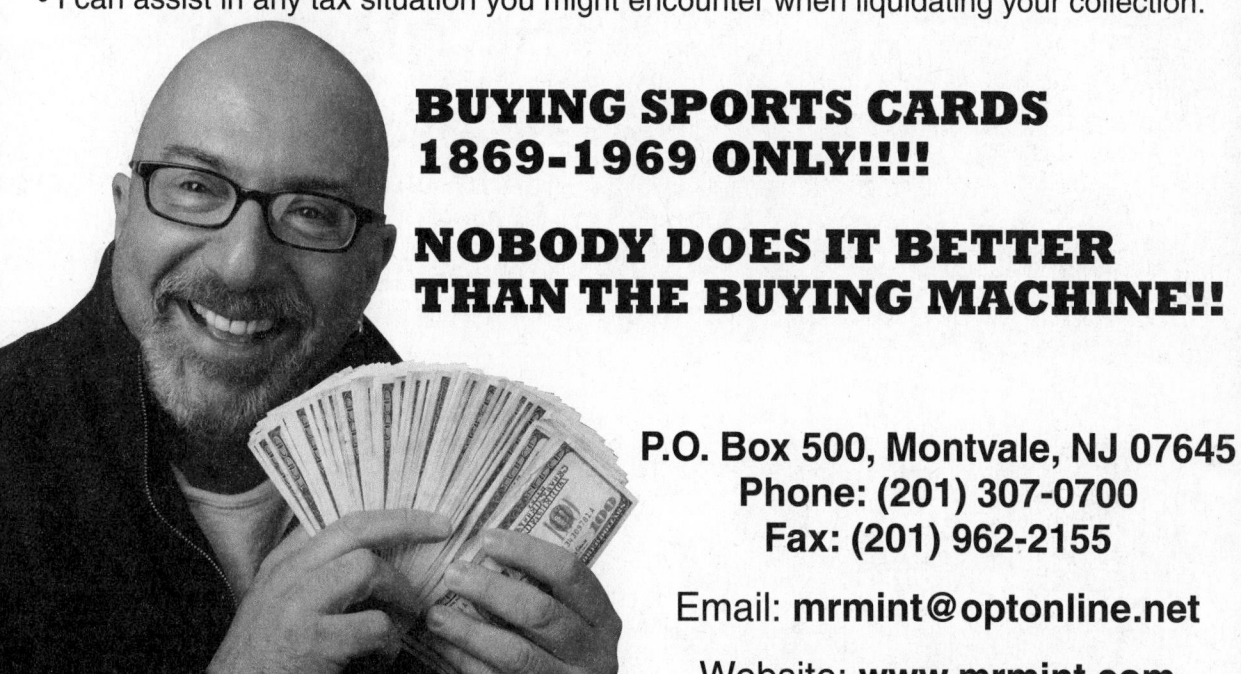

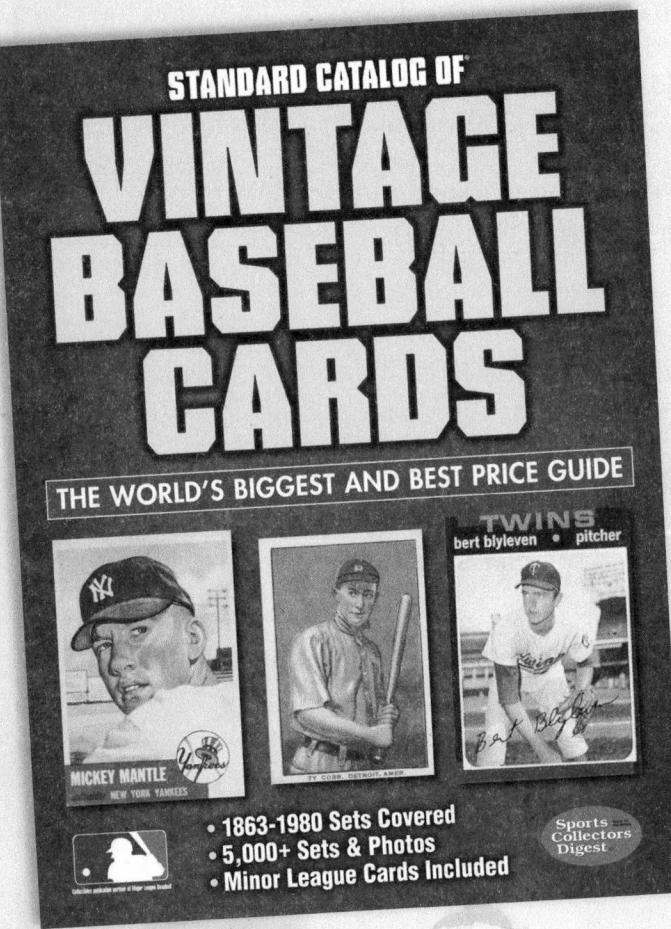

The Authority in Antiques & Collectibles

For nearly 30 years, Antique Trader Antiques & Collectibles has served as the leading source for information on antiques and collectibles. Eric Bradley brings you 816 pages full of pictures, pricing information, and more on this amazingly diverse and glorious market.

In This Antiques Price Guide You'll Find:

- Expert advice along with market and collecting trends
- 4,500 high quality color images
- Vetted values and pricing guide information

Antique Trader Antiques & Collectibles is the undisputed best-selling annual guide in the hobby.

Item # U4566 • Retail: $22.99

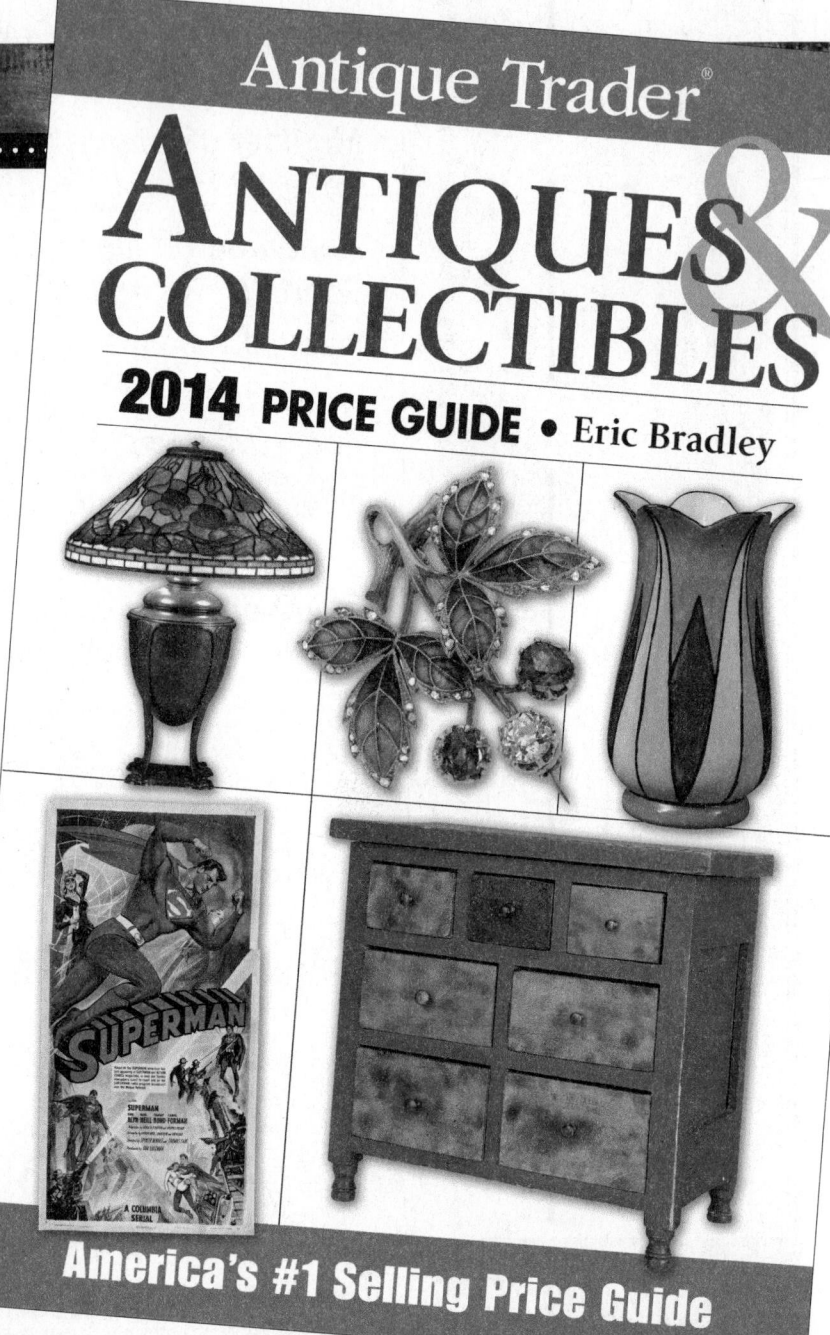

Antique Trader®

ANTIQUES & COLLECTIBLES

2014 PRICE GUIDE • Eric Bradley

America's #1 Selling Price Guide

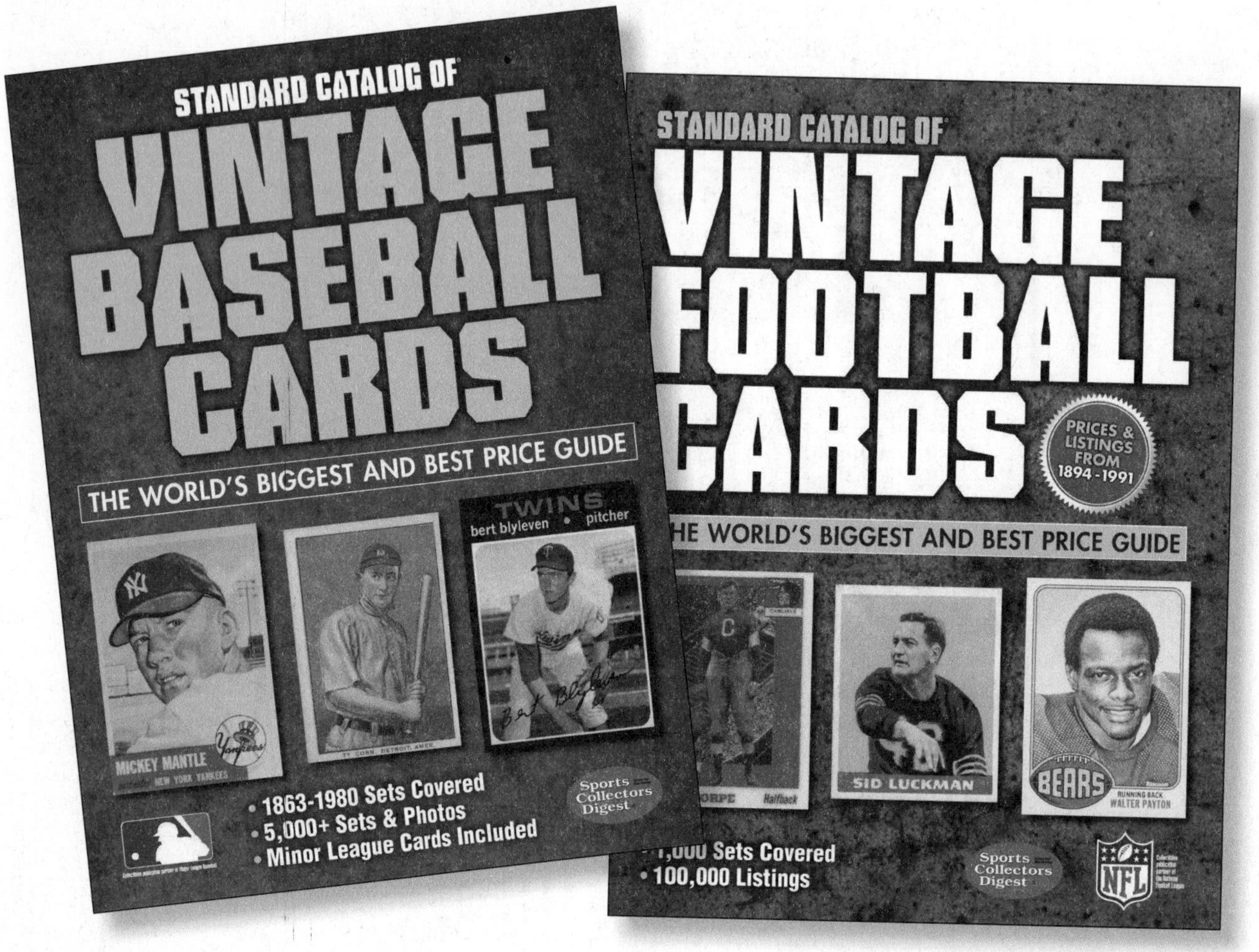

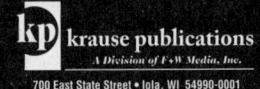

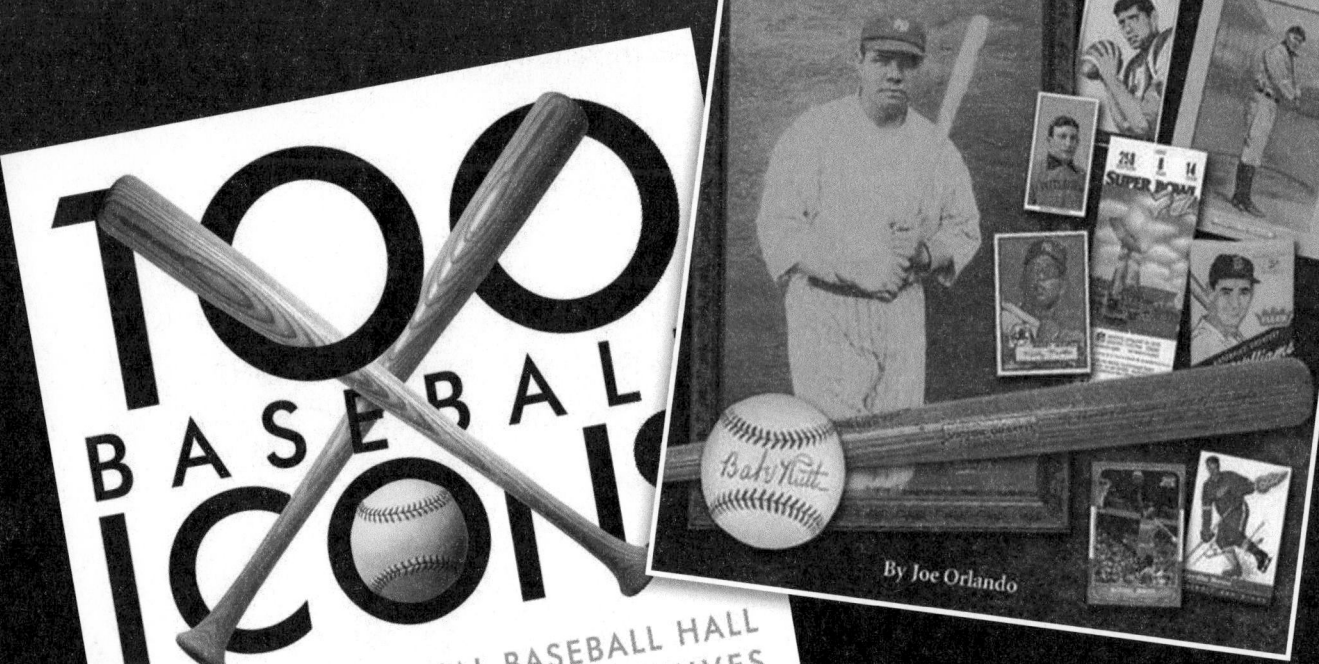

STANDARD CATALOG OF®
VINTAGE BASEBALL CARDS

Collectibles publication partner of Major League Baseball®

Sports Collectors Digest

Voice for the Hobby

Published by

Krause Publications, a division of F+W Media, Inc.
700 East State Street • Iola, WI 54990-0001
715-445-2214 • 888-457-2873
www.krausebooks.com

To order books or other products call toll-free 1-800-258-0929
or visit us online at www.krausebooks.com

ISBN-13: 978-1-4402-3849-9
ISBN-10: 1-4402-3849-9

Cover Design by Kevin Ulrich
Designed by Sandi Carpenter
Edited by Tom Bartsch

Printed in the United States of America

Acknowledgments

Hundreds of individuals have made countless valuable contributions that have been incorporated into the Standard Catalog of Baseball Cards. While all cannot be acknowledged, special appreciation is extended to the following principal contributors who have exhibited a special dedication by creating, revising or verifying listings and technical data, reviewing market valuations or providing cards to be illustrated.

Rob Adesso • Ken Agona • Gary Agostino • Lisa Albano • Dan Albaugh • Tom Akins • Will Allison • Mark Anker • Ellis Anmuth • Steve Applebaum • Tom Atkins • Bill Atkinson

Rand Bailey • Bill Ballew • Andy Baran • Gary Bartolett • Judy Bartolett • Bob Bartosz • John Beisiegel • Karen Bell • Dr. Charles E. Belles • Dave Berman • Cathy Black • Jerry A. Blum • Ralph Blunt Jr. • Mike Bodner • Jeff Bossak • Bill Bossert • Bob Bostoff • Brian Boston • Jim Boushley • Mark Bowers • Mike Boyd • Roland Bracken • John Brigandi • Scott Brockelman • Lou Brown • Dan Bruner • Greg Bussineau

Billy Caldwell • Len Caprisecca • Tony Carrafiell • Brian Cataquet • Lee Champion • Dwight Chapin • Lou Chericoni • Ryan Christoff • Jim Clarke • Shane Cohen • Rich Cole • Paul Conan Jr. • Charles Conlon • Eric Cooper • Bill Cornell • Bryan Couling • Bob Crabill • Clyde Cripe • Al Cristafulli • Jim Cumpton • Robert Curtiss

Pete D'Luhosch • Tom Daniels • Stuart Dansinger • James Davis • Dick DeCourcy • Ken Degnan • Dan DeKing • Mike Del Gado • Bill Diebold • Larry Dluhy • Brett Domue • John Dorsey

Curtis Earl • Eric Eichelkraut • Mark Elliott • Jeff Emerson • Brian Engles • Shirley Eross • John B. Esch • Joe Esposito • Dan Even • Doak Ewing

Julian Fernandez • David Festberg • Robert Fisk • Jay Finglass • Nick Flaviano • Rick Fleury • Jeff Fritsch • Larry Fritsch

Gary Gagen • Richard Galasso • Tom Galic • Richard R. Gallagher • Chris Gallutia • Tony Galovich • Phillip Garrou • Gary Gatanis • Frank Giffune • Richard Gilkeson • Gerald J. Glasser • Philip Glazer • Matthew Glidden • Keith David Goldfarb • Jack Goodman • Bill Goodwin • Dick Goddard • Barry Gordon • Howard Gordon • Mike Gordon • Sean Gottlieb • Bob Gray • Wayne Grove • Gerry Guenther • Don Guilbert • Tom Guilfoile

David Hall • Joel Hall • Walter Hall • Gary Hamilton • Ed Hans • Tom Harbin • Michael Harrington • Don Harrison • Rich Hawksley • Herbert Hecht • Bill Henderson • Mike Henderson • Kathy Henry • Pete Henrici • Steve Hershkowitz • Bob Hicks • Gregg Hitesman • John Hoffman • Dennis Hollenbeck • Jack Horkan • Jim Horne • Brent Horton • Ron Hosmer • Marvin Huck • Brad Hudecek

Bob Ivanjack

Robert Jacobsen • David Jenkins • Donn Jennings • Scott Jensen • Andrew Jerome • Jim Johnston • Stewart Jones • Larry Jordan

Judy Kay • Allan Kaye • Michael Keedy • Frank Keetz • Mark Kemmerle • Rick Keplinger • John King • John Kitleson • Terry Knouse • Bob Koehler • David Kohler • A.F. Kokol • Dan Kravitz

Steve Lacasse • Jason Lange • Mark K. Larson • Lee Lasseigne • William Lawrence • Scott Lawson • Richard Leech • Morley Leeking • Tom Leon • Don Lepore • Rod Lethbridge • Scott Letts • David Levin • Stuart Leviton • Howie Levy • Hal Lewis • Rob Lifson • Lew Lipset • Jeff Litteral • Dick Lloyd • Chuck Lobenthal • Leon Luckey • Chuck Lumb

Mark Macrae • Paul Marchant • Robert Marek • Bob Marotto • Art Martineau • Bob Marquette • Richard Masson • Bill Mastro • Ralph Maya • Dan McKee • Fred McKie • Tony McLaughlin • Don McPherson • Doug McWilliams • John Mehlin • Bill Mendel • H. Dexter • Joe Merkel • Blake Meyer • Louis Middleton • Bob Miller • Jay Miller • Keith Mitchell • J.A. Monaco • Robert Montgomery • Joe Moreno • Brian Morris • Mike Mosier • Scott Mosley • Mike Mowrey • Peter Mudavin • Mark Murphy • David Musser

Frank Nagy • Steve Neimand • Roger Neufeldt • Tim Newcomb • Joe Newman • Bill Nicolls • Chuck Nobriga • Mark Nochta • Wayne Nochta

Bud Obermeyer • Jeff Obermeyer • Keith Olbermann

D.J. Panaia • Joe Pasternack • Marty Perry • Tom Pfirrman • Dan Piepenbrok • Stan Pietruska • Paul Pollard • Harvey Poris • Don "Barefoot" Post

Pat Quinn

Ed Ranson • Fred Rapaport • Jim Resseque • Steve Rice • Mike Rich • Bob Richardson • Al Richter • Gavin Riley • Mark Rios • Ron Ritzler • Tom Reid • Bob Robles • Mike Rodell • Scott Roemer • Mike Rogers • Chris Ronan • Rocky Rosato • Alan Rosen • John Rumierz • Bob Rund • Moe Ryan

Len Samworth • Jon Sands • Kevin Savage • Stephen Schauer • Allan Schoenberger • Dave Schwartz • Robert Scott • Larry Serota • 707 Sports Cards • Jim Sexton • Corey Shanus • Max Silberman • Al Simeone • Paul Sjolin • Barry Sloate • Joe Smith • Mark Soltan • John Spalding • Kevin Spears • Gene Speranza • Nigel Spill • Mike Spillane • Jerry Spillman • David Spivack • Dana Sprague • Don Steinbach • Paul Stewart • Dan Stickney • Larry Stone • Ken Stough • Al Strumpf • Doug Stultz • Jim Suckow • Rich Suen • Joe Szeremet

J.J. Teaparty • Erik Teller • Lee Temanson • K.J. Terplak • Mark Theotikos • Dick Tinsley • Gary Tkac • Bud Tompkins • Joseph Tonely • Scott Torrey • Dan Tripper

Rich Unruh • Jack Urban

Glen Van Aken • Frank Van Damme • Brian Van Horn

Geno Wagner • Frank Wakefield • Pete Waldman • Eric Waller • Tony Walls • Gary Walter • Frank Ward • Adam Warshaw • Dave Weber • Ken Weimer • Jeff Weiss • Richard Weiss • Dale Weselowski • E.C. Wharton-Tigar • Charles Williamson • Jay Wolt • Frank Wozny • Bill Wright

Rhett Yeakley • Rhys Yeakley • Kit Young • Ted Zanidakis

How To Use This Catalog

This catalog has been uniquely designed to serve the needs of collectors and dealers at all levels from beginning to advanced. It provides a comprehensive guide to more than 140 years of baseball card issues, arranged so that even the most novice hobbyist can consult it with confidence and ease.

The following explanations summarize the general practices used in preparing this catalog's listings. However, because of specialized requirements which may vary from card set to card set, these must not be considered ironclad. Where these standards have been set aside, appropriate notations are usually incorporated.

ARRANGEMENT

The most important feature in identifying and pricing a baseball card is its set of origin. Therefore the main body of this catalog, covering cards issued from 1863-1980, has been alphabetically arranged within specific eras of issue according to the name by which the set is most popularly known to collectors, or by which it can be most easily identified by a person examining a card.

Previous editions of this catalog relied heavily upon card set identification numbers originated in Jefferson Burdick's pioneering "American Card Catalog." However, since that work was last updated more than 40 years ago, its numbering system has become arcane and is little used by the present generation of hobbyists. Where practical, sets which were listed in previous editions by their ACC designations have been reclassified alphabetically by a more readily identifiable signpost, such as manufacturer's name. Most of those sets however continue to bear the ACC catalog number in the set heading.

Among card issuers that produced sets for more than a single year, their sets are then listed chronologically, from earliest to most recent, again within specific eras.

Within each set, the cards are listed by their designated card number, or in the absence of card numbers, alphabetically according to the last name of the player pictured. Listing numbers found in parentheses indicate the number does not appear on the card. Certain cards which fall outside the parameters of the normal card numbering for a specific set may be found at the beginning or end of the listings for that set.

Listings are generally arranged in two major sections – major league and minor league issues.

MAJOR LEAGUE ISSUES

The main body of the book details major league baseball card issues from 1863 through 1980, focusing on the Vintage Era (1863-1980). In general, this will include issues that picture one or more baseball players, usually contemporary with their playing days, printed on paper or cardboard in a variety of shapes and sizes and given away as a premium with the purchase of another product or service.

Included within each era's listings are related non-card collectibles featuring baseball players which do not fit under the definition previously given for baseball cards. These include many items on which players are depicted on materials other than paper or cardboard, such as pins, coins, silks, leathers, patches, felts, pennants, metallic ingots, statues, figurines, limited-edition artworks and others.

Also presented herein are foreign issues, one of the growth areas of the baseball card hobby in recent years. These encompass the various issues from countries outside of North America, particularly Latin America. Since the 1920s a variety of baseball cards, stamps and stickers have emanated from the Caribbean, South America and elsewhere chronicling the various winter baseball leagues that have flourished there, often stocked with former and future major league stars and, in the early years, providing the only contemporary cards of many U.S. and Latin Negro Leagues players.

MINOR LEAGUE ISSUES (1867-1969)

Prior to 1970 virtually all minor league baseball cards were issued as single cards rather than as complete sets. Like contemporary major league cards they were usually intended as premiums given away with the purchase of goods and services.

The listings which follow offer individual card prices in three grades of preservation to allow accurate valuations of superstar and other special interest cards, along with cards that were short-printed or otherwise are scarce.

IDENTIFICATION

While most modern baseball cards are well identified on front, back or both, as to date and issue, such has not always been the case. In general, the back of the card is more useful in identifying the set of origin than the front. The issuer or sponsor's name will usually appear on the back since, after all, baseball cards were first produced as a promotional item to stimulate sales of other products. As often as not, that issuer's name is the name by which the set is known to collectors and under which it will be found listed in this catalog.

In some difficult cases, identifying a baseball card's general age, if not specific year of issue, can usually be accomplished by studying the biological or statistical information on the back of the card. The last year mentioned in either the biography or stats is usually the year which preceded the year of issue.

Over the years there have been many cards issued that bear no identification features at all with which to pinpoint the issuer. In such cases, they are cataloged by the names under which they are best known in the hobby. Many of the strip-card issues of the 1920s, for example, remain listed under the "W" catalog number where they were originally enumerated in the "American Card Catalog."

It is the ultimate goal, through the use of cross listings and more detailed indexes, to allow a person holding a card in his hand to find the catalog listing for that card with the greatest ease.

PHOTOGRAPHS

Wherever possible a photograph of the front and back of at least one representative card from most of the sets listed in this catalog has been incorporated into the listings to assist identification. (Persons who can provide sample cards for photography purposes for those sets which are missing photos in this volume are encouraged to contact the editor.)

Photographs have been printed in reduced size. The actual size of cards in each set is usually given in the introductory text preceding its listing, unless the card is the current standard size (2.5" by 3.5").

DATING

The dating of baseball cards by year of issue on the front or back of the card itself is a relatively new phenomenon. In most cases, to accurately determine a date of issue for an unidentified card, it must be studied for clues. As mentioned, the biography, career summary or statistics on the back of the card are the best way to pinpoint a year of issue. In most cases, the year of issue will be the year after the last season mentioned on the card.

Luckily for today's collector, earlier generations have done much of the research in determining year of issue for those cards that bear no clues. The painstaking task of matching the players' listed and/or pictured team against their career records often allowed an issue date to be determined.

In some cases, particular card sets were issued over a period of more than one calendar year, but since they are collected together as a single set, their specific year of issue is not important. Such sets will be listed with their complete known range of issue years.

There remain some early issues for which an exact year of issue cannot be reliably pinpointed. In those cases a "best guess" date or one in the middle of the possible range has been used to identify the issue; such cases are usually noted in the introductory text.

NUMBERING

While many baseball card issues as far back as the 1880s have featured card numbers assigned by the issuer to facilitate the collecting of a complete set, the practice has by no means been universal. Even today, not every set bears card numbers.

Logically, those baseball cards that were numbered by their manufacturer are presented in that numerical order within the listings of this catalog whenever possible. In a few cases, complete player checklists were obtained from earlier published sources that did not note card numbers, and so numbers have been arbitrarily assigned. Many other unnumbered issues have been assigned catalog numbers to facilitate their universal identification within the hobby, especially when buying and selling by mail. Among some issues for which the complete checklist remains unknown and for which new discoveries are still being reported, gaps have been left in the assigned numbering to facilitate future additions.

In all cases, numbers that have been assigned, or which otherwise do not appear on the card through error or by design, are shown in this catalog within parentheses. In virtually all cases, unless a more natural system suggested itself by the unique matter of a particular set, the assignment of numbers by the cataloging staff has been done by alphabetical arrangement of the players' last names or the card's principal title.

Significant collectible variations for any particular card are noted within the listings by the application of a suffix letter. In instances of variations, the suffix "a" is assigned to the variation which was created first, when it can be so identified.

NAMES

The identification of a player by full name on the front of his baseball card has been a common practice only since the 1920s. Prior to that, the player's last name and team were the usual information found on the card front.

As a general – though not universally applied – practice, the listings in this volume present the player's name exactly as it appears on the front of the card. If the player's full name only appears on the back, rather than on the front of the card, the listing may correspond to that designation.

A player's name checklisted in bold italic type indicates a rookie card as defined later in this introduction.

Cards that contain misspelled first or last names, or even wrong initials, will usually have included in their listings the incorrect information, with a correction accompanying in parentheses. This extends also to cases where the name on the card does not correspond to the player actually pictured.

In some cases, to facilitate efficient presentations, to maintain ease of use for the reader, or to allow for proper computer sorting of data, a player's name or card title may be listed other than as it actually appears on the card.

GRADING

It is necessary that some sort of card grading standard be used so that buyer and seller (especially when dealing through the Internet or by mail) may reach an informed agreement on the value of a card.

Pre-1981 cards are generally priced in the three grades of preservation in which those cards are most commonly encountered in the daily buying and selling in the hobby marketplace. They are listed in grades of Near Mint (NR MT), Excellent (EX) and Very Good (VG), reflecting the basic fact that few cards were able to survive for 25, 50 or even 100 years in close semblance to the condition of their issue.

The pricing of cards in these three conditions will allow readers to accurately price cards which fall in intermediate grades, such as EX-MT, or VG-EX.

Although grades below Very Good are not generally priced in this volume, close approximations of low-grade card values may be figured on the following formula: Good condition cards are valued at about 50 percent of VG price, with Fair cards about 50 percent of Good.

Cards in Poor condition have little or no market value except in the cases of the rarest and most expensive cards. In such cases, value has to be negotiated individually.

Modern (1981-date) issues, which have been preserved in top condition in considerable numbers, are listed only in the grade of Near Mint-to-Mint (NM/M). Earlier editions of this book priced such cards under the heading of Mint condition. However, the rise of independent grading services in the past decade and their use of the NM/M designation to describe the vast majority of new card specimens has influenced the marketplace to the extent that only a small percentage of cards, even fresh from the pack, can meet the strict standards for a true Mint example. The switch to a NM/M designation is part of the catalog's commitment to accurately reflect the current conditions of the card market.

As with older cards, values for lower-grade cards from 1981-date may be generally figured by using a figure of 75 percent of the NM/M price for Near Mint specimens, and 40 percent of the Mint price for Excellent cards.

For the benefit of the reader, we present herewith the grading guide which was originally formulated in 1981 by Baseball Cards magazine and Sports Collectors Digest, and has been continually refined since that time.

These grading definitions have been used in the pricing of cards in this book, but they are by no means a universally-accepted grading standard.

The potential buyer of a baseball card should keep that in mind when encountering cards of nominally the same grade, but at a price which differs widely from that quoted in this book.

Ultimately, the collector must formulate his/her own personal grading standards in deciding whether cards available for purchase meet the needs of their collection.

No collector is required to adhere to the grading standards presented herewith – nor to any other published grading standards.

Mint (MT): A perfect card. Well-centered, with parallel borders that appear equal to the naked eye. Four sharp, square corners. No creases, edge dents, surface scratches, paper flaws, loss of luster, yellowing or fading, regardless of age. No imperfectly printed card – out of register, badly cut or ink flawed – or card stained by contact with gum, wax or other substances can be considered truly Mint, even if new out of the pack. Generally, to be considered in Mint condition, a card's borders must exist in a ratio of no greater than 60/40 side to side and top to bottom.

Near Mint/Mint (NM/M): A nearly perfect card. Well-centered, with at least three sharp, square corners. No creases, edge dents, surface scratches, paper flaws, loss of luster, yellowing or fading, regardless of age. No imperfectly printed card – out of register, badly cut or ink flawed – or card stained by contact with gum, wax or other substances can be considered Near Mint/ Mint, even if new out of the pack. Generally, to be considered in NM/M condition, a card's borders must exist in a ratio of no greater than 65/35 side to side and top to bottom.

Near Mint (NR MT): At first glance, a Near Mint card appears perfect; upon closer examination, however, a minor flaw will be discovered. On well-centered cards, at least two of the four corners must be perfectly sharp; the others showing a minor imperfection upon close inspection. A slightly off-center card with one or more borders being noticeably unequal – no worse than in a ratio of 70/30 S/S or T/B – would also fit this grade.

Excellent (EX): Corners are still fairly sharp with only moderate wear. Card borders may be off-center as much as 80/20. No creases. May have very minor gum, wax or product stains, front or back. Surfaces may show slight loss of luster from rubbing across other cards.

Very Good (VG): Show obvious handling. Corners rounded and/ or perhaps showing minor creases. Other minor creases may be visible. Surfaces may exhibit loss of luster, but all printing is intact. May show major gum, wax or other packaging stains. No major creases, tape marks or extraneous markings or writing. All four borders visible, though the ratio may be as poor as 95/5. Exhibits honest wear.

Good (G): A well-worn card, but exhibits no intentional damage or abuse. May have major or multiple creases and/ or corners rounded well beyond the border. A Good card will generally sell for about 50 percent the value of a card in Very Good condition.

Fair (F or Fr.): Shows excessive wear, along with damage or abuse. Will show all the wear characteristics of a Good card, along with such damage as thumb tack holes in or near margins, evidence of having been taped or pasted, perhaps small tears around the edges, or creases so heavy as to break the cardboard. Backs may show minor added pen or pencil writing, or be missing small bits of paper. Still, basically a complete card. A Fair card will generally sell for 50 percent the value of a Good specimen.

Poor (P): A card that has been tortured to death. Corners or other areas may be torn off. Card may have been trimmed, show holes from a paper punch or have been used for BB gun practice. Front may have extraneous pen or pencil writing, or other defacement. Major portions of front or back design may be missing. Not a pretty sight.

In addition to these terms, collectors may encounter intermediate grades, such as VG-EX or EX-MT. These cards usually have characteristics of both the lower and higher grades, and are generally priced midway between those two values.

With the rise in popularity of third-party authentication/grading services since the mid-1990s, it must be stressed that the grades and corresponding values presented in this book are for "raw" cards – cards which have not been independently graded. Depending on the reputation of the certification firm, cards that have been graded and encased in plastic slabs may sell for a significant premium over the values found here. This is especially true of high-grade specimens of vintage cards that in certified grades of Near Mint/Mint, Mint or Gem Mint may bring multiples of "catalog" value. Even collector-grade vintage cards can command a premium when authenticated, graded and slabbed because potential buyers may feel more secure in such cards' authenticity and freedom from tampering.

ROOKIE CARDS

While the status (and automatic premium value) that a player's rookie card carries has fluctuated in recent years, and though the hobby still has not reached a universal definition of a rookie card, many significant vintage-era rookie cards are noted in this catalog's listings by the use of bold italic type. Conversely, many significant modern-era rookie cards are noted in this catalog's listings by the use of RC or (RC). Beginning with products issued in 2006, cards with an (RC) logo indicate the featured player has a rookie card issued prior to that year. For purposes of this catalog, a player's rookie card is considered to be any card in a nationally distributed, licensed Major League base (non-insert) set from a major manufacturer in the first year in which that player appears on a card, regardless of whether that player has yet appeared in a Major League game or is technically a rookie according to MLB definition.

VALUATIONS

Values quoted in this book represent the current retail market at the time of compilation (Summer, 2013). The quoted values are the result of a unique system of evaluation and verification created by the catalog's editors. Utilizing specialized computer analysis and drawing upon recommendations provided through their daily involvement in the publication of the hobby's leading sports collectors' periodicals, as well as the input of consultants, dealers and collectors, each listing is, in the final analysis, the interpretation of that data by one or more of the editors.

It should be stressed, however, that this book is intended to serve only as an aid in evaluating cards; actual market conditions are constantly changing. Because this volume is intended to reflect the national market, users will find regional price variances caused by demand differences.

Publication of this book is not intended as a solicitation to buy or sell the listed cards by the editors, publisher or contributors.

Again, the values here are retail prices – what a collector can expect to pay when buying a card from a dealer. The wholesale price, that which a collector can expect to receive from a dealer when selling cards, will be significantly lower.

Many dealers operate on a 100 percent mark-up, generally paying about 50 percent of a card's retail value for cards that they are purchasing for inventory. On some high-demand cards, dealers will pay 100 percent or more of retail value, anticipating continued price increases. Conversely, for many low-demand cards, such as common (non-star) players' cards, dealers may pay as little as 10 percent or even less of retail with many base-brand cards of recent years having no resale value at all.

SET PRICES

Collectors may note that the complete set prices for newer issues quoted in these listings are usually significantly lower than the total of the value of the individual cards that comprise the set. This reflects two factors in the baseball card market. First, a seller is often willing to take a lower composite price for a complete set as a "volume discount" and to avoid carrying in inventory a large number of common-player or other lower-demand cards.

Second, to a degree, the value of common cards can be said to be inflated as a result of having a built-in overhead charge to justify the dealer's time in sorting cards, carrying them in stock and filling orders. This accounts for the fact that even brand new base-brand baseball cards, which cost the dealer around 2 cents each when bought in bulk, carry individual price tags of 5 cents or higher.

Some set prices shown, especially for vintage cards in top condition, are merely theoretical in that it is unlikely that a complete set exists in that condition. In general among older cards the range of conditions found in even the most painstakingly assembled complete set make the set values quoted useful only as a starting point for price negotiations.

ERRORS/VARIATIONS

It is often hard for the beginning collector to understand that an error on a baseball card, in and of itself, does not necessarily add premium value to that card. It is usually only when the correcting of an error in a subsequent printing creates a variation that premium value attaches to an error.

Minor errors, such as wrong stats or personal data, misspellings, inconsistencies, etc. – usually affecting the back of the card – are very common, especially in recent years. Unless a corrected variation was also printed, these errors are not noted in the listings of this book because they are not generally perceived by collectors to have premium value.

On the other hand, major effort has been expended to include the most complete listings ever for collectible variation cards. Many scarce and valuable variations are included in these listings because they are widely collected and often have significant premium value.

COUNTERFEITS/REPRINTS

As the value of baseball cards has risen in the past 25+ years, certain cards and sets have become too expensive for the average collector to obtain. This, along with changes in the technology of color printing, has given rise to increasing numbers of counterfeit and reprint cards.

While both terms describe essentially the same thing – a modern-day copy that attempts to duplicate as closely as possible an original baseball card – there are differences that are important to the collector.

Generally a counterfeit is made with the intention of deceiving somebody into believing it is genuine, and thus paying large amounts of money for it. The counterfeiter takes every pain to try to make their fakes look as authentic as possible.

A reprint, on the other hand, while it may have been made to look as close as possible to an original card, is made with the intention of allowing collectors to buy them as substitutes for cards they may never be otherwise able to afford. The big difference is that a reprint is generally marked as such, usually on the back of the card.

In other cases, like the Topps 1952 reprint set and later Archives issues, the replicas are printed in a size markedly different from the originals, or utilizing current technology that differs from that available in the past. Collectors should be aware, however, that unscrupulous persons will sometimes cut off or otherwise obliterate the distinguishing word – "Reprint," "Copy," – or modern copyright date on the back of a reprint card in an attempt to pass it as genuine.

A collector's best defense against reprints and counterfeits is to acquire a knowledge of the look and feel of genuine baseball cards of various eras and issues.

UNLISTED CARDS

Persons encountering cards which are not listed in this reference should not immediately infer that they have something rare and/or valuable. With hundreds of thousands of baseball cards issued over the past century and thousands more being issued each year, this catalog's comprehensiveness will always remain relative. This is especially true in the area of sets released regionally, and the vast universe of foreign and collectors' issues for which coverage has only recently begun. Readers who have cards or sets that are not covered in this edition are invited to correspond with the editor for purposes of adding to the compilation work now in progress. A photocopy or scan of the card's front and back will assist in determining its status. For questions relating to vintage era cards, contact: Tom Bartsch, 700 E. State St., Iola, WI 54990; e-mail tom.bartsch@fwmedia.com. Major contributions will be acknowledged in future editions.

Abbreviation Key

IS: Interleague Showdown

OPS: Overprinted "Promotional Sample"

ED: Expansion Draft

AS: All-Star

HL: Hit List

RC: Rookie Class

RC or (RC): Rookie Card

UPT: Unlimited Potential/Talent

SF: Star Factor

SP: Short Print

DT: Double Team

GLS: Gold Leaf Stars

CC: Curtain Calls

GLR: Gold Leaf Rookies

TP: Top Performers

FF: Future Foundation

DK: Diamond King

RR: Rated Rookie

DP: Double Print

IA: In Action

PC: Promo Card

SR: Star Rookie

STANDARD CATALOG OF®
VINTAGE BASEBALL CARDS

Collectibles publication partner of Major League Baseball®

Sports Collectors Digest

Voice for the Hobby

Published by

Krause Publications, a division of F+W Media, Inc.
700 East State Street • Iola, WI 54990-0001
715-445-2214 • 888-457-2873
www.krausebooks.com

To order books or other products call toll-free 1-800-258-0929
or visit us online at www.krausebooks.com

ISBN-13: 978-1-4402-3849-9
ISBN-10: 1-4402-3849-9

Cover Design by Kevin Ulrich
Designed by Sandi Carpenter
Edited by Tom Bartsch

Printed in the United States of America

1976 A & P Brewers

The Aaron and Yount cards from this regional issue support the set price. The set was issued by the A & P grocery chain. Oversize - 5-7/8" x 9" - cards (actually printed on semigloss paper) were given out at the stores in 1976 in series of four with the purchase of select weekly grocery specials. Players are pictured in tight capless portraits. Each photo has a black facsimile autograph; backs are blank. The unnumbered cards are checklisted here in alphabetical order.

		NM	E	VG
	Complete Set (16):	35.00	17.50	10.50
	Common Player:	3.00	1.50	.90
(1)	Henry Aaron	20.00	10.00	6.00
(2)	Pete Broberg	3.00	1.50	.90
(3)	Jim Colborn	3.00	1.50	.90
(4)	Mike Hegan	3.00	1.50	.90
(5)	Tim Johnson	3.00	1.50	.90
(6)	Von Joshua	3.00	1.50	.90
(7)	Sixto Lezcano	3.00	1.50	.90
(8)	Don Money	3.00	1.50	.90
(9)	Charlie Moore	3.00	1.50	.90
(10)	Darrell Porter	3.00	1.50	.90
(11)	George Scott	3.00	1.50	.90
(12)	Bill Sharp	3.00	1.50	.90
(13)	Jim Slaton	3.00	1.50	.90
(14)	Bill Travers	3.00	1.50	.90
(15)	Robin Yount	10.00	5.00	3.00
(16)	County Stadium	3.00	1.50	.90

1976 A & P Royals

Identical in format to the Brewers' set issued around Milwaukee, these 5-7/8" x 9" photos picture players without their caps in posed portraits. The cards were given away four per week with the purchase of selected grocery item specials. Cards have a Players Association logo in the upper-left corner, and a black facsimile autograph on front. Backs are blank. The unnumbered cards are checklisted here alphabetically.

		NM	E	VG
	Complete Set (16):	40.00	20.00	12.00
	Common Player:	3.00	1.50	.90
(1)	Doug Bird	3.00	1.50	.90
(2)	George Brett	20.00	10.00	6.00
(3)	Steve Busby	3.00	1.50	.90
(4)	Al Cowens	3.00	1.50	.90
(5)	Al Fitzmorris	3.00	1.50	.90
(6)	Dennis Leonard	3.00	1.50	.90
(7)	Buck Martinez	3.00	1.50	.90
(8)	John Mayberry	3.00	1.50	.90
(9)	Hal McRae	4.50	2.25	1.25
(10)	Amos Otis	4.50	2.25	1.25
(11)	Fred Patek	3.00	1.50	.90
(12)	Tom Poquette	3.00	1.50	.90
(13)	Mel Rojas	3.00	1.50	.90
(14)	Tony Solaita	3.00	1.50	.90
(15)	Paul Splittorff	3.00	1.50	.90
(16)	Jim Wohlford	3.00	1.50	.90

1968 Aamco Roger Maris Postcard

The cited date is approximate on this large-format (about 6" x 9") postcard. The borderless front has a color pose of the reigning home run king with the legend, "It's a real pennant winner!" The postcard format back is directed at auto service professionals, encouraging them to refer transmission problems to a local Aamco facility. A color Aamco logo is at bottom-left.

	NM	E	VG
Roger Maris	150.00	75.00	45.00

1954 ABC Freight Postcard

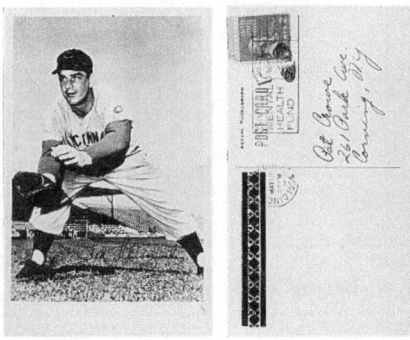

So far only one player is known in this black-and-white glossy postcard issue. The front has a posed photo with facsimile autograph. The wide white border at bottom was likely to accomodate an authentic signature. The divided back carries in its upper-left corner the two-line message "You can't miss by playing ball with / ABC Freight Forwarding Corp." However, on the sole known specimen, that message has been obliterated by being overprinted with a decorative black design. Format is 3-1/2" x 5-7/16".

		NM	E	VG
(1)	Ted Kluszewski (Batting)	150.00	75.00	45.00
(2)	Ted Kluszewski (Fielding)	150.00	75.00	45.00

1932 Abdulla Tobacco

Babe Ruth, Amerika

Along with several other contemporary card issues from Germany, Babe Ruth is the lone representative from American baseball in this series of 200 cards. Cards are 1-11/16" x 2-1/2" and feature sepia-tone photos on front, with the celebrity's name and nation printed in the white border at bottom. Backs are in German and include a card number.

		NM	E	VG
196	Babe Ruth	1,750	875.00	525.00

1949-1950 Acebo y Cia

These small (about 1-1/2" x 1-3/4") Cuban cards were issued in matchboxes, probably over more than one season, as some players are known in photo variations. Fronts have a black-and-white or duotone photo, bordered, with the player name in plain type. Backs have player information presented in one of several different styles, or are blank-backed. It is likely this checklist, which includes a significant contingent of American players, is not complete.

		NM	E	VG
	Common Player:	100.00	50.00	30.00
(1)	Bob Addis	100.00	50.00	30.00
(2)	Luis Aloma	100.00	50.00	30.00
(3)	Ferrel (Ferrell) Anderson	100.00	50.00	30.00
(4)	Bill Antonello	100.00	50.00	30.00
(5)	Mario Arencibia	100.00	50.00	30.00
(6)	Maurice Atwright	100.00	50.00	30.00
(7)	Wesley Bailey	100.00	50.00	30.00
(8)	Vic Barnhart	100.00	50.00	30.00
(9)	Carlos Blanco	100.00	50.00	30.00
(10)	Herberto Blanco	100.00	50.00	30.00
(11)	Adolfo Cabrera	100.00	50.00	30.00
(12)	Emilio Cabrera	100.00	50.00	30.00
(13)	Lorenzo "Chiquitin" Cabrera	100.00	50.00	30.00
(14)	Rafael Villa Cabrera	100.00	50.00	30.00
(15)	Samuel Calderone	100.00	50.00	30.00
(16)	Avelino Canizares	100.00	50.00	30.00
(17)	Clemente "Sungo" Carreras	100.00	50.00	30.00
(18)	Jack Cassini	100.00	50.00	30.00
(19)	Aristonico Cocorreoso	100.00	50.00	30.00
(20)	Carlos Colas	100.00	50.00	30.00
(21)	Kevin (Chuck) Connors	450.00	225.00	135.00
(22)	Sandalio "Potrellilo" Consuegra	125.00	62.00	37.00
(23)	Agustin Cordeiro	100.00	50.00	30.00
(24)	Reinaldo Cordeiro	100.00	50.00	30.00
(25)	Reinaldo Cordeiro	100.00	50.00	30.00
(26)	Alejandro Crespo	100.00	50.00	30.00
(27)	Raymond "Talua" Dandridge	500.00	250.00	150.00
(28)	Jose "Pipo" de la Noval	100.00	50.00	30.00
(29)	Carlos "Yiqui" De Souza	100.00	50.00	30.00
(30)	Mario Diaz	100.00	50.00	30.00
(31)	Lino Donoso	100.00	50.00	30.00
(32)	Claro Duany	100.00	50.00	30.00
(33)	Gumersindo Elba	100.00	50.00	30.00
(34)	Paul (Al) Epperly	100.00	50.00	30.00
(35)	Roberto "Tarzan" Estalella	125.00	65.00	35.00
(36)	Jose Ma. Fernandez	100.00	50.00	30.00
(37)	Jose Ma. Fernandez Jr.	100.00	50.00	30.00
(38)	Rodolfo Fernandez	100.00	50.00	30.00
(39)	Thomas Fine	100.00	50.00	30.00
(40)	Andres Fleitas	100.00	50.00	30.00
(41)	Pedro Formental	100.00	50.00	30.00
(42)	"Sojito" Gallardo	100.00	50.00	30.00
(43)	Chicuelo Garcia	100.00	50.00	30.00
(44)	Manuel "Cocaina" Garcia	150.00	75.00	45.00
(45)	Pablo Garcia	100.00	50.00	30.00
(46)	Silvio Garcia	100.00	50.00	30.00
(47)	Lloyd Gearhart (Reverse image.)	100.00	50.00	30.00
(48)	Lloyd Gearhart (Corrected)	100.00	50.00	30.00
(49)	(Al) Gerheauser	100.00	50.00	30.00
(50)	Albert Gionfrido (Gionfriddo)	125.00	65.00	35.00
(51)	Leonardo Goicochea	100.00	50.00	30.00
(52)	Enrique Gonzalez	100.00	50.00	30.00
(53)	Hiram Gonzalez	100.00	50.00	30.00
(54)	Miguel Angel Gonzalez	125.00	65.00	35.00
(55)	Fermin Guerra	100.00	50.00	30.00
(56)	Wes Hamner	100.00	50.00	30.00
(57)	Eugene Handley	100.00	50.00	30.00
(58)	Rollie Hemsley	100.00	50.00	30.00
(59)	Salvador Hernandez	100.00	50.00	30.00
(60)	Clarence Hicks	100.00	50.00	30.00
(61)	Manuel "Chino" Hidalgo	100.00	50.00	30.00
(62)	Bob Hooper	100.00	50.00	30.00
(63)	Amado Ibanez	100.00	50.00	30.00
(64)	Don Lenhardt	100.00	50.00	30.00

(65)	Vicente Lopez	100.00	50.00	30.00
(66)	Raul Lopez	100.00	50.00	30.00
(67)	"Tony" Lorenzo	100.00	50.00	30.00
(68)	Adolfo Luque	150.00	75.00	45.00
(69)	John Bill Maldovan	100.00	50.00	30.00
(70)	Max Manning	250.00	125.00	75.00
(71)	Conrado Marrero	125.00	65.00	35.00
(72)	Rogelio "Limonar" Martinez (Pitching)	100.00	50.00	30.00
(73)	Rogelio "Limonar" Martinez (Portrait)	100.00	50.00	30.00
(74)	Agapito Mayor	100.00	50.00	30.00
(75)	Lester McCrabb	100.00	50.00	30.00
(76)	Guillermo "Willy" Miranda	125.00	65.00	35.00
(77)	Rene Monteagudo	100.00	50.00	30.00
(78)	Julio "Jiqui" Moreno	100.00	50.00	30.00
(79)	Ernesto Morrilla	100.00	50.00	30.00
(80)	Howie Moss	100.00	50.00	30.00
(81)	Rafael Sam Noble	100.00	50.00	30.00
(82)	Regino Otero	100.00	50.00	30.00
(83)	Oliverio Ortiz	100.00	50.00	30.00
(84)	Roberto Ortiz (Batting)	100.00	50.00	30.00
(85)	Roberto Ortiz (Portrait)	100.00	50.00	30.00
(86)	Pedro Pages	100.00	50.00	30.00
(87)	Leonard Pearson	250.00	125.00	75.00
(88)	Eddie Pellagrin (Pellagrini)	100.00	50.00	30.00
(89)	Conrado Perez	100.00	50.00	30.00
(90)	Damon Phillips	100.00	50.00	30.00
(91)	Jose "Pototo" Piloto	100.00	50.00	30.00
(92)	William Powell	100.00	50.00	30.00
(93)	Al Prendergast	100.00	50.00	30.00
(94)	Napoleon Reyes (Holding bat.)	100.00	50.00	30.00
(95)	Napoleon Reyes (No bat.)	100.00	50.00	30.00
(96)	Donald Richmond	100.00	50.00	30.00
(97)	Hector Rodriguez	100.00	50.00	30.00
(98)	Oscar Rodriguez	100.00	50.00	30.00
(99)	Julio Rojo	100.00	50.00	30.00
(100)	Octavio Rubert	100.00	50.00	30.00
(101)	Arturo Seijas	100.00	50.00	30.00
(102)	Raymond Shore (Arms crossed.)	100.00	50.00	30.00
(103)	Raymond Shore (Pose unrecorded.)	100.00	50.00	30.00
(104)	Ford Smith	100.00	50.00	30.00
(105)	Rene Solis	100.00	50.00	30.00
(106)	Roberto Fernandez Tapanes	100.00	50.00	30.00
(107)	Don Thompson	100.00	50.00	30.00
(108)	Gilberto Torres	100.00	50.00	30.00
(109)	Quincy Trouppe	150.00	75.00	45.00
(110)	Christian Van Cuyk	100.00	50.00	30.00
(111)	John Van Cuyk	100.00	50.00	30.00
(112)	Ben Wade	100.00	50.00	30.00
(113)	Archie Wilson	100.00	50.00	30.00
(114)	Edward Wright	100.00	50.00	30.00
(115)	Adrian Zabala	100.00	50.00	30.00

1970 Action Cartridge

This set of boxes with baseball players' pictures on them was issued by Action Films Inc. of Mountain View, Calif., in 1970-71. The boxes, measuring 2-5/8" x 6" x 1" deep, contained 8mm film cartridges of various professional athletes demonstrating playing tips. The movie series include 12 baseball players. (Other sports represented were football, golf, tennis, hockey and skiing, a total of 40, in all). Boxes feature color player portraits inside an oval and include a facsimile autograph. The values listed are for complete boxes or player panels, without the movie cartridge.

		NM	E	VG
	Complete Set (12):	275.00	135.00	85.00
	Common Player:	9.00	4.50	2.75
	Box w/Cartridge: 2X			
	Viewer:	60.00	30.00	20.00
1	Tom Seaver	40.00	20.00	12.00
2	Dave McNally	9.00	4.50	2.75
3	Bill Freehan	9.00	4.50	2.75
4	Willie McCovey	25.00	12.50	7.50
5	Glenn Beckert, Don Kessinger	9.00	4.50	2.75
6	Brooks Robinson	30.00	15.00	9.00
7	Hank Aaron	60.00	30.00	18.00
8	Reggie Jackson	45.00	22.50	13.50
9	Pete Rose	50.00	25.00	15.00
10	Lou Brock	25.00	12.50	7.50
11	Willie Davis	9.00	4.50	2.75
12	Rod Carew	25.00	12.50	7.50

1933-1934 Adams Hat Stores

In the early 1930s a men's haberdasher issued a series of colorized 8" x 10" portrait photos of baseball players and other celebrities dressed in suit-and-tie and wearing a hat. Above a facsimile autograph on front is a testimonial for Adams Hats. Backs are stamped, "Property of Adams Hat Stores, Inc." The location of the issuing store or stores in unknown. Only the ballplayers are listed here.

		NM	E	VG
	Complete Set (3):	1,750	875.00	525.00
	Common Player:	600.00	300.00	180.00
(1)	Carl Hubbell	600.00	300.00	180.00
(2)	Lefty Gomez	600.00	300.00	180.00
(3)	John McGraw	600.00	300.00	180.00

1913 A Fan For A Fan

These cardboard novelties were produced by the American Tobacco Co. as a premium with the purchase of a 5-cent bag of Bull Durham tobacco. About 7-1/4" in diameter, the bursting baseball and portrait are printed in color with a facsimile autograph. The handle is about 5" long. The back has only a printed baseball's stitching design. The known fans are listed here alphabetically. Modern counterfeits are known. They usually lack the baseball "stitching" on back and have a slot in the cardboard for the stick.

		NM	E	VG
	Complete Set (5):	30,000	16,000	9,750
	Common Player:	2,400	1,200	725.00
(1)	Frank Baker	4,500	2,250	1,350
(2)	Hal Chase	3,600	1,800	1,100
(3)	Ty Cobb	15,000	7,500	4,500
(4)	Larry Doyle	2,400	1,200	725.00
(5)	Christy Mathewson	5,500	2,750	1,650

1939 African Tobacco

The unlikely venue of the "other" U.S.A. (Union of South Africa) is the provenance of this rare Babe Ruth card. The African Tobacco Co. issued a set of 100 cards in a series titled "The World of Sport." The cards were issued in both a large (2-1/4" x 3-1/4") and small (1-3/4" x 2-1/2") format. Fronts have a black-and-white photo of Ruth, with a white border all around. Backs are printed in both English and Afrikaner.

		NM	E	VG
34	Babe Ruth (Large)	1,250	625.00	375.00
34	Babe Ruth (Small)	1,250	625.00	375.00

1924-1925 Aguilitas Segundas

This set is known to collectors as Aguilitas Segundas for the top line of the ad on back. In reality, this second series cigarette card issue was issued several years before the Aguilitas first series counterpart. About 1-1/2" x 2-3/8", the cards have round black-and-white player portrait photos in a debossed rectangular area on glossy stock. Beneath the photo is a player name or nickname, with "BASE BALL" below. The ballplayers are a subset of a 900-card issue which included movie and stage stars, soccer players, boxers and other subjects. All baseball players are known within the num erical range of 841 through 899, though only four cards are known above #880, and none between #880-895. The known ballplayers comprise 44, many of whom were stars of the Negro Leagues, including several Hall of Famers and some who appear on no other career-contemporary cards. Cards are checklisted with the name as shown on the card, further identification, where necessary, is listed parenthetically. Many surviving specimens show evidence of having been glued into an album which largely accounts for their survival in the area's hot, humid climate. Examples are rarely seen in condition approaching Excellent.

		EX	VG
	Common Player:	125.00	75.00
841	(Pablo "Champion") Mesa	125.00	75.00
842	A. (Armando) Marsans	125.00	75.00
843	C. (Cristobal) Torriente	4,500	2,700
844	Merito Acosta	125.00	75.00
845	Cheo Ramos	125.00	75.00
846	Joe (John Henry "Pop" Lloyd	7,500	4,500
847	(Herman Matias) Rios	125.00	75.00
848	(Lucas) Boada	125.00	75.00
849	(Jose) Mendez	3,750	2,250
850	(Valentin) Dreke	175.00	100.00
851	(Eugenio) Morin	125.00	75.00
852	Mayari (Esteban "Mayari" Montalvo)	125.00	75.00
853	(Valentin) Dreke	175.00	105.00
854	(Julio) Rojo	125.00	75.00
855	(Rafael) Almeida	125.00	75.00
856	(Emilio) Palmero	125.00	75.00
857	(Adolfo) Luque	250.00	150.00
858	(Isidro) Fabre	125.00	75.00
859	(Manuel) Cueto	125.00	75.00
860	Dibu (Pedro Dibut)	125.00	75.00
861	Cheo Ramos	125.00	75.00
862	(Jesse) Hubbard	375.00	225.00

863	Kakin (Gonzalez)	125.00	75.00
864	(Jose Maria) Fernandez	125.00	75.00
865	(Snake) Henry	225.00	135.00
866	Cruje (Ernie Krueger)	225.00	135.00
867	(Manuel) Parrado	125.00	75.00
868	(Chuck) Dressen	125.00	75.00
869	(Oscar) Charleston	7,500	4,500
870	Sam (John Henry "Pop") Lloyd	7,500	4,500
871	Mc. Key (Raleigh "Biz" Mackey)	3,750	2,250
872	P. (Eusebio "Papo") Gonzalez	125.00	75.00
873	(Clint) Thomas	300.00	180.00
874	(Dobie) Moore	300.00	180.00
875	(Frank) Duncan	300.00	180.00
876	O. (Oscar) Rodriguez	125.00	75.00
877	Lopito (Jose "Lopito" Lopez)	125.00	75.00
878	E. (Eustaquio "Bombin") Pedroso	500.00	300.00
879	(Dick) Lundy	1,375	825.00
880	Sirike (Valentin "Sirique" Gonzalez)	120.00	65.00
895	(Oscar) Tuero	120.00	65.00
897	(Alejandro) Oms	600.00	360.00
898	Peter (Jesse Petty)	110.00	65.00
899	(Danny) Clark	120.00	65.00

1926-1927 Aguilitas

 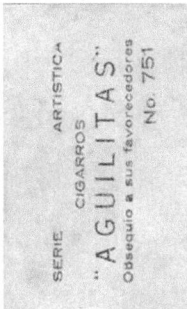

Uniforms worn by some of the players indicate this set was produced after the related series known as "Segundas," or Second Series. The baseball players - all Cuban nationals - are among 100 athletes (including soccer players and boxers) in a 900-card multi-subject set issued in packs of Aguilitas cigarettes. The cards are printed in black-and-white on glossy stock. On front is a large square portrait or action pose. In the bottom border is "BASE-BALL" with the player name and position below. Names as shown on the cards are presented in this checklist, with further identification as necessary provided parenthetically. Several of the cards are duplicated in the series with different card numbers. Like most contemporary Latin American issues, surviving examples are seldom found in high-grade and often with evidence of having been in an album.

		E	VG
	Common Player:	85.00	50.00
751	Cheo Hernandez	85.00	50.00
752	(Jose Maria) Fernandez	100.00	60.00
756	R. (Ricardo) Torres	85.00	50.00
759	Jacinto Calvo	85.00	50.00
761	E. (Emilio) Palmero	85.00	50.00
763	Champion (Pablo) Mesa	125.00	75.00
769	C. (Carlos) Zarza	85.00	50.00
771	Fernando Rios	85.00	50.00
772	J. (Joseito) Rodriguez	85.00	50.00
774	(Juanelo) Mirabal (Same as #824.)	125.00	75.00
776	L. (Lalo) Rodriguez	85.00	50.00
777	A. (Adolfo) Luque	175.00	100.00
778	Alejandro Oms	1,250	750.00
779	(Armando) Marsans (Same as #829.)	185.00	110.00
782a	A. (Alfredo) Cabrera	85.00	50.00
782b	Daniel Blanco (Same as #832.)	85.00	50.00
787	B. (Bartolo) Portuando	125.00	75.00
791	A. (Agustin) Navarro	85.00	50.00
796	R. (Raphael "Busta") Quintana	85.00	50.00
797	(Roberto) Puig (Same as #847.)	85.00	50.00
817	(Oscar) Levis	85.00	50.00
819	Raul Atan	85.00	50.00
821	(Jose) Pepin Perez	85.00	50.00
822	(Isidro) Fabre	100.00	60.00
823	(Bienvenido "Hooks") Jimenez	125.00	75.00
824	(Juanelo) Mirabal (Same as #774.)	125.00	75.00
825	Tomas Calvo	85.00	50.00
826	(Pelayo) Chacon	125.00	75.00
829	(Armando) Marsans (Same as #779.)	185.00	110.00
832	Daniel Blanco (Same as #782.)	85.00	50.00
836	(Valentin) Dreke	125.00	75.00

838	(Jose) Echarri	85.00	50.00
839	Miguel Angel (Gonzalez)	150.00	90.00
841	(Oscar) Estrada	150.00	90.00
846	Acosta (Jose Acosta)	150.00	90.00
847	(Roberto) Puig (Same as #797.)	85.00	50.00
849	(Cesar) Alvarez	85.00	50.00

1954 Alaga Syrup Willie Mays Postcard

The year of issue on this one-card set is approximate. In 3-1/4" x 5-1/2" format the black-and-white card has a borderless portrait on front with a facsimile autograph. Back has an ad for Alaga Syrup, along with standard postcard elements.

		NM	E	VG
(1)	Willie Mays	800.00	400.00	240.00

1944-45 Albertype Hall of Fame Plaque Postcards - Type 1

 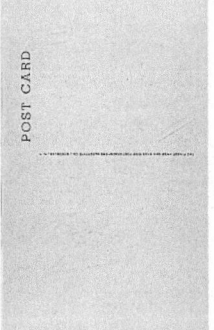

From 1944-1952, Albertype was the official producer of the Baseball Hall of Fame's postcards available for public sale. The 3-1/2" x 5-1/2" black-and-white cards depict the bronze plaque of each inductee. Fronts have a white border. Postcard-style backs have a bit of player data and identification of the specific producer. In the first type of Albertype plaque postcards, issued 1944-45, the line of type beneath the plaque photo has an abbreviation for New York. Later Albertypes spelled out the state name. The unnumbered cards are checklisted here alphabetically.

		NM	E	VG
	Complete Set (38):	800.00	400.00	240.00
	Common Player:	20.00	10.00	6.00
(1)	G.C. Alexander	25.00	12.50	7.50
(2)	Adrian Anson	20.00	10.00	6.00
(3)	Roger Bresnahan	20.00	10.00	6.00
(4)	Dan Brouthers	20.00	10.00	6.00
(5)	Morgan Bulkeley	20.00	10.00	6.00
(6)	Alexander Cartwright	20.00	10.00	6.00
(7)	Henry Chadwick	20.00	10.00	6.00
(8)	Fred Clarke	20.00	10.00	6.00
(9)	Ty Cobb	40.00	20.00	12.00
(10)	Eddie Collins	20.00	10.00	6.00
(11)	Jimmy Collins	20.00	10.00	6.00
(12)	Charles A. Comiskey	20.00	10.00	6.00
(13)	Candy Cummings	20.00	10.00	6.00
(14)	Ed Delahanty	20.00	10.00	6.00
(15)	Hugh Duffy	20.00	10.00	6.00
(16)	Buck Ewing	20.00	10.00	6.00
(17)	Lou Gehrig	50.00	25.00	15.00
(18)	Rogers Hornsby	20.00	10.00	6.00
(19)	Hughie Jennings	20.00	10.00	6.00
(20)	Ban Johnson	20.00	10.00	6.00
(21)	Walter Johnson	30.00	15.00	9.00
(22)	Willie Keeler	20.00	10.00	6.00
(23)	King Kelly	20.00	10.00	6.00
(24)	Nap Lajoie	20.00	10.00	6.00

(25)	Kenesaw Landis	20.00	10.00	6.00
(26)	Connie Mack	20.00	10.00	6.00
(27)	Christy Mathewson	30.00	15.00	9.00
(28)	John McGraw	20.00	10.00	6.00
(29)	Jim O'Rourke	20.00	10.00	6.00
(30)	Chas. Radbourn	20.00	10.00	6.00
(31)	Wilbert Robinson	20.00	10.00	6.00
(32)	Babe Ruth	65.00	32.00	19.50
(33)	George Sisler	20.00	10.00	6.00
(34)	Al Spalding	20.00	10.00	6.00
(35)	Tris Speaker	20.00	10.00	6.00
(36)	Honus Wagner	30.00	15.00	9.00
(37)	George Wright	20.00	10.00	6.00
(38)	Cy Young	30.00	15.00	9.00

1946-52 Albertype Hall of Fame Plaque Postcards - Type 2

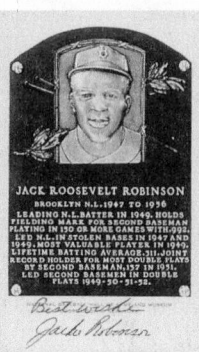

From 1944-1952, Albertype was the official producer of the Baseball Hall of Fame's postcards available for public sale. The 3-1/2" x 5-1/2" black-and-white cards depict the bronze plaque of each inductee. Fronts have a white border. Postcard-style backs have a bit of biographical data and identification of the specific issuer. In the second series of Albertype plaque postcards, issued 1946-52, the line of type beneath the plaque photo spells out the New York state name. The unnumbered cards are checklisted here alphabetically. Those cards found only in this series are noted with an asterisk. Because the Foxx and Ott cards were first issued in 1951, and the Paul Waner, Heilmann and 1864 Knickerbocker Nine in 1952, they are scarcer than those issued earlier.

		NM	E	VG
	Complete Set (63):	1,325	675.00	425.00
	Common Player:	20.00	10.00	6.00
(1)	G.C. Alexander	25.00	12.50	7.50
(2)	Adrian Anson	20.00	10.00	6.00
(3)	Roger Bresnahan	20.00	10.00	6.00
(4)	Dan Brouthers	20.00	10.00	6.00
(5)	Mordecai Brown (*)	25.00	12.50	7.50
(6)	Morgan Bulkeley	20.00	10.00	6.00
(7)	Jesse Burkett (*)	25.00	12.50	7.50
(8)	Alexander Cartwright	20.00	10.00	6.00
(9)	Henry Chadwick	20.00	10.00	6.00
(10)	Frank Chance (*)	25.00	12.50	7.50
(11)	Jack Chesbro (*)	25.00	12.50	7.50
(12)	Fred Clarke	20.00	10.00	6.00
(13)	Ty Cobb	40.00	20.00	12.00
(14)	Mickey Cochrane (*)	25.00	12.50	7.50
(15)	Eddie Collins	20.00	10.00	6.00
(16)	Jimmy Collins	20.00	10.00	6.00
(17)	Charles A. Comiskey	20.00	10.00	6.00
(18)	Candy Cummings	20.00	10.00	6.00
(19)	Ed Delahanty	20.00	10.00	6.00
(20)	Hugh Duffy	20.00	10.00	6.00
(21)	Johnny Evers (*)	25.00	12.50	7.50
(22)	Buck Ewing	20.00	10.00	6.00
(23)	James E. (Jimmy) Foxx (*)	45.00	22.00	13.50
(24)	Frankie Frisch (*)	25.00	12.50	7.50
(25)	Lou Gehrig	50.00	25.00	15.00
(26)	Charlie Gehringer (*)	25.00	12.50	7.50
(27)	Clark Griffith (*)	25.00	12.50	7.50
(28)	Lefty Grove (*)	25.00	12.50	7.50
(29)	Harry Heilmann (*)	40.00	20.00	12.00
(30)	Rogers Hornsby	20.00	10.00	6.00
(31)	Carl Hubbell (*)	25.00	12.50	7.50
(32)	Hughie Jennings	20.00	10.00	6.00
(33)	Ban Johnson	20.00	10.00	6.00
(34)	Walter Johnson	30.00	15.00	9.00
(35)	Willie Keeler	20.00	10.00	6.00
(36)	King Kelly	20.00	10.00	6.00
(37)	Nap Lajoie	20.00	10.00	6.00
(38)	Kenesaw Landis	20.00	10.00	6.00
(39)	Connie Mack	20.00	10.00	6.00
(40)	Christy Mathewson	30.00	15.00	9.00
(41)	Tommy McCarthy (*)	25.00	12.50	7.50
(62)	Joe McGinnity (*)	25.00	12.50	7.50
(43)	John McGraw	20.00	10.00	6.00

		NM	E	VG
(44)	Kid Nichols (*)	25.00	12.50	7.50
(45)	Jim O'Rourke	20.00	10.00	6.00
(46)	Mel Ott (*)	35.00	17.50	10.50
(47)	Herb Pennock (*)	25.00	12.50	7.50
(48)	Ed Plank (*)	25.00	12.50	7.50
(49)	Chas. Radbourn	20.00	10.00	6.00
(50)	Wilbert Robinson	20.00	10.00	6.00
(51)	Babe Ruth	65.00	32.00	19.50
(52)	George Sisler	20.00	10.00	6.00
(53)	Al Spalding	20.00	10.00	6.00
(54)	Tris Speaker	20.00	10.00	6.00
(55)	Joe Tinker (*)	25.00	12.50	7.50
(56)	Pie Traynor (*)	25.00	12.50	7.50
(57)	Rube Waddell (*)	25.00	12.50	7.50
(58)	Honus Wagner	30.00	15.00	9.00
(59)	Ed Walsh (*)	25.00	12.50	7.50
(60)	Paul Waner (*)	35.00	17.50	10.50
(61)	George Wright	20.00	10.00	6.00
(62)	Cy Young	30.00	15.00	9.00
(63)	Knickerbocker Nine 1864	35.00	17.50	10.50

1970 Carl Aldana Orioles

Belanger

Little is known about the distribution or origin of this 12-card regional set, which was available in 1970 in the Baltimore area. Measuring 3-1/4" x 2-1/8", the unnumbered cards picture members of the Baltimore Orioles and include two poses of Brooks Robinson. The cards feature line drawings of the players surrounded by a plain border. The player's last name appears below the portrait sketch. The set was named after Carl Aldana, who supplied the artwork for the cards.

		NM	E	VG
Complete Set (12):		125.00	65.00	40.00
Common Player:		12.00	6.00	3.50
(1)	Mark Belanger	12.00	6.00	3.50
(2)	Paul Blair	12.00	6.00	3.50
(3)	Mike Cuellar	12.00	6.00	3.50
(4)	Ellie Hendricks	12.00	6.00	3.50
(5)	Dave Johnson	12.00	6.00	3.50
(6)	Dave McNally	12.00	6.00	3.50
(7)	Jim Palmer	45.00	22.50	13.50
(8)	Boog Powell	25.00	12.50	7.50
(9)	Brooks Robinson (Diving - face showing.)	40.00	20.00	12.00
(10)	Brooks Robinson (Diving - back showing.)	40.00	20.00	12.00
(11)	Frank Robinson	60.00	30.00	18.00
(12)	Earl Weaver	15.00	7.50	4.50

1971 Carl Aldana

Lang

Devoid of any indication of when produced or by whom, this set of obscure players of the 1940s and 1950s was a collectors' issue from Carl Aldana circa 1971. The cards are blank-backed, about 2-1/8" x 2-3/4". Fronts have a red background with an artwork player portrait in blue. The player's last name and card number are in dark blue, his first name in white. For a few of the players, this is their only known baseball card.

		NM	E	VG
Complete Set (16):		125.00	60.00	37.50
Common Player:		10.00	5.00	3.00
1	Wally Hood	10.00	5.00	3.00
2	Jim Westlake	10.00	5.00	3.00
3	Stan McWilliams	10.00	5.00	3.00
4	Les Fleming	10.00	5.00	3.00
5	John Ritchey	10.00	5.00	3.00
6	Steve Nagy	10.00	5.00	3.00
7	Ken Gables	10.00	5.00	3.00
8	Maurice Fisher	10.00	5.00	3.00
9	Don Lang	10.00	5.00	3.00
10	Harry Malmburg (Malmberg)	10.00	5.00	3.00
11	Jack Conway	10.00	5.00	3.00
12	Don White	10.00	5.00	3.00
13	Dick Lajeskie	10.00	5.00	3.00
14	Walt Judnich	10.00	5.00	3.00
15	Joe Kirrene	10.00	5.00	3.00
16	Ed Sauer	10.00	5.00	3.00

1940s Alerta Antonio Alcalde Premium Pictures

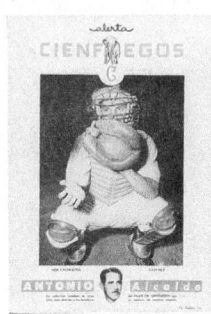

There are still gaps in the hobby's knowledge of this late-1940s/early-1950s Cuban issue. Evidently a premium used in a contest conducted by a newspaper or sports periodical, these pictures are printed on semi-gloss paper in an 8" x 11" format. Featured on front are black-and-white posed action or portrait photos. The team name and symbol are above and a portrait, presumably of Antonio, is at bottom. Pictures are highlighted by color graphics: blue for Almendares, green for Cienfuegos, red for Havana and orange for Marianao. Backs are blank, but are sometimes seen with a round rubber-stamped "Alerta" logo or red boxed "ANTONIO, ALCALDE." The unnumbered pictures are listed here alphabetically within team. The pictures include many American players and those who spent time in the major leagues.

		NM	E	VG
Complete Set (72):		2,000	1,000	400.00
Common Player:		30.00	15.00	6.00
ALMENDARES SCORPIONS				
(1)	Bill Antonello	35.00	17.50	7.00
(2)	Francisco Campos	35.00	17.50	7.00
(3)	Avelino Canizares	30.00	15.00	6.00
(4)	Yiqui De Souza	30.00	15.00	6.00
(5)	Rodolfo Fernandez	30.00	15.00	6.00
(6)	Andres Fleitas	30.00	15.00	6.00
(7)	Al Gionfriddo	35.00	17.50	7.00
(8)	Fermin Guerra	35.00	17.50	7.00
(9)	Bob Hooper	35.00	17.50	7.00
(10)	Vincente Lopez	30.00	15.00	6.00
(11)	Conrado Marrero	35.00	17.50	7.00
(12)	Agapito Mayor	30.00	15.00	6.00
(13)	Willy Miranda	35.00	17.50	7.00
(14)	Rene Monteagudo	35.00	17.50	7.00
(15)	Roberto Ortiz	35.00	17.50	7.00
(16)	Hector Rodriguez	35.00	17.50	7.00
(17)	Octavio Rubert	30.00	15.00	6.00
(18)	Rene Solis	30.00	15.00	6.00
CIENFUEGOS ELEPHANTS				
(1)	Bob Addis	35.00	17.50	7.00
(2)	Sam Calderone	35.00	17.50	7.00
(3)	Jack Cassini	35.00	17.50	7.00
(4)	Alejandro Crespo	35.00	17.50	7.00
(5)	Paul (Al) Epperly	35.00	17.50	7.00
(6)	Thomas Fine	35.00	17.50	7.00
(7)	Pedro Formental (Formenthal)	30.00	15.00	6.00
(8)	Francisco Gallardo	30.00	15.00	6.00
(9)	Lloyd Gearhart	35.00	17.50	7.00
(10)	Leonardo Goicochea	30.00	15.00	6.00
(11)	Salvador Hernandez	35.00	17.50	7.00
(12)	Clarence (Buddy) Hicks	35.00	17.50	7.00
(13)	Max Manning	45.00	22.00	9.00
(14)	San (Ray) Noble	35.00	17.50	7.00
(15)	Regino Otero	35.00	17.50	7.00
(16)	Pedro Pages	30.00	15.00	6.00
(17)	Napoleon Reyes	35.00	17.50	7.00
(18)	Ernie Shore	35.00	17.50	7.00

		NM	E	VG
(19)	Adrian Zabala	35.00	17.50	7.00
HAVANA LIONS				
(1)	Ferrell Anderson	35.00	17.50	7.00
(2)	Wess Bailey	30.00	15.00	6.00
(3)	Vic Barnhart	35.00	17.50	7.00
(4)	Herberto Blanco	30.00	15.00	6.00
(5)	Emilio Cabrera	30.00	15.00	6.00
(6)	Pedro Formental (Formenthal)	30.00	15.00	6.00
(7)	Al Gerheauser	35.00	17.50	7.00
(8)	Miguel Angel Gonzalez	60.00	30.00	12.00
(9)	Chino Hidalgo	30.00	15.00	6.00
(10)	Jimmy Lenhart	30.00	15.00	6.00
(11)	Adolfo Luque	60.00	30.00	12.00
(12)	Max Manning	45.00	22.50	9.00
(13)	Julio Moreno	35.00	17.50	7.00
(14)	Lenox Pearson	45.00	22.50	9.00
(15)	Don Richmond	35.00	17.50	7.00
(16)	John Ford Smith	30.00	15.00	6.00
(17)	Don Thompson	35.00	17.50	7.00
(18)	Gilberto Torres	35.00	17.50	7.00
MARIANAO TIGERS				
(1)	Mario Arencibia	30.00	15.00	6.00
(2)	Carlos Blanco	30.00	15.00	6.00
(3)	Chiquitin Cabbera	30.00	15.00	6.00
(4)	Sandalio Consuegra	35.00	17.50	7.00
(5)	Reinaldo Cordeiro	30.00	15.00	6.00
(6)	Talua (Ray) Dandridge	350.00	175.00	75.00
(7)	Mario Diaz	30.00	15.00	6.00
(8)	Claro Duany	35.00	17.50	7.00
(9)	Roberto Estalella	35.00	17.50	7.00
(10)	Chicuelo Garcia	30.00	15.00	6.00
(11)	Wesley Hamner	35.00	17.50	7.00
(12)	Rollie Hemsley	35.00	17.50	7.00
(13)	Amado Ibanez	30.00	15.00	6.00
(14)	Limonar (Rogelio) Martinez	35.00	17.50	7.00
(15)	Don Phillips	30.00	15.00	6.00
(16)	Bartholomew (Jim) Prendergast	35.00	17.50	7.00
(17)	John (Quincy) Trouppe	100.00	50.00	30.00

1904 Allegheny Card Co.

By definition the rarest card issue of the early 20th Century is this baseball game set featuring only National League players. It is thought that the sole known boxed set was produced as a prototype and never actually reached distribution. The issue contains 104 player cards and a "Ball Counter" card for each team. Cards are in playing-card format, about 2-1/2" x 3-1/2" with rounded corners. Backs are printed in red with baseball equipment pictured. Fronts are printed in blue with a circular player portrait at center. Team name is at top, with player's last name (occasionally with initials and occasionally misspelled) beneath. The unique boxed set was discovered in the late 1980s. It was sold at auction in 1991 for $26,400, and again in 1995 for $11,000, after which it was broken up for individual card sales. The checklist is presented here in alphabetical order. All cards appear to have been hand-cut.

		NM	E	VG
Common Player:		1,000	500.00	300.00
(1)	Ed Abbaticchio	1,000	500.00	300.00
(2)	Harry Aubrey	1,000	500.00	300.00
(3)	Charlie Babb	1,000	500.00	300.00
(4)	George Barclay	1,000	500.00	300.00
(5)	Shad Barry	1,000	500.00	300.00
(6)	Bill Beagen ((Bergen))	1,000	500.00	300.00
(7)	Ginger Beaumont	1,000	500.00	300.00
(8)	Jake Beckley	2,500	875.00	525.00
(9)	Frank Bowerman	1,000	500.00	300.00
(10)	Dave Brain	1,000	500.00	300.00
(11)	Kitty Bransfield	1,000	500.00	300.00
(12)	Roger Bresnahan	2,500	875.00	525.00
(13)	Mordecai Brown	2,500	875.00	525.00
(14)	George Browne	1,000	500.00	300.00
(15)	Al Buckenberger	1,000	500.00	300.00
(16)	Jimmy Burke	1,000	500.00	300.00
(17)	Fred Carisch	1,000	500.00	300.00
(18)	Pat Carney	1,000	500.00	300.00

(19)	Doc Casey	1,000	500.00	300.00
(20)	Frank Chance	3,500	1,750	1,050
(21)	Fred Clarke	2,500	875.00	525.00
(22)	Dick Cooley	1,000	500.00	300.00
(23)	Bill Dahlen	1,750	500.00	300.00
(24)	Tom Daly	1,000	500.00	300.00
(25)	Charlie Dexter	1,000	500.00	300.00
(26)	Johnny Dobbs	1,000	500.00	300.00
(27)	Mike Donlin	1,000	500.00	300.00
(28)	Patsy Donovan	1,000	500.00	300.00
(29)	Red Dooin	1,000	500.00	300.00
(30)	Klondike Douglas (Douglass)	1,000	500.00	300.00
(31)	Jack Doyle	1,000	500.00	300.00
(32)	Bill Duggleby	1,000	500.00	300.00
(33)	Jack Dunn	1,000	500.00	270.00
(34)	Johnny Evers	3,000	875.00	525.00
(35)	John Farrel (Farrell)	1,000	500.00	300.00
(36)	Tim Flood	1,000	500.00	300.00
(37)	Chick Fraser	1,000	500.00	300.00
(38)	Ned Garver	1,000	500.00	300.00
(39)	Doc Gessler	1,000	500.00	300.00
(40)	Billy Gilbert	1,000	500.00	300.00
(41)	Kid Gleason	2,500	500.00	300.00
(42)	Ed Greminger (Gremminger)	1,000	500.00	300.00
(43)	Jim Hackett	1,000	500.00	300.00
(44)	Noodles Hahn	1,000	500.00	300.00
(45)	Ed. Hanlon	2,500	875.00	525.00
(46)	Jack Harper	1,000	500.00	300.00
(47)	Rudy Hulswitt	1,000	500.00	300.00
(48)	Fred Jacklitsch	1,000	500.00	300.00
(49)	Davy Jones	1,000	500.00	300.00
(50)	Oscar Jones	1,000	500.00	300.00
(51)	Bill Keister	1,000	500.00	300.00
(52)	Joe Kelley	2,500	875.00	525.00
(53)	Brickyard Kennedy	1,000	500.00	300.00
(54)	Johnny Kling	1,000	500.00	300.00
(55)	Otto Kruger (Krueger)	1,000	500.00	300.00
(56)	Tommy Leach	1,000	500.00	300.00
(57)	Sam Leever	1,000	500.00	300.00
(58)	Bobby Lowe	1,750	875.00	525.00
(59)	Carl Lundgren	1,000	500.00	300.00
(60)	Christy Mathewson	8,500	4,250	2,550
(61)	Tom McCreery	1,000	500.00	300.00
(62)	Chappie McFarland	1,000	500.00	300.00
(63)	Dan McGann	1,000	500.00	300.00
(64)	Iron Man McGinnity	2,500	875.00	525.00
(65)	John McGraw	2,500	875.00	525.00
(66)	Jock Menefee	1,000	500.00	300.00
(67)	Sam Mertes	1,000	500.00	300.00
(68)	Fred Mitchell	1,000	500.00	300.00
(69)	Pat Moran	1,000	500.00	300.00
(70)	Ed Murphy	1,000	500.00	300.00
(71)	Jack O'Neill	1,000	500.00	300.00
(72)	Mike O'Neill	1,000	500.00	300.00
(73)	Heinie Peitz	1,000	500.00	300.00
(74)	Ed Phelps	1,000	500.00	300.00
(75)	Deacon Phillippe	1,000	500.00	300.00
(76)	Togie Pittinger	1,000	500.00	300.00
(77)	Ed Poole	1,000	500.00	300.00
(78)	Tommy Raub	1,000	500.00	300.00
(79)	Bill Reidy	1,000	500.00	300.00
(80)	Claude Ritchie	1,000	500.00	300.00
(81)	Lew Ritter	1,000	500.00	300.00
(82)	Frank Roth	1,000	500.00	300.00
(83)	Jack Ryan	1,000	500.00	300.00
(84)	Jimmy Scheckard (Sheckard)	1,000	500.00	300.00
(85)	Jimmy Sebring	1,000	500.00	300.00
(86)	Frank Selee	7,500	2,000	1,200
(87)	Cy Seymour	1,000	500.00	300.00
(88)	Harry Smith	1,000	500.00	300.00
(89)	Homer Smoot	1,000	500.00	300.00
(90)	Tully Sparks	1,000	500.00	300.00
(91)	Joe Stanley	1,000	500.00	300.00
(92)	Harry Steinfeldt	1,000	500.00	300.00
(93)	Sammy Strang	1,000	500.00	300.00
(94)	Jack Suthoff (Sutthoff)	1,000	500.00	300.00
(95)	Jack Taylor	1,000	500.00	300.00
(96)	Luther Taylor	1,750	875.00	525.00
(97)	Roy Thomas	1,000	500.00	300.00
(98)	Joe Tinker	1,750	875.00	525.00
(99)	Fred Tinney (Tenney)	1,000	500.00	300.00
(100)	Honus Wagner	12,500	6,250	3,750
(101)	Jack Warner	1,000	500.00	300.00
(102)	Jake Weimer	1,000	500.00	300.00
(103)	Vic Willis	1,750	875.00	525.00
(104)	Harry Wolverton	1,000	500.00	300.00
(105)	Boston Ball Counter	165.00	80.00	50.00
(106)	Brooklyn Ball Counter	165.00	80.00	50.00
(107)	Chicago Ball Counter	165.00	80.00	50.00
(108)	Cincinnati Ball Counter	165.00	80.00	50.00
(109)	New York Ball Counter	165.00	80.00	50.00
(110)	Philadelpia Ball Counter	165.00	80.00	50.00
(111)	Pittsburgh Ball Counter	165.00	80.00	50.00
(112)	St. Louis Ball Counter	165.00	80.00	50.00

1888 Allen & Ginter Girl Baseball Players (N48, N508)

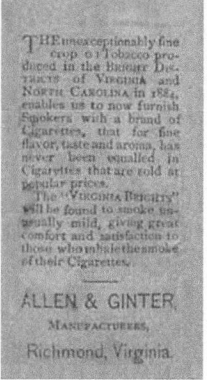

At least three different brands of cigarette advertising can be found on the several different styles of photographic cards depicting women in baseball uniforms. About 1-1/2" x 2-5/8", the cards picture models, rather than real ballplayers. The sepia-toned full-length photos are usually captioned with a position and a number and have a small square or other device advertising a particular brand. Some Dixie- and Virginia Brights-brand cards are known with advertising on back but most cards are blank-backed. As many as 36 different photos are thought to exist.

	NM	E	VG
Ad Backs: 2X			
Common Player	750.00	375.00	225.00

1888 Allen & Ginter World's Champions (N28)

This 50-card set was titled "The World's Champions" and includes 10 baseball players and 40 other sports personalities such as John L. Sullivan and Buffalo Bill Cody. The approximately 1-1/2" x 2-3/4" color cards were inserted in boxes of Allen & Ginter cigarettes. The card fronts are color lithographs on white card stock, and are considered among the most attractive cards ever produced. All card backs have a complete checklist for this unnumbered set, which includes six eventual Hall of Famers.

	NM	E	VG
Complete Set (10):	22,500	11,250	6,750
Common Player:	850.00	400.00	200.00
(1) Adrian C. Anson	6,000	2,500	1,000
(2) Chas. W. Bennett	850.00	400.00	200.00
(3) R.L. Caruthers	850.00	400.00	200.00
(4) John Clarkson	2,750	975.00	450.00
(5) Charles Comiskey	3,750	1,000	475.00
(6) Capt. John Glasscock	850.00	400.00	200.00
(7) Timothy Keefe	2,750	975.00	450.00
(8) Mike Kelly	3,500	1,200	500.00
(9) Joseph Mulvey	850.00	400.00	200.00
(10) John Ward	2,750	975.00	450.00

1888 Allen & Ginter World's Champions (N29)

Building on the success of its first series of tobacco cards, Allen & Ginter issued a second series of "World's Champions" in 1888. Once again, 50 of these approximately 1-1/2" x 2-3/4" color cards were produced, in virtually the same format. Only six baseball players are included in this set. The most obvious difference from the first series cards is the absence of the Allen & Ginter name on the card fronts.

	NM	E	VG
Complete Set (6):	9,350	4,675	2,750
Common Player:	1,000	425.00	200.00
(1) Wm. Ewing	3,500	1,500	700.00
(2) Jas. H. Fogarty (Middle initial actually G.)	1,000	425.00	200.00
(3) Charles H. Getzin (Getzien)	1,000	425.00	200.00
(4) Geo. F. Miller	1,000	425.00	200.00
(5) John Morrell (Morrill)	1,150	475.00	225.00
(6) James Ryan	1,000	425.00	200.00

1888 Allen & Ginter World's Champions (N43)

Presumably issued in a larger-than-standard cigarette package, the 50 cards designated N43 in the "American Card Catalog" are enhanced versions of the Allen & Ginter World's Champions (N29) series of 1888. As with the N29 set, six of the athletes in N43 are baseball players. The larger cards measure about 3-1/4" x 2-7/8" compared to the 1-1/4" x 2-3/4" size of the N29s. The larger format allows for the use of baseball-related color lithography to the right and left of the central player portrait. Like the N29 cards, backs of the N43 A&Gs present the entire "Series Two" checklist along with advertising of the Richmond tobacco company. Only the baseball players are cataloged here.

	NM	E	VG
Complete Set (6):	26,400	14,000	7,700
Common Player:	3,850	1,500	1,000
(1) Wm. Ewing	8,500	3,825	2,375
(2) Jas. H. Fogarty (Middle initial actually G.)	3,850	1,500	1,000
(3) Charles H. Getzin (Getzien)	3,850	1,500	1,000
(4) Geo. F. Miller	3,850	1,500	1,000
(5) John Morrell (Morrill)	4,000	1,800	1,125
(6) James Ryan	3,850	1,500	1,000

1888 Allen & Ginter World's Champions Album (A16)

By redeeming 50 of the coupons found in boxes of A&G cigarettes, a lithographed album could be obtained in which to house the 50 cards of the World's Champions, Series 1 (N28). About 6" x 8", the album features an ornately decorated cover reproducing the cards of the cards of the day's top athletes, John L. Sullivan and Monte Ward. The back cover is blank. Inside, secured by means of string ties at three places, are 12 dual-sided color pages on which to glue the cards in the series. The album had its own designation in the American Card Catalog, A16.

	NM	E	VG
World's Champions Album (A16)	4,000	2,000	1,200

1888 Allen & Ginter World's Champions Album (A17)

By redeeming 50 of the coupons found in boxes of A&G cigarettes, a lithographed album could be obtained in which to house the 50 cards of The World's Champions, Series 2 (N29). About 6" x 8", the album features a handsomely decorated cover of a trumpeteer. The back cover is also in color with A&G's pipe-smoking man logo. Inside, secured by means of string ties at three places, are 12 dual-sided color pages on which to glue the cards in the series. The album had its own designation in the American Card Catalog, A16.

	NM	E	VG
World's Champions Album (A17)	4,000	2,000	1,000

1954 All-Star Photo Pack

The method of distribution for this series of 6" x 8-3/4" blank-back, black-and-white player photos is speculative, though it is most likely they were sold in photo packs at concession stands. Photos, mostly posed action shots, are bordered in white and have the player name in a white strip near the bottom.

		NM	E	VG
Complete Set (24):		400.00	200.00	120.00
Common Player:		10.00	5.00	3.00
(1)	Bobby Avila	10.00	5.00	3.00
(2)	Ernie Banks	25.00	12.50	7.50
(3)	Larry "Yogi" Berra	25.00	12.50	7.50
(4)	Ray Boone	10.00	5.00	3.00
(5)	Roy Campanella	25.00	12.50	7.50
(6)	Alvin Dark	10.00	5.00	3.00
(7)	Mike Garcia	10.00	5.00	3.00
(8)	Al Kaline	20.00	10.00	6.00
(9)	Ralph Kiner	15.00	7.50	4.50
(10)	Ted Kluszewski	15.00	7.50	4.50
(11)	Harvey Kuenn	10.00	5.00	3.00
(12)	Mickey Mantle	90.00	45.00	27.50
(13)	Ed Mathews	20.00	10.00	6.00
(14)	Willie Mays	50.00	25.00	15.00
(15)	Orestes Minoso	12.50	6.25	3.75
(16)	Stan Musial	35.00	17.50	10.00
(17)	Don Newcombe	12.50	6.25	3.75
(18)	Allie Reynolds	12.50	6.25	3.75
(19)	Robin Roberts	15.00	7.50	4.50
(20)	Eddie Robinson	10.00	5.00	3.00
(21)	Jackie Robinson	45.00	22.50	13.50
(22)	Al Schoendienst	15.00	7.50	4.50
(23)	Duke Snider	20.00	10.00	6.00
(24)	Ted Williams	80.00	40.00	24.00

1910 All Star Base-Ball

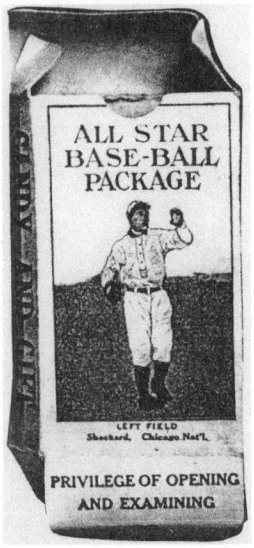

This rare set was issued circa 1910 by candy maker J.H. Dockman & Son. The cards, measuring approximately 1-7/8" x 3-3/8", were printed on the front and back of boxes of candy sold as "All Star Base-Ball Package." There are two players on each box; one on front (with a thumbnail notch at top), the other on back. The cards consist of drawings that bear no resemblance to the player named. In fact, the artwork on these cards crudely reproduces the images from the T3 Turkey Red cabinet series, giving a different player's name to each of the borrowed images. Many are found which were cut from the box immediately below the "PACKAGE" line, while others were cut to the full size of the panel. Values shown here presume the latter format.

		NM	E	VG
Complete Set (24):		50,000	25,000	12,500
Common Player:		2,000	1,200	600.00
(1)	Johnny Bates	2,000	1,200	600.00
(2)	Heinie Beckendorf	2,000	1,200	600.00
(3)	Joe Birmingham	2,000	1,200	600.00
(4)	Roger Bresnahan	4,000	2,500	1,200
(5)	Al Burch	2,000	1,200	600.00
(6)	Donie Bush	2,000	1,200	600.00
(7)	Frank Chance	4,000	2,500	1,200
(8)	Ty Cobb	10,000	5,000	3,000
(9)	Wid Conroy	2,000	1,200	600.00
(10)	Jack Coombs	2,000	1,200	600.00
(11)	George Gibson	2,000	1,200	600.00
(12)	Dick Hoblitzel	2,000	1,200	600.00
(13)	Johnny Kling	2,000	1,200	600.00
(14)	Frank LaPorte	2,000	1,200	600.00
(15)	Ed Lennox	2,000	1,200	600.00
(16)	Connie Mack	4,000	2,500	1,200
(17)	Christy Mathewson	4,500	2,750	1,500
(18)	Matty McIntyre	2,000	1,200	600.00
(19)	Al Schweitzer	2,000	1,200	600.00
(20)	Jimmy Sheckard	2,000	1,200	600.00
(21)	Bill Sweeney	2,000	1,200	600.00
(22)	Terry Turner	2,000	1,200	600.00
(23)	Hans Wagner	9,000	4,500	2,700
(24)	Harry Wolter	2,000	1,200	600.00

1950 All-Star Baseball "Pin-Ups"

This set of ten 7" diameter black-and-white player photos was issued in the form of a booklet, with the individual pictures perforated to be punched out. Each picture has a hole at the top for hanging. The front and back cover of the book are identical and picture Ted Williams, along with a list of the players inside. Backs of each player picture have how-to

tips for playing a specific position, hitting, base stealing, etc. Published by Garden City Publishing Co., Inc., the book carried a cover price of 50 cents. The unnumbered pictures are checklisted here alphabetically.

		NM	E	VG
Complete Book:		1,250	625.00	375.00
Complete Set, Singles (10):		800.00	400.00	240.00
Common Player:		25.00	12.50	7.50
(1)	Joe DiMaggio	200.00	100.00	60.00
(2)	Jim Hegan	25.00	12.50	7.50
(3)	Gil Hodges	75.00	37.50	22.50
(4)	George Kell	35.00	17.50	10.00
(5)	Ralph Kiner	45.00	22.50	13.50
(6)	Stan Musial	100.00	50.00	30.00
(7)	Mel Parnell	25.00	12.50	7.50
(8)	Phil Rizzuto	75.00	37.50	22.50
(9)	Jackie Robinson	150.00	75.00	45.00
(10)	Ted Williams	150.00	75.00	45.00

1971 Allstate Insurance

This four-card series was distributed as part of an internal sales promotion for Allstate Insurance. Graphic artist Ray Lending, an Allstate employee, created the 2-1/2" x 3-1/4" cards in duo-tone black and green on white. Card fronts show the players in batting stance, with the player name in one of the upper corners and the "Hall of Fame Series" logo printed across the bottom of the card. The card backs carry the player's full name and position, followed by a brief career summary, biography, and Career Highlights chart listing major league totals. "1971 Charger" and "Hall of Fame Series" are printed at the bottom of the card back. 8,000 sets were distributed.

		NM	E	VG
Complete Set (4):		400.00	200.00	120.00
Common Player:		50.00	25.00	15.00
(1)	Ty Cobb	50.00	25.00	15.00
(2)	Stan Musial	50.00	25.00	15.00
(3)	Babe Ruth	200.00	100.00	60.00
(4)	Ted Williams	150.00	75.00	45.00

1946-1947 Almanaque Deportivo

Former and future Major Leaguers mix with Negro Leaguers and Caribbean stars in this issue. Apparently sold in sheets of four, well-cut examples of these cards measure a nominal 1-7/8" x 2-1/2" and are printed in color on thin paper. Player identification is on the back of the card, usually with career notes and a large advertisement from one of many different sponsors. A colorful album was issued to house the set. Like all Cuban cards of the era, specimens surviving in grades of VG or better are scarce.

		E	VG
Complete Set (160):		3,000	1,800
Common Player:		17.50	10.00
Album:		200.00	120.00
A-1	Adolfo Luque	30.00	20.00
A-2	Tomas de la Cruz	17.50	10.00
A-3	Roberto Ortiz	22.50	13.50
A-4	Evelio Martinez	17.50	10.00
A-5	Jess Jessup	45.00	27.50

A-6	Santos Amaro	17.50	10.00
A-7	Rene Gonzalez	17.50	10.00
A-8	Buck O'Neil	310.00	185.00
A-9	J. (Lefty) Gaines	45.00	27.50
A-10	Max Lanier	22.50	13.50
A-11	George Hausmann	17.50	10.00
A-12	Avelino Canizares	17.50	10.00
A-13	Calampio Leon	17.50	10.00
A-14	Conrado Marrero	25.00	15.00
A-15	Alberto Leal	17.50	10.00
A-16	Lloyd Davenport	45.00	27.50
A-17	Teodoro Oxamendi	17.50	10.00
A-18	Santiago Ulrich	17.50	10.00
A-19	Lazaro Salazar	50.00	30.00
A-20	Cheo Ramos	17.50	10.00
A-21	Jorge Comellas	17.50	10.00
A-22	Agapito Mayor	17.50	10.00
A-23	Hector Rodriguez	22.50	13.50
A-24	Joe Williams	17.50	10.00
A-25	Andres Fleitas	17.50	10.00
C-1	Martin Dihigo	250.00	150.00
C-2	Alejandro Carrasquel	17.50	10.00
C-3	Adrian Zabala	17.50	10.00
C-4	Jimmy Roy	17.50	10.00
C-5	Napoleon Reyes	40.00	25.00
C-6	Stanislas Bread	17.50	10.00
C-7	Roland Gladu	17.50	10.00
C-8	Roy Zimmerman	17.50	10.00
C-9	Max Manning	62.50	37.50
C-10	Myron Hayworth	17.50	10.00
C-11	Pedro Miro	17.50	10.00
C-12	Jose Luis Colas	17.50	10.00
C-13	Conrado Perez	17.50	10.00
C-14	Luis Tiant Sr.	22.50	13.50
C-15	Ramon Heredia	17.50	10.00
C-16	Vinicio Garcia	17.50	10.00
C-17	(Walt) Nothe	17.50	10.00
C-18	Danny Gardella	17.50	10.00
C-19	Alejandro Crespo	30.00	20.00
C-20	Ray Noble	17.50	10.00
C-21	Pedro Pages	17.50	10.00
F-1	Napoleon y C. Blanco (Action)	17.50	10.00
F-2	Chanquilon y H. Rodriguez (Action)	17.50	10.00
F-3	Estalella y Fleitas (Action)	17.50	10.00
F-4	Castano y Kimbro (Action)	17.50	10.00
H-1	Miguel Angel Gonzalez	27.50	16.50
H-2	Pedro (Natilla) Jimenez	17.50	10.00
H-3	Fred Martin	17.50	10.00
H-4	James Lamarque	40.00	25.00
H-5	Salvador Hernandez	17.50	10.00
H-6	S. (Hank) Thompson	25.00	15.00
H-7	Antonio Ordenana	17.50	10.00
H-8	Manuel Garcia	17.50	10.00
H-9	Alberto Hernandez	17.50	10.00
H-10	Terry McDuffie	22.50	13.50
H-11	Louis Frank Klein	17.50	10.00
H-12	Herberto Blanco	17.50	10.00
H-13	H.(Henry) Kimbro	75.00	45.00
H-14	Rene Monteagudo	17.50	10.00
H-15	Lennox Pearson	50.00	30.00
H-16	Carlos Blanco	17.50	10.00
H-17	Pedro Formental	27.50	16.50
H-18	William Bell	17.50	10.00
H-19	Raul Navarro	17.50	10.00
H-20	Lazaro Medina	17.50	10.00
L-1	Julio Moreno	17.50	10.00
L-2	Daniel Parra	17.50	10.00
L-3	Rogelio Martinez	17.50	10.00
L-4	J. Antonio Zardon	17.50	10.00
L-5	Julian Acosta	17.50	10.00
L-6	Orlando Suarez	17.50	10.00
L-7	Manuel Hidalgo	17.50	10.00
L-8	Fermin Guerra	17.50	10.00
L-9	Regino Otero	17.50	10.00
L-10	Jorge Juan Torres	17.50	10.00
L-11	Valeriano Fano	17.50	10.00
L-12	Amado Ibanez	17.50	10.00
L-13	"Atares" Garcia	17.50	10.00
L-14	Armando Gallart	17.50	10.00
L-15	Perdo Dunabeitia	17.50	10.00
L-16	Oscar del Calvo	17.50	10.00
L-17	Johnny Davis	50.00	30.00
L-18	Emilio Cabrera	17.50	10.00
L-19	Lee Holleman	17.50	10.00
L-20	Antonio Napoles	17.50	10.00
L-21	Pedro Diaz	17.50	10.00
L-22	Lazaro Bernal	17.50	10.00
L-23	Hector Arago	17.50	10.00
L-24	Oscar Garmendia	17.50	10.00
L-25	Barney Serrell	45.00	27.50
L-26	Armando Marsans	27.50	16.50
L-27	Mario Diaz	17.50	10.00
L-28	Raymond Dandridge	175.00	105.00
L-29	Leon Tredway	17.50	10.00
L-30	Orestes Perera	17.50	10.00
L-31	Armando Vazquez	17.50	10.00
L-32	Cleveland Clark	25.00	15.00

L-33	Johnny Williams	45.00	27.50
L-34	Clarence Iott	17.50	10.00
L-35	Gilberto Torres	17.50	10.00
L-36	George Brown	17.50	10.00
L-37	Wayne Johnson	17.50	10.00
L-38	Miguel Angel Carmona	17.50	10.00
L-39	Leovigildo Xiques	17.50	10.00
L-40	Rafael Rivas	17.50	10.00
L-41	Joaquin Gutierrez	17.50	10.00
L-42	Miguel Lastra	17.50	10.00
L-43	Francisco Quicutis	17.50	10.00
L-44	Silvio Garcia	45.00	27.50
L-45	Angel Fleitas	17.50	10.00
L-46	Eddy Chandler	17.50	10.00
L-47	Gilberto Castillo	17.50	10.00
L-48	Isidoro Leon	17.50	10.00
L-49	Antonio Rodriguez	17.50	10.00
L-50	Laniel Hooker	45.00	27.50
L-51	Charles Perez	17.50	10.00
L-52	Ruben Garcia	17.50	10.00
L-53	Raquel Antunez	17.50	10.00
L-54	Claro Duany	22.50	13.50
L-55	Bucker (Booker) McDaniels	45.00	27.50
L-56	Francisco Jimenez	17.50	10.00
L-57	Luis Minsal	17.50	10.00
L-58	Rogelio Linares	17.50	10.00
L-59	Isasio Gonzalez	17.50	10.00
L-60	Manolo Parrado	17.50	10.00
L-61	Jose Maria Fernandez	17.50	10.00
L-62	Rogelio Valdes	17.50	10.00
L-63	R. Franco	17.50	10.00
L-64	J. Cedan	17.50	10.00
L-65	Jacinto Roque	17.50	10.00
L-66	Pablo Garcia	17.50	10.00
M-1	Pipo de la Noval	17.50	10.00
M-2	J. Valenzuela	17.50	10.00
M-3	Oliverio Ortiz	17.50	10.00
M-4	Antonio Castanos	17.50	10.00
M-5	Sandalio Consuegra	22.50	13.50
M-6	(Jim) Lindsey	17.50	10.00
M-7	Roberto Estalella	17.50	10.00
M-8	Lino Donoso	17.50	10.00
M-9	Paul Calvert	17.50	10.00
M-10	Gilberto Valdivia	17.50	10.00
M-11	Orestes Minoso	65.00	37.50
M-12	J. Cabrera	17.50	10.00
M-13	Manuel Godinez	17.50	10.00
M-14	Frank Casanovas	17.50	10.00
M-15	Roberto Avila	30.00	20.00
M-16	Pedro Orta	17.50	10.00
M-17	Feliciano Castro	17.50	10.00
M-18	Mario Arencibia	17.50	10.00
M-19	Antonio Diaz	17.50	10.00
M-20	Aristonico Correoso	17.50	10.00
M-21	Angel Gonzalez	17.50	10.00
M-22	Murray Franklin	17.50	10.00
M-23	Francisco Campos	17.50	10.00
M-24	Angel Castro	17.50	10.00

1894 Alpha Photo-Engraving Baltimore Orioles

The rarest baseball card set of the 1890s (each card is known in only a single example) is the Baltimore Orioles team set issued by the Alpha Photo-Engraving Co. of that city. The round-corner 2-3/8" x 3-7/16" cards feature black-and-white photos of the National League champions in formalwear. Last-name identification is in a strip below the photo and a white border surrounds both. On the red-and-white backs a large ad for the producer is at center, while small baseball batter figures are in each corner surrounded by a leafy background. The unnumbered cards are checklisted here alphabetically, though the list may not be complete; one glaring omission is Hall of Fame outfielder Willie Keeler. In early 2006 the set was sold and broken up. Each card was authenticated and graded by SGC, with grades ranging from Fair to Very Good.

		NM
Common Player:		8,000
(1)	Frank Bonner	8,000
(2)	Steve Brodie	8,000
(3)	Dan Brouthers	60,000
(4)	Duke Esper	8,000
(5)	Kid Gleason	60,000
(6)	Ned Hanlon	60,000
(7)	Bill Hawke	8,000
(8)	George Hemming	8,000
(9)	Hughie Jennings	100,000
(10)	Joe Kelley	100,000
(11)	John McGraw	200,000
(12)	Sadie McMahon	8,000
(13)	Heinie Reitz	8,000
(14)	Wilbert Robinson	60,000

1916 Altoona Tribune

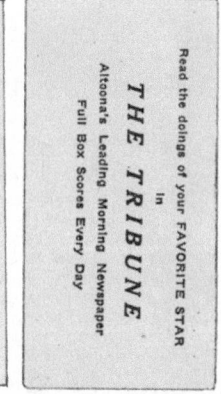

This Pennsylvania daily newspaper was one of several regional advertisers to use this black-and-white, 1-5/8" x 3" 200-card set for promotional purposes. The Altoona issue shares the checklist of the 1916 M101-4 Blank Backs. Type card and superstar collectors will pay a significant premium for a Tribune version of a specific card.

PREMIUM:
Common player: 5-8X
Hall of Famer: 4-6X

(See 1916 M101-4 Blank Backs for checklist and base card values.)

1909-11 American Beauty Cigarettes

Two versions of the American Beauty Cigarettes advertising on the backs of T206 can be found; with and without a decorative border surrounding the typography, which is printed in green. All "350 Subjects" American Beauty cards originated from Factory No. 25 in Virginia. American Beauty T206s may be a bit narrower than the standard 1-7/16". Among T205, AB backs may be found printed in either black or green, the latter somewhat scarcer. See T205, T206 for checklist and base acrd values.

PREMIUM:
T205: 1.5-2.5X
T206 350 Series: 2-4X
T206 460 Series: 3-5X

1934 American Boy Gum

The date cited is approximate, based on the fact that the only two cards known thus far in this issue are of Detroit players who were on the Tigers 1934 A.L. pennant winners and 1935 World Series champions. About the size of contemporary Goudey cards, 2-3/8" x 2-7/8" these cards are crudely printed. Backs offer a wrapper redemption for a foreign coin. The issue may have originated in Detroit as the only known examples were found in Windsor, Ont.

VALUES UNDETERMINED
Fred Marberry
Schoolboy Rowe

1908 American Caramel (E91, Set A)

Issued by Philadelphia's American Caramel Co., 1908-1910, the E91 set of Base Ball Caramels has limited popularity with collectors because many of the color drawings show "generic" players rather than the named major leaguers; the same artwork was used to depict two or three different players. The player's name, position and team appear in the white border at bottom. The cards measure approximately 1-1/2" x 2-3/4" and were issued in three separate series. They can be differentiated by their backs, which checklist the cards. Set A lists the Athletics in the upper-left, the Giants at upper-right and the Cubs below. Set B lists the Cubs and Athletics on top with the Giants below, and Set C lists Pittsburg and Washington on top with Boston below. A line indicating the cards were "Manufactured Only by the American Caramel Co." appears at the bottom.

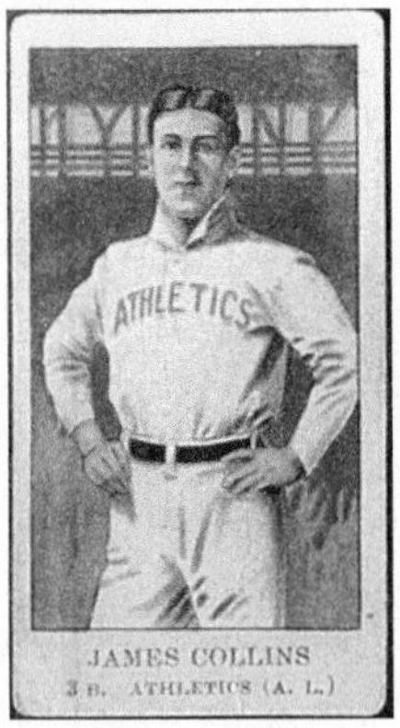
JAMES COLLINS
3 B. ATHLETICS (A. L.)

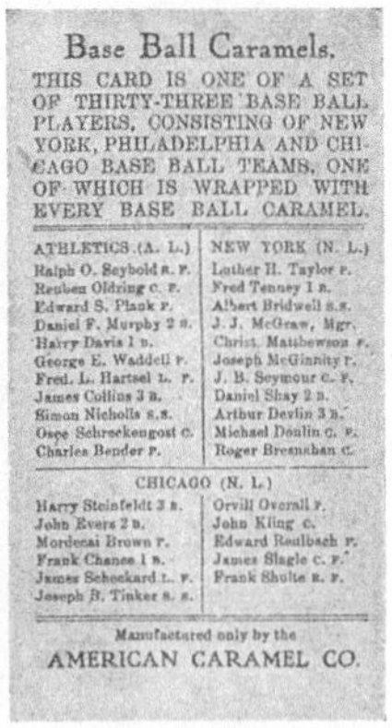
Base Ball Caramels.
THIS CARD IS ONE OF A SET OF THIRTY-THREE BASE BALL PLAYERS, CONSISTING OF NEW YORK, PHILADELPHIA AND CHICAGO BASE BALL TEAMS, ONE OF WHICH IS WRAPPED WITH EVERY BASE BALL CARAMEL.
ATHLETICS (A. L.)
Ralph O. Seybold R. F.
Reuben Oldring C. F.
Edward S. Plank P.
Daniel F. Murphy 2 B.
Harry Davis 1 B.
George E. Waddell P.
Fred. L. Hartsel L. F.
James Collins 3 B.
Simon Nicholls S.S.
Osee Schreckengost C.
Charles Bender P.
NEW YORK (N. L.)
Luther H. Taylor P.
Fred Tenney 1 B.
Albert Bridwell S.S.
J. J. McGraw, Mgr.
Christ. Matthewson P.
Joseph McGinnity P.
J. B. Seymour C. F.
Daniel Shay 2 B.
Arthur Devlin 3 B.
Michael Donlin C. F.
Roger Bresnahan C.
CHICAGO (N. L.)
Harry Steinfeldt 3 B.
John Evers 2 B.
Mordecai Brown P.
Frank Chance 1 B.
James Scheckard L. F.
Joseph B. Tinker S. S.
Orvill Overall P.
John Kling C.
Edward Reulbach P.
James Slagle C. F.
Frank Shulte R. F.
Manufactured only by the
AMERICAN CARAMEL CO.

		NM	E	VG
Complete Set (33):		10,000	4,000	2,500
Common Player:		200.00	75.00	40.00
(1)	Charles Bender	425.00	175.00	100.00
(2)	Roger Bresnahan	600.00	300.00	180.00
(3)	Albert Bridwell	200.00	75.00	45.00
(4)	Mordecai Brown	425.00	175.00	100.00
(5)	Frank Chance	425.00	175.00	100.00
(6)	James Collins	425.00	175.00	100.00
(7)	Harry Davis	200.00	75.00	40.00
(8)	Arthur Devlin	200.00	75.00	40.00
(9)	Michael Donlin	200.00	75.00	40.00
(10)	John Evers	425.00	175.00	100.00
(11)	Frederick L. Hartsel	200.00	75.00	40.00
(12)	John Kling	200.00	75.00	40.00
(13)	Christopher Matthewson (Mathewson)	1,750	785.00	435.00
(14)	Joseph McGinnity	425.00	175.00	100.00
(15)	John J. McGraw	425.00	175.00	100.00
(16)	Daniel F. Murphy	200.00	75.00	40.00
(17)	Simon Nicholls	200.00	75.00	40.00
(18)	Reuben Oldring	200.00	75.00	40.00
(19)	Orvill Overall (Orval)	200.00	75.00	40.00
(20)	Edward S. Plank	900.00	450.00	270.00
(21)	Edward Reulbach	200.00	75.00	40.00
(22)	James Scheckard (Sheckard)	200.00	75.00	40.00
(23)	Osee Schreckengost (Ossee)	200.00	75.00	40.00
(24)	Ralph O. Seybold	200.00	75.00	40.00
(25)	J. Bentley Seymour	200.00	75.00	40.00
(26)	Daniel Shay	200.00	75.00	40.00
(27)	Frank Shulte (Schulte)	200.00	75.00	40.00
(28)	James Slagle	200.00	75.00	40.00
(29)	Harry Steinfeldt	200.00	75.00	40.00
(30)	Luther H. Taylor	400.00	160.00	100.00
(31)	Fred Tenney	200.00	75.00	40.00
(32)	Joseph B. Tinker	425.00	175.00	100.00
(33)	George Edward Waddell	425.00	175.00	100.00

1909-11 American Caramel (E90-1)

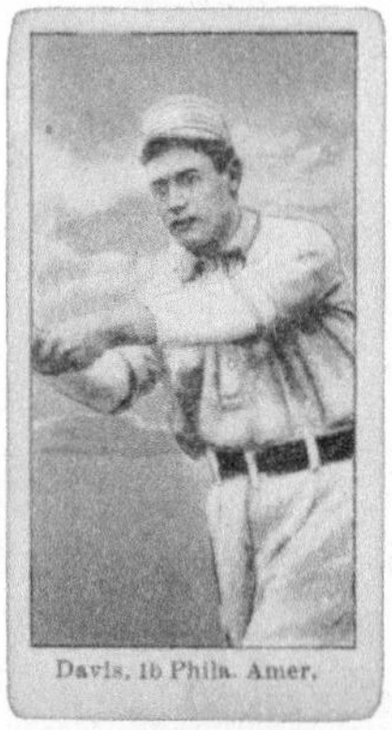
Davis, 1b Phila. Amer.

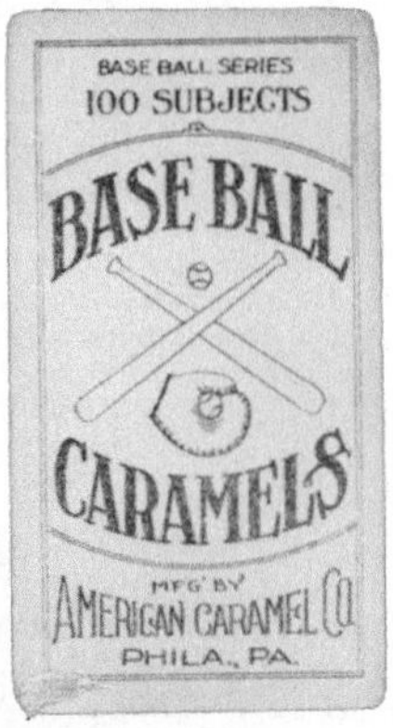
BASE BALL SERIES
100 SUBJECTS
BASE BALL
CARAMELS
MFG BY
AMERICAN CARAMEL CO
PHILA., PA.

The E90-1 set was issued by the American Caramel Co. from 1909 through 1911, with the bulk of the set being produced in the first year. The cards, which nominally measure 1-1/2" x 2-3/4" (with the usual tolerances for original cutting variations), were issued with sticks of caramel candy. They are color renderings of photographs. Backs state that 100 subjects are included in the set though more actually do exist. There are several levels of scarcity in the set, those levels being mostly determined by the year the cards were issued. For the reader's covenience, the players' first names have been added in the checklist that follows. The complete set price includes all variations.

		NM	E	VG
Complete Set (120):		250,000	125,000	75,000
Common Player:		400.00	125.00	40.00
(1)	Bill Bailey	400.00	125.00	40.00
(2)	Home Run Baker	1,750	875.00	525.00
(3)	Jack Barry	600.00	200.00	60.00
(4)	George Bell	500.00	175.00	60.00
(5)	Harry Bemis	1,000	350.00	150.00
(6)	Chief Bender	1,750	875.00	525.00
(7)	Bob Bescher	1,000	350.00	150.00
(8)	Cliff Blankenship	500.00	175.00	60.00
(9)	John Bliss	500.00	175.00	60.00
(10)	Bill Bradley	400.00	125.00	40.00
(11)	Kitty Bransfield ("P" on shirt.)	900.00	450.00	270.00
(12)	Kitty Bransfield (No "P.")	1,950	975.00	585.00
(13)	Roger Bresnahan	1,750	875.00	525.00
(14)	Al Bridwell	400.00	125.00	40.00
(15)	Buster Brown (Boston)	2,000	500.00	200.00
(16)	Mordecai Brown (Chicago)	800.00	250.00	80.00
(17)	Donie Bush	400.00	125.00	40.00
(18)	John Butler	500.00	175.00	60.00
(19)	Howie Camnitz	500.00	175.00	60.00
(20)	Frank Chance	1,750	875.00	525.00
(21)	Hal Chase	1,350	675.00	405.00
(22)	Fred Clarke (Philadelphia)	1,750	875.00	525.00
(23)	Fred Clarke (Pittsburgh)	5,000	1,250	500.00
(24)	Wally Clement	1,000	350.00	150.00
(25)	"Ty" Cobb	12,500	4,500	1,500
(26)	Eddie Collins	1,750	875.00	525.00
(27)	Frank Corridon	400.00	125.00	40.00
(28)	Sam Crawford	1,750	875.00	525.00
(29)	Lou Criger	400.00	125.00	40.00
(30)	George Davis	2,500	700.00	350.00
(31)	Harry Davis	400.00	125.00	40.00
(32)	Ray Demmitt	800.00	250.00	80.00
(33)	Mike Donlin	600.00	200.00	70.00
(34)	Wild Bill Donovan	500.00	175.00	60.00
(35)	Red Dooin	400.00	125.00	40.00
(36)	Patsy Dougherty	1,000	350.00	150.00
(37)	Hugh Duffy	5,000	1,250	500.00
(38)	Jimmy Dygert	400.00	125.00	40.00
(39)	Rube Ellis	400.00	125.00	40.00
(40)	Clyde Engle	500.00	175.00	60.00
(41)	Art Fromme	800.00	250.00	80.00
(42)	George Gibson (Back view.)	1,000	350.00	150.00
(43)	George Gibson (Front view.)	600.00	200.00	70.00
(44)	Peaches Graham	6,000	2,750	1,550
(45)	Eddie Grant	600.00	200.00	70.00
(46)	Dolly Gray	600.00	200.00	70.00
(47)	Bob Groom	400.00	125.00	40.00
(48)	Charley Hall	1,750	805.00	455.00
(49)	Roy Hartzell (Fielding)	400.00	125.00	40.00
(50)	Roy Hartzell (Batting)	600.00	200.00	70.00
(51)	Heinie Heitmuller	400.00	125.00	40.00
(52)	Harry Howell (Follow-through.)	400.00	125.00	40.00
(53)	Harry Howell (Wind-up.)	800.00	250.00	80.00
(54)	Tex Irwin (Erwin)	600.00	200.00	70.00
(55)	Frank Isbell	400.00	125.00	40.00
(56)	Joe Jackson	90,000	40,000	17,750
(57)	Hughie Jennings	1,150	575.00	345.00
(58)	Buck Jordon (Jordan)	400.00	125.00	40.00
(59)	Addie Joss (Portrait)	3,000	1,500	900.00
(60)	Addie Joss (Pitching)	4,500	2,200	1,350
(61)	Ed Karger	1,500	500.00	200.00
(62)	Willie Keeler (Portrait, pink background.)	1,750	875.00	525.00
(63)	Willie Keeler (Portrait, red background.)	5,000	1,250	500.00
(64)	Willie Keeler (Throwing)	6,000	3,000	1,800
(65)	John Knight	600.00	200.00	70.00
(66)	Harry Krause	400.00	125.00	40.00
(67)	Nap Lajoie	3,000	1,500	900.00
(68)	Tommy Leach (Throwing)	1,000	350.00	150.00
(69)	Tommy Leach (Batting)	600.00	200.00	70.00
(70)	Sam Leever	600.00	200.00	70.00
(71)	Hans Lobert	1,500	500.00	200.00
(72)	Harry Lumley	400.00	125.00	40.00
(73)	Rube Marquard	1,500	400.00	150.00
(74)	Christy Matthewson (Mathewson)	7,500	2,600	1,000
(75)	Stuffy McInnes (McInnis)	400.00	125.00	40.00
(76)	Harry McIntyre	400.00	125.00	40.00
(77)	Larry McLean	1,000	350.00	150.00
(78)	George McQuillan	400.00	125.00	40.00
(79)	Dots Miller	500.00	175.00	60.00
(80)	Fred Mitchell (New York)	400.00	125.00	40.00
(81)	Mike Mitchell (Cincinnati)	16,500	7,600	4,300
(82)	George Mullin	400.00	125.00	40.00
(83)	Rebel Oakes	2,400	1,200	725.00
(84)	Paddy O'Connor	800.00	250.00	80.00
(85)	Charley O'Leary	400.00	125.00	40.00
(86)	Orval Overall	800.00	250.00	80.00
(87)	Jim Pastorius	400.00	125.00	40.00
(88)	Ed Phelps	400.00	125.00	40.00
(89)	Eddie Plank	2,000	920.00	520.00
(90)	Lew Richie	600.00	200.00	70.00
(91)	Germany Schaefer	500.00	175.00	60.00
(92)	Biff Schlitzer	800.00	250.00	80.00
(93)	Johnny Seigle (Siegle)	1,500	500.00	200.00
(94)	Dave Shean	1,500	500.00	200.00
(95)	Jimmy Sheckard	600.00	200.00	70.00
(96)	Tris Speaker	10,000	2,000	800.00
(97)	Jake Stahl	6,000	2,750	1,550
(98)	Oscar Stanage	400.00	125.00	40.00
(99)	George Stone (No hands visible.)	400.00	125.00	40.00
(100)	George Stone (Left hand visible.)	600.00	200.00	70.00
(101)	George Stovall	500.00	175.00	60.00
(102)	Ed Summers	400.00	200.00	120.00
(103)	Bill Sweeney (Boston)	6,250	3,125	1,875
(104)	Jeff Sweeney (New York)	400.00	125.00	40.00
(105)	Jesse Tannehill (Chicago A.L.)	400.00	125.00	40.00
(106)	Lee Tannehill (Chicago N.L.)	400.00	125.00	40.00
(107)	Fred Tenney	800.00	250.00	80.00
(108)	Ira Thomas (Philadelphia)	400.00	125.00	40.00
(109)	Roy Thomas (Boston)	400.00	125.00	40.00
(110)	Joe Tinker	1,100	505.00	285.00
(111)	Bob Unglaub	400.00	125.00	40.00
(112)	Jerry Upp	1,500	500.00	200.00
(113)	Honus Wagner (Batting)	10,000	4,000	2,000
(114)	Honus Wagner (Throwing)	15,000	7,500	3,000
(115)	Bobby Wallace	1,750	875.00	525.00
(116)	Ed Walsh	10,000	2,000	800.00
(117)	Vic Willis	1,750	875.00	525.00
(118)	Hooks Wiltse	600.00	200.00	70.00
(119)	Cy Young (Cleveland)	10,000	5,000	3,000
(120)	Cy Young (Boston)	6,000	3,000	1,800

1909 American Caramel (E91, Set B)

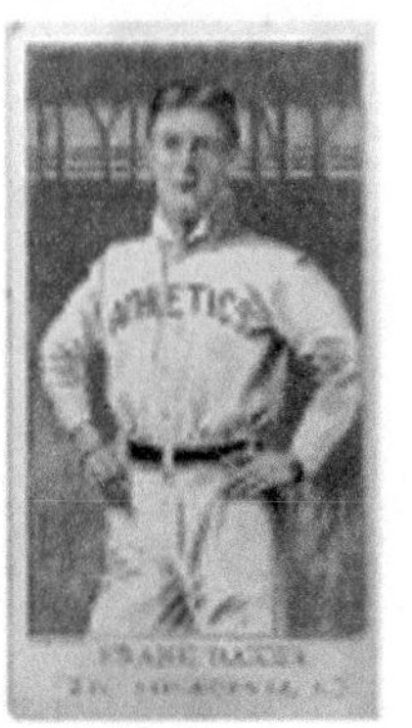

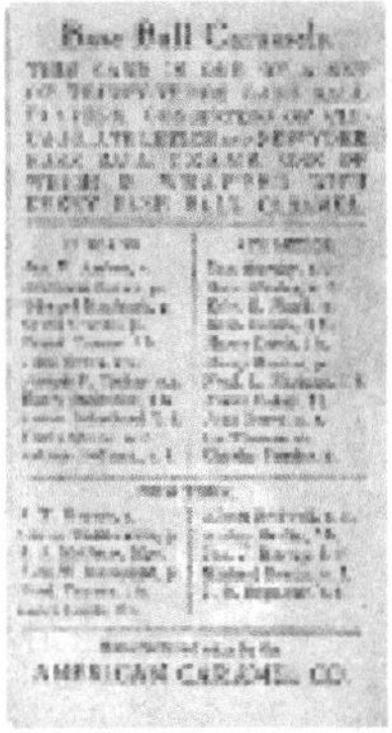

		NM	E	VG
Complete Set (33):		9,500	4,000	2,400
Common Player:		200.00	75.00	40.00
(1)	James Archer	200.00	75.00	40.00
(2)	Frank Baker	425.00	175.00	100.00
(3)	John Barry	200.00	75.00	40.00
(4)	Charles Bender	425.00	175.00	100.00
(5)	Albert Bridwell	200.00	75.00	40.00
(6)	Mordecai Brown	425.00	175.00	100.00
(7)	Frank Chance	425.00	175.00	100.00
(8)	Edw. Collins	425.00	175.00	100.00
(9)	Harry Davis	200.00	75.00	40.00
(10)	Arthur Devlin	200.00	75.00	40.00
(11)	Michael Donlin	200.00	75.00	40.00
(12)	Larry Doyle	200.00	75.00	40.00
(13)	John Evers	425.00	175.00	100.00
(14)	Robt. Ganley	200.00	75.00	40.00
(15)	Frederick L. Hartsel	200.00	75.00	40.00
(16)	Arthur Hoffman (Hofman)	200.00	75.00	40.00
(17)	Harry Krause	200.00	75.00	40.00
(18)	Rich. W. Marquard	425.00	175.00	100.00
(19)	Christopher Matthewson (Mathewson)	1,350	675.00	405.00
(20)	John J. McGraw	900.00	175.00	100.00
(21)	J.T. Meyers	200.00	75.00	40.00
(22)	Dan Murphy	200.00	75.00	40.00
(23)	Jno. J. Murray	200.00	75.00	40.00
(24)	Orvill Overall (Orval)	200.00	75.00	40.00
(25)	Edward S. Plank	900.00	450.00	270.00
(26)	Edward Reulbach	1,150	75.00	40.00

		NM	E	VG
(27)	James Scheckard (Sheckard)	200.00	75.00	40.00
(28)	J. Bentley Seymour	200.00	75.00	40.00
(29)	Harry Steinfeldt	200.00	75.00	40.00
(30)	Frank Shulte (Schulte)	200.00	75.00	40.00
(31)	Fred Tenney	200.00	75.00	40.00
(32)	Joseph B Tinker	425.00	175.00	100.00
(33)	Ira Thomas	200.00	75.00	40.00

1910 American Caramel (E91, Set C)

		NM	E	VG
Complete Set (33):		11,000	4,400	2,850
Common Player:		200.00	75.00	40.00
(1)	W.J. Barbeau	200.00	75.00	40.00
(2)	Geo. Browne	200.00	75.00	40.00
(3)	Robt. Chech (Charles)	200.00	75.00	40.00
(4)	Fred Clarke	425.00	175.00	100.00
(5)	Wid Conroy	200.00	75.00	40.00
(6)	James Delehanty (Delahanty)	200.00	75.00	40.00
(7)	Jon A. Donohue (Donahue)	200.00	75.00	40.00
(8)	P. Donahue	200.00	75.00	40.00
(9)	Geo. Gibson	200.00	75.00	40.00
(10)	Robt. Groom	200.00	75.00	40.00
(11)	Harry Hooper	425.00	175.00	100.00
(12)	Tom Hughes	200.00	75.00	40.00
(13)	Walter Johnson	1,150	575.00	345.00
(14)	Edwin Karger	3,500	75.00	40.00
(15)	Tommy Leach	200.00	75.00	40.00
(16)	Sam'l Leever	200.00	75.00	40.00
(17)	Harry Lord	200.00	75.00	40.00
(18)	Geo. F. McBride	200.00	75.00	40.00
(19)	Ambr. McConnell	200.00	75.00	40.00
(20)	Clyde Milan	200.00	75.00	40.00
(21)	J.B. Miller	200.00	75.00	40.00
(22)	Harry Niles	200.00	75.00	40.00
(23)	Chas. Phillipi (Phillippe)	200.00	75.00	40.00
(24)	T.H. Speaker	650.00	275.00	125.00
(25)	Jacob Stahl	200.00	75.00	40.00
(26)	Chas. E. Street	200.00	75.00	40.00
(27)	Allen Storke	200.00	75.00	40.00
(28)	Robt. Unglaub	200.00	75.00	40.00
(29)	C. Wagner	200.00	75.00	40.00
(30)	Hans Wagner	3,500	1,750	1,050
(31)	Victor Willis	425.00	175.00	100.00
(32)	Owen Wilson	200.00	75.00	40.00
(33)	Jos. Wood	300.00	125.00	75.00

1910 American Caramel Die-cuts (E125)

Issued circa 1910 by the American Caramel Co., this set of die-cut cards is so rare that it wasn't even known to exist until the late 1960s. Apparently inserted in boxes of caramels, these cards, which are die-cut figures of baseball players, vary in size but are all relatively large - some measuring 7"

high and 4" wide. Players from the Athletics, Red Sox, Giants and Pirates are known with a team checklist appearing on the back.

		NM	E	VG
Common Player:		2,600	1,300	780.00
(1)	Babe Adams	2,600	1,300	780.00
(2)	Red Ames	2,600	1,300	780.00
(3)	Home Run Baker	5,000	2,250	1,500
(4)	Jack Barry	2,600	1,300	780.00
(5)	Chief Bender	5,625	2,530	1,690
(6)	Al Bridwell	2,600	1,300	780.00
(7)	Bobby Byrne	2,600	1,300	780.00
(8)	Bill Carrigan	2,600	1,300	780.00
(9)	Ed Cicotte	2,600	1,300	780.00
(10)	Fred Clark (Clarke)	5,000	2,250	1,500
(11)	Eddie Collins	5,000	2,250	1,500
(12)	Harry Davis	2,600	1,300	780.00
(13)	Art Devlin	2,600	1,300	780.00
(14)	Josh Devore	2,600	1,300	780.00
(15)	Larry Doyle	2,600	1,300	780.00
(16)	John Flynn	2,600	1,300	780.00
(17)	George Gibson	2,600	1,300	780.00
(18)	Topsy Hartzell (Hartsel)	2,600	1,300	780.00
(19)	Harry Hooper	5,000	2,250	1,500
(20)	Harry Krause	2,600	1,300	780.00
(21)	Tommy Leach	2,600	1,300	780.00
(22)	Harry Lord	2,600	1,300	780.00
(23)	Christy Mathewson	18,750	8,440	5,625
(24)	Amby McConnell	2,600	1,300	780.00
(25)	Fred Merkle	2,600	1,300	780.00
(26)	Dots Miller	2,600	1,300	780.00
(27)	Danny Murphy	2,600	1,300	780.00
(28)	Red Murray	2,600	1,300	780.00
(29)	Harry Niles	2,600	1,300	780.00
(30)	Rube Oldring	2,600	1,300	780.00
(31)	Eddie Plank	18,750	8,440	5,625
(32)	Cy Seymour	2,600	1,300	780.00
(33)	Tris Speaker (Batting)	11,250	5,065	3,375
(34)	Tris Speaker (Fielding)	11,250	5,065	3,375
(35)	Jake Stahl	2,600	1,300	780.00
(36)	Ira Thomas	2,600	1,300	780.00
(37)	Heinie Wagner	2,600	1,300	780.00
(38)	Honus Wagner (Batting)	25,000	11,250	7,500
(39)	Honus Wagner (Throwing)	25,000	11,250	7,500
(40)	Art Wilson	2,600	1,300	780.00
(41)	Owen Wilson	2,600	1,300	780.00
(42)	Hooks Wiltse	2,600	1,300	780.00

1910 American Caramel Pirates (E90-2)

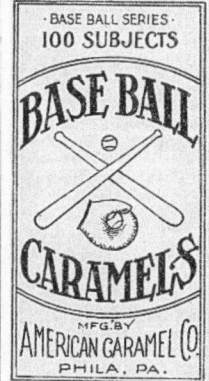

WAGNER, PITTSBURG

Closely related to the E90-1 American Caramel set, the E90-2 set consists of 11 cards featuring members of the 1909 champion Pittsburgh Pirates. The cards measure a nominal 1-1/2" x 2-5/8", though tolerances must be allowed for original cutting variations common to the era. They display a color lithograph on front set upon a solid color background of either red, green blue or pink. The player's name and "Pittsburg" appear in blue capital letters in the border beneath the portrait. The backs are identical to those in the E90-1 set, depicting a drawing of a ball, glove and crossed bats with the words "Base Ball Caramels" and a reference to "100 Subjects."

		NM	E	VG
Complete Set (11):		35,000	17,500	10,500
Common Player:		1,200	550.00	250.00
(1)	Babe Adams	1,200	550.00	250.00
(2)	Fred Clarke	2,750	1,350	825.00
(3)	George Gibson	1,200	550.00	250.00
(4)	Ham Hyatt	1,200	550.00	250.00
(5)	Tommy Leach	1,200	550.00	250.00
(6)	Sam Leever	1,200	550.00	250.00
(7)	Nick Maddox	1,200	550.00	250.00
(8)	Dots Miller	1,200	550.00	250.00
(9)	Deacon Phillippe	1,200	550.00	250.00
(10)	Honus Wagner	22,500	8,500	4,500
(11)	Owen Wilson	1,200	550.00	250.00

1910 American Caramel White Sox/Cubs (E90-3)

Evers, 2. b. Cubs

Similar in size (nominally 1-1/2" x 2-3/4", but with the usual tolerances for cutting variations on cards of the era) and style to the more popular E90-1 set, the E90-3 set was issued by the American Caramel Co. in 1910. The 20-card, color lithograph set includes 11 Chicago Cubs and nine White Sox. The fronts of the cards have a similar design to the E90-1 set, although different pictures were used. The backs can be differentiated by two major changes: The bottom of the card indicates the American Caramel Co. of "Chicago," rather than Philadelphia, and the top of the card contains the phrase "All The Star Players," rather than "100 Subjects."

		NM	E	VG
Complete Set (20):		47,500	24,000	14,000
Common Player:		1,700	850.00	425.00
(1)	Jimmy Archer	1,700	850.00	350.00
(2)	Lena Blackburne	1,700	850.00	350.00
(3)	Mordecai Brown	3,000	1,500	550.00
(4)	Frank Chance	3,000	1,500	550.00
(5)	King Cole	1,700	850.00	350.00
(6)	Patsy Dougherty	1,700	850.00	350.00
(7)	Johnny Evers	3,000	1,500	550.00
(8)	Chick Gandil	7,500	3,700	2,200
(9)	Ed Hahn	1,700	850.00	425.00
(10a)	Solly Hofman	1,700	850.00	350.00
(10b)	Solly Hofman (Broken "m" in last name gives appearance of "Hofnlan.")	3,600	1,750	900.00
(11)	Orval Overall	1,700	850.00	350.00
(12)	Fred Payne	1,700	850.00	425.00
(13)	Billy Purtell	1,700	850.00	350.00
(14)	Wildfire Schulte	1,700	850.00	350.00
(15)	Jimmy Sheckard	1,700	850.00	350.00
(16)	Frank Smith	1,700	850.00	350.00
(17)	Harry Steinfeldt	1,700	850.00	350.00
(18)	Joe Tinker	3,000	1,500	550.00
(19)	Ed Walsh	3,000	1,500	550.00
(20)	Rollie Zeider	1,700	850.00	350.00

1915 American Caramel (E106)

Chase, 1b. Buffalo Feds

This card is one of a set of forty-eight leading Baseball Players in the National, American and Federal Leagues. One card is given with every piece of Baseball Caramel manufactured by the AMERICAN CARAMEL CO. YORK PA UNDER THE FAMOUS BRAND OF THE P. C. W.

This 48-card set, designated E106 by the American Card Catalog, was produced by the American Caramel Co., of York, Pa., in 1915 and includes players from the National, American and Federal Leagues. Cards measure 1-1/2" x 2-3/4". The set is related to the E90-1 and E92 sets, from which the artwork is taken, but this issue has a glossy coating on front, which makes the cards very susceptible to cracking.

		NM	E	VG
Complete Set (48):		95,000	50,000	30,000
Common Player:		700.00	350.00	200.00
(1)	Jack Barry	700.00	350.00	200.00
(2)	Chief Bender (White hat.)	1,300	650.00	400.00
(3)	Chief Bender (Striped hat.)	1,300	650.00	400.00
(4)	Bob Bescher	700.00	350.00	200.00
(5)	Roger Bresnahan	1,300	650.00	400.00
(6)	Al Bridwell	700.00	350.00	200.00
(7)	Donie Bush	700.00	350.00	200.00
(8)	Hal Chase (Portrait)	700.00	350.00	200.00
(9)	Hal Chase (Catching)	700.00	350.00	200.00
(10)	Ty Cobb (W/bat, facing front.)	12,500	6,250	3,750
(11)	Ty Cobb (Batting, facing to side.)	12,000	6,000	3,600
(12)	Eddie Collins	1,300	650.00	400.00
(13)	Sam Crawford	1,300	650.00	400.00
(14)	Ray Demmitt	700.00	350.00	200.00
(15)	Wild Bill Donovan	700.00	350.00	200.00
(16)	Red Dooin	700.00	350.00	200.00
(17)	Mickey Doolan	700.00	350.00	200.00
(18)	Larry Doyle	700.00	350.00	200.00
(19)	Clyde Engle	700.00	350.00	200.00
(20)	Johnny Evers	1,300	650.00	400.00
(21)	Art Fromme	700.00	350.00	200.00
(22)	George Gibson (Catching, back view.)	700.00	350.00	200.00
(23)	George Gibson (Catching, front view.)	700.00	350.00	200.00
(24)	Roy Hartzell	700.00	350.00	200.00
(25)	Fred Jacklitsch	700.00	350.00	200.00
(26)	Hugh Jennings	1,300	650.00	400.00
(27)	Otto Knabe	700.00	350.00	200.00
(28)	Nap Lajoie	1,300	650.00	400.00
(29)	Hans Lobert	700.00	350.00	200.00
(30)	Rube Marquard	1,300	650.00	400.00
(31)	Christy Matthewson (Mathewson)	7,500	3,750	2,250
(32)	John McGraw	1,300	650.00	400.00
(33)	George McQuillan	700.00	350.00	200.00
(34)	Dots Miller	700.00	350.00	200.00
(35)	Danny Murphy	700.00	350.00	200.00
(36)	Rebel Oakes	700.00	350.00	200.00
(37)	Eddie Plank	3,750	1,875	1,125
(38)	Germany Schaefer	700.00	350.00	200.00
(39)	Tris Speaker	3,000	1,500	900.00
(40)	Oscar Stanage	700.00	350.00	200.00
(41)	George Stovall	700.00	350.00	200.00
(42)	Jeff Sweeney	700.00	350.00	200.00
(43)	Joe Tinker (Portrait)	1,300	650.00	400.00
(44)	Joe Tinker (Batting)	1,300	650.00	400.00
(45)	Honus Wagner (Batting)	12,500	6,250	3,750
(46)	Honus Wagner (Throwing)	9,000	4,500	2,700
(47)	Hooks Wiltse	700.00	350.00	200.00
(48)	Heinie Zimmerman	700.00	350.00	200.00

1921 American Caramel Series of 80 (E121)

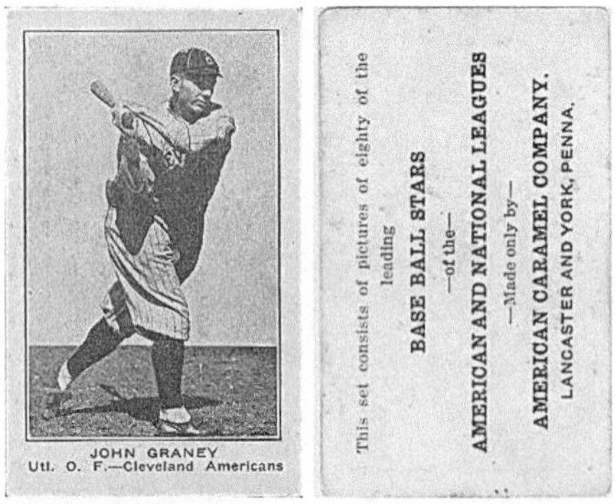

Issued circa 1921, possibly over more than one year, the set designated as E121 Series of 80 actually comprises more than 100 different players and numerous variations. The unnumbered cards, measuring about 2" x 3-1/4" are printed in black-and-white with posed action photos on front. Cards in the set can be found with one of four different backs, though it is currently unrecorded which backs are found with which fronts. The most common backs have the top line ending with "the", and are found in three varieties. On Type 1 backs, "This" on the top line is aligned with the "A" of "AMERICAN" on the fifth line, and the last line is printed in a sans-serif font. On Type 2 backs, "This" on the top line is aligned with the "E" of "AMERICAN" on the fifth line, the last line is printed in a sans-serif font, and the back printed is oriented at a 180-degree rotation from the other types. Type 3 backs have the last line in a serif font. Type 4 backs have the top line ending with "eighty" and are found only with the bottom line in the serif font. A number of players and front variations that had been listed in previous checklists, but the existence of which cannot be verified, have been removed from this list.

		NM	E	VG
Complete Set (122):		52,500	21,500	10,000
Common Player:		150.00	60.00	30.00
(1)	G.C. Alexander (Arms above head. Existence now questioned.)			
(2)	Grover Alexander (Right arm forward.)	1,500	600.00	300.00
(3)	Jim Bagby Sr.	150.00	60.00	30.00
(4a)	J. Franklin Baker	400.00	160.00	80.00
(4b)	Frank Baker (Existence now questioned.)			
(5)	Dave Bancroft (Batting)	400.00	160.00	80.00
(6)	Dave Bancroft (Leaping)	400.00	160.00	80.00
(7)	Ping Bodie	150.00	60.00	30.00
(8)	George Burns	150.00	60.00	30.00
(9)	Geo. J. Burns	150.00	60.00	30.00
(10)	Owen Bush	150.00	60.00	30.00
(11)	Max Carey (Batting)	400.00	160.00	80.00
(12)	Max Carey (Hands at hips.)	400.00	160.00	80.00
(13)	Cecil Causey	150.00	60.00	30.00
(14)	Ty Cobb (Throwing, looking front. Existence now questioned.)			
(15a)	Ty Cobb (Throwing, looking right, Mgr. on front.)	1,800	725.00	360.00
(15b)	Ty Cobb (Throwing, looking right, Manager on front.)	3,250	1,600	975.00
(16)	Eddie Collins	600.00	300.00	180.00
(17)	"Rip" Collins	150.00	60.00	30.00
(18)	Jake Daubert	150.00	60.00	30.00
(19)	George Dauss	150.00	60.00	30.00
(20)	Charles Deal (Dark uniform.)	150.00	60.00	30.00
(21)	Charles Deal (White uniform.)	150.00	60.00	30.00
(22)	William Doak	150.00	60.00	30.00
(23)	Bill Donovan	150.00	60.00	30.00
(24)	"Phil" Douglas (Existence now questioned.)			
(25a)	Johnny Evers (Manager)	400.00	160.00	80.00
(25b)	Johnny Evers (Mgr.)	400.00	160.00	80.00
(26)	Urban Faber (Dark uniform.)	400.00	160.00	80.00
(27)	Urban Faber (White uniform.)	400.00	160.00	80.00
(28)	William Fewster (First name actually Wilson.)	150.00	60.00	30.00
(29)	Eddie Foster	150.00	60.00	30.00
(30)	Frank Frisch	400.00	160.00	80.00
(31)	W.L. Gardner	150.00	60.00	30.00
(32a)	Alexander Gaston (No position on front. Existence now questioned.)			
(32b)	Alexander Gaston (Position on front. Existence now questioned.)			
(33)	"Kid" Gleason	150.00	60.00	30.00
(34)	"Mike" Gonzalez	150.00	60.00	30.00
(35)	Hank Gowdy	150.00	60.00	30.00
(36)	John Graney	150.00	60.00	30.00
(37)	Tom Griffith	150.00	60.00	30.00
(38)	Heinie Groh	150.00	60.00	30.00
(39)	Harry Harper	150.00	60.00	30.00
(40)	Harry Heilman (Heilmann)	400.00	160.00	80.00
(41)	Walter Holke (Portrait)	150.00	60.00	30.00
(42)	Walter Holke (Throwing)	150.00	60.00	30.00
(43)	Charles Hollacher (Hollocher)	150.00	60.00	30.00
(44)	Harry Hooper	400.00	160.00	80.00
(45)	Rogers Hornsby	1,600	800.00	480.00
(46)	Waite Hoyt	400.00	160.00	80.00
(47)	Miller Huggins	400.00	160.00	80.00
(48)	Wm. C. Jacobson	150.00	60.00	30.00
(49)	Hugh Jennings	400.00	160.00	80.00
(50)	Walter Johnson (Throwing)	1,750	875.00	525.00
(51)	Walter Johnson (Hands at chest.)	1,600	800.00	475.00
(52)	James Johnston	150.00	60.00	30.00
(53)	Joe Judge	150.00	60.00	30.00
(54)	George Kelly	400.00	160.00	80.00
(55)	Dick Kerr	150.00	60.00	30.00
(56)	P.J. Kilduff	150.00	60.00	30.00
(57a)	Bill Killifer (Incorrect name.)	150.00	60.00	30.00
(57b)	Bill Killefer (Correct name.)	150.00	60.00	30.00
(58)	John Lavan	150.00	60.00	30.00
(59)	"Nemo" Leibold	150.00	60.00	30.00
(60)	Duffy Lewis	150.00	60.00	30.00
(61)	Al. Mamaux	150.00	60.00	30.00
(62)	"Rabbit" Maranville	400.00	160.00	80.00
(63a)	Carl May (Mays)	200.00	80.00	40.00
(63b)	Carl Mays (Correct name.)	200.00	80.00	40.00
(64)	John McGraw	400.00	160.00	80.00
(65)	Jack McInnis	150.00	60.00	30.00
(66)	M.J. McNally	150.00	60.00	30.00
(67)	Emil Muesel (Photo is Lou DeVormer.)	150.00	60.00	30.00
(68)	R. Meusel	150.00	60.00	30.00
(69)	Clyde Milan	150.00	60.00	30.00
(70)	Elmer Miller	150.00	60.00	30.00
(71)	Otto Miller	150.00	60.00	30.00
(72)	Guy Morton	150.00	60.00	30.00
(73)	Eddie Murphy	150.00	60.00	30.00
(74)	"Hy" Myers	150.00	60.00	30.00
(75)	Arthur Nehf	150.00	60.00	30.00
(76)	Steve O'Neill	150.00	60.00	30.00
(77a)	Roger Peckinbaugh (Incorrect name.)	150.00	60.00	30.00
(77b)	Roger Peckinpaugh (Correct name.)	150.00	60.00	30.00
(78a)	Jeff Pfeffer (Brooklyn)	150.00	60.00	30.00
(78b)	Jeff Pfeffer (St. Louis)	150.00	60.00	30.00
(79)	Walter Pipp	250.00	100.00	50.00
(80)	Jack Quinn	150.00	60.00	30.00
(81)	John Rawlings	150.00	60.00	30.00
(82)	E.C. Rice	650.00	620.00	195.00
(83)	Eppa Rixey, Jr.	400.00	160.00	80.00
(84)	Tom Rogers	150.00	60.00	30.00
(85)	Robert Roth	150.00	60.00	30.00
(86a)	Ed. Roush (C.F.)	400.00	160.00	80.00
(86b)	Ed. Roush (L.F.)	400.00	160.00	80.00
(87a)	Babe Ruth	19,500	9,750	5,850
(87b)	"Babe" Ruth	17,500	7,000	3,500
(87c)	George Ruth	19,000	7,600	3,800
(88)	"Bill" Ryan	150.00	60.00	30.00
(89)	"Slim" Sallee (Glove showing.)	150.00	60.00	30.00
(90)	"Slim" Sallee (No glove showing.)	150.00	60.00	30.00
(91)	Ray Schalk	400.00	160.00	80.00
(92)	Walter Schang	150.00	60.00	30.00
(93a)	Fred Schupp (Name incorrect. Existence now questioned.)			
(93b)	Ferd Schupp (Name correct.)	150.00	60.00	30.00
(94)	Everett Scott	150.00	60.00	30.00
(95)	Hank Severeid	150.00	60.00	30.00
(96)	Robert Shawkey	150.00	60.00	30.00
(97a)	Pat Shea (Existence now questioned.)			
(97b)	"Pat" Shea	150.00	60.00	30.00
(98)	George Sisler (Batting)	400.00	160.00	80.00
(99)	George Sisler (Throwing)	400.00	160.00	80.00
(100)	Earl Smith	150.00	60.00	30.00
(101)	Frank Snyder	150.00	60.00	30.00
(102a)	Tris Speaker (Mgr.)	800.00	325.00	160.00
(102b)	Tris Speaker (Manager - large projection.)	800.00	325.00	160.00
(102c)	Tris Speaker (Manager - small projection. Existence now questioned.)			
(103)	Milton Stock	150.00	60.00	30.00
(104)	Amos Strunk	150.00	60.00	30.00
(105)	Zeb Terry	150.00	60.00	30.00
(106)	Chester Thomas	150.00	60.00	30.00
(107)	Fred Toney (Trees in background.)	150.00	60.00	30.00
(108)	Fred Toney (No trees.)	150.00	60.00	30.00
(109)	George Tyler	150.00	60.00	30.00
(110)	Jim Vaughn (Dark hat.)	150.00	60.00	30.00
(111)	Jim Vaughn (White hat.)	150.00	60.00	30.00
(112)	Bob Veach (Glove in air.)	150.00	60.00	30.00
(113)	Bob Veach (Arms crossed.)	150.00	60.00	30.00
(114)	Oscar Vitt	150.00	60.00	30.00
(115)	W. Wambsganss (Photo actually Fred Coumbe.)	150.00	60.00	30.00
(116)	Aaron Ward	150.00	60.00	30.00
(117)	Zach Wheat	400.00	160.00	80.00
(118)	George Whitted	150.00	60.00	30.00
(119)	Fred Williams	150.00	60.00	30.00
(120)	Ivy B. Wingo	150.00	60.00	30.00
(121)	Joe Wood	600.00	300.00	180.00
(122)	"Pep" Young	150.00	60.00	30.00

1922 American Caramel Series of 120 (E121)

Produced by American Caramel Co., the E121 Series of 120 has back advertising that claims that the set contained 120 subjects. Identical in design to the E121 Series of 80 set except for the card backs, the black-and-white cards measure about 2" x 3-1/4". Numerous variations are found in the set, most involving a change in the player's name, team or position. The complete set price does not include variations. A number of cards and variations previously listed in this set have been deleted, as their existence has never been confirmed. Gaps have been left to accommodate additions.

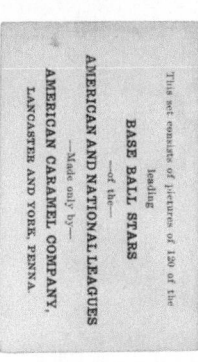

ELMER SMITH
O. F.—Boston Americans

AMERICAN AND NATIONAL LEAGUES
AMERICAN CARAMEL COMPANY,
LANCASTER AND YORK, PENNA.

leading
BASE BALL STARS
—of the—
Made only by—

This set consists of pictures of 120 of the

	NM	E	VG
Complete Set (123):	95,000	47,000	28,000
Common Player:	100.00	40.00	15.00
(1) Chas. "Babe" Adams	100.00	40.00	15.00
(2) G.C. Alexander	750.00	300.00	150.00
(3) Jim Bagby Sr.	100.00	40.00	15.00
(4) Dave Bancroft	400.00	160.00	80.00
(5) Turner Barber	100.00	40.00	15.00
(6a) Carlson L. Bigbee	100.00	40.00	15.00
(6b) L. Bigbee	100.00	40.00	15.00
(7) "Bullet Joe" Bush	100.00	40.00	15.00
(8) Max Carey	400.00	160.00	80.00
(9) Cecil Causey	100.00	40.00	15.00
(10) Ty Cobb (Batting)	5,750	2,875	1,725
(11) Ty Cobb (Throwing)	4,250	2,100	1,250
(12) Eddie Collins	400.00	160.00	80.00
(13) A. Wilbur Cooper	100.00	40.00	15.00
(14) Stanley Coveleskie (Coveleski)	400.00	160.00	80.00
(15) Dave Danforth	100.00	40.00	15.00
(16) Jake Daubert	100.00	40.00	15.00
(17) George Dauss	100.00	40.00	15.00
(18) Dixie Davis	100.00	40.00	15.00
(19) Lou DeVormer ((Photo actually Irish Meusel.))	100.00	40.00	15.00
(20) William Doak	100.00	40.00	15.00
(22) Phil Douglas	100.00	40.00	15.00
(23) Urban Faber	400.00	160.00	80.00
(24) Bib Falk (Bibb)	100.00	40.00	15.00
(25) Wm: Fewster (First name actually Wilson.)	100.00	40.00	158.00
(26) Max Flack	100.00	40.00	15.00
(27) Ira Falgstead (Flagstead)	100.00	40.00	15.00
(28) Frank Frisch	400.00	160.00	80.00
(29) W.L. Gardner	100.00	40.00	15.00
(30) Alexander Gaston	100.00	40.00	15.00
(31) E.P. Gharrity	100.00	40.00	15.00
(32) George Gibson	100.00	40.00	15.00
(33) Chas. "Whitey" Glazner	100.00	40.00	15.00
(34) "Kid" Gleason	100.00	40.00	15.00
(35) Hank Gowdy	100.00	40.00	15.00
(36) John Graney	100.00	40.00	15.00
(37) Tom Griffith	100.00	40.00	15.00
(38) Chas. Grimm	100.00	40.00	15.00
(39) Heine Groh	100.00	40.00	15.00
(40) Jess Haines	400.00	160.00	80.00
(41) Harry Harper	100.00	40.00	15.00
(43) Harry Heilmann (Name correct, batting.)	600.00	240.00	120.00
(44) Clarence Hodge	100.00	40.00	15.00
(45) Walter Holke (Portrait)	100.00	40.00	15.00
(47) Charles Hollocher	100.00	40.00	15.00
(48) Harry Hooper	400.00	160.00	80.00
(49a) Rogers Hornsby (2B.)	1,100	450.00	225.00
(49b) Rogers Hornsby (O.F.)	1,100	450.00	225.00
(50) Waite Hoyt	400.00	160.00	80.00
(51) Miller Huggins	400.00	160.00	80.00
(52) Walter Johnson	1,350	550.00	275.00
(53) Joe Judge	100.00	40.00	15.00
(54) George Kelly	400.00	160.00	80.00
(55) Dick Kerr	100.00	40.00	15.00
(56) P.J. Kilduff	100.00	40.00	15.00
(57) Bill Killifer (Killefer) (Batting)	100.00	40.00	15.00
(58) Bill Killifer (Killefer) (Throwing)	100.00	40.00	15.00
(59) John Lavan	100.00	40.00	15.00
(60) Walter Mails	100.00	40.00	15.00
(61) "Rabbit" Maranville	400.00	160.00	80.00
(62) Elwood Martin	100.00	40.00	15.00
(63) Carl Mays	200.00	80.00	40.00
(64) John J. McGraw	400.00	160.00	80.00
(65) Jack McInnis	100.00	40.00	15.00
(66) M.J. McNally	100.00	40.00	15.00
(67) Emil Meusel (Photo actually Lou DeVormer.)	100.00	40.00	15.00
(68) R. Meusel	100.00	40.00	15.00
(69) Clyde Milan	100.00	40.00	15.00
(70) Elmer Miller	100.00	40.00	15.00
(71) Otto Miller	100.00	40.00	15.00
(72) Johnny Mostil	100.00	40.00	15.00
(73) Eddie Mulligan	100.00	40.00	15.00
(74a) Hy Myers	100.00	40.00	15.00
(75) Earl Neale	300.00	120.00	60.00
(76) Arthur Nehf	100.00	40.00	15.00
(77) Leslie Nunamaker	100.00	40.00	15.00
(78) Joe Oeschger	100.00	40.00	15.00
(80) Steve O'Neill	100.00	40.00	15.00
(81) D.B. Pratt	100.00	40.00	15.00
(82a) John Rawlings (2B.)	100.00	40.00	15.00
(82b) John Rawlings (Utl.)	100.00	40.00	15.00
(83) E.S. Rice (Initials actually E.C.)	400.00	160.00	80.00
(84) Eppa J. Rixey	400.00	160.00	80.00
(86) Wilbert Robinson	400.00	160.00	80.00
(87) Tom Rogers	100.00	40.00	15.00
(88a) Ed Rounnel (Rommel)	100.00	40.00	15.00
(88b) Ed. Rommel	100.00	40.00	15.00
(89) Ed Roush	400.00	160.00	80.00
(90) "Muddy" Ruel	100.00	40.00	15.00
(91) Walter Ruether	100.00	40.00	15.00
(92) "Babe" Ruth (Photo montage)	8,000	4,000	2,400
(93) "Babe" Ruth (Holding bird.)	6,500	3,200	1,950
(94) "Babe" Ruth (Holding ball.)	8,000	4,000	2,400
(95) Bill Ryan	100.00	40.00	15.00
(96) Ray Schalk (Catching)	400.00	160.00	80.00
(97) Ray Schalk (Batting)	400.00	160.00	80.00
(98) Wally Schang	100.00	40.00	15.00
(99) Everett Scott	100.00	40.00	15.00
(101) Joe Sewell	400.00	160.00	80.00
(102) Robert Shawkey	100.00	40.00	15.00
(103) Pat Shea	100.00	40.00	15.00
(104) Earl Sheely	100.00	40.00	15.00
(105) Urban Schocker	100.00	40.00	15.00
(106) George Sisler (Batting)	400.00	160.00	80.00
(108) Earl Smith	100.00	40.00	15.00
(109) Elmer Smith	100.00	40.00	15.00
(110) Frank Snyder	100.00	40.00	15.00
(111) Bill Southworth	400.00	200.00	120.00
(112) Tris Speaker	600.00	240.00	120.00
(113) Milton J. Stock	100.00	40.00	15.00
(114) Amos Strunk	100.00	40.00	15.00
(115) Zeb Terry	100.00	40.00	15.00
(116) Fred Toney	100.00	40.00	15.00
(117) George Topocer (Toporcer)	100.00	40.00	15.00
(118) Bob Veach	100.00	40.00	15.00
(119) Oscar Vitt	100.00	40.00	15.00
(120) Curtis Walker	100.00	40.00	15.00
(121) W. Wambsganss (Photo actually Fred Coumbe.)	100.00	40.00	15.00
(122) Aaron Ward	100.00	40.00	15.00
(123) Zach Wheat	400.00	160.00	80.00
(124) George Whitted (Pittsburgh)	100.00	40.00	15.00
(125) Fred Williams	100.00	40.00	15.00
(126) Ivy B. Wingo	100.00	40.00	15.00
(127) Ross Young (Youngs)	400.00	160.00	80.00

1922 American Caramel Series of 240 (E120)

WASHINGTON AMERICANS
"SENATORS"
MANAGER—CLYDE MILAN

WALTER JOHNSON	PITCHER
TOM PHILLIPS	PITCHER
GEORGE MOGRIDGE	PITCHER
HARRY COURTNEY	PITCHER
J. T. ZACHARY	PITCHER
ED GHARRITY	CATCHER
VAL PICINICH	CATCHER
JOE JUDGE	FIRST BASE
STANLEY HARRIS	SECOND BASE
ROGER PECKINPAUGH	SHORT STOP
HOWARD SHANKS	THIRD BASE
LEON GOSLIN	OUTFIELD
SAM RICE	OUTFIELD
CLYDE MILAN	OUTFIELD
EARL SMITH	OUTFIELD

THIS PICTURE IS ONE OF A SERIES OF 240 PICTURES OF BASEBALL STARS—15 PLAYERS IN EACH OF THE 16 MAJOR LEAGUE TEAMS. WE SUPPLY HANDSOME BLANK ALBUMS TO HOLD 120 PICTURES—ONE FOR AMERICAN LEAGUE, ONE FOR NATIONAL LEAGUE—10 CENTS EACH POSTPAID.

AMERICAN CARAMEL CO.
LANCASTER, PA.   YORK, PA.

WALTER JOHNSON
PITCHER, WASHINGTON AMERICANS

One of the most popular sets of the 1920s candy cards, the 1922 E120s were produced by the American Caramel Co. and distributed with sticks of caramel candy. The unnumbered cards measure 2" x 3-1/2". Cards depicting players from the American League are printed in brown ink on thin cream cardboard; National Leaguers are printed in green on blue-green stock. Backs carry team checklists. Many of the E120 photos were used in other sets of the era. A pair of 11-1/2" x 10-1/2" albums, holding 120 cards each and stamped American or National League were also issued.

	NM	E	VG
Complete Set (240):	80,000	40,000	24,000
Common Player:	110.00	50.00	30.00
Album:	225.00	110.00	65.00
(1) Charles (Babe) Adams	175.00	70.00	35.00
(2) Eddie Ainsmith	175.00	70.00	35.00
(3) Vic Aldridge	175.00	70.00	35.00
(4) Grover C. Alexander	1,350	675.00	405.00
(5) Jim Bagby Sr.	175.00	70.00	35.00
(6) Frank (Home Run) Baker	500.00	200.00	100.00
(7) Dave (Beauty) Bancroft	500.00	200.00	100.00
(8) Walt Barbare	175.00	70.00	35.00
(9) Turner Barber	175.00	70.00	35.00
(10) Jess Barnes	175.00	70.00	35.00
(11) Clyde Barnhart	175.00	70.00	35.00
(12) John Bassler	175.00	70.00	35.00
(13) Will Bayne	175.00	70.00	35.00
(14) Walter (Huck) Betts	175.00	70.00	35.00
(15) Carson Bigbee	175.00	70.00	35.00
(16) Lu Blue	175.00	70.00	35.00
(17) Norman Boeckel	175.00	70.00	35.00
(18) Sammy Bohne	400.00	160.00	80.00
(19) George Burns	175.00	70.00	35.00
(20) George Burns	175.00	70.00	35.00
(21) "Bullet Joe" Bush	175.00	70.00	35.00
(22) Leon Cadore	175.00	70.00	35.00
(23) Marty Callaghan	175.00	70.00	35.00
(24) Frank Calloway (Callaway)	175.00	70.00	35.00
(25) Max Carey	500.00	200.00	100.00
(26) Jimmy Caveney	175.00	70.00	35.00
(27) Virgil Cheeves	175.00	70.00	35.00
(28) Vern Clemons	175.00	70.00	35.00
(29) Ty Cob (Cobb)	4,500	2,250	1,350
(30) Bert Cole	175.00	70.00	35.00
(31) Eddie Collins	500.00	200.00	100.00
(32) John (Shano) Collins	175.00	70.00	35.00
(33) T.P. (Pat) Collins	175.00	70.00	35.00
(34) Wilbur Cooper	175.00	70.00	35.00
(35) Harry Courtney	175.00	70.00	35.00
(36) Stanley Coveleskie (Coveleski)	500.00	200.00	100.00
(37) Elmer Cox	175.00	70.00	35.00
(38) Sam Crane	175.00	70.00	35.00
(39) Walton Cruise	175.00	70.00	35.00
(40) Bill Cunningham	175.00	70.00	35.00
(41) George Cutshaw	175.00	70.00	35.00
(42) Dave Danforth	175.00	70.00	35.00
(43) Jake Daubert	175.00	70.00	35.00
(44) George Dauss	175.00	70.00	35.00
(45) Frank (Dixie) Davis	175.00	70.00	35.00
(46) Hank DeBerry	175.00	70.00	35.00
(47) Albert Devormer (Lou DeVormer)	175.00	70.00	35.00
(48) Bill Doak	175.00	70.00	35.00
(49) Pete Donohue	175.00	70.00	35.00
(50) "Shufflin" Phil Douglas	175.00	70.00	35.00
(51) Joe Dugan	175.00	70.00	35.00
(52) Louis (Pat) Duncan	175.00	70.00	35.00
(53) Jimmy Dykes	175.00	70.00	35.00
(54) Howard Ehmke	300.00	150.00	90.00
(55) Frank Ellerbe	175.00	70.00	35.00
(56) Urban (Red) Faber	500.00	200.00	100.00
(57) Bib Falk (Bibb)	175.00	70.00	35.00
(58) Dana Fillingim	175.00	70.00	35.00
(59) Max Flack	175.00	70.00	35.00
(60) Ira Flagstead	175.00	70.00	35.00
(61) Art Fletcher	175.00	70.00	35.00
(62) Horace Ford	175.00	70.00	35.00
(63) Jack Fournier	175.00	70.00	35.00
(64) Frank Frisch	500.00	200.00	100.00
(65) Ollie Fuhrman	175.00	70.00	35.00
(66) Clarance Galloway	175.00	70.00	35.00
(67) Larry Gardner	175.00	70.00	35.00
(68) Walter Gerber	175.00	70.00	35.00
(69) Ed Gharrity	175.00	70.00	35.00
(70) John Gillespie	175.00	70.00	35.00
(71) Chas. (Whitey) Glazner	175.00	70.00	35.00
(72) Johnny Gooch	175.00	70.00	35.00
(73) Leon Goslin	500.00	200.00	100.00
(74) Hank Gowdy	175.00	70.00	35.00
(75) John Graney	175.00	70.00	35.00
(76) Tom Griffith	175.00	70.00	35.00
(77) Burleigh Grimes	500.00	200.00	100.00
(78) Oscar Ray Grimes	175.00	70.00	35.00
(79) Charlie Grimm	175.00	70.00	35.00
(80) Heinie Groh	175.00	70.00	35.00
(81) Jesse Haines	500.00	200.00	100.00
(82) Earl Hamilton	175.00	70.00	35.00
(83) Gene (Bubbles) Hargrave	175.00	70.00	35.00
(84) Bryan Harris (Harriss)	175.00	70.00	35.00
(85) Joe Harris	175.00	70.00	35.00

(86)	Stanley Harris	500.00	200.00	100.00
(87)	Chas. (Dowdy) Hartnett	500.00	200.00	100.00
(88)	Bob Hasty	175.00	70.00	35.00
(89)	Joe Hauser	225.00	90.00	45.00
(90)	Clif Heathcote	175.00	70.00	35.00
(91)	Harry Heilmann	500.00	200.00	100.00
(92)	Walter (Butch) Henline	175.00	70.00	35.00
(93)	Clarence (Shovel) Hodge	175.00	70.00	35.00
(94)	Walter Holke	175.00	70.00	35.00
(95)	Charles Hollocher	175.00	70.00	35.00
(96)	Harry Hooper	500.00	200.00	100.00
(97)	Rogers Hornsby	900.00	360.00	180.00
(98)	Waite Hoyt	500.00	200.00	100.00
(99)	Wilbur Hubbell (Wilbert)	175.00	70.00	35.00
(100)	Bernard (Bud) Hungling	175.00	70.00	35.00
(101)	Will Jacobson	175.00	70.00	35.00
(102)	Charlie Jamieson	175.00	70.00	35.00
(103)	Ernie Johnson	175.00	70.00	35.00
(104)	Sylvester Johnson	175.00	70.00	35.00
(105)	Walter Johnson	1,800	900.00	550.00
(106)	Jimmy Johnston	175.00	70.00	35.00
(107)	W.R. (Doc) Johnston	175.00	70.00	35.00
(108)	"Deacon" Sam Jones	175.00	70.00	35.00
(109)	Bob Jones	175.00	70.00	35.00
(110)	Percy Jones	175.00	70.00	35.00
(111)	Joe Judge	175.00	70.00	35.00
(112)	Ben Karr	175.00	70.00	35.00
(113)	Johnny Kelleher	175.00	70.00	35.00
(114)	George Kelly	500.00	200.00	100.00
(115)	Lee King	175.00	70.00	35.00
(116)	Wm (Larry) Kopff (Kopf)	175.00	70.00	35.00
(117)	Marty Krug	175.00	70.00	35.00
(118)	Johnny Lavan	175.00	70.00	35.00
(119)	Nemo Leibold	175.00	70.00	35.00
(120)	Roy Leslie	175.00	70.00	35.00
(121)	George Leverette (Leverett)	175.00	70.00	35.00
(122)	Adolfo Luque	175.00	70.00	35.00
(123)	Walter Mails	175.00	70.00	35.00
(124)	Al Mamaux	175.00	70.00	35.00
(125)	"Rabbit" Maranville	500.00	200.00	100.00
(126)	Cliff Markle	175.00	70.00	35.00
(127)	Richard (Rube) Marquard	500.00	200.00	100.00
(128)	Carl Mays	200.00	80.00	40.00
(129)	Hervey McClellan (Harvey)	175.00	70.00	35.00
(130)	Austin McHenry	175.00	70.00	35.00
(131)	"Stuffy" McInnis	175.00	70.00	35.00
(132)	Martin McManus	175.00	70.00	35.00
(133)	Mike McNally	175.00	70.00	35.00
(134)	Hugh McQuillan	175.00	70.00	35.00
(135a)	Lee Meadows (Philadelphia back)	175.00	70.00	35.00
(135b)	Lee Meadows (Pittsburgh back)	250.00	100.00	50.00
(136)	Mike Menosky	175.00	70.00	35.00
(137)	Bob (Dutch) Meusel	175.00	70.00	35.00
(138)	Emil (Irish) Meusel	175.00	70.00	35.00
(139)	Clyde Milan	175.00	70.00	35.00
(140)	Edmund (Bing) Miller	175.00	70.00	35.00
(141)	Elmer Miller	175.00	70.00	35.00
(142)	Lawrence (Hack) Miller	175.00	70.00	35.00
(143)	Clarence Mitchell	175.00	70.00	35.00
(144)	George Mogridge	175.00	70.00	35.00
(145)	Roy Moore	175.00	70.00	35.00
(146)	John L. Mokan	175.00	70.00	35.00
(147)	John Morrison	175.00	70.00	35.00
(148)	Johnny Mostil	175.00	70.00	35.00
(149)	Elmer Myers	175.00	70.00	35.00
(150)	Hy Myers	175.00	70.00	35.00
(151)	Roliene Naylor (Roleine)	175.00	70.00	35.00
(152)	Earl "Greasy" Neale	175.00	70.00	35.00
(153)	Art Nehf	175.00	70.00	35.00
(154)	Les Nunamaker	175.00	70.00	35.00
(155)	Joe Oeschger	175.00	70.00	35.00
(156)	Bob O'Farrell	175.00	70.00	35.00
(157)	Ivan Olson	175.00	70.00	35.00
(158)	George O'Neil	175.00	70.00	35.00
(159)	Steve O'Neill	175.00	70.00	35.00
(160)	Frank Parkinson	175.00	70.00	35.00
(161)	Roger Peckinpaugh	175.00	70.00	35.00
(162)	Herb Pennock	500.00	200.00	100.00
(163)	Ralph (Cy) Perkins	175.00	70.00	35.00
(164)	Will Pertica	175.00	70.00	35.00
(165)	Jack Peters	175.00	70.00	35.00
(166)	Tom Phillips	175.00	70.00	35.00
(167)	Val Picinich	175.00	70.00	35.00
(168)	Herman Pillette	175.00	70.00	35.00
(169)	Ralph Pinelli	175.00	70.00	35.00
(170)	Wallie Pipp	175.00	70.00	35.00
(171)	Clark Pittenger (Clarke)	175.00	70.00	35.00
(172)	Raymond Powell	175.00	70.00	35.00
(173)	Derrill Pratt	175.00	70.00	35.00
(174)	Jack Quinn	175.00	70.00	35.00
(175)	Joe (Goldie) Rapp	175.00	70.00	35.00
(176)	John Rawlings	175.00	70.00	35.00
(177)	Walter (Dutch) Reuther (Ruether)	175.00	70.00	35.00
(178)	Sam Rice	500.00	200.00	100.00
(179)	Emory Rigney	175.00	70.00	35.00
(180)	Jimmy Ring	175.00	70.00	35.00
(181)	Eppa Rixey	500.00	200.00	100.00
(182)	Charles Robertson	175.00	70.00	35.00
(183)	Ed Rommel	175.00	70.00	35.00
(184)	Eddie Roush	500.00	200.00	100.00
(185)	Harold (Muddy) Ruel (Herold)	175.00	70.00	35.00
(186)	Babe Ruth	18,500	9,250	5,550
(187)	Ray Schalk	500.00	200.00	100.00
(188)	Wallie Schang	175.00	70.00	35.00
(189)	Ray Schmandt	175.00	70.00	35.00
(190)	Walter Schmidt	175.00	70.00	35.00
(191)	Joe Schultz	175.00	70.00	35.00
(192)	Everett Scott	175.00	70.00	35.00
(193)	Henry Severeid	175.00	70.00	35.00
(194)	Joe Sewell	500.00	200.00	100.00
(195)	Howard Shanks	175.00	70.00	35.00
(196)	Bob Shawkey	175.00	70.00	35.00
(197)	Earl Sheely	175.00	70.00	35.00
(198)	Will Sherdel	175.00	70.00	35.00
(199)	Ralph Shinners	175.00	70.00	35.00
(200)	Urban Shocker	175.00	70.00	35.00
(201)	Charles (Chick) Shorten	175.00	70.00	35.00
(202)	George Sisler	500.00	200.00	100.00
(203)	Earl Smith (N.Y. Giants)	175.00	70.00	35.00
(204)	Earl Smith (Washington)	175.00	70.00	35.00
(205)	Elmer Smith	175.00	70.00	35.00
(206)	Jack Smith	175.00	70.00	35.00
(207)	Sherrod Smith	175.00	70.00	35.00
(208)	Colonel Snover	175.00	70.00	35.00
(209)	Frank Snyder	175.00	70.00	35.00
(210)	Al Sothoron	175.00	70.00	35.00
(211)	Bill Southworth	500.00	250.00	150.00
(212)	Tris Speaker	900.00	360.00	180.00
(213)	Arnold Statz	175.00	70.00	35.00
(214)	Milton Stock	175.00	70.00	35.00
(215)	Amos Strunk	175.00	70.00	35.00
(216)	Jim Tierney	175.00	70.00	35.00
(217)	John Tobin	175.00	70.00	35.00
(218)	Fred Toney	175.00	70.00	35.00
(219)	George Toporcer	175.00	70.00	35.00
(220)	Harold (Pie) Traynor	500.00	200.00	100.00
(221)	George Uhle	175.00	70.00	35.00
(222)	Elam Vangilder	175.00	70.00	35.00
(223)	Bob Veach	175.00	70.00	35.00
(224)	Clarence (Tillie) Walker	175.00	70.00	35.00
(225)	Curtis Walker	175.00	70.00	35.00
(226)	Al Walters	175.00	70.00	35.00
(227)	Bill Wambsganss	175.00	70.00	35.00
(228)	Aaron Ward	175.00	70.00	35.00
(229)	John Watson	175.00	70.00	35.00
(230)	Frank Welch	175.00	70.00	35.00
(231)	Zach Wheat	500.00	200.00	100.00
(232)	Fred (Cy) Williams	175.00	70.00	35.00
(233)	Kenneth Williams	175.00	70.00	35.00
(234)	Ivy Wingo	175.00	70.00	35.00
(235)	Joe Wood	400.00	160.00	80.00
(236)	Lawrence Woodall	175.00	70.00	35.00
(237)	Russell Wrightstone	175.00	70.00	35.00
(238)	Everett Yaryan	175.00	70.00	35.00
(239)	Ross Young (Youngs)	500.00	200.00	100.00
(240)	J.T. Zachary	175.00	70.00	35.00

1922 American Caramel Series of 80 (E122)

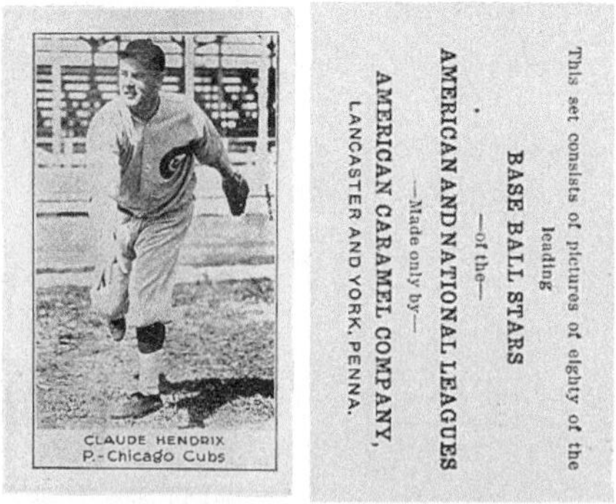
CLAUDE HENDRIX
P.-Chicago Cubs
This set consists of pictures of eighty of the leading
BASE BALL STARS
—of the—
AMERICAN AND NATIONAL LEAGUES
—Made only by—
AMERICAN CARAMEL COMPANY,
LANCASTER AND YORK, PENNA.

Known as E122 in the American Card Catalog, this set is actually a parallel of the E121 American Caramel set. The cards are nearly identical to E121's "Series of 80," except the player's name, position and team are printed inside a gray rectangle at the bottom of the card, and the photos have a more coarse appearance. At 2" x 3-1/4", the E122s are slightly shorter than E121s.

		NM	E	VG
	Complete Set (81):	40,000	20,000	12,000
	Common Player:	100.00	40.00	25.00
(1)	Grover Alexander	1,450	725.00	435.00
(2)	Jim Bagby Sr.	150.00	60.00	30.00
(3)	J. Franklin Baker	400.00	160.00	80.00
(4)	Dave Bancroft	400.00	160.00	80.00
(5)	Ping Bodie	150.00	60.00	30.00
(6)	George Burns	150.00	60.00	30.00
(7)	Geo. J. Burns	150.00	60.00	30.00
(8)	Owen Bush	150.00	60.00	30.00
(9)	Max Carey	400.00	160.00	80.00
(10)	Cecil Causey	150.00	60.00	30.00
(11)	Ty Cobb	1,900	760.00	380.00
(12)	Eddie Collins	400.00	160.00	80.00
(13)	Jake Daubert	150.00	60.00	30.00
(14)	George Dauss	150.00	60.00	30.00
(15)	Charles Deal	150.00	60.00	30.00
(16)	William Doak	150.00	60.00	30.00
(17)	Bill Donovan	150.00	60.00	30.00
(18)	Johnny Evers	400.00	160.00	80.00
(19)	Urban Faber	400.00	160.00	80.00
(20)	Eddie Foster	150.00	60.00	30.00
(21)	W.L. Gardner	150.00	60.00	30.00
(22)	"Kid" Gleason	150.00	60.00	30.00
(23)	Hank Gowdy	150.00	60.00	30.00
(24)	John Graney	150.00	60.00	30.00
(25)	Tom Griffith	150.00	60.00	30.00
(26)	Sam Harris (Stan "Bucky")	400.00	160.00	80.00
(27)	Harry Heilman (Heilmann)	400.00	160.00	80.00
(28)	Walter Holke	150.00	60.00	30.00
(29)	Charles Hollacher (Hollocher)	150.00	60.00	30.00
(30)	Harry Hooper	400.00	160.00	80.00
(31)	Rogers Hornsby	600.00	240.00	120.00
(32)	Wm. C. Jacobson	150.00	60.00	30.00
(33)	Walter Johnson	1,100	450.00	225.00
(34)	James Johnston	150.00	60.00	30.00
(35)	Joe Judge	150.00	60.00	30.00
(36)	George Kelly	400.00	160.00	80.00
(37)	Dick Kerr	150.00	60.00	30.00
(38)	P.J. Kilduff	150.00	60.00	30.00
(39)	Bill Killefer	150.00	60.00	30.00
(40)	John Lavan	150.00	60.00	30.00
(41)	Duffy Lewis	150.00	60.00	30.00
(42)	Perry Lipe	150.00	60.00	30.00
(43)	Al. Mamaux	150.00	60.00	30.00
(44)	"Rabbit" Maranville	400.00	160.00	80.00
(45)	Carl May (Mays)	200.00	80.00	40.00
(46)	John McGraw	400.00	160.00	80.00
(47)	Jack McInnis	150.00	60.00	30.00
(48)	Clyde Milan	150.00	60.00	30.00
(49)	Otto Miller	150.00	60.00	30.00
(50)	Guy Morton	150.00	60.00	30.00
(51)	Eddie Murphy	150.00	60.00	30.00
(52)	"Hy" Myers	150.00	60.00	30.00
(53)	Steve O'Neill	150.00	60.00	30.00
(54)	Roger Peckinbaugh (Peckinpaugh)	150.00	60.00	30.00
(55)	Jeff Pfeffer	150.00	60.00	30.00
(56)	Walter Pipp	175.00	70.00	35.00
(57)	E.C. Rice	400.00	160.00	80.00
(58)	Eppa Rixey, Jr.	400.00	160.00	80.00
(59)	Babe Ruth	15,000	7,500	4,500
(60)	"Slim" Sallee	150.00	60.00	30.00
(61)	Ray Schalk	400.00	160.00	80.00
(62)	Walter Schang	150.00	60.00	30.00
(63a)	Fred Schupp (Name incorrect.)	150.00	60.00	30.00
(63b)	Ferd Schupp (Name correct.)	150.00	60.00	30.00
(64)	Everett Scott	150.00	60.00	30.00
(65)	Hank Severeid	150.00	60.00	30.00
(66)	George Sisler (Batting)	400.00	160.00	80.00
(67)	George Sisler (Throwing)	400.00	160.00	80.00
(68)	Tris Speaker	750.00	300.00	150.00
(69)	Milton Stock	150.00	60.00	30.00
(70)	Amos Strunk	150.00	60.00	30.00
(71)	Chester Thomas	150.00	60.00	30.00
(72)	George Tyler	150.00	60.00	30.00
(73)	Jim Vaughn	150.00	60.00	30.00
(74)	Bob Veach	150.00	60.00	30.00
(75)	Oscar Vitt	150.00	60.00	30.00
(76)	W. Wambsganss	150.00	60.00	30.00
(77)	Zach Wheat	400.00	160.00	80.00
(78)	Fred Williams	150.00	60.00	30.00
(79)	Ivy B. Wingo	150.00	60.00	30.00
(80)	Joe Wood	150.00	60.00	30.00
(81)	Pep Young	150.00	60.00	30.00

1927 American Caramel Series of 60 (E126)

Issued in 1927 by the American Caramel Co., of Lancaster, Pa., this obscure 60-card set was one of the last of the caramel card issues. Measuring 2" x 3-1/4", the cards differ from most sets of the period because they are numbered. The back of each card includes an offer for an album to house the set which includes players from all 16 major league teams. The set has the American Card Catalog designation E126.

	NM	E	VG
Complete Set (60):	36,500	14,500	7,250
Common Player:	125.00	55.00	30.00
1 John Gooch	200.00	80.00	40.00
2 Clyde L. Barnhart	200.00	80.00	40.00
3 Joe Busch (Bush)	200.00	80.00	40.00
4 Lee Meadows	200.00	80.00	40.00
5 E.T. Cox	200.00	80.00	40.00
6 "Red" Faber	750.00	370.00	220.00
7 Aaron Ward	200.00	80.00	40.00
8 Ray Schalk	750.00	370.00	220.00
9 "Specs" Toporcer ("Specs")	200.00	80.00	40.00
10 Bill Southworth	750.00	370.00	220.00
11 Allen Sothoron	200.00	80.00	40.00
12 Will Sherdel	200.00	80.00	40.00
13 Grover Alexander	1,500	750.00	450.00
14 Jack Quinn	200.00	80.00	40.00
15 C. Galloway	200.00	80.00	40.00
16 "Eddie" Collins	750.00	370.00	220.00
17 "Ty" Cobb	4,200	2100.00	1,260
18 Percy Jones	200.00	80.00	40.00
19 Chas. Grimm	200.00	80.00	40.00
20 "Bennie" Karr	200.00	80.00	40.00
21 Charlie Jamieson	200.00	80.00	40.00
22 Sherrod Smith	200.00	80.00	40.00
23 Virgil Cheeves	200.00	80.00	40.00
24 James Ring	200.00	80.00	40.00
25 "Muddy" Ruel	200.00	80.00	40.00
26 Joe Judge	200.00	80.00	40.00
27 Tris Speaker	1,500	750.00	450.00
28 Walter Johnson	2,500	1,250	750.00
29 E.C. "Sam" Rice	750.00	370.00	220.00
30 Hank DeBerry	200.00	80.00	40.00
31 Walter Henline	200.00	80.00	40.00
32 Max Carey	750.00	370.00	220.00
33 Arnold J. Statz	200.00	80.00	40.00
34 Emil Meusel	200.00	80.00	40.00
35 T.P. "Pat" Collins	200.00	80.00	40.00
36 Urban Shocker	200.00	80.00	40.00
37 Bob Shawkey	200.00	80.00	40.00
38 "Babe" Ruth	16,000	8,000	4,800
39 Bob Meusel	200.00	80.00	40.00
40 Alex Ferguson	200.00	80.00	40.00
41 "Stuffy" McInnis	200.00	80.00	40.00
42 "Cy" Williams	200.00	80.00	40.00
43 Russel Wrightstone (Russell)	200.00	80.00	40.00
44 John Tobin	200.00	80.00	40.00
45 Wm. C. Jacobson	200.00	80.00	40.00
46 Bryan "Slim" Harriss	200.00	80.00	40.00
47 Elam Vangilder	200.00	80.00	40.00
48 Ken Williams	200.00	80.00	40.00
49 Geo. R. Sisler	1,500	750.00	450.00
50 Ed Brown	200.00	80.00	40.00
51 Jack Smith	200.00	80.00	40.00
52 Dave Bancroft	750.00	370.00	220.00
53 Larry Woodall	200.00	80.00	40.00
54 Lu Blue	200.00	80.00	40.00
55 Johnny Bassler	200.00	80.00	40.00
56 "Jakie" May	200.00	80.00	40.00
57 Horace Ford	200.00	80.00	40.00
58 "Curt" Walker	200.00	80.00	40.00
59 "Artie" Nehf	200.00	80.00	40.00
60 Geo. Kelly	600.00	240.00	120.00

1908 American League Pub. Co. Postcards

This set of black-and-white postcards was produced by the American League Publishing Co., Cleveland. The 3-1/2" x 5" cards have a large player posed-action photo against a white background and a small oval portrait photo in one of the top corners. A box at bottom contains some biographical data. The otherwise blank back has postcard indicia printed in black. As might be expected, all but two of the players in the known checklist were contemporary members of the

Cleveland ballclub. A few cards have been seen with red or green overprinting on front "Collister & Sayle, Athletic Outfitters, Cleveland, O.", with a schedule printed on back.

	NM	E	VG
Complete Set (16):	15,000	7,500	4,500
Common Player:	350.00	175.00	100.00
(1) Harry Bay	350.00	175.00	100.00
(2) Harry Bemis	350.00	175.00	100.00
(3) Charles Berger	350.00	175.00	100.00
(4) Joseph Birmingham	350.00	175.00	100.00
(5) W. Bradley	350.00	175.00	100.00
(6) Tyrus R. Cobb	6,000	3,000	1,800
(7) Walter Clarkson	350.00	175.00	100.00
(8) Elmer Flick	600.00	300.00	180.00
(9) C.T. Hickman	350.00	175.00	100.00
(10) William Hinchman	350.00	175.00	100.00
(11) Addie Joss	900.00	450.00	270.00
(12) Glen Liebhardt (Glenn)	350.00	175.00	100.00
(13) Nap Lajoie	900.00	450.00	270.00
(14) George Nill	350.00	175.00	100.00
(15) George Perring	350.00	175.00	100.00
(16) Honus Wagner	2,100	1,050	625.00

1950 American Nut & Chocolate Pennants (F150)

Although there is nothing on these small (1-7/8" x 4") felt pennants to identify the issuer, surviving ads show that the American Nut & Chocolate Co. of Boston sold them as a set of 22 for 50 cents. The pennants of American League players are printed in blue on white, while National Leaguers are printed in red on white. The pennants feature crude line-art drawings of the players at left, along with a facsimile autograph. A 10% variation in the size of the printing on the Elliott and Sain pennants has been noted, and may exist on others, as well. An approximately 17" x 7" version of the Ted Williams pennant is known and was available as a mail-in premium. Other players may also exist in that format. The checklist here is arranged alphabetically.

	NM	E	VG
Complete Set (22):	1,800	900.00	550.00
Common Player:	65.00	32.50	20.00
(1) Ewell Blackwell	65.00	32.50	20.00
(2) Harry Brecheen	65.00	32.50	20.00
(3) Phil Cavarretta	65.00	32.50	20.00
(4) Bobby Doerr	100.00	50.00	30.00
(5) Bob Elliott	65.00	32.50	20.00
(6) Boo Ferriss	65.00	32.50	20.00
(7) Joe Gordon	100.00	50.00	30.00
(8) Tommy Holmes	65.00	32.50	20.00
(9) Charles Keller	65.00	32.50	20.00
(10) Ken Keltner	65.00	32.50	20.00
(11) Ralph Kiner	100.00	50.00	30.00
(12) Whitey Kurowski	65.00	32.50	20.00
(13) Johnny Pesky	65.00	32.50	20.00
(14) Pee Wee Reese	130.00	65.00	40.00
(15) Phil Rizzuto	130.00	65.00	40.00
(16) Johnny Sain	65.00	32.50	20.00
(17) Enos Slaughter	100.00	50.00	30.00
(18) Warren Spahn	100.00	50.00	30.00
(19) Vern Stephens	65.00	32.50	20.00
(20) Earl Torgeson	65.00	32.50	20.00
(21) Dizzy Trout	65.00	32.50	20.00
(22) Ted Williams	300.00	150.00	90.00
(22) Ted Williams (17" x 7")	1,100	550.00	325.00

1968 American Oil Sweepstakes

One of several contemporary sweepstakes run by gas stations, this game required matching right- and left-side game pieces of the same athletic figure (or sporty auto) to win the stated prize. Naturally one side or the other was distributed in extremely limited quantities to avoid paying out too many prizes. Cards were given away in perforated pairs with a qualifying gasoline purchase. Uncut pairs carry a small premium over single cards. Data on which card halves were the rare part needed for redemption is incomplete and would have an effect on the collector value of surviving specimens. Individual game pieces measure 2-9/16" x 2-1/8" and are printed in color. Only the baseball players in the set are listed here.

	NM	E	VG
(1a) Mickey Mantle (Action, left side, $10.)	40.00	20.00	12.00
(1b) Mickey Mantle (Portrait, right side, $10.)	30.00	15.00	9.00
(2a) Willie Mays (Action, left side, $10.)	40.00	20.00	12.00
(2b) Willie Mays (Portrait, right side, $10.)	25.00	12.50	7.50
(3a) Babe Ruth (Action, left side, $1.)	40.00	20.00	12.00
(3b) Babe Ruth (Portrait, right side, $1.)	25.00	12.50	7.50

1962 American Tract Society

These full-color cards, which carry religious messages on the back, were issued in 1962 by the American Tract Society, an interdenominational, non-sectarian publisher of Christian literature in the United States since 1825. Known as "Tra-cards," the cards measure 2-3/4" x 3-1/2" and feature color photographs on the fronts. The set includes religious scenes along with photos of various celebrities and sports stars, including baseball players Felipe Alou, Bobby Richardson, Jerry Kindall and Al Worthington. (There are two poses each of Alou and Kindall.) The backs carry rather lengthy, first-person religious testimonials from the players. The cards are numbered on the back in the lower right corner.

	NM	E	VG
Complete Set (6):	70.00	35.00	20.00
Common Player:	10.00	5.00	3.00
43 Bobby Richardson	25.00	12.50	7.50
51a Jerry Kindall (Cleveland)	10.00	5.00	3.00
51b Jerry Kindall (Minnesota)	10.00	5.00	3.00
52a Felipe Alou (Kneeling)	15.00	7.50	4.50
52b Felipe Alou (Batting)	15.00	7.50	4.50
66 Al Worthington	10.00	5.00	3.00

1973 John B. Anderson Former Greats

This set of postcard-sized black-and-white cards features the artwork of John B. Anderson, a New York collector. Each card includes a facsimile autograph on front; backs are blank. The unnumbered cards are checklisted here in alphabetical order.

	NM	E	VG
Complete Set (12):	30.00	15.00	9.00
Common Player:	4.00	2.00	1.25

(1)	Ty Cobb	6.00	3.00	1.75
(2)	Mickey Cochrane	4.00	2.00	1.25
(3)	Roberto Clemente	10.00	5.00	3.00
(4)	Lou Gehrig	10.00	5.00	3.00
(5)	Frank Frisch	4.00	2.00	1.25
(6)	Gil Hodges	6.00	3.00	1.75
(7)	Rogers Hornsby	4.00	2.00	1.25
(8)	Connie Mack	4.00	2.00	1.25
(9)	Christy Mathewson	6.00	3.00	1.75
(10)	Jackie Robinson	10.00	5.00	3.00
(11)	Babe Ruth	10.00	5.00	3.00
(12)	Pie Traynor	4.00	2.00	1.25

1977 John B. Anderson Aaron-Mays

This collectors' set of postcard size, black-and-white drawings is a collectors issue. Cards are blank-backed.

		NM	E	VG
Complete Set (4):		5.00	2.50	1.50
Common Card:		2.00	1.00	.60
(1)	Hank Aaron (Arm in air.)	2.00	1.00	.60
(2)	Hank Aaron (Portrait)	2.00	1.00	.60
(3)	Willie Mays (Giants)	2.00	1.00	.60
(4)	Willie Mays (Mets)	2.00	1.00	.60

1977 John B. Anderson New York Teams

Joe DiMaggio

Stars and local favorites of the three New York teams of the 1940s and 1950s are featured in this set of collectors' cards. The 3-1/2" x 5-1/2" blank-back, black-and-white cards feature artwork by John B. Anderson. The unnumbered cards are checklisted here in alphabetical order.

		NM	E	VG
Complete Set (24):		45.00	27.50	13.50
Common Player:		4.00	2.00	1.25
(1)	Yogi Berra	6.00	3.00	1.75
(2)	Ralph Branca	4.00	2.00	1.25
(3)	Dolf Camilli	4.00	2.00	1.25
(4)	Roy Campanella	6.00	3.00	1.75
(5)	Jerry Coleman	4.00	2.00	1.25
(6)	Frank Crosetti	4.00	2.00	1.25
(7)	Bill Dickey	4.00	2.00	1.25
(8)	Joe DiMaggio	15.00	7.50	4.50
(9)	Sid Gordon	4.00	2.00	1.25
(10)	Babe Herman	4.00	2.00	1.25
(11)	Carl Hubbell	4.00	2.00	1.25
(12)	Billy Johnson	4.00	2.00	1.25
(13)	Ernie Lombardi	4.00	2.00	1.25
(14)	Willard Marshall	4.00	2.00	1.25
(15)	Willie Mays	10.00	5.00	3.00
(16)	Joe McCarthy	4.00	2.00	1.25
(17)	Joe Medwick	4.00	2.00	1.25
(18)	Joe Moore	4.00	2.00	1.25
(19)	Andy Pafko	4.00	2.00	1.25
(20)	Jackie Robinson	10.00	5.00	3.00
(21)	Red Ruffing	4.00	2.00	1.25
(22)	Bill Terry	4.00	2.00	1.25
(23)	Hoyt Wilhelm	4.00	2.00	1.25
(24)	Gene Woodling	4.00	2.00	1.25

1904 Anonymous Studio Cabinets

Collins

The origins of this series of cabinet photos are unknown, as is the full extent of the issue. It is known that the portraits are the uncredited work of Boston photographer Carl Horner. Sixteen pieces were sold in the 1991 Copeland Auction, though only the players listed here have been reliably checklisted. The cabinets measure about 5-3/8" x 6-7/8" and have black or dark gray borders. Some pieces are reported to have slate-blue blank backs. The player's last name is presented in the lower-left corner in black or white outline script. The unnumbered cards are checklisted here in alphabetical order.

		NM	E	VG
Common Player:		750.00	375.00	225.00
(1)	Jake Beckley	2,000	1,000	600.00
(2)	Roger Bresnahan	2,000	1,000	600.00
(3)	Jimmy Collins	2,000	1,000	600.00
(4)	Tommy Corcoran	750.00	370.00	220.00
(5)	Lave Cross	750.00	370.00	220.00
(6)	Hugh Duffy	2,000	1,000	600.00
(7)	Clark Griffith	2,000	1,000	600.00
(8)	Danny Hoffman	750.00	370.00	220.00
(9)	James "Ducky" Holmes	750.00	370.00	220.00
(10)	Iron Man McGinity (McGinnity)	2,000	1,000	600.00
(11)	John McGraw	2,000	1,000	600.00
(12)	Matty McIntyre	750.00	370.00	220.00

1912 Anonymous T207

While most T207s are found with one of five different cigarette brands advertised on back, there is a less commonly encountered type with no such ad. They are known as Anonymous backs. Two types are known, one originating from Factory 3 in Louisiana and one from Virginia's Factory 25. The latter is much scarcer though commands little additional premium.

(See 1912 T207 for checklist and price guide.)

1925 Anonymous Postcards

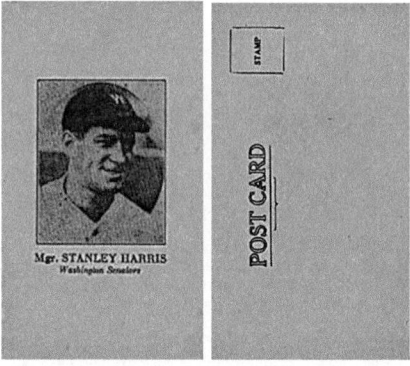

Mgr. STANLEY HARRIS
Washington Senators

POST CARD

STAMP

The date attributed is speculative based on the limited number of known subjects. These 3-1/4" x 5-1/2" cards. have a square portrait photo at center in black-and-white. With the exception of Babe Ruth, all known subjects were managers in 1925. The subject is identified by name (in either all-caps or upper- and lower-case, team, and, sometimes, title "Mgr." At least two styles of undivided backs have been found, with an ornate "POST CARD" device at top and a stamp box. The cards are printed on low-grade cardboard. Collector uncertainty as to the origins of the cards and the potential supply has kept market prices down.

	NM	E	VG
Common Player:	300.00	150.00	90.00
Tyrus Cobb	400.00	200.00	120.00
Mgr. Tyrus Cobb	400.00	200.00	120.00
Stanley Harris	200.00	100.00	60.00
Walter Johnson	300.00	150.00	90.00
John McGraw	200.00	100.00	60.00
"Bill" McKechnie	200.00	100.00	60.00
Wilbert Robinson	200.00	100.00	60.00
Babe Ruth	600.00	300.00	180.00

1940s Anonymous Premium Photos

These pictures were issued circa 1946-47. They can be found printed either on paper stock or glossy photo stock. There is no indication on these 8" x 10" black-and-white photos as to who produced them or for what purpose. The blank-backed, white-bordered pictures have the player identified with a sometimes-misspelled script signature. It is not known if this checklist is complete.

Harry Heilman

		NM	E	VG
Complete Set (12):		300.00	150.00	90.00
Common Player:		20.00	10.00	6.00
(1)	Ty Cobb	40.00	20.00	12.00
(2)	Dizzy Dean	25.00	12.50	7.50
(3)	Joe DiMaggio	45.00	22.00	13.50
(4)	Bob Feller	25.00	12.50	7.50
(5)	Lou Gehrig	40.00	20.00	12.00
(6)	Harry Heilman (Heilmann)	20.00	10.00	6.00
(7)	Roger (Rogers) Hornsby	25.00	12.50	7.50
(8)	Carl Hubbell	20.00	10.00	6.00
(9)	Walter Johnson	25.00	12.50	7.50
(10)	Connie Mack	20.00	10.00	6.00
(11)	Christy Mathewson	30.00	15.00	9.00
(12)	Bob Meusel	20.00	10.00	6.00
(13)	Irish Emil Meusel	20.00	10.00	6.00
(14)	Johnny Mize	20.00	10.00	6.00
(15)	Babe Ruth	50.00	25.00	15.00
(16)	babe Ruth/Lou Gehrig	40.00	20.00	12.00
(17)	Zack Wheat	20.00	10.00	6.00

1949-1950 Ansco Almendares Scorpions

This set of the Cuban Professional League champions of the 1949-50 season was sponsored by Ansco Cameras and Film, whose logo appears on front. Some cards have on back a rubber-stamp with the name of an Havana photo studio, which may have distributed the cards. The cards are actual black-and-white photos on glossy photo paper, measuring about 3" x 3-7/8". The Scorpions had many former and future major leaguers on their roster. Cards are listed alphabetically here.

		NM	E	VG
Complete Set (20):		3,250	1,625	975.00
Common Player:		150.00	60.00	40.00
(1)	Bill Antonello	175.00	70.00	45.00
(2)	Zungo Cabrera	150.00	60.00	40.00
(3)	Tony Castanos	150.00	60.00	40.00
(4)	Avelino Canizares	150.00	60.00	40.00
(5)	Kevin (Chuck) Connors	450.00	180.00	110.00
(6)	Andres Fleitas	150.00	60.00	40.00
(7)	Al Gionfriddo	175.00	70.00	45.00
(8)	Fermin Guerra	150.00	60.00	40.00
(9)	Gene Handley	150.00	60.00	40.00
(10)	Bob Hooper	150.00	60.00	40.00
(11)	Vincente Lopez	150.00	60.00	40.00
(12)	Conrado Marrero	175.00	70.00	45.00
(13)	Agapito Mayor	150.00	60.00	40.00
(14)	Willie Miranda	175.00	70.00	45.00
(15)	Rene Monteagudo	150.00	60.00	40.00
(16)	Roberto Ortiz	150.00	60.00	40.00
(17)	Hector Rodriguez	150.00	60.00	40.00
(18)	Octavio Rubert	150.00	60.00	40.00
(19)	Rene Solis	150.00	60.00	40.00
(20)	Ed Wright	150.00	60.00	40.00

1961-62 Apple Fresh Milk Minnesota Twins

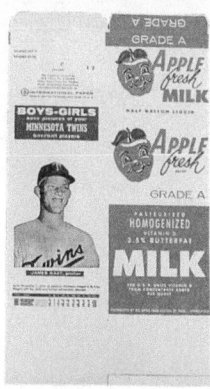

(See 1961, 1962 Cloverleaf Dairy Minnesota Twins.)

1971 Arco

In 1971, players from four major league teams in the east were featured in a set of facsimile autographed color photos in a gas station giveaway program. Following the promotion, leftover pictures were sold directly to collectors in the pages of the existing hobby media. The photos share an 8" x 10" format, with virtually all of the players being pictured without caps. Red, white and blue stars flank the player name in the bottom border. Black-and-white backs have career summary and stats, personal data, team sponsor and union logos and an ad for frames for the pictures. The unnumbered photos are listed here alphabetically within team.

		NM	E	VG
Complete Set (49):		175.00	90.00	50.00
Common Player:		3.00	1.50	.90
	RED SOX TEAM SET:	60.00	30.00	18.00
(1)	Luis Aparicio	10.00	5.00	3.00
(2)	Ken Brett	4.00	2.00	1.25
(3)	Billy Conigliaro	4.00	2.00	1.25
(4)	Ray Culp	4.00	2.00	1.25
(5)	Doug Griffin	4.00	2.00	1.25
(6)	Bob Montgomery	4.00	2.00	1.25
(7)	Gary Peters	4.00	2.00	1.25
(8)	George Scott	5.00	2.50	1.50
(9)	Sonny Siebert	4.00	2.00	1.25
(10)	Reggie Smith	5.00	2.50	1.50
(11)	Ken Tatum	4.00	2.00	1.25
(12)	Carl Yastrzemski	15.00	7.50	4.50
	YANKEES TEAM SET:	65.00	32.50	20.00
(1)	Jack Aker	6.00	3.00	1.75
(2)	Stan Bahnsen	6.00	3.00	1.75
(3)	Frank Baker	6.00	3.00	1.75
(4)	Danny Cater	6.00	3.00	1.75
(5)	Horace Clarke	6.00	3.00	1.75
(6)	John Ellis	6.00	3.00	1.75
(7)	Gene Michael	6.00	3.00	1.75
(8)	Thurman Munson	12.00	6.00	3.50
(9)	Bobby Murcer	7.50	3.75	2.25
(10)	Fritz Peterson	6.00	3.00	1.75
(11)	Mel Stottlemyre	6.00	3.00	1.75
(12)	Roy White	7.50	3.75	2.25
	PHILLIES TEAM SET:	40.00	20.00	12.00
(1)	Larry Bowa	3.00	1.50	.90
(2)	Jim Bunning	10.00	5.00	3.00
(3)	Roger Freed	3.00	1.50	.90
(4)	Terry Harmon	3.00	1.50	.90
(5)	Larry Hisle	3.00	1.50	.90
(6)	Joe Hoerner	3.00	1.50	.90
(7)	Deron Johnson	3.00	1.50	.90
(8)	Tim McCarver	5.00	2.50	1.50
(9)	Don Money	3.00	1.50	.90
(10)	Dick Selma	3.00	1.50	.90
(11)	Chris Short	3.00	1.50	.90
(12)	Tony Taylor	3.00	1.50	.90
(13)	Rick Wise	3.00	1.50	.90

	PIRATES TEAM SET:	50.00	25.00	15.00
(1)	Gene Alley	3.00	1.50	.90
(2)	Steve Blass	3.00	1.50	.90
(3)	Roberto Clemente	30.00	15.00	9.00
(4)	Dave Giusti	3.00	1.50	.90
(5)	Richie Hebner	3.00	1.50	.90
(6)	Bill Mazeroski	7.50	3.75	2.25
(7)	Bob Moose	3.00	1.50	.90
(8)	Al Oliver	4.50	2.25	1.25
(9)	Bob Robertson	3.00	1.50	.90
(10)	Manny Sanguillen	3.00	1.50	.90
(11)	Willie Stargell	7.50	3.75	2.25
(12)	Luke Walker	3.00	1.50	.90

1980-81 Argus Publishing Reggie Jackson

 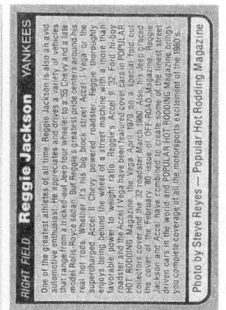

Some of the cars from Reggie Jackson's collection of hot rods and vintage vehicles were featured on a series of promotional cards issued by the publisher of Hot Rodding and Super Chevy magazines. The standard-size color cards have photos of Jackson with his cars on front, along with magazine and other logos. Backs have information on Jackson's cars. It was reported 10,000 of each were produced for distribution at automotive trade shows and a California drag strip.

		NM	E	VG
Complete Set (3):		80.00	40.00	24.00
(1)	1980 SEMA Show (Reggie Jackson) (1932 Ford highboy)	40.00	20.00	12.00
2	1981 SEMA (Reggie Jackson) (1932 Ford 5-window)	20.00	10.00	6.00
3	1981 Super Chevy Sunday (Reggie Jackson) (1955 Chevrolet)	20.00	10.00	6.00

1955 Armour Coins

In 1955, Armour inserted a plastic "coin" into packages of hot dogs. A raised profile of a ballplayer is on front along with the player's name and team. On back, between a diamond diagram and crossed bats are name, team, position, birthplace and date, batting and throwing preference, and 1954 hitting or pitching record. The coins measure 1-1/2" in diameter and are unnumbered. They can be found in a variety of colors, some of which are much scarcer than others and elicit higher prices from Armour specialists who have studied their relative scarcities. Values shown are for coins in the most common colors (aqua, blue, green, orange and red). Each 1955 coin can be found in two different "busts tilts" in which the tip of the cap and back point of the bust point to distinctly different areas of the rim. These variations are too arcane for the average collector. The complete set price includes only the most common variations.

		NM	E	VG
Complete Set (24):		800.00	400.00	240.00
Common Player:		15.00	8.00	4.00
(1a)	John "Johnny" Antonelli ("New York Giants" on back.)	75.00	37.00	22.00
(1b)	John "Johnny" Antonelli ("N.Y. Giants" on back.)	15.00	8.00	4.00
(2)	Larry "Yogi" Berra	40.00	20.00	12.00
(3)	Delmar "Del" Crandall	15.00	8.00	4.00
(4)	Lawrence "Larry" Doby	30.00	15.00	9.00

(5a)	James "Jim" Finigan ("Ouincy" on back)	15.00	8.00	4.00
(5b)	James "Jim" Finigan ("Quincy" on back)	15.00	8.00	4.00
(6)	Edward "Whitey" Ford	50.00	25.00	15.00
(7a)	James "Junior" Gilliam ("bats L or R,")	40.00	20.00	12.00
(7b)	James "Junior" Gilliam ("bats L - R," thick lips, wide gap between "BROOKLYN" and "DODGERS")	75.00	37.00	22.00
(7c)	James "Junior" Gilliam ("bats L - R," thin lips, narrow gap between "BROOKLYN" and "DODGERS")	75.00	37.00	22.00
(8a)	Harvey "Kitten" Haddix (Narrow gap between "LOUIS" and "CARDINALS")	40.00	20.00	12.00
(8b)	Harvey "Kitten" Haddix (Wide gap between "LOUIS" and "CARDINALS")	15.00	8.00	4.00
(9a)	Ranson "Randy" Jackson (Ransom) ("nfielder" on back)	125.00	65.00	40.00
(9b)	Ranson "Randy" Jackson (Ransom) ("Infielder" on back.)	40.00	20.00	12.00
(10a)	Jack "Jackie" Jensen ("Boston Reb Sox")	30.00	15.00	9.00
(10b)	Jack "Jackie" Jensen ("Boston Red Sox")	50.00	25.00	15.00
(11)	Theodore "Ted" Kluszewski	15.00	8.00	4.00
(12a)	Harvey E. Kuenn (line on back is bats/throws. Widely spaced letters in name; last)	100.00	50.00	30.00
(12b)	Harvey E. Kuenn (Widely spaced letters in name; last line on back is 1954 average.)	50.00	25.00	15.00
(12c)	Harvey E. Kuenn (back is 1954 average. Condensed letters in name; last line on)	50.00	25.00	15.00
(13a)	Charles "Mickey" Mantel (Incorrect spelling.)	125.00	65.00	40.00
(13b)	Charles "Mickey" Mantle (Corrected) ("bats L or R")	400.00	200.00	120.00
(13c)	Charles "Mickey" Mantle (Corrected) ("bats L - R")	800.00	400.00	240.00
(14)	Donald "Don" Mueller (SP)	40.00	20.00	12.00
(15)	Harold "Pee Wee" Reese	40.00	20.00	12.00
(16)	Allie P. Reynolds	15.00	8.00	4.00
(17)	Albert "Flip" Rosen	15.00	8.00	4.00
(18)	Curtis "Curt" Simmons	15.00	8.00	4.00
(19a)	Edwin "Duke" Snider (No decimal before 341)	100.00	50.00	30.00
(19b)	Edwin "Duke" Snider (Decimal before 341)	100.00	50.00	30.00
(20)	Warren Spahn	40.00	20.00	12.00
(21)	Frank Thomas (SP)	40.00	20.00	12.00
(22a)	Virgil "Fire" Trucks (WHITESOX)	15.00	8.00	4.00
(22b)	Virgil "Fire" Trucks (WHITE SOX)	150.00	75.00	45.00
(23)	Robert "Bob" Turley	15.00	8.00	4.00
(24)	James "Mickey" Vernon	15.00	8.00	4.00

1958 Armour S.F. Giants Tabs

In the Giants' first season on the West Coast, packages of Armour hot dogs in the Bay Area could be found with a small (about 2" x 1-5/8") lithographed tin player "tab" enclosed. In team colors of black, white and orange the tabs have black-and-white portraits at center, around which is a round, square or diamond shaped device bearing the team name and other graphic touches. At the sides are wings with baseballs or caps printed thereon. A 1/2" tab is at top with a slotted panel at bottom. The tab of one piece could be inserted into the slot of another to create a chain of these pieces, or the top tab could be folded over a shirt pocket to wear the item as a badge. The unnumbered pieces are checklisted here alphabetically. NM values quoted are for unbent pieces only.

	NM	E	VG
Complete Set (10):	2,750	1,350	825.00
Common Player:	250.00	125.00	75.00
(1) Johnny Antonelli	250.00	125.00	75.00
(2) Curt Barclay	250.00	125.00	75.00
(3) Ray Crone	250.00	125.00	75.00
(4) Whitey Lockman	250.00	125.00	75.00
(5a) Willie Mays (Portrait in circle.)	500.00	250.00	150.00
(5b) Willie Mays (Portrait in diamond.)	500.00	250.00	150.00
(6) Don Mueller	250.00	125.00	75.00
(7) Danny O'Connell	250.00	125.00	75.00
(8) Hank Sauer	250.00	125.00	75.00
(9) Daryl Spencer	250.00	125.00	75.00
(10) Bobby Thomson	250.00	125.00	75.00

1959 Armour Bacon K.C. Athletics

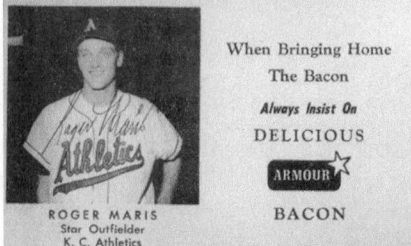

ROGER MARIS
Star Outfielder
K. C. Athletics

Not so much a baseball card set as a handful of related single-card issues used at player promotional appearances, a total of four cards are currently known of this issue. Measuring either 5-1/2" x 3-1/4" or 5-1/2" x 4", the horizontal-format cards are printed in black-and-white on paper stock and are blank-backed. A posed player photo appears at left, with an ad for Armour bacon at right. Cards were given out at player appearances at local supermarkets. To date, all known specimens have been found autographed and are priced as such.

	NM	E	VG
Complete Set (4):	2,500	1,250	750.00
Common Player:	75.00	37.00	22.00
(1) Harry Chiti	75.00	37.50	22.50
(2) Whitey Herzog	90.00	45.00	27.50
(3) Roger Maris (Photo to waist.)	1,00.00	500.00	300.00
(4) Roger Maris (Hands on knees.)	1,400	700.00	425.00

1959 Armour Coins

After a three-year layoff, Armour again inserted plastic "coins" into its hot dog packages. The coins retained their 1-1/2" size but did not include as much detailed information as in 1955. Missing from the coins' backs is information such as birthplace and date, team, and batting and throwing preference. The fronts contain the player's name and, unlike 1955, only the team nickname is given. The set consists of 20 coins which come in a myriad of colors. Common colors are navy blue, royal blue, medium green, orange and red. Many other colors are known, many of them scarce and of extra value to Armour specialists. In 1959 Armour had a mail-in offer of 10 coins for $1, which accounts for half of the coins in the set being much amore plentiful than the others.

	NM	E	VG
Complete Set (20):	400.00	200.00	120.00
Common Player:	15.00	7.50	4.50

(1) Hank Aaron	30.00	15.00	9.00
(2) John Antonelli	15.00	7.50	4.50
(3) Richie Ashburn	30.00	15.00	9.00
(4) Ernie Banks	30.00	15.00	9.00
(5) Don Blasingame	15.00	7.50	4.50
(6) Bob Cerv	15.00	7.50	4.50
(7) Del Crandall	15.00	7.50	4.50
(8) Whitey Ford	25.00	12.50	7.50
(9) Nellie Fox	20.00	10.00	6.00
(10) Jackie Jensen	20.00	10.00	6.00
(11) Harvey Kuenn	30.00	15.00	9.00
(12) Frank Malzone	20.00	10.00	6.00
(13) Johnny Podres	30.00	15.00	9.00
(14) Frank Robinson	30.00	15.00	9.00
(15) Roy Sievers	15.00	7.50	4.50
(16) Bob Skinner	15.00	7.50	4.50
(17) Frank Thomas	15.00	7.50	4.50
(18) Gus Triandos	15.00	7.50	4.50
(19) Bob Turley	20.00	10.00	6.00
(20) Mickey Vernon	15.00	7.50	4.50

1960 Armour Coins

The 1960 Armour coin issue is identical in number and style to the 1959 set. The unnumbered coins, 1-1/2" in diameter, once again came in a variety of colors. Common colors for 1960 are pale blue, royal blue, red, red-orange, light green, dark green and yellow. Values shown are for common-colored pieces. Scarcer colors exist and may be of premium value to specialists. The Bud Daley coin is very scarce, although it is not known why. Theories for the scarcity center on broken molding equipment, contract disputes, or that the coin was only inserted in a test product that quickly proved to be unsuccessful. As in 1959, a mail-in offer for 10 free coins was made available by Armour. The complete set price includes only the most common variations. Many 1960 Armour coins are found with only partial rims on back (Mantle is particularly susceptible to this condition). Coins without full back rims can grade no higher than VG.

	NM	E	VG
Complete Set (20):	1,100	550.00	325.00
Common Player:	12.50	6.25	3.75
(1a) Hank Aaron (Braves)	25.00	12.50	7.50
(1b) Hank Aaron (Milwaukee Braves)	40.00	20.00	12.00
(2) Bob Allison	20.00	10.00	6.00
(3) Ernie Banks	30.00	15.00	9.00
(4) Ken Boyer	12.50	6.25	3.75
(5) Rocky Colavito	35.00	17.50	10.50
(6) Gene Conley	12.50	6.25	3.75
(7) Del Crandall	12.50	6.25	3.75
(8) Bud Daley	750.00	375.00	225.00
(9a) Don Drysdale (L.A condensed.)	35.00	17.50	10.50
(9b) Don Drysdale (Space between L. and A.)	25.00	12.50	7.50
(10) Whitey Ford	20.00	10.00	6.00
(11) Nellie Fox	15.00	7.50	4.50
(12) Al Kaline	20.00	10.00	6.00
(13a) Frank Malzone (Red Sox)	12.50	6.25	3.75
(13b) Frank Malzone (Boston Red Sox)	20.00	10.00	6.00
(14) Mickey Mantle	75.00	37.50	22.50
(15) Ed Mathews	20.00	10.00	6.00
(16) Willie Mays	50.00	25.00	15.00
(17) Vada Pinson	12.50	6.25	3.75
(18) Dick Stuart	12.50	6.25	3.75
(19) Gus Triandos	12.50	6.25	3.75
(20) Early Wynn	12.50	6.25	3.75

1908 Art Post Card Co. Our Home Team

This set of team post cards presents players from five Midwestern teams in a foldout format. The cover of the accordian-fold novelty is in orange and green. A 3-1/2" x 5-1/2" postcard depicts a ballfield and various pieces of baseball equipment. Printed on a large baseball is "Our Home Team." Folded inside are a number of 2" x 2-1/4" panels with one or two player photos printed on each side. Each player is identified, though misspelled names are common.

	NM	E	VG
Complete Set (5):	5,500	2,750	1,650
Common Team Card:	800.00	400.00	250.00
(1) Chicago Cubs(Three Finger Brown, Frank Chance, Johnny Evers, Chick Fraser, Solly Hofman, Johnny Kling, Carl Lundgren, Pat Moran, Jake Pfeister, Ed Reulbach, Wildfire Schulte, Jimmy Sheckard, Jimmy Slagle, Harry Steinfeldt, Joe Tinker, Heinie Zimmerman)	1,200	600.00	360.00
(2) Chicago White Sox(Nick Altrock, John Anderson, Jake Atz, George Davis, Jiggs Donohue (Donahue), Patsy Dougherty, Eddie Hahn, Frank Isbell, Fielder Jones, Frank Owen, George Rohe, Billy Sullivan, Lee Tannehill, Ed Walsh, Doc White)	1,850	925.00	550.00
(3) Detroit Tigers(William Caughlin (Coughlin), Ty Cobb, Sam Crawford, Wild Bill Donovan, Red Downs, Hughie Jennings, Davy Jones, Red Killefer, Ed Killian, Matty McIntyre, George Mullin, Charley O'Leary, Fred Payne, Claude Rossman, Germany Schaefer, Boss Schmidt, George Suggs, Ed Summers, Ira Thomas, George Winter, Ed Willett)	2,000	1,000	600.00
(4) St. Louis Browns(Bob Bailey, Bert Blue, Dode Criss, Bill Dinneen, Hobe Ferris, Bill Graham, Roy Hartzell, Danny Hoffman, Harry Howell, Charlie Jones, Tom Jones, Jimmy McAleer, Jack O'Connor, Barney Pelty, Jack Powell, Al Schweitzer, Tubby Spencer, George Stone, Rube Waddell, Bobby Wallace, Jimmy Williams, Joe Yeager)	950.00	475.00	285.00
(5) St. Louis Cardinals	800.00	400.00	240.00

1953-55 Artvue Hall of Fame Plaque Postcards - Type 1

From 1953-1963, Artvue was the official producer of the Baseball Hall of Fame's cards available for public sale. The 3-1/2" x 5-1/2" black-and-white cards depict the bronze plaque of each inductee. Fronts have a white border. Postcard-style backs have a bit of player data and identification of the specific producer. On Type 1 Artvue cards, issued 1953-55, the bolt holes in the four corners of the plaque are open. The Type 2 Artvues have baseball bolts in each corner of the plaque. The unnumbered cards are checklisted here alphabetically.

		NM	E	VG
Complete Set (79):		2,000	1,000	600.00
Common Player:		30.00	15.00	9.00
(1)	G.C. Alexander	30.00	15.00	9.00
(2)	Adrian Anson	30.00	15.00	9.00
(3)	Frank Baker	30.00	15.00	9.00
(4)	Ed Barrow	30.00	15.00	9.00
(5)	Chief Bender	30.00	15.00	9.00
(6)	Roger Bresnahan	30.00	15.00	9.00
(7)	Dan Brouthers	30.00	15.00	9.00
(8)	Mordecai Brown	30.00	15.00	9.00
(9)	Morgan Bulkeley	30.00	15.00	9.00
(10)	Jesse Burkett	30.00	15.00	9.00
(11)	Alexander Cartwright	30.00	15.00	9.00
(12)	Henry Chadwick	30.00	15.00	9.00
(13)	Frank Chance	30.00	15.00	9.00
(14)	Jack Chesbro	30.00	15.00	9.00
(15)	Fred Clarke	30.00	15.00	9.00
(16)	Ty Cobb	80.00	40.00	24.00
(17)	Mickey Cochrane	30.00	15.00	9.00
(18)	Eddie Collins	30.00	15.00	9.00
(19)	Jimmy Collins	30.00	15.00	9.00
(20)	Charles Comiskey	30.00	15.00	9.00
(21)	Tom Connolly	30.00	15.00	9.00
(22)	Candy Cummings	30.00	15.00	9.00
(23)	Dizzy Dean	30.00	15.00	9.00
(24)	Ed Delahanty	30.00	15.00	9.00
(25)	Bill Dickey	30.00	15.00	9.00
(26)	Joe DiMaggio	80.00	40.00	24.00
(27)	Hugh Duffy	30.00	15.00	9.00
(28)	Johnny Evers	30.00	15.00	9.00
(29)	Buck Ewing	30.00	15.00	9.00
(30)	Jimmie Foxx	30.00	15.00	9.00
(31)	Frankie Frisch	30.00	15.00	9.00
(32)	Lou Gehrig	90.00	45.00	27.50
(33)	Charlie Gehringer	30.00	15.00	9.00
(34)	Clark Griffith	30.00	15.00	9.00
(35)	Lefty Grove	30.00	15.00	9.00
(36)	Gabby Hartnett	30.00	15.00	9.00
(37)	Harry Heilmann	30.00	15.00	9.00
(38)	Rogers Hornsby	30.00	15.00	9.00
(39)	Carl Hubbell	30.00	15.00	9.00
(40)	Hughie Jennings	30.00	15.00	9.00
(41)	Ban Johnson	30.00	15.00	9.00
(42)	Walter Johnson	60.00	30.00	18.00
(43)	Willie Keeler	30.00	15.00	9.00
(44)	King Kelly	30.00	15.00	9.00
(45)	Bill Klem	30.00	15.00	9.00
(46)	Nap Lajoie	30.00	15.00	9.00
(47)	Kenesaw Landis	30.00	15.00	9.00
(48)	Ted Lyons	30.00	15.00	9.00
(49)	Connie Mack	30.00	15.00	9.00
(50)	Rabbit Maranville	30.00	15.00	9.00
(51)	Christy Mathewson	60.00	30.00	18.00
(52)	Tommy McCarthy	30.00	15.00	9.00
(53)	Joe McGinnity	30.00	15.00	9.00
(54)	John McGraw	30.00	15.00	9.00
(55)	Kid Nichols	30.00	15.00	9.00
(56)	Jim O'Rourke	30.00	15.00	9.00
(57)	Mel Ott	30.00	15.00	9.00
(58)	Herb Pennock	30.00	15.00	9.00
(59)	Ed Plank	30.00	15.00	9.00
(60)	Chas. Radbourn	30.00	15.00	9.00
(61)	Wilbert Robinson	30.00	15.00	9.00
(62)	Babe Ruth	120.00	60.00	35.00
(63)	Ray Schalk	30.00	15.00	9.00
(64)	Al Simmons	30.00	15.00	9.00
(65)	George Sisler	30.00	15.00	9.00
(66)	Al Spalding	30.00	15.00	9.00
(67)	Tris Speaker	30.00	15.00	9.00
(68)	Bill Terry	30.00	15.00	9.00
(69)	Joe Tinker	30.00	15.00	9.00
(70)	Pie Traynor	30.00	15.00	9.00
(71)	Dazzy Vance	30.00	15.00	9.00
(72)	Rube Waddell	30.00	15.00	9.00
(73)	Honus Wagner	60.00	30.00	18.00
(74)	Bobby Wallace	30.00	15.00	9.00
(75)	Ed Walsh	30.00	15.00	9.00
(76)	Paul Waner	30.00	15.00	9.00
(77)	George Wright	30.00	15.00	9.00
(78)	Harry Wright	30.00	15.00	9.00
(79)	Cy Young	60.00	30.00	18.00

1956-63 Artvue Hall of Fame Plaque Postcards - Type 2

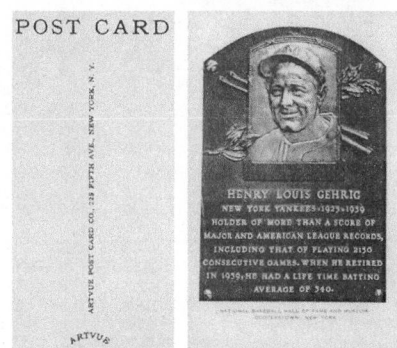

From 1953-1963, Artvue was the official producer of the Baseball Hall of Fame's postcards available for public sale. The 3-1/2" x 5-1/2" black-and-white cards depict the bronze plaque of each inductee. Fronts have a white border. Postcard-style backs have a bit of player data and identification of the specific producer. On Type 2 Artvue cards, issued 1956-63, there are baseball bolts in each corner of the plaque. The unnumbered cards are checklisted here alphabetically. Players unique to Type 2 are noted with an asterisk.

		NM	E	VG
Complete Set (94):		2,000	1,000	600.00
Common Player:		25.00	12.50	7.50
(1)	G.C. Alexander	25.00	12.50	7.50
(2)	Adrian Anson	25.00	12.50	7.50
(3)	Frank Baker	25.00	12.50	7.50
(4)	Ed Barrow	25.00	12.50	7.50
(5)	Chief Bender	25.00	12.50	7.50
(6)	Roger Bresnahan	25.00	12.50	7.50
(7)	Dan Brouthers	25.00	12.50	7.50
(8)	Mordecai Brown	25.00	12.50	7.50
(9)	Morgan Bulkeley	25.00	12.50	7.50
(10)	Jesse Burkett	25.00	12.50	7.50
(11)	Max Carey (*)	25.00	12.50	7.50
(12)	Alexander Cartwright	25.00	12.50	7.50
(13)	Henry Chadwick	25.00	12.50	7.50
(14)	Frank Chance	25.00	12.50	7.50
(15)	Jack Chesbro	25.00	12.50	7.50
(16)	Fred Clarke	25.00	12.50	7.50
(17)	John Clarkson (*)	25.00	12.50	7.50
(18)	Ty Cobb	60.00	30.00	18.00
(19)	Mickey Cochrane	25.00	12.50	7.50
(20)	Eddie Collins	25.00	12.50	7.50
(21)	Jimmy Collins	25.00	12.50	7.50
(22)	Charles Comiskey	25.00	12.50	7.50
(23)	Tom Connolly	25.00	12.50	7.50
(24)	Sam Crawford (*)	25.00	12.50	7.50
(25)	Joe Cronin (*)	25.00	12.50	7.50
(26)	Candy Cummings	25.00	12.50	7.50
(27)	Dizzy Dean	25.00	12.50	7.50
(28)	Ed Delahanty	25.00	12.50	7.50
(29)	Bill Dickey	25.00	12.50	7.50
(30)	Joe DiMaggio	80.00	40.00	24.00
(31)	Hugh Duffy	25.00	12.50	7.50
(32)	Johnny Evers	25.00	12.50	7.50
(33)	Buck Ewing	25.00	12.50	7.50
(34)	Bob Feller (*)	25.00	12.50	7.50
(35)	Elmer Flick (*)	25.00	12.50	7.50
(36)	Jimmie Foxx	25.00	12.50	7.50
(37)	Frank Frisch	25.00	12.50	7.50
(38)	Lou Gehrig	80.00	40.00	24.00
(39)	Charlie Gehringer	25.00	12.50	7.50
(40)	Hank Greenberg (*)	25.00	12.50	7.50
(41)	Clark Griffith	25.00	12.50	7.50
(42)	Lefty Grove	25.00	12.50	7.50
(43)	Billy Hamilton (*)	25.00	12.50	7.50
(44)	Gabby Hartnett	25.00	12.50	7.50
(45)	Harry Heilmann	25.00	12.50	7.50
(46)	Rogers Hornsby	25.00	12.50	7.50
(47)	Carl Hubbell	25.00	12.50	7.50
(48)	Hughie Jennings	25.00	12.50	7.50
(49)	Ban Johnson	25.00	12.50	7.50
(50)	Walter Johnson	40.00	20.00	12.00
(51)	Willie Keeler	25.00	12.50	7.50
(52)	King Kelly	25.00	12.50	7.50
(53)	Bill Klem	25.00	12.50	7.50
(54)	Nap Lajoie	25.00	12.50	7.50
(55)	Kenesaw Landis	25.00	12.50	7.50
(56)	Ted Lyons	25.00	12.50	7.50
(57)	Connie Mack	25.00	12.50	7.50
(58)	Rabbit Maranville	25.00	12.50	7.50
(59)	Christy Mathewson	40.00	20.00	12.00
(60)	Joe McCarthy (*)	25.00	12.50	7.50
(61)	Tommy McCarthy	25.00	12.50	7.50
(62)	Joe McGinnity	25.00	12.50	7.50
(63)	John McGraw	25.00	12.50	7.50
(64)	Bill McKechnie (*)	25.00	12.50	7.50
(65)	Kid Nichols	25.00	12.50	7.50
(66)	Jim O'Rourke	25.00	12.50	7.50
(67)	Mel Ott	25.00	12.50	7.50
(68)	Herb Pennock	25.00	12.50	7.50
(69)	Ed Plank	25.00	12.50	7.50
(70)	Charles Radbourn	25.00	12.50	7.50
(71)	Sam Rice (*)	25.00	12.50	7.50
(72)	Eppa Rixey (*)	25.00	12.50	7.50
(73)	Jackie Robinson (*)	40.00	20.00	12.00
(74)	Wilbert Robinson	25.00	12.50	7.50
(75)	Edd Roush (*)	25.00	12.50	7.50
(76)	Babe Ruth	120.00	60.00	35.00
(77)	Ray Schalk	25.00	12.50	7.50
(78)	Al Simmons	25.00	12.50	7.50
(79)	George Sisler	25.00	12.50	7.50
(80)	Albert Spalding	25.00	12.50	7.50
(81)	Tris Speaker	25.00	12.50	7.50
(82)	Bill Terry	25.00	12.50	7.50
(83)	Joe Tinker	25.00	12.50	7.50
(84)	Pie Traynor	25.00	12.50	7.50
(85)	Dazzy Vance	25.00	12.50	7.50
(86)	Rube Waddell	25.00	12.50	7.50
(87)	Honus Wagner	40.00	20.00	12.00
(88)	Bobby Wallace	25.00	12.50	7.50
(89)	Ed Walsh	25.00	12.50	7.50
(90)	Paul Waner	25.00	12.50	7.50
(91)	Zack Wheat (*)	25.00	12.50	7.50
(92)	George Wright	25.00	12.50	7.50
(93)	Harry Wright	25.00	12.50	7.50
(94)	Cy Young	40.00	20.00	12.00

1967 Ashland Oil Grand Slam Baseball

These baseball player folders were issued in conjunction with a sweepstakes conducted at Ashland gas stations, which offered a bicycle in exchange for a completed "Baseball Player Photo Album." To avoid giving away too many bikes, the Jim Maloney card was short-printed. The cards were originally issued in the form of a sealed tri-folder. When opened to 7-1/2" x 2", a blue duotone player portrait photo is pictured at center. Back of the panel offers contest rules. The unnumbered panels are listed here in alphabetical order. Prices are for complete tri-fold panels.

		NM	E	VG
Complete Set (11, no Maloney):		300.00	150.00	90.00
Common Player:		20.00	10.00	6.00
Album:		150.00	75.00	45.00
(1)	Jim Bunning	30.00	15.00	9.00
(2)	Elston Howard	25.00	12.50	7.50
(3)	Al Kaline	50.00	25.00	15.00
(4)	Harmon Killebrew	30.00	15.00	9.00
(5)	Ed Kranepool	20.00	10.00	6.00
(6)	Jim Maloney (SP (Value undetermined.))			
(7)	Bill Mazeroski	30.00	15.00	9.00
(8)	Frank Robinson	40.00	20.00	12.00
(9)	Ron Santo	25.00	12.50	7.50
(10)	Joe Torre	25.00	12.50	7.50
(11)	Leon Wagner	20.00	10.00	6.00
(12)	Pete Ward	20.00	10.00	6.00

1895 Ashman Studio Cabinets

The date attributed is speculative and about at the mid-point of the sole known subject's tenure with the Baltimore Orioles of the National League. In typical cabinet format, about 4-1/2" x 6-1/2", the card features a sepia-toned portrait photo attached to a blank-back, cream-colored thick cardboard mount bearing the advertising at bottom of the Balitmore photographer's studio. It is unknown whether cabinets of any of McGraw's teammates or adversaries were also produced.

	NM	E	VG
John McGraw	10,000	5,000	3,000

1933 Astra Margarine

One of several "foreign" Babe Ruth cards issued during his prime was included in a 112-card set produced as premiums for Astra Margarine in Germany. Ruth is the only major league ballplayer in the issue. Cards are in full color, measuring 2-3/4" x 4-1/8". Backs of the unnumbered cards are printed in German. Three types of backs can be found on the Ruth card. Type 1, has the Astra name nearly centered. The Type 2 back has the brand name printed closer to the bottom of the card, with only four lines of type under it. Type 3 is a variation of Type 2 on which the appropriate page number (83) of the accompanying album is mentioned on the line immediately above "Handbuch des Sports" near the top. One card was given with the purchase of each 1/2 pound of margarine and the album could be ordered by mail. See also Sanella Margarine.

		NM	E	VG
Type 1	Babe Ruth (Astra centered.)	1,500	750.00	450.00
Type 2	Babe Ruth (Astra at bottom.)	1,750	875.00	525.00
Type 3	Babe Ruth (Astra at bottom w/83.)	3,500	1,750	1,000

1978 Atlanta Nobis Center

In conjunction with a May 1978 card show to benefit the training/rehabilitation center supported by Hall of Fame linebacker Tommy Nobis, this collectors' set was issued. Most of the players on the 2-1/2" x 3-1/2" cards are former stars of the Boston, Milwaukee or Atlanta Braves, though players from a few other teams and footballer Nobis are also included; several of the players appeared at the show as autograph guests. The cards are in the style of 1959 Topps, with black-and-white player photos in a circle at center and a light green background. The career summary on back is in black-and-white. The unnumbered cards are checklisted here in alphabetical order.

		NM	E	VG
Complete Set (24):		50.00	25.00	15.00
Common Player:		3.00	1.50	.90
(1)	Hank Aaron	12.00	6.00	3.50
(2)	Joe Adcock	3.00	1.50	.90
(3)	Felipe Alou	3.00	1.50	.90
(4)	Frank Bolling	3.00	1.50	.90
(5)	Orlando Cepeda	4.00	2.00	1.25
(6)	Ty Cline	3.00	1.50	.90
(7)	Tony Cloninger	3.00	1.50	.90
(8)	Del Crandall	3.00	1.50	.90
(9)	Fred Haney	3.00	1.50	.90
(10)	Pat Jarvis	3.00	1.50	.90
(11)	Ernie Johnson	3.00	1.50	.90
(12)	Ken Johnson	3.00	1.50	.90
(13)	Denny Lemaster	3.00	1.50	.90
(14)	Eddie Mathews	4.00	2.00	1.25
(15)	Lee Maye	3.00	1.50	.90
(16)	Denis Menke	3.00	1.50	.90
(17)	Felix Millan	3.00	1.50	.90
(18)	Johnny Mize	4.00	2.00	1.20
(19)	Tommy Nobis	3.00	1.50	.90
(20)	Gene Oliver	3.00	1.50	.90
(21)	Johnny Sain	3.50	1.75	1.00
(22)	Warren Spahn	4.00	2.00	1.20
(23)	Joe Torre	4.00	2.00	1.20
(24)	Bob Turley	3.50	1.75	1.00

1968 Atlantic Oil Play Ball Game Cards

Because some of the cards were redeemable either alone or in combination for cash awards, and thus were issued in lesser quantities, completion of this game issue was difficult from Day 1. Fifty different players are known in the issue, along with a number of variations. The majority of the cards can be found with card backs either explaining the game rules or picturing a pitcher throwing to a batter. The cards were issued in two-card panels, designed to be separated into a pair of 2-1/2" x 3-1/2" cards. For lack of an MLB license, the color player photos at center have the uniform logos removed. Printed at top is the face value of the particular card, while the player's name, team and league are printed in the bottom border. A large player number is printed in a white circle at bottom-right. American Leaguers' cards are bordered in red, while the National League cards have blue borders.

		NM	E	VG
Complete Set (Non-winners) (40):		350.00	175.00	100.00
Common Player:		6.00	3.00	1.50
Instant Winner Card:		30.00	15.00	9.00
AMERICAN LEAGUE				
1a	Tony Oliva	6.00	3.00	1.75
1b	Brooks Robinson	15.00	7.50	4.50
1c	Pete Ward	6.00	3.00	1.75
2a	Max Alvis	6.00	3.00	1.75
2b	Campy Campaneris	6.00	3.00	1.75
2c	Jim Fregosi	6.00	3.00	1.75
2d	Al Kaline	20.00	10.00	6.00
2e	Tom Tresh	6.00	3.00	1.75
3	Bill Freehan ($2,500 winner)	300.00	150.00	90.00
4	Tommy Davis ($100 winner)	100.00	50.00	30.00
5a	Norm Cash	7.50	3.75	2.25
5b	Frank Robinson	15.00	7.50	4.50
5c	Carl Yastrzemski	25.00	12.50	7.50
6a	Joe Pepitone	7.50	3.75	2.25
6b	Boog Powell	10.00	5.00	3.00
6c	George Scott	6.00	3.00	1.75
6d	Fred Valentine	6.00	3.00	1.75
7	Tom McCraw ($10 winner)	75.00	37.00	22.00
8	Andy Etchebarren ($5 winner)	50.00	25.00	15.00
9a	Dean Chance	6.00	3.00	1.75
9b	Joel Horlen	6.00	3.00	1.75
9c	Jim Lonborg	6.00	3.00	1.75
9d	Sam McDowell	6.00	3.00	1.75
10	Earl Wilson ($1 winner)	35.00	17.50	10.50
11	Jose Santiago	6.00	3.00	1.75
NATIONAL LEAGUE				
1a	Bob Aspromonte	6.00	3.00	1.75
1b	Lou Brock	12.00	6.00	3.50
1c	Johnny Callison	6.00	3.00	1.75
1d	Pete Rose	25.00	12.50	7.50
1e	Maury Wills	7.50	3.75	2.25
2	Tommie Agee ($2,500 winner)	300.00	150.00	90.00
3a	Felipe Alou	7.50	3.75	2.25
3b	Jim Hart	6.00	3.00	1.75
3c	Vada Pinson	7.50	3.75	2.25
4a	Hank Aaron	25.00	12.50	7.50
4b	Orlando Cepeda	10.00	5.00	3.00
4c	Willie McCovey	12.00	6.00	3.50
4d	Ron Santo	9.00	4.50	2.75
5	Ernie Banks ($100 winner)	450.00	225.00	135.00
6	Ron Fairly ($10 winner)	75.00	37.50	22.50
7a	Roberto Clemente	75.00	37.50	22.50
7b	Roger Maris	25.00	12.50	7.50
7c a	Ron Swoboda (Collect w/ N.L. #6, win $10.)	6.00	3.00	1.75
7c b	Ron Swoboda (Collect w/ N.L. #8, win $5.)	45.00	22.00	13.50
8	Billy Williams ($5 winner)	95.00	47.00	28.00
9a	Jim Bunning	9.00	4.50	2.75
9b	Bob Gibson	12.00	6.00	3.50
9c	Jim Maloney	6.00	3.00	1.75
9d	Mike McCormick	6.00	3.00	1.75
10	Milt Pappas	6.00	3.00	1.75
11	Claude Osteen ($1 winner)	35.00	17.50	10.00

1969 Atlantic-Richfield Boston Red Sox

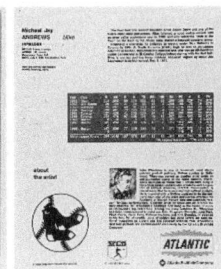

One of many larger-format (8" x 10") baseball premiums sponsored as gas station giveaways in the late 1960s and early 1970s was this set of Boston Red Sox player pictures by celebrity artist John Wheeldon sponsored by the Atlantic-Richfield Oil Co. Done in pastel colors, the pictures feature large portraits and smaller action pictures of the player against a bright background. A facsimile autograph is pencilled in beneath the pictures, and the player's name is printed in the white bottom border. Backs are printed in black-and-white and include biographical and career data, full major and minor legaue stats, a self-portrait and biography of the artist and the logos of the team, players' association and sponsor. The unnumbered pictures are checklisted here alphabetically.

		NM	E	VG
Complete Set (12):		75.00	35.00	25.00
Common Player:		6.00	3.00	1.75
(1)	Mike Andrews	6.00	3.00	1.75
(2)	Tony Conigliaro	10.00	5.00	3.00
(3)	Ray Culp	6.00	3.00	1.75
(4)	Russ Gibson	6.00	3.00	1.75
(5)	Dalton Jones	6.00	3.00	1.75
(6)	Jim Lonborg	8.00	4.00	2.50
(7)	Sparky Lyle	8.00	4.00	2.50
(8)	Syd O'Brien	6.00	3.00	1.75
(9)	George Scott	8.00	4.00	2.50
(10)	Reggie Smith	8.00	4.00	2.50
(11)	Rico Petrocelli	8.00	4.00	2.50
(12)	Carl Yastrzemski	25.00	12.50	7.50

1962 Auravision Records

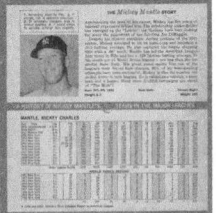

Similar in design and format to the 16-record set which was issued in 1964, this test issue can be differentiated by the stats on the back. On the 1962 record, Mantle is shown in a stadium-background pose, as compared to a clouded sky on the 1964 record. Where Gentile and Colavito are shown in the uniform of K.C. A's on the 1964 records, they are shown as a Tiger (Colavito) and Oriole (Gentile) on the earlier version. The set is checklisted here alphabetically.

	NM	E	VG
Complete Set (8):	300.00	150.00	90.00
Common Player:	15.00	7.50	4.50

(1)	Ernie Banks	30.00	15.00	9.00
(2)	Rocky Colavito	25.00	12.50	7.50
(3)	Whitey Ford	30.00	15.00	9.00
(4)	Jim Gentile	15.00	7.50	4.50
(5)	Mickey Mantle	125.00	62.50	37.50
(6)	Roger Maris	35.00	17.50	10.50
(7)	Willie Mays	50.00	25.00	15.00
(8)	Warren Spahn	30.00	15.00	9.00

1964 Auravision Records

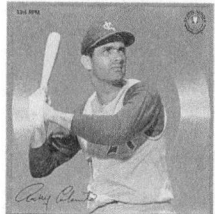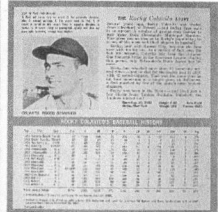

Never a candidate for the Billboard "Hot 100," this series of baseball picture records is popular with collectors due to the high-quality photos on front and back. On the grooved front side of the 6-3/4" x 6-3/4" plastic-laminated cardboard record is a color player photo with facsimile autograph, Sports Record trophy logo and 33-1/3 RPM notation. A color border surrounds the photo and is carried over to the unrecorded back side. There is another photo on back, along with a career summary and complete major and minor league stats and instructions for playing the record. In the bottom border is a copyright notice by Sports Champions Inc., and a notice that the Auravision Record is a product of Columbia Records. A hole at center of the record could be punched out for playing and the records featured a five-minute interview with the player by sportscaster Marty Glickman. The records were originally a mail-in premium available through an offer on Milk Duds candy boxes and Meadow Gold milk. Large quantities of the records made their way into the hobby as remainders. For early-1960s baseball items they remain reasonably priced today. The unnumbered records are checklisted here alphabetically. The Mays record is unaccountably much scarcer than the others.

		NM	E	VG
Complete Set (16):		150.00	75.00	45.00
Common Player:		6.00	3.00	1.75
(1)	Bob Allison	6.00	3.00	1.75
(2)	Ernie Banks	9.00	4.50	2.75
(3)	Ken Boyer	6.00	3.00	1.75
(4)	Rocky Colavito	7.50	3.75	2.25
(5)	Don Drysdale	9.00	4.50	2.75
(6)	Whitey Ford	10.00	5.00	3.00
(7)	Jim Gentile	6.00	3.00	1.75
(8)	Al Kaline	10.00	5.00	3.00
(9)	Sandy Koufax	20.00	10.00	6.00
(10)	Mickey Mantle	25.00	12.50	7.50
(11)	Roger Maris	12.50	6.25	3.75
(12)	Willie Mays (SP)	60.00	30.00	18.00
(13)	Bill Mazeroski	9.00	4.50	2.75
(14)	Frank Robinson	9.00	4.50	2.75
(15)	Warren Spahn	9.00	4.50	2.75
(16)	Pete Ward	6.00	3.00	1.75

1945 Autographs Game

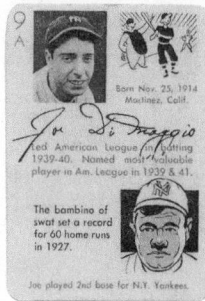

Politicians, movie stars and athletes are among the celebrities featured in this game from Leister Game Co. The 2-1/2" x 3-1/2" cards are printed in red and black on white and were found in pairs. The celebrity whose signature was reproduced on the card was seen in a photograph and top, while his paired partner was shown at bottom in an artist's depiction. Only two baseball players are included in the set.

		NM	E	VG
Complete Boxed Set (55):		650.00	325.00	195.00
9A	Joe DiMaggio, Babe Ruth (DiMaggio signature.)	75.00	37.50	22.50
9A	Babe Ruth, Joe DiMaggio (Ruth signature.)	150.00	75.00	45.00

B

1914 B18 Blankets

These 5-1/4"-square flannels were issued in 1914 wrapped around several popular brands of tobacco. The flannels, whose American Card Catalog designation is B18, picked up the nickname blankets because many of them were sewn together to form bed covers or throws. Different color combinations on the flannels exist for all 10 teams included in the set. The complete set price includes only the lowest-priced variation for each of the 90 players.

		NM	E	VG
Complete Set (90):		7,000	3,500	2,000
Complete Set W/Variations (201):		55,000	27,500	16,500
Common Player:		40.00	20.00	12.00
(1a)	Babe Adams (Purple pennants.)	80.00	40.00	25.00
(1b)	Babe Adams (Red pennants.)	130.00	65.00	40.00
(2a)	Sam Agnew (Purple basepaths.)	80.00	40.00	25.00
(2b)	Sam Agnew (Red basepaths.)	125.00	65.00	35.00
(3a)	Eddie Ainsmith (Green pennants.)	40.00	20.00	12.00
(3b)	Eddie Ainsmith (Brown pennants.)	40.00	20.00	12.00
(4a)	Jimmy Austin (Purple basepaths.)	80.00	40.00	25.00
(4b)	Jimmy Austin (Red basepaths.)	90.00	45.00	27.00
(5a)	Del Baker (White infield.)	40.00	20.00	12.00
(5b)	Del Baker (Brown infield.)	250.00	125.00	75.00
(5c)	Del Baker (Red infield.)	3,000	1,500	900.00
(6a)	Johnny Bassler (Purple pennants.)	90.00	45.00	27.00
(6b)	Johnny Bassler (Yellow pennants.)	125.00	65.00	35.00
(7a)	Paddy Bauman (Baumann) (White infield.)	40.00	20.00	12.00
(7b)	Paddy Bauman (Baumann) (Brown infield.)	250.00	125.00	75.00
(7c)	Paddy Bauman (Baumann) (Red infield.)	3,000	1,500	900.00
(8a)	Luke Boone (Blue infield.)	40.00	20.00	12.00
(8b)	Luke Boone (Green infield.)	40.00	20.00	12.00
(9a)	George Burns (Brown basepaths.)	40.00	20.00	12.00
(9b)	George Burns (Green basepaths.)	40.00	20.00	12.00
(10a)	Tioga George Burns (White infield.)	40.00	20.00	12.00
(10b)	Tioga George Burns (Brown infield.)	250.00	125.00	75.00
(10c)	Tioga George Burns (Red infield.)	1,650	825.00	495.00
(11a)	Max Carey (Purple pennants.)	150.00	75.00	45.00
(11b)	Max Carey (Red pennants.)	175.00	85.00	55.00
(12a)	Marty Cavanaugh (Kavanagh) (White infield.)	40.00	20.00	12.00
(12b)	Marty Cavanaugh (Kavanagh) (Brown infield.)	250.00	125.00	75.00
(12c)	Marty Cavanaugh (Kavanagh) (Red infield.)	3,000	1,500	900.00
(12d)	Marty Kavanaugh (Kavanagh)	200.00	100.00	60.00
(13a)	Frank Chance (Green infield.)	100.00	50.00	30.00
(13b)	Frank Chance (Brown pennants, blue infield.)	100.00	50.00	30.00
(13c)	Frank Chance (Yellow pennants, blue infield.)	450.00	225.00	135.00
(14a)	Ray Chapman (Purple pennants.)	125.00	65.00	35.00
(14b)	Ray Chapman (Yellow pennants.)	200.00	100.00	60.00
(15a)	Ty Cobb (White infield.)	500.00	250.00	150.00
(15b)	Ty Cobb (Brown infield.)	900.00	450.00	270.00
(15c)	Ty Cobb (Red infield.)	17,500	8,750	5,250
(16a)	King Cole (Blue infield.)	40.00	20.00	12.00
(16b)	King Cole (Green infield.)	40.00	20.00	12.00
(17a)	Joe Connolly (White infield.)	40.00	20.00	12.00
(17b)	Joe Connolly (Brown infield.)	250.00	125.00	75.00
(17c)	Joe Connolly (Red infield.)	3,000	1,500	900.00
(18a)	Harry Coveleski (White infield.)	40.00	20.00	12.00
(18b)	Harry Coveleski (Brown infield.)	250.00	125.00	75.00
(18c)	Harry Coveleski (Red infield.)	3,000	1,500	900.00
(19a)	George Cutshaw (Blue infield.)	40.00	20.00	12.00
(19b)	George Cutshaw (Green infield.)	40.00	20.00	12.00
(20a)	Jake Daubert (Blue infield.)	45.00	22.50	13.50
(20b)	Jake Daubert (Green infield.)	45.00	22.50	13.50
(21a)	Ray Demmitt (White infield.)	40.00	20.00	12.00
(21b)	Ray Demmitt (Brown infield.)	300.00	150.00	90.00
(21c)	Ray Demmitt (Red infield.)	3,000	1,500	900.00
(22a)	Bill Doak (Purple pennants.)	80.00	40.00	24.00
(22b)	Bill Doak (Yellow pennants.)	125.00	65.00	35.00
(23a)	Cozy Dolan (Purple pennants.)	80.00	40.00	25.00
(23b)	Cozy Dolan (Yellow pennants.)	150.00	75.00	45.00
(24a)	Larry Doyle (Brown basepaths.)	45.00	22.50	13.50
(24b)	Larry Doyle (Green basepaths.)	45.00	22.50	13.50
(25a)	Art Fletcher (Brown basepaths.)	40.00	20.00	12.00
(25b)	Art Fletcher (Green basepaths.)	40.00	20.00	12.00
(26a)	Eddie Foster (Brown pennants.)	40.00	20.00	12.00
(26b)	Eddie Foster (Green pennants.)	40.00	20.00	12.00
(27a)	Del Gainor (White infield.)	50.00	25.00	15.00
(27b)	Del Gainor (Brown infield.)	250.00	150.00	75.00
(28a)	Chick Gandil (Brown pennants.)	100.00	50.00	30.00
(28b)	Chick Gandil (Green pennants.)	125.00	65.00	35.00
(29a)	George Gibson (Purple pennants.)	80.00	40.00	25.00
(29b)	George Gibson (Red pennants.)	90.00	45.00	27.00
(30a)	Hank Gowdy (White infield.)	40.00	20.00	12.00
(30b)	Hank Gowdy (Brown infield.)	250.00	125.00	75.00
(30c)	Hank Gowdy (Red infield.)	3,000	1,500	900.00
(31a)	Jack Graney (Purple pennants.)	90.00	45.00	27.00
(31b)	Jack Graney (Yellow pennants.)	125.00	65.00	35.00
(32a)	Eddie Grant (Brown basepaths.)	40.00	20.00	12.00
(32b)	Eddie Grant (Green basepaths.)	40.00	20.00	12.00
(33a)	Tommy Griffith (White infield, green pennants.)	40.00	20.00	12.00
(33b)	Tommy Griffith (White infield, red pennants.)	1,500	750.00	450.00
(33c)	Tommy Griffith (Brown infield.)	125.00	65.00	35.00
(33d)	Tommy Griffith (Red infield.)	3,000	1,500	900.00

		NM	E	VG
(34a)	Earl Hamilton (Purple basepaths.)	80.00	40.00	25.00
(34b)	Earl Hamilton (Red basepaths.)	90.00	45.00	27.00
(35a)	Roy Hartzell (Blue infield.)	40.00	20.00	12.00
(35b)	Roy Hartzell (Green infield.)	40.00	20.00	12.00
(36a)	Miller Huggins (Purple pennants.)	160.00	80.00	45.00
(36b)	Miller Huggins (Yellow pennants.)	245.00	120.00	75.00
(37a)	John Hummel (Blue infield.)	40.00	20.00	12.00
(37b)	John Hummel (Green infield.)	40.00	20.00	12.00
(38a)	Ham Hyatt (Purple pennants.)	80.00	40.00	24.00
(38b)	Ham Hyatt (Red pennants.)	90.00	45.00	27.00
(39a)	Joe Jackson (Purple pennants.)	1,500	750.00	450.00
(39b)	Joe Jackson (Yellow pennants.)	1,100	550.00	330.00
(40a)	Bill James (White infield.)	40.00	20.00	12.00
(40b)	Bill James (Brown infield.)	160.00	80.00	50.00
(40c)	Bill James (Red infield.)	3,000	1,500	900.00
(41a)	Walter Johnson (Brown pennants.)	300.00	150.00	90.00
(41b)	Walter Johnson (Green pennants.)	275.00	135.00	80.00
(42a)	Ray Keating (Blue infield.)	40.00	20.00	12.00
(42b)	Ray Keating (Green infield.)	40.00	20.00	12.00
(43a)	Joe Kelley (Kelly) (Purple pennants.)	90.00	45.00	27.00
(43b)	Joe Kelley (Kelly) (Red pennants.)	90.00	45.00	27.00
(44a)	Ed Konetchy (Purple pennants.)	60.00	30.00	18.00
(44b)	Ed Konetchy (Red pennants.)	90.00	45.00	27.00
(45a)	Nemo Leibold (Purple pennants.)	75.00	37.50	22.00
(45b)	Nemo Leibold (Yellow pennants.)	150.00	75.00	45.00
(46a)	Fritz Maisel (Blue infield.)	40.00	20.00	12.00
(46b)	Fritz Maisel (Green infield.)	40.00	20.00	12.00
(47a)	Les Mann (White infield.)	40.00	20.00	12.00
(47b)	Les Mann (Brown infield.)	250.00	125.00	75.00
(47c)	Les Mann (Red infield.)	1,650	825.00	495.00
(48a)	Rabbit Maranville (White infield.)	130.00	65.00	39.00
(48b)	Rabbit Maranville (Brown infield.)	250.00	125.00	75.00
(48c)	Rabbit Maranville (Red infield.)	4,500	2,200	1,350
(49a)	Bill McAllister (McAllester) (Purple basepaths.)	80.00	40.00	25.00
(49b)	Bill McAllister (McAllester) (Red basepaths.)	100.00	50.00	30.00
(50a)	George McBride (Brown pennants.)	40.00	20.00	12.00
(50b)	George McBride (Green pennants.)	40.00	20.00	12.00
(51a)	Chief Meyers (Brown basepaths.)	40.00	20.00	12.00
(51b)	Chief Meyers (Green basepaths.)	40.00	20.00	12.00
(52a)	Clyde Milan (Brown pennants.)	40.00	20.00	12.00
(52b)	Clyde Milan (Green pennants.)	40.00	20.00	12.00
(53a)	J. Miller (Purple pennants.)	80.00	40.00	25.00
(53b)	J. Miller (Yellow pennants.)	125.00	65.00	35.00
(54a)	Otto Miller (Blue infield.)	40.00	20.00	12.00
(54b)	Otto Miller (Green infield.)	40.00	20.00	12.00
(55a)	Willie Mitchell (Purple pennants.)	80.00	40.00	25.00
(55b)	Willie Mitchell (Yellow pennants.)	150.00	75.00	45.00
(56a)	Danny Moeller (Brown pennants.)	40.00	20.00	12.00
(56b)	Danny Moeller (Green pennants.)	40.00	20.00	12.00
(57a)	Ray Morgan (Brown pennants.)	40.00	20.00	12.00
(57b)	Ray Morgan (Green pennants.)	40.00	20.00	12.00
(58a)	George Moriarty (White infield.)	40.00	20.00	12.00
(58b)	George Moriarty (Brown infield.)	250.00	125.00	75.00
(58c)	George Moriarty (Red infield.)	3,000	1,500	900.00
(59a)	Mike Mowrey (Purple pennants.)	80.00	40.00	25.00
(59b)	Mike Mowrey (Red pennants.)	90.00	45.00	27.00
(60a)	Red Murray (Brown basepaths.)	40.00	20.00	12.00
(60b)	Red Murray (Green basepaths.)	40.00	20.00	12.00
(61a)	Ivy Olson (Purple pennants.)	80.00	40.00	25.00
(61b)	Ivy Olson (Yellow pennants.)	160.00	80.00	50.00
(62a)	Steve O'Neill (Purple pennants.)	75.00	37.50	22.00
(62b)	Steve O'Neill (Red pennants.)	150.00	75.00	45.00
(62c)	Steve O'Neill (Yellow pennants.)	150.00	75.00	45.00
(63a)	Marty O'Toole (Purple pennants.)	80.00	40.00	25.00
(63b)	Marty O'Toole (Red pennants.)	90.00	45.00	27.00
(64a)	Roger Peckinpaugh (Blue infield.)	45.00	22.50	13.50
(64b)	Roger Peckinpaugh (Green infield.)	45.00	22.50	13.50
(65a)	Hub Perdue (White infield.)	40.00	20.00	12.00
(65b)	Hub Perdue (Brown infield.)	250.00	125.00	75.00
(65c)	Hub Purdue (Red infield.)	3,000	1,500	900.00
(66a)	Del Pratt (Purple basepaths.)	80.00	40.00	25.00
(66b)	Del Pratt (Red basepaths.)	90.00	45.00	27.00
(67a)	Hank Robinson (Purple pennants.)	80.00	40.00	25.00
(67b)	Hank Robinson (Yellow pennants.)	130.00	65.00	40.00
(68a)	Nap Rucker (Blue infield.)	40.00	20.00	12.00
(68b)	Nap Rucker (Green infield.)	40.00	20.00	12.00
(69a)	Slim Sallee (Purple pennants.)	100.00	50.00	30.00
(69b)	Slim Sallee (Yellow pennants.)	150.00	75.00	45.00
(70a)	Howard Shanks (Brown pennants.)	40.00	20.00	12.00
(70b)	Howard Shanks (Green pennants.)	40.00	20.00	12.00
(71a)	Burt Shotton (Purple basepaths.)	80.00	40.00	25.00
(71b)	Burt Shotton (Red basepaths.)	75.00	37.50	22.00
(72a)	Red Smith (Blue infield.)	40.00	20.00	12.00
(72b)	Red Smith (Green infield.)	40.00	20.00	12.00
(73a)	Fred Snodgrass (Brown basepaths.)	40.00	20.00	12.00
(73b)	Fred Snodgrass (Green basepaths.)	40.00	20.00	12.00
(74a)	Bill Steele (Purple pennants.)	80.00	40.00	24.00
(74b)	Bill Steele (Yellow pennants.)	150.00	75.00	45.00
(75a)	Casey Stengel (Blue infield.)	100.00	50.00	30.00
(75b)	Casey Stengel (Green infield.)	100.00	50.00	30.00
(76a)	Jeff Sweeney (Blue infield.)	40.00	20.00	12.00
(76b)	Jeff Sweeney (Green infield.)	40.00	20.00	12.00
(77a)	Jeff Tesreau (Brown basepaths.)	40.00	20.00	12.00
(77b)	Jeff Tesreau (Green basepaths.)	40.00	20.00	12.00
(78a)	Terry Turner (Purple pennants.)	80.00	40.00	25.00
(78b)	Terry Turner (Yellow pennants.)	150.00	75.00	45.00
(79a)	Lefty Tyler (White infield.)	40.00	20.00	12.00
(79b)	Lefty Tyler (Brown infield.)	250.00	125.00	75.00
(79c)	Lefty Tyler (Red infield.)	3,000	1,500	900.00
(80a)	Jim Viox (Purple pennants.)	80.00	40.00	25.00
(80b)	Jim Viox (Red pennants.)	90.00	45.00	27.00
(81a)	Bull Wagner (Blue infield.)	40.00	20.00	12.00
(81b)	Bull Wagner (Green infield.)	40.00	20.00	12.00
(82a)	Bobby Wallace (Purple basepaths.)	150.00	75.00	45.00
(82b)	Bobby Wallace (Red basepaths.)	150.00	75.00	45.00
(83a)	Dee Walsh (Purple basepaths.)	80.00	40.00	25.00
(83b)	Dee Walsh (Red basepaths.)	90.00	45.00	27.00
(84a)	Jimmy Walsh (Blue infield.)	40.00	20.00	12.00
(84b)	Jimmy Walsh (Green infield.)	40.00	20.00	12.00
(85a)	Bert Whaling (White infield.)	40.00	20.00	12.00
(85b)	Bert Whaling (Brown infield.)	250.00	125.00	75.00
(85c)	Bert Whaling (Red infield.)	3,000	1,500	900.00
(86a)	Zach Wheat (Blue infield.)	125.00	65.00	35.00
(86b)	Zach Wheat (Green infield.)	100.00	50.00	30.00
(87a)	Possum Whitted (Purple pennants.)	80.00	40.00	25.00
(87b)	Possum Whitted (Yellow pennants.)	125.00	65.00	35.00
(88a)	Gus Williams (Purple basepaths.)	80.00	40.00	25.00
(88b)	Gus Williams (Red basepaths.)	90.00	45.00	27.00
(89a)	Owen Wilson (Purple pennants.)	80.00	40.00	25.00
(89b)	Owen Wilson (Yellow pennants.)	150.00	75.00	45.00
(90a)	Hooks Wiltse (Brown basepaths.)	40.00	20.00	12.00
(90b)	Hooks Wiltse (Green basepaths.)	40.00	20.00	12.00

1949 Baas Cheri-Cola

Only five of these premium issues have ever been cataloged so it's unknown how many comprise a set. The 7-5/8" x 9-1/2" pictures feature black-and-white player photos on front, with the player's name printed in white script. On back, printed in red, is an ad for Baas Cheri-Cola Drink. The un-numbered pictures are checklisted in alphabetical order.

		NM	E	VG
Common Player:		125.00	65.00	40.00
(1)	Bobby Doerr	450.00	220.00	135.00
(2)	Bob Feller	750.00	370.00	225.00
(3)	Ken Keltner	375.00	185.00	110.00
(4)	John Sain	375.00	185.00	110.00
(5)	Ted Williams	1,800	900.00	550.00

1930 Baguer Chocolate

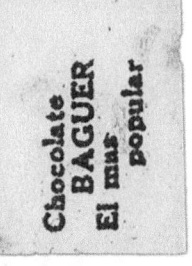

This rare Cuban issue was apparently current between the start of the 1930 season and the redemption expiration date of Jan. 31, 1931. The set consists of 90 black-and-white player photos, about 5/8" x 7/8". The pictures have white borders and a white strip at the bottom of photo with some form of the player's name. Backs are printed in red, "Chocolate BAGUER El mas popular." An album was issued to collect the pictures and when full it could be exchanged for baseball equipment, toys or candy. The unnumbered cards are checklisted here in alphabetical order.

		NM	E	VG
Complete Set (90):		5,500	3,750	2,200
Common Player:		30.00	20.00	12.00
Album:		75.00	52.00	30.00
(1)	George Bancroft (Dave)	65.00	45.00	25.00
(2)	Clyde Beck	30.00	20.00	12.00
(3)	Larry Benton	30.00	20.00	12.00
(4)	Max Bishop	30.00	20.00	12.00
(5)	Clarence Blair	30.00	20.00	12.00
(6)	Fred Blake	30.00	20.00	12.00
(7)	Mitchell Blake (SP)	80.00	55.00	30.00
(8)	Joe Boley	30.00	20.00	12.00
(9)	Jim Bottomley	65.00	45.00	25.00
(10)	George Burns	30.00	20.00	12.00
(11)	Guy Bush	30.00	20.00	12.00
(12)	Mickey Cochrane	75.00	50.00	30.00
(13)	Eddie Collins	75.00	50.00	30.00
(14)	Kiki Cuyler	65.00	45.00	25.00

		NM	E	VG
(15)	Jimmy Dikes (Dykes)	30.00	20.00	12.00
(16)	Leo Dixon	30.00	20.00	12.00
(17)	Pete Donohue	30.00	20.00	12.00
(18)	Taylor Douthit	30.00	20.00	12.00
(19)	George Earnshaw	30.00	20.00	12.00
(20)	R. Elliot (Jumbo Elliott)	30.00	20.00	12.00
(21)	Joe (Woody) English	30.00	20.00	12.00
(22)	Urban Faber	65.00	45.00	25.00
(23)	Lewis Fonseca	30.00	20.00	12.00
(24)	Jimmy Foxx	275.00	190.00	110.00
(25)	Walter French	30.00	20.00	12.00
(26)	Frankie Frisch	75.00	50.00	30.00
(27)	Lou Gehrig	600.00	420.00	240.00
(28)	Walter Gerber	30.00	20.00	12.00
(29)	Miguel A. Gonzalez	65.00	45.00	25.00
(30)	Goose Goslin	65.00	45.00	25.00
(31)	W. Grampp (Henry)	30.00	20.00	12.00
(32)	Burleigh Grimes	65.00	45.00	25.00
(33)	Charlie Grimm	30.00	20.00	12.00
(34)	Lefty Grove	75.00	50.00	30.00
(35)	Geo. Haas	30.00	20.00	12.00
(36)	(Bill) Hallahan	30.00	20.00	12.00
(37)	Stanley Harris	65.00	45.00	25.00
(38)	Geo. (Charles "Gabby") Hartnett	65.00	45.00	25.00
(39)	Cliff Heathcote	30.00	20.00	12.00
(40)	Babe Herman	30.00	20.00	12.00
(41)	Andy High	30.00	20.00	12.00
(42)	Rogers Hornsby	100.00	70.00	40.00
(43)	Dan Howley	30.00	20.00	12.00
(44)	Travis Jackson	65.00	45.00	25.00
(45)	Walter Johnson	250.00	175.00	100.00
(46)	Fred Lindstrom	65.00	45.00	25.00
(47)	Alfonso Lopez	75.00	50.00	30.00
(48)	Red Lucas	30.00	20.00	12.00
(49)	(Dolf) Luque	65.00	45.00	25.00
(50)	Pat Malone	30.00	20.00	12.00
(51)	Harry (Heinie) Manush	65.00	45.00	25.00
(52)	Fred Marberry	30.00	20.00	12.00
(53)	Joe McCarthy	65.00	45.00	25.00
(54)	J.J. McGraw	65.00	45.00	25.00
(55)	G. Mc. Millan (Norman McMillan)	30.00	20.00	12.00
(56)	Bing Miller	30.00	20.00	12.00
(57)	J. (Johnny) Moore	30.00	20.00	12.00
(58)	Buddy Myers (Myer)	30.00	20.00	12.00
(59)	Bob O'Farrell	30.00	20.00	12.00
(60)	Melvin Ott	75.00	50.00	30.00
(61)	Herb Pennock	65.00	45.00	25.00
(62)	Cy Perkins	30.00	20.00	12.00
(63)	Jack Quinn	30.00	20.00	12.00
(64)	Chas. Rhen (Rhem)	30.00	20.00	12.00
(65)	Harry Rice	30.00	20.00	12.00
(66)	Sam Rice	65.00	45.00	35.00
(67)	Lance Richbourg	30.00	20.00	12.00
(68)	W. (Wilbert) Robinson	65.00	45.00	25.00
(69)	Eddie Rommell (Rommel)	30.00	20.00	12.00
(70)	Charles Root	30.00	20.00	12.00
(71)	Muddy Ruel	30.00	20.00	12.00
(72)	Babe Ruth	900.00	630.00	360.00
(73)	Wally Schang	30.00	20.00	12.00
(74)	Bill Shores	30.00	20.00	12.00
(75)	Al Simmons	65.00	45.00	25.00
(76)	Geo. Sisler	75.00	50.00	30.00
(77)	Earl Smith	30.00	20.00	12.00
(78)	Riggs Stephenson	30.00	20.00	12.00
(79)	Joe (Walter "Lefty") Stewart	30.00	20.00	12.00
(80)	H. Summa	30.00	20.00	12.00
(81)	Bill Terry	65.00	45.00	25.00
(82)	Fresco Thompson	30.00	20.00	12.00
(83)	Charley Tolson	30.00	20.00	12.00
(84)	'Pie' Traynor	65.00	45.00	25.00
(85)	Dazzy Vance	65.00	45.00	25.00
(86)	Rube Walberg	30.00	20.00	12.00
(87)	'Hack' Wilson	65.00	45.00	25.00
(88)	Jimmy Wilson	30.00	20.00	12.00
(89)	Glenn Wright	30.00	20.00	12.00
(90)	Tom Zachary	30.00	20.00	12.00

1941 Ballantine Coasters

National League pitcher-catcher pairs are featured on this set of drink coasters issued by Ballantine Ale & Beer. The 4-1/2" diameter composition coasters are printed in black with orange, blue or red highlights. Fronts have line draw-ings of the batterymates and a few words about the previous or coming season. Backs have a Ballentine's ad. It is unknown whether there are more than these three coasters in the series.

		NM	E	VG
Common Coaster:		35.00	17.50	10.00
(1)	Bob Klinger, Virgil Davis (Pirates)	35.00	17.50	10.00
(2a)	Lon Warneke, Gus Mancuso (Cardinals) ("AT THE GAME IT'S . . ." above portraits.))	35.00	17.50	10.00
(2b)	Lon Warneke, Gus Mancuso (Cardinals) ("At the Game it's" below portraits.))	35.00	17.50	10.00
(3)	Whit Wyatt, Mickey Owen (Dodgers)	35.00	17.50	10.00

1911 Baltimore News Newsboys Series

This scarce version of E94 carries on its back the notation, "Baltimore News Newsboy Series" and offers $1 to the first 35 boys completing the full set. Unlike the Close Candy Co. cards, the newspaper version is found only with the light blue background on front. The issue was designated M131 in the American Card Catalog.

		NM	E	VG
Common Player:		3,000	1,500	1,000
(1)	Jimmy Austin	3,000	1,500	1,000
(2)	Johnny Bates	3,000	1,500	1,000
(3)	Bob Bescher	3,000	1,500	1,000
(4)	Bobby Byrne	3,000	1,500	1,000
(5)	Frank Chance	7,500	3,750	2,250
(6)	Ed Cicotte	6,000	3,000	1,800
(7)	Ty Cobb	75,000	37,500	22,500
(8)	Sam Crawford	7,500	3,750	2,250
(9)	Harry Davis	3,000	1,500	1,000
(10)	Art Devlin	3,000	1,500	1,000
(11)	Josh Devore	3,000	1,500	1,000
(12)	Mickey Doolan	3,000	1,500	1,000
(13)	Patsy Dougherty	3,000	1,500	1,000
(14)	Johnny Evers	7,500	3,750	2,250
(15)	Eddie Grant	3,000	1,500	1,000
(16)	Hugh Jennings	7,500	3,750	2,250
(17)	Red Kleinow	3,000	1,500	1,000
(18)	Joe Lake	3,000	1,500	1,000
(19)	Nap Lajoie	9,000	4,500	2,700
(20)	Tommy Leach	3,000	1,500	1,000
(21)	Hans Lobert	3,000	1,500	1,000
(22)	Harry Lord	3,000	1,500	1,000
(23)	Sherry Magee	3,000	1,500	1,000
(24)	John McGraw	11,250	5,625	3,375
(25)	Earl Moore	3,000	1,500	1,000
(26)	Red Murray	3,000	1,500	1,000
(27)	Tris Speaker	13,500	6,750	4,050
(28)	Terry Turner	3,000	1,500	1,000
(29)	Honus Wagner	55,500	27,750	16,650
(30)	"Old" Cy. Young	22,500	11,250	6,750

1914 Baltimore News Terrapins

Players from both of Baltimore's professional baseball teams are included in this set of schedule cards from the local newspaper. That season fans could support the Orioles of the International League or the Terrapins of the Federal League. The newspaper's cards are 2-5/8" x 3-5/8", monochrome printed in either red or blue with a wide border. Players are pictured in full-length posed action photos with the backgrounds erased in favor of a few artificial shadows. The player name, position and league are shown on front. Backs have a schedule "AT HOME" and "ABROAD" of the appropriate team with an ad for the paper at top and a curious line at bottom which reads, "This Card is Given to," with space for

a signature. The unnumbered cards are checklisted here in alphabetical order, though it is presumed the checklist is incomplete. Only the Federal Leaguers' cards are listed here; the Orioles will be found in the minor league section of this catalog.

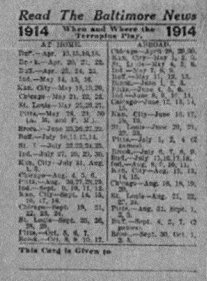

		NM	E	VG
Common Player:		8,800	4,400	2,640
(1)	Neal Ball	8,800	4,400	2,640
(2)	Mike Doolan	8,800	4,400	2,640
(3)	Happy Finneran	8,800	4,400	2,640
(4)	Fred Jacklitch (Jacklitsch)	8,800	4,400	2,640
(5)	Otto Knabe	8,800	4,400	2,640
(6)	Benny Meyers (Meyer)	8,800	4,400	2,640
(7)	Jack Quinn	8,800	4,400	2,640
(8)	Hack Simmons	8,800	4,400	2,640
(9)	Frank Smith	8,800	4,400	2,640
(10)	George Suggs	8,800	4,400	2,640
(11)	Harry (Swats) Swacina	8,800	4,400	2,640
(12)	Ducky Yount	8,800	4,400	2,640
(13)	Guy Zinn	8,800	4,400	2,640

1954 Baltimore Orioles Picture Pack

This appears to be a team-issued photo pack in the O's first season after moving from St. Louis. The black-and-white poses are 6" x 8" in format, bordered in white and blank-backed. Pictures have a facsimile autograph on front. At least three versions of the photo pack were issued over the course of the season to reflect roster changes. It is unknown whether this checklist is complete.

		NM	E	VG
Complete Set (33):		600.00	300.00	180.00
Common Player:		20.00	10.00	6.00
(1)	Cal Abrams	20.00	10.00	6.00
(2)	Neil Berry	20.00	10.00	6.00
(3)	Vern Bickford	20.00	10.00	6.00
(4)	Jim Brideweser	20.00	10.00	6.00
(5)	Bob Chakales	20.00	10.00	6.00
(6)	Gil Coan	20.00	10.00	6.00
(7)	Joe Coleman	20.00	10.00	6.00
(8)	Clint Courtney	20.00	10.00	6.00
(9)	Chuck Diering	20.00	10.00	6.00
(10)	Jim Dyck	20.00	10.00	6.00
(11)	Howie Fox	20.00	10.00	6.00
(12)	Jim Fridley (Batting)	20.00	10.00	6.00
(13)	Jim Fridley (Portrait)	20.00	10.00	6.00
(14)	Jehosie Heard	25.00	12.50	7.50
(15)	Bill Hunter	20.00	10.00	6.00
(16)	Darrell Johnson	20.00	10.00	6.00
(17)	Dick Kokos	20.00	10.00	6.00
(18)	Lou Kretlow	20.00	10.00	6.00
(19)	Dick Kryhoski	20.00	10.00	6.00
(20)	Don Larsen	40.00	20.00	12.00
(21)	Don Lenhardt	20.00	10.00	6.00
(22)	Dick Littlefield	20.00	10.00	6.00
(23)	Sam Mele	20.00	10.00	6.00
(24)	Les Moss	20.00	10.00	6.00
(25)	Ray Murray	20.00	10.00	6.00
(26)	Billy O'Dell	20.00	10.00	6.00
(27)	Duane Pillette	20.00	10.00	6.00
(28)	Vern Stephens	20.00	10.00	6.00
(29)	Marlin Stuart	20.00	10.00	6.00
(30)	Bob Turley	40.00	20.00	12.00
(31)	Eddie Waitkus	20.00	10.00	6.00
(32)	Vic Wertz	25.00	12.50	7.50
(33)	Bob Young	20.00	10.00	6.00

1960 Baltimore Orioles Scrapbook

This set of O's cutouts was printed during spring training prior to the 1960 season, though in what newspaper and how many per day is unknown. The pictures are printed in black-and-white in a size of about 3-1/2" x 6-3/8". Each picture has a dotted line to define its borders. Within are a player portrait photo, facsimile autograph, biographical details and a career summary.

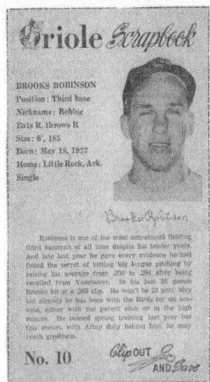

	NM	EX	VG
Complete Set (49):	250.00	125.00	75.00
Common Player:	6.00	3.00	1.75
1 Marvin Breeding	6.00	3.00	1.75
2 Paul Richards	6.00	3.00	1.75
3 Barry Shetrone	6.00	3.00	1.75
4 Fred Valentine	6.00	3.00	1.75
5 Jerry Adair	6.00	3.00	1.75
6 Raymond Barker	6.00	3.00	1.75
7 Leo Burke	6.00	3.00	1.75
8 Ronald Hansen	6.00	3.00	1.75
9 David Nicholson	6.00	3.00	1.75
10 Brooks Robinson	20.00	10.00	6.00
11 Wesley Stock	6.00	3.00	1.75
12 Dean Chance	9.00	4.50	2.50
13 William Gardner	6.00	3.00	1.75
14 Hal Brown	6.00	3.00	1.75
15 Arne Thorsland	6.00	3.00	1.75
16 John Fisher	6.00	3.00	1.75
17 John "Boog" Powell	15.00	7.50	4.50
18 Bobbie Lee Mabe	6.00	3.00	1.75
19 Alfred Nagel	6.00	3.00	1.75
20 Robert Saverine	6.00	3.00	1.75
21 Arnold Portocarrero	6.00	3.00	1.75
22 Walter Coleman	6.00	3.00	1.75
23 Bob Boyd	6.00	3.00	1.75
24 Albert Pearson	6.00	3.00	1.75
25 Gene Woodling	6.00	3.00	1.75
26 William Hoeft	6.00	3.00	1.75
27 Gus Triandos	6.00	3.00	1.75
28 Myron Ginsberg	6.00	3.00	1.75
29 Willie Tasby	6.00	3.00	1.75
30 Gene Green	6.00	3.00	1.75
31 John Powers	6.00	3.00	1.75
32 Art Quirk	6.00	3.00	1.75
33 Charles Staniland	6.00	3.00	1.75
34 Bob Riedel	6.00	3.00	1.75
35 Milt Pappas	6.00	3.00	1.75
36 Steve Barber	6.00	3.00	1.75
37 Gordon Jones	6.00	3.00	1.75
38 Walter Dropo	6.00	3.00	1.75
39 Billy Klaus	6.00	3.00	1.75
40 Jackie Brandt	6.00	3.00	1.75
41 Hoyt Wilhelm	12.00	6.00	3.75
42 Jerry Walker	6.00	3.00	1.75
43 Al Pilarcik	6.00	3.00	1.75
44 John Anderson	6.00	3.00	1.75
45 Charles Estrada	6.00	3.00	1.75
46 Luman Harris	6.00	3.00	1.75
47 Harry Brecheen	6.00	3.00	1.75
48 James A. Adair	6.00	3.00	1.75
49 Clinton D. Courtney	6.00	3.00	1.75

1958 Baltimore Orioles Team Issue

CLIFFORD CONNIE JOHNSON
(CONNIE)

These blank-backed, black-and-white cards are approximately postcard size at 3-1/4" x 5-1/2" and feature posed

portraits of the players printed on semi-gloss cardboard. The unnumbered cards are checklisted here alphabetically.

		NM	E	VG
Complete Set (16):		165.00	82.00	49.00
Common Player:		12.00	6.00	3.50
(1)	Bob Boyd	12.00	6.00	3.50
(2)	Harry Brecheen	12.00	6.00	3.50
(3)	Hal Brown	12.00	6.00	3.50
(4)	Jim Busby	12.00	6.00	3.50
(5)	Foster Castleman	12.00	6.00	3.50
(6)	Billy Gardner	12.00	6.00	3.50
(7)	Connie Johnson	12.00	6.00	3.50
(8)	Ken Lehman	12.00	6.00	3.50
(9)	Willie Miranda	12.00	6.00	3.50
(10)	Bob Nieman	12.00	6.00	3.50
(11)	Paul Richards	12.00	6.00	3.50
(12)	Brooks Robinson	36.00	18.00	11.00
(13)	Gus Triandos	12.00	6.00	3.50
(14)	Dick Williams	12.00	6.00	3.50
(15)	Gene Woodling	18.00	9.00	5.50
(16)	George Zuverink	12.00	6.00	3.50

1970 Baltimore Orioles Traffic Safety

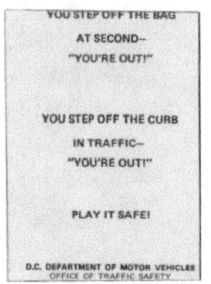

Similar in concept and design to the much more common Washington Senators safety issue of the same year, the Orioles cards are printed on yellow paper in 2-1/2" x 3-7/8" format. Fronts have player photo, name, team and position; backs have a safety message and notice of sponsorship by the D.C. Department of Motor Vehicles Office of Traffic Safety.

		NM	E	VG
Complete Set (10):		25.00	12.50	7.50
Common Player:		2.50	1.25	.75
(1)	Mark Bellanger (Belanger)	2.50	1.25	.75
(2)	Paul Blair	2.50	1.25	.75
(3)	Don Buford	2.50	1.25	.75
(4)	Mike Cuellar (Back in Spanish.)	4.00	2.00	1.25
(5)	Dave Johnson	2.50	1.25	.75
(6)	Dave McNally	2.50	1.25	.75
(7)	Boog Powell	5.00	2.50	1.50
(8)	Merv Rettenmund	2.50	1.25	.75
(9)	Brooks Robinson	10.00	5.00	3.00
(10)	Earl Weaver	3.50	1.75	1.00

1971 Bank of Montreal Rusty Staub

This 4" x 6" color card was issued by the Bank of Montreal, probably in conjunction with an autograph appearance by the popular Expos slugger. The front has a photo of the player working on his war club. The team and sponsor's logo are at top-right. On back are the player's stats.

	NM	E	VG
Rusty Staub	32.50	16.00	10.00

1913 Tom Barker Game (WG6)

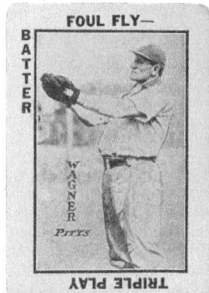

Nearly identical in format to "The National Game" card set, this issue features a different back design of a red-and-white line art representation of a batter. Fronts of the round-cornered, 2-1/2" x 3-1/2" cards have a black-and-white player

pose, or game action photo, along with two game scenarios used when playing the card game. There are nine action photos in the set. Player cards are checklisted here alphabetically. The set originally sold for 50 cents. The set was reprinted in the 1980s.

		NM	E	VG
Complete Set (54):		5,000	2,500	1,500
Common Player:		48.00	24.00	15.00
Game Box:		78.00	36.00	18.00
(1)	Grover Alexander	360.00	162.00	90.00
(2)	Frank Baker	120.00	54.00	30.00
(3)	Chief Bender	120.00	54.00	30.00
(4)	Bob Bescher	48.00	24.00	15.00
(5)	Joe Birmingham	48.00	24.00	15.00
(6)	Roger Bresnahan	120.00	54.00	30.00
(7)	Nixey Callahan	48.00	24.00	15.00
(8)	Bill Carrigan	48.00	24.00	15.00
(9)	Frank Chance	120.00	54.00	30.00
(10)	Hal Chase	78.00	36.00	19.00
(11)	Fred Clarke	120.00	54.00	30.00
(12)	Ty Cobb	810.00	360.00	210.00
(13)	Sam Crawford	120.00	54.00	30.00
(14)	Jake Daubert	48.00	24.00	15.00
(15)	Red Dooin	48.00	24.00	15.00
(16)	Johnny Evers	120.00	54.00	30.00
(17)	Vean Gregg	48.00	24.00	15.00
(18)	Clark Griffith	120.00	54.00	30.00
(19)	Dick Hoblitzel	48.00	24.00	15.00
(20)	Miller Huggins	120.00	54.00	30.00
(21)	Joe Jackson	1,920	870.00	480.00
(22)	Hughie Jennings	120.00	54.00	30.00
(23)	Walter Johnson	420.00	180.00	110.00
(24)	Ed Konetchy	48.00	24.00	15.00
(25)	Nap Lajoie	120.00	54.00	30.00
(26)	Connie Mack	120.00	54.00	30.00
(27)	Rube Marquard	120.00	54.00	30.00
(28)	Christy Mathewson	420.00	180.00	110.00
(29)	John McGraw	120.00	54.00	30.00
(30)	Chief Meyers	48.00	24.00	15.00
(31)	Clyde Milan	48.00	24.00	15.00
(32)	Marty O'Toole	48.00	24.00	15.00
(33)	Nap Rucker	48.00	24.00	15.00
(34)	Tris Speaker	160.00	75.00	40.00
(35)	George Stallings	48.00	24.00	15.00
(36)	Bill Sweeney	48.00	24.00	15.00
(37)	Joe Tinker	120.00	54.00	30.00
(38)	Honus Wagner	720.00	330.00	180.00
(39)	Ed Walsh	120.00	54.00	30.00
(40)	Zach Wheat	120.00	54.00	30.00
(41)	Ivy Wingo	48.00	24.00	15.00
(42)	Joe Wood	72.00	33.00	18.00
(43)	Cy Young	420.00	180.00	100.00
(---)	**Rules card**	48.00	24.00	15.00
(---)	**Score card**	48.00	24.00	15.00
	ACTION PHOTO CARDS			
(A1)	Batter swinging, looking forward.	18.00	8.10	4.50
(A2)	Batter swinging, looking back.	18.00	8.10	4.50
(A3)	Runner sliding, fielder at bag.	18.00	8.10	4.50
(A4)	Runner sliding, umpire behind.	48.00	24.00	15.00
(A5)	Runner sliding, hugging base.	18.00	8.10	4.50
(A6)	Sliding play at plate, umpire at left.	18.00	8.10	4.50
(A7)	Sliding play at plate, umpire at right.	18.00	8.10	4.50
(A8)	Play at plate, runner standing.	18.00	8.10	4.50
(A9)	Runner looking backwards.	18.00	8.10	4.50

1974-80 Bob Bartosz Postcards

DAVEY JOHNSON

Through the last half of the 1970s, Bob Bartosz, who was a photographer coving the Phillies for a New Jersey daily newspaper, produced a series of player postcards. Most cards were produced at the request of the players for use in handling fan requests. Generally, no more than 500 cards of each player were ever produced. Most of the cards are in black-and-white with player name in a white stripe. Three cards were done in color. Size varies, but averages about 3-5/8" x 5-1/2". Back designs also vary, with most simply having Bartosz' credit line vertically at center. The unnumbered cards are checklisted here in alphabetical order.

		NM	E	VG
	Complete Set (32):			
	Common Player:	3.00	1.50	.90

BLACK-AND-WHITE POSTCARDS

		NM	E	VG
(1)	Hank Aaron (16th career grand slam)	7.50	3.75	2.25
(2)	Richie Ashburn (5th Delaware Valley Show)	3.00	1.50	.90
(3)	James Cool Papa Bell	3.00	1.50	.90
(4)	Bob Boone	4.00	2.00	1.25
(5)	Jimmie Crutchfield	3.00	1.50	.90
(6)	Barry Foote	3.00	1.50	.90
(7)	Steve Garvey	4.00	2.00	1.25
(8)	Tommy Hutton (Phillies)	3.00	1.50	.90
(9)	Tommy Hutton (Blue Jays)	3.00	1.50	.90
(10)	Dane Iorg	3.00	1.50	.90
(11)	Davey Johnson	3.00	1.50	.90
(12)	Jay Johnstone	3.00	1.50	.90
(13)	Dave Kingman (Stadium background.)	3.00	1.50	.90
(14)	Dave Kingman (Black background.)	3.00	1.50	.90
(15)	Greg Luzinski (Both feet show.)	3.00	1.50	.90
(16)	Greg Luzinski (Only left foot shows.)	3.00	1.50	.90
(17)	Jerry Martin (Phillies)	3.00	1.50	.90
(18)	Jerry Martin (Cubs)	3.00	1.50	.90
(19)	Tim McCarver	4.00	2.00	1.25
(20)	John Montefusco	3.00	1.50	.90
(21)	Jerry Mumphrey	3.00	1.50	.90
(22)	Phil Niekro	4.00	2.00	1.25
(23)	Robin Roberts (Hall of Fame induction.)	3.00	1.50	.90
(24)	Robin Roberts (4th Delaware Valley Show)	3.00	1.50	.90
(25)	Steve Swisher	3.00	1.50	.90
(26)	Tony Taylor (Uniform number visible.)	3.00	1.50	.90
(27)	Tony Taylor (Number is covered.)	3.00	1.50	.90
(28)	Tom Underwood	3.00	1.50	.90
(29)	Billy Williams (N.L. umpire.)	3.00	1.50	.90
(30)	1974 National League All-Stars	4.00	2.00	1.25

COLOR POSTCARDS

		NM	E	VG
(1)	Greg Luzinski	7.50	3.75	2.25
(2)	Bill Madlock	7.50	3.75	2.25
(3)	Jason Thompson	6.00	3.00	1.75

1978 Bob Bartosz Baseball Postcards

Newspaper photographer Bob Bartosz produced a book of postcards in 1978 combining player poses, action shots and stadium photos. Two dozen cards are printed in 4" x 5-1/2" black-and-white format and perforated on pages of four in the 8-1/2" x 11" book. Backs have standard postcard indicia and are numbered with a "BB" prefix and titled, all printing in black.

		NM	E	VG
	Complete Book (24):	30.00	15.00	9.00
	Common Player:	1.50	.70	.45
1	25th anniversary of the 1950 Phillies (Group photo at old-timers game.)	1.50	.70	.45
2	Aaron and Mays at Cooperstown(Hank Aaron, Willie Mays)	4.00	2.00	1.25

		NM	E	VG
3	Willie Mays	7.50	3.75	2.25
4	Aaron signing autographs(Hank Aaron)	3.00	1.50	.90
5	Dizzy Dean (Old-timers action sequence.)	2.50	1.25	.70
6	Jack Russell Stadium, Clearwater, Fla.	1.50	.70	.45
7	Paddy Livingston	1.50	.70	.45
8	Bob Feller (Old-timers game.)	2.50	1.25	.70
9	Hall of Fame Game at Doubleday Field	1.50	.70	.45
10	Doubleday Field at Cooperstown, N.Y.	1.50	.70	.45
11	Three Rivers Stadium, Pittsburgh	1.50	.70	.45
12	Hall of Fame Game at Doubleday Field	1.50	.70	.45
13	Shibe Park from the air	1.50	.70	.45
14	Olympic Stadium, Montreal	1.50	.70	.45
15	A tree grows at home plate (Shibe Park - 1974)	1.50	.70	.45
16	The Bleachers, Wrigley Field	1.50	.70	.45
17	Another Home Run(Hank Aaron)	2.50	1.25	.70
18	Home Run King(Hank Aaron)	2.25	1.25	.70
19	Autograph Time - 1950 (Phillies signing balls.)	1.50	.70	.45
20	The Champs (1976 Phillies)	1.50	.70	.45
21	Last Day - Shibe Park, 1977	1.50	.70	.45
22	Connie Mack Stadium, Philadelphia	1.50	.70	.45
23	Shibe Park	1.50	.70	.45
24	Shibe Park	1.50	.70	.45

1911 Baseball Bats

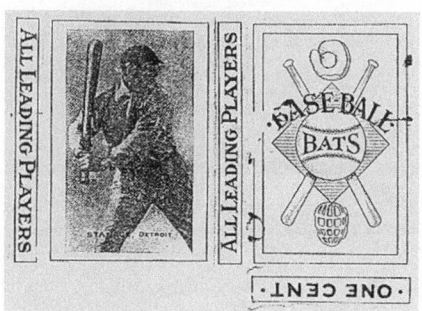

Issued circa 1911, cards in this rare 47-card issue were printed on the back panel of "Baseball Bats" penny candy. The cards themselves measure approximately 1-3/8" x 2-3/8" and feature a black-and-white player photo surrounded by an orange or white border. Player's name and team are printed in small, black capital letters near the bottom of the photo. Cards are blank-backed.

		NM	E	VG
	Complete Set (50):	40,000	20,000	12,000
	Common Player:	550.00	275.00	165.00
(1)	Red Ames	550.00	275.00	165.00
(2)	Home Run Baker	1,100	550.00	330.00
(3)	Jack Barry	550.00	275.00	165.00
(4)	Ginger Beaumont	550.00	275.00	165.00
(5)	Chief Bender	1,100	550.00	330.00
(6)	Al Bridwell	550.00	275.00	165.00
(7)	Mordecai Brown	1,100	550.00	330.00
(8)	Bill Corrigan (Carrigan)	550.00	275.00	165.00
(9)	Frank Chance	1,100	550.00	330.00
(10)	Hal Chase	850.00	425.00	250.00
(11)	Ed Cicotte	925.00	460.00	275.00
(12)	Fred Clark (Clarke)	1,100	550.00	330.00
(13)	Ty Cobb	6,000	4,000	2,000
(14)	King Cole	550.00	275.00	165.00
(15)	Eddie Collins	1,100	550.00	330.00
(16)	Sam Crawford	1,100	550.00	330.00
(17)	Lou Criger	550.00	275.00	165.00
(18)	Harry Davis	550.00	275.00	165.00
(19)	Jim Delehanty	550.00	275.00	165.00
(20)	Art Devlin	550.00	275.00	165.00
(21)	Josh Devore	550.00	275.00	165.00
(22)	Wild Bill Donovan	550.00	275.00	165.00
(23)	Larry Doyle	550.00	275.00	165.00
(24)	Johnny Evers	1,100	550.00	330.00
(25)	John Flynn	550.00	275.00	165.00
(26)	George Gibson	550.00	275.00	165.00
(27)	Solly Hoffman (Hofman)	550.00	275.00	165.00
(28)	Walter Johnson	2,200	1,100	660.00
(29)	Johnny Kling	550.00	275.00	165.00
(30)	Nap Lajoie	1,100	550.00	330.00

		NM	E	VG
(31)	Christy Mathewson	3,000	2,000	1,000
(32)	Matty McIntyre	550.00	275.00	165.00
(33)	Fred Merkle	550.00	275.00	165.00
(34)	Danny Murphy	550.00	275.00	165.00
(35)	Tom Needham	550.00	275.00	165.00
(36)	Harry Niles	550.00	275.00	165.00
(37)	Rube Oldring	550.00	275.00	165.00
(38)	Wildfire Schulte	550.00	275.00	165.00
(39)	Cy Seymour	550.00	275.00	165.00
(40)	Jimmy Sheckard	550.00	275.00	165.00
(41)	Tris Speaker	2,400	1,600	1,000
(42)	Oscar Stanage (Batting - front view.)	550.00	275.00	165.00
(43)	Oscar Stanage (Batting - side view.)	550.00	275.00	165.00
(44)	Ira Thomas	550.00	275.00	165.00
(45)	Joe Tinker	1,100	550.00	330.00
(46)	Heinie Wagner	550.00	275.00	165.00
(47)	Honus Wagner	4,500	2,250	1,350
(48)	Ed Walsh	1,100	550.00	330.00
(49)	Art Wilson	550.00	275.00	165.00
(50)	Owen Wilson	550.00	275.00	165.00

1887-1893 Baseball Currency

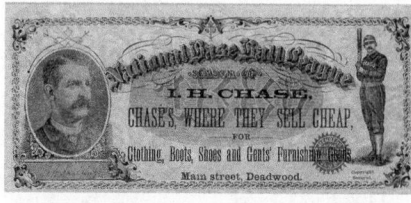

Because of their similarity in size (about 7-3/4" x 3-3/8"), design and color to then-circulating U.S. paper money, this form of advertising flyer was thought to catch the attention of the general public. The notes were printed in black-and-green (some 1889 Chicago notes are printed in black-and-red) on white. Fronts have at left a large oval portrait of the team's president or manager. At right on the Chicago and Detroit notes is a full-figure rendering of an unnamed Cap Anson. On the St. Louis notes, there is a picture of the Wilman Trophy indicative of the team's 1886 World's Championship. On the 1893 note, National League President N.E. Young is pictured at left, with a grouping of baseball equipment at right. In the center is a large ornate date with either "National Base Ball League" or "National / Base Ball Association" at top in gothic typography. Backs have black-and-white woodcuts of the team's players on a decorative green (or red) background. The notes were originally printed with large open spaces on front and back so that advertising messages could be over-printed by local merchants. The value of the notes can be affected by the location of a specific advertiser and/or the content of his message. Sports collectors compete with numismatists for examples of these advertising pieces.

	NM	E	VG
1887 Chicago White Stockings (Front: Pres. A.G. Spalding. Back: Cap Anson, Mark Baldwin, John Clarkson, Tom Daily (Daly), Dell Darling, Silver Flint, Lou Hardie, Fred Pfeffer, Jimmy Ryan, Marty Sullivan, Billy Sunday, Ed Williamson.)	2,300	1,150	750.00
1887 Detroit Wolverines (Front: Manager Bill Watkins. Back: Lady Baldwin, Charlie Bennett, Fatty Briody, Dan Brouthers, Fred Dunlap, Charlie Ganzel, Ned Hanlon,Hardy Richardson, Jack Rowe, Sam Thompson, Stump Weidman (Wiedman), Deacon White.)	2,600	1,300	775.00
1887 St. Louis Browns (Front: Pres. Chris Von Der Ahe. Back: Jack Boyle, Doc Bushong, Bob Caruthers, Charlie Comiskey, Dave Foutz, Bill Gleason, Arlie Latham, Tip O'Neil (O'Neill), Yank Robinson, Curt Welch.)	4,000	2,000	1,200

1888 Chicago White Stockings (Front: Pres. A.G. Spalding. Back: Cap Anson, Mark Baldwin, John Clarkson, Tom Daily (Daly), Dell Darling, Silver Flint, Lou Hardie, Fred Pfeffer, Jimmy Ryan, Marty Sullivan, Billy Sunday, Ed Williamson.)   2,600   1,300   750.00

1888 Detroit Wolverines (Front: Manager Bill Watkins. Back: Lady Baldwin, Charlie Bennett, Fatty Briody, Dan Brouthers, Fred Dunlap, Charlie Ganzel, Ned Hanlon, Hardy Richardson, Jack Rowe, Sam Thompson, Stump Weidman (Wiedman), Deacon White.)   2,600   1,300   775.00

1888 Detroit Wolverines (Front: Manager Bill Watkins. Back: Lady Baldwin, Charlie Bennett, Fatty Briody, Dan Brouthers, Fred Dunlap, Charlie Ganzel, Ned Hanlon, Hardy Richardson, Jack Rowe, Sam Thompson, Stump Weidman (Wiedman), Deacon White.)   2,600   1,300   775.00

1888 St. Louis Browns (Front: Pres. Chris Von Der Ahe. Back: Jack Boyle, Charles Comiskey, Silver King, Arlie Latham, Harry Lyons, Tommy McCarthy, Chippy McGarr, Jocko Milligan, Tip O'Neill, Yank Robinson.)   6,000   3,000   1,800

1889 Chicago White Stockings (Front: Pres. A.G. Spalding. Back: Cap Anson, Mark Baldwin, Tom Burns, Tom Daily (Daly), Dell Darling, Silver Flint, Bob Pettit, Fred Pfeffer, Jimmy Ryan, Marty Sullivan, George Van Haltren, Ed Williamson.)   2,600   1,300   750.00

1893 National League All-Stars (Front: Pres. N.E. Young. Back: Bob Allen, Cap Anson, Mark Baldwin, John Clarkson, Charles Comiskey, Dave Foutz, King Kelly, Billy Nash, Jim O'Rourke, Fred Pfeffer, George Van Haltren, John Ward.)(VALUE UNDETERMINED)

1979 Baseball Favorites "1953 Bowman"

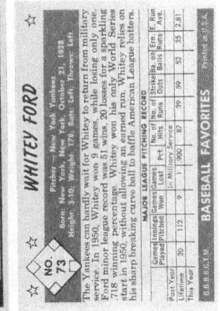

This collectors' series was designed to represent an extension of the 64-card 1953 Bowman black-and-white card issue. This series uses the same design on its 2-1/2" x 3-3/4" format. Fronts have a black-and-white player photo with no extraneous graphics. Backs are printed in red and black and offer career highlights, stats and biographical data, written as if in 1953. Many of the players in this collectors' edition originally appeared in Bowman's 1953 color series. Issue price was about $7.

		NM	E	VG
Complete Set (16):		30.00	15.00	9.00
Common Player:		1.00	.50	.30
65	Monte Irvin	1.00	.50	.30
66	Early Wynn	1.00	.50	.30
67	Robin Roberts	1.00	.50	.30
68	Stan Musial	4.00	2.00	1.20
69	Ernie Banks	3.00	1.50	.90
70	Willie Mays	6.00	3.00	1.80
71	Yogi Berra	4.00	2.00	1.25
72	Mickey Mantle	15.00	7.50	4.50
73	Whitey Ford	1.25	.60	.40
74	Bob Feller	1.00	.50	.30
75	Ted Williams	5.00	2.50	1.50
76	Satchel Paige	4.00	2.00	1.20
77	Jackie Robinson	4.00	2.00	1.20
78	Ed Mathews	1.00	.50	.30
79	Warren Spahn	1.00	.50	.30
80	Ralph Kiner	1.00	.50	.30

1964 Baseball Greats Postcard

Four of California's star players are pictured on this standard-format (5-1/2" x 3-1/2") color postcard in a pair of two-player poses. Each player's facsimile autograph appears on front. Back is in typical postcard format with player identification, a stamp box and vertical center divider with publisher and distributor information. (See also Baseball Stars - Present and Future.)

	NM	E	VG
Don Drysdale, Dean Chance, Willie Mays, Sandy Koufax	40.00	20.00	12.00

1910-57 Baseball Magazine Player Posters

Beginning shortly after its 1908 debut, Baseball Magazine produced a lengthy series of player posters which it offered as premiums to readers. Ranging in size from 9" x 12-1/4" to 9" x 20" (and a series of super-size 1957s), the posters feature poses of top players in sepia tones bordered in white. In the bottom border over the years appeared various formats of player identification, copyright information and promotion for the magazine. The unnumbered posters are listed here alphabetically by year. Some posters were reprinted over the years and there may exist pose variations as well as posters which have escaped this list. Names shown here may not coincide with the form in which they actually appear on the posters. Inaccuracies in, or incompleteness of, the checklist is the likely result of its having been compiled from ads appearing in the magazine. The posters were listed in the American Card Catalog as M114.

		NM	E	VG
	1910			
(1)	Ty Cobb	350.00	175.00	105.00
(2)	Johnny Evers	150.00	75.00	45.00
(3)	Hughie Jennings	100.00	50.00	30.00
(4)	Honus Wagner	300.00	150.00	90.00
	1912			
(1)	Babe Adams	60.00	30.00	18.00
(2)	Howie Camnitz	60.00	30.00	18.00
(3)	Frank Chance	125.00	62.00	37.00
(4)	Claude Hendrix	60.00	30.00	18.00
(5)	Marty O'Toole	60.00	30.00	18.00
(6)	Boston Red Sox Team	250.00	125.00	75.00
(7)	New York Giants Team	250.00	125.00	75.00
	1913			
(1)	Jimmy Archer	60.00	30.00	18.00
(2)	Jack Barry	60.00	30.00	18.00
(3)	Joe Bush	60.00	30.00	18.00
(4)	Sam Crawford	100.00	50.00	30.00
(5)	Eddie Collins	125.00	62.00	37.00
(6)	Jake Daubert	60.00	30.00	18.00
(7)	Larry Doyle	60.00	30.00	18.00
(8)	Art Fletcher	60.00	30.00	18.00
(9)	Joe Jackson	1,000	500.00	300.00
(10)	Walter Johnson	250.00	125.00	75.00
(11)	Nap Lajoie	200.00	100.00	60.00
(12)	Connie Mack	100.00	50.00	30.00
(13)	Fritz Maisel	60.00	30.00	18.00
(14)	Rube Marquard	100.00	50.00	30.00
(15)	Christy Mathewson	250.00	125.00	75.00
(16)	John McGraw	125.00	62.00	37.00
(17)	Stuffy McInnis	60.00	30.00	18.00
(18)	"Chief" Meyers	60.00	30.00	18.00
(19)	Red Murray	60.00	30.00	18.00
(20)	Eddie Plank	125.00	62.00	37.00
(21)	"Nap" Rucker	60.00	30.00	18.00
(22)	Reb Russell	60.00	30.00	18.00
(23)	Tris Speaker	125.00	62.00	37.00
(24)	Ed Walsh	100.00	50.00	30.00
(25)	Smokey Joe Wood	75.00	37.00	22.00
(26)	Boston Braves Team	250.00	125.00	75.00
(27)	Philadelphia Athletics Team	250.00	125.00	75.00
	1914			
(1)	Home Run Baker	100.00	50.00	30.00
(2)	Larry Cheney	60.00	30.00	18.00
(3)	Joe Connolly	60.00	30.00	18.00
(4)	Hank Gowdy	60.00	30.00	18.00
(5)	Bill James	60.00	30.00	18.00
(6)	Jimmy Lavender	60.00	30.00	18.00
(7)	Rabbit Maranville	100.00	50.00	30.00
(8)	Dick Rudolph	60.00	30.00	18.00
(9)	Wally Schang	60.00	30.00	18.00
(10)	Bob Shawkey	60.00	30.00	18.00
(11)	Jimmy Sheckard	60.00	30.00	18.00
(12)	Charles Schmidt	60.00	30.00	18.00
(13)	Wildfire Schulte	60.00	30.00	18.00
(14)	Lefty Tyler	60.00	30.00	18.00
(15)	Boston Braves Team	200.00	100.00	60.00
(16)	Chicago Cubs Team	200.00	100.00	60.00
(17)	Chicago Whales Team	250.00	125.00	75.00
(18)	Cincinnati Reds Team	200.00	100.00	60.00
(19)	Cleveland Indians Team	200.00	100.00	60.00
(20)	Detroit Tigers Team	200.00	100.00	60.00
(21)	New York Yankees Team	200.00	100.00	60.00
(22)	St. Louis Browns Team	200.00	100.00	60.00
(22)	St. Louis Cardinals Team	200.00	100.00	60.00
(24)	Washington Senators Team	200.00	100.00	60.00
	1915			
(1)	Grover Alexander	125.00	62.00	37.00
(2)	Chief Bender	100.00	50.00	30.00
(3)	Harry Hooper	100.00	50.00	30.00
(4)	Duffy Lewis	60.00	30.00	18.00
(5)	Tris Speaker	100.00	50.00	30.00
(6)	Boston Red Sox Team	200.00	100.00	60.00
(7)	Chicago White Sox Team	200.00	100.00	60.00
(8)	Philadelphia Athletics Team	200.00	100.00	60.00
(9)	Philadelphia Phillies Team	200.00	100.00	60.00
(10)	St. Louis Cardinals Team	200.00	100.00	60.00
	1916			
(1)	Larry Gardner	50.00	25.00	15.00
(2)	Buck Herzog	50.00	25.00	15.00
(3)	Rogers Hornsby	75.00	37.00	22.00
(4)	Walter Johnson	160.00	80.00	48.00
(5)	Fielder Jones	50.00	25.00	15.00
(6)	Benny Kauff	50.00	25.00	15.00
(7)	Dave Robertson	50.00	25.00	15.00
(8)	Babe Ruth (Pitching)	300.00	150.00	90.00
(9)	George Sisler	75.00	37.00	22.00
(10)	Zack Wheat	75.00	37.00	22.00
(11)	Boston Red Sox Team	150.00	75.00	45.00
(12)	Brooklyn Dodgers Team	100.00	50.00	30.00
(13)	Philadelphia Phillies Team	100.00	50.00	30.00
	1917			
(1)	George Burns	50.00	25.00	15.00
(2)	Ed Cicotte	150.00	75.00	45.00
(3)	Art Fletcher	50.00	25.00	15.00
(4)	Red Faber	50.00	25.00	15.00
(5)	Happy Felsch	150.00	75.00	45.00
(6)	Ferd Schupp	50.00	25.00	15.00
(7)	Ray Schalk	50.00	25.00	15.00

(8)	Buck Weaver	150.00	75.00	45.00
(9)	Chicago White Sox Team	250.00	125.00	75.00
(10)	New York Giants Team	150.00	75.00	45.00
1918				
(1)	Home Run Baker	75.00	37.00	22.00
1919				
(1)	Ed Cicotte	75.00	37.00	22.00
(2)	Chicago White Sox Team	400.00	200.00	120.00
(3)	Cincinnati Reds Team	125.00	62.00	37.00
1920				
(1)	Jim Bagby Sr.	30.00	15.00	9.00
(2)	Dave Bancroft	45.00	22.00	13.50
(3)	Max Carey	45.00	22.00	13.50
(4)	Harry Coveleski	45.00	22.00	13.50
(5)	Hod Eller	30.00	15.00	9.00
(6)	Burleigh Grimes	45.00	22.00	13.50
(7)	Heinie Groh	30.00	15.00	9.00
(8)	Rogers Hornsby	45.00	22.00	13.50
(9)	Walter Johnson	75.00	37.00	22.00
(10)	Dick Kerr	30.00	15.00	9.00
(11)	Pat Moran	30.00	15.00	9.00
(12)	Duster Mails	30.00	15.00	9.00
(13)	Hy Myers	30.00	15.00	9.00
(14)	Steve O'Neill	30.00	15.00	9.00
(15)	Edd Roush	45.00	22.00	13.50
(16)	Dutch Ruether	30.00	15.00	9.00
(17)	Babe Ruth (Batting, no stands in background.)	800.00	400.00	240.00
(18)	Ray Schalk	45.00	22.00	13.50
(19)	Earl Smith	30.00	15.00	9.00
(20)	Sherrod Smith	30.00	15.00	9.00
(21)	Tris Speaker	45.00	22.00	13.50
(22)	Hippo Vaughn	30.00	15.00	9.00
(23)	Bobby Veach	30.00	15.00	9.00
(24)	Bill Wambsganss	30.00	15.00	9.00
(25)	Brooklyn Dodgers Team	125.00	62.00	37.00
(26)	Cleveland Indians Team	125.00	62.00	37.00
1921				
(1)	Dave Bancroft	45.00	22.00	13.50
(2)	Wilbur Cooper	30.00	15.00	9.00
(3)	Phil Douglas	30.00	15.00	9.00
(4)	Frank Frisch	50.00	25.00	15.00
(5)	Harry Heilmann	45.00	22.00	13.50
(6)	Waite Hoyt	45.00	22.00	13.50
(7)	George Kelly	45.00	22.00	13.50
(8)	Carl Mays	45.00	22.00	13.50
(9)	Mike McNally	30.00	15.00	9.00
(10)	Irish Meusel	30.00	15.00	9.00
(11)	Bob Meusel	30.00	15.00	9.00
(12)	Art Nehf	30.00	15.00	9.00
(13)	Wally Schang	30.00	15.00	9.00
(14)	Walter Schmidt	30.00	15.00	9.00
(15)	Frank Snyder	30.00	15.00	9.00
(16)	Aaron Ward	30.00	15.00	9.00
(17)	Ross Youngs	45.00	22.00	13.50
(18)	New York Giants Team	100.00	50.00	30.00
(19)	New York Yankees Team	300.00	150.00	90.00
(20)	Pittsburgh Pirates Team	100.00	50.00	30.00
1922 - NONE				
1923				
(1)	New York Giants Team	90.00	45.00	27.00
(2)	New York Yankees Team	200.00	100.00	60.00
1924				
(1)	Johnny Bassler	30.00	15.00	9.00
(2)	Jim Bottomley	45.00	22.00	13.50
(3)	Kiki Cuyler	45.00	22.00	13.50
(4)	Joe Dugan	30.00	15.00	9.00
(5)	Bibb Falk	30.00	15.00	9.00
(6)	Jack Fournier	30.00	15.00	9.00
(7)	Goose Goslin	45.00	22.00	13.50
(8)	Sam Harris	30.00	15.00	9.00
(9)	Gabby Hartnett	45.00	22.00	13.50
(10)	Travis Jackson	45.00	22.00	13.50
(11)	Baby Doll Jacobson	30.00	15.00	9.00
(12)	Charlie Jamieson	30.00	15.00	9.00
(13)	Herb Pennock	45.00	22.00	13.50
(14)	Sam Rice	45.00	22.00	13.50
(15)	Eppa Rixey	45.00	22.00	13.50
(16)	Muddy Ruel	30.00	15.00	9.00
(17)	Hollis Thurston	30.00	15.00	9.00
(18)	Pie Traynor	45.00	22.00	13.50
(19)	Dazzy Vance	45.00	22.00	13.50
(20)	Kenny Williams	30.00	15.00	9.00
(21)	New York Giants Team	90.00	45.00	27.00
(22)	Washington Senators Team	90.00	45.00	27.00
1925				
(1)	Vic Aldridge	30.00	15.00	9.00
(2)	Mickey Cochrane	45.00	22.00	13.50
(3)	Ted Lyons	45.00	22.00	13.50
(4)	Eddie Rommel	30.00	15.00	9.00
(5)	Al Simmons	45.00	22.00	13.50
(6)	Glenn Wright	30.00	15.00	9.00
(7)	Pittsburgh Pirates Team	90.00	45.00	27.00
(8)	Washington Senators Team	90.00	45.00	27.00
1926				
(1)	Les Bell	30.00	15.00	9.00

(2)	George H. Burns	30.00	15.00	9.00
(3)	Hughie Critz	30.00	15.00	9.00
(4)	Henry (Lou) Gehrig (Portrait)	250.00	125.00	75.00
(5)	Ray Kremer	30.00	15.00	9.00
(6)	Bob O'Farrell	30.00	15.00	9.00
(7)	Tommy Thevenow	30.00	15.00	9.00
(8)	George Uhle	30.00	15.00	9.00
(9)	Hack Wilson	45.00	22.00	13.50
(10)	New York Yankees Team	250.00	125.00	75.00
(11)	St. Louis Cardinals Team	90.00	45.00	27.00
1927				
(1)	Carmen Hill	30.00	15.00	9.00
(2)	Tony Lazzeri	45.00	22.00	13.50
(3)	Fred Lindstrom	45.00	22.00	13.50
(4)	Charlie Root	30.00	15.00	9.00
(5)	Lloyd Waner	45.00	22.00	13.50
(6)	Paul Waner	45.00	22.00	13.50
(7)	New York Yankees Team	200.00	100.00	60.00
(8)	Pittsburgh Pirates Team	90.00	45.00	27.00
1928				
(1)	Jimmie Foxx	60.00	30.00	18.00
1929				
(1)	Guy Bush	30.00	15.00	9.00
(2)	Lefty Grove	45.00	22.00	13.50
(3)	Chicago Cubs Team	125.00	62.00	37.00
(4)	Philadelphia Athletics Team	90.00	45.00	27.00
1930				
(1)	George Earnshaw	30.00	15.00	9.00
(2)	Wes Ferrell	30.00	15.00	9.00
(3)	Charley Gelbert	30.00	15.00	9.00
(4)	Babe Herman	30.00	15.00	9.00
(5)	Chuck Klein	45.00	22.00	13.50
(6)	Philadelphia Athletics Team	90.00	45.00	27.00
(7)	St. Louis Cardinals Team	90.00	45.00	27.00
1931				
(1)	Earl Averill	45.00	22.00	13.50
(2)	Ed Brandt	30.00	15.00	9.00
(3)	Ben Chapman	30.00	15.00	9.00
(4)	Joe Cronin	45.00	22.00	13.50
(5)	Bill Hallahan	30.00	15.00	9.00
(6)	Pepper Martin	40.00	20.00	12.00
1932 - NONE				
1933				
(1)	Dizzy Dean	75.00	37.00	22.00
(2)	Lou Gehrig (Batting)	225.00	110.00	67.00
(3)	Carl Hubbell	60.00	30.00	18.00
(4)	Heinie Manush	45.00	22.00	13.50
(5)	Mel Ott	45.00	22.00	13.50
(6)	Babe Ruth (Batting, stands in background.)	250.00	125.00	75.00
(7)	Hal Schumacher	30.00	15.00	9.00
(8)	Lon Warneke	30.00	15.00	9.00
(9)	New York Giants Team	90.00	45.00	27.00
(10)	Washington Senators Team	90.00	45.00	27.00
1934				
(1)	Dick Bartell	30.00	15.00	9.00
(2)	Paul Dean	45.00	22.00	13.50
(3)	Lefty Gomez	45.00	22.00	13.50
(4)	Rogers Hornsby	45.00	22.00	13.50
(5)	Ducky Medwick	45.00	22.00	13.50
(6)	Van Lingle Mungo	30.00	15.00	9.00
(7)	Schoolboy Rowe	30.00	15.00	9.00
(8)	Arky Vaughan	45.00	22.00	13.50
(9)	Lloyd Waner	45.00	22.00	13.50
(10)	Paul Waner	45.00	22.00	13.50
(11)	Detroit Tigers Team	100.00	50.00	30.00
1935				
(1)	Wally Berger	30.00	15.00	9.00
(2)	Ripper Collins	30.00	15.00	9.00
(3)	Charley Gehringer	45.00	22.00	13.50
(4)	Hank Greenberg	60.00	30.00	18.00
(5)	Mel Harder	30.00	15.00	9.00
(6)	Billy Herman	45.00	22.00	13.50
(7)	Buddy Myer	30.00	15.00	9.00
(8)	Al Simmons	45.00	22.00	13.50
(9)	Bill Terry	45.00	22.00	13.50
(10)	Joe Vosmik	30.00	15.00	9.00
(11)	Chicago Cubs Team	100.00	50.00	30.00
(12)	Detroit Tigers Team	90.00	45.00	27.00
1936				
(1)	Luke Appling	45.00	22.00	13.50
(2)	Frank Demaree	30.00	15.00	9.00
(3)	Paul Derringer	30.00	15.00	9.00
(4)	Joe DiMaggio	80.00	40.00	24.00
(5)	Vern Kennedy	30.00	15.00	9.00
(6)	Ernie Lombardi	45.00	22.00	13.50
(7)	Joe Moore	30.00	15.00	9.00
(8)	Terry Moore	30.00	15.00	9.00
(9)	Moose Solters	30.00	15.00	9.00
(10)	Hal Trosky	30.00	15.00	9.00
(11)	Bill Werber	30.00	15.00	9.00
(12)	New York Giants Team	100.00	50.00	30.00
(13)	New York Yankees Team	200.00	100.00	60.00
1937				

(1)	Cy Blanton	30.00	15.00	9.00
(2)	Dolph Camilli	30.00	15.00	9.00
(3)	Joe Cronin	45.00	22.00	13.50
(4)	Bill Dickey	50.00	25.00	15.00
(5)	Bob Feller	50.00	25.00	15.00
(6)	Stan Hack	30.00	15.00	9.00
(7)	Buddy Hassett	30.00	15.00	9.00
(8)	Bill Lee	30.00	15.00	9.00
(9)	Buddy Lewis	30.00	15.00	9.00
(10)	Johnny Mize	45.00	22.00	13.50
(11)	Jimmy Ripple	30.00	15.00	9.00
(12)	Charles Ruffing	45.00	22.00	13.50
(13)	Cecil Travis	30.00	15.00	9.00
(14)	Gee Walker	30.00	15.00	9.00
1938				
(1)	Ethan Allen	30.00	15.00	9.00
(2)	Clay Bryant	30.00	15.00	9.00
(3)	Harlond Clift	30.00	15.00	9.00
(4)	Frank Crosetti	35.00	17.50	10.50
(5)	Harry Danning	30.00	15.00	9.00
(6)	Bobby Doerr	45.00	22.00	13.50
(7)	Augie Galan	30.00	15.00	9.00
(8)	Ival Goodman	30.00	15.00	9.00
(9)	Joe Gordon	30.00	15.00	9.00
(10)	Tommy Henrich	35.00	17.50	10.50
(11)	Mike Kreevich	30.00	15.00	9.00
(12)	Frank McCormick	30.00	15.00	9.00
(13)	Babe Phelps	30.00	15.00	9.00
(14)	Johnny Rizzo	30.00	15.00	9.00
(15)	Red Rolfe	30.00	15.00	9.00
(16)	Johnny Vander Meer	35.00	17.50	10.50
(17)	Rudy York	30.00	15.00	9.00
1939				
(1)	Morrie Arnovich	30.00	15.00	9.00
(2)	Jimmie Foxx	45.00	22.00	13.50
(3)	Luke Hamlin	30.00	15.00	9.00
(4)	Bob Johnson	35.00	17.50	10.50
(5)	Charlie Keller	35.00	17.50	10.50
(6)	Ken Keltner	35.00	17.50	10.50
(7)	Emil "Dutch" Leonard	30.00	15.00	9.00
(8)	Bobo Newsom	30.00	15.00	9.00
(9)	Don Padgett	30.00	15.00	9.00
(10)	Bucky Walters	30.00	15.00	9.00
(11)	Ted Williams	120.00	60.00	36.00
1940 (9-1/2" x 12")				
(1)	George Case	20.00	10.00	6.00
(2)	Babe Dahlgren	20.00	10.00	6.00
(3)	Elbie Fletcher	20.00	10.00	6.00
(4)	Cookie Lavagetto	20.00	10.00	6.00
(5)	Barney McCosky	20.00	10.00	6.00
(6)	Bill McGee	20.00	10.00	6.00
(7)	Ducky Medwick	40.00	20.00	12.00
(8)	Eddie Miller	20.00	10.00	6.00
(9)	Hugh Mulcahy	20.00	10.00	6.00
(10)	Claude Passeau	20.00	10.00	6.00
(11)	Rip Radcliff	20.00	10.00	6.00
(12)	Jim Tabor	20.00	10.00	6.00
(13)	Eugene "Junior" Thompson	20.00	10.00	6.00
(14)	Mike Tresh	20.00	10.00	6.00
(15)	Roy Weatherly	20.00	10.00	6.00
(16)	Norm "Babe" Young	20.00	10.00	6.00
1941 (9-1/2" x 12")				
(1)	Sam Chapman	20.00	10.00	6.00
(2)	Ty Cobb	60.00	30.00	18.00
(3)	Mort Cooper	20.00	10.00	6.00
(4)	Dom DiMaggio	40.00	20.00	12.00
(5)	Jeff Heath	20.00	10.00	6.00
(6)	Thornton Lee	20.00	10.00	6.00
(7)	Danny Litwhiler	20.00	10.00	6.00
(8)	Al Lopez	40.00	20.00	12.00
(9)	Christy Mathewson	60.00	30.00	18.00
(10)	Joe McCarthy	40.00	20.00	12.00
(11)	Bill Nicholson	20.00	10.00	6.00
(12)	Pete Reiser	20.00	10.00	6.00
(13)	Elmer Riddle	20.00	10.00	6.00
(14)	Phil Rizzuto	60.00	30.00	18.00
(15)	Johnny Rucker	20.00	10.00	6.00
(16)	Hans Wagner	60.00	30.00	18.00
1942 (9-1/2" x 12")				
(1)	Jim Bagby Jr.	20.00	10.00	6.00
(2)	Ernie Bonham	20.00	10.00	6.00
(3)	Lou Boudreau	40.00	20.00	12.00
(4)	Tommy Bridges	20.00	10.00	6.00
(5)	Jimmy Brown	20.00	10.00	6.00
(6)	Dolph Camilli	20.00	10.00	6.00
(7)	Walker Cooper	20.00	10.00	6.00
(8)	Bob Elliott	20.00	10.00	6.00
(9)	Lou Gehrig (Batting)	100.00	50.00	30.00
(10)	Tex Hughson	20.00	10.00	6.00
(11)	Eddie Joost	20.00	10.00	6.00
(12)	Don Kolloway	20.00	10.00	6.00
(13)	Phil Marchildon	20.00	10.00	6.00
(14)	Clyde McCullough	20.00	10.00	6.00
(15)	George McQuinn	20.00	10.00	6.00
(16)	Cliff Melton	20.00	10.00	6.00
(17)	Lou Novikoff	20.00	10.00	6.00
(18)	Mickey Owen	20.00	10.00	6.00
(19)	Pee Wee Reese	50.00	25.00	15.00

(20)	Stan Spence	20.00	10.00	6.00
(21)	Vern Stephens	20.00	10.00	6.00
(22)	Virgil Trucks	20.00	10.00	6.00
(23)	Fred "Dixie" Walker	20.00	10.00	6.00
(24)	Max West	20.00	10.00	6.00

1943 (9-1/2" x 12")

(1)	Hiram Bithorn	20.00	10.00	6.00
(2)	Spud Chandler	20.00	10.00	6.00
(3)	Al Javery	20.00	10.00	6.00
(4)	Bill Johnson	20.00	10.00	6.00
(5)	Kenesaw Landis	40.00	20.00	12.00
(6)	Tony Lupien	20.00	10.00	6.00
(7)	Marty Marion	25.00	12.50	7.50
(8)	Stan Musial	60.00	30.00	18.00
(9)	Bobo Newsom	20.00	10.00	6.00
(10)	Babe Ruth (Portrait)	80.00	40.00	24.00
(11)	Rip Sewell	20.00	10.00	6.00
(12)	Joe Schultz	20.00	10.00	6.00
(13)	Dizzy Trout	20.00	10.00	6.00
(14)	Mickey Vernon	20.00	10.00	6.00
(15)	Dick Wakefield	20.00	10.00	6.00
(16)	Mickey Witek	20.00	10.00	6.00
(17)	Early Wynn	40.00	20.00	12.00
(18)	New York Yankees Team	90.00	45.00	27.00
(19)	St. Louis Cardinals Team	90.00	45.00	27.00

1944 (9-1/2" x 12")

(1)	Augie Galan	20.00	10.00	6.00
(2)	Johnny Hopp	20.00	10.00	6.00
(3)	Jack Kramer	20.00	10.00	6.00
(4)	Johnny Lindell	20.00	10.00	6.00
(5)	Ray Mueller	20.00	10.00	6.00
(6)	Hal Newhouser	40.00	20.00	12.00
(7)	Nelson Potter	20.00	10.00	6.00
(8)	Ray Sanders	20.00	10.00	6.00
(9)	"Snuffy" Stirnweiss	20.00	10.00	6.00
(10)	Jim Tobin	20.00	10.00	6.00
(11)	Thurman Tucker	20.00	10.00	6.00
(12)	Bill Voiselle	20.00	10.00	6.00
(13)	Ted Wilks	20.00	10.00	6.00
(14)	Detroit Tigers Team	90.00	45.00	27.00
(15)	St. Louis Browns Team	90.00	45.00	27.00
(16)	St. Louis Cardinals Team	90.00	45.00	27.00

1945 (9-1/2" x 12")

(1)	Phil Cavarretta	20.00	10.00	6.00
(2)	Russ Christopher	20.00	10.00	6.00
(3)	Tony Cuccinello	20.00	10.00	6.00
(4)	Boo Ferriss	20.00	10.00	6.00
(5)	Hal Gregg	20.00	10.00	6.00
(6)	Steve Gromek	20.00	10.00	6.00
(7)	Ducky Medwick	40.00	20.00	12.00
(8)	George Myatt	20.00	10.00	6.00
(9)	Frank Overmire	20.00	10.00	6.00
(10)	Andy Pafko	25.00	12.50	7.50
(11)	Red Schoendienst	40.00	20.00	12.00
(12)	Chicago Cubs Team	90.00	45.00	27.00
(13)	Detroit Tigers Team	75.00	37.00	22.00

1946

(1)	Joe Beggs	20.00	10.00	6.00
(2)	Johnny Berardino	25.00	12.50	7.50
(3)	Bill Bevens	20.00	10.00	6.00
(4)	Harry Brecheen	20.00	10.00	6.00
(5)	Mickey Harris	20.00	10.00	6.00
(6)	Kirby Higbe	20.00	10.00	6.00
(7)	Dave Koslo	20.00	10.00	6.00
(8)	Whitey Kurowski	20.00	10.00	6.00
(9)	Vic Lombardi	20.00	10.00	6.00
(10)	Phil Masi	20.00	10.00	6.00
(11)	Mike McCormick	20.00	10.00	6.00
(12)	Johnny Mize	40.00	20.00	12.00
(13)	Hal Newhouser	40.00	20.00	12.00
(14)	Johnny Pesky	20.00	10.00	6.00
(15)	Howie Pollett	20.00	10.00	6.00
(16)	Jerry Priddy	20.00	10.00	6.00
(17)	Aaron Robinson	20.00	10.00	6.00
(18)	Enos Slaughter	40.00	20.00	12.00
(19)	Eddie Stanky	20.00	10.00	6.00
(20)	Hal Wagner	20.00	10.00	6.00
(21)	Rudy York	20.00	10.00	6.00
(22)	Boston Red Sox Team	75.00	37.00	22.00
(23)	St. Louis Cardinals Team	75.00	37.00	22.00

1947

(1)	Ewell Blackwell	20.00	10.00	6.00
(2)	Ralph Branca	20.00	10.00	6.00
(3)	Billy Cox	20.00	10.00	6.00
(4)	Bob Dillinger	20.00	10.00	6.00
(5)	Joe Dobson	20.00	10.00	6.00
(6)	Joe Gordon	20.00	10.00	6.00
(7)	Hank Greenberg	45.00	22.00	13.50
(8)	Clint Hartung	20.00	10.00	6.00
(9)	Jim Hegan	20.00	10.00	6.00
(10)	Larry Jansen	20.00	10.00	6.00
(11)	George Kell	40.00	20.00	12.00
(12)	Ken Keltner	20.00	10.00	6.00
(13)	Ralph Kiner	40.00	20.00	12.00
(14)	Willard Marshall	20.00	10.00	6.00
(15)	Walt Masterson	20.00	10.00	6.00
(16)	"Red" Munger	20.00	10.00	6.00
(17)	Don Newcombe	25.00	12.50	7.50

(18)	Hal Newhouser	40.00	20.00	12.00
(19)	Joe Page	20.00	10.00	6.00
(20)	Babe Ruth (Portrait)	100.00	50.00	30.00
(21)	Warren Spahn	40.00	20.00	12.00
(22)	Harry Taylor	20.00	10.00	6.00
(23)	Harry "The Hat" Walker	20.00	10.00	6.00
(24)	Brooklyn Dodgers Team	100.00	50.00	30.00
(25)	New York Yankees Team	150.00	75.00	45.00

1948

(1)	Richie Ashburn	40.00	20.00	12.00
(2)	Rex Barney	20.00	10.00	6.00
(3)	Gene Bearden	20.00	10.00	6.00
(4)	Lou Brissie	20.00	10.00	6.00
(5)	Alvin Dark	20.00	10.00	6.00
(6)	Larry Doby	40.00	20.00	12.00
(7)	Carl Furillo	25.00	12.50	7.50
(8)	Frank Gustine	20.00	10.00	6.00
(9)	Fred Hutchinson	20.00	10.00	6.00
(10)	Sheldon Jones	20.00	10.00	6.00
(11)	Bob Lemon	40.00	20.00	12.00
(12)	Hank Majeski	20.00	10.00	6.00
(13)	Barney McCosky	20.00	10.00	6.00
(14)	Mel Parnell	20.00	10.00	6.00
(15)	Carl Scheib	20.00	10.00	6.00
(16)	Al Zarilla	20.00	10.00	6.00
(17)	Boston Braves Team	75.00	37.00	22.00
(18)	Cleveland Indians Team	75.00	37.00	22.00

1949

(1)	Hoot Evers	20.00	10.00	6.00
(2)	Bob Feller	40.00	20.00	12.00
(3)	Billy Goodman	20.00	10.00	6.00
(4)	Sid Gordon	20.00	10.00	6.00
(5)	Gil Hodges	40.00	20.00	12.00
(6)	Art Houtteman	20.00	10.00	6.00
(7)	Dale Mitchell	20.00	10.00	6.00
(8)	Vic Raschi	20.00	10.00	6.00
(9)	Robin Roberts	40.00	20.00	12.00
(10)	Ray Scarborough	20.00	10.00	6.00
(11)	Duke Snider	50.00	25.00	15.00
(12)	Vic Wertz	20.00	10.00	6.00
(13)	Ted Williams	75.00	37.00	22.00
(14)	Brooklyn Dodgers Team	90.00	45.00	27.00
(15)	New York Yankees Team	90.00	45.00	27.00

1950

(1)	Hank Bauer	15.00	7.50	4.50
(2)	Yogi Berra	30.00	15.00	9.00
(3)	Walt Dropo	12.00	6.00	3.50
(4)	Del Ennis	12.00	6.00	3.50
(5)	Johnny Groth	12.00	6.00	3.50
(6)	Granny Hamner	12.00	6.00	3.50
(7)	Ted Kluszewski	15.00	7.50	4.50
(8)	Johnny Lipon	12.00	6.00	3.50
(9)	Hank Sauer	12.00	6.00	3.50
(10)	Earl Torgeson	12.00	6.00	3.50
(11)	New York Yankees Team	50.00	25.00	15.00
(12)	Philadelphia Phillies Team	35.00	17.50	10.50

1951

(1)	Grover Alexander	15.00	7.50	4.50
(2)	Chico Carrasquel	15.00	7.50	4.50
(3)	Bubba Church	12.00	6.00	3.50
(4)	Alvin Dark	12.00	6.00	3.50
(5)	Luke Easter	12.00	6.00	3.50
(6)	Carl Erskine	15.00	7.50	4.50
(7)	Ned Garver	12.00	6.00	3.50
(8)	Rogers Hornsby	15.00	7.50	4.50
(9)	Walter Johnson	25.00	12.50	7.50
(10)	Tony Lazzeri	15.00	7.50	4.50
(11)	Whitey Lockman	12.00	6.00	3.50
(12)	Ed Lopat	15.00	7.50	4.50
(13)	Sal Maglie	12.00	6.00	3.50
(14)	Willie Mays	150.00	75.00	45.00
(15)	Gil McDougald	20.00	10.00	6.00
(16)	Irv Noren	12.00	6.00	3.50
(17)	Eddie Robinson	12.00	6.00	3.50
(18)	Jackie Robinson	125.00	62.00	37.00
(19)	Red Rolfe	12.00	6.00	3.50
(20)	Tris Speaker	20.00	10.00	6.00
(21)	Eddie Stanky	12.00	6.00	3.50
(22)	Clyde Vollmer	12.00	6.00	3.50
(23)	Wes Westrum	12.00	6.00	3.50
(24)	Cy Young	25.00	12.50	7.50
(25)	New York Giants Team	40.00	20.00	12.00
(26)	New York Yankees Team	60.00	30.00	18.00

1952

(1)	Bobby Avila	12.00	6.00	3.50
(2)	Lou Boudreau	20.00	10.00	6.00
(3)	Jim Busby	12.00	6.00	3.50
(4)	Roy Campanella	30.00	15.00	9.00
(5)	Gil Coan	12.00	6.00	3.50
(6)	Walker Cooper	12.00	6.00	3.50
(7)	Al Corwin	12.00	6.00	3.50
(8)	Murry Dickson	12.00	6.00	3.50
(9)	Leo Durocher	20.00	10.00	6.00
(10)	Bob Elliott	12.00	6.00	3.50
(11)	Ferris Fain	12.00	6.00	3.50
(12)	Jimmie Foxx	20.00	10.00	6.00
(13)	Mike Garcia	12.00	6.00	3.50
(14)	Hank Greenberg	25.00	12.50	7.50

(15)	Solly Hemus	12.00	6.00	3.50
(16)	Monte Irvin	20.00	10.00	6.00
(17)	Sam Jethroe	12.00	6.00	3.50
(18)	Ellis Kinder	12.00	6.00	3.50
(19)	Dick Kryhoski	12.00	6.00	3.50
(20)	Clem Labine	15.00	7.50	4.50
(21)	Mickey Mantle	200.00	100.00	60.00
(22)	Connie Marrero	12.00	6.00	3.50
(23)	Cass Michaels	12.00	6.00	3.50
(24)	Minnie Minoso	15.00	7.50	4.50
(25)	Don Mueller	12.00	6.00	3.50
(26)	Mel Parnell	12.00	6.00	3.50
(27)	Allie Reynolds	15.00	7.50	4.50
(28)	"Preacher" Roe	15.00	7.50	4.50
(29)	Saul Rogovin	12.00	6.00	3.50
(30)	Al Rosen	15.00	7.50	4.50
(31)	Red Schoendienst	20.00	10.00	6.00
(32)	Andy Seminick	12.00	6.00	3.50
(33)	Bobby Shantz	12.00	6.00	3.50
(34)	Duke Snider	25.00	12.50	7.50
(35)	Gerry Staley	12.00	6.00	3.50
(36)	Gene Stephens	12.00	6.00	3.50
(37)	Max Surkont	12.00	6.00	3.50
(38)	Bobby Thomson	12.00	6.00	3.50
(39)	Elmer Valo	12.00	6.00	3.50
(40)	Eddie Waitkus	12.00	6.00	3.50
(41)	Gene Woodling	15.00	7.50	4.50
(42)	Eddie Yost	12.00	6.00	3.50
(43)	Gus Zernial	12.00	6.00	3.50
(44)	Brooklyn Dodgers Team	50.00	25.00	15.00
(45)	New York Yankees Team	75.00	37.00	22.00

1953

(1)	Joe Black	15.00	7.50	4.50
(2)	Billy Cox	12.00	6.00	3.50
(3)	Billy Loes	12.00	6.00	3.50
(4)	Billy Martin	15.00	7.50	4.50
(5)	Eddie Mathews	25.00	12.50	7.50
(6)	George Shuba	12.00	6.00	3.50
(7)	Hoyt Wilhelm	20.00	10.00	6.00

1954

(1)	Joe Adcock	12.00	6.00	3.50
(2)	Johnny Antonelli	12.00	6.00	3.50
(3)	Gus Bell	12.00	6.00	3.50
(4)	Jim Greengrass	12.00	6.00	3.50
(5)	Bob Grim	12.00	6.00	3.50
(6)	Frank House	12.00	6.00	3.50
(7)	Jackie Jensen	12.00	6.00	3.50
(8)	Al Kaline	25.00	12.50	7.50
(9)	Harvey Kuenn	15.00	7.50	4.50
(10)	Willie Miranda	12.00	6.00	3.50
(11)	Wally Moon	12.00	6.00	3.50
(12)	Ray Moore	12.00	6.00	3.50
(13)	Don Mossi	12.00	6.00	3.50
(14)	Stan Musial	30.00	15.00	9.00
(15)	Hal Naragon	12.00	6.00	3.50
(16)	Chet Nichols	12.00	6.00	3.50
(17)	Billy Pierce	12.00	6.00	3.50
(18)	Arnie Portocarrero	12.00	6.00	3.50
(19)	James "Dusty" Rhodes	12.00	6.00	3.50
(20)	Babe Ruth	50.00	25.00	15.00
(21)	Dean Stone	12.00	6.00	3.50
(22)	Bob Turley	15.00	7.50	4.50
(23)	Jim Wilson	12.00	6.00	3.50
(24)	New York Giants Team	50.00	25.00	15.00

1955

(1)	Gene Conley	12.00	6.00	3.50
(2)	Elston Howard	15.00	7.50	4.50
(3)	Hank Sauer	12.00	6.00	3.50

1956

(1)	Hank Bauer	15.00	7.50	4.50
(2)	Yogi Berra	25.00	12.50	7.50
(3)	Ray Boone	12.00	6.00	3.50
(4)	Ken Boyer	15.00	7.50	4.50
(5)	Tom Brewer	12.00	6.00	3.50
(6)	Bob Buhl	12.00	6.00	3.50
(7)	Nellie Fox	20.00	10.00	6.00
(8)	Bob Keegan	12.00	6.00	3.50
(9)	Don Larsen	15.00	7.50	4.50
(10)	Jim Lemon	12.00	6.00	3.50
(11)	Danny O'Connell	12.00	6.00	3.50
(12)	Jim Pendleton	12.00	6.00	3.50
(13)	Bob Rush	12.00	6.00	3.50
(14)	Roy Sievers	12.00	6.00	3.50
(15)	Gus Zernial	12.00	6.00	3.50

1957

(1)	Hank Aaron	30.00	15.00	9.00
(2)	Joe Adcock	12.00	6.00	3.50
(3)	Luis Arroyo	12.00	6.00	3.50
(4)	Ed Bailey	12.00	6.00	3.50
(5)	Ernie Banks	25.00	12.50	7.50
(6)	Roy Campanella	20.00	10.00	6.00
(7)	Billy Cox	12.00	6.00	3.50
(8)	Del Crandall	12.00	6.00	3.50
(9)	Whitey Ford	25.00	12.50	7.50
(10)	Bob Friend	12.00	6.00	3.50
(11)	Carl Furillo	15.00	7.50	4.50
(12)	Granny Hamner	12.00	6.00	3.50
(13)	Gil Hodges	15.00	7.50	4.50

		NM	E	VG
(14)	Billy Hoeft	12.00	6.00	3.50
(15)	Walter Johnson	25.00	12.50	7.50
(16)	George Kell	20.00	10.00	6.00
(17)	Ted Kluszewski	20.00	10.00	6.00
(18)	Johnny Kucks	12.00	6.00	3.50
(19)	Harvey Kuenn	12.00	6.00	3.50
(20)	Clem Labine	12.00	6.00	3.50
(21)	Vern Law	12.00	6.00	3.50
(22)	Brooks Lawrence	12.00	6.00	3.50
(23)	Bob Lemon	20.00	10.00	6.00
(24)	Sherman Lollar	12.00	6.00	3.50
(25)	Billy Martin	15.00	7.50	4.50
(25)	Eddie Mathews	20.00	10.00	6.00
(26)	Charlie Maxwell	12.00	6.00	3.50
(27)	Willie Mays	60.00	30.00	18.00
(28)	Gil McDougald	15.00	7.50	4.50
(29)	Willie Miranda	12.00	6.00	3.50
(30)	Jimmy Piersall	12.00	6.00	3.50
(31)	Pee Wee Reese	25.00	12.50	7.50
(32)	"Rip" Repulski	12.00	6.00	3.50
(33)	Robin Roberts	20.00	10.00	6.00
(34)	Frank Robinson	30.00	15.00	9.00
(35)	Al Rosen	12.00	6.00	3.50
(36)	Babe Ruth	60.00	30.00	18.00
(37)	Herb Score	15.00	7.50	4.50
(38)	Enos Slaughter	20.00	10.00	6.00
(39)	Warren Spahn	20.00	10.00	6.00
(40)	Johnny Temple	12.00	6.00	3.50
(41)	Mickey Vernon	12.00	6.00	3.50

1957 (17-1/2" x 20")

		NM	E	VG
(1)	Johnny Antonelli	30.00	15.00	9.00
(2)	Hank Bauer	45.00	22.00	13.50
(3)	Frank House	30.00	15.00	9.00
(4)	Jackie Jensen	35.00	17.50	10.00
(5)	Al Kaline	45.00	22.00	13.50
(6)	Bob Lemon	35.00	17.50	10.00
(7)	Chet Nichols	30.00	15.00	9.00
(8)	Al Rosen	30.00	15.00	9.00
(9)	Dean Stone	30.00	15.00	9.00
(10)	Bob Turley	35.00	17.50	10.00
(11)	Mickey Vernon	30.00	15.00	9.00

1915 Baseball Magazine Premiums

Two of the 1915 editions of Baseball Magazine were issued with attached premiums inside featuring color portraits of star players. The approximately 6-1/2" x 9-3/4" premiums featured artwork by frequent cover artist J.F. Kernan, printed on heavy glossy paper designed to be removed for display.

	NM	E	VG
Honus Wagner (Premium (Feb.))	1,000	500.00	300.00
Christy Mathewson (Premium (April))	750.00	375.00	225.00

1947-52 Baseball Player Charms

The date of issue for this novelty item is conjectural, based on known player selection. Packaged in plastic bubbles for sale in vending machines, these charms are found in several different shapes - rectangle, octagon, etc. - and colors of plastic. A black-and-white photo appears at center with a loop at top for hanging. Some players are found with slight variations in the photo cropping. Size also varies but is about 3/4" x 1". Players are not identified on the charm and there is no number. The checklist here is in alphabetical order, and likely not complete.

		NM	E	VG
Common Player:		20.00	10.00	6.00
(1)	Yogi Berra	45.00	22.00	13.50
(2)	Ewell Blackwell	20.00	10.00	6.00
(3)	Roy Campanella	45.00	22.00	13.50
(4)	Joe DiMaggio	75.00	37.00	22.00
(5)	Del Ennis	75.00	37.00	22.00
(6)	Carl Erskine	20.00	10.00	6.00
(7)	Bob Feller	25.00	12.50	7.50
(8)	Carl Furillo	22.50	11.00	6.75
(9)	Lou Gehrig	65.00	32.00	19.50
(9)	Sid Gordon	20.00	10.00	6.00
(11)	Hank Greenberg	45.00	22.00	13.50
(12)	Ralph Kiner	20.00	10.00	6.00
(13)	Whitey Lockman	20.00	10.00	6.00
(14)	Stan Musial	55.00	27.00	16.50
(15)	Andy Pafko	20.00	10.00	6.00
(16)	Mel Parnell	20.00	10.00	6.00
(17)	Pee Wee Reese	35.00	17.50	10.50
(18)	Phil Rizzuto	30.00	15.00	9.00
(19)	Jackie Robinson	65.00	32.00	19.50
(20)	Babe Ruth	95.00	47.00	28.00
(21)	Johnny Schmitz	20.00	10.00	6.00
(22)	Duke Snider	35.00	17.50	10.50
(23)	Wally Westlake	20.00	10.00	6.00
(24)	Ted Williams	60.00	30.00	18.00

1961 Baseball Player Key Chains

The maker of these postage-stamp size (1-1/8" x 1-1/2") black-and-white, blank-back "cards" is unknown. From the inclusion of numerous journeyman Pirates players in the set, it probably has a Pittsburgh origin. Possibly intended for sale at stadium souvenir counters, they were made to be inserted into clear plastic key chain novelties, and have a semi-gloss front surface. Unnumbered, they are checklisted here alphabetically.

		NM	E	VG
Complete Set (69):		400.00	200.00	120.00
Common Player:		5.00	2.50	1.50
(1)	Hank Aaron	15.00	7.50	4.50
(2)	Bob Allison	5.00	2.50	1.50
(3)	George Altman	5.00	2.50	1.50
(4)	Luis Aparicio	7.50	3.75	2.25
(5)	Richie Ashburn	7.50	3.75	2.25
(6)	Ernie Banks	10.00	5.00	3.00
(7)	Earl Battey	5.00	2.50	1.50
(8)	Hank Bauer	6.00	3.00	1.75
(9)	Gus Bell	5.00	2.50	1.50
(10)	Yogi Berra	10.00	5.00	3.00
(11)	Ken Boyer	6.00	3.00	1.75
(12)	Lew Burdette	5.00	2.50	1.50
(13)	Smoky Burgess	5.00	2.50	1.50
(14)	Orlando Cepeda	7.50	3.75	2.25
(15)	Gino Cimoli	5.00	2.50	1.50
(16)	Roberto Clemente	20.00	10.00	6.00
(17)	Del Crandall	5.00	2.50	1.50
(18)	Dizzy Dean	9.00	4.50	2.75
(19)	Don Drysdale	7.50	3.75	2.25
(20)	Sam Esposito	5.00	2.50	1.50
(21)	Roy Face	5.00	2.50	1.50
(22)	Nelson Fox	7.50	3.75	2.25
(23)	Bob Friend	5.00	2.50	1.50
(24)	Lou Gehrig	12.50	6.25	3.75
(25)	Joe Gibbon	5.00	2.50	1.50
(26)	Jim Gilliam	6.00	3.00	1.75
(27)	Fred Green	5.00	2.50	1.50
(28)	Pumpsie Green	5.00	2.50	1.50
(29)	Dick Groat	6.00	3.00	1.75
(30)	Harvey Haddix	5.00	2.50	1.50
(31)	Don Hoak	5.00	2.50	1.50
(32)	Glen Hobbie	5.00	2.50	1.50
(33)	Frank Howard	6.00	3.00	1.75
(34)	Jackie Jensen	5.00	2.50	1.50

		NM	E	VG
(35)	Sam Jones	5.00	2.50	1.50
(36)	Al Kaline	9.00	4.50	2.75
(37)	Harmon Killebrew	7.50	3.75	2.25
(38)	Harvey Kuenn	5.00	2.50	1.50
(39)	Norm Larker	5.00	2.50	1.50
(40)	Vernon Law	5.00	2.50	1.50
(41)	Mickey Mantle	30.00	15.00	9.00
(42)	Roger Maris	12.00	6.00	3.50
(43)	Eddie Mathews	7.50	3.75	2.25
(44)	Willie Mays	12.00	6.00	3.50
(45)	Bill Mazeroski	7.50	3.75	2.25
(46)	Willie McCovey	7.50	3.75	2.25
(47)	Lindy McDaniel	5.00	2.50	1.50
(48)	Roy McMillan	5.00	2.50	1.50
(49)	Minnie Minoso	6.00	3.00	1.75
(50)	Danny Murtaugh	5.00	2.50	1.50
(51)	Stan Musial	12.00	6.00	3.50
(52)	Rocky Nelson	5.00	2.50	1.50
(53)	Bob Oldis	5.00	2.50	1.50
(54)	Vada Pinson	6.00	3.00	1.75
(55)	Vic Power	5.00	2.50	1.50
(56)	Robin Roberts	7.50	3.75	2.25
(57)	Pete Runnels	5.00	2.50	1.50
(58)	Babe Ruth	20.00	10.00	6.00
(59)	Ron Santo	6.00	3.00	1.75
(60)	Dick Schofield	5.00	2.50	1.50
(61)	Bob Skinner	5.00	2.50	1.50
(62)	Hal Smith	5.00	2.50	1.50
(63)	Duke Snider	9.00	4.50	2.75
(64)	Warren Spahn	7.50	3.75	2.25
(65)	Dick Stuart	5.00	2.50	1.50
(66)	Willie Tasby	5.00	2.50	1.50
(67)	Tony Taylor	5.00	2.50	1.50
(68)	Bill Virdon	5.00	2.50	1.50
(69)	Ted Williams	17.50	9.00	5.00

1978 Baseball Player Patches

These card-size (about 2-1/2" x 3-1/4") cloth patches feature embroidered player portraits on a white background with a color border. Uniform logos are not present. The patches originally sold for $2.50 apiece from the Penn Emblem Co., Philadelphia, though the company's name is not found on the patches. The unnumbered patches are listed here in alphabetical order.

		NM	E	VG
Complete Set (103):		525.00	265.00	160.00
Common Player:		4.50	2.25	1.35
(1)	Buddy Bell	4.50	2.25	1.35
(2)	Johnny Bench	15.00	7.50	4.50
(3)	Vida Blue	4.50	2.25	1.35
(4)	Bobby Bonds	4.50	2.25	1.35
(5)	Bob Boone	4.50	2.25	1.35
(6)	Larry Bowa	4.50	2.25	1.35
(7)	George Brett	18.00	9.00	5.50
(8)	Lou Brock	13.50	6.75	4.00
(9)	Rick Burleson	4.50	2.25	1.35
(10)	Jeff Burroughs	4.50	2.25	1.35
(11)	Bert Campaneris	4.50	2.25	1.35
(12)	John Candelaria	4.50	2.25	1.35
(13)	Rod Carew	13.50	6.75	4.00
(14)	Steve Carlton	13.50	6.75	4.00
(15)	Gary Carter	11.25	5.50	3.25
(16)	Dave Cash	4.50	2.25	1.35
(17)	Cesar Cedeno	4.50	2.25	1.35
(18)	Ron Cey	4.50	2.25	1.35
(19)	Chris Chambliss	4.50	2.25	1.35
(20)	Jack Clark	4.50	2.25	1.35
(21)	Dave Concepcion	4.50	2.25	1.35
(22)	Cecil Cooper	4.50	2.25	1.35
(23)	Jose Cruz	4.50	2.25	1.35
(24)	Andre Dawson	4.50	2.25	1.35
(25)	Dan Driessen	4.50	2.25	1.35
(26)	Rawly Eastwick	4.50	2.25	1.35
(27)	Dwight Evans	4.50	2.25	1.35
(28)	Mark Fidrych	4.50	2.25	1.25
(29)	Rollie Fingers	11.25	5.50	3.25
(30)	Carlton Fisk	13.50	6.75	4.00
(31)	George Foster	4.50	2.25	1.35
(32)	Steve Garvey	9.00	4.50	2.70
(33)	Rich Gossage	4.50	2.25	1.35

(34)	Bobby Grich	4.50	2.25	1.35
(35)	Ross Grimsley	4.50	2.25	1.35
(36)	Ron Guidry	4.50	2.25	1.35
(37)	Mike Hargrove	4.50	2.25	1.35
(38)	Keith Hernandez	4.50	2.25	1.35
(39)	Larry Hisle	4.50	2.25	1.35
(40)	Bob Horner	4.50	2.25	1.35
(41)	Roy Howell	4.50	2.25	1.35
(42)	"Catfish" Hunter	11.25	5.50	3.25
(43)	Reggie Jackson	12.00	6.00	3.50
(44)	Tommy John	6.00	3.00	1.80
(45)	Jim Kern	4.50	2.25	1.35
(46)	Chet Lemon	4.50	2.25	1.35
(47)	Davey Lopes	4.50	2.25	1.35
(48)	Greg Luzinski	4.50	2.25	1.35
(49)	Fred Lynn	4.50	2.25	1.35
(50)	Garry Maddox	4.50	2.25	1.35
(51)	Bill Madlock	4.50	2.25	1.35
(52)	Jon Matlack	4.50	2.25	1.35
(53)	John Mayberry	4.50	2.25	1.35
(54)	Lee Mazzilli	4.50	2.25	1.35
(55)	Rick Monday	4.50	2.25	1.35
(56)	Don Money	4.50	2.25	1.35
(57)	Willie Montanez	4.50	2.25	1.35
(58)	John Montefusco	4.50	2.25	1.35
(59)	Joe Morgan	13.50	6.75	4.00
(60)	Thurman Munson	7.50	3.75	2.25
(61)	Bobby Murcer	4.50	2.25	1.35
(62)	Graig Nettles	4.50	2.25	1.35
(63)	Phil Niekro	7.50	3.75	2.25
(64)	Al Oliver	4.50	2.25	1.35
(65)	Amos Otis	4.50	2.25	1.35
(66)	Jim Palmer	13.50	6.75	4.00
(67)	Dave Parker	4.50	2.25	1.35
(68)	Fred Patek	4.50	2.25	1.35
(69)	Tony Perez	11.25	5.50	3.25
(70)	Lou Piniella	8.00	4.00	2.40
(71)	Biff Pocoroba	4.50	2.25	1.35
(72)	Darrell Porter	4.50	2.25	1.35
(73)	Rick Reuschel	4.50	2.25	1.35
(74)	Jim Rice	9.00	4.50	2.70
(75a)	Pete Rose (Red border.)	12.00	6.00	3.50
(75b)	Pete Rose (Blue border.)	12.00	6.00	3.50
(76)	Joe Rudi	4.50	2.25	1.35
(77)	Rick Reuschel	4.50	2.25	1.35
(78)	Nolan Ryan	22.50	11.25	6.75
(79)	Manny Sanguillen	4.50	2.25	1.35
(80)	Mike Schmidt	18.00	9.00	5.40
(81)	George Scott	4.50	2.25	1.35
(82)	Tom Seaver	20.25	10.00	6.00
(83)	Ted Simmons	4.50	2.25	1.35
(84)	Reggie Smith	4.50	2.25	1.35
(85)	Willie Stargell	20.25	10.00	6.00
(86)	Rennie Stennett	4.50	2.25	1.35
(87)	Jim Sundberg	4.50	2.25	1.35
(88)	Bruce Sutter	7.50	3.75	2.25
(89)	Frank Tanana	4.50	2.25	1.35
(90)	Garry Templeton	4.50	2.25	1.35
(91)	Gene Tenace	4.50	2.25	1.35
(92)	Jason Thompson	4.50	2.25	1.35
(93)	Luis Tiant	4.50	2.25	1.35
(94)	Joe Torre	4.50	2.25	1.25
(95)	Ellis Valentine	4.50	2.25	1.35
(96)	Bob Watson	4.50	2.25	1.35
(97)	Frank White	4.50	2.25	1.35
(98)	Lou Whitaker	4.50	2.25	1.35
(99)	Bump Wills	4.50	2.25	1.35
(100)	Dave Winfield	20.25	10.00	6.00
(101)	Butch Wynegar	4.50	2.25	1.35
(102)	Carl Yastrzemski	18.00	9.00	5.40
(103)	Richie Zisk	4.50	2.25	1.35

1892 Base Ball Scenes (N360)

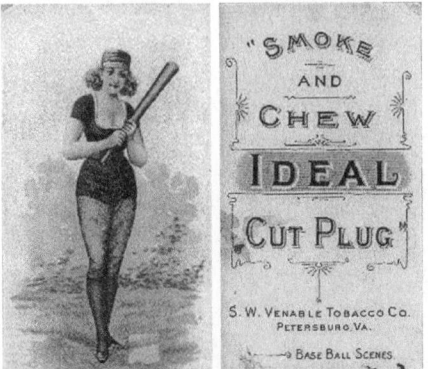

The N360 American Card Catalog designation covers the several tobacco manufacturers who issued this type of card to advertise various brands. Obviously, the cards do not pic- ture actual ballplayers, but rather have on their fronts color lithographs of attractive women in baseball uniforms and in game action. Approximately 2-3/16" x 3-15/16" most cards have a tiny line of type at bottom carrying a Donaldson Bros., N.Y., copyright. Those cards issued to promote the Little Rhody Cut Plus brand have a script ad message on front and a monthly schedule of the 12-team National League on back. Advertising for the various brands of tobacco companies may be printed directly on the card back, on a paper label pasted over another ad or overprinted on a previously printed ad. Cards are known with these manufacturers and brands. S.W. Venable: Cockade, Gay Head, Helmet, Ideal and Pluck; G.F. Young & Bro.: Little Rhody, and M.T. Coffey. Nine different poses are known for the card fronts.

	NM	E	VG
Common Card:	800.00	400.00	240.00

1911 Baseball Scorecard Fan

This unusual player collectible is a combination fan and scorecard published circa 1911. The cardboard scorecard is about 10-1/2" x 9" and stapled to an approximately 11" long wooden handle. Printed in black-and-white, there are 16 player portraits at top, separated by a baseball. At center is the portrait of young lady and at bottom is a ball-in-mitt photo. The fans can be found with various local advertising overprinted on front or back: Barton's Barber Shop, Ira P. File Ice Cream and Confectionery, Maine's Bliss School of Business, Poole Pianos, Kemper pharmacy, etc. The players are identified by last name and for lack of uniform details, specific identification of a few of them is speculative.

	NM	E	VG
Germany Schaeffer (Schaefer), Bobby Wallace, Billy Sullivan, Hal Chase, George Moriarty, Harry Lord, Harry Davis, Nap Lajoie, Mickey Doolan, Clark Griffith, Bill Dahlen, Jeff Sweeney, Frank Chance, Art Devlin, Fred Clark (Clarke), Roger Bresnahan	1,500	750.00	400.00

1913 Base Ball Series Notebooks

The issue date cited is conjectural, based on writing found in a surviving specimen of this child's notebook. The 8" x 10" notebook has on its cover a baseball diamond and bleachers drawing in white on a beige background. Printed above and below the artwork are full-color reproductions of five baseball cards from the Philadelphia Caramel issues of 1909 (E95) and 1910 (E96). The cover is printed on thinner stock the original cards and has no printing on the reverse side. This has led to cut copies of these cards being misidentified as proofs. Because similar blank-back, thin stock cards are known of other players, it is possible other notebook covers may exist.

	NM	E	VG
Complete Notebook:			
Fred Clark (Clarke)(E96), Nap Lajoie (E96), Jake Pfeister (E96), Honus Wagner (E95), Ed Willetts (Willett)(E95)	750.00	375.00	225.00
OBSERVED SINGLES			
Harry Krause (E95)	100.00	40.00	20.00

1948 Baseball's Great Hall of Fame Exhibits

Titled "Baseball's Great Hall of Fame," this 32-player set features black and white player photos against a gray background. The photos are accented by Greek columns on either side with brief player information printed at the bottom. The blank-backed cards are unnumbered and are listed here alphabetically. The cards measure 3-3/8" x 5-3/8". Collectors should be aware that 24 cards from this set were reprinted on whiter stock in 1974.

		NM	E	VG
Complete Set (33):		500.00	250.00	150.00
Common Player:		7.50	3.75	2.25
(1)	Grover Cleveland Alexander	15.00	7.50	4.50
(2)	Roger Bresnahan	7.50	3.75	2.25
(3)	Frank Chance	7.50	3.75	2.25
(4)	Jack Chesbro	7.50	3.75	2.25
(5)	Fred Clarke	7.50	3.75	2.25
(6)	Ty Cobb	75.00	37.00	22.00
(7)	Mickey Cochrane	7.50	3.75	2.25
(8)	Eddie Collins	7.50	3.75	2.25
(9)	Hugh Duffy	7.50	3.75	2.25
(10)	Johnny Evers	7.50	3.75	2.25
(11)	Frankie Frisch	7.50	3.75	2.25
(12)	Lou Gehrig	35.00	17.50	10.00
(13)	Clark Griffith	7.50	3.75	2.25
(14)	Robert "Lefty" Grove	7.50	3.75	2.25
(15)	Rogers Hornsby	10.00	5.00	3.00
(16)	Carl Hubbell	7.50	3.75	2.25
(17)	Hughie Jennings	7.50	3.75	2.25
(18)	Walter Johnson	15.00	7.50	4.50
(19)	Willie Keeler	7.50	3.75	2.25
(20)	Napoleon Lajoie	7.50	3.75	2.25
(21)	Connie Mack	7.50	3.75	2.25
(22)	Christy Matthewson (Mathewson)	20.00	10.00	6.00
(23)	John J. McGraw	7.50	3.75	2.25
(24)	Eddie Plank	7.50	3.75	2.25
(25)	Babe Ruth (Batting)	60.00	30.00	18.00
(26)	Babe Ruth (Standing with bats.)	250.00	125.00	75.00
(27)	George Sisler	7.50	3.75	2.25
(28)	Tris Speaker	10.00	5.00	3.00
(29)	Joe Tinker	7.50	3.75	2.25
(30)	Rube Waddell	7.50	3.75	2.25
(31)	Honus Wagner	25.00	12.50	7.50
(32)	Ed Walsh	7.50	3.75	2.25
(33)	Cy Young	15.00	7.50	4.50

1974 Baseball's Great Hall of Fame Exhibits

Two dozen of the cards from the 1948 issue were reprinted in 1974 by the original publisher, Exhibit Supply Co., Chicago. The 1974 reissues are in the same 3-3/8" x 5-3/8" format as the originals, and in the same design. They are blank-backed and printed on a thinner, slicker cardboard stock than the 1948 cards. The reprints can be found printed in black, blue or brown. The unnumbered cards are checklisted here alphabetically.

		NM	E	VG
Complete Set (24):		20.00	10.00	6.00
Common Player:		3.00	1.50	.90
(1)	Grover Cleveland Alexander	3.50	1.75	1.00
(2)	Roger Bresnahan	3.00	1.50	.90
(3)	Frank Chance	3.00	1.50	.90
(4)	Jack Chesbro	3.00	1.50	.90
(5)	Fred Clarke	3.00	1.50	.90
(6)	Ty Cobb	10.00	5.00	3.00
(7)	Mickey Cochrane	3.00	1.50	.90
(8)	Eddie Collins	3.00	1.50	.90
(9)	Johnny Evers	3.00	1.50	.90
(10)	Frankie Frisch	3.00	1.50	.90
(11)	Clark Griffith	3.00	1.50	.90
(12)	Robert "Lefty" Grove	3.00	1.50	.90
(13)	Rogers Hornsby	4.00	2.00	1.25
(14)	Hughie Jennings	3.00	1.50	.90
(15)	Walter Johnson	5.00	2.50	1.50
(16)	Connie Mack	3.00	1.50	.90
(17)	Christy Mathewson	5.00	2.50	1.50
(18)	John McGraw	3.00	1.50	.90
(19)	George Sisler	3.00	1.50	.90
(20)	Joe Tinker	3.00	1.50	.90
(21)	Rube Waddell	3.00	1.50	.90
(22)	Honus Wagner	6.00	3.00	1.75
(23)	Ed Walsh	3.00	1.50	.90
(24)	Cy Young	5.00	2.50	1.50

1977 Baseball's Great Hall of Fame Exhibits

A second set of "Baseball's Great Hall of Fame" exhibit cards was produced in 1977, most cards featuring more recent players than the 1948 cards. The cards were produced in the same 3-3/8" x 5-3/8" blank-back, black-and-white design as the 1948 cards, and are a genuine product of Exhibit Supply Co., Chicago. The new cards were printed on an extremely high grade of semi-gloss cardboard, in contrast to the earlier versions. Production was announced at 500,000 cards. The unnumbered cards are checklisted here alphabetically.

		NM	E	VG
Complete Set (32):		35.00	17.50	10.00
Common Player:		2.00	1.00	.60
(1)	Luke Appling	2.00	1.00	.60
(2)	Ernie Banks	3.00	1.50	.90
(3)	Yogi Berra	3.00	1.50	.90
(4)	Roy Campanella	3.00	1.50	.90
(5)	Roberto Clemente	9.00	4.50	2.75
(6)	Alvin Dark	2.00	1.00	.60
(7)	Joe DiMaggio	9.00	4.50	2.75
(8)	Bob Feller	2.00	1.00	.60
(9)	Whitey Ford	2.00	1.00	.60
(10)	Jimmie Foxx	2.00	1.00	.60
(11)	Lou Gehrig	9.00	4.50	2.75
(12)	Charlie Gehringer	2.00	1.00	.60
(13)	Hank Greenberg	2.50	1.25	.70
(14)	Gabby Hartnett	2.00	1.00	.60
(15)	Carl Hubbell	2.00	1.00	.60
(16)	Al Kaline	2.00	1.00	.60
(17)	Mickey Mantle	15.00	7.50	4.50
(18)	Willie Mays	6.00	3.00	1.75
(19)	Johnny Mize	2.00	1.00	.60
(20)	Stan Musial	4.00	2.00	1.25
(21)	Mel Ott	2.00	1.00	.60
(22)	Satchel Paige	2.50	1.25	.70
(23)	Robin Roberts	2.00	1.00	.60
(24)	Jackie Robinson	6.00	3.00	1.75
(25)	Babe Ruth	12.00	6.00	3.50
(26)	Duke Snider	2.00	1.00	.60
(27)	Warren Spahn	2.00	1.00	.60
(28)	Tris Speaker	2.00	1.00	.60
(29)	Honus Wagner	3.00	1.50	.90
(30)	Ted Williams	6.00	3.00	1.75
(31)	Rudy York	2.00	1.00	.60
(32)	Cy Young	2.00	1.00	.60

1912 Base Ball Stars Series

This set of blank-backed, black-and-white 6" x 9" pictures features the contestants of the 1912 World Series - the Red Sox and Giants. It is possible these pictures were sold at the ballparks during the Series. The checklist here is probably incomplete. The unnumbered pictures have been listed alphabetically within team.

		NM	E	VG
Common Player:		450.00	225.00	135.00
	BOSTON RED SOX			
(1)	Hugh Bedient	450.00	225.00	135.00
(2)	Joe Wood	480.00	240.00	145.00
	N.Y. GIANTS			
(1)	Rube Marquard	525.00	260.00	150.00
(2)	Christy Mathewson	1,050	525.00	315.00
(3)	Jeff Tesreau	450.00	225.00	135.00

1964 Baseball Stars - Present and Future Photocard

This large-format (11" x 8-1/2") color card features three group photos of top stars of the day. In addition to the photos, there are facsimile autographs of each player on the bright yellow background. Back is blank. (See also Baseball Greats Postcard.)

	NM	E	VG
Sheet:	35.00	17.50	105.00

Dean Chance, Don Drysdale, Dick Farrell, Jim Fregosi, Sandy Koufax, Willie Mays, Joe Pepitone, Dick Radatz

1938 Baseball Tabs

The issuer and manner of distribution for these baseball tabs is unknown. About 3/4" diameter, with bendable wings at each side, the points of which could be stuck through fabric and thus attached to a cap or jacket, the tabs have black-and-white player portraits on a baseball-style background in one of several colors. Most of the player first names have parentheses around them. The team tabs have a large nickname at center and the city and league at bottom. The inclusion of American Association teams argues for distribution in the upper Midwest. The unnumbered tabs are listed here in alphabetical order.

		NM	E	VG
Complete Set (53):		3,000	1,500	900.00
Common Player:		50.00	25.00	15.50
Common Team:		50.00	25.00	15.00
(1)	Luke Appling	75.00	37.00	22.00
(2)	Earl Averill	75.00	37.00	22.00
(3)	Phil Cavarretta	50.00	25.00	15.00
(4)	Dizzy Dean	100.00	50.00	30.00
(5)	Paul Derringer	50.00	25.00	15.00
(6)	Bill Dickey	90.00	45.00	27.00
(7)	Joe DiMaggio	450.00	225.00	135.00
(8)	Bob Feller	75.00	37.00	22.00
(9)	Lou Fette	50.00	25.00	15.00
(10)	Jimmie Foxx	100.00	50.00	30.00
(11)	Lou Gehrig	375.00	185.00	110.00
(12)	Charley Gehringer	75.00	37.00	22.00
(13)	Lefty Gomez	75.00	37.00	22.00
(14)	Hank Greenberg	90.00	45.00	27.00
(15)	Lefty Grove	75.00	37.00	22.00
(16)	Mule Haas	50.00	25.00	15.00
(17)	Gabby Hartnett	75.00	37.00	22.00
(18)	Rollie Hemsley	50.00	25.00	15.00
(19)	Carl Hubbell	75.00	37.00	22.00
(20)	Chuck Klein	75.00	37.00	22.00
(21)	Red Kress	50.00	25.00	15.00
(22)	Push-Em-Up-Tony Lazzeri	75.00	37.00	22.00
(23)	Ted Lyons	75.00	37.00	22.00
(24)	Joe Medwick	75.00	37.00	22.00
(25)	Van Lingle Mungo	50.00	25.00	15.00
(26)	Rip Radcliff	50.00	25.00	15.00
(27)	Schoolboy Rowe	50.00	25.00	15.00
(28)	Al Simmons	75.00	37.00	22.00
(29)	Little Poison Waner	75.00	37.00	22.00
(30)	Athletics (Philadelphia)	50.00	25.00	15.00
(31)	Bees (Boston)	50.00	25.00	15.00
(32)	Blues (Kansas City)	50.00	25.00	15.00
(33)	Brewers (Milwaukee)	50.00	25.00	15.00
(34)	Browns (St. Louis)	50.00	25.00	15.00
(35)	Cardinals (St. Louis)	50.00	25.00	15.00
(36)	Colonels (Louisville)	50.00	25.00	15.00
(37)	Cubs (Chicago)	50.00	25.00	15.00
(38)	Dodgers (Brooklyn)	50.00	25.00	15.00
(39)	Giants (New York)	50.00	25.00	15.00
(40)	Indians (Cleveland)	50.00	25.00	15.00
(41)	Indians (Indianapolis)	50.00	25.00	15.00
(42)	Millers (Minneapolis)	50.00	25.00	15.00
(43)	Mud-Hens (Toledo)	50.00	25.00	15.00
(44)	Nationals (Washington)	50.00	25.00	15.00
(45)	Phillies (Philadelphia)	50.00	25.00	15.00
(46)	Pirates (Pittsburgh)	50.00	25.00	15.00
(47)	Red Birds (Columbus)	50.00	25.00	15.00
(48)	Reds (Cincinnati)	50.00	25.00	15.00
(49)	Red Sox (Boston)	50.00	25.00	15.00
(50)	Saints (St. Paul)	50.00	25.00	15.00
(51)	Tigers (Detroit)	50.00	25.00	15.00
(52)	White Sox (Chicago)	50.00	25.00	15.00
(53)	Yankees (New York)	65.00	32.00	19.50

1934-36 Batter-Up (R318)

National Chicle's 192-card "Batter-Up" set was issued over a three-year period. The blank-backed cards are die-cut, enabling collectors of the era to fold the top of the card over so that it could stand upright on its own support. The cards can be found in black-and-white or a variety of color tints. Card numbers 1-80 measure 2-3/8" x 3-1/4" in size, while the high-numbered cards (#81-192) measure 2-3/8" x 3" (1/4" smaller in height). The high-numbered cards are significantly more difficult to find than the lower numbers. The set's ACC designation is R318.

		NM	E	VG
Complete Set (192):		33,750	16,875	10,125
Common Player (1-80):		180.00	90.00	54.00
Common Player (81-192):		335.00	165.00	100.00
1	Wally Berger	315.00	155.00	95.00
2	Ed Brandt	175.00	90.00	50.00
3	Al Lopez	565.00	280.00	165.00
4	Dick Bartell	175.00	90.00	50.00
5	Carl Hubbell	600.00	300.00	180.00
6	Bill Terry	565.00	280.00	165.00
7	Pepper Martin	175.00	90.00	50.00
8	Jim Bottomley	565.00	280.00	165.00
9	Tommy Bridges	180.00	90.00	54.00
10	Rick Ferrell	565.00	280.00	165.00
11	Ray Benge	180.00	90.00	54.00
12	Wes Ferrell	180.00	90.00	54.00
13	Bill Cissell	180.00	90.00	54.00
14	Pie Traynor	565.00	280.00	165.00
15	Roy Mahaffey	180.00	90.00	54.00
16	Chick Hafey	565.00	280.00	165.00
17	Lloyd Waner	565.00	280.00	165.00
18	Jack Burns	180.00	90.00	54.00
19	Buddy Myer	180.00	90.00	54.00
20	Bob Johnson	180.00	90.00	54.00
21	Arky Vaughn (Vaughan)	565.00	280.00	165.00
22	Red Rolfe	180.00	90.00	54.00
23	Lefty Gomez	565.00	280.00	165.00
24	Earl Averill	565.00	280.00	165.00
25	Mickey Cochrane	565.00	280.00	165.00
26	Van Mungo	180.00	90.00	54.00
27	Mel Ott	750.00	375.00	225.00
28	Jimmie Foxx	975.00	485.00	290.00
29	Jimmy Dykes	180.00	90.00	54.00
30	Bill Dickey	565.00	280.00	165.00
31	Lefty Grove	565.00	280.00	165.00
32	Joe Cronin	565.00	280.00	165.00
33	Frankie Frisch	565.00	280.00	165.00
34	Al Simmons	565.00	280.00	165.00
35	Rogers Hornsby	865.00	430.00	260.00
36	Ted Lyons	565.00	280.00	165.00
37	Rabbit Maranville	565.00	280.00	165.00
38	Jimmie Wilson	180.00	90.00	54.00
39	Willie Kamm	180.00	90.00	54.00
40	Bill Hallahan	180.00	90.00	54.00

41	Gus Suhr	180.00	90.00	54.00
42	Charlie Gehringer	565.00	280.00	165.00
43	Joe Heving	180.00	90.00	54.00
44	Adam Comorosky	180.00	90.00	54.00
45	Tony Lazzeri	775.00	280.00	165.00
46	Sam Leslie	180.00	90.00	54.00
47	Bob Smith	180.00	90.00	54.00
48	Willis Hudlin	180.00	90.00	54.00
49	Carl Reynolds	180.00	90.00	54.00
50	Fred Schulte	180.00	90.00	54.00
51	Cookie Lavagetto	180.00	90.00	54.00
52	Hal Schumacher	180.00	90.00	54.00
53	Doc Cramer	180.00	90.00	54.00
54	Si Johnson	180.00	90.00	54.00
55	Ollie Bejma	180.00	90.00	54.00
56	Sammy Byrd	180.00	90.00	54.00
57	Hank Greenberg	750.00	500.00	300.00
58	Bill Knickerbocker	180.00	90.00	54.00
59	Billy Urbanski	180.00	90.00	54.00
60	Ed Morgan	180.00	90.00	54.00
61	Eric McNair	180.00	90.00	54.00
62	Ben Chapman	180.00	90.00	54.00
63	Roy Johnson	180.00	90.00	54.00
64	"Dizzy" Dean	750.00	375.00	225.00
65	Zeke Bonura	180.00	90.00	54.00
66	Firpo Marberry	180.00	90.00	54.00
67	Gus Mancuso	180.00	90.00	54.00
68	Joe Vosmik	180.00	90.00	54.00
69	Earl Grace	180.00	90.00	54.00
70	Tony Piet	180.00	90.00	54.00
71	Rollie Hemsley	180.00	90.00	54.00
72	Fred Fitzsimmons	180.00	90.00	54.00
73	Hack Wilson	565.00	280.00	165.00
74	Chick Fullis	180.00	90.00	54.00
75	Fred Frankhouse	180.00	90.00	54.00
76	Ethan Allen	180.00	90.00	54.00
77	Heinie Manush	565.00	280.00	165.00
78	Rip Collins	180.00	90.00	54.00
79	Tony Cuccinello	180.00	90.00	54.00
80	Joe Kuhel	300.00	150.00	90.00
81	Thomas Bridges	335.00	165.00	100.00
82	Clinton Brown	335.00	165.00	100.00
83	Albert Blanche	335.00	165.00	100.00
84	"Boze" Berger	335.00	165.00	100.00
85	Goose Goslin	750.00	375.00	225.00
86	Vernon Gomez	800.00	400.00	240.00
87	Joe Glen (Glenn)	335.00	165.00	100.00
88	Cy Blanton	335.00	165.00	100.00
89	Tom Carey	335.00	165.00	100.00
90	Ralph Birkhofer	335.00	165.00	100.00
91	Frank Gabler	335.00	165.00	100.00
92	Dick Coffman	335.00	165.00	100.00
93	Ollie Bejma	335.00	165.00	100.00
94	Leroy Earl Parmalee	335.00	165.00	100.00
95	Carl Reynolds	335.00	165.00	100.00
96	Ben Cantwell	335.00	165.00	100.00
97	Curtis Davis	335.00	165.00	100.00
98	Wallace Moses, Billy Webb	750.00	375.00	225.00
99	Ray Benge	335.00	165.00	100.00
100	"Pie" Traynor	750.00	375.00	225.00
101	Phil. Cavarretta	335.00	165.00	100.00
102	"Pep" Young	335.00	165.00	100.00
103	Willis Hudlin	335.00	165.00	100.00
104	Mickey Haslin	335.00	165.00	100.00
105	Oswald Bluege	335.00	165.00	100.00
106	Paul Andrews	335.00	165.00	100.00
107	Edward A. Brandt	335.00	165.00	100.00
108	Dan Taylor	335.00	165.00	100.00
109	Thornton T. Lee	335.00	165.00	100.00
110	Hal Schumacher	335.00	165.00	100.00
111	Minter Hayes, Ted Lyons	825.00	415.00	250.00
112	Odell Hale	335.00	165.00	100.00
113	Earl Averill	750.00	375.00	225.00
114	Italo Chelini	335.00	165.00	100.00
115	Ivy Andrews, Jim Bottomley	975.00	485.00	290.00
116	Bill Walker	335.00	165.00	100.00
117	Bill Dickey	1,125	565.00	340.00
118	Gerald Walker	335.00	165.00	100.00
119	Ted Lyons	750.00	375.00	225.00
120	Elden Auker (Eldon)	335.00	165.00	100.00
121	Wild Bill Hallahan	335.00	165.00	100.00
122	Freddy Lindstrom	750.00	375.00	225.00
123	Oral C. Hildebrand	335.00	165.00	100.00
124	Luke Appling	750.00	375.00	225.00
125	"Pepper" Martin	750.00	375.00	225.00
126	Rick Ferrell	750.00	375.00	225.00
127	Ival Goodman	335.00	165.00	100.00
128	Joe Kuhel	335.00	165.00	100.00
129	Ernest Lombardi	750.00	375.00	225.00
130	Charles Gehringer	750.00	375.00	225.00
131	Van L. Mungo	500.00	250.00	150.00
132	Larry French	335.00	165.00	100.00
133	"Buddy" Myer	335.00	165.00	100.00
134	Mel Harder	335.00	165.00	100.00
135	Augie Galan	335.00	165.00	100.00
136	"Gabby" Hartnett	750.00	375.00	225.00

137	Stan Hack	335.00	165.00	100.00
138	Billy Herman	750.00	375.00	225.00
139	Bill Jurges	335.00	165.00	100.00
140	Bill Lee	335.00	165.00	100.00
141	"Zeke" Bonura	335.00	165.00	100.00
142	Tony Piet	335.00	165.00	100.00
143	Paul Dean	650.00	325.00	200.00
144	Jimmy Foxx	1,275	635.00	380.00
145	Joe Medwick	750.00	375.00	225.00
146	Rip Collins	335.00	165.00	100.00
147	Melo Almada	335.00	165.00	100.00
148	Allan Cooke	335.00	165.00	100.00
149	Moe Berg	940.00	470.00	282.00
150	Adolph Camilli	335.00	165.00	100.00
151	Oscar Melillo	335.00	165.00	100.00
152	Bruce Campbell	335.00	165.00	100.00
153	Lefty Grove	940.00	470.00	282.00
154	John Murphy	335.00	165.00	100.00
155	Luke Sewell	335.00	165.00	100.00
156	Leo Durocher	750.00	375.00	225.00
157	Lloyd Waner	750.00	375.00	225.00
158	Guy Bush	335.00	165.00	100.00
159	Jimmy Dykes	335.00	165.00	100.00
160	Steve O'Neill	335.00	165.00	100.00
161	Gen. Crowder	335.00	165.00	100.00
162	Joe Cascarella	335.00	165.00	100.00
163	"Bud" Hafey	335.00	165.00	100.00
164	"Gilly" Campbell	335.00	165.00	100.00
165	Ray Hayworth	335.00	165.00	100.00
166	Frank Demaree	335.00	165.00	100.00
167	John Babich	335.00	165.00	100.00
168	Marvin Owen	335.00	165.00	100.00
169	Ralph Kress	335.00	165.00	100.00
170	"Mule" Haas	335.00	165.00	100.00
171	Frank Higgins	335.00	165.00	100.00
172	Walter Berger	335.00	165.00	100.00
173	Frank Frisch	750.00	375.00	225.00
174	Wess Ferrell (Wes)	335.00	165.00	100.00
175	Pete Fox	335.00	165.00	100.00
176	John Vergez	335.00	165.00	100.00
177	William Rogell	335.00	165.00	100.00
178	"Don" Brennan	335.00	165.00	100.00
179	James Bottomley	750.00	375.00	225.00
180	Travis Jackson	750.00	375.00	225.00
181	Robert Rolfe	335.00	165.00	100.00
182	Frank Crosetti	600.00	300.00	180.00
183	Joe Cronin	750.00	375.00	225.00
184	"Schoolboy" Rowe	500.00	250.00	150.00
185	"Chuck" Klein	750.00	375.00	225.00
186	Lon Warneke	335.00	165.00	100.00
187	Gus Suhr	335.00	165.00	100.00
188	Ben Chapman	335.00	165.00	100.00
189	Clint. Brown	375.00	185.00	115.00
190	Paul Derringer	375.00	185.00	115.00
191	John Burns	375.00	185.00	115.00
192	John Broaca	675.00	335.00	200.00

1934-36 Batter-Up Premiums

The identity of these premium pictures and their association with National Chicle's Batter-Up bubblegum card set was not recognized by most collectors until the mid-2000s. These are the pictures that were mentioned on the wrappers of the high-number series of Batter-Up cards, and were apparently designed to be handed out by the retailer to the purchaser of each penny pack of gum. The 5" x 8" photos are printed in a dark red duotone on thin glossy stock. The back is blank. The pictures on the premiums are the same as on the player's Batter-Up card. The extent of the premium checklist is unknown.

	NM	EX	VG
Common Player:	1,200.	725.00	350.00
Joe Vosmik	1,200.	725.00	350.00
Paul Waner	2,000.	1,200.	600.00

1958 Bazooka "My Favorite Team" Patches

These screen-printed felt patches were available via a mail-in offer found in Topps baseball cards. Approximately 5" in diameter, they were intended to be sewn on jackets, caps, etc.

		NM	E	VG
Complete Set (16):		450.00	225.00	135.00
Common Patch:		30.00	15.00	9.00
(1)	Baltimore Orioles	30.00	15.00	9.00
(2)	Boston Red Sox	35.00	17.50	10.50
(3)	Chicago Cubs	45.00	22.00	13.50
(4)	Chicago White Sox	30.00	15.00	9.00
(5)	Cincinnati Reds	30.00	15.00	9.00
(6)	Cleveland Indians	30.00	15.00	9.00
(7)	Detroit Tigers	30.00	15.00	9.00
(8)	Kansas City A's	30.00	15.00	9.00
(9)	Los Angeles Dodgers	40.00	20.00	12.00
(10)	Milwaukee Braves	35.00	17.50	10.50
(11)	New York Yankees	50.00	25.00	15.00
(12)	Philadelphia Phillies	30.00	15.00	9.00
(13)	Pittsburgh Pirates	30.00	15.00	9.00
(14)	San Francisco Giants	40.00	20.00	12.00
(15)	St. Louis Cardinals	30.00	15.00	9.00
(16)	Washington Senators	35.00	17.50	10.50

1959 Bazooka

The 1959 Bazooka set, consisting of 23 full-color, unnumbered cards, was printed on boxes of one-cent Topps bubble gum. The blank-backed cards measure 2-13/16" x 4-15/16", when properly cut. Nine cards were first issued, with 14 being added to the set later. The nine more plentiful cards are #'s 1, 5, 8, 9, 14, 15, 16, 17 and 22. Complete boxes would command double the price shown.

		NM	E	VG
Complete Set (23):		10,500	5,250	3,150
Common Player:		120.00	60.00	35.00
(1a)	Hank Aaron (Name in white.)	575.00	290.00	175.00
(1b)	Hank Aaron (Name in yellow.)	550.00	275.00	165.00
(2)	Richie Ashburn (SP)	500.00	250.00	150.00
(3)	Ernie Banks (SP)	800.00	400.00	240.00
(4)	Ken Boyer (SP)	350.00	175.00	105.00
(5)	Orlando Cepeda	225.00	110.00	65.00
(6)	Bob Cerv (SP)	350.00	175.00	105.00
(7)	Rocky Colavito (SP)	425.00	215.50	125.00
(8)	Del Crandall	120.00	60.00	35.00
(9)	Jim Davenport	120.00	60.00	35.00
(10)	Don Drysdale (SP)	500.00	250.00	150.00
(11)	Nellie Fox (SP)	500.00	250.00	150.00
(12)	Jackie Jensen (SP)	350.00	175.00	105.00
(13)	Harvey Kuenn (SP)	350.00	175.00	105.00
(14)	Mickey Mantle	1,800	900.00	540.00
(15)	Willie Mays	800.00	400.00	240.00
(16)	Bill Mazeroski	250.00	125.00	75.00
(17)	Roy McMillan	120.00	60.00	35.00

		NM	E	VG
(18)	Billy Pierce (SP)	350.00	175.00	105.00
(19)	Roy Sievers (SP)	350.00	175.00	105.00
(20)	Duke Snider (SP)	850.00	425.00	250.00
(21)	Gus Triandos (SP)	350.00	175.00	105.00
(22)	Bob Turley	225.00	110.00	65.00
(23)	Vic Wertz (SP)	350.00	175.00	10 5.00

1959 Bazooka Pennants

These screen-printed felt pennants were available via a mail-in offer found in Topps baseball cards. Approximately 15" long and 5" wide, they have a "COPYRIGHT BAZOOKA" bar near the wide end.

		NM	E	VG
Complete Set (16):		600.00	300.00	180.00
Common Team:		40.00	20.00	12.00
(1)	Baltimore Orioles	40.00	20.00	12.00
(2)	Boston Red Sox	40.00	20.00	12.00
(3)	Chicago Cubs	40.00	20.00	12.00
(4)	Chicago White Sox	45.00	22.50	13.50
(5)	Cincinnati Redlegs	40.00	20.00	12.00
(6)	Cleveland Indians	40.00	20.00	12.00
(7)	Detroit Tigers	40.00	20.00	12.00
(8)	Kansas City A's	40.00	20.00	12.00
(9)	Los Angeles Dodgers	45.00	22.50	13.50
(10)	Milwaukee Braves	40.00	20.00	12.00
(11)	New York Yankees	50.00	25.00	15.00
(12)	Philadelphia Phillies	40.00	20.00	12.00
(13)	Pittsburgh Pirates	40.00	20.00	12.00
(14)	San Francisco Giants	40.00	20.00	12.00
(15)	St. Louis Cardinals	40.00	20.00	12.00
(16)	Washington Senators	40.00	20.00	12.00

1960 Bazooka

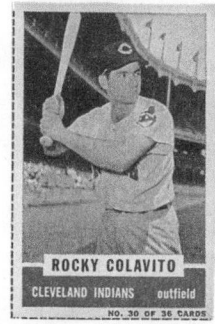

Three-card panels were printed on the bottoms of Bazooka bubble gum boxes in 1960. The blank-backed set is comprised of 36 cards with the card number located at the bottom of each full-color card. Individual cards measure 1-13/16" x 2-3/4"; the panels measure 2-3/4" x 5-1/2".

		NM	E	VG
Complete Panel Set (12):		2,200	1,100	650.00
Complete Singles Set (36):		2,000	1,000	600.00
Common Player:		15.00	7.50	4.50
	Panel (1)	125.00	62.00	37.00
1	Ernie Banks	90.00	45.00	27.00
2	Bud Daley	15.00	7.50	4.50
3	Wally Moon	15.00	7.50	4.50
	Panel (2)	200.00	100.00	60.00
4	Hank Aaron	150.00	75.00	45.00
5	Milt Pappas	15.00	7.50	4.50
6	Dick Stuart	15.00	7.50	4.50
	Panel (3)	325.00	160.00	97.00
7	Roberto Clemente	200.00	100.00	60.00
8	Yogi Berra	90.00	45.00	27.00
9	Ken Boyer	25.00	12.50	7.50
	Panel (4)	100.00	50.00	30.00
10	Orlando Cepeda	50.00	25.00	15.00
11	Gus Triandos	15.00	7.50	4.50
12	Frank Malzone	15.00	7.50	4.50
	Panel (5)	200.00	100.00	60.00
13	Willie Mays	150.00	75.00	45.00
14	Camilo Pascual	15.00	7.50	4.50
15	Bob Cerv	15.00	7.50	4.50
	Panel (6)	125.00	62.00	37.00
16	Vic Power	15.00	7.50	4.50
17	Larry Sherry	15.00	7.50	4.50
18	Al Kaline	75.00	37.00	22.00
	Panel (7)	200.00	100.00	60.00

		NM	E	VG
19	Warren Spahn	75.00	37.00	22.00
20	Harmon Killebrew	75.00	37.00	22.00
21	Jackie Jensen	25.00	12.50	7.50
	Panel (8)	175.00	87.00	52.00
22	Luis Aparicio	50.00	25.00	15.00
23	Gil Hodges	50.00	25.00	15.00
24	Richie Ashburn	50.00	25.00	15.00
	Panel (9)	125.00	62.00	37.00
25	Nellie Fox	50.00	25.00	15.00
26	Robin Roberts	50.00	25.00	15.00
27	Joe Cunningham	15.00	7.50	4.50
	Panel (10)	200.00	100.00	60.00
28	Early Wynn	50.00	25.00	15.00
29	Frank Robinson	75.00	37.00	22.00
30	Rocky Colavito	50.00	25.00	15.00
	Panel (11)	750.00	375.00	225.00
31	Mickey Mantle	500.00	250.00	150.00
32	Glen Hobbie	15.00	7.50	4.50
33	Roy McMillan	15.00	7.50	4.50
	Panel (12)	60.00	30.00	18.00
34	Harvey Kuenn	15.00	7.50	4.50
35	Johnny Antonelli	15.00	7.50	4.50
36	Del Crandall	15.00	7.50	4.50

1960 Bazooka Hot Iron Transfers

Team logo transfers were available via a mail-in offer found on cards inserted into packs of 1960 Topps. Varying in size and shape, but generally about 5" square, the transfers were packaged in a colorful envelope which provided instructions for ironing the logo to a t-shirt or other cloth surface. Unlike earlier Bazooka mail-in premiums, the gum is not named on the transfers. Values shown are for transfers without the envelope. Envelopes, which carried the name and logo of the team inside, are valued about the same as the transfer itself.

		NM	E	VG
Complete Set (16):		300.00	150.00	90.00
Common Team:		20.00	10.00	6.00
Envelope: 1X				
(1)	Baltimore Orioles	20.00	10.00	6.00
(2)	Boston Red Sox	20.00	10.00	6.00
(3)	Chicago Cubs	20.00	10.00	6.00
(4)	Chicago White Sox	20.00	10.00	6.00
(5)	Cincinnati Redlegs	20.00	10.00	6.00
(6)	Cleveland Indians	20.00	10.00	6.00
(7)	Detroit Tigers	20.00	10.00	6.00
(8)	Kansas City A's	20.00	10.00	6.00
(9)	Los Angeles Dodgers	22.50	11.00	6.75
(10)	Milwaukee Braves	20.00	10.00	6.00
(11)	New York Yankees	25.00	12.50	7.50
(12)	Philadelphia Phillies	20.00	10.00	6.00
(13)	Pittsburgh Pirates	22.50	11.00	6.75
(14)	San Francisco Giants	20.00	10.00	6.00
(15)	St. Louis Cardinals	20.00	10.00	6.00
(16)	Washington Senators	20.00	10.00	6.00

1961 Bazooka

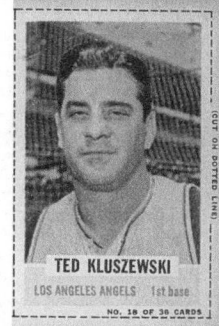

Similar in design to the 1960 Bazooka set, the 1961 edition consists of 36 cards printed in panels of three on the bottom of Bazooka bubble gum boxes. The full-color cards, which measure 1-13/16" x 2-3/4" individually and 2-3/4" x 5-1/2" as panels, are numbered 1 through 36. The backs are blank.

		NM	E	VG
Complete Set, Panels (12):		1,500	750.00	450.00
Complete Set, Singles (36):		1,200	600.00	350.00
Common Player:		12.00	6.00	3.50
	Panel (1)	750.00	375.00	225.00
1	Art Mahaffey	12.00	6.00	3.50
2	Mickey Mantle	400.00	200.00	120.00
3	Ron Santo	25.00	12.50	7.50
	Panel (2)	225.00	110.00	65.00
4	Bud Daley	12.00	6.00	3.50
5	Roger Maris	100.00	50.00	30.00
6	Eddie Yost	12.00	6.00	3.50
	Panel (3)	75.00	37.50	22.50
7	Minnie Minoso	15.00	7.50	4.50
8	Dick Groat	13.50	7.00	4.00
9	Frank Malzone	12.00	6.00	3.50
	Panel (4)	100.00	50.00	30.00
10	Dick Donovan	12.00	6.00	3.50
11	Ed Mathews	45.00	22.50	13.50
12	Jim Lemon	12.00	6.00	3.50
	Panel (5)	75.00	37.50	22.50
13	Chuck Estrada	12.00	6.00	3.50
14	Ken Boyer	15.00	7.50	4.50
15	Harvey Kuenn	12.00	6.00	3.50
	Panel (6)	100.00	50.00	30.00
16	Ernie Broglio	12.00	6.00	3.50
17	Rocky Colavito	25.00	12.50	7.50
18	Ted Kluszewski	25.00	12.50	7.50
	Panel (7)	250.00	125.00	75.00
19	Ernie Banks	100.00	50.00	30.00
20	Al Kaline	45.00	22.50	13.50
21	Ed Bailey	12.00	6.00	3.50
	Panel (8)	250.00	125.00	75.00
22	Jim Perry	12.00	6.00	3.50
23	Willie Mays	100.00	50.00	30.00
24	Bill Mazeroski	40.00	20.00	12.00
	Panel (9)	100.00	50.00	30.00
25	Gus Triandos	12.00	6.00	3.50
26	Don Drysdale	45.00	22.50	13.50
27	Frank Herrera	12.00	6.00	3.50
	Panel (10)	100.00	50.00	30.00
28	Earl Battey	12.00	6.00	3.50
29	Warren Spahn	45.00	22.50	13.50
30	Gene Woodling	12.00	6.00	3.50
	Panel (11)	100.00	50.00	30.00
31	Frank Robinson	45.00	22.50	13.50
32	Pete Runnels	12.00	6.00	3.50
33	Woodie Held	12.00	6.00	3.50
	Panel (12)	100.00	50.00	30.00
34	Norm Larker	12.00	6.00	3.50
35	Luis Aparicio	35.00	17.50	10.00
36	Bill Tuttle	12.00	6.00	3.50

1962 Bazooka

In 1962, Bazooka increased the size of its set to 45 full-color cards. The set is unnumbered and was printed in panels of three on the bottoms of bubble gum boxes. Individual cards measure 1-13/16" x 2-3/4" in size, with panels at 2-3/4" x 5-1/2". In the checklist that follows the cards have been numbered alphabetically, using the name of the player who appears on the left end of the panel. Panels (1), (11) and (15) were issued in much shorter supply and command a higher price.

		NM	E	VG
Complete Set, Panels (15):		4,000	2,000	1,200
Complete Set, Singles (45):		3,750	1,850	1,100
Common Player:		12.50	6.25	3.75
	Panel (1)	850.00	425.00	255.00
(1)	Bob Allison	160.00	80.00	45.00
(2)	Ed Mathews	400.00	200.00	120.00
(3)	Vada Pinson	200.00	100.00	60.00
	Panel (2)	100.00	50.00	30.00
(4)	Earl Battey	12.50	6.25	3.75
(5)	Warren Spahn	45.00	22.50	13.50
(6)	Lee Thomas	12.50	6.25	3.75
	Panel (3)	75.00	40.00	25.00
(7)	Orlando Cepeda	30.00	15.00	9.00

(8) Woodie Held	12.50	6.25	3.75
(9) Bob Aspromonte	12.50	6.25	3.75
Panel (4)	200.00	100.00	60.00
(10) Dick Howser	12.50	6.25	3.75
(11) Roberto Clemente	125.00	65.00	35.00
(12) Al Kaline	45.00	22.50	13.50
Panel (5)	125.00	65.00	35.00
(13) Joey Jay	12.50	6.25	3.75
(14) Roger Maris	85.00	42.50	25.00
(15) Frank Howard	15.00	7.50	4.50
Panel (6)	175.00	90.00	50.00
(16) Sandy Koufax	125.00	65.00	35.00
(17) Jim Gentile	12.50	6.25	3.75
(18) Johnny Callison	12.50	6.25	3.75
Panel (7)	50.00	25.00	15.00
(19) Jim Landis	12.50	6.25	3.75
(20) Ken Boyer	13.00	6.50	4.00
(21) Chuck Schilling	12.50	6.25	3.75
Panel (8)	575.00	285.00	175.00
(22) Art Mahaffey	12.50	6.25	3.75
(23) Mickey Mantle	350.00	175.00	105.00
(24) Dick Stuart	13.50	6.75	4.00
Panel (9)	100.00	50.00	30.00
(25) Ken McBride	12.50	6.25	3.75
(26) Frank Robinson	45.00	22.50	13.50
(27) Gil Hodges	30.00	15.00	9.00
Panel (10)	175.00	85.00	50.00
(28) Milt Pappas	12.50	6.25	3.75
(29) Hank Aaron	125.00	65.00	35.00
(30) Luis Aparicio	30.00	15.00	9.00
Panel (11)	900.00	450.00	275.00
(31) Johnny Romano	160.00	80.00	50.00
(32) Ernie Banks	500.00	250.00	150.00
(33) Norm Siebern	160.00	80.00	50.00
Panel (12)	75.00	35.00	25.00
(34) Ron Santo	20.00	10.00	6.00
(35) Norm Cash	15.00	7.50	4.50
(36) Jimmy Piersall	15.00	7.50	4.50
Panel (13)	175.00	85.00	50.00
(37) Don Schwall	12.50	6.25	3.75
(38) Willie Mays	125.00	65.00	35.00
(39) Norm Larker	12.50	6.25	3.75
Panel (14)	110.00	55.00	35.00
(40) Bill White	12.50	6.25	3.75
(41) Whitey Ford	50.00	25.00	15.00
(42) Rocky Colavito	30.00	15.00	9.00
Panel (15)	750.00	375.00	225.00
(43) Don Zimmer	200.00	100.00	60.00
(44) Harmon Killebrew	350.00	175.00	100.00
(45) Gene Woodling	160.00	80.00	50.00

8 Dick Farrell (Portrait)	10.00	5.00	3.00
9 Hank Aaron (Glove in front.)	90.00	45.00	27.50
Panel (4)	200.00	100.00	60.00
10 Dick Donovan	10.00	5.00	3.00
11 Jim Gentile (Batting)	10.00	5.00	3.00
12 Willie Mays (Bat in front.)	90.00	45.00	22.50
Panel (5)	125.00	65.00	35.00
13 Camilo Pascual (Hands at waist.)	10.00	5.00	3.00
14 Roberto Clemente (Portrait)	90.00	45.00	22.50
15 Johnny Callison (Pinstriped uniform.)	10.00	5.00	3.00
Panel (6)	150.00	75.00	45.00
16 Carl Yastrzemski (Kneeling)	60.00	30.00	18.00
17 Don Drysdale	35.00	17.50	10.00
18 Johnny Romano (Portrait)	10.00	5.00	3.00
Panel (7)	45.00	22.50	13.50
19 Al Jackson	10.00	5.00	3.00
20 Ralph Terry	10.00	5.00	3.00
21 Bill Monbouquette	10.00	5.00	3.00
Panel (8)	150.00	75.00	45.00
22 Orlando Cepeda	35.00	17.50	10.00
23 Stan Musial	75.00	40.00	25.00
24 Floyd Robinson (No pinstripes.)	10.00	5.00	3.00
Panel (9)	45.00	22.50	13.50
25 Chuck Hinton (Batting)	10.00	5.00	3.00
26 Bob Purkey	10.00	5.00	3.00
27 Ken Hubbs	12.50	6.25	3.75
Panel (10)	75.00	40.00	25.00
28 Bill White	10.00	5.00	3.00
29 Ray Herbert	10.00	5.00	3.00
30 Brooks Robinson (Glove in front.)	40.00	20.00	12.00
Panel (11)	100.00	50.00	30.00
31 Frank Robinson (Batting)	40.00	20.00	12.00
32 Lee Thomas	10.00	5.00	3.00
33 Rocky Colavito (Detroit)	30.00	15.00	9.00
Panel (12)	90.00	45.00	27.50
34 Al Kaline (Kneeling)	45.00	22.50	13.50
35 Art Mahaffey	10.00	5.00	3.00
36 Tommy Davis (Follow-through.)	10.00	5.00	3.00

17 Babe Ruth	65.00	32.50	20.00
18 Connie Mack	13.50	6.75	4.00
19 Hank Greenberg	20.00	10.00	6.00
20 John McGraw	13.50	6.75	4.00
21 Johnny Evers	13.50	6.75	4.00
22 Al Simmons	13.50	6.75	4.00
23 Jimmy Collins	13.50	6.75	4.00
24 Tris Speaker	13.50	6.75	4.00
25 Frank Chance	13.50	6.75	4.00
26 Fred Clarke	13.50	6.75	4.00
27 Wilbert Robinson	13.50	6.75	4.00
28 Dazzy Vance	13.50	6.75	4.00
29 Grover Alexander	16.00	8.00	4.75
30 Kenesaw Landis	13.50	6.75	4.00
31 Willie Keeler	13.50	6.75	4.00
32 Rogers Hornsby	16.00	8.00	4.75
33 Hugh Duffy	13.50	6.75	4.00
34 Mickey Cochrane	13.50	6.75	4.00
35 Ty Cobb	60.00	30.00	18.00
36 Mel Ott	13.50	6.75	4.00
37 Clark Griffith	13.50	6.75	4.00
38 Ted Lyons	13.50	6.75	4.00
39 Cap Anson	13.50	6.75	4.00
40 Bill Dickey	13.50	6.75	4.00
41 Eddie Collins	13.50	6.75	4.00

1964 Bazooka

The 1964 Bazooka set is identical in design and size to the previous year's effort. However, different photographs were used from year to year. The 1964 set consists of 36 full-color, blank-backed cards numbered 1 through 36. Individual cards measure 1-9/16" x 2-1/2"; three-card panels measure 2-1/2" x 4-11/16". Sheets of 10 full-color baseball stamps were inserted in each box of bubble gum.

	NM	E	VG
Complete Set, Panels (12):	1,400	700.00	425.00
Complete Set, Singles (36):	950.00	475.00	275.00
Common Player:	10.00	5.00	3.00
Panel (1)	225.00	110.00	70.00
1 Mickey Mantle (Bat on shoulder.)	200.00	100.00	60.00
2 Dick Groat	10.00	5.00	3.00
3 Steve Barber	10.00	5.00	3.00
Panel (2)	75.00	37.00	22.00
4 Ken McBride	10.00	5.00	3.00
5 Warren Spahn (Cap to waist.)	35.00	17.50	10.50
6 Bob Friend	10.00	5.00	3.00
Panel (3)	150.00	75.00	45.00
7 Harmon Killebrew (Portrait)	35.00	17.50	10.50
8 Dick Farrell (Hands above head.)	10.00	5.00	3.00
9 Hank Aaron (Glove to left.)	75.00	37.50	22.50
Panel (4)	150.00	75.00	45.00
10 Rich Rollins	10.00	5.00	3.00
11 Jim Gentile (Portrait)	10.00	5.00	3.00
12 Willie Mays (Looking to left.)	75.00	37.50	22.50
Panel (5)	150.00	75.00	45.00
13 Camilo Pascual (Follow-through.)	10.00	5.00	3.00
14 Roberto Clemente (Throwing)	75.00	37.50	22.50
15 Johnny Callison (Batting, screen showing.)	10.00	5.00	3.00
Panel (6)	125.00	62.00	37.00
16 Carl Yastrzemski (Batting)	40.00	20.00	12.00
17 Billy Williams (Kneeling)	30.00	15.00	9.00
18 Johnny Romano (Batting)	10.00	5.00	3.00
Panel (7)	65.00	32.50	20.00
19 Jim Maloney	10.00	5.00	3.00
20 Norm Cash	12.50	6.25	3.75
21 Willie McCovey	30.00	15.00	9.00

1963 Bazooka

The 1963 Bazooka issue reverted to a 12-panel, 36-card set, but saw a change in the size of the cards. Individual cards measure 1-9/16" x 2-1/2", while panels are 2-1/2" x 4-11/16". The card design was altered also, with the player's name, team and position situated in a white oval at the bottom of the card. The full-color, blank-backed set is numbered 1-36. The complete set was counterfeited circa 2002, with many cards sold in "FGA" certified slabs, depressing the value of cards not graded by a major certification company.

	NM	E	VG
Complete Set, Panels (12):	1,750	875.00	525.00
Complete Set, Singles (36):	1,200	600.00	350.00
Common Player:	10.00	5.00	3.00
Panel (1)	450.00	225.00	135.00
1 Mickey Mantle (Batting righty.)	350.00	175.00	105.00
2 Bob Rodgers	10.00	5.00	3.00
3 Ernie Banks	60.00	30.00	18.00
Panel (2)	95.00	50.00	30.00
4 Norm Siebern	10.00	5.00	3.00
5 Warren Spahn (Portrait)	35.00	17.50	10.00
6 Bill Mazeroski	25.00	12.50	7.50
Panel (3)	175.00	90.00	50.00
7 Harmon Killebrew (Batting)	50.00	25.00	15.00

1963 Bazooka All-Time Greats

Consisting of 41 cards, the Bazooka All-Time Greats set was issued as inserts (five per box) in boxes of Bazooka bubble gum. A black-and-white portrait photo of the player is placed inside a gold plaque within a white border. Card backs contain a brief biography of the player. The numbered cards measure 1-9/16" x 2-1/2". Cards can be found with silver fronts instead of gold; the silver are worth double the values listed.

	NM	E	VG
Complete Set (41):	675.00	335.00	200.00
Common Player:	13.50	6.75	4.00
Silver: 2.5X			
1 Joe Tinker	13.50	6.75	4.00
2 Harry Heilmann	13.50	6.75	4.00
3 Jack Chesbro	13.50	6.75	4.00
4 Christy Mathewson	30.00	15.00	9.00
5 Herb Pennock	13.50	6.75	4.00
6 Cy Young	30.00	15.00	9.00
7 Ed Walsh	13.50	6.75	4.00
8 Nap Lajoie	13.50	6.75	4.00
9 Eddie Plank	13.50	6.75	4.00
10 Honus Wagner	35.00	17.50	10.00
11 Chief Bender	13.50	6.75	4.00
12 Walter Johnson	30.00	15.00	9.00
13 Three-Fingered Brown	13.50	6.75	4.00
14 Rabbit Maranville	13.50	6.75	4.00
15 Lou Gehrig	60.00	30.00	18.00
16 Ban Johnson	13.50	6.75	4.00

		NM	E	VG
	Panel (8)	40.00	20.00	12.00
22	Jim Fregosi (Batting)	10.00	5.00	3.00
23	George Altman	10.00	5.00	3.00
24	Floyd Robinson (Pinstriped uniform.)	10.00	5.00	3.00
	Panel (9)	40.00	20.00	12.00
25	Chuck Hinton (Portrait)	10.00	5.00	3.00
26	Ron Hunt (Batting)	10.00	5.00	3.00
27	Gary Peters (Pitching)	10.00	5.00	3.00
	Panel (10)	90.00	45.00	27.00
28	Dick Ellsworth	10.00	5.00	3.00
29	Elston Howard (W/ bat.)	20.00	10.00	6.00
30	Brooks Robinson (Kneeling w/ glove.)	35.00	17.50	10.50
	Panel (11)	175.00	87.00	52.00
31	Frank Robinson (Uniform number shows.)	35.00	17.50	10.50
32	Sandy Koufax (Glove in front.)	75.00	37.50	22.50
33	Rocky Colavito (Kansas City)	25.00	12.50	7.50
	Panel (12)	90.00	45.00	27.00
34	Al Kaline (Holding two bats.)	40.00	20.00	12.00
35	Ken Boyer (Cap to waist.)	10.00	5.00	3.00
36	Tommy Davis (Batting)	10.00	5.00	3.00

1964 Bazooka Stamps

Occasionally mislabeled "Topps Stamps," the 1964 Bazooka stamps were produced by Topps, but found only in boxes of Bazooka bubble gum. Issued in sheets of 10, 100 color stamps make up the set. Each stamp measures 1" x 1-1/2" in size. While the stamps are not individually numbered, the sheets are numbered one through 10. The stamps are commonly found as complete sheets of 10 and are priced in that fashion in the checklist that follows.

		NM	E	VG
	Complete Sheet Set (10x10):	750.00	375.00	225.00
	Common Sheet:	35.00	17.50	10.00
	Common Stamp:	4.00	2.00	1.25
1	Max Alvis, Ed Charles, Dick Ellsworth, Jimmie Hall, Frank Malzone, Milt Pappas, Vada Pinson, Tony Taylor, Pete Ward, Bill White	35.00	17.50	10.50
2	Bob Aspromonte, Larry Jackson, Willie Mays, Al McBean, Bill Monbouquette, Bobby Richardson, Floyd Robinson, Frank Robinson, Norm Siebern, Don Zimmer	80.00	40.00	25.00
3	Ernie Banks, Roberto Clemente, Curt Flood, Jesse Gonder, Woody Held, Don Lock, Dave Nicholson, Joe Pepitone, Brooks Robinson, Carl Yastrzemski	120.00	60.00	35.00
4	Hank Aguirre, Jim Grant, Harmon Killebrew, Jim Maloney, Juan Marichal, Bill Mazeroski, Juan Pizarro, Boog Powell, Ed Roebuck, Ron Santo	85.00	45.00	25.00
5	Jim Bouton, Norm Cash, Orlando Cepeda, Tommy Harper, Chuck Hinton, Albie Pearson, Ron Perranoski, Dick Radatz, Johnny Romano, Carl Willey	45.00	25.00	15.00
6	Steve Barber, Jim Fregosi, Tony Gonzalez, Mickey Mantle, Jim O'Toole, Gary Peters, Rich Rollins, Warren Spahn, Dick Stuart, Joe Torre	165.00	80.00	50.00

		NM	E	VG
7	Felipe Alou, George Altman, Ken Boyer, Rocky Colavito, Jim Davenport, Tommy Davis, Bill Freehan, Bob Friend, Ken Johnson, Billy Moran	40.00	20.00	12.00
8	Earl Battey, Ernie Broglio, Johnny Callison, Donn Clendenon, Don Drysdale, Jim Gentile, Elston Howard, Claude Osteen, Billy Williams, Hal Woodeshick	55.00	27.50	16.50
9	Hank Aaron, Jack Baldschun, Wayne Causey, Moe Drabowsky, Dick Groat, Frank Howard, Al Jackson, Jerry Lumpe, Ken McBride, Rusty Staub	65.00	32.50	19.50
10	Vic Davalillo, Dick Farrell, Ron Hunt, Al Kaline, Sandy Koufax, Eddie Mathews, Willie McCovey, Camilo Pascual, Lee Thomas	85.00	45.00	25.00

1965 Bazooka

The 1965 Bazooka set is identical to the 1963 and 1964 sets. Different players were added each year and different photographs were used for those players being included again. Individual cards cut from the boxes measure 1-9/16" x 2-1/2". Complete three-card panels measure 2-1/2" x 4-11/16." Cards are again blank-backed.

		NM	E	VG
	Complete Set, Panels (12):	1,300	650.00	400.00
	Complete Set, Singles (36):	900.00	450.00	275.00
	Common Player:	10.00	5.00	3.00
	Panel (1)	350.00	175.00	105.00
1	Mickey Mantle (Batting lefty.)	300.00	150.00	90.00
2	Larry Jackson	10.00	5.00	3.00
3	Chuck Hinton	10.00	5.00	3.00
	Panel (2)	40.00	20.00	12.00
4	Tony Oliva	12.50	6.25	3.75
5	Dean Chance	10.00	5.00	3.00
6	Jim O'Toole	10.00	5.00	3.00
	Panel (3)	125.00	65.00	35.00
7	Harmon Killebrew (Bat on shoulder.)	35.00	17.50	10.50
8	Pete Ward	10.00	5.00	3.00
9	Hank Aaron (Batting)	75.00	37.50	22.50
	Panel (4)	125.00	62.00	37.00
10	Dick Radatz	10.00	5.00	3.00
11	Boog Powell	12.50	6.25	3.75
12	Willie Mays (Looking down.)	75.00	37.50	22.50
	Panel (5)	250.00	125.00	75.00
13	Bob Veale	10.00	5.00	3.00
14	Roberto Clemente (Batting)	100.00	50.00	30.00
15	Johnny Callison (Batting, no screen in background.)	10.00	5.00	3.00
	Panel (6)	60.00	30.00	18.00
16	Joe Torre	15.00	7.50	4.50
17	Billy Williams (Batting)	25.00	12.50	7.50
18	Bob Chance	10.00	5.00	3.00
	Panel (7)	50.00	25.00	15.00
19	Bob Aspromonte	10.00	5.00	3.00
20	Joe Christopher	10.00	5.00	3.00
21	Jim Bunning	25.00	12.50	7.50
	Panel (8)	75.00	37.50	22.50
22	Jim Fregosi	10.00	5.00	3.00
23	Bob Gibson	30.00	15.00	9.00

		NM	E	VG
24	Juan Marichal	25.00	12.50	7.50
	Panel (9)	40.00	20.00	12.00
25	Dave Wickersham	10.00	5.00	3.00
26	Ron Hunt (Throwing)	10.00	5.00	3.00
27	Gary Peters (Portrait)	10.00	5.00	3.00
	Panel (10)	85.00	42.50	25.00
28	Ron Santo	15.00	7.50	4.50
29	Elston Howard (W/ glove.)	12.50	6.25	3.75
30	Brooks Robinson (Portrait)	35.00	17.50	10.50
	Panel (11)	200.00	100.00	60.00
31	Frank Robinson (Portrait)	35.00	17.50	10.50
32	Sandy Koufax (Hands over head.)	100.00	50.00	30.00
33	Rocky Colavito (Cleveland)	20.00	10.00	6.00
	Panel (12)	75.00	37.00	22.00
34	Al Kaline (Portrait)	35.00	17.50	10.50
35	Ken Boyer (Portrait)	10.00	5.00	3.00
36	Tommy Davis (Fielding)	10.00	5.00	3.00

1966 Bazooka

The 1966 Bazooka set was increased to 48 cards. Printed in panels of three on the bottoms of boxes of bubble gum, the full-color cards are blank-backed and numbered. Individual cards measure 1-9/16" x 2-1/2"; panels measure 2-1/2" x 4-11/16". Most of those 1966 Bazooka cards which have the same player/number combination as 1967 share the same photo and are indistinguishable as singles or panels; year of issue for complete boxes can be distinguished by the small photo on front of Koufax (1966) or Mantle (1967).

		NM	E	VG
	Complete Set, Panels (16):	2,200	1,100	650.00
	Complete Set, Singles (48):	1,500	750.00	450.00
	Common Player:	10.00	5.00	3.00
	Panel (1)	175.00	85.00	50.00
1	Sandy Koufax	100.00	50.00	30.00
2	Willie Horton	13.50	6.75	4.00
3	Frank Howard	13.50	6.75	4.00
	Panel (2)	60.00	30.00	18.00
4	Richie Allen	16.50	8.25	5.00
5	Mel Stottlemyre	10.00	5.00	3.00
6	Tony Conigliaro	20.00	10.00	6.00
	Panel (3)	400.00	200.00	120.00
7	Mickey Mantle	300.00	150.00	90.00
8	Leon Wagner	10.00	5.00	3.00
9	Ed Kranepool	10.00	5.00	3.00
	Panel (4)	120.00	60.00	36.00
10	Juan Marichal	35.00	17.50	10.00
11	Harmon Killebrew	50.00	25.00	15.00
12	Johnny Callison	10.00	5.00	3.00
	Panel (5)	100.00	50.00	30.00
13	Roy McMillan	10.00	5.00	3.00
14	Willie McCovey	40.00	20.00	12.00
15	Rocky Colavito	30.00	15.00	9.00
	Panel (6)	150.00	75.00	45.00
16	Willie Mays	80.00	40.00	24.00
17	Sam McDowell	10.00	5.00	3.00
18	Vern Law	10.00	5.00	3.00
	Panel (7)	80.00	40.00	24.00
19	Jim Fregosi	10.00	5.00	3.00
20	Ron Fairly	10.00	5.00	3.00
21	Bob Gibson	40.00	20.00	12.00
	Panel (8)	110.00	55.00	35.00
22	Carl Yastrzemski	60.00	30.00	18.00
23	Bill White	10.00	5.00	3.00
24	Bob Aspromonte	10.00	5.00	3.00
	Panel (9)	150.00	75.00	45.00
25	Dean Chance (California)	10.00	5.00	3.00
26	Roberto Clemente	100.00	50.00	30.00
27	Tony Cloninger	10.00	5.00	3.00
	Panel (10)	135.00	65.00	40.00
28	Curt Blefary	10.00	5.00	3.00
29	Milt Pappas	10.00	5.00	3.00
30	Hank Aaron	80.00	40.00	24.00
	Panel (11)	130.00	65.00	40.00

#	Player	NM	E	VG
31	Jim Bunning	40.00	20.00	12.00
32	Frank Robinson (Portrait)	50.00	25.00	15.00
33	Bill Skowron	13.50	6.75	4.00
	Panel (12)	100.00	50.00	30.00
34	Brooks Robinson	50.00	25.00	15.00
35	Jim Wynn	10.00	5.00	3.00
36	Joe Torre	17.50	8.75	5.25
	Panel (13)	225.00	110.00	65.00
37	Jim Grant	10.00	5.00	3.00
38	Pete Rose	135.00	65.00	40.00
39	Ron Santo	20.00	10.00	6.00
	Panel (14)	90.00	45.00	27.50
40	Tom Tresh	13.50	6.75	4.00
41	Tony Oliva	13.50	6.75	4.00
42	Don Drysdale	40.00	20.00	12.00
	Panel (15)	40.00	20.00	12.00
43	Pete Richert	10.00	5.00	3.00
44	Bert Campaneris	10.00	5.00	3.00
45	Jim Maloney	10.00	5.00	3.00
	Panel (16)	130.00	65.00	40.00
46	Al Kaline	50.00	25.00	15.00
47	Eddie Fisher	10.00	5.00	3.00
48	Billy Williams	40.00	20.00	12.00

1967 Bazooka

The 1967 Bazooka set is identical in design to the sets of 1964-1966. Printed in panels of three on the bottoms of bubble gum boxes, the set is made up of 48 full-color, blank-backed, numbered cards. Individual cards measure 1-9/16" x 2-1/2"; complete panels measure 2-1/2" x 4-11/16". Most of those 1967 Bazooka cards which have the same player/number combination as 1966 share the same photo and are indistinguishable as singles or panels; complete boxes can be distinguished by the small photo on front of Koufax (1966) or Mantle (1967).

#	Player	NM	E	VG
	Complete Set, Panels (18):	3,900	1,950	1,200
	Complete Set, Singles (48):	2,400	1,200	720.00
	Common Player:	16.00	8.00	5.00
	Panel (1)	65.00	35.00	20.00
1	Rick Reichardt	16.00	8.00	5.00
2	Tommie Agee	16.00	8.00	5.00
3	Frank Howard	20.00	10.00	6.00
	Panel (2)	90.00	45.00	25.00
4	Richie Allen	30.00	15.00	10.00
5	Mel Stottlemyre	20.00	10.00	6.00
6	Tony Conigliaro	20.00	10.00	6.00
	Panel (3)	975.00	500.00	300.00
7	Mickey Mantle	650.00	325.00	200.00
8	Leon Wagner	16.00	8.00	5.00
9	Gary Peters	16.00	8.00	5.00
	Panel (4)	240.00	120.00	75.00
10	Juan Marichal	80.00	40.00	25.00
11	Harmon Killebrew	100.00	50.00	30.00
12	Johnny Callison	16.00	8.00	5.00
	Panel (5)	220.00	110.00	70.00
13	Denny McLain	35.00	20.00	12.00
14	Willie McCovey	80.00	40.00	25.00
15	Rocky Colavito	50.00	25.00	15.00
	Panel (6)	240.00	120.00	75.00
16	Willie Mays	150.00	75.00	40.00
17	Sam McDowell	16.00	8.00	5.00
18	Jim Kaat	20.00	10.00	6.00
	Panel (7)	160.00	80.00	50.00
19	Jim Fregosi	16.00	8.00	5.00
20	Ron Fairly	16.00	8.00	5.00
21	Bob Gibson	80.00	40.00	25.00
	Panel (8)	200.00	100.00	60.00
22	Carl Yastrzemski	100.00	50.00	30.00
23	Bill White	16.00	8.00	5.00
24	Bob Aspromonte	16.00	8.00	5.00
	Panel (9)	280.00	140.00	85.00
25	Dean Chance (Minnesota)	16.00	8.00	5.00
26	Roberto Clemente	150.00	80.00	50.00
27	Tony Cloninger	16.00	8.00	5.00
	Panel (10)	240.00	120.00	75.00
28	Curt Blefary	16.00	8.00	5.00
29	Phil Regan	16.00	8.00	5.00
30	Hank Aaron	150.00	75.00	45.00
	Panel (11)	280.00	140.00	85.00
31	Jim Bunning	80.00	40.00	25.00
32	Frank Robinson (Batting)	100.00	50.00	30.00
33	Ken Boyer	16.00	8.00	5.00
	Panel (12)	200.00	100.00	60.00
34	Brooks Robinson	100.00	50.00	30.00
35	Jim Wynn	16.00	8.00	5.00
36	Joe Torre	30.00	15.00	10.00
	Panel (13)	450.00	225.00	135.00
37	Tommy Davis	16.00	8.00	5.00
38	Pete Rose	250.00	125.00	75.00
39	Ron Santo	35.00	20.00	12.00
	Panel (14)	160.00	80.00	50.00
40	Tom Tresh	20.00	10.00	6.00
41	Tony Oliva	20.00	10.00	6.00
42	Don Drysdale	80.00	40.00	25.00
	Panel (15)	65.00	35.00	20.00
43	Pete Richert	16.00	8.00	5.00
44	Bert Campaneris	16.00	8.00	5.00
45	Jim Maloney	16.00	8.00	5.00
	Panel (16)	280.00	140.00	85.00
46	Al Kaline	100.00	50.00	30.00
47	Matty Alou	16.00	8.00	5.00
48	Billy Williams	80.00	40.00	25.00

1968 Bazooka

The design of the 1968 Bazooka set is radically different from previous years. The player cards are situated on the sides of the boxes with the box back containing "Tipps From The Topps." Four unnumbered player cards, measuring 1-1/4" x 3-1/8", are featured on each box. The box back includes a small player photo plus illustrated tips on various aspects of the game of baseball. Boxes are numbered 1-15 on the top panels. There are 56 different player cards in the set, with four of the cards (Agee, Drysdale, Rose, Santo) being used twice to round out the set of 15 boxes.

#	Player	NM	E	VG
	Complete Box Set (15):	4,250	2,125	1,250
	Complete Singles Set (60):	3,000	1,500	900.00
	Common Player:	10.00	5.00	3.00
	Box 1 - Bunting	275.00	135.00	80.00
1	Maury Wills	15.00	7.50	4.50
(1)	Clete Boyer	15.00	7.50	4.50
(2)	Paul Casanova	10.00	5.00	3.00
(3)	Al Kaline	65.00	32.50	20.00
(4)	Tom Seaver	80.00	40.00	25.00
	Box 2 - Batting	250.00	125.00	75.00
2	Carl Yastrzemski	80.00	40.00	25.00
(5)	Matty Alou	10.00	5.00	3.00
(6)	Bill Freehan	10.00	5.00	3.00
(7)	Jim Hunter	45.00	22.50	13.50
(8)	Jim Lefebvre	10.00	5.00	3.00
	Box 3 - Stealing Bases	175.00	85.00	50.00
3	Bert Campaneris	10.00	5.00	3.00
(9)	Bobby Knoop	10.00	5.00	3.00
(10)	Tim McCarver	15.00	7.50	4.50
(11)	Frank Robinson	65.00	32.50	20.00
(12)	Bob Veale	10.00	5.00	3.00
	Box 4 - Sliding	100.00	50.00	30.00
4	Maury Wills	15.00	7.50	4.50
(13)	Joe Azcue	10.00	5.00	3.00
(14)	Tony Conigliaro	15.00	7.50	4.50
(15)	Ken Holtzman	10.00	5.00	3.00
(16)	Bill White	10.00	5.00	3.00
	Box 5 - The Double Play	315.00	155.00	95.00
5	Julian Javier	10.00	5.00	3.00
(17)	Hank Aaron	175.00	87.00	52.00
(18)	Juan Marichal	45.00	22.50	13.50
(19)	Joe Pepitone	17.50	9.00	5.00
(20)	Rico Petrocelli	15.00	7.50	4.50
	Box 6 - Playing 1st Base	375.00	185.00	110.00
6	Orlando Cepeda	50.00	25.00	15.00
(21)	Tommie Agee	10.00	5.00	3.00
(22a)	Don Drysdale (No period after "A" in team name.)	40.00	20.00	12.00
(22b)	Don Drysdale (Period after "A.")	40.00	20.00	12.00
(23)	Pete Rose	175.00	87.00	52.00
(24)	Ron Santo	17.50	9.00	5.00
	Box 7 - Playing 2nd Base	225.00	110.00	65.00
7	Bill Mazeroski	50.00	25.00	15.00
(25)	Jim Bunning	45.00	22.50	13.50
(26)	Frank Howard	15.00	7.50	4.50
(27)	John Roseboro	10.00	5.00	3.00
(28)	George Scott	10.00	5.00	3.00
	Box 8 - Playing 3rd Base	275.00	135.00	80.00
8	Brooks Robinson	65.00	32.50	20.00
(29)	Tony Gonzalez	10.00	5.00	3.00
(30)	Willie Horton	15.00	7.50	4.50
(31)	Harmon Killebrew	65.00	32.50	20.00
(32)	Jim McGlothlin	10.00	5.00	3.00
	Box 9 - Playing Shortstop	150.00	75.00	45.00
9	Jim Fregosi	10.00	5.00	3.00
(33)	Max Alvis	10.00	5.00	3.00
(34)	Bob Gibson	45.00	22.50	13.50
(35)	Tony Oliva	15.00	7.50	4.50
(36)	Vada Pinson	15.00	7.50	4.50
	Box 10 - Catching	160.00	80.00	45.00
10	Joe Torre	17.50	9.00	5.00
(37)	Dean Chance	10.00	5.00	3.00
(38)	Tommy Davis	10.00	5.00	3.00
(39)	Ferguson Jenkins	45.00	22.00	13.50
(40)	Rick Monday	10.00	5.00	3.00
	Box 11 - Pitching	850.00	425.00	255.00
11	Jim Lonborg	15.00	7.50	4.50
(41)	Curt Flood	15.00	7.50	4.50
(42)	Joel Horlen	10.00	5.00	3.00
(43)	Mickey Mantle	650.00	325.00	195.00
(44)	Jim Wynn	10.00	5.00	3.00
	Box 12 - Fielding the Pitcher's Position	375.00	185.00	110.00
12	Mike McCormick	10.00	5.00	3.00
(45)	Roberto Clemente	200.00	100.00	60.00
(46)	Al Downing	10.00	5.00	3.00
(47)	Don Mincher	10.00	5.00	3.00
(48)	Tony Perez	45.00	22.00	13.50
	Box 13 - Coaching	225.00	110.00	65.00
13	Frank Crosetti	15.00	7.50	4.50
(49)	Rod Carew	55.00	27.50	16.50
(50)	Willie McCovey	55.00	27.50	16.50
(51)	Ron Swoboda	10.00	5.00	3.00
(52)	Earl Wilson	10.00	5.00	3.00
	Box 14 - Playing the Outfield	250.00	125.00	75.00
14	Willie Mays	175.00	87.00	52.00
(53)	Richie Allen	15.00	7.50	4.50
(54)	Gary Peters	10.00	5.00	3.00
(55)	Rusty Staub	17.50	9.00	5.00
(56)	Billy Williams	50.00	25.00	15.00
	Box 15 - Base Running	375.00	185.00	110.00
15	Lou Brock	55.00	27.50	16.50
(57)	Tommie Agee	10.00	5.00	3.00
(58)	Don Drysdale	40.00	20.00	12.00
(59)	Pete Rose	175.00	87.00	52.00
(60)	Ron Santo	17.50	9.00	5.00

1969-70 Bazooka

Issued over a two-year span, the 1969-70 Bazooka set utilized the box bottom and sides. The bottom, entitled "Baseball Extra," features an historic event in baseball; the 3" x 6-1/4" panels are numbered 1-12. Two "All-Time Great" cards were located on each side of the box. These cards are not numbered and have no distinct borders; individual cards measure 1-1/4" x 3-1/8". The prices in the checklist that follows are for complete boxes only. Cards/panels cut from the boxes have a greatly reduced value - 25 percent of the complete box prices for all cut pieces.

		NM	E	VG
	Complete Set (12):	500.00	250.00	150.00
	Common Box:	35.00	17.50	10.50
1	No-Hit Duel By Toney & Vaughn(Mordecai Brown, Ty Cobb, Willie Keeler, Eddie Plank)	50.00	25.00	15.00
2	Alexander Conquers Yanks(Rogers Hornsby, Ban Johnson, Walter Johnson, Al Simmons)	35.00	17.50	10.50
3	Yanks' Lazzeri Sets AL Record(Grover Alexander, Chief Bender, Christy Mathewson, Cy Young)	40.00	20.00	12.00
4	HR Almost Hit Out Of Stadium(Hugh Duffy, Lou Gehrig, Tris Speaker, Joe Tinker)	35.00	17.50	10.50
5	4 Consecutive Homers By Lou(Frank Chance, Mickey Cochrane, John McGraw, Babe Ruth)	55.00	27.00	16.50
6	No-Hit Game By Walter Johnson(Johnny Evers, Walter Johnson, John McGraw, Cy Young)	35.00	17.50	10.50
7	Twelve RBIs By Bottomley(Ty Cobb, Eddie Collins, Johnny Evers, Lou Gehrig)	55.00	27.00	16.50
8	Ty Ties Record(Mickey Cochrane, Eddie Collins, Mel Ott, Honus Wagner)	35.00	17.50	10.50
9	Babe Ruth Hits 3 HRs In Game(Cap Anson, Jack Chesbro, Al Simmons, Tris Speaker)	55.00	27.00	16.50
10	Calls Shot In Series Game(Nap Lajoie, Connie Mack, Rabbit Maranville, Ed Walsh)	55.00	27.00	16.50
11	Ruth's 60th HR Sets New Record(Frank Chance, Nap Lajoie, Mel Ott, Joe Tinker)	55.00	27.00	16.50
12	Double Shutout By Ed Reulbach(Rogers Hornsby, Rabbit Maranville, Christy Mathewson, Honus Wagner)	35.00	17.50	10.50

1	Tim McCarver	12.50	6.25	3.75
2	Frank Robinson	35.00	17.50	10.00
3	Bill Mazeroski	30.00	15.00	9.00
	Panel (2)	100.00	50.00	30.00
4	Willie McCovey	30.00	15.00	9.00
5	Carl Yastrzemski	40.00	20.00	12.00
6	Clyde Wright	7.50	3.75	2.25
	Panel (3)	60.00	30.00	18.00
7	Jim Merritt	7.50	3.75	2.25
8	Luis Aparicio	25.00	12.50	7.50
9	Bobby Murcer	12.50	6.25	3.75
	Panel (4)	30.00	15.00	9.00
10	Rico Petrocelli	7.50	3.75	2.25
11	Sam McDowell	7.50	3.75	2.25
12	Cito Gaston	7.50	3.75	2.25
	Panel (5)	85.00	42.50	25.00
13	Ferguson Jenkins	25.00	12.50	7.50
14	Al Kaline	35.00	17.50	10.00
15	Ken Harrelson	7.50	3.75	2.25
	Panel (6)	115.00	55.00	35.00
16	Tommie Agee	7.50	3.75	2.25
17	Harmon Killebrew	35.00	17.50	10.00
18	Reggie Jackson	45.00	22.50	13.50
	Panel (7)	60.00	30.00	18.00
19	Juan Marichal	25.00	12.50	7.50
20	Frank Howard	10.00	5.00	3.00
21	Bill Melton	7.50	3.75	2.25
	Panel (8)	125.00	65.00	35.00
22	Brooks Robinson	35.00	17.50	10.00
23	Hank Aaron	60.00	30.00	18.00
24	Larry Dierker	7.50	3.75	2.25
	Panel (9)	60.00	30.00	18.00
25	Jim Fregosi	7.50	3.75	2.25
26	Billy Williams	30.00	15.00	9.00
27	Dave McNally	7.50	3.75	2.25
	Panel (10)	65.00	32.50	20.00
28	Rico Carty	7.50	3.75	2.25
29	Johnny Bench	35.00	17.50	10.00
30	Tommy Harper	7.50	3.75	2.25
	Panel (11)	110.00	55.00	30.00
31	Bert Campaneris	7.50	3.75	2.25
32	Pete Rose	50.00	25.00	15.00
33	Orlando Cepeda	25.00	12.50	7.50
	Panel (12)	65.00	32.50	20.00
34	Maury Wills	7.50	3.75	2.25
35	Tom Seaver	35.00	17.50	10.00
36	Tony Oliva	10.00	5.00	3.00
	Panel (13)	120.00	60.00	35.00
37	Bill Freehan	7.50	3.75	2.25
38	Roberto Clemente	75.00	37.50	22.50
39	Claude Osteen	7.50	3.75	2.25
	Panel (14)	65.00	32.50	20.00
40	Rusty Staub	12.50	6.25	3.75
41	Bob Gibson	30.00	15.00	9.00
42	Amos Otis	7.50	3.75	2.25
	Panel (15)	55.00	27.50	16.50
43	Jim Wynn	7.50	3.75	2.25
44	Richie Allen	20.00	10.00	6.00
45	Tony Conigliaro	15.00	7.50	4.50
	Panel (16)	110.00	55.00	35.00
46	Randy Hundley	7.50	3.75	2.25
47	Willie Mays	60.00	30.00	18.00
48	Jim Hunter	25.00	12.50	7.50

(3)	Reggie Jackson	70.00	35.00	25.00
	Panel (2)	160.00	80.00	50.00
(4)	Bert Campaneris	8.00	4.00	2.50
(5)	Pete Rose	75.00	40.00	25.00
(6)	Orlando Cepeda	35.00	20.00	12.00
	Panel (3)	100.00	50.00	30.00
(7)	Rico Carty	8.00	4.00	2.50
(8)	Johnny Bench	60.00	30.00	20.00
(9)	Tommy Harper	8.00	4.00	2.50
	Panel (4)	140.00	70.00	45.00
(10)	Bill Freehan	8.00	4.00	2.50
(11)	Roberto Clemente	90.00	45.00	25.00
(12)	Claude Osteen	8.00	4.00	2.50
	Panel (5)	85.00	40	25.00
(13)	Jim Fregosi	8.00	4.00	2.50
(14)	Billy Williams	40.00	25.00	15.00
(15)	Dave McNally	8.00	4.00	2.50
	Panel (6)	160.00	80.00	50.00
(16)	Randy Hundley	8.00	4.00	2.50
(17)	Willie Mays	75.00	40.00	25.00
(18)	Jim Hunter	35.00	20.00	12.00
	Panel (7)	80.00	40.00	25.00
(19)	Juan Marichal	40.00	20.00	12.00
(20)	Frank Howard	12.00	6.00	4.00
(21)	Bill Melton	8.00	4.00	2.50
	Panel (8)	150.00	75.00	45.00
(22)	Willie McCovey	45.00	25.00	15.00
(23)	Carl Yastrzemski	60.00	30.00	20.00
(24)	Clyde Wright	8.00	4.00	2.50
	Panel (9)	80.00	40.00	25.00
(25)	Jim Merritt	8.00	4.00	2.50
(26)	Luis Aparicio	40.00	20.00	12.00
(27)	Bobby Murcer	15.00	8.00	5.00
	Panel (10)	40.00	20.00	12.00
(28)	Rico Petrocelli	8.00	4.00	2.50
(29)	Sam McDowell	8.00	4.00	2.50
(30)	Cito Gaston	8.00	4.00	2.50
	Panel (11)	175.00	90.00	50.00
(31)	Brooks Robinson	60.00	30.00	20.00
(32)	Hank Aaron	75.00	40.00	25.00
(33)	Larry Dierker	8.00	4.00	2.50
	Panel (12)	90.00	45.00	25.00
(34)	Rusty Staub	12.00	6.00	4.00
(35)	Bob Gibson	45.00	25.00	15.00
(36)	Amos Otis	12.00	6.00	4.00

1930 Becker Bros. Theatre

Only recently brought to light, the issue date attributed here is uncertain and may be clarified if and when additions to the checklist are made. About postcard size, the cards have sepia portraits of Philadelphia A's players on front, identified in the white border at bottom. Backs have advertising for the theatre, including a list of upcoming features.

		NM	E	VG
	Common Player:	150.00	75.00	45.00
(1)	Max Bishop	150.00	75.00	45.00
(2)	Mickey Cochrane	250.00	125.00	75.00
(3)	Sammy Hale	150.00	75.00	45.00
(4)	Jimmie Foxx	300.00	150.00	90.00
(5)	Al Simmons	250.00	125.00	75.00

1958 Bell Brand Dodgers

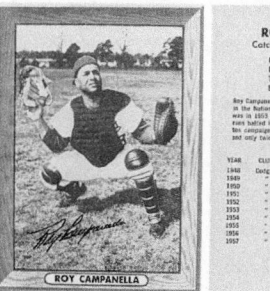
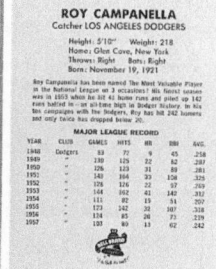

Celebrating the Dodgers first year of play in Los Angeles, Bell Brand inserted 10 different unnumbered cards in their bags of potato chips and corn chips. The cards, which measure 3" x 4", have a sepia-colored photo inside a 1/4" green woodgrain border. The card backs feature statistical and biographical information and include the Bell Brand logo. Roy Campanella is included in the set despite a career-ending car wreck that prevented him from ever playing in Los Angeles.

		NM	E	VG
	Complete Set (10):	6,500	3,200	1,950
	Common Player:	125.00	65.00	35.00
1	Roy Campanella	450.00	200.00	120.00
2	Gino Cimoli (SP)	1,200	600.00	360.00
3	Don Drysdale	400.00	175.00	100.00
4	Junior Gilliam	125.00	65.00	35.00

1971 Bazooka Numbered Set

The 1971 Bazooka numbered set is a proof set produced by the company after the unnumbered set was released. The set is comprised of 48 cards as opposed to the 36 cards which make up the unnumbered set. Issued in panels of three, the 12 cards not found in the unnumbered set are #1-3, 13-15, 34-36 and 43-45. All other cards are identical to those found in the unnumbered set. The cards, which measure 2" x 2-5/8", contain full-color photos and are blank-backed.

	NM	E	VG
Complete Panel Set (16):	1,300	655.00	400.00
Complete Singles Set (48):	950.00	475.00	275.00
Common Player:	7.50	3.75	2.25
Panel (1)	100.00	50.00	30.00

1971 Bazooka Unnumbered Set

This Bazooka set was issued in 1971, consisting of 36 full-color, blank-backed, unnumbered cards. Printed in panels of three on the bottoms of bubble gum boxes, individual cards measure 2" x 2-5/8"; complete panels measure 2-5/8" x 5-5/16". In the checklist that follows, the cards have been numbered by panel using the name of the player who appears on the left end of the panel.

		NM	E	VG
	Complete Panel Set (12):	1,050	525.00	320.00
	Complete Singles Set (36):	900.00	450.00	270.00
	Common Player:	8.00	4.00	2.50
	Panel (1)	160.00	80.00	50.00
(1)	Tommie Agee	8.00	4.00	2.50
(2)	Harmon Killebrew	55.00	30.00	20.00

		NM	E	VG
5	Gil Hodges	350.00	175.00	105.00
6	Sandy Koufax	2,000	1,000	600.00
7	Johnny Podres (SP)	600.00	300.00	180.00
8	Pee Wee Reese	450.00	200.00	120.00
9	Duke Snider	900.00	450.00	270.00
10	Don Zimmer	125.00	65.00	40.00

1958 Bell Brand Dodgers Ad Posters

These point-of-purchase in-store displays were created to draw attention to the snack company's premiere baseball card offering. The posters were printed in tete-a-tete pairs designed to be hung over a string. Each single panel measures about 22" x 36", and, like the cards, is printed in green and sepia on white stock.

	NM	E	VG
Bell Brand Dodgers Ad Posters(Don Drysdale)	2,400	1,200	725.00
Bell Brand Dodgers Ad Posters(Gil Hodges)	2,000	1,000	600.00
Bell Brand Dodgers Ad Posters(Junior Gilliam)	1,200	600.00	350.00
Bell Brand Dodgers Ad Posters(Pee Wee Reese)	2,500	1,250	750.00

1960 Bell Brand Dodgers

 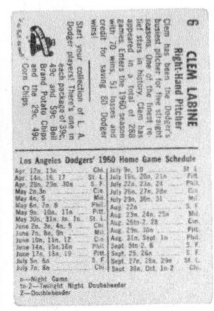

Bell Brand returned with a baseball card set in 1960 that was entirely different in style to their previous effort. The cards, which measure 2-1/2" x 3-1/2", feature beautiful, full-color photos. The backs carry a short player biography, the 1960 Dodgers home schedule, and the Bell Brand logo. Twenty different numbered cards were inserted in various size bags of potato chips and corn chips. Although sealed in cellophane, the cards were still subject to grease stains. Cards #'s 6, 12 and 18 are the scarcest in the set.

		NM	E	VG
Complete Set (20):		1,500	750.00	450.00
Common Player:		45.00	22.50	13.50
1	Norm Larker	45.00	22.50	13.50
2	Duke Snider	150.00	75.00	45.00
3	Danny McDevitt	45.00	22.50	13.50
4	Jim Gilliam	50.00	25.00	15.00
5	Rip Repulski	45.00	22.50	13.50
6	Clem Labine (SP)	90.00	45.00	27.50
7	John Roseboro	45.00	22.50	13.50
8	Carl Furillo	60.00	30.00	18.00
9	Sandy Koufax	300.00	150.00	90.00
10	Joe Pignatano	45.00	22.50	13.50
11	Chuck Essegian	45.00	22.50	13.50
12	John Klippstein (SP)	150.00	75.00	45.00
13	Ed Roebuck	45.00	22.50	13.50
14	Don Demeter	45.00	22.50	13.50
15	Roger Craig	45.00	22.50	13.50
16	Stan Williams	45.00	22.50	13.50
17	Don Zimmer	60.00	30.00	18.00
18	Walter Alston (SP)	100.00	50.00	30.00
19	Johnny Podres	60.00	30.00	18.00
20	Maury Wills	75.00	37.50	22.50

1961 Bell Brand Dodgers

The 1961 Bell Brand set is identical in format to the previous year, although printed on thinner stock. Cards can be distinguished from the 1960 set by the 1961 schedule on the backs. The cards, which measure 2-7/16" x 3-1/2", are numbered by the player's uniform number. Twenty different cards were inserted into various size potato chip and corn chip packages, each card being sealed in a cellophane wrapper.

 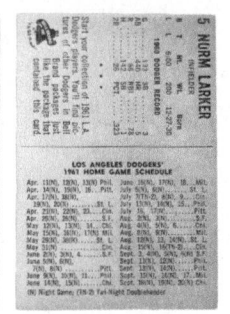

		NM	E	VG
Complete Set (20):		1,750	875.00	525.00
Common Player:		50.00	25.00	15.00
3	Willie Davis	60.00	30.00	18.00
4	Duke Snider	175.00	85.00	50.00
5	Norm Larker	50.00	25.00	15.00
8	John Roseboro	50.00	25.00	15.00
9	Wally Moon	50.00	25.00	15.00
11	Bob Lillis	50.00	25.00	15.00
12	Tom Davis	60.00	30.00	18.00
14	Gil Hodges	150.00	75.00	45.00
16	Don Demeter	50.00	25.00	15.00
19	Jim Gilliam	60.00	30.00	18.00
22	John Podres	60.00	30.00	18.00
24	Walter Alston	75.00	37.50	22.50
30	Maury Wills	110.00	55.00	30.00
32	Sandy Koufax	425.00	210.00	125.00
34	Norm Sherry	60.00	30.00	18.00
37	Ed Roebuck	50.00	25.00	15.00
38	Roger Craig	50.00	25.00	15.00
40	Stan Williams	50.00	25.00	15.00
43	Charlie Neal	50.00	25.00	15.00
51	Larry Sherry	60.00	30.00	18.00

1962 Bell Brand Dodgers

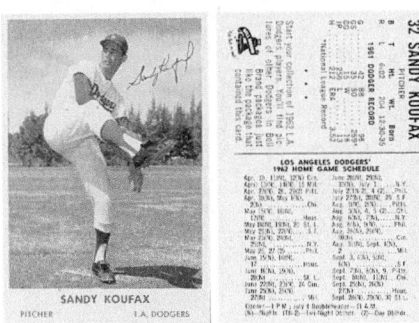

The 1962 Bell Brand set is identical in style to the previous two years and cards can be distinguished by the 1962 Dodgers schedule on the back. Each card measures 2-7/16" x 3-1/2" and is numbered by the player's uniform number. Printed on glossy stock, the 1962 set was less susceptible to grease stains.

		NM	E	VG
Complete Set (20):		1,700	850.00	500.00
Common Player:		50.00	25.00	15.00
3	Willie Davis	50.00	25.00	15.00
4	Duke Snider	200.00	100.00	60.00
6	Ron Fairly	50.00	25.00	15.00
8	John Roseboro	50.00	25.00	15.00
9	Wally Moon	50.00	25.00	15.00
12	Tom Davis	50.00	25.00	15.00
16	Ron Perranoski	50.00	25.00	15.00
19	Jim Gilliam	55.00	27.50	16.50
20	Daryl Spencer	50.00	25.00	15.00
22	John Podres	55.00	27.50	16.50
24	Walter Alston	75.00	37.50	22.50
25	Frank Howard	55.00	27.50	16.50
30	Maury Wills	90.00	45.00	27.50
32	Sandy Koufax	250.00	125.00	75.00
34	Norm Sherry	60.00	30.00	18.00
37	Ed Roebuck	50.00	25.00	15.00
40	Stan Williams	50.00	25.00	15.00

		NM	E	VG
51	Larry Sherry	60.00	30.00	18.00
53	Don Drysdale	125.00	65.00	35.00
56	Lee Walls	50.00	25.00	15.00

1962 Bell Brand Dodgers Ad Poster

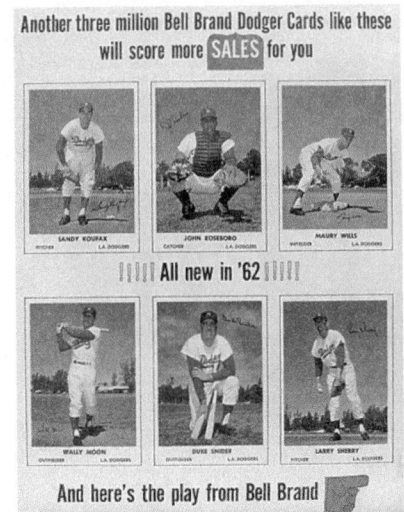

This 8-1/2" x 11-1/2" color poster was distributed to retailers to solicit sales of Bell Brand items. The sheet has actual size pictures of six of the cards from the set. On back is retailer information.

	NM	E	VG
1962 Bell Brand Ad Poster(Koufax, Roseboro, Wills, Moon, Snider, Sherry)	750.00	370.00	220.00

1951 Berk Ross

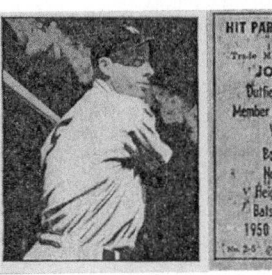

Entitled "Hit Parade of Champions," the 1951 Berk Ross set features 72 stars of various sports. The cards, which measure 2-1/16" x 2-1/2" and have tinted color photographs, were issued in four boxes containing two-card panels. The issue is divided into four subsets with the first ten players of each series being baseball players. Only the baseball players are listed in the checklist that follows. Complete panels are valued 50 percent higher than the sum of the individual cards.

		NM	E	VG
Complete Boxed Set (72):		1,700	850.00	500.00
Complete Baseball Set (40):		1,700	850.00	500.00
Common Player:		13.50	6.75	4.00
1-1	Al Rosen	16.00	8.00	5.00
1-2	Bob Lemon	20.00	10.00	6.00
1-3	Phil Rizzuto	50.00	25.00	15.00
1-4	Hank Bauer	16.00	8.00	5.00
1-5	Billy Johnson	13.50	6.75	4.00
1-6	Jerry Coleman	13.50	6.75	4.00
1-7	Johnny Mize	25.00	12.50	7.50
1-8	Dom DiMaggio	20.00	10.00	6.00
1-9	Richie Ashburn	30.00	15.00	9.00
1-10	Del Ennis	13.50	6.75	4.00
2-1	Stan Musial	150.00	75.00	45.00
2-2	Warren Spahn	25.00	12.50	7.50
2-3	Tommy Henrich	16.00	8.00	5.00
2-4	Larry "Yogi" Berra	100.00	50.00	30.00
2-5	Joe DiMaggio	300.00	150.00	90.00
2-6	Bobby Brown	13.50	6.75	4.00
2-7	Granville Hamner	13.50	6.75	4.00
2-8	Willie Jones	13.50	6.75	4.00
2-9	Stanley Lopata	13.50	6.75	4.00
2-10	Mike Goliat	13.50	6.75	4.00
3-1	Ralph Kiner	20.00	10.00	6.00

		NM	E	VG
3-2	Billy Goodman	13.50	6.75	4.00
3-3	Allie Reynolds	16.00	8.00	5.00
3-4	Vic Raschi	16.00	8.00	5.00
3-5	Joe Page	13.50	6.75	4.00
3-6	Eddie Lopat	13.50	6.75	4.00
3-7	Andy Seminick	13.50	6.75	4.00
3-8	Dick Sisler	13.50	6.75	4.00
3-9	Eddie Waitkus	13.50	6.75	4.00
3-10	Ken Heintzelman	13.50	6.75	4.00
4-1	Gene Woodling	16.00	8.00	5.00
4-2	Cliff Mapes	13.50	6.75	4.00
4-3	Fred Sanford	13.50	6.75	4.00
4-4	Tommy Byrne	13.50	6.75	4.00
4-5	Eddie (Whitey) Ford	180.00	90.00	55.00
4-6	Jim Konstanty	13.50	6.75	4.00
4-7	Russ Meyer	13.50	6.75	4.00
4-8	Robin Roberts	20.00	10.00	6.00
4-9	Curt Simmons	13.50	6.75	4.00
4-10	Sam Jethroe	13.50	6.75	4.00

1952 Berk Ross

Although the card size is different (2" x 3"), the style of the fronts and backs of the 1952 Berk Ross set is similar to the previous year's effort. Seventy-two unnumbered cards make up the set. Rizzuto is included twice in the set and the Blackwell and Fox cards have transposed backs. The cards were issued individually rather than as two-card panels like in 1951.

		NM	E	VG
Complete Set (72):		5,000	2,500	1,500
Common Player:		25.00	12.50	7.50
(1)	Richie Ashburn	50.00	25.00	15.00
(2)	Hank Bauer	30.00	15.00	9.00
(3)	Larry "Yogi" Berra	175.00	85.00	50.00
(4)	Ewell Blackwell (Photo actually Nelson Fox.)	75.00	37.50	22.50
(5)	Bobby Brown	25.00	12.50	7.50
(6)	Jim Busby	25.00	12.50	7.50
(7)	Roy Campanella	140.00	70.00	40.00
(8)	Chico Carrasquel	25.00	12.50	7.50
(9)	Jerry Coleman	25.00	12.50	7.50
(10)	Joe Collins	25.00	12.50	7.50
(11)	Alvin Dark	25.00	12.50	7.50
(12)	Dom DiMaggio	35.00	17.50	10.00
(13)	Joe DiMaggio	400.00	200.00	120.00
(14)	Larry Doby	40.00	20.00	12.00
(15)	Bobby Doerr	40.00	20.00	12.00
(16)	Bob Elliot (Elliott)	25.00	12.50	7.50
(17)	Del Ennis	25.00	12.50	7.50
(18)	Ferris Fain	25.00	12.50	7.50
(19)	Bob Feller	100.00	50.00	30.00
(20)	Nelson Fox (Photo actually Ewell Blackwell.)	125.00	60.00	35.00
(21)	Ned Garver	25.00	12.50	7.50
(22)	Clint Hartung	25.00	12.50	7.50
(23)	Jim Hearn	25.00	12.50	7.50
(24)	Gil Hodges	75.00	37.50	22.50
(25)	Monte Irvin	40.00	20.00	12.00
(26)	Larry Jansen	25.00	12.50	7.50
(27)	George Kell	40.00	20.00	12.00
(28)	Sheldon Jones	25.00	12.50	7.50
(29)	Monte Kennedy	25.00	12.50	7.50
(30)	Ralph Kiner	40.00	20.00	12.00
(31)	Dave Koslo	25.00	12.50	7.50
(32)	Bob Kuzava	25.00	12.50	7.50

		NM	E	VG
(33)	Bob Lemon	40.00	20.00	12.00
(34)	Whitey Lockman	25.00	12.50	7.50
(35)	Eddie Lopat	25.00	12.50	7.50
(36)	Sal Maglie	25.00	12.50	7.50
(37)	Mickey Mantle	2,000	1,000	500.00
(38)	Billy Martin	90.00	45.00	27.50
(39)	Willie Mays	500.00	250.00	150.00
(40)	Gil McDougal (McDougald)	30.00	15.00	9.00
(41)	Orestes Minoso	30.00	15.00	9.00
(42)	Johnny Mize	50.00	25.00	15.00
(43)	Tom Morgan	25.00	12.50	7.50
(44)	Don Mueller	25.00	12.50	7.50
(45)	Stan Musial	250.00	125.00	75.00
(46)	Don Newcombe	35.00	17.50	10.00
(47)	Ray Noble	25.00	12.50	7.50
(48)	Joe Ostrowski	25.00	12.50	7.50
(49)	Mel Parnell	25.00	12.50	7.50
(50)	Vic Raschi	25.00	12.50	7.50
(51)	Pee Wee Reese	125.00	65.00	35.00
(52)	Allie Reynolds	30.00	15.00	9.00
(53)	Bill Rigney	25.00	12.50	7.50
(54)	Phil Rizzuto (Bunting)	90.00	45.00	27.00
(55)	Phil Rizzuto (Swinging)	200.00	100.00	60.00
(56)	Robin Roberts	40.00	20.00	12.00
(57)	Eddie Robinson	25.00	12.50	7.50
(58)	Jackie Robinson	325.00	160.00	100.00
(59)	Elwin "Preacher" Roe	25.00	12.50	7.50
(60)	Johnny Sain	30.00	15.00	9.00
(61)	Albert "Red" Schoendienst	40.00	20.00	12.00
(62)	Duke Snider	140.00	70.00	40.00
(63)	George Spencer	25.00	12.50	7.50
(64)	Eddie Stanky	25.00	12.50	7.50
(65)	Henry Thompson	25.00	12.50	7.50
(66)	Bobby Thomson	30.00	15.00	9.00
(67)	Vic Wertz	25.00	12.50	7.50
(68)	Waldon Westlake	25.00	12.50	7.50
(69)	Wes Westrum	25.00	12.50	7.50
(70)	Ted Williams	450.00	225.00	135.00
(71)	Gene Woodling	30.00	15.00	9.00
(72)	Gus Zernial	25.00	12.50	7.50

1916 BF2 Felt Pennants

Issued circa 1916, this unnumbered set consists of 97 felt pennants with a small black-and-white player photo glued to each. The triangular pennants measure approximately 2-7/8" across the top and taper to a length of about 5-3/4" long, while the collins are 1-3/4" x 1-1/4" and appear to be identical to photos used for M101-4/M101-5 issues of the same period. The pennants list the player's name and team. The pennants were given away as premiums with the purchase of five-cent loaves of Ferguson Bakery bread in the Roxbury, Mass., area.

(See 1916 Ferguson Bakery Felt Pennants for checklist and values.)

1936-37 BF3 Felt Player/Team Pennants

The checklists for these series of felt pennants issued circa 1936-1938 are not complete, and new examples are still being reported. The pennants do not carry any manufacturer's name although packages found with various pieces attribute the issues to Red Ball Sales, a gum company in Chicago, and Grandpa Brands Co., Cincinnati, another gum company. One pennant was given away with the purchase of a stick of gum, and at least one wrapper indicates large format (28" x 12") versions of the Red Ball pennants could be had in a redemption program. The pennants vary in size slightly but generally measure approximately 2-1/2" x 4-1/2" and were issued in various styles and colors. Most of the printing is white, although some pennants have been found with other colors of printing, and the same pennant is often found in more than one color combination. The pennants feature both individual players and teams, including some minor league clubs. The pennants were grouped together in the American Card Catalog under the designation of BF3. Advanced collectors have categorized the pennants into a number of basic design types, depending on what elements are included on the pennant. The unnumbered felts are listed alphabetically within type. Gaps have been left in the assigned numbers to accommodate future discoveries.

	NM	E	VG
Common Pennant:	25.00	12.50	7.50

1937 BF104 Blankets

A throwback to the 1914 B18 blankets, little is known about these 3-1/2"-square felts. They were designated as BF104 in the American Card Catalog. The issuer and manner of distribution remain a mystery. Subjects are depicted in either portrait or action artwork. This checklist likely is not complete.

		NM	E	VG
Common Player:		300.00	150.00	90.00
(1)	Moe Berg	500.00	250.00	150.00
(2)	Cy Blanton	300.00	150.00	90.00
(3)	Earle Brucker	300.00	150.00	90.00
(4)	Mickey Cochrane	600.00	300.00	180.00
(5)	Joe Cronin	600.00	300.00	180.00
(6)	Tony Cuccinello	300.00	150.00	90.00
(7)	Dizzy Dean	1,200	600.00	360.00
(8)	Frank Demaree	300.00	150.00	90.00
(9)	Jimmie Foxx	900.00	450.00	275.00
(10)	Larry French	300.00	150.00	90.00
(11)	Frankie Frisch	600.00	300.00	180.00
(12)	Hank Greenberg	1,000	500.00	300.00
(13)	Hank Greenberg	1,000	500.00	300.00
(14)	Gabby Hartnett	600.00	300.00	180.00
(15)	Billy Herman	600.00	300.00	180.00
(16)	Woody Jensen	300.00	150.00	90.00
(17)	Billy Jurges	300.00	150.00	90.00
(18)	Harry Kelly (Kelley)	300.00	150.00	90.00
(19)	Thornton Lee	300.00	150.00	90.00
(20)	Danny MacFayden	300.00	150.00	90.00
(21)	Connie Mack	600.00	300.00	180.00
(22)	Stu Martin	300.00	150.00	90.00
(23)	Joe Medwick	600.00	300.00	180.00
(24)	Ray Mueller	300.00	150.00	90.00
(25)	L. Newsome	300.00	150.00	90.00
(26)	L. Newsome	300.00	150.00	90.00
(27)	Monty Stratton	405.00	200.00	120.00
(28)	Pie Traynor	600.00	300.00	180.00
(29)	Jim Turner	300.00	150.00	90.00
(30)	Bill Werber	300.00	150.00	90.00
(31)	Jack Wilson	300.00	150.00	90.00
(32)	Rudy York	300.00	150.00	90.00

1956 Big League Stars Statues

While the plastic statues in this set are virtually identical to the set issued in 1955 by Dairy Queen, the packaging of the Big League Stars statues on a card with all the usual elements of a baseball card makes them more collectible. The DQ versions of the statues are white, while the Big League versions are bronze colored. The statues measure about 3" tall and were sold in a 4" x 5" cardboard and plastic blister pack for about 19 cents. Complete league sets were also sold in a large package. The singles package features the player's name in a large banner near the top with his team printed below and line drawings of ballplayers in action around the statue. Backs have a player portrait photo with facsimile autograph, position, team, previous year and career stats and a career summary. A perforated tab at bottom can be pulled out to make a stand for the display. Most packages are found with the hole at top punched out to allow for hanging on a hook. Besides singles, larger packages of nine National or American league statues were also sold in a window-box. The set is checklisted alphabetically.

		NM	E	VG
Complete Set (18):		5,200	2,600	1,500
Common Player:		60.00	30.00	18.00

UNOPENED PACKAGED STATUES

(1)	John Antonelli	220.00	110.00	65.00
(2)	Bob Avila	220.00	110.00	65.00
(3)	Yogi Berra	675.00	340.00	200.00
(4)	Roy Campanella	675.00	340.00	200.00
(5)	Larry Doby	300.00	150.00	100.00
(6)	Del Ennis	220.00	110.00	65.00
(7)	Jim Gilliam	250.00	125.00	75.00
(8)	Gil Hodges	675.00	340.00	200.00
(9)	Harvey Kuenn	220.00	110.00	65.00
(10)	Bob Lemon	250.00	125.00	75.00
(11)	Mickey Mantle	3,400	1,700	1,000
(12)	Ed Mathews	500.00	250.00	150.00
(13)	Minnie Minoso	220.00	110.00	65.00
(14)	Stan Musial	1,000	500.00	300.00
(15)	Pee Wee Reese	675.00	340.00	200.00
(16)	Al Rosen	220.00	110.00	65.00
(17)	Duke Snider	675.00	340.00	200.00
(18a)	Mickey Vernon (Senators)	220.00	110.00	65.00
(18b)	Mickey Vernon (Red Sox)	220.00	110.00	65.00

STATUES

(1)	John Antonelli	40.00	20.00	12.00
(2)	Bob Avila	40.00	20.00	12.00
(3)	Yogi Berra	150.00	75.00	45.00
(4)	Roy Campanella	150.00	75.00	45.00
(5)	Larry Doby	60.00	30.00	18.00
(6)	Del Ennis	40.00	20.00	12.00
(7)	Jim Gilliam	50.00	25.00	15.00
(8)	Gil Hodges	125.00	62.00	37.00
(9)	Harvey Kuenn	40.00	20.00	12.00
(10)	Bob Lemon	60.00	30.00	18.00
(11)	Mickey Mantle	300.00	150.00	90.00
(12)	Ed Mathews	100.00	50.00	30.00
(13)	Minnie Minoso	50.00	25.00	15.00
(14)	Stan Musial	200.00	100.00	60.00
(15)	Pee Wee Reese	150.00	75.00	45.00
(16)	Al Rosen	45.00	22.00	13.50
(17)	Duke Snider	150.00	75.00	45.00
(18)	Mickey Vernon (Senators)	40.00	20.00	12.00
(18b)	Mickey Vernon (Red Sox)	220.00	110.00	65.00

PACKAGE/CARD ONLY

(1)	John Antonelli	75.00	37.50	23.00
(2)	Bob Avila	75.00	37.50	23.00
(3)	Yogi Berra	225.00	115.00	70.00
(4)	Roy Campanella	225.00	115.00	70.00
(5)	Larry Doby	75.00	37.50	22.00
(6)	Del Ennis	75.00	37.50	23.00
(7)	Jim Gilliam	65.00	32.50	20.00
(8)	Gil Hodges	125.00	65.00	39.00
(9)	Harvey Kuenn	75.00	37.50	23.00
(10)	Bob Lemon	75.00	37.50	22.00
(11)	Mickey Mantle	1,800	900.00	540.00
(12)	Ed Mathews	125.00	62.50	37.50
(13)	Minnie Minoso	75.00	37.50	22.00
(14)	Stan Musial	265.00	130.00	80.00
(15)	Pee Wee Reese	225.00	115.00	70.00
(16)	Al Rosen	75.00	37.50	23.00
(17)	Duke Snider	225.00	115.00	70.00
(18a)	Mickey Vernon (Senators)	75.00	37.50	23.00
(18)	Mickey Vernon	75.00	37.50	23.00
(18a)	Mickey Vernon (White Sox)	75.00	37.50	23.00

1978 Big T/Tastee Freeze Discs

One player from each major league team was selected for inclusion in this discs set distributed by Big T family restaurants and Tastee Freeze stands in North Carolina, and possibly other parts of the country. The 3-3/8" diameter discs have a sepia-toned player portrait photo at center within a white diamond and surrounded by a brightly colored border with four colored stars at top. Licensed by the Players Association through Michael Schecter Associates, the photos have had

uniform logos removed. Backs are printed in red, white and blue and have the sponsor's logos and a line of 1977 stats, along with a card number.

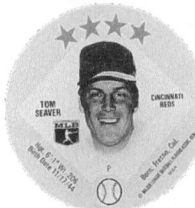 

		NM	E	VG
Complete Set (26):		30.00	15.00	9.00
Common Player:		2.00	1.00	.60

1	Buddy Bell	2.00	1.00	.60
2	Jim Palmer	8.00	4.00	2.50
3	Steve Garvey	5.00	2.50	1.50
4	Jeff Burroughs	2.00	1.00	.60
5	Greg Luzinski	2.00	1.00	.60
6	Lou Brock	8.00	4.00	2.50
7	Thurman Munson	5.00	2.50	1.50
8	Rod Carew	8.00	4.00	2.50
9	George Brett	20.00	10.00	6.00
10	Tom Seaver	15.00	7.50	4.50
11	Willie Stargell	8.00	4.00	2.50
12	Jerry Koosman	2.00	1.00	.60
13	Bill North	2.00	1.00	.60
14	Richie Zisk	2.00	1.00	.60
15	Bill Madlock	2.00	1.00	.60
16	Carl Yastrzemski	15.00	7.50	4.50
17	Dave Cash	2.00	1.00	.60
18	Bob Watson	2.00	1.00	.60
19	Dave Kingman	2.00	1.00	.60
20	Gene Tenace	2.00	1.00	.60
21	Ralph Garr	2.00	1.00	.60
22	Mark Fidrych	4.00	2.00	1.25
23	Frank Tanana	2.00	1.00	.60
24	Larry Hisle	2.00	1.00	.60
25	Bruce Bochte	2.00	1.00	.60
26	Bob Bailor	2.00	1.00	.60

1955-60 Bill and Bob Braves Postcards

One of the most popular and scarce of the 1950s color postcard series is the run of Milwaukee Braves known as "Bill and Bobs." While some of the cards do carry a photo credit acknowledging the pair, and a few add a Bradenton, Fla., (spring training home of the Braves) address, little else is known about the issuer. The cards themselves appear to have been purchased by the players to honor photo and autograph requests. Several of the cards carry facsimile autographs pre-printed on the front. The cards feature crisp full-color photos on their borderless fronts. Postcard backs have a variety of printing including card numbers, photo credits, a Kodachrome logo and player name. Some cards are found with some of those elements, some with none. There is some question whether Frank Torre's card is actually a Bill and Bob product, because it is 1/16" narrower than the standard 3-1/2" x 5-1/2" format of the other cards, features the player with a Pepsi bottle in his hand and is rubber-stamped on back with a Pepsi bottler's address. The Torre card is usually collected with the rest of the set.

		NM	E	VG
Complete Set (20):		4,600	2,300	1,350
Common Player:		100.00	50.00	30.00

(1)	Hank Aaron	1,200	600.00	360.00
(2)	Joe Adcock (Fielding)	185.00	90.00	55.00
(3)	Joe Adcock (Bat on shoulder.)	185.00	90.00	55.00
(4)	Joe Adcock (Kneeling with two bats.)	145.00	75.00	45.00
(5)	Billy Bruton (Kneeling)	185.00	90.00	55.00
(6)	Billy Bruton (Throwing)	250.00	125.00	75.00
(7)	Bob Buhl	100.00	50.00	30.00
(8)	Lou Burdette	100.00	50.00	30.00
(9)	Gene Conley	100.00	50.00	30.00
(10)	Wes Covington (Kneeling, one bat.)	145.00	75.00	45.00
(11)	Wes Covington (Kneeling, seven bats.)	145.00	75.00	45.00
(12)	Del Crandall (Kneeling, one bat.)	135.00	65.00	40.00
(13)	Del Crandall (Kneeling, two bats.)	135.00	65.00	40.00
(14)	Chuck Dressen	145.00	75.00	45.00
(15)	Charlie Grimm	245.00	120.00	75.00
(16)	Fred Haney	235.00	115.00	70.00
(17)	Bob Keely	185.00	90.00	55.00
(18)	Eddie Mathews	400.00	200.00	120.00
(19)	Warren Spahn	500.00	250.00	150.00
(20)	Frank Torre	245.00	120.00	75.00

1923-24 Billiken

 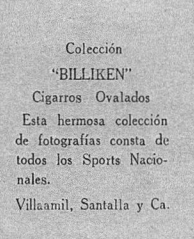

Apparently issued as a premium with its Billiken brand cigars, these cards were issued by Villaamil, Santalla y Ca. About 2" x 2-5/8", the cards have black-and-white posed photos surrounded with a white border. Below the picture the player's last name and team are presented in typewriter style. Among the scarcest and most popular of the pre-war Cuban issues, the set features many players from the Negro Leagues. Counterfeits are known.

		NM	E	VG
Common Player:		800.00	325.00	160.00

ALMENDARES

(1)	Bernardo Baro	1,200	480.00	240.00
(2)	Manuel Cueto	900.00	360.00	180.00
(3)	Valentin Dreke	1,200	480.00	240.00
(4)	Isidro Fabre	900.00	360.00	180.00
(5)	Jose Maria Fernandez	900.00	360.00	180.00
(6)	Oscar Fuhr	800.00	325.00	160.00
(7)	Bienvenido "Hooks" Gimenez (Jimenez)	1,200	480.00	240.00
(8)	"Snake" Henry (Henry)	1,000	400.00	200.00
(9)	Ramon "Mike" Herrera	800.00	325.00	160.00
(10)	Jesse Hubbard	1,500	600.00	300.00
(11)	Armando Marsans	1,800	720.00	360.00
(12)	Jackie May (Jakie)	900.00	360.00	180.00
(13)	Eugenio Morin	800.00	325.00	160.00
(14)	Joseito Rodriguez	800.00	325.00	160.00
(15)	Nip Winters	2,000	800.00	400.00

HABANA

(16)	Eufemio Abreu	900.00	360.00	180.00
(17)	John Bischoff	800.00	325.00	160.00
(18)	Clark	800.00	325.00	160.00
(19)	Andy Cooper	5,000	2,000	1,000
(20)	Mack Eglefton (Eggleston)	1,300	520.00	260.00
(21)	Bienvenido "Hooks" Gimenez (Jimenez)	1,200	480.00	240.00
(22)	Marcelino Guerra	800.00	325.00	160.00
(23)	Oscar Levis	900.00	360.00	180.00
(24)	John Henry "Pop" Lloid (Lloyd)	19,500	9,750	5,850
(25)	Juanelo Mirabal	900.00	360.00	180.00
(26)	Bartolo Portuando (Portuondo)	1,200	480.00	240.00
(27)	Raphael "Busta" Quintana	800.00	325.00	160.00
(28)	Buster Ross	800.00	325.00	160.00
(29)	Clint Thomas	1,500	600.00	300.00
(30)	Edgar Westley (Wesley)	1,500	600.00	300.00

MARIANAO

(31)	Merito Acosta	800.00	325.00	160.00
(32)	Jose Acostica	800.00	325.00	160.00
(33)	D. Brown	800.00	325.00	160.00
(34)	E. Brown	800.00	325.00	160.00
(35)	Rogelio Crespo	800.00	325.00	160.00
(36)	Harry Deberry	800.00	325.00	160.00
(37)	Charlie Dressen	900.00	360.00	180.00
(38)	Freddie Fitzsmann (Fitzsimmons)	800.00	325.00	160.00
(39)	Griffin	800.00	325.00	160.00

		NM	E	VG
(40)	Ernie Krueger	800.00	325.00	160.00
(41)	Slim Love	800.00	325.00	160.00
(42)	Jose "Pepin" Perez	800.00	325.00	160.00
(43)	Rgal (Rigal)	800.00	325.00	160.00
(44)	Hank Sceiber (Schreiber)	800.00	325.00	160.00
(45)	Cristobal Torriente	19,500	9,750	5,850
	SANTA CLARA			
(46)	Oscar Charleston	19,500	9,750	5,850
(47)	Rube Currie	1,500	600.00	300.00
(48)	Pedro Dibut	900.00	360.00	180.00
(49)	Eddie Douglas (Douglass)	1,500	600.00	300.00
(50)	Frank Duncan	1,500	600.00	300.00
(51)	Oliver Marcell (Marcelle)	5,000	2,000	1,000
(52)	Mayari (Esteban Montalvo)	900.00	360.00	180.00
(53)	Jose Mendez	6,000	2,400	1,200
(54)	Augustin "Tinti" Molina	800.00	325.00	160.00
(55)	Dobie Moore	1,500	600.00	300.00
(56)	Alejandro Oms	2,000	800.00	400.00
(57)	Herman Rios	900.00	360.00	180.00
(58)	Julio Rojo	900.00	360.00	180.00
(59)	Red Ryan	1,200	480.00	240.00
(60)	Frank Wardfield (Warfield)	1,500	600.00	300.00

1916 Block and Kuhl Co.

 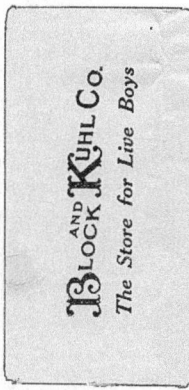

Best known for its use as a promotional medium for The Sporting News, this 200-card set can be found with ads on the back for several local and regional businesses. Among them is the Block and Kuhl department store, Peoria, Ill. Type card and superstar collectors can expect to pay a significant premium for individual cards with Block and Kuhl's advertising. The checklist is believed to generally parallel the 1916 M101-4 Blank Backs. Cards measure 1-5/8" x 3" and are printed in black-and-white.

(See 1916 M101-4 Blank Backs for checklist.)

1911 Blome's Chocolates (E94)

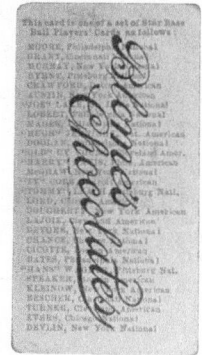

Advertising for Blome's Chocolates overprinted in purple on the back of these cards is one of several brands produced bu George Close Candy Co. Type collectors will pay a premium of up to 5-7X for a Blome's version as opposed to the generic Close Candy version of the same player.

(See 1911 George Close Candy Co. for checklist and base card values.)

1933 Blue Bird Babe Ruth

A small hoard of the (a) cards appeared in the market in early 1994 making available a card which had previously been virtually unknown. Printed in black-and-white on thin card stock, the piece measures 3-7/8" x 5-7/8". The photo on front was used in modified form on several other early-1930s issues. The back offers balls and gloves available for redemption with soft drink bottle caps and cash. The discovery of the (b) version came in 1999.

		NM	E	VG
(1a)	Babe Ruth (Batting follow-through, front view.)	2,000	1,000	600.00
(1b)	Babe Ruth (Batting follow-through, side view.)	7,500	3,700	2,200

1930 Blue Ribbon Malt Chicago Cubs

These player pictures were originally printed on a 40" x 12" advertising piece by Blue Ribbon Malt. The black-and-white pictures have facsimile autographs on front and measure 3-1/2" high by 1-7/16" to 3" wide.

		NM	E	VG
	Complete Uncut Sheet:	500.00	250.00	150.00
(1)	Clyde Beck			
(2)	Lester Bell			
(3)	Clarence Blair			
(4)	Fred Blake			
(5)	Jimmie Burke			
(6)	Guy Bush			
(7)	Hazen "Kiki" Cuyler			
(8)	Woody English			
(9)	Eddie Farrell			
(10)	Charlie Grimm			
(11)	Leo "Gabby" Hartnett			
(12)	Clift Heathcote			
(13)	Rogers Hornsby			
(14)	George L. Kelly			
(15)	Pierce "Pat" Malone			
(16)	Joe McCarthy			
(17)	Lynn Nelson			
(18)	Bob Osborn			
(19)	Jess Petty			
(20)	Charlie Root			
(21)	Ray Schalk			
(22)	John Schulte			
(23)	Al Shealy			
(24)	Riggs Stephenson			
(25)	Dan Taylor			
(26)	Zack Taylor			
(27)	Bud Teachout			
(28)	Lewis "Hack" Wilson			

1930 Blue Ribbon Malt Chicago White Sox

These player pictures were originally printed on a 40" x 12" advertising piece by Blue Ribbon Malt. However, if cut from the piece, there is no identification of the issuer. The black-and-white pictures have facsimile autographs on front and measure 3-1/2" high by 1-7/16" to 2-7/8" wide.

		NM	E	VG
	Complete Uncut Sheet:	1,000	500.00	300.00
(1)	"Chick" Autry			
(2)	"Red" Barnes			
(3)	Moe Berg			
(4)	Garland Braxton			

(5)	Donie Bush
(6)	Pat Caraway
(7)	Bill Cissell
(8)	"Bud" Clancy
(9)	Clyde Crouse
(10)	U.C. Faber
(11)	Bob Fothergill
(12)	Frank J. "Dutch" Henry
(13)	Smead Jolley
(14)	Bill "Willie" Kamm
(15)	Bernard "Mike" Kelly
(16)	Johnny Kerr
(17)	Ted Lyons
(18)	Harold McKain
(19)	"Jim" Moore
(20)	"Greg" Mulleavy
(21)	Carl N. Reynolds
(22)	Blondy Ryan
(23)	"Benny" Tate
(24)	Tommy Thomas
(25)	Ed Walsh, Jr.
(26)	Johnny Watwood
(27)	Bob Weiland

1930 Blue Ribbon Malt Premiums

The manner of distribution for this series is unknown. And, while the name of the sponsor does not appear, the similarity to other Blue Ribbon Malt issues pinpoints their source. The premiums are a 5" x 7" black-and-white photo (sometimes, but not always, mounted on a heavy gray cardboard 6-1/4" x 8-3/4" backing). A facsimile autograph is on the photo. This incomplete checklist is presented alphabetically by team.

		NM	E	VG
	Common Player:	225.00	110.00	65.00
	CHICAGO CUBS			
(1)	Clyde Beck	225.00	110.00	65.00
(2)	Lester Bell	225.00	110.00	65.00
(3)	Clarence Blair	225.00	110.00	65.00
(4)	Fred Blake	225.00	110.00	65.00
(5)	Jimmy Burke	225.00	110.00	65.00
(6)	Guy Bush	225.00	110.00	65.00
(7)	Hal Carlson	225.00	110.00	65.00
(8)	Hazen "Kiki" Cuyler	300.00	150.00	90.00
(9)	Woody English	225.00	110.00	65.00
(10)	Charlie Grimm	225.00	110.00	65.00
(11)	Leo "Gabby" Hartnett	300.00	150.00	90.00
(12)	Cliff Heathcote	225.00	110.00	65.00
(13)	Rogers Hornsby	800.00	400.00	240.00
(14)	Perce "Pat" Malone	225.00	110.00	65.00
(15)	Joe McCarthy	275.00	135.00	80.00
(16)	Malcolm Moss	225.00	110.00	65.00
(17)	Lynn Nelson	225.00	110.00	65.00
(18)	Bob Osborn	225.00	110.00	65.00
(19)	Charles Root	225.00	110.00	65.00
(20)	Ray Schalk	275.00	135.00	80.00
(21)	John Schulte	225.00	110.00	65.00
(22)	Al Shealy	225.00	110.00	65.00
(23)	Riggs Stephenson	225.00	110.00	65.00
(24)	Dan Taylor	225.00	110.00	65.00
(25)	Zack Taylor	225.00	110.00	65.00
(26)	Chas. J. Tolson	225.00	110.00	65.00
(27)	Hal Totten (Announcer)	225.00	110.00	65.00
(28)	Lewis "Hack" Wilson	350.00	175.00	105.00
	CHICAGO WHITE SOX			
(1)	Donie Bush	225.00	110.00	65.00
(2)	Bill Cissell	225.00	110.00	65.00
(4)	Red Faber	275.00	135.00	85.00
(5)	Smead Jolley	225.00	110.00	65.00
(7)	Willie Kamm	225.00	110.00	65.00
(9)	Ted Lyons	275.00	135.00	85.00
(11)	Carl Reynolds	225.00	110.00	65.00
(13)	Art Shires	225.00	110.00	65.00
(15)	Tommy Thomas	225.00	110.00	65.00
(16)	Johnny Watwood	225.00	110.00	65.00

1931 Blue Ribbon Malt

Players of the Chicago Cubs and White Sox are featured in this series of 4-7/8" x 6-7/8" black-and-white photos. Each blank-backed photo is bordered in white with "Compliments of BLUE RIBBON MALT-America's Biggest Seller" printed in the bottom border and a facsimile autograph across the photo. It is likely players other than those listed here were also issued.

	NM	E	VG
Common Player:	90.00	45.00	27.00
(1) Lu Blue	90.00	45.00	27.00
(2) Lew Fonseca	90.00	45.00	27.00
(3) Vic Frazier	90.00	45.00	27.00
(4) John Kerr	90.00	45.00	27.00
(5) Bob Smith	90.00	45.00	27.00
(6) Billy Sullivan	90.00	45.00	27.00
(7) Lewis "Hack" Wilson	125.00	62.00	37.00

1931 Blum's Baseball Bulletin Premiums

The year of issue presented is speculative, based on biographical information on the specimens seen thus far. This series of 9-1/2" x 13-5/8" (Small) or 11-1/2" x 13-3/4" (Large) pictures was printed on premium stock with black-and-white pictures and text bordered in red or green baseballs. A credit line at bottom says the series was "Compiled by Fred J. Blum, Publisher, Blum's Baseball Bulletin." The number of players with a connection to Rochester, N.Y., indicates Blum's firm must have been located there. The checklist here is likely incomplete.

	NM	E	VG
Common Player:	200.00	100.00	60.00
(1) Edward T. Collins (S)	300.00	150.00	90.00
(2) Jacob E. Daubert (S)	200.00	100.00	60.00
(3) William E. Donovan (L)	200.00	100.00	60.00
(4) John J. Evers (S)	300.00	150.00	90.00
(5) Lou Gehrig (L)	350.00	175.00	105.00
(6) Henry K. Groh (L)	200.00	100.00	60.00
(7) Lefty Grove (L)	400.00	200.00	120.00
(8) Walter Johnson (S)	500.00	250.00	150.00
(9) Napoleon Lajoie (S)	350.00	175.00	105.00
(10) Walter J.V. Maranville (S)	300.00	150.00	90.00
(11) James (Wicky) McAvoy (L)	200.00	100.00	60.00
(12) Rochester 1911 (Team composite.) (L)	200.00	100.00	60.00
(13) William H. Southworth (L)	300.00	150.00	90.00
(14) Tristam Speaker (S)	475.00	240.00	140.00
(15) George Toporcer (L)	200.00	100.00	60.00
(16) Arthur C. (Dazzy) Vance	400.00	200.00	120.00

1961-1963 Bobbin' Head Dolls

Some of the top stars of the day were caricatured in the first generation of bobbin' head dolls. Additionally, Mantle and Maris were depicted in a pair of color 5" x 7" advertising photos depicting the home run heroes of 1961 holding their dolls. The players are pictured in belt-to-cap photos wearing road uniforms and posed in a stadium setting. Backs are blank.

	NM	E	VG
	500.00	250.00	150.00
Roberto Clemente (Picture box.)	1,000	500.00	300.00
Mickey Mantle (Ad photo.)	650.00	325.00	195.00
Mickey Mantle (Large or small picture box.)	750.00	375.00	225.00
Roger Maris (Ad photo.)	325.00	160.00	97.5
Roger Maris (Large or small picture box.)	900.00	450.00	275.00

1947 Bond Bread

Tommy Holmes

These cards were issued as singles by "Homogenized" Bond Bread in 1947, but had their origins in 12-card boxed sets printed by Aarco Playing Card Co., Chicago, and sold as "Collectors & Traders Sports Stars Subjects." The Bond Bread cards are in the original format of 2-1/4" x 3-3/8" black-and-white cards printed on round-cornered blank-backed stock. The borderless fronts have portraits or posed action photos with the player name in facsimile autograph or script typography. At some point after the original Bond Bread issue, half of the cards were reprinted in a square-cornered 2-1/4" x 3-1/2" size on slightly different stock, for purposes unknown. A large quantity of these 24 cards was found in a New York warehouse in the 1980s. To complicate the situation, the square-cornered cards were illegally counterfeited sometime after 2000, often sold in high-graded slabs by fraudulent grading companies. The issue was designated in the American Card Catalog as W571/D305.

	NM	E	VG
Complete Set (48):	1,600	800.00	475.00
Common Player:	15.00	7.50	4.50
(1) Rex Barney (SP)	20.00	10.00	6.00
(2) Yogi Berra (SP)	75.00	37.50	22.50
(3) Ewell Blackwell	15.00	7.50	4.50
(4) Lou Boudreau	20.00	10.00	6.00
(5) Ralph Branca (SP)	20.00	10.00	6.00
(6) Harry Brecheen	15.00	7.50	4.50
(7) Dom DiMaggio (SP)	50.00	25.00	15.00
(8) Joe DiMaggio (SP)	275.00	135.00	85.00
(9) Bobbie Doerr (Bobby)	20.00	10.00	6.00
(10) Bruce Edwards (SP)	20.00	10.00	6.00
(11) Bob Elliott	15.00	7.50	4.50
(12) Del Ennis	15.00	7.50	4.50
(13) Bob Feller	25.00	12.50	7.50
(14) Carl Furillo (SP)	35.00	17.50	10.00
(15) Cid Gordon (Sid)(SP)	20.00	10.00	6.00
(16) Joe Gordon	15.00	7.50	4.50
(17) Joe Hatten (SP)	20.00	10.00	6.00
(18) Gil Hodges (SP)	75.00	37.50	22.50
(19) Tommy Holmes	15.00	7.50	4.50
(20) Larry Janson (Jansen) (SP)	20.00	10.00	6.00
(21) Sheldon Jones (SP)	20.00	10.00	6.00
(22) Edwin Joost (SP)	20.00	10.00	6.00
(23) Charlie Keller (SP)	20.00	10.00	6.00
(24) Ken Keltner	15.00	7.50	4.50
(25) Buddy Kerr (SP)	20.00	10.00	6.00
(26) Ralph Kiner	20.00	10.00	6.00
(27) John Lindell (SP)	20.00	10.00	6.00
(28) Whitey Lockman (SP)	20.00	10.00	6.00
(29) Willard Marshall (SP)	20.00	10.00	6.00
(30) Johnny Mize	20.00	10.00	6.00
(31) Stan Musial	60.00	30.00	18.00
(32) Andy Pafko	15.00	7.50	4.50
(33) Johnny Pesky	15.00	7.50	4.50
(34) Pee Wee Reese (SP)	125.00	65.00	35.00
(35) Phil Rizzuto	30.00	15.00	9.00
(36) Aaron Robinson	15.00	7.50	4.50
(37) Jackie Robinson	90.00	45.00	27.50
(38) John Sain	15.00	7.50	4.50
(39) Enos Slaughter	20.00	10.00	6.00
(40) Vern Stephens	15.00	7.50	4.50
(41) George Tebbetts (SP)	20.00	10.00	6.00
(42) Bob Thomson (SP)	25.00	12.50	7.50
(43) Johnny Vandermeer (VanderMeer) (SP)	20.00	10.00	6.00
(44) Ted Williams	90.00	45.00	27.00
BOXERS			
(45) Primo Carnera	15.00	7.50	4.50
(46) Marcel Cerdan (SP)	40.00	20.00	12.00
(47) Jake LaMotta (SP)	60.00	30.00	18.00
(48) Joe Louis	30.00	15.00	9.00

1947 Bond Bread Exhibits

Walker Cooper

The manner of distribution of these variants of the "Bond Bread" (W571 / D305) baseball cards is believed to have been via penny arcade dispensers. The cards can be found in two sizes, about 3-3/8" x 5-3/8" (nearly the same as contemporary Exhibit Supply Co. cards), and about 3" x 5". Over 75 percent of the baseball players known in the base Bond Bread set have been reported in this format, plus one player, Walker Cooper, not in the base set. The four W571/D305 boxers have not yet been reported in this format.

	NM	E	VG
Complete Set (33):	1,250	625.00	375.00
Common Player:	25.00	12.50	7.50
(1) Rex Barney			
(2) Yogi Berra			
(3) Ewell Blackwell	25.00	12.50	7.50
(4) Lou Boudreau	30.00	15.00	9.00
(5) Ralph Branca			
(6) Harry Brecheen	25.00	12.50	7.50
(--) Walker Cooper	50.00	25.00	15.00
(7) Dom DiMaggio	30.00	15.00	9.00
(8) Joe DiMaggio	200.00	100.00	60.00
(9) Bobbie Doerr (Bobby)	35.00	17.50	10.00
(10) Bruce Edwards			
(11) Bob Elliott	25.00	12.50	7.50
(12) Del Ennis	25.00	12.50	7.50
(13) Bob Feller	40.00	20.00	12.00
(14) Carl Furillo	100.00	50.00	30.00
(15) Cid Gordon (Sid)			
(16) Joe Gordon	25.00	12.50	7.50
(17) Joe Hatten			
(18) Gil Hodges	90.00	45.00	27.50
(19) Tommy Holmes	25.00	12.50	7.50
(20) Larry Janson (Jansen)	25.00	12.50	7.50
(21) Sheldon Jones	25.00	12.50	7.50
(22) Edwin Joost	25.00	12.50	7.50
(23) Charlie Keller			
(24) Ken Keltner	25.00	12.50	7.50
(25) Buddy Kerr	25.00	12.50	7.50
(26) Ralph Kiner	30.00	15.00	9.00
(27) John Lindell	25.00	12.50	7.50
(28) Whitey Lockman	25.00	12.50	7.50
(29) Willard Marshall			
(30) Johnny Mize	30.00	15.00	9.00
(31) Stan Musial	75.00	37.50	22.50
(32) Andy Pafko	25.00	12.50	7.50
(33) Johnny Pesky	25.00	12.50	7.50
(34) Pee Wee Reese	100.00	50.00	30.00
(35) Phil Rizzuto	50.00	25.00	15.00
(36) Aaron Robinson	25.00	12.50	7.50
(37) Jackie Robinson	175.00	90.00	55.00

		NM	E	VG
(38)	John Sain	25.00	12.50	7.50
(39)	Enos Slaughter	30.00	15.00	9.00
(40)	Vern Stephens	25.00	12.50	7.50
(41)	George Tebbetts	25.00	12.50	7.50
(42)	Bob Thomson			
(43)	Johnny Vandermeer (VanderMeer)	25.00	12.50	7.50
(44)	Ted Williams	175.00	85.00	55.00

1947 Bond Bread Jackie Robinson

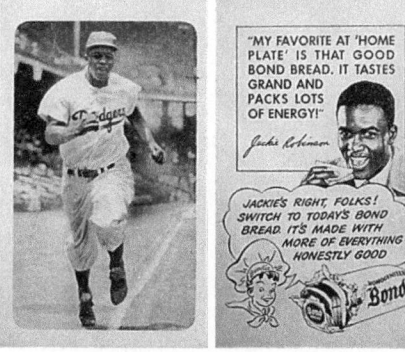

The modern major leagues' first black player is featured in this set issued by Bond Bread in 1947. The cards, measuring 2-1/4" x 3-1/2", are black-and-white photos of Robinson in various action and portrait poses. The unnumbered cards bear three different backs advertising Bond Bread. Four cards use a horizontal format. Card #6 was issued in greater quantities and perhaps was a promotional card; its back is the only one containing a short biography of Robinson.

		NM	E	VG
Complete Set (13):		85,000	42,500	25,000
Common Card:		6,750	3,400	2,000
(1)	Jackie Robinson (Awaiting pitch.)	6,750	3,400	2,000
(2)	Jackie Robinson (Batting, white shirt sleeves.)	6,750	3,400	2,000
(3)	Jackie Robinson (Batting, no shirt sleeves.)	6,750	3,400	2,000
(4)	Jackie Robinson (Leaping, scoreboard in background.)	6,750	3,400	2,000
(5)	Jackie Robinson (Leaping, no scoreboard.)	6,750	3,400	2,000
(6)	Jackie Robinson (Portrait, facsimile autograph.)	6,750	3,400	2,000
(7)	Jackie Robinson (Portrait, holding glove in air.)	6,750	3,400	2,000
(8)	Jackie Robinson (Running down baseline.)	6,750	3,400	2,000
(9)	Jackie Robinson (Running to catch ball.)	6,750	3,400	2,000
(10)	Jackie Robinson (Sliding)	6,750	3,400	2,000
(11)	Jackie Robinson (Stretching for throw, ball in glove.)	6,750	3,400	2,000
(12)	Jackie Robinson (Stretching for throw, no ball visible.)	6,750	3,400	2,000
(13)	Jackie Robinson (Throwing)	6,750	3,400	2,000

1947 Bond Bread Perforated, Dual-Sided

The manner of distribtion for this variant of the "Bond Bread" (W571/D305) cards is unknown, although anec-

dotal evidence suggests a connection with Bar Nunn show stores. About the size of the commonly seen blank-backed baseball cards (2-1/4" x 3-1/2"), these differ in that they have two, three or four sides perforated, indicating they were issued in sheet form. Also, this group has, instead of a blank back, another picture. Most of the pictures seen thus far are of Western movie stars. Only a few are named on the cards, but they include John Wayne, Hopalong Cassidy, Gene Autry and Noah Berry. The only non-Western back seen is Michigan quarterback Bob Chappius, paired with Tommy Holmes. Thus far, none of the short-printed Bond Bread cards have been seen in this format. Assigned numbers correspond to the Bond Bread set.

		NM	E	VG
Complete Set (24):		550.00	275.00	165.00
Common Card:				
(3)	Ewell Blackwell	15.00	7.50	4.50
(4)	Lou Boudreau	22.50	11.00	6.75
(6)	Harry Brecheen	15.00	7.50	4.50
(9)	Bobbie Doerr (Bobby)	22.50	11.00	6.75
(11)	Bob Elliott	15.00	7.50	4.50
(12)	Del Ennis	15.00	7.50	4.50
(13)	Bob Feller	25.00	12.50	7.50
(16)	Joe Gordon	15.00	7.50	4.50
(19)	Tommy Holmes	15.00	7.50	4.50
(24)	Ken Keltner	15.00	7.50	4.50
(26)	Ralph Kiner	22.50	11.00	6.75
(30)	Johnny Mize	22.50	11.00	6.75
(31)	Stan Musial	60.00	30.00	18.00
(32)	Andy Pafko	15.00	7.50	4.50
(33)	Johnny Pesky	15.00	7.50	4.50
(35)	Phil Rizzuto	30.00	15.00	9.00
(36)	Aaron Robinson	15.00	7.50	4.50
(37)	Jackie Robinson	110.00	55.00	35.00
(38)	John Sain	15.00	7.50	4.50
(39)	Enos Slaughter	22.50	11.00	6.75
(40)	Vern Stephens	15.00	7.50	4.50
(44)	Ted Williams	110.00	55.00	35.00
	BOXERS			
(45)	Primo Carnera	15.00	7.50	4.50
(48)	Joe Louis	30.00	15.00	9.00

1947 Bond Bread Premiums

While there is no empirical evidence, it is believed these 6-5/8" x 9" black-and-white, blank-back player pictures are associated with the Bond Bread card issue, since they share the same photos and script names, right down to the misspellings. They were possibly made available to bread buyers as some sort of premium. The checklist presented here is the same as that of the card issue. Though not all of the premium pictures have been confirmed, it is reasonable to presume their existence.

		NM	E	VG
Common Player:		40.00	20.00	12.00
(1)	Rex Barney	40.00	20.00	12.00
(2)	Yogi Berra	150.00	75.00	45.00
(3)	Ewell Blackwell	40.00	20.00	12.00
(4)	Lou Boudreau	75.00	37.50	22.50
(5)	Ralph Branca	60.00	30.00	18.00
(6)	Harry Brecheen	40.00	20.00	12.00
(7)	Dom DiMaggio	60.00	30.00	18.00
(8)	Joe DiMaggio	600.00	300.00	180.00
(9)	Bobbie Doerr (Bobby)	60.00	30.00	18.00
(10)	Bruce Edwards	40.00	20.00	12.00
(11)	Bob Elliott	40.00	20.00	12.00
(12)	Del Ennis	50.00	25.00	15.00
(13)	Bob Feller	150.00	75.00	45.00
(14)	Carl Furillo	60.00	30.00	18.00
(15)	Cid Gordon (Sid)	40.00	20.00	12.00
(16)	Joe Gordon	40.00	20.00	12.00
(17)	Joe Hatten	40.00	20.00	12.00
(18)	Gil Hodges	100.00	50.00	30.00
(19)	Tommy Holmes	40.00	20.00	12.00
(20)	Larry Janson (Jansen)	40.00	20.00	12.00
(21)	Sheldon Jones	40.00	20.00	12.00
(22)	Edwin Joost	40.00	20.00	12.00

		NM	E	VG
(23)	Charlie Keller	45.00	22.50	13.50
(24)	Ken Keltner	40.00	20.00	12.00
(25)	Buddy Kerr	40.00	20.00	12.00
(26)	Ralph Kiner	75.00	37.50	22.50
(27)	John Lindell	40.00	20.00	12.00
(28)	Whitey Lockman	40.00	20.00	12.00
(29)	Willard Marshall	40.00	20.00	12.00
(30)	Johnny Mize	75.00	37.50	22.50
(31)	Stan Musial	300.00	150.00	90.00
(32)	Andy Pafko	40.00	20.00	12.00
(33)	Johnny Pesky	40.00	20.00	12.00
(34)	Pee Wee Reese	150.00	75.00	45.00
(35)	Phil Rizzuto	150.00	75.00	45.00
(36)	Aaron Robinson	40.00	20.00	12.00
(37)	Jackie Robinson	1,000	500.00	300.00
(38)	John Sain	50.00	25.00	15.00
(39)	Enos Slaughter	75.00	37.50	22.50
(40)	Vern Stephens	40.00	20.00	12.00
(41)	George Tebbetts	40.00	20.00	12.00
(42)	Bob Thomson	60.00	30.00	18.00
(43)	Johnny Vandermeer	40.00	20.00	12.00
(44)	Ted Williams	350.00	175.00	100.00
	BOXERS			
(45)	Primo Carnera	45.00	22.50	13.50
(46)	Marcel Cerdan	40.00	20.00	12.00
(47)	Jake LaMotta	60.00	30.00	18.00
(48)	Joe Louis	75.00	37.50	22.50

1957 Borden's Dodgers Ticket Promotions

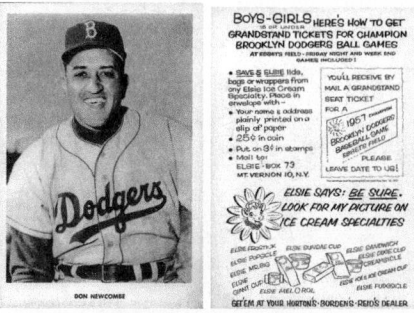

In their final season in Brooklyn, the Dodgers partnered with Borden's to offer grandstand seat tickets to those redeeming five wrappers from various Elsie-branded dairy treats. The offer was promoted on the back of what appear to be contemporary team-issued picture pack photos. On the backs of the 5" x 7" black-and-white pictures is an illustrated advertisement providing details of the offer. This checklist is very likely incomplete.

		NM	EX	VG
(1)	Gino Cimoli	150.00	75.00	45.00
(2)	Sandy Koufax	750.00	500.00	350.00
(3)	Don Newcombe	250.00	125.00	75.00

1912 Boston American Series Red Sox Postcards

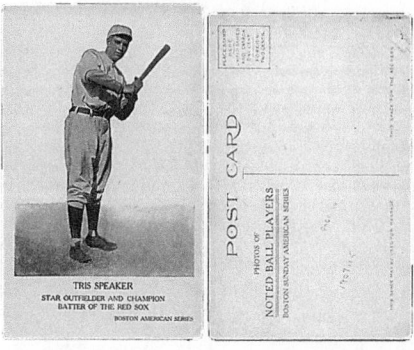

Star players from the World Champion Red Sox are featured in two sets of postcards issued by one of the city's daily newspapers. This set carries the notation "Boston American Series" at bottom right and is approximately 3-1/2" x 5-1/2". The cards are printed in sepia tones with a cream border. At bottom is the player name and position on two lines. Backs have typical postcard markings and a three-line notation, "PHOTOS OF / NOTED BALL PLAYERS / BOSTON SUNDAY AMERICAN SERIES."

	NM	E	VG
Complete Set (6):	2,400	1,200	725.00
Common Player:	400.00	200.00	120.00

(1)	Forrest Cady	400.00	200.00	120.00
(2)	Hub Perdue	400.00	200.00	120.00
(3)	Tris Speaker	750.00	370.00	220.00
(4)	Jake Stahl	400.00	200.00	120.00
(5)	Heinie Wagner	400.00	200.00	120.00
(6)	Joe Wood	400.00	200.00	120.00

1912 Boston Daily American Souvenir Postcards

TRIS SPEAKER
STAR OUTFIELDER AND CHAMPION
BATTER OF THE RED SOX
BOSTON AMERICAN SERIES

HEINIE WAGNER
CAPTAIN OF RED SOX.
Boston Daily American Souvenir
96

A second style of postcard issued by a local newspaper to honor the World Champions is labeled at bottom-left "Boston American Souvenir." The 3-1/2" x 5-1/2" cards are printed in black on a cream-colored stock. The player name and position are printed inside the photo frame. In the bottom-right border is a union logo and the number "96." The back has standard postcard markings.

		NM	E	VG
Common Player:		450.00	225.00	135.00
(1)	Forrest Cady	450.00	225.00	135.00
(2)	Ray Collins	450.00	225.00	135.00
(3)	Rabbit Maranville	600.00	300.00	180.00
(4)	Heinie Wagner	450.00	225.00	135.00
(5)	Joe Wood	500.00	250.00	150.00

1936 Boston American Sport Stamps

BOSTON AMERICAN
SPORT
STAMP
H. LAVAGETTO, 2B, PIRATES
Harry Lavagetto — Cookie joined the Pittsburgh Pirates at their spring training camp in 1934 . . . and immediately caught on at the keystone sack . . . such associates as Arky Vaughan and Gus Suhr have helped him to hold down his job . . . bats and throws right-handed and is a very classy fielder . . . batted .290 last season . . . 22 years old . . . stands 5 feet 11½

Similar to several contemporary issues, the Sport Stamps were printed on the pages of the daily newspaper over the course of the season. About 2" x 3-1/2", depending on the length of the biography and how well they were cut off the paper, they are printed in black-and-white. A tightly cropped player portrait is centered on a 2" x 2-5/8" stamp design with the paper's name above and the player's name, position and team below. This checklist may not be complete. Two of the players (Castleman, R. Johnson) have the paper at top listed as "SUNDAY ADVERTISER." Many of the stamps were issued in pairs, and at least a couple of football players are known, as well as the listed baseball players.

		NM	E	VG
Common Player:		12.00	6.00	3.50
(1)	J. (John) Allen	12.00	6.00	3.50
(2)	I. (Ivy) Andrews	12.00	6.00	3.50
(3)	E. (Elden)(Eldon) Auker	12.00	6.00	3.50
(4)	E. (Earl) Averill	20.00	10.00	6.00
(5)	R. (Richard) Bartell	12.00	6.00	3.50
(6)	R. (Roy) Bell	12.00	6.00	3.50
(7)	R. (Raymond) Benge	12.00	6.00	3.50
(8)	M. (Morris) Berg	30.00	15.00	9.00
(9)	Walter Berger	12.00	6.00	3.50
(10)	C. (Charles) Berry	12.00	6.00	3.50
(11)	(George) Blaeholder	12.00	6.00	3.50
(12)	A. (Albert) Blanche	12.00	6.00	3.50
(13)	D. (Darrell) Blanton	12.00	6.00	3.50
(14)	O. (Oswald) Bleuge (Bluege)	12.00	6.00	3.50
(15)	W. (William) Bolton	12.00	6.00	3.50
(16)	H. (Henry) Bonura	12.00	6.00	3.50
(17)	J. (James) Bottomley	20.00	10.00	6.00
(18)	J. (Joseph) Bowman	12.00	6.00	3.50
(19)	E. (Edward) Brandt	12.00	6.00	3.50
(20)	C. (Clinton) Brown	12.00	6.00	3.50
(21)	J. (John) Burnett	12.00	6.00	3.50
(22)	G. (Guy) Bush	12.00	6.00	3.50
(23)	A. (Albert) Butcher	12.00	6.00	3.50
(24)	E. (Earl) Caldwell	12.00	6.00	3.50
(25)	D. (Dolph) Camilli	12.00	6.00	3.50
(26)	B. (Bruce) Campbell	12.00	6.00	3.50
(27)	J. (Joseph) Cascarella	12.00	6.00	3.50
(28)	C. (Clyde) Castleman	12.00	6.00	3.50
(29)	P. (Philip) Cavarretta	12.00	6.00	3.50
(30)	W. (William) Chapman	12.00	6.00	3.50
(31)	L. (Louis) Chiozza	12.00	6.00	3.50
(32)	H. (Harland)(Harlond) Clift	12.00	6.00	3.50
(33)	G. (Gordon) Cochrane	25.00	12.50	7.50
(34)	J. (James) Collins	12.00	6.00	3.50
(35)	A. (Allen) Cooke	12.00	6.00	3.50
(36)	J. (Joseph) Coscarart	12.00	6.00	3.50
(37)	Roger Cramer	12.00	6.00	3.50
(38)	J. (Joseph) Cronin	20.00	10.00	6.00
(39)	F. (Frank) Crosetti	15.00	7.50	4.50
(40)	A. (Alvin) Crowder	12.00	6.00	3.50
(41)	A. (Anthony) Cuccinello	12.00	6.00	3.50
(42)	H. (Hazen) Cuyler	20.00	10.00	6.00
(43)	H. (Harry) Danning	12.00	6.00	3.50
(44)	V. (Virgil) Davis	12.00	6.00	3.50
(45)	J. (Jerome) Dean	35.00	17.50	10.50
(46)	P. (Paul) Dean	16.00	8.00	4.75
(47)	J. (Joseph) Demaree	12.00	6.00	3.50
(48)	Paul Derringer	12.00	6.00	3.50
(49)	G. (George) Dickey	12.00	6.00	3.50
(50)	W. (William) Dickey	25.00	12.50	7.50
(51)	L. (Leo) Durocher	20.00	10.00	6.00
(52)	J. (James) Dykes	12.00	6.00	3.50
(53)	G. (George) Earnshaw	12.00	6.00	3.50
(54)	E. (Elmwood)(Elwood) English	12.00	6.00	3.50
(55)	R. (Robert) Feller	25.00	12.50	7.50
(56)	R. (Richard) Ferrell	20.00	10.00	6.00
(57)	Wes Ferrell	12.00	6.00	3.50
(58)	(Louis) Finney	12.00	6.00	3.50
(59)	F. (Fred) Fitzsimmons	12.00	6.00	3.50
(60)	Jimmy Foxx	30.00	15.00	9.00
(61)	(Fred) Frankhouse	12.00	6.00	3.50
(62)	L. (Lawrence) French	12.00	6.00	3.50
(63)	(Frank) Frisch	20.00	10.00	6.00
(64)	A. (August) Galan	12.00	6.00	3.50
(65)	H. (Heny)(Henry) Gehrig	60.00	30.00	18.00
(66)	C. (Charles) Gehringer	20.00	10.00	6.00
(67)	(Charles) Gelbert	12.00	6.00	3.50
(68)	A. (Angelo) Giuliani	12.00	6.00	3.50
(69)	V. (Vernon) Gomez	20.00	10.00	6.00
(70)	L. (Leon) Goslin	20.00	10.00	6.00
(71)	R. (Robert) Grace	12.00	6.00	3.50
(72)	C. (Charles) Grimm	12.00	6.00	3.50
(73)	Robert Grove	25.00	12.50	7.50
(74)	G. (George) Haas	12.00	6.00	3.50
(75)	I. (Irving) Hadley	12.00	6.00	3.50
(76)	M. (Melvin) Harder	12.00	6.00	3.50
(77)	C. (Charles) Hartnett	20.00	10.00	6.00
(78)	M. (Minter) Hayes	12.00	6.00	3.50
(79)	R. (Ralston) Hemsley	12.00	6.00	3.50
(80)	F. (Floyd) Herman	12.00	6.00	3.50
(81)	(Michael) Higgins	12.00	6.00	3.50
(82)	M. (Myril) Hoag	12.00	6.00	3.50
(83)	E. (Elon) Hogsett	12.00	6.00	3.50
(84)	R. (Rogers) Hornsby	25.00	12.50	7.50
(85)	W. (Waite) Hoyt	20.00	10.00	6.00
(86)	W. (Willis) Hudlin	12.00	6.00	3.50
(87)	T. (Travis) Jackson	20.00	10.00	6.00
(88)	R. (Robert) Johnson	12.00	6.00	3.50
(89)	R. (Roy) Johnson	12.00	6.00	3.50
(90)	B. (Baxter) Jordan	12.00	6.00	3.50
(91)	W. (William) Jurgess (Jurges)	12.00	6.00	3.50
(92)	(Lloyd) Kennedy	12.00	6.00	3.50
(93)	C. (Charles) Klein	20.00	10.00	6.00
(94)	(William) Knickerbocker	12.00	6.00	3.50
(95)	J. (John) Knott	12.00	6.00	3.50
(96)	M. (Mark) Koenig	12.00	6.00	3.50
(97)	J. (Joseph) Kuhel	12.00	6.00	3.50
(98)	L. (Lynford) Lary	12.00	6.00	3.50
(99)	H. (Harry) Lavagetto	12.00	6.00	3.50
(100)	A. (Anthony) Lazzeri	20.00	10.00	6.00
(101)	W. (William) Lee	12.00	6.00	3.50
(102)	H. (Henry) Leiber	12.00	6.00	3.50
(103)	Wm. (William) Lewis	12.00	6.00	3.50
(104)	E. (Edward) Linke	12.00	6.00	3.50
(105)	E. (Ernest) Lombardi	20.00	10.00	6.00
(106)	Al Lopez	20.00	10.00	6.00
(107)	C. (Charles) Lucas	12.00	6.00	3.50
(108)	T. (Theodore) Lyons	20.00	10.00	6.00
(109)	Dan MacFayden	12.00	6.00	3.50
(110)	P. (Percy)(Perce) Malone	12.00	6.00	3.50
(111)	A. (Augustus) Mancuso	12.00	6.00	3.50
(112)	(John) Martin	15.00	7.50	4.50
(113)	J. (Joseph) Medwick	12.00	6.00	3.50
(114)	E. (Edmund) Miller	12.00	6.00	3.50
(115)	J. (John) Mize	20.00	10.00	6.00
(116)	Gene Moore	12.00	6.00	3.50
(117)	R. (Randolph) Moore	12.00	6.00	3.50
(118)	V. (Van Lingle) Mungo	12.00	6.00	3.50
(119)	C. (Charles) Myer	12.00	6.00	3.50
(120)	A. (Alfred) Niemiec	12.00	6.00	3.50
(121)	(Fred) Ostermueller	12.00	6.00	3.50
(122)	M. (Melvin) Ott	25.00	12.50	7.50
(123)	L. (LeRoy) Parmelee	12.00	6.00	3.50
(124)	A. (Anthony) Piet	12.00	6.00	3.50
(125)	A. (Alvin) Powell	12.00	6.00	3.50
(126)	F. (Frank) Pytlak	12.00	6.00	3.50
(127)	R. (Ray) Radcliff	12.00	6.00	3.50
(128)	R. (Robert) Reis	12.00	6.00	3.50
(129)	(Carl) Reynolds	12.00	6.00	3.50
(130)	J. (John) Rhodes	12.00	6.00	3.50
(131)	R. (Robert) Rolfe	12.00	6.00	3.50
(132)	C. (Charles) Root	12.00	6.00	3.50
(133)	L. (Lynwood) Rowe	12.00	6.00	3.50
(134)	C. (Charles) Ruffing	20.00	10.00	6.00
(135)	F. (Fred) Schulte	12.00	6.00	3.50
(136)	H. (Harold) Schumacher	12.00	6.00	3.50
(137)	J. (James) Sewell	12.00	6.00	3.50
(138)	A. (Aloysius) Simmons	20.00	10.00	6.00
(139)	J. (Julius) Soulters (Solters)	12.00	6.00	3.50
(140)	G. (George) Stainback	12.00	6.00	3.50
(141)	J. (Johnathan)(John) Stone	12.00	6.00	3.50
(142)	J. (Joseph) Stripp	12.00	6.00	3.50
(143)	W. (William) Terry	20.00	10.00	6.00
(144)	T. (Thomas) Thevenow	12.00	6.00	3.50
(145)	A. (Alphonse) Thomas	12.00	6.00	3.50
(146)	C. (Cecil) Travis	12.00	6.00	3.50
(147)	H. (Harold) Traynor	20.00	10.00	6.00
(148)	H. (Harold) Trosky	12.00	6.00	3.50
(149)	R. (Russell) Van Atta	12.00	6.00	3.50
(150)	F. (Floyd) Vaughan	20.00	10.00	6.00
(151)	J. (Joseph) Vosmik	12.00	6.00	3.50
(152)	G. (Gerald) Walker	12.00	6.00	3.50
(153)	W. (William) Walter	12.00	6.00	3.50
(154)	L. (Lloyd) Waner	20.00	10.00	6.00
(155)	P. (Paul) Waner	20.00	10.00	6.00
(156)	L. (Lonnie) Warneke	12.00	6.00	3.50
(157)	G. (George) Watkins	12.00	6.00	3.50
(158)	J. (Joyner) White	12.00	6.00	3.50
(159)	(Burgess) Whitehead	12.00	6.00	3.50
(160)	(Earl) Whitehill	12.00	6.00	3.50
(161)	A. (Arthur) Whitney	12.00	6.00	3.50
(162)	J. (Jack) Wilson	12.00	6.00	3.50
(163)	J. (James) Wilson	12.00	6.00	3.50

1932 Boston Braves Photo Pack

This set of player pictures was sold in an envelope titled "Sixteen Rotogravure Pictures of the Boston Braves," though the known checklist for the set contains only 15 subjects, the picture of manager Bill McKechnie having been included twice. It is possible the duplicate manager's picture was substituted for an as-yet unknown player whose photo was removed after he left the team. Gowell Studios is credited on the pictures with providing the photography for the pictures. The blank-backed, sepia-toned pictures are in a format of 9" x 12".

		NM	EX	VG
Complete Set (16):		500.00	250.00	150.00
Common Player:		35.00	17.50	10.00
(1)	Wally Berger	35.00	17.50	10.00
(2)	Huck Betts	35.00	17.50	10.00
(3)	Eddie Brandt	35.00	17.50	10.00
(4)	Bobby Brown	35.00	17.50	10.00
(5)	Ben Cantwell	35.00	17.50	10.00
(6)	Pinky Hargrave	35.00	17.50	10.00
(7)	Fritz Knothe	35.00	17.50	10.00

(8)	Fred Leach	35.00	17.50	10.00
(9)	Rabbit Maranville	60.00	30.00	17.50
(10)	Bill McKechnie	60.00	30.00	17.50
(12)	Randy Moore	35.00	17.50	10.00
(13)	Art Shires	35.00	17.50	10.00
(14)	Al Spohrer	35.00	17.50	10.00
(15)	Bill Urbankski	35.00	17.50	10.00
(16)	Red Worthington	35.00	17.50	10.00

1912 Boston Garter

If it weren't for the checklist printed on the back of the few known specimens, the extent of this extremely rare issue would be unknown. Many of the cards mentioned on the back have yet to be seen. Issued by the George Frost Co. of Boston, and packed one card per box of a dozen garters, the approximately 4" x 8-1/4" cards are printed in color lithography on the front, and black-and-white on the back. Fronts have a picture of the player standing near his locker or sitting in a chair, dressing in his uniform. The issuer's Boston-brand garter is prominently shown below the player's boxer shorts. A window in the background displays a cityscape or ballpark scene. There was a card issued for one player on each of the 16 major league teams of the day. Large-format (21-1/2" x 11-1/4") cardboard window display posters which reproduce pairs of the cards are sometimes seen in the hobby.

		NM	E	VG
	Common Player:	30,000	12,000	7,250
(1)	Bob Bescher	30,000	12,000	7,250
(2)	Roger Bresnahan	40,000	13,750	8,250
(3)	Frank Chance	40,000	15,000	9,000
(4)	Hal Chase	30,000	12,500	7,500
(5)	Fred Clarke	40,000	13,750	8,250
(6)	Eddie Collins	40,000	13,750	8,250
(7)	Charles Dooin	30,000	12,000	7,250
(8)	Hugh Jennings	40,000	13,750	8,250
(9)	Walter Johnson	60,000	17,500	10,500
(10)	Johnny Kling	30,000	12,000	7,250
(11)	Larry Lajoie	45,000	15,000	9,000
(12)	Frank LaPorte	30,000	12,000	7,250
(13)	Christy Mathewson	75,000	37,500	22,500
(14)	Nap Rucker	30,000	12,000	7,250
(15)	Tris Speaker	45,000	15,000	9,000
(16)	Ed Walsh	40,000	13,750	8,250

1914 Boston Garter - Color

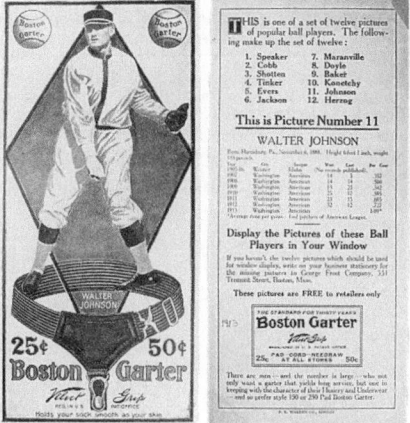

The second of what are presumed to have been three annual issue by the George Frost Co., Boston, contains 12

cards. The colorful lithograph fronts have a player picture in front of a ballpark diagram. A large Boston-brand garter appears at the bottom. Baseballs with the Boston Garter name appear in each upper corner. Black-and-white backs have a checklist for the set, career statistics for the player pictured and details on the cards' availability. Retailers received one card per box of dozen garters and could write to the company to complete the set. About 4" x 8-1/4", they were intended to be displayed in shop windows.

		NM	E	VG
	Common Player:	25,000	12,500	7,500
1	Tris Speaker	75,000	37,000	22,000
2	Ty Cobb	125,000	62,500	37,500
3	Burt Shotten (Shotton)	15,000	7,500	4,500
4	Joe Tinker	40,000	20,000	12,000
5	Johnny Evers	15,000	6,250	3,750
6	Joe Jackson	150,000	75,000	45,000
7	Rabbit Maranville	40,000	20,000	12,000
8	Larry Doyle	15,000	7,500	4,500
9	Frank Baker	40,000	20,000	12,000
10	Ed Konetchy	15,000	7,500	4,500
11	Walter Johnson	75,000	37,000	22,000
12	Buck Herzog	15,000	7,500	4,500

1914 Boston Garter - Sepia

The 1914 date attributed to this 10-card set may or may not be accurate. Since the company's other two known issues can be reliably dated and were produced using the color lithographic process, it is presumed that the use of photographs would have come later. Fronts of the approximately 3-3/4" x 6-1/4" cards feature a green duo-tone photo of the player. His last name appears in white script at the bottom, along with a baseball with the Boston Garter name. Backs have a checklist of the set and information on how retail store owners can send for additional cards to supplement those which were packaged one per box of a dozen garters.

		NM	E	VG
	Complete Set (10):	140,000	70,000	42,500
	Common Player:	15,000	7,500	4,500
1	Christy Mathewson	35,000	20,000	12,500
2	Red Murray	7,500	3,750	2,250
3	Eddie Collins	15,000	7,500	4,500
4	Hugh Jennings	15,000	7,500	4,500
5	Hal Chase	12,000	6,000	3,600
6	Bob Bescher	7,500	3,750	2,250
7	Red Dooin	7,500	3,750	2,250
8	Larry Lajoie	15,000	7,500	4,500
9	Tris Speaker	20,000	10,000	6,000
10	Heinie Zimmerman	7,500	3,750	2,250

1909 Boston Herald Supplements

Members of the Red Sox and Braves were featured in this series of supplements in the Boston Sunday Herald. About 7-1/4" x 9-3/4", the blank-back, posed-action pictures are se-

pia toned. A black box at bottom has player identification, an issue date and a note to "See Story on Sporting Page." While the pictures themselves are numbered, this checklist, almost certainly incomplete, is arranged alphabetically. Some of the pictures show cross-town rivals on the same piece.

		NM	E	VG
(1)	Chick Autry	200.00	100.00	60.00
	BOSTON BRAVES			
(2)	Johnny Bates	200.00	100.00	60.00
(3)	Ginger Beaumont	200.00	100.00	60.00
(4)	Beals Becker	200.00	100.00	60.00
(5)	Frank Bowerman	200.00	100.00	60.00
(6)	Jack Coffey	200.00	100.00	60.00
(6)	Jack Coffey	200.00	100.00	60.00
(7)	Bill Dahlen	200.00	100.00	60.00
(8)	Peaches Graham	200.00	100.00	60.00
(9)	Al Mattern	200.00	100.00	60.00
(10)	Harry Smith	200.00	100.00	60.00
(11)	Bill Sweeney	200.00	100.00	60.00
(12)	("Tom") Thomas H. Tuckey	200.00	100.00	60.00
	BOSTON RED SOX			
(1)	Charlie Chech	200.00	100.00	60.00
(2)	Bill Carrigan	200.00	100.00	60.00
(3)	Pat Donahue	200.00	100.00	60.00
(4)	"Doc" (Harry H.) Gessler	200.00	100.00	60.00
(5)	Harry Hooper	300.00	150.00	90.00
(6)	Harry Lord	200.00	100.00	60.00
(7)	Amby McConnell	200.00	100.00	60.00
(8)	Harry Niles	200.00	100.00	60.00
(9)	Tris Speaker	600.00	300.00	180.00
	BOSTON BRAVES/RED SOX			
(1)	Johnny Bates, Harry Hooper	150.00	75.00	45.00
(2)	Ginger Beaumont, Tris Speaker	150.00	75.00	45.00
(3)	Ed Cicotte, Tommy Tuckey	200.00	100.00	60.00
(4)	Bill Dahlen, Heinie Wagner	150.00	75.00	45.00
(5)	Doc Gessler, Frank Bowerman	150.00	75.00	45.00
(6)	Harry Lord, Unknown Brave	150.00	75.00	45.00
(7)	Amby McConnell, Jack Coffey	150.00	75.00	45.00
(8)	Harry Smith, Pat Donahue	150.00	75.00	45.00
(9)	Jake Stahl, Chick Autrey (Autry)	150.00	75.00	45.00

1908 Boston Oyster House Chicago Cubs

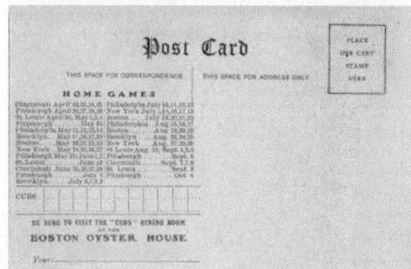

Located in Chicago, not Boston, this restaurant featured, according to its advertising, "The 'Cubs' Dining Room." In keeping with that theme, the business adopted as a promotion the set of Cubs/Teddy Bear postcards issued the previous year by Grignon, a local publisher. The restaurant version has on its back a 1908 Cubs home schedule and rudimentary scorecard, along with standard postcard markings.

	NM	E	VG
Common Player:	500.00	250.00	150.00
Stars: 1X			

(See 1907 Grignon Chicago Cubs postcards for checklist and base values.)

1908 Boston Red Sox Foldout Postcard

At first glance this standard-size (about 5-1/2" x 3-1/2") postcard reveals on its front only portrait photos of the the owners and grounds of the Boston Red Sox, with a cotter-pinned baseball at left printed in red. Hidden behind the ball, however, is an accordian-folded strip of black-and-white player photos, printed front-to-back, in a size of about 1-1/8" x 1-3/4".

	NM	E	VG
1908 Boston Red Sox	4,500	2,250	1,350

1910 Boston Red Sox Cabinets

Details are lacking on this high-quality photographic issue depicting the 1910 Red Sox. The sepia photos picture the players in full-length poses and are glued to cardboard mattes. There is no identification on the pieces, nor on the decorative paper folders in which they were apparently originally sold.

	NM	E	VG
Common Player:	350.00	175.00	100.00
(1) Hugh Bradley	350.00	175.00	100.00
(2) Bill Carrigan	350.00	175.00	100.00
(3) Ed Cicotte	1,000	500.00	300.00
(4) Ray Collins	350.00	175.00	100.00
(5) Clyde Engle	350.00	175.00	100.00
(6) Larry Gardner	350.00	175.00	100.00
(7) Charley Hall	350.00	175.00	100.00
(8) Harry Hooper	750.00	375.00	225.00
(9) Ben Hunt	350.00	175.00	100.00
(10) Duffy Lewis	500.00	250.00	150.00
(11) Tom Madden	350.00	175.00	100.00
(12) Doc Moskiman	350.00	175.00	100.00
(13) Harry Smith	350.00	175.00	100.00
(14) Tris Speaker	1,000	500.00	300.00
(15) Jake Stahl	350.00	175.00	100.00
(16) Heinie Wagner	350.00	175.00	100.00

1912 Boston Red Sox Tattoos

This set of tattoos is similar to a number of other issues of the era, most of which were made in Germany. This issue features members of the World Champion Boston Red Sox. Approximately 1-3/8" x 1-3/4", the tattoos are printed in mirror-image in bright colors. Images are crude line art with no resemblance to the actual players. Players are identified at bottom by at least a last name. A position is designated at the background of the picture. These items were issued on a perforated sheet. "Collins" may represent retired Red Sox Jimmy Collins or 1912 pitcher Ray Collins. The unnumbered tattoos are listed here alphabetically, though the listing may not be complete.

	NM	E	VG
Complete Set (13):	475.00	235.00	140.00
Common Player:	35.00	17.50	10.00
(1) Hugh Bedient	35.00	17.50	10.00
(2) Hick Cady	35.00	17.50	10.00
(3) Collins	35.00	17.50	10.00
(4) Clyde Engle	35.00	17.50	10.00
(5) Charley Hall	35.00	17.50	10.00
(6) Martin Krug	35.00	17.50	10.00
(7) Jerry McCarthy (Mascot)	35.00	17.50	10.00
(8) Les Nunamaker	35.00	17.50	10.00
(9) Larry Pape	35.00	17.50	10.00
(10) Tris Speaker	125.00	65.00	35.00
(11) Jake Stahl	35.00	17.50	10.00
(12) Heinie Wagner	35.00	17.50	10.00
(13) Joe Wood	50.00	25.00	15.00

1940 Boston Red Sox Photo Pack

Approximately 6" x 9", these blank-back, black-and-white pictures depict the BoSox in (usually) neck-to-cap poses. The pictures are bordered in white and there is a facsimile autograph on each photo.

	NM	E	VG
Complete Set (25):	300.00	150.00	75.00
Common Player:	8.00	4.00	2.50
(1) Jim Bagby Jr.	8.00	4.00	2.50
(2) Bill Butland	8.00	4.00	2.50
(3) Tom Carey	8.00	4.00	2.50
(4) Doc Cramer	8.00	4.00	2.50
(5) Joe Cronin	15.00	7.50	4.50
(6) Gene Desautels	8.00	4.00	2.50
(7) Emerson Dickman	8.00	4.00	2.50
(8) Dom DiMaggio	15.00	7.50	4.50
(9) Bobby Doerr	15.00	7.50	4.50
(10) Lou Finney	8.00	4.00	2.50
(11) Jimmie Foxx	35.00	17.50	10.00
(12) Denny Galehouse	8.00	4.00	2.50
(13) Joe Glenn	8.00	4.00	2.50
(14) Lefty Grove	30.00	15.00	9.00
(15) Mickey Harris	8.00	4.00	2.50
(16) Herbie Hash	8.00	4.00	2.50
(17) Joe Heving	8.00	4.00	2.50
(18) Leo Nonnenkamp	8.00	4.00	2.50
(19) Fritz Ostermueller	8.00	4.00	2.50
(20) Mickey Owen	8.00	4.00	2.50
(21) John Peacock	8.00	4.00	2.50
(22) Jim Tabor	8.00	4.00	2.50
(23) Charles Wagner	8.00	4.00	2.50
(24) Ted Williams	60.00	30.00	18.00
(25) Jack Wilson	8.00	4.00	2.50

1941 Boston Red Sox Photo Pack

Approximately 6" x 9", these blank-back, black-and-white pictures depict the BoSox in informal poses, most leaning on the dugout top step. The pictures are bordered in white and there is a facsimile autograph on each photo. It is possible this checklist (arranged alphabetically) is incomplete as other players may have been added to or deleted from the set to conform to roster changes during the season.

	NM	E	VG
Complete Set (25):	200.00	100.00	60.00
Common Player:	8.00	4.00	2.50
(1) Paul Campbell	8.00	4.00	2.50
(2) Tom Carey	8.00	4.00	2.50
(3) Joe Cronin	20.00	10.00	6.00
(4) Emerson Dickman	8.00	4.00	2.50
(5) Dom DiMaggio	15.00	7.50	4.50
(6) Joe Dobson	8.00	4.00	2.50
(7) Bobby Doerr	12.00	6.00	3.50
(8) Lou Finney	8.00	4.00	2.50
(9) Bill Fleming	8.00	4.00	2.50
(10) Pete Fox	8.00	4.00	2.50
(11) Jimmie Foxx	30.00	15.00	9.00
(12) Lefty Grove	25.00	12.50	7.50
(13) Mickey Harris	8.00	4.00	2.50
(14) Tex Hughson	8.00	4.00	2.50
(15) Earl Johnson	8.00	4.00	2.50
(16) Lefty Judd	8.00	4.00	2.50
(17) Dick Newsome	8.00	4.00	2.50
(18) Skeeter Newsome	8.00	4.00	2.50
(19) John Peacock	8.00	4.00	2.50
(20) Frank Pytlak	8.00	4.00	2.50
(21) Mike Ryba	8.00	4.00	2.50
(22) Stan Spence	8.00	4.00	2.50
(23) Jim Tabor	8.00	4.00	2.50
(24) Charlie Wagner	8.00	4.00	2.50
(25) Ted Williams	50.00	25.00	15.00
(26) Jack Wilson	8.00	4.00	2.50

1942 Boston Red Sox Photo Pack

In a format of approximately 6-1/2" x 9", these team-issued player portraits are blank-backed, black-and-white with a white border. Most photos are chest-to-cap presentations and all have a facsimile autograph. Some of the players in the issue can be seen wearing the "HEALTH" patch which MLB adopted during World War II. This checklist may not be complete as it is possible some players were added or deleted from the set to reflect mid-season roster moves.

	NM	E	VG
Complete Set (25):	275.00	135.00	85.00
Common Player:	10.00	5.00	3.00
(1) Mace Brown	10.00	5.00	3.00
(2) Bill Butland	10.00	5.00	3.00
(3) Paul Campbell	10.00	5.00	3.00
(4) Tom Carey	10.00	5.00	3.00
(5) Ken Chase	10.00	5.00	3.00
(6) Bill Conroy	10.00	5.00	3.00
(7) Joe Cronin	20.00	10.00	6.00
(8) Dom DiMaggio	20.00	10.00	6.00
(9) Joe Dobson	10.00	5.00	3.00
(10) Bobby Doerr	20.00	10.00	6.00
(11) Lou Finney	10.00	5.00	3.00
(12) Pete Fox	10.00	5.00	3.00
(13) Jimmie Foxx	40.00	20.00	12.00
(14) Tex Hughson	10.00	5.00	3.00
(15) Oscar Judd	10.00	5.00	3.00
(16) Tony Lupien	10.00	5.00	3.00
(17) Dick Newsome	10.00	5.00	3.00
(18) Skeeter Newsome	10.00	5.00	3.00
(19) John Peacock	10.00	5.00	3.00
(20) Johnny Pesky	10.00	5.00	3.00
(21) Mike Ryba	10.00	5.00	3.00
(22) Jim Tabor	10.00	5.00	3.00
(23) Yank Terry	10.00	5.00	3.00
(24) Charlie Wagner	10.00	5.00	3.00
(25) Ted Williams	60.00	30.00	18.00

1943 Boston Red Sox Photo Pack

In a format of approximately 6-1/2" x 9", these team-issued player portraits are blank-backed, black-and-white with a white border. Most photos are chest-to-cap presentations and all have a facsimile autograph. Some of the players in the issue can be seen wearing the "HEALTH" patch which MLB adopted during World War II. This checklist may not be complete as it is possible some players were added or deleted from the set to reflect mid-season roster moves.

	NM	E	VG
Complete Set (24):	125.00	65.00	40.00
Common Player:	8.00	4.00	2.50
(1) Mace Brown	8.00	4.00	2.50
(2) Ken Chase	8.00	4.00	2.50
(3) Bill Conroy	8.00	4.00	2.50
(4) Joe Cronin	15.00	7.50	4.50
(5) Joe Dobson	8.00	4.00	2.50
(6) Bobby Doerr	15.00	7.50	4.50
(7) Pete Fox	8.00	4.00	2.50
(8) Ford Garrison	8.00	4.00	2.50
(9) Tex Hughson	8.00	4.00	2.50
(10) Oscar Judd	8.00	4.00	2.50
(11) Andy Karl	8.00	4.00	2.50
(12) Eddie Lake	8.00	4.00	2.50

(13)	John Lazor	8.00	4.00	2.50
(14)	Lou Lucier	10.00	5.00	3.00
(15)	Tony Lupien	8.00	4.00	2.50
(16)	Dee Miles	8.00	4.00	2.50
(17)	Dick Newsome	8.00	4.00	2.50
(18)	Skeeter Newsome	8.00	4.00	2.50
(19)	Roy Partee	8.00	4.00	2.50
(20)	John Peacock	8.00	4.00	2.50
(21)	Mike Ryba	8.00	4.00	2.50
(22)	Al Simmons	15.00	7.50	4.50
(23)	Jim Tabor	8.00	4.00	2.50
(24)	Yank Terry	8.00	4.00	2.50

1946 Boston Red Sox Photo Pack

The American League champion Red Sox are featured in this team-issue photo pack. The player portraits are printed in black-and-white on heavy paper in 6-1/2" x 9" format. The photos have a white border and a facsimile autograph on front. Backs are blank. The unnumbered pictures are listed here in alphabetical order.

		NM	E	VG
Complete Set (25):		225.00	110.00	65.00
Common Player:		6.00	3.00	1.75
(1)	Ernie Andres	6.00	3.00	1.75
(2)	Jim Bagby Sr.	6.00	3.00	1.75
(3)	Mace Brown	6.00	3.00	1.75
(4)	Joe Cronin	12.00	6.00	3.50
(5)	Leon Culbertston	6.00	3.00	1.75
(6)	Mel Deutsch	6.00	3.00	1.75
(7)	Dom DiMaggio	10.00	5.00	3.00
(8)	Joe Dobson	6.00	3.00	1.75
(9)	Bobby Doerr	12.00	6.00	3.50
(10)	Boo Ferriss	6.00	3.00	1.75
(11)	Mickey Harris	6.00	3.00	1.75
(12)	Randy Heflin	6.00	3.00	1.75
(13)	Tex Hughson	6.00	3.00	1.75
(14)	Earl Johnson	6.00	3.00	1.75
(15)	Ed McGah	6.00	3.00	1.75
(16)	George Metkovich	6.00	3.00	1.75
(17)	Roy Partee	6.00	3.00	1.75
(18)	Eddie Pellagrini	6.00	3.00	1.75
(19)	Johnny Pesky	7.50	3.75	2.25
(20)	Rip Russell	6.00	3.00	1.75
(21)	Mike Ryba	6.00	3.00	1.75
(22)	Charlie Wagner	6.00	3.00	1.75
(23)	Hal Wagner	6.00	3.00	1.75
(24)	Ted Williams	60.00	30.00	18.00
(25)	Rudy York	6.00	3.00	1.75

1947 Boston Red Sox Photo Pack

In the same 6-1/2" x 9" format which the team had used for its photo packs since 1942, this set of black-and-white, blank-back pictures features (usually) chest-to-cap portraits with white borders, a dark background and a facsimile autograph within the picture. Some of the photos were re-used from previous years' issues, or were re-issued in subsequent years. The unnumbered pictures are checklisted here in alphabetical order. This list may or may not be complete; it is possible other players' photos were added or deleted to reflect seasonal roster changes.

		NM	E	VG
Complete Set (25):		200.00	100.00	60.00
Common Player:		6.00	3.00	1.75
(1)	Joe Cronin	15.00	7.50	4.50
(2)	Leon Culberson	6.00	3.00	1.75
(3)	Dom DiMaggio	12.50	6.25	3.75
(4)	Joseph Dobson	6.00	3.00	1.75
(5)	Bobby Doerr	15.00	7.50	4.50
(6)	Harry Dorish	6.00	3.00	1.75
(7)	Dave "Boo" Ferriss	6.00	3.00	1.75
(8)	Tommy Fine	6.00	3.00	1.75
(9)	Don Gutteridge	6.00	3.00	1.75
(10)	Mickey Harris	6.00	3.00	1.75
(11)	Tex Hughson	6.00	3.00	1.75
(12)	Earl Johnson	6.00	3.00	1.75
(13)	Bob Klinger	6.00	3.00	1.75
(14)	Sam Mele	6.00	3.00	1.75
(15)	Wally Moses	6.00	3.00	1.75
(16)	Johnny Murphy	6.00	3.00	1.75
(17)	Mel Parnell	6.00	3.00	1.75
(18)	Roy Partee	6.00	3.00	1.75
(19)	Eddie Pellagrini	6.00	3.00	1.75
(20)	Johnny Pesky	7.50	3.75	2.25
(21)	Rip Russell	6.00	3.00	1.75
(22)	Birdie Tebbetts	6.00	3.00	1.75
(23)	Ted Williams	60.00	30.00	18.00
(24)	Rudy York	6.00	3.00	1.75
(25)	Bill Zuber	6.00	3.00	1.75

1948 Boston Red Sox Photo Pack

In the same 6-1/2" x 9" format which the team had used for its photo packs since 1942, this set of black-and-white, blank-back pictures features (usually) chest-to-cap portraits with white borders, a dark background and a facsimile autograph within the picture. Some of the photos were re-used from previous years' issues, or were re-issued in subsequent years. The unnumbered pictures are checklisted here in alphabetical order. This list may or may not be complete; it is possible other players' photos were added or deleted to reflect seasonal roster changes.

		NM	E	VG
Complete Set (25):		200.00	100.00	60.00
Common Player:		6.00	3.00	1.75
(1)	Matt Batts	6.00	3.00	1.75
(2)	Dom DiMaggio	15.00	7.50	4.50
(3)	Joseph Dobson	6.00	3.00	1.75
(4)	Bobby Doerr	15.00	7.50	4.50
(5)	Harry Dorish	6.00	3.00	1.75
(6)	Dave "Boo" Ferriss	6.00	3.00	1.75
(7)	Dennis Galehouse	6.00	3.00	1.75
(8)	Billy Goodman	6.00	3.00	1.75
(9)	Mickey Harris	6.00	3.00	1.75
(10)	Bill Hitchcock	6.00	3.00	1.75
(11)	Earl Johnson	6.00	3.00	1.75
(12)	Jake Jones	6.00	3.00	1.75
(13)	Ellis Kinder	6.00	3.00	1.75
(14)	Jack Kramer	6.00	3.00	1.75
(15)	Joe McCarthy	15.00	7.50	4.50
(16)	Maurice McDermott	6.00	3.00	1.75
(17)	Sam Mele	6.00	3.00	1.75
(18)	Wally Moses	6.00	3.00	1.75
(19)	Mel Parnell	6.00	3.00	1.75
(20)	Johnny Pesky	7.50	3.75	2.25
(21)	Stan Spence	6.00	3.00	1.75
(22)	Vern Stephens	6.00	3.00	1.75
(23)	Chuck Stobbs	6.00	3.00	1.75
(24)	Birdie Tebbetts	6.00	3.00	1.75
(25)	Ted Williams	60.00	30.00	18.00

1949 Boston Red Sox Photo Pack

In the same 6-1/2" x 9" format the team used for its photo packs since 1942, this set of black-and-white, blank-back pictures features (usually) chest-to-cap portraits with white borders, a dark background and a facsimile autograph within the picture. Some of the photos were re-used from previous years' issues, or were re-issued in subsequent years. The unnumbered pictures are checklisted here in alphabetical order.

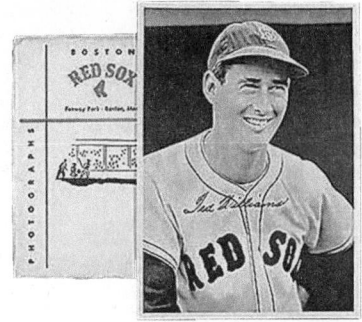

		NM	E	VG
Complete Set (25):		200.00	100.00	60.00
Common Player:		6.00	3.00	1.80
(1)	Matt Batts	6.00	3.00	1.80
(2)	Merrill Combs	6.00	3.00	1.80
(3)	Dom DiMaggio	15.00	7.50	4.50
(4)	Joe Dobson	6.00	3.00	1.80
(5)	Bobby Doerr	15.00	7.50	4.50
(6)	David "Boo" Ferris	6.00	3.00	1.80
(7)	Bill Goodman	6.00	3.00	1.80
(8)	Mickey Harris	6.00	3.00	1.80
(9)	Billy Hitchcock	6.00	3.00	1.80
(10)	Tex Hughson	6.00	3.00	1.80
(11)	Earl Johnson	6.00	3.00	1.80
(12)	Ellis Kinder	6.00	3.00	1.80
(13)	Jack Kramer	6.00	3.00	1.80
(14)	Joe McCarthy	15.00	7.50	4.50
(15)	Sam Mele	6.00	3.00	1.80
(16)	Tommy O'Brien	6.00	3.00	1.80
(17)	Mel Parnell	6.00	3.00	1.80
(18)	Johnny Pesky	6.00	3.00	1.80
(19)	Frank Quinn	6.00	3.00	1.80
(20)	Vern Stephens	6.00	3.00	1.80
(21)	Chuck Stobbs	6.00	3.00	1.80
(22)	Lou Stringer	6.00	3.00	1.80
(23)	Birdie Tebbetts	6.00	3.00	1.80
(24)	Ted Williams	60.00	30.00	18.00
(25)	Al Zarilla	6.00	3.00	1.80

1950 Boston Red Sox Photo Pack

In the same approximately 6-1/2" x 9" format which the team had used for its photo packs since the 1940s, this set of black-and-white, blank-back pictures features (usually) chest-to-cap portraits with white borders, a dark background and a facsimile autograph within the photo. Some of the photos were re-used from previous years' issues. The unnumbered pictures are checklisted here in alphabetical order. This list may or may not be complete; it is possible other players' photos were added or deleted to reflect seasonal roster changes.

		NM	E	VG
Complete Set (25):		150.00	75.00	40.00
Common Player:		4.00	2.00	1.25
(1)	Matt Batts	4.00	2.00	1.25
(2)	Earle Combs	7.50	3.75	2.25
(3)	Dom DiMaggio	9.00	4.50	2.75
(4)	Joe Dobson	4.00	2.00	1.25
(5)	Bobby Doerr	9.00	4.50	2.75
(6)	Walt Dropo	12.00	6.00	3.50
(7)	Bill Goodman	4.00	2.00	1.25
(8)	Earl Johnson	4.00	2.00	1.25
(9)	Ken Keltner	4.00	2.00	1.25
(10)	Ellis Kinder	4.00	2.00	1.25
(11)	Walt Masterson	4.00	2.00	1.25
(12)	Joe McCarthy	9.00	4.50	2.75
(13)	Maurice McDermott	4.00	2.00	1.25
(14)	Al Papai	4.00	2.00	1.25
(15)	Mel Parnell	4.00	2.00	1.25
(16)	Johnny Pesky	4.00	2.00	1.25

		NM	E	VG
(17)	Buddy Rosar	4.00	2.00	1.25
(18)	Charley Schanz	4.00	2.00	1.25
(19)	Vern Stephens	4.00	2.00	1.25
(20)	Chuck Stobbs	4.00	2.00	1.25
(21)	Lou Stringer	4.00	2.00	1.25
(22)	Birdie Tebbetts	4.00	2.00	1.25
(23)	Ted Williams	30.00	15.00	9.00
(24)	Tom Wright	4.00	2.00	1.25
(25)	Al Zarilla	4.00	2.00	1.25

1953 Boston Red Sox Photo Pack

In the same approximately 6-1/2" x 9" format which the team had used for its photo packs since the 1940s, this set of black-and-white, blank-back pictures features (usually) chest-to-cap portraits with white borders and a facsimile autograph within the photo. Some of the photos were re-used from previous years' issues. The unnumbered pictures are checklisted here in alphabetical order. This list may or may not be complete; it is possible other players' photos were added or deleted to reflect seasonal roster changes.

		NM	E	VG
Complete Set (30):		120.00	60.00	35.00
Common Player:		4.00	2.00	1.25
(1)	Milt Bolling	4.00	2.00	1.25
(2)	Lou Boudreau	9.00	4.50	2.75
(3)	Harold Brown	4.00	2.00	1.25
(4)	Bill Consolo	4.00	2.00	1.25
(5)	Dom DiMaggio	15.00	7.50	4.50
(6)	Hoot Evers	4.00	2.00	1.25
(7)	Ben Flowers	4.00	2.00	1.25
(8)	Hershell Freeman	4.00	2.00	1.25
(9)	Dick Gernert	4.00	2.00	1.25
(10)	Bill Goodman	4.00	2.00	1.25
(11)	Marv Grissom	4.00	2.00	1.25
(12)	Ken Holcombe	4.00	2.00	1.25
(13)	Sid Hudson	4.00	2.00	1.25
(14)	George Kell	9.00	4.50	2.75
(15)	Bill Kennedy	4.00	2.00	1.25
(16)	Ellis Kinder	4.00	2.00	1.25
(17)	Ted Lepcio	4.00	2.00	1.25
(18)	Johnny Lipon	4.00	2.00	1.25
(19)	Maurice McDermott	4.00	2.00	1.25
(20)	John Merson	4.00	2.00	1.25
(21)	Gus Niarhos	4.00	2.00	1.25
(22)	Willard Nixon	4.00	2.00	1.25
(23)	Mel Parnell	4.00	2.00	1.25
(24)	Jim Piersall	6.00	3.00	1.75
(25)	Gene Stephens	4.00	2.00	1.25
(26)	Tommy Umphlett	4.00	2.00	1.25
(27)	Bill Werle	4.00	2.00	1.25
(28)	Sam White	4.00	2.00	1.25
(29)	Del Wilber	4.00	2.00	1.25
(30)	Al Zarilla	4.00	2.00	1.25

1954 Boston Red Sox Photo Pack

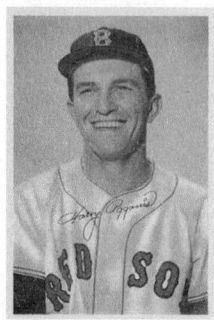

In the same approximately 6-1/2" x 9" format which the team had used for its photo packs since the 1940s, this set

of black-and-white, blank-back pictures features (usually) chest-to-cap portraits with white borders and a facsimile autograph within the photo. Some of the photos were re-used from previous years' issues. The unnumbered pictures are checklisted here in alphabetical order. This list may or may not be complete; it is possible other players' photos were added or deleted to reflect seasonal roster changes. The set was sold in a red and white paper envelope.

		NM	E	VG
Complete Set (30):		125.00	62.50	37.50
Common Player:		4.00	2.00	1.25
(1)	Harry Agganis	15.00	7.50	4.50
(2)	Milt Bolling	4.00	2.00	1.25
(3)	Lou Boudreau	9.00	4.50	2.75
(4)	Tom Brewer	4.00	2.00	1.25
(5)	Harold Brown	4.00	2.00	1.25
(6)	Truman Clevenger	4.00	2.00	1.25
(7)	Bill Consolo	4.00	2.00	1.25
(8)	Joe Dobson	4.00	2.00	1.25
(9)	Hoot Evers	4.00	2.00	1.25
(10)	Dick Gernert	4.00	2.00	1.25
(11)	Bill Goodman	4.00	2.00	1.25
(12)	Bill Henry	4.00	2.00	1.25
(13)	Tom Herrin	4.00	2.00	1.25
(14)	Sid Hudson	4.00	2.00	1.25
(15)	Jackie Jensen	6.00	3.00	1.75
(16)	George Kell	9.00	4.50	2.75
(17)	Leo Kiely	4.00	2.00	1.25
(18)	Ellis Kinder	4.00	2.00	1.25
(19)	Ted Lepcio	4.00	2.00	1.25
(20)	Charlie Maxwell	4.00	2.00	1.25
(21)	Willard Nixon	4.00	2.00	1.25
(22)	Karl Olsen	4.00	2.00	1.25
(23)	Mickey Owen	4.00	2.00	1.25
(24)	Mel Parnell	4.00	2.00	1.25
(25)	Jim Piersall	6.00	3.00	1.75
(26)	Frank Sullivan	4.00	2.00	1.25
(27)	Bill Werle	4.00	2.00	1.25
(28)	Sammy White	4.00	2.00	1.25
(29)	Ted Williams	30.00	15.00	9.00
(30)	Del Wilber	4.00	2.00	1.25

1957 Boston Red Sox Photo Pack

JIMMY PIERSALL

In approximately the same 5" x 7" black-and-white, blank-back format as the later Jay Publishing issues, this team issue is distinguished by the lack of a team name in the bottom border. Some of the photos were re-used in the following year's issue. Sets were originally sold in a manila envelope for 25 cents.

		NM	E	VG
Complete Set (12):		45.00	22.00	13.50
Common Player:		3.00	1.50	.90
(1)	Tom Brewer	3.00	1.50	.90
(2)	Dick Gernert	3.00	1.50	.90
(3)	Mike Higgins	3.00	1.50	.90
(4)	Jackie Jensen	4.50	2.25	1.25
(5)	Frank Malzone	3.00	1.50	.90
(6)	Gene Mauch	4.50	2.25	1.25
(7)	Jimmy Piersall	4.50	2.25	1.25
(8)	Dave Sisler	3.00	1.50	.90
(9)	Frank Sullivan	3.00	1.50	.90
(10)	Mickey Vernon	3.00	1.50	.90
(11)	Sammy White	3.00	1.50	.90
(12)	Ted Williams	20.00	10.00	6.00

1958 Boston Red Sox Photo Pack

In approximately the same 5" x 7" black-and-white, blank-back format as the contemporary Jay Publishing issues, this team issue is distinguished by the lack of a team name in the bottom border. Some of the photos were re-used from the previous year's issue. Sets were originally sold in a manila envelope for 25 cents.

		NM	E	VG
Complete Set (12):		45.00	22.00	13.50
Common Player:		3.00	1.50	.90
(1)	Ken Aspromonte	3.00	1.50	.90
(2)	Tom Brewer	3.00	1.50	.90
(3)	Mike Higgins	3.00	1.50	.90
(4)	Jack Jensen	4.50	2.25	1.25
(5)	Frank Malzone	3.00	1.50	.90
(6)	Will Nixon	3.00	1.50	.90
(7)	Jim Piersall	4.50	2.25	1.25
(8)	Pete Runnels	3.00	1.50	.90
(9)	Gene Stephens	3.00	1.50	.90
(10)	Frank Sullivan	3.00	1.50	.90
(11)	Sam White	3.00	1.50	.90
(12)	Ted Williams	20.00	10.00	6.00

1959 Boston Red Sox Photo Pack

In approximately the same 5" x 7" black-and-white, blank-back format as the contemporary Jay Publishing issues, this team issue is distinguished by the lack of a team name in the bottom border. Some of the photos were re-used from the previous years' issues. Sets were originally sold in a manila envelope for 25 cents.

		NM	E	VG
Complete Set (12):		45.00	22.00	13.50
Common Player:		3.00	1.50	.90
(1)	Tom Brewer	3.00	1.50	.90
(2)	Don Buddin	3.00	1.50	.90
(3)	Dick Gernert	3.00	1.50	.90
(4)	Mike Higgins	3.00	1.50	.90
(5)	Jack Jensen	4.50	2.25	1.25
(6)	Frank Malzone	3.00	1.50	.90
(7)	Jim Piersall	4.50	2.25	1.25
(8)	Pete Runnels	3.00	1.50	.90
(9)	Gene Stephens	3.00	1.50	.90
(10)	Frank Sullivan	3.00	1.50	.90
(11)	Sam White	3.00	1.50	.90
(12)	Ted Williams	20.00	10.00	6.00

1960 Boston Red Sox Photo Pack

In approximately the same 5" x 7" black-and-white, blank-back format as the contemporary Jay Publishing issues, this team issue is distinguished by the lack of a team name in the bottom border. Some of the photos were re-used from the previous years' issues. Sets were originally sold in a manila envelope for 25 cents. The fact that more than 12 players are known indicates there were some changes in specific contents over the course of the season to reflect roster changes.

		NM	E	VG
Complete Set (14):		50.00	25.00	15.00
Common Player:		3.00	1.50	.90
(1)	Tom Brewer	3.00	1.50	.90
(2)	Don Buddin	3.00	1.50	.90
(3)	Jerry Casale	3.00	1.50	.90
(4)	Ike Delock	3.00	1.50	.90
(5)	Pumpsie Green	3.00	1.50	.90
(6)	Bill Jurges	3.00	1.50	.90
(7)	Frank Malzone	3.00	1.50	.90
(8)	Pete Runnels	3.00	1.50	.90
(9)	Ed Sadowski	3.00	1.50	.90
(10)	Gene Stephens	3.00	1.50	.90
(11)	Willie Tasby	3.00	1.50	.90
(12)	Bobby Thomson	3.00	1.50	.90
(13)	Vic Wertz	3.00	1.50	.90
(14)	Ted Williams	20.00	10.00	6.00

1968 Boston Red Sox Team Issue

About 5-1/2" x 7-1/2", these black-and-white player pictures have posed photos, bordered in white, with a facsimile autograph. Backs are blank. The alphabetized checklist here is likely incomplete.

		NM	E	VG
Complete Set (8):		15.00	7.50	4.50
Common Player:		2.00	1.00	.60
(1a)	Mike Andrews ("B" on cap.)	2.00	1.00	.60
(1b)	Mike Andrews (No "B.")	2.00	1.00	.60

		NM	E	VG
(2)	Darrell Brandon	2.00	1.00	.60
(3)	Bobby Doerr	3.00	1.50	.90
(4)	Ken Harrelson	2.50	1.25	.70
(5)	Jim Lonborg	2.50	1.25	.70
(6)	Rico Petrocelli	3.00	1.50	.90
(7)	Reggie Smith	2.50	1.25	.70
(8)	Dick Williams	2.00	1.00	.60

1969 Boston Red Sox Team Issue

This team-issue photo pack features black-and-white portrait photos on a 4-1/4" x 7" blank-back format, similar to the team's 1971 issue. The player's name and team nickname are designated in the white border at top. The unnumbered cards are checklisted here in alphabetical order.

		NM	E	VG
Complete Set (12):		60.00	30.00	15.00
Common Player:		4.00	2.00	1.25
(1)	Mike Andrews	4.00	2.00	1.25
(2)	Tony Conigliaro	9.00	4.50	2.75
(3)	Russ Gibson	4.00	2.00	1.25
(4)	Dalton Jones	4.00	2.00	1.25
(5)	Bill Landis	4.00	2.00	1.25
(6)	Jim Lonborg	5.00	2.50	1.50
(7)	Sparky Lyle	4.00	2.00	1.25
(8)	Rico Petrocelli	5.00	2.50	1.50
(9)	George Scott	5.00	2.50	1.50
(10)	Reggie Smith	4.00	2.00	1.25
(11)	Dick Williams	4.00	2.00	1.25
(12)	Carl Yastrzemski	15.00	7.50	4.50

1978 Boston Red Sox of the 1950s-1960s

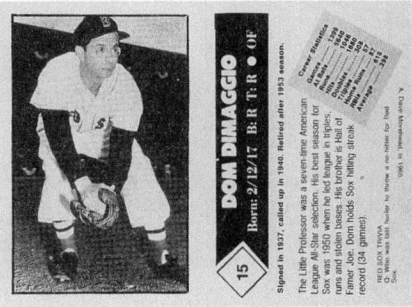

The date of actual issue, the name of the issuer and even the "official" title of this collectors' edition card set is currently unknown. The 2-1/2" x 3-1/2" cards are printed in black-and-white on front and backs. Fronts have the style of the 1953 Bowmans, with only a player photo and a white border. Backs are reminiscent of the 1955 Bowman, with player identification, career highlights, stats and a Red Sox trivia question. Cards #1-64 concentrate on the 1950s, cards #65-128 feature 1960s players.

		NM	E	VG
Complete Set (128):		100.00	50.00	30.00
Common Player:		4.00	2.00	1.25
1	Harry Agganis	12.00	6.00	3.50
2	Ken Aspromonte	4.00	2.00	1.25
3	Bobby Avila	4.00	2.00	1.25
4	Frank Baumann	4.00	2.00	1.25
5	Lou Berberet	4.00	2.00	1.25
6	Milt Bolling	4.00	2.00	1.25
7	Lou Boudreau	6.00	3.00	1.75
8	Ted Bowsfield	4.00	2.00	1.25
9	Tom Brewer	4.00	2.00	1.25
10	Don Buddin	4.00	2.00	1.25
11	Jerry Casale	4.00	2.00	1.25
12	Billy Consolo	4.00	2.00	1.25
13	Pete Daley	4.00	2.00	1.25
14	Ike Delock	4.00	2.00	1.25
15	Dom DiMaggio	9.00	4.50	2.75
16	Bobby Doerr	6.00	3.00	1.75
17	Walt Dropo	5.00	2.50	1.50
18	Arnie Earley	4.00	2.00	1.25
19	Hoot Evers	4.00	2.00	1.25
20	Mike Fornieles	4.00	2.00	1.25
21	Gary Geiger	4.00	2.00	1.25
22	Don Gile	4.00	2.00	1.25
23	Joe Ginsberg	4.00	2.00	1.25
24	Billy Goodman	4.00	2.00	1.25
25	Pumpsie Green	4.00	2.00	1.25
26	Grady Hatton	4.00	2.00	1.25
27	Billy Herman	5.00	2.50	1.50
28	Jackie Jensen	5.00	2.50	1.50
29	George Kell	6.00	3.00	1.75
30	Marty Keough	4.00	2.00	1.25
31	Leo Kiely	4.00	2.00	1.25
32	Ellis Kinder	4.00	2.00	1.25
33	Billy Klaus	4.00	2.00	1.25
34	Don Lenhardt	4.00	2.00	1.25
35	Ted Lepcio	4.00	2.00	1.25
36	Frank Malzone	4.00	2.00	1.25
37	Gene Mauch	4.00	2.00	1.25
38	Maury McDermott	4.00	2.00	1.25
39	Bill Monbouquette	4.00	2.00	1.25
40	Chet Nichols	4.00	2.00	1.25
41	Willard Nixon	4.00	2.00	1.25
42	Jim Pagliaroni	4.00	2.00	1.25
43	Mel Parnell	4.00	2.00	1.25
44	Johnny Pesky	4.00	2.00	1.25
45	Jimmy Piersall	5.00	2.50	1.50
46	Bob Porterfield	4.00	2.00	1.25
47	Pete Runnels	4.00	2.00	1.25
48	Dave Sisler	4.00	2.00	1.25
49	Riverboat Smith	4.00	2.00	1.25
50	Gene Stephens	4.00	2.00	1.25
51	Vern Stephens	4.00	2.00	1.25
52	Chuck Stobbs	4.00	2.00	1.25
53	Dean Stone	4.00	2.00	1.25
54	Frank Sullivan	4.00	2.00	1.25
55	Haywood Sullivan	4.00	2.00	1.25
56	Birdie Tebbetts	4.00	2.00	1.25
57	Mickey Vernon	4.00	2.00	1.25
58	Vic Wertz	4.00	2.00	1.25
59	Sammy White	4.00	2.00	1.25
60	Ted Williams	20.00	10.00	6.00
61	Ted Wills	4.00	2.00	1.25
62	Earl Wilson	4.00	2.00	1.25
63	Al Zarilla	4.00	2.00	1.25
64	Norm Zauchin	4.00	2.00	1.25
65	Ted Williams, Carl Yastrzemski	12.00	6.00	3.50
66	Dick Williams, Carl Yastrzemski, Jim Lonborg, George Scott	10.00	5.00	3.00
67	Tony Conigliaro, Billy Conigliaro	9.00	4.50	2.75
68	Jerry Adair	4.00	2.00	1.25
69	Mike Andrews	4.00	2.00	1.25
70	Gary Bell	4.00	2.00	1.25
71	Dennis Bennett	4.00	2.00	1.25
72	Ed Bressoud	4.00	2.00	1.25
73	Ken Brett	4.00	2.00	1.25
74	Lu Clinton	4.00	2.00	1.25
75	Billy Conigliaro	5.00	2.50	1.50
76	Tony Conigliaro	6.00	3.00	1.75
77	Gene Conley	4.00	2.00	1.25
78	Ray Culp	4.00	2.00	1.25
79	Dick Ellsworth	4.00	2.00	1.25
80	Joe Foy	4.00	2.00	1.25
81	Russ Gibson	4.00	2.00	1.25
82	Jim Gosger	4.00	2.00	1.25
83	Lennie Green	4.00	2.00	1.25
84	Ken Harrelson	4.00	2.00	1.25
85	Tony Horton	4.00	2.00	1.25
86	Elston Howard	5.00	2.50	1.50
87	Dalton Jones	4.00	2.00	1.25
88	Eddie Kasko	4.00	2.00	1.25
89	Joe Lahoud	4.00	2.00	1.25
90	Jack Lamabe	4.00	2.00	1.25
91	Jim Lonborg	5.00	2.50	1.50
92	Sparky Lyle	5.00	2.50	1.50
93	Felix Mantilla	4.00	2.00	1.25
94	Roman Mejias	4.00	2.00	1.25
95	Don McMahon	4.00	2.00	1.25
96	Dave Morehead	4.00	2.00	1.25
97	Gerry Moses	4.00	2.00	1.25
98	Mike Nagy	4.00	2.00	1.25
99	Russ Nixon	4.00	2.00	1.25
100	Gene Oliver	4.00	2.00	1.25
101	Dan Osinski	4.00	2.00	1.25
102	Rico Petrocelli	5.00	2.50	1.50
103	Juan Pizarro	4.00	2.00	1.25
104	Dick Radatz	4.00	2.00	1.25
105	Vicente Romo	4.00	2.00	1.25
106	Mike Ryan	4.00	2.00	1.25
107	Jose Santiago	4.00	2.00	1.25
108	Chuck Schilling	4.00	2.00	1.25
109	Dick Schofield	4.00	2.00	1.25
110	Don Schwall	4.00	2.00	1.25
111	George Scott	4.00	2.00	1.25
112	Norm Siebern	4.00	2.00	1.25
113	Sonny Siebert	4.00	2.00	1.25
114	Reggie Smith	4.00	2.00	1.25
115	Bill Spanswick	4.00	2.00	1.25
116	Tracy Stallard	4.00	2.00	1.25
117	Lee Stange	4.00	2.00	1.25
118	Jerry Stephenson	4.00	2.00	1.25
119	Dick Stuart	4.00	2.00	1.25
120	Tom Sturdivant	4.00	2.00	1.25
121	Jose Tartabull	4.00	2.00	1.25
122	George Thomas	4.00	2.00	1.25
123	Lee Thomas	4.00	2.00	1.25
124	Bob Tillman	4.00	2.00	1.25
125	Gary Waslewski	4.00	2.00	1.25
126	Dick Williams	4.00	2.00	1.25
127	John Wyatt	4.00	2.00	1.25
128	Carl Yastrzemski	12.00	6.00	3.50

1979 Boston Red Sox Team Issue

The origins of this Boston Red Sox card set are unclear. It may have been a team issue. The wide white bottom border beneath the black-and-white photo on the 2-1/2" x 3-1/2" cards may have been intended for autographing. Backs have player personal data and complete major and minor league stats. The checklist here, listed alphabetically, may not be complete.

		NM	E	VG
Complete Set (24):		50.00	25.00	15.00
Common Player:		3.00	1.50	.90
(1)	Gary Allenson	3.00	1.50	.90
(2)	Jack Brohamer	3.00	1.50	.90
(3)	Tom Burgmeier	3.00	1.50	.90
(4)	Rick Burleson	3.00	1.50	.90
(5)	Bill Campbell	3.00	1.50	.90
(6)	Dick Drago	3.00	1.50	.90
(7)	Dennis Eckersley	12.00	6.00	3.50
(8)	Dwight Evans	4.50	2.25	1.25
(9)	Carlton Fisk	15.00	7.50	4.50
(10)	Andy Hassler	3.00	1.50	.90
(11)	Butch Hobson	3.00	1.50	.90
(12)	Fred Lynn	7.50	3.75	2.25
(13)	Bob Montgomery	3.00	1.50	.90
(14)	Mike O'Berry	3.00	1.50	.90
(15)	Jerry Remy	3.00	1.50	.90
(16)	Steve Renko	3.00	1.50	.90
(17)	Jim Rice	15.00	7.50	4.50
(18)	George Scott	4.50	2.25	1.25
(19)	Bob Stanley	3.00	1.50	.90
(20)	Mike Torrez	3.00	1.50	.90
(21)	Larry Wolfe	3.00	1.50	.90
(22)	Jim Wright	3.00	1.50	.90
(23)	Carl Yastrzemski	20.00	10.00	6.00
(24)	Gary Hancock, Stan Papi (Two-sided.)	3.00	1.50	.90

1917 Boston Store

One of several regional advertisers to use this 200-card set as a promotional medium was this Chicago department store. While variations are known of cards #76, 90, 121, 146, and 190 in the Collins-McCarthy ad-back version of this set, it is unclear whether those variations also exist in the Boston Store issue. The American Card Catalog listed these 2" x 3-1/4" black-and-white cards as H801-8.

		NM	E	VG
Complete Set (200):		160,000	80,000	47,500
Common Player:		300.00	150.00	90.00
1	Sam Agnew	300.00	150.00	90.00
2	Grover Alexander	1,600	800.00	480.00
3	W.S. Alexander (W.E.)	300.00	150.00	90.00
4	Leon Ames	300.00	150.00	90.00
5	Fred Anderson	300.00	150.00	90.00
6	Ed Appleton	300.00	150.00	90.00
7	Jimmy Archer	300.00	150.00	90.00
8	Jimmy Austin	300.00	150.00	90.00
9	Jim Bagby Sr.	300.00	150.00	90.00

10	H.D. Baird	300.00	150.00	90.00
11	J. Franklin Baker	1,200	600.00	350.00
12	Dave Bancroft	1,200	600.00	350.00
13	Jack Barry	300.00	150.00	90.00
14	Joe Benz	300.00	150.00	90.00
15	Al Betzel	300.00	150.00	90.00
16	Ping Bodie	300.00	150.00	90.00
17	Joe Boehling	300.00	150.00	90.00
18	Eddie Burns	300.00	150.00	90.00
19	George Burns	300.00	150.00	90.00
20	Geo. J. Burns	300.00	150.00	90.00
21	Joe Bush	300.00	150.00	90.00
22	Owen Bush	300.00	150.00	90.00
23	Bobby Byrne	300.00	150.00	90.00
24	Forrest Cady	300.00	150.00	90.00
25	Max Carey	600.00	300.00	180.00
26	Ray Chapman	600.00	300.00	180.00
27	Larry Cheney	300.00	150.00	90.00
28	Eddie Cicotte	1,800	900.00	550.00
29	Tom Clarke	300.00	150.00	90.00
30	Ty Cobb	13,000	6,500	4,000
31	Eddie Collins	1,200	600.00	350.00
32	"Shauno" Collins (Shano)	300.00	150.00	90.00
33	Fred Coumbe	300.00	150.00	90.00
34	Harry Coveleskie (Coveleski)	300.00	150.00	90.00
35	Gavvy Cravath	300.00	150.00	90.00
36	Sam Crawford	1,200	600.00	350.00
37	Geo. Cutshaw	300.00	150.00	90.00
38	Jake Daubert	300.00	150.00	90.00
39	Geo. Dauss	300.00	150.00	90.00
40	Charles Deal	300.00	150.00	90.00
41	"Wheezer" Dell	300.00	150.00	90.00
42	William Doak	300.00	150.00	90.00
43	Bill Donovan	300.00	150.00	90.00
44	Larry Doyle	300.00	150.00	90.00
45	Johnny Evers	1,200	600.00	350.00
46	Urban Faber	1,200	600.00	350.00
47	"Hap" Felsch	3,000	1,500	900.00
48	Bill Fischer	300.00	150.00	90.00
49	Ray Fisher	300.00	150.00	90.00
50	Art Fletcher	300.00	150.00	90.00
51	Eddie Foster	300.00	150.00	90.00
52	Jacques Fournier	300.00	150.00	90.00
53	Del Gainer (Gainor)	300.00	150.00	90.00
54	Bert Gallia	300.00	150.00	90.00
55	"Chic" Gandil (Chick)	900.00	450.00	270.00
56	Larry Gardner	300.00	150.00	90.00
57	Joe Gedeon	300.00	150.00	90.00
58	Gus Getz	300.00	150.00	90.00
59	Frank Gilhooley	300.00	150.00	90.00
60	Wm. Gleason	300.00	150.00	90.00
61	M.A. Gonzales (Gonzalez)	400.00	200.00	120.00
62	Hank Gowdy	300.00	150.00	90.00
63	John Graney	300.00	150.00	90.00
64	Tom Griffith	300.00	150.00	90.00
65	Heinie Groh	300.00	150.00	90.00
66	Bob Groom	300.00	150.00	90.00
67	Louis Guisto	300.00	150.00	90.00
68	Earl Hamilton	300.00	150.00	90.00
69	Harry Harper	300.00	150.00	90.00
70	Grover Hartley	300.00	150.00	90.00
71	Harry Heilmann	1,200	600.00	350.00
72	Claude Hendrix	300.00	150.00	90.00
73	Olaf Henriksen	300.00	150.00	90.00
74	John Henry	300.00	150.00	90.00
75	"Buck" Herzog	300.00	150.00	90.00
76a	Hugh High (White stockings, photo actually Claude Williams.)	1,600	800.00	475.00
76b	Hugh High (Black stockings, correct photo.)	400.00	200.00	120.00
77	Dick Hoblitzell	300.00	150.00	90.00
78	Walter Holke	300.00	150.00	90.00
79	Harry Hooper	1,200	600.00	350.00
80	Rogers Hornsby	1,500	750.00	450.00
81	Ivan Howard	300.00	150.00	90.00
82	Joe Jackson	60,000	30,000	18,000
83	Harold Janvrin	300.00	150.00	90.00
84	William James	300.00	150.00	90.00
85	C. Jamieson	300.00	150.00	90.00
86	Hugh Jennings	1,200	600.00	350.00
87	Walter Johnson	2,200	1,100	650.00
88	James Johnston	300.00	150.00	90.00
89	Fielder Jones	300.00	150.00	90.00
90a	Joe Judge (Bat on right shoulder, photo actually Ray Morgan.)	1,600	800.00	475.00
90b	Joe Judge (Bat on left shoulder, correct photo.)	400.00	200.00	120.00
91	Hans Lobert	300.00	150.00	90.00
92	Benny Kauff	300.00	150.00	90.00
93	Wm. Killefer Jr.	300.00	150.00	90.00
94	Ed. Konetchy	300.00	150.00	90.00
95	John Lavan	300.00	150.00	90.00
96	Jimmy Lavender	300.00	150.00	90.00
97	"Nemo" Leibold	300.00	150.00	90.00
98	H.B. Leonard	300.00	150.00	90.00
99	Duffy Lewis	300.00	150.00	90.00
100	Tom Long	300.00	150.00	90.00
101	Wm. Louden	300.00	150.00	90.00
102	Fred Luderus	300.00	150.00	90.00
103	Lee Magee	300.00	150.00	90.00
104	Sherwood Magee	300.00	150.00	90.00
105	Al Mamaux	300.00	150.00	90.00
106	Leslie Mann	300.00	150.00	90.00
107	"Rabbit" Maranville	1,200	600.00	350.00
108	Rube Marquard	1,200	600.00	350.00
109	Armando Marsans	480.00	240.00	150.00
110	J. Erskine Mayer	300.00	150.00	90.00
111	George McBride	300.00	150.00	90.00
112	Lew McCarty	300.00	120.00	90.00
113	John J. McGraw	1,200	600.00	350.00
114	Jack McInnis	300.00	150.00	90.00
115	Lee Meadows	300.00	150.00	90.00
116	Fred Merkle	300.00	150.00	90.00
117	"Chief" Meyers	300.00	150.00	90.00
118	Clyde Milan	300.00	150.00	90.00
119	Otto Miller	300.00	150.00	90.00
120	Clarence Mitchell	300.00	150.00	90.00
121a	Ray Morgan (Bat on left shoulder, photo actually Joe Judge.)	1,600	800.00	475.00
121b	Ray Morgan (Bat on right shoulder, correct photo.)	400.00	200.00	120.00
122	Guy Morton	300.00	150.00	90.00
123	"Mike" Mowrey	300.00	150.00	90.00
124	Elmer Myers	300.00	150.00	90.00
125	"Hy" Myers	300.00	150.00	90.00
126	A.E. Neale	600.00	300.00	180.00
127	Arthur Nehf	300.00	150.00	90.00
128	J.A. Niehoff	300.00	150.00	90.00
129	Steve O'Neill	300.00	150.00	90.00
130	"Dode" Paskert	300.00	150.00	90.00
131	Roger Peckinpaugh	400.00	200.00	120.00
132	"Pol" Perritt	300.00	150.00	90.00
133	"Jeff" Pfeffer	300.00	150.00	90.00
134	Walter Pipp	300.00	150.00	90.00
135	Derril Pratt (Derrill)	300.00	150.00	90.00
136	Bill Rariden	300.00	150.00	90.00
137	E.C. Rice	1,200	600.00	350.00
138	Wm. A. Ritter (Wm. H.)	300.00	150.00	90.00
139	Eppa Rixey	1,200	600.00	350.00
140	Davey Robertson	300.00	150.00	90.00
141	"Bob" Roth	300.00	150.00	90.00
142	Ed. Roush	1,200	600.00	350.00
143	Clarence Rowland	300.00	150.00	90.00
144	Dick Rudolph	300.00	150.00	90.00
145	William Rumler	300.00	150.00	90.00
146a	Reb Russell (Pitching follow-thru, photo actually Mellie Wolfgang.)	1,600	800.00	350.00
146b	Reb Russell (Hands at side, correct photo.)	400.00	200.00	120.00
147	"Babe" Ruth	50,000	25,000	15,000
148	Vic Saier	300.00	150.00	90.00
149	"Slim" Sallee	300.00	150.00	90.00
150	Ray Schalk	1,000	500.00	300.00
151	Walter Schang	300.00	150.00	90.00
152	Frank Schulte	300.00	150.00	90.00
153	Ferd Schupp	300.00	150.00	90.00
154	Everett Scott	300.00	150.00	90.00
155	Hank Severeid	300.00	150.00	90.00
156	Howard Shanks	300.00	150.00	90.00
157	Bob Shawkey	300.00	150.00	90.00
158	Jas. Sheckard	300.00	150.00	90.00
159	Ernie Shore	300.00	150.00	90.00
160	C.H. Shorten	300.00	150.00	90.00
161	Burt Shotton	300.00	150.00	90.00
162	Geo. Sisler	1,600	800.00	475.00
163	Elmer Smith	300.00	150.00	90.00
164	J. Carlisle Smith	300.00	150.00	90.00
165	Fred Snodgrass	300.00	150.00	90.00
166	Tris Speaker	1,500	750.00	450.00
167	Oscar Stanage	300.00	150.00	90.00
168	Charles Stengel	1,200	600.00	350.00
169	Milton Stock	300.00	150.00	90.00
170	Amos Strunk	300.00	150.00	90.00
171	"Zeb" Terry	300.00	150.00	90.00
172	"Jeff" Tesreau	300.00	150.00	90.00
173	Chester Thomas	300.00	150.00	90.00
174	Fred Toney	300.00	150.00	90.00
175	Terry Turner	300.00	150.00	90.00
176	George Tyler	300.00	150.00	90.00
177	Jim Vaughn	300.00	150.00	90.00
178	Bob Veach	300.00	150.00	90.00
179	Oscar Vitt	300.00	150.00	90.00
180	Hans Wagner	6,000	3,000	1,800
181	Clarence Walker	300.00	150.00	90.00
182	Jim Walsh	300.00	150.00	90.00
183	Al Walters	300.00	150.00	90.00
184	W. Wambsganss	300.00	150.00	90.00
185	Buck Weaver	2,400	1,200	725.00
186	Carl Weilman	300.00	150.00	90.00
187	Zack Wheat	1,200	600.00	350.00
188	Geo. Whitted	300.00	150.00	90.00
189	Joe Wilhoit	300.00	150.00	90.00
190a	Claude Williams (Black stockings, photo actually Hugh High.)	2,400	1,200	725.00
190b	Claude Williams (White stockings, correct photo.)	3,000	1,500	900.00
191	Fred Williams	300.00	150.00	90.00
192	Art Wilson	300.00	150.00	90.00
193	Lawton Witt	300.00	150.00	90.00
194	Joe Wood	400.00	200.00	120.00
195	William Wortman	300.00	150.00	90.00
196	Steve Yerkes	300.00	150.00	90.00
197	Earl Yingling	300.00	150.00	90.00
198	"Pep" Young (Photo actually Ralph Young.)	300.00	150.00	90.00
199	Rollie Zeider	300.00	150.00	90.00
200	Henry Zimmerman	300.00	150.00	90.00

1972 Bowery Bank Joe DiMaggio

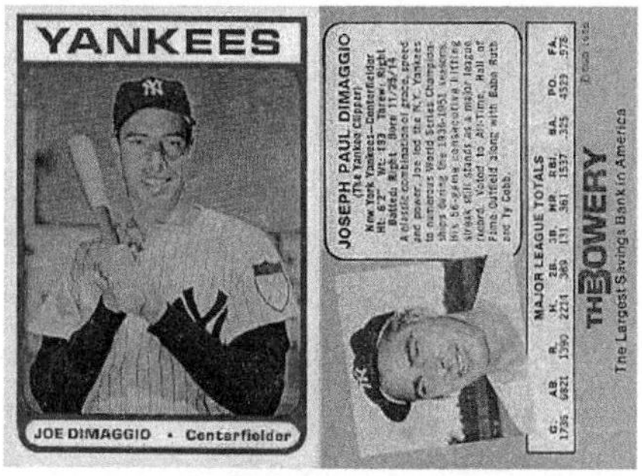

These cards were issued to promote the New York City bank's relationship with spokesman Joe DiMaggio. The 2-1/2" x 3-1/2" cards have a posed color photo on front. The back has a black-and-white portrait, biographical data, career highlights and stats on a pink background.

	NM	E	VG
Joe DiMaggio	17.50	9.00	5.00

1948 Bowman

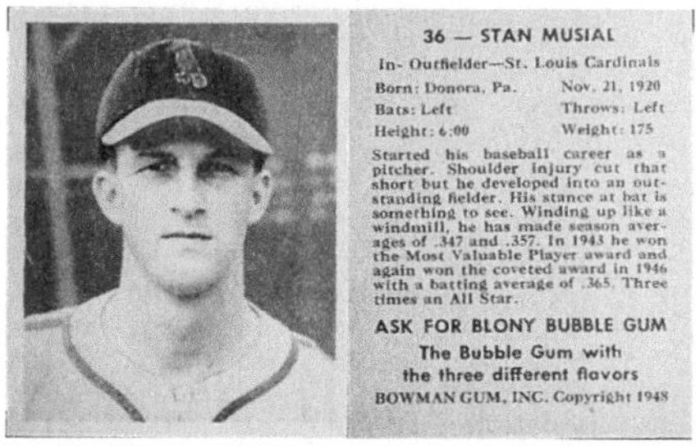

Bowman Gum Co.'s premiere set of 1948 was one of the first major issues of the post-war period. Forty-eight black-and-white cards comprise the set, with each card card measuring 2-1/16" x 2-1/2". The card backs, printed in black ink on gray stock, include the card number and the player's name, team, position, and a short biography. Twelve cards (marked with an "SP") were printed in short supply when they were removed from the 36-card printing sheet to make room for the set's high numbers (#37-48).

		NM	E	VG
Complete Set (48):		4,250	2,100	1,250
Common Player (1-36):		50.00	25.00	15.00
Common Player (37-48):		120.00	60.00	35.00
1	Bob Elliott **RC**	150.00	60.00	18.00
2	Ewell Blackwell **RC**	140.00	70.00	40.00
3	Ralph Kiner **RC**	200.00	100.00	60.00
4	Johnny Mize	100.00	50.00	30.00
5	Bob Feller	400.00	200.00	120.00
6	Yogi Berra **RC**	700.00	350.00	210.00
7	Pete Reiser (SP)	200.00	100.00	60.00
8	Phil Rizzuto **RC** (SP)	400.00	200.00	120.00
9	Walker Cooper	50.00	25.00	15.00
10	Buddy Rosar	50.00	25.00	15.00
11	Johnny Lindell	50.00	25.00	15.00
12	Johnny Sain **RC**	120.00	60.00	35.00
13	Willard Marshall **RC** (SP)	120.00	60.00	36.00

14	Allie Reynolds **RC**	120.00	60.00	35.00
15	Eddie Joost	50.00	25.00	15.00
16	Jack Lohrke (SP)	120.00	60.00	36.00
17	Enos Slaughter	200.00	100.00	60.00
18	Warren Spahn **RC**	475.00	240.00	140.00
19	Tommy Henrich	120.00	60.00	36.00
20	Buddy Kerr (SP)	120.00	60.00	36.00
21	Ferris Fain **RC**	80.00	40.00	24.00
22	Floyd (Bill) Bevens (SP)	120.00	60.00	36.00
23	Larry Jansen	50.00	25.00	15.00
24	Emil (Dutch) Leonard (SP)	120.00	60.00	36.00
25	Barney McCoskey (McCosky)	50.00	25.00	15.00
26	Frank Shea (SP)	120.00	60.00	36.00
27	Sid Gordon	50.00	25.00	15.00
28	Emil Verban (SP)	120.00	60.00	36.00
29	Joe Page **RC** (SP)	250.00	130.00	70.00
30	Whitey Lockman **RC** (SP)	150.00	75.00	45.00
31	Bill McCahan	50.00	25.00	15.00
32	Bill Rigney **RC**	50.00	25.00	15.00
33	Billy Johnson	50.00	25.00	15.00
34	Sheldon Jones (SP)	120.00	60.00	36.00
35	Snuffy Stirnweiss	50.00	25.00	15.00
36	Stan Musial **RC**	900.00	450.00	270.00
37	Clint Hartung	120.00	60.00	36.00
38	Red Schoendienst **RC**	400.00	200.00	120.00
39	Augie Galan	120.00	60.00	36.00
40	Marty Marion **RC**	200.00	100.00	60.00
41	Rex Barney	135.00	65.00	40.00
42	Ray Poat	120.00	60.00	36.00
43	Bruce Edwards	160.00	80.00	48.00
44	Johnny Wyrostek	120.00	60.00	36.00
45	Hank Sauer	120.00	60.00	36.00
46	Herman Wehmeier	120.00	60.00	36.00
47	Bobby Thomson **RC**	280.00	140.00	80.00
48	Dave Koslo	300.00	150.00	90.00

1949 Bowman

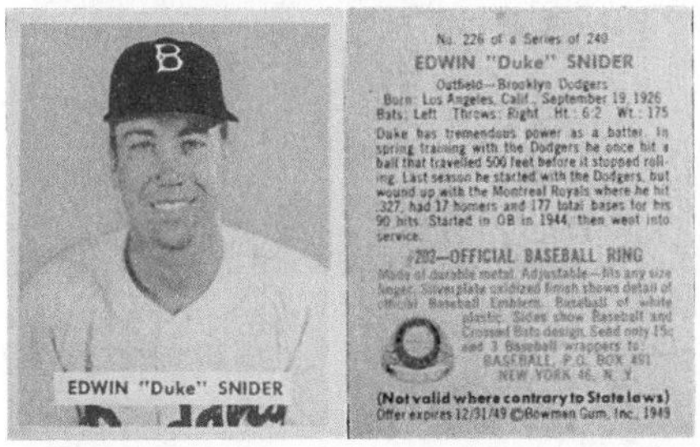

In 1949, Bowman increased the size of its issue to 240 numbered cards. The 2-1/16" x 2-1/2" cards are black-and-white photos overprinted with team uniform colors on a background of various solid pastel colors. Beginning with card #109 in the set, Bowman added the players' names on the card fronts. Twelve cards (#4, 78, 83, 85, 88, 98, 109, 124, 127, 132 and 143), which were produced in the first four series of printings, were reprinted in the seventh series with either a card front or back modification. These variations are noted in the checklist. Cards #1-3 and 5-73 can be found with either white or gray backs. The complete set value shown here does not include the higher priced variation cards.

	NM	E	VG
Complete Set (240):	18,000	9,000	5,500
Common Player (1-144):	40.00	20.00	12.00
Common Player (145-240):	75.00	37.00	22.00

1	Vernon Bickford	200.00	15.00	9.00
2	"Whitey" Lockman	40.00	20.00	12.00
3	Bob Porterfield	40.00	20.00	12.00
4a	Jerry Priddy (No name on front.)	40.00	20.00	12.00
4b	Jerry Priddy (Name on front.)	80.00	40.00	24.00
5	Hank Sauer	40.00	20.00	12.00
6	Phil Cavarretta	40.00	20.00	12.00
7	Joe Dobson	40.00	20.00	12.00
8	Murry Dickson	40.00	20.00	12.00
9	Ferris Fain	40.00	20.00	12.00
10	Ted Gray	40.00	20.00	12.00
11	Lou Boudreau **RC**	90.00	45.00	27.00
12	Cass Michaels	40.00	20.00	12.00
13	Bob Chesnes	40.00	20.00	12.00
14	Curt Simmons **RC**	100.00	50.00	30.00
15	Ned Garver **RC**	50.00	25.00	15.00
16	Al Kozar	40.00	20.00	12.00
17	Earl Torgeson	40.00	20.00	12.00
18	Bobby Thomson	75.00	37.00	22.00
19	Bobby Brown **RC**	75.00	37.00	22.00
20	Gene Hermanski	40.00	20.00	12.00
21	Frank Baumholtz	40.00	20.00	12.00
22	Harry "P-Nuts" Lowrey	40.00	20.00	12.00
23	Bobby Doerr **RC**	65.00	32.00	19.50
24	Stan Musial	400.00	200.00	120.00
25	Carl Scheib	40.00	20.00	12.00
26	George Kell **RC**	90.00	45.00	27.00
27	Bob Feller	250.00	125.00	75.00
28	Don Kolloway	40.00	20.00	12.00
29	Ralph Kiner	95.00	47.00	27.00
30	Andy Seminick	40.00	20.00	12.00
31	Dick Kokos	40.00	20.00	12.00
32	Eddie Yost	40.00	20.00	12.00
33	Warren Spahn	250.00	125.00	62.50
34	Dave Koslo	40.00	20.00	12.00
35	Vic Raschi **RC**	75.00	37.00	22.00
36	Pee Wee Reese **RC**	180.00	90.00	55.00
37	John Wyrostek	40.00	20.00	12.00
38	Emil Verban	40.00	20.00	12.00
39	Bill Goodman	40.00	20.00	12.00
40	"Red" Munger	40.00	20.00	12.00
41	Lou Brissie	40.00	20.00	12.00
42	"Hoot" Evers	40.00	20.00	12.00
43	Dale Mitchell	40.00	20.00	12.00
44	Dave Philley	40.00	20.00	12.00
45	Wally Westlake	40.00	20.00	12.00
46	Robin Roberts **RC**	250.00	125.00	62.50
47	Johnny Sain	50.00	25.00	15.00
48	Willard Marshall	40.00	20.00	12.00
49	Frank Shea	45.00	22.00	13.50
50	Jackie Robinson **RC**	1,250	625.00	375.00
51	Herman Wehmeier	40.00	20.00	12.00
52	Johnny Schmitz	40.00	20.00	12.00
53	Jack Kramer	40.00	20.00	12.00
54	Marty Marion	45.00	22.00	13.50
55	Eddie Joost	40.00	20.00	12.00
56	Pat Mullin	40.00	20.00	12.00
57	Gene Bearden	40.00	20.00	12.00
58	Bob Elliott	40.00	20.00	12.00
59	Jack Lohrke	40.00	20.00	12.00
60	Yogi Berra	350.00	175.00	87.50
61	Rex Barney	45.00	22.00	13.50
62	Grady Hatton	40.00	20.00	12.00
63	Andy Pafko	40.00	20.00	12.00
64	Dom DiMaggio **RC**	75.00	37.50	22.50
65	Enos Slaughter	80.00	40.00	24.00
66	Elmer Valo	40.00	20.00	12.00
67	Alvin Dark **RC**	60.00	30.00	18.00
68	Sheldon Jones	40.00	20.00	12.00
69	Tommy Henrich	55.00	27.50	16.50
70	Carl Furillo **RC**	150.00	75.00	37.50
71	Vern Stephens	40.00	20.00	12.00
72	Tommy Holmes	40.00	20.00	12.00
73	Billy Cox	45.00	22.50	13.50
74	Tom McBride	40.00	20.00	12.00
75	Eddie Mayo	40.00	20.00	12.00
76	Bill Nicholson	40.00	20.00	12.00
77	Ernie Bonham	40.00	20.00	12.00
78a	Sam Zoldak (No name on front.)	40.00	20.00	12.00
78b	Sam Zoldak (Name on front.)	80.00	40.00	24.00
79	Ron Northey	40.00	20.00	12.00
80	Bill McCahan	40.00	20.00	12.00
81	Virgil "Red" Stallcup	40.00	20.00	12.00
82	Joe Page	45.00	22.00	13.50
83a	Bob Scheffing (No name on front.)	40.00	20.00	12.00
83b	Bob Scheffing (Name on front.)	80.00	40.00	24.00
84	Roy Campanella **RC**	550.00	270.00	165.00
85a	Johnny Mize (No name on front.)	85.00	42.50	25.00
85b	Johnny Mize (Name on front.)	130.00	65.00	40.00
86	Johnny Pesky	40.00	20.00	12.00
87	Randy Gumpert	40.00	20.00	12.00
88a	Bill Salkeld (No name on front.)	40.00	20.00	12.00
88b	Bill Salkeld (Name on front.)	80.00	40.00	84.00
89	Mizell Platt	40.00	20.00	12.00
90	Gil Coan	40.00	20.00	12.00
91	Dick Wakefield	40.00	20.00	12.00
92	Willie Jones	40.00	20.00	12.00
93	Ed Stevens	40.00	20.00	12.00
94	Mickey Vernon **RC**	45.00	22.00	13.50
95	Howie Pollett	40.00	20.00	12.00
96	Taft Wright	40.00	20.00	12.00
97	Danny Litwhiler	40.00	20.00	12.00
98a	Phil Rizzuto (No name on front.)	225.00	110.00	65.00
98b	Phil Rizzuto (Name on front.)	280.00	190.00	85.00
99	Frank Gustine	40.00	20.00	12.00
100	Gil Hodges **RC**	300.00	150.00	75.00
101	Sid Gordon	40.00	20.00	12.00
102	Stan Spence	40.00	20.00	12.00
103	Joe Tipton	40.00	20.00	12.00
104	Ed Stanky **RC**	60.00	30.00	18.00
105	Bill Kennedy	40.00	20.00	12.00
106	Jake Early	40.00	20.00	12.00
107	Eddie Lake	40.00	20.00	12.00
108	Ken Heintzelman	40.00	20.00	12.00
109a	Ed Fitz Gerald (Script name on back.)	40.00	20.00	12.00
109b	Ed Fitz Gerald (Printed name on back.)	80.00	40.00	24.00
110	Early Wynn **RC**	150.00	75.00	37.50
111	Red Schoendienst	90.00	45.00	27.00
112	Sam Chapman	40.00	20.00	12.00
113	Ray Lamanno	40.00	20.00	12.00
114	Allie Reynolds	65.00	32.50	20.00
115	Emil "Dutch" Leonard	40.00	20.00	12.00
116	Joe Hatten	40.00	20.00	12.00
117	Walker Cooper	40.00	20.00	12.00
118	Sam Mele	40.00	20.00	12.00
119	Floyd Baker	40.00	20.00	12.00
120	Cliff Fannin	40.00	20.00	12.00
121	Mark Christman	40.00	20.00	12.00
122	George Vico	40.00	20.00	12.00
123	Johnny Blatnick	40.00	20.00	12.00
124a	Danny Murtaugh (Script name on back.)	40.00	20.00	12.00
124b	Danny Murtaugh (Printed name on back.)	80.00	40.00	24.00
125	Ken Keltner	40.00	20.00	12.00
126a	Al Brazle (Script name on back.)	40.00	20.00	12.00
126b	Al Brazle (Printed name on back.)	80.00	40.00	24.00
127a	Henry Majeski (Script name on back.)	40.00	20.00	12.00
127b	Henry Majeski (Printed name on back.)	80.00	40.00	24.00
128	Johnny Vander Meer	50.00	25.00	15.00
129	Billy Johnson	45.00	22.00	13.50
130	Harry "The Hat" Walker	45.00	22.00	13.50
131	Paul Lehner	40.00	20.00	12.00
132a	Al Evans (Script name on back.)	40.00	20.00	12.00
132b	Al Evans (Printed name on back.)	80.00	40.00	24.00
133	Aaron Robinson	40.00	20.00	12.00
134	Hank Borowy	40.00	20.00	12.00
135	Stan Rojek	40.00	20.00	12.00
136	Hank Edwards	40.00	20.00	12.00
137	Ted Wilks	40.00	20.00	12.00
138	"Buddy" Rosar	40.00	20.00	12.00
139	Hank "Bow-Wow" Arft	40.00	20.00	12.00
140	Ray Scarborough	40.00	20.00	12.00
141	"Tony Lupien	40.00	20.00	12.00
142	Eddie Waitkus	40.00	20.00	12.00
143a	Bob Dillinger (Script name on back.)	40.00	20.00	12.00
143b	Bob Dillinger (Printed name on back.)	80.00	40.00	24.00
144	Mickey Haefner	40.00	20.00	12.00
145	"Blix" Donnelly	75.00	37.00	22.00
146	Mike McCormick	75.00	37.00	22.00
147	Elmer Singleton	75.00	37.00	22.00
148	Bob Swift	75.00	37.00	22.00
149	Roy Partee	75.00	37.00	22.00
150	Allie Clark	75.00	37.00	22.00
151	Mickey Harris	75.00	37.00	22.00
152	Clarence Maddern	75.00	37.00	22.00
153	Phil Masi	75.00	37.00	22.00
154	Clint Hartung	75.00	37.00	22.00
155	Mickey Guerra	75.00	37.00	22.00
156	Al Zarilla	75.00	37.00	22.00
157	Walt Masterson	75.00	37.00	22.00
158	Harry Brecheen	75.00	37.00	22.00
159	Glen Moulder	75.00	37.00	22.00
160	Jim Blackburn	75.00	37.00	22.00
161	"Jocko" Thompson	75.00	37.00	22.00
162	Preacher Roe **RC**	120.00	60.00	30.00
163	Clyde McCullough	75.00	37.00	22.00
164	Vic Wertz **RC**	85.00	42.00	25.00
165	"Snuffy" Stirnweiss	75.00	37.00	22.00
166	Mike Tresh	75.00	37.00	22.00
167	Boris "Babe" Martin	75.00	37.00	22.00
168	Doyle Lade	75.00	37.00	22.00
169	Jeff Heath	75.00	37.00	22.00
170	Bill Rigney	75.00	37.00	22.00
171	Dick Fowler	75.00	37.00	22.00
172	Eddie Pellagrini	75.00	37.00	22.00
173	Eddie Stewart	75.00	37.00	22.00
174	Terry Moore **RC**	125.00	65.00	35.00
175	Luke Appling **RC**	125.00	62.50	37.50
176	Ken Raffensberger	75.00	37.00	22.00
177	Stan Lopata	75.00	37.00	22.00
178	Tommy Brown	75.00	37.00	22.00
179	Hugh Casey	75.00	37.00	22.00
180	Connie Berry	75.00	37.00	22.00
181	Gus Niarhos	75.00	37.00	22.00
182	Hal Peck	75.00	37.00	22.00
183	Lou Stringer	75.00	37.00	22.00
184	Bob Chipman	75.00	37.00	22.00
185	Pete Reiser	90.00	45.00	27.00
186	"Buddy" Kerr	75.00	37.00	22.00

187	Phil Marchildon	75.00	37.00	22.00
188	Karl Drews	75.00	37.00	22.00
189	Earl Wooten	75.00	37.00	22.00
190	Jim Hearn **RC**	90.00	45.00	27.00
191	Joe Haynes	75.00	37.00	22.00
192	Harry Gumbert	75.00	37.00	22.00
193	Ken Trinkle	75.00	37.00	22.00
194	Ralph Branca	120.00	60.00	35.00
195	Eddie Bockman	75.00	37.00	22.00
196	Fred Hutchinson **RC**	75.00	37.00	22.00
197	Johnny Lindell	75.00	37.00	22.00
198	Steve Gromek	75.00	37.00	22.00
199	"Tex" Hughson	75.00	37.00	22.00
200	Jess Dobernic	75.00	37.00	22.00
201	Sibby Sisti	75.00	37.00	22.00
202	Larry Jansen	75.00	37.00	22.00
203	Barney McCosky	75.00	37.00	22.00
204	Bob Savage	75.00	37.00	22.00
205	Dick Sisler	75.00	37.00	22.00
206	Bruce Edwards	75.00	37.00	22.00
207	Johnny Hopp	75.00	37.00	22.00
208	"Dizzy" Trout	75.00	37.00	22.00
209	Charlie Keller	100.00	50.00	30.00
210	Joe Gordon	75.00	37.00	22.00
211	Dave "Boo" Ferris	75.00	37.00	22.00
212	Ralph Hamner	75.00	37.00	22.00
213	Charles "Red" Barrett	75.00	37.00	22.00
214	Richie Ashburn **RC**	575.00	270.00	165.00
215	Kirby Higbe	75.00	37.00	22.00
216	"Schoolboy" Rowe	75.00	37.00	22.00
217	Marino Pieretti	75.00	37.00	22.00
218	Dick Kryhoski	75.00	37.00	22.00
219	Virgil "Fire" Trucks **RC**	90.00	45.00	27.00
220	Johnny McCarthy	75.00	37.00	22.00
221	Bob Muncrief	75.00	37.00	22.00
222	Alex Kellner	75.00	37.00	22.00
223	Bob Hofman	75.00	37.00	22.00
224	Satchel Paige **RC**	1,450	725.00	435.00
225	Gerry Coleman **RC**	90.00	45.00	27.00
226	Duke Snider **RC**	925.00	400.00	240.00
227	Fritz Ostermueller	75.00	37.00	22.00
228	Jackie Mayo	75.00	37.00	22.00
229	Ed Lopat **RC**	90.00	45.00	27.00
230	Augie Galan	75.00	37.00	22.00
231	Earl Johnson	75.00	37.00	22.00
232	George McQuinn	75.00	37.00	22.00
233	Larry Doby **RC**	325.00	160.00	97.50
234	"Rip" Sewell	75.00	37.00	22.00
235	Jim Russell	75.00	37.00	22.00
236	Fred Sanford	75.00	37.00	22.00
237	Monte Kennedy	75.00	37.00	22.00
238	Bob Lemon **RC**	225.00	110.00	65.00
239	Frank McCormick	75.00	37.00	22.00
240	Norm "Babe" Young (Photo actually Bobby Young.)	140.00	45.00	25.00

1950 Bowman

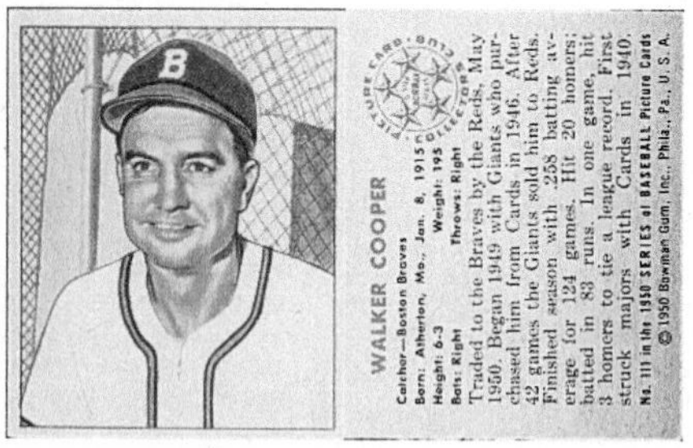

The quality of the 1950 Bowman issue showed a marked improvement over the company's previous efforts. The cards are color art reproductions of actual photographs and measure 2-1/16" x 2-1/2". Backs include the same type of information found in the previous year's issue but are designed in a horizontal format. Cards found in the first two series (#1-72) are the scarcer of the issue. The backs of the final 72 cards (#181-252) can be found with or without the copyright line at the bottom of the card, the "without" version being the less common.

	NM	E	VG
Complete Set (252):	12,500	6,000	3,500
Common Player (1-72):	60.00	30.00	18.00
Common Player (73-252):	25.00	12.50	7.50

1	Mel Parnell	700.00	87.50	43.75
2	Vern Stephens	60.00	30.00	18.00
3	Dom DiMaggio	130.00	65.00	40.00
4	Gus Zernial **RC**	90.00	45.00	27.50
5	Bob Kuzava	60.00	30.00	18.00
6	Bob Feller	300.00	150.00	90.00
7	Jim Hegan	60.00	30.00	18.00
8	George Kell	125.00	65.00	35.00
9	Vic Wertz	60.00	30.00	18.00
10	Tommy Henrich	75.00	37.50	22.50
11	Phil Rizzuto	325.00	162.50	81.25
12	Joe Page	75.00	37.00	22.00
13	Ferris Fain	60.00	30.00	18.00
14	Alex Kellner	80.00	30.00	18.00
15	Al Kozar	60.00	30.00	18.00
16	Roy Sievers **RC**	90.00	45.00	27.50
17	Sid Hudson	60.00	30.00	18.00
18	Eddie Robinson	60.00	30.00	18.00
19	Warren Spahn	300.00	150.00	75.00
20	Bob Elliott	60.00	30.00	18.00
21	Pee Wee Reese	300.00	150.00	75.00
22	Jackie Robinson	1,200	600.00	300.00
23	Don Newcombe **RC**	140.00	70.00	35.00
24	Johnny Schmitz	60.00	30.00	18.00
25	Hank Sauer	60.00	30.00	18.00
26	Grady Hatton	60.00	30.00	18.00
27	Herman Wehmeier	60.00	30.00	18.00
28	Bobby Thomson	100.00	50.00	30.00
29	Ed Stanky	65.00	32.00	19.50
30	Eddie Waitkus	60.00	30.00	18.00
31	Del Ennis **RC**	80.00	40.00	24.00
32	Robin Roberts	165.00	80.00	47.50
33	Ralph Kiner	125.00	60.00	35.00
34	Murry Dickson	60.00	30.00	18.00
35	Enos Slaughter	125.00	60.00	35.00
36	Eddie Kazak	60.00	30.00	18.00
37	Luke Appling	100.00	50.00	30.00
38	Bill Wight	60.00	30.00	18.00
39	Larry Doby	125.00	62.50	31.25
40	Bob Lemon	125.00	60.00	35.00
41	"Hoot" Evers	60.00	30.00	18.00
42	Art Houtteman	60.00	30.00	18.00
43	Bobby Doerr	100.00	50.00	30.00
44	Joe Dobson	60.00	30.00	18.00
45	Al Zarilla	60.00	30.00	18.00
46	Yogi Berra	400.00	200.00	100.00
47	Jerry Coleman	65.00	32.00	19.50
48	Lou Brissie	60.00	30.00	18.00
49	Elmer Valo	60.00	30.00	18.00
50	Dick Kokos	60.00	30.00	18.00
51	Ned Garver	60.00	30.00	18.00
52	Sam Mele	60.00	30.00	18.00
53	Clyde Vollmer	60.00	30.00	18.00
54	Gil Coan	60.00	30.00	18.00
55	"Buddy" Kerr	60.00	30.00	18.00
56	Del Crandell **RC** (Crandall)	75.00	37.00	22.00
57	Vernon Bickford	60.00	30.00	18.00
58	Carl Furillo	80.00	40.00	24.00
59	Ralph Branca	75.00	37.00	22.00
60	Andy Pafko	60.00	30.00	18.00
61	Bob Rush	60.00	30.00	18.00
62	Ted Kluszewski **RC**	125.00	62.50	37.50
63	Ewell Blackwell	60.00	30.00	18.00
64	Alvin Dark	60.00	30.00	18.00
65	Dave Koslo	60.00	30.00	18.00
66	Larry Jansen	60.00	30.00	18.00
67	Willie Jones	60.00	30.00	18.00
68	Curt Simmons	60.00	30.00	18.00
69	Wally Westlake	60.00	30.00	18.00
70	Bob Chesnes	60.00	30.00	18.00
71	Red Schoendienst	75.00	37.00	22.00
72	Howie Pollet	60.00	30.00	18.00
73	Willard Marshall	25.00	12.50	7.50
74	Johnny Antonelli **RC**	40.00	20.00	12.00
75	Roy Campanella	300.00	150.00	75.00
76	Rex Barney	25.00	12.50	7.50
77	Duke Snider	300.00	150.00	75.00
78	Mickey Owen	25.00	12.50	7.50
79	Johnny Vander Meer	25.00	12.50	7.50
80	Howard Fox	25.00	12.50	7.50
81	Ron Northey	25.00	12.50	7.50
82	"Whitey" Lockman	25.00	12.50	7.50
83	Sheldon Jones	25.00	12.50	7.50
84	Richie Ashburn	125.00	62.50	31.25
85	Ken Heintzelman	25.00	12.50	7.50
86	Stan Rojek	25.00	12.50	7.50
87	Bill Werle	25.00	12.50	7.50
88	Marty Marion	30.00	15.00	9.00
89	George Munger	25.00	12.50	7.50
90	Harry Brecheen	25.00	12.50	7.50
91	Cass Michaels	25.00	12.50	7.50
92	Hank Majeski	25.00	12.50	7.50
93	Gene Bearden	25.00	12.50	7.50
94	Lou Boudreau	70.00	35.00	20.00
95	Aaron Robinson	25.00	12.50	7.50
96	Virgil "Fire" Trucks	25.00	12.50	7.50
97	Maurice McDermott	25.00	12.50	7.50
98	Ted Williams **RC**	1,100	550.00	275.00
99	Billy Goodman	25.00	12.50	7.50
100	Vic Raschi	50.00	25.00	15.00
101	Bobby Brown	55.00	27.50	16.50
102	Billy Johnson	30.00	15.00	9.00
103	Eddie Joost	25.00	12.50	7.50
104	Sam Chapman	25.00	12.50	7.50
105	Bob Dillinger	25.00	12.50	7.50
106	Cliff Fannin	25.00	12.50	7.50
107	Sam Dente	25.00	12.50	7.50
108	Ray Scarborough	25.00	12.50	7.50
109	Sid Gordon	25.00	12.50	7.50
110	Tommy Holmes	25.00	12.50	7.50
111	Walker Cooper	25.00	12.50	7.50
112	Gil Hodges	125.00	60.00	35.00
113	Gene Hermanski	25.00	12.50	7.50
114	Wayne Terwilliger **RC**	25.00	12.50	7.50
115	Roy Smalley	25.00	12.50	7.50
116	Virgil "Red" Stallcup	25.00	12.50	7.50
117	Bill Rigney	25.00	12.50	7.50
118	Clint Hartung	25.00	12.50	7.50
119	Dick Sisler	25.00	12.50	7.50
120	Jocko Thompson	25.00	12.50	7.50
121	Andy Seminick	25.00	12.50	7.50
122	Johnny Hopp	25.00	12.50	7.50
123	Dino Restelli	25.00	12.50	7.50
124	Clyde McCullough	25.00	12.50	7.50
125	Del Rice	25.00	12.50	7.50
126	Al Brazle	25.00	12.50	7.50
127	Dave Philley	25.00	12.50	7.50
128	Phil Masi	25.00	12.50	7.50
129	Joe Gordon	25.00	12.50	7.50
130	Dale Mitchell	25.00	12.50	7.50
131	Steve Gromek	25.00	12.50	7.50
132	Mickey Vernon	25.00	12.50	7.50
133	Don Kolloway	25.00	12.50	7.50
134	"Dizzy" Trout	25.00	12.50	7.50
135	Pat Mullin	25.00	12.50	7.50
136	"Buddy" Rosar	25.00	12.50	7.50
137	Johnny Pesky	25.00	12.50	7.50
138	Allie Reynolds	60.00	30.00	18.00
139	Johnny Mize	65.00	32.50	20.00
140	Pete Suder	25.00	12.50	7.50
141	Joe Coleman	25.00	12.50	7.50
142	Sherman Lollar **RC**	25.00	12.50	7.50
143	Eddie Stewart	25.00	12.50	7.50
144	Al Evans	25.00	12.50	7.50
145	Jack Graham	25.00	12.50	7.50
146	Floyd Baker	25.00	12.50	7.50
147	Mike Garcia **RC**	30.00	15.00	9.00
148	Early Wynn	70.00	35.00	20.00
149	Bob Swift	25.00	12.50	7.50
150	George Vico	25.00	12.50	7.50
151	Fred Hutchinson	25.00	12.50	7.50
152	Ellis Kinder	25.00	12.50	7.50
153	Walt Masterson	25.00	12.50	7.50
154	Gus Niarhos	30.00	15.00	9.00
155	Frank "Spec" Shea	30.00	15.00	9.00
156	Fred Sanford	30.00	15.00	9.00
157	Mike Guerra	25.00	12.50	7.50
158	Paul Lehner	25.00	12.50	7.50
159	Joe Tipton	25.00	12.50	7.50
160	Mickey Harris	25.00	12.50	7.50
161	Sherry Robertson	25.00	12.50	7.50
162	Eddie Yost	25.00	12.50	7.50
163	Earl Torgeson	25.00	12.50	7.50
164	Sibby Sisti	25.00	12.50	7.50
165	Bruce Edwards	25.00	12.50	7.50
166	Joe Hatten	25.00	12.50	7.50
167	Preacher Roe	50.00	25.00	15.00
168	Bob Scheffing	25.00	12.50	7.50
169	Hank Edwards	25.00	12.50	7.50
170	Emil Leonard	25.00	12.50	7.50
171	Harry Gumbert	25.00	12.50	7.50
172	Harry Lowrey	25.00	12.50	7.50
173	Lloyd Merriman	25.00	12.50	7.50
174	Henry Thompson **RC**	30.00	15.00	9.00
175	Monte Kennedy	25.00	12.50	7.50
176	"Blix" Donnelly	25.00	12.50	7.50
177	Hank Borowy	25.00	12.50	7.50
178	Eddy Fitz Gerald	25.00	12.50	7.50
179	Charles Diering	25.00	12.50	7.50
180	Harry "The Hat" Walker	25.00	12.50	7.50
181	Marino Pieretti	25.00	12.50	7.50
182	Sam Zoldak	25.00	12.50	7.50
183	Mickey Haefner	25.00	12.50	7.50
184	Randy Gumpert	25.00	12.50	7.50
185	Howie Judson	25.00	12.50	7.50
186	Ken Keltner	25.00	12.50	7.50
187	Lou Stringer	25.00	12.50	7.50
188	Earl Johnson	25.00	12.50	7.50
189	Owen Friend	25.00	12.50	7.50
190	Ken Wood	25.00	12.50	7.50
191	Dick Starr	25.00	12.50	7.50
192	Bob Chipman	25.00	12.50	7.50
193	Pete Reiser	30.00	15.00	9.00
194	Billy Cox	35.00	17.50	10.00
195	Phil Cavarretta	25.00	12.50	7.50
196	Doyle Lade	25.00	12.50	7.50
197	Johnny Wyrostek	25.00	12.50	7.50
198	Danny Litwhiler	25.00	12.50	7.50
199	Jack Kramer	25.00	12.50	7.50
200	Kirby Higbe	25.00	12.50	7.50
201	Pete Castiglione	25.00	12.50	7.50
202	Cliff Chambers	25.00	12.50	7.50
203	Danny Murtaugh	25.00	12.50	7.50

204	Granny Hamner	25.00	12.50	7.50
205	Mike Goliat	25.00	12.50	7.50
206	Stan Lopata	25.00	12.50	7.50
207	Max Lanier	25.00	12.50	7.50
208	Jim Hearn	25.00	12.50	7.50
209	Johnny Lindell	25.00	12.50	7.50
210	Ted Gray	25.00	12.50	7.50
211	Charlie Keller	30.00	15.00	9.00
212	Gerry Priddy	25.00	12.50	7.50
213	Carl Scheib	25.00	12.50	7.50
214	Dick Fowler	25.00	12.50	7.50
215	Ed Lopat	50.00	25.00	15.00
216	Bob Porterfield	30.00	15.00	9.00
217	Casey Stengel **RC**	70.00	35.00	20.00
218	Cliff Mapes	30.00	15.00	9.00
219	Hank Bauer **RC**	70.00	35.00	20.00
220	Leo Durocher **RC**	60.00	30.00	18.00
221	Don Mueller	25.00	12.50	7.50
222	Bobby Morgan	25.00	12.50	7.50
223	Jimmy Russell	25.00	12.50	7.50
224	Jack Banta	25.00	12.50	7.50
225	Eddie Sawyer	25.00	12.50	7.50
226	Jim Konstanty **RC**	30.00	15.00	9.00
227	Bob Miller	25.00	12.50	7.50
228	Bill Nicholson	25.00	12.50	7.50
229	Frank Frisch	50.00	25.00	15.00
230	Bill Serena	25.00	12.50	7.50
231	Preston Ward	25.00	12.50	7.50
232	Al Rosen **RC**	55.00	27.50	16.50
233	Allie Clark	25.00	12.50	7.50
234	Bobby Shantz **RC**	45.00	22.50	13.50
235	Harold Gilbert	25.00	12.50	7.50
236	Bob Cain	25.00	12.50	7.50
237	Bill Salkeld	25.00	12.50	7.50
238	Nippy Jones	25.00	12.50	7.50
239	Bill Howerton	25.00	12.50	7.50
240	Eddie Lake	25.00	12.50	7.50
241	Neil Berry	25.00	12.50	7.50
242	Dick Kryhoski	25.00	12.50	7.50
243	Johnny Groth	25.00	12.50	7.50
244	Dale Coogan	25.00	12.50	7.50
245	Al Papai	25.00	12.50	7.50
246	Walt Dropo **RC**	35.00	17.50	10.00
247	Irv Noren **RC**	35.00	17.50	10.00
248	Sam Jethroe **RC**	40.00	20.00	12.00
249	"Snuffy" Stirnweiss	25.00	12.50	7.50
250	Ray Coleman	25.00	12.50	7.50
251	Les Moss	25.00	12.50	7.50
252	Billy DeMars	65.00	15.00	7.50

1951 Bowman

In 1951, Bowman increased the number of cards in its set for the third consecutive year when it issued 324 cards. The cards are, like 1950, color art reproductions of actual photographs but now measure 2-1/16" x 3-1/8" in size. The player's name is in a black strip on front. Several of the pictures are enlargements of the 1950 version. The high-numbered series (#253-324), which includes the rookie cards of Mantle and Mays, are the scarcest of the issue.

	NM	E	VG
Complete Set (324):	20,000	9,500	5,500
Common Player (1-252):	20.00	10.00	6.00
Common Player (253-324):	40.00	20.00	12.00

1	Whitey Ford **RC**	2,000	700.00	275.00
2	Yogi Berra	450.00	220.00	135.00
3	Robin Roberts	100.00	50.00	25.00
4	Del Ennis	20.00	10.00	6.00
5	Dale Mitchell	20.00	10.00	6.00
6	Don Newcombe	50.00	25.00	12.50
7	Gil Hodges	150.00	75.00	45.00
8	Paul Lehner	20.00	10.00	6.00
9	Sam Chapman	20.00	10.00	6.00
10	Red Schoendienst	75.00	37.50	22.50
11	"Red" Munger	20.00	10.00	6.00
12	Hank Majeski	20.00	10.00	6.00
13	Ed Stanky	22.50	11.00	6.50
14	Alvin Dark	20.00	10.00	6.00
15	Johnny Pesky	20.00	10.00	6.00
16	Maurice McDermott	20.00	10.00	6.00
17	Pete Castiglione	20.00	10.00	6.00
18	Gil Coan	20.00	10.00	6.00
19	Sid Gordon	20.00	10.00	6.00
20	Del Crandall	20.00	10.00	6.00
21	"Snuffy" Stirnweiss	20.00	10.00	6.00
22	Hank Sauer	20.00	10.00	6.00
23	"Hoot" Evers	20.00	10.00	6.00
24	Ewell Blackwell	20.00	10.00	6.00
25	Vic Raschi	40.00	20.00	12.00
26	Phil Rizzuto	175.00	87.50	43.75
27	Jim Konstanty	20.00	10.00	6.00
28	Eddie Waitkus	20.00	10.00	6.00
29	Allie Clark	20.00	10.00	6.00
30	Bob Feller	125.00	62.50	31.25
31	Roy Campanella	300.00	150.00	75.00
32	Duke Snider	300.00	150.00	75.00
33	Bob Hooper	20.00	10.00	6.00
34	Marty Marion	25.00	12.50	7.50
35	Al Zarilla	20.00	10.00	6.00
36	Joe Dobson	20.00	10.00	6.00
37	Whitey Lockman	20.00	10.00	6.00
38	Al Evans	20.00	10.00	6.00
39	Ray Scarborough	20.00	10.00	6.00
40	Gus Bell **RC**	30.00	15.00	9.00
41	Eddie Yost	20.00	10.00	6.00
42	Vern Bickford	20.00	10.00	6.00
43	Billy DeMars	20.00	10.00	6.00
44	Roy Smalley	20.00	10.00	6.00
45	Art Houtteman	20.00	10.00	6.00
46	George Kell	50.00	25.00	15.00
47	Grady Hatton	20.00	10.00	6.00
48	Ken Raffensberger	20.00	10.00	6.00
49	Jerry Coleman	22.50	11.00	6.50
50	Johnny Mize	60.00	30.00	18.00
51	Andy Seminick	20.00	10.00	6.00
52	Dick Sisler	20.00	10.00	6.00
53	Bob Lemon	50.00	25.00	15.00
54	Ray Boone **RC**	35.00	17.50	10.00
55	Gene Hermanski	20.00	10.00	6.00
56	Ralph Branca	50.00	25.00	15.00
57	Alex Kellner	20.00	10.00	6.00
58	Enos Slaughter	50.00	25.00	15.00
59	Randy Gumpert	20.00	10.00	6.00
60	"Chico" Carrasquel	20.00	10.00	6.00
61	Jim Hearn	20.00	10.00	6.00
62	Lou Boudreau	45.00	22.50	13.50
63	Bob Dillinger	20.00	10.00	6.00
64	Bill Werle	20.00	10.00	6.00
65	Mickey Vernon	20.00	10.00	6.00
66	Bob Elliott	20.00	10.00	6.00
67	Roy Sievers	20.00	10.00	6.00
68	Dick Kokos	20.00	10.00	6.00
69	Johnny Schmitz	20.00	10.00	6.00
70	Ron Northey	20.00	10.00	6.00
71	Jerry Priddy	20.00	10.00	6.00
72	Lloyd Merriman	20.00	10.00	6.00
73	Tommy Byrne	20.00	10.00	6.00
74	Billy Johnson	20.00	10.00	6.00
75	Russ Meyer	20.00	10.00	6.00
76	Stan Lopata	20.00	10.00	6.00
77	Mike Goliat	20.00	10.00	6.00
78	Early Wynn	60.00	30.00	18.00
79	Jim Hegan	20.00	10.00	6.00
80	Pee Wee Reese	200.00	100.00	50.00
81	Carl Furillo	55.00	27.50	16.50
82	Joe Tipton	20.00	10.00	6.00
83	Carl Scheib	20.00	10.00	6.00
84	Barney McCosky	20.00	10.00	6.00
85	Eddie Kazak	20.00	10.00	6.00
86	Harry Brecheen	20.00	10.00	6.00
87	Floyd Baker	20.00	10.00	6.00
88	Eddie Robinson	20.00	10.00	6.00
89	Henry Thompson	20.00	10.00	6.00
90	Dave Koslo	20.00	10.00	6.00
91	Clyde Vollmer	20.00	10.00	6.00
92	Vern Stephens	20.00	10.00	6.00
93	Danny O'Connell	20.00	10.00	6.00
94	Clyde McCullough	20.00	10.00	6.00
95	Sherry Robertson	20.00	10.00	6.00
96	Sandy Consuegra	20.00	10.00	600
97	Bob Kuzava	20.00	10.00	6.00
98	Willard Marshall	20.00	10.00	6.00
99	Earl Torgeson	20.00	10.00	6.00
100	Sherman Lollar	20.00	10.00	6.00
101	Owen Friend	20.00	10.00	6.00
102	Emil "Dutch" Leonard	20.00	10.00	6.00
103	Andy Pafko	20.00	10.00	6.00
104	Virgil "Fire" Trucks	20.00	10.00	6.00
105	Don Kolloway	20.00	10.00	6.00
106	Pat Mullin	20.00	10.00	6.00
107	Johnny Wyrostek	20.00	10.00	6.00
108	Virgil Stallcup	20.00	10.00	6.00
109	Allie Reynolds	45.00	22.50	13.50
110	Bobby Brown	30.00	15.00	9.00
111	Curt Simmons	20.00	10.00	6.00
112	Willie Jones	20.00	10.00	6.00
113	Bill "Swish" Nicholson	20.00	10.00	6.00
114	Sam Zoldak	20.00	10.00	6.00
115	Steve Gromek	20.00	10.00	6.00
116	Bruce Edwards	20.00	10.00	6.00
117	Eddie Miksis	20.00	10.00	6.00
118	Preacher Roe	50.00	25.00	12.50
119	Eddie Joost	20.00	10.00	6.00
120	Joe Coleman	20.00	10.00	6.00
121	Gerry Staley	20.00	10.00	6.00
122	Joe Garagiola **RC**	100.00	50.00	25.00
123	Howie Judson	20.00	10.00	6.00
124	Gus Niarhos	20.00	10.00	6.00
125	Bill Rigney	20.00	10.00	6.00
126	Bobby Thomson	50.00	25.00	15.00
127	Sal Maglie **RC**	75.00	37.50	22.50
128	Ellis Kinder	20.00	10.00	6.00
129	Matt Batts	20.00	10.00	6.00
130	Tom Saffell	20.00	10.00	6.00
131	Cliff Chambers	20.00	10.00	6.00
132	Cass Michaels	20.00	10.00	6.00
133	Sam Dente	20.00	10.00	6.00
134	Warren Spahn	150.00	75.00	37.50
135	Walker Cooper	20.00	10.00	6.00
136	Ray Coleman	20.00	10.00	6.00
137	Dick Starr	20.00	10.00	6.00
138	Phil Cavarretta	20.00	10.00	6.00
139	Doyle Lade	20.00	10.00	6.00
140	Eddie Lake	20.00	10.00	6.00
141	Fred Hutchinson	20.00	10.00	6.00
142	Aaron Robinson	20.00	10.00	6.00
143	Ted Kluszewski	75.00	30.00	18.00
144	Herman Wehmeier	20.00	10.00	6.00
145	Fred Sanford	20.00	10.00	6.00
146	Johnny Hopp	20.00	10.00	6.00
147	Ken Heintzelman	20.00	10.00	6.00
148	Granny Hamner	20.00	10.00	6.00
149	"Bubba" Church	20.00	10.00	6.00
150	Mike Garcia	20.00	10.00	6.00
151	Larry Doby	70.00	35.00	20.00
152	Cal Abrams	22.50	11.00	6.50
153	Rex Barney	22.50	11.00	6.50
154	Pete Suder	20.00	10.00	6.00
155	Lou Brissie	20.00	10.00	6.00
156	Del Rice	20.00	10.00	6.00
157	Al Brazle	20.00	10.00	6.00
158	Chuck Diering	20.00	10.00	6.00
159	Eddie Stewart	20.00	10.00	6.00
160	Phil Masi	20.00	10.00	6.00
161	Wes Westrum	20.00	10.00	6.00
162	Larry Jansen	20.00	10.00	6.00
163	Monte Kennedy	20.00	10.00	6.00
164	Bill Wight	20.00	10.00	6.00
165	Ted Williams	800.00	400.00	200.00
166	Stan Rojek	20.00	10.00	6.00
167	Murry Dickson	20.00	10.00	6.00
168	Sam Mele	20.00	10.00	6.00
169	Sid Hudson	20.00	10.00	6.00
170	Sibby Sisti	20.00	10.00	6.00
171	Buddy Kerr	20.00	10.00	6.00
172	Ned Garver	20.00	10.00	6.00
173	Hank Arft	20.00	10.00	6.00
174	Mickey Owen	20.00	10.00	6.00
175	Wayne Terwilliger	20.00	10.00	6.00
176	Vic Wertz	20.00	10.00	6.00
177	Charlie Keller	20.00	10.00	6.00
178	Ted Gray	20.00	10.00	6.00
179	Danny Litwhiler	20.00	10.00	6.00
180	Howie Fox	20.00	10.00	6.00
181	Casey Stengel	100.00	50.00	25.00
182	Tom Ferrick	20.00	10.00	6.00
183	Hank Bauer	35.00	17.50	10.00
184	Eddie Sawyer	20.00	10.00	6.00
185	Jimmy Bloodworth	20.00	10.00	6.00
186	Richie Ashburn	100.00	50.00	30.00
187	Al Rosen	35.00	17.50	10.00
188	Roberto Avila **RC**	25.00	12.50	7.50
189	Erv Palica	20.00	10.00	6.00
190	Joe Hatten	20.00	10.00	6.00
191	Billy Hitchcock	20.00	10.00	6.00
192	Hank Wyse	20.00	10.00	6.00
193	Ted Wilks	20.00	10.00	6.00
194	Harry "Peanuts" Lowrey	20.00	10.00	6.00
195	Paul Richards	20.00	10.00	6.00
196	Bill Pierce **RC**	32.50	16.00	10.00
197	Bob Cain	20.00	10.00	6.00
198	Monte Irvin **RC**	150.00	75.00	45.00
199	Sheldon Jones	20.00	10.00	6.00
200	Jack Kramer	20.00	10.00	6.00
201	Steve O'Neill	20.00	10.00	6.00
202	Mike Guerra	20.00	10.00	6.00
203	Vernon Law **RC**	40.00	20.00	12.00
204	Vic Lombardi	20.00	10.00	6.00
205	Mickey Grasso	20.00	10.00	6.00
206	Connie Marrero	20.00	10.00	6.00
207	Billy Southworth	35.00	17.50	10.50
208	"Blix" Donnelly	20.00	10.00	6.00
209	Ken Wood	20.00	10.00	6.00
210	Les Moss	20.00	10.00	6.00
211	Hal Jeffcoat	20.00	10.00	6.00
212	Bob Rush	20.00	10.00	6.00
213	Neil Berry	20.00	10.00	6.00
214	Bob Swift	20.00	10.00	6.00
215	Kent Peterson	20.00	10.00	6.00
216	Connie Ryan	20.00	10.00	6.00
217	Joe Page	27.50	13.50	8.00
218	Ed Lopat	32.50	16.00	10.00
219	Gene Woodling **RC**	40.00	20.00	12.00
220	Bob Miller	20.00	10.00	6.00
221	Dick Whitman	20.00	10.00	6.00
222	Thurman Tucker	20.00	10.00	6.00
223	Johnny Vander Meer	25.00	12.50	7.50
224	Billy Cox	27.50	13.50	8.00
225	Dan Bankhead **RC**	30.00	15.00	9.00
226	Jimmy Dykes	20.00	10.00	6.00
227	Bobby Shantz	22.50	11.00	6.50
228	Cloyd Boyer **RC**	20.00	10.00	6.00

229	Bill Howerton	20.00	10.00	6.00
230	Max Lanier	20.00	10.00	6.00
231	Luis Aloma	20.00	10.00	6.00
232	Nellie Fox **RC**	200.00	100.00	60.00
233	Leo Durocher	40.00	20.00	12.00
234	Clint Hartung	20.00	10.00	6.00
235	Jack Lohrke	20.00	10.00	6.00
236	"Buddy" Rosar	20.00	10.00	6.00
237	Billy Goodman	20.00	10.00	6.00
238	Pete Reiser	22.50	11.00	6.50
239	Bill MacDonald	20.00	10.00	6.00
240	Joe Haynes	20.00	10.00	6.00
241	Irv Noren	20.00	10.00	6.00
242	Sam Jethroe	20.00	10.00	6.00
243	Johnny Antonelli	20.00	10.00	6.00
244	Cliff Fannin	20.00	10.00	6.00
245	John Berardino	25.00	12.50	7.50
246	Bill Serena	20.00	10.00	6.00
247	Bob Ramazotti	20.00	10.00	6.00
248	Johnny Klippstein **RC**	20.00	10.00	6.00
249	Johnny Groth	20.00	10.00	6.00
250	Hank Borowy	20.00	10.00	6.00
251	Willard Ramsdell	20.00	10.00	6.00
252	"Dixie" Howell	20.00	10.00	6.00
253	Mickey Mantle **RC**	11,000	3,500	1,750
254	Jackie Jensen **RC**	100.00	50.00	25.00
255	Milo Candini	40.00	20.00	12.00
256	Ken Silvestri	40.00	20.00	12.00
257	Birdie Tebbetts	40.00	20.00	12.00
258	Luke Easter **RC**	45.00	22.50	13.50
259	Charlie Dressen	40.00	20.00	12.00
260	Carl Erskine **RC**	100.00	50.00	25.00
261	Wally Moses	40.00	20.00	12.00
262	Gus Zernial	40.00	20.00	12.00
263	Howie Pollet	40.00	20.00	12.00
264	Don Richmond	40.00	20.00	12.00
265	Steve Bilko **RC**	40.00	20.00	12.00
266	Harry Dorish	40.00	20.00	12.00
267	Ken Holcombe	40.00	20.00	12.00
268	Don Mueller	40.00	20.00	12.00
269	Ray Noble	40.00	20.00	12.00
270	Willard Nixon	40.00	20.00	12.00
271	Tommy Wright	40.00	20.00	12.00
272	Billy Meyer	40.00	20.00	12.00
273	Danny Murtaugh	40.00	20.00	12.00
274	George Metkovich	40.00	20.00	12.00
275	Bucky Harris	50.00	25.00	15.00
276	Frank Quinn	40.00	20.00	12.00
277	Roy Hartsfield	40.00	20.00	12.00
278	Norman Roy	40.00	20.00	12.00
279	Jim Delsing	40.00	20.00	12.00
280	Frank Overmire	40.00	20.00	12.00
281	Al Widmar	40.00	20.00	12.00
282	Frank Frisch	55.00	27.50	16.50
283	Walt Dubiel	40.00	20.00	12.00
284	Gene Bearden	40.00	20.00	12.00
285	Johnny Lipon	40.00	20.00	12.00
286	Bob Usher	40.00	20.00	12.00
287	Jim Blackburn	40.00	20.00	12.00
288	Bobby Adams	40.00	20.00	12.00
289	Cliff Mapes	50.00	25.00	15.00
290	Bill Dickey **RC**	150.00	75.00	37.50
291	Tommy Henrich	55.00	27.50	16.50
292	Eddie Pellagrini	40.00	20.00	12.00
293	Ken Johnson	40.00	20.00	12.00
294	Jocko Thompson	40.00	20.00	12.00
295	Al Lopez	100.00	50.00	25.00
296	Bob Kennedy	40.00	20.00	12.00
297	Dave Philley	40.00	20.00	12.00
298	Joe Astroth	40.00	20.00	12.00
299	Clyde King	50.00	25.00	15.00
300	Hal Rice	40.00	20.00	12.00
301	Tommy Glaviano	40.00	20.00	12.00
302	Jim Busby	40.00	20.00	12.00
303	Marv Rotblatt	40.00	20.00	12.00
304	Allen Gettel	40.00	20.00	12.00
305	Willie Mays **RC**	3,000	1,100	650.00
306	Jim Piersall **RC**	120.00	60.00	30.00
307	Walt Masterson	40.00	20.00	12.00
308	Ted Beard	40.00	20.00	12.00
309	Mel Queen	40.00	20.00	12.00
310	Erv Dusak	40.00	20.00	12.00
311	Mickey Harris	40.00	20.00	12.00
312	Gene Mauch **RC**	50.00	25.00	15.00
313	Ray Mueller	40.00	20.00	12.00
314	Johnny Sain	45.00	22.50	13.50
315	Zack Taylor	40.00	20.00	12.00
316	Duane Pillette	40.00	20.00	12.00
317	Smoky Burgess **RC**	60.00	30.00	18.00
318	Warren Hacker	40.00	20.00	12.00
319	Red Rolfe	40.00	20.00	12.00
320	Hal White	40.00	20.00	12.00
321	Earl Johnson	40.00	20.00	12.00
322	Luke Sewell	40.00	20.00	12.00
323	Joe Adcock **RC**	100.00	50.00	25.00
324	Johnny Pramesa	125.00	62.50	31.25

1952 Bowman

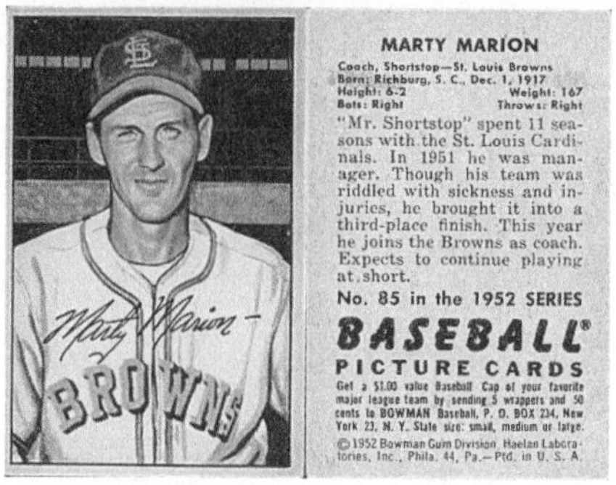
Marty Marion
BROWNS
MARTY MARION
Coach, Shortstop—St. Louis Browns
Born: Richburg, S. C., Dec. 1, 1917
Height: 6-2
Weight: 167
Bats: Right
Throws: Right
"Mr. Shortstop" spent 11 seasons with the St. Louis Cardinals. In 1951 he was manager. Though his team was riddled with sickness and injuries, he brought it into a third-place finish. This year he joins the Browns as coach. Expects to continue playing at short.
No. 85 in the 1952 SERIES
BASEBALL®
PICTURE CARDS
Get a $1.00 value Baseball Cap of your favorite major league team by sending 5 wrappers and 50 cents to BOWMAN Baseball, P. O. BOX 234, New York 23, N. Y. State size: small, medium or large.
© 1952 Bowman Gum Division Haelan Laboratories, Inc., Phila. 44, Pa.—Ptd. in U. S. A.

Bowman reverted to a 252-card set in 1952, but retained the card size (2-1/16" x 3-1/8") employed the preceding year. The cards, which are color art reproductions of actual photographs, feature a facsimile autograph on front.

		NM	E	VG
	Complete Set (252):	10,000	5,000	3,000
	Common Player (1-216):	25.00	12.50	7.50
	Common Player (217-252):	40.00	20.00	12.00
1	Yogi Berra	750.00	370.00	220.00
2	Bobby Thomson	60.00	30.00	15.00
3	Fred Hutchinson	20.00	10.00	6.00
4	Robin Roberts	75.00	37.00	22.00
5	Minnie Minoso **RC**	120.00	60.00	30.00
6	Virgil "Red" Stallcup	25.00	12.50	7.50
7	Mike Garcia	25.00	12.50	7.50
8	Pee Wee Reese	125.00	62.50	37.50
9	Vern Stephens	25.00	12.50	7.50
10	Bob Hooper	25.00	12.50	7.50
11	Ralph Kiner	50.00	25.00	12.50
12	Max Surkont	25.00	12.50	7.50
13	Cliff Mapes	25.00	12.50	7.50
14	Cliff Chambers	25.00	12.50	7.50
15	Sam Mele	25.00	12.50	7.50
16	Omar Lown	25.00	12.50	7.50
17	Ed Lopat	55.00	27.50	16.50
18	Don Mueller	25.00	12.50	7.50
19	Bob Cain	25.00	12.50	7.50
20	Willie Jones	25.00	12.50	7.50
21	Nellie Fox	100.00	50.00	25.00
22	Willard Ramsdell	25.00	12.50	7.50
23	Bob Lemon	60.00	30.00	18.00
24	Carl Furillo	50.00	25.00	15.00
25	Maurice McDermott	25.00	12.50	7.50
26	Eddie Joost	25.00	12.50	7.50
27	Joe Garagiola	30.00	15.00	9.00
28	Roy Hartsfield	25.00	12.50	7.50
29	Ned Garver	25.00	12.50	7.50
30	Red Schoendienst	45.00	22.50	13.50
31	Eddie Yost	25.00	12.50	7.50
32	Eddie Miksis	25.00	12.50	7.50
33	Gil McDougald **RC**	60.00	30.00	18.00
34	Al Dark	25.00	12.50	7.50
35	Granny Hamner	25.00	12.50	7.50
36	Cass Michaels	25.00	12.50	7.50
37	Vic Raschi	30.00	15.00	9.00
38	Whitey Lockman	25.00	12.50	7.50
39	Vic Wertz	25.00	12.50	7.50
40	"Bubba" Church	25.00	12.50	7.50
41	"Chico" Carrasquel	25.00	12.50	7.50
42	Johnny Wyrostek	25.00	12.50	7.50
43	Bob Feller	150.00	75.00	37.50
44	Roy Campanella	250.00	125.00	62.50
45	Johnny Pesky	25.00	12.50	7.50
46	Carl Scheib	25.00	12.50	7.50
47	Pete Castiglione	25.00	12.50	7.50
48	Vernon Bickford	25.00	12.50	7.50
49	Jim Hearn	25.00	12.50	7.50
50	Gerry Staley	25.00	12.50	7.50
51	Gil Coan	25.00	12.50	7.50
52	Phil Rizzuto	150.00	75.00	37.50
53	Richie Ashburn	120.00	60.00	30.00
54	Billy Pierce	25.00	12.50	7.50
55	Ken Raffensberger	25.00	12.50	7.50
56	Clyde King	25.00	12.50	7.50
57	Clyde Vollmer	25.00	12.50	7.50
58	Hank Majeski	25.00	12.50	7.50
59	Murry Dickson	25.00	12.50	7.50
60	Sid Gordon	25.00	12.50	7.50
61	Tommy Byrne	25.00	12.50	7.50
62	Joe Presko	25.00	12.50	7.50
63	Irv Noren	25.00	12.50	7.50
64	Roy Smalley	25.00	12.50	7.50
65	Hank Bauer	50.00	25.00	15.00
66	Sal Maglie	25.00	12.50	7.50
67	Johnny Groth	25.00	12.50	7.50
68	Jim Busby	25.00	12.50	7.50
69	Joe Adcock	25.00	12.50	7.50
70	Carl Erskine	40.00	20.00	12.00
71	Vernon Law	25.00	12.50	7.50
72	Earl Torgeson	25.00	12.50	7.50
73	Jerry Coleman	30.00	15.00	9.00
74	Wes Westrum	25.00	12.50	7.50
75	George Kell	45.00	22.50	13.50
76	Del Ennis	25.00	12.50	7.50
77	Eddie Robinson	25.00	12.50	7.50
78	Lloyd Merriman	25.00	12.50	7.50
79	Lou Brissie	25.00	12.50	7.50
80	Gil Hodges	100.00	50.00	30.00
81	Billy Goodman	25.00	12.50	7.50
82	Gus Zernial	25.00	12.50	7.50
83	Howie Pollet	25.00	12.50	7.50
84	Sam Jethroe	25.00	12.50	7.50
85	Marty Marion	30.00	15.00	9.00
86	Cal Abrams	25.00	12.50	7.50
87	Mickey Vernon	25.00	12.50	7.50
88	Bruce Edwards	25.00	12.50	7.50
89	Billy Hitchcock	25.00	12.50	7.50
90	Larry Jansen	25.00	12.50	7.50
91	Don Kolloway	25.00	12.50	7.50
92	Eddie Waitkus	25.00	12.50	7.50
93	Paul Richards	25.00	12.50	7.50
94	Luke Sewell	25.00	12.50	7.50
95	Luke Easter	25.00	12.50	7.50
96	Ralph Branca	40.00	20.00	12.00
97	Willard Marshall	25.00	12.50	7.50
98	Jimmy Dykes	25.00	12.50	7.50
99	Clyde McCullough	25.00	12.50	7.50
100	Sibby Sisti	25.00	12.50	7.50
101	Mickey Mantle	1,850	850.00	525.00
102	Peanuts Lowrey	25.00	15.00	7.50
103	Joe Haynes	25.00	12.50	7.50
104	Hal Jeffcoat	25.00	12.50	7.50
105	Bobby Brown	35.00	17.50	10.00
106	Randy Gumpert	25.00	12.50	7.50
107	Del Rice	25.00	12.50	7.50
108	George Metkovich	25.00	12.50	7.50
109	Tom Morgan	30.00	15.00	9.00
110	Max Lanier	25.00	12.50	7.50
111	"Hoot" Evers	25.00	12.50	7.50
112	"Smoky" Burgess	25.00	12.50	7.50
113	Al Zarilla	25.00	12.50	7.50
114	Frank Hiller	25.00	12.50	7.50
115	Larry Doby	60.00	30.00	18.00
116	Duke Snider	200.00	100.00	60.00
117	Bill Wight	25.00	12.50	7.50
118	Ray Murray	25.00	12.50	7.50
119	Bill Howerton	25.00	12.50	7.50
120	Chet Nichols	25.00	12.50	7.50
121	Al Corwin	25.00	12.50	7.50
122	Billy Johnson	25.00	12.50	7.50
123	Sid Hudson	25.00	12.50	7.50
124	Birdie Tebbetts	25.00	12.50	7.50
125	Howie Fox	25.00	12.50	7.50
126	Phil Cavarretta	25.00	12.50	7.50
127	Dick Sisler	25.00	12.50	7.50
128	Don Newcombe	50.00	25.00	15.00
129	Gus Niarhos	25.00	12.50	7.50
130	Allie Clark	25.00	12.50	7.50
131	Bob Swift	25.00	12.50	7.50
132	Dave Cole	25.00	12.50	7.50
133	Dick Kryhoski	25.00	12.50	7.50
134	Al Brazle	25.00	12.50	7.50
135	Mickey Harris	25.00	12.50	7.50
136	Gene Hermanski	25.00	12.50	7.50
137	Stan Rojek	25.00	12.50	7.50
138	Ted Wilks	25.00	12.50	7.50
139	Jerry Priddy	25.00	12.50	7.50
140	Ray Scarborough	25.00	12.50	7.50
141	Hank Edwards	25.00	12.50	7.50
142	Early Wynn	45.00	22.50	13.50
143	Sandy Consuegra	25.00	12.50	7.50
144	Joe Hatten	25.00	12.50	7.50
145	Johnny Mize	80.00	40.00	24.00
146	Leo Durocher	45.00	22.50	13.50
147	Marlin Stuart	25.00	12.50	7.50
148	Ken Heintzelman	25.00	12.50	7.50
149	Howie Judson	25.00	12.50	7.50
150	Herman Wehmeier	25.00	12.50	7.50
151	Al Rosen	30.00	15.00	9.00
152	Billy Cox	40.00	20.00	12.00
153	Fred Hatfield	25.00	12.50	7.50
154	Ferris Fain	25.00	12.50	7.50
155	Billy Meyer	25.00	12.50	7.50
156	Warren Spahn	120.00	60.00	30.00
157	Jim Delsing	25.00	12.50	7.50
158	Bucky Harris	30.00	15.00	9.00
159	Dutch Leonard	20.00	10.00	6.00
160	Eddie Stanky	25.00	12.50	7.50
161	Jackie Jensen	45.00	22.50	13.50
162	Monte Irvin	55.00	27.50	16.50
163	Johnny Lipon	25.00	12.50	7.50
164	Connie Ryan	25.00	12.50	7.50
165	Saul Rogovin	25.00	12.50	7.50
166	Bobby Adams	25.00	12.50	7.50
167	Bob Avila	25.00	12.50	7.50

168	Preacher Roe	35.00	17.50	10.00
169	Walt Dropo	25.00	12.50	7.50
170	Joe Astroth	25.00	12.50	7.50
171	Mel Queen	25.00	12.50	7.50
172	Ebba St. Claire	25.00	12.50	7.50
173	Gene Bearden	25.00	12.50	7.50
174	Mickey Grasso	25.00	12.50	7.50
175	Ransom Jackson	25.00	12.50	7.50
176	Harry Brecheen	25.00	12.50	7.50
177	Gene Woodling	35.00	17.50	10.00
178	Dave Williams	25.00	12.50	7.50
179	Pete Suder	25.00	12.50	7.50
180	Eddie Fitz Gerald	25.00	12.50	7.50
181	Joe Collins	30.00	15.00	9.00
182	Dave Koslo	25.00	12.50	7.50
183	Pat Mullin	25.00	12.50	7.50
184	Curt Simmons	25.00	12.50	7.50
185	Eddie Stewart	25.00	12.50	7.50
186	Frank Smith	25.00	12.50	7.50
187	Jim Hegan	25.00	12.50	7.50
188	Charlie Dressen	30.00	15.00	9.00
189	Jim Piersall	30.00	15.00	9.00
190	Dick Fowler	25.00	12.50	7.50
191	Bob Friend **RC**	30.00	15.00	9.00
192	John Cusick	25.00	12.50	7.50
193	Bobby Young	25.00	12.50	7.50
194	Bob Porterfield	25.00	12.50	7.50
195	Frank Baumholtz	25.00	12.50	7.50
196	Stan Musial	450.00	225.00	135.00
197	Charlie Silvera **RC**	40.00	20.00	12.00
198	Chuck Diering	25.00	12.50	7.50
199	Ted Gray	25.00	12.50	7.50
200	Ken Silvestri	25.00	12.50	7.50
201	Ray Coleman	25.00	12.50	7.50
202	Harry Perkowski	25.00	12.50	7.50
203	Steve Gromek	25.00	12.50	7.50
204	Andy Pafko	25.00	12.50	7.50
205	Walt Masterson	25.00	12.50	7.50
206	Elmer Valo	25.00	12.50	7.50
207	George Strickland	25.00	12.50	7.50
208	Walker Cooper	25.00	12.50	7.50
209	Dick Littlefield	25.00	12.50	7.50
210	Archie Wilson	25.00	12.50	7.50
211	Paul Minner	25.00	12.50	7.50
212	Solly Hemus	25.00	12.50	7.50
213	Monte Kennedy	25.00	12.50	7.50
214	Ray Boone	25.00	12.50	7.50
215	Sheldon Jones	25.00	12.50	7.50
216	Matt Batts	25.00	12.50	7.50
217	Casey Stengel	125.00	60.00	35.00
218	Willie Mays	1,350	600.00	300.00
219	Neil Berry	40.00	20.00	12.00
220	Russ Meyer	40.00	20.00	12.00
221	Lou Kretlow	40.00	20.00	12.00
222	"Dixie" Howell	40.00	20.00	12.00
223	Harry Simpson **RC**	45.00	22.50	13.50
224	Johnny Schmitz	40.00	20.00	12.00
225	Del Wilber	40.00	20.00	12.00
226	Alex Kellner	40.00	20.00	12.00
227	Clyde Sukeforth	40.00	20.00	12.00
228	Bob Chipman	40.00	20.00	12.00
229	Hank Arft	40.00	20.00	12.00
230	Frank Shea	40.00	20.00	12.00
231	Dee Fondy **RC**	40.00	20.00	12.00
232	Enos Slaughter	100.00	50.00	25.00
233	Bob Kuzava	50.00	25.00	15.00
234	Fred Fitzsimmons	40.00	20.00	12.00
235	Steve Souchock	40.00	20.00	12.00
236	Tommy Brown	40.00	20.00	12.00
237	Sherman Lollar	40.00	20.00	12.00
238	Roy McMillan **RC**	40.00	20.00	12.00
239	Dale Mitchell	40.00	20.00	12.00
240	Billy Loes **RC**	45.00	22.50	13.50
241	Mel Parnell	40.00	20.00	12.00
242	Everett Kell	40.00	20.00	12.00
243	"Red" Munger	40.00	20.00	12.00
244	Lew Burdette **RC**	60.00	30.00	18.00
245	George Schmees	40.00	20.00	12.00
246	Jerry Snyder	40.00	20.00	12.00
247	John Pramesa	40.00	20.00	12.00
248a	Bill Werle (. after G and most of W missing))	40.00	20.00	12.00
248b	Bill Werle (Full signature.)	40.00	20.00	12.00
249	Henry Thompson	40.00	20.00	12.00
250	Ike Delock	40.00	20.00	12.00
251	Jack Lohrke	40.00	20.00	12.00
252	Frank Crosetti	125.00	62.50	31.25

1952 Bowman Proofs

Coincident to Topps issue of its "Giant Size" baseball cards in 1952, Bowman began experimenting with up-sizing its card issues from the then-current 2-1/16" x 3-1/8". A group of proof cards was produced using 12 players from the '52 Bowman set. The proofs are 2-1/2" x 3-3/4", overall about 45% larger than the issued '52s. Each proof is found in two types, black-and-white and color. Both have blank-backs except for hand-written notes with the player's name, team and card number in the '52 set. Many of the proofs feature slight differences from the issued versions, such as uniform changes, elimination of background elements or picture cropping. The color proofs include a facsimile autograph. A small group of these proof cards entered the hobby early in the 1980s when a former Bowman executive disposed of his hobby card files. The proofs are numbered according to their number within the 1952 Bowman set.

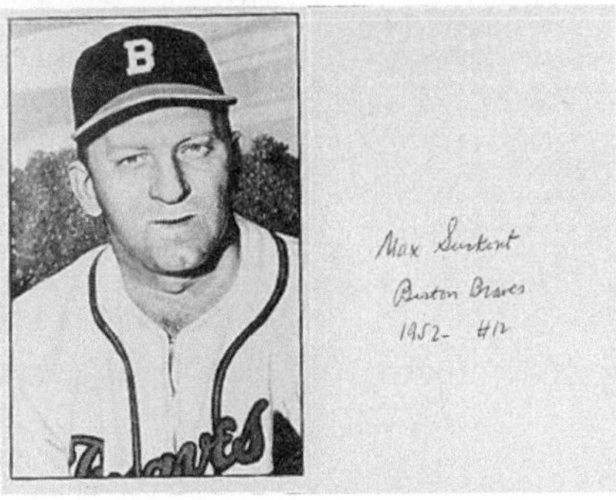

		NM	E	VG
Common Player, B/W:		1,200	600.00	360.00
Common Player, Color:		1,800	900.00	550.00
1	Yogi Berra (B/W)	4,000	2,000	1,200
1	Yogi Berra (Color)	6,400	3,200	2,000
2	Bobby Thomson (B/W)	1,200	600.00	360.00
2	Bobby Thomson (Color)	4,000	2,000	1,200
3	Fred Hutchinson (B/W)	1,600	800.00	500.00
3	Fred Hutchinson (Color)	1,800	900.00	550.00
4	Robin Roberts (B/W)	2,900	1,450	875.00
4	Robin Roberts (Color)	4,800	2,400	1,500
10	Bob Hooper (B/W)	1,600	800.00	500.00
10	Bob Hooper (Color)	1,800	900.00	550.00
11	Ralph Kiner (B/W)	2,900	1,450	875.00
11	Ralph Kiner (Color)	4,800	2,400	1,500
12	Max Surkont (B/W)	1,600	800.00	500.00
12	Max Surkont (Color)	1,800	900.00	550.00
13	Cliff Mapes (B/W)	1,600	800.00	500.00
13	Cliff Mapes (Color)	1,800	900.00	550.00
14	Cliff Chambers (B/W)	1,600	800.00	500.00
14	Cliff Chambers (Color)	1,800	900.00	550.00
34	Alvin Dark (B/W)	1,600	800.00	500.00
34	Alvin Dark (Color)	1,800	900.00	550.00
39	Vic Wertz (B/W)	1,600	800.00	500.00
39	Vic Wertz (Color)	1,800	900.00	550.00
142	Early Wynn (B/W)	2,600	1,300	800.00
142	Early Wynn (Color)	4,800	2,400	1,450
176	Harry Brecheen (B/W)	1,600	800.00	500.00
176	Harry Brecheen (Color)	1,800	900.00	550.00

1953 Bowman

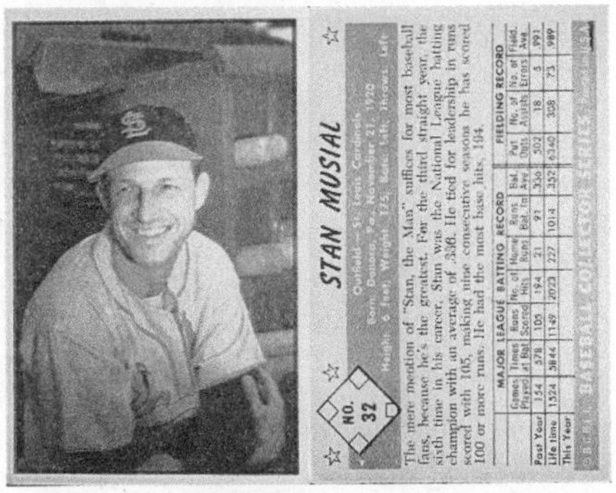

The first set of contemporary major league players featuring actual color photographs, the 160-card 1953 Bowman color set remains one of the most popular issues of the postwar era. The set is greatly appreciated for its uncluttered look; card fronts that contain no names, teams or facsimile autographs. Bowman increased the size of the cards to 2-1/2" x 3-3/4" to better compete with Topps' larger format. Bowman copied an idea from the 1952 Topps set and developed card backs that gave player career and previous-year statistics. The high-numbered cards (#113-160) are the scarcest of the set, with #113-128 being especially scarce.

		NM	E	VG
Complete Set (160):		18,000	9,000	5,500
Common Player (1-112):		40.00	20.00	12.00
Common Player (113-160):		90.00	45.00	25.00
1	Davey Williams	175.00	87.50	43.75
2	Vic Wertz	45.00	17.50	10.00
3	Sam Jethroe	40.00	20.00	12.00
4	Art Houtteman	40.00	20.00	12.00
5	Sid Gordon	40.00	20.00	12.00
6	Joe Ginsberg	40.00	20.00	12.00
7	Harry Chiti	40.00	20.00	12.00
8	Al Rosen	55.00	27.50	16.50
9	Phil Rizzuto	250.00	125.00	62.50
10	Richie Ashburn	150.00	75.00	37.50
11	Bobby Shantz	40.00	20.00	12.00
12	Carl Erskine	50.00	25.00	15.00
13	Gus Zernial	40.00	20.00	12.00
14	Billy Loes	55.00	27.50	16.50
15	Jim Busby	40.00	20.00	12.00
16	Bob Friend	40.00	20.00	12.00
17	Gerry Staley	40.00	20.00	12.00
18	Nellie Fox	150.00	75.00	37.50
19	Al Dark	40.00	20.00	12.00
20	Don Lenhardt	40.00	20.00	12.00
21	Joe Garagiola	50.00	25.00	15.00
22	Bob Porterfield	40.00	20.00	12.00
23	Herman Wehmeier	40.00	20.00	12.00
24	Jackie Jensen	45.00	22.50	13.50
25	"Hoot" Evers	40.00	20.00	12.00
26	Roy McMillan	40.00	20.00	12.00
27	Vic Raschi	70.00	35.00	20.00
28	"Smoky" Burgess	45.00	22.50	13.50
29	Roberto Avila	40.00	20.00	12.00
30	Phil Cavarretta	40.00	20.00	12.00
31	Jimmy Dykes	40.00	20.00	12.00
32	Stan Musial	550.00	270.00	165.00
33	Pee Wee Reese	700.00	350.00	210.00
34	Gil Coan	40.00	20.00	12.00
35	Maury McDermott	40.00	20.00	12.00
36	Minnie Minoso	85.00	42.50	25.00
37	Jim Wilson	40.00	20.00	12.00
38	Harry Byrd	40.00	20.00	12.00
39	Paul Richards	40.00	20.00	12.00
40	Larry Doby	100.00	50.00	25.00
41	Sammy White	40.00	20.00	12.00
42	Tommy Brown	40.00	20.00	12.00
43	Mike Garcia	40.00	20.00	12.00
44	Hank Bauer, Yogi Berra, Mickey Mantle	775.00	387.50	232.50
45	Walt Dropo	40.00	20.00	12.00
46	Roy Campanella	350.00	175.00	87.50
47	Ned Garver	40.00	20.00	12.00
48	Hank Sauer	40.00	20.00	12.00
49	Eddie Stanky	40.00	20.00	12.00
50	Lou Kretlow	40.00	20.00	12.00
51	Monte Irvin	55.00	27.50	16.50
52	Marty Marion	45.00	22.50	13.50
53	Del Rice	40.00	20.00	12.00
54	"Chico" Carrasquel	40.00	20.00	12.00
55	Leo Durocher	70.00	35.00	20.00
56	Bob Cain	40.00	20.00	12.00
57	Lou Boudreau	75.00	37.50	22.50
58	Willard Marshall	40.00	20.00	12.00
59	Mickey Mantle	1,450	725.00	435.00
60	Granny Hamner	40.00	20.00	12.00
61	George Kell	60.00	30.00	18.00
62	Ted Kluszewski	90.00	45.00	27.50
63	Gil McDougald	100.00	50.00	25.00
64	Curt Simmons	40.00	20.00	12.00
65	Robin Roberts	125.00	62.50	31.25
66	Mel Parnell	40.00	20.00	12.00
67	Mel Clark	40.00	20.00	12.00
68	Allie Reynolds	80.00	40.00	20.00
69	Charlie Grimm	40.00	20.00	12.00
70	Clint Courtney	40.00	20.00	12.00
71	Paul Minner	40.00	20.00	12.00
72	Ted Gray	40.00	20.00	12.00
73	Billy Pierce	40.00	20.00	12.00
74	Don Mueller	40.00	20.00	12.00
75	Saul Rogovin	40.00	20.00	12.00
76	Jim Hearn	40.00	20.00	12.00
77	Mickey Grasso	40.00	20.00	12.00
78	Carl Furillo	80.00	40.00	25.00
79	Ray Boone	40.00	20.00	12.00
80	Ralph Kiner	115.00	55.00	35.00
81	Enos Slaughter	100.00	50.00	25.00
82	Joe Astroth	40.00	20.00	12.00
83	Jack Daniels	40.00	20.00	12.00
84	Hank Bauer	80.00	40.00	25.00
85	Solly Hemus	40.00	20.00	12.00
86	Harry Simpson	40.00	20.00	12.00
87	Harry Perkowski	40.00	20.00	12.00
88	Joe Dobson	40.00	20.00	12.00
89	Sandalio Consuegra	40.00	20.00	12.00
90	Joe Nuxhall	40.00	20.00	12.00
91	Steve Souchock	40.00	20.00	12.00
92	Gil Hodges	300.00	150.00	75.00
93	Billy Martin, Phil Rizzuto	300.00	150.00	75.00
94	Bob Addis	40.00	20.00	12.00
95	Wally Moses	40.00	20.00	12.00
96	Sal Maglie	65.00	32.50	20.00
97	Eddie Mathews **RC**	350.00	175.00	87.50
98	Hector Rodriquez	40.00	20.00	12.00
99	Warren Spahn	350.00	175.00	87.50
100	Bill Wight	40.00	20.00	12.00
101	Red Schoendienst	100.00	50.00	25.00

102	Jim Hegan	40.00	20.00	12.00
103	Del Ennis	40.00	20.00	12.00
104	Luke Easter	40.00	20.00	12.00
105	Eddie Joost	40.00	20.00	12.00
106	Ken Raffensberger	40.00	20.00	12.00
107	Alex Kellner	40.00	20.00	12.00
108	Bobby Adams	40.00	20.00	12.00
109	Ken Wood	40.00	20.00	12.00
110	Bob Rush	40.00	20.00	12.00
111	Jim Dyck	40.00	20.00	12.00
112	Toby Atwell	40.00	20.00	12.00
113	Karl Drews	90.00	45.00	25.00
114	Bob Feller	475.00	240.00	140.00
115	Cloyd Boyer	90.00	45.00	25.00
116	Eddie Yost	90.00	45.00	25.00
117	Duke Snider	600.00	300.00	150.00
118	Billy Martin **RC**	400.00	200.00	100.00
119	Dale Mitchell	90.00	45.00	25.00
120	Marlin Stuart	90.00	45.00	25.00
121	Yogi Berra	650.00	320.00	195.00
122	Bill Serena	90.00	45.00	25.00
123	Johnny Lipon	90.00	45.00	25.00
124	Charlie Dressen	100.00	50.00	25.00
125	Fred Hatfield	90.00	45.00	25.00
126	Al Corwin	90.00	45.00	25.00
127	Dick Kryhoski	90.00	45.00	25.00
128	"Whitey" Lockman	90.00	45.00	25.00
129	Russ Meyer	95.00	47.50	27.50
130	Cass Michaels	90.00	45.00	25.00
131	Connie Ryan	90.00	45.00	25.00
132	Fred Hutchinson	90.00	45.00	25.00
133	Willie Jones	90.00	45.00	25.00
134	Johnny Pesky	90.00	45.00	25.00
135	Bobby Morgan	95.00	47.50	27.50
136	Jim Brideweser	100.00	50.00	30.00
137	Sam Dente	90.00	45.00	25.00
138	"Bubba" Church	90.00	45.00	25.00
139	Pete Runnels	90.00	45.00	25.00
140	Alpha Brazle	90.00	45.00	25.00
141	Frank "Spec" Shea	90.00	45.00	25.00
142	Larry Miggins	90.00	45.00	25.00
143	Al Lopez **RC**	100.00	50.00	25.00
144	Warren Hacker	90.00	45.00	25.00
145	George Shuba	125.00	60.00	35.00
146	Early Wynn	200.00	100.00	50.00
147	Clem Koshorek	90.00	45.00	25.00
148	Billy Goodman	90.00	45.00	25.00
149	Al Corwin	90.00	45.00	25.00
150	Carl Scheib	90.00	45.00	25.00
151	Joe Adcock	90.00	45.00	25.00
152	Clyde Vollmer	90.00	45.00	25.00
153	Whitey Ford	800.00	400.00	240.00
154	Omar "Turk" Lown	90.00	45.00	25.00
155	Allie Clark	90.00	45.00	25.00
156	Max Surkont	90.00	45.00	25.00
157	Sherman Lollar	90.00	45.00	25.00
158	Howard Fox	90.00	45.00	25.00
159	Mickey Vernon (Photo actually Floyd Baker.)	95.00	47.50	27.50
160	Cal Abrams	500.00	250.00	125.00

1953 Bowman Black & White

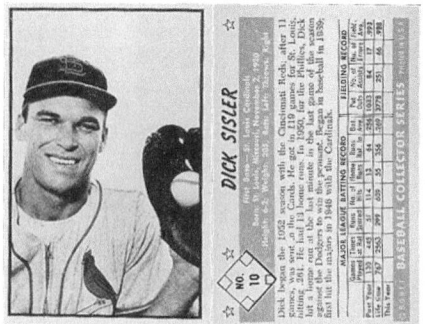

The 1953 Bowman black-and-white set is similar in all respects to the 1953 Bowman color cards, except that it lacks color. Sixty-four cards, which measure 2-1/2" x 3-3/4", comprise the set.

		NM	E	VG
Complete Set (64):		4,500	2,125	1,275
Common Player:		55.00	25.00	15.00
1	Gus Bell	150.00	75.00	37.50
2	Willard Nixon	65.00	30.00	15.00
3	Bill Rigney	55.00	25.00	15.00
4	Pat Mullin	55.00	25.00	15.00
5	Dee Fondy	55.00	25.00	15.00
6	Ray Murray	55.00	25.00	15.00
7	Andy Seminick	55.00	25.00	15.00
8	Pete Suder	55.00	25.00	15.00

9	Walt Masterson	55.00	25.00	15.00
10	Dick Sisler	55.00	25.00	15.00
11	Dick Gernert	55.00	25.00	15.00
12	Randy Jackson	55.00	25.00	15.00
13	Joe Tipton	55.00	25.00	15.00
14	Bill Nicholson	55.00	25.00	15.00
15	Johnny Mize	125.00	62.50	31.25
16	Stu Miller	55.00	25.00	15.00
17	Virgil Trucks	55.00	25.00	15.00
18	Billy Hoeft	55.00	25.00	15.00
19	Paul LaPalme	55.00	25.00	15.00
20	Eddie Robinson	55.00	25.00	15.00
21	Clarence "Bud" Podbielan	55.00	25.00	15.00
22	Matt Batts	55.00	25.00	15.00
23	Wilmer Mizell	55.00	25.00	15.00
24	Del Wilber	55.00	25.00	15.00
25	Johnny Sain	100.00	50.00	30.00
26	Preacher Roe	90.00	45.00	25.00
27	Bob Lemon	175.00	87.50	43.75
28	Hoyt Wilhelm **RC**	125.00	62.50	31.25
29	Sid Hudson	55.00	25.00	15.00
30	Walker Cooper	55.00	25.00	15.00
31	Gene Woodling	100.00	50.00	30.00
32	Rocky Bridges	55.00	25.00	15.00
33	Bob Kuzava	55.00	25.00	15.00
34	Ebba St. Clair (St. Claire)	55.00	25.00	15.00
35	Johnny Wyrostek	55.00	25.00	15.00
36	Jim Piersall	90.00	45.00	25.00
37	Hal Jeffcoat	55.00	25.00	15.00
38	Dave Cole	55.00	25.00	15.00
39	Casey Stengel	400.00	200.00	120.00
40	Larry Jansen	55.00	25.00	15.00
41	Bob Ramazotti	55.00	25.00	15.00
42	Howie Judson	55.00	25.00	15.00
43a	Hal Bevan (Birth year 1950.)	55.00	25.00	15.00
43b	Hal Bevan (Birth year 1930.)	120.00	60.00	35.00
44	Jim Delsing	55.00	25.00	15.00
45	Irv Noren	100.00	50.00	30.00
46	Bucky Harris	100.00	50.00	35.00
47	Jack Lohrke	55.00	25.00	15.00
48	Steve Ridzik	55.00	25.00	15.00
49	Floyd Baker	55.00	25.00	15.00
50	Emil "Dutch" Leonard	55.00	25.00	15.00
51	Lew Burdette	75.00	35.00	20.00
52	Ralph Branca	100.00	50.00	30.00
53	Morris Martin	55.00	25.00	15.00
54	Bill Miller	55.00	25.00	15.00
55	Don Johnson	55.00	25.00	15.00
56	Roy Smalley	55.00	25.00	15.00
57	Andy Pafko	55.00	25.00	15.00
58	Jim Konstanty	55.00	25.00	15.00
59	Duane Pillette	55.00	25.00	15.00
60	Billy Cox	80.00	40.00	20.00
61	Tom Gorman	80.00	40.00	25.00
62	Keith Thomas	55.00	25.00	15.00
63	Steve Gromek	55.00	25.00	15.00
64	Andy Hansen	75.00	25.00	15.00

1953 Bowman Color Proofs

Four subjects are known to have survived in proof form created prior to the production of Bowman's landmark 1953 color card set. In the same 2-1/2" x 3-3/4" size as the issued cards, the proofs are blank-backed and lack the black frame line separating the picture from the white border. The Enos Slaughter card is otherwise identical to the issued version. The Spahn was changed to a different, more close-up picture for the issued card. The "Dodgers In Action" card was never issued, nor was the Ferris Fain card, probably due to Fain's trade from the A's to the White Sox prior to the 1953 season.

		NM	E	VG
(1)	Dodgers In Action	5,000	2,500	1,500
(2)	Ferris Fain	3,750	1,850	1,110
(3)	Enos Slaughter	1,750	875.00	525.00
(4)	Warren Spahn	4,250	2,100	1,250

1954 Bowman

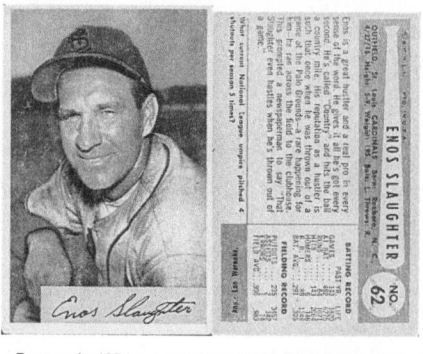

Bowman's 1954 set consists of 224 full-color cards that measure 2-1/2" x 3-3/4". It is believed that contractual problems caused the withdrawal of card #66 (Ted Williams) from the set, creating one of the most sought-after scarcities of the postwar era. The Williams card was replaced by Jim Piersall (who is also #210) in subsequent print runs. The set contains over 40 variations, most involving statistical errors on the card backs that were corrected. On most cards neither variation carries a premium value as both varieties appear to have been printed in equal amounts. The complete set price that follows does not include all variations or #66 Williams.

		NM	E	VG
Complete Set (224):		5,000	2,400	1,400
Common Player (1-128):		10.00	5.00	3.00
Common Player (129-224):		12.00	6.00	3.50
1	Phil Rizzuto	125.00	62.50	37.50
2	Jack Jensen	50.00	25.00	12.50
3	Marion Fricano	10.00	5.00	3.00
4	Bob Hooper	10.00	5.00	3.00
5	Billy Hunter	10.00	5.00	3.00
6	Nellie Fox	60.00	30.00	18.00
7	Walter Dropo	10.00	5.00	3.00
8	Jim Busby	10.00	5.00	3.00
9	Dave Williams	10.00	5.00	3.00
10a	Carl Erskine (Two black loops in u-l) (Value Undetermined)			
10b	Carl Erskine (No black loops)	10.00	5.00	3.00
11	Sid Gordon	10.00	5.00	3.00
12a	Roy McMillan (551/1290 At Bat)	12.00	6.00	3.50
12b	Roy McMillan (557/1296 At Bat)	15.00	7.50	4.50
13	Paul Minner	10.00	5.00	3.00
14	Gerald Staley	10.00	5.00	3.00
15	Richie Ashburn	75.00	37.50	18.75
16	Jim Wilson	10.00	5.00	3.00
17	Tom Gorman	12.50	6.25	3.75
18	"Hoot" Evers	10.00	5.00	3.00
19	Bobby Shantz	10.00	5.00	3.00
20	Artie Houtteman	10.00	5.00	3.00
21	Vic Wertz	10.00	5.00	3.00
22a	Sam Mele (213/1661 Putouts)	12.00	6.00	3.50
22b	Sam Mele (217/1665 Putouts)	15.00	7.50	4.50
23	Harvey Kuenn **RC**	20.00	10.00	6.00
24	Bob Porterfield	10.00	5.00	3.00
25a	Wes Westrum (1.000/.987 Field Avg.)	12.00	6.00	3.50
25b	Wes Westrum (.982/.986 Field Avg.)	15.00	7.50	4.50
26a	Billy Cox (1.000/.960 Field Avg.)	15.00	7.50	4.50
26b	Billy Cox (.972/.960 Field Avg.)	20.00	10.00	6.00
27	Dick Cole	10.00	5.00	3.00
28a	Jim Greengrass (Birthplace Addison, N.J.)	20.00	10.00	6.00
28b	Jim Greengrass (Birthplace Addison, N.Y.)	12.00	6.00	3.50
29	Johnny Klippstein	10.00	5.00	3.00
30	Del Rice	10.00	5.00	3.00
31	"Smoky" Burgess	10.00	5.00	3.00
32	Del Crandall	10.00	5.00	3.00
33a	Vic Raschi (No trade line.)	27.50	13.50	8.25
33b	Vic Raschi (Traded line.)	50.00	25.00	15.00
34	Sammy White	10.00	5.00	3.00
35a	Eddie Joost (Quiz answer is 8.)	12.00	6.00	3.50
35b	Eddie Joost (Quiz answer is 33.)	15.00	7.50	4.50
36	George Strickland	10.00	5.00	3.00

37	Dick Kokos	10.00	5.00	3.00
38a	Minnie Minoso (.895/.961 Field Avg.)	25.00	12.50	7.50
38b	Minnie Minoso (.963/.963 Field Avg.)	30.00	15.00	9.00
39	Ned Garver	10.00	5.00	3.00
40	Gil Coan	10.00	5.00	3.00
41a	Alvin Dark (.986/.960 Field Avg.)	12.00	6.00	3.50
41b	Alvin Dark (.968/.960 Field Avg.)	15.00	7.50	4.50
42	Billy Loes	15.00	7.50	4.50
43a	Bob Friend (20 shutouts in quiz question)	12.00	6.00	3.50
43b	Bob Friend (16 shutouts in quiz question)	15.00	7.50	4.50
44	Harry Perkowski	10.00	5.00	3.00
45	Ralph Kiner	35.00	17.50	10.00
46	"Rip" Repulski	10.00	5.00	3.00
47a	Granny Hamner (.970/.953 Field Avg.)	12.00	6.00	3.50
47b	Granny Hamner (.953/.951 Field Avg.)	15.00	7.50	4.50
48	Jack Dittmer	10.00	5.00	3.00
49	Harry Byrd	12.50	6.25	3.75
50	George Kell	30.00	15.00	9.00
51	Alex Kellner	10.00	5.00	3.00
52	Joe Ginsberg	10.00	5.00	3.00
53a	Don Lenhardt (.969/.984 Field Avg.)	12.00	6.00	3.50
53b	Don Lenhardt (.966/.983 Field Avg.)	15.00	7.50	4.50
54	"Chico" Carrasquel	10.00	5.00	3.00
55	Jim Delsing	10.00	5.00	3.00
56	Maurice McDermott	10.00	5.00	3.00
57	Hoyt Wilhelm	27.50	13.50	8.25
58	Pee Wee Reese	100.00	50.00	25.00
59	Bob Schultz	10.00	5.00	3.00
60	Fred Baczewski	10.00	5.00	3.00
61a	Eddie Miksis (.954/.962 Field Avg.)	12.00	6.00	3.50
61b	Eddie Miksis (.954/.961 Field Avg.)	15.00	7.50	4.50
62	Enos Slaughter	35.00	17.50	10.00
63	Earl Torgeson	10.00	5.00	3.00
64	Eddie Mathews	80.00	40.00	20.00
65	Mickey Mantle	1,250	700.00	450.00
66a	Ted Williams	2,350	900.00	400.00
66b	Jimmy Piersall	60.00	30.00	18.00
67a	Carl Scheib (.306 Pct. with two lines under bio)	25.00	12.50	7.50
67b	Carl Scheib (.306 Pct. with one line under bio)	12.00	6.00	3.50
67c	Carl Scheib (.300 Pct.)	15.00	7.50	4.50
68	Bob Avila	10.00	5.00	3.00
69	Clinton Courtney	10.00	5.00	3.00
70	Willard Marshall	10.00	5.00	3.00
71	Ted Gray	10.00	5.00	3.00
72	Ed Yost	10.00	5.00	3.00
73	Don Mueller	10.00	5.00	3.00
74	Jim Gilliam RC	35.00	17.50	10.00
75	Max Surkont	10.00	5.00	3.00
76	Joe Nuxhall	10.00	5.00	3.00
77	Bob Rush	10.00	5.00	3.00
78	Sal Yvars	10.00	5.00	3.00
79	Curt Simmons	10.00	5.00	3.00
80a	Johnny Logan (106 Runs)	12.00	6.00	3.50
80b	Johnny Logan (100 Runs)	15.00	7.50	4.50
81a	Jerry Coleman (1.000/.975 Field Avg.)	15.00	7.50	4.50
81b	Jerry Coleman (.952/.975 Field Avg.)	20.00	10.00	6.00
82a	Bill Goodman (.965/.986 Field Avg.)	12.00	6.00	3.50
82b	Bill Goodman (.972/.985 Field Avg.)	15.00	7.50	4.50
83	Ray Murray	10.00	5.00	3.00
84	Larry Doby	45.00	22.50	13.50
85a	Jim Dyck (.926/.956 Field Avg.)	12.00	6.00	3.50
85b	Jim Dyck (.947/.960 Field Avg.)	15.00	7.50	4.50
86	Harry Dorish	10.00	5.00	3.00
87	Don Lund	10.00	5.00	3.00
88	Tommy Umphlett	10.00	5.00	3.00
89	Willie Mays	500.00	250.00	125.00
90	Roy Campanella	150.00	75.00	37.50
91	Cal Abrams	10.00	5.00	3.00
92	Ken Raffensberger	10.00	5.00	3.00
93a	Bill Serena (.983/.966 Field Avg.)	12.00	6.00	3.50
93b	Bill Serena (.977/.966 Field Avg.)	15.00	7.50	4.50
94a	Solly Hemus (476/1343 Assists)	12.00	6.00	3.50
94b	Solly Hemus (477/1343 Assists)	15.00	7.50	4.50

95	Robin Roberts	40.00	20.00	12.00
96	Joe Adcock	10.00	5.00	3.00
97	Gil McDougald	20.00	10.00	6.00
98	Ellis Kinder	10.00	5.00	3.00
99a	Peter Suder (.985/.974 Field Avg.)	12.00	6.00	3.50
99b	Peter Suder (.978/.974 Field Avg.)	15.00	7.50	4.50
100	Mike Garcia	10.00	5.00	3.00
101	Don Larsen RC	40.00	20.00	12.00
102	Bill Pierce	10.00	5.00	3.00
103a	Stephen Souchock (144/1192 Putouts)	12.00	6.00	3.50
103b	Stephen Souchock (147/1195 Putouts)	15.00	7.50	4.50
104	Frank Spec Shea	10.00	5.00	3.00
105a	Sal Maglie (Quiz answer is 8.)	20.00	10.00	6.00
105b	Sal Maglie (Quiz answer is 1904.)	30.00	15.00	9.00
106	Clem Labine	20.00	10.00	6.00
107	Paul LaPalme	10.00	5.00	3.00
108	Bobby Adams	10.00	5.00	3.00
109	Roy Smalley	10.00	5.00	3.00
110	Red Schoendienst	30.00	15.00	9.00
111	Murry Dickson	10.00	5.00	3.00
112	Andy Pafko	10.00	5.00	3.00
113	Allie Reynolds	20.00	10.00	6.00
114	Willard Nixon	10.00	5.00	3.00
115	Don Bollweg	10.00	5.00	3.00
116	Luke Easter	10.00	5.00	3.00
117	Dick Kryhoski	10.00	5.00	3.00
118	Bob Boyd	10.00	5.00	3.00
119	Fred Hatfield	10.00	5.00	3.00
120	Mel Hoderlein	10.00	5.00	3.00
121	Ray Katt	10.00	5.00	3.00
122	Carl Furillo	30.00	15.00	9.00
123	Toby Atwell	10.00	5.00	3.00
124a	Gus Bell (15/27 Errors)	12.00	6.00	3.50
124b	Gus Bell (11/26 Errors)	15.00	7.50	4.50
125	Warren Hacker	10.00	5.00	3.00
126	Cliff Chambers	10.00	5.00	3.00
127	Del Ennis	10.00	5.00	3.00
128	Ebba St. Claire	10.00	5.00	3.00
129	Hank Bauer	35.00	17.50	10.00
130	Milt Bolling	12.00	6.00	3.50
131	Joe Astroth	12.00	6.00	3.50
132	Bob Feller	75.00	37.50	18.75
133	Duane Pillette	12.00	6.00	3.50
134	Luis Aloma	12.00	6.00	3.50
135	Johnny Pesky	12.00	6.00	3.50
136	Clyde Vollmer	12.00	6.00	3.50
137	Al Corwin	12.00	6.00	3.50
138a	Gil Hodges (.993/.991 Field Avg.)	80.00	40.00	20.00
138b	Gil Hodges (.992/.991 Field Avg.)	100.00	50.00	30.00
139a	Preston Ward (.961/.992 Field Avg.)	15.00	7.50	4.50
139b	Preston Ward (.990/.992 Field Avg.)	17.50	8.75	5.25
140a	Saul Rogovin (7-12 Won/Lost with 2 Strikeouts)	15.00	7.50	4.50
140b	Saul Rogovin (7-12 Won/Lost with 62 Strikeouts)	17.50	8.75	5.25
140c	Saul Rogovin (8-12 Won/Lost)	40.00	20.00	12.00
141	Joe Garagiola	30.00	15.00	9.00
142	Al Brazle	12.00	6.00	3.50
143	Willie Jones	12.00	6.00	3.50
144	Ernie Johnson RC	30.00	15.00	9.00
145a	Billy Martin (.985/.983 Field Avg.)	80.00	40.00	20.00
145b	Billy Martin (.983/.982 Field Avg.)	90.00	45.00	25.00
146	Dick Gernert	12.00	6.00	3.50
147	Joe DeMaestri	12.00	6.00	3.50
148	Dale Mitchell	12.00	6.00	3.50
149	Bob Young	12.00	6.00	3.50
150	Cass Michaels	12.00	6.00	3.50
151	Pat Mullin	12.00	6.00	3.50
152	Mickey Vernon	12.00	6.00	3.50
153a	"Whitey" Lockman (100/331 Assists)	15.00	7.50	4.50
153b	"Whitey" Lockman (102/333 Assists)	17.50	8.75	5.25
154	Don Newcombe	50.00	25.00	12.50
155	Frank Thomas RC	25.00	12.50	7.50
156a	Rocky Bridges (320/467 Assists)	15.00	7.50	4.50
156b	Rocky Bridges (328/475 Assists)	17.50	8.75	5.25
157	Omar Lown	12.00	6.00	3.50
158	Stu Miller	12.00	6.00	3.50
159	John Lindell	12.00	6.00	3.50
160	Danny O'Connell	12.00	6.00	3.50
161	Yogi Berra	175.00	87.50	43.75
162	Ted Lepcio	12.00	6.00	3.50

163a	Dave Philley (152 Games, no traded line)	50.00	25.00	15.00
163b	Dave Philley (152 Games, traded line)	22.50	11.00	6.75
163c	Dave Philley (157 Games, traded line)	27.50	13.50	8.25
164	Early Wynn	45.00	22.50	13.50
165	Johnny Groth	12.00	6.00	3.50
166	Sandy Consuegra	12.00	6.00	3.50
167	Bill Hoeft	12.00	6.00	3.50
168	Edward Fitz Gerald	12.00	6.00	3.50
169	Larry Jansen	12.00	6.00	3.50
170	Duke Snider	240.00	120.00	60.00
171	Carlos Bernier	12.00	6.00	3.50
172	Andy Seminick	12.00	6.00	3.50
173	Dee Fondy	12.00	6.00	3.50
174a	Pete Castiglione (.966/.959 Field Avg.)	15.00	7.50	4.50
174b	Pete Castiglione (.970/.959 Field Avg.)	17.50	8.75	5.25
175	Mel Clark	12.00	6.00	3.50
176	Vernon Bickford	12.00	6.00	3.50
177	Whitey Ford	125.00	62.50	31.25
178	Del Wilber	12.00	6.00	3.50
179a	Morris Martin (44 ERA)	15.00	7.50	4.50
179b	Morris Martin (4.44 ERA)	17.50	8.75	5.25
180	Joe Tipton	12.00	6.00	3.50
181	Les Moss	12.00	6.00	3.50
182	Sherman Lollar	12.00	6.00	3.50
183	Matt Batts	12.00	6.00	3.50
184	Mickey Grasso	12.00	6.00	3.50
185a	Daryl Spencer RC (.941/.944 Field Avg.)	15.00	7.50	4.50
185b	Daryl Spencer RC (.933/.936 Field Avg.)	17.50	8.75	5.25
186	Russ Meyer	15.00	7.50	4.50
187	Vern Law	12.00	6.00	3.50
188	Frank Smith	12.00	6.00	3.50
189	Ransom Jackson	12.00	6.00	3.50
190	Joe Presko	12.00	6.00	3.50
191	Karl Drews	12.00	6.00	3.50
192	Lew Burdette	12.00	6.00	3.50
193	Eddie Robinson	15.00	7.50	4.50
194	Sid Hudson	12.00	6.00	3.50
195	Bob Cain	12.00	6.00	3.50
196	Bob Lemon	30.00	15.00	9.00
197	Lou Kretlow	12.00	6.00	3.50
198	Virgil Trucks	12.00	6.00	3.50
199	Steve Gromek	12.00	6.00	3.50
200	Connie Marrero	12.00	6.00	3.50
201	Bob Thomson	20.00	10.00	6.00
202	George Shuba	15.00	7.50	4.50
203	Vic Janowicz	25.00	12.50	7.50
204	Jack Collum	12.00	6.00	3.50
205	Hal Jeffcoat	12.00	6.00	3.50
206	Steve Bilko	12.00	6.00	3.50
207	Stan Lopata	12.00	6.00	3.50
208	Johnny Antonelli	12.00	6.00	3.50
209	Gene Woodling (Photo reversed.)	35.00	17.50	10.00
210	Jimmy Piersall	35.00	17.50	10.00
211	Jim Robertson	12.00	6.00	3.50
212a	Owen Friend (.964/.957 Field Avg.)	15.00	7.50	4.50
212b	Owen Friend (.967/.958 Field Avg.)	17.50	8.75	5.25
213	Dick Littlefield	12.00	6.00	3.50
214	Ferris Fain	12.00	6.00	3.50
215	Johnny Bucha	12.00	6.00	3.50
216a	Jerry Snyder (.988/.988 Field Avg.)	15.00	7.50	4.50
216b	Jerry Snyder (.968/.968 Field Avg.)	17.50	8.75	5.25
217a	Henry Thompson (.956/.951 Field Avg.)	15.00	7.50	4.50
217b	Henry Thompson (.958/.952 Field Avg.)	17.50	8.75	5.25
218a	Preacher Roe (black loop at top)	40.00	20.00	12.00
218b	Preacher Roe (no black loop (value undetermined))			
219	Hal Rice	12.00	6.00	3.50
220	Hobie Landrith	12.00	6.00	3.50
221	Frank Baumholtz	12.00	6.00	3.50
222	Memo Luna	15.00	7.50	4.50
223	Steve Ridzik	12.00	6.00	3.50
224	Billy Bruton	45.00	12.00	5.00

1955 Bowman

Bowman produced its final baseball card set as an independent card maker in 1955, a popular issue that has color player photographs placed inside a television set design. The set consists of 320 cards measuring 2-1/2" x 3-3/4". High-numbered cards (#225-320) appear to have replaced certain low-numbered cards on the press sheets and are scarcer. The high series includes 31 umpire cards.

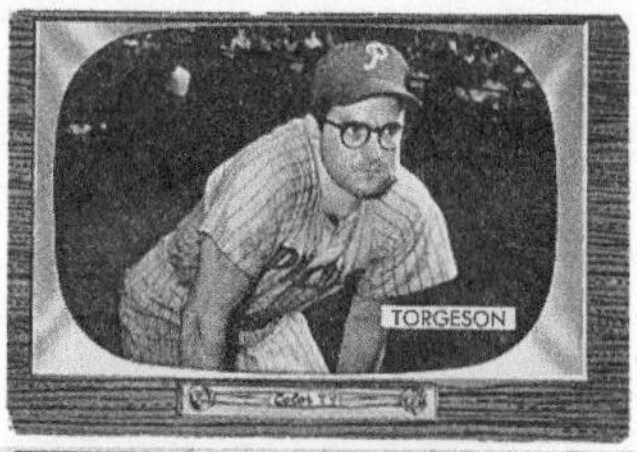

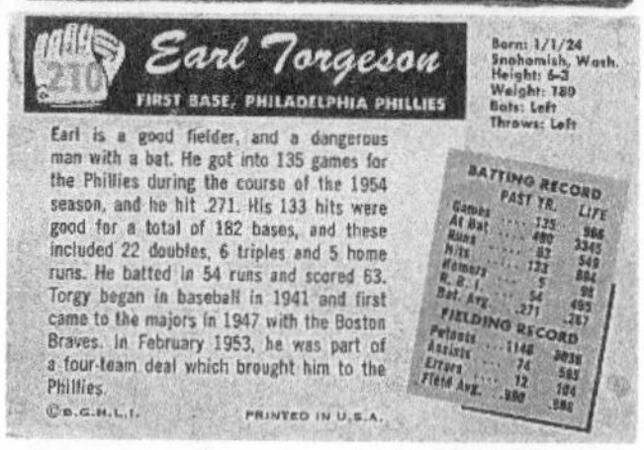

		NM	E	VG
Complete Set (320):		7,000	3,500	2,000
Common Player (1-224):		12.50	6.25	3.75
Common Player (225-320):		25.00	12.50	7.50
1	Hoyt Wilhelm	100.00	50.00	25.00
2	Al Dark	15.00	7.50	4.50
3	Joe Coleman	12.50	6.25	3.75
4	Eddie Waitkus	12.50	6.25	3.75
5	Jim Robertson	12.50	6.25	3.75
6	Pete Suder	12.50	6.25	3.75
7	Gene Baker	12.50	6.25	3.75
8	Warren Hacker	12.50	6.25	3.75
9	Gil McDougald	25.00	12.50	7.50
10	Phil Rizzuto	125.00	62.50	31.25
11	Billy Bruton	12.50	6.25	3.75
12	Andy Pafko	12.50	6.25	3.75
13	Clyde Vollmer	12.50	6.25	3.75
14	Gus Keriazakos	12.50	6.25	3.75
15	Frank Sullivan **RC**	12.50	6.25	3.75
16	Jim Piersall	12.50	6.25	3.75
17	Del Ennis	12.50	6.25	3.75
18	Stan Lopata	12.50	6.25	3.75
19	Bobby Avila	12.50	6.25	3.75
20	Al Smith	12.50	6.25	3.75
21	Don Hoak **RC**	15.00	7.50	4.50
22	Roy Campanella	125.00	62.50	31.25
23	Al Kaline **RC**	150.00	75.00	37.50
24	Al Aber	12.50	6.25	3.75
25	Minnie Minoso	30.00	15.00	9.00
26	Virgil Trucks	12.50	6.25	3.75
27	Preston Ward	12.50	6.25	3.75
28	Dick Cole	12.50	6.25	3.75
29	Red Schoendienst	25.00	12.50	7.50
30	Bill Sarni	12.50	6.25	3.75
31	Johnny Temple	12.50	6.25	3.75
32	Wally Post	12.50	6.25	3.75
33	Nellie Fox	60.00	30.00	15.00
34	Clint Courtney	12.50	6.25	3.75
35	Bill Tuttle	12.50	6.25	3.75
36	Wayne Belardi	12.50	6.25	3.75
37	Pee Wee Reese	100.00	50.00	30.00
38	Early Wynn	25.00	12.50	7.50
39	Bob Darnell	15.00	7.50	4.50
40	Vic Wertz	12.50	6.25	3.75
41	Mel Clark	12.50	6.25	3.75
42	Bob Greenwood	12.50	6.25	3.75
43	Bob Buhl	12.50	6.25	3.75
44	Danny O'Connell	12.50	6.25	3.75
45	Tom Umphlett	12.50	6.25	3.75
46	Mickey Vernon	12.50	6.25	3.75
47	Sammy White	12.50	6.25	3.75
48a	Milt Bolling (Frank Bolling back.)	20.00	10.00	6.00
48b	Milt Bolling (Milt Bolling back.)	20.00	10.00	6.00
49	Jim Greengrass	12.50	6.25	3.75
50	Hobie Landrith	12.50	6.25	3.75
51	Elvin Tappe	12.50	6.25	3.75
52	Hal Rice	12.50	6.25	3.75
53	Alex Kellner	12.50	6.25	3.75
54	Don Bollweg	12.50	6.25	3.75
55	Cal Abrams	12.50	6.25	3.75
56	Billy Cox	12.50	6.25	3.75
57	Bob Friend	12.50	6.25	3.75
58	Frank Thomas	12.50	6.25	3.75
59	Whitey Ford	100.00	50.00	25.00
60	Enos Slaughter	30.00	15.00	9.00
61	Paul LaPalme	12.50	6.25	3.75
62	Royce Lint	12.50	6.25	3.75
63	Irv Noren	15.00	7.50	4.50
64	Curt Simmons	12.50	6.25	3.75
65	Don Zimmer **RC**	30.00	15.00	9.00
66	George Shuba	15.00	7.50	4.50
67	Don Larsen	30.00	15.00	9.00
68	Elston Howard **RC**	80.00	40.00	24.00
69	Bill Hunter	15.00	7.50	4.50
70	Lew Burdette	12.50	6.25	3.75
71	Dave Jolly	12.50	6.25	3.75
72	Chet Nichols	12.50	6.25	3.75
73	Eddie Yost	12.50	6.25	3.75
74	Jerry Snyder	12.50	6.25	3.75
75	Brooks Lawrence	12.50	6.25	3.75
76	Tom Poholsky	12.50	6.25	3.75
77	Jim McDonald	12.50	6.25	3.75
78	Gil Coan	12.50	6.25	3.75
79	Willie Miranda	12.50	6.25	3.75
80	Lou Limmer	12.50	6.25	3.75
81	Bob Morgan	12.50	6.25	3.75
82	Lee Walls	12.50	6.25	3.75
83	Max Surkont	12.50	6.25	3.75
84	George Freese	12.50	6.25	3.75
85	Cass Michaels	12.50	6.25	3.75
86	Ted Gray	12.50	6.25	3.75
87	Randy Jackson	12.50	6.25	3.75
88	Steve Bilko	12.50	6.25	3.75
89	Lou Boudreau	25.00	12.50	7.50
90	Art Ditmar	12.50	6.25	3.75
91	Dick Marlowe	12.50	6.25	3.75
92	George Zuverink	12.50	6.25	3.75
93	Andy Seminick	12.50	6.25	3.75
94	Hank Thompson	12.50	6.25	3.75
95	Sal Maglie	12.50	6.25	3.75
96	Ray Narleski	12.50	6.25	3.75
97	John Podres **RC**	30.00	15.00	9.00
98	Jim Gilliam	27.50	13.50	8.25
99	Jerry Coleman	15.00	7.50	4.50
100	Tom Morgan	15.00	7.50	4.50
101a	Don Johnson (Ernie Johnson (Braves) on front.)	60.00	30.00	18.00
101b	Don Johnson (Don Johnson (Orioles) on front.)	27.50	13.50	8.25
102	Bobby Thomson	17.50	8.75	5.25
103	Eddie Mathews	80.00	40.00	20.00
104	Bob Porterfield	12.50	6.25	3.75
105	Johnny Schmitz	12.50	6.25	3.75
106	Del Rice	12.50	6.25	3.75
107	Solly Hemus	12.50	6.25	3.75
108	Lou Kretlow	12.50	6.25	3.75
109	Vern Stephens	12.50	6.25	3.75
110	Bob Miller	12.50	6.25	3.75
111	Steve Ridzik	12.50	6.25	3.75
112	Granny Hamner	12.50	6.25	3.75
113	Bob Hall	12.50	6.25	3.75
114	Vic Janowicz	12.50	6.25	3.75
115	Roger Bowman	12.50	6.25	3.75
116	Sandy Consuegra	12.50	6.25	3.75
117	Johnny Groth	12.50	6.25	3.75
118	Bobby Adams	12.50	6.25	3.75
119	Joe Astroth	12.50	6.25	3.75
120	Ed Burtschy	12.50	6.25	3.75
121	Rufus Crawford	12.50	6.25	3.75
122	Al Corwin	12.50	6.25	3.75
123	Marv Grissom	12.50	6.25	3.75
124	Johnny Antonelli	12.50	6.25	3.75
125	Paul Giel	12.50	6.25	3.75
126	Billy Goodman	12.50	6.25	3.75
127	Hank Majeski	12.50	6.25	3.75
128	Mike Garcia	12.50	6.25	3.75
129	Hal Naragon	12.50	6.25	3.75
130	Richie Ashburn	50.00	25.00	15.00
131	Willard Marshall	12.50	6.25	3.75
132a	Harvey Kueen (Misspelled last name.)	25.00	12.50	7.50
132b	Harvey Kuenn (Corrected)	35.00	17.50	10.00
133	Charles King	12.50	6.25	3.75
134	Bob Feller	80.00	40.00	20.00
135	Lloyd Merriman	12.50	6.25	3.75
136	Rocky Bridges	12.50	6.25	3.75
137	Bob Talbot	12.50	6.25	3.75
138	Davey Williams	12.50	6.25	3.75
139	Billy & Bobby Shantz	15.00	7.50	4.50
140	Bobby Shantz	12.50	6.25	3.75
141	Wes Westrum	12.50	6.25	3.75
142	Rudy Regalado	12.50	6.25	3.75
143	Don Newcombe	25.00	12.50	7.50
144	Art Houtteman	12.50	6.25	3.75
145	Bob Nieman	12.50	6.25	3.75
146	Don Liddle	12.50	6.25	3.75
147	Sam Mele	12.50	6.25	3.75
148	Bob Chakales	12.50	6.25	3.75
149	Cloyd Boyer	12.50	6.25	3.75
150	Bill Klaus	12.50	6.25	3.75
151	Jim Brideweser	12.50	6.25	3.75
152	Johnny Klippstein	12.50	6.25	3.75
153	Eddie Robinson	15.00	7.50	4.50
154	Frank Lary **RC**	12.50	6.25	3.75
155	Gerry Staley	12.50	6.25	3.75
156	Jim Hughes	15.00	7.50	4.50
157a	Ernie Johnson (Don Johnson (Orioles) picture on front.)	15.00	7.50	4.50
157b	Ernie Johnson (Ernie Johnson (Braves) picture on front.)	30.00	15.00	9.00
158	Gil Hodges	40.00	20.00	12.00
159	Harry Byrd	12.50	6.25	3.75
160	Bill Skowron	40.00	20.00	12.00
161	Matt Batts	12.50	6.25	3.75
162	Charlie Maxwell **RC**	12.50	6.25	3.75
163	Sid Gordon	12.50	6.25	3.75
164	Toby Atwell	12.50	6.25	3.75
165	Maurice McDermott	12.50	6.25	3.75
166	Jim Busby	12.50	6.25	3.75
167	Bob Grim	15.00	7.50	4.50
168	Yogi Berra	125.00	62.50	31.25
169	Carl Furillo	27.50	13.50	8.25
170	Carl Erskine	25.00	12.50	7.50
171	Robin Roberts	32.50	16.00	10.00
172	Willie Jones	12.50	6.25	3.75
173	"Chico" Carrasquel	12.50	6.25	3.75
174	Sherman Lollar	12.50	6.25	3.75
175	Wilmer Shantz	12.50	6.25	3.75
176	Joe DeMaestri	12.50	6.25	3.75
177	Willard Nixon	12.50	6.25	3.75
178	Tom Brewer	12.50	6.25	3.75
179	Hank Aaron	300.00	150.00	75.00
180	Johnny Logan	12.50	6.25	3.75
181	Eddie Miksis	12.50	6.25	3.75
182	Bob Rush	12.50	6.25	3.75
183	Ray Katt	12.50	6.25	3.75
184	Willie Mays	275.00	137.50	68.75
185	Vic Raschi	12.50	6.25	3.75
186	Alex Grammas	12.50	6.25	3.75
187	Fred Hatfield	12.50	6.25	3.75
188	Ned Garver	12.50	6.25	3.75
189	Jack Collum	12.50	6.25	3.75
190	Fred Baczewski	12.50	6.25	3.75
191	Bob Lemon	30.00	15.00	9.00
192	George Strickland	12.50	6.25	3.75
193	Howie Judson	12.50	6.25	3.75
194	Joe Nuxhall	12.50	6.25	3.75
195a	Erv Palica (No traded line.)	30.00	15.00	9.00
195b	Erv Palica (Traded line.)	125.00	60.00	35.00
196	Russ Meyer	15.00	7.50	4.50
197	Ralph Kiner	35.00	17.50	10.00
198	Dave Pope	12.50	6.25	3.75
199	Vernon Law	12.50	6.25	3.75
200	Dick Littlefield	12.50	6.25	3.75
201	Allie Reynolds	25.00	12.50	7.50
202	Mickey Mantle	750.00	375.00	225.00
203	Steve Gromek	12.50	6.25	3.75
204a	Frank Bolling (Milt Bolling back.)	45.00	22.50	13.50
204b	Frank Bolling (Frank Bolling back.)	30.00	15.00	9.00
205	"Rip" Repulski	12.50	6.25	3.75
206	Ralph Beard	12.50	6.25	3.75
207	Frank Shea	12.50	6.25	3.75
208	Ed Fitz Gerald	12.50	6.25	3.75
209	"Smoky" Burgess	12.50	6.25	3.75
210	Earl Torgeson	12.50	6.25	3.75
211	John "Sonny" Dixon	12.50	6.25	3.75
212	Jack Dittmer	12.50	6.25	3.75
213	George Kell	30.00	15.00	9.00
214	Billy Pierce	12.50	6.25	3.75
215	Bob Kuzava	12.50	6.25	3.75
216	Preacher Roe	15.00	7.50	4.50
217	Del Crandall	12.50	6.25	3.75
218	Joe Adcock	12.50	6.25	3.75
219	"Whitey" Lockman	12.50	6.25	3.75
220	Jim Hearn	12.50	6.25	3.75
221	Hector "Skinny" Brown	12.50	6.25	3.75
222	Russ Kemmerer	12.50	6.25	3.75
223	Hal Jeffcoat	12.50	6.25	3.75
224	Dee Fondy	12.50	6.25	3.75
225	Paul Richards	25.00	12.50	7.50
226	W.F. McKinley (Umpire)	30.00	15.00	9.00
227	Frank Baumholtz	25.00	12.50	7.50
228	John M. Phillips	25.00	12.50	7.50
229	Jim Brosnan	25.00	12.50	7.50
230	Al Brazle	25.00	12.50	7.50
231	Jim Konstanty	25.00	12.50	7.50
232	Birdie Tebbetts	25.00	12.50	7.50
233	Bill Serena	25.00	12.50	7.50
234	Dick Bartell	25.00	12.50	7.50
235	J.A. Paparella (Umpire)	30.00	15.00	9.00
236	Murry Dickson	25.00	12.50	7.50
237	Johnny Wyrostek	25.00	12.50	7.50
238	Eddie Stanky	25.00	12.50	7.50
239	Edwin A. Rommel (Umpire)	30.00	15.00	9.00
240	Billy Loes	25.00	12.50	7.50
241	John Pesky	25.00	12.50	7.50
242	Ernie Banks **RC**	350.00	175.00	87.50
243	Gus Bell	25.00	12.50	7.50
244	Duane Pillette	25.00	12.50	7.50
245	Bill Miller	25.00	12.50	7.50

246	Hank Bauer	45.00	22.50	13.50
247	Dutch Leonard	25.00	12.50	7.50
248	Harry Dorish	25.00	12.50	7.50
249	Billy Gardner	25.00	12.50	7.50
250	Larry Napp (Umpire)	30.00	15.00	9.00
251	Stan Jok	25.00	12.50	7.50
252	Roy Smalley	25.00	12.50	7.50
253	Jim Wilson	25.00	12.50	7.50
254	Bennett Flowers	25.00	12.50	7.50
255	Pete Runnels	25.00	12.50	7.50
256	Owen Friend	25.00	12.50	7.50
257	Tom Alston	25.00	12.50	7.50
258	John W. Stevens (Umpire)	30.00	15.00	9.00
259	Don Mossi **RC**	35.00	17.50	10.00
260	Edwin H. Hurley (Umpire)	30.00	15.00	9.00
261	Walt Moryn	25.00	12.50	7.50
262	Jim Lemon	25.00	12.50	7.50
263	Eddie Joost	25.00	12.50	7.50
264	Bill Henry	25.00	12.50	7.50
265	Al Barlick (Umpire)	60.00	30.00	15.00
266	Mike Fornieles	25.00	12.50	7.50
267	George Honochick (Umpire)	50.00	25.00	15.00
268	Roy Lee Hawes	25.00	12.50	7.50
269	Joe Amalfitano	25.00	12.50	7.50
270	Chico Fernandez	25.00	12.50	7.50
271	Bob Hooper	25.00	12.50	7.50
272	John Flaherty (Umpire)	30.00	15.00	9.00
273	"Bubba" Church	25.00	12.50	7.50
274	Jim Delsing	25.00	12.50	7.50
275	William T. Grieve (Umpire)	30.00	15.00	9.00
276	Ike Delock	25.00	12.50	7.50
277	Ed Runge (Umpire)	30.00	15.00	9.00
278	Charles Neal **RC**	35.00	17.50	10.00
279	Hank Soar (Umpire)	30.00	15.00	9.00
280	Clyde McCullough	25.00	12.50	7.50
281	Charles Berry (Umpire)	30.00	15.00	9.00
282	Phil Cavarretta	25.00	12.50	7.50
283	Nestor Chylak (Umpire)	60.00	30.00	15.00
284	William A. Jackowski (Umpire)	30.00	15.00	9.00
285	Walt Dropo	25.00	12.50	7.50
286	Frank Secory (Umpire)	30.00	15.00	9.00
287	Ron Mrozinski	25.00	12.50	7.50
288	Dick Smith	25.00	12.50	7.50
289	Art Gore (Umpire)	30.00	15.00	9.00
290	Hershell Freeman	25.00	12.50	7.50
291	Frank Dascoli (Umpire)	30.00	15.00	9.00
292	Marv Blaylock	25.00	12.50	7.50
293	Thomas D. Gorman (Umpire)	30.00	15.00	9.00
294	Wally Moses	25.00	12.50	7.50
295	Lee Ballanfant (Umpire)	30.00	15.00	9.00
296	Bill Virdon **RC**	30.00	15.00	9.00
297	"Dusty" Boggess (Umpire)	30.00	15.00	9.00
298	Charlie Grimm	25.00	12.50	7.50
299	Lonnie Warneke (Umpire)	30.00	15.00	9.00
300	Tommy Byrne	30.00	15.00	9.00
301	William Engeln (Umpire)	30.00	15.00	9.00
302	Frank Malzone **RC**	30.00	15.00	9.00
303	Jocko Conlan (Umpire)	60.00	30.00	15.00
304	Harry Chiti	25.00	12.50	7.50
305	Frank Umont (Umpire)	30.00	15.00	9.00
306	Bob Cerv	30.00	15.00	9.00
307	"Babe" Pinelli (Umpire)	25.00	12.50	7.50
308	Al Lopez	35.00	17.50	10.00
309	Hal Dixon (Umpire)	30.00	15.00	9.00
310	Ken Lehman	30.00	15.00	9.00
311	Larry Goetz (Umpire)	30.00	15.00	9.00
312	Bill Wight	25.00	12.50	7.50
313	Augie Donatelli (Umpire)	30.00	15.00	9.00
314	Dale Mitchell	25.00	12.50	7.50
315	Cal Hubbard (Umpire)	70.00	35.00	21.00
316	Marion Fricano	25.00	12.50	7.50
317	Bill Summers (Umpire)	30.00	15.00	9.00
318	Sid Hudson	25.00	12.50	7.50
319	Al Schroll	25.00	12.50	7.50
320	George Susce, Jr.	60.00	30.00	15.00

1956 Bowman Prototypes

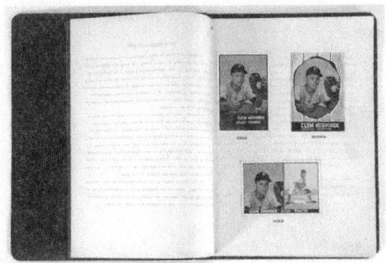

To gauge consumer demand for a 1956 baseball card set that it never issued, Bowman produced a "Baseball Card Preference Study" report. The report survives today in the form of a 24-page notebook that includes samples of the three designs apparently preferred by the pre-teen boys surveyed. All three cards are glued to one page of the report and all feature the photo of Pirates catcher Clem Koshorek used in the 1953 Bowman set. It is believed only two of the reports survive.

(Sold for $10,440 in 5/05 auction.)

1963 George Brace All Time Chicago Cubs

The year of issue attributed here is only theoretical. The set consists of a window envelope which contains 18 5-1/4" x 7" black-and-white photos of former Cubs greats by famed Chicago baseball photographer George Brace. The blank-backed unnumbered pictures have player identification in the white border at bottom. They are checklisted here alphabetically.

		NM	E	VG
	Complete Set (18):	50.00	25.00	15.00
	Common Player:	7.50	3.75	2.25
(1)	Grover Cleveland Alexander	10.00	5.00	3.00
(2)	Cap Anson	10.00	5.00	3.00
(3)	Three Finger Brown	9.00	4.50	2.75
(4)	Frank Chance	9.00	4.50	2.75
(5)	Johnny Evers	9.00	4.50	2.75
(6)	Charlie Grimm	7.50	3.75	2.25
(7)	Stan Hack	7.50	3.75	2.25
(8)	Gabby Hartnett	7.50	3.75	2.25
(9)	Billy Herman	7.50	3.75	2.25
(10)	Charlie Hollocher	7.50	3.75	2.25
(11)	Billy Jurges	7.50	3.75	2.25
(12)	Johnny Kling	7.50	3.75	2.25
(13)	Joe McCarthy	7.50	3.75	2.25
(14)	Ed Reulbach	7.50	3.75	2.25
(15)	Albert Spalding	7.50	3.75	2.25
(16)	Joe Tinker	9.00	4.50	2.75
(17)	Hippo Vaughn	7.50	3.75	2.25
(18)	Hack Wilson	9.00	4.50	2.75

1908-11 H.H. Bregstone Browns/Cardinals Post Cards (PC743)

Among the rarest of the early 20th Century baseball player postcards are those of the St. Louis Browns and Cardinals from H.H. Bregstone, also of St. Louis. The 3-1/2" x 5-1/2" cards feature sepia player photos that are borderless at top and sides. At bottom is a box with the player's name, team, position, league and the issuer's address. Backs are standard postcard format. The unnumbered cards are checklisted here alphabetically within team. With a single exception (Gregory), all of the Browns players are from 1909, while the range of Cardinals spans the era 1908-1911.

	NM	E	VG
Complete Set, Browns (22):	19,000	9,500	5,700
Complete Set, Cardinals (34):	36,000	18,000	11,000
Common Player:	1,000	500.00	300.00

ST. LOUIS BROWNS

(1)	Bill Bailey	1,000	500.00	300.00
(2)	Lou Criger	1,000	500.00	300.00
(3)	Dode Criss	1,000	500.00	300.00
(4)	Bill Dineen	1,000	500.00	300.00
(5)	Hobe Ferris	1,000	500.00	300.00
(6)	Bill Graham	1,000	500.00	300.00
(7)	B Gregory	1,000	500.00	300.00
(8)	Art Griggs	1,000	500.00	300.00
(9)	Roy Hartzell	1,000	500.00	300.00
(10)	Danny Hoffman	1,000	500.00	300.00
(11)	Harry Howell	1,000	500.00	300.00
(12)	Tom Jones	1,000	500.00	300.00
(13)	Jimmy McAleer	1,000	500.00	300.00
(14)	Ham Patterson	1,000	500.00	300.00
(15)	Barney Pelty	1,000	500.00	300.00
(16)	Al Schweitzer	1,000	500.00	300.00
(17)	Wib Smith	1,000	500.00	300.00
(18)	Jim Stephens	1,000	500.00	300.00
(19)	George Stone	1,000	500.00	300.00
(20)	Rube Waddell	1,500	750.00	450.00
(21)	Bobby Wallace	1,500	750.00	450.00
(22)	Jimmy Williams	1,000	500.00	300.00

ST. LOUIS CARDINALS

(1)	Jap Barbeau	1,000	500.00	300.00
(2)	Shad Barry	1,000	500.00	300.00
(3)	Fred Beebe	1,000	500.00	300.00
(4)	Frank Betcher	1,000	500.00	300.00
(5)	Jack Bliss	1,000	500.00	300.00
(6)	Roger Bresnahan	1,600	800.00	480.00
(7)	Bobby Byrne	1,000	500.00	300.00
(8)	Chappie Charles	1,000	500.00	300.00
(9)	Frank Corridon	1,000	500.00	300.00
(10)	Joe Delahanty	1,400	700.00	420.00
(11)	Rube Ellis	1,000	500.00	300.00
(12)	Steve Evans	1,000	500.00	300.00
(13)	Art Fromme	1,000	500.00	300.00
(14)	Rube Geyer	1,000	500.00	300.00
(15)	Billy Gilbert	1,000	500.00	300.00
(16)	Bob Harmon	1,000	500.00	300.00
(17)	Irv Higginbotham	1,000	500.00	300.00
(18)	Tom Higgins	1,000	500.00	300.00
(19)	Art Hoelskoetter	1,000	500.00	300.00
(20)	Miller Huggins	1,500	750.00	450.00
(21)	Rudy Hulswitt	1,000	500.00	300.00
(22)	Adam Johnson	1,000	500.00	300.00
(23)	Ed Konetchy	1,000	500.00	300.00
(24)	Johnny Lush	1,000	500.00	300.00
(25)	Lee Magee	1,000	500.00	300.00
(26)	Stoney McGlynn	1,000	500.00	300.00
(27)	Rebel Oakes	1,000	500.00	300.00
(28)	Bill O'Hara	1,000	500.00	300.00
(29)	Patsy O'Rourke	1,000	500.00	300.00
(30)	Ed Phelps	1,000	500.00	300.00
(31)	Charlie Rhodes	1,000	500.00	300.00
(32)	Elmer Rieger	1,000	500.00	300.00
(33)	Slim Sallee	1,000	500.00	300.00
(34)	Vic Willis	1,500	750.00	450.00

1903-1904 Breisch-Williams

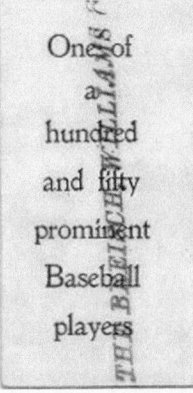

Many veteran collectors now believe that Breisch Williams Confectionary Co. of Oxford, Pa., was just one of several firms that used the black-and-white card issue cataloged as E107 as a premium. A relatively small percentage of E107s are found with a purple rubber-stamped "THE BREISCH-WILLIAMS CO" message diagonally on back. It is speculated the stamp may have been used to "cancel" cards there were returned in a prize redemption program. The overprinted cards currently carry a premium of 2-3X the value of blank-backed or "One of a ..." E107s. With only a single known exception, all Breisch-Williams stamped cards are of Type 1.

(See E107 Type 1 and Type 2 for checklist and base value information.)

1909-10 C.A. Briggs Co. (E97)

CY. YOUNG. BOSTON, NAT'L

This card is one of a set of 30 BALL PLAYERS Cards, as follows:

AUSTIN, New York American.
BRADLEY, Cleveland American
BIRMINGHAM, Cleveland American
BRANSFIELD, Philadelphia National
CAMNITZ, Pittsburg National
CARRIGAN, Boston American
DURHAM, New York National
DYGERT, Philadelphia American
DOOLAN, Philadelphia National
DEVORE, New York National
DAVIS, Philadelphia American
HEMPHILL, New York American
HEINCHMAN, Cleveland American
HARTSEL, Philadelphia American
KROH, Chicago National
KLEINOW, New York American
KELLY, Boston National
KEELER, New York National
McINTYRE, Detroit American
McCONNELL, Boston American
MOORE, Philadelphia National
MULLIN, Detroit American
MURRAY, New York National
MEYERS, New York National
NICHOLS, Cleveland American
ROSSMAN, Detroit American
SULLIVAN, Chicago American
STEINFELDT, Chicago American
SCHLEI, New York National
CY. YOUNG, Cleveland American

C.A.BRIGGS CO., Lozenge Makers
Boston, Mass.

Measuring approximately 1-1/2" x 2-3/4", this set is nearly identical to several other candy issues of the same period. Designated as E97 in the American Card Catalog, the set was issued in 1909-1910 by "C.A. Briggs Co., Lozenge Makers of Boston, Mass." The front of the card shows a tinted player photo, with the player's last name, position and team printed below. Backs are printed in brown and checklist the 30 players in the set alphabetically. The C.A. Briggs Co. name appears at the bottom. Black-and-white examples of this set have also been found on a thin paper stock with blank backs and are believed to be "proof cards." They are valued about 2-3X the figures shown here. Five variations are also found in the set. The more expensive variations are not included in the complete set price.

		NM	E	VG
Complete Set (30):		60,000	24,000	12,000
Common Player:		1,500	750.00	450.00
Proofs: 1.5-2X				
(1)	Jimmy Austin	1,500	750.00	450.00
(2)	Joe Birmingham	1,500	750.00	450.00
(3)	Bill Bradley	1,500	750.00	450.00
(4)	Kitty Bransfield	1,500	750.00	450.00
(5)	Howie Camnitz	1,500	750.00	450.00
(6)	Bill Carrigan	1,500	750.00	450.00
(7)	Harry Davis	1,500	750.00	450.00
(8)	Josh Devore	1,500	750.00	450.00
(9a)	Mickey Dolan (Doolan)	4,500	2,200	1,350
(9b)	Mickey Doolan	1,500	750.00	450.00
(10)	Bull Durham	1,500	750.00	450.00
(11)	Jimmy Dygert	1,500	750.00	450.00
(12a)	Topsy Hartsell (Hartsel)	4,000	1,500	750.00
(12b)	Topsy Hartsel	1,500	750.00	450.00
(13)	Bill Heinchman (Hinchman)	1,500	750.00	450.00
(14)	Charlie Hemphill	1,500	750.00	450.00
(15)	Wee Willie Keeler	8,000	3,200	1,600
(16)	Joe Kelly (Kelley)	8,000	3,200	1,600
(17)	Red Kleinow	1,500	750.00	450.00
(18)	Rube Kroh	1,500	750.00	450.00
(19)	Matty McIntyre	1,500	750.00	450.00
(20)	Amby McConnell	1,500	750.00	450.00
(21)	Chief Meyers	1,500	750.00	450.00
(22)	Earl Moore	1,500	750.00	450.00
(23)	George Mullin	1,500	750.00	450.00
(24)	Red Murray	1,500	750.00	450.00
(25a)	Simon Nichols (Nicholls) (Philadelphia)	10,000	5,000	2,000
(25b)	Simon Nichols (Nicholls) (Cleveland)	4,000	1,500	750.00
(26)	Claude Rossman	4,000	1,500	750.00
(27)	Admiral Schlei	2,500	1,000	500.00
(28a)	Harry Steinfeld (Name incorrect.)	4,400	1,800	900.00
(28b)	Harry Steinfeldt (Name correct.)	4,400	1,800	900.00
(29a)	Dennis Sullivan (Chicago)	1,500	750.00	450.00
(29b)	Dennis Sullivan (Boston)	10,000	5,000	3,000
(30a)	Cy. Young (Cleveland) (Picture actually Irv Young.)	7,500	3,700	2,200
(30b)	Cy. Young (Boston) (Picture actually Irv Young.)	10,000	5,000	3,000

1933 C.A. Briggs Co. Babe Ruth

24. BASEBALL
The national summer sport of the United States. Origin obscure, but believed derived from old English game of "Rounders." Professional Baseball started in 1882, first college league 1870. 1932 World Series won by New York Americans (Yankees) defeating in four straight games Chicago Nationals (Cubs). Babe Ruth, idol of baseball, has again signed up with Yankees for 1933, at a salary of $52,000.

This is one of a series of 31 sport pictures. Obtain the set, return to C. A. Briggs Company, Cambridge, Mass., and receive FREE, your choice of either a Baseball, Bat or Mit, or 1 lb. Assorted Chocolates. Your cards will be returned to you.

Stars in a variety of sports are featured in this series of candy issues. Card #24 has a drawing on front against a red background. The player bears more than a passing resemblance to Babe Ruth and on the back of the 2-3/8" x 2-7/8" card, along with a short history of baseball, Babe Ruth and his $52,000 contract for 1933 are mentioned. At bottom are details for redeeming a set of the 31 cards for baseball equipment or a pound of chocolates.

		NM	E	VG
24	Baseball(Babe Ruth)	3,000	1,500	900.00

1953-54 Briggs Meats

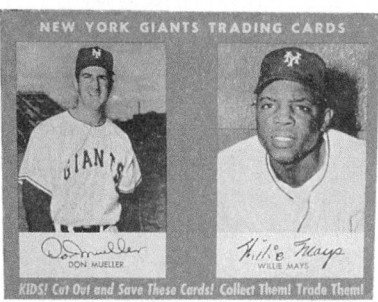

NEW YORK GIANTS TRADING CARDS

DON MUELLER — WILLIE MAYS

KIDS! Cut Out and Save These Cards! Collect Them! Trade Them!

The Briggs Meat set was issued over a two-year span (1953-54) and features 28 players from the Washington Senators and 12 from the New York teams. The set was issued in two-card panels on hot dog packages sold in the Washington, D.C. vicinity. The color cards, which are blank-backed and measure 2-1/4" x 3-1/2", are printed on waxed cardboard. Pictures of the New York players can also be found on cards in the 1954 Dan-Dee Potato Chips and 1953-1955 Stahl-Meyer Franks sets. There is a slight difference in style between the Senators cards and those of the New York players. The white panel beneath the photo of the Washington players includes a facsimile autograph plus a few biographical details about the player. The New York players' cards have only the player's name and facsimile signature in that panel. Many of the Senators cards command a premium for scarcity.

		NM	E	VG
Common Player:		1,000	500.00	300.00
(1)	Hank Bauer	1,250	625.00	375.00
(2)	James Busby	1,000	500.00	300.00
(3)	Tommy Byrne	1,000	500.00	300.00
(4)	Gil Coan (SP)	6,500	3,250	1,950
(5)	John Dixon (SP)	3,500	1,750	1,050
(6)	Carl Erskine	1,000	500.00	200.00
(7)	Edward Fitzgerald (Fitz Gerald)	1,000	500.00	300.00
(8)	Newton Grasso (SP)	6,500	3,250	1,950
(9)	Melvin Hoderlein	1,000	500.00	300.00
(10)	Gil Hodges	3,500	1,750	1,050
(11)	Monte Irvin	1,750	875.00	525.00
(12)	Jackie Jensen/SP	1,100	550.00	325.00
(13)	Whitey Lockman	1,000	500.00	300.00
(14)	Mickey Mantle	17,500	8,750	5,250
(15)	Conrado Marrero	1,000	500.00	300.00
(16)	Walter Masterson/SP	1,000	500.00	300.00
(17)	Carmen Mauro/SP	1,000	500.00	300.00
(18)	Willie Mays	13,500	6,750	4,050
(19)	Mickey McDermott	1,000	500.00	300.00
(20)	Gil McDougald	3,000	1,050	900.00
(21)	Julio Moreno/SP	1,000	500.00	300.00
(22)	Don Mueller	1,000	500.00	300.00
(23)	Don Newcombe	1,200	600.00	350.00
(24)	Robert Oldis	1,000	500.00	300.00
(25)	Erwin Porterfield	1,000	500.00	300.00
(26)	Phil Rizzuto	4,250	2,125	1,275
(27)	James Runnels	3,000	1,500	900.00
(28)	John Schmitz	2,000	1,000	600.00
(29)	Angel Scull	1,000	500.00	300.00
(30)	Frank Shea	1,000	500.00	300.00
(31)	Albert Sima/SP	1,000	500.00	300.00

(32)	Duke Snider	7,500	3,750	2,250
(33)	Charles Stobbs	1,000	500.00	300.00
(34)	Willard Terwilliger	2,000	1,000	600.00
(35)	Joe Tipton	1,000	500.00	300.00
(36)	Thomas Umphlett	1,000	500.00	300.00
(37)	Gene Verble/SP	1,000	500.00	300.00
(38)	James Vernon	3,000	1,500	900.00
(39)	Clyde Vollmer	1,000	500.00	300.00
(40)	Edward Yost	1,000	500.00	300.00

1947 Brillantina Sol de Oro Managers

The approximately 6" x 8" black-and-white pictures were issued in conjunction with a contest run by an Havana shampoo company. Fronts have photos of the managers of Cuba's four professional teams, bordered in white, with a facsimile autograph and message. A sponsor's credit line is in the bottom border. Backs have further promotional copy for the shampoo and rules of the contest.

		NM	E	VG
Complete Set (4):		600.00	300.00	180.00
Common Player:		150.00	75.00	45.00
(1)	Salvador Hernandez	150.00	75.00	45.00
(2)	Adolfo Luque	250.00	125.00	75.00
(3)	Napoleon Reyes	200.00	100.00	60.00
(4)	Lazaro Salazar	150.00	75.00	45.00

1909-12 Broad Leaf Cigarettes

Cards with the Broad Leaf brand advertising on back can be found among the three most popular cigarette card issues circa 1910: T205 Gold Border, T206 White Border and T207 Brown Background. Two types are seen in T206, one that mentions "350 Subjects" and another, much rarer, that mentions "460 Subjects." Because some of the scarcer cards in T207 are often found with Broadleaf (as it was then spelled) backs, it is not practical to quote a value multiplier; premiums for such cards have already been factored into the prices under T207. In T205, Broad Leaf backs can be found printed in either black or brown-olive green.

PREMIUMS:
T205: 6-7X
T206 350 Subjects: 8-10X
T206 460 Subjects, Common: 50-75X
T206 460 Subjects, HoF:25-40X

(See T205, T206, T207 for checklists.)

1974 Broder N.Y. Mets Tour of Japan

Veteran collector Ed Broder who was stationed with the U.S. Army in Japan, produced this collectors' issue chronicling the goodwill tour undertaken by the National League Champion N.Y. Mets. Nominally measuring about 1-7/8" x 3", cards have borderless black-and-white photos on front with no player identification or other graphics. Backs have player name, team and "1974 New York Mets Tour of Japan" in typewriter font along with a team logo. The unnumbered cards are checklisted here alphabetically.

	NM	E	VG
Complete Set (20):	60.00	30.00	18.00
Common Player:	4.00	2.00	1.25
(1) Yogi Berra	20.00	10.00	6.00
(2) Wayne Garrett	8.00	4.00	2.50
(3) Ron Hodges	8.00	4.00	2.50
(4) Tsuneo Horiuchi	8.00	4.00	2.50
(5) Kazumasa Kono	4.00	2.00	1.25
(6) Jerry Koosman	8.00	4.00	2.50
(7) Ed Kranepool, John Milner, unidentified Japanese player, Joe Torre	4.00	2.00	1.25
(8) Jon Matlack	8.00	4.00	2.50
(9) Felix Millan	8.00	4.00	2.50
(10) John Milner	8.00	4.00	2.50
(11) Shigeo Nagashima	10.00	5.00	3.00
(12) Sadaharu Oh	15.00	7.50	4.50
(13) Tom Seaver	40.00	20.00	12.00
(14) Yososhi Sekimoto	4.00	2.00	1.25
(15) Tamio Suetsugu	4.00	2.00	1.25
(16) Kazumi Takahashi	4.00	2.00	1.25
(17) Yoshima Takahashi	4.00	2.00	1.25
(18) George Theodore	8.00	4.00	2.50
(19) Joe Torre, Kazuyoshi Yamamoto	15.00	7.50	4.50
(20) Kazuyoshi Yamamoto, Tetsuhara Kawakami	10.00	5.00	3.00

1975 Broder 1962 "Original" N.Y. Mets

Veteran collector Ed Broder produced this collectors' issue. Nominally measuring about 2" x 3", cards have borderless black-and-white photos on front with only the player name for identification. Backs are blank. The unnumbered cards are checklisted here alphabetically.

	NM	E	VG
Complete Set (15):	50.00	25.00	15.00
Common Player:	5.00	2.50	1.50
(1) Richie Ashburn	10.00	5.00	3.00
(2) Gus Bell	5.00	2.50	1.50
(3) Roger Craig	5.00	2.50	1.50
(4) Gil Hodges	10.00	5.00	3.00
(5) Rogers Hornsby	7.50	3.75	2.25
(6) Sherman Jones	5.00	2.50	1.50
(7) Rod Kanehl	5.00	2.50	1.50
(8) Clem Labine	5.00	2.50	1.50
(9) Hobie Landrith	5.00	2.50	1.50
(10) R.G. Miller	5.00	2.50	1.50
(11) Wilmer Mizell	5.00	2.50	1.50
(12) Charley Neal	5.00	2.50	1.50
(13) Casey Stengal (Stengel)	7.50	3.75	2.25
(14) Frank Thomas	5.00	2.50	1.50
(15) Marv Throneberry	5.00	2.50	1.50

1975 Broder All-Time N.Y. Mets

Veteran collector Ed Broder produced this collectors' issue. Nominally measuring about 1-7/8" x 3-1/8", cards have borderless black-and-white photos on front. Some cards have the dates of their tenure with the team on front. The unnumbered cards are checklisted here alphabetically.

	NM	E	VG
Complete Set (12):	45.00	22.50	13.50
Common Player:	4.00	2.00	1.25
(1) Yogi Berra	7.50	3.75	2.25
(2) Bud Harrelson	4.00	2.00	1.25
(3) Jim Hickman	4.00	2.00	1.25
(4) Al Jackson	4.00	2.00	1.25
(5) Cleon Jones	4.00	2.00	1.25
(6) Jerry Koosman	4.00	2.00	1.25
(7) Ed Kranepool	4.00	2.00	1.25
(8) Tug McGraw	4.00	2.00	1.25
(9) Nolan Ryan	15.00	7.50	4.50
(10) Tom Seaver	9.00	4.50	2.75
(11) Warren Spahn	6.00	3.00	1.75
(12) Casey Stengal (Stengel)	6.00	3.00	1.75

1975 Broder Major League Postcards

This series of 3-1/8" x 5-1/8", borderless, blank-back pictures was advertised as the first in a proposed series designed to accommodate player autographs. Only California Angels and Montreal Expos players are included. The cards are printed on thin cardboard and feature close-up portraits with the player name in black type.

	NM	E	VG
Complete Set (9):	25.00	12.50	7.50
Common Player:	3.00	1.50	.90
(1) Tim Foli	3.00	1.50	.90
(2) Barry Foote	3.00	1.50	.90
(3) Mike Jorgensen	3.00	1.50	.90
(4) Larry Lintz	3.00	1.50	.90
(5) Dave McNally	3.00	1.50	.90
(6) Steve Rodgers (Rogers)	3.00	1.50	.90
(7) Nolan Ryan	10.00	5.00	3.00
(8) Bill Singer	3.00	1.50	.90
(9) Dick Williams	3.00	1.50	.90

1975 Broder Major Leagues - The 1950's

Veteran collector Ed Broder produced this collectors' issue. Nominally measuring about 2" x 3", cards have borderless black-and-white photos on front with only the player name for identification. Backs are blank. The unnumbered cards are checklisted here alphabetically. The set is notable in that a number of familiar players are pictured with teams not seen on their Topps and Bowman cards. The set sold originally for $2.20.

	NM	E	VG
Complete Set (28):	100.00	50.00	30.00
Common Player:	4.00	2.00	1.25
(1) Bobby Adams	4.00	2.00	1.25
(2) Richie Ashburn	6.50	3.25	2.00
(3) Ken Aspromonte	4.00	2.00	1.25
(4) Ray Boone	5.00	2.50	1.50
(5) Lou Boudreau	6.50	3.25	2.00
(6) Smoky Burgess	4.00	2.00	1.25
(7) Phil Cavaretta (Cavarretta)	4.00	2.00	1.25
(8) Gene Conley	4.00	2.00	1.25
(9) Del Crandell (Crandall)	4.00	2.00	1.25
(10) Bob Friend	4.00	2.00	1.25
(11) Harvey Haddix	4.00	2.00	1.25
(12) Fred Haney	4.00	2.00	1.25
(13) Ted Kluszewski	5.00	2.50	1.50
(14) Jim Konstanty	4.00	2.00	1.25
(15) Sandy Koufax	7.50	3.75	2.25
(16) Harvey Kuenn	4.00	2.00	1.25
(17) Bob Lemon	6.00	3.00	1.75
(18) Marty Marion	4.00	2.00	1.25
(19) Minnie Minoso	5.00	2.50	1.50
(20) Stan Musial	7.00	3.50	2.00
(21) Albie Pearson	4.00	2.00	1.25
(22) Paul Richards	4.00	2.00	1.25
(23) Hank Sauer	4.00	2.00	1.25
(24) Herb Score	4.00	2.00	1.25
(25) Bob Skinner	4.00	2.00	1.25
(26) Enos Slaughter	6.00	3.00	1.75
(27) Gus Triandos	4.00	2.00	1.25
(28) Gus Zernial	4.00	2.00	1.25

1978 Broder Photocards

This collectors' issue features late 1970s photos of some of the game's stars from the 1920s-1960s. Cards are printed in 3-1/2" x 5-1/2", blank-back, black-and-white format on thick grayback card stock. Cards were printed four to a sheet and often found on uncut sheets.

lloyd waner

	NM	E	VG
Complete Set (20):	40.00	20.00	12.00
Common Player:	3.00	1.50	.90
(1) Walt Alston	3.00	1.50	.90
(2) Luke Appling	3.00	1.50	.90
(3) Ernie Banks	4.50	2.25	1.25
(4) Yogi Berra	4.50	2.25	1.25
(5) Bill Dickey	4.00	2.00	1.25
(6) Bob Feller (Pitching)	4.00	2.00	1.25
(7) Bob Feller (Portrait)	4.00	2.00	1.25
(8) Billy Herman	3.00	1.50	.90
(9) Bob Lemon	3.00	1.50	.90
(10) Mickey Mantle	6.00	3.00	1.75
(11) Willie Mays (Batting)	5.00	2.50	1.50
(12) Willie Mays (Portrait)	5.00	2.50	1.50
(13) Johnny Mize	3.00	1.50	.90
(14) Pee Wee Reese	4.00	2.00	1.25
(15) Allie Reynolds	3.00	1.50	.90
(16) Brooks Robinson	4.00	2.00	1.25
(17) Enos Slaughter	3.00	1.50	.90
(18) Warren Spahn	3.00	1.50	.90
(19) Lloyd Waner	3.00	1.50	.90
(20) Ted Williams	5.00	2.50	1.50

1940 Brooklyn Dodgers Picture Pack

Rookie Pee Wee Reese appears in this team-issued set of black-and-white pictures. The 6" x 9" pictures have player portraits surrounded by a white border. A facsimile autograph appears on front. Backs are blank. The unnumbered pictures are checklisted here in alphabetical order. Because of roster changes, it is possible the specific makeup of the packs may have changed once or more the course of the season. Some of the pictures were reused in subsequent years' offerings.

	NM	E	VG
Complete Set (25):	150.00	75.00	45.00
Common Player:	8.00	4.00	2.50
(1) Dolf Camilli	8.00	4.00	2.50
(2) Tex Carleton	8.00	4.00	2.50
(3) Hugh Casey	8.00	4.00	2.50
(4) Pete Coscarart	8.00	4.00	2.50
(5) Curt Davis	8.00	4.00	2.50
(6) Leo Durocher	12.00	6.00	3.50
(7) Fred Fitzsimmons	8.00	4.00	2.50
(8) Herman Franks	8.00	4.00	2.50
(9) Joe Gallagher	8.00	4.00	2.50
(10) Charlie Gilbert	8.00	4.00	2.50
(11) Luke Hamlin	8.00	4.00	2.50
(12) Johnny Hudson	8.00	4.00	2.50
(13) Newt Kimball	8.00	4.00	2.50
(14) Cookie Lavagetto	8.00	4.00	2.50
(15) Gus Mancuso	8.00	4.00	2.50
(16) Joe Medwick	12.00	6.00	3.50
(17) Van Lingle Mungo	10.00	5.00	3.00
(18) Babe Phelps	8.00	4.00	2.50
(19) Tot Pressnell	8.00	4.00	2.50
(20) Pee Wee Reese	24.00	12.00	7.25
(21) Vito Tamulis	8.00	4.00	2.50
(22) Joe Vosmik	8.00	4.00	2.50
(23) Dixie Walker	8.00	4.00	2.50
(24) Jimmy Wasdell	8.00	4.00	2.50
(25) Whitlow Wyatt	8.00	4.00	2.50

1941 Brooklyn Dodgers Picture Pack

This team-issued set of 6" x 9" black-and-white pictures has player portraits surrounded by a white border. A facsimile autograph appears on front. Backs are blank. The unnumbered pictures are checklisted here in alphabetical order. Because of roster changes, it is possible the specific makeup of the packs may have changed once or more over the course of the season and that there may have been players issued other than those listed here. Some of the pictures were reused the 1940 offering. Team-issued pictures of 1940-41 can be differentiated from later years by their ballpark backgrounds.

		NM	E	VG
Complete Set (25):		185.00	95.00	55.00
Common Player:		10.00	5.00	3.00
(1)	Mace Brown	10.00	5.00	3.00
(2)	Dolph Camilli	10.00	5.00	3.00
(3)	Hugh Casey	10.00	5.00	3.00
(4)	Pete Coscarart	10.00	5.00	3.00
(5)	Curt Davis	10.00	5.00	3.00
(6)	Leo Durocher	15.00	7.50	4.50
(7)	Fred Fitzsimmons	10.00	5.00	3.00
(8)	Luke Hamlin	10.00	5.00	3.00
(9)	Billy Herman	15.00	7.50	4.50
(10)	Kirby Higbe	10.00	5.00	3.00
(11)	Newt Kimball	10.00	5.00	3.00
(12)	Harry "Cookie" Lavagetto	10.00	5.00	3.00
(13)	Joe Medwick	15.00	7.50	4.50
(14)	Mickey Owen	10.00	5.00	3.00
(15)	Babe Phelps	10.00	5.00	3.00
(16)	Pee Wee Reese	25.00	12.50	7.50
(17)	Pete Reiser	10.00	5.00	3.00
(18)	Lew Riggs	10.00	5.00	3.00
(19)	Bill Swift	10.00	5.00	3.00
(20)	Vito Tamulis	10.00	5.00	3.00
(21)	Joe Vosmik	10.00	5.00	3.00
(22)	Dixie Walker	10.00	5.00	3.00
(23)	Jimmy Wasdell	10.00	5.00	3.00
(24)	Kemp Wicker	10.00	5.00	3.00
(25)	Whit Wyatt	10.00	5.00	3.00

1942 Brooklyn Dodgers Picture Pack

This set of 6" x 9" black-and-white team-issued pictures features player portrait photos in a studio setting. The pictures have a white border all around, and there is a facsimile autograph on front. Backs are blank. The unnumbered pictures are checklisted here alphabetically. Pictures from the 1942 and 1943 photo packs are indistinguishable except for player selection.

		NM	E	VG
Complete Set (25):		150.00	75.00	45.00
Common Player:		8.00	4.00	2.50
(1)	Johnny Allen	8.00	4.00	2.50
(2)	Frenchy Bordagaray	8.00	4.00	2.50
(3)	Dolf Camilli	8.00	4.00	2.50
(4)	Hugh Casey	8.00	4.00	2.50
(5)	Curt Davis	8.00	4.00	2.50
(6)	Leo Durocher	12.00	6.00	3.50
(7)	Larry French	8.00	4.00	2.50
(8)	Augie Galan	8.00	4.00	2.50
(9)	Ed Head	8.00	4.00	2.50
(10)	Billy Herman	12.00	6.00	3.50
(11)	Kirby Higbe	8.00	4.00	2.50
(12)	Alex Kampouris	8.00	4.00	2.50
(13)	Newt Kimball	8.00	4.00	2.50
(14)	Joe Medwick	12.00	6.00	3.50
(15)	Mickey Owen	8.00	4.00	2.50
(16)	Pee Wee Reese	16.00	8.00	4.75
(17)	Pete Reiser	10.00	5.00	3.00
(18)	Lew Riggs	8.00	4.00	2.50
(19)	Johnny Rizzo	8.00	4.00	2.50
(20)	Schoolboy Rowe	10.00	5.00	3.00
(21)	Billy Sullivan	8.00	4.00	2.50
(22)	Arky Vaughan	12.00	6.00	3.50
(23)	Dixie Walker	8.00	4.00	2.50
(24)	Les Webber	8.00	4.00	2.50
(25)	Whitlow Wyatt	8.00	4.00	2.50

1943 Brooklyn Dodgers Picture Pack

This set of 6" x 9" black-and-white team-issued pictures features player portrait photos in a studio setting. The pictures have a white border all around, and there is a facsimile autograph on front. Backs are blank. The unnumbered pictures are checklisted here alphabetically. Pictures from the 1942 and 1943 photo packs are indistinguishable except for player selection.

		NM	E	VG
Complete Set (25):		150.00	75.00	45.00
Common Player:		8.00	4.00	2.50
(1)	Johnny Allen	8.00	4.00	2.50
(2)	Frenchy Bordagaray	8.00	4.00	2.50
(3)	Bob Bragan	10.00	5.00	3.00
(4)	Dolf Camilli	8.00	4.00	2.50
(5)	Johnny Cooney	8.00	4.00	2.50
(6)	John Corriden	8.00	4.00	2.50
(7)	Curt Davis	8.00	4.00	2.50
(8)	Leo Durocher	12.00	6.00	3.50
(9)	Fred Fitzsimmons	8.00	4.00	2.50
(10)	Augie Galan	8.00	4.00	2.50
(11)	Al Glossop	8.00	4.00	2.50
(12)	Ed Head	8.00	4.00	2.50
(13)	Billy Herman	12.00	6.00	3.50
(14)	Kirby Higbe	8.00	4.00	2.50
(15)	Max Macon	8.00	4.00	2.50
(16)	Joe Medwick	12.00	6.00	3.50
(17)	Rube Melton	8.00	4.00	2.50
(18)	Dee Moore	8.00	4.00	2.50
(19)	"Buck" Newsom	10.00	5.00	3.00
(20)	Mickey Owen	8.00	4.00	2.50
(21)	Arky Vaughan	12.00	6.00	3.50
(22)	Dixie Walker	8.00	4.00	2.50
(23)	Paul Waner	12.00	6.00	3.50
(24)	Les Webber	8.00	4.00	2.50
(25)	Whitlow Wyatt	8.00	4.00	2.50

1946 Brooklyn Dodgers Picture Pack

This team-issued set of player portrait pictures is in a blank-back 6-1/2" x 9" format. A facsimile autograph appears on front. Like many souvenir-stand photo packs of the era, it is possible the specific contents of this product may have changed during the course of the season as players joined and left the team.

		NM	E	VG
Complete Set (25):		125.00	65.00	40.00
Common Player:		6.00	3.00	1.80
(1)	Andy Anderson	6.00	3.00	1.80
(2)	Henry Behrman	6.00	3.00	1.80
(3)	Ralph Branca	6.00	3.00	1.80
(4)	Hugh Casey	6.00	3.00	1.80
(5)	Leo Durocher	9.00	4.50	2.75
(6)	Carl Furillo	12.00	6.00	3.50
(7)	Augie Galan	6.00	3.00	1.80
(8)	Hal Gregg	6.00	3.00	1.80
(9)	Joe Hatten	6.00	3.00	1.80
(10)	Al Head	6.00	3.00	1.80
(11)	Art Herring	6.00	3.00	1.80
(12)	Billy Herman	9.00	4.50	2.75
(13)	Gene Hermanski	6.00	3.00	1.80
(14)	Kirby Higbe	6.00	3.00	1.80
(15)	Harry "Cookie" Lavagetto	6.00	3.00	1.80
(16)	Vic Lombardi	6.00	3.00	1.80
(17)	Pee Wee Reese	12.00	6.00	3.50
(18)	Pete Reiser	6.00	3.00	1.80
(19)	Stan Rojek	6.00	3.00	1.80
(20)	Mike Sandlock	6.00	3.00	1.80
(21)	Eddie Stanky	7.50	3.75	2.25
(22)	Ed Stevens	6.00	3.00	1.80
(23)	Dixie Walker	6.00	3.00	1.80
(24)	Les Webber	6.00	3.00	1.80
(25)	Dick Whitman	6.00	3.00	1.80

1947 Brooklyn Dodgers Picture Pack

This team-issued set of player portrait pictures is in a blank-back 6-1/2" x 9" format. A facsimile autograph appears on front. Like many souvenir-stand photo packs of the era, it is possible the specific contents of this product may have changed during the course of the season as players joined and left the team.

		NM	E	VG
Complete Set (25):		350.00	175.00	105.00
Common Player:		9.00	4.50	2.75
(1)	Ray Blades	9.00	4.50	2.75
(2)	Bobby Bragan	9.00	4.50	2.75
(3)	Ralph Branca	9.00	4.50	2.75
(4)	Tommy Brown	9.00	4.50	2.75
(5)	Hugh Casey	9.00	4.50	2.75
(6)	Ed Chandler	9.00	4.50	2.75
(7)	Carl Furillo	20.00	10.00	6.00
(8)	Hal Gregg	9.00	4.50	2.75
(9)	Joe Hatten	9.00	4.50	2.75
(10)	Gene Hermanski	9.00	4.50	2.75
(11)	Gil Hodges	40.00	20.00	12.00
(12)	Spider Jorgensen	9.00	4.50	2.75
(13)	Clyde King	9.00	4.50	2.75
(14)	Vic Lombardi	9.00	4.50	2.75
(15)	Rube Melton	9.00	4.50	2.75
(16)	Eddie Miksis	9.00	4.50	2.75
(17)	Pee Wee Reese	30.00	15.00	9.00
(18)	Pete Reiser	9.00	4.50	2.75
(19)	Jackie Robinson	80.00	40.00	24.00
(20)	Stan Rojek	9.00	4.50	2.75
(21)	Burt Shotton	9.00	4.50	2.75
(22)	Duke Snider	40.00	20.00	12.00
(23)	Eddie Stanky	12.50	6.25	3.75
(24)	Harry Taylor	9.00	4.50	2.75
(25)	Dixie Walker	9.00	4.50	2.75

1948 Brooklyn Dodgers Picture Pack

This team-issued set of player portrait pictures is in a blank-back 6-1/2" x 9" format. A facsimile autograph appears on front. Like many souvenir-stand photo packs of the era, it is possible the specific contents of this product may have changed during the course of the season as players joined and left the team, and that pictures were re-used from year-to-year.

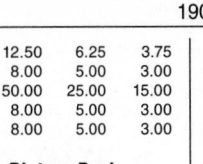

		NM	E	VG
Complete Set (26):		300.00	150.00	95.00
Common Player:		8.00	4.00	2.50
(1)	Rex Barney	8.00	4.00	2.50
(2)	Ray Blades	8.00	4.00	2.50
(3)	Bobby Bragan	8.00	4.00	2.50
(4)	Ralph Branca	8.00	4.00	2.50
(5)	Tommy Brown	8.00	4.00	2.50
(6)	Hugh Casey	8.00	4.00	2.50
(7)	Billy Cox	8.00	4.00	2.50
(8)	Leo Durocher	15.00	7.50	4.50
(9)	Bruce Edwards	8.00	4.00	2.50
(10)	Carl Furillo	20.00	10.00	6.00
(11)	Joe Hatten	8.00	4.00	2.50
(12)	Gene Hermanski	8.00	4.00	2.50
(13)	Gil Hodges	30.00	15.00	9.00
(14)	Spider Jorgensen	8.00	4.00	2.50
(15)	Don Lund	8.00	4.00	2.50
(16)	Eddie Miksis	8.00	4.00	2.50
(17)	Jake Pitler	8.00	4.00	2.50
(18)	Pee Wee Reese	25.00	12.50	7.50
(19)	Pete Reiser	8.00	4.00	2.50
(20)	Jackie Robinson	65.00	32.00	19.50
(21)	Preacher Roe	12.00	6.00	3.50
(22)	Burt Shotton	8.00	4.00	2.50
(23)	Clyde Sukeforth	8.00	4.00	2.50
(24)	Harry Taylor	8.00	4.00	2.50
(25)	Arky Vaughan	15.00	7.50	4.50
(26)	Preston Ward	8.00	4.00	2.50

1949 Brooklyn Dodgers Picture Pack

This team-issued set of player portrait pictures is in a blank-back 6-1/2" x 9" format. A facsimile autograph appears on front. Like many souvenir-stand photo packs of the era, it is possible the specific contents of this product may have changed during the course of the season as players joined and left the team, and that pictures were re-used from year-to-year.

		NM	E	VG
Complete Set (25):		575.00	300.00	160.00
Common Player:		8.00	5.00	3.00
(1)	Jack Banta	8.00	5.00	3.00
(2)	Rex Barney	8.00	5.00	3.00
(3)	Ralph Branca	12.50	6.25	3.75
(4)	Tommy Brown	8.00	5.00	3.00
(5)	Roy Campanella	200.00	100.00	60.00
(6)	Billy Cox	8.00	5.00	3.00
(7)	Bruce Edwards	8.00	5.00	3.00
(8)	Carl Furillo	20.00	10.00	6.00
(9)	Joe Hatten	8.00	5.00	3.00
(10)	Gene Hermanski	8.00	5.00	3.00
(11)	Gil Hodges	40.00	20.00	12.00
(12)	Johnny Hopp	8.00	5.00	3.00
(13)	Spider Jorgensen	8.00	5.00	3.00
(14)	Mike McCormick	8.00	5.00	3.00
(15)	Eddie Miksis	8.00	5.00	3.00
(16)	Don Newcombe	100.00	50.00	30.00
(17)	Erv Palica	8.00	5.00	3.00
(18)	Jake Pitler	8.00	5.00	3.00
(19)	Pee Wee Reese	50.00	25.00	15.00
(20)	Jackie Robinson	75.00	37.00	22.00

(21)	Preacher Roe	12.50	6.25	3.75
(22)	Burt Shotton	8.00	5.00	3.00
(23)	Duke Snider	50.00	25.00	15.00
(24)	Milt Stock	8.00	5.00	3.00
(25)	Clyde Sukeforth	8.00	5.00	3.00

1955 Brooklyn Dodgers Picture Pack

This set of approximately 5" x 7" blank-back, black-and-white pictures was a souvenir stand item at Ebbets Field. Player photos are chest-to-cap portraits surrounded by a white border with the player name at bottom in all-caps, followed by the team nickname in upper- and lower-case type. The unnumbered pictures are listed here alphabetically. The set was sold for 25 cents in a white paper envelope with "WORLD CHAMPION Dodgers" printed in blue.

		NM	E	VG
Complete Set (12):		100.00	50.00	30.00
Common Player:		8.00	4.00	2.50
(1)	Walter Alston	8.00	4.00	2.50
(2)	Roy Campanella	20.00	10.00	6.00
(3)	Carl Erskine	8.00	4.00	2.50
(4)	Carl Furillo	10.00	5.00	3.00
(5)	Gil Hodges	16.00	8.00	4.75
(6)	Randy Jackson	8.00	4.00	2.50
(7)	Clem Labine	8.00	4.00	2.50
(8)	Don Newcombe	8.00	4.00	2.50
(9)	Johnny Podres	8.00	4.00	2.50
(10)	Peewee Reese	13.50	6.75	4.00
(11)	Jackie Robinson	24.00	12.00	7.25
(12)	Duke Snider	16.00	8.00	4.75

1956 Brooklyn Dodgers Picture Pack

DON DRYSDALE, Dodgers

This set of 5" x 7" blank-back, black-and-white pictures was a souvenir stand item at Ebbets Field. Player photos are surrounded by a white border with the player name at bottom in all-caps, followed by the team nickname in upper- and lower-case type. The unnumbered pictures are listed here alphabetically. The same photos were offered in a 50-piece Yankees-Dodgers "World Series Picture Portfolio."

		NM	E	VG
Complete Set (25):		250.00	125.00	75.00
Common Player:		10.00	5.00	3.00
(1)	Walter Alston	12.50	6.25	3.75
(2)	Sandy Amoros	12.50	6.25	3.75
(3)	Joe Becker	10.00	5.00	3.00
(4)	Don Bessent	10.00	5.00	3.00
(5)	Roy Campanella	30.00	15.00	9.00
(6)	Roger Craig	10.00	5.00	3.00
(7)	Don Drysdale	25.00	12.50	7.50
(8)	Carl Erskine	12.50	6.25	3.75
(9)	Chico Fernandez	10.00	5.00	3.00
(10)	Carl Furillo	15.00	7.50	4.50
(11)	Jim Gilliam	15.00	7.50	4.50
(12)	Billy Herman	12.50	6.25	3.75
(13)	Gil Hodges	25.00	12.50	7.50
(14)	Randy Jackson	10.00	5.00	3.00
(15)	Sandy Koufax	35.00	17.50	10.50
(16)	Clem Labine	12.50	6.25	3.75
(17)	Sal Maglie	10.00	5.00	3.00
(18)	Charlie Neal	10.00	5.00	3.00
(19)	Don Newcombe	12.50	6.25	3.75
(20)	Jake Pitler	10.00	5.00	3.00
(21)	Peewee Reese	20.00	10.00	6.00
(22)	Jackie Robinson	35.00	17.50	10.50
(23)	Ed Roebuck	10.00	5.00	3.00
(24)	Duke Snider	25.00	12.50	7.50
(25)	Al Walker	10.00	5.00	3.00

1957 Brooklyn Dodgers Picture Pack

In their final year in Brooklyn, the Dodgers issued this souvenir-stand picture pack, offered for 25 cents. The pictures are 5" x 7", blank-back, black-and-white. Player portraits are surrounded by a white border with the player name at bottom in all-caps and "Dodgers" in upper- and lower-case type. The unnumbered pictures are listed here alphabetically.

		NM	E	VG
Complete Set (12):		125.00	65.00	40.00
Common Player:		10.00	5.00	3.00
(1)	Walter Alston	15.00	7.50	4.50
(2)	Roy Campanella	25.00	12.50	7.50
(3)	Carl Furillo	15.00	7.50	4.50
(4)	Jim Gilliam	15.00	7.50	4.50
(5)	Gil Hodges	20.00	10.00	6.00
(6)	Randy Jackson	10.00	5.00	3.00
(7)	Clem Labine	10.00	5.00	3.00
(8)	Sal Maglie	10.00	5.00	3.00
(9)	Don Newcombe	12.50	6.25	3.75
(10)	Johnny Podres	15.00	7.50	4.50
(11)	Peewee Reese	20.00	10.00	6.00
(12)	Duke Snider	20.00	10.00	6.00

1953-55 Brown & Bigelow

Some of baseball's biggest stars, either as they appeared in the mid-1950s or as spirit images, instruct All-American boys in the skills of baseball on this series of cards. Produced by the St. Paul firm of Brown & Bigelow, the 2-1/4" x 3-1/2", round-cornered cards can be found either as playing cards or with schedules printed on the back. The cards could be customized by local sponsors in a panel at the bottom of the artwork. The Medcalf artwork is also seen on contemporary wall and desk calendars and other printed items.

		NM	E	VG
	UNOPENED DECKS			
(1)	Ty Cobb	45.00	22.50	13.50
(2)	Lou Gehrig	50.00	25.00	15.00
(3)	Connie Mack	30.00	15.00	9.00
(4)	John McGraw	30.00	15.00	9.00
(5)	Babe Ruth	65.00	32.50	20.00
(6)	Honus Wagner	40.00	20.00	12.00
	SINGLE CARDS			
(1)	Ty Cobb	6.00	3.00	1.75
(2)	Lou Gehrig	8.00	4.00	2.50
(3)	Connie Mack	4.00	2.00	1.25
(4)	John McGraw	4.00	2.00	1.25
(5)	Babe Ruth	10.00	5.00	3.00
(6)	Honus Wagner	5.00	2.50	1.50

1911-14 Brunners Bread (D304)

(See 1911-1914 General Baking Co. for checklist and values.)

1908-1910 Brush Detroit Tigers Postcards

The makers of this short-lived (1907-11) automobile evidently engaged members of the hometown team to endorse their product. The 3-1/2" x 5-3/8" black-and-white postcards have a bordered photo on front showing a Tigers player (in uniform or suit) with the auto. A few lines of poetry about the player complete the design. Backs have typical postcard format. It is likely the checklist here is incomplete.

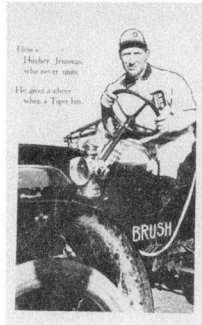

		NM	E	VG
(1)	Ty Cobb	8,000	4,000	2,400
(2)	William Coughlin	1,500	750.00	450.00
(3)	Bill Donovan	750.00	375.00	225.00
(4)	Hughie Jennings ((Hands			
	on steering wheel.))	3,000	1,500	900.00
(5)	Hughie Jennings ((Hands			
	in air.))	3,000	1,500	900.00
(6)	Matty McIntyre	1,500	750.00	450.00
(7)	George Mullin	1,500	750.00	450.00
(8)	Germany Schaefer,			
	Charley O'Leary	1,500	750.00	450.00
(9)	Charlie Schmidt	1,500	750.00	450.00
(10)	Ira Thomas	1,500	750.00	450.00

1979 Bubble Yum Toronto Blue Jays

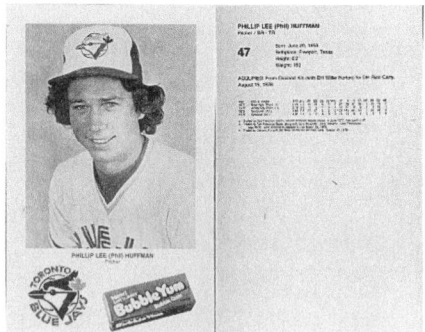

Members of the Toronto Blue Jays in the team's third season are featured in this set of 5-1/2" x 8-1/2" black-and-white player pictures. Fronts feature player portraits identified by their full name and position. In the wide bottom border are team and sponsor logos. Backs have player biographical data, major and minor league stats, acquisition information and career highlights. Cards are numbered by uniform number.

		NM	E	VG
	Complete Set (20):	65.00	32.50	20.00
	Common Player:	4.00	2.00	1.25
1	Bob Bailor	4.00	2.00	1.25
4	Alfredo Griffin	4.00	2.00	1.25
7	Roy Hartsfield	4.00	2.00	1.25
9	Rick Cerone	4.00	2.00	1.25
10	John Mayberry	4.00	2.00	1.25
11	Luis Gomez	4.00	2.00	1.25
13	Roy Howell	4.00	2.00	1.25
18	Jim Clancy	4.00	2.00	1.25
19	Otto Velez	4.00	2.00	1.25
20	Al Woods	4.00	2.00	1.25
21	Rico Carty	4.00	2.00	1.25
22	Rick Bosetti	4.00	2.00	1.25
23	Dave Lemanczyk	4.00	2.00	1.25
24	Tom Underwood	4.00	2.00	1.25
31	Bobby Doerr	6.00	3.00	1.75
34	Jesse Jefferson	4.00	2.00	1.25
38	Balor Moore	4.00	2.00	1.25
44	Tom Buskey	4.00	2.00	1.25
46	Dave Freisleben	4.00	2.00	1.25
47	Phil Huffman	4.00	2.00	1.25

1976 Buckmans Discs

One of several regional sponsors of player disc sets in 1976 was Buckmans Ice Cream Village in Rochester, N.Y. The discs are 3-3/8" diameter with a black-and-white player portrait photo in the center of the baseball design. A line of red stars is above, while the left and right panels feature one of several bright colors. Produced by Michael Schecter Associates under license from the Major League Baseball Players Association, the player photos have had uniform and cap logos removed. Backs are printed in red and purple. The un-numbered checklist here is presented in alphabetical order.

		NM	E	VG
	Complete Set (70):	60.00	30.00	18.00
	Common Player:	.75	.40	.25
(1)	Henry Aaron	6.00	3.00	1.75
(2)	Johnny Bench	3.50	1.75	1.00
(3)	Vida Blue	.75	.40	.25
(4)	Larry Bowa	.75	.40	.25
(5)	Lou Brock	2.50	1.25	.70
(6)	Jeff Burroughs	.75	.40	.25
(7)	John Candelaria	.75	.40	.25
(8)	Jose Cardenal	.75	.40	.25
(9)	Rod Carew	2.50	1.25	.70
(10)	Steve Carlton	2.50	1.25	.70
(11)	Dave Cash	.75	.40	.25
(12)	Cesar Cedeno	.75	.40	.25
(13)	Ron Cey	.75	.40	.25
(14)	Carlton Fisk	2.50	1.25	.70
(15)	Tito Fuentes	.75	.40	.25
(16)	Steve Garvey	2.00	1.00	.60
(17)	Ken Griffey	.75	.40	.25
(18)	Don Gullett	.75	.40	.25
(19)	Willie Horton	.75	.40	.25
(20)	Al Hrabosky	.75	.40	.25
(21)	Catfish Hunter	2.50	1.25	.70
(22)	Reggie Jackson (A's)	5.00	2.50	1.50
(23)	Randy Jones	.75	.40	.25
(24)	Jim Kaat	.75	.40	.25
(25)	Don Kessinger	.75	.40	.25
(26)	Dave Kingman	.75	.40	.25
(27)	Jerry Koosman	.75	.40	.25
(28)	Mickey Lolich	.75	.40	.25
(29)	Greg Luzinski	.75	.40	.25
(30)	Fred Lynn	.75	.40	.25
(31)	Bill Madlock	.75	.40	.25
(32)	Carlos May (White Sox)	.75	.40	.25
(33)	John Mayberry	.75	.40	.25
(34)	Bake McBride	.75	.40	.25
(35)	Doc Medich	.75	.40	.25
(36)	Andy Messersmith			
	(Dodgers)	.75	.40	.25
(37)	Rick Monday	.75	.40	.25
(38)	John Montefusco	.75	.40	.25
(39)	Jerry Morales	.75	.40	.25
(40)	Joe Morgan	2.50	1.25	.70
(41)	Thurman Munson	2.50	1.25	.70
(42)	Bobby Murcer	.75	.40	.25
(43)	Al Oliver	.75	.40	.25
(44)	Jim Palmer	2.50	1.25	.70
(45)	Dave Parker	.75	.40	.25
(46)	Tony Perez	2.50	1.25	.70
(47)	Jerry Reuss	.75	.40	.25
(48)	Brooks Robinson	3.00	1.50	.90
(49)	Frank Robinson	3.00	1.50	.90
(50)	Steve Rogers	.75	.40	.25
(51)	Pete Rose	6.00	3.00	1.75
(52)	Nolan Ryan	20.00	10.00	6.00
(53)	Manny Sanguillen	.75	.40	.25
(54)	Mike Schmidt	5.00	2.50	1.50
(55)	Tom Seaver	3.00	1.50	.90
(56)	Ted Simmons	.75	.40	.25
(57)	Reggie Smith	.75	.40	.25
(58)	Willie Stargell	2.50	1.25	.70
(59)	Rusty Staub	.75	.40	.25
(60)	Rennie Stennett	.75	.40	.25
(61)	Don Sutton	2.50	1.25	.70
(62)	Andy Thornton (Cubs)	.75	.40	.25
(63)	Luis Tiant	.75	.40	.25
(64)	Joe Torre	1.50	.70	.45
(65)	Mike Tyson	.75	.40	.25
(66)	Bob Watson	.75	.40	.25
(67)	Wilbur Wood	.75	.40	.25
(68)	Jimmy Wynn	.75	.40	.25
(69)	Carl Yastrzemski	3.50	1.75	1.00
(70)	Richie Zisk	.75	.40	.25

1916 Bucyrus Brewing Co. (M101-4)

One of a dozen or so firms that utilized Felix Mendelsohn's baseball card issue as an advertising medium was this Ohio brewery. Unlike the other companies, however, Bucyrus did not issue individual cards, but only a 42" x 28" uncut sheet containing all 200 cards and labeled "1916 - BASEBALL'S HALL OF FAME - 1916." If cut from the sheet, the single cards would be indistinguishable from the blank-back version of M101-4.

	NM	E	VG
Complete Uncut Sheet:	35,000	25,000	15,000

(for checklist. See 1916 M101-4 Blank Backs)

1950 Buitoni Macaroni Joe DiMaggio Pins

At least two styles of 1-1/2" diameter pinback buttons are known from the Yankee Clipper's association with a New York pasta company. One style has a black-and-white portrait photo at the center of a red-stiched baseball design. Printed in red at top is "JOE DiMAGGIO / TV CLUB." At bottom is the program sponsor's name. Another style has a photo of the player with a bat over his shoulder on a yellow background. "JOE DiMAGGIO CLUB" is at top, "BUITONI/ FOODS CORP." at bottom, both in red. Each style was reproduced in 2-1/4" size early in the 21st Century; those replicas have no collectible value.

	NM	E	VG
Joe DiMaggio (Portrait)	750.00	375.00	220.00
Joe DiMaggio (W/ bat.)	1,200	600.00	360.00

1932 Bulgaria Sport Tobacco

Despite the name of the sponsoring issuer, this set of cards is a product of Germany. Only a single major league ballplayer is pictured among the 272 cards in the set: Babe Ruth, who shares a card with boxing great Max Schmeling in a photo taken in the U.S. The black-and-white cards in the set measure 1-5/8" x 2-3/8" and have backs printed in German, including a card number.

		NM	E	VG
256	Babe Ruth, Max Schmeling	250.00	125.00	75.00

1952-1953 Burger Beer Cincinnati Reds

Whether or not they were a promotional issue of Burger Beer (they are not marked as to issuer), advanced collectors of 1950s Reds memorabilia ascribe these 8" x 10-1/2" black-and-white photos to the long-time Reds sponsor because of their similarity to later Burger editions. The blank-back photos have portraits or posed action shots surrounded with white borders. In the wide bottom border is a C Reds logo, with the player name and (usually) position at right in all-capitals. The Clyde King picture, which can be reliably dated to 1953, his only season with the Reds, is a portrait drawing, rather than a photo, and has no position listed. The unnumbered pictures are listed here alphabetically and the checklist presented is likely incomplete.

Common Player:	NM 30.00	E 15.00	VG 9.00
(1) Joe Adcock (Fielding)	40.00	20.00	12.00
(2) Bob Borkowski (Batting follow-through.)	30.00	15.00	9.00
(3) Jim Greengrass	30.00	15.00	9.00
(4) Grady Hatton (Portrait)	30.00	15.00	9.00
(5) Niles Jordan (Portrait)	30.00	15.00	9.00
(6) Clyde King (Portrait art.)	30.00	15.00	9.00
(7) Willard Marshall (Batting follow-through.)	30.00	15.00	9.00
(8) Ed Pellagrini (Portrait)	30.00	15.00	9.00
(9) Bud Podbielan (Portrait)	30.00	15.00	9.00
(10) Frank Smith	30.00	15.00	9.00
(11) John Temple (Batting follow-through.)	30.00	15.00	9.00
(12) Herm Wehmeier	30.00	15.00	9.00

1954 Burger Beer Cincinnati Reds

Burger Beer was one of the Reds' broadcast sponsors and (presumably) stadium concessionaires in the 1950s and 1960s. In that period they produced several distinctive styles of Reds' player pictures, though the manner of distribution is unknown The pictures may have been given as point-of-purchase handouts, or possibly used to satisfy fan requests for a favorite player's picture. This issue of 8-1/2" x 11" pictures can be distinguished by the appearance, on either front or back, of the advertising message, "Courtesy of Burger Brewing Co." Players are identified only by name, in heavy upper- and lower-case typography. This checklist is likely incomplete and gaps have been left in the assigned numbering for future additions.

Common Player:	NM 30.00	EX 15.00	VG 9.00
(1) Bobby Adams	30.00	15.00	9.00
(2) Fred Baczewski	30.00	15.00	9.00
(3) Dick Bartell (coach)	30.00	15.00	9.00
(5) Bob Borkowski	30.00	15.00	9.00
(9) Jim Greengrass	30.00	15.00	9.00
(10) Charley Harmon	30.00	15.00	9.00
(11) Waite Hoyt (announcer)	30.00	15.00	9.00
(17) Andy Serminick	30.00	15.00	9.00
(18) Birdie Tebbetts (manager)	30.00	15.00	9.00

1955 Burger Beer Cincinnati Reds

The evidence attributing these 8" x 10" black-and-white player pictures to one of the team's radio sponsors, Burger Beer, is apocryphal, based largely on the format, which is similar to the company's 1956-64 promotional issues. This series has player portraits or poses bordered in white. In the bottom border, flanked by team logos are two or three lines of capital-letter typography with the player's name, position and, sometimes, team. Backs are blank. This checklist is likely not complete.

1956-1957 Burger Beer Cincinnati Reds

Common Player:	NM 30.00	E 15.00	VG 9.00
(1) Bobby Adams	30.00	15.00	9.00
(2) Dr. Wayne Anderson (trainer)	30.00	15.00	9.00
(3) Fred Baczewski	30.00	15.00	9.00
(4) Ed Bailey	30.00	15.00	9.00
(5) Gus Bell	30.00	15.00	9.00
(6) Rocky Bridges	30.00	15.00	9.00
(7) Jackie Collum	30.00	15.00	9.00
(8) Art Fowler	30.00	15.00	9.00
(9) Jim Greengrass	30.00	15.00	9.00
(10) Charlie Harmon	30.00	15.00	9.00
(11) Ray Jablonski	30.00	15.00	9.00
(12) Johnny Klippstein	30.00	15.00	9.00
(13) Ted Kluszewski	45.00	22.00	13.50
(14) Roy McMillan	30.00	15.00	9.00
(15) Rudy Minarcin	30.00	15.00	9.00
(16) Joe Nuxhall	45.00	22.00	13.50
(17) Harry Perkowski	45.00	22.00	13.50
(18) Wally Post	30.00	15.00	9.00
(19) Frank Smith	30.00	15.00	9.00
(20) Gerry Staley	30.00	15.00	9.00
(21) Birdie Tebbetts	30.00	15.00	9.00
(22) Johnny Temple	30.00	15.00	9.00

1956-1957 Burger Beer Cincinnati Reds

The 1956 and 1957 series of 8-1/2" x 11" black-and-white player photos from one of the Reds' broadcast sponsors can be distinguished from later issues by the presence of an advertising slogan at the bottom of the otherwise blank black, "COURTESY OF BURGER - A FINER BEER YEAR AFTER YEAR." Players are identified on the bottom front border in large capital letters. Because at least one player is known in both portrait and posed action photos, poses other than portraits are indicated in parentheses.

Common Player:	NM 30.00	E 15.00	VG 9.00
(1) Ed Bailey (Portrait to top button.)	30.00	15.00	9.00
(2) Ed. Bailey (Portrait to chest showing number.)	30.00	15.00	9.00
(3) Gus Bell (Portrait to chest showing number.)	30.00	15.00	9.00
(4) Gus Bell (Portrait to top button.)	30.00	15.00	9.00
(5) Joe Black	30.00	15.00	9.00
(6) Smoky Burgess (Batting)	35.00	17.50	10.50
(7) George Crowe (Batting)	30.00	15.00	9.00
(8) Chuck Harmon (Fielding)	30.00	15.00	9.00
(9) Don Hoak	30.00	15.00	9.00
(10) Waite Hoyt (Broadcaster)	30.00	15.00	9.00
(11) Ray Jablonski (Throwing)	30.00	15.00	9.00
(12) Hal Jeffcoat (Follow-through.)	30.00	15.00	9.00
(13) Ted Kluszewski (Batting)	50.00	25.00	15.00
(14) Ted Kluszewski (Portrait to top button.)	50.00	25.00	15.00
(15) Brooks Lawrence (Follow-through.)	30.00	15.00	9.00
(16) Roy McMillan (Batting)	30.00	15.00	9.00
(17) Roy McMillan (Fielding)	30.00	15.00	9.00

(18) Roy McMillan (Portrait to second button.)	30.00	15.00	9.00
(19) Jackie Moran (Broadcaster)	30.00	15.00	9.00
(20) Joe Nuxhall	30.00	15.00	9.00
(21) Wally Post (portrait)	30.00	15.00	9.00
(22) Wally Post (batting)	30.00	15.00	9.00
(22) Frank Robinson (Fielding)	150.00	75.00	45.00
(23) Frank Robinson (Portrait, white cap.)	125.00	62.00	37.00
(24) Birdie Tebbetts	30.00	15.00	9.00
(25) Johnny Temple (Portrait to second button.)	30.00	15.00	9.00
(26) Johnny Temple (Portrait to chest showing number.)	30.00	15.00	9.00
(27) Johnny Temple (Throw)	30.00	15.00	9.00
(28) Bob Thurman (Batting)	30.00	15.00	9.00

1958-1959 Burger Beer Cincinnati Reds

The 1958-1959 series of 8-1/2" x 11" black-and-white player photos can be distinguished by the presence of an advertising slogan at the bottom of the otherwise blank black, "COURTESY OF SPARKLE * BREWED BURGER BEER / HAVE FUN - HAVE A BURGER." Players are identified by first and last name, or by last name only on the bottom front border in large capital letters. The team name may or may not appear, as well.

Common Player:	NM 30.00	E 15.00	VG 9.00
(1) Bailey (Portrait)	30.00	15.00	9.00
(2) Ed. Bailey (Portrait)	30.00	15.00	9.00
(3) Gus Bell (Portrait, dark cap.)	30.00	15.00	9.00
(4) Waite Hoyt (At microphone.)	30.00	15.00	9.00
(6) Jerry Lynch (Portrait)	30.00	15.00	9.00
(7) Roy McMillan (Portrait)	30.00	15.00	9.00
(8) (Don) Newcombe (Portrait)	30.00	15.00	9.00
(9) Joe Nuxhall (Follow-through.)	30.00	15.00	9.00
(11) (Vada) Pinson (Portrait)	45.00	22.00	13.50
(12) (Bob) Purkey (Portrait)	30.00	15.00	9.00
(13) Frank Robinson (Batting, dark cap.)	125.00	62.00	37.00
(14) Frank Robinson (Fielding)	125.00	62.00	37.00
(15) (Frank) Robinson (Portrait, white cap.)	125.00	62.00	37.00
(16) Manager Mayo Smith (Adjusting cap.)	30.00	15.00	9.00
(17) John Temple (Portrait)	30.00	15.00	9.00
(18) Frank Thomas (Batting)	30.00	15.00	9.00
(19) (Frank) Thomas (Portrait)	30.00	15.00	9.00

1960-64 Burger Beer Cincinnati Reds

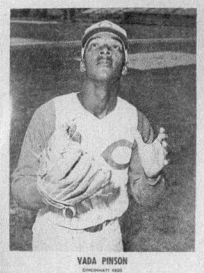

The sponsor is not identified, nor the year of issue published on these 8-1/2" x 11" player photos. Uniform and cap styles can give some idea of when the photos were taken. Photos are black-and-white portraits or action poses surrounded by white borders with the player and team names at bottom. Backs are blank. The unnumbered photos are listed here in alphabetical order. Some photos were re-issued year after year with only minor changes in cropping; these are not listed separately. This checklist will likely remain incomplete for some time. Gaps have been in the assigned numbering to accommodate future additions.

		NM	E	VG
	Common Player:	15.00	7.50	4.50
(1)	Ed. Bailey (Portrait, white cap.)	15.00	7.50	4.50
(2)	Ed. Bailey (Portrait, Dark Cap.)	40.00	20.00	12.00
(3)	Gus Bell (Batting)	15.00	7.50	4.50
(4)	Gus Bell (Fielding fly ball.)	15.00	7.50	4.50
(5)	Gus Bell (Portrait)	15.00	7.50	4.50
(6)	Don Blasingame/Portrait	15.00	7.50	4.50
(7)	Gordon Coleman (Bat behind cap.)	15.00	7.50	4.50
(8)	Gordon Coleman (Bat behind shoulder.)	15.00	7.50	4.50
(9)	Gordon Coleman (Fielding)	15.00	7.50	4.50
(10)	John Edwards (Portrait, light tower in background.)			
(11)	John Edwards (Portrait, no tower.)	15.00	7.50	4.50
(12)	Gene Freese (Fielding)	15.00	7.50	4.50
(13)	Don Hoak (Dark Cap)	35.00	17.50	10.50
(14)	Jay Hook (Follow-through.)	15.00	7.50	4.50
(15)	Waite Hoyt (Portrait at microphone.) (Announcer, lg, sm letters.)	15.00	7.50	4.50
(16)	Waite Hoyt (Portrait w/ folder.) (Announcer)	15.00	7.50	4.50
(17)	Fred Hutchinson (Portrait, C on vest.)	15.00	7.50	4.50
(18)	Fred Hutchinson (Portrait, half of "1" and "C.")	15.00	7.50	4.50
(19)	Fred Hutchinson (Portrait, C Reds on vest.)	15.00	7.50	4.50
(20)	Fred. Hutchinson (Only top of chest emblem shows.)	15.00	7.50	4.50
(21)	Joey Jay (Follow-through.)	15.00	7.50	4.50
(22)	Joey Jay (Portrait)	15.00	7.50	4.50
(23)	Hal Jeffcoat (follow thru)	15.00	7.50	4.50
(24)	Eddie Kasko (Batting)	15.00	7.50	4.50
(25)	Eddie Kasko (steps on bag)	15.00	7.50	4.50
(26)	Gene Kelly (Announcer)	15.00	7.50	4.50
(27)	Brooks Lawrence (follow thru)	15.00	7.50	4.50
(29)	Roy McMillan (Fielding)	15.00	7.50	4.50
(28)	Jerry Lynch (Batting)	15.00	7.50	4.50
(29)	Jim Maloney (Portrait)	15.00	7.50	4.50
(30)	Roy McMillan (Batting)	15.00	7.50	4.50
(31)	Don Newcombe (Wind-up.)	20.00	10.00	6.00
(32)	Joe Nuxhall (Follow-through, long-sleeve undershirt.)	15.00	7.50	4.50
(33)	Joe Nuxhall (Follow-through, short-sleeve undershirt.)	15.00	7.50	4.50
(34)	Jim O'Toole (Portrait)	15.00	7.50	4.50
(35)	Jim O'Toole (Wind-up, 2)	15.00	7.50	4.50
(36)	Jim O'Toole (Follow-through, 2 ver)	15.00	7.50	4.50
(37)	Don Pavletich (Portrait)	15.00	7.50	4.50
(38)	Vada Pinson (Batting, light tower on left.)	20.00	10.00	6.00
(39)	Vada Pinson (Batting, light tower on right)	20.00	10.00	6.00
(40)	Vada Pinson (Catching fly ball.)	20.00	10.00	6.00
(41)	Vada Pinson (Hands on knees.)	20.00	10.00	6.00
(42)	Wally Post (Batting)	15.00	7.50	4.50
(43)	Wally Post (Portrait)	15.00	7.50	4.50
(44)	Bob Purkey (Pitching, right foot visible.)	15.00	7.50	4.50
(45)	Bob Purkey (Pitching, right foot not visible.)	15.00	7.50	4.50
(46)	Bob Purkey (Portrait, teeth don't show.)	15.00	7.50	4.50
(47)	Bob Purkey (Portrait, teeth show.)	15.00	7.50	4.50
(48)	Frank Robinson (Batting, dark cap.)	45.00	22.00	13.50
(49)	Frank Robinson (Batting, white cap.)	45.00	22.00	13.50
(50)	Frank Robinson (Fielding fly ball, dark cap.)	45.00	22.00	13.50
(51)	Frank Robinson (Fielding fly ball, white cap.)	45.00	22.00	13.50

		NM	E	VG
(52)	Frank Robinson (Portrait, pinstripes, black background.)	45.00	22.00	13.50
(53)	Frank Robinson (Portrait, pinstripes, natural sky background.)	45.00	22.00	13.50
(54)	Frankie Robinson (Portrait to chest.)	45.00	22.00	13.50
(55)	Pete Rose (Portrait to chest.)	200.00	100.00	60.00
(56)	Johnny Temple (Portrait, Dark Cap.)	25.00	12.50	7.50

1977 Burger Chef Funmeal Discs

The largest of the disc sets produced by Michael Schechter Associates is the 216-piece issue for the Burger Chef fast food restaurant chain. The discs were issued nine-per-team on a cardboard tray accompanying a 69-cent Funmeal for kids. The 2-3/8" discs could be punched out of the tray. They share the basic design of other MSA discs of the era. A black-and-white player photo is in the center of a baseball design. Because the discs were licensed only by the Players Association, the player photos have had cap logos airbrushed away. The left and right side panels are in one of several bright colors. Backs feature a Burger Chef cartoon character in color. The individual discs are unnumbered.

		NM	E	VG
	Complete Set, Trays (24):	100.00	50.00	30.00
	Complete Set, Singles (216):	90.00	45.00	27.00
	Common Player:	.75	.35	.20
1A	**Cincinnati Reds** (Full tray.)	20.00	10.00	6.00
(1A1)	Johnny Bench	4.50	2.25	1.25
(1A2)	Dave Concepcion	.75	.35	.20
(1A3)	Dan Driessen	.75	.35	.20
(1A4)	George Foster	.75	.35	.20
(1A5)	Cesar Geronimo	.75	.35	.20
(1A6)	Ken Griffey	1.25	.60	.40
(1A7)	Joe Morgan	3.50	1.75	1.00
(1A8)	Gary Nolan	.75	.35	.20
(1A9)	Pete Rose	7.50	3.75	2.25
2A	**St. Louis Cardinals** (Full tray.)	10.00	5.00	3.00
(2A1)	Lou Brock	3.50	1.75	1.00
(2A2)	John Denny	.75	.35	.20
(2A3)	Pete Falcone	.75	.35	.20
(2A4)	Keith Hernandez	.75	.40	.25
(2A5)	Al Hrabosky	.75	.35	.20
(2A6)	Bake McBride	.75	.35	.20
(2A7)	Ken Reitz	.75	.35	.20
(2A8)	Ted Simmons	.75	.35	.20
(2A9)	Mike Tyson	.75	.35	.20
3A	**Detroit Tigers** (Full tray.)	8.00	4.00	2.50
(3A1)	Mark Fidrych	1.50	.70	.45
(3A2)	Bill Freehan	.75	.35	.20
(3A3)	John Hiller	.75	.35	.20
(3A4)	Willie Horton	.75	.35	.20
(3A5)	Ron LeFlore	.75	.35	.20
(3A6)	Ben Oglivie	.75	.35	.20
(3A7)	Aurelio Rodriguez	.75	.35	.20
(3A8)	Rusty Staub	1.25	.60	.40
(3A9)	Jason Thompson	.75	.35	.20
4A	**Cleveland Indians** (Full tray.)	8.00	4.00	2.50
(4A1)	Buddy Bell	.75	.35	.20
(4A2)	Frank Duffy	.75	.35	.20
(4A3)	Dennis Eckersley	2.75	1.50	.80
(4A4)	Ray Fosse	.75	.35	.20
(4A5)	Wayne Garland	.75	.35	.20
(4A6)	Duane Kuiper	.75	.35	.20
(4A7)	Dave LaRoche	.75	.35	.20
(4A8)	Rick Manning	.75	.35	.20
(4A9)	Rick Waits	.75	.35	.20
5A	**Chicago White Sox** (Full tray.)	8.00	4.00	2.50
(5A1)	Jack Brohamer	.75	.35	.20
(5A2)	Bucky Dent	1.00	.50	.30
(5A3)	Ralph Garr	.75	.35	.20
(5A4)	Bart Johnson	.75	.35	.20
(5A5)	Lamar Johnson	.75	.35	.20
(5A6)	Chet Lemon	.75	.35	.20
(5A7)	Jorge Orta	.75	.35	.20
(5A8)	Jim Spencer	.75	.35	.20
(5A9)	Richie Zisk	.75	.35	.20

		NM	E	VG
6A	**Chicago Cubs** (Full tray.)	8.00	4.00	2.50
(6A1)	Bill Bonham	.75	.35	.20
(6A2)	Bill Buckner	1.25	.60	.40
(6A3)	Ray Burris	.75	.35	.20
(6A4)	Jose Cardenal	.75	.35	.20
(6A5)	Bill Madlock	.75	.35	.20
(6A6)	Jerry Morales	.75	.35	.20
(6A7)	Rick Reuschel	.75	.35	.20
(6A8)	Manny Trillo	.75	.35	.20
(6A9)	Joe Wallis	.75	.35	.20
7A	**Minnesota Twins** (Full tray.)	10.00	5.00	3.00
(7A1)	Lyman Bostock	.75	.35	.20
(7A2)	Rod Carew	3.50	1.75	1.00
(7A3)	Mike Cubbage	.75	.35	.20
(7A4)	Dan Ford	.75	.35	.20
(7A5)	Dave Goltz	.75	.35	.20
(7A6)	Larry Hisle	.75	.35	.20
(7A7)	Tom Johnson	.75	.35	.20
(7A8)	Bobby Randall	.75	.35	.20
(7A9)	Butch Wynegar	.75	.35	.20
8A	**Houston Astros** (Full tray.)	8.00	4.00	2.50
(8A1)	Enos Cabell	.75	.35	.20
(8A2)	Cesar Cedeno	.75	.35	.20
(8A3)	Jose Cruz	.75	.35	.20
(8A4)	Joe Ferguson	.75	.35	.20
(8A5)	Ken Forsch	.75	.35	.20
(8A6)	Roger Metzger	.75	.35	.20
(8A7)	J.R. Richard	.75	.35	.20
(8A8)	Leon Roberts	.75	.35	.20
(8A9)	Bob Watson	.75	.35	.20
1B	**Baltimore Orioles** (Full tray.)	15.00	7.50	4.50
(1B1)	Mark Belanger	.75	.35	.20
(1B2)	Paul Blair	.75	.35	.20
(1B3)	Al Bumbry	.75	.35	.20
(1B4)	Doug DeCinces	.75	.35	.20
(1B5)	Ross Grimsley	.75	.35	.20
(1B6)	Lee May	.75	.35	.20
(1B7)	Jim Palmer	3.50	1.75	1.00
(1B8)	Brooks Robinson	4.50	2.25	1.25
(1B9)	Ken Singleton	.75	.35	.20
2B	**Boston Red Sox** (Full tray.)	15.00	7.50	4.50
(2B1)	Rick Burleson	.75	.35	.20
(2B2)	Dwight Evans	.75	.40	.25
(2B3)	Carlton Fisk	3.50	1.75	1.00
(2B4)	Fergie Jenkins	2.75	1.50	.80
(2B5)	Bill Lee	.75	.35	.20
(2B6)	Fred Lynn	.75	.40	.25
(2B7)	Jim Rice	1.50	.70	.45
(2B8)	Luis Tiant	.75	.35	.20
(2B9)	Carl Yastrzemski	4.50	2.25	1.25
3B	**Kansas City Royals** (Full tray.)	13.50	6.75	4.00
(3B1)	Doug Bird	.75	.35	.20
(3B2)	George Brett	6.00	3.00	1.75
(3B3)	Dennis Leonard	.75	.35	.20
(3B4)	John Mayberry	.75	.35	.20
(3B5)	Hal McRae	.75	.35	.20
(3B6)	Amos Otis	.75	.35	.20
(3B7)	Fred Patek	.75	.35	.20
(3B8)	Tom Poquette	.75	.35	.20
(3B9)	Paul Splittorff	.75	.35	.20
4B	**Milwaukee Brewers** (Full tray.)	10.00	5.00	3.00
(4B1)	Jerry Augustine	.75	.35	.20
(4B2)	Sal Bando	.75	.35	.20
(4B3)	Von Joshua	.75	.35	.20
(4B4)	Sixto Lezcano	.75	.35	.20
(4B5)	Charlie Moore	.75	.35	.20
(4B6)	Ed Rodriguez	.75	.35	.20
(4B7)	Jim Slaton	.75	.35	.20
(4B8)	Bill Travers	.75	.35	.20
(4B9)	Robin Yount	3.50	1.75	1.00
5B	**Texas Rangers** (Full tray.)	10.00	5.00	3.00
(5B1)	Juan Beniquez	.75	.35	.20
(5B2)	Bert Blyleven	.75	.35	.20
(5B3)	Bert Campaneris	.75	.35	.20
(5B4)	Tom Grieve	.75	.35	.20
(5B5)	Mike Hargrove	.75	.35	.20
(5B6)	Toby Harrah	.75	.35	.20
(5B7)	Gaylord Perry	2.75	1.50	.80
(5B8)	Lenny Randle	.75	.35	.20
(5B9)	Jim Sundberg	.75	.35	.20
6B	**Atlanta Braves** (Full tray.)	8.00	4.00	2.50
(6B1)	Jeff Burroughs	.75	.35	.20
(6B2)	Darrel Chaney	.75	.35	.20
(6B3)	Gary Matthews	.75	.35	.20
(6B4)	Andy Messersmith	.75	.35	.20
(6B5)	Willie Montanez	.75	.35	.20
(6B6)	Phil Niekro	2.75	1.50	.80
(6B7)	Tom Paciorek	.75	.35	.20
(6B8)	Jerry Royster	.75	.35	.20
(6B9)	Dick Ruthven	.75	.35	.20
7B	**Pittsburgh Pirates** (Full tray.)	10.00	5.00	3.00
(7B1)	John Candelaria	.75	.35	.20
(7B2)	Duffy Dyer	.75	.35	.20

(7B3)	Al Oliver	1.25	.60	.40
(7B4)	Dave Parker	.75	.40	.25
(7B5)	Jerry Reuss	.75	.35	.20
(7B6)	Bill Robinson	.75	.35	.20
(7B7)	Willie Stargell	3.50	1.75	1.00
(7B8)	Rennie Stennett	.75	.35	.20
(7B9)	Frank Taveras	.75	.35	.20
8B	**New York Yankees** (Full tray.)	20.00	10.00	6.00
(8B1)	Chris Chambliss	.75	.35	.20
(8B2)	Don Gullett	.75	.35	.20
(8B3)	Catfish Hunter	2.75	1.50	.80
(8B4)	Reggie Jackson	5.00	2.50	1.50
(8B5)	Thurman Munson	4.50	2.25	1.25
(8B6)	Graig Nettles	.75	.35	.20
(8B7)	Willie Randolph	.75	.35	.20
(8B8)	Mickey Rivers	.75	.35	.20
(8B9)	Roy White	.75	.35	.20
1C	**California Angels** (Full tray.)	25.00	12.50	7.50
(1C1)	Bobby Bonds	.75	.35	.20
(1C2)	Dave Chalk	.75	.35	.20
(1C3)	Bobby Grich	.75	.35	.20
(1C4)	Paul Hartzell	.75	.35	.20
(1C5)	Ron Jackson	.75	.35	.20
(1C6)	Jerry Remy	.75	.35	.20
(1C7)	Joe Rudi	.75	.35	.20
(1C8)	Nolan Ryan	16.00	8.00	4.75
(1C9)	Frank Tanana	.75	.35	.20
2C	**Oakland A's** (Full tray.)	8.00	4.00	2.50
(2C1)	Stan Bahnsen	.75	.35	.20
(2C2)	Vida Blue	.75	.35	.20
(2C3)	Phil Garner	.75	.35	.20
(2C4)	Paul Lindblad	.75	.35	.20
(2C5)	Mike Norris	.75	.35	.20
(2C6)	Bill North	.75	.35	.20
(2C7)	Manny Sanguillen	.75	.35	.20
(2C8)	Mike Torrez	.75	.35	.20
(2C9)	Claudell Washington	.75	.35	.20
3C	**Los Angeles Dodgers** (Full tray.)	10.00	5.00	3.00
(3C1)	Ron Cey	.75	.35	.20
(3C2)	Steve Garvey	2.00	1.00	.60
(3C3)	Davey Lopes	.75	.35	.20
(3C4)	Rick Monday	.75	.35	.20
(3C5)	Doug Rau	.75	.35	.20
(3C6)	Rick Rhoden	.75	.35	.20
(3C7)	Reggie Smith	.75	.35	.20
(3C8)	Don Sutton	2.75	1.50	.80
(3C9)	Steve Yeager	.75	.35	.20
4C	**Montreal Expos** (Full tray.)	10.00	5.00	3.00
(4C1)	Gary Carter	3.00	1.50	.90
(4C2)	Dave Cash	.75	.35	.20
(4C3)	Tim Foli	.75	.35	.20
(4C4)	Barry Foote	.75	.35	.20
(4C5)	Larry Parrish	.75	.35	.20
(4C6)	Tony Perez	3.00	1.50	.90
(4C7)	Steve Rogers	.75	.35	.20
(4C8)	Del Unser	.75	.35	.20
(4C9)	Ellis Valentine	.75	.35	.20
5C	**New York Mets** (Full tray.)	13.50	6.75	4.00
(5C1)	Bud Harrelson	.75	.35	.20
(5C2)	Dave Kingman	1.00	.50	.30
(5C3)	Jerry Koosman	.75	.35	.20
(5C4)	Ed Kranepool	.75	.35	.20
(5C5)	Skip Lockwood	.75	.35	.20
(5C6)	Jon Matlack	.75	.35	.20
(5C7)	Felix Millan	.75	.35	.20
(5C8)	Tom Seaver	4.50	2.25	1.25
(5C9)	John Stearns	.75	.35	.20
6C	**Philadelphia Phillies** (Full tray.)	15.00	7.50	4.50
(6C1)	Bob Boone	1.00	.50	.30
(6C2)	Larry Bowa	.75	.35	.20
(6C3)	Steve Carlton	3.50	1.75	1.00
(6C4)	Jay Johnstone	.75	.35	.20
(6C5)	Jim Kaat	1.25	.60	.40
(6C6)	Greg Luzinski	.75	.40	.25
(6C7)	Garry Maddox	.75	.35	.20
(6C8)	Tug McGraw	1.25	.60	.40
(6C9)	Mike Schmidt	6.00	3.00	1.75
7C	**San Diego Padres** (Full tray.)	10.00	5.00	3.00
(7C1)	Rollie Fingers	2.75	1.50	.80
(7C2)	George Hendrick	.75	.35	.20
(7C3)	Enzo Hernandez	.75	.35	.20
(7C4)	Mike Ivie	.75	.35	.20
(7C5)	Randy Jones	.75	.35	.20
(7C6)	Butch Metzger	.75	.35	.20
(7C7)	Dave Rader	.75	.35	.20
(7C8)	Gene Tenace	.75	.35	.20
(7C9)	Dave Winfield	3.50	1.75	1.00
8C	**San Francisco Giants** (Full tray.)	8.00	4.00	2.50
(8C1)	Jim Barr	.75	.35	.20
(8C2)	Willie Crawford	.75	.35	.20
(8C3)	Larry Herndon	.75	.35	.20
(8C4)	Randy Moffitt	.75	.35	.20

(8C5)	John Montefusco	.75	.35	.20
(8C6)	Bobby Murcer	.75	.35	.20
(8C7)	Marty Perez	.75	.35	.20
(8C8)	Chris Speier	.75	.35	.20
(8C9)	Gary Thomasson	.75	.35	.20

1977 Burger King Tigers

This series of color 8" x 10" player portraits was given away one per week at Detroit area Burger Kings. Backs are blank and there is no player identification on the front. The photos are checklisted here alphabetically.

		NM	E	VG
	Complete Set (4):	40.00	20.00	12.00
	Common Player:	10.00	5.00	3.00
(1)	Mark Fidrych (Holding glove.)	15.00	7.50	4.50
(2)	Ron LeFlore (Black guy w/bat.)	10.00	5.00	3.00
(3)	Dave Rozema (Winding up.)	10.00	5.00	3.00
(4)	Mickey Stanley (White guy w/bat.)	10.00	5.00	3.00

1977 Burger King Yankees

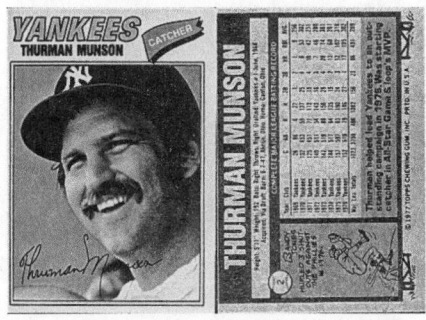

The first Topps-produced set for Burger King restaurants was issued in the New York area, featuring the A.L. champion Yankees. Twenty-two players plus an unnumbered checklist were issued at the beginning of the promotion with card #23 (Lou Piniella) being added to the set later. The "New York Post" reported production of the first 22 player cards at about 170,000 of each. The Piniella card was issued in limited quantities. Cards are 2-1/2" x 3-1/2" and have fronts identical to the regular 1977 Topps set except for numbers 2, 6, 7, 13, 14, 15, 17, 20 and 21. These cards feature different poses or major picture-cropping variations. It should be noted that very minor cropping variations between the regular Topps sets and the Burger King issues exist throughout the years the sets were produced.

		NM	E	VG
	Complete Set w/Piniella (24):	20.00	10.00	6.00
	Complete Set no Piniella (23):	13.50	6.75	4.00
	Common Player:	.25	.13	.08
1	Yankees Team (Billy Martin)	.75	.40	.25
2	Thurman Munson	5.00	2.50	1.50
3	Fran Healy	.25	.13	.08
4	Catfish Hunter	1.50	.70	.45
5	Ed Figueroa	.25	.13	.08
6	Don Gullett	.25	.13	.08
7	Mike Torrez	.25	.13	.08
8	Ken Holtzman	.25	.13	.08
9	Dick Tidrow	.25	.13	.08
10	Sparky Lyle	.40	.20	.12
11	Ron Guidry	.45	.25	.14
12	Chris Chambliss	.25	.13	.08
13	Willie Randolph	.45	.25	.14
14	Bucky Dent	.45	.25	.14
15	Graig Nettles	.60	.30	.20
16	Fred Stanley	.25	.13	.08

17	Reggie Jackson	5.00	2.50	1.50
18	Mickey Rivers	.25	.13	.08
19	Roy White	.40	.20	.12
20	Jim Wynn	.40	.20	.12
21	Paul Blair	.25	.13	.08
22	Carlos May	.25	.13	.08
23	Lou Piniella	15.00	7.50	4.50
---	**Checklist**	.05	.03	.02

1978 Burger King Astros

 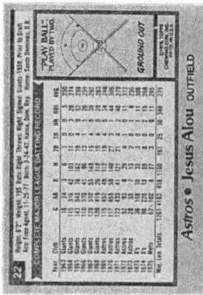

Burger King restaurants in the Houston area distributed a Topps-produced set showcasing the Astros. Cards are standard 2-1/2" x 3-1/2" and are numbered 1-22, plus and unnumbered checklist. Fronts are identical to the regular 1978 Topps set with the exception of card numbers 21, Dave Bergman, who appeared on a Rookie Outfielders cards in the '78 Topps set; and 22, Jesus Alou, who did not have a card in the regular issue. Although not noted in the following checklist, it should be remembered that very minor picture-cropping variations between the regular Topps issues and the 1977-1980 Burger King sets do exist.

		NM	E	VG
	Complete Set (23):	15.00	7.50	4.50
	Common Player:	.75	.40	.25
1	Bill Virdon	.90	.45	.25
2	Joe Ferguson	.75	.40	.25
3	Ed Herrmann	.75	.40	.25
4	J.R. Richard	1.50	.70	.45
5	Joe Niekro	1.25	.60	.40
6	Floyd Bannister	.75	.40	.25
7	Joaquin Andujar	.75	.40	.25
8	Ken Forsch	.75	.40	.25
9	Mark Lemongello	.75	.40	.25
10	Joe Sambito	.75	.40	.25
11	Gene Pentz	.75	.40	.25
12	Bob Watson	.90	.45	.25
13	Julio Gonzalez	.75	.40	.25
14	Enos Cabell	.75	.40	.25
15	Roger Metzger	.75	.40	.25
16	Art Howe	.90	.45	.25
17	Jose Cruz	1.00	.50	.30
18	Cesar Cedeno	1.00	.50	.30
19	Terry Puhl	.75	.40	.25
20	Wilbur Howard	.75	.40	.25
21	Dave Bergman	.75	.40	.25
22	Jesus Alou	1.00	.50	.30
---	**Checklist**	.10	.05	.03

1978 Burger King Rangers

 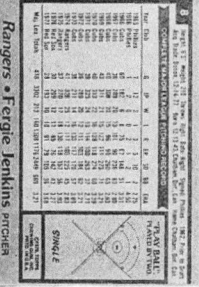

Issued by Burger King restaurants in the Dallas-Fort Worth area, this Topps-produced set features the Texas Rangers. Cards are standard 2-1/2" x 3-1/2" and identical in style to the regular 1978 Topps set with the following exceptions: #'s 5, 8, 10, 12, 17, 21 and 22. An unnumbered checklist card was included with the set.

		NM	E	VG
	Complete Set (23):	15.00	7.50	4.50
	Common Player:	.75	.40	.25
1	Billy Hunter	.75	.40	.25

		NM	E	VG
2	Jim Sundberg	.75	.40	.25
3	John Ellis	.75	.40	.25
4	Doyle Alexander	.75	.40	.25
5	Jon Matlack	.75	.40	.25
6	Dock Ellis	.75	.40	.25
7	George Medich	.75	.40	.25
8	Fergie Jenkins	6.00	3.00	1.75
9	Len Barker	.75	.40	.25
10	Reggie Cleveland	.75	.40	.25
11	Mike Hargrove	1.00	.50	.30
12	Bump Wills	1.00	.50	.30
13	Toby Harrah	1.00	.50	.30
14	Bert Campaneris	1.00	.50	.30
15	Sandy Alomar	1.00	.50	.30
16	Kurt Bevacqua	.75	.40	.25
17	Al Oliver	1.50	.70	.45
18	Juan Beniquez	.75	.40	.25
19	Claudell Washington	.75	.40	.25
20	Richie Zisk	.75	.40	.25
21	John Lowenstein	.75	.40	.25
22	Bobby Thompson	.75	.40	.25
---	Checklist	.10	.05	.03

1978 Burger King Tigers

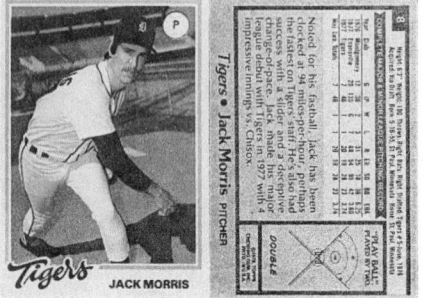

JACK MORRIS

Rookie cards of Morris, Trammell and Whitaker make the Topps-produced 1978 Burger King Detroit Tigers issue the most popular of the BK sets. Twenty-two player cards and an unnumbered checklist make up the set which was issued in the Detroit area. Cards measure 2-1/2" x 3-1/2", and are identical to the regular 1978 Topps issue with the following exceptions: #'s 6, 7, 8, 13, 15 and 16. Numerous minor picture-cropping variations between the regular Topps issues and the Burger King sets appear from 1977-1980; these minor variations are not noted in the following checklist.

		NM	E	VG
Complete Set (23):		25.00	12.50	7.50
Common Player:		.75	.40	.25
1	Ralph Houk	.90	.45	.25
2	Milt May	.75	.40	.25
3	John Wockenfuss	.75	.40	.25
4	Mark Fidrych	2.50	1.25	.70
5	Dave Rozema	.75	.40	.25
6	Jack Billingham	.75	.40	.25
7	Jim Slaton	.75	.40	.25
8	Jack Morris	3.00	1.50	.90
9	John Hiller	.75	.40	.25
10	Steve Foucault	.75	.40	.25
11	Milt Wilcox	.75	.40	.25
12	Jason Thompson	.75	.40	.25
13	Lou Whitaker	6.00	3.00	1.75
14	Aurelio Rodriguez	.75	.40	.25
15	Alan Trammell	10.00	5.00	3.00
16	Steve Dillard	.75	.40	.25
17	Phil Mankowski	.75	.40	.25
18	Steve Kemp	.75	.40	.25
19	Ron LeFlore	.90	.45	.25
20	Tim Corcoran	.75	.40	.25
21	Mickey Stanley	.75	.40	.25
22	Rusty Staub	.90	.45	.25
---	Checklist	.10	.05	.03

1978 Burger King Yankees

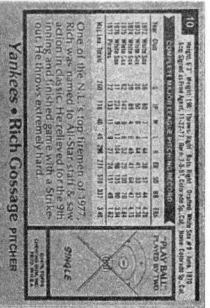

RICH GOSSAGE

Produced by Topps for Burger King outlets in the New York area for the second year in a row, the 1978 Yankees set contains 22 cards plus an unnumbered checklist. The cards are numbered 1 through 22 and are the standard size of 2-1/2" x 3-1/2". The cards feature the same pictures found in the regular 1978 Topps set except for numbers 10, 11 and 16. Only those variations containing different poses or major picture-cropping differences are noted. Numerous minor picture-cropping variations, that are very insignificant in nature, exist between the regular Topps sets and the Burger King issues of 1977-1980.

		NM	E	VG
Complete Set (23):		15.00	7.50	4.50
Common Player:		.50	.25	.15
1	Billy Martin	1.50	.70	.45
2	Thurman Munson	5.00	2.50	1.50
3	Cliff Johnson	.50	.25	.15
4	Ron Guidry	1.00	.50	.30
5	Ed Figueroa	.50	.25	.15
6	Dick Tidrow	.50	.25	.15
7	Catfish Hunter	2.00	1.00	.60
8	Don Gullett	.50	.25	.15
9	Sparky Lyle	1.00	.50	.30
10	Rich Gossage	1.50	.70	.45
11	Rawly Eastwick	.50	.25	.15
12	Chris Chambliss	.50	.25	.15
13	Willie Randolph	1.00	.50	.30
14	Graig Nettles	1.00	.50	.30
15	Bucky Dent	1.00	.50	.30
16	Jim Spencer	.50	.25	.15
17	Fred Stanley	.50	.25	.15
18	Lou Piniella	1.25	.60	.40
19	Roy White	1.00	.50	.30
20	Mickey Rivers	.50	.25	.15
21	Reggie Jackson	6.00	3.00	1.75
22	Paul Blair	.50	.25	.15
---	Checklist	.10	.05	.03

1979 Burger King Phillies

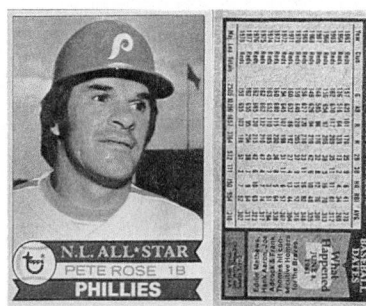

N.L. ALL-STAR
PETE ROSE 1B
PHILLIES

Twenty-two Phillies players are featured in the 1979 Burger King issue given out in the Philadelphia area. The Topps-produced set, measuring 2-1/2" x 3-1/2", also includes an unnumbered checklist. Cards are identical to the regular 1979 Topps set except #1, 11, 12, 13, 14, 17 and 22, which have different poses. Very minor picture-cropping variations between the regular Topps issues and the Burger King sets can be found throughout the four years the cards were produced, but only those variations featuring major changes are noted in the checklists.

		NM	E	VG
Complete Set (23):		7.50	3.75	2.25
Common Player:		.25	.13	.08
1	Danny Ozark	.25	.13	.08
2	Bob Boone	.45	.25	.14
3	Tim McCarver	.50	.25	.15
4	Steve Carlton	1.50	.70	.45
5	Larry Christenson	.25	.13	.08
6	Dick Ruthven	.25	.13	.08
7	Ron Reed	.25	.13	.08
8	Randy Lerch	.25	.13	.08
9	Warren Brusstar	.25	.13	.08
10	Tug McGraw	.40	.20	.12
11	Nino Espinosa	.25	.13	.08
12	Doug Bird	.25	.13	.08
13	Pete Rose	3.00	1.50	.90
14	Manny Trillo	.25	.13	.08
15	Larry Bowa	.40	.20	.12
16	Mike Schmidt	3.00	1.50	.90
17	Pete Mackanin	.25	.13	.08
18	Jose Cardenal	.25	.13	.08
19	Greg Luzinski	.25	.13	.08
20	Garry Maddox	.25	.13	.08
21	Bake McBride	.25	.13	.08
22	Greg Gross	.25	.13	.08
---	Checklist	.08	.04	.02

1979 Burger King Yankees

LUIS TIANT P
YANKEES

The New York Yankees were featured in a Topps-produced Burger King set for the third consecutive year in 1979. Once again, 22 numbered player cards and an unnumbered checklist made up the set. Cards measure 2-1/2" x 3-1/2", and are identical to the 1979 Topps regular set except for #4, 8, 9 and 22 which included new poses. Numerous minor picture cropping variations between the regular Topps issue and the Burger King sets of 1977-1980 exist.

		NM	E	VG
Complete Set (23):		7.50	3.75	2.25
Common Player:		.25	.13	.08
1	Yankees Team(Bob Lemon)	.75	.40	.25
2	Thurman Munson	2.50	1.25	.70
3	Cliff Johnson	.25	.13	.08
4	Ron Guidry	.60	.30	.20
5	Jay Johnstone	.40	.20	.12
6	Catfish Hunter	1.25	.60	.40
7	Jim Beattie	.25	.13	.08
8	Luis Tiant	.40	.20	.12
9	Tommy John	.75	.40	.25
10	Rich Gossage	.60	.30	.20
11	Ed Figueroa	.25	.13	.08
12	Chris Chambliss	.25	.13	.08
13	Willie Randolph	.40	.20	.12
14	Bucky Dent	.40	.20	.12
15	Graig Nettles	.40	.20	.12
16	Fred Stanley	.25	.13	.08
17	Jim Spencer	.25	.13	.08
18	Lou Piniella	.60	.30	.20
19	Roy White	.40	.20	.12
20	Mickey Rivers	.25	.13	.08
21	Reggie Jackson	4.00	2.00	1.25
22	Juan Beniquez	.25	.13	.08
---	Checklist	.06	.03	.02

1980 Burger King Phillies

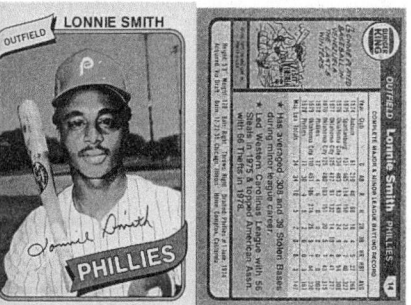

LONNIE SMITH
OUTFIELD
PHILLIES

Philadelphia-area Burger King outlets issued a 23-card set featuring the Phillies for the second in a row in 1980. The Topps-produced set, measuring 2-1/2" x 3-1/2", contains 22 player cards and an unnumbered checklist. Fronts are identical in design to the regular 1980 Topps sets with the following exceptions: #1, 3, 8, 14 and 22 feature new poses. Very minor picture-cropping variations between the regular Topps issues and the Burger King sets exist in all years. Those minor differences are not noted in the checklists. The 1980 Burger King sets were the first to include the Burger King logo on the card backs.

		NM	E	VG
Complete Set (23):		6.00	3.00	1.75
Common Player:		.10	.05	.03
1	Dallas Green	.15	.08	.05
2	Bob Boone	.50	.25	.15
3	Keith Moreland	.25	.13	.08
4	Pete Rose	2.50	1.25	.70
5	Manny Trillo	.10	.05	.03
6	Mike Schmidt	2.50	1.25	.70
7	Larry Bowa	.20	.10	.06
8	John Vukovich	.10	.05	.03

9	Bake McBride	.10	.05	.03
10	Garry Maddox	.10	.05	.03
11	Greg Luzinski	.25	.13	.08
12	Greg Gross	.10	.05	.03
13	Del Unser	.10	.05	.03
14	Lonnie Smith	.40	.20	.12
15	Steve Carlton	1.00	.50	.30
16	Larry Christenson	.10	.05	.03
17	Nino Espinosa	.10	.05	.03
18	Randy Lerch	.10	.05	.03
19	Dick Ruthven	.10	.05	.03
20	Tug McGraw	.15	.08	.05
21	Ron Reed	.10	.05	.03
22	Kevin Saucier	.10	.05	.03
---	Checklist	.05	.03	.02

1980 Burger King Pitch, Hit & Run

In 1980, Burger King issued, in conjunction with its "Pitch, Hit & Run" promotion, a Topps-produced set featuring pitchers (card #s 1-11), hitters (#s 12-22), and base stealers (#s 23-33). Fronts, which carry the Burger King logo, are identical in design to the regular 1980 Topps set except for numbers 1, 4, 5, 7, 9, 10, 16, 17, 18, 22, 23, 27, 28, 29 and 30, which feature different poses. Cards measure 2-1/2" x 3-1/2" in size. An unnumbered checklist was included with the set.

		NM	E	VG
	Complete Set (34):	10.00	5.00	3.00
	Common Player:	.10	.05	.03
1	Vida Blue	.10	.05	.03
2	Steve Carlton	1.00	.50	.30
3	Rollie Fingers	.65	.35	.20
4	Ron Guidry	.25	.13	.08
5	Jerry Koosman	.10	.05	.03
6	Phil Niekro	.65	.35	.20
7	Jim Palmer	1.00	.50	.30
8	J.R. Richard	.10	.05	.03
9	Nolan Ryan	4.00	2.00	1.25
10	Tom Seaver	1.00	.50	.30
11	Bruce Sutter	1.00	.50	.30
12	Don Baylor	.10	.05	.03
13	George Brett	2.00	1.00	.60
14	Rod Carew	1.00	.50	.30
15	George Foster	.10	.05	.03
16	Keith Hernandez	.10	.05	.03
17	Reggie Jackson	1.50	.70	.45
18	Fred Lynn	.10	.05	.03
19	Dave Parker	.10	.05	.03
20	Jim Rice	1.00	.50	.30
21	Pete Rose	3.00	1.50	.90
22	Dave Winfield	1.00	.50	.30
23	Bobby Bonds	.10	.05	.03
24	Enos Cabell	.10	.05	.03
25	Cesar Cedeno	.10	.05	.03
26	Julio Cruz	.10	.05	.03
27	Ron LeFlore	.10	.05	.03
28	Dave Lopes	.10	.05	.03
29	Omar Moreno	.10	.05	.03
30	Joe Morgan	1.00	.50	.30
31	Bill North	.10	.05	.03
32	Frank Taveras	.10	.05	.03
33	Willie Wilson	.10	.05	.03
---	Checklist	.05	.03	.02

1916 Burgess-Nash Clothiers

This 200-card set can be found with ads on the back for several local and regional businesses. Among them is Burgess-Nash clothiers, from Omaha, Neb. Type card and superstar collectors can expect to pay a significant premium for cards with the Burgess-Nash advertising, compared to the generic M101-4 Blank Backs values. Cards measure about 1-5/8" x 3" and are printed in black-and-white.

PREMIUM: 12-15X

(See 1916 M101-4 Blank Backs for checklist.)

1935 George Burke Detroit Tigers Photo Stamps

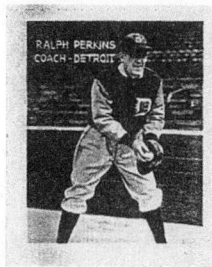

This team set of black-and-white, 1-1/16" x 1-1/4" photo stamps was produced by baseball photographer George Burke. The set was printed on two sheets of 12 players each. Each stamp has the player's name, position abbreviation and city in black or white typography. The blank-backed ungummed stamps of the 1935 World's Champs are checklisted here in alphabetical order.

		NM	E	VG
	Complete Set (24):	325.00	160.00	95.00
	Common Player:	10.00	5.00	3.00
(1)	Elden Auker	10.00	5.00	3.00
(2)	Del Baker	10.00	5.00	3.00
(3)	Tom Bridges	10.00	5.00	3.00
(4)	Herman Clifton	10.00	5.00	3.00
(5)	Mickey Cochrane	30.00	15.00	9.00
(6)	Alvin Crowder	10.00	5.00	3.00
(7)	Ervin Fox	10.00	5.00	3.00
(8)	Charles Gehringer	30.00	15.00	9.00
(9)	Leon Goslin	30.00	15.00	9.00
(10)	Henry Greenberg	45.00	22.50	13.50
(11)	Raymond Hayworth	10.00	5.00	3.00
(12)	Elon Hogsett	10.00	5.00	3.00
(13)	Roxie Lawson	10.00	5.00	3.00
(14)	Marvin Owen	10.00	5.00	3.00
(15)	Ralph Perkins	10.00	5.00	3.00
(16)	Frank Reiber	10.00	5.00	3.00
(17)	Wm. Rogell	10.00	5.00	3.00
(18)	Lynwood Rowe	12.50	6.25	3.75
(19)	Henry Schuble	10.00	5.00	3.00
(20)	Hugh Shelley	10.00	5.00	3.00
(21)	Victor Sorrell	10.00	5.00	3.00
(22)	Joseph Sullivan	10.00	5.00	3.00
(23)	Gerald Walker	10.00	5.00	3.00
(24)	Joyner White	10.00	5.00	3.00

1935-37 George Burke Postage Stamp Photos

These small (3/4" x 1") black-and-white stamps were produced by Chicago baseball portraitist George Burke for sale to individual players for use in answering fan mail. The stamps were not a big seller, though the checklist presented alphabetically here is surely incomplete. The unnumbered stamps, which are blank-backed, were not self-adhesive and were printed in sheets of at least six of the same player. Some of the photo-stamps have facsimile autographs, others do not.

	NM	E	VG
Common Player:	10.00	5.00	3.00
Luke Appling	20.00	10.00	6.00
Jimmy Austin	10.00	5.00	3.00
Dick Bartell	10.00	5.00	3.00
Huck Betts	10.00	5.00	3.00
George Blaeholder	10.00	5.00	3.00
Jim Bottomley	20.00	10.00	6.00
Earl Browne	10.00	5.00	3.00
Irving Burns	10.00	5.00	3.00
Sam Byrd	10.00	5.00	3.00
Gilly Campbell	10.00	5.00	3.00
James (Tex) Carleton	10.00	5.00	3.00
Hugh Casey	10.00	5.00	3.00
James "Rip" Collins	10.00	5.00	3.00
Earle Combs	20.00	10.00	6.00
Adam Comorosky	10.00	5.00	3.00
Jocko Conlan	20.00	10.00	6.00
Kiki Cuyler	20.00	10.00	6.00
Paul Derringer	10.00	5.00	3.00
Jim DeShong	10.00	5.00	3.00
Bill Dickey	20.00	10.00	6.00
Bill Dietrich	10.00	5.00	3.00
Carl Doyle	10.00	5.00	3.00
Chuck Dressen	10.00	5.00	3.00
Jimmy Dykes	10.00	5.00	3.00
Hank Erickson	10.00	5.00	3.00
Wes Ferrell	10.00	5.00	3.00
Arthur Fletcher	10.00	5.00	3.00
Jimmie Foxx (Facsimile autograph.)	40.00	20.00	12.00
Jimmie Foxx (No autograph.)	40.00	20.00	12.00
Larry French	10.00	5.00	3.00
Benny Frey	10.00	5.00	3.00
Tony Freitas	10.00	5.00	3.00
Frankie Frisch	20.00	10.00	6.00
Ed Gharrity	10.00	5.00	3.00
Lefty Gomez	20.00	10.00	6.00
Charlie Grimm	10.00	5.00	3.00
Stan Hack	10.00	5.00	3.00
Chick Hafey	20.00	10.00	6.00
Mel Harder	10.00	5.00	3.00
Bucky Harris	20.00	10.00	6.00
Gabby Hartnett	20.00	10.00	6.00
Roy Henshaw	10.00	5.00	3.00
Babe Herman	15.00	7.50	4.50
Billy Herman	20.00	10.00	6.00
Leroy Herrmann	10.00	5.00	3.00
Myril Hoag	10.00	5.00	3.00
Al Hollingsworth	10.00	5.00	3.00
Carl Hubbell	30.00	15.00	9.00
Bob Johnson	10.00	5.00	3.00
Douglas Johnson	10.00	5.00	3.00
Si Johnson	10.00	5.00	3.00
George L. Kelly	20.00	10.00	6.00
Chuck Klein	20.00	10.00	6.00
Mark Koenig	10.00	5.00	3.00
Tony Lazzeri	30.00	15.00	9.00
Bill Lee	10.00	5.00	3.00
Dutch Leonard	10.00	5.00	3.00
Ernie Lombardi	20.00	10.00	6.00
Al Lopez	20.00	10.00	6.00
Adolfo Luque	15.00	7.50	4.50
Earle Mack	10.00	5.00	3.00
Roy Mahaffey	10.00	5.00	3.00
Gus Mancuso	10.00	5.00	3.00
Rabbit Maranville	20.00	10.00	6.00
Johnny Marcum	10.00	5.00	3.00
Joe McCarthy	20.00	10.00	6.00
Eric McNair	10.00	5.00	3.00
Van Lingle Mungo	10.00	5.00	3.00
Skeeter Newsome	10.00	5.00	3.00
Mel Ott	40.00	20.00	12.00
Claude Passeau	10.00	5.00	3.00
Monte Pearson	10.00	5.00	3.00
Raymond Pepper	10.00	5.00	3.00
Charlie Root	10.00	6.00	3.00
Red Ruffing	20.00	10.00	6.00
George Selkirk	10.00	5.00	3.00
Joe Sewell	20.00	10.00	6.00
Luke Sewell	10.00	5.00	3.00
Al Simmons	20.00	10.00	6.00
Casey Stengel	20.00	10.00	6.00
Riggs Stephenson	10.00	5.00	3.00
Alan Strange	10.00	5.00	3.00
Gus Suhr	10.00	5.00	3.00
Billy Sullivan	10.00	5.00	3.00
Dan Taylor	10.00	5.00	3.00
Fay Thomas	10.00	5.00	3.00
Hal Trosky	10.00	5.00	3.00
Honus Wagner	40.00	20.00	12.00

	NM	E	VG
Rube Walberg	10.00	5.00	3.00
Paul Waner	20.00	10.00	6.00
Lon Warneke	10.00	5.00	3.00
Harold Warstler	10.00	5.00	3.00
Billy Webb	10.00	5.00	3.00
Whitlow Wyatt	10.00	5.00	3.00

1933 Butter Cream (R306)

 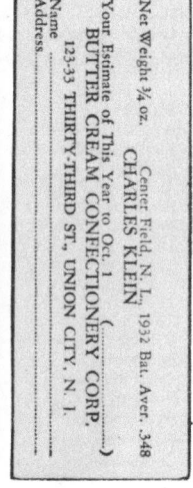

The 1933 Butter Cream set consists of unnumbered, black-and-white cards which measure 1-1/4" x 3-1/2". Backs feature a contest in which the collector was to estimate players' statistics by a specific date. Two different backs are known: 1) Estimate through Sept. 1 and no company address, and 2) Estimate through Oct. 1 with the Butter Cream address. The ACC designation for the set is R306.

		NM	E	VG
Complete Set w/o Ruth (29):		25,000	12,500	6,000
Common Player:		750.00	375.00	165.00
(1)	Earl Averill	1,200	600.00	350.00
(2)	Ed. Brandt	750.00	375.00	165.00
(3)	Guy T. Bush	750.00	375.00	165.00
(4)	Gordon Cochrane	1,200	600.00	350.00
(5)	Joe Cronin	1,200	600.00	350.00
(6)	George Earnshaw	750.00	375.00	165.00
(7)	Wesley Ferrell	750.00	375.00	165.00
(8)	"Jimmy" E. Foxx	4,500	2,250	1,350
(9)	Frank C. Frisch	1,200	600.00	350.00
(10)	Charles M. Gelbert	750.00	375.00	165.00
(11)	"Lefty" Robert M. Grove	1,500	750.00	450.00
(12)	Leo Charles Hartnett	1,200	600.00	350.00
(13)	"Babe" Herman	750.00	375.00	165.00
(14)	Charles Klein	1,200	600.00	350.00
(15)	Ray Kremer	750.00	375.00	165.00
(16)	Fred C. Linstrom (Lindstrom)	1,200	600.00	350.00
(17)	Ted A. Lyons	1,200	600.00	350.00
(18)	"Pepper" John L. Martin	900.00	450.00	200.00
(19)	Robert O'Farrell	750.00	375.00	165.00
(20)	Ed. A. Rommel	750.00	375.00	165.00
(21)	Charles Root	750.00	375.00	165.00
(22)	Harold "Muddy" Ruel (Herold)	750.00	375.00	165.00
(23)	Babe Ruth	45,000	22,500	13,500
(24)	"Al" Simmons	1,200	600.00	350.00
(25)	"Bill" Terry	1,200	600.00	350.00
(26)	George E. Uhle	750.00	375.00	165.00
(27)	Lloyd J. Waner	1,200	600.00	350.00
(28)	Paul G. Waner	1,200	600.00	350.00
(29)	Hack Wilson	1,200	600.00	350.00
(30)	Glen. Wright	750.00	375.00	165.00

1934 Butterfinger (R310)

Cards in this set were available as a premium with Butterfinger and other candy products. The unnumbered cards measure approximately 7-3/4" x 9-1/2". The black-and-white cards feature a player photo with facsimile autograph. Similar cards in a 6-1/2" x 8-1/2" format are a companion Canadian issue.

		NM	E	VG
Complete Set (65):		6,500	3,250	2,000
Common Player:		60.00	30.00	18.00
Cardboard Ad Variety: 4X				
(1)	Earl Averill	110.00	55.00	35.00
(2)	Richard Bartell	60.00	30.00	18.00
(3)	Larry Benton	60.00	30.00	18.00
(4)	Walter Berger	60.00	30.00	18.00
(5)	Jim Bottomly (Bottomley)	110.00	55.00	35.00
(6)	Ralph Boyle	60.00	30.00	18.00
(7)	Tex Carleton	60.00	30.00	18.00
(8)	Owen T. Carroll	60.00	30.00	18.00
(9)	Ben Chapman	60.00	30.00	18.00
(10)	Gordon (Mickey) Cochrane	110.00	55.00	35.00
(11)	James Collins	60.00	30.00	18.00
(12)	Joe Cronin	110.00	55.00	35.00
(13)	Alvin Crowder	60.00	30.00	18.00
(14)	"Dizzy" Dean	240.00	120.00	75.00
(15)	Paul Derringer	60.00	30.00	18.00
(16)	William Dickey	125.00	62.00	37.00
(17)	Leo Durocher	110.00	55.00	35.00
(18)	George Earnshaw	60.00	30.00	18.00
(19)	Richard Ferrell	110.00	55.00	35.00
(20)	Lew Fonseca	60.00	30.00	18.00
(21a)	Jimmy Fox (Name incorrect.)	225.00	110.00	70.00
(21b)	Jimmy Foxx (Name correct.)	185.00	95.00	55.00
(22)	Benny Frey	60.00	30.00	18.00
(23)	Frankie Frisch	110.00	55.00	35.00
(24)	Lou Gehrig	900.00	450.00	270.00
(25)	Charles Gehringer	110.00	55.00	35.00
(26)	Vernon Gomez	110.00	55.00	35.00
(27)	Ray Grabowski	60.00	30.00	18.00
(28)	Robert (Lefty) Grove	150.00	75.00	45.00
(29)	George (Mule) Haas	60.00	30.00	18.00
(30)	"Chick" Hafey	110.00	55.00	35.00
(31)	Stanley Harris	110.00	55.00	35.00
(32)	J. Francis Hogan	60.00	30.00	18.00
(33)	Ed Holley	60.00	30.00	18.00
(34)	Rogers Hornsby	150.00	75.00	45.00
(35)	Waite Hoyt	110.00	55.00	35.00
(36)	Walter Johnson	250.00	125.00	75.00
(37)	Jim Jordan	60.00	30.00	18.00
(38)	Joe Kuhel	60.00	30.00	18.00
(39)	Hal Lee	60.00	30.00	18.00
(40)	Gus Mancuso	60.00	30.00	18.00
(41)	Henry Manush	110.00	55.00	35.00
(42)	Fred Marberry	60.00	30.00	18.00
(43)	Pepper Martin	85.00	45.00	25.00
(44)	Oscar Melillo	60.00	30.00	18.00
(45)	Johnny Moore	60.00	30.00	18.00
(46)	Joe Morrissey	60.00	30.00	18.00
(47)	Joe Mowrey	60.00	30.00	18.00
(48)	Bob O'Farrell	60.00	30.00	18.00
(49)	Melvin Ott	125.00	65.00	35.00
(50)	Monte Pearson	60.00	30.00	18.00
(51)	Carl Reynolds	60.00	30.00	18.00
(52)	Charles Ruffing	110.00	55.00	35.00
(53)	Babe Ruth	1,000	500.00	300.00
(54)	John "Blondy" Ryan	60.00	30.00	18.00
(55)	Al Simmons	110.00	55.00	35.00
(56)	Al Spohrer	60.00	30.00	18.00
(57)	Gus Suhr	60.00	30.00	18.00
(58)	Steve Swetonic	60.00	30.00	18.00
(59)	Dazzy Vance	110.00	55.00	35.00
(60)	Joe Vosmik	60.00	30.00	18.00
(61)	Lloyd Waner	110.00	55.00	35.00
(62)	Paul Waner	110.00	55.00	35.00
(63)	Sam West	60.00	30.00	18.00
(64)	Earl Whitehill	60.00	30.00	18.00
(65)	Jimmy Wilson	60.00	30.00	18.00

1934 Butterfinger - Canadian (V94)

Similar to the U.S. issue, though smaller in size at 6-1/2" x 8-1/2", these black-and-white paper cards include a number of players not found in the U.S. issue. Like the "regular" Butterfinger cards, each of the Canadian pieces includes a facsimile autograph on the front; backs are blank. The existence of Canadian versions of Lou Gehrig and Babe Ruth are now questionable.

		NM	E	VG
Complete Set (58):		3,500	1,750	1,100
Common Player:		50.00	25.00	15.00
(1)	Earl Averill	100.00	50.00	30.00
(2)	Larry Benton	50.00	25.00	15.00
(3)	Jim Bottomly (Bottomley)	100.00	50.00	30.00
(4)	Tom Bridges	50.00	25.00	15.00
(5)	Bob Brown	50.00	25.00	15.00
(6)	Owen T. Carroll	50.00	25.00	15.00
(7)	Gordon (Mickey) Cochrane	100.00	50.00	30.00
(8)	Roger Cramer	50.00	25.00	15.00
(9)	Joe Cronin	100.00	50.00	30.00
(10)	Alvin Crowder	50.00	25.00	15.00
(11)	"Dizzy" Dean	185.00	95.00	55.00
(12)	Edward Delker	50.00	25.00	15.00
(13)	William Dickey	125.00	62.00	37.00
(14)	Richard Ferrell	100.00	50.00	30.00
(15)	Lew Fonseca	50.00	25.00	15.00
(16a)	Jimmy Fox (Name incorrect.)	145.00	75.00	45.00
(16b)	Jimmy Foxx (Name correct.)	145.00	75.00	45.00
(17)	Chick Fullis	50.00	25.00	15.00
(19)	Charles Gehringer	100.00	50.00	30.00
(20)	Vernon Gomez	100.00	50.00	30.00
(21)	Robert (Lefty) Grove	125.00	62.00	37.00
(22)	George (Mule) Haas	50.00	25.00	15.00
(23)	"Chick" Hafey	100.00	50.00	30.00
(24)	Stanley Harris	100.00	50.00	30.00
(25)	Frank Higgins	50.00	25.00	15.00
(26)	J. Francis Hogan	50.00	25.00	15.00
(27)	Ed Holley	50.00	25.00	15.00
(28)	Waite Hoyt	100.00	50.00	30.00
(29)	Jim Jordan	50.00	25.00	15.00
(30)	Hal Lee	50.00	25.00	15.00
(31)	Gus Mancuso	50.00	25.00	15.00
(32)	Oscar Melillo	50.00	25.00	15.00
(33)	Austin Moore	50.00	25.00	15.00
(34)	Randy Moore	50.00	25.00	15.00
(35)	Joe Morrissey	50.00	25.00	15.00
(36)	Joe Mowrey	50.00	25.00	15.00
(37)	Bobo Newsom	50.00	25.00	15.00
(38)	Ernie Orsatti	50.00	25.00	15.00
(39)	Carl Reynolds	50.00	25.00	15.00
(40)	Walter Roettger	50.00	25.00	15.00
(42)	John "Blondy" Ryan	50.00	25.00	15.00
(43)	John Salveson	50.00	25.00	15.00
(44)	Al Simmons	100.00	50.00	30.00
(45)	Al Smith	50.00	25.00	15.00
(46)	Harold Smith	50.00	25.00	15.00
(47)	Allyn Stout	50.00	25.00	15.00
(48)	Fresco Thompson	50.00	25.00	15.00
(49)	Art Veltman	50.00	25.00	15.00
(50)	Johnny Vergez	50.00	25.00	15.00
(51)	Gerald Walker	50.00	25.00	15.00
(52)	Paul Waner	100.00	50.00	30.00
(53)	Burgess Whitehead	50.00	25.00	15.00
(54)	Earl Whitehill	50.00	25.00	15.00
(55)	Robert Weiland	50.00	25.00	15.00
(56)	Jimmy Wilson	50.00	25.00	15.00
(57)	Bob Worthington	50.00	25.00	15.00
(58)	Tom Zachary	50.00	25.00	15.00

1911-14 Butter Krust Bread (D304)

(See 1911-14 General Baking Co. for checklist and values.)

1933 Button Gum

(See 1933 Cracker Jack.)

C

1909 Cabanas

In conjunction with a post-season visit by the A.L. Champion Detroit Tigers (who without Hall of Famer Ty Cobb and Sam Crawford won only four of 12 games from the locals), Cabanas brand cigarettes issued this set. About 1-1/2" x 2-1/4" the cards feature black-and-white portrait photos. Players from the Almendares team have a blue frame and some colorized blue details on their uniforms, Havana players are in red, the Tigers are in gray. Printed on backs of the cards is (roughly translated) "The best way to form a valuable collection of baseball players of the Cuban clubs and the foreign visitors is to smoke Cabanas." It is unknown whether the checklists presented here alphabetically are complete.

		NM	E	VG
Common Cuban Player:		600.00	300.00	175.00
Common Tigers Player:		900.00	450.00	275.00
ALMENDARES B.B.C.				
(1)	Rafael Almeida	700.00	350.00	210.00
(2)	Armando Cabanas	700.00	350.00	210.00
(3)	Alfredo Cabrera	600.00	300.00	175.00
(4)	Regino "Mamelo" Garcia	1,150	575.00	345.00
(5a)	Heliodoro Hidalgo (C.F.)	1,150	575.00	345.00
(5b)	Heliodoro Hidalgo (C.F. Jabuco)	1,150	575.00	345.00
(6)	Armando Marsans	700.00	350.00	210.00
(7)	Esteban Prats	600.00	300.00	175.00
(8)	Carlos "Bebe" Royer	700.00	350.00	210.00
HABANA B.B.C.				
(1)	Luis Bustamante	2,250	1,125	675.00
(2)	Luis "Chico" Gonzalez	600.00	300.00	175.00
(3)	Valentin "Sirique" Gonzalez	600.00	300.00	175.00
(4)	Ricardo Hernandez	600.00	300.00	175.00
(5)	Preston "Pete" Hill (VALUE UNDETERMINED)			
(6)	Angel D. Mesa	600.00	300.00	175.00
(7)	Augustin "Tinti" Molina	700.00	350.00	210.00
(8)	Carlos "Chino" Moran	600.00	300.00	175.00
(9)	Luis "Mulo" Padron	3,500	1,750	1,050
(10)	Elilio Palomino	600.00	300.00	175.00
(11)	Pastor H. Pareda	600.00	300.00	180.00
(12)	Agustin Parpetti	2,000	1,000	600.00
(13)	Inocencio Perez	600.00	300.00	175.00
(14)	Bruce Petway	7,500	3,750	2,250
(15)	Gonzalo Sanchez	600.00	300.00	175.00
DETROIT TIGERS				
(1)	C. Beckendorff (Beckendorf)	900.00	450.00	275.00
(2)	Owen (Donie) Bush	900.00	450.00	275.00
(3)	Hopke	900.00	450.00	275.00
(4)	David Jones	900.00	450.00	275.00
(5)	William Lelivelt	900.00	450.00	275.00
(6)	Matty Mc. Intyre	900.00	450.00	275.00
(7)	George Moriarty	900.00	450.00	275.00
(8)	George Mullin	900.00	450.00	275.00
(9)	Frank O'Laughlin (O'Loughlin) (Umpire)	1,800	900.00	550.00
(10)	Charles O'Leary	900.00	450.00	275.00
(11)	Charles Schmidt	900.00	450.00	275.00
(12)	Edgar Willetts (Willett)	900.00	450.00	275.00

1955 Cain's Jimmy Piersall

The date of issue is speculative for these promotional postcards. The borderless black-and-white photo on the front of the 3-1/2" x 5-1/2" cards shows the popular BoSox star in a fielding pose. A blue facsimile autograph is printed at top. The postcard-format back has a drawing of the product beneath an advertising message bearing Piersall's signature. Similar cards advertising Colonial Meats are also known.

	NM	E	VG
Autographed:	300.00	150.00	90.00
Jimmy Piersall (Mayonnaise.)	125.00	62.50	37.50
Jimmy Piersall (Potato chips.)	125.00	62.50	37.50
Jimmy Piersall (Riviera dressing.)	125.00	62.50	37.50

1965 California Angels Matchbook Covers

These 1-1/2" x 4-1/2" matchbooks can be found with the advertising of two different banks printed on them; both are products of the local Universal Match Corp., and are printed in black and gold on white on front, with the inside surface in black-and-white. The County National Bank version has the player portrait photo within a plain black frame. Inside, the CNB matchbooks have player identification and personal data and 1964 stats. There is also an offer to redeem 15 different players' matchbooks for two free game tickets. The Santa Ana Savings matchbooks have the same player information and ads for the bank and the Angels' radio station. The player photos on front of the Santa Ana matchbooks have a gold frame. Values shown are for complete but empty covers, with the striker surface intact. Complete matchbooks with matches bring about 2X the values quoted.

		NM	E	VG
Complete Set (15):		120.00	60.00	35.00
Common Player:		10.00	5.00	3.00
(1)	Dean Chance	12.50	6.25	3.75
(2)	Lu Clinton	10.00	5.00	3.00
(3)	Jim Fregosi	10.00	5.00	3.00
(4)	Ed Kirkpatrick	10.00	5.00	3.00
(5)	Bobby Knoop	10.00	5.00	3.00
(6)	Barry Latman	10.00	5.00	3.00
(7)	Bob Lee	10.00	5.00	3.00
(8)	Ken McBride	10.00	5.00	3.00
(9)	Fred Newman	10.00	5.00	3.00
(10)	Jimmy Piersall	20.00	10.00	6.00
(11)	Rick Reichardt	10.00	5.00	3.00
(12)	Bill Rigney	10.00	5.00	3.00
(13)	Bob Rodgers	10.00	5.00	3.00
(14)	Tom Satriano	10.00	5.00	3.00
(15)	Willie Smith	10.00	5.00	3.00

1976 California Pacific Bank

Whether these are a legitimate promotional issue or a made-for-collectors set is unknown. The cards may have been created for use at autograph appearances at a Fullerton, Calif., bank. About 3-5/8" x 5", though the size varies, the black-and-white blank-back cards have player photos on front (some of which are reproductions of team-issued photos) and a promotional message describing the bank's "Big League Service." Two poses of Steve Carlton are known.

		NM	E	VG
Complete Set (7):		60.00	30.00	18.00
Common Player:		5.00	2.50	1.50
(1)	Steve Busby	5.00	2.50	1.50
(2)	Steve Carlton	15.00	7.50	4.50
(3)	Steve Carlton	15.00	7.50	4.50
(4)	Bill Russell	5.00	2.50	1.50
(5)	Mike Schmidt	20.00	10.00	6.00
(6)	Ted Simmons	5.00	2.50	1.50
(7)	Don Sutton	10.00	5.00	3.00

1950 Callahan Hall of Fame

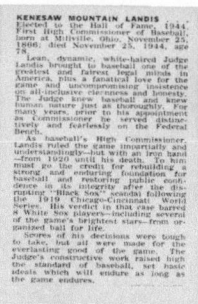

These cards, which feature artist Mario DeMarco's drawings of Hall of Famers, were produced from 1950 through 1956 and sold by the Baseball Hall of Fame in Cooperstown and at major league ballparks. The cards measure 1-3/4" x 2-1/2" and include a detailed player biography on the back. When introduced in 1950 the set included all members of the Hall of Fame up to that time, and then new cards were added each year as more players were elected. Therefore, cards of players appearing in all previous editions are more common than those players who appeared in just one or two years. When the set was discontinued in 1956 it consisted of 82 cards, which is now considered a complete set. The cards are not numbered and are listed here alphabetically. B.E. Callahan of Chicago, the publisher of "Who's Who in Baseball," produced the card set.

		NM	E	VG
Original 1950 Boxed Set (62):		500.00	250.00	150.00
Complete Set (82):		750.00	370.00	220.00
Common Player:		6.00	3.00	1.75
(1)	Grover Alexander	25.00	12.50	7.50
(2)	"Cap" Anson	15.00	7.50	4.50
(3)	J. Franklin "Home Run" Baker	150.00	75.00	45.00
(4)	Edward G. Barrow	35.00	17.50	10.00
(5a)	Charles "Chief" Bender (Bio ends " . . . immortal name for him.")	25.00	12.50	7.50
(5b)	Charles "Chief" Bender (Bio ends " . . . died in 1954.")	35.00	17.50	10.00
(6)	Roger Bresnahan	10.00	5.00	3.00
(7)	Dan Brouthers	15.00	7.50	4.50
(8)	Mordecai Brown	10.00	5.00	3.00
(9)	Morgan G. Bulkeley	10.00	5.00	3.00
(10)	Jesse Burkett	16.00	8.00	4.75
(11)	Alexander Cartwright	12.50	6.25	3.75
(12)	Henry Chadwick	12.00	6.00	3.50
(13)	Frank Chance	16.00	8.00	4.75
(14)	Albert B. Chandler	225.00	115.00	70.00
(15)	Jack Chesbro	7.50	3.75	2.25
(16)	Fred Clarke	10.00	5.00	3.00
(17)	Ty Cobb	50.00	25.00	15.00
(18a)	Mickey Cochran (Name incorrect.)	10.00	5.00	3.00
(18b)	Mickey Cochrane (Name correct.)	12.00	6.00	3.50
(19a)	Eddie Collins (had every . . . " Second paragraph of bio begins "Eddie)	9.00	4.50	2.75
(19b)	Eddie Collins (brilliant . . . " Second paragraph of bio begins "He was)	13.50	6.75	4.00
(20)	Jimmie Collins	12.50	6.25	3.75
(21)	Charles A. Comiskey	12.50	6.25	3.75
(22)	Tom Connolly	50.00	25.00	15.00
(23)	Candy Cummings	9.00	4.50	2.75
(24)	Dizzy Dean	45.00	22.50	13.50
(25)	Ed Delahanty	6.00	3.00	1.75
(26a)	Bill Dickey (was right-handed all the way." First paragraph of bio ends " . . . He)	75.00	37.00	22.00
(26b)	Bill Dickey (during his final year." First paragraph of bio ends " . . .)	35.00	17.50	10.50
(27)	Joe DiMaggio	180.00	90.00	54.00
(28)	Hugh Duffy	7.50	3.75	2.25
(29)	Johnny Evers	13.50	6.75	4.00
(30)	Buck Ewing	10.00	5.00	3.00
(31)	Jimmie Foxx	20.00	10.00	6.00
(32)	Frank Frisch	6.00	3.00	1.75
(33)	Lou Gehrig	85.00	42.50	25.00
(34a)	Charles Gehringer (White cap.)	9.00	4.50	2.75
(34b)	Charlie Gehringer (Dark cap.)	11.00	5.50	3.25
(35)	Clark Griffith	6.00	3.00	1.75
(36)	Lefty Grove	10.00	5.00	3.00

		NM	E	VG
(37)	Leo "Gabby" Hartnett	40.00	20.00	12.00
(38)	Harry Heilmann	30.00	15.00	9.00
(39)	Rogers Hornsby	16.00	8.00	4.75
(40)	Carl Hubbell	12.00	6.00	3.50
(41)	Hughey Jennings	6.00	3.00	1.75
(42)	Ban Johnson	7.50	3.75	2.25
(43)	Walter Johnson	10.00	5.00	3.00
(44)	Willie Keeler	7.50	3.75	2.25
(45)	Mike Kelly	10.00	5.00	3.00
(46)	Bill Klem	50.00	25.00	15.00
(47)	Napoleon Lajoie	11.00	5.50	3.25
(48)	Kenesaw M. Landis	6.00	3.00	1.75
(49)	Ted Lyons	100.00	50.00	30.00
(50)	Connie Mack	12.00	6.00	3.50
(51)	Walter Maranville	20.00	10.00	6.00
(52)	Christy Mathewson	25.00	12.50	7.50
(53)	Tommy McCarthy	12.50	6.25	3.75
(54)	Joe McGinnity	6.00	3.00	1.75
(55)	John McGraw	10.00	5.00	3.00
(56)	Charles Nichols	16.00	8.00	4.75
(57)	Jim O'Rourke	9.00	4.50	2.75
(58)	Mel Ott	16.00	8.00	4.75
(59)	Herb Pennock	9.00	4.50	2.75
(60)	Eddie Plank	10.00	5.00	3.00
(61)	Charles Radbourne	10.00	5.00	3.00
(62)	Wilbert Robinson	6.00	3.00	1.75
(63)	Babe Ruth	100.00	50.00	30.00
(64)	Ray "Cracker" Schalk	30.00	15.00	9.00
(65)	Al Simmons	60.00	30.00	18.00
(66a)	George Sisler (Bio ends "Sisler today is . . . ")	13.50	6.75	4.00
(66b)	George Sisler (Bio ends "Sisler was chosen as . . . ")	9.00	4.50	2.75
(67)	A. G. Spalding	10.00	5.00	3.00
(68)	Tris Speaker	16.00	8.00	4.75
(69)	Bill Terry	30.00	15.00	9.00
(70)	Joe Tinker	10.00	5.00	3.00
(71)	"Pie" Traynor	10.00	5.00	3.00
(72)	Clarence A. "Dazzy" Vance	30.00	15.00	9.00
(73)	Rube Waddell	9.00	4.50	2.75
(74)	Hans Wagner	30.00	15.00	9.00
(75)	Bobby Wallace	13.50	6.75	4.00
(76)	Ed Walsh	10.00	5.00	3.00
(77a)	Paul Waner (Complete black frame line around picture.)	9.00	4.50	2.75
(77b)	Paul Waner (Bottom missing on black frame line around picture.)	40.00	20.00	12.00
(78)	George Wright	15.00	7.50	4.50
(79)	Harry Wright	40.00	20.00	12.00
(80)	Cy Young	12.50	6.25	3.75
(---)	Museum Exterior View (No date at top of list on back.)	35.00	17.50	10.00
(---)	Museum Exterior View (Date "1954" on top of list on back.)	60.00	30.00	18.00
(---)	Museum Interior View (men.) Back copy ends, ". . . to all baseball)	30.00	15.00	9.00
(---)	Museum Interior View (concluded." Back copy ends " . . . playing days are)	13.50	6.75	4.00

1898 Cameo Pepsin Gum Pins (1896-97 Whitehead & Hoag Pins)

(The following has been updated courtesy of Keith Olbermann in 2012, with the new proposed titles in parenthesis above).

The first large set of baseball player pins is this issue from Whitehead & Hoag, advertising Cameo Pepsin Gum. The 1-1/4" pins have a sepia player portrait photo at center, with name and team at top left and right. It is very difficult to find pins with clear pictures as they tend to darken or fade with time. Pins were issued with a paper inset in back advertising the gum, but are often found with the paper missing. It is likely that there will be future additions to this checklist. The unnumbered pins are presented here in alphabetical order. Those with a "*" are known with both Whitehead & Hoag or Cameo backs.

		NM	E	VG
	Common Player:	1,300	650.00	400.00
(1)	John Anderson (Brooklyn)	1,300	650.00	400.00
(2)	Cap Anson (Chicago)	3,300	1,300	800.00
(3)	Jimmy Bannon (Boston)	1,300	650.00	400.00
(4)	Billy Barnie(Brooklyn)	1,300	650.00	400.00
(5)	Marty Bergen (Boston)	1,300	650.00	400.00
(6)	Beville (Indianapolis)	1,300	650.00	400.00
(7)	Louis Bierbauer (Pittsburg)	1,300	650.00	400.00
(8)	Frank Bowerman (Balt.)	1,300	650.00	400.00
(9)	Ted Breitenstein (Cincinnati*)	1,300	650.00	400.00
(10)	Herbert "Buttons" Briggs (Chicago)	1,300	650.00	400.00
(11a)	Richard Brown (Cincinnati on shirt)	1,300	650.00	400.00
(11b)	Richard Brown (no name readable on shirt)	1,300	650.00	400.00
(12)	Eddie Burk (Burke) (Cincinnati)	1,300	650.00	400.00
(13a)	Jesse Burkett (Cleveland) ("Cameo Pepsin Pin" ad)	4,000	2,000	1,200
(13b)	Jesse Burkett (Cleveland) ("On Time Starch, Soda, and Yeast" ad)	4,000	2,000	1,200
(14)	Frank "Buster" Burrell (Brooklyn)	1,300	650.00	400.00
(15)	Jimmy Canavan (Brooklyn)	1,300	650.00	400.00
(16)	Cupid Childs (Cleveland)	1,300	650.00	400.00
(17)	William (Dad) Clark (Clarke) (N.Y.)	1,300	650.00	400.00
(18)	Boileryard Clark (Clarke) (Balt.)	1,300	650.00	400.00
(19)	Jack Clements (Phila.)	1,300	650.00	400.00
(20)	James Corkman (Cockman) (Indianapolis)	1,300	650.00	400.00
(21)	Archibald B. Cole (Cedar Rapids)	1,300	650.00	400.00
(22)	Jimmy Collins (Boston)	2,850	1,300	800.00
(23)	Tommy Corcoran (Cincinnati)	1,300	650.00	400.00
(24)	Lave Cross (Phila.)	1,300	650.00	400.00
(25)	Nig Cuppy Cleveland)	1,300	650.00	400.00
(26)	Bill Dahlen Chicago)	1,300	650.00	400.00
(27a)	Bill Dammon (Dammann) (Cincinnati) ("Cameo Pepsin Pin" ad)	1,300	650.00	400.00
(27b)	Bill Dammon (Dammann) ("On Time Starch, Soda and Yeast" ad)	1,300	650.00	400.00
(28)	Dan Daub (Brooklyn)	1,300	650.00	400.00
(29)	George Decker (Chicago)	1,300	650.00	400.00
(30)	Ed Delahanty (Phila.)	3,300	1,300	800.00
(31)	Cozy Dolan (Boston)*	1,300	650.00	400.00
(32)	Tim Donahue (Chicago)	1,300	650.00	400.00
(33)	Frank Donnelly (Cedar Rapids)	1,300	650.00	400.00
(34)	Patsy Donovan (Pittsburg)	1,300	650.00	400.00
(35)	Hugh Duffy (Boston)	2,850	1,300	800.00
(36)	Jack Dunn (Brooklyn)	1,300	650.00	400.00
(37)	Frank Dwyer (Cincinnati)*	1,300	650.00	400.00
(38a)	Bones Ely (Pittsburgh) (thick lettering)	1,300	650.00	400.00
(38b)	Bones Ely (thin lettering)	1,300	650.00	650.00
(39)	Bill Everett (Everitt) (Chicago)	1,300	650.00	400.00
(40a)	Buck Ewing (Cincinnati) ("Mgr." just touches cap)	5,000	2,500	1,500
(40b)	Buck Ewing ("Mgr." does not touch cap)	5,000	2,500	1,500
(41)	James Fields (Buffalo)	1,300	650.00	400.00
(42)	Chauncey Fisher (Brooklyn)	1,300	650.00	400.00
(43)	Al Fisher (Brooklyn)	1,300	650.00	400.00
(44)	Tim Flood (Cedar Rapids)	1,300	650.00	400.00
(45)	Frank Foreman (Indianapolis)	1,300	650.00	400.00
(46)	James Franklin (Owner - Buffalo)	1,300	650.00	400.00
(47)	William Fuller (Cedar Rapids)	1,300	650.00	400.00
(48)	Charlie Ganzel (Boston)	1,300	650.00	400.00
(49)	Jot Goar (Pittsburgh) *	1,300	650.00	400.00
(50)	Jot Goar (Indianapolis)	1,300	650.00	400.00
(51)	Bill Gray (Indianapolis)*	1,300	650.00	400.00
(52)	Mike Griffin (Brooklyn)	1,300	650.00	400.00
(53)	Clark Griffith (Chicago)	2,650	1,300	800.00
(54)	John Grim (Brooklyn)*	1,300	650.00	400.00
(55)	Billy Hamilton (Boston)	2,750	1,375	825.00
(56)	Joseph Harrington (Boston)	1,300	650.00	400.00
(57a)	Bill Hart (right side background brown, "Mgr. Chicago" barely readable, photo borders visible on both sides)	1,300	650.00	400.00
(57b)	Bill Hart (right side background gray, "Mgr. Chicago" easily readable, no photo borders visible)*	1,300	650.00	400.00
(58a)	Charles Hastings (Pittsburg) (thick lettering)	1,300	650.00	400.00
(58b)	Charles Hastings (thin lettering)	1,300	650.00	400.00
(59)	Pink Hawley (Pittsburg)*	1,300	650.00	400.00
(60)	Belden Hill (Cedar Rapids)	1,300	650.00	400.00
(61)	Bill Hoffer (Balt.)	1,300	650.00	400.00
(62)	George Hogriever (Indianapolis)	1,300	650.00	400.00
(63)	Bug Holliday (Cincinnati)	1,300	650.00	400.00
(64)	Elmer Horton (Balt.)	1,300	650.00	400.00
(65a)	Dummy Hoy ("Cincinnati" readable on shirt)	2,450	1,550	900.00
(66b)	Dummy Hoy (Cincinnati) (no name readable on shirt)	2,450	1,550	900.00
(66a)	Jim Hughey (Pittsburg) (Cropping line visible under "Pittsburg")	1,300	650.00	400.00
(66b)	Jim Hughey (no cropping line visible under "Pittsburg")*	1,300	650.00	400.00
(67)	Edwin Hutchinson (Cedar Rapids)	1,300	650.00	400.00
(68)	Charlie Irwin (Cincinnati)	1,300	650.00	400.00
(69)	Hughie Jennings (Balt.)	2,650	1,300	800.00
(70)	Willie Keeler (Baltimore)	2,650	1,300	800.00
(71)	Brickyard Kennedy (Brooklyn)	1,300	650.00	400.00
(72)	A.F. Kennedy (Cedar Rapids)	1,300	650.00	400.00
(73)	Frank Killen (Pittsburg, thick lettering)	1,300	650.00	400.00
(73b)	Frank Killen (Pittsburg, thin lettering)	1,300	650.00	400.00
(74)	Malachi Kittredge (Chicago)	1,300	650.00	400.00
(75)	Candy LaChance (Brooklyn)	1,300	650.00	400.00
(76)	Bill Lange (Chicago)	1,300	650.00	400.00
(77)	Herman Long (Boston)	1,300	650.00	400.00
(78)	Bobby Lowe (Boston)	1,300	650.00	400.00
(79a)	Denny Lyons (Pittsburg) (Cropping line visible under "Pittsburg")	1,300	650.00	400.00
(79b)	Denny Lyons (No cropping line visible under "Pittsburg")*	1,300	650.00	400.00
(80)	Connie Mack (Pittsburg)	3,300	1,300	800.00
(81)	Louis Mahaffy (Mahaffey) (Cedar Rapids)	1,300	650.00	400.00
(82)	Willard Mains (Boston)	1,300	650.00	400.00
(83)	Jimmy McAleer (Cleveland)	1,300	650.00	400.00
(84)	Barry McCormick (Chicago)	1,300	650.00	400.00
(85)	McDougal (Cedar Rapids)	1,300	650.00	400.00
(86)	Chippy McGarr (Cleveland)	1,300	650.00	400.00
(87)	John McGraw (Balt.)	1,750	1,100	650.00
(88)	Ed McKean (Cleveland)	1,300	650.00	400.00
(89)	Sadie McMann (McMahon) (Brooklyn)	1,300	650.00	400.00
(90)	Bid McPhee (Cincinnati)	4,200	2,450	1,100
(91a)	Bill Merritt (Pittsburg) (Beckley's head visible in front of "Pittsburg" uniform lettering)	1,300	650.00	400.00
(91b)	Bill Merritt (Pittsburg) (Beckley's head, "Pittsburg" uniform lettering erased)	1,300	650.00	400.00
(92a)	Dusty Miller (Cincinnati) ("Cameo Pepsin Pin" ad)	1,300	650.00	400.00
(92b)	Dusty Miller (Cincinnati) ("On Time Starch, Soda, and Yeast" ad)	1,300	650.00	400.00
(93)	Frank Motz (Indianapolis)	1,300	650.00	400.00

(94a) Kid Nichols (Boston, thick lettering) — 2,750 — 1,375 — 825.00
(94b) Kid Nichols (Boston, thin lettering) — 2,750 — 1,375 — 825.00
(95) Tom O'Brien (Balt.) — 1,300 — 650.00 — 400.00
(96) Jack O'Connor (Cleveland)* — 1,300 — 650.00 — 400.00
(97) John Pappaulan (Pappalau) (R.F., Cleveland)) — 1,300 — 650.00 — 400.00
(98) Harley Payne (Brooklyn) — 1,300 — 650.00 — 400.00
(99) Heinie Peitz (Cincinnati)* — 1,300 — 650.00 — 400.00
(100) Silver Bill Phillips (Indianapolis) — 1,300 — 650.00 — 400.00
(101) Arlie Pond (Baltimore) — 1,300 — 650.00 — 400.00
(102) Jack Powell (Cleveland)* — 1,300 — 650.00 — 400.00
(103) Joe Quinn (Balt.) — 1,300 — 650.00 — 400.00
(104) Bill Reidy (Milwaukee) — 1,300 — 650.00 — 400.00
(105) Heinie Reitz (Baltimore) — 1,300 — 650.00 — 400.00
(106) Billy Rhines (Cincinnati) — 1,300 — 650.00 — 400.00
(107) Claude Richie (Ritchey) (Cincinnati)* — 1,300 — 650.00 — 400.00
(108) Jack Rowe (Buffalo) — 1,300 — 650.00 — 400.00
(109) Jimmy Ryan (Chicago)* — 1,300 — 650.00 — 400.00
(110a) Jack (John) Ryan (Boston, thick lettering)) — 1,300 — 650.00 — 400.00
(110b) Jack (John) Ryan (Boston, thin lettering) — 1,300 — 650.00 — 400.00
(111) Pop Schreiver (Schriver) (Cincinnati)* — 1,300 — 650.00 — 400.00
(112) Cy Seymour (N.Y.) — 1,300 — 650.00 — 400.00
(113) Billy Shindle (Brooklyn) — 1,300 — 650.00 — 400.00
(114) Harry T. Smith (Buffalo) — 1,300 — 650.00 — 400.00
(115) Elmer Smith (Pittsburg)* — 1,300 — 650.00 — 400.00
(116) Broadway Aleck Smith (Brooklyn) — 1,300 — 650.00 — 400.00
(117) Germany Smith (Brooklyn) — 1,300 — 650.00 — 400.00
(118) Louis Sockalexis (Cleveland) — 2,000 — 1,300 — 650.00
(119) George Speer (Milwaukee) — 1,300 — 650.00 — 400.00
(120) Jake Stentzel (Stenzel) (Balt.)* — 1,300 — 650.00 — 400.00
(121) Jack Stivetts (Boston) — 1,300 — 650.00 — 400.00
(122) Joe Sugden (Pittsburg)* — 1,300 — 650.00 — 400.00
(123) Jim "Suter" Sullivan (Buffalo) — 1,300 — 650.00 — 400.00
(124) Patsy Tebeau (Cleveland)* — 1,300 — 650.00 — 400.00
(125) Fred Tenney (Boston) — 1,300 — 650.00 — 400.00
(126) Adonis Terry (Chicago)* — 1,300 — 650.00 — 400.00
(127) Tommy Tucker (Boston) — 1,300 — 650.00 — 400.00
(128) William Urquhart (Buffalo) — 1,300 — 650.00 — 400.00
(129) Edward Van Buren (Cedar Rapids) — 1,300 — 650.00 — 400.00
(130a) Farmer Vaughn ("Cincinnati" readable on shirt) — 1,300 — 650.00 — 400.00
(130b) Farmer Vaughn (Cincinnati) (no name readable on shirt) — 1,300 — 650.00 — 400.00
(131) Bobby Wallace (Cleveland) — 2,650 — 1,300 — 800.00
(132) Bill Watkins (Indianapolis) — 1,300 — 650.00 — 400.00
(133) William Weaver (Milwaukee) — 1,300 — 650.00 — 400.00
(134) Robert Wood (Indianapolis) — 1,300 — 650.00 — 400.00
(135) Cy Young (Cleveland)* — 6,000 — 3,000 — 1,800
(136) Chief Zimmer (Cleveland) — 1,300 — 625.00 — 400.00
(137) 1897 Baltimore Base Ball Club ("champions of '96") — 1,400 — 700.00 — 400.00
(138) Brooklyn B.B. Club — 1,400 — 700.00 — 400.00
(139a) Buffalo B.B. Club (dated 1897; no photographer's credit) — 1,400 — 700.00 — 400.00
(139b) Buffalo B.B. Club (no date; photographer's credit) — 1,400 — 700.00 — 400.00
(140) Indianapolis B.B. Club — 1,400 — 700.00 — 400.00
(141) New Castle B.B. Club — 1,400 — 700.00 — 400.00
(142) Pittsburg B.B. Club* — 1,400 — 700.00 — 400.00
(143) Toronto B.B. Club* — 1,400 — 700.00 — 400.00

1958 Roy Campanella Career Summary Card

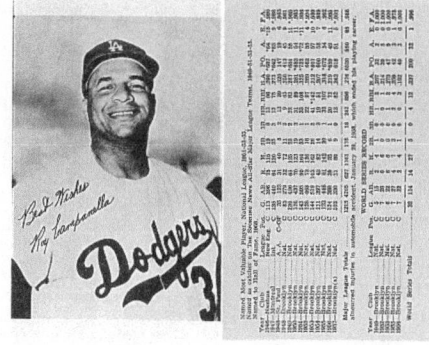

This card was probably produced to allow Campy to respond to fan mail following his career-ending auto wreck in 1957. The 3-1/8" x 5" card is printed in black-and-white on thin semi-gloss cardboard. Front has a portrait photo and facsimile autograph, with a white stripe at top and bottom. The back has a career statistical summary, apparently taken from a contemporary Baseball Register.

	NM	E	VG
Roy Campanella	30.00	15.00	9.00

1974 Capital Publishing Co.

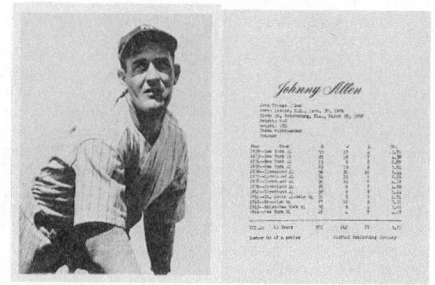

This ambitious collectors issue offered more than 100 cards of "old-timers" in an attractive 4-1/8" x 5-1/4" format. Card fronts have black-and-white photos with white borders all-around. Backs have player identification, biographical data and major league stats.

	NM	E	VG
Complete Set (104):	200.00	100.00	60.00
Common Player:	6.00	3.00	1.75
1 Babe Ruth	15.00	7.50	4.50
2 Lou Gehrig	10.00	5.00	3.00
3 Ty Cobb	9.00	4.50	2.75
4 Jackie Robinson	7.50	3.75	2.25
5 Roger Connor	6.00	3.00	1.75
6 Harry Heilmann	6.00	3.00	1.75
7 Clark Griffith	6.00	3.00	1.75
8 Ed Walsh	6.00	3.00	1.75
9 Hugh Duffy	6.00	3.00	1.75
10 Russ Christopher	6.00	3.00	1.75
11 Snuffy Stirnweiss	6.00	3.00	1.75
12 Willie Keeler	6.00	3.00	1.75
13 Buck Ewing	6.00	3.00	1.75
14 Tony Lazzeri	6.00	3.00	1.75
15 King Kelly	6.00	3.00	1.75
16 Jimmy McAleer	6.00	3.00	1.75
17 Frank Chance	6.00	3.00	1.75
18 Sam Zoldak	6.00	3.00	1.75
19 Christy Mathewson	7.50	3.75	2.25
20 Eddie Collins	6.00	3.00	1.75
21 Cap Anson	6.00	3.00	1.75
22 Steve Evans	6.00	3.00	1.75
23 Mordecai Brown	6.00	3.00	1.75
24 Don Black	6.00	3.00	1.75
25 Home Run Baker	6.00	3.00	1.75
26 Jack Chesbro	6.00	3.00	1.75
27 Gil Hodges	6.00	3.00	1.75
28 Dan Brouthers	6.00	3.00	1.75
29 Don Hoak	6.00	3.00	1.75
30 Herb Pennock	6.00	3.00	1.75
31 Vern Stephens	6.00	3.00	1.75
32 Cy Young	7.50	3.75	2.25
33 Ed Cicotte	7.50	3.75	2.25
34 Sam Jones	6.00	3.00	1.75
35 Ed Waitkus	6.00	3.00	1.75
36 Roger Bresnahan	6.00	3.00	1.75
37 Fred Merkle	6.00	3.00	1.75
38 Ed Delehanty (Delahanty)	6.00	3.00	1.75
39 Tris Speaker	6.00	3.00	1.75
40 Fred Clarke	6.00	3.00	1.75
41 Johnny Evers	6.00	3.00	1.75
42 Mickey Cochrane	6.00	3.00	1.75
43 Nap Lajoie	6.00	3.00	1.75
44 Charles Comiskey	6.00	3.00	1.75
45 Sam Crawford	6.00	3.00	1.75
46 Ban Johnson	6.00	3.00	1.75
47 Ray Schalk	6.00	3.00	1.75
48 Pat Moran	6.00	3.00	1.75
49 Walt Judnich	6.00	3.00	1.75
50 Bill Killefer	6.00	3.00	1.75
51 Jimmie Foxx	6.00	3.00	1.75
52 Red Rolfe	6.00	3.00	1.75
53 Howie Pollett	6.00	3.00	1.75
54 Wally Pipp	6.00	3.00	1.75
55 Chief Bender	6.00	3.00	1.75
56 Connie Mack	6.00	3.00	1.75
57 Bump Hadley	6.00	3.00	1.75
58 Al Simmons	6.00	3.00	1.75
59 Hughie Jennings	6.00	3.00	1.75
60 Johnny Allen	6.00	3.00	1.75
61 Fred Snodgrass	6.00	3.00	1.75
62 Heinie Manush	6.00	3.00	1.75
63 Dazzy Vance	6.00	3.00	1.75
64 George Sisler	6.00	3.00	1.75
65 Jim Bottomley	6.00	3.00	1.75
66 Ray Chapman	6.00	3.00	1.75
67 Hal Chase	6.00	3.00	1.75
68 Jack Barry	6.00	3.00	1.75
69 George Burns	6.00	3.00	1.75
70 Jim Barrett	6.00	3.00	1.75
71 Grover Alexander	6.00	3.00	1.75
72 Elmer Flick	6.00	3.00	1.75
73 Jake Flowers	6.00	3.00	1.75
74 Al Orth	6.00	3.00	1.75
75 Cliff Aberson	6.00	3.00	1.75
76 Moe Berg	7.50	3.75	2.25
77 Bill Bradley	6.00	3.00	1.75
78 Max Bishop	6.00	3.00	1.75
79 Jimmy Austin	6.00	3.00	1.75
80 Beals Becker	6.00	3.00	1.75
81 Jack Clements	6.00	3.00	1.75
82 Cy Blanton	6.00	3.00	1.75
83 Garland Braxton	6.00	3.00	1.75
84 Red Ames	6.00	3.00	1.75
85 Hippo Vaughn	6.00	3.00	1.75
86 Ray Caldwell	6.00	3.00	1.75
87 Clint Brown	6.00	3.00	1.75
88 Joe Jackson	15.00	7.50	4.50
89 Pete Appleton	6.00	3.00	1.75
90 Ed Brandt	6.00	3.00	1.75
91 Walter Johnson	7.50	3.75	2.25
92 Dizzy Dean	6.00	3.00	1.75
93 Nick Altrock	6.00	3.00	1.75
94 Buck Weaver	7.50	3.75	2.25
95 George Blaeholder	6.00	3.00	1.75
96 Jim Bagby Sr.	6.00	3.00	1.75
97 Ted Blankenship	6.00	3.00	1.75
98 Babe Adams	6.00	3.00	1.75
99 Lefty Williams	7.50	3.75	2.25
100 Tommy Bridges	6.00	3.00	1.75
101 Rube Benton	6.00	3.00	1.75
102 Unknown	6.00	3.00	1.75
103 Max Butcher	6.00	3.00	1.75
104 Chick Gandil	7.50	3.75	2.25

1945-46 Caramelo Deportivo Cuban League

One of the better-known of Cuba's baseball card issues is the 100-card set issued by Caramelo Deportivo (Sporting Caramels) covering the 1945-46 Cuban winter league season. Printed in black-and-white on very thin 1-7/8" x 2-5/8" paper, the cards were intended to be pasted into an album issued for the purpose. Fronts have a card number, but no player identification; backs have the player's name, a few biographical and career details and an ad for the issuer, in as many as three different configurations. Many former and future Major Leaguers and stars of the U.S. Negro Leagues will be found on this checklist; sometimes providing the only cards issued contemporary with their playing careers.

		NM	E	VG
	Complete Set, No Reyes (99):	6,500	3,250	1,950
	Common Player:	25.00	12.50	7.50
	Album:	200.00	100.00	60.00
1	Caramelo Deportivo Title Card	7.50	3.75	2.25
2	Action Scene	12.50	6.25	3.75
3	Amado Maestri (Umpire)	25.00	12.50	7.50
4	Bernardino Rodriguez (Umpire)	25.00	12.50	7.50
5	Quico Magrinat (Umpire)	25.00	12.50	7.50
6	Cuco Conder (Announcer)	25.00	12.50	7.50
7	Marianao Team Banner	10.00	5.00	3.00
8	Armando Marsans	75.00	37.50	22.00
9	Jose Fernandez	25.00	12.50	7.50
10	Jose Luis Colas	25.00	12.50	7.50
11	"Charlotio" Orta (Charolito)	25.00	12.50	7.50
12	Barney Serrell	50.00	25.00	15.00
13	Claro Duany	30.00	15.00	9.00
14	Antonio Castanos	25.00	12.50	7.50
15	Virgilio Arteaga	25.00	12.50	7.50
16	Gilberto Valdivia	25.00	12.50	7.50
17	Jugo Cabrera	25.00	12.50	7.50
18	Lazaro Salazar	75.00	37.50	22.00
19	Julio Moreno	25.00	12.50	7.50
20	Oliverio Ortiz	25.00	12.50	7.50
21	Lou Knerr	25.00	12.50	7.50
22	Francisco Campos	25.00	12.50	7.50
23	Red Adams	25.00	12.50	7.50
24	Sandalio Consuegra	25.00	12.50	7.50
25	Ray Dandridge	1,500	750.00	450.00
26	Booker McDaniels	40.00	20.00	12.00
27	Orestes Minoso	675.00	335.00	200.00
28	Daniel Parra	25.00	12.50	7.50
29	Roberto Estalella	25.00	12.50	7.50
30	Raymond Brown	1,900	950.00	575.00
31	Havana Team Banner	10.00	5.00	3.00
32	Miguel Gonzalez	40.00	20.00	12.00
33	Julio Rojo	25.00	12.50	7.50
34	Herberto Blanco	25.00	12.50	7.50
35	Pedro Formenthal	30.00	15.00	9.00
36	Rene Monteagudo	25.00	12.50	7.50
37	Carlos Blanco	25.00	12.50	7.50
38	Salvandor Hernandez	25.00	12.50	7.50
39	Rogelio Linares	25.00	12.50	7.50
40	Antonio Ordenana	25.00	12.50	7.50
41	Pedro Jiminez	25.00	12.50	7.50
42	Charley Kaiser	25.00	12.50	7.50
43	Manuel "Cocaina" Garcia	80.00	40.00	24.00
44	Sagua Hernandez	25.00	12.50	7.50
45	Lou Klein	25.00	12.50	7.50
46	Manuel Hidalgo	25.00	12.50	7.50
47	Dick Sisler	35.00	17.50	10.00
48	Jim Rebel	25.00	12.50	7.50
49	Raul Navarro	25.00	12.50	7.50
50	Pedero Medina	25.00	12.50	7.50
51	Charlie (Terries) McDuffie	75.00	37.50	22.00
52	Fred Martin	25.00	12.50	7.50
53	Julian Acosta	25.00	12.50	7.50
54	Cienfuegos Team Banner	10.00	5.00	3.00
55	Adolfo Luque	125.00	62.00	37.00
56	Jose Ramos	25.00	12.50	7.50
57	Conrado Perez	25.00	12.50	7.50
58	Antonio Rodriguez	25.00	12.50	7.50
59	Alejandro Crespo	30.00	15.00	9.00
60	Roland Gladu	25.00	12.50	7.50
61	Pedro Pages	25.00	12.50	7.50
62	Silvio Garcia	80.00	40.00	24.00
63	Carlos Colas	25.00	12.50	7.50
64	Salvatore Maglie	125.00	60.00	35.00
65	Martin Dihigo	4,500	2,200	1,350
66	Luis Tiant Sr.	185.00	90.00	55.00
67	Jim Roy	25.00	12.50	7.50
68	Ramon Roger	25.00	12.50	7.50
69	Adrian Zabala	25.00	12.50	7.50
70	Armando Gallart	25.00	12.50	7.50
71	Jose Zardon	25.00	12.50	7.50
72	Ray Berres	25.00	12.50	7.50
73	Napoleon Reyes (SP)	2,400	1,200	725.00
74	Jose Gomez	25.00	12.50	7.50
75	Loevigildo Xiques	25.00	12.50	7.50
76	Almendares Team Banner	10.00	5.00	3.00
77	Reinaldo Coreiro	25.00	12.50	7.50
78	Bartalo Portaundo (Bartolo Portuondo)	25.00	12.50	7.50
79	Jacinto Roque	25.00	12.50	7.50
80	Hector Arago	25.00	12.50	7.50
81	Gilberto Torres	30.00	15.00	9.00
82	Roberto Ortiz	30.00	15.00	9.00
83	Hector Rodriguez	25.00	12.50	7.50
84	Chifian Clark	40.00	20.00	12.00
85	Fermin Guerra	30.00	15.00	9.00
86	Jorge Comellas	25.00	12.50	7.50
87	Regino Otero	25.00	12.50	7.50
88	Tomas de la Cruz	30.00	15.00	9.00
89	Mario Diaz	25.00	12.50	7.50
90	Luis Aloma	25.00	12.50	7.50
91	Lloyd Davenport	40.00	20.00	12.00
92	Agapito Mayor	25.00	12.50	7.50
93	Ramon Bragana	100.00	50.00	30.00
94	Avelino Canizares	25.00	12.50	7.50
95	Santiago Ulrich	25.00	12.50	7.50
96	Beto Avila	50.00	25.00	15.00
97	Santos Amaro	30.00	15.00	9.00
98	Andres Fleitas	25.00	12.50	7.50
99	Limonar Martinez	25.00	12.50	7.50
100	Juan Montero	25.00	12.50	7.50

1946-47 Caramelo Deportivo Cuban League

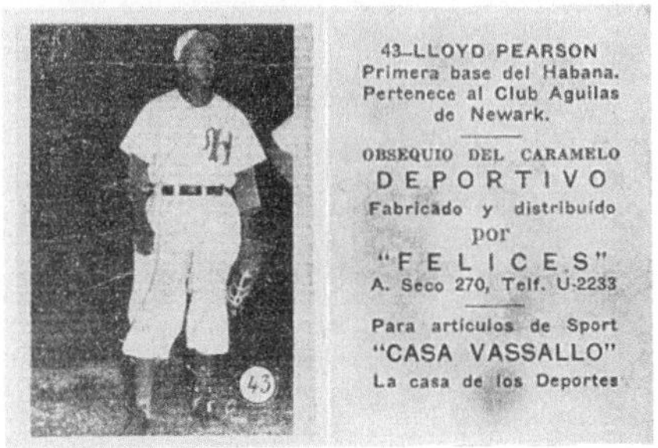

Following its 100-card issue of the previous Cuban winter league season, this candy company issued a 185-card set for 1946-47. Besides more players, extra cards included banners, stadiums, managers, umpires and sportscasters. Printed on paper stock and intended to be pasted into an accompanying album, the cards measure about 1-7/8" x 2-1/2", though inconsistent cutting creates both over- and undersized cards. Fronts have black-and-white player photos and a circle with a card number. Photos are often fuzzy or dark, indicative of their having been picked up from another source, such as a newspaper. Backs repeat the card number and have the player name at top, along with his Cuban League and, frequently, U.S. professional affiliation. Some 60 of the players in the set played in the segregated Negro Leagues of the era. A large ad for the candy and its sellers appear at bottom of the back. Because of the thin stock and placement in albums, these cards are usually found creased and/or with back damage.

		NM	E	VG
	Complete Set (185):	12,000	6,000	3,600
	Common Player:	50.00	25.00	15.00
	Album:	250.00	125.00	75.00
1	Introduction Card	25.00	12.50	7.50
2	New El Cerro Stadium	25.00	12.50	7.50
3	Stadium La Tropical	25.00	12.50	7.50
4	Maestri, Bernardino and Magrinat (El Cerro umpires.)	50.00	25.00	15.00
5	La Tropical umpires(Atan, Lopez, Vidal and Morales)	50.00	25.00	15.00
6	Cuco Conde (Announcer)	25.00	12.50	7.50
7	Cienfuegos Team Banner	25.00	12.50	7.50
8	Martin Dihigo	750.00	375.00	225.00
9a	Napoleon Reyes	60.00	30.00	18.00
9b	Napoleon Reyes	60.00	30.00	18.00
10	Adrian Zabala	50.00	25.00	15.00
11	Roland Gladu	50.00	25.00	15.00
12	Alejandro Crespo	100.00	50.00	30.00
13	Alejandro Carrasquel	50.00	25.00	15.00
14	Napoleon Heredia	50.00	25.00	15.00
15	Andres Mesa	50.00	25.00	15.00
16	Pedro Pages	50.00	25.00	15.00
17	Danny Gardella	50.00	25.00	15.00
18	Conrado Perez	50.00	25.00	15.00
19	Myron Hayworth	50.00	25.00	15.00
20	Pedro Miro	50.00	25.00	15.00
21	Guillermo Vargas	50.00	25.00	15.00
22	Hoot Gibson	50.00	25.00	15.00
23	Rafael Noble	55.00	27.50	16.50
24	Ramon Roger	50.00	25.00	15.00
25	Luis Arango	50.00	25.00	15.00
26	Roy Zimmerman	50.00	25.00	15.00
27	Luis Tiant Sr.	125.00	65.00	35.00
28	Jean Roy	55.00	27.50	16.50
29	Stanislov Bread	50.00	25.00	15.00
30	Walter Nothe	50.00	25.00	15.00
31	Vinicio Garcia	50.00	25.00	15.00
32	Dan (Max) Manning	200.00	100.00	60.00
33	Habana Lions Team Banner	25.00	12.50	7.50
34	Miguel A. Gonzalez	80.00	40.00	24.00
35	Pedro Formental	100.00	50.00	30.00
36	Ray Navarro	50.00	25.00	15.00
37	Pedro Jiminez	50.00	25.00	15.00
38	Rene Monteagudo	50.00	25.00	15.00
39	Salvador Hernandez	50.00	25.00	15.00
40	Hugh (Terris) Mc. Duffie	70.00	35.00	20.00
41	Herberto Blanco	50.00	25.00	15.00
42	Harry (Henry) Kimbro	130.00	65.00	40.00
43	Lloyd (Lennie) Pearson	180.00	90.00	55.00
44	W. Bell	55.00	27.50	16.50
45	Carlos Blanco	50.00	25.00	15.00
46	Hank Thompson	70.00	35.00	20.00
47	Manuel ("Cocaina") Garcia	150.00	75.00	45.00
48	Alberto Hernandez	50.00	25.00	15.00
49	Tony Ordenana	50.00	25.00	15.00
50	Lazaro Medina	50.00	25.00	15.00
51	Fred Martin	50.00	25.00	15.00
52	Eddie (Jim) Lamarque	150.00	75.00	45.00
53	Juan Montero	50.00	25.00	15.00
54	Lou Klein	50.00	25.00	15.00
55	Pablo Garcia	50.00	25.00	15.00
56	Julio Rojo	50.00	25.00	15.00
57	Almendares Team Banner	25.00	12.50	7.50
58	Adolfo Luque	90.00	45.00	27.50
59	Cheo Ramos	50.00	25.00	15.00
60	Avelino Canizares	50.00	25.00	15.00
61	George Hausmann	50.00	25.00	15.00
62	Homero Ariosa	50.00	25.00	15.00
63	Santos Amaro	50.00	25.00	15.00
64	Hank Robinson	60.00	30.00	18.00
65	Lazaro Salazar	200.00	100.00	60.00
66	Andres Fleitas	50.00	25.00	15.00
67	Hector Rodriguez	80.00	40.00	24.00
68	Jorge Comellas	50.00	25.00	15.00
69	Lloyd Davenport	130.00	65.00	40.00
70	Tomas de la Cruz	50.00	25.00	15.00
71a	Roberto Ortiz	80.00	40.00	24.00
71b	Roberto Ortiz	50.00	25.00	15.00
72	Jess (Gentry) Jessup	130.00	65.00	40.00
73	Agapito Mayor	50.00	25.00	15.00
74	William	50.00	25.00	15.00
75	Santiago Ullrich	50.00	25.00	15.00
76	Coty Leal	50.00	25.00	15.00
77	Max Lanier	55.00	27.50	16.50
78	Buck O'Neill	800.00	400.00	240.00
79	Mario Ariosa	50.00	25.00	15.00
80	Lefty Gaines	130.00	65.00	40.00
81	Marianao Team Banner	25.00	12.50	7.50
82	Armando Marsans	80.00	40.00	24.00
83	Antonio Castanos	50.00	25.00	15.00
84	Orestes Minoso	200.00	100.00	60.00
85	Murray Franklin	50.00	25.00	15.00
86	Roberto Estalella	50.00	25.00	15.00
87	A. Castro	50.00	25.00	15.00
88	Gilberto Valdivia	50.00	25.00	15.00
89	Baffeth (Lloyd "Pepper" Bassett)	130.00	65.00	40.00
90	Oliverio Ortiz	50.00	25.00	15.00
91	Francisco Campos	50.00	25.00	15.00
92	Sandalio Consuegra	65.00	32.50	20.00
93	Lorenzo Cabrera	50.00	25.00	15.00
94	Roberto Avila	80.00	40.00	24.00
95	Chanquilon Diaz	50.00	25.00	15.00
96	Pedro Orta	50.00	25.00	15.00
97	Cochihuila Valenzuela	50.00	25.00	15.00
98	Ramon Carneado	50.00	25.00	15.00
99	Aristonico Correoso	50.00	25.00	15.00
100	Daniel Doy	50.00	25.00	15.00
101	Joe Lindsay	50.00	25.00	15.00
102	Habana Reds Team Banner	25.00	12.50	7.50
103	Gilberto Torres	50.00	25.00	15.00
104	Oscar Rodriguez	50.00	25.00	15.00
105	Isidoro Leon	50.00	25.00	15.00
106	Julio Moreno	50.00	25.00	15.00
107	Chulungo del Monte	50.00	25.00	15.00
108	Len Hooker	100.00	50.00	30.00
109	Antonio Napoles	50.00	25.00	15.00
110	Orlando Suarez	50.00	25.00	15.00
111	Guillermo Monje	50.00	25.00	15.00
112	Isasio Gonzalez	50.00	25.00	15.00
113	Regino Otero	50.00	25.00	15.00
114	Angel Fleitas	50.00	25.00	15.00
115	Jorge Torres	50.00	25.00	15.00
116	Claro Duany	100.00	50.00	30.00
117	Charles Perez	50.00	25.00	15.00
118	Francisco Quicutis	50.00	25.00	15.00
119	Lazaro Bernal	50.00	25.00	15.00
120	Tommy Warren	50.00	25.00	15.00
121	Clarence Iott	55.00	27.00	16.50
122	P. Newcomb (Don Newcombe)	600.00	300.00	180.00
123	Gilberto Castillo	50.00	25.00	15.00
124	Matanzas Team Banner	25.00	12.50	7.50
125	Silvio Garcia	200.00	100.00	60.00
126	Bartolo Portuondo	50.00	25.00	15.00
127	Pedro Arango	50.00	25.00	15.00
128	Yuyo Acosta	50.00	25.00	15.00
129	Jose Cendan	50.00	25.00	15.00
130	Eddie Chandler	50.00	25.00	15.00
131	Rogelio Martinez	50.00	25.00	15.00

132	Atares Garcia	50.00	25.00	15.00
133	Manuel Godinez	50.00	25.00	15.00
134	John Williams	130.00	65.00	40.00
135	Emilio Cabrera	50.00	25.00	15.00
136	Barney Serrell	130.00	65.00	40.00
137	Armando Gallart	50.00	25.00	15.00
138	Ruben Garcia	50.00	25.00	15.00
139	Loevigildo Xiques	50.00	25.00	15.00
140	Chifian (Chiflan) Clark	130.00	65.00	40.00
141	Jacinto Roque	50.00	25.00	15.00
142	John (Johnny) Davis	150.00	75.00	45.00
143	Norman Wilson	50.00	25.00	15.00
144	Camaguey Team Banner	25.00	12.50	7.50
145	Antonio Rodriguez	50.00	25.00	15.00
146	Manuel Parrado	50.00	25.00	15.00
147	Leon Treadway	50.00	25.00	15.00
148	Amado Ibanez	50.00	25.00	15.00
149	Teodoro Oxamendi	50.00	25.00	15.00
150	Adolfo Cabrera	50.00	25.00	15.00
151	Oscar Garmendia	50.00	25.00	15.00
152	Hector Arago	50.00	25.00	15.00
153	Evelio Martinez	50.00	25.00	15.00
154	Raquel Antunez	50.00	25.00	15.00
155	Lino Donoso	50.00	25.00	15.00
156	Eliecer Alvarez	50.00	25.00	15.00
157	George Brown	50.00	25.00	15.00
158	Roberto Johnson	50.00	25.00	15.00
159	Rafael Franco	50.00	25.00	15.00
160	Miguel A. Carmona	50.00	25.00	15.00
161	Lilo Fano	50.00	25.00	15.00
162	Orestes Pereda	50.00	25.00	15.00
163	Pedro Diaz	50.00	25.00	15.00
164	Oriente Team Banner	25.00	12.50	7.50
165	Fermin Guerra	50.00	25.00	15.00
166	Jose M. Fernandez	50.00	25.00	15.00
167	Cando Lopez	50.00	25.00	15.00
168	Conrado Marrero	60.00	30.00	18.00
169	Oscar del Calvo	50.00	25.00	15.00
170	Booker McDaniels	150.00	75.00	45.00
171	Rafael Rivas	50.00	25.00	15.00
172	Daniel Parra	50.00	25.00	15.00
173	L. Holleman	50.00	25.00	15.00
174	Rogelio Valdes	50.00	25.00	15.00
175	Raymond Dandridge	950.00	475.00	285.00
176	Manuel Hidalgo	50.00	25.00	15.00
177	Miguel Lastra	50.00	25.00	15.00
178	Luis Minsal	50.00	25.00	15.00
179	Andres Vazquez	50.00	25.00	15.00
180	Jose A. Zardon	50.00	25.00	15.00
181	Jose Luis Colas	50.00	25.00	15.00
182	Rogelio Linares	50.00	25.00	15.00
183	Mario Diaz	50.00	25.00	15.00
184	R. Verdes	50.00	25.00	15.00
185	Indio Jiminez	50.00	25.00	15.00

1948-1949 Caramelos El Indio

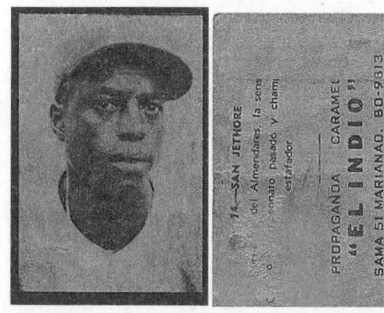

Perhaps the rarest of the late-1940s Cuban caramel cards is this issue picturing members of the island's four-team professional winter league. Measuring 1-5/8" x 2-7/16", the cards are printed in black-and-white on thick paper stock. Front photos are bordered in black with no player identification. On back at top is a card number and player name, along with a few words about the player. At bottom is an ad for the sponsor. Many American players, including Negro Leaguers, are included in the issue. The set is arranged alphabetically by team. An album was available in which to mount the cards. As with most contemporary Cuban issues, low-grade survivors are the norm, with Good condition being about the best seen, making the pricing here somewhat hypothetical.

	NM	E	VG
Common Player:	200.00	100.00	60.00
Album:	300.00	150.00	90.00

1	Fermin Guerra	275.00	135.00	80.00
2	Rodolfo Fernandez	200.00	100.00	60.00
3	Reinaldo Cordeiro	200.00	100.00	60.00
4	Andres Fleitas	200.00	100.00	60.00
5	Tango Suarez	200.00	100.00	60.00
6	Ken Connors (Kevin "Chuck")	600.00	300.00	180.00

7	Rene Gonzalez	200.00	100.00	60.00
8	Jinny Bloodwrth (Jimmy Bloodworth)	275.00	135.00	80.00
9	Sojito Gallardo	200.00	100.00	60.00
10	Hector Rodriguez	275.00	135.00	80.00
11	Avelino Canizares	200.00	100.00	60.00
12	Gilberto Torres	200.00	100.00	60.00
13	Monte Yrving (Monte Irvin)	1,600	800.00	475.00
14	San Jethore (Sam Jethroe)	325.00	160.00	100.00
15	Al Gionfrido (Gionfriddo)	275.00	135.00	80.00
16	Santos Amaro	275.00	135.00	80.00
17	Hiram Gonzalez	200.00	100.00	60.00
18	Conrado Marrero	275.00	135.00	80.00
19	Jorge Comellas	200.00	100.00	60.00
20	Agapito Mayor	200.00	100.00	60.00
21	Octavio Rubert	200.00	100.00	60.00
22	Tata Solis	200.00	100.00	60.00
23	Morris Martin	275.00	135.00	80.00
24	Cyde (Clyde) King	275.00	135.00	80.00
25	Miguel Angel Gonzalez	325.00	160.00	100.00
26	Joseito Rodriguez	200.00	100.00	60.00
27	Sungo Carreras	200.00	100.00	60.00
28	Hank Anderson	275.00	135.00	80.00
29	Emilio Cabrera	200.00	100.00	60.00
30	Lennox Pearson	325.00	160.00	100.00
31	Herberto Blanco	200.00	100.00	60.00
32	Pablo Garcia	200.00	100.00	60.00
33	Chino Hidalgo	200.00	100.00	60.00
34	Amado Ibanez	200.00	100.00	60.00
35	Carlos Blanco	200.00	100.00	60.00
36	Henry Thompson	275.00	135.00	80.00
37	Henry Kimbro	275.00	135.00	80.00
38	Pedro Formental	275.00	135.00	80.00
39	Saguita Hernandez	200.00	100.00	60.00
40	Francisco Quicutis	200.00	100.00	60.00
41	George Stancer (Stanceu)	275.00	135.00	80.00
42	Jim Yockin (Yochim)	275.00	135.00	80.00
43	Tony Lorenzo	200.00	100.00	60.00
44	Rafael Rivas	200.00	100.00	60.00
45	Jose Cerdan	200.00	100.00	60.00
46	Cocaina Garcia	325.00	160.00	100.00
47	Bill Schuster	275.00	135.00	80.00
48	Oliverio Ortiz	200.00	100.00	60.00
49	Salvador Hernandez	200.00	100.00	60.00
50	Oscar Rodriguez	200.00	100.00	60.00
51	Julio Rojo	200.00	100.00	60.00
52	Ray Noble	250.00	125.00	75.00
53	Regino Otero	200.00	100.00	60.00
54	Peter Coscarat (Coscarart)	275.00	135.00	80.00
55	Jimmy Redmond	275.00	135.00	80.00
56	Mc. Quillan (Glenn McQuillen)	275.00	135.00	80.00
57	Stan Bread	275.00	135.00	80.00
58	Armando Gallart	200.00	100.00	60.00
59	Angel Fleitas	200.00	100.00	60.00
60	Pedro Pages	200.00	100.00	60.00
61	Alejandro Crespo	275.00	135.00	80.00
62	Jose Luis Colas	200.00	100.00	60.00
63	Conrado Perez	200.00	100.00	60.00
64	Coaker Tripletl (Triplett)	275.00	135.00	80.00
65	Pedro Dunabeitia	200.00	100.00	60.00
66	Maik Sukont (Max Surkont)	275.00	135.00	80.00
67	Max Mamming (Manning)	525.00	260.00	150.00
68	Jom Mikan	275.00	135.00	80.00
69	Herman Bess (Besse)	275.00	135.00	80.00
70	Wito (Luis) Aloma	275.00	135.00	80.00
71	Raul Lopez	200.00	100.00	60.00
72	Silvio Garcia	300.00	150.00	90.00
73	Gilberto Torres	200.00	100.00	60.00
74	Pipo de la Noval	200.00	100.00	60.00
75	Jose Maria Fernandez	200.00	100.00	60.00
76	Vitico Munoz	200.00	100.00	60.00
77	Luis Suarez	200.00	100.00	60.00
78	Wilfredo Salas	200.00	100.00	60.00
79	Julio Moreno	200.00	100.00	60.00
80	Bill Harrington	275.00	135.00	80.00
81	Oreste (Minnie) Minoso	525.00	260.00	150.00
82	Clarence Hicks	275.00	135.00	80.00
83	Pedro Ballester	200.00	100.00	60.00
84	Jose Hawerton	200.00	100.00	60.00
85	Ramon Roger	200.00	100.00	60.00
86	M Arenciba	200.00	100.00	60.00
87	Louis Kahn	275.00	135.00	80.00
88	Mario Diaz	200.00	100.00	60.00
89	Chiquitin Cabrera	200.00	100.00	60.00
90	Beto Avila	275.00	135.00	80.00
91	Cisco Campos	200.00	100.00	60.00
92	Johnny Simmons	275.00	135.00	80.00
93	Claro Duany	275.00	135.00	80.00
94	Clyde (Dave) Barnhill	800.00	400.00	240.00
95	Clarence Beer	275.00	135.00	80.00
96	Joaquin Gutierrez	200.00	100.00	60.00

1955 Carling Beer Cleveland Indians

Apparently the first of a line of premium photos which extended into the early 1960s. Measuring 8-1/2" x 12" and printed in black-and-white on semi-gloss thin card stock, these photocards are blank-backed. The 1955 Carling photos are identifiable from the 1956 issue, with which they share a "DBL" prefix to the card number in the lower-right corner, by the phrase "Great Champions" appearing just under the player photo.

	NM	E	VG
Complete Set (10):	750.00	375.00	225.00
Common Player:	60.00	30.00	18.00
96A	Ralph Kiner	110.00	55.00	35.00
96Ba	Larry Doby	100.00	50.00	30.00
96C	Al Rosen	75.00	37.50	22.50
96D	Mike Garcia	60.00	30.00	18.00
96E	Early Wynn	90.00	45.00	27.50
96F	Bob Feller	150.00	75.00	45.00
96G	Jim Hegan	60.00	30.00	18.00
96H	George Strickland	60.00	30.00	18.00
96K	Bob Lemon	90.00	45.00	27.50
96L	Art Houtteman	60.00	30.00	18.00

1956 Carling Beer Cleveland Indians

This set was sponsored by Carling Black Label Beer. The oversized (8-1/2" x 12") cards feature black-and-white posed photos with the player's name in a white strip and a Carling ad at the bottom of the card front. Backs are blank. Like the cards issued in 1955, the 1956 set carries a DBL 96 series indication in the lower-right corner and lists brewery locations as Cleveland, St. Louis and Belleville, Ill. Unlike the '55 photocards, however, the first line under the player photo on the 1956 issue is "Premium Quality." Cards numbered DBL 96I and DBL 96J are unknown.

	NM	E	VG
Complete Set (10):	900.00	450.00	275.00
Common Player:	60.00	30.00	18.00
96A	Al Smith	60.00	30.00	18.00
96B	Herb Score	120.00	60.00	35.00
96C	Al Rosen	90.00	45.00	27.50
96D	Mike Garcia	60.00	30.00	18.00
96E	Early Wynn	120.00	60.00	35.00
96F	Bob Feller	200.00	100.00	60.00
96G	Jim Hegan	60.00	30.00	18.00
96H	George Strickland	60.00	30.00	18.00
96K	Bob Lemon	120.00	60.00	35.00
96L	Art Houtteman	60.00	30.00	18.00

1957 Carling Beer Cleveland Indians

The fact that Kerby Farrell managed the Indians only in 1957 pinpoints the year of issue for those Carling Beer photocards which carry a DBL 179 series number in the lower-right corner. Following the black-and-white, blank-backed 8-1/2" x 12" format of earlier issues, the 1957 Carlings list on the bottom line breweries at Cleveland; Frankenmuth, Mich.; Natick, Mass., and, Belleville, Ill. Cards numbered DBL 179I and DBL 179J are currently unknown.

	NM	E	VG
Complete Set (10):	900.00	450.00	275.00
Common Player:	60.00	30.00	18.00
179A Vic Wertz	60.00	30.00	18.00
179B Early Wynn	100.00	50.00	30.00
179C Herb Score	90.00	45.00	27.50
179D Bob Lemon	100.00	50.00	30.00
179E Ray Narleski	60.00	30.00	18.00
179F Jim Hegan	60.00	30.00	18.00
179G Bob Avila	60.00	30.00	18.00
179H Al Smith	60.00	30.00	18.00
179K Kerby Farrell	60.00	30.00	18.00
179L Rocky Colavito	300.00	150.00	90.00

1958 Carling Beer Cleveland Indians

Identical in format to earlier issues, the 1958 premium photos can be distinguished by the card number printed in the lower-right corner. Cards in the 1958 series have numbers which begin with a DBL 2 or DBL 217 prefix.

	NM	E	VG
Complete Set (10):	725.00	360.00	215.00
Common Player:	60.00	30.00	18.00
2 Vic Wertz	60.00	30.00	18.00
217 Minnie Minoso	100.00	50.00	30.00
217B Gene Woodling	60.00	30.00	18.00
217C Russ Nixon	60.00	30.00	18.00
217D Bob Lemon	120.00	60.00	35.00
217E Bobby Bragan	60.00	30.00	18.00
217F Cal McLish	60.00	30.00	18.00
217G Rocky Colavito	150.00	75.00	45.00
217H Herb Score	100.00	50.00	30.00
217J Chico Carrasquel	60.00	30.00	18.00

1959 Carling Beer Cleveland Indians

The appearance of Billy Martin among Carling photocards labeled with a DBL 266 prefix fixes the year of issue to 1959, the fiery second baseman's only year with the Tribe. Once again the 8-1/2" x 12" black-and-white, blank-backed cards follow the format of previous issues. Breweries listed on the bottom of the 1959 Carlings are Cleveland; Atlanta; Frankenmuth, Mich.; Natick, Mass.; Belleville, Ill., and, Tacoma, Wash.

	NM	E	VG
Complete Set (6):	600.00	300.00	180.00
Common Player:	75.00	37.50	22.50
266A Vic Power	75.00	37.50	22.50
266B Minnie Minoso	100.00	50.00	30.00
266C Herb Score	100.00	50.00	30.00
266D Rocky Colavito	150.00	75.00	45.00
266E Jimmy Piersall	100.00	50.00	30.00
266F Billy Martin	150.00	75.00	45.00

1961 Carling Beer Cleveland Indians

Totally different player selection and the use of an LB prefix to the number in the lower-right corner define the 1961 issue from Carling Beer. Otherwise the photocards share the same 8-1/2" x 12" black-and-white format with earlier issues. The blank-backed cards of the 1961 issue list only a single

brewery, Cleveland, at the bottom of the ad portion of the issues. The checklist here is arranged alphabetically. Cards numbered LB 420I and LB420J are unknown.

	NM	E	VG
Complete Set (10):	600.00	300.00	180.00
Common Player:	60.00	30.00	18.00
420A Jimmy Piersall	100.00	50.00	30.00
420B Willie Kirkland	60.00	30.00	18.00
420C Johnny Antonelli	60.00	30.00	18.00
420D John Romano	60.00	30.00	18.00
420E Woodie Held	60.00	30.00	18.00
420F Tito Francona	60.00	30.00	18.00
420G Jim Perry	90.00	45.00	27.50
420H Bubba Phillips	60.00	30.00	18.00
420K John Temple	60.00	30.00	18.00
420L Vic Power	60.00	30.00	18.00

1909-11 Carolina Brights

Among the last of the T206 cards printed, those with Carolina Brights advertising on back are scarce and command a significant premium. The advertising on back is printed in black.

PREMIUMS:
Common Player: 6-8X
Typical Hall of Famer: 5-8X

(See T206 for checklist and base card values.)

1976 Carousel Discs

One of several regional sponsors of player disc sets in 1976 was the Michigan snack bar chain, Carousel. The sponsor's discs are unique in that they do not have pre-printed backs, but rather have a black rubber-stamp on the otherwise blank back. To date more than 20 such stamps have been seen, reportedly from New Jersey to Alaska. The discs are 3-3/8" diameter with a black-and-white player portrait photo in the center of the baseball design. A line of red stars is above, while the left and right panels feature one of several bright colors. Produced by Michael Schecter Associates under license from the Major League Baseball Players Association, the player photos have had uniform and cap logos removed. The unnumbered checklist here is presented in alphabetical order.

		NM	E	VG
Complete Set (70):		70.00	35.00	21.00
Common Player:		4.00	2.00	1.25
(1)	Henry Aaron	25.00	12.50	7.50
(2)	Johnny Bench	15.00	7.50	4.50
(3)	Vida Blue	4.00	2.00	1.25
(4)	Larry Bowa	4.00	2.00	1.25
(5)	Lou Brock	10.00	5.00	3.00
(6)	Jeff Burroughs	4.00	2.00	1.25
(7)	John Candelaria	4.00	2.00	1.25
(8)	Jose Cardenal	4.00	2.00	1.25
(9)	Rod Carew	10.00	5.00	3.00
(10)	Steve Carlton	10.00	5.00	3.00
(11)	Dave Cash	4.00	2.00	1.25
(12)	Cesar Cedeno	4.00	2.00	1.25
(13)	Ron Cey	4.00	2.00	1.25
(14)	Carlton Fisk	10.00	5.00	3.00
(15)	Tito Fuentes	4.00	2.00	1.25
(16)	Steve Garvey	7.00	3.50	2.00
(17)	Ken Griffey	4.00	2.00	1.25
(18)	Don Gullett	4.00	2.00	1.25
(19)	Willie Horton	4.00	2.00	1.25

(20)	Al Hrabosky	4.00	2.00	1.25
(21)	Catfish Hunter	10.00	5.00	3.00
(22a)	Reggie Jackson (A's)	15.00	7.50	4.50
(22b)	Reggie Jackson (Orioles)	20.00	10.00	6.00
(23)	Randy Jones	4.00	2.00	1.25
(24)	Jim Kaat	4.00	2.00	1.25
(25)	Don Kessinger	4.00	2.00	1.25
(26)	Dave Kingman	3.50	1.75	1.00
(27)	Jerry Koosman	4.00	2.00	1.25
(28)	Mickey Lolich	4.00	2.00	1.25
(29)	Greg Luzinski	4.00	2.00	1.25
(30)	Fred Lynn	4.00	2.00	1.25
(31)	Bill Madlock	4.00	2.00	1.25
(32a)	Carlos May (White Sox)	6.00	3.00	1.75
(32b)	Carlos May (Yankees)	4.00	2.00	1.25
(33)	John Mayberry	4.00	2.00	1.25
(34)	Bake McBride	4.00	2.00	1.25
(35)	Doc Medich	4.00	2.00	1.25
(36a)	Andy Messersmith (Dodgers)	6.00	3.00	1.75
(36b)	Andy Messersmith (Braves)	4.00	2.00	1.25
(37)	Rick Monday	4.00	2.00	1.25
(38)	John Montefusco	4.00	2.00	1.25
(39)	Jerry Morales	4.00	2.00	1.25
(40)	Joe Morgan	10.00	5.00	3.00
(41)	Thurman Munson	9.00	4.50	2.75
(42)	Bobby Murcer	4.00	2.00	1.25
(43)	Al Oliver	4.00	2.00	1.25
(44)	Jim Palmer	10.00	5.00	3.00
(45)	Dave Parker	4.00	2.00	1.25
(46)	Tony Perez	10.00	5.00	3.00
(47)	Jerry Reuss	4.00	2.00	1.25
(48)	Brooks Robinson	12.00	6.00	3.50
(49)	Frank Robinson	12.00	6.00	3.50
(50)	Steve Rogers	4.00	2.00	1.25
(51)	Pete Rose	25.00	12.50	7.50
(52)	Nolan Ryan	30.00	15.00	9.00
(53)	Manny Sanguillen	4.00	2.00	1.25
(54)	Mike Schmidt	24.00	12.00	7.25
(55)	Tom Seaver	10.00	5.00	3.00
(56)	Ted Simmons	4.00	2.00	1.25
(57)	Reggie Smith	4.00	2.00	1.25
(58)	Willie Stargell	10.00	5.00	3.00
(59)	Rusty Staub	3.50	1.75	1.00
(60)	Rennie Stennett	4.00	2.00	1.25
(61)	Don Sutton	10.00	5.00	3.00
(62a)	Andy Thornton (Cubs)	6.00	3.00	1.75
(62b)	Andy Thornton (Expos)	4.00	2.00	1.25
(63)	Luis Tiant	4.00	2.00	1.25
(64)	Joe Torre	6.00	3.00	1.75
(65)	Mike Tyson	4.00	2.00	1.25
(66)	Bob Watson	4.00	2.00	1.25
(67)	Wilbur Wood	4.00	2.00	1.25
(68)	Jimmy Wynn	4.00	2.00	1.25
(69)	Carl Yastrzemski	12.00	6.00	3.50
(70)	Richie Zisk	4.00	2.00	1.25

1973 Norm Cash Day Card

As part of the Tiger Stadium festivities on August 12, this 7" x 5" color card was given to fans. Besides an action photo of the feared slugger, his facsimile autograph appears.

	NM	E	VG
Norm Cash	12.50	6.25	3.75

1939 Centennial of Baseball Stamps

Part of the pagentry surrounding the 1939 centennial of the fabled beginnings of baseball was this set of player and history stamps and an accompanying 36-page album. The single stamps measure about 1-5/8" x 2-1/8" and are blank-backed. Stamps #1-13 deal with the game's history; most feature artwork by famed baseball artist and former major league pitcher Al Demaree. Stamps #14-25 feature photos of the game's greats in tombstone frames surrounded by colorful borders.

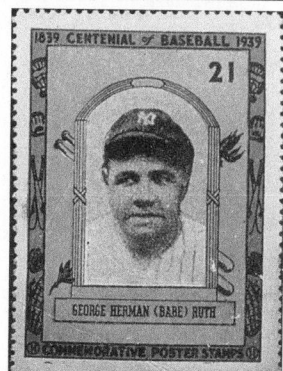

	NM	E	VG
Complete Set, w/Album (25):	1,000	500.00	300.00
Common Player:	50.00	25.00	15.00
Common Historical:	20.00	10.00	6.00
Uncut Stamp Sheet (25):	1,000	500.00	300.00
Album:	80.00	40.00	25.00

		NM	E	VG
1	Abner Doubleday	50.00	25.00	15.00
2	1849 Knickerbockers	50.00	25.00	15.00
3	Ball/bat Standards	20.00	10.00	6.00
4	1858 Brooklyn vs. New York Series	50.00	25.00	15.00
5	1859 Amherst vs. Williams Series	20.00	10.00	6.00
6	Curve Ball(Arthur Cummings)	50.00	25.00	15.00
7	First Admission Fee	20.00	10.00	6.00
8	First Professional Players	50.00	25.00	15.00
9	First No-Hitter(George Bradley)	50.00	25.00	15.00
10	Morgan G. Bulkeley	50.00	25.00	15.00
11	First World's Champions	50.00	25.00	15.00
12	Byron Bancroft (Ban) Johnson	50.00	25.00	15.00
13	**First Night Game**	20.00	10.00	6.00
14	Grover Cleveland Alexander	60.00	30.00	18.00
15	Tyrus Raymond Cobb	150.00	75.00	45.00
16	Eddie Collins	50.00	25.00	15.00
17	Wee Willie Keeler	50.00	25.00	15.00
18	Walter Perry Johnson	75.00	37.50	22.50
19	Napoleon (Larry) Lajoie	50.00	25.00	15.00
20	Christy Mathewson	75.00	37.50	22.50
21	George Herman (Babe) Ruth	300.00	150.00	90.00
22	George Sisler	50.00	25.00	15.00
23	Tristam E. (Tris) Speaker	60.00	30.00	18.00
24	Honus Wagner	100.00	50.00	30.00
25	Denton T. (Cy) Young	75.00	37.50	22.50

1952 Central National Bank of Cleveland

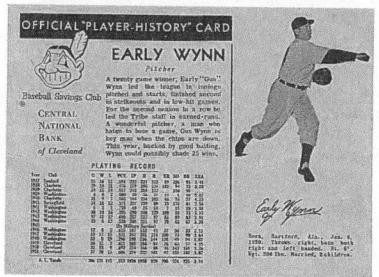

The scope of this issue is undetermined. It is possible a player card was given as a premium for deposits in the bank's "Baseball Savings Club." The cards are about 6-3/4" x 4-3/4", printed in dark blue on cream-colored stock with a blank back. Titled "OFFICIAL "PLAYER-HISTORY" CARD," it features an action pose, facsimile signature, personal data, career summary and complete stats.

	NM	E	VG
Common Player:	100.00	50.00	30.00
Early Wynn	200.00	100.00	60.00

1929 Certified's Ice Cream Pins

Unless or until further players are seen in this series, the date of issue will have to remain uncertain. Apparently given away by Wrigley Field's ice cream concessionaire, these 1" diameter pin-backs feature player portraits and typography in sepia tones lithographed on a white background.

		NM	E	VG
Complete Set (5):		2,600	1,300	775.00
Common Player:		450.00	225.00	135.00
(1)	Joe Bush	450.00	225.00	135.00
(2)	Kiki Cuyler	600.00	300.00	180.00
(3)	Rogers Hornsby	725.00	360.00	215.00
(4)	Riggs Stephenson	450.00	225.00	135.00
(5)	Hack Wilson	600.00	300.00	180.00

1964 Challenge the Yankees Game

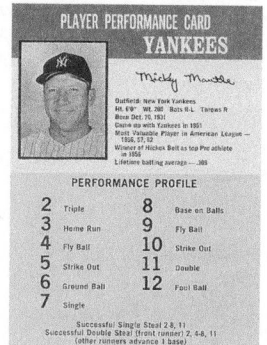

The 50 player cards in this set were part of a boxed dice baseball game produced by Hassenfeld Bros. of Pawtucket, R.I. Cards are approximately 4" x 5-1/2" and blank-backed, featuring a small black-and-white photo, a facsimile autograph and a few biographical details and stats. Player selection is virtually the same for the games issued in 1964 and 1965, and the only way to distinguish cards from each year is to study the stats. Cards are unnumbered and are checklisted below in alphabetical order.

		NM	E	VG
Complete Boxed Set:		1,200	600.00	350.00
Complete Card Set (50):		850.00	425.00	250.00
Common Player:		9.00	4.50	2.75
(1)	Hank Aaron	150.00	75.00	45.00
(2)	Yogi Berra	45.00	22.50	13.50
(3)	Johnny Blanchard	9.00	4.50	2.75
(4)	Jim Bouton	20.00	10.00	6.00
(5)	Clete Boyer	15.00	7.50	4.50
(6)	Marshall Bridges	9.00	4.50	2.75
(7)	Harry Bright	9.00	4.50	2.75
(8)	Tom Cheney	9.00	4.50	2.75
(9)	Del Crandall	9.00	4.50	2.75
(10)	Al Downing	9.00	4.50	2.75
(11)	Whitey Ford	40.00	20.00	12.00
(12)	Tito Francona	9.00	4.50	2.75
(13)	Jake Gibbs	9.00	4.50	2.75
(14)	Pedro Gonzalez	9.00	4.50	2.75
(15)	Dick Groat	9.00	4.50	2.75
(16)	Steve Hamilton	9.00	4.50	2.75
(17)	Elston Howard	20.00	10.00	6.00
(18)	Al Kaline	45.00	22.50	13.50
(19)	Tony Kubek	30.00	15.00	9.00
(20)	Phil Linz	9.00	4.50	2.75
(21)	Hector Lopez	9.00	4.50	2.75
(22)	Art Mahaffey	9.00	4.50	2.75
(23)	Frank Malzone	9.00	4.50	2.75
(24)	Mickey Mantle	400.00	200.00	120.00
(25)	Juan Marichal	30.00	15.00	9.00
(26)	Roger Maris	75.00	37.50	22.50
(27)	Eddie Mathews	30.00	15.00	9.00
(28)	Bill Mazeroski	30.00	15.00	9.00
(29)	Ken McBride	9.00	4.50	2.75
(30)	Willie McCovey	30.00	15.00	9.00
(31)	Tom Metcalf	9.00	4.50	2.75
(32)	Jim O'Toole	9.00	4.50	2.75
(33)	Milt Pappas	9.00	4.50	2.75
(34)	Joe Pepitone	15.00	7.50	4.50
(35)	Ron Perranoski	9.00	4.50	2.75
(36)	Johnny Podres	9.00	4.50	2.75
(37)	Dick Radatz	9.00	4.50	2.75
(38)	Hal Reniff	9.00	4.50	2.75
(39)	Bobby Richardson	30.00	15.00	9.00
(40)	Rich Rollins	9.00	4.50	2.75
(41)	Ron Santo	20.00	10.00	6.00
(42)	Moose Skowron	20.00	10.00	6.00
(43)	Duke Snider	30.00	15.00	9.00
(44)	Bill Stafford	9.00	4.50	2.75
(45)	Ralph Terry	9.00	4.50	2.75
(46)	Tom Tresh	15.00	7.50	4.50
(47)	Pete Ward	9.00	4.50	2.75
(48)	Carl Warwick	9.00	4.50	2.75
(49)	Stan Williams	9.00	4.50	2.75
(50)	Carl Yastrzemski	75.00	37.50	22.50

1965 Challenge the Yankees Game

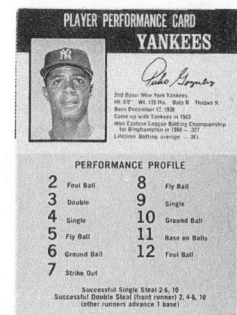

The player cards in this set were part of a boxed dice baseball game produced by Hassenfeld Bros. of Pawtucket, R.I. Cards are approximately 4" x 5-1/2" and blank-backed, featuring a small black-and-white photo, a facsimile autograph and a few biographical details and stats. Player selection is virtually the same for the games issued in 1964 and 1965, and the only way to distinguish cards from each year is to study the stats. Cards are unnumbered and are checklisted below in alphabetical order. The card of Yankee pitcher Rollie Sheldon was apparently withdrawn following his May 3 trade to Kansas City and is scarcer than the rest of the set.

		NM	E	VG
Complete Boxed Set:		1,500	750.00	450.00
Complete Card Set (50):		1,000	500.00	300.00
Common Player:		10.00	5.00	3.00
(1)	Henry Aaron	125.00	62.00	37.00
(2)	Johnny Blanchard	10.00	5.00	3.00
(3)	Jim Bouton	12.50	6.25	3.75
(4)	Clete Boyer	12.50	6.25	3.75
(5)	Leon Carmel	10.00	5.00	3.00
(6)	Joe Christopher	10.00	5.00	3.00
(7)	Vic Davalillo	10.00	5.00	3.00
(8)	Al Downing	10.00	5.00	3.00
(9)	Whitey Ford	50.00	25.00	15.00
(10)	Bill Freehan	10.00	5.00	3.00
(11)	Jim Gentile	10.00	5.00	3.00
(12)	Jake Gibbs	10.00	5.00	3.00
(13)	Pedro Gonzalez	10.00	5.00	3.00
(14)	Dick Groat	10.00	5.00	3.00
(15)	Steve Hamilton	10.00	5.00	3.00
(16)	Elston Howard	20.00	10.00	6.00
(17)	Al Kaline	50.00	25.00	15.00
(18)	Tony Kubek	25.00	12.50	7.50
(19)	Phil Linz	10.00	5.00	3.00
(20)	Don Lock	10.00	5.00	3.00
(21)	Hector Lopez	10.00	5.00	3.00
(22)	Art Mahaffey	10.00	5.00	3.00
(23)	Frank Malzone	10.00	5.00	3.00
(24)	Mickey Mantle	350.00	175.00	100.00
(25)	Juan Marichal	40.00	20.00	12.00
(26)	Roger Maris	90.00	45.00	27.00
(27)	Eddie Mathews	50.00	25.00	15.00
(28)	Bill Mazeroski	40.00	20.00	12.00
(29)	Ken McBride	10.00	5.00	3.00
(30)	Tim McCarver	15.00	7.50	4.50
(31)	Willie McCovey	40.00	20.00	12.00
(32)	Tom Metcalf	10.00	5.00	3.00
(33)	Pete Mikkelsen	10.00	5.00	3.00
(34)	Jim O'Toole	10.00	5.00	3.00
(35)	Milt Pappas	10.00	5.00	3.00
(36)	Joe Pepitone	12.50	6.25	3.75
(37)	Ron Perranoski	10.00	5.00	3.00
(38)	Johnny Podres	12.50	6.25	3.75
(39)	Dick Radatz	10.00	5.00	3.00
(40)	Pedro Ramos	10.00	5.00	3.00
(41)	Hal Reniff	10.00	5.00	3.00
(42)	Bobby Richardson	25.00	12.50	7.50
(43)	Rich Rollins	10.00	5.00	3.00
(44)	Ron Santo	20.00	10.00	6.00
(45)	Rollie Sheldon (SP)	75.00	37.00	22.00
(46)	Bill Stafford	10.00	5.00	3.00
(47)	Mel Stottlemyre	12.50	6.25	3.75
(48)	Tom Tresh	12.50	6.25	3.75
(49)	Pete Ward	10.00	5.00	3.00
(50)	Carl Yaztrzemski	75.00	37.00	22.00

1947 Champ Hats Premiums

The attributed date is speculative, based on the limited known player selection. These 8" x 10" sepia photo cards have player pictures in uniform. In the wide bottom border is: "(Player Name) says:" and an ad message. Backs are blank.

		NM	E	VG
Common Player:		250.00	125.00	75.00
(1)	Mickey Vernon	250.00	125.00	75.00
(2)	Dixie Walker	250.00	125.00	75.00

1957-1962 Charcoal Steak House Ted Kluszewski

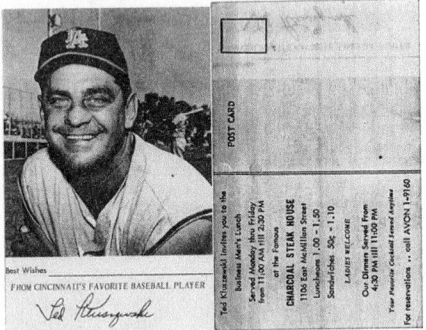

The true scope of this issue combined with the related Ted Kluszewski Steak House cards (see also) is not known. Based on cards showing Klu in Reds and Angels uniforms, it is possible examples may yet be seen in Pirates and White Sox uniforms. About 4" x 6", the black-and-white cards have a facsimile signature of Kluszewski on front. The back is in postcard style and advertises the Cincinnati restaurant he operated with Jack Stayin.

	NM	E	VG
Ted Kluszewski (Angels)	75.00	40.00	25.00

1961 Chemstrand Iron-On Patches

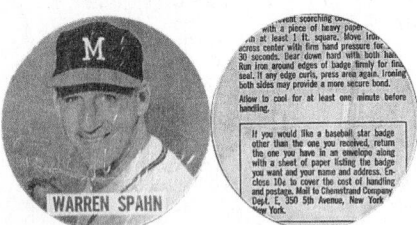

These colorful 2-1/2" diameter cloth patches were included with the purchase of a boy's sport shirt for a short period in 1961. The patches were issued in a cello package with instructions for ironing it onto the shirt. The package also offered the opportunity to trade the player patch for a different star.

		NM	E	VG
Complete Set (9):		825.00	400.00	225.00
Common Player:		60.00	30.00	20.00
(1)	Ernie Banks	125.00	60.00	35.00
(2)	Yogi Berra	125.00	60.00	35.00
(3)	Nellie Fox	90.00	45.00	25.00
(4)	Dick Groat	60.00	30.00	20.00
(5)	Al Kaline	90.00	45.00	25.00
(6)	Harmon Killebrew	90.00	45.00	25.00
(7)	Frank Malzone	60.00	30.00	20.00
(8)	Willie Mays	180.00	90.00	50.00
(9)	Warren Spahn	90.00	45.00	25.00

1976 Chevrolet Baseball Centennial Prints

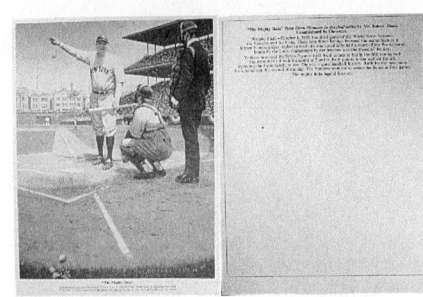

In conjunction with the centennial of organized baseball, Chevrolet commissioned a set of paintings by artist Robert Thom which were reproduced in an 8-1/2" x 11" format and distributed by local auto dealers. Fronts carry the picture's title in the white border at bottom. Backs have a description of the picture on front.

		NM	E	VG
Complete Set (4):		40.00	20.00	12.00
Common Print:		8.00	4.00	2.50
(1)	The First Game (1876)	8.00	4.00	2.50
(2)	The Gashouse Gang(Pepper Martin, Bill Werber)	8.00	4.00	2.50
(3)	The Mighty Babe(Babe Ruth)	15.00	7.50	4.50
(4)	The Record Breaker(Hank Aaron)	12.50	6.25	3.75

1908 Chicago Cubs/White Sox Postcards

The issuer of this postcard set is unknown. The only identification on the card is a dollar sign within a shield which apears near the center on back, along with standard postcard indicia. Fronts of the 3-7/16" x 5-3/8" cards have black-and-white player photos on a gray background. A plain strip at bottom has the player's name on a top line; his position and team on a second line. The checklist presented here is probably not complete.

		NM	E	VG
Complete Set, Cubs (11):		3,000	1,500	900.00
Complete Set, White Sox (9):		3,500	1,750	1,000
Common Player:		200.00	100.00	60.00
CUBS				
(1)	Mordecai Brown	600.00	300.00	180.00
(2)	Frank Chance	600.00	300.00	180.00
(3)	Johnny Evers	600.00	300.00	180.00
(4)	Solly Hoffman (Hofman)	200.00	100.00	60.00
(5)	John Kling	200.00	100.00	60.00
(6)	"Jack" Pfiester	200.00	100.00	60.00
(7)	Edw. Reulbach	200.00	100.00	60.00
(8)	James Sheckard	200.00	100.00	60.00
(9)	Harry Steinfeldt	200.00	100.00	60.00
(10)	Joe Tinker	600.00	300.00	180.00
(11)	Chicago National League, Cubs. (Team photo.)	500.00	250.00	150.00
WHITE SOX				
(1)	"Nic" Altrock	400.00	200.00	120.00
(2)	"Jakey" Atz	500.00	250.00	150.00
(3)	Geo. Davis	600.00	300.00	180.00
(4)	"Jiggs" Donahue	300.00	150.00	90.00
(5)	"Pat" Dougherty	300.00	150.00	90.00
(6)	"Eddie" Hahn	300.00	150.00	90.00
(7)	Frank Isbell	300.00	150.00	90.00
(8)	Fielder Jones	300.00	150.00	90.00
(9)	"Ed" Walsh	650.00	325.00	195.00

1931 Chicago Cubs Picture Pack

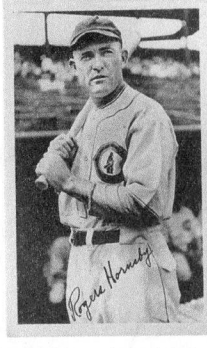

In the second-year of team-issued photo packs during the 1930s-1940s was this set of 1931 Cubs. The 6-1/8" x 9-1/2" sepia-toned pictures have facsimile autographs across the front and a white border around. Backs are blank. Like all the team's other photo packs, it is possible the specific make-up of the 30 pictures in each set changed as personnel came and went during the season. A number of non-playing team personnel are also in the set.

		NM	E	VG
Complete Set (35):		450.00	225.00	135.00
Common Player:		12.50	6.25	3.75
(1)	Ed Baecht	12.50	6.25	3.75
(2)	Clyde Beck	12.50	6.25	3.75
(3)	Les Bell	12.50	6.25	3.75
(4)	Clarence Blair	12.50	6.25	3.75
(5)	John F. Blake	12.50	6.25	3.75
(6)	Guy Bush	12.50	6.25	3.75
(7)	Kiki Cuyler	30.00	15.00	9.00
(8)	Woody English	12.50	6.25	3.75
(9)	Earl Grace	12.50	6.25	3.75
(10)	Charlie Grimm	15.00	7.50	4.50
(11)	Gabby Hartnett	30.00	15.00	9.00
(12)	Rollie Hemsley	12.50	6.25	3.75
(13)	Rogers Hornsby	60.00	30.00	18.00
(14)	Bill Jurges	12.50	6.25	3.75
(15)	Pat Malone	12.50	6.25	3.75
(16)	Jakie May	12.50	6.25	3.75
(17)	John Moore	12.50	6.25	3.75
(18)	Charley O'Leary	12.50	6.25	3.75
(19)	Charlie Root	15.00	7.50	4.50
(20)	Ray Schalk	30.00	15.00	9.00
(21)	Bob Smith	12.50	6.25	3.75
(22)	Riggs Stephenson	15.00	7.50	4.50
(23)	Les Sweetland	12.50	6.25	3.75
(24)	Dan Taylor	12.50	6.25	3.75
(25)	Zack Taylor	12.50	6.25	3.75
(26)	Bud Teachout	12.50	6.25	3.75
(27)	Lon Warneke	12.50	6.25	3.75
(28)	Hack Wilson	45.00	22.00	13.50
Non-Playing Personnel				
(29)	Margaret Donahue	12.50	6.25	3.75
(30)	Bob Lewis (Traveling secretary.)	12.50	6.25	3.75
(31)	Andy Lotshaw (Trainer)	12.50	6.25	3.75
(32)	John Seys	12.50	6.25	3.75
(33)	William Veeck (President)	45.00	22.00	13.50
(34)	W.M. Walker (VP)	12.50	6.25	3.75
(35)	P.K. Wrigley	12.50	6.25	3.75
(36)	William Wrigley (Owner)	17.50	8.75	5.25

1932 Chicago Cubs Picture Pack

This is one of many Cubs team issues of player pictures in the 1930s-1940s. The large format (6-1/8" x 9-1/4"), set features action poses of the players in black-and-white on a black background. A bit of the ground at the players' feet is also included in the photo portion. A white facsimile autograph in the black background identifies the player. Backs are blank. The unnumbered pictures are checklisted here in alphabetical order. Some pictures of non-playing personnel were also issued.

		NM	E	VG
	Complete Set (35):	325.00	165.00	100.00
	Common Player:	12.50	6.25	3.75
(1)	Guy Bush	12.50	6.25	3.75
(2)	Gilly Campbell	12.50	6.25	3.75
(3)	Red Corriden	12.50	6.25	3.75
(4)	Kiki Cuyler	25.00	12.50	7.50
(5)	Frank Demaree	12.50	6.25	3.75
(6)	Woody English	12.50	6.25	3.75
(7)	Burleigh Grimes	25.00	12.50	7.50
(8)	Charlie Grimm	12.50	6.25	3.75
(9)	Marv Gudat	12.50	6.25	3.75
(10)	Stan Hack	15.00	7.50	4.50
(11)	Gabby Hartnett	25.00	12.50	7.50
(12)	Rollie Hemsley	12.50	6.25	3.75
(13)	Billy Herman	25.00	12.50	7.50
(14)	LeRoy Herrmann	12.50	6.25	3.75
(15)	Billy Jurges	12.50	6.25	3.75
(16)	Mark Koenig	12.50	6.25	3.75
(17)	Pat Malone	12.50	6.25	3.75
(18)	Jake May	12.50	6.25	3.75
(19)	Johnny Moore	12.50	6.25	3.75
(20)	Charley O'Leary	12.50	6.25	3.75
(21)	Lance Richbourg	12.50	6.25	3.75
(22)	Charlie Root	15.00	7.50	4.50
(23)	Bob Smith	12.50	6.25	3.75
(24)	Riggs Stephenson	15.00	7.50	4.50
(25)	Harry Taylor	12.50	6.25	3.75
(26)	Zack Taylor	12.50	6.25	3.75
(27)	Bud Tinning	12.50	6.25	3.75
(28)	Lon Warneke	12.50	6.25	3.75
	Non-playing Personnel			
(29)	Marge Donahue	12.50	6.25	3.75
(30)	Bob Lewis (Traveling secretary.)	12.50	6.25	3.75
(31)	John Seys	12.50	6.25	3.75
(32)	Bill Veeck (President)	25.00	12.50	7.50
(33)	W.M. Walker	12.50	6.25	3.75
(34)	Phil Wrigley	12.50	6.25	3.75
(35)	William Wrigley	12.50	6.25	3.75

1932 Chicago Cubs Team Issue

Because of its similarity in format to the team's picture pack issue of 1932, it is presumed this card set was also a team production. The blank-back cards are about 2-1/4" x 2-1/2" with player poses and a bit of ground underfoot set against a white background which has a facsimile autograph. This checklist is incomplete and arranged alphabetically.

	NM	E	VG
Common Player:	300.00	150.00	90.00
Charlie Grimm	300.00	150.00	90.00
Marv Gudat	300.00	150.00	90.00
Stanley C. Hack	350.00	175.00	100.00
Rolly Hemsley	300.00	150.00	90.00
Jakie May	300.00	150.00	90.00
Bud Tinning	300.00	150.00	90.00

1933 Chicago Cubs Picture Pack

Likely a concession stand souvenir item, this large format (5-7/8" x 8-7/8"), set features action poses of the players in black-and-white on a black background. A bit of the ground at the players' feet is also included in the photo portion. A white facsimile autograph in the black background identifies the player. Backs are blank. The unnumbered pictures are checklisted here in alphabetical order. Some pictures of non-playing personnel were included.

		NM	E	VG
	Complete Set (30):	275.00	135.00	85.00
	Common Player:	12.50	6.25	3.75
(1)	Guy Bush	12.50	6.25	3.75
(2)	Gilly Campbell	12.50	6.25	3.75
(3)	John M. Corriden	12.50	6.25	3.75
(4)	Kiki Cuyler	25.00	12.50	7.50
(5)	J. Frank Demaree	12.50	6.25	3.75
(6)	Woody English	12.50	6.25	3.75
(7)	Burleigh A. Grimes	25.00	12.50	7.50
(8)	Charlie Grimm	12.50	6.25	3.75
(9)	Leo "Gabby" Hartnett	25.00	12.50	7.50
(10)	Harvey Hendrick	12.50	6.25	3.75
(11)	Roy Henshaw	12.50	6.25	3.75
(12)	Babe Herman	15.00	7.50	4.50
(13)	William Herman	25.00	12.50	7.50
(14)	William Jurges	12.50	6.25	3.75
(15)	Mark Koenig	12.50	6.25	3.75
(16)	Perce "Pat" Malone	12.50	6.25	3.75
(17)	Lynn Nelson	12.50	6.25	3.75
(18)	Charlie Root	15.00	7.50	4.50
(19)	John Schulte	12.50	6.25	3.75
(20)	Riggs Stephenson	15.00	7.50	4.50
(21)	Zack Taylor	12.50	6.25	3.75
(22)	Bud Tinning	12.50	6.25	3.75
(23)	L. Warneke	12.50	6.25	3.75
	Non-playing Personnel			
(24)	Margaret Donahue	12.50	6.25	3.75
(25)	Robert C. Lewis (Traveling secretary.)	12.50	6.25	3.75
(26)	John O. Seys	12.50	6.25	3.75
(27)	William L. Veeck (President)	25.00	12.50	7.50
(28)	W.M. Walker	12.50	6.25	3.75
(29)	Philip K. Wrigley	12.50	6.25	3.75
(30)	Wm. Wrigley	12.50	6.25	3.75

1936 Chicago Cubs Picture Pack

Nearly identical in format to the 1933 issue, these 5-7/8" x 8-7/8" pictures are printed in black-and-white on a black background with (usually) a white facsimile autograph. Backs are blank. The specific make-up of photo packs sold at Wrigley Field may have changed over the course of the season as players came and went. The unnumbered pictures are checklisted here in alphabetical order.

		NM	E	VG
	Complete Set (34):	240.00	120.00	72.00
	Common Player:	9.00	4.50	2.75
(1)	Ethan Allen	9.00	4.50	2.75
(2)	Clay Bryant	9.00	4.50	2.75
(3)	Tex Carleton	9.00	4.50	2.75
(4)	Phil Cavarretta	12.00	6.00	3.50
(5)	John Corriden	9.00	4.50	2.75
(6)	Frank Demaree	9.00	4.50	2.75
(7)	Curt Davis	9.00	4.50	2.75
(8)	Woody English	9.00	4.50	2.75
(9)	Larry French	9.00	4.50	2.75
(10)	Augie Galan	9.00	4.50	2.75
(11)	Johnny Gill	9.00	4.50	2.75
(12)	Charlie Grimm	12.00	6.00	3.50
(13)	Stan Hack	12.00	6.00	3.50
(14)	Gabby Hartnett	18.00	9.00	5.50
(15)	Roy Henshaw	9.00	4.50	2.75
(16)	Billy Herman	18.00	9.00	5.50
(17)	Roy Johnson	9.00	4.50	2.75
(18)	Bill Jurges	9.00	4.50	2.75
(19)	Chuck Klein	18.00	9.00	5.50
(20)	Fabian Kowalik	9.00	4.50	2.75
(21)	Bill Lee	9.00	4.50	2.75
(22)	Gene Lillard	9.00	4.50	2.75
(23)	Ken O'Dea	9.00	4.50	2.75
(24)	Charlie Root	12.00	6.00	3.50
(25)	Clyde Shoun	9.00	4.50	2.75
(26)	Tuck Stainback	9.00	4.50	2.75
(27)	Walter Stephenson	9.00	4.50	2.75
(28)	Lon Warneke	9.00	4.50	2.75
	Non-playing personnel			
(29)	Margaret Donahue	9.00	4.50	2.75
(30)	Bob Lewis (Traveling secretary.)	9.00	4.50	2.75
(31)	Andy Lotshaw (Trainer)	9.00	4.50	2.75
(32)	John O. Seys	9.00	4.50	2.75
(33)	Charles Weber	9.00	4.50	2.75
(34)	Wrigley Field	18.00	9.00	5.50

1939 Chicago Cubs Picture Pack

The use of a textured paper stock for these 6-1/2" x 9" pictures helps identify the 1939 team issue. The pictures once again feature sepia portrait photos with a white border. A facsimile autograph is at bottom. Backs are blank. The specific make-up of photo packs sold at Wrigley Field may have changed over the course of the season as players came and went. The unnumbered pictures are checklisted here in alphabetical order.

		NM	E	VG
	Complete Set (25):	225.00	115.00	65.00
	Common Player:	9.00	4.50	2.75
(1)	Dick Bartell	9.00	4.50	2.75
(2)	Clay Bryant	9.00	4.50	2.75
(3)	Phil Cavarretta	12.00	6.00	3.50
(4)	John Corriden	9.00	4.50	2.75
(5)	Dizzy Dean	40.00	20.00	12.00
(6)	Larry French	9.00	4.50	2.75
(7)	Augie Galan	9.00	4.50	2.75
(8)	Bob Garbark	9.00	4.50	2.75
(9)	Jim Gleeson	9.00	4.50	2.75
(10)	Stan Hack	12.00	6.00	3.50
(11)	Gabby Hartnett	20.00	10.00	6.00
(12)	Billy Herman	20.00	10.00	6.00
(13)	Roy Johnson	9.00	4.50	2.75
(14)	Bill Lee	9.00	4.50	2.75
(15)	Hank Leiber	9.00	4.50	2.75
(16)	Gene Lillard	9.00	4.50	2.75
(17)	Gus Mancuso	9.00	4.50	2.75
(18)	Bobby Mattick	9.00	4.50	2.75
(19)	Vance Page	9.00	4.50	2.75
(20)	Claude Passeau	9.00	4.50	2.75
(21)	Carl Reynolds	9.00	4.50	2.75
(22)	Charlie Root	12.00	6.00	3.50
(23)	Glenn "Rip" Russell	9.00	4.50	2.75
(24)	Jack Russell	9.00	4.50	2.75
(25)	Earl Whitehill	9.00	4.50	2.75

1940 Chicago Cubs Picture Pack

The 1940 team-issue is identical in format to the 1939s: 6-1/2" x 9", printed on rough-surfaced paper stock with black-and-white portraits surrounded by a wide border and a facsimile autograph on front. Study of the uniforms, however, may help differentiate the issue from 1939, as the 1940 uniforms have no stripe on the shoulders. It is possible that 1939 pictures continued to be issued in the 1940 photo packs and that specific make-up of the packs changed with the team's roster. The blank-back pictures are unnumbered and checklisted here in alphabetical order.

		NM	E	VG
	Complete Set (25):	80.00	40.00	24.00
	Common Player:	9.00	4.50	2.75
(1)	Dick Bartell	9.00	4.50	2.75
(2)	Clay Bryant	9.00	4.50	2.75
(3)	Phil Cavarretta	12.00	6.00	3.50
(4)	John Corriden	9.00	4.50	2.75
(5)	Bob Collins	9.00	4.50	2.75
(6)	"Del" Dallessandro	9.00	4.50	2.75
(7)	Larry French	9.00	4.50	2.75
(8)	Augie Galan	9.00	4.50	2.75
(9)	Jim Gleeson	9.00	4.50	2.75
(10)	Stan Hack	12.00	6.00	3.50
(11)	Gabby Hartnett	20.00	10.00	6.00
(12)	Billy Herman	20.00	10.00	6.00
(13)	Roy Johnson	9.00	4.50	2.75
(14)	Bill Lee	9.00	4.50	2.75
(15)	Hank Leiber	9.00	4.50	2.75
(16)	Bobby Mattick	9.00	4.50	2.75
(17)	Jake Mooty	9.00	4.50	2.75
(18)	Bill Nicholson	9.00	4.50	2.75
(19)	Vance Page	9.00	4.50	2.75
(20)	Claude Passeau	9.00	4.50	2.75
(21)	Ken Raffensberger	9.00	4.50	2.75
(22)	Bill Rogell	9.00	4.50	2.75
(23)	Charlie Root	9.00	4.50	2.75
(24)	Rip Russell	9.00	4.50	2.75
(25)	Al Todd	9.00	4.50	2.75

1941 Chicago Cubs Picture Pack

A change of paper stock to a smooth finish helps differentiate the 1941 team-issue from previous years' offerings. Size remains at 6-1/2" x 9" with sepia player portraits surrounded by a white border and overprinted with a facsimile autograph. Backs are blank on these unnumbered photos. The pictures are listed here in alphabetical order.

		NM	E	VG
Complete Set (25):		190.00	95.00	57.00
Common Player:		9.00	4.50	2.75
(1)	Phil Cavarretta	12.00	6.00	3.50
(2)	Dom Dallessandro	9.00	4.50	2.75
(3)	Paul Erickson	9.00	4.50	2.75
(4)	Larry French	9.00	4.50	2.75
(5)	Augie Galan	9.00	4.50	2.75
(6)	Greek George	9.00	4.50	2.75
(7)	Charlie Gilbert	9.00	4.50	2.75
(8)	Stan Hack	12.00	6.00	3.50
(9)	Johnny Hudson	9.00	4.50	2.75
(10)	Bill Lee	9.00	4.50	2.75
(11)	Hank Leiber	9.00	4.50	2.75
(12)	Clyde McCullough	9.00	4.50	2.75
(13)	Jake Mooty	9.00	4.50	2.75
(14)	Bill Myers	9.00	4.50	2.75
(15)	Bill Nicholson	9.00	4.50	2.75
(16)	Lou Novikoff	9.00	4.50	2.75
(17)	Vern Olsen	9.00	4.50	2.75
(18)	Vance Page	9.00	4.50	2.75
(19)	Claude Passeau	9.00	4.50	2.75
(20)	Tot Pressnell	9.00	4.50	2.75
(21)	Charlie Root	12.00	6.00	3.50
(22)	Bob Scheffing	9.00	4.50	2.75
(23)	Lou Stringer	9.00	4.50	2.75
(24)	Bob Sturgeon	9.00	4.50	2.75
(25)	Cubs Staff(Dizzy Dean, Charlie Grimm, Dick Spalding, Jimmie Wilson)	12.00	6.00	3.50

1942 Chicago Cubs Picture Pack

The relatively small number of photos in this team-issued set indicates it may have been issued as a supplement to update earlier photo packs with players who were new to the Cubs. In the same 6-1/2" x 9" format as previous issues, the 1942s are printed in sepia on a smooth-surfaced paper. A facsimile autograph graces the front and the portrait photo is surrounded by a border. Backs are blank and the pictures are not numbered. The checklist here is in alphabetical order.

		NM	E	VG
Complete Set (26):		175.00	90.00	55.00
Common Player:		9.00	4.50	2.75
(1)	Hiram Bithorn	12.00	6.00	3.50
(2)	Phil Cavarretta	9.00	4.50	2.75
(3)	"Del" Dallassandro	9.00	4.50	2.75
(4)	Paul Erickson	9.00	4.50	2.75
(5)	Bill Fleming	9.00	4.50	2.75
(6)	Charlie Gilbert	9.00	4.50	2.75
(7)	Stan Hack	15.00	7.50	4.50
(8)	Ed Hanyzewski	9.00	4.50	2.75
(9)	Chico Hernandez	9.00	4.50	2.75

(10)	Bill Lee	9.00	4.50	2.75
(11)	Harry Lowrey	9.00	4.50	2.75
(12)	Clyde McCullough	9.00	4.50	2.75
(13)	Lennie Merullo	9.00	4.50	2.75
(14)	Jake Mooty	9.00	4.50	2.75
(15)	Bill Nicholson	9.00	4.50	2.75
(16)	Lou Novikoff	9.00	4.50	2.75
(17)	Vern Olsen	9.00	4.50	2.75
(18)	Claude Passeau	9.00	4.50	2.75
(19)	Tot Pressnell	9.00	4.50	2.75
(20)	Glen "Rip" Russell	9.00	4.50	2.75
(21)	Bob Scheffing	9.00	4.50	2.75
(22)	Johnny Schmitz	9.00	4.50	2.75
(23)	Lou Stringer	9.00	4.50	2.75
(24)	Bob Sturgeon	9.00	4.50	2.75
(25)	Kiki Cuyler, Dick Spalding, Jimmie Wilson	9.00	4.50	2.75
(26)	Jimmie Wilson, Dick Spalding, Charlie Grimm, Dizzy Dean	15.00	7.50	4.50

1943 Chicago Cubs Picture Pack

It is impossible to differentiate pictures from the 1943 issue from those of early years and of 1944, since many pictures were reused and the format is identical: 6-1/2" x 9", black-and-white portrait photos with facsimile autograph and white borders. Backs are blank and the photos are not numbered. They are checklisted here alphabetically.

		NM	E	VG
Complete Set (25):		215.00	105.00	65.00
Common Player:		9.00	4.50	2.75
(1)	Dick Barrett	9.00	4.50	2.75
(2)	Heinz Becker	9.00	4.50	2.75
(3)	Hiram Bithorn	12.00	6.00	3.50
(4)	Phil Cavarretta	9.00	4.50	2.75
(5)	"Del" Dallasandro	9.00	4.50	2.75
(6)	Paul Derringer	9.00	4.50	2.75
(7)	Paul Erickson	9.00	4.50	2.75
(8)	Bill Fleming	9.00	4.50	2.75
(9)	Stan Hack	12.00	6.00	3.50
(10)	Ed Hanyzewski	9.00	4.50	2.75
(11)	Chico Hernandez	9.00	4.50	2.75
(12)	Bill Lee	9.00	4.50	2.75
(13)	Peanuts Lowrey	9.00	4.50	2.75
(14)	Stu Martin	9.00	4.50	2.75
(15)	Clyde McCullough	9.00	4.50	2.75
(16)	Len Merullo	9.00	4.50	2.75
(17)	Bill Nicholson	9.00	4.50	2.75
(18)	Lou Novikoff	9.00	4.50	2.75
(19)	Claude Passeau	9.00	4.50	2.75
(20)	Ray Prim	9.00	4.50	2.75
(21)	Eddie Stanky	12.00	6.00	3.50
(22)	Al Todd	9.00	4.50	2.75
(23)	Lon Warneke	9.00	4.50	2.75
(24)	Hank Wyse	9.00	4.50	2.75
(25)	Cubs Coaches(Kiki Cuyler, Dick Spalding, Jimmie Wilson)	9.00	4.50	2.75

1944 Chicago Cubs Picture Pack

A slight size reduction, to 6" x 8-1/2", helps identify the team's 1944 photo pack. The pictures feature black-and-white portrait photos with a white border. A facsimile autograph is at bottom. Backs are blank. The specific make-up of photo packs sold at Wrigley Field may have changed over the course of the season as players came and went. The unnumbered pictures are checklisted here in alphabetical order.

		NM	E	VG
Complete Set (25):		215.00	105.00	65.00
Common Player:		9.00	4.50	2.75
(1)	Heinz Becker	9.00	4.50	2.75
(2)	John Burrows	9.00	4.50	2.75
(3)	Phil Cavarretta	12.00	6.00	3.50
(4)	"Del" Dallessandro	9.00	4.50	2.75
(5)	Paul Derringer	9.00	4.50	2.75
(6)	Roy Easterwood	9.00	4.50	2.75
(7)	Paul Erickson	9.00	4.50	2.75
(8)	Bill Fleming	9.00	4.50	2.75
(9)	Jimmie Foxx	30.00	15.00	9.00
(10)	Ival Goodman	9.00	4.50	2.75
(11)	Ed Hanyzewski	9.00	4.50	2.75
(12)	Billy Holm	9.00	4.50	2.75
(13)	Don Johnson	9.00	4.50	2.75
(14)	Garth Mann	9.00	4.50	2.75
(15)	Len Merullo	9.00	4.50	2.75
(16)	John Miklos	9.00	4.50	2.75
(17)	Bill Nicholson	9.00	4.50	2.75
(18)	Lou Novikoff	9.00	4.50	2.75
(19)	Andy Pafko	12.00	6.00	3.50
(20)	Ed Sauer	9.00	4.50	2.75
(21)	Bill Schuster	9.00	4.50	2.75
(22)	Eddie Stanky	12.00	6.00	3.50
(23)	Hy Vandenberg	9.00	4.50	2.75
(24)	Hank Wyse	9.00	4.50	2.75
(25)	Tony York	9.00	4.50	2.75

1924 Chicago Evening American Cubs/ White Sox Pins

These 1-3/8" diameter pins were issued by the Chicago Evening American newspaper to promote its peach-colored sports section. Rather crude blue-and-white line drawings of the players are at center, within an orange peach with the player's name at bottom. Borders are either white or dark blue. The pins were produced by Greenduck Metal Stamping of Chicago.

		NM	E	VG
Complete Set (12):		3,500	1,750	1,000
Common Player:		200.00	100.00	65.00
(1)	Grover Alexander	750.00	375.00	225.00
(2)	Eddie Collins	450.00	225.00	135.00
(3)	"Red" Faber	350.00	175.00	105.00
(4)	Ray Grimes	200.00	100.00	65.00
(5)	Charlie Hollocher	200.00	100.00	65.00
(6)	Harry Hooper	350.00	175.00	105.00
(7)	Willie Kamm	200.00	100.00	65.00
(8)	Bill Killefer	200.00	100.00	65.00
(9)	Bob O'Farrell	200.00	100.00	65.00
(10)	Charlie Robertson	200.00	100.00	65.00
(11)	Ray Schalk	350.00	175.00	100.00
(12)	Jigger Statz	200.00	100.00	65.00

1930 Chicago Evening American Pins

Members of the Cubs and White Sox are featured on this series of pins issued by one of the local daily newspapers. Player portraits are featured in black-and-white on a white background over these 1-1/4" celluloid pins. Above the picture are the player's position, last name and team; below is the sponsor's name. The unnumbered pins are listed here in alphabetical order within team.

	NM	E	VG
Complete Set (20):	6,500	3,250	1,950
Common Player:	250.00	125.00	75.00

Chicago Cubs Team Set (11):

		NM	E	VG
		3,500	1,750	1,000
(1)	Les Bell	250.00	125.00	75.00
(2)	Guy Bush	250.00	125.00	75.00
(3)	Kiki Cuyler	350.00	175.00	100.00
(4)	Woody English	250.00	125.00	75.00
(5)	Charlie Grimm	250.00	125.00	75.00
(6)	Gabby Hartnett	350.00	175.00	100.00
(7)	Rogers Hornsby	750.00	375.00	225.00
(8)	Joe McCarthy	350.00	175.00	100.00
(9)	Charlie Root	250.00	125.00	75.00
(10)	Riggs Stephenson	250.00	125.00	75.00
(11)	Hack Wilson	400.00	200.00	120.00

Chicago White Sox Team Set (9):

		NM	E	VG
		3,000	1,500	900.00
(1)	Moe Berg	1,000	500.00	300.00
(2)	Bill Cissel (Cissell)	250.00	125.00	75.00
(3)	Red Faber	350.00	175.00	105.00
(4)	Bill Hunnefield	250.00	125.00	75.00
(5)	Smead Jolley	250.00	125.00	75.00
(6)	Willie Kamm	250.00	125.00	75.00
(7)	Jimmy Moore	250.00	125.00	75.00
(8)	Carl Reynolds	250.00	125.00	75.00
(9)	Art Shires	250.00	125.00	75.00

1930 Chicago Herald and Examiner Babe Ruth Premium

This premium picture with a black-and-white batting pose of Ruth was issued by a Chicago newspaper. Two sizes are known, approximately 8-1/2" x 11-1/2" and 5" x 7". The pictures are blank-back. The year attributed is speculative.

	NM	E	VG
Babe Ruth (Large)	1,350	625.00	400.00
Babe Ruth (Small)	1,350	625.00	400.00

1976 Chicagoland Collectors Association Chicago Greats

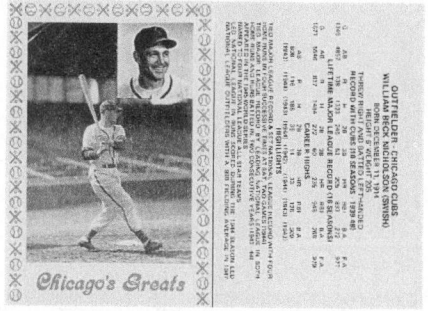

Former stars of the Cubs and White Sox are featured in this collectors issue produced in conjunction with an early sports card and memorabilia show in Chicago. The 2-1/2" x 3-1/2" cards feature black-and-white action photos at center of most cards, with a portrait photo inset at top. Graphics around the front are in red. Backs have detailed career summaries. A starting team, manager and president for each of the Chicago teams is represented in the issue. Complete sets were originally sold for about $2 with uncut sheets sold for $6.

		NM	E	VG
Complete Set (25):		15.00	7.50	4.50
Common Player:		2.00	1.00	.60
(1)	Luke Appling	2.00	1.00	.60
(2)	Ernie Banks	6.00	3.00	1.75
(3)	Zeke Bonura	2.00	1.00	.60
(4)	Phil Cavarretta	2.00	1.00	.60
(5)	Jimmy Dykes	2.00	1.00	.60

(6)	Red Faber, Ted Lyons	2.00	1.00	.60
(7)	Nellie Fox	4.00	2.00	1.25
(8)	Larry French	2.00	1.00	.60
(9)	Charlie Grimm	2.00	1.00	.60
(10)	Gabby Hartnett	2.00	1.00	.60
(11)	Billy Herman	2.00	1.00	.60
(12)	Mike Kreevich	2.00	1.00	.60
(13)	Sherman Lollar	2.00	1.00	.60
(14)	Al Lopez	2.00	1.00	.60
(15)	Minnie Minoso	3.00	1.50	.90
(16)	Wally Moses	2.00	1.00	.60
(17)	Bill Nicholson	2.00	1.00	.60
(18)	Claude Passeau	2.00	1.00	.60
(19)	Billy Pierce	2.00	1.00	.60
(20)	Ron Santo	2.00	1.00	.60
(21)	Hank Sauer	2.00	1.00	.60
(22)	Riggs Stephenson	2.00	1.00	.60
(23)	Bill Veeck	2.00	1.00	.60
(24)	P.K. Wrigley	2.00	1.00	.60
(25)	Checklist	2.00	1.00	.60

1915 Chicago Tribune Supplements

As the 1915 baseball season opened, the Chicago Sunday Tribune ran supplements in its April 4 and April 11 editions featuring pictures of Chicago players. The black-and-white pictures are 8" x 11". Saier is pictured in uniform, the others are in street clothes. Printed in the white border beneath each photo is "Supplement to The Chicago Sunday Tribune, April 4 (or) 11, 1915." Each picture bears a facsimile autograph of the player and is blank-backed.

		NM	E	VG
Complete Set (4):		400.00	200.00	120.00
Common Player:		50.00	25.00	15.00
(1)	Roger Bresnahan (April 11)	100.00	50.00	30.00
(2)	Eddie Collins (April 11)	100.00	50.00	30.00
(3)	Vic Saier (April 11)	50.00	25.00	15.00
(4)	Joe Tinker (April 4)	150.00	75.00	45.00

1917 Chicago White Sox Team Issue

This set of the World Champion White Sox (including several of the notorious Black Sox) was produced by Davis Printing Works in Chicago and apparently sold as a complete boxed set by the team. Individual cards measure about 1-11/16" x 2-3/4". Fronts feature full-length black-and-white photos of the players on a light background with a white border. Player name and position are in black beneath the picture. Backs are blank. To date, only one set is known to exist. It sold at auction in 1991 for $45,100, again in 1997 for $46,000 and in 2001 for $50,330. The unnumbered cards are checklisted here alphabetically.

Complete Set (25):
Value undetermined.

(1)	Joe Benz
(2)	Eddie Cicotte
(3)	Eddie Collins
(4)	Shano Collins
(5)	Charles Comiskey

(6)	Dave Danforth
(7)	Red Faber
(8)	Happy Felsch
(9)	Chick Gandil
(10)	Kid Gleason
(11)	Joe Jackson
(12)	Joe Jenkins
(13)	Ted Jourdan
(14)	Nemo Leibold
(15)	Byrd Lynn
(16)	Fred McMullin
(17)	Eddie Murphy
(18)	Swede Risberg
(19)	Pants Rowland
(20)	Reb Russell
(21)	Ray Schalk
(22)	James Scott
(23)	Buck Weaver
(24)	Lefty Williams
(25)	Mellie Wolfgang

1940 Chicago White Sox Photo Pack

This set of souvenir photos was produced by Andy Lotshaw, who was a Cubs trainer. The 5-1/2" x 6-3/4" pictures have a sepia pose bordered in white, with a facsimile autograph. Backs are blank. The unnumbered pictures are checklisted here in alphabetical order.

		NM	E	VG
Complete Set (25):		300.00	150.00	90.00
Common Player:		15.00	7.50	4.50
(1)	Pete Appleton	15.00	7.50	4.50
(2)	Luke Appling	30.00	15.00	9.00
(3)	Clint Brown	15.00	7.50	4.50
(4)	Bill Dietrich	15.00	7.50	4.50
(5)	Jimmy Dykes	15.00	7.50	4.50
(6)	Mule Haas	15.00	7.50	4.50
(7)	Jack Hayes	15.00	7.50	4.50
(8)	Bob Kennedy	15.00	7.50	4.50
(9)	Jack Knott	15.00	7.50	4.50
(10)	Mike Kreevich	15.00	7.50	4.50
(11)	Joe Kuhel	15.00	7.50	4.50
(12)	Thornton Lee	15.00	7.50	4.50
(13)	Ted Lyons	25.00	12.50	7.50
(14)	Eric McNair	15.00	7.50	4.50
(15)	John Rigney	15.00	7.50	4.50
(16)	Larry Rosenthal	15.00	7.50	4.50
(17)	Ken Silvestri	15.00	7.50	4.50
(18)	Eddie Smith	15.00	7.50	4.50
(19)	J. Solters	15.00	7.50	4.50
(20)	Monty Stratton	20.00	10.00	6.00
(21)	Mike Tresh	15.00	7.50	4.50
(22)	Tom Turner	15.00	7.50	4.50
(23)	Skeeter Webb	20.00	10.00	6.00
(24)	Ed Weiland	15.00	7.50	4.50
(25)	Taft Wright	15.00	7.50	4.50

1948 Chicago White Sox Photo Pack

The last-place White Sox of 1948 are immortalized in this team-issued set of player photos. Individual players are pictured in a 6-1/2" x 9" portrait photo with a thin white border around. A facsimile autograph also appears on front. Backs are blank. A team photo was also included in the set. The photo pack was sold in a large white envelope with a red and blue team logo. The unnumbered pictures are checklisted here in alphabetical order.

		NM	E	VG
Complete Set (30):		180.00	90.00	54.00
Common Player:		7.50	3.75	2.25
(1)	Luke Appling	18.00	9.00	5.50
(2)	Floyd Baker	7.50	3.75	2.25
(3)	Fred Bradley	7.50	3.75	2.25
(4)	Earl Caldwell	7.50	3.75	2.25
(5)	Red Faber	15.00	7.50	4.50
(6)	Bob Gillespie	7.50	3.75	2.25

		NM	E	VG
(7)	Jim Goodwin	12.00	6.00	3.50
(8)	Orval Grove	7.50	3.75	2.25
(9)	Earl Harrist	7.50	3.75	2.25
(10)	Joe Haynes	7.50	3.75	2.25
(11)	Ralph Hodgin	7.50	3.75	2.25
(12)	Howie Judson	7.50	3.75	2.25
(13)	Bob Kennedy	7.50	3.75	2.25
(14)	Don Kolloway	7.50	3.75	2.25
(15)	Tony Lupien	7.50	3.75	2.25
(16)	Ted Lyons	15.00	7.50	4.50
(17)	Cass Michaels	7.50	3.75	2.25
(18)	Bing Miller	7.50	3.75	2.25
(19)	Buster Mills	7.50	3.75	2.25
(20)	Glen Moulder	7.50	3.75	2.25
(21)	Frank Papish	7.50	3.75	2.25
(22)	Ike Pearson	7.50	3.75	2.25
(23)	Dave Philley	7.50	3.75	2.25
(24)	Aaron Robinson	7.50	3.75	2.25
(25)	Mike Tresh	7.50	3.75	2.25
(26)	Jack Wallaesa	7.50	3.75	2.25
(27)	Ralph Weigel	7.50	3.75	2.25
(28)	Bill Wight	7.50	3.75	2.25
(29)	Taft Wright	7.50	3.75	2.25
(30)	**Team Picture**	18.00	9.00	5.50

1960-64 Chicago White Sox Ticket Stubs

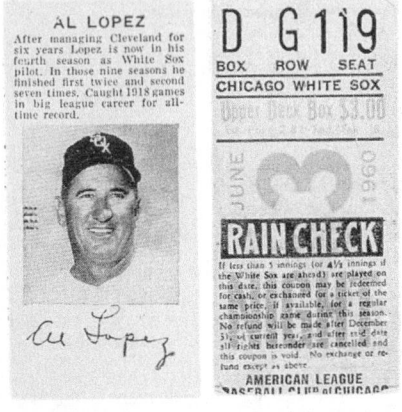

From 1960-64 tickets to White Sox home games at Comiskey Park were issued bearing player photos. Along with the photos on the backs of the 1-5/16" x 2-5/8" ticket stubs are career information and facsimile autographs. Photos were generally re-used from year to year and color variations, depending on the type of ticket, are known. Players from each year are listed here alphabetically.

		NM	E	VG
Complete Set (113):		2,250	1,125	675.00
Common Player:		30.00	15.00	9.00
60-1	Luis Aparicio	75.00	37.00	22.00
60-2	Earl Battey	30.00	15.00	9.00
60-3	Frank Baumann	30.00	15.00	9.00
60-4	Dick Donovan	30.00	15.00	9.00
60-5	Nelson Fox	75.00	37.00	22.00
60-6	Gene Freese	30.00	15.00	9.00
60-7	Ted Kluszewski	60.00	30.00	18.00
60-8	Jim Landis	30.00	15.00	9.00
60-9	Barry Latman	30.00	15.00	9.00
60-10	Sherm Lollar	30.00	15.00	9.00
60-11	Al Lopez	45.00	22.00	13.50
60-12	Turk Lown	30.00	15.00	9.00
60-13	Orestes Minoso	50.00	25.00	15.00
60-14	Bill Pierce	30.00	15.00	9.00
60-15	Jim Rivera	30.00	15.00	9.00
60-16	Bob Shaw	30.00	15.00	9.00
60-17	Roy Sievers	30.00	15.00	9.00
60-18	Al Smith	30.00	15.00	9.00
60-19	Gerry Staley	30.00	15.00	9.00
60-20	Early Wynn	45.00	22.00	13.50
61-1	Luis Aparicio	75.00	37.00	22.00
61-2	Frank Baumann	30.00	15.00	9.00
61-3	Camilo Carreon	30.00	15.00	9.00
61-4	Sam Esposito	30.00	15.00	9.00
61-5	Nelson Fox	75.00	37.00	22.00
61-6	Billy Goodman	30.00	15.00	9.00
61-7	Jim Landis	30.00	15.00	9.00
61-8	Sherman Lollar	30.00	15.00	9.00
61-9	Al Lopez	45.00	22.00	13.50
61-10	J.C. Martin	30.00	15.00	9.00
61-11	Cal McLish	30.00	15.00	9.00
61-12	Orestes Minoso	50.00	25.00	15.00
61-13	Bill Pierce	30.00	15.00	9.00
61-14	Juan Pizarro	30.00	15.00	9.00
61-15	Bob Roselli	30.00	15.00	9.00
61-16	Herb Score	35.00	17.50	10.50
61-17	Bob Shaw	30.00	15.00	9.00
61-18	Roy Sievers	30.00	15.00	9.00
61-19	Al Smith	30.00	15.00	9.00
61-20	Gerry Staley	30.00	15.00	9.00
61-21	Early Wynn	45.00	22.00	13.50
62-1	Luis Aparicio	75.00	37.00	22.00
62-2	Frank Baumann	30.00	15.00	9.00
62-3	John Buzhardt	30.00	15.00	9.00
62-4	Camilo Carreon	30.00	15.00	9.00
62-5	Joe Cunningham	30.00	15.00	9.00
62-6	Bob Farley	30.00	15.00	9.00
62-7	Eddie Fisher	30.00	15.00	9.00
62-8	Nelson Fox	75.00	37.00	22.00
62-9	Jim Landis	30.00	15.00	9.00
62-10	Sherm Lollar	30.00	15.00	9.00
62-11	Al Lopez	45.00	22.00	13.50
62-12	Turk Lown	30.00	15.00	9.00
62-13	J.C. Martin	30.00	15.00	9.00
62-14	Cal McLish	30.00	15.00	9.00
62-15	Gary Peters	30.00	15.00	9.00
62-16	Juan Pizarro	30.00	15.00	9.00
62-17	Floyd Robinson	30.00	15.00	9.00
62-18	Bob Roselli	30.00	15.00	9.00
62-19	Herb Score	35.00	17.50	10.50
62-20	Al Smith	30.00	15.00	9.00
62-21	Charles Smith	30.00	15.00	9.00
62-22	Early Wynn	45.00	22.00	13.50
63-1	Frank Baumann	30.00	15.00	9.00
63-2	John Buzhardt	30.00	15.00	9.00
63-3	Camilo Carreon	30.00	15.00	9.00
63-4	Joe Cunningham	30.00	15.00	9.00
63-5	Dave DeBusschere	40.00	20.00	12.00
63-6	Eddie Fisher	30.00	15.00	9.00
63-7	Nelson Fox	75.00	37.00	22.00
63-8	Ron Hansen	30.00	15.00	9.00
63-9	Ray Herbert	30.00	15.00	9.00
63-10	Mike Hershberger	30.00	15.00	9.00
63-11	Joe Horlen	30.00	15.00	9.00
63-12	Grover Jones	30.00	15.00	9.00
63-13	Mike Joyce	30.00	15.00	9.00
63-14	Frank Kreutzer	30.00	15.00	9.00
63-15	Jim Landis	30.00	15.00	9.00
63-16	Sherman Lollar	30.00	15.00	9.00
63-17	Al Lopez	45.00	22.00	13.50
63-18	J.C. Martin	30.00	15.00	9.00
63-19	Charlie Maxwell	30.00	15.00	9.00
63-20	Dave Nicholson	30.00	15.00	9.00
63-21	Juan Pizarro	30.00	15.00	9.00
63-22	Floyd Robinson	30.00	15.00	9.00
63-23	Charley Smith	30.00	15.00	9.00
63-24	Pete Ward	30.00	15.00	9.00
63-25	Al Weis	30.00	15.00	9.00
63-26	Hoyt Wilhelm	45.00	22.00	13.50
63-27	Dom Zanni	30.00	15.00	9.00
64-1	Fritz Ackley	30.00	15.00	9.00
64-2	Frank Baumann	30.00	15.00	9.00
64-3	Don Buford	30.00	15.00	9.00
64-4	John Buzhardt	30.00	15.00	9.00
64-5	Camilo Carreon	30.00	15.00	9.00
64-6	Joe Cunningham	30.00	15.00	9.00
64-7	Dave DeBusschere	40.00	20.00	12.00
64-8	Eddie Fisher	30.00	15.00	9.00
64-9	Jim Golden	30.00	15.00	9.00
64-10	Ron Hansen	30.00	15.00	9.00
64-11	Ray Herbert	30.00	15.00	9.00
64-12	Mike Hershberger	30.00	15.00	9.00
64-13	Joe Horlen	30.00	15.00	9.00
64-14	Jim Landis	30.00	15.00	9.00
64-15	Al Lopez	45.00	22.00	13.50
64-16	J.C. Martin	30.00	15.00	9.00
64-17	Dave Nicholson	30.00	15.00	9.00
64-18	Gary Peters	30.00	15.00	9.00
64-19	Juan Pizarro	30.00	15.00	9.00
64-20	Floyd Robinson	30.00	15.00	9.00
64-21	Gene Stephens	30.00	15.00	9.00
64-22	Pete Ward	30.00	15.00	9.00
64-23	Al Weis	30.00	15.00	9.00
64-24	Hoyt Wilhelm	45.00	22.00	13.50

1899 Chickering Studio Boston Beaneaters Cabinets

These oversize (8-7/8" x 9-7/8") cabinet cards feature virtually every regular on the 1899 National League runners-up and this checklist may not be complete. The cards feature chest-up, capless sepia portraits of the players, glued to either black or gray cardboard mounts with the advertising of Boston's Elmer Chickering Studio in silver or gold leaf at bottom. Players are identified by first and last name in fancy black script at the bottom of the photo. Backs are blank.

		NM	E	VG
Common Player:		3,000	650.00	425.00
(1)	Harvey Bailey	3,000	650.00	425.00
(2)	Martin Bergen	3,000	650.00	425.00
(3)	William Clarke	3,000	650.00	425.00
(4)	Jimmy Collins	7,500	2,700	1,725
(5)	Hugh Duffy	9,000	3,200	1,900
(6)	Billy Hamilton	7,500	3,000	1,800
(7)	Frank Killen	3,000	650.00	425.00
(8)	Ted Lewis	3,000	650.00	425.00
(9)	Herman Long	7,500	2,425	1,450
(10)	Bobby Lowe	3,000	1,125	675.00
(11)	Jouett Meekin	7,500	1,500	900.00
(12)	Charles Nichols	9,000	3,200	1,875
(13)	Fred Tenney	3,000	650.00	425.00

1900 Chickering Studio Cabinets

The extent of this issue of standard-format (about 4-1/4" x 6-1/2") cabinets is unknown. Fronts have a studio pose with a decorative studio logo in the bottom border. Backs have a large ad for the renowned Boston photographer.

		NM	E	VG
Common Player:		1,500	750.00	450.00
(1)	Win Mercer	1,500	750.00	450.00
(2)	Kid Nichols	9,000	4,500	2,750

1956-1957 Chicle Peloteros

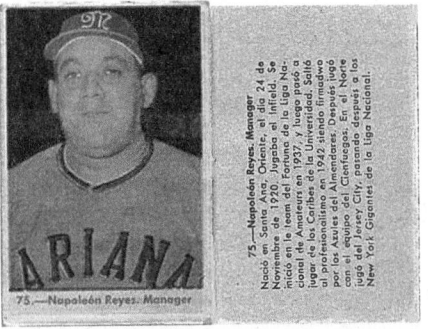

One of the few gumcard issues from Cuba, this set took a cue from American companies by skip-numbering the set to keep youngsters buying gum in search of cards that did not exist. The cards measure about 2" x 3". Fronts have color portrait photos bordered in white with the player name and card number in a colored strip below. Backs are in black-and-white with a few biographical notes and career highlights. The cards are printed on thick gray stock. A colorful album to house the cards was also produced.

		NM	E	VG
Complete Set (40):		2,750	1,375	850.00
Common Player:		60.00	30.00	18.00
Album:		100.00	50.00	30.00
2	Emilio Cabrera	60.00	30.00	18.00
4	Conrado Marrero	100.00	50.00	30.00
5	Silvio Garcia	250.00	125.00	75.00
6	Russel (Russell) Nixon	75.00	37.50	22.50
7	Enrique Izquierdo	60.00	30.00	18.00
8	Lou Skinner	60.00	30.00	18.00
9	Robert Mc Kee	60.00	30.00	18.00

		NM	E	VG
10	Gonzalo Naranjo	60.00	30.00	18.00
11	Trompoloco Rodriguez	60.00	30.00	18.00
12	Evelio Hernandez	60.00	30.00	18.00
26	Oscar Rodriguez	60.00	30.00	18.00
27	Jose (Cheo) Ramos	60.00	30.00	18.00
28	Napoleon Heredia	60.00	30.00	18.00
29	Camilo Pascual	150.00	75.00	45.00
30	Pedro Ramos	90.00	45.00	27.50
31	Rene Gutierrez	60.00	30.00	18.00
32	Julio (Jiqui) Moreno	65.00	32.50	20.00
33	Bud Daley	65.00	32.50	20.00
34	Dick Tomaneck (Tomanek)	60.00	30.00	18.00
35	Rafael Noble	65.00	32.50	20.00
50	Gilberto Torres	60.00	30.00	18.00
51	Salvador Hernandez	60.00	30.00	18.00
52	Pipo de la Noval	60.00	30.00	18.00
53	Juan Soler	60.00	30.00	18.00
54	Oscar Sierra	60.00	30.00	18.00
55	Billy Muffet (Muffett)	60.00	30.00	18.00
56	Robert Bluaylock (Blaylock)	60.00	30.00	18.00
57	Edwin Mayers	60.00	30.00	18.00
58	Vicente Amor	60.00	30.00	18.00
59	Raul Sanchez	60.00	30.00	18.00
75	Napoleon Reyes	90.00	45.00	27.50
76	Jose Maria Fernandez	90.00	45.00	27.50
77	Juan Izaguirre	60.00	30.00	18.00
79	Rene Friol	60.00	30.00	18.00
80	Asdrubal Baro	60.00	30.00	18.00
82	Juan Delis	60.00	30.00	18.00
83	Julio Becquer	60.00	30.00	18.00
84	Rodolfo Arias	60.00	30.00	18.00
86	Patricio Quintana	60.00	30.00	18.00
87	Aldo Salvent	60.00	30.00	18.00

1972 Chicago Cubs & Chicago White Sox Color Caricatures

Produced by Chi-Foursome, Inc., these color caricatures were intended for sale at gas stations and supermarkets, but were never released at these locations. Apparently, only a small quantity was sold at Wrigley Field, and it is believed only about 3,000 of each player was produced. The caricatures were produced on 11" x 14" textured cardboard stock, with a facsimile autograph next to each player on front. Backs are blank.

	NM	E	VG
CUBS	10.00	5.00	3.00
Complete Set (15):	100.00	50.00	30.00
Common Player:	10.00	5.00	3.00

1977 Chilly Willee Discs

Virtually identical in format to the several locally sponsored disc sets of the previous year, these 3-3/8" diameter player discs were given away at participating frozen drink stands. Discs once again feature black-and-white player portrait photos in the center of a baseball design. The left and right panels are in one of several bright colors. Licensed by the Players Association through Mike Schechter Associates, the player photos carry no uniform logos. Backs are printed in blue and red. The unnumbered discs are checklisted here alphabetically.

	NM	E	VG
Complete Set (70):	65.00	32.50	20.00
Common Player:	1.00	.50	.30

(1)	Sal Bando	1.00	.50	.30
(2)	Buddy Bell	1.00	.50	.30
(3)	Johnny Bench	5.00	2.50	1.50
(4)	Larry Bowa	1.00	.50	.30
(5)	Steve Braun	1.00	.50	.30
(6)	George Brett	12.00	6.00	3.50
(7)	Lou Brock	5.00	2.50	1.50
(8)	Jeff Burroughs	1.00	.50	.30
(9)	Bert Campaneris	1.00	.50	.30
(10)	John Candelaria	1.00	.50	.30
(11)	Jose Cardenal	1.00	.50	.30
(12)	Rod Carew	5.00	2.50	1.50
(13)	Steve Carlton	5.00	2.50	1.50
(14)	Dave Cash	1.00	.50	.30
(15)	Cesar Cedeno	1.00	.50	.30
(16)	Ron Cey	1.00	.50	.30
(17)	Dave Concepcion	1.00	.50	.30
(18)	Dennis Eckersley	5.00	2.50	1.50
(19)	Mark Fidrych	2.50	1.25	.70
(20)	Rollie Fingers	4.00	2.00	1.25
(21)	Carlton Fisk	5.00	2.50	1.50
(22)	George Foster	1.00	.50	.30
(23)	Wayne Garland	1.00	.50	.30
(24)	Ralph Garr	1.00	.50	.30
(25)	Steve Garvey	2.00	1.00	.60
(26)	Cesar Geronimo	1.00	.50	.30
(27)	Bobby Grich	1.00	.50	.30
(28)	Ken Griffey Sr.	1.00	.50	.30
(29)	Don Gullett	1.00	.50	.30
(30)	Mike Hargrove	1.00	.50	.30
(31)	Al Hrabosky	1.00	.50	.30
(32)	Catfish Hunter	4.00	2.00	1.25
(33)	Reggie Jackson	10.00	5.00	3.00
(34)	Randy Jones	1.00	.50	.30
(35)	Dave Kingman	1.00	.50	.30
(36)	Jerry Koosman	1.00	.50	.30
(37)	Dave LaRoche	1.00	.50	.30
(38)	Greg Luzinski	1.00	.50	.30
(39)	Fred Lynn	1.00	.50	.30
(40)	Bill Madlock	1.00	.50	.30
(41)	Rick Manning	1.00	.50	.30
(42)	Jon Matlock	1.00	.50	.30
(43)	John Mayberry	1.00	.50	.30
(44)	Hal McRae	1.00	.50	.30
(45)	Andy Messersmith	1.00	.50	.30
(46)	Rick Monday	1.00	.50	.30
(47)	John Montefusco	1.00	.50	.30
(48)	Joe Morgan	5.00	2.50	1.50
(49)	Thurman Munson	4.00	2.00	1.25
(50)	Bobby Murcer	1.00	.50	.30
(51)	Bill North	1.00	.50	.30
(52)	Jim Palmer	5.00	2.50	1.50
(53)	Tony Perez	5.00	2.50	1.50
(54)	Jerry Reuss	1.00	.50	.30
(55)	Brooks Robinson	5.00	2.50	1.50
(56)	Pete Rose	10.00	5.00	3.00
(57)	Joe Rudi	1.00	.50	.30
(58)	Nolan Ryan	20.00	10.00	6.00
(59)	Manny Sanguillen	1.00	.50	.30
(60)	Mike Schmidt	12.00	6.00	3.50
(61)	Tom Seaver	5.00	2.50	1.50
(62)	Bill Singer	1.00	.50	.30
(63)	Willie Stargell	5.00	2.50	1.50
(64)	Rusty Staub	1.50	.70	.45
(65)	Luis Tiant	1.00	.50	.30
(66)	Bob Watson	1.00	.50	.30
(67)	Butch Wynegar	1.00	.50	.30
(68)	Carl Yastrzemski	5.00	2.50	1.50
(69)	Robin Yount	5.00	2.50	1.50
(70)	Richie Zisk	1.00	.50	.30

1929 Churchman's Cigarettes

Though he is identified nowhere on this English cigarette card, the home run swing of Babe Ruth on the front is unmistakable. The last of a set of 25 "Sports & Games in Many

Lands" series, the approximately 2-5/8" x 1-3/8" cards have color artwork on the front and green-and-white backs. The back of the baseball card provides a short history of "The great national sport of the U.S.A."

		NM	E	VG
25	Baseball, U.S.A.(Babe Ruth)	350.00	175.00	100.00

1963 Cincinnati Enquirer Reds' Scrapbook

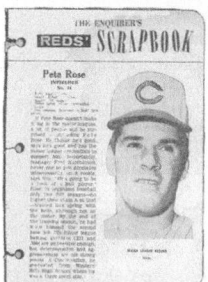

One of the city's newspapers carried this series that could be out of the newspaper and saved. The black-and-white clippings feature a player photo, stats, career notes and biographical data.

		NM	E	VG
	Complete Set (33):	150.00	75.00	45.00
	Common Player:	3.00	1.50	.90
(1)	Don Blasingame	3.00	1.50	.90
(2)	Harry Bright	3.00	1.50	.90
(3)	Jim Brosnan	3.00	1.50	.90
(4)	Leo Cardenas	3.00	1.50	.90
(5)	Gerry Coleman	3.00	1.50	.90
(6)	John Edwards	3.00	1.50	.90
(7)	Sam Ellis	3.00	1.50	.90
(8)	Hank Foiles	3.00	1.50	.90
(9)	Gene Freese	3.00	1.50	.90
(10)	Jesse Gonder	3.00	1.50	.90
(11)	Tommy Harper	3.00	1.50	.90
(12)	Bill Henry	3.00	1.50	.90
(13)	Ken Hunt	3.00	1.50	.90
(14)	Fred Hutchinson	3.00	1.50	.90
(15)	Joey Jay	3.00	1.50	.90
(16)	Eddie Kasko	3.00	1.50	.90
(17)	Marty Keough	3.00	1.50	.90
(18)	Johnny Klippstein	3.00	1.50	.90
(19)	Jerry Lynch	3.00	1.50	.90
(20)	Jim Maloney	3.00	1.50	.90
(21)	Joe Nuxhall	4.50	2.25	1.25
(22)	Jim O'Toole	3.00	1.50	.90
(23)	Jim Owens	3.00	1.50	.90
(24)	Don Pavletich	3.00	1.50	.90
(25)	Vada Pinson	6.00	3.00	1.75
(26)	Wally Post	3.00	1.50	.90
(27)	Bob Purkey	3.00	1.50	.90
(28)	Frank Robinson	20.00	10.00	6.00
(29)	Pete Rose	90.00	45.00	27.00
(30)	Dave Sisler	3.00	1.50	.90
(31)	John Tsitouris	3.00	1.50	.90
(32)	Ken Walters	3.00	1.50	.90
(33)	Al Worthington	3.00	1.50	.90

1980 Cincinnati Enquirer Cincinnati Reds

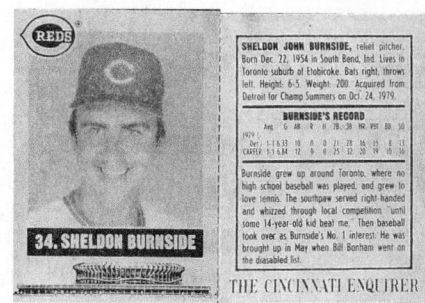

This set of paper "cards" was printed within the pages of the Cincinnati Enquirer newspaper. The 2-1/4" x 3" cards are printed in black-and-white (both front and back) on newsprint. Dotted lines show where the cards were to be cut. Fronts have a player photo and a drawing of Riverfront Stadium. The team logo is in an upper corner and player identification in a black band towards the bottom. Backs have biographical and career details along with stats. Cards are checklisted here according to the uniform numbers printed on front.

		NM	E	VG
Complete Set (32):		100.00	50.00	30.00
Common Player:		3.00	1.50	.90
2	Russ Nixon	3.00	1.50	.90
3	John McNamara	3.00	1.50	.90
4	Harry Dunlop	3.00	1.50	.90
5	Johnny Bench	9.00	4.50	2.75
6	Bill Fischer	3.00	1.50	.90
7	Hector Cruz	3.00	1.50	.90
9	Vic Correll	3.00	1.50	.90
11	Ron Plaza	3.00	1.50	.90
12	Harry Spilman	3.00	1.50	.90
13	Dave Concepcion	3.00	1.50	.90
15	George Foster	3.00	1.50	.90
16	Ron Oester	3.00	1.50	.90
19	Don Werner	3.00	1.50	.90
20	Cesar Geronimo	3.00	1.50	.90
22	Dan Driessen	3.00	1.50	.90
23	Rick Auerbach	3.00	1.50	.90
25	Ray Knight	3.00	1.50	.90
26	Junior Kennedy	3.00	1.50	.90
28	Sam Mejias	3.00	1.50	.90
29	Dave Collins	3.00	1.50	.90
30	Ken Griffey	3.00	1.50	.90
31	Paul Moskau	3.00	1.50	.90
34	Sheldon Burnside	3.00	1.50	.90
35	Frank Pastore	3.00	1.50	.90
36	Mario Soto	3.00	1.50	.90
37	Dave Tomlin	3.00	1.50	.90
40	Doug Bair	3.00	1.50	.90
41	Tom Seaver	7.50	3.75	2.25
42	Bill Bonham	3.00	1.50	.90
44	Charlie Leibrandt	3.00	1.50	.90
47	Tom Hume	3.00	1.50	.90
51	Mike LaCoss	3.00	1.50	.90

1938 Cincinnati Post Reds

Over the course of several weeks during the summer of 1938, daily editions of the Cincinnati Post sports section carried a set of player portraits designed to be cut out and saved. The pieces measure 6" x 11" and feature a large photo with facsimile autograph, topped by a headline and carrying a short biography below. Everything is in black-and-white. The unnumbered series is checklisted here in alphabetical order.

		NM	E	VG
Complete Set (25):		450.00	225.00	135.00
Common Player:		20.00	10.00	6.00
(1)	Wally Berger	30.00	15.00	9.00
(2)	Joe Cascarella	20.00	10.00	6.00
(3)	Harry Craft	20.00	10.00	6.00
(4)	Dusty Cooke	20.00	10.00	6.00
(5)	Peaches Davis	20.00	10.00	6.00
(6)	Paul Derringer	25.00	12.50	7.50
(7)	Linus (Junior) Frey	20.00	10.00	6.00
(8)	Lee Gamble	20.00	10.00	6.00
(9)	Ival Goodman	20.00	10.00	6.00
(10)	Hank Gowdy	20.00	10.00	6.00
(11)	Lee Grissom	20.00	10.00	6.00
(12)	Willard Hershberger	25.00	12.50	7.50
(13)	Don Lang	20.00	10.00	6.00
(14)	Ernie Lombardi	35.00	17.50	10.50
(15)	Buck McCormick	20.00	10.00	6.00
(16)	Bill McKechnie	35.00	17.50	10.50
(17)	Whitey Moore	20.00	10.00	6.00
(18)	Billy Myers	20.00	10.00	6.00
(19)	Clifford Richardson	20.00	10.00	6.00
(20)	Lewis Riggs	20.00	10.00	6.00
(21)	Edd Roush	35.00	17.50	10.50
(22)	Gene Schott	20.00	10.00	6.00
(23)	Johnny Vander Meer	30.00	15.00	9.00
(24)	Bucky Walter	20.00	10.00	6.00
(25)	James Weaver	20.00	10.00	6.00

1919-20 Cincinnati Reds Postcards

ADOLFO LUQUE, Pitcher
Cincinnati "Reds" World's Champions 1919

Two versions of each of the cards in this issue are known. Picturing members of the 1919 World Champions, the foils of the Black Sox scandal, these 3-1/2" x 5-1/2" cards have black-and-white player poses on front. In the white border at bottom (or occasionally, at top) are two lines of type. The top line has the player name and position. The second line can be found in two versions. One reads, "Cincinnati 'Reds' - Champions of National League" the other, presumably a second printing following the World Series, reads, "Cincinnati 'Reds' World's Champions 1919." Backs are printed with standard postcard indicia. Some cards have been found with the advertising of Mt. Union Dairy on the back. The unnumbered cards are checklisted here in alphabetical order.

		NM	E	VG
Complete Set (24):		3,000	1,500	900.00
Common Player:		150.00	75.00	45.00
(1)	Nick Allen	150.00	75.00	45.00
(2)	Rube Bressler	150.00	75.00	45.00
(3)	Jake Daubert	150.00	75.00	45.00
(4)	Pat Duncan	150.00	75.00	45.00
(5)	Hod Eller	150.00	75.00	45.00
(6)	Ray Fisher	150.00	75.00	45.00
(7)	Eddie Gerner	150.00	75.00	45.00
(8)	Heinie Groh	150.00	75.00	45.00
(9)	Larry Kopf	150.00	75.00	45.00
(10)	Adolfo Luque	175.00	85.00	50.00
(11)	Sherwood Magee	150.00	75.00	45.00
(12)	Roy Mitchell	150.00	75.00	45.00
(13)	Pat Moran	150.00	75.00	45.00
(14)	Greasy Neale	200.00	100.00	60.00
(15)	Bill Rariden	150.00	75.00	45.00
(16)	Morris Rath	150.00	75.00	45.00
(17)	Walter Reuther (Ruether)	150.00	75.00	45.00
(18)	Jimmy Ring	150.00	75.00	45.00
(19)	Eddie Roush	400.00	200.00	120.00
(20)	Harry Sallee	150.00	75.00	45.00
(21)	Hank Schreiber	150.00	75.00	45.00
(22)	Charles See	150.00	75.00	45.00
(23)	Jimmy Smith	150.00	75.00	45.00
(24)	Ivy Wingo	150.00	75.00	45.00

1938 Cincinnati Reds Team Issue

EDDIE ROUSH, Coach

This set of 2" x 3" cards were sold as a boxed set at the ballpark. Fronts feature a black-and-white photo of the player with his name and position in a red strip beneath the picture. Backs have the player's name, position and a generally flattering description of the player's talents. The cards are not numbered. In the American Card Catalog, this issue was designated W711-1.

		NM	E	VG
Complete Set (23):		1,000	500.00	300.00
Common Player:		40.00	20.00	12.00
(1)	Wally Berger ("... in a trade with the Giants in June.")	40.00	20.00	12.00
(2)	Joe Cascarella	40.00	20.00	12.00
(3)	Allen "Dusty" Cooke	40.00	20.00	12.00
(4)	Harry Craft	40.00	20.00	12.00
(5)	Ray "Peaches" Davis	40.00	20.00	12.00
(6)	Paul Derringer ("Won 22 games...this season.")	40.00	20.00	12.00
(7)	Linus Frey ("... only 25 now.")	40.00	20.00	12.00
(8)	Lee Gamble ("... Syracuse last year.")	40.00	20.00	12.00
(9)	Ival Goodman (No mention of 30 homers.)	40.00	20.00	12.00
(10)	Harry "Hank" Gowdy	40.00	20.00	12.00
(11)	Lee Grissom (No mention of 1938.)	40.00	20.00	12.00
(12)	Willard Hershberger	100.00	50.00	30.00
(13)	Ernie Lombardi (No mention of 1938 MVP.)	200.00	100.00	60.00
(14)	Frank McCormick	40.00	20.00	12.00
(15)	Bill McKechnie ("Last year he led ...")	200.00	100.00	60.00

		NM	E	VG
(16)	Lloyd "Whitey" Moore ("... last year with Syracuse.")	40.00	20.00	12.00
(17)	Billy Myers ("... in his fourth year.")	40.00	20.00	12.00
(18)	Lee Riggs ("... in his fourth season ...")	40.00	20.00	12.00
(19)	Eddie Roush	200.00	100.00	60.00
(20)	Gene Schott	40.00	20.00	12.00
(21)	Johnny Vander Meer (Portrait)	75.00	37.00	22.00
(22)	Wm. "Bucky" Walter ("... won 14 games ...")	40.00	20.00	12.00
(23)	Jim Weaver	40.00	20.00	12.00

1939 Cincinnati Reds Team Issue

PAUL DERRINGER
Pitcher

This big Kentuckian has been one of the National League's greatest hurlers since he came up with the St. Louis Cardinals in 1931. He was the league's leading hurler as a rookie and started the first game of the 1931 World Series. Came to the Reds in 1933. Won 22 games for the Reds in 1935 and 21 last year.

An updating by one season of the team-issued 1938 W711-1 set, most of the players and poses on the 2" x 3" cards remained the same. A close study of the career summary on the card's back is necessary to determine which year of issue is at hand. The Livengood card is believed to have been withdrawn from distribution early and is scarce.

		NM	E	VG
Complete Set (27):		1,250	625.00	375.00
Common Player:		40.00	20.00	12.00
(1)	Wally Berger ("... in a trade with the Giants in June, 1938.")	40.00	20.00	12.00
(2)	Nino Bongiovanni	40.00	20.00	12.00
(3)	Stanley "Frenchy" Bordagaray	40.00	20.00	12.00
(4)	Harry Craft	40.00	20.00	12.00
(5)	Ray "Peaches" Davis	40.00	20.00	12.00
(6)	Paul Derringer ("Won 21 games ... last year.")	45.00	22.00	13.50
(7)	Linus Frey ("... only 26 now.")	40.00	20.00	12.00
(8)	Lee Gamble ("... Syracuse in 1937.")	40.00	20.00	12.00
(9)	Ival Goodman (Mentions hitting 30 homers.)	40.00	20.00	12.00
(10)	Harry "Hank" Gowdy	40.00	20.00	12.00
(11)	Lee Grissom (Mentions 1938.)	40.00	20.00	12.00
(12)	Willard Hershberger	100.00	50.00	30.00
(13)	Eddie Joost	40.00	20.00	12.00
(14)	Wes Livengood	250.00	125.00	75.00
(15)	Ernie Lombardi (Mentions MVP of 1938.)	225.00	110.00	67.00
(16)	Frank McCormick	40.00	20.00	12.00
(17)	Bill McKechnie ("In 1937 he led ...")	200.00	100.00	60.00
(18)	Lloyd "Whitey" Moore ("... in 1937 with Syracuse.")	40.00	20.00	12.00
(19)	Billy Myers ("... in his fifth year ...")	40.00	20.00	12.00
(20)	Lee Riggs ("... in his fifth season...")	40.00	20.00	12.00
(21)	Les Scarsella	40.00	20.00	12.00
(22)	Eugene "Junior" Thompson	40.00	20.00	12.00
(23)	Johnny Vander Meer (Pitching)	50.00	25.00	15.00
(24)	Wm. "Bucky" Walters ("Won 15 games ...")	40.00	20.00	12.00
(25)	Jim Weaver	40.00	20.00	12.00
(26)	Bill Werber	40.00	20.00	12.00
(27)	Jimmy Wilson	40.00	20.00	12.00

1940 Cincinnati Reds Team Issue

Another early Reds team issue, this set of black-and-white 2-1/8" x 2-5/8" cards is unnumbered and features player portrait photos on the front. Name, position, biographical information and five years' worth of stats are on the back. The Reds were World Champions in 1940 (defeating Detroit), and the set features several special World Series cards, making it one of the first to feature events as well as individuals. The set was listed in the American Card Catalog as W711-2.

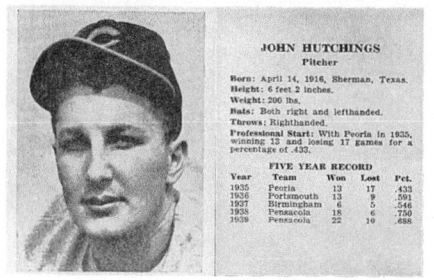

		NM	E	VG
	Complete Set (32):	900.00	450.00	275.00
	Common Player:	25.00	12.50	7.50
(1)	Morris Arnovich	25.00	12.50	7.50
(2)	William (Bill) Baker	25.00	12.50	7.50
(3)	Joseph Beggs	25.00	12.50	7.50
(4)	Harry Craft	25.00	12.50	7.50
(5)	Paul Derringer	25.00	12.50	7.50
(6)	Linus Frey	25.00	12.50	7.50
(7)	Ival Goodman	25.00	12.50	7.50
(8)	Harry (Hank) Gowdy	25.00	12.50	7.50
(9)	Witt Guise	25.00	12.50	7.50
(10)	Harry (Socko) Hartman	25.00	12.50	7.50
(11)	Willard Hershberger	35.00	17.50	10.50
(12)	John Hutchings	25.00	12.50	7.50
(13)	Edwin Joost	25.00	12.50	7.50
(14)	Ernie Lombardi	60.00	30.00	18.00
(15)	Frank McCormick	25.00	12.50	7.50
(16)	Myron McCormick	25.00	12.50	7.50
(17)	William Boyd McKechnie	60.00	30.00	18.00
(18)	Lloyd (Whitey) Moore	25.00	12.50	7.50
(19)	William (Bill) Myers	25.00	12.50	7.50
(20)	Lewis Riggs	25.00	12.50	7.50
(21)	Elmer Riddle	25.00	12.50	7.50
(22)	James A. Ripple	25.00	12.50	7.50
(23)	Milburn Shoffner	25.00	12.50	7.50
(24)	Eugene Thompson	25.00	12.50	7.50
(25)	James Turner	25.00	12.50	7.50
(26)	John Vander Meer	30.00	15.00	9.00
(27)	Wm. (Bucky) Walters	25.00	12.50	7.50
(28)	William (Bill) Werber	25.00	12.50	7.50
(29)	James Wilson	25.00	12.50	7.50
(30)	The Cincinnati Reds World Champions	25.00	12.50	7.50
(31a)	Tell the World About the Cincinnati Reds	25.00	12.50	7.50
(31b)	Tell the World About the Cincinnsti Red/World's Champions	25.00	12.50	7.50
(32)	Results 1940 World's Series	25.00	12.50	7.50

1954-1955 Cincinnati Reds Postcards

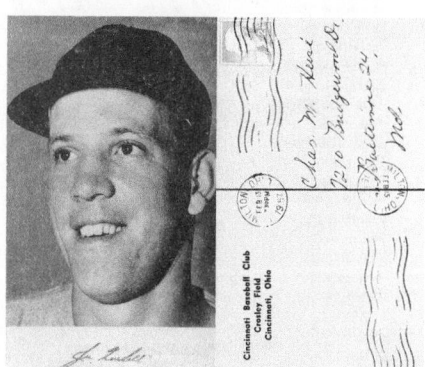

The first team-issued Redlegs postcards of the modern era were produced during the 1954 and 1955 seasons for use by players in answering fan requests for pictures and autographs. The cards are 3-1/2" x 5-5/8", printed in black-and-white on non-glossy cardboard stock. Fronts have poses which are borderless at top and sides. At bottom is a 3/4" white strip which is either blank or which has the player and team name printed. Many cards are found with stamped facsimile autographs, and/or authentically signed. Backs have a vertical line at center. At top-left is: "Cincinnati Baseball Club / Crosley Field / Cincinnati, Ohio." While there is no stamp box on the back, many of the cards have been postally used. The issue was listed in the "American Card Catalog" as PC746.

	NM	E	VG
Common Player:	15.00	7.50	4.50

		NM	E	VG
(1)	Bobby Adams (Fielding)	15.00	7.50	4.50
(2)	Bobby Adams (Portrait to neck.)	15.00	7.50	4.50
(3)	Dr. Wayne Anderson (Trainer)(Chest-up.))	30.00	15.00	9.00
(4)	Fred Baczewski (Ready to pitch.)	15.00	7.50	4.50
(5)	Ed Bailey (Batting to waist.)	15.00	7.50	4.50
(6)	Dick Bartell (Portrait to neck.)	15.00	7.50	4.50
(7)	Dick Bartell (Portrait to shoulders.)	15.00	7.50	4.50
(8)	Matt Batts (Batting follow-through.)	15.00	7.50	4.50
(9)	Gus Bell (Portrait to neck.)	15.00	7.50	4.50
(10)	Gus Bell (Waist up, ready to hit.)	15.00	7.50	4.50
(11)	Joe Black (Standing in dugout.)	15.00	7.50	4.50
(12)	Bob Borkowski (Batting follow-through.)	15.00	7.50	4.50
(13)	Buzz Boyle (Scout) (Chest-up in suit.))	40.00	20.00	12.00
(14)	Rocky Bridges (Portrait to neck.)	15.00	7.50	4.50
(15)	Smoky Burgess (Portrait to neck.)	15.00	7.50	4.50
(16)	Jackie Collum (Pitching follow-through.)	15.00	7.50	4.50
(17)	Jackie Collum (Portrait to neck.)	15.00	7.50	4.50
(18)	Powell Crosley, Jr. (Portrait)(President)	15.00	7.50	4.50
(19)	Jimmy Dykes (Standing in dugout.)	15.00	7.50	4.50
(20)	Nino Escalera (Portrait to neck.)	15.00	7.50	4.50
(21)	Tom Ferrick (Portrait to neck.)	15.00	7.50	4.50
(22)	Art Fowler (Hands over head.)	15.00	7.50	4.50
(23)	Art Fowler (Portrait to neck.)	15.00	7.50	4.50
(24)	Hershell Freeman (Portrait to shoulders.)	15.00	7.50	4.50
(26)	Jim Greengrass (Waist-up, batting.)	15.00	7.50	4.50
(27)	Don Gross (Portrait to neck.)	15.00	7.50	4.50
(28)	Charley Harmon (Batting to belt.)	15.00	7.50	4.50
(29)	Ray Jablonski (Batting to belt.)	15.00	7.50	4.50
(30)	Howie Judson (Portrait to neck.)	15.00	7.50	4.50
(31)	Johnny Klippstein (Pitching follow-through.)	15.00	7.50	4.50
(32)	Ted Kluszewski (Batting, cut out sleeves.)	30.00	15.00	9.00
(33)	Ted Kluszewski (Batting to belt.)	30.00	15.00	9.00
(34)	Ted Kluszewski (Batting follow-through, full length.)	30.00	15.00	9.00
(35)	Ted Kluszewski (Batting follow-through to waist.)	30.00	15.00	9.00
(36)	Ted Kluszewski (Batting follow-through, #18 on back.)	30.00	15.00	9.00
(37)	Ted Kluszewski (Stretching at 1B.)	30.00	15.00	9.00
(38)	Ted Kluszewski (Standing w/ four bats.)	30.00	15.00	9.00
(39)	Ted Kluszewski (Portrait to neck, looking right.)	30.00	15.00	9.00
(40)	Ted Kluszewski (Portrait to shoulders, leaning right.)	30.00	15.00	9.00
(41)	Hobie Landrith (Catching)	15.00	7.50	4.50
(42)	Hobie Landrith (Pose to neck.)	15.00	7.50	4.50
(43)	William McKechnie, Jr. (Portrait)(Farm club supervisor.))	15.00	7.50	4.50
(44)	Roy McMillan (Portrait to neck.)	15.00	7.50	4.50
(45)	Roy McMillan (Ready to hit.)	15.00	7.50	4.50
(46)	Lloyd Merriman (Ready to hit.)	15.00	7.50	4.50
(47)	Rudy Minarcin (Portrait to neck.)	15.00	7.50	4.50
(48)	Rudy Minarcin (Portrait to shoulders, chain.)	15.00	7.50	4.50
(49)	Joe Nuxhall (Portrait to neck.)	15.00	7.50	4.50
(51)	Joe Nuxhall (Pitching follow-through.)	15.00	7.50	4.50
(52)	Stan Palys (Batting follow-through.)	15.00	7.50	4.50
(53)	Harry Perkowski (Portrait to neck.)	15.00	7.50	4.50
(54)	Bud Podbielan (Ready to pitch, belt visible.)	15.00	7.50	4.50
(55)	Bud Podbielan (Ready to pitch, no belt.)	15.00	7.50	4.50
(56)	Wally Post (Ready to hit to belt, fans in back.)	22.50	11.00	6.75
(57)	Wally Post (Ready to hit to hips.)	22.50	11.00	6.75
(58)	Wally Post (Batting follow-through, pole on left.)	22.50	11.00	6.75
(59)	Wally Post (Batting follow-through, no pole.)	22.50	11.00	6.75
(60)	Wally Post (Portrait to neck.)	22.50	11.00	6.75
(61)	Ken Raffensberger (Pitching wind-up.)	15.00	7.50	4.50
(62)	Steve Ridzik (Portrait to neck.)	15.00	7.50	4.50
(63)	Connie Ryan (Portrait to neck.)	15.00	7.50	4.50
(64)	Moe Savransky (Portrait to neck.)	15.00	7.50	4.50
(65)	Andy Seminick (Batting follow-through.)	15.00	7.50	4.50
(66)	Al Silvera (Portrait to shoulders.)	15.00	7.50	4.50
(67)	Frank Smith (Ready to pitch.)	15.00	7.50	4.50
(68)	Milt Smith (Portrait to shoulders.)	15.00	7.50	4.50
(69)	Gerry Staley (Ready to pitch.)	15.00	7.50	4.50
(70)	Birdie Tebbetts (Portrait to neck.)	15.00	7.50	4.50
(71)	Birdie Tebbetts (Portrait to shoulders.)	15.00	7.50	4.50
(72)	Johnny Temple (Portrait to neck, mouth closed.)	15.00	7.50	4.50
(73)	Johnny Temple (Portrait to neck, mouth open.)	15.00	7.50	4.50
(74)	Bob Thurman (Batting follow-through.)	15.00	7.50	4.50
(76)	Corky Valentine (Pitching follow-through.)	15.00	7.50	4.50
(77)	Herm Wehmeier (Portrait to neck.)	15.00	7.50	4.50
(78)	George Zuverink (Portrait to neck.)	15.00	7.50	4.50
(79)	Crosley Field	15.00	7.50	4.50

1956 Cincinnati Reds Postcards

After a number of years issuing printed postcards for players to answer fan mail, the team began a three-year run of glossy black-and-white photographic card sets in 1956. About 3-1/2" x 5-3/4", the cards usually feature portrait photos, though some action poses are also seen. The pictures are bordered in white with a 1" or so border at bottom with the player and team names. Differentiating the 1956s from similarly formatted issues in 1957-1958 is best done on back. The 1956 cards are divided-back with "Post Card" at top. At right, in the stamp box, is "Place Postage Stamp Here" and, at bottom, "This space for address." Cards are numbered here alphabetically, with gaps left in the assigned numbering for future additions.

	NM	E	VG
Complete Set (31):	350.00	175.00	105.00
Common Player:	10.00	5.00	3.00

(1)	Tom Acker	10.00	5.00	3.00
(2)	Ed Bailey	10.00	5.00	3.00
(3)	Gus Bell	10.00	5.00	3.00
(4)	Joe Black	10.00	5.00	3.00
(5)	"Rocky" Bridges	10.00	5.00	3.00
(6)	"Smoky" Burgess	12.50	6.25	3.75
(7)	George Crowe	10.00	5.00	3.00
(8)	Jim Dyck	10.00	5.00	3.00
(9)	Jimmy Dykes	10.00	5.00	3.00
(11)	Bruce Edwards (Non-'56 back.)	10.00	5.00	3.00
(12)	Tom Ferrick	10.00	5.00	3.00
(13)	Joe Frazier	10.00	5.00	3.00
(14)	Hersh Freeman	10.00	5.00	3.00
(15)	Alex Grammas	10.00	5.00	3.00
(16)	Don Gross	10.00	5.00	3.00
(17)	Ray Jablonski	10.00	5.00	3.00
(18)	Larry Jansen	10.00	5.00	3.00
(19)	Hal Jeffcoat	10.00	5.00	3.00
(21)	Johnny Klippstein	10.00	5.00	3.00
(22)	Ted Kluszewski	20.00	10.00	6.00
(23)	Brooks Lawrence	10.00	5.00	3.00
(24)	Frank McCormick	10.00	5.00	3.00
(25)	Roy McMillan	10.00	5.00	3.00
(26)	Joe Nuxhall	12.50	6.25	3.75
(27)	Stan Palys ('56 back)	10.00	5.00	3.00
(28)	Stan Palys (Non-'56 back.)	10.00	5.00	3.00
(29)	Wally Post	10.00	5.00	3.00
(31)	Frank Robinson	75.00	37.00	22.00
(32)	"Birdie" Tebbetts	10.00	5.00	3.00
(33)	Johnny Temple	10.00	5.00	3.00
(34)	Bob Thurman	10.00	5.00	3.00

1957 Cincinnati Reds Picture Pack

FRANK ROBINSON, Redlegs

Similar in format to the Jay Publishing photo packs, this appears to be a team-issued souvenir item, with many of the pictures having been seen in other team-related contexts. The black-and-white, blank-backed pictures measure 5" x 7". They can be differentiated from contemporary Jay photos by the fact that only the team nickname, "Redlegs," appears, rather than city and team. Player names are in all-caps.

		NM	E	VG
Complete Set (12):		45.00	22.50	13.50
Common Player:		4.00	2.00	1.25
(1)	Ed Bailey	4.00	2.00	1.25
(2)	Gus Bell	4.00	2.00	1.25
(3)	Smoky Burgess	4.00	2.00	1.25
(4)	Hersh Freeman	4.00	2.00	1.25
(5)	Ted Kluszewski	7.50	3.75	2.25
(6)	Brooks Lawrence	4.00	2.00	1.25
(7)	Roy McMillan	4.00	2.00	1.25
(8)	Joe Nuxhall	4.00	2.00	1.25
(9)	Wally Post	4.00	2.00	1.25
(10)	Frank Robinson	15.00	7.50	4.50
(11)	Birdie Tebbetts	4.00	2.00	1.25
(12)	Johnny Temple	4.00	2.00	1.25

1957 Cincinnati Reds Postcards

JOHNNY KLIPPSTEIN
Cincinnati Redlegs

The second in a long run of glossy-front, black-and-white annual postcard issues, the 1957 can often be distinguished from the 1956 and 1958 cards by the appearance of players in sleeveless uniforms with dark undershirts. Even more distinguishing is that the 1957s, on back, have "PHOTO POST CARD" across the top, and lack the notice "This Space for Address" which appeared on the 1956 cards. The '57s can also be identified by "Divolite Peerless" which appears in the postage-stamp box. The 3-1/2" x 5-3/4" cards have white borders. At bottom is 1" white space with the player name and "Cincinnati Redlegs" and space for an autograph. The unnumbered cards are checklisted here in alphabetical order.

		NM	E	VG
Complete Set (34):		300.00	150.00	90.00
Common Player:		9.00	4.50	2.75
(1)	Tom Acker	9.00	4.50	2.75
(2)	Ed Bailey	9.00	4.50	2.75
(3)	Gus Bell	9.00	4.50	2.75
(4)	"Rocky" Bridges	9.00	4.50	2.75
(5)	"Smoky" Burgess	11.00	5.50	3.25
(6)	George Crowe	9.00	4.50	2.75
(7)	Bobby Durnbaugh	9.00	4.50	2.75
(8)	Jimmy Dykes	9.00	4.50	2.75
(9)	Tom Ferrick	9.00	4.50	2.75
(10)	Art Fowler	9.00	4.50	2.75
(11)	Hersh Freeman	9.00	4.50	2.75
(12)	Alex Grammas	9.00	4.50	2.75
(13)	Don Gross	9.00	4.50	2.75
(14)	Warren Hacker	9.00	4.50	2.75
(15)	Bobby Henrich	9.00	4.50	2.75
(16)	Don Hoak	11.00	5.50	3.25
(17)	Hal Jeffcoat	9.00	4.50	2.75
(18)	Johnny Klippstein	9.00	4.50	2.75
(19)	Ted Kluszewski (Batting)	18.00	9.00	5.50
(20)	Ted Kluszewski (Portrait)	18.00	9.00	5.50
(21)	Brooks Lawrence	9.00	4.50	2.75
(22)	Jerry Lynch	9.00	4.50	2.75
(23)	Frank McCormick	9.00	4.50	2.75
(24)	Roy McMillan	9.00	4.50	2.75
(25)	Joe Nuxhall	9.00	4.50	2.75
(26)	Wally Post	9.00	4.50	2.75
(27)	Frank Robinson	45.00	22.00	13.50
(28)	Raul Sanchez	9.00	4.50	2.75
(29)	Art Schult	9.00	4.50	2.75
(30)	"Birdie" Tebbetts	9.00	4.50	2.75
(31)	Johnny Temple	9.00	4.50	2.75
(32)	Bob Thurman	9.00	4.50	2.75
(33)	Pete Whisenant (Batting)	9.00	4.50	2.75
(34)	Pete Whisenant (Portrait)	9.00	4.50	2.75

1958 Cincinnati Reds Postcards

WALT DROPO
Cincinnati Redlegs

Cards from the third of a long run of glossy-front, black-and-white annual postcard issues can be most often distinguished from similarly formatted 1956-57 cards by the appearance of players in white uniforms with white caps. Two back styles are known. One, like the 1957 issue, has a postage box with "Divolite Peerless" inside and one without the box, but with "Post Card" and "Actual Photograph." Both have a vertical dividing line. The 3-1/2" x 5-3/4" cards have white borders. At bottom is 1" white space with the player name and "Cincinnati Redlegs" and space for an autograph. The unnumbered cards are checklisted here in alphabetical order, though this list may not be complete as several stars are unknown in this style.

		NM	E	VG
Complete Set (30):		300.00	150.00	90.00
Common Player:		9.00	4.50	2.75
(1)	Tom Acker	9.00	4.50	2.75
(2)	Dr. Wayne Anderson (Trainer)	9.00	4.50	2.75
(3)	Ed Bailey	9.00	4.50	2.75
(4)	Steve Bilko	9.00	4.50	2.75
(5)	"Smoky" Burgess	11.00	5.50	3.25
(6)	George Crowe	9.00	4.50	2.75
(7)	Walt Dropo	9.00	4.50	2.75
(8)	Jimmie Dykes	9.00	4.50	2.75
(9)	Tom Ferrick	9.00	4.50	2.75
(10)	Dee Fondy	9.00	4.50	2.75
(11)	Alex Grammas	9.00	4.50	2.75
(12)	Harvey Haddix	9.00	4.50	2.75
(13)	Hal Jeffcoat	9.00	4.50	2.75
(14)	Alex Kellner	9.00	4.50	2.75
(15)	Johnny Klippstein	9.00	4.50	2.75
(16)	Turk Lown	9.00	4.50	2.75
(17)	Jerry Lynch	9.00	4.50	2.75
(18)	Roy McMillan	9.00	4.50	2.75
(19)	Ed Miksis (Pinstripes)	9.00	4.50	2.75
(20)	Joe Nuxhall	10.00	5.00	3.00
(21)	Vada Pinson	15.00	7.50	4.50
(22)	Bob Purkey	9.00	4.50	2.75
(23)	Charley Rabe	9.00	4.50	2.75
(24)	John Riddle	9.00	4.50	2.75
(25)	Willard Schmidt	9.00	4.50	2.75
(26)	Manager "Birdie" Tebbetts (Portrait to neck.)	9.00	4.50	2.75
(27)	Manager "Birdie" Tebbetts (Portrait, white background, #1 shows.)	9.00	4.50	2.75
(28)	Johnny Temple	9.00	4.50	2.75
(29)	Bob Thurman	9.00	4.50	2.75
(30)	Pete Whisenant	9.00	4.50	2.75

1969 Citgo Coins

This 20-player set of small (about 1" in diameter) metal coins was issued by Citgo in 1969 to commemorate professional baseball's 100th anniversary. The brass-coated coins, susceptible to oxidation, display the player in a crude portrait with his name across the top. The backs honor the 100th anniversary of pro ball. The coins are unnumbered but are generally checklisted according to numbers that appear on a red, white and blue paper display folder that was available from Citgo by mail.

		NM	E	VG
Complete Set (20):		80.00	40.00	25.00
Common Player:		2.00	1.00	.60
Cardboard Display Folder:		30.00	15.00	9.00
Unopened Pack:		12.00		
1	Denny McLain	2.50	1.25	.70
2	Dave McNally	2.00	1.00	.60
3	Jim Lonborg	2.00	1.00	.60
4	Harmon Killebrew	6.50	3.25	2.00
5	Mel Stottlemyre	2.00	1.00	.60
6	Willie Horton	2.00	1.00	.60
7	Jim Fregosi	2.00	1.00	.60
8	Rico Petrocelli	2.00	1.00	.60
9	Stan Bahnsen	2.00	1.00	.60
10	Frank Howard	2.50	1.25	.70
11	Joe Torre	2.50	1.25	.70
12	Jerry Koosman	2.00	1.00	.60
13	Ron Santo	3.50	1.75	1.00
14	Pete Rose	20.00	10.00	6.00
15	Rusty Staub	2.00	1.00	.60
16	Henry Aaron	20.00	10.00	6.00
17	Richie Allen	3.50	1.75	1.00
18	Ron Swoboda	2.00	1.00	.60
19	Willie McCovey	6.50	3.25	2.00
20	Jim Bunning	5.00	2.50	1.50

1969 Citgo New York Mets

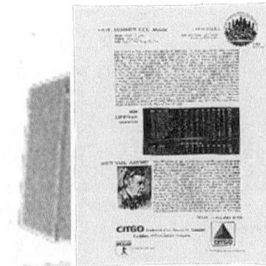

One of several regional issues in the Mets World Championship season of 1969, this set of 8" x 10" player portraits was sponsored by Citgo, whose gas stations distributed the pictures with fuel purchases. Fronts feature large portraits and smaller action pictures of the player, done in pastels, set against a bright pastel background. The paintings are the work of noted celebrity artist John Wheeldon. Beneath the pictures is a facsimile autograph. The player's name is printed in the bottom border. Backs are printed in black-and-white and include biography and career details, full major and minor league stats and a self-portrait and biography of the artist. Logos of the Mets, the Players Association and the sponsor complete the back design. The unnumbered player pictures are checklisted here in alphabetical order.

	NM	E	VG
Complete Set (8):	65.00	32.00	19.50
Common Player:	6.50	3.25	2.00
(1) Tommie Agee	8.00	4.00	2.50
(2) Ken Boswell	6.50	3.25	2.00
(3) Gary Gentry	6.50	3.25	2.00
(4) Jerry Grote	6.50	3.25	2.00
(5) Cleon Jones	6.50	3.25	2.00
(6) Jerry Koosman	8.00	4.00	2.50
(7) Ed Kranepool	6.50	3.25	2.00
(8) Tom Seaver	25.00	12.50	7.50

1975 Clark & Sons Baseball Favorites

To commemorate the firm's 10 years in business and the Boston Red Sox first pennant since 1967, Clark & Sons Locksmiths of Rhode Island issued this set of Red Sox greats. Two versions were issued. The first has a "324 Waterman Avenue, Providence" address on back. A second printing corrected the errors to "324A Waterman Avenue, East Providence" and added a wavy line around the photo and name on front. Cards measure 2-1/2" x 3-5/8" and are printed in black-and-white.

	NM	E	VG
Complete Set (4):	12.50	6.25	3.75
Common Player:	1.25	.60	.40
1 Bobby Doerr	2.00	1.00	.60
2 Ted Williams	10.00	5.00	3.00
3 Dom DiMaggio	2.50	1.25	.70
4 Johnny Pesky	1.25	.60	.40

1921 Clark's Bread

It is not known to what extent this set's checklist of base cards and possible variations parallels the contemporary blank-back 1921-1922 W575-1 strip cards. The cards measure about 2" x 3-1/4" and are printed in black-and-white. It is unknown into which region the bread cards might have been issued. Collectors have been known to pay a premium of 10X for this version.

	NM	E	VG
Common Player:	1,200	600.00	350.00
Hal of Famers: 4-6X			

(See 1921 American Caramel Series of 80 or 1922 W575-1 for checklists and base card values.)

1972 Classic Cards

 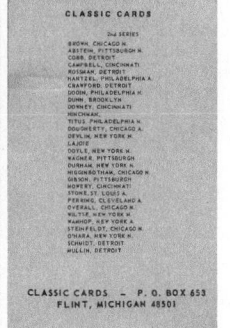

The set depicts players from 1900-1909 in sepiatone photos printed on thin, cream-colored card stock by the Flint, MI company not related to the 1990s card maker of the same name. The first series features sequentially numbered cards, the remainder marked only with a series number. Card size is 2-3/4" x 4-1/2" for the first series and 2-3/4" x 4-1/4" for the last three 30-card series.

	NM	E	VG
Complete Set (120):	50.00	25.00	10.00
Common Player:	2.00	1.00	.60
1 Griffith, Cincinnati	2.00	1.00	.60
2 Johnson, Washington	2.00	1.00	.60
3 Ganley, Washington	2.00	1.00	.60
4 Tinker, Chicago	2.00	1.00	.60
5 Chance, Chicago	2.00	1.00	.60
6 Conroy, Washington	2.00	1.00	.60
7 Bresnahan, N.Y.	2.00	1.00	.60
8 Powell, Pittsburgh	2.00	1.00	.60
9 Pfeister, Chicago	2.00	1.00	.60
10 McCarthy, Boston	2.00	1.00	.60
11 McConnell, Boston	2.00	1.00	.60
12 Jennings, Detroit	2.00	1.00	.60
13 Lennox, Brooklyn	2.00	1.00	.60
14 McCormick, N.Y.	2.00	1.00	.60
15 Merkle, N.Y.	2.00	1.00	.60
16 Hoblitzell, Cincinnati	2.00	1.00	.60
17 Dahlen, Boston	2.00	1.00	.60
18 Chance, Chicago	2.00	1.00	.60
19 Ferguson, Boston	2.00	1.00	.60
20 Camnitz, Pittsburgh	2.00	1.00	.60
21 N.Y.(Neal Ball)	2.00	1.00	.60
22 Hemphill, N.Y.	2.00	1.00	.60
23 Baker, Philadelphia	2.00	1.00	.60
24 Mathewson, N.Y.	5.00	2.50	1.50
25 Burch, Brooklyn	2.00	1.00	.60
26 Grant, Philadelphia	2.00	1.00	.60
27 Ames, N.Y.	2.00	1.00	.60
28 Newton, N.Y.	2.00	1.00	.60
29 Moran, Chicago	2.00	1.00	.60
30 Lajoie, Cleveland	2.00	1.00	.60
(31) Abstein, Pittsburgh	2.00	1.00	.60
(32) Brown, Chicago	2.00	1.00	.60
(33) Campbell, Cincinnati	2.00	1.00	.60
(34) Cobb, Detroit	5.00	2.50	1.50
(35) Crawford, Detroit	2.00	1.00	.60
(36) Devlin, N.Y.	2.00	1.00	.60
(37) Dooin, Philadelphia	2.00	1.00	.60
(38) Dougherty, Chicago	2.00	1.00	.60
(39) Downey, Cincinnati	2.00	1.00	.60
(40) Doyle, New York	2.00	1.00	.60
(41) Dunn, Brooklyn	2.00	1.00	.60
(42) Durham, N.Y.	2.00	1.00	.60
(43) Gibson, Pittsburgh	2.00	1.00	.60
(44) Hartzel, Philadelphia	2.00	1.00	.60
(45) Higginbotham, Chicago	2.00	1.00	.60
(46) Hinchman	2.00	1.00	.60
(47) Lajoie	2.00	1.00	.60
(48) Mowery, Cincinnati	2.00	1.00	.60
(49) Mullin, Detroit	2.00	1.00	.60
(50) O'Hara, New York	2.00	1.00	.60
(51) Overall, Chicago	2.00	1.00	.60
(52) Perring, Cleveland	2.00	1.00	.60
(53) Rossman, Detroit	2.00	1.00	.60
(54) Schmidt, Detroit	2.00	1.00	.60
(55) Steinfeldt, Chicago	2.00	1.00	.60
(56) Stone, St. Louis	2.00	1.00	.60
(57) Titus, Philadelphia	2.00	1.00	.60
(58) Wagner, Pittsburgh	2.00	1.00	.60
(59) Wamhow, N.Y.	2.00	1.00	.60
(60) Wiltse, New York	2.00	1.00	.60
(61) Barger, Brooklyn	2.00	1.00	.60
(62) Bergen, Brooklyn	2.00	1.00	.60
(63) Bowerman, Boston	2.00	1.00	.60
(64) Bransfeld, Philadelphia	2.00	1.00	.60
(65) Bresnahan, St. Louis	2.00	1.00	.60
(66) Coakley, Chicago	2.00	1.00	.60
(67) Donovan, Detroit	2.00	1.00	.60
(68) Elberfeld, New York	2.00	1.00	.60
(69) Evers, Chicago	2.00	1.00	.60
(70) Fromme, Cincinnati	2.00	1.00	.60
(71) Herzog, N.Y.	2.00	1.00	.60
(72) Hummel, Cincinnati	2.00	1.00	.60
(73) Jordan, Brooklyn	2.00	1.00	.60
(74) Keeler, New York	2.00	1.00	.60
(75) Lumley, Brooklyn	2.00	1.00	.60
(76) Maddox, Pittsburgh	2.00	1.00	.60
(77) McGinnity, New York	2.00	1.00	.60
(78) McGraw, New York	2.00	1.00	.60
(79) McIntyre, Brooklyn	2.00	1.00	.60
(80) Moriarity, New York	2.00	1.00	.60
(81) Pastorius, Brooklyn	2.00	1.00	.60
(82) Purtell, Chicago	2.00	1.00	.60
(83) Schulte, Chicago	2.00	1.00	.60
(84) Sebring, Brooklyn	2.00	1.00	.60
(85) Smith, Washington	2.00	1.00	.60
(86) Speaker, Boston	5.00	2.50	1.50
(87) Spencer, Boston	2.00	1.00	.60
(88) Tuckey, Boston	2.00	1.00	.60
(89) Vaughn, New York	2.00	1.00	.60
(90) Wheat, Brooklyn	2.00	1.00	.60
(91) Altzier, Chicago	2.00	1.00	.60
(92) Bender, Philadelphia	2.00	1.00	.60
(93) Cincinnati(Bob Ewing)	2.00	1.00	.60
(94) Bresnahan, St. Louis	2.00	1.00	.60
(95) Chappelle, Boston	2.00	1.00	.60
(96) Chase, New York	2.00	1.00	.60
(97) Daley, Cincinnati	2.00	1.00	.60
(98) Davis, Chicago	2.00	1.00	.60
(99) Delahanty, St. Louis	2.00	1.00	.60
(100) Donohue, Washington	2.00	1.00	.60
(101) Doyle, New York	2.00	1.00	.60
(102) Ellis, St. Louis	2.00	1.00	.60
(103) Graham, St. Louis	2.00	1.00	.60
(104) Herzog, New York	2.00	1.00	.60
(105) Hyatt, Pittsburgh	2.00	1.00	.60
(106) Konetchy, St. Louis	2.00	1.00	.60
(107) Lake, New York	2.00	1.00	.60
(108) Lord, Boston	2.00	1.00	.60
(109) New York(Luther Taylor)	2.00	1.00	.60
(110) McLean, Cincinnati	2.00	1.00	.60
(111) Needham, Chicago	2.00	1.00	.60
(112) Pearce, Cincinnati	2.00	1.00	.60
(113) Powell, Pittsburgh	2.00	1.00	.60
(114) Purtell, Chicago	2.00	1.00	.60
(115) Schreck, Philadelphia	2.00	1.00	.60
(116) Storke, Pittsburgh	2.00	1.00	.60
(117) Strunk, Philadelphia	2.00	1.00	.60
(118) Summers, Detroit	2.00	1.00	.60
(119) Thomas, Philadelphia	2.00	1.00	.60
(120) Wagner, Boston	2.00	1.00	.60

1973 Roberto Clemente Memorial Postcard

This collectors' issue postcard was isused as a memorial. In standard 3-1/2" x 5-1/2" format with a postcard-style back, the black-and-white card has printed in the wide bottom border, the player's name, dates of his birth and death and, "In Memory OF A COURAGEOUS HUMAN BEING." On back is a credit line to Allied Printing.

	NM	E	VG
Roberto Clemente	25.00	12.50	7.50

1913 Cleveland Indians Schedule Postcards

The extent to which the team may have used this type of postcard to announce forthcoming home series is unknown. It can be assumed other cards with other players featured were issued during the course of the season. About 7" x 3-1/2", the card has a portrait photo on the left end of its black-and-white front. On back, in red and black, are details of upcoming series and ticket outlet information.

	NM	E	VG
Joe Birmingham	900.00	450.00	275.00
Ray Chapman	1,350	675.00	400.00
Jack Graney	900.00	450.00	275.00
Joe Jackson, Fred Clarke (Pirates exhibition game.)	2,500	1,250	750.00
Doc Johnston	900.00	450.00	275.00
Willie Mitchell	900.00	450.00	275.00

1937 Cleveland Press Indians Album

These newspaper cut-outs from the 1937 Cleveland Press depict Cleveland Indians players and coaches staff. Published at the start of their new season. Each cut-out has a paragraph at the bottom highlighting the player's performance in the 1936 season. The cut-outs measure 3-1/2 wide but measure between 7-9 inches long depending on the length of text and photo.

		NM	E	VG
Complete Set (29):		300.00	150.00	75.00
Common player:		10.00	5.00	2.50
1	Frank Pytlak	10.00	5.00	2.50
2	Roy Weatherly	10.00	5.00	2.50
3	Roy Hughes	10.00	5.00	2.50
4	Bruce Campbell	10.00	5.00	2.50
5	Lyn Lary	10.00	5.00	2.50
6	Julius Solters	15.00	7.50	4.50
7	Earl Averill	15.00	7.50	4.50
8	Mel Harder	10.00	5.00	2.50
9	Tom Drake	10.00	5.00	2.50
10	Billy Sullivan	10.00	5.00	2.50
11	Whitlow Wyatt	10.00	5.00	2.50
12	Denny Galehouse	10.00	5.00	2.50
13	Earl Whitehill	10.00	5.00	2.50
14	Willis Hudlin	10.00	5.00	2.50
15	Odell Hale	10.00	5.00	2.50
16	Carl Fischer	10.00	5.00	2.50
17	Joe Becker	10.00	5.00	2.50
18	Bob Feller	30.00	15.00	9.00
19	Hal Trosky	15.00	7.50	4.50
20	Jeff Heath	10.00	5.00	2.50
21	Ivy Paul Andrews	10.00	5.00	2.50
22	Lloyd Brown	10.00	5.00	2.50
23	Johnny Allen	10.00	5.00	2.50
24	Joe Heving	10.00	5.00	2.50
25	John Kroner	10.00	5.00	2.50
26	George Uhle	10.00	5.00	2.50
27	Wally Schang	10.00	5.00	2.50
28	Max Weisman	10.00	5.00	2.50
29	Steve O'Neill	10.00	5.00	2.50

1947 Cleveland Indians Picture Pack

The first of several annual issues of player photo packs, the 1947 version offered "autographed photos" of all players on the team's roster as of July 1. All players were presented in studio quality portraits in 6" x 8-1/2" format, lithographed on heavy paper with a facsimile autograph. A thin white border surrounds the photo. Backs are blank. The photos were sold in sets for 50 cents. The unnumbered pictures are checklisted here alphabetically.

	NM	E	VG
Complete Set (25):	100.00	50.00	30.00
Common player:	3.00	1.50	.90

		NM	E	VG
(1)	Don Black	4.00	2.00	1.25
(2)	Eddie Bockman	3.00	1.50	.90
(3)	Lou Boudreau	9.00	4.50	2.75
(4)	Jack Conway	3.00	1.50	.90
(5)	Larry Doby	25.00	12.50	7.50
(6)	Hank Edwards	3.00	1.50	.90
(7)	"Red" Embree	3.00	1.50	.90
(8)	Bob Feller	25.00	12.50	7.50
(9)	Les Fleming	3.00	1.50	.90
(10)	Allen Gettel	3.00	1.50	.90
(11)	Joe Gordon	9.00	4.50	2.75
(12)	Steve Gromek	3.00	1.50	.90
(13)	Mel Harder	4.50	2.25	1.25
(14)	Jim Hegan	3.00	1.50	.90
(15)	Ken Keltner	4.50	2.25	1.25
(16)	Ed Klieman	3.00	1.50	.90
(17)	Bob Lemon	9.00	4.50	2.75
(18)	Al Lopez	9.00	4.50	2.75
(19)	George Metkovich	3.00	1.50	.90
(20)	Dale Mitchell	4.00	2.00	1.25
(21)	Hal Peck	3.00	1.50	.90
(22)	Eddie Robinson	3.00	1.50	.90
(23)	Hank Ruszkowski	3.00	1.50	.90
(24)	Pat Seerey	3.00	1.50	.90
(25)	Bryan Stephens	3.00	1.50	.90
(26)	Les Willis	3.00	1.50	.90

1948-52 Cleveland Indians Pencil Clips

These celluloid and steel pencil clips were sold at the ballpark to be used on pencils given away with scorecards. The round button portion of the clip is about 3/4" in diameter, while the clip itself is a little over 1-1/2". Black-and-white player portraits are centered in a colored border with the team name at top and player name at bottom. While many of the same players and photos were used year after year, issue date of the clips can be determined by the border color. In 1951-1952, when blue borders were used, the year is distinguished by the presence (1951) or absence (1952) of a white union logo on back.

		NM	E	VG
Common Player:		35.00	17.50	10.50
	1948 (Black)			
(1)	Gene Bearden	35.00	17.50	10.50
(2)	John Berardino	40.00	20.00	12.00
(3)	Don Black	35.00	17.50	10.50
(4)	Lou Boudreau	45.00	22.00	13.50
(5)	Russ Christopher	35.00	17.50	10.50
(6)	Allie Clark	35.00	17.50	10.50
(7)	Larry Doby	60.00	30.00	18.00
(8)	Hank Edwards	35.00	17.50	10.50
(9)	Bob Feller	50.00	25.00	15.00
(10)	Al Gettel	35.00	17.50	10.50
(11)	Joe Gordon	45.00	22.00	13.50
(12)	Walt Judnich	35.00	17.50	10.50
(13)	Ken Keltner	35.00	17.50	10.50
(14)	Bob Lemon	45.00	22.00	13.50
(15)	Dale Mitchell	35.00	17.50	10.50
(16)	Bob Muncrief	35.00	17.50	10.50
(17)	Eddie Robinson	35.00	17.50	10.50
(18)	Pat Seerey	35.00	17.50	10.50
(19)	Joe Tipton	35.00	17.50	10.50
(20)	Thurman Tucker	35.00	17.50	10.50
	1949 (Brown)			
(1)	Gene Bearden	35.00	17.50	10.50
(2)	Ray Boone	35.00	17.50	10.50
(3)	Lou Boudreau	45.00	22.00	13.50
(4)	Allie Clark	35.00	17.50	10.50
(5)	Larry Doby	55.00	27.00	16.50
(6)	Bob Feller	50.00	25.00	15.00
(7)	Mike Garcia	35.00	17.50	10.50
(8)	Joe Gordon	45.00	22.00	13.50
(9)	Steve Gromek	35.00	17.50	10.50
(10)	Jim Hegan	35.00	17.50	10.50
(11)	Ken Keltner	35.00	17.50	10.50
(12)	Bob Kennedy	35.00	17.50	10.50
(13)	Bob Lemon	45.00	22.00	13.50
(14)	Dale Mitchell	35.00	17.50	10.50
(15)	Satchel Paige	125.00	62.00	37.00
(16)	Mike Tresh	35.00	17.50	10.50
(17)	Bill Veeck	45.00	22.00	13.50
(18)	Mickey Vernon	35.00	17.50	10.50
(19)	Early Wynn	45.00	22.00	13.50
(20)	Sam Zoldak	35.00	17.50	10.50
	1950 (White)			
(1)	Bobby Avila	35.00	17.50	10.50
(2)	Al Benton	35.00	17.50	10.50
(3)	Ray Boone	35.00	17.50	10.50
(4)	Lou Boudreau	45.00	22.00	13.50
(5)	Larry Doby	55.00	27.00	16.50
(6)	Luke Easter	40.00	20.00	12.00
(7)	Bob Feller	50.00	25.00	15.00
(8)	Mike Garcia	40.00	20.00	12.00
(9)	Steve Gromek	35.00	17.50	10.50
(10)	Jim Hegan	35.00	17.50	10.50
(11)	Bob Kennedy	35.00	17.50	10.50
(12)	Bob Lemon	45.00	22.00	13.50
(13)	Dale Mitchell	35.00	17.50	10.50
(14)	Ray Murray	35.00	17.50	10.50
(15)	Al Rosen	40.00	20.00	12.00
(16)	Thurman Tucker	35.00	17.50	10.50
(17)	Dick Weik	35.00	17.50	10.50
(18)	Early Wynn	45.00	22.00	13.50
	1950 (Blue w/union logo.)			
(1)	Bobby Avila	35.00	17.50	10.50
(2)	Ray Boone	35.00	17.50	10.50
(3)	Larry Doby	55.00	27.00	16.50
(4)	Luke Easter	40.00	20.00	12.00
(5)	Bob Feller	50.00	25.00	15.00
(6)	Jim Hegan	35.00	17.50	10.50
(7)	Bob Kennedy	35.00	17.50	10.50
(8)	Bob Lemon	45.00	22.00	13.50
(9)	Al Lopez	45.00	22.00	13.50
(10)	Dale Mitchell	35.00	17.50	10.50
(11)	Al Rosen	40.00	20.00	12.00
(12)	Early Wynn	45.00	22.00	13.50
	1952 (Blue, no logo.)			
(1)	Bobby Avila	35.00	17.50	10.50
(2)	Lou Brissie	35.00	17.50	10.50
(3)	Bob Chakales	35.00	17.50	10.50
(4)	Merrill Combs	35.00	17.50	10.50
(5)	Larry Doby	55.00	27.00	16.50
(6)	Luke Easter	40.00	20.00	12.00
(7)	Bob Feller	50.00	25.00	15.00
(8)	Mike Garcia	40.00	20.00	12.00
(9)	Steve Gromek	35.00	17.50	10.50
(10)	Jim Hegan	35.00	17.50	10.50
(11)	Sam Jones	35.00	17.50	10.50
(12)	Bob Lemon	45.00	22.00	13.50
(13)	Barney McCosky	35.00	17.50	10.50
(14)	Dale Mitchell	35.00	17.50	10.50
(15)	Pete Reiser	35.00	17.50	10.50
(16)	Al Rosen	45.00	22.50	13.50
(17)	Harry Simpson	35.00	17.50	10.50
(18)	Birdie Tebbetts	35.00	17.50	10.50
(19)	Early Wynn	45.00	22.00	13.50

1948 Cleveland Indians Picture Pack

For its second year of production as a souvenir sales item, the Indians picture pack utilized the basic format of the previous year: black-and-white photos with a white border and facsimile autograph. Backs were again blank. The 1948 set can be differentiated from the 1947 issue by its size; at 6-1/2" x 9", the '48s are larger by a half-inch horizontally and vertically. The unnumbered pictures are checklisted here in alphabetical order. The specific content of the packs may have changed over the course of the season with roster moves.

		NM	E	VG
Complete Set (33):		300.00	150.00	90.00
Common Player:		6.00	3.00	1.75
(1)	Gene Bearden	6.00	3.00	1.75
(2)	Johnny Berardino	12.00	6.00	3.50
(3)	Don Black	7.50	3.75	2.25

		NM	EX	VG
(4)	Lou Boudreau	20.00	10.00	6.00
(5)	Russ Christopher	6.00	3.00	1.75
(6)	Allie Clark	6.00	3.00	1.75
(7)	Larry Doby	25.00	12.50	7.50
(8)	Hank Edwards	6.00	3.00	1.75
(9)	Bob Feller	25.00	12.50	7.50
(10)	Joe Gordon	6.00	3.00	1.75
(11)	Hank Greenberg (GM, in uniform.)	40.00	20.00	12.00
(12)	Hank Greenberg (GM, in civies.)	20.00	10.00	6.00
(13)	Steve Gromek	6.00	3.00	1.75
(14)	Mel Harder	6.00	3.00	1.75
(15)	Jim Hegan	6.00	3.00	1.75
(16)	Walt Judnich	6.00	3.00	1.75
(17)	Ken Keltner	6.00	3.00	1.75
(18)	Bob Kennedy	6.00	3.00	1.75
(19)	Ed Klieman	6.00	3.00	1.75
(20)	Bob Lemon	20.00	10.00	6.00
(21)	Al Lopez	20.00	10.00	6.00
(22)	Bill McKechnie	20.00	10.00	6.00
(23)	Dale Mitchell	6.00	3.00	1.75
(24)	Bob Muncrief	6.00	3.00	1.75
(25)	Satchel Paige	60.00	30.00	18.00
(26)	Hal Peck	6.00	3.00	1.75
(27)	Eddie Robinson	6.00	3.00	1.75
(28)	Muddy Ruel	6.00	3.00	1.75
(29)	Joe Tipton	6.00	3.00	1.75
(30)	Thurman Tucker	6.00	3.00	1.75
(31)	Bill Veeck (Owner)	20.00	10.00	6.00
(32)	Sam Zoldak	6.00	3.00	1.75
(33)	Cleveland Municipal Stadium	9.00	4.50	2.75

1949 Cleveland Indians Display Photos

BOB FELLER - P. CLEVELAND INDIANS

Members of the Tribe are pictured (in the same poses found on their photo-pack issues) on these large-format (11" x 14") display photos, said to have been used for in-stadium promotions. It is possible there are others besides those checklisted here.

		NM	E	VG
Complete Set (11):		650.00	325.00	200.00
Common Player:		40.00	20.00	12.00
(1)	Ray Boone	45.00	22.00	13.50
(2)	Larry Doby	100.00	50.00	30.00
(3)	Luke Easter	50.00	25.00	15.00
(4)	Bob Feller	125.00	62.00	37.00
(5)	Jim Hegan	40.00	20.00	12.00
(6)	Bob Kennedy	40.00	20.00	12.00
(7)	Bob Lemon	75.00	37.00	22.00
(8)	Al Lopez	75.00	37.00	22.00
(9)	Dale Mitchell	40.00	20.00	12.00
(10)	Al Rosen	50.00	25.00	15.00
(11)	Early Wynn	75.00	37.00	22.00

1949 Cleveland Indians Picture Pack (3)

In addition to the "Autographed Photos" picture packs issued in 1949 (Portrait and Action versions), a third photo pack was issued, presumably also available at Municipal Stadium and other souvenir outlets. Like most Indians' picture packs of the era, the player photos are in a 6-1/2" x 9" black-and-white, blank-back format with narrow white bor-

ders. This set is a mix of portrait and action photos, some of which are found in other Indians' photo packs. The principal difference in this set is that rather than having a facsimile player autograph on front, this set uses script versions of the player names, in either black or white. It is likely this checklist is not complete as Indians' photo packs of the era generally contained 25-33 pictures, and several of the team's stars are not represented in this list. Gaps have been left in the assigned numbering to accommodate future additions.

		NM	EX	VG
Common Player:		5.00	2.50	1.50
(2)	Gene Bearden	5.00	2.50	1.50
(4)	Ray Boone	5.00	2.50	1.50
(5)	Lou Boudreau	15.00	7.50	4.50
(6)	Allie Clark	5.00	2.50	1.50
(9)	Bob Feller	20.00	10.00	6.00
(11)	Mike Garcia	5.00	2.50	1.50
(12)	Joe Gordon	15.00	7.50	4.50
(13)	Steve Gromek	5.00	2.50	1.50
(14)	Jim Hegan	5.00	2.50	1.50
(17)	Dale Mitchell	5.00	2.50	1.50
(19)	Satchell (Satchel) Paige	25.00	12.50	7.50
(20)	Frank Papish	5.00	2.50	1.50
(22)	Thurman Tucker	5.00	2.50	1.50
(23)	Mickey Vernon	5.00	2.50	1.50
(25)	Sam Zoldak	5.00	2.50	1.50

1949 Cleveland Indians Picture Pack - Action

Posed action photos are the focus of this team-issued picture pack. The black-and-white 6-1/2" x 9" photos feature white borders all around and a facsimile autograph on front. Backs are blank. The set was sold in a red and white paper envelope labeled "World Champion Cleveland Indians Autographed Action Photos." Backs are blank. The unnumbered pictures are checklisted here alphabetically. Unmarked reprints of this team-issue, complete with mailing envelope, were made in the late 1980s.

		NM	E	VG
Complete Set (30):		175.00	90.00	55.00
Common Player:		4.00	2.00	1.25
(1)	Bob Avila	6.00	3.00	1.75
(2)	Gene Bearden	4.00	2.00	1.25
(3)	Al Benton	4.00	2.00	1.25
(4)	John Berardino	12.00	6.00	3.50
(5)	Ray Boone	6.00	3.00	1.75
(6)	Lou Boudreau	16.00	8.00	4.75
(7)	Allie Clark	4.00	2.00	1.25
(8)	Larry Doby	17.50	8.75	5.25
(9)	Bob Feller	20.00	10.00	6.00
(10)	Mike Garcia	6.00	3.00	1.75
(11)	Joe Gordon	16.00	8.00	4.75
(12)	Hank Greenberg (GM)	12.00	6.00	3.50
(13)	Steve Gromek	4.00	2.00	1.25
(14)	Jim Hegan	4.00	2.00	1.25
(15)	Ken Keltner	4.00	2.00	1.25
(16)	Bob Kennedy	4.00	2.00	1.25
(17)	Bob Lemon	12.00	6.00	3.50
(18)	Dale Mitchell	4.00	2.00	1.25
(19)	Satchel Paige	40.00	20.00	12.00
(20)	Frank Papish	4.00	2.00	1.25
(21)	Hal Peck	4.00	2.00	1.25
(22)	Al Rosen	8.00	4.00	2.50
(23)	Mike Tresh	4.00	2.00	1.25
(24)	Thurman Tucker	4.00	2.00	1.25
(25)	Bill Veeck (Owner)	12.00	6.00	3.50
(26)	Mickey Vernon	6.00	3.00	1.75
(27)	Early Wynn	12.00	6.00	3.50
(28)	Sam Zoldak	4.00	2.00	1.25
(29)	Indians coaches(Mel Harder, Steve O'Neill, Bill McKechnie, Muddy Ruel, George Susce)	4.00	2.00	1.25
30)	Municipal Stadium	6.00	3.00	1.75

1949 Cleveland Indians Picture Pack - Portraits

		NM	E	VG
Complete Set (20):		75.00	40.00	25.00
Common Player:		3.00	1.50	.90
(1)	Bob Avila	4.50	2.25	1.25
(2)	Gene Bearden	3.00	1.50	.90
(3)	John Berardino	4.50	2.25	1.25
(4)	Lou Boudreau	7.50	3.75	2.25
(5)	Larry Doby	10.00	5.00	3.00
(6)	Bob Feller	12.50	6.25	3.75
(7)	Mike Garcia	4.50	2.25	1.25
(8)	Joe Gordon	7.50	3.75	2.25
(9)	Steve Gromek	3.00	1.50	.90
(10)	Jim Hegan	3.00	1.50	.90
(11)	Ken Keltner	3.00	1.50	.90
(12)	Bob Kennedy	3.00	1.50	.90
(13)	Bob Lemon	5.00	2.50	1.50
(14)	Dale Mitchell	3.00	1.50	.90
(15)	Satchel Paige	30.00	15.00	9.00
(16)	Hal Peck	3.00	1.50	.90
(17)	Thurman Tucker	3.00	1.50	.90
(18)	Mickey Vernon	4.00	2.00	1.25
(19)	Early Wynn	5.00	2.50	1.50
(20)	Sam Zoldak	3.00	1.50	.90

1949 Cleveland Indians Sun Picture Camera

Lou Boudreau

These novelty cards are self-developing photoprints sold by the team in packages of four that included negatives and pieces of photo-sensitive paper which were used to make the 1-7/8" x 2" black-and-white blank-back pictures. Because existing negatives could be used to make many new prints, values for the prints themselves are low. Prices quoted here are for negative/print combinations.

		NM	E	VG
Complete Set Negatives/Prints (20):		3,000	1,500	900.00
Common Negative/Print:		125.00	65.00	35.00
(1)	Gene Bearden	125.00	65.00	35.00
(2)	Al Benton	125.00	65.00	35.00
(3)	Ray Boone	125.00	65.00	35.00
(4)	Lou Boudreau	200.00	100.00	60.00
(5)	Allie Clark	125.00	65.00	35.50
(6)	Larry Doby	250.00	125.00	75.00
(7)	Bob Feller	250.00	125.00	75.00
(8)	Mike Garcia	135.00	70.00	40.00
(9)	Joe Gordon	200.00	100.00	60.00
(10)	Steve Gromek	125.00	65.00	35.00
(11)	Jim Hegan	125.00	65.00	35.00
(12)	Ken Keltner	135.00	70.00	40.00
(13)	Bob Kennedy	125.00	65.00	35.00
(14)	Bob Lemon	200.00	100.00	60.00
(15)	Dale Mitchell	125.00	65.00	35.00
(16)	Hal Peck	125.00	65.00	35.00
(17)	Satchel Paige	400.00	200.00	120.00
(18)	Thurman Tucker	125.00	65.00	35.00
(19)	Mickey Vernon	125.00	65.00	35.00
(20)	Early Wynn	200.00	100.00	60.00

1950 Cleveland Indians Picture Pack

Similar in format to previous years' issues, these 6-1/2" x 9" black-and-white player poses have a white border and fac-simile autograph on front. Backs are blank. The unnumbered photos are checklisted here alphabetically. It is possible the contents of specific picture packs changed over the course of the season to reflect roster moves.

		NM	E	VG
Complete Set (27):		160.00	80.00	50.00
Common Player:		4.00	2.00	1.20
(1)	Bobby Avila	5.00	2.50	1.50
(2)	Gene Bearden	4.00	2.00	1.20
(3)	Al Benton	4.00	2.00	1.20
(4)	Ray Boone	5.00	2.50	1.50
(5)	Lou Boudreau	12.00	6.00	3.50
(6)	Allie Clark	4.00	2.00	1.20
(7)	Larry Doby	17.50	8.75	5.25
(8)	Luke Easter	6.00	3.00	1.75
(9)	Bob Feller	20.00	10.00	6.00
(10)	Jess Flores	4.00	2.00	1.20
(11)	Mike Garcia	5.00	2.50	1.50
(12)	Joe Gordon	12.00	6.00	3.50
(13)	Hank Greenberg (GM)	12.00	6.00	3.50
(14)	Steve Gromek	4.00	2.00	1.20
(15)	Jim Hegan	4.00	2.00	1.20
(16)	Bob Kennedy	4.00	2.00	1.20
(17)	Bob Lemon	12.00	6.00	3.50
(18)	Dale Mitchell	4.00	2.00	1.20
(19)	Ray Murray	4.00	2.00	1.20
(20)	Chick Pieretti	4.00	2.00	1.20
(21)	Al Rosen	6.00	3.00	1.75
(22)	Dick Rozek	4.00	2.00	1.20
(23)	Ellis Ryan (Owner)	4.00	2.00	1.20
(24)	Thurman Tucker	4.00	2.00	1.20
(25)	Early Wynn	12.00	6.00	3.50
(26)	Sam Zoldak	4.00	2.00	1.20
(27)	Cleveland Municipal Stadium	8.00	4.00	2.50

1950 Cleveland Indians Picture Pack (2)

In addition to the "Autographed Photos" picture pack is-sued in 1950, a second photo pack was issued, presumably also available at Municipal Stadium and other souvenir out-lets. Like most Indians' picture packs of the era, the player photos are in a 6-1/2" x 9" black-and-white, blank-back for-mat with narrow white borders. This set is a mix of portrait and action photos, some of which are found in other Indians' photo packs. The principal difference in this set is that rather than having a facsimile player autograph on front, this set uses script versions of the player names, in either black or white. The set was sold in a white paper envelope with red and black artwork at left depicting Chief Wahoo and several of the photos.

		NM	EX	VG
Complete Set (25):		150.00	75.00	45.00
Common Player:		5.00	2.50	1.50
(1)	Bobby Avila	5.00	2.50	1.50
(2)	Gene Bearden	5.00	2.50	1.50
(3)	Al Benton	5.00	2.50	1.50
(4)	Ray Boone	5.00	2.50	1.50
(5)	Lou Boudreau	15.00	7.50	4.50
(6)	Allie Clark	5.00	2.50	1.50
(7)	Larry Doby	15.00	7.50	4.50

(8)	Luke Easter	5.00	2.50	1.50
(9)	Bob Feller	20.00	10.00	6.00
(10)	Jesse Flores	5.00	2.50	1.50
(11)	Mike Garcia	5.00	2.50	1.50
(12)	Joe Gordon	15.00	7.50	4.50
(13)	Steve Gromek	5.00	2.50	1.50
(14)	Jim Hegan	5.00	2.50	1.50
(15)	Bob Kennedy	5.00	2.50	1.50
(16)	Bob Lemon	15.00	7.50	4.50
(17)	Dale Mitchell	5.00	2.50	1.50
(18)	Ray Murray	5.00	2.50	1.50
(19)	Chick Pieretti	5.00	2.50	1.50
(20)	Al Rosen	9.00	4.50	2.50
(21)	Dick Rozek	5.00	2.50	1.50
(22)	Thurman Tucker	5.00	2.50	1.50
(23)	Dick Weik	5.00	2.50	1.50
(24)	Early Wynn	15.00	7.50	4.50
(25)	Sam Zoldak	5.00	2.50	1.50

1951 Cleveland Indians Picture Pack

While this set of Indians pictures shares the 6-1/2" x 9" for-mat of the Tribe's other team issues of the era, it is unique in its use of a much glossier front surface. Pictures are, with the exception of the manager, game-action or posed-action in black-and-white, bordered in white and with a facsimile auto-graph. Backs are blank. It is unknown whether this checklist is complete or whether players were added or removed to reflect in-season roster changes.

		NM	E	VG
Complete Set (26):		150.00	75.00	45.00
Common Player:		4.00	2.00	1.25
(1)	Bob Avila	4.00	2.00	1.25
(2)	Gene Bearden	4.00	2.00	1.25
(3)	Ray Boone	6.00	3.00	1.75
(4)	Lou Brissie	4.00	2.00	1.25
(5)	Bob Chakales	4.00	2.00	1.25
(6)	Sam Chapman	4.00	2.00	1.25
(7)	Merrill Combs	4.00	2.00	1.25
(8)	Larry Doby	15.00	7.50	4.50
(9)	Luke Easter	6.00	3.00	1.75
(10)	Red Fahr	4.00	2.00	1.25
(11)	Bob Feller	20.00	10.00	6.00
(12)	Mike Garcia	6.00	3.00	1.75
(13)	Steve Gromek	4.00	2.00	1.25
(14)	Jim Hegan	4.00	2.00	1.25
(15)	Bob Kennedy	4.00	2.00	1.25
(16)	Bob Lemon	12.50	6.25	3.75
(17)	Al Lopez	12.50	6.25	3.75
(18)	Milt Neilsen	4.00	2.00	1.25
(19)	Al Rosen	8.00	4.00	2.50
(20)	Dick Rozek	4.00	2.00	1.25
(21)	Harry Simpson	4.00	2.00	1.25
(22)	Snuffy Stirnweiss	4.00	2.00	1.25
(23)	Birdie Tebbetts	4.00	2.00	1.25
(24)	Johnny Vander Meer	6.00	3.00	1.75
(25)	Early Wynn	12.50	6.25	3.75
(26)	George Zuverink	4.00	2.00	1.25

1952 Cleveland Indians Picture Pack (Fine Pen)

One of two different black-and-white photo packs issued by the Indians in 1952, this set is differentiated by the ap-pearance of finer facsimile autographs than those seen on the other set. The photos are also slightly larger, at 6-1/2" x 9", on blank-backed heavy paper stock. The set was sold in a red and white paper envelope titled Cleveland Indians 1952 Autographed Photos.

	NM	E	VG
Complete Set (25):	160.00	80.00	50.00
Common Player:	6.00	3.00	2.00

(1)	Bobby Avila	6.00	3.00	2.00
(2)	Ray Boone	6.00	3.00	2.00
(3)	Lou Brissie	6.00	3.00	2.00
(4)	Bob Chakales	6.00	3.00	2.00
(5)	Merril (Merrill) Combs	6.00	3.00	2.00
(6)	Larry Doby	20.00	10.00	6.00
(7)	Luke Easter	6.00	3.00	2.00
(8)	Bob Feller	20.00	10.00	6.00
(9)	Jim Fridley	6.00	3.00	2.00
(10)	Mike Garcia	6.00	3.00	2.00
(11)	Steve Gromek	6.00	3.00	2.00
(12)	Mickey Harris	6.00	3.00	2.00
(13)	Jim Hegan	6.00	3.00	2.00
(14)	Bob Kennedy	6.00	3.00	2.00
(15)	Bob Lemon	12.00	6.00	4.00
(16)	Al Lopez	12.00	6.00	4.00
(17)	Dale Mitchell	6.00	3.00	2.00
(18)	Pete Reiser	6.00	3.00	2.00
(19)	Al "Flip" Rosen	6.00	3.00	2.00
(20)	Dick Rozek	6.00	3.00	2.00
(21)	Harry Simpson	6.00	3.00	2.00
(22)	George Strinweiss	6.00	3.00	2.00
(23)	Birdie Tebbetts	6.00	3.00	2.00
(24)	Early Wynn	12.00	6.00	4.00
(25)	George Zuvernick	6.00	3.00	2.00

1952 Cleveland Indians Picture Pack (Wide Pen)

Like the 1951 Picture Pack, these pictures contain action poses, but are slightly smaller at 6" x 8-3/4". Unnumbered prints here are checklisted alphabetically.

		NM	E	VG
Complete Set (24):		150.00	75.00	45.00
Common Player:		6.00	3.00	2.00
(1)	Bobby Avila	6.00	3.00	2.00
(2)	Johnny Bernardino	6.00	3.00	2.00
(3)	Ray Boone	6.00	3.00	2.00
(4)	Lou Brissie	6.00	3.00	2.00
(5)	Merril (Merrill) Combs	6.00	3.00	2.00
(6)	Larry Doby	12.00	6.00	4.00
(7)	Luke Easter	6.00	3.00	2.00
(8)	Bob Feller	20.00	10.00	6.00
(9)	Jim Fridley	6.00	3.00	2.00
(10)	Mike Garcia	6.00	3.00	2.00
(11)	Steve Gromek	6.00	3.00	2.00
(12)	Mickey Harris	6.00	3.00	2.00
(13)	Jim Hegan	6.00	3.00	2.00
(14)	Sam Jones	6.00	3.00	2.00
(15)	Bob Lemon	12.00	6.00	4.00
(16)	Dale Mitchell	6.00	3.00	2.00
(17)	Barney McCosky	6.00	3.00	2.00
(18)	Pete Reiser	6.00	3.00	2.00
(19)	Al Rosen	6.00	3.00	2.00
(20)	Dick Rozek	6.00	3.00	2.00
(21)	Harry Simpson	6.00	3.00	2.00
(22)	Birdie Tebbets (Tebbetts)	6.00	3.00	2.00
(23)	Joe Tipton	6.00	3.00	2.00
(24)	Early Wynn	12.00	6.00	4.00

1954 Cleveland Indians Picture Pack

Because many of the pictures found in the championship season picture pack are the same poses found in earlier is-sues, size can be used to differentiate the years of issue. For 1954, the pictures were down-sized slightly in height, to a 6" x 8-3/4" format, and printed on heavier paper than in previ-ous years. Each of the portraits, poses and action photos are bordered in white and include a facsimile autograph. The unnumbered pictures are checklisted here alphabetically.

		NM	E	VG
	Complete Set (27):	125.00	65.00	40.00
	Common Player:	4.00	2.00	1.25
(1)	Bobby Avila	4.00	2.00	1.25
(2)	Sam Dente	4.00	2.00	1.25
(3)	Larry Doby	10.00	5.00	3.00
(4)	Bob Feller	15.00	7.50	4.50
(5)	Mike Garcia	4.00	2.00	1.25
(6)	Bill Glynn	4.00	2.00	1.25
(7)	Mike Hegan	4.00	2.00	1.25
(8)	Bob Hooper	4.00	2.00	1.25
(9)	Dave Hoskins	4.00	2.00	1.25
(10)	Art Houtteman	4.00	2.00	1.25
(11)	Bob Lemon	7.50	3.75	2.25
(12)	Al Lopez	7.50	3.75	2.25
(13)	Hank Majeski	4.00	2.00	1.25
(14)	Dale Mitchell	4.00	2.00	1.25
(15)	Don Mossi	6.00	3.00	1.75
(16)	Hal Naragon	4.00	2.00	1.25
(17)	Ray Narleski	4.00	2.00	1.25
(18)	Hal Newhouser	7.50	3.75	2.25
(19)	Dave Philley	4.00	2.00	1.25
(20)	Dave Pope	4.00	2.00	1.25
(21)	Rudy Regaldo	4.00	2.00	1.25
(22)	Al Rosen	6.00	3.00	1.75
(23)	Al Smith	4.00	2.00	1.25
(24)	George Strickland	4.00	2.00	1.25
(25)	Vic Wertz	4.00	2.00	1.25
(26)	Wally Westlake	4.00	2.00	1.25
(27)	Early Wynn	7.50	3.75	2.25

1955 Cleveland Indians Postcards

These team-issued black-and-white player postcards can be distinguished from earlier and later issues by the uniformity of the photos. All pictures are head-and-shoulder portraits against a white background. Players are wearing caps with Chief Wahoo inside a "C." Some cards are found with a notation on back, "Pub. by Ed Wood, Forestville, Calif." Cards were sent out to fans by the team and/or player and are usually found with an autograph on front.

		NM	E	VG
	Complete Set (29):	400.00	200.00	120.00
	Common Player:	12.00	6.00	3.50
(1)	Bob Avila	15.00	7.50	4.50
(2)	Tony Cuccinello	12.00	6.00	3.50
(3)	Bud Daley	12.00	6.00	3.50
(4)	Sam Dente	12.00	6.00	3.50
(5)	Larry Doby	18.00	9.00	5.50
(6)	Bob Feller	30.00	15.00	9.00
(7)	Hank Foiles	12.00	6.00	3.50
(8)	Mike Garcia	12.00	6.00	3.50
(9)	Mel Harder	12.00	6.00	3.50
(10)	Jim Hegan	12.00	6.00	3.50
(11)	Art Houtteman	12.00	6.00	3.50
(12)	Ralph Kiner	20.00	10.00	6.00
(13)	Red Kress	12.00	6.00	3.50
(14)	Ken Kuhn	12.00	6.00	3.50
(15)	Bob Lemon	18.00	9.00	5.50
(16)	Bill Lobe	12.00	6.00	3.50
(17)	Dale Mitchell	12.00	6.00	3.50
(18)	Don Mossi	12.00	6.00	3.50
(19)	Hal Naragon	12.00	6.00	3.50
(20)	Ray Narleski	12.00	6.00	3.50
(21)	Dave Philley	12.00	6.00	3.50
(22)	Al Rosen	15.00	7.50	4.50
(23)	Herb Score	24.00	12.00	7.25
(24)	Al Smith	12.00	6.00	3.50
(25)	George Strickland	12.00	6.00	3.50
(26)	Vic Wertz	12.00	6.00	3.50
(27)	Wally Westlake	12.00	6.00	3.50
(28)	Bill Wright	12.00	6.00	3.50
(29)	Early Wynn	18.00	9.00	5.50

1956 Cleveland Indians Picture Pack

The Indians used a mix of styles in its souvenir picture pack for 1956. About 6-1/2" x 9", with white borders and blank backs, the pictures have a mix of portraits and posed action photos. Some pictures have a facsimile autograph while others have the players name in a white strip.

		NM	E	VG
	Complete Set (23):	90.00	45.00	27.50
	Common Player:	4.00	2.00	1.25
(1)	Earl Averill	4.00	2.00	1.25
(2)	Bob Avila	4.00	2.00	1.25
(3)	Jim Busby	4.00	2.00	1.25
(4)	Alphonso "Chico" Carrasquel	4.00	2.00	1.25
(5)	Rocky Colavito	20.00	10.00	6.00
(6)	Bud Daley	15.00	7.50	4.50
(7)	Mike Garcia	4.00	2.00	1.25
(8)	Jim Hegan	4.00	2.00	1.25

(9)	Kenny Kuhn	4.00	2.00	1.25
(10)	Bob Lemon	7.50	3.75	2.25
(11)	Sam Mele	4.00	2.00	1.25
(12)	Dale Mitchell	4.00	2.00	1.25
(13)	Don Mossi	4.00	2.00	1.25
(14)	Hal Naragon	4.00	2.00	1.25
(15)	Ray Narleski	4.00	2.00	1.25
(16)	Al "Flip" Rosen	5.00	2.50	1.50
(17)	Herb Score	7.50	3.75	2.25
(18)	Al Smith	4.00	2.00	1.25
(19)	George Strickland	4.00	2.00	1.25
(20)	Vic Wertz	4.00	2.00	1.25
(21)	Gene Woodling	4.00	2.00	1.25
(22)	Early Wynn	7.50	3.75	2.25
(23)	Indians Coaches Mel Harder, Bill Labe, Tony Cuccinello, Red Kress	7.50	3.75	2.25

1957 Cleveland Indians Picture Pack

This set of "Official Autographed Pictures" issued in 1957 was sold at Municipal Stadium and other souvenir outlets for 50 cents. The player photos are in a 6-1/2" x 9" black-and-white, blank-back format with narrow white borders, printed on thin semi-gloss stock. About half the photos are identical to those issued in 1956. A facsimile player autograph on front identifies the photo.

		NM	EX	VG
	Complete Set: (24)	150.00	75.00	45.00
	Common Player:	6.00	3.00	2.00
(1)	Bob Avila	6.00	3.00	2.00
(2)	Jim Busby	6.00	3.00	2.00
(3)	Alphonso "Chico" Carrasquel	6.00	3.00	2.00
(4)	Rocky Colavito	20.00	10.00	6.00
(5)	Bud Daley	12.00	6.00	4.00
(6)	Kirby Farrell	6.00	3.00	2.00
(7)	Mike Garcia	6.00	3.00	2.00
(8)	Jim Hegan	6.00	3.00	2.00
(9)	Ken Kuhn	6.00	3.00	2.00
(10)	Bob Lemon	9.00	4.50	2.50
(11)	Roger Maris	25.00	12.50	9.00
(12)	Don Mossi	6.00	3.00	2.00
(13)	Hal Naragon	6.00	3.00	2.00
(14)	Ray Narleski	6.00	3.00	2.00
(15)	Russ Nixon	6.00	3.00	2.00
(16)	Stan Pitula	6.00	3.00	2.00
(17)	Lawrence Raines	6.00	3.00	2.00
(18)	Herb Score	9.00	4.50	2.50
(19)	Al Smith	6.00	3.00	2.00
(20)	George Strickland	6.00	3.00	2.00
(21)	Dick Tomanek	6.00	3.00	2.00
(22)	Vic Wertz	6.00	3.00	2.00
(23)	Gene Woodling	6.00	3.00	2.00
(24)	Early Wynn	12.00	6.00	4.00

1958 Cleveland Indians Picture Pack

This set of "Official Autographed Pictures" issued in 1958 was sold at Municipal Stadium and other souvenir outlets for 50 cents. The player photos are in a 6-1/2" x 9" black-and-white, blank-back format with narrow white borders, printed on thin semi-gloss stock. A facsimile player autograph on front identifies the photo. The players were pictured in their new striped uniforms.

		NM	EX	VG
	Complete Set: (24)	125.00	65.00	35.00
	Common Player:	5.00	2.50	1.50
(1)	Bob Avila	5.00	2.50	1.50
(2)	Bobby Bragan	5.00	2.50	1.50
(3)	Dick Brown	5.00	2.50	1.50
(4)	Alphonso "Chico" Carrasquel	5.00	2.50	1.50
(5)	Rocky Colavito	9.00	4.50	2.50
(6)	Larry Doby	12.00	6.00	4.00
(7)	Mike Garcia	6.00	3.00	2.00
(8)	Gary Geiger	6.00	3.00	1.75
(9)	Jim Grant	6.00	3.00	1.75
(10)	Bill Harrell	5.00	2.50	1.50
(11)	Roger Maris	25.00	12.50	9.00
(12)	Cal McLish	5.00	2.50	1.50
(13)	Minnie Minoso	7.50	3.75	2.25
(14)	Bill Moran	5.00	2.50	1.50
(15)	Don Mossi	5.00	2.50	1.50
(16)	Ray Narleski	5.00	2.50	1.50
(17)	Russ Nixon	5.00	2.50	1.50
(18)	J.W. Porter	5.00	2.50	1.50
(19)	Herb Score	7.50	3.75	2.25
(20)	Dick Tomanek	5.00	2.50	1.50
(21)	Mickey Vernon	5.00	2.50	1.50
(22)	Preston Ward	5.00	2.50	1.50
(23)	Hoyt Wilhelm	12.00	6.00	4.00
(24)	Indians Coaches (Red Kress, Bobby Bragan Eddie Stanky, Mel Harder)	5.00	2.50	1.50

1959 Cleveland Indians Picture Pack

A continuation of the team's tradition of issuing player picture packs, this set of "Official Autographed Pictures" issued in 1959 was sold at Municipal Stadium and other souvenir outlets for 50 cents. The player photos are in a 6-1/2" x 9" black-and-white, blank-back format with narrow white borders. A facsimile player autograph on front identifies the photo.

		NM	EX	VG
	Complete Set: (28)	125.00	65.00	35.00
	Common Player:	5.00	2.50	1.50
(1)	Gary Bell	5.00	2.50	1.50
(2)	Jim Bolger	5.00	2.50	1.50
(3)	Dick Brodowski	5.00	2.50	1.50
(4)	Dick Brown	5.00	2.50	1.50
(5)	Al Cicotte	5.00	2.50	1.50
(6)	Rocky Colavito	9.00	4.50	2.50
(7)	Don Ferrarese	5.00	2.50	1.50
(8)	Tito Francona	5.00	2.50	1.50
(10)	Mike Garcia (name printed)	6.00	3.00	1.75
(11)	Joe Gordon	9.00	4.50	2.50
(12)	Jim "Mudcat" Grant	6.00	3.00	1.75
(13)	Mel Harder	5.00	2.50	1.50
(14)	Carroll Hardy	5.00	2.50	1.50
(15)	Woody Held	5.00	2.50	1.50
(16)	Frank Lane	5.00	2.50	1.50
(17)	Billy Martin	7.50	3.75	2.25
(18)	Cal McLish	5.00	2.50	1.50
(19)	Minnie Minoso	7.50	3.75	2.25
(20)	Hal Naragon	5.00	2.50	1.50
(21)	Russ Nixon	5.00	2.50	1.50
(22)	Jim Perry	6.00	3.00	1.75
(23)	Jimmy Piersall	6.00	3.00	1.75
(24)	Vic Power	6.00	3.00	1.75
(25)	Herb Score	7.50	3.75	2.25
(26)	George Strickland	5.00	2.50	1.50
(27)	Mickey Vernon	5.00	2.50	1.75
(28)	Ray Webster	5.00	2.50	1.50

1960 Cleveland Indians Picture Pack

A continuation of the team's tradition of issuing player picture packs, this set of "Official Autographed Pictures" issued in 1960 was sold at Municipal Stadium and other souvenir outlets for 50 cents, in a black-and-gold paper envelope. The player photos are in a 6-1/2" x 9" black-and-white, blank-back format with narrow white borders. A facsimile player autograph on front identifies the photo.

		NM	EX	VG
	Complete Set: (23)	100.00	50.00	30.00
	Common Player:	5.00	2.50	1.50
(1)	Ken Aspromonte	5.00	2.50	1.50
(2)	Gary Bell	5.00	2.50	1.50
(3)	John Briggs	5.00	2.50	1.50
(4)	Hank Foiles	5.00	2.50	1.50
(5)	Tito Francona	5.00	2.50	1.50
(6)	Joe Gordon	9.00	4.50	2.50
(7)	Bob Hale	5.00	2.50	1.50
(8)	Wynn Hawkins	5.00	2.50	1.50
(9)	Woody Held	5.00	2.50	1.50
(10)	John Klippstein	5.00	2.50	1.50
(11)	Harvey Kuenn	5.00	2.50	1.50
(12)	Frank Lane	5.00	2.50	1.50
(13)	Barry Latman	5.00	2.50	1.50
(14)	Mike Lee	5.00	2.50	1.50
(15)	Bobby Locke	5.00	2.50	1.50
(16)	Jim Perry	6.00	3.00	1.75
(17)	John "Bubba" Phillips	5.00	2.50	1.50
(18)	Jimmy Piersall	6.00	3.00	1.75
(19)	Vic Power	6.00	3.00	1.75
(20)	John Romano	6.00	3.00	1.75
(21)	Dick Stigman	5.00	2.50	1.50
(22)	George Strickland	5.00	2.50	1.75
(23)	John Temple	5.00	2.50	1.50

1961 Cleveland Indians Picture Pack

A continuation of the team's tradition of issuing player picture packs, this set of "Official Autographed Pictures" issued in 1961 was sold at Municipal Stadium and other souvenir outlets for 50 cents, in a black-and-gold paper envelope. The player photos are in a 6-1/2" x 9" black-and-white, blank-back format with narrow white borders. A facsimile player autograph on front identifies the photo.

		NM	EX	VG
	Complete Set: (22)	100.00	50.00	30.00
	Common Player:	5.00	2.50	1.50
(1)	John Antonelli	5.00	2.50	1.50
(2)	Ken Aspromonte	5.00	2.50	1.50
(3)	Gary Bell	5.00	2.50	1.50
(4)	Walter Bond	5.00	2.50	1.50
(5)	Mike de la Hoz	5.00	2.50	1.50
(6)	James Dykes	5.00	2.50	1.50
(7)	Tito Francona	5.00	2.50	1.50
(8)	Jim Grant	5.00	2.50	1.50
(9)	Wynn Hawkins	5.00	2.50	1.50
(10)	Woodie Held	5.00	2.50	1.50
(11)	Willie Kirkland	5.00	2.50	1.50
(12)	Barry Latman	5.00	2.50	1.50
(13)	Bobby Locke	5.00	2.50	1.50
(14)	Jim Perry	6.00	3.00	1.75
(15)	Bubba Phillips	5.00	2.50	1.50
(16)	Jimmy Piersall	6.00	3.00	1.75
(17)	Vic Power	6.00	3.00	1.75
(18)	John Romano	6.00	3.00	1.75
(19)	Dick Stigman	5.00	2.50	1.50
(20)	John Temple	5.00	2.50	1.50
(21)	Manager and coaches (Mel McGaha, Mel Harder, Jimmie Dykes, Luke Appling)	5.00	2.50	1.50
(22)	Home of the Cleveland Indians (Cleveland Stadium)	5.00	2.50	1.50

1962 Cleveland Indians Picture Pack

A change to a very thin paper stock with very little gloss marked the final Cleveland Indians picture pack of the era. This set of "Official Autographed Pictures" issued in 1962 was sold at Municipal Stadium and other souvenir outlets for 50 cents, in a black-printed manila paper envelope. The player photos are in a 6-1/2" x 9" black-and-white, blank-back format with narrow white borders. A facsimile player autograph on front identifies the photo.

		NM	EX	VG
	Complete Set: (22)	90.00	45.00	25.00
	Common Player:	5.00	2.50	1.50
(1)	Bob Allen	5.00	2.50	1.50
(2)	Gary Bell	5.00	2.50	1.50
(3)	Ty Cline	5.00	2.50	1.50
(4)	Dan Dillard	5.00	2.50	1.50
(5)	Dick Donovan	5.00	2.50	1.50
(6)	Howard "Doc" Edwards	5.00	2.50	1.50
(7)	Chuck Essegian	5.00	2.50	1.50
(8)	Tito Francona	5.00	2.50	1.50
(9)	Frank Funk	5.00	2.50	1.50
(10)	Jim Grant	5.00	2.50	1.50
(11)	Gene Green	5.00	2.50	1.50
(12)	Woodie Held	5.00	2.50	1.50
(13)	Jerry Kindall	5.00	2.50	1.50
(14)	Willie Kirkland	5.00	2.50	1.50
(15)	Barry Latman	5.00	2.50	1.50
(16)	Al Luplow	5.00	2.50	1.50
(17)	Mel McGaha	5.00	2.50	1.50
(18)	Jim Perry	6.00	3.00	1.75
(19)	Bubba Phillips	5.00	2.50	1.50
(20)	Pedro Ramos	6.00	3.00	1.75
(21)	John Romano	6.00	3.00	1.75
(22)	Manager and coaches (Ray Katt, Salty Parker, Mel Harder, Mel McGaha)	5.00	2.50	1.50

1967 Cleveland Indians "Yearbook"

ROCKY COLAVITO

The 1967 Cleveland Indians "Yearbook" wasn't what the hobby generally thinks of in regards to that term. Rather, the 1967 Cleveland Indians Yearbook was a 7" x 9" folder that held, loose-leaf style, a set of player photos and a few other specialty pictures. Each picture was printed on heavy paper stock, about 6-3/16" x 8-11/16". Most of the player pictures were color poses, though a few were in black and white. Fronts have a white border with the player name at bottom. Backs are in black-and-white with an informal player photo, complete stats, biographical details and career highlights.

		NM	EX	VG
	Complete Yearbook:	80.00	40.00	25.00
	Common Player:	3.00	1.50	.90
(1)	Bob Allen	3.00	1.50	.90
(2)	Max Alvis	3.00	1.50	.90
(3)	Joe Azcue	3.00	1.50	.90
(4)	Steve Bailey	3.00	1.50	.90
(5)	Basebells Night at the Stadium (b/w)	3.00	1.50	.90
(6)	Gary Bell	3.00	1.50	.90
(7)	Richard Booker	3.00	1.50	.90
(8)	Larry Brown	3.00	1.50	.90
(9)	Rocky Colavito	15.00	7.50	4.50
(10)	George Culver (b/w)	3.00	1.50	.90
(11)	Vic Davalillo	3.00	1.50	.90
(12)	Vern Fuller	3.00	1.50	.90
(13)	Gus Gil	3.00	1.50	.90
(14)	Pedro Gonzalez	3.00	1.50	.90
(15)	Steve Hargan	3.00	1.50	.90
(16)	Chuck Hinton	3.00	1.50	.90
(17)	Indians Field Leaders (George Strickland, Del Rice, Mgr. Joe Altobelli, Pat Mullin, Clay Bryant)	3.00	1.50	.90
(18)	Jack Kralick	3.00	1.50	.90
(19)	Lee Maye	3.00	1.50	.90
(20)	Sam McDowell	5.00	2.50	1.50
(21)	John O'Donoghue	3.00	1.50	.90
(22)	Dick Radatz	3.00	1.50	.90
(23)	Vincente Romo (b/w)	3.00	1.50	.90
(24)	Chico Salmon	3.00	1.50	.90
(25)	Sonny Siebert	3.00	1.50	.90
(26)	Duke Sims	3.00	1.50	.90
(27)	Willie Smith (b/w)	3.00	1.50	.90
(28)	Luis Tiant	5.00	2.50	1.50
(29)	Leon Wagner	3.00	1.50	.90
(30)	Wahoo Club (Al Rosen, Larry Brown)	3.00	1.50	.90
(31)	Fred Whitfield	3.00	1.50	.90

1884 Climax Poster

"Representatives of Professional Baseball in America" is the title of this sepia-toned lithograph produced by Lorillard tobacco as a premium for its Climax Red Tin Tag Plug chew. About 26" x 20", the poster depicts 16 top stars, managers and executives in street-clothed portraits on a background of ballplayers, equipment and ballparks.

	NM	E	VG
1884 Climax Representatives of Baseball	25,000	12,500	7,500

1911 George Close Candy Co. (E94)

This 1911 issue is nearly identical to several contemporary candy and caramel sets. Issued by The George Close Co. of Cambridge, Mass., the approximately 1-1/2" x 2-3/4" cards feature color-tinted black-and-white player photos. Each card can be found with any of seven different background colors (blue, gold, green, olive, red, violet and yellow). Backs carry a set checklist. Eleven different back variations are known to exist. One variation contains just the checklist without any advertising, while 10 other variations include overprinted backs advertising various candy products manufactured by Close. The set carries the ACC designation E94.

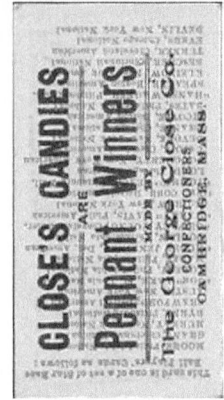

BYRNE, PITTSBURGH

		NM	E	VG
	Complete Set (30):	103,500	52,000	31,000
	Common Player:	1,800	900.00	350.00
	Advertising Backs: 3-5X			
(1)	Jimmy Austin	1,800	900.00	350.00
(2)	Johnny Bates	1,800	900.00	350.00
(3)	Bob Bescher	1,800	900.00	350.00
(4)	Bobby Byrne	1,800	900.00	350.00
(5)	Frank Chance	3,000	1,500	600.00
(6)	Ed Cicotte	3,000	1,500	600.00
(7)	Ty Cobb	40,000	20,000	12,000
(8)	Sam Crawford	3,000	1,500	600.00
(9)	Harry Davis	1,800	900.00	350.00
(10)	Art Devlin	1,800	900.00	350.00
(11)	Josh Devore	1,800	900.00	350.00
(12)	Mickey Doolan	1,800	900.00	350.00
(13)	Patsy Dougherty	1,800	900.00	350.00
(14)	Johnny Evers	3,000	1,500	600.00
(15)	Eddie Grant	1,800	900.00	350.00
(16)	Hugh Jennings	3,000	1,500	600.00
(17)	Red Kleinow	1,800	900.00	350.00
(18)	Joe Lake	1,800	900.00	350.00
(19)	Nap Lajoie	3,000	1,500	600.00
(20)	Tommy Leach	1,800	900.00	350.00
(21)	Hans Lobert	1,800	900.00	350.00
(22)	Harry Lord	1,800	900.00	350.00
(23)	Sherry Magee	1,800	900.00	350.00
(24)	John McGraw	3,000	1,500	600.00
(25)	Earl Moore	1,800	900.00	350.00
(26)	Red Murray	1,800	900.00	350.00
(27)	Tris Speaker	4,000	2,000	800.00
(28)	Terry Turner	1,800	900.00	350.00
(29)	Honus Wagner	22,500	10,000	3,600
(30)	"Old" Cy. Young	15,000	7,500	3,000

1961 Cloverleaf Dairy Minnesota Twins

These unnumbered cards picture members of the debut Minnesota Twins team. Measuring approximately 3-3/4" x 7-3/4", the cards were actually side panels from Cloverleaf (and Apple Fresh brand) Milk cartons. Complete cartons are valued at about twice the prices listed. The card includes a black-and-white player photo with name, position, personal data and year-by-year statistics appearing below. Green graphics highlight the panels. Some pictures were reissued in 1962 but can be differentiated from the 1961 set by the stats at bottom.

		NM	E	VG
	Complete Set (17):	1,125	550.00	335.00
	Common Player:	75.00	37.00	22.00
(1)	Earl Battey	75.00	37.00	22.00
(2)	Reno Bertoia	75.00	37.00	22.00

		NM	E	VG
(3)	Billy Gardner	75.00	37.00	22.00
(4)	Paul Giel	75.00	37.00	22.00
(5)	Lenny Green	75.00	37.00	22.00
(6)	Jim Kaat	80.00	40.00	24.00
(7)	Jack Kralick	75.00	37.00	22.00
(8)	Don Lee	75.00	37.00	22.00
(9)	Jim Lemon	75.00	37.00	22.00
(10)	Billy Martin	90.00	45.00	27.00
(11)	Don Mincher	75.00	37.00	22.00
(12)	Camilo Pascual	80.00	40.00	24.00
(13)	Pedro Ramos	75.00	37.00	22.00
(14)	Chuck Stobbs	75.00	37.00	22.00
(15)	Bill Tuttle	75.00	37.00	22.00
(16)	Jose Valdivielso	75.00	37.00	22.00
(17)	Zoilo Versalles	80.00	40.00	24.00

1962 Cloverleaf Dairy Minnesota Twins

These unnumbered cards picture members of the Minnesota Twins. Measuring approximately 3-3/4" x 7-3/4", the cards were actually side panels from Cloverleaf (and Apple Fresh brand) Milk cartons. Complete cartons are valued at about twice the prices listed. The card includes a black-and-white player photo with name, position, personal data and year-by-year statistics appearing below. Green graphics highlight the panels. Some pictures were reissued in 1962 but can be differentiated from the 1961 set by the stats at bottom.

		NM	E	VG
Complete Set (24):		1,400	700.00	425.00
Common Player:		75.00	37.00	22.00
(1)	Bernie Allen	75.00	37.00	22.00
(2)	George Banks	75.00	37.00	22.00
(3)	Earl Battey	75.00	37.00	22.00
(4)	Joe Bonikowski	75.00	37.00	22.00
(5)	John Goryl	75.00	37.00	22.00
(6)	Lenny Green	75.00	37.00	22.00
(7)	Jim Kaat	80.00	40.00	24.00
(8)	Jack Kralick	75.00	37.00	22.00
(9)	Jim Lemon	75.00	37.00	22.00
(10)	Georges Maranda	75.00	37.00	22.00
(11)	Orlando Martinez	75.00	37.00	22.00
(12)	Don Mincher	75.00	37.00	22.00
(13)	Ray Moore	75.00	37.00	22.00
(14)	Hal Naragon	75.00	37.00	22.00
(15)	Camilo Pascual	80.00	40.00	24.00
(16)	Vic Power	80.00	40.00	24.00
(17)	Rich Rollins	75.00	37.00	22.00
(18)	Theodore Sadowski	75.00	37.00	22.00
(19)	Albert Stange	75.00	37.00	22.00
(20)	Dick Stigman	75.00	37.00	22.00
(21)	Bill Tuttle	75.00	37.00	22.00
(22)	Zoilo Versalles	80.00	40.00	24.00
(23)	Gerald Zimmerman	75.00	37.00	22.00
(24)	Manager and Coaches (Floyd Baker, Edward Fitz Gerald, Gordon Maltzberger, Sam Mele, George Strickland)	75.00	37.00	22.00

1912 Ty Cobb Postcard

There is no indication of a publisher on this card, nor that it is part of a multi-player series. In standard postcard format of 5-1/2" x 3-1/2", the card has a black-and-white photograph of a smiling Cobb and a caption in the bottom border, "TY COBB WORLDS'S GREATEST BALL PLAYER AND HIS FAVORITE BAT." The divided back has standard postcard markings.

	NM	E	VG
Ty Cobb	3,500	1,750	1,000

1947 Coca-Cola All Time Sports Favorite

In 1947 Coke produced a series of 10 All Time Sports Favorite cardboard signs. On heavy cardboard with a framed look, the 13" x 15" signs have color artwork at center. In the bottom border are a few words about the athlete, along with a Coke bottle and round red logo. Only one baseball player appears in the series.

	NM	E	VG
Ty Cobb	2,000	1,000	600.00

1952 Coca-Cola Playing Tips

While more widely distributed than the three test cards, the 10-card set of playing tips cards is still scarce today. Issued in the metropolitan New York region, the cards include only players from the Yankees, Giants and Dodgers. Fronts feature color paintings of players in action, though the artwork bears little actual resemblance to the players named. The phrase "Coke is a natural" is in the background on pennants, panels, etc. The player's name, team and position are included in the picture. In the portion of the card meant to be inserted into the soda-bottle carton, the home schedule of the player's team for 1952 is presented. Printed in red on back are tips for playing the position of the pictured player. Cards are irregularly shaped, measuring about 3-1/2" at their widest point, and 7-1/2" in length. The unnumbered cards are checklisted here in alphabetical order.

		NM	E	VG
Complete Set (10):		2,100	1,050	625.00
Common Player:		160.00	80.00	50.00
(1)	Hank Bauer	275.00	135.00	82.00
(2)	Carl Furillo	350.00	175.00	105.00
(3)	Gil Hodges	450.00	225.00	135.00
(4)	Ed Lopat	190.00	95.00	57.00
(5)	Gil McDougald	250.00	125.00	75.00
(6)	Don Mueller	150.00	75.00	45.00
(7)	Pee Wee Reese	450.00	225.00	135.00
(8)	Bobby Thomson (3B)	250.00	125.00	75.00
(9)	Bobby Thomson (Hitting)	350.00	175.00	105.00
(10)	Wes Westrum	150.00	75.00	45.00

1952 Coca-Cola Playing Tips Test Cards

Apparently a regional issue to test the concept of baseball playing tips cards inserted into cartons of soda bottles, these test cards have a number of differences to the version which was more widely issued. The test cards feature a colorful drawing of the player with a bottle of Coke, along with his name in script and his team. Backs are printed in red on gray cardboard. Rizzuto's card has been seen with three different playing tips. Mays' card has a biography instead of a playing tip. The cards are irregularly shaped, measuring about 3-1/2" at their widest point, and about 7-1/2" in length.

See tips on how to play baseball on back of this card.

		NM	E	VG
Complete Set (4):		16,000	8,000	4,800
(1)	Willie Mays	6,500	3,200	1,950
(2)	Phil Rizzuto (Bunting tips.)	4,500	2,200	1,350
(3)	Phil Rizzuto (Pitching tips.)	4,500	2,200	1,350
(4)	Phil Rizzuto (SS fielding tips.)	4,500	2,200	1,350

1953 Coca-Cola Signs

The attributed date is approximate, based on the uniforms in which the players are pictured. It is possible the series was issued over more than one year. The signs vary in size from about 10" x 12" to 12" x 15" and are made of cardboard. Some are die-cut to produce an irregular shape. Players are pictured in color artwork holding a bottle of Coke with one of several styles of Coca-Cola logo in the background.

		NM	E	VG
Common Player:		750.00	375.00	225.00
(1)	Bill Bruton	1,600	800.00	480.00
(2)	Roy Campanella	5,000	2,500	1,500
(3)	Larry Doby	3,000	1,500	900.00
(4)	Monte Irvin	3,000	1,500	900.00
(5)	Satchel Paige	8,000	4,000	2,400
(6)	Phil Rizzuto	3,000	1,500	900.00

1967-68 Coca-Cola Bottle Caps

Over two seasons, bottles of Coke products (Coca-Cola, Fresca, Tab, Sprite and Fanta) were sealed with caps bearing the pictures of major league ballplayers. The 1" diameter caps have a small baseball symbol on the top of the cap. Inside, protected by a clear plastic liner, is a black-and-white portrait photo of a player. (Most photos have cap insignia blacked out.) His team nickname is printed at top, his name at bottom and his position at right (1967 only in team issues, 1967-68 in All-Stars). To the left of the picture is an identification number, usually with a letter prefix. In areas with major league baseball teams, regional issues of the caps featured local players with a letter prefix to the number. Also released in those areas were American League or National League All-Star sets, with cap number preceded by an "A" or "N." In areas not served by major league teams, a 35-cap All-Star series with no prefix letter was issued. While most caps were identical in both years of issue, some player team changes, etc., were reflected in updated caps in 1968. Severe bending by bottle openers and rust are specific detriments to condition often found on these caps. Collectors usually save these caps without regard to which specific brand of soda appears on top, though obviously the Coca-Cola pieces are much more common. Cap-saver sheets were available which, when filled, could be exchanged for a team set of photocards (see 1967 Dexter Press Premiums) or other prizes.

	NM	E	VG
Complete Set (580):	4,000	2,000	1,200
Common Player:	5.00	2.50	1.50
Playing Tips (16):	3.00	1.50	.90

Sprite, Fresca, Tab + 10 Percent

		NM	E	VG
	MAJOR LEAGUE ALL-STARS			
1	Richie Allen	7.50	3.75	2.25
2	Pete Rose	32.50	16.00	9.75
3	Brooks Robinson	25.00	12.50	7.50
4	Marcelino Lopez	5.00	2.50	1.50
5	Rusty Staub	5.00	2.50	1.50
6	Ron Santo	7.50	3.75	2.25
7	Jim Nash	5.00	2.50	1.50
8	Jim Fregosi	5.00	2.50	1.50
9	Paul Casanova	5.00	2.50	1.50
10	Willie Mays	45.00	22.50	13.50
11	Willie Stargell	15.00	7.50	4.50
12	Tony Oliva	7.50	3.75	2.25
13	Joe Pepitone	7.50	3.75	2.25
14	Juan Marichal	12.00	6.00	3.50
15	Jim Bunning	12.00	6.00	3.50
16	Claude Osteen	5.00	2.50	1.50
17	Carl Yastrzemski	25.00	12.50	7.50
18	Harmon Killebrew	25.00	12.50	7.50
19	Hank Aaron	45.00	22.50	13.50
20	Joe Torre	7.50	3.75	2.25
21	Ernie Banks	25.00	12.50	7.50
22	Al Kaline	25.00	12.50	7.50
23	Frank Robinson	25.00	12.50	7.50
24	Max Alvis	5.00	2.50	1.50
25	Elston Howard	7.50	3.75	2.25
26	Gaylord Perry	12.00	6.00	3.50
27	Bill Mazeroski	12.00	6.00	3.50
28	Ron Swoboda	5.00	2.50	1.50
29	Vada Pinson	7.50	3.75	2.25
30	Joe Morgan	25.00	12.50	7.50
31	Cleon Jones	5.00	2.50	1.50
32	Willie Horton	5.00	2.50	1.50
33	Leon Wagner	5.00	2.50	1.50
34	George Scott	5.00	2.50	1.50
35	Ed Charles	5.00	2.50	1.50
	NATIONAL LEAGUE ALL-STARS			
N7	Tom Seaver	15.00	7.00	4.50
N19	Hank Aaron	40.00	20.00	12.00
N20	Jim Bunning	10.00	5.00	3.00
N21	Joe Torre	6.00	3.00	1.75
N22	Claude Osteen	5.00	2.50	1.50
N23	Ron Santo	6.00	3.00	1.75
N24	Joe Morgan	20.00	10.00	6.00
N25	Richie Allen	6.00	3.00	1.75
N26	Ron Swoboda	5.00	2.50	1.50
N27	Ernie Banks	20.00	10.00	6.00
N28	Bill Mazeroski	12.00	6.00	3.50
N29	Willie Stargell	12.00	6.00	3.50
N30	Pete Rose	25.00	12.50	7.50
N31	Gaylord Perry	10.00	5.00	3.00
N32	Rusty Staub	5.00	2.50	1.50
N33	Vada Pinson	6.00	3.00	1.75
N34	Juan Marichal	10.00	5.00	3.00
N35	Cleon Jones	5.00	2.50	1.50
	AMERICAN LEAGUE ALL-STARS			
A19	Al Kaline	20.00	10.00	6.00
A20	Frank Howard	5.00	2.50	1.50
A21	Brooks Robinson	20.00	10.00	6.00
A22	George Scott	5.00	2.50	1.50
A23	Willie Horton	5.00	2.50	1.50
A24	Jim Fregosi	5.00	2.50	1.50
A25	Ed Charles	5.00	2.50	1.50
A26	Harmon Killebrew	20.00	10.00	6.00
A27	Tony Oliva	6.00	3.00	1.75
A28	Joe Pepitone	6.00	3.00	1.75
A29	Elston Howard	6.00	3.00	1.75
A30	Jim Nash	5.00	2.50	1.50
A31	Marcelino Lopez	5.00	2.50	1.50
A32	Frank Robinson	20.00	10.00	6.00
A33	Leon Wagner	5.00	2.50	1.50
A34	Max Alvis	5.00	2.50	1.50
A35	Paul Casanova	5.00	2.50	1.50
	PLAYING TIPS			
19	SS fields ball . . .	3.00	1.50	.90
20	2b relays . . .	3.00	1.50	.90
21	1b completes DP	3.00	1.50	.90
22	Pitcher fields bunt . . .	3.00	1.50	.90
23	2b relays . . .	3.00	1.50	.90
24	1b complete DP	3.00	1.50	.90
25	CF makes catch . . .	3.00	1.50	.90
26	Catcher tags runner	3.00	1.50	.90
	1967 ATLANTA BRAVES			
B1	Gary Geiger	5.00	2.50	1.50
B2	Ty Cline	5.00	2.50	1.50
B3	Hank Aaron	45.00	22.50	13.50
B4	Gene Oliver	5.00	2.50	1.50
B5	Tony Cloninger	5.00	2.50	1.50
B6	Denis Menke	5.00	2.50	1.50
B7	Denny Lemaster	5.00	2.50	1.50
B8	Woody Woodward	5.00	2.50	1.50
B9	Joe Torre	7.50	3.75	2.25
B10	Ken Johnson	5.00	2.50	1.50
B11	Bob Bruce	5.00	2.50	1.50
B12	Felipe Alou	7.50	3.75	2.25
B13	Clete Boyer	5.00	2.50	1.50
B14	Wade Blasingame	5.00	2.50	1.50
B15	Don Schwall	5.00	2.50	1.50
B16	Dick Kelley	5.00	2.50	1.50
B17	Rico Carty	6.00	3.00	1.75
B18	Mack Jones	5.00	2.50	1.50
	1968 ATLANTA BRAVES			
B1	Cecil Upshaw	5.00	2.50	1.50
B2	Tito Francona	5.00	2.50	1.50
B3	Hank Aaron	40.00	20.00	12.00
B4	Pat Jarvis	5.00	2.50	1.50
B5	Tony Cloninger	5.00	2.50	1.50
B6	Phil Niekro	15.00	7.50	4.50
B7	Felix Millan	5.00	2.50	1.50
B8	Woody Woodward	5.00	2.50	1.50
B9	Joe Torre	7.50	3.75	2.25
B10	Ken Johnson	5.00	2.50	1.50
B11	Marty Martinez	5.00	2.50	1.50
B12	Felipe Alou	7.50	3.75	2.25
B13	Clete Boyer	5.00	2.50	1.50
B14	Sonny Jackson	5.00	2.50	1.50
B15	Deron Johnson	5.00	2.50	1.50
B16	Claude Raymond	5.00	2.50	1.50
B17	Rico Carty	6.00	3.00	1.75
B18	Mack Jones	5.00	2.50	1.50
	1967 BALTIMORE ORIOLES			
O1	Dave McNally	5.00	2.50	1.50
O2	Luis Aparicio	20.00	10.00	6.00
O3	Paul Blair	5.00	2.50	1.50
O4	Frank Robinson	25.00	12.50	7.50
O5	Jim Palmer	30.00	15.00	9.00
O6	Russ Snyder	5.00	2.50	1.50
O7	Stu Miller	5.00	2.50	1.50
O8	Dave Johnson	5.00	2.50	1.50
O9	Andy Etchebarren	5.00	2.50	1.50
O10	Brooks Robinson	25.00	12.50	7.50
O11	John Powell	12.00	6.00	3.50
O12	Sam Bowens	5.00	2.50	1.50
O13	Curt Blefary	5.00	2.50	1.50
O14	Ed Fisher	5.00	2.50	1.50
O15	Wally Bunker	5.00	2.50	1.50
O16	Moe Drabowsky	5.00	2.50	1.50
O17	Larry Haney	5.00	2.50	1.50
O18	Tom Phoebus	5.00	2.50	1.50
	1968 BALTIMORE ORIOLES			
O1	Dave McNally	5.00	2.50	1.50
O2	Jim Hardin	5.00	2.50	1.50
O3	Paul Blair	5.00	2.50	1.50
O4	Frank Robinson	25.00	12.50	7.50
O5	Bruce Howard	5.00	2.50	1.50
O6	John O'Donoghue	5.00	2.50	1.50
O7	Dave May	5.00	2.50	1.50
O8	Dave Johnson	5.00	2.50	1.50
O9	Andy Etchebarren	5.00	2.50	1.50
O10	Brooks Robinson	25.00	12.50	7.50
O11	John Powell	8.00	4.00	2.50
O12	Pete Richert	5.00	2.50	1.50
O13	Curt Blefary	5.00	2.50	1.50
O14	Mark Belanger	6.00	3.00	1.75
O15	Wally Bunker	5.00	2.50	1.50
O16	Don Buford	5.00	2.50	1.50
O17	Larry Haney	5.00	2.50	1.50
O18	Tom Phoebus	5.00	2.50	1.50
	1967 BOSTON RED SOX			
R1	Lee Stange	5.00	2.50	1.50
R2	Carl Yastrzemski	30.00	15.00	9.00
R3	Don Demeter	5.00	2.50	1.50
R4	Jose Santiago	5.00	2.50	1.50
R5	Darrell Brandon	5.00	2.50	1.50
R6	Joe Foy	5.00	2.50	1.50
R7	Don McMahon	5.00	2.50	1.50
R8	Dalton Jones	5.00	2.50	1.50
R9	Mike Ryan	5.00	2.50	1.50
R10	Bob Tillman	5.00	2.50	1.50
R11	Rico Petrocelli	6.00	3.00	1.75
R12	George Scott	5.00	2.50	1.50
R13	George Smith	5.00	2.50	1.50
R14	Dennis Bennett	5.00	2.50	1.50
R15	Hank Fischer	5.00	2.50	1.50
R16	Jim Lonborg	6.00	3.00	1.75
R17	Jose Tartabull	5.00	2.50	1.50
R18	George Thomas	5.00	2.50	1.50
	1968 BOSTON RED SOX			
R1	Lee Stange	5.00	2.50	1.50
R2	Gary Waslewski	5.00	2.50	1.50
R3	Gary Bell	5.00	2.50	1.50
R4	John Wyatt	5.00	2.50	1.50
R5	Darrell Brandon	5.00	2.50	1.50
R6	Joe Foy	5.00	2.50	1.50
R7	Ray Culp	5.00	2.50	1.50
R8	Dalton Jones	5.00	2.50	1.50
R9	Gene Oliver	5.00	2.50	1.50
R10	Jose Santiago	5.00	2.50	1.50
R11	Rico Petrocelli	6.00	3.00	1.75
R12	George Scott	5.00	2.50	1.50
R13	Mike Andrews	5.00	2.50	1.50
R14	Dick Ellsworth	5.00	2.50	1.50
R15	Norm Siebern	5.00	2.50	1.50
R16	Jim Lonborg	6.00	3.00	1.75
R17	Jerry Adair	5.00	2.50	1.50
R18	Elston Howard	5.00	2.50	1.50
	1967 CALIFORNIA ANGELS			
L19	Len Gabrielson	5.00	2.50	1.50
L20	Jackie Hernandez	5.00	2.50	1.50
L21	Paul Schaal	5.00	2.50	1.50
L22	Lew Burdette	5.00	2.50	1.50
L23	Jimmie Hall	5.00	2.50	1.50
L24	Fred Newman	5.00	2.50	1.50
L25	Don Mincher	5.00	2.50	1.50
L26	Bob Rodgers	5.00	2.50	1.50
L27	Jack Sanford	5.00	2.50	1.50
L28	Bobby Knoop	5.00	2.50	1.50
L29	Jose Cardenal	5.00	2.50	1.50
L30	Jim Fregosi	5.00	2.50	1.50
L31	George Brunet	5.00	2.50	1.50
L32	Marcelino Lopez	5.00	2.50	1.50
L33	Minnie Rojas	5.00	2.50	1.50
L34	Jay Johnstone	5.00	2.50	1.50
L35	Ed Kirkpatrick	5.00	2.50	1.50
	1967 CHICAGO CUBS			
C1	Ferguson Jenkins	15.00	7.50	4.50
C2	Ernie Banks	30.00	15.00	9.00
C3	Glenn Beckert	5.00	2.50	1.50
C4	Bob Hendley	5.00	2.50	1.50
C5	John Boccabella	5.00	2.50	1.50
C6	Ron Campbell	5.00	2.50	1.50
C7	Ray Culp	5.00	2.50	1.50
C8	Adolfo Phillips	5.00	2.50	1.50
C9	Don Bryant	5.00	2.50	1.50
C10	Randy Hundley	5.00	2.50	1.50
C11	Ron Santo	6.00	3.00	1.75
C12	Lee Thomas	5.00	2.50	1.50
C13	Billy Williams	25.00	12.50	7.50
C14	Ken Holtzman	5.00	2.50	1.50
C15	Cal Koonce	5.00	2.50	1.50
C16	Curt Simmons	5.00	2.50	1.50
C17	George Altman	5.00	2.50	1.50
C18	Bryon Browne	5.00	2.50	1.50
	CHICAGO WHITE SOX			
L1	Gary Peters	5.00	2.50	1.50
L2	Jerry Adair	5.00	2.50	1.50
L3	Al Weis	5.00	2.50	1.50
L4	Pete Ward	5.00	2.50	1.50
L5	Hoyt Wilhelm	15.00	7.50	4.50
L6	Don Buford	5.00	2.50	1.50
L7	John Buzhardt	5.00	2.50	1.50
L8	Wayne Causey	5.00	2.50	1.50
L9	Jerry McNertney	5.00	2.50	1.50
L10	Ron Hansen	5.00	2.50	1.50
L11	Tom McCraw	5.00	2.50	1.50
L12	Jim O'Toole	5.00	2.50	1.50
L13	Bill Skowron	6.00	3.00	1.75
L14	Joel Horlen	5.00	2.50	1.50
L15	Tommy John	12.00	6.00	3.50
L16	Bob Locker	5.00	2.50	1.50
L17	Ken Berry	5.00	2.50	1.50
L18	Tommie Agee	5.00	2.50	1.50
	1967 CINCINNATI REDS			
F1	Floyd Robinson	5.00	2.50	1.50
F2	Leo Cardenas	5.00	2.50	1.50
F3	Gordy Coleman	5.00	2.50	1.50
F4	Tommy Harper	5.00	2.50	1.50
F5	Tommy Helms	5.00	2.50	1.50
F6	Deron Johnson	5.00	2.50	1.50
F7	Jim Maloney	5.00	2.50	1.50
F8	Tony Perez	25.00	12.50	7.50
F9	Don Pavletich	5.00	2.50	1.50
F10	John Edwards	5.00	2.50	1.50
F11	Vada Pinson	7.50	3.75	2.25
F12	Chico Ruiz	5.00	2.50	1.50
F13	Pete Rose	40.00	20.00	12.00
F14	Bill McCool	5.00	2.50	1.50
F15	Joe Nuxhall	5.00	2.50	1.50
F16	Milt Pappas	5.00	2.50	1.50
F17	Art Shamsky	5.00	2.50	1.50
F18	Dick Simpson	5.00	2.50	1.50
	1967 CLEVELAND INDIANS			
I1	Luis Tiant	6.00	3.00	1.75
I2	Max Alvis	5.00	2.50	1.50
I3	Larry Brown	5.00	2.50	1.50

I4	Rocky Colavito	10.00	5.00	3.00
I5	John O'Donoghue	5.00	2.50	1.50
I6	Pedro Gonzalez	5.00	2.50	1.50
I7	Gary Bell	5.00	2.50	1.50
I8	Sonny Siebert	5.00	2.50	1.50
I9	Joe Azcue	5.00	2.50	1.50
I10	Lee Maye	5.00	2.50	1.50
I11	Chico Salmon	5.00	2.50	1.50
I12	Leon Wagner	5.00	2.50	1.50
I13	Fred Whitfield	5.00	2.50	1.50
I14	Jack Kralick	5.00	2.50	1.50
I15	Sam McDowell	6.00	3.00	1.75
I16	Dick Radatz	5.00	2.50	1.50
I17	Vic Davalillo	5.00	2.50	1.50
I18	Chuck Hinton	5.00	2.50	1.50
	1968 CLEVELAND INDIANS			
I1	Luis Tiant	6.00	3.00	1.75
I2	Max Alvis	5.00	2.50	1.50
I3	Larry Brown	5.00	2.50	1.50
I4	Tommy Harper	5.00	2.50	1.50
I5	Vern Fuller	5.00	2.50	1.50
I6	Jose Cardenal	5.00	2.50	1.50
I7	Dave Nelson	5.00	2.50	1.50
I8	Sonny Siebert	5.00	2.50	1.50
I9	Joe Azcue	5.00	2.50	1.50
I10	Lee Maye	5.00	2.50	1.50
I11	Chico Salmon	5.00	2.50	1.50
I12	Leon Wagner	5.00	2.50	1.50
I13	Eddie Fisher	5.00	2.50	1.50
I14	Stan Williams	5.00	2.50	1.50
I15	Sam McDowell	6.00	3.00	1.75
I16	Steve Hargan	5.00	2.50	1.50
I17	Vic Davalillo	5.00	2.50	1.50
I18	Duke Sims	5.00	2.50	1.50
	1967 DETROIT TIGERS			
T1	Larry Sherry	5.00	2.50	1.50
T2	Norm Cash	7.50	3.75	2.25
T3	Jerry Lumpe	5.00	2.50	1.50
T4	Dave Wickersham	5.00	2.50	1.50
T5	Joe Sparma	5.00	2.50	1.50
T6	Dick McAuliffe	5.00	2.50	1.50
T7	Fred Gladding	5.00	2.50	1.50
T8	Jim Northrup	5.00	2.50	1.50
T9	Bill Freehan	5.00	2.50	1.50
T10	Earl Wilson	5.00	2.50	1.50
T11	Dick Tracewski	5.00	2.50	1.50
T12	Don Wert	5.00	2.50	1.50
T13	Jake Wood	5.00	2.50	1.50
T14	Mickey Lolich	6.00	3.00	1.75
T15	Johnny Podres	5.00	2.50	1.50
T16	Bill Monbouquette	5.00	2.50	1.50
T17	Al Kaline	30.00	15.00	9.00
T18	Willie Horton	5.00	2.50	1.50
	1968 DETROIT TIGERS			
T1	Ray Oyler	5.00	2.50	1.50
T2	Norm Cash	7.50	3.75	2.25
T3	Mike Marshall	5.00	2.50	1.50
T4	Mickey Stanley	5.00	2.50	1.50
T5	Joe Sparma	5.00	2.50	1.50
T6	Dick McAuliffe	5.00	2.50	1.50
T7	Gates Brown	5.00	2.50	1.50
T8	Jim Northrup	5.00	2.50	1.50
T9	Bill Freehan	5.00	2.50	1.50
T10	Earl Wilson	5.00	2.50	1.50
T11	Dick Tracewski	5.00	2.50	1.50
T12	Don Wert	5.00	2.50	1.50
T13	Dennis Ribant	5.00	2.50	1.50
T14	Mickey Lolich	6.00	3.00	1.75
T15	Denny McLain	12.00	6.00	3.50
T16	Ed Mathews	25.00	12.50	7.50
T17	Al Kaline	30.00	15.00	9.00
T18	Willie Horton	5.00	2.50	1.50
	1967 HOUSTON ASTROS			
H1	Dave Giusti	5.00	2.50	1.50
H2	Bob Aspromonte	5.00	2.50	1.50
H3	Ron Davis	5.00	2.50	1.50
H4	Claude Raymond	5.00	2.50	1.50
H5	Barry Latman	5.00	2.50	1.50
H6	Chuck Harrison	5.00	2.50	1.50
H7	Bill Heath	5.00	2.50	1.50
H8	Sonny Jackson	5.00	2.50	1.50
H9	John Bateman	5.00	2.50	1.50
H10	Ron Brand	5.00	2.50	1.50
H11	Aaron Pointer	5.00	2.50	1.50
H12	Joe Morgan	25.00	12.50	7.50
H13	Rusty Staub	6.00	3.00	1.75
H14	Mike Cuellar	5.00	2.50	1.50
H15	Larry Dierker	5.00	2.50	1.50
H16	Dick Farrell	5.00	2.50	1.50
H17	Jim Landis	5.00	2.50	1.50
H18	Ed Mathews	25.00	12.50	7.50
	1968 HOUSTON ASTROS			
H1	Dave Giusti	5.00	2.50	1.50
H2	Bob Aspromonte	5.00	2.50	1.50
H3	Ron Davis	5.00	2.50	1.50
H4	Julio Gotay	5.00	2.50	1.50
H5	Fred Gladding	5.00	2.50	1.50
H6	Lee Thomas	5.00	2.50	1.50
H7	Wade Blasingame	5.00	2.50	1.50
H8	Denis Menke	5.00	2.50	1.50
H9	John Bateman	5.00	2.50	1.50
H10	Ron Brand	5.00	2.50	1.50
H11	Doug Rader	5.00	2.50	1.50
H12	Joe Morgan	25.00	12.50	7.50
H13	Rusty Staub	6.00	3.00	1.75
H14	Mike Cuellar	5.00	2.50	1.50
H15	Larry Dierker	5.00	2.50	1.50
H16	Denny Lemaster	5.00	2.50	1.50
H17	Jim Wynn	5.00	2.50	1.50
H18	Don Wilson	5.00	2.50	1.50
	1967 KANSAS CTIY ATHLETICS			
K1	Jim Nash	5.00	2.50	1.50
K2	Bert Campaneris	5.00	2.50	1.50
K3	Ed Charles	5.00	2.50	1.50
K4	Wes Stock	5.00	2.50	1.50
K5	John Odom	5.00	2.50	1.50
K6	Ossie Chavarria	5.00	2.50	1.50
K7	Jack Aker	5.00	2.50	1.50
K8	Dick Green	5.00	2.50	1.50
K9	Phil Roof	5.00	2.50	1.50
K10	Rene Lacheman	5.00	2.50	1.50
K11	Mike Hershberger	5.00	2.50	1.50
K12	Joe Nossek	5.00	2.50	1.50
K13	Roger Repoz	5.00	2.50	1.50
K14	Chuck Dobson	5.00	2.50	1.50
K15	Jim Hunter	15.00	7.50	4.50
K16	Lew Krausse	5.00	2.50	1.50
K17	Danny Cater	5.00	2.50	1.50
K18	Jim Gosger	5.00	2.50	1.50
	1967 LOS ANGELES DODGERS			
L1	Phil Regan	5.00	2.50	1.50
L2	Bob Bailey	5.00	2.50	1.50
L3	Ron Fairly	5.00	2.50	1.50
L4	Joe Moeller	5.00	2.50	1.50
L5	Don Sutton	15.00	7.50	4.50
L6	Ron Hunt	5.00	2.50	1.50
L7	Jim Brewer	5.00	2.50	1.50
L8	Lou Johnson	5.00	2.50	1.50
L9	John Roseboro	5.00	2.50	1.50
L10	Jeff Torborg	5.00	2.50	1.50
L11	John Kennedy	5.00	2.50	1.50
L12	Jim Lefebvre	5.00	2.50	1.50
L13	Wes Parker	5.00	2.50	1.50
L14	Bob Miller	5.00	2.50	1.50
L15	Claude Osteen	5.00	2.50	1.50
L16	Ron Perranoski	5.00	2.50	1.50
L17	Willie Davis	5.00	2.50	1.50
L18	Al Ferrera	5.00	2.50	1.50
	1968 LOS ANGELES DODGERS			
L1	Phil Regan	5.00	2.50	1.50
L2	Bob Bailey	5.00	2.50	1.50
L3	Ron Fairly	5.00	2.50	1.50
L4	Jim Brewer	5.00	2.50	1.50
L5	Don Sutton	15.00	7.50	4.50
L6	Tom Haller	5.00	2.50	1.50
L7	Rocky Colavito	12.00	6.00	3.50
L8	Jim Grant	5.00	2.50	1.50
L9	Jim Campanis	5.00	2.50	1.50
L10	Jeff Torborg	5.00	2.50	1.50
L11	Zoilo Versalles	6.00	3.00	1.75
L12	Jim Lefebvre	5.00	2.50	1.50
L13	Wes Parker	5.00	2.50	1.50
L14	Bill Singer	5.00	2.50	1.50
L15	Claude Osteen	5.00	2.50	1.50
L16	Len Gabrielson	5.00	2.50	1.50
L17	Willie Davis	5.00	2.50	1.50
L18	Al Ferrera	5.00	2.50	1.50
	1967 MINNESOTA TWINS			
M1	Ron Kline	5.00	2.50	1.50
M2	Bob Allison	6.00	3.00	1.75
M3	Earl Battey	5.00	2.50	1.50
M4	Jim Merritt	5.00	2.50	1.50
M5	Jim Perry	6.00	3.00	1.75
M6	Harmon Killebrew	25.00	12.50	7.50
M7	Dave Boswell	5.00	2.50	1.50
M8	Rich Rollins	5.00	2.50	1.50
M9	Jerry Zimmerman	5.00	2.50	1.50
M10	Al Worthington	5.00	2.50	1.50
M11	Cesar Tovar	5.00	2.50	1.50
M12	Sandy Valdespino	5.00	2.50	1.50
M13	Zoilo Versalles	6.00	3.00	1.75
M14	Dean Chance	6.00	3.00	1.75
M15	Jim Grant	5.00	2.50	1.50
M16	Jim Kaat	9.00	4.50	2.75
M17	Tony Oliva	10.00	5.00	3.00
M18	Andy Kosco	5.00	2.50	1.50
	1968 MINNESOTA TWINS			
M1	Rich Reese	5.00	2.50	1.50
M2	Bob Allison	6.00	3.00	1.75
M3	Ron Perranoski	5.00	2.50	1.50
M4	John Roseboro	5.00	2.50	1.50
M5	Jim Perry	6.00	3.00	1.75
M6	Harmon Killebrew	25.00	12.50	7.50
M7	Dave Boswell	5.00	2.50	1.50
M8	Rich Rollins	5.00	2.50	1.50
M9	Jerry Zimmerman	5.00	2.50	1.50
M10	Al Worthington	5.00	2.50	1.50
M11	Cesar Tovar	5.00	2.50	1.50
M12	Jim Merritt	5.00	2.50	1.50
M13	Bob Miller	5.00	2.50	1.50
M14	Dean Chance	6.00	3.00	1.75
M15	Ted Uhlaender	5.00	2.50	1.50
M16	Jim Kaat	9.00	4.50	2.75
M17	Tony Oliva	10.00	5.00	3.00
M18	Rod Carew	40.00	20.00	12.00
	1967 NEW YORK METS			
V19	Chuck Hiller	5.00	2.50	1.50
V20	Johnny Lewis	5.00	2.50	1.50
V21	Ed Kranepool	5.00	2.50	1.50
V22	Al Luplow	5.00	2.50	1.50
V23	Don Cardwell	5.00	2.50	1.50
V24	Cleon Jones	5.00	2.50	1.50
V25	Bob Shaw	5.00	2.50	1.50
V26	John Stephenson	5.00	2.50	1.50
V27	Ron Swoboda	5.00	2.50	1.50
V28	Ken Boyer	6.00	3.00	1.75
V29	Ed Bressoud	5.00	2.50	1.50
V30	Tommy Davis	5.00	2.50	1.50
V31	Roy McMillan	5.00	2.50	1.50
V32	Jack Fisher	5.00	2.50	1.50
V33	Tug McGraw	6.00	3.00	1.75
V34	Jerry Grote	5.00	2.50	1.50
V35	Jack Hamilton	5.00	2.50	1.50
	1967 NEW YORK YANKEES			
V1	Mel Stottlemyre	5.00	2.50	1.50
V2	Ruben Amaro	5.00	2.50	1.50
V3	Jake Gibbs	5.00	2.50	1.50
V4	Dooley Womack	5.00	2.50	1.50
V5	Fred Talbot	5.00	2.50	1.50
V6	Horace Clarke	5.00	2.50	1.50
V7	Jim Bouton	6.00	3.00	1.75
V8	Mickey Mantle	125.00	60.00	35.00
V9	Elston Howard	7.50	3.75	2.25
V10	Hal Reniff	5.00	2.50	1.50
V11	Charley Smith	5.00	2.50	1.50
V12	Bobby Murcer	6.00	3.00	1.75
V13	Joe Pepitone	6.00	3.00	1.75
V14	Al Downing	5.00	2.50	1.50
V15	Steve Hamilton	5.00	2.50	1.50
V16	Fritz Peterson	5.00	2.50	1.50
V17	Tom Tresh	6.00	3.00	1.75
V18	Roy White	6.00	3.00	1.75
	1967 PHILADELPHIA PHILLIES			
P1	Richie Allen	7.50	3.75	2.25
P2	Bob Wine	5.00	2.50	1.50
P3	Johnny Briggs	5.00	2.50	1.50
P4	John Callison	5.00	2.50	1.50
P5	Doug Clemens	5.00	2.50	1.50
P6	Dick Groat	5.00	2.50	1.50
P7	Dick Ellsworth	5.00	2.50	1.50
P8	Phil Linz	5.00	2.50	1.50
P9	Clay Dalrymple	5.00	2.50	1.50
P10	Bob Uecker	10.00	5.00	3.00
P11	Cookie Rojas	5.00	2.50	1.50
P12	Tony Taylor	5.00	2.50	1.50
P13	Bill White	5.00	2.50	1.50
P14	Larry Jackson	5.00	2.50	1.50
P15	Chris Short	5.00	2.50	1.50
P16	Jim Bunning	15.00	7.50	4.50
P17	Tony Gonzalez	5.00	2.50	1.50
P18	Don Lock	5.00	2.50	1.50
	1967 PITTSBURGH PIRATES			
E1	Al McBean	5.00	2.50	1.50
E2	Gene Alley	5.00	2.50	1.50
E3	Donn Clendenon	5.00	2.50	1.50
E4	Bob Veale	5.00	2.50	1.50
E5	Pete Mikkelsen	5.00	2.50	1.50
E6	Bill Mazeroski	20.00	10.00	6.00
E7	Steve Blass	5.00	2.50	1.50
E8	Manny Mota	5.00	2.50	1.50
E9	Jim Pagliaroni	5.00	2.50	1.50
E10	Jesse Gonder	5.00	2.50	1.50
E11	Jose Pagan	5.00	2.50	1.50
E12	Willie Stargell	25.00	12.50	7.50
E13	Maury Wills	9.00	4.50	2.75
E14	Elroy Face	5.00	2.50	1.50
E15	Woodie Fryman	5.00	2.50	1.50
E16	Vern Law	5.00	2.50	1.50
E17	Matty Alou	5.00	2.50	1.50
E18	Roberto Clemente	60.00	30.00	18.00
	1967 SAN FRANCISCO GIANTS			
G1	Bob Bolin	5.00	2.50	1.50
G2	Ollie Brown	5.00	2.50	1.50
G3	Jim Davenport	5.00	2.50	1.50
G4	Tito Fuentes	5.00	2.50	1.50
G5	Norm Siebern	5.00	2.50	1.50
G6	Jim Hart	5.00	2.50	1.50
G7	Juan Marichal	15.00	7.50	4.50
G8	Hal Lanier	5.00	2.50	1.50
G9	Tom Haller	5.00	2.50	1.50
G10	Bob Barton	5.00	2.50	1.50
G11	Willie McCovey	20.00	10.00	6.00
G12	Mike McCormick	5.00	2.50	1.50
G13	Frank Linzy	5.00	2.50	1.50

		NM	E	VG
G14	Ray Sadecki	5.00	2.50	1.50
G15	Gaylord Perry	15.00	7.50	4.50
G16	Lindy McDaniel	5.00	2.50	1.50
G17	Willie Mays	60.00	30.00	18.00
G18	Jesus Alou	5.00	2.50	1.50

1968 SAN FRANCISCO GIANTS

G1	Bob Bolin	5.00	2.50	1.50
G2	Ollie Brown	5.00	2.50	1.50
G3	Jim Davenport	5.00	2.50	1.50
G4	Bob Barton	5.00	2.50	1.50
G5	Jack Hiatt	5.00	2.50	1.50
G6	Jim Hart	5.00	2.50	1.50
G7	Juan Marichal	15.00	7.50	4.50
G8	Hal Lanier	5.00	2.50	1.50
G9	Ron Hunt	5.00	2.50	1.50
G10	Ron Herbel	5.00	2.50	1.50
G11	Willie McCovey	20.00	10.00	6.00
G12	Mike McCormick	5.00	2.50	1.50
G13	Frank Linzy	5.00	2.50	1.50
G14	Ray Sadecki	5.00	2.50	1.50
G15	Gaylord Perry	15.00	7.50	4.50
G16	Lindy McDaniel	5.00	2.50	1.50
G17	Willie Mays	60.00	30.00	18.00
G18	Jesus Alou	5.00	2.50	1.50

1967 WASHINGTON SENATORS

S1	Bob Humphreys	5.00	2.50	1.50
S2	Bernie Allen	5.00	2.50	1.50
S3	Ed Brinkman	5.00	2.50	1.50
S4	Pete Richert	5.00	2.50	1.50
S5	Camilo Pascual	5.00	2.50	1.50
S6	Frank Howard	7.50	3.75	2.25
S7	Casey Cox	5.00	2.50	1.50
S8	Jim King	5.00	2.50	1.50
S9	Paul Casanova	5.00	2.50	1.50
S10	Dick Lines	5.00	2.50	1.50
S11	Dick Nen	5.00	2.50	1.50
S12	Ken McMullen	5.00	2.50	1.50
S13	Bob Saverine	5.00	2.50	1.50
S14	Jim Hannan	5.00	2.50	1.50
S15	Darold Knowles	5.00	2.50	1.50
S16	Phil Ortega	5.00	2.50	1.50
S17	Ken Harrelson	5.00	2.50	1.50
S18	Fred Valentine	5.00	2.50	1.50

1971 Coca-Cola Houston Astros

The constitution and distribution of these Coke premium pictures is unknown. Players are pictured in pastel drawings on the semi-gloss fronts of these 8" x 11" sheets. (The punch holes on the photographed card are not original.) A black facsimile autograph appears in the lower portion of the drawing and the player's name is printed in black in the white bottom border. Backs are printed in blue and red with a background photo of the Astrodome. Data on back includes biographical information, complete pro record and career summary. The unnumbered cards are checklisted here in alphabetical order; but this list is probably not complete.

		NM	E	VG
Complete Set (12):		50.00	25.00	15.00
Common Player:		5.00	2.50	1.50
(1)	Jesus Alou	5.00	2.50	1.50
(2)	Wade Blasingame (SP)	9.00	4.50	2.75
(3)	Cesar Cedeno	7.50	3.75	2.25
(4)	Larry Dierker	7.50	3.75	2.25
(5)	John Edwards	5.00	2.50	1.50
(6)	Denis Menke	5.00	2.50	1.50
(7)	Roger Metzger	5.00	2.50	1.50
(8)	Joe Morgan	15.00	7.50	4.50
(9)	Doug Rader	5.00	2.50	1.50
(10)	Bob Watson	5.00	2.50	1.50
(11)	Don Wilson	5.00	2.50	1.50
(12)	Jim Wynn (SP)	12.00	6.00	3.50

1978 Coca-Cola/WPLO Atlanta Braves

Co-sponsored by Coke and a local radio station, this set of Braves cards is rendered in blue-and-white line art portraits in a 3" x 4-1/4" format. A soda discount coupon was distributed with the set.

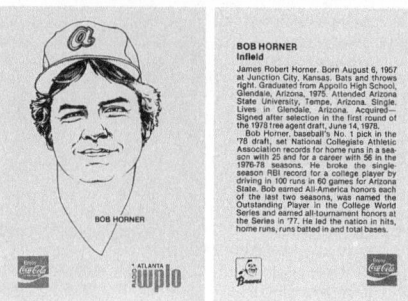

		NM	E	VG
Complete Set (14):		30.00	15.00	9.00
Common Player:		3.00	1.50	.90
(1)	Barry Bonnell	3.00	1.50	.90
(2)	Jeff Burroughs	3.00	1.50	.90
(3)	Rick Camp	3.00	1.50	.90
(4)	Gene Garber	3.00	1.50	.90
(5)	Rod Gilbreath	3.00	1.50	.90
(6)	Bob Horner	4.50	2.25	1.25
(7)	Glenn Hubbard	3.00	1.50	.90
(8)	Gary Matthews	3.00	1.50	.90
(9)	Larry McWilliams	3.00	1.50	.90
(10)	Dale Murphy	9.00	4.50	2.75
(11)	Phil Niekro	5.00	2.50	1.50
(12)	Rowland Office	3.00	1.50	.90
(13)	Biff Pocoroba	3.00	1.50	.90
(14)	Jerry Royster	3.00	1.50	.90

1979 Coca-Cola/7-Eleven MVPs

The co-MVPs of the National League for 1979 are pictured on this 5" x 7" blank-back photo card. A red band at top identifies the player and the award. At bottom are Coke and 7-Eleven logos.

	NM	E	VG
Keith Hernandez, Willie Stargell	6.00	3.00	1.80

1909 "Colgan's Chips" Square Proofs

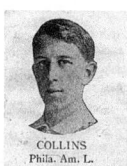

Though widely identified as being connected to the Colgan's Chips disc issues of 1909-1912, there is nothing to tie these square cards to the gum company except for the shared use of player photos. The squares measure about 1-3/8" x 1-3/4" and are blank-backed. Black-and-white player portrait photos have a last name and team identification beneath. Many, but not all, of the surviving specimens have paper and/or glue residue on back, leading to speculation they may have been part of an advertising piece. The extent of the checklist is unknown, with verified examples listed here.

		NM	E	VG
Common Player:		250.00	120.00	80.00
(1)	Red Ames	250.00	120.00	80.00
(2)	Charlie Babb (Memphis)	250.00	120.00	80.00
(3)	Baerwald (Memphis)	250.00	124.00	74.00
(4)	Home Run Baker	800.00	400.00	240.00
(5)	Johnny Bates	250.00	120.00	80.00
(6)	Ginger Beaumont (Boston)	250.00	120.00	80.00
(7)	Beals Becker	250.00	120.00	80.00
(8)	Roger Bresnahan	800.00	400.00	240.00
(9)	Al Bridwell	250.00	120.00	80.00
(10)	Lew Brockett	250.00	124.00	74.00
(11)	Al Burch	250.00	120.00	80.00
(12)	Donie Bush	250.00	120.00	80.00
(13)	Howie Camnitz	250.00	120.00	80.00
(14)	Frank Chance	800.00	400.00	240.00
(15)	Fred Clarke (Pittsburg)	800.00	400.00	240.00
(16)	Ty Cobb	6,000	3,000	1,800
(17)	Eddie Collins	800.00	400.00	240.00
(18)	Dode Criss	250.00	120.00	80.00
(19)	Jake Daubert (Memphis)	250.00	120.00	80.00
(20)	Harry Davis (Philadelphia)	250.00	120.00	80.00
(21)	Ray Demmett (Demmitt) (New York)	250.00	120.00	80.00
(22)	Clyde Engle (New York)	250.00	120.00	80.00
(23)	Steve Evans	250.00	120.00	80.00
(24)	Johnny Evers	800.00	400.00	240.00
(25)	Harry Gaspar	250.00	120.00	80.00
(26)	Gus Getz (Boston)	250.00	120.00	80.00
(27)	George Gibson	250.00	120.00	80.00
(28)	George Gibson	250.00	120.00	80.00
(29)	Harry Hooper (Boston A.L.)	800.00	400.00	240.00
(30)	Hugh Jennings	800.00	400.00	240.00
(31)	Addie Joss	800.00	400.00	240.00
(32)	Otto Knabe	250.00	120.00	80.00
(33)	James Lafitte	250.00	120.00	80.00
(34)	Bill Lelivelt	250.00	120.00	80.00
(35)	Bill Ludwig (Milwaukee)	250.00	120.00	80.00
(36)	Nick Maddox	250.00	120.00	80.00
(37)	Dots Miller	250.00	120.00	80.00
(38)	Mike Mitchell	250.00	120.00	80.00
(39)	Danny Murphy	250.00	120.00	80.00
(40)	Heinie Peitz	250.00	120.00	80.00
(41)	Jake Pfiester	250.00	120.00	80.00
(42)	Bill Schardt (Milwaukee)	250.00	120.00	80.00
(43)	Cy Seymour (New York)	250.00	124.00	74.00
(44)	Fred Snodgrass	250.00	120.00	80.00
(45)	Bob Spade (Cincinnati)	250.00	120.00	80.00
(46)	Bob Unglaub	250.00	120.00	80.00
(47)	Rube Waddell (St. Louis)	800.00	400.00	240.00
(48)	Honus Wagner (Pittsburg)	3,000	1,500	900.00
(49)	Owen Wilson	250.00	120.00	80.00
(50)	Hooks Wiltse	250.00	120.00	80.00
(51)	Woods (Buffalo)	250.00	120.00	80.00

1909-1911 Colgan's Chips Stars of the Diamond (E254)

This unusual set of 1-7/16"-diameter round cards was issued over a three-year period by the Colgan Gum Co., Louisville, Ky. The cards were inserted in five-cent tins of Colgan's Mint Chips and Violet Chips brands of gum. The borderless cards feature a black-and-white player portrait on the front along with the player's last name, team and league. On more than a dozen cards, variations are known in the size of the photo and/or lettering on front. Since they cannot be identified without another card to compare with, they are noted here only with an asterisk. The card back identifies the set as "Stars of the Diamond" and carries advertising for Colgan's Gum. Some backs are seen with a line of type at the bottom stating, "208 IN PRESENT SERIES." Over 225 different players were pictured over the three-year period, but because of team changes and other notable variations, at least 289 different cards exist. This issue was catalogued as E254 in the American Card Catalog. A number of cards and variations which had been listed in earlier editions of this catalog have been eliminated for lack of proof of their existence. Gaps have been left in the assigned numbering to accommodate future additions. Persons with "Stars of the Diamond" players or variations that do no appear on this list should contact the editor. Recent hobby finds suggest a rare variation with violet- printed backs exist, perhaps packaged with "Violet Chips." Further confirmation is required before pricing data will be established.

		NM	E	VG
Common Player:		75.00	35.00	20.00
Round Tin Package:		30.00	15.00	9.00
(1)	Ed Abbaticchio	75.00	35.00	20.00
(2)	Fred Abbott	75.00	35.00	20.00
(3a)	Bill Abstein (Pittsburg)	75.00	35.00	20.00
(3b)	Bill Abstein (Jersey City)	75.00	35.00	20.00
(4)	Babe Adams	75.00	35.00	20.00

(5)	Doc Adkins	75.00	35.00	20.00
(6a)	Dave Altizer (Cincinnati)	75.00	35.00	20.00
(6b)	Dave Altizer (Minneapolis)	75.00	35.00	20.00
(7)	Nick Altrock	95.00	50.00	30.00
(8)	Red Ames	75.00	35.00	20.00
(9a)	Jimmy Austin (New York)	75.00	35.00	20.00
(9b)	Jimmy Austin (St. Louis)	75.00	35.00	20.00
(10a)	Charlie Babb (Memphis)	75.00	35.00	20.00
(10b)	Charlie Babb (Norfolk)	75.00	35.00	20.00
(11)	Baerwald	75.00	35.00	20.00
(12)	Bill Bailey	75.00	35.00	20.00
(13)	Home Run Baker (*)	215.00	110.00	65.00
(14)	Jack Barry (*)	75.00	35.00	20.00
(15a)	Bill Bartley (Curved letters.)	75.00	35.00	20.00
(15b)	Bill Bartley (Horizontal letters.)	75.00	35.00	20.00
(16a)	Johnny Bates (Cincinnati)	75.00	35.00	20.00
(16b)	Johnny Bates (Philadelphia, black letters.)	75.00	35.00	20.00
(16c)	Johnny Bates (Philadelphia, white letters.)	75.00	35.00	20.00
(17)	Dick Bayless	75.00	35.00	20.00
(18a)	Ginger Beaumont (Boston)	75.00	35.00	20.00
(18b)	Ginger Beaumont (Chicago)	75.00	35.00	20.00
(18c)	Ginger Beaumont (St. Paul)	75.00	35.00	20.00
(19)	Beals Becker	75.00	35.00	20.00
(20)	George Bell	75.00	35.00	20.00
(21a)	Harry Bemis (Cleveland)	75.00	35.00	20.00
(21b)	Harry Bemis (Columbus)	75.00	35.00	20.00
(22a)	Heinie Berger (Cleveland)	75.00	35.00	20.00
(22b)	Heinie Berger (Columbus)	75.00	35.00	20.00
(23)	Beumiller	75.00	35.00	20.00
(24)	Joe Birmingham	75.00	35.00	20.00
(25)	Kitty Bransfield	75.00	35.00	20.00
(26)	Roger Bresnahan	215.00	110.00	65.00
(27)	Al Bridwell	75.00	35.00	20.00
(28)	Lew Brockett	75.00	35.00	20.00
(29)	Al Burch (*)	75.00	35.00	20.00
(30)	Burke	75.00	35.00	20.00
(31)	Donie Bush	75.00	35.00	20.00
(32)	Bill Byers	75.00	35.00	20.00
(33)	Howie Cammitz (Camnitz)	75.00	35.00	20.00
(34a)	Charlie Carr (Indianapolis)	75.00	35.00	20.00
(34b)	Charlie Carr (Utica)	75.00	35.00	20.00
(35)	Frank Chance	215.00	110.00	65.00
(36)	Hal Chase	150.00	80.00	40.00
(37)	Bill Clancy (Clancey)	75.00	35.00	20.00
(38a)	Fred Clarke (Pittsburg)	215.00	110.00	65.00
(38b)	Fred Clarke (Pittsburgh)	215.00	110.00	65.00
(39)	Tommy Clarke (Cincinnati)	75.00	35.00	20.00
(40)	Bill Clymer	75.00	35.00	20.00
(41)	Ty Cobb (*)	2,000	875.00	525.00
(42)	Eddie Collins	215.00	110.00	65.00
(43)	Bunk Congalton	75.00	35.00	20.00
(44)	Wid Conroy	75.00	35.00	20.00
(45)	Ernie Courtney	75.00	35.00	20.00
(46a)	Harry Coveleski (Cincinnati)	75.00	35.00	20.00
(46b)	Harry Coveleski (Chattanooga)	75.00	35.00	20.00
(47)	Doc Crandall	75.00	35.00	20.00
(48)	Gavvy Cravath	75.00	35.00	20.00
(49)	Dode Criss	75.00	35.00	20.00
(50a)	Jake Daubert (Memphis)	75.00	35.00	20.00
(50b)	Jake Daubert (Brooklyn)	75.00	35.00	20.00
(51)	Harry Davis (Philadelphia)	75.00	35.00	20.00
(52)	Davis (St. Paul)	75.00	35.00	20.00
(53)	Frank Delahanty	75.00	35.00	20.00
(54a)	Ray Demmett (Demmitt) (New York)	75.00	35.00	20.00
(54b)	Ray Demmett (Demmitt) (Montreal)	75.00	35.00	20.00
(55)	Art Devlin	75.00	35.00	20.00
(56)	Wild Bill Donovan	75.00	35.00	20.00
(57)	Mickey Doolin (Doolan)	75.00	35.00	20.00
(58)	Patsy Dougherty	75.00	35.00	20.00
(59)	Tom Downey	75.00	35.00	20.00
(60)	Larry Doyle	75.00	35.00	20.00
(61)	Jack Dunn	95.00	50.00	30.00
(62)	Dick Eagan (Egan)	75.00	35.00	20.00
(63a)	Kid Elberfield (Elberfeld) (Washington)	75.00	35.00	20.00
(63b)	Kid Elberfield (Elberfeld) (New York)	75.00	35.00	20.00
(64)	Rube Ellis	75.00	35.00	20.00
(65)	Clyde Engle (Boston)	75.00	35.00	20.00
(66)	Steve Evans (Horizontal letters.)	75.00	35.00	20.00
(67)	Johnny Evers	215.00	110.00	65.00
(68)	Cecil Ferguson	75.00	35.00	20.00
(69)	Hobe Ferris	75.00	35.00	20.00
(70)	Field (Montreal) (Photo actually Michael Joyce)	75.00	35.00	20.00
(71)	Fitzgerald	75.00	35.00	20.00
(72a)	Patsy Flaherty (Kansas City)	75.00	35.00	20.00
(72b)	Patsy Flaherty (Atlanta)	75.00	35.00	20.00
(73)	Jack Flater	75.00	35.00	20.00
(74a)	Elmer Flick (Cleveland)	215.00	110.00	65.00
(74b)	Elmer Flick (Toledo)	215.00	110.00	65.00
(75a)	James Freck (Frick, Baltimore)	90.00	45.00	30.00
(75b)	James Freck (Frick, Toronto)	75.00	35.00	20.00
(76)	Jerry Freeman (Photo actually Buck Freeman.)	75.00	35.00	20.00
(77)	Art Fromme (*)	75.00	35.00	20.00
(78a)	Larry Gardner (Boston)	75.00	35.00	20.00
(78b)	Larry Gardner (New York)	75.00	35.00	20.00
(79)	Harry Gaspar	75.00	35.00	20.00
(80a)	Gus Getz (Boston)	75.00	35.00	20.00
(80b)	Gus Getz (Indianapolis)	75.00	35.00	20.00
(81)	George Gibson	75.00	35.00	20.00
(82a)	Moose Grimshaw (Toronto)	75.00	35.00	20.00
(82b)	Moose Grimshaw (Louisville)	75.00	35.00	20.00
(83)	Ed Hahn	75.00	35.00	20.00
(84)	John Halla (*)	75.00	35.00	20.00
(85)	Ed Hally (Holly)	75.00	35.00	20.00
(86)	Charlie Hanford	75.00	35.00	20.00
(87)	Topsy Hartsel	75.00	35.00	20.00
(88a)	Roy Hartzell (St. Louis)	75.00	35.00	20.00
(88b)	Roy Hartzell (New York)	75.00	35.00	20.00
(89)	Weldon Henley	75.00	35.00	20.00
(91)	Harry Hinchman	75.00	35.00	20.00
(92)	Solly Hofman	75.00	35.00	20.00
(93a)	Harry Hooper (Boston Na'l)	215.00	110.00	65.00
(93b)	Harry Hooper (Boston Am. L.)	240.00	120.00	75.00
(94)	Howard (*)	75.00	35.00	20.00
(95a)	Hughes (No name in uniform.)	75.00	35.00	20.00
(95b)	Hughes (Name and team name in uniform.)	75.00	35.00	20.00
(96b)	Rudy Hulswitt (St. Louis)	75.00	35.00	20.00
(96c)	Rudy Hulswitt (Chattanooga)	75.00	35.00	20.00
(97)	John Hummel	75.00	35.00	20.00
(98)	George Hunter	75.00	35.00	20.00
(99)	Hugh Jennings	215.00	110.00	65.00
(100)	Davy Jones	75.00	35.00	20.00
(101)	Tom Jones	75.00	35.00	20.00
(102a)	Tim Jordon (Jordan, Brooklyn)	75.00	35.00	20.00
(102b)	Tim Jordon (Jordan, Atlanta)	75.00	35.00	20.00
(102c)	Tim Jordon (Jordan, Louisville)	75.00	35.00	20.00
(103)	Addie Joss	325.00	120.00	75.00
(104)	Al Kaiser	75.00	35.00	20.00
(105)	Joe Kelly (Kelley)	215.00	110.00	65.00
(106)	Bill Killefer (*)	75.00	35.00	20.00
(107a)	Ed Killian (Detroit)	75.00	35.00	20.00
(107b)	Ed Killian (Toronto)	75.00	35.00	20.00
(108)	Otto Knabe	75.00	35.00	20.00
(109)	Jack Knight	75.00	35.00	20.00
(111)	Ed Konetchy	75.00	35.00	20.00
(112)	Rube Kroh	75.00	35.00	20.00
(113)	James Lafitte	75.00	35.00	20.00
(114)	Lakoff	75.00	35.00	20.00
(115)	Frank Lange	75.00	35.00	20.00
(116a)	Frank LaPorte (St. Louis)	75.00	35.00	20.00
(116b)	Frank LaPorte (New York)	75.00	35.00	20.00
(117)	Tommy Leach	75.00	35.00	20.00
(118)	Bill Lelivelt	75.00	35.00	20.00
(119a)	Jack Lewis (Milwaukee)	75.00	35.00	20.00
(119b)	Jack Lewis (Indianapolis)	75.00	35.00	20.00
(120a)	Vive Lindaman (Boston)	75.00	35.00	20.00
(120b)	Vive Lindaman (Louisville)	75.00	35.00	20.00
(120c)	Vive Lindaman (Indianapolis)	75.00	35.00	20.00
(121)	Bris Lord	75.00	35.00	20.00
(122a)	Harry Lord (Boston)	75.00	35.00	20.00
(122b)	Harry Lord (Chicago)	75.00	35.00	20.00
(123)	Bill Ludwig (Milwaukee)	75.00	35.00	20.00
(124)	Nick Maddox	75.00	35.00	20.00
(125a)	Manser (Jersey City)	75.00	35.00	20.00
(125b)	Manser (Rochester)	75.00	35.00	20.00
(126)	Al Mattern	75.00	35.00	20.00
(127)	Bill Matthews	75.00	35.00	20.00
(128)	George McBride	75.00	35.00	20.00
(129)	Joe McCarthy (Toledo)	215.00	110.00	65.00
(130)	McConnell	75.00	35.00	20.00
(131)	Moose McCormick	75.00	35.00	20.00
(132)	Dan McGann	75.00	35.00	20.00
(133)	Jim McGinley	75.00	35.00	20.00
(134)	Iron Man McGinnity	215.00	110.00	65.00
(135a)	Matty McIntyre (Detroit)	75.00	35.00	20.00
(135b)	Matty McIntyre (Chicago)	75.00	35.00	20.00
(136)	Larry McLean (*)(Three photo size variations known.)	75.00	35.00	20.00
(137)	Fred Merkle	75.00	35.00	20.00
(138a)	Merritt (Buffalo)	75.00	35.00	20.00
(138b)	Merritt (Jersey City)	75.00	35.00	20.00
(139)	Meyer (Newark)	75.00	35.00	20.00
(140)	Chief Meyers (New York)	75.00	35.00	20.00
(141)	Clyde Milan	75.00	35.00	20.00
(142)	Dots Miller	75.00	35.00	20.00
(143)	Mike Mitchell	75.00	35.00	20.00
(144)	Moran	75.00	35.00	20.00
(145a)	Bill Moriarty (Louisville)	75.00	35.00	20.00
(145b)	Bill Moriarty (Omaha)	75.00	35.00	20.00
(146)	George Moriarty	75.00	35.00	20.00
(147a)	George Mullen (Name incorrect.)	75.00	35.00	20.00
(147b)	George Mullin (Name correct.)	75.00	35.00	20.00
(148a)	Simmy Murch (Chattanooga)	75.00	35.00	20.00
(148b)	Simmy Murch (Indianapolis)	75.00	35.00	20.00
(149)	Danny Murphy	75.00	35.00	20.00
(150a)	Red Murray (New York, white letters.)	75.00	35.00	12.00
(150b)	Red Murray (St. Paul)	75.00	35.00	20.00
(151)	Billy Nattress (*)	75.00	35.00	20.00
(152a)	Red Nelson (St. Louis)	75.00	35.00	20.00
(152b)	Red Nelson (Toledo)	75.00	35.00	20.00
(153)	Rebel Oakes	75.00	35.00	20.00
(154)	Fred Odwell	75.00	35.00	20.00
(155a)	Al Orth (New York)	75.00	35.00	20.00
(155b)	Al Orth (Indianapolis)	75.00	35.00	20.00
(156)	Fred Osborn	75.00	35.00	20.00
(157)	Orval Overall	75.00	35.00	20.00
(158)	Owens	75.00	35.00	20.00
(159)	Fred Parent	75.00	35.00	20.00
(161a)	Dode Paskert (Cincinnati)	75.00	35.00	20.00
(161b)	Dode Paskert (Philadelphia)	75.00	35.00	20.00
(162)	Heinie Peitz	75.00	35.00	20.00
(163)	Bob Peterson	75.00	35.00	20.00
(164)	Jake Pfeister	75.00	35.00	20.00
(165)	Deacon Phillipe (Phillippe)	75.00	35.00	20.00
(166a)	Ollie Pickering (Louisville)	75.00	35.00	20.00
(166b)	Ollie Pickering (Minneapolis)	75.00	35.00	20.00
(166c)	Ollie Pickering (Omaha)	75.00	35.00	20.00
(167a)	Billy Purtell (Chicago)	75.00	35.00	20.00
(167b)	Billy Purtell (Boston)	75.00	35.00	20.00
(168)	Bugs Raymond	75.00	35.00	20.00
(169)	Pat Regan (Ragan)	75.00	35.00	20.00
(170)	Barney Reilly	75.00	35.00	20.00
(171)	Duke Reilly (Reilley)	75.00	35.00	20.00
(172)	Ed Reulbach	75.00	35.00	20.00
(173)	Claude Ritchey	75.00	35.00	20.00
(174)	Lou Ritter	75.00	35.00	20.00
(175)	William "Rabbit" Robinson (Louisville)	75.00	35.00	20.00
(176)	Rock	75.00	35.00	20.00
(177a)	Jack Rowan (Cincinnati)	75.00	35.00	20.00
(177b)	Jack Rowan (Philadelphia)	75.00	35.00	20.00
(178)	Nap Rucker	75.00	35.00	20.00
(179a)	Dick Rudolph (New York)	75.00	35.00	20.00
(179b)	Dick Rudolph (Toronto)	75.00	35.00	20.00
(180)	Jack Ryan ((St. Paul) (Photo actually Jimmy Ryan.))	75.00	35.00	20.00
(181)	Slim Sallee	75.00	35.00	20.00
(182a)	Bill Schardt (Birmingham)	75.00	35.00	20.00
(182b)	Bill Schardt (Milwaukee)	75.00	35.00	20.00
(183)	Jimmy Scheckard (Sheckard)	75.00	35.00	20.00
(184a)	George Schirm (Birmingham)	75.00	35.00	20.00
(184b)	George Schirm (Buffalo)	75.00	35.00	20.00
(185)	Larry Schlafly	75.00	35.00	20.00
(186)	Wildfire Schulte	75.00	35.00	20.00
(187a)	James Seabaugh (Looking to left, photo actually Julius Weisman.)	75.00	35.00	20.00
(187b)	James Seabaugh (Looking straight ahead, correct photo.)	75.00	35.00	20.00
(188)	Selby (*)	75.00	35.00	20.00

(189a)	Cy Seymour (New York)	75.00	35.00	20.00
(189b)	Cy Seymour (Baltimore)	75.00	35.00	20.00
(190)	Hosea Siner	75.00	35.00	20.00
(191)	G. Smith	75.00	35.00	20.00
(192a)	Sid Smith (Atlanta)	75.00	35.00	20.00
(192b)	Sid Smith (Buffalo)	75.00	35.00	20.00
(193)	Fred Snodgrass	75.00	35.00	20.00
(194a)	Bob Spade (Cincinnati)	75.00	35.00	20.00
(194b)	Bob Spade (Newark)	75.00	35.00	20.00
(195a)	Tully Sparks (Philadelphia)	75.00	35.00	20.00
(195b)	Tully Sparks (Richmond)	75.00	35.00	20.00
(196)	Tris Speaker (Boston Am.)	260.00	120.00	80.00
(197)	Tubby Spencer	75.00	35.00	20.00
(198)	Jake Stahl	75.00	35.00	20.00
(199)	John Stansberry (Stansbury)	75.00	35.00	20.00
(200)	Harry Steinfeldt (*)	75.00	35.00	20.00
(201)	George Stone	75.00	35.00	20.00
(202)	George Stovall	75.00	35.00	20.00
(203)	Gabby Street	75.00	35.00	20.00
(204a)	Sullivan (Louisville)	75.00	35.00	20.00
(204b)	Sullivan (Omaha)	75.00	35.00	20.00
(205a)	Ed Summers (No white in uniform.)	75.00	35.00	20.00
(205b)	Ed Summers (White in uniform.)	75.00	35.00	20.00
(206)	Suter	75.00	35.00	20.00
(207)	Lee Tannehill	75.00	35.00	20.00
(208)	Taylor	75.00	35.00	20.00
(209)	Joe Tinker	215.00	110.00	65.00
(210)	John Titus	75.00	35.00	20.00
(211)	Terry Turner	75.00	35.00	20.00
(212a)	Bob Unglaub (Washington)	75.00	35.00	20.00
(212b)	Bob Unglaub (Lincoln)	75.00	35.00	20.00
(213a)	Rube Waddell (St. Louis)	215.00	110.00	65.00
(213b)	Rube Waddell (Minneapolis)	215.00	110.00	65.00
(213c)	Rube Waddell (Newark)	215.00	110.00	65.00
(214)	Honus Wagner (*)	1,650	825.00	495.00
(215)	Walker	75.00	35.00	20.00
(216)	Waller	75.00	35.00	20.00
(217)	Clarence Wauner (Wanner)	75.00	35.00	20.00
(218)	Julius Weisman (Name correct.)	75.00	35.00	20.00
(219)	Jack White (Buffalo)	75.00	35.00	20.00
(220)	Kirby White (Boston)	75.00	35.00	20.00
(221)	Julius Wiesman (Weisman)	75.00	35.00	20.00
(222)	Ed Willett	75.00	35.00	20.00
(223)	Otto Williams	75.00	35.00	20.00
(224)	Owen Wilson	75.00	35.00	20.00
(225)	Hooks Wiltse	75.00	35.00	20.00
(226a)	Orville Woodruff (Indianapolis)	75.00	35.00	20.00
(226b)	Orville Woodruff (Louisville)	75.00	35.00	20.00
(227)	Woods	75.00	35.00	20.00
(228)	Cy Young	570.00	280.00	170.00
(229)	Bill Zimmerman	75.00	35.00	20.00
(230)	Heinie Zimmerman	75.00	35.00	20.00

1912 Colgan's Chips Red Borders (E270)

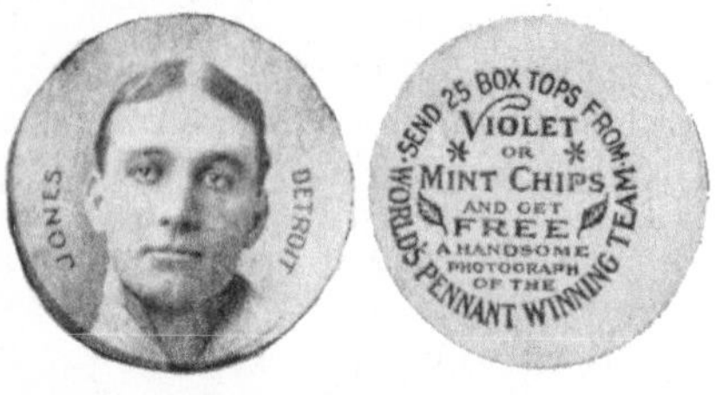

This set, issued in 1912 by Colgan Gum Co., Louisville, Ky., is very similar to the 1909-11 Colgan's release. Measuring about 1-3/8" in diameter, the black-and-white player pictures were inserted in tins of Colgan's Mint and Violet Chips gum. They are differentiated from the earlier issues by their distinctive red borders and by the back of the cards, which advises collectors to "Send 25 Box Tops" for a photo of the "World's Pennant Winning Team." The issue is designated as the E270 Red Border set in the American Card Catalog. A Red Border card of Gavvy Cravath previous cataloged is now believed not to exist.

		NM	E	VG
	Complete Set (181):	50,000	25,000	14,400
	Common Player:	350.00	175.00	105.00
(1)	Ed Abbaticchio	350.00	175.00	105.00
(2)	Fred Abbott	350.00	175.00	105.00
(3)	Babe Adams	350.00	175.00	105.00
(4)	Doc Adkins	350.00	175.00	105.00
(5)	Red Ames	350.00	175.00	105.00
(6)	Charlie Babb	350.00	175.00	105.00
(7)	Rudy Baerwald	375.00	200.00	120.00
(8)	Bill Bailey	350.00	175.00	105.00
(9)	Home Run Baker	600.00	300.00	180.00
(10)	Jack Barry	350.00	175.00	105.00
(11)	Johnny Bates	350.00	175.00	105.00
(12)	Dick Bayless	350.00	175.00	105.00
(13)	Ginger Beaumont	350.00	175.00	105.00
(14)	Beals Becker	350.00	175.00	105.00
(15)	George Bell	350.00	175.00	105.00
(16)	Harry Bemis	350.00	175.00	105.00
(17)	Heinie Berger	350.00	175.00	105.00
(18)	Beumiller	350.00	175.00	105.00
(19)	Joe Birmingham	350.00	175.00	105.00
(20)	Kitty Bransfield	350.00	175.00	105.00
(21)	Roger Bresnahan	750.00	370.00	220.00
(22)	Lew Brockett	350.00	175.00	105.00
(23)	Al Burch	350.00	175.00	105.00
(24)	Donie Bush	350.00	175.00	105.00
(25)	Bill Byers	350.00	175.00	105.00
(26)	Howie Cammitz (Camnitz)	350.00	175.00	105.00
(27)	Charlie Carr	350.00	175.00	105.00
(28)	Frank Chance	750.00	370.00	220.00
(29)	Hal Chase	700.00	350.00	210.00
(30)	Fred Clarke (Pittsburg)	750.00	370.00	220.00
(31)	Tommy Clarke (Cincinnati)	350.00	175.00	105.00
(32)	Bill Clymer	350.00	175.00	105.00
(33)	Ty Cobb	6,500	3,250	1,950
(34)	Eddie Collins	750.00	370.00	220.00
(35)	Wid Conroy	350.00	175.00	105.00
(36)	Harry Coveleski	350.00	175.00	105.00
(37)	Dode Criss	350.00	175.00	105.00
(38)	Jake Daubert	350.00	175.00	105.00
(39)	Harry Davis (Philadelphia)	350.00	175.00	105.00
(40)	Davis (St. Paul)	350.00	175.00	105.00
(41)	Frank Delahanty	350.00	175.00	105.00
(42)	Ray Demmett (Demmitt)	350.00	175.00	105.00
(43)	Art Devlin	350.00	175.00	105.00
(44)	Wild Bill Donovan	350.00	175.00	105.00
(45)	Mickey Doolin (Doolan)	350.00	175.00	105.00
(46)	Patsy Dougherty	350.00	175.00	105.00
(47)	Tom Downey	350.00	175.00	105.00
(48)	Larry Doyle	350.00	175.00	105.00
(49)	Jack Dunn	350.00	175.00	105.00
(50)	Dick Eagan (Egan)	350.00	175.00	105.00
(51)	Kid Elberfield (Elberfeld)	350.00	175.00	105.00
(52)	Rube Ellis	350.00	175.00	105.00
(53)	Steve Evans	350.00	175.00	105.00
(54)	Johnny Evers	750.00	370.00	220.00
(55)	Cecil Ferguson	350.00	175.00	105.00
(56)	Hobe Ferris	350.00	175.00	105.00
(57)	Fisher	350.00	175.00	105.00
(58)	Fitzgerald	350.00	175.00	105.00
(59)	Elmer Flick	750.00	370.00	220.00
(60)	James Freck (Frick)	350.00	175.00	105.00
(61)	Art Fromme	350.00	175.00	105.00
(62)	Larry Gardner	350.00	175.00	105.00
(63)	Harry Gaspar	350.00	175.00	105.00
(64)	George Gibson	350.00	175.00	105.00
(65)	Moose Grimshaw	350.00	175.00	105.00
(66)	John Halla	350.00	175.00	105.00
(67)	Ed Hally (Holly)	350.00	175.00	105.00
(68)	Charlie Hanford	350.00	175.00	105.00
(69)	Topsy Hartsel	350.00	175.00	105.00
(70)	Roy Hartzell	350.00	175.00	105.00
(71)	Weldon Henley (Two sizes photo variations noted.)	350.00	175.00	105.00
(72)	Harry Hinchman	350.00	175.00	105.00
(73)	Solly Hofman	350.00	175.00	105.00
(74)	Harry Hooper	750.00	370.00	220.00
(75)	Howard	350.00	175.00	105.00
(76)	Hughes	350.00	175.00	105.00
(77)	Rudy Hulswitt	350.00	175.00	105.00
(78)	John Hummel	350.00	175.00	105.00
(79)	George Hunter	350.00	175.00	105.00
(80)	Hugh Jennings	750.00	370.00	220.00
(81)	Davy Jones	350.00	175.00	105.00
(82)	Tom Jones	350.00	175.00	105.00
(83)	Tim Jordon (Jordan)	375.00	185.00	110.00
(84)	Joe Kelly (Kelley)	750.00	370.00	220.00
(85)	Bill Killefer	375.00	185.00	110.00
(86)	Ed Killian	375.00	185.00	110.00
(87)	Otto Knabe	375.00	185.00	110.00
(88)	Jack Knight	375.00	185.00	110.00
(89)	Ed Konetchy	375.00	185.00	110.00
(90)	Rube Kroh	375.00	185.00	110.00
(91)	LaCrosse (Photo actually Bill Schardt.)	350.00	175.00	105.00
(92)	Frank LaPorte	350.00	175.00	105.00
(93)	Tommy Leach	350.00	175.00	105.00
(94)	Jack Lelivelt	350.00	175.00	105.00
(95)	Jack Lewis	350.00	175.00	105.00
(96)	Vive Lindaman	350.00	175.00	105.00
(97)	Bris Lord	350.00	175.00	105.00
(98)	Harry Lord	350.00	175.00	105.00
(99)	Bill Ludwig	350.00	175.00	105.00
(100)	Nick Maddox	350.00	175.00	105.00
(101)	Manser	350.00	175.00	105.00
(102)	Al Mattern	350.00	175.00	105.00
(103)	George McBride	350.00	175.00	105.00
(104)	Joe McCarthy (Toledo)	750.00	370.00	220.00
(105)	McConnell	350.00	175.00	105.00
(106)	Moose McCormick	350.00	175.00	105.00
(107)	Dan McGann	350.00	175.00	105.00
(108)	Jim McGinley	350.00	175.00	105.00
(109)	Iron Man McGinnity	750.00	370.00	220.00
(110)	Matty McIntyre	350.00	175.00	105.00
(111)	Larry McLean	350.00	175.00	105.00
(112)	Fred Merkle	350.00	175.00	105.00
(113)	Merritt	350.00	175.00	105.00
(114)	Meyer (Newark)	350.00	175.00	105.00
(115)	Chief Meyers	350.00	175.00	105.00
(116)	Clyde Milan	350.00	175.00	105.00
(117)	Dots Miller	350.00	175.00	105.00
(118)	Mike Mitchell	350.00	175.00	105.00
(119)	Bill Moriarty (Omaha)	350.00	175.00	105.00
(120)	George Moriarty (Detroit)	350.00	175.00	105.00
(121)	George Mullen (Mullin)	350.00	175.00	105.00
(122)	Simmy Murch (Chattanooga)	350.00	175.00	105.00
(123)	Simmy Murch (Indianapolis)	350.00	175.00	105.00
(124)	Danny Murphy	350.00	175.00	105.00
(125)	Red Murray	350.00	175.00	105.00
(126)	Red Nelson	350.00	175.00	105.00
(127)	Rebel Oakes	350.00	175.00	105.00
(128)	Rebel Oakes (Columbus)	350.00	175.00	105.00
(129)	Rebel Oakes ((Indianapolis))	350.00	175.00	105.00
(130)	Orval Overall	350.00	175.00	105.00
(131)	Owens	350.00	175.00	105.00
(132)	Fred Parent	350.00	175.00	105.00
(133)	Dode Paskert	350.00	175.00	105.00
(134)	Bob Peterson	350.00	175.00	105.00
(135)	Jake Pfeister (Pfiester)	350.00	175.00	105.00
(136)	Deacon Phillipe (Phillippe)	350.00	175.00	105.00
(137)	Heinie Pietz (Peitz)	350.00	175.00	105.00
(138)	Ollie Pickering	350.00	175.00	105.00
(139)	Bugs Raymond	350.00	175.00	105.00
(140)	Pat Regan (Ragan)	350.00	175.00	105.00
(141)	Ed Reulbach	350.00	175.00	105.00
(142)	Robinson	350.00	175.00	105.00
(143)	Rock	350.00	175.00	105.00
(144)	Jack Rowan	350.00	175.00	105.00
(145)	Nap Rucker	350.00	175.00	105.00
(146)	Dick Rudolph	350.00	175.00	105.00
(147)	Slim Sallee	350.00	175.00	105.00
(148)	Jimmy Scheckard (Sheckard)	350.00	175.00	105.00
(149)	George Schirm	350.00	175.00	105.00
(150)	Wildfire Schulte	350.00	175.00	105.00
(151)	James Seabaugh	350.00	175.00	105.00
(152)	Selby	350.00	175.00	105.00
(153)	Cy Seymour	350.00	175.00	105.00
(154)	Hosea Siner	350.00	175.00	105.00
(155)	Sid Smith	350.00	175.00	105.00
(156)	Fred Snodgrass	350.00	175.00	105.00
(157)	Bob Spade	350.00	175.00	105.00
(158)	Tully Sparks	350.00	175.00	105.00
(159)	Tris Speaker	1,125	562.50	337.50
(160)	Tubby Spencer	350.00	175.00	105.00
(161)	John Stausberry (Stansbury)	350.00	175.00	105.00
(162)	Harry Steinfeldt	350.00	175.00	105.00
(163)	George Stone	350.00	175.00	105.00
(164)	George Stovall	350.00	175.00	105.00
(165)	Gabby Street	350.00	175.00	105.00
(166)	Sullivan (Omaha)	350.00	175.00	105.00
(167)	John Sullivan (Louisville)	350.00	175.00	105.00
(168)	Ed Summers	350.00	175.00	105.00
(169)	Joe Tinker	750.00	370.00	220.00
(170)	John Titus	350.00	175.00	105.00
(171)	Terry Turner	350.00	175.00	105.00
(172)	Bob Unglaub	350.00	175.00	105.00
(173)	Rube Waddell	750.00	370.00	220.00
(174)	Walker	350.00	175.00	105.00
(175)	Waller	350.00	175.00	105.00
(176)	Kirby White (Boston)	350.00	175.00	105.00
(177)	Jack White (Buffalo)	350.00	175.00	105.00
(178)	Julius Wiesman (Weisman)	350.00	175.00	105.00
(179)	Otto Williams	350.00	175.00	105.00
(180)	Hooks Wiltse	350.00	175.00	105.00
(181)	Orville Woodruff	350.00	175.00	105.00
(182)	Woods	350.00	175.00	105.00
(183)	Cy Young	2,340	1,170	700.00
(184)	Bill Zimmerman	350.00	175.00	105.00
(185)	Heinie Zimmerman	350.00	175.00	105.00

1913 Colgan's Chips Tin Tops

Except for the backs, these round black-and-white cards (about 1-7/16" in diameter) are identical to the 1909-11 Colgan's Chips issue, and were inserted in tin cannisters of Colgan's Mint Chips and Violet Chips. The front features a portrait photo along with the player's last name, team and, where necessary, league. The back advises collectors to "Send 25 Tin Tops" and a two-cent stamp to receive a photo of the "World's Pennant Winning Team." The set carries the designation E270 in the American Card Catalog.

		NM	E	VG
Complete Set (222):		60,000	30,000	18,000
Common Player:		180.00	90.00	54.00
(1)	Ed Abbaticchio	180.00	90.00	54.00
(2)	Doc Adkins	180.00	90.00	54.00
(3)	Joe Agler	180.00	90.00	54.00
(4)	Eddie Ainsmith	180.00	90.00	54.00
(5)	Whitey Alperman	180.00	90.00	54.00
(6a)	Red Ames (New York)	180.00	90.00	54.00
(6b)	Red Ames (Cincinnati)	180.00	90.00	54.00
(7)	Jimmy Archer	180.00	90.00	54.00
(8a)	Tommy Atkins (Atlanta)	180.00	90.00	54.00
(8b)	Tommy Atkins (Ft. Wayne)	180.00	90.00	54.00
(9a)	Jake Atz (New Orleans)	180.00	90.00	54.00
(9b)	Jake Atz (Providence)	180.00	90.00	54.00
(10)	Jimmy Austin	180.00	90.00	54.00
(11)	Home Run Baker	360.00	180.00	110.00
(12)	Home Run Baker	360.00	180.00	110.00
(13)	Johnny Bates	180.00	90.00	54.00
(14)	Beck (Buffalo)	180.00	90.00	54.00
(15)	Beebe	180.00	90.00	54.00
(16)	Harry Bemis	180.00	90.00	54.00
(17)	Bob Bescher	180.00	90.00	54.00
(18)	Beumiller (Louisville)	180.00	90.00	54.00
(19)	Joe Birmingham	180.00	90.00	54.00
(22)	Al Bridwell	180.00	90.00	54.00
(20)	Bliss	180.00	90.00	54.00
(21)	Roger Bresnahan	360.00	180.00	110.00
(25)	Burns	180.00	90.00	54.00
(23)	George Brown (Browne)	180.00	90.00	54.00
(24)	Al Burch	180.00	90.00	54.00
(26)	Donie Bush	180.00	90.00	54.00
(27)	Bobby Byrne	180.00	90.00	54.00
(28)	Nixey Callahan	180.00	90.00	54.00
(29)	Howie Camnitz	180.00	90.00	54.00
(30)	Billy Campbell	180.00	90.00	54.00
(31)	Charlie Carr	180.00	90.00	54.00
(32)	Jay Cashion	180.00	90.00	54.00
(33)	Frank Chance	360.00	180.00	110.00
(34)	Hal Chase	220.00	110.00	65.00
(35)	Ed Cicotte	270.00	135.00	80.00
(36)	Clarke (Indianapolis)	180.00	90.00	54.00
(37)	Fred Clarke (Pittsburg)	360.00	180.00	110.00
(38)	Tommy Clarke (Cincinnati)	180.00	90.00	54.00
(39)	Clemons	180.00	90.00	54.00
(40)	Bill Clymer	180.00	90.00	54.00
(41)	Ty Cobb	2,400	1,200	720.00
(42)	Eddie Collins	360.00	180.00	110.00
(43a)	Bunk Congalton (Omaha)	180.00	90.00	54.00
(43b)	Bunk Congalton (Toledo)	180.00	90.00	54.00
(44)	Cook	180.00	90.00	54.00
(45)	Jack Coombs	180.00	90.00	54.00
(46)	Corcoran	180.00	90.00	54.00
(47)	Corcoran	180.00	90.00	54.00
(48)	Gavvy Cravath	180.00	90.00	54.00
(49)	Sam Crawford	360.00	180.00	110.00
(50)	Bill Dahlen	180.00	90.00	54.00
(51)	Bert Daniels	180.00	90.00	54.00
(52a)	Jake Daubert	180.00	90.00	54.00
(52b)	Jake Daubert ((White cap.))	180.00	90.00	54.00
(53a)	Josh Devore (Cincinnati)	180.00	90.00	54.00
(53b)	Josh Devore (New York)	180.00	90.00	54.00
(54)	Mike Donlin	180.00	90.00	54.00
(55)	Wild Bill Donovan	180.00	90.00	54.00
(56)	Red Dooin	180.00	90.00	54.00
(57)	Mickey Doolan	180.00	90.00	54.00
(58)	Larry Doyle	180.00	90.00	54.00
(59)	Delos Drake	180.00	90.00	54.00
(60)	Dick Egan	180.00	90.00	54.00
(61)	Kid Elberfield (Elberfeld)	180.00	90.00	54.00
(62)	Roy Ellam	180.00	90.00	54.00
(63)	Elliott	180.00	90.00	54.00
(64)	Rube Ellis	180.00	90.00	54.00
(65)	Elwert	180.00	90.00	54.00
(66)	Clyde Engle	180.00	90.00	54.00
(67)	Jimmy Esmond	180.00	90.00	54.00
(68)	Steve Evans	180.00	90.00	54.00
(69)	Johnny Evers	360.00	180.00	110.00
(70)	Hobe Ferris	180.00	90.00	54.00
(71)	Russ Ford	180.00	90.00	54.00
(72)	Ed Foster	180.00	90.00	54.00
(73)	Friel	180.00	90.00	54.00
(74)	John Frill	180.00	90.00	54.00
(75)	Art Fromme	180.00	90.00	54.00
(76)	Gus Getz (Newark)	180.00	90.00	54.00
(77)	George Gibson	180.00	90.00	54.00
(78)	Graham	180.00	90.00	54.00
(79a)	Eddie Grant (Cincinnati)	180.00	90.00	54.00
(79b)	Eddie Grant (New York)	180.00	90.00	54.00
(80)	Gravath	180.00	90.00	54.00
(81)	Grief	180.00	90.00	54.00
(82)	Bob Groom	180.00	90.00	54.00
(83)	Topsy Hartsel	180.00	90.00	54.00
(84)	Roy Hartzell	180.00	90.00	54.00
(85)	Harry Hinchman	180.00	90.00	54.00
(86)	Dick Hoblitzell	180.00	90.00	54.00
(87a)	Happy Hogan (St. Louis)	180.00	90.00	54.00
(87b)	Happy Hogan (San Francisco)	180.00	90.00	54.00
(88)	Harry Hooper	360.00	180.00	110.00
(89)	Miller Huggins	360.00	180.00	110.00
(90a)	Hughes (Milwaukee)	180.00	90.00	54.00
(90b)	Hughes (Rochester)	180.00	90.00	54.00
(91)	Rudy Hulswitt	180.00	90.00	54.00
(92)	John Hummel	180.00	90.00	54.00
(93)	George Hunter	180.00	90.00	54.00
(94)	Shoeless Joe Jackson	20,000	4,800	2,880
(95)	Jameson (Buffalo)	180.00	90.00	54.00
(96)	Hugh Jennings	360.00	180.00	110.00
(97)	Pete Johns	180.00	90.00	54.00
(98)	Walter Johnson	780.00	390.00	235.00
(99)	Davy Jones (Toledo)	180.00	90.00	54.00
(100)	Tim Jordan	180.00	90.00	54.00
(101)	Bob Keefe	180.00	90.00	54.00
(102)	Wee Willie Keeler	360.00	180.00	110.00
(103)	Joe Kelly (Kelley)	360.00	180.00	110.00
(104)	Ed Killian	180.00	90.00	54.00
(105)	Bill Killifer (Killefer)	180.00	90.00	54.00
(106)	Johnny Kling (Boston)	180.00	90.00	54.00
(107)	Klipfer	180.00	90.00	54.00
(108)	Otto Knabe	180.00	90.00	54.00
(109)	Jack Knight	180.00	90.00	54.00
(110)	Ed Konetchy	180.00	90.00	54.00
(111)	Paul Krichell	180.00	90.00	54.00
(112)	James Lafitte	180.00	90.00	54.00
(113)	Nap Lajoie	360.00	180.00	110.00
(114)	Frank Lange	180.00	90.00	54.00
(115)	Lee	180.00	90.00	54.00
(116)	Jack Lewis	180.00	90.00	54.00
(117)	Harry Lord	180.00	90.00	54.00
(118)	Johnny Lush	180.00	90.00	54.00
(119)	Madden	180.00	90.00	54.00
(120)	Nick Maddox	180.00	90.00	54.00
(121)	Sherry Magee	180.00	90.00	54.00
(122)	Manser	180.00	90.00	54.00
(123a)	Frank Manusch (Manush) (New Orleans)	180.00	90.00	54.00
(123b)	Frank Manusch (Toledo)	180.00	90.00	54.00
(124)	Rube Marquard	360.00	180.00	110.00
(125)	McAllister	180.00	90.00	54.00
(126)	George McBride	180.00	90.00	54.00
(127)	McCarthy (Newark)	180.00	90.00	54.00
(128)	Joe McCarthy (Toledo)	360.00	180.00	110.00
(129)	McConnell	180.00	90.00	54.00
(130)	Moose McCormick	180.00	90.00	54.00
(131)	Larry McLean	180.00	90.00	54.00
(132)	Fred Merkle	180.00	90.00	54.00
(133)	Chief Meyers	180.00	90.00	54.00
(134)	Clyde Milan	180.00	90.00	54.00
(135)	Miller (Columbus)	180.00	90.00	54.00
(136)	Dots Miller (Pittsburg)	180.00	90.00	54.00
(137)	Clarence Mitchell	180.00	90.00	54.00
(138)	Mike Mitchell	180.00	90.00	54.00
(139)	Roy Mitchell	180.00	90.00	54.00
(140)	Carlton Molesworth	180.00	90.00	54.00
(141)	Herbie Moran	180.00	90.00	54.00
(142)	George Moriarty	180.00	90.00	54.00
(143)	George Mullen (Mullin)	180.00	90.00	54.00
(144)	Danny Murphy	180.00	90.00	54.00
(145)	Murray (Buffalo)	180.00	90.00	54.00
(146)	Jim Murray	180.00	90.00	54.00
(147)	Niles ((Indianapolis))	180.00	90.00	54.00
(148)	Jake Northrop	180.00	90.00	54.00
(149)	Rebel Oakes	180.00	90.00	54.00
(150)	Rube Oldring	180.00	90.00	54.00
(151)	Steve O'Neil (O'Neill)	180.00	90.00	54.00
(152)	O'Rourke	180.00	90.00	54.00
(153)	Owens (Minneapolis)	180.00	90.00	54.00
(154)	Larry Pape	180.00	90.00	54.00
(155)	Fred Parent	180.00	90.00	54.00
(156)	Dode Paskert	180.00	90.00	54.00
(157)	Heinie Peitz	180.00	90.00	54.00
(158)	Perry	180.00	90.00	54.00
(159)	Billy Purtell	180.00	90.00	54.00
(160)	Bill Rariden	180.00	90.00	54.00
(161)	Morrie Rath	180.00	90.00	54.00
(162)	Bugs Raymond	180.00	90.00	54.00
(163)	Ed Reulbach	180.00	90.00	54.00
(164)	Nap Rucker	180.00	90.00	54.00
(165)	Dick Rudolph	180.00	90.00	54.00
(166)	Bud Ryan	180.00	90.00	54.00
(167)	Slim Sallee	180.00	90.00	54.00
(168)	Ray Schalk	180.00	90.00	54.00
(169)	Schardt ((Indianapolis))	180.00	90.00	54.00
(170)	Jimmy Scheckard (Sheckard)	180.00	90.00	54.00
(171)	Wildfire Schulte	180.00	90.00	54.00
(172)	Wildfire Schulte	180.00	90.00	54.00
(173)	Bob Shawkey	180.00	90.00	54.00
(174)	Skeeter Shelton	180.00	90.00	54.00
(175)	Burt Shotten (Shotton)	180.00	90.00	54.00
(176)	Sisson ((Atlanta))	180.00	90.00	54.00
(177)	Smith (Montreal)	180.00	90.00	54.00
(178a)	Sid Smith (Atlanta)	180.00	90.00	54.00
(178b)	Sid Smith (Newark)	180.00	90.00	54.00
(179)	Fred Snodgrass	180.00	90.00	54.00
(180)	Tris Speaker	540.00	270.00	160.00
(181)	Jake Stahl	180.00	90.00	54.00
(182)	John Stansberry (Stansbury)	180.00	90.00	54.00
(183)	John Stansberry (Stansbury)	180.00	90.00	54.00
(184)	Amos Strunk	180.00	90.00	54.00
(185)	Sullivan	180.00	90.00	54.00
(186)	Suter	180.00	90.00	54.00
(187)	Harry Swacina	180.00	90.00	54.00
(188)	Bill Sweeney	180.00	90.00	54.00
(189)	Jeff Sweeney	180.00	90.00	54.00
(190)	Lee Tannehill	180.00	90.00	54.00
(191)	Dummy Taylor (Topeka)	300.00	150.00	90.00
(192)	Jim Thorpe	12,000	3,900	2,340
(193)	Joe Tinker	360.00	180.00	110.00
(194a)	John Titus (Boston)	180.00	90.00	54.00
(194b)	John Titus (Philadelphia)	180.00	90.00	54.00
(195)	Terry Turner	180.00	90.00	54.00
(195)	Viebahn	180.00	90.00	54.00
(196)	Bob Unglaub	180.00	90.00	54.00
(197)	Rube Waddell	360.00	180.00	110.00
(198)	Honus Wagner	2,500	750.00	450.00
(199)	Bobby Wallace	360.00	180.00	110.00
(200)	Ed Walsh	360.00	180.00	110.00
(201)	Jack Warhop	180.00	90.00	54.00
(202a)	Harry Welchouce (Welchonce) (Nashville)	180.00	90.00	54.00
(202b)	Harry Welchouce (Welchonce) (Nashville)	180.00	90.00	54.00
(203)	Zach Wheat	360.00	180.00	110.00
(204)	Kirb. White	180.00	90.00	54.00
(205)	Kaiser Wilhelm	180.00	90.00	54.00
(206a)	Ed Willett	180.00	90.00	54.00
(206b)	Ed Willett ((White cap.))	180.00	90.00	54.00
(207)	Otto Williams	180.00	90.00	54.00
(208)	Owen Wilson	180.00	90.00	54.00
(209)	Hooks Wiltse	180.00	90.00	54.00
(210)	Joe Wood	180.00	90.00	54.00
(211)	Orville Woodruff	180.00	90.00	54.00
(212)	Joe Yeager	180.00	90.00	54.00
(213)	Bill Zimmerman	180.00	90.00	54.00
(214)	Heinie Zimmerman	180.00	90.00	54.00

1947 Collectors & Traders Sport Star Subjects

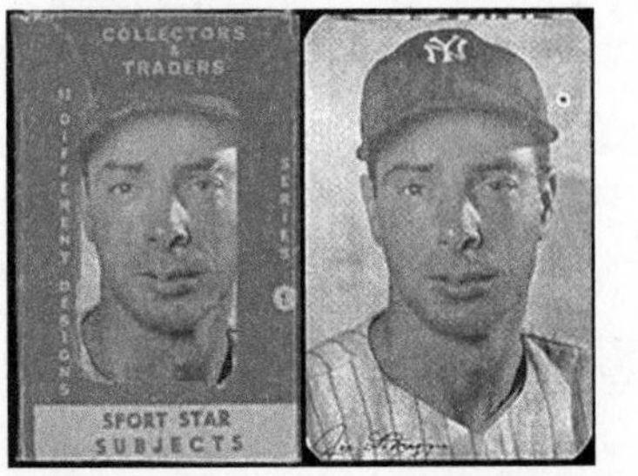

This set was the origination point for the Bond Bread insert cards and related other issues. The cards were produced by Aarco Playing Card Co., Chicago. They were originally sold in window-boxed series of 12 cards each comprising 11 baseball players and a boxer. The individual cards are printed in black-and-white on 3-3/8" x 2-1/4" blank-back cardboard with rounded corners.

	NM	EX	VG
Complete Boxed Set (48):	4,500	2,250	1,350

(See 1947 Bond Bread for checklist and single card values.)

1917 Collins-McCarthy (E135)

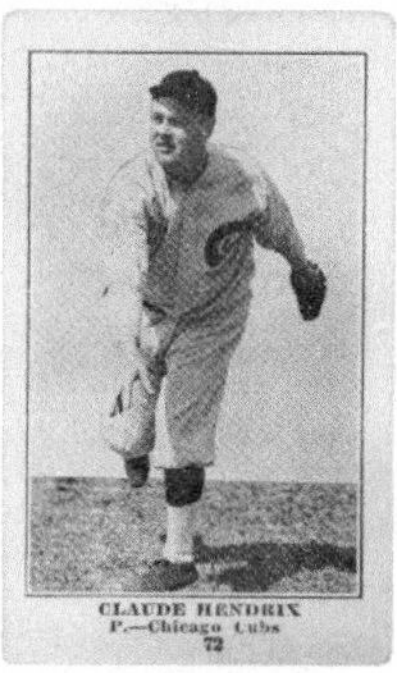

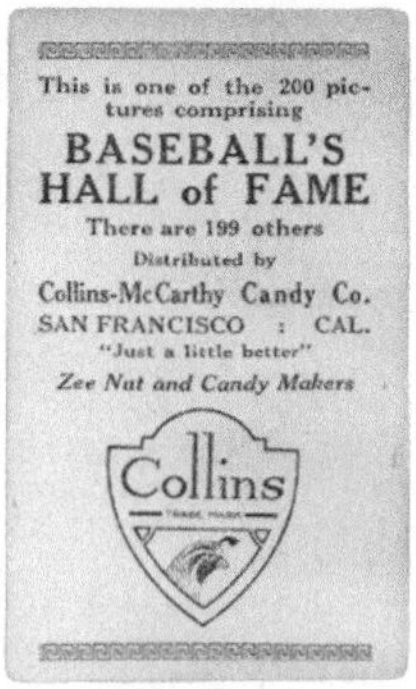

Produced by the Collins-McCarthy Candy Co. of San Francisco, the 200-card, black-and-white set represents the company's only venture into issuing non-Pacific Coast League players. The cards, numbered alphabetically, measure 2" x 3-1/4" and are printed on thin stock. Though the set is entitled "Baseball's Hall of Fame," many nondescript players appear in the issue. The complete set price does not include the more expensive variations. The same cards can be found with the advertising of other regional issuers on back, or blank-backed. Blank backs are much more scarce.

		NM	E	VG
Common Player:		300.00	150.00	90.00
1	Sam Agnew	300.00	150.00	90.00
2	Grover Alexander	2,000	1,000	600.00
3	W.S. Alexander (W.E.)	300.00	150.00	90.00
4	Leon Ames	300.00	150.00	90.00
5	Fred Anderson	300.00	150.00	90.00
6	Ed Appleton	300.00	150.00	90.00
7	Jimmy Archer	300.00	150.00	90.00
8	Jimmy Austin	300.00	150.00	90.00
9	Jim Bagby Sr.	300.00	150.00	90.00
10	H.D. Baird	300.00	150.00	90.00
11	J. Franklin Baker	4,000	2,000	1,200
12	Dave Bancroft	4,000	2,000	1,200
13	Jack Barry	300.00	150.00	90.00
14	Joe Benz	300.00	150.00	90.00
15	Al Betzel	300.00	150.00	90.00
16	Ping Bodie	300.00	150.00	90.00
17	Joe Boehling	300.00	150.00	90.00
18	Eddie Burns	300.00	150.00	90.00
19	George Burns	300.00	150.00	90.00
20	Geo. J. Burns	300.00	150.00	90.00
21	Joe Bush	300.00	150.00	90.00
22	Owen Bush	300.00	150.00	90.00
23	Bobby Byrne	300.00	150.00	90.00
24	Forrest Cady	300.00	150.00	90.00
25	Max Carey	2,000	1,000	600.00
26	Ray Chapman	350.00	175.00	105.00
27	Larry Cheney	300.00	150.00	90.00
28	Eddie Cicotte	2,000	1,000	600.00
29	Tom Clarke	300.00	150.00	90.00
30	Ty Cobb	30,000	15,000	9,000
31	Eddie Collins	4,000	2,000	1,200
32	"Shauno" Collins (Shano)	300.00	150.00	90.00
33	Fred Coumbe	300.00	150.00	90.00
34	Harry Coveleskie (Coveleski)	300.00	150.00	90.00
35	Gavvy Cravath	300.00	150.00	90.00
36	Sam Crawford	4,000	2,000	1,200
37	Geo. Cutshaw	300.00	150.00	90.00
38	Jake Daubert	300.00	150.00	90.00
39	Geo. Dauss	300.00	150.00	90.00
40	Charles Deal	300.00	150.00	90.00
41	"Wheezer" Dell	300.00	150.00	90.00
42	William Doak	300.00	150.00	90.00
43	Bill Donovan	300.00	150.00	90.00
44	Larry Doyle	300.00	150.00	90.00
45	Johnny Evers	2,000	1,000	600.00
46	Urban Faber	2,000	1,000	600.00
47	"Hap" Felsch	2,000	1,000	600.00
48	Bill Fischer	300.00	150.00	90.00
49	Ray Fisher	300.00	150.00	90.00
50	Art Fletcher	300.00	150.00	90.00
51	Eddie Foster	300.00	150.00	90.00
52	Jacques Fournier	300.00	150.00	90.00
53	Del Gainer (Gainor)	300.00	150.00	90.00
54	Bert Gallia	300.00	150.00	90.00
55	"Chic" Gandil (Chick)	2,000	1,000	600.00
56	Larry Gardner	300.00	150.00	90.00
57	Joe Gedeon	300.00	150.00	90.00
58	Gus Getz	300.00	150.00	90.00
59	Frank Gilhooley	300.00	150.00	90.00
60	Wm. Gleason	300.00	150.00	90.00
61	M.A. Gonzales (Gonzalez)	330.00	165.00	100.00
62	Hank Gowdy	300.00	150.00	90.00
63	John Graney	300.00	150.00	90.00
64	Tom Griffith	300.00	150.00	90.00
65	Heinie Groh	300.00	150.00	90.00
66	Bob Groom	300.00	150.00	90.00
67	Louis Guisto	300.00	150.00	90.00
68	Earl Hamilton	300.00	150.00	90.00
69	Harry Harper	300.00	150.00	90.00
70	Grover Hartley	300.00	150.00	90.00
71	Harry Heilmann	10,000	5,000	3,000
72	Claude Hendrix	300.00	150.00	90.00
73	Olaf Henriksen	300.00	150.00	90.00
74	John Henry	300.00	150.00	90.00
75	"Buck" Herzog	300.00	150.00	90.00
76a	Hugh High (White stockings, photo actually Claude Williams.)	400.00	200.00	120.00
76b	Hugh High (Black stockings, correct photo.)	350.00	175.00	105.00
77	Dick Hoblitzell	300.00	150.00	90.00
78	Walter Holke	300.00	150.00	90.00
79	Harry Hooper	2,000	1,000	600.00
80	Rogers Hornsby	15,000	7,500	4,500
81	Ivan Howard	300.00	150.00	90.00
82	Joe Jackson	60,000	30,000	18,000
83	Harold Janvrin	300.00	150.00	90.00
84	William James	300.00	150.00	90.00
85	C. Jamieson	300.00	150.00	90.00
86	Hugh Jennings	2,000	1,000	600.00
87	Walter Johnson	15,000	7,500	4,500
88	James Johnston	300.00	150.00	90.00
89	Fielder Jones	300.00	150.00	90.00
90a	Joe Judge (Bat on right shoulder, photo actually Ray Morgan.)	400.00	200.00	120.00
90b	Joe Judge (Bat on left shoulder, correct photo.)	350.00	175.00	105.00
91	Hans Lobert	300.00	150.00	90.00
92	Benny Kauff	300.00	150.00	90.00
93	Wm. Killefer Jr.	300.00	150.00	90.00
94	Ed. Konetchy	300.00	150.00	90.00
95	John Lavan	300.00	150.00	90.00
96	Jimmy Lavender	300.00	150.00	90.00
97	"Nemo" Leibold	300.00	150.00	90.00
98	H.B. Leonard	300.00	150.00	90.00
99	Duffy Lewis	300.00	150.00	90.00
100	Tom Long	300.00	150.00	90.00
101	Wm. Louden	300.00	150.00	90.00
102	Fred Luderus	300.00	150.00	90.00
103	Lee Magee	300.00	150.00	90.00
104	Sherwood Magee	300.00	150.00	90.00
105	Al Mamaux	300.00	150.00	90.00
106	Leslie Mann	300.00	150.00	90.00
107	"Rabbit" Maranville	4,000	2,000	1,200
108	Rube Marquard	4,000	2,000	1,200
109	Armando Marsans	330.00	165.00	100.00
110	J. Erskine Mayer	300.00	150.00	90.00
111	George McBride	300.00	150.00	90.00
112	Lew McCarty	300.00	150.00	90.00
113	John J. McGraw	2,000	1,000	600.00
114	Jack McInnis	300.00	150.00	90.00
115	Lee Meadows	300.00	150.00	90.00
116	Fred Merkle	300.00	150.00	90.00
117	"Chief" Meyers	300.00	150.00	90.00
118	Clyde Milan	300.00	150.00	90.00
119	Otto Miller	300.00	150.00	90.00
120	Clarence Mitchell	300.00	150.00	90.00
121a	Ray Morgan (Bat on left shoulder, photo actually Joe Judge.)	400.00	200.00	120.00
121b	Ray Morgan (Bat on right shoulder, correct photo.)	350.00	175.00	105.00
122	Guy Morton	300.00	150.00	90.00
123	"Mike" Mowrey	300.00	150.00	90.00
124	Elmer Myers	300.00	150.00	90.00
125	"Hy" Myers	300.00	150.00	90.00
126	A.E. Neale	750.00	370.00	220.00
127	Arthur Nehf	300.00	150.00	90.00
128	J.A. Niehoff	300.00	150.00	90.00
129	Steve O'Neill	300.00	150.00	90.00
130	"Dode" Paskert	300.00	150.00	90.00
131	Roger Peckinpaugh	300.00	150.00	90.00
132	"Pol" Perritt	300.00	150.00	90.00
133	"Jeff" Pfeffer	300.00	150.00	90.00
134	Walter Pipp	300.00	150.00	90.00
135	Derril Pratt (Derrill)	300.00	150.00	90.00
136	Bill Rariden	300.00	150.00	90.00
137	E.C. Rice	4,000	2,000	1,200
138	Wm. A. Ritter (Wm. H.)	300.00	150.00	90.00
139	Eppa Rixey	2,000	1,000	600.00
140	Davey Robertson	300.00	150.00	90.00
141	"Bob" Roth	300.00	150.00	90.00
142	Ed. Roush	2,000	1,000	600.00
143	Clarence Rowland	300.00	150.00	90.00
144	Dick Rudolph	300.00	150.00	90.00
145	William Rumler	300.00	150.00	90.00
146a	Reb Russell (Pitching follow-thru, photo actually Mellie Wolfgang.)	400.00	200.00	120.00
146b	Reb Russell (Hands at side, correct photo.)	350.00	175.00	105.00
147	"Babe" Ruth	25,000	12,500	7,500
148	Vic Saier	300.00	150.00	90.00
149	"Slim" Sallee	300.00	150.00	90.00
150	Ray Schalk	2,000	1,000	600.00
151	Walter Schang	300.00	150.00	90.00
152	Frank Schulte	300.00	150.00	90.00
153	Ferd Schupp	300.00	150.00	90.00
154	Everett Scott	300.00	150.00	90.00
155	Hank Severeid	300.00	150.00	90.00
156	Howard Shanks	300.00	150.00	90.00
157	Bob Shawkey	300.00	150.00	90.00
158	Jas. Sheckard	300.00	150.00	90.00
159	Ernie Shore	300.00	150.00	90.00
160	C.H. Shorten	300.00	150.00	90.00
161	Burt Shotton	300.00	150.00	90.00
162	Geo. Sisler	4,000	2,000	1,200
163	Elmer Smith	300.00	150.00	90.00
164	J. Carlisle Smith	300.00	150.00	90.00
165	Fred Snodgrass	300.00	150.00	90.00
166	Tris Speaker	4,000	2,000	1,200
167	Oscar Stanage	300.00	150.00	90.00
168	Charles Stengel	6,000	3,000	1,800
169	Milton Stock	300.00	150.00	90.00
170	Amos Strunk	300.00	150.00	90.00
171	"Zeb" Terry	300.00	150.00	90.00
172	"Jeff" Tesreau	300.00	150.00	90.00
173	Chester Thomas	300.00	150.00	90.00
174	Fred Toney	300.00	150.00	90.00
175	Terry Turner	300.00	150.00	90.00
176	George Tyler	300.00	150.00	90.00
177	Jim Vaughn	300.00	150.00	90.00
178	Bob Veach	300.00	150.00	90.00
179	Oscar Vitt	300.00	150.00	90.00
180	Hans Wagner	20,000	10,000	6,000
181	Clarence Walker	300.00	150.00	90.00
182	Jim Walsh	300.00	150.00	90.00
183	Al Walters	300.00	150.00	90.00
184	W. Wambsganss	300.00	150.00	90.00
185	Buck Weaver	2,000	1,000	600.00
186	Carl Weilman	300.00	150.00	90.00
187	Zack Wheat	4,000	2,000	1,200
188	Geo. Whitted	300.00	150.00	90.00
189	Joe Wilhoit	300.00	150.00	90.00
190a	Claude Williams (Black stockings, photo actually Hugh High.)	1,200	600.00	350.00
190b	Claude Williams (White stockings, correct photo.)	1,500	750.00	450.00
191	Fred Williams	300.00	150.00	90.00
192	Art Wilson	300.00	150.00	90.00
193	Lawton Witt	300.00	150.00	90.00
194	Joe Wood	300.00	150.00	90.00
195	William Wortman	300.00	150.00	90.00
196	Steve Yerkes	300.00	150.00	90.00
197	Earl Yingling	300.00	150.00	90.00
198	"Pep" (Ralph) Young	300.00	150.00	90.00
199	Rollie Zeider	300.00	150.00	90.00
200	Henry Zimmerman	300.00	150.00	90.00

1954 Colonial Meats Jimmy Piersall

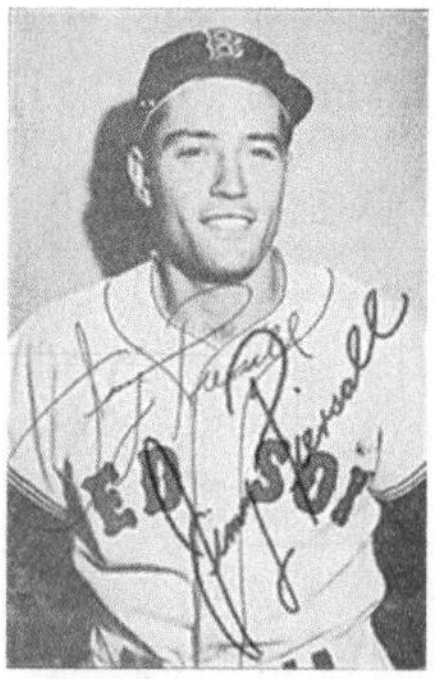

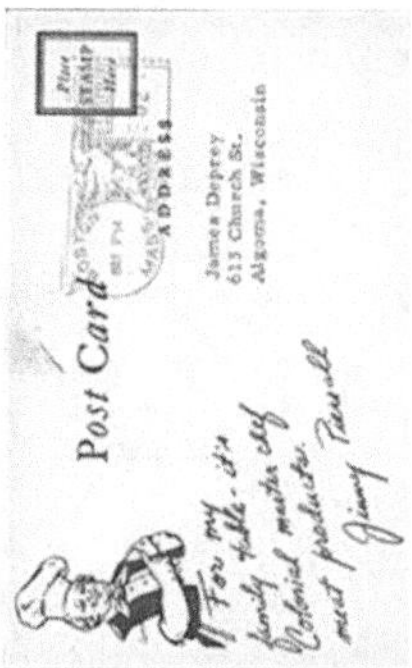

These promotional postcards are known in at least two varieties. Each of the 3-1/2" x 5-1/2" cards shows the popular BoSox star in a portrait pose with facsimile autograph. The postcard-format back has at left a cartoon butcher and an advertising message bearing Piersall's signature. Similar cards advertising Cain's grocery products are also known.

	NM	E	VG
Autographed: 2-3X	300.00	150.00	90.00

		NM	E	VG
(1)	Jimmy Piersall (Chest-to-cap, back printed in black.)	125.00	65.00	35.00
(2)	Jimmy Piersall (Waist-to-cap, back printed in black and blue.)	125.00	65.00	35.00

1888 Conly Cabinets

Contemporary, but much less numerous than, the Old Judge cabinet cards is this issue from a Boston photo studio. Carrying an April, 1888, copyright date, the 4-1/4" x 6-1/2" have sepia photos of the players in action poses. Backs have decorative advertising for the studio. The extent of the checklist is unknown.

	NM	E	VG
John Clarkson (Ball in hands at chest.)	3,000	1,200	725.00
John Clarkson (Ball in hands at chest.)	3,000	1,200	725.00
John Clarkson (Right arm at back.)	3,000	1,200	725.00
John Clarkson (Right arm extended.)	3,000	1,200	725.00

1891 Conly Studio Cabinets

The extent of this issue from a Boston photo studio is unknown. The checklist begins here with three players from the Boston Reds American Associations champions. The 4-1/4" x 6-1/2" cards have a sepia portrait photo of the player in street clothes. Back has decorative advertising for the studio.

		NM	E	VG
Common Player:		1,000	500.00	300.00
(1)	Duke Farrell	1,200	500.00	300.00
(2)	George Haddock	1,200	500.00	300.00
(3)	Cub Stricker	1,200	500.00	300.00

1910 Coupon Cigarettes Type 1 (T213)

Though they feature the same pictures used in the contemporary T206 tobacco issue, Coupon Cigarette cards make up three distinct sets, produced between 1910 and 1919. Type 1 Coupon cards feature a mix of players from the National and American Leagues, and the Southern League. Nominally the traditional 1-7/16" x 2-1/8" cigarette-card size, fronts of the Coupons are identical to the more popular T206 series. Backs, however, clearly identify the cards as being a product of Coupon Cigarettes and allow the collector to easily differentiate among the three types. Type 1 cards, produced in 1910, carry a general advertisement for Coupon "Mild" Cigarettes, with no mention of price. Distribution of the Coupons was limited to the Louisiana area, making the set very difficult to checklist and even moreso to collect. Numerous variations further complicate the situation. It is quite possible the checklists here are incomplete and additions will surface in the future. Type 1 cards are considered the rar-

est of the Coupon issues, and, because they were printed on a thinner stock, they are especially difficult to find in top condition.

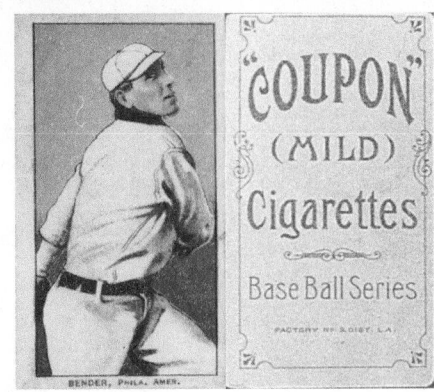

		NM	E	VG
Complete Set (68):		30,000	15,000	8,500
Common Player:		450.00	170.00	85.00
(1)	Harry Bay	450.00	170.00	85.00
(2)	Beals Becker	450.00	170.00	85.00
(3)	Chief Bender	1,275	500.00	250.00
(4)	Bernhard	450.00	170.00	85.00
(5)	Ted Breitenstein	450.00	170.00	85.00
(6)	Bobby Byrne	450.00	170.00	85.00
(7)	Billy Campbell	450.00	170.00	85.00
(8)	Scoops Carey	1,275	500.00	250.00
(9)	Frank Chance	1,275	500.00	250.00
(10)	Chappy Charles	450.00	170.00	85.00
(11)	Hal Chase (Portrait)	625.00	250.00	125.00
(12)	Hal Chase (Throwing)	625.00	250.00	125.00
(13)	Ty Cobb	11,625	4,650	2,325
(14)	Bill Cranston	450.00	170.00	85.00
(15)	Birdie Cree	450.00	170.00	85.00
(16)	Wild Bill Donovan	450.00	170.00	85.00
(17)	Mickey Doolan	450.00	170.00	85.00
(18)	Jean Dubuc	450.00	170.00	85.00
(19)	Joe Dunn	450.00	170.00	85.00
(20)	Roy Ellam	450.00	170.00	85.00
(21)	Clyde Engle	450.00	170.00	85.00
(22)	Johnny Evers	1,275	500.00	250.00
(23)	Art Fletcher	450.00	170.00	85.00
(24)	Charlie Fritz	450.00	170.00	85.00
(25)	Ed Greminger	450.00	170.00	85.00
(26)	Bill Hart (Little Rock)	450.00	170.00	85.00
(27)	Jimmy Hart (Montgomery)	450.00	170.00	85.00
(28)	Topsy Hartsel	450.00	170.00	85.00
(29)	Gordon Hickman	450.00	170.00	85.00
(30)	Danny Hoffman	450.00	170.00	85.00
(31)	Harry Howell	450.00	170.00	85.00
(32)	Miller Huggins (Hands at mouth.)	1,275	500.00	250.00
(33)	Miller Huggins (Portrait)	1,275	500.00	250.00
(34)	George Hunter	450.00	170.00	85.00
(35)	A.O. "Dutch" Jordan	450.00	170.00	85.00
(36)	Ed Killian	450.00	170.00	85.00
(37)	Otto Knabe	450.00	170.00	85.00
(38)	Frank LaPorte	450.00	170.00	85.00
(39)	Ed Lennox	450.00	170.00	85.00
(40)	Harry Lentz (Sentz)	450.00	170.00	85.00
(41)	Rube Marquard	1,275	500.00	250.00
(42)	Doc Marshall	450.00	170.00	85.00
(43)	Christy Mathewson	3,225	1,300	650.00
(44)	George McBride	450.00	170.00	85.00
(45)	Pryor McElveen	450.00	170.00	85.00
(46)	Matty McIntyre	450.00	170.00	85.00
(47)	Mike Mitchell	450.00	170.00	85.00
(48)	Carlton Molesworth	450.00	170.00	85.00
(49)	Mike Mowrey	450.00	170.00	85.00
(50)	Chief Myers (Meyers) (Batting)	450.00	170.00	85.00
(51)	Chief Myers (Meyers) (Fielding)	450.00	170.00	85.00
(52)	Dode Paskert	450.00	170.00	85.00
(53)	Hub Perdue	450.00	170.00	85.00
(54)	Arch Persons	450.00	170.00	85.00
(55)	Ed Reagan	450.00	170.00	85.00
(56)	Bob Rhoades (Rhoads)	450.00	170.00	85.00
(57)	Ike Rockenfeld	450.00	170.00	85.00
(58)	Claude Rossman	450.00	170.00	85.00
(59)	Boss Schmidt	450.00	170.00	85.00
(60)	Sid Smith	450.00	170.00	85.00
(61)	Charlie Starr	450.00	170.00	85.00
(62)	Gabby Street	450.00	170.00	85.00
(63)	Ed Summers	450.00	170.00	85.00
(64)	Jeff Sweeney	450.00	170.00	85.00
(65)	Ira Thomas	450.00	170.00	85.00
(66)	Woodie Thornton	450.00	170.00	85.00
(67)	Ed Willett	450.00	170.00	85.00
(68)	Owen Wilson	450.00	170.00	85.00

1914-16 Coupon Cigarettes Type 2 (T213)

Though they feature the same photos used in the contemporary T206 tobacco issue, Coupon Cigarette cards make up three distinct sets, produced between 1910 and 1919. Type 2 Coupons feature a mix of players from the three major leagues (National, American and Federal), and several minor leagues. The 1-7/16" x 2-5/8" Coupon fronts are virtually identical, except for the use of blue typography, to the more popular T206 series. Backs, however, clearly identify the cards as being a product of Coupon Cigarettes and allow the collector to easily differentiate among the three types. Type 2 cards, issued from 1914 to 1916, contain the words "MILD and SWEET" and "20 for 5 cents." Distribution of the Coupon cards was limited to the Louisiana area, making the set difficult to checklist and even moreso to collect. Numerous variations further complicate the situation. It is quite possible the checklists here are incomplete and additions will surface in the future. Although Type 2 cards are the most common, they were printed with a "glossy" coating, making them susceptible to cracking and creasing.

		NM	E	VG
Complete Set (188):		80,000	36,000	17,500
Common Player:		275.00	125.00	60.00
(1)	Red Ames (Cincinnati)	275.00	125.00	60.00
(2)	Red Ames (St. Louis)	275.00	125.00	60.00
(3)	Home Run Baker (Phila. Amer.)	550.00	245.00	120.00
(4)	Home Run Baker (Philadelphia Amer.)	600.00	275.00	130.00
(5)	Home Run Baker (New York)	550.00	245.00	120.00
(6)	Cy Barger	275.00	125.00	60.00
(7)	Chief Bender (Trees in background, Philadelphia Amer.)	550.00	245.00	120.00
(8)	Chief Bender (Trees in background, Baltimore.)	550.00	245.00	120.00
(9)	Chief Bender (Trees in background, Philadelphia Nat.)	550.00	245.00	120.00
(10)	Chief Bender (No trees, Philadelphia Amer.)	550.00	245.00	120.00
(11)	Chief Bender (No trees, Baltimore.)	550.00	245.00	120.00
(12)	Chief Bender (No trees, Philadelphia Natl.)	550.00	240.00	120.00
(13)	Bill Bradley	275.00	125.00	60.00
(14)	Roger Bresnahan (Chicago)	550.00	245.00	120.00
(15)	Roger Bresnahan (Toledo)	550.00	245.00	120.00
(16)	Al Bridwell (St. Louis)	275.00	125.00	60.00
(17)	Al Bridwell (Nashville)	275.00	125.00	60.00
(18)	Mordecai Brown (Chicago)	550.00	245.00	120.00
(19)	Mordecai Brown (St. Louis)	550.00	245.00	120.00
(20)	Bobby Byrne	275.00	125.00	60.00
(21)	Howie Camnitz (Arm at side.)	275.00	125.00	60.00
(22)	Howie Camnitz (Pittsburgh, hands above head.)	275.00	125.00	60.00
(23)	Howie Camnitz (Savannah, hands above head.)	275.00	125.00	60.00
(24)	Billy Campbell	275.00	125.00	60.00
(25)	Frank Chance (Batting, New York.)	550.00	245.00	120.00
(26)	Frank Chance (Los Angeles, batting.)	600.00	270.00	130.00
(27)	Frank Chance (New York, portrait.)	550.00	245.00	120.00
(28)	Frank Chance (Los Angeles, portrait.)	600.00	270.00	130.00
(29)	Bill Chapelle (Brooklyn, "R" on shirt.)	275.00	125.00	60.00
(30)	Larry Chapelle (Chappel) (Cleveland, no "R" on shirt, photo actually Bill Chapelle.)	275.00	125.00	60.00
(31)	Hal Chase (Chicago, holding trophy.)	365.00	165.00	80.00
(32)	Hal Chase (Buffalo, holding trophy.)	365.00	165.00	80.00
(33)	Hal Chase (Chicago, portrait, blue background.)	365.00	165.00	80.00
(34)	Hal Chase (Buffalo, portrait, blue background.)	365.00	165.00	80.00
(35)	Hal Chase (Chicago, throwing.)	365.00	165.00	80.00
(36)	Hal Chase (Buffalo, throwing.)	365.00	165.00	80.00

(37)	Ty Cobb (Portrait)	7,250	3,250	1,600
(38)	Ty Cobb (Bat off shoulder.)	6,000	2,700	1,325
(39)	Eddie Collins (Philadelphia, "A" on shirt.)	600.00	270.00	130.00
(40)	Eddie Collins (Chicago, "A" on shirt.)	600.00	270.00	130.00
(41)	Eddie Collins (Chicago, no "A" on shirt.)	600.00	270.00	130.00
(42)	Doc Crandall (St. Louis Fed.)	275.00	125.00	60.00
(43)	Doc Crandall (St. Louis Amer.)	275.00	125.00	60.00
(44)	Sam Crawford	550.00	245.00	120.00
(45)	Birdie Cree	275.00	125.00	60.00
(46)	Harry Davis (Phila. Amer.)	275.00	125.00	60.00
(47)	Harry Davis (Philadelphia Amer.)	275.00	125.00	60.00
(48)	Ray Demmitt (Chicago Amer. (New York uniform.))	275.00	125.00	60.00
(49)	Ray Demmitt (Chicago Amer. (St. Louis uniform.))	275.00	125.00	60.00
(50)	Josh Devore (Philadelphia)	275.00	125.00	60.00
(51)	Josh Devore (Chillicothe)	275.00	125.00	60.00
(52)	Mike Donlin (New York)	275.00	125.00	60.00
(53)	Mike Donlin (.300 batter 7 years)	275.00	125.00	60.00
(54)	Wild Bill Donovan	275.00	125.00	60.00
(55)	Mickey Doolan (Baltimore, batting.)	275.00	125.00	60.00
(56)	Mickey Doolan (Chicago, batting.)	275.00	125.00	60.00
(57)	Mickey Doolan (Baltimore, fielding.)	275.00	125.00	60.00
(58)	Mickey Doolan (Chicago, fielding.)	275.00	125.00	60.00
(59)	Tom Downey	275.00	125.00	60.00
(60)	Larry Doyle (Batting)	275.00	125.00	60.00
(61)	Larry Doyle (Portrait)	275.00	125.00	60.00
(62)	Jean Dubuc	275.00	125.00	60.00
(63)	Jack Dunn (Picture is Joe Dunn.)	275.00	125.00	60.00
(64)	Kid Elberfield (Elberfeld) (Brooklyn)	275.00	125.00	60.00
(65)	Kid Elberfield (Elberfeld) (Chatanooga)	275.00	125.00	60.00
(66)	Steve Evans	275.00	125.00	60.00
(67)	Johnny Evers	550.00	245.00	120.00
(68)	Russ Ford	275.00	125.00	60.00
(69)	Art Fromme	275.00	125.00	60.00
(70)	Chick Gandil (Washington)	1,000	450.00	220.00
(71)	Chick Gandil (Cleveland)	550.00	245.00	120.00
(72)	Rube Geyer	275.00	125.00	60.00
(73)	Clark Griffith	550.00	245.00	120.00
(74)	Bob Groom	275.00	125.00	60.00
(75)	Buck Herzog ("B" on shirt.)	300.00	135.00	66.00
(76)	Buck Herzog (No "B" on shirt.)	400.00	180.00	88.00
(77)	Dick Hoblitzell (Cincinnati)	275.00	125.00	60.00
(78)	Dick Hoblitzell (Boston Nat.)	275.00	125.00	60.00
(79)	Dick Hoblitzell (Boston Amer.)	275.00	125.00	60.00
(80)	Solly Hofman	275.00	125.00	60.00
(81)	Solly Hofman (Hofman)	275.00	125.00	60.00
(82)	Miller Huggins (Hands at mouth.)	550.00	245.00	120.00
(83)	Miller Huggins (Portrait)	550.00	245.00	120.00
(84)	John Hummel (Brooklyn Nat.)	275.00	125.00	60.00
(85)	John Hummel (Brooklyn)	275.00	125.00	60.00
(86)	Hughie Jennings (Both hands showing.)	550.00	245.00	120.00
(87)	Hughie Jennings (One hand showing.)	550.00	245.00	120.00
(88)	Walter Johnson	2,500	1,125	550.00
(89)	Tim Jordan (Toronto)	275.00	125.00	60.00
(90)	Tim Jordan (Ft. Worth)	275.00	125.00	60.00
(91)	Joe Kelley (New York)	550.00	245.00	120.00
(92)	Joe Kelley (Toronto)	550.00	245.00	120.00
(93)	Otto Knabe	275.00	125.00	60.00
(94)	Ed Konetchy (Pittsburgh Nat.)	275.00	125.00	60.00
(95)	Ed Konetchy (Pittsburgh Fed.)	275.00	125.00	60.00
(96)	Ed Konetchy (Boston)	275.00	125.00	60.00
(97)	Harry Krause	275.00	125.00	60.00
(98)	Nap Lajoie (Phila. Amer.)	550.00	245.00	120.00
(99)	Nap Lajoie (Philadelphia Amer.)	550.00	245.00	120.00
(100)	Nap Lajoie (Cleveland)	2,000	1,000	600.00
(101)	Tommy Leach (Chicago)	275.00	125.00	60.00
(102)	Tommy Leach (Cincinnati)	275.00	125.00	60.00
(103)	Tommy Leach (Rochester)	275.00	125.00	60.00
(104)	Ed Lennox	275.00	125.00	60.00
(105)	Sherry Magee (Phila. Nat.)	275.00	125.00	60.00
(106)	Sherry Magee (Philadelphia Nat.)	275.00	125.00	60.00
(107)	Sherry Magee (Boston)	275.00	125.00	60.00
(108)	Rube Marquard (New York, pitching, "NY" on shirt.)	600.00	270.00	130.00
(109)	Rube Marquard (Brooklyn, pitching, no "NY" on shirt.)	550.00	245.00	120.00
(110)	Rube Marquard (New York, portrait, "NY" on shirt.)	550.00	245.00	120.00
(111)	Rube Marquard (Brooklyn, portrait, no "NY" on shirt.)	550.00	245.00	120.00
(112)	Christy Mathewson	3,000	1,350	660.00
(113)	John McGraw (Glove at side.)	550.00	245.00	120.00
(114)	John McGraw (Portrait)	550.00	245.00	120.00
(115)	Larry McLean	275.00	125.00	60.00
(116)	George McQuillan (Pittsburgh)	275.00	125.00	60.00
(117)	George McQuillan (Phila. Nat.)	275.00	125.00	60.00
(118)	George McQuillan (Philadelphia Nat.)	275.00	125.00	60.00
(119)	Fred Merkle	275.00	125.00	60.00
(120)	Chief Meyers (New York, fielding.)	275.00	125.00	60.00
(121)	Chief Meyers (Brooklyn, fielding.)	275.00	125.00	60.00
(122)	Chief Meyers (New York, portrait.)	275.00	125.00	60.00
(123)	Chief Meyers (Brooklyn, portrait.)	275.00	125.00	60.00
(124)	Dots Miller	275.00	125.00	60.00
(125)	Mike Mitchell	275.00	125.00	60.00
(126)	Mike Mowrey (Pittsburgh Nat.)	275.00	125.00	60.00
(127)	Mike Mowrey (Pittsburgh Fed.)	275.00	125.00	60.00
(128)	Mike Mowrey (Brooklyn)	275.00	125.00	60.00
(129)	George Mullin (Indianapolis)	275.00	125.00	60.00
(130)	George Mullin (Newark)	275.00	125.00	60.00
(131)	Danny Murphy	275.00	125.00	60.00
(132)	Red Murray (New York)	275.00	125.00	60.00
(133)	Red Murray (Chicago)	275.00	125.00	60.00
(134)	Red Murray (Kansas City)	275.00	125.00	60.00
(135)	Tom Needham	275.00	125.00	60.00
(136)	Rebel Oakes	275.00	125.00	60.00
(137)	Rube Oldring (Phila. Amer.)	275.00	125.00	60.00
(138)	Rube Oldring (Philadelphia Amer.)	275.00	125.00	60.00
(139)	Dode Paskert (Phila. Nat.)	275.00	125.00	60.00
(140)	Dode Paskert (Philadelphia Nat.)	275.00	125.00	60.00
(141)	Billy Purtell	275.00	125.00	60.00
(142)	Jack Quinn (Baltimore)	275.00	125.00	60.00
(143)	Jack Quinn (Vernon)	275.00	125.00	60.00
(144)	Ed Reulbach (Brooklyn Nat.)	275.00	125.00	60.00
(145)	Ed Reulbach (Brooklyn Fed.)	275.00	125.00	60.00
(146)	Ed Reulbach (Pittsburgh)	275.00	125.00	60.00
(147)	Nap Rucker (Brooklyn)	275.00	125.00	60.00
(148)	Nap Rucker (Brooklyn Nat.)	275.00	125.00	60.00
(149)	Dick Rudolph	275.00	125.00	60.00
(150)	Germany Schaefer (Washington, "W" on shirt.)	275.00	125.00	60.00
(151)	Germany Schaefer (K.C. Fed., "W" on shirt.)	275.00	125.00	60.00
(152)	Germany Schaefer (New York, no "W" on shirt.)	275.00	125.00	60.00
(153)	Admiral Schlei (Batting)	275.00	125.00	60.00
(154)	Admiral Schlei (Portrait)	275.00	125.00	60.00
(155)	Boss Schmidt	275.00	125.00	60.00
(156)	Wildfire Schulte	275.00	125.00	60.00
(157)	Frank Smith	275.00	125.00	60.00
(158)	Tris Speaker	2,400	1,200	725.00
(159)	George Stovall	275.00	125.00	60.00
(160)	Gabby Street (Catching)	275.00	125.00	60.00
(161)	Gabby Street (Portrait)	275.00	125.00	60.00
(162)	Ed Summers	275.00	125.00	60.00
(163)	Bill Sweeney (Boston)	275.00	125.00	60.00
(164)	Bill Sweeney (Chicago)	275.00	125.00	60.00
(165)	Jeff Sweeney (New York)	275.00	125.00	60.00
(166)	Jeff Sweeney (Richmond)	275.00	125.00	60.00
(167)	Ira Thomas (Phila. Amer.)	275.00	125.00	60.00
(168)	Ira Thomas (Philadelphia Amer.)	275.00	125.00	60.00
(169)	Joe Tinker (Chicago Fed., bat off shoulder.)	550.00	245.00	120.00
(170)	Joe Tinker (Chicago Nat., bat off shoulder.)	550.00	245.00	120.00
(171)	Joe Tinker (Chicago Fed., bat off shoulder.)	550.00	245.00	120.00
(172)	Joe Tinker (Chicago Nat., bat off shoulder.)	550.00	245.00	120.00
(173)	Heinie Wagner	275.00	125.00	60.00
(174)	Jack Warhop (New York, "NY" on shirt.)	275.00	125.00	60.00
(175)	Jack Warhop (St. Louis, no "NY" on shirt.)	275.00	125.00	60.00
(176)	Zach Wheat (Brooklyn)	550.00	245.00	120.00
(177)	Zach Wheat (Brooklyn Nat.)	550.00	245.00	120.00
(178)	Kaiser Wilhelm	275.00	125.00	60.00
(179)	Ed Willett (St. Louis)	275.00	125.00	60.00
(180)	Ed Willett (Memphis)	275.00	125.00	60.00
(181)	Owen Wilson	275.00	125.00	60.00
(182)	Hooks Wiltse (New York, pitching.)	275.00	125.00	60.00
(183)	Hooks Wiltse (Brooklyn, pitching.)	275.00	125.00	60.00
(184)	Hooks Wiltse (Jersey City, pitching.)	275.00	125.00	60.00
(185)	Hooks Wiltse (New York, portrait.)	275.00	125.00	60.00
(186)	Hooks Wiltse (Brooklyn, portrait.)	275.00	125.00	60.00
(187)	Hooks Wiltse (Jersey City, portrait.)	275.00	125.00	60.00
(188)	Heinie Zimmerman	275.00	125.00	60.00

1919 Coupon Cigarettes Type 3 (T213)

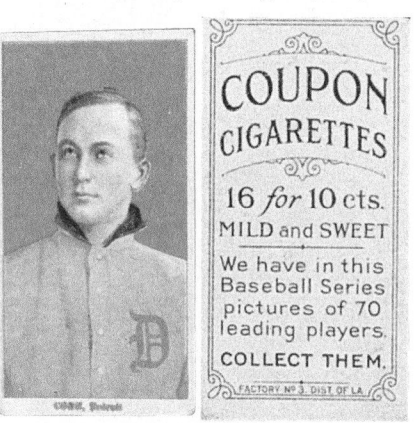

Though using the same photos seen in the contemporary T206 tobacco issue, Coupon Cigarette cards comprise three distinct sets produced between 1910 and 1919. Coupon cards feature a mix of players from the National and American Leagues, and several minor leagues. Slightly smaller than the usual cigarette-card format, Type 3 Coupons nominally measure 1-3/8" x 2-9/16", but are more prone to original size deviations than Type 1 or Type 2 Coupons. Except for the blue ink used in the player identification line, the fronts of the Coupon cards are virtually identical to the more popular T206 series. Backs, however, clearly identify the cards as being a product of Coupon Cigarettes and allow the collector to easily differentiate among the three types. Type 3 cards, issued in 1919, advertise "16 for 10 cts." and mention "70 leading players." Distribution of the Coupon cards was limited to the Louisiana area, making the set difficult to checklist and even more difficult to collect. Numerous variations further complicate the situation. It is quite possible the checklists here are incomplete and additions will surface in the future. While most Type 3 Coupons mention on their backs, "FACTORY No. 3, DIST OF LA," some have been seen with that designation blacked out and an overprint applied citing "FACTORY No. 8, DIST OF LA."

		NM	E	VG
Complete Set (70):		60,000	30,000	18,000
Common Player:		600.00	300.00	180.00
(1)	Red Ames	600.00	300.00	180.00
(2)	Home Run Baker	1,200	600.00	350.00
(3)	Chief Bender (No trees in background.)	1,200	600.00	350.00
(4)	Chief Bender (Trees in background.)	1,200	600.00	350.00
(5)	Roger Bresnahan	1,200	600.00	350.00
(6)	Al Bridwell	600.00	300.00	180.00

(7)	Miner Brown	1,200	600.00	350.00
(8)	Bobby Byrne	600.00	300.00	180.00
(9)	Frank Chance (Batting)	1,200	600.00	350.00
(10)	Frank Chance (Portrait)	1,200	600.00	350.00
(11)	Hal Chase (Holding trophy.)	900.00	450.00	270.00
(12)	Hal Chase (Portrait)	900.00	450.00	270.00
(13)	Hal Chase (Throwing)	900.00	450.00	270.00
(14)	Ty Cobb (Batting)	7,500	3,750	2,250
(15)	Ty Cobb (Portrait)	7,500	3,750	2,250
(16)	Eddie Collins	1,200	600.00	350.00
(17)	Sam Crawford	1,200	600.00	350.00
(18)	Harry Davis	600.00	300.00	180.00
(19)	Mike Donlin	600.00	300.00	180.00
(20)	Wild Bill Donovan	600.00	300.00	180.00
(21)	Mickey Doolan (Batting)	600.00	300.00	180.00
(22)	Mickey Doolan (Fielding)	600.00	300.00	180.00
(23)	Larry Doyle (Batting)	600.00	300.00	180.00
(24)	Larry Doyle (Portrait)	600.00	300.00	180.00
(25)	Jean Dubuc	600.00	300.00	180.00
(26)	Jack Dunn	600.00	300.00	180.00
(27)	Kid Elberfeld	600.00	300.00	180.00
(28)	Johnny Evers	1,200	600.00	350.00
(29)	Chick Gandil	1,100	550.00	330.00
(30)	Clark Griffith	1,200	600.00	350.00
(31)	Buck Herzog	600.00	300.00	180.00
(32)	Dick Hoblitzell	600.00	300.00	180.00
(33)	Miller Huggins (Hands at mouth.)	1,200	600.00	350.00
(34)	Miller Huggins (Portrait)	1,200	600.00	350.00
(35)	John Hummel	600.00	300.00	180.00
(36)	Hughie Jennings (Both hands showing.)	1,200	600.00	350.00
(37)	Hughie Jennings (One hand showing.)	1,200	600.00	350.00
(38)	Walter Johnson	1,800	900.00	550.00
(39)	Tim Jordan	600.00	300.00	180.00
(40)	Joe Kelley	1,200	600.00	180.00
(41)	Ed Konetchy	600.00	300.00	180.00
(42)	Larry Lajoie	1,200	600.00	350.00
(43)	Sherry Magee	600.00	300.00	180.00
(44)	Rube Marquard	1,200	600.00	350.00
(45)	Christy Mathewson	4,200	2,100	1,260
(47)	John McGraw (Glove at side.)	1,200	600.00	350.00
(48)	John McGraw (Portrait)	1,200	600.00	135030.00
(49)	George McQuillan	600.00	300.00	180.00
(50)	Fred Merkle	600.00	300.00	180.00
(51)	Dots Miller	600.00	300.00	180.00
(52)	Mike Mowrey	600.00	300.00	180.00
(53)	Chief Myers (Meyers) (Brooklyn)	600.00	300.00	180.00
(54)	Chief Myers (Meyers) (New Haven)	600.00	300.00	180.00
(55)	Dode Paskert	600.00	300.00	180.00
(56)	Jack Quinn	600.00	300.00	180.00
(57)	Ed Reulbach	600.00	300.00	180.00
(58)	Nap Rucker	600.00	300.00	180.00
(59)	Dick Rudolph	600.00	300.00	180.00
(60)	Herman Schaeffer (Schaefer)	600.00	300.00	180.00
(61)	Wildfire Schulte	600.00	300.00	180.00
(62)	Tris Speaker	3,200	1,600	960.00
(63)	Gabby Street (Catching)	600.00	300.00	180.00
(64)	Gabby Street (Portrait)	600.00	300.00	180.00
(65)	Jeff Sweeney	600.00	300.00	180.00
(66)	Ira Thomas	600.00	300.00	180.00
(67)	Joe Tinker	1,200	600.00	350.00
(68)	Zach Wheat	1,200	600.00	350.00
(69)	Geo. Wiltse	600.00	300.00	180.00
(70)	Heinie Zimmerman	600.00	300.00	180.00

1919 Coupon Cigarettes Type 3, Factory 8 Overprint

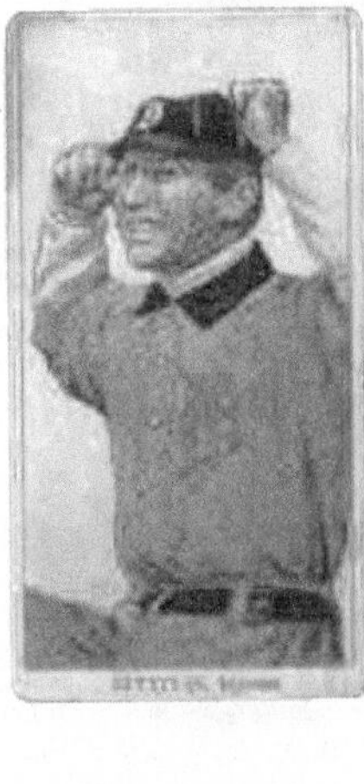

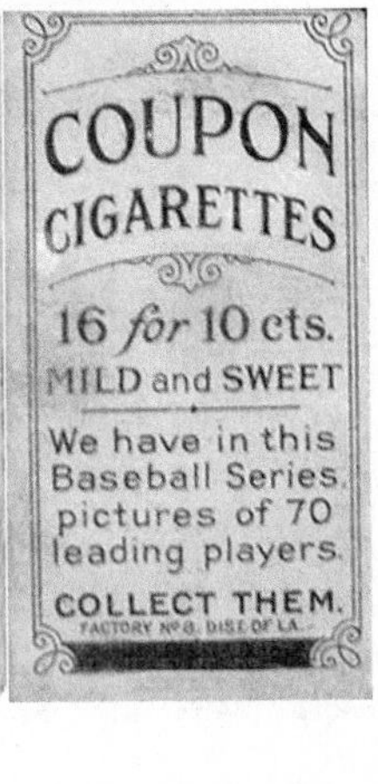

Of interest to specialty collectors is a variation of Type 3 Coupon cards on which the normal "FACTORY No. 3 . . . " line at bottom back has been blacked out and a "FACTORY No. 8 . . . " designation overprinted. The extent of the overprint checklist is unknown and at least one card (Cobb, bat off shoulder) is found as a Factory 8, but not yet verified to exist as a Factory 3 version.

	NM	E	VG
Common Player:	600.00	300.00	180.00
Hall of Famers: 5-7X			

Chief Bender (No trees.)
Ty Cobb (Bat off shoulder.)
Eddie Collins
Jean Dubuc
Hughie Jennings (Both hands showing.)
Rube Marquard
John McGraw (Portrait)

1914 Cracker Jack (E145)

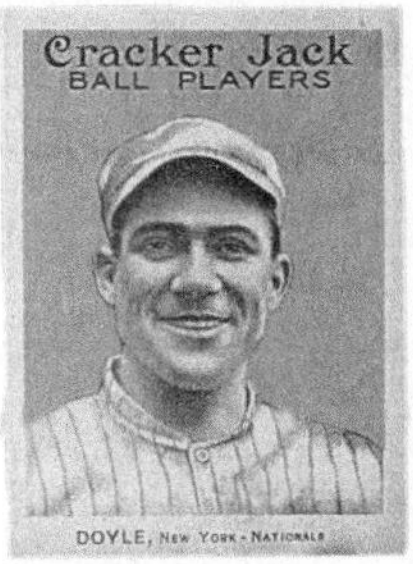

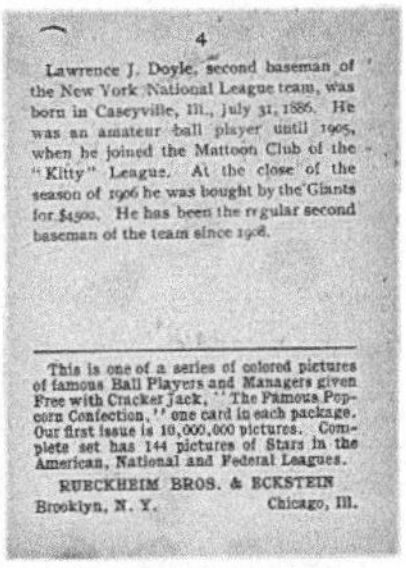
4

Lawrence J. Doyle, second baseman of the New York National League team, was born in Caseyville, Ill., July 31, 1886. He was an amateur ball player until 1905, when he joined the Mattoon Club of the "Kitty" League. At the close of the season of 1906 he was bought by the Giants for $4500. He has been the regular second baseman of the team since 1908.

This is one of a series of colored pictures of famous Ball Players and Managers given Free with Cracker Jack, "The Famous Popcorn Confection," one card in each package. Our first issue is 10,000,000 pictures. Complete set has 144 pictures of Stars in the American, National and Federal Leagues.

RUECKHEIM BROS. & ECKSTEIN
Brooklyn, N. Y. Chicago, Ill.

The 1914 Cracker Jack set, whose ACC designation is E145-1, is one of the most popular of the "E" card sets and features baseball stars from the American, National and Federal leagues. The 2-1/4" x 3" cards, are printed on thin stock and were inserted in boxes of Cracker Jack. The 1914 issue consists of 144 cards with tinted color photographs on a red background. Numbered backs feature a short biography plus an advertisement. The advertising on the low-numbered cards in the set indicates that 10 million cards were issued, while the high-numbered cards boast that 15 million were printed.

		NM	E	VG
Complete Set (144):		375,000	115,000	45,000
Common Player:		850.00	360.00	100.00
1	Otto Knabe	2,000	325.00	125.00
2	Home Run Baker	3,250	1,250	650.00
3	Joe Tinker	3,500	1,350	675.00
4	Larry Doyle	850.00	360.00	100.00
5	Ward Miller	850.00	360.00	100.00
6	Eddie Plank	3,500	1,300	600.00
7	Eddie Collins	2,500	1,250	550.00
8	Rube Oldring	850.00	360.00	100.00
9	Artie Hoffman (Hofman)	850.00	360.00	100.00
10	Stuffy McInnis	850.00	360.00	100.00
11	George Stovall	850.00	360.00	100.00
12	Connie Mack	3,250	1,250	650.00
13	Art Wilson	850.00	360.00	100.00
14	Sam Crawford	2,300	760.00	345.00
15	Reb Russell	850.00	360.00	100.00
16	Howie Camnitz	850.00	360.00	100.00
17a	Roger Bresnahan (No number on back.)	7,500	2,475	1,125
17b	Roger Bresnahan (Number on back.)	3,000	1,250	750.00
18	Johnny Evers	2,500	1,250	750.00
19	Chief Bender	2,500	1,250	750.00
20	Cy Falkenberg	850.00	360.00	100.00
21	Heinie Zimmerman	850.00	360.00	100.00
22	Smokey Joe Wood	1,500	495.00	225.00
23	Charles Comiskey	2,500	1,250	750.00
24	George Mullen (Mullin)	850.00	360.00	100.00
25	Mike Simon	850.00	360.00	100.00
26	Jim Scott	850.00	360.00	100.00
27	Bill Carrigan	850.00	360.00	100.00
28	Jack Barry	850.00	360.00	100.00
29	Vean Gregg	850.00	360.00	100.00
30	Ty Cobb	30,000	10,000	4,500
31	Heinie Wagner	850.00	360.00	100.00
32	Mordecai Brown	2,500	1,250	750.00
33	Amos Strunk	850.00	360.00	100.00
34	Ira Thomas	850.00	360.00	100.00
35	Harry Hooper	2,500	1,250	750.00
36	Ed Walsh	2,500	1,250	750.00
37	Grover C. Alexander	9,000	2,975	1,350
38	Red Dooin	850.00	360.00	100.00
39	Chick Gandil	1,700	850.00	500.00
40	Jimmy Austin	850.00	360.00	100.00
41	Tommy Leach	850.00	360.00	100.00
42	Al Bridwell	850.00	360.00	100.00
43	Rube Marquard	3,900	1,300	585.00
44	Jeff Tesreau	850.00	360.00	100.00
45	Fred Luderus	850.00	360.00	100.00
46	Bob Groom	850.00	360.00	100.00
47	Josh Devore	850.00	360.00	100.00
48	Harry Lord	850.00	360.00	100.00
49	Dots Miller	850.00	360.00	100.00
50	John Hummell (Hummel)	850.00	360.00	100.00
51	Nap Rucker	850.00	360.00	100.00
52	Zach Wheat	2,500	1,250	750.00
53	Otto Miller	850.00	360.00	100.00
54	Marty O'Toole	850.00	360.00	100.00
55	Dick Hoblitzel (Hoblitzell)	850.00	360.00	100.00
56	Clyde Milan	850.00	360.00	100.00
57	Walter Johnson	9,500	3,800	1,675
58	Wally Schang	850.00	360.00	100.00
59	Doc Gessler	850.00	360.00	100.00
60	Rollie Zeider	850.00	360.00	100.00
61	Ray Schalk	2,500	1,250	750.00
62	Jay Cashion	850.00	360.00	100.00
63	Babe Adams	850.00	360.00	100.00
64	Jimmy Archer	850.00	360.00	100.00
65	Tris Speaker	6,500	3,200	1,950
66	Nap Lajoie	6,500	3,200	1,950
67	Doc Crandall	850.00	360.00	100.00
68	Honus Wagner	16,500	5,450	2,475
69	John McGraw	2,500	1,250	750.00
70	Fred Clarke	2,300	760.00	345.00
71	Chief Meyers	850.00	360.00	100.00
72	Joe Boehling	850.00	360.00	100.00
73	Max Carey	2,500	1,250	750.00
74	Frank Owens	850.00	360.00	100.00
75	Miller Huggins	2,500	1,250	750.00
76	Claude Hendrix	850.00	360.00	100.00
77	Hughie Jennings	2,500	1,250	750.00
78	Fred Merkle	850.00	360.00	100.00
79	Ping Bodie	850.00	360.00	100.00
80	Ed Reulbach	850.00	360.00	100.00
81	Jim Delehanty (Delahanty)	850.00	360.00	100.00
82	Gavvy Cravath	850.00	360.00	100.00
83	Russ Ford	850.00	360.00	100.00
84	Elmer Knetzer	850.00	360.00	100.00
85	Buck Herzog	850.00	360.00	100.00
86	Burt Shotten	850.00	360.00	100.00
87	Hick Cady	850.00	360.00	100.00
88	Christy Mathewson	120,000	60,000	20,000
89	Larry Cheney	850.00	360.00	100.00
90	Frank Smith	850.00	360.00	100.00
91	Roger Peckinpaugh	900.00	295.00	135.00
92	Al Demaree	850.00	360.00	100.00
93	Del Pratt	19,000	8,500	3,000
94	Eddie Cicotte	2,200	725.00	330.00
95	Ray Keating	850.00	360.00	100.00
96	Beals Becker	850.00	360.00	100.00
97	Rube Benton	850.00	360.00	100.00
98	Frank Laporte (LaPorte)	850.00	360.00	100.00
99	Frank Chance	6,500	3,200	1,950
100	Tom Seaton	850.00	360.00	100.00
101	Wildfire Schulte	850.00	360.00	100.00
102	Ray Fisher	850.00	360.00	100.00
103	Joe Jackson	55,000	23,000	11,000
104	Vic Saier	850.00	360.00	100.00
105	Jimmy Lavender	850.00	360.00	100.00
106	Joe Birmingham	850.00	360.00	100.00
107	Tom Downey	850.00	360.00	100.00
108	Sherry Magee	850.00	360.00	100.00
109	Fred Blanding	850.00	360.00	100.00
110	Bob Bescher	850.00	360.00	100.00
111	Nixey Callahan	850.00	360.00	100.00
112	Jeff Sweeney	850.00	360.00	100.00
113	George Suggs	850.00	360.00	100.00
114	George Moriarity (Moriarty)	850.00	360.00	100.00
115	Ad Brennan	850.00	360.00	100.00
116	Rollie Zeider	850.00	360.00	100.00
117	Ted Easterly	850.00	360.00	100.00
118	Ed Konetchy	850.00	360.00	100.00
119	George Perring	850.00	360.00	100.00
120	Mickey Doolan	850.00	360.00	100.00
121	Hub Perdue	850.00	360.00	100.00
122	Donie Bush	850.00	360.00	100.00
123	Slim Sallee	850.00	360.00	100.00
124	Earle Moore (Earl)	850.00	360.00	100.00
125	Bert Niehoff	850.00	360.00	100.00
126	Walter Blair	850.00	360.00	100.00
127	Butch Schmidt	850.00	360.00	100.00
128	Steve Evans	850.00	360.00	100.00
129	Ray Caldwell	850.00	360.00	100.00
130	Ivy Wingo	850.00	360.00	100.00
131	George Baumgardner	850.00	360.00	100.00
132	Les Nunamaker	850.00	360.00	100.00
133	Branch Rickey	5,000	2,300	750.00
134	Armando Marsans	900.00	295.00	135.00
135	Bill Killifer (Killefer)	850.00	360.00	100.00
136	Rabbit Maranville	3,500	1,800	600.00
137	Bill Rariden	850.00	360.00	100.00
138	Hank Gowdy	850.00	360.00	100.00
139	Rebel Oakes	850.00	360.00	100.00

140	Danny Murphy	850.00	360.00	100.00
141	Cy Barger	850.00	360.00	100.00
142	Gene Packard	850.00	360.00	100.00
143	Jake Daubert	850.00	360.00	100.00
144	Jimmy Walsh	1,800	550.00	200.00

1915 Cracker Jack (E145)

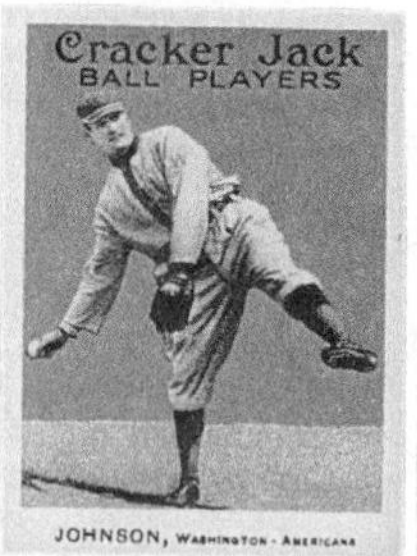

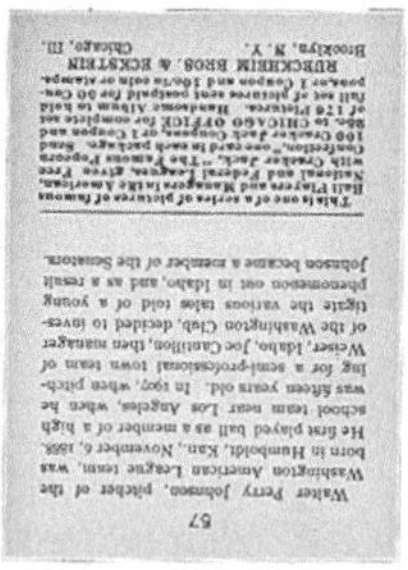

The 1915 Cracker Jack set (E145-2) is a reissue of the 1914 edition with some card additions and deletions, team designation changes, and new poses. A total of 176 cards comprise the set. Cards can be distinguished as either 1914 or 1915 by the advertising on the backs. The 1914 cards call the set complete at 144 pictures; the 1915 version notes 176 pictures. Backs of 1915 Cracker Jack cards are printed upside-down in relation to the front. A complete set and an album were available from the company.

	NM	E	VG
Complete Set (176):	150,000	60,000	30,000
Common Player (1-144):	300.00	110.00	65.00
Common Player (145-176):	325.00	130.00	65.00
Album:	750.00	375.00	225.00

1	Otto Knabe	1,400	475.00	125.00
2	Home Run Baker	1,200	600.00	350.00
3	Joe Tinker	1,250	625.00	375.00
4	Larry Doyle	300.00	110.00	65.00
5	Ward Miller	300.00	110.00	65.00
6	Eddie Plank	2,000	1,000	600.00
7	Eddie Collins	1,200	480.00	240.00
8	Rube Oldring	300.00	110.00	65.00
9	Artie Hoffman (Hofman)	300.00	110.00	65.00
10	Stuffy McInnis	300.00	110.00	65.00
11	George Stovall	300.00	110.00	65.00
12	Connie Mack	1,100	450.00	225.00
13	Art Wilson	300.00	110.00	65.00
14	Sam Crawford	1,100	450.00	225.00
15	Reb Russell	300.00	110.00	65.00
16	Howie Camnitz	300.00	110.00	65.00
17	Roger Bresnahan	1,100	450.00	225.00
18	Johnny Evers	1,100	450.00	225.00
19	Chief Bender	1,350	675.00	405.00
20	Cy Falkenberg	300.00	110.00	65.00
21	Heinie Zimmerman	300.00	110.00	65.00
22	Smokey Joe Wood	800.00	325.00	160.00
23	Charles Comiskey	1,100	450.00	225.00
24	George Mullen (Mullin)	300.00	110.00	65.00
25	Mike Simon	300.00	110.00	65.00
26	Jim Scott	300.00	110.00	65.00
27	Bill Carrigan	300.00	110.00	65.00
28	Jack Barry	300.00	110.00	65.00
29	Vean Gregg	300.00	110.00	65.00
30	Ty Cobb	12,000	5,000	1,750
31	Heinie Wagner	300.00	110.00	65.00
32	Mordecai Brown	2,000	1,000	600.00
33	Amos Strunk	300.00	110.00	65.00
34	Ira Thomas	300.00	110.00	65.00
35	Harry Hooper	1,100	450.00	225.00
36	Ed Walsh	1,100	450.00	225.00
37	Grover C. Alexander	3,750	1,875	1,125
38	Red Dooin	300.00	110.00	65.00
39	Chick Gandil	800.00	325.00	160.00
40	Jimmy Austin	300.00	110.00	65.00
41	Tommy Leach	300.00	110.00	65.00
42	Al Bridwell	300.00	110.00	65.00
43	Rube Marquard	1,100	450.00	225.00
44	Jeff Tesreau	300.00	110.00	65.00
45	Fred Luderus	300.00	110.00	65.00
46	Bob Groom	300.00	110.00	65.00
47	Josh Devore	300.00	110.00	65.00
48	Steve O'Neill	300.00	110.00	65.00
49	Dots Miller	300.00	110.00	65.00
50	John Hummell (Hummel)	300.00	110.00	65.00
51	Nap Rucker	300.00	110.00	65.00
52	Zach Wheat	1,750	875.00	525.00
53	Otto Miller	300.00	110.00	65.00
54	Marty O'Toole	300.00	110.00	65.00
55	Dick Hoblitzel (Hoblitzell)	300.00	110.00	65.00
56	Clyde Milan	300.00	110.00	65.00
57	Walter Johnson	6,000	2,500	900.00
58	Wally Schang	300.00	110.00	65.00
59	Doc Gessler	300.00	110.00	65.00
60	Oscar Dugey	300.00	110.00	65.00
61	Ray Schalk	1,200	600.00	350.00
62	Willie Mitchell	300.00	110.00	65.00
63	Babe Adams	300.00	110.00	65.00
64	Jimmy Archer	300.00	110.00	65.00
65	Tris Speaker	1,700	680.00	340.00
66	Nap Lajoie	2,100	1,050	625.00
67	Doc Crandall	300.00	110.00	65.00
68	Honus Wagner	9,000	4,000	900.00
69	John McGraw	1,100	450.00	225.00
70	Fred Clarke	1,100	450.00	225.00
71	Chief Meyers	300.00	110.00	65.00
72	Joe Boehling	300.00	110.00	65.00
73	Max Carey	1,100	450.00	225.00
74	Frank Owens	300.00	110.00	65.00
75	Miller Huggins	1,100	450.00	225.00
76	Claude Hendrix	300.00	110.00	65.00
77	Hughie Jennings	1,100	450.00	225.00
78	Fred Merkle	300.00	110.00	65.00
79	Ping Bodie	300.00	110.00	65.00
80	Ed Reulbach	300.00	110.00	65.00
81	Jim Delehanty (Delahanty)	300.00	110.00	65.00
82	Gavvy Cravath	300.00	110.00	65.00
83	Russ Ford	300.00	110.00	65.00
84	Elmer Knetzer	300.00	110.00	65.00
85	Buck Herzog	300.00	110.00	65.00
86	Burt Shotten	300.00	110.00	65.00
87	Hick Cady	300.00	110.00	65.00
88	Christy Mathewson	10,000	3,600	1,200
89	Larry Cheney	300.00	110.00	65.00
90	Frank Smith	300.00	110.00	65.00
91	Roger Peckinpaugh	350.00	140.00	70.00
92	Al Demaree	300.00	110.00	65.00
93	Del Pratt	300.00	110.00	65.00
94	Eddie Cicotte	1,000	400.00	200.00
95	Ray Keating	300.00	110.00	65.00
96	Beals Becker	300.00	110.00	65.00
97	Rube Benton	300.00	110.00	65.00
98	Frank Laporte (LaPorte)	300.00	110.00	65.00
99	Hal Chase	600.00	240.00	120.00
100	Tom Seaton	300.00	110.00	65.00
101	Wildfire Schulte	300.00	110.00	65.00
102	Ray Fisher	300.00	110.00	65.00
103	Joe Jackson	24,000	9,000	3,000
104	Vic Saier	300.00	110.00	65.00
105	Jimmy Lavender	300.00	110.00	65.00
106	Joe Birmingham	300.00	110.00	65.00
107	Tom Downey	300.00	110.00	65.00
108	Sherry Magee	300.00	110.00	65.00
109	Fred Blanding	300.00	110.00	65.00
110	Bob Bescher	300.00	110.00	65.00
111	Herbie Moran	300.00	110.00	65.00
112	Ed Sweeney	300.00	110.00	65.00
113	George Suggs	300.00	110.00	65.00
114	George Moriarity (Moriarty)	300.00	110.00	65.00
115	Ad Brennan	300.00	110.00	65.00
116	Rollie Zeider	300.00	110.00	65.00
117	Ted Easterly	300.00	110.00	65.00
118	Ed Konetchy	300.00	110.00	65.00
119	George Perring	300.00	110.00	65.00
120	Mickey Doolan	300.00	110.00	65.00
121	Hub Perdue	300.00	110.00	65.00
122	Donie Bush	300.00	110.00	65.00
123	Slim Sallee	300.00	110.00	65.00
124	Earle Moore (Earl)	300.00	110.00	65.00
125	Bert Niehoff	300.00	110.00	65.00
126	Walter Blair	300.00	110.00	65.00
127	Butch Schmidt	300.00	110.00	65.00
128	Steve Evans	300.00	110.00	65.00
129	Ray Caldwell	300.00	110.00	65.00
130	Ivy Wingo	300.00	110.00	65.00
131	George Baumgardner	300.00	110.00	65.00
132	Les Nunamaker	300.00	110.00	65.00
133	Branch Rickey	1,100	450.00	225.00
134	Armando Marsans	425.00	175.00	85.00
135	Bill Killifer (Killefer)	300.00	110.00	65.00
136	Rabbit Maranville	1,100	450.00	225.00
137	Bill Rariden	300.00	110.00	65.00
138	Hank Gowdy	300.00	110.00	65.00
139	Rebel Oakes	300.00	110.00	65.00
140	Danny Murphy	300.00	110.00	65.00
141	Cy Barger	300.00	110.00	65.00
142	Gene Packard	300.00	110.00	65.00
143	Jake Daubert	300.00	110.00	65.00
144	Jimmy Walsh	300.00	110.00	65.00
145	Ted Cather	325.00	130.00	65.00
146	Lefty Tyler	325.00	130.00	65.00
147	Lee Magee	325.00	130.00	65.00
148	Owen Wilson	325.00	130.00	65.00
149	Hal Janvrin	325.00	130.00	65.00
150	Doc Johnston	325.00	130.00	65.00
151	Possum Whitted	325.00	130.00	65.00
152	George McQuillen (McQuillan)	325.00	130.00	65.00
153	Bill James	325.00	130.00	65.00
154	Dick Rudolph	325.00	130.00	65.00
155	Joe Connolly	325.00	130.00	65.00
156	Jean Dubuc	325.00	130.00	65.00
157	George Kaiserling	325.00	130.00	65.00
158	Fritz Maisel	325.00	130.00	65.00
159	Heinie Groh	325.00	130.00	65.00
160	Benny Kauff	325.00	130.00	65.00
161	Edd Rousch (Roush)	1,250	500.00	250.00
162	George Stallings	325.00	130.00	65.00
163	Bert Whaling	325.00	130.00	65.00
164	Bob Shawkey	325.00	130.00	65.00
165	Eddie Murphy	325.00	130.00	65.00
166	Bullet Joe Bush	325.00	130.00	65.00
167	Clark Griffith	1,250	500.00	250.00
168	Vin Campbell	325.00	130.00	65.00
169	Ray Collins	325.00	130.00	65.00
170	Hans Lobert	325.00	130.00	65.00
171	Earl Hamilton	325.00	130.00	65.00
172	Erskine Mayer	450.00	180.00	90.00
173	Tilly Walker	325.00	130.00	65.00
174	Bobby Veach	325.00	130.00	65.00
175	Joe Benz	325.00	130.00	65.00
176	Hippo Vaughn	1,100	200.00	75.00

1933 Cracker Jack Pins (PR4)

Although no manufacturer is indicated on the pins themselves, the manufacturer has been identified as Button Gum Co., Chicago, but there is still some indication that Cracker Jack inserted this 25-player set in their products circa 1933. Each pin measures 13/16" in diameter and features a line drawing of a player portrait. The unnumbered pins are printed in blue and gray with backgrounds found in either yellow or gray.

	NM	E	VG
Complete Set (25):	1,600	800.00	475.00
Common Player:	35.00	17.50	10.00

(1)	Charles Berry	35.00	17.50	10.00
(2)	Bill Cissell	35.00	17.50	10.00
(3)	KiKi Cuyler	60.00	30.00	18.00
(4)	Dizzy Dean	100.00	50.00	30.00
(5)	Wesley Ferrell	35.00	17.50	10.00
(6)	Frank Frisch	60.00	30.00	18.00
(7)	Lou Gehrig	250.00	125.00	75.00
(8)	Vernon Gomez	60.00	30.00	18.00
(9)	Goose Goslin	60.00	30.00	18.00
(10)	George Grantham	35.00	17.50	10.00
(11)	Charley Grimm	35.00	17.50	10.00
(12)	Lefty Grove	75.00	37.00	22.00
(13)	Gabby Hartnett	60.00	30.00	18.00
(14)	Travis Jackson	60.00	30.00	18.00
(15)	Tony Lazzeri	60.00	30.00	18.00
(16)	Ted Lyons	60.00	30.00	18.00
(17)	Rabbit Maranville	60.00	30.00	18.00
(18)	Carl Reynolds	35.00	17.50	10.00
(19)	Charles Ruffing	60.00	30.00	18.00
(20)	Al Simmons	60.00	30.00	18.00
(21)	Gus Suhr	35.00	17.50	10.00
(22)	Bill Terry	60.00	30.00	18.00
(23)	Dazzy Vance	60.00	30.00	18.00
(24)	Paul Waner	60.00	30.00	18.00
(25)	Lon Warneke	35.00	17.50	10.00

1979 Larry Crain Prints

"Baseball's Greatest Team," as voted during baseball's centennial, was featured on a set of 8-1/2" x 11" black-and-white prints by artist Larry Crain. Each print is signed and numbered by the artist. The set of 11 was originally sold for $25.

	NM	E	VG
Complete Set (11):	25.00	12.50	7.50
Common Player:	3.00	1.50	.90

(1)	Yogi Berra	3.00	1.50	.90
(2)	Joe DiMaggio	5.00	2.50	1.50
(3)	Lou Gehrig	4.00	2.00	1.25
(4)	Rogers Hornsby	3.00	1.50	.90
(5)	Walter Johnson	3.00	1.50	.90
(6)	Willie Mays	4.00	2.00	1.25
(7)	Brooks Robinson	3.00	1.50	.90
(8)	Babe Ruth	5.00	2.50	1.50
(9)	Warren Spahn	3.00	1.50	.90
(10)	Casey Stengel	3.00	1.50	.90
(11)	Honus Wagner	3.00	1.50	.90

1976 Crane Potato Chips Discs

This unnumbered 70-card set of player discs was issued with Crane Potato Chips in 1976. The front of the discs are designed to look like a baseball with the player's black-and-white portrait in the center and vital data in side panels containing one of several bright colors. Discs measure 3-3/8" in diameter. This is the most common among several regionally issued sets sharing the same card fronts with different ads on back. The discs were produced by Michael Schechter Associates under license from the players' union. All uniform and cap logos have been deleted from the discs' photos. The unnumbered discs are checklisted here in alphabetical order. Several of the discs have team variations reflecting player moves. These are known only among the Crane discs and have not been verified in the issues of other advertisers.

		NM	E	VG
	Complete Set (70):	37.50	18.50	11.00
	Common Player:	1.50	.75	..45
(1)	Henry Aaron	13.50	6.75	4.00
(2)	Johnny Bench	6.00	3.00	1.75
(3)	Vida Blue	1.50	.75	.45
(4)	Larry Bowa	1.50	.75	.45
(5)	Lou Brock	4.50	2.25	1.25
(6)	Jeff Burroughs	1.50	.75	.45
(7)	John Candelaria	1.50	.75	.45
(8)	Jose Cardenal	1.50	.75	.45
(9)	Rod Carew	4.50	2.25	1.25
(10)	Steve Carlton	4.50	2.25	1.25
(11)	Dave Cash	1.50	.75	.45
(12)	Cesar Cedeno	1.50	.75	.45
(13)	Ron Cey	1.50	.75	.45
(14)	Carlton Fisk	4.50	2.25	1.25
(15)	Tito Fuentes	1.50	.75	.45
(16)	Steve Garvey	3.00	1.50	.90
(17)	Ken Griffey	1.50	.75	.45
(18)	Don Gullett	1.50	.75	.45
(19)	Willie Horton	1.50	.75	.45
(20)	Al Hrabosky	1.50	.75	.45
(21)	Catfish Hunter	4.50	2.25	1.25
(22a)	Reggie Jackson (A's)	9.00	4.50	2.75
(22b)	Reggie Jackson (Orioles)	22.50	11.25	6.75
(23)	Randy Jones	1.50	.75	.45
(24)	Jim Kaat	1.50	.75	.45
(25)	Don Kessinger	1.50	.75	.45
(26)	Dave Kingman	1.50	.75	.45
(27)	Jerry Koosman	1.50	.75	.45
(28)	Mickey Lolich	1.50	.75	.45
(29)	Greg Luzinski	1.50	.75	.45
(30)	Fred Lynn	1.50	.75	.45
(31)	Bill Madlock	1.50	.75	.45
(32a)	Carlos May (White Sox)	1.50	.75	.45
(32b)	Carlos May (Yankees)	1.50	.75	.45
(33)	John Mayberry	1.50	.75	.45
(34)	Bake McBride	1.50	.75	.45
(35)	Doc Medich	1.50	.75	.45
(36a)	Andy Messersmith (Dodgers)	1.50	.75	.45
(36b)	Andy Messersmith (Braves)	1.50	.75	.45
(37)	Rick Monday	1.50	.75	.45
(38)	John Montefusco	1.50	.75	.45
(39)	Jerry Morales	1.50	.75	.45
(40)	Joe Morgan	4.50	2.25	1.25
(41)	Thurman Munson	4.50	2.25	1.25
(42)	Bobby Murcer	1.50	.75	.45
(43)	Al Oliver	1.50	.75	.45
(44)	Jim Palmer	4.50	2.25	1.25
(45)	Dave Parker	1.50	.75	.45
(46)	Tony Perez	4.50	2.25	1.25
(47)	Jerry Reuss	1.45	.75	.45
(48)	Brooks Robinson	5.00	2.50	1.50
(49)	Frank Robinson	5.00	2.50	1.50
(50)	Steve Rogers	1.50	.75	.45
(51)	Pete Rose	12.00	6.00	3.50
(52)	Nolan Ryan	22.50	11.25	6.75
(53)	Manny Sanguillen	1.50	.75	.45
(54)	Mike Schmidt	9.00	4.50	2.70
(55)	Tom Seaver	6.00	3.00	1.80
(56)	Ted Simmons	1.50	.75	.45
(57)	Reggie Smith	1.50	.75	.45
(58)	Willie Stargell	4.50	2.25	1.25
(59)	Rusty Staub	1.50	.75	.45
(60)	Rennie Stennett	1.50	.75	.45
(61)	Don Sutton	4.50	2.25	1.25
(62a)	Andy Thornton (Cubs)	1.50	.75	.45
(62b)	Andy Thornton (Expos)	1.50	.75	.45
(63)	Luis Tiant	1.50	.75	.45
(64)	Joe Torre	3.00	1.50	.90
(65)	Mike Tyson	1.50	.75	.45
(66)	Bob Watson	1.50	.75	.45
(67)	Wilbur Wood	1.50	.75	.45
(68)	Jimmy Wynn	1.50	.75	.45
(69)	Carl Yastrzemski	6.00	3.00	1.75
(70)	Richie Zisk	1.50	.75	.45

1913 Cravats Felt Pennants

Little is known about this felt pennant issue, including the complete checklist. The name "Cravats" in the baseball above the player picture may represent the issuer, or describe the issue; the word "cravat" is an arcane term for a triangular piece of cloth. The pennants measure 4-1/8" across the top and are 9" long. Background colors are dark, with all printing in white. At center is a line art represntation of the player, with his name horizontally beneath and his team nickname vertically at bottom. At top is a bat and ball logo with the "Cravats" name. Most specimens are seen with a metal ring reinforcing the hole punched at top center. The known checklist points to 1913 as the most probable year of issue.

		NM	E	VG
	Common Player:	500.00	250.00	150.00
(1)	Eddie Ainsmith	500.00	250.00	150.00
(2)	"Home Run" Baker	900.00	450.00	270.00
(3)	Hugh Bedient	500.00	250.00	150.00
(4)	C.A. Bender	900.00	450.00	270.00
(5)	Ray Caldwell	500.00	250.00	150.00
(6)	Jack Coombs	500.00	250.00	150.00
(7)	C.S. Dooin	500.00	250.00	150.00
(8)	Lawrence Doyle	500.00	250.00	150.00
(9)	Ed Konethy (Konetchy)	500.00	250.00	150.00
(10)	James Lavender	500.00	250.00	150.00
(11)	John J. McGraw	900.00	450.00	270.00
(12)	Stuffy McInnes (McInnis)	500.00	250.00	150.00
(13)	Christy Mathewson	2,300	1,150	700.00
(14)	J.T. (Chief) Meyer (Meyers)	500.00	250.00	150.00
(15)	Nap Rucker	500.00	250.00	150.00
(16)	Tris Speaker	1,200	600.00	350.00
(17)	Ed Sweeney	500.00	250.00	125.00
(18)	Jeff Tesreau	500.00	250.00	150.00
(19)	Ira Thomas	500.00	250.00	150.00
(20)	Joe Tinker	900.00	450.00	270.00
(21)	Ed Walsh	900.00	450.00	270.00

1922 Cream Nut/Goodie Bread

According to the advertising on back this set should comprise half of the known players from the generic W573 strip card issue. The black-and-white cards, about 2-1/16" x

3-3/8", share their format and player selection not only with W573, but also E120 American Caramel. Printed horizontally on the backs is: "Ask Your Dealer for / CREAM NUT or GOODIE BREAD / and get / A BASE BALL STAR / 120 Different Subjects." The location of the issuing entity, the specific manner of distribution and the checklist are unknown as only a handful of this particular ad-back series have survived. Collectors will pay a premium for this version above the normal W573 blank-back.

	NM	E	VG
Common Player:	800.00	400.00	240.00

Hall of Famers: 8-10X

(See 1922 W573.)

1909 Croft's Candy (E92)

 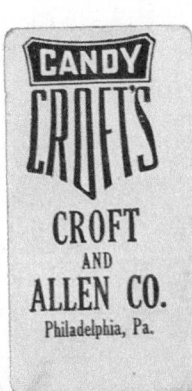

Wagner, s.s. Pittsburg Nat'l

Because they share the format and pictures with several related issues (Croft's Cocoa, Dockman Gum, Nadja Caramels, etc.) this set shared the E92 designation in the American Card Catalog. It is more logical to present these sets as separate issues, based on the advertising which appears on back. Fronts of the 1-1/2" x 2-3/4" cards feature a color lithograph of the player. His last name, position and team are printed in black in the border below. Backs have a shield-shaped logo for Croft's Candy, a product of Croft & Allen Co., Philadelphia. Backs can be found printed in black, in blue (scarcer) or in red (extremely rare). Cards are unnumbered and the checklist is presented here alphabetically.

		NM	E	VG
	Complete Set (50):	125,000	50,000	25,000
	Common Player:	1,100	550.00	330.00
	Blue Back: 1.5-2.5X			
	Red Back: 10-12X			
(1)	Jack Barry	1,110	550.00	330.00
(2)	Harry Bemis	1,065	425.00	220.00
(3)	Chief Bender (Striped cap.)	4,000	2,000	1,200
(4)	Chief Bender (White cap.)	3,600	1,800	1,080
(5)	Bill Bergen	1,110	550.00	330.00
(6)	Bob Bescher	1,100	550.00	330.00
(7)	Al Bridwell	1,100	550.00	330.00
(8)	Doc Casey	1,100	550.00	330.00
(9)	Frank Chance	3,600	1,800	1,080
(10)	Hal Chase	2,000	815.00	405.00
(11)	Ty Cobb	18,750	7,500	3,750
(12)	Eddie Collins	3,600	1,800	1,080
(13)	Sam Crawford	3,300	1,650	990.00
(14)	Harry Davis	1,100	550.00	330.00
(15)	Art Devlin	1,100	550.00	330.00
(16)	Wild Bill Donovan	1,100	550.00	330.00
(17)	Red Dooin	1,100	550.00	330.00
(18)	Mickey Doolan	1,100	550.00	330.00
(19)	Patsy Dougherty	1,100	550.00	330.00
(20)	Larry Doyle (Throwing)	1,100	550.00	330.00
(21)	Larry Doyle (With bat.)	1,100	550.00	330.00
(22)	Johnny Evers	3,600	1,800	1,080
(23)	George Gibson	1,1100.00	550.00	330.00
(24)	Topsy Hartsel	1,100	550.00	330.00
(25)	Fred Jacklitsch	1,100	550.00	330.00
(26)	Hugh Jennings	3,300	1,650	990.00
(27)	Red Kleinow	1,100	550.00	330.00
(28)	Otto Knabe	1,100	550.00	330.00
(29)	Jack Knight	1,100	550.00	330.00
(30)	Nap Lajoie	4,100	2,050	1,230
(31)	Hans Lobert	1,100	550.00	330.00
(32)	Sherry Magee	1,100	550.00	330.00
(33)	Christy Matthewson (Mathewson)	9,750	3,875	1,850
(34)	John McGraw	3,300	1,650	990.00
(35)	Larry McLean	1,100	550.00	330.00
(36)	Dots Miller (Batting)	1,100	550.00	330.00
(37)	Dots Miller (Fielding)	1,500	600.00	300.00
(38)	Danny Murphy	1,100	550.00	330.00

(39)	Bill O'Hara	4,000	2,000	1,200
(40)	Germany Schaefer	1,100	550.00	330.00
(41)	Admiral Schlei	1,100	550.00	330.00
(42)	Boss Schmidt	1,100	550.00	330.00
(43)	Johnny Seigle (Siegle)	1,100	550.00	330.00
(44)	Dave Shean	1,100	550.00	330.00
(45)	Boss Smith (Schmidt)	1,100	550.00	330.00
(46)	Joe Tinker	3,600	1,800	1,080
(47)	Honus Wagner (Batting)	15,000	6,000	3,000
(48)	Honus Wagner (Throwing)	15,000	6,000	3,000
(49)	Cy Young	8,125	3,250	1,625
(50)	Heinie Zimmerman	1,100	550.00	330.00

1909 Croft's Cocoa (E92)

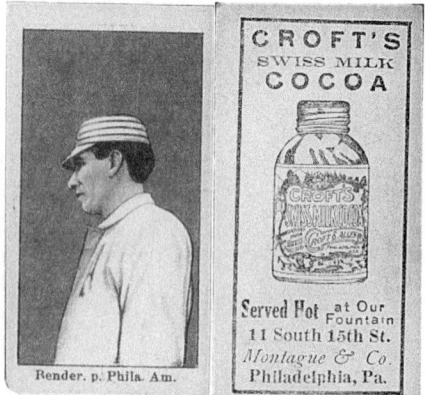

Render. p. Phila. Am.

Like related issues once cataloged together as E92 (Croft's Candy, Dockman Gum, Nadja Caramels, etc.), these 1-1/2" x 2-3/4" cards feature a color player lithograph on front, which his name, position and team printed in the white border below. Backs have an ad for Crofts Swiss Milk Cocoa of Philadelphia. The checklist, presented here alphabetically, is identical to that of Croft's Candy.

		NM	E	VG
Complete Set (50):		100,000	50,000	30,000
Common Player:		800.00	400.00	240.00
(1)	Jack Barry	800.00	400.00	240.00
(2)	Harry Bemis	800.00	400.00	240.00
(3)	Chief Bender (Striped hat.)	3,000	1,200	600.00
(4)	Chief Bender (White hat.)	1,800	720.00	360.00
(5)	Bill Bergen	800.00	400.00	240.00
(6)	Bob Bescher	800.00	400.00	240.00
(7)	Al Bridwell	800.00	400.00	240.00
(8)	Doc Casey	800.00	40.00	240.00
(9)	Frank Chance	1,650	660.00	330.00
(10)	Hal Chase	1,240	495.00	250.00
(11)	Ty Cobb	22,500	9,000	5,000
(12)	Eddie Collins	1,650	675.00	340.00
(13)	Sam Crawford	1,650	675.00	340.00
(14)	Harry Davis	800.00	400.00	240.00
(15)	Art Devlin	800.00	400.00	240.00
(16)	Wild Bill Donovan	800.00	400.00	240.00
(17)	Red Dooin	800.00	400.00	240.00
(18)	Mickey Doolan	800.00	400.00	240.00
(19)	Patsy Dougherty	800.00	400.00	240.00
(20)	Larry Doyle (Throwing)	800.00	400.00	240.00
(21)	Larry Doyle (With bat.)	800.00	400.00	240.00
(22)	Johnny Evers	3,150	1,260	640.00
(23)	George Gibson	800.00	400.00	240.00
(24)	Topsy Hartsel	800.00	400.00	240.00
(25)	Fred Jacklitsch	800.00	400.00	240.00
(26)	Hugh Jennings	1,650	675.00	340.00
(27)	Red Kleinow	800.00	400.00	240.00
(28)	Otto Knabe	800.00	400.00	240.00
(29)	Jack Knight	1,240	495.00	250.00
(30)	Nap Lajoie	2,025	825.00	415.00
(31)	Hans Lobert	800.00	400.00	240.00
(32)	Sherry Magee	800.00	400.00	240.00
(33)	Christy Matthewson (Mathewson)	10,125	4,050	2,500
(34)	John McGraw	1,650	675.00	340.00
(35)	Larry McLean	800.00	400.00	240.00
(36)	Dots Miller (Batting)	800.00	400.00	240.00
(37)	Dots Miller (Fielding)	1,240	495.00	250.00
(38)	Danny Murphy	800.00	400.00	240.00
(39)	Bill O'Hara	800.00	400.00	240.00
(40)	Germany Schaefer	800.00	400.00	240.00
(41)	Admiral Schlei	800.00	400.00	240.00
(42)	Boss Schmidt	800.00	400.00	240.00
(43)	Johnny Seigle (Siegle)	1,000	500.00	300.00
(44)	Dave Shean	800.00	400.00	240.00
(45)	Boss Smith (Schmidt)	800.00	400.00	240.00
(46)	Joe Tinker	1,650	675.00	340.00
(47)	Honus Wagner (Batting)	11,000	5,500	3,300

(48)	Honus Wagner (Throwing)	11,000	5,500	3,300
(49)	Cy Young	6,000	3,000	1,800
(50)	Heinie Zimmerman	800.00	400.00	240.00

1969 Crown Brooks Robinson

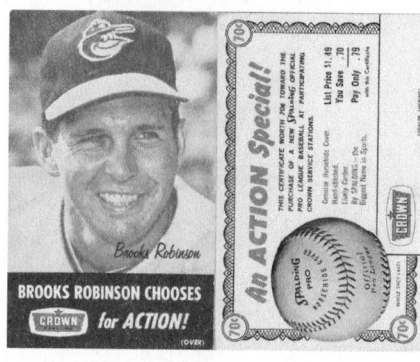

The attributed date is speculative. This 3-9/16" x 5-11/16" card feaures a black-and-white portrait photo on front with the player name in blue scrip. A blue panel at bottom has the gas company's logo and an ad slogan. On back is a black, red and white coupon offering a discount on a baseball. A blank panel at bottom was intended for use by individual service stations to print their name and address.

	NM	E	VG
Brooks Robinson	150.00	75.00	45.00

1977-78 Cubic Corp. Sports Deck Playing Cards

Playing cards featuring pencil drawings of stars in various sports were produced on a limited basis in the late 1970s by Cubic Corp. of San Diego. The cards are standard bridge size (2-1/4" x 3-1/2") with rounded corners and feature the artwork of Al Landsman along with a facsimile autograph within a colored frame. Each deck has the same athlete on the back and sold for $1.60. There is no indication of the manufacturer on individual cards, it is only found on the box. It is believed most of the decks were only produced in limited sample quantities. Similar cards were produced for Pepsi and are listed thereunder. Only the baseball players are checklisted here, in alphabetical order.

		NM	E	VG
(1)	Johnny Bench (Boxed deck.)	17.50	8.75	5.25
(1)	Johnny Bench (Single card.)	.50	.25	.15
(2)	Lou Gehrig (Boxed deck.)	25.00	12.50	7.50
(2)	Lou Gehrig (Single card.)	1.50	.70	.45
(3)	Catfish Hunter (Boxed deck.)	15.00	7.50	4.50
(3)	Catfish Hunter (Single card.)	.50	.25	.15
(4)	Randy Jones (Boxed deck.)	10.00	5.00	3.00
(4)	Randy Jones (Single card.)	.50	.25	.15
(5)	Mickey Mantle (Boxed deck.)	40.00	20.00	12.00
(5)	Mickey Mantle (Single card.)	4.00	2.00	1.25
(6)	Butch Metzger (Boxed deck.)	10.00	5.00	3.00
(6)	Butch Metzger (Single card.)	.50	.25	.15
(7)	Joe Morgan (Boxed deck.)	12.50	6.25	3.75
(7)	Joe Morgan (Single card.)	.50	.25	.15
(8)	Stan Musial (Boxed deck.)	25.00	12.50	7.50
(8)	Stan Musial (Single card.)	1.50	.70	.45
(9)	Jackie Robinson (Boxed deck.)	25.00	12.50	7.50
(9)	Jackie Robinson (Single card.)	1.50	.70	.45
(10)	Pete Rose (Boxed deck.)	35.00	17.50	10.00
(10)	Pete Rose (Single card.)	1.00	.50	.30
(11)	Babe Ruth (Boxed deck.)	30.00	15.00	9.00
(11)	Babe Ruth (Single card.)	3.00	1.50	.90

(12)	Tom Seaver (Boxed deck.)	30.00	15.00	9.00
(12)	Tom Seaver (Single card.)	1.00	.50	.30
(13)	Frank Tanana (Boxed deck.)	10.00	5.00	3.00
(13)	Frank Tanana (Single card.)	.50	.25	.15
(14)	Phillies logo/autographs (Boxed deck.)	10.00	5.00	3.00
(14)	Phillies logo/autographs (Single card.)	1.00	.50	.30

1911 Cullivan's Fireside Philadelphia A's (T208)

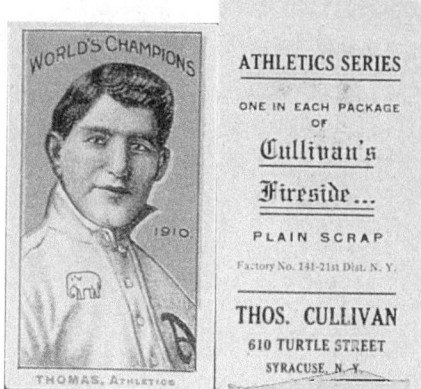

The 1911 T208 Firesides, an 18-card Philadelphia Athletics set issued by the Thomas Cullivan Tobacco Company of Syracuse, N.Y., is among the rarest of all 20th Century tobacco issues. Cullivan issued the set to commemorate the Athletics' 1910 Championship season, and, except for pitcher Jack Coombs, the checklist includes nearly all key members of the club, including manager Connie Mack. The cards are the standard size for tobacco issues, about 1-1/2" x 2-5/8". The front of each card features a player portrait set against a colored background. The player's name and the word "Athletics" appear at the bottom, while "World's Champions 1910" is printed along the top. Backs advertise the set as the "Athletics Series" and advise that one card is included in each package of "Cullivan's Fireside Plain Scrap" tobacco. The same checklist was used for a similar Athletics set issued by Rochester Baking/Williams Baking (D359). Blank-backed versions are also known to exist.

		NM	E
Common Player:		6,000	3,300
(1)	Home Run Baker	16,000	10,000
(2)	Jack Barry	6,000	3,300
(3)	Chief Bender	16,000	10,000
(4)	Eddie Collins	30,000	18,000
(5)	Harry Davis	6,000	3,300
(6)	Jimmy Dygert	40,000	24,000
(7)	Topsy Hartsel	6,000	3,300
(8)	Harry Krause	6,000	3,300
(9)	Jack Lapp	6,000	3,300
(10)	Paddy Livingston	6,000	3,300
(11)	Bris Lord	6,000	3,300
(12)	Connie Mack	16,000	10,000
(13)	Cy Morgan	6,000	3,300
(14)	Danny Murphy	6,000	3,300
(15)	Rube Oldring	18,000	11,500
(16)	Eddie Plank	25,000	16,500
(17)	Amos Strunk	6,000	3,300
(18)	Ira Thomas	6,000	3,000

1964+ Curteichcolor Hall of Fame Plaque Postcards

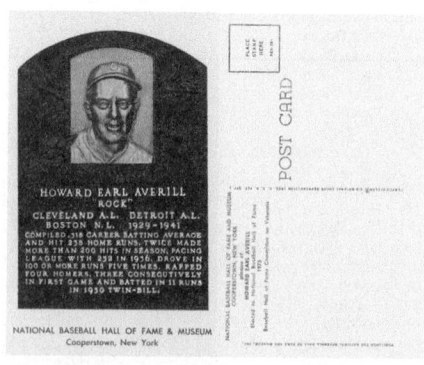

(See Hall of Fame Yellow Plaque Postcards for checklist, price data.)

1909-12 Cycle Cigarettes

Ward Miller

Ward Miller, outfielder for the Chicago Nationals, was considered the most valuable performer in the minor leagues in 1911. As a member of the Montreal team of the Eastern League he batted .332, fielded .958 and stole 63 bases in 156 games. There was quite a scramble for his services and Chicago secured him. Miller had a trial in the National League in 1910 when the Chicago club brought him up from the minors and released him to Cincinnati from where he went to Montreal. He is an Illinois boy and started out in 1906 with the Rock Island team of the Three-Eye League.

Cycle brand advertising found on the backs of T205, T206 and T207 cards generally indicates a slightly greater degree of scarcity than the most common back variations from those sets. While a value multiplier can generate a ballpark approximation of value for most cards from T205 and T206, it is not practical for T207s because all Cycle cards from that set are scarce and much of that scarcity has already been factored into the individual player prices quoted in the base T207 listings.

PREMIUMS:
T205: 1.5-2.5X
T206 350 Series: 1-1.5X
T206 460 Series: 1.5-2X

(See T205, T206, T207 for checklists and base card values.)

D

1959 Dad's Cookies Exhibits

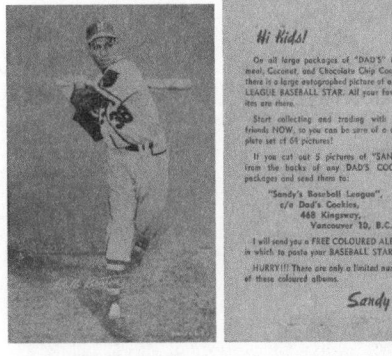

Hi Kids!

On all large packages of "DAD'S" Oatmeal, Coconut, and Chocolate Chip Cookies, there is a large autographed picture of a BIG LEAGUE BASEBALL STAR. All your favourites are there.

Start collecting and trading with your friends NOW, so you can be sure of a complete set of 64 pictures!

If you cut out 5 pictures of "SANDY" from the backs of any DAD'S COOKIE packages and send them to:

"Sandy's Baseball League",
c/o Dad's Cookies,
468 Kingsway,
Vancouver 10, B.C.

I will send you a FREE COLOURED ALBUM in which to paste your BASEBALL STARS.

HURRY!!! There are only a limited number of these coloured albums.

Sandy

A Vancouver bakery that issued several type of hockey cards in later years created this set of baseball cards by overprinting the usually blank backs of the 64 cards in Exhibit Supply Co.'s 1959 issue. Cards measure 3-3/8" x 5-3/8" and are printed in reddish-gray-brown. The back indicates an album was available to house the set.

	NM	E	VG
Complete Set (64):	6,000	3,000	1,800
Common Player:	70.00	35.00	21.00
(1) Hank Aaron	400.00	200.00	120.00
(2) Joe Adcock (Script name.)	70.00	35.00	21.00
(3) Johnny Antonelli (Giants)	70.00	35.00	21.00
(4) Luis Aparicio (Portrait)	160.00	80.00	47.50
(5) Richie Ashburn (Phillies)	200.00	100.00	60.00
(6) Ed Bailey (With cap.)	70.00	35.00	21.00
(7) Ernie Banks (Bat on shoulder, script name.)	300.00	150.00	90.00
(8) Hank Bauer (N.Y. cap.)	100.00	50.00	30.00
(9) Yogi Berra	300.00	150.00	90.00
(10) Don Blasingame	70.00	35.00	21.00
(11) Bill Bruton	70.00	35.00	21.00

(12)	Lew Burdette (Pitching, side view.)	70.00	35.00	21.00
(13)	Chico Carrasquel (Portrait)	70.00	35.00	21.00
(14)	Orlando Cepeda (To chest.)	160.00	80.00	47.50
(15)	Bob Cerv (A's cap.)	70.00	35.00	21.00
(16)	Delmar Crandall	70.00	35.00	21.00
(17)	Alvin Dark (Cubs)	70.00	35.00	21.00
(18)	Larry Doby	160.00	80.00	47.50
(19)	Dick Donovan (Sox cap.)	70.000	35.00	21.00
(20)	Don Drysdale (Portrait)	180.00	90.00	55.00
(21)	Del Ennis	70.00	35.00	21.00
(22)	Whitey Ford (Pitching)	250.00	125.00	75.00
(23)	Nelson Fox	160.00	80.00	47.50
(24)	Bob Friend	70.00	35.00	21.00
(25)	Billy Goodman (Batting)	70.00	35.00	21.00
(26)	Whitey Herzog	70.00	35.00	21.00
(27)	Gil Hodges (LA on cap.)	150.00	75.00	45.00
(28)	Elston Howard	100.00	50.00	30.00
(29)	Jackie Jensen	100.00	50.00	30.00
(30)	Al Kaline (Portrait w/ two bats.)	200.00	100.00	60.00
(31)	Harmon Killebrew (Batting)	200.00	100.00	60.00
(32)	Billy Klaus	70.00	35.00	21.00
(33)	Ted Kluzewski (Kluszewski) (Pirates uniform.)	120.00	60.00	35.00
(34)	Tony Kubek (Light background.)	120.00	60.00	35.00
(35)	Harvey Kuenn (D on cap.)	70.00	35.00	21.00
(36)	Don Larsen	70.00	35.00	21.00
(37)	Johnny Logan	70.00	35.00	21.00
(38)	Dale Long (C on cap.)	70.00	35.00	21.00
(39)	Mickey Mantle (Batting, no pinstripes, "c k" of "Mickey" separated.)	700.00	350.00	220.00
(40)	Eddie Mathews	200.00	100.00	60.00
(41)	Willie Mays (Portrait)	400.00	200.00	120.00
(42)	Bill Mazeroski (Portrait)	160.00	80.00	47.50
(43)	Lindy McDaniel	70.00	35.00	21.00
(44)	Gil McDougald	90.00	45.00	27.00
(45)	Orestes Minoso (C on cap.)	90.00	45.00	27.00
(46)	Stan Musial	350.00	175.00	105.00
(47)	Don Newcombe (Plain jacket.)	90.00	45.00	27.00
(48)	Andy Pafko ((Yours truly.) (Plain uniform.))	70.00	35.00	21.00
(49)	Billy Pierce	70.00	35.00	21.00
(50)	Robin Roberts (Script name.)	160.00	80.00	47.50
(51)	Carl Sawatski (P on cap.)	70.00	35.00	21.00
(52)	Herb Score (C on cap.)	70.00	35.00	21.00
(53)	Roy Sievers (Portrait, W on cap, light background.)	70.00	35.00	21.00
(54)	Curt Simmons	70.00	35.00	21.00
(55)	Bill Skowron	100.00	50.00	30.00
(56)	Duke Snider (LA on cap.)	200.00	100.00	60.00
(57)	Warren Spahn (M on cap.)	200.00	100.00	60.00
(58)	Frankie Thomas (Photo actually Bob Skinner.)	100.00	50.00	30.00
(59)	Earl Torgeson (Plain uniform.)	70.00	35.00	21.00
(60)	Gus Triandos	70.00	35.00	21.00
(61)	Vic Wertz (Portrait)	70.00	35.00	21.00
(62)	Ted Williams (Sincerely yours.) (#9 not showing))	400.00	200.00	120.00
(63)	Gene Woodling (Script name.)	70.00	35.00	21.00
(64)	Gus Zernial (Script name.)	70.00	35.00	21.00

1972 Daily Juice Co.

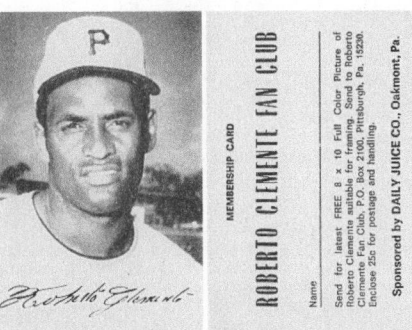

This one-card "set" was regionally issued to Roberto Clemente Fan Club members. Large numbers of the cards found their way into the hobby, including in uncut sheet form. The

cards feature a full-color front black-and-white back. The card measures the standard 2-1/2" in width but is somewhat longer, at 3-3/4". This unnumbered card remains about the least expensive baseball card that was issued during Clemente's lifetime.

	NM	E	VG
Uncut Sheet (30):	200.00	100.00	60.00
1 Roberto Clemente	15.00	7.50	4.50

1950s Dairy Council Curt Simmons Postcard

Issued by "The Dairy Council," probably locally, this black-and-white postcard features an action-pose photo of the star Phillies pitcher. There is a white facsimile autograph on front. Back of the 3-3/4" x 5-3/4" card has another facsimile autograph and the legend, "Dairy Council and the Philadelphia Phillies join me in wishing you good luck and good health."

	NM	E	VG
Curt Simmons	200.00	100.00	60.00

1976 Dairy Isle Discs

One of several regional sponsors of player disc sets in 1976 was the upstate New York area chain, Dairy Isle. The discs are 3-3/8" diameter with a black-and-white player portrait photo in the center of the baseball design. A line of red stars is above, while the left and right panels feature one of several bright colors. Produced by Michael Schecter Associates under license from the Major League Baseball Players Association, the player photos have had uniform and cap logos removed. Backs are printed in red and purple. The unnumbered checklist here is presented in alphabetical order.

	NM	E	VG
Complete Set (70):	90.00	45.00	27.00
Common Player:	2.00	1.00	.60
(1) Henry Aaron	20.00	10.00	6.00
(2) Johnny Bench	9.00	4.50	2.70
(3) Vida Blue	2.00	1.00	.60
(4) Larry Bowa	2.00	1.00	.60
(5) Lou Brock	8.00	4.00	2.50
(6) Jeff Burroughs	2.00	1.00	.60
(7) John Candelaria	2.00	1.00	.60
(8) Jose Cardenal	2.00	1.00	.60
(9) Rod Carew	8.00	4.00	2.50
(10) Steve Carlton	8.00	4.00	2.50
(11) Dave Cash	2.00	1.00	.60
(12) Cesar Cedeno	2.00	1.00	.60
(13) Ron Cey	2.00	1.00	.60
(14) Carlton Fisk	8.00	4.00	2.50
(15) Tito Fuentes	2.00	1.00	.60
(16) Steve Garvey	6.00	3.00	1.75
(17) Ken Griffey	2.00	1.00	.60
(18) Don Gullett	2.00	1.00	.60
(19) Willie Horton	2.00	1.00	.60
(20) Al Hrabosky	2.00	1.00	.60
(21) Catfish Hunter	8.00	4.00	2.50
(22) Reggie Jackson (A's)	12.00	6.00	3.50
(23) Randy Jones	2.00	1.00	.60
(24) Jim Kaat	2.00	1.00	.60
(25) Don Kessinger	2.00	1.00	.60
(26) Dave Kingman	2.00	1.00	.60
(27) Jerry Koosman	2.00	1.00	.60
(28) Mickey Lolich	2.00	1.00	.60

(29)	Greg Luzinski	2.00	1.00	.60
(30)	Fred Lynn	2.00	1.00	.60
(31)	Bill Madlock	2.00	1.00	.60
(32)	Carlos May (White Sox)	2.00	1.00	.60
(33)	John Mayberry	2.00	1.00	.60
(34)	Bake McBride	2.00	1.00	.60
(35)	Doc Medich	2.00	1.00	.60
(36)	Andy Messersmith	2.00	1.00	.60
(37)	Rick Monday	2.00	1.00	.60
(38)	John Montefusco	2.00	1.00	.60
(39)	Jerry Morales	2.00	1.00	.60
(40)	Joe Morgan	8.00	4.00	2.50
(41)	Thurman Munson	6.00	3.00	1.75
(42)	Bobby Murcer	2.00	1.00	.60
(43)	Al Oliver	2.00	1.00	.60
(44)	Jim Palmer	8.00	4.00	2.50
(45)	Dave Parker	2.00	1.00	.60
(46)	Tony Perez	8.00	4.00	2.50
(47)	Jerry Reuss	2.00	1.00	.60
(48)	Brooks Robinson	9.00	4.50	2.75
(49)	Frank Robinson	9.00	4.50	2.75
(50)	Steve Rogers	2.00	1.00	.60
(51)	Pete Rose	20.00	10.00	60.00
(52)	Nolan Ryan	40.00	20.00	12.00
(53)	Manny Sanguillen	2.00	1.00	.60
(54)	Mike Schmidt	12.00	6.00	3.50
(55)	Tom Seaver	9.00	4.50	2.75
(56)	Ted Simmons	2.00	1.00	.60
(57)	Reggie Smith	2.00	1.00	.60
(58)	Willie Stargell	8.00	4.00	2.50
(59)	Rusty Staub	2.50	1.25	.70
(60)	Rennie Stennett	2.00	1.00	.60
(61)	Don Sutton	8.00	4.00	2.50
(62)	Andy Thornton (Cubs)	2.00	1.00	.60
(63)	Luis Tiant	2.00	1.00	.60
(64)	Joe Torre	6.00	3.00	1.75
(65)	Mike Tyson	2.00	1.00	.60
(66)	Bob Watson	2.00	1.00	.60
(67)	Wilbur Wood	2.00	1.00	.60
(68)	Jimmy Wynn	2.00	1.00	.60
(69)	Carl Yastrzemski	9.00	4.50	2.75
(70)	Richie Zisk	2.00	1.00	.60

1977 Dairy Isle Discs

Virtually identical in format to the 1976 issue (substituting red and blue for the back ad in 1977, instead of the previous year's red and purple), these 3-3/8" diameter player discs were given away at Dairy Isle outlets. Discs once again feature black-and-white player portrait photos in the center of a baseball design. The left and right panels are in one of several bright colors. Licensed by the players' association through Mike Schechter Associates, the player photos carry no uniform logos. The unnumbered discs are checklisted here alphabetically.

		NM	E	VG
Complete Set (70):		60.00	30.00	18.00
Common Player:		2.00	1.00	.60
(1)	Sal Bando	2.00	1.00	.60
(2)	Buddy Bell	2.00	1.00	.60
(3)	Johnny Bench	9.00	4.50	2.75
(4)	Larry Bowa	2.00	1.00	.60
(5)	Steve Braun	2.00	1.00	.60
(6)	George Brett	20.00	10.00	6.00
(7)	Lou Brock	7.00	3.50	2.00
(8)	Jeff Burroughs	2.00	1.00	.60
(9)	Bert Campaneris	2.00	1.00	.60
(10)	John Candelaria	2.00	1.00	.60
(11)	Jose Cardenal	2.00	1.00	.60
(12)	Rod Carew	14.00	7.00	4.25
(13)	Steve Carlton	7.50	3.50	2.00
(14)	Dave Cash	2.00	1.00	.60
(15)	Cesar Cedeno	2.00	1.00	.60
(16)	Ron Cey	2.00	1.00	.60
(17)	Dave Concepcion	2.00	1.00	.60
(18)	Dennis Eckersley	7.00	3.50	2.00
(19)	Mark Fidrych	2.00	1.00	.60
(20)	Rollie Fingers	7.00	3.50	2.00
(21)	Carlton Fisk	7.00	3.50	2.00
(22)	George Foster	2.00	1.00	.60
(23)	Wayne Garland	2.00	1.00	.60
(24)	Ralph Garr	2.00	1.00	.60
(25)	Steve Garvey	7.00	3.50	2.00
(26)	Cesar Geronimo	2.00	1.00	.60
(27)	Bobby Grich	2.00	1.00	.60

(28)	Ken Griffey	2.00	1.00	.60
(29)	Don Gullett	2.00	1.00	.60
(30)	Mike Hargrove	2.00	1.00	.60
(31)	Al Hrabosky	2.00	1.00	.60
(32)	Jim Hunter	7.00	3.50	2.00
(33)	Reggie Jackson	9.00	4.50	2.50
(34)	Randy Jones	1.00	.50	.30
(35)	Dave Kingman	1.00	.50	.30
(36)	Jerry Koosman	1.00	.50	.30
(37)	Dave LaRoche	1.00	.50	.30
(38)	Greg Luzinski	1.00	.50	.30
(39)	Fred Lynn	1.00	.50	.30
(40)	Bill Madlock	1.00	.50	.30
(41)	Rick Manning	1.00	.50	.30
(42)	Jon Matlack	1.00	.50	.30
(43)	John Mayberry	1.00	.50	.30
(44)	Hal McRae	1.00	.50	.30
(45)	Andy Messersmith	2.00	1.00	.60
(46)	Rick Monday	2.00	1.00	.60
(47)	John Montefusco	2.00	1.00	.60
(48)	Joe Morgan	7.00	3.50	2.00
(49)	Thurman Munson	5.00	2.50	1.50
(50)	Bobby Murcer	2.00	1.00	.60
(51)	Bill North	2.00	1.00	.60
(52)	Jim Palmer	7.00	3.50	2.00
(53)	Tony Perez	7.00	3.50	2.00
(54)	Jerry Reuss	2.00	1.00	.60
(55)	Brooks Robinson	9.00	4.50	2.75
(56)	Pete Rose	10.00	5.00	3.00
(57)	Joe Rudi	1.00	.50	.30
(58)	Nolan Ryan	15.00	7.50	4.50
(59)	Manny Sanguillen	1.00	.50	.30
(60)	Mike Schmidt	6.00	3.00	1.75
(61)	Tom Seaver	4.50	2.25	1.25
(62)	Bill Singer	1.00	.50	.30
(63)	Willie Stargell	7.00	3.50	2.00
(64)	Rusty Staub	2.50	1.25	.70
(65)	Luis Tiant	2.00	1.00	.60
(66)	Bob Watson	2.00	1.00	.60
(67)	Butch Wynegar	2.00	1.00	.60
(68)	Carl Yastrzemski	9.00	4.50	2.75
(69)	Robin Yount	7.00	3.50	2.00
(70)	Richie Zisk	2.00	1.00	.60

1950s Dairylea Mickey Mantle Decal

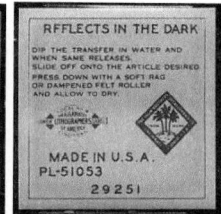

There is currently no way to specify the year of release for this decal, though a release date in the late 1950s seems like a reasonable assumption. About 2-1/4" square, these decals feature glow-in-the-dark ink in red and green on front. The back is printed in blue on an orange background. There seems to have been a small hoard of these decals discovered circa 2009. Dairylea was a milk producers' cooperative in Orange County, just north and west of New York City.

	NM	EX	VG
Mickey Mantle	150.00	90.00	45.00

1956 Dairy Queen Stars Statues

This set is identical in composition and manufacture to the carded figures sold as Big League Stars (see listing). The DQ versions of the statues are white, while the Big League versions are bronze colored. The statues measure about 3" tall and were evidently sold or given away with a purchase at the chain of ice cream shops.

	NM	E	VG
Complete Set (18):	1,100	550.00	350.00
Common Player:	40.00	20.00	12.00

(1)	John Antonelli	40.00	20.00	12.00
(2)	Bob Avila	40.00	20.00	12.00
(3)	Yogi Berra	100.00	50.00	30.00
(4)	Roy Campanella	100.00	50.00	30.00
(5)	Larry Doby	65.00	32.50	20.00
(6)	Del Ennis	40.00	20.00	12.00
(7)	Jim Gilliam	40.00	20.00	12.00
(8)	Gil Hodges	75.00	37.50	22.50
(9)	Harvey Kuenn	40.00	20.00	12.00
(10)	Bob Lemon	50.00	25.00	15.00
(11)	Mickey Mantle	325.00	160.00	100.00
(12)	Ed Mathews	75.00	37.50	22.50
(13)	Minnie Minoso	40.00	20.00	12.00
(14)	Stan Musial	160.00	80.00	50.00
(15)	Pee Wee Reese	100.00	50.00	30.00
(16)	Al Rosen	40.00	20.00	12.00
(17)	Duke Snider	100.00	50.00	30.00
(18)	Mickey Vernon	40.00	20.00	12.00

1954 Dan-Dee Potato Chips

Issued in bags of potato chips, the cards in this 29-card set are commonly found with grease stains despite their waxed surface. The unnumbered cards, which measure 2-1/2" x 3-5/8", feature color pictures. Backs have player statistical and biographical information. The set consists mostly of players from the Indians and Pirates. Photos of the Yankees players were also used for the Briggs Meats and Stahl-Meyer Franks sets.

	NM	E	VG
Complete Set (29):	8,750	4,400	2,600
Common Player:	140.00	70.00	40.00
(1) Bob Avila	140.00	70.00	40.00
(2) Hank Bauer	170.00	85.00	50.00
(3) Walker Cooper (SP)	475.00	250.00	150.00
(4) Larry Doby	175.00	90.00	50.00
(5) Luke Easter	160.00	80.00	50.00
(6) Bob Feller	450.00	225.00	140.00
(7) Bob Friend	140.00	70.00	40.00
(8) Mike Garcia	140.00	70.00	40.00
(9) Sid Gordon	140.00	70.00	40.00
(10) Jim Hegan	140.00	70.00	40.00
(11) Gil Hodges	575.00	300.00	175.00
(12) Art Houtteman	140.00	70.00	40.00
(13) Monte Irvin	175.00	90.00	50.00
(14) Paul LaPalm (LaPalme)	140.00	70.00	40.00
(15) Bob Lemon	175.00	90.00	50.00
(16) Al Lopez	175.00	90.00	50.00
(17) Mickey Mantle	3,000	1,500	900.00
(18) Dale Mitchell	140.00	70.00	40.00
(19) Phil Rizzuto	320.00	160.00	100.00
(20) Curtis Roberts	140.00	70.00	40.00
(21) Al Rosen	160.00	80.00	50.00
(22) Red Schoendienst	175.00	90.00	50.00
(23) Paul Smith (SP)	500.00	250.00	150.00
(24) Duke Snider	600.00	300.00	180.00
(25) George Strickland	140.00	70.00	40.00
(26) Max Surkont	140.00	70.00	40.00
(27) Frank Thomas (SP)	300.00	150.00	90.00
(28) Wally Westlake	140.00	70.00	40.00
(29) Early Wynn	175.00	90.00	50.00

1977 Tom Daniels Burleigh Grimes

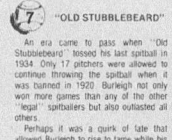

The career of Hall of Fame spitballer Burleigh Grimes is traced in this collectors' issue. The 2-1/2" x 3-1/2" cards have black-and-white photos from Grimes' collection, bordered in bright blue. A card title is in black in the bottom border. Backs are printed in black and blue on white and have a description of the front photo. One card in each set is authentically autographed by Grimes. Price at issue was $3.50; uncut sheets were also available.

	NM	E	VG
Complete Set (16):	10.00	5.00	3.00
Common Card:	1.00	.50	.30
1 Dodger Manager 1937-38	1.00	.50	.30
2 "Lord Burleigh"	1.00	.50	.30
3 Last Spitballers	1.00	.50	.30
4 Grimes, Hornsby, McGraw, Roush	1.00	.50	.30
5 Winning Combination	1.00	.50	.30
6 World Champion	1.00	.50	.30
7 "Old Stubblebeard"	1.00	.50	.30
8 Grimes Meets McCarthy	1.00	.50	.30
9 Dodger Greats	1.00	.50	.30
10 "The Babe"	2.00	1.00	.60
11 Dodger Strategists	1.00	.50	.30
12 Bender and Grimes	1.00	.50	.30
13 Number '270'	1.00	.50	.30
14 The Origin	1.00	.50	.30
15 1964 HoF Inductees	1.00	.50	.30
16 "Lord Burleigh" 1977	1.00	.50	.30

1910 Darby Chocolates (E271)

The 1910 Darby Chocolates cards are among the rarest of all candy cards. The cards were printed on boxes of "Pennant" Chocolates, two players per box - one each on front and back. The cards feature black-and-white player action photos outlined with a thick dark shadow. The boxes are accented with orange or green graphics. Most of the known examples of this set were not found until 1982 when a group in fire-damaged condition was inadvertently subjected to restoration. Values shown here are for cards in untampered-with state of preservation. Values for restored cards must be adjusted significantly downward. This checklist may or may not be complete.

	NM	E	VG
Common Player:	12,000	6,000	3,500
(1) Jimmy Archer	12,000	6,000	3,600
(2) Chief Bender	16,000	8,000	4,800
(3) Bob Bescher	12,000	6,000	3,600
(4) Roger Bresnahan	16,000	8,000	4,800
(5) Al Bridwell	12,000	6,000	3,600
(6) Mordicai Brown (Mordecai)	16,000	8,000	4,800
(7) "Eddie" Cicotte	13,500	6,750	4,000
(8) Fred Clark (Clarke)	12,000	6,000	3,600
(9) Ty. Cobb (Batting)	30,000	15,000	9,000
(10) "Ty" Cobb (Fielding)	30,000	15,000	9,000
(11) King Cole	12,000	6,000	3,600
(12) E. Collins	16,000	8,000	4,800
(13) Wid Conroy	12,000	6,000	3,600
(14) "Sam" Crawford	16,000	8,000	4,800
(15) Bill Dahlin (Dahlen)	12,000	6,000	3,600
(16) Bill Donovan	12,000	6,000	3,600
(17) "Pat" Dougherty	12,000	6,000	3,600
(18) Kid Elberfeld	12,000	6,000	3,600
(19) "Johnny" Evers	16,000	8,000	4,800
(20) Charlie Herzog	12,000	6,000	3,600
(21) Hughie Jennings	16,000	8,000	4,800
(22) Walter Johnson	20,000	10,000	6,000
(23) Ed Konetchy	12,000	6,000	3,600
(24) Tommy Leach	12,000	6,000	3,600
(25) Fred Luderous (Luderus)	12,000	6,000	3,600
(26) "Mugsy" McGraw	16,000	8,000	4,800
(27) "Mike" Mowery (Mowrey)	12,000	6,000	3,600
(28) Jack Powell	12,000	6,000	3,600
(29) Slim Sallee	12,000	6,000	3,600
(30) James Scheckard (Sheckard)	12,000	6,000	3,600
(31) Walter Snodgrass	12,000	6,000	3,600
(32) "Tris" Speaker	17,500	8,750	5,250
(33) Charlie Suggs	12,000	6,000	3,600
(34) Fred Tenney	12,000	6,000	3,600
(35) "Jim" Vaughn	12,000	6,000	3,600
(36) "Hans" Wagner	40,000	13,750	8,250

1911 Harry Davis Day Postcard

HARRY DAVIS DAY
SHIBE PARK
WEDNESDAY, MAY 31st

In his final season with the Philadelphia Athletics, the star first baseman of the famed $100,000 Infield was honored with a "day" at Shibe Park. This standard-size black-and-white postcard was created to remind fans to attend the event. A pre-printed message on back over the facsimile signature of Connie Mack urges fans to "show our appreciation of what Captain Davis has done for baseball and the city of his birth."

	NM	E	VG
Harry Davis	750.00	375.00	225.00

1970 Dayton Daily News Bubble-Gumless Cards

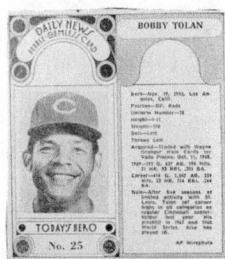

These "cards" are actually newspaper clippings which were issued on a daily basis during the baseball season by the Ohio newspaper. Labeled "Today's Hero," the clippings measure approximately 3-1/2" x 4" and are printed in black-and-white. At left is a portrait photo of the player, at right are personal data, stats and career highlights. At least two All-star versions of these paper cards were issued. They differ from the regular format in their use of red background printing and an "All-Star" designation in place of a card number. At least two All-star versions of these paper cards were issued. They differ from the regular format in their use of red background printing and an "All-Star" designation in place of a card number.

	NM	E	VG
Complete Set (160):	2,000	1,000	600.00
Common Player:	9.00	4.50	2.75
1 Pete Rose	40.00	20.00	12.00
2 Johnny Bench	20.00	10.00	6.00
3 Maury Wills	12.00	6.00	3.50
4 Harmon Killebrew	20.00	10.00	6.00
5 Frank Robinson	20.00	10.00	6.00
6 Willie Mays	60.00	30.00	18.00
7 Hank Aaron	60.00	30.00	18.00
8 Tom Seaver	20.00	10.00	6.00
9 Sam McDowell	9.00	4.50	2.75
10 Rico Petrocelli	9.00	4.50	2.75
11a Tony Perez (Dark cap.)	20.00	10.00	6.00
11b Tony Perez (Light cap.)	20.00	10.00	6.00
12 Hoyt Wilhelm	15.00	7.50	4.50
13 Alex Johnson	9.00	4.50	2.75
14 Gary Nolan	9.00	4.50	2.75
15 Al Kaline	25.00	12.50	7.50
16 Bob Gibson	15.00	7.50	4.50
17 Larry Dierker	9.00	4.50	2.75
18 Ernie Banks	30.00	15.00	9.00
19 Lee May	9.00	4.50	2.75
20 Claude Osteen	9.00	4.50	2.75
21 Tony Horton	9.00	4.50	2.75
22 Mack Jones	9.00	4.50	2.75
23 Wally Bunker	9.00	4.50	2.75
24 Bill Hands	9.00	4.50	2.75

25 Bobby Tolan	9.00	4.50	2.75
26 Jim Wynn	9.00	4.50	2.75
27 Tom Haller	9.00	4.50	2.75
28 Carl Yastrzemski	25.00	12.50	7.50
29 Jim Merritt	9.00	4.50	2.75
30 Tony Oliva	12.00	6.00	3.50
31 Reggie Jackson	40.00	20.00	12.00
32 Bob Clemente	90.00	45.00	27.00
33 Tommy Helms	9.00	4.50	2.75
34 Boog Powell	12.00	6.00	3.50
35 Mickey Lolich	9.00	4.50	2.75
36 Frank Howard	12.00	6.00	3.50
37 Jim McGlothlin	9.00	4.50	2.75
38 Rusty Staub	12.00	6.00	3.50
39 Mel Stottlemyre	9.00	4.50	2.75
40 Rico Carty	9.00	4.50	2.75
41 Nate Colbert	9.00	4.50	2.75
42 Wayne Granger	9.00	4.50	2.75
43 Mike Hegan	9.00	4.50	2.75
44 Jerry Koosman	9.00	4.50	2.75
45 Jim Perry	9.00	4.50	2.75
46 Pat Corrales	9.00	4.50	2.75
47 Dick Bosman	9.00	4.50	2.75
48 Bert Campaneris	9.00	4.50	2.75
49 Larry Hisle	9.00	4.50	2.75
50 Bernie Carbo	9.00	4.50	2.75
51 Wilbur Wood	9.00	4.50	2.75
52 Dave McNally	9.00	4.50	2.75
53 Andy Messersmith	9.00	4.50	2.75
54 Jimmy Stewart	9.00	4.50	2.75
55 Luis Aparicio	15.00	7.50	4.50
56 Mike Cuellar	9.00	4.50	2.75
57 Bill Grabarkewitz	9.00	4.50	2.75
58 Dick Dietz	9.00	4.50	2.75
59 Dave Concepcion	9.00	4.50	2.75
60 Gary Gentry	9.00	4.50	2.75
61 Don Money	9.00	4.50	2.75
62 Rod Carew	20.00	10.00	6.00
63 Denis Menke	9.00	4.50	2.75
64 Hal McRae	9.00	4.50	2.75
65 Felipe Alou	9.00	4.50	2.75
66 Richie Hebner	9.00	4.50	2.75
67 Don Sutton	15.00	7.50	4.50
68 Wayne Simpson	9.00	4.50	2.75
69 Art Shamsky	9.00	4.50	2.75
70 Luis Tiant	9.00	4.50	2.75
71 Clay Carroll	9.00	4.50	2.75
72 Jim Hickman	9.00	4.50	2.75
73 Clarence Gaston	9.00	4.50	2.75
74 Angel Bravo	9.00	4.50	2.75
75 Jim Hunter	15.00	7.50	4.50
76 Lou Piniella	10.00	5.00	3.00
77 Jim Bunning	15.00	7.50	4.50
78 Don Gullett	9.00	4.50	2.75
79 Dan Cater	9.00	4.50	2.75
80 Richie Allen	13.50	6.75	4.00
81 Jim Bouton	10.00	5.00	3.00
82 Jim Palmer	15.00	7.50	4.50
83 Woody Woodward	9.00	4.50	2.75
84 Tom Agee	9.00	4.50	2.75
85 Carlos May	9.00	4.50	2.75
86 Ray Washburn	9.00	4.50	2.75
87 Denny McLain	10.00	5.00	3.00
88 Lou Brock	15.00	7.50	4.50
89 Ken Henderson	9.00	4.50	2.75
90 Roy White	9.00	4.50	2.75
91 Chris Cannizzaro	9.00	4.50	2.75
92 Willie Horton	9.00	4.50	2.75
93 Jose Cardenal	9.00	4.50	2.75
94 Jim Fregosi	9.00	4.50	2.75
95 Richie Hebner	9.00	4.50	2.75
96 Tony Conigliaro	10.00	5.00	3.00
97 Tony Cloninger	9.00	4.50	2.75
98 Mike Epstein	9.00	4.50	2.75
99 Ty Cline	9.00	4.50	2.75
100 Tommy Harper	9.00	4.50	2.75
101 Jose Azcue	9.00	4.50	2.75
102a Glenn Beckert	9.00	4.50	2.75
102b Ray Fosse	9.00	4.50	2.75
103 Glenn Beckert	9.00	4.50	2.75
104 Gerry Moses	9.00	4.50	2.75
105 Bud Harrelson	9.00	4.50	2.75
106 Joe Torre	13.50	6.75	4.00
107 Dave Johnson	9.00	4.50	2.75
108 Don Kessinger	9.00	4.50	2.75
109 Bill Freehan	9.00	4.50	2.75
110 Sandy Alomar	9.00	4.50	2.75
111 Matty Alou	9.00	4.50	2.75
112 Joe Morgan	15.00	7.50	4.50
113 John Odom	9.00	4.50	2.75
114 Amos Otis	9.00	4.50	2.75
115 Jay Johnstone	9.00	4.50	2.75
116 Ron Perranoski	9.00	4.50	2.75
117 Manny Mota	9.00	4.50	2.75
118 Billy Conigliaro	9.00	4.50	2.75
119 Leo Cardenas	9.00	4.50	2.75
120 Rich Reese	9.00	4.50	2.75
121 Ron Santo	12.00	6.00	3.50

122	Gene Michael	9.00	4.50	2.75
123	Milt Pappas	9.00	4.50	2.75
124	Joe Pepitone	10.00	5.00	3.00
125	Jose Cardenal	9.00	4.50	2.75
126	Jim Northrup	9.00	4.50	2.75
127	Wes Parker	9.00	4.50	2.75
128	Fritz Peterson	9.00	4.50	2.75
129	Phil Regan	9.00	4.50	2.75
130	John Callison	9.00	4.50	2.75
131	Cookie Rojas	9.00	4.50	2.75
132	Claude Raymond	9.00	4.50	2.75
133	Darrel Chaney	9.00	4.50	2.75
134	Gary Peters	9.00	4.50	2.75
135	Del Unser	9.00	4.50	2.75
136	Joey Foy	9.00	4.50	2.75
137	Luke Walker	9.00	4.50	2.75
138	Bill Mazeroski	15.00	7.50	4.50
139	Tony Taylor	9.00	4.50	2.75
140	Leron Lee	9.00	4.50	2.75
141	Jesus Alou	9.00	4.50	2.75
142	Donn Clendenon	9.00	4.50	2.75
143	Merv Rettenmund	9.00	4.50	2.75
144	Bob Moose	9.00	4.50	2.75
145	Jim Kaat	10.00	5.00	3.00
146	Randy Hundley	9.00	4.50	2.75
147	Jim McAndrew	9.00	4.50	2.75
148	Manny Sanguillen	9.00	4.50	2.75
149	Bob Allison	9.00	4.50	2.75
150	Jim Maloney	9.00	4.50	2.75
151	Don Buford	9.00	4.50	2.75
152	Gene Alley	9.00	4.50	2.75
153	Cesar Tovar	9.00	4.50	2.75
154	Brooks Robinson	20.00	10.00	6.00
155	Milt Wilcox	9.00	4.50	2.75
156	Willie Stargell	20.00	10.00	6.00
157	Paul Blair	9.00	4.50	2.75
158	Andy Etchebarren	9.00	4.50	2.75
159	Mark Belanger	9.00	4.50	2.75
160	Elrod Hendricks	9.00	4.50	2.75
	All-Star Johnny Bench	30.00	15.00	9.00
	All-Star Tony Perez	25.00	12.50	7.50

1938 Dizzy Dean's Service Station

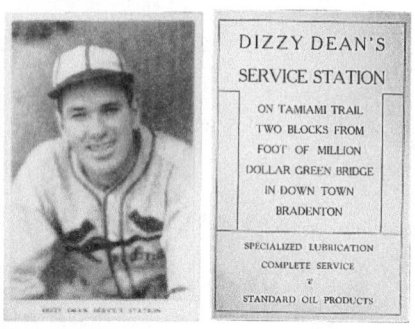

The date of issue of this one-card set is only a guess. The 4" x 6" black-and-white card advertises Dean's service station in Florida.

	NM	E	VG
Dizzy Dean	350.00	175.00	100.00

1973 Dean's Photo Service San Diego Padres

A true rookie-year issue for Dave Winfield is included in this set of 5-1/2" x 8-1/2" black-and-white, blank-backed player photos sponsored by Dean's Photo Service and given away by the team in five six-card series at various home games. Pictures have posed player portraits surrounded by a white border. Beneath are the name and position, with team and sponsor logos at bottom. The set is checklisted here alphabetically.

		NM	E	VG
		80.00	40.00	24.00
Complete Set (31):		80.00	40.00	24.00
Common Player:		4.00	2.00	1.25
(1)	Steve Arlin	4.00	2.00	1.25
(2)	Mike Caldwell	4.00	2.00	1.25
(3)	Dave Campbell	4.00	2.00	1.25
(4)	Nate Colbert	4.00	2.00	1.25
(5)	Mike Corkins	4.00	2.00	1.25
(6)	Pat Corrales	4.00	2.00	1.25
(7)	Jim Davenport	4.00	2.00	1.25
(8)	Dave Garcia	4.00	2.00	1.25
(9)	Clarence Gaston	4.00	2.00	1.25
(10)	Bill Greif	4.00	2.00	1.25
(11)	John Grubb	4.00	2.00	1.25
(12)	Enzo Hernandez	4.00	2.00	1.25
(13)	Randy Jones	4.00	2.00	1.25
(14)	Fred Kendall	4.00	2.00	1.25
(15)	Clay Kirby	4.00	2.00	1.25
(16)	Leron Lee	4.00	2.00	1.25
(17)	Dave Marshall	4.00	2.00	1.25
(18)	Don Mason	4.00	2.00	1.25
(19)	Jerry Morales	4.00	2.00	1.25
(20)	Ivan Murrell	4.00	2.00	1.25
(21)	Fred Norman	4.00	2.00	1.25
(22)	Johnny Podres	4.00	2.00	1.25
(23)	Dave Roberts	4.00	2.00	1.25
(24)	Vicente Romo	4.00	2.00	1.25
(25)	Gary Ross	4.00	2.00	1.25
(26)	Bob Skinner	4.00	2.00	1.25
(27)	Derrel Thomas	4.00	2.00	1.25
(28)	Rich Troedson	4.00	2.00	1.25
(29)	Whitey Wietelmann	4.00	2.00	1.25
(30)	Dave Winfield	25.00	12.50	7.50
(31)	Don Zimmer	5.00	2.50	1.50

1974 Dean's Photo Service San Diego Padres

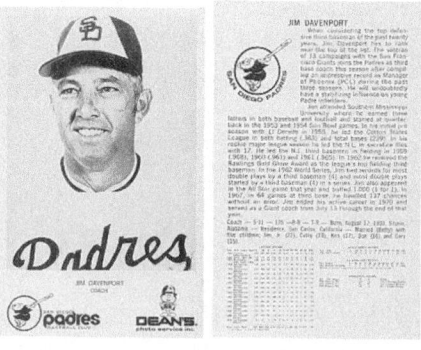

This issue shares the same basic format as the years which preceded it and succeeded it. Fronts of the 5-1/2" x 8-1/2" cards have a large player portrait or pose at top, with the player's name and position below. In the wide white border at bottom are the team and sponsor's logos. Backs, for the first time, have a lengthy career summary, personal data and full professional stats. All printing is in black-and-white. The unnumbered cards are checklisted here alphabetically.

		NM	E	VG
Complete Set (30):		70.00	35.00	21.00
Common Player:		4.00	2.00	1.25
(1)	Matty Alou	4.00	2.00	1.25
(2)	Bob Barton	4.00	2.00	1.25
(3)	Glenn Beckert	4.00	2.00	1.25
(4)	Jack Bloomfield	4.00	2.00	1.25
(5)	Nate Colbert	4.00	2.00	1.25
(6)	Mike Corkins	4.00	2.00	1.25
(7)	Jim Davenport	4.00	2.00	1.25
(8)	Dave Freisleben	4.00	2.00	1.25
(9)	Cito Gaston	4.00	2.00	1.25
(10)	Bill Greif	4.00	2.00	1.25
(11)	Johnny Grubb	4.00	2.00	1.25
(12)	Larry Hardy	4.00	2.00	1.25
(13)	Enzo Hernandez	4.00	2.00	1.25
(14)	Dave Hilton	4.00	2.00	1.25
(15)	Randy Jones	4.00	2.00	1.25
(16)	Fred Kendall	4.00	2.00	1.25
(17)	Gene Locklear	4.00	2.00	1.25
(18)	Willie McCovey	10.00	5.00	3.00
(19)	John McNamara	4.00	2.00	1.25
(20)	Rich Morales	4.00	2.00	1.25
(21)	Bill Posedel	4.00	2.00	1.25
(22)	Dave Roberts	4.00	2.00	1.25
(23)	Vicente Romo	4.00	2.00	1.25
(24)	Dan Spillner	4.00	2.00	1.25
(25)	Bob Tolan	4.00	2.00	1.25
(26)	Derrel Thomas	4.00	2.00	1.25
(27)	Rich Troedson	4.00	2.00	1.25
(28)	Whitey Wietelmann	4.00	2.00	1.25
(29)	Bernie Williams	4.00	2.00	1.25
(30)	Dave Winfield	15.00	7.50	4.50

1975 Dean's Photo Service San Diego Padres

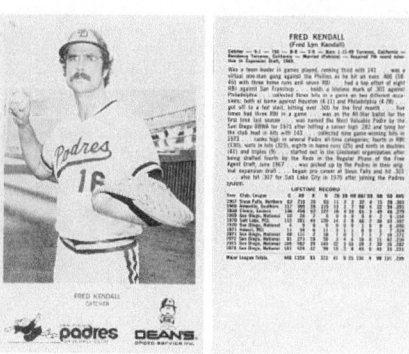

Player biographical data and stats continued on the backs of the cards in the 1975 series sponsored by Dean's. Once again the black-and-white pictures were in 5-1/2" x 8-1/2" format. Fronts have the player photo at top, with his name and position beneath. At bottom are the team and sponsor logos. The Padres logo consists of a cartoon character robed monk in various baseball poses. The pictures were given away at autograph nights during the season. The unnumbered photos are checklisted here in alphabetical order.

		NM	E	VG
Complete Set (30):		60.00	30.00	18.00
Common Player:		4.00	2.00	1.25
(1)	Jim Davenport	4.00	2.00	1.25
(2)	Bob Davis	4.00	2.00	1.25
(3)	Rich Folkers	4.00	2.00	1.25
(4)	Alan Foster	4.00	2.00	1.25
(5)	Dave Freisleben	4.00	2.00	1.25
(6)	Danny Frisella	4.00	2.00	1.25
(7)	Tito Fuentes	4.00	2.00	1.25
(8)	Bill Greif	4.00	2.00	1.25
(9)	Johnny Grubb	4.00	2.00	1.25
(10)	Enzo Hernandez	4.00	2.00	1.25
(11)	Randy Hundley (Blank back.)	4.00	2.00	1.25
(12)	Mike Ivie	4.00	2.00	1.25
(13)	Jerry Johnson	4.00	2.00	1.25
(14)	Randy Jones	4.00	2.00	1.25
(15)	Fred Kendall	4.00	2.00	1.25
(16)	Ted Kubiak	4.00	2.00	1.25
(17)	Gene Locklear	4.00	2.00	1.25
(18)	Willie McCovey	10.00	5.00	3.00
(19)	Joe McIntosh	4.00	2.00	1.25
(20)	John McNamara	4.00	2.00	1.25
(21)	Tom Morgan	4.00	2.00	1.25
(22)	Dick Sharon	4.00	2.00	1.25
(23)	Dick Sisler	4.00	2.00	1.25
(24)	Dan Spillner	4.00	2.00	1.25
(25)	Brent Strom	4.00	2.00	1.25
(26)	Bobby Tolan	4.00	2.00	1.25
(27)	Dave Tomlin	4.00	2.00	1.25
(28)	Hector Torres (Blank back.)	4.00	2.00	1.25
(29)	Whitey Wietelmann	4.00	2.00	1.25
(30)	Dave Winfield	15.00	7.50	4.50

1976 Dean's Photo Service San Diego Padres

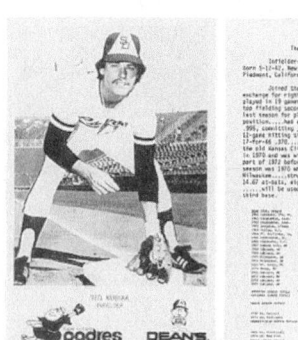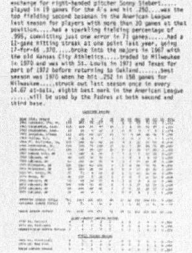

The last of four black-and-white team sets which were sponsored by Dean's was issued in 1976. The format was little different than previous years. Cards are 5-1/2" x 8-1/2" black-and-white. Fronts have a player portrait or pose surrounded by a white border. At bottom front are team and sponsor logos. Backs have personal data, a career summary and complete professional stats. The unnumbered cards are checklisted in alphabetical order.

		NM	E	VG
	Complete Set (30):	60.00	30.00	18.00
	Common Player:	4.00	2.00	1.25
(1)	Joe Amalfitano	4.00	2.00	1.25
(2)	Roger Craig	4.00	2.00	1.25
(3)	Bob Davis	4.00	2.00	1.25
(4)	Willie Davis	4.00	2.00	1.25
(5)	Rich Folkers	4.00	2.00	1.25
(6)	Alan Foster	4.00	2.00	1.25
(7)	Dave Freisleben	4.00	2.00	1.25
(8)	Tito Fuentes	4.00	2.00	1.25
(9)	John Grubb	4.00	2.00	1.25
(10)	Enzo Hernandez	4.00	2.00	1.25
(11)	Mike Ivie	4.00	2.00	1.25
(12)	Jerry Johnson	4.00	2.00	1.25
(13)	Randy Jones	4.00	2.00	1.25
(14)	Fred Kendall	4.00	2.00	1.25
(15)	Ted Kubiak	4.00	2.00	1.25
(16)	Willie McCovey	10.00	5.00	3.00
(17)	John McNamara	4.00	2.00	1.25
(18)	Luis Melendez	4.00	2.00	1.25
(19)	Butch Metzger	4.00	2.00	1.25
(20)	Doug Rader	4.00	2.00	1.25
(21)	Merv Rettenmund	4.00	2.00	1.25
(22)	Ken Reynolds	4.00	2.00	1.25
(23)	Dick Sisler	4.00	2.00	1.25
(24)	Dan Spillner	4.00	2.00	1.25
(25)	Brent Strom	4.00	2.00	1.25
(26)	Dave Tomlin	4.00	2.00	1.25
(27)	Hector Torres	4.00	2.00	1.25
(28)	Jerry Turner	4.00	2.00	1.25
(29)	Whitey Wietelmann	4.00	2.00	1.25
(30)	Dave Winfield	15.00	7.50	4.50

1978 Dearborn Show

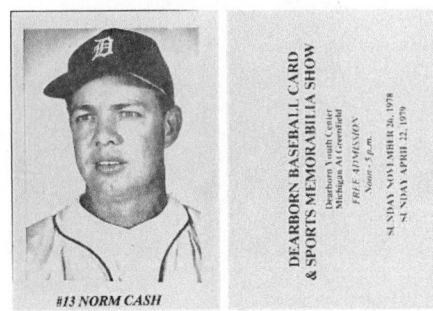

#13 NORM CASH

DEARBORN BASEBALL CARD & SPORTS MEMORABILIA SHOW

Former members of the Detroit Tigers, some of whom were scheduled to appear as autograph guests, are featured in this collectors' issue produced in conjunction with the 1978 Dearborn Baseball Card & Sports Memorabilia Show. The 2-5/8" x 3-5/8" cards have black-and-white player photos on front with the player name and card number in the white border at bottom. Backs, also in black-and-white, advertise the fall, 1978, and spring, 1979 shows.

		NM	E	VG
	Complete Set (18):	60.00	30.00	18.00
	Common Player:	4.00	2.00	1.25
1	Rocky Colavito	15.00	7.50	4.50
2	Ervin Fox	4.00	2.00	1.25
3	Lynwood Rowe	4.00	2.00	1.25
4	Gerald Walker	4.00	2.00	1.25
5	Leon Goslin	4.00	2.00	1.25
6	Harvey Kuenn	6.00	3.00	1.75
7	Frank Howard	6.00	3.00	1.75
8	Woodie Fryman	4.00	2.00	1.25
9	Don Wert	4.00	2.00	1.25
10	Jim Perry	4.00	2.00	1.25
11	Mayo Smith	4.00	2.00	1.25
12	Al Kaline	20.00	10.00	6.00
13	Norm Cash	12.00	6.00	3.50
14	Mickey Cochrane	9.00	4.50	2.75
15	Fred Marberry	4.00	2.00	1.25
16	Bill Freehan	6.00	3.00	1.75
17	Charlie Gehringer	9.00	4.50	2.75
18	Jim Northrup	4.00	2.00	1.25

1971 Dell Today's Team Stamps

This issue was produced as a series of individual team (plus one All-Star) albums. The 8-1/2" x 10-7/8" booklets offer team and league histories and stats, photos of all-time team stars and two pages of 12 player stamps each. Each stamp is 1-7/8" x 2-15/16" and has a posed color photo and black facsimile autograph on front. Backs have the player name, biographical details and a few career highlights, along with an underprint of the team logo. The stamps are perforated for easy seperation, though there are no spaces in the 12-page album for their housing once removed from the sheet. The team albums were sold individually (39 cents) as well

as in six-team divisional sets ($2). The checklist is arranged alphabetically by team within league; individual stamps are unnumbered.

JACK DiLAURO

Pitcher — Bats right and left, throws right. Born 1943. Height 6-2. Weight 185. Relieved 42 times in 1970. Has good breaking ball and control. Good fielding pitcher who demonstrated ability to win three straight years in Triple-A ball. Originally signed by Tigers.

		NM	E	VG
	Complete Set, Albums (25):	225.00	110.00	65.00
	Complete Set, Stamps (600):	175.00	90.00	50.00
	Common Player:	1.00	.50	.30
	Complete All-Star Album:	20.00	10.00	6.00
(1)	Hank Aaron	7.50	3.75	2.25
(2)	Luis Aparicio	2.50	1.25	.70
(3)	Ernie Banks	5.00	2.50	1.50
(4)	Johnny Bench	3.00	1.50	.90
(5)	Rico Carty	1.00	.50	.30
(6)	Roberto Clemente	10.00	5.00	3.00
(7)	Bob Gibson	2.50	1.25	.70
(8)	Willie Horton	1.00	.50	.30
(9)	Frank Howard	1.50	.70	.45
(10)	Reggie Jackson	6.00	3.00	1.75
(11)	Fergie Jenkins	1.50	.70	.45
(12)	Alex Johnson	1.00	.50	.30
(13)	Al Kaline	3.00	1.50	.90
(14)	Harmon Killebrew	3.00	1.50	.90
(15)	Willie Mays	7.50	3.75	2.25
(16)	Sam McDowell	1.00	.50	.30
(17)	Denny McLain	1.50	.70	.45
(18)	Boog Powell	1.50	.70	.45
(19)	Brooks Robinson	3.00	1.50	.90
(20)	Frank Robinson	3.00	1.50	.90
(21)	Pete Rose	7.50	3.75	2.25
(22)	Tom Seaver	3.00	1.50	.90
(23)	Rusty Staub	1.50	.70	.45
(24)	Carl Yastrzemski	3.00	1.50	.90
	Complete Atlanta Braves Album:	15.00	7.50	4.50
(1)	Hank Aaron	7.50	3.75	2.25
(2)	Tommie Aaron	1.00	.50	.30
(3)	Hank Allen	1.00	.50	.30
(4)	Clete Boyer	1.50	.70	.45
(5)	Oscar Brown	1.00	.50	.30
(6)	Rico Carty	1.00	.50	.30
(7)	Orlando Cepeda	2.50	1.25	.70
(8)	Bob Didier	1.00	.50	.30
(9)	Ralph Garr	1.00	.50	.30
(10)	Gil Garrido	1.00	.50	.30
(11)	Ron Herbel	1.00	.50	.30
(12)	Sonny Jackson	1.00	.50	.30
(13)	Pat Jarvis	1.00	.50	.30
(14)	Larry Jaster	1.00	.50	.30
(15)	Hal King	1.00	.50	.30
(16)	Mike Lum	1.00	.50	.30
(17)	Felix Millan	1.00	.50	.30
(18)	Jim Nash	1.00	.50	.30
(19)	Phil Niekro	2.00	1.00	.60
(20)	Bob Priddy	1.00	.50	.30
(21)	Ron Reed	1.00	.50	.30
(22)	George Stone	1.00	.50	.30
(23)	Cecil Upshaw	1.00	.50	.30
(24)	Hoyt Wilhelm	2.00	1.00	.60
	Complete Chicago Cubs Album:	15.00	7.50	4.50
(1)	Ernie Banks	5.00	2.50	1.50
(2)	Glenn Beckert	1.00	.50	.30
(3)	Danny Breeden	1.00	.50	.30
(4)	Johnny Callison	1.00	.50	.30
(5)	Jim Colborn	1.00	.50	.30
(6)	Joe Decker	1.00	.50	.30
(7)	Bill Hands	1.00	.50	.30
(8)	Jim Hickman	1.00	.50	.30
(9)	Ken Holtzman	1.00	.50	.30
(10)	Randy Hundley	1.00	.50	.30
(11)	Fergie Jenkins	2.00	1.00	.60
(12)	Don Kessinger	1.00	.50	.30
(13)	J.C. Martin	1.00	.50	.30
(14)	Bob Miller	1.00	.50	.30
(15)	Milt Pappas	1.00	.50	.30
(16)	Joe Pepitone	1.00	.50	.30
(17)	Juan Pizarro	1.00	.50	.30

(18)	Paul Popovich	1.00	.50	.30
(19)	Phil Regan	1.00	.50	.30
(20)	Roberto Rodriguez	1.00	.50	.30
(21)	Ken Rudolph	1.00	.50	.30
(22)	Ron Santo	1.50	.70	.45
(23)	Hector Torres	1.00	.50	.30
(24)	Billy Williams	2.50	1.25	.70
	Complete Cincinnati Reds Album:	20.00	10.00	6.00
(1)	Johnny Bench	3.00	1.50	.90
(2)	Angel Bravo	1.00	.50	.30
(3)	Bernie Carbo	1.00	.50	.30
(4)	Clay Carroll	1.00	.50	.30
(5)	Darrel Chaney	1.00	.50	.30
(6)	Ty Cline	1.00	.50	.30
(7)	Tony Cloninger	1.00	.50	.30
(8)	Dave Concepcion	1.00	.50	.30
(9)	Pat Corrales	1.00	.50	.30
(10)	Greg Garrett	1.00	.50	.30
(11)	Wayne Granger	1.00	.50	.30
(12)	Don Gullett	1.00	.50	.30
(13)	Tommy Helms	1.00	.50	.30
(14)	Lee May	1.00	.50	.30
(15)	Jim McGlothlin	1.00	.50	.30
(16)	Hal McRae	1.00	.50	.30
(17)	Jim Merritt	1.00	.50	.30
(18)	Gary Nolan	1.00	.50	.30
(19)	Tony Perez	2.50	1.25	.70
(20)	Pete Rose	7.50	3.75	2.25
(21)	Wayne Simpson	1.00	.50	.30
(22)	Jimmy Stewart	1.00	.50	.30
(23)	Bobby Tolan	1.00	.50	.30
(24)	Woody Woodward	1.00	.50	.30
	Complete Houston Astros Album:	10.00	5.00	3.00
(1)	Jesus Alou	1.00	.50	.30
(2)	Jack Billingham	1.00	.50	.30
(3)	Ron Cook	1.00	.50	.30
(4)	George Culver	1.00	.50	.30
(5)	Larry Dierker	1.00	.50	.30
(6)	Jack DiLauro	1.00	.50	.30
(7)	Johnny Edwards	1.00	.50	.30
(8)	Fred Gladding	1.00	.50	.30
(9)	Tom Griffin	1.00	.50	.30
(10)	Skip Guinn	1.00	.50	.30
(11)	Jack Hiatt	1.00	.50	.30
(12)	Denny Lemaster	1.00	.50	.30
(13)	Marty Martinez	1.00	.50	.30
(14)	John Mayberry	1.00	.50	.30
(15)	Denis Menke	1.00	.50	.30
(16)	Norm Miller	1.00	.50	.30
(17)	Joe Morgan	2.50	1.25	.70
(18)	Doug Rader	1.00	.50	.30
(19)	Jim Ray	1.00	.50	.30
(20)	Scipio Spinks	1.00	.50	.30
(21)	Bob Watkins	1.00	.50	.30
(22)	Bob Watson	1.00	.50	.30
(23)	Don Wilson	1.00	.50	.30
(24)	Jim Wynn	1.00	.50	.30
	Complete Los Angeles Dodgers Album:	12.50	6.25	3.75
(1)	Rich Allen	1.50	.70	.45
(2)	Jim Brewer	1.00	.50	.30
(3)	Bill Buckner	1.00	.50	.30
(4)	Willie Crawford	1.00	.50	.30
(5)	Willie Davis	1.00	.50	.30
(6)	Al Downing	1.00	.50	.30
(7)	Steve Garvey	6.00	3.00	1.75
(8)	Billy Grabarkewitz	1.00	.50	.30
(9)	Tom Haller	1.00	.50	.30
(10)	Jim Lefebvre	1.00	.50	.30
(11)	Pete Mikkelsen	1.00	.50	.30
(12)	Joe Moeller	1.00	.50	.30
(13)	Manny Mota	1.00	.50	.30
(14)	Claude Osteen	1.00	.50	.30
(15)	Wes Parker	1.00	.50	.30
(16)	Jose Pena	1.00	.50	.30
(17)	Bill Russell	1.00	.50	.30
(18)	Duke Sims	1.00	.50	.30
(19)	Bill Singer	1.00	.50	.30
(20)	Mike Strahler	1.00	.50	.30
(21)	Bill Sudakis	1.00	.50	.30
(22)	Don Sutton	2.00	1.00	.60
(23)	Jeff Torborg	1.00	.50	.30
(24)	Maury Wills	1.00	.50	.30
	Complete Montreal Expos Album:	10.00	5.00	3.00
(1)	Bob Bailey	1.00	.50	.30
(2)	John Bateman	1.00	.50	.30
(3)	John Boccabella	1.00	.50	.30
(4)	Ron Brand	1.00	.50	.30
(5)	Boots Day	1.00	.50	.30
(6)	Jim Fairey	1.00	.50	.30
(7)	Ron Fairly	1.00	.50	.30
(8)	Jim Gosger	1.00	.50	.30
(9)	Don Hahn	1.00	.50	.30
(10)	Ron Hunt	1.00	.50	.30
(11)	Mack Jones	1.00	.50	.30

(12)	Jose Laboy	1.00	.50	.30
(13)	Mike Marshall	1.00	.50	.30
(14)	Dan McGinn	1.00	.50	.30
(15)	Carl Morton	1.00	.50	.30
(16)	John O'Donoghue	1.00	.50	.30
(17)	Adolfo Phillips	1.00	.50	.30
(18)	Claude Raymond	1.00	.50	.30
(19)	Steve Renko	1.00	.50	.30
(20)	Marv Staehle	1.00	.50	.30
(21)	Rusty Staub	1.25	.60	.40
(22)	Bill Stoneman	1.00	.50	.30
(23)	Gary Sutherland	1.00	.50	.30
(24)	Bobby Wine	1.00	.50	.30
	Complete New York Mets Album:	25.00	12.50	7.50
(1)	Tommie Agee	1.00	.50	.30
(2)	Bob Aspromonte	1.00	.50	.30
(3)	Ken Boswell	1.00	.50	.30
(4)	Dean Chance	1.00	.50	.30
(5)	Donn Clendenon	1.00	.50	.30
(6)	Duffy Dyer	1.00	.50	.30
(7)	Dan Frisella	1.00	.50	.30
(8)	Wayne Garrett	1.00	.50	.30
(9)	Gary Gentry	1.00	.50	.30
(10)	Jerry Grote	1.00	.50	.30
(11)	Bud Harrelson	1.00	.50	.30
(12)	Cleon Jones	1.00	.50	.30
(13)	Jerry Koosman	1.00	.50	.30
(14)	Ed Kranepool	1.00	.50	.30
(15)	Dave Marshall	1.00	.50	.30
(16)	Jim McAndrew	1.00	.50	.30
(17)	Tug McGraw	1.00	.50	.30
(18)	Nolan Ryan	20.00	10.00	6.00
(19)	Ray Sadecki	1.00	.50	.30
(20)	Tom Seaver	3.00	1.50	.90
(21)	Art Shamsky	1.00	.50	.30
(22)	Ron Swoboda	1.00	.50	.30
(23)	Ron Taylor	1.00	.50	.30
(24)	Al Weis	1.00	.50	.30
	Complete Philadelphia Phillies Album:	10.00	5.00	3.00
(1)	Larry Bowa	1.00	.50	.30
(2)	Johnny Briggs	1.00	.50	.30
(3)	Bryon Browne	1.00	.50	.30
(4)	Jim Bunning	2.00	1.00	.60
(5)	Billy Champion	1.00	.50	.30
(6)	Mike Compton	1.00	.50	.30
(7)	Denny Doyle	1.00	.50	.30
(8)	Roger Freed	1.00	.50	.30
(9)	Woody Fryman	1.00	.50	.30
(10)	Oscar Gamble	1.00	.50	.30
(11)	Terry Harmon	1.00	.50	.30
(12)	Larry Hisle	1.00	.50	.30
(13)	Joe Hoerner	1.00	.50	.30
(14)	Deron Johnson	1.00	.50	.30
(15)	Barry Lersch	1.00	.50	.30
(16)	Tim McCarver	1.50	.70	.45
(17)	Don Money	1.00	.50	.30
(18)	Mike Ryan	1.00	.50	.30
(19)	Dick Selma	1.00	.50	.30
(20)	Chris Short	1.00	.50	.30
(21)	Ron Stone	1.00	.50	.30
(22)	Tony Taylor	1.00	.50	.30
(23)	Rick Wise	1.00	.50	.30
(24)	Billy Wilson	1.00	.50	.30
	Complete Pittsburgh Pirates Album:	30.00	15.00	9.00
(1)	Gene Alley	1.00	.50	.30
(2)	Steve Blass	1.00	.50	.30
(3)	Nelson Briles	1.00	.50	.30
(4)	Jim Campanis	1.00	.50	.30
(5)	Dave Cash	1.00	.50	.30
(6)	Roberto Clemente	10.00	5.00	3.00
(7)	Vic Davalillo	1.00	.50	.30
(8)	Dock Ellis	1.00	.50	.30
(9)	Jim Grant	1.00	.50	.30
(10)	Dave Giusti	1.00	.50	.30
(11)	Richie Hebner	1.00	.50	.30
(12)	Jackie Hernandez	1.00	.50	.30
(13)	Johnny Jeter	1.00	.50	.30
(14)	Lou Marone	1.00	.50	.30
(15)	Jose Martinez	1.00	.50	.30
(16)	Bill Mazeroski	2.50	1.25	.70
(17)	Bob Moose	1.00	.50	.30
(18)	Al Oliver	1.25	.60	.40
(19)	Jose Pagan	1.00	.50	.30
(20)	Bob Robertson	1.00	.50	.30
(21)	Manny Sanguillen	1.00	.50	.30
(22)	Willie Stargell	2.50	1.25	.70
(23)	Bob Veale	1.00	.50	.30
(24)	Luke Walker	1.00	.50	.30
	Complete San Diego Padres Album:	10.00	5.00	3.00
(1)	Jose Arcia	1.00	.50	.30
(2)	Bob Barton	1.00	.50	.30
(3)	Fred Beene	1.00	.50	.30
(4)	Ollie Brown	1.00	.50	.30
(5)	Dave Campbell	1.00	.50	.30

(6)	Chris Cannizzaro	1.00	.50	.30
(7)	Nate Colbert	1.00	.50	.30
(8)	Mike Corkins	1.00	.50	.30
(9)	Tommy Dean	1.00	.50	.30
(10)	Al Ferrara	1.00	.50	.30
(11)	Rod Gaspar	1.00	.50	.30
(12)	Cito Gaston	1.00	.50	.30
(13)	Enzo Hernandez	1.00	.50	.30
(14)	Clay Kirby	1.00	.50	.30
(15)	Don Mason	1.00	.50	.30
(16)	Ivan Murrell	1.00	.50	.30
(17)	Gerry Nyman	1.00	.50	.30
(18)	Tom Phoebus	1.00	.50	.30
(19)	Dave Roberts	1.00	.50	.30
(20)	Gary Ross	1.00	.50	.30
(21)	Al Santorini	1.00	.50	.30
(22)	Al Severinsen	1.00	.50	.30
(23)	Ron Slocum	1.00	.50	.30
(24)	Ed Spiezio	1.00	.50	.30
	Complete San Francisco Giants Album:	12.50	6.25	3.75
(1)	Bobby Bonds	1.25	.60	.40
(2)	Ron Bryant	1.00	.50	.30
(3)	Don Carrithers	1.00	.50	.30
(4)	John Cumberland	1.00	.50	.30
(5)	Mike Davison	1.00	.50	.30
(6)	Dick Dietz	1.00	.50	.30
(7)	Tito Fuentes	1.00	.50	.30
(8)	Russ Gibson	1.00	.50	.30
(9)	Jim Ray Hart	1.00	.50	.30
(10)	Bob Heise	1.00	.50	.30
(11)	Ken Henderson	1.00	.50	.30
(12)	Steve Huntz	1.00	.50	.30
(13)	Frank Johnson	1.00	.50	.30
(14)	Jerry Johnson	1.00	.50	.30
(15)	Hal Lanier	1.00	.50	.30
(16)	Juan Marichal	2.00	1.00	.60
(17)	Willie Mays	7.50	3.75	2.25
(18)	Willie McCovey	2.50	1.25	.70
(19)	Don McMahon	1.00	.50	.30
(20)	Jim Moyer	1.00	.50	.30
(21)	Gaylord Perry	2.00	1.00	.60
(22)	Frank Reberger	1.00	.50	.30
(23)	Rich Robertson	1.00	.50	.30
(24)	Bernie Williams	1.00	.50	.30
	Complete St. Louis Cardinals Album:	10.00	5.00	3.00
(1)	Matty Alou	1.00	.50	.30
(2)	Jim Beauchamp	1.00	.50	.30
(3)	Frank Bertaina	1.00	.50	.30
(4)	Lou Brock	2.50	1.25	.70
(5)	George Brunet	1.00	.50	.30
(6)	Jose Cardenal	1.00	.50	.30
(7)	Steve Carlton	2.50	1.25	.70
(8)	Moe Drabowsky	1.00	.50	.30
(9)	Bob Gibson	2.50	1.25	.70
(10)	Joe Hague	1.00	.50	.30
(11)	Julian Javier	1.00	.50	.30
(12)	Leron Lee	1.00	.50	.30
(13)	Frank Linzy	1.00	.50	.30
(14)	Dal Maxvill	1.00	.50	.30
(15)	Jerry McNertney	1.00	.50	.30
(16)	Fred Norman	1.00	.50	.30
(17)	Milt Ramirez	1.00	.50	.30
(18)	Dick Schofield	1.00	.50	.30
(19)	Mike Shannon	1.00	.50	.30
(20)	Ted Sizemore	1.00	.50	.30
(21)	Bob Stinson	1.00	.50	.30
(22)	Carl Taylor	1.00	.50	.30
(23)	Joe Torre	1.50	.70	.45
(24)	Mike Torrez	1.00	.50	.30
	Complete Baltimore Orioles Album:	15.00	7.50	4.50
(1)	Mark Belanger	1.00	.50	.30
(2)	Paul Blair	1.00	.50	.30
(3)	Don Buford	1.00	.50	.30
(4)	Terry Crowley	1.00	.50	.30
(5)	Mike Cuellar	1.00	.50	.30
(6)	Clay Dalrymple	1.00	.50	.30
(7)	Pat Dobson	1.00	.50	.30
(8)	Andy Etchebarren	1.00	.50	.30
(9)	Dick Hall	1.00	.50	.30
(10)	Jim Hardin	1.00	.50	.30
(11)	Elrod Hendricks	1.00	.50	.30
(12)	Grant Jackson	1.00	.50	.30
(13)	Dave Johnson	1.00	.50	.30
(14)	Dave Leonhard	1.00	.50	.30
(15)	Marcelino Lopez	1.00	.50	.30
(16)	Dave McNally	1.00	.50	.30
(17)	Curt Motton	1.00	.50	.30
(18)	Jim Palmer	2.00	1.00	.60
(19)	Boog Powell	1.00	.50	.30
(20)	Merv Rettenmund	1.00	.50	.30
(21)	Brooks Robinson	3.00	1.50	.90
(22)	Frank Robinson	3.00	1.50	.90
(23)	Pete Richert	1.00	.50	.30
(24)	Chico Salmon	1.00	.50	.30

	Complete Boston Red Sox Album:	15.00	7.50	4.50
(1)	Luis Aparicio	2.50	1.25	.70
(2)	Bobby Bolin	1.00	.50	.30
(3)	Ken Brett	1.00	.50	.30
(4)	Billy Conigliaro	1.00	.50	.30
(5)	Ray Culp	1.00	.50	.30
(6)	Mike Flore	1.00	.50	.30
(7)	John Kennedy	1.00	.50	.30
(8)	Cal Koonce	1.00	.50	.30
(9)	Joe Lahoud	1.00	.50	.30
(10)	Bill Lee	1.00	.50	.30
(11)	Jim Lonborg	1.00	.50	.30
(12)	Sparky Lyle	1.00	.50	.30
(13)	Mike Nagy	1.00	.50	.30
(14)	Don Pavletich	1.00	.50	.30
(15)	Gary Peters	1.00	.50	.30
(16)	Rico Petrocelli	1.00	.50	.30
(17)	Vicente Romo	1.00	.50	.30
(18)	Tom Satriano	1.00	.50	.30
(19)	George Scott	1.00	.50	.30
(20)	Sonny Siebert	1.00	.50	.30
(21)	Reggie Smith	1.00	.50	.30
(22)	Jarvis Tatum	1.00	.50	.30
(23)	Ken Tatum	1.00	.50	.30
(24)	Carl Yastrzemski	3.00	1.50	.90
	Complete California Angels Album:	10.00	5.00	3.00
(1)	Sandy Alomar	1.00	.50	.30
(2)	Joe Azcue	1.00	.50	.30
(3)	Ken Berry	1.00	.50	.30
(4)	Gene Brabender	1.00	.50	.30
(5)	Billy Cowan	1.00	.50	.30
(6)	Tony Conigliaro	1.50	.70	.45
(7)	Eddie Fisher	1.00	.50	.30
(8)	Jim Fregosi	1.00	.50	.30
(9)	Tony Gonzales (Gonzalez)	1.00	.50	.30
(10)	Alex Johnson	1.00	.50	.30
(11)	Fred Lasher	1.00	.50	.30
(12)	Jim Maloney	1.00	.50	.30
(13)	Rudy May	1.00	.50	.30
(14)	Ken McMullen	1.00	.50	.30
(15)	Andy Messersmith	1.00	.50	.30
(16)	Gerry Moses	1.00	.50	.30
(17)	Syd O'Brien	1.00	.50	.30
(18)	Mel Queen	1.00	.50	.30
(19)	Roger Repoz	1.00	.50	.30
(20)	Archie Reynolds	1.00	.50	.30
(21)	Chico Ruiz	1.00	.50	.30
(22)	Jim Spencer	1.00	.50	.30
(23)	Clyde Wright	1.00	.50	.30
(24)	Billy Wynne	1.00	.50	.30
	Complete Chicago White Sox Album:	10.00	5.00	3.00
(1)	Luis Alvarado	1.00	.50	.30
(2)	Mike Andrews	1.00	.50	.30
(3)	Tom Egan	1.00	.50	.30
(4)	Steve Hamilton	1.00	.50	.30
(5)	Ed Hermann	1.00	.50	.30
(6)	Joel Horlen	1.00	.50	.30
(7)	Tommy John	1.25	.60	.40
(8)	Bart Johnson	1.00	.50	.30
(9)	Jay Johnstone	1.00	.50	.30
(10)	Duane Josephson	1.00	.50	.30
(11)	Pat Kelly	1.00	.50	.30
(12)	Bobby Knoop	1.00	.50	.30
(13)	Carlos May	1.00	.50	.30
(14)	Lee Maye	1.00	.50	.30
(15)	Tom McGraw	1.00	.50	.30
(16)	Bill Melton	1.00	.50	.30
(17)	Rich Morales	1.00	.50	.30
(18)	Tom Murphy	1.00	.50	.30
(19)	Don O'Riley	1.00	.50	.30
(20)	Rick Reichardt	1.00	.50	.30
(21)	Bill Robinson	1.00	.50	.30
(22)	Bob Spence	1.00	.50	.30
(23)	Walt Williams	1.00	.50	.30
(24)	Wilbur Wood	1.00	.50	.30
	Complete Cleveland Indians Album:	10.00	5.00	3.00
(1)	Rick Austin	1.00	.50	.30
(2)	Buddy Bradford	1.00	.50	.30
(3)	Larry Brown	1.00	.50	.30
(4)	Lou Camilli	1.00	.50	.30
(5)	Vince Colbert	1.00	.50	.30
(6)	Ray Fosse	1.00	.50	.30
(7)	Alan Foster	1.00	.50	.30
(8)	Roy Foster	1.00	.50	.30
(9)	Rich Hand	1.00	.50	.30
(10)	Steve Hargan	1.00	.50	.30
(11)	Ken Harrelson	1.00	.50	.30
(12)	Jack Heidemann	1.00	.50	.30
(13)	Phil Hennigan	1.00	.50	.30
(14)	Dennis Higgins	1.00	.50	.30
(15)	Chuck Hinton	1.00	.50	.30
(16)	Tony Horton	1.00	.50	.30
(17)	Ray Lamb	1.00	.50	.30

(18)	Eddie Leon	1.00	.50	.30
(19)	Sam McDowell	1.00	.50	.30
(20)	Graig Nettles	1.25	.60	.40
(21)	Mike Paul	1.00	.50	.30
(22)	Vada Pinson	1.25	.60	.40
(23)	Ken Suarez	1.00	.50	.30
(24)	Ted Uhlaender	1.00	.50	.30
	Complete Detroit Tigers Album:	10.00	5.00	3.00
(1)	Ed Brinkman	1.00	.50	.30
(2)	Gates Brown	1.00	.50	.30
(3)	Ike Brown	1.00	.50	.30
(4)	Les Cain	1.00	.50	.30
(5)	Norm Cash	1.50	.70	.45
(6)	Joe Coleman	1.00	.50	.30
(7)	Bill Freehan	1.00	.50	.30
(8)	Cesar Gutierrez	1.00	.50	.30
(9)	John Hiller	1.00	.50	.30
(10)	Willie Horton	1.00	.50	.30
(11)	Dalton Jones	1.00	.50	.30
(12)	Al Kaline	3.00	1.50	.90
(13)	Mike Kilkenny	1.00	.50	.30
(14)	Mickey Lolich	1.00	.50	.30
(15)	Dick McAuliffe	1.00	.50	.30
(16)	Joe Niekro	1.00	.50	.30
(17)	Jim Northrup	1.00	.50	.30
(18)	Daryl Patterson	1.00	.50	.30
(19)	Jimmie Price	1.00	.50	.30
(20)	Bob Reed	1.00	.50	.30
(21)	Aurelio Rodriguez	1.00	.50	.30
(22)	Fred Scherman	1.00	.50	.30
(23)	Mickey Stanley	1.00	.50	.30
(24)	Tom Timmermann	1.00	.50	.30
	Complete Kansas City Royals Album:	10.00	5.00	3.00
(1)	Ted Abernathy	1.00	.50	.30
(2)	Wally Bunker	1.00	.50	.30
(3)	Tom Burgmeier	1.00	.50	.30
(4)	Bill Butler	1.00	.50	.30
(5)	Bruce Dal Canton	1.00	.50	.30
(6)	Dick Drago	1.00	.50	.30
(7)	Bobby Floyd	1.00	.50	.30
(8)	Gail Hopkins	1.00	.50	.30
(9)	Joe Keough	1.00	.50	.30
(10)	Ed Kirkpatrick	1.00	.50	.30
(11)	Tom Matchick	1.00	.50	.30
(12)	Jerry May	1.00	.50	.30
(13)	Aurelio Monteagudo	1.00	.50	.30
(14)	Dave Morehead	1.00	.50	.30
(15)	Bob Oliver	1.00	.50	.30
(16)	Amos Otis	1.00	.50	.30
(17)	Fred Patek	1.00	.50	.30
(18)	Lou Piniella	1.25	.60	.40
(19)	Cookie Rojas	1.00	.50	.30
(20)	Jim Rooker	1.00	.50	.30
(21)	Paul Schaal	1.00	.50	.30
(22)	Rich Severson	1.00	.50	.30
(23)	George Spriggs	1.00	.50	.30
(24)	Carl Taylor	1.00	.50	.30
	Complete Milwaukee Brewers Album:	10.00	5.00	3.00
(1)	Dave Baldwin	1.00	.50	.30
(2)	Dick Ellsworth	1.00	.50	.30
(3)	John Gelnar	1.00	.50	.30
(4)	Tommy Harper	1.00	.50	.30
(5)	Mike Hegan	1.00	.50	.30
(6)	Bob Humphreys	1.00	.50	.30
(7)	Andy Kosco	1.00	.50	.30
(8)	Lew Krausse	1.00	.50	.30
(9)	Ted Kubiak	1.00	.50	.30
(10)	Skip Lockwood	1.00	.50	.30
(11)	Dave May	1.00	.50	.30
(12)	Bob Meyer	1.00	.50	.30
(13)	John Morris	1.00	.50	.30
(14)	Marty Pattin	1.00	.50	.30
(15)	Roberto Pena	1.00	.50	.30
(16)	Eduardo Rodriguez	1.00	.50	.30
(17)	Phil Roof	1.00	.50	.30
(18)	Ken Sanders	1.00	.50	.30
(19)	Ted Savage	1.00	.50	.30
(20)	Russ Snyder	1.00	.50	.30
(21)	Bob Tillman	1.00	.50	.30
(22)	Bill Voss	1.00	.50	.30
(23)	Danny Walton	1.00	.50	.30
(24)	Floyd Wicker	1.00	.50	.30
	Complete Minnesota Twins Album:	15.00	7.50	4.50
(1)	Brant Alyea	1.00	.50	.30
(2)	Bert Blyleven	1.00	.50	.30
(3)	Dave Boswell	1.00	.50	.30
(4)	Leo Cardenas	1.00	.50	.30
(5)	Rod Carew	2.50	1.25	.70
(6)	Tom Hall	1.00	.50	.30
(7)	Jim Holt	1.00	.50	.30
(8)	Jim Kaat	1.00	.50	.30
(9)	Harmon Killebrew	2.50	1.25	.70
(10)	Charlie Manuel	1.00	.50	.30
(11)	George Mitterwald	1.00	.50	.30

(12)	Tony Oliva	1.25	.60	.40
(13)	Ron Perranoski	1.00	.50	.30
(14)	Jim Perry	1.00	.50	.30
(15)	Frank Quilici	1.00	.50	.30
(16)	Rich Reese	1.00	.50	.30
(17)	Rick Renick	1.00	.50	.30
(18)	Danny Thompson	1.00	.50	.30
(19)	Luis Tiant	1.00	.50	.30
(20)	Tom Tischinski	1.00	.50	.30
(21)	Cesar Tovar	1.00	.50	.30
(22)	Stan Williams	1.00	.50	.30
(23)	Dick Woodson	1.00	.50	.30
(24)	Bill Zepp	1.00	.50	.30
	Complete New York Yankees Album:	15.00	7.50	4.50
(1)	Jack Aker	1.00	.50	.30
(2)	Stan Bahnsen	1.00	.50	.30
(3)	Curt Blefary	1.00	.50	.30
(4)	Bill Burbach	1.00	.50	.30
(5)	Danny Cater	1.00	.50	.30
(6)	Horace Clarke	1.00	.50	.30
(7)	John Ellis	1.00	.50	.30
(8)	Jake Gibbs	1.00	.50	.30
(9)	Ron Hansen	1.00	.50	.30
(10)	Mike Kekich	1.00	.50	.30
(11)	Jerry Kenney	1.00	.50	.30
(12)	Ron Klimkowski	1.00	.50	.30
(13)	Steve Kline	1.00	.50	.30
(14)	Mike McCormick	1.00	.50	.30
(15)	Lindy McDaniel	1.00	.50	.30
(16)	Gene Michael	1.00	.50	.30
(17)	Thurman Munson	1.50	.70	.45
(18)	Bobby Murcer	1.25	.60	.40
(19)	Fritz Peterson	1.00	.50	.30
(20)	Mel Stottlemyre	1.00	.50	.30
(21)	Pete Ward	1.00	.50	.30
(22)	Gary Waslewski	1.00	.50	.30
(23)	Roy White	1.00	.50	.30
(24)	Ron Woods	1.00	.50	.30
	Complete Oakland A's Album:	15.00	7.50	4.50
(1)	Felipe Alou	1.00	.50	.30
(2)	Sal Bando	1.00	.50	.30
(3)	Vida Blue	1.00	.50	.30
(4)	Bert Campaneris	1.00	.50	.30
(5)	Ron Clark	1.00	.50	.30
(6)	Chuck Dobson	1.00	.50	.30
(7)	Dave Duncan	1.00	.50	.30
(8)	Frank Fernandez	1.00	.50	.30
(9)	Rollie Fingers	2.00	1.00	.60
(10)	Dick Green	1.00	.50	.30
(11)	Steve Hovley	1.00	.50	.30
(12)	Catfish Hunter	2.00	1.00	.60
(13)	Reggie Jackson	6.00	3.00	1.75
(14)	Marcel Lacheman	1.00	.50	.30
(15)	Paul Lindblad	1.00	.50	.30
(16)	Bob Locker	1.00	.50	.30
(17)	Don Mincher	1.00	.50	.30
(18)	Rick Monday	1.00	.50	.30
(19)	John Odom	1.00	.50	.30
(20)	Jim Roland	1.00	.50	.30
(21)	Joe Rudi	1.00	.50	.30
(22)	Diego Segui	1.00	.50	.30
(23)	Bob Stickels	1.00	.50	.30
(24)	Gene Tenace	1.00	.50	.30
	Complete Washington Senators Album:	12.50	6.25	3.75
(1)	Bernie Allen	1.00	.50	.30
(2)	Dick Bosman	1.00	.50	.30
(3)	Jackie Brown	1.00	.50	.30
(4)	Paul Casanova	1.00	.50	.30
(5)	Casey Cox	1.00	.50	.30
(6)	Tim Cullen	1.00	.50	.30
(7)	Mike Epstein	1.00	.50	.30
(8)	Curt Flood	1.25	.60	.40
(9)	Joe Foy	1.00	.50	.30
(10)	Jim French	1.00	.50	.30
(11)	Bill Gogolewski	1.00	.50	.30
(12)	Tom Grieve	1.00	.50	.30
(13)	Joe Grzenda	1.00	.50	.30
(14)	Frank Howard	1.25	.60	.40
(15)	Joe Janeski	1.00	.50	.30
(16)	Darold Knowles	1.00	.50	.30
(17)	Elliott Maddox	1.00	.50	.30
(18)	Denny McLain	1.25	.60	.40
(19)	Dave Nelson	1.00	.50	.30
(20)	Horacio Pina	1.00	.50	.30
(21)	Jim Shellenback	1.00	.50	.30
(22)	Ed Stroud	1.00	.50	.30
(23)	Del Unser	1.00	.50	.30
(24)	Don Wert	1.00	.50	.30

1933 DeLong (R333)

The DeLong Co. of Boston was among the first to sell baseball cards with gum, issuing a set of 24 cards in 1933. DeLong cards measure about 1-15/16" x 2-15/16", with black-and-white player photos on a color background. The photos show the players in various action poses and positions them in the middle of a miniature stadium setting so that they appear to be giants. Most of the cards are vertically designed, but a few are horizontal. Backs were by Austen Lake, editor of the Boston Transcript, and contain tips to help youngsters become better ballplayers. The ACC designation for this set is R333.

	NM	E	VG
Complete Set (24):	30,000	8,000	4,000
Common Player:	700.00	280.00	140.00

		NM	E	VG
1	"Marty" McManus	900.00	280.00	140.00
2	Al Simmons	950.00	385.00	190.00
3	Oscar Melillo	700.00	280.00	140.00
4	William (Bill) Terry	950.00	385.00	190.00
5	Charlie Gehringer	950.00	385.00	190.00
6	Gordon (Mickey) Cochrane	950.00	385.00	190.00
7	Lou Gehrig	9,000	3,080	1,260
8	Hazen S. (Kiki) Cuyler	950.00	385.00	190.00
9	Bill Urbanski	700.00	280.00	140.00
10	Frank J. (Lefty) O'Doul	750.00	395.00	195.00
11	Freddie Lindstrom	950.00	385.00	190.00
12	Harold (Pie) Traynor	950.00	385.00	190.00
13	"Rabbit" Maranville	950.00	385.00	190.00
14	Vernon "Lefty" Gomez	950.00	385.00	190.00
15	Riggs Stephenson	700.00	280.00	140.00
16	Lon Warneke	700.00	280.00	140.00
17	Pepper Martin	700.00	280.00	140.00
18	Jimmy Dykes	700.00	280.00	140.00
19	Chick Hafey	950.00	385.00	190.00
20	Joe Vosmik	700.00	280.00	140.00
21	Jimmy Foxx (Jimmie)	2,100	800.00	475.00
22	Charles (Chuck) Klein	950.00	385.00	190.00
23	Robert (Lefty) Grove	1,250	595.00	300.00
24	"Goose" Goslin	950.00	385.00	190.00

1934 Al Demaree Die-cuts (R304)

Among the rarest 1930s gum cards are those issued by Dietz Gum Co., a Chicago confectioner, in packages of "Ball Players in Action Chewing Gum." The cards are so rare that the complete checklist may never be known. The set was cataloged as R304 in the American Card Catalog. The cards feature photographic portraits of players set upon cartoon bodies drawn by former major league pitcher Demaree. The photo and artwork are generally in black-and-white, while the players on some teams have blue or red uniform details printed on. The cards can be folded to create a stand-up figure, but did not have a background to be cut or torn away, as is common with most die-cut baseball cards. Unfolded, the cards measure 6-1/2" long and from 1-5/8" to 1-3/4" wide, depending on pose.

		NM	E	VG
Common Player:		1,000	500.00	300.00
1	Lyn Lary	1,000	500.00	300.00
3	Earle Combs	2,20000	1,100	650.00
4	Babe Ruth	16,000	8,000	4,750
5	Sam Byrd	1,200	600.00	360.00
6	Tony Lazzeri	1,650	825.00	495.00
7	Frank Crosetti	1,500	750.00	450.00
9	Lou Gehrig	15,000	7,5000.00	4,500
10	Lefty Gomez	1,650	825.00	495.00
11	Mule Haas	1,000	500.00	300.00
12	Evar Swenson	1,000	500.00	300.00
13	Marv Shea	1,000	500.00	300.00
14	Al Simmons (Throwing)	1,650	825.00	495.00
15	Jack Hayes	1,000	500.00	300.00
16	Al Simmons (Batting)	1,650	825.00	495.00
17	Jimmy Dykes	1,000	500.00	300.00
18	Luke Appling	1,650	825.00	495.00
19	Ted Lyons	1,650	825.00	495.00
20	Red Kress	1,000	500.00	300.00
21	Gee Walker	1,000	500.00	300.00
22	Charlie Gehringer	1,650	825.00	495.00
23	Mickey Cochrane (Catching)	1,650	825.00	495.00
24	Mickey Cochrane (Batting)	1,650	825.00	495.00
25	Pete Fox	1,000	500.00	300.00
26	Firpo Marberry	1,000	500.00	300.00
28	Mickey Owen	1,000	500.00	300.00
29	Hank Greenberg	4,500	2,250	1,250
30	Goose Goslin	1,650	825.00	495.00
31	Earl Averill	1,650	825.00	495.00
32	Frankie Pytlak	1,000	500.00	300.00
33	Willie Kamm	1,000	500.00	300.00
34	Johnny Burnett	1,000	500.00	300.00
35	Joe Vosmik	1,000	500.00	300.00
36	Dick Porter	1,000	500.00	300.00
38	Harley Boss	1,000	500.00	300.00
39	Joe Vismik	1,000	500.00	300.00
40	Orel Hildebrand	1,000	500.00	300.00
41	Jack Burns	1,000	500.00	300.00
42	Frank Grube	1,000	500.00	300.00
43	Oscar Mellilo	1,000	500.00	300.00
44	Sam West	1,000	500.00	300.00
45	Ray Pepper	1,000	500.00	300.00
46	Bruce Campbell	1,000	500.00	300.00
47	Sam West	1,000	500.00	300.00
48	Art Scharein	1,000	500.00	300.00
49	George Blaeholder	1,000	500.00	300.00
50	Rogers Hornsby	3,750	1,875	1,125
51	Eric McNair	1,000	500.00	300.00
52	Bob Johnson	1,000	500.00	300.00
53	Pinky Higgins	1,000	500.00	300.00
54	Jimmie Foxx	4,500	2,250	1,250
56	Dib Williams	1,000	500.00	300.00
57	Lou Finney	1,000	500.00	300.00
60	Roy Mahaffey	1,000	500.00	300.00
61	Ossie Bluege	1,000	500.00	300.00
62	Luke Sewell	1,000	500.00	300.00
63	John Stone	1,000	500.00	300.00
64	Joe Cronin	1,650	825.00	495.00
65	Joe Cronin/btg.	1,650	825.00	495.00
66	Buddy Myer	1,000	500.00	300.00
67	Earl Whitehill	1,000	500.00	300.00
68	Fred Schulte	1,000	500.00	300.00
70	Joe Kuhel	1,000	500.00	300.00
71	Ed Morgan	1,000	500.00	300.00
73	Rick Ferrell	1,650	825.00	495.00
74	Carl Reynolds	1,000	500.00	300.00
76	Bill Cissell	1,000	500.00	300.00
77	Johnny Hodapp	1,000	500.00	300.00
78	Dusty Cooke	1,000	500.00	300.00
79	Lefty Grove	3,200	1,600	960.00
80	Max Bishop	1,000	500.00	300.00
81	Hughie Critz	1,000	500.00	300.00
82	Gus Mancuso	1,000	500.00	300.00
83	Kiddo Davis	1,000	500.00	300.00
84	Blondy Ryan	1,000	500.00	300.00
86	Travis Jackson	1,650	825.00	495.00
87	Mel Ott	11,000	5,500	3,250
89	Bill Terry	1,650	825.00	495.00
90	Carl Hubbell	3,000	1,500	900.00
91	Tony Cuccinello	1,000	500.00	300.00
92	Al Lopez	1,650	825.00	495.00
94	Johnny Frederick	1,000	500.00	300.00
95	Glenn Wright	1,000	500.00	300.00
96	Hack Wilson	1,650	825.00	495.00
97	Danny Taylor	1,000	500.00	300.00
98	Van Mungo	1,000	500.00	300.00
99	John Frederick	1,000	500.00	300.00
100	Sam Leslie	1,000	500.00	300.00
101	Sparky Adams	1,000	500.00	300.00
102a	Mark Koenig	1,000	500.00	300.00
102b	Ernie Lombardi	1,650	825.00	495.00
104	Tony Piet	1,000	500.00	300.00
105	Chick Hafey/btg.	1,650	825.00	495.00
107	Syl Johnson	1,000	500.00	300.00
108	Jim Bottomley	1,650	825.00	495.00
109	Chick Hafey	1,650	825.00	495.00
110	Adam Comorosky	1,000	500.00	300.00
111	Dick Bartell	1,000	500.00	300.00
112	Harvey Hendrick	1,000	500.00	300.00
114	Fritz Knothe	1,000	500.00	300.00
115	Don Hurst (Batting)	1,000	500.00	300.00
117	Prince Oana	1,800	900.00	550.00
118	Ed Holley	1,000	500.00	300.00
120	Don Hurst (Throwing)	1,000	500.00	300.00
121	Spud Davis	1,000	500.00	300.00
122	George Watkins	1,000	500.00	300.00
123	Frankie Frisch	1,650	825.00	495.00
124	Pepper Martin (Batting)	1,000	500.00	300.00
125	Ripper Collins	1,000	500.00	300.00
126	Dizzy Dean	4,000	2,000	1,200
127	Pepper Martin (Fielding)	1,000	500.00	300.00
128	Joe Medwick	1,650	825.00	495.00
129	Leo Durocher	1,650	825.00	495.00
130	Ernie Orsatti	1,000	500.00	300.00
131	Buck Jordan	1,000	500.00	300.00
132	Shanty Hogan	1,000	500.00	300.00
133a	Wes Shulmerich (Schulmerich)	1,000	500.00	300.00
133b	Randy Moore	1,000	500.00	300.00
134	Billy Urbanski	1,000	500.00	300.00
135	Wally Berger	1,000	500.00	300.00
136	Pinky Whitney	1,000	500.00	300.00
137	Wally Berger	1,000	500.00	300.00
139	Rabbit Maranville	1,650	825.00	495.00
140	Ben Cantwell	1,000	500.00	300.00
141	Gus Suhr	1,000	500.00	300.00
142	Earl Grace	1,000	500.00	300.00
143	Fred Lindstrom	2,200	1,100	650.00
144	Arky Vaughan	1,650	825.00	495.00
145	Pie Traynor (btg.)	1,650	825.00	495.00
146	Tommy Thevenow	1,000	500.00	300.00
147	Lloyd Waner	1,650	825.00	495.00
148	Paul Waner	1,650	825.00	495.00
149	Pie Traynor (Throwing)	1,650	825.00	495.00
150	Larry French	1,000	500.00	300.00
151	Kiki Cuyler	1,650	825.00	495.00
152	Gabby Hartnett	1,650	825.00	495.00
153	Chuck Klein (Throwing)	1,650	825.00	495.00
154	Chuck Klein	1,650	825.00	495.00
155	Bill Jurges	1,000	500.00	300.00
155b	Jimmie Foxx	4,000	2,000	1,200
156	Woody English	1,000	500.00	300.00
157	Lonnie Warnecke	1,000	500.00	300.00
158	Billy Herman	1,650	825.00	495.00
159	Babe Herman	1,200	600.00	350.00
160	Charlie Grimm	1,000	500.00	300.00
161	Cy Rigler (Umpire)	2,200	1,100	660.00
162	Bill Klem (Umpire)	2,500	1,250	750.00
163	Cy Pfirman (Umpire)	1,000	500.00	300.00
165	Bill Dineen (Dinneen) (Umpire)	1,200	600.00	350.00
166	Charlie Moran (Umpire)	1,000	500.00	300.00
167	George Hildebrand (Umpire)	1,000	500.00	300.00

1932 Charles Denby Cigars Cubs

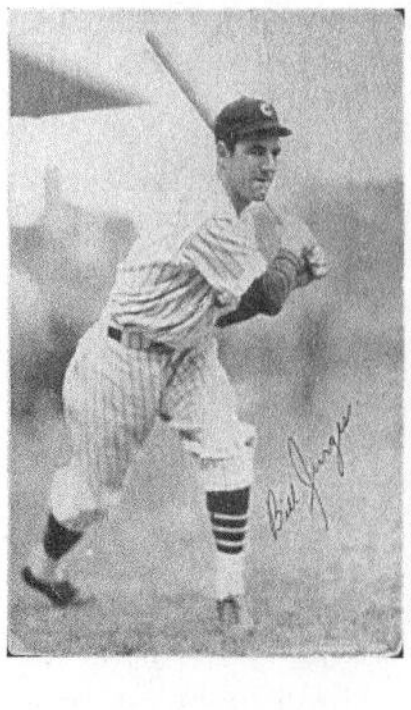

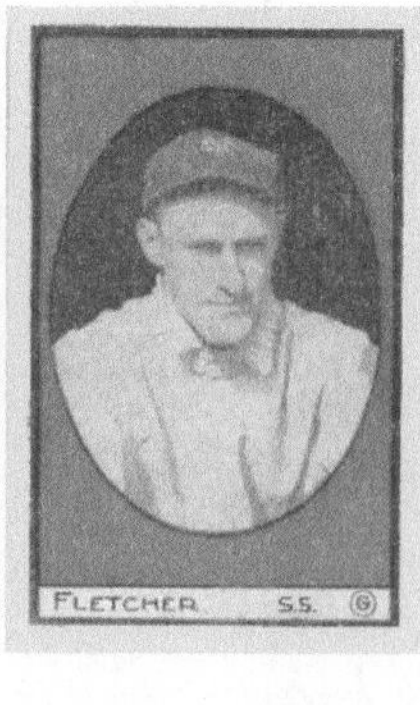

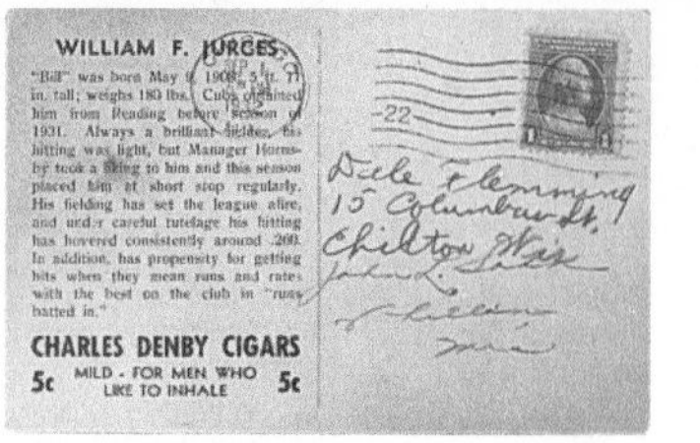

This series of Chicago Cubs postcards was issued by the Fendrich Cigar Co., Evansville, Ind., to promote its Charles Denby brand in 1932. It is the last major tobacco-card issue produced before World War II. The cards are a standard postcard size (5-1/4" x 3-3/8") and feature a glossy black-and-white player photo with a facsimile autograph. In typical postcard style, the back of the card is divided in half, with a printed player profile on the left and room for the mailing address on the right. The back also includes an advertisement for Charles Denby Cigars, the mild five-cent cigar "for men who like to inhale." Eight players are known but more may exist.

		NM	E	VG
Complete Set (8):		3,750	1,850	1,100
Common Player:		500.00	200.00	100.00
(1)	Hazen Cuyler	625.00	250.00	125.00
(2)	Elwood English	500.00	200.00	100.00
(3)	Charles J. Grimm	500.00	200.00	100.00
(4)	William Herman	750.00	300.00	150.00
(5)	Rogers Hornsby	1,000	400.00	200.00
(6)	William F. Jurges	500.00	200.00	100.00
(7)	Riggs Stephenson	500.00	200.00	100.00
(8)	Lonnie Warneke	500.00	200.00	100.00

1950-51 Denia Puerto Rican League

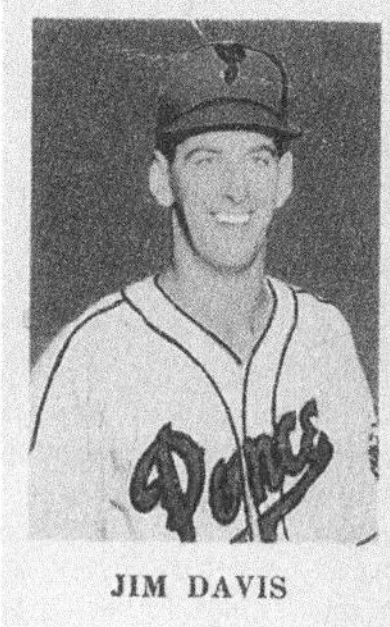

This issue was produced in conjunction with the 1950-51 Puerto Rican League winter season. Measurements vary slightly from a norm of about 1-3/4" x 2-1/8". Cards have colorized portrait photos with blank backs, probably intended to be glued into an album. Cards are unnumbered. This checklist is alphabetized, with gaps left for what is believed to be 57 uncataloged cards. Some of the players are veterans of the Negro Leagues and American major and minor leagues. Black-and-white reprints of the cards are known. A few cards have been found with a prize-redemption stamp on back.

		NM	E	VG
Common Player:		125.00	65.00	40.00
(1)	Alberto Alberdeston	125.00	65.00	40.00
	Luis Arroyo	100.00	40.00	20.00
(2)	Jaime Almendro	125.00	65.00	40.00
	Joe Atkins	100.00	40.00	20.00
(3)	Yiyo Alonso	125.00	65.00	40.00
	Sammy Bankhead	110.00	45.00	22.50
(4)	Luis (Tite) Arroyo	150.00	75.00	45.00
	Carlos Bernier	100.00	40.00	20.00
(5)	Pedro J. Arroyo	125.00	65.00	40.00
	Hiram Bithorn	100.00	40.00	20.00
(6)	Joe Atkins	150.00	75.00	45.00
	Raymond Brown	300.00	120.00	60.00
(7)	Eugene Baker	200.00	100.00	60.00
	Willard Brown	300.00	120.00	60.00
(8)	Dan Bankhead	200.00	100.00	60.00
	Perucho Cepeda	155.00	65.00	35.00
(9)	Sammy Bankhead	1,200	600.00	360.00
	Jim Davis	100.00	40.00	20.00
(10)	Ramon Bayron	125.00	65.00	40.00
	Leon Day	375.00	150.00	75.00
(11)	Hiram Bithorn	200.00	100.00	60.00
	Luicius Easter	125.00	50.00	25.00
(12)	Rafael Blasini	125.00	65.00	40.00
	Ruben Gomez	100.00	40.00	20.00
(13)	Bob Boyd	150.00	75.00	45.00
	Johnny Logan	100.00	40.00	20.00
(14)	Roger Breard	125.00	65.00	40.00

		NM	E	VG
	Emilio Navarro	100.00	40.00	20.00
(15)	Stan Breard	125.00	65.00	40.00
	Arnie Portocarrero	100.00	40.00	20.00
(16)	Barney Brown	1,000	500.00	300.00
	Vic Power	125.00	50.00	25.00
(17)	Raymond Brown	2,000	1,000	600.00
	Luis Rentas	100.00	40.00	20.00
(18)	Willard Brown	2,000	1,000	600.00
	Miguel A. Rivera	100.00	40.00	20.00
(19)	Jose A. Burgos	125.00	65.00	40.00
	Ministro Rodriguez	100.00	40.00	20.00
(20)	Joe Buzas	125.00	65.00	40.00
	Jose Santiago	100.00	40.00	20.00
(21)	Luis R. Cabrera	125.00	65.00	40.00
	Barney Serrell	100.00	40.00	20.00
(22)	Rafael Casanovas	125.00	65.00	40.00
	Bob Thurman	100.00	40.00	20.00
(23)	N. Zurdo Castro	125.00	65.00	40.00
	Artie Wilson	225.00	90.00	45.00
(24)	Perucho Cepeda	800.00	400.00	240.00
(25)	T. Gomez Checo	125.00	65.00	40.00
(26)	Al Cihoki (Cihocki)	125.00	65.00	40.00
(27)	Buster Clarkson	250.00	125.00	75.00
(28)	Francisco Coimbre	800.00	400.00	240.00
(29)	Eugene Collins	350.00	175.00	105.00
(30)	Monchile Concepcion	150.00	75.00	45.00
(31)	Charlie Corin	125.00	65.00	40.00
(32)	Herminio Cortfu	125.00	65.00	40.00
(33)	Johnny Cox	125.00	65.00	40.00
(34)	George Crowe	200.00	100.00	60.00
(35)	Jim Davis	125.00	65.00	40.00
(36)	Johnny Davis	450.00	225.00	135.00
(37)	Piper Davis	450.00	225.00	135.00
(38)	Leon Day	6,000	3,000	1,800
(39)	Ellis "Cot" Deal	150.00	75.00	45.00
(40)	Jack Dittmer	125.00	65.00	40.00
(41)	Verdes Drake	150.00	75.00	45.00
(42)	Saturnino Escalera	125.00	65.00	40.00
(43)	C. Guillaro Estrella	125.00	65.00	40.00
(44)	S. Federico	125.00	65.00	40.00
(45)	Dumbo Fernandez	125.00	65.00	40.00
(46)	Elias Frias	125.00	65.00	40.00
(47)	Les Fusselmann (Fusselman)	125.00	65.00	40.00
(48)	Felipe Garcia	125.00	65.00	40.00
(49)	(Carden) Gillenwater	125.00	65.00	40.00
(50)	Jim Gilliam	250.00	125.00	75.00
(51)	Ruben Gomez	200.00	100.00	60.00
(52)	Faelo Gonzalez	125.00	65.00	40.00
(53)	Gely Goyco	125.00	65.00	40.00
(54)	Jack Harshmann (Harshman)	125.00	65.00	40.00
(55)	Rudy Hernandez	125.00	65.00	40.00
(56)	Roy Hughes	125.00	65.00	40.00
(57)	Pachy Irizarry	125.00	65.00	40.00
(58)	Indian (Indio) Jiminez	125.00	65.00	40.00
(59)	Sam Jones	125.00	65.00	40.00
(60)	Walt Judnich	125.00	65.00	40.00
(61)	Russ Kearns	125.00	65.00	40.00
(62)	Billy Klaus	150.00	75.00	45.00
(63)	Jim Lamarque	350.00	175.00	105.00
(64)	Red Lynn	125.00	65.00	40.00
(65)	Bob Malloy	125.00	65.00	40.00
(66)	Clifford Mapes	125.00	65.00	40.00
(67)	Canena Marquez	450.00	225.00	135.00
(68)	Achin Matos	125.00	65.00	40.00
(69)	Benny Meyers	125.00	65.00	40.00
(70)	Henry Miller	150.00	75.00	45.00
(71)	Oscar Mir Flores	125.00	65.00	40.00
(72)	Jose E. Montalvo	125.00	65.00	40.00
(73)	Willie Morales	125.00	65.00	40.00
(74)	Gallego Munoz	125.00	65.00	40.00
(75)	Earl Naylor	125.00	65.00	40.00
(76)	Ernest Nevel	125.00	65.00	40.00
(77)	Don Nicholas	125.00	65.00	40.00
(78)	John O'Donnell	125.00	65.00	40.00
(79)	Guayuvin Olivo	150.00	75.00	45.00
(80)	Miguel Payano	125.00	65.00	40.00
(81)	Les Peden	125.00	65.00	40.00
(82)	Juan Perez	125.00	65.00	40.00
(83)	Palomo Perez	125.00	65.00	40.00
(84)	German Pizarro	125.00	65.00	40.00
(85)	Dave Pope	150.00	75.00	45.00
(86)	Milton Ralat	125.00	65.00	40.00
(87)	Enrique Reinoso	125.00	65.00	40.00
(88)	Roberto Rivera	125.00	65.00	40.00
(89)	Julio Rodriguez	125.00	65.00	40.00
(90)	Pedro Rodriguez	125.00	65.00	40.00
(91)	Domingo Rosello	125.00	65.00	40.00
(92)	Joe Rossi	125.00	65.00	40.00
(93)	Miguel Rueda	125.00	65.00	40.00
(94)	Ramon Salgado	125.00	65.00	40.00
(95)	Juan Sanchez	125.00	65.00	40.00
(96)	Carlos M. Santiago	125.00	65.00	40.00
(97)	Jose G. Santiago	125.00	65.00	40.00
(98)	V. Scarpatte	125.00	65.00	40.00
(99)	Jose Seda	125.00	65.00	40.00
(100)	Barney Serrell	350.00	175.00	105.00
(101)	Al Smith	200.00	100.00	60.00
(102)	Jose St. Clair	125.00	65.00	40.00
(103)	Tetelo Sterling	125.00	65.00	40.00
(104)	Russ Sullivan	125.00	65.00	40.00
(105)	Lonnie Summers	150.00	75.00	45.00
(106)	Jim Tabor	125.00	65.00	40.00
(107)	Bert Thiel	125.00	65.00	40.00
(108)	Valmy Thomas	125.00	65.00	40.00
(109)	Bob Thurman	350.00	175.00	105.00
(110)	Tiant Tineo	125.00	65.00	40.00
(111)	Gilberto Torres	125.00	65.00	40.00
(112)	Manuel Traboux	125.00	65.00	40.00
(113)	Joe Tuminelli	125.00	65.00	40.00
(114)	Jose L. Velazquez	125.00	65.00	40.00
(115)	Ben Wade	150.00	75.00	45.00
(116)	Johnny Williams	250.00	125.00	75.00
(117)	Marvin Williams	150.00	75.00	45.00
(118)	Artie Wilson	450.00	225.00	135.00
(119)	Pedrin Zorrilla	125.00	65.00	40.00
(120)	Pito entrevista a Hornsby	300.00	150.00	90.00
(121)	El galardon del triunfo	125.00	65.00	40.00
(122)	Fanaticos de alta posicion	125.00	65.00	40.00
(123)	VOLO LA VERJA	125.00	65.00	40.00

1950-51 Denia Puerto Rican League - Action

115- Gilliam dió out a Casanovas

These 2-1/2" x 3-1/2" cards are part of a set of about 150 covering many different sports. The pictures are colorized photographs and the cards are blank-backed, intended to be glued into an album. The number of baseball subjects is not known. Confirmed subjects are listed here, with identified players listed parenthetically.

		NM	E	VG
	Common Card:	50.00	25.00	15.00
1	Tetelo tambien joronea. (Tetelo Vargas)	85.00	40.00	25.00
2	Taborn saca en home. (Earl Taborn)	50.00	25.00	15.00
3	Se la aguo la blanqueada.	50.00	25.00	15.00
4	R. Blasini se lesiona. (Rafael Blasini)	50.00	25.00	15.00
5	Atkins mofa, Polaco safe. (Joe Atkins)	50.00	25.00	15.00
6	CERCADO-	50.00	25.00	15.00
7	Pitcher se desliza - safe.	50.00	25.00	15.00
8	Fdo. Ramos tras homer(Fernando Ramos)	50.00	25.00	15.00
9	Wilson safe en terecera. (Artie Wilson)	110.00	55.00	32.50
10	Tiro malo - SAFE.	50.00	25.00	15.00
11	VILLODAS LO ESPERA - OUT.(Luis Villodas)	50.00	25.00	15.00
12	Perry da out a Gilliam -(Alonso Perry, Jim Gilliam)	85.00	40.00	25.00
13	Safe en primera -	50.00	25.00	15.00
14	Medina obsequia a Brown.(Medina Chapman, Willard Brown)	200.00	100.00	60.00
15	Tiro malo, Almendaro anota.(Jaime Almendro)	50.00	25.00	15.00
16	Ramos toco primero - OUT.(Fernando Ramos)	50.00	25.00	15.00
17	Brazo contra brazo -	50.00	25.00	15.00
18	Pedroso felicitado tras homer -(Fernando Pedroso)	50.00	25.00	15.00
19	QUE PASA, CEFO?(Cefo Conde)	50.00	25.00	15.00
20	Canena estafa home -(Canena Marquez)	65.00	30.00	20.00
21	Buen slide - SAFE.	50.00	25.00	15.00
22	Mucha vista, Powell.(Bill Powell)	50.00	25.00	15.00
23	OUT FORZADO.	50.00	25.00	15.00
24	Alomar out en home. (Guinea Alomar)	50.00	25.00	15.00
25	Regreso a base - SAFE.	50.00	25.00	15.00
26	Pitcher trata sorprender - SAFE.	50.00	25.00	15.00
27	LOS RECUERDA USTED?	50.00	25.00	15.00
28	Leo Thomas sale de juego.(Leo Thomas)	50.00	25.00	15.00
29	Atkins es felicitado por tribu.(Joe Atkins)	50.00	25.00	15.00
30	Trio campeonil cagueno(Manuel Hernandez, Quincy Trouppe, Chet Brewer)	135.00	65.00	40.00
31	Llegando y llegando.	50.00	25.00	15.00
32	El fotografoen accion -	50.00	25.00	15.00
33	El fotografo en accion	50.00	25.00	15.00
34	No me toques Arroyito - OUT.(Luis "Tite" Arroyo)	50.00	25.00	15.00
35	Taborn propina out.(Earl Taborn)	50.00	25.00	15.00
36	El Mucaro conecta homer -(Bob Thurman)	65.00	30.00	20.00
37	PANTALONES Y FALDAS.(Jose G. Santiago)	50.00	25.00	15.00
38	Buzas en la derrota.(Joe Buzas)	50.00	25.00	15.00
39	El Gran Jurado se reune. (Raymond Brown)	135.00	65.00	40.00
40	Canena se desliza -(Canena Marquez)	65.00	30.00	20.00
41	Que dijo el umpire?	50.00	25.00	15.00
42	Bernier sabe escurrirse -(Carlos Bernier)	50.00	25.00	15.00
43	Se la escapo, la bola - SAFE.	50.00	25.00	15.00
44	Squeeze play perfecto.	50.00	25.00	15.00
45	Cuidado, que la lleva!	50.00	25.00	15.00
46	Que el umpire diga -	50.00	25.00	15.00
47	Pepe Lucas boto la bola. (Pepe Lucas)	50.00	25.00	15.00
48	Gachito se apunta hit.	50.00	25.00	15.00
49	Peloteros o Luchadores?	50.00	25.00	15.00
50	Otoniel lo toca - OUT. (Otoniel Ortiz)	50.00	25.00	15.00
51	Premian a Jorge Rosas. (Jorge Rosas)	50.00	25.00	15.00
52	Markland dio homerun -(Jim Markland)	50.00	25.00	15.00
53	Blasini safe en primera. (Rafael Blasini)	50.00	25.00	15.00
54	Graham conecto homer -(Jack Graham)	50.00	25.00	15.00
55	Penalver se prepara - SAFE.	50.00	25.00	15.00
56	No quiere riesgos	50.00	25.00	15.00
57	Bin Torres esquiva - SAFE.(Bin Torres)	50.00	25.00	15.00
58	Mutua embestida- SAFE.	50.00	25.00	15.00
59	Lo sacaron a media base.	50.00	25.00	15.00
60	Llego transqueando.	50.00	25.00	15.00
61	Quedate quieto - dice el coach.	50.00	25.00	15.00
62	Buscando en vano su presa -	50.00	25.00	15.00
63	Besando la base?	50.00	25.00	15.00
64	Pescaron al Jueyito. (Jueyito Andrade)	50.00	25.00	15.00
65	Greco da tremendo toletazo.	50.00	25.00	15.00
66	Thomas catcher, Wallaesa al bate. (Valmy Thomas, Jack Wallaesa)	50.00	25.00	15.00
67	Trofeos de TRIPLE CAMPEON.	50.00	25.00	15.00
74	H. Reyes lanza, Sanchez Batea.(Herminio Reyes, Juan Sanchez)	50.00	25.00	15.00
77	Wilson apacigua a Bernier . . .(Artie Wilson, Carlos Bernier)	85.00	40.00	25.00
78	Cogida de cuatro estrellas . . .	50.00	25.00	15.00
80	Davis out de Gachito - Wallaesa . . .(Johnny Davis, Jack Wallaesa)	50.00	25.00	15.00
81	Arroyo busca double-play.(Pedro J. Arroyo)	50.00	25.00	15.00
82	Ruben sale por lesion. (Ruben Gomez)	50.00	25.00	15.00
83	SAFE EN EL PLATO.	50.00	25.00	15.00
84	Buen esfuerzo, pero en vano . . .	50.00	25.00	15.00
85	ESTAS TRISTE, JONES?(Sam Jones)	50.00	25.00	15.00
87	Equipo ESTRELLAS NATIVAS	50.00	25.00	15.00

88	Arroyo batea, Scarpatte recibe(Pedro J. Arroyo, V. Scarpatte)	50.00	25.00	15.00
93	Cihoki recoge . . . out(Al Cihocki)	50.00	25.00	15.00
95	El arbitro pensativo . . . out.	50.00	25.00	15.00
97	Buena atrapada . . . del fotografo.	50.00	25.00	15.00
103	Villodas da hit. . .(Luis Villodas)	50.00	25.00	15.00
106	HIT EL BATAZO . . .	50.00	25.00	15.00
110	LO COGIERON LLEGANDO . . .	50.00	25.00	15.00
115	Gilliam dio out a Casanovas(Jim Gilliam, Rafael Casanovas)	85.00	40.00	25.00
124	Canena pone fuera a Bernier . . .(Canena Marquez, Carlos Bernier)	50.00	25.00	15.00
137	Terminado el swing . . .	50.00	25.00	15.00

1909 Derby Cigars N.Y. Giants

Although there is no advertising on these cards to indicate their origin, it is believed that this set was issued by Derby Cigars, a product of American Tobacco Co. A dozen different subjects, all New York Giants, have been found. The cards, many of which appear to be hand-cut measure about 1-3/4" x 2-3/4". The cards feature an oval black-and-white player portrait on a red background. The player's name and position are in a white strip at bottom.

		NM	E	VG
Complete Set (12):		45,000	22,500	13,500
Common Player:		3,700	1,850	1,100
(1)	Josh Devore	3,700	1,850	1,100
(2)	Larry Doyle	3,700	1,850	1,100
(3)	Art Fletcher	3,700	1,850	1,100
(4)	Buck Herzog	3,700	1,850	1,100
(5)	Rube Marquard	5,500	2,700	1,650
(6)	Christy Mathewson	12,500	6,250	3,750
(7)	Fred Merkle	3,700	1,850	1,100
(8)	Chief Meyers	3,700	1,850	1,100
(9)	Red Murray	3,700	1,850	1,100
(10)	John McGraw	5,500	2,700	1,650
(11)	Fred Snodgrass	3,700	1,850	1,100
(12)	Hooks Wiltse	3,700	1,850	1,100

1977 Detroit Caesars Discs

Virtually identical in format to the several locally sponsored disc sets of the previous year, these 3-3/8" diameter player discs were sponsored by a professional slow-pitch softball team. Discs once again feature black-and-white player portrait photos in the center of a baseball design. The left and right panels are in one of several bright colors. Licensed by the Players Association through Mike Schechter Associates, the player photos carry no uniform logos. Backs are printed in green. The unnumbered discs are checklisted here alphabetically.

	NM	E	VG
Complete Set (70):	125.00	65.00	35.00
Common Player:	2.50	1.25	.75

(1)	Sal Bando	2.50	1.25	.75
(2)	Buddy Bell	2.50	1.25	.75
(3)	Johnny Bench	6.00	3.00	1.75
(4)	Larry Bowa	2.50	1.25	.75
(5)	Steve Braun	2.50	1.25	.75
(6)	George Brett	15.00	7.50	4.50
(7)	Lou Brock	6.00	3.00	1.75
(8)	Jeff Burroughs	2.50	1.25	.75
(9)	Bert Campaneris	2.50	1.25	.75
(10)	John Candelaria	2.50	1.25	.75
(11)	Jose Cardenal	2.50	1.25	.75
(12)	Rod Carew	4.50	2.25	1.25
(13)	Steve Carlton	4.50	2.25	1.25
(14)	Dave Cash	2.50	1.25	.75
(15)	Cesar Cedeno	2.50	1.25	.75
(16)	Ron Cey	2.50	1.25	.75
(17)	Dave Concepcion	2.50	1.25	.75
(18)	Dennis Eckersley	3.00	1.50	.90
(19)	Mark Fidrych	5.00	2.50	1.50
(20)	Rollie Fingers	5.00	2.50	1.50
(21)	Carlton Fisk	6.00	3.00	1.75
(22)	George Foster	2.50	1.25	.75
(23)	Wayne Garland	2.50	1.25	.75
(24)	Ralph Garr	2.50	1.25	.75
(25)	Steve Garvey	4.00	2.00	1.25
(26)	Cesar Geronimo	2.50	1.25	.75
(27)	Bobby Grich	2.50	1.25	.75
(28)	Ken Griffey Sr.	2.50	1.25	.75
(29)	Don Gullett	2.50	1.25	.75
(30)	Mike Hargrove	2.50	1.25	.75
(31)	Al Hrabosky	2.50	1.25	.75
(32)	Jim Hunter	5.00	2.50	1.50
(33)	Reggie Jackson	9.00	4.50	2.75
(34)	Randy Jones	2.50	1.25	.75
(35)	Dave Kingman	3.50	1.75	1.00
(36)	Jerry Koosman	2.50	1.25	.75
(37)	Dave LaRoche	2.50	1.25	.75
(38)	Greg Luzinski	2.50	1.25	.75
(39)	Fred Lynn	2.50	1.25	.75
(40)	Bill Madlock	2.50	1.25	.75
(41)	Rick Manning	2.50	1.25	.75
(42)	Jon Matlock	2.50	1.25	.75
(43)	John Mayberry	2.50	1.25	.75
(44)	Hal McRae	2.50	1.25	.75
(45)	Andy Messersmith	2.50	1.25	.75
(46)	Rick Monday	2.50	1.25	.75
(47)	John Montefusco	2.50	1.25	.75
(48)	Joe Morgan	6.00	3.00	1.75
(49)	Thurman Munson	5.00	2.50	1.50
(50)	Bobby Murcer	2.50	1.25	.75
(51)	Bill North	2.50	1.25	.75
(52)	Jim Palmer	6.00	3.00	1.75
(53)	Tony Perez	5.00	2.50	1.50
(54)	Jerry Reuss	2.50	1.25	.75
(55)	Brooks Robinson	5.00	2.50	1.50
(56)	Pete Rose	15.00	7.50	4.50
(57)	Joe Rudi	2.50	1.25	.75
(58)	Nolan Ryan	30.00	15.00	9.00
(59)	Manny Sanguillen	2.50	1.25	.75
(60)	Mike Schmidt	15.00	7.50	4.50
(61)	Tom Seaver	7.50	3.75	2.25
(62)	Bill Singer	2.50	1.25	.75
(63)	Willie Stargell	6.00	3.00	1.75
(64)	Rusty Staub	3.50	1.75	1.00
(65)	Luis Tiant	2.50	1.25	.75
(66)	Bob Watson	2.50	1.25	.75
(67)	Butch Wynegar	2.50	1.25	.75
(68)	Carl Yastrzemski	7.50	3.75	2.25
(69)	Robin Yount	6.00	3.00	1.75
(70)	Richie Zisk	2.50	1.25	.75

1908 Detroit Free Press Tigers Postcards

Most of the stars of the 1907-09 American League Champion Detroit Tigers are found in this set of postcards issued by a local newspaper and reportedly sold at the stadium for $1 a set. The cards are 3-1/2" x 5-1/4", printed in black-and-white. Fronts have a border around the photo with the line, "Copyright by the Detroit Free Press, 1908" beneath the photo. At bottom is the player's last name in capital letters with

his position in parentheses. Backs have standard postcard indicia. The unnumbered cards are checklisted here alphabetically. It is possible this list is not complete.

		NM	E	VG
Complete Set (11):		12,500	6,250	3,750
Common Player:		400.00	200.00	120.00
(1)	Ty Cobb	8,000	4,000	2,400
(2)	Sam Crawford	1,500	750.00	450.00
(3)	Wild Bill Donovan	400.00	200.00	120.00
(4)	Hughie Jennings	1,500	750.00	450.00
(5)	Ed Killian	400.00	200.00	120.00
(6)	Matty McIntyre	400.00	200.00	120.00
(7)	George Mullen (Mullin)	400.00	200.00	120.00
(8)	Charley O'Leary	400.00	200.00	120.00
(9)	Boss Schmidt	400.00	200.00	120.00
(10)	Ed Summer (Summers)	400.00	200.00	120.00
(11)	Ed Willett	400.00	200.00	120.00

1935 Detroit Free Press Tigers

Colorized photos with brightly colored backgrounds and borders are featured in this series of newspaper pictures featuring the World Champion Detroit Tigers. About 9" x 11", the pictures are blank-backed. These premiums were issued every Sunday between April 28-Aug. 25. The unnumbered pictures are checklisted here in alphabetical order. In the American Card Catalog, the set carried the designation M120.

		NM	E	VG
Complete Set (18):		750.00	370.00	220.00
Common Player:		40.00	20.00	12.00
(1)	Eldon Auker	40.00	20.00	12.00
(2)	Tommy Bridges	40.00	20.00	12.00
(3)	Flea Clifton	40.00	20.00	12.00
(4)	Gordon Stanley (Mickey) Cochrane	100.00	50.00	30.00
(5)	Alvin Crowder	40.00	20.00	12.00
(6)	Pete Fox	40.00	20.00	12.00
(7)	Charles Gehringer	75.00	37.50	22.50
(8)	Goose Goslin	75.00	37.50	22.50
(9)	Henry Greenberg	125.00	65.00	35.00
(10)	Ray Hayworth	40.00	20.00	12.00
(11)	Elon Hogsett	40.00	20.00	12.00
(12)	Marvin Owen	40.00	20.00	12.00
(13)	Billy Rogell	40.00	20.00	12.00
(14)	Lynwood (Schoolboy) Rowe	45.00	22.50	13.50
(15)	Victor ("Vic") Sorrell	40.00	20.00	12.00
(16)	Joe Sullivan	40.00	20.00	12.00
(17)	Jerry Walker	40.00	20.00	12.00
(18)	Jo-Jo White	40.00	20.00	12.00

1968 Detroit Free Press Bubblegumless Tiger Cards

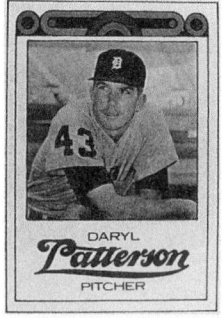

The World Champion Tigers are featured in this series of newspaper inserts published in August, 1968, by the "Detroit Magazine" rotogravure section of the Sunday "Detroit Free Press." The full-color fronts and the backs were printed on separate pages to allow them to be cut out and pasted on cardboard to make a baseball card. Backs are horizontally formatted and include a drawing of the player at left; biographical data and recent stats at right. Card elements measure 2-1/2" x 3-1/2". Values quoted are for front/back pairs. Unmatched fronts are priced at 45 percent of the prices shown; backs should be priced at 30 percent.

		NM	E	VG
Complete Set, Uncut Pages:		250.00	125.00	75.00
Complete Set, Singles (28):		200.00	100.00	60.00
Common Player:		10.00	5.00	3.00
(1)	Gates Brown	10.00	5.00	3.00
(2)	Norm Cash	15.00	7.50	4.50
(3)	Tony Cuccinello	10.00	5.00	3.00
(4)	Pat Dobson	10.00	5.00	3.00
(5)	Bill Freehan	12.50	6.25	3.75
(6)	John Hiller	10.00	5.00	3.00
(7)	Willie Horton	10.00	5.00	3.00
(8)	Al Kaline	35.00	17.50	10.50
(9)	Fred Lasher	10.00	5.00	3.00
(10)	Mickey Lolich	15.00	7.50	4.50
(11)	Tom Matchick	10.00	5.00	3.00
(12)	Dick McAuliffe	10.00	5.00	3.00
(13)	Denny McLain	12.50	6.25	3.75
(14)	Don McMahon	10.00	5.00	3.00
(15)	Wally Moses	10.00	5.00	3.00
(16)	Jim Northrup	10.00	5.00	3.00
(17)	Ray Oyler	10.00	5.00	3.00
(18)	Daryl Patterson	10.00	5.00	3.00
(19)	Jim Price	10.00	5.00	3.00
(20)	Johnny Sain	10.00	5.00	3.00
(21)	Mayo Smith	10.00	5.00	3.00
(22)	Joe Sparma	10.00	5.00	3.00
(23)	Mickey Stanley	10.00	5.00	3.00
(24)	Dick Tracewski	10.00	5.00	3.00
(25)	Jon Warden	10.00	5.00	3.00
(26)	Don Wert	10.00	5.00	3.00
(27)	Earl Wilson	10.00	5.00	3.00
(28)	Jon Wyatt (John)	10.00	5.00	3.00

1978 Detroit Free Press Tigers

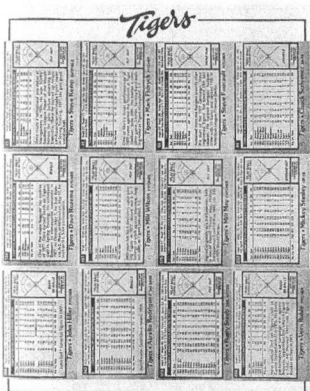

In its Sunday color magazine of April 16, 1978, the newspaper printed presumably authorized reproductions of all 1978 Topps cards which featured members of the Detroit Tigers. The magazine has a cover photo of Mark Fidrych. In the centerspread, reproduced in color, are pictures of the fronts of 20 Tigers cards. Two pages later the cards of three departed Tigers, five multi-player rookie cards and the team card are printed, also in full color. Three more pages have the backs of the cards, printed in black-and-white, rather than the orange-and-blue of genuine Topps cards. Instructions with the article invited readers to cut out the fronts and backs and paste them onto pieces of cardboard to make their own cards. Values shown are for complete front/back pairs.

		NM	E	VG
Complete Magazine:		60.00	30.00	20.00
Complete Set, Singles (28):		30.00	15.00	9.00
Common Player:		3.00	1.50	.90
21		3.00	1.50	.90
45	Mark Fidrych	6.00	3.00	1.75
68	Steve Foucault	3.00	1.50	.90
94	Chuck Scrivener	3.00	1.50	.90
124	Dave Rozema	3.00	1.50	.90
151	Milt Wilcox	3.00	1.50	.90
176	Milt May	3.00	1.50	.90
232	Mickey Stanley	3.00	1.50	.90
258	John Hiller	3.00	1.50	.90
286	Ben Oglivie	3.00	1.50	.90
342	Aurelio Rodriguez	3.00	1.50	.90
370	Rusty Staub	6.00	3.00	1.75
385	Tito Fuentes	3.00	1.50	.90
404	Tigers team card (Color checklist back.)	6.00	3.00	1.75
456	Vern Ruhle	3.00	1.50	.90
480	Ron LeFlore	3.50	1.75	1.00
515	Tim Corcoran	3.00	1.50	.90
536	Roric Harrison	3.00	1.50	.90
559	Phil Mankowski	3.00	1.50	.90
607	Fernando Arroyo	3.00	1.50	.90
633	Tom Veryzer	3.00	1.50	.90
660	Jason Thompson	3.00	1.50	.90
684	Ralph Houk	3.50	1.75	1.00
701	Tom Hume, Larry Landreth, Steve McCatty, Bruce Taylor (Rookie Pitchers)	3.00	1.50	.90
703	Larry Andersen, Tim Jones, Mickey Mahler, Jack Morris (Rookie Pitchers)	7.50	3.75	2.25
704	Garth Iorg, Dave Oliver, Sam Perlozzo, Lou Whitaker (Rookie 2nd Basemen)	9.00	4.50	2.75
707	Mickey Klutts, Paul Molitor, Alan Trammell, U.L. Washington (Rookie Shortstops)	20.00	10.00	6.00
708	Bo Diaz, Dale Murphy, Lance Parrish, Ernie Whitt (Rookie Catchers)	10.00	5.00	3.00
723	Johnny Wockenfuss	3.00	1.50	.90

1907 Detroit Seamless Steel Tubes Co. Ty Cobb Postcard

It is unclear whether this postcard of the budding Tigers star was a proprietary issue of a local steel company or a more generic postcard on which different advertising messages could be imprinted. The 3-1/2" x 5-1/2" black-and-white postcard has on front a full-length pose of Cobb, with a few biographical details. The back is pre-printed with postcard markings including a one-cent "stamp" and pictorial seal of the U.S.

Ty Cobb (Sold in 3/10 auction for $14,100 SGC-graded as Fair. Similar result in 2012 auction.)

1934 Detroit Tigers Team Issue

This set of blank-back, postcard-sized black-and-white player photo cards is presumed to have been a team issue. A recently-discovered poster associates them with Detroit retailer Newton Annis Furs. Photos have white borders with the wider top border having three stipes. Player name and position are printed within the picture. The unnumbered cards are checklisted here alphabetically. Envelopes in which some of the cards were sold specify 10 "Tiger Photos" for 10 cents.

		NM	E	VG
Complete Set (23):		1,200	600.00	350.00
Common Player:		60.00	30.00	18.00
(1)	Eldon Auker	120.00	60.00	35.00
(2)	Del Baker	120.00	60.00	35.00
(3)	Tommy Bridges	120.00	60.00	35.00
(4)	Mickey Cochrane	300.00	150.00	90.00
(5)	General Crowder	120.00	60.00	35.00
(6)	Frank Doljack	120.00	60.00	35.00
(7)	Carl Fischer	120.00	60.00	35.00
(8)	Pete Fox	120.00	60.00	35.00
(9)	Charlie Gehringer	300.00	150.00	90.00
(10)	Goose Goslin	300.00	150.00	90.00
(11)	"Hank" Greenberg	500.00	250.00	150.00
(12)	Luke Hamlin	120.00	60.00	35.00
(13)	Ray Hayworth	120.00	60.00	35.00
(14)	Elon Hogsett	120.00	60.00	35.00
(15)	Firpo Marberry	120.00	60.00	35.00
(16)	Marvin Owen	120.00	60.00	35.00
(17)	Cy Perkins	120.00	60.00	35.00
(18)	Billy Rogell	120.00	60.00	35.00
(19)	Schoolboy Rowe	120.00	60.00	35.00
(20)	Heinie Schuble	120.00	60.00	35.00
(21)	Vic Sorrell	120.00	60.00	35.00
(22)	Gee Walker	120.00	60.00	35.00
(23)	Jo-Jo White	120.00	60.00	35.00

1964 Detroit Tigers Milk Bottle Caps

These small (1-5/16" diameter) cardboard milk bottle caps feature line drawings of the 1964 Tigers. The caps are printed in dark blue and orange on front and blank on back. The unnumbered caps are checklisted here in alphabetical order. A wire staple is found in most caps. The caps were reportedly produced for Twin Pines Dairy for use on bottles of chocolate milk.

		NM	E	VG
Complete Set (14):		800.00	400.00	240.00
Common Player:		50.00	25.00	15.00
(1)	Hank Aguirre	50.00	25.00	15.00
(2)	Billy Bruton	50.00	25.00	15.00
(3)	Norman Cash	100.00	50.00	30.00
(4)	Don Demeter	50.00	25.00	15.00
(5)	Chuck Dressen	50.00	25.00	15.00
(6)	Bill Freehan	70.00	35.00	21.00
(7)	Al Kaline	300.00	150.00	90.00
(8)	Frank Lary	50.00	25.00	15.00
(9)	Jerry Lumpe	50.00	25.00	15.00
(10)	Dick McAuliffe	50.00	25.00	15.00
(11)	Bubba Phillips	50.00	25.00	15.00
(12)	Ed Rakow	50.00	25.00	15.00
(13)	Phil Regan	50.00	25.00	15.00
(14)	Dave Wickersham	50.00	25.00	15.00

1936 Detroit Times Sports Stamps

Printed as part of the regular newspaper page, these feature items have a stamp-design photo element of about 2" x 2-1/2" atop a biographical and career summary. These stamps were printed between June and August and include stars of other sports such as boxing, football, hockey, golf, etc."

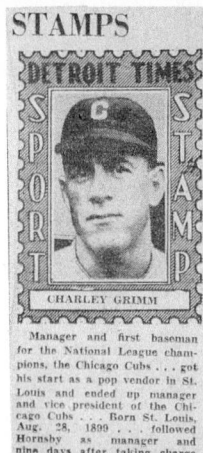

STAMPS

DETROIT TIMES

CHARLEY GRIMM

Manager and first baseman for the National League champions, the Chicago Cubs . . . got his start as a pop vendor in St. Louis and ended up manager and vice president of the Chicago Cubs . . . Born St. Louis, Aug. 28, 1899 . . . followed Hornsby as manager and nine days after taking charge had the team in first place.

	NM	E	VG
Common Player:	15.00	7.50	4.50
(1) Eldon Auker	15.00	7.50	4.50
(2) Del Baker	15.00	7.50	4.50
(3) Tommy Bridges	15.00	7.50	4.50
(4) Jack Burns	15.00	7.50	4.50
(5) Ty Cobb	40.00	20.00	12.00
(6) Mickey Cochrane (Dark cap.)	20.00	10.00	6.00
(7) Mickey Cochrane (White cap.)	20.00	10.00	6.00
(8) Joe Cronin	20.00	10.00	6.00
(9) Alvin Crowder	15.00	7.50	4.50
(10a) Dizzy Dean (Bio first line "Star pitcher of.")	30.00	15.00	9.00
(10b) Dizzy Dean (Bio "of" on second line.)	30.00	15.00	9.00
(11) Paul Dean	15.00	7.50	4.50
(12) Wes Ferrell	15.00	7.50	4.50
(13) Pete Fox	15.00	7.50	4.50
(14) Jimmy Foxx	30.00	15.00	9.00
(15) Frank Frisch	20.00	10.00	6.00
(16a) Lou Gehrig (Bio first line "...slugging first.")	40.00	20.00	12.00
(16b) Lou Gehrig (Bio first line "slugging.")	40.00	20.00	12.00
(17) Charles Gehringer	20.00	10.00	6.00
(18) Chas. Gehringer	20.00	10.00	6.00
(19) Lefty Gomez	20.00	10.00	6.00
(20a) Goose Goslin (White cap.)	20.00	10.00	6.00
(20b) Goose Goslin (Dark cap.)	20.00	10.00	6.00
(21) Hank Greenberg	20.00	10.00	6.00
(22) Charley Grimm	15.00	7.50	4.50
(23) Ray Hayworth	15.00	7.50	4.50
(24) Elon Hogsett	15.00	7.50	4.50
(25) Walter Johnson	30.00	15.00	9.00
(26) Chuck Klein	20.00	10.00	6.00
(27) Connie Mack	20.00	10.00	6.00
(28) Heinie Manush	20.00	10.00	6.00
(29) Van Lingle Mungo	15.00	7.50	4.50
(30) Glenn Myatt	15.00	7.50	4.50
(31) Steve O'Neill	15.00	7.50	4.50
(32) Billy Rogell	15.00	7.50	4.50
(33a) Schoolboy Rowe (White cap.)	15.00	7.50	4.50
(33b) Schoolboy Rowe (Dark cap.)	15.00	7.50	4.50
(34) Babe Ruth	40.00	20.00	12.00
(35) Al Simmons	30.00	15.00	9.00
(36) Vic Sorrell	15.00	7.50	4.50
(37) Tris Speaker	30.00	15.00	9.00
(38) Casey Stengel	20.00	10.00	6.00
(39) Joe Sullivan	15.00	7.50	4.50
(40) Bill Terry	15.00	7.50	4.50
(41) Joe Vosmik	15.00	7.50	4.50
(42) Gerry Walker	15.00	7.50	4.50
(43) Lon Warneke	15.00	7.50	4.50
(44) Jo Jo White	15.00	7.50	4.50
(45) Earl Whitehill	15.00	7.50	4.50
(46) Jimmy Wilson	15.00	7.50	4.50

1966 Dexter Press California Angels

Less well-known than the New York firm's premium issues for Coca-Cola are Dexter Press' team issues. Sold for 50 cents in a cellophane bag with a colorful cardboard header the team issues are in the same basic design as the premium cards of 1967, but measure only 4" x 5-7/8". Though they were sold in sets of eight, more individual cards exist for the known teams, so it is evident there was some exchange of cards within the sets over the course of the sales period. Cards have color player poses with a black facsimile autograph at top and with or wihout a white border around. Backs

are printed in blue with personal data and career highlights at top and copyright information at bottom. The cards are checklisted here alphabetically.

 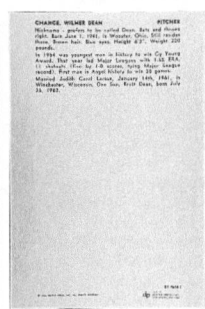

	NM	E	VG
Complete Set (17):	100.00	50.00	30.00
Common Player:	10.00	5.00	3.00
(1) Jose Cardenal	10.00	5.00	3.00
(2) George Brunet	10.00	5.00	3.00
(3) Dean Chance	12.00	6.00	3.50
(4) Jim Fregosi	10.00	5.00	3.00
(5) Ed Kirkpatrick	10.00	5.00	3.00
(6) Bob Knoop	10.00	5.00	3.00
(7) Bob Lee	10.00	5.00	3.00
(8) Marcelino Lopez	10.00	5.00	3.00
(9) Fred Newman	10.00	5.00	3.00
(10) Albie Pearson	10.00	5.00	3.00
(11) Jim Piersall	13.50	6.75	4.00
(12) Rick Reichardt	10.00	5.00	3.00
(13) Bob Rodgers	10.00	5.00	3.00
(14) Paul Schaal	10.00	5.00	3.00
(15) Norm Siebern	10.00	5.00	3.00
(16) Willie Smith	10.00	5.00	3.00
(17) Anaheim Stadium	10.00	5.00	3.00

1966 Dexter Press California Angels 8x10

The extent to which this larger format premium parallels the smaller set is currently unknown.

	NM	E	VG
Common Player:	10.00	5.00	3.00
(1) Dean Chance	15.00	7.50	4.50
(2) Willie Smith	10.00	5.00	3.00
(3) Team Photo	10.00	5.00	3.00

1966 Dexter Press California Angels Booklet

HOME OF THE CALIFORNIA ANGELS

20 NATURAL COLOR VIEWS SAVE THIS MINIATURE FOR YOUR SCRAPBOOK

ANAHEIM CALIFORNIA

This souvenir-stand bound booklet offered pictures of the 1966 California Angels in two different sizes. Each 8-1/8" x 3-1/2" page features a pair of identical color photo cards. A postcard-size (3-1/2" x 5-1/2") portrait has a facsimile autograph of the player at top, attached by perforations to a 2-1/4" x 3-1/2" card, which in turn is perforated into the bound end of the book. Booklets originally sold for 50 cents. The unnumbered cards are checklisted here in alphabetical order.

	NM	E	VG
Complete Booket:	150.00	75.00	45.00
Complete Set, Large (10):	60.00	30.00	18.00
Complete Set, Small (10):	40.00	20.00	12.00
Common Player, Large:	8.00	4.00	2.40
Common Player, Small:	6.00	3.00	1.80
Large Format (3-1/2" x 5-1/2")			
(1) Jose Cardenal	8.00	4.00	2.50
(2) Dean Chance	8.00	4.00	2.50
(3) Jim Fregosi	8.00	4.00	2.50
(4) Bob Knoop	8.00	4.00	2.50
(5) Albie Pearson	8.00	4.00	2.50
(6) Rick Reichardt	8.00	4.00	2.50
(7) Bob Rodgers	8.00	4.00	2.50
(8) Paul Schaal	8.00	4.00	2.50
(9) Willie Smith	8.00	4.00	2.50
(10) **Anaheim Stadium**	8.00	4.00	2.50
Small Format (2-1/4" x 3-1/2")			
(1) Jose Cardenal	6.00	3.00	1.80
(2) Dean Chance	6.00	3.00	1.80
(3) Jim Fregosi	6.00	3.00	1.80
(4) Bob Knoop	6.00	3.00	1.80
(5) Albie Pearson	6.00	3.00	1.80
(6) Rick Reichardt	6.00	3.00	1.80
(7) Bob Rodgers	6.00	3.00	1.80
(8) Paul Schaal	6.00	3.00	1.80
(9) Willie Smith	6.00	3.00	1.80
(10) **Anaheim Stadium**	6.00	3.00	1.80

1966-67 Dexter Press N.Y. Yankees

Less commonly encountered than the later Dexter Press/ Coca-Cola premium issues are the team-set photocards produced by the New York firm. Cards were sold in bagged sets with a colorful cardboard header. Virtually identical in design to the 5-1/2" x 7" premium cards of 1967, the team-set pictures measure 4" x 5-7/8" with a white border around, and a black facsimile autograph at the top of, color player poses. Backs are printed in blue with a few biographical details at top and copyright information at bottom. The unnumbered cards are checklisted here in alphabetical order.

	NM	E	VG
Complete Set (12):	200.00	100.00	60.00
Common Player:	15.00	7.50	4.50
(1) Jim Bouton	17.50	8.75	5.25
(2) Horace Clarke	15.00	7.50	4.50
(3) Al Downing	15.00	7.50	4.50
(4) Whitey Ford	20.00	10.00	6.00
(5) Steve Hamilton	15.00	7.50	4.50
(6) Elston Howard	17.50	8.75	5.25
(7) Mickey Mantle	60.00	30.00	18.00
(8) Joe Pepitone	17.50	8.75	5.25
(9) Bill Robinson	15.00	7.50	4.50
(10) Mel Stottlemyre	15.00	7.50	4.50
(11) Tom Tresh	17.50	8.75	5.25
(12) Steve Whitaker	15.00	7.50	4.50

1967 Dexter Press Premiums

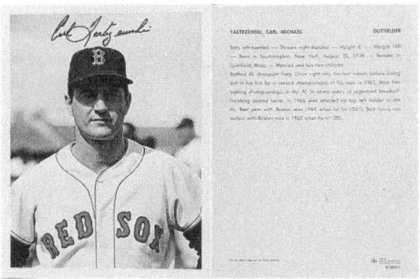

Among the most attractive baseball collectibles issued during the 1960s were the cards produced by Dexter Press and issued in team sets as a premium by Coca-Cola. Eighteen of the 20 Major League teams participated in the promotion (only one California Angels player and no St. Louis Cardinals). The cards are in 5-1/2" x 7" glossy format. All of the color photos are waist-to-cap poses shot during spring training, and all cards feature a black facsimile autograph at the top of the photo. The cards have a 1/4" white border around the picture. Backs are printed in blue on white and include a few biographical details and career highlights. Nine of the 12 players in the All-Star issue can be differentiated from the same players' cards in the team sets by the lengthier biographies on back. The bios on the cards of Bunning, Mays and Santo are the same in both versions. While each of the cards has a number printed on back in the lower-right, they are checklisted here alphabetically within team. Sixteen of the Dexter Press premiums were issued in a smaller, borderless sticker set in 1983; it is an unauthorized collector issue.

	NM	E	VG
Complete Set (229):	1,500	750.00	450.00
Common Player:	5.00	2.50	1.50
KANSAS CITY ATHLETICS			

(3) Jim Fregosi	6.00	3.00	1.80
(4) Bob Knoop	6.00	3.00	1.80
(5) Albie Pearson	6.00	3.00	1.80
(6) Rick Reichardt	6.00	3.00	1.80
(7) Bob Rodgers	6.00	3.00	1.80
(8) Paul Schaal	6.00	3.00	1.80
(9) Willie Smith	6.00	3.00	1.80
(10) **Anaheim Stadium**	6.00	3.00	1.80

(26) Jack Aker 5.00 2.50 1.50

ATLANTA BRAVES

(38) Hank Aaron 25.00 12.50 7.50

CHICAGO CUBS

(50) George Altman 5.00 2.50 1.50

LOS ANGELES DODGERS

(62) Bob Bailey 5.00 2.50 1.50

SAN FRANCISCO GIANTS

(74) Jesus Alou 5.00 2.50 1.50

CLEVELAND INDIANS

(86) Max Alvis 5.00 2.50 1.50

NEW YORK METS

(98) Ed Bressoud 5.00 2.50 1.50

CHICAGO WHITE SOX

(206) Tommie Agee 5.00 2.50 1.50

NEW YORK YANKEES

(218) Jim Bouton 6.00 3.00 1.75

ALL-STARS

(3) Willie Davis 5.00 2.50 1.50
(4) Al Kaline 10.00 5.00 3.00
(5) Harmon Killebrew 10.00 5.00 3.00
(6) Willie Mays 12.50 6.25 3.75
(7) Joe Pepitone 6.00 3.00 1.75
(8) Brooks Robinson 10.00 5.00 3.00
(9) Frank Robinson 10.00 5.00 3.00

KANSAS CITY ATHLETICS

(27) Campy Campaneris 5.00 2.50 1.50

ATLANTA BRAVES

(39) Felipe Alou 6.00 3.00 1.75

CHICAGO CUBS

(51) Ernie Banks 18.00 9.00 5.50

LOS ANGELES DODGERS

(63) Willie Davis 5.00 2.50 1.50

SAN FRANCISCO GIANTS

(75) Ollie Brown 5.00 2.50 1.50

CLEVELAND INDIANS

(87) Joe Azcue 5.00 2.50 1.50

NEW YORK METS

(99) Ken Boyer 7.00 3.50 2.00

CHICAGO WHITE SOX

(207) Ken Berry 5.00 2.50 1.50

NEW YORK YANKEES

(219) Horace Clarke 5.00 2.50 1.50

ALL-STARS

(3) Willie Davis 5.00 2.50 1.50

KANSAS CITY ATHLETICS

(28) Danny Cater 5.00 2.50 1.50

ATLANTA BRAVES

(40) Wade Blasingame 5.00 2.50 1.50

CHICAGO CUBS

(52) Glen Beckert (Glenn) 5.00 2.50 1.50

LOS ANGELES DODGERS

(64) Ron Fairly 5.00 2.50 1.50

SAN FRANCISCO GIANTS

(76) Jim Davenport 5.00 2.50 1.50

CLEVELAND INDIANS

(88) Gary Bell 5.00 2.50 1.50

CHICAGO WHITE SOX

(208) Don Buford 5.00 2.50 1.50

NEW YORK YANKEES

(220) Al Downing 5.00 2.50 1.50

HOUSTON ASTROS

(21) Sonny Jackson 5.00 2.50 1.50
(22) Jim Landis 5.00 2.50 1.50
(23) Eddie Mathews 10.00 5.00 3.00
(24) Joe Morgan 12.00 6.00 3.50
(25) Rusty Staub 7.50 3.75 2.25

ALL-STARS

(4) Al Kaline 10.00 5.00 3.00

KANSAS CITY ATHLETICS

(29) Ed Charles 5.00 2.50 1.50

ATLANTA BRAVES

(41) Clete Boyer 5.00 2.50 1.50

CHICAGO CUBS

(53) John Boccabella 5.00 2.50 1.50

LOS ANGELES DODGERS

(65) Ron Hunt 5.00 2.50 1.50

SAN FRANCISCO GIANTS

(77) Tito Fuentes 5.00 2.50 1.50

CLEVELAND INDIANS

(89) Larry Brown 5.00 2.50 1.50

CHICAGO WHITE SOX

(209) Ron Hansen 5.00 2.50 1.50

NEW YORK YANKEES

(221) Steve Hamilton 5.00 2.50 1.50

KANSAS CITY ATHLETICS

(26) Jack Aker 5.00 2.50 1.50
(27) Campy Campaneris 5.00 2.50 1.50
(28) Danny Cater 5.00 2.50 1.50
(29) Ed Charles 5.00 2.50 1.50
(30) Ossie Chavarria 5.00 2.50 1.50
(31) Dick Green 5.00 2.50 1.50
(32) Mike Hershberger 5.00 2.50 1.50
(33) Lew Krausse 5.00 2.50 1.50
(34) Jim Nash 5.00 2.50 1.50
(35) Joe Nossek 5.00 2.50 1.50
(36) Roger Repoz 5.00 2.50 1.50
(37) Phil Roof 5.00 2.50 1.50

ALL-STARS

(5) Harmon Killebrew 10.00 5.00 3.00

KANSAS CITY ATHLETICS

(30) Ossie Chavarria 5.00 2.50 1.50

ATLANTA BRAVES

(42) Bob Bruce 5.00 2.50 1.50

CHICAGO CUBS

(54) Ray Culp 5.00 2.50 1.50

LOS ANGELES DODGERS

(66) Lou Johnson 5.00 2.50 1.50

SAN FRANCISCO GIANTS

(78) Tom Haller 5.00 2.50 1.50

CLEVELAND INDIANS

(90) Rocky Colavito 7.50 3.75 2.25

CHICAGO WHITE SOX

(210) Joel Horlen 5.00 2.50 1.50

NEW YORK YANKEES

(222) Elston Howard 7.50 3.75 2.25

ATLANTA BRAVES

(38) Hank Aaron 25.00 12.50 7.50
(39) Felipe Alou 6.00 3.00 1.75
(40) Wade Blasingame 5.00 2.50 1.50
(41) Clete Boyer 5.00 2.50 1.50
(42) Bob Bruce 5.00 2.50 1.50
(43) Ty Cline 5.00 2.50 1.50
(44) Tony Cloninger 5.00 2.50 1.50
(45) Ken Johnson 5.00 2.50 1.50
(46) Dennis Menke 5.00 2.50 1.50
(47) Gene Oliver 5.00 2.50 1.50
(48) Joe Torre 7.50 3.75 2.25
(49) Woody Woodward 5.00 2.50 1.50

ALL-STARS

(6) Willie Mays 12.50 6.25 3.75

KANSAS CITY ATHLETICS

(31) Dick Green 5.00 2.50 1.50

ATLANTA BRAVES

(43) Ty Cline 5.00 2.50 1.50

CHICAGO CUBS

(55) Ken Holtzman 5.00 2.50 1.50

LOS ANGELES DODGERS

(67) John Kennedy 5.00 2.50 1.50

SAN FRANCISCO GIANTS

(79) Jim Hart 5.00 2.50 1.50

CLEVELAND INDIANS

(91) Vic Davalillo 5.00 2.50 1.50

CHICAGO WHITE SOX

(211) Tommy John 6.00 3.00 1.75

NEW YORK YANKEES

(223) Mickey Mantle 40.00 20.00 12.00

CHICAGO CUBS

(50) George Altman 5.00 2.50 1.50
(51) Ernie Banks 18.00 9.00 5.50
(52) Glen Beckert (Glenn) 5.00 2.50 1.50
(53) John Boccabella 5.00 2.50 1.50
(54) Ray Culp 5.00 2.50 1.50
(55) Ken Holtzman 5.00 2.50 1.50
(56) Randy Hundley 5.00 2.50 1.50
(57) Cal Koonce 5.00 2.50 1.50
(58) Adolfo Phillips 5.00 2.50 1.50
(59) Ron Santo 6.00 3.00 1.75
(60) Lee Thomas 5.00 2.50 1.50
(61) Billy Williams 10.00 5.00 3.00

ALL-STARS

(7) Joe Pepitone 6.00 3.00 1.75

KANSAS CITY ATHLETICS

(32) Mike Hershberger 5.00 2.50 1.50

ATLANTA BRAVES

(44) Tony Cloninger 5.00 2.50 1.50

CHICAGO CUBS

(56) Randy Hundley 5.00 2.50 1.50

LOS ANGELES DODGERS

(68) Jim Lefebvre 5.00 2.50 1.50

SAN FRANCISCO GIANTS

(80) Hal Lanier 5.00 2.50 1.50

CLEVELAND INDIANS

(92) Pedro Gonzalez 5.00 2.50 1.50

CHICAGO WHITE SOX

(212) Bob Locker 5.00 2.50 1.50

NEW YORK YANKEES

(224) Joe Pepitone 6.00 3.00 1.75

LOS ANGELES DODGERS

(62) Bob Bailey 5.00 2.50 1.50
(63) Willie Davis 5.00 2.50 1.50
(64) Ron Fairly 5.00 2.50 1.50
(65) Ron Hunt 5.00 2.50 1.50
(66) Lou Johnson 5.00 2.50 1.50
(67) John Kennedy 5.00 2.50 1.50
(68) Jim Lefebvre 5.00 2.50 1.50
(69) Claude Osteen 5.00 2.50 1.50
(70) Wes Parker 5.00 2.50 1.50
(71) Ron Perranoski 5.00 2.50 1.50
(72) Phil Regan 5.00 2.50 1.50
(73) Don Sutton 7.50 3.75 2.25

ALL-STARS

(8) Brooks Robinson 10.00 5.00 3.00

HOUSTON ASTROS

(21) Sonny Jackson 5.00 2.50 1.50

KANSAS CITY ATHLETICS

(33) Lew Krausse 5.00 2.50 1.50

ATLANTA BRAVES

(45) Ken Johnson 5.00 2.50 1.50

CHICAGO CUBS

(57) Cal Koonce 5.00 2.50 1.50

LOS ANGELES DODGERS

(69) Claude Osteen 5.00 2.50 1.50

SAN FRANCISCO GIANTS

(81) Willie Mays 15.00 7.50 4.50

CLEVELAND INDIANS

(93) Chuck Hinton 5.00 2.50 1.50

CHICAGO WHITE SOX

(213) Tommy McCraw 5.00 2.50 1.50

NEW YORK YANKEES

(225) Fritz Peterson 5.00 2.50 1.50

SAN FRANCISCO GIANTS

(74) Jesus Alou 5.00 2.50 1.50
(75) Ollie Brown 5.00 2.50 1.50
(76) Jim Davenport 5.00 2.50 1.50
(77) Tito Fuentes 5.00 2.50 1.50
(78) Tom Haller 5.00 2.50 1.50
(79) Jim Hart 5.00 2.50 1.50
(80) Hal Lanier 5.00 2.50 1.50
(81) Willie Mays 15.00 7.50 4.50
(82) Mike McCormick 5.00 2.50 1.50
(83) Willie McCovey 12.00 6.00 3.50
(84) Gaylord Perry 8.00 4.00 2.50
(85) Norman Siebern 5.00 2.50 1.50

ALL-STARS

(9) Frank Robinson 10.00 5.00 3.00

HOUSTON ASTROS

(22) Jim Landis 5.00 2.50 1.50

KANSAS CITY ATHLETICS

(34) Jim Nash 5.00 2.50 1.50

ATLANTA BRAVES

(46) Dennis Menke 5.00 2.50 1.50

CHICAGO CUBS

(58) Adolfo Phillips 5.00 2.50 1.50

LOS ANGELES DODGERS

(70) Wes Parker 5.00 2.50 1.50

SAN FRANCISCO GIANTS

(82) Mike McCormick 5.00 2.50 1.50

CLEVELAND INDIANS

(94) Sam McDowell 6.00 3.00 1.75

MINNESOTA TWINS

(202) Rich Rollins 5.00 2.50 1.50

CHICAGO WHITE SOX

(214) Jerry McNertney 5.00 2.50 1.50

NEW YORK YANKEES

		NM	E	VG
(226)	Charley Smith	5.00	2.50	1.50

CLEVELAND INDIANS

(86)	Max Alvis	5.00	2.50	1.50
(87)	Joe Azcue	5.00	2.50	1.50
(88)	Gary Bell	5.00	2.50	1.50
(89)	Larry Brown	5.00	2.50	1.50
(90)	Rocky Colavito	7.50	3.75	2.25
(91)	Vic Davalillo	5.00	2.50	1.50
(92)	Pedro Gonzalez	5.00	2.50	1.50
(93)	Chuck Hinton	5.00	2.50	1.50
(94)	Sam McDowell	6.00	3.00	1.75
(95)	Luis Tiant	6.00	3.00	1.75
(96)	Leon Wagner	5.00	2.50	1.50
(97)	Fred Whitfield	5.00	2.50	1.50

HOUSTON ASTROS

(23)	Eddie Mathews	10.00	5.00	3.00

KANSAS CITY ATHLETICS

(35)	Joe Nossek	5.00	2.50	1.50

ATLANTA BRAVES

(47)	Gene Oliver	5.00	2.50	1.50

CHICAGO CUBS

(59)	Ron Santo	6.00	3.00	1.75

LOS ANGELES DODGERS

(71)	Ron Perranoski	5.00	2.50	1.50

SAN FRANCISCO GIANTS

(83)	Willie McCovey	12.00	6.00	3.50

CLEVELAND INDIANS

(95)	Luis Tiant	6.00	3.00	1.75

MINNESOTA TWINS

(203)	Ted Uhlaender	5.00	2.50	1.50

CHICAGO WHITE SOX

(215)	Jim O'Toole	5.00	2.50	1.50

NEW YORK YANKEES

(227)	Mel Stottlemyre	6.00	3.00	1.75

NEW YORK METS

(98)	Ed Bressoud	5.00	2.50	1.50
(99)	Ken Boyer	7.00	3.50	2.00

HOUSTON ASTROS

(24)	Joe Morgan	12.00	6.00	3.50

KANSAS CITY ATHLETICS

(36)	Roger Repoz	5.00	2.50	1.50

ATLANTA BRAVES

(48)	Joe Torre	7.50	3.75	2.25

CHICAGO CUBS

(60)	Lee Thomas	5.00	2.50	1.50

LOS ANGELES DODGERS

(72)	Phil Regan	5.00	2.50	1.50

SAN FRANCISCO GIANTS

(84)	Gaylord Perry	8.00	4.00	2.50

CLEVELAND INDIANS

(96)	Leon Wagner	5.00	2.50	1.50

MINNESOTA TWINS

(204)	Sandy Valdespino	5.00	2.50	1.50

CHICAGO WHITE SOX

(216)	Bill "Moose" Skowron	7.00	3.50	2.00

NEW YORK YANKEES

(228)	Tom Tresh	6.00	3.00	1.75

HOUSTON ASTROS

(25)	Rusty Staub	7.50	3.75	2.25

KANSAS CITY ATHLETICS

(37)	Phil Roof	5.00	2.50	1.50

ATLANTA BRAVES

(49)	Woody Woodward	5.00	2.50	1.50

CHICAGO CUBS

(61)	Billy Williams	10.00	5.00	3.00

LOS ANGELES DODGERS

(73)	Don Sutton	7.50	3.75	2.25

SAN FRANCISCO GIANTS

(85)	Norman Siebern	5.00	2.50	1.50

CLEVELAND INDIANS

(97)	Fred Whitfield	5.00	2.50	1.50

MINNESOTA TWINS

(205)	Zoilo Versalles	5.00	2.50	1.50

CHICAGO WHITE SOX

(217)	Pete Ward	5.00	2.50	1.50

NEW YORK YANKEES

(229)	Roy White	6.00	3.00	1.75

MINNESOTA TWINS

(201)	Tony Oliva	8.00	4.00	2.50
(202)	Rich Rollins	5.00	2.50	1.50
(203)	Ted Uhlaender	5.00	2.50	1.50
(204)	Sandy Valdespino	5.00	2.50	1.50
(205)	Zoilo Versalles	5.00	2.50	1.50

CHICAGO WHITE SOX

(206)	Tommie Agee	5.00	2.50	1.50
(207)	Ken Berry	5.00	2.50	1.50
(208)	Don Buford	5.00	2.50	1.50
(209)	Ron Hansen	5.00	2.50	1.50
(210)	Joel Horlen	5.00	2.50	1.50
(211)	Tommy John	6.00	3.00	1.75
(212)	Bob Locker	5.00	2.50	1.50
(213)	Tommy McCraw	5.00	2.50	1.50
(214)	Jerry McNertney	5.00	2.50	1.50
(215)	Jim O'Toole	5.00	2.50	1.50
(216)	Bill "Moose" Skowron	7.00	3.50	2.00
(217)	Pete Ward	5.00	2.50	1.50

NEW YORK YANKEES

(218)	Jim Bouton	6.00	3.00	1.75
(219)	Horace Clarke	5.00	2.50	1.50
(220)	Al Downing	5.00	2.50	1.50
(221)	Steve Hamilton	5.00	2.50	1.50
(222)	Elston Howard	7.50	3.75	2.25
(223)	Mickey Mantle	40.00	20.00	12.00
(224)	Joe Pepitone	6.00	3.00	1.75
(225)	Fritz Peterson	5.00	2.50	1.50
(226)	Charley Smith	5.00	2.50	1.50
(227)	Mel Stottlemyre	6.00	3.00	1.75
(228)	Tom Tresh	6.00	3.00	1.75
(229)	Roy White	6.00	3.00	1.75

1967 Dexter Press Team Posters

These 17" x 11" color card-stock posters reproduce the 12 cards (or on the Cubs sheet, four additional players) found in the 1967 Dexter Press premium team sets, in images about 2" x 3". The cards are pictured on a solid color background with color team logos. Printed on back are player identification and biographical information. Dexter Press copyright and credit lines are at bottom. It is not known whether other teams involved in the premium program can also be found in poster format.

	NM	E	VG
California Angels	270.00	135.00	80.00
Chicago Cubs	360.00	180.00	110.00
Chicago White Sox	270.00	135.00	80.00
N.Y. Mets	360.00	180.00	110.00
N.Y. Yankees	600.00	300.00	180.00
Washington Senators	360.00	180.00	110.00

1968 Dexter Press Postcards

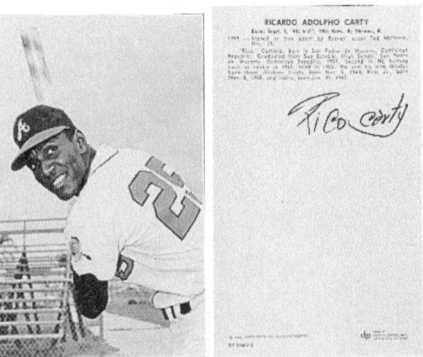

In its second year of printing premium cards for Coca-Cola, Dexter Press changed format and greatly reduced the number of participating teams and players. Only six teams were represented by 12-card sets, while an additional four teams had one or two players included. For 1968, Dexter Press produced its premiums in postcard (3-1/2" x 5-1/2") size. The cards featured borderless color player poses on front. Backs were printed in blue on white and included a facsimile autograph, biographical details and career highlights. Cards carry a Dexter Press serial number on back, but are checklisted here alphabetically within team.

		NM	E	VG
Complete Set (77):		500.00	250.00	150.00
Common Player:		4.00	2.00	1.25

PHILADELPHIA PHILLIES

(50)	Dick Allen	9.00	4.50	2.75

PITTSBURGH PIRATES

(51)	Roberto Clemente	25.00	12.50	7.50

BOSTON RED SOX

(53)	Jerry Adair	4.00	2.00	1.25

DETROIT TIGERS

(65)	Bill Freehan	6.00	3.00	1.75

MINNESOTA TWINS

(66)	Bob Allison	4.00	2.00	1.25

PITTSBURGH PIRATES

(52)	Bill Mazeroski	10.00	5.00	3.00

BOSTON RED SOX

(54)	Mike Andrews	4.00	2.00	1.25

MINNESOTA TWINS

(67)	Dave Boswell	4.00	2.00	1.25

HOUSTON ASTROS

(5)	Mike Cuellar	4.00	2.00	1.25
(6)	Ron Davis	4.00	2.00	1.25
(7)	Dave Giusti	4.00	2.00	1.25
(8)	Julio Gotay	4.00	2.00	1.25
(9)	Denny Lemaster	4.00	2.00	1.25

BOSTON RED SOX

(55)	Gary Bell	4.00	2.00	1.25

MINNESOTA TWINS

(68)	Rod Carew	10.00	5.00	3.00

HOUSTON ASTROS

(5)	Mike Cuellar	4.00	2.00	1.25

BOSTON RED SOX

(56)	Darrell Brandon	4.00	2.00	1.25

MINNESOTA TWINS

(69)	Dean Chance	4.00	2.00	1.25

HOUSTON ASTROS

(6)	Ron Davis	4.00	2.00	1.25

BOSTON RED SOX

(57)	Dick Ellsworth	4.00	2.00	1.25

MINNESOTA TWINS

(70)	Jim Kaat	4.00	2.00	1.25

BALTIMORE ORIOLES

(44)	Dave Johnson	4.00	2.00	1.25
(45)	Dave McNally	4.00	2.00	1.25
(46)	Tom Phoebus	4.00	2.00	1.25
(47)	Boog Powell	5.00	2.50	1.50
(48)	Brooks Robinson	12.00	6.00	3.50
(49)	Frank Robinson	12.00	6.00	3.50

HOUSTON ASTROS

(7)	Dave Giusti	4.00	2.00	1.25

BOSTON RED SOX

(58)	Joe Foy	4.00	2.00	1.25

MINNESOTA TWINS

(71)	Harmon Killebrew	10.00	5.00	3.00

PHILADELPHIA PHILLIES

(50)	Dick Allen	9.00	4.50	2.75

HOUSTON ASTROS

(8)	Julio Gotay	4.00	2.00	1.25

BOSTON RED SOX

(59)	Dalton Jones	4.00	2.00	1.25

MINNESOTA TWINS

(72)	Russ Nixon	4.00	2.00	1.25

PITTSBURGH PIRATES

(51)	Roberto Clemente	25.00	12.50	7.50
(52)	Bill Mazeroski	10.00	5.00	3.00

HOUSTON ASTROS

(9)	Denny Lemaster	4.00	2.00	1.25

BALTIMORE ORIOLES

(45)	Dave McNally	4.00	2.00	1.25

BOSTON RED SOX

(60)	Jim Lonborg	5.00	2.50	1.50

MINNESOTA TWINS

(73)	Tony Oliva	6.00	3.00	1.75

BOSTON RED SOX

(53)	Jerry Adair	4.00	2.00	1.25

(54)	Mike Andrews	4.00	2.00	1.25
(55)	Gary Bell	4.00	2.00	1.25
(56)	Darrell Brandon	4.00	2.00	1.25
(57)	Dick Ellsworth	4.00	2.00	1.25
(58)	Joe Foy	4.00	2.00	1.25
(59)	Dalton Jones	4.00	2.00	1.25
(60)	Jim Lonborg	5.00	2.50	1.50
(61)	Dave Morehead	4.00	2.00	1.25
(62)	Rico Petrocelli	4.00	2.00	1.25
(63)	George Scott	4.00	2.00	1.25
(64)	John Wyatt	4.00	2.00	1.25

BALTIMORE ORIOLES

(46)	Tom Phoebus	4.00	2.00	1.25

BOSTON RED SOX

(61)	Dave Morehead	4.00	2.00	1.25

MINNESOTA TWINS

(74)	Rich Rollins	4.00	2.00	1.25

DETROIT TIGERS

(65)	Bill Freehan	6.00	3.00	1.75

BALTIMORE ORIOLES

(47)	Boog Powell	5.00	2.50	1.50

BOSTON RED SOX

(62)	Rico Petrocelli	4.00	2.00	1.25

MINNESOTA TWINS

(75)	John Roseboro	4.00	2.00	1.25
(66)	Bob Allison	4.00	2.00	1.25
(67)	Dave Boswell	4.00	2.00	1.25
(68)	Rod Carew	10.00	5.00	3.00
(69)	Dean Chance	4.00	2.00	1.25
(70)	Jim Kaat	4.00	2.00	1.25
(71)	Harmon Killebrew	10.00	5.00	3.00
(72)	Russ Nixon	4.00	2.00	1.25
(73)	Tony Oliva	6.00	3.00	1.75
(74)	Rich Rollins	4.00	2.00	1.25
(75)	John Roseboro	4.00	2.00	1.25
(76)	Cesar Tovar	4.00	2.00	1.25
(77)	Ted Uhlaender	4.00	2.00	1.25

BALTIMORE ORIOLES

(48)	Brooks Robinson	12.00	6.00	3.50

BOSTON RED SOX

(63)	George Scott	4.00	2.00	1.25

MINNESOTA TWINS

(76)	Cesar Tovar	4.00	2.00	1.25

BALTIMORE ORIOLES

(49)	Frank Robinson	12.00	6.00	3.50

BOSTON RED SOX

(64)	John Wyatt	4.00	2.00	1.25

MINNESOTA TWINS

(77)	Ted Uhlaender	4.00	2.00	1.25

1979 Dexter Press Hall of Fame Plaque Postcards

(See Hall of Fame (Dexter Press) for checklist, value data.)

1960 Diamond Associates Postcards

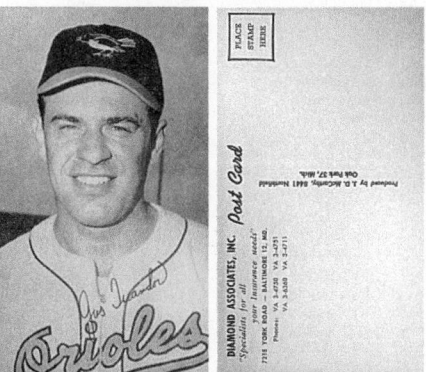

Based on the uniform style depicted on front, the actual year of issue for this card could be anywhere between 1958-1962. Produced by photographer J.D. McCarthy, apparently for the star catcher's off-season business, the 3-1/4" x 5-1/2" black-and-white card has a facsimile autograph on front. The postcard-style back has the address and phone numbers of the insurance company.

	NM	E	VG
Gus Triandos	30.00	15.00	9.00

1940 Diamond Dust Punchboard Cards

These paper cards are the consolation prizes from a popular gambling device of the Depression era, the punchboard. For five cents a customer could choose one of 624 holes on the punchboard and push a wood or metal punch through the paper on front, driving out the back a 1" x about 1-3/4" picture of a baseball player. Fifteen of the players were $1 winners and were produced in much shorter supply than the others; any which were redeemed would probably have been destroyed. The pictures are printed on ribbed paper to assist in fitting them into the board. They are pictures taken from the photos on contemporary "Salutation" Exhibit cards, though without uniform logos. They are printed in bright colors with the player name in a color bar at bottom. Backs are blank. The unnumbered cards are listed here in alphabetical order, with an asterisk indicating winners. The punchboard itself is highly collectible, with colorful baseball graphics and player pictures and names. Earlier and later versions of Diamond Dust punchboards are also known, but have not been checklisted.

		NM	E	VG
	Complete Set (33):	850.00	425.00	250.00
	Common Player:	15.00	7.50	4.50
	Complete Unused Punchboard:	1,200	600.00	350.00
(1)	Luke Appling (*)	45.00	22.00	13.50
(2)	Earl Averill (*)	45.00	22.00	13.50
(3)	Adolf Camilli	15.00	7.50	4.50
(4)	Harland Clift (Harlond)	15.00	7.50	4.50
(5)	Joe Cronin (*) (Unconfirmed)	45.00	22.00	13.50
(6)	Tony Cuccinello	15.00	7.50	4.50
(7)	Dizzy Dean	35.00	17.50	10.50
(8)	Bill Dickey (*)	50.00	25.00	15.00
(9)	Joe DiMaggio (*)	125.00	62.00	37.00
(10)	Bob Feller	30.00	15.00	9.00
(11)	Jimmie Foxx (*)	45.00	22.00	13.50
(12)	Charlie Gehringer (*)	45.00	22.00	13.50
(13)	Lefty Gomez	25.00	12.50	7.50
(14)	Hank Greenberg	30.00	15.00	9.00
(15)	Lefty Grove	25.00	12.50	7.50
(16)	Gabby Hartnett	15.00	7.50	4.50
(17)	Carl Hubbell	25.00	12.50	7.50
(18)	Bob Johnson	15.00	7.50	4.50
(19)	Chuck Klein	25.00	12.50	7.50
(20)	Bill Lee	15.00	7.50	4.50
(21)	Ernie Lombardi (*)	45.00	22.00	13.50
(22)	Frank McCormick (*)	25.00	12.50	7.50
(23)	Joe Medwick	25.00	12.50	7.50
(24)	Johnny Mize (*)	45.00	22.00	13.50
(25)	Buck Newson (Newsom)	15.00	7.50	4.50
(26)	Mel Ott (*)	45.00	22.00	13.50
(27)	Johnny Rizzo (*)	25.00	12.50	7.50
(28)	Red Ruffing (*) (Unconfirmed)	45.00	22.00	13.50
(29)	Cecil Travis	15.00	7.50	4.50
(30)	Johnny Vander Meer	15.00	7.50	4.50
(31)	Arky Vaughan (*)	45.00	22.00	13.50
(32)	Lon Warneke	15.00	7.50	4.50
(33)	Rudy York (*) (Unconfirmed)	25.00	12.50	7.50

1979 Diamond Greats

Card collector, dealer and later Donruss photographer Jack Wallin produced this collectors' issue. Cards are in the 2-1/2" x 3-1/2" format, printed in black-and-white and blank-backed. Besides the player photo on front, there is identification and a line of career stats. Four 100-card series were issued. Series 1 concentrates on Yankees, Giants, Senators and Dodgers. Series 2 comprises the Cubs, White Sox, Cardinals and Browns. The third series features Braves, Red Sox, Reds and Indians. Series 4 concentrates on the Phillies, A's, Pirates and Tigers.

Roy Sievers

		NM	E	VG
	Complete Set (400):	275.00	135.00	85.00
	Series 1 (1-100):	60.00	30.00	18.00
	Series 2 (101-200):	50.00	25.00	15.00
	Series 3 (201-300):	50.00	25.00	15.00
	Series 4 (301-400):	50.00	25.00	15.00
	Common Player:	2.00	1.00	.60
1	Joe DiMaggio	12.00	6.00	3.50
2	Ben Chapman	2.00	1.00	.60
3	Joe Dugan	2.00	1.00	.60
4	Bobby Shawkey	2.00	1.00	.60
5	Joe Sewell	2.00	1.00	.60
6	George Pipgras	2.00	1.00	.60
7	George Selkirk	2.00	1.00	.60
8	Babe Dahlgren	2.00	1.00	.60
9	Spud Chandler	2.00	1.00	.60
10	Duffy Lewis	2.00	1.00	.60
11	Lefty Gomez	3.00	1.50	.90
12	Atley Donald	2.00	1.00	.60
13	Whitey Witt	2.00	1.00	.60
14	Marius Russo	2.00	1.00	.60
15	Buddy Rosar	2.00	1.00	.60
16	Russ Van Atta	2.00	1.00	.60
17	Johnny Lindell	2.00	1.00	.60
18	Bobby Brown	2.00	1.00	.60
19	Tony Kubek	2.50	1.25	.70
20	Joe Beggs	2.00	1.00	.60
21	Don Larsen	2.50	1.25	.70
22	Andy Carey	2.00	1.00	.60
23	Johnny Kucks	2.00	1.00	.60
24	Elston Howard	2.50	1.25	.70
25	Roger Maris	4.00	2.00	1.25
26	Rube Marquard	2.50	1.25	.70
27	Sam Leslie	2.00	1.00	.60
28	Freddy Leach	2.00	1.00	.60
29	Fred Fitzsimmons	2.00	1.00	.60
30	Bill Terry	2.50	1.25	.70
31	Joe Moore	2.00	1.00	.60
32	Waite Hoyt	2.00	1.00	.60
33	Travis Jackson	2.00	1.00	.60
34	Gus Mancuso	2.00	1.00	.60
35	Carl Hubbell	3.00	1.50	.90
36	Bill Voiselle	2.00	1.00	.60
37	Hank Leiber	2.00	1.00	.60
38	Burgess Whitehead	2.00	1.00	.60
39	Johnny Mize	3.00	1.50	.90
40	Bill Lohrman	2.00	1.00	.60
41	Bill Rigney	2.00	1.00	.60
42	Cliff Melton	2.00	1.00	.60
43	Willard Marshall	2.00	1.00	.60
44	Wes Westrum	2.00	1.00	.60
45	Monte Irvin	3.00	1.50	.90
46	Marv Grissom	2.00	1.00	.60
47	Clyde Castleman	2.00	1.00	.60
48	Harry Gumbert	2.00	1.00	.60
49	Daryl Spencer	2.00	1.00	.60
50	Willie Mays	9.00	4.50	2.75
51	Sam West	2.00	1.00	.60
52	Fred Schulte	2.00	1.00	.60
53	Cecil Travis	2.00	1.00	.60
54	Tommy Thomas	2.00	1.00	.60
55	Dutch Leonard	2.00	1.00	.60
56	Jimmy Wasdell	2.00	1.00	.60
57	Doc Cramer	2.00	1.00	.60
58	Harland Clift (Harlond)	2.00	1.00	.60
59	Ken Chase	2.00	1.00	.60
60	Buddy Lewis	2.00	1.00	.60
61	Ossie Bluege	2.00	1.00	.60
62	Chuck Stobbs	2.00	1.00	.60
63	Jimmy DeShong	2.00	1.00	.60
64	Roger Wolff	2.00	1.00	.60
65	Luke Sewell	2.00	1.00	.60
66	Sid Hudson	2.00	1.00	.60
67	Jack Russell	2.00	1.00	.60
68	Walt Masterson	2.00	1.00	.60
69	George Myatt	2.00	1.00	.60
70	Monte Weaver	2.00	1.00	.60
71	Cliff Bolton	2.00	1.00	.60
72	Ray Scarborough	2.00	1.00	.60
73	Albie Pearson	2.00	1.00	.60
74	Gil Coan	2.00	1.00	.60

75	Roy Sievers	2.00	1.00	.60
76	Burleigh Grimes	2.00	1.00	.60
77	Charlie Hargreaves	2.00	1.00	.60
78	Babe Herman	2.00	1.00	.60
79	Fred Frankhouse	2.00	1.00	.60
80	Al Lopez	2.00	1.00	.60
81	Lonny Frey	2.00	1.00	.60
82	Dixie Walker	2.00	1.00	.60
83	Kirby Higbe	2.00	1.00	.60
84	Bobby Bragan	2.00	1.00	.60
85	Leo Durocher	2.00	1.00	.60
86	Woody English	2.00	1.00	.60
87	Preacher Roe	2.00	1.00	.60
88	Vic Lombardi	2.00	1.00	.60
89	Clyde Sukeforth	2.00	1.00	.60
90	Pee Wee Reese	5.00	2.50	1.50
91	Joe Hatten	2.00	1.00	.60
92	Gene Hermanski	2.00	1.00	.60
93	Ray Benge	2.00	1.00	.60
94	Duke Snider	5.00	2.50	1.50
95	Walter Alston	2.00	1.00	.60
96	Don Drysdale	3.00	1.50	.90
97	Andy Pafko	2.00	1.00	.60
98	Don Zimmer	2.00	1.00	.60
99	Carl Erskine	2.00	1.00	.60
100	Dick Williams	2.00	1.00	.60
101	Charlie Grimm	2.00	1.00	.60
102	Clarence Blair	2.00	1.00	.60
103	Johnny Moore	2.00	1.00	.60
104	Clay Bryant	2.00	1.00	.60
105	Billy Herman	2.00	1.00	.60
106	Hy Vandenberg	2.00	1.00	.60
107	Lennie Merullo	2.00	1.00	.60
108	Hank Wyse	2.00	1.00	.60
109	Dom Dallessandro	2.00	1.00	.60
110	Al Epperly	2.00	1.00	.60
111	Bill Nicholson	2.00	1.00	.60
112	Vern Olsen	2.00	1.00	.60
113	Johnny Schmitz	2.00	1.00	.60
114	Bob Scheffing	2.00	1.00	.60
115	Bob Rush	2.00	1.00	.60
116	Roy Smalley	2.00	1.00	.60
117	Ransom Jackson	2.00	1.00	.60
118	Cliff Chambers	2.00	1.00	.60
119	Harry Chiti	2.00	1.00	.60
120	Johnny Klippstein	2.00	1.00	.60
121	Gene Baker	2.00	1.00	.60
122	Walt Moryn	2.00	1.00	.60
123	Dick Littlefield	2.00	1.00	.60
124	Bob Speake	2.00	1.00	.60
125	Hank Sauer	2.00	1.00	.60
126	Monty Stratton	2.50	1.25	.70
127	Johnny Kerr	2.00	1.00	.60
128	Milt Gaston	2.00	1.00	.60
129	Eddie Smith	2.00	1.00	.60
130	Larry Rosenthal	2.00	1.00	.60
131	Orval Grove	2.00	1.00	.60
132	Johnny Hodapp	2.00	1.00	.60
133	Johnny Rigney	2.00	1.00	.60
134	Willie Kamm	2.00	1.00	.60
135	Ed Lopat	2.00	1.00	.60
136	Smead Jolley	2.00	1.00	.60
137	Ralph Hodgin	2.00	1.00	.60
138	Ollie Bejma	2.00	1.00	.60
139	Zeke Bonura	2.00	1.00	.60
140	Al Hollingsworth	2.00	1.00	.60
141	Thurman Tucker	2.00	1.00	.60
142	Cass Michaels	2.00	1.00	.60
143	Bill Wight	2.00	1.00	.60
144	Don Lenhardt	2.00	1.00	.60
145	Sammy Esposito	2.00	1.00	.60
146	Jack Harshman	2.00	1.00	.60
147	Turk Lown	2.00	1.00	.60
148	Jim Landis	2.00	1.00	.60
149	Bob Shaw	2.00	1.00	.60
150	Minnie Minoso	2.50	1.25	.70
151	Les Bell	2.00	1.00	.60
152	Taylor Douthit	2.00	1.00	.60
153	Jack Rothrock	2.00	1.00	.60
154	Terry Moore	2.00	1.00	.60
155	Max Lanier	2.00	1.00	.60
156	Don Gutteridge	2.00	1.00	.60
157	Stu Martin	2.00	1.00	.60
158	Stan Musial	5.00	2.50	1.50
159	Frank Crespi	2.00	1.00	.60
160	Johnny Hopp	2.00	1.00	.60
161	Ernie Koy	2.00	1.00	.60
162	Joe Garagiola	3.00	1.50	.90
163	Ed Kazak	2.00	1.00	.60
164	Joe Orengo	2.00	1.00	.60
165	Howie Krist	2.00	1.00	.60
166	Enos Slaughter	3.00	1.50	.90
167	Ray Sanders	2.00	1.00	.60
168	Walker Cooper	2.00	1.00	.60
169	Nippy Jones	2.00	1.00	.60
170	Dick Sisler	2.00	1.00	.60
171	Harvey Haddix	2.00	1.00	.60
172	Solly Hemus	2.00	1.00	.60
173	Ray Jablonski	2.00	1.00	.60
174	Alex Grammas	2.00	1.00	.60
175	Joe Cunningham	2.00	1.00	.60
176	Debs Garms	2.00	1.00	.60
177	Chief Hogsett	2.00	1.00	.60
178	Alan Strange	2.00	1.00	.60
179	Rick Ferrell	2.00	1.00	.60
180	Jack Kramer	2.00	1.00	.60
181	Jack Knott	2.00	1.00	.60
182	Bob Harris	2.00	1.00	.60
183	Billy Hitchcock	2.00	1.00	.60
184	Jim Walkup	2.00	1.00	.60
185	Roy Cullenbine	2.00	1.00	.60
186	Bob Muncrief	2.00	1.00	.60
187	Chet Laabs	2.00	1.00	.60
188	Vern Kennedy	2.00	1.00	.60
189	Bill Trotter	2.00	1.00	.60
190	Denny Galehouse	2.00	1.00	.60
191	Al Zarilla	2.00	1.00	.60
192	Hank Arft	2.00	1.00	.60
193	Nelson Potter	2.00	1.00	.60
194	Ray Coleman	2.00	1.00	.60
195	Bob Dillinger	2.00	1.00	.60
196	Dick Kokos	2.00	1.00	.60
197	Bob Cain	2.00	1.00	.60
198	Virgil Trucks	2.00	1.00	.60
199	Duane Pillette	2.00	1.00	.60
200	Bob Turley	2.00	1.00	.60
201	Wally Berger	2.00	1.00	.60
202	John Lanning	2.00	1.00	.60
203	Buck Jordan	2.00	1.00	.60
204	Jim Turner	2.00	1.00	.60
205	Johnny Cooney	2.00	1.00	.60
206	Hank Majeski	2.00	1.00	.60
207	Phil Masi	2.00	1.00	.60
208	Tony Cuccinello	2.00	1.00	.60
209	Whitey Wietelmann	2.00	1.00	.60
210	Lou Fette	2.00	1.00	.60
211	Vince DiMaggio	2.50	1.25	.70
212	Huck Betts	2.00	1.00	.60
213	Red Barrett	2.00	1.00	.60
214	Pinkey Whitney	2.00	1.00	.60
215	Tommy Holmes	2.00	1.00	.60
216	Ray Berres	2.00	1.00	.60
217	Mike Sandlock	2.00	1.00	.60
218	Max Macon	2.00	1.00	.60
219	Sibby Sisti	2.00	1.00	.60
220	Johnny Beazley	2.00	1.00	.60
221	Bill Posedel	2.00	1.00	.60
222	Connie Ryan	2.00	1.00	.60
223	Del Crandall	2.00	1.00	.60
224	Bob Addis	2.00	1.00	.60
225	Warren Spahn	3.00	1.50	.90
226	Johnny Pesky	2.00	1.00	.60
227	Dom DiMaggio	2.50	1.25	.70
228	Emerson Dickman	2.00	1.00	.60
229	Bobby Doerr	2.00	1.00	.60
230	Tony Lupien	2.00	1.00	.60
231	Roy Partee	2.00	1.00	.60
232	Stan Spence	2.00	1.00	.60
233	Jim Bagby	2.00	1.00	.60
234	Buster Mills	2.00	1.00	.60
235	Fabian Gaffke	2.00	1.00	.60
236	George Metkovich	2.00	1.00	.60
237	Tom McBride	2.00	1.00	.60
238	Charlie Wagner	2.00	1.00	.60
239	Eddie Pellagrini	2.00	1.00	.60
240	Harry Dorish	2.00	1.00	.60
241	Ike Delock	2.00	1.00	.60
242	Mel Parnell	2.00	1.00	.60
243	Matt Batts	2.00	1.00	.60
244	Gene Stephens	2.00	1.00	.60
245	Milt Bolling	2.00	1.00	.60
246	Charlie Maxwell	2.00	1.00	.60
247	Willard Nixon	2.00	1.00	.60
248	Sammy White	2.00	1.00	.60
249	Dick Gernert	2.00	1.00	.60
250	Rico Petrocelli	2.00	1.00	.60
251	Edd Roush	2.00	1.00	.60
252	Mark Koenig	2.00	1.00	.60
253	Jimmy Outlaw	2.00	1.00	.60
254	Ethan Allen	2.00	1.00	.60
255	Tony Freitas	2.00	1.00	.60
256	Frank McCormick	2.00	1.00	.60
257	Bucky Walters	2.00	1.00	.60
258	Harry Craft	2.00	1.00	.60
259	Nate Andrews	2.00	1.00	.60
260	Ed Lukon	2.00	1.00	.60
261	Elmer Riddle	2.00	1.00	.60
262	Lee Grissom	2.00	1.00	.60
263	Johnny Vander Meer	2.00	1.00	.60
264	Eddie Joost	2.00	1.00	.60
265	Kermit Wahl	2.00	1.00	.60
266	Ival Goodman	2.00	1.00	.60
267	Clyde Vollmer	2.00	1.00	.60
268	Grady Hatton	2.00	1.00	.60
269	Ted Kluszewski	3.00	1.50	.90
270	Johnny Pramesa	2.00	1.00	.60
271	Joe Black	2.50	1.25	.70
272	Roy McMillan	2.00	1.00	.60
273	Wally Post	2.00	1.00	.60
274	Joe Nuxhall	2.00	1.00	.60
275	Jerry Lynch	2.00	1.00	.60
276	Stan Coveleski	2.00	1.00	.60
277	Bill Wambsganss	2.00	1.00	.60
278	Bruce Campbell	2.00	1.00	.60
279	George Uhle	2.00	1.00	.60
280	Earl Averill	2.00	1.00	.60
281	Whit Wyatt	2.00	1.00	.60
282	Oscar Grimes	2.00	1.00	.60
283	Roy Weatherly	2.00	1.00	.60
284	Joe Dobson	2.00	1.00	.60
285	Bob Feller	3.00	1.50	.90
286	Jim Hegan	2.00	1.00	.60
287	Mel Harder	2.00	1.00	.60
288	Ken Keltner	2.00	1.00	.60
289	Red Embree	2.00	1.00	.60
290	Al Milnar	2.00	1.00	.60
291	Lou Boudreau	2.00	1.00	.60
292	Ed Klieman	2.00	1.00	.60
293	Steve Gromek	2.00	1.00	.60
294	George Strickland	2.00	1.00	.60
295	Gene Woodling	2.00	1.00	.60
296	Hank Edwards	2.00	1.00	.60
297	Don Mossi	2.00	1.00	.60
298	Eddie Robinson	2.00	1.00	.60
299	Sam Dente	2.00	1.00	.60
300	Herb Score	2.00	1.00	.60
301	Dolf Camilli	2.00	1.00	.60
302	Jack Warner	2.00	1.00	.60
303	Ike Pearson	2.00	1.00	.60
304	Johnny Peacock	2.00	1.00	.60
305	Gene Corbett	2.00	1.00	.60
306	Walt Millies	2.00	1.00	.60
307	Vance Dinges	2.00	1.00	.60
308	Joe Marty	2.00	1.00	.60
309	Hugh Mulcahey	2.00	1.00	.60
310	Boom Boom Beck	2.00	1.00	.60
311	Charley Schanz	2.00	1.00	.60
312	John Bolling	2.00	1.00	.60
313	Danny Litwhiler	2.00	1.00	.60
314	Emil Verban	2.00	1.00	.60
315	Andy Semenick	2.00	1.00	.60
316	John Antonelli	2.00	1.00	.60
317	Robin Roberts	3.00	1.50	.90
318	Richie Ashburn	3.00	1.50	.90
319	Curt Simmons	2.00	1.00	.60
320	Murry Dickson	2.00	1.00	.60
321	Jim Greengrass	2.00	1.00	.60
322	Gene Freese	2.00	1.00	.60
323	Bobby Morgan	2.00	1.00	.60
324	Don Demeter	2.00	1.00	.60
325	Eddie Sawyer	2.00	1.00	.60
326	Bob Johnson	2.00	1.00	.60
327	Ace Parker	3.00	1.50	.90
328	Joe Hauser	2.00	1.00	.60
329	Walt French	2.00	1.00	.60
330	Tom Ferrick	2.00	1.00	.60
331	Bill Werber	2.00	1.00	.60
332	Walt Masters	2.00	1.00	.60
333	Les McCrabb	2.00	1.00	.60
334	Ben McCoy	2.00	1.00	.60
335	Eric Tipton	2.00	1.00	.60
336	Al Rubeling	2.00	1.00	.60
337	Nick Etten	2.00	1.00	.60
338	Carl Scheib	2.00	1.00	.60
339	Dario Lodigiani	2.00	1.00	.60
340	Earle Brucker	2.00	1.00	.60
341	Al Brancato	2.00	1.00	.60
342	Lou Limmer	2.00	1.00	.60
343	Elmer Valo	2.00	1.00	.60
344	Bob Hooper	2.00	1.00	.60
345	Joe Astroth	2.00	1.00	.60
346	Pete Suder	2.00	1.00	.60
347	Dave Philley	2.00	1.00	.60
348	Gus Zernial	2.00	1.00	.60
349	Bobby Shantz	2.00	1.00	.60
350	Joe DeMaestri	2.00	1.00	.60
351	Fred Lindstrom	2.00	1.00	.60
352	Red Lucas	2.00	1.00	.60
353	Clyde Barnhart	2.00	1.00	.60
354	Nick Strincevich	2.00	1.00	.60
355	Lloyd Waner	2.00	1.00	.60
356	Guy Bush	2.00	1.00	.60
357	Joe Bowman	2.00	1.00	.60
358	Al Todd	2.00	1.00	.60
359	Mace Brown	2.00	1.00	.60
360	Larry French	2.00	1.00	.60
361	Elbie Fletcher	2.00	1.00	.60
362	Woody Jensen	2.00	1.00	.60
363	Rip Sewell	2.00	1.00	.60
364	Johnny Dickshot	2.00	1.00	.60
365	Pete Coscarart	2.00	1.00	.60
366	Bud Hafey	2.00	1.00	.60
367	Ken Heintzelman	2.00	1.00	.60
368	Wally Westlake	2.00	1.00	.60

369	Frank Gustine	2.00	1.00	.60
370	Smoky Burgess	2.00	1.00	.60
371	Dick Groat	2.00	1.00	.60
372	Vern Law	2.00	1.00	.60
373	Bob Skinner	2.00	1.00	.60
374	Don Cardwell	2.00	1.00	.60
375	Bob Friend	2.00	1.00	.60
376	Frank O'Rourke	2.00	1.00	.60
377	Birdie Tebbetts	2.00	1.00	.60
378	Charlie Gehringer	3.00	1.50	.90
379	Eldon Auker	2.00	1.00	.60
380	Tuck Stainback	2.00	1.00	.60
381	Chet Morgan	2.00	1.00	.60
382	Johnny Lipon	2.00	1.00	.60
383	Paul Richards	2.00	1.00	.60
384	Johnny Gorsica	2.00	1.00	.60
385	Ray Hayworth	2.00	1.00	.60
386	Jimmy Bloodworth	2.00	1.00	.60
387	Gene Desautels	2.00	1.00	.60
388	Jo Jo White	2.00	1.00	.60
389	Boots Poffenberger	2.00	1.00	.60
390	Barney McCosky	2.00	1.00	.60
391	Dick Wakefield	2.00	1.00	.60
392	Johnny Groth	2.00	1.00	.60
393	Steve Souchock	2.00	1.00	.60
394	George Vico	2.00	1.00	.60
395	Hal Newhouser	2.00	1.00	.60
396	Ray Herbert	2.00	1.00	.60
397	Jim Bunning	2.00	1.00	.60
398	Frank Lary	2.00	1.00	.60
399	Harvey Kuenn	2.00	1.00	.60
400	Eddie Mathews	3.00	1.50	.90

1911 Diamond Gum Pins (PE2)

The World's Champion Philadelphia A's are well represented and specially marked in this series of small 1" diameter pins. The sepia-toned center portion of the pin has a player portrait photo with his last name, team and league in white at left and right. Around that is a metallic blue border with a white inscription; either "World's Champions" on the A's players, or "Free with Diamond Gum" on the other players.

		NM	E	VG
Complete Set (32):		30,000	15,000	9,000
Common Player:		500.00	250.00	150.00
(1)	Babe Adams	500.00	250.00	150.00
(2)	Home Run Baker	1,600	800.00	475.00
(3)	Chief Bender	1,600	800.00	475.00
(4)	Mordecai Brown	1,600	800.00	475.00
(5)	Donie Bush	500.00	250.00	150.00
(6)	Bill Carrigan	500.00	250.00	150.00
(7)	Frank Chance	1,600	800.00	475.00
(8)	Hal Chase	800.00	400.00	240.00
(9)	Ty Cobb	3,250	1,600	975.00
(10)	Eddie Collins	1,600	800.00	475.00
(11)	George Davis	500.00	250.00	150.00
(12)	Red Dooin	500.00	250.00	150.00
(13)	Larry Doyle	500.00	250.00	150.00
(14)	Johnny Evers	1,600	800.00	475.00
(15)	Miller Huggins	1,600	800.00	475.00
(16)	Hughie Jennings	1,600	800.00	475.00
(17)	Nap Lajoie	1,600	800.00	475.00
(18)	Harry Lord	500.00	250.00	150.00
(19)	Christy Mathewson	2,000	1,000	600.00
(20)	Dots Miller, Herbie Moran (Rochester)	500.00	250.00	150.00
(21)	George Mullen (Mullin)	500.00	250.00	150.00
(22)	Danny Murphy	500.00	250.00	150.00
(23)	Orval Overall	500.00	250.00	150.00
(24)	Eddie Plank	1,600	800.00	475.00
(25)	Ralph Savage (Rochester)	500.00	250.00	150.00
(26)	Ryan Savidge (Rochester)	500.00	250.00	150.00
(27)	Hack Simmons	500.00	250.00	150.00
(28)	Chet Spencer	500.00	250.00	150.00
(29)	Ira Thomas	500.00	250.00	150.00
(30)	Joe Tinker	1,600	800.00	475.00
(31)	Honus Wagner	3,000	1,500	900.00
(32)	Cy Young	2,000	1,000	600.00

1934 Diamond Matchbooks - Silver Border

During much of the Great Depression, the hobby of matchbook collecting swept the country. Generally selling at two for a penny, the matchbooks began to feature photos and artwork to attract buyers. In the late 1930s, several series of sports subjects were issued by Diamond Match Co., of New York City. The first issue was a set of 200 baseball players known to collectors as "silver border" for the color of the photo frame on of the approximately 1-1/2" x 4-1/8" (open) matchbooks. Player portrait or posed photos are printed in sepia on front, and can be found bordered in either red, green, blue or orange (though it is unclear whether all players can actually be found in the red version), theoretically creating an 800-piece color variation set. The player's name and team are printed on the "saddle" and there is a career summary on back, along with a design of glove, ball and bats. Matchbooks are commonly collected with the matches removed and the striker at back-bottom intact. Pieces without the striker are valued at 50 percent of these listed prices. Complete covers with matches bring a premium of 2-3X. The players are listed here alphabetically.

		NM	E	VG
Complete Set (200):		4,500	2,250	1,350
Common Player:		20.00	10.00	6.00
(1)	Earl Adams	20.00	10.00	6.00
(2)	Ethan Allen	20.00	10.00	6.00
(3)	Eldon L. Auker	20.00	10.00	6.00
(4)	Delmar David Baker	20.00	10.00	6.00
(5)	Richard "Dick" Bartell	20.00	10.00	6.00
(6)	Walter Beck	20.00	10.00	6.00
(7)	Herman Bell	20.00	10.00	6.00
(8)	Ray Benge	20.00	10.00	6.00
(9)	Larry J. Benton	20.00	10.00	6.00
(10)	Louis W. Berger	20.00	10.00	6.00
(11)	Walter "Wally" Berger	20.00	10.00	6.00
(12)	Ray Berres	20.00	10.00	6.00
(13)	Charlie Berry	20.00	10.00	6.00
(14)	Walter M. "Huck" Betts	20.00	10.00	6.00
(15)	Ralph Birkofer	20.00	10.00	6.00
(16)	George F. Blaeholder	20.00	10.00	6.00
(17)	Jim Bottomley	40.00	20.00	12.00
(18a)	Ralph Boyle (Photo actually Virgil Davis, white cap.)	20.00	10.00	6.00
(18b)	Ralph Boyle (Correct photo, cark cap.)	20.00	10.00	6.00
(19)	Ed Brandt	20.00	10.00	6.00
(20)	Don Brennan	20.00	10.00	6.00
(21)	Irving (Jack) Burns	20.00	10.00	6.00
(22)	Guy "Joe" Bush	20.00	10.00	6.00
(23)	Adolph Camilli	20.00	10.00	6.00
(24)	Ben Cantwell	20.00	10.00	6.00
(25)	Tex Carleton	20.00	10.00	6.00
(26)	Owen Carroll	20.00	10.00	6.00
(27)	Louis Chiozza	20.00	10.00	6.00
(28)	Watson Clark	20.00	10.00	6.00
(29)	James A. Collins	20.00	10.00	6.00
(30)	Phil Collins	20.00	10.00	6.00
(31)	Edward J. Connolly	20.00	10.00	6.00
(32)	Raymond F. Coombs	20.00	10.00	6.00
(33)	Roger Cramer	20.00	10.00	6.00
(34)	Clifford Crawford	20.00	10.00	6.00
(35)	Hugh M. Critz	20.00	10.00	6.00
(36)	Alvin Crowder	20.00	10.00	6.00
(37)	Tony Cuccinello	20.00	10.00	6.00
(38)	Hazen "Kiki" Cuyler	40.00	20.00	12.00
(39)	Virgil Davis	20.00	10.00	6.00
(40)	Jerome "Dizzy" Dean	80.00	40.00	24.00
(41)	Paul Dean	35.00	17.50	10.50
(42)	Edward Delker	20.00	10.00	6.00
(43)	Paul Derringer	20.00	10.00	6.00
(44)	Eugene DeSautel	20.00	10.00	6.00
(45)	William J. Dietrich	20.00	10.00	6.00
(46)	Frank F. Doljack	20.00	10.00	6.00
(47)	Edward F. Durham	20.00	10.00	6.00
(48)	Leo Durocher	40.00	20.00	12.00
(49)	Jim Elliott	20.00	10.00	6.00
(50)	Charles D. English	20.00	10.00	6.00
(51)	Elwood G. English	20.00	10.00	6.00
(52)	Richard Ferrell	40.00	20.00	12.00
(53)	Wesley Ferrell (EXISTENCE DOUBTED)			
(54)	Charles W. Fischer	20.00	10.00	6.00
(55)	Freddy Fitzsimmons	20.00	10.00	6.00
(56)	Lew Fonseca	20.00	10.00	6.00
(57)	Fred Frankhouse	20.00	10.00	6.00
(58)	John Frederick	20.00	10.00	6.00
(59)	Benny Frey (Reds)	20.00	10.00	6.00
(60)	Linus Frey (Dodgers)	20.00	10.00	6.00
(61)	Frankie Frisch	45.00	22.00	13.50
(62)	Chick Fullis	20.00	10.00	6.00
(63)	August Galan	20.00	10.00	6.00
(64)	Milton Galatzer	120.00	60.00	36.00
(65)	Dennis W. Galehouse	20.00	10.00	6.00
(66)	Milton Gaston	20.00	10.00	6.00
(67)	Chas. Gehringer	45.00	22.00	13.50
(68)	Edward P. Gharrity	20.00	10.00	6.00
(69)	George Gibson	20.00	10.00	6.00
(70)	Isidore Goldstein	250.00	125.00	75.00
(71)	"Hank" Gowdy	20.00	10.00	6.00
(72)	Earl Grace	20.00	10.00	6.00
(73)	Chas. Grimm (Fielding)	20.00	10.00	6.00
(74)	Chas. Grimm (Portrait)	20.00	10.00	6.00
(75)	Frank T. Grube	20.00	10.00	6.00
(76)	Richard Gyselman	20.00	10.00	6.00
(77)	Stanley C. Hack	25.00	12.50	7.50
(78)	Irving Hadley	20.00	10.00	6.00
(79)	Charles "Chick" Hafey	40.00	20.00	12.00
(80)	Harold A. Haid	20.00	10.00	6.00
(81)	Jesse Haines	40.00	20.00	12.00
(82)	Odell A. Hale	20.00	10.00	6.00
(83)	Bill Hallahan	20.00	10.00	6.00
(84)	Luke D. Hamlin	20.00	10.00	6.00
(85)	Roy Hansen	20.00	10.00	6.00
(86)	Melvin Harder	20.00	10.00	6.00
(87)	William M. Harris	20.00	10.00	6.00
(88)	Gabby Hartnett	40.00	20.00	12.00
(89)	Harvey Hendrick	20.00	10.00	6.00
(90)	Floyd "Babe" Herman	25.00	12.50	7.50
(91)	William Herman	40.00	20.00	12.00
(92)	J. Francis Hogan	20.00	10.00	6.00
(93)	Elon Hogsett	20.00	10.00	6.00
(94)	Waite Hoyt	40.00	20.00	12.00
(95)	Carl Hubbell	50.00	25.00	15.00
(96)	Silas K. Johnson	20.00	10.00	6.00
(97)	Sylvester Johnson	20.00	10.00	6.00
(98)	Roy M. Joiner	20.00	10.00	6.00
(99)	Baxter Jordan	20.00	10.00	6.00
(100)	Arndt Jorgens	20.00	10.00	6.00
(101)	William F. Jurges	20.00	10.00	6.00
(102)	Vernon Kennedy	20.00	10.00	6.00
(103)	John F. Kerr	20.00	10.00	6.00
(104)	Charles "Chuck" Klein	40.00	20.00	12.00
(105)	Theodore Kleinhans	20.00	10.00	6.00
(106)	Bill Klem (Umpire)	125.00	65.00	35.00
(107)	Robert G. Kline	20.00	10.00	6.00
(108)	William Knickerbocker	20.00	10.00	6.00
(109)	Jack H. Knott	20.00	10.00	6.00
(110)	Mark Koenig	20.00	10.00	6.00
(111)	William Lawrence	20.00	10.00	6.00
(112)	Thornton S. Lee	20.00	10.00	6.00
(113)	Wm. C. "Bill" Lee	20.00	10.00	6.00
(114)	Emil Leonard	20.00	10.00	6.00
(115)	Ernest Lombardi	40.00	20.00	12.00
(116)	Alfonso Lopez	40.00	20.00	12.00
(117)	Red Lucas	20.00	10.00	6.00
(118)	Ted Lyons	40.00	20.00	12.00
(119)	Daniel MacFayden	20.00	10.00	6.00
(120)	Ed. Majeski	20.00	10.00	6.00
(121)	Leroy Mahaffey	20.00	10.00	6.00
(122)	Pat Malone	20.00	10.00	6.00
(123)	Leo Mangum	20.00	10.00	6.00
(124)	Rabbit Maranville	40.00	20.00	12.00
(125)	Charles K. Marrow	20.00	10.00	6.00
(126)	William McKechnie	40.00	20.00	12.00
(127)	Justin McLaughlin	20.00	10.00	6.00
(128)	Marty McManus	20.00	10.00	6.00
(129)	Eric McNair	20.00	10.00	6.00
(130)	Joe Medwick	40.00	20.00	12.00
(131)	Jim Mooney	20.00	10.00	6.00
(132)	Joe Moore	20.00	10.00	6.00
(133)	John Moore	20.00	10.00	6.00
(134)	Randy Moore	20.00	10.00	6.00
(135)	Joe Morrissey	20.00	10.00	6.00
(136)	Joseph Mowrey	20.00	10.00	6.00
(137)	Fred W. Muller	20.00	10.00	6.00
(138)	Van Mungo	25.00	12.50	7.50
(139)	Glenn Myatt	20.00	10.00	6.00
(140a)	Lynn Nelson (Photo actually Eugene DeSautel, no "C" on cap.)	20.00	10.00	6.00
(140b)	Lynn Nelson (Correct photo, "C" on cap.)	20.00	10.00	6.00
(141)	Henry Oana	60.00	30.00	18.00
(142)	Lefty O'Doul	35.00	17.50	10.50
(143)	Robert O'Farrell	20.00	10.00	6.00
(144)	Ernest Orsatti	20.00	10.00	6.00
(145)	Fritz R. Ostermueller	20.00	10.00	6.00
(146)	Melvin Ott	45.00	22.00	13.50
(147)	Roy Parmelee	20.00	10.00	6.00
(148)	Ralph Perkins	20.00	10.00	6.00
(149)	Frank Pytlak	20.00	10.00	6.00
(150)	Ernest C. Quigley (Umpire)	45.00	22.00	13.50
(151)	George Rensa	20.00	10.00	6.00
(152)	Harry Rice	20.00	10.00	6.00
(153)	Walter Roettger	20.00	10.00	6.00
(154)	William G. Rogell	20.00	10.00	6.00
(155)	Edwin A. Rommel	20.00	10.00	6.00
(156)	Charlie Root	20.00	10.00	6.00
(157)	John Rothrock	20.00	10.00	6.00
(158)	Jack Russell	20.00	10.00	6.00
(159)	Blondy Ryan	20.00	10.00	6.00
(160)	Alexander (Al) Schacht	35.00	17.50	10.50

(161)	Wesley Schultmerick	20.00	10.00	6.00
(162)	Truett B. Sewell	20.00	10.00	6.00
(163)	Gordon Slade	20.00	10.00	6.00
(164)	Bob Smith	20.00	10.00	6.00
(165)	Julius J. Solters	20.00	10.00	6.00
(166)	Glenn Spencer	20.00	10.00	6.00
(167)	Al Spohrer	20.00	10.00	6.00
(168)	George Stainback	20.00	10.00	6.00
(169)	Albert "Dolly" Stark (Umpire)	40.00	20.00	12.00
(170)	Casey Stengel	50.00	25.00	15.00
(171)	Riggs Stephenson	20.00	10.00	6.00
(172)	Walter C. Stewart	20.00	10.00	6.00
(173)	Lin Storti	20.00	10.00	6.00
(174)	Allyn (Fish Hook) Stout	20.00	10.00	6.00
(175)	Joe Stripp	20.00	10.00	6.00
(176)	Gus Suhr	20.00	10.00	6.00
(177)	Billy Sullivan, Jr.	20.00	10.00	6.00
(178)	Benny Tate	20.00	10.00	6.00
(179)	Danny Taylor	20.00	10.00	6.00
(180)	Tommy Thevenow	20.00	10.00	6.00
(181)	Bud Tinning	20.00	10.00	6.00
(182)	Cecil Travis	20.00	10.00	6.00
(183)	Forest F. Twogood	20.00	10.00	6.00
(184)	Bill Urbanski	20.00	10.00	6.00
(185)	Dazzy Vance	40.00	20.00	12.00
(186)	Arthur Veltman (SP)	100.00	50.00	30.00
(187)	John L. Vergez	20.00	10.00	6.00
(188)	Gerald (Jerry) Walker	20.00	10.00	6.00
(189)	William H. Walker	20.00	10.00	6.00
(190)	Lloyd Waner	40.00	20.00	12.00
(191)	Paul Waner	40.00	20.00	12.00
(192)	Lon Warnecke	20.00	10.00	6.00
(193)	Harold B. Warstler	20.00	10.00	6.00
(194)	Bill Werber	20.00	10.00	6.00
(195)	Joyner White	20.00	10.00	6.00
(196)	Arthur Whitney	20.00	10.00	6.00
(197)	James Wilson	20.00	10.00	6.00
(198)	Lewis (Hack) Wilson	40.00	20.00	12.00
(199)	Ralph L. Winegarner	20.00	10.00	6.00
(200)	Thomas Zachary	20.00	10.00	6.00

1935 Diamond Matchbooks - Black Border

Only 24 players were issued in the 1935 Diamond Matchbook baseball series. Similar in design to the 1934 issue, these 1-1/2" x 4-1/8" matchbooks have sepia player portrait photos on front, framed in either red, green or blue. The overall borders of the cover are black. Backs of the 1935 issue feature a career summary overprinted on a silhouetted batting figure. The "saddle" has the player name and team superimposed on a baseball. These matchbooks are commonly collected with the matches removed and the striker at back-bottom intact. Pieces without the striker are valued at 50 percent of these listed prices. Complete covers with matches bring a premium of 2-3X. The players are listed here alphabetically.

		NM	E	VG
Complete Set (24):		850.00	425.00	250.00
Common Player:		25.00	12.50	7.50
(1)	Ethan Allen (Red)	25.00	12.50	7.50
(2)	Walter Berger (Red)	25.00	12.50	7.50
(3)	Tommy Carey (Blue)	25.00	12.50	7.50
(4)	Louis Chiozza (Blue)	25.00	12.50	7.50
(5)	Jerome (Dizzy) Dean (Green)	65.00	32.50	20.00
(6)	Frankie Frisch (Red)	50.00	25.00	15.00
(7)	Charles Grimm (Blue)	25.00	12.50	7.50
(8)	Charles Hafey (Red)	40.00	20.00	12.00
(9)	J. Francis Hogan (Red)	25.00	12.50	7.50
(10)	Carl Hubbell (Green)	50.00	25.00	15.00
(11)	Charles Klein (Green)	40.00	20.00	12.00
(12)	Ernest Lombardi (Blue)	40.00	20.00	12.00
(13)	Alfonso Lopez (Blue)	40.00	20.00	12.00
(14)	Rabbit Maranville (Green)	40.00	20.00	12.00
(15)	Joe Moore (Red)	25.00	12.50	7.50
(16)	Van Mungo (Green)	25.00	12.50	7.50
(17)	Melvin (Mel) Ott (Blue)	50.00	25.00	15.00
(18)	Gordon Slade (Green)	25.00	12.50	7.50
(19)	Casey Stengel (Green)	50.00	25.00	15.00
(20)	Tommy Thevenow (Red)	25.00	12.50	7.50
(21)	Lloyd Waner (Red)	40.00	20.00	12.00
(22)	Paul Waner (Green)	50.00	25.00	15.00
(23)	Lon Warnecke (Blue)	25.00	12.50	7.50
(24)	James Wilson (Blue)	25.00	12.50	7.50

1935-36 Diamond Matchbooks

By the career summaries on back of these covers it is evident this series was issued over a two-year period. Measuring about 1-1/2" x 4-1/8", the fronts have posed player photos printed in sepia. Borders can be found in red, green or blue, and it is believed that most, if not all, players, can be found in those three color varieties. Matchbooks in this series do not have the team name on back beneath the player name, as is the case on later series. Collectors generally prefer matchbooks to be complete with striker surface on bottom-back, though with matches removed. Values shown should be halved for covers without strikers. Complete with matches, covers will sell for a 2-3X premium over the values shown.

		NM	E	VG
Complete Set (156):		3,500	1,750	1,000
Common Player:		20.00	10.00	6.00
(1)	Ethan Allen	20.00	10.00	6.00
(2)	Melo Almada	30.00	15.00	9.00
(3)	Eldon Auker	20.00	10.00	6.00
(4)	Dick Bartell	20.00	10.00	6.00
(5)	Aloysius Bejma	20.00	10.00	6.00
(6)	Ollie Bejma	20.00	10.00	6.00
(7)	Roy Chester Bell	20.00	10.00	6.00
(8)	Louis Berger	20.00	10.00	6.00
(9)	Walter Berger	20.00	10.00	6.00
(10)	Ralph Birkofer	20.00	10.00	6.00
(11)	Max Bishop	20.00	10.00	6.00
(12)	George Blaeholder	20.00	10.00	6.00
(13)	Henry (Zeke) Bonura	20.00	10.00	6.00
(14)	Jim Bottomley	35.00	17.50	10.50
(15)	Ed Brandt	20.00	10.00	6.00
(16)	Don Brennan	20.00	10.00	6.00
(17)	Lloyd Brown	20.00	10.00	6.00
(18)	Walter G. Brown	20.00	10.00	6.00
(19)	Claiborne Bryant	20.00	10.00	6.00
(20)	Jim Bucher	20.00	10.00	6.00
(21)	John Burnett	20.00	10.00	6.00
(22)	Irving Burns	20.00	10.00	6.00
(23)	Merritt Cain	20.00	10.00	6.00
(24)	Ben Cantwell	20.00	10.00	6.00
(25)	Tommy Carey	20.00	10.00	6.00
(26)	Tex Carleton	20.00	10.00	6.00
(27)	Joseph Cascarella	20.00	10.00	6.00
(28)	Thomas H. Casey	20.00	10.00	6.00
(29)	George Caster	20.00	10.00	6.00
(30)	Phil Cavarretta	20.00	10.00	6.00
(31)	Louis Chiozza	20.00	10.00	6.00
(32)	Edward Cihocki	20.00	10.00	6.00
(33)	Herman E. Clifton	20.00	10.00	6.00
(34)	Richard Coffman	20.00	10.00	6.00
(35)	Edward P. Coleman	20.00	10.00	6.00
(36)	James A. Collins	20.00	10.00	6.00
(37)	John Conlan	40.00	20.00	12.00
(38)	Roger Cramer	20.00	10.00	6.00
(39)	Hugh M. Critz	20.00	10.00	6.00
(40)	Alvin Crowder	20.00	10.00	6.00
(41)	Tony Cuccinello	20.00	10.00	6.00
(42)	Hazen "Kiki" Cuyler	35.00	17.50	10.50
(43)	Virgil Davis	20.00	10.00	6.00
(44)	Jerome Dean	75.00	37.00	22.00
(45)	Paul Derringer	20.00	10.00	6.00
(46)	James DeShong	20.00	10.00	6.00
(47)	William Dietrich	20.00	10.00	6.00
(48)	Leo Durocher	35.00	17.50	10.50
(49)	George Earnshaw	20.00	10.00	6.00
(50)	Elwood English	20.00	10.00	6.00
(51)	Louis Finney	20.00	10.00	6.00
(52)	Charles Fischer	20.00	10.00	6.00
(53)	Freddy Fitzsimmons	20.00	10.00	6.00
(54)	Benny Frey	20.00	10.00	6.00
(55)	Linus B. Frey	20.00	10.00	6.00
(56)	Frankie Frisch	40.00	20.00	12.00
(57)	August Galan	20.00	10.00	6.00
(58)	Milton Galatzer	20.00	10.00	6.00
(59)	Dennis Galehouse	20.00	10.00	6.00
(60)	Debs Garms	20.00	10.00	6.00
(61)	Angelo J. Giuliani	20.00	10.00	6.00
(62)	Earl Grace	20.00	10.00	6.00
(63)	Charles Grimm	20.00	10.00	6.00
(64)	Frank Grube	20.00	10.00	6.00
(65)	Stanley Hack	25.00	12.50	7.50
(66)	Irving "Bump" Hadley	20.00	10.00	6.00
(67)	Odell Hale	20.00	10.00	6.00
(68)	Bill Hallahan	20.00	10.00	6.00
(69)	Roy Hansen	20.00	10.00	6.00
(70)	Melvin Harder	20.00	10.00	6.00
(71)	Charles Hartnett	35.00	17.50	10.50
(72)	"Gabby" Hartnett	35.00	17.50	10.50
(73)	Clyde Hatter	20.00	10.00	6.00
(74)	Raymond Hayworth	20.00	10.00	6.00
(75)	Raymond Hayworth (W/ chest protector.)	20.00	10.00	6.00
(76)	William Herman	35.00	17.50	10.50
(77)	Gordon Hinkle	20.00	10.00	6.00
(78)	George Hockette	20.00	10.00	6.00
(79)	James Holbrook	20.00	10.00	6.00
(80)	Alex Hooks	20.00	10.00	6.00
(81)	Waite Hoyt	35.00	17.50	10.50
(82)	Carl Hubbell	40.00	20.00	12.00
(83)	Roy M. Joiner	20.00	10.00	6.00
(84)	Sam Jones	20.00	10.00	6.00
(85)	Baxter Jordan	20.00	10.00	6.00
(86)	Arndt Jorgens	20.00	10.00	6.00
(87)	William F. Jurges	20.00	10.00	6.00
(88)	William Kamm	20.00	10.00	6.00
(89)	Vernon Kennedy	20.00	10.00	6.00
(90)	John Kerr	20.00	10.00	6.00
(91)	Charles Klein	40.00	20.00	12.00
(92)	Ted Kleinhans	20.00	10.00	6.00
(93)	Wm. Knickerbocker (Thighs-up.)	20.00	10.00	6.00
(94)	Wm. Knickerbocker (Waist-up.)	20.00	10.00	6.00
(95)	Jack Knott	20.00	10.00	6.00
(96)	Mark Koenig	20.00	10.00	6.00
(97)	Fabian L. Kowalik	20.00	10.00	6.00
(98)	Ralph Kress	20.00	10.00	6.00
(99)	Wm. C. "Bill" Lee	20.00	10.00	6.00
(100)	Louis Legett	20.00	10.00	6.00
(101)	Emil "Dutch" Leonard	20.00	10.00	6.00
(102)	Fred Lindstrom	35.00	17.50	10.50
(103)	Edward Linke (Pole in background.)	20.00	10.00	6.00
(104)	Edward Linke (No pole.)	20.00	10.00	6.00
(105)	Ernest Lombardi	35.00	17.50	10.50
(106)	Al Lopez	35.00	17.50	10.50
(107)	John Marcum	20.00	10.00	6.00
(108)	William McKechnie	35.00	17.50	10.50
(109)	Eric McNair	20.00	10.00	6.00
(110)	Joe Medwick	35.00	17.50	10.50
(111)	Oscar Melillo	20.00	10.00	6.00
(112)	John Michaels	20.00	10.00	6.00
(113)	Joe Moore	20.00	10.00	6.00
(114)	John Moore	20.00	10.00	6.00
(115)	Wallace Moses	20.00	10.00	6.00
(116)	Joseph Milligan	20.00	10.00	6.00
(117)	Van Mungo	25.00	12.50	7.50
(118)	Glenn Myatt	20.00	10.00	6.00
(119)	James O'Dea	20.00	10.00	6.00
(120)	Ernest Orsatti	20.00	10.00	6.00
(121)	Fred Ostermueller	20.00	10.00	6.00
(122)	Melvin "Mel" Ott	40.00	20.00	12.00
(123)	LeRoy Parmelee	20.00	10.00	6.00
(124)	Monte Pearson	20.00	10.00	6.00
(125)	Raymond Pepper	20.00	10.00	6.00
(126)	Raymond Phelps	20.00	10.00	6.00
(127)	George Pipgras	20.00	10.00	6.00
(128)	Frank Pytlak	20.00	10.00	6.00
(129)	Gordon Rhodes	20.00	10.00	6.00
(130)	Charlie Root	20.00	10.00	6.00
(131)	John Rothrock	20.00	10.00	6.00
(132)	Herold "Muddy" Ruel	20.00	10.00	6.00
(133)	Jack Saltzgaver	20.00	10.00	6.00
(134)	Fred Schulte	20.00	10.00	6.00
(135)	George Selkirk	20.00	10.00	6.00
(136)	Mervyn Shea	20.00	10.00	6.00
(137)	Al Spohrer	20.00	10.00	6.00
(138)	George Stainback	20.00	10.00	6.00
(139)	Casey Stengel	40.00	20.00	12.00
(140)	Walter Stephenson	20.00	10.00	6.00
(141)	Lee Stine	20.00	10.00	6.00
(142)	John Stone	20.00	10.00	6.00
(143)	Gus Suhr	20.00	10.00	6.00
(144)	Tommy Thevenow	20.00	10.00	6.00
(145)	Fay Thomas	20.00	10.00	6.00
(146)	Leslie Tietje	20.00	10.00	6.00
(147)	Bill Urbanski	20.00	10.00	6.00
(148)	William H. Walker	20.00	10.00	6.00
(149)	Lloyd Waner	40.00	20.00	12.00

		NM	E	VG
(150)	Paul Waner	40.00	20.00	12.00
(151)	Lon Warnecke	20.00	10.00	6.00
(152)	Harold Warstler	20.00	10.00	6.00
(153)	Bill Werber	20.00	10.00	6.00
(154)	Vernon Wiltshere	20.00	10.00	6.00
(155)	James Wilson	20.00	10.00	6.00
(156)	Ralph Winegarner	20.00	10.00	6.00

1936 Diamond Matchbooks - Chicago Cubs

This short series of baseball player matchbooks can each be found with borders of red, green or blue. Except for Dean, all photos are portraits, printed in sepia or black-and-white. Dean and Paul Waner are the only subjects in the set who were not members of the Chicago Cubs. This series can be differentiated from 1935-36 Diamond Matchbooks only by studying the career summary and stats on back. About 1-1/2" x 4-1/8", these matchbooks are commonly collected with the matches removed and the striker at back-bottom intact. Pieces without the striker are valued at 50 percent of these listed prices. Complete covers with matches bring a premium of 2-3X. The players are listed here alphabetically.

		NM	E	VG
	Complete Set (23):	350.00	175.00	100.00
	Common Player:	12.50	6.25	3.75
(1)	Claiborne Bryant	12.50	6.25	3.75
(2)	Tex Carleton	12.50	6.25	3.75
(3)	Phil Cavarretta	12.50	6.25	3.75
(4)	James A. Collins	12.50	6.25	3.75
(5)	Curt Davis	12.50	6.25	3.75
(6)	Jerome "Dizzy" Dean	50.00	25.00	15.00
(7)	Frank Demaree	12.50	6.25	3.75
(8)	Larry French	12.50	6.25	3.75
(9)	Linus R. Frey	12.50	6.25	3.75
(10)	August Galan	12.50	6.25	3.75
(11)	Bob Garbark	12.50	6.25	3.75
(12)	Stanley Hack	15.00	7.50	4.50
(13)	Charles Hartnett	30.00	15.00	9.00
(14)	William Herman	30.00	15.00	9.00
(15)	William F. Jurges	12.50	6.25	3.75
(16)	William C. "Bill" Lee	12.50	6.25	3.75
(17)	Joe Marty	12.50	6.25	3.75
(18)	James K. O'Dea	12.50	6.25	3.75
(19)	LeRoy Parmelee	12.50	6.25	3.75
(20)	Charlie Root	12.50	6.25	3.75
(21)	Clyde Shoun	12.50	6.25	3.75
(22)	George Stainback	12.50	6.25	3.75
(23)	Paul Waner	40.00	20.00	12.00

1936 Diamond Matchbooks - Team on Back

This is the smallest series of baseball player matchbooks, with only 13 subjects, each found with borders of red, green or blue. Player poses on front are printed in sepia (except one variation of Grimm that is in black-and-white). This series can be differentiated from contemporary series by the appearance of the player's team name on back, beneath his name. Backs have a career summary. About 1-1/2" x 4-1/8", these matchbooks are commonly collected with the matches removed and the striker at back bottom intact. Pieces without the striker are valued at 50 percent of these listed prices. Complete covers with matches bring a premium of 2-3X. The players are listed here alphabetically.

		NM	E	VG
	Complete Set (13):	350.00	175.00	100.00
	Common Player:	20.00	10.00	6.00
(1)	Tommy Carey	20.00	10.00	6.00
(2)	Tony Cuccinello	20.00	10.00	6.00
(3)	Freddy Fitzsimmons	20.00	10.00	6.00
(4)	Frank Frisch	45.00	22.00	13.50
(5a)	Charles Grimm (Home uniform, b/w.)	20.00	10.00	6.00
(5b)	Charlie Grimm (Home uniform, sepia.)	20.00	10.00	6.00
(6)	Charlie Grimm (Road uniform.)	20.00	10.00	6.00
(7)	Carl Hubbell	45.00	22.00	13.50
(8)	Baxter Jordan	20.00	10.00	6.00
(9)	Chuck Klein	45.00	22.00	13.50
(10)	Al Lopez	35.00	17.50	10.50
(11)	Joe Medwick	35.00	17.50	10.50
(12)	Van Lingle Mungo	25.00	12.50	7.50
(13)	Mel Ott	45.00	22.00	13.50

1889 Diamond S Cigars Boston N.L.

(See 1889 Number 7 Cigars for checklist and value information.)

1934-36 Diamond Stars (R327)

Issued from 1934-36, the Diamond Stars set (ACC designation R327) consists of 108 cards. Produced by National Chicle, the cards measure 2-3/8" x 2-7/8" and are color art renderings of actual photographs on art deco backgrounds.

The year of issue can usually be determined by the player's statistics found on the reverse of the card. Backs also feature either a player biography or a playing tip. Some cards can be found with either green or blue printing on the backs. The complete set price does not include the higher priced variations which make up the 170-card "master" set.

	NM	E	VG
Complete Set (108):	22,500	9,000	4,000
Complete Set (170):	35,000	14,000	6,250
Common Player (1-84):	125.00	62.50	37.50
Common Player (85-96):	200.00	85.00	45.00
Common Player (97-108):	500.00	245.00	120.00
1a	"Lefty" Grove (1934 green back)	5,000	2,500	1,500
1b	"Lefty" Grove (1935 green back)	5,000	2,500	1,500
2a	Al Simmons (1934 green back)	850.00	420.00	250.00
2b	Al Simmons (1935 green back)	850.00	420.00	250.00
2c	Al Simmons (1936 blue back)	900.00	450.00	270.00
3a	"Rabbit" Maranville (1934 green back)	450.00	220.00	135.00
3b	"Rabbit" Maranville (1935 green back)	450.00	220.00	135.00
4a	"Buddy" Myer (1934 green back)	125.00	62.50	37.50
4b	"Buddy" Myer (1935 green back)	125.00	62.50	37.50
4c	"Buddy" Myer (1936 blue back)	130.00	65.00	40.00
5a	Tom Bridges (1934 green back)	125.00	62.50	37.50
5b	Tom Bridges (1935 green back)	125.00	62.50	37.50
5c	Tom Bridges (1936 blue back)	130.00	65.00	40.00
6a	Max Bishop (1934 green back)	125.00	62.50	37.50
6b	Max Bishop (1935 green back)	125.00	62.50	37.50
7a	Lew Fonseca (1934 green back)	125.00	62.50	37.50
7b	Lew Fonseca (1935 green back)	125.00	62.50	37.50
8a	Joe Vosmik (1934 green back)	125.00	62.50	37.50
8b	Joe Vosmik (1935 green back)	125.00	62.50	37.50
8c	Joe Vosmik (1936 blue back)	130.00	65.00	40.00
9a	"Mickey" Cochrane (1934 green back)	450.00	220.00	135.00
9b	"Mickey" Cochrane (1935 green back)	450.00	220.00	135.00
9c	"Mickey" Cochrane (1936 blue back)	525.00	210.00	105.00
10a	Roy Mahaffey (1934 green back)	125.00	62.50	37.50
10b	Roy Mahaffey (1935 green back)	125.00	62.50	37.50
10c	Roy Mahaffey (1936 blue back)	130.00	65.00	40.00
11a	Bill Dickey (1934 green back)	525.00	210.00	105.00
11b	Bill Dickey (1935 green back)	525.00	210.00	105.00
12a	Dixie Walker (1934 green back)	125.00	62.50	37.50
12b	Dixie Walker (1935 green back)	125.00	62.50	37.50
12c	Dixie Walker (1936 blue back)	130.00	65.00	40.00
13a	George Blaeholder (1934 green back)	125.00	62.50	37.50
13b	George Blaeholder (1935 green back)	125.00	62.50	37.50
14a	Bill Terry (1934 green back)	450.00	220.00	135.00
14b	Bill Terry (1935 green back)	450.00	220.00	135.00
15a	Dick Bartell (1934 green back)	125.00	62.50	37.50
15b	Dick Bartell (1935 green back)	125.00	62.50	37.50
16a	Lloyd Waner (1934 green back)	450.00	220.00	135.00
16b	Lloyd Waner (1935 green back)	450.00	220.00	135.00
16c	Lloyd Waner (1936 blue back)	550.00	270.00	165.00
17a	Frankie Frisch (1934 green back)	450.00	220.00	135.00
17b	Frankie Frisch (1935 green back)	450.00	220.00	135.00

18a	"Chick" Hafey (1934 green back)	450.00	220.00	135.00
18b	"Chick" Hafey (1935 green back)	450.00	220.00	135.00
19a	Van Mungo (1934 green back)	315.00	125.00	65.00
19b	Van Mungo (1935 green back)	315.00	125.00	65.00
20a	"Shanty" Hogan (1934 green back)	125.00	62.50	37.50
20b	"Shanty" Hogan (1935 green back)	125.00	62.50	37.50
21a	Johnny Vergez (1934 green back)	125.00	62.50	37.50
21b	Johnny Vergez (1935 green back)	125.00	62.50	37.50
22a	Jimmy Wilson (1934 green back)	125.00	62.50	37.50
22b	Jimmy Wilson (1935 green back)	125.00	62.50	37.50
22c	Jimmy Wilson (1936 blue back)	130.00	65.00	40.00
23a	Bill Hallahan (1934 green back)	125.00	62.50	37.50
23b	Bill Hallahan (1935 green back)	125.00	62.50	37.50
24a	"Sparky" Adams (1934 green back)	125.00	62.50	37.50
24b	"Sparky" Adams (1935 green back)	125.00	62.50	37.50
25	Walter Berger	125.00	62.50	37.50
26a	"Pepper" Martin (1935 green back)	150.00	75.00	45.00
26b	"Pepper" Martin (1936 blue back)	175.00	70.00	35.00
27	"Pie" Traynor	200.00	85.00	45.00
28	"Al" Lopez	200.00	85.00	45.00
29	Robert Rolfe	125.00	62.50	37.50
30a	"Heinie" Manush (1935 green back)	200.00	85.00	45.00
30b	"Heinie" Manush (1936 blue back)	225.00	112.50	67.50
31a	"Kiki" Cuyler (1935 green back)	200.00	85.00	45.00
31b	"Kiki" Cuyler (1936 blue back)	225.00	112.50	67.50
32	Sam Rice	200.00	85.00	45.00
33	"Schoolboy" Rowe	125.00	50.00	20.00
34	Stanley Hack	125.00	50.00	20.00
35	Earle Averill	200.00	85.00	45.00
36a	Earnie Lombardi	550.00	270.00	165.00
36b	Ernie Lombardi	250.00	125.00	75.00
37	"Billie" Urbanski	125.00	62.50	37.50
38	Ben Chapman	125.00	62.50	37.50
39	Carl Hubbell	300.00	150.00	90.00
40	"Blondy" Ryan	125.00	62.50	37.50
41	Harvey Hendrick	125.00	62.50	37.50
42	Jimmy Dykes	125.00	62.50	37.50
43	Ted Lyons	200.00	85.00	45.00
44	Rogers Hornsby	525.00	210.00	105.00
45	"Jo Jo" White	125.00	62.50	37.50
46	"Red" Lucas	125.00	62.50	37.50
47	Cliff Bolton	125.00	62.50	37.50
48	"Rick" Ferrell	200.00	85.00	45.00
49	"Buck" Jordan	125.00	62.50	37.50
50	"Mel" Ott	300.00	150.00	90.00
51	John Whitehead	125.00	62.50	37.50
52	George Stainback	125.00	62.50	37.50
53	Oscar Melillo	125.00	62.50	37.50
54a	"Hank" Greenburg (Greenberg)	1,600	800.00	475.00
54b	"Hank" Greenberg	800.00	400.00	240.00
55	Tony Cuccinello	125.00	62.50	37.50
56	"Gus" Suhr	125.00	62.50	37.50
57	Cy Blanton	125.00	62.50	37.50
58	Glenn Myatt	125.00	62.50	37.50
59	Jim Bottomley	200.00	85.00	45.00
60	Charley "Red" Ruffing	200.00	85.00	45.00
61	"Billie" Werber	125.00	62.50	37.50
62	Fred M. Frankhouse	125.00	62.50	37.50
63	"Stonewall" Jackson	200.00	85.00	45.00
64	Jimmie Foxx	550.00	270.00	165.00
65	"Zeke" Bonura	125.00	62.50	37.50
66	"Ducky" Medwick	200.00	85.00	45.00
67	Marvin Owen	125.00	62.50	37.50
68	"Sam" Leslie	125.00	62.50	37.50
69	Earl Grace	125.00	62.50	37.50
70	"Hal" Trosky	125.00	62.50	37.50
71	"Ossie" Bluege	125.00	62.50	37.50
72	"Tony" Piet	125.00	62.50	37.50
73a	"Fritz" Ostermueller (1935 green back)	125.00	62.50	37.50
73b	"Fritz" Ostermueller (1935 blue back)	125.00	62.50	37.50
73c	"Fritz" Ostermueller (1936 blue back)	130.00	65.00	40.00
74a	Tony Lazzeri (1935 green back)	375.00	185.00	110.00

74b	Tony Lazzeri (1935 blue back)	375.00	185.00	110.00
74c	Tony Lazzeri (1936 blue back)	385.00	155.00	77.00
75a	Irving Burns (1935 green back)	125.00	62.50	37.50
75b	Irving Burns (1935 blue back)	125.00	62.50	37.50
75c	Irving Burns (1936 blue back)	130.00	65.00	40.00
76a	Bill Rogell (1935 green back)	125.00	62.50	37.50
76b	Bill Rogell (1935 blue back)	130.00	65.00	40.00
76c	Bill Rogell (1936 blue back)	130.00	65.00	40.00
77a	Charlie Gehringer (1935 green back)	350.00	140.00	70.00
77b	Charlie Gehringer (1935 blue back)	350.00	140.00	70.00
77c	Charlie Gehringer (1936 blue back)	375.00	185.00	110.00
78a	Joe Kuhel (1935 green back)	125.00	62.50	37.50
78b	Joe Kuhel (1935 blue back)	125.00	62.50	37.50
78c	Joe Kuhel (1936 blue back)	130.00	65.00	40.00
79a	Willis Hudlin (1935 green back)	125.00	62.50	37.50
79b	Willis Hudlin (1935 blue back)	125.00	62.50	37.50
79c	Willis Hudlin (1936 blue back)	130.00	65.00	40.00
80a	Louis Chiozza (1935 green back)	125.00	62.50	37.50
80b	Louis Chiozza (1935 blue back)	125.00	62.50	37.50
80c	Louis Chiozza (1936 blue back)	130.00	65.00	40.00
81a	Bill DeLancey (1935 green back)	125.00	62.50	37.50
81b	Bill DeLancey (1935 blue back)	125.00	62.50	37.50
81c	Bill DeLancey (1936 blue back)	130.00	65.00	40.00
82a	John Babich (1935 green back)	125.00	62.50	37.50
82b	John Babich (1935 blue back)	125.00	62.50	37.50
82c	John Babich (1936 blue back)	130.00	65.00	40.00
83a	Paul Waner (1935 green back)	200.00	85.00	45.00
83b	Paul Waner (1935 blue back)	200.00	85.00	45.00
83c	Paul Waner (1936 blue back)	225.00	85.00	45.00
84a	Sam Byrd (1935 green back)	125.00	62.50	37.50
84b	Sam Byrd (1935 blue back)	125.00	62.50	37.50
84c	Sam Byrd (1936 blue back)	130.00	65.00	40.00
85	Julius Solters	200.00	85.00	45.00
86	Frank Crosetti	350.00	140.00	70.00
87	Steve O'Neil (O'Neill)	200.00	85.00	45.00
88	Geo. Selkirk	200.00	85.00	45.00
89	Joe Stripp	200.00	85.00	45.00
90	Ray Hayworth	200.00	85.00	45.00
91	Bucky Harris	450.00	220.00	135.00
92	Ethan Allen	200.00	85.00	45.00
93	Alvin Crowder	200.00	85.00	45.00
94	Wes Ferrell	200.00	85.00	45.00
95	Luke Appling	455.00	185.00	90.00
96	Lew Riggs	200.00	85.00	45.00
97	"Al" Lopez	800.00	400.00	240.00
98	"Schoolboy" Rowe	500.00	245.00	120.00
99	"Pie" Traynor	800.00	400.00	240.00
100	Earle Averill (Earl)	800.00	400.00	240.00
101	Dick Bartell	500.00	245.00	120.00
102	Van Mungo	600.00	300.00	180.00
103	Bill Dickey	900.00	450.00	270.00
104	Robert Rolfe	750.00	370.00	220.00
105	"Ernie" Lombardi	800.00	400.00	240.00
106	"Red" Lucas	500.00	245.00	120.00
107	Stanley Hack	600.00	300.00	180.00
108	Walter Berger	1,120	280.00	135.00

1924 Diaz Cigarettes

Because they were printed in Cuba and feature only pitchers, the 1924 Diaz Cigarette cards are among the rarest and most intriguing of all tobacco issues. Produced in Havana for the Diaz brand, the black-and-white cards measure 1-3/4" x 2-1/2" and were printed on a semi-gloss stock. The player's name and position are listed at the bottom of the card, while his team and league appear at the top. According to the card

backs, printed in Spanish, the set consists of 136 cards - all major league pitchers. But to date only the cards checklisted here have been discovered, and several of them never played in the major leagues.

		NM	E	VG
Common Player:		900.00	360.00	180.00
1	Walter P. Johnson	5,250	2,200	1,100
2	Waite C. Hoyt	1,500	600.00	300.00
3	Grover C. Alexander	2,250	900.00	450.00
4	Thomas Sheehan	900.00	360.00	180.00
5	Pete Donohue	900.00	360.00	180.00
6	Herbert J. Pennock	1,350	550.00	275.00
7				
8	Carl Mays	1,100	450.00	225.00
9				
10	Allan S. Sothoron (Allen)	900.00	360.00	180.00
11	Wm. Piercy	900.00	360.00	180.00
12	Curtis Fullerton	900.00	360.00	180.00
13	Hollis Thurston	900.00	360.00	180.00
14	George Walberg	900.00	360.00	180.00
15	Fred Heimach	900.00	360.00	180.00
16	Sherrod M. Smith	900.00	360.00	180.00
17	Warren H. Ogden	900.00	360.00	180.00
18	Ernest P. Osborne (Earnest)	900.00	360.00	180.00
19	Walter H. Ruether	900.00	360.00	180.00
20	Burleigh A. Grimes	1,350	550.00	275.00
21	Joseph Genewich	900.00	360.00	180.00
22	Victor Aldridge	900.00	360.00	180.00
23	Arnold E. Stone	900.00	360.00	180.00
24	Lester C. Howe	900.00	360.00	180.00
25	George K. Murry (Murray)	900.00	360.00	180.00
26	Herman Pillette	900.00	360.00	180.00
27	John D. Couch	900.00	360.00	180.00
28	Tony C. Kaufmann	900.00	360.00	180.00
29	Frank (Jake) May	900.00	360.00	180.00
30	Howard J. Ehmke	900.00	360.00	180.00
31				
32				
33	Gorham V. Leverett	900.00	360.00	180.00
34	Bryan Harris	900.00	360.00	180.00
35	Paul F. Schreiber	900.00	360.00	180.00
36	Dewey Hinkle	900.00	360.00	180.00
37	Arthur C. Vance	1,350	550.00	275.00
38	Jesse J. Haines	1,350	550.00	275.00
39	Earl Hamilton	900.00	360.00	180.00
40	A. Wilbur Cooper	900.00	360.00	180.00
41	Thomas F. Long	900.00	360.00	180.00
42	Alex Ferguson	900.00	360.00	180.00
43	Chester Ross	900.00	360.00	180.00
44	John J. Quinn (Middle initial actually P.)	900.00	360.00	180.00
45	Ray C. Kolp	900.00	360.00	180.00
46	Arthur N. Nehf	900.00	360.00	180.00
47				
48				
49	Edwin A. Rommel	900.00	360.00	180.00
50	Theodore A. Lyons	1,350	550.00	275.00
51	Roy Meeker	900.00	360.00	180.00
52	John D. Stuart	900.00	360.00	180.00
53	Joseph Oeschger	900.00	360.00	180.00
54	Wayland Dean	900.00	360.00	180.00
55	Guy Morton	900.00	360.00	180.00
56	William L. Doak	900.00	360.00	180.00
57	Edward J. Pfeffer	900.00	360.00	180.00
58	Sam Gray	900.00	360.00	180.00
59				
60	Godfrey Brogan	900.00	360.00	180.00
61				
62a	Howard E. Baldwin	900.00	360.00	180.00
62b	Richard W. Marquard	1,750	875.00	525.00
63	Bert Lewis	900.00	360.00	180.00
64				
65	Dennis Burns	900.00	360.00	180.00
66	Roline C. Naylor (Roleine)	900.00	360.00	180.00
67	Walter H. Huntzinger	900.00	360.00	180.00
68	S. F. Baumgartner	900.00	360.00	180.00
69				
70	Clarence E. Mitchell	900.00	360.00	180.00

71				
72	Charles F. Clazner			
	(Glazner)	900.00	360.00	180.00
73				
74				
75	Dennis J. Gearin	900.00	360.00	180.00
76	Jonathan T. Zachary	900.00	360.00	180.00
77				
78	Jess F. Winter (Jesse			
	Winters)	900.00	360.00	180.00
79	Charles Ruffing	1,350	550.00	275.00
80	John W. Cooney	900.00	360.00	180.00
81	Leslie J. Bush (Middle			
	initial A.)	900.00	360.00	180.00
82	William Harris	900.00	360.00	180.00
83	Joseph B. Shaute	900.00	360.00	180.00
84	George W. Pipgras	900.00	360.00	180.00
85	Eppa J. Rixey	1,350	550.00	275.00
86	William L. Sherdel	900.00	360.00	180.00
87	John C. Benton	900.00	360.00	180.00
88	Arthur R. Decatur	900.00	360.00	180.00
89	Harry G. Shriver	900.00	360.00	180.00
90	John D. Morrison	900.00	360.00	180.00
91	Walter M. Betts	900.00	360.00	180.00
92	Oscar Roettger	900.00	360.00	180.00
93				
94	Mike Cvengros	900.00	360.00	180.00
95	Leo L. Dickerman	900.00	360.00	180.00
96	Philip B. Weinart	2,400	960.00	480.00
97	Nicholas Dumovich	900.00	360.00	180.00
98				
99	Timothy A. McNamara	900.00	360.00	180.00
100	Allan Russell	900.00	360.00	180.00
101	Ted Blankenship	900.00	360.00	180.00
102	Howard E. Baldwin	900.00	360.00	180.00
103	Frank T. Davis	900.00	360.00	180.00
104	James C. Edwards	900.00	360.00	180.00
105	Hubert F. Pruett	900.00	360.00	180.00
106	Richard Rudolph	900.00	360.00	180.00
107				
108	Claude Jonnard	900.00	360.00	180.00
109				
110				
111	John M. Bentley (Initial			
	actually N.)	900.00	360.00	180.00
112	Wilfred D. Ryan	900.00	360.00	180.00
113	George D. Metivier	900.00	360.00	180.00
114				
115	Sylvester Johnson	900.00	360.00	180.00
116	O.L. Fuhr	900.00	360.00	180.00
117				
118	Stanley Coveleski	1,350	550.00	275.00
119	Dave C. Danforth	900.00	360.00	180.00
120	Elam Van Gilder	900.00	360.00	180.00
121	Bert Cole	900.00	360.00	180.00
122	Kenneth E. Holoway			
	(Holloway)	900.00	360.00	180.00
123	Charles Robertson	900.00	360.00	180.00
124				
125	George Dauss	900.00	360.00	180.00
126				
127				
128				
129	Phillip Bedgood	900.00	360.00	180.00
130	Fred Wingfield	900.00	360.00	180.00
131	George Mogridge	900.00	360.00	180.00
132	J. Martina	900.00	360.00	180.00
133	B.F. Speece	900.00	360.00	180.00
134	Harold Carlson	900.00	360.00	180.00
135	Wilbert W. Hubbell	900.00	360.00	180.00
136	Milton Gaston	900.00	360.00	180.00

(The following pitchers are known to have been
included in the set, though their card numbers
are unknown. They are listed here alphabetically,
though the names may be different on the cards.)

---	Jess L. Barnes	900.00	360.00	180.00
---	Virgil E. Barnes	900.00	360.00	180.00
---	William Bayne	900.00	360.00	180.00
---	Lawrence J. Benton	900.00	360.00	180.00
---	Warren Collins (Rip)	900.00	360.00	180.00
---	Joubert Davenport (Lum)	900.00	360.00	180.00
---	Urban C. Faber	900.00	360.00	180.00
---	Robert K. Hasty	900.00	360.00	180.00
---	Frank J. Henry	900.00	360.00	180.00
---	Samuel P. Jones	900.00	360.00	180.00
---	Adolfo Luque	1,200	600.00	350.00
---	Fred Marberry	900.00	360.00	180.00
---	Richard W. Marquard	900.00	360.00	180.00
---	Walter H. McGrew (Slim)	900.00	360.00	180.00
---	Herbert McQuaid	900.00	360.00	180.00
---	Hugh A. McQuillan	900.00	360.00	180.00
---	Lee Meadows	900.00	360.00	180.00
---	Louis A. North	900.00	360.00	180.00
---	George W. Pipgras	900.00	360.00	180.00
---	James J. Ring	900.00	360.00	180.00
---	Robert Shawkey	900.00	360.00	180.00
---	Urban J. Shocker	900.00	360.00	180.00
---	George Uhle	900.00	360.00	180.00

---	John R. Watson	900.00	360.00	180.00
---	Ed L. Wells	900.00	360.00	180.00
---	Byron W. Yarrison	900.00	360.00	180.00
---	Paul V. Zahniser	900.00	360.00	180.00

1962 Dickson Orde & Co.

SPORTS
OF THE
COUNTRIES
(A Series of 25)
No. 11
AMERICA
Everyone knows that America
is a great Baseball playing
country, where an almost
fanatical enthusiasm is displayed. The game is very
similar to "Rounders" in
its basic rules but it re-
quires players of great
strength and skill in judg-
ment. The best known Baseball player of all time is
Babe Ruth, whose record of
714 home runs has never
been equalled.

DICKSON ORDE &
CO. LTD.
Farnham : Surrey : England

One of several English tobacco cards to include baseball among a series of world's sports, this card is of marginal interest to U.S. collectors because its color front pictures (from the back) a batter who could be Babe Ruth as part of a baseball scene on the front of the 2-5/8" x 1-3/8" card. The short description of baseball on the card's black-and-white back does mention Ruth. The "Sports of the Countries" series comprises 25 cards.

		NM	E	VG
11	America (Babe Ruth)	25.00	12.50	7.50

1980 Did You Know . . . ?

DID YOU KNOW............?

Mickey WITEK—
THE N.Y. GIANTS 2ND
BASEMAN IN 1943 —
BANGED OUT 195 HITS!

MEL '80

This collectors' edition was produced by artist Mel (?) Anderson. The blank-backed 3-1/4" x 6-3/8" cards have black-and-white drawings of ballplayers and a "Did You Know" trivia fact. The unnumbered cards are checklisted here alphabetically.

		NM	E	VG
	Complete Set (30):	25.00	12.50	7.50
	Common Player:	2.00	1.00	.60
(1)	Richie Ashburn	4.00	2.00	1.25
(2)	Hank Bauer	2.50	1.25	.70
(3)	Ewell "The Whip"			
	Blackwell	2.50	1.25	.70
(4)	Johnny Callison	2.00	1.00	.60
(5)	Roger "Doc" Cramer	2.00	1.00	.60
(6)	Harry Danning	2.00	1.00	.60
(7)	Ferris Fain	2.00	1.00	.60
(8)	Ned Garver	2.00	1.00	.60
(9)	Harvey Haddix	2.00	1.00	.60
(10)	Clint Hartung	2.00	1.00	.60
(11)	"Bobo" Holloman	2.00	1.00	.60
(12)	Ron Hunt	2.00	1.00	.60
(13)	Howard "Spud" Krist	2.00	1.00	.60
(14)	Emil "Dutch" Leonard	2.00	1.00	.60
(15)	Buddy Lewis	2.00	1.00	.60
(16)	Jerry Lynch	2.00	1.00	.60
(17)	Roy McMillan	2.00	1.00	.60
(18)	Johnny Mize	3.00	1.50	.90
(19)	Hugh Mulcahy	2.00	1.00	.60
(20)	Hal Newhouser	2.00	1.00	.60
(21)	Jim Perry	2.00	1.00	.60
(22)	Phil Rizzuto	4.00	2.00	1.25
(23)	Bobby Shantz	2.00	1.00	.60
(24)	Roy Sievers	2.00	1.00	.60
(25)	Nick Testa	3.00	1.50	.90
(26)	Cecil Travis	2.00	1.00	.60
(27)	Elmer "Valient" Valo	2.00	1.00	.60
(28)	Bill Werber	2.00	1.00	.60
(29)	Mickey Witek	2.00	1.00	.60
(30)	Hal Woodeshick	2.00	1.00	.60

1907 Dietsche Chicago Cubs Postcards (PC765-2)

This series of early Cubs postcards was published by the same Detroit printer who issued Tigers postcard series from 1907-09. The Dietsche Cubs postcards are scarcer than the Tigers issues because they were only offered for sale in Detroit in conjunction with the 1907 World Series between the Tigers and Cubs, and few people bought the visiting team's cards. The 3-1/2" x 5-1/2" black-and-white cards have most of the photographic background blacked out on front. The player's last name may or may not appear on the front. Postcard style backs include a short career summary and a dated copyright line. The 15-card sets originally sold for 25 cents.

		NM	E	VG
	Complete Set (15):	6,000	3,000	1,800
	Common Player:	350.00	175.00	105.00
(1)	Mordecai Brown	500.00	200.00	100.00
(2)	Frank L. Chance	500.00	200.00	100.00
(3)	John Evers	500.00	200.00	100.00
(4)	Arthur F. Hoffman			
	(Hofman)	350.00	175.00	105.00
(5)	John Kling	350.00	175.00	105.00
(6)	Carl Lundgren	350.00	175.00	105.00
(7)	Patrick J. Moran	350.00	175.00	105.00
(8)	Orval Overall	350.00	175.00	105.00
(9)	John A. Pfeister	350.00	175.00	105.00
(10)	Edw. M. Ruelbach	350.00	175.00	105.00
(11)	Frank M. Schulte	350.00	175.00	105.00
(12)	James T. Sheckard	350.00	175.00	105.00
(13)	James Slagle	350.00	175.00	105.00
(14)	Harry Steinfeldt	350.00	175.00	105.00
(15)	Joseph B. Tinker	500.00	200.00	100.00

1907-09 Dietsche Detroit Tigers Postcards (PC765-1)

Three apparent annual issues (1907-09) of the home team by Detroit postcard publisher A.C. Dietsche, these 3-1/2" x 5-1/2" black-and-white postcards have most of the photographic background on front blackened out. The player's last name usually appears on the front of the 1908 and 1909 cards. On back, along with the postcard legalities are a short player biography and a dated copyright line. The postcards were sold in sets of 15 cards for 25 cents.

	NM	E	VG
Common Player:	150.00	60.00	30.00

Series 1 - 1907

		NM	E	VG
	Complete Set (16):	8,000	2,800	1,400
(1)	Tyrus R. Cobb (Batting)	3,000	1,500	900.00
(2)	Tyrus R. Cobb (Fielding)	4,000	2,000	1,200
(3)	William Coughlin	150.00	60.00	30.00
(4)	Samuel S. Crawford	325.00	130.00	65.00
(5)	William E. Donovan	150.00	60.00	30.00
(6)	Jerome W. Downs	150.00	60.00	30.00
(7)	Hughie A. Jennings	325.00	130.00	65.00
(8)	David Jones	150.00	60.00	30.00
(9)	Edward H. Killian	150.00	60.00	30.00
(10)	George J. Mullin	150.00	60.00	30.00
(11)	Charles O'Leary	150.00	60.00	30.00
(12)	Fred T. Payne	150.00	60.00	30.00
(13)	Claude Rossman	150.00	60.00	30.00
(14)	Herman W. Schaefer	150.00	60.00	30.00
(15)	Charles Schmidt	150.00	60.00	30.00
(16)	Edward Siever	150.00	60.00	30.00

Series 2 - 1908

		NM	E	VG
	Complete Set (22):	9,000	4,400	2,200
(1)	Henry Beckendorf	200.00	100.00	60.00
(2)	Owen Bush	200.00	100.00	60.00
(3)	Tyrus R. Cobb	4,500	2,200	1,350
(4)	William Coughlin	200.00	100.00	60.00
(5)	Sam Crawford	450.00	220.00	135.00
(6)	William E. Donovan	200.00	100.00	60.00
(7)	Jerome W. Downs	200.00	100.00	60.00
(8)	Hughie A. Jennings	450.00	220.00	135.00
(9)	Tom Jones	200.00	100.00	60.00
(10)	Edward H. Killian	200.00	100.00	60.00
(11)	Matthew McIntyre	200.00	100.00	60.00
(12)	George J. Moriarty	200.00	100.00	60.00
(13)	George J. Mullin	200.00	100.00	60.00
(14)	Charles O'Leary	200.00	100.00	60.00
(15)	Fred T. Payne	200.00	100.00	60.00
(16)	Germany Schaefer	200.00	100.00	60.00
(17)	Charles Schmidt	200.00	100.00	60.00
(18)	Oscar Stanage	200.00	100.00	60.00
(19)	Oren Edgar Summers	200.00	100.00	60.00
(20)	Ira Thomas	200.00	100.00	60.00
(21)	Edgar Willett	200.00	100.00	60.00
(22)	George Winter	180.00	70.00	35.00

Series 3 - 1909

		NM	E	VG
	Complete Set (4):	900.00	300.00	150.00
(1)	James Delehanty	225.00	112.50	67.50
(2)	Tom Jones	200.00	100.00	60.00
(3)	Ralph Works	200.00	100.00	60.00
(4)	Detroit Tigers Team	300.00	125.00	60.00

1907 Dietsche Posters

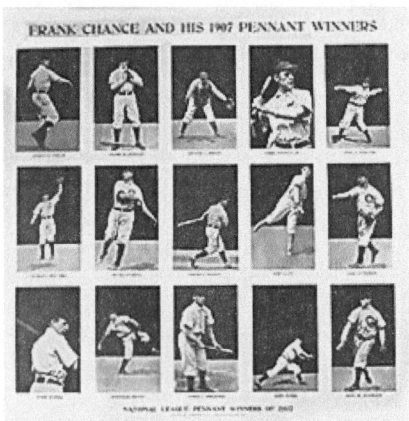

The images found on the Dietsche postcards were conglomerated on a pair of black-and-white cardboard posters. About 22" square, the posters are headlined: "FRANK CHANCE AND HIS 1907 PENNANT WINNERS" and "HUGHIE JENNINGS AND HIS GREAT 1907 TIGERS."

	NM	E	VG
1907 Chicago Cubs	1,000	500.00	300.00
1907 Detroit Tigers	1,000	500.00	300.00

1934 Dietz Gum Ball Players in Action

See 1934 Al Demaree Die-cuts (R304).

1942 Joe DiMaggio Candy Box Card

With no maker's name visible, this crudely executed war-era card is believed to have been printed on a candy box. In a format of 2-7/16" x 3-3/16" it is printed in blue and orange on white, is perforated on the sides and blank-backed.

	NM	E	VG
Joe DiMaggio	150.00	75.00	45.00

1950 Joe DiMaggio Oriental Tour Postcard

 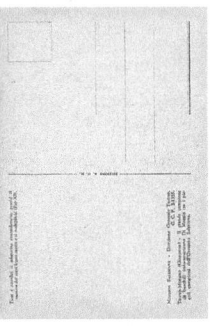

In the post-season of 1950, during the Korean War, Joe DiMaggio led a goodwill tour of the Orient, including stops to visit the troops and to baseball-related destinations in Japan. This Italian postcard shows DiMaggio and Lefty O'Doul in a colorized photo surrounded by Japanese schoolboy ballplayers. The postcard-style back describes the scene. The card measures about 6" x 4".

	NM	E	VG
Joe DiMaggio	125.00	65.00	40.00

1951 Joe DiMaggio Baseball Shoes

 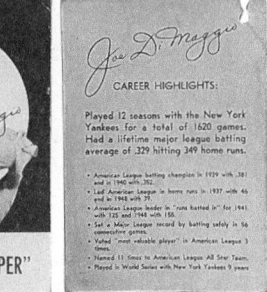

This 2-1/2" x 3-1/2" card was included with DiMaggio brand baseball shoes. A hole punched in the upper-left corner allowed the card to be attached to the shoe strings. Front has an action pose of DiMaggio printed in black-and-white on a dark green background. A facsimile autograph is at center. At bottom is printed: "THE YANKEE CLIPPER." The back has another facsimile signature and the player's career highlights through the 1950 season.

	NM	E	VG
Joe DiMaggio (Hang-tag card.)	140.00	70.00	40.00
Joe DiMaggio (Complete box, shoes, tag.)	650.00	325.00	200.00

1972-83 Dimanche/Derniere Heure Photos

From 1972-74, and 1977-83, the Montreal magazine Dimanche / Derniere Heure (loosely translated, "Sunday / Latest Hour," issued color photos of Expos (and a few other) players. The 8-1/2" x 11" photos are printed on semi-gloss paper stock that is punched for a three-ring binder. Fronts have a large color photo with player data, stats and career highlights printed in black beneath - all in French. At left or top is usually the issue date in which the photo was included in the magazine. Backs are blank.

	NM	E	VG
Common Player:	5.00	2.50	1.50

(Stars are valued up to $50.)

1972 Dimanche/Derniere Heure Expos

		NM	E	VG
	Complete Set (27):	155.00	78.00	47.00
	Common Player:	5.00	2.50	1.50
(1)	Bill Stoneman (April 9)	5.00	2.50	1.50
(2)	John Boccabella (April 16)	5.00	2.50	1.50
(3)	Gene Mauch (April 23)	5.00	2.50	1.50
(4)	Ron Hunt (April 30)	5.00	2.50	1.50
(5)	Steve Renko (May 7)	5.00	2.50	1.50
(6)	Boots Day (May 14)	5.00	2.50	1.50
(7)	Bob Bailey (May 21)	5.00	2.50	1.50
(8)	Ernie McAnally (May 28)	5.00	2.50	1.50
(9)	Ken Singleton (June 4)	5.00	2.50	1.50
(10)	Ron Fairly (June 11)	5.00	2.50	1.50
(11)	Ron Woods (June 18)	5.00	2.50	1.50
(12)	Mike Jorgensen (June 25)	5.00	2.50	1.50
(13)	Bobby Wine (July 2)	5.00	2.50	1.50
(14)	Mike Torrez (July 9)	5.00	2.50	1.50
(15)	Terry Humphrey (July 16)	5.00	2.50	1.50
(16)	Jim Fairey (July 23)	5.00	2.50	1.50
(17)	Tim Foli (July 30)	5.00	2.50	1.50
(18)	Clyde Mashore (Aug. 6)	5.00	2.50	1.50
(19)	Tim McCarver (Aug. 13)	9.00	4.50	2.75
(20)	Hector Torres (Aug. 20)	5.00	2.50	1.50
(21)	Tom Walker (Aug. 27)	5.00	2.50	1.50
(22)	Cal McLish (Sept. 3)	5.00	2.50	1.50
(23)	Balor Moore (Sept. 10)	5.00	2.50	1.50
(24)	John Strohmayer (Sept. 17)	5.00	2.50	1.50
(25)	Larry Doby (Sept. 24)	12.00	6.00	3.50
(26)	Hal Breeden (Oct. 1)	5.00	2.50	1.50
(27)	Mike Marshall (Oct. 8)	5.00	2.50	1.50

1973 Dimanche/Derniere Heure National Leaguers

		NM	E	VG
	Complete Set (16):	185.00	90.00	55.00
	Common Player:	6.00	3.00	1.75
(1)	Roberto Clemente (April 15)	25.00	12.50	7.50
(2)	Coco Laboy (April 22)	6.00	3.00	1.75
(3)	Rusty Staub (April 29)	8.00	4.00	2.50
(4)	Johnny Bench (May 6)	12.50	6.25	3.75
(5)	Ferguson Jenkins (May 13)	9.00	4.50	2.75
(6)	Bob Gibson (May 20)	10.00	5.00	3.00

(7)	Hank Aaron (May 27)	20.00	10.00	6.00
(8)	Willie Montanez (June 3)	6.00	3.00	1.75
(9)	Willie McCovey (June 10)	10.00	5.00	3.00
(10)	Willie Davis (June 17)	6.00	3.00	1.75
(11)	Steve Carlton (June 24)	10.00	5.00	3.00
(12)	Willie Stargell (July 1)	10.00	5.00	3.00
(13)	Dave Bristol (July 8)	6.00	3.00	1.75
(14)	Larry Bowa (July 15)	6.00	3.00	1.75
(15)	Pete Rose (July 22)	20.00	10.00	6.00
(16)	Pepe Frias (July 29)	6.00	3.00	1.75

1974 Dimanche/Derniere Heure Expos

		NM	E	VG
Complete Set (10):		40.00	20.00	12.00
Common Player:		5.00	2.50	1.50
(1)	Dennis Blair	5.00	2.50	1.50
(2)	Don Carrithers	5.00	2.50	1.50
(3)	Jim Cox	5.00	2.50	1.50
(4)	Willie Davis	5.00	2.50	1.50
(5)	Don Demola	5.00	2.50	1.50
(6)	Barry Foote	5.00	2.50	1.50
(7)	Larry Lintz	5.00	2.50	1.50
(8)	John Montague	5.00	2.50	1.50
(9)	Steve Rogers	5.00	2.50	1.50
(10)	Chuck Taylor	5.00	2.50	1.50

1977 Dimanche/Derniere Heure Expos

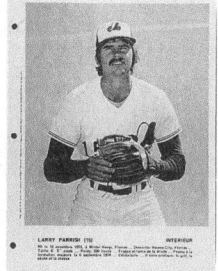

		NM	E	VG
Complete Set (26):		125.00	62.00	37.00
Common Player:		5.00	2.50	1.50
(1)	Steve Rogers (April 24)	5.00	2.50	1.50
(2)	Tim Foli (May 1)	5.00	2.50	1.50
(3)	Dick Williams (May 8)	5.00	2.50	1.50
(4)	Larry Parrish (May 15)	5.00	2.50	1.50
(5)	Jose Morales (May 22)	5.00	2.50	1.50
(6)	Don Stanhouse (May 29)	5.00	2.50	1.50
(7)	Gary Carter (June 5)	10.00	5.00	3.00
(8)	Ellis Valentine (June 12)	5.00	2.50	1.50
(9)	Dave Cash (June 19)	5.00	2.50	1.50
(10)	Jackie Brown (June 26)	5.00	2.50	1.50
(11)	Barry Foote (July 3)	5.00	2.50	1.50
(12)	Dan Warthen (July 10)	5.00	2.50	1.50
(13)	Tony Perez (July 17)	10.00	5.00	3.00
(14)	Wayne Garrett (July 24)	5.00	2.50	1.50
(15)	Bill Atkinson (July 31)	5.00	2.50	1.50
(16)	Joe Kerrigan (Aug. 7)	5.00	2.50	1.50
(17)	Mickey Vernon (Aug. 14)	5.00	2.50	1.50
(18)	Jeff Terpko (Aug. 21)	5.00	2.50	1.50
(19)	Andre Dawson (Aug. 28)	10.00	5.00	3.00
(20)	Del Unser (Sept. 4)	5.00	2.50	1.50
(21)	Stan Bahnsen (Sept. 11)	5.00	2.50	1.50
(22)	Warren Cromartie (Sept. 18)	5.00	2.50	1.50
(23)	Santo Alcala (Sept. 25)	5.00	2.50	1.50
(24)	Wayne Twitchell (Oct. 2)	5.00	2.50	1.50
(25)	Pepe Frias (Oct. 9)	5.00	2.50	1.50
(26)	Sam Mejias (Oct. 16)	5.00	2.50	1.50

1978 Dimanche/Derniere Heure Expos

		NM	E	VG
Complete Set (13):		62.00	31.00	18.50
Common Player:		5.00	2.50	1.50
(1)	Ross Grimsley (May 7)	5.00	2.50	1.50

(2)	Chris Speier (May 14)	5.00	2.50	1.50
(3)	Norm Sherry (May 21)	5.00	2.50	1.50
(4)	Hal Dues (May 28)	5.00	2.50	1.50
(5)	Rudy May (June 4)	5.00	2.50	1.50
(6)	Stan Papi (June 11)	5.00	2.50	1.50
(7)	Darold Knowles (June 18)	5.00	2.50	1.50
(8)	Bob Reece (June 25)	5.00	2.50	1.50
(9)	Dan Schatzeder (July 2)	5.00	2.50	1.50
(10)	Jim Brewer (July 9)	5.00	2.50	1.50
(11)	Mike Garman (July 16)	5.00	2.50	1.50
(12)	Woodie Fryman (July 23)	5.00	2.50	1.50
(13)	Ed Hermann	5.00	2.50	1.50

1979 Dimanche/Derniere Heure Expos

		NM	E	VG
Complete Set (8):		35.00	17.50	10.50
Common Player:		5.00	2.50	1.50
(1)	Bill Lee (May 6)	5.00	2.50	1.50
(2)	Elias Sosa (May 13)	5.00	2.50	1.50
(3)	Tommy Hutton (May 20)	5.00	2.50	1.50
(4)	Tony Solaita (May 27)	5.00	2.50	1.50
(5)	Rodney Scott (June 3)	5.00	2.50	1.50
(6)	Duffy Dyer (June 10)	5.00	2.50	1.50
(7)	Jim Mason (June 17)	5.00	2.50	1.50
(8)	Ken Macha (June 24)	5.00	2.50	1.50

1980 Dimanche/Derniere Heure Expos

		NM	E	VG
Complete Set (23):		125.00	62.00	37.00
Common Player:		5.00	2.50	1.50
(1)	Steve Rogers (April 20)	5.00	2.50	1.50
(2)	Dick Williams (April 27)	5.00	2.50	1.50
(3)	Bill Lee (May 4)	5.00	2.50	1.50
(4)	Jerry White (May 11)	5.00	2.50	1.50
(5)	Scott Sanderson (May 18)	5.00	2.50	1.50
(6)	Ron LeFlore (May 25)	5.00	2.50	1.50
(7)	Elias Sosa (June 1)	5.00	2.50	1.50
(8)	Ellis Valentine (June 8)	5.00	2.50	1.50
(9)	Rodney Scott (June 22)	5.00	2.50	1.50
(10)	Woodie Fryman (June 29)	5.00	2.50	1.50
(11)	Chris Speier (July 6)	5.00	2.50	1.50
(12)	Warren Cromartie (July 13)	5.00	2.50	1.50
(13)	Stan Bahnsen (July 20)	5.00	2.50	1.50
(14)	Tommy Hutton (July 27)	5.00	2.50	1.50
(15)	Bill Almon (Aug. 3)	5.00	2.50	1.50
(16)	Fred Norman (Aug. 10)	5.00	2.50	1.50
(17)	Andre Dawson (Aug. 17)	10.00	5.00	3.00
(18)	John Tamargo (Aug. 24)	5.00	2.50	1.50
(19)	Larry Parrish (Aug. 31)	5.00	2.50	1.50
(20)	David Palmer (Sept. 7)	5.00	2.50	1.50
(21)	Tony Bernazard (Sept. 14)	5.00	2.50	1.50
(22)	Gary Carter (Sept. 21)	10.00	5.00	3.00
(23)	Ken Macha (Sept. 28)	5.00	2.50	1.50

1888 Dixie Cigarettes Girl Baseball Players (N48)

(See 1888 Allen & Ginter Girl Baseball Players.)

1937 Dixie Lids

This unnumbered set of Dixie cup ice cream tops was issued in 1937 and consists of 24 different lids, although only six picture sports stars; four of whom are baseball players. The lids are found in two different sizes, either 2-11/16" in diameter or 2-5/16" in diameter. The 1937 Dixie lids have their "picture" side printed in black or dark red. The reverse carries the advertising of one of many local dairies which packaged the ice cream treats. The lids must have the small tab still intact to command top value.

		NM	E	VG
Complete Set (4):		700.00	350.00	210.00
Common Player:		180.00	90.00	55.00
(1)	Charles Gehringer	180.00	90.00	55.00
(2)	Charles ("Gabby") Hartnett	180.00	90.00	55.00
(3)	Carl Hubbell (Mouth closed.)	195.00	95.00	55.00
(4)	Joe Medwick	180.00	90.00	55.00

1937 Dixie Lids Premiums

Issued as a premium offer in conjunction with the 1937 Dixie lids, this unnumbered set of color 8" x 10" pictures was printed on heavy paper and features the same subjects as the Dixie lids set. The 1937 Dixie premiums have a distinctive dark green band along the left margin containing the player's name. The back has smaller photos of the player in action with a large star at the top and a player write-up. The 1937 premiums are easily distinguished from the 1938 issue by the use of yellow ink for the names in the left border. A "My Scrapbook of Stars" album was issued in which to house the 24 sports and movie stars issued in the series.

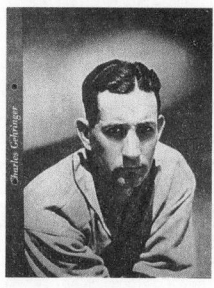 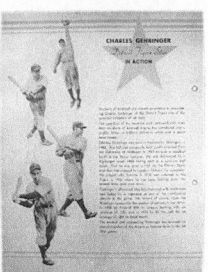

		NM	E	VG
Complete Set (4):		500.00	250.00	150.00
Common Player:		150.00	75.00	45.00
Album:		300.00	150.00	90.00
(2)	Charles Gehringer	150.00	75.00	45.00
(3)	Charles (Gabby) Hartnett	150.00	75.00	45.00
(4)	Carl Hubbell	175.00	87.00	52.00
(5)	Joe (Ducky) Medwick	150.00	75.00	45.00

1938 Dixie Lids

Similar to its set of the previous year, the 1938 Dixie lids set is a 24-subject set that includes six sports stars - four of whom are baseball players. The lids are found in two sizes, either 2-11/16" in diameter or 2-5/16" in diameter. The 1938 Dixie Lids have their "picture" side printed in blue ink. The reverse carries advertising from one of many local dairies which packaged the ice cream cups. Dixie lids must have the small tab still intact to command top value.

		NM	E	VG
Complete Set (4):		600.00	300.00	180.00
Common Player:		80.00	40.00	25.00

		NM	E	VG
(1)	Bob Feller	200.00	100.00	60.00
(2)	Jimmie Foxx	200.00	100.00	60.00
(3)	Carl Hubbell (Mouth open.)	175.00	85.00	50.00
(4)	Wally Moses	80.00	40.00	25.00

1938 Dixie Lids Premiums

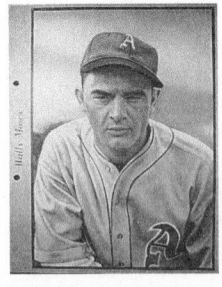 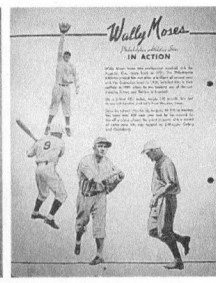

Issued in conjunction with the 1938 Dixie cup lids, this unnumbered set of 8" x 10" pictures contains the same subjects. A colored border surrounds the entire picture with the player's name in black at left. The back contains smaller photos of the player in action with his name in script at the top and a short write-up. A "My Scrapbook of Stars" album was issued in which to house the 24 sports and movie stars that comprise the complete series.

		NM	E	VG
Complete Set (4):		425.00	210.00	125.00
Common Player:		62.00	31.00	18.50
Album:		300.00	150.00	90.00
(1)	Bob Feller	125.00	62.00	37.00
(2)	Jimmy Foxx	125.00	62.00	37.00
(3)	Carl Hubbell	125.00	62.00	37.00
(4)	Wally Moses	60.00	30.00	18.00

1952 Dixie Lids

After a 14-year break, another Dixie lid set, featuring 24 baseball players, appeared in 1952. The unnumbered lids are found in three sizes, the most common being 2-11/16" in diameter. Somewhat scarcer, and carrying a modest premium over the values listed, are lids in sizes of 2-1/4" or 3-3/16". All are printed with a blue tint on their "picture" side. The backs carry advertising from one of the many local or regional dairies which packaged the ice cream treats. The Dixie lids of the 1950s can be distinguished from earlier issues because the bottom of the photo is squared off to accomodate the player's name. Dixie lids must contain the small tab to command top value.

		NM	E	VG
Complete Set (24):		5,500	2,750	1,650
Common Player:		200.00	100.00	60.00
(1)	Richie Ashburn	325.00	160.00	95.00
(2)	Tommy Byrne	200.00	100.00	60.00
(3)	Chico Carrasquel	200.00	100.00	60.00
(4)	Pete Castiglione	200.00	100.00	60.00
(5)	Walker Cooper	200.00	100.00	60.00
(6)	Billy Cox	225.00	110.00	65.00
(7)	Ferris Fain	200.00	100.00	60.00
(8)	Bobby Feller	350.00	175.00	100.00
(9)	Nelson Fox	325.00	160.00	95.00
(10)	Monte Irvin	275.00	135.00	80.00
(11)	Ralph Kiner	275.00	135.00	80.00
(12)	Cass Michaels	200.00	100.00	60.00
(13)	Don Mueller	200.00	100.00	60.00
(14)	Mel Parnell	200.00	100.00	60.00
(15)	Allie Reynolds	225.00	110.00	65.00
(16)	Preacher Roe	225.00	110.00	65.00
(17)	Connie Ryan	200.00	100.00	60.00
(18)	Hank Sauer	200.00	100.00	60.00
(19)	Al Schoendienst	275.00	135.00	80.00
(20)	Andy Seminick	200.00	100.00	60.00
(21)	Bobby Shantz	200.00	100.00	60.00
(22)	Enos Slaughter	275.00	135.00	80.00
(23)	Virgil Trucks	200.00	100.00	60.00
(24)	Gene Woodling	250.00	125.00	75.00

1952 Dixie Lids Premiums

This unnumbered set of 24 player photos was issued as a premium in conjunction with the 1952 Dixie cup lids and features the same subjects. The player's team and facsimile autograph appear along the bottom of the 8" x 10" blank-backed photo, which was printed on heavy paper. The 1952 Dixie premiums show the player's 1951 season statistics in the lower right corner.

		NM	E	VG
Complete Set (24):		2,250	1,125	675.00
Common Player:		90.00	45.00	25.00
(1)	Richie Ashburn	225.00	110.00	65.00
(2)	Tommy Byrne	90.00	45.00	25.00
(3)	Chico Carrasquel	90.00	45.00	25.00
(4)	Pete Castiglione	90.00	45.00	25.00
(5)	Walker Cooper	90.00	45.00	25.00
(6)	Billy Cox	100.00	50.00	30.00
(7)	Ferris Fain	90.00	45.00	25.00
(8)	Bob Feller	225.00	110.00	65.00
(9)	Nelson Fox	200.00	100.00	60.00
(10)	Monte Irvin	125.00	60.00	35.00
(11)	Ralph Kiner	125.00	60.00	35.00
(12)	Cass Michaels	90.00	45.00	25.00
(13)	Don Mueller	90.00	45.00	25.00
(14)	Mel Parnell	90.00	45.00	25.00
(15)	Allie Reynolds	100.00	50.00	30.00
(16)	Preacher Roe	100.00	50.00	30.00
(17)	Connie Ryan	90.00	45.00	25.00
(18)	Hank Sauer	90.00	45.00	25.00
(19)	Al Schoendienst	125.00	60.00	35.00
(20)	Andy Seminick	90.00	45.00	25.00
(21)	Bobby Shantz	90.00	45.00	25.00
(22)	Enos Slaughter	125.00	60.00	35.00
(23)	Virgil Trucks	90.00	45.00	25.00
(24)	Gene Woodling	100.00	50.00	30.00

1953 Dixie Lids

The 1953 Dixie lids set again consists of 24 unnumbered players and is identical in design to the 1952 set. Lids are either 2-1/4" or 2-11/16"in diameter and must include the small tab to command top value. Backs of the lids may be found with advertising of many local or regional dairies which packaged the ice cream cups.

		NM	E	VG
Complete Set (24):		4,000	2,000	1,200
Common Player:		120.00	60.00	35.00
(1)	Richie Ashburn	250.00	125.00	75.00
(2)	Chico Carrasquel	120.00	60.00	35.00
(3)	Billy Cox	130.00	65.00	40.00
(4)	Ferris Fain	120.00	60.00	35.00
(5)	Nelson Fox	200.00	100.00	60.00
(6a)	Sid Gordon (Boston)	240.00	120.00	70.00
(6b)	Sid Gordon (Milwaukee)	120.00	60.00	35.00
(7)	Warren Hacker	120.00	60.00	35.00
(8)	Monte Irvin	200.00	100.00	60.00
(9)	Jackie Jensen	180.00	90.00	55.00
(10a)	Ralph Kiner (Pittsburgh)	350.00	175.00	100.00
(10b)	Ralph Kiner (Chicago)	200.00	100.00	60.00
(11)	Ted Kluszewski	200.00	100.00	60.00
(12)	Bob Lemon	200.00	100.00	60.00
(13)	Don Mueller	120.00	60.00	35.00
(14)	Mel Parnell	120.00	60.00	35.00
(15)	Jerry Priddy	120.00	60.00	35.00
(16)	Allie Reynolds	130.00	65.00	40.00

(17)	Preacher Roe	130.00	65.00	40.00
(18)	Hank Sauer	120.00	60.00	35.00
(19)	Al Schoendienst	200.00	100.00	60.00
(20)	Bobby Shantz	120.00	60.00	35.00
(21)	Enos Slaughter	200.00	100.00	60.00
(22a)	Warren Spahn (Boston)	550.00	275.00	165.00
(22b)	Warren Spahn (Milwaukee)	500.00	250.00	150.00
(23a)	Virgil Trucks (Chicago)	250.00	125.00	75.00
(23b)	Virgil Trucks (St. Louis)	150.00	75.00	45.00
(24)	Gene Woodling	130.00	65.00	40.00

1953 Dixie Lids Premiums

This set of 8" x 10" photos was issued as a premium in conjunction with the 1953 Dixie lids set and includes the same subjects. A premium picture could be obtained in exchange for 12 lids. The player's team and facsimile autograph are at the bottom of the unnumbered, blank-backed photos. His 1952 season stats are shown in the lower right corner.

		NM	E	VG
Complete Set (24):		3,000	1,500	900.00
Common Player:		100.00	50.00	30.00
(1)	Richie Ashburn	250.00	125.00	75.00
(2)	Chico Carrasquel	100.00	50.00	30.00
(3)	Billy Cox	120.00	60.00	35.00
(4)	Ferris Fain	100.00	50.00	30.00
(5)	Nelson Fox	200.00	100.00	60.00
(6)	Sid Gordon	100.00	50.00	30.00
(7)	Warren Hacker	100.00	50.00	30.00
(8)	Monte Irvin	180.00	90.00	55.00
(9)	Jack Jensen	120.00	60.00	35.00
(10)	Ralph Kiner	180.00	90.00	55.00
(11)	Ted Kluszewski	180.00	90.00	55.00
(12)	Bob Lemon	180.00	90.00	55.00
(13)	Don Mueller	100.00	50.00	30.00
(14)	Mel Parnell	100.00	50.00	30.00
(15)	Jerry Priddy	100.00	50.00	30.00
(16)	Allie Reynolds	120.00	60.00	35.00
(17)	Preacher Roe	120.00	60.00	35.00
(18)	Hank Sauer	100.00	50.00	30.00
(19)	Al Schoendienst	180.00	90.00	55.00
(20)	Bobby Shantz	120.00	60.00	35.00
(21)	Enos Slaughter	180.00	90.00	55.00
(22)	Warren Spahn	260.00	130.00	75.00
(23)	Virgil Trucks	100.00	50.00	30.00
(24)	Gene Woodling	120.00	60.00	35.00

1954 Dixie Lids

The 1954 Dixie lids set consists of 18 players. Each player is found in both a "left" and "right" version. The picture side features a black-and-white photo. The lids usually measure 2-11/16" in diameter, although two other sizes (2-1/4" and 3-3/16") also exist and are valued at a significant premium above the prices listed. The 1954 Dixie lids are similar to earlier issues, except they carry an offer for a "3-D Starviewer" around the outside edge. The small tabs must be attached to command top value. The lids are unnumbered. Backs can be found with advertising from many local or regional dairies which packaged the ice cream cups.

	NM	E	VG
Complete Set (18):	2,000	1,000	600.00
Common Player:	120.00	60.00	35.00
2-1/4" or 3-3/16": 2-3X			

(1)	Richie Ashburn	250.00	125.00	75.00
(2)	Clint Courtney	120.00	60.00	35.00
(3)	Sid Gordon	120.00	60.00	35.00
(4)	Billy Hoeft	120.00	60.00	35.00
(5)	Monte Irvin	200.00	100.00	60.00
(6)	Jackie Jensen	130.00	65.00	40.00
(7)	Ralph Kiner	200.00	100.00	60.00
(8)	Ted Kluszewski	200.00	100.00	60.00
(9)	Gil McDougald	130.00	65.00	40.00
(10)	Minny Minoso	130.00	65.00	40.00
(11)	Danny O'Connell	120.00	60.00	35.00
(12)	Mel Parnell	120.00	60.00	35.00
(13)	Preacher Roe	130.00	65.00	40.00
(14)	Al Rosen	130.00	65.00	40.00
(15)	Al Schoendienst	200.00	100.00	60.00
(16)	Enos Slaughter	200.00	100.00	60.00
(17)	Gene Woodling	130.00	65.00	40.00
(18)	Gus Zernial	120.00	60.00	35.00

1909 Dockman & Sons Gum (E92)

Base Ball Gum.

THIS CARD IS ONE OF A SET OF

50 Base Ball Players

PROMINENT MEMBERS OF NATIONAL AND AMERICAN LEAGUES, ONE OF WHICH IS WRAPPED WITH EVERY PACKAGE OF BASE BALL GUM.

Manufactured only by JOHN H. DOCKMAN & SONS

Once cataloged as a part of the E92 compendium, the John Dockman & Sons Gum card issue differs from the Croft's Candy/Cocoa sets in that it has 10 fewer cards. Otherwise the format (1-1/2" x 2-3/4") and color litho player pictures are identical. Beneath the player picture on front is his last name, position and team. Backs, which describe the set as having 50 cards, are an ad for the gum company. Cards are checklisted here alphabetically.

		NM	E	VG
Complete Set (40):		50,000	20,000	10,000
Common Player:		1,000	500.00	300.00
(1)	Harry Bemis	1,000	500.00	300.00
(2)	Chief Bender	2,400	1,200	725.00
(3)	Bill Bergen	1,000	500.00	300.00
(4)	Bob Bescher	1,000	500.00	300.00
(5)	Al Bridwell	1,000	500.00	300.00
(6)	Doc Casey	1,000	500.00	300.00
(7)	Frank Chance	2,100	1,050	625.00
(8)	Hal Chase	1,250	625.00	375.00
(9)	Sam Crawford	2,100	1,050	625.00
(10)	Harry Davis	1,000	500.00	300.00
(11)	Art Devlin	1,000	500.00	300.00
(12)	Wild Bill Donovan	1,000	500.00	300.00
(13)	Mickey Doolan	1,000	500.00	300.00
(14)	Patsy Dougherty	1,000	500.00	300.00
(15)	Larry Doyle (Throwing)	1,000	500.00	300.00
(16)	Larry Doyle (With bat.)	1,000	500.00	300.00
(17)	George Gibson	1,000	500.00	300.00
(18)	Topsy Hartsel	1,000	500.00	300.00
(19)	Hugh Jennings	2,100	1,050	625.00
(20)	Red Kleinow	1,000	500.00	300.00
(21)	Nap Lajoie	2,400	1,200	725.00
(22)	Hans Lobert	1,000	500.00	300.00
(23)	Sherry Magee	1,000	500.00	300.00
(24)	Christy Matthewson (Mathewson)	8,000	4,000	2,400
(25)	John McGraw	2,100	1,050	625.00
(26)	Larry McLean	1,000	500.00	300.00
(27)	Dots Miller	1,000	500.00	300.00
(28)	Danny Murphy	1,000	500.00	300.00
(29)	Bill O'Hara	1,000	500.00	300.00
(30)	Germany Schaefer	1,000	500.00	300.00
(31)	Admiral Schlei	1,000	500.00	300.00
(32)	Boss Schmidt	1,000	500.00	300.00
(33)	Johnny Seigle	1,000	500.00	300.00
(34)	Dave Shean	1,000	500.00	300.00
(35)	Boss Smith (Schmidt)	1,000	500.00	300.00
(36)	Joe Tinker	2,100	1,050	625.00
(37)	Honus Wagner (Batting)	12,000	6,000	3,500
(38)	Honus Wagner (Throwing)	12,000	6,000	3,500
(39)	Cy Young	4,750	2,400	1,400
(40)	Heinie Zimmerman	1,000	500.00	300.00

1969-1972 Dodge Postcards

1969 Dodge Polara 500

Bill's Best Catch of the Year... Dodge Fever

Bill Freehan
Detroit All-Star Catcher

Between 1969-1972 Dodge issued a series of black-and-white promotional postcards featuring sports figures endorsing the car company's line-up. Player portrait photos on front are combined with a photo of one of the cars and some extraneous sales copy. Divided backs of the 5-1/2" x 3-1/2" cards have a couple sentences of career summary or highlights and a sales pitch. Only the baseball players are listed here, though stars from football, basketball, golf, hockey and racing were also included in the series.

		NM	E	VG
Common Player:		15.00	7.50	4.50
(1)	Lou Brock (1970)	60.00	30.00	18.00
(2)	Lou Brock (1971)	60.00	30.00	18.00
(3)	Bill Freehan (1969)	30.00	15.00	9.00
(5)	Bill Freehan (1971)	15.00	7.50	4.50
(6)	Bill Freehan (1972)	15.00	7.50	4.50
(7)	Bill Freehan (1972)	15.00	7.50	4.50
(8)	Bill Freehan (1972)	15.00	7.50	4.50
(9)	Joe Garagiola (1970)	35.00	17.50	10.50
(10)	Mickey Lolich (1969)	15.00	7.50	4.50

1888-1889 Dogs Head Cabinets (N173)

DOGS HEAD & OLD JUDGE CIGARETTES

(See 1888-1889 Old Judge Cabinets.)

1950 Dominican Republic

151 Phill Rizzuto

Selection of known Major League players makes 1950 the best guess for year of issue of this Caribbean card set. Like many contemporary Latin issues, these were probably produced to be collected in an accompanying album. Printed on fragile paper in blue, red or green duo-tones, the cards measure about 1-5/8" x 2-3/8" and are blank-backed. The set may or may not be complete at 292, the highest number currently known. Players featured in the issue are drawn from the Dominican and Cuban winter leagues (including Negro Leagues and minor league players) as well as the majors. In the bottom border beneath the player photo is a card number and name. Names are frequently misspelled and this list may not have succeeded in correcting all of them, particularly the Latino players. It is hoped that gaps in the checklist will eventually be filled with confirmed specimens. Many of the photos

on these cards appear to have been lifted - some even with the typography intact - from Bowman baseball cards of the era. Some, perhaps all, of the cards were printed in more than one color.

		VG
1	Guillermo Estrella	10.00
2	Benitez Redondo	10.00
3	Vidal Lopez	10.00
4	R. del Monte y C.	10.00
5		
6		
7	Juan Delfin Garcia	10.00
8	J. Raf. Carretero	10.00
9	J. Benjamin (Papo)	10.00
10		
11	Rufo E. Felix	10.00
12	Gallego Munoz	10.00
13	Julio A. Lara	10.00
14		
15		
16	Rafael Espada	10.00
17	Aladino Paez	10.00
18		
19	Pepe Lucas	10.00
20	Manolete Caceres	10.00
21	E.A. Lantigua	10.00
22	Olmedo Suarez	10.00
23	Chucho Ramos	10.00
24	Gullabin Olivo	10.00
25	Jose Luis Velazquez	10.00
26		
27	Felle Delgado	10.00
28		
29		
30	Alcibades Colon	10.00
31	Horacio Martinez	10.00
32	Ramon Burgos	10.00
33	Carlos A. Piallo	10.00
34	W.E. Springfield	10.00
35	Fiquito Suarez	10.00
36		
37		
38	Rafael Ortiz	10.00
39		
40		
41	Tetelo Vargas	10.00
42	Miguel Rueda	10.00
43	Hector Salazar	10.00
44		
45	Rafael Vargas	10.00
46		
47		
48		
49		
50	Gerard Thorne	10.00
51	Bienvenido Arias	10.00
52	Son Howell	15.00
53		
54		
55		
56		
57	P. Mateo (Richard)	10.00
58		
59		
60	Martin Dihigo	150.00
61		
62		
63		
64		
65	Octavio Blanco	10.00
66	Daniel Rodriguez	10.00
67		
68	Luis Villodas	10.00
69	Miguel Aracena	10.00
70	Amor Diaz	10.00
71	Juan B. Perdomo	10.00
72	Julio Martinez	10.00
73	Fernando Bueno	10.00
74	Rene Gutierrez	10.00
75	Israel Hernandez	10.00
76	Tomas Gomez Checo	10.00
77		
78	Miguel Tian Tineo	10.00
79	Rafael Valdez	10.00
80	Calampio Leon	10.00
81	Leonardo Coicochea	10.00
82	Herberto Blanco	10.00
83		
84	Rogelio Martinez	10.00
85		
86		
87	Silvio Garcia	10.00
88		
89	Napoleon Reyes	15.00
90		
91		
92		

93	Claro Duane (Duany)	10.00
94		
95		
96	Regino Otero	10.00
97	Avelino Canizares	10.00
98	Sandalio Consuegra	25.00
99	Roberto R. Topane	10.00
100	Jaok Cassin (Jack Cassini)	20.00
101	Jaime B. Prendesgart (Jim Prendergast)	20.00
102	Pablo Garcia	10.00
103		
104		
105		
106	Alejandro Crespo	20.00
107	Hiran Gonzalez	10.00
108	Rafael Noble	20.00
109		
110	Jose R. Lopez	10.00
111		
112		
113	Gilberto Torres	10.00
114		
115	Patato Pascual	10.00
116		
117		
118		
119	Gilberto Valdivia	10.00
120	Svdor. Hernandez	10.00
121		
122		
123		
124	Pedro Formental (Formenthal)	10.00
125		
126		
127		
128		
129		
130		
131		
132		
133		
134		
135	H. Wilson	25.00
136		
137		
138		
139	Carl Hubbell	35.00
140		
141		
142	Cocaina Garcia	10.00
143		
144		
145		
146		
147		
148		
149		
150		
151	Phill Rizzuto (Phil)	75.00
152	Bill Mc Cahan	20.00
153		
154	Allie Reynolds	55.00
155	Gill Coan (Gil)	20.00
156		
157	Mizell Platt	20.00
158		
159	Al S. "Red" (Schoendienst)	50.00
160	Jack Lorke (Lohrke)	20.00
161		
162		
163	Bill Nicholson	20.00
164	Sam Mele	20.00
165	Bob Schiffino (Scheffing)	20.00
166		
167		
168		
169	Harri Gumbert (Harry)	20.00
170		
171	Johnny Wyrostek	20.00
172		
173		
174		
175		
176		
177	Ken Keltner	25.00
178		
179	Harry Walker	25.00
180		
181		
182		
183		
184		
185	Sibby Sisti	20.00
186		
187	Eddie Waiticus (Waitkus)	25.00
188	Eddie Lake	20.00
189		

190	Hank Arft	20.00
191		
192		
193		
194	Walker Cooper	20.00
195	Al Brazle	20.00
196	Sam Champmann (Chapman)	20.00
197		
198	Doyle Lade	20.00
199		
200	Henry Eduards (Edwards)	20.00
201		
202		
203	N.Y. "Baby" (Norman "Babe" Young)	20.00
204		
205		
206	Bob Feller	75.00
207	Ralph Branca	35.00
208		
209		
210		
211	Larry (Yogi) Berra	75.00
212	Eddie Joost	20.00
213		
214		
215		
216		
217		
218		
219	Gil Hodges	55.00
220		
221		
222		
223	James, Vernon (Mickey)	25.00
224		
225		
226		
227		
228		
229		
230		
231		
232		
233		
234	Pete Raiser (Reiser)	30.00
235		
236	Bob Elliot	20.00
237		
238	Lou Boudreau	45.00
239	Danny Murtany (Photo is Joe Gordon.)	25.00
240	Jakie Robinson (Jackie)	125.00
241		
242		
243	Tommy Henrick (Henrich)	25.00
244	Pee Wee Reese	55.00
245	Bobby Brower (Brown)	25.00
246		
247		
248	Enos Slaughter	35.00
249		
250		
251	Tommy Henrich	25.00
252	George Koslo (Dave)	20.00
253	Frank Gustino (Gustine)	20.00
254		
255		
256		
257	Bill Rigney	20.00
258		
259	Rex Barney	25.00
260		
261	Mark Christman	20.00
262	Whetey Lockman (Whitey)	20.00
263		
264	Ralph Kiner	55.00
265		
266	Cliff Fannin	20.00
267	Joe Page	25.00
268		
269		
270		
271	Johnny Sain	30.00
272		
273		
274		
275		
276		
277		
278		
279	Joe Dobson	20.00
280		
281	Carrol Lockman (Whitey)	20.00
282		
283	Monte Kennedy	20.00
284		
285		
286	Carlos Bernier	20.00

287		
288		
289	Buster Clarkson	20.00
290	Williard Brown (Willard)	25.00
291	Jim Rivera	25.00
292	Saturnino Escalera	20.00

1958 Dominican Republic

The date of issue is speculative, based on the known winter ball career of the sole card known. The identity of the issuer and manner of distribution is unknown, though from their wide borders it is possible these were printed on some type of box or package and intended to be cut out and possibly placed into an album, as is customary with many Latin American baseball card issues. The cards are nominally about 2" x 2-1/2" and are printed in sepia on thin, blank-back cardboard. As with many issues of the era and area, when these cards are found they are usually in wretched condition.

VG

Felipe R. Alou 35.00

1959 Dominican Republic

The date of issue is speculative. The identity of the issuer and manner of distribution is unknown, though they appear to have been sold in strips or panels and intended to be separated and possibly placed into an album, as is customary with many Latin American baseball cards. The cards are nominally about 2-1/8" x 3-1/4" and printed in black or blue on thin, blank-back cardboard. As with many issues of the era and area, when these cards are found they are usually in wretched condition. These players certainly represent only a portion of the checklist.

VG

Walter James 15.00
Osvaldo Virgil 25.00

1966 Dominican Republic

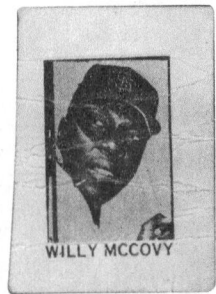

The date of issue is speculative, based on the fact these cards "borrowed" their images from 1965 Topps cards. The identity of the issuer and manner of distribution is unknown, though from their wide borders it is possible these were printed on some type of box or package and intended to be cut out and possibly placed into an album, as is customary with many Latin American baseball card issues. The cards are nominally about 1-3/4" x 2-1/2" and are printed in red on thin, blank-back cardboard. As with many issues of the era and area, when these cards are found they are usually in wretched condition. These players probably represent only a portion of the checklist which may or may not comprise only Major League players.

		VG
(1)	Sandy Koufax	200.00
(2)	Juan Marichal	100.00
(3)	Willy Mays (Willie)	200.00
(4)	Willy McCovy (Willie McCovey)	45.00

1937 Donut Co. of American Thrilling Moments

The official title of this multi-subject card set is "Thrilling Moments in the Lives of Famous Americans." The cards, about 1-7/8" x 2-7/8", were printed in groups of 18 on donut boxes. Each card is printed in black-and-white on a single background color. The cards themselves do not name the famous American depicted, but his biography is found in the album which was issued to house the set. Cards are blank-backed. There is only a single baseball played in the 72-card set.

	NM	E	VG
Beloved Baseball Idol of All Boys (Babe Ruth)	4,000	1,600	800.00

1952-55 Dormand Postcards

This mid-1950s issue features only selected players from the Yankees, Brooklyn Dodgers, White Sox and Philadelphia A's. Apparently produced on order by the players by Louis Dormand, a Long Island, N.Y., photographer, the cards were used to honor fan requests for photos and autographs. All cards have a facsimile autograph printed in front. Otherwise the fronts of these 3-1/2" x 5-1/2" postcards feature only sharp color photos with no border. Backs, printed in blue or green, feature a few player biographical and career details, one or two lines identifying the producer and usually product and series numbers. Most have a Kodachrome logo. Some cards do not have all of these elements and several are found blank-backed. The Gil Hodges card is considerably scarcer than the others in the set, with those of Jim Konstanty, Elston Howard, and Casey Stengel also seldom seen. Besides the standard-sized cards listed below, there are oversize versions of Rizzuto's and Mantle's cards. A variation of Johnny Sain's card shows his Arkansas Chevrolet dealership in a photo above the player's picture. The complete set price includes only the standard-size cards.

	NM	E	VG
Common Player:	25.00	12.50	7.50
101a Phil Rizzuto (Large autograph upper right, orange sky)	40.00	20.00	12.00
101b Phil Rizzuto (Small autograph, upper right, blue sky)	45.00	22.50	13.50
101c Phil Rizzuto (large autograph, diagonal)	50.00	25.00	15.00
101d Phil Rizzuto (9" x 12")	55.00	27.50	16.50
102 Yogi Berra (four back types)	65.00	32.50	20.00
103 Ed Lopat (two back types)	30.00	15.00	9.00
104 Hank Bauer (Small autograph)	30.00	15.00	9.00
104 Hank Bauer (Large autograph)	60.00	30.00	18.00
105 Joe Collins (Patch, left shoulder, autograph at top.)	60.00	30.00	18.00

105	Joe Collins (Patch left shoulder, autograph at bottom.)	60.00	30.00	18.00
105	Joe Collins (No patch on sleeve, auto at top)	40.00	20.00	12.00
105	Joe Collins (Kneel, patch, autograph upper right)	60.00	30.00	18.00
105	Joe Collins (kneel, patch, autograph lower left)	60.00	30.00	18.00
106	Ralph Houk	30.00	15.00	9.00
107	Bill Miller	27.50	13.50	8.25
108	Ray Scarborough	35.00	17.50	10.00
109	Allie Reynolds (2 back types)	25.00	12.50	7.50
110	Gil McDougald (Small autograph, green grass)	25.00	12.50	7.50
110	Gil McDougald (Large autograph, brownish grass)	25.00	12.50	7.50
111	Mickey Mantle (Bat on shoulder, blue back.)	100.00	50.00	30.00
111	Mickey Mantle (Bat on shoulder, green back.)	100.00	50.00	30.00
111	Mickey Mantle (Batting stance, 3-1/2" x 5-1/2".)	200.00	100.00	60.00
111	Mickey Mantle (Bat on shoulder, 6" x 9".)	550.00	275.00	165.00
111	Mickey Mantle (Bat on shoulder, 9" x 12".)	1,200	600.00	360.00
112	Johnny Mize (two back types)	90.00	45.00	27.50
113	Casey Stengel (Autograph at top.)	165.00	80.00	50.00
113	Casey Stengel (Autograph at bottom.)	165.00	80.00	50.00
114	Bobby Shantz (Autograph parallel to top.)	40.00	20.00	12.00
114	Bobby Shantz (Autograph angles downward.)	75.00	37.00	22.00
115	Whitey Ford (two back types)	60.00	30.00	18.00
116	Johnny Sain (Beginning windup.)	35.00	17.50	10.00
116	Johnny Sain (Leg kick.)	25.00	12.50	7.50
116	Johnny Sain (Clipped version, with auto dealership ad.)	150.00	75.00	45.00
117	Jim McDonald (two color variations known)	25.00	12.50	7.50
118	Gene Woodling (two color variations known)	25.00	12.50	7.50
119	Charlie Silvera	30.00	15.00	9.00
120	Don Bollweg	25.00	12.50	7.50
121	Billy Pierce (two color variations known)	30.00	15.00	9.00
122	Chico Carrasquel (three cropping variations known)	25.00	12.50	7.50
123	Willie Miranda (two color variations known)	25.00	12.50	7.50
124	Carl Erskine (two cropping variations known)	65.00	32.50	20.00
125	Roy Campanella	150.00	75.00	45.00
126	Jerry Coleman	25.00	12.50	7.50
127	Pee Wee Reese	50.00	25.00	15.00
128	Carl Furillo (three color variations known)	50.00	25.00	15.00
129	Gil Hodges	75.00	37.50	22.50
130	Billy Martin (two color and cropping variations known)	30.00	15.00	9.00
131	NOT ISSUED			
132	Irv Noren	35.00	17.50	10.50
133	Enos Slaughter	175.00	87.50	52.50
134	Tom Gorman (two cropping variations known)	25.00	12.50	7.50
135	Ed Robinson	35.00	17.50	10.00
136	Frank Crosetti	150.00	75.00	45.00
137	NOT ISSUED			
138	Jim Konstanty	150.00	75.00	45.00
139	Elston Howard (two cropping variations known)	150.00	75.00	45.00
140	Bill Skowron (two cropping variations known)	400.00	200.00	120.00

1941 Double Play (R330)

Issued by Gum Products Inc., Cambridge, Mass., this set comprises 75 numbered cards with two consecutive numbers per card featuring 150 (130 different) players. The blank-backed cards measure about 3-1/8" x 2-1/2". Most feature sepia-toned portrait photos. Cards 81-82 through 99-100 have vertical "in action" photos of 40 of the players who

also appear in portraits. The last 50 cards in the series are scarcer than the early numbers. Cards which have been cut in half to form single cards have little collector value.

JOE DI MAGGIO New York Yankees. Center fielder. Born Nov. 25, 1914. Bats right. Throws right. Height 6 ft. Weight 195 lbs. Batted .352. No. 63 Double Play

CHARLEY KELLER New York Yankees. Left fielder. Born Sept. 12, 1916. Bats left. Throws right. Height 5 ft. 10 in. Wt. 190 lbs. Batted .286. No. 64 Double Play

	NM	E	VG
Complete Set (75):	10,000	4,000	2,000
Common Player (1/2-99/100):	70.00	25.00	12.50
Common Player (101/102-149/150):	90.00	35.00	15.00
1-2 Larry French, Vance Page	90.00	30.00	15.00
3-4 Billy Herman, Stanley Hack	125.00	50.00	25.00
5-6 Linus Frey, John Vander Meer	75.00	30.00	15.00
7-8 Paul Derringer, Bucky Walters	70.00	25.00	12.50
9-10 Frank McCormick, Bill Werber	70.00	25.00	12.50
11-12 Jimmy Ripple, Ernie Lombardi	85.00	35.00	15.00
13-14 Alex Kampouris, John Wyatt	70.00	25.00	12.50
15-16 Mickey Owen, Paul Waner	110.00	45.00	20.00
17-18 Cookie Lavagetto, Harold Reiser	75.00	30.00	15.00
19-20 Jimmy Wasdell, Dolph Camilli	70.00	25.00	12.50
21-22 Dixie Walker, Ducky Medwick	110.00	45.00	20.00
23-24 Harold Reese, Kirby Higbe	600.00	240.00	120.00
25-26 Harry Danning, Cliff Melton	70.00	25.00	12.50
27-28 Harry Gumbert, Burgess Whitehead	70.00	25.00	12.50
29-30 Joe Orengo, Joe Moore	70.00	25.00	12.50
31-32 Mel Ott, Babe Young	200.00	80.00	40.00
33-34 Lee Handley, Arky Vaughan	110.00	45.00	20.00
35-36 Bob Klinger, Stanley Brown	70.00	25.00	12.50
37-38 Terry Moore, Gus Mancuso	70.00	25.00	12.50
39-40 Johnny Mize, Enos Slaughter	700.00	280.00	140.00
41-42 Jimmy Brown, Sibby Sisti	70.00	25.00	12.50
43-44 Max West, Carvel Rowell	70.00	25.00	12.50
45-46 Danny Litwhiler, Merrill May	70.00	25.00	12.50
47-48 Frank Hayes, Al Brancato	70.00	25.00	12.50
49-50 Bob Johnson, Bill Nagel	70.00	25.00	12.50
51-52 Buck Newsom, Hank Greenberg	200.00	80.00	40.00
53-54 Barney McCosky, Charley Gehringer	140.00	55.00	25.00
55-56 Pinky Higgins, Dick Bartell	70.00	25.00	12.50
57-58 Ted Williams, Jim Tabor	650.00	260.00	130.00
59-60 Joe Cronin, Jimmy Foxx	275.00	110.00	55.00
61-62 Lefty Gomez, Phil Rizzuto	675.00	275.00	135.00
63-64 Joe DiMaggio, Charley Keller	850.00	420.00	250.00
65-66 Red Rolfe, Bill Dickey	125.00	50.00	25.00
67-68 Joe Gordon, Red Ruffing	120.00	45.00	25.00
69-70 Mike Tresh, Luke Appling	110.00	45.00	20.00
71-72 Moose Solters, John Rigney	70.00	25.00	12.50
73-74 Buddy Meyer, Ben Chapman (Myer)	70.00	25.00	12.50
75-76 Cecil Travis, George Case	70.00	25.00	12.50
77-78 Joe Krakauskas, Bob Feller	200.00	80.00	40.00
79-80 Ken Keltner, Hal Trosky	70.00	25.00	12.50
81-82 Ted Williams, Joe Cronin (In action)	550.00	220.00	110.00
83-84 Joe Gordon, Charley Keller (In action)	135.00	67.50	40.50
85-86 Hank Greenberg, Red Ruffing (In action.)	225.00	90.00	45.00

		NM	E	VG
87-88	Hal Trosky, George Case (In action.)	70.00	25.00	12.50
89-90	Mel Ott, Burgess Whitehead (In action.)	210.00	85.00	40.00
91-92	Harry Danning, Harry Gumbert (In action.)	70.00	25.00	12.50
93-94	Babe Young, Cliff Melton (In action.)	70.00	25.00	12.50
95-96	Jimmy Ripple, Bucky Walters (In action.)	70.00	25.00	12.50
97-98	Stanley Hack, Bob Klinger (In action.)	70.00	25.00	12.50
99-	Johnny Mize, Dan			
100	Litwhiler (In action.)	135.00	55.00	25.00
101-	Dom Dallessandro, Augie			
102	Galan	70.00	25.00	12.50
103-	Bill Lee, Phil Cavarretta			
104		90.00	35.00	15.00
105-	Lefty Grove, Bobby Doerr			
106		225.00	112.50	67.50
107-	Frank Pytlak, Dom			
108	DiMaggio	115.00	45.00	20.00
109-	Gerald Priddy, John			
110	Murphy	90.00	35.00	15.00
111-	Tommy Henrich, Marius			
112	Russo	100.00	40.00	20.00
113-	Frank Crosetti, John			
114	Sturm	100.00	40.00	20.00
115-	Ival Goodman, Myron			
116	McCormick	90.00	35.00	15.00
117-	Eddie Joost, Ernie Koy			
118		90.00	35.00	15.00
119-	Lloyd Waner, Hank			
120	Majeski	125.00	50.00	25.00
121-	Buddy Hassett, Eugene			
122	Moore	90.00	35.00	15.00
123-	Nick Etten, John Rizzo			
124		90.00	35.00	15.00
125-	Sam Chapman, Wally			
126	Moses	90.00	35.00	15.00
127-	John Babich, Richard			
128	Siebert	90.00	35.00	15.00
129-	Nelson Potter, Benny			
130	McCoy	90.00	25.00	15.00
131-	Clarence Campbell, Louis			
132	Boudreau	125.00	50.00	25.00
133-	Rolly Hemsley, Mel			
134	Harder	90.00	35.00	15.00
135-	Gerald Walker, Joe			
136	Heving	90.00	35.00	15.00
137-	John Rucker, Ace Adams			
138		90.00	35.00	15.00
139-	Morris Arnovich, Carl			
140	Hubbell	225.00	90.00	45.00
141-	Lew Riggs, Leo Durocher			
142		135.00	55.00	25.00
143-	Fred Fitzsimmons, Joe			
144	Vosmik	90.00	35.00	15.00
145-	Frank Crespi, Jim Brown			
146		90.00	35.00	15.00
147-	Don Heffner, Harland Clift			
148	(Harlond)	90.00	35.00	15.00
149-	Debs Garms, Elbie			
150	Fletcher	90.00	35.00	15.00

1976 Douglas Cool Papa Bell

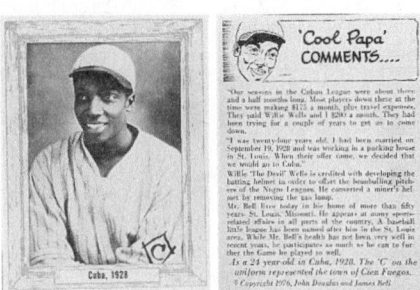

This collectors' issue was produced following the 1974 induction of James "Cool Papa" Bell into the Hall of Fame. Collector John Douglas collaborated with Bell to produce the set chronicling Bell's career (1922-46) in the Negro and Latin American pro leagues. Fronts have vintage sepia-toned photos of Bell surrounded by a yellow, green or orange wood-grain frame with a title plaque at bottom. Backs are in brown-and-white with a drawing of Bell at top and autobiographical material at center. A description of the photo and copyright data are at bottom. The unnumbered cards are checklisted here alphabetically by their titles.

	NM	E	VG
Complete Set (13):	10.00	5.00	3.00
Common Card:	1.00	.50	.30

(1)	Amazing Speed	1.00	.50	.30
(2)	Brock Sets SB Record	1.00	.50	.30
(3)	Cool Papa	1.00	.50	.30
(4)	Cuba, 1928	1.00	.50	.30
(5)	Great Fielder, Too	1.00	.50	.30
(6)	HOF, Cooperstown	1.00	.50	.30
(7)	HOF Favorite	1.00	.50	.30
(8)	Induction Day, 1974	1.00	.50	.30
(9)	Monarchs' Manager	1.00	.50	.30
(10)	On Deck in Cuba	1.00	.50	.30
(11)	The Mexican Leagues	1.00	.50	.30
(12)	Touring Havana	1.00	.50	.30
(13)	With Josh Gibson	1.00	.50	.30

1977 Douglas Johnny Mize

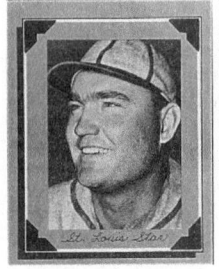 

In an effort to promote Johnny Mize for induction to the Hall of Fame, John Douglas created this collectors' issue. The Big Cat's career is traced on a series of 3-1/4" x 3-7/8" cards with black-and-white photos on a greenish-brown background. Black-and-white backs have a drawing of Mize at top with lengthy narrative below. The unnumbered cards are checklisted here by the title which appears on the front. Mize was selected for the Hall of Fame in 1981.

	NM	E	VG
Complete Set (20):	9.00	4.50	2.75
Common Card:	1.00	.50	.30

(1)	Marshall	1.00	.50	.30
(2)	Call for Phillip Morris	1.00	.50	.30
(3)	Cardinal Slugger	1.00	.50	.30
(4)	Card's Big Stick	1.00	.50	.30
(5)	Early Photo - 1913	1.00	.50	.30
(6)	51 Homers, 1947	1.00	.50	.30
(7)	Home Run, 1952 Series	1.00	.50	.30
(8)	June 16, 1953	1.00	.50	.30
(9)	Louisville Poster - 1947	1.00	.50	.30
(10)	Mize, Happy Chandler, Bucky Harris	1.00	.50	.30
(11)	Mize, Reynolds, Johnson	1.00	.50	.30
(12)	N.L. Homer Champ 1948	1.00	.50	.30
(13)	Series MVP - 1952	1.00	.50	.30
(14)	St. Louis Star	1.00	.50	.30
(15)	The Navy - 1943	1.00	.50	.30
(16)	Vu-Master Slide	1.00	.50	.30
(17)	With Enos Slaughter	1.00	.50	.30
(18)	With Roy Rogers	1.00	.50	.30
(19)	With Terry Moore	1.00	.50	.30
(20)	Woodling, Raschi, Mize - 1952	1.00	.50	.30

1978 Dover Publications Great Players Postcards

This set of 32 collectors' issue postcards was originally issued in the form of an 8" x 11" booklet from which individual cards could be separated. The 3-7/8" x 5-1/2" cards are perforated on two sides, depending on their placement on a four-card page. Fronts have borderless sepia photos. Black-and-white backs have standard postcard indicia, copyright data, player identification and a brief career summary. The unnumbered cards are checklisted here alphabetically.

	NM	E	VG

			NM	E	VG
	Complete Set, Booklet:		7.50	3.75	2.25
	Complete Set, Singles (32):		7.50	3.75	2.25
	Common Player:		.50	.25	.15
(1)	Grover Cleveland Alexander		.60	.30	.20
(2)	Chief Bender		.50	.25	.15
(3)	Roger Bresnahan		.50	.25	.15
(4)	Bullet Joe Bush		.50	.25	.15
(5)	Frank Chance		.50	.25	.15
(6)	Ty Cobb		1.25	.60	.40
(7)	Eddie Collins		.50	.25	.15
(8)	Stan Coveleski		.50	.25	.15
(9)	Sam Crawford		.50	.25	.15
(10)	Frankie Frisch		.50	.25	.15
(11)	Goose Goslin		.50	.25	.15
(12)	Harry Heilmann		.50	.25	.15
(13)	Rogers Hornsby		.75	.40	.25
(14)	Joe Jackson		4.00	2.00	1.25
(15)	Hughie Jennings		.50	.25	.15
(16)	Walter Johnson		1.00	.50	.30
(17)	Sad Sam Jones		.50	.25	.15
(18)	Rabbit Maranville		.50	.25	.15
(19)	Rube Marquard		.50	.25	.15
(20)	Christy Mathewson		1.00	.50	.30
(21)	John McGraw		.50	.25	.15
(22)	Herb Pennock		.50	.25	.15
(23)	Eddie Plank		.50	.25	.15
(24)	Edd Roush		.50	.25	.15
(25)	Babe Ruth		4.00	2.00	1.25
(26)	George Sisler		.50	.25	.15
(27)	Tris Speaker		.75	.40	.25
(28)	Casey Stengel		.50	.25	.15
(29)	Joe Tinker		.50	.25	.15
(30)	Pie Traynor		.50	.25	.15
(31)	Dazzy Vance		.50	.25	.15
(32)	Cy Young		.75	.40	.25

1925 Drake's

Among a series of 64 movie stars packaged with Drake's Cake in the mid-1920s was a card of Babe Ruth, who did some movie work for Universal Pictures at the time. The 2-7/16" x 4-3/16" black-and-white card has a portrait of Ruth on front, with his name, studio and card number in the bottom border. Backs have been seen with at least two styles of advertising, one for Drake's Cake and one for Yankee Cake.

		NM	E	VG
61	Babe Ruth	3,750	1,875	1,125

1950 Drake's

Entitled "TV Baseball Series," the 1950 Drake's Baker-ies set pictures 36 different players on a television screen format. The cards, 2-1/2" x 2-1/2", contain black-and-white photos surrounded by a black border. Backs carry a player biography plus an advertisement advising collectors to look for the cards in packages of Oatmeal or Jumble cookies.

		NM	E	VG
	Complete Set (36):	9,975	5,000	3,000
	Common Player:	200.00	100.00	60.00
1	Elwin "Preacher" Roe	340.00	170.00	100.00
2	Clint Hartung	200.00	100.00	60.00

		NM	E	VG
3	Earl Torgeson	200.00	100.00	60.00
4	Leland "Lou" Brissie	200.00	100.00	60.00
5	Edwin "Duke" Snider	675.00	340.00	200.00
6	Roy Campanella	675.00	340.00	200.00
7	Sheldon "Available" Jones	200.00	100.00	60.00
8	Carroll "Whitey" Lockman	200.00	100.00	60.00
9	Bobby Thomson	240.00	120.00	75.00
10	Dick Sisler	200.00	100.00	60.00
11	Gil Hodges	400.00	200.00	120.00
12	Eddie Waitkus	200.00	100.00	60.00
13	Bobby Doerr	350.00	175.00	100.00
14	Warren Spahn	400.00	200.00	120.00
15	John "Buddy" Kerr	200.00	100.00	60.00
16	Sid Gordon	200.00	100.00	60.00
17	Willard Marshall	200.00	100.00	60.00
18	Carl Furillo	400.00	200.00	120.00
19	Harold "Pee Wee" Reese	540.00	270.00	160.00
20	Alvin Dark	200.00	100.00	60.00
21	Del Ennis	200.00	100.00	60.00
22	Ed Stanky	200.00	100.00	60.00
23	Tommy "Old Reliable" Henrich	240.00	120.00	75.00
24	Larry "Yogi" Berra	675.00	350.00	200.00
25	Phil "Scooter" Rizzuto	675.00	350.00	200.00
26	Jerry Coleman	200.00	100.00	60.00
27	Joe Page	200.00	100.00	60.00
28	Allie Reynolds	240.00	120.00	75.00
29	Ray Scarborough	200.00	100.00	60.00
30	George "Birdie" Tebbetts	200.00	100.00	60.00
31	Maurice "Lefty" McDermott	200.00	100.00	60.00
32	Johnny Pesky	200.00	100.00	60.00
33	Dom "Little Professor" DiMaggio	250.00	125.00	75.00
34	Vern "Junior" Stephens	200.00	100.00	60.00
35	Bob Elliott	200.00	100.00	60.00
36	Enos "Country" Slaughter	440.00	220.00	130.00

1909-11 Drum Cigarettes

Other than Ty Cobb brand, Drum is the rarest of the various cigarette advertisements to be found on the backs of T206. Typography on the back is printed in a plum color. Multipliers shown are for "common" players; Hall of Fame players and other high-demand cards command a lesser premium relative to common-brand backs. Among T205 backs, Drum, printed in brown, ranks as the scarcest of the brands.

PREMIUMS
T205 Common Players:
15-25X
T205 Hall of Famers: 15-25X
T206 Common Players:
35-50X
T206 Hall of Famers: 35-50X

(See T205, T206 for checklists and base card values.)

1972 Don Drysdale's Restaurant Postcards

The date cited is taken from the postmark of an observed example. The actual span during which the cards were current is unknown. These versions of J.D. McCarthy postcards have on their 3-1/4" x 5-1/2" fronts a borderless black-and-white pose. The salutation and facsimile autograph are incuse printed in blue ink. Postcard style backs are known in three styles. One advertises Don Drysdale's Dugout in Santa Ana, Calif., another advertises his Club 53 in Kona, Hawaii, while a third advertises Don Drysdale's Dugout and the Whaler's Pub on Maui.

	NM	E	VG
Don Drysdale	25.00	12.50	7.50

1914-15 J.H. Dugan Calendar Cabinets

Newly presented in 2013, this set is named for the Rutland, Vt., advertiser whose name appears on each of the 12 cabinet cards that comprise the set. Each card measures 4-3/4" by 3-1/2". The reverse of each card features a brief player biography with height, weight and playing statistics. Two punch holes resides at the top of each card for a binder never issued. List alphabetically with calendar month in parenthesis. The set sold in a 1990s auction for $82,000. Heritage Auctions sold a set in Fall 2013, too late for results here.

		NM	E	VG

Complete Set (12):

1	Jimmy Archer (December 1914)	
2	Frank Baker (November 1914)	
3	Jack Barry (March 1915)	
4	Chief Bender (June 1914)	
5	Ty Cobb (October 1914)	
6	Eddie Collins (September 1914)	
7	Joe Jackson (April 1915)	
8	Walter Johnson (August 1914)	
9	Christy Mathewson (July 1914)	
10	John McInnes (May 1915)	
11	Wallie Schang (January 1915)	
12	Tris Speaker (February 1915)	

1965 Dugan Bros. Casey Stengel

 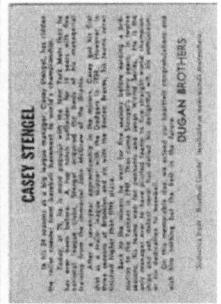

In celebration of the Ol' Perfesser's 75th birthday, the N.Y. Mets held a birthday party for him at Shea Stadium on July 25. This approximately 2-1/2" x 3-1/2" card was given to each of the 40,000+ fans in attendance, sponsored by Dugan Bros., a local bakery which also provided a birthday cake for the occasion. Unfortunately, Stengel was unable to attend the fete; early that morning he broke his hip leaving a nightclub, ending his managerial career. The card is printed in blue on white. The back provides career highlights.

	NM	E	VG
Casey Stengel	40.00	20.00	12.00

1888 Duke Talk of the Diamond (N135)

One of the more obscure 19th Century tobacco issues is a 25-card set issued by Honest Long Cut Tobacco in the late 1880's. Titled "Talk of the Diamond," the set features full-color cards measuring 4-1/8" x 2-1/2". Each card features a cartoon-like drawing illustrating a popular baseball term or expression. The left portion of the card pictures an unspecified player in a fielding position, and some of the artwork for that part of the set was borrowed from the more popular Buchner Gold Coin set (N284) issued about the same time. Because the "Talk of the Diamond" set does not feature in-

dividual players, it has never really captured the attention of baseball card collectors. It does, however, hold interest as a novelty item of the period. It carries an N135 American Card Catalog designation.

	NM	E	VG
Complete Set (25):	9,350	3,850	1,925
Common Card:	385.00	155.00	75.00
(1) A Base Tender	400.00	155.00	75.00
(2) A Big Hit	400.00	155.00	75.00
(3) A Chronic Kicker	400.00	155.00	75.00
(4) A Foul Balk	400.00	155.00	75.00
(5) A Foul Catch	400.00	155.00	75.00
(6) A Good Catch	400.00	155.00	75.00
(7) A Good Throw	400.00	155.00	75.00
(8) A Heavy Batter	400.00	155.00	75.00
(9) A Home Run	400.00	155.00	75.00
(10) A Hot Ball	400.00	155.00	75.00
(11) A Low Ball	400.00	155.00	75.00
(12) A Pitcher in the Box	400.00	155.00	75.00
(13) A Regular Ball	400.00	155.00	75.00
(14) A Rounder	400.00	155.00	75.00
(15) A Short Stop	400.00	155.00	75.00
(16) After the Ball	400.00	155.00	75.00
(17) Going for Third Base	400.00	155.00	75.00
(18) He Serves the Ball	400.00	155.00	75.00
(19) Left Field	400.00	155.00	75.00
(20) Left on Base	400.00	155.00	75.00
(21) Lively Game	400.00	155.00	75.00
(22) No Game	400.00	155.00	75.00
(23) Out	400.00	155.00	75.00
(24) Stealing a Base	400.00	155.00	75.00
(25) Three out-All out	400.00	155.00	75.00

1889 Duke's Terrors of America

 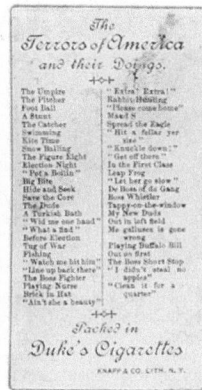

Officially titled "The Terrors of America and their Doings," this set of tobacco inserts features color artwork of boys in all manners of activities, some mischievous. Several of the cards picture the lads playing sports, including baseball. The cards were issued in three sizes. The smallest measure 1-7/16" x 2-3/4" and have an ad on the checklist back for Duke's Cigarettes. A slightly larger 1-3/4" x 3-1/8" version advertises Duke's Mixture. The largest features the card design on an ornate background and measures 2-1/2" x 4-3/16", advertising Honest Long Cut on back.

	NM	E	VG
Duke's Cigarettes	80.00	40.00	24.00
Duke's Mixture	100.00	50.00	30.00
Honest Long Cut	200.00	100.00	60.00

1969 Dunkin' Donuts Chicago Cubs Bumper Stickers

This series of Cubs novelty collectibles was the first of two annual presentations. The stickers measure about 8" x 4" and have at their left end a photographic portrait of a player at one end of an artwork at bat on a black background. At right is a baseball design with the sponsor's logo. A second version exists with "Cub Power" in place of the DD advertising. The unnumbered stickers are checklisted here alphabetically.

		NM	E	VG
Complete Set (6):		350.00	175.00	100.00
Common Player:		30.00	15.00	9.00
(1)	Ernie Banks	125.00	65.00	35.00
(2)	Glenn Beckert	30.00	15.00	9.00
(3)	Randy Hundley	30.00	15.00	9.00
(4)	Don Kessinger	30.00	15.00	9.00
(5)	Ron Santo	60.00	30.00	18.00
(6)	Billy Williams	75.00	37.00	22.00

1970 Dunkin' Donuts Chicago Cubs Bumper Stickers

This series of Cubs novelty collectibles was the second of two annual presentations. The stickers measure about 8" x 4" and have at their left end a photographic portrait (without cap) of a player in a vaguely baseball-like design. In upper-left is a blue facsimile autograph. At right is "Cubs are no. 1," at bottom is a DD credit line. Basic color scheme of the graphics is red, white and blue. The unnumbered stickers are checklisted here alphabetically.

		NM	E	VG
Complete Set (6):		350.00	175.00	100.00
Common Player:		30.00	15.00	9.00
(1)	Ernie Banks	125.00	62.00	37.00
(2)	Glenn Beckert	30.00	15.00	9.00
(3)	Randy Hundley	30.00	15.00	9.00
(4)	Don Kessinger	30.00	15.00	9.00
(5)	Ron Santo	60.00	30.00	18.00
(6)	Billy Williams	75.00	37.00	22.00

1947 DuPont Cavalcade of America Premium

This 6" x 9" black-and-white card was distributed by NBC radio in conjunction with one of its weekly programs, which featured Babe Ruth on Sept. 29, 1947. The front has a bordered photo of Ruth in his classic batting follow-through. The back has information about the broadcast and details "The Babe's 54 Major League Records."

	NM	E	VG
Babe Ruth	500.00	250.00	150.00

1972 Durochrome Chicago White Sox Decals

While they are technically stickers rather than decals, this set of six White Sox was given away during the course of half a dozen "Decal Days" at Comiskey Park, as listed on the peel-off back. The stickers measure 3-9/16" x 4-9/16" and feature posed action photos of the players in their vintage red-trimmed uniforms. Fronts have a facsimile autograph and, in the bottom border, the team name. Backs are printed in green and have a few vital statistics, an ad by the manufacturer and an enigmatic row of numbers at the bottom. The unnumbered stickers are checklisted here in alphabetical order.

		NM	E	VG
Complete Set (6):		60.00	30.00	18.00
Common Player:		9.00	4.50	2.75
(1)	Richard Allen	25.00	12.50	7.50
(2)	Ed Hermann	9.00	4.50	2.75
(3)	Bart Johnson	9.00	4.50	2.75
(4)	Carlos May	9.00	4.50	2.75
(5)	Bill Melton	9.00	4.50	2.75
(6)	Wilbur Wood	9.00	4.50	2.75

E

1914 E. & S. Publishing Co.

Currently, a dozen players have been reported from this issue. Front of the 5-1/2" x 3-3/4" postcards has a large portrait or action picture of the player at center, with a number of cartoons around. The printing is in blue ink. The back is done in ornate typography with copyright line, stamp box, etc. Other players may yet be discovered.

		NM	E	VG
(1)	"Jimmie" Archer	300.00	150.00	90.00
(2)	Joe Benz	300.00	150.00	90.00
(3)	Frank Chance	300.00	150.00	90.00
(4)	Ty Cobb	4,500	2,250	1,350
(5)	Miller Huggins	600.00	300.00	180.00
(6)	Joe Jackson	6,000	3,000	1,800
(7)	James Lavender	300.00	150.00	90.00
(8)	Christy Mathewson	2,500	1,250	750.00
(9)	"Tex" Russell	300.00	150.00	90.00
(10)	Frank Schulte	300.00	150.00	90.00
(11)	Jim Scott	300.00	150.00	90.00
(12)	Art Wilson	300.00	150.00	90.00

1908-09 E91 American Caramel Co.

(See 1908-09 American Caramel Co. for checklists, values.)

1909 E92 Nadja Caramels

(See 1909 Nadja Caramels.)

1910 E93 Standard Caramel Co.

(See 1910 Standard Caramel Co. for checklist, values.)

1911 E94

(See 1911 George Close Candy Co. for checklist and value data.)

1909 E95 Philadelphia Caramel

(See 1909 Philadelphia Caramel for checklist, price guide.)

1910 E96 Philadelphia Caramel

(See 1910 Philadelphia Caramel for checklist, values.)

1910 E98 "Set of 30"

This set of 30 subjects was issued in 1910 and is closely related to several other early candy issues that are nearly identical. The cards measure 1-1/2" x 2-3/4" and feature color lithograph player pictures. The backs, printed in brown, contain a checklist of the set but no advertising or other information indicating the manufacturer. The set was designated E98 by the "American Card Catalog." While the cards are unnumbered, they are listed here according to the numbers on the back checklist. Some or all of the cards may be found with different colored backgrounds. Mathewson's card is the only one in set with the caption in serif type.

		NM	E	VG
Complete Set (30):		125,000	62,500	37,500
Common Player:		1,500	480.00	180.00
(1)	Christy Matthewson (Mathewson)	12,000	6,000	3,500
(2)	John McGraw	4,000	2,000	1,200
(3)	Johnny Kling	1,500	480.00	200.00
(4)	Frank Chance	4,000	2,000	1,200
(5)	"Hans" Wagner	17,500	8,750	5,250
(6)	Fred Clarke	4,000	2,000	1,200
(7)	Roger Bresnahan	4,000	2,000	1,200
(8)	Hal Chase	2,000	800.00	350.00
(9)	Russ Ford	1,500	750.00	450.00
(10)	"Ty" Cobb	18,000	9,000	5,500
(11)	Hughey Jennings	4,000	2,000	1,200
(12)	Chief Bender	4,000	2,000	1,200
(13)	Ed Walsh	2,750	1,500	400.00
(14)	"Cy" Young (Picture actually Irv Young.)	9,000	3,000	1,500
(15)	Al Bridwell	1,500	480.00	180.00
(16)	Miner Brown	4,000	2,000	1,200
(17)	George Mullin	1,500	480.00	180.00
(18)	Chief Meyers	1,500	480.00	180.00
(19)	Hippo Vaughn	3,500	1,750	400.00
(20)	Red Dooin	1,500	480.00	180.00
(21)	Fred Tenny (Tenney)	3,000	1,500	400.00
(22)	Larry McLean	1,500	480.00	180.00
(23)	Nap Lajoie	5,000	2,500	1,000
(24)	Joe Tinker	4,000	2,000	1,200
(25)	Johnny Evers	4,000	2,000	1,200
(26)	Harry Davis	1,500	480.00	180.00
(27)	Eddie Collins	4,000	2,000	1,200
(28)	Bill Dahlen	3,000	1,500	500.00
(29)	"Connie" Mack	6,000	3,000	1,800
(30)	Jack Coombs	3,500	1,750	400.00

1909 E101 "Set of 50"

Cobb, c.f. Detroit Am.

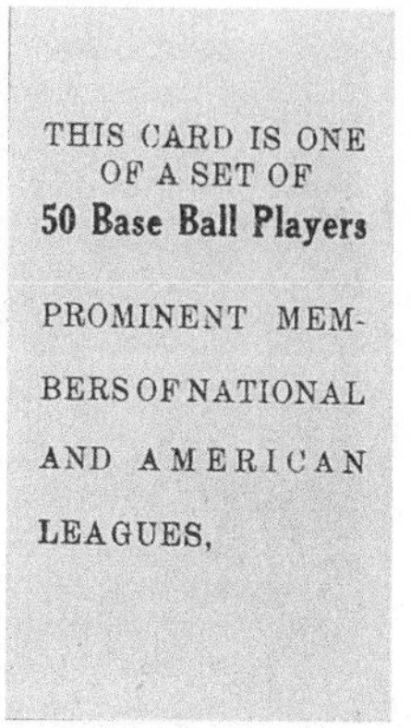
THIS CARD IS ONE
OF A SET OF
50 Base Ball Players
PROMINENT MEM-
BERS OF NATIONAL
AND AMERICAN
LEAGUES,

This 50-card set is closely related to the E92 issues by Nadja, Croft's, Dockman, etc. The fronts of the 1-1/2"x2-3/4" E101 cards are identical to the E92 set, but the back is "anonymous," containing no advertising or other information regarding the set's sponsor. The backs read simply "This card is one of a set of 50 Base Ball Players Prominent Members of National and American Leagues."

	NM	E	VG
Complete Set (50):	60,000	20,000	10,000
Common Player:	750.00	375.00	220.00
(1) Jack Barry	750.00	375.00	220.00
(2) Harry Bemis	750.00	375.00	220.00
(3) Chief Bender (White hat.)	2,800	1,400	700.00
(4) Chief Bender (Striped hat.)	3,200	1,600	950.00
(5) Bill Bergen	750.00	375.00	220.00
(6) Bob Bescher	750.00	350.00	220.00
(7) Al Bridwell	1,200	600.00	375.00
(8) Doc Casey	750.00	375.00	220.00
(9) Frank Chance	3,200	1,600	950.00
(10) Hal Chase	2,400	1,200	650.00
(11) Ty Cobb	15,000	7,500	4,000
(12) Eddie Collins	3,700	1,500	750.00
(13) Sam Crawford	3,200	1,600	950.00
(14) Harry Davis	1,200	600.00	375.00
(15) Art Devlin	750.00	375.00	220.00
(16) Wild Bill Donovan	750.00	375.00	220.00
(17) Red Dooin	750.00	375.00	220.00
(18) Mickey Doolan	750.00	375.00	220.00
(19) Patsy Dougherty	750.00	375.00	220.00
(20) Larry Doyle (With bat.)	750.00	375.00	220.00
(21) Larry Doyle (Throwing)	750.00	375.00	220.00
(22) Johnny Evers	3,200	1,600	950.00
(23) George Gibson	750.00	375.00	220.00
(24) Topsy Hartsel	750.00	375.00	220.00
(25) Fred Jacklitsch	750.00	375.00	220.00
(26) Hugh Jennings	3,200	1,600	950.00
(27) Red Kleinow	750.00	375.00	220.00
(28) Otto Knabe	750.00	375.00	220.00
(29) Jack Knight	750.00	375.00	220.00
(30) Nap Lajoie	3,200	1,600	950.00
(31) Hans Lobert	750.00	375.00	220.00
(32) Sherry Magee	750.00	375.00	220.00
(33) Christy Matthewson (Mathewson)	10,500	5,200	3,000
(34) John McGraw	3,200	1,600	950.00
(35) Larry McLean	750.00	375.00	220.00
(36) Dots Miller (Batting)	750.00	375.00	220.00
(37) Dots Miller (Fielding)	750.00	375.00	220.00
(38) Danny Murphy	750.00	375.00	220.00
(39) Bill O'Hara	750.00	375.00	220.00
(40) Germany Schaefer	1,200	600.00	300.00
(41) Admiral Schlei	750.00	375.00	220.00
(42) Boss Schmidt	750.00	375.00	220.00
(43) Johnny Seigle	1,200	600.00	300.00
(44) Dave Shean	750.00	375.00	220.00
(45) Boss Smith (Schmidt)	750.00	375.00	220.00
(46) Joe Tinker	3,200	1,600	950.00
(47) Honus Wagner (Batting)	13,500	7,000	4,000
(48) Honus Wagner (Throwing)	13,500	7,000	4,000
(49) Cy Young	9,500	5,000	2,800
(50) Heinie Zimmerman	750.00	375.00	220.00

1909 E102 "Set of 25"

One of many similar early candy card sets, this set - designated as E102 in the American Card Catalog - was published no earlier than mid-1909. The producer of the set is unknown. Measuring approximately 1-1/2" x 2-3/4", the set is almost identical in design to the E101 set and other closely related issues. The set consists of 25 players, which are checklisted on the back of the card. Four of the players have been found in two variations, resulting in 29 different cards. Because there is no advertising on the cards, the set can best be identified by the words - "This Picture is one of a Set of Twenty-five Base Ball Players, as follows" - which appears on the back of each card.

Wagner, s.s. Pittsburg Nat'l

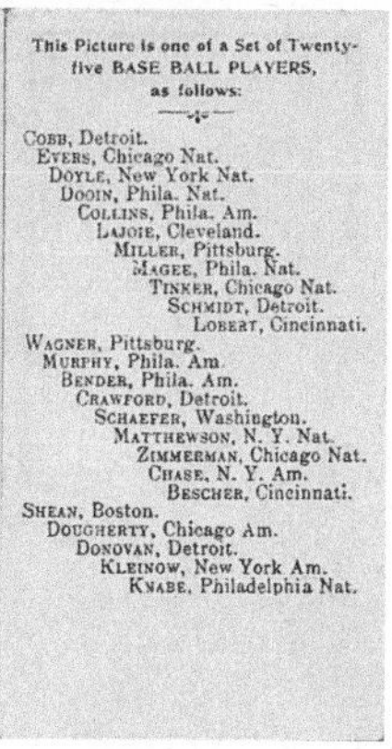
This Picture is one of a Set of Twenty-five BASE BALL PLAYERS, as follows:
Cobb, Detroit.
Evers, Chicago Nat.
Doyle, New York Nat.
Dooin, Phila. Nat.
Collins, Phila. Am.
Lajoie, Cleveland.
Miller, Pittsburg.
Magee, Phila. Nat.
Tinker, Chicago Nat.
Schmidt, Detroit.
Lobert, Cincinnati.
Wagner, Pittsburg.
Murphy, Phila. Am.
Bender, Phila. Am.
Crawford, Detroit.
Schaefer, Washington.
Matthewson, N. Y. Nat.
Zimmerman, Chicago Nat.
Chase, N. Y. Am.
Bescher, Cincinnati.
Shean, Boston.
Dougherty, Chicago Am.
Donovan, Detroit.
Kleinow, New York Am.
Knabe, Philadelphia Nat.

	NM	E	VG
Complete Set (29):	55,000	22,000	11,000
Common Player:	850.00	350.00	175.00
(1) Chief Bender	1,450	575.00	290.00
(2) Bob Bescher	850.00	350.00	175.00
(3) Hal Chase	900.00	360.00	180.00
(4) Ty Cobb	15,000	6,000	3,000
(5) Eddie Collins	1,450	575.00	290.00
(6) Sam Crawford	1,450	575.00	290.00
(7) Wild Bill Donovan	850.00	350.00	175.00
(8) Red Dooin	850.00	350.00	175.00
(9) Patsy Dougherty	850.00	350.00	175.00
(10) Larry Doyle (Batting)	850.00	350.00	175.00
(11) Larry Doyle (Throwing)	850.00	350.00	175.00
(12) Johnny Evers	1,450	575.00	290.00
(13) Red Kleinow	850.00	350.00	175.00
(14) Otto Knabe	850.00	350.00	175.00
(15) Nap Lajoie	1,825	725.00	365.00
(16) Hans Lobert	850.00	350.00	175.00
(17) Sherry Magee	850.00	350.00	175.00
(18) Christy Matthewson (Mathewson)	11,500	5,750	3,450
(19) Dots Miller (Batting)	850.00	350.00	175.00
(20) Dots Miller (Fielding)	1,650	650.00	325.00
(21) Danny Murphy	850.00	350.00	175.00
(22) Germany Schaefer	850.00	350.00	175.00
(23) Boss Schmidt	850.00	350.00	175.00
(24) Dave Shean	850.00	350.00	175.00
(25) Boss Smith (Schmidt)	850.00	350.00	175.00
(26) Joe Tinker	1,450	575.00	290.00
(27) Honus Wagner (Batting)	12,500	6,250	3,750
(28) Honus Wagner (Throwing)	12,500	6,250	3,750
(29) Heinie Zimmerman	850.00	350.00	175.00

1910 E104 Nadja Caramels

(See 1910 Nadja Caramels.)

1915 E106 American Caramel Co.

(See 1915 American Caramel Co.)

1903-1904 E107 Type 1

Identified by the American Card Catalog as E107, this set is significant because it was one of the first major baseball card sets since the 1880s. It established the pattern for most of the tobacco and candy cards that followed over the next two decades. Measuring approximately 1-3/8" x 2-5/8", cards feature black-and-white player photos with the name, position and team in the bottom border. Most are found either with black back printing reading, "One of a hundred and fifty prominent Baseball players," or blank-backed, in about equal numbers. Also found are cards with a purple diagonal overprint stating "THE BREISCH-WILLIAMS CO." Type 1 consists of 147 known different players, plus 11 additional variations. The Type 2 cards are thicker than those of Type 1 and some (Keeler and Delehanty) cards have captions different from those found in Type 1. Values shown for EX and NM grades are mostly theoretical, as few cards are known in better than VG condition.

	NM	EX	VG
Common Player: 9,000 4,500 2,700			
Breisch-Williams Overprint: 2-3X			
(1a) John Anderson (St. Louis)	9,000	4,500	2,700
(1b) John Anderson (New York)	9,000	4,500	2,700
(2) Jimmy Barret (Barrett)	9,000	4,500	2,700
(3) Ginger Beaumont	9,000	4,500	2,700
(4) Fred Beck	9,000	4,500	2,700
(5) Jake Beckley	30,000	15,000	9,000
(6) Harry Bemis	9,000	4,500	2,700
(7) Chief Bender	30,000	15,000	9,000
(8) Bill Bernhard	9,000	4,500	2,700
(9) Harry Bey (Bay)	9,000	4,500	2,700
(10) Bill Bradley	9,000	4,500	2,700
(11) Fritz Buelow	9,000	4,500	2,700
(12) Nixey Callahan	9,000	4,500	2,700
(13) Scoops Carey	9,000	4,500	2,700
(14) Charley Carr	9,000	4,500	2,700
(15) Bill Carrick	9,000	4,500	2,700
(16) Doc Casey	10,500	4,080	2,040
(17) Frank Chance	30,000	15,000	9,000
(18) Jack Chesbro	30,000	15,000	9,000
(19) Boileryard Clark (Clarke)	9,000	4,500	2,700
(20) Fred Clarke	30,000	15,000	9,000
(21) Jimmy Collins	30,000	15,000	9,000
(22) Duff Cooley	9,000	4,500	2,700
(23) Tommy Corcoran	9,000	4,500	2,700
(24) Bill Coughlan (Coughlin)	9,000	4,500	2,700
(25) Lou Criger	9,000	4,500	2,700
(26) Lave Cross	9,000	4,500	2,700
(27) Monte Cross	9,000	4,500	2,700
(28a) Bill Dahlen (Brooklyn)	9,000	4,500	2,700
(28b) Bill Dahlen (New York)	17,000	4,080	2,040
(29) Tom Daly	9,000	4,500	2,700
(30) George Davis	30,000	15,000	9,000
(31) Harry Davis	9,000	4,500	2,700
(32) Ed Delehanty (Delahanty)	30,000	15,000	9,000
(33) Gene DeMont (DeMontreville)	9,000	4,500	2,700
(34a) Pop Dillon (Detroit)	9,000	4,500	2,700
(34b) Pop Dillon (Brooklyn)	16,200	8,100	4,800
(35) Bill Dineen (Dinneen)	9,000	4,500	2,700
(36) Red Donahue	9,000	4,500	2,700
(37) Mike Donlin	9,000	4,500	2,700
(38) Patsy Donovan	9,000	4,500	2,700
(39) Patsy Dougherty (Photo actually Tom Hughes.)	9,000	4,500	2,700
(40) Klondike Douglass	9,000	4,500	2,700
(41a) Jack Doyle (Brooklyn)	9,000	4,500	2,700
(41b) Jack Doyle (Philadelphia)	9,000	4,500	2,700
(42) Lew Drill	9,000	4,500	2,700
(43) Jack Dunn	9,000	4,500	2,700
(44a) Kid Elberfield (Elberfeld) (Detroit)	9,000	4,500	2,700
(44b) Kid Elberfield (Elberfeld) (No team designation.)	9,000	4,500	2,700
(45) Duke Farrell	9,000	4,500	2,700
(46) Hobe Ferris	9,000	4,500	2,700
(47) Elmer Flick	30,000	15,000	9,000
(48) Buck Freeman	9,000	4,500	2,700
(49) Bill Freil (Friel)	9,000	4,500	2,700
(50) Dave Fultz	9,000	4,500	2,700
(51) Ned Garvin	9,000	4,500	2,700
(52) Billy Gilbert	9,000	4,500	2,700
(53) Harry Gleason	9,000	4,500	2,700
(54a) Kid Gleason (New York)	9,000	4,500	2,700
(54b) Kid Gleason (Philadelphia)	9,000	4,500	2,700
(55) John Gochnauer (Gochnaur)	9,000	4,500	2,700
(56) Danny Green	9,000	4,500	2,700
(57) Noodles Hahn	9,000	4,500	2,700
(58) Bill Hallman	9,000	4,500	2,700
(59) Ned Hanlon	30,000	15,000	9,000
(60) Dick Harley	9,000	4,500	2,700
(61) Jack Harper	9,000	4,500	2,700
(62) Topsy Hartsell (Hartsel)	9,000	4,500	2,700
(63) Emmet Heidrick	9,000	4,500	2,700
(64) Charlie Hemphill	9,000	4,500	2,700
(65) Weldon Henley	9,000	4,500	2,700
(66) Piano Legs Hickman	9,000	4,500	2,700
(67) Harry Howell	9,000	4,500	2,700
(68) Frank Iasbel (Isbell)	9,000	4,500	2,700
(69) Fred Jacklitzch (Jacklitsch)	9,000	4,500	2,700
(70) Fielder Jones (Chicago)	9,000	4,500	2,700
(71) Charlie Jones (Boston)	9,000	4,500	2,700
(72) Addie Joss	30,000	15,000	9,000
(73) Mike Kahoe	9,000	4,500	2,700
(74) Wee Willie Keeler	30,000	15,000	9,000
(75) Joe Kelley	30,000	15,000	9,000
(76) Brickyard Kennedy	9,000	4,500	2,700
(77) Frank Kitson	9,000	4,500	2,700
(78a) Malachi Kittredge (Boston)	9,000	4,500	2,700
(78b) Malachi Kittredge (Washington)	9,000	4,500	2,700
(79) Candy LaChance	9,000	4,500	2,700
(80) Nap Lajoie	30,000	15,000	9,000
(81) Tommy Leach	9,000	4,500	2,700
(82a) Watty Lee (Washington)	9,000	4,500	2,700
(82b) Watty Lee (Pittsburg)	9,000	4,500	2,700
(83) Sam Leever	9,000	4,500	2,700
(84) Herman Long	9,000	4,500	2,700
(85a) Billy Lush (Detroit)	9,000	4,500	2,700
(85b) Billy Lush (Cleveland)	9,000	4,500	2,700
(86) Christy Mathewson	125,000	62,500	37,500
(87) Sport McAllister	9,000	4,500	2,700

(88)	Jack McCarthy	9,000	4,500	2,700
(89)	Barry McCormick	9,000	4,500	2,700
(90)	Ed McFarland (Chicago)	9,000	4,500	2,700
(91)	Herm McFarland (New York)	9,000	4,500	2,700
(92)	Joe McGinnity	30,000	15,000	9,000
(93)	John McGraw	30,000	15,000	9,000
(94a)	Deacon McGuire (Brooklyn)	9,000	4,500	2,700
(94b)	Deacon McGuire (New York)	17,000	4,080	2,040
(95)	Jock Menefee	9,000	4,500	2,700
(96)	Sam Mertes	9,000	4,500	2,700
(97)	Roscoe Miller (Picture actually George Mullin.)	9,000	4,500	2,700
(98)	Fred Mitchell	9,000	4,500	2,700
(99)	Earl Moore	9,000	4,500	2,700
(100)	Danny Murphy	9,000	4,500	2,700
(101)	Jack O'Connor	9,000	4,500	2,700
(102)	Al Orth	9,000	4,500	2,700
(103)	Dick Padden	9,000	4,500	2,700
(104)	Freddy Parent	9,000	4,500	2,700
(105)	Roy Patterson	9,000	4,500	2,700
(106)	Heinie Peitz	9,000	4,500	2,700
(107)	Deacon Phillipi (Phillippe)	9,000	4,500	2,700
(108)	Wiley Piatt	9,000	4,500	2,700
(109)	Ollie Pickering	9,000	4,500	2,700
(110)	Eddie Plank	78,000	39,000	24,000
(111a)	Ed Poole (Cincinnati)	9,000	4,500	2,700
(111b)	Ed Poole (Brooklyn)	9,000	4,500	2,700
(112a)	Jack Powell (St. Louis)	9,000	4,500	2,700
(112b)	Jack Powell (New York)	9,000	4,500	2,700
(113)	Mike Powers	9,000	4,500	2,700
(114)	Claude Ritchie (Ritchey)	9,000	4,500	2,700
(115)	Jimmy Ryan	9,000	4,500	2,700
(116)	Ossee Schreckengost	9,000	4,500	2,700
(117)	Kip Selbach	9,000	4,500	2,700
(118)	Socks Seybold	9,000	4,500	2,700
(119)	Jimmy Sheckard	9,000	4,500	2,700
(120)	Ed Siever	9,000	4,500	2,700
(121)	Harry Smith	9,000	4,500	2,700
(122)	Tully Sparks	9,000	4,500	2,700
(123)	Jake Stahl	9,000	4,500	2,700
(124)	Harry Steinfeldt	9,000	4,500	2,700
(125)	Sammy Strang	9,000	4,500	2,700
(126)	Willie Sudhoff	9,000	4,500	2,700
(127)	Joe Sugden	9,000	4,500	2,700
(128)	Billy Sullivan	9,000	4,500	2,700
(129)	Jack Taylor	9,000	4,500	2,700
(130)	Fred Tenney	9,000	4,500	2,700
(131)	Roy Thomas	9,000	4,500	2,700
(132a)	Jack Thoney (Cleveland)	9,000	4,500	2,700
(132b)	Jack Thoney (New York)	9,000	4,500	2,700
(133)	Jack Townsend	9,000	4,500	2,700
(134)	George Van Haltren	9,000	4,500	2,700
(135)	Rube Waddell	30,000	15,000	9,000
(136)	Honus Wagner	360,000	180,000	108,000
(137)	Bobby Wallace	30,000	15,000	9,000
(138)	Jack Warner	9,000	4,500	2,700
(139)	Jimmy Wiggs	9,000	4,500	2,700
(140)	Jimmy Williams	9,000	4,500	2,700
(141)	Vic Willis	30,000	15,000	9,000
(142)	Hooks Wiltse	9,000	4,500	2,700
(143)	George Winters (Winter)	9,000	4,500	2,700
(144)	Bob Wood	9,000	4,500	2,700
(145)	Joe Yeager	9,600	4,800	2,880
(146)	Cy Young	125,000	62,500	37,500
(147)	Chief Zimmer	9,000	4,500	2,700

1903-1904 E107 Type 2

Many of the Type 2 E107 cards seen to date do not measure the nominal 1-3/8" x 2-5/8" of the Type 1 cards, often having been cut more narrowly. Once thought to have been cut from an advertising piece, it now appears these were a regular production issue, as at least one specimen has been found with the purple diagonal overprint stating "THE BREISCHWILLIAMS CO." Type 2 cards are printed on a thicker and more gray card stock than Type 1 and at least a few (Keeler and Delehanty) cards have captions different from those found in Type 1. NM values are principally theoretical as few cards in known in conditions better than EX.

		NM	EX	VG
	Common Player:	6,000	3,000	1,800
(1)	Ed Delehanty (Delahanty)	33,500	17,000	10,000
(2)	Jack Doyle	6,000	3,000	1,800
(3)	Wee Willie Keeler	33,500	17,000	10,000
(4)	Nap Lajoie	33,500	17,000	10,000
(5)	Tommy Leach	6,000	3,000	1,800
(6)	Socks Seybold	6,000	3,000	1,800
(7)	Fred Tenney	6,000	3,000	1,800
(8)	Rube Waddell	33,500	17,000	10,000

1922 E120 American Caramel Series of 240

(See 1922 American Caramel Series of 240.)

1921-22 E121 American Caramel Series of 80/120

(See 1921 American Caramel Series of 80, Series of 120.)

1922 E122 American Caramel Series of 80

(See 1922 American Caramel Series of 80 for checklist, values.)

1910 E125 American Caramel Die-Cuts

(See 1910 American Caramel Die-Cuts for checklist, values.)

1927 E126 American Caramel Series of 60

(See 1927 American Caramel Series of 60.)

1927 E210 York Caramels

(See York Caramels.)

1921 E253 Oxford Confectionery

(See 1921 Oxford Confectionery.)

1909-11 E90-1, E90-2, E90-3 American Caramel

(See 1909-11 American Caramel Co. for checklists, values.)

1940s Eagle Hall of Fame

The date of this issue can only be approximated, probably in the late 1940s. The 9-1/4" x 11-1/4" cards have high-gloss sepia photos on thick cardboard. A wood-look frame and identification plaques are pictured around the central photo. Backs are blank. The pictures were issued by the Carnegie (Pa.) Aerie of the Eagles, lodge #1134, according to the bottom "plaque." At top is "Eagle Hall of Fame." Presumably the four ballplayers and two boxers known were all members of that fraternal order. The unnumbered pieces are checklisted alphabetically.

		NM	E	VG
	Complete Set (6):	700.00	350.00	210.00
	Common Player:	40.00	20.00	12.00
(1)	Bob Fitzsimmons (Boxer)	40.00	20.00	12.00
(2)	Lefty Grove	150.00	75.00	45.00
(3)	Connie Mack	150.00	75.00	45.00
(4)	Stan Musial	200.00	100.00	60.00
(5)	John Sullivan (Boxer)	75.00	37.00	22.00
(6)	Honus Wagner	175.00	87.00	52.00
(7)	Cy Young	175.00	87.00	52.00

1979 Early Red Sox Favorites

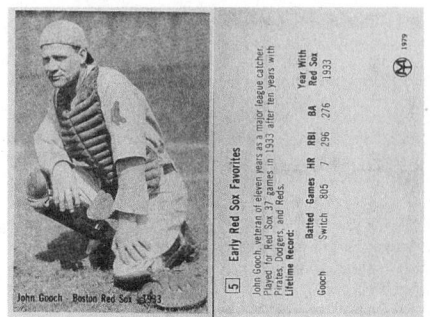

This collectors' issue from Maine features players of the 1920s-1930s Red Sox. Cards are printed in black-and-white in a 2-5/8" x 3-3/4" format. Front photos are bordered in white and have identification of the players overprinted in black. Backs have a few stats, highlights or an explanation of the photo on front. Many cards feature more than one player.

		NM	E	VG
	Complete Set (24):	40.00	20.00	12.00
	Common Player:	4.00	2.00	1.25
1	New Fenway Park	4.00	2.00	1.25
2	Mrs. Tom Yawkey and Mrs. Eddie Collins	4.00	2.00	1.25
3	Red Sox Outfielders - 1932(Tom Oliver, Earl Webb, Jack Rothrock)	4.00	2.00	1.25
4	Red Sox Ace Pitchers(John Marcum, Wes Ferrell, Lefty Grove, Fritz Ostermueller)	4.00	2.00	1.25
5	John Gooch	4.00	2.00	1.25
6	Red Sox Recruits at Sarasota, Fla.(Joe Cronin)	4.00	2.00	1.25
7	Danny MacFayden	4.00	2.00	1.25
8	Dale Alexander	4.00	2.00	1.25
9	Robert (Fatsy) Fothergill	4.00	2.00	1.25
10	Red Sox Sunday Morning Workout	4.00	2.00	1.25
11	Jimmie Foxx (Signing ball for Mrs. Yawkey.)	6.00	3.00	1.75
12	Lefty Grove (Presented keys to new car.)	6.00	3.00	1.75
13	"Fireball" Lefty Grove	6.00	3.00	1.75
14	Praciticng Base Stealing(Jack Rothrock, Urban Pickering)	4.00	2.00	1.25
15	Tom Daly, Al Schacht, Herb Pennock	4.00	2.00	1.25
16	Eddie Collins, Heinie Manush	6.00	3.00	1.75
17	Tris Speaker	6.00	3.00	1.75
18	Home Run Star(Jimmie Foxx)	6.00	3.00	1.75
19	Smead Jolley	4.00	2.00	1.25
20	Hal Trosky, Jimmie Foxx	4.00	2.00	1.25
21	Herold "Muddy" Ruel, Wilcy "Fireman" Moore	4.00	2.00	1.25
22	Bob Quinn, Shano Collins	4.00	2.00	1.25
23	Tom Oliver	4.00	2.00	1.25
24	Joe Cronin, Herb Pennock, Buetter	4.00	2.00	1.25

1966 East Hills Pirates

Stores in the East Hills Shopping Center, a large mall located in suburban Pittsburgh, distributed cards from this 25-card full-color set in 1966. The cards, which measure 3-1/4" x 4-1/4", are blank-backed and are numbered by the players' uniform numbers. The numbers appear in the lower right corners of the cards.

		NM	E	VG
	Complete Set (25):	75.00	37.00	22.00
	Common Player:	2.50	1.25	.70
3	Harry Walker	2.50	1.25	.70
7	Bob Bailey	2.50	1.25	.70
8	Willie Stargell	10.00	5.00	3.00
9	Bill Mazeroski	10.00	5.00	3.00
10	Jim Pagliaroni	2.50	1.25	.70
11	Jose Pagan	2.50	1.25	.70
12	Jerry May	2.50	1.25	.70
14	Gene Alley	2.50	1.25	.70
15	Manny Mota	2.50	1.25	.70
16	Andy Rodgers	2.50	1.25	.70
17	Donn Clendenon	2.50	1.25	.70
18	Matty Alou	2.50	1.25	.70

19	Pete Mikkelsen	2.50	1.25	.70
20	Jesse Gonder	2.50	1.25	.70
21	Bob Clemente	60.00	30.00	18.00
22	Woody Fryman	2.50	1.25	.70
24	Jerry Lynch	2.50	1.25	.70
25	Tommie Sisk	2.50	1.25	.70
26	Roy Face	2.50	1.25	.70
28	Steve Blass	2.50	1.25	.70
32	Vernon Law	3.50	1.75	1.00
34	Al McBean	2.50	1.25	.70
39	Bob Veale	2.50	1.25	.70
43	Don Cardwell	2.50	1.25	.70
45	Gene Michael	2.50	1.25	.70

1933 Eclipse Import

Issued in 1933, this set was sold in eight-card strips. Numbered from 401 through 424, the cards measure 2-7/16" x 2-7/8". The design features a crude colored drawing of the player on the front. The back of the card displays the card number at the top followed by the player's name, team and a brief write-up. Card numbers 403, 413, and 414 are missing and probably correspond to the three unnumbered cards in the set. The set carries an American Card Catalog designation of R337.

		NM	E	VG
	Complete Set (24):	12,500	6,250	3,750
	Common Player:	200.00	100.00	60.00
401	Johnny Vergez	200.00	100.00	60.00
402	Babe Ruth	7,500	3,700	2,200
403	Not Issued			
404	George Pipgras	200.00	100.00	60.00
405	Bill Terry	450.00	220.00	135.00
406	George Connally	200.00	100.00	60.00
407	Watson Clark	200.00	100.00	60.00
408	"Lefty" Grove	500.00	250.00	150.00
409	Henry Johnson	200.00	100.00	60.00
410	Jimmy Dykes	200.00	100.00	60.00
411	Henry Hine Schuble	200.00	100.00	60.00
412	Dave Harris	450.00	220.00	135.00
413	Not Issued			
414	Not Issued			
415	Al Simmons	450.00	220.00	135.00
416	Henry "Heinie" Manush	450.00	220.00	135.00
417	Glen Myatt (Glenn)	200.00	100.00	60.00
418	Babe Herman	175.00	70.00	35.00
419	Frank Frisch	450.00	220.00	135.00
420	Tony Lazzeri	450.00	220.00	135.00
421	Paul Waner	450.00	220.00	135.00
422	Jimmy Wilson	200.00	100.00	60.00
423	Charles Grimm	200.00	100.00	60.00
424	Dick Bartell	200.00	100.00	60.00
----	Jimmy Fox (Jimmie Foxx)	600.00	240.00	120.00
----	Roy Johnson	200.00	100.00	60.00
----	Pie Traynor	450.00	220.00	135.00

1942 Editorial Bruguera Babe Ruth

The Babe is the only baseball player appearing is this 12-card series of "Figuras deportivas de fama mundial" (World famous sports figures) issued in Spain. The cards are blank-backed, about 4-3/4" x 3-1/2", with color artwork on front.

	NM	E	VG
Babe Ruth	450.00	220.00	135.00

1930s Edwards, Ringer & Bigg Cigarettes

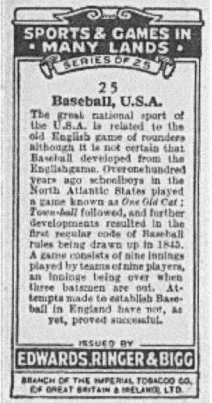

Though he is identified nowhere on this English cigarette card, the home run swing of Babe Ruth on the front is unmistakable. The last card in a set of 25 "Sports & Games in Many Lands" series, the approximately 2-5/8" x 1-3/8" cards have color artwork on the front and green-and-white backs. The back of the baseball card provides a short history of "The great national sport of the U.S.A." The card is nearly identical to the much more common 1929 Churchman's brand, except for the ads on back and the lack on the later card of the Churchman's name on top-right front.

		NM	E	VG
25	Baseball, U.S.A.(Babe Ruth)	400.00	200.00	120.00

1909-11 El Principe de Gales Cigarettes

PREMIUMS:
Commons: 1-2X
Hall of Famers: 1-2X

(See T206 for checklist and base card values.)

1976 English's Chicken Baltimore Orioles Lids

It is uncertain whether the checklist presented here is complete. These 8-3/8" diameter fried chicken bucket lids are printed on heavy waxed cardboard in black-and-white. Cap logos have been airbrushed off. A few previous seasons' stats are printed to the left and right of the player photo.

		NM	E	VG
	Complete Set (5):	400.00	200.00	125.00
	Common Player:	20.00	10.00	6.00
(1)	Mike Cuellar	20.00	10.00	6.00
(2)	Ken Holtzman	20.00	10.00	6.00

(3)	Lee May	20.00	10.00	6.00
(4)	Jim Palmer	100.00	50.00	30.00
(5)	Brooks Robinson	300.00	150.00	90.00

1963-1973 Equitable Sports Hall of Fame

This series of black-and-white art prints was produced over more than a decade. About 8" x 11", the prints feature the artwork of Robert Riger or George Loh, reproduced from ads for the life insurance company. Nearly 95 pieces honoring athletes from many sports were produced. Only the baseball players are listed here.

		NM	E	VG
	Common Player:	6.00	3.00	1.80
(1)	Ernie Banks	7.50	3.75	2.25
(2)	Roy Campanella	7.50	3.75	2.25
(3)	Johnny Evers	6.00	3.00	1.80
(4)	Bob Feller	6.00	3.00	1.80
(5)	Lou Gehrig	10.00	5.00	3.00
(6)	Lefty Grove	6.00	3.00	1.80
(7)	Tommy Henrich	6.00	3.00	1.80
(8)	Carl Hubbell	6.00	3.00	1.80
(9)	Al Kaline	6.00	3.00	1.80
(10)	Jerry Koosman	6.00	3.00	1.80
(11)	Mickey Mantle	15.00	7.50	4.50
(12)	Eddie Mathews	6.00	3.00	1.80
(13)	Willie Mays	9.00	4.50	2.75
(14)	Stan Musial	9.00	4.50	2.75
(15)	Pee Wee Reese	6.00	3.00	1.80
(16)	Allie Reynolds	6.00	3.00	1.80
(17)	Robin Roberts	6.00	3.00	1.80
(18)	Brooks Robinson	6.00	3.00	1.80
(19)	Red Ruffing	6.00	3.00	1.80
(20)	Babe Ruth	12.50	6.25	3.75
(21)	Warren Spahn	6.00	3.00	1.80

1954 Esskay Hot Dogs Orioles

Measuring 2-1/4" x 3-1/2", the 1954 Esskay Hot Dogs set features the Baltimore Orioles. The unnumbered color cards were issued in panels of two on packages of hot dogs and are usually found with grease stains. The cards have waxed fronts with blank backs on a white stock. Complete boxes of Esskay Hot Dogs are scarce and command a price of 2-3 times greater than the single card values.

		E	VG
	Complete Set (34):	56,000	34,000
	Common Player:	1,875	1,125
(1)	Neil Berry	1,875	1,125
(2)	Michael Blyzka	1,875	1,125
(3)	Harry Brecheen	1,875	1,125
(4)	Gil Coan	1,875	1,125
(5)	Joe Coleman	1,875	1,125
(6)	Clinton Courtney	1,875	1,125
(7)	Charles E. Diering	1,875	1,125
(8)	Jimmie Dykes	1,875	1,125
(9)	Frank J. Fanovich	1,875	1,125
(10)	Howard Fox	1,875	1,125
(11)	Jim Fridley	1,875	1,125
(12)	Vinicio "Chico" Garcia	1,875	1,125
(13)	Jehosie Heard	2,500	1,500

(14)	Darrell Johnson	1,875	1,125
(15)	Bob Kennedy	1,875	1,125
(16)	Dick Kokos	1,875	1,125
(17)	Dave Koslo	1,875	1,125
(18)	Lou Kretlow	1,875	1,125
(19)	Richard D. Kryhoski	1,875	1,125
(20)	Don Larsen	3,100	1,875
(21)	Donald E. Lenhardt	1,875	1,125
(22)	Richard Littlefield	1,875	1,125
(23)	Sam Mele	1,875	1,125
(24)	Les Moss	1,875	1,125
(25)	Ray L. Murray	1,875	1,125
(26)	"Bobo" Newson (Stadium lights in background.)	2,200	1,300
(27)	Tom Oliver	1,875	1,125
(28)	Duane Pillette	1,875	1,125
(29)	Francis M. Skaff	1,875	1,125
(30)	Marlin Stuart	1,875	1,125
(31)	Robert L. Turley	2,800	1,700
(32)	Eddie Waitkus	1,875	1,125
(33)	Vic Wertz	1,875	1,125
(34)	Robert G. Young	1,875	1,125

1955 Esskay Hot Dogs Orioles

For the second consecutive year, Esskay Meats placed baseball cards of Orioles players on their boxes of hot dogs. The unnumbered, color cards measure 2-1/4" x 3-1/2" and can be distinguished from the previous year by their unwaxed fronts and blank gray backs. Many of the same photos from 1954 were used with only minor picture-cropping differences. For 1955, only one player card per box was printed. The space which was occupied by the second player card in 1954 carried a prize redemption coupon on 1955 boxes.

		E	VG
Complete Set (26):		47,000	28,500
Common Player:		1,875	1,125
(1)	Cal Abrams	1,875	1,125
(2)	Robert S. Alexander	1,875	1,125
(3)	Harry Byrd	1,875	1,125
(4)	Gil Coan	1,875	1,125
(5)	Joseph P. Coleman	1,875	1,125
(6)	William R. Cox	1,875	1,125
(7)	Charles E. Diering	1,875	1,125
(8)	Walter A. Evers	1,875	1,125
(9)	Don Johnson	1,875	1,125
(10)	Robert D. Kennedy	1,875	1,125
(11)	Lou Kretlow	1,875	1,125
(12)	Robert L. Kuzava	1,875	1,125
(13)	Fred Marsh	1,875	1,125
(14)	Charles Maxwell	1,875	1,125
(15)	Jimmie McDonald	1,875	1,125
(16)	Bill Miller	1,875	1,125
(17)	Willy Miranda	1,875	1,125
(18)	Raymond L. Moore	1,875	1,125
(19)	John Lester Moss	1,875	1,125
(20)	"Bobo" Newsom (No stadium lights in background.)	1,875	1,125
(21)	Duane Pillette	1,875	1,125
(22)	Harold W. Smith	1,875	1,125
(23)	Gus Triandos	1,875	1,125
(24)	Edward S. Waitkus	1,875	1,125
(25)	Eugene R. Woodling	2,200	1,300
(26)	Robert G. Young	1,875	1,125

1972 Esso Hispanic Coins

Little is known of these coins, except that they were distributed in Puerto Rico. Even the sponsor, Esso Oil Co., is not mentioned anywhere on the pieces. Made of aluminum and 1-1/4" in diameter, coin fronts have a portrait of the player with his name above. Backs are in Spanish and have the player's position, team, height, weight, date and place of birth. The coins of Tony Perez and, to a lesser extent, Rod Carew are scarcer than the others. A person receiving a Perez coin was able to exchange it for a full tank of gas. In 2006, a brass-finish Roberto Clemente coin was first reported, probably also a short-printed exchange coin.

		NM	E	VG
Complete Set (13):		325.00	160.00	95.00
Common Player:		12.00	6.00	3.50
(1)	Luis Aparicio	25.00	12.50	7.50
(2)	Rod Carew	50.00	25.00	15.00
(3)	Rico Carty	12.00	6.00	3.50
(4)	Cesar Cedeno	12.00	6.00	3.50
(5)	Orlando Cepeda	20.00	10.00	6.00
(6)	Roberto Clemente	125.00	62.50	37.50
(7)	Mike Cuellar	12.00	6.00	3.50
(8)	Juan Marichal	20.00	10.00	6.00
(9)	Felix Millan	12.00	6.00	3.50
(10)	Guillermo Montanez	12.00	6.00	3.50
(11)	Tony Oliva	15.00	7.50	4.50
(12a)	Tany Perez (Tony)	75.00	37.50	22.50
(12b)	Tony Perez	75.00	37.50	22.50
(13)	Manny Sanguillen	12.00	6.00	3.50

1909 E-UNC Candy

The attributed date is speculative, based on the only season in which all of the known players on this surely incomplete checklist played with the teams listed on their cards. It is also speculative to list these as a candy or caramel card issue becxause nothing is currently to their maker or issuer, if indeed they were issued and are not prototypes for one of more of the E-card sets that followed in the 1910s. All known cards appear to be hand-cut in approximately 1-1/2" x 2-3/4 "size that was to become the standard for many carmel issues. Cards have blanks backs and blue captions giving the player name, team and league, where necessary.

		VG
(1)	Al Bridwell	750.00
(4)	Moose McCormick	750.00
(5)	Bill O'Hara	750.00
(6)	Hans Wagner	4,500

1910 E-UNC Candy

Little is known about these 1910-era cards except that they appear to have been cut from a candy box. Printed in blue or red duo-tone and blank-backed, the cards measure about 2-3/4" per side. A 1-3/8" x 2-1/2" central image has a player photo with a diamond design around. Player identification is in a white strip at bottom.

		NM	E	VG
Common Player:		1,000	500.00	300.00
(1)	"Ty" Cobb	6,000	3,000	1,800
(2)	Eddie Collins	1,000	500.00	300.00

(3)	Johnny Evers	1,000	500.00	300.00
(4)	"Christy" Mathewson	2,000	1,000	600.00
(5)	"Honus" Wagner	3,500	1,750	1,050
(6)	"Cy" Young (Photo actually Irv Young)	750.00	370.00	220.00

1936 E-UNC Candy

These cards appear to be a secondary use of the center portions of the 1936 S and S Game cards, having the same player photos and data in a size which varies from about 1-3/4" to 1-7/8" wide and between 2-3/8" and 2-1/2" tall. These differ in that instead of the green backs found on most of the game cards, these have plain backs which are sometimes found with a rubber-stamped message to present the card for a free gift or candy bar. These stamps indicate the cards were used as a prize premium in an as yet unidentified candy company's promotion. With more than half of the S and S players known in this candy company version, it is not unreasonable to assume the checklists for both sets are the same.

		NM	E	VG
Complete Set (52):		3,250	1,600	975.00
Common Player:		45.00	22.50	13.50
(1)	Luke Appling	100.00	50.00	30.00
(2)	Earl Averill	100.00	50.00	30.00
(3)	Zeke Bonura	45.00	22.50	13.50
(4)	Dolph Camilli	45.00	22.50	13.50
(5)	Ben Cantwell	45.00	22.50	13.50
(6)	Phil Cavaretta (Cavarretta)	45.00	22.50	13.50
(7)	Rip Collins	45.00	22.50	13.50
(8)	Joe Cronin	100.00	50.00	30.00
(9)	Frank Crosetti	60.00	30.00	18.00
(10)	Kiki Cuyler	100.00	50.00	30.00
(11)	Virgil Davis	45.00	22.50	13.50
(12)	Frank Demaree	45.00	22.50	13.50
(13)	Paul Derringer	45.00	22.50	13.50
(14)	Bill Dickey	150.00	75.00	45.00
(15)	Woody English	45.00	22.50	13.50
(16)	Fred Fitzsimmons	45.00	22.50	13.50
(17)	Richard Ferrell	100.00	50.00	30.00
(18)	Pete Fox	45.00	22.50	13.50
(19)	Jimmy Foxx	175.00	87.50	52.50
(20)	Larry French	45.00	22.50	13.50
(21)	Frank Frisch	150.00	75.00	45.00
(22)	August Galan	45.00	22.50	13.50
(23)	Chas. Gehringer	150.00	75.00	45.00
(24)	John Gill	45.00	22.50	13.50
(25)	Charles Grimm	45.00	22.50	13.50
(26)	Mule Haas	45.00	22.50	13.50
(27)	Stanley Hack	45.00	22.50	13.50
(28)	Bill Hallahan	45.00	22.50	13.50
(29)	Melvin Harder	45.00	22.50	13.50
(30)	Gabby Hartnett	100.00	50.00	30.00
(31)	Ray Hayworth	45.00	22.50	13.50
(32)	Ralston Hemsley	45.00	22.50	13.50
(33)	Bill Herman	100.00	50.00	30.00
(34)	Frank Higgins	45.00	22.50	13.50
(35)	Carl Hubbell	160.00	80.00	47.50
(36)	Bill Jurges	45.00	22.50	13.50
(37)	Vernon Kennedy	45.00	22.50	13.50
(38)	Chuck Klein	100.00	50.00	30.00
(39)	Mike Kreevich	45.00	22.50	13.50
(40)	Bill Lee	45.00	22.50	13.50
(41)	Jos. Medwick	100.00	50.00	30.00
(42)	Van Mungo	45.00	22.50	13.50
(43)	James O'Dea	45.00	22.50	13.50
(44)	Mel Ott	160.00	80.00	47.50
(45)	Rip Radcliff	45.00	22.50	13.50
(46)	Pie Traynor	100.00	50.00	30.00
(47)	Arky Vaughan (Vaughn)	100.00	50.00	30.00
(48)	Joe Vosmik	45.00	22.50	13.50
(49)	Lloyd Waner	100.00	50.00	30.00
(50)	Paul Waner	90.00	45.00	25.00
(51)	Lon Warneke	45.00	22.50	13.50
(52)	Floyd Young	45.00	22.50	13.50

1949 Eureka Sportstamps

The commissioner of baseball, president of the National League and 198 N.L. players are included in this issue. The stamps were issued on team sheets measuring 7-1/2" x 10", with individual stamps measuring 1-1/2" x 2". An album issued with the set provided short player biographies. The stamps feature colorized posed player action photos. At bottom is a yellow strip with the player's name, stamp number and copyright line. Stamps are numbered alphabetically within teams.

	NM	E	VG
Complete Set (200):	900.00	450.00	275.00
Common Player:	5.00	2.50	1.50
Album w/mounted stamps:	400.00	200.00	120.00
Album:	75.00	37.50	22.00

		NM	E	VG
1	Albert B. (Happy) Chandler	15.00	7.50	4.50
2	Ford Frick	5.00	2.50	1.50
3	Billy Southworth	5.00	2.50	1.50
4	Johnny Antonelli	5.00	2.50	1.50
5	Red Barrett	5.00	2.50	1.50
6	Clint Conatser	5.00	2.50	1.50
7	Alvin Dark	5.00	2.50	1.50
8	Bob Elliott	5.00	2.50	1.50
9	Glenn Elliott	5.00	2.50	1.50
10	Elbie Fletcher	5.00	2.50	1.50
11	Bob Hall	5.00	2.50	1.50
12	Jeff Heath	5.00	2.50	1.50
13	Bobby Hogue	5.00	2.50	1.50
14	Tommy Holmes	5.00	2.50	1.50
15	Al Lakeman	5.00	2.50	1.50
16	Phil Masi	5.00	2.50	1.50
17	Nelson Potter	5.00	2.50	1.50
18	Pete Reiser	10.00	5.00	3.00
19	Rick Rickert	5.00	2.50	1.50
20	Connie Ryan	5.00	2.50	1.50
21	Jim Russell	5.00	2.50	1.50
22	Johnny Sain	10.00	5.00	3.00
23	Bill Salkeld	5.00	2.50	1.50
24	Sibby Sisti	5.00	2.50	1.50
25	Warren Spahn	25.00	12.50	7.50
26	Eddie Stanky	5.00	2.50	1.50
27	Bill Voiselle	5.00	2.50	1.50
28	Bert Shotton	5.00	2.50	1.50
29	Jack Banta	5.00	2.50	1.50
30	Rex Barney	7.50	3.75	2.25
31	Ralph Branca	15.00	7.50	4.50
32	Tommy Brown	5.00	2.50	1.50
33	Roy Campanella	40.00	20.00	12.00
34	Billy Cox	7.50	3.75	2.25
35	Bruce Edwards	5.00	2.50	1.50
36	Carl Furillo	20.00	10.00	6.00
37	Joe Hatten	5.00	2.50	1.50
38	Gene Hermanski	5.00	2.50	1.50
39	Gil Hodges	25.00	12.50	7.50
40	Johnny Jorgensen	5.00	2.50	1.50
41	Lefty Martin	5.00	2.50	1.50
42	Mike McCormick	5.00	2.50	1.50
43	Eddie Miksis	5.00	2.50	1.50
44	Paul Minner	5.00	2.50	1.50
45	Sam Narron	10.00	5.00	3.00
46	Don Newcombe	20.00	10.00	6.00
47	Jake Pitler	5.00	2.50	1.50
48	Pee Wee Reese	35.00	17.50	10.50
49	Jackie Robinson	50.00	25.00	15.00
50	Duke Snider	40.00	20.00	12.00
51	Dick Whitman	5.00	2.50	1.50
52	Forrest Burgess	10.00	5.00	3.00
53	Phil Cavaretta	5.00	2.50	1.50
54	Bob Chipman	5.00	2.50	1.50
55	Walter Dubiel	5.00	2.50	1.50
56	Hank Edwards	5.00	2.50	1.50
57	Frankie Gustine	5.00	2.50	1.50
58	Hal Jeffcoat	5.00	2.50	1.50
59	Emil Kush	5.00	2.50	1.50
60	Doyle Lade	5.00	2.50	1.50
61	Dutch Leonard	5.00	2.50	1.50
62	Peanuts Lowrey	5.00	2.50	1.50
63	Gene Mauch	7.50	3.75	2.25
64	Cal McLish	5.00	2.50	1.50
65	Rube Novotney	5.00	2.50	1.50
66	Andy Pafko	5.00	2.50	1.50
67	Bob Ramazzotti	5.00	2.50	1.50
68	Herman Reich	5.00	2.50	1.50
69	Bob Rush	5.00	2.50	1.50
70	Johnny Schmitz	5.00	2.50	1.50
71	Bob Scheffing	5.00	2.50	1.50
72	Roy Smalley	5.00	2.50	1.50
73	Emil Verban	5.00	2.50	1.50
74	Al Walker	5.00	2.50	1.50
75	Harry Walker	5.00	2.50	1.50
76	Bucky Walters	5.00	2.50	1.50
77	Bob Adams	5.00	2.50	1.50
78	Ewell Blackwell	5.00	2.50	1.50
79	Jimmy Bloodworth	5.00	2.50	1.50
80	Walker Cooper	5.00	2.50	1.50
81	Tony Cuccinello	5.00	2.50	1.50
82	Jess Dobernic	5.00	2.50	1.50
83	Eddie Erautt	5.00	2.50	1.50
84	Frank Fanovich	5.00	2.50	1.50
85	Howie Fox	5.00	2.50	1.50
86	Grady Hatton	5.00	2.50	1.50
87	Homer Howell	5.00	2.50	1.50
88	Ted Kluszewski	20.00	10.00	6.00
89	Danny Litwhiler	5.00	2.50	1.50
90	Everett Lively	5.00	2.50	1.50
91	Lloyd Merriman	5.00	2.50	1.50
92	Phil Page	5.00	2.50	1.50
93	Kent Peterson	5.00	2.50	1.50
94	Ken Raffensberger	5.00	2.50	1.50
95	Luke Sewell	5.00	2.50	1.50
96	Virgil Stallcup	5.00	2.50	1.50
97	Johnny Vander Meer	10.00	5.00	3.00
98	Herman Wehmeier	5.00	2.50	1.50
99	Johnny Wyrostek	5.00	2.50	1.50
100	Benny Zientara	5.00	2.50	1.50
101	Leo Durocher	12.50	6.25	3.75
102	Hank Behrman	5.00	2.50	1.50
103	Augie Galan	5.00	2.50	1.50
104	Sid Gordon	5.00	2.50	1.50
105	Bert Haas	5.00	2.50	1.50
106	Andy Hansen	5.00	2.50	1.50
107	Clint Hartung	5.00	2.50	1.50
108	Kirby Higbe	5.00	2.50	1.50
109	George Hausman	5.00	2.50	1.50
110	Larry Jansen	5.00	2.50	1.50
111	Sheldon Jones	5.00	2.50	1.50
112	Monte Kennedy	5.00	2.50	1.50
113	Buddy Kerr	5.00	2.50	1.50
114	Dave Koslo	5.00	2.50	1.50
115	Joe Lafata	5.00	2.50	1.50
116	Whitey Lockman	5.00	2.50	1.50
117	Jack Lohrke	5.00	2.50	1.50
118	Willard Marshall	5.00	2.50	1.50
119	Bill Milne	5.00	2.50	1.50
120	Johnny Mize	15.00	7.50	4.50
121	Don Mueller	5.00	2.50	1.50
122	Ray Mueller	5.00	2.50	1.50
123	Bill Rigney	5.00	2.50	1.50
124	Bobby Thomson	7.50	3.75	2.25
125	Sam Webb	5.00	2.50	1.50
126	Wesley Westrum	5.00	2.50	1.50
127	Eddie Sawyer	5.00	2.50	1.50
128	Richie Ashburn	30.00	15.00	9.00
129	Benny Bengough	5.00	2.50	1.50
130	Charlie Bicknell	5.00	2.50	1.50
131	Buddy Blattner	5.00	2.50	1.50
132	Hank Borowy	5.00	2.50	1.50
133	Ralph Caballero	5.00	2.50	1.50
134	Blix Donnelly	5.00	2.50	1.50
135	Del Ennis	5.00	2.50	1.50
136	Granville Hamner	5.00	2.50	1.50
137	Ken Heintzelman	5.00	2.50	1.50
138	Stan Hollmig	5.00	2.50	1.50
139	Willie Jones	5.00	2.50	1.50
140	Jim Konstanty	5.00	2.50	1.50
141	Stan Lopata	5.00	2.50	1.50
142	Jackie Mayo	5.00	2.50	1.50
143	Bill Nicholson	5.00	2.50	1.50
144	Robin Roberts	60.00	30.00	18.00
145	Schoolboy Rowe	5.00	2.50	1.50
146	Andy Seminick	5.00	2.50	1.50
147	Ken Silvestri	5.00	2.50	1.50
148	Curt Simmons	5.00	2.50	1.50
149	Dick Sisler	5.00	2.50	1.50
150	Ken Trinkle	5.00	2.50	1.50
151	Eddie Waitkus	5.00	2.50	1.50
152	Bill Meyer	5.00	2.50	1.50
153	Monte Basgall	5.00	2.50	1.50
154	Eddie Bockman	5.00	2.50	1.50
155	Ernie Bonham	5.00	2.50	1.50
156	Hugh Casey	5.00	2.50	1.50
157	Pete Castiglione	5.00	2.50	1.50
158	Cliff Chambers	5.00	2.50	1.50
159	Murry Dickson	5.00	2.50	1.50
160	Ed Fitz Gerald	5.00	2.50	1.50
161	Les Fleming	5.00	2.50	1.50
162	Hal Gregg	5.00	2.50	1.50
163	Goldie Holt	5.00	2.50	1.50
164	Johnny Hopp	5.00	2.50	1.50
165	Ralph Kiner	20.00	10.00	6.00
166	Vic Lombardi	5.00	2.50	1.50
167	Clyde McCullough	5.00	2.50	1.50
168	Danny Murtaugh	5.00	2.50	1.50
169	Bill Posedel	5.00	2.50	1.50
170	Elmer Riddle	5.00	2.50	1.50
171	Stan Rojek	5.00	2.50	1.50
172	Rip Sewell	5.00	2.50	1.50
173	Eddie Stevens	5.00	2.50	1.50
174	Dixie Walker	5.00	2.50	1.50
175	Bill Werle	5.00	2.50	1.50
176	Wally Westlake	5.00	2.50	1.50
177	Eddie Dyer	5.00	2.50	1.50
178	Bill Baker	5.00	2.50	1.50
179	Al Brazle	5.00	2.50	1.50
180	Harry Brecheen	5.00	2.50	1.50
181	Chuck Diering	5.00	2.50	1.50
182	Joe Garagiola	13.50	6.75	4.00
183	Tom Galviano	5.00	2.50	1.50
184	Jim Hearn	5.00	2.50	1.50
185	Ken Johnson	5.00	2.50	1.50
186	Nippy Jones	5.00	2.50	1.50
187	Ed Kazak	5.00	2.50	1.50
188	Lou Klein	5.00	2.50	1.50
189	Marty Marion	5.00	2.50	1.50
190	George Munger	5.00	2.50	1.50
191	Stan Musial	45.00	22.00	13.50
192	Spike Nelson	5.00	2.50	1.50
193	Howie Pollet	5.00	2.50	1.50
194	Bill Reeder	5.00	2.50	1.50
195	Del Rice	5.00	2.50	1.50
196	Ed Sauer	5.00	2.50	1.50
197	Red Schoendienst	20.00	10.00	6.00
198	Enos Slaughter	20.00	10.00	6.00
199	Ted Wilks	5.00	2.50	1.50
200	Ray Yochim	5.00	2.50	1.50

1914 Evening Sun N.Y. Giants

The World's Champion 1913 N.Y. Giants are featured in this set of newspaper supplements titled, "Evening Sun's Gallery of Famous Baseball Players." It is believed the paper was published in Norwich, N.Y. Slightly larger than 9" x 12", the supplements feature black-and-white portraits by Lawrence Semon, who also produced a contemporary series of baseball postcards.

		NM	E	VG
Complete Set (21):		8,000	4,000	2,400
Common Player:		200.00	100.00	60.00
(1)	George Burns	200.00	100.00	60.00
(2)	Doc Crandall	200.00	100.00	60.00
(3)	Al Demaree	200.00	100.00	60.00
(4)	Art Fletcher	200.00	100.00	60.00
(5)	Art Fromme	200.00	100.00	60.00
(6)	Grover Hartley	200.00	100.00	60.00
(7)	Buck Herzog	200.00	100.00	60.00
(8)	Rube Marquard	400.00	200.00	120.00
(9)	Christy Mathewson	2,400	1,200	725.00
(10)	Moose McCormick	200.00	100.00	60.00
(11)	John McGraw	400.00	200.00	120.00
(12)	Fred Merkle	200.00	100.00	60.00
(13)	Chief Meyers	200.00	100.00	60.00
(14)	Red Murray	200.00	100.00	60.00
(15)	Wilbert Robinson	400.00	200.00	120.00
(16)	Arthur Shafer	200.00	100.00	60.00
(17)	Fred Snodgrass	200.00	100.00	60.00
(18)	Jeff Tesreau	200.00	100.00	60.00
(19)	Jim Thorpe	2,500	1,250	750.00
(20)	Art Wilson	200.00	100.00	60.00
(21)	Hooks Wiltse	200.00	100.00	60.00

1916 Everybody's

DICK RUDOLPH
P—Boston Braves
149

EVERYBODY'S
BOYS' CLOTHING DEPARTMENT
Fourth Floor

Where "Everybody's" department store was located is unknown, but in 1916 they chose to use baseball cards to promote their boy's wear department. The approximately 1-5/8" x 3" black-and-white cards share the format and checklist with the much more common M101-4 blank-back version and several other regional advertisers. Everybody's is one of the scarcest advertising backs to be found in this issue and the cards command a premium from type-card and superstar collectors. There are four styles of typography on back.

Premium:15-25X

(See 1916 M101-4 Blank Backs for checklist and base card values.)

1921 Exhibits

The Exhibit Supply Company of Chicago issued the first in a long series of postcard-size (3-3/8" x 5-3/8") baseball cards in 1921. The Exhibit cards were commonly sold in "penny arcade" vending machines. The 1921 series consists of 64 cards and includes four players from each of the 16 major league teams. The cards feature black-and-white photos with the player's name printed in a fancy script. The player's position and team appear below the name in small, hand-lettered capital letters. American League is designated as "AM.L.," which can help differentiate the 1921 series from future years. Some of the cards contain white borders while others do not. All have blank backs. There are various spelling errors in the picture legends.

		NM	E	VG
	Complete Set (64):	15,000	7,500	4,500
	Common Player:	75.00	35.00	20.00
(1)	Chas. B. Adams	75.00	35.00	20.00
(2)	Grover C. Alexander	275.00	135.00	80.00
(3)	David Bancroft	175.00	85.00	50.00
(4)	Geo. J. Burns	75.00	35.00	20.00
(5)	Owen Bush	75.00	35.00	20.00
(6)	Max J. Carey	175.00	85.00	50.00
(7)	Ty R. Cobb	1,250	625.00	375.00
(8)	Eddie T. Collins	175.00	85.00	50.00
(9)	John Collins	75.00	35.00	20.00
(10)	Stanley Coveleskie (Coveleski)	200.00	100.00	60.00
(11)	Walton E. Cruise	75.00	35.00	20.00
(12)	Jacob E. Daubert	75.00	35.00	20.00
(13)	George Dauss	75.00	35.00	20.00
(14)	Charles A. Deal	75.00	35.00	20.00
(15)	Joe A. Dugan	75.00	35.00	20.00
(16)	James Dykes	75.00	35.00	20.00
(17)	U.C. "Red" Faber	175.00	85.00	50.00
(18)	J.F. Fournier	75.00	35.00	20.00
(19)	Frank F. Frisch	175.00	85.00	50.00
(20)	W.L. Gardner	75.00	35.00	20.00
(21)	H.M. "Hank" Gowdy	75.00	35.00	20.00
(22)	Burleigh A. Grimes	200.00	100.00	60.00
(23)	Heinie Groh	75.00	35.00	20.00
(24)	Jesse Haines	200.00	100.00	60.00
(25)	Sam Harris (Stanley)	200.00	100.00	60.00
(26)	Walter L. Holke	75.00	35.00	20.00
(27)	Charles J. Hollicher (Hollocher)	75.00	35.00	20.00
(28)	Rogers Hornsby	325.00	160.00	95.00
(29)	James H. Johnson (Johnston)	75.00	35.00	20.00
(30)	Walter P. Johnson	750.00	375.00	225.00
(31)	Sam P. Jones	75.00	35.00	20.00
(32)	Geo. L. Kelly	200.00	100.00	60.00
(33)	Dick Kerr	75.00	35.00	20.00
(34)	William L. Killifer (Killefer)	75.00	35.00	20.00
(35)	Ed Konetchy	75.00	35.00	20.00
(36)	John "Doc" Lavan	75.00	35.00	20.00
(37)	Walter J. Maranville	500.00	250.00	150.00
(38)	Carl W. Mays	75.00	35.00	20.00
(39)	J. "Stuffy" McInnis	75.00	35.00	20.00
(40)	Rollie C. Naylor	75.00	35.00	20.00
(41)	A. Earl Neale (Earle)	125.00	60.00	35.00
(42)	Ivan M. Olsen	75.00	35.00	20.00
(43)	S.F. "Steve" O'Neil (O'Neill)	75.00	35.00	20.00
(44)	Robert (Roger) Peckinpaugh	300.00	150.00	90.00
(45)	Ralph "Cy" Perkins	75.00	35.00	20.00
(46)	Raymond R. Powell	75.00	35.00	20.00
(47)	Joe "Goldie" Rapp	75.00	35.00	20.00
(48)	Edgar S. Rice	450.00	220.00	135.00
(49)	Jimmy Ring	75.00	35.00	20.00
(50)	Geo. H. "Babe" Ruth	5,000	2,500	1,500
(51)	Ray W. Schalk	450.00	220.00	135.00
(52)	Wallie Schang	75.00	35.00	20.00
(53)	Everett Scott	75.00	35.00	20.00
(54)	H.S. Shanks (Photo actually Wally Schang.)	75.00	35.00	20.00
(55)	Urban Shocker	75.00	35.00	20.00
(56)	Geo. H. Sisler	175.00	85.00	50.00
(57)	Tris Speaker	900.00	450.00	270.00
(58)	John Tobin	75.00	35.00	20.00
(59)	Robt. Veach	75.00	35.00	20.00
(60)	Zack D. Wheat	175.00	85.00	50.00
(61)	Geo. B. Whitted	75.00	35.00	20.00
(62)	Cy Williams	75.00	35.00	20.00
(63)	Kenneth R. Williams	75.00	35.00	20.00
(64)	Ivy B. Wingo	75.00	35.00	20.00

1922 Eastern Exhibit Supply Co.

Postcard-style backs differentiate these cards from the more common Exhibit Supply Co., cards from Chicago. This 20-card series was produced by a Philadelphia company, although on some cards, the Eastern Exhibit copyright line on back has been blacked out and that of the Chicago company printed beneath it. The sepia tone, or more rarely black-and-white cards measure 3-3/8" x 5-5/8".

	Complete Set (20):	7,500	3,700	2,200
	Common Player:	20.00	80.00	40.00
	Black-and-White: 3-5X			
(1)	Grover Alexander	200.00	100.00	60.00
(2)	Dave Bancroft	125.00	65.00	35.00
(3)	Jesse Barnes	80.00	40.00	20.00
(4)	Joe Bush	80.00	40.00	20.00
(5)	Ty Cobb	750.00	375.00	225.00
(6)	Eddie Collins	125.00	65.00	35.00
(7)	Urban Faber	125.00	65.00	35.00
(8)	Clarence Galloway	80.00	40.00	20.00
(9)	Heinie Groh	80.00	40.00	20.00
(10)	Harry Heilmann	350.00	175.00	105.00
(11)	Charlie Hollocher	80.00	40.00	20.00
(12)	Rogers Hornsby	200.00	100.00	60.00
(13)	Walter Johnson	750.00	370.00	220.00
(14)	Eddie Rommel	80.00	40.00	20.00
(15)	Babe Ruth	2,500	1,250	750.00
(16)	Ray Schalk	125.00	65.00	35.00
(17)	Wallie Schang	80.00	40.00	20.00
(18)	Tris Speaker	200.00	100.00	60.00
(19)	Zach Wheat	125.00	65.00	35.00
(20)	Kenneth Williams	80.00	40.00	20.00

1922 Exhibits

The Exhibit Supply Co. continued the 3-3/8" x 5-3/8" format in 1922 but doubled the number of cards in the series to 128, including eight players from each team. All but nine of the players who appeared in the 1921 series are pictured in the 1922 set, along with 74 new players. The cards again display black-and-white photos with blank backs. Some photos have white borders. The player's name appears in script with the postition and team below in small block capital letters. American League is designated as "A.L." Again, there are several spelling errors and incorrect player identifications. Only the 74 new additions are included in this checklist.

Moses Yellowhorse
PITTSBURGH, N.L.

		NM	E	VG
	Complete Set (74):	7,500	3,750	2,250
	Common Player:	85.00	40.00	25.00
(1)	Jim Bagby Sr.	85.00	40.00	25.00
(2)	J. Frank Baker	150.00	75.00	45.00
(3)	Walter Barbare	85.00	40.00	25.00
(4)	Turner Barber	85.00	40.00	25.00
(5)	John Bassler	85.00	40.00	25.00
(6)	Carlson L. Bigbee (Carson)	85.00	40.00	25.00
(7)	Sam Bohne	125.00	62.50	37.50
(8)	Geo. Burns	85.00	40.00	25.00
(9)	George Burns	85.00	40.00	25.00
(10)	Jeo Bush (Joe)	85.00	40.00	25.00
(11)	Leon Cadore	85.00	40.00	25.00
(12)	Jim Caveney	85.00	40.00	25.00
(13)	Wilbur Cooper	85.00	40.00	25.00
(14)	George Cutshaw	85.00	40.00	25.00
(15)	Dave Danforth	85.00	40.00	25.00
(16)	Bill Doak	85.00	40.00	25.00
(17)	Joe Dugan	85.00	40.00	25.00
(18)	Pat Duncan	85.00	40.00	25.00
(19)	Howard Emke (Ehmke)	85.00	40.00	25.00
(20)	Wm. Evans (Umpire)	375.00	185.00	110.00
(21)	Bib Falk (Bibb)	85.00	40.00	25.00
(22)	Dana Fillingin (Fillingim)	85.00	40.00	25.00
(23)	Ira Flagstead	85.00	40.00	25.00
(24)	(Art) Fletcher	85.00	40.00	25.00
(25)	(Wally) Gerber	85.00	40.00	25.00
(26)	Ray Grimes	85.00	40.00	25.00
(27)	Harry Heilman (Heilmann)	150.00	75.00	45.00
(28)	George Hildebrand (Umpire)	200.00	100.00	60.00
(29)	Wibur Hubbell (Wilbert)	85.00	40.00	25.00
(30)	Bill Jacobson	85.00	40.00	25.00
(31)	E.R. Johnson	85.00	40.00	25.00
(32)	Joe Judge	85.00	40.00	25.00
(33)	Bill Klem (Umpire)	450.00	220.00	135.00
(34)	Harry Liebold (Leibold)	85.00	40.00	25.00
(35)	Walter Mails	85.00	40.00	25.00
(36)	Geo. Maisel	85.00	40.00	25.00
(37)	Lee Meadows	85.00	40.00	25.00
(38)	Clyde Milam (Milan)	85.00	40.00	25.00
(39)	Ed (Bing) Miller	85.00	40.00	25.00
(40)	Hack Miller	85.00	40.00	25.00
(41)	George Moriarty (Umpire)	500.00	250.00	150.00
(42)	Robert Muesel (Meusel)	85.00	40.00	25.00
(43)	Harry Myers	85.00	40.00	25.00
(44)	Arthur Nehf	85.00	40.00	25.00
(45)	Joe Oeschger	85.00	40.00	25.00
(46)	Geo. O'Neil	85.00	40.00	25.00
(47)	Roger Peckinpaugh	85.00	40.00	25.00
(48)	Val Picinich	85.00	40.00	25.00
(49)	Bill Piercy	85.00	40.00	25.00
(50)	Derrill Pratt	85.00	40.00	25.00
(51)	Jack Quinn	85.00	40.00	25.00
(52)	Walter Reuther (Ruether)	85.00	40.00	25.00
(53)	Charles Rigler (Umpire)	200.00	100.00	60.00
(54)	Eppa Rixey	150.00	75.00	45.00
(55)	Chas. Robertson	85.00	40.00	25.00
(56)	Everett Scott	85.00	40.00	25.00
(57)	Earl Sheely	85.00	40.00	25.00
(58)	Earl Smith (portrait)	85.00	40.00	25.00
(59)	Earl Smith (Standing) (Photo actually Brad Kocher.))	85.00	40.00	25.00
(60)	Elmer Smith	85.00	40.00	25.00
(61)	Jack Smith (Photo actually Jimmy Smith.)	85.00	40.00	25.00
(62)	Sherrod Smith	85.00	40.00	25.00
(63)	Frank Snyder	85.00	40.00	25.00
(64)	Allan Sothoron (Allen)	85.00	40.00	25.00
(65)	Arnold Statz	85.00	40.00	25.00
(66)	Milton Stock	85.00	40.00	25.00
(67)	James Tierney	85.00	40.00	25.00
(68)	George Toporcer	85.00	40.00	25.00
(69)	Clarence (Tilly) Walker	85.00	40.00	25.00
(70)	Curtis Walker	85.00	40.00	25.00

		NM	E	VG
(71)	Aaron Ward	85.00	40.00	25.00
(72)	Joe Wood	100.00	50.00	30.00
(73)	Moses Yellowhorse	400.00	300.00	200.00
(74)	Ross Young (Youngs)	150.00	75.00	45.00

1923-24 Exhibits

The Exhibit cards for 1923 and 1924 are generally collected as a single 128-card series. The format remained basically the same as the previous year, 3-3/8" x 5-3/8", with black-and-white photos (some surrounded by a white border) and blank backs. The player's name is again shown in script with the position and team printed below in a small, square block-type style. Many of the same photos were used from previous years, although some are cropped differently, and some players have new team designations, background changes, team emblems removed, borders added or taken away, and other minor changes. Fifty-eight new cards are featured, including 38 players pictured for the first time in an Exhibit set. Only the 58 new cards are included in this checklist. The Babe Ruth card, which differs from the 1921 issue in the addition of a white border, is very rare with only a handful known.

		NM	E	VG
Complete Set (59):		25,000	12,500	7,500
Common Player:		225.00	110.00	65.00
(1)	Clyde Barnhart	225.00	110.00	65.00
(2)	Ray Blades	225.00	110.00	65.00
(3)	James Bottomley	400.00	200.00	120.00
(4)	George Burns	225.00	110.00	65.00
(5)	Dan Clark	225.00	110.00	65.00
(6)	Bill Doak	225.00	110.00	65.00
(7)	Joe Dugan	225.00	110.00	65.00
(8)	Howard J. Ehmke	225.00	110.00	65.00
(9)	Ira Flagstead	225.00	110.00	65.00
(10)	J.F. Fournier	225.00	110.00	65.00
(11)	Howard Freigan (Freigau)	225.00	110.00	65.00
(12)	C.E. Galloway	225.00	110.00	65.00
(13)	Joe Genewich	225.00	110.00	65.00
(14)	Mike Gonzales (Gonzalez)	275.00	135.00	82.00
(15)	H.M. "Hank" Gowdy	225.00	110.00	65.00
(16)	Charles Grimm	225.00	110.00	65.00
(17)	Heinie Groh	225.00	110.00	65.00
(18)	Chas. L. Harnett (Hartnett)	400.00	200.00	120.00
(19)	George Harper	225.00	110.00	65.00
(20)	Slim Harris (Harriss)	225.00	110.00	65.00
(21)	Clifton Heathcote	225.00	110.00	65.00
(22)	Andy High	225.00	110.00	65.00
(23)	Walter L. Holke	225.00	110.00	65.00
(24)	Charles D. Jamieson	225.00	110.00	65.00
(25)	Willie Kamm	225.00	110.00	65.00
(26)	Tony Kaufmann	225.00	110.00	65.00
(27)	Dudley Lee	225.00	110.00	65.00
(28)	Harry Liebold (Leibold)	225.00	110.00	65.00
(29)	Aldofo Luque	225.00	110.00	65.00
(30)	W.C. (Wid) Matthews	225.00	110.00	65.00
(31)	John J. McGraw	400.00	200.00	120.00
(32)	J. "Stuffy" McInnis	225.00	110.00	65.00
(33)	Johnny Morrison	225.00	110.00	65.00
(34)	John A. Mostil	225.00	110.00	65.00
(35)	J.F. O'Neill (Should be S.F.)	225.00	110.00	65.00
(36)	Ernest Padgett	225.00	110.00	65.00
(37)	Val Picinich	225.00	110.00	65.00
(38)	Bill Piercy	225.00	110.00	65.00
(39)	Herman Pillette	225.00	110.00	65.00
(40)	Wallie Pipp	275.00	135.00	82.00
(41)	Raymond R. Powell (Black background.)	225.00	110.00	65.00
(43)	Del. Pratt	225.00	110.00	65.00
(44)	E.E. Rigney	225.00	110.00	65.00
(45)	Eddie Rommel	225.00	110.00	65.00
(46)	Geo. H. "Babe" Ruth	12,000	6,500	5,000
(47)	Muddy Ruel	225.00	110.00	65.00
(48)	J.H. Sand	225.00	110.00	65.00
(49)	Henry Severeid	225.00	110.00	65.00

(50)	Joseph Sewell	400.00	200.00	120.00
(51)	Al. Simmons	1,000	500.00	300.00
(52)	R.E. Smith	225.00	110.00	65.00
(53)	Sherrod Smith	225.00	110.00	65.00
(54)	Casey Stengel	500.00	400.00	300.00
(55)	J.R. Stevenson (Stephenson)	225.00	110.00	65.00
(56)	James Tierney	225.00	110.00	65.00
(57)	Robt. Veach	225.00	110.00	65.00
(58)	L. Woodall	225.00	110.00	65.00
(59)	Russell G. Wrighstone	225.00	110.00	65.00

1925-31 Postcard-Back Exhibits

These cards can be found with plain backs; postcard backs including the legend: "This Side for Correspondence"; and postcard backs including the legend "Not to be used in Exhibit machines". Some printings also have the legend "Made in U.S.A.' added to the backs. Cards will rarely be found with a coupon on the back corner. The fronts are borderless photos that generally have the player's name, team, and league designation handwritten across the fronts. Over the years of issue, players were added to and removed from the set and corrections were made to account for team changes, resulting in significant short-prints and variations. Cards can be found in a variety of colors. The "plain background" cards designated below are "cut-outs" of previous images reused against plain backgrounds.

		NM	E	VG
Common Player:		90.00	45.00	25.00
(1)	Virgie Barnes	90.00	45.00	25.00
(2)	Johnny Bassler	90.00	45.00	25.00
(3)	Sammy Bohne	200.00	100.00	60.00
(4)	Jim Bottomley	450.00	220.00	135.00
(5)	Ty Cobb (Detroit)	1,500	750.00	450.00
(6)	Ty Cobb (Athletics)	1,500	750.00	450.00
(7)	Mickey Cochrane	400.00	200.00	120.00
(8)	Urban Faber (Photo background.)	250.00	125.00	75.00
(9)	Urban Faber (Plain background.)	500.00	250.00	150.00
(10)	Jack Fournier	90.00	45.00	25.00
(11)	Jimmy Foxx	750.00	370.00	220.00
(12)	Frank Frisch (New York)	400.00	200.00	120.00
(13)	Frank Frisch (St. Louis)	450.00	225.00	135.00
(14)	Lou Gehrig (Batting, photo background.)	2,000	1,000	600.00
(15)	Lou Gehrig (Batting, plain background.)	4,000	2,000	1,200
(16)	Lou Gehrig (Portrait)	2,000	1,000	600.00
(17)	Tom Griffith	90.00	45.00	25.00
(18)	Heinie Groh	90.00	45.00	25.00
(19)	Lefty Grove	500.00	250.00	150.00
(20)	George Haas	90.00	45.00	25.00
(21)	Stanley Harris	400.00	200.00	120.00
(22)	Charlie Hartnett (Photo background.)	250.00	125.00	75.00
(23)	Charlie Hartnett (Plain background.)	500.00	250.00	150.00
(24)	Harry Heilmann	400.00	200.00	120.00
(25)	Rogers Hornsby (St. Louis)	600.00	300.00	180.00
(26)	Rogers Hornsby (Boston)	600.00	300.00	180.00
(27)	Rogers Hornsby (Chicago)	600.00	300.00	180.00
(28)	Walter Johnson	600.00	300.00	180.00
(29)	Jimmy Johnston	90.00	45.00	25.00
(30)	Joe Judge	90.00	45.00	25.00
(31)	George Kelly	400.00	200.00	120.00
(32)	Chuck Klein	250.00	125.00	75.00
(33)	Hugh McQuillan	180.00	90.00	54.00
(34)	"Bob" Meusel	90.00	45.00	25.00
(35)	Bing Miller	90.00	45.00	25.00
(36)	Lefty O'Doul	150.00	75.00	45.00
(37)	Roger Peckinpaugh (Washington)	250.00	125.00	75.00
(38)	Roger Peckinpaugh (Cleveland)	500.00	300.00	200.00
(39)	Ralph Pinelli	90.00	45.00	25.00
(40)	Walter Pipp	125.00	60.00	35.00
(41)	Jimmy Ring	90.00	45.00	25.00
(42)	Eppa Rixey	400.00	200.00	120.00
(43)	Ed Rouch (Edd Roush) (Cincinnati)	400.00	200.00	120.00
(44)	Ed Rouch (Edd Roush) (New York)	500.00	250.00	150.00
(45)	Babe Ruth (Pose)	3,500	1,750	1,050
(46)	Babe Ruth (Batting follow-through.)	3,250	1,600	975.00
(47)	John Sand	90.00	45.00	25.00
(48)	Everett Scott	180.00	90.00	54.00
(49)	Al Simmons (View from side, "AM.L.")	500.00	250.00	150.00
(50)	Al Simmons (View from front, "A.L.")	400.00	200.00	120.00
(51)	George Sisler (Photo background.)	400.00	200.00	120.00

(52)	George Sisler (Plain background.)	500.00	250.00	150.00
(53)	Jack Smith	90.00	45.00	25.00
(54)	Tris Speaker (Photo background.)	600.00	300.00	180.00
(55)	Tris Speaker (Plain background.)	750.00	370.00	220.00
(56)	Phil Todt (Photo background.)	90.00	45.00	25.00
(57)	Phil Todt (Plain background.)	180.00	90.00	54.00
(58)	Specs Toporcer	180.00	90.00	54.00
(59)	Pie Traynor	400.00	200.00	120.00
(60)	Dazzy Vance	400.00	200.00	120.00
(61)	Rube Walberg	90.00	45.00	25.00
(62)	Paul Waner (Batting, photo background.)	400.00	200.00	120.00
(63)	Paul Waner (Batting, plain background.)	500.00	250.00	150.00
(64)	Paul Waner (Portrait)	400.00	200.00	120.00
(65)	Zack Wheat	400.00	200.00	120.00
(66)	Cy Williams	90.00	45.00	25.00
(67)	Hack Wilson	400.00	200.00	120.00
(68)	Jimmy Wilson (Photo background.)	90.00	45.00	25.00
(69)	Jimmy Wilson (Plain background.)	180.00	90.00	54.00

1925-31 Postcard-Back Four-on-One Exhibits

The Exhibit Supply Company experimented with a four-on-one format in the late 1920s, ultimately adopting the format for several years from 1929-1938 for its main issues. This group of cards contains seven known cards in two distinct formats; a mixed subjects group containing two baseball players and two boxers or two entertainers; and a group containing four baseball players. The mixed subjects group was issued first, very likely circa 1926-1928 and is the rarer of the two. The all-baseball group certainly was issued as late as 1931 based on the team designations of certain players. Examples have been found with blank backs, postcard backs, and a postcard back with coupon (1 known), and in a variety of colors. Some cards have been found with two contrasting colors used, primarily blue and orange.

		NM	E	VG
(1)	Lou Gehrig, Lefty Grove, Pete Donahue, Gordon Cochrane	2,200	1,100	650.00
(2)	Lefty O'Doul, Dazzy Vance, Hughey Critz, Art Shires	650.00	325.00	195.00
(3)	Eugene Criqui (Boxer), Dave Shade (Boxer), Joe Judge, Ty Cobb	3,000	1,500	900.00
(4)	Joe Judge, Ty Cobb, Charlie Chaplin (Actor), Marie Prevost (Actress)	2,500	1,250	750.00
(5)	Joe Judge, Paul Waner, Willie Kamm, Travis Jackson	750.00	375.00	225.00
(6)	Bucky Harris, Heinie Groh, Jack Dempsey (Boxer), Rocky Kansas (Boxer)	750.00	375.00	225.00
(7)	Walter Johnson, Al Simmons, Gene Tunney (Boxer), Benny Leonard (Boxer)	2,500	1,250	750.00
(8)	Babe Ruth, Rogers Hornsby, Mickey Walker (Boxer), Georges Carpentier (Boxer)	3,500	1,750	1,000
(9)	Charles Klein, Eddy Collins, Geo. Kelly, Bing Miller	750.00	375.00	225.00

1925 Champions Babe Ruth Exhibit

This is part of a (presumably) 32-card multi-sport "World's Champions" issue and the only baseball player in the set. The 3-3/8" x 5-3/8" card is printed in black-and-white and has a blank back.

	NM	E	VG
Babe Ruth	4,250	2,100	1,250

1925 Exhibits

The 1925 series of Exhibits contains 128 unnumbered cards, each measuring 3-3/8" x 5-3/8". The player's name (in all capital letters), position and team (along with a line reading "Made in U.S.A.") are printed in a small white box in a lower corner of the card. Most of the photos are vertical, however a few are horizontal. There are several misspellings in the set. Lou Gehrig's first baseball card appears in this issue. The cards are listed here in alphabetical order.

	NM	E	VG
Complete Set (128):	60,000	30,000	18,000
Common Player:	125.00	65.00	35.00
(1) Sparky Adams	125.00	65.00	35.00
(2) Grover C. Alexander	400.00	200.00	120.00
(3) David Bancroft	300.00	150.00	90.00
(4) Jesse Barnes	125.00	65.00	35.00
(5) John Bassler	125.00	65.00	35.00
(6) Lester Bell	125.00	65.00	35.00
(7) Lawrence Benton	125.00	65.00	35.00
(8) Carson Bigbee	125.00	65.00	35.00
(9) Max Bishop	125.00	65.00	35.00
(10) Raymond Blates (Blades)	125.00	65.00	35.00
(11) Oswald Bluege	125.00	65.00	35.00
(12) James Bottomly (Bottomley)	400.00	200.00	120.00
(13) Raymond Bressler	125.00	65.00	35.00
(14) John Brooks	125.00	65.00	35.00
(15) Maurice Burrus	125.00	65.00	35.00
(16) Max Carey	400.00	200.00	120.00
(17) Tyrus Cobb	2,000	1,000	600.00
(18) Eddie Collins	400.00	200.00	120.00
(19) Stanley Coveleski	400.00	200.00	120.00
(20) Hugh M. Critz	125.00	65.00	35.00
(21) Hazen Cuyler	400.00	200.00	120.00
(22) George Dauss	125.00	65.00	35.00
(23) I.M. Davis	125.00	65.00	35.00
(24) John H. DeBerry	125.00	65.00	35.00
(25) Art Decatur	125.00	65.00	35.00
(26) Peter Donohue	125.00	65.00	35.00
(27) Charles Dressen	125.00	65.00	35.00
(28) James J. Dykes	125.00	65.00	35.00
(29) Howard Ehmke	125.00	65.00	35.00
(30) Bib Falk (Bibb)	125.00	65.00	35.00
(31) Wilson Fewster	125.00	65.00	35.00
(32) Max Flack	125.00	65.00	35.00
(33) Ira Flagstead	125.00	65.00	35.00
(34) Jacques F. Fournier	125.00	65.00	35.00
(35) Howard Freigau	125.00	65.00	35.00
(36) Frank Frisch	400.00	200.00	120.00
(37) Henry L. Gehrig	17,500	8,750	5,250
(38) Joseph Genewich	125.00	65.00	35.00
(39) Walter Gerber	125.00	65.00	35.00
(40) Frank Gibson	125.00	65.00	35.00
(41) Leon Goslin	400.00	200.00	120.00
(42) George Grantham	125.00	65.00	35.00
(43) Samuel Gray	125.00	65.00	35.00
(44) Burleigh A. Grimes	400.00	200.00	120.00
(45) Charles Grimm	125.00	65.00	35.00
(46) Heine Groh (Heinie)	125.00	65.00	35.00
(47) Samuel Hale	125.00	65.00	35.00
(48) George Harper	125.00	65.00	35.00
(49) David Harris	125.00	65.00	35.00
(50) Stanley Harris	400.00	200.00	120.00
(51) Leo Hartnett	400.00	200.00	120.00
(52) Nelson Hawks	125.00	65.00	35.00
(53) Harry Heilmann	400.00	200.00	120.00
(54) Walter Henline	125.00	65.00	35.00
(55) Walter Holke	125.00	65.00	35.00
(56) Harry Hooper	400.00	200.00	120.00
(57) Rogers Hornsby	1,500	750.00	450.00
(58) Wilbur Hubbell	125.00	65.00	35.00
(59) Travis C. Jackson	400.00	200.00	120.00
(60) William Jacobson	125.00	65.00	35.00
(61) Charles Jamieson	125.00	65.00	35.00
(62) James H. Johnson (Johnston)	125.00	65.00	35.00
(63) Walter Johnson	2,500	1,250	750.00
(64) Joseph Judge	125.00	65.00	35.00
(65) Willie Kamm	125.00	65.00	35.00
(66) Ray Kremer	125.00	65.00	35.00
(67) Walter Lutzke	125.00	65.00	35.00
(68) Walter Maranville	400.00	200.00	120.00
(69) John ("Stuffy") McInnes (McInnis)	125.00	65.00	35.00
(70) Martin McManus	125.00	65.00	35.00
(71) Earl McNeely	125.00	65.00	35.00
(72) Emil Meusel	125.00	65.00	35.00
(73) Edmund (Bing) Miller	125.00	65.00	35.00
(74) John Mokan	125.00	65.00	35.00
(75) Clarence Mueller	125.00	65.00	35.00
(76) Robert W. Muesel (Meusel)	125.00	65.00	35.00
(77) Glenn Myatt	125.00	65.00	35.00
(78) Arthur Nehf	125.00	65.00	35.00
(79) George O'Neil	125.00	65.00	35.00
(80) Frank O'Rourke	125.00	65.00	35.00
(81) Ralph Perkins	125.00	65.00	35.00
(82) Valentine Picinich	125.00	65.00	35.00
(83) Walter C. Pipp	125.00	65.00	35.00
(84) John Quinn	125.00	65.00	35.00
(85) Emory Rigney	125.00	65.00	35.00
(86) Eppa Rixey	400.00	200.00	120.00
(87) Edwin Rommel	125.00	65.00	35.00
(88) Ed (Edd) Roush	400.00	200.00	120.00
(89) Harold Ruel (Herold)	125.00	65.00	35.00
(90) Charles Ruffing	400.00	200.00	120.00
(91) George H. "Babe" Ruth	7,500	3,700	2,200
(92) John Sand	125.00	65.00	35.00
(93) Henry Severid (Severeid)	125.00	65.00	35.00
(94) Joseph Sewell	400.00	200.00	120.00
(95) Ray Shalk (Schalk)	400.00	200.00	120.00
(96) Walter H. Shang (Schang)	125.00	65.00	35.00
(97) J.R. Shawkey	125.00	65.00	35.00
(98) Earl Sheely	125.00	65.00	35.00
(99) William Sherdell (Sherdel)	125.00	65.00	35.00
(100) Urban J. Shocker	125.00	65.00	35.00
(101) George Sissler (Sisler)	1,350	675.00	405.00
(102) Earl Smith	125.00	65.00	35.00
(103) Sherrod Smith	125.00	65.00	35.00
(104) Frank Snyder	125.00	65.00	35.00
(105) Wm. H. Southworth	125.00	65.00	35.00
(106) Tristram Speaker	3,500	1,750	1,050
(107) Milton J. Stock	125.00	65.00	35.00
(108) Homer Summa	125.00	65.00	35.00
(109) William Terry	225.00	110.00	65.00
(110) Hollis Thurston	125.00	65.00	35.00
(111) John Tobin	125.00	65.00	35.00
(112) Philip Todt	125.00	65.00	35.00
(113) George Torporcer (Toporcer)	125.00	65.00	35.00
(114) Harold Traynor	400.00	200.00	120.00
(115) A.C. "Dazzy" Vance	400.00	200.00	120.00
(116) Robert Veach (Photo actually Ernest Vache.)	125.00	65.00	35.00
(117) William Wambsganss	125.00	65.00	35.00
(118) Aaron Ward	125.00	65.00	35.00
(119) A.J. Weis	125.00	65.00	35.00
(120) Frank Welch	125.00	65.00	35.00
(121) Zack Wheat	400.00	200.00	120.00
(122) Fred Williams	125.00	65.00	35.00
(123) Kenneth Williams	125.00	65.00	35.00
(124) Ernest Wingard	125.00	65.00	35.00
(125) Ivy Wingo	125.00	65.00	35.00
(126) Al Wings (Wingo)	125.00	65.00	35.00
(127) Larry Woodall	125.00	65.00	35.00
(128) Glen Wright (Glenn)	125.00	65.00	35.00

1926 Exhibits

The 1926 Exhibit cards are the same size (3-3/8" x 5-3/8") as previous Exhibit issues but are easily distinguished because of their blue-gray color. The set consists of 128 cards, 91 of which are identical to the photos in the 1925 series. The 37 new photos do not include the boxed caption used in 1925. The cards are unnumbered and are listed here alphabetically.

	NM	E	VG
Complete Set (128):	30,000	15,000	9,000
Common Player:	125.00	60.00	35.00
(1) Sparky Adams	125.00	60.00	35.00
(2) David Bancroft	400.00	200.00	120.00
(3) John Bassler	125.00	60.00	35.00
(4) Lester Bell	125.00	60.00	35.00
(5) John M. Bentley	125.00	60.00	35.00
(6) Lawrence Benton	125.00	60.00	35.00
(7) Carson Bigbee	125.00	60.00	35.00
(8) George Bischoff (Team actually Boston A.L.)	125.00	60.00	35.00
(9) Max Bishop	125.00	60.00	35.00
(10) J. Fred Blake	125.00	60.00	35.00
(11) Ted Blankenship	125.00	60.00	35.00
(12) Raymond Blates (Blades)	125.00	60.00	35.00
(13) Lucerne A. Blue (Luzerne)	125.00	60.00	35.00
(14) Oswald Bluege	125.00	60.00	35.00
(15) James Bottomly (Bottomley)	400.00	200.00	120.00
(16) Raymond Bressler	125.00	60.00	35.00
(17) Geo. H. Burns	125.00	60.00	35.00
(18) Maurice Burrus	125.00	60.00	35.00
(19) John Butler	125.00	60.00	35.00
(20) Max Carey	400.00	200.00	120.00
(21) Tyrus Cobb	1,400	700.00	425.00
(22) Eddie Collins	400.00	200.00	120.00
(23) Patrick T. Collins	125.00	60.00	35.00
(24) Earl B. Combs (Earle)	225.00	110.00	65.00
(25) James E. Cooney	125.00	60.00	35.00
(26) Stanley Coveleski	400.00	200.00	120.00
(27) Hugh M. Critz	125.00	60.00	35.00
(28) Hazen Cuyler	400.00	200.00	120.00
(29) George Dauss	125.00	60.00	35.00
(30) Peter Donohue	125.00	60.00	35.00
(31) Charles Dressen	125.00	60.00	35.00
(32) James J. Dykes	125.00	60.00	35.00
(33) Bib Falk (Bibb)	125.00	60.00	35.00
(34) Edward S. Farrell	125.00	60.00	35.00
(35) Wilson Fewster	125.00	60.00	35.00
(36) Ira Flagstead	125.00	60.00	35.00
(37) Howard Freigau	125.00	60.00	35.00
(38) Bernard Friberg	125.00	60.00	35.00
(39) Frank Frisch	400.00	200.00	120.00
(40) Jacques F. Furnier (Fournier)	125.00	60.00	35.00
(41) Joseph Galloway (Clarence)(Photo reversed.))	125.00	60.00	35.00
(42) Henry L. Gehrig	2,350	1,175	725.00
(43) Charles Gehringer	500.00	250.00	150.00
(44) Joseph Genewich	125.00	60.00	35.00
(45) Walter Gerber	125.00	60.00	35.00
(46) Leon Goslin	400.00	200.00	120.00
(47) George Grantham	125.00	60.00	35.00
(48) Burleigh A. Grimes	200.00	100.00	60.00
(49) Charles Grimm	125.00	60.00	35.00
(50) Fred Haney	125.00	60.00	35.00
(51) Wm. Hargrave	125.00	60.00	35.00
(52) George Harper	125.00	60.00	35.00
(53) Stanley Harris	200.00	100.00	60.00
(54) Leo Hartnett	200.00	100.00	60.00
(55) Joseph Hauser	125.00	60.00	35.00
(56) C.E. Heathcote	125.00	60.00	35.00
(57) Harry Heilmann	400.00	200.00	120.00
(58) Walter Henline	125.00	60.00	35.00
(59) Ramon Herrera	125.00	60.00	35.00
(60) Andrew A. High	125.00	60.00	35.00
(61) Rogers Hornsby	450.00	225.00	135.00
(62) Clarence Huber	125.00	60.00	35.00
(63) Wm. Hunnefield (Photo actually Tommy Thomas.)	125.00	60.00	35.00
(64) William Jacobson	125.00	60.00	35.00
(65) Walter Johnson	600.00	300.00	180.00
(66) Joseph Judge	125.00	60.00	35.00
(67) Willie Kamm	125.00	60.00	35.00
(68) Ray Kremer	125.00	60.00	35.00
(69) Anthony Lazzeri	500.00	250.00	150.00
(70) Frederick Lindstrom	450.00	225.00	125.00
(71) Walter Lutzke	125.00	60.00	35.00
(72) John Makan (Mokan)	125.00	60.00	35.00
(73) Walter Maranville	400.00	200.00	125.00
(74) Martin McManus	125.00	60.00	35.00
(75) Earl McNeely	125.00	60.00	35.00
(76) Hugh A. McQuillan	125.00	60.00	35.00
(77) Douglas McWeeny	125.00	60.00	35.00
(78) Oscar Melillo	125.00	60.00	35.00

(79)	Edmund (Bind)(Bing) Miller	125.00	60.00	35.00
(80)	Clarence Mueller	125.00	60.00	35.00
(81)	Robert W. Muesel (Meusel)	125.00	60.00	35.00
(82)	Joseph W. Munson	125.00	60.00	35.00
(83)	Emil Musel (Meusel)	125.00	60.00	35.00
(84)	Glenn Myatt	125.00	60.00	35.00
(85)	Bernie F. Neis	125.00	60.00	35.00
(86)	Robert O'Farrell	125.00	60.00	35.00
(87)	George O'Neil	125.00	60.00	35.00
(88)	Frank O'Rourke	125.00	60.00	35.00
(89)	Ralph Perkins	125.00	60.00	35.00
(90)	Walter C. Pipp	135.00	65.00	40.00
(91)	Emory Rigney	125.00	60.00	35.00
(92)	James J. Ring	125.00	60.00	35.00
(93)	Eppa Rixey	200.00	100.00	60.00
(94)	Edwin Rommel	125.00	60.00	35.00
(95)	Ed. Roush	200.00	100.00	60.00
(96)	Harold Ruel (Herold)	125.00	60.00	35.00
(97)	Charles Ruffing	400.00	200.00	125.00
(98)	Geo. H. "Babe" Ruth	1,875	935.00	560.00
(99)	John Sand	125.00	60.00	35.00
(100)	Joseph Sewell	200.00	100.00	60.00
(101)	Ray Shalk (Schalk)	400.00	200.00	125.00
(102)	J.R. Shawkey	125.00	60.00	35.00
(103)	Earl Sheely	125.00	60.00	35.00
(104)	William Sherdell (Sherdel)	125.00	60.00	35.00
(105)	Urban J. Shocker	125.00	60.00	35.00
(106)	George Sissler (Sisler)	400.00	200.00	125.00
(107)	Earl Smith	125.00	60.00	35.00
(108)	Sherrod Smith	125.00	60.00	35.00
(109)	Frank Snyder	125.00	60.00	35.00
(110)	Tristram Speaker	425.00	210.00	125.00
(111)	Fred Spurgeon	125.00	60.00	35.00
(112)	Homer Summa	125.00	60.00	35.00
(113)	Edward Taylor	125.00	60.00	35.00
(114)	J. Taylor	125.00	60.00	35.00
(115)	William Terry	400.00	200.00	120.00
(116)	Hollis Thurston	125.00	60.00	35.00
(117)	Philip Todt	125.00	60.00	35.00
(118)	George Torporcer (Toporcer)	125.00	60.00	35.00
(119)	Harold Traynor	400.00	200.00	120.00
(120)	Wm. Wambsganss	125.00	60.00	35.00
(121)	John Warner	125.00	60.00	35.00
(122)	Zach Wheat	400.00	200.00	120.00
(123)	Kenneth Williams	125.00	60.00	35.00
(124)	Ernest Wingard	125.00	60.00	35.00
(125)	Fred Wingfield	125.00	60.00	35.00
(126)	Ivy Wingo	125.00	60.00	35.00
(127)	Glen Wright (Glenn)	125.00	60.00	35.00
(128)	Russell Wrightstone	125.00	60.00	35.00

1927 Exhibits

The Exhibit Supply Co. issued a set of 64 cards in 1927, each measuring 3-3/8" x 5-3/8". The set can be identified from earlier issues by its light green tint. The player's name and team appear in capital letters in one lower corner, while "Ex. Sup. Co., Chgo." and "Made in U.S.A." appear in the other. All 64 photos used in the 1927 set were borrowed from previous issues, but 13 players are listed with new teams. There are several misspellings and other labeling errors in the set. The unnumbered cards are listed here in alphabetical order. Cards will rarely be found with a corner coupon in purple printed or stamped on the back of the card.

		NM	E	VG
Complete Set (64):		25,000	12,500	7,500
Common Player:		75.00	35.00	20.00
(1)	Sparky Adams	75.00	35.00	20.00
(2)	Grover C. Alexander	250.00	125.00	75.00
(3)	David Bancroft	150.00	75.00	45.00
(4)	John Bassler	75.00	35.00	20.00
(5)	John M. Bentley (Middle initial actually N.)	75.00	35.00	20.00
(6)	Fred Blankenship (Ted)	75.00	35.00	20.00
(7)	James Bottomly (Bottomley)	150.00	75.00	45.00
(8)	Raymond Bressler	75.00	35.00	20.00
(9)	Geo. H. Burns	75.00	35.00	20.00
(10)	John Buttler (Butler)	75.00	35.00	20.00
(11)	Tyrus Cobb	4,000	2,000	1,200
(12)	Eddie Collins	150.00	75.00	45.00
(13)	Hazen Cuyler	150.00	75.00	45.00
(14)	George Daus (Dauss)	75.00	35.00	20.00
(15)	A.R. Decatur	75.00	35.00	20.00
(16)	Wilson Fewster	75.00	35.00	20.00
(17)	Ira Flagstead	75.00	35.00	20.00
(18)	Henry L. Gehrig	6,500	3,200	1,950
(19)	Charles Gehringer	150.00	75.00	45.00
(20)	Joseph Genewich	75.00	35.00	20.00
(21)	Leon Goslin	150.00	75.00	45.00
(22)	Burleigh A. Grimes	150.00	75.00	45.00
(23)	Charles Grimm	75.00	35.00	20.00
(24)	Fred Haney	75.00	35.00	20.00
(25)	Wm. Hargrave	75.00	35.00	20.00
(26)	George Harper	75.00	35.00	20.00
(27)	Leo Hartnett	150.00	75.00	45.00
(28)	Clifton Heathcote	75.00	35.00	20.00
(29)	Harry Heilman (Heillmann)	150.00	75.00	45.00
(30)	Walter Henline	75.00	35.00	20.00
(31)	Andrew High	75.00	35.00	20.00
(32)	Rogers Hornsby	250.00	125.00	75.00
(33)	Wm. Hunnefield (Photo actually Tommy Thomas.)	75.00	35.00	20.00
(34)	Walter Johnson	650.00	325.00	195.00
(35)	Willie Kamm	75.00	35.00	20.00
(36)	Ray Kremer	75.00	35.00	20.00
(37)	Anthony Lazzeri	150.00	75.00	45.00
(38)	Fredrick Lindstrom (Frederick)	150.00	75.00	45.00
(39)	Walter Lutzke	75.00	35.00	20.00
(40)	John "Stuffy" McInnes (McInnis)	75.00	35.00	20.00
(41)	John Mokan	75.00	35.00	20.00
(42)	Robert W. Muesel (Meusel)	75.00	35.00	20.00
(43)	Glenn Myatt	75.00	35.00	20.00
(44)	Bernie Neis	75.00	35.00	20.00
(45)	Robert O'Farrell	75.00	35.00	20.00
(46)	Walter C. Pipp	100.00	50.00	30.00
(47)	Eppa Rixey	150.00	75.00	45.00
(48)	Harold Ruel (Herold)	75.00	35.00	20.00
(49)	Geo. H. "Babe" Ruth	8,000	4,000	2,400
(50)	Ray Schalk	150.00	75.00	45.00
(51)	George Sissler (Sisler)	150.00	75.00	45.00
(52)	Earl Smith	75.00	35.00	20.00
(53)	Wm. H. Southworth	75.00	35.00	20.00
(54)	Tristam Speaker (Tristram)	250.00	125.00	75.00
(55)	J. Taylor	75.00	35.00	20.00
(56)	Philip Todt	75.00	35.00	20.00
(57)	Harold Traynor	150.00	75.00	45.00
(58)	William Wambsganns (Wambsganss)	75.00	35.00	20.00
(59)	Zach Wheat	150.00	75.00	45.00
(60)	Kenneth Williams	75.00	35.00	20.00
(61)	Ernest Wingard	75.00	35.00	20.00
(62)	Fred Wingfield	75.00	35.00	20.00
(63)	Ivy Wingo	75.00	35.00	20.00
(64)	Russell Wrightstone	75.00	35.00	20.00

1928 Exhibits

The Exhibit Supply Co. switched to a blue tint for the photos in its 64-card set in 1928. There are 36 new photos in the set, including 24 new players. Four players from the previous year are shown with new teams and 24 of the cards are identical to the 1927 series, except for the color of the card. They are blank backed, or found with a purple printed or stamped corner coupon on the back. The photos are captioned in the same style as the 1927 set. The set again includes some misspelling and incorrect labels. The cards are unnumbered and are listed here in alphabetical order.

		NM	E	VG
Complete Set (64):		12,000	6,000	3,600
Common Player:		100.00	50.00	30.00
(1)	Grover C. Alexander	500.00	250.00	150.00
(2)	David Bancroft	250.00	125.00	75.00
(3)	Virgil Barnes	100.00	50.00	30.00
(4)	Francis R. Blades	100.00	50.00	30.00
(5)	L.A. Blue	100.00	50.00	30.00
(6)	Edward W. Brown	100.00	50.00	30.00
(7)	Max G. Carey	250.00	125.00	75.00
(8)	Chalmer W. Cissell	100.00	50.00	30.00
(9)	Gordon S. Cochrane	250.00	125.00	75.00
(10)	Pat Collins	100.00	50.00	30.00
(11)	Hugh M. Critz	100.00	50.00	30.00
(12)	Howard Ehmke	100.00	50.00	30.00
(13)	E. English	100.00	50.00	30.00
(14)	Bib Falk (Bibb)	100.00	50.00	30.00
(15)	Ira Flagstead	100.00	50.00	30.00
(16)	Robert Fothergill	100.00	50.00	30.00
(17)	Frank Frisch	250.00	125.00	75.00
(18)	Lou Gehrig	2,000	1,000	600.00
(19)	Leon Goslin	250.00	125.00	75.00
(20)	Eugene Hargrave	100.00	50.00	30.00
(21)	Charles R. Hargraves (Hargreaves)	100.00	50.00	30.00
(22)	Stanley Harris	250.00	125.00	75.00
(23)	Bryan "Slim" Harriss	100.00	50.00	30.00
(24)	Leo Hartnett	250.00	125.00	75.00
(25)	Joseph Hauser	100.00	50.00	30.00
(26)	Fred Hoffman (Hofmann)	100.00	50.00	30.00
(27)	J. Francis Hogan	100.00	50.00	30.00
(28)	Rogers Hornsby	360.00	180.00	120.00
(29)	Chas. Jamieson	100.00	50.00	30.00
(30)	Sam Jones	100.00	50.00	30.00
(31)	Ray Kremer	100.00	50.00	30.00
(32)	Fred Leach	100.00	50.00	30.00
(33)	Fredrick Lindstrom (Frederick)	250.00	125.00	75.00
(34)	Adolph Luque (Adolfo)	120.00	60.00	40.00
(35)	Theodore Lyons	250.00	125.00	75.00
(36)	Harry McCurdy	100.00	50.00	30.00
(37)	Glenn Myatt	100.00	50.00	30.00
(38)	John Ogden (Photo actually Warren Ogden.)	100.00	50.00	30.00
(39)	James Ring	100.00	50.00	30.00
(40)	A.C. Root (Should be C.H.)	100.00	50.00	30.00
(41)	Edd. Roush	250.00	125.00	75.00
(42)	Harold Ruel (Herold)	100.00	50.00	30.00
(43)	Geo. H. "Babe" Ruth	2,500	1,250	750.00
(44)	Henry Sand	100.00	50.00	30.00
(45)	Fred Schulte	100.00	50.00	30.00
(46)	Joseph Sewell	250.00	125.00	75.00
(47)	Walter Shang (Schang)	100.00	50.00	30.00
(48)	Urban J. Shocker	100.00	50.00	30.00
(49)	Al. Simmons	250.00	125.00	75.00
(50)	Earl Smith	100.00	50.00	30.00
(51)	Robert Smith	100.00	50.00	30.00
(52)	Jack Tavener	100.00	50.00	30.00
(53)	J. Taylor	100.00	50.00	30.00
(54)	Philip Todt	100.00	50.00	30.00
(55)	Geo. Uhle	100.00	50.00	30.00
(56)	Arthur "Dazzy" Vance	250.00	125.00	75.00
(57)	Paul Waner	250.00	125.00	75.00
(58)	Earl G. Whitehill (Middle intial actually O.)	100.00	50.00	30.00
(59)	Fred Williams	100.00	50.00	30.00
(60)	James Wilson	100.00	50.00	30.00
(61)	L.R. (Hack) Wilson	250.00	125.00	75.00
(62)	Lawrence Woodall	100.00	50.00	30.00
(63)	Glen Wright (Glenn)	100.00	50.00	30.00
(64)	William A. Zitzman (Zitzmann)	100.00	50.00	30.00

1929-30 Four-on-One Exhibits

Although the size of the card remained the same, the Exhibit Supply Co. of Chicago began putting four players' pictures on each card in 1929 - a practice that would continue for the next decade. Known as "four-on-one" cards, the players are identified by name and team at the bottom of the photos, which are separated by borders. The 32 cards in the 1929-30 series have postcard backs and were printed in a wide range of color combinations of black, brown and blue ink on blue, orange, green, red, white, and yellow backgrounds. Most of the backs are uncolored, however, cards with a black on red front have been seen with red backs, and cards with blue on yellow fronts have been seen with yellow backs. There are numerous spelling and caption errors in the set, and the player identified as Babe Herman is actually Jesse Petty.

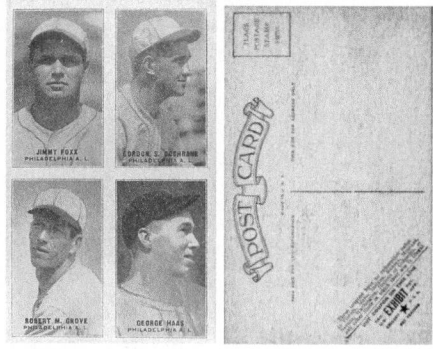

		NM	E	VG
Complete Set (32):		7,500	3,700	2,200
Common Card:		65.00	32.00	20.00
(1)	Earl J. Adams, R. Bartell, Earl Sheely, Harold Traynor	150.00	75.00	45.00
(2)	Dale Alexander, C. Gehringer, G.F. McManus (Should be M.J.), H.F. Rice	150.00	75.00	45.00
(3)	Grover C. Alexander, James Bottomly (Bottomley), Frank Frisch, James Wilson	250.00	125.00	75.00
(4)	Martin G. Autrey (Autry), Alex Metzler, Carl Reynolds, Alphonse Thomas	65.00	32.50	20.00
(5)	Earl Averill, B.A. Falk, K. Holloway, L. Sewell	150.00	75.00	45.00
(6)	David Bancroft, Del L. Bisonette (Bissonette), John H. DeBerry, Floyd C. Herman (Photo actually Jesse Petty.)	150.00	75.00	45.00
(7)	C.E. Beck, Leo Hartnett, Rogers Hornsby, L.R. (Hack) Wilson	200.00	100.00	60.00
(8)	Ray Benge, Lester L. Sweetland, A.C. Whitney, Cy. Williams	65.00	32.50	20.00
(9)	Benny Bengough, Earl B. Coombs (Combs), Waite Hoyt, Anthony Lazzeri	200.00	100.00	60.00
(10)	L. Benton, Melvin Ott, Andrew Reese, William Terry	150.00	75.00	45.00
(11)	Max Bishop, James Dykes, Samuel Hale, Homer Summa	65.00	32.50	20.00
(12)	L.A. Blue, O. Melillo, F.O. Rourke (Frank O'Rourke), F. Schulte	65.00	32.50	20.00
(13)	Oswald Bluege, Leon Goslin, Joseph Judge, Harold Ruel (Herold)	150.00	75.00	45.00
(14)	Chalmer W. Cissell, John W. Clancy, Willie Kamm, John L. Kerr (Kerr's middle initial actually "F.")	65.00	32.50	20.00
(15)	Gordon S. Cochrane, Jimmy Foxx, Robert M. Grove, George Haas	250.00	125.00	75.00
(16)	Pat Collins, Joe Dugan, Edward Farrel (Farrell), George Sisler	150.00	75.00	45.00
(17)	H.M. Critz, G.L. Kelly, V.J. Picinich, W.C. Walker	150.00	75.00	45.00
(18)	Nick Cullop, D'Arcy Flowers, Harvey Hendrick, Arthur "Dazzy" Vance	150.00	75.00	45.00
(19)	Hazen Cuyler, E. English, C.J. Grimm, C.H. Root	150.00	75.00	45.00
(20)	Taylor Douthit, Chas. M. Gilbert (Gelbert), Chas. J. Hafey, Fred G. Haney	150.00	75.00	45.00
(21)	Leo Durocher, Henry L. Gehrig, Mark Koenig, Geo. H. "Babe" Ruth	1,400	700.00	400.00
(22)	L.A. Fonseca, Carl Lind, J. Sewell, J. Tavener	150.00	75.00	45.00
(23)	H.E. Ford, C.F. Lucas, C.A. Pittenger, E.V. Purdy	65.00	32.50	20.00
(24)	Bernard Friberg, Donald Hurst, Frank O'Doul, Fresco Thompson	65.00	32.50	20.00
(25)	S. Gray, R. Kress, H. Manush, W.H. Shang (Schang)	150.00	75.00	45.00
(26)	Charles R. Hargreaves, Ray Kremer, Lloyd Waner, Paul Waner	150.00	75.00	45.00
(27)	George Harper, Fred Maguire, Lance Richbourg, Robert Smith	65.00	32.50	20.00
(28)	Jack Hayes, Sam P. Jones, Chas. M. Myer, Sam Rice	150.00	75.00	45.00
(29)	Harry E. Heilman (Heilmann), C.N. Richardson, M.J. Shea, G.E. Uhle	150.00	75.00	45.00
(30)	J.A. Heving, R.R. Reeves (Should be R.E.), J. Rothrock, C.H. Ruffing	150.00	75.00	45.00
(31)	J.F. Hogan, T.C. Jackson, Fred Lindstrom, J.D. Welsh	150.00	75.00	45.00
(32)	W.W. Regan, H. Rhyne, D. Taitt, P.J. Todt	65.00	32.50	20.00

1929 Exhibit "Star Picture Stamps"

This series of movie star Exhibit cards includes pictures of other celebrities who were featured in contemporary movies. Produced by Exhibit Supply Co. of Chicago, whose advertising appears on the postcard-style back, the 5-3/8" x 3-3/8" card has a variety of colors on the front which pictures the stars in the format of eight "Star Pictures Stamps." On this card, Ruth is pictured in the uniform he wore in the 1927 film "The Babe Comes Home."

	NM	E	VG
Babe Ruth (W/Tom Mix, Charles Lindbergh, Charlie Chaplin, Jack Dempsey, Harold Lloyd, Douglas Fairbanks and Al Jolson.)	750.00	375.00	225.00

1931-32 Babe Ruth Exhibit

The rarest Exhibit card to feature Babe Ruth, this circa 1931 issue has a photographic portrait of him in dress clothes, and is part of a 32-card movie stars series. Found in black-and-white or various color tints, this approximately 3-1/2" x 5-1/2" card has a facsimile autograph in white on front. It can be found with either a postcard-style back or a back offering premium merchandise.

	NM	E	VG
Babe Ruth	3,500	1,750	1,050

1931-32 Four-on-One Exhibits

The 1931-1932 series issued by the Exhibit Co. again consisted of 32 cards, each picturing four players. The series can be differentiated from the previous year by the coupon backs, which list various premiums available (including kazoos, toy pistols and other prizes). The cards again were printed in various color combinations, including; black on green, blue on green, black on orange, black on red, blue on white and black on yellow. There are numerous spelling and caption errors in the series. The Babe Herman/Jesse Petty error of the previous year was still not corrected, and the card of Rick Ferell not only misspells his name ("Farrel"), but also pictures the wrong player (Edward Farrell).

		NM	E	VG
Complete Set (32):		7,500	3,700	2,200
Common Card:		90.00	45.00	27.00
(1)	Earl J. Adams, James Bottomly (Bottomley), Frank Frisch, James Wilson	150.00	75.00	45.00
(2)	Dale Alexander, C. Gehringer, G.F. McManus (Should be M.J.), G.E. Uhle	150.00	75.00	45.00
(3)	L.L. Appling (Should be L.B.), Chalmer W. Cissell, Willie Kamm, Ted Lyons	150.00	75.00	45.00
(4)	Buzz Arlett, Ray Benge, Chuck Klein, A.C. Whitney	150.00	75.00	45.00
(5)	Earl Averill, B.A. Falk, L.A. Fonseca, L. Sewell	150.00	75.00	45.00
(6)	Richard Bartell, Bernard Friberg, Donald Hurst, Harry McCurdy	90.00	45.00	27.00
(7)	Walter Berger, Fred Maguire, Lance Richbourg, Earl Sheely	90.00	45.00	27.00
(8)	Chas. Berry, Robt. Reeves, R.R. Reeves (Should be R.E.), J. Rothrock	90.00	45.00	27.00
(9)	Del L. Bisonette (Bissonette), Floyd C. Herman (Photo - J. Petty, Jack Quinn, Glenn Wright)	90.00	45.00	27.00
(10)	L.A. Blue, Smead Jolley, Carl Reynolds, Henry Tate	90.00	45.00	27.00
(11)	O. Bluege, Joe Judge, Chas. M. Myer, Sam Rice	150.00	75.00	45.00
(12)	John Boley, James Dykes, E.J. Miller, Al. Simmons	150.00	75.00	45.00
(13)	Gordon S. Cochrane, Jimmy Foxx, Robert M. Grove, George Haas	450.00	220.00	135.00
(14)	Adam Comorosky, Gus Suhr, T.J. Thevenow, Harold Traynor	150.00	75.00	45.00
(15)	Earl B. Coombs (Combs), W. Dickey, Anthony Lazzeri, H. Pennock	225.00	110.00	65.00
(16)	H.M. Critz, J.F. Hogan, T.C. Jackson, Fred Lindstrom	150.00	75.00	45.00
(17)	Joe Cronin, H. Manush, F. Marberry, Roy Spencer	150.00	75.00	45.00
(18)	Nick Cullop, Les Durocher (Leo), Harry Heilmann, W.C. Walker	150.00	75.00	45.00
(19)	Hazen Cuyler, E. English, C.J. Grimm, C.H. Root	150.00	75.00	45.00
(20)	Taylor Douthit, Chas. M. Gilbert (Gelbert), Chas. J. Hafey, Bill Hallahan	90.00	45.00	27.00

(21) Richard Farrel (Ferrell), S. Gray, R. Kress, W. Stewart (Photo actually Ed Farrell.) 90.00 45.00 27.00
(22) W. Ferrell, J. Goldman, Hunnefield, Ed Morgan 125.00 62.50 37.50
(23) Fred Fitzsimmons, Robert O'Farrell, Melvin Ott, William Terry 150.00 75.00 45.00
(24) D'Arcy Flowers, Frank O'Doul, Fresco Thompson, Arthur "Dazzy" Vance 150.00 75.00 45.00
(25) H.E. Ford (Should be H.H.), Gooch, C.F. Lucas, W. Roettger 90.00 45.00 27.00
(26) E. Funk, W. Hoyt, Mark Koenig, Wallie Schang 90.00 45.00 27.00
(27) Henry L. Gehrig, Lyn Lary, James Reese (Photo actually Andy Reese.), Geo. H. "Babe" Ruth 2,200 1,100 650.00
(28) George Grantham, Ray Kremer, Lloyd Waner, Paul Waner 150.00 75.00 45.00
(29) Leon Goslin, O. Melillo, F.O. Rourke (Frank O'Rourke), F. Schulte 150.00 75.00 45.00
(30) Leo Hartnett, Rogers Hornsby, J.R. Stevenson (Stephenson), L.R. (Hack) Wilson 200.00 100.00 60.00
(31) D. MacFayden, H. Rhyne, Bill Sweeney, E.W. Webb 90.00 45.00 27.00
(32) Walter Maranville, Randolph Moore, Alfred Spohrer, J.T. Zachary 150.00 75.00 45.00

1933 Four-on-One Exhibits

The 1933 series of four-on-one Exhibits consists of 16 cards with blank backs. Color combinations include: blue on green, black on orange, black on red, blue on white and black on yellow. Most have a plain, white back, although the black on yellow cards are also found with a yellow back. Most of the pictures used are reprinted from previous series, and there are some spelling and caption errors, including the Richard Ferrell/Edward Farrel mixup from the previous year. Al Lopez is shown as "Vincent" Lopez.

	NM	E	VG
Complete Set (16):	6,000	3,000	1,800
Common Card:	85.00	40.00	25.00

(1) Earl J. Adams, Frank Frisch, Chas. Gilbert (Gelbert), Bill Hallahan 150.00 75.00 45.00
(2) Earl Averill, W. Ferrell, Ed Morgan, L. Sewell 150.00 75.00 45.00
(3) Richard Bartell, Ray Benge, Donald Hurst, Chuck Klein 150.00 75.00 45.00
(4) Walter Berger, Walter Maranville, Alfred Spohrer, J.T. Zachary 150.00 75.00 45.00
(5) Charles Berry, L.A. Blue, Ted Lyons, Bob Seeds 150.00 75.00 45.00
(6) Chas. Berry, D. MacFayden, H. Rhyne, E.W. Webb 85.00 40.00 25.00
(7) Mickey Cochrane, Jimmy Foxx, Robert M. Grove, Al. Simmons 450.00 225.00 135.00
(8) H.M. Critz, Fred Fitzsimmons, Fred Lindstrom, Robert O'Farrell 150.00 75.00 45.00
(9) W. Dickey, Anthony Lazzeri, H. Pennock, George H. "Babe" Ruth 2,250 1,125 675.00

(10) Taylor Douthit, George Grantham, Chas. J. Hafey, C.F. Lucas 150.00 75.00 45.00
(11) E. English, C.J. Grimm, C.H. Root, J.R. Stevenson (Stephenson) 85.00 40.00 25.00
(12) Richard Farrel (Farrell), Leon Goslin, S. Gray, O. Melillo (photo actually Ed Farrell) 150.00 75.00 45.00
(13) C. Gehringer, "Muddy" Ruel, Jonathan Stone (first name - John, G.E. Uhle 150.00 75.00 45.00
(14) Joseph Judge, H. Manush, F. Marberry, Roy Spencer 150.00 75.00 45.00
(15) Vincent Lopez (Al), Frank O'Doul, Arthur "Dazzy" Vance, Glenn Wright 150.00 75.00 45.00
(16) Gus Suhr, Tom J. Thevenow, Lloyd Waner, Paul Waner 150.00 75.00 45.00

1934 Four-on-One Exhibits

This 16-card series issued by the Exhibit Co. in 1934 is again blank-backed and continues the four-on-one format in a 3-3/8" x 5-3/8" size. The 1934 series can be differentiated from previous years by the more subdued colors of the cards, which include lighter shades of blue, brown, green and violet - all printed on white card stock. Many new photos were also used in the 1934 series. Of the 64 players included, 25 appear for the first time and another 16 were given new poses. Spelling was improved, but Al Lopez is still identified as "Vincent."

	NM	E	VG
Complete Set (16):	3,300	1,650	1,000
Common Card:	100.00	50.00	30.00

(1) Luke Appling, George Earnshaw, Al Simmons, Evar Swanson 150.00 75.00 45.00
(2) Earl Averill, W. Ferrell, Willie Kamm, Frank Pytlak 150.00 75.00 45.00
(3) Richard Bartell, Donald Hurst, Wesley Schulmerich, Jimmy Wilson 100.00 50.00 30.00
(4) Walter Berger, Ed Brandt, Frank Hogan, Bill Urbanski 100.00 50.00 30.00
(5) Jim Bottomley, Chas. J. Hafey, Botchi Lombardi, Tony Piet 150.00 75.00 45.00
(6) Irving Burns, Irving Hadley, Rollie Hemsley, O. Melillo 100.00 50.00 30.00
(7) Bill Cissell, Rick Ferrell, Lefty Grove, Roy Johnson 150.00 75.00 45.00
(8) Mickey Cochrane, C. Gehringer, Goose Goslin, Fred Marberry 150.00 75.00 45.00
(9) George Cramer (Roger), Jimmy Foxx, Frank Higgins, Slug Mahaffey 180.00 90.00 55.00
(10) Joe Cronin, Alvin Crowder, Joe Kuhel, H. Manush 150.00 75.00 45.00
(11) W. Dickey, Lou Gehrig, Vernon Gomez, Geo. H. "Babe" Ruth 1,700 850.00 500.00
(12) E. English, C.J. Grimm, Chas. Klein, Lon Warneke 150.00 75.00 45.00

(13) Frank Frisch, Bill Hallahan, Pepper Martin, John Rothrock 150.00 75.00 45.00
(14) Carl Hubbell, Mel Ott, Blondy Ryan, Bill Terry 180.00 90.00 55.00
(15) Leonard Koenecke, Sam Leslie, Vincent Lopez (Al), Glenn Wright 150.00 75.00 45.00
(16) T.J. Thevenow, Pie Traynor, Lloyd Waner, Paul Waner 150.00 75.00 45.00

1935 Four-on-One Exhibits

Continuing with the same four-on-one format, the Exhibit Supply Co. issued another 16-card series in 1935. All cards were printed in a slate-blue color with a blank back. Seventeen of the players included in the 1935 series appear for the first time. While another 11 are shown with new poses. There are several spelling and caption errors. Babe Ruth appears in a regular Exhibit issue for the last time.

	NM	E	VG
Complete Set (16):	5,000	2,500	1,500
Common Card:	75.00	35.00	20.00

(1) Earl Averill, Mel Harder, Willie Kamm, Hal Trosky 125.00 60.00 35.00
(2) Walter Berger, Ed Brandt, Frank Hogan, "Babe" Ruth 2,000 1,000 600.00
(3) Henry Bonura, Jimmy Dykes, Ted Lyons, Al Simmons 125.00 60.00 35.00
(4) Jimmy Bottomley, Paul Derringer, Chas. J. Hafey, Botchi Lombardi 125.00 60.00 35.00
(5) Irving Burns, Rollie Hemsley, O. Melillo, L.N. Newson 75.00 35.00 20.00
(6) Guy Bush, Pie Traynor, Floyd Vaughn (Vaughan), Paul Waner 125.00 60.00 35.00
(7) Mickey Cochrane, C. Gehringer, Goose Goslin, Linwood Rowe (Lynwood) 125.00 60.00 35.00
(8) Phil Collins, John "Blondy" Ryan, Geo. Watkins, Jimmy Wilson 75.00 35.00 20.00
(9) George Cramer (Roger), Jimmy Foxx, Bob Johnson, Slug Mahaffey 150.00 75.00 45.00
(10) Hughie Critz, Carl Hubbell, Mel Ott, Bill Terry 150.00 75.00 45.00
(11) Joe Cronin, Rick Ferrell, Lefty Grove, Billy Werber 145.00 70.00 40.00
(12) Tony Cuccinello, Vincent Lopez (Al), Van Mungo, Dan Taylor (photo actually George Puccinelli) 125.00 60.00 35.00
(13) Jerome "Dizzy" Dean, Paul Dean, Frank Frisch, Pepper Martin 325.00 160.00 95.00
(14) W. Dickey, Lou Gehrig, Vernon Gomez, Tony Lazzeri 900.00 450.00 275.00
(15) C.J. Grimm, Gabby Hartnett, Chas. Klein, Lon Warneke 125.00 60.00 35.00
(16) H. Manush, Buddy Meyer (Myer), Fred Schulte, Earl Whitehill 125.00 60.00 35.00

1936 Four-on-One Exhibits

The 1936 series of four-on-one cards again consisted of 16 cards in either green or slate blue with plain, blank backs. The series can be differentiated from the previous year's Exhibit cards by the line "PTD. IN U.S.A." at the bottom. Of the 64 players pictured, 16 appear for the first time and another nine are shown in new poses. The series is again marred by several spelling and caption errors.

	NM	E	VG
Complete Set (16):	3,000	1,500	900.00
Common Card:	80.00	40.00	25.00
(1) Paul Andrews, Harland Clift (Harlond), Rollie Hemsley, Sammy West	80.00	40.00	25.00
(2) Luke Appling, Henry Bonura, Jimmy Dykes, Ted Lyons	100.00	50.00	30.00
(3) Earl Averill, Mel Harder, Hal Trosky, Joe Vosmik	100.00	50.00	30.00
(4) Walter Berger, Danny MacFayden, Bill Urbanski, Pinky Whitney	80.00	40.00	25.00
(5) Charles Berry, Frank Higgins, Bob Johnson, Puccinelli	80.00	40.00	25.00
(6) Ossie Bluege, Buddy Meyer (Myer), L.N. Newsom, Earl Whitehill	80.00	40.00	25.00
(7) Stan. Bordagaray, Dutch Brandt, Fred Lindstrom, Van Mungo	100.00	50.00	30.00
(8) Guy Bush, Pie Traynor, Floyd Vaughn (Vaughan), Paul Waner	100.00	50.00	30.00
(9) Dolph Camilli, Curt Davis, Johnny Moore, Jimmy Wilson	80.00	40.00	25.00
(10) Mickey Cochrane, C. Gehringer, Goose Goslin, Linwood Rowe (Lynwood)	100.00	50.00	30.00
(11) Joe Cronin, Rick Ferrell, Jimmy Foxx, Lefty Grove	175.00	85.00	50.00
(12) Jerome "Dizzy" Dean, Paul Dean, Frank Frisch, Joe "Ducky" Medwick	300.00	150.00	90.00
(13) Paul Derringer, Babe Herman, Alex Kampouris, Botchi Lombardi	100.00	50.00	30.00
(14) Augie Galan, Gabby Hartnett, Billy Herman, Lon Warneke	100.00	50.00	30.00
(15) Lou Gehrig, Vernon Gomez, Tony Lazzeri, Red Ruffing	1,300	650.00	390.00
(16) Carl Hubbell, Gus Mancuso, Mel Ott, Bill Terry	125.00	60.00	35.00

1937 Four-on-One Exhibits

The 1937 four-on-one Exhibit cards were printed in either green or bright blue. The backs are again blank. The 1937 cards are difficult to distinguish from the 1936 series, because both contain the "PTD. IN U.S.A." line along the bottom. Of the 64 photos, 47 are re-issues from previous series.

	NM	E	VG
Complete Set (16):	2,750	1,350	825.00
Common Card:	125.00	65.00	40.00
(1) Earl Averill, Bob Feller, Frank Pytlak, Hal Trosky	300.00	150.00	90.00
(2) Luke Appling, Henry Bonura, Jimmy Dykes, Vernon Kennedy	250.00	125.00	70.00
(3) Walter Berger, Alfonso Lopez, Danny MacFayden, Bill Urbanski	250.00	125.00	75.00
(4) Cy Blanton, Gus Suhr, Floyd Vaughn (Vaughan), Paul Waner	250.00	125.00	75.00
(5) Dolph Camilli, Johnny Moore, Wm. Walters, Pinky Whitney	125.00	65.00	40.00
(6) Harland Clift (Harlond), Rollie Hemsley, Orval Hildebrand (Oral), Sammy West	25.00	65.00	40.00
(7) Mickey Cochrane, C. Gehringer, Goose Goslin, Linwood Rowe (Lynwood)	250.00	125.00	75.00
(8) Joe Cronin, Rick Ferrell, Jimmy Foxx, Lefty Grove	300.00	150.00	90.00
(9) Jerome "Dizzy" Dean, Stuart Martin, Joe "Ducky" Medwick, Lon Warneke	350.00	175.00	100.00
(10) Paul Derringer, Botchi Lombardi, Lew Riggs, Phil Weintraub	250.00	125.00	75.00
(11) Joe DiMaggio, Lou Gehrig, Vernon Gomez, Tony Lazzeri	2,700	1,350	800.00
(12) E. English, Johnny Moore, Van Mungo, Gordon Phelps	125.00	65.00	40.00
(13) Augie Galan, Gabby Hartnett, Billy Herman, Bill Lee	250.00	125.00	75.00
(14) Carl Hubbell, Sam Leslie, Gus. Mancuso, Mel Ott	250.00	125.00	75.00
(15) Bob Johnson, Harry Kelly (Kelley), Wallace Moses, Billy Weber (Werber)	125.00	65.00	40.00
(16) Joe Kuhel, Buddy Meyer (Myer), L.N. Newsom, Jonathan Stone (First name actually John.)	125.00	65.00	40.00

1938 Four-on-One Exhibits

The Exhibit Co. used its four-on-one format for the final time in 1938, issuing another 16-card series. The cards feature brown printing on white stock with the line "MADE IN U.S.A." appearing along the bottom. The backs are blank. Twelve players appeared for the first time and three others are shown in new poses. Again, there are several spelling and caption mistakes.

	NM	E	VG
Complete Set (16):	5,000	2,500	1,500
Common Card:	125.00	65.00	40.00
(1) Luke Appling, Mike Kreevich, Ted Lyons, L. Sewell	200.00	100.00	60.00
(2) Morris Arnovich, Chas. Klein, Wm. Walters, Pinky Whitney	125.00	65.00	40.00
(3) Earl Averill, Bob Feller, Odell Hale, Hal Trosky	250.00	125.00	75.00
(4) Beau Bell, Harland Clift (Harlond), L.N. Newsom, Sammy West	125.00	64.00	40.00
(5) Cy Blanton, Gus Suhr, Floyd Vaughn (Vaughan), Paul Waner	200.00	100.00	60.00
(6) Tom Bridges, C. Gehringer, Hank Greenberg, Rudy York	200.00	100.00	60.00
(7) Dolph Camilli, Leo Durocher, Van Mungo, Gordon Phelps	200.00	100.00	60.00
(8) Joe Cronin, Jimmy Foxx, Lefty Grove, Joe Vosmik	250.00	125.00	75.00
(9) Tony Cuccinello, Vince DiMaggio, Roy Johnson, Danny MacFayden (Photo actually George Puccinelli.)	140.00	70.00	40.00
(10) Jerome "Dizzy" Dean, Augie Galan, Gabby Hartnett, Billy Herman	300.00	150.00	90.00
(11) Paul Derringer, Ival Goodman, Botchi Lombardi, Lew Riggs	200.00	100.00	60.00
(12) W. Dickey, Joe DiMaggio, Lou Gehrig, Vernon Gomez	2,000	1,000	600.00
(13) Rick Ferrell, W. Ferrell, Buddy Meyer (Myer), Jonathan Stone (First name actually John.)	200.00	100.00	60.00
(14) Carl Hubbell, Hank Leiber, Mel Ott, Jim Ripple	200.00	100.00	60.00
(15) Bob Johnson, Harry Kelly (Kelley), Wallace Moses, Billy Weber (Werber)	125.00	65.00	40.00
(16) Stuart Martin, Joe "Ducky" Medwick, Johnny Mize, Lon Warneke	200.00	100.00	60.00

1939-46 Salutation Exhibits

Referred to as "Exhibits" because they were issued by the Exhibit Supply Co. of Chicago, Ill., the bulk of this group was produced over an eight-year span, though production and sale of some players' cards continued well into the period of the 1947-66 Exhibits. These cards are frequently called "Salutations" because of the personalized greeting found on the card. The black-and-white cards, which measure 3-3/8" x 5-3/8", are unnumbered and blank-backed. Most Exhibits were sold through vending machines for a penny. The complete set price includes all variations.

		NM	E	VG
	Complete Set (83):	6,500	3,250	1,950
	Common Player:	15.00	7.50	4.50
(1)	Luke Appling ("Made In U.S.A." in left corner.)	20.00	10.00	6.00
(2)	Luke Appling ("Made In U.S.A." in right corner.)	45.00	22.50	13.50
(3)	Earl Averill	400.00	200.00	120.00
(4)	Charles "Red" Barrett	20.00	10.00	6.00
(5)	Henry "Hank" Borowy	15.00	7.50	4.50
(6)	Lou Boudreau (Large projection, small projection. Look at the feet and bat top.)	25.00	12.50	7.50
(7)	Adolf Camilli	30.00	15.00	9.00
(8)	Phil Cavarretta	15.00	7.50	4.50
(9)	Harland Clift (Harlond)	20.00	10.00	6.00
(10)	Tony Cuccinello	50.00	30.00	20.00
(11)	Dizzy Dean	140.00	70.00	45.00
(12)	Paul Derringer	20.00	10.00	6.00
(13)	Bill Dickey ("Made In U.S.A." in left corner.)	35.00	17.50	10.00
(14)	Bill Dickey ("Made In U.S.A." in right corner.)	55.00	27.50	16.50
(15)	Joe DiMaggio (Issued into the 1950s.)	150.00	75.00	45.00
(16)	Bob Elliott	15.00	7.50	4.50
(17)	Bob Feller (Portrait)	120.00	60.00	35.00
(18)	Bob Feller (Pitching)	50.00	25.00	15.00
(19)	Dave Ferriss	45.00	22.50	13.50
(20)	Jimmy Foxx	75.00	37.50	22.50
(21)	Lou Gehrig	1,750	875.00	525.00
(22)	Charlie Gehringer	150.00	100.00	50.00
(23)	Vernon Gomez	300.00	150.00	100.00
(24)	Joe Gordon (Cleveland)	40.00	20.00	12.00
(25)	Joe Gordon (New York)	25.00	12.50	7.50
(26)	Hank Greenberg (Truly yours.)	75.00	37.00	22.00
(27)	Hank Greenberg (Very truly yours.)	160.00	80.00	50.00
(28)	Robert Grove	50.00	25.00	15.00
(29)	Gabby Hartnett	350.00	225.00	150.00
(30)	Buddy Hassett	20.00	10.00	6.00
(31)	Jeff Heath (Large projection.)	25.00	12.50	7.50
(32)	Jeff Heath (Small projection.)	25.00	12.50	7.50
(33)	Kirby Higbe	20.00	10.00	6.00
(34)	Tommy Holmes (Yours truly: with and without "An Exhibit Card.")	15.00	7.50	4.50
(35)	Tommy Holmes (Sincerely yours.)	130.00	65.00	40.00
(36)	Carl Hubbell	40.00	20.00	12.00
(37)	Bob Johnson	40.00	20.00	12.00
(38)	Charles Keller ("MADE IN U.S.A." left corner.)	25.00	12.50	7.50
(39)	Charles Keller ("MADE IN U.S.A." right corner.)	15.00	7.50	4.50
(40)	Ken Keltner	25.00	12.50	7.50
(41)	Chuck Klein	350.00	225.00	150.00
(42)	Mike Kreevich	300.00	200.00	100.00
(43)	Joe Kuhel	20.00	10.00	6.00
(44)	Bill Lee	20.00	10.00	6.00
(45)	Ernie Lombardi (Cordially)	325.00	160.00	95.00
(46)	Ernie Lombardi (Cordially yours: Large projection, small projection. Look at the cropping on the lead foot.)	20.00	10.00	6.00
(47)	Martin Marion ("An Exhibit Card" in lower-left.)	20.00	10.00	6.00
(48)	Marty Marion (No "An Exhibit Card.")	20.00	10.00	6.00
(49)	Merrill May	25.00	12.50	7.50
(50)	Frank McCormick ("Made In U.S.A." in left corner.)	30.00	15.00	9.00
(51)	Frank McCormick ("Made In U.S.A." in right corner.)	15.00	7.50	4.50
(52)	George McQuinn ("Made In U.S.A." in left corner.)	20.00	10.00	6.00
(53)	George McQuinn ("Made In U.S.A." in right corner.)	15.00	7.50	4.50
(54)	Joe Medwick	55.00	27.50	16.50
(55)	Johnny Mize ("Made In U.S.A." in left corner.)	35.00	17.50	10.00
(56)	Johnny Mize ("Made In U.S.A." in right corner.)	20.00	10.00	6.00
(57)	Hugh Mulcahy	150.00	75.00	45.00
(58)	Hal Newhouser	30.00	15.00	9.00

(59)	Buck Newson (Newsom)	275.00	135.00	80.00
(60)	Louis (Buck) Newsom	15.00	7.50	4.50
(61)	Mel Ott ("Made In U.S.A." in left corner.)	40.00	20.00	12.00
(62)	Mel Ott ("Made In U.S.A." in right corner.)	25.00	12.50	7.50
(63)	Andy Pafko ("C" on cap.)	20.00	10.00	6.00
(64)	Andy Pafko (Plain cap.)	15.00	7.50	4.50
(65)	Claude Passeau	15.00	7.50	4.50
(66)	Howard Pollet ("Made In U.S.A." in left corner.)	20.00	10.00	6.00
(67)	Howard Pollet ("Made In U.S.A." in right corner.)	15.00	7.50	4.50
(68)	Pete Reiser ("Made In U.S.A." in left corner.)	45.00	22.50	13.50
(69)	Pete Reiser ("Made In U.S.A." in right corner.)	20.00	10.00	6.00
(70)	Johnny Rizzo	300.00	200.00	100.00
(71)	Glenn Russell	75.00	37.50	22.00
(72)	George Stirnweiss	20.00	10.00	6.00
(73)	Cecil Travis	45.00	20.00	12.50
(74)	Paul Trout	15.00	7.50	4.50
(75)	Johnny Vander Meer	65.00	32.50	20.00
(76)	Arky Vaughn (Vaughan)	50.00	25.00	15.00
(77)	Fred "Dixie" Walker ("D" on cap.)	20.00	10.00	6.00
(78)	Fred "Dixie" Walker ("D" blanked out.)	60.00	30.00	18.00
(79)	"Bucky" Walters	30.00	15.00	9.00
(80)	Lon Warneke	20.00	10.00	6.00
(81)	Ted Williams (#9 shows)	750.00	370.00	220.00
(82)	Ted Williams (#9 not showing: large projection, small projection. Look at the space from the bottom of the foot at the right side to the card bottom.)	100.00	50.00	30.00
(83)	Rudy York (large projection, small projection.)	20.00	10.00	6.00

1947-66 Exhibits

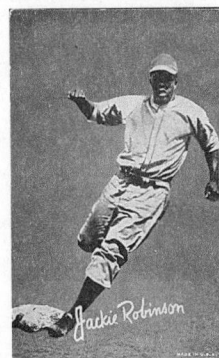

Produced by the Exhibit Supply Co. of Chicago, these issues cover a span of 20 years. Each unnumbered, black-and-white card is printed on heavy cardboard measuring 3-3/8" x 5-3/8" and is blank-backed. The company issued new sets each year, with many players being repeated year after year. Other players appeared in only one or two years, thereby creating levels of scarcity. Many cards can be found with minor variations in the wording and placement of the credit line at bottom. Some pieces have been found printed on a semi-gloss paper stock, perhaps as proofs. Their value is 50 percent or less than the issued version.

		NM	E	VG
	Common Player:	9.00	4.50	2.75
(1)	Hank Aaron	65.00	32.00	19.50
(2)	Joe Adcock (White signature.)	9.00	4.50	2.75
(3)	Joe Adcock (Black signature.)	10.00	5.00	3.00
(4)	Max Alvis	30.00	15.00	9.00
(5)	Johnny Antonelli (Braves)	9.00	4.50	2.75
(6)	Johnny Antonelli (Giants)	10.00	5.00	3.00
(7)	Luis Aparicio (Portrait)	12.00	6.00	3.50
(8)	Luis Aparicio (Batting)	17.50	8.75	5.25
(9)	Luke Appling (With and without "An Exhibit Card.")	20.00	10.00	6.00
(10)	Ritchie Ashburn (Phillies, first name incorrect. With and without "An Exhibit Card.")	12.00	6.00	3.50
(11)	Richie Ashburn (Phillies, first name correct.)	12.00	6.00	3.50

(12)	Richie Ashburn (Cubs)	17.50	8.75	5.25
(13)	Bob Aspromonte	9.00	4.50	2.75
(14)	Toby Atwell	9.00	4.50	2.75
(15)	Ed Bailey (With cap.)	10.00	5.00	3.00
(16)	Ed Bailey (No cap.)	9.00	4.50	2.75
(17)	Gene Baker	9.00	4.50	2.75
(18)	Ernie Banks (Bat on shoulder, script signature.)	55.00	27.50	16.50
(19)	Ernie Banks (Bat on shoulder, plain signature.)	17.50	8.75	5.25
(20)	Ernie Banks (Portrait)	30.00	15.00	9.00
(21)	Steve Barber	9.00	4.50	2.75
(22)	Earl Battey	10.00	5.00	3.00
(23)	Matt Batts	9.00	4.50	2.75
(24)	Hank Bauer (N.Y. cap.)	10.00	5.00	3.00
(25)	Hank Bauer (Plain cap.)	45.00	22.00	13.50
(26)	Frank Baumholtz	9.00	4.50	2.75
(27)	Gene Bearden (With and without "An Exhibit Card.")	9.00	4.50	2.75
(28)	Joe Beggs	15.00	7.50	4.50
(29)	Larry "Yogi" Berra	60.00	30.00	18.00
(30a)	Yogi Berra ("MADE IN U.S.A." lower-right.)	35.00	17.50	10.00
(30b)	Yogi Berra ("PRINTED IN U.S.A." lower-right. With and without "An Exhibit Card.")	35.00	17.50	10.00
(31)	Steve Bilko	10.00	5.00	3.00
(32)	Ewell Blackwell (Pitching)	10.00	5.00	3.00
(33)	Ewell Blackwell (Portrait)	9.00	4.50	2.75
(34)	Don Blasingame (St. Louis cap.)	9.00	4.50	2.75
(35)	Don Blasingame (Plain cap.)	17.50	8.75	5.25
(36)	Ken Boyer	12.00	6.00	3.50
(37)	Ralph Branca (With and without "An Exhibit Card.")	12.00	6.00	3.50
(38)	Jackie Brandt	40.00	20.00	12.00
(39)	Harry Brecheen	9.00	4.50	2.75
(40)	Tom Brewer	13.50	6.75	4.00
(41)	Lou Brissie	10.00	5.00	3.00
(42)	Bill Bruton	9.00	4.50	2.75
(43)	Lew Burdette (Pitching, side view.)	9.00	4.50	2.75
(44)	Lew Burdette (Pitching, front view.)	10.00	5.00	3.00
(45)	Johnny Callison	12.50	6.25	3.75
(46)	Roy Campanella	25.00	12.50	7.50
(47)	Chico Carrasquel (Portrait)	15.00	7.50	4.50
(48)	Chico Carrasquel (Leaping)	9.00	4.50	2.75
(49)	George Case	13.50	6.75	4.00
(50)	Hugh Casey	40.00	30.00	20.00
(51)	Norm Cash	12.00	6.00	3.50
(52)	Orlando Cepeda (Portrait)	15.00	7.50	4.50
(53)	Orlando Cepeda (Batting)	15.00	7.50	4.50
(54)	Bob Cerv (A's cap.)	12.00	6.00	3.50
(55)	Bob Cerv (Plain cap.)	20.00	10.00	6.00
(56)	Dean Chance	9.00	4.50	2.75
(57)	Spud Chandler	40.00	30.00	20.00
(58)	Tom Cheney	9.00	4.50	2.75
(59)	Bubba Church	10.00	5.00	3.00
(60)	Roberto Clemente	50.00	25.00	15.00
(61)	Rocky Colavito (Portrait)	35.00	17.50	10.00
(62)	Rocky Colavito (Batting)	25.00	12.50	7.50
(63)	Choo Choo Coleman	12.00	6.00	3.50
(64)	Gordy Coleman	35.00	17.50	10.50
(65)	Jerry Coleman	10.00	5.00	3.00
(66)	Mort Cooper	35.00	17.50	10.00
(67)	Walker Cooper (With and without "Made in USA")	9.00	4.50	2.75
(68)	Roger Craig	12.00	6.00	3.50
(69)	Delmar Crandall	9.00	4.50	2.75
(70)	Joe Cunningham (Batting)	40.00	20.00	12.00
(71)	Joe Cunningham (Portrait)	65.00	32.00	19.50
(72)	Guy Curtwright (Curtright)	10.00	5.00	3.00
(73)	Bud Daley	35.00	17.50	10.00
(74)	Alvin Dark (Braves)	125.00	62.50	37.50
(75)	Alvin Dark (Giants)	10.00	5.00	3.00
(76)	Alvin Dark (Cubs)	12.00	6.00	3.50
(77)	Murray Dickson (Murry)	25.00	12.50	7.50
(78)	Bob Dillinger (With and without "An Exhibit Card.")	12.00	6.00	3.50
(79)	Dom DiMaggio	25.00	12.50	7.50
(80)	Joe Dobson	25.00	15.00	10.00

No.	Player			
(81a)	Larry Doby (Three forms: Without "An Exhibit Card," with "An Exhibit Card," and with "An Exhibit Card" scratched out.)	40.00	20.00	12.00
(81b)	Larry Doby (Bat well off right border.)	25.00	12.50	7.50
(82a)	Bobby Doerr ("AN EXHIBIT CARD" lower-left.)	15.00	7.50	4.50
(82b)	Bobby Doerr (No "AN EXHIBIT CARD.")	15.00	7.50	4.50
(83)	Dick Donovan (Plain cap.)	12.00	6.00	3.50
(84)	Dick Donovan (Sox cap.)	9.00	4.50	2.75
(85)	Walter Dropo	9.00	4.50	2.75
(86)	Don Drysdale (Glove at waist.)	20.00	10.00	6.00
(87)	Don Drysdale (Portrait)	35.00	17.50	10.00
(88)	Luke Easter	15.00	7.50	4.50
(89)	Bruce Edwards	15.00	7.50	4.50
(90)	Del Ennis	15.00	7.50	4.50
(91)	Al Evans	15.00	7.50	4.50
(92)	Walter Evers	9.00	4.50	2.75
(93)	Ferris Fain (Fielding)	12.00	6.00	3.50
(94)	Ferris Fain (Portrait)	15.00	7.50	4.50
(95)	Dick Farrell	9.00	4.50	2.75
(96)	Ed "Whitey" Ford	30.00	15.00	9.00
(97)	Whitey Ford (Pitching)	30.00	15.00	9.00
(98)	Whitey Ford (Portrait)	175.00	85.00	50.00
(99)	Dick Fowler	12.50	6.25	3.75
(100)	Nelson Fox	25.00	12.50	7.50
(101)	Tito Francona	9.00	4.50	2.75
(102)	Bob Friend	9.00	4.50	2.75
(103)	Carl Furillo	25.00	12.50	7.50
(104)	Augie Galan	30.00	15.00	9.00
(105)	Jim Gentile	9.00	4.50	2.75
(106)	Tony Gonzalez	9.00	4.50	2.75
(107)	Billy Goodman (Leaping)	17.50	8.75	5.25
(108)	Billy Goodman (Batting)	12.00	6.00	3.50
(109)	Ted Greengrass (Jim)	9.00	4.50	2.75
(110)	Dick Groat	10.00	5.00	3.00
(111)	Steve Gromek	9.00	4.50	2.75
(112)	Johnny Groth	9.00	4.50	2.75
(113)	Orval Grove	15.00	7.50	4.50
(114)	Frank Gustine (Pirates uniform.)	20.00	10.00	6.00
(115)	Frank Gustine (Plain uniform.)	10.00	5.00	3.00
(116)	Berthold Haas	20.00	10.00	6.00
(117)	Grady Hatton	10.00	5.00	3.00
(118)	Jim Hegan	9.00	4.50	2.75
(119)	Tom Henrich	25.00	12.50	7.50
(120)	Ray Herbert	15.00	7.50	4.50
(121)	Gene Hermanski	10.00	5.00	3.00
(122)	Whitey Herzog	12.00	6.00	3.50
(123)	Kirby Higbe	30.00	15.00	9.00
(124)	Chuck Hinton	9.00	4.50	2.75
(125)	Don Hoak	15.00	7.50	4.50
(126)	Gil Hodges ("B" on cap.)	12.50	6.25	3.75
(127)	Gil Hodges ("LA" on cap.)	25.00	12.50	7.50
(128)	Johnny Hopp	25.00	15.00	8.00
(129)	Elston Howard	12.00	6.00	3.50
(130)	Frank Howard	15.00	7.50	4.50
(131)	Ken Hubbs	30.00	15.00	9.00
(132)	Tex Hughson	25.00	15.00	8.00
(133)	Fred Hutchinson	60.00	30.00	18.00
(134)	Monty Irvin (Monte)	12.00	6.00	3.50
(135)	Joey Jay	9.00	4.50	2.75
(136)	Jackie Jensen	45.00	22.50	13.50
(137)	Sam Jethroe	10.00	5.00	3.00
(138)	Bill Johnson	30.00	15.00	9.00
(139)	Walter Judnich	13.50	6.75	4.00
(140)	Al Kaline (Kneeling)	25.00	12.50	7.50
(141)	Al Kaline (Portrait w/ two bats.)	17.50	8.75	5.25
(142)	George Kell	20.00	10.00	6.00
(143)	Charley Keller (With and without "An Exhibit Card.")	12.50	6.25	3.75
(144)	Alex Kellner	15.00	7.50	4.50
(145)	Kenn (Ken) Keltner	10.00	5.00	3.00
(146)	Harmon Killebrew (With bat.)	50.00	25.00	15.00
(147)	Harmon Killebrew (Throwing)	40.00	20.00	12.00
(148)	Harmon Killibrew (Killebrew) (Portrait)	50.00	25.00	15.00
(149)	Ellis Kinder	9.00	4.50	2.75
(150)	Ralph Kiner	25.00	12.50	7.50
(151)	Billy Klaus	30.00	15.00	9.00
(152)	Ted Kluzewski (Kluszewski) (Batting)	17.50	8.75	5.25
(153)	Ted Kluzewski (Kluszewski) (Pirates uniform.)	12.00	6.00	3.50
(154)	Ted Kluzewski (Kluszewski) (Plain uniform.)	50.00	25.00	15.00
(155)	Don Kolloway	20.00	10.00	6.00
(156)	Jim Konstanty	10.00	5.00	3.00
(157)	Sandy Koufax	40.00	20.00	12.00
(158)	Ed Kranepool	55.00	27.50	16.50
(159)	Tony Kubek (Light background.)	16.00	8.00	4.75
(160)	Tony Kubek (Dark background.)	45.00	22.50	13.50
(161)	Harvey Kuenn ("D" on cap.)	30.00	15.00	9.00
(162)	Harvey Kuenn (Plain cap.)	16.00	8.00	4.75
(163)	Harvey Kuenn ("SF" on cap.)	24.00	12.00	7.25
(164)	Whitey Kurowski	30.00	15.00	9.00
(165)	Eddie Lake	25.00	15.00	8.00
(166)	Jim Landis	9.00	4.50	2.75
(167)	Don Larsen	10.00	5.00	3.00
(168)	Bob Lemon (Glove not visible.)	15.00	7.50	4.50
(169)	Bob Lemon (Glove partially visible.)	25.00	12.50	7.50
(170)	Buddy Lewis	25.00	12.50	7.50
(171)	Johnny Lindell	35.00	17.50	10.00
(172)	Phil Linz	25.00	12.50	7.50
(173)	Don Lock	25.00	12.50	7.50
(174)	Whitey Lockman	9.00	4.50	2.75
(175)	Johnny Logan	9.00	4.50	2.75
(176)	Dale Long ("P" on cap.)	9.00	4.50	2.75
(177)	Dale Long ("C" on cap.)	20.00	10.00	6.00
(178)	Ed Lopat	10.00	5.00	3.00
(179)	Harry Lowery (Name misspelled.)	10.00	5.00	3.00
(180)	Harry Lowrey (Name correct.)	10.00	5.00	3.00
(181)	Sal Maglie	9.00	4.50	2.75
(182)	Art Mahaffey	10.00	5.00	3.00
(183)	Hank Majeski	9.00	4.50	2.75
(184)	Frank Malzone	16.00	8.00	4.75
(185)	Mickey Mantle (Batting, full-length.)	140.00	70.00	40.00
(186)	Mickey Mantle (Batting, waist-up, "ck" in "Mickey" connected.)	100.00	50.00	30.00
(187)	Mickey Mantle (Batting, waist-up, "c k" in "Mickey" not connected.)	175.00	85.00	50.00
(188)	Mickey Mantle (Portrait)	600.00	300.00	180.00
(189)	Martin Marion	20.00	10.00	6.00
(190)	Roger Maris	25.00	12.50	7.50
(191)	Willard Marshall (With and without "An Exhibit Card.")	10.00	5.00	3.00
(192)	Eddie Matthews (Name incorrect.)	24.00	12.00	7.25
(193)	Eddie Mathews (Name correct.)	45.00	22.00	13.50
(194)	Ed Mayo	10.00	5.00	3.00
(195)	Willie Mays (Batting)	45.00	22.50	13.50
(196)	Willie Mays (Portrait)	60.00	30.00	18.00
(197)	Bill Mazeroski (Portrait)	16.00	8.00	4.75
(198)	Bill Mazeroski (Batting)	16.00	8.00	4.75
(199)	Ken McBride	15.00	7.50	4.50
(200)	Barney McCaskey (McCosky)	13.50	6.75	4.00
(201)	Barney McCoskey (McCosky)	200.00	100.00	50.00
(202)	Lindy McDaniel	9.00	4.50	2.75
(203a)	Gil McDougald ("MADE IN U.S.A." lower-right.)	20.00	10.00	6.00
(203b)	Gil McDougald ("PRINTED IN U.S.A." lower-right.)	15.00	7.50	4.50
(204)	Albert Mele	30.00	15.00	9.00
(205)	Sam Mele	20.00	10.00	6.00
(206)	Orestes Minoso ("C" on cap.)	12.50	6.25	3.75
(207)	Orestes Minoso (Sox on cap.)	9.00	4.50	2.75
(208)	Dale Mitchell	9.00	4.50	2.75
(209)	Wally Moon	12.00	6.00	3.50
(210)	Don Mueller	10.00	5.00	3.00
(211)	Stan Musial ("Made in USA" and "Printed in USA")	60.00	30.00	18.00
(212)	Stan Musial (Batting)	70.00	35.00	20.00
(213)	Charley Neal	15.00	7.50	4.50
(214)	Don Newcombe (Shaking hands.)	25.00	12.50	7.50
(215)	Don Newcombe (Dodgers on jacket.)	9.00	4.50	2.75
(216)	Don Newcombe (Plain jacket.)	10.00	5.00	3.00
(217)	Hal Newhouser	35.00	17.50	10.00
(218)	Ron Northey	20.00	10.00	6.00
(219)	Bill O'Dell	9.00	4.50	2.75
(220)	Joe Page	20.00	10.00	6.00
(221)	Satchel Paige	90.00	45.00	25.00
(222)	Milt Pappas	9.00	4.50	2.75
(223)	Camilo Pascual	9.00	4.50	2.75
(224)	Albie Pearson	25.00	12.50	7.50
(225)	Johnny Pesky	9.00	4.50	2.75
(226)	Gary Peters	25.00	12.50	7.50
(227)	Dave Philley	9.00	4.50	2.75
(228)	Billy Pierce	9.00	4.50	2.75
(229)	Jimmy Piersall	15.00	7.50	4.50
(230)	Vada Pinson	12.50	6.25	3.75
(231)	Bob Porterfield	9.00	4.50	2.75
(232)	John "Boog" Powell	45.00	22.50	13.50
(233)	Vic Raschi	15.00	7.50	4.50
(234)	Harold "Peewee" Reese (Fielding, ball partially visible.)	45.00	22.00	13.50
(235)	Harold "Peewee" Reese (Fielding, ball not visible.)	25.00	12.50	7.50
(236)	Del Rice	12.50	6.25	3.75
(237)	Bobby Richardson	125.00	60.00	35.00
(238)	Phil Rizzuto (Has a small and large projection. The large projection is known in two forms: with "An Exhibit Card," and with "An Exhibit Card" scratched out.)	25.00	12.50	7.50
(239)	Robin Roberts (White signature.)	14.50	7.25	4.25
(240)	Robin Roberts (Black signature.)	25.00	12.50	7.50
(241)	Brooks Robinson	25.00	12.50	7.50
(242)	Eddie Robinson	9.00	4.50	2.75
(243)	Floyd Robinson	17.50	8.75	5.25
(244)	Frankie Robinson	50.00	25.00	15.00
(245)	Jackie Robinson	50.00	25.00	15.00
(246)	Preacher Roe	35.00	17.50	10.00
(247)	Bob Rogers (Rodgers)	30.00	15.00	9.00
(248)	Richard Rollins	25.00	12.50	7.50
(249)	Pete Runnels	13.50	6.75	4.00
(250)	John Sain	12.50	6.25	3.75
(251)	Ron Santo	25.00	12.50	7.50
(252)	Henry Sauer	10.00	5.00	3.00
(253)	Carl Sawatski ("M" on cap.)	9.00	4.50	2.75
(254)	Carl Sawatski ("P" on cap.)	9.00	4.50	2.75
(255)	Carl Sawatski (Plain cap.)	17.50	8.75	5.25
(256)	Johnny Schmitz	10.00	5.00	3.00
(257)	Red Schoendeinst (Schoendienst) (Fielding, name in white.)	25.00	12.50	7.50
(258)	Red Schoendeinst (Schoendienst) (Fielding, name in red-brown.)	30.00	15.00	9.00
(259)	Red Schoendinst (Schoendienst) (Batting)	12.50	6.25	3.75
(260)	Herb Score ("C" on cap.)	15.00	7.50	4.50
(261)	Herb Score (Plain cap.)	17.50	8.75	5.25
(262)	Andy Seminick	9.00	4.50	2.75
(263)	Rip Sewell	20.00	10.00	6.00
(264)	Norm Siebern	9.00	4.50	2.75
(265)	Roy Sievers (Batting)	15.00	7.50	4.50
(266)	Roy Sievers (Portrait, "W" on cap, light background.)	12.00	6.00	3.50
(267)	Roy Sievers (Portrait, "W" on cap, dark background.)	17.50	8.75	5.25
(268)	Roy Sievers (Portrait, plain cap.)	20.00	10.00	6.00
(269)	Curt Simmons	10.00	5.00	3.00
(270)	Dick Sisler	10.00	5.00	3.00
(271)	Bill Skowron	12.50	6.25	3.75
(272)	Bill "Moose" Skowron	65.00	32.50	20.00
(273)	Enos Slaughter	20.00	10.00	6.00
(274)	Duke Snider ("B" on cap.)	22.50	11.00	6.75
(275)	Duke Snider ("LA" on cap.)	20.00	10.00	6.00
(276)	Warren Spahn ("B" on cap.)	20.00	10.00	6.00
(277)	Warren Spahn ("M" on cap.)	20.00	10.00	6.00
(278)	Stanley Spence	16.00	8.00	4.75
(279)	Ed Stanky (Plain uniform. With and without "An Exhibit Card.")	17.50	8.75	5.25
(280)	Ed Stanky (Giants uniform.)	10.00	5.00	3.00
(281)	Vern Stephens (Batting)	10.00	5.00	3.00
(282)	Vern Stephens (Portrait)	10.00	5.00	3.00
(283)	Ed Stewart	10.00	5.00	3.00
(284)	Snuffy Stirnweiss	12.50	6.25	3.75
(285)	George "Birdie" Tebbetts	17.50	8.75	5.25

		NM	E	VG
(286)	Frankie Thomas (Photo actually Bob Skinner.)	35.00	17.50	10.00
(287)	Frank Thomas (Portrait, "Best Wishes.")	16.00	8.00	4.75
(288)	Lee Thomas	9.00	4.50	2.75
(289)	Bobby Thomson (With and without "An Exhibit Card")	25.00	12.50	7.50
(290)	Earl Torgeson (Braves uniform.)	9.00	4.50	2.75
(291)	Earl Torgeson (Plain uniform.)	10.00	5.00	3.00
(292)	Gus Triandos	12.00	6.00	3.50
(293)	Virgil Trucks	9.00	4.50	2.75
(294)	Johnny Vandermeer (VanderMeer)	25.00	12.50	7.50
(295)	Emil Verban	12.00	6.00	3.50
(296)	Mickey Vernon (Throwing)	15.00	7.50	4.50
(297)	Mickey Vernon (Batting)	9.00	4.50	2.75
(298)	Bill Voiselle	30.00	15.00	9.00
(299)	Leon Wagner	6.50	3.25	1.75
(300)	Eddie Waitkus (Throwing, Chicago uniform.)	40.00	20.00	12.00
(301)	Eddie Waitkus (Throwing, plain uniform.)	10.00	5.00	3.00
(302)	Eddie Waitkus (Portrait)	15.00	7.50	4.50
(303)	Dick Wakefield	10.00	5.00	3.00
(304)	Harry Walker	40.00	20.00	12.00
(305)	Bucky Walters	20.00	10.00	6.00
(306)	Pete Ward	75.00	37.50	22.50
(307)	Herman Wehmeier	10.00	5.00	3.00
(308)	Vic Wertz (Batting)	9.00	4.50	2.75
(309)	Vic Wertz (Portrait)	9.00	4.50	2.75
(310)	Wally Westlake	10.00	5.00	3.00
(311)	Wes Westrum	17.50	8.75	5.25
(312)	Billy Williams	20.00	10.00	6.00
(313)	Maurice Wills	15.00	7.50	4.50
(314)	Gene Woodling (White signature.)	9.00	4.50	2.75
(315)	Gene Woodling (Black signature.)	12.00	6.00	3.50
(316)	Taffy Wright	10.00	5.00	3.00
(317)	Carl Yastrazemski (Yastrzemski)	200.00	100.00	60.00
(318)	Al Zarilla	12.50	6.25	3.75
(319)	Gus Zernial (White signature.)	9.00	4.50	2.75
(320)	Gus Zernial (Black signature.)	12.00	6.00	3.50
(321)	Braves Team - 1948	50.00	25.00	15.00
(322)	Dodgers Team - 1949	75.00	37.50	22.50
(323)	Dodgers Team - 1952	65.00	32.50	20.00
(324)	Dodgers Team - 1955	175.00	87.50	52.50
(325)	Dodgers Team - 1956	60.00	30.00	18.00
(326)	Giants Team - 1951	125.00	62.50	37.50
(327)	Giants Team - 1954	75.00	37.00	22.00
(328)	Indians Team - 1948	55.00	27.50	16.50
(329)	Indians Team - 1954	75.00	37.00	22.00
(330)	Phillies Team - 1950	40.00	20.00	12.00
(331)	Yankees Team - 1949	110.00	55.00	32.50
(332)	Yankees Team - 1950	120.00	60.00	35.00
(333)	Yankees Team - 1951	120.00	60.00	35.00
(334)	Yankees Team - 1952	75.00	37.00	22.00
(335)	Yankees Team - 1955	75.00	37.00	22.00
(336)	Yankees Team - 1956	75.00	37.00	22.00

1953 Canadian Exhibits

This Canadian-issued set consists of 64 cards and includes both major leaguers and players from the Montreal Royals of the International League. The cards are slightly smaller than the U.S. exhibit cards, measuring 3-1/4" x 5-1/4", and are numbered. The blank-backed cards were printed on gray stock. Card numbers 1-32 have a green or red tint, while card numbers 33-64 have a blue or reddish-brown tint.

	NM	E	VG
Complete Set (64):	1,750	875.00	525.00
Common Player (1-32):	30.00	15.00	9.00

Common Player (33-64):		18.00	9.00	5.50
1	Preacher Roe	40.00	20.00	12.00
2	Luke Easter	40.00	20.00	12.00
3	Gene Bearden	30.00	15.00	9.00
4	Chico Carrasquel	40.00	20.00	12.00
5	Vic Raschi	40.00	20.00	12.00
6	Monty (Monte) Irvin	60.00	30.00	18.00
7	Henry Sauer	30.00	15.00	9.00
8	Ralph Branca	40.00	20.00	12.00
9	Ed Stanky	40.00	20.00	12.00
10	Sam Jethroe	30.00	15.00	9.00
11	Larry Doby	60.00	30.00	18.00
12	Hal Newhouser	60.00	30.00	18.00
13	Gil Hodges	100.00	50.00	30.00
14	Harry Brecheen	30.00	15.00	9.00
15	Ed Lopat	40.00	20.00	12.00
16	Don Newcombe	50.00	25.00	15.00
17	Bob Feller	120.00	60.00	36.00
18	Tommy Holmes	30.00	15.00	9.00
19	Jackie Robinson	130.00	70.00	40.00
20	Roy Campanella	110.00	50.00	30.00
21	Harold "Peewee" Reese	100.00	50.00	30.00
22	Ralph Kiner	120.00	60.00	36.00
23	Dom DiMaggio	50.00	25.00	15.00
24	Bobby Doerr	60.00	30.00	18.00
25	Phil Rizzuto	100.00	50.00	30.00
26	Bob Elliott	30.00	15.00	9.00
27	Tom Henrich	40.00	20.00	12.00
28	Joe DiMaggio	400.00	200.00	120.00
29	Harry Lowery (Lowrey)	30.00	15.00	9.00
30	Ted Williams	150.00	75.00	45.00
31	Bob Lemon	b0.00	40.00	24.00
32	Warren Spahn	100.00	50.00	30.00
33	Don Hoak	50.00	25.00	15.00
34	Bob Alexander	30.00	15.00	9.00
35	John Simmons	30.00	15.00	9.00
36	Steve Lembo	30.00	15.00	9.00
37	Norman Larker	40.00	20.00	12.00
38	Bob Ludwick	30.00	15.00	9.00
39	Walter Moryn	40.00	20.00	12.00
40	Charlie Thompson	30.00	15.00	9.00
41	Ed Roebuck	40.00	20.00	12.00
42	Russell Rose	30.00	15.00	9.00
43	Edmundo (Sandy) Amoros	50.00	25.00	15.00
44	Bob Milliken	30.00	15.00	9.00
45	Art Fabbro	30.00	15.00	9.00
46	Spook Jacobs	30.00	15.00	9.00
47	Carmen Mauro	30.00	15.00	9.00
48	Walter Fiala	30.00	15.00	9.00
49	Rocky Nelson	30.00	15.00	9.00
50	Tom La Sorda (Lasorda)	120.00	60.00	36.00
51	Ronnie Lee	30.00	15.00	9.00
52	Hampton Coleman	30.00	15.00	9.00
53	Frank Marchio	30.00	15.00	9.00
54	William Sampson	30.00	15.00	9.00
55	Gil Mills	30.00	15.00	9.00
56	Al Ronning	30.00	15.00	9.00
57	Stan Musial	150.00	75.00	45.00
58	Walker Cooper	18.00	9.00	5.50
59	Mickey Vernon	18.00	9.00	5.50
60	Del Ennis	18.00	9.00	5.50
61	Walter Alston	80.00	40.00	24.00
62	Dick Sisler	18.00	9.00	5.50
63	Billy Goodman	18.00	9.00	5.50
64	Alex Kellner	18.00	9.00	5.50

1955 Exhibits - Post Card Backs

For an unkown purpose, the 64 Exhibit cards issued in 1955 (including many re-issued from earlier years) were produced in a very limited edition with a post card back, as opposed to the blank-back format usually found on the 3-3/8" x 5-3/8" cards. The postcard back can be found with or without the words "A Mutoscope Card."

	NM	E	VG
Complete Set (64):	6,000	3,000	1,800
Common Player:	50.00	30.00	20.00

		NM	E	VG
(1)	Joe Adcock	50.00	25.00	15.00
(2)	Ritchie (Richie) Ashburn	90.00	45.00	27.00
(3)	Toby Atwell	50.00	25.00	15.00
(4)	Gene Baker	50.00	25.00	15.00
(5)	Ernie Banks (Bat on shoulder, printed name.)	150.00	75.00	45.00
(6)	Matt Batts	50.00	25.00	15.00
(7)	Frank Baumholtz	50.00	25.00	15.00
(8)	Yogi Berra	150.00	75.00	45.00
(9)	Steve Bilko	50.00	25.00	15.00
(10)	Roy Campanella	125.00	62.00	37.00
(11)	Chico Carrasquel (Leaping)	50.00	25.00	15.00
(12)	Alvin Dark (Giants)	50.00	25.00	15.00
(13)	Larry Doby	90.00	45.00	27.00
(14)	Walter Dropo	50.00	25.00	15.00
(15)	Del Ennis	50.00	25.00	15.00
(16)	Ferris Fain (Portrait)	90.00	45.00	27.00
(17)	Bob Feller (Yours truly.)	200.00	100.00	60.00
(18)	Billy Goodman (Leaping)	90.00	45.00	27.00
(19)	Ted (Jim) Greengrass	50.00	25.00	15.00
(20)	Steve Gromek	50.00	25.00	15.00
(21)	Johnny Groth	50.00	25.00	15.00
(22)	Jim Hegan	50.00	25.00	15.00
(23)	Gene Hermanski	50.00	25.00	15.00
(24)	Gil Hodges (B on cap.)	100.00	50.00	30.00
(25)	Monty (Monte) Irvin	90.00	45.00	27.00
(26)	Al Kaline (Kneeling)	150.00	75.00	45.00
(27)	George Kell	90.00	45.00	27.00
(28)	Alex Kellner	50.00	25.00	15.00
(29)	Ted Kluszewski (Kluszewski) (Batting)	125.00	62.00	37.00
(30)	Bob Lemon (Glove not showing.)	90.00	45.00	27.00
(31)	Whitey Lockman	50.00	25.00	15.00
(32)	Ed Lopat	60.00	30.00	18.00
(33)	Sal Maglie	50.00	25.00	15.00
(34)	Mickey Mantle (Batting, waist-up.)	800.00	400.00	240.00
(35)	Ed Matthews (Mathews)	125.00	62.00	37.00
(36)	Willie Mays (Batting)	400.00	200.00	120.00
(37)	Gil McDougald	60.00	30.00	18.00
(38)	Sam Mele	50.00	25.00	15.00
(39)	Orestes Minoso (C on cap.)	90.00	45.00	27.00
(40)	Dale Mitchell	50.00	25.00	15.00
(41)	Stan Musial (Kneeling)	200.00	100.00	60.00
(42)	Andy Pafko (Yours truly.) (C on cap.))	50.00	25.00	15.00
(43)	Bob Porterfield	50.00	25.00	15.00
(44)	Vic Raschi	50.00	25.00	15.00
(45)	Harold "Peewee" Reese	125.00	62.00	37.00
(46)	Phil Rizzuto	125.00	62.00	37.00
(47)	Robin Roberts	90.00	45.00	27.00
(48)	Jackie Robinson	300.00	150.00	90.00
(49)	Henry Sauer	50.00	25.00	15.00
(50)	Johnny Schmitz	50.00	25.00	15.00
(51)	Red Schoendinst (Schoendienst)	90.00	45.00	27.00
(52)	Andy Seminick	50.00	25.00	15.00
(53)	Duke Snider (B on cap.)	125.00	62.00	37.00
(54)	Warren Spahn (B on cap.)	125.00	62.00	37.00
(55)	Vern Stephens (Portrait)	50.00	25.00	15.00
(56)	Earl Torgeson (Braves uniform.)	50.00	25.00	15.00
(57)	Virgil Trucks	50.00	25.00	15.00
(58)	Mickey Vernon (Batting)	50.00	25.00	15.00
(59)	Eddie Waitkus	50.00	25.00	15.00
(60)	Vic Wertz (Batting)	50.00	25.00	15.00
(61)	Gene Woodling	50.00	25.00	15.00
(62)	Gus Zernial	50.00	25.00	15.00
(63)	Champions	300.00	150.00	90.00
(64)	Champions	300.00	150.00	90.00

1959 Exhibits - Dad's Cookies

(See 1959 Dad's Cookies.)

1961 Exhibits - Wrigley Field

JOHN JOSEPH EVERS

Distributed at Chicago's Wrigley Field circa 1961, this 24-card set features members of the Baseball Hall of Fame. The cards measure 3-3/8" x 5-3/8" and include the player's full name along the bottom. They were printed on gray stock and have a postcard back or blank back. The set is unnumbered.

		NM	E	VG
Complete Set (24):		750.00	375.00	225.00
Common Player:		10.00	5.00	3.00
(1)	Grover Cleveland Alexander	15.00	7.50	4.50
(2)	Adrian Constantine Anson	12.50	6.25	3.75
(3)	John Franklin Baker	10.00	5.00	3.00
(4)	Roger Phillip Bresnahan	10.00	5.00	3.00
(5)	Mordecai Peter Brown	10.00	5.00	3.00
(6)	Frank Leroy Chance	10.00	5.00	3.00
(7)	Tyrus Raymond Cobb	145.00	75.00	45.00
(8)	Edward Trowbridge Collins	10.00	5.00	3.00
(9)	James J. Collins	10.00	5.00	3.00
(10)	John Joseph Evers	10.00	5.00	3.00
(11)	Henry Louis Gehrig	145.00	75.00	45.00
(12)	Clark C. Griffith	10.00	5.00	3.00
(13)	Walter Perry Johnson	25.00	12.50	7.50
(14)	Anthony Michael Lazzeri	10.00	5.00	3.00
(15)	James Walter Vincent Maranville	10.00	5.00	3.00
(16)	Christopher Mathewson	30.00	15.00	9.00
(17)	John Joseph McGraw	10.00	5.00	3.00
(18)	Melvin Thomas Ott	10.00	5.00	3.00
(19)	Herbert Jeffries Pennock	10.00	5.00	3.00
(20)	George Herman Ruth	180.00	90.00	55.00
(21)	Aloysius Harry Simmons	10.00	5.00	3.00
(22)	Tristram Speaker	25.00	12.50	7.50
(23)	Joseph B. Tinker	10.00	5.00	3.00
(24)	John Peter Wagner	40.00	20.00	12.00

1962 Statistic Back Exhibits

In 1962, the Exhibit Supply Co. added career statistics to the yearly set they produced. The black-and-white, unnumbered cards measure 3-3/8" x 5-3/8". The statistics found on the back are printed in black or red.

		NM	E	VG
Complete Set (32):		500.00	250.00	150.00
Common Player:		6.00	3.00	1.75
Red Backs: 1.5X				
(1)	Hank Aaron	35.00	17.50	10.00
(2)	Luis Aparicio	15.00	7.50	4.50
(3)	Ernie Banks	25.00	12.50	7.50
(4)	Larry "Yogi" Berra	25.00	12.50	7.50
(5)	Ken Boyer	7.50	3.75	2.25
(6)	Lew Burdette	6.00	3.00	1.75
(7)	Norm Cash	7.50	3.75	2.25
(8)	Orlando Cepeda	15.00	7.50	4.50

(9)	Roberto Clemente	50.00	25.00	15.00
(10)	Rocky Colavito	15.00	7.50	4.50
(11)	Ed "Whitey" Ford	17.50	8.75	5.25
(12)	Nelson Fox	15.00	7.50	4.50
(13)	Tito Francona	6.00	3.00	1.75
(14)	Jim Gentile	6.00	3.00	1.75
(15)	Dick Groat	6.00	3.00	1.75
(16)	Don Hoak	6.00	3.00	1.75
(17)	Al Kaline	17.50	8.75	5.25
(18)	Harmon Killebrew	17.50	8.75	5.25
(19)	Sandy Koufax	30.00	15.00	9.00
(20)	Jim Landis	6.00	3.00	1.75
(21)	Art Mahaffey	6.00	3.00	1.75
(22)	Frank Malzone	6.00	3.00	1.75
(23)	Mickey Mantle	100.00	50.00	30.00
(24)	Roger Maris	17.50	8.75	5.25
(25)	Eddie Mathews	17.50	8.75	5.25
(26)	Willie Mays	35.00	17.50	10.00
(27)	Wally Moon	6.00	3.00	1.75
(28)	Stan Musial	30.00	15.00	9.00
(29)	Milt Pappas	6.00	3.00	1.75
(30)	Vada Pinson	7.50	3.75	2.25
(31)	Norm Siebern	6.00	3.00	1.75
(32)	Warren Spahn	17.50	8.75	5.25

1963 Statistic Back Exhibits

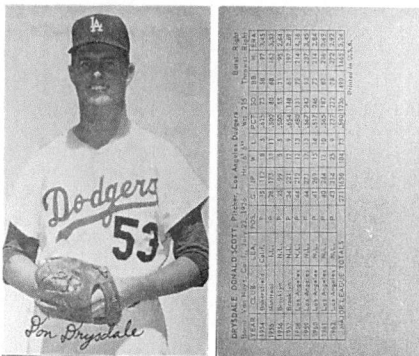

The Exhibit Supply Co. issued a 64-card set with career statistics on the backs of the cards in 1963. The unnumbered, black-and-white cards are printed on thick cardboard and measure 3-3/8" x 5-3/8" in size. The statistics on the back are only found printed in red.

		NM	E	VG
Complete Set (64):		900.00	450.00	275.00
Common Player:		7.50	3.75	2.25
(1)	Hank Aaron	35.00	17.50	10.00
(2)	Luis Aparicio	15.00	7.50	4.50
(3)	Bob Aspromonte	7.50	3.75	2.25
(4)	Ernie Banks	25.00	12.50	7.50
(5)	Steve Barber	7.50	3.75	2.25
(6)	Earl Battey	7.50	3.75	2.25
(7)	Larry "Yogi" Berra	25.00	12.50	7.50
(8)	Ken Boyer	9.00	4.50	2.75
(9)	Lew Burdette	7.50	3.75	2.25
(10)	Johnny Callison	7.50	3.75	2.25
(11)	Norm Cash	9.00	4.50	2.75
(12)	Orlando Cepeda	15.00	7.50	4.50
(13)	Dean Chance	7.50	3.75	2.25
(14)	Tom Cheney	7.50	3.75	2.25
(15)	Roberto Clemente	40.00	20.00	12.00
(16)	Rocky Colavito	15.00	7.50	4.50
(17)	Choo Choo Coleman	7.50	3.75	2.25
(18)	Roger Craig	7.50	3.75	2.25
(19)	Joe Cunningham	7.50	3.75	2.25
(20)	Don Drysdale	15.00	7.50	4.50
(21)	Dick Farrell	7.50	3.75	2.25
(22)	Ed "Whitey" Ford	20.00	10.00	6.00
(23)	Nelson Fox	15.00	7.50	4.50
(24)	Tito Francona	7.50	3.75	2.25
(25)	Jim Gentile	7.50	3.75	2.25
(26)	Tony Gonzalez	7.50	3.75	2.25
(27)	Dick Groat	7.50	3.75	2.25
(28)	Ray Herbert	7.50	3.75	2.25
(29)	Chuck Hinton	7.50	3.75	2.25
(30)	Don Hoak	7.50	3.75	2.25
(31)	Frank Howard	9.00	4.50	2.75
(32)	Ken Hubbs	12.00	6.00	3.50
(33)	Joey Jay	7.50	3.75	2.25
(34)	Al Kaline	15.00	7.50	4.50
(35)	Harmon Killebrew	15.00	7.50	4.50
(36)	Sandy Koufax	30.00	15.00	9.00
(37)	Harvey Kuenn	7.50	3.75	2.25
(38)	Jim Landis	7.50	3.75	2.25
(39)	Art Mahaffey	7.50	3.75	2.25
(40)	Frank Malzone	7.50	3.75	2.25
(41)	Mickey Mantle	150.00	75.00	45.00
(42)	Roger Maris	15.00	7.50	4.50
(43)	Eddie Mathews	15.00	7.50	4.50
(44)	Willie Mays	35.00	17.50	10.00
(45)	Bill Mazeroski	15.00	7.50	4.50
(46)	Ken McBride	7.50	3.75	2.25
(47)	Wally Moon	7.50	3.75	2.25
(48)	Stan Musial	30.00	15.00	9.00
(49)	Charlie Neal	7.50	3.75	2.25
(50)	Bill O'Dell	7.50	3.75	2.25
(51)	Milt Pappas	7.50	3.75	2.25
(52)	Camilo Pascual	7.50	3.75	2.25
(53)	Jimmy Piersall	9.00	4.50	2.75
(54)	Vada Pinson	9.00	4.50	2.75
(55)	Brooks Robinson	20.00	10.00	6.00
(56)	Frankie Robinson	20.00	10.00	6.00
(57)	Pete Runnels	7.50	3.75	2.25
(58)	Ron Santo	9.00	4.50	2.75
(59)	Norm Siebern	7.50	3.75	2.25
(60)	Warren Spahn	20.00	10.00	6.00
(61)	Lee Thomas	7.50	3.75	2.25
(62)	Leon Wagner	7.50	3.75	2.25
(63)	Billy Williams	15.00	7.50	4.50
(64)	Maurice Wills	13.50	6.75	4.00

1980 Hall of Fame Exhibits

Satchel Paige

Following the purchase of the "remains" of the Exhibit Supply Co., by a collector in the late 1970s, this set of Exhibits was issued in 1980. The set utilizies photos from earlier issues in the same 3-3/8" x 5-3/8" size. Each card has a notation in white at the bottom, "An Exhibit Card 1980 Hall Of Fame," to distinguish them from the older version. Sets could be purchased printed in sepia, red or blue for $5. The unnumbered cards are checklisted here alphabetically.

		NM	E	VG
Complete Set (32):		25.00	12.50	7.50
Common Player:		2.00	1.00	.60
(1)	Grover Cleveland Alexander	2.50	1.25	.70
(2)	Lou Boudreau	2.00	1.00	.60
(3)	Roger Bresnahan	2.00	1.00	.60
(4)	Roy Campanella	2.00	1.00	.60
(5)	Frank Chance	2.00	1.00	.60
(6)	Ty Cobb	5.00	2.50	1.50
(7)	Mickey Cochrane	2.00	1.00	.60
(8)	Dizzy Dean	2.50	1.25	.70
(9)	Joe DiMaggio	6.00	3.00	1.75
(10)	Bill Dickey	2.00	1.00	.60
(11)	Johnny Evers	2.00	1.00	.60
(12)	Jimmy Foxx	2.50	1.25	.70
(13)	Vernon Gomez	2.00	1.00	.60
(14)	Robert "Lefty" Grove	2.00	1.00	.60
(15)	Hank Greenberg	2.50	1.25	.70
(16)	Rogers Hornsby	2.00	1.00	.60
(17)	Carl Hubbell	2.00	1.00	.60
(18)	Hughie Jennings	2.00	1.00	.60
(19)	Walter Johnson	2.50	1.25	.70
(20)	Napoleon Lajoie	2.00	1.00	.60
(21)	Bob Lemon	2.00	1.00	.60
(22)	Mickey Mantle	12.00	6.00	3.50
(23)	Christy Mathewson	2.00	1.00	.60
(24)	Mel Ott	2.00	1.00	.60
(25)	Satchel Paige	2.50	1.25	.70
(26)	Jackie Robinson	4.00	2.00	1.25
(27)	Babe Ruth	9.00	4.50	2.75
(28)	Tris Speaker	2.00	1.00	.60
(29)	Joe Tinker	2.00	1.00	.60
(30)	Honus Wagner	3.00	1.50	.90
(31)	Ted Williams	4.00	2.00	1.25
(32)	Cy Young	2.50	1.25	.70

1980 Exhibits

Following the purchase of the "remains" of the Exhibit Supply Co., by a collector in the late 1970s, this set of Exhibits was issued in 1980. The set utilizied photos from earlier issues in the same 3-3/8" x 5-3/8" size. Each card carries a notation in white at the bottom, "An Exhibit Card 1980," to distinguish them from the older version. Sets could be purchased printed in sepia, red or blue, at $4.50 per set. A total of 5,000 sets were reported printed. The unnumbered cards are checklisted here alphabetically.

		NM	E	VG
	Complete Set (32):	40.00	20.00	12.00
	Common Player:	2.00	1.00	.60
(1)	Johnny Antonelli	2.00	1.00	.60
(2)	Richie Ashburn	2.00	1.00	.60
(3)	Earl Averill	2.00	1.00	.60
(4)	Ernie Banks	4.00	2.00	1.25
(5)	Ewell Blackwell	2.00	1.00	.60
(6)	Lou Brock	2.00	1.00	.60
(7)	Dean Chance	2.00	1.00	.60
(8)	Roger Craig	2.00	1.00	.60
(9)	Lou Gehrig	20.00	10.00	6.00
(10)	Gil Hodges	2.00	1.00	.60
(11)	Jack Jensen	2.00	1.00	.60
(12)	Willie Keeler	2.00	1.00	.60
(13)	George Kell	2.00	1.00	.60
(14)	Alex Kellner	2.00	1.00	.60
(15)	Harmon Killebrew	2.00	1.00	.60
(16)	Dale Long	2.00	1.00	.60
(17)	Sal Maglie	2.00	1.00	.60
(18)	Roger Maris	4.00	2.00	1.25
(19)	Willie Mays	13.50	6.75	4.00
(20)	Minnie Minoso	2.00	1.00	.60
(21)	Stan Musial	10.00	5.00	3.00
(22)	Billy Pierce	2.00	1.00	.60
(23)	Jimmy Piersall	2.00	1.00	.60
(24)	Eddie Plank	2.00	1.00	.60
(25)	Pete Reiser	2.00	1.00	.60
(26)	Brooks Robinson	2.00	1.00	.60
(27)	Pete Runnels	2.00	1.00	.60
(28)	Herb Score	2.00	1.00	.60
(29)	Warren Spahn	2.00	1.00	.60
(30)	Billy Williams	2.00	1.00	.60
(31)	1948 Boston Braves Team	3.00	1.50	.90
(32)	1948 Cleveland Indians Team	3.00	1.50	.90

F

1961 F & M Bank Minnesota Twins Matchbook Covers

The star players on the inaugural Twins team are featured in this series of matchbook covers. The 1-1/2" x 4-7/16" matchbooks are printed in black, red and blue on white, and include a player portrait (players are shown wearing Washington Senators caps) and team logo on front. The sponsoring bank's picture and logo are on back. Inside the front cover are a few details about the player. Values shown are for complete but empty covers, with the striker surface intact. Complete matchbooks with matches bring about 2X the values quoted.

		NM	E	VG
	Complete Set (10):	140.00	70.00	40.00
	Common Player:	24.00	12.00	7.50
(1)	Bob Allison	24.00	12.00	7.50
(2)	Earl Battey	18.00	9.00	5.50
(3)	Reno Bertoia	15.00	7.50	4.50
(4)	Billy Gardner	15.00	7.50	4.50
(5)	Lenny Green	15.00	7.50	4.50
(6)	Harmon Killebrew	40.00	20.00	12.00
(7)	Cookie Lavagetto	15.00	7.50	4.50
(8)	Jim Lemon	24.00	12.00	7.00
(9)	Camilo Pascual	24.00	12.00	7.00
(10)	Pedro Ramos	15.00	7.50	4.50

1962 F & M Bank Minnesota Twins Matchbook Covers

The '62 Twins are featured in this series of matchbook covers. The 1-1/2" x 4-7/16" matchbooks are printed in black, red and blue on white, and include a player portrait (new players who did not appear in the 1961 set are shown in Twins caps) and team logo on front. The sponsoring bank's picture and logo are on back. Inside the front cover are a few details about the player. Values shown are for complete but empty covers, with the striker surface intact. Complete matchbooks with matches bring about 2X the values quoted.

		NM	E	VG
	Complete Set (10):	150.00	75.00	45.00
	Common Player:	15.00	7.50	4.50
(1)	Bob Allison	24.00	12.00	7.00
(2)	Earl Battey	18.00	9.00	5.50
(3)	Lenny Green	15.00	7.50	4.50
(4)	Jim Kaat	24.00	12.00	7.00
(5)	Harmon Killebrew	40.00	20.00	12.00
(6)	Jack Kralick	15.00	7.50	4.50
(7)	Jim Lemon	24.00	12.00	7.00
(8)	Camilo Pascual	24.00	12.00	7.00
(9)	Pedro Ramos	15.00	7.50	4.50
(10)	Zoilo Versalles	24.00	12.00	7.00

1966 Fairway Minnesota Twins

Color portraits of Twins favorites comprise this regional issue from a local grocery chain. The 8" x 10" glossy pictures have blue facsimile autographs on front and a white border. Black-and-white backs have a lengthy career summary, biographical data and full major and minor league stats. The unnumbered pictures are checklisted here in alphabetical order. There are no markings on the picture to identify the Fairway store.

		NM	E	VG
	Complete Set (17):	175.00	85.00	55.00
	Common Player:	7.50	3.75	2.25
(1)	Bernie Allen	7.50	3.75	2.25
(2)	Bob Allison	13.50	6.75	4.00
(3)	Earl Battey	10.00	5.00	3.00
(4)	Jim Grant	7.50	3.75	2.25
(5)	Jimmie Hall	7.50	3.75	2.25
(6)	Jim Kaat	15.00	7.50	4.50
(7)	Harmon Killebrew	30.00	15.00	9.00
(8)	Jim Merritt	7.50	3.75	2.25
(9)	Don Mincher	7.50	3.75	2.25
(10)	Tony Oliva	15.00	7.50	4.50
(11)	Camilo Pascual	10.00	5.00	3.00
(12)	Jim Perry	10.00	5.00	3.00
(13)	Frank Quilici	7.50	3.75	2.25
(14)	Rich Rollins	7.50	3.75	2.25
(15)	Sandy Valdespino	7.50	3.75	2.25
(16)	Zoilo Versalles	13.50	6.75	4.00
(17)	Al Worthington	7.50	3.75	2.25

1964 Falstaff Beer

This 6" x 4" black-and-white postcard pictures the principal radio announcers for the CBS "Game of the Week" sponsored by the brewing company and was probably used to respond to fan requests for autographs. Facsimile signatures of the Hall of Famers are featured on front.

	NM	E	VG
"Dizzy" Dean, "Pee Wee Reese"	20.00	10.00	6.00

1977 Family Fun Centers Padres

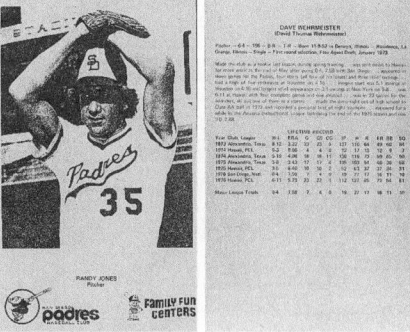

For 1977, Family Fun Centers, a chain of mini theme parks, took over sponsorship of the Padres annual issue of black-and-white player photos. The 5-1/2" x 8-1/2" photos have a large player pose at top-center, with his name and position below. In the bottom corners are team and sponsor logos. Backs have biographical data, complete stats and career highlights. Players are checklisted here alphabetically.

		NM	E	VG
	Complete Set (33):	90.00	45.00	27.50
	Common Player:	4.50	2.25	1.25
(1)	Billy Almon	4.50	2.25	1.25
(2)	Joey Amalfitano	4.50	2.25	1.25
(3)	Tucker Ashford	4.50	2.25	1.25
(4)	Mike Champion	4.50	2.25	1.25
(5)	Roger Craig	4.50	2.25	1.25
(6)	Alvin Dark	4.50	2.25	1.25
(7)	Bob Davis	4.50	2.25	1.25
(8)	Rollie Fingers	12.50	6.25	3.75
(9)	Dave Freisleben	4.50	2.25	1.25
(10)	Tom Griffin	4.50	2.25	1.25
(11)	George Hendrick	4.50	2.25	1.25
(12)	Mike Ivie	4.50	2.25	1.25
(13)	Randy Jones	4.50	2.25	1.25

(14)	John McNamara	4.50	2.25	1.25
(15)	Bob Owchinko	4.50	2.25	1.25
(16)	Merv Rettenmund	4.50	2.25	1.25
(17)	Gene Richards	4.50	2.25	1.25
(18)	Dave Roberts	4.50	2.25	1.25
(19)	Jackie Robinson (Blank back.)	25.00	12.50	7.50
(20)	Rick Sawyer	4.50	2.25	1.25
(21)	Pat Scanlon	4.50	2.25	1.25
(22)	Bob Shirley	4.50	2.25	1.25
(23)	Bob Skinner	4.50	2.25	1.25
(24)	Dan Spillner	4.50	2.25	1.25
(25)	Gary Sutherland	4.50	2.25	1.25
(26)	Gene Tenace	4.50	2.25	1.25
(27)	Dave Tomlin	4.50	2.25	1.25
(28)	Jerry Turner	4.50	2.25	1.25
(29)	Bobby Valentine	4.50	2.25	1.25
(30)	Dave Wehrmeister	4.50	2.25	1.25
(31)	Whitey Wietelmann	4.50	2.25	1.25
(32)	Don Williams	4.50	2.25	1.25
(33)	Dave Winfield	15.00	7.50	4.50

1978 Family Fun Centers Angels

The players, manager and coaches of the '78 Angels are featured in this set of 3-1/2" x 5-1/2" sepia-tone cards. The unnumbered cards are checklisted here alphabetically.

NOLAN RYAN

		NM	E	VG
	Complete Set (38):	90.00	45.00	25.00
	Common Player:	2.50	1.25	.70
(1)	Don Aase	2.50	1.25	.70
(2)	Mike Barlow	2.50	1.25	.70
(3)	Don Baylor	3.50	1.75	1.00
(4)	Lyman Bostock	2.50	1.25	.70
(5)	Ken Brett	2.50	1.25	.70
(6)	Dave Chalk	2.50	1.25	.70
(7)	Bob Clear	2.50	1.25	.70
(8)	Brian Downing	2.50	1.25	.70
(9)	Ron Fairly	2.50	1.25	.70
(10)	Gil Flores	2.50	1.25	.70
(11)	Dave Frost	2.50	1.25	.70
(12)	Dave Garcia	2.50	1.25	.70
(13)	Bobby Grich	2.50	1.25	.70
(14)	Tom Griffin	2.50	1.25	.70
(15)	Marv Grissom	2.50	1.25	.70
(16)	Ike Hampton	2.50	1.25	.70
(17)	Paul Hartzell	2.50	1.25	.70
(18)	Terry Humphrey	2.50	1.25	.70
(19)	Ron Jackson	2.50	1.25	.70
(20)	Chris Knapp	2.50	1.25	.70
(21)	Ken Landreaux	2.50	1.25	.70
(22)	Carney Lansford	2.50	1.25	.70
(23)	Dave LaRoche	2.50	1.25	.70
(24)	John McNamara	2.50	1.25	.70
(25)	Dyar Miller	2.50	1.25	.70
(26)	Rick Miller	2.50	1.25	.70
(27)	Balor Moore	2.50	1.25	.70
(28)	Rance Mulliniks	2.50	1.25	.70
(29)	Floyd Rayford	2.50	1.25	.70
(30)	Jimmie Reese	4.00	2.00	1.25
(31)	Merv Rettenmund	2.50	1.25	.70
(32)	Joe Rudi	2.50	1.25	.70
(33)	Nolan Ryan	45.00	22.50	13.50
(34)	Bob Skinner	2.50	1.25	.70
(35)	Tony Solaita	2.50	1.25	.70
(36)	Frank Tanana	2.50	1.25	.70
(37)	Dickie Thon	2.50	1.25	.70
---	Header Card	.70	.35	.20

1978 Family Fun Centers Padres

In conjunction with the Padres' hosting of the 1978 All-Star Game, Family Fun Centers issued this set of cards covering the players, coaches, announcers and even the owner. The 3-1/2" x 5-1/2" cards have a plaque look with a 3" x 3-1/4" posed color photo set on a wood background. The player's name is in a gold box at bottom, with the team and sponsor's logos in between. Backs are in black-and-white with a player portrait photo and facsimile autograph at bottom, a few biographical details and career stats at top and an essay in the middle titled, "My Greatest Thrill in Baseball." A uniform number appears at top-left. The set is checklisted here in alphabetical order.

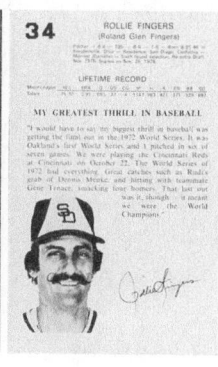

		NM	E	VG
	Complete Set (39):	75.00	37.50	22.50
	Common Player:	3.00	1.50	.90
(1)	Bill Almon	3.00	1.50	.90
(2)	Tucker Ashford	3.00	1.50	.90
(3)	Chuck Baker	3.00	1.50	.90
(4)	Dave Campbell (Announcer)	3.00	1.50	.90
(5)	Mike Champion	3.00	1.50	.90
(6)	Jerry Coleman (Announcer)	3.00	1.50	.90
(7)	Roger Craig	3.00	1.50	.90
(8)	John D'Acquisto	3.00	1.50	.90
(9)	Bob Davis	3.00	1.50	.90
(10)	Chuck Estrada	3.00	1.50	.90
(11)	Rollie Fingers	9.00	4.50	2.75
(12)	Dave Freisleben	3.00	1.50	.90
(13)	Oscar Gamble	3.00	1.50	.90
(14)	Fernando Gonzalez	3.00	1.50	.90
(15)	Billy Herman	4.00	2.00	1.25
(16)	Randy Jones	3.00	1.50	.90
(17)	Ray Kroc (owner)	5.00	2.50	1.50
(18)	Mark Lee	3.00	1.50	.90
(19)	Mickey Lolich	3.00	1.50	.90
(20)	Bob Owchinko	3.00	1.50	.90
(21)	Broderick Perkins	3.00	1.50	.90
(22)	Gaylord Perry	9.00	4.50	2.75
(23)	Eric Rasmussen	3.00	1.50	.90
(24)	Don Reynolds	3.00	1.50	.90
(25)	Gene Richards	3.00	1.50	.90
(26)	Dave Roberts	3.00	1.50	.90
(27)	Phil Roof	3.00	1.50	.90
(28)	Bob Shirley	3.00	1.50	.90
(29)	Ozzie Smith	60.00	30.00	18.00
(30)	Dan Spillner	3.00	1.50	.90
(31)	Rick Sweet	3.00	1.50	.90
(32)	Gene Tenace	3.00	1.50	.90
(33)	Derrel Thomas	3.00	1.50	.90
(34)	Jerry Turner	3.00	1.50	.90
(35)	Dave Wehrmeister	3.00	1.50	.90
(36)	Whitey Wietelmann	3.00	1.50	.90
(37)	Don Williams	3.00	1.50	.90
(38)	Dave Winfield	15.00	7.50	4.50
(39)	All-Star Game	3.00	1.50	.90

1979 Family Fun Centers Padres

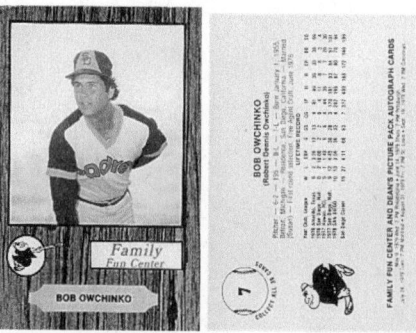

Each card features a posed color photo against a wood-grain border. Fronts have player identification, the Padres mascot and the logo of one of the sponsors - Family Fun Centers or Dean's Photo Service. Black-and-white backs have player personal data, major and minor league stats, a notation to "COLLECT ALL 36 CARDS" and a list of distribution dates. The 3-1/4" x 4-3/4" cards were issued in 12-1/2" x 9-1/2" perforated panels of six cards plus a coupon from each sponsor. Panels were given out one per month May through September at promotional games, making the set difficult to complete. Cards #25-30 have not been confirmed as issued.

		NM	E	VG
	Complete Set (30):	60.00	30.00	18.00
	Common Player:	3.00	1.50	.90
1	Roger Craig	3.00	1.50	.90
2	John D'Acquisto	3.00	1.50	.90
3	Ozzie Smith	25.00	12.50	7.50
4	KGB Chicken	4.00	2.00	1.25
5	Gene Richards	3.00	1.50	.90
6	Jerry Turner	3.00	1.50	.90
7	Bob Owchinko	3.00	1.50	.90
8	Gene Tenace	3.00	1.50	.90
9	Whitey Wietelmann	3.00	1.50	.90
10	Bill Almon	3.00	1.50	.90
11	Dave Winfield	15.00	7.50	4.50
12	Mike Hargrove	3.00	1.50	.90
13	Fernando Gonzalez	3.00	1.50	.90
14	Barry Evans	3.00	1.50	.90
15	Steve Mura	3.00	1.50	.90
16	Chuck Estrada	3.00	1.50	.90
17	Bill Fahey	3.00	1.50	.90
18	Gaylord Perry	6.00	3.00	1.75
19	Dan Briggs	3.00	1.50	.90
20	Billy Herman	4.00	2.00	1.25
21	Mickey Lolich	3.00	1.50	.90
22	Broderick Perkins	3.00	1.50	.90
23	Fred Kendall	3.00	1.50	.90
24	Rollie Fingers	6.00	3.00	1.75
31	Bobby Tolan	3.00	1.50	.90
32	Doug Rader	3.00	1.50	.90
33	Dave Campbell	3.00	1.50	.90
34	Jay Johnstone	3.00	1.50	.90
35	Mark Lee	3.00	1.50	.90
36	Bob Shirley	3.00	1.50	.90

1980 Family Fun Centers Padres

Six Padres players or staff are featured on these 13" x 10" or 12-1/2" x 9-1/2" coupon sheets. At the right end of each glossy paper sheet is a group of coupons and advertising for the recreation centers, printed in black, yellow and green. At left are six photos. Each of the 3" x 4" photos has a color player pose. At either top or bottom, depending on placement on the sheet, is the player name in black, "FAMILY FUN CENTER" in green and a red building logo. Backs are blank and the sheets are not perforated.

		NM	E	VG
	Complete Set (7):	80.00	40.00	24.00
	Common Sheet:	7.00	3.50	2.00
(1)	Kurt Bevacqua, Dave Cash, Paul Dade, Rollie Fingers, Don Williams, Dave Winfield	20.00	10.00	6.00
(2)	Ed Brinkman, Dave Edwards, Jack Krol, Luis Salazar, Craig Stimac, John Urrea	7.00	3.50	2.00
(3)	Jerry Coleman, John D'Acquisto, Bill Fahey, Randy Jones, Gene Richards, Ozzie Smith	30.00	15.00	9.00
(4)	Dave Campbell, Juan Eichelberger, Barry Evans, Bobby Tolan, Jerry Turner, Rick Wise	7.00	3.50	2.00
(5)	John Curtis, Al Heist, Gary Lucas, Willie Montanez, Aurelio Rodriguez, Gene Tenace	7.00	3.50	2.00
(6)	Eddie Doucette, Chuck Estrada, Tim Flannery, Eric Rasmussen, Bob Shirley, San Diego Chicken	10.00	5.00	3.00

(7)	Von Joshua, Fred			
	Kendall, Dennis			
	Kinney, Jerry			
	Mumphrey, Steve			
	Mura, Dick Phillips	7.00	3.50	2.00

1916 Famous and Barr Clothiers

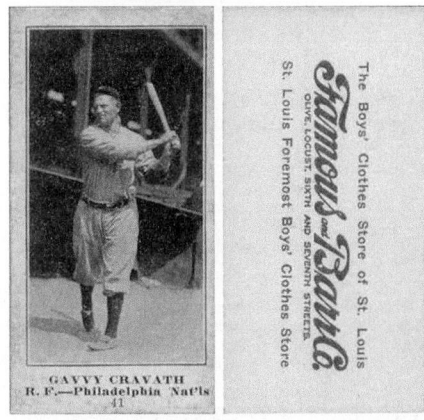

GAVVY CRAVATH
R. F.—Philadelphia Nat'ls
41

The Boys' Clothes Store of St. Louis
Famous and Barr Co.
OLIVE, LOCUST, SIXTH AND SEVENTH STREETS.
St. Louis Foremost Boys' Clothes Store

This is among the most complex of the regional advertising-backed card sets that utilized the fronts generated by Felix Mendelsohn because players have been found that parallel both the M101-5 and M101-4 issues. Additionally, the advertising for the St. Louis clothing store on the backs can be found reading both top-to-bottom and bottom-to-top in relation to the front, the latter usually found on a card stock that is whiter than the related issues. Like the related issues, the Famous and Barr cards are printed in black-and-white in a size of approximately 1-5/8"x3". Because of the mixing of M101-5 and M101-4 fronts, the exact composition of the Famous and Barr set is known and checklist additions can be expected.

	NM	E	VG
Common Player:	125.00	50.00	25.00
1 Babe Adams	190.00	65.00	25.00
2 Sam Agnew	125.00	50.00	25.00
3 Eddie Ainsmith	125.00	50.00	25.00
4 Grover Alexander	2,150	1,075	645.00
5 Leon Ames	125.00	50.00	25.00
6 Jimmy Archer	125.00	50.00	25.00
7 Jimmy Austin	125.00	50.00	25.00
8a J. Franklin Baker	800.00	400.00	240.00
8b H.D. Baird (3rd B.)	125.00	50.00	25.00
8c H.D. Baird ((C.F.))	125.00	50.00	25.00
9 Dave Bancroft	800.00	400.00	240.00
10 Jack Barry	125.00	50.00	25.00
11 Zinn Beck	125.00	50.00	25.00
12 Lute Boone	125.00	50.00	25.00
13 Joe Benz	125.00	50.00	25.00
14 Bob Bescher	125.00	50.00	25.00
15 Al Betzel	125.00	50.00	25.00
16 Roger Bresnahan	800.00	400.00	240.00
17 Eddie Burns	125.00	50.00	25.00
18 Geo. J. Burns	125.00	50.00	25.00
19 Joe Bush	125.00	50.00	25.00
20 Owen Bush	125.00	50.00	25.00
21 Art Butler	125.00	50.00	25.00
22 Bobbie Byrne	125.00	50.00	25.00
23a Forrest Cady (MAY NOT EXIST)			
23b Mordecai Brown	800.00	400.00	240.00
24 Jimmy Callahan	125.00	50.00	25.00
25 Ray Caldwell	125.00	50.00	25.00
26 Max Carey	800.00	400.00	240.00
27 George Chalmers	125.00	50.00	25.00
28 Frank Chance	800.00	400.00	240.00
29 Ray Chapman	155.00	65.00	30.00
30 Larry Cheney	125.00	50.00	25.00
31 Eddie Cicotte	1,200	600.00	350.00
32 Tom Clarke	125.00	50.00	25.00
33 Eddie Collins	800.00	400.00	240.00
34 "Shauno" Collins	125.00	50.00	25.00
35 Charles Comisky (Comiskey)	800.00	400.00	240.00
36 Joe Connolly	125.00	50.00	25.00
37 Luther Cook	125.00	50.00	25.00
38 Jack Coombs	125.00	50.00	25.00
39 Dan Costello	125.00	50.00	25.00
40 Harry Coveleskie (Coveleski)	125.00	50.00	25.00
41 Gavvy Cravath	125.00	50.00	25.00
42 Sam Crawford	800.00	400.00	240.00
43 Jean Dale	125.00	50.00	25.00
44 Jake Daubert	125.00	50.00	25.00
45 Geo. A. Davis Jr.	125.00	50.00	25.00
46 Charles Deal	125.00	50.00	25.00

47 Al Demaree	125.00	50.00	25.00
48 William Doak	125.00	50.00	25.00
49 Bill Donovan	125.00	50.00	25.00
50 Charles Dooin	125.00	50.00	25.00
51 Mike Doolan	125.00	50.00	25.00
52 Larry Doyle	125.00	50.00	25.00
53 Jean Dubuc	125.00	50.00	25.00
54 Oscar Dugey	125.00	50.00	25.00
55 Johnny Evers	800.00	400.00	240.00
56 Urban Faber	800.00	400.00	240.00
57 "Hap" Felsch	1,000	400.00	200.00
58 Bill Fischer	125.00	50.00	25.00
59 Ray Fisher	125.00	50.00	25.00
60 Max Flack	125.00	50.00	25.00
61 Art Fletcher	125.00	50.00	25.00
62 Eddie Foster	125.00	50.00	25.00
63 Jacques Fournier	125.00	50.00	25.00
64 Del Gainer (Gainor)	125.00	50.00	25.00
65 Larry Gardner	125.00	50.00	25.00
66 Joe Gedeon	125.00	50.00	25.00
67 Gus Getz	125.00	50.00	25.00
68 Geo. Gibson	125.00	50.00	25.00
69 Wilbur Good	125.00	50.00	25.00
70 Hank Gowdy	125.00	50.00	25.00
71 John Graney	125.00	50.00	25.00
72 Tom Griffith	125.00	50.00	25.00
73 Heinie Groh	125.00	50.00	25.00
74 Earl Hamilton	125.00	50.00	25.00
75 Bob Harmon	125.00	50.00	25.00
76 Roy Hartzell	125.00	50.00	25.00
77 Claude Hendrix	125.00	50.00	25.00
78 Olaf Henriksen	125.00	50.00	25.00
79 John Henry	125.00	50.00	25.00
80 "Buck" Herzog	125.00	50.00	25.00
81 Hugh High	125.00	50.00	25.00
82 Dick Hoblitzell	125.00	50.00	25.00
83 Harry Hooper	800.00	400.00	240.00
84 Ivan Howard	125.00	50.00	25.00
85 Miller Huggins	800.00	400.00	240.00
86 Joe Jackson	25,000	10,000	5,000
87 William James	125.00	50.00	25.00
88 Harold Janvrin	125.00	50.00	25.00
89 Hugh Jennings	800.00	400.00	240.00
90 Walter Johnson	2,190	875.00	440.00
91 Fielder Jones	125.00	50.00	25.00
92 Bennie Kauff	125.00	50.00	25.00
93 Wm. Killefer Jr.	125.00	50.00	25.00
94 Ed. Konetchy	125.00	50.00	25.00
95 Napoleon Lajoie	800.00	400.00	240.00
96 Jack Lapp	125.00	50.00	25.00
97a John Lavan (Correct spelling.)	125.00	50.00	25.00
97b John Lavin ((Incorret spelling.) (MAY NOT EXIST))			
98 Jimmy Lavender	125.00	50.00	25.00
99 "Nemo" Leibold	125.00	50.00	25.00
100 H.B. Leonard	125.00	50.00	25.00
101 Duffy Lewis	125.00	50.00	25.00
102 Hans Lobert	125.00	50.00	25.00
103 Tom Long	125.00	50.00	25.00
104 Fred Luderus	125.00	50.00	25.00
105 Connie Mack	800.00	400.00	240.00
106 Lee Magee	125.00	50.00	25.00
107 Al. Mamaux	125.00	50.00	25.00
108 Leslie Mann	125.00	50.00	25.00
109 "Rabbit" Maranville	800.00	400.00	240.00
110 Rube Marquard	080.00	400.00	240.00
111 Armando Marsans	155.00	65.00	30.00
112 J. Erskine Mayer	155.00	65.00	30.00
113 George McBride	125.00	50.00	25.00
114 John J. McGraw	800.00	400.00	240.00
115 Jack McInnis	125.00	50.00	25.00
116 Fred Merkle	125.00	50.00	25.00
117 Chief Meyers	125.00	50.00	25.00
118 Clyde Milan	125.00	50.00	25.00
119 Otto Miller	125.00	50.00	25.00
120 Willie Mitchel (Mitchell)	125.00	50.00	25.00
121 Fred Mollwitz	125.00	50.00	25.00
122 J. Herbert Moran	125.00	50.00	25.00
123 Pat Moran	125.00	50.00	25.00
124 Ray Morgan	125.00	50.00	25.00
125 Geo. Moriarty	125.00	50.00	25.00
126 Guy Morton	125.00	50.00	25.00
127 Ed. Murphy (Photo actually Danny Murphy.)	125.00	50.00	25.00
128 John Murray	125.00	50.00	25.00
129 "Hy" Myers	125.00	50.00	25.00
130 J.A. Niehoff	125.00	50.00	25.00
131 Leslie Nunamaker	125.00	50.00	25.00
132 Rube Oldring	125.00	50.00	25.00
133 Oliver O'Mara	125.00	50.00	25.00
134 Steve O'Neill	125.00	50.00	25.00
135 "Dode" Paskert	125.00	50.00	25.00
136 Roger Peckinpaugh (Photo actually Gavvy Cravath.)	125.00	50.00	25.00

137 E.J. Pfeffer (Photo actually Jeff Pfeffer.)	125.00	50.00	25.00
138 Geo. Pierce (Pearce)	125.00	50.00	25.00
139 Walter Pipp	125.00	50.00	25.00
140 Derril Pratt (Derrill)	125.00	50.00	25.00
141 Bill Rariden	125.00	50.00	25.00
142 Eppa Rixey	800.00	400.00	240.00
143 Davey Robertson	125.00	50.00	25.00
144 Wilbert Robinson	800.00	400.00	240.00
145 Bob Roth	125.00	50.00	25.00
146 Ed. Roush	800.00	400.00	240.00
147 Clarence Rowland	125.00	50.00	25.00
148 "Nap" Rucker	125.00	50.00	25.00
149 Dick Rudolph	125.00	50.00	25.00
150 Reb Russell	125.00	50.00	25.00
151 Babe Ruth	68,750	27,500	13,750
152 Vic Saier	125.00	50.00	25.00
153 "Slim" Sallee	125.00	50.00	25.00
154 "Germany" Schaefer	125.00	50.00	25.00
155 Ray Schalk	800.00	400.00	240.00
156 Walter Schang	125.00	50.00	25.00
157 Chas. Schmidt	125.00	50.00	25.00
158 Frank Schulte	125.00	50.00	25.00
159 Jim Scott	125.00	50.00	25.00
160 Everett Scott	125.00	50.00	25.00
161 Tom Seaton	125.00	50.00	25.00
162 Howard Shanks	125.00	50.00	25.00
163 Bob Shawkey (Photo actually Jack McInnis.)	125.00	50.00	25.00
164 Ernie Shore	125.00	50.00	25.00
165 Burt Shotton	125.00	50.00	25.00
166 George Sisler	800.00	400.00	240.00
167 J. Carlisle Smith	125.00	50.00	25.00
168 Fred Snodgrass	125.00	50.00	25.00
169 Geo. Stallings	125.00	50.00	25.00
170 Oscar Stanage (Photo actually Chas. Schmidt.)	125.00	50.00	25.00
171 Charles Stengel	815.00	325.00	165.00
172 Milton Stock	125.00	50.00	25.00
173 Amos Strunk (Photo actually Olaf Henriksen.)	125.00	50.00	25.00
174 Billy Sullivan	125.00	50.00	25.00
175 Chas. Tesreau	125.00	50.00	25.00
176 Jim Thorpe	20,000	10,000	6,000
177 Joe Tinker	800.00	400.00	240.00
178a Fred Toney	125.00	50.00	25.00
178b Jim Vaughn	125.00	50.00	25.00
179 Terry Turner	125.00	50.00	25.00
180 Jim Vaughn	125.00	50.00	25.00
181 Bob Veach	125.00	50.00	25.00
182a James Voix	125.00	50.00	25.00
182b Hans Wagner	6,500	3,200	1,950
183 Oscar Vitt	125.00	50.00	25.00
184 Hans Wagner	6,500	3,200	1,950
185 Clarence Walker (Photo not Walker.)	125.00	50.00	25.00
186 Zach Wheat	800.00	400.00	240.00
187 Ed. Walsh	800.00	400.00	240.00
188 Buck Weaver	800.00	400.00	240.00
189 Carl Weilman	125.00	50.00	25.00
190 Geo. Whitted	125.00	50.00	25.00
191 Fred Williams	125.00	50.00	25.00
192 Art Wilson	125.00	50.00	25.00
193 J. Owen Wilson	125.00	50.00	25.00
194 Ivy Wingo	125.00	50.00	25.00
195 "Mel" Wolfgang	125.00	50.00	25.00
196 Joe Wood	600.00	300.00	180.00
197 Steve Yerkes	125.00	50.00	25.00
198 Rollie Zeider	125.00	50.00	25.00
199 Heiny Zimmerman	125.00	50.00	25.00
200 Ed. Zwilling	125.00	50.00	25.00

1906 Fan Craze - American League

One of the earliest 20th Century baseball card sets, this issue from the Fan Craze Co. of Cincinnati was designed as a deck of playing cards and was intended to be used as a baseball table game. Separate sets were issued for the National League, with backs printed in red, and the American League, which are blue-backed. Both sets feature black-and-white player portraits in an oval vignette with the player's name and team below. The top of the card indicates one of many various baseball plays, such as "Single," "Out at First," "Strike," "Stolen Base," etc. The unnumbered cards measure 2-1/2" x 3-1/2". An ad card identifies the set as "An Artistic Constellation of Great Stars." Sears sold the set for 48 cents, postpaid.

		NM	E	VG
	Complete Set (51):	8,250	4,125	2,475
	Complete Boxed Set:	9,350	4,675	2,750
	Common Player:	120.00	60.00	35.00
	Ad/Header Card:	120.00	60.00	35.00
(1)	Nick Altrock	110.00	55.00	35.00
(2)	Jim Barrett	120.00	60.00	35.00
(3)	Harry Bay	120.00	60.00	35.00
(4)	Albert Bender	375.00	185.00	110.00
(5)	Bill Bernhardt	120.00	60.00	35.00
(6)	W. Bradley	120.00	60.00	35.00
(7)	Jack Chesbro	350.00	175.00	105.00
(8)	Jimmy Collins	350.00	175.00	105.00
(9)	Sam Crawford	350.00	175.00	105.00
(10)	Lou Criger	120.00	60.00	35.00
(11)	Lave Cross	120.00	60.00	35.00
(12)	Monte Cross	120.00	60.00	35.00
(13)	Harry Davis	120.00	60.00	35.00
(14)	Bill Dinneen	120.00	60.00	35.00
(15)	Pat (Bill) Donovan	120.00	60.00	35.00
(16)	Pat Dougherty	120.00	60.00	35.00
(17)	Norman Elberfield (Elberfeld)	120.00	60.00	35.00
(18)	Hoke Ferris (Hobe)	120.00	60.00	35.00
(19)	Elmer Flick	350.00	175.00	105.00
(20)	Buck Freeman	120.00	60.00	35.00
(21)	Fred Glade	120.00	60.00	35.00
(22)	Clark Griffith	350.00	175.00	105.00
(23)	Charley Hickman	120.00	60.00	35.00
(24)	Wm. Holmes	120.00	60.00	35.00
(25)	Harry Howell	120.00	60.00	35.00
(26)	Frank Isbel (Isbell)	120.00	60.00	35.00
(27)	Albert Jacobson	120.00	60.00	35.00
(28)	Ban Johnson	375.00	185.00	110.00
(29)	Fielder Jones	120.00	60.00	35.00
(30)	Adrian Joss	500.00	250.00	150.00
(31)	Billy Keeler	350.00	175.00	105.00
(32)	Napolean Lajoie	650.00	320.00	195.00
(33)	Connie Mack	375.00	185.00	110.00
(34)	Jimmy McAleer	120.00	60.00	35.00
(35)	Jim McGuire	120.00	60.00	35.00
(36)	Earl Moore	120.00	60.00	35.00
(37)	George Mullen (Mullin)	120.00	60.00	35.00
(38)	Billy Owen (Frank Owens)	120.00	60.00	35.00
(39)	Fred Parent	120.00	60.00	35.00
(40)	Case Patten	120.00	60.00	35.00
(41)	Ed Plank	650.00	320.00	195.00
(42)	Ossie Schreckengost	120.00	60.00	35.00
(43)	Jake Stahl	120.00	60.00	35.00
(44)	Fred (George) Stone	120.00	60.00	35.00
(45)	Wm. Sudhoff	120.00	60.00	35.00
(46)	Roy (Terry) Turner	120.00	60.00	35.00
(47)	G.E. Waddell	350.00	175.00	105.00
(48)	Bob Wallace	350.00	175.00	105.00
(49)	G. Harris White	120.00	60.00	35.00
(50)	Geo. Winters (Winter)	120.00	60.00	35.00
(51)	Cy Young	1,100	550.00	325.00

1906 Fan Craze - National League

Identical in size and format to the American League set of two years previous, this set of unnumbered cards was issued by the Fan Craze Co. of Cincinnati in 1906 and was designed like a deck of playing cards. The cards were intended to be used in playing a baseball table game. The National League cards are printed with red backs and black-and-white player photos on front. Sears sold the set for 48 cents postpaid.

		NM	E	VG
	Complete Set (54):	11,000	5,500	3,300
	Complete Boxed Set:	17,600	8,800	5,225
	Common Player:	75.00	32.00	19.50
	Ad/Header Card:	75.00	32.00	19.50

		NM	E	VG
(1)	Leon Ames	75.00	32.00	19.50
(2)	Clarence Beaumont	75.00	32.00	19.50
(3)	Jake Beckley	330.00	165.00	100.00
(4)	Billy Bergen	75.00	32.00	19.50
(5)	Roger Bresnahan	330.00	165.00	100.00
(6)	George Brown (Browne)	75.00	32.00	19.50
(7)	Mordacai Brown	330.00	165.00	100.00
(8)	Jas. Casey	75.00	32.00	19.50
(9)	Frank Chance	330.00	165.00	100.00
(10)	Fred Clarke	330.00	165.00	100.00
(11)	Thos. Corcoran	75.00	32.00	19.50
(12)	Bill Dahlen	75.00	32.00	19.50
(13)	Mike Donlin	75.00	32.00	19.50
(14)	Charley Dooin	75.00	32.00	19.50
(15)	Mickey Doolin (Doolan)	75.00	32.00	19.50
(16)	Hugh Duffy	330.00	165.00	100.00
(17)	John E. Dunleavy	75.00	32.00	19.50
(18)	Bob Ewing	75.00	32.00	19.50
(19)	"Chick" Fraser	75.00	32.00	19.50
(20)	J. Edward (Edward H.) Hanlon	330.00	165.00	100.00
(21)	G.E. Howard	75.00	32.00	19.50
(22)	Miller Huggins	330.00	165.00	100.00
(23)	Joseph Kelley	330.00	165.00	100.00
(24)	John Kling	75.00	32.00	19.50
(25)	Tommy Leach	75.00	32.00	19.50
(26)	Harry Lumley	75.00	32.00	19.50
(27)	Carl Lundgren	75.00	32.00	19.50
(28)	Bill Maloney	75.00	32.00	19.50
(29)	Dan McGann	75.00	32.00	19.50
(30)	Joe McGinnity	330.00	165.00	100.00
(31)	John J. McGraw	330.00	165.00	100.00
(32)	Harry McIntire (McIntyre)	75.00	32.00	19.50
(33)	Charley Nichols	550.00	275.00	165.00
(34)	Mike O'Neil (O'Neill)	75.00	32.00	19.50
(35)	Orville (Orval) Overall	75.00	32.00	19.50
(36)	Frank Pfeffer	75.00	32.00	19.50
(37)	Deacon Phillippe	75.00	32.00	19.50
(38)	Charley Pittinger	75.00	32.00	19.50
(39)	Harry C. Pulliam	75.00	32.00	19.50
(40)	Claude Ritchey	75.00	32.00	19.50
(41)	Ed Ruelbach (Reulbach)	75.00	32.00	19.50
(42)	J. Bentley Seymour	75.00	32.00	19.50
(43)	Jim Sheckard	75.00	32.00	19.50
(44)	Jack Taylor	75.00	32.00	19.50
(45)	Luther H. Taylor	220.00	110.00	65.00
(46)	Fred Tenny (Tenney)	75.00	32.00	19.50
(47)	Harry Theilman (Jake Thielman)	75.00	32.00	19.50
(48)	Roy Thomas	75.00	32.00	19.50
(49)	Hans Wagner	5,000	2,065	1,240
(50)	Jake Weimer	75.00	32.00	19.50
(51)	Bob Wicker	75.00	32.00	19.50
(52)	Victor Willis	330.00	165.00	100.00
(53)	Lew (George "Hooks") Wiltsie	75.00	32.00	19.50
(54)	Irving Young	75.00	32.00	19.50

1922 Fans Cigarettes (T231)

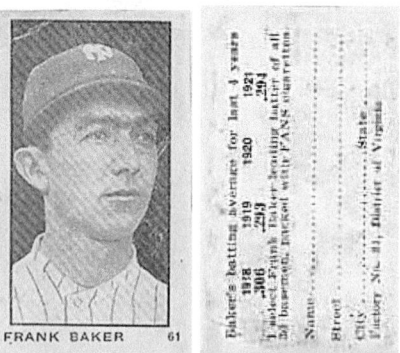

More mystery surrounds this obscure set than any other tobacco issue. In fact, the only evidence of its existence until 1992 was a photocopy of a single card of Pittsburgh Pirates outfielder Carson Bigbee. Even the owner of the card is unknown. Cards measure approximately 2-1/2" x 1-1/2" and are black-and-white. Adding to the mystery is the number "85" which appears in the lower right corner on the front of the card, apparently indicating there were at least that many cards in the set. In 1992 card "61" was reported. Card backs displays the player's batting averages for each season from 1918 through 1921 and includes the line: "I select (name) leading batter of all (position), packed with FANS cigarettes." The statement is followed by blanks for a person to fill in his name and address, as if the card were some sort of "ballot." With only one specimen known of each, these are among the rarest baseball cards in the hobby. Their American Card Catalog designation is T231.

VALUES UNDETERMINED

61	Frank Baker
85	Carson Bigbee

1939 Father & Son Shoes

Chuck Klein, outfielder, Phillies
Compliments Father & Son Shoes

This set features Phillies and A's players and was distributed in the Philadelphia area in 1939 by Father & Son Shoes stores. The unnumbered black and white cards measure 3" x 4". The player's name, position and team appear below the photo, along with the line "Compliments of Fathers & Son Shoes." The backs are blank. The checklist, arranged here alphabetically, may be incomplete.

		NM	E	VG
	Complete Set (17):	5,000	2,500	1,500
	Common Player:	450.00	220.00	135.00
(1)	Morrie Arnovich	450.00	220.00	135.00
(2)	Earl Brucker	450.00	220.00	135.00
(3)	George Caster	450.00	220.00	135.00
(4)	Sam Chapman	450.00	220.00	135.00
(5)	Spud Davis	450.00	220.00	135.00
(6)	Joe Gantenbein	450.00	220.00	135.00
(7)	Bob Johnson	450.00	220.00	135.00
(8)	Chuck Klein	1,125	565.00	340.00
(9)	Herschel Martin	450.00	220.00	135.00
(10)	Merrill May	300.00	150.00	90.00
(11)	Wally Moses	450.00	220.00	135.00
(12)	Emmett Mueller	450.00	220.00	135.00
(13)	Hugh Mulcahy	450.00	220.00	135.00
(14)	Skeeter Newsome	450.00	220.00	135.00
(15)	Claude Passeau	450.00	220.00	135.00
(16)	George Scharien (Scharein)	450.00	220.00	135.00
(17)	Dick Siebert	450.00	220.00	135.00

1913-1915 Fatima Posters

These blank-back, black-and-white (1913) or b/w with a color picture of a cigarette pack (1914-15) window posters were produced by Pictorial News Co. of New York for distribution by Fatima Cigarettes, whose advertising appears in the lower-right corner of the 12-1/2" x 19" pictures. To the left of the advertising are a couple of sentences about the player(s) pictured (usually in an action pose). The pictures are numbered, but there is currently no idea as to the extent of the issue.

		NM	E	VG
6	Bermuda	1,200	600.00	360.00
15	Christy Mathewson	6,000	3,000	2,000
22	Ty Cobb	7,500	3,500	2,500
31	in National Race	1,000	500.00	300.00
33	Joe Jackson	4,500	2,250	1,350
35	Have to Beat (Chief Bender, Jack Coombs, Eddie Plank)	450.00	225.00	135.00
36	League Race	650.00	325.00	200.00
43	Chicago Cubs team	1,200	600.00	360.00
45	(Various action photos.)	250.00	125.00	75.00
51	Walter Johnson	5,500	2,750	1,650

		NM	E	VG
56	Series Battles(Christy Mathewson, Rube Marquard, Jeff Tesreau, Al Demaree, Chief Bender, Boardwalk Brown, Byron Houck, Eddie Plank)	650.00	325.00	195.00
105	Down in Marlin(Mathewson, Snodgrass, Fletcher, etc.)	325.00	160.00	95.00
153	(1914 Philadelphia A's)	1,500	750.00	450.00
226	Big League Baseball	7,500	3,750	2,250
259	(1915 Philadelphia Phillies)	2,500	1,250	750.00
260	(1915 Red Sox)	3,500	1,750	1,050

1913 Fatima Premiums

Among the rarest of the tobacco cards are the large-format (21" x 13") versions of the T200 Fatima team photos which could be obtained by redeeming 40 coupons from cigarette packs. The premium-size team photos are virtually identical to the smaller cards, except they do not carry the Fatima advertising on the front. Because of their large size, the premiums are seldom seen in top grade. The complete set price is quoted as a hypothetical proposition only; none is known.

		NM	E	VG
	Common Card:	15,000	4,500	2,200
(1)	Boston Nationals	16,000	5,000	2,500
(2)	Brooklyn Nationals	16,000	5,000	2,500
(3)	Chicago Nationals	20,000	6,000	3,000
(4)	Cincinnati Nationals	15,000	4,500	2,200
(5)	New York Nationals	16,000	5,000	2,500
(6)	Philadelphia Nationals	15,000	4,500	2,200
(7)	Pittsburg Nationals	20,000	6,000	3,000
(8)	St. Louis Nationals	15,000	4,500	2,200
(9)	Boston Americans	25,000	7,500	3,750
(10)	Chicago Americans	16,000	5,000	2,500
(11)	Cleveland Americans	25,000	12,500	7,500
(12)	Detroit Americans	25,000	12,500	7,500
(13)	New York Americans	25,000	7,500	3,750
(14)	Philadelphia Americans	20,000	6,000	3,000
(15)	St. Louis Americans	20,000	6,000	3,000
(16)	Washington Americans	15,000	4,500	2,200

1913 Fatima Team Cards (T200)

Issued by the Ligget & Myers Tobacco Co. in 1913 with Fatima brand cigarettes, the T200 set consists of eight National and eight American League team cards. The cards measure 2-5/8" x 4-3/4" and are glossy photographs on paper stock. Although it is unknown why, several of the cards are more difficult to obtain than others. The team cards feature 369 different players, managers and mascots. The card backs contain an offer for an enlarged copy (13" x 21") of a team card, minus the advertising on front, in exchange for 40 Fatima cigarette coupons.

		NM	E	VG
	Complete Set (16):	40,000	12,000	6,000
	Common Card:	1,200	375.00	180.00
(1)	Boston Nationals	4,000	1,200	600.00
(2)	Brooklyn Nationals	2,000	600.00	300.00
(3)	Chicago Nationals	1,200	375.00	180.00
(4)	Cincinnati Nationals	2,250	1,125	675.00
(5)	New York Nationals	2,200	660.00	330.00
(6)	Philadelphia Nationals	1,200	375.00	180.00
(7)	Pittsburg Nationals	1,500	450.00	225.00
(8)	St. Louis Nationals	3,000	1,500	900.00
(9)	Boston Americans	3,000	1,500	900.00
(10)	Chicago Americans	2,000	600.00	300.00
(11)	Cleveland Americans	4,750	2,400	1,400
(12)	Detroit Americans	5,750	2,875	1,725
(13)	New York Americans	4,500	1,350	675.00
(14)	Philadelphia Americans	2,100	1,050	625.00
(15)	St. Louis Americans	3,200	1,000	500.00
(16)	Washington Americans	4,200	1,300	650.00

1914 Fatima (T222)

Unlike the typical 20th Century tobacco card issues, the T222 Fatima cards are glossy photographs on a thin paper stock and measure a larger 2-1/2" x 4-1/2". According to the back of the card, the set includes "100 photographs of famous Baseball Players, American Athletic Champions and Photoplay stars." The baseball portion of the set appears to be complete at 52. The set includes players from 13 of the 16 major league teams (no Red Sox, White Sox or Pirates). Most cards are seen with a small black number from 2-9 or 12-15 beneath the player's name. The same number can be found on up to seven cards. Cards with numbers 12-15 are considered short-prints and so designated in this alphabetical checklist.

		NM	E	VG
	Complete Set (52):	137,500	56,250	28,125
	Common Player:	1,440	565.00	280.00
(1)	Grover Alexander	20,000	4,500	2,250
(2)	Jimmy Archer	1,440	565.00	280.00
(3)	Jimmy Austin (SP)	3,440	1,375	690.00
(4)	Jack Barry	1,440	565.00	280.00
(5)	George Baumgardner (SP)	3,440	1,375	690.00
(6)	Rube Benton	1,440	565.00	280.00
(7)	Roger Bresnahan	4,500	1,815	905.00
(8)	Boardwalk Brown	1,440	565.00	280.00
(9)	George Burns	1,440	565.00	280.00
(10)	Bullet Joe Bush	1,440	565.00	280.00
(11)	George Chalmers	1,440	565.00	280.00
(12)	Frank Chance	4,500	1,815	905.00
(13)	Al Demaree	1,440	565.00	280.00
(14)	Art Fletcher	1,440	565.00	280.00
(15)	Earl Hamilton (SP)	3,440	1,375	690.00
(16)	John Henry (SP)	3,440	1,375	690.00
(17)	Byron Houck	1,440	565.00	280.00
(18)	Miller Huggins	4,500	1,815	905.00
(19)	Hughie Jennings	4,500	1,815	905.00
(20)	Walter Johnson (SP)	17,500	8,750	5,250
(21)	Ray Keating (SP)	3,440	1,375	690.00
(22)	Jack Lapp	1,440	565.00	280.00
(23)	Tommy Leach	1,440	565.00	280.00
(24)	Nemo Leibold (SP)	3,440	1,375	690.00
(25)	Jack Lelivelt (SP)	3,440	1,375	690.00
(26)	Hans Lobert (SP)	3,440	1,375	690.00
(27)	Lee Magee (SP)	3,440	1,375	690.00
(28)	Sherry Magee (SP)	3,440	1,375	690.00
(29)	Fritz Maisel	1,440	565.00	280.00
(30)	Rube Marquard	4,500	1,815	905.00
(31)	George McBride (SP)	3,440	1,375	690.00
(32)	Stuffy McInnis	1,440	565.00	280.00
(33)	Larry McLean	1,440	565.00	280.00
(34)	Ray Morgan (SP)	3,440	1,375	690.00
(35)	Eddie Murphy	1,440	565.00	280.00
(36)	Red Murray	1,440	565.00	280.00
(37)	Rube Oldring	1,440	565.00	280.00
(38)	Bill Orr	1,440	565.00	280.00
(39)	Hub Perdue	1,440	565.00	280.00
(40)	Art Phelan	1,440	565.00	280.00
(41)	Ed Reulbach	1,440	565.00	280.00
(42)	Vic Saier	1,140	565.00	280.00
(43)	Slim Sallee	1,440	565.00	280.00
(44)	Wally Schang	1,440	565.00	280.00
(45)	Wildfire Schulte (SP)	3,440	1,375	690.00
(46)	J.C. "Red" Smith (SP)	3,440	1,375	690.00
(47)	Amos Strunk	1,440	565.00	280.00
(48)	Bill Sweeney	1,440	565.00	280.00
(49)	Lefty Tyler	1,440	565.00	280.00
(50)	Ossie Vitt	1,440	565.00	280.00
(51)	Ivy Wingo	1,440	565.00	280.00
(52)	Heinie Zimmerman	1,440	565.00	280.00

1981 FBI Food Discs

These 2-7/8" discs were issued in pairs on the bottoms of cardboard six-pack contains of Bantam (and possibly other brands) soft drinks in Canada. Black-and-white player portraits at center have had the cap logos airbrushed away. A green-and-orange FBI logo is at top, with the player's name at bottom. Unlike the 1982 FBI issue, there is no copyright date on the 1981 discs. The MLB Players Association logo flanks the portrait at left, with the players position (in English and French) at right, along with his team's city. The team nickname apparently appears only on those discs that have more than one team in a city. The unnumbered discs are checklisted here in alphabetical order. This list is certainly incomplete and the set probably comprises at least 30 discs. Because of their appearance on the bottom of a box, many discs suffer from scuffing on the front, or show indentations from the soda cans. A premium of 25-50 percent attaches to intact boxes or panels.

	NM/M
Rick Bosetti	25.00
Warren Cromartie	25.00
Steve Garvey	35.00
Larry Hisle	25.00
Reggie Jackson	75.00
Pete Rose	400.00
Nolan Ryan	400.00
Gary (Garry) Templeton	25.00

1955 Felin's Franks

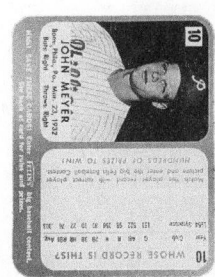

Because of the relatively few specimens in collectors' hands, it is believed this hot dog issue was never actually released. The 4" x 3-5/8" round-cornered panels have a red border front and back with a color player photo on the left side of the front. At right-front are the 1954 stats of a player different than that pictured. Each half of the front shares a large black number. According to the card back, hot dog buyers were supposed to match the pictures and stats of 30 different players to have a chance to win prizes.

		NM	E	VG
	Common Player:	1,250	625.00	375.00
1	Mayo Smith	1,250	625.00	375.00
2	(Probably coach Benny Bengough.)			
3	Wally Moses	1,250	625.00	375.00
4	Whit Wyatt	1,250	625.00	375.00
5	Maje McDonnell	1,250	625.00	375.00
6	Wiechec (Trainer)	750.00	375.00	225.00
7	Murry Dickson	1,250	625.00	375.00
8	Earl Torgeson	1,250	625.00	375.00
9	Bobby Morgan	1,250	625.00	375.00
10	John Meyer	1,250	625.00	375.00
11	Bob Miller	1,250	625.00	375.00
12	Jim Owens	1,250	625.00	375.00
13	Steve Ridzik	1,250	625.00	375.00
14	Robin Roberts	3,750	1,850	1,100
15	(Probably Curt Simmons.)			
16	Herm Wehmeier	1,250	625.00	375.00
17	Smoky Burgess	1,250	625.00	375.00
18	Stan Lopata	1,250	625.00	375.00

19	Gus Niarhos	1,250	625.00	375.00
20	Floyd Baker	1,250	625.00	375.00
21	Marv Blaylock	1,250	625.00	375.00
22	Granny Hamner	1,250	625.00	375.00
23	Willie Jones	1,250	625.00	375.00
24	Ted Kazanski	1,250	625.00	375.00
25	Unknown			
26	Richie Ashburn	4,500	2,200	1,350
27	Joe Lonnett	1,250	625.00	375.00
28	Mel Clark	1,250	625.00	375.00
29	Bob Greenwood	1,250	625.00	375.00
30	Unknown			

1913 Fenway Breweries/Tom Barker Game

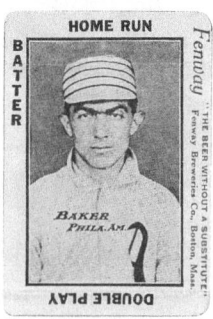

Presumably distributed as a promotion for its Fenway brand of beer, a specially labeled boxed set of the Tom Barker baseball game cards was issued. Only the box, the Score Card and the card of Frank "Home Run" Baker are found bearing the red advertising overprint.

	NM	E	VG
Complete Set (54):	6,000	3,000	1,800
Frank Baker	350.00	175.00	5105.00
Score Card	40.00	20.00	12.00

1916 Ferguson Bakery Felt Pennants (BF2)

Issued circa 1916, this unnumbered set consists of 97 felt pennants with a small black-and-white player photo glued to each. The triangular pennants measure approximately 2-7/8" across the wide top and taper to a length of about 6". The photos are about 1-1/4" x 1-3/4" and appear to be identical to photos used for The Sporting News issues of the same period. The pennants list the player's name and team. The pennants were given away as premiums with the purchase of five-cent loaves of Ferguson Bakery Bread in the Roxbury, Mass. area. It is believed that each player can be found on several different colors of background felt.

		NM	E	VG
Complete Set (97):		27,500	13,500	8,250
Common Player:		175.00	85.00	50.00
(1)	Grover Alexander	600.00	300.00	180.00
(2)	Jimmy Archer	175.00	85.00	50.00
(3)	J. Franklin Baker	450.00	225.00	135.00
(4)	Dave Bancroft	450.00	225.00	135.00
(5)	Jack Barry	175.00	85.00	50.00
(6)	"Chief" Bender	450.00	225.00	135.00
(7)	Joe Benz	175.00	85.00	50.00
(8)	Mordecai Brown	450.00	225.00	135.00
(9)	Geo. J. Burns	175.00	85.00	50.00
(10)	"Donie" Bush	175.00	85.00	50.00
(11)	Forrest Cady	175.00	85.00	50.00
(12)	Max Carey	450.00	225.00	135.00
(13)	Ray Chapman	300.00	150.00	90.00
(14)	Ty Cobb	1,800	900.00	550.00
(15)	Eddie Collins	450.00	225.00	135.00
(16)	"Shauno" Collins	175.00	85.00	50.00
(17)	Charles Comiskey	450.00	225.00	135.00
(18)	Harry Coveleskie (Coveleski)	175.00	85.00	50.00
(19)	Gavvy Cravath	175.00	85.00	50.00
(20)	Sam Crawford	450.00	225.00	135.00
(21)	Jake Daubert	175.00	85.00	50.00
(22)	Josh Devore	175.00	85.00	50.00
(23)	Charles Dooin	175.00	85.00	50.00
(24)	Larry Doyle	175.00	85.00	50.00
(25)	Jean Dubuc	175.00	85.00	50.00
(26)	Johnny Evers	450.00	225.00	135.00
(27)	Urban Faber	450.00	225.00	135.00
(28)	Eddie Foster	175.00	85.00	50.00
(29)	Del Gainer (Gainor)	175.00	85.00	50.00
(30)	"Chic" Gandil	375.00	185.00	110.00
(31)	Joe Gedeon	175.00	85.00	50.00
(32)	Hank Gowdy	175.00	85.00	50.00
(33)	Earl Hamilton	175.00	85.00	50.00
(34)	Claude Hendrix	175.00	85.00	50.00
(35)	Buck Herzog	175.00	85.00	50.00
(36)	Harry Hooper	450.00	225.00	135.00
(37)	Miller Huggins	450.00	225.00	135.00
(38)	Joe Jackson	3,500	1,750	1,000
(39)	William James	175.00	85.00	50.00
(40)	Hugh Jennings	450.00	225.00	135.00
(41)	Walter Johnson	900.00	450.00	275.00
(42)	Fielder Jones	175.00	85.00	50.00
(43)	Joe Judge	175.00	85.00	50.00
(44)	Benny Kauff	175.00	85.00	50.00
(45)	Wm. Killefer	175.00	85.00	50.00
(46)	Napoleon Lajoie	450.00	225.00	135.00
(47)	Jack Lapp	175.00	85.00	50.00
(48)	John Lavan	175.00	85.00	50.00
(49)	Jimmy Lavender	175.00	85.00	50.00
(50)	"Dutch" Leonard	175.00	85.00	50.00
(51)	Duffy Lewis	175.00	85.00	50.00
(52)	Hans Lobert	175.00	85.00	50.00
(53)	Fred Luderus	175.00	85.00	50.00
(54)	Connie Mack	450.00	225.00	135.00
(55)	Sherwood Magee	175.00	85.00	50.00
(56)	Al Mamaux	175.00	85.00	50.00
(57)	"Rabbit" Maranville	450.00	225.00	135.00
(58)	Rube Marquard	450.00	225.00	135.00
(59)	George McBride	175.00	85.00	50.00
(60)	John J. McGraw	450.00	225.00	135.00
(61)	Jack McInnis	175.00	85.00	50.00
(62)	Fred Merkle	175.00	85.00	50.00
(63)	Chief Meyers	175.00	85.00	50.00
(64)	Clyde Milan	175.00	85.00	50.00
(65)	Otto Miller	175.00	85.00	50.00
(66)	Pat Moran	175.00	85.00	50.00
(67)	Ray Morgan	175.00	85.00	50.00
(68)	Guy Morton	175.00	85.00	50.00
(69)	Ed. Murphy	175.00	85.00	50.00
(70)	Rube Oldring	175.00	85.00	50.00
(71)	"Dode" Paskert	175.00	85.00	50.00
(72)	Walter Pipp	175.00	85.00	50.00
(73)	Clarence Rowland	175.00	85.00	50.00
(74)	"Nap" Rucker	175.00	85.00	50.00
(75)	Dick Rudolph	175.00	85.00	50.00
(76)	Reb Russell	175.00	85.00	50.00
(77)	Vic Saier	175.00	85.00	50.00
(78)	"Slim" Sallee	175.00	85.00	50.00
(79)	Ray Schalk	450.00	225.00	135.00
(80)	Walter Schang	175.00	85.00	50.00
(81)	Frank Schulte	175.00	85.00	50.00
(82)	Jim Scott	175.00	85.00	50.00
(83)	George Sisler	450.00	225.00	135.00
(84)	Geo. Stallings	175.00	85.00	50.00
(85)	Oscar Stanage	175.00	85.00	50.00
(86)	"Jeff" Tesreau	175.00	85.00	50.00
(87)	Joe Tinker	450.00	225.00	135.00
(88)	Geo. Tyler	175.00	85.00	50.00
(89)	Jim Vaughn	175.00	85.00	50.00
(90)	Bobby Veach	175.00	85.00	50.00
(91)	Hans Wagner	1,350	675.00	400.00
(92)	Ed. Walsh	450.00	225.00	135.00
(93)	Buck Weaver	750.00	375.00	225.00
(94)	Ivy Wingo	175.00	85.00	50.00
(95)	Joe Wood	350.00	175.00	100.00
(96)	"Pep" Young	175.00	85.00	50.00
(97)	Heiny Zimmerman	175.00	85.00	50.00

1916 Ferguson Bakery Photo Prize Pennants

As part of its baseball insert and premium program, the Roxbury, Mass., bakery issued this series of large (9" x 24") felt pennants bearing a black-and-white player photo (3" x 5"). The colorful pennants are decorated with baseball graphics and have player and team identification. The pennants were a premium for redeeming 50 tickets from five-cent loaves of bread. Examples of the large-format pennants are so scarce only a handful of players are checklisted thus far.

		NM	E	VG
Common Player:		9,000	4,500	2,750
(1)	Grover Alexander	15,000	7,500	4,500
(2)	Jack Barry	9,000	4,500	2,750
(3)	Ty Cobb	20,000	10,000	6,000
(4)	Eddie Collins	9,000	4,500	2,750
(4)	Bill Donovan	9,000	4,500	2,750
(5)	Miller Huggins	12,500	6,250	3,750
(6)	John McGraw	12,500	6,250	3,750
(8)	Joe Tinker	9,000	4,500	2,750

1957 Fine Arts Studio

The date of issue on this card is theoretical with no real evidence present on the piece. Published by Fine Arts Studio of Cleveland, the 3-1/2" x 5-1/2" card has a borderless color photo on front. Player identification is on back with standard postcard markings and credit lines to the publisher and printer (Dexter Press of New York).

	NM	E	VG
75062 Richie Ashburn	100.00	50.00	30.00

1959 First Federal Savings Famous Senators Matchbooks

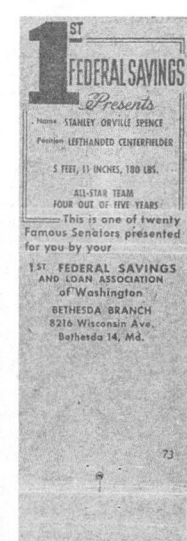

Star Senators of the 20th Century are featured in this series of matchbook covers. The 1-1/2" x 4-1/2" matchbooks include a black-and-white player portrait photo and team logo on front. The sponsoring bank's advertising is on back. Player identification and information are printed inside. Values shown are for complete but empty covers, with the striker surface intact. Complete matchbooks with matches bring about 2X the values quoted.

		NM	E	VG
Complete Set (20):		325.00	160.00	95.00
Common Player:		15.00	7.50	4.50
(1)	Nick Altrock	15.00	7.50	4.50
(2)	Ossie Bluege	15.00	7.50	4.50
(3)	Joe Cronin	20.00	10.00	6.00
(4)	Alvin Crowder	15.00	7.50	4.50
(5)	Goose Goslin	20.00	10.00	6.00
(6)	Clark Griffith	20.00	10.00	6.00
(7)	Bucky Harris	20.00	10.00	6.00
(8)	Walter Johnson	45.00	22.00	13.50
(9)	Joe Judge	15.00	7.50	4.50
(10)	Harmon Killebrew	25.00	12.50	7.50
(11)	Joe Kuhel	15.00	7.50	4.50
(12)	Buddy Lewis	15.00	7.50	4.50
(13)	Clyde Milan	15.00	7.50	4.50
(14)	Buddy Myer	15.00	7.50	4.50
(15)	Roger Peckinpaugh	15.00	7.50	4.50
(16)	Sam Rice	20.00	10.00	6.00
(17)	Roy Sievers	15.00	7.50	4.50
(18)	Stanley Spence	15.00	7.50	4.50
(19)	Mickey Vernon	15.00	7.50	4.50
(20)	Samuel West	15.00	7.50	4.50

1953 First National Super Market Boston Red Sox

Four of the early 1950s Red Sox appear in this series issued by a Boston grocery chain. The cards may have been distributed in conjunction with players' in-store appearances. The cards measure 3-3/4" x 5" and are printed in black-and-white. A facsimile autograph appears on the front. Backs have the sponsor's advertising. The unnumbered cards are checklisted here alphabetically. See also 1953 Stop & Shop Boston Red Sox.

		NM	E	VG
Complete Set (4):		2,500	1,250	750.00
Common Player:		750.00	375.00	225.00
(1)	Billy Goodman	750.00	375.00	225.00
(2)	Ellis Kinder	750.00	375.00	225.00
(3)	Mel Parnell	750.00	375.00	225.00
(4)	Sammy White	750.00	375.00	225.00

1951 Fischer's Bread Labels

This set of end-labels from loaves of bread consists of 32 player photos, each measuring approximately 2-3/4" square. The labels include the player's name, team and position, along with a few words about him. The bakery's slogan "Bread For Energy" appears in a dark band along the bottom. The set, which is unnumbered, was distributed in the Northeast.

		NM	E	VG
Complete Set (32):		25,000	10,000	5,000
Common Player:		750.00	375.00	225.00
(1)	Vern Bickford	750.00	300.00	150.00
(2)	Ralph Branca	825.00	325.00	175.00
(3)	Harry Brecheen	750.00	300.00	150.00
(4)	"Chico" Carrasquel	750.00	300.00	150.00
(5)	Cliff Chambers	750.00	300.00	150.00
(6)	"Hoot" Evers	750.00	300.00	150.00
(7)	Ned Garver	750.00	300.00	150.00
(8)	Billy Goodman	750.00	300.00	150.00
(9)	Gil Hodges	1,350	550.00	275.00
(10)	Larry Jansen	750.00	300.00	150.00
(11)	Willie Jones	750.00	300.00	150.00
(12)	Eddie Joost	750.00	300.00	150.00
(13)	George Kell	1,250	500.00	250.00
(14)	Alex Kellner	750.00	300.00	150.00
(15)	Ted Kluszewski	1,200	480.00	240.00
(16)	Jim Konstanty	750.00	300.00	150.00
(17)	Bob Lemon	1,250	500.00	250.00
(18)	Cass Michaels	750.00	300.00	150.00
(19)	Johnny Mize	1,250	500.00	250.00
(20)	Irv Noren	750.00	300.00	150.00
(21)	Andy Pafko	750.00	300.00	150.00
(22)	Joe Page	750.00	300.00	150.00
(23)	Mel Parnell	750.00	300.00	150.00
(24)	Johnny Sain	825.00	330.00	165.00
(25)	"Red" Schoendienst	1,250	500.00	250.00
(26)	Roy Sievers	750.00	300.00	150.00
(27)	Roy Smalley	750.00	300.00	150.00
(28)	Herman Wehmeier	750.00	300.00	150.00
(29)	Bill Werle	750.00	300.00	150.00
(30)	Wes Westrum	750.00	300.00	150.00
(31)	Early Wynn	1,250	500.00	250.00
(32)	Gus Zernial	750.00	300.00	150.00

1970 Flavor-est Milk Milwaukee Brewers

Mike Hershberger

While purporting to be a dairy issue, this is actually a collectors' set produced by Illinois hobbyist Bob Solon. The cards picture members of the 1970 Brewers in their first year in Milwaukee. Posed action photos and portraits are printed in blue-and-white on a 2-3/8" x 4-1/4" format. The pictures are borderless at top and sides. At bottom is a white strip with the player name. Backs have a dairy ad. The unnumbered cards are checklisted here alphabetically. Ironically, this set was later reissued in a marked reprint.

		NM	E	VG
Complete Set (24):		25.00	12.50	7.50
Common Player:		2.50	1.25	.70
(1)	Gene Brabender	2.50	1.25	.70
(2)	Dave Bristol	2.50	1.25	.70
(3)	Wayne Comer	2.50	1.25	.70
(4)	Cal Ermer	2.50	1.25	.70
(5)	Greg Goossen	2.50	1.25	.70
(6)	Tom Harper	3.50	1.75	1.00
(7)	Mike Hegan	3.50	1.75	1.00
(8)	Mike Hershberger	2.50	1.25	.70
(9)	Steve Hovley	2.50	1.25	.70
(10)	John Kennedy	2.50	1.25	.70
(11)	Lew Krausse	2.50	1.25	.70
(12)	Ted Kubiak	2.50	1.25	.70
(13)	Bob Locker	2.50	1.25	.70
(14)	Roy McMillan	2.50	1.25	.70
(15)	Jerry McNertney	2.50	1.25	.70
(16)	Bob Meyer	2.50	1.25	.70
(17)	John Morris	2.50	1.25	.70
(18)	John O'Donoghue	2.50	1.25	.70
(19)	Marty Pattin	2.50	1.25	.70
(20)	Rich Rollins	2.50	1.25	.70
(21)	Phil Roof	2.50	1.25	.70
(22)	Ted Savage	2.50	1.25	.70
(23)	Russ Snyder	2.50	1.25	.70
(24)	Dan Walton	3.50	1.75	1.00

1923 Fleer

While only a few specimens are known to date, from the print on the back it can be presumed that all 60 of the baseball players from the blank-back strip card set cataloged as W515 were also issued with Fleer advertising on the verso. Several cards are also known with boxers, indicating another 60 cards of non-baseball athletes and other famous people were also produced. The 1-5/8" x 2-3/8" cards feature crude color line art of the player on front, with a black-and-white ad on back. The cards pre-date by more than a decade Fleer's "Cops and Robbers" set of 1935, and are some 35 years in advance of Fleer's first modern baseball issue.

		NM	E	VG
Complete Set (60):		15,000	7,500	4,500
Common Player:		175.00	85.00	50.00
1	Bill Cunningham	175.00	85.00	50.00
2	Al Mamaux	175.00	85.00	50.00
3	"Babe" Ruth	1,325	660.00	400.00
4	Dave Bancroft	350.00	175.00	105.00
5	Ed Rommel	175.00	85.00	50.00
6	"Babe" Adams	175.00	85.00	50.00
7	Clarence Walker	175.00	85.00	50.00
8	Waite Hoyt	350.00	175.00	105.00
9	Bob Shawkey	175.00	85.00	50.00
10	"Ty" Cobb	1,000	500.00	300.00
11	George Sisler	350.00	175.00	105.00
12	Jack Bentley	175.00	85.00	50.00
13	Jim O'Connell	175.00	85.00	50.00
14	Frank Frisch	350.00	175.00	105.00
15	Frank Baker	350.00	175.00	105.00
16	Burleigh Grimes	350.00	175.00	105.00
17	Wally Schang	175.00	85.00	50.00
18	Harry Heilman (Heilmann)	350.00	175.00	105.00
19	Aaron Ward	175.00	85.00	50.00
20	Carl Mays	200.00	100.00	60.00
21	The Meusel Bros.(Bob Meusel, Irish Meusel)	225.00	110.00	67.00
22	Arthur Nehf	175.00	85.00	50.00
23	Lee Meadows	175.00	85.00	50.00
24	"Casey" Stengel	375.00	185.00	110.00
25	Jack Scott	175.00	85.00	50.00
26	Kenneth Williams	175.00	85.00	50.00
27	Joe Bush	175.00	85.00	50.00
28	Tris Speaker	400.00	200.00	120.00
29	Ross Young (Youngs)	350.00	175.00	105.00
30	Joe Dugan	175.00	85.00	50.00
31	The Barnes Bros.(Jesse Barnes, Virgil Barnes)	200.00	100.00	60.00
32	George Kelly	350.00	175.00	105.00
33	Hugh McQuillen (McQuillan)	175.00	85.00	50.00
34	Hugh Jennings	350.00	175.00	105.00
35	Tom Griffith	175.00	85.00	50.00
36	Miller Huggins	350.00	175.00	105.00
37	"Whitey" Witt	175.00	85.00	50.00
38	Walter Johnson	500.00	250.00	150.00
39	"Wally" Pipp	200.00	100.00	60.00
40	"Dutch" Reuther (Ruether)	175.00	85.00	50.00
41	Jim Johnston	175.00	85.00	50.00
42	Willie Kamm	175.00	85.00	50.00
43	Sam Jones	175.00	85.00	50.00
44	Frank Snyder	175.00	85.00	50.00
45	John McGraw	350.00	175.00	105.00
46	Everett Scott	175.00	85.00	50.00
47	"Babe" Ruth	1,325	660.00	400.00
48	Urban Shocker	175.00	85.00	50.00
49	Grover Alexander	400.00	200.00	120.00
50	"Rabbit" Maranville	350.00	175.00	105.00
51	Ray Schalk	350.00	175.00	105.00
52	"Heinie" Groh	175.00	85.00	50.00
53	Wilbert Robinson	350.00	175.00	105.00
54	George Burns	175.00	85.00	50.00
55	Rogers Hornsby	400.00	200.00	120.00
56	Zack Wheat	350.00	175.00	105.00
57	Eddie Roush	350.00	175.00	105.00
58	Eddie Collins	350.00	175.00	105.00

| 59 | Charlie Hollocher | 175.00 | 85.00 | 50.00 |
| 60 | Red Faber | 350.00 | 175.00 | 105.00 |

1959 Fleer Ted Williams

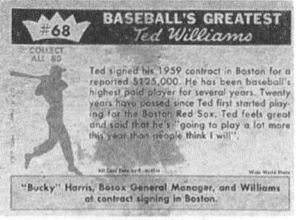

This 80-card 1959 Fleer set tells of the life of baseball great Ted Williams, from his childhood years up to 1958. The full-color cards measure 2-1/2" x 3-1/2" in size and make use of both horizontal and vertical formats. The card backs, all designed horizontally, contain a continuing biography of Williams. Card #68 was withdrawn from the set early in production and is scarce. Counterfeit cards of #68 have been produced and can be distinguished by a cross-hatch pattern which appears over the photo on the card fronts.

		NM	E	VG
Complete Set (80):		1,250	625.00	312.50
Common Card:		15.00	7.50	3.75
Wax Pack (6):		400.00		
1	The Early Years	100.00	50.00	25.00
2	Ted's Idol (Babe Ruth)	120.00	60.00	30.00
3	Practice Makes Perfect	15.00	7.50	3.75
4	1934 - Ted Learns The Fine Points	15.00	7.50	3.75
5	Ted's Fame Spreads - 1935-36	15.00	7.50	3.75
6	Ted Turns Professional	20.00	10.00	6.00
7	1936 - From Mound To Plate	15.00	7.50	3.75
8	1937 - First Full Season	15.00	7.50	3.75
9	(With Eddie Collins.)	15.00	7.50	3.75
10	1938 - Gunning As A Pastime	15.00	7.50	3.75
11	(With Jimmie Foxx.)	30.00	15.00	9.00
12	1939 - Burning Up The Minors	20.00	10.00	6.00
13	1939 - Ted Shows He Will Stay	15.00	7.50	3.75
14	Outstanding Rookie of 1939	20.00	10.00	6.00
15	1940 - Williams Licks Sophomore Jinx	20.00	10.00	6.00
16	1941 - Williams' Greatest Year	15.00	7.50	3.75
17	1941 - How Ted Hit .400	35.00	17.50	10.50
18	1941 - All-Star Hero	15.00	7.50	3.75
19	1942 - Ted Wins Triple Crown	15.00	7.50	3.75
20	1942 - On To Naval Training	15.00	7.50	3.75
21	1943 - Honors For Williams	15.00	7.50	3.75
22	1944 - Ted Solos	15.00	7.50	3.75
23	1944 - Williams Wins His Wings	15.00	7.50	3.75
24	1945 - Sharpshooter	15.00	7.50	3.75
25	1945 - Ted Is Discharged	15.00	7.50	3.75
26	1946 - Off To A Flying Start	15.00	7.50	3.75
27	July 9, 1946 - One Man Show	15.00	7.50	3.75
28	July 14, 1946 - The Williams Shift	15.00	7.50	3.75
29	July 21, 1946, Ted Hits For The Cycle	20.00	10.00	6.00
30	1946 - Beating The Williams Shift	15.00	7.50	3.75
31	Oct. 1946 - Sox Lose The Series	15.00	7.50	3.75
32	1946 - Most Valuable Player	15.00	7.50	3.75
33	1947 - Another Triple Crown For Ted	15.00	7.50	3.75
34	1947 - Ted Sets Runs-Scored Record	15.00	7.50	3.75

35	1948 - The Sox Miss The Pennant	15.00	7.50	3.75
36	1948 - Banner Year For Ted	15.00	7.50	3.75
37	1949 - Sox Miss Out Again	15.00	7.50	3.75
38	1949 - Power Rampage	15.00	7.50	3.75
39	(With Joe Cronin and Eddie Collins.)	15.00	7.50	3.75
40	July 11, 1950 - Ted Crashes Into Wall	15.00	7.50	3.75
41	1950 - Ted Recovers	15.00	7.50	3.75
42	1951 - Williams Slowed By Injury	15.00	7.50	3.75
43	1951 - Leads Outfielders In Double Play	15.00	7.50	3.75
44	1952 - Back To The Marines	15.00	7.50	3.75
45	1952 - Farewell To Baseball?	15.00	7.50	3.75
46	1952 - Ready For Combat	15.00	7.50	3.75
47	1953 - Ted Crash Lands Jet	15.00	7.50	3.75
48	July 14, 1953 - Ted Returns	15.00	7.50	3.75
49	1953 - Smash Return	15.00	7.50	3.75
50	March 1954 - Spring Injury	15.00	7.50	3.75
51	May 16, 1954 - Ted Is Patched Up	15.00	7.50	3.75
52	1954 - Ted's Comeback	15.00	7.50	3.75
53	1954 - Ted's Comeback Is A Sucess	15.00	7.50	3.75
54	Dec. 1954, Fisherman Ted Hooks a Big On	15.00	7.50	3.75
55	(With Joe Cronin.)	15.00	7.50	3.75
56	1955 - 2,000th Major League Hit	15.00	7.50	3.75
57	1956 - Ted Reaches 400th Homer	15.00	7.50	3.75
58	1957 - Williams Hits .388	15.00	7.50	3.75
59	1957 - Hot September For Ted	15.00	7.50	3.75
60	1957 - More Records For Ted	15.00	7.50	3.75
61	1957 - Outfielder Ted	15.00	7.50	3.75
62	1958 - 6th Batting Title For Ted	15.00	7.50	3.75
63	Ted's All-Star Record	35.00	17.50	10.00
64	1958 - Daughter And Famous Daddy	15.00	7.50	3.75
65	August 30, 1958	15.00	7.50	3.75
66	1958 - Powerhouse	15.00	7.50	3.75
67	(With Sam Snead.)	20.00	10.00	6.00
68	Jan. 23, 1959 - Ted Signs For 1959	850.00	420.00	250.00
69	A Future Ted Williams?	15.00	7.50	3.75
70	Ted Williams & Jim Thorpe	30.00	15.00	9.00
71	Ted's Hitting Fundamentals #1	15.00	7.50	3.75
72	Ted's Hitting Fundamentals #2	15.00	7.50	3.75
73	Ted's Hitting Fundamentals #3	15.00	7.50	3.75
74	Here's How!	15.00	7.50	3.75
75	(With Babe Ruth, Eddie Collins.)	30.00	15.00	9.00
76	Ted's Remarkable "On Base" Record	15.00	7.50	3.75
77	Ted Relaxes	15.00	7.50	3.75
78	Honors For Williams	15.00	7.50	3.75
79	Where Ted Stands	25.00	12.50	7.50
80	Ted's Goals For 1959	40.00	15.00	9.00

1960 Fleer Baseball Greats

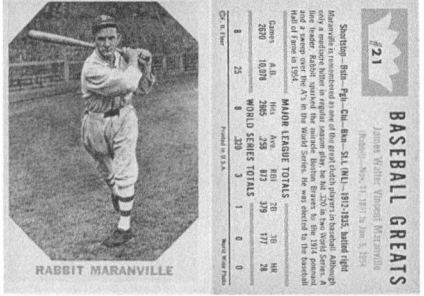

The 1960 Fleer Baseball Greats set consists of 78 cards of the game's top players from the past, plus a card of Ted Williams, who was in his final major league season. The cards are standard size (2-1/2" x 3-1/2") and feature color photos inside blue, green, red or yellow borders. The card backs carry a short player biography plus career hitting or pitching statistics. Unissued cards with a Pepper Martin back (#80), but with another player pictured on the front, exist. All

have been either cancelled with a slit cut out of the bottom, or show evidence of having been hand-cut from a sheet.

		NM	E	VG
Complete Set (79):		500.00	250.00	125.00
Common Player:		6.00	3.00	1.50
Wax Pack:		300.00		
1	Nap Lajoie	22.50	7.50	4.00
2	Christy Mathewson	16.00	8.00	5.00
3	Babe Ruth	100.00	50.00	25.00
4	Carl Hubbell	6.00	3.00	1.50
5	Grover Cleveland Alexander	15.00	7.50	4.50
6	Walter Johnson	20.00	10.00	6.00
7	Chief Bender	6.00	3.00	1.50
8	Roger Bresnahan	6.00	3.00	1.50
9	Mordecai Brown	6.00	3.00	1.50
10	Tris Speaker	6.00	3.00	1.50
11	Arky Vaughan	6.00	3.00	1.50
12	Zack Wheat	6.00	3.00	1.50
13	George Sisler	6.00	3.00	1.50
14	Connie Mack	6.00	3.00	1.50
15	Clark Griffith	6.00	3.00	1.50
16	Lou Boudreau	6.00	3.00	1.50
17	Ernie Lombardi	6.00	3.00	1.50
18	Heinie Manush	6.00	3.00	1.50
19	Marty Marion	6.00	3.00	1.50
20	Eddie Collins	6.00	3.00	1.50
21	Rabbit Maranville	6.00	3.00	1.50
22	Joe Medwick	6.00	3.00	1.50
23	Ed Barrow	6.00	3.00	1.50
24	Mickey Cochrane	6.00	3.00	1.50
25	Jimmy Collins	6.00	3.00	1.50
26	Bob Feller	13.50	6.75	4.00
27	Luke Appling	6.00	3.00	1.50
28	Lou Gehrig	100.00	50.00	25.00
29	Gabby Hartnett	6.00	3.00	1.50
30	Chuck Klein	6.00	3.00	1.50
31	Tony Lazzeri	6.00	3.00	1.50
32	Al Simmons	6.00	3.00	1.50
33	Wilbert Robinson	6.00	3.00	1.50
34	Sam Rice	6.00	3.00	1.50
35	Herb Pennock	6.00	3.00	1.50
36	Mel Ott	6.00	3.00	1.50
37	Lefty O'Doul	6.00	3.00	1.50
38	Johnny Mize	6.00	3.00	1.50
39	Bing Miller	6.00	3.00	1.50
40	Joe Tinker	6.00	3.00	1.50
41	Frank Baker	6.00	3.00	1.50
42	Ty Cobb	50.00	25.00	12.50
43	Paul Derringer	6.00	3.00	1.50
44	Cap Anson	6.00	3.00	1.50
45	Jim Bottomley	6.00	3.00	1.50
46	Eddie Plank	6.00	3.00	1.50
47	Cy Young	16.00	8.00	5.00
48	Hack Wilson	6.00	3.00	1.50
49	Ed Walsh	6.00	3.00	1.50
50	Frank Chance	6.00	3.00	1.50
51	Dazzy Vance	6.00	3.00	1.50
52	Bill Terry	6.00	3.00	1.50
53	Jimmy Foxx	15.00	7.50	4.50
54	Lefty Gomez	6.00	3.00	1.50
55	Branch Rickey	6.00	3.00	1.50
56	Ray Schalk	6.00	3.00	1.50
57	Johnny Evers	6.00	3.00	1.50
58	Charlie Gehringer	6.00	3.00	1.50
59	Burleigh Grimes	6.00	3.00	1.50
60	Lefty Grove	6.00	3.00	1.50
61	Rube Waddell	6.00	3.00	1.50
62	Honus Wagner	15.00	7.50	4.50
63	Red Ruffing	6.00	3.00	1.50
64	Judge Landis	6.00	3.00	1.50
65	Harry Heilmann	6.00	3.00	1.50
66	John McGraw	6.00	3.00	1.50
67	Hughie Jennings	6.00	3.00	1.50
68	Hal Newhouser	6.00	3.00	1.50
69	Waite Hoyt	6.00	3.00	1.50
70	Bobo Newsom	6.00	3.00	1.50
71	Earl Averill	6.00	3.00	1.50
72	Ted Williams	80.00	40.00	20.00
73	Warren Giles	6.00	3.00	1.50
74	Ford Frick	6.00	3.00	1.50
75	Ki Ki Cuyler	6.00	3.00	1.50
76	Paul Waner	6.00	3.00	1.50
77	Pie Traynor	6.00	3.00	1.50
78	Lloyd Waner	6.00	3.00	1.50
79	Ralph Kiner	6.00	3.00	1.50
80	Pepper Martin (Unissued, slit-cancelled proof, Lefty Grove, Joe Tinker or Eddie Collins on front.)	3,000	1,500	900.00
80	Pepper Martin (Unissued hand-cut proof. Lefty Grove, Eddie Collins or Joe Tinker on front.)	4,000	2,000	1,200

1960-62 Fleer Team Logo Decals

These colorful team logo decals were pack inserts in Fleer's 1960-62 baseball card issues. The decals measure 2-1/4" x 3". Those issued in 1960 have a blue background on front. The 1961-62 decals have a white background on front. Backs have advertising for Fleer bubblegum and instructions on applying the decals. The 1961 decals have back printing in blue; the 1962s are in red.

	NM	E	VG
Complete Set, 1960 (16):	100.00	50.00	30.00
Complete Set, 1961 (18):	100.00	50.00	30.00
Complete Set, 1962 (20):	250.00	125.00	75.00
1960 team decal, blue background	9.00	4.50	2.75
1961 decal, white background, blue back	4.50	2.25	1.25
1962 decal, white background, red back	9.00	4.50	2.75

1961 Fleer Baseball Greats

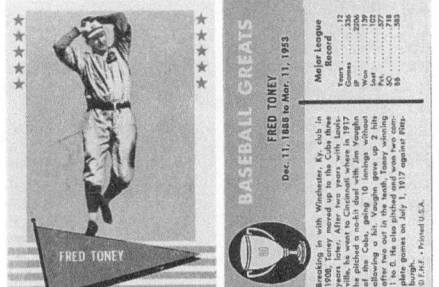

In 1961, Fleer issued another set utilizing the Baseball Greats theme. The 154-card set was issued in two series and features a color (or colorized) player portrait against a colored background. The player's name is located in a pennant at bottom. Card backs feature orange and black on white stock and contain player biographical and statistical information. The cards measure 2-1/2" x 3-1/2" in size. Five-cent wax packs included five cards plus a team logo decal and sticker.

	NM	E	VG
Complete Set (154):	1,400	700.00	425.00
Common Player:	10.00	5.00	3.00
Wax Pack (5+1+1):	265.00		

1	Checklist(Frank Baker, Ty Cobb, Zach Wheat)	65.00	35.00	20.00
2	G.C. Alexander	12.00	6.00	3.00
3	Nick Altrock	10.00	5.00	3.00
4	Cap Anson	10.00	5.00	3.00
5	Earl Averill	10.00	5.00	3.00
6	Home Run Baker	10.00	5.00	3.00
7	Dave Bancroft	10.00	5.00	3.00
8	Chief Bender	10.00	5.00	3.00
9	Jim Bottomley	10.00	5.00	3.00
10	Roger Bresnahan	10.00	5.00	3.00
11	Mordecai Brown	10.00	5.00	3.00
12	Max Carey	10.00	5.00	3.00
13	Jack Chesbro	10.00	5.00	3.00
14	Ty Cobb	65.00	35.00	20.00
15	Mickey Cochrane	10.00	5.00	3.00
16	Eddie Collins	10.00	5.00	3.00
17	Earle Combs	10.00	5.00	3.00
18	Charles Comiskey	10.00	5.00	3.00
19	Ki Ki Cuyler	10.00	5.00	3.00
20	Paul Derringer	10.00	5.00	3.00
21	Howard Ehmke	10.00	5.00	3.00
22	Billy Evans	10.00	5.00	3.00
23	Johnny Evers	10.00	5.00	3.00
24	Red Faber	10.00	5.00	3.00
25	Bob Feller	12.00	6.00	4.00
26	Wes Ferrell	10.00	5.00	3.00
27	Lew Fonseca	10.00	5.00	3.00
28	Jimmy Foxx	12.00	6.00	3.00
29	Ford Frick	10.00	5.00	3.00
30	Frankie Frisch	10.00	5.00	3.00
31	Lou Gehrig	125.00	60.00	40.00
32	Charlie Gehringer	10.00	5.00	3.00
33	Warren Giles	10.00	5.00	3.00
34	Lefty Gomez	10.00	5.00	3.00
35	Goose Goslin	10.00	5.00	3.00
36	Clark Griffith	10.00	5.00	3.00
37	Burleigh Grimes	10.00	5.00	3.00
38	Lefty Grove	10.00	5.00	3.00
39	Chick Hafey	10.00	5.00	3.00
40	Jesse Haines	10.00	5.00	3.00
41	Gabby Hartnett	10.00	5.00	3.00
42	Harry Heilmann	10.00	5.00	3.00
43	Rogers Hornsby	10.00	5.00	3.00
44	Waite Hoyt	10.00	5.00	3.00
45	Carl Hubbell	10.00	5.00	3.00
46	Miller Huggins	10.00	5.00	3.00
47	Hughie Jennings	10.00	5.00	3.00
48	Ban Johnson	10.00	5.00	3.00
49	Walter Johnson	15.00	8.00	5.00
50	Ralph Kiner	10.00	5.00	3.00
51	Chuck Klein	10.00	5.00	3.00
52	Johnny Kling	10.00	5.00	3.00
53	Judge Landis	10.00	5.00	3.00
54	Tony Lazzeri	10.00	5.00	3.00
55	Ernie Lombardi	10.00	5.00	3.00
56	Dolf Luque	10.00	5.00	3.00
57	Heinie Manush	10.00	5.00	3.00
58	Marty Marion	10.00	5.00	3.00
59	Christy Mathewson	15.00	8.00	5.00
60	John McGraw	10.00	5.00	3.00
61	Joe Medwick	10.00	5.00	3.00
62	Bing Miller	10.00	5.00	3.00
63	Johnny Mize	10.00	5.00	3.00
64	Johnny Mostil	10.00	5.00	3.00
65	Art Nehf	10.00	5.00	3.00
66	Hal Newhouser	10.00	5.00	3.00
67	Bobo Newsom	10.00	5.00	3.00
68	Mel Ott	10.00	5.00	3.00
69	Allie Reynolds	10.00	5.00	3.00
70	Sam Rice	10.00	5.00	3.00
71	Eppa Rixey	10.00	5.00	3.00
72	Edd Roush	10.00	5.00	3.00
73	Schoolboy Rowe	10.00	5.00	3.00
74	Red Ruffing	10.00	5.00	3.00
75	Babe Ruth	150.00	75.00	40.00
76	Joe Sewell	10.00	5.00	3.00
77	Al Simmons	10.00	5.00	3.00
78	George Sisler	10.00	5.00	3.00
79	Tris Speaker	10.00	5.00	3.00
80	Fred Toney	10.00	5.00	3.00
81	Dazzy Vance	10.00	5.00	3.00
82	Jim Vaughn	10.00	5.00	3.00
83	Big Ed Walsh	10.00	5.00	3.00
84	Lloyd Waner	10.00	5.00	3.00
85	Paul Waner	10.00	5.00	3.00
86	Zach Wheat	10.00	5.00	3.00
87	Hack Wilson	10.00	5.00	3.00
88	Jimmy Wilson	10.00	5.00	3.00
89	Checklist(George Sisler, Pie Traynor)	75.00	40.00	25.00
90	Babe Adams	10.00	5.00	3.00
91	Dale Alexander	10.00	5.00	3.00
92	Jim Bagby Sr.	10.00	5.00	3.00
93	Ossie Bluege	10.00	5.00	3.00
94	Lou Boudreau	10.00	5.00	3.00
95	Tommy Bridges	10.00	5.00	3.00
96	Donnie Bush (Donie)	10.00	5.00	3.00
97	Dolph Camilli	10.00	5.00	3.00
98	Frank Chance	10.00	5.00	3.00
99	Jimmy Collins	10.00	5.00	3.00
100	Stanley Coveleskie (Coveleski)	10.00	5.00	3.00
101	Hughie Critz	10.00	5.00	3.00
102	General Crowder	10.00	5.00	3.00
103	Joe Dugan	10.00	5.00	3.00
104	Bibb Falk	10.00	5.00	3.00
105	Rick Ferrell	10.00	5.00	3.00
106	Art Fletcher	10.00	5.00	3.00
107	Dennis Galehouse	10.00	5.00	3.00
108	Chick Galloway	10.00	5.00	3.00
109	Mule Haas	10.00	5.00	3.00
110	Stan Hack	10.00	5.00	3.00
111	Bump Hadley	10.00	5.00	3.00
112	Billy Hamilton	10.00	5.00	3.00
113	Joe Hauser	10.00	5.00	3.00
114	Babe Herman	10.00	5.00	3.00
115	Travis Jackson	10.00	5.00	3.00
116	Eddie Joost	10.00	5.00	3.00
117	Addie Joss	10.00	5.00	3.00
118	Joe Judge	10.00	5.00	3.00
119	Joe Kuhel	10.00	5.00	3.00
120	Nap Lajoie	10.00	5.00	3.00
121	Dutch Leonard	10.00	5.00	3.00
122	Ted Lyons	10.00	5.00	3.00
123	Connie Mack	10.00	5.00	3.00
124	Rabbit Maranville	10.00	5.00	3.00
125	Fred Marberry	10.00	5.00	3.00
126	Iron Man McGinnity	10.00	5.00	3.00
127	Oscar Melillo	10.00	5.00	3.00
128	Ray Mueller	10.00	5.00	3.00
129	Kid Nichols	10.00	5.00	3.00
130	Lefty O'Doul	10.00	5.00	3.00
131	Bob O'Farrell	10.00	5.00	3.00
132	Roger Peckinpaugh	10.00	5.00	3.00
133	Herb Pennock	10.00	5.00	3.00
134	George Pipgras	10.00	5.00	3.00
135	Eddie Plank	10.00	5.00	3.00
136	Ray Schalk	10.00	5.00	3.00
137	Hal Schumacher	10.00	5.00	3.00
138	Luke Sewell	10.00	5.00	3.00
139	Bob Shawkey	10.00	5.00	3.00
140	Riggs Stephenson	10.00	5.00	3.00
141	Billy Sullivan	10.00	5.00	3.00
142	Bill Terry	10.00	5.00	3.00
143	Joe Tinker	10.00	5.00	3.00
144	Pie Traynor	10.00	5.00	3.00
145	George Uhle	10.00	5.00	3.00
146	Hal Troskey (Trosky)	10.00	5.00	3.00
147	Arky Vaughan	10.00	5.00	3.00
148	Johnny Vander Meer	10.00	5.00	3.00
149	Rube Waddell	10.00	5.00	3.00
150	Honus Wagner	65.00	35.00	20.00
151	Dixie Walker	10.00	5.00	3.00
152	Ted Williams	150.00	75.00	40.00
153	Cy Young	15.00	8.00	5.00
154	Ross Young (Youngs)	10.00	5.00	3.00

1961 Fleer World Champions Pennant Decals

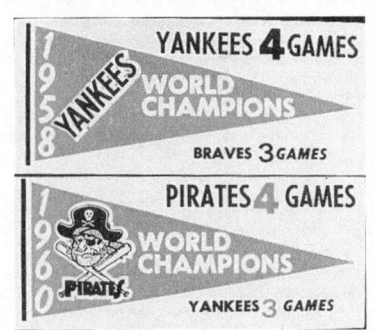

The winner of each World Series from 1913-1960 is honored in this pack insert. The 3" x 1-1/4" decals have a large red or blue pennant at center, with a team name or logo and the "WORLD CHAMPIONS" notation. The year of the Series win is at left on the pennant. The number of games won by each team is at top and bottom on right. Backs offer instructions for applying the decals.

	NM	E	VG
Complete Set (48):	300.00	150.00	90.00
Common Decal:	6.00	3.00	1.75

(1)	1913 - A's	6.00	3.00	1.75
(2)	1914 - Braves	6.00	3.00	1.75
(3)	1915 - Red Sox	6.00	3.00	1.75
(4)	1916 - Red Sox	6.00	3.00	1.75
(5)	1917 - White Sox	6.00	3.00	1.75
(6)	1918 - Red Sox	6.00	3.00	1.75
(7)	1919 - Reds	9.00	4.50	2.75
(8)	1920 - Indians	6.00	3.00	1.75
(9)	1921 - Giants	6.00	3.00	1.75
(10)	1922 - Giants	6.00	3.00	1.75
(11)	1923 - Yankees	7.50	3.75	2.25
(12)	1924 - Senators	6.00	3.00	1.75
(13)	1925 - Yankees	7.50	3.75	2.25
(14)	1926 - Cardinals	6.00	3.00	1.75
(14)	1927 - Yankees	7.50	3.75	2.25
(14)	1928 - Yankees	7.50	3.75	2.25
(15)	1929 - A's	6.00	3.00	1.75
(16)	1930 - A's	6.00	3.00	1.75
(17)	1931 - Cardinals	6.00	3.00	1.75
(18)	1932 - Yankees	7.50	3.75	2.25
(19)	1933 - Giants	6.00	3.00	1.75
(20)	1934 - Cardinals	6.00	3.00	1.75
(21)	1935 - Tigers	6.00	3.00	1.75
(22)	1936 - Yankees	7.50	3.75	2.25
(23)	1937 - Yankees	7.50	3.75	2.25
(24)	1938 - Yankees	7.50	3.75	2.25
(25)	1939 - Yankees	7.50	3.75	2.25
(26)	1940 - Reds	6.00	3.00	1.75
(27)	1941 - Yankees	7.50	3.75	2.25
(28)	1942 - Cardinals	6.00	3.00	1.75
(29)	1943 - Yankees	7.50	3.75	2.25
(30)	1944 - Cardinals	6.00	3.00	1.75
(31)	1945 - Tigers	6.00	3.00	1.75
(32)	1946 - Cardinals	6.00	3.00	1.75
(33)	1947 - Yankees	7.50	3.75	2.25
(34)	1948 - Indians	6.00	3.00	1.75

(35)	1949 - Yankees	7.50	3.75	2.25
(36)	1950 - Yankees	7.50	3.75	2.25
(37)	1951 - Yankees	7.50	3.75	2.25
(38)	1952 - Yankees	7.50	3.75	2.25
(41)	1953 - Yankees	7.50	3.75	2.25
(42)	1954 - Giants	6.00	3.00	1.75
(43)	1955 - Dodgers	9.00	4.50	2.75
(44)	1956 - Yankees	7.50	3.75	2.25
(45)	1957 - Braves	7.50	3.75	2.25
(46)	1958 - Yankees	7.50	3.75	2.25
(47)	1959 - Dodgers	9.00	4.50	2.75
(48)	1960 - Pirates	9.00	4.50	2.75

1963 Fleer

 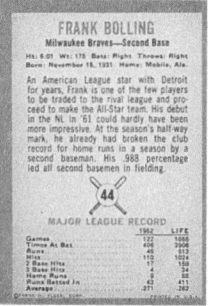

A lawsuit by Topps stopped Fleer's 1963 set at one series of 66 cards. Issued with a cookie rather than gum, the set features color photos of current players. The card backs include statistical information for 1962 and career plus a brief player biography. The cards, which measure 2-1/2" x 3-1/2", are numbered 1-66. An unnumbered checklist was issued with the set and is included in the complete set price in the checklist that follows. The checklist and #46 Adcock are scarce.

		NM	E	VG
	Complete Set (67):	1,800	900.00	550.00
	Common Player:	15.00	7.50	4.50
	Wax Pack:	1,000		
1	Steve Barber	50.00	25.00	15.00
2	Ron Hansen	15.00	7.50	4.50
3	Milt Pappas	15.00	7.50	4.50
4	Brooks Robinson	75.00	37.00	22.00
5	Willie Mays	150.00	75.00	45.00
6	Lou Clinton	15.00	7.50	4.50
7	Bill Monbouquette	15.00	7.50	4.50
8	Carl Yastrzemski	120.00	60.00	40.00
9	Ray Herbert	15.00	7.50	4.50
10	Jim Landis	15.00	7.50	4.50
11	Dick Donovan	15.00	7.50	4.50
12	Tito Francona	15.00	7.50	4.50
13	Jerry Kindall	15.00	7.50	4.50
14	Frank Lary	15.00	7.50	4.50
15	Dick Howser	15.00	7.50	4.50
16	Jerry Lumpe	15.00	7.50	4.50
17	Norm Siebern	15.00	7.50	4.50
18	Don Lee	15.00	7.50	4.50
19	Albie Pearson	15.00	7.50	4.50
20	Bob Rodgers	15.00	7.50	4.50
21	Leon Wagner	15.00	7.50	4.50
22	Jim Kaat	20.00	10.00	6.00
23	Vic Power	15.00	7.50	4.50
24	Rich Rollins	15.00	7.50	4.50
25	Bobby Richardson	20.00	10.00	6.00
26	Ralph Terry	15.00	7.50	4.50
27	Tom Cheney	15.00	7.50	4.50
28	Chuck Cottier	15.00	7.50	4.50
29	Jimmy Piersall	15.00	7.50	4.50
30	Dave Stenhouse	15.00	7.50	4.50
31	Glen Hobbie	15.00	7.50	4.50
32	Ron Santo	30.00	15.00	9.00
33	Gene Freese	15.00	7.50	4.50
34	Vada Pinson	15.00	7.50	4.50
35	Bob Purkey	15.00	7.50	4.50
36	Joe Amalfitano	15.00	7.50	4.50
37	Bob Aspromonte	15.00	7.50	4.50
38	Dick Farrell	15.00	7.50	4.50
39	Al Spangler	15.00	7.50	4.50
40	Tommy Davis	15.00	7.50	4.50
41	Don Drysdale	60.00	30.00	18.00
42	Sandy Koufax	240.00	120.00	70.00
43	Maury Wills RC	120.00	60.00	40.00
44	Frank Bolling	15.00	7.50	4.50
45	Warren Spahn	60.00	30.00	18.00
46	Joe Adcock (SP)	125.00	62.50	37.50
47	Roger Craig	15.00	7.50	4.50
48	Al Jackson	15.00	7.50	4.50
49	Rod Kanehl	15.00	7.50	4.50
50	Ruben Amaro	15.00	7.50	4.50
51	John Callison	15.00	7.50	4.50
52	Clay Dalrymple	15.00	7.50	4.50
53	Don Demeter	15.00	7.50	4.50
54	Art Mahaffey	15.00	7.50	4.50
55	"Smoky" Burgess	15.00	7.50	4.50
56	Roberto Clemente	150.00	75.00	45.00
57	Elroy Face	15.00	7.50	4.50
58	Vernon Law	15.00	7.50	4.50
59	Bill Mazeroski	25.00	12.00	7.00
60	Ken Boyer	15.00	7.50	4.50
61	Bob Gibson	75.00	37.00	22.00
62	Gene Oliver	15.00	7.50	4.50
63	Bill White	15.00	7.50	4.50
64	Orlando Cepeda	30.00	15.00	9.00
65	Jimmy Davenport	15.00	7.50	4.50
66	Billy O'Dell	25.00	12.00	8.00
---	(SP)	550.00	275.00	160.00

1966 Fleer All Star Match Baseball

This seldom-seen issue was produced in the years when Fleer was locked out of the "regular" baseball card market. Standard 2-1/2" x 3-1/2" format cards are designed for playing a baseball match game. Backs have a portion of a black-and-white photo of Dodger pitcher Don Drysdale, which can be assembled in jigsaw puzzle fashion. Fronts are printed in red, blue, yellow and black, and numbered F1-F66. Because single cards have little collector appeal, the value of a set is considerably higher than the sum of the parts.

	NM	E	VG
Complete Set (66):	400.00	200.00	120.00
Common Card:	6.00	3.00	1.75
Wax Pack:	200.00		

Don Drysdale

1968-70 Fleer Major League Baseball Patches

From 1968-70, Fleer sold bubblegum in wax packs which also included four team logo/quiz cards and half a dozen cloth patches, all for a dime. The 2-9/16" x 4-1/16" cards are blank-back and have on front a color team logo at top and three baseball trivia questions at bottom. The cloth patches are about 2-1/2" x 3-5/16" and are die-cut to allow the team logos and nameplates to be removed from the paper backing and stuck on jackets, etc.

	NM	E	VG
Complete Set Logo Cards (24):	18.00	9.00	5.50
Common Logo Card:	1.50	.70	.45
Complete Set Cloth Patches (29):	35.00	17.50	10.00
Common Cloth Patch:	1.50	.75	.45
Wax Pack:	2.00		
Wax Box (24):	30.00		

LOGO/QUIZ CARDS
(1)	Atlanta Braves	1.50	.70	.45
(2)	Baltimore Orioles	1.50	.70	.45
(3)	Boston Red Sox	1.50	.70	.45
(4)	California Angels	1.50	.70	.45
(5)	Chicago Cubs	1.50	.70	.45
(6)	Chicago White Sox	1.50	.70	.45
(7)	Cincinnati Reds	1.50	.70	.45
(8)	Cleveland Indians	1.50	.70	.45
(9)	Detroit Tigers	1.50	.70	.45
(10)	Houston Astros	1.50	.70	.45
(11)	Kansas City Royals	1.50	.70	.45
(12)	Los Angeles Dodgers	1.50	.70	.45
(13)	Minnesota Twins	1.50	.70	.45
(14)	Montreal Expos	2.50	1.25	.70
(15)	New York Mets	3.00	1.50	.90
(16)	New York Yankees	4.00	2.00	1.25
(17)	Oakland A's	2.50	1.25	.70
(18)	Philadelphia Phillies	1.50	.70	.45
(19)	Pittsburgh Pirates	1.50	.70	.45
(20)	San Diego Padres	2.50	1.25	.70
(21)	San Francisco Giants	1.50	.70	.45
(22)	Seattle Pilots	6.00	3.00	1.75
(23)	St. Louis Cardinals	1.50	.70	.45
(24)	Washington Senators	1.50	.70	.45

TEAM LOGO CLOTH PATCHES
(1)	Atlanta Braves	1.50	.70	.45
(2)	Baltimore Orioles	1.50	.70	.45
(3)	Boston Red Sox	1.50	.70	.45
(4)	California Angels	1.50	.70	.45
(5)	Chicago Cubs	1.50	.70	.45
(6)	Chicago White Sox	1.50	.70	.45
(7)	Cincinnati Reds	1.50	.70	.45
(8)	(Indian head)	1.50	.70	.45
(9)	(Batting Indian.)	1.50	.70	.45
(10)	Detroit Tigers	1.50	.70	.45
(11)	Houston Astros	1.50	.70	.45
(12)	Kansas City Royals	1.50	.70	.45
(13)	Los Angeles Dodgers	1.50	.70	.45
(14)	(M)	1.50	.70	.45
(15)	(Batting keg.)	1.50	.70	.45
(16)	Minnesota Twins	1.50	.70	.45
(17)	Montreal Expos	2.00	1.00	.60
(18)	New York Mets	2.00	1.00	.60
(19)	New York Yankees	3.00	1.50	.90
(20)	(Plain ball.)	2.00	1.00	.60
(21)	("The SWINGIN,'" white shoes, on ball.)	1.50	.70	.45
(22)	Philadelphia Phillies	1.50	.70	.45
(23)	Pittsburgh Pirates	1.50	.70	.45
(24)	San Diego Padres	2.00	1.00	.60
(25)	San Francisco Giants	1.50	.70	.45
(26)	Seattle Pilots	3.00	1.50	.90
(27)	St. Louis Cardinals	1.50	.70	.45
(28)	Washington Senators	1.50	.70	.45
(29)	Major League Baseball	1.50	.70	.45

1969 Fleer Cap Plaques

This set of novelty plaques features 3D impressions of each team's cap on thin plastic stock in a 3" x 4" format. Each cap plaque was sold in a wrapper with an easel backing board, surviving specimens of which are quite scarce. No cap plaque was issued for the expansion Montreal Expos.

		NM	E	VG
	Complete Set (23):	1,200	600.00	350.00
	Common Plaque:	45.00	22.50	13.50
	Easel Backing Board:	22.00	11.00	6.50
	Unopened Pack:	45.00		
(1)	Atlanta Braves	50.00	25.00	15.00
(2)	Baltimore Orioles	60.00	30.00	18.00
(3)	Boston Red Sox	50.00	25.00	15.00
(4)	California Angels	45.00	22.50	13.50
(5)	Chicago Cubs	60.00	30.00	18.00
(6)	Chicago White Sox	45.00	22.50	13.50
(7)	Cincinnati Reds	45.00	22.50	13.50
(8)	Cleveland Indians	45.00	22.50	13.50
(9)	Detroit Tigers	45.00	22.50	13.50
(10)	Houston Astros	45.00	22.50	13.50
(11)	Kansas City Royals	45.00	22.50	13.50
(12)	Los Angeles Dodgers	50.00	25.00	15.00
(13)	Minnesota Twins	45.00	22.50	13.50
(14)	New York Mets	75.00	37.50	22.50

		NM	E	VG
(15)	New York Yankees	115.00	55.00	35.00
(16)	Oakland A's	60.00	30.00	18.00
(17)	Philadelphia Phillies	45.00	22.50	13.50
(18)	Pittsburgh Pirates	50.00	25.00	15.00
(19)	San Diego Padres	45.00	22.50	13.50
(20)	San Francisco Giants	45.00	22.50	13.50
(21)	Seattle Pilots	125.00	62.50	37.00
(22)	St. Louis Cardinals	50.00	25.00	15.00
(23)	Washington Senators	50.00	25.00	15.00

1970 Fleer Team Logo Decals

These colorful team logo decals were pack inserts in Fleer's 1970 World Series issue. The decals measure 2-7/16" x 2-3/4". Backs have instructions for applying the decals.

		NM	E	VG
Complete Set (24):		90.00	45.00	27.50
Common Team:		7.50	3.75	2.25
(1)	Atlanta Braves	7.50	3.75	2.25
(2)	Baltimore Orioles	9.00	4.50	2.75
(3)	Boston Red Sox	7.50	3.75	2.25
(4)	California Angels	7.50	3.75	2.25
(5)	Chicago Cubs	7.50	3.75	2.25
(6)	Chicago White Sox	7.50	3.75	2.25
(7)	Cincinnati Reds	7.50	3.75	2.25
(8)	Cleveland Indians	7.50	3.75	2.25
(9)	Detroit Tigers	7.50	3.75	2.25
(10)	Houston Astros	7.50	3.75	2.25
(11)	Kansas City Royals	7.50	3.75	2.25
(12)	Los Angeles Dodgers	7.50	3.75	2.25
(13)	Milwaukee Brewers	7.50	3.75	2.25
(14)	Minnesota Twins	7.50	3.75	2.25
(15)	Montreal Expos	7.50	3.75	2.25
(16)	New York Mets	7.50	3.75	2.25
(17)	New York Yankees	9.00	4.50	2.75
(18)	Oakland A's	7.50	3.75	2.25
(19)	Philadelphia Phillies	7.50	3.75	2.25
(20)	Pittsburgh Pirates	9.00	4.50	2.75
(21)	San Diego Padres	7.50	3.75	2.25
(22)	San Francisco Giants	7.50	3.75	2.25
(23)	St. Louis Cardinals	7.50	3.75	2.25
(24)	Washington Senators	10.00	5.00	3.00

1970 Fleer World Series

Utilizing the artwork done by Robert Laughlin a few years earlier for a privately marketed set, Fleer offered the first of two World Series highlights sets in 1970. Cards have color front with light blue backs. No card was issued for the 1904 World Series because no Series was played. Cards are checklisted in chronological order.

		NM	E	VG
Complete Set (66):		150.00	75.00	45.00
Common Card:		1.50	.70	.45
Wax Pack:		35.00		
1	1903 Red Sox/Pirates	2.50	1.25	.70
2	(Christy Mathewson)	2.50	1.25	.70

3	1906 White Sox/Cubs	1.50	.70	.45
4	1907 Cubs/Tigers	1.50	.70	.45
5	(Tinker/Evers/Chance)	3.00	1.50	.90
6	(Honus Wagner/Ty Cobb)	7.50	3.75	2.25
7	(Chief Bender/Jack Coombs)	2.00	1.00	.60
8	(John McGraw)	2.00	1.00	.60
9	1912 Red Sox/Giants	2.00	1.00	.60
10	1913 A's/Giants	1.50	.70	.45
11	1914 Braves/A's	2.00	1.00	.60
12	(Babe Ruth)	5.00	2.50	1.50
13	(Babe Ruth)	5.00	2.50	1.50
14	1917 White Sox/Giants	1.50	.70	.45
15	1918 Red Sox/Cubs	1.50	.70	.45
16	1919 Reds/White Sox	3.00	1.50	.90
17	(Stan Coveleski)	2.00	1.00	.60
18	(Kenesaw Landis)	2.00	1.00	.60
19	(Heinie Groh)	2.00	1.00	.60
20	(Babe Ruth)	7.50	3.75	2.25
21	(John McGraw)	2.50	1.25	.70
22	(Walter Johnson)	3.00	1.50	.90
23	(Grover Cleveland Alexander/Tony Lazzeri)	3.00	1.50	.90
24	1927 Yankees/Pirates	2.50	1.25	.70
25	(Babe Ruth/Lou Gehrig)	7.50	3.75	2.25
26	1929 A's/Cubs	1.50	.70	.45
27	1930 A's/Cardinals	1.50	.70	.45
28	(Pepper Martin)	2.00	1.00	.60
29	(Babe Ruth/Lou Gehrig)	7.50	3.75	2.25
30	1933 Giants/Senators (Mel Ott)	2.50	1.25	.70
31	1934 Cardinals/Tigers	1.50	.70	.45
32	1935 Tigers/Cubs (Charlie Gehringer/ Tommy Bridges)	2.00	1.00	.60
33	1936 Yankees/Giants	2.00	1.00	.60
34	1937 Yankees/Giants (Carl Hubbell)	2.50	1.25	.70
35	1938 Yankees/Cubs (Lou Gehrig)	4.00	2.00	1.25
36	1939 Yankees/Reds	1.50	.70	.45
37	1940 Reds/Tigers (Mike McCormick)	1.50	.70	.45
38	1941 Yankees/Dodgers	2.00	1.00	.60
39	1942 Cardinals/Yankees	1.50	.70	.45
40	1943 Yankees/Cardinals	1.50	.70	.45
41	1944 Cardinals/Browns	2.00	1.00	.60
42	1945 Tigers/Cubs (Hank Greenberg)	2.50	1.25	.70
43	1946 Cardinals/Red Sox (Enos Slaughter)	2.00	1.00	.60
44	1947 Yankees/Dodgers (Al Gionfriddo)	2.00	1.00	.60
45	1948 Indians/Braves	1.50	.70	.45
46	(Allie Reynolds/Preacher Roe)	2.00	1.00	.60
47	1950 Yankees/Phillies	2.00	1.00	.60
48	1951 Yankees/Giants	1.50	.70	.45
49	(Johnny Mize/Duke Snider)	2.50	1.25	.70
50	(Carl Erskine)	2.00	1.00	.60
51	(Johnny Antonelli)	1.50	.70	.45
52	1955 Dodgers/Yankees	2.00	1.00	.60
53	1956 Yankees/Dodgers	2.00	1.00	.60
54	(Lew Burdette)	3.00	1.50	.90
55	(Bob Turley)	1.50	.70	.45
56	(Chuck Essegian)	2.00	1.00	.60
57	1960 Pirates/Yankees	2.00	1.00	.60
58	(Whitey Ford)	2.00	1.00	.60
59	1962 Giants/Yankees	1.50	.70	.45
60	(Bill Skowron)	1.50	.70	.45
61	(Bobby Richardson)	2.00	1.00	.60
62	1965 Dodgers/Twins	2.00	1.00	.60
63	1966 Orioles/Dodgers	1.50	.70	.45
64	1967 Cardinals/Red Sox	1.50	.70	.45
65	1968 Tigers/Cardinals	2.00	1.00	.60
66	1969 Mets/Orioles	4.50	2.25	1.25

1971-80 Fleer World Series

(The 1952 World Series card reproduced at top)

1952 WORLD SERIES

New York AL 4 — Brooklyn NL 3

The Yankees took their fourth consecutive world championship to tie their predecessors of Joe McCarthy. While absorbing their sixth straight Series setback, the Dodgers carried the Bombers to seven game and even had a 3-2 game lead. Johnny Mize hit .400 and slammed three homers, in consecutive games. Duke Snider hit .345 and clouted four round-trippers, tying the Series mark. Reynolds and Raschi each won two for New York; each fanned 18. The Yankee center fielder hit the first two of 18 Series homers.

1. Brooklyn 4, New York 2
2. New York 7, Brooklyn 1
3. Brooklyn 5, New York 3
4. New York 2, Brooklyn 0
5. Brooklyn 6, New York 5 (11)
6. New York 3, Brooklyn 2
7. New York 4, Brooklyn 2

#50 by R. G. Laughlin   Mfd. by Fleer Corp., Phila. Pa. 19141
Official Insignia 1968 © Major League Baseball Promotion Corp.

New artwork by Robert Laughlin is featured in the second of Fleer's World Series highlights sets. Fronts feature color art with backs printed in black. It appears as if the original set issued in 1971 was updated intermittently.

		NM	E	VG
Complete Set (68):		135.00	65.00	40.00
Complete Set (75):		350.00	175.00	100.00
Common Card:		2.00	1.00	.60
Wax Pack:		30.00		
1	1903 Red Sox/Pirates (Cy Young)	6.00	3.00	1.75
2	1904 No World Series (John McGraw)	5.00	2.50	1.50
3	1905 Giants/A's (Christy Mathewson/Chief Bender)	5.00	2.50	1.50
4	1906 White Sox/Cubs	2.00	1.00	.60
5	1907 Cubs/Tigers	2.00	1.00	.60
6	1908 Cubs/Tigers (Ty Cobb)	5.00	2.50	1.50
7	1909 Pirates/Tigers	2.50	1.25	.70
8	1910 A's/Cubs (Eddie Collins)	2.50	1.25	.70
9	1911 A's/Giants (Home Run Baker)	2.50	1.25	.70
10	1912 Red Sox/Giants	2.00	1.00	.60
11	1913 A's/Giants (Christy Mathewson)	3.00	1.50	.90
12	1914 Braves/A's	2.00	1.00	.60
13	1915 Red Sox/Phillies (Grover Cleveland Alexander)	3.00	1.50	.90
14	1916 Red Sox/Dodgers (Jack Coombs)	2.00	1.00	.60
15	1917 White Sox/Giants (Red Faber)	2.50	1.25	.70
16	1918 Red Sox/Cubs (Babe Ruth)	6.00	3.00	1.75
17	1919 Reds/White Sox	4.00	2.00	1.25
18	1920 Indians/Dodgers (Elmer Smith)	2.50	1.25	.70
19	1921 Giants/Yankees (Waite Hoyt)	4.00	2.00	1.25
20	1922 Giants/Yankees (Art Nehf)	2.50	1.25	.70
21	1923 Yankees/Giants (Herb Pennock)	2.50	1.25	.70
22	1924 Senators/Giants (Walter Johnson)	4.00	2.00	1.25
23	1925 Pirates/Senators (Walter Johnson/Ki Ki Cuyler)	4.00	2.00	1.25
24	1926 Cardinals/Yankees (Rogers Hornsby)	4.00	2.00	1.25
25	1927 Yankees/Pirates	2.50	1.25	.70
26	1928 Yankees/Cardinals (Lou Gehrig)	5.00	2.50	1.50
27	1929 A's/Cubs (Howard Ehmke)	2.00	1.00	.60
28	1930 A's/Cardinals (Jimmie Foxx)	3.00	1.50	.90
29	1931 Cardinals/A's (Pepper Martin)	2.50	1.25	.70
30	1932 Yankees/Cubs (Babe Ruth)	6.00	3.00	1.75
31	1933 Giants/Senators (Carl Hubbell)	3.00	1.50	.90
32	1934 Cardinals/Tigers	2.00	1.00	.60
33	1935 Tigers/Cubs (Mickey Cochrane)	2.50	1.25	.70
34	1936 Yankees/Giants (Red Rolfe)	2.50	1.25	.70
35	1937 Yankees/Giants (Tony Lazerri)	4.00	2.00	1.25
36	1938 Yankees/Cubs	3.00	1.50	.90
37	1939 Yankees/Reds	3.00	1.50	.90
38	1940 Reds/Tigers (Mike McCormick)	2.00	1.00	.60
39	1941 Yankees/Dodgers (Charlie Keller)	2.50	1.25	.70
40	1942 Cardinals/Yankees (Whitey Kurowski/ Johnny Beazley)	2.00	1.00	.60
41	1943 Yankees/Cardinals (Spud Chandler)	2.00	1.00	.60

42	1944 Cardinals/Browns (Mort Cooper)	2.50	1.25	.70
43	1945 Tigers/Cubs (Hank Greenberg)	3.00	1.50	.90
44	1946 Cardinals/Red Sox (Enos Slaughter)	2.50	1.25	.70
45	1947 Yankees/Dodgers (Johnny Lindell/Hugh Casey)	2.50	1.25	.70
46	1948 Indians/Braves	2.00	1.00	.60
47	1949 Yankees/Dodgers (Preacher Roe)	2.00	1.00	.60
48	1950 Yankees/Phillies (Allie Reynolds)	2.50	1.25	.70
49	1951 Yankees/Giants (Ed Lopat)	2.50	1.25	.70
50	1952 Yankees/Dodgers (Johnny Mize)	2.50	1.25	.70
51	1953 Yankees/Dodgers	2.50	1.25	.70
52	1954 Giants/Indians	2.00	1.00	.60
53	1955 Dodgers/Yankees (Duke Snider)	4.00	2.00	1.25
54	1956 Yankees/Dodgers	2.50	1.25	.70
55	1957 Braves/Yankees	2.50	1.25	.70
56	1958 Yankees/Braves (Hank Bauer)	2.50	1.25	.70
57	1959 Dodgers/White Sox (Duke Snider)	3.00	1.50	.90
58	1960 Pirates/Yankees (Bill Skowron/Bobby Richardson)	2.50	1.25	.70
59	1961 Yankees/Reds (Whitey Ford)	2.50	1.25	.70
60	1962 Yankees/Giants	2.00	1.00	.60
61	1963 Dodgers/Yankees	2.00	1.00	.60
62	1964 Cardinals/Yankees	2.50	1.25	.70
63	1965 Dodgers/Twins	2.50	1.25	.70
64	1966 Orioles/Dodgers	2.00	1.00	.60
65	1967 Cardinals/Red Sox	2.00	1.00	.60
66	1968 Tigers/Cardinals	2.50	1.25	.70
67	1969 Mets/Orioles	6.00	3.00	1.75
68	1970 Orioles/Reds	5.00	2.50	1.50
69	1971 Pirates/Orioles (Roberto Clemente)	35.00	17.50	10.00
70	1972 A's/Reds	15.00	7.50	4.50
71	1973 A's/Mets	15.00	7.50	4.50
(72)	1974 A's/Dodgers	50.00	25.00	15.00
(73)	1975 Reds/Red Sox	50.00	25.00	15.00
(74)	1976 Reds/Yankees	50.00	25.00	15.00
(75)	1977 Yankees/Dodgers	50.00	25.00	15.00

1973 Fleer Team Logo Decals

These colorful team logo decals were pack inserts in Fleer's "Wildest Days and Plays." The decals measure 4" x 2-11/16". Backs have instructions for applying the decals.

		NM	E	VG
Complete Set (24):		110.00	55.00	33.00
Common Team:		9.00	4.50	2.75
(1)	Atlanta Braves	9.00	4.50	2.75
(2)	Baltimore Orioles	9.00	4.50	2.75
(3)	Boston Red Sox	9.00	4.50	2.75
(4)	California Angels	9.00	4.50	2.75
(5)	Chicago Cubs	9.00	4.50	2.75
(6)	Chicago White Sox	9.00	4.50	2.75
(7)	Cincinnati Reds	9.00	4.50	2.75
(8)	Cleveland Indians	9.00	4.50	2.75
(9)	Detroit Tigers	9.00	4.50	2.75
(10)	Houston Astros	9.00	4.50	2.75
(11)	Kansas City Royals	9.00	4.50	2.75
(12)	Los Angeles Dodgers	9.00	4.50	2.75
(13)	Milwaukee Brewers	9.00	4.50	2.75
(14)	Minnesota Twins	9.00	4.50	2.75
(15)	Montreal Expos	9.00	4.50	2.75
(16)	New York Mets	12.00	6.00	3.50
(17)	New York Yankees	10.00	5.00	3.00
(18)	Oakland A's	10.00	5.00	3.00
(19)	Philadelphia Phillies	9.00	4.50	2.75
(20)	Pittsburgh Pirates	11.00	5.50	3.25
(21)	San Diego Padres	9.00	4.50	2.75
(22)	San Francisco Giants	9.00	4.50	2.75
(23)	St. Louis Cardinals	9.00	4.50	2.75
(24)	Texas Rangers	12.00	6.00	3.50

1973 Fleer Team Signs

Each of the major league teams was represented in this issue of thick oversized (7-3/4" x 11-1/2") team logo signs. The blank-back signs have rounded corners and a grommeted hole at top-center for hanging. The unnumbered signs are checklisted here alphabetically.

		NM	E	VG
Complete Set (24):		35.00	17.50	10.00
Common Team:		4.00	2.00	1.25
(1)	Atlanta Braves	4.00	2.00	1.25
(2)	Baltimore Orioles	4.00	2.00	1.25
(3)	Boston Red Sox	4.00	2.00	1.25
(4)	California Angels	4.00	2.00	1.25
(5)	Chicago Cubs	4.00	2.00	1.25
(6)	Chicago White Sox	4.00	2.00	1.25
(7)	Cincinnati Reds	5.00	2.50	1.50
(8)	Cleveland Indians	4.00	2.00	1.25
(9)	Detroit Tigers	4.00	2.00	1.25
(10)	Houston Astros	4.00	2.00	1.25
(11)	Kansas City Royals	4.00	2.00	1.25
(12)	Los Angeles Dodgers	4.00	2.00	1.25
(13)	Milwaukee Brewers	4.00	2.00	1.25
(14)	Minnesota Twins	4.00	2.00	1.25
(15)	Montreal Expos	4.00	2.00	1.25
(16)	New York Mets	5.00	2.50	1.50
(17)	New York Yankees	5.00	2.50	1.50
(18)	Oakland A's	5.00	2.50	1.50
(19)	Philadelphia Phillies	4.00	2.00	1.25
(20)	Pittsburgh Pirates	4.00	2.00	1.25
(21)	St. Louis Cardinals	4.00	2.00	1.25
(22)	San Francisco Giants	4.00	2.00	1.25
(23)	San Diego Padres	4.00	2.00	1.25
(24)	Texas Rangers	4.00	2.00	1.25

1974 Fleer Wildest Days and Plays

 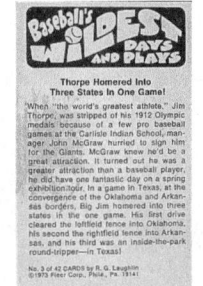

This 42-card set highlights unusual plays and happenings in baseball history, with the fronts featuring artwork by R.G. Laughlin. The cards are 2-1/2" x 4" and printed with color on the front and in red on the back. Original retail price was about $3.25.

		NM	E	VG
Complete Set (42):		35.00	17.50	10.00
Common Player:		1.50	.70	.45
1	Cubs and Phillies Score 49 Runs in Game	1.50	.70	.45
2	Frank Chance Five HBP's in One Day	2.00	1.00	.60
3	Jim Thorpe Homered Into Three States	2.00	1.00	.60
4	Eddie Gaedel Midget in Majors	2.00	1.00	.60
5	Most Tied Game Ever	1.50	.70	.45
6	Seven Errors in One Inning	1.50	.70	.45
7	Four 20-Game Winners But No Pennant	1.50	.70	.45
8	Dummy Hoy Umpire Signals Strikes	2.00	1.00	.60
9	Fourteen Hits in One Inning	1.50	.70	.45
10	Yankees Not Shut Out for Two Years	1.50	.70	.45
11	Buck Weaver 17 Straight Fouls	2.00	1.00	.60
12	George Sisler Greatest Thrill	1.50	.70	.45
13	Wrong-Way Baserunner	1.50	.70	.45
14	Kiki Cuyler Sits Out Series	1.50	.70	.45
15	Grounder Climbed Wall	1.50	.70	.45
16	Gabby Street Washington Monument	1.50	.70	.45
17	Mel Ott Ejected Twice	2.00	1.00	.60
18	Shortest Pitching Career	1.50	.70	.45
19	Three Homers in One Inning	1.50	.70	.45
20	Bill Byron Singing Umpire	1.50	.70	.45
21	Fred Clarke Walking Steal of Home	1.50	.70	.45
22	Christy Mathewson 373rd Win Discovered	2.00	1.00	.60
23	Hitting Through the Unglaub Arc	1.50	.70	.45
24	Jim O'Rourke Catching at 52	1.50	.70	.45
25	Fired for Striking Out in Series	1.50	.70	.45
26	Eleven Run Inning on One Hit	1.50	.70	.45
27	58 Innings in 3 Days	1.50	.70	.45
28	Homer on Warm-up Pitch	1.50	.70	.45
29	Giants Win 26 Straight But Finish Fourth	1.50	.70	.45
30	Player Who Stole First Base	1.50	.70	.45
31	Ernie Shore Perfect Game in Relief	1.50	.70	.45
32	Greatest Comeback	1.50	.70	.45
33	All-Time Flash-in-the-Pan	1.50	.70	.45
34	Pruett Fanned Ruth 19 Out of 31	2.00	1.00	.60
35	Fixed Batting Race(Ty Cobb, Nap Lajoie)	2.00	1.00	.60
36	Wild Pitch Rebound Play	1.50	.70	.45
37	17 Straight Scoring Innings	1.50	.70	.45
38	Wildest Opening Day	1.50	.70	.45
39	Baseball's Strike One	1.50	.70	.45
40	Opening Day No-Hitter That Didn't Count	1.50		.45
41	Jimmie Foxx 6 Straight Walks in One Game	2.00	1.00	.60
42	Entire Team Hit and Scored in Inning	1.50	.70	.45

1975 Fleer Pioneers of Baseball

 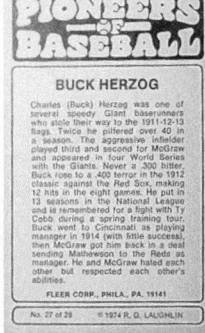

This 28-card set did not draw a great deal of interest in the hobby. The cards are slightly oversized (2-1/2" x 4") and feature sepia-toned photographs of old baseball players. The backs feature information about the player and the card number. A "Pioneers of Baseball" banner appears at the top of the card back. Each 10-cent pack included one card and one each cloth team pennant and patch, plus a stick of gum.

		NM	E	VG
Complete Set (28):		20.00	10.00	6.00
Common Player:		1.50	.75	.45
Wax Pack:		6.00		
Wax Box (24):		65.00		
1	Cap Anson	1.50	.75	.45
2	Harry Wright	1.50	.75	.45
3	Buck Ewing	1.50	.75	.45
4	A.G. Spalding	1.50	.75	.45
5	Old Hoss Radbourn	1.50	.75	.45
6	Dan Brouthers	1.50	.75	.45
7	Roger Bresnahan	1.50	.75	.45
8	Mike Kelly	1.50	.75	.45
9	Ned Hanton	1.50	.75	.45
10	Ed Delahanty	1.50	.75	.45
11	Pud Galvin	1.50	.75	.45

12	Amos Rusie	1.50	.75	.45
13	Tommy McCarthy	1.50	.75	.45
14	Ty Cobb	6.00	3.00	1.75
15	John McGraw	1.50	.75	.45
16	Home Run Baker	1.50	.75	.45
17	Johnny Evers	1.50	.75	.45
18	Nap Lajoie	1.50	.75	.45
19	Cy Young	2.50	1.25	.70
20	Eddie Collins	1.50	.75	.45
21	John Glasscock	1.50	.75	.45
22	Hal Chase	1.50	.75	.45
23	Mordecai Brown	1.50	.75	.45
24	Jake Daubert	1.50	.75	.45
25	Mike Donlin	1.50	.75	.45
26	John Clarkson	1.50	.75	.45
27	Buck Herzog	1.50	.75	.45
28	Art Nehf	1.50	.75	.45

1976 Fleer Baseball Firsts

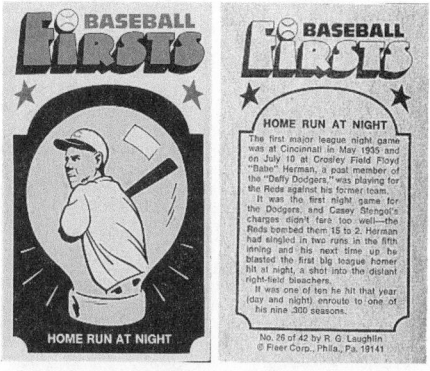

This 42-card set from Fleer is titled "Baseball Firsts" and features several historical moments in baseball, as captured through the artwork of sports artist R.G. Laughlin. The cards are 2-1/2" x 4" and are numbered on the back, which is gray card stock with black printing. The set is not licensed by Major League Baseball.

		NM	E	VG
Complete Set (42):		80.00	40.00	25.00
Common Player:		2.00	1.00	.60
1	Slide	2.00	1.00	.60
2	Spring Training	2.00	1.00	.60
3	Bunt	2.00	1.00	.60
4	Catcher's Mask	2.00	1.00	.60
5	Four Straight Homers (Lou Gehrig)	10.00	5.00	3.00
6	Radio Broadcast	2.00	1.00	.60
7	Numbered Uniforms	2.00	1.00	.60
8	Shin Guards	2.00	1.00	.60
9	Players Association	2.00	1.00	.60
10	Knuckleball	2.00	1.00	.60
11	Player With Glasses	2.00	1.00	.60
12	Baseball Cards	12.00	6.00	3.50
13	Standardized Rules	2.00	1.00	.60
14	Grand Slam	2.00	1.00	.60
15	Player Fined	2.00	1.00	.60
16	Presidential Opener	2.00	1.00	.60
17	Player Transaction	2.00	1.00	.60
18	All-Star Game	2.00	1.00	.60
19	Scoreboard	2.00	1.00	.60
20	Cork-center Ball	2.00	1.00	.60
21	Scorekeeping	2.00	1.00	.60
22	Domed Stadium	2.00	1.00	.60
23	Batting Helmet	2.00	1.00	.60
24	Fatality	4.00	2.00	1.25
25	Unassisted Triple Play	2.00	1.00	.60
26	Home Run at Night	2.00	1.00	.60
27	Black Major Leaguer	4.00	2.00	1.25
28	Pinch Hitter	2.00	1.00	.60
29	Million Dollar World Series	2.00	1.00	.60
30	Tarpaulin	2.00	1.00	.60
31	Team Initials	2.00	1.00	.60
32	Pennant Playoff	2.00	1.00	.60
33	Glove	2.00	1.00	.60
34	Curve Ball	2.00	1.00	.60
35	Night Game	2.00	1.00	.60
36	Admission Charge	2.00	1.00	.60
37	Farm System	2.00	1.00	.60
38	Telecast	2.00	1.00	.60
39	Commissioner	2.00	1.00	.60
40	.400 Hitter	2.00	1.00	.60
41	World Series	2.00	1.00	.60
42	Player Into Service	2.00	1.00	.60

1980 Fleer World Series/Team Logo Stickers

World Series cards similar to previous Fleer issues of the 1970s were issued in a new version in 1980. Wax packs containing five stickercards and a piece of bubblegum were offered for a nickel. Each card/sticker combination carried a World Series cartoon card from one of the Autumn Classics from 1940-1979. Unlike the earlier Fleer-Laughlin W.S. cards, these are backed with a team-logo sticker, some of which bear the team's 1979 record, and some of which do not.

		NM	E	VG
Complete Set (40):		50.00	25.00	15.00
Common Card:		1.50	.75	.45
Wax Pack (5):		4.00		
Wax Box (36):		80.00		
(1)	1940 Reds/Tigers (Mike McCormick)	1.50	.75	.45
(2)	1941 Yankees/Dodgers (Charlie Keller)	2.25	1.25	.75
(3)	1942 Cardinals/Yankees (Whitey Kurowski/Johnny Beazley)	2.25	1.25	.75
(4)	1943 Yankees/Cardinals (Spud Chandler)	2.25	1.25	.75
(5)	1944 Cardinals/Browns (Mort Cooper)	2.25	1.25	.75
(6)	1945 Tigers/Cubs (Hank Greenberg)	3.00	1.50	.90
(7)	1946 Cardinals/Red Sox (Enos Slaughter)	1.50	.75	.45
(8)	1947 Yankees/Dodgers (Johnny Lindell/Hugh Casey)	3.00	1.50	.90
(9)	1948 Indians/Braves	1.50	.75	.45
(10)	1949 Yankees/Dodgers (Preacher Roe)	3.00	1.50	.90
(11)	1950 Yankees/Phillies (Allie Reynolds)	3.00	1.50	.90
(12)	1951 Yankees/Giants (Ed Lopat)	3.00	1.50	.90
(13)	1952 Yankees/Dodgers (Johnny Mize)	4.00	2.00	1.25
(14)	1953 Yankees/Dodgers	4.00	2.00	1.25
(15)	1954 Giants/Indians	3.00	1.50	.90
(16)	1955 Dodgers/Yankees (Duke Snider)	4.50	2.25	1.25
(17)	1956 Yankees/Dodgers	4.00	2.00	1.25
(18)	1957 Braves/Yankees	4.00	2.00	1.25
(19)	1958 Yankees/Braves (Hank Bauer)	3.00	1.50	.90
(20)	1959 Dodgers/White Sox (Duke Snider)	3.00	1.50	.90
(21)	1960 Pirates/Yankees (Bill Skowron/Bobby Richardson)	4.50	2.25	1.25
(22)	1961 Yankees/Reds (Whitey Ford)	3.00	1.50	.90
(23)	1962 Yankees/Giants	3.00	1.50	.90
(24)	1963 Dodgers/Yankees	3.00	1.50	.90
(25)	1964 Cardinals/Yankees	3.00	1.50	.90
(26)	1965 Dodgers/Twins	1.50	.75	.45
(27)	1966 Orioles/Dodgers	1.50	.75	.45
(28)	1967 Cardinals/Red Sox	1.50	.75	.45
(29)	1968 Tigers/Cardinals	1.50	.75	.45
(30)	1969 Mets/Orioles	4.00	2.00	1.25
(31)	1970 Orioles/Reds	1.50	.75	.45
(32)	1971 Pirates/Orioles	1.50	.75	.45
(33)	1972 A's/Reds	1.50	.75	.45
(34)	1973 A's/Mets	1.50	.75	.45
(35)	1974 A's/Dodgers	1.50	.75	.45
(36)	1975 Reds/Red Sox	2.25	1.25	.75
(37)	1976 Reds/Yankees	1.50	.75	.45
(38)	1977 Yankees/Dodgers	2.25	1.25	.75
(39)	1978 Yankees/Dodgers	2.25	1.25	.75
(40)	1979 Pirates/Orioles	2.25	1.25	.75

1983 Fleer Famous Feats

This 40-card set by sports artist R.G. Laughlin is over-sized, 2-1/2" x 4". It features the pen and ink work of the artist, with several colors added to the front. The backs are printed in blue on white card stock. The Major League Baseball logo appears on the front of the card, one of the few Laughlin issues to do so. Selling price at issue was about $3.

		NM	E	VG
Complete Set (40):		40.00	20.00	12.00
Common Player:		1.50	.75	.45
1	Joe McGinnity	2.00	1.00	.60
2	Rogers Hornsby	3.50	1.75	1.00
3	Christy Mathewson	4.00	2.00	1.25
4	Dazzy Vance	2.00	1.00	.60
5	Lou Gehrig	7.50	3.75	2.25
6	Jim Bottomley	2.00	1.00	.60
7	Johnny Evers	2.00	1.00	.60
8	Walter Johnson	4.00	2.00	1.25
9	Hack Wilson	2.00	1.00	.60
10	Wilbert Robinson	2.00	1.00	.60
11	Cy Young	3.50	1.75	1.00
12	Rudy York	1.50	.75	.45
13	Grover C. Alexander	2.00	1.00	.60
14	Fred Toney, Hippo Vaughn	1.50	.75	.45
15	Ty Cobb	7.50	3.75	2.25
16	Jimmie Foxx	3.50	1.75	1.00
17	Hub Leonard	1.50	.75	.45
18	Eddie Collins	2.00	1.00	.60
19	Joe Oeschger, Leon Cadore	1.50	.75	.45
20	Babe Ruth	9.00	4.50	2.75
21	Honus Wagner	4.00	2.00	1.25
22	Red Rolfe	1.50	.75	.45
23	Ed Walsh	2.00	1.00	.60
24	Paul Waner	2.00	1.00	.60
25	Mel Ott	2.50	1.25	.70
26	Eddie Plank	2.00	1.00	.60
27	Sam Crawford	2.00	1.00	.60
28	Napoleon Lajoie	2.00	1.00	.60
29	Ed Reulbach	1.50	.75	.45
30	Pinky Higgins	1.50	.75	.45
31	Bill Klem	2.00	1.00	.60
32	Tris Speaker	3.00	1.50	.90
33	Hank Gowdy	1.50	.75	.45
34	Lefty O'Doul	1.50	.75	.45
35	Lloyd Waner	2.00	1.00	.60
36	Chuck Klein	2.00	1.00	.60
37	Deacon Phillippe	1.50	.75	.45
38	Ed Delahanty	2.00	1.00	.60
39	Jack Chesbro	2.00	1.00	.60
40	Willie Keeler	2.00	1.00	.60

1986 Fleer Baseball's Famous Feats

Yet another incarnation of Robert Laughlin's "Baseball's Famous Feats" cartoon artwork is this 22-card issue, in standard 2-1/2" x 3-1/2" format. The player art is backed with team logo and pennant stickers, creating a huge variety of possible front/back combinations. The cards are licensed by Major League Baseball and numbered on the front.

		NM/M
Complete Set (22):		6.00
Common Player:		.75
1	Grover Cleveland Alexander	.75
2	Jimmy (Jimmie) Foxx	1.00
3	Ty Cobb	1.50
4	Walter Johnson	1.00
5	Hack Wilson	.75
6	Tris Speaker	1.00
7	Hank Gowdy	.75
8	Bill Klem	.75
9	Ed Reulbach	.75
10	Fred Toney, Hippo Vaughn	.75
11	Joe Oeschger, Leon Cadore	.75
12	Lloyd Waner	.75
13	Eddie Plank	.75

14	Deacon Phillippe		.75
15	Ed Dalahanty (Delahanty)		.75
16	Eddie Collins		.75
17	Jack Chesbro		.75
18	Red Rolfe		.75
19	Ed Walsh		.75
20	Honus Wagner		1.25
21	Nap Lajoie		.75
22	Cy Young		1.00

1952 Fleet-Wing Cleveland Indians Pictures

Very similar in format to contemporary team-issued picture pack photos, this set of player premium pictures was issued by a Northern Ohio gas station chain. The pictures are 6" x 9" (slightly narrower than picture pack photos) printed in black-and-white on blank-back paper stock that is heavier than usually found in the picture packs. Players are identified by a facsimile autograph. Pictures were given away with a $1 purchase at participating gas stations. A 32-page album to house the set was also issued.

		NM	EX	VG
Complete Set (16):		200.00	100.00	60.00
Common Player:		12.00	6.00	3.50
Album		150.00	75.00	45.00
(1)	Bob Avila	12.00	6.00	3.50
(2)	Ray Boone	12.00	6.00	3.50
(3)	Lou Brissie	12.00	6.00	3.50
(4)	Larry Doby	25.00	12.50	7.50
(5)	Luke Easter	12.00	6.00	3.50
(6)	Bob Feller	25.00	12.50	7.50
(7)	Mike Garcia	12.00	6.00	3.50
(8)	Jim Hegan	12.00	6.00	3.50
(9)	Bob Kennedy	12.00	6.00	3.50
(10)	Bob Lemon	20.00	10.00	6.00
(11)	Al Lopez	20.00	10.00	6.00
(12)	Dale Mitchell	12.00	6.00	3.50
(13)	Al Rosen	12.00	6.00	3.50
(14)	Harry Simpson	12.00	6.00	3.50
(15)	Birdie Tebbetts	12.00	6.00	3.50
(16)	Early Wynn	20.00	10.00	6.00

1916 Fleischmann Bakery (D381)

These cards were issued by a New York City bakery, presumably given away with the purchase of bread or other goods. The blank-back cards are printed in black-and-white in a 2-3/4" x 5-3/8" format. Fronts have player photos with the name, team and position in two lines beneath. Most cards have an Underwood & Underwood copyright notice on the picture. At bottom is a coupon that could be redeemed for an album to house the cards. Prices shown here are for cards without the coupon. Cards with coupon are valued at about the premium shown below. Cards are checklisted here in

alphabetical order. Some cards can be found with differing sizes of the player's photo and/or with wrong and corrected photos. A nearly identical issue was produced contemporarily by Ferguson Bread. The two can be distinguished by the two-line identification on front of the Fleischmann cards, and one-line identification on Fergusons.

		NM	E	VG
Common Player:		400.00	200.00	100.00
With Coupon: 8-10X				
(1)	Babe Adams	400.00	200.00	100.00
(2)	Grover Alexander	700.00	300.00	150.00
(3)	Walt E. Alexander	400.00	200.00	100.00
(4)	Frank Allen	400.00	200.00	100.00
(5)	Fred Anderson	400.00	200.00	100.00
(6)	Dave Bancroft	550.00	225.00	110.00
(7)	Jack Barry	400.00	200.00	100.00
(8a)	Beals Becker (No uniform logo.)	400.00	200.00	100.00
(8b)	Beals Becker (Partial uniform logo.)	400.00	200.00	100.00
(9)	Eddie Burns	400.00	200.00	100.00
(10)	George J. Burns	400.00	200.00	100.00
(11)	Bobby Byrne	400.00	200.00	100.00
(12)	Ray Caldwell	400.00	200.00	100.00
(13)	James Callahan	400.00	200.00	100.00
(14)	William Carrigan	400.00	200.00	100.00
(15)	Larry Cheney	400.00	200.00	100.00
(16a)	Tom Clark (No hand/glove.)	400.00	200.00	100.00
(16b)	Tom Clark (Hand and glove show.)	400.00	200.00	100.00
(17)	Ty Cobb	2,900	1,450	725.00
(18a)	Ray W. Collins (Partial top button.)	400.00	200.00	100.00
(18b)	Ray W. Collins (Full top button.)	400.00	200.00	100.00
(19)	Jack Coombs	400.00	200.00	100.00
(20)	A. Wilbur Cooper	400.00	200.00	100.00
(21)	George Cutshaw	400.00	200.00	100.00
(22)	Jake Daubert	400.00	200.00	100.00
(23)	Wheezer Dell	400.00	200.00	100.00
(24)	Bill Donovan	400.00	200.00	100.00
(25)	Larry Doyle	400.00	200.00	100.00
(26)	R.J. Egan	400.00	200.00	100.00
(27)	Johnny Evers	550.00	225.00	110.00
(28)	Ray Fisher	400.00	200.00	100.00
(29)	Harry Gardner (Larry)	400.00	200.00	100.00
(30)	Joe Gedeon	400.00	200.00	100.00
(31)	Larry Gilbert	400.00	200.00	100.00
(32)	Frank Gilhooley	400.00	200.00	100.00
(33)	Hank Gowdy	400.00	200.00	100.00
(34)	Sylvanus Gregg	400.00	200.00	100.00
(35)	Tom Griffith	400.00	200.00	100.00
(36)	Heinie Groh	400.00	200.00	100.00
(37)	Bob Harmon	400.00	200.00	100.00
(38)	Roy A. Hartzell	400.00	200.00	100.00
(39)	Claude Hendrix	400.00	200.00	100.00
(40)	Olaf Henriksen	400.00	200.00	100.00
(41)	Buck Herzog	400.00	200.00	100.00
(42)	Hugh High	400.00	200.00	100.00
(43)	Dick Hoblitzell	400.00	200.00	100.00
(44)	Herb Hunter	400.00	200.00	100.00
(45)	Harold Janvrin	400.00	200.00	100.00
(46)	Hugh Jennings	550.00	225.00	110.00
(47)	John Johnston	400.00	200.00	100.00
(48)	Erving Kantlehner	400.00	200.00	100.00
(49)	Benny Kauff	400.00	200.00	100.00
(50a)	Ray Keating (Error, striped cap, photo is Kocher.)	400.00	200.00	100.00
(50b)	Ray Keating (Correct, "NY" on cap.)	400.00	200.00	100.00
(51)	Wade Killefer	400.00	200.00	100.00
(52a)	Elmer Knetzer (Error, no "B" on cap, photo is Konetchy.)	400.00	200.00	100.00
(52b)	Elmer Knetzer (Correct, "B" on cap.)	400.00	200.00	100.00
(53a)	B.W. Kocher (Error, "NY" on cap, photo is Keating.)	400.00	200.00	100.00
(53b)	B.W. Kocher (Correct, striped cap.)	400.00	200.00	100.00
(54a)	Ed. Konetchy (Error, "B" on cap, photo is Knetzer.)	400.00	200.00	100.00
(54b)	Ed. Konetchy (Correct, no "B" on cap.)	400.00	200.00	100.00
(55)	Fred Lauderous (Luderous)	400.00	200.00	100.00
(56)	Dutch Leonard	400.00	200.00	100.00
(57)	Duffy Lewis	400.00	200.00	100.00
(58)	Slim Love	400.00	200.00	100.00
(59)	Albert L. Mamaux	400.00	200.00	100.00
(60)	Rabbit Maranville	550.00	225.00	110.00
(61)	Rube Marquard	540.00	215.00	110.00
(62)	Christy Mathewson	1,900	950.00	475.00

		NM	E	VG
(63)	Bill McKechnie	550.00	225.00	110.00
(64)	Chief Meyer (Meyers)	400.00	200.00	100.00
(65)	Otto Miller	400.00	200.00	100.00
(66)	Fred Mollwitz	400.00	200.00	100.00
(67)	Herbie Moran	400.00	200.00	100.00
(68)	Mike Mowrey	400.00	200.00	100.00
(69)	Dan Murphy	400.00	200.00	100.00
(70)	Art Nehf	400.00	200.00	100.00
(71)	Rube Oldring	400.00	200.00	100.00
(72)	Oliver O'Mara	400.00	200.00	100.00
(73)	Dode Paskert	400.00	200.00	100.00
(74)	D.C. Pat Ragan	400.00	200.00	100.00
(75)	William A. Rariden	400.00	200.00	100.00
(76)	Davis Robertson	400.00	200.00	100.00
(77)	Wm. Rodgers	400.00	200.00	100.00
(78)	Edw. F. Rousch (Roush)	550.00	225.00	110.00
(79)	Nap Rucker	400.00	200.00	100.00
(80)	Dick Rudolph	400.00	200.00	100.00
(81)	Wally Schang	400.00	200.00	100.00
(82)	Rube Schauer	400.00	200.00	100.00
(83)	Pete Schneider	400.00	200.00	100.00
(84)	Ferd Schupp	400.00	200.00	100.00
(85)	Ernie Shore	400.00	200.00	100.00
(86)	Red Smith	400.00	200.00	100.00
(87)	Fred Snodgrass	400.00	200.00	100.00
(88)	Tris Speaker	700.00	350.00	175.00
(89)	George Stallings	400.00	200.00	100.00
(90)	C.D. Stengle (Casey Stengel)	600.00	300.00	150.00
(91)	Sailor Stroud	400.00	200.00	100.00
(92)	Amos Strunk	400.00	200.00	100.00
(93)	Chas. (Jeff) Tesreau	400.00	200.00	100.00
(94a)	Chester D. Thomas (One button shows.)	400.00	200.00	100.00
(94b)	Chester D. Thomas (Two buttons.)	400.00	200.00	100.00
(95)	Fred Toney	400.00	200.00	100.00
(96)	Walt Tragesser	400.00	200.00	100.00
(97)	Honus Wagner	5,000	1,000	500.00
(98)	Carl Weilman	400.00	200.00	100.00
(99)	Zack Wheat	550.00	225.00	110.00
(100)	George Whitted	400.00	200.00	100.00
(101)	Arthur Wilson	400.00	200.00	100.00
(102)	Ivy Wingo	400.00	200.00	100.00
(103)	Joe Wood	500.00	250.00	125.00

1940s Ford Babe Ruth Premium

The exact date of this premium photo's issue is unknown. The approximately 5" x 6-1/2" blank-back, black-and-white photo features Ruth in an oft-seen batting pose. In the wide white border at bottom is printed, "CONSULTANT / FORD MOTOR COMPANY / AMERICAN LEGION JUNIOR BASEBALL."

	NM	E	VG
Babe Ruth	300.00	150.00	90.00

1961 Ford Pittsburgh Pirates Prints

The year after the team's dramatic World Series win over the Yankees, Pittsburgh area Ford dealers distributed a set of six player prints. The blank-back, 11-7/8" x 14-3/4" prints feature action drawings of the players by artist Robert Riger. Some of the prints are horizontal in format, some are vertical. A Ford Motor Co. copyright line appears in the lower-left corner and a line at bottom center identifies the player in the form of a title for the picture. The unnumbered prints are listed here in alphabetical order. The pictures were reprinted by an unauthorized party circa 1998.

		NM	E	VG
Complete Set (6):		125.00	65.00	35.00
Common Player:		15.00	7.50	4.50
(1)	BOB FRIEND COMES IN WITH THE FAST ONE(Bob Friend)	15.00	7.50	4.50
(2)	CLEMENTE LINES ONE OVER SECOND(Roberto Clemente)	75.00	37.50	22.00
(3)	GROAT CUTS DOWN A BRAVE STEAL(Dick Groat)	15.00	7.50	4.50
(4)	HOAK HANDLES A HOT SHOT AT THIRD(Don Hoak)	15.00	7.50	4.50
(5)	MAZ GETS THE BIG HIT(Bill Mazeroski)	30.00	15.00	9.00
(6)	THE LAW(Vern Law)	15.00	7.50	4.50

1962 Ford Detroit Tigers Postcards

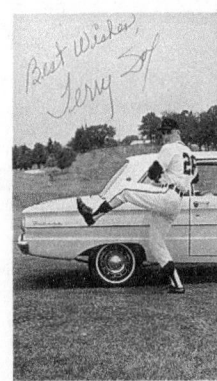

Because baseball card collectors have to compete with auto memorabilia hobbyists for these scarce cards, they are among the most valuable postcard issues of the early 1960s. In 3-1/4" x 5-1/2" postcard format, the full-color cards feature photos taken on a golf course of players posed in front of various new Fords. White backs have a name, position and team, with a box for a stamp. Probably given out in conjunction with autograph appearances at car dealers (they are frequently found autographed), the set lacks some of the team's biggest stars (Al Kaline, Norm Cash), and includes coaches and even trainer Jack Homel. Probably because of lack of demand, the coaches' and trainer's cards are the scarcest to find today. The unnumbered cards are checklisted here alphabetically.

		NM	E	VG
Complete Set (16):		1,425	710.00	425.00
Common Player:		60.00	30.00	18.00
(1)	Hank Aguirre	90.00	45.00	27.50
(2)	Steve Boros	120.00	60.00	35.00
(3)	Dick Brown	90.00	45.00	27.50
(4)	Jim Bunning	150.00	75.00	45.00
(5)	Phil Cavaretta	135.00	65.00	40.00
(6)	Rocky Colavito	185.00	90.00	55.00
(7)	Terry Fox	60.00	30.00	18.00
(8)	Purn Goldy	75.00	37.50	22.50
(9)	Jack Homel	135.00	65.00	40.00
(10)	Ron Kline	90.00	45.00	27.50
(11)	Don Mossi	60.00	30.00	18.00
(12)	George Myatt	120.00	60.00	35.00
(13)	Ron Nischwitz	90.00	45.00	27.50
(14)	Larry Osborne	60.00	30.00	18.00
(15)	Phil Regan	90.00	45.00	27.50
(16)	Mike Roarke	135.00	65.00	40.00

1938 Foto Fun

Sponsored by Poll-Parrott Shoes, this set was an early attempt at a self-developing player photocard (a technology that Topps used in the 1940s-50s) used a black-and-white negative and a piece of photo paper to create a blue-tint photo that could be placed in a gold cardboard frame. The back of the 2-3/4" x 3-5/8" frame is printed in brown and gives instructions for developing the photo. The checklist of the un-numbered cards, presented here alphabetically, may or may not be complete at 93.

		NM	E	VG
Common Player:		160.00	80.00	45.00
(1)	Luke Appling	375.00	185.00	110.00
(2)	Morris Arnovich	160.00	80.00	45.00
(3)	Eldon Auker	160.00	80.00	45.00
(4)	Jim Bagby Jr.	160.00	80.00	45.00
(5)	Red Barrett	160.00	80.00	45.00
(6)	Roy Bell	160.00	80.00	45.00
(7)	Wally Berger	160.00	80.00	45.00
(8)	Oswald Bluege	160.00	80.00	45.00
(9)	Frenchy Bordagaray	160.00	80.00	45.00
(10)	Tom Bridges	160.00	80.00	45.00
(11)	Dolf Camilli	160.00	80.00	45.00
(12)	Ben Chapman	160.00	80.00	45.00
(13)	Harland Clift (Harlond)	160.00	80.00	45.00
(14)	Harry Craft	160.00	80.00	45.00
(15)	Roger Cramer	160.00	80.00	45.00
(16)	Joe Cronin	375.00	185.00	110.00
(17)	Tony Cuccinello	160.00	80.00	45.00
(18)	Kiki Cuyler	375.00	185.00	110.00
(19)	Ellsworth Dahlgren	160.00	80.00	45.00
(20)	Harry Danning	160.00	80.00	45.00
(21)	Frank Demaree	160.00	80.00	45.00
(22)	Gene Desautels	160.00	80.00	45.00
(23)	Jim Deshong	160.00	80.00	45.00
(24)	Bill Dickey	450.00	225.00	135.00
(25)	Lou Fette	160.00	80.00	45.00
(26)	Lou Finney	160.00	80.00	45.00
(27)	Larry French	160.00	80.00	45.00
(28)	Linus Frey	160.00	80.00	45.00
(29)	Augie Galan	160.00	80.00	45.00
(30)	Debs Garms	160.00	80.00	45.00
(31)	Charles Gehringer	450.00	225.00	135.00
(32)	Lefty Gomez	450.00	225.00	135.00
(33)	Ival Goodman	160.00	80.00	45.00
(34)	Lee Grissom	160.00	80.00	45.00
(35)	Stan Hack	180.00	90.00	55.00
(36)	Irving Hadley	160.00	80.00	45.00
(37)	Rollie Hemsley	160.00	80.00	45.00
(38)	Tommy Henrich	160.00	80.00	45.00
(39)	Billy Herman	375.00	185.00	110.00
(40)	Willard Hershberger	160.00	80.00	45.00
(41)	Michael Higgins	160.00	80.00	45.00
(42)	Oral Hildebrand	160.00	80.00	45.00
(43)	Carl Hubbell	450.00	225.00	135.00
(44)	Willis Hudlin	160.00	80.00	45.00
(45)	Mike Kreevich	160.00	80.00	45.00
(46)	Ralph Kress	160.00	80.00	45.00
(47)	John Lanning	160.00	80.00	45.00
(48)	Lyn Lary	160.00	80.00	45.00
(49)	Cookie Lavagetto	160.00	80.00	45.00
(50)	Thornton Lee	160.00	80.00	45.00
(51)	Ernie Lombardi	375.00	185.00	110.00
(52)	Al Lopez	375.00	185.00	110.00
(53)	Ted Lyons	375.00	185.00	110.00
(54)	Danny MacFayden	160.00	80.00	45.00
(55)	Max Macon	160.00	80.00	45.00
(56)	Pepper Martin	250.00	125.00	75.00
(57)	Joe Marty	160.00	80.00	45.00
(58)	Frank McCormick	160.00	80.00	45.00
(59)	Bill McKechnie	375.00	185.00	110.00
(60)	Joe Medwick	375.00	185.00	110.00
(61)	Cliff Melton	160.00	80.00	45.00
(62)	Charley Meyer (Myer)	160.00	80.00	45.00
(63)	John Mize	450.00	225.00	135.00
(64)	Terry Moore	180.00	90.00	55.00
(65)	Whitey Moore	160.00	80.00	45.00
(66)	Emmett Mueller	160.00	80.00	45.00
(67)	Hugh Mulcahy	160.00	80.00	45.00
(68)	Van L. Mungo	160.00	80.00	45.00
(69)	Johnny Murphy	160.00	80.00	45.00
(70)	Lynn Nelson	160.00	80.00	45.00
(71)	Mel Ott	450.00	225.00	135.00
(72)	Monte Pearson	160.00	80.00	45.00
(73)	Bill Rogell	160.00	80.00	45.00
(74)	George Selkirk	160.00	80.00	45.00
(75)	Milt Shofner	160.00	80.00	45.00
(76)	Al Simmons	375.00	185.00	110.00
(77)	Clyde Shoun	160.00	80.00	45.00
(78)	Gus Suhr	160.00	80.00	45.00
(79)	Billy Sullivan	160.00	80.00	45.00
(80)	Cecil Travis	160.00	80.00	45.00
(81)	Pie Traynor	375.00	185.00	110.00
(82)	Hal Trosky	160.00	80.00	45.00
(83)	Jim Turner	160.00	80.00	45.00
(84)	Johnny Vander Meer	160.00	80.00	45.00
(85)	Oscar Vitt	160.00	80.00	45.00
(86)	Gerald Walker	160.00	80.00	45.00
(87)	Paul Waner	375.00	185.00	110.00
(88)	Rabbit Warstler	160.00	80.00	45.00
(89)	Bob Weiland	160.00	80.00	45.00
(90)	Burgess Whitehead	160.00	80.00	45.00
(91)	Earl Whitehill	160.00	80.00	45.00
(92)	Rudy York	160.00	80.00	45.00
(93)	Del Young	160.00	80.00	45.00

1887 Four Base Hits

Although the exact origin of this set is still in doubt, the Four Base Hits cards are among the rarest and most sought after of all 19th century tobacco issues. There is some speculation that the cards, measuring 2-1/4" x 3-7/8", were produced by Charles Gross & Co. because of their similarity to the Kalamazoo Bats issues, but there is also some evidence to support the theory that they were issued by August Beck & Co., producer of the Yum Yum set. The Four Base Hits cards feature sepia-toned photos with the player's name and position below the picture, and the words "Smoke Four Base Hits. Four For 10 Cents." along the bottom. The card labeled "Daily" is a double error. The name should have been spelled "Daly," but the card actually pictures Billy Sunday. Many of the cards on this surely incomplete checklist are known to survive in only a single example; few in grades above VG.

		NM	E	VG
Common Player:		35,000	15,000	
(1)	John Clarkson ((Possibly Unique))	175,000	100,000	
(2)	Tido Daily ((Daly) (Photo is Billy Sunday))	35,000	20,000	
(3)	Pat Deasley	35,000	20,000	
(4)	Mike Dorgan	35,000	20,000	
(5)	Buck Ewing ((Possibly Unique))	225,000	125,000	
(6)	Pete Gillespie	35,000	20,000	
(7)	Frank Hankinson	35,000	20,000	
(8)	King Kelly ((Two known))	350,000	200,000	
(9)	Tim Keefe ((Three known))	125,000	90,000	
(10)	Al Mays	35,000	20,000	
(11)	Jim Mutrie	40,000	25,000	
(12)	Jim O'Rourke ((Two known))	135,000	95,000	
(13)	Chief Roseman	35,000	20,000	
(14)	Marty Sullivan	35,000	20,000	
(15)	Rip Van Haltren ((Two known))	45,000	30,000	
(15)	John Ward ((Two known))	165,000	100,000	
(15)	Mickey Welch ((Two known))	125,000	90,000	

1960s Nellie Fox Bowl Postcard

This specially marked version of a typical J.D. McCarthy postcard advertises on back the White Sox second baseman's bowling enterprise in Chambersburg, Pa. The card is black-and-white with a facsimile autograph on front.

	NM	E	VG
Nellie Fox	35.00	17.50	10.50

1907 F.P. Burke Frank Chance Postcard

This novelty postcard is one of many baseball-themed postcards issued by Chicago publisher F.P. Burke. The black-and-white card is about standard (3-1/2" x 5-1/2") postcard size with typical postcard markings on the back.

	NM	EX	VG
Frank Chance	1,500.	750.00	450.00

1980 Franchise Babe Ruth

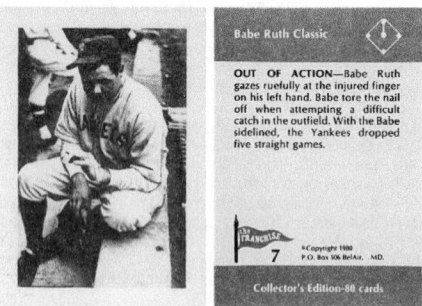

The first in a series of collectors' issues relative to Maryland baseball, this 80-card set chronicles the life - on and off the field - of Babe Ruth. Fronts of the 2-1/2" x 3-1/2" cards have black-and-white photos surrounded by wide white borders. Backs are printed in red and black and include a caption and description of the front photo. At the time of issue, the set sold for about $8.

	NM	E	VG
Complete Set (80):	35.00	17.50	10.00
Common Card:	1.00	.50	.30

1-80	Babe Ruth

1961 Franklin Milk

While it is not part of the contemporary Cloverleaf Dairy milk carton Minnesota Twins issues, this carton is often collected alongside the others. Printed in red and blue, the portion of the milk carton advertising Harmon Killebrew's radio show measures about 4" x 4-1/2".

		NM	E	VG
(1)	Harmon Killebrew (Complete carton.)	1,600	800.00	480.00
(1)	Harmon Killebrew (Cut panel.)	250.00	125.00	75.00

1964 Freihofer's Philadelphia Phillies

The attributed date is speculative, based on the players checklisted from this issue. These 8" x 10" pictures feature studio poses and are printed on heavy, non-glossy paper. A white border surrounds the photo, with the player name in typewriter-style all-caps at bottom. Backs are blank. Two styles of advertising have been seen imprinted on the pictures. Type 1 pictures have a bakery logo as part of the legend "ANOTHER FAVORITE / FROM FREIHOFER'S / that's who!" Type 2 pictures have a script inscription: "Best WISHES to a / Fellow Freihofer's Booster."

	NM	E	VG
TYPE 1 (Logo)			
Ruben Amaro	50.00	25.00	15.00
Wes Covington	50.00	25.00	15.00
TYPE 2 (No logo.)			
Wes Covington	30.00	15.00	9.00

1963 French Bauer Reds Milk Caps

This regional set of cardboard milk bottle caps was issued in the Cincinnati area in 1963 and features 30 members of the Cincinnati Reds. The unnumbered, blank-backed discs are approximately 1-1/4" in diameter and feature rather crude drawings of the players with their names in script alongside the artwork and the words "Visit Beautiful Crosley Field/See The Reds in Action" along the outside. An album was issued to house the set. Some caps have been seen with incorrect picture/name combinations.

		NM	E	VG
Complete Set (30):		1,300	650.00	400.00
Common Player:		25.00	12.50	7.50
Album:		100.00	50.00	30.00
(1)	Don Blasingame	25.00	12.50	7.50
(2)	Leo Cardenas	25.00	12.50	7.50
(3)	Gordon Coleman	25.00	12.50	7.50
(4)	Wm. O. DeWitt	25.00	12.50	7.50
(5)	John Edwards	25.00	12.50	7.50
(6)	Jesse Gonder	25.00	12.50	7.50
(7)	Tommy Harper	25.00	12.50	7.50
(8)	Bill Henry	25.00	12.50	7.50
(9)	Fred Hutchinson	25.00	12.50	7.50
(10)	Joey Jay	25.00	12.50	7.50
(11)	Eddie Kasko	25.00	12.50	7.50
(12)	Marty Keough	25.00	12.50	7.50
(13)	Jim Maloney	25.00	12.50	7.50
(14)	Joe Nuxhall	30.00	15.00	9.00
(15)	Reggie Otero	25.00	12.50	7.50
(16)	Jim O'Toole	25.00	12.50	7.50
(17)	Jim Owens	25.00	12.50	7.50
(18)	Vada Pinson	30.00	15.00	9.00
(19)	Bob Purkey	25.00	12.50	7.50
(20)	Frank Robinson	125.00	60.00	35.00
(21)	Dr. Richard Rohde	25.00	12.50	7.50
(22)	Pete Rose	500.00	250.00	150.00
(23)	Ray Shore	25.00	12.50	7.50
(24)	Dick Sisler	25.00	12.50	7.50
(25)	Bob Skinner	25.00	12.50	7.50
(26)	John Tsitorius	25.00	12.50	7.50
(27)	Jim Turner	25.00	12.50	7.50
(28)	Ken Walters	25.00	12.50	7.50
(29)	Al Worthington	25.00	12.50	7.50
(30)	Dom Zanni	25.00	12.50	7.50

1946 Friedman's Dodger Aces Postcard

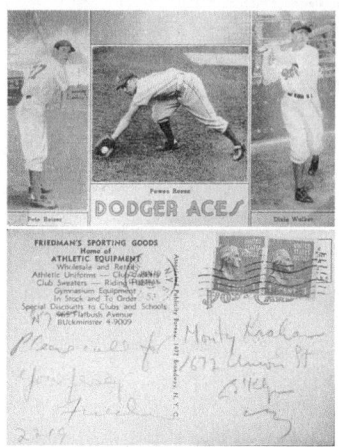

The date of issue is conjectural and could actually have been anytime in the 1940s until 1947, though the cards continued to be used at least into 1953 according to postally used examples. The 5-1/2" x 3-1/2" postcard has a linen finish on front and features color posed action photos of three Dodgers stars. Backs have information about the sporting goods store, a postage stamp box and a credit line to Associated Publicity Bureau.

	NM	E	VG
Dodger Aces(Pete Reiser, Pewee (Pee Wee) Reese, Dixie Walker)	35.00	17.50	10.50

1960-61 Fritos Ticket Folders

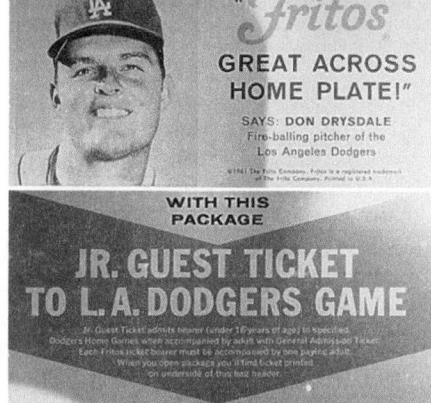

Only a few players are known in this issue of folders which includes a "Jr. Guest Ticket" to selected Dodgers games. About 5-5/8" x 3", the folder has a black-and-white player portrait on front and is highlighted in red and yellow. When opened, the folder has advertising for Fritos corn chips (or other Firtos-Lay brands) and a Dodgers home schedule. Others may exist.

		NM	E	VG
Common Player:		90.00	45.00	25.00
(1)	Don Drysdale (1960) (Crispies advertising.))	250.00	125.00	75.00
(1)	Don Drysdale (1961)	200.00	100.00	60.00
(2)	Gil Hodges (1960)	200.00	100.00	60.00
(3)	Frank Howard (1961)	90.00	45.00	25.00
(4)	Wally Moon (1960)	150.00	75.00	45.00
(5)	Charley Neal (1960)	150.00	75.00	45.00
(6)	Larry Sherry (1960)	150.00	75.00	45.00

1977 Fritsch One-Year Winners

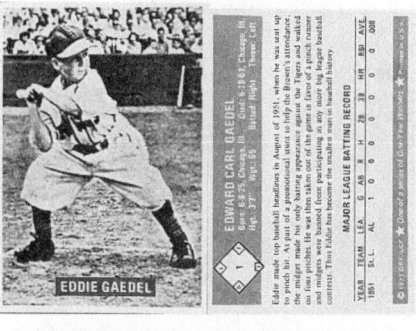

EDDIE GAEDEL

First printed in 1977, this collector's issue features players with brief, but often well-known, major league baseball careers. Because of the timing or duration of their playing days, few ever appeared on a major baseball card issue. The 2-1/2" x 3-1/2" cards have black-and-white photos on front, bordered in green, with the player name in white within a green strip at bottom. Backs are printed in black, red and white in similitude of the 1953 Bowman backs and contain personal data, stats and career highlights.

		NM	E	VG
Complete Set (18):		12.00	6.00	3.50
Common Player:		1.00	.50	.30
1	Eddie Gaedel	5.00	2.50	1.50
2	Chuck Connors	3.00	1.50	.90
3	Joe Brovia	1.00	.50	.30
4	Ross Grimsley	1.00	.50	.30
5	Bob Thorpe	1.00	.50	.30
6	Pete Gray	5.00	2.50	1.50
7	Cy Buker	1.00	.50	.30
8	Ted Fritsch	2.00	1.00	.60
9	Ron Necciai	1.00	.50	.30
10	Nino Escalera	1.00	.50	.30
11	Bobo Holloman	1.00	.50	.30
12	Tony Roig	1.00	.50	.30
13	Paul Pettit	1.00	.50	.30
14	Paul Schramka	1.00	.50	.30
15	Hal Trosky	1.00	.50	.30
16	Floyd Wooldridge	1.00	.50	.30
17	Jim Westlake	1.00	.50	.30
18	Leon Brinkopf	1.00	.50	.30

1979 Fritsch One-Year Winners

PIDGE BROWNE

Players with short major-league careers, few of whom appeared on contemporary baseball cards, are featured in the second collectors' series of "One-Year Winners." The cards are numbered contiguously from the end of the 1977 issue and share a back format printed in red, white and black. Fronts of the 1979 issue have a white border and feature color player photos with a shadow box beneath carrying the name.

		NM	E	VG
Complete Set (36):		40.00	20.00	12.00
Common Player:		3.00	1.50	.90
19	Daryl Robertson	3.00	1.50	.90
20	Gerry Schoen	3.00	1.50	.90
21	Jim Brenneman	3.00	1.50	.90
22	Pat House	3.00	1.50	.90
23	Ken Poulsen	3.00	1.50	.90
24	Arlo Brunsberg	3.00	1.50	.90
25	Jay Hankins	3.00	1.50	.90
26	Chuck Nieson	3.00	1.50	.90
27	Dick Joyce	3.00	1.50	.90
28	Jim Ellis	3.00	1.50	.90
29	John Duffie	3.00	1.50	.90
30	Vern Holtgrave	3.00	1.50	.90
31	Bill Bethea	3.00	1.50	.90
32	Joe Moock	3.00	1.50	.90
33	John Hoffman	3.00	1.50	.90
34	Jorge Rubio	3.00	1.50	.90

35	Fred Rath	3.00	1.50	.90
36	Jess Hickman	3.00	1.50	.90
37	Tom Fisher	3.00	1.50	.90
38	Dick Scott	3.00	1.50	.90
39	Jim Hibbs	3.00	1.50	.90
40	Paul Gilliford	3.00	1.50	.90
41	Bob Botz	3.00	1.50	.90
42	Jack Kubiszyn	3.00	1.50	.90
43	Rich Rusteck	3.00	1.50	.90
44	Roy Gleason	3.00	1.50	.90
45	Glenn Vaughn	3.00	1.50	.90
46	Bill Graham	3.00	1.50	.90
47	Dennis Musgraves	3.00	1.50	.90
48	Ron Henry	3.00	1.50	.90
49	Mike Jurewicz	3.00	1.50	.90
50	Pidge Browne	3.00	1.50	.90
51	Ron Keller	3.00	1.50	.90
52	Doug Gallagher	3.00	1.50	.90
53	Dave Thies	3.00	1.50	.90
54	Don Eaddy	3.00	1.50	.90

1928 Fro-joy (F52)

George Herman ("Babe") Ruth

"The Sultan of Swat," who holds the world's record for home-run hits in a single season with 60 circuit clouts during the regular playing season of 1927, topped by 2 more against Pittsburgh during the World's Series games last year.

Boys—Girls:

Fro-joy Ice Cream, in Fro-joy Cones, builds bone and strength. Eat one every day.

Chock-full of
"YOUTH UNITS"

PICTURE NO. 1

This is the first in a series of six pictures of "Babe" Ruth being given free with Fro-joy Cones during Fro-joy Cone Week, August 6-11th, 1928. The complete set can be exchanged for a large reproduction of "Babe" Ruth's autographed photo. Ask your dealer for a FREE circular giving full details.

Capitalizing on the extreme popularity of Babe Ruth, these cards were given away with ice cream cones during the Aug. 6-11, 1928, "Fro-joy Cone Week." The 2-1/16" x 4" cards have black-and-white photos on front with a title and a few sentences explaining the photo. Backs contain advertising for Fro-joy Ice Cream and Cones. An uncut sheet along with a large-format action photo of Ruth was available in a mail-in redemption offer. Virtually all uncut sheets offered in the market today, and all color Fro-joy cards are modern counterfeits. Purchase of an uncut sheet without the original mailing envelope and/or premium picture is not advised. Cards graded by a major authentication firm carry a significant premium due to the prevalence of single-card counterfeits in the market.

		NM	E	VG
Complete Set (6):		3,450	1,625	975.00
Uncut Sheet:		2,900	1,450	870.00
1	George Herman ("Babe") Ruth	1,150	575.00	345.00
2	Look Out, Mr. Pitcher!	500.00	250.00	150.00
3	Bang! The Babe Lines One Out!	500.00	250.00	150.00
4	When the "Babe" Comes Home	500.00	250.00	150.00
5	"Babe" Ruth's Grip!	325.00	160.00	97.50
6	Ruth is a Crack Fielder	500.00	250.00	150.00

1928 Fro-joy Premium Photo

This 8-1/2" x 10" photo of Babe Ruth was given away when a complete set of individual Fro-joy Babe Ruth cards was sent in for redemption. It is extremely scarce in its own right and is vital for verification of the authenticity of uncut Fro-joy card sheets. The premium photo is printed in blue in the debossed center area of a cream-colored card. A facsimile autograph of Ruth adorns the image.

	NM	E	VG
Babe Ruth	1,200	600.00	360.00

1969 Fud's Photography Montreal Expos

Compliments of

JOSE LABOY

FUD'S PHOTOGRAPHY

This collectors' issue was produced by Bob Solon sometime after 1969. The 3-1/2" x 3" black-and-white horizontal cards have action photos of the players with a white strip in the lower-right corner bearing the name. In the white border at top is "Compliments of," while the purported photo studio name is centered at bottom. Backs are blank. The unnumbered cards are checklisted here alphabetically.

		NM	E	VG
Complete Set (14):		40.00	20.00	12.00
Common Player:		4.00	2.00	1.25
(1)	Bob Bailey	4.00	2.00	1.25
(2)	John Bateman	4.00	2.00	1.25
(3)	Don Bosch	4.00	2.00	1.25
(4)	Jim Grant	4.00	2.00	1.25
(5)	Mack Jones	4.00	2.00	1.25
(6)	Jose Laboy	4.00	2.00	1.25
(7)	Dan McGinn	4.00	2.00	1.25
(8)	Cal McLish	4.00	2.00	1.25
(9)	Carl Morton	4.00	2.00	1.25
(10)	Manny Mota	6.00	3.00	1.75
(11)	Rusty Staub	9.00	4.50	2.75
(12)	Gary Sutherland	4.00	2.00	1.25
(13)	Mike Wegener	4.00	2.00	1.25
(14)	Floyd Wicker	4.00	2.00	1.25

G

1888 G & B Chewing Gum (E223)

GALVIN Pitcher.
NATIONAL LEAGUE
G & B. N.Y.

This set, issued with G&B Chewing Gum, produced in New York City by Green & Blackwell, is the first baseball card issued with candy or gum and the only 19th Century candy issue. The cards in the G&B set are small, measuring approximately 1-1/16" x 2-1/8", and nearly identical in format to the August Beck Yum Yum tobacco issue (N403). Many of the photos and pictures were shared between the sets. The player's name and position appear in thin capital letters below the photo, followed by either "National League" or "American League" (actually referring to the American Association). At the very bottom of the card, the manufacturer, "G & B N.Y." is indicated. Some of the "National League" cards also include the words "Chewing Gum" under the league designation. The set was assigned the ACC number E223. All of the action poses and some of the portraits are line drawings rather than photographs. Gaps have been left in the assigned numbering to accommodate future additions.

		NM	E	VG
Common Player:		10,000	4,000	2,500
(3)	Cap Anson (Batting)	25,000	10,000	6,250
(4)	Cap Anson (Photo portrait.)	37,500	15,000	9,375
(7)	Lady Baldwin (Detroit) (Left arm extended.)	10,000	4,000	2,500
(9)	Mark Baldwin (Chicago) (Bat at side.))	10,000	4,000	2,500
(10)	Mark Baldwin (Chicago) (Photo portrait.))	31,250	12,500	7,815
(13)	Sam Barkley (Line portrait.)	10,000	4,000	2,500
(15)	Steve Brady (Photo portrait.)	31,250	12,500	7,815
(17)	Dan Brouthers (Pose unrecorded.)	31,250	12,500	7,815
(19)	Willard (California) Brown (Photo portrait.)	31,250	12,500	7,815
(20)	Willard (California) Brown (Line art.)	10,000	4,000	2,500
(23)	Charles Buffington (Buffinton)(Photo portrait.)	31,250	12,500	7,815
(25)	Tom Burns (Photo portrait.)	31,250	12,500	7,815
(27)	Doc Bushong (Line portrait.)	10,000	4,000	2,500
(29)	Bob Caruthers (Line portrait.)	10,000	4,000	2,500
(33)	John Clarkson (Photo portrait.)	37,500	15,000	9,375
(35)	John Coleman (Photo portrait.)	31,250	12,500	7,815
(37)	Charlie Comiskey (Line portrait.)	18,750	7,500	4,690
(39)	Roger Connor (Batting)	18,750	7,500	4,690
(40)	Roger Connor (Photo portrait.)	37,500	15,000	9,375
(43)	Con Daily (Photo portrait.)	31,250	12,500	7,815
(45)	Tom Deasley (Photo portrait.)	31,250	12,500	7,815
(47)	Jim Donahue (Photo portrait.)	31,250	12,500	7,815
(49)	Mike Dorgan (Photo portrait.)	31,250	12,500	7,815
(51)	Dude Esterbrook (Photo portrait.)	31,250	12,500	7,815
(53)	Buck Ewing (Photo portrait.)	37,500	15,000	9,375
(54)	Buck Ewing (With bat.)	18,750	7,500	4,690
(57)	Charlie Ferguson (Right arm head-high.)	10,000	4,000	2,500
(59)	Silver Flint (Photo portrait.)	15,625	6,250	3,905
(61)	Pud Galvin (Ball in hands at front.)	18,750	7,500	4,690
(63)	Charlie Getzein (Getzien) (Throwing))	10,000	4,000	2,500
(65)	Jack Glasscock (Line art.)	10,000	4,000	2,500
(67)	Will Gleason (Batting)	10,000	4,000	2,500
(69)	Ed Greer (Photo portrait.)	31,250	12,500	7,815
(71)	Frank Hankinson (Photo portrait.)	31,250	12,500	7,815
(73)	Ned Hanlon (Batting)	18,750	7,500	4,690
(75)	Pete Hotaling (Batting)	15,625	6,250	3,905
(77)	Spud Johnson (Batting)	10,000	4,000	2,500
(79)	Tim Keefe (Ball in hands above waist.)	18,750	7,500	4,690
(80)	Tim Keefe (Batting)	18,750	7,500	4,690
(81)	Tim Keefe (Photo portrait.)	37,500	15,000	9,375
(83)	King Kelly (Batting)	25,000	10,000	6,250
(84)	King Kelly (Photo, standing by urn.)	100,000	20,000	12,500
(87)	Gus Krock (Photo portrait.)	31,250	12,500	7,815
(89)	Arlie Latham (Line portrait.)	10,000	4,000	2,500
(91)	Connie Mack (Throwing)	37,500	15,000	9,375
(93)	Kid Madden (Pitching)	10,000	4,000	2,500
(95)	Al Mays (Photo portrait.)	31,250	12,500	7,815

(97)	Jumbo McGinnis (Line portrait.)	10,000	4,000	2,500
(99)	Doggie Miller (Leaning on bat.)	10,000	4,000	2,500
(101)	John Morrill (Bat at side.)	10,000	4,000	2,500
(103)	James Mutrie (Photo portrait.)	31,250	12,500	7,815
(105)	Hugh Nicoll (Nicol)(Line portrait.))	10,000	4,000	2,500
(107)	Tip O'Neill (Line portrait.))	10,000	4,000	2,500
(109)	Jim O'Rourke (Photo portrait.)	37,500	15,000	9,375
(111)	Dave Orr (Batting)	10,000	4,000	2,500
(112)	Dave Orr (Photo portrait.)	31,250	12,500	7,815
(115)	Fred Pfeffer (Bat on shoulder.)	10,000	4,000	2,500
(117)	Henry Porter (Pitching)	10,000	4,000	2,500
(119)	Al Reache (Reach) (Line portrait.) (Possibly unique; value undetermined.))			
(121)	Danny Richardson (Batting)	10,000	4,000	2,500
(122)	Danny Richardson (Photo portrait.)	31,250	12,500	7,815
(125)	Yank Robinson (Line portrait.)	10,000	4,000	2,500
(127)	Chief Roseman (Photo portrait.)	31,250	12,500	7,815
(129)	Jimmy Ryan (Photo portrait.)	31,250	12,500	7,815
(130)	Jimmy Ryan (Throwing)	10,000	4,000	2,500
(133)	Pop Smith (Photo portrait.)	31,250	12,500	7,815
(137)	Bill Sowders (Ball in hands at chest.)	10,000	4,000	2,500
(138)	Bill Sowders (Throwing)	10,000	4,000	2,500
(139)	Albert Spaulding (Spalding) (Line portrait.) (Possibly unique; value undetermined.))			
(141)	Marty Sullivan (Line portrait.)	10,000	4,000	2,500
(143)	Billy Sunday (Fielding)	15,620	6,250	3,905
(144)	Billy Sunday (Photo portrait.)	34,375	13,750	8,595
(145)	Ezra Sutton (Batting)	10,000	4,000	2,500
(149)	Sam Thompson (Batting)	18,750	7,500	4,690
(153)	Mike Tiernan (Batting)	10,000	4,000	2,500
(154)	Mike Tiernan (Photo portrait.)	31,250	12,500	7,815
(157)	Larry Twitchell (Photo portrait.)	31,250	12,500	7,815
(159)	Rip Van Haltren (Photo portrait.)	31,250	12,500	7,815
(161)	Chris Von Der Ahe (Line portrait.)	10,000	4,000	2,500
(165)	John Ward (Photo portrait.)	37,500	15,000	9,375
(169)	Mickey Welch (Ball in hands above waist.)	18,750	7,500	4,690
(170)	Mickey Welch (Right arm extended forward.)	18,750	7,500	4,690
(171)	Mickey Welch (Photo portrait.)	37,500	15,000	9,375
(173)	Curt Welsh (Welch)	10,000	4,000	2,500
(177)	Jim Whitney	10,000	4,000	2,500
(181)	Pete Wood (Throwing)	10,000	4,000	2,500

1966 H.F. Gardner Postcards

Baseball players (and track legend Jesse Owens) who were born in Alabama are featured in this issue credited on some of the cards' backs to a Bessemer, Ala., firm, Scenic South Card Co. Fronts feature borderless color photos attributed to H.F. Gardner. The date given is somewhat arbitrary based on the mention of the Atlanta Braves on the back of

a card. Cards are in standard 3-1/2" x 5-1/2" postcard size and format. A brief biography of the athletes appears on the back, along with the credits. The Aarons and Williams cards were found in a warehouse in 1999, driving down their prices.

		NM	E	VG
Complete Set (5):		20.00	10.00	6.00
Common Player:		3.00	1.50	.90
(1)	Hank Aaron, Tommie Aaron	15.00	7.50	4.50
(2)	Bill Bruton	3.50	1.75	1.00
(3)	Lee Maye	3.50	1.75	1.00
(4)	Jesse Owens	4.50	2.25	1.25
(5)	Billy Williams	3.00	1.50	.90

1922 Gassler's American Maid Bread

These 2" x 3-1/4" black-and-white cards are one of several versions of the W575-1 strip cards with custom-printed advertising on the backs. It is unknown whether each card in the W575-1 checklist can be found with the Gassler's back.

	NM	E	VG
Common Player:	150.00	75.00	45.00
Stars: 4-6X			

(See W575-1 for checklist; Gassler values 3X-4X.)

1962 Gehl's Ice Cream

Issued only in the Milwaukee area to promote sales of Gold-Mine brand ice cream, the six cards in this black-and-white set all feature Roger Maris, who the previous year had broken Babe Ruth's season home run record. The 4" x 5" cards are blank backed and each has a facsimile autograph on front reading "To My / Gold Mine Pal / Roger Maris." The cards are unnumbered; a description of each is provided in the checklist.

		NM	E	VG
Complete Set (6):		1,600	800.00	480.00
Common Card:		400.00	200.00	120.00
(1)	Roger Maris (Bat on shoulder, close-up.)	400.00	200.00	120.00
(2)	Roger Maris (Bat on shoulder, photo to waist.)	400.00	200.00	120.00
(3)	Roger Maris (Batting stance.)	400.00	200.00	120.00
(4)	Roger Maris ("Hitting My 61st," ballpark photo.)	325.00	160.00	100.00
(5)	Roger Maris (Holding bat in hands.)	400.00	200.00	120.00
(6)	Roger Maris (Portrait in warm-up jacket.)	400.00	200.00	120.00

1941 Lou Gehrig Memorial Ticket

On July 4, 1941, just a month after his death, the N.Y. Yankees scheduled special memorial ceremonies for the Iron Horse. Tickets for the event picture Gehrig and were issued in several colors and price ranges based on seat location. Most often found in stub form of about 3-3/8" x 2-1/2", full tickets are also occasionally seen, probably because a rainout on July 4 forced the ceremonies to the following Sunday.

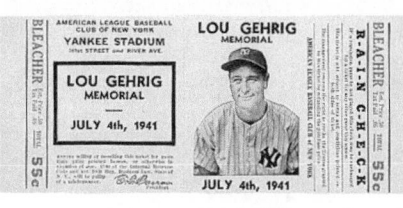

	NM	E	VG
Lou Gehrig (Ticket stub.)	1,800	900.00	550.00
Lou Gehrig (Full ticket.)	5,250	2,625	1,575

Lou Gehrig Never Forgotten Pin

This 1-3/4" celluloid pinback button was issued following the 1941 death of Lou Gehrig. A black-and-white portrait of the smiling Iron Horse is bordered in black with white inscriptions. The pin has been extensively and illicitly reproduced since the late 1980s; the modern replicas have no collectible value.

	NM	E	VG
Lou Gehrig	1,250	625.00	375.00

1911-14 General Baking Co. (D304)

This issue by a bakery based in Buffalo, N.Y., is similar in design to contemporary tobacco and candy cards, but is larger in size, at 1-3/4" x 2-1/2". Fronts feature a color lithograph with the player's name and team below in capital letters. Some players who changed teams in 1913-14 are found with the team name obliterated at bottom by a black line. Five different back styles are known, listed here by the principal brand name: 1) Brunners, 2) Butter Krust, 3) General Baking Co., 4) Weber Bakery, 5) Martens Bakery. The complete set price does not include "no-team" variations. Modern counterfeits of the issue are widely seen in the hobby market.

		NM	E	VG
Complete Set (25):		100,000	50,000	30,000
Common Player:		1,200	600.00	350.00
(1)	J. Frank Baker	3,500	1,750	1,050
(2)	Jack Barry	1,500	750.00	450.00
(3)	George Bell	1,600	800.00	480.00
(4)	Charles Bender	4,500	2,200	1,350
(5a)	Frank Chance (Chicago)	4,500	2,200	1,350
(5b)	Frank Chance (No team.)	5,000	2,500	1,500
(6a)	Hal Chase (N.Y.)	1,750	875.00	525.00
(6b)	Hal Chase (No team.)	2,500	1,250	750.00
(7)	Ty Cobb	35,000	17,500	10,500
(8)	Eddie Collins	5,000	2,500	1,500
(9a)	Otis Crandall (N.Y.)	1,600	800.00	480.00
(9b)	Otis Crandall (No team.)	2,400	1,200	725.00
(10)	Sam Crawford	4,000	2,000	1,200
(11a)	John Evers (Chicago)	4,000	2,000	1,200
(11b)	John Evers (No team.)	4,500	2,200	1,350
(12)	Arthur Fletcher	1,600	800.00	480.00
(13a)	Charles Herzog (N.Y.)	1,600	800.00	480.00
(13b)	Charles Herzog (No team.)	2,400	1,200	725.00
(14)	M. (Billy) Kelly	1,600	800.00	475.00
(15)	Napoleon Lajoie	4,000	2,000	1,200

(16)	Rube Marquard	5,250	2,625	1,575
(17)	Christy Mathewson	7,500	3,700	2,200
(18)	Fred Merkle	1,600	800.00	480.00
(19)	"Chief" Meyers	1,600	800.00	480.00
(20)	Marty O'Toole	1,600	800.00	480.00
(21)	Nap. Rucker	1,600	800.00	480.00
(22)	Arthur Shafer	1,600	800.00	480.00
(23)	Fred Tenny (Tenney)	1,200	600.00	350.00
(24)	Honus Wagner	15,000	7,500	4,500
(25)	Cy Young	7,500	3,700	2,200

1915 General Baking Co. (D303)

Cobb, c. f. Detroit Americans

Issued in 1915 by the General Baking Co., these unnumbered cards measure 1-1/2" x 2-3/4". The player pictures and format of the cards are identical to the E106 set, but the D303 cards are easily identified by the advertisement for General Baking on the back.

		NM	E	VG
Complete Set (51):		80,000	32,000	16,000
Common Player:		1,600	800.00	300.00
(1)	Jack Barry	1,600	800.00	300.00
(2)	Chief Bender (Blue background.)	3,000	1,700	800.00
(3)	Chief Bender (Green background.)	3,000	1,750	800.00
(4)	Bob Bescher (New York)	1,600	800.00	300.00
(5)	Bob Bescher (St. Louis)	1,600	800.00	300.00
(6)	Roger Bresnahan	3,000	1,750	800.00
(7)	Al Bridwell	1,600	800.00	300.00
(8)	Donie Bush	1,600	800.00	300.00
(9)	Hal Chase (Catching)	1,800	800.00	360.00
(10)	Hal Chase (Portrait)	1,800	900.00	360.00
(11)	Ty Cobb (Batting)	20,000	10,000	4,000
(12)	Ty Cobb (Leaning on bat.)	30,000	15,000	6,000
(13)	Eddie Collins	3,000	1,700	800.00
(14)	Sam Crawford	3,000	1,700	800.00
(15)	Ray Demmitt	1,600	800.00	300.00
(16)	Wild Bill Donovan	1,600	800.00	300.00
(17)	Red Dooin	1,600	800.00	300.00
(18)	Mickey Doolan	1,600	800.00	300.00
(19)	Larry Doyle	1,600	800.00	300.00
(20)	Clyde Engle	1,600	800.00	300.00
(21)	Johnny Evers	3,000	1,700	800.00
(22)	Art Fromme	1,600	800.00	300.00
(23)	George Gibson (Catching, back view.)	1,600	800.00	300.00
(24)	George Gibson (Catching, front view.)	1,600	800.00	300.00
(25)	Roy Hartzell	1,600	800.00	300.00
(26)	Fred Jacklitsch	1,600	800.00	300.00
(27)	Hugh Jennings	3,000	1,750	800.00
(28)	Otto Knabe	1,600	800.00	300.00
(29)	Nap Lajoie	4,000	2,000	1,000
(30)	Hans Lobert	1,600	800.00	300.00
(31)	Rube Marquard	3,000	1,500	900.00
(32)	Christy Mathewson	12,500	6,250	3,750
(33)	John McGraw	3,000	1,500	900.00
(34)	George McQuillan	1,600	800.00	300.00
(35)	Dots Miller	1,600	800.00	300.00
(36)	Danny Murphy	1,600	800.00	300.00
(37)	Rebel Oakes	1,600	800.00	300.00
(38)	Eddie Plank (No position on front.)	3,000	1,700	750.00
(39)	Eddie Plank (Position on front.)	6,000	3,000	1,500
(40)	Germany Schaefer	1,600	800.00	300.00
(41)	Boss Smith (Schmidt)	1,600	800.00	300.00
(42)	Tris Speaker	8,000	3,500	1,500
(43)	Oscar Stanage	1,600	800.00	300.00
(44)	George Stovall	1,600	800.00	300.00
(45)	Jeff Sweeney	1,600	800.00	300.00
(46)	Joe Tinker (Batting)	2,000	1,200	600.00
(47)	Joe Tinker (Portrait)	2,000	1,200	600.00

(48)	Honus Wagner (Batting)	20,000	10,000	4,000
(49)	Honus Wagner (Throwing)	30,000	15,000	6,000
(50)	Hooks Wiltse	1,600	800.00	300.00
(51)	Heinie Zimmerman	1,600	800.00	300.00

1908 General Photo Co. St. Louis Browns Postcards

The extent of this postcard issue by a hometown printer is unknown. It is likely other single-player postcards were issued. Approximately 3-1/2" x 5-1/2", the cards are black-and-white with a credit line on bottom: "Photo by General Photo Co., 610 Granite Bldg., St. Louis." On the team photo card, players are identified below the group photo.

		NM	E	VG
(1)	Harry Howell	1,500	750.00	450.00
(2)	"Rube" Waddell	1,500	750.00	450.00
(3)	St. Louis Browns - 1908	1,000	500.00	300.00

1948 Gentle's Bread Boston Braves

These 3" x 9" waxed-paper end labels were found on loaves of Gentle's bread. Printed in blue and red, the labels depict action poses of the National League Champion '48 Braves. A facsimile autograph appears with the photo. Backs are blank. The unnumbered labels are checklisted here alphabetically.

		NM	E	VG
Complete Set (9):		3,000	1,500	900.00
Common Player:		400.00	200.00	120.00
(1)	Alvin Dark	450.00	225.00	135.00
(2)	Bob Elliott	400.00	200.00	120.00
(3)	Tommy Heath	400.00	200.00	120.00

(4)	Tommy Holmes	400.00	200.00	120.00
(5)	Phil Masi	400.00	200.00	120.00
(6)	John Sain	450.00	225.00	135.00
(7)	Warren Spahn	600.00	300.00	180.00
(8)	Eddie Stanky	450.00	225.00	135.00
(9)	Earl Torgeson	400.00	200.00	120.00

1956 Gentry Magazine Ty Cobb

In issue #20 of Gentry magazine, dated Fall, 1956, a feature article on card collecting was enhanced with the inclusion of an original Ty Cobb card tipped onto an interior page. Measuring about 4" x 2-1/4" and blank-backed, the color card is similar in design to the T205 tobacco card issue.

	NM	E	VG
Complete Magazine:	125.00	65.00	40.00
Ty Cobb	90.00	45.00	27.00

1909-10 German Baseball Stamps

A marginal notation "Made in Germany" on one of the stamps in this series identifies its origins. Little else in known of them. The stamps measure about 1-3/8" to 1-1/2" by 1-3/4" to 1-7/8". They are printed in bright colors on a pink background with name and team in blue. Because of their European origins, there are many mistakes in player and team names. The crude pictures are not representative of the player named. Unnumbered stamps are listed here in alphabetical order. It is evident several different configurations of 35-stamp sheets must have been issued.

		NM	E	VG
Complete Sheet (35):		1,150	575.00	345.00
Complete Set (41):		1,300	650.00	400.00
Common Player:		65.00	32.50	20.00
(1)	Ginger Beaumont	65.00	32.50	20.00
(2)	Frank Bowerman	65.00	32.50	20.00
(3)	Kitty Bransfield	65.00	32.50	20.00
(4)	Al Bridwell	65.00	32.50	20.00
(5a)	Roger Bresnahan (Light shirt.)	100.00	50.00	30.00
(5b)	Roger Bresnahan (Dark shirt.)	100.00	50.00	30.00
(6)	Bill Carrigan	65.00	32.50	20.00
(7)	Hal Chase	80.00	40.00	24.00
(8)	Eddie Collins	100.00	50.00	30.00
(9)	Harry Davis	65.00	32.50	20.00
(10)	Wild Bill Donovan	65.00	32.50	20.00
(11)	Larry Doyle	65.00	32.50	20.00
(12)	Jean Dubuc	65.00	32.50	20.00
(13)	Kid Elberfield (Elberfeld)	65.00	32.50	20.00
(14)	Dick Hoblitzell	65.00	32.50	20.00
(15)	Solly Hoffman (Hofman)	65.00	32.50	20.00
(16)	Tim Jordan	65.00	32.50	20.00
(17)	Willie Keeler	100.00	50.00	30.00
(18)	Nap Lajoie	100.00	50.00	30.00
(19)	Tommy Leach	65.00	32.50	20.00
(20)	Christy Mathewson	325.00	160.00	100.00
(21)	Dots Miller	65.00	32.50	20.00
(22)	John McGraw	100.00	50.00	30.00

(23)	Eddie Plank	100.00	50.00	30.00
(24)	Jack Rowan	65.00	32.50	20.00
(25)	Nap Rucker	65.00	32.50	20.00
(26)	Shannon (Boston)	65.00	32.50	20.00
(27)	Frank Smith	65.00	32.50	20.00
(28)	Tris Speaker	120.00	60.00	35.00
(29)	Jake Stahl	65.00	32.50	20.00
(30)	Lee Tannehill	65.00	32.50	20.00
(31)	Fred Tenney	65.00	32.50	20.00
(32)	Ira Thomas	65.00	32.50	20.00
(33)	Joe Tinker	100.00	50.00	30.00
(34)	Honus Wagner	285.00	140.00	85.00
(35)	Jimmy Williams	65.00	32.50	20.00
(36)	Cy Young	165.00	85.00	50.00
(37)	Baseball	15.00	7.50	4.50
(38)	Bat	15.00	7.50	4.50
(39)	Body Protector	15.00	7.50	4.50
(40)	Catcher's Mask	15.00	7.50	4.50
(41)	Crossed Bats	15.00	7.50	4.50
(42)	Glove	15.00	7.50	4.50

1923 German Baseball Transfers

With crude artwork lifted from the W515 strip card set, this issue of baseball player (and boxer) transfers was produced in Germany. Approximately 1-3/16" x 1-1/2", the stamps are printed in red on a green background. All of the design, except for the "MADE IN GERMANY" notation in the white bottom margin, is in mirror-image, befitting their use as tattoos or transfers. Two of the baseball players are double-prints. The unnumbered stamps (baseball only) are checklisted here alphabetically.

		NM	E	VG
Complete Baseball Set (13):		500.00	250.00	150.00
Complete Sheet (25):		600.00	300.00	180.00
Common Player:		40.00	20.00	12.00
(1)	Grover Alexander	45.00	22.00	13.50
(2)	Dave Bancroft	40.00	20.00	12.00
(3)	George (J.) Burns	30.00	15.00	9.00
(4)	"Ty" Cobb	150.00	75.00	45.00
(5)	Red Faber (DP)	25.00	12.50	7.50
(6)	Arthur Nehf	30.00	15.00	9.00
(7)	"Babe" Ruth	200.00	100.00	60.00
(8)	Ray Schalk	40.00	20.00	12.00
(9)	Everett Scott	30.00	15.00	9.00
(10)	Bob Shawkey	30.00	15.00	9.00
(11)	Tris Speaker	45.00	22.00	13.50
(12)	"Casey" Stengel	45.00	22.00	13.50
(13)	Zack Wheat (DP)	30.00	15.00	9.00

1922 Lou Gertenrich

One of the most attractive advertising backs of the 1920s is found on this version of the 1922 issue which is most often found with American Caramel ads on back. Gertenrich had a three-game major league career between 1901-1903, supporting his advertising claim of "The Baseball Player Candy Manufacturer." Probably originating in Chicago, these cards are 2" x 3-1/2" black-and-white. The set shares the checklist with the American Caramel Co. (E121) set of 120. Because of the scarcity and appeal of this regional issue, the Gentenrich versions carry a substantial premium for type-card and

superstar collectors.

	NM	E	VG
Common Player:	600.00	300.00	175.00
Stars: 2-3X			

(See 1922 American Caramel Series of 120 for checklist.)

1888 Gilbert & Bacon Cabinets

The known range of this cabinet card issue comprises mostly members of the 1888 Philadelphia Athletics and Phillies. The posed action photos on the approximately 4-1/4" x 6-1/2" cards are the same pictures seen on many of the players' Old Judge and Old Judge cabinet cards. The G&B cabinets have an embossed Goodwin & Co. copyright seal. An elaborate typescript Gilbert & Bacon studio logo is found in the bottom-left border, with the city named at right. Backs have an ornate studio logo.

		NM	E	VG
Common Player:		3,000	1,200	700.00
(1)	Louis Bierbauer	3,000	1,200	700.00
(2)	Bill Blair	3,000	1,200	700.00
(3)	Charlie Ferguson (Ball in hands at chest.)	3,000	1,200	700.00
(4)	Charlie Ferguson (Batting)	3,000	1,200	700.00
(5)	Charlie Ferguson (Throwing)	3,000	1,200	700.00
(6)	Kid Gleason	3,000	1,200	700.00
(7)	John Henry	3,000	1,200	700.00
(8)	Henry Larkin	3,000	1,200	700.00
(9)	Denny Lyons	3,000	1,200	700.00
(11)	Deacon McGuire (Bat behind head.)	3,000	1,200	700.00
(12)	Deacon McGuire (Bat on shoulder.)	3,000	1,200	700.00
(13)	Deacon McGuire (Fielding, hands at waist.)	3,000	1,200	700.00
(14)	Deacon McGuire (Fielding, hands head-high.)	3,000	1,200	700.00
(15)	Deacon McGuire (Throwing)	3,000	1,200	700.00
(16)	George Pinkney (Bat at 45-degree angle.)	3,000	1,200	700.00
(17)	George Pinkney (Bat at 60-degree angle.)	3,000	1,200	700.00
(18)	George Pinkney (Bat nearly horizontal.)	3,000	1,200	700.00
(19)	George Pinkney (Fielding fly ball.)	3,000	1,200	700.00
(21)	George Pinkney (Fielding line drive.)	3,000	1,200	700.00
(22)	George Pinkney (Throwing)	3,000	1,200	700.00
(23)	Ben Sanders (Ball in hands at chest.)	3,000	1,200	700.00
(24)	Ben Sanders (Batting)	3,000	1,200	700.00
(25)	Ben Sanders (Fielding fly ball.)	3,000	1,200	700.00
(26)	Ben Sanders (Throwing)	3,000	1,200	700.00
(27)	Harry Stovey	3,000	1,200	700.00
(28)	Michael Sullivan	3,000	1,200	700.00
(29)	Gus Weyhing	3,000	1,200	700.00
(31)	John Weyhing	3,000	1,200	700.00
(32)	Harry Wright	7,500	3,700	2,200

1916 Gimbels

This version of the 1916 M101-5 and M101-4 Blank Backs can be found with three slightly different styles of typography on back.

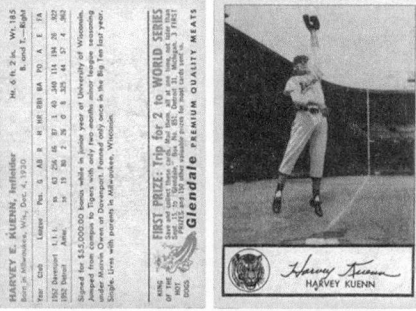

	NM	E	VG
Common Player:	225.00	112.50	67.50
Stars: 2-3X			

(See 1916 M101-5 and M101-4 Blank Backs for checklists and base pricing. An SGC-graded Good #151 Babe Ruth sold at auction for $17,834 in 7/09.)

1953 Glendale Hot Dogs Tigers

Glendale Meats issued these unnumbered, full- color cards (2-5/8" x 3-3/4") in packages of hot dogs Featuring only Detroit Tigers players, the card fronts contain a player picture with his name, a facsimile autograph, and the Tigers logo. Backs carry player statistical and biographical information plus an offer for a trip for two to the World Series. Collectors were advised to mail all the cards they had saved to Glendale Meats. The World Series trip plus 150 other prizes were to be given to the individuals sending in the most cards. As with most cards issued with food products, high-grade cards are tough to find because of the cards' susceptibility to stains. The Houtteman card is extremely scarce.

	NM	E	VG
Complete Set (28):	55,000	27,500	16,500
Common Player:	1,800	900.00	550.00
Ad Booklet:	40,000	20,000	12,000
(1) Matt Batts	1,800	900.00	550.00
(2) Johnny Bucha	1,800	900.00	550.00
(3) Frank Carswell	1,800	900.00	550.00
(4) Jim Delsing	1,800	900.00	550.00
(5) Walt Dropo	1,800	900.00	550.00
(6) Hal Erickson	1,800	900.00	550.00
(7) Paul Foytack	1,800	900.00	550.00
(8) Owen Friend	1,800	900.00	550.00
(9) Ned Garver	1,800	900.00	550.00
(10) Joe Ginsberg	1,800	900.00	550.00
(11) Ted Gray	1,800	900.00	550.00
(12) Fred Hatfield	1,800	900.00	550.00
(13) Ray Herbert	1,800	900.00	550.00
(14) Bill Hitchcock	1,800	900.00	550.00
(15) Bill Hoeft	1,800	900.00	550.00
(16) Art Houtteman	8,000	4,000	2,400
(17) Milt Jordan	1,800	900.00	550.00
(18) Harvey Kuenn	2,500	1,250	750.00
(19) Don Lund	1,800	900.00	550.00
(20) Dave Madison	1,800	900.00	550.00
(21) Dick Marlowe	1,800	900.00	550.00
(22) Pat Mullin	1,800	900.00	550.00
(23) Bob Nieman	1,800	900.00	550.00
(24) Johnny Pesky	1,800	900.00	550.00
(25) Jerry Priddy	1,800	900.00	550.00
(26) Steve Souchock	1,800	900.00	550.00
(27) Russ Sullivan	1,800	900.00	550.00
(28) Bill Wight	2,200	1,100	600.00

1916 Globe Clothing Store (H801-9)

This 200-card set can be found with ads on the back for several local and regional businesses. Among them is the Globe clothing store in St. Louis. Type card, team- and single-player collectors may pay a modest premium for individual cards with the Globe store's advertising over the parallel 1916 M101-4 Blank Backs values. This version carries an "American Card Catalog" designation of H801-9. Cards measure 1-5/8" x 3" and are printed in black-and-white.

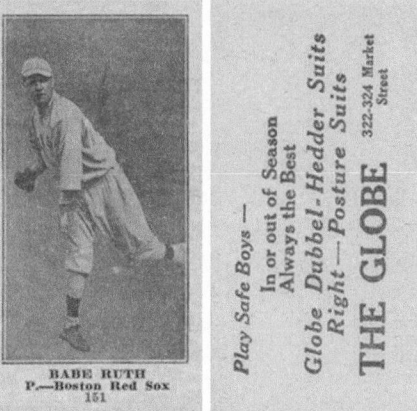

	NM	E	VG
Common Player:	400.00	200.00	120.00
Stars: 3-5X			

(See 1916 M101-4 Blank Backs for checklist and base values.)

1969 Globe Imports Playing Cards

Largely ignored by collectors for more than 35 years, this issue has little to offer any but the most avid superstar collector. Printed in black-and-white on very thin white cardboard, either with blank backs, or with red-and-white checkerboard patterned backs, the cards measure 1-5/8" x 2-1/4". Muddy player action photos are at center of each card, with the player's name reversed out of a black strip at the bottom. It is likely this set was issued over a period of more than one year. The plain-back version was probably issued first, and has photos which include cap and jersey logos. The checked-back version seems to have been a later issue with many of the cards showing uniform logos airbrushed away. The photo quality of the checked-back cards is also much poorer than the plain-backs. A few players were substituted between the issues, and there may be more yet to be reported. The Babe Ruth AD card listed here is actually part of a multi-topic deck in similar format issued contemprarily with the baseball decks.

	NM	E	VG
Complete Set (52+Joker):	20.00	10.00	6.00
Common Player:	.25	.15	.10
PLAIN BACK			
HEARTS			
2 Chris Short	.25	.15	.10
3 Tony Conigliaro	.75	.40	.25
4 Bill Freehan	.25	.15	.10
5 Willie McCovey	2.00	1.00	.60
6 Joel Horlen	.25	.15	.10
7 Ernie Banks	2.00	1.00	.60
8 Jim Wynn	.25	.15	.10
9 Brooks Robinson	2.00	1.00	.60
10 Orlando Cepeda	1.00	.50	.30
J Al Kaline	2.00	1.00	.60
Q Gene Alley	.25	.15	.10
K Rusty Staub	.75	.40	.25
A Willie Mays	4.00	2.00	1.25
CLUBS			
2 Reggie Smith	.25	.15	.10
3 Mike McCormick	.25	.15	.10
4 Tony Oliva	.50	.25	.15
5 Bud Harrelson	.25	.15	.10
6 Rick Reichardt	.25	.15	.10
7 Billy Williams	1.00	.50	.30
8 Pete Rose	6.00	3.00	1.75
9 Jim Maloney	.25	.15	.10
10 Tim McCarver	.75	.40	.25
J Max Alvis	.25	.15	.10
Q Ron Swoboda	.25	.15	.10
K Johnny Callison	.25	.15	.10

	NM	E	VG
A Richie Allen	.75	.40	.25
DIAMONDS			
2 Paul Casanova	.25	.15	.10
3 Juan Marichal	1.00	.50	.30
4 Jim Fregosi	.25	.15	.10
5 Earl Wilson	.25	.15	.10
6 Tony Horton	.25	.15	.10
7 Harmon Killebrew	2.00	1.00	.60
8 Tom Seaver	3.00	1.50	.90
9 Curt Flood	.75	.40	.25
10 Frank Robinson	2.00	1.00	.60
J Bob Aspromonte	.25	.15	.10
Q Lou Brock	2.00	1.00	.60
K Jim Lonborg	.25	.15	.10
A(a) Bob Gibson	2.00	1.00	.60
A(b) Babe Ruth	12.00	6.00	3.60
SPADES			
2 Cesar Tovar	.25	.15	.10
3 Rick Monday	.25	.15	.10
4 Richie Allen	.75	.40	.25
5 Mel Stottlemyre	.50	.25	.15
6 Tommy John	.75	.40	.25
7 Don Mincher	.25	.15	.10
8 Chico Cardenas	.25	.15	.10
9 Willie Davis	.25	.15	.10
10 Bert Campaneris	.25	.15	.10
J Ron Santo	.75	.40	.25
Q Al Ferrera	.25	.15	.10
K Clete Boyer	.50	.25	.15
A(a) Don Drysdale	3.00	1.50	.90
A(b) Mickey Mantle	40.00	20.00	12.00
CHECKERBOARD BACK			
HEARTS			
2 Chris Short	.25	.15	.10
3 Tony Conigliaro	.75	.40	.25
4 Bill Freehan	.25	.15	.10
5 Willie McCovey	2.00	1.00	.60
6 Joel Horlen	.25	.15	.10
7 Ernie Banks	2.00	1.00	.60
8 Jim Wynn	.25	.15	.10
9 Brooks Robinson	2.00	1.00	.60
10 Orlando Cepeda	1.00	.50	.30
J Al Kaline	2.00	1.00	.60
Q Gene Alley	.25	.15	.10
K Rusty Staub	.75	.40	.25
A Willie Mays	6.00	3.00	1.75
CLUBS			
2 Reggie Smith	.25	.15	.10
3 Jerry Koosman	.25	.15	.10
4 Tony Oliva	.50	.25	.15
5 Bud Harrelson	.25	.15	.10
6 Rick Reichardt	.25	.15	.10
7 Billy Williams	1.00	.50	.30
8 Pete Rose	6.00	3.00	1.75
9 Jim Maloney	.25	.15	.10
10 Tim McCarver	.75	.40	.25
J Max Alvis	.25	.15	.10
Q Ron Swoboda	.25	.15	.10
K Johnny Callison	.25	.15	.10
A Richie Allen	.75	.40	.25
DIAMONDS			
2 Paul Casanova	.25	.15	.10
3 Juan Marichal	1.00	.50	.30
4 Jim Fregosi	.25	.15	.10
5 Earl Wilson	.25	.15	.10
7 Tony Horton	.25	.15	.10
7 Harmon Killebrew	2.00	1.00	.60
8 Tom Seaver	3.00	1.50	.90
9 Curt Flood	.75	.40	.25
10 Frank Robinson	2.00	1.00	.60
J Bob Aspromonte	.25	.15	.10
Q Lou Brock	2.00	1.00	.60
K Jim Lonborg	.25	.15	.10
A Bob Gibson	2.00	1.00	.60
SPADES			
2 Denny McLain	.50	.25	.15
3 Rick Monday	.25	.15	.10
4 Richie Allen	.75	.40	.25
5 Mel Stottlemyre	.50	.25	.15
6 Tommy John	.75	.40	.25
7 Don Mincher	.25	.15	.10
8 Chico Cardenas	.25	.15	.10
9 Willie Davis	.25	.15	.10
10 Bert Campaneris	.25	.15	.10
J Ron Santo	.75	.40	.25
Q Al Ferrera	.25	.15	.10
K Clete Boyer	.50	.25	.15
A Ken Harrelson	.25	.15	.10

1887 Gold Coin (Buchner) (N284)

Issued circa 1887, the N284 issue was produced by D. Buchner & Co. for its Gold Coin brand of chewing tobacco. Actually, the series was not comprised only of baseball players - actors, jockeys, firemen and policemen were also included. The cards, which measure 1-3/4" x 3", are color drawings. The set is not a popular one among collectors as the drawings do not in all cases represent the players designated on the cards. In most instances, players at a given position share the same drawing depicted on the card front. Three different card backs are found, all advising collectors to save the valuable chewing tobacco wrappers. Wrappers could be redeemed for various prizes.

KENNEDY, PITCHER, LACROSSE.

	NM	E	VG
Complete Set (143):	200,000	60,000	30,000
Common Player:	1,200	360.00	180.00
(1) Ed Andrews (Hands at neck.)	1,200	360.00	180.00
(2) Ed Andrews (Hands waist high.)	1,200	360.00	180.00
(3) Cap Anson (Hands outstretched.)	6,000	1,800	900.00
(4) Cap Anson (Left hand on hip.)	8,000	2,400	1,200
(5) Tug Arundel	1,200	360.00	180.00
(6) Sam Barkley (Pittsburg)	1,200	360.00	180.00
(7) Sam Barkley (St. Louis)	1,200	360.00	180.00
(8) Charley Bassett	1,200	360.00	180.00
(9) Charlie Bastian	815.00	365.00	165.00
(10) Ed Beecher	1,200	360.00	180.00
(11) Charlie Bennett	1,200	360.00	180.00
(12) Henry Boyle	1,200	360.00	180.00
(13) Dan Brouthers (Hands outstretched.)	4,700	1,400	700.00
(14) Dan Brouthers (With bat.)	4,700	1,400	700.00
(15) Tom Brown	1,200	360.00	180.00
(16) Jack Burdock	1,200	360.00	180.00
(17) Oyster Burns (Baltimore)	1,200	360.00	180.00
(18) Tom Burns (Chicago)	1,200	360.00	180.00
(19) Doc Bushong	1,200	360.00	180.00
(20) John Cahill	1,200	360.00	180.00
(21) Cliff Carroll (Washington)	1,200	360.00	180.00
(22) Fred Carroll (Pittsburgh)	1,200	360.00	180.00
(23) Bob Carruthers (Caruthers)	1,200	360.00	180.00
(24) Dan Casey	1,200	360.00	180.00
(25) John Clarkson (Ball at chest.)	4,200	1,250	625.00
(26) John Clarkson (Arm oustretched.)	4,700	1,400	700.00
(27) Jack Clements	1,200	360.00	180.00
(28) John Coleman	1,200	360.00	180.00
(29) Charles Comiskey	5,200	1,600	800.00
(30) Roger Connor (Hands outstretched chest-level, "New York.")	4,200	1,250	625.00
(31) Roger Connor (Hands oustreteched face-level, "N.Y.")	4,700	1,400	700.00
(32) John Corbett	1,200	360.00	180.00
(33) Sam Craig (Crane)	1,200	360.00	180.00
(34) Sam Crane	1,200	360.00	180.00
(35) John Crowley	1,200	360.00	180.00
(36) Ed Cushmann (Cushman)	1,200	360.00	180.00
(37) Ed Dailey (Daily)	1,200	360.00	180.00
(38) Con Daley (Daily)	1,200	360.00	180.00
(39) Pat Deasley	1,200	360.00	180.00
(40) Jerry Denny (Hands on knees.)	1,200	360.00	180.00
(41) Jerry Denny (Hands on thighs.)	1,200	360.00	180.00
(42) Jim Donnelly	1,200	360.00	180.00
(43) Jim Donohue (Donahue)	1,200	360.00	180.00
(44) Mike Dorgan (Right field.)	1,200	360.00	180.00
(45) Mike Dorgan (Batter.)	1,200	360.00	180.00
(46) Fred Dunlap	1,200	360.00	180.00
(47) Dude Esterbrook	1,200	360.00	180.00
(48) Buck Ewing (Ready to tag.)	4,200	1,250	625.00
(49) Buck Ewing (Hands at neck.)	4,700	1,400	700.00
(50) Sid Farrar	1,200	360.00	180.00
(51) Jack Farrell (Ready to tag.)	1,200	360.00	180.00
(52) Jack Farrell (Hands at knees.)	1,200	360.00	180.00

(53) Charlie Ferguson	1,200	360.00	180.00
(54) Silver Flint	1,200	360.00	180.00
(55) Jim Fogerty (Fogarty)	1,200	360.00	180.00
(56) Tom Forster	1,200	360.00	180.00
(57) Dave Foutz	1,200	360.00	180.00
(58) Chris Fulmer	1,200	360.00	180.00
(59) Joe Gerhardt	1,200	360.00	180.00
(60) Charlie Getzein (Getzien)	1,200	360.00	180.00
(61) Pete Gillespie (Left field.)	1,200	360.00	180.00
(62) Pete Gillespie (Batter.)	1,200	360.00	180.00
(63) Barney Gilligan	1,200	360.00	180.00
(64) Jack Glasscock (Fielding grounder.)	1,200	360.00	180.00
(65) Jack Glasscock (Hands on knees.)	1,200	360.00	180.00
(66) Will Gleason	1,200	360.00	180.00
(67) George Gore	1,200	360.00	180.00
(68) Frank Hankinson	1,200	360.00	180.00
(69) Ned Hanlon	4,200	1,250	625.00
(70) Jim Hart	1,200	360.00	180.00
(71) Egyptian Healy	1,200	360.00	180.00
(72) Paul Hines (Centre field.)	1,200	360.00	180.00
(73) Paul Hines (Batter.)	1,200	360.00	180.00
(74) Joe Hornung	1,200	360.00	180.00
(75) Arthur Irwin	1,200	360.00	180.00
(76) Dick Johnston	1,200	360.00	180.00
(77) Tim Keefe (Ball in hand.)	4,250	1,250	625.00
(78) Tim Keefe (Ball out of hand.)	4,700	1,400	700.00
(79) King Kelly (Right field.)	5,200	1,500	750.00
(80) King Kelly (Catcher.)	5,200	1,500	750.00
(81) Ted Kennedy	1,200	360.00	180.00
(82) Matt Kilroy	1,200	360.00	180.00
(83) Arlie Latham	1,200	360.00	180.00
(84) Jimmy Manning	1,200	360.00	180.00
(85) Bill McClellan	1,200	360.00	180.00
(86) Jim McCormick	1,200	360.00	180.00
(87) Jack McGeachy	1,200	360.00	180.00
(88) Jumbo McGinnis	1,200	360.00	180.00
(89) George Meyers (Myers)	1,200	360.00	180.00
(90) Doggie Miller	1,200	360.00	180.00
(91) John Morrill (Hands outstretched.)	1,200	360.00	180.00
(92) John Morrill (Hands at neck.)	1,200	360.00	180.00
(93) Tom Morrissy (Morrissey)	1,200	360.00	180.00
(94) Joe Mulvey (Hands on knees.)	1,200	360.00	180.00
(95) Joe Mulvey (Hands above head.)	1,200	360.00	180.00
(96) Al Myers	1,200	360.00	180.00
(97) Candy Nelson	1,200	360.00	180.00
(98) Hugh Nichol	1,200	360.00	180.00
(99) Billy O'Brien	815.00	365.00	165.00
(100) Tip O'Neil (O'Neill)	1,200	360.00	180.00
(101) Orator Jim O'Rourke (Hands cupped.)	4,700	1,400	700.00
(102) Orator Jim O'Rourke (Hands on thighs.)	4,700	1,400	700.00
(103) Dave Orr	1,200	360.00	180.00
(104) Jimmy Peoples	1,200	360.00	180.00
(105) Fred Pfeffer	1,200	360.00	180.00
(106) Bill Phillips	1,200	360.00	180.00
(107) Mark Polhemus	1,200	360.00	180.00
(108) Henry Porter	1,200	360.00	180.00
(109) Blondie Purcell	1,200	360.00	180.00
(110) Old Hoss Radbourn (Hands at chest.)	4,250	1,250	625.00
(111) Old Hoss Radbourn (Hands above waist.)	4,700	1,400	700.00
(112) Danny Richardson (New York, hands at knees.)	1,200	360.00	180.00
(113) Danny Richardson (New York, foot on base.)	1,200	360.00	180.00
(114) Hardy Richardson (Detroit, hands at right shoulder.)	1,200	360.00	180.00
(115) Hardy Richardson (Detroit, right hand above head.)	1,200	360.00	180.00
(116) Yank Robinson	1,200	360.00	180.00
(117) George Rooks	1,200	360.00	180.00
(118) Chief Rosemann (Roseman)	1,200	360.00	180.00
(119) Jimmy Ryan	1,200	360.00	180.00
(120) Emmett Seery (Hands at right shoulder.)	1,200	360.00	180.00
(121) Emmett Seery (Hands outstretched.)	1,200	360.00	180.00
(122) Otto Shomberg (Schomberg)	1,200	360.00	180.00
(123) Pap Smith	1,200	360.00	180.00
(124) Joe Strauss	1,200	360.00	180.00
(125) Danny Sullivan (St. Louis)	1,200	360.00	180.00
(126) Marty Sullivan (Chicago)	1,200	360.00	180.00
(127) Billy Sunday	2,400	700.00	350.00
(128) Ezra Sutton	1,200	360.00	180.00

(129) Sam Thompson (Hand at belt.)	4,250	1,250	625.00
(130) Sam Thompson (Hands chest high.)	4,700	1,400	700.00
(131) Chris Von Der Ahe	4,250	1,250	625.00
(132) John Ward (Fielding grounder.)	4,250	1,250	625.00
(133) John Ward (Hands by knee.)	4,700	1,400	700.00
(134) John Ward (Hands on knees.)	4,700	1,400	700.00
(135) Curt Welch	1,200	360.00	180.00
(136) Deacon White	1,200	360.00	180.00
(137) Art Whitney (Pittsburgh)	1,200	360.00	180.00
(138) Jim Whitney (Washington)	1,200	360.00	180.00
(139) Ned Williamson (Fielding grounder.)	1,200	360.00	180.00
(140) Ned Williamson (Hands at chest.)	1,200	360.00	180.00
(141) Medoc Wise	1,200	360.00	180.00
(142) George Wood (Hands at right shoulder.)	1,200	360.00	180.00
(143) George Wood (Stealing base.)	1,200	360.00	180.00

1960 Gold Mine Bucks

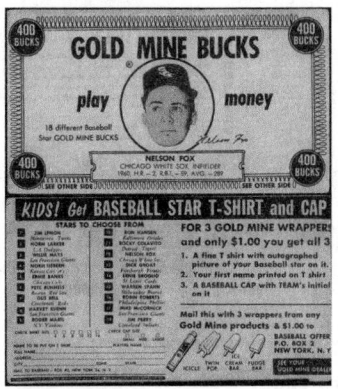

This (possible) series of play money is one of the scarcest regional issues of the early 1960s. In recent years only a single example, Nellie Fox, has been confirmed, though the back of the piece offers a checklist of 18 players that may have been issued. Until other players from that list are confirmed in this format, it is possible that only the Fox "money" was issued, and the list only represents the players available on the autographed t-shirt redemption specified on the back. The known note is about 5-1/2" x 3-1/8", printed in black on gold paper. The note has a player portrait in a circle at center, with a facsimile autograph and a few 1960 stats. Whether any of the other possible player notes were printed in "denominations" other than "400 Bucks" is unknown.

	NM	EX	VG
Complete Set (18):	(Value undetermined)		
Common Player:	(Value undetermined)		
1 Jim Lemon	(Unconfirmed)		
2 Norm Larker	(Unconfirmed)		
3 Willie Mays	(Unconfirmed)		
4 Norm Siebern	(Unconfirmed)		
5 Ernie Banks	(Unconfirmed)		
6 Pete Runnels	(Unconfirmed)		
7 Gus Bell	(Unconfirmed)		
8 Harvey Kuenn	(Unconfirmed)		
9 Roger Maris	(Unconfirmed)		
10 Ron Hansen	(Unconfirmed)		
11 Rocky Colavito	(Unconfirmed)		
12 Nellie Fox	(Value undetermined)		
13 Dick Groat	(Unconfirmed)		
14 Ernie Broglio	(Unconfirmed)		
15 Warren Spahn	(Unconfirmed)		
16 Robin Roberts	(Unconfirmed)		
17 Mike McCormick	(Unconfirmed)		
18 Jim Perry	(Unconfirmed)		

1961 Golden Press

The 1961 Golden Press set features 33 players, all enshrined in the Baseball Hall of Fame. The full color cards measure 2-1/2" x 3-1/2" and came in a booklet with perforations so that they could be easily removed. Full books with the cards intact would command 50 percent over the set price in the checklist that follows. Card numbers 1-3 and 28-33 are slightly higher in price as they were located on the book's front and back covers, making them more susceptible to scuffing and wear. Cards in a larger (2-3/4" x 3-5/8"), apparently unperforated format are also known, though their method of distribution is unclear.

DIZZY DEAN
pitcher

⭐ 8
Jerome Hanna Dean
"Dizzy"
1930-1941 St. Louis, Chicago NL

During his first full five years in the major leagues, Dean won 120 games, for an average of 24 per year. In 1934 he reached his peak when he won 30 games, and lost only 7. That year Dizzy and his brother Paul each beat the Detroit Tigers twice to bring the World Series championship to St. Louis' Gas House Gang. Dean was the last major league pitcher to win 30 games. In the 1937 all-star game, a line drive hit Dean's toe and curtailed his brilliant pitching career.

Lifetime Record 12 yrs.

G	IP	W	L	PCT	SHO	SO
317	1966	150	83	.644	26	1155

Elected to Hall of Fame 1953

		NM	E	VG
	Complete Set (33):	100.00	50.00	30.00
	Complete Set in Book:	175.00	85.00	50.00
	Common Player:	3.00	1.50	.90
1	Mel Ott	3.00	1.50	.90
2	Grover Cleveland Alexander	5.00	2.50	1.50
3	Babe Ruth	40.00	20.00	12.00
4	Hank Greenberg	5.00	2.50	1.50
5	Bill Terry	3.00	1.50	.90
6	Carl Hubbell	3.00	1.50	.90
7	Rogers Hornsby	4.00	2.00	1.25
8	Dizzy Dean	5.00	2.50	1.50
9	Joe DiMaggio	20.00	10.00	6.00
10	Charlie Gehringer	3.00	1.50	.90
11	Gabby Hartnett	3.00	1.50	.90
12	Mickey Cochrane	3.00	1.50	.90
13	George Sisler	3.00	1.50	.90
14	Joe Cronin	3.00	1.50	.90
15	Pie Traynor	3.00	1.50	.90
16	Lou Gehrig	20.00	10.00	6.00
17	Lefty Grove	3.00	1.50	.90
18	Chief Bender	3.00	1.50	.90
19	Frankie Frisch	3.00	1.50	.90
20	Al Simmons	3.00	1.50	.90
21	Home Run Baker	3.00	1.50	.90
22	Jimmy Foxx	4.00	2.00	1.25
23	John McGraw	3.00	1.50	.90
24	Christy Mathewson	10.00	5.00	3.00
25	Ty Cobb	20.00	10.00	6.00
26	Dazzy Vance	3.00	1.50	.90
27	Bill Dickey	3.00	1.50	.90
28	Eddie Collins	3.00	1.50	.90
29	Walter Johnson	9.00	4.50	2.75
30	Tris Speaker	4.00	2.00	1.25
31	Nap Lajoie	3.00	1.50	.90
32	Honus Wagner	12.00	6.00	3.50
33	Cy Young	9.00	4.50	2.75

1955 Golden Stamp Books

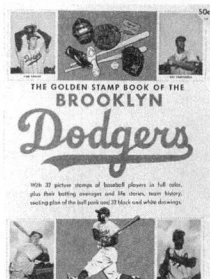

The 1954 World Series contestants, Cleveland and the Giants, along with the popular Dodgers and Braves are featured in this set of stamp books. The 32-page albums measure about 8-1/2" x 11" and include drawings and write-ups for each of the 32 players and managers featured. Other pages of the album include team histories, stats, etc. Sheets of 16 color stamps each are bound into the front and back of the album. Individual stamps measure about 2" x 2-5/8" and are unnumbered. Values shown are for complete albums with the stamps not pasted in; albums with stamps affixed to the pages are worth about 50 percent. The players for each team are listed in the order in which they appear in the album.

		NM	E	VG
	Complete Set (4):	500.00	250.00	150.00
	Common Stamp:	5.00	2.50	1.50
S-1	**NEW YORK GIANTS ALBUM**	125.00	65.00	35.00
(1)	1954 Team Photo	5.00	2.50	1.50
(2)	Leo Durocher	6.00	3.00	1.75
(3)	Johnny Antonelli	5.00	2.50	1.50
(4)	Sal Maglie	5.00	2.50	1.50
(5)	Ruben Gomez	5.00	2.50	1.50
(6)	Hoyt Wilhelm	6.00	3.00	1.75
(7)	Marv Grissom	5.00	2.50	1.50
(8)	Jim Hearn	5.00	2.50	1.50
(9)	Paul Giel	5.00	2.50	1.50
(10)	Al Corwin	5.00	2.50	1.50
(11)	George Spencer	5.00	2.50	1.50
(12)	Don Liddle	5.00	2.50	1.50
(13)	Windy McCall	5.00	2.50	1.50
(14)	Al Worthington	5.00	2.50	1.50
(15)	Wes Westrum	5.00	2.50	1.50
(16)	Whitey Lockman	5.00	2.50	1.50
(17)	Dave Williams	5.00	2.50	1.50
(18)	Hank Thompson	5.00	2.50	1.50
(19)	Alvin Dark	5.00	2.50	1.50
(20)	Monte Irvin	7.50	3.75	2.25
(21)	Willie Mays	50.00	25.00	15.00
(22)	Don Mueller	5.00	2.50	1.50
(23)	Dusty Rhodes	5.00	2.50	1.50
(24)	Ray Katt	5.00	2.50	1.50
(25)	Joe Amalfitano	5.00	2.50	1.50
(26)	Bill Gardner	5.00	2.50	1.50
(27)	Foster Castleman	5.00	2.50	1.50
(28)	Bobby Hofman	5.00	2.50	1.50
(29)	Bill Taylor	5.00	2.50	1.50
(30)	Manager and Coaches	5.00	2.50	1.50
(31)	Bobby Weinstein (Batboy)	5.00	2.50	1.50
(32)	Polo Grounds	5.00	2.50	1.50
S-2	**MILWAUKEE BRAVES ALBUM**	125.00	65.00	35.00
(1)	1954 Team Photo	5.00	2.50	1.50
(2)	Charlie Grimm	5.00	2.50	1.50
(3)	Warren Spahn	7.50	3.75	2.25
(4)	Lew Burdette	5.00	2.50	1.50
(5)	Chet Nichols	5.00	2.50	1.50
(6)	Gene Conley	5.00	2.50	1.50
(7)	Bob Buhl	5.00	2.50	1.50
(8)	Jim Wilson	5.00	2.50	1.50
(9)	Dave Jolly	5.00	2.50	1.50
(10)	Ernie Johnson	5.00	2.50	1.50
(11)	Joey Jay	5.00	2.50	1.50
(12)	Dave Koslo	5.00	2.50	1.50
(13)	Charlie Gorin	5.00	2.50	1.50
(14)	Ray Crone	5.00	2.50	1.50
(15)	Del Crandall	5.00	2.50	1.50
(16)	Joe Adcock	5.00	2.50	1.50
(17)	Jack Dittmer	5.00	2.50	1.50
(18)	Eddie Mathews	15.00	7.50	4.50
(19)	Johnny Logan	5.00	2.50	1.50
(20)	Andy Pafko	5.00	2.50	1.50
(21)	Bill Bruton	5.00	2.50	1.50
(22)	Bobby Thomson	5.00	2.50	1.50
(23)	Charlie White	5.00	2.50	1.50
(24)	Danny O'Connell	5.00	2.50	1.50
(25)	Hank Aaron	50.00	25.00	15.00
(26)	Jim Pendleton	5.00	2.50	1.50
(27)	George Metkovich	5.00	2.50	1.50
(28)	Mel Roach	5.00	2.50	1.50
(29)	John Cooney	5.00	2.50	1.50
(30)	Bucky Walters	5.00	2.50	1.50
(31)	Charles Lacks (Trainer)	5.00	2.50	1.50
(32)	Milwaukee County Stadium	5.00	2.50	1.50
S-3	**BROOKLYN DODGERS ALBUM**	200.00	100.00	60.00
(1)	Walter Alston	6.00	3.00	1.75
(2)	Don Newcombe	6.00	3.00	1.75
(3)	Carl Erskine	5.00	2.50	1.50
(4)	Johnny Podres	5.00	2.50	1.50
(5)	Billy Loes	5.00	2.50	1.50
(6)	Russ Meyer	5.00	2.50	1.50
(7)	Jim Hughes	5.00	2.50	1.50
(8)	Sandy Koufax	100.00	50.00	30.00
(9)	Joe Black	5.00	2.50	1.50
(10)	Karl Spooner	5.00	2.50	1.50
(11)	Clem Labine	5.00	2.50	1.50
(12)	Roy Campanella	15.00	7.50	4.50
(13)	Gil Hodges	12.00	6.00	3.50
(14)	Jim Gilliam	6.00	3.00	1.75
(15)	Jackie Robinson	50.00	25.00	15.00
(16)	Pee Wee Reese	15.00	7.50	4.50
(17)	Duke Snider	15.00	7.50	4.50
(18)	Carl Furillo	6.00	3.00	1.75
(19)	Sandy Amoros	5.00	2.50	1.50
(20)	Frank Kellert	5.00	2.50	1.50
(21)	Don Zimmer	6.00	3.00	1.75
(22)	Al Walker	5.00	2.50	1.50
(23)	Tommy Lasorda	7.50	3.75	2.25
(24)	Ed Roebuck	5.00	2.50	1.50
(25)	Don Hoak	5.00	2.50	1.50
(26)	George Shuba	5.00	2.50	1.50
(27)	Billy Herman	6.00	3.00	1.75
(28)	Jake Pitler	5.00	2.50	1.50
(29)	Joe Becker	5.00	2.50	1.50
(30)	Doc Wendler (Trainer), Carl Furillo	5.00	2.50	1.50
(31)	Charlie Di Giovanna (Batboy)	5.00	2.50	1.50
(32)	Ebbets Field	5.00	2.50	1.50
S-4	**CLEVELAND INDIANS ALBUM**	100.00	50.00	30.00
(1)	Al Lopez	6.00	3.00	1.75
(2)	Bob Lemon	6.00	3.00	1.75
(3)	Early Wynn	6.00	3.00	1.75
(4)	Mike Garcia	5.00	2.50	1.50
(5)	Bob Feller	12.00	6.00	3.50
(6)	Art Houtteman	5.00	2.50	1.50
(7)	Herb Score	7.50	3.75	2.25
(8)	Don Mossi	7.50	3.75	2.25
(9)	Ray Narleski	5.00	2.50	1.50
(10)	Jim Hegan	5.00	2.50	1.50
(11)	Vic Wertz	5.00	2.50	1.50
(12)	Bobby Avila	5.00	2.50	1.50
(13)	George Strickland	5.00	2.50	1.50
(14)	Al Rosen	5.00	2.50	1.50
(15)	Larry Doby	6.00	3.00	1.75
(16)	Ralph Kiner	7.50	3.75	2.25
(17)	Al Smith	5.00	2.50	1.50
(18)	Wally Westlake	5.00	2.50	1.50
(19)	Hal Naragon	5.00	2.50	1.50
(20)	Hank Foiles	5.00	2.50	1.50
(21)	Hank Majeski	5.00	2.50	1.50
(22)	Bill Wight	5.00	2.50	1.50
(23)	Sam Dente	5.00	2.50	1.50
(24)	Dave Pope	5.00	2.50	1.50
(25)	Dave Philley	5.00	2.50	1.50
(26)	Dale Mitchell	5.00	2.50	1.50
(27)	Hank Greenberg (GM)	10.00	5.00	3.00
(28)	Mel Harder	5.00	2.50	1.50
(29)	Ralph Kress	5.00	2.50	1.50
(30)	Tony Cuccinello	5.00	2.50	1.50
(31)	Bill Lobe	5.00	2.50	1.50
(32)	Cleveland Municipal Stadium	5.00	2.50	1.50

1934 Gold Medal Foods (R313A)

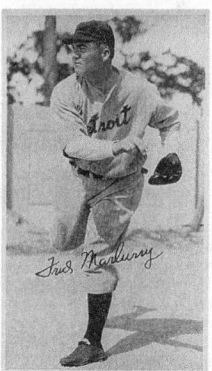

This set of unnumbered, blank-backed cards was issued by Gold Medal Foods (the Minneapolis parent company of Wheaties) to commemorate the 1934 World Series. The black-and-white cards measure 3-1/4" x 5-3/8". The checklist comprises six members each of the Detroit Tigers and St. Louis Cardinals, who were participants in the '34 World Series.

		NM	E	VG
	Complete Set (12):	1,000	500.00	300.00
	Common Player:	60.00	30.00	18.00
(1)	Tommy Bridges	60.00	30.00	18.00
(2)	Mickey Cochrane	90.00	45.00	27.50
(3)	Dizzy Dean	350.00	175.00	100.00
(4)	Paul Dean	75.00	37.50	22.50
(5)	Frank Frisch	90.00	45.00	27.50
(6)	"Goose" Goslin	90.00	45.00	27.50
(7)	William Hallahan	60.00	30.00	18.00
(8)	Fred Marberry	60.00	30.00	18.00
(9)	Johnny "Pepper" Martin	60.00	30.00	18.00
(10)	Joe Medwick	90.00	45.00	27.50
(11)	William Rogell	60.00	30.00	18.00
(12)	"Jo Jo" White	60.00	30.00	18.00

1930s Goodrich Tire Mickey Cochrane

Without postmarked examples for verification, the issue date of this promotional postcard can only be estimated. Front of the 5-1/4" x 3-1/4" postcard has line art of Cochrane and his endorsement for the company's tires. The card is printed in yellow, orange and black. The lower-right quadrant was likely left blank to allow local tire retailers to place their advertisement. Back of the card has a pre-printed one-cent stamp.

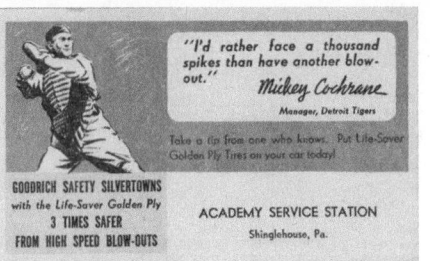

	NM	E	VG
Mickey Cochrane	100.00	50.00	30.00

1889 Goodwin & Co. Baseball Album (A35)

As a mail-in redemption premium for 75 coupons from its Old Judge and Dog's Head cigarette brands, Goodwin offered this 12-page lithographed album. In an unusual 8-1/4" diameter format, the pages have a single hole punched the side and are attached by a fancy tasseled cord allowing them to be fanned out for viewing. Front and back covers of the album depict a baseball, with the inside covers advertising the cigarettes, as does the sixth page of the album. The nine other pages depict in vivid color either single stars of the game or groups of four players, with an emphasis on the N.Y. Giants champions of 1888. Backs of the pages offer player stats for the previous season and schedules for various leagues for 1889. Because these albums are sometimes offered as single pages, they are priced as such here.

		NM	E	VG
	Complete Album:	20,000	10,000	6,000
(1)	Front Cover	225.00	110.00	65.00
(2)	Mickey Welch, John Ward, Buck Ewing, Tim Keefe	1,100	550.00	330.00
(3)	Cap Anson	4,000	1,500	900.00
(4)	Jim O'Rourke, Danny Richardson, Roger Connor, George Gore	1,200	460.00	275.00
(5)	Mike "King" Kelly	3,000	1,500	900.00
(6)	Advertising	350.00	100.00	60.00
(7)	John Ward	2,125	1,050	635.00
(8)	Mike Slattery, Pat Murphy, Gil Hatfield, Ed Crane	750.00	375.00	225.00
(9)	Charles Comiskey	2,125	1,050	635.00
(10)	Willard Brown, Bill George, Elmer Foster, Michael Tiernan	850.00	425.00	255.00
(11)	Jim Mutrie, Lidell Titcomb, Art Whitney, Willie Breslin - Mascot	875.00	435.00	260.00
(12)	Back Cover	200.00	100.00	60.00

1888 Goodwin Champions

Issued in 1888 by New York's Goodwin & Co., the 50-card "Champions" set includes eight baseball players - seven from the National League and one from the American Association. The full-color cards, which measure 1-1/2" x 2-5/8",

were inserted in packages of Old Judge and Gypsy Queen Cigarettes. A small ad for the cards lists all 50 subjects of the "Champions" set, which also included popular billiards players, bicyclists, marksmen, pugilists, runners, wrestlers, college football stars, weightlifters, and Wild West star Buffalo Bill Cody. Four of the eight baseball players in the set (Anson, Kelly, Keefe and Brouthers) are Hall of Famers. The cards feature very attractive player portraits, making the "Champions" set among the most beautiful of all the 19th Century tobacco inserts. All cards can be found with or without a tiny line of type at the bottom of the back which reads, "Geo. S. Harris & Sons, Lith., Phila." Trademarked cards are 3-5X scarcer, but currently carry little or no premium value.

		NM	EX	VG
	Complete Set (8):	50,000	25,000	15,000
	Common Player:	3,000	1,400	650.00
	Album:	17,500	8,750	5,250
(1)	Ed Andrews	3,000	1,400	650.00
(2)	Cap Anson	20,000	8,000	3,250
(3)	Dan Brouthers	5,250	2,800	1,000
(4)	Bob Caruthers	3,000	1,400	650.00
(5)	Fred Dunlap	3,000	1,400	650.00
(6)	Jack Glasscock	3,000	1,400	650.00
(7)	Tim Keefe	5,500	3,000	1,000
(8)	King Kelly	11,000	4,000	1,700

1933 Goudey (R319)

Goudey Gum Co.'s first baseball card issue was a 239-card effort in 1933. The cards are color art reproductions of either portrait or action photos. The numbered cards measure 2-3/8" x 2-7/8" and carry a short player biography on the reverse. Card #106 (Napoleon Lajoie) is listed in the set though it was not actually issued until 1934. The card is very scarce and is unique in that it carries a 1934 design front and a 1933 back. The Lajoie card is not included in the complete set prices quoted here. The ACC designation for the set is R319. Grading companies and auction houses have found a few examples of these cards with blue printing on the backs instead of the customary green.

		NM	E	VG
	Complete Set (239):	110,000	37,500	19,500
	Common Player (1-40):	300.00	150.00	90.00
	Common Player (41-44):	175.00	87.50	52.50
	Common Player (45-52):	200.00	70.00	35.00
	Common Player (53-240):	175.00	87.50	52.50
1	Benny Bengough	5,500	750.00	175.00
2	Arthur (Dazzy) Vance	1,000	500.00	300.00
3	Hugh Critz	650.00	325.00	195.00
4	Henry "Heinie" Schuble	650.00	325.00	195.00
5	Floyd (Babe) Herman	600.00	300.00	180.00
6a	Jimmy Dykes (Age is 26 in bio.)	350.00	175.00	105.00
6b	Jimmy Dykes (Age is 36 in bio.)	350.00	175.00	105.00
7	Ted Lyons	900.00	450.00	250.00
8	Roy Johnson	300.00	150.00	90.00
9	Dave Harris	300.00	150.00	90.00
10	Glenn Myatt	300.00	150.00	90.00
11	Billy Rogell	300.00	150.00	90.00
12	George Pipgras	300.00	87.00	90.00
13	Lafayette Thompson	300.00	150.00	90.00
14	Henry Johnson	300.00	150.00	90.00
15	Victor Sorrell	300.00	150.00	90.00
16	George Blaeholder	300.00	150.00	90.00
17	Watson Clark	300.00	150.00	90.00
18	Herold (Muddy) Ruel	300.00	150.00	90.00
19	Bill Dickey	900.00	315.00	160.00
20	Bill Terry	1,250	435.00	225.00
21	Phil Collins	300.00	150.00	90.00
22	Harold (Pie) Traynor	1,250	435.00	225.00
23	Hazen (Ki-Ki) Cuyler	1,250	435.00	225.00
24	Horace Ford	300.00	150.00	90.00
25	Paul Waner	1,750	610.00	315.00
26	Chalmer Cissell	300.00	150.00	90.00
27	George Connally	300.00	150.00	90.00
28	Dick Bartell	300.00	150.00	90.00
29	Jimmy Foxx	2,500	1,175	500.00
30	Frank Hogan	300.00	150.00	90.00
31	Tony Lazzeri	1,250	435.00	225.00
32	John (Bud) Clancy	300.00	150.00	90.00
33	Ralph Kress	300.00	150.00	90.00
34	Bob O'Farrell	300.00	150.00	90.00
35	Al Simmons	1,250	435.00	225.00
36	Tommy Thevenow	300.00	150.00	90.00
37	Jimmy Wilson	300.00	150.00	90.00
38	Fred Brickell	300.00	150.00	90.00
39	Mark Koenig	300.00	87.00	90.00
40	Taylor Douthit	300.00	150.00	90.00
41	Gus Mancuso	175.00	82.50	52.50
42	Eddie Collins	475.00	165.00	85.00
43	Lew Fonseca	175.00	87.50	52.50
44	Jim Bottomley	425.00	150.00	75.00
45	Larry Benton	200.00	70.00	35.00
46	Ethan Allen	200.00	70.00	35.00
47a	Henry "Heinie" Manush ((Chain-link fence at top left.))	600.00	210.00	110.00
47b	Henry "Heinie" Manush ((No fence.))	600.00	210.00	110.00
48	Marty McManus	200.00	70.00	35.00
49	Frank Frisch	800.00	280.00	145.00
50	Ed Brandt	200.00	70.00	35.00
51	Charlie Grimm	200.00	70.00	35.00
52	Andy Cohen	225.00	80.00	40.00
53	George Herman (Babe) Ruth	15,500	5,900	2,400
54	Ray Kremer	175.00	87.50	52.50
55	Perce (Pat) Malone	175.00	87.50	52.50
56	Charlie Ruffing	425.00	150.00	80.00
57	Earl Clark	175.00	87.50	52.50
58	Frank (Lefty) O'Doul	350.00	120.00	65.00
59	Edmund (Bing) Miller	175.00	87.50	52.50
60	Waite Hoyt	600.00	300.00	180.00
61	Max Bishop	175.00	87.50	52.50
62	"Pepper" Martin	275.00	90.00	52.50
63	Joe Cronin	425.00	150.00	75.00
64	Burleigh Grimes	425.00	150.00	75.00
65	Milton Gaston	175.00	87.50	52.50
66	George Grantham	175.00	87.50	52.50
67	Guy Bush	175.00	87.50	52.50
68	Horace Lisenbee	175.00	87.50	52.50
69	Randy Moore	175.00	87.50	52.50
70	Floyd (Pete) Scott	175.00	87.50	52.50
71	Robert J. Burke	175.00	87.50	52.50
72	Owen Carroll	175.00	87.50	52.50
73	Jesse Haines	425.00	150.00	75.00
74	Eppa Rixey	425.00	150.00	75.00
75	Willie Kamm	175.00	87.50	52.50
76	Gordon (Mickey) Cochrane	475.00	165.00	85.00
77	Adam Comorosky	175.00	87.50	52.50
78	Jack Quinn	175.00	87.50	52.50
79	Urban (Red) Faber	425.00	150.00	75.00
80	Clyde Manion	175.00	87.50	52.50
81	Sam Jones	175.00	87.50	52.50
82	Dibrell Williams	175.00	87.50	52.50
83	Pete Jablonowski	175.00	87.50	52.50
84	Glenn Spencer	175.00	87.50	52.50
85	John Henry "Heinie" Sand	175.00	87.50	52.50
86	Phil Todt	175.00	87.50	52.50
87	Frank O'Rourke	175.00	87.50	52.50
88	Russell Rollings	175.00	87.50	52.50
89	Tris Speaker	825.00	415.00	250.00
90	Jess Petty	175.00	87.50	52.50
91	Tom Zachary	175.00	87.50	52.50
92	Lou Gehrig	4,250	2,000	800.00
93	John Welch	175.00	87.50	52.50
94	Bill Walker	175.00	87.50	52.50
95	Alvin Crowder	175.00	87.50	52.50
96	Willis Hudlin	175.00	87.50	52.50
97	Joe Morrissey	175.00	87.50	52.50
98	Walter Berger	175.00	87.50	52.50
99	Tony Cuccinello	175.00	87.50	52.50
100	George Uhle	175.00	87.50	52.50
101	Richard Coffman	175.00	87.50	52.50
102	Travis C. Jackson	425.00	150.00	75.00
103	Earl Combs (Earle)	600.00	300.00	180.00
104	Fred Marberry	175.00	87.50	52.50
105	Bernie Friberg	175.00	87.50	52.50
106	Napoleon (Larry) Lajoie	40,000	24,000	12,000
107	Henry (Heinie) Manush	425.00	150.00	75.00
108	Joe Kuhel	175.00	87.50	52.50
109	Joe Cronin	425.00	150.00	75.00
110	Leon (Goose) Goslin (Portrait)	600.00	300.00	180.00
111	Monte Weaver	175.00	87.50	52.50
112	Fred Schulte	175.00	87.50	52.50
113	Oswald Bluege	175.00	87.50	52.50
114	Luke Sewell	175.00	87.50	52.50
115	Cliff Heathcote	175.00	87.50	52.50
116	Eddie Morgan	175.00	87.50	52.50
117	Walter (Rabbit) Maranville	425.00	150.00	75.00
118	Valentine J. (Val) Picinich	175.00	87.50	52.50
119	Rogers Hornsby	1,450	725.00	425.00
120	Carl Reynolds	175.00	87.50	52.50

121	Walter Stewart	175.00	87.50	52.50
122	Alvin Crowder	175.00	87.50	52.50
123	Jack Russell (Orange background, white cap.)	175.00	87.50	52.50
124	Earl Whitehill	175.00	87.50	52.50
125	Bill Terry	425.00	150.00	75.00
126	Joe Moore	175.00	87.50	52.50
127	Melvin Ott	650.00	325.00	195.00
128	Charles (Chuck) Klein	450.00	155.00	80.00
129	Harold Schumacher	175.00	87.50	52.50
130	Fred Fitzsimmons	175.00	87.50	52.50
131	Fred Frankhouse	175.00	87.50	52.50
132	Jim Elliott	175.00	87.50	52.50
133	Fred Lindstrom	425.00	150.00	75.00
134	Edgar (Sam) Rice	425.00	150.00	75.00
135	Elwood (Woody) English	175.00	87.50	52.50
136	Flint Rhem	175.00	87.50	52.50
137	Fred (Red) Lucas	175.00	87.50	52.50
138	Herb Pennock	415.00	145.00	75.00
139	Ben Cantwell	175.00	87.50	52.50
140	Irving (Bump) Hadley	175.00	87.50	52.50
141	Ray Benge	175.00	87.50	52.50
142	Paul Richards	175.00	87.50	52.50
143	Glenn Wright	175.00	87.50	52.50
144	George Herman (Babe) Ruth (Double-print; replaced card #106 on press sheet.)	9,500	3,400	1,800
145	George Walberg	175.00	87.50	52.50
146	Walter Stewart	175.00	87.50	52.50
147	Leo Durocher	450.00	200.00	120.00
148	Eddie Farrell	175.00	87.50	52.50
149	George Herman (Babe) Ruth	11,000	4,600	2,000
150	Ray Kolp	175.00	87.50	52.50
151	D'Arcy (Jake) Flowers	175.00	87.50	52.50
152	James (Zack) Taylor	175.00	87.50	52.50
153	Charles (Buddy) Myer	175.00	87.50	52.50
154	Jimmy Foxx	2,000	750.00	450.00
155	Joe Judge	175.00	87.50	52.50
156	Danny Macfayden (MacFayden)	175.00	87.50	52.50
157	Sam Byrd	175.00	87.50	52.50
158	Morris (Moe) Berg	600.00	300.00	180.00
159	Oswald Bluege	175.00	87.50	52.50
160	Lou Gehrig	5,250	2,000	900.00
161	Al Spohrer	175.00	87.50	52.50
162	Leo Mangum	175.00	87.50	52.50
163	Luke Sewell	175.00	87.50	52.50
164	Lloyd Waner	450.00	155.00	75.00
165	Joe Sewell	450.00	155.00	75.00
166	Sam West	175.00	87.50	52.50
167	Jack Russell (Name on two lines, see also #123p.)	175.00	87.50	52.50
168	Leon (Goose) Goslin (Name on one line, see also #110p.)	600.00	210.00	110.00
169	Al Thomas	175.00	87.50	52.50
170	Harry McCurdy	175.00	87.50	52.50
171	Charley Jamieson	175.00	87.50	52.50
172	Billy Hargrave	175.00	87.50	52.50
173	Roscoe Holm	175.00	87.50	52.50
174	Warren (Curley) Ogden	175.00	87.50	52.50
175	Dan Howley	175.00	87.50	52.50
176	John Ogden	175.00	87.50	52.50
177	Walter French	175.00	87.50	52.50
178	Jackie Warner	175.00	87.50	52.50
179	Fred Leach	175.00	87.50	52.50
180	Eddie Moore	175.00	87.50	52.50
181	George Herman (Babe) Ruth	7,000	3,750	1,500
182	Andy High	175.00	87.50	52.50
183	George Walberg	175.00	87.50	52.50
184	Charley Berry	175.00	87.50	52.50
185	Bob Smith	175.00	87.50	52.50
186	John Schulte	175.00	87.50	52.50
187	Henry (Heinie) Manush	425.00	150.00	75.00
188	Rogers Hornsby	1,200	425.00	215.00
189	Joe Cronin	425.00	150.00	75.00
190	Fred Schulte	175.00	87.50	52.50
191	Ben Chapman	175.00	87.50	52.50
192	Walter Brown	175.00	87.50	52.50
193	Lynford Lary	175.00	87.50	52.50
194	Earl Averill	425.00	150.00	75.00
195	Evar Swanson	175.00	87.50	52.50
196	Leroy Mahaffey	175.00	87.50	52.50
197	Richard (Rick) Ferrell	425.00	150.00	75.00
198	Irving (Jack) Burns	175.00	87.50	52.50
199	Tom Bridges	175.00	87.50	52.50
200	Bill Hallahan	175.00	87.50	52.50
201	Ernie Orsatti	175.00	87.50	52.50
202	Charles Leo (Gabby) Hartnett	425.00	150.00	75.00
203	Lonnie Warneke	175.00	87.50	52.50
204	Jackson Riggs Stephenson	175.00	87.50	52.50
205	Henry (Heinie) Meine	175.00	87.50	52.50
206	Gus Suhr	175.00	87.50	52.50
207	Melvin Ott	1,300	400.00	200.00
208	Byrne (Bernie) James	175.00	87.50	52.50
209	Adolfo Luque	200.00	70.00	36.00
210	Virgil Davis	175.00	87.50	52.50
211	Lewis (Hack) Wilson	700.00	250.00	140.00
212	Billy Urbanski	175.00	87.50	52.50
213	Earl Adams	175.00	87.50	52.50
214	John Kerr	175.00	87.50	52.50
215	Russell Van Atta	175.00	87.50	52.50
216	Vernon Gomez	425.00	150.00	75.00
217	Frank Crosetti	275.00	96.00	49.00
218	Wesley Ferrell	175.00	87.50	52.50
219	George (Mule) Haas	175.00	87.50	52.50
220	Robert (Lefty) Grove	825.00	275.00	140.00
221	Dale Alexander	175.00	87.50	52.50
222	Charley Gehringer	600.00	210.00	110.00
223	Jerome (Dizzy) Dean	1,200	500.00	275.00
224	Frank Demaree	175.00	87.50	52.50
225	Bill Jurges	175.00	87.50	52.50
226	Charley Root	175.00	87.50	52.50
227	Bill Herman	425.00	150.00	75.00
228	Tony Piet	175.00	87.50	52.50
229	Floyd Vaughan	425.00	150.00	75.00
230	Carl Hubbell	1,100	455.00	230.00
231	Joe Moore	175.00	87.50	52.50
232	Frank (Lefty) O'Doul	300.00	150.00	90.00
233	Johnny Vergez	175.00	87.50	52.50
234	Carl Hubbell	725.00	255.00	130.00
235	Fred Fitzsimmons	175.00	87.50	52.50
236	George Davis	175.00	87.50	52.50
237	Gus Mancuso	175.00	87.50	52.50
238	Hugh Critz	175.00	87.50	52.50
239	Leroy Parmelee	175.00	87.50	52.50
240	Harold Schumacher	350.00	75.00	35.00

1933 Goudey Proofs

Over the years a number of fully printed proof cards of the 1933 Goudey set have been reported. All are either unique or nearly so, and usually vary only subtly, such as a different card number on back, from the regularly issued version. Because of their rarity, no values can be assigned. The most recent sale of a 1933 Goudey proof card was of a non-Hall of Famer in certified Excellent condition for $10,023 in 2010.

106 Leo Durocher
110 Leon (Goose) Goslin (Same picture as #168 but name in two lines on front.)
123 Jack Russell (Same picture as #167 but name in one line on front.)
123 Luke Sewell
124 Al Spohrer
128 George Walberg

1933-34 Goudey Premiums (R309-1)

Consisting of just four unnumbered cards, this set of black-and-white photos was printed on heavy cardboard and issued as a premium by the Goudey Gum Co. in 1933. Cards (1), (2), and (4) were issued in 1933 and card (3) was issued in 1934. The cards measure 5-1/2" x 8-13/16" and are accented with a gold, picture-frame border and an easel on the back. Besides the game's greatest player, the set has team photos of the 1933 All-Star squads from each league and the World's Champion 1933 N.Y. Giants.

		NM	E	VG
Complete Set (4):		3,250	1,625	975.00
Common Card:		600.00	300.00	180.00
(1)	American League All Stars	650.00	325.00	195.00
(2)	National League All Stars	600.00	300.00	180.00
(4)	George Herman (Babe) Ruth	1,350	675.00	405.00

1934 Goudey (R320)

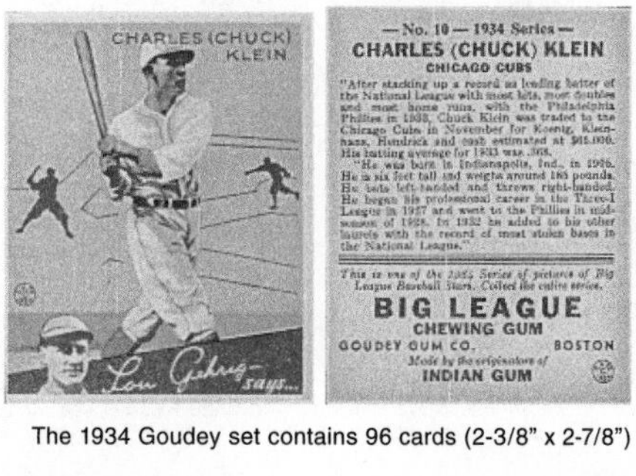

The 1934 Goudey set contains 96 cards (2-3/8" x 2-7/8") that feature color art reproductions of player photographs. Card fronts have two different designs; one featuring a small portrait photo of Lou Gehrig with the the words "Lou Gehrig says..." inside a blue strip at the bottom, while the other design carries a red "Chuck Klein says..." strip and also has his photo. The card backs contain a short player biography that purports to have been written by Gehrig or Klein. The ACC designation for the set is R320. Albums, blue for N.L., magenta for A.L., were given away to the person who bought the last penny pack in each box of high-numbers or who mailed 50 wrappers to the gum company.

		NM	E	VG
Complete Set (96):		30,000	11,000	5,250
Common Player (1-48):		120.00	45.00	20.00
Common Player (49-72):		160.00	55.00	25.00
Common Player (73-96):		250.00	100.00	50.00
Album:		500.00	250.00	150.00
1	Jimmy Foxx	4,000	600.00	210.00
2	Gordon (Mickey) Cochrane	550.00	220.00	110.00
3	Charlie Grimm	120.00	45.00	20.00
4	Elwood (Woody) English	120.00	45.00	20.00
5	Ed Brandt	120.00	45.00	20.00
6	Jerome (Dizzy) Dean	1,600	400.00	190.00
7	Leo Durocher	350.00	140.00	70.00
8	Tony Piet	120.00	45.00	20.00
9	Ben Chapman	120.00	45.00	20.00
10	Charles (Chuck) Klein	350.00	140.00	70.00
11	Paul Waner	350.00	140.00	70.00
12	Carl Hubbell	350.00	140.00	70.00
13	Frank Frisch	350.00	140.00	70.00
14	Willie Kamm	120.00	45.00	20.00
15	Alvin Crowder	120.00	45.00	20.00
16	Joe Kuhel	120.00	45.00	20.00
17	Hugh Critz	120.00	45.00	20.00
18	Henry (Heinie) Manush	350.00	140.00	70.00
19	Robert (Lefty) Grove	625.00	225.00	110.00
20	Frank Hogan	120.00	45.00	20.00
21	Bill Terry	350.00	140.00	70.00
22	Floyd Vaughan	350.00	140.00	70.00
23	Charley Gehringer	475.00	190.00	95.00
24	Ray Benge	120.00	45.00	20.00
25	Roger Cramer	120.00	45.00	20.00
26	Gerald Walker	120.00	45.00	20.00
27	Luke Appling	350.00	140.00	70.00
28	Ed. Coleman	120.00	45.00	20.00
29	Larry French	120.00	45.00	20.00
30	Julius Solters	120.00	45.00	20.00
31	Baxter Jordan	120.00	45.00	20.00
32	John (Blondy) Ryan	120.00	45.00	20.00
33	Frank (Don) Hurst	120.00	45.00	20.00
34	Charles (Chick) Hafey	350.00	140.00	70.00
35	Ernie Lombardi	350.00	140.00	70.00
36	Walter (Huck) Betts	120.00	45.00	20.00
37	Lou Gehrig	5,8000	2,000	950.00
38	Oral Hildebrand	120.00	45.00	20.00
39	Fred Walker	120.00	45.00	20.00
40	John Stone	120.00	45.00	20.00
41	George Earnshaw	120.00	45.00	20.00
42	John Allen	120.00	45.00	20.00
43	Dick Porter	120.00	45.00	20.00
44	Tom Bridges	120.00	45.00	20.00
45	Oscar Melillo	120.00	45.00	20.00
46	Joe Stripp	120.00	45.00	20.00
47	John Frederick	120.00	45.00	20.00
48	James (Tex) Carleton	120.00	45.00	20.00
49	Sam Leslie	160.00	55.00	25.00
50	Walter Beck	160.00	55.00	25.00
51	Jim (Rip) Collins	160.00	55.00	25.00
52	Herman Bell	160.00	55.00	25.00
53	George Watkins	160.00	55.00	25.00
54	Wesley Schulmerich	160.00	55.00	25.00
55	Ed Holley	160.00	55.00	25.00
56	Mark Koenig	160.00	55.00	25.00
57	Bill Swift	160.00	55.00	25.00
58	Earl Grace	160.00	55.00	25.00
59	Joe Mowry	160.00	55.00	25.00
60	Lynn Nelson	160.00	55.00	25.00
61	Lou Gehrig	4,850	1,700	925.00
62	Henry Greenberg	1,300	550.00	275.00
63	Minter Hayes	160.00	55.00	25.00
64	Frank Grube	160.00	55.00	25.00
65	Cliff Bolton	160.00	55.00	25.00
66	Mel Harder	160.00	55.00	25.00
67	Bob Weiland	160.00	55.00	25.00
68	Bob Johnson	160.00	55.00	25.00
69	John Marcum	160.00	55.00	25.00
70	Ervin (Pete) Fox	160.00	55.00	25.00
71	Lyle Tinning	160.00	55.00	25.00
72	Arndt Jorgens	160.00	55.00	25.00
73	Ed Wells	250.00	100.00	50.00
74	Bob Boken	250.00	100.00	50.00
75	Bill Werber	250.00	100.00	50.00
76	Hal Trosky	250.00	100.00	50.00
77	Joe Vosmik	250.00	100.00	50.00
78	Frank (Pinkey) Higgins	250.00	100.00	50.00
79	Eddie Durham	250.00	100.00	50.00

80	Marty McManus	250.00	100.00	50.00
81	Bob Brown	250.00	100.00	50.00
82	Bill Hallahan	250.00	100.00	50.00
83	Jim Mooney	250.00	100.00	50.00
84	Paul Derringer	250.00	100.00	50.00
85	Adam Comorosky	250.00	100.00	50.00
86	Lloyd Johnson	250.00	100.00	50.00
87	George Darrow	250.00	100.00	50.00
88	Homer Peel	250.00	100.00	50.00
89	Linus Frey	250.00	100.00	50.00
90	Hazen (Ki-Ki) Cuyler	525.00	100.00	50.00
91	Dolph Camilli	250.00	100.00	50.00
92	Steve Larkin	250.00	100.00	50.00
93	Fred Ostermueller	250.00	100.00	50.00
94	Robert A. (Red) Rolfe	400.00	160.00	80.00
95	Myril Hoag	250.00	100.00	50.00
96	Jim DeShong	525.00	160.00	60.00

1935 Goudey 4-in-1 (R321)

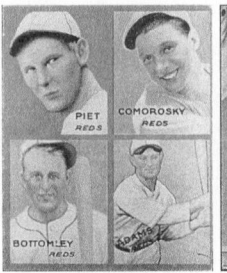

The 1935 Goudey set features color portraits of four players (usually) from the same team on each card. Thirty-six card fronts make up the set with 114 front/back combinations existing. The card backs form nine different puzzles: 1) Tigers Team, 2) Chuck Klein, 3) Frankie Frisch, 4) Mickey Cochrane, 5) Joe Cronin, 6) Jimmy Foxx, 7) Al Simmons, 8) Indians Team, and 9) Senators Team. The cards, which measure 2-3/8" x 2-7/8", have an ACC designation of R321. The numbering has been assigned for this checklist on the basis of alphabetical order of the players found on each card front.

		NM	E	VG
Complete Set (36):		11,000	4,400	2,200
Complete Set (114):		62,500	25,000	12,500
Common Card:		125.00	50.00	25.00
(1)	Sparky Adams, Jim Bottomley, Adam Comorosky, Tony Piet	300.00	120.00	60.00
(2)	Ethan Allen, Fred Brickell, Bubber Jonnard, Jimmie Wilson	125.00	30.00	15.00
(3)	Johnny Allen, Jimmie Deshong, Red Rolfe, Dixie Walker (DeShong)	125.00	30.00	15.00
(4)	Luke Appling, Jimmie Dykes, George Earnshaw, Luke Sewell	300.00	120.00	60.00
(5)	Earl Averill, Oral Hildebrand, Willie Kamm, Hal Trosky	300.00	120.00	60.00
(6)	Dick Bartell, Hughie Critz, Gus Mancuso, Mel Ott	300.00	120.00	60.00
(7)	Ray Benge, Fred Fitzsimmons, Mark Koenig, Tom Zachary	125.00	30.00	15.00
(8)	Larry Benton, Ben Cantwell, Flint Rhem, Al Spohrer	125.00	30.00	15.00
(9)	Charlie Berry, Bobby Burke, Red Kress, Dazzy Vance	300.00	120.00	60.00
(10)	Max Bishop, Bill Cissell, Joe Cronin, Carl Reynolds	300.00	120.00	60.00
(11)	George Blaeholder, Dick Coffman, Oscar Melillo, Sammy West	125.00	30.00	15.00
(12)	Cy Blanton, Babe Herman, Tom Padden, Gus Suhr	125.00	30.00	15.00
(13)	Zeke Bonura, Mule Haas, Jackie Hayes, Ted Lyons	300.00	120.00	60.00
(14)	Jim Bottomley, Adam Comorosky, Willis Hudlin, Glenn Myatt	300.00	120.00	60.00
(15)	Ed Brandt, Fred Frankhouse, Shanty Hogan, Gene Moore	125.00	50.00	25.00
(16)	Ed Brandt, Rabbit Maranville, Marty McManus, Babe Ruth	3,250	1,000	450.00
(17)	Tommy Bridges, Mickey Cochrane, Charlie Gehringer, Billy Rogell	350.00	140.00	70.00
(18)	Jack Burns, Frank Grube, Rollie Hemsley, Bob Weiland	125.00	30.00	15.00
(19)	Guy Bush, Waite Hoyt, Lloyd Waner, Paul Waner	350.00	140.00	70.00
(20)	Sammy Byrd, Danny MacFayden, Pepper Martin, Bob O'Farrell	125.00	30.00	15.00
(21a)	Gilly Campbell, Ival Goodman, Alex Kampouris, Billy Meyers (Myers) (no "Meyers")	200.00	80.00	40.00
(21b)	Gilly Campbell, Ival Goodman, Alex Kampouris, Billy Meyers (Myers)	150.00	60.00	30.00
(22)	Tex Carleton, Dizzy Dean, Frankie Frisch, Ernie Orsatti	650.00	260.00	130.00
(23)	Watty Clark, Lonny Frey, Sam Leslie, Joe Stripp	125.00	30.00	15.00
(24)	Mickey Cochrane, Willie Kamm, Muddy Ruel, Al Simmons	350.00	140.00	70.00
(25)	Ed Coleman, Doc Cramer, Bob Johnson, Johnny Marcum	125.00	30.00	15.00
(26)	General Crowder, Goose Goslin, Firpo Marberry, Heinie Schuble	300.00	120.00	60.00
(27)	Kiki Cuyler, Woody English, Burleigh Grimes, Chuck Klein	350.00	140.00	70.00
(28)	Bill Dickey, Tony Lazzeri, Pat Malone, Red Ruffing	400.00	160.00	80.00
(29)	Rick Ferrell, Wes Ferrell, Fritz Ostermueller, Bill Werber	300.00	120.00	60.00
(30)	Pete Fox, Hank Greenberg, Schoolboy Rowe, Gee Walker	350.00	140.00	70.00
(31)	Jimmie Foxx, Pinky Higgins, Roy Mahaffey, Dib Williams	400.00	160.00	80.00
(32)	Bump Hadley, Lyn Lary, Heinie Manush, Monte Weaver	300.00	120.00	60.00
(33)	Mel Harder, Bill Knickerbocker, Lefty Stewart, Joe Vosmik	125.00	30.00	15.00
(34)	Travis Jackson, Gus Mancuso, Hal Schumacher, Bill Terry	300.00	120.00	60.00
(35)	Joe Kuhel, Buddy Meyer, John Stone, Earl Whitehill (Myer)	125.00	30.00	15.00
(36)	Red Lucas, Tommy Thevenow, Pie Traynor, Glenn Wright	300.00	120.00	60.00

1935 Goudey Premiums (R309-2)

The black-and-white photos in this set were issued as a premium by retailers in exchange for coupons from 10 Goudey wrappers in 1935. The pictures measure 5-1/2" x 9" (or a bit longer), and are printed on thin, glossy paper. The unnumbered set includes three team collages and players, whose names are written in script in the "wide pen" style.

		NM	E	VG
Complete Set (16):		5,000	2,500	1,500
Common Player:		275.00	135.00	82.00
(1)	Elden Auker	275.00	135.00	82.00
(2)	Johnny Babich	275.00	135.00	82.00
(3)	Dick Bartell	275.00	135.00	82.00
(4)	Lester R. Bell	275.00	135.00	82.00
(5)	Wally Berger	275.00	135.00	82.00
(6)	Mickey Cochrane	400.00	200.00	120.00
(7)	Ervin Fox, Leon "Goose" Goslin, Gerald Walker	325.00	160.00	97.00
(8)	Vernon Gomez	400.00	200.00	120.00
(9)	Hank Greenberg	500.00	250.00	150.00
(10)	Oscar Melillo	275.00	135.00	82.00
(11)	Mel Ott	400.00	200.00	120.00
(12)	Schoolboy Rowe	275.00	135.00	82.00
(13)	Vito Tamulis	275.00	135.00	82.00
(14)	Boston Red Sox	300.00	150.00	90.00
(15)	Cleveland Indians	300.00	150.00	90.00
(16)	Washington Senators	300.00	150.00	90.00

1935 Goudey Puzzle-Backs

Each of the 36 card fronts in 1935 Goudey can be found with from two to four different backs that could be used to assemble a six-piece (single player) or 12-piece (team photo or composite) puzzle. This listing checklists the different backs found with each front as well as the cards that comprise each of the nine puzzles. The numbers given for each puzzle piece correspond to the assigned numbers of the card fronts.

		NM	E	VG
	Sparky Adams, Jim Bottomley, Adam Comorosky, Tony Piet			
1H	Tigers, H			
3F	Frisch, F			
4F	Cochrane, F			
5F	Cronin, F			
	Ethan Allen, Fred Brickell, Bubber Jonnard, Jimmie Wilson			
1E	Tigers, E			
3C	Frisch, C			
5C	Cronin, C			
6C	Foxx, C			
	Johnny Allen, Jimmie Deshong, Red Rolfe, Dixie Walker (DeShong)			
8E	Indians, E			
9E	Senators, E			
	Luke Appling, Jimmie Dykes, George Earnshaw, Luke Sewell			
1I	Tigers, I			
2F	Klein, F			
6F	Foxx, F			
7F	Simmons, F			
	Earl Averill, Oral Hildebrand, Willie Kamm, Hal Trosky			
1L	Tigers, L			
2E	Klein, E			
6E	Foxx, E			
7E	Simmons, E			
	Dick Bartell, Hughie Critz, Gus Mancuso, Mel Ott			
2A	Klein, A			
4A	Cochrane, A			
7A	Simmons, A			
	Ray Benge, Fred Fitzsimmons, Mark Koenig, Tom Zachary			
8A	Indians, A			
9A	Senators, A			
	Larry Benton, Ben Cantwell, Flint Rhem, Al Spohrer			
8L	Indians, L			
9L	Senators, L			
	Charlie Berry, Bobby Burke, Red Kress, Dazzy Vance			
2C	Klein, C			
4C	Cochrane, C			
7C	Simmons, C			
	Max Bishop, Bill Cissell, Joe Cronin, Carl Reynolds			
1G	Tigers, G			
3E	Frisch, E			
5E	Cronin, E			
6E	Foxx, E			
	George Blaeholder, Dick Coffman, Oscar Melillo, Sammy West			
1F	Tigers, F			
3D	Frisch, D			
5D	Cronin, D			
6D	Foxx, D			
	Cy Blanton, Babe Herman, Tom Padden, Gus Suhr			
8K	Indians, K			
9K	Senators, K			
	Zeke Bonura, Mule Haas, Jackie Hayes, Ted Lyons			
8B	Indians, B			
9B	Senators, B			
	Jim Bottomley, Adam Comorosky, Willis Hudlin, Glenn Myatt			
1K	Tigers, K			
3B	Frisch, B			
5B	Cronin, B			
6B	Foxx, B			
	Ed Brandt, Fred Frankhouse, Shanty Hogan, Gene Moore			

2E	Klein, E
4E	Cochrane, E
7E	Simmons, E
	Ed Brandt, Rabbit Maranville, Marty McManus, Babe Ruth
1J	Tigers, J
3A	Frisch, A
4A	Cochrane, A
5A	Cronin, A
	Tommy Bridges, Mickey Cochrane, Charlie Gehringer, Billy Rogell
1D	Tigers, D
2D	Klein, D
6D	Foxx, D
7D	Simmons, D
	Jack Burns, Frank Grube, Rollie Hemsley, Bob Weiland
8C	Indians, C
9C	Senators, C
	Guy Bush, Waite Hoyt, Lloyd Waner, Paul Waner
1E	Tigers, E
3C	Frisch, C
4C	Cochrane, C
5C	Cronin, C
	Sammy Byrd, Danny MacFayden, Pepper Martin, Bob O'Farrell
2F	Klein, F
4F	Cochrane, F
7F	Simmons, F
	Gilly Campbell, Ival Goodman, Alex Kampouris, Billy Meyers (Myers)
8D	Indians, D
9D	Senators, D
	Tex Carleton, Dizzy Dean, Frankie Frisch, Ernie Orsatti
1A	Tigers, A
2A	Klein, A
6A	Foxx, A
7A	Simmons, A
	Watty Clark, Lonny Frey, Sam Leslie, Joe Stripp
1G	Tigers, G
3E	Frisch, E
4E	Cochrane, E
5E	Cronin, E
	Mickey Cochrane, Willie Kamm, Muddy Ruel, Al Simmons
1J	Tigers, J
3A	Frisch, A
5A	Cronin, A
6A	Foxx, A
	Ed Coleman, Doc Cramer, Bob Johnson, Johnny Marcum
8J	Indians, J
9J	Senators, J
	General Crowder, Goose Goslin, Firpo Marberry, Heinie Schuble
1H	Tigers, H
3F	Frisch, F
5F	Cronin, F
6F	Foxx, F
	Kiki Cuyler, Woody English, Burleigh Grimes, Chuck Klein
1F	Tigers, F
3D	Frisch, D
4D	Cochrane, D
5D	Cronin, D
	Bill Dickey, Tony Lazzeri, Pat Malone, Red Ruffing
2D	Klein, D
4D	Cochrane, D
7D	Simmons, D
	Rick Ferrell, Wes Ferrell, Fritz Ostermueller, Bill Werber
8G	Indians, G
9G	Senators, G
	Pete Fox, Hank Greenberg, Schoolboy Rowe, Gee Walker
8F	Indians, F
9F	Senators, F
	Jimmie Foxx, Pinky Higgins, Roy Mahaffey, Dib Williams
1B	Tigers, B
2B	Klein, B
6B	Foxx, B
7B	Simmons, B
	Bump Hadley, Lyn Lary, Heinie Manush, Monte Weaver
1C	Tigers, C
2C	Klein, C
6C	Foxx, C
7C	Simmons, C
	Mel Harder, Bill Knickerbocker, Lefty Stewart, Joe Vosmik
8I	Indians, I
9I	Senators, I
	Travis Jackson, Gus Mancuso, Hal Schumacher, Bill Terry
1K	Tigers, K

3B	Frisch, B
4B	Cochrane, B
5B	Cronin, B
	Joe Kuhel, Buddy Meyer, John Stone, Earl Whitehill (Myer)
8H	Indians, H
9H	Senators, H
	Red Lucas, Tommy Thevenow, Pie Traynor, Glenn Wright
2B	Klein, B
4B	Cochrane, B
7B	Simmons, B
	Picture 1, Detroit Tigers Team Photo
A (22)	
B (31)	
C (32)	
D (17)	
E (2)	
E (19)	
F (11)	
F (27)	
G (10)	
G (23)	
H (1)	
H (26)	
I (4)	
J (16)	
J (24)	
K (14)	
K (34)	
L (5)	
	Picture 2, Chuck Klein
A (6)	
A (22)	
B (31)	
B (36)	
C (9)	
C (32)	
D (17)	
D (28)	
E (5)	
E (15)	
F (4)	
F (20)	
	Picture 3, Frankie Frisch
A (16)	
A (24)	
B (14)	
B (34)	
C (2)	
C (19)	
D (11)	
D (27)	
E (10)	
E (23)	
F (1)	
F (26)	
	Picture 4, Gordon (Mickey) Cochrane
A (6)	
A (16)	
B (34)	
B (36)	
C (9)	
C (19)	
D (27)	
D (28)	
E (15)	
E (23)	
F (1)	
F (20)	
	Picture 5, Joe Cronin
A (16)	
A (24)	
B (14)	
B (34)	
C (2)	
C (19)	
D (11)	
D (27)	
E (10)	
E (23)	
F (1)	
F (26)	
	Picture 6, Jimmy (Jimmie) Foxx
A (22)	
A (24)	
B (14)	
B (31)	
C (2)	
C (32)	
D (11)	
D (17)	
E (5)	
E (10)	
F (4)	
F (26)	
	Picture 7, Al Simmons
A (6)	

A (22)	
B (31)	
B (36)	
C (9)	
C (32)	
D (17)	
D (28)	
E (5)	
E (15)	
F (4)	
F (20)	
	Picture 8, Cleve. Indians Composite
A (7)	
B (13)	
C (18)	
D (21)	
E (3)	
F (30)	
G (34)	
H (35)	
I (32)	
J (25)	
K (12)	
L (8)	
	Picture 9, Wash. Senators Composite
A (7)	
B (13)	
C (18)	
D (21)	
E (3)	
F (30)	
G (29)	
H (35)	
I (33)	
J (25)	
K (12)	
L (8)	

1936 Goudey "Wide Pen" Premiums (R314)

The premium cards originally listed in the American Card Catalog as R314 are known to generations of collectors as "Wide Pens" because of the distinctive, thick style of cursive printing used for the facsimile autographs. Current thinking is that the issue is actually comprised of several distinct types issued over the course of at least two years and sharing a basic 3-1/4" x 5-1/2" black-and-white unnumbered format. Dates attributed are speculative.

1936 Goudey "Wide Pen" Premiums - Type 1

These in-store premiums are known to collectors as "Wide Pens" because of the distinctive, thick style of cursive printing used for the facsimile autographs. Cards have a 3-1/4" x 5-1/2" black-and-white, unnumbered format. Type 1 cards have bordered photos with "LITHO IN U.S.A." in the bottom border.

		NM	E	VG
Complete Set (120):		9,000	3,750	1,250
Common Player:		60.00	25.00	15.00
(1)	Ethan Allen (Kneeling)	60.00	25.00	15.00
(2)	Earl Averill (Portrait)	90.00	38.00	23.00
(3)	Dick Bartell (Portrait)	60.00	25.00	15.00
(4)	Dick Bartell (Sliding)	60.00	25.00	15.00
(5)	Walter Berger (Portrait)	60.00	25.00	15.00
(6)	Geo. Blaeholder (Portrait)	60.00	25.00	15.00
(7)	"Cy" Blanton (Portrait)	60.00	25.00	15.00
(8)	"Cliff" Bolton (Portrait)	60.00	25.00	15.00
(9)	Stan Bordagaray (Portrait)	60.00	25.00	15.00
(10)	Tommy Bridges (Portrait)	60.00	25.00	15.00
(11)	Bill Brubaker (Portrait)	60.00	25.00	15.00
(12)	Sam Byrd (Portrait)	60.00	25.00	15.00
(13)	Dolph Camilli (Portrait)	60.00	25.00	15.00
(14)	Clydell Castleman (Pitching)	60.00	25.00	15.00

(15)	Clydell Castleman (Portrait)	60.00	25.00	15.00
(16)	"Phil" Cavaretta (Cavarretta) (Fielding)	60.00	25.00	15.00
(17)	Ben Chapman, Bill Werber	75.00	31.00	19.50
(18)	"Mickey" Cochrane (Portrait)	100.00	42.00	26.00
(19)	Earl Coombs (Earle Combs)(Batting)	90.00	38.00	23.00
(20)	Joe Coscarart (Portrait)	60.00	25.00	15.00
(21)	Joe Cronin (Kneeling)	90.00	38.00	23.00
(22)	Frank Crosetti (Batting)	65.00	27.00	17.00
(23)	Tony Cuccinello (Portrait)	60.00	25.00	15.00
(24)	"Kiki" Cuyler (Portrait)	90.00	38.00	23.00
(25)	Curt Davis (Pitching)	60.00	25.00	15.00
(26)	Virgil Davis (Catching)	60.00	25.00	15.00
(27)	Paul Derringer (Portrait)	60.00	25.00	15.00
(28)	"Bill" Dickey (Catching)	100.00	42.00	26.00
(29)	Joe DiMaggio, Joe McCarthy	850.00	355.00	220.00
(30)	Jimmy Dykes (Kneeling)	60.00	25.00	15.00
(31)	"Rick" Ferrell (Catching)	90.00	38.00	23.00
(32)	"Wes" Ferrell (Portrait)	60.00	25.00	15.00
(33)	Rick Ferrell, Wes Ferrell	100.00	42.00	26.00
(34)	Lou Finney (Portrait)	60.00	25.00	15.00
(35)	Ervin "Pete" Fox (Portrait)	60.00	25.00	15.00
(36)	Tony Freitas (Portrait)	60.00	25.00	15.00
(37)	Lonnie Frey (Batting)	60.00	25.00	15.00
(38)	Frankie Frisch (Portrait)	90.00	38.00	23.00
(39)	"Augie" Galan (Portrait)	60.00	25.00	15.00
(40)	Charles Gehringer (Portrait)	100.00	42.00	26.00
(41)	Charlie Gelbert (Portrait)	60.00	25.00	15.00
(42)	"Lefty" Gomez (Portrait)	100.00	42.00	26.00
(43)	"Goose" Goslin (Portrait)	90.00	38.00	23.00
(44)	Earl Grace (Catching)	60.00	25.00	15.00
(45)	Hank Greenberg (Portrait)	260.00	110.00	68.00
(46)	"Mule" Haas (Batting)	60.00	25.00	15.00
(47)	Odell Hale (Portrait)	60.00	25.00	15.00
(48)	Bill Hallahan (Portrait)	60.00	25.00	15.00
(49)	"Mel" Harder (Portrait)	60.00	25.00	15.00
(50)	"Bucky" Harris (Portrait)	90.00	38.00	23.00
(51)	"Gabby" Hartnett (Catching)	90.00	38.00	23.00
(52)	Ray Hayworth (Catching)	60.00	25.00	15.00
(53)	"Rolly" Hemsley (Catching)	60.00	25.00	15.00
(54)	Babe Herman (Portrait)	75.00	31.00	19.50
(55)	Frank Higgins (Portrait)	60.00	25.00	15.00
(56)	Oral Hildebrand (Portrait)	60.00	25.00	15.00
(57)	Myril Hoag (Portrait)	60.00	25.00	15.00
(58)	Waite Hoyt (Pitching)	90.00	38.00	23.00
(59)	Woody Jensen (Batting)	60.00	25.00	15.00
(60)	Bob Johnson (Batting)	60.00	25.00	15.00
(61)	"Buck" Jordan (Portrait)	60.00	25.00	15.00
(62)	Alex Kampouris (Portrait)	60.00	25.00	15.00
(63)	"Chuck" Klein (Portrait)	90.00	38.00	23.00
(64)	Joe Kuhel (Portrait)	60.00	25.00	15.00
(65)	Lyn Lary (Portrait)	60.00	25.00	15.00
(66)	Harry Lavagetto (Portrait)	60.00	25.00	15.00
(67)	Sam Leslie (Portrait)	60.00	25.00	15.00
(68)	Freddie Lindstrom (Portrait)	90.00	38.00	23.00
(69)	Ernie Lombardi (Throwing)	90.00	38.00	23.00
(70)	"Al" Lopez (Throwing)	90.00	38.00	23.00
(71)	Dan MacFayden (Portrait)	60.00	25.00	15.00
(72)	John Marcum (Pitching)	60.00	25.00	15.00
(73)	"Pepper" Martin (Portrait)	75.00	31.00	19.50
(74)	Eric McNair (Portrait)	60.00	25.00	15.50
(75)	"Ducky" Medwick (Kneeling)	90.00	38.00	23.00
(76)	Gene Moore (Portrait)	60.00	25.00	15.00
(77)	Randy Moore (Portrait)	60.00	25.00	15.00
(78)	Terry Moore (Portrait)	60.00	25.00	15.00
(79)	Edw. Moriarty (Portrait)	60.00	25.00	15.00
(80)	"Wally" Moses (Portrait)	60.00	25.00	15.00
(81)	"Buddy" Myer (Batting)	60.00	25.00	15.00
(82)	"Buck" Newsom (Portrait)	60.00	25.00	15.00
(83)	Steve O'Neill, Frank Pytlak	60.00	25.00	15.00
(84)	Fred Ostermueller (Portrait)	60.00	25.00	15.00
(85)	Marvin Owen (Portrait)	60.00	25.00	15.00
(86)	Tommy Padden (Portrait)	60.00	25.00	15.00
(87)	Ray Pepper (Batting)	60.00	25.00	15.00
(88)	Tony Piet (Portrait)	60.00	25.00	15.00
(89)	"Rabbit" Pytlak (Throwing)	60.00	25.00	15.00
(90)	"Rip" Radcliff (Portrait)	60.00	25.00	15.00
(91)	Bobby Reis (Portrait)	60.00	25.00	15.00
(92)	"Lew" Riggs (Fielding)	60.00	25.00	15.00
(93)	Bill Rogell (Portrait)	60.00	25.00	15.00
(94)	"Red" Rolfe (Portrait)	60.00	25.00	15.00
(95)	"Schoolboy" Rowe (Portrait)	65.00	27.00	17.00
(96)	Al Schacht (Portrait)	75.00	31.00	19.50
(97)	"Luke" Sewell (Catching)	60.00	25.00	15.00
(98)	Al Simmons (Portrait)	90.00	38.00	23.00
(99)	John Stone (Portrait)	60.00	25.00	15.00
(100)	Gus Suhr (Fielding)	60.00	25.00	15.00
(101)	Joe Sullivan (Portrait)	60.00	25.00	15.00
(102)	Bill Swift (Portrait)	60.00	25.00	15.00
(103)	Vito Tamulis (Portrait)	60.00	25.00	15.00
(104)	Dan Taylor (Portrait)	60.00	25.00	15.00
(105)	Cecil Travis (Portrait)	60.00	25.00	15.00
(106)	Hal Trosky (Portrait)	60.00	25.00	15.00
(107)	"Bill" Urbanski (Portrait)	60.00	25.00	15.00
(108)	Russ Van Atta (Portrait)	60.00	25.00	15.00
(109)	"Arky" Vaughan (Portrait)	90.00	38.00	23.00
(110)	Gerald Walker (Portrait)	60.00	25.00	15.00
(111)	"Buck" Walter (Walters) (Portrait)	60.00	25.00	15.00
(113)	Paul Waner (Portrait)	90.00	38.00	23.00
(114)	"Lon" Warneke (Portrait)	60.00	25.00	15.00
(115)	"Rabbit" Warstler (Batting)	60.00	25.00	15.00
(116)	Bill Werber (Portrait)	60.00	25.00	15.00
(117)	"Jo Jo" White (Portrait)	60.00	25.00	15.00
(118)	Burgess Whitehead (Portrait)	60.00	25.00	15.00
(119)	John Whitehead (Portrait)	60.00	25.00	15.00
(120)	Whitlow Wyatt (Portrait)	60.00	25.00	15.00

1936 Goudey "Wide Pen" Premiums - Type 2

These 3-1/4" x 5-1/2" black-and-white, unnumbered cards are known as "Wide Pens" because of the distinctive cursive printing of the facsimile autographs. Type 2 and Type 3 cards share their photos. Type 2 cards have borders, but no "LITHO IN U.S.A." line. Some Type 2 cards also share their photos with Type 1, but have a different projection (size). Those are indicated parenthetically with an asterisk.

		NM	E	VG
	Complete Set (24):	2,700	1,250	750.00
	Common Player:	90.00	40.00	25.00
(1)	Mel Almada (Kneeling)	110.00	49.00	27.00
(2)	Lucius Appling (Portrait)	135.00	61.00	34.00
(3)	Henry Bonura (Portrait)	90.00	40.00	25.00
(4)	Ben Chapman, Bill Werber	120.00	54.00	30.00
(5)	Herman Clifton (Batting)	90.00	40.00	25.00
(6)	Roger "Doc" Cramer (Portrait)	90.00	40.00	25.00
(7)	Joe Cronin (Kneeling*)	135.00	61.00	34.00
(8)	Jimmy Dykes (Kneeling*)	90.00	40.00	25.00
(9)	Erwin "Pete" Fox (Ervin) (Portrait*)	90.00	40.00	25.00
(10)	Jimmy Foxx (Portrait)	260.00	115.00	65.00
(11)	Hank Greenberg (Portrait*)	350.00	155.00	87.00
(12)	Oral Hildebrand (Portrait*)	90.00	40.00	25.00
(13)	Alex Hooks (Fielding)	90.00	40.00	25.00
(14)	Willis Hudlin (Throwing)	90.00	40.00	25.00
(15)	Bill Knickerbocker (Portrait)	90.00	40.00	25.00
(16)	Heine (Heinie) Manush (Portrait)	135.00	61.00	34.00
(17)	Steve O'Neill (Portrait)	90.00	40.00	25.00
(18)	Marvin Owen (Portrait*)	90.00	40.00	25.00
(19)	Al Simmons (Bats on shoulder.)	135.00	61.00	34.00
(20)	Lem "Moose" Solters (Batting)(First name actually Julius.)	90.00	40.00	25.00
(21)	Hal Trosky (Batting)	90.00	40.00	25.00
(22)	Joe Vosmik (Batting)	90.00	40.00	25.00
(23)	Joe Vosmik (Portrait)	90.00	40.00	25.00
(24)	Earl Whitehill (Throwing)	90.00	40.00	25.00

1936 Goudey "Wide Pen" Premiums - Type 3

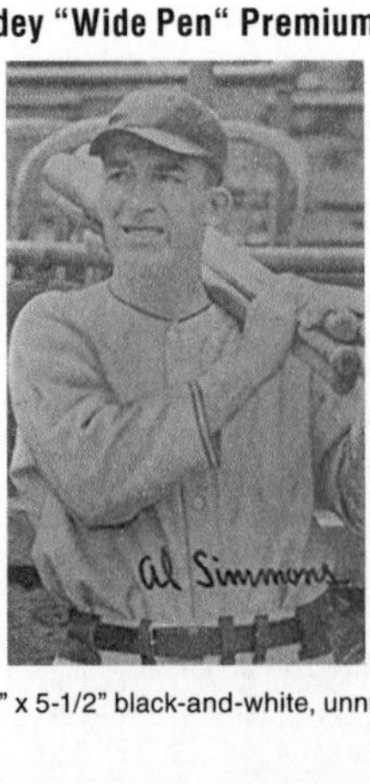

These 3-1/4" x 5-1/2" black-and-white, unnumbered cards are known as "Wide Pens" because of the distinctive cursive printing of the facsimile autographs. Type 2 and Type 3 cards share their photos. Type 3 cards are borderless and some also share their photos with Type 1, but have a different projection (size). Those are indicated parenthetically with an asterisk.

		NM	E	VG
	Complete Set (24):	2,700	1,250	750.00
	Common Player:	90.00	40.00	25.00
(1)	Mel Almada (Kneeling)	120.00	54.00	30.00
(2)	Lucius Appling (Portrait)	135.00	61.00	34.00
(3)	Henry Bonura (Portrait)	90.00	40.00	25.00
(4)	Ben Chapman, Bill Werber	120.00	54.00	30.00
(5)	Herman Clifton (Batting)	90.00	40.00	25.00
(6)	Roger "Doc" Cramer (Portrait)	90.00	40.00	25.00
(7)	Joe Cronin (Kneeling*)	135.00	61.00	34.00
(8)	Jimmy Dykes (Kneeling*)	90.00	40.00	25.00
(9)	Erwin "Pete" Fox (Ervin) (Portrait*)	90.00	40.00	25.00
(10)	Jimmy Foxx (Portrait)	260.00	115.00	65.00
(11)	Hank Greenberg (Portrait*)	350.00	155.00	87.00
(12)	Oral Hildebrand (Portrait*)	90.00	40.00	25.00
(13)	Alex Hooks (Fielding)	90.00	40.00	25.00
(14)	Willis Hudlin (Throwing)	90.00	40.00	25.00
(15)	Bill Knickerbocker (Portrait)	90.00	40.00	25.00
(16)	Heine (Heinie) Manush (Portrait)	135.00	61.00	34.00
(17)	Steve O'Neill (Portrait)	90.00	40.00	25.00
(18)	Marvin Owen (Portrait*)	90.00	40.00	25.00
(19)	Al Simmons (Bats on shoulder.)	135.00	61.00	34.00
(20)	Lem "Moose" Solters (Batting)(First name actually Julius.)	90.00	40.00	25.00
(21)	Hal Trosky (Batting)	90.00	40.00	25.00
(22)	Joe Vosmik (Batting)	90.00	40.00	25.00
(23)	Joe Vosmik (Portrait)	90.00	40.00	25.00
(24)	Earl Whitehill (Throwing)	90.00	40.00	25.00

1936 Goudey (R322)

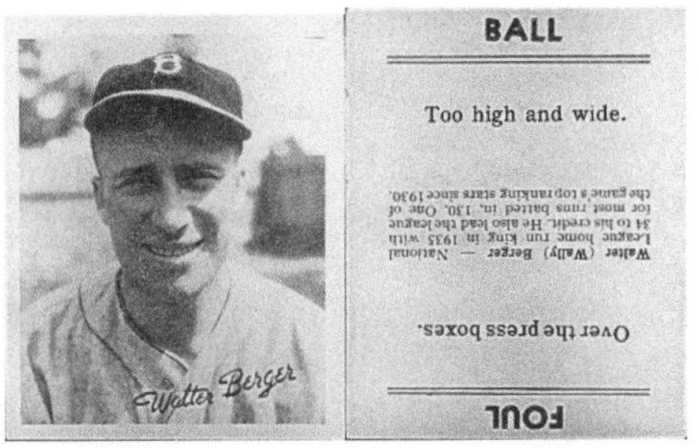

The 1936 Goudey set consists of black-and-white cards measuring 2-3/8" x 2-7/8". A facsimile autograph is positioned on the card fronts. Backs contain a brief player biography and were designed to be used to play a baseball game. Different game situations (out, single, double, etc.) are given on each card. Numerous front/back combinations exist in the set. The ACC designation for the set is R322.

		NM	E	VG
	Complete Set (25):	2,625	1,300	785.00
	Common Player:	80.00	40.00	25.00
(1)	Walter Berger	80.00	40.00	25.00
(2)	Henry Bonura	80.00	40.00	25.00
(3)	Stan Bordagaray	80.00	40.00	25.00
(4)	Bill Brubaker	80.00	40.00	25.00
(5)	Dolf Camilli	80.00	40.00	25.00
(6)	Clydell Castleman	80.00	40.00	25.00
(7)	"Mickey" Cochrane	175.00	85.00	50.00
(8)	Joe Coscarart	80.00	40.00	25.00
(9)	Frank Crosetti	110.00	55.00	30.00
(10)	"Kiki" Cuyler	140.00	70.00	40.00
(11)	Paul Derringer	80.00	40.00	25.00
(12)	Jimmy Dykes	80.00	40.00	25.00
(13)	"Rick" Ferrell	140.00	70.00	40.00
(14)	"Lefty" Gomez	175.00	85.00	50.00
(15)	Hank Greenberg	275.00	135.00	80.00
(16)	"Bucky" Harris	140.00	70.00	40.00
(17)	"Rolly" Hemsley	80.00	40.00	25.00
(18)	Frank Higgins	80.00	40.00	25.00
(19)	Oral Hildebrand	80.00	40.00	25.00
(20)	"Chuck" Klein	140.00	70.00	40.00
(21)	"Pepper" Martin	110.00	55.00	30.00
(22)	"Buck" Newsom	80.00	40.00	25.00
(23)	Joe Vosmik	80.00	40.00	25.00
(24)	Paul Waner	140.00	70.00	40.00
(25)	Bill Werber	80.00	40.00	25.00

1937 Goudey "Wide Pen" Premiums - Type 4

These premium cards are known to generations of collectors as "Wide Pens" because of the distinctive, thick style of cursive typography used for the facsimile autographs. They have a 3-1/4" x 5-1/2" black-and-white, unnumbered format. Type 4 cards are printed on a paper stock usually described as "creamy." They are bordered, but do not have a "LITHO IN U.S.A." line. Type 5 cards share the creamy paper stock of Type 4, and may have been part of the same issue, which would indicate Canadian origins. An asterisk after the pose indicates a photo shared with Type 1, though possibly of a larger or smaller projection.

	NM	E	VG
Complete Set (36):	6,750	3,000	1,800
Common Player:	90.00	40.00	25.00
(1) "Luke" Appling (Batting)	135.00	61.00	34.00
(2) Earl Averill (Portrait*)	135.00	61.00	34.00
(3) "Cy" Blanton (Pitching)	90.00	40.00	25.00
(4) "Zeke" Bonura (Batting)	90.00	40.00	25.00
(5) Tom Bridges (Throwing)	90.00	40.00	25.00
(6) Tommy Bridges (Portrait*)	90.00	40.00	25.00
(7) Mickey Cochrane (Portrait*)	135.00	61.00	34.00
(8) Joe Cronin (Kneeling*)	135.00	61.00	34.00
(9) "Joe" DiMaggio (Portrait)	3,000	1,000	625.00
(10) "Bobby" Doeer (Doerr) (Batting)	135.00	61.00	34.00
(11) Jimmy Dykes (Fielding)	90.00	40.00	25.00
(12) "Bob" Feller (Pitching)	300.00	135.00	75.00
(13) "Elbie" Fletcher (Fielding)	90.00	40.00	25.00
(14) Erwin "Pete" Fox (Ervin) (Portrait*)	90.00	40.00	25.00
(15) Pete Fox (Batting)	90.00	40.00	25.00
(16) "Gus" Galan (Batting)	90.00	40.00	25.00
(17) Charles Gehringer (Portrait*)	135.00	61.00	34.00
(18) Hank Greenberg (Portrait*)	225.00	100.00	56.00
(19) "Goose" Goslin (Portrait*)	135.00	61.00	34.00
(20) Mel Harder (Portrait)	90.00	40.00	25.00
(21) "Gabby" Hartnett (Catching*)	135.00	61.00	34.00
(22) Ray Hayworth (Catching*)	90.00	40.00	25.00
(23) "Pinky" Higgins (Batting)	90.00	40.00	25.00
(24) Carl Hubbell (Pitching)	135.00	61.00	34.00
(25) "Wally" Moses (Batting)	90.00	40.00	25.00
(26) Lou Newsom (Portrait)	90.00	40.00	25.00
(27) Marvin Owen (Portrait*)	90.00	40.00	25.00
(28) Bill Rogell (Portrait*)	90.00	40.00	25.00
(29) "Schoolboy" Rowe (Pitching)	90.00	40.00	25.00
(30) "Schoolboy" Rowe (Portrait*)	90.00	40.00	25.00
(31) Al Simmons (Portrait*)	135.00	61.00	34.00
(32) Julius Solters (Batting)	90.00	40.00	25.00
(33) "Hal" Trosky (Batting)	90.00	40.00	25.00
(34) Joe Vosmik (Kneeling)	90.00	40.00	25.00
(35) "Jo Jo" White (Portrait*)	90.00	40.00	25.00
(36) Johnnie Whitehead (Pitching)	90.00	40.00	25.00

1937 Goudey "Wide Pen" Premiums - Type 5

These premium cards are known as "Wide Pens" because of the distinctive, thick style of cursive printing used for the facsimile autographs. they have a 3-1/4" x 5-1/2" black-and-white, unnumbered format. The photos are bordered, but do not have a "LITHO IN U.S.A." line. Type 5 cards are printed on a paper stock usually described as "creamy" and may have been part of the same issue as Type 4. Type 5 is comprised only of Toronto and Montreal (International League) players.

	NM	E	VG
Complete Set (39):	4,750	2,400	1,350
Common Player:	135.00	65.00	35.00

(1)	Buddy Bates	135.00	65.00	35.00
(2)	Del Bisonette (Portrait)	135.00	65.00	35.00
(3)	Lincoln Blakely	135.00	65.00	35.00
(4)	Isaac J. Boone	135.00	65.00	35.00
(5)	John H. Burnett (Batting)	135.00	65.00	35.00
(6)	Leon Chagon	135.00	65.00	35.00
(7)	Gus Dugas (Portrait)	135.00	65.00	35.00
(8)	Henry N. Erickson (Catching)	135.00	65.00	35.00
(9)	Art Funk (Portrait)	135.00	65.00	35.00
(10)	George Granger (Portrait)	135.00	65.00	35.00
(11)	Thomas G. Heath	135.00	65.00	35.00
(12)	Phil Hensiek (Portrait)	135.00	65.00	35.00
(13)	Leroy Herrmann (Throwing)	135.00	65.00	35.00
(14)	Henry Johnson	135.00	65.00	35.00
(15)	Hal King (Portrait)	135.00	65.00	35.00
(16)	Charles F. Lucas (Portrait)	135.00	65.00	35.00
(17)	Edward S. Miller (Batting) (Middle initial actually R.)	135.00	65.00	35.00
(18)	Jake F. Mooty (Pitching)	135.00	65.00	35.00
(19)	Guy Moreau (Portrait, street clothes.)	135.00	65.00	35.00
(20)	George Murray (Portrait)	135.00	65.00	35.00
(21)	Glenn Myatt	135.00	65.00	35.00
(22)	Lauri Myllykangas	135.00	65.00	35.00
(23)	Francis J. Nicholas (Pitching)	135.00	65.00	35.00
(24)	Bill O'Brien (Montreal trainer)	135.00	65.00	35.00
(25)	Thomas Oliver (Batting)	135.00	65.00	35.00
(26)	James Pattison	135.00	65.00	35.00
(27)	Crip Polli (Portrait)	135.00	65.00	35.00
(28)	Harlin Pool (Bats)	135.00	65.00	35.00
(29)	Walter Purcey (Pitching)	135.00	65.00	35.00
(30)	Bill Rhiel	135.00	65.00	35.00
(31)	Ben Sankey	135.00	65.00	35.00
(32)	Les Scarcella (Scarsella) (Kneeling)	135.00	65.00	35.00
(33)	Bob Seeds (Portrait)	135.00	65.00	35.00
(34)	Frank Shaugnessy (Portrait)	135.00	65.00	35.00
(35)	Harry Smythe (Portrait)	135.00	65.00	35.00
(36)	Ben Tate (Portrait)	135.00	65.00	35.00
(37)	Fresco Thompson (Portrait)	135.00	65.00	35.00
(38)	Charles Wilson (Portrait)	135.00	65.00	35.00
(39)	Francis Wistert (Pitching)	135.00	65.00	35.00

1937 Goudey Knot Hole League

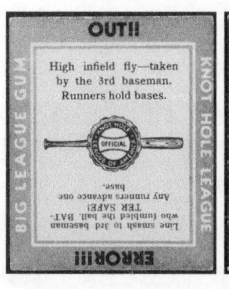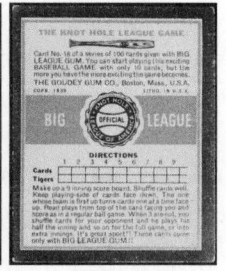

Though they do not picture or name any players, the fact these game cards were issued by Goudey makes them collectible for many hobbyists. While they carry a copyright date of 1935, the cards were not issued until 1937. About 2-3/8" x 2-7/8", and printed in red, white and blue, the cards were intended to be used to play a baseball game using the situations printed on the fronts. Despite advertising a series of 100 cards, only 24 were actually issued. The cards were designated R325 in the American Card Catalog.

	NM	E	VG
Complete Set (24):	450.00	180.00	90.00
Common Card:	25.00	10.00	5.00

1	Double / Foul	25.00	10.00	5.00
2	Steals Home!! / Strike	25.00	10.00	5.00
3	Ball / Out	25.00	10.00	5.00
4	Strike / Ball	25.00	10.00	5.00
5	Strike / Wild Pitch	25.00	10.00	5.00
6	Ball / Out	25.00	10.00	5.00
7	Bunt - Scratch Hit!! / Stolen Base !!	25.00	10.00	5.00
8	Hit by Pitched Ball / Out	25.00	10.00	5.00
9	Foul / Ball	25.00	10.00	5.00
10	Foul / Double!	25.00	10.00	5.00
11	Out / Ball	25.00	10.00	5.00
12	Foul / Force Out	25.00	10.00	5.00
13	Out / Single	25.00	10.00	5.00
14	Strike / Ball	25.00	10.00	5.00
15	Foul Tip / Strike!	25.00	10.00	5.00
16	Three Bagger / Out	25.00	10.00	5.00
17	Ball / Out	25.00	10.00	5.00
18	Out!! / Error!!!	25.00	10.00	5.00
19	Strike / Foul	25.00	10.00	5.00
20	Out / Double Play	25.00	10.00	5.00
21	!!Home Run!! / Ball	25.00	10.00	5.00
22	Out / Strike	25.00	10.00	5.00
23	Ball / Out	25.00	10.00	5.00
24	Lout!! / Error!!!	25.00	10.00	5.00

1937 Goudey Thum Movies

These 2" x 3" baseball novelty booklets create the illusion of baseball action in motion when the pages are rapidly flipped. The booklets are numbered on the top of the back page. Thum Movies were listed in the American Card Catalog as R342.

	NM	E	VG
Complete Set (13):	1,750	875.00	525.00
Common Player:	70.00	35.00	20.00

1	John Irving Burns	70.00	35.00	20.00
2	Joe Vosmik	70.00	35.00	20.00
3	Mel Ott	225.00	110.00	65.00
4	Joe DiMaggio	525.00	260.00	155.00
5	Wally Moses	70.00	35.00	20.00
6	Van Lingle Mungo	70.00	35.00	20.00
7	Luke Appling	100.00	50.00	30.00
8	Bob Feller	225.00	110.00	65.00
9	Paul Derringer	70.00	35.00	20.00
10	Paul Waner	100.00	50.00	30.00
11	Joe Medwick	100.00	50.00	30.00
12	James Emory Foxx	225.00	110.00	65.00
13	Wally Berger	70.00	35.00	20.00

1938 Goudey (R323)

Sometimes referred to as the Goudey Heads-Up set, this issue begins numbering (#241) where the 1933 Goudey set left off. On the card fronts, a photo is used for the player's head with the body being a cartoon drawing. Twenty-four different players are pictured twice in the set. Cards #241-264 feature plain backgrounds on the fronts. Cards #265-288 contain the same basic design and photo but include small drawings and comments within the background. Backs have player statistical and biographical information. The ACC designation for the issue is R323.

	NM	E	VG
Complete Set (48):	29,000	11,500	5,750
Common Player (241-264):	200.00	85.00	30.00
Common Player (265-288):	225.00	100.00	35.00

241	Charlie Gehringer	600.00	250.00	100.00
242	Ervin Fox	300.00	100.00	40.00
243	Joe Kuhel	200.00	85.00	30.00
244	Frank DeMaree	200.00	85.00	30.00
245	Frank Pytlak	200.00	85.00	30.00
246a	Ernie Lombardi (Red Sox)	800.00	320.00	160.00
246b	Ernie Lombardi (Reds followed by black baseball.)	450.00	180.00	90.00
246c	Ernie Lombardi (Reds)	350.00	140.00	70.00
247	Joe Vosmik	200.00	85.00	30.00
248	Dick Bartell	200.00	85.00	30.00
249	Jimmy Foxx	1,000	500.00	300.00
250	Joe DiMaggio	5,000	2,000	1,100
251	Bump Hadley	200.00	85.00	30.00
252	Zeke Bonura	200.00	85.00	30.00
253	Hank Greenberg	1,100	450.00	225.00
254	Van Lingle Mungo	300.00	120.00	60.00
255	Julius Solters	200.00	85.00	30.00
256	Vernon Kennedy	200.00	85.00	30.00
257	Al Lopez	425.00	200.00	85.00
258	Bobby Doerr	500.00	200.00	85.00
259	Bill Werber	200.00	85.00	30.00
260	Rudy York	200.00	85.00	30.00
261	Rip Radcliff	200.00	85.00	30.00
262	Joe Ducky Medwick	425.00	200.00	85.00
263	Marvin Owen	200.00	85.00	30.00
264	Bob Feller	2,000	700.00	300.00
265	Charlie Gehringer	600.00	200.00	100.00
266	Ervin Fox	225.00	100.00	35.00

267	Joe Kuhel	225.00	100.00	35.00
268	Frank DeMaree	225.00	100.00	35.00
269	Frank Pytlak	225.00	100.00	35.00
270	Ernie Lombardi	500.00	225.00	100.00
271	Joe Vosmik	225.00	100.00	35.00
272	Dick Bartell	225.00	100.00	35.00
273	Jimmy Foxx	1,200	500.00	200.00
274	Joe DiMaggio	5,250	2,200	1,200
275	Bump Hadley	225.00	100.00	35.00
276	Zeke Bonura	225.00	100.00	35.00
277	Hank Greenberg	1,300	600.00	300.00
278	Van Lingle Mungo	225.00	100.00	35.00
279	Julius Solters	225.00	100.00	35.00
280	Vernon Kennedy	225.00	100.00	35.00
281	Al Lopez	500.00	225.00	90.00
282	Bobby Doerr	550.00	250.00	100.00
283	Bill Werber	225.00	100.00	35.00
284	Rudy York	225.00	100.00	35.00
285	Rip Radcliff	225.00	100.00	35.00
286	Joe Ducky Medwick	600.00	250.00	100.00
287	Marvin Owen	225.00	100.00	35.00
288	Bob Feller	1,750	875.00	525.00

1938 Goudey Big League Baseball Movies

Probably issued in both 1937-38, according to the biographies on back, this set of "flip movies" was comprised of small (2" x 3") booklets whose pages produced a movie effect when flipped rapidly, similar to a penny arcade novelty popular at the time. There are 13 players in the set; each movie having two cleary labeled parts. The cover of the booklets identify the set as "Big League Baseball Movies." They carry the American Card Catalog designation R326.

		NM	E	VG
	Complete Set (26):	3,750	1,875	1,125
	Common Player:	75.00	37.50	22.50
1a	John Irving Burns (Part 1)	75.00	37.50	22.50
1b	John Irving Burns (Part 2)	75.00	37.50	22.50
2a	Joe Vosmik (Part 1)	75.00	37.50	22.50
2b	Joe Vosmik (Part 2)	75.00	37.50	22.50
3a	Mel Ott (Part 1)	185.00	95.00	55.00
3b	Mel Ott (Part 2)	185.00	95.00	55.00
4a	Joe DiMaggio (Part 1, Joe DiMaggio cover photo.)	475.00	235.00	140.00
4aa	Joe DiMaggio (Part 1, Vince DiMaggio cover photo.)	375.00	185.00	110.00
4b	Joe DiMaggio (Part 2, Joe DiMaggio cover photo.)	475.00	235.00	140.00
4ba	Joe DiMaggio (Part 2, Vince DiMaggio cover photo.)	375.00	185.00	110.00
5a	Wally Moses (Part 1)	75.00	37.50	22.50
5b	Wally Moses (Part 2)	75.00	37.50	22.50
6a	Van Lingle Mungo (Part 1)	75.00	37.50	22.50
6b	Van Lingle Mungo (Part 2)	75.00	37.50	22.50
7a	Luke Appling (Part 1)	110.00	55.00	35.00
7b	Luke Appling (Part 2)	110.00	55.00	35.00
8a	Bob Feller (Part 1)	225.00	110.00	65.00
8b	Bob Feller (Part 2)	225.00	110.00	65.00
9a	Paul Derringer (Part 1)	75.00	37.50	22.50
9b	Paul Derringer (Part 2)	75.00	37.50	22.50
10a	Paul Waner (Part 1)	110.00	55.00	35.00
10b	Paul Waner (Part 2)	110.00	55.00	35.00
11a	Joe Medwick (Part 1)	110.00	55.00	35.00
11b	Joe Medwick (Part 2)	110.00	55.00	35.00
12a	James Emory Foxx (Part 1)	260.00	130.00	75.00
12b	James Emory Foxx (Part 2)	260.00	130.00	75.00
13a	Wally Berger (Part 1)	75.00	37.50	22.50
13b	Wally Berger (Part 2)	75.00	37.50	22.50

1939 Goudey Premiums (R303-A)

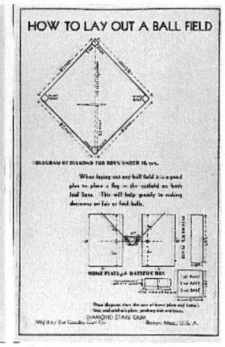

Although this unnumbered set of paper premiums has the name "Diamond Stars Gum" on the back, it is not related to National Chicle's Diamond Stars card sets. Rather, this 48-player set was a premium issued by the Goudey Gum Co. Each premium photo measures 4" x 6-3/16" and is printed in a brown-toned sepia. The front of the photo includes a facsimile autograph, while the back contains drawings that illustrate various baseball tips. These pictures are soemtimes found with top and bottom border trimmed to a depth of 5-3/4" for distribution in Canada.

		NM	E	VG
	Complete Set (48):	6,000	2,400	1,200
	Common Player:	75.00	30.00	15.00
(1)	Luke Appling	135.00	55.00	25.00
(2)	Earl Averill	135.00	55.00	25.00
(3)	Wally Berger	75.00	30.00	15.00
(4)	Darrell Blanton	75.00	30.00	15.00
(5)	Zeke Bonura	75.00	30.00	15.00
(6)	Mace Brown	75.00	30.00	15.00
(7)	George Case	75.00	30.00	15.00
(8)	Ben Chapman	75.00	30.00	15.00
(9)	Joe Cronin	135.00	55.00	25.00
(10)	Frank Crosetti	90.00	36.00	18.00
(11)	Paul Derringer	75.00	30.00	15.00
(12)	Bill Dickey	150.00	60.00	30.00
(13)	Joe DiMaggio	650.00	260.00	130.00
(14)	Bob Feller	225.00	90.00	45.00
(15)	Jimmy (Jimmie) Foxx	235.00	95.00	45.00
(16)	Charles Gehringer	135.00	55.00	25.00
(17)	Lefty Gomez	135.00	55.00	25.00
(18)	Ival Goodman	75.00	30.00	15.00
(19)	Joe Gordon	135.00	55.00	25.00
(20)	Hank Greenberg	175.00	70.00	35.00
(21)	Buddy Hassett	75.00	30.00	15.00
(22)	Jeff Heath	75.00	30.00	15.00
(23)	Tom Henrich	75.00	30.00	15.00
(24)	Billy Herman	135.00	54.00	27.00
(25)	Frank Higgins	75.00	30.00	15.00
(26)	Fred Hutchinson	75.00	30.00	15.00
(27)	Bob Johnson	75.00	30.00	15.00
(28)	Ken Keltner	75.00	30.00	15.00
(29)	Mike Kreevich	75.00	30.00	15.00
(30)	Ernie Lombardi	135.00	55.00	25.00
(31)	Gus Mancuso	75.00	30.00	15.00
(32)	Eric McNair	75.00	30.00	15.00
(33)	Van Mungo	75.00	30.00	15.00
(34)	Buck Newsom	75.00	30.00	15.00
(35)	Mel Ott	150.00	55.00	25.00
(36)	Marvin Owen	75.00	30.00	15.00
(37)	Frank Pytlak	75.00	30.00	15.00
(38)	Woodrow Rich	75.00	30.00	15.00
(39)	Charley Root	75.00	30.00	15.00
(40)	Al Simmons	135.00	55.00	25.00
(41)	James Tabor	75.00	30.00	15.00
(42)	Cecil Travis	75.00	30.00	15.00
(43)	Hal Trosky	75.00	30.00	15.00
(44)	Arky Vaughan	135.00	55.00	25.00
(45)	Joe Vosmik	75.00	30.00	15.00
(46)	Lon Warneke	75.00	30.00	15.00
(47)	Ted Williams	2,000	1,000	600.00
(48)	Rudy York	75.00	30.00	15.00

1939 Goudey Premiums (R303-B)

Although larger (4-3/4" x 7-1/4" to 7-3/8"), the photos in this 24-player set are identical to those in the R303-A issue of the same year, and the format of the set is unchanged. The set, designated as R303-B in the American Card Catalog, can be found in both black-and-white and sepia-toned, with backs printed in brown.

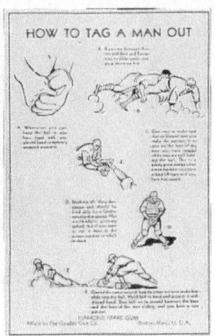

		NM	E	VG
	Complete Set (24):	2,500	1,000	500.00
	Common Player:	60.00	24.00	12.00
(1)	Luke Appling	90.00	35.00	15.00
(2)	George Case	60.00	25.00	12.00
(3)	Ben Chapman	60.00	25.00	12.00
(4)	Joe Cronin	90.00	35.00	15.00
(5)	Bill Dickey	110.00	45.00	20.00
(6)	Joe DiMaggio	850.00	425.00	250.00
(7)	Bob Feller	150.00	60.00	30.00
(8)	Jimmy (Jimmie) Foxx	175.00	70.00	35.00
(9)	Lefty Gomez	90.00	35.00	15.00
(10)	Ival Goodman	60.00	25.00	12.00
(11)	Joe Gordon	90.00	45.00	27.00
(12)	Hank Greenberg	125.00	50.00	25.00
(13)	Jeff Heath	60.00	25.00	12.00
(14)	Billy Herman	90.00	35.00	15.00
(15)	Frank Higgins	60.00	25.00	12.00
(16)	Ken Keltner	60.00	25.00	12.00
(17)	Mike Kreevich	60.00	25.00	12.00
(18)	Ernie Lombardi	90.00	35.00	15.00
(19)	Gus Mancuso	60.00	25.00	12.00
(20)	Mel Ott	110.00	45.00	20.00
(21)	Al Simmons	90.00	35.00	15.00
(22)	Arky Vaughan	90.00	35.00	15.00
(23)	Joe Vosmik	60.00	25.00	12.00
(24)	Rudy York	60.00	25.00	12.00

1941 Goudey (R324)

Goudey Gum's last set was issued in 1941. The 2-3/8" x 2-7/8" (size approximate due to imprecise cutting) cards feature black-and-white photos set against blue, green, red or yellow backgrounds. The player's name, team and position plus the card number are supposed to be situated in a box at the bottom of the card. However, due to vagaries of cutting, some or all of the bottom printing might appear at the top of the card, greatly reducing its value. The card backs are blank. The ACC designation for the set is R324.

		NM	E	VG
	Complete Set (33):	10,000	5,000	3,000
	Common Player:	250.00	100.00	50.00
1	Hugh Mulcahy	250.00	100.00	50.00
2	Harland Clift	250.00	100.00	50.00
3	Louis Chiozza	250.00	100.00	50.00
4	Warren (Buddy) Rosar	250.00	100.00	50.00
5	George McQuinn	250.00	100.00	50.00
6	Emerson Dickman	250.00	100.00	50.00
7	Wayne Ambler	250.00	100.00	50.00
8	Bob Muncrief	250.00	100.00	50.00
9	Bill Dietrich	250.00	100.00	50.00
10	Taft Wright	250.00	100.00	50.00
11	Don Heffner	250.00	100.00	50.00
12	Fritz Ostermueller	250.00	100.00	50.00
13	Frank Hayes	250.00	100.00	50.00
14	John (Jack) Kramer	250.00	100.00	50.00
15	Dario Lodigiani	275.00	110.00	55.00
16	George Case	250.00	100.00	50.00
17	Vito Tamulis	250.00	100.00	50.00
18	Whitlow Wyatt	250.00	100.00	50.00
19	Bill Posedel	250.00	100.00	50.00
20	Carl Hubbell	750.00	370.00	220.00
21	Harold Warstler (SP)	650.00	320.00	195.00
22	Joe Sullivan (SP)	650.00	320.00	195.00

23	Norman (Babe) Young (SP)	650.00	320.00	195.00
24	Stanley Andrews (SP)	650.00	320.00	195.00
25	Morris Arnovich (SP)	700.00	260.00	90.00
26	Elburt Fletcher	250.00	100.00	50.00
27	Bill Crouch	275.00	110.00	55.00
28	Al Todd	250.00	100.00	50.00
29	Debs Garms	250.00	100.00	50.00
30	Jim Tobin	250.00	100.00	50.00
31	Chester Ross	250.00	100.00	50.00
32	George Coffman	250.00	100.00	50.00
33	Mel Ott	1,500	750.00	450.00

1955 Robert Gould All Stars Cards

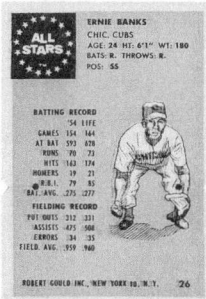

One of three issues of miniature plastic player statues is-sued in the mid-Fifties was the All Stars series by Robert Gould Inc. of New York. The white plastic statues, which sold for about a quarter, came rubber-banded to a baseball card. The card measures 2-1/2" x 3-1/2" with a white border. A rather crude black-and-white line drawing of the player is set against a green background. There are a few biographi-cal details and 1954 and lifetime stats. An "All Stars" logo is in an upper corner, while the card number is at lower-right. The cards are blank-backed. All cards have a pair of notches at the sides and two punch holes to hold the rubber band. Prices shown here are for the cards alone. A 2-5/8" x 3-5/8" album reproducing all 28 player cards was also issued.

		NM	E	VG
Complete Set, Cards (28):		17,000	8,500	5,000
Common Player:		500.00	250.00	150.00
Album:		400.00	200.00	120.00
1	Willie Mays	2,200	1,100	660.00
2	Gus Zernial	500.00	250.00	150.00
3	Red Schoendienst	650.00	325.00	200.00
4	Chico Carrasquel	500.00	250.00	150.00
5	Jim Hegan	500.00	250.00	150.00
6	Curt Simmons	500.00	250.00	150.00
7	Bob Porterfield	500.00	250.00	150.00
8	Jim Busby	500.00	250.00	150.00
9	Don Mueller	500.00	250.00	150.00
10	Ted Kluszewski	600.00	300.00	200.00
11	Ray Boone	500.00	250.00	150.00
12	Smoky Burgess	500.00	250.00	150.00
13	Bob Rush	500.00	250.00	150.00
14	Early Wynn	600.00	300.00	180.00
15	Bill Bruton	500.00	250.00	150.00
16	Gus Bell	500.00	250.00	150.00
17	Jim Finigan	500.00	250.00	150.00
18	Granny Hamner	500.00	250.00	150.00
19	Hank Thompson	500.00	250.00	150.00
20	Joe Coleman	500.00	250.00	150.00
21	Don Newcombe	550.00	275.00	160.00
22	Richie Ashburn	650.00	325.00	200.00
23	Bobby Thomson	500.00	250.00	150.00
24	Sid Gordon	500.00	250.00	150.00
25	Gerry Coleman	500.00	250.00	150.00
26	Ernie Banks	1,700	850.00	500.00
27	Billy Pierce	500.00	250.00	150.00
28	Mel Parnell	500.00	250.00	150.00

1955 Robert Gould All Stars Statues

One of three issues of miniature plastic player statues was issued in the mid-Fifties was the All Stars series by Robert Gould Inc. of New York. The white plastic statues, which sold for about a quarter, came rubber-banded to a baseball card. Depending on pose, they vary in size from around 2" to 2-1/2". The figures have a round base with the player's name. Prices shown here are for the statues alone. The statues were also sold in seven-player boxed sets labeled "A" through "D."

		NM	E	VG
Complete Set, Statues (28):		3,000	1,500	900.00
Common Player:		80.00	40.00	25.00
1	Willie Mays	600.00	300.00	180.00
2	Gus Zernial	80.00	40.00	25.00
3	Red Schoendienst	150.00	75.00	45.00
4	Chico Carrasquel	80.00	40.00	25.00
5	Jim Hegan	80.00	40.00	25.00
6	Curt Simmons	80.00	40.00	25.00
7	Bob Porterfield	80.00	40.00	25.00
8	Jim Busby	80.00	40.00	25.00
9	Don Mueller	80.00	40.00	25.00
10	Ted Kluszewski	100.00	50.00	30.00
11	Ray Boone	80.00	40.00	25.00
12	Smoky Burgess	80.00	40.00	25.00
13	Bob Rush	80.00	40.00	25.00
14	Early Wynn	120.00	60.00	40.00
15	Bill Bruton	80.00	40.00	25.00
16	Gus Bell	80.00	40.00	25.00
17	Jim Finigan	80.00	40.00	25.00
18	Granny Hamner	80.00	40.00	25.00
19	Hank Thompson	80.00	40.00	25.00
20	Joe Coleman	80.00	40.00	25.00
21	Don Newcombe	90.00	45.00	30.00
22	Richie Ashburn	150.00	75.00	45.00
23	Bobby Thomson	90.00	45.00	30.00
24	Sid Gordon	80.00	40.00	25.00
25	Gerry Coleman	80.00	40.00	25.00
26	Ernie Banks	480.00	240.00	150.00
27	Billy Pierce	80.00	40.00	25.00
28	Mel Parnell	80.00	40.00	25.00

1978 Grand Slam

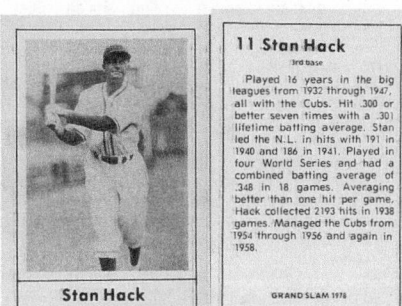

This collectors' edition card set was produced by Jack Wallin. The black-and-white 2-1/4" x 3-1/4" cards have player poses or action photos on front, with the name in the white border at bottom. Backs have a career summary.

		NM	E	VG
Complete Set (200):		120.00	60.00	35.00
Common Player:		2.00	1.00	.60
1	Leo Durocher	2.00	1.00	.60
2	Bob Lemon	2.00	1.00	.60
3	Earl Averill	2.00	1.00	.60
4	Dale Alexander	2.00	1.00	.60
5	Hank Greenberg	12.00	6.00	3.50
6	Waite Hoyt	2.00	1.00	.60
7	Al Lopez	2.00	1.00	.60
8	Lloyd Waner	2.00	1.00	.60
9	Bob Feller	2.00	1.00	.60
10	Guy Bush	2.00	1.00	.60
11	Stan Hack	2.00	1.00	.60
12	Zeke Bonura	2.00	1.00	.60
13	Wally Moses	2.00	1.00	.60
14	Fred Fitzsimmons	2.00	1.00	.60
15	Johnny Vander Meer	2.00	1.00	.60
16	Riggs Stephenson	2.00	1.00	.60
17	Bucky Walters	2.00	1.00	.60
18	Charlie Grimm	2.00	1.00	.60
19	Phil Cavarretta	2.00	1.00	.60
20	Wally Berger	2.00	1.00	.60
21	Joe Sewell	2.00	1.00	.60
22	Edd Roush	2.00	1.00	.60
23	Johnny Mize	2.00	1.00	.60
24	Bill Dickey	2.00	1.00	.60
25	Lou Boudreau	2.00	1.00	.60
26	Bill Terry	2.00	1.00	.60
27	Willie Kamm	2.00	1.00	.60
28	Charlie Gehringer	2.00	1.00	.60
29	Stan Coveleski	2.00	1.00	.60

30	Larry French	2.00	1.00	.60
31	George Kelly	2.00	1.00	.60
32	Terry Moore	2.00	1.00	.60
33	Billy Herman	2.00	1.00	.60
34	Babe Herman	2.00	1.00	.60
35	Carl Hubbell	2.00	1.00	.60
36	Buck Leonard	2.00	1.00	.60
37	Gus Suhr	2.00	1.00	.60
38	Burleigh Grimes	2.00	1.00	.60
39	Al Fonseca	2.00	1.00	.60
40	Travis Jackson	2.00	1.00	.60
41	Enos Slaughter	2.00	1.00	.60
42	Fred Lindstrom	2.00	1.00	.60
43	Rick Ferrell	2.00	1.00	.60
44	Cookie Lavagetto	2.00	1.00	.60
45	Stan Musial	12.00	6.00	3.50
46	Hal Trosky	2.00	1.00	.60
47	Hal Newhouser	2.00	1.00	.60
48	Paul Dean	2.00	1.00	.60
49	George Halas	6.00	3.00	1.75
50	Jocko Conlan	2.00	1.00	.60
51	Joe DiMaggio	30.00	15.00	9.00
52	Bobby Doerr	2.00	1.00	.60
53	Carl Reynolds	2.00	1.00	.60
54	Pete Reiser	2.00	1.00	.60
55	Frank McCormick	2.00	1.00	.60
56	Mel Harder	2.00	1.00	.60
57	George Uhle	2.00	1.00	.60
58	Doc Cramer	2.00	1.00	.60
59	Taylor Douthit	2.00	1.00	.60
60	Cecil Travis	2.00	1.00	.60
61	James Bell	2.00	1.00	.60
62	Charlie Keller	2.00	1.00	.60
63	Bill Hallahan	2.00	1.00	.60
64	Debs Garms	2.00	1.00	.60
65	Rube Marquard	2.00	1.00	.60
66	Rube Walberg	2.00	1.00	.60
67	Augie Galan	2.00	1.00	.60
68	George Pipgras	2.00	1.00	.60
69	Hal Schumacher	2.00	1.00	.60
70	Dolf Camilli	2.00	1.00	.60
71	Paul Richards	2.00	1.00	.60
72	Judy Johnson	2.00	1.00	.60
73	Frank Crosetti	2.00	1.00	.60
74	Harry Lowery	2.00	1.00	.60
75	Walter Alston	2.00	1.00	.60
76	Dutch Leonard	2.00	1.00	.60
77	Barney McCosky	2.00	1.00	.60
78	Joe Dobson	2.00	1.00	.60
79	George Kell	2.00	1.00	.60
80	Ted Lyons	2.00	1.00	.60
81	Johnny Pesky	2.00	1.00	.60
82	Hank Borowy	2.00	1.00	.60
83	Ewell Blackwell	2.00	1.00	.60
84	Pee Wee Reese	12.00	6.00	3.50
85	Monte Irvin	2.00	1.00	.60
86	Joe Moore	2.00	1.00	.60
87	Joe Wood	2.00	1.00	.60
88	Babe Dahlgren	2.00	1.00	.60
89	Bibb Falk	2.00	1.00	.60
90	Ed Lopat	2.00	1.00	.60
91	Rip Sewell	2.00	1.00	.60
92	Marty Marion	2.00	1.00	.60
93	Taft Wright	2.00	1.00	.60
94	Allie Reynolds	2.00	1.00	.60
95	Harry Walker	2.00	1.00	.60
96	Tex Hughson	2.00	1.00	.60
97	George Selkirk	2.00	1.00	.60
98	Dom DiMaggio	10.00	5.00	3.00
99	Walker Cooper	2.00	1.00	.60
100	Phil Rizzuto	10.00	5.00	3.00
101	Robin Roberts	2.00	1.00	.60
102	Joe Adcock	2.00	1.00	.60
103	Hank Bauer	2.00	1.00	.60
104	Frank Baumholtz	2.00	1.00	.60
105	Ray Boone	2.00	1.00	.60
106	Smoky Burgess	2.00	1.00	.60
107	Walt Dropo	2.00	1.00	.60
108	Alvin Dark	2.00	1.00	.60
109	Carl Erskine	2.00	1.00	.60
110	Dick Donovan	2.00	1.00	.60
111	Dee Fondy	2.00	1.00	.60
112	Mike Garcia	2.00	1.00	.60
113	Bob Friend	2.00	1.00	.60
114	Ned Garver	2.00	1.00	.60
115	Billy Goodman	2.00	1.00	.60
116	Larry Jansen	2.00	1.00	.60
117	Jackie Jensen	2.00	1.00	.60
118	John Antonelli	2.00	1.00	.60
119	Ted Kluszewski	2.00	1.00	.60
120	Harvey Kuenn	2.00	1.00	.60
121	Clem Labine	2.00	1.00	.60
122	Red Schoendienst	2.00	1.00	.60
123	Don Larsen	2.00	1.00	.60
124	Vern Law	2.00	1.00	.60
125	Charlie Maxwell	2.00	1.00	.60
126	Wally Moon	2.00	1.00	.60
127	Bob Nieman	2.00	1.00	.60

		NM	E	VG
128	Don Newcombe	2.00	1.00	.60
129	Wally Post	2.00	1.00	.60
130	Johnny Podres	2.00	1.00	.60
131	Vic Raschi	2.00	1.00	.60
132	Dusty Rhodes	2.00	1.00	.60
133	Jim Rivera	2.00	1.00	.60
134	Pete Runnels	2.00	1.00	.60
135	Hank Sauer	2.00	1.00	.60
136	Roy Sievers	2.00	1.00	.60
137	Bobby Shantz	2.00	1.00	.60
138	Curt Simmons	2.00	1.00	.60
139	Bob Skinner	2.00	1.00	.60
140	Bill Skowron	2.00	1.00	.60
141	Warren Spahn	2.00	1.00	.60
142	Gerry Staley	2.00	1.00	.60
143	Frank Thomas	2.00	1.00	.60
144	Bobby Thomson	2.00	1.00	.60
145	Bob Turley	2.00	1.00	.60
146	Vic Wertz	2.00	1.00	.60
147	Bill Virdon	2.00	1.00	.60
148	Gene Woodling	2.00	1.00	.60
149	Eddie Yost	2.00	1.00	.60
150	Sandy Koufax	25.00	12.50	7.50
151	Lefty Gomez	2.00	1.00	.60
152	Al Rosen	2.00	1.00	.60
153	Vince DiMaggio	2.00	1.00	.60
154	Bill Nicholson	2.00	1.00	.60
155	Mark Koenig	2.00	1.00	.60
156	Max Lanier	2.00	1.00	.60
157	Ken Keltner	2.00	1.00	.60
158	Whit Wyatt	2.00	1.00	.60
159	Marv Owen	2.00	1.00	.60
160	Red Lucas	2.00	1.00	.60
161	Babe Phelps	2.00	1.00	.60
162	Pete Donohue	2.00	1.00	.60
163	Johnny Cooney	2.00	1.00	.60
164	Glenn Wright	2.00	1.00	.60
165	Willis Hudlin	2.00	1.00	.60
166	Tony Cuccinello	2.00	1.00	.60
167	Bill Bevens	2.00	1.00	.60
168	Dave Ferris	2.00	1.00	.60
169	Whitey Kurowski	2.00	1.00	.60
170	Buddy Hassett	2.00	1.00	.60
171	Ossie Bluege	2.00	1.00	.60
172	Hoot Evers	2.00	1.00	.60
173	Thornton Lee	2.00	1.00	.60
174	Virgil Davis	2.00	1.00	.60
175	Bob Shawkey	2.00	1.00	.60
176	Smead Jolley	2.00	1.00	.60
177	Andy High	2.00	1.00	.60
178	George McQuinn	2.00	1.00	.60
179	Mickey Vernon	2.00	1.00	.60
180	Birdie Tebbetts	2.00	1.00	.60
181	Jack Kramer	2.00	1.00	.60
182	Don Kolloway	2.00	1.00	.60
183	Claude Passeau	2.00	1.00	.60
184	Frank Shea	2.00	1.00	.60
185	Bob O'Farrell	2.00	1.00	.60
186	Bob Johnson	2.00	1.00	.60
187	Ival Goodman	2.00	1.00	.60
188	Mike Kreevich	2.00	1.00	.60
189	Joe Stripp	2.00	1.00	.60
190	Mickey Owen	2.00	1.00	.60
191	Hughie Critz	2.00	1.00	.60
192	Ethan Allen	2.00	1.00	.60
193	Billy Rogell	2.00	1.00	.60
194	Joe Kuhel	2.00	1.00	.60
195	Dale Mitchell	2.00	1.00	.60
196	Eldon Auker	2.00	1.00	.60
197	Johnny Beazley	2.00	1.00	.60
198	Spud Chandler	2.00	1.00	.60
199	Ralph Branca	2.00	1.00	.60
200	Joe Cronin	2.00	1.00	.60

1957-58 Graphics Arts Service Detroit Tigers Postcards

This series of Tigers postcards was issued over a two-year span by a Cincinnati printer. The 3-3/16" x 5-7/16" cards have a black-and-white borderless player photo on front with or without a facsimile autograph. Backs have standard postcard indicia, including the producer's name and address.

		NM	E	VG
Complete Set (22):		1,500	750.00	450.00
Common Player:		60.00	30.00	18.00
(1)	Al Aber	60.00	30.00	18.00
(2)	Hank Aguirre	60.00	30.00	18.00
(3)	Reno Bertoia (Fielding)	60.00	30.00	18.00
(4)	Reno Bertoia (Portrait)	60.00	30.00	18.00
(5)	Frank Bolling	60.00	30.00	18.00
(6)	Jim Bunning	120.00	60.00	35.00
(7)	Jack Dittmer	60.00	30.00	18.00
(8)	Paul Foytack	60.00	30.00	18.00
(9)	Jim Hegan	60.00	30.00	18.00
(10)	Tommy Henrich	80.00	40.00	24.00
(11)	Billy Hoeft	60.00	30.00	18.00
(12)	Frank House	60.00	30.00	18.00
(13)	Al Kaline	180.00	90.00	55.00
(14)	Harvey Kuenn	80.00	40.00	24.00
(15)	Don Lee	60.00	30.00	18.00
(16)	Billy Martin	90.00	45.00	25.00
(17)	Tom Morgan	60.00	30.00	18.00
(18)	J.W. Porter	60.00	30.00	18.00
(19)	Ron Samford	60.00	30.00	18.00
(20)	Bob Shaw	60.00	30.00	18.00
(21)	Lou Sleater	60.00	30.00	18.00
(22)	Tim Thompson	60.00	30.00	18.00

1888 Gray Studio Cabinets

The posed action photos on the approximately 4-1/4" x 6-1/2" cards are the same pictures seen on many of the players' Old Judge and Old Judge cabinet cards. Gray cabinets are found with two fancy logotypes at lower-left. On one, the tail of the "y" underscores the "Gra," while on the other, fancy decorations bookend the studio name. The Boston address of the studio is at lower-right. Players are not identified on the cards, and the backs are blank.

		NM	E	VG
Common Player:		1,500	700.00	450.00
(1)	Charlie Buffinton (Batting)	1,500	700.00	450.00
(2)	Charlie Buffinton (Right arm forward.)	1,500	700.00	450.00
(3)	Dan Casey (Arms at sides.)	1,500	700.00	450.00
(4)	Dan Casey (Ball in hands at chest.)	1,500	700.00	450.00
(5)	Dan Casey (Left arm outstretched.)	1,500	700.00	450.00
(6)	Jack Clements (Batting)	1,500	700.00	450.00
(7)	Jack Clements (Fielding, hands chest-high.)	1,500	700.00	450.00
(8)	Jack Clements (Hands on knees.)	1,500	700.00	450.00
(12)	Ed Daily (Batting)	1,500	700.00	450.00
(13)	Ed Daily (Holding ball in front of face.)	1,500	700.00	450.00
(14)	Ed Daily (Throwing)	1,500	700.00	450.00
(16)	Sid Farrar (Arms crossed.)	1,500	700.00	450.00
(17)	Sid Farrar (Fielding grounder.)	1,500	700.00	450.00
(18)	Sid Farrar (Fielding fly ball.)	1,500	700.00	450.00
(19)	Sid Farrar (Right hand on belt buckle.)	1,500	700.00	450.00
(21)	Charlie Ferguson (Ball in hands at chest.)	1,500	700.00	450.00
(22)	Charlie Ferguson (Batting)	1,500	700.00	450.00
(23)	Charlie Ferguson (Tagging Tommy McCarthy.)	1,800	900.00	550.00
(24)	Charlie Ferguson (Throwing, right arm back.)	1,500	700.00	450.00
(26)	Jim Fogarty (Batting)	1,500	700.00	450.00
(27)	Jim Fogarty (Fielding grounder.)	1,500	700.00	450.00
(28)	Jim Fogarty (Fielding, hands at neck.)	1,500	700.00	450.00
(29)	Jim Fogarty (Fielding on the run.)	1,500	700.00	450.00
(32)	Tom Gunning (Fielding, hands at knees.)	1,500	700.00	450.00
(33)	Arthur Irwin (Batting)	1,500	700.00	450.00
(34)	Arthur Irwin (Fielding, hands chest-high.)	1,500	700.00	450.00
(35)	Arthur Irwin (Throwing)	1,500	700.00	450.00
(39)	Tommy McCarthy (Batting)	3,000	1,500	900.00
(40)	Tommy McCarthy (Fielding, hands chest-high.)	3,000	1,500	900.00
(41)	Tommy McCarthy (Tagging baserunner.)	3,000	1,500	900.00
(42)	Tommy McCarthy (Throwing)	3,000	1,500	900.00
(44)	Deacon McGuire (Batting)	1,500	700.00	450.00
(45)	Deacon McGuire (Fielding, hands chest-high.)	1,500	700.00	450.00
(48)	Joe Mulvey (Batting)	1,500	700.00	450.00
(49)	Joe Mulvey (Fielding, hands at waist.)	1,500	700.00	450.00
(50)	Joe Mulvey (Watching ball.)	1,500	700.00	450.00
(60)	George Wood (Batting)	1,500	700.00	450.00
(61)	George Wood (Fielding fly ball.)	1,500	700.00	450.00
(62)	George Wood (Fielding grounder.)	1,500	700.00	450.00
(63)	George Wood (Throwing)	1,500	700.00	450.00

1975-76 Great Plains Greats

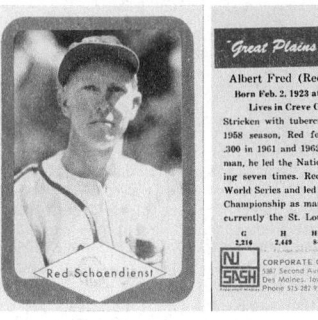

This collectors' issue was issued in two series in conjunction with shows conducted by the Great Plains Sports Collectors Association. Cards are about 2-5/8" x 3-3/4". Fronts have black-and-white photos with heavy colored frames and white borders. Player name is overprinted on a diamond at bottom. Backs have a career summary and stats, and a sponsor's ad. The 1975 issue (#1-24) was sponsored by Sheraton Inns; the 1976 cards (#25-42) were sponsored by Nu-Sash Corp.

		NM	E	VG
Complete Set (43):		20.00	10.00	6.00
Common Player:		1.00	.50	.30
1	Bob Feller	2.00	1.00	.60
2	Carl Hubbell	1.00	.50	.30
3	Jocko Conlan	1.00	.50	.30
4	Hal Trosky	1.00	.50	.30
5	Allie Reynolds	1.00	.50	.30
6	Burleigh Grimes	1.00	.50	.30
7	Jake Beckley	1.00	.50	.30
8	Al Simmons	1.00	.50	.30
9	Paul Waner	1.00	.50	.30
10	Chief Bender	1.00	.50	.30
11	Fred Clarke	1.00	.50	.30
12	Jim Bottomley	1.00	.50	.30
13	Dave Bancroft	1.00	.50	.30
14	Bing Miller	1.00	.50	.30
15	Walter Johnson	2.50	1.25	.70
16	Grover Alexander	2.50	1.25	.70
17	Bob Johnson	1.00	.50	.30
18	Roger Maris	2.50	1.25	.70
19	Ken Keltner	1.00	.50	.30
20	Red Faber	1.00	.50	.30
21	"Cool Papa" Bell	1.00	.50	.30
22	Yogi Berra	2.50	1.25	.70
23	Fred Lindstrom	1.00	.50	.30
24	Ray Schalk	1.00	.50	.30
---	Checklist	.10	.05	.03
25	Lloyd Waner	1.00	.50	.30
26	Johnny Hopp	1.00	.50	.30
27	Mel Harder	1.00	.50	.30
28	Dutch Leonard	1.00	.50	.30
29	Bob O'Farrell	1.00	.50	.30
30	Cap Anson	1.00	.50	.30
31	Dazzy Vance	1.00	.50	.30
32	Red Schoendienst	1.00	.50	.30
33	George Pipgras	1.00	.50	.30
34	Harvey Kuenn	1.00	.50	.30
35	Red Ruffing	1.00	.50	.30
36	Roy Sievers	1.00	.50	.30
37	Ken Boyer	1.00	.50	.30
38	Al Smith	1.00	.50	.30
39	Casey Stengel	1.00	.50	.30
40	Bob Gibson	1.50	.70	.45
41	Mickey Mantle	10.00	5.00	3.00
42	Denny McLain	1.00	.50	.30

1908-1909 Greenfield's Chocolates Postcards

These special advertising versions of the Rose Co. post-cards were produced circa 1908-09. The 3-1/2" x 5-1/2" cards feature a black-and-white player portrait photo at center, surrounded by an embossed round gold frame. The player's surname and (usually) team are in a white panel under the photo. The background is green and includes crossed bats and a baseball, a diamond diagram and pictures of a fielder and batter. The postcard-format back is printed in black-and-white with a TRC logo at bottom-center. Printed at left in ornate typography is advertising for the New York confectioner. Two back styles are known apparently the result of the candy company's move from Fifth Ave. to Barclay St. (or vice versa) during the issuing period. It is unknown how many of the player postcards in the Rose Co. series can be found with this advertising on back. (See 1908-1909 Rose Company Postcards for checklist and base values.)

PREMIUM: 3-5X

(See 1908-1909 Rose Company Postcards for checklist and base values.)

1916 Green-Joyce

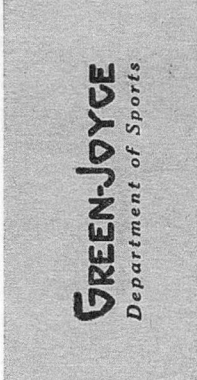

BOB BESCHER
L. F.—St. Louis Cardinals.
15

Best known for its use as a promotional medium for The Sporting News, this 200-card set can be found with blank backs or with ads on the back for several local and regional businesses. Among them is Green-Joyce "Department of Sports, " location Columbus, OH. Type-card and superstar collectors can expect to pay a premiu, for individual cards with Green- Joyce advertising as opposed to the more common M101-4 blank-back values. Cards measure 1-5/8" x 3" and are printed in black-and-white.

(See 1916 M101-4 Blank Backs for checklist and base values.)

1928 Greiners Bread

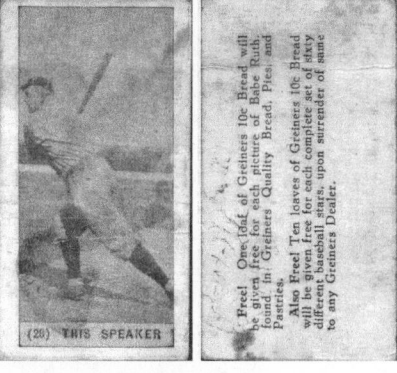

(26) THIS SPEAKER

This set of approximately 1-3/8" x 2-1/2" black-and-white cards appears to parallel the strip card set cataloged as 1928 W502. The difference lies in the advertising that appears on the back of this version for the bakery products. The location of Greiners bakery is unknown.

Common Player: (Value undetermined)
Stars: (Value undetermined)

1969 Greiner Tires Pittsburgh Pirates

One of the scarcer of the many Pirates regionals of the late 1960s is this eight-card issue. Printed on heavy paper in black-and-white, the 5-1/2" x 8-1/2" cards are blank-backed and unnumbered. They are checklisted here alphabetically. Some sources say the Matty Alou card is scarcer than the rest of the set.

		NM	E	VG
Complete Set (8):		80.00	40.00	24.00
Common Player:		4.50	2.25	1.25
(1)	Gene Alley	4.50	2.25	1.25
(2)	Matty Alou	30.00	15.00	9.00
(3)	Steve Blass	4.50	2.25	1.25
(4)	Roberto Clemente	30.00	15.00	9.00
(5)	Jerry May	4.50	2.25	1.25
(6)	Bill Mazeroski	12.50	6.25	3.75
(7)	Larry Shepard	4.50	2.25	1.25
(8)	Willie Stargell	12.50	6.25	3.75

1974 Greyhound Heroes on the Base Paths

The first of three annual baseball card folders honoring the stolen base leaders and runners-up in each league, this 20" x 9" five-panel sheet features six 4" x 3" cards printed in black-and-white with sepia graphics. Backs are printed in black, brown and white. Besides the cards, the folder contains information about the bus company's award, as well as major league stolen base records and base-stealing tips. Besides individual cards of the 1974 winner and runner-up in each league, the folder has cards picturing all winners and runners-up since 1965.

		NM	E	VG
Complete Set, Folder:		10.00	5.00	3.00
Complete Set, Singles:		8.00	4.00	2.50
Common Player:		2.00	1.00	.60
(1)	Lou Brock	4.00	2.00	1.25
(2)	Rod Carew	4.00	2.00	1.25
(3)	Davey Lopes	2.00	1.00	.60
(4)	Bill North	2.00	1.00	.60

(5)	A.L. Winners/Runners-Up(Don Buford, Bert Campaneris, Rod Carew, Tommy Harper, Dave Nelson, Bill North, Amos Otis, Fred Patek)	2.00	1.00	.60
(6)	N.L. Winners/Runners-Up(Lou Brock, Jose Cardenal, Sonny Jackson, Davey Lopes, Joe Morgan, Bobby Tolan, Maury Wills)	2.00	1.00	.60

1975 Greyhound Heroes on the Base Paths

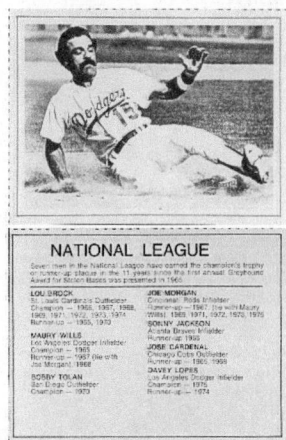

Six perforated 3-7/8" x 3" cards are featured on this folded five-panel 20" x 9" sheet honoring top base stealers in both leagues for the 1975 season. Four of the cards have each league's SB leader and runner-up in a black-and-white portrait photo with blue background. Backs are printed in black, blue and white and include major league stats. There are also two action photo cards with lists on the back of each year's winner and runner-up for the Greyhound Stolen Base Awards since 1965.

		NM	E	VG
Complete Set, Folder:		7.00	3.50	2.00
Complete Set, Singles:		4.00	2.00	1.25
Common Player:		1.50	.70	.45
(1)	Davey Lopes	1.50	.70	.45
(2)	Davey Lopes (Action)	1.50	.70	.45
(3)	Joe Morgan	2.50	1.25	.70
(4)	Bill North (Action)	1.50	.70	.45
(5)	Mickey Rivers	1.50	.70	.45
(6)	Claudell Washington	1.50	.70	.45

1976 Greyhound Heroes on the Base Paths

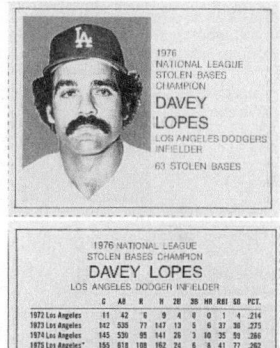

The last of three annual baseball card folders honoring the stolen base leaders and runners-up in each league, this 20" x 9" five-panel sheet features six 4" x 3" cards printed in black-and-white with sepia graphics. Backs are printed in black, brown and white. Besides the cards, the folder contains information about the bus company's award, as well as major league stolen base records and base-stealing tips. Besides individual cards of the 1974 winner and runner-up in each league, the folder includes two action-photo cards listing all winners and runners-up since 1965.

	NM	E	VG
Complete Set, Folder:	6.00	3.00	1.75
Complete Set, Singles:	5.00	2.50	1.50
Common Player:	1.50	.70	.45
(1) Ronald Le Flore	1.50	.70	.45
(2) Davey Lopes	1.50	.70	.45
(3) Davey Lopes (Action)	1.50	.70	.45
(4) Joe Morgan	3.00	1.50	.90
(5) Bill North	1.50	.70	.45
(6) Bill North (Action)	1.50	.70	.45

1907 Grignon Chicago Cubs Postcards

The eventual 1907 World Champion Cubs are featured in this set of novelty postcards. Fronts of the 3-1/2" x 5-1/2" horizontal cards have a green background with white border. The central figure on each is a teddy bear in a baseball pose. In an upper corner is a black-and-white circular portrait of one of the Cubs, with identification below. A line of infield chatter - i.e., "This is a Cinch" - completes the design. Backs have standard postcard markings and some have been seen with advertising for local businesses. The unnumbered cards are checklisted here alphabetically.

	NM	E	VG
Complete Set (16):	14,500	7,250	4,350
Common Player:	900.00	450.00	270.00
(1) Mordecai Brown	1,600	800.00	480.00
(2) Frank Chance	1,600	800.00	480.00
(3) John Evers	1,600	800.00	480.00
(4) Arthur Hofman	900.00	450.00	270.00
(5) John Kling	900.00	450.00	270.00
(6) Carl Lundgren	900.00	450.00	270.00
(7) Pat Moran	900.00	450.00	270.00
(8) Orvie Overall	900.00	450.00	270.00
(9) Jack Pfeister	900.00	450.00	270.00
(10) Ed Reulbach	900.00	450.00	270.00
(11) Frank Schulte	900.00	450.00	270.00
(12) James Sheckard	900.00	450.00	270.00
(13) James Slagle	900.00	450.00	270.00
(14) Harry Steinfeldt	900.00	450.00	270.00
(15) Jack Taylor	900.00	450.00	270.00
(16) Joe Tinker	1,600	800.00	480.00

"1959-60" Gulf Oil Corp.

These fantasy/fraud cards were first reported in the hobby in 1999, though the copyright line on back purports to date them from 1959-1960. Two types of cards were produced, one series of eight featuring line-art portraits, the other featuring re-screened photos taken from team photo packs and similar sources. Cards are 2-1/2" x 3-1/2" printed in black-and-white. The unnumbered cards are checklisted here alphabetically within series. Because the cards were illegally produced in violation of player rights and team copyrights, no collector value is attributed.

	NM	E	VG
Complete Set (16):			
Complete Set (16):			
	Artwork Series		
(1)	Ty Cobb		
(2)	Bill Dickey		
(3)	Joe DiMaggio		
(4)	Lou Gehrig		
(5)	Rogers Hornsby		
(6)	Walter Johnson		
(7)	Babe Ruth		
(8)	Pie Traynor		
	Photo Series		
(1)	Don Drysdale		
(2)	Bob Gibson		
(3)	Sandy Koufax		
(4)	Mickey Mantle		
(5)	Roger Maris		
(6)	Willie Mays		
(7)	Willie McCovey		
(8)	Stan Musial		

1956 Gum Products Adventure

This series of 100 cards depicts all manner of action and adventure scenes, including several sports subjects, one of which is a baseball player. The card depicts Boston U. quarterback and Boston Red Sox prospect Harry Agganis, who died unexpectedly in 1955. The 3-1/2" x 2-1/2" horizontal card has a central portrait artwork of Agganis as a Red Sox, surrounded by other scenes from his personal and sporting life. The black-and-white back has a short biography.

	NM	E	VG
55 Harry Agganis (Boston's Golden Greek)	25.00	12.50	7.50

1948 Gunther Beer Washington Senators Postcards

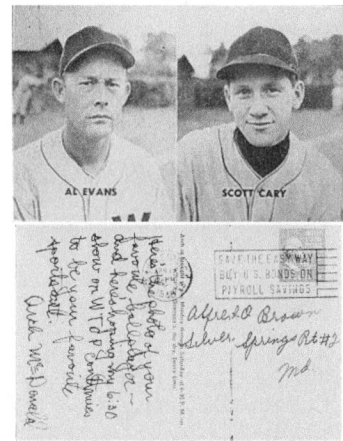

These postcards were apparently made available by writing to the radio voice of the Senators, Arch McDonald. A pre-printed message on the left side of the back urges the fan to keep listening to McDonald's program, sponsored by "Gunther's, the dry, beery beer." The black-and-white cards measure 3-1/2" x 5-1/2" and feature portrait photos of the Washington players. Most cards have two players side-by-side while manager Joe Kuhel has his own card. Player names are in heavy black letters across their chests. The cards are unnumbered and it is possible others will surface.

	NM	E	VG
Complete Set (13):	3,500	1,750	1,050
Common Card:	285.00	140.00	85.00
(1) Joe Kuhel	285.00	140.00	85.00
(2) Gil Coan, Mickey Vernon	285.00	140.00	85.00
(3) Mark Christman, Clarence Difani	285.00	140.00	85.00
(4) Al Evans, Scott Cary	285.00	140.00	85.00
(5) Tom Ferrick, Harold Keller	285.00	140.00	85.00
(6) Mickey Haefner, Forrest Thompson	285.00	140.00	85.00
(7) Sid Hudson, Al Kozar	285.00	140.00	85.00
(7) Sid Hudson, Al Kozar	285.00	140.00	85.00
(8) Walter Masterson, Rick Ferrell	600.00	300.00	180.00
(10) Marino Pieretti, Leon Culberson	285.00	140.00	85.00
(11) Sherrard Robertson, Eddie Lyons	285.00	140.00	85.00

		NM	E	VG
(12)	Ray Scarborough, Kenneth McCreight	285.00	140.00	85.00
(13)	Early Wynn, Eddie Yost	850.00	420.00	250.00

1923-1924 Tomas Gutierrez

The largest of the Cuban baseball card issues of the 1920s, this is also one of the scarcest and most popular. Printed in dark brown (some backs are in black) on sepia paper, the 1-5/8" x 2-3/8" cards were inserted into packs of Diaz cigarettes. Cards have portrait photos on front with team name at top and the player name (sometimes misspelled and sometimes a nickname) and position below. Backs, which can be found in three styles, have the card number and an offer for an album. It is the album offer which accounts for much of this issue's scarcity. The album was a hardcover, ornate book with pictures of each card pre-printed. It is believed that the album was available by turning in a complete set of the cards, which were not returned. Adding to the set's popularity is its inclusion of many Negro Leagues players including future Hall of Famers Oscar Charleston and Pop Lloyd. Following the checklist are the names of cards known to exist from their presence in the album, but whose number is unknown.

		NM	E	VG
Complete Set (85): VALUE UNDETERMINED				
Common Player:		350.00	140.00	70.00
Album:		4,500	2,250	1,350
	SANTA CLARA			
1	(Agustin) "Tinti" Molina	350.00	140.00	70.00
2	Julio Rojo	450.00	180.00	90.00
3	Frank Duncan	1,750	700.00	350.00
4	Eustaquio "Bombin" Pedroso	2,250	900.00	450.00
5	Dave Brown	2,250	900.00	450.00
6	Pedro Dibut	450.00	180.00	90.00
7	Rube Currie	1,750	700.00	350.00
8	Jose Mendez	6,000	2,400	1,200
9	Esteban "Mayari" Montalvo	850.00	340.00	170.00
10	Frank Warfield	1,750	700.00	350.00
11	Oliver Marcelle	2,250	900.00	450.00
12	Dobie Moore	1,750	700.00	350.00
13	Herman Matias Rios	350.00	140.00	70.00
14	Oscar Charleston	30,000	15,000	9,000
15	Alejandro Oms	2,250	900.00	450.00
16	Pablo "Champion" Mesa	850.00	340.00	170.00
17	Bill Holland	2,250	900.00	450.00
18	Oscar "Heavy" Johnson	2,250	900.00	450.00
	ALMENDARES			
19	Eugenio Morin	350.00	140.00	70.00
20	Snake Henry	350.00	140.00	70.00
21	Manuel Cueto	350.00	140.00	70.00
22	Jesse Hubbard	850.00	340.00	170.00
23	Kakin Gonzalez	350.00	140.00	70.00
24	Jose Maria Fernandez	350.00	140.00	70.00
25	Oscar Rodriguez	350.00	140.00	70.00
26	Lucas Boada	350.00	140.00	70.00
27	Eusebio "Papo" Gonzalez	350.00	140.00	70.00
28	Ramon "Paito" Herrera	350.00	140.00	70.00
29	Bernardo Baro	850.00	340.00	170.00
30	Armando Marsans	1,200	480.00	240.00
31	Isidro Fabre	850.00	340.00	170.00
32	Oscar Fuhr	350.00	140.00	70.00
33	Valentin Dreke	850.00	340.00	170.00
34	Joseito Rodriguez	350.00	140.00	70.00
35	Jose "Cheo" Ramos	350.00	140.00	70.00
36	Willis "Pud" Flournoy	1,200	480.00	240.00
37	Oscar Tuero	350.00	140.00	70.00
38	Rafael Almeida	850.00	340.00	170.00
40	Chuck Dressen	60.00	300.00	180.00
39	Almendares Pennant	350.00	140.00	70.00
	MARIANAO			
41	Don Brown	350.00	140.00	70.00
42	Merito Acosta	350.00	140.00	70.00
43	(Ed) Morris	350.00	140.00	70.00
44	Ernie Krueger	350.00	140.00	70.00
45	Pepin Perez	350.00	140.00	70.00

		NM	E	VG
46	(Harry) McCurdy	350.00	140.00	70.00
47	Jose "Acostica" Acosta	350.00	140.00	70.00
48	Jacinto Calvo	350.00	140.00	70.00
49	(Eddie) Brown	350.00	140.00	70.00
50	(Rosy) Ryan	350.00	140.00	70.00
51	Rogelio Crespo	350.00	140.00	70.00
52	Hank Deberry	350.00	140.00	70.00
53	(Art) Phelan	350.00	140.00	70.00
54	Jess Petty	500.00	250.00	150.00
55	(Jimmy) Cooney	350.00	140.00	70.00
58	Maianaro Pennant	350.00	140.00	70.00
59	Bienvenido	350.00	140.00	70.00
56a	H. Scheiber (Hank Schreiber) (Infilllder)	350.00	140.00	70.00
56b	H. Scheiber (Hank Schreiber) (Infilllder)	350.00	140.00	70.00
57	E. Palmero	350.00	140.00	70.00
---	Otis Brannan	350.00	140.00	70.00
---	Emilio Palmero	350.00	140.00	70.00

HAVANA

		NM	E	VG
60	Buste Ross	350.00	140.00	70.00
61	Juanelo Mirabal	350.00	140.00	70.00
62	Cristobal Torriente	17,500	7,000	3,500
63	John Henry "Pop" Lloyd	30,000	15,000	9,000
64	Oscar Levis	700.00	280.00	140.00
65	Pelayo Chacon	850.00	340.00	170.00
66	Eufemio Abreu	350.00	140.00	70.00
67	Mack Eggleston	850.00	340.00	170.00
68	(Tauca "Manzanillo") Campos	350.00	140.00	70.00
69	Raphael "Busta" Quintana	350.00	140.00	70.00
70	Merven "Red" Ryan	850.00	340.00	170.00
71	(Danny) Clark	350.00	140.00	70.00
72	Clint Thomas	1,000	400.00	200.00
73	Adolfo Luque	1,200	480.00	240.00
74	Marcelino Guerra	350.00	140.00	70.00
75	Bartolo Portuondo	850.00	340.00	170.00
76	Andy Cooper	8,000	4,000	2,400
77	(John) Bischoff	350.00	140.00	70.00
78	Edgar Wesley	1,750	700.00	350.00
79	Havana Pennant	350.00	140.00	70.00
---	Jacinto Calvo	300.00	120.00	60.00

MISCELLANEOUS

		NM	E	VG
80	Hector Magrinat (Umpire)	350.00	140.00	70.00
81	Valentin "Sirique" Gonzalez (Umpire)	350.00	140.00	70.00
82	Slim Love (Marianao)	350.00	140.00	70.00
83	Cristobal Torriente (Marianao)	22,500	11,2500.00	6,750
84				
85	Jakie May (Almendares)	450.00	180.00	90.00

1887 Gypsy Queen (N175)

The 1887 Gypsy Queen set is very closely related to the N172 Old Judge set and employs the same photos. Gypsy Queens are easily identified by the advertising along the top. A line near the bottom lists the player's name, position and team, followed by an 1887 copyright line and words "Cigarettes" and "Goodwin & Co. N.Y." Although the checklist is still considered incomplete, some 140 different poses have been discovered so far. Gypsy Queens were issued in two distinct sizes, the more common version measuring 1-1/2" x 2-1/2" (same as Old Judge) and a larger size measuring 2" x 3-1/2" which are considered extremely rare. The large Gypsy Queens are identical in format to the smaller size; the nine known examples are designated here.

		NM	E	VG
Common Player:		4,500	2,225	1,200
(13 1)	J. (Tug) Arundel (Fielding)	4,500	2,225	1,200
(13 2)	J. (Tug) Arundel (Battling)	4,500	2,225	1,200
(17)	Mark Baldwin	4,500	2,225	1,200

		NM	E	VG
(19 1)	Sam Barkley (Fielding)	4,500	2,225	1,200
(19 2)	Sam Barkley (Tagging player.)	4,500	2,225	1,200
(19 3)	Sam Barkley (Throwing)	4,500	2,225	1,200
(35)	Henry Boyle (Right arm outstretched.)	4,500	2,225	1,200
(43 1)	Dan Brouthers (Looking at ball.)	9,000	4,500	2,700
(43 2)	Dan Brouthers (Looking to right.)	9,000	4,500	2,700
(44 1)	Tom Brown (Pittsburgh, bat at side.)	4,500	2,225	1,200
(44 2)	Tom Brown (Pittsburgh, catching.)	4,500	2,225	1,200
(45L)	Willard (California) Brown (N.Y., large, throwing.)	20,000	10,000	6,000
(45 1)	Willard (California) Brown (N.Y., throwing.)	4,500	2,225	1,200
(45 2)	Willard (California) Brown (N.Y., wearing mask.)	4,750	2,375	1,425
(50)	Charlie Buffington (Buffinton) (Bat at 45 degrees.)	4,500	2,225	1,200
(51)	Ernie Burch (Fielding, hands above head, outdoors.)	5,500	2,750	1,650
(53)	Jack Burdock (Fielding grounder.)	4,500	2,225	1,200
(55)	Watch Burnham	4,500	2,225	1,200
(59)	Tom Burns	4,500	2,225	1,200
(60)	Doc Bushong (Brown's Champions)	6,500	3,250	1,950
(61)	John (Patsy) Cahill	4,500	2,225	1,200
(68)	Fred Carroll (Bat at side.)	4,500	2,225	1,200
(71)	Bob Caruthers	4,500	2,225	1,200
(72 1)	Dan Casey (Hands at chest.)	4,500	2,225	1,200
(72 2)	Dan Casey (Left arm extended.)	4,500	2,225	1,200
(79 1)	Jack Clements (Hands on knees.)	4,500	2,225	1,200
(79 2)	Jack Clements (With bat.)	4,500	2,225	1,200
(83)	John Coleman (Bat at side.)	4,500	2,225	1,200
(86)	Charlie Comiskey	9,000	4,500	2,750
(88 1)	Roger Connor ((Hands on knees.))	30,000	15,450	9,300
(88 2)	Roger Connor ((Bat at 45 degrees.))	9,000	4,500	2,700
(89)	Dick Conway	4,500	2,225	1,200
(94)	Larry Corcoran	4,500	2,225	1,200
(97 1)	Sam Crane (Fielding grounder.)	4,500	2,225	1,200
(97 2)	Sam Crane (With bat.)	4,500	2,225	1,200
(109)	Ed Dailey	4,500	2,225	1,200
(113)	Abner Dalrymple (Right arm cap-high.)	4,500	2,225	1,200
(117)	Dell Darling	4,500	2,225	1,200
(121 1)	Pat Dealey (Bat at side.)	4,500	2,225	1,200
(121 2)	Pat Dealey (Bat on shoulder.)	4,500	2,225	1,200
(125L)	Jerry Denny (Large, with bat.)	20,000	10,000	6,000
(125 1)	Jerry Denny (Catching)	4,500	2,225	1,200
(125 2)	Jerry Denny (With bat.)	4,500	2,225	1,200
(130)	Jim Donnelly (Bat at 45 degrees.)	4,500	2,225	1,200
(133)	Mike Dorgan (Arms crossed.)	4,500	2,225	1,200
(149L)	Buck Ewing (Large, catching fly ball.)	32,000	15,450	9,300
(149 1)	Buck Ewing (Bat at 45 degrees.)	9,000	4,500	2,700
(149 2)	Buck Ewing (Fielding fly ball.)	9,000	4,500	2,700
(149 3)	Buck Ewing (Fielding ground ball.)	9,000	4,500	2,700
(156 1)	Jack Farrell (Bat at side.)	4,500	2,225	1,200
(156 2)	Jack Farrell (Bat in air.)	4,500	2,225	1,200
(156 3)	Jack Farrell (Fielding)	4,500	2,225	1,200
(156 4)	Jack Farrell (Hands on thighs.)	4,500	2,225	1,200
(158 1)	Charlie Ferguson (Hands at chest.)	4,500	2,225	1,200
(158 2)	Charlie Ferguson (Right arm extended back.)	6,500	3,200	1,950
(158 3)	Charlie Ferguson (Tagging player.)	4,500	2,225	1,200
(158 4)	Charlie Ferguson (With bat.)	4,500	2,225	1,200
(161 1)	Jocko Fields (Catching)	4,500	2,225	1,200

		NM	E	VG
(161 2)	Jocko Fields (Tagging player.)	5,000	2,500	1,500
(161 3)	Jocko Fields (Throwing)	4,500	2,225	1,200
(167 1)	Jim Fogarty (Bat on shoulder.)	4,500	2,225	1,200
(167 2)	Jim Fogarty (Fielding fly ball.)	4,500	2,225	1,200
(171)	Dave Foutz (Brown's Champions)	6,500	3,250	1,950
(178)	John Gaffney (Bending to right.)	4,500	2,225	1,200
(181 1)	Pud Galvin (Leaning on bat.)	12,000	6,000	3,600
(181 2)	Pud Galvin (Without bat.)	12,000	6,000	3,600
(184 1)	Emil Geiss (Hands above waist.)	4,500	2,225	1,200
(184 2)	Emil Geiss (Right hand extended.)	4,500	2,225	1,200
(191 1)	Pete Gillespie (Fielding)	4,500	2,225	1,200
(191 2)	Pete Gillespie (With bat.)	4,500	2,225	1,200
(192)	Barney Gilligan	4,500	2,225	1,200
(194 1)	Jack Glasscock (Hands on knees.)	4,750	2,400	1,400
(194 2)	Jack Glasscock (Throwing)	4,750	2,400	1,400
(194 3)	Jack Glasscock (With bat.)	4,750	2,400	1,400
(195)	Bill Gleason (Brown's Champions)	6,500	3,250	1,950
(199 1)	George Gore (Fielding)	4,500	2,225	1,200
(199 2)	George Gore (Hand at head level.)	4,500	2,225	1,200
(202)	Ed Greer (Batting, outdoors.)	5,500	2,750	1,650
(207 1)	Tom Gunning (Stooping to catch low ball on left.)	4,500	2,225	1,200
(207 2)	Tom Gunning (Bending, hands by right knee.)	4,500	2,225	1,200
(215 1)	Ned Hanlon (Catching)	9,000	4,500	2,700
(215 2)	Ned Hanlon (Bat at 45 degrees.)	9,000	4,500	2,700
(218 1)	John Harkins (Hands above waist, outdoors.)	5,500	2,750	1,650
(218 2)	John Harkins (Throwing, outdoors.)	5,500	2,750	1,650
(223)	Egyptian Healey (Healy) (Batting)	4,500	2,225	1,200
(232)	Paul Hines (Hands at sides.)	4,500	2,225	1,200
(241)	Joe Horning (Hornung) (Bat at 45 degrees.)	4,500	2,225	1,200
(244)	Nat Hudson (Brown's Champions)	6,500	3,200	1,950
(248 1)	Arthur Irwin (Batting)	4,500	2,225	1,200
(248 2)	Arthur Irwin (Fielding, hands below knees.)	4,500	2,225	1,200
(253 1)	Dick Johnston (Catching)	4,500	2,225	1,200
(253 2)	Dick Johnston (With bat.)	4,500	2,225	1,200
(256L)	Tim Keefe (Large, ball in hands at chest.)	33,000	16,500	10,000
(256 1)	Tim Keefe (Ball in hands at chest.)	9,000	4,500	2,700
(256 2)	Tim Keefe (Hands above waist, facing front.)	9,000	4,500	2,700
(256 3)	Tim Keefe (Right hand extended at head level.)	9,000	4,500	2,700
(256 4)	Tim Keefe (With bat.)	9,000	4,500	2,700
(DP 13)	(Fielding Ball, Danny Richardson sliding. ("Keefe and Richardson Stealing 2d, N.Y.'s")	12,000	6,000	3,600
(261L)	King Kelly (Large, bat horizontal.)	55,000	27,000	16,500
(261 1)	King Kelly (Fielding, hands chest-high.)	18,000	9,000	5,400
(261 2)	King Kelly (Portrait)	18,000	9,000	5,400
(261 4)	King Kelly (With bat.)	12,500	6,250	3,750
(262)	Rudy Kemmler	4,500	2,225	1,200
(273 1)	Bill Krieg (Fielding thigh-high ball.)	4,500	2,225	1,200
(273 2)	Bill Krieg (With bat.)	4,500	2,225	1,200
(278)	Arlie Latham	4,500	2,225	1,200
(302 1)	Mike Mattimore (Hands above head.)	4,500	2,225	1,200
(302 2)	Mike Mattimore (Hands at neck.)	4,500	2,225	1,200
(302 3)	Mike Mattimore (Sliding)	4,500	2,225	1,200
(307 1)	Tommy McCarthy (Catching)	9,000	4,500	2,700

(307 2)	Tommy McCarthy (Sliding)	9,000	4,500	2,700
(307 3)	Tommy McCarthy (With bat.)	9,000	4,500	2,700
(309)	Bill McClellan	4,500	2,225	1,200
(311 1)	Jim McCormick (Ball in hands at chest.)	4,500	2,225	1,200
(311 2)	Jim McCormick (Bat at 45 degrees.)	4,500	2,225	1,200
(316 1)	Jack McGeachy (Bat at 45 degrees.)	4,500	2,225	1,125
(316 2)	Jack McGeachy (Fielding ball over head.)	5,150	2,600	1,550
(318 1)	Deacon McGuire (Batting)	4,500	2,225	1,200
(318 2)	Deacon McGuire (Catching)	4,500	2,225	1,200
(321)	Alex McKinnon (Fielding, hands waist-high.)	4,500	2,225	1,200
(326 1)	Jim McTamany (Bat on shoulder, outdoors.)	5,500	2,750	1,650
(326 2)	Jim McTamany (Fielding, outdoors.)	5,500	2,750	1,650
(330)	Doggie Miller	4,500	2,225	1,200
(336)	John Morrell (Morrill) (Hands on hips.)	5,000	2,500	1,500
(339)	Joe Mulvey (Fiedling ball at waist.)	4,500	2,225	1,200
(344 1)	Al Myers (Washington, bat vertical.)	4,500	2,225	1,200
(344 2)	Al Myers (Washington, hands on knees.)	4,500	2,225	1,200
(344 3)	Al Myers (Portrait, with arms folded.)	4,500	2,225	1,200
(345 1)	George Myers (Indianapolis, stooping.)	4,500	2,225	1,200
(345 2)	George Myers (Indianapolis, with bat.)	4,500	2,225	1,200
(347)	Billy Nash (Portrait)	4,500	2,225	1,200
(353)	Hugh Nicol (Brown's Champions)	9,000	4,500	2,700
(358)	Jack O'Brien (Bat over shoulder, outdoors.)	4,500	2,225	1,200
(362 1)	Hank O'Day (Ball in hand.)	4,500	2,225	1,200
(362 2)	Hank O'Day (With bat.)	4,500	2,225	1,200
(365)	Tip O'Neill (Brown's Champions)	6,500	3,250	1,950
(366)	Orator Jim O'Rourke (Fielding)	9,000	4,500	2,700
(367)	Tom O'Rourke (Bat at 45 degrees.)	4,500	2,225	1,200
(371)	Jimmy Peeples (Catching, outdoors.)	4,500	2,225	1,200
(374)	Fred Pfeffer (Throwing)	4,500	2,225	1,200
(378)	George Pinkney (Pinckney)	4,500	2,225	1,200
(380)	Henry Porter (Throwing, right hand cap-high, outdoors.)	5,500	2,750	1,650
(386)	Old Hoss Radbourn (With bat.)	9,000	4,500	2,700
(393L)	Danny Richardson (N.Y., large, bat at 45 degrees.)	24,200	12,000	7,200
(393 1)	Danny Richardson (N.Y., bat at 45 degrees.)	4,500	2,225	1,200
(393 2)	Danny Richardson (N.Y., moving to left, arms at sides.)	4,500	2,225	1,200
(394)	Hardy Richardson (Detroit)	4,500	2,225	1,200
(396)	John Roach (Batting)	4,500	2,225	1,200
(399)	Yank Robinson (Brown's Champions)	6,000	3,000	1,800
(403)	Jack Rowe (Bat at side.)	4,500	2,225	1,200
(405)	Jimmy Ryan (Ball in hands at chest.)	4,500	2,225	1,200
(415 1)	Emmett Seery (Arms folded.)	4,500	2,225	1,200
(415 2)	Emmett Seery (Ball in hands.)	4,500	2,225	1,200
(415 3)	Emmett Seery (Catching)	4,500	2,225	1,200
(425 1)	George Shoch (Batting, w/umpire.)	4,500	2,225	1,200
(425 2)	George Schoch (Shoch) (Fielding, hands head high.)	4,500	2,225	1,200
(426)	Otto Shomberg (Schomberg)(Ball in hands at shoulder.)	4,500	2,225	1,200
(435)	Pop Smith	4,500	2,225	1,200

(446 1)	Bill Stemmyer (Stemmeyer) (Ball in hands at chest.)	4,500	2,225	1,200
(446 2)	Bill Stemmyer (Stemmeyer) (With bat.)	4,500	2,225	1,200
(459 1)	Ezra Sutton (Fielding)	4,500	2,225	1,200
(459 2)	Ezra Sutton (Throwing)	4,500	2,225	1,200
(459 3)	Ezra Sutton (With bat.)	4,500	2,225	1,200
(460)	Ed Swartwood (Kneeling to field, outdoors.)	5,500	2,750	1,650
(464)	Pop Tate (Fielding)	4,500	2,225	1,200
(467)	William "Adonis" Terry ((Batting outdoors.)	4,500	2,225	1,200
(468 1)	Sam Thompson (Arms folded.)	9,000	4,500	2,700
(468 2)	Sam Thompson (Bat at side.)	9,000	4,500	2,700
(468 3)	Sam Thompson (Swinging at ball.)	9,000	4,500	2,700
(469L)	Mike Tiernan (Large, fielding fly ball.)	20,000	10,000	6,000
(469)	Mike Tiernan (Fielding grounder.)	4,500	2,225	1,200
(472)	Steve Toole (With bat, outdoors.)	5,500	2,750	1,650
(480 1)	Larry Twitchell (Hands by chest.)	4,500	2,225	1,200
(480 2)	Larry Twitchell (Right hand extended.)	4,500	2,225	1,200
(489)	Chris Von Der Ahe	4,800	2,400	1,375
(491L)	John Ward (Large, throwing.)	32,000	15,450	9,300
(491)	John Ward	14,500	7,250	4,350
(493)	Bill Watkins (Portrait)	4,500	2,225	1,200
(498)	Curt Welch	4,500	2,225	1,200
(511 1)	Art Whitney (Pittsburgh, bending.)	4,500	2,225	1,200
(511 2)	Art Whitney (Pittsburgh, with bat.)	4,500	2,225	1,200
(513)	Jim Whitney (Washington, throwing, r. hand waist-high.)	4,500	2,225	1,200
(515)	Ned Williamson (Throwing)	4,750	2,850	1,710
(519)	Sam Wise	4,500	2,225	1,200
(521 1)	George Wood (Batting)	4,500	2,225	1,200
(521 2)	George Wood (Throwing)	4,500	2,225	1,200

H

1922 Haffner's Big-Tayto-Loaf Bread

The bakery ad on the back is all that sets this issue apart from the blank-back W575-1 and several other versions with different sponsors named on back. The cards are 2" x 3-1/4" black-and-white. It is unknown whether each of the cards in the W575-1 checklist can be found in the Haffner's version.

PREMIUMS:
Common Players: 5-6X
Hall of Famers: 3-4X

(See W575-1 for checklist and card values.)

1951 Hage's Ice Cream Cleveland Indians

Similar in format to the Pacific Coast League cards produced by the dairy from 1949-51, these cards feature former members of the San Diego Padres, then a farm club of the Indians. Cards measure 2-5/8" x 3-1/8" and are printed in tones of sepia and green. Fronts have posed action photos similar to those found on contemporary Num Num and team photo pack pictures. A small white box on front has the player name and "CLEVELAND." There is a white border around the front photo. Backs are blank and unnumbered; the cards are presented here in alphabetical order.

		NM	E	VG
Complete Set (10):		5,000	2,500	1,500
Common Player:		850.00	425.00	250.00
(1)	Ray Boone	850.00	425.00	250.00
(2)	Allie Clark	850.00	425.00	250.00
(3)	Luke Easter	900.00	450.00	270.00
(4)	Jesse Flores	850.00	425.00	250.00
(5)	Johnny Gorsica	400.00	200.00	100.00
(6)	Dennis Luby (fielding)	375.00	185.00	110.00
(7)	Al Olsen	850.00	425.00	250.00
(8)	Al Rosen	900.00	450.00	270.00
(9)	Harry Simpson	850.00	425.00	250.00
(10)	George Zuverink	850.00	425.00	250.00

1888 Joseph Hall Cabinets

These cabinet-sized (6-1/2" x 4-1/2") cards feature team photos taken by Joseph Hall, a well-known photographer of the day. Extremely rare, all have Hall's name beneath the photo and some include his Brooklyn address. The team is identified in large capital letters with the individual players identified in smaller type on both sides. Fourteen teams are known to date, but others may also exist, and Hall may have produced similar team cabinets in other years as well.

		NM	E	VG
Common Team:		6,000	3,000	1,800
(1)	Athletic Ball Club, 1888	12,000	6,000	3,600
(2)	Baltimore Ball Club, 1888	16,800	8,400	5,000
(3)	Boston Ball Club, 1888	18,000	9,000	5,400
(4)	Brooklyn Ball Club, 1888	21,000	10,500	6,300
(5)	Chicago Ball Club, 1888	42,000	21,000	12,000
(6)	Cincinnati Ball Club, 1888	18,000	9,000	5,400
(7)	Cleveland Ball Club, 1888	15,000	7,500	4,500
(8)	Detroit Ball Club, 1888	19,200	9,600	5,800
(9)	Indianapolis Ball Club, 1888	18,000	9,000	5,400
(10)	Kansas City Ball Club, 1888	22,500	11,250	6,750
(11)	Louisville Ball Club, 1888	15,000	7,500	4,500
(12)	New York Ball Club, League Champions - (Wearing baseball uniforms.)	27,000	13,500	8,100
(13)	New York Ball Club, 1888 (Wearing tuxedos.)	22,000	11,000	6,660
(14)	St. Louis Baseball Club, 1888	15,000	7,500	4,500
(15)	Washington Baseball Club, 1888	48,000	24,000	14,400

1888 Joseph Hall Imperial Cabinets

Besides the standard-sized team-photo cabinet cards, super-sized versions of some (possibly all) teams were also available in a format known to collectors as an imperial cabinet. The large pictures use the same photos as the regular cabinets, enlarged to sizes as diverse as approximately 13" x 10" and 24" x 19" and mounted on heavy black or white backing boards. Printed on the mount in gold are the team name, date, player names and the Joseph Hall studio identification. Only those teams which have actually been observed in this format are listed here, with values generally set by their infrequent appearances in hobby auctions.

	NM	E	VG
Cincinnati Ball Club, 1888 (13" x 10")	13,750	6,350	3,750
New York Ball Club/1888 ((13" x 10"))	20,625	9,525	5,625
St. Louis Ball Club - 1888 (24" x 19")	13,750	6,350	3,750

1888-1889 Joseph Hall N.Y. Giants Cabinets

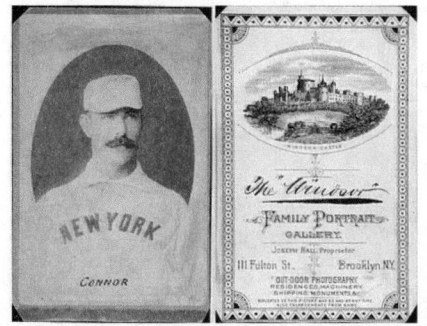

Among the several baseball related photographic cards produced by the Brooklyn studio of Joesph Hall was this series of individual player cabinets of the 1888-1889 N.Y. Giants. Approximately 4" x 6-1/4", these cards were likely produced for sale to the public, though virtually every example known in the hobby today is unique. The card fronts have oval portraits of the players, with their name penned in below. In most cases the portraits are the same as those used on the S.F. Hess tobacco card set of 1889. The black-and-white backs of the cabinets have an engraving of Windsor Castle at top, with advertising for the studio below, all in an ornate border. This checklist is known to be incomplete.

	VG
Roger Connor	4,500
Tim Keefe	4,500
Jim O'Rourke	4,500
Mickey Welch	4,500

1939-43 Hall of Fame Sepia Postcards

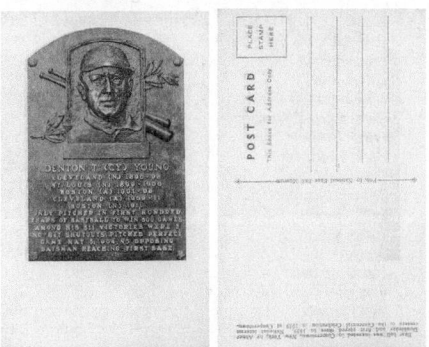

The first Hall of Fame postcards were issued in two types between 1939-1943. They share an identical format and are differentiated by the typography on back, one set having been issued prior to the Hall of Fame's opening in June, 1939, and a later version issued after the opening. The 3-1/2" x 5-1/2" cards are similar in format to the later series printed in black-and-white and various colors, but this initial effort is printed in sepia on a cream-colored background. Most fronts picture the plaque of one of the 25 first inductees, with a wide bottom border to accomodate an autograph. Designated Type 1, this issue has a back caption which ends with, "National interest centers in the Centennial Celebration in 1939 at Cooperstown." The later version, Type 2, ends its description, "The National Base Ball Museum and Hall of Fame and Doubleday Field are maintained here as a Shrine

to the national game." On both types, vertically at centers is a credit line "Pub. by National Base Ball Museum." At right are a stamp box and line for the mailing address. The unnumbered cards are listed here in alphabetical order within type.

	NM	E	VG
Complete Set, Type 1 (35):	3,750	1,850	1,100
Complete Set, Type 2 (37):	3,250	1,625	975.00
Common Card:	60.00	30.00	18.00
TYPE 1			
(1) G.C. Alexander	100.00	50.00	30.00
(2) Adrian Anson	100.00	50.00	30.00
(3) Morgan Bulkeley	100.00	50.00	30.00
(4) Alexander Cartwright	100.00	50.00	30.00
(5) Henry Chadwick	100.00	50.00	30.00
(6) Ty Cobb	225.00	110.00	65.00
(7) Eddie Collins	100.00	50.00	30.00
(8) Chas. Comiskey	100.00	50.00	30.00
(9) Candy Cummings	100.00	50.00	30.00
(10) Buck Ewing	100.00	50.00	30.00
(11) Ban Johnson	100.00	50.00	30.00
(12) Walter Johnson	175.00	85.00	50.00
(13) Willie Keeler	100.00	50.00	30.00
(14) Napoleon Lajoie	100.00	50.00	30.00
(15) Connie Mack	100.00	50.00	30.00
(16) Christy Mathewson	175.00	85.00	50.00
(17) John McGraw	100.00	50.00	30.00
(18) Chas. Radbourne	100.00	50.00	30.00
(19) Babe Ruth	450.00	225.00	135.00
(20) George Sisler	100.00	50.00	30.00
(21) Al Spalding	100.00	50.00	30.00
(22) Tris Speaker	100.00	50.00	30.00
(23) Honus Wagner	200.00	100.00	60.00
(24) George Wright	100.00	50.00	30.00
(25) Cy Young	150.00	75.00	45.00
(26) The Abner Doubleday Baseball	50.00	25.00	15.00
(27) Abner Doubleday, Major Gen'l	50.00	25.00	15.00
(28) Doubleday Field in its Original State	50.00	25.00	15.00
(29) Doubleday Field in 1938	50.00	25.00	15.00
(30) Exhibition Game on Doubleday Field	50.00	25.00	15.00
(31) Exterior - Ntl. Baseball Hall of Fame (no title on front)	50.00	25.00	15.00
(32) Interior - Ntl. Baseball Museum	50.00	25.00	15.00
(33) The Bust of Christy Mathewson	50.00	25.00	15.00
(34) Entrance of the Hall of Fame	50.00	25.00	15.00
(35) Ntl. Baseball Museum "Immortals"	50.00	25.00	15.00
TYPE 2			
(1) G.C. Alexander	100.00	50.00	30.00
(2) Adrian Anson	100.00	50.00	30.00
(3) Morgan Bulkeley	100.00	50.00	30.00
(4) Alexander Cartwright	100.00	50.00	30.00
(5) Henry Chadwick	100.00	50.00	30.00
(6) Ty Cobb	225.00	110.00	65.00
(7) Eddie Collins	100.00	50.00	30.00
(8) Charles Comiskey	100.00	50.00	30.00
(9) Candy Cummings	100.00	50.00	30.00
(10) Buck Ewing	100.00	50.00	30.00
(11) Lou Gehrig	300.00	150.00	90.00
(12) Rogers Hornsby	125.00	65.00	35.00
(13) Ban Johnson	100.00	50.00	30.00
(14) Walter Johnson	175.00	85.00	50.00
(15) Willie Keeler	100.00	50.00	30.00
(16) Napoleon Lajoie	100.00	50.00	30.00
(17) Connie Mack	100.00	50.00	30.00
(18) Christy Mathewson	175.00	85.00	50.00
(19) John McGraw	100.00	50.00	30.00
(20) Chas. Radbourne	100.00	50.00	30.00
(21) Babe Ruth	450.00	225.00	135.00
(22) George Sisler	100.00	50.00	30.00
(23) Al Spalding	100.00	50.00	30.00
(24) Tris Speaker	100.00	50.00	30.00
(25) Honus Wagner	200.00	100.00	60.00
(26) George Wright	100.00	50.00	30.00
(27) Cy Young	150.00	75.00	45.00
(28) The Abner Doubleday Baseball	50.00	25.00	15.00
(29) Abner Doubleday, Major Gen'l	50.00	25.00	15.00
(30) Doubleday Field in its Original State	50.00	25.00	15.00
(31) Doubleday Field in 1938	50.00	25.00	15.00
(32) Exhibition Game on Doubleday Field	50.00	25.00	15.00
(33) Exterior - Ntl. Baseball Hall of Fame	50.00	25.00	15.00
(34) Interior - Ntl. Baseball Hall of Fame	50.00	25.00	15.00
(35) The Bust of Christy Mathewson	50.00	25.00	15.00
(36) Entrance of the Hall of Fame	50.00	25.00	15.00
(37) Ntl. Baseball Museum - "Immortals"	50.00	25.00	15.00

1944-63 Hall of Fame Black-and-White Plaque Postcards

(See listings cataloged under Albertype and Artvue.)

1963 Hall of Fame Picture Pack

The attributed date is only approximate for this set of 5" x 7" black-and-white, blank-back pictures sold by the Hall of Fame. In the wide border beneath the player photo are identification, teams and years played, a few stats and induction year along with an HoF logo. Some of the same pictures were repeated in the later version of the issue.

	NM	E	VG
Complete Set (24):	40.00	20.00	12.00
Common Player:	3.00	1.50	.90
(1) Grover Alexander	4.00	2.00	1.25
(2) Ty Cobb	6.00	3.00	1.75
(3) Mickey Cochrane	3.00	1.50	.90
(4) Eddie Collins	3.00	1.50	.90
(5) Joe Cronin	3.00	1.50	.90
(6) Bill Dickey	3.00	1.50	.90
(7) Joe DiMaggio	7.50	3.75	2.25
(8) Bob Feller	4.00	2.00	1.25
(9) Frank Frisch	3.00	1.50	.90
(10) Lou Gehrig	7.50	3.75	2.25
(11) Rogers Hornsby	3.00	1.50	.90
(12) Walter Johnson	4.00	2.00	1.25
(13) Connie Mack	3.00	1.50	.90
(14) Christy Mathewson	4.00	2.00	1.25
(15) John McGraw	3.00	1.50	.90
(16) Jackie Robinson	5.00	2.50	1.50
(17) Babe Ruth	10.00	5.00	3.00
(18) George Sisler	3.00	1.50	.90
(19) Tris Speaker	3.00	1.50	.90
(20) Bill Terry	3.00	1.50	.90
(21) Pie Traynor	3.00	1.50	.90
(22) Honus Wagner	4.00	2.00	1.25
(23) Paul Waner	3.00	1.50	.90
(24) Cy Young	4.00	2.00	1.25

1973 Hall of Fame Picture Pack

This set of 5" x 6-3/4" black-and-white player photos picture "Baseball's Greats Enshrined at Cooperstown, N.Y." Player career data is printed in the wide white border at bottom and there is a Hall of Fame logo at lower-left. The unnumbered pictures are listed here in alphabetical order.

	NM	E	VG
Complete Set (20):	20.00	10.00	6.00
Common Player:	2.00	1.00	.60
(1) Yogi Berra	3.00	1.50	.90
(2) Roy Campanella	3.00	1.50	.90
(3) Ty Cobb	4.00	2.00	1.25
(4) Joe Cronin	2.50	1.25	.70

(5)	Dizzy Dean	3.00	1.50	.90
(6)	Joe DiMaggio	7.50	3.75	2.25
(7)	Bob Feller	3.00	1.50	.90
(8)	Lou Gehrig	7.50	3.75	2.25
(9)	Rogers Hornsby	3.00	1.50	.90
(10)	Sandy Koufax	5.00	2.50	1.50
(11)	Christy Mathewson	3.00	1.50	.90
(12)	Stan Musial	3.00	1.50	.90
(13)	Satchel Paige	3.00	1.50	.90
(14)	Jackie Robinson	5.00	2.50	1.50
(15)	Babe Ruth	10.00	5.00	3.00
(16)	Warren Spahn	2.50	1.25	.70
(17)	Casey Stengel	3.00	1.50	.90
(18)	Honus Wagner	3.00	1.50	.90
(19)	Ted Williams	5.00	2.50	1.50
(20)	Cy Young	3.00	1.50	.90

1979 Hall of Fame (Dexter Press) Plaque Postcards

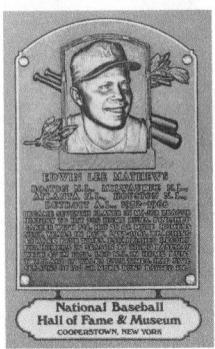

This short-lived series, begun no later than 1979, features the Hall of Fame inductees' plaques on bright backgrounds of red, orange, blue and green. Because of the cards' color and finish, they are difficult to autograph.

		NM	E	VG
Complete Set (53):		350.00	175.00	105.00
Common Player:		6.00	3.00	1.75
(1)	Grover Alexander	6.00	3.00	1.75
(2)	Lou Boudreau	6.00	3.00	1.75
(3)	Roy Campanella	10.00	5.00	3.00
(4)	Roberto Clemente	20.00	10.00	6.00
(5)	Ty Cobb	15.00	7.50	4.50
(6)	Stan Coveleski	6.00	3.00	1.75
(7)	Sam Crawford	6.00	3.00	1.75
(8)	Martin Dihigo	6.00	3.00	1.75
(9)	Joe DiMaggio	22.50	11.00	6.75
(10)	Billy Evans	6.00	3.00	1.75
(11)	Johnny Evers	6.00	3.00	1.75
(12)	Red Faber	6.00	3.00	1.75
(13)	Elmer Flick	6.00	3.00	1.75
(14)	Ford Frick	6.00	3.00	1.75
(15)	Frank Frisch	6.00	3.00	1.75
(16)	Pud Galvin	6.00	3.00	1.75
(17)	Lou Gehrig	20.00	10.00	6.00
(18)	Warren Giles	6.00	3.00	1.75
(19)	Will Harridge	6.00	3.00	1.75
(20)	Harry Heilmann	6.00	3.00	1.75
(21)	Harry Hooper	6.00	3.00	1.75
(22)	Waite Hoyt	6.00	3.00	1.75
(23)	Miller Huggins	6.00	3.00	1.75
(24)	Judy Johnson	6.00	3.00	1.75
(25)	Addie Joss	6.00	3.00	1.75
(26)	Tim Keefe	6.00	3.00	1.75
(27)	Willie Keeler	6.00	3.00	1.75
(28)	George Kelly	6.00	3.00	1.75
(29)	Sandy Koufax	15.00	7.50	4.50
(30)	Nap Lajoie	6.00	3.00	1.75
(31)	Pop Lloyd	6.00	3.00	1.75
(32)	Connie Mack	6.00	3.00	1.75
(33)	Larry MacPhail	6.00	3.00	1.75
(34)	Mickey Mantle	25.00	12.50	7.50
(35)	Heinie Manush	6.00	3.00	1.75
(36)	Eddie Mathews	6.00	3.00	1.75
(37)	Willie Mays	15.00	7.50	4.50
(38)	Ducky Medwick	6.00	3.00	1.75
(39)	Stan Musial	12.00	6.00	3.50
(40)	Herb Pennock	6.00	3.00	1.75
(41)	Edd Roush	6.00	3.00	1.75
(42)	Babe Ruth	25.00	12.50	7.50
(43)	Amos Rusie	6.00	3.00	1.75
(44)	Ray Schalk	6.00	3.00	1.75
(45)	Al Simmons	6.00	3.00	1.75
(46)	Albert Spalding	6.00	3.00	1.75
(47)	Joe Tinker	6.00	3.00	1.75
(48)	Pie Traynor	6.00	3.00	1.75
(49)	Dazzy Vance	6.00	3.00	1.75
(50)	Lloyd Waner	6.00	3.00	1.75

(51)	Ted Williams	20.00	10.00	6.00
(52)	Hack Wilson	6.00	3.00	1.75
(53)	Ross Youngs	6.00	3.00	1.75

1979 HoF (Dexter Press) Plaque Postcards - Autographed

		NM	E	VG
(2)	Lou Boudreau	30.00	27.00	22.00
(3)	Roy Campanella (Value Undetermined)			
(6)	Stan Coveleski	50.00	45.00	37.00
(9)	Joe DiMaggio	350.00	315.00	260.00
(22)	Waite Hoyt	100.00	90.00	75.00
(24)	Judy Johnson	65.00	60.00	50.00
(28)	George Kelly	75.00	65.00	55.00
(29)	Sandy Koufax	150.00	135.00	110.00
(34)	Mickey Mantle	400.00	360.00	300.00
(36)	Eddie Mathews	50.00	45.00	37.00
(37)	Willie Mays	50.00	45.00	37.00
(39)	Stan Musial	25.00	22.00	18.50
(41)	Edd Roush	50.00	45.00	37.00
(50)	Lloyd Waner	50.00	45.00	37.00
(51)	Ted Williams	300.00	270.00	225.00

1964-date Hall of Fame Yellow Plaque Postcards

 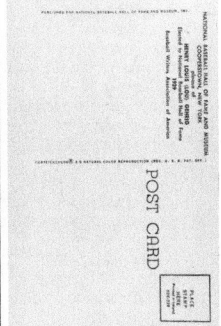

Since 1964 a number of related series of Hall of Fame Plaque Postcards have been produced by a pair of printers. The 3-1/2" x 5-1/2" postcards were first produced by Curteichcolor and, later, by Mike Roberts Color Productions. Like earlier HoF postcards, these series feature a color photo of an inductee's plaque on a yellow background. Black-and-white backs have a variety of player information, postcard indicia, copyright data and credit lines. Few hobbyists attempt to collect these by issuer, rather trying to assemble a complete set of each player regardless of who did the printing and when. Prior to 1977, single postcards sold for five cents at the HoF gift shop; in 1977 the price doubled to a dime, with complete sets (about 150) selling for $6. Today a complete set is available from the Hall of Fame for about $45, with singles at 25 cents apiece.

Complete Set (281)	45.00	22.00	13.50
Common Player:	.50	.50	.25
Hank Aaron	.50	.50	.25
Grover Alexander	.50	.50	.25
Walter Alston	.50	.50	.25
Sparky Anderson	.50	.50	.25
Cap Anson	.50	.50	.25
Luis Aparicio	.50	.50	.25
Luke Appling	.50	.50	.25
Richie Ashburn	.50	.50	.25
Earl Averill	.50	.50	.25
Frank Baker	.50	.50	.25
Dave Bancroft	.50	.50	.25
Ernie Banks	.50	.50	.25
Al Barlick	.50	.50	.25
Ed Barrow	.50	.50	.25
Jake Beckley	.50	.50	.25
Cool Papa Bell	.50	.50	.25
Johnny Bench	.50	.50	.25
Chief Bender	.50	.50	.25
Yogi Berra	.50	.50	.25
Wade Boggs	.50	.50	.25
Jim Bottomley	.50	.50	.25
Lou Boudreau	.50	.50	.25
Roger Bresnahan	.50	.50	.25
George Brett	.50	.50	.25
Lou Brock	.50	.50	.25
Dan Brouthers	.50	.50	.25
Mordecai Brown	.50	.50	.25
Ray Brown	.50	.25	.15
Willard Brown	.50	.25	.15
Morgan Bulkeley	.50	.50	.25
Jim Bunning	.50	.50	.25
Jesse Burkett	.50	.50	.25

Roy Campanella	.50	.50	.25
Rod Carew	.50	.50	.25
Max Carey	.50	.50	.25
Steve Carlton	.50	.50	.25
Gary Carter	.50	.50	.25
Alexander Cartwright	.50	.50	.25
Orlando Cepeda	.50	.50	.25
Henry Chadwick	.50	.50	.25
Frank Chance	.50	.50	.25
A.B. (Happy) Chandler	.50	.50	.25
Oscar Charleston	.50	.50	.25
Jack Chesbro	.50	.50	.25
Nestor Chylak	.50	.50	.25
Fred Clarke	.50	.50	.25
John Clarkson	.50	.50	.25
Roberto Clemente	.50	.50	.25
Ty Cobb	.50	.50	.25
Mickey Cochrane	.50	.50	.25
Eddie Collins	.50	.50	.25
Jimmy Collins	.50	.50	.25
Earle Combs	.50	.50	.25
Charles Comiskey	.50	.50	.25
Jocko Conlan	.50	.50	.25
Tom Connolly	.50	.50	.25
Roger Connor	.50	.50	.25
Andy Cooper	.50	.25	.15
Stan Coveleski	.50	.50	.25
Sam Crawford	.50	.50	.25
Joe Cronin	.50	.50	.25
Candy Cummings	.50	.50	.25
Kiki Cuyler	.50	.50	.25
Ray Dandridge	.50	.50	.25
George Davis	.50	.50	.25
Leon Day	.50	.50	.25
Dizzy Dean	.50	.50	.25
Ed Delahanty	.50	.50	.25
Bill Dickey	.50	.50	.25
Martin Dihigo	.50	.50	.25
Joe DiMaggio	.50	.50	.25
Larry Doby	.50	.50	.25
Bobby Doerr	.50	.50	.25
Barney Dreyfuss	.50	.25	.15
Don Drysdale	.50	.50	.25
Hugh Duffy	.50	.50	.25
Leo Durocher	.50	.50	.25
Dennis Eckersley	.50	.25	.15
Billy Evans	.50	.50	.25
Johnny Evers	.50	.50	.25
Buck Ewing	.50	.50	.25
Red Faber	.50	.50	.25
Bob Feller	.50	.50	.25
Rick Ferrell	.50	.50	.25
Rollie Fingers	.50	.50	.25
Carlton Fisk	.50	.50	.25
Elmer Flick	.50	.50	.25
Whitey Ford	.50	.50	.25
Bill Foster	.50	.50	.25
Rube Foster	.50	.50	.25
Nellie Fox	.50	.50	.25
Jimmie Foxx	.50	.50	.25
Ford Frick	.50	.50	.25
Frank Frisch	.50	.50	.25
Pud Galvin	.50	.50	.25
Lou Gehrig	.50	.50	.25
Charlie Gehringer	.50	.50	.25
Bob Gibson	.50	.50	.25
Josh Gibson	.50	.50	.25
Warren Giles	.50	.50	.25
Lefty Gomez	.50	.50	.25
Goose Goslin	.50	.50	.25
Rich "Goose" Gossage	.50	.25	.15
Frank Grant	.50	.25	.15
Hank Greenberg	.50	.50	.25
Clark Griffith	.50	.50	.25
Burleigh Grimes	.50	.50	.25
Lefty Grove	.50	.50	.25
Tony Gwynn	.50	.25	.15
Chick Hafey	.50	.50	.25
Jesse Haines	.50	.50	.25
Billy Hamilton	.50	.50	.25
Ned Hanlon	.50	.50	.25
Will Harridge	.50	.50	.25
Bucky Harris	.50	.50	.25
Gabby Hartnett	.50	.50	.25
Harry Heilmann	.50	.50	.25
Billy Herman	.50	.50	.25
Pete Hill	.50	.25	.15
Harry Hooper	.50	.50	.25
Rogers Hornsby	.50	.50	.25
Waite Hoyt	.50	.50	.25
Cal Hubbard	.50	.50	.25
Carl Hubbell	.50	.50	.25
Miller Huggins	.50	.50	.25
William Hulbert	.50	.50	.25
Catfish Hunter	.50	.50	.25
Monte Irvin	.50	.50	.25
Reggie Jackson	.50	.50	.25
Travis Jackson	.50	.50	.25

Name			
Fergie Jenkins	.50	.50	.25
Hughie Jennings	.50	.50	.25
Ban Johnson	.50	.50	.25
Judy Johnson	.50	.50	.25
Walter Johnson	.50	.50	.25
Addie Joss	.50	.50	.25
Al Kaline	.50	.50	.25
Tim Keefe	.50	.50	.25
Willie Keeler	.50	.50	.25
George Kell	.50	.50	.25
Joe Kelley	.50	.50	.25
George Kelly	.50	.50	.25
Mike "King" Kelly	.50	.50	.25
Harmon Killebrew	.50	.50	.25
Ralph Kiner	.50	.50	.25
Chuck Klein	.50	.50	.25
Bill Klem	.50	.50	.25
Sandy Koufax	.50	.50	.25
Bowie Kuhn	.50	.25	.15
Nap Lajoie	.50	.25	.15
Kenesaw M. Landis	.50	.50	.25
Tommy Lasorda	.50	.50	.25
Tony Lazzeri	.50	.50	.25
Bob Lemon	.50	.50	.25
Buck Leonard	.50	.50	.25
Freddie Lindstrom	.50	.50	.25
Pop Lloyd	.50	.50	.25
Ernie Lombardi	.50	.50	.25
Al Lopez	.50	.50	.25
Ted Lyons	.50	.50	.25
Connie Mack	.50	.50	.25
Biz Mackey	.50	.25	.15
Larry MacPhail	.50	.50	.25
Effa "Effie" Manley	.50	.25	.15
Mickey Mantle	.50	.50	.25
Heinie Manush	.50	.50	.25
Rabbit Maranville	.50	.50	.25
Juan Marichal	.50	.50	.25
Rube Marquard	.50	.50	.25
Eddie Mathews	.50	.50	.25
Christy Mathewson	.50	.50	.25
Willie Mays	.50	.50	.25
Bill Mazeroski	.50	.50	.25
Joe McCarthy	.50	.50	.25
Tommy McCarthy	.50	.50	.25
Willie McCovey	.50	.50	.25
Joe McGinnity	.50	.50	.25
Bill McGowan	.50	.50	.25
John McGraw	.50	.50	.25
Bill McKechnie	.50	.50	.25
Lee MacPhail	.50	.50	.25
Bid McPhee	.50	.50	.25
Ducky Medwick	.50	.50	.25
Jose Mendez	.50	.25	.15
Johnny Mize	.50	.50	.25
Paul Molitor	.50	.25	.15
Joe Morgan	.50	.50	.25
Stan Musial	.50	.50	.25
Hal Newhouser	.50	.50	.25
Kid Nichols	.50	.50	.25
Phil Niekro	.50	.50	.25
Walter O'Malley	.50	.25	.15
Jim O'Rourke	.50	.50	.25
Mel Ott	.50	.50	.25
Satchel Paige	.50	.50	.25
Jim Palmer	.50	.50	.25
Herb Pennock	.50	.50	.25
Tony Perez	.50	.50	.25
Gaylord Perry	.50	.50	.25
Ed Plank	.50	.50	.25
Alex Pompez	.50	.25	.15
Cum Posey	.50	.25	.15
Kirby Puckett	.50	.50	.25
Charles Radbourne	.50	.50	.25
Pee Wee Reese	.50	.50	.25
Sam Rice	.50	.50	.25
Cal Ripken Jr.	.50	.25	.15
Branch Rickey	.50	.50	.25
Eppa Rixey	.50	.50	.25
Phil Rizzuto	.50	.50	.25
Robin Roberts	.50	.50	.25
Brooks Robinson	.50	.50	.25
Frank Robinson	.50	.50	.25
Jackie Robinson	.50	.50	.25
Wilbert Robinson	.50	.50	.25
Bullet Rogan	.50	.50	.25
Edd Roush	.50	.50	.25
Red Ruffing	.50	.50	.25
Amos Rusie	.50	.50	.25
Babe Ruth	.50	.50	.25
Nolan Ryan	.50	.50	.25
Ryne Sandberg	.50	.25	.15
Louis Santop	.50	.25	.15
Ray Schalk	.50	.50	.25
Mike Schmidt	.50	.50	.25
Red Schoendienst	.50	.50	.25
Tom Seaver	.50	.50	.25
Frank Selee	.50	.50	.25

Name			
Joe Sewell	.50	.50	.25
Al Simmons	.50	.50	.25
George Sisler	.50	.50	.25
Enos Slaughter	.50	.50	.25
Hilton Smith	.50	.50	.25
Ozzie Smith	.50	.50	.25
Duke Snider	.50	.50	.25
Billy Southworth	.50	.25	.15
Warren Spahn	.50	.50	.25
Albert Spalding	.50	.50	.25
Tris Speaker	.50	.50	.25
Willie Stargell	.50	.50	.25
Turkey Stearnes	.50	.50	.25
Casey Stengel	.50	.50	.25
Mule Suttles	.50	.25	.15
Don Sutton	.50	.50	.25
Ben Taylor	.50	.25	.15
Bill Terry	.50	.50	.25
Sam Thompson	.50	.50	.25
Joe Tinker	.50	.50	.25
Cristobal Torriente	.50	.25	.15
Paul Traynor	.50	.50	.25
Dazzy Vance	.50	.50	.25
Arky Vaughan	.50	.50	.25
Bill Veeck	.50	.50	.25
Rube Waddell	.50	.50	.25
Honus Wagner	.50	.50	.25
Bobby Wallace	.50	.50	.25
Ed Walsh	.50	.50	.25
Lloyd Waner	.50	.50	.25
Paul Waner	.50	.50	.25
Monte Ward	.50	.50	.25
Earl Weaver	.50	.50	.25
George Weiss	.50	.50	.25
Mickey Welch	.50	.50	.25
Willie Wells	.50	.50	.25
Zack Wheat	.50	.50	.25
Sol White	.50	.25	.15
Hoyt Wilhelm	.50	.50	.25
J.L. Wilkinson	.50	.25	.15
Billy Williams	.50	.50	.25
Dick Williams	.50	.25	.15
Joe Williams	.50	.50	.25
Ted Williams	.50	.50	.25
.50			
Vic Willis	.50	.50	.25
Hack Wilson	.50	.50	.25
Jud Wilson	.50	.25	.15
Dave Winfield	.50	.50	.25
George Wright	.50	.50	.25
Harry Wright	.50	.50	.25
Early Wynn	.50	.50	.25
Carl Yastrzemski	.50	.50	.25
Tom Yawkey	.50	.50	.25
Cy Young	.50	.50	.25
Ross Youngs	.50	.50	.25
Robin Yount	.50	.50	.25

1964-date Hall of Fame Yellow Plaque Postcards - Autographed

This listing represents the Curteichcolor and Mike Roberts yellow Hall of Fame plaque postcards which are known to exist, or in a few cases are theoretically possible. Value of genuinely autographed HoF plaque postcards is not so much dependent on star status of the player, but on perception of how many such cards could exist given the time the player remained alive and in good health following his selection at Cooperstown. Players who died or were incapacitated shortly after induction may have more valuable autographed cards than currently living players of greater renown. Values quoted are for cards autographed on front; cards signed on the back can be worth 50 percent less.

	NM	E	VG
Hank Aaron	55.00	45.00	35.00
Walter Alston	150.00	120.00	90.00
Sparky Anderson	55.00	45.00	35.00
Luis Aparicio	15.00	12.00	9.00

	NM	E	VG
Luke Appling	20.00	16.00	12.00
Richie Ashburn	55.00	45.00	35.00
Earl Averill	50.00	40.00	30.00
Dave Bancroft	1,600	800.00	480.00
Ernie Banks	45.00	35.00	25.00
Al Barlick	25.00	12.50	7.50
Cool Papa Bell	50.00	40.00	30.00
Johnny Bench	45.00	36.00	27.00
Yogi Berra	25.00	20.00	15.00
Wade Boggs	50.00	40.00	30.00
Lou Boudreau	15.00	12.00	9.00
George Brett	125.00	100.00	75.00
Lou Brock	30.00	24.00	18.00
Jim Bunning	40.00	32.00	24.00
Roy Campanella (Value Undetermined)			
Rod Carew	50.00	40.00	30.00
Max Carey	60.00	50.00	35.00
Steve Carlton	35.00	30.00	20.00
Gary Carter	100.00	80.00	60.00
Orlando Cepeda	35.00	30.00	20.00
A.B. (Happy) Chandler	20.00	16.00	12.00
Earle Combs	300.00	240.00	180.00
Jocko Conlan	25.00	20.00	15.00
Stan Coveleski	30.00	24.00	18.00
"Stanislaus Kowalewski"	150.00	120.00	90.00
Sam Crawford	600.00	480.00	360.00
Joe Cronin	50.00	40.00	30.00
Ray Dandridge	15.00	12.00	9.00
Dizzy Dean	250.00	125.00	75.00
Bill Dickey	50.00	40.00	30.00
Joe DiMaggio	175.00	87.50	52.50
Larry Doby	90.00	70.00	55.00
Bobby Doerr	7.50	6.00	4.50
Don Drysdale	45.00	35.00	25.00
Dennis Eckersley	75.00	60.00	45.00
Red Faber	165.00	130.00	100.00
Bob Feller	7.50	6.00	4.50
Rick Ferrell	15.00	12.00	9.00
Rollie Fingers	20.00	16.00	12.00
Carlton Fisk	80.00	65.00	45.00
Elmer Flick	600.00	480.00	360.00
Whitey Ford	40.00	20.00	12.00
Jimmie Foxx (Usually signed on back.)	1,750	1,400	1,050
Ford Frick	225.00	180.00	135.00
Frank Frisch	250.00	125.00	75.00
Charlie Gehringer	30.00	24.00	18.00
Bob Gibson	30.00	24.00	18.00
Lefty Gomez	35.00	30.00	20.00
Goose Goslin (Usually signed on back; value of such $750-1,000.)	2,250	1,800	1,350
Hank Greenberg	175.00	140.00	100.00
Burleigh Grimes	35.00	30.00	20.00
Lefty Grove	160.00	130.00	95.00
Tony Gwynn	150.00	120.00	90.00
Chick Hafey	725.00	580.00	435.00
Jesse Haines	125.00	100.00	75.00
Bucky Harris	325.00	260.00	195.00
Gabby Hartnett	725.00	580.00	435.00
Billy Herman	12.00	9.50	7.25
Harry Hooper	235.00	190.00	140.00
Waite Hoyt	40.00	32.00	24.00
Cal Hubbard	650.00	325.00	195.00
Carl Hubbell (Pre-stroke.)	40.00	32.00	24.00
Carl Hubbell (Post-stroke.)	25.00	20.00	15.00
Catfish Hunter	35.00	17.50	10.50
Monte Irvin	10.00	8.00	6.00
Reggie Jackson	75.00	60.00	45.00
Travis Jackson	30.00	24.00	18.00
Fergie Jenkins	15.00	12.00	9.00
Judy Johnson	35.00	17.50	10.50
Al Kaline	20.00	16.00	12.00
George Kell	7.50	6.00	4.50
George Kelly	40.00	32.00	24.00
Harmon Killebrew	25.00	20.00	15.00
Ralph Kiner	15.00	12.00	9.00
Sandy Koufax	150.00	100.00	75.00
Tommy Lasorda	100.00	80.00	60.00
Bob Lemon	12.00	9.50	7.25
Buck Leonard (Post-stroke autographed cards worth 50 percent.)	15.00	12.00	9.00
Freddie Lindstrom	75.00	60.00	45.00
Al Lopez	40.00	32.00	24.00
Ted Lyons	45.00	35.00	25.00
Lee MacPhail	35.00	28.00	21.00
Mickey Mantle	235.00	190.00	140.00
Heinie Manush	325.00	260.00	195.00
Juan Marichal	15.00	12.00	9.00
Rube Marquard	45.00	32.00	24.00
Eddie Mathews	25.00	20.00	15.00
Willie Mays	50.00	40.00	30.00
Bill Mazeroski	50.00	40.00	30.00
Joe McCarthy	80.00	65.00	45.00

	NM	E	VG
Willie McCovey	35.00	28.00	21.00
Bill McKechnie (Possible, not likely.)			
Ducky Medwick	150.00	125.00	90.00
Johnny Mize	15.00	12.00	9.00
Paul Molitor	90.00	75.00	55.00
Joe Morgan	30.00	24.00	18.00
Eddie Murray	125.00	100.00	75.00
Stan Musial	40.00	35.00	25.00
Hal Newhouser	15.00	12.00	9.00
Phil Niekro	35.00	30.00	20.00
Satchel Paige	300.00	275.00	190.00
Jim Palmer	20.00	16.00	12.00
Tony Perez	50.00	40.00	30.00
Gaylord Perry	25.00	20.00	15.00
Kirby Puckett	125.00	100.00	75.00
Pee Wee Reese	45.00	35.00	25.00
Sam Rice	185.00	150.00	110.00
Cal Ripken Jr.	100.00	80.00	60.00
Phil Rizzuto	30.00	24.00	18.00
Robin Roberts	25.00	20.00	15.00
Brooks Robinson	12.50	10.00	7.50
Frank Robinson	35.00	30.00	25.00
Jackie Robinson (Often signed on back; value of such $550.)	1,000	900.00	800.00
Edd Roush	30.00	24.00	18.00
Red Ruffing	200.00	160.00	120.00
Nolan Ryan	65.00	50.00	40.00
Ryne Sandberg	60.00	45.00	35.00
Ray Schalk	450.00	360.00	270.00
Mike Schmidt	80.00	65.00	50.00
Red Schoendienst	30.00	24.00	18.00
Tom Seaver	40.00	32.00	24.00
Joe Sewell	15.00	12.00	9.00
George Sisler	200.00	160.00	120.00
Enos Slaughter	10.00	8.00	6.00
Ozzie Smith	95.00	75.00	55.00
Duke Snider	35.00	30.00	25.00
Warren Spahn	35.00	30.00	25.00
Willie Stargell	50.00	40.00	30.00
Casey Stengel	225.00	180.00	135.00
Bruce Sutter	60.00	45.00	35.00
Don Sutton	40.00	32.00	24.00
Bill Terry	25.00	20.00	15.00
Pie Traynor	950.00	880.00	710.00
Lloyd Waner	30.00	24.00	18.00
Paul Waner (Possible, not likely.)			
Earl Weaver	35.00	30.00	20.00
George Weiss (Possible, not likely.)			
Zack Wheat	450.00	360.00	270.00
Hoyt Wilhelm	15.00	12.00	9.00
Billy Williams	15.00	12.00	9.00
Ted Williams	200.00	160.00	120.00
Dave Winfield	100.00	80.00	60.00
Early Wynn	25.00	20.00	15.00
Carl Yastrzemski	55.00	45.00	35.00
Robin Yount	150.00	120.00	90.00

1908 Hall's Studio N.Y. Giants Cabinets

Members of the N.Y. Giants are pictured in this series of approximately 4-1/2" x 6-1/2" cabinet photos from New York City photographer, Hall's Studio. The players are all identically posed bare-headed in white shirts buttoned at the collar. It is unknown whether this checklist is complete.

	NM	E	VG
Common Player:	600.00	300.00	180.00
(1) Al Bridwell	600.00	300.00	180.00
(2) Doc Crandall	600.00	300.00	180.00
(3) Larry Doyle	600.00	300.00	180.00
(4) Buck Herzog	600.00	300.00	180.00
(5) Rube Marquard	800.00	400.00	240.00
(6) John McGraw	800.00	400.00	240.00
(7) Fred Merkle	600.00	300.00	180.00

1961 Harmony Milk Pittsburgh Pirates

The PIRATES train on HARMONY MILK

The attributed year of issue is approximate and subject to change if and when further players are added to the checklist. These premium photos are 8" x 10" in format, round-cornered with blank backs.

	NM	E	VG
Common Player:	175.00	90.00	50.00
(1) Roberto Clemente	600.00	300.00	180.00
(2) Dick Groat	175.00	90.00	50.00
(3) Don Hoak	175.00	90.00	50.00
(4) Vern Law	175.00	90.00	50.00
(5) Danny Murtaugh	175.00	90.00	50.00

1928 Harrington's Ice Cream

Sharing the same format and checklist with several other (Tharp's, Yeungling's, Sweetman, etc.) contemporary ice cream sets this 60-card set from a Dushore, Pa., dairy includes all of the top stars of the day. Cards are printed in black-and-white on a 1-3/8" x 2-1/2" format. The player's name and a card number appear either in a strip within the frame of the photo, or printed in the border beneath the photo. Card backs have a redemption offer that includes an ice cream bar in exchange for a Babe Ruth card, or a gallon of ice cream for a complete set of 60.

	NM	E	VG
Complete Set (No #48 Smith) (59):	20,000	8,000	4,000
Common Player:	90.00	35.00	20.00
1 Burleigh Grimes	350.00	140.00	70.00
2 Walter Reuther (Ruether)	90.00	35.00	20.00
3 Joe Dugan	90.00	35.00	20.00
4 Red Faber	350.00	140.00	70.00
5 Gabby Hartnett	350.00	140.00	70.00
6 Babe Ruth	7,000	3,500	2,100
7 Bob Meusel	90.00	35.00	20.00
8 Herb Pennock	350.00	140.00	70.00
9 George Burns	90.00	35.00	20.00
10 Joe Sewell	350.00	140.00	70.00
11 George Uhle	90.00	35.00	20.00
12 Bob O'Farrell	90.00	35.00	20.00
13 Rogers Hornsby	600.00	300.00	180.00
14 "Pie" Traynor	350.00	140.00	70.00
15 Clarence Mitchell	90.00	35.00	20.00
16 Eppa Jepha Rixey	350.00	140.00	70.00
17 Carl Mays	125.00	50.00	25.00
18 Adolfo Luque	100.00	40.00	20.00
19 Dave Bancroft	350.00	140.00	70.00
20 George Kelly	350.00	140.00	70.00
21 Earl (Earle) Combs	350.00	140.00	70.00
22 Harry Heilmann	350.00	140.00	70.00
23 Ray W. Schalk	350.00	140.00	70.00
24 Johnny Mostil	90.00	35.00	20.00
25 Hack Wilson	350.00	140.00	70.00
26 Lou Gehrig	6,000	1,400	700.00
27 Ty Cobb	5,000	2,500	1,500
28 Tris Speaker	450.00	180.00	90.00
29 Tony Lazzeri	350.00	140.00	70.00
30 Waite Hoyt	350.00	140.00	70.00
31 Sherwood Smith	90.00	35.00	20.00
32 Max Carey	350.00	140.00	70.00
33 Eugene Hargrave	90.00	35.00	20.00
34 Miguel L. Gonzalez (Middle initial A.)	100.00	40.00	20.00
35 Joe Judge	90.00	35.00	20.00
36 E.C. (Sam) Rice	350.00	140.00	70.00
37 Earl Sheely	90.00	35.00	20.00
38 Sam Jones	90.00	35.00	20.00
39 Bib (Bibb) A. Falk	90.00	35.00	20.00
40 Willie Kamm	90.00	35.00	20.00
41 Stanley Harris	350.00	140.00	70.00
42 John J. McGraw	350.00	140.00	70.00
43 Artie Nehf	90.00	35.00	20.00
44 Grover Alexander	450.00	180.00	90.00
45 Paul Waner	350.00	140.00	70.00
46 William H. Terry	350.00	140.00	70.00
47 Glenn Wright	90.00	35.00	20.00
48 Earl Smith (Printed in green only. Value undetermined.)			
49 Leon (Goose) Goslin	350.00	140.00	70.00
50 Frank Frisch	350.00	140.00	70.00
51 Joe Harris	90.00	35.00	20.00
52 Fred (Cy) Williams	90.00	35.00	20.00
53 Eddie Roush	350.00	140.00	70.00
54 George Sisler	350.00	140.00	70.00
55 Ed. Rommel	90.00	35.00	20.00
56 Rogers Peckinpaugh (Roger)	90.00	35.00	20.00
57 Stanley Coveleskie (Coveleski)	350.00	140.00	70.00
58 Lester Bell	90.00	35.00	20.00
59 L. Waner	350.00	140.00	70.00
60 John P. McInnis	90.00	35.00	20.00

1930-1931 Harrison Studio Homestead Grays Postcards

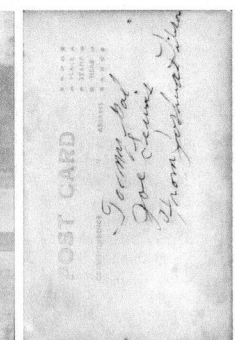

Whether the famed Negro League powerhouse team, the Homestead Grays, were in Little Rock, Ark., for spring training or on a barnstorming tour, they became the subjects of a series of postcards from the local photographer, Harrison Studio. The cards are in standard postcard format, featuring borderless black-and-white photographic poses. It is likely the checklist here is incomplete.

(1) Josh Gibson (Front/back autographed card sold at auction 4/06 for $81,200.)
(2) Vic Harris
(3) Ted Page
(4) Ambrose Reed
(5) Homestead Grays 1930 Team Photo
(6) Homestead Grays 1931 Team Photo

1911-12 Hassan Cigarettes

Prior to its sole sponsorship of the T202 Triplefolders set of 1912, Hassan was one of 10 American Tobacco Co. brands advertising on the backs of 1911 T205 Gold Borders. Two different factories are noted on these backs, No. 30 and No. 649, the former being slightly scarcer, though currently no more valuable. Hassan backs in T205 are printed in green and command a 1.5-2x premium in the market.

(See T202, T205.)

1952 Hawthorn-Mellody Chicago White Sox Pins

This issue was sponsored by a local dairy. The 1-3/8" diameter pins have sepia lithographs of the players with "Club of Champs" printed above. A non-pictorial membership button is also part of the set. The unnumbered pins are listed here in alphabetical order.

	NM	E	VG
Complete Set (11):	400.00	200.00	120.00
Common Player:	35.00	17.50	10.50
(1) Ray Coleman	35.00	17.50	10.50
(2) Sam Dente	35.00	17.50	10.50
(3) Joe Dobson	35.00	17.50	10.50
(4) Nelson Fox	80.00	40.00	24.00
(5) Sherman Lollar	45.00	22.00	13.50
(6) Bill Pierce	45.00	22.00	13.50
(7) Eddie Robinson	35.00	17.50	10.50
(8) Hector Rodriguez	35.00	17.50	10.50
(9) Eddie Stewart	35.00	17.50	10.50
(10) Al Zarilla	35.00	17.50	10.50
(11) Member's pin	15.00	7.50	4.50

1959 R.H. Hayes Postcards

Whether there are any other player postcards distributed by R.H. Hayes of Kansas is unknown. Produced for Hayes by Dexter Press, which issued cards for Coke in later years, the 3-1/2" x 5-1/2" postcard has a borderless color photo on front with a facsimile autograph at bottom. The postcard back has credit lines for Hayes and Dexter and a short biography of the player.

	NM	E	VG
(1) Hank Bauer	45.00	22.50	13.50

1911 Helmar Stamps (T332)

A collectible departure from the traditional tobacco cards of the period, Helmar Cigarettes in 1911 issued a series of small major league baseball player "stamps." The stamps, each measuring approximately 1-1/8" x 1-3/8", feature a black and white player portrait surrounded by a colorful, ornate frame. The stamps were originally issued in a 2" x 2-1/2" glassine envelope which advertised the Helmar brand and promoted "Philately - the Popular European Rage." To date, 181 different player stamps have been found. The set includes as many as 50 different frame designs. The Helmar stamp set has been assigned a T332 designation by the American Card Catalog.

	NM	E	VG
Complete Set (180):	8,000	4,000	2,400
Common Player:	50.00	25.00	15.00
(1) Babe Adams	50.00	25.00	15.00
(2) Red Ames	50.00	25.00	15.00
(3) Jimmy Archer	50.00	25.00	15.00
(4) Jimmy Austin	50.00	25.00	15.00
(5) Home Run Baker	100.00	50.00	30.00
(6) Neal Ball	50.00	25.00	15.00
(7) Cy Barger	50.00	25.00	15.00
(8) Jack Barry	50.00	25.00	15.00
(9) Johnny Bates	50.00	25.00	15.00
(10) Fred Beck	50.00	25.00	15.00
(11) Beals Becker	50.00	25.00	15.00
(12) George Bell	50.00	25.00	15.00
(13) Chief Bender	100.00	50.00	30.00
(14) Bob Bescher	50.00	25.00	15.00
(15) Joe Birmingham	50.00	25.00	15.00
(16) John Bliss	50.00	25.00	15.00
(17) Bruno Block	50.00	25.00	15.00
(18) Ping Bodie	50.00	25.00	15.00
(19) Roger Bresnahan	100.00	50.00	30.00
(20) Al Bridwell	50.00	25.00	15.00
(21) Lew Brockett	50.00	25.00	15.00
(22) Mordecai Brown	100.00	50.00	30.00
(23) Bill Burns	50.00	25.00	15.00
(24) Donie Bush	50.00	25.00	15.00
(25) Bobby Byrne	50.00	25.00	15.00
(26) Nixey Callahan	50.00	25.00	15.00
(27) Howie Camnitz	50.00	25.00	15.00
(28) Max Carey	100.00	50.00	30.00
(29) Bill Carrigan	50.00	25.00	15.00
(30) Frank Chance	100.00	50.00	30.00
(31) Hal Chase	50.00	25.00	15.00
(32) Ed Cicotte	80.00	40.00	24.00
(33) Fred Clarke	100.00	50.00	30.00
(34) Tommy Clarke	50.00	25.00	15.00
(35) Ty Cobb	750.00	375.00	225.00
(36) King Cole	50.00	25.00	15.00
(37) Eddie Collins (Philadelphia)	100.00	50.00	30.00
(38) Shano Collins (Chicago)	50.00	25.00	15.00
(39) Wid Conroy	50.00	25.00	15.00
(40) Doc Crandall	50.00	25.00	15.00
(41) Sam Crawford	100.00	50.00	30.00
(42) Birdie Cree	50.00	25.00	15.00
(43) Bill Dahlen	50.00	25.00	15.00
(44) Jake Daubert	50.00	25.00	15.00
(45) Harry Davis	50.00	25.00	15.00
(46) Jim Delahanty	50.00	25.00	15.00
(47) Art Devlin	50.00	25.00	15.00
(48) Josh Devore	50.00	25.00	15.00
(49) Mike Donlin	50.00	25.00	15.00
(50) Wild Bill Donovan	50.00	25.00	15.00
(51) Red Dooin	50.00	25.00	15.00
(52) Mickey Doolan	50.00	25.00	15.00
(53) Patsy Dougherty	50.00	25.00	15.00
(54) Tom Downey	50.00	25.00	15.00
(55) Larry Doyle	50.00	25.00	15.00
(56) Louis Drucke	50.00	25.00	15.00
(57) Clyde Engle	50.00	25.00	15.00
(58) Tex Erwin	50.00	25.00	15.00
(59) Steve Evans	50.00	25.00	15.00
(60) Johnny Evers	100.00	50.00	30.00
(61) Jack Ferry	50.00	25.00	15.00
(62) Ray Fisher	50.00	25.00	15.00
(63) Art Fletcher	50.00	25.00	15.00
(64) Russ Ford	50.00	25.00	15.00
(65) Art Fromme	50.00	25.00	15.00
(66) Earl Gardner	50.00	25.00	15.00
(67) Harry Gaspar	50.00	25.00	15.00
(68) George Gibson	50.00	25.00	15.00
(69) Roy Golden	50.00	25.00	15.00
(70) Hank Gowdy	50.00	25.00	15.00
(71) Peaches Graham	50.00	25.00	15.00
(72) Eddie Grant	50.00	25.00	15.00
(73) Dolly Gray	50.00	25.00	15.00
(74) Clark Griffith	100.00	50.00	30.00
(75) Bob Groom	50.00	25.00	15.00
(76) Bob Harmon	50.00	25.00	15.00
(77) Grover Hartley	50.00	25.00	15.00
(78) Arnold Hauser	50.00	25.00	15.00
(79) Buck Herzog	50.00	25.00	15.00
(80) Dick Hoblitzell	50.00	25.00	15.00
(81) Solly Hoffman (Hofman)	50.00	25.00	15.00
(82) Miller Huggins	100.00	50.00	30.00
(83) Long Tom Hughes	50.00	25.00	15.00
(84) John Hummel	50.00	25.00	15.00
(85) Hughie Jennings	100.00	50.00	30.00
(86) Walter Johnson	275.00	135.00	82.00
(87) Davy Jones	50.00	25.00	15.00
(88) Johnny Kling	50.00	25.00	15.00
(89) Otto Knabe	50.00	25.00	15.00
(90) Jack Knight	50.00	25.00	15.00
(91) Ed Konetchy	50.00	25.00	15.00
(92) Harry Krause	50.00	25.00	15.00
(93) Nap Lajoie	175.00	87.00	45.00
(94) Joe Lake	50.00	25.00	15.00
(95) Frank LaPorte	50.00	25.00	15.00
(96) Tommy Leach	50.00	25.00	15.00
(97) Lefty Leifield	50.00	25.00	15.00
(98) Ed Lennox	50.00	25.00	15.00
(99) Paddy Livingston	50.00	25.00	15.00
(100) Hans Lobert	50.00	25.00	15.00
(101) Harry Lord	50.00	25.00	15.00
(102) Fred Luderus	50.00	25.00	15.00
(103) Sherry Magee	50.00	25.00	15.00
(104) Rube Marquard	100.00	50.00	30.00
(105) Christy Mathewson	300.00	150.00	90.00
(106) Al Mattern	50.00	25.00	15.00
(107) George McBride	50.00	25.00	15.00
(108) Amby McConnell	50.00	25.00	15.00
(109) John McGraw	100.00	50.00	30.00
(110) Harry McIntire (McIntyre)	50.00	25.00	15.00
(111) Matty McIntyre	50.00	25.00	15.00
(112) Larry McLean	50.00	25.00	15.00
(113) Fred Merkle	50.00	25.00	15.00
(114) Chief Meyers	50.00	25.00	15.00
(115) Clyde Milan	50.00	25.00	15.00
(116) Dots Miller	50.00	25.00	15.00
(117) Mike Mitchell	50.00	25.00	15.00
(118) Earl Moore	50.00	25.00	15.00
(119) Pat Moran	50.00	25.00	15.00
(120) George Moriarty	50.00	25.00	15.00
(121) Mike Mowrey	50.00	25.00	15.00
(122) George Mullin	50.00	25.00	15.00
(123) Danny Murphy	50.00	25.00	15.00
(124) Red Murray	50.00	25.00	15.00
(125) Tom Needham	50.00	25.00	15.00
(126) Rebel Oakes	50.00	25.00	15.00
(127) Rube Oldring	50.00	25.00	15.00
(128) Marty O'Toole	50.00	25.00	15.00
(129) Fred Parent	50.00	25.00	15.00
(130) Dode Paskert	50.00	25.00	15.00
(131) Barney Pelty	50.00	25.00	15.00
(132) Eddie Phelps	50.00	25.00	15.00
(133) Jack Powell	50.00	25.00	15.00
(134) Jack Quinn	50.00	25.00	15.00
(135) Ed Reulbach	50.00	25.00	15.00
(136) Lew Richie	50.00	25.00	15.00
(137) Reggie Richter	50.00	25.00	15.00
(138) Jack Rowan	50.00	25.00	15.00
(139) Nap Rucker	50.00	25.00	15.00
(140) Slim Sallee	50.00	25.00	15.00
(141) Doc Scanlan	50.00	25.00	15.00
(142) Germany Schaefer	50.00	25.00	15.00
(143) Boss Schmidt	50.00	25.00	15.00
(144) Wildfire Schulte	50.00	25.00	15.00
(145) Jim Scott	50.00	25.00	15.00
(146) Tillie Shafer	50.00	25.00	15.00
(147) Dave Shean	50.00	25.00	15.00
(148) Jimmy Sheckard	50.00	25.00	15.00
(149) Mike Simon	50.00	25.00	15.00
(150) Fred Snodgrass	50.00	25.00	15.00
(151) Tris Speaker	125.00	62.00	37.00
(152) Oscar Stanage	50.00	25.00	15.00
(153) Bill Steele	50.00	25.00	15.00
(154) Harry Stovall	50.00	25.00	15.00
(155) Gabby Street	50.00	25.00	15.00
(156) George Suggs	50.00	25.00	15.00
(157) Billy Sullivan	50.00	25.00	15.00
(158) Bill Sweeney	50.00	25.00	15.00
(159) Jeff Sweeney	50.00	25.00	15.00
(160) Lee Tannehill	50.00	25.00	15.00
(161) Ira Thomas	50.00	25.00	15.00
(162) Joe Tinker	100.00	50.00	30.00
(163) John Titus	50.00	25.00	15.00
(164) Fred Toney	50.00	25.00	15.00
(165) Terry Turner	50.00	25.00	15.00
(166) Hippo Vaughn	50.00	25.00	15.00
(167) Heinie Wagner	50.00	25.00	15.00
(168) Bobby Wallace	100.00	50.00	30.00
(169) Ed Walsh	100.00	50.00	30.00
(170) Jack Warhop	50.00	25.00	15.00
(171) Zach Wheat	100.00	50.00	30.00
(172) Doc White	50.00	25.00	15.00
(173) Ed Willett	50.00	25.00	15.00
(174) Art Wilson (New York)	50.00	25.00	15.00
(175) Owen Wilson (Pittsburgh)	50.00	25.00	15.00
(176) Hooks Wiltse	50.00	25.00	15.00
(177) Harry Wolter	50.00	25.00	15.00
(178) Harry Wolverton	50.00	25.00	15.00
(179) Cy Young	400.00	200.00	120.00
(180) Irv Young	50.00	25.00	15.00

1920-21 Hendler's Ice Cream

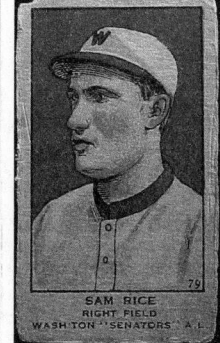

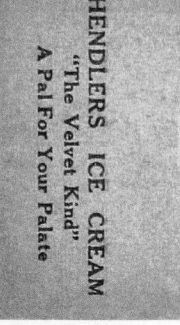

This Baltimore-area regional issue is a parallel to the 120-card strip card set known as W514, though it is not known whether all or only some of the W514 cards can be found with the ice cream company's advertising printed in blue on the backs. The cards were originally issued in strips of 10, cut horizontally from larger sheets. Well-cut cards should measure about 1-3/8" x 2-1/2." The back printing on each card has the same two top lines: HENDLERS ICE CREAM / "The Velvet Kind", with the third line being one of five currently know ad slogans. See W514 for checklist and base price information.

	NM	EX	VG
Common Player:	500.00	200.00	100.00

Stars: 4-6X corresponding W514

1910 Hermes Ice Cream Pirates Pins

The World's Champion Pittsburgh Pirates are featured on this colorful set of 1-1/4" pins. Sepia player portraits at center have a yellow border around with a blue banner at bottom and a skull and crossbones. The players are not identified on the buttons, making them difficult to collect.

	NM	E	VG
Complete Set (12):	18,000	9,000	5,400
Common Player:	1,100	550.00	330.00
(1) Bill Abstein	1,100	550.00	330.00
(2) Red Adams	1,100	550.00	330.00
(3) Bobby Byrne	1,100	550.00	330.00
(4) Howie Camnitz	1,100	550.00	330.00
(5) Fred Clarke	1,100	550.00	330.00
(6) George Gibson	1,100	550.00	330.00
(7) Tommy Leach	1,100	550.00	330.00
(8) Sam Leever	1,100	550.00	330.00
(9) Dots Miller	1,100	550.00	330.00
(10) Mike Simon	1,100	550.00	330.00
(11) Honus Wagner	8,000	4,000	2,400
(12) Owen Wilson	1,100	550.00	330.00

1916 Herpolsheimer Co.

 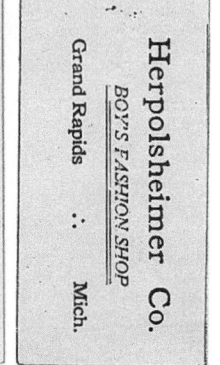

Advertising for a Michigan clothier is all that differentiates these cards from the more common Sporting News or blank-back M101-4 and M101-5 versions and those of other regional advertisers. The cards are black-and-white in 1-5/8" x 3" format. The Herpolsheimer cards command a significant premium from type-card and superstar collectors.

PREMIUMS:
Common Players: 3-4X
Hall of Famers: 2-3X

(See 1916 M101-4 and M101-5 Blank Backs for checklists and price guides.) (A certified NM Babe Ruth sold at auction for $82,250 in May 2010.)

1921 Herpolsheimer's

Evidently prepared for, but never actually issued by, a Grand Rapids, Mich., department store, this issue shares a basic format with the blank-backed strip card set designated W575-1 and the American Caramel Co. E121 Series of 80, although the known checklist for the Herpolsheimers includes cards that have not been verified in either or both of those sets. It is also not known to what extent the variations in

---

W575-1/E121 are found among the Michigan store's version. The 2-1/16" x 3-3/8" black-and-white cards are each currently known in only one copy each. The checklist here is likely incomplete; gaps have been left in the assigned numbering to accommodate future additions. All known examples originated froma series of eBay auctions in late 2004, with each card having a dollar sign and numeral penciled on back..

		NM
Common Player:		350.00
(3)	Grover Alexander	1,100
(5)	Jim Bagby	350.00
(11)	J. Franklin Baker	750.00
(13)	Ping Bodie	350.00
(15)	George Burns	350.00
(16)	Geo. J. Burns	350.00
(18)	Owen Bush	350.00
(21)	Ty Cobb	4,000
(22)	Eddie Collins	750.00
(28)	George Dauss	350.00
(29)	Dave Davenport	350.00
(30)	Charles Deal	350.00
(33)	William Doak	350.00
(34)	Bill Donovan (Pitching)	350.00
(39)	Urban Faber (Dark uniform.)	750.00
(45)	Art Fletcher	350.00
(47)	Jacques Fournier	350.00
(49)	W.L. Gardner	350.00
(52)	"Kid" Gleason	350.00
(54)	Hank Gowdy	350.00
(55)	John Graney (L.F.)	350.00
(57)	Tom Griffith	350.00
(67)	John Henry	350.00
(74)	Rogers Hornsby (2nd B.)	2,000
(79)	Hugh Jennings	500.00
(80)	Walter Johnson	4,500
(82)	James Johnston	350.00
(84)	Joe Judge (Batting)	350.00
(89)	P.J. Kilduff	350.00
(93)	"Nemo" Leibold	350.00
(94)	Duffy Lewis	350.00
(95)	Al Mamaux	350.00
(96)	"Rabbit" Maranville	750.00
(101)	John McGraw (Manager)	750.00
(102)	Jack McInnis	350.00
(107)	Clyde Milan	350.00
(109)	Otto Miller	350.00
(112)	Guy Morton	350.00
(115)	Eddie Murphy	350.00
(116)	"Hy" Myers (C.F.)	350.00
(123)	Steve O'Neill	350.00
(124)	Roger Peckinbaugh (Peckinpaugh)	350.00
(125)	Jeff Pfeffer (Brooklyn)	350.00
(133)	E.C. Rice	350.00
(134)	Eppa Rixey, Jr.	750.00
(145)	Babe Ruth (R.F.)	10,000
(149)	"Slim" Sallee (Glove showing.)	350.00
(151)	Ray Schalk (Bunting)	750.00
(153)	Walter Schang	350.00
(155)	Everett Scott (Boston)	350.00
(173)	Tris Speaker (Manager)	1,625
(175)	Charles Stengel (Batting)	750.00
(177)	Milton Stock	350.00
(178)	Amos Strunk (R.F.)	350.00
(181)	Zeb Terry (White uniform.)	350.00
(182)	Chester Thomas	350.00
(183)	Fred Toney (Both feet on ground.)	350.00
(186)	George Tyler	350.00
(187)	Jim Vaughn (Dark cap.)	350.00
(190)	Bob Veach (Arms folded.)	350.00
(191)	Oscar Vitt (3rd B.)	350.00
(193)	W. Wambsganss	350.00
(194)	Carl Weilman	350.00
(195)	Zach Wheat	750.00
(196)	George Whitted	350.00
(198)	Ivy B. Wingo	350.00
(200)	Joe Wood	675.00
(202)	"Pep" (Ralph) Young	350.00

1888 S.F. Hess (N338-2)

The most popular of the S.F. Hess & Co. issues, this 21-card set was issued in 1889 and pictures 16 players from the New York Giants, two New York Mets players, two from St. Louis and one from Detroit. The cards measure 2-3/4" x 1-1/2" and feature sepia-toned photographs, most of which are enclosed in ovals with a dark background. The player's name is printed in capital letters just beneath the photo, and the S.F. Hess & Co. logo appears at the bottom (without using the Creole Cigarette brand name).

		NM	E	VG
Common Player:		7,900	3,950	2,500
(1)	Bill Brown	7,900	3,950	2,500
(2)	Roger Conner (Connor)	20,000	10,000	6,000
(3)	Ed Crane	7,900	3,950	2,500
(4)	Buck Ewing	21,000	10,500	6,200
(5)	Elmer Foster	7,900	3,950	2,500
(6)	Wm. George	7,900	3,950	2,500
(7)	Joe Gerhardt	7,900	3,950	2,500
(8)	Chas. Getzein (Getzien)	7,900	3,950	2,500
(9)	Geo. Gore	7,900	3,950	2,500
(10)	Gil Hatfield	7,900	3,950	2,500
(11)	Tim Keefe	20,000	10,000	6,000
(12)	Arlie Latham	7,900	3,950	2,500
(13)	Pat Murphy	7,900	3,950	2,500
(14)	Jim Mutrie	7,900	3,950	2,500
(15)	Dave Orr	7,900	3,950	2,500
(16)	Danny Richardson	7,900	3,950	2,500
(17)	Mike Slattery	7,900	3,950	2,500
(18)	Silent Mike Tiernan	7,900	3,950	2,500
(19)	Lidell Titcomb	7,900	3,950	2,500
(20)	Johnny Ward	20,000	10,000	6,000
(21)	Curt Welch	7,900	3,950	2,500
(22)	Mickey Welch	20,000	10,000	6,000
(23)	Arthur Whitney	7,900	3,950	2,500

1909-11 Hindu Cigarettes

Hindu backs are among the more difficult to find among the various cigarette-brand ads seen on T205 and T206 cards. T206s are usually found with the ad printed in brown ink. Much scarcer are those with the ad in red. Fewer than 50 T205s have ever been seen with the Hindu ad on back, printed in brown. Multipliers shown are for "common" player cards. It is noteworthy that more than a few T206 Hindus are found with the cryptic "7C" or "FC" in crayon or grease pencil on the back.

PREMIUMS
T205: 15-20X
T206 Brown Commons: 6-8X
T206 Brown Hall of Famers: 4-6X
T206 Brown Southern Leaguers: 2.5-3.5X
T206 Red Commons: 8-16X
T206 Red Hall of Famers: 10-12X

(See T205, T206 for checklists and base card values.)

1958 Hires Root Beer

Like most baseball cards issued with a tab in the 1950s, the Hires cards are extremely scarce today in their original form. The basic card was attached to a wedge-shaped tab that served the dual purpose of offering a fan club membership and of holding the card into the cardboard carton of soda bottles with which it was distributed. Measurements of the card vary somewhat, from about 2-3/8" to 2-5/8" wide and 3-3/8" to 3-5/8" tall (without tab). The tab extends for another 3-1/2". Numbering of the Hires set begins at 10 and goes through 76, with card #69 never issued, making a set complete at 66 cards.

PEE WEE REESE
INFIELD—Los Angeles Dodgers

JOIN THE HIRES BASEBALL CLUB TODAY!

Learn how to play baseball from the BIG LEAGUERS! How to pitch! Catch! Judge plays! Just paste 10c to the Hires bottle cap picture on the reverse side and send with 2 Hires bottle caps to:

CHARLES E. HIRES COMPANY
P.O. Box 300, Haddonfield, New Jersey

LOOK WHAT YOU GET:

1 Hires "How to Play Baseball Book".
2 Valuable membership card.

Printed in U.S.A.

Pee Wee Reese
LOS ANGELES DODGERS

To: HIRES BASEBALL CLUB
BOX 500
HADDONFIELD, NEW JERSEY

	NM	E	VG
Complete Set, W/Tab (66):	5,250	2,650	1,550
Common Player, W/Tab:	60.00	30.00	18.00
Complete Set, No Tab (66):	3,250	1,600	975.00
Common Player, No Tab:	35.00	17.50	10.00

WITH TAB

#	Player	NM	E	VG
10	Richie Ashburn	165.00	80.00	50.00
11	Chico Carrasquel	60.00	30.00	18.00
12	Dave Philley	60.00	30.00	18.00
13	Don Newcombe	110.00	55.00	35.00
14	Wally Post	60.00	30.00	18.00
15	Rip Repulski	60.00	30.00	18.00
16	Chico Fernandez	60.00	30.00	18.00
17	Larry Doby	95.00	50.00	25.00
18	Hector Brown	60.00	30.00	18.00
19	Danny O'Connell	60.00	30.00	18.00
20	Granny Hamner	60.00	30.00	18.00
21	Dick Groat	60.00	30.00	18.00
22	Ray Narleski	60.00	30.00	18.00
23	Pee Wee Reese	165.00	85.00	50.00
24	Bob Friend	60.00	30.00	18.00
25	Willie Mays	500.00	250.00	150.00
26	Bob Nieman	60.00	30.00	18.00
27	Frank Thomas	60.00	30.00	18.00
28	Curt Simmons	60.00	30.00	18.00
29	Stan Lopata	60.00	30.00	18.00
30	Bob Skinner	60.00	30.00	18.00
31	Ron Kline	60.00	30.00	18.00
32	Willie Miranda	60.00	30.00	18.00
33	Bob Avila	60.00	30.00	18.00
34	Clem Labine	90.00	45.00	27.50
35	Ray Jablonski	60.00	30.00	18.00
36	Bill Mazeroski	110.00	55.00	35.00
37	Billy Gardner	60.00	30.00	18.00
38	Pete Runnels	60.00	30.00	18.00
39	Jack Sanford	60.00	30.00	18.00
40	Dave Sisler	60.00	30.00	18.00
41	Don Zimmer	90.00	45.00	27.00
42	Johnny Podres	90.00	45.00	27.50
43	Dick Farrell	60.00	30.00	18.00
44	Hank Aaron	425.00	210.00	125.00
45	Bill Virdon	60.00	30.00	18.00
46	Bobby Thomson	75.00	37.50	22.50
47	Willard Nixon	60.00	30.00	18.00
48	Billy Loes	60.00	30.00	18.00
49	Hank Sauer	60.00	30.00	18.00
50	Johnny Antonelli	60.00	30.00	18.00
51	Daryl Spencer	60.00	30.00	18.00
52	Ken Lehman	75.00	37.50	22.50
53	Sammy White	60.00	30.00	18.00
54	Charley Neal	75.00	37.50	22.50
55	Don Drysdale	165.00	80.00	50.00
56	Jack Jensen	65.00	32.50	20.00
57	Ray Katt	60.00	30.00	18.00
58	Franklin Sullivan	60.00	30.00	18.00
59	Roy Face	60.00	30.00	18.00
60	Willie Jones	60.00	30.00	18.00
61	Duke Snider (SP)	250.00	125.00	75.00
62	Whitey Lockman	60.00	30.00	18.00
63	Gino Cimoli	75.00	37.00	22.50
64	Marv Grissom	60.00	30.00	18.00
65	Gene Baker	60.00	30.00	18.00
66	George Zuverink	60.00	30.00	18.00
67	Ted Kluszewski	135.00	70.00	40.00
68	Jim Busby	60.00	30.00	18.00
69	Not issued			
70	Curt Barclay	60.00	30.00	18.00
71	Hank Foiles	60.00	30.00	18.00
72	Gene Stephens	60.00	30.00	18.00
73	Al Worthington	60.00	30.00	18.00
74	Al Walker	60.00	30.00	18.00
75	Bob Boyd	60.00	30.00	18.00
76	Al Pilarcik	60.00	30.00	18.00

NO TAB

#	Player			
10	Richie Ashburn	110.00	55.00	35.00
11	Chico Carrasquel	35.00	17.50	10.00
12	Dave Philley	35.00	17.50	10.00
13	Don Newcombe	65.00	32.50	20.00
14	Wally Post	35.00	17.50	10.00
15	Rip Repulski	35.00	17.50	10.00
16	Chico Fernandez	35.00	17.50	10.00
17	Larry Doby	75.00	37.50	22.50
18	Hector Brown	35.00	17.50	10.00
19	Danny O'Connell	35.00	17.50	10.00
20	Granny Hamner	35.00	17.50	10.00
21	Dick Groat	35.00	17.50	10.00
22	Ray Narleski	35.00	17.50	10.00
23	Pee Wee Reese	100.00	50.00	30.00
24	Bob Friend	35.00	17.50	10.00
25	Willie Mays	200.00	100.00	60.00
26	Bob Nieman	35.00	17.50	10.00
27	Frank Thomas	35.00	17.50	10.00
28	Curt Simmons	35.00	17.50	10.00
29	Stan Lopata	35.00	17.50	10.00
30	Bob Skinner	35.00	17.50	10.00
31	Ron Kline	35.00	17.50	10.00
32	Willie Miranda	35.00	17.50	10.00
33	Bob Avila	35.00	17.50	10.00
34	Clem Labine	45.00	22.50	13.50
35	Ray Jablonski	35.00	17.50	10.00
36	Bill Mazeroski	75.00	37.50	22.50
37	Billy Gardner	35.00	17.50	10.00
38	Pete Runnels	35.00	17.50	10.00
39	Jack Sanford	35.00	17.50	10.00
40	Dave Sisler	35.00	17.50	10.00
41	Don Zimmer	45.00	22.50	13.50
42	Johnny Podres	45.00	22.50	13.50
43	Dick Farrell	35.00	17.50	10.00
44	Hank Aaron	200.00	100.00	60.00
45	Bill Virdon	35.00	17.50	10.00
46	Bobby Thomson	45.00	22.50	13.50
47	Willard Nixon	35.00	17.50	10.00
48	Billy Loes	35.00	17.50	10.00
49	Hank Sauer	35.00	17.50	10.00
50	Johnny Antonelli	35.00	17.50	10.00
51	Daryl Spencer	35.00	17.50	10.00
52	Ken Lehman	40.00	20.00	12.00
53	Sammy White	35.00	17.50	10.00
54	Charley Neal	40.00	20.00	12.00
55	Don Drysdale	75.00	37.50	22.50
56	Jack Jensen	40.00	20.00	12.00
57	Ray Katt	35.00	17.50	10.00
58	Franklin Sullivan	35.00	17.50	10.00
59	Roy Face	35.00	17.50	10.00
60	Willie Jones	35.00	17.50	10.00
61	Duke Snider (SP)	180.00	90.00	55.00
62	Whitey Lockman	35.00	17.50	10.00
63	Gino Cimoli	40.00	20.00	10.00
64	Marv Grissom	35.00	17.50	10.00
65	Gene Baker	35.00	17.50	10.00
66	George Zuverink	35.00	17.50	10.00
67	Ted Kluszewski	75.00	37.50	22.50
68	Jim Busby	35.00	17.50	10.00
69	**NOT ISSUED**			
70	Curt Barclay	35.00	17.50	10.00
71	Hank Foiles	35.00	17.50	10.00
72	Gene Stephens	35.00	17.50	10.00
73	Al Worthington	35.00	17.50	10.00
74	Al Walker	35.00	17.50	10.00
75	Bob Boyd	35.00	17.50	10.00
76	Al Pilarcik	35.00	17.50	10.00

1958 Hires Root Beer Test Set

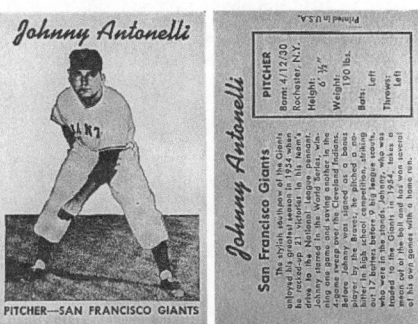

Johnny Antonelli
PITCHER—SAN FRANCISCO GIANTS

Among the scarcest of the regional issues of the late 1950s is the eight-card test issue which preceded the Hires Root Beer set of 66 cards. The test cards differ from the regular issue in that they have sepia-toned, rather than color pictures, which are set against plain yellow or orange backgrounds (much like the 1958 Topps), instead of viewed through a knothole. Like the regular Hires cards, the 2-5/16" x 3-1/2" cards were issued with an attached wedge-shaped tab of like size. The tab offered membership in Hires' baseball fan club, and served to hold the card into the carton of bottled root beer with which it was given away.

	NM	E	VG
Complete Set, W/Tab (8):	10,000	4,000	2,000
Common Player, W/Tab:	725.00	290.00	145.00
Complete Set, No Tab (8):	3,000	1,200	600.00
Common Player, No Tab:	250.00	100.00	50.00

WITH TAB

#	Player			
(1)	Johnny Antonelli	725.00	290.00	145.00
(2)	Jim Busby	725.00	290.00	145.00
(3)	Chico Fernandez	725.00	290.00	145.00
(4)	Bob Friend	725.00	290.00	145.00
(5)	Vern Law	725.00	290.00	145.00
(6)	Stan Lopata	725.00	290.00	145.00
(7)	Willie Mays	5,000	2,000	1,000
(8)	Al Pilarcik	725.00	290.00	145.00

NO TAB

#	Player			
(1)	Johnny Antonelli	250.00	100.00	50.00
(2)	Jim Busby	250.00	100.00	50.00
(3)	Chico Fernandez	250.00	100.00	50.00
(4)	Bob Friend	250.00	100.00	50.00
(5)	Vern Law	250.00	100.00	50.00
(6)	Stan Lopata	250.00	100.00	50.00
(7)	Willie Mays	2,100	1,075	645.00
(8)	Al Pilarcik	250.00	100.00	50.00

1951 Hirsch Clothing stores Chicago Cubs Premiums

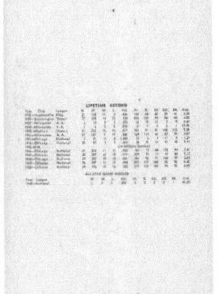

These Cubs player pictures were issued by a Chicago area clothing emporium. This type of premium was often issued in conjunction with player autograph appearances at retail outlets. The pictures are 5-1/2" x 8," printed in black-and-white on semi-glossy thin cardboard stock. Backs have year-by-year stats. Each photo has a facsimile autograph. Printed in the wide bottom border is "COMPLIMENTS OF HIRSCH CLOTHING STORES". Whether this checklist represents the entirety of the issue, or there are players yet to be reported, is not known.

	NM	EX	VG
(1) Hank Sauer	40.00	25.00	80.00
(2) Johnny Schmitz	25.00		80.00 40.00
(3) Bob Schultz	40.00	25.00	80.00

1951-52 Hit Parade of Champions

(See 1951-52 Berk Ross.)

1953 H-O Instant Oatmeal Records

Baseball playing tips from several star New York players are featured in this set of box-top premium records. For 25 cents and two oatmeal box tops, a set of three of the four records could be ordered by mail. The records are 4-3/4" in diameter and have a color player portrait with facsimile autograph on the back side, while the grooved recording side has an action pose in black-and-white.

	NM	E	VG
Complete Set (4):	1,050	525.00	315.00
Common Player:	160.00	80.00	48.00
(1) Roy Campanella	350.00	175.00	105.00
(2) "Whitey" Lockman	175.00	87.00	52.00
(3) Allie Reynolds	225.00	110.00	67.00
(4) Duke Snider	350.00	175.00	105.00

1977 Holiday Inn Discs

Virtually identical in format to the several locally sponsored disc sets of the previous year, these 3-3/8" diameter player discs were given away five at a time with the purchase of a children's dinner at some 72 participating Holiday Inns in the Midwest. Discs once again feature black-and-white player portrait photos in the center of a baseball design. The left and right panels are in one of several bright colors. Licensed by the Players Association through Mike Schechter Associates, the player photos carry no uniform logos. Backs are printed in green. The unnumbered discs are checklisted here alphabetically.

	NM	E	VG
Complete Set (70):	160.00	80.00	45.00
Common Player:	2.00	1.00	.60
(1) Sal Bando	2.00	1.00	.60
(2) Buddy Bell	2.00	1.00	.60
(3) Johnny Bench	6.00	3.00	1.75
(4) Larry Bowa	2.00	1.00	.60
(5) Steve Braun	2.00	1.00	.60
(6) George Brett	20.00	10.00	6.00
(7) Lou Brock	6.00	3.00	1.75
(8) Jeff Burroughs	2.00	1.00	.60
(9) Bert Campaneris	2.00	1.00	.60
(10) John Candelaria	2.00	1.00	.60
(11) Jose Cardenal	2.00	1.00	.60
(12) Rod Carew	6.00	3.00	1.75
(13) Steve Carlton	6.00	3.00	1.75
(14) Dave Cash	2.00	1.00	.60
(15) Cesar Cedeno	2.00	1.00	.60
(16) Ron Cey	2.00	1.00	.60
(17) Dave Concepcion	2.00	1.00	.60
(18) Dennis Eckersley	5.00	2.50	1.50
(19) Mark Fidrych	3.00	1.50	.90
(20) Rollie Fingers	5.00	2.50	1.50
(21) Carlton Fisk	6.00	3.00	1.75
(22) George Foster	2.00	1.00	.60
(23) Wayne Garland	2.00	1.00	.60
(24) Ralph Garr	2.00	1.00	.60
(25) Steve Garvey	4.00	2.00	1.25
(26) Cesar Geronimo	2.00	1.00	.60
(27) Bobby Grich	2.00	1.00	.60
(28) Ken Griffey Sr.	2.50	1.25	.70
(29) Don Gullett	2.00	1.00	.60
(30) Mike Hargrove	2.00	1.00	.60
(31) Al Hrabosky	2.00	1.00	.60
(32) Jim Hunter	5.00	2.50	1.50
(33) Reggie Jackson	10.00	5.00	3.00
(34) Randy Jones	2.00	1.00	.60
(35a) Dave Kingman (Mets)	2.50	1.25	.70
(35b) Dave Kingman (Padres)	4.00	2.00	1.25
(36) Jerry Koosman	2.00	1.00	.60
(37) Dave LaRoche	2.00	1.00	.60
(38) Greg Luzinski	2.00	1.00	.60
(39) Fred Lynn	2.00	1.00	.60
(40) Bill Madlock	2.00	1.00	.60
(41) Rick Manning	2.00	1.00	.60
(42) Jon Matlock	2.00	1.00	.60
(43) John Mayberry	2.00	1.00	.60
(44) Hal McRae	2.00	1.00	.60
(45) Andy Messersmith	2.00	1.00	.60
(46) Rick Monday	2.00	1.00	.60
(47) John Montefusco	2.00	1.00	.60
(48) Joe Morgan	6.00	3.00	1.75
(49) Thurman Munson	4.00	2.00	1.25
(50) Bobby Murcer	2.00	1.00	.60
(51) Bill North	2.00	1.00	.60
(52) Jim Palmer	6.00	3.00	1.75
(53) Tony Perez	5.00	2.50	1.50
(54) Jerry Reuss	2.00	1.00	.60
(55) Brooks Robinson	6.00	3.00	1.75
(56) Pete Rose	15.00	7.50	4.50
(57) Joe Rudi	2.00	1.00	.60
(58) Nolan Ryan	40.00	20.00	12.00
(59) Manny Sanguillen	2.00	1.00	.60
(60) Mike Schmidt	15.00	7.50	4.50
(61) Tom Seaver	6.00	3.00	1.75
(62) Bill Singer	2.00	1.00	.60
(63) Willie Stargell	6.00	3.00	1.75
(64) Rusty Staub	3.00	1.50	.90
(65) Luis Tiant	2.00	1.00	.60
(66) Bob Watson	2.00	1.00	.60
(67) Butch Wynegar	2.00	1.00	.60
(68) Carl Yastrzemski	7.50	3.75	2.25
(69) Robin Yount	6.00	3.00	1.75
(70) Richie Zisk	2.00	1.00	.60

1925 Holland World's Champions Washington Senators

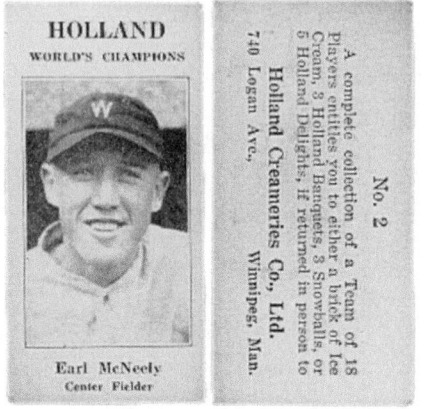

The World's Champion Washington Senators were featured on a set issued in Winnipeg, Manitoba, of all places. The 1-1/2" x 3" cards have player portrait photos printed in blue on front. The black-printed back has a card number and details of a redemption offer of cards for ice cream. Like many such offers it appears as if card #16 was intentionally withheld or minimally distributed, making it very scarce today.

	NM	E	VG
Complete Set, No #16 (17):	35,000	17,500	10,250
Common Player:	1,850	925.00	555.00
1 Ralph Miller	1,850	925.00	555.00
2 Earl McNeely	1,850	925.00	555.00
3 Allan Russell	1,850	925.00	555.00
4 Ernest Shirley	1,850	925.00	555.00
5 Sam Rice	2,500	1,250	750.00
6 Muddy Ruel	1,850	925.00	555.00
7 Ossie Bluege	1,850	925.00	555.00
8 Nemo Leibold	1,850	925.00	555.00
9 Paul Zahniser	1,850	925.00	555.00
10 Firpo Marberry	1,850	925.00	555.00
11 Warren Ogden	1,850	925.00	555.00
12 George Mogridge	1,850	925.00	555.00
13 Tom Zachary	1,850	925.00	555.00
14 Goose Goslin	2,500	1,250	750.00
15 Joe Judge	1,850	925.00	555.00
16 Roger Peckinpaugh	5,000	2,500	1,500
17 Bucky Harris	2,500	1,250	750.00
18 Walter Johnson	7,750	3,875	2,325

1916 Holmes to Homes Bread

Most often found with blank backs, this 200-card set can also be found with ads on the back for several local and regional businesses. Among them is Holmes to Homes Milk-Made Bread, location unknown. Type card collectors and superstar collectors can expect to pay a significant premium for individual cards with Holmes to Homes advertising. Cards measure 1-5/8" x 3" and are printed in black-and-white.

PREMIUM: 15-25X

(See 1916 M101-5 Blank Backs for checklist and base value information.)

1920 Holsum Bread

Issued by the Weil Baking Co., New Orleans, which produced several sets in the 1910s, this issue shares a format, but not the checklist of the 1921 American Caramel Co. set known as E121, Series of 80, and the contemporary W575-1 blank-back strip cards. To what extent the base cards and known variations in those set are found among the Holsum version is unknown. The Holsum cards differ from E121 primarily in the advertising on the back and sometimes in photo and/or caption details. The approximately 2" x 3-1/4" black-and-white cards are much scarcer than the caramel version. The trial checklist presented here is incomplete.

		NM	E	VG
Common Player:		350.00	175.00	100.00
(4)	Jimmy Austin	350.00	175.00	100.00
(2)	Grover Alexander	1,000	500.00	300.00
(7)	Dave Bancroft	600.00	300.00	180.00
(13)	Jack Barry	350.00	175.00	100.00
(16)	Ping Bodie	350.00	175.00	100.00
(19)	George Burns	350.00	175.00	100.00
(20)	Geo S. Burns	350.00	175.00	100.00
(26)	Ray Chapman	425.00	210.00	125.00
(23)	Max Carey	600.00	300.00	180.00
(28)	Eddie Cicotte	600.00	300.00	180.00
(30)	Eddie Collins	750.00	370.00	220.00
(37)	Geo. Cutshaw	350.00	175.00	100.00
(32)	Harry Coveleskie	350.00	175.00	100.00
(42)	Charles Deal (Dark uniform.)	350.00	175.00	100.00
(39)	George Dauss	350.00	175.00	100.00
(45)	Johnny Evers	600.00	300.00	180.00
(44)	Williams Doak	350.00	175.00	100.00
(46)	Urban Faber (Dark uniform.)	600.00	300.00	180.00
(50)	Art Fletcher	350.00	175.00	100.00
(51)	Eddie Foster	350.00	175.00	100.00
(52)	Jacques Fournier	350.00	175.00	100.00
(64)	Hank Gowdy	350.00	175.00	100.00
(70)	Tom Griffith	350.00	175.00	100.00
(56)	W.L. Gardner	350.00	175.00	100.00
(80)	Rogers Hornsby	1,250	625.00	375.00
(66)	John Graney	350.00	175.00	100.00
(68)	John Henry	350.00	175.00	100.00
(69)	"Buck" Herzog	350.00	175.00	100.00
(85)	Joe Jackson (VALUE UNDETERMINED) (A certified Poor card sold at auction for $19,618 in June 2010)			
(88)	Walter Johnson (Hands at chest.)	2,000	1,000	600.00
(93)	Wm. Killefer Jr.	350.00	175.00	100.00
(71)	Harry Hooper	600.00	300.00	180.00
(95)	John Lavan	350.00	175.00	100.00
(89)	James Johnston	350.00	175.00	100.00
(97)	H.B. Leonard	350.00	175.00	100.00
(91)	Joe Judge	350.00	175.00	100.00
(99)	Duffy Lewis	350.00	175.00	100.00
(92)	P.J. Kilduff	350.00	175.00	100.00
(105)	Al Mamaux	350.00	175.00	100.00
(110)	John McGraw	600.00	300.00	180.00
(107)	"Rabbit" Maranville	600.00	300.00	180.00
(115)	Clyde Milan	350.00	175.00	100.00
(116)	Otto Miller	350.00	175.00	100.00
(120)	Ray Morgan	350.00	175.00	100.00
(122)	Guy Morton	350.00	175.00	100.00
(124)	"Hy" Myers	350.00	175.00	100.00

(127)	Arthur Nehf	350.00	175.00	100.00
(129)	Steve O'Neill	350.00	175.00	100.00
(132)	Roger Peckinpaugh	400.00	200.00	120.00
(133)	Jeff Pfeffer	350.00	175.00	100.00
(136)	Bill Rariden	350.00	175.00	100.00
(140)	"Bob" Roth	350.00	175.00	100.00
(138)	Davey Robertson	350.00	175.00	100.00
(153)	Walter Schang	350.00	175.00	100.00
(142)	Edd Rousch	600.00	300.00	180.00
(155)	Everett Scott	350.00	175.00	100.00
(150)	Slim Sallee	350.00	175.00	100.00
(162)	Geo. Sisler	600.00	300.00	180.00
(159)	Hank Severied	350.00	175.00	100.00
(164)	J. Carlisle Smith	350.00	175.00	100.00
(166)	Tris Speaker	1,250	625.00	375.00
(168)	Charles Stengel	600.00	300.00	180.00
(169)	Milton Stock	350.00	175.00	100.00
(170)	Amos Strunk (Batting, Chicago Americans.)	350.00	175.00	100.00
(171)	Amos Strunk (Arms at side, Chicago White Sox.)	350.00	175.00	100.00
(173)	Chester Thomas	350.00	175.00	100.00
(174)	Fred Toney	350.00	175.00	100.00
(175)	Jim Vaughn (Plain uniform)	350.00	175.00	100.00
(178)	Bob Veach	350.00	175.00	100.00
(184)	W. Wambsganss	350.00	175.00	100.00
(186)	Carl Weilman	350.00	175.00	100.00
(187)	Zack Wheat	600.00	300.00	180.00
(192)	Ivy Wingo	350.00	175.00	100.00
(190)	Claude Williams (White stockings, correct photo.)	2,500	1,250	750.00
(202)	Pep Young	350.00	175.00	100.00

1959 Home Run Derby

GIL HODGES
LOS ANGELES DODGERS

This 20-card unnumbered set was produced by American Motors to publicize the Home Run Derby television program. The cards measure approximately 3-1/4" x 5-1/4" and feature black-and-white player photos on blank-backed white stock. The player name and team are printed beneath the photo. This set was reprinted (marked as such) in 1988 by Card Collectors' Co. of New York. An advertising poster is sometimes seen which is essentially an uncut sheet of the cards with a promotional message at bottom.

		NM	E	VG
Complete Set (20):		17,500	8,7500.00	5,000
Common Player:		300.00	150.00	90.00
Advertising Poster:		6,200	3,100	1,900
(1)	Hank Aaron	1,600	800.00	500.00
(2)	Bob Allison	300.00	150.00	90.00
(3)	Ernie Banks	1,250	650.00	400.00
(4)	Ken Boyer	350.00	175.00	100.00
(5)	Bob Cerv	300.00	150.00	90.00
(6)	Rocky Colavito	600.00	300.00	180.00
(7)	Gil Hodges	600.00	300.00	180.00
(8)	Jackie Jensen	300.00	150.00	90.00
(9)	Al Kaline	1,100	650.00	325.00
(10)	Harmon Killebrew	1,100	650.00	325.00
(11)	Jim Lemon	300.00	150.00	90.00
(12)	Mickey Mantle	3,500	1,750	1,050
(13)	Ed Mathews	1,000	500.00	300.00
(14)	Willie Mays	1,600	800.00	500.00
(15)	Wally Post	300.00	150.00	90.00
(16)	Frank Robinson	825.00	400.00	240.00
(17)	Mark Scott (host)	600.00	300.00	180.00
(18)	Duke Snider	1,200	600.00	375.00
(19)	Dick Stuart	300.00	150.00	90.00
(20)	Gus Triandos	300.00	150.00	90.00

1894 Honest (Duke) Cabinets (N142)

These color cabinet cards, which measure 6" x 9-1/2", were produced by W.H. Duke for its Honest tobacco brand. The player name is centered at the bottom of the card front. The brand name "Honest" is located in the lower-left corner with the words "New York" in the lower-right corner. Three bicyclists are also part of the set.

		NM	E	VG
Complete Set (4):		100,000	50,000	30,000
Common Player:		16,000	8,000	4,800
(1)	G.S. Davis	24,200	12,100	7,260
(2)	E.J. Delahanty	35,300	17,600	10,560
(3)	W.M. Nash	16,000	8,000	4,800
(4)	W. Robinson	36,850	18,425	11,055

1911-12 Honest Long Cut Tobacco

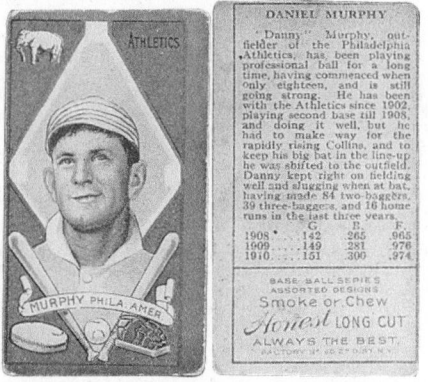

Advertising, printed in black, for Honest Long Cut tobacco is among the more commonly found on the backs of T205 Gold Border cards of 1911. The brand also advertised on the multi-sport T227 Series of Champions in 1912.

(See T205, T227 for checklists and values.)

1927 Honey Boy

The date of issue for this rare Canadian issue is conjectural. These black-and-white 1-5/8" x 2-3/8" cards were issued by the Purity Ice Cream Company in Winnipeg, Canada, and were redeemable as a set of 21 for a brick of "Delicious Honey Boy Ice Cream." Besides the major leaguers in the set, there are also cards of local amateurs and semi-pros, including hockey Hall of Famer Steamer Maxwell and Chicago Blackhawks star Cecil Browne. The major leaguers are not identified by team, nor do their photos have team insignias present. When redeemed, cards were punch-cancelled. Values shown are for uncancelled cards; cards exhibiting the punch-holes would be worth about 50 percent of the indicated figures.

		NM	E	VG
Complete Set (21):		24,000	12,000	7,500
Common (Major League) Player:		900.00	450.00	275.00
1	"Steamer" Maxwell (Arenas)	2,000	1,000	600.00
2	Cecil Browne (Dominion Express)	400.00	200.00	120.00
3	Carson McVey (Transcona)	400.00	200.00	120.00
4	Sam Perlman (Tigers)	400.00	200.00	120.00
5	"Snake" Siddle (Arenas)	400.00	200.00	120.00
6	Eddie Cass (Columbus)	400.00	200.00	120.00
7	Jimmy Bradley (Columbus)	400.00	200.00	120.00
8	Gordon Caslake (Dominion Express)	400.00	200.00	120.00
9	Ward McVey (Tigers)	400.00	200.00	120.00
10	"Tris" Speaker	3,800	1,900	1,140
11	George Sisler	2,000	1,000	600.00
12	E. Meusel	900.00	450.00	275.00
13	Ed. Roush	2,000	1,000	600.00
14	"Babe" Ruth	22,500	11,250	6,750
15	Harry Heilmann	2,000	1,000	600.00
16	Heinie Groh	900.00	450.00	275.00
17	Eddie Collins	2,000	1,000	600.00
18	Grover Alexander	3,250	1,600	975.00
19	Dave Bancroft	2,000	1,000	600.00
20	Frank Frisch	2,000	1,000	600.00
21	George Burns	900.00	450.00	275.00

1905-1909 Carl Horner Cabinets

Carl Horner was the premier baseball portraitist of the early 20th Century. From his Boston studio came the images of the day's stars and journeymen which live on today on some of the most popular baseball cards of the era - including the famed T206 Honus Wagner. Highly collectible in their own right are the cabinet photos produced by the studio. Because of rarity, values can be determined only on those rare occasions when an example comes onto the market. Because the body of his work was accomplished over a number of years, mounting style and other technical details of the generally 5-1/2" x 7" cabinets may vary. Because the players are not identified on the cabinet, identification can be a problem, though quite often a contemporary notation of the player's name can be found written on back.

	NM	E	VG
Common Player:	1,200	600.00	350.00
Walter Johnson	15,000	6,000	3,600
Honus Wagner	20,000	8,000	4.800.00

1959 Hostess Bob Turley

The date attributed to this card is speculative. The 3-1/2" x 4-3/8" black-and-white card has an action pose of the Yankees pitcher on front surrounded by a white border. On back is a list of Hostess Cakes products.

	NM	E	VG
Bob Turley	200.00	100.00	60.00

1975 Hostess

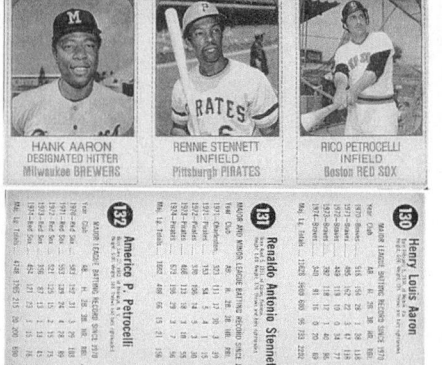

HANK AARON
DESIGNATED HITTER
Milwaukee BREWERS

RENNIE STENNETT
INFIELD
Pittsburgh PIRATES

RICO PETROCELLI
INFIELD
Boston RED SOX

The first of what would become five annual issues, the 1975 Hostess set consists of 50 three-card panels which formed the bottom of boxes of family-size snack cake products. Unlike many similar issues, the Hostess cards do not share common borders, so it was possible to cut them neatly and evenly from the box. Well-cut single cards measure 2-1/4" x 3-1/4", while a three-card panel measures 7-1/4" x 3-1/4". Because some of the panels were issued on packages of less popular snack cakes, they are somewhat scarcer today. Since the hobby was quite well-developed when the Hostess cards were first issued, there is no lack of complete panels. Even unused complete boxes are available today. Some of the photos in this issue also appear on Topps cards of the era.

		NM	E	VG
Complete Panel Set (50):		350.00	175.00	100.00
Complete Set, Singles (150):		165.00	80.00	50.00
Common Panel:		5.00	2.50	1.50
Common Player:		1.00	.50	.30
	Panel (1)	5.00	2.50	1.50
1	Bobby Tolan	1.00	.50	.30
2	Cookie Rojas	1.00	.50	.30
3	Darrell Evans	1.25	.60	.40
	Panel (2)	10.00	5.00	3.00
4	Sal Bando	1.00	.50	.30
5	Joe Morgan	5.00	2.50	1.50
6	Mickey Lolich	1.25	.60	.40
	Panel (3)	10.00	5.00	3.00
7	Don Sutton	4.50	2.25	1.25
8	Bill Melton	1.00	.50	.30
9	Tim Foli	1.00	.50	.30
	Panel (4)	5.00	2.50	1.50
10	Joe Lahoud	1.00	.50	.30
11a	Bert Hooten (Incorrect spelling.)	1.50	.70	.45
11b	Burt Hooton (Corrected)	1.00	.50	.30
12	Paul Blair	1.00	.50	.30
	Panel (5)	5.00	2.50	1.50
13	Jim Barr	1.00	.50	.30
14	Toby Harrah	1.00	.50	.30
15	John Milner	1.00	.50	.30
	Panel (6)	5.00	2.50	1.50
16	Ken Holtzman	1.00	.50	.30
17	Cesar Cedeno	1.00	.50	.30
18	Dwight Evans	1.00	.50	.30
	Panel (7)	10.00	5.00	3.00
19	Willie McCovey	5.00	2.50	1.50
20	Tony Oliva	1.25	.60	.40
21	Manny Sanguillen	1.00	.50	.30
	Panel (8)	10.00	5.00	3.00
22	Mickey Rivers	1.00	.50	.30
23	Lou Brock	5.00	2.50	1.50
24	Graig Nettles	1.50	.70	.45
	Panel (9)	5.00	2.50	1.50
25	Jim Wynn	1.00	.50	.30
26	George Scott	1.00	.50	.30
27	Greg Luzinski	1.00	.50	.30
	Panel (10)	15.00	7.50	4.50
28	Bert Campaneris	1.00	.50	.30
29	Pete Rose	12.50	6.25	3.75
30	Buddy Bell	1.00	.50	.30
	Panel (11)	5.00	2.50	1.50
31	Gary Matthews	1.00	.50	.30
32	Fred Patek	1.00	.50	.30
33	Mike Lum	1.00	.50	.30
	Panel (12)	5.00	2.50	1.50
34	Ellie Rodriguez	1.00	.50	.30
35	Milt May	1.00	.50	.30
36	Willie Horton	1.00	.50	.30
	Panel (13)	10.00	5.00	3.00
37	Dave Winfield	5.00	2.50	1.50
38	Tom Grieve	1.00	.50	.30
39	Barry Foote	1.00	.50	.30

	Panel (14)	5.00	2.50	1.50
40	Joe Rudi	1.00	.50	.30
41	Bake McBride	1.00	.50	.30
42	Mike Cuellar	1.00	.50	.30
	Panel (15)	5.00	2.50	1.50
43	Garry Maddox	1.00	.50	.30
44	Carlos May	1.00	.50	.30
45	Bud Harrelson	1.00	.50	.30
	Panel (16)	10.00	5.00	3.00
46	Dave Chalk	1.00	.50	.30
47	Dave Concepcion	1.00	.50	.30
48	Carl Yastrzemski	7.50	3.75	2.25
	Panel (17)	10.00	5.00	3.00
49	Steve Garvey	3.00	1.50	.90
50	Amos Otis	1.00	.50	.30
51	Ricky Reuschel	1.00	.50	.30
	Panel (18)	10.00	5.00	3.00
52	Rollie Fingers	4.50	2.25	1.25
53	Bob Watson	1.00	.50	.30
54	John Ellis	1.00	.50	.30
	Panel (19)	10.00	5.00	3.00
55	Bob Bailey	1.00	.50	.30
56	Rod Carew	6.00	3.00	1.75
57	Richie Hebner	1.00	.50	.30
	Panel (20)	20.00	10.00	6.00
58	Nolan Ryan	15.00	7.50	4.50
59	Reggie Smith	1.00	.50	.30
60	Joe Coleman	1.00	.50	.30
	Panel (21)	10.00	5.00	3.00
61	Ron Cey	1.00	.50	.30
62	Darrell Porter	1.00	.50	.30
63	Steve Carlton	5.00	2.50	1.50
	Panel (22)	5.00	2.50	1.50
64	Gene Tenace	1.00	.50	.30
65	Jose Cardenal	1.00	.50	.30
66	Bill Lee	1.00	.50	.30
	Panel (23)	5.00	2.50	1.50
67	Davey Lopes	1.00	.50	.30
68	Wilbur Wood	1.00	.50	.30
69	Steve Renko	1.00	.50	.30
	Panel (24)	10.00	5.00	3.00
70	Joe Torre	3.00	1.50	.90
71	Ted Sizemore	1.00	.50	.30
72	Bobby Grich	1.00	.50	.30
	Panel (25)	12.50	6.25	3.75
73	Chris Speier	1.00	.50	.30
74	Bert Blyleven	1.25	.60	.40
75	Tom Seaver	6.00	3.00	1.75
	Panel (26)	5.00	2.50	1.50
76	Nate Colbert	1.00	.50	.30
77	Don Kessinger	1.00	.50	.30
78	George Medich	1.00	.50	.30
	Panel (27)	20.00	10.00	6.00
79	Andy Messersmith	1.00	.50	.30
80	Robin Yount	12.50	6.25	3.75
81	Al Oliver	1.25	.60	.40
	Panel (28)	15.00	7.50	4.50
82	Bill Singer	1.00	.50	.30
83	Johnny Bench	6.00	3.00	1.75
84	Gaylord Perry	4.50	2.25	1.25
	Panel (29)	5.00	2.50	1.50
85	Dave Kingman	1.00	.50	.30
86	Ed Herrmann	1.00	.50	.30
87	Ralph Garr	1.00	.50	.30
	Panel (30)	12.50	6.25	3.75
88	Reggie Jackson	7.50	3.75	2.25
89a	Doug Radar (Incorrect spelling.)	1.50	.70	.45
89b	Doug Rader (Corrected)	1.00	.50	.30
90	Elliott Maddox	1.00	.50	.30
	Panel (31)	5.00	2.50	1.50
91	Bill Russell	1.00	.50	.30
92	John Mayberry	1.00	.50	.30
93	Dave Cash	1.00	.50	.30
	Panel (32)	5.00	2.50	1.50
94	Jeff Burroughs	1.00	.50	.30
95	Ted Simmons	1.00	.50	.30
96	Joe Decker	1.00	.50	.30
	Panel (33)	10.00	5.00	3.00
97	Bill Buckner	1.25	.60	.40
98	Bobby Darwin	1.00	.50	.30
99	Phil Niekro	4.50	2.25	1.25
	Panel (34)	5.00	2.50	1.50
100	Mike Sundberg (Jim)	1.00	.50	.30
101	Greg Gross	1.00	.50	.30
102	Luis Tiant	1.00	.50	.30
	Panel (35)	5.00	2.50	1.50
103	Glenn Beckert	1.00	.50	.30
104	Hal McRae	1.00	.50	.30
105	Mike Jorgensen	1.00	.50	.30
	Panel (36)	5.00	2.50	1.50
106	Mike Hargrove	1.00	.50	.30
107	Don Gullett	1.00	.50	.30
108	Tito Fuentes	1.00	.50	.30
	Panel (37)	5.00	2.50	1.50
109	Johnny Grubb	1.00	.50	.30
110	Jim Kaat	1.25	.60	.40
111	Felix Millan	1.00	.50	.30

	Panel (38)	5.00	2.50	1.50
112	Don Money	1.00	.50	.30
113	Rick Monday	1.00	.50	.30
114	Dick Bosman	1.00	.50	.30
	Panel (39)	10.00	5.00	3.00
115	Roger Metzger	1.00	.50	.30
116	Fergie Jenkins	4.50	2.25	1.25
117	Dusty Baker	1.25	.60	.40
	Panel (40)	10.00	5.00	3.00
118	Billy Champion	1.00	.50	.30
119	Bob Gibson	5.00	2.50	1.50
120	Bill Freehan	1.00	.50	.30
	Panel (41)	5.00	2.50	1.50
121	Cesar Geronimo	1.00	.50	.30
122	Jorge Orta	1.00	.50	.30
123	Cleon Jones	1.00	.50	.30
	Panel (42)	10.00	5.00	3.00
124	Steve Busby	1.00	.50	.30
125a	Bill Madlock (Pitcher)	1.50	.70	.45
125b	Bill Madlock (Infield)	1.00	.50	.30
126	Jim Palmer	5.00	2.50	1.50
	Panel (43)	10.00	5.00	3.00
127	Tony Perez	5.00	2.50	1.50
128	Larry Hisle	1.00	.50	.30
129	Rusty Staub	1.25	.60	.40
	Panel (44)	20.00	10.00	6.00
130	Hank Aaron	13.50	6.75	4.00
131	Rennie Stennett	1.00	.50	.30
132	Rico Petrocelli	1.00	.50	.30
	Panel (45)	15.00	7.50	4.50
133	Mike Schmidt	12.50	6.25	3.75
134	Sparky Lyle	1.00	.50	.30
135	Willie Stargell	5.00	2.50	1.50
	Panel (46)	10.00	5.00	3.00
136	Ken Henderson	1.00	.50	.30
137	Willie Montanez	1.00	.50	.30
138	Thurman Munson	5.00	2.50	1.50
	Panel (47)	5.00	2.50	1.50
139	Richie Zisk	1.00	.50	.30
140	George Hendricks (Hendrick)	1.00	.50	.30
141	Bobby Murcer	1.50	.70	.45
	Panel (48)	15.00	7.50	4.50
142	Lee May	1.00	.50	.30
143	Carlton Fisk	5.00	2.50	1.50
144	Brooks Robinson	6.00	3.00	1.75
	Panel (49)	5.00	2.50	1.50
145	Bobby Bonds	1.25	.60	.40
146	Gary Sutherland	1.00	.50	.30
147	Oscar Gamble	1.00	.50	.30
	Panel (50)	10.00	5.00	3.00
148	Jim Hunter	4.50	2.25	1.25
149	Tug McGraw	1.25	.60	.40
150	Dave McNally	1.00	.50	.30

1975 Hostess Twinkies

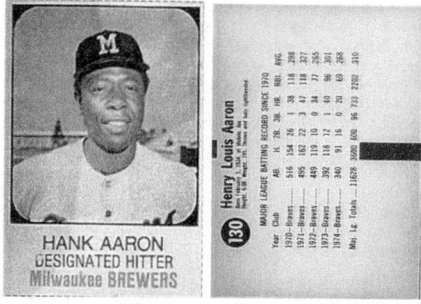

HANK AARON
DESIGNATED HITTER
Milwaukee BREWERS

Believed to have been issued only in selected markets, and on a limited basis at that, the 1975 Hostess Twinkie set features 60 of the cards from the "regular" Hostess set of that year. The cards were issued one per pack with the popular snack cake. Cards #1-36 are a direct pick-up from the Hostess set, while the remaining 24 cards in the set were selected from the more popular names in the remainder of the Hostess issue - with an emphasis on West Coast players. Thus, after card #36 the '75 Twinkie cards are skip-numbered from 40-136. In identical 2-1/4" x 3-1/4" size, the Twinkie cards differ from the Hostess issue only in the presence of small black bars at top and bottom center of the back of the card. While cards actually issued with snack cakes are virtually always found with brown stains, enough unissued cards were leaked into the hobby to provide clean examples for those willing to search them out and pay the price.

		NM	E	VG
Complete Set (60):		800.00	325.00	80.00
Common Player:		4.00	1.50	.40
1	Bobby Tolan	4.00	1.50	.40
2	Cookie Rojas	4.00	1.50	.40
3	Darrell Evans	4.00	1.50	.40
4	Sal Bando	4.00	1.50	.40

#	Player	NM	E	VG
5	Joe Morgan	24.00	9.50	2.50
6	Mickey Lolich	6.00	2.50	.60
7	Don Sutton	20.00	8.00	2.00
8	Bill Melton	4.00	1.50	.40
9	Tim Foli	4.00	1.50	.40
10	Joe Lahoud	4.00	1.50	.40
11	Bert Hooten (Burt Hooton)	4.00	1.50	.40
12	Paul Blair	4.00	1.50	.40
13	Jim Barr	4.00	1.50	.40
14	Toby Harrah	4.00	1.50	.40
15	John Milner	4.00	1.50	.40
16	Ken Holtzman	4.00	1.50	.40
17	Cesar Cedeno	4.00	1.50	.40
18	Dwight Evans	4.00	1.50	.40
19	Willie McCovey	24.00	9.50	2.50
20	Tony Oliva	8.00	3.25	.80
21	Manny Sanguillen	4.00	1.50	.40
22	Mickey Rivers	4.00	1.50	.40
23	Lou Brock	24.00	9.50	2.50
24	Graig Nettles	6.00	2.50	.60
25	Jim Wynn	4.00	1.50	.40
26	George Scott	4.00	1.50	.40
27	Greg Luzinski	4.00	1.50	.40
28	Bert Campaneris	4.00	1.50	.40
29	Pete Rose	80.00	32.00	8.00
30	Buddy Bell	4.00	1.50	.40
31	Gary Matthews	4.00	1.50	.40
32	Fred Patek	4.00	1.50	.40
33	Mike Lum	4.00	1.50	.40
34	Ellie Rodriguez	4.00	1.50	.40
35	Milt May (Photo actually Lee May.)	4.00	1.50	.40
36	Willie Horton	4.00	1.50	.40
40	Joe Rudi	4.00	1.50	.40
43	Garry Maddox	4.00	1.50	.40
46	Dave Chalk	4.00	1.50	.40
49	Steve Garvey	15.00	6.00	1.50
52	Rollie Fingers	20.00	8.00	2.00
58	Nolan Ryan	100.00	40.00	10.00
61	Ron Cey	4.00	1.50	.40
64	Gene Tenace	4.00	1.50	.40
65	Jose Cardenal	4.00	1.50	.40
67	Dave Lopes	4.00	1.50	.40
68	Wilbur Wood	4.00	1.50	.40
73	Chris Speier	4.00	1.50	.40
77	Don Kessinger	4.00	1.50	.40
79	Andy Messersmith	4.00	1.50	.40
80	Robin Yount	40.00	16.00	4.00
82	Bill Singer	4.00	1.50	.40
103	Glenn Beckert	4.00	1.50	.40
110	Jim Kaat	6.00	2.50	.60
112	Don Money	4.00	1.50	.40
113	Rick Monday	4.00	1.50	.40
122	Jorge Orta	4.00	1.50	.40
125	Bill Madlock	4.00	1.50	.40
130	Hank Aaron	75.00	30.00	7.50
136	Ken Henderson	4.00	1.50	.40

1976 Hostess

The second of five annual Hostess issues, the 1976 cards carried a "Bicentennial" color theme, with red, white and blue stripes at the bottom of the 2-1/4" x 3-1/4" cards. Like other Hostess issues, the cards were printed in panels of three as the bottom of family-size boxes of snack cake products. This leads to a degree of scarcity for some of the 150 cards in the set; those which were found on less-popular brands. A well-trimmed three-card panel measures 7-1/4" x 3-1/4". Some of the photos used in the 1976 Hostess set can also be found on Topps issues of the era. A "Hostess All-Star Team" album with spaces for 18 cards was available. Card backs can be found printed in black or brown, although it is not known if all cards can be found in both colors.

	NM	E	VG
Complete Panel Set (50):	300.00	150.00	90.00
Complete Set, Singles (150):	250.00	125.00	75.00
Common Panel:	5.00	2.50	1.50
Common Player:	.75	.40	.25
Album:	20.00	10.00	6.00

#	Player	NM	E	VG
	Panel (1)	20.00	10.00	6.00
1	Fred Lynn	1.00	.50	.30
2	Joe Morgan	5.00	2.50	1.50
3	Phil Niekro	4.00	2.00	1.25
	Panel (2)	10.00	5.00	3.00
4	Gaylord Perry	4.00	2.00	1.25
5	Bob Watson	.75	.40	.25
6	Bill Freehan	.75	.40	.25
	Panel (3)	10.00	5.00	3.00
7	Lou Brock	5.00	2.50	1.50
8	Al Fitzmorris	.75	.40	.25
9	Rennie Stennett	.75	.40	.25
	Panel (4)	10.00	5.00	3.00
10	Tony Oliva	1.00	.50	.30
11	Robin Yount	5.00	2.50	1.50
12	Rick Manning	.75	.40	.25
	Panel (5)	7.00	3.50	2.00
13	Bobby Grich	.75	.40	.25
14	Terry Forster	.75	.40	.25
15	Dave Kingman	1.00	.50	.30
	Panel (6)	10.00	5.00	3.00
16	Thurman Munson	4.50	2.25	1.25
17	Rick Reuschel	.75	.40	.25
18	Bobby Bonds	1.00	.50	.30
	Panel (7)	10.00	5.00	3.00
19	Steve Garvey	3.50	1.75	1.00
20	Vida Blue	.75	.40	.25
21	Dave Rader	.75	.40	.25
	Panel (8)	10.00	5.00	3.00
22	Johnny Bench	5.00	2.50	1.50
23	Luis Tiant	.75	.40	.25
24	Darrell Evans	.75	.40	.25
	Panel (9)	7.00	3.50	2.00
25	Larry Dierker	.75	.40	.25
26	Willie Horton	.75	.40	.25
27	John Ellis	.75	.40	.25
	Panel (10)	7.00	3.50	2.00
28	Al Cowens	.75	.40	.25
29	Jerry Reuss	.75	.40	.25
30	Reggie Smith	.75	.40	.25
	Panel (11)	10.00	5.00	3.00
31	Bobby Darwin	.75	.40	.25
32	Fritz Peterson	.75	.40	.25
33	Rod Carew	5.00	2.50	1.50
	Panel (12)	20.00	10.00	6.00
34	Carlos May	.75	.40	.25
35	Tom Seaver	6.00	3.00	1.75
36	Brooks Robinson	6.00	3.00	1.75
	Panel (13)	7.00	3.50	2.00
37	Jose Cardenal	.75	.40	.25
38	Ron Blomberg	.75	.40	.25
39	Lee Stanton	.75	.40	.25
	Panel (14)	7.00	3.50	2.00
40	Dave Cash	.75	.40	.25
41	John Montefusco	.75	.40	.25
42	Bob Tolan	.75	.40	.25
	Panel (15)	7.00	3.50	2.00
43	Carl Morton	.75	.40	.25
44	Rick Burleson	.75	.40	.25
45	Don Gullett	.75	.40	.25
	Panel (16)	7.00	3.50	2.00
46	Vern Ruhle	.75	.40	.25
47	Cesar Cedeno	.75	.40	.25
48	Toby Harrah	.75	.40	.25
	Panel (17)	10.00	5.00	3.00
49	Willie Stargell	5.00	2.50	1.50
50	Al Hrabosky	.75	.40	.25
51	Amos Otis	.75	.40	.25
	Panel (18)	7.00	3.50	2.00
52	Bud Harrelson	.75	.40	.25
53	Jim Hughes	.75	.40	.25
54	George Scott	.75	.40	.25
	Panel (19)	10.00	5.00	3.00
55	Mike Vail	.75	.40	.25
56	Jim Palmer	5.00	2.50	1.50
57	Jorge Orta	.75	.40	.25
	Panel (20)	7.00	3.50	2.00
58	Chris Chambliss	.75	.40	.25
59	Dave Chalk	.75	.40	.25
60	Ray Burris	.75	.40	.25
	Panel (21)	10.00	5.00	3.00
61	Bert Campaneris	.75	.40	.25
62	Gary Carter	5.00	2.50	1.50
63a	Ron Cey	.75	.40	.25
63b	Ron Cey (Reversed negatives, unissued proof.)	35.00	17.50	10.50
	Panel (22)	27.50	13.50	8.25
64	Carlton Fisk	5.00	2.50	1.50
65	Marty Perez	.75	.40	.25
66	Pete Rose	12.00	6.00	3.50
	Panel (23)	7.00	3.50	2.00
67	Roger Metzger	.75	.40	.25
68	Jim Sundberg	.75	.40	.25
69	Ron LeFlore	.75	.40	.25
	Panel (24)	7.00	3.50	2.00
70	Ted Sizemore	.75	.40	.25
71	Steve Busby	.75	.40	.25
72	Manny Sanguillen	.75	.40	.25
	Panel (25)	10.00	5.00	3.00
73	Larry Hisle	.75	.40	.25
74	Pete Broberg	.75	.40	.25
75	Boog Powell	3.00	1.50	.90
	Panel (26)	8.00	4.00	2.50
76	Ken Singleton	.75	.40	.25
77	Rich Gossage	1.25	.60	.40
78	Jerry Grote	.75	.40	.25
	Panel (27)	35.00	17.50	10.50
79	Nolan Ryan	16.00	8.00	4.75
80	Rick Monday	.75	.40	.25
81	Graig Nettles	1.25	.60	.40
	Panel (28)	27.50	13.50	8.25
82	Chris Speier	.75	.40	.25
83	Dave Winfield	5.00	2.50	1.50
84	Mike Schmidt	7.50	3.75	2.25
	Panel (29)	10.00	5.00	3.00
85	Buzz Capra	.75	.40	.25
86	Tony Perez	5.00	2.50	1.50
87	Dwight Evans	.75	.40	.25
	Panel (30)	7.00	3.50	2.00
88	Mike Hargrove	.75	.40	.25
89	Joe Coleman	.75	.40	.25
90	Greg Gross	.75	.40	.25
	Panel (31)	7.00	3.50	2.00
91	John Mayberry	.75	.40	.25
92	John Candelaria	.75	.40	.25
93	Bake McBride	.75	.40	.25
	Panel (32)	20.00	10.00	6.00
94	Hank Aaron	12.00	6.00	3.50
95	Buddy Bell	.75	.40	.25
96	Steve Braun	.75	.40	.25
	Panel (33)	7.00	3.50	2.00
97	Jon Matlack	.75	.40	.25
98	Lee May	.75	.40	.25
99	Wilbur Wood	.75	.40	.25
	Panel (34)	7.00	3.50	2.00
100	Bill Madlock	.75	.40	.25
101	Frank Tanana	.75	.40	.25
102	Mickey Rivers	.75	.40	.25
	Panel (35)	10.00	5.00	3.00
103	Mike Ivie	.75	.40	.25
104	Rollie Fingers	4.00	2.00	1.25
105	Davey Lopes	.75	.40	.25
	Panel (36)	7.00	3.50	2.00
106	George Foster	.75	.40	.25
107	Denny Doyle	.75	.40	.25
108	Earl Williams	.75	.40	.25
	Panel (37)	7.00	3.50	2.00
109	Tom Veryzer	.75	.40	.25
110	J.R. Richard	.75	.40	.25
111	Jeff Burroughs	.75	.40	.25
	Panel (38)	17.50	8.75	5.25
112	Al Oliver	1.00	.50	.30
113	Ted Simmons	.75	.40	.25
114	George Brett	7.50	3.75	2.25
	Panel (39)	7.00	3.50	2.00
115	Frank Duffy	.75	.40	.25
116	Bert Blyleven	.75	.40	.25
117	Darrell Porter	.75	.40	.25
	Panel (40)	8.00	4.00	2.50
118	Don Baylor	1.00	.50	.30
119	Bucky Dent	.75	.40	.25
120	Felix Millan	.75	.40	.25
	Panel (41)	8.00	4.00	2.50
121a	Mike Cuellar	.75	.40	.25
121b	Andy Messersmith (Unissued proof.)	25.00	12.50	7.50
122	Gene Tenace	.75	.40	.25
123	Bobby Murcer	1.25	.60	.40
	Panel (42)	10.00	5.00	3.00
124	Willie McCovey	5.00	2.50	1.50
125	Greg Luzinski	.75	.40	.25
126	Larry Parrish	.75	.40	.25
	Panel (43)	8.00	4.00	2.50
127	Jim Rice	2.00	1.00	.60
128	Dave Concepcion	.75	.40	.25
129	Jim Wynn	.75	.40	.25
	Panel (44)	7.00	3.50	2.00
130	Tom Grieve	.75	.40	.25
131	Mike Cosgrove	.75	.40	.25
132	Dan Meyer	.75	.40	.25
	Panel(45)	7.00	3.50	2.00
133	Dave Parker	1.00	.50	.30
134	Don Kessinger	.75	.40	.25
135	Hal McRae	.75	.40	.25
	Panel (46)	13.50	6.75	4.00
136	Don Money	.75	.40	.25
137	Dennis Eckersley	5.00	2.50	1.50
138a	Fergie Jenkins	4.00	2.00	1.25
138b	Johnny Briggs (Unissued proof.)	25.00	12.50	7.50
	Panel (47)	10.00	5.00	3.00
139	Mike Torrez	.75	.40	.25
140	Jerry Morales	.75	.40	.25
141	Jim Hunter	4.00	2.00	1.25
	Panel (48)	7.00	3.50	2.00

		NM	E	VG
142	Gary Matthews	.75	.40	.25
143	Randy Jones	.75	.40	.25
144	Mike Jorgensen	.75	.40	.25
	Panel (49)	17.50	8.75	5.25
145	Larry Bowa	.75	.40	.25
146	Reggie Jackson	7.50	3.75	2.25
147	Steve Yeager	.75	.40	.25
	Panel (50)	13.50	6.75	4.00
148	Dave May	.75	.40	.25
149	Carl Yastrzemski	6.00	3.00	1.75
150	Cesar Geronimo	.75	.40	.25

1976 Hostess Twinkies

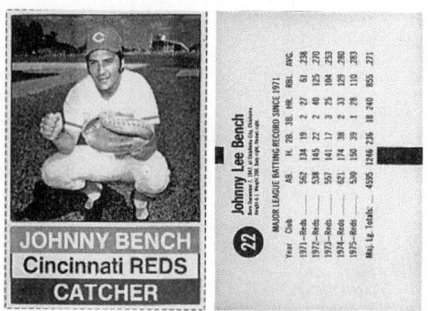

The 60 cards in this regionally issued (test markets only) set closely parallel the first 60 cards in the numerical sequence of the "regular" 1976 Hostess issue. The singular difference is the appearance on the back of a black band toward the center of the card at top and bottom. Also unlike the three-card panels of the regular Hostess issue, the 2-1/4" x 3-1/4" Twinkie cards were issued singly, as the cardboard stiffener for the cellophane-wrapped snack cakes. While cards actually issued with snack cakes are virtually always found with brown stains, enough unissued cards were leaked into the hobby to provide clean examples for those willing to search them out and pay the price.

		NM	E	VG
	Complete Set (60):	500.00	200.00	50.00
	Common Player:	4.00	1.50	.40
1	Fred Lynn	4.00	1.50	.40
2	Joe Morgan	24.00	9.50	2.50
3	Phil Niekro	20.00	8.00	2.00
4	Gaylord Perry	20.00	8.00	2.00
5	Bob Watson	4.00	1.50	.40
6	Bill Freehan	4.00	1.50	.40
7	Lou Brock	24.00	9.50	2.50
8	Al Fitzmorris	4.00	1.50	.40
9	Rennie Stennett	4.00	1.50	.40
10	Tony Oliva	6.00	2.50	.60
11	Robin Yount	24.00	9.50	2.50
12	Rick Manning	4.00	1.50	.40
13	Bobby Grich	4.00	1.50	.40
14	Terry Forster	4.00	1.50	.40
15	Dave Kingman	5.00	2.00	.50
16	Thurman Munson	15.00	6.00	1.50
17	Rick Reuschel	4.00	1.50	.40
18	Bobby Bonds	4.00	1.50	.40
19	Steve Garvey	12.00	4.75	1.25
20	Vida Blue	4.00	1.50	.40
21	Dave Rader	4.00	1.50	.40
22	Johnny Bench	24.00	9.50	2.50
23	Luis Tiant	4.00	1.50	.40
24	Darrell Evans	4.00	1.50	.40
25	Larry Dierker	4.00	1.50	.40
26	Willie Horton	4.00	1.50	.40
27	John Ellis	4.00	1.50	.40
28	Al Cowens	4.00	1.50	.40
29	Jerry Reuss	4.00	1.50	.40
30	Reggie Smith	4.00	1.50	.40
31	Bobby Darwin	4.00	1.50	.40
32	Fritz Peterson	4.00	1.50	.40
33	Rod Carew	24.00	9.50	2.50
34	Carlos May	4.00	1.50	.40
35	Tom Seaver	30.00	12.00	3.00
36	Brooks Robinson	24.00	9.50	2.50
37	Jose Cardenal	4.00	1.50	.40
38	Ron Blomberg	4.00	1.50	.40
39	Lee Stanton	4.00	1.50	.40
40	Dave Cash	4.00	1.50	.40
41	John Montefusco	4.00	1.50	.40
42	Bob Tolan	4.00	1.50	.40
43	Carl Morton	4.00	1.50	.40
44	Rick Burleson	4.00	1.50	.40
45	Don Gullett	4.00	1.50	.40
46	Vern Ruhle	4.00	1.50	.40
47	Cesar Cedeno	4.00	1.50	.40
48	Toby Harrah	4.00	1.50	.40
49	Willie Stargell	24.00	9.50	2.50
50	Al Hrabosky	4.00	1.50	.40
51	Amos Otis	4.00	1.50	.40
52	Bud Harrelson	4.00	1.50	.40
53	Jim Hughes	4.00	1.50	.40
54	George Scott	4.00	1.50	.40
55	Mike Vail	4.00	1.50	.40
56	Jim Palmer	20.00	8.00	2.00
57	Jorge Orta	4.00	1.50	.40
58	Chris Chambliss	4.00	1.50	.40
59	Dave Chalk	4.00	1.50	.40
60	Ray Burris	4.00	1.50	.40

1976 Hostess Unissued Proofs

To help prevent a recurrence of the errors which plagued Hostess' debut set in 1975, the company prepared proof sheets of the cards before they were printed onto the bottoms of snack cake boxes. Probably to have ready substitutes in case problems were found, or a card had to be withdrawn at the last minute, there were seven players printed in proof version that were never issued on boxes. In addition, changes to cards #61, 121 and 138 were made between the proof stage and issued versions (they are detailed in the 1976 Hostess listings). The proofs share the format and 2-1/4" x 3-1/4" size of the issued cards.

		NM	E	VG
	Complete Set (9):	400.00	200.00	120.00
	Common Player:	40.00	20.00	12.00
151	Fergie Jenkins (Issued as #138.)	75.00	37.50	22.50
152	Mike Cuellar (Issued as #121.)	40.00	20.00	12.00
153	Tom Murphy	40.00	20.00	12.00
154	Dusty Baker	40.00	20.00	12.00
155	Barry Foote	40.00	20.00	12.00
156	Steve Carlton	100.00	50.00	30.00
157	Richie Zisk	40.00	20.00	12.00
158	Ken Holtzman	40.00	20.00	12.00
159	Cliff Johnson	40.00	20.00	12.00

1977 Hostess

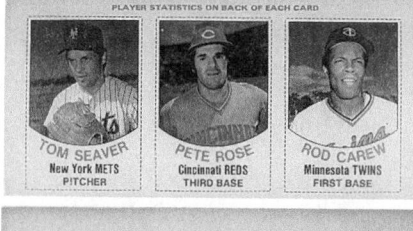

The third of five consecutive annual issues, the 1977 Hostess cards retained the same card size - 2-1/4" x 3-1/4", set size - 150 cards, and mode of issue - three cards on a 7-1/4" x 3-1/4" panel, as the previous two efforts. Because they were issued as the bottom panel of snack cake boxes, and because some brands of Hostess products were more popular than others, certain cards in the set are scarcer than others. A fold-out (to 8-1/2" x 22") All-Star Team album was available.

	NM	E	VG
Complete Panel Set (50):	500.00	250.00	150.00
Complete Set, Singles (150):	300.00	150.00	90.00
Common Panel:	4.00	2.00	1.25

		NM	E	VG
	Common Player:	.75	.40	.25
	Album:	20.00	10.00	6.00
	Panel (1)	20.00	10.00	6.00
1	Jim Palmer	3.00	1.50	.90
2	Joe Morgan	3.00	1.50	.90
3a	Reggie Jackson	5.00	2.50	1.50
3b	Rod Carew (Unissued proof.)	20.00	10.00	6.00
	Panel (2)	25.00	12.50	7.50
4	Carl Yastrzemski	3.50	1.75	1.00
5	Thurman Munson	2.50	1.25	.70
6	Johnny Bench	3.50	1.75	1.00
	Panel (3)	30.00	15.00	9.00
7	Tom Seaver	3.00	1.50	.90
8	Pete Rose	7.50	3.75	2.25
9a	Rod Carew	3.00	1.50	.90
9b	Reggie Jackson (Unissued proof.)	75.00	37.00	22.00
	Panel (4)	4.00	2.00	1.25
10	Luis Tiant	.75	.40	.25
11	Phil Garner	.75	.40	.25
12	Sixto Lezcano	.75	.40	.25
	Panel (5)	4.00	2.00	1.25
13	Mike Torrez	.75	.40	.25
14	Davey Lopes	.75	.40	.25
15	Doug DeCinces	.75	.40	.25
	Panel (6)	4.00	2.00	1.25
16	Jim Spencer	.75	.40	.25
17	Hal McRae	.75	.40	.25
18	Mike Hargrove	.75	.40	.25
	Panel (7)	4.00	2.00	1.25
19	Willie Montanez	.75	.40	.25
20	Roger Metzger	.75	.40	.25
21	Dwight Evans	.75	.40	.25
	Panel (8)	5.00	2.50	1.50
22	Steve Rogers	.75	.40	.25
23	Jim Rice	1.25	.60	.40
24	Pete Falcone	.75	.40	.25
	Panel (9)	6.00	3.00	1.75
25	Greg Luzinski	.75	.40	.25
26	Randy Jones	.75	.40	.25
27	Willie Stargell	3.00	1.50	.90
	Panel (10)	5.00	2.50	1.50
28	John Hiller	.75	.40	.25
29	Bobby Murcer	.75	.40	.25
30	Rick Monday	.75	.40	.25
	Panel (11)	6.00	3.00	1.75
31	John Montefusco	.75	.40	.25
32	Lou Brock	3.00	1.50	.90
33	Bill North	.75	.40	.25
	Panel (12)	15.00	7.50	4.50
34	Robin Yount	3.00	1.50	.90
35	Steve Garvey	1.00	.50	.30
36	George Brett	5.00	2.50	1.50
	Panel (13)	4.00	2.00	1.25
37	Toby Harrah	.75	.40	.25
38	Jerry Royster	.75	.40	.25
39	Bob Watson	.75	.40	.25
	Panel (14)	5.00	2.50	1.50
40	George Foster	.75	.40	.25
41	Gary Carter	3.00	1.50	.90
42	John Denny	.75	.40	.25
	Panel (15)	20.00	10.00	6.00
43	Mike Schmidt	5.00	2.50	1.50
44	Dave Winfield	3.00	1.50	.90
45	Al Oliver	.90	.45	.25
	Panel (16)	4.00	2.00	1.25
46	Mark Fidrych	.75	.40	.25
47	Larry Herndon	.75	.40	.25
48	Dave Goltz	.75	.40	.25
	Panel (17)	4.00	2.00	1.25
49	Jerry Morales	.75	.40	.25
50	Ron LeFlore	.75	.40	.25
51	Fred Lynn	.75	.40	.25
	Panel (18)	4.00	2.00	1.25
52	Vida Blue	.75	.40	.25
53	Rick Manning	.75	.40	.25
54	Bill Buckner	.75	.40	.25
	Panel (19)	4.00	2.00	1.25
55	Lee May	.75	.40	.25
56	John Mayberry	.75	.40	.25
57	Darrel Chaney	.75	.40	.25
	Panel (20)	4.00	2.00	1.25
58	Cesar Cedeno	.75	.40	.25
59	Ken Griffey	.75	.40	.25
60	Dave Kingman	.75	.40	.25
	Panel (21)	4.00	2.00	1.25
61	Ted Simmons	.75	.40	.25
62	Larry Bowa	.75	.40	.25
63	Frank Tanana	.75	.40	.25
	Panel (22)	4.00	2.00	1.25
64	Jason Thompson	.75	.40	.25
65	Ken Brett	.75	.40	.25
66	Roy Smalley	.75	.40	.25
	Panel (23)	4.00	2.00	1.25
67	Ray Burris	.75	.40	.25
68	Rick Burleson	.75	.40	.25

#	Player			
69	Buddy Bell	.75	.40	.25
	Panel (24)	5.00	2.50	1.50
70	Don Sutton	2.50	1.25	.70
71	Mark Belanger	.75	.40	.25
72	Dennis Leonard	.75	.40	.25
	Panel (25)	5.00	2.50	1.50
73	Gaylord Perry	2.50	1.25	.70
74	Dick Ruthven	.75	.40	.25
75	Jose Cruz	.75	.40	.25
	Panel (26)	4.00	2.00	1.25
76	Cesar Geronimo	.75	.40	.25
77	Jerry Koosman	.75	.40	.25
78	Garry Templeton	.75	.40	.25
	Panel (27)	25.00	12.50	7.50
79	Jim Hunter	2.50	1.25	.70
80	John Candelaria	.75	.40	.25
81	Nolan Ryan	10.00	5.00	3.00
	Panel (28)	4.00	2.00	1.25
82	Rusty Staub	.90	.45	.25
83	Jim Barr	.75	.40	.25
84	Butch Wynegar	.75	.40	.25
	Panel (29)	4.00	2.00	1.25
85	Jose Cardenal	.75	.40	.25
86	Claudell Washington	.75	.40	.25
87	Bill Travers	.75	.40	.25
	Panel (30)	4.00	2.00	1.25
88	Rick Waits	.75	.40	.25
89	Ron Cey	.75	.40	.25
90	Al Bumbry	.75	.40	.25
	Panel (31)	4.00	2.00	1.25
91	Bucky Dent	.90	.45	.25
92	Amos Otis	.75	.40	.25
93	Tom Grieve	.75	.40	.25
	Panel (32)	4.00	2.00	1.25
94	Enos Cabell	.75	.40	.25
95	Dave Concepcion	.75	.40	.25
96	Felix Millan	.75	.40	.25
	Panel (33)	4.00	2.00	1.25
97	Bake McBride	.75	.40	.25
98	Chris Chambliss	.75	.40	.25
99	Butch Metzger	.75	.40	.25
	Panel (34)	4.00	2.00	1.25
100	Rennie Stennett	.75	.40	.25
101	Dave Roberts	.75	.40	.25
102	Lyman Bostock	.75	.40	.25
	Panel (35)	6.00	3.00	1.75
103	Rick Reuschel	.75	.40	.25
104	Carlton Fisk	3.00	1.50	.90
105	Jim Slaton	.75	.40	.25
	Panel (36)	5.00	2.50	1.50
106	Dennis Eckersley	2.50	1.25	.70
107	Ken Singleton	.75	.40	.25
108	Ralph Garr	.75	.40	.25
	Panel (37)	5.00	2.50	1.50
109	Freddie Patek	.75	.40	.25
110	Jim Sundberg	.75	.40	.25
111	Phil Niekro	2.50	1.25	.70
	Panel (38)	4.00	2.00	1.25
112	J.R. Richard	.75	.40	.25
113	Gary Nolan	.75	.40	.25
114	Jon Matlack	.75	.40	.25
	Panel (39)	7.50	3.75	2.25
115	Keith Hernandez	.75	.40	.25
116	Graig Nettles	.90	.45	.25
117	Steve Carlton	3.00	1.50	.90
	Panel (40)	4.00	2.00	1.25
118	Bill Madlock	.75	.40	.25
119	Jerry Reuss	.75	.40	.25
120	Aurelio Rodriguez	.75	.40	.25
	Panel (41)	4.00	2.00	1.25
121	Dan Ford	.75	.40	.25
122	Ray Fosse	.75	.40	.25
123	George Hendrick	.75	.40	.25
	Panel (42)	4.00	2.00	1.25
124	Alan Ashby	.75	.40	.25
125	Joe Lis	.75	.40	.25
126	Sal Bando	.75	.40	.25
	Panel (43)	5.00	2.50	1.50
127	Richie Zisk	.75	.40	.25
128	Rich Gossage	.75	.40	.25
129	Don Baylor	.75	.40	.25
	Panel (44)	4.00	2.00	1.25
130	Dave McKay	.75	.40	.25
131	Bobby Grich	.75	.40	.25
132	Dave Pagan	.75	.40	.25
	Panel (45)	4.00	2.00	1.25
133	Dave Cash	.75	.40	.25
134	Steve Braun	.75	.40	.25
135	Dan Meyer	.75	.40	.25
	Panel (46)	5.00	2.50	1.50
136	Bill Stein	.75	.40	.25
137	Rollie Fingers	2.50	1.25	.70
138	Brian Downing	.75	.40	.25
	Panel (47)	4.00	2.00	1.25
139	Bill Singer	.75	.40	.25
140	Doyle Alexander	.75	.40	.25
141	Gene Tenace	.75	.40	.25
	Panel (48)	4.00	2.00	1.25
142	Gary Matthews	.75	.40	.25
143	Don Gullett	.75	.40	.25
144	Wayne Garland	.75	.40	.25
	Panel (49)	4.00	2.00	1.25
145	Pete Broberg	.75	.40	.25
146	Joe Rudi	.75	.40	.25
147	Glenn Abbott	.75	.40	.25
	Panel (50)	4.00	2.00	1.25
148	George Scott	.75	.40	.25
149	Bert Campaneris	.75	.40	.25
150	Andy Messersmith	.75	.40	.25

1977 Hostess Twinkies

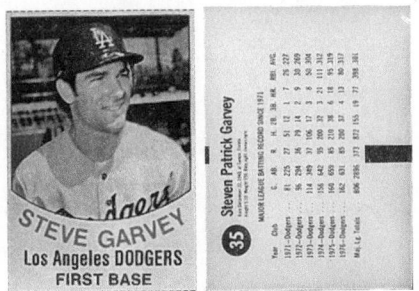

The 1977 Hostess Twinkie issue, at 150 different cards, is the largest of the single-panel Twinkie sets. It is also the most obscure. The cards, which measure 2-1/4" x 3-1/4" but are part of a larger panel, were found not only with Twinkies, but with Hostess Cupcakes as well. Cards #1-30 and 111-150 are Twinkies panels and #31-135 are Cupcakes panels. Complete Cupcakes panels are approximately 2-1/4" x 4-1/2" in size, while complete Twinkies panels measure 3-1/8" x 4-1/4". The photos used in the set are identical to those in the 1977 Hostess three-card panel set. The main difference is the appearance of a black band at the center of the card back. While cards actually issued with snack cakes are virtually always found with brown stains, enough unissued cards were leaked into the hobby to provide clean examples for those willing to search them out and pay the price.

#	Player	NM	E	VG
	Complete Set (150):	725.00	300.00	75.00
	Common Player:	4.00	1.50	.40
1	Jim Palmer	25.00	10.00	2.50
2	Joe Morgan	25.00	10.00	2.50
3	Reggie Jackson	40.00	16.00	4.00
4	Carl Yastrzemski	32.50	13.00	3.25
5	Thurman Munson	15.00	6.00	1.50
6	Johnny Bench	25.00	10.00	2.50
7	Tom Seaver	25.00	10.00	2.50
8	Pete Rose	65.00	26.00	6.50
9	Rod Carew	25.00	10.00	2.50
10	Luis Tiant	4.00	1.50	.40
11	Phil Garner	4.00	1.50	.40
12	Sixto Lezcano	4.00	1.50	.40
13	Mike Torrez	4.00	1.50	.40
14	Dave Lopes	4.00	1.50	.40
15	Doug DeCinces	4.00	1.50	.40
16	Jim Spencer	4.00	1.50	.40
17	Hal McRae	4.00	1.50	.40
18	Mike Hargrove	4.00	1.50	.40
19	Willie Montanez	4.00	1.50	.40
20	Roger Metzger	4.00	1.50	.40
21	Dwight Evans	4.00	1.50	.40
22	Steve Rogers	4.00	1.50	.40
23	Jim Rice	12.50	5.00	1.25
24	Pete Falcone	4.00	1.50	.40
25	Greg Luzinski	4.00	1.50	.40
26	Randy Jones	4.00	1.50	.40
27	Willie Stargell	25.00	10.00	2.50
28	John Hiller	4.00	1.50	.40
29	Bobby Murcer	4.00	1.50	.40
30	Rick Monday	4.00	1.50	.40
31	John Montefusco	4.00	1.50	.40
32	Lou Brock	25.00	10.00	2.50
33	Bill North	4.00	1.50	.40
34	Robin Yount	25.00	10.00	2.50
35	Steve Garvey	12.50	5.00	1.25
36	George Brett	40.00	16.00	4.00
37	Toby Harrah	4.00	1.50	.40
38	Jerry Royster	4.00	1.50	.40
39	Bob Watson	4.00	1.50	.40
40	George Foster	4.00	1.50	.40
41	Gary Carter	25.00	10.00	2.50
42	John Denny	4.00	1.50	.40
43	Mike Schmidt	40.00	16.00	4.00
44	Dave Winfield	25.00	10.00	2.50
45	Al Oliver	4.00	1.50	.40
46	Mark Fidrych	6.50	2.50	.60
47	Larry Herndon	4.00	1.50	.40
48	Dave Goltz	4.00	1.50	.40
49	Jerry Morales	4.00	1.50	.40
50	Ron LeFlore	4.00	1.50	.40
51	Fred Lynn	4.00	1.50	.40
52	Vida Blue	4.00	1.50	.40
53	Rick Manning	4.00	1.50	.40
54	Bill Buckner	4.00	1.50	.40
55	Lee May	4.00	1.50	.40
56	John Mayberry	4.00	1.50	.40
57	Darrel Chaney	4.00	1.50	.40
58	Cesar Cedeno	4.00	1.50	.40
59	Ken Griffey	4.00	1.50	.40
60	Dave Kingman	6.50	2.50	.60
61	Ted Simmons	4.00	1.50	.40
62	Larry Bowa	4.00	1.50	.40
63	Frank Tanana	4.00	1.50	.40
64	Jason Thompson	4.00	1.50	.40
65	Ken Brett	4.00	1.50	.40
66	Roy Smalley	4.00	1.50	.40
67	Ray Burris	4.00	1.50	.40
68	Rick Burleson	4.00	1.50	.40
69	Buddy Bell	4.00	1.50	.40
70	Don Sutton	20.00	8.00	2.00
71	Mark Belanger	4.00	1.50	.40
72	Dennis Leonard	4.00	1.50	.40
73	Gaylord Perry	20.00	8.00	2.00
74	Dick Ruthven	4.00	1.50	.40
75	Jose Cruz	4.00	1.50	.40
76	Cesar Geronimo	4.00	1.50	.40
77	Jerry Koosman	4.00	1.50	.40
78	Garry Templeton	4.00	1.50	.40
79	Catfish Hunter	20.00	8.00	2.00
80	John Candelaria	4.00	1.50	.40
81	Nolan Ryan	100.00	40.00	10.00
82	Rusty Staub	6.50	2.50	.60
83	Jim Barr	4.00	1.50	.40
84	Butch Wynegar	4.00	1.50	.40
85	Jose Cardenal	4.00	1.50	.40
86	Claudell Washington	4.00	1.50	.40
87	Bill Travers	4.00	1.50	.40
88	Rick Waits	4.00	1.50	.40
89	Ron Cey	4.00	1.50	.40
90	Al Bumbry	4.00	1.50	.40
91	Bucky Dent	4.00	1.50	.40
92	Amos Otis	4.00	1.50	.40
93	Tom Grieve	4.00	1.50	.40
94	Enos Cabell	4.00	1.50	.40
95	Dave Concepcion	4.00	1.50	.40
96	Felix Millan	4.00	1.50	.40
97	Bake McBride	4.00	1.50	.40
98	Chris Chambliss	4.00	1.50	.40
99	Butch Metzger	4.00	1.50	.40
100	Rennie Stennett	4.00	1.50	.40
101	Dave Roberts	4.00	1.50	.40
102	Lyman Bostock	4.00	1.50	.40
103	Rick Reuschel	4.00	1.50	.40
104	Carlton Fisk	25.00	10.00	2.50
105	Jim Slaton	4.00	1.50	.40
106	Dennis Eckersley	20.00	8.00	2.00
107	Ken Singleton	4.00	1.50	.40
108	Ralph Garr	4.00	1.50	.40
109	Freddie Patek	4.00	1.50	.40
110	Jim Sundberg	4.00	1.50	.40
111	Phil Niekro	20.00	8.00	2.00
112	J. R. Richard	4.00	1.50	.40
113	Gary Nolan	4.00	1.50	.40
114	Jon Matlack	4.00	1.50	.40
115	Keith Hernandez	4.00	1.50	.40
116	Graig Nettles	4.00	1.50	.40
117	Steve Carlton	25.00	10.00	2.50
118	Bill Madlock	4.00	1.50	.40
119	Jerry Reuss	4.00	1.50	.40
120	Aurelio Rodriguez	4.00	1.50	.40
121	Dan Ford	4.00	1.50	.40
122	Ray Fosse	4.00	1.50	.40
123	George Hendrick	4.00	1.50	.40
124	Alan Ashby	4.00	1.50	.40
125	Joe Lis	4.00	1.50	.40
126	Sal Bando	4.00	1.50	.40
127	Richie Zisk	4.00	1.50	.40
128	Rich Gossage	4.00	1.50	.40
129	Don Baylor	6.50	2.50	.60
130	Dave McKay	4.00	1.50	.40
131	Bob Grich	4.00	1.50	.40
132	Dave Pagan	4.00	1.50	.40
133	Dave Cash	4.00	1.50	.40
134	Steve Braun	4.00	1.50	.40
135	Dan Meyer	4.00	1.50	.40
136	Bill Stein	4.00	1.50	.40
137	Rollie Fingers	20.00	8.00	2.00
138	Brian Downing	4.00	1.50	.40
139	Bill Singer	4.00	1.50	.40
140	Doyle Alexander	4.00	1.50	.40
141	Gene Tenace	4.00	1.50	.40
142	Gary Matthews	4.00	1.50	.40
143	Don Gullett	4.00	1.50	.40
144	Wayne Garland	4.00	1.50	.40
145	Pete Broberg	4.00	1.50	.40
146	Joe Rudi	4.00	1.50	.40

147	Glenn Abbott	4.00	1.50	.40
148	George Scott	4.00	1.50	.40
149	Bert Campaneris	4.00	1.50	.40
150	Andy Messersmith	4.00	1.50	.40

1977 Hostess Unissued Proofs

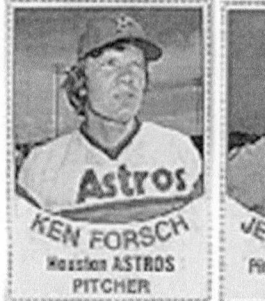 

The reason for the existence of these rare Hostess proofs is unknown, but there seems little doubt that they were never actually circulated; perhaps being held in reserve in case the cards actually printed on product boxes had to be replaced. The 10 cards were printed on a sheet in three-card panels, like the issued Hostess cards, plus a single of Briles. The proofs share the format of the issued cards, and the 2-1/4" x 3-1/4" size. Besides these "high number" proofs, there also exist numbering-variation proofs of cards #3, 9, 65 and 119 (see 1977 Hostess listings).

	NM	E	VG
Complete Set (10):	400.00	200.00	120.00
Common Single:	40.00	20.00	12.00

151	Ed Kranepool	40.00	20.00	12.00
152	Ross Grimsley	40.00	20.00	12.00
153	Ken Brett (#65 in regular-issue set)	40.00	20.00	12.00
154	Rowland Office	40.00	20.00	12.00
155	Rick Wise	40.00	20.00	12.00
156	Paul Splittorff	40.00	20.00	12.00
157	Jerry Augustine	40.00	20.00	12.00
158	Ken Forsch	40.00	20.00	12.00
159	Jerry Reuss	40.00	20.00	12.00
160	Nelson Briles	40.00	20.00	12.00

1978 Hostess

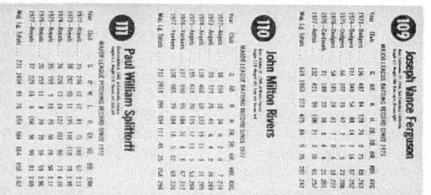

Other than the design on the front of the card, there was little different about the 1978 Hostess cards from the three years' issues which had preceded it, or the one which followed. The 2-1/4" x 3-1/4" cards were printed in panels of three (7-1/4" x 3-1/4") as the bottom of family-sized boxes of snack cakes. The 1978 set was again complete at 150 cards. Like other years of Hostess issues, there are scarcities within the 1978 set that are the result of those panels having been issued with less-popular brands of snack cakes.

	NM	E	VG
Complete Panel Set (50):	275.00	135.00	80.00
Complete Set, Singles (150):	225.00	110.00	65.00
Common Panel:	6.00	3.00	1.75
Common Player:	.75	.40	.25
Album:	25.00	12.50	7.50

	Panel (1)	6.00	3.00	1.75
1	Butch Hobson	.75	.40	.25
2	George Foster	.75	.40	.25
3	Bob Forsch	.75	.40	.25
	Panel (2)	13.50	6.75	4.00
4	Tony Perez	4.00	2.00	1.25
5	Bruce Sutter	4.00	2.00	1.25
6	Hal McRae	.75	.40	.25
	Panel (3)	7.50	3.75	2.25
7	Tommy John	1.25	.60	.40
8	Greg Luzinski	.75	.40	.25
9	Enos Cabell	.75	.40	.25
	Panel (4)	10.00	5.00	3.00
10	Doug DeCinces	.75	.40	.25
11	Willie Stargell	4.50	2.25	1.25
12	Ed Halicki	.75	.40	.25
	Panel (5)	6.00	3.00	1.75
13	Larry Hisle	.75	.40	.25
14	Jim Slaton	.75	.40	.25
15	Buddy Bell	.75	.40	.25
	Panel (6)	6.00	3.00	1.75
16	Earl Williams	.75	.40	.25
17	Glenn Abbott	.75	.40	.25
18	Dan Ford	.75	.40	.25
	Panel (7)	6.00	3.00	1.75
19	Gary Matthews	.75	.40	.25
20	Eric Soderholm	.75	.40	.25
21	Bump Wills	.75	.40	.25
	Panel (8)	6.00	3.00	1.75
22	Keith Hernandez	.75	.40	.25
23	Dave Cash	.75	.40	.25
24	George Scott	.75	.40	.25
	Panel (9)	20.00	10.00	6.00
25	Ron Guidry	1.25	.60	.40
26	Dave Kingman	.75	.40	.25
27	George Brett	9.00	4.50	2.75
	Panel (10)	6.00	3.00	1.75
28	Bob Watson	.75	.40	.25
29	Bob Boone	.90	.45	.25
30	Reggie Smith	.75	.40	.25
	Panel (11)	45.00	22.00	13.50
31	Eddie Murray	18.50	9.25	5.50
32	Gary Lavelle	.75	.40	.25
33	Rennie Stennett	.75	.40	.25
	Panel (12)	6.00	3.00	1.75
34	Duane Kuiper	.75	.40	.25
35	Sixto Lezcano	.75	.40	.25
36	Dave Rozema	.75	.40	.25
	Panel (13)	6.00	3.00	1.75
37	Butch Wynegar	.75	.40	.25
38	Mitchell Page	.75	.40	.25
39	Bill Stein	.75	.40	.25
	Panel (14)	6.00	3.00	1.75
40	Elliott Maddox	.75	.40	.25
41	Mike Hargrove	.75	.40	.25
42	Bobby Bonds	.75	.40	.25
	Panel (15)	20.00	10.00	6.00
43	Garry Templeton	.75	.40	.25
44	Johnny Bench	4.50	2.25	1.25
45	Jim Rice	1.50	.70	.45
	Panel (16)	17.50	8.75	5.25
46	Bill Buckner	.75	.40	.25
47	Reggie Jackson	9.00	4.50	2.75
48	Freddie Patek	.75	.40	.25
	Panel (17)	10.00	5.00	3.00
49	Steve Carlton	4.50	2.25	1.25
50	Cesar Cedeno	.75	.40	.25
51	Steve Yeager	.75	.40	.25
	Panel (18)	6.00	3.00	1.75
52	Phil Garner	.75	.40	.25
53	Lee May	.75	.40	.25
54	Darrell Evans	.75	.40	.25
	Panel (19)	6.00	3.00	1.75
55	Steve Kemp	.75	.40	.25
56a	Dusty Baker	.90	.45	.25
56b	Andre Thornton (Unissued proof.)	18.00	9.00	5.50
57	Ray Fosse	.75	.40	.25
	Panel (20)	6.00	3.00	1.75
58	Manny Sanguillen	.75	.40	.25
59	Tom Johnson	.75	.40	.25
60	Lee Stanton	.75	.40	.25
	Panel (21)	10.00	5.00	3.00
61	Jeff Burroughs	.75	.40	.25
62	Bobby Grich	.75	.40	.25
63	Dave Winfield	4.50	2.25	1.25
	Panel (22)	6.00	3.00	1.75
64	Dan Driessen	.75	.40	.25
65	Ted Simmons	.75	.40	.25
66	Jerry Remy	.75	.40	.25
	Panel (23)	6.00	3.00	1.75
67	Al Cowens	.75	.40	.25
68	Sparky Lyle	.75	.40	.25
69	Manny Trillo	.75	.40	.25
	Panel (24)	9.00	4.50	2.75
70	Don Sutton	4.00	2.00	1.25
71	Larry Bowa	.75	.40	.25
72	Jose Cruz	.75	.40	.25
	Panel (25)	10.00	5.00	3.00
73	Willie McCovey	4.50	2.25	1.25
74	Bert Blyleven	.75	.40	.25
75	Ken Singleton	.75	.40	.25
	Panel (26)	6.00	3.00	1.75
76	Bill North	.75	.40	.25
77	Jason Thompson	.75	.40	.25
78	Dennis Eckersley	4.00	2.00	1.25
	Panel (27)	6.00	3.00	1.75
79	Jim Sundberg	.75	.40	.25
80	Jerry Koosman	.75	.40	.25
81	Bruce Bochte	.75	.40	.25
	Panel (28)	45.00	22.00	13.50
82	George Hendrick	.75	.40	.25
83	Nolan Ryan	20.00	10.00	6.00
84	Roy Howell	.75	.40	.25
	Panel (29)	10.00	5.00	3.00
85	Butch Metzger	.75	.40	.25
86	George Medich	.75	.40	.25
87	Joe Morgan	4.50	2.25	1.25
	Panel (30)	6.00	3.00	1.75
88	Dennis Leonard	.75	.40	.25
89	Willie Randolph	.90	.45	.25
90	Bobby Murcer	.90	.45	.25
	Panel (31)	6.00	3.00	1.75
91	Rick Manning	.75	.40	.25
92	J.R. Richard	.75	.40	.25
93	Ron Cey	.75	.40	.25
	Panel (32)	6.00	3.00	1.75
94	Sal Bando	.75	.40	.25
95	Ron LeFlore	.75	.40	.25
96	Dave Goltz	.75	.40	.25
	Panel (33)	6.00	3.00	1.75
97	Dan Meyer	.75	.40	.25
98	Chris Chambliss	.75	.40	.25
99	Biff Pocoroba	.75	.40	.25
	Panel (34)	6.00	3.00	1.75
100	Oscar Gamble	.75	.40	.25
101	Frank Tanana	.75	.40	.25
102	Lenny Randle	.75	.40	.25
	Panel (35)	6.00	3.00	1.75
103	Tommy Hutton	.75	.40	.25
104	John Candelaria	.75	.40	.25
105	Jorge Orta	.75	.40	.25
	Panel (36)	6.00	3.00	1.75
106	Ken Reitz	.75	.40	.25
107	Bill Campbell	.75	.40	.25
108	Dave Concepcion	.75	.40	.25
	Panel (37)	6.00	3.00	1.75
109	Joe Ferguson	.75	.40	.25
110	Mickey Rivers	.75	.40	.25
111	Paul Splittorff	.75	.40	.25
	Panel (38)	20.00	10.00	6.00
112	Davey Lopes	.75	.40	.25
113	Mike Schmidt	9.00	4.50	2.75
114	Joe Rudi	.75	.40	.25
	Panel (39)	10.00	5.00	3.00
115	Milt May	.75	.40	.25
116	Jim Palmer	4.50	2.25	1.25
117	Bill Madlock	.75	.40	.25
	Panel (40)	6.00	3.00	1.75
118	Roy Smalley	.75	.40	.25
119	Cecil Cooper	.75	.40	.25
120	Rick Langford	.75	.40	.25
	Panel (41)	9.00	4.50	2.75
121	Ruppert Jones	.75	.40	.25
122	Phil Niekro	4.00	2.00	1.25
123	Toby Harrah	.75	.40	.25
	Panel (42)	6.00	3.00	1.75
124	Chet Lemon	.75	.40	.25
125	Gene Tenace	.75	.40	.25
126	Steve Henderson	.75	.40	.25
	Panel (43)	35.00	17.50	10.50
127	Mike Torrez	.75	.40	.25
128	Pete Rose	10.00	5.00	3.00
129	John Denny	.75	.40	.25
	Panel (44)	6.00	3.00	1.75
130	Darrell Porter	.75	.40	.25
131	Rick Reuschel	.75	.40	.25
132	Graig Nettles	.90	.45	.25
	Panel (45)	6.00	3.00	1.75
133	Garry Maddox	.75	.40	.25
134	Mike Flanagan	.75	.40	.25
135	Dave Parker	.75	.40	.25
	Panel (46)	10.00	5.00	3.00
136	Terry Whitfield	.75	.40	.25
137	Wayne Garland	.75	.40	.25
138	Robin Yount	4.50	2.25	1.25
	Panel (47)	20.00	10.00	6.00
139a	Gaylord Perry (San Diego)	4.00	2.00	1.25
139b	Gaylord Perry (Texas, unissued proof.)	30.00	15.00	9.00
140	Rod Carew	4.50	2.25	1.25
141	Wayne Gross	.75	.40	.25
	Panel (48)	9.00	4.50	2.75
142	Barry Bonnell	.75	.40	.25
143	Willie Montanez	.75	.40	.25
144	Rollie Fingers	4.00	2.00	1.25
	Panel (49)	35.00	17.50	10.50
145	Lyman Bostock	.75	.40	.25
146	Gary Carter	4.50	2.25	1.25
147	Ron Blomberg	.75	.40	.25

Panel (50)	30.00	15.00	9.00
148 Bob Bailor	.75	.40	.25
149 Tom Seaver	5.00	2.50	1.50
150 Thurman Munson	4.00	2.00	1.25

1978 Hostess Unissued Proofs

Different versions of two of the issued cards (see 1978 Hostess #56, 139) plus 10 players who do not appear on the snack cake boxes constitute the proof set for '78 Hostess. The unissued proofs are identical in format to the cards actually issued and measure 2-1/4" x 3-1/4" at the dotted lines.

	NM	E	VG
Complete Set (10):	450.00	225.00	135.00
Common Player:	50.00	25.00	15.00
151 Bill Robinson	50.00	25.00	15.00
152 Lou Piniella	75.00	37.50	22.50
153 Lamar Johnson	50.00	25.00	15.00
154 Mark Belanger	50.00	25.00	15.00
155 Ken Griffey	75.00	37.50	22.50
156 Ken Forsch	50.00	25.00	15.00
157 Ted Sizemore	50.00	25.00	15.00
158 Don Baylor	50.00	25.00	15.00
159 Dusty Baker	60.00	30.00	18.00
160 Al Oliver	75.00	37.50	22.50

1979 Hostess

The last of five consecutive annual issues, the 1979 Hostess set retained the 150-card set size, 2-1/4" x 3-1/4" single-card size and 7-1/4" x 3-1/4" three-card panel format from the previous years. The cards were printed as the bottom panel on family-size boxes of Hostess snack cakes. Some panels, which were printed on less-popular brands, are somewhat scarcer today than the rest of the set. Like all Hostess issues, because the hobby was in a well-developed state at the time of issue, the 1979s survive today in complete panels and complete unused boxes for collectors who like original packaging.

	NM	E	VG
Complete Panel Set (50):	250.00	125.00	75.00
Complete Singles Set (150):	175.00	85.00	50.00
Common Panel:	4.50	2.25	1.25
Common Single Player:	.75	.40	.25
Panel (1)	7.50	3.75	2.25
1 John Denny	.75	.40	.25
2a Jim Rice ("d-of, unissued proof)	15.00	7.50	4.50
2b Jim Rice ("dh-of")	1.50	.70	.45
3 Doug Bair	.75	.40	.25
Panel (2)	6.00	3.00	1.75
4 Darrell Porter	.75	.40	.25
5 Ross Grimsley	.75	.40	.25
6 Bobby Murcer	1.00	.50	.30
Panel (3)	25.00	12.50	7.50
7 Lee Mazzilli	.75	.40	.25
8 Steve Garvey	1.50	.70	.45
9 Mike Schmidt	6.00	3.00	1.75
Panel (4)	12.00	6.00	3.50
10 Terry Whitfield	.75	.40	.25
11 Jim Palmer	2.50	1.25	.70
12 Omar Moreno	.75	.40	.25
Panel (5)	5.00	2.50	1.50
13 Duane Kuiper	.75	.40	.25
14 Mike Caldwell	.75	.40	.25
15 Steve Kemp	.75	.40	.25
Panel (6)	5.00	2.50	1.50
16 Dave Goltz	.75	.40	.25
17 Mitchell Page	.75	.40	.25
18 Bill Stein	.75	.40	.25
Panel (7)	5.00	2.50	1.50
19 Gene Tenace	.75	.40	.25
20 Jeff Burroughs	.75	.40	.25
21 Francisco Barrios	.75	.40	.25
Panel (8)	7.50	3.75	2.25
22 Mike Torrez	.75	.40	.25
23 Ken Reitz	.75	.40	.25
24 Gary Carter	2.50	1.25	.70
Panel (9)	9.00	4.50	2.75
25 Al Hrabosky	.75	.40	.25
26 Thurman Munson	1.50	.70	.45
27 Bill Buckner	.75	.40	.25

Panel (10)	6.00	3.00	1.75
28 Ron Cey	.75	.40	.25
29 J.R. Richard	.75	.40	.25
30 Greg Luzinski	.75	.40	.25
Panel (11)	5.00	2.50	1.50
31 Ed Ott	.75	.40	.25
32 Denny Martinez	.75	.40	.25
33 Darrell Evans	.75	.40	.25
Panel (12)	5.00	2.50	1.50
34 Ron LeFlore	.75	.40	.25
35 Rick Waits	.75	.40	.25
36 Cecil Cooper	.75	.40	.25
Panel (13)	15.00	7.50	4.50
37 Leon Roberts	.75	.40	.25
38a Rod Carew (Large head.) (Botton of collar trim doesnot show.))	3.00	1.50	.90
38b Rod Carew (Small head.) (Bottom of collar trim shows.))	3.00	1.50	.90
39 John Henry Johnson	.75	.40	.25
Panel (14)	5.00	2.50	1.50
40 Chet Lemon	.75	.40	.25
41 Craig Swan	.75	.40	.25
42 Gary Matthews	.75	.40	.25
Panel (15)	5.00	2.50	1.50
43 Lamar Johnson	.75	.40	.25
44 Ted Simmons	.75	.40	.25
45 Ken Griffey	.75	.40	.25
Panel (16)	6.00	3.00	1.75
46 Freddie Patek	.75	.40	.25
47 Frank Tanana	.75	.40	.25
48 Rich Gossage	1.00	.50	.30
Panel (17)	5.00	2.50	1.50
49 Burt Hooton	.75	.40	.25
50 Ellis Valentine	.75	.40	.25
51 Ken Forsch	.75	.40	.25
Panel (18)	6.00	3.00	1.75
52 Bob Knepper	.75	.40	.25
53 Dave Parker	.75	.40	.25
54 Doug DeCinces	.75	.40	.25
Panel (19)	20.00	10.00	6.00
55 Robin Yount	3.00	1.50	.90
56 Rusty Staub	1.00	.50	.30
57 Gary Alexander	.75	.40	.25
Panel (20)	5.00	2.50	1.50
58 Julio Cruz	.75	.40	.25
59 Matt Keough	.75	.40	.25
60 Roy Smalley	.75	.40	.25
Panel (21)	15.00	7.50	4.50
61 Joe Morgan	3.00	1.50	.90
62 Phil Niekro	2.00	1.00	.60
63 Don Baylor	.75	.40	.25
Panel (22)	20.00	10.00	6.00
64 Dwight Evans	.75	.40	.25
65 Tom Seaver	3.00	1.50	.90
66 George Hendrick	.75	.40	.25
Panel (23)	25.00	12.50	7.50
67 Rick Reuschel	.75	.40	.25
68 George Brett	6.00	3.00	1.75
69 Lou Piniella	1.00	.50	.30
Panel (24)	12.00	6.00	3.50
70 Enos Cabell	.75	.40	.25
71 Steve Carlton	2.50	1.25	.70
72 Reggie Smith	.75	.40	.25
Panel (25)	5.00	2.50	1.50
73 Rick Dempsey	.75	.40	.25
74 Vida Blue	.75	.40	.25
75 Phil Garner	.75	.40	.25
Panel (26)	5.00	2.50	1.50
76 Rick Manning	.75	.40	.25
77 Mark Fidrych	1.00	.50	.30
78 Mario Guerrero	.75	.40	.25
Panel (27)	5.00	2.50	1.50
79 Bob Stinson	.75	.40	.25
80 Al Oliver	.75	.40	.25
81 Doug Flynn	.75	.40	.25
Panel (28)	7.50	3.75	2.25
82 John Mayberry	.75	.40	.25
83 Gaylord Perry	2.00	1.00	.60
84 Joe Rudi	.75	.40	.25
Panel (29)	5.00	2.50	1.50
85 Dave Concepcion	.75	.40	.25
86 John Candelaria	.75	.40	.25
87 Pete Vuckovich	.75	.40	.25
Panel (30)	5.00	2.50	1.50
88 Ivan DeJesus	.75	.40	.25
89 Ron Guidry	.75	.40	.25
90 Hal McRae	.75	.40	.25
Panel (31)	6.00	3.00	1.75
91 Cesar Cedeno	.75	.40	.25
92 Don Sutton	2.00	1.00	.60
93 Andre Thornton	.75	.40	.25
Panel (32)	5.00	2.50	1.50
94 Roger Erickson	.75	.40	.25
95 Larry Hisle	.75	.40	.25
96 Jason Thompson	.75	.40	.25
Panel (33)	5.00	2.50	1.50

97 Jim Sundberg	.75	.40	.25
98 Bob Horner	.75	.40	.25
99 Ruppert Jones	.75	.40	.25
Panel (34)	60.00	30.00	18.00
100 Willie Montanez	.75	.40	.25
101 Nolan Ryan	12.00	6.00	3.50
102 Ozzie Smith	15.00	7.50	4.50
Panel (35)	12.00	6.00	3.50
103 Eric Soderholm	.75	.40	.25
104 Willie Stargell	2.50	1.25	.70
105a Bob Bailor (Photo reversed, unissued proof.)	.75	.40	.25
105b Bob Bailor (Photo corrected.)	.75	.40	.25
Panel (36)	12.50	6.25	3.75
106 Carlton Fisk	2.50	1.25	.70
107 George Foster	.75	.40	.25
108 Keith Hernandez	.75	.40	.25
Panel (37)	5.00	2.50	1.50
109 Dennis Leonard	.75	.40	.25
110 Graig Nettles	1.00	.50	.30
111 Jose Cruz	.75	.40	.25
Panel (38)	5.00	2.50	1.50
112 Bobby Grich	.75	.40	.25
113 Bob Boone	.75	.40	.25
114 Davey Lopes	.75	.40	.25
Panel (39)	15.00	7.50	4.50
115 Eddie Murray	3.00	1.50	.90
116 Jack Clark	.75	.40	.25
117 Lou Whitaker	.75	.40	.25
Panel (40)	20.00	10.00	6.00
118 Miguel Dilone	.75	.40	.25
119 Sal Bando	.75	.40	.25
120 Reggie Jackson	6.00	3.00	1.75
Panel (41)	15.00	7.50	4.50
121 Dale Murphy	2.00	1.00	.60
122 Jon Matlack	.75	.40	.25
123 Bruce Bochte	.75	.40	.25
Panel (42)	12.50	6.25	3.75
124 John Stearns	.75	.40	.25
125 Dave Winfield	3.00	1.50	.90
126 Jorge Orta	.75	.40	.25
Panel (43)	25.00	12.50	7.50
127 Garry Templeton	.75	.40	.25
128 Johnny Bench	3.00	1.50	.90
129 Butch Hobson	.75	.40	.25
Panel (44)	6.00	3.00	1.75
130 Bruce Sutter	2.50	1.25	.70
131 Bucky Dent	.75	.40	.25
132 Amos Otis	.75	.40	.25
Panel (45)	5.00	2.50	1.50
133 Bert Blyleven	.75	.40	.25
134 Larry Bowa	.75	.40	.25
135 Ken Singleton	.75	.40	.25
Panel (46)	5.00	2.50	1.50
136 Sixto Lezcano	.75	.40	.25
137 Roy Howell	.75	.40	.25
138 Bill Madlock	.75	.40	.25
Panel (47)	5.00	2.50	1.50
139 Dave Revering	.75	.40	.25
140 Richie Zisk	.75	.40	.25
141 Butch Wynegar	.75	.40	.25
Panel (48)	25.00	12.50	7.50
142 Alan Ashby	.75	.40	.25
143 Sparky Lyle	.75	.40	.25
144 Pete Rose	7.50	3.75	2.25
Panel (49)	6.00	3.00	1.75
145 Dennis Eckersley	2.50	1.25	.70
146 Dave Kingman	.75	.40	.25
147 Buddy Bell	.75	.40	.25
Panel (50)	5.00	2.50	1.50
148 Mike Hargrove	.75	.40	.25
149 Jerry Koosman	.75	.40	.25
150 Toby Harrah	.75	.40	.25

1979 Hostess Unissued Proofs

Identical in format to the 150 cards which were issued on boxes of Hostess snack cakes, these cards were possibly prepared in the event trades of players in the issued set required quick replacement. The reason these cards were never released is unknown. Cards measure 2-1/4" x 3-1/4" at the dotted-line borders. While some of the proofs are numbered on back, others have no card number.

		NM	E	VG
Complete Set (17):		1,100	550.00	330.00
Common Player:		50.00	25.00	15.00
151	Dusty Baker	60.00	30.00	18.00
152	Mark Belanger	60.00	30.00	18.00
154	Al Cowens	50.00	25.00	15.00
155	Dan Driessen	50.00	25.00	15.00
157	Steve Henderson	50.00	25.00	15.00
159	Tommy John	75.00	37.50	22.50
160	Garry Maddox	50.00	25.00	15.00
(161)	Willie McCovey	250.00	125.00	75.00
(162)	Scott McGregor	50.00	25.00	15.00
(163)	Bill Nahorodny	50.00	25.00	15.00
(164)	Terry Puhl	50.00	25.00	15.00
(165)	Willie Randolph	50.00	25.00	15.00
(166)	Jim Slaton	50.00	25.00	15.00
(167)	Paul Splittorff	50.00	25.00	15.00
(168)	Frank Taveras	50.00	25.00	15.00
(169)	Alan Trammell	125.00	65.00	35.00
(170)	Bump Wills	50.00	25.00	15.00

1971 House of Jazz

Controversy has dogged this card set since the first reports of its existence in the early 1970s. The legitimacy of the issue has been questioned though certain hobby journalists traced the cards to a record store which supposedly gave them away with music purchases, along with similar cards depicting musicians. The 2-3/8" x 3-1/2" cards are printed in black-and-white with round corners. Backs of some, but not all, cards have a blue-and-white address sticker for "HOUSE OF JAZZ, LTD." The unnumbered cards are checklisted here in alphabetical order.

		NM	E	VG
Complete Set (35):		200.00	100.00	60.00
Common Player:		5.00	2.50	1.50
(1)	John Antonelli	5.00	2.50	1.50
(2)	Richie Ashburn	6.00	3.00	1.75
(3)	Ernie Banks	6.50	3.25	2.00
(4)	Hank Bauer	5.00	2.50	1.50
(5)	Joe DiMaggio	15.00	7.50	4.50
(6)	Bobby Doerr	5.00	2.50	1.50
(7)	Herman Franks	5.00	2.50	1.50
(8)	Lou Gehrig	15.00	7.50	4.50
(9)	Granny Hamner	5.00	2.50	1.50
(10)	Al Kaline	6.50	3.25	2.00
(11)	Harmon Killebrew	6.00	3.00	1.75
(12)	Jim Konstanty	5.00	2.50	1.50
(13)	Bob Lemon	5.00	2.50	1.50
(14)	Ed Lopat	5.00	2.50	1.50
(15)	Stan Lopata	5.00	2.50	1.50
(16)	Peanuts Lowrey	5.00	2.50	1.50
(17)	Mickey Mantle	35.00	17.50	10.00
(18)	Phil Marchildon	5.00	2.50	1.50
(19)	Walt Masterson	5.00	2.50	1.50
(20)	Ed Mathews	6.00	3.00	1.75
(21)	Willie Mays	10.00	5.00	3.00
(22)	Don Newcombe	5.00	2.50	1.50
(23)	Joe Nuxhall	5.00	2.50	1.50
(24)	Satchel Paige	7.50	3.75	2.25
(25)	Roy Partee	5.00	2.50	1.50
(26)	Jackie Robinson	7.50	3.75	2.25
(27)	Babe Ruth	20.00	10.00	6.00
(28)	Carl Scheib	5.00	2.50	1.50
(29)	Bobby Shantz	5.00	2.50	1.50
(30)	Burt Shotton	5.00	2.50	1.50
(31)	Duke Snider	6.50	3.25	2.00
(32)	Warren Spahn	6.00	3.00	1.75
(33)	Johnny Temple	5.00	2.50	1.50
(34)	Ted Williams	10.00	5.00	3.00
(35)	Early Wynn	5.00	2.50	1.50

1967 Houston Astros Team Issue

 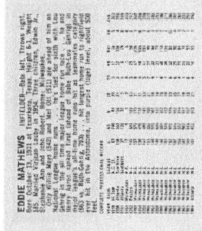

This set of 12 player cards was issued by the Houston Astros, though the exact nature of the promotion is not known. Individual cards of 2-5/8" x 3-1/8" were printed on a perforated sheet about 9" x 10-1/2". Fronts have a posed color photo with a black facsimile autograph. Backs are printed in black on white with a yellow color block behind the player data and career notes. Full major and minor league stats are at bottom. The unnumbered cards are checklisted here in alphabetical order.

		NM	E	VG
Complete Set, Sheet:		65.00	32.50	20.00
Complete Set, Singles (12):		65.00	32.50	20.00
Common Player:		8.00	4.00	2.50
(1)	Bob Aspromonte	8.00	4.00	2.50
(2)	John Bateman	8.00	4.00	2.50
(3)	Mike Cuellar	8.00	4.00	2.50
(4)	Larry Dierker	8.00	4.00	2.50
(5)	Dave Giusti	8.00	4.00	2.50
(6)	Grady Hatton	8.00	4.00	2.50
(7)	Bill Heath	8.00	4.00	2.50
(8)	Sonny Jackson	8.00	4.00	2.50
(9)	Ed Mathews	20.00	10.00	6.00
(10)	Joe Morgan	20.00	10.00	6.00
(11)	Rusty Staub	12.50	6.25	3.75
(12)	Jim Wynn	8.00	4.00	2.50

1962 Houston Colt .45s Booklets

 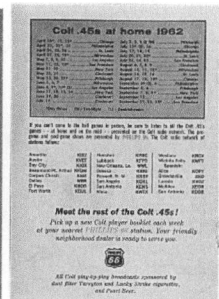

To introduce the members of the new Houston National League team, Phillips 66 gasoline sponsored (along with the team's cigarette and beer broadcast sponsors) this set of 24 player profile booklets given away one per week during the season. Fronts of the 16-page 5-3/8" x 7-7/16" booklets feature a blue and white action photo of the player on a bright orange background. Black and white graphics complete the design. The player's name appears in a Texas map outline. Backs have the 1962 Houston Colt .45s home-game schedule and details of the team's statewide radio network. Inside the booklet are a complete biography, stats and both posed and action photos of the players, along with families, teammates, etc. Because of player trades during the season, and lessened demand for some of the non-player booklets, some of the series are quite scarce. Each of the booklets can be found with different sponsors logos on front.

		NM	E	VG
Complete Set (24):		240.00	120.00	72.00
Common Booklet:		15.00	7.50	4.50
(1)	Joe Amalfitano	15.00	7.50	4.50
(2)	Bob Aspromonte	15.00	7.50	4.50
(3)	Bob Bruce	15.00	7.50	4.50
(4)	Jim Campbell	18.00	9.00	5.50
(5)	Harry Craft	15.00	7.50	4.50
(6)	Dick Farrell	15.00	7.50	4.50
(7)	Dave Giusti	15.00	7.50	4.50
(8)	Jim Golden	15.00	7.50	4.50
(9)	J.C. Hartman	18.00	9.00	5.50
(10)	Ken Johnson	15.00	7.50	4.50
(11)	Norm Larker	15.00	7.50	4.50
(12)	Bob Lillis	15.00	7.50	4.50
(13)	Don McMahon	15.00	7.50	4.50
(14)	Roman Mejias	15.00	7.50	4.50
(15)	Jim Pendleton	18.00	9.00	5.50
(16)	Paul Richards (GM)	15.00	7.50	4.50

(17)	Bobby Shantz	30.00	15.00	9.00
(18)	Hal Smith	15.00	7.50	4.50
(19)	Al Spangler	15.00	7.50	4.50
(20)	Jim Umbricht	15.00	7.50	4.50
(21)	Carl Warwick	15.00	7.50	4.50
(22)	Hal Woodeshick	15.00	7.50	4.50
(23)	Coaches(James Adair, Bobby Bragan, Cot Deal, Luman Harris)	25.00	12.50	7.50
(24)	Announcers(Rene Cardenas, Orlando Diego, Gene Elston, Al Helfer, Lowell Passe, Guy Savage)	19.00	9.50	5.75

1953-1955 Howard Photo Service Postcards

Little is known about these postcards. Player and team combinations on the known pieces suggest a range of issue dates between 1953 and 1955. The 3-1/2" x 5-5/8" cards have a glossy black-and-white front photo. A rubber-stamp on the back attributes the card to "Howard Photo Service, N.Y.C." The specific pose on the second Turley card is not known. It is possible other cards may yet be discovered.

		NM	E	VG
Common Player:		20.00	10.00	6.00
(1)	Ned Garver	20.00	10.00	6.00
(2)	Billy Hitchcock	20.00	10.00	6.00
(3)	Dave Madison	20.00	10.00	6.00
(4)	Willie Mays	165.00	85.00	50.00
(5)	Willie Mays (Seven-Up ad on back.)	950.00	475.00	285.00
(6)	Bob Turley (Follow-through.)	30.00	15.00	9.00
(7)	Bob Turley (Wind-up.)	30.00	15.00	9.00

1976 HRT/RES 1942 Play Ball

 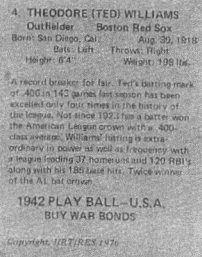

TED WILLIAMS – Of
Boston Red Sox

This "phantom" continuation of the Play Ball series of 1939-41 was the creation of Ted Taylor and Bob Schmierer, whose initials appear in the copyright line on back. The 2-1/2" x 3-1/8" cards feature black-and-white photos on front and were printed on gray clay-content cardboard in a near replication of the stock found on the vintage Play Ball series. Backs were also done in style reminiscent of 1940s issues. Besides player data and career summaries, backs have a "1942 PLAY BALL - U.S.A." title line and either a "Buy War Bonds" or "'Keep Baseball Going' - FDR" slogan above the 1976 copyright line. The pair produced a number of other original and reprint issues in the 1970s. All of the others carry advertisements for their "Philly" card shows.

		NM	E	VG
Complete Set (36):		30.00	15.00	9.00
Common Card:		1.00	.50	.30
1	Lou Gehrig	4.00	7.50	3.75
2	Joe DiMaggio	4.00	7.50	3.75
3	Phil Rizzuto	1.50	3.00	1.50
4	Ted Williams	3.00	6.00	3.00
5	Charles Wagner	.50	1.00	.50
6	Thornton Lee	.50	1.00	.50
7	Taft Wright	.50	1.00	.50

		NM	E	VG
8	Jeff Heath	.50	1.00	.50
9	Roy Mack	.50	1.00	.50
10	Pat Mullin	.50	1.00	.50
11	Al Benton	.50	1.00	.50
12	Bob Harris	.50	1.00	.50
13	Roy Cullenbine	.50	1.00	.50
14	Cecil Travis	.50	1.00	.50
15	Buck Newsom	.50	1.00	.50
16	Eddie Collins Jr.	.50	1.00	.50
17	Dick Siebert	.50	1.00	.50
18	Dee Miles	.50	1.00	.50
19	Pete Reiser	.50	1.00	.50
20	Dolph Camilli	.50	1.00	.50
21	Curt Davis	.50	1.00	.50
22	Spud Krist	.50	1.00	.50
23	Frank Crespi	.50	1.00	.50
24	Elmer Riddle	.50	1.00	.50
25	Bucky Walters	.50	1.00	.50
26	Vince DiMaggio	.75	1.50	.70
27	Max Butcher	.50	1.00	.50
28	Mel Ott	1.50	3.00	1.50
29	Bob Carpenter	.50	1.00	.50
30	Claude Passeau	.50	1.00	.50
31	Dom Dallessandro	.50	1.00	.50
32	Casey Stengel	1.50	3.00	1.50
33	Alva Javery	.50	1.00	.50
34	Hans Lobert	.50	1.00	.50
35	Nick Etten	.50	1.00	.50
36	John Podgajny	.50	1.00	.50

1976-77 HRT/RES 1947 Bowman

Advertised as "The Set That Never Was," this collectors' issue from Ted Taylor and Bob Schmierer used a 2-1/8" x 2-1/2" black-and-white format and gray cardboard stock to replicate the feel of the first post-WWII baseball cards. The set was issued in three series with advertising on back promoting the second (1976) and third (1977) annual EPSCC "Philly" shows. Series one (#1-49) was issued in 1976; series two (#50-81) and three (#82-113) were 1977 issues.

		NM	E	VG
Complete Set (113):		90.00	45.00	27.50
Common Player:		1.00	.50	.30
1	Bobby Doerr	1.00	.50	.30
2	Stan Musial	3.00	1.50	.90
3	Babe Ruth	7.50	3.75	2.25
4	Joe DiMaggio	6.00	3.00	1.75
5	Andy Pafko	1.00	.50	.30
6	Johnny Pesky	1.00	.50	.30
7	Gil Hodges	1.50	.70	.45
8	Tommy Holmes	1.00	.50	.30
9	Ralph Kiner	1.00	.50	.30
10	Yogi Berra	2.00	1.00	.60
11	Bob Feller	1.50	.70	.45
12	Joe Gordon	1.00	.50	.30
13	Eddie Joost	1.00	.50	.30
14	Del Ennis	1.00	.50	.30
15	Johnny Mize	1.00	.50	.30
16	Pee Wee Reese	1.25	.60	.40
17	Jackie Robinson	4.00	2.00	1.25
18	Enos Slaughter	1.00	.50	.30
19	Vern Stephens	1.00	.50	.30
20	Bobby Thomson	1.00	.50	.30
21	Ted Williams	6.00	3.00	1.75
22	Bob Elliott	1.00	.50	.30
23	Mickey Vernon	1.00	.50	.30
24	Ewell Blackwell	1.00	.50	.30
25	Lou Boudreau	1.00	.50	.30
26	Ralph Branca	1.00	.50	.30
27	Harry Breechen (Brecheen)	1.00	.50	.30
28	Dom DiMaggio	1.00	.50	.30
29	Bruce Edwards	1.00	.50	.30
30	Sam Chapman	1.00	.50	.30
31	George Kell	1.00	.50	.30
32	Jack Kramer	1.00	.50	.30
33	Hal Newhouser	1.00	.50	.30
34	Charlie Keller	1.00	.50	.30
35	Ken Keltner	1.00	.50	.30
36	Hank Greenberg	1.25	.60	.40
37	Howie Pollet	1.00	.50	.30
38	Luke Appling	1.00	.50	.30
39	Pete Suder	1.00	.50	.30

		NM	E	VG
40	Johnny Sain	1.00	.50	.30
41	Phil Cavaretta (Cavaretta)	1.00	.50	.30
42	Johnny Vander Meer	1.00	.50	.30
43	Mel Ott	1.00	.50	.30
44	Walker Cooper	1.00	.50	.30
45	Birdie Tebbetts	1.00	.50	.30
46	George Stirnweiss	1.00	.50	.30
47	Connie Mack	1.00	.50	.30
48	Jimmie Foxx	1.00	.50	.30
49	Checklist(Joe DiMaggio, Babe Ruth)	1.50	.70	.45
(50)	Honus Wagner T206 Card (First series.)	1.00	.50	.30
51	Ted Taylor (First series.)	1.00	.50	.30
52	Bob Schmierer (First series.)	1.00	.50	.30
50	Schoolboy Rowe (Second series.)	1.00	.50	.30
51	Andy Seminick (Second series.)	1.00	.50	.30
52	Fred Walker (Second series.)	1.00	.50	.30
53	Virgil Trucks	1.00	.50	.30
54	Dizzy Trout	1.00	.50	.30
55	Walter Evers	1.00	.50	.30
56	Thurman Tucker	1.00	.50	.30
57	Fritz Ostermueller	1.00	.50	.30
58	Augie Galan	1.00	.50	.30
59	Norman Young	1.00	.50	.30
60	Skeeter Newsome	1.00	.50	.30
61	Jack Lohrke	1.00	.50	.30
62	Rudy York	1.00	.50	.30
63	Tex Hughson	1.00	.50	.30
64	Sam Mele	1.00	.50	.30
65	Fred Hutchinson	1.00	.50	.30
66	Don Black	1.00	.50	.30
67	Les Fleming	1.00	.50	.30
68	George McQuinn	1.00	.50	.30
69	Mike McCormick	1.00	.50	.30
70	Mickey Witek	1.00	.50	.30
71	Blix Donnelly	1.00	.50	.30
72	Elbie Fletcher	1.00	.50	.30
73	Hal Gregg	1.00	.50	.30
74	Dick Whitman	1.00	.50	.30
75	Johnny Neun	1.00	.50	.30
76	Doyle Lade	1.00	.50	.30
77	Ron Northey	1.00	.50	.30
78	Walker Cooper	1.00	.50	.30
79	Warren Spahn	1.00	.50	.30
80	Happy Chandler	1.00	.50	.30
81	Checklist(Connie Mack, Roy Mack, Connie Mack III)	1.00	.50	.30
82	Earle Mack	1.00	.50	.30
83	Buddy Rosar	1.00	.50	.30
84	Walt Judnich	1.00	.50	.30
85	Bob Kennedy	1.00	.50	.30
86	Mike Tresh	1.00	.50	.30
87	Sid Hudson	1.00	.50	.30
88	Eugene Thompson	1.00	.50	.30
89	Bill Nicholson	1.00	.50	.30
90	Stan Hack	1.00	.50	.30
91	Terry Moore	1.00	.50	.30
92	Ted Lyons	1.00	.50	.30
93	Barney McCosky	1.00	.50	.30
94	Stan Spence	1.00	.50	.30
95	Larry Jansen	1.00	.50	.30
96	Whitey Kurowski	1.00	.50	.30
97	Honus Wagner	1.50	.70	.45
98	Billy Herman	1.00	.50	.30
99	Jim Tabor	1.00	.50	.30
100	Phil Marchildon	1.00	.50	.30
101	Dave Ferriss	1.00	.50	.30
102	Al Zarilla	1.00	.50	.30
103	Bob Dillinger	1.00	.50	.30
104	Bob Lemon	1.00	.50	.30
105	Jim Hegan	1.00	.50	.30
106	Johnny Lindell	1.00	.50	.30
107	Willard Marshall	1.00	.50	.30
108	Walt Masterson	1.00	.50	.30
109	Carl Scheib	1.00	.50	.30
110	Bobby Brown	1.00	.50	.30
111	Cy Block	1.00	.50	.30
112	Sid Gordon	1.00	.50	.30
113	Checklist(Ty Cobb, Babe Ruth, Tris Speaker)	1.50	.70	.45

1977 HRT/RES Philadelphia 'Favorites'

This collectors' issue was produced by promoters Ted Taylor and Bob Schmierer to promote their third annual "Philly Show" in 1977. Printed in black-and-white on front and back, the 2-3/8" x 3-5/8" cards feature former Philadelphia A's and Phillies player photos on front, and an ad for the show on back. Cards were given away at area malls and sporting events to promote the show. Complete sets were originally sold for $2.75.

		NM	E	VG
Complete Set (25):		30.00	15.00	9.00
Common Player:		2.00	1.00	.60
1	Connie Mack	.50	2.00	1.00	.60
2	Larry Lajoie	.50	2.50	1.25	.70
3	Eddie Collins	.50	2.00	1.00	.60
4	Lefty Grove	.50	2.50	1.25	.70
5	Al Simmons	.50	2.00	1.00	.60
6	Jimmie Foxx	.50	3.00	1.50	.90
7	Frank Baker	.50	2.00	1.00	.60
8	Ferris Fain	.50	2.00	1.00	.60
9	Jimmy Dykes	.50	2.00	1.00	.60
10	Willie Jones	.50	2.00	1.00	.60
11	Del Ennis	.50	2.00	1.00	.60
12	Granny Hamner	.50	2.00	1.00	.60
13	Andy Seminick	.50	2.00	1.00	.60
14	Robin Roberts	.75	4.00	2.00	1.25
15	Ed Delahanty	.50	2.00	1.00	.60
16	Gavvy Cravath	.50	2.00	1.00	.60
17	Cy Williams	.50	2.00	1.00	.60
18	Chuck Klein	.50	2.00	1.00	.60
19	Rich Ashburn	.75	4.00	2.00	1.25
20	Bobby Shantz	.50	2.00	1.00	.60
21	Gus Zernial	.50	2.00	1.00	.60
22	Eddie Sawyer	.50	2.00	1.00	.60
23	Grover Alexander	.50	2.00	1.00	.60
24	Wally Moses	.50	2.00	1.00	.60
25	Connie Mack Stadium	.50	2.00	1.00	.60

1978 HRT/RES 1939 Father and Son Reprints

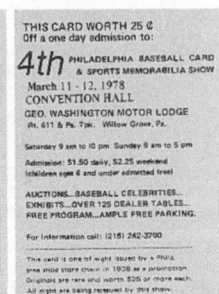

Reprints of scarce 1939 Father and Son Shoes stores cards of local ballplayers (minus the original advertising on front) were created by Ted Taylor and Bob Schmierer to promote their fourth "Philly Show" in March, 1978. The 3" x 4" cards have black-and-white player photos on front. Backs carry an ad for the show and information about the reprints.

		NM	E	VG
Complete Set (8):		7.50	3.75	2.25
Common Player:		1.00	.50	.30
(1)	Sam Chapman	.50	1.00	.50
(2)	Chuck Klein	.75	1.50	.70
(3)	Herschel Martin	.50	1.00	.50
(4)	Wally Moses	.50	1.00	.50
(5)	Hugh Mulcahy	.50	1.00	.50
(6)	Skeeter Newsome	.50	1.00	.50
(7)	George Scharien (Scharein)	.50	1.00	.50
(8)	Dick Siebert	.50	1.00	.50

1979 HRT/RES 1950 Phillies/A's "Doubleheaders"

Though their names or initials do not appear on the cards, this collectors' set was issued by Ted Taylor and Bob Schmierer to promote the March and September 1979, "Philly Shows," the sixth and seventh in the show's history. Borrowing from the format of the 1941 "Doubleheaders" bubblegum card issue, these 2-1/2" x 2-1/8" cards depict members of the 1950 Phillies "Whiz Kids" and the 1950 A's, the last team managed by Connie Mack. Fronts are printed in blue and white, backs in maroon and white. The dual-player cards feature various ads on back, while the managers' cards have a team narrative. The unnumbered cards are checklisted here alphabetically within team, by the last name of the player on the left.

	NM	E	VG
Complete Set (30):	25.00	12.50	7.50
Common Card:	1.50	.70	.45

1910 H.C. Hubel Ty Cobb Postcard

This novelty postcard pictures a super-sized Ty Cobb on a city streetscape. The card is about standard postcard size at 3-3/8" x 5-3/8", printed in sepia tones. Printed in the lower-left corner is "TY COBB, MAKING A HIT ON CAMPUS. / DETROIT / COPY'R'D BY H.C. HUBEL, ST. CLAIR, MICH. / 1910." The back has typical postcard markings.

	NM	EX	VG
Ty Cobb	4,000	2,000	1,200

1957-1959 Hudepohl Beer Cincinnati Reds

These 8" x 10" black-and-white photos were distributed by Hudepohl Beer, although the brewery or brand is not mentioned on the pictures. They are identical in format to the team-issued publicity photos. The Hudepohl pictures differ from the team-issue in that the beer pictures have a semi-gloss finish and no printing on the back, while the team pictures have a glossy surface and a four-line warning on back not to use them for advertising purposes. The pictures have portrait or posed action photos, sometimes with the background removed. They are bordered in white with the player and team name at bottom. The type style is sans-serif for 1957 pictures, and serifed in 1959. Years of issue have been attributed according to corresponding team-issue photos and uniforms pictured. Because so many of the Hudepohl pictures are found autographed, it is possible they were distributed in conjunction with player promotional appearances. This checklist may well not be complete.

	NM	E	VG
Common Player:	20.00	10.00	6.00
1957 (Redlegs, sans-serif.)			
Ed. Bailey (Batting)	20.00	10.00	6.00
George Crowe (Batting)	20.00	10.00	6.00
Ted Kluszewski (Batting)	35.00	17.50	10.50
Brooks Lawrence (Follow-through.)	20.00	10.00	6.00
Roy McMillan (Batting)	20.00	10.00	6.00
Joe Nuxhall (Follow-through.)	25.00	12.50	7.50
Manager "Birdie" Tebbetts (Portrait)	20.00	10.00	6.00
1959 (Reds, serif.)			
Brooks Lawrence (Portrait)	20.00	10.00	6.00

1960 Hudepohl Beer Cincinnati Reds

These 8" x 10" black-and-white photos were distributed by Hudepohl Beer, although the brewery or brand is not mentioned on the pictures. Similar in format to the team-issued publicity photos, the Hudepohl pictures differ in that they have a semi-gloss finish and no printing on the back, while the team pictures have a glossy surface and a four-line warning on back

not to use them for advertising purposes. The pictures have portrait or posed action photos, sometimes with the background removed. They are bordered in white with the player and team name at bottom in a light sans-serif type. Years of issue have been attributed according to corresponding team-issue photos and uniforms pictured. Because so many of the Hudepohl pictures are found autographed, it is possible they were distributed in conjunction with player promotional appearances. This checklist may not be complete.

	NM	E	VG
Common Player:	20.00	10.00	6.00
(1) Ed. Bailey	20.00	10.00	6.00
(2) Gus Bell	20.00	10.00	6.00
(3) Jerry Lynch	20.00	10.00	6.00
(4) Roy McMillan	20.00	10.00	6.00
(5) Don Newcombe	20.00	10.00	6.00
(6) Joe Nuxhall	25.00	12.50	7.50
(7) Vada Pinson	30.00	15.00	9.00
(8) Frank Robinson	85.00	42.00	25.00

1907 Geo. W. Hull Chicago White Sox Postcards

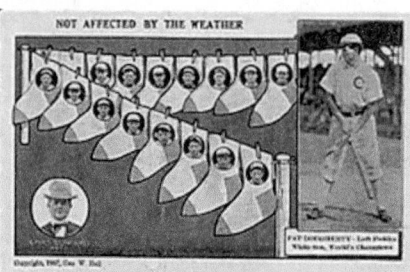

Members of the World Champion White Sox are featured on this single-team issue. Horizontal in format, the black-and-white cards measure about 5-1/2" x 3-1/2". All of the cards share a basic design of a player action posed photo at right, with his name, position, and "White Sox, World's Champions" in a white box beneath. The main part of the card pictures a clothesline full of white socks, each of which has a small round portrait photo of one of the players - 15 in all. In a larger portrait at lower-left is team owner Charles Comiskey. In the white border at top, each card has a witty statement such as "String of World-Beaters" and "Not Worn By Ladies, But Admired By Them." In the bottom border is, "Copyright 1907, Geo. W. Hull." Backs have been seen with a schedule of home games and with an ad from the Morrison Hotel and Boston Oyster House of Chicago.

	NM	E	VG
Complete Set (16):	12,000	6,000	3600
Common Player:	700.00	350.00	210.00
(1) Nick Altrock	700.00	350.00	210.00
(2) George Davis	1,150	575.00	345.00
(3) Jiggs Donahue	700.00	350.00	210.00
(4) Pat Dougherty	700.00	350.00	210.00
(5) Eddie Hahn	700.00	350.00	210.00
(6) Frank Isbell	700.00	350.00	210.00
(7) Fielder Jones	700.00	350.00	210.00
(8) Ed McFarland	700.00	350.00	210.00
(9) Frank Owens	700.00	350.00	210.00
(10) Roy Patterson	700.00	350.00	210.00
(11) George Rohe	700.00	350.00	210.00
(12) Frank Smith	700.00	350.00	210.00
(13) Billy Sullivan	700.00	350.00	210.00
(14) Lee Tannehill	700.00	350.00	210.00
(15) Eddie Walsh	1,100	550.00	330.00
(16) Doc White	700.00	350.00	210.00

1953 Hunter Wieners Cardinals

From the great era of the regionally issued hot dog cards in the mid-1950s, the 1953 Hunter wieners set of St. Louis Cardinals is among the rarest today. Originally issued in two-card panels, the cards are most often found as 2-1/4" x 3-1/4" singles today when they can be found at all. The cards feature a light blue facsimile autograph printed over the stat box at the bottom. They are blank-backed.

	NM	E	VG
Complete Set (26):	20,000	10,000	6,000
Common Player:	600.00	300.00	180.00
(1) Steve Bilko	600.00	300.00	180.00
(2) Cloyd Boyer	600.00	300.00	180.00
(3) Al Brazle	600.00	300.00	180.00
(4) Cliff Chambers	600.00	300.00	180.00
(5) Michael Clark	600.00	300.00	180.00
(6) Jack Crimian	600.00	300.00	180.00
(7) Lester Fusselman	600.00	300.00	180.00
(8) Harvey Haddix	650.00	320.00	200.00
(9) Solly Hemus	600.00	300.00	180.00
(10) Ray Jablonski	600.00	300.00	180.00
(11) William Johnson	600.00	300.00	180.00
(12) Harry Lowrey	600.00	300.00	180.00
(13) Lawrence Miggins	600.00	300.00	180.00
(14) Stuart Miller	600.00	300.00	180.00
(15) Wilmer Mizell	600.00	300.00	180.00
(16) Stanley Musial	6,000	3,000	1,800
(17) Joseph Presko	600.00	300.00	180.00
(18) Delbert Rice	600.00	300.00	180.00
(19) Harold Rice	600.00	300.00	180.00
(20) Willard Schmidt	600.00	300.00	180.00
(21) Albert Schoendienst	1,300	650.00	400.00
(22) Richard Sisler	600.00	300.00	180.00
(23) Enos Slaughter	1,300	650.00	400.00
(24) Gerald Staley	600.00	300.00	180.00
(25) Edward Stanky	650.00	320.00	200.00
(26) John Yuhas	600.00	300.00	180.00

1954 Hunter Wieners Cardinals

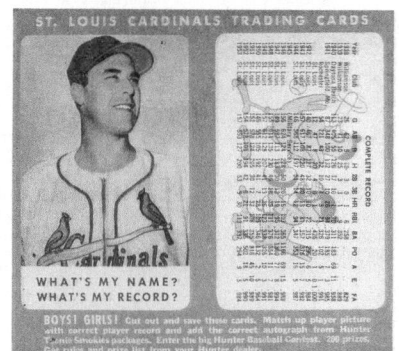

A nearly impossible set to complete today by virtue of the method of its issue, the 1954 Hunter hot dog set features what would traditionally be the front and back of a normal baseball card on two different cards. The "front," has a color photo with a box at bottom challenging the collector to name the player and quote his stats. The "back" features cartoon Cardinals in action, and contains the answers. However, because both parts were printed on a single panel. Because most of the back (non-picture) portions of the panels were thrown away years ago, it is a formidable challenge to complete a '54 Hunter set today. There is no back printing on the 2-1/4" x 3-1/2" cards.

	NM	E	VG
Complete Set (30):	18,000	9,000	5,500
Common Player:	500.00	250.00	150.00
(1) Tom Alston	500.00	250.00	150.00
(2) Steve Bilko	500.00	250.00	150.00
(3) Al Brazle	500.00	250.00	150.00
(4) Tom Burgess	500.00	250.00	150.00
(5) Cot Deal	500.00	250.00	150.00
(6) Alex Grammas	500.00	250.00	150.00
(7) Harvey Haddix	500.00	250.00	150.00
(8) Solly Hemus	500.00	250.00	150.00
(9) Ray Jablonski	500.00	250.00	150.00
(10) Royce Lint	500.00	250.00	150.00
(11) Peanuts Lowrey	500.00	250.00	150.00
(12) Memo Luna	500.00	250.00	150.00
(13) Stu Miller	500.00	250.00	150.00
(14) Stan Musial	4,000	2,000	1,200
(15) Tom Poholsky	500.00	250.00	150.00
(16) Bill Posedel	500.00	250.00	150.00
(17) Joe Presko	500.00	250.00	150.00
(18) Dick Rand	500.00	250.00	150.00
(19) Vic Raschi	500.00	250.00	150.00
(20) Rip Repulski	500.00	250.00	150.00
(21) Del Rice	500.00	250.00	150.00
(22) John Riddle	500.00	250.00	150.00
(23) Mike Ryba	500.00	250.00	150.00

(24)	Red Schoendienst	1,000	500.00	300.00
(25)	Dick Schofield	550.00	270.00	165.00
(26)	Enos Slaughter	1,000	500.00	300.00
(27)	Gerry Staley	500.00	250.00	150.00
(28)	Ed Stanky	500.00	250.00	150.00
(29)	Ed Yuhas	500.00	250.00	150.00
(30)	Sal Yvars	500.00	250.00	150.00

1955 Hunter Wieners Cardinals

The 1955 team set of St. Louis Cardinals, included with packages of Hunter hot dogs, features the third format change in three years of issue. For 1955, the cards were printed in a tall, narrow (2" wide with the height tapering from 4-3/4" at left to 4-1/2" at right) format, two to a panel. The cards feature both a posed action photo and a portrait photo, along with a facsimile autograph and brief biographical data on the front. There is no back printing, as the cards were part of the wrapping for packages of hot dogs.

		NM	E	VG
Complete Set (31):		22,000	11,000	6,500
Common Player:		500.00	250.00	150.00
(1)	Thomas Edison Alston	500.00	250.00	150.00
(2)	Kenton Lloyd Boyer	1,350	675.00	400.00
(3)	Harry Lewis Elliott	500.00	250.00	150.00
(4)	John Edward Faszholz	500.00	250.00	150.00
(5)	Joseph Filmore Frazier	500.00	250.00	150.00
(6)	Alexander Pete Grammas	500.00	250.00	150.00
(7)	Harvey Haddix	500.00	250.00	150.00
(8)	Solly Joseph Hemus	500.00	250.00	150.00
(9)	Lawrence Curtis Jackson	500.00	250.00	150.00
(10)	Tony R. Jacobs	500.00	250.00	150.00
(11)	Gordon Bassett Jones	500.00	250.00	150.00
(12)	Paul Edmore LaPalme	500.00	250.00	150.00
(13)	Brooks Ulysses Lawrence	500.00	250.00	150.00
(14)	Wallace Wade Moon	800.00	400.00	250.00
(15)	Stanley Frank Musial	5,400	2,700	1,625
(16)	Thomas George Poholsky	500.00	250.00	150.00
(17)	William John Posedel	500.00	250.00	150.00
(18)	Victor Angelo John Raschi	500.00	250.00	150.00
(19)	Eldon John Repulski	500.00	250.00	150.00
(20)	Delbert Rice	500.00	250.00	150.00
(21)	John Ludy Riddle	500.00	250.00	150.00
(22)	William F. Sarni	500.00	250.00	150.00
(23)	Albert Fred Schoendienst	1,100	550.00	325.00
(24)	Richard John Schofield (Actually John Richard.)	500.00	250.00	150.00
(25)	Frank Thomas Smith	500.00	250.00	150.00
(26)	Edward R. Stanky	550.00	275.00	165.00
(27)	Robert Loyd Stephenson	500.00	275.00	150.00
(28)	Bobby Gene Tiefenauer	250.00	125.00	75.00
(29)	William Charles Virdon	800.00	400.00	240.00
(30)	Frederick E. Walker	500.00	250.00	150.00
(31)	Floyd Lewis Woolridge	500.00	250.00	150.00

1941 Huskies

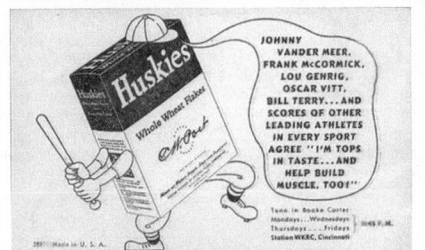

This advertising card was issued by Huskies Whole Wheat Flakes cereal. In black-and-white, the card measures about 5-1/2" x 3-1/2". Facsimile autographs appear on the borderless front photo.

	NM	E	VG
John Vander Meer, Frank McCormick	125.00	65.00	40.00

1976 Icee Drinks Reds

Issued in 1976 in the Cincinnati area by Icee Drinks, this 12-card set of semi-circular cards features members of the Reds. The cards measure approximately 2" in diameter with the bottom of the disc squared off. The cards were originally issued as soft drink lids. Fronts have a portrait photo in black-and-white, with uniform logos removed. Backs are blank. The cards are unnumbered. A 7" x 12" cap saver sheet was also available; it does not picture the players.

		NM	E	VG
Complete Set (12):		60.00	30.00	18.00
Common Player:		2.00	1.00	.60
Saver Sheet:		27.00	13.50	8.00
(1)	Johnny Bench	10.00	5.00	3.00
(2)	Dave Concepcion	2.25	1.25	.70
(3)	Rawly Eastwick	2.00	1.00	.60
(4)	George Foster	2.25	1.25	.70
(5)	Cesar Geronimo	2.00	1.00	.60
(6)	Ken Griffey	2.50	1.25	.70
(7)	Don Gullett	2.00	1.00	.60
(8)	Will McEnaney	2.00	1.00	.60
(9)	Joe Morgan	6.00	3.00	1.75
(10)	Gary Nolan	2.00	1.00	.60
(11)	Tony Perez	4.00	2.00	1.25
(12)	Pete Rose	27.50	13.50	8.25

1963 I.D.L. Drug Store Pittsburgh Pirates

This set of 26 black-and-white cards was regionally distributed. The 4" x 5" semi-gloss cards are blank-backed and unnumbered. The checklist is arranged alphabetically. Johnny Logan's card is considered scarce and may have been pulled from distribution early.

		NM	E	VG
Complete Set (27):		450.00	220.00	130.00
Common Player:		15.00	7.70	4.50
(1)	Bob Bailey	15.00	7.50	4.50
(2)	Forrest "Smoky" Burgess	15.00	7.50	4.50
(3)	Don Cardwell	15.00	7.50	4.50
(4)	Roberto Clemente	150.00	75.00	45.00
(5)	Donn Clendenon	20.00	10.00	6.00
(6)	Roy Face	15.00	7.50	4.50
(7)	Earl Francis	15.00	7.50	4.50
(8)	Bob Friend	15.00	7.50	4.50
(9)	Joe Gibbon	15.00	7.50	4.50
(10)	Julio Gotay	15.00	7.50	4.50
(11)	Harvey Haddix	15.00	7.50	4.50
(12)	Johnny Logan (SP)	30.00	15.00	9.00
(13)	Bill Mazeroski	50.00	25.00	15.00
(14)	Al McBean	15.00	7.50	4.50
(15)	Danny Murtaugh	15.00	7.50	4.50
(16)	Sam Narron	15.00	7.50	4.50
(17)	Ron Northey	15.00	7.50	4.50
(18)	Frank Oceak	15.00	7.50	4.50
(19)	Jim Pagliaroni	15.00	7.50	4.50
(20)	Ted Savage	15.00	7.50	4.50
(21)	Dick Schofield	15.00	7.50	4.50
(22)	Bob Skinner (SP)	30.00	15.00	9.00
(23)	Willie Stargell	50.00	25.00	15.00
(24)	Tom Sturdivant	15.00	7.50	4.50
(25)	Virgil "Fire" Trucks	15.00	7.50	4.50
(26)	Bob Veale	15.00	7.50	4.50
(27)	Bill Virdon	15.00	7.50	4.50

1916 Indianapolis Brewing Co.

Best known in blank-back form or with ads on back for The Sporting News, this 200-card set can be found with the imprint of several other local and regional businesses. Among them is the Indianapolis Brewing Co. Type-card and superstar collectors can expect to pay a significant premium for individual cards with Indianapolis Brewing advertising. The checklist parallels that of the 1916 M101-4 Blank Backs. Cards measure 1-5/8" x 3" and are printed in black-and-white. The brewery originally advertised the set on its "Facts for Fans" booklet, at a cost of 25 cents.

		NM	E	VG
Complete Set (200):		96,000	48,000	28,800
Common Player:		275.00	135.00	82.50
1	Babe Adams	360.00	120.00	75.00
2	Sam Agnew	275.00	135.00	82.50
3	Eddie Ainsmith	275.00	135.00	82.50
4	Grover Alexander	900.00	450.00	270.00
5	Leon Ames	275.00	135.00	82.50
6	Jimmy Archer	275.00	135.00	82.50
7	Jimmy Austin	275.00	135.00	82.50
8	H.D. Baird	275.00	135.00	82.50
9	J. Franklin Baker	540.00	270.00	160.00
10	Dave Bancroft	540.00	270.00	160.00
11	Jack Barry	275.00	135.00	82.50
12	Zinn Beck	275.00	135.00	82.50
13	"Chief" Bender	540.00	270.00	160.00
14	Joe Benz	275.00	135.00	82.50
15	Bob Bescher	275.00	135.00	82.50
16	Al Betzel	275.00	135.00	82.50
17	Mordecai Brown	540.00	270.00	160.00
18	Eddie Burns	275.00	135.00	82.50
19	George Burns	275.00	135.00	82.50
20	Geo. J. Burns	275.00	135.00	82.50
21	Joe Bush	275.00	135.00	82.50
22	"Donie" Bush	275.00	135.00	82.50
23	Art Butler	275.00	135.00	82.50
24	Bobbie Byrne	275.00	135.00	82.50
25	Forrest Cady	275.00	135.00	82.50
26	Jimmy Callahan	275.00	135.00	82.50
27	Ray Caldwell	275.00	135.00	82.50
28	Max Carey	540.00	270.00	160.00

29	George Chalmers	275.00	135.00	82.50
30	Ray Chapman	300.00	150.00	90.00
31	Larry Cheney	275.00	135.00	82.50
32	Eddie Cicotte	540.00	270.00	160.00
33	Tom Clarke	275.00	135.00	82.50
34	Eddie Collins	540.00	270.00	160.00
35	"Shauno" Collins	275.00	135.00	82.50
36	Charles Comiskey	540.00	270.00	160.00
37	Joe Connolly	240.00	120.00	75.00
38	Ty Cobb	6,500	3,200	1,950
39	Harry Coveleskie (Coveleski)	275.00	135.00	82.50
40	Gavvy Cravath	275.00	135.00	82.50
41	Sam Crawford	540.00	270.00	160.00
42	Jean Dale	275.00	135.00	82.50
43	Jake Daubert	275.00	135.00	82.50
44	Charles Deal	275.00	135.00	82.50
45	Al Demaree	275.00	135.00	82.50
46	Josh Devore	275.00	135.00	82.50
47	William Doak	275.00	135.00	82.50
48	Bill Donovan	275.00	135.00	82.50
49	Charles Dooin	275.00	135.00	82.50
50	Mike Doolan	275.00	135.00	82.50
51	Larry Doyle	275.00	135.00	82.50
52	Jean Dubuc	275.00	135.00	82.50
53	Oscar Dugey	275.00	135.00	82.50
54	Johnny Evers	540.00	270.00	160.00
55	Urban Faber	540.00	270.00	160.00
56	"Hap" Felsch	800.00	400.00	240.00
57	Bill Fischer	275.00	135.00	82.50
58	Ray Fisher	275.00	135.00	82.50
59	Max Flack	275.00	135.00	82.50
60	Art Fletcher	275.00	135.00	82.50
61	Eddie Foster	275.00	135.00	82.50
62	Jacques Fournier	275.00	135.00	82.50
63	Del Gainer (Gainor)	275.00	135.00	82.50
64	"Chic" Gandil	540.00	270.00	160.00
65	Larry Gardner	275.00	135.00	82.50
66	Joe Gedeon	275.00	135.00	82.50
67	Gus Getz	275.00	135.00	82.50
68	Geo. Gibson	275.00	135.00	82.50
69	Wilbur Good	275.00	135.00	82.50
70	Hank Gowdy	275.00	135.00	82.50
71	John Graney	275.00	135.00	82.50
72	Clark Griffith	540.00	270.00	160.00
73	Tom Griffith	275.00	135.00	82.50
74	Heinie Groh	275.00	135.00	82.50
75	Earl Hamilton	275.00	135.00	82.50
76	Bob Harmon	275.00	135.00	82.50
77	Roy Hartzell	275.00	135.00	82.50
78	Claude Hendrix	275.00	135.00	82.50
79	Olaf Henriksen	275.00	135.00	82.50
80	John Henry	275.00	135.00	82.50
81	"Buck" Herzog	275.00	135.00	82.50
82	Hugh High	275.00	135.00	82.50
83	Dick Hoblitzell	275.00	135.00	82.50
84	Harry Hooper	540.00	270.00	160.00
85	Ivan Howard	275.00	135.00	82.50
86	Miller Huggins	540.00	270.00	160.00
87	Joe Jackson	20,000	7,500	4,500
88	William James	275.00	135.00	82.50
89	Harold Janvrin	275.00	135.00	82.50
90	Hugh Jennings	540.00	270.00	160.00
91	Walter Johnson	2,500	1,250	750.00
92	Fielder Jones	275.00	135.00	82.50
93	Joe Judge	275.00	135.00	82.50
94	Bennie Kauff	275.00	135.00	82.50
95	Wm. Killefer Jr.	275.00	135.00	82.50
96	Ed. Konetchy	275.00	135.00	82.50
97	Napoleon Lajoie	750.00	370.00	220.00
98	Jack Lapp	275.00	135.00	82.50
99	John Lavan	275.00	135.00	82.50
100	Jimmy Lavender	275.00	135.00	82.50
101	"Nemo" Leibold	275.00	135.00	82.50
102	H.B. Leonard	275.00	135.00	82.50
103	Duffy Lewis	275.00	135.00	82.50
104	Hans Lobert	275.00	135.00	82.50
105	Tom Long	275.00	135.00	82.50
106	Fred Luderus	275.00	135.00	82.50
107	Connie Mack	540.00	270.00	160.00
108	Lee Magee	275.00	135.00	82.50
109	Sherwood Magee	275.00	135.00	82.50
110	Al. Mamaux	275.00	135.00	82.50
111	Leslie Mann	275.00	135.00	82.50
112	"Rabbit" Maranville	540.00	270.00	160.00
113	Rube Marquard	540.00	270.00	160.00
114	J. Erskine Mayer	360.00	180.00	110.00
115	George McBride	275.00	135.00	82.50
116	John J. McGraw	540.00	270.00	160.00
117	Jack McInnis	275.00	135.00	82.50
118	Fred Merkle	275.00	135.00	82.50
119	Chief Meyers	275.00	135.00	82.50
120	Clyde Milan	275.00	135.00	82.50
121	John Miller	275.00	135.00	82.50
122	Otto Miller	275.00	135.00	82.50
123	Willie Mitchell	275.00	135.00	82.50
124	Fred Mollwitz	275.00	135.00	82.50
125	Pat Moran	275.00	135.00	82.50

126	Ray Morgan	275.00	135.00	82.50
127	Geo. Moriarty	275.00	135.00	82.50
128	Guy Morton	275.00	135.00	82.50
129	Mike Mowrey	275.00	135.00	82.50
130	Ed. Murphy	275.00	135.00	82.50
131	"Hy" Myers	275.00	135.00	82.50
132	J.A. Niehoff	275.00	135.00	82.50
133	Rube Oldring	275.00	135.00	82.50
134	Oliver O'Mara	275.00	135.00	82.50
135	Steve O'Neill	275.00	135.00	82.50
136	"Dode" Paskert	275.00	135.00	82.50
137	Roger Peckinpaugh	275.00	135.00	82.50
138	Walter Pipp	275.00	135.00	82.50
139	Derril Pratt (Derrill)	275.00	135.00	82.50
140	Pat Ragan	275.00	135.00	82.50
141	Bill Rariden	275.00	135.00	82.50
142	Eppa Rixey	540.00	270.00	160.00
143	Davey Robertson	275.00	135.00	82.50
144	Wilbert Robinson	540.00	270.00	160.00
145	Bob Roth	275.00	135.00	82.50
146	Ed. Roush	540.00	270.00	160.00
147	Clarence Rowland	275.00	135.00	82.50
148	"Nap" Rucker	275.00	135.00	82.50
149	Dick Rudolph	275.00	135.00	82.50
150	Reb Russell	275.00	135.00	82.50
151	Babe Ruth	24,000	12,000	7,200
152	Vic Saier	275.00	135.00	82.50
153	"Slim" Sallee	275.00	135.00	82.50
154	Ray Schalk	540.00	270.00	160.00
155	Walter Schang	275.00	135.00	82.50
156	Frank Schulte	275.00	135.00	82.50
157	Everett Scott	275.00	135.00	82.50
158	Jim Scott	240.00	120.00	75.00
159	Tom Seaton	275.00	135.00	82.50
160	Howard Shanks	275.00	135.00	82.50
161	Bob Shawkey	275.00	135.00	82.50
162	Ernie Shore	275.00	135.00	82.50
163	Burt Shotton	275.00	135.00	82.50
164	Geo. Sisler	540.00	270.00	160.00
165	J. Carlisle Smith	275.00	135.00	82.50
166	Fred Snodgrass	275.00	135.00	82.50
167	Geo. Stallings	275.00	135.00	82.50
168	Oscar Stanage	275.00	135.00	82.50
169	Charles Stengel	540.00	270.00	160.00
170	Milton Stock	275.00	135.00	82.50
171	Amos Strunk	275.00	135.00	82.50
172	Billy Sullivan	275.00	135.00	82.50
173	"Jeff" Tesreau	275.00	135.00	82.50
174	Joe Tinker	540.00	270.00	160.00
175	Fred Toney	275.00	135.00	82.50
176	Terry Turner	275.00	135.00	82.50
177	George Tyler	275.00	135.00	82.50
178	Jim Vaughn	275.00	135.00	82.50
179	Bob Veach	275.00	135.00	82.50
180	James Viox	275.00	135.00	82.50
181	Oscar Vitt	275.00	135.00	82.50
182	Hans Wagner	5,500	2,700	1,650
183	Clarence Walker	275.00	135.00	82.50
184	Ed. Walsh	540.00	270.00	160.00
185	W. Wambsganss (Photo actually Fritz Coumbe.)	275.00	135.00	82.50
186	Buck Weaver	2,400	1,200	725.00
187	Carl Weilman	275.00	135.00	82.50
188	Zach Wheat	540.00	270.00	160.00
189	Geo. Whitted	275.00	135.00	82.50
190	Fred Williams	275.00	135.00	82.50
191	Art Wilson	275.00	135.00	82.50
192	J. Owen Wilson	275.00	135.00	82.50
193	Ivy Wingo	275.00	135.00	82.50
194	"Mel" Wolfgang	275.00	135.00	82.50
195	Joe Wood	450.00	220.00	135.00
196	Steve Yerkes	275.00	135.00	82.50
197	"Pep" Young	275.00	135.00	82.50
198	Rollie Zeider	275.00	135.00	82.50
199	Heiny Zimmerman	275.00	135.00	82.50
200	Ed. Zwilling	275.00	135.00	82.50

1923 Curtis Ireland Candy (E123)

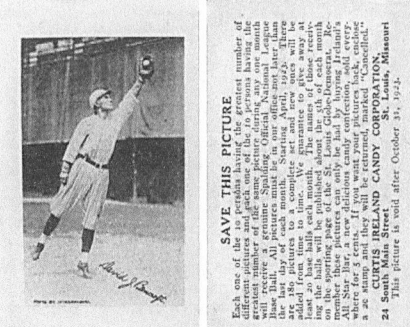

This set, identified in the ACC as E123, was issued in 1923 by the Curtis Ireland Candy Corp. of St. Louis and was distributed with Ireland's "All Star Bars." Except for the backs, the Ireland set is identical to the Willard Chocolate V100 set of the same year. Measuring 3-1/4" x 2-1/16", the cards feature sepia-toned photos with the player's name in script on the front. The backs advertise a contest which required the collector to mail in the cards in exchange for prizes, which probably explains their relative scarcity.

		NM	E	VG
Complete Set (180):		250,000	50,000	30,000
Common Player:		1,200	360.00	180.00
(1)	Chas. B Adams	1,200	360.00	180.00
(2)	Grover C. Alexander	2,000	600.00	300.00
(3)	J.P. Austin	1,200	360.00	180.00
(4)	J.C. Bagby Sr.	1,200	360.00	180.00
(5)	J. Franklin Baker	1,800	550.00	275.00
(6)	David J. Bancroft	1,800	550.00	275.00
(7)	Turner Barber	1,200	360.00	180.00
(8)	Jesse L. Barnes	1,200	360.00	180.00
(9)	J.C. Bassler	1,200	360.00	180.00
(10)	L.A. Blue	1,200	360.00	180.00
(11)	Norman D. Boeckel	600.00	240.00	150.00
(12)	F.L. Brazil (Brazill)	1,200	360.00	180.00
(13)	G.H. Burns	1,200	360.00	180.00
(14)	Geo. J. Burns	1,200	360.00	180.00
(15)	Leon Cadore	1,200	360.00	180.00
(16)	Max G. Carey	900.00	360.00	225.00
(17)	Harold G. Carlson	600.00	240.00	150.00
(18)	Lloyd R. Christenberry (Christenbury)	1,200	360.00	180.00
(19)	Vernon J. Clemons	1,200	360.00	180.00
(20)	T.R. Cobb	17,000	5,400	2,600
(21)	Bert Cole	1,200	360.00	180.00
(22)	John F. Collins	1,200	360.00	180.00
(23)	S. Coveleskie (Coveleski)	1,800	550.00	275.00
(24)	Walton E. Cruise	1,200	360.00	180.00
(25)	G.W. Cutshaw	1,200	360.00	180.00
(26)	Jacob E. Daubert	1,200	360.00	180.00
(27)	Geo. Dauss	1,200	360.00	180.00
(28)	F.T. Davis	1,200	360.00	180.00
(29)	Chas. A. Deal	1,200	360.00	180.00
(30)	William L. Doak	1,200	360.00	180.00
(31)	William E. Donovan	1,200	360.00	180.00
(32)	Hugh Duffy	1,800	550.00	275.00
(33)	J.A. Dugan	1,200	360.00	180.00
(34)	Louis B. Duncan	1,200	360.00	180.00
(35)	James Dykes	1,200	360.00	180.00
(36)	H.J. Ehmke	1,200	360.00	180.00
(37)	F.R. Ellerbe	1,200	360.00	180.00
(38)	E.G. Erickson	1,200	360.00	180.00
(39)	John J. Evers	1,800	550.00	275.00
(40)	U.C. Faber	1,800	550.00	275.00
(41)	B.A. Falk	1,200	360.00	180.00
(42)	Max Flack	1,200	360.00	180.00
(43)	Lee Fohl	1,200	360.00	180.00
(44)	Jacques F. Fournier	1,200	360.00	180.00
(45)	Frank F. Frisch	1,800	550.00	275.00
(46)	C.E. Galloway	1,200	360.00	180.00
(47)	W.C. Gardner	1,200	360.00	180.00
(48)	E.P. Gharrity	1,200	360.00	180.00
(49)	Geo. Gibson	1,200	360.00	180.00
(50)	Wm. Gleason	1,200	360.00	180.00
(51)	William Gleason	1,200	360.00	180.00
(52)	Henry M. Gowdy	1,200	360.00	180.00
(53)	I.M. Griffin	1,200	360.00	180.00
(54)	Thomas Griffith	1,200	360.00	180.00
(55)	Burleigh A. Grimes	1,800	550.00	275.00
(56)	Charles J. Grimm	1,200	360.00	180.00
(57)	Jesse J. Haines	1,800	550.00	275.00
(58)	S.R. Harris	1,800	550.00	275.00
(59)	W.B. Harris	1,200	360.00	180.00
(60)	R.K. Hasty	1,200	360.00	180.00
(61)	H.E. Heilman (Heilmann)	1,800	550.00	275.00
(62)	Walter J. Henline	1,200	360.00	180.00
(63)	Walter L. Holke	1,200	360.00	180.00
(64)	Charles J. Hollocher	1,200	360.00	180.00
(65)	H.B. Hooper	1,800	550.00	275.00
(66)	Rogers Hornsby	2,500	750.00	375.00
(67)	W.C. Hoyt	1,800	550.00	275.00
(68)	Miller Huggins	1,800	550.00	275.00
(69)	W.C. Jacobsen (Jacobson)	1,200	360.00	180.00
(70)	C.D. Jamieson	1,200	360.00	180.00
(71)	Ernest Johnson	1,200	360.00	180.00
(72)	W.P. Johnson	4,500	1,350	700.00
(73)	James H. Johnston	1,200	360.00	180.00
(74)	R.W. Jones	1,200	360.00	180.00
(75)	Samuel Pond Jones	1,200	360.00	180.00
(76)	J.I. Judge	1,200	360.00	180.00
(77)	James W. Keenan	1,200	360.00	180.00
(78)	Geo. L. Kelly	1,800	550.00	275.00
(79)	Peter J. Kilduff	1,200	360.00	180.00
(80)	William Killefer	1,200	360.00	180.00
(81)	Lee King	1,200	360.00	180.00
(82)	Ray Kolp	1,200	360.00	180.00
(83)	John Lavan	1,200	360.00	180.00
(84)	H.L. Leibold	1,200	360.00	180.00

(Image caption, card back text:) SAVE THIS PICTURE — Each one of the 10 penants having the greatest number of different pictures and the greatest number of the same picture during any one month will receive a genuine Spalding Official National League Base Ball. All pictures must be in by the last day of each month. Starting April, 1923. There are 180 pictures to a complete set and new ones will be added from time to time so that your collection will never be complete. The names of those receiving the balls will be published about the 15th of each month. All Star Bars, a new delicious candy confection, sold everywhere. These pictures can only be had by buying Ireland's All Star Bars at your candy dealer's or news-stand. Pictures must be in good condition to be counted. Offer void after October 31, 1923. CURTIS IRELAND CANDY CORPORATION, 24 South Main Street, St. Louis, Missouri. This picture is void after October 31, 1923.

(85)	Connie Mack	1,800	550.00	275.00
(86)	J.W. Mails	1,200	550.00	180.00
(87)	Walter J. Maranville	1,800	550.00	275.00
(88)	Richard W. Marquard	1,800	550.00	275.00
(89)	C.W. Mays	1,300	360.00	180.00
(90)	Geo. F. McBride	1,200	360.00	180.00
(91)	H.M. McClellan	1,200	360.00	180.00
(92)	John J. McGraw	1,800	550.00	275.00
(93)	Austin B. McHenry	1,200	360.00	180.00
(94)	J. McInnis	1,200	360.00	180.00
(95)	Douglas McWeeney (McWeeny)	1,200	360.00	180.00
(96)	M. Menosky	1,200	360.00	180.00
(97)	Emil F. Meusel	1,200	360.00	180.00
(98)	R. Meusel	1,200	360.00	180.00
(99)	Henry W. Meyers	1,200	360.00	180.00
(100)	J.C. Milan	1,200	360.00	180.00
(101)	John K. Miljus	1,200	360.00	180.00
(102)	Edmund J. Miller	1,200	360.00	180.00
(103)	Elmer Miller	1,200	360.00	180.00
(104)	Otto L. Miller	1,200	360.00	180.00
(105)	Fred Mitchell	1,200	360.00	180.00
(106)	Geo. Mogridge	1,200	360.00	180.00
(107)	Patrick J. Moran	1,200	360.00	180.00
(108)	John D. Morrison	1,200	360.00	180.00
(109)	J.A. Mostil	1,200	360.00	180.00
(110)	Clarence F. Mueller	1,200	360.00	180.00
(111)	A. Earle Neale	1,200	360.00	180.00
(112)	Joseph Oeschger	1,200	360.00	180.00
(113)	Robert J. O'Farrell	1,200	360.00	180.00
(114)	J.C. Oldham	1,200	360.00	180.00
(115)	I.M. Olson	1,200	360.00	180.00
(116)	Geo. M. O'Neil	1,200	360.00	180.00
(117)	S.F. O'Neill	1,200	360.00	180.00
(118)	Frank J. Parkinson	1,200	360.00	180.00
(119)	Geo. H. Paskert	1,200	360.00	180.00
(120)	R.T. Peckinpaugh	1,200	360.00	180.00
(121)	H.J. Pennock	1,800	550.00	275.00
(122)	Ralph Perkins	1,200	360.00	180.00
(123)	Edw. J. Pfeffer	1,200	360.00	180.00
(124)	W.C. Pipp	1,200	360.00	180.00
(125)	Charles Elmer Ponder	1,200	360.00	180.00
(126)	Raymond R. Powell	1,200	360.00	180.00
(127)	D.B. Pratt	1,200	360.00	180.00
(128)	Joseph Rapp	1,200	360.00	180.00
(129)	John H. Rawlings	1,200	360.00	180.00
(130)	E.S. Rice (Should be E.C.)	1,800	550.00	275.00
(131)	Branch Rickey	2,000	600.00	300.00
(132)	James J. Ring	1,200	360.00	180.00
(133)	Eppa J. Rixey	1,800	550.00	275.00
(134)	Davis A. Robertson	1,200	360.00	180.00
(135)	Edwin Rommel	1,200	360.00	180.00
(136)	Edd J. Roush	1,800	550.00	275.00
(137)	Harold Ruel (Herold)	1,200	360.00	180.00
(138)	Allen Russell	1,200	360.00	180.00
(139)	G.H. Ruth	25,000	7,500	3,800
(140)	Wilfred D. Ryan	1,200	360.00	180.00
(141)	Henry F. Sallee	1,200	360.00	180.00
(142)	W.H. Schang	1,200	360.00	180.00
(143)	Raymond H. Schmandt	1,200	360.00	180.00
(144)	Everett Scott	1,200	360.00	180.00
(145)	Henry Severeid	1,200	380.00	150.00
(146)	Jos. W. Sewell	1,800	550.00	275.00
(147)	Howard S. Shanks	1,200	360.00	180.00
(148)	E.H. Sheely	1,200	360.00	180.00
(149)	Ralph Shinners	1,200	360.00	180.00
(150)	U.J. Shocker	1,200	360.00	180.00
(151)	G.H. Sisler	1,800	550.00	275.00
(152)	Earl L. Smith	1,200	360.00	180.00
(153)	Earl S. Smith	1,200	360.00	180.00
(154)	Geo. A. Smith	1,200	360.00	180.00
(155)	J.W. Smith	1,200	360.00	180.00
(156)	Tris E. Speaker	2,700	800.00	400.00
(157)	Arnold Staatz	1,200	360.00	180.00
(158)	J.R. Stephenson	1,200	360.00	180.00
(159)	Milton J. Stock	1,200	360.00	180.00
(160)	John L. Sullivan	1,200	360.00	180.00
(161)	H.F. Tormahlen	1,200	360.00	180.00
(162)	Jas. A. Tierney	1,200	360.00	180.00
(163)	J.T. Tobin	1,200	360.00	180.00
(164)	Jas. L. Vaughn	1,200	360.00	180.00
(165)	R.H. Veach	1,200	360.00	180.00
(166)	C.W. Walker	1,200	360.00	180.00
(167)	A.L. Ward	1,200	360.00	180.00
(168)	Zack D. Wheat	1,800	550.00	275.00
(169)	George B. Whitted	1,200	360.00	180.00
(170)	Irvin K. Wilhelm	1,200	360.00	180.00
(171)	Roy H. Wilkinson	1,200	360.00	180.00
(172)	Fred C. Williams	1,200	360.00	180.00
(173)	K.R. Williams	1,200	360.00	180.00
(174)	Sam'l W. Wilson	1,200	360.00	180.00
(175)	Ivy B. Wingo	1,200	360.00	180.00
(176)	L.W. Witt	1,200	360.00	180.00
(177)	Joseph Wood	1,300	360.00	180.00
(178)	E. Yaryan	1,200	360.00	180.00
(179)	R.S. Young	1,200	360.00	180.00
(180)	Ross Young (Youngs)	1,800	550.00	275.00

1967 Irvindale Dairy Atlana Braves

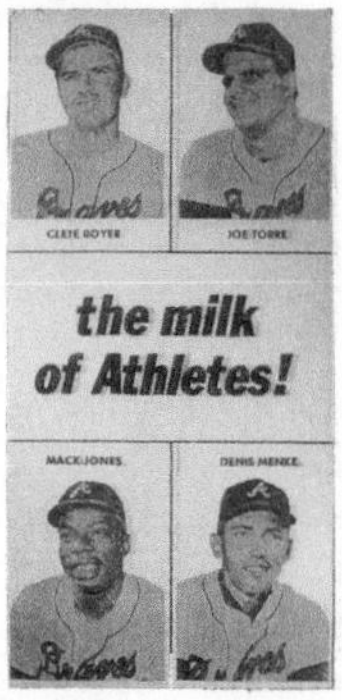

This quartet of Brav es was printed in shades of deep red on the white background of a milk carton panel. Well-cut individual pieces measure 1-3/4" x 2-5/8" and are blank-backed.

		NM	E	VG
Complete Set, Panel:		250.00	125.00	75.00
Complete Set, Singles:		175.00	85.00	45.00
Common Player:		40.00	20.00	12.00
(1)	Clete Boyer	40.00	20.00	12.00
(2)	Mack Jones	40.00	20.00	12.00
(3)	Denis Menke	40.00	20.00	12.00
(4)	Joe Torre	60.00	30.00	18.00

1976 Isaly's/Sweet William discs

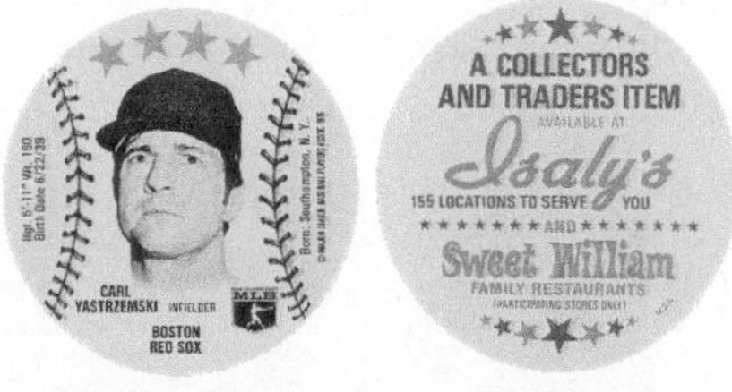

One of several regional sponsors of player disc sets in 1976 was the Pittsburgh area dairy store chain, Isaly's, and the Sweet William restaurants. The discs are 3-3/8" diameter with a black-and-white player portrait photo in the center of the baseball design. A line of red stars is above, while the left and right panels feature one of several bright colors. Produced by Michael Schecter Associates under license from the Major League Baseball Players Association, the player photos have had uniform and cap logos removed. Backs are printed in red and purple. The unnumbered checklist here is presented in alphabetical order.

		NM	E	VG
Complete Set (70):		15.00	7.50	4.50
Common Player:		.50	.25	.15
(1)	Henry Aaron	4.00	2.00	1.25
(2)	Johnny Bench	2.00	1.00	.60
(3)	Vida Blue	.50	.25	.15
(4)	Larry Bowa	.50	.25	.15
(5)	Lou Brock	2.00	1.00	.60
(6)	Jeff Burroughs	.50	.25	.15
(7)	John Candelaria	.50	.25	.15
(8)	Jose Cardenal	.50	.25	.15
(9)	Rod Carew	2.00	1.00	.60
(10)	Steve Carlton	2.00	1.00	.60
(11)	Dave Cash	.50	.25	.15
(12)	Cesar Cedeno	.50	.25	.15
(13)	Ron Cey	.50	.25	.15
(14)	Carlton Fisk	2.00	1.00	.60
(15)	Tito Fuentes	.50	.25	.15
(16)	Steve Garvey	1.50	.70	.45
(17)	Ken Griffey	.50	.25	.15
(18)	Don Gullett	.50	.25	.15
(19)	Willie Horton	.50	.25	.15
(20)	Al Hrabosky	.50	.25	.15
(21)	Catfish Hunter	2.00	1.00	.60
(22)	Reggie Jackson (A's)	3.00	1.50	.90
(23)	Randy Jones	.50	.25	.15
(24)	Jim Kaat	.50	.25	.15
(25)	Don Kessinger	.50	.25	.15
(26)	Dave Kingman	.50	.25	.15
(27)	Jerry Koosman	.50	.25	.15
(28)	Mickey Lolich	.50	.25	.15
(29)	Greg Luzinski	.50	.25	.15
(30)	Fred Lynn	.50	.25	.15
(31)	Bill Madlock	.50	.25	.15
(32)	Carlos May (White Sox)	.50	.25	.15
(33)	John Mayberry	.50	.25	.15
(34)	Bake McBride	.50	.25	.15
(35)	Doc Medich	.50	.25	.15
(36)	Andy Messersmith (Dodgers)	.50	.25	.15
(37)	Rick Monday	.50	.25	.15
(38)	John Montefusco	.50	.25	.15
(39)	Jerry Morales	.50	.25	.15
(40)	Joe Morgan	2.00	1.00	.60
(41)	Thurman Munson	2.00	1.00	.60
(42)	Bobby Murcer	.50	.25	.15
(43)	Al Oliver	.50	.25	.15
(44)	Jim Palmer	2.00	1.00	.60
(45)	Dave Parker	.50	.25	.15
(46)	Tony Perez	2.00	1.00	.60
(47)	Jerry Reuss	.50	.25	.15
(48)	Brooks Robinson	2.00	1.00	.60
(49)	Frank Robinson	2.00	1.00	.60
(50)	Steve Rogers	.50	.25	.15
(51)	Pete Rose	6.00	3.00	1.75
(52)	Nolan Ryan	12.00	6.00	3.50
(53)	Manny Sanguillen	.50	.25	.15
(54)	Mike Schmidt	3.00	1.50	.90
(55)	Tom Seaver	2.00	1.00	.60
(56)	Ted Simmons	.50	.25	.15
(57)	Reggie Smith	.50	.25	.15
(58)	Willie Stargell	2.00	1.00	.60
(59)	Rusty Staub	.75	.40	.25
(60)	Rennie Stennett	.50	.25	.15
(61)	Don Sutton	2.00	1.00	.60
(62)	Andy Thornton (Cubs)	.50	.25	.15
(63)	Luis Tiant	.50	.25	.15
(64)	Joe Torre	1.50	.70	.45
(65)	Mike Tyson	.50	.25	.15
(66)	Bob Watson	.50	.25	.15
(67)	Wilbur Wood	.50	.25	.15
(68)	Jimmy Wynn	.50	.25	.15
(69)	Carl Yastrzemski	2.50	1.25	.70
(70)	Richie Zisk	.50	.25	.15

1976 ISCA Hoosier Hot-Stove All-Stars

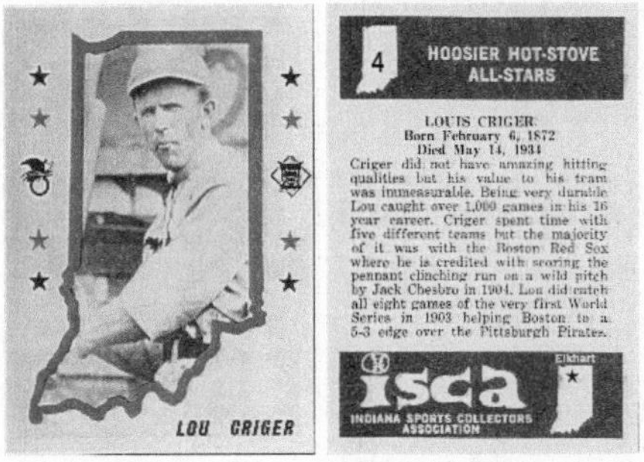

Famous native Hoosier ballplayers are featured in this collectors' issue from the Indiana Sports Collectors Assn. The 2-5/8" x 3-5/8" cards have black-and-white player photos on front framed in the state's outline. Red and blue graphics on a white background complete the design. Backs are in black and blue on white and include a career summary. A star on the state map at bottom indicates where the player was born.

		NM	E	VG
Complete Set (26):		15.00	7.50	4.50
Common Player:		2.00	1.00	.60
1	Edd Roush	2.00	1.00	.60
2	Sam Thompson	2.00	1.00	.60
3	Chuck Klein	2.00	1.00	.60
4	Lou Criger	2.00	1.00	.60
5	Amos Rusie	2.00	1.00	.60
6	Billy Herman	2.00	1.00	.60
7	George Dauss	2.00	1.00	.60
8	Tom Thevenow	2.00	1.00	.60
9	Mordecai Brown	2.00	1.00	.60
10	Freddie Fitzsimmons	2.00	1.00	.60
11	Art Nehf	2.00	1.00	.60
12	Carl Erskine	3.00	1.50	.90
13	Don Larsen	3.00	1.50	.90
14	Gil Hodges	6.00	3.00	1.75
15	Pete Fox	2.00	1.00	.60
16	Butch Henline	2.00	1.00	.60
17	Doc Crandall	2.00	1.00	.60
18	Dizzy Trout	2.00	1.00	.60
19	Donie Bush	2.00	1.00	.60
20	Max Carey	2.00	1.00	.60
21	Eugene Hargrave, William Hargrave	2.00	1.00	.60
22	Sam Rice	2.00	1.00	.60
23	Babe Adams	2.00	1.00	.60
24	Cy Williams	2.00	1.00	.60
25	1913 Indianapolis Federal League Team	2.00	1.00	.60
26	Paul Frisz	2.00	1.00	.60

J

1912 J=K Candy

Originally printed on the front and back of candy boxes which advertised "100 Principal League Players," the extent of this series is currently unknown and the checklist presented here is almost certainly incomplete. The blank-back, black-and-white (some have a bit of color tinting) cards can be found in two sizes, 1-7/8" x 3-1/2" if printed on the box front, or 1-7/8" x 2-7/8" if printed on back. Player photos are framed with an ornate-cornered border. In a plaque at bottom, all in capital letters, are the player's name, position, team and league; the latter three designations are abbreviated. Gaps have been left in the assigned numbering to accommodate future discoveries.

	NM	E	VG
Type I Common:	2,000	1,200	750.00
Type II Common:	3,000	1,500	1,000
(1) Hugh Bedient	2,000	1,200	750.00
(2) Hick Cady	2,000	1,200	750.00
(3) Bill Carrigan (Type II)	3,000	1,500	1,000
(4) Hal Chase	2,500	1,250	800.00
(5) Eddie Collins	3,000	1,500	900.00
(6) Doc Crandall	2,000	1,200	750.00
(7) Lou Criger	2,000	1,200	750.00
(8) Harry Davis	2,000	1,200	750.00
(9) Jim Delahanty	2,000	1,200	750.00
(10) Art Devlin	2,000	1,200	750.00
(11) Josh Devore (Type II)	3,000	1,500	1,000
(12) Larry Doyle	2,000	1,200	750.00
(13) Larry Gardner	2,000	1,200	750.00
(14) George Gibson	2,000	1,200	750.00
(15) Charley Hall	2,000	1,200	750.00
(16) Topsy Hartsel	2,000	1,200	750.00
(17) Buck Herzog (Type II)	3,000	1,500	1,000
(18) Solly Hofman	2,000	1,200	750.00
(19) Johnny Kling	3,000	1,500	1,000
(20) Marty Krug	2,000	1,200	750.00
(21) Napoleon Lajoie	6,500	3,200	1,950
(22) Duffy Lewis	2,000	1,200	750.00
(23) Rube Marquard	6,000	3,000	1,800
(24) Christy Mathewson	9,000	4,500	2,700
(25) John McGraw	3,000	1,500	900.00
(26) Red Murray	2,000	1,200	750.00
(27) Harry Niles	2,000	1,200	750.00
(28) Orval Overall	2,000	1,200	750.00
(29) Larry Pape	2,000	1,200	750.00
(30) Ed Reulbach	2,000	1,200	750.00
(31) Cy Seymour	2,000	1,200	750.00
(32) Jimmy Sheckard	2,000	1,200	750.00
(33) Hack Simmons	2,000	1,200	750.00
(34) Tris Speaker (Type II)	7,500	3,750	2,250
(35) Jake Stahl	2,000	1,200	750.00
(36) Oscar Stanage	2,000	1,200	750.00
(37) Harry Steinfeldt	2,000	1,200	750.00
(38) Jeff Tesreau (Type II)	3,000	1,500	1,000
(39) Ira Thomas	2,000	1,200	750.00
(40) Joe Tinker	3,000	1,500	1,000
(41) Honus Wagner (Type II)	25,000	12,500	7,500
(42) Ed Walsh	3,000	1,500	1,000
(43) Owen Wilson	2,000	1,200	750.00

1969 Jack In The Box California Angels

This regional issue was distributed a few cards per week at the chain's fast food restaurants. Blank-back cards are printed in black-and-white on thin white stock in a 1-15/16" x 3-1/2" format. The checklist for the unnumbered cards is presented here alphabetically.

HOYT WILHELM
Pitcher
Career Record, 2.47 ERA

	NM	E	VG
Complete Set (13):	30.00	15.00	9.00
Common Player:	3.00	1.50	.90
(1) Sandy Alomar	3.00	1.50	.90
(2) Joe Azcue	3.00	1.50	.90
(3) Jim Fregosi	3.50	1.75	1.00
(4) Lou Johnson	3.00	1.50	.90
(5) Jay Johnstone	6.00	3.00	1.75
(6) Rudy May	3.00	1.50	.90
(7) Jim McGlothlin	3.00	1.50	.90
(8) Andy Messersmith	3.00	1.50	.90
(9) Tom Murphy	3.00	1.50	.90
(10) Rick Reichardt	3.00	1.50	.90
(11) Aurelio Rodriguez	3.00	1.50	.90
(12) Jim Spencer	3.00	1.50	.90
(13) Hoyt Wilhelm	10.00	5.00	3.00

1971 Jack In The Box California Angels

Rudy May
CALIFORNIA ANGELS
P

Unlike the legitimate issue of 1969, this is an unauthorized collectors issue with no official connection to either the team of the fast food restaurant chain. The cards are printed in horizontal format on 4" x 2-1/2" manila paper in black ink. Fronts have a player portrait photo at left. Stacked at right are the player's name, team, position and Jack in the Box logo. Backs are blank. The set is checklisted here in alphabetical order.

	NM	E	VG
Complete Set (10):	25.00	12.50	7.50
Common Player:	3.00	1.50	.90
(1) Sandy Alomar	3.00	1.50	.90
(2) Ken Berry	3.00	1.50	.90
(3) Tony Conigliaro	15.00	7.50	4.50
(4) Jim Fregosi	3.00	1.50	.90
(5) Alex Johnson	3.00	1.50	.90
(6) Rudy May	3.00	1.50	.90
(7) Andy Messersmith	3.00	1.50	.90
(8) "Lefty" Phillips	3.00	1.50	.90
(9) Jim Spencer	3.00	1.50	.90
(10) Clyde Wright	3.00	1.50	.90

1970 Jack in the Box Pittsburgh Pirates

DAVE GIUSTI
Pittsburgh Pirates P
1969: 22g. 3-7 3.60

Though this set is known within the hobby as the "Jack in the Box" Pirates, it bears no such advertising and has no actual connection to the restaurant chain; they are a collector's issue. The black-and-white cards measure 2" x 3-1/2" and are blank-backed. Beneath the photo on front is the player identification and a few stats from the 1969 season.

	NM	E	VG
Complete Set (12):	35.00	17.50	10.00
Common Player:	3.00	1.50	.90
(1) Gene Alley	3.00	1.50	.90
(2) Dave Cash	3.00	1.50	.90
(3) Dock Ellis	3.00	1.50	.90
(4) Dave Giusti	3.00	1.50	.90
(5) Jerry May	3.00	1.50	.90
(6) Bill Mazeroski	12.50	6.25	3.75
(7) Al Oliver	6.00	3.00	1.75
(8) Jose Pagan	3.00	1.50	.90
(9) Fred Patek	3.00	1.50	.90
(10) Bob Robertson	3.00	1.50	.90
(11) Manny Sanguillen	4.50	2.25	1.25
(12) Willie Stargell	12.50	6.25	3.75

1954 Bill Jacobellis N.Y. Giants

James (Dusty) Rhodes

In the Giants' championship season, New York photographer Bill Jacobellis produced this set of player/team pictures, probably to be sold at the Polo Grounds souvenir stands. The black-and-white pictures are blank-backed and measure about 8-1/4" x 10-1/2", printed on semi-gloss paper. The player name is centered in bold type in the white bottom border; at right is "Bill Jacobellis Photo." The unnumbered pictures are listed here in alphabetical order.

	NM	E	VG
Complete Set (8):	110.00	55.00	32.50
Common Player:	12.50	6.25	3.75
(1) John Antonelli	12.50	6.25	3.75
(2) Alvin Dark	12.50	6.25	3.75
(3) Ruben Gomez	12.50	6.25	3.75
(4) Whitey Lockman	12.50	6.25	3.75
(5) Willie Mays	60.00	30.00	18.00
(6) Don Mueller	12.50	6.25	3.75
(7) James (Dusty) Rhodes	12.50	6.25	3.75
(8) N.Y. Giants of 1954	20.00	10.00	6.00

1958-1965 Jay Publishing Picture Packs

JOHN CALLISON, Philadelphia Phillies

The name "Picture Packs" has been used to describe this massive series of 5" x 7" black-and-white player photos issued by Jay Publishing's Big League Books division over the eight-year period from 1958-1965. The company also produced yearbooks for various major league teams during that period; many of the photos used in the yearbooks also appear in the Picture Packs. Picture Pack sets consist of 12 player/manager photos with name, city and team nickname in the bottom border. They were available by mail, at the ballparks and in stores. They were sold in either plain brown or white envelopes, or in clear plastic. Most were printed on a glossy, slick paper stock, although the quality of the paper may vary from team to team and year to year. The photos were issued anonymously, with no indication of the producer or year of issue. Two different types were issued, differentiated by the typeface used in the captions. Type 1 photos, issued from 1958 through 1961, were printed with a sans-serif style typeface, while Type 2 photos, issued from 1962 through 1965, used a serif typeface. Besides team sets there were a few special picture packs such as All-Stars, old-timers and World Series participants. Some years' team-set packs were updated (sometimes more than once) to reflect roster changes. Many pictures were reused from year to year.

	NM	E	VG
Typical Team Set:	40.00	20.00	12.00
Common Player:	3.00	1.50	.90
Typical Hall of Famer:	10.00	5.00	3.00
Superstars:	20.00	10.00	6.00

1962 Jell-O

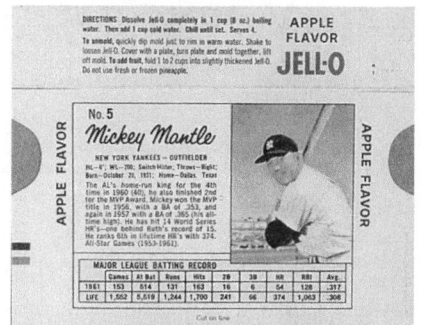

Virtually identical in content to the 1962 Post cereal cards, the '62 Jell-O set of 197 was only issued in the Midwest. Players and card numbers are identical in the two sets, except Brooks Robinson (#29), Ted Kluszewski (#82) and Smoky Burgess (#176) were not issued in the Jell-O version. The Jell-O cards are easy to distinguish from the Post of that year by the absence of the red oval Post logo and red or blue border around the stat box. Cards which have been neatly trimmed from the box on which they were printed will measure 3-3/8" by just under 2-1/2". Cards of some non-star players can be very scarce because they originally appeared on a limited number of boxes, or unpopular flavors or sizes.

	NM	E	VG
Complete Set (197):	4,250	2,125	1,065
Common Player:	5.00	2.50	1.25
1 Bill Skowron	30.00	12.00	7.50
2 Bobby Richardson	500.00	200.00	125.00
3 Cletis Boyer	30.00	12.00	7.50
4 Tony Kubek	35.00	14.00	9.00
5 Mickey Mantle	300.00	150.00	75.00
6 Roger Maris	125.00	50.00	30.00
7 Yogi Berra	60.00	30.00	15.00
8 Elston Howard	30.00	12.00	7.50
9 Whitey Ford	60.00	25.00	15.00
10 Ralph Terry	25.00	10.00	6.25
11 John Blanchard	30.00	12.00	7.50
12 Luis Arroyo	15.00	6.00	3.75
13 Bill Stafford	30.00	12.00	7.50
14 Norm Cash	20.00	8.00	5.00
15 Jake Wood	5.00	2.50	1.25
16 Steve Boros	5.00	2.50	1.25
17 Chico Fernandez	5.00	2.50	1.25
18 Billy Bruton	5.00	2.50	1.25
19 Ken Aspromonte	5.00	2.50	1.25
20 Al Kaline	75.00	30.00	17.50
21 Dick Brown	5.00	2.50	1.25
22 Frank Lary	5.00	2.50	1.25
23 Don Mossi	5.00	2.50	1.25
24 Phil Regan	5.00	2.50	1.25
25 Charley Maxwell	5.00	2.50	1.25
26 Jim Bunning	30.00	12.00	7.50
27 Jim Gentile	5.00	2.50	1.25
28 Marv Breeding	5.00	2.50	1.25
29 Not Issued			
30 Ron Hansen	5.00	2.50	1.25
31 Jackie Brandt	50.00	20.00	12.50
32 Dick Williams	5.00	2.50	1.25
33 Gus Triandos	5.00	2.50	1.25
34 Milt Pappas	5.00	2.50	1.25
35 Hoyt Wilhelm	30.00	12.00	7.50
36 Chuck Estrada	5.00	2.50	1.25
37 Vic Power	5.00	2.50	1.25
38 Johnny Temple	5.00	2.50	1.25
39 Bubba Phillips	30.00	12.00	7.50
40 Tito Francona	5.00	2.50	1.25
41 Willie Kirkland	5.00	2.50	1.25
42 John Romano	5.00	2.50	1.25
43 Jim Perry	15.00	6.00	3.75
44 Woodie Held	5.00	2.50	1.25
45 Chuck Essegian	5.00	2.50	1.25

46 Roy Sievers	15.00	6.00	3.75
47 Nellie Fox	40.00	16.00	10.00
48 Al Smith	15.00	6.00	3.75
49 Luis Aparicio	40.00	16.00	10.00
50 Jim Landis	5.00	2.50	1.25
51 Minnie Minoso	25.00	10.00	6.25
52 Andy Carey	30.00	12.00	7.50
53 Sherman Lollar	5.00	2.50	1.25
54 Bill Pierce	5.00	2.50	1.25
55 Early Wynn	50.00	20.00	12.50
56 Chuck Schilling	60.00	30.00	15.00
57 Pete Runnels	5.00	2.50	1.25
58 Frank Malzone	20.00	8.00	5.00
59 Don Buddin	15.00	6.00	3.75
60 Gary Geiger	5.00	2.50	1.25
61 Carl Yastrzemski	200.00	100.00	50.00
62 Jackie Jensen	60.00	24.00	15.00
63 Jim Pagliaroni	30.00	12.00	7.50
64 Don Schwall	5.00	2.50	1.25
65 Dale Long	5.00	2.50	1.25
66 Chuck Cottier	20.00	8.00	5.00
67 Billy Klaus	30.00	12.00	7.50
68 Coot Veal	5.00	2.50	1.25
69 Marty Keough	60.00	25.00	15.00
70 Willie Tasby	60.00	25.00	15.00
71 Gene Woodling	5.00	2.50	1.25
72 Gene Green	60.00	25.00	15.00
73 Dick Donovan	15.00	6.00	3.75
74 Steve Bilko	25.00	10.00	6.25
75 Rocky Bridges	30.00	12.00	7.50
76 Eddie Yost	15.00	6.00	3.75
77 Leon Wagner	15.00	6.00	3.75
78 Albie Pearson	15.00	6.00	3.75
79 Ken Hunt	20.00	8.00	5.00
80 Earl Averill	75.00	30.00	17.50
81 Ryne Duren	15.00	6.00	3.75
82 Not Issued			
83 Bob Allison	15.00	6.00	3.75
84 Billy Martin	20.00	8.00	5.00
85 Harmon Killebrew	75.00	30.00	17.50
86 Zoilo Versalles	15.00	6.00	3.75
87 Lennie Green	50.00	25.00	12.50
88 Bill Tuttle	60.00	25.00	15.00
89 Jim Lemon	90.00	45.00	22.50
90 Earl Battey	30.00	12.00	7.50
91 Camilo Pascual	25.00	10.00	6.25
92 Norm Siebern	5.00	2.50	1.25
93 Jerry Lumpe	5.00	2.50	1.25
94 Dick Howser	15.00	6.00	3.75
95 Gene Stephens	60.00	25.00	15.00
96 Leo Posada	15.00	6.00	3.75
97 Joe Pignatano	15.00	6.00	3.75
98 Jim Archer	15.00	6.00	3.75
99 Haywood Sullivan	30.00	12.00	7.50
100 Art Ditmar	5.00	2.50	1.25
101 Gil Hodges	80.00	40.00	20.00
102 Charlie Neal	15.00	6.00	3.75
103 Daryl Spencer	15.00	6.00	3.75
104 Maury Wills	30.00	12.00	7.50
105 Tommy Davis	30.00	12.00	7.50
106 Willie Davis	15.00	6.00	3.75
107 John Roseboro	60.00	25.00	15.00
108 John Podres	30.00	12.00	7.50
109 Sandy Koufax	80.00	40.00	20.00
110 Don Drysdale	50.00	25.00	12.50
111 Larry Sherry	75.00	37.50	18.75
112 Jim Gilliam	30.00	12.00	7.50
113 Norm Larker	60.00	25.00	15.00
114 Duke Snider	70.00	35.00	17.50
115 Stan Williams	60.00	25.00	15.00
116 Gordon Coleman	70.00	35.00	17.50
117 Don Blasingame	30.00	12.00	7.50
118 Gene Freese	50.00	20.00	12.50
119 Ed Kasko	60.00	25.00	15.00
120 Gus Bell	30.00	12.00	7.50
121 Vada Pinson	15.00	6.00	3.75
122 Frank Robinson	40.00	15.00	10.00
123 Bob Purkey	15.00	6.00	3.75
124 Joey Jay	15.00	6.00	3.75
125 Jim Brosnan	15.00	6.00	3.75
126 Jim O'Toole	15.00	6.00	3.75
127 Jerry Lynch	15.00	6.00	3.75
128 Wally Post	15.00	6.00	3.75
129 Ken Hunt	15.00	6.00	3.75
130 Jerry Zimmerman	15.00	6.00	3.75
131 Willie McCovey	60.00	25.00	15.00
132 Jose Pagan	30.00	12.00	7.50
133 Felipe Alou	15.00	6.00	3.75
134 Jim Davenport	15.00	6.00	3.75
135 Harvey Kuenn	15.00	6.00	3.75
136 Orlando Cepeda	50.00	20.00	12.50
137 Ed Bailey	15.00	6.00	3.75
138 Sam Jones	15.00	6.00	3.75
139 Mike McCormick	15.00	6.00	3.75
140 Juan Marichal	60.00	25.00	15.00
141 Jack Sanford	15.00	6.00	3.75
142 Willie Mays	80.00	40.00	20.00
143 Stu Miller	70.00	35.00	17.50

144 Joe Amalfitano	15.00	6.00	3.75
145 Joe Adcock	15.00	6.00	3.75
146 Frank Bolling	30.00	12.00	7.50
147 Ed Mathews	75.00	37.50	18.75
148 Roy McMillan	5.00	2.50	1.25
149 Hank Aaron	75.00	37.50	18.75
150 Gino Cimoli	30.00	12.00	7.50
151 Frank J. Thomas	5.00	2.50	1.25
152 Joe Torre	60.00	25.00	15.00
153 Lou Burdette	15.00	6.00	3.75
154 Bob Buhl	5.00	2.50	1.25
155 Carlton Willey	5.00	2.50	1.25
156 Lee Maye	50.00	20.00	12.50
157 Al Spangler	60.00	25.00	15.00
158 Bill White	80.00	40.00	20.00
159 Ken Boyer	55.00	27.50	13.75
160 Joe Cunningham	15.00	6.00	3.75
161 Carl Warwick	15.00	6.00	3.75
162 Carl Sawatski	65.00	32.50	16.25
163 Lindy McDaniel	5.00	2.50	1.25
164 Ernie Broglio	15.00	6.00	3.75
165 Larry Jackson	5.00	2.50	1.25
166 Curt Flood	25.00	10.00	6.25
167 Curt Simmons	60.00	25.00	15.00
168 Alex Grammas	30.00	12.00	7.50
169 Dick Stuart	15.00	6.00	3.75
170 Bill Mazeroski	60.00	25.00	15.00
171 Don Hoak	15.00	6.00	3.75
172 Dick Groat	15.00	6.00	3.75
173 Roberto Clemente	180.00	70.00	45.00
174 Bob Skinner	30.00	12.00	7.50
175 Bill Virdon	60.00	25.00	15.00
176 **Not Issued**			
177 Elroy Face	15.00	6.00	3.75
178 Bob Friend	15.00	6.00	3.75
179 Vernon Law	30.00	12.00	7.50
180 Harvey Haddix	60.00	25.00	15.00
181 Hal Smith	30.00	12.00	7.50
182 Ed Bouchee	50.00	20.00	12.50
183 Don Zimmer	60.00	25.00	15.00
184 Ron Santo	35.00	15.00	9.00
185 Andre Rodgers	5.00	2.50	1.25
186 Richie Ashburn	50.00	20.00	12.50
187 George Altman	5.00	2.50	1.25
188 Ernie Banks	50.00	20.00	12.50
189 Sam Taylor	5.00	2.50	1.25
190 Don Elston	5.00	2.50	1.25
191 Jerry Kindall	50.00	20.00	12.50
192 Pancho Herrera	5.00	2.50	1.25
193 Tony Taylor	5.00	2.50	1.25
194 Ruben Amaro	30.00	12.00	7.50
195 Don Demeter	5.00	2.50	1.25
196 Bobby Gene Smith	60.00	25.00	15.00
197 Clay Dalrymple	5.00	2.50	1.25
198 Robin Roberts	60.00	25.00	15.00
199 Art Mahaffey	5.00	2.50	1.25
200 John Buzhardt	5.00	2.50	1.25

1963 Jell-O

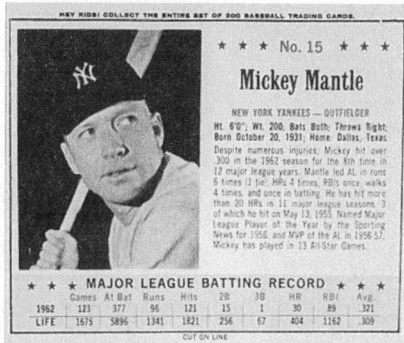

Like the other Post and Jell-O issues of the era, the '63 Jell-O set includes many scarce cards; primarily those which were printed as the backs of less popular brands and sizes of the gelatin dessert. Slightly smaller than the virtually identical Post cereal cards of the same year, the 200 cards in the Jell-O issue measure 3-3/8" x 2-1/2". The easiest way to distinguish 1963 Jell-O cards from Post cards is by the red line that separates the 1962 stats from the lifetime stats. On Post cards, the line extends almost all the way to the side borders, on the Jell-O cards, the line begins and ends much closer to the stats. The high value of some non-star players' cards can be attributed to scarcity caused by the cards having originally been printed on unpopular flavors or sizes.

	NM	E	VG
Complete Set (200):	6,000	3,000	1,800
Common Player:	7.50	3.00	2.00
1 Vic Power	15.00	6.00	3.50

#	Player			
2	Bernie Allen	65.00	25.00	15.00
3	Zoilo Versalles	65.00	25.00	15.00
4	Rich Rollins	7.50	3.00	2.00
5	Harmon Killebrew	100.00	30.00	15.00
6	Lenny Green	35.00	15.00	10.00
7	Bob Allison	15.00	6.00	3.50
8	Earl Battey	55.00	22.50	13.50
9	Camilo Pascual	10.00	4.00	2.50
10	Jim Kaat	60.00	25.00	15.00
11	Jack Kralick	7.50	3.00	2.00
12	Bill Skowron	65.00	25.00	15.00
13	Bobby Richardson	80.00	35.00	18.00
14	Cletis Boyer	7.50	3.00	2.00
15	Mickey Mantle	125.00	62.50	31.25
16	Roger Maris	40.00	15.00	10.00
17	Yogi Berra	30.00	12.00	7.50
18	Elston Howard	35.00	15.00	10.00
19	Whitey Ford	20.00	8.00	5.00
20	Ralph Terry	7.50	3.00	2.00
21	John Blanchard	30.00	12.00	7.50
22	Bill Stafford	25.00	10.00	6.00
23	Tom Tresh	7.50	3.00	2.00
24	Steve Bilko	7.50	3.00	2.00
25	Bill Moran	7.50	3.00	2.00
26	Joe Koppe	7.50	3.00	2.00
27	Felix Torres	7.50	3.00	2.00
28	Leon Wagner	10.00	4.00	2.50
29	Albie Pearson	7.50	3.00	2.00
30	Lee Thomas	7.50	3.00	2.00
31	Bob Rodgers	65.00	25.00	15.00
32	Dean Chance	7.50	3.00	2.00
33	Ken McBride	35.00	15.00	10.00
34	George Thomas	35.00	15.00	10.00
35	Joe Cunningham	60.00	25.00	15.00
36	Nelson Fox	12.50	5.00	3.00
37	Luis Aparicio	12.50	5.00	3.00
38	Al Smith	7.50	3.00	2.00
39	Floyd Robinson	7.50	3.00	2.00
40	Jim Landis	7.50	3.00	2.00
41	Charlie Maxwell	7.50	3.00	2.00
42	Sherman Lollar	15.00	6.00	3.50
43	Early Wynn	20.00	8.00	5.00
44	Juan Pizarro	75.00	30.00	17.50
45	Ray Herbert	50.00	20.00	12.50
46	Norm Cash	17.50	7.00	4.50
47	Steve Boros	35.00	15.00	10.00
48	Dick McAuliffe	7.50	3.00	2.00
49	Bill Bruton	15.00	6.00	3.75
50	Rocky Colavito	25.00	10.00	6.00
51	Al Kaline	30.00	12.00	7.50
52	Dick Brown	35.00	15.00	10.00
53	Jim Bunning	15.00	6.00	3.50
54	Hank Aguirre	7.50	3.00	2.00
55	Frank Lary	40.00	15.00	10.00
56	Don Mossi	40.00	15.00	10.00
57	Jim Gentile	7.50	3.00	2.00
58	Jackie Brandt	7.50	3.00	2.00
59	Brooks Robinson	30.00	12.00	7.50
60	Ron Hansen	7.50	3.00	2.00
61	Jerry Adair	100.00	50.00	25.00
62	John Powell	9.00	3.50	2.25
63	Russ Snyder	35.00	15.00	10.00
64	Steve Barber	7.50	3.00	2.00
65	Milt Pappas	40.00	15.00	10.00
66	Robin Roberts	10.00	4.00	2.50
67	Tito Francona	7.50	3.00	2.00
68	Jerry Kindall	35.00	15.00	10.00
69	Woodie Held	7.50	3.00	2.00
70	Bubba Phillips	7.50	3.00	2.00
71	Chuck Essegian	7.50	3.00	2.00
72	Willie Kirkland	35.00	15.00	10.00
73	Al Luplow	35.00	15.00	10.00
74	Ty Cline	55.00	27.50	13.75
75	Dick Donovan	7.50	3.00	2.00
76	John Romano	7.50	3.00	2.00
77	Pete Runnels	12.50	5.00	3.00
78	Ed Bressoud	100.00	40.00	25.00
79	Frank Malzone	7.50	3.00	2.00
80	Carl Yastrzemski	100.00	40.00	25.00
81	Gary Geiger	7.50	3.00	2.00
82	Lou Clinton	40.00	15.00	10.00
83	Earl Wilson	7.50	3.00	2.00
84	Bill Monbouquette	7.50	3.00	2.00
85	Norm Siebern	7.50	3.00	2.00
86	Jerry Lumpe	9.00	3.50	2.00
87	Manny Jimenez	9.00	3.50	2.25
88	Gino Cimoli	12.50	5.00	3.00
89	Ed Charles	70.00	35.00	17.50
90	Ed Rakow	7.50	3.00	2.00
91	Bob Del Greco	125.00	62.50	31.25
92	Haywood Sullivan	40.00	15.00	10.00
93	Chuck Hinton	7.50	3.00	2.00
94	Ken Retzer	35.00	15.00	10.00
95	Harry Bright	30.00	12.00	7.50
96	Bob Johnson	10.00	4.00	2.50
97	Dave Stenhouse	35.00	15.00	10.00
98	Chuck Cottier	7.50	3.00	2.00
99	Tom Cheney	9.00	3.50	2.00
100	Claude Osteen	75.00	30.00	17.50
101	Orlando Cepeda	15.00	6.00	3.50
102	Charley Hiller	35.00	15.00	10.00
103	Jose Pagan	35.00	15.00	10.00
104	Jim Davenport	7.50	3.00	2.00
105	Harvey Kuenn	7.50	3.00	2.00
106	Willie Mays	60.00	30.00	15.00
107	Felipe Alou	7.50	3.00	2.00
108	Tom Haller	35.00	15.00	10.00
109	Juan Marichal	25.00	10.00	6.00
110	Jack Sanford	12.50	5.00	3.00
111	Bill O'Dell	7.50	3.00	2.00
112	Willie McCovey	100.00	40.00	25.00
113	Lee Walls	35.00	15.00	10.00
114	Jim Gilliam	60.00	25.00	15.00
115	Maury Wills	10.00	4.00	2.50
116	Ron Fairly	7.50	3.00	2.00
117	Tommy Davis	7.50	3.00	2.00
118	Duke Snider	20.00	8.00	5.00
119	Willie Davis	20.00	8.00	5.00
120	John Roseboro	7.50	3.00	2.00
121	Sandy Koufax	50.00	20.00	12.50
122	Stan Williams	50.00	25.00	12.50
123	Don Drysdale	12.50	5.00	3.00
124	Daryl Spencer	7.50	3.00	2.00
125	Gordy Coleman	7.50	3.00	2.00
126	Don Blasingame	50.00	20.00	12.50
127	Leo Cardenas	7.50	3.00	2.00
128	Eddie Kasko	80.00	35.00	20.00
129	Jerry Lynch	7.50	3.00	2.00
130	Vada Pinson	7.50	3.00	2.00
131	Frank Robinson	20.00	8.00	5.00
132	John Edwards	40.00	15.00	10.00
133	Joey Jay	7.50	3.00	2.00
134	Bob Purkey	7.50	3.00	2.00
135	Marty Keough	95.00	47.50	23.75
136	Jim O'Toole	40.00	15.00	10.00
137	Dick Stuart	7.50	3.00	2.00
138	Bill Mazeroski	12.50	5.00	3.00
139	Dick Groat	7.50	3.00	2.00
140	Don Hoak	7.50	3.00	2.00
141	Bob Skinner	12.50	5.00	3.00
142	Bill Virdon	7.50	3.00	2.00
143	Roberto Clemente	350.00	150.00	75.00
144	Smoky Burgess	7.50	3.00	2.00
145	Bob Friend	7.50	3.00	2.00
146	Al McBean	50.00	20.00	12.50
147	ElRoy Face	7.50	3.00	2.00
148	Joe Adcock	7.50	3.00	2.00
149	Frank Bolling	7.50	3.00	2.00
150	Roy McMillan	7.50	3.00	2.00
151	Eddie Mathews	12.50	5.00	3.00
152	Hank Aaron	50.00	20.00	12.50
153	Del Crandall	35.00	15.00	10.00
154	Bob Shaw	7.50	3.00	2.00
155	Lew Burdette	7.50	3.00	2.00
156	Joe Torre	50.00	20.00	12.50
157	Tony Cloninger	100.00	50.00	25.00
158	Bill White	7.50	3.00	2.00
159	Julian Javier	60.00	25.00	15.00
160	Ken Boyer	9.00	3.50	2.00
161	Julio Gotay	75.00	30.00	17.50
162	Curt Flood	25.00	10.00	6.00
163	Charlie James	65.00	25.00	15.00
164	Gene Oliver	50.00	20.00	12.50
165	Ernie Broglio	15.00	6.00	3.50
166	Bob Gibson	135.00	67.50	33.75
167	Lindy McDaniel	35.00	15.00	10.00
168	Ray Washburn	7.50	3.00	2.00
169	Ernie Banks	40.00	15.00	10.00
170	Ron Santo	15.00	6.00	3.50
171	George Altman	7.50	3.00	2.00
172	Billy Williams	100.00	40.00	25.00
173	Andre Rodgers	75.00	30.00	17.50
174	Ken Hubbs	15.00	6.00	3.75
175	Don Landrum	60.00	25.00	15.00
176	Dick Bertell	65.00	25.00	15.00
177	Roy Sievers	7.50	3.00	2.00
178	Tony Taylor	35.00	15.00	10.00
179	John Callison	7.50	3.00	2.00
180	Don Demeter	7.50	3.00	2.00
181	Tony Gonzalez	80.00	40.00	20.00
182	Wes Covington	50.00	20.00	12.50
183	Art Mahaffey	7.50	3.00	2.00
184	Clay Dalrymple	7.50	3.00	2.00
185	Al Spangler	7.50	3.00	2.00
186	Roman Mejias	7.50	3.00	2.00
187	Bob Aspromonte	200.00	100.00	50.00
188	Norm Larker	7.50	3.00	2.00
189	Johnny Temple	7.50	3.00	2.00
190	Carl Warwick	35.00	15.00	10.00
191	Bob Lillis	35.00	15.00	10.00
192	Dick Farrell	90.00	45.00	22.50
193	Gil Hodges	15.00	6.00	3.50
194	Marv Throneberry	7.50	3.00	2.00
195	Charlie Neal	75.00	30.00	17.50
196	Frank Thomas	25.00	10.00	6.00
197	Richie Ashburn	15.00	6.00	3.50
198	Felix Mantilla	60.00	25.00	15.00
199	Rod Kanehl	35.00	15.00	10.00
200	Roger Craig	75.00	30.00	17.50

1969 Jewel Food Chicago Cubs

This set of premium pictures was issued by the midwest regional home-delivery food service. The pictures are 6" x 9" color poses with white borders and blank backs. A facsimile autograph appears on front.

		NM	E	VG
Complete Set (20):		125.00	65.00	35.00
Common Player:		6.00	3.00	1.80
(1)	Ted Abernathy	6.00	3.00	1.80
(2)	Hank Aguirre	6.00	3.00	1.80
(3)	Ernie Banks	30.00	15.00	9.00
(4)	Glenn Beckert	7.50	3.75	2.25
(5)	Bill Hands	6.00	3.00	1.80
(6)	Jim Hickman	6.00	3.00	1.80
(7)	Kenny Holtzman	6.00	3.00	1.75
(8)	Randy Hundley	7.50	3.75	2.25
(9)	Fergie Jenkins	12.50	6.25	3.75
(10)	Don Kessinger	7.50	3.75	2.25
(11)	Rich Nye	6.00	3.00	1.80
(12)	Paul Popovich	6.00	3.00	1.80
(13)	Jim Qualls	6.00	3.00	1.80
(14)	Phil Regan	6.00	3.00	1.80
(15)	Ron Santo	15.00	7.50	4.50
(16)	Dick Selma	6.00	3.00	1.80
(17)	Willie Smith	6.00	3.00	1.80
(18)	Al Spangler	6.00	3.00	1.80
(19)	Billy Williams	15.00	7.50	4.50
(20)	Don Young	6.00	3.00	1.80

1977 Jewel Food Chicago Cubs/White Sox

Once again in 1977, Jewel grocery stores in the Chicago area offered photos of local players with specific product purchases over a four-week period. The 5-7/8" x 9" color photos are printed on heavy paper. Fronts have player poses, a facsimile signature and the MLB Players Association logo in the upper-left corner. Backs are blank. The pictures are not numbered and are checklisted here alphabetically within team. It was reported 12,000 of each picture were produced.

		NM	E	VG
Complete Set, Cubs (16):		12.00	6.00	3.50
Complete Set, White Sox (16):		12.00	6.00	3.50
Common Player:		1.50	.70	.45
	CHICAGO CUBS			
(1)	Larry Biittner	1.50	.70	.45
(2)	Bill Bonham	1.50	.70	.45
(3)	Bill Buckner	2.50	1.25	.70
(4)	Ray Burris	1.50	.70	.45
(5)	Jose Cardenal	1.50	.70	.45
(6)	Gene Clines	1.50	.70	.45
(7)	Ivan DeJesus	1.50	.70	.45

(8)	Willie Hernandez	1.50	.70	.45
(9)	Mike Krukow	1.50	.70	.45
(10)	George Mitterwald	1.50	.70	.45
(11)	Jerry Morales	1.50	.70	.45
(12)	Bobby Murcer	2.50	1.25	.70
(13)	Steve Ontiveros	1.50	.70	.45
(14)	Rick Reuschel	1.50	.70	.45
(15)	Bruce Sutter	3.50	1.75	1.00
(16)	Manny Trillo	1.50	.70	.45

CHICAGO WHITE SOX

(1)	Alan Bannister	1.50	.70	.45
(2)	Francisco Barrios	1.50	.70	.45
(3)	Jim Essian	1.50	.70	.45
(4)	Oscar Gamble	1.50	.70	.45
(5)	Ralph Garr	1.50	.70	.45
(6)	Lamar Johnson	1.50	.70	.45
(7)	Chris Knapp	1.50	.70	.45
(8)	Ken Kravec	1.50	.70	.45
(9)	Lerrin LaGrow	1.50	.70	.45
(10)	Chet Lemon	1.50	.70	.45
(11)	Jorge Orta	1.50	.70	.45
(12)	Eric Soderholm	1.50	.70	.45
(13)	Jim Spencer	1.50	.70	.45
(14)	Steve Stone	2.50	1.25	.70
(15)	Wilbur Wood	1.50	.70	.45
(16)	Richie Zisk	1.50	.70	.45

1949 Jimmy Fund Boston Braves Die-cuts

The reigning National League champions undertook the support of the Jimmy Fund, a Boston charity for children's cancer research, with a set of die-cut counter cards accompanying contributions boxes. Between about 6" and 8" at the base, and up to a foot tall, these heavy cardboard pieces feature sepia-toned player action photos in front of a large baseball on which is written, "THANK YOU! in behalf of 'JIMMY.'" with a facsimile signature below. Backs have a fold-out easel to stand the card up, and a notation that following the fund drive, the card should be given to the largest contributor at that location.

		NM	E	VG
	Complete Set (25):	17,500	8,750	5,250
	Common Player:	750.00	375.00	225.00
(1)	Johnny Antonelli	750.00	375.00	225.00
(2)	Red Barrett	750.00	375.00	225.00
(3)	Vern Bickford	750.00	375.00	225.00
(4)	Jimmy Brown	750.00	375.00	225.00
(5)	Clint Conatser	750.00	375.00	225.00
(6)	Al Dark	750.00	375.00	225.00
(7)	Bob Elliott	750.00	375.00	225.00
(8)	Glenn Elliott	750.00	375.00	225.00
(9)	Bob Hall	750.00	375.00	225.00
(10)	Bobby Hogue	750.00	375.00	225.00
(11)	Tommy Holmes	750.00	375.00	225.00
(12)	Phil Masi	750.00	375.00	225.00
(13)	Pete Reiser	750.00	375.00	225.00
(14)	Marv Rickert	750.00	375.00	225.00
(15)	Jim Russell	750.00	375.00	225.00
(16)	Connie Ryan	750.00	375.00	225.00
(17)	Johnny Sain	850.00	425.00	255.00
(18)	Bill Salkeld	750.00	375.00	225.00
(19)	Sibby Sisti	750.00	375.00	225.00
(20)	Billy Southworth	950.00	475.00	285.00
(21)	Warren Spahn	1,200	600.00	360.00
(22)	Eddie Stanky	750.00	375.00	225.00
(23)	Don Thompson	750.00	375.00	225.00
(24)	Earl Torgeson	750.00	375.00	225.00
(25)	Bill Voiselle	750.00	375.00	225.00

1978 JJH Reading Remembers

This collectors' issue was created to honor baseball players (and a few others) who were born, lived in or played in Berks County, Pa., particularly in Reading. The cards are 3" x 4" featuring borderless sepia photos on front. Most of the photos picture players in big league uniforms. Backs are in black-and-white and have career stats and summaries. A number of major leaguers who did not have cards contemporary with their careers are found in this set. Cards are numbered by uniform number. Production was reported as 1,000 sets.

		NM	E	VG
	Complete Set (23):	25.00	12.50	7.50
	Common Player:	2.00	1.00	.60
1	Whitey Kurowski	2.00	1.00	.60
6	Carl Furillo	5.00	2.50	1.50
9	Roger Maris	10.00	5.00	3.00
12	Stan Wetzel	2.00	1.00	.60
17	Doug Clemens	2.00	1.00	.60
18	Randy Gumpert	2.00	1.00	.60
18	Ty Stofflet (Softball)	2.00	1.00	.60
21	George Eyrich	2.00	1.00	.60
23	Vic Wertz	2.00	1.00	.60
24	Lenny Moore (Football)	2.00	1.00	.60
25	Dick Gernert	2.00	1.00	.60
27	Herb Score	2.00	1.00	.60
27	Charlie Wagner	2.00	1.00	.60
28	Carl Mathias	2.00	1.00	.60
32	Jesse Levan	2.00	1.00	.60
34	Betz Klopp	2.00	1.00	.60
36	Robin Roberts	9.00	4.50	2.75
39	Bob Katz	2.00	1.00	.60
39	Harry Schaeffer	2.00	1.00	.60
40	Tommy Brown (Baseball/ Football)	1.50	.70	.45
46	Dom Dallessandro	2.00	1.00	.60
---	Lauer's Park	2.00	1.00	.60
---	John Updike (Author)	2.00	1.00	.60

1950s J.J.K. Copyart Postcards

Issued from about 1950 through at least 1956, this series of glossy black-and-white player postcards appears to have been produced on order of the individual players to respond to fan requests for pictures and/or autographs. Fronts have player poses bordered in white in about 3-1/2" x 5-1/2" format; most have facsimile autographs. Backs have typical postcard layout with a credit line to J.J.K. Copyart Photographers of New York City. Some players are known in more than one pose.

		NM	E	VG
	Common Player:	15.00	7.50	4.50

BOSTON/MILWAUKEE BRAVES

(1)	Del Crandall	15.00	7.50	4.50
(2)	Tommy Holmes	15.00	7.50	4.50
(3)	Willard Marshall	15.00	7.50	4.50
(4)	Eddie Mathews	60.00	30.00	18.00
(5)	Eddie Mathews	60.00	30.00	18.00
(6)	Danny O'Connell	15.00	7.50	4.50
(7)	Sibby Sisti	15.00	7.50	4.50
(8)	Eddie Stanky	25.00	12.50	7.50

BROOKLYN DODGERS

(1)	Jackie Robinson	200.00	100.00	60.00

NEW YORK GIANTS

(1)	Johnny Antonelli	15.00	7.50	4.50
(2)	Johnny Antonelli	15.00	7.50	4.50
(3)	Sam Calderone	15.00	7.50	4.50
(4)	Jim Hearn	15.00	7.50	4.50
(5)	Jim Hearn	15.00	7.50	4.50
(6)	Larry Jansen	15.00	7.50	4.50
(7)	Whitey Lockman	15.00	7.50	4.50
(8)	Whitey Lockman	15.00	7.50	4.50
(9)	Don Mueller	15.00	7.50	4.50
(10)	Bill Rigney	15.00	7.50	4.50
(11)	Bill Rigney	15.00	7.50	4.50
(12)	Hank Sauer	15.00	7.50	4.50
(13)	Red Schoendienst	30.00	15.00	9.00
(14)	Daryl Spencer	15.00	7.50	4.50
(15)	Eddie Stanky	25.00	12.50	7.50
(16)	Wes Westrum	15.00	7.50	4.50
(17)	Wes Westrum	15.00	7.50	4.50
(18)	Hoyt Wilhelm	30.00	15.00	9.00
(19)	Al Worthington	15.00	7.50	4.50

PHILADELPHIA PHILLIES

(1)	Del Ennis	15.00	7.50	4.50
(2)	Robin Roberts	30.00	15.00	9.00
(3)	Curt Simmons	15.00	7.50	4.50

1973 Johnny Pro Orioles

This regional set of large (4-1/4" x 7-1/4") die-cut cards was issued by Johnny Pro Enterprises Inc. of Baltimore and features only Orioles. The cards were designed to be punched out and folded to make baseball player figures that can stand up. The full-color die-cut figures appear against a green background. The cards are numbered according to the player's uniform number, which appears in a white box along with his name and position. The backs are blank. Three players (Robinson, Grich, and Palmer) appear in two poses each, and cards of Orlando Pena were not die-cut. Values listed are for complete cards not punched out. Cards originally sold for 15 cents apiece.

		NM	E	VG
	Complete Set (28):	200.00	100.00	60.00
	Common Player:	5.00	2.50	1.50
1	Al Bumbry	5.00	2.50	1.50
2	Rich Coggins	5.00	2.50	1.50
3a	Bobby Grich (Batting)	5.00	2.50	1.50
3b	Bobby Grich (Fielding)	5.00	2.50	1.50
4	Earl Weaver	6.00	3.00	1.75
5a	Brooks Robinson (Batting)	30.00	15.00	9.00
5b	Brooks Robinson (Fielding)	25.00	12.50	7.50
6	Paul Blair	4.00	2.00	1.25
7	Mark Belanger	4.00	2.00	1.25
8	Andy Etchebarren	5.00	2.50	1.50
10	Elrod Hendricks	5.00	2.50	1.50
11	Terry Crowley	5.00	2.50	1.50
12	Tommy Davis	5.00	2.50	1.50
13	Doyle Alexander	5.00	2.50	1.50
14	Merv Rettenmund	5.00	2.50	1.50
15	Frank Baker	5.00	2.50	1.50
19	Dave McNally	5.00	2.50	1.50
21	Larry Brown	5.00	2.50	1.50
22a	Jim Palmer (Follow-through.)	15.00	7.50	4.50
22b	Jim Palmer (Wind-up)	30.00	15.00	9.00
23	Grant Jackson	5.00	2.50	1.50
25	Don Baylor	6.00	3.00	1.75
26	Boog Powell	10.00	5.00	3.00
27	Orlando Pena	8.00	4.00	2.50
32	Earl Williams	5.00	2.50	1.50
34	Bob Reynolds	5.00	2.50	1.50
35	Mike Cuellar	5.00	2.50	1.50
39	Eddie Watt	5.00	2.50	1.50

1974 Johnny Pro Phillies

LARRY BOWA
Infielder

Although slightly smaller (3-3/4" x 7-1/8") and featuring members of the Phillies, this set is very similar to the 1973 Johnny Pro Orioles set. The full-color die-cut player figures are set against a white background. Again, the set is numbered according to the player's uniform number. The values listed are for complete cards.

		NM	E	VG
Complete Set (12):		100.00	50.00	30.00
Common Player:		3.00	1.50	.90
8	Bob Boone	7.50	3.75	2.25
10	Larry Bowa	7.50	3.75	2.25
16	Dave Cash	3.00	1.50	.90
19	Greg Luzinski	5.00	2.50	1.50
20	Mike Schmidt	50.00	25.00	15.00
22	Mike Anderson	3.00	1.50	.90
24	Bill Robinson	3.00	1.50	.90
25	Del Unser	3.00	1.50	.90
27	Willie Montanez	3.00	1.50	.90
32	Steve Carlton	25.00	12.50	7.50
37	Ron Schueler	3.00	1.50	.90
41	Jim Lonborg	3.00	1.50	.90

1922 Henry A. Johnson Wholesale Confectioner

JOE JUDGE
1st B.—Washington Americans

To compete with other candy issues featuring baseball cards as premiums, Alameda, Calif., confectioner Henry A. Johnson purchased uncut sheets of the blank-back strip cards known as W575-1, overprinted their backs and packaged them with his Likem brand candy bars. The advertising on back gives the firm's name, address and telephone number. Collectors can expect to pay a premium of about 3X for this version. Only the type style shown here can definitely be traced to the 1920s. Other styles of typography are known to have been applied in the 1980s and later.

	NM	E	VG
Common Player:	85.00	42.50	25.00
Stars: 5-7X			

(See W575-1 for checklist and base card values.)

1953 Johnston Cookies Braves

The first and most common of three annual issues, the '53 Johnstons were inserted into boxes of cookies on a regional basis. Complete sets were also available via a mail-in offer from the company, whose factory sits in the shadow of Milwaukee County Stadium. While at first glance appearing to be color photos, the pictures on the 25 cards in the set are actually well-done colorizations of black-and-white pho-

tos. Cards measure 2-9/16" x 3-5/8". Write-ups on the backs were "borrowed" from the Braves' 1953 yearbook.

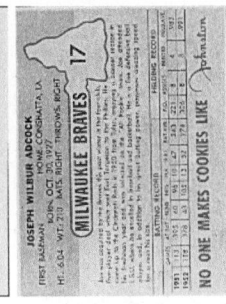

JOE ADCOCK

		NM	E	VG
Complete Set (25):		500.00	250.00	150.00
Common Player:		15.00	7.50	4.50
1	Charlie Grimm	15.00	7.50	4.50
2	John Antonelli	15.00	7.50	4.50
3	Vern Bickford	15.00	7.50	4.50
4	Bob Buhl	15.00	7.50	4.50
5	Lew Burdette	15.00	7.50	4.50
6	Dave Cole	15.00	7.50	4.50
7	Ernie Johnson	15.00	7.50	4.50
8	Dave Jolly	15.00	7.50	4.50
9	Don Liddle	15.00	7.50	4.50
10	Warren Spahn	150.00	75.00	45.00
11	Max Surkont	15.00	7.50	4.50
12	Jim Wilson	15.00	7.50	4.50
13	Sibby Sisti	15.00	7.50	4.50
14	Walker Cooper	15.00	7.50	4.50
15	Del Crandall	15.00	7.50	4.50
16	Ebba St. Claire	15.00	7.50	4.50
17	Joe Adcock	15.00	7.50	4.50
18	George Crowe	15.00	7.50	4.50
19	Jack Dittmer	15.00	7.50	4.50
20	Johnny Logan	15.00	7.50	4.50
21	Ed Mathews	150.00	75.00	45.00
22	Bill Bruton	15.00	7.50	4.50
23	Sid Gordon	15.00	7.50	4.50
24	Andy Pafko	15.00	7.50	4.50
25	Jim Pendleton	15.00	7.50	4.50

1954 Johnston Cookies Braves

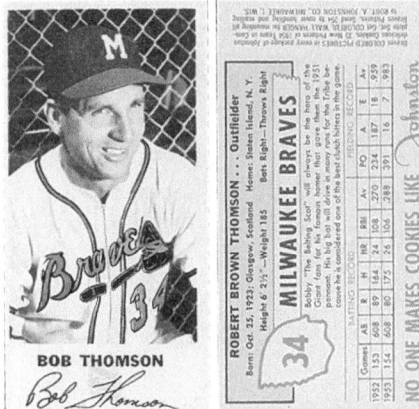

BOB THOMSON

In its second of three annual issues, Johnston's increased the number of cards in its 1954 Braves issue to 35, and switched to an unusual size, a narrow format, 2" x 3-7/8". Cards are listed here by uniform number. After his early-season injury (which gave Hank Aaron a chance to play regularly), Bobby Thomson's card was withdrawn, accounting for its scarcity and high value. Uncut sheets of 42 cards (including seven double-prints) in a size of about 12-1/2" x 27-3/4" are not uncommon. A 21-1/2" x 31" wall-hanging display poster with die-cuts into which cards could be inserted was available as a premium offer.

		NM	E	VG
Complete Set (35):		1,500	750.00	450.00
Common Player:		25.00	12.00	7.00
Uncut Sheet:		3,450	1,725	1,035
Display Poster:		500.00	250.00	150.00
1	Del Crandall	25.00	12.00	7.00
3	Jim Pendleton	25.00	12.00	7.00
4	Danny O'Connell	25.00	12.00	7.00
5	Henry Aaron	700.00	275.00	125.00
6	Jack Dittmer	25.00	12.00	7.00
9	Joe Adcock	25.00	12.00	7.00
10	Robert Buhl	25.00	12.00	7.00

		NM	E	VG
11	Phillip Paine (Phillips) (DP)	25.00	12.00	7.00
12	Ben Johnson	25.00	12.00	7.00
13	Sibby Sisti	25.00	12.00	7.00
15	Charles Gorin	25.00	12.00	7.00
16	Chet Nichols	25.00	12.00	7.00
17	Dave Jolly (DP)	25.00	12.00	7.00
19	Jim Wilson (DP)	25.00	12.00	7.00
20	Ray Crone	25.00	12.00	7.00
21	Warren Spahn (DP)	125.00	50.00	30.00
22	Gene Conley	25.00	12.00	7.00
23	Johnny Logan (DP)	25.00	12.00	7.00
24	Charlie White	25.00	12.00	7.00
27	George Metkovich	25.00	12.00	7.00
28	John Cooney	25.00	12.00	7.00
29	Paul Burris	25.00	12.00	7.00
31	Wm. Walters (DP)	25.00	12.00	7.00
32	Ernest T. Johnson	25.00	12.00	7.00
33	Lew Burdette	25.00	12.00	7.00
34	Bob Thomson (SP)	365.00	175.00	95.00
35	Robert Keely	25.00	12.00	7.00
38	Billy Bruton	25.00	12.00	7.00
40	Charles Grimm	25.00	12.00	7.00
41	Ed Mathews	100.00	50.00	30.00
42	Sam Calderone (DP)	25.00	12.00	7.00
47	Joey Jay	25.00	12.00	7.00
48	Andy Pafko	25.00	12.00	7.00
---	Dr. Charles Lacks (Asst. trainer.)	25.00	12.00	7.00
---	Joseph F. Taylor (Asst. trainer.)	25.00	12.00	7.00

1955 Johnston Cookies Braves

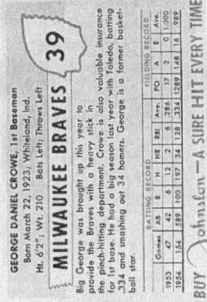

GEORGE CROWE

A third change in size and format was undertaken in the final year of Braves sets produced by Johnston's. The 35 cards in the 1955 set were issued in six fold-out panels of six cards each (Andy Pafko was double-printed). As in 1954, cards are numbered by uniform number, except those of the team equipment manager, trainer and road secretary (former Boston star Duffy Lewis). Single cards measure 2-7/8" x 4". Besides including panels in boxes of cookies, the '55 Johnstons could be ordered for five cents per panel by mail. The scarcest of the Johnston's issues, the 1955 set can be found today still in complete panels, or as single cards.

		NM	E	VG
Complete Folder Set (6):		1,500	750.00	450.00
Complete Singles Set (35):		1,500	750.00	450.00
Common Player:		30.00	20.00	12.00
Common Folder:		200.00	100.00	60.00
1	Del Crandall	30.00	20.00	12.00
Series 1 Folder		475.00	240.00	140.00
	Hank Aaron, Lew Burdette, Del Crandall, Charlie Gorin, Bob Keely, Danny O'Connell			
3	Jim Pendleton	30.00	20.00	12.00
Series 2 Folder		160.00	80.00	45.00
	Joe Adcock, Joe Jay, Dr. Charles K. Lacks, Chet Nichols, Andy Pafko, Charlie White			
4	Danny O'Connell	30.00	20.00	12.00
Series 3 Folder		175.00	90.00	50.00
	Gene Conley, George Crowe, Jim Pendleton, Roy Smalley, Warren Spahn, Joe Taylor			
6	Jack Dittmer	30.00	20.00	12.00
Series 4 Folder		160.00	80.00	45.00
	Billy Bruton, John Cooney, Dave Jolly, Dave Koslo, Johnny Logan, Andy Pafko			
9	Joe Adcock	30.00	20.00	12.00
Series 5 Folder		190.00	95.00	55.00
	Ray Crone, Ernie Johnson, Duffy Lewis, Eddie Mathews, Phil Paine, Chuck Tanner			
10	Bob Buhl	30.00	20.00	12.00
Series 6 Folder		160.00	80.00	45.00
	Bob Buhl, Jack Dittmer, Charlie Grimm, Bobby Thomson, Bucky Walters, Jim Wilson			
11	Phil Paine	30.00	20.00	12.00
12	Ray Crone	30.00	20.00	12.00

15	Charlie Gorin	30.00	20.00	12.00
16	Dave Jolly	30.00	20.00	12.00
17	Chet Nichols	30.00	20.00	12.00
18	Chuck Tanner	30.00	20.00	12.00
19	Jim Wilson	30.00	20.00	12.00
20	Dave Koslo	30.00	20.00	12.00
21	Warren Spahn	100.00	50.00	30.00
22	Gene Conley	30.00	20.00	12.00
23	John Logan	30.00	20.00	12.00
24	Charlie White	30.00	20.00	12.00
28	Johnny Cooney	30.00	20.00	12.00
30	Roy Smalley	30.00	20.00	12.00
31	Bucky Walters	30.00	20.00	12.00
32	Ernie Johnson	30.00	20.00	12.00
33	Lew Burdette	30.00	20.00	12.00
34	Bobby Thomson	35.00	17.50	10.50
35	Bob Keely	30.00	20.00	12.00
38	Billy Bruton	30.00	20.00	12.00
39	George Crowe	30.00	20.00	12.00
40	Charlie Grimm	30.00	20.00	12.00
41	Eddie Mathews	100.00	50.00	30.00
44	Hank Aaron	450.00	225.00	135.00
47	Joe Jay	30.00	20.00	12.00
48	Andy Pakfo	30.00	20.00	12.00
----	Dr. Charles K. Lacks	30.00	20.00	12.00
---	Duffy Lewis	30.00	20.00	12.00
---	Joe Taylor	30.00	20.00	12.00

1976 Jerry Jonas Productions All Time Greats

This card set was produced only in prototype form with an estimated 50 of each printed. The cards were designed to introduce a baseball card promotion to team executives at their annual World Series meeting. The 2-3/4" x 3-3/4" cards have black-and-white player photos at center with colored borders reminiscent of the 1975 Topps cards. Backs are printed in black on blue and feature biographical data, career highlights and stats along with a credit line to Jerry Jones Productions. The proposed promotion was never adopted. The unnumbered cards are checklisted here in alphabetical order.

		NM	E	VG
Complete Set, Uncut Sheet:		225.00	110.00	70.00
Complete Set, Singles (8):		225.00	110.00	70.00
Common Player:		15.00	7.50	4.50
(1)	Grover Alexander	15.00	7.50	4.50
(2)	Rogers Hornsby	15.00	7.50	4.50
(3)	Sandy Koufax	75.00	37.00	22.00
(4)	Willie Mays	50.00	25.00	15.00
(5)	Stan Musial	25.00	12.50	7.50
(6)	Mel Ott	15.00	7.50	4.50
(7)	Robin Roberts	15.00	7.50	4.50
(8)	Honus Wagner	15.00	7.50	4.50

1911 Jones, Keyser & Arras Cabinets

Contemporary with the better-known Sporting Life, Turkey Red and Pinkerton cabinet photos, this series of baseball player cabinets was issued by the New York City studio of Jones, Keyser & Arras, whose address appears on the back of the card. The 4-1/2" x 7-1/4" cabinets have photos glued to stiff gray cardboard mounts. Both photo and mount are numbered within the known range of 301-349, making it likely there are 50 baseball players in the series. Most known subjects are from the three New York teams of the era. Photos carry at bottom a stylized J, K & A logo, a 1911 copyright and a number. That number is repeated in the bottom border of the mount, along with the player's last name and the team/league. Several photos are known which have been removed from the mount, making identification difficult.

		NM	E	VG
Common Player:		2,400	1,200	720.00
301	Russ Ford	2,400	1,200	720.00
303	John Warhop	2,400	1,200	720.00
304	Bill Dahlen	2,400	1,200	720.00
306	Zack Wheat	4,000	2,000	1,200
307	Al Bridwell	2,400	1,200	720.00
308	Red Murray	2,400	1,200	720.00
310	Fred Snodgrass	2,400	1,200	720.00
311	Red Ames	2,400	1,200	720.00
312	Fred Merkle	2,400	1,200	720.00
313	Art Devlin	2,400	1,200	720.00
314	Hooks Wiltse	2,400	1,200	720.00
315	Josh Devore	2,400	120.00	720.00
316	Eddie Collins	4,000	2,000	1,200
317	Ed Reulbach	2,400	1,200	720.00
318	Jimmy Scheckard (Sheckard)	2,400	120.00	720.00
320	Frank Schulte	2,400	1,200	720.00
321	Solly Hofman	2,400	1,200	720.00
322	Bill Bergen	2,400	1,200	720.00
323	George Bell	2,400	1,200	720.00
324	Nap Rucker	2,400	120.00	720.00
325	Fred Clarke	4,000	2,000	1,200
326	Clark Griffith, Mgr.	4,000	2,000	1,200
327	Roger Bresnahan	4,000	2,000	1,200
328	Fred Tenney	2,400	1,200	720.00
329	Harry Lord	2,400	1,200	720.00
331	Walter Johnson	12,000	6,000	3,600
332	Nap Lajoie	4,000	2,000	1,200
333	Joe Tinker	4,000	2,000	1,200
334	Mordecai Brown	4,000	2,000	1,200
336	Jimmy Archer	2,400	1,200	720.00
338	Nixey Callahan	2,400	1,200	720.00
340	Hal Chase	3,500	1,750	1,050
341	Larry Doyle	2,400	1,200	720.00
342	Chief Meyers	2,400	1,200	720.00
343	Christy Mathewson	12,000	6,000	3,600
344	Bugs Raymond	2,400	1,200	720.00
345	John J. McGraw, Mgr.	4,000	2,000	1,200
346	Honus Wagner	15,000	7,500	4,500
347	Ty Cobb	25,000	12,500	7,500
348	Johnny Evers	4,000	2,000	1,200
349	Frank Chance	4,000	2,000	1,200

1863 Jordan & Co.

Because this card pictures a ballplayer on front with advertising on back, it has been described as the world's first baseball card. The 2-7/16" x 4-1/16" card doubled as a ticket to a benefit (to the players!) series of matches between New York and Brooklyn teams and all-stars at Hoboken, N.J., in Sept., 1863. The ticket cards were sold for 50 cents apiece, twice the cost of regular admission. According to surviving records, photos of four different players were used on the tickets.

(1)	William Crossley ((1/08 auction, $7,100))
(2)	William Hammond (12/04 auction, $19,364)
(3)	Sam Wright (Unknown)
(4)	Harry Wright (Clipped-corners, 7/00 auction, $83,545.)

1931 Josetti Tobacco

This is one of several early 1930s German cigarette cards to picture Babe Ruth. In this case he is pictured on the 1-5/8" x 2-3/8" black-and-white card with American comedic actor Harold Lloyd. The card is part of a numbered set of 272 movie star cards. Backs are printed in German. The card can be found with Ruth's first name printed as George or as Babe.

		NM	E	VG
151a	George Ruth, Harold Lloyd	450.00	225.00	135.00
151b	Babe Ruth, Harold Lloyd	450.00	225.00	135.00

1910 Ju-Ju Drums (E286)

Issued in 1910 with Ju Ju Drum Candy, this extremely rare set of circular baseball cards is very similar in design to the more common Colgan's Chips cards. About the size of a silver dollar (1-7/16" in diameter) the cards display a player photo on the front with the player's name and team printed below in a semi-circle design. The backs carry advertising for Ju-Ju Drums. The checklist contains 45 different players to date, but the issue - known as E286 in the American Card Catalog - is so rare that others are likely to exist.

		NM	E	VG
Complete Set (45):		90,000	45,000	27,000
Common Player:		1,500	750.00	450.00
(1)	Eddie Ainsmith	1,500	750.00	450.00
(2)	Jimmy Austin	1,500	750.00	450.00
(3)	Chief Bender	5,500	2,750	1,650
(4)	Bob Bescher	1,500	750.00	450.00
(5)	Bruno Bloch (Block)	1,500	750.00	450.00
(6)	Frank Burke	1,500	750.00	450.00
(7)	Donie Bush	1,500	750.00	450.00
(8)	Frank Chance	4,000	2,000	1,200
(9)	Harry Cheek	1,500	750.00	450.00
(10)	Ed Cicotte	3,000	1,500	900.00
(11)	Ty Cobb	20,000	10,000	6,000
(12)	King Cole	1,500	750.00	450.00
(13)	Jack Coombs	1,500	750.00	450.00
(14)	Bill Dahlen	1,500	750.00	450.00
(15)	Bert Daniels	1,500	750.00	450.00
(16)	Harry Davis	1,500	750.00	450.00
(17)	Larry Doyle	1,500	750.00	350.00
(18)	Rube Ellis	1,500	750.00	450.00
(19)	Cecil Ferguson	1,500	750.00	450.00
(20)	Russ Ford	1,500	750.00	450.00
(21)	Bob Harnion (Harmon)	1,500	750.00	450.00
(22)	Ham Hyatt	1,500	750.00	450.00
(23)	Red Kellifer (Killifer)	1,500	750.00	450.00
(24)	Art Kruger (Krueger)	1,500	750.00	450.00
(25)	Tommy Leach	1,500	750.00	450.00
(26)	Harry Lumley	1,500	750.00	450.00
(27)	Christy Mathewson	10,000	5,000	3,000
(28)	John McGraw	3,750	1,875	1,125
(29)	Deacon McGuire	1,500	750.00	450.00
(30)	Chief Meyers	1,500	750.00	450.00
(31)	Otto Miller	1,500	750.00	450.00
(32)	Charlie Mullen	1,500	750.00	450.00
(33)	Tom Needham	1,500	750.00	450.00
(34)	Rube Oldring	1,500	750.00	450.00
(35)	Barney Pelty	1,500	750.00	450.00
(36)	Ed Reulbach	1,500	750.00	450.00
(37)	Jack Rowan	1,500	750.00	450.00
(38)	Dave Shean	1,500	750.00	450.00

		NM	E	VG
(39)	Tris Speaker	7,500	3,750	2,250
(40)	Ed Sweeney	1,500	750.00	450.00
(41)	Honus Wagner	12,500	6,250	3,750
(42)	Jimmy Walsh	1,500	750.00	450.00
(43)	Kirby White	1,500	750.00	450.00
(44)	Ralph Works	1,500	750.00	450.00
(45)	Elmer Zacher	1,500	750.00	450.00

1893 Just So Tobacco

This set is so rare that only a dozen or so examples are known, although it is possible others remain to be reported. The set features only members of the Cleveland club, known then as the "Spiders." Measuring 2-1/2" x 3-7/8", these sepia-colored cards were printed on heavy paper. The player appears in a portrait photo with his name beneath and an ad for Just So Tobacco at bottom. The existence of this set wasn't even established until the 1960s, and for 15 years only two subjects were known. In 1981 and 1989 several more cards were discovered. To date only one or two copies of each of the known cards have turned up in collectors' hands, making it among the rarest of all baseball card issues.

		NM	E
Common Player:		30,000	19,000
(1)	F.W. Boyd	30,000	19,000
(2)	Burkette (Jesse Burkett) (Unique. Trimmed and restored. Value undetermined.)		
(3)	C.L. Childs ("Cupid")	30,000	19,000
(4)	John Clarkson (Unique. Value undetermined.)		
(5)	J.O. Connor (Jack O'Connor)	30,000	19,000
(6)	G. Cuppy	30,000	19,000
(7)	G.W. Davies	30,000	19,000
(8)	W. Ewing (Unique. Value undetermined.) (A Poor card sold for $17,625 at auction in May 2010.)		
(9)	C.M. Hastings	30,000	19,000
(10)	E.J. McKean	30,000	19,000
(11)	CAPt Tebeau ("Patsy")	30,000	19,000
(12)	J.K. Virtue	30,000	19,000
(13)	T.C. Williams	30,000	19,000
(14)	D.T. Young (Cy)(Unique. Value undetermined.)		
(15)	C.L. Zimmer ("Chief")	30,000	19,000

K

1950s Kabaya Caramel Babe Ruth

This card was part of a series produced by an Okayama, Japan candy company. The card measures about 1-1/2" x 2-1/8" with color artwork of Ruth on front. On back is Japanese script within the design of an open book.

	NM	E	VG
Babe Ruth	1,200	600.00	350.00

1955 Kahn's Wieners Reds

The first of what would become 15 successive years of baseball card issues by the Kahn's meat company of Cincinnati is also the rarest. The set consists of six Cincinnati Redlegs player cards, 3-1/4" x 4". Printed in black and white, with blank backs, the '55 Kahn's cards were distributed at a one-day promotional event at a Cincinnati amusement park, where the featured players were on hand to sign autographs. Like the other Kahn's issues through 1963, the '55 cards have a 1/2" white panel containing an advertising message below the player photo. These cards are sometimes found with this portion cut off, greatly reducing the value of the card.

		NM	E	VG
Complete Set (6):		13,000	6,500	4,000
Common Player:		2,000	1,000	600.00
(1)	Gus Bell	2,500	1,250	750.00
(2)	Ted Kluszewski	2,900	1,450	870.00
(3)	Roy McMillan	2,000	1,000	600.00
(4)	Joe Nuxhall	2,000	1,000	600.00
(5)	Wally Post	2,000	1,000	600.00
(6)	Johnny Temple	2,000	1,000	600.00

1956 Kahn's Wieners Reds

In 1956, Kahn's expanded its baseball card program to include 15 Redlegs players, and began issuing the cards one per pack in packages of hot dogs. Because the cards were packaged in direct contact with the meat, they are often found today in stained condition. In 3-1/4" x 4" format, black and white with blank backs, the '56 Kahn's cards can be distinguished from later issues by the presence of full stadium photographic backgrounds behind the player photos. Like all Kahn's issues, the 1956 set is unnumbered; the checklists are arranged alphabetically for convenience. The set features the first-ever baseball card of Hall of Famer Frank Robinson.

		NM	E	VG
Complete Set (15):		3,250	1,625	1,000
Common Player:		150.00	75.00	45.00
(1)	Ed Bailey	150.00	75.00	45.00
(2)	Gus Bell	175.00	90.00	55.00
(3)	Joe Black	225.00	110.00	65.00
(4)	"Smoky" Burgess	200.00	100.00	60.00
(5)	Art Fowler	150.00	75.00	45.00
(6)	Hershell Freeman	150.00	75.00	45.00
(7)	Ray Jablonski	150.00	75.00	45.00
(8)	John Klippstein	150.00	75.00	45.00
(9)	Ted Kluszewski	365.00	180.00	110.00
(10)	Brooks Lawrence	150.00	75.00	45.00
(11)	Roy McMillan	150.00	75.00	45.00
(12)	Joe Nuxhall	150.00	75.00	45.00
(13)	Wally Post	150.00	75.00	45.00
(14)	Frank Robinson	1,000	500.00	300.00
(15)	Johnny Temple	150.00	75.00	45.00

1957 Kahn's Wieners

In its third season of baseball card issue, Kahn's kept the basic 3-1/4" x 4" format, with black-and-white photos and blank backs. The issue was expanded to 28 players, all Pirates or Reds. The last of the blank-backed Kahn's sets until 1966, the 1957 Reds players can be distinguished from the 1956 issue by the general lack of background photo detail, in favor of a neutral light gray background. The Dick Groat card appears with two name variations, a facsimile autograph, "Richard Groat," and a printed "Dick Groat." Both Groat varieties are included in the complete set price.

		NM	E	VG
Complete Set (29):		4,000	2,000	1,200
Common Player:		80.00	40.00	24.00
(1)	Tom Acker	80.00	40.00	24.00
(2)	Ed Bailey	80.00	40.00	24.00
(3)	Gus Bell	100.00	50.00	30.00
(4)	Smoky Burgess	100.00	50.00	30.00
(5)	Roberto Clemente	1,250	625.00	375.00
(6)	George Crowe	80.00	40.00	24.00
(7)	Elroy Face	80.00	40.00	24.00
(8)	Hershell Freeman	80.00	40.00	24.00
(9)	Robert Friend	80.00	40.00	24.00
(10a)	Dick Groat	190.00	95.00	55.00
(10b)	Richard Groat	190.00	95.00	55.00
(11)	Don Gross	80.00	40.00	24.00
(12)	Warren Hacker	80.00	40.00	24.00
(13)	Don Hoak	80.00	40.00	24.00
(14)	Hal Jeffcoat	80.00	40.00	24.00
(15)	Ron Kline	80.00	40.00	24.00
(16)	John Klippstein	80.00	40.00	24.00
(17)	Ted Kluszewski	225.00	110.00	65.00
(18)	Brooks Lawrence	80.00	40.00	24.00
(19)	Dale Long	80.00	40.00	24.00
(20)	Bill Mazeroski	325.00	160.00	95.00
(21)	Roy McMillan	80.00	40.00	24.00
(22)	Joe Nuxhall	80.00	40.00	24.00
(23)	Wally Post	80.00	40.00	24.00
(24)	Frank Robinson	300.00	150.00	90.00
(25)	Johnny Temple	80.00	40.00	24.00
(26)	Frank Thomas	80.00	40.00	24.00
(27)	Bob Thurman	80.00	40.00	24.00
(28)	Lee Walls	80.00	40.00	24.00

1958 Kahn's Wieners

Long-time Cincinnati favorite Wally Post became the only Philadelphia Phillies ballplayer to appear in the 15-year run of Kahn's issues when he was traded in 1958, but included as part of the otherwise exclusively Pirates-Reds set. Like previous years, the '58 Kahn's were 3-1/4" x 4", with black and white player photos. Unlike previous years, however, the cards had printing on the back, a story by the pictured player, titled "My Greatest Thrill in Baseball." Quite similar to the 1959 issue, the '58 Kahn's can be distinguished by the fact that the top line of the advertising panel at bottom has the word "Wieners" in 1958, but not in 1959. Several of cards in the set appear to have been short-printed.

		NM	E	VG
Complete Set (29):		4,500	2,250	1,350
Common Player:		100.00	50.00	30.00
(1)	Ed Bailey	100.00	50.00	30.00
(2)	Gene Baker	100.00	50.00	30.00
(3)	Gus Bell	110.00	55.00	35.00
(4)	Smoky Burgess	110.00	55.00	35.00

		NM	E	VG
(5)	Roberto Clemente	900.00	450.00	275.00
(6)	George Crowe	100.00	50.00	30.00
(7)	Elroy Face	100.00	50.00	30.00
(8)	Henry Foiles	100.00	50.00	30.00
(9)	Dee Fondy	100.00	50.00	30.00
(10)	Robert Friend	100.00	50.00	30.00
(11)	Richard Groat	110.00	55.00	35.00
(12)	Harvey Haddix	100.00	50.00	30.00
(13)	Don Hoak	110.00	55.00	35.00
(14)	Hal Jeffcoat	110.00	55.00	35.00
(15)	Ronald L. Kline	110.00	55.00	35.00
(16)	Ted Kluszewski	200.00	100.00	60.00
(17)	Vernon Law	100.00	50.00	30.00
(18)	Brooks Lawrence	100.00	50.00	30.00
(19)	Bill Mazeroski	300.00	150.00	90.00
(20)	Roy McMillan	100.00	50.00	30.00
(21)	Joe Nuxhall	100.00	50.00	30.00
(22)	Wally Post	300.00	150.00	90.00
(23)	John Powers	100.00	50.00	30.00
(24)	Robert T. Purkey	100.00	50.00	30.00
(25)	Charles Rabe	300.00	150.00	90.00
(26)	Frank Robinson	600.00	300.00	180.00
(27)	Robert Skinner	100.00	50.00	30.00
(28)	Johnny Temple	100.00	50.00	30.00
(29)	Frank Thomas	300.00	150.00	90.00

1959 Kahn's Wieners

 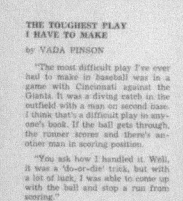

A third team was added to the Kahn's lineup in 1959, the Cleveland Indians joining the Pirates and Reds. Again printed in black-and-white in the 3-1/4" x 4" size, the 1959 Kahn's cards can be differentiated from the previous issue by the lack of the word "Wieners" on the top line of the advertising panel at bottom. Backs again featured a story written by the pictured player, such as "The Toughest Play I Had to Make," "My Most Difficult Moment in Baseball," etc. A number of the cards were short-printed.

		NM	E	VG
Complete Set (38):		6,000	3,000	1,800
Common Player:		75.00	37.50	22.50
(1)	Ed Bailey	75.00	37.50	22.50
(2)	Gary Bell	75.00	37.50	22.50
(3)	Gus Bell	75.00	37.50	22.50
(4)	Richard Brodowski	500.00	250.00	150.00
(5)	Forrest Burgess	75.00	37.50	22.50
(6)	Roberto Clemente	850.00	425.00	255.00
(7)	Rocky Colavito	325.00	160.00	100.00
(8)	ElRoy Face	75.00	37.50	22.50
(9)	Robert Friend	75.00	37.50	22.50
(10)	Joe Gordon	75.00	37.50	22.50
(11)	Jim Grant	75.00	37.50	22.50
(12)	Richard M. Groat	90.00	45.00	27.00
(13)	Harvey Haddix	450.00	225.00	135.00
(14)	Woodie Held	450.00	225.00	135.00
(15)	Don Hoak	75.00	37.50	22.50
(16)	Ronald Kline	75.00	37.50	22.50
(17)	Ted Kluszewski	200.00	100.00	60.00
(18)	Vernon Law	75.00	37.50	22.50
(19)	Jerry Lynch	75.00	37.50	22.50
(20)	Billy Martin	115.00	55.00	35.00
(21)	Bill Mazeroski	250.00	125.00	75.00
(22)	Cal McLish	450.00	225.00	135.00
(23)	Roy McMillan	75.00	37.50	22.50
(24)	Minnie Minoso	80.00	40.00	24.00
(25)	Russell Nixon	75.00	37.50	22.50
(26)	Joe Nuxhall	75.00	37.50	22.50
(27)	Jim Perry	75.00	37.50	22.50
(28)	Vada Pinson	200.00	100.00	60.00
(29)	Vic Power	75.00	37.50	22.50
(30)	Robert Purkey	75.00	37.50	22.50
(31)	Frank Robinson	235.00	120.00	75.00
(32)	Herb Score	75.00	37.50	22.50
(33)	Robert Skinner	75.00	37.50	22.50
(34)	George Strickland	275.00	135.00	85.00
(35)	Richard L. Stuart	75.00	37.50	22.50
(36)	John Temple	75.00	37.50	22.50
(37)	Frank Thomas	75.00	37.50	22.50
(38)	George A. Witt	75.00	37.50	22.50

1960 Kahn's Wieners

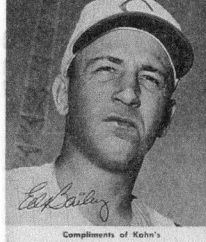 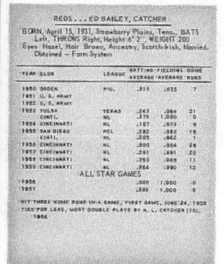

Three more teams joined the Kahn's roster in 1960, the Chicago Cubs, Chicago White Sox and St. Louis Cardinals. Again 3-1/4" x 4" with black-and-white photos, the 1960 Kahn's cards featured for the first time player stats and personal data on the back, except Harvey Kuenn, which was issued with blank back, probably because of the lateness of his trade to the Indians.

		NM	E	VG
Complete Set (42):		3,000	1,500	900.00
Common Player:		40.00	20.00	12.00
(1)	Ed Bailey	40.00	20.00	12.00
(2)	Gary Bell	40.00	20.00	12.00
(3)	Gus Bell	45.00	22.50	13.50
(4)	Forrest Burgess	45.00	22.50	13.50
(5)	Gino N. Cimoli	40.00	20.00	12.00
(6)	Roberto Clemente	725.00	360.00	215.00
(7)	ElRoy Face	40.00	20.00	12.00
(8)	Tito Francona	40.00	20.00	12.00
(9)	Robert Friend	40.00	20.00	12.00
(10)	Jim Grant	40.00	20.00	12.00
(11)	Richard Groat	40.00	20.00	12.00
(12)	Harvey Haddix	40.00	20.00	12.00
(13)	Woodie Held	40.00	20.00	12.00
(14)	Bill Henry	40.00	20.00	12.00
(15)	Don Hoak	40.00	20.00	12.00
(16)	Jay Hook	40.00	20.00	12.00
(17)	Eddie Kasko	40.00	20.00	12.00
(18)	Ronnie Kline	50.00	25.00	15.00
(19)	Ted Kluszewski	300.00	150.00	90.00
(20)	Harvey Kuenn	200.00	100.00	60.00
(21)	Vernon S. Law	45.00	22.50	13.50
(22)	Brooks Lawrence	40.00	20.00	12.00
(23)	Jerry Lynch	40.00	20.00	12.00
(24)	Billy Martin	90.00	45.00	27.00
(25)	Bill Mazeroski	150.00	75.00	45.00
(26)	Cal McLish	40.00	20.00	12.00
(27)	Roy McMillan	40.00	20.00	12.00
(28)	Don Newcombe	45.00	22.50	13.50
(29)	Russ Nixon	40.00	20.00	12.00
(30)	Joe Nuxhall	40.00	20.00	12.00
(31)	James J. O'Toole	40.00	20.00	12.00
(32)	Jim Perry	45.00	22.00	13.50
(33)	Vada Pinson	65.00	32.50	20.00
(34)	Vic Power	40.00	20.00	12.00
(35)	Robert T. Purkey	40.00	20.00	12.00
(36)	Frank Robinson	200.00	100.00	60.00
(37)	Herb Score	45.00	22.50	13.50
(38)	Robert R. Skinner	40.00	20.00	12.00
(39)	Richard L. Stuart	40.00	20.00	12.00
(40)	John Temple	40.00	20.00	12.00
(41)	Frank Thomas	50.00	25.00	15.00
(42)	Lee Walls	40.00	20.00	12.00

1961 Kahn's Wieners

After a single season, the Chicago and St. Louis teams dropped out of the Kahn's program, but the 1961 set was larger than ever, at 43 cards. The same basic format - 3-1/4" x 4" size, black-and-white photos and statistical information on the back - was retained. For the first time in '61, the meat company made complete sets of the Kahn's cards available to collectors via a mail-in offer. This makes the 1961 and later Kahn's cards considerably easier to obtain than the earlier issues.

1962 Kahn's Wieners

		NM	E	VG
Complete Set (43):		2,650	1,300	800.00
Common Player:		40.00	20.00	12.00
(1)	John A. Antonelli	40.00	20.00	12.00
(2)	Ed Bailey	40.00	20.00	12.00
(3)	Gary Bell	40.00	20.00	12.00
(4)	Gus Bell	45.00	22.00	13.50
(5)	James P. Brosnan	40.00	20.00	12.00
(6)	Forrest Burgess	45.00	22.00	13.50
(7)	Gino Cimoli	40.00	20.00	12.00
(8)	Roberto Clemente	825.00	410.00	245.00
(9)	Gordon Coleman	40.00	20.00	12.00
(10)	Jimmie Dykes	40.00	20.00	12.00
(11)	ElRoy Face	40.00	20.00	12.00
(12)	Tito Francona	40.00	20.00	12.00
(13)	Gene L. Freese	40.00	20.00	12.00
(14)	Robert Friend	40.00	20.00	12.00
(15)	Jim Grant	40.00	20.00	12.00
(16)	Richard M. Groat	40.00	20.00	12.00
(17)	Harvey Haddix	40.00	20.00	12.00
(18)	Woodie Held	40.00	20.00	12.00
(19)	Don Hoak	40.00	20.00	12.00
(20)	Jay Hook	40.00	20.00	12.00
(21)	Joe Jay	40.00	20.00	12.00
(22)	Eddie Kasko	40.00	20.00	12.00
(23)	Willie Kirkland	40.00	20.00	12.00
(24)	Vernon S. Law	40.00	20.00	12.00
(25)	Jerry Lynch	40.00	20.00	12.00
(26)	Jim Maloney	40.00	20.00	12.00
(27)	Bill Mazeroski	150.00	75.00	45.00
(28)	Wilmer D. Mizell	40.00	20.00	12.00
(29)	Glenn R. Nelson	40.00	20.00	12.00
(30)	James J. O'Toole	40.00	20.00	12.00
(31)	Jim Perry	40.00	20.00	12.00
(32)	John M. Phillips	40.00	20.00	12.00
(33)	Vada E. Pinson Jr.	55.00	27.00	16.50
(34)	Wally Post	40.00	20.00	12.00
(35)	Vic Power	40.00	20.00	12.00
(36)	Robert T. Purkey	40.00	20.00	12.00
(37)	Frank Robinson	250.00	125.00	75.00
(38)	John A. Romano Jr.	40.00	20.00	12.00
(39)	Dick Schofield	40.00	20.00	12.00
(40)	Robert Skinner	40.00	20.00	12.00
(41)	Hal Smith	40.00	20.00	12.00
(42)	Richard Stuart	40.00	20.00	12.00
(43)	John E. Temple	40.00	20.00	12.00

1962 Kahn's Wieners

 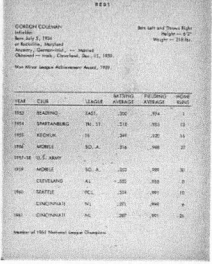

Besides the familiar Reds, Pirates and Indians players in the 1962 Kahn's set, a fourth team was added, the Minnesota Twins, though the overall size of the set was decreased from the previous year, to 38 players in 1962. The cards retained the 3-1/4" x 4" black-and-white format of previous years. The '62 Kahn's set is awash in variations. Besides the photo and front design variations on the Bell, Purkey and Power cards, each Cleveland player can be found with two back variations, listing the team either as "Cleveland" or "Cleveland Indians." The complete set values listed below include all variations.

		NM	E	VG
Complete Set (51):		2,250	1,125	675.00
Common Player:		15.00	7.50	4.50
(1a)	Gary Bell (Cleveland Indians back.)	100.00	50.00	30.00
(1b)	Gary Bell (Cleveland back.)	35.00	17.50	10.00
(2)	James P. Brosnan	15.00	7.50	4.50
(3)	Forrest Burgess	30.00	15.00	9.00
(4)	Leonardo Cardenas	15.00	7.50	4.50
(5)	Roberto Clemente	300.00	150.00	90.00
(6a)	Ty Cline (Cleveland Indians back.)	70.00	35.00	20.00
(6b)	Ty Cline (Cleveland back.)	30.00	15.00	9.00
(7)	Gordon Coleman	15.00	7.50	4.50
(8)	Dick Donovan	30.00	15.00	9.00
(9)	John Edwards	15.00	7.50	4.50
(10a)	Tito Francona (Cleveland Indians back.)	70.00	35.00	20.00

		NM	E	VG
(10b)	Tito Francona (Cleveland back.)	30.00	15.00	9.00
(11)	Gene Freese	15.00	7.50	4.50
(12)	Robert B. Friend	20.00	10.00	6.00
(13)	Joe Gibbon	75.00	37.50	22.50
(14a)	Jim Grant (Cleveland Indians back.)	70.00	35.00	20.00
(14b)	Jim Grant (Cleveland back.)	30.00	15.00	9.00
(15)	Richard M. Groat	40.00	20.00	12.00
(16)	Harvey Haddix	15.00	7.50	4.50
(17a)	Woodie Held (Cleveland Indians back.)	70.00	35.00	20.00
(17b)	Woodie Held (Cleveland back.)	30.00	15.00	9.00
(18)	Bill Henry	15.00	7.50	4.50
(19)	Don Hoak	15.00	7.50	4.50
(20)	Ken Hunt	15.00	7.50	4.50
(21)	Joseph R. Jay	15.00	7.50	4.50
(22)	Eddie Kasko	15.00	7.50	4.50
(23a)	Willie Kirkland (Cleveland Indians back.)	70.00	35.00	20.00
(23b)	Willie Kirkland (Cleveland back.)	30.00	15.00	9.00
(24a)	Barry Latman (Cleveland Indians back.)	70.00	35.00	20.00
(24b)	Barry Latman (Cleveland back.)	30.00	15.00	9.00
(25)	Jerry Lynch	15.00	7.50	4.50
(26)	Jim Maloney	20.00	10.00	6.00
(27)	Bill Mazeroski	100.00	50.00	30.00
(28)	Jim O'Toole	15.00	7.50	4.50
(29a)	Jim Perry (Cleveland Indians back.)	70.00	35.00	20.00
(29b)	Jim Perry (Cleveland back.)	30.00	15.00	9.00
(30a)	John M. Phillips (Cleveland Indians back.)	70.00	35.00	20.00
(30b)	John M. Phillips (Cleveland back.)	30.00	15.00	9.00
(31)	Vada E. Pinson	30.00	15.00	9.00
(32)	Wally Post	15.00	7.50	4.50
(33a)	Vic Power (Cleveland Indians back.)	70.00	35.00	20.00
(33b)	Vic Power (Cleveland back.)	30.00	15.00	9.00
(33c)	Vic Power (Minnesota Twins back.)	150.00	75.00	45.00
(34a)	Robert T. Purkey (No autograph.)	150.00	75.00	45.00
(34b)	Robert T. Purkey (With autograph.)	35.00	17.50	10.00
(35)	Frank Robinson	100.00	50.00	30.00
(36a)	John Romano (Cleveland Indians back.)	70.00	35.00	20.00
(36b)	John Romano (Cleveland back.)	30.00	15.00	9.00
(37)	Dick Stuart	15.00	7.50	4.50
(38)	Bill Virdon	15.00	7.50	4.50

1963 Kahn's Wieners

In 1963, for the first time since Kahn's began issuing baseball cards in 1955, the design underwent a significant change, white borders were added to the top and sides of player photo. Also, the card size was changed to 3-3/16" x 4-1/4". Statistical and personal data continued to be printed on the card backs. Joining traditional Reds, Pirates and Indians personnel in the 1963 set were a handful of New York Yankees and Dick Groat, in his new identity as a St. Louis Cardinal.

		NM	E	VG
	Complete Set (30):	2,400	1,200	750.00
	Common Player:	60.00	30.00	20.00
(1)	Robert Bailey	60.00	30.00	20.00
(2)	Don Blasingame	60.00	30.00	20.00
(3)	Clete Boyer	120.00	60.00	40.00
(4)	Forrest Burgess	75.00	40.00	25.00
(5)	Leonardo Cardenas	60.00	30.00	20.00
(6)	Roberto Clemente	420.00	220.00	125.00
(7)	Don Clendennon (Donn Clendenon)	60.00	30.00	20.00
(8)	Gordon Coleman	60.00	30.00	20.00
(9)	John A. Edwards	60.00	30.00	20.00
(10)	Gene Freese	60.00	30.00	25.00
(11)	Robert B. Friend	60.00	30.00	20.00
(12)	Joe Gibbon	60.00	30.00	20.00
(13)	Dick Groat	120.00	60.00	40.00
(14)	Harvey Haddix	60.00	30.00	20.00
(15)	Elston Howard	120.00	60.00	40.00
(16)	Joey Jay	60.00	30.00	20.00
(17)	Eddie Kasko	60.00	30.00	20.00
(18)	Tony Kubek	120.00	60.00	40.00
(19)	Jerry Lynch	60.00	30.00	20.00
(20)	Jim Maloney	75.00	40.00	25.00
(21)	Bill Mazeroski	180.00	90.00	50.00
(22)	Joe Nuxhall	75.00	40.00	25.00
(23)	Jim O'Toole	60.00	30.00	20.00
(24)	Vada E. Pinson	120.00	60.00	40.00
(25)	Robert T. Purkey	60.00	30.00	20.00
(26)	Bob Richardson	120.00	60.00	40.00
(27)	Frank Robinson	250.00	125.00	75.00
(28)	Bill Stafford	75.00	40.00	25.00
(29)	Ralph W. Terry	75.00	40.00	25.00
(30)	Bill Virdon	75.00	40.00	25.00

1964 Kahn's Wieners

After nearly a decade of virtually identical card issues, the 1964 Kahn's issue was an abrupt change. In a new size, 3" x 3-1/2", the nearly square cards featured a borderless color photo. The only other design element on the front of the card was a facsimile autograph. The advertising slogan which had traditionally appeared on the front of the card was moved to the back, where it joined the player's stats and personal data. The teams in the 1964 issue once again reverted to the Reds, Pirates and Indians.

		NM	E	VG
	Complete Set (31):	1,150	600.00	350.00
	Common Player:	20.00	10.00	6.00
(1)	Max Alvis	20.00	10.00	6.00
(2)	Bob Bailey	20.00	10.00	6.00
(3)	Leonardo Cardenas	20.00	10.00	6.00
(4)	Roberto Clemente	300.00	150.00	90.00
(5)	Donn A. Clendenon	20.00	10.00	6.00
(6)	Victor Davalillo	20.00	10.00	6.00
(7)	Dick Donovan	20.00	10.00	6.00
(8)	John A. Edwards	20.00	10.00	6.00
(9)	Robert Friend	20.00	10.00	6.00
(10)	Jim Grant	20.00	10.00	6.00
(11)	Tommy Harper	20.00	10.00	6.00
(12)	Woodie Held	20.00	10.00	6.00
(13)	Joey Jay	20.00	10.00	6.00
(14)	Jack Kralick	20.00	10.00	6.00
(15)	Jerry Lynch	20.00	10.00	6.00
(16)	Jim Maloney	20.00	10.00	6.00
(17)	Bill Mazeroski	75.00	37.50	22.00
(18)	Alvin McBean	20.00	10.00	6.00
(19)	Joe Nuxhall	20.00	10.00	6.00
(20)	Jim Pagliaroni	20.00	10.00	6.00
(21)	Vada E. Pinson Jr.	35.00	17.50	10.00
(22)	Robert T. Purkey	20.00	10.00	6.00
(23)	Pedro Ramos	20.00	10.00	6.00
(24)	Frank Robinson	75.00	37.50	22.50
(25)	John Romano	20.00	10.00	6.00
(26)	Pete Rose	250.00	125.00	75.00
(27)	John Tsitouris	20.00	10.00	6.00
(28)	Robert A. Veale Jr.	20.00	10.00	6.00
(29)	Bill Virdon	20.00	10.00	6.00
(30)	Leon Wagner	20.00	10.00	6.00
(31)	Fred Whitfield	20.00	10.00	6.00

1965 Kahn's Wieners

There was little change for the Kahn's issue in 1965 beyond the addition of Milwaukee Braves players to the Reds, Pirates and Indians traditionally included in the set. At 45 players, the 1965 issue was the largest of the Kahn's sets. Once again in 3" x 3-1/2" size, the 1965s retained the borderless color photo design of the previous season. A look at the stats on the back will confirm the year of issue, allowing differentiation between the 1964 and 1965 cards.

		NM	E	VG
	Complete Set (45):	1,750	875.00	520.00
	Common Player:	20.00	10.00	6.00
(1)	Hank Aaron	180.00	90.00	50.00
(2)	Max Alvis	20.00	10.00	6.00
(3)	Jose Azcue	20.00	10.00	6.00
(4)	Bob Bailey	20.00	10.00	6.00
(5)	Frank Bolling	20.00	10.00	6.00
(6)	Leonardo Cardenas	20.00	10.00	6.00
(7)	Rico Ricardo Carty	20.00	10.00	6.00
(8)	Donn A. Clendenon	20.00	10.00	6.00
(9)	Tony Cloninger	20.00	10.00	6.00
(10)	Gordon Coleman	20.00	10.00	6.00
(11)	Victor Davalillo	20.00	10.00	6.00
(12)	John A. Edwards	20.00	10.00	6.00
(13)	Sam Ellis	20.00	10.00	6.00
(14)	Robert Friend	20.00	10.00	6.00
(15)	Tommy Harper	20.00	10.00	6.00
(16)	Chuck Hinton	20.00	10.00	6.00
(17)	Dick Howser	20.00	10.00	6.00
(18)	Joey Jay	20.00	10.00	6.00
(19)	Deron Johnson	20.00	10.00	6.00
(20)	Jack Kralick	20.00	10.00	6.00
(21)	Denny Lemaster	20.00	10.00	6.00
(22)	Jerry Lynch	20.00	10.00	6.00
(23)	Jim Maloney	20.00	10.00	6.00
(24)	Lee Maye	20.00	10.00	6.00
(25)	Bill Mazeroski	80.00	40.00	25.00
(26)	Alvin McBean	20.00	10.00	6.00
(27)	Bill McCool	20.00	10.00	6.00
(28)	Sam McDowell	20.00	10.00	6.00
(29)	Donald McMahon	20.00	10.00	6.00
(30)	Denis Menke	20.00	10.00	6.00
(31)	Joe Nuxhall	20.00	10.00	6.00
(32)	Gene Oliver	20.00	10.00	6.00
(33)	Jim O'Toole	20.00	10.00	6.00
(34)	Jim Pagliaroni	20.00	10.00	6.00
(35)	Vada E. Pinson Jr.	35.00	20.00	12.00
(36)	Frank Robinson	140.00	70.00	40.00
(37)	Pete Rose	400.00	200.00	120.00
(38)	Willie Stargell	80.00	40.00	25.00
(39)	Ralph W. Terry	20.00	10.00	6.00
(40)	Luis Tiant	30.00	15.00	9.00
(41)	Joe Torre	35.00	20.00	12.00
(42)	John Tsitouris	20.00	10.00	6.00
(43)	Robert A. Veale Jr.	20.00	10.00	6.00
(44)	Bill Virdon	20.00	10.00	6.00
(45)	Leon Wagner	20.00	10.00	6.00

1966 Kahn's Wieners

The fourth new format in five years greeted collectors with the introduction of Kahn's 1966 issue. The design consists of a color photo bordered by white and yellow vertical stripes. The player's name is printed above the photo, and a facsimile autograph appears across the photo. As printed, the cards are 2-13/16" x 4-9/16" in size. The player photo area is about 2-13/16" x x 2-11/16", separated at top by a dotted line from an advertising panel with a red rose logo and the word "Kahn's" and at bottom from a dotted line by an irregularly shaped piece marked "CUT ALONG DOTTED LINES." Naturally, many of the cards are found today with the top and/or bottom portion cut off. Values listed here are for complete uncut cards; those without the ad portion and bottom panel are valued at 50 percent or less. Players from the Cincinnati Reds, Pittsburgh Pirates, Cleveland Indians and Atlanta Braves were included in the set. Since the cards are blank-backed, collectors must learn to differentiate player poses to determine year of issue for some cards.

		NM	E	VG
Complete Set (32):		1,250	625.00	375.00
Common Player:		15.00	7.50	4.50
(1)	Henry Aaron	200.00	100.00	60.00
(2)	Felipe Alou	20.00	10.00	6.00
(3)	Max Alvis	15.00	7.50	4.50
(4)	Robert Bailey	15.00	7.50	4.50
(5)	Wade Blasingame	15.00	7.50	4.50
(6)	Frank Bolling	15.00	7.50	4.50
(7)	Leo Cardenas	15.00	7.50	4.50
(8)	Roberto Clemente	400.00	200.00	120.00
(9)	Tony Cloninger	15.00	7.50	4.50
(10)	Vic Davalillo	15.00	7.50	4.50
(11)	John Edwards	15.00	7.50	4.50
(12)	Sam Ellis (White cap.)	15.00	7.50	4.50
(13)	Pedro Gonzalez	15.00	7.50	4.50
(14)	Tommy Harper	15.00	7.50	4.50
(15)	Deron Johnson	15.00	7.50	4.50
(16)	Mack Jones	15.00	7.50	4.50
(17)	Denny Lemaster	15.00	7.50	4.50
(18)	Jim Maloney (White cap.)	15.00	7.50	4.50
(19)	Bill Mazeroski	90.00	45.00	27.00
(20)	Bill McCool	15.00	7.50	4.50
(21)	Sam McDowell	25.00	12.50	7.50
(22)	Denis Menke	15.00	7.50	4.50
(23)	Joe Nuxhall	15.00	7.50	4.50
(24)	Jim Pagliaroni	15.00	7.50	4.50
(25)	Milt Pappas	15.00	7.50	4.50
(26)	Vada Pinson	25.00	12.50	7.50
(27)	Pete Rose (Right hand in glove.)	250.00	125.00	75.00
(28)	Sonny Siebert	15.00	7.50	4.50
(29)	Willie Stargell	90.00	45.00	27.00
(30)	Joe Torre	25.00	12.50	7.50
(31)	Bob Veale	15.00	7.50	4.50
(32)	Fred Whitfield	15.00	7.50	4.50

1967 Kahn's Wieners

Retaining the 1966 format, the '67 Kahn's set was expanded to 41 players by adding several New York Mets to the previous season's lineup of Reds, Pirates, Indians and Braves. Making this set especially challenging for collectors is the fact that some cards are found in a smaller size and/or with different colored stripes bordering the color player photo. On the majority of cards, the size remained about 2-13/16" x 4-9/16" (with ad at top and bottom panel; about 2-13/16" x 2-11/16" when cut on dotted lines). However, because of packing in different products, some cards can be found in 2-13/16" x 3-1/4" size (with ad; 2-13/16" x 2-1/8" without ad). The border stripe variations are listed below. Values quoted are for complete uncut cards; values drop by 50 percent or more for cards without the ad and/or bottom panels. All variation cards are included in the valuations given for the complete set.

		NM	E	VG
Complete Set (51):		1,800	900.00	550.00
Common Player:		20.00	10.00	6.00
(1a)	Henry Aaron (Large size.)	125.00	65.00	35.00
(1b)	Henry Aaron (Small size.)	125.00	65.00	35.00
(2)	Gene Alley	20.00	10.00	6.00
(3a)	Felipe Alou ((Large size.))	25.00	12.50	7.50
(3b)	Felipe Alou ((Small size.))	25.00	12.50	7.50
(4a)	Matty Alou (Yellow & white striped border.)	25.00	12.50	7.50
(4b)	Matty Alou (Red & white striped border.)	30.00	15.00	9.00
(5)	Max Alvis	20.00	10.00	6.00
(6a)	Ken Boyer (Yellow & white striped border.)	30.00	15.00	9.00
(6b)	Ken Boyer (Red, white & green striped border.)	35.00	17.50	10.00
(7)	Leo Cardenas	20.00	10.00	6.00
(8)	Rico Carty	20.00	10.00	6.00
(9)	Tony Cloninger	20.00	10.00	6.00

(10)	Tommy Davis	20.00	10.00	6.00
(11)	John Edwards	20.00	10.00	6.00
(12a)	Sam Ellis (Large size.) (Red cap.))	20.00	10.00	6.00
(12b)	Sam Ellis (Small size.) (Red cap.))	30.00	15.00	9.00
(13)	Jack Fisher	20.00	10.00	6.00
(14)	Steve Hargan	20.00	10.00	6.00
(15)	Tom Harper	20.00	10.00	6.00
(16a)	Tom Helms (Large size.)	20.00	10.00	6.00
(16b)	Tom Helms (Small size.)	35.00	17.50	10.00
(17)	Deron Johnson	20.00	10.00	6.00
(18)	Ken Johnson	20.00	10.00	6.00
(19)	Cleon Jones	20.00	10.00	6.00
(20a)	Ed Kranepool (Yellow & white striped border.)	20.00	10.00	6.00
(20b)	Ed Kranepool (Red & white striped border.)	30.00	15.00	9.00
(21a)	James Maloney (Yellow & white striped border.)	25.00	12.50	7.50
(21b)	James Maloney (Red & white striped border.)	30.00	15.00	9.00
(22)	Lee May	20.00	10.00	6.00
(23a)	Wm. Mazeroski (Large size.)	75.00	37.50	22.50
(23b)	Wm. Mazeroski (Small size.)	75.00	37.50	22.50
(24)	Wm. McCool	20.00	10.00	6.00
(25)	Sam McDowell (Blue sleeves.)	25.00	12.50	7.50
(26)	Dennis Menke (Denis)	20.00	10.00	6.00
(27)	Jim Pagliaroni	20.00	10.00	6.00
(28)	Don Pavletich	20.00	10.00	6.00
(29)	Tony Perez	60.00	30.00	18.00
(30)	Vada Pinson	30.00	15.00	9.00
(31)	Dennis Ribant	20.00	10.00	6.00
(32)	Pete Rose (Batting)	275.00	135.00	85.00
(33)	Art Shamsky	20.00	10.00	6.00
(34)	Bob Shaw	20.00	10.00	6.00
(35)	Sonny Siebert	20.00	10.00	6.00
(36)	Wm. Stargell (First name actually Wilver.)	80.00	40.00	24.00
(37a)	Joe Torre (Large size.)	35.00	17.50	10.00
(37b)	Joe Torre (Small size.)	35.00	17.50	10.00
(38)	Bob Veale	20.00	10.00	6.00
(39)	Leon Wagner	20.00	10.00	6.00
(40a)	Fred Whitfield (Large size.)	20.00	10.00	6.00
(40b)	Fred Whitfield (Small size.)	20.00	10.00	6.00
(41)	Woody Woodward	20.00	10.00	6.00

1968 Kahn's Wieners

The number of card size and stripe color variations increased with the 1968 Kahn's issue, though the basic card format was retained. Basic size is about 2-13/16" x 4-9/16" with top ad panel and bottom panel intact; 2-13/16" x 2-11/16" with ad and bottom panels cut off. Color photos are bordered by yellow and white vertical stripes. In addition to the basic issue, a number of the cards appear in a smaller, 2-13/16" x 3-1/4", size, while some appear with variations in the color of border stripes. One card, Maloney, can be found with a top portion advertising Blue Mountain brand meats, as well as Kahn's. The 1968 set features the largest number of teams represented in any Kahn's issue: Braves, Cubs, White Sox, Reds, Indians, Tigers, Mets and Pirates. Values quoted are for complete uncut cards, those without the ad and/or bottom panel are worth 50 percent or less. Complete set prices include all variations.

		NM	E	VG
Complete Set (56):		4,500	2,200	1,350
Common Player:		40.00	20.00	12.00
(1a)	Hank Aaron (Large size.)	200.00	100.00	60.00
(1b)	Hank Aaron (Small size.)	250.00	125.00	75.00
(2)	Tommy Agee	40.00	20.00	12.00
(3a)	Gene Alley (Large size.)	40.00	20.00	12.00
(3b)	Gene Alley (Small size.)	60.00	30.00	18.00
(4)	Felipe Alou	50.00	25.00	15.00

(5a)	Matty Alou (Yellow striped border.)	50.00	25.00	15.00
(5b)	Matty Alou (Red striped border.)	50.00	25.00	15.00
(6a)	Max Alvis (Large size.)	40.00	20.00	12.00
(6b)	Max Alvis (Small size.)	60.00	30.00	18.00
(7)	Gerry Arrigo	40.00	20.00	12.00
(8)	John Bench	550.00	275.00	165.00
(9a)	Clete Boyer (Large size.)	40.00	20.00	12.00
(9b)	Clete Boyer (Small size.)	60.00	30.00	18.00
(10)	Larry Brown	40.00	20.00	12.00
(11a)	Leo Cardenas (Large size.)	40.00	20.00	12.00
(11b)	Leo Cardenas (Small size.)	60.00	30.00	18.00
(12a)	Bill Freehan (Large size.)	60.00	30.00	18.00
(12b)	Bill Freehan (Small size.)	60.00	30.00	18.00
(13)	Steve Hargan	40.00	20.00	12.00
(14)	Joel Horlen	40.00	20.00	12.00
(15)	Tony Horton	60.00	30.00	18.00
(16)	Willie Horton	50.00	25.00	15.00
(17)	Ferguson Jenkins	150.00	75.00	45.00
(18)	Deron Johnson	40.00	20.00	12.00
(19)	Mack Jones	40.00	20.00	12.00
(20)	Bob Lee	40.00	20.00	12.00
(21a)	Jim Maloney (Large size, rose logo.)	50.00	25.00	15.00
(21b)	Jim Maloney (Large size, Blue Mountain logo.)	120.00	60.00	35.00
(21c)	Jim Maloney (Small size, yellow & white striped border.)	60.00	30.00	18.00
(21d)	Jim Maloney (Small size, yellow, white & green striped border.)	60.00	30.00	18.00
(22a)	Lee May (Large size.)	50.00	25.00	15.00
(22b)	Lee May (Small size.)	60.00	30.00	18.00
(23a)	Wm. Mazeroski (Large size.)	100.00	50.00	30.00
(23b)	Wm. Mazeroski (Small size.)	130.00	65.00	40.00
(24)	Dick McAuliffe	40.00	20.00	12.00
(25)	Bill McCool	40.00	20.00	12.00
(26a)	Sam McDowell (Yellow striped border.)	50.00	25.00	15.00
(26b)	Sam McDowell (Red striped border.)	60.00	30.00	18.00
(27a)	Tony Perez (Yellow striped border.)	90.00	45.00	27.00
(27b)	Tony Perez (Red striped border.)	100.00	50.00	30.00
(28)	Gary Peters	40.00	20.00	12.00
(29a)	Vada Pinson (Large size.)	60.00	30.00	18.00
(29b)	Vada Pinson (Small size.)	60.00	30.00	18.00
(30)	Chico Ruiz	40.00	20.00	12.00
(31a)	Ron Santo (Yellow striped border.)	60.00	30.00	18.00
(31b)	Ron Santo (Red striped border.)	80.00	40.00	24.00
(32)	Art Shamsky	40.00	20.00	12.00
(33)	Luis Tiant (Arms above head.)	40.00	20.00	12.00
(34a)	Joe Torre (Large size.)	60.00	30.00	18.00
(34b)	Joe Torre (Small size.)	70.00	35.00	21.00
(35a)	Bob Veale (Large size.)	40.00	20.00	12.00
(35b)	Bob Veale (Small size.)	60.00	30.00	18.00
(36)	Leon Wagner	40.00	20.00	12.00
(37)	Billy Williams	150.00	75.00	45.00
(38)	Earl Wilson	40.00	20.00	12.00

1969 Kahn's Wieners

In its 15th consecutive year of baseball card issue, Kahn's continued the format adopted in 1966. The basic 22 players' cards were printed in about 2-13/16" x 4-9/16" size (with ad panel at top and bottom panel; 2-13/16" x 2-11/16" without panels) and are blanked-backed. Teams represented in the set are the Braves, Cubs, White Sox, Reds, Cardinals, Indians and Pirates. Cards feature a color photo and facsimile autograph bordered by yellow and white vertical stripes. At top is an ad panel consisting of the Kahn's red rose logo. However, because some cards were produced for inclusion in packages other than the standard hot dogs, a number of variations in card size and stripe color were created, as noted in the listings. The smaller size cards, 2-13/16" x 3-1/4" with top and bottom panels; 3/16" x 2-1/8" without panels, were created by more closely cropping the player photo at top and bottom. Values quoted are for complete uncut cards with both panels intact; deduct a minimum 50 percent for cards wihtout the ad and/or bottom panel. Complete set values include all variations. For years an (18b) (red-striped border) Ron Santo had been documented. Recent evidence now suggests that such a variations does not exist.

		NM	E	VG
	Complete Set (29):	1,200	600.00	375.00
	Common Player:	25.00	12.50	7.50
(1a)	Hank Aaron (Large size.)	125.00	62.00	37.00
(1b)	Hank Aaron (Small size.)	140.00	70.00	42.00
(2)	Matty Alou	25.00	12.50	7.50
(3)	Max Alvis	25.00	12.50	7.50
(4)	Gerry Arrigo	25.00	12.50	7.50
(5)	Steve Blass	25.00	12.50	7.50
(6)	Clay Carroll (Follow-through.)	25.00	12.50	7.50
(7)	Tony Cloninger	25.00	12.50	7.50
(8)	George Culver	25.00	12.50	7.50
(9)	Joel Horlen (Follow-through.)	25.00	12.50	7.50
(10)	Tony Horton (Batting)	35.00	17.50	10.50
(11)	Alex Johnson	25.00	12.50	7.50
(12a)	Jim Maloney (Large size.) (Arms at sides.))	30.00	15.00	9.00
(12b)	Jim Maloney (Small size.) (Arms at sides.))	35.00	17.50	10.50
(13a)	Lee May (Yellow striped border.) (Foot on bag.))	30.00	15.00	9.00
(13b)	Lee May (Red striped border.) (Foot on bag.))	35.00	17.50	10.50
(14a)	Bill Mazeroski (Yellow striped border.)	50.00	25.00	15.00
(14b)	Bill Mazeroski (Red striped border.)	55.00	27.00	16.50
(15a)	Sam McDowell (Yellow striped border.) (Right leg raised.))	30.00	15.00	9.00
(15b)	Sam McDowell (Red striped border.) (Right leg raised.))	35.00	17.50	10.50
(16a)	Tony Perez (Large size.) (Glove on base.))	60.00	30.00	18.00
(16b)	Tony Perez (Small size.) (Glove on base.))	75.00	37.50	22.50
(17)	Gary Peters (Follow-through.)	25.00	12.50	7.50
(18a)	Ron Santo (Yellow striped border.)	50.00	25.00	15.00
(18b)	Ron Santo (Red striped border. Now believed not to exist.)			
(19)	Luis Tiant (Arms at knees.)	25.00	12.50	7.50
(20)	Joe Torre	35.00	17.50	10.50
(21)	Bob Veale	25.00	12.50	7.50
(22)	Billy Williams (Bat behind head.)	80.00	40.00	24.00

1970s Kahn's Kielbasa Singles Carl Yastrzemski

The exact year or years of this label's issue are not known. The 4-7/8" x 3-1/8" cardboard package insert has a color portrait photo of baseball's most famous Polish player endorsing the polish sausage product.

	NM	E	VG
Carl Yastrzemski	15.00	7.50	4.50

1886-88 Kalamazoo Bats (N690)

		NM	E	VG
	Common Player:	11,000	5,500	3,250
	Advertising-back: 1.5X			
(1)	Ed Andrews	11,000	5,500	3,250
(2)	Charles Bastian, Denny Lyons	11,000	5,500	3,250
(3)	Lou Bierbauer	11,000	5,500	3,250
(4)	Lou Bierbauer, Bill Gallagher	11,000	5,500	3,250
(5)	Charles Buffington (Buffinton)	11,000	5,500	3,250
(6)	Dan Casey	11,000	5,500	3,250
(7)	Jack Clements	11,000	5,500	3,250
(8)	Roger Connor (Possibly Unique)	65,000	24,000	16,000
(9)	Larry Corcoran	24,000	12,000	7,250
(10)	Ed Cushman	24,000	12,000	7,250
(11)	Pat Deasley	24,000	12,000	7,250
(12)	Jim Devlin	11,000	5,500	3,250
(13)	Jim Donahue	24,000	12,000	7,250
(14)	Mike Dorgan	24,000	12,000	7,250
(15)	Dude Esterbrooke ((Esterbrook))	24,000	12,000	7,250
(16)	Buck Ewing ((Possibly unique))	85,000	27,000	18,000
(17)	Sid Farrar	11,000	5,500	3,250
(18)	Charlie Ferguson	11,000	5,500	3,250
(19)	Jim Fogarty	11,000	5,500	3,250
(20)	Jim Fogarty, Deacon McGuire	11,000	5,500	3,250
(21)	Elmer Foster	24,000	12,000	7,250
(22)	Whitey Gibson	11,000	5,500	3,250
(23)	Pete Gillespie	24,000	12,000	7,250
(24)	Tom Gunning	11,000	5,500	3,250
(25)	Arthur Irwin	11,000	5,500	3,250
(26)	Arthur Irwin, Al Maul	11,000	5,500	3,250
(27)	Tim Keefe	65,000	21,000	14,000
(28)	Henry Larkin	11,000	5,500	3,250
(29)	Henry Larkins (Larkin), Jocko Milligan	11,000	5,500	3,250
(30)	Jack Lynch	24,000	12,000	7,250
(31)	Denny Lyons (Athletics)	11,000	5,500	3,250
(32)	Harry Lyons (Phila.)	11,000	5,500	3,250
(33)	Harry Lyons, Billy Taylor	11,000	5,500	3,250
(34)	Fred Mann	11,000	5,500	3,250
(35)	Charlie Mason	11,000	5,500	3,250
(36)	Bobby Mathews	20,000	12,500	
(37)	Al Maul	11,000	5,500	3,250
(38)	Al Mays	24,000	12,000	7,250
(39)	Chippy McGan (McGarr)	11,000	5,500	3,250
(40)	Deacon McGuire (Fielding)	11,000	5,500	3,250
(41)	Deacon McGuire (Throwing)	11,000	5,500	3,250
(42)	Tom McLaughlin	24,000	12,000	7,250
(43)	Jocko Milligan, Harry Stowe (Stovey)	11,000	5,500	3,250
(44)	Joseph Mulvey	11,000	5,500	3,250
(45)	Candy Nelson	24,000	12,000	7,250
(46)	Orator Jim O'Rourke (Possibly unique)	75,000	21,000	14,000
(47)	Dave Orr	24,000	12,000	7,250
(48)	Tom Poorman	11,000	5,500	3,250
(49)	Danny Richardson	24,000	12,000	7,250
(50)	Wilbert Robinson	15,000	7,500	4,500
(51)	Wilbert Robinson, Fred Mann	15,000	7,500	4,500
(52)	Chief Roseman	24,000	12,000	7,250
(53)	Ed Seward	20,000	10,000	6,000
(54)	Harry Stowe (Stovey) (Hands on hips.)	75,000	21,000	14,000
(55)	Harry Stowe (Stovey) (Hands outstretched.)	11,000	5,500	3,250
(56)	George Townsend	11,000	5,500	3,250
(57)	Jocko Milligan, George Townsend	12,500	6,250	3,750

(58)	John Ward (Possibly unique)	100,000	28,500	19,000
(59)	Gus Weyhing	24,000	12,000	7,250
(60)	George Wood	11,000	5,500	3,250
(61)	Harry Wright	40,000	15,000	25,000

1887 Kalamazoo Bats Cabinets (N690-1)

This extremely rare issue of cabinet cards was issued as a premium by Charles Gross & Co. of Philadelphia, makers of the Kalamazoo Bats brand of cigarettes. Two distinct types have been found, both measuring 4-1/4" x 6-1/2". One variety displays the photo on a black mount with the words "Smoke Kalamazoo Bats" embossed in gold to the left. The other contains no advertising, although there is an oval embossment on the card, along with the words "Chas. Gross & Co." and an 1887 copyright line. These cards also have a distinctive pink color on the back of the cardboard mount. Because of the rarity of Kalamazoo Bats cabinets, and uncertainty as to completeness of this checklist, gaps have been left in the assigned numbering.

		NM	E	VG
	Common Player:	15,000	7,500	4,500
(1)	Ed Andrews	15,000	7,500	4,500
(2)	Charles Bastian, Daniel Casey, Billy Taylor	15,000	7,500	4,500
(3)	Charles Bastian, Denny Lyons	15,000	7,500	4,500
(4)	Louis Bierbauer, Gallagher	15,000	7,500	4,500
(5)	Charles Buffington (Buffinton)	15,000	7,500	4,500
(6)	Daniel Casey	15,000	7,500	4,500
(7)	Jack Clements	15,000	7,500	4,500
(8)	Jim Devlin	15,000	7,500	4,500
(9)	Sid Farrar	15,000	7,500	4,500
(10)	Charlie Ferguson	15,000	7,500	4,500
(11)	Jim Fogarty	15,000	7,500	4,500
(12)	Whitey Gibson	15,000	7,500	4,500
(13)	Tom Gunning	15,000	7,500	4,500
(14)	Arthur Irwin	15,000	7,500	4,500
(15)	Arthur Irwin, Al Maul	15,000	7,500	4,500
(16)	Henry Larkins (Larkin), Jocko Milligan	15,000	7,500	4,500
(17)	Harry Lyons	15,000	7,500	4,500
(18)	Harry Lyons, Billy Taylor	15,000	7,500	4,500
(19)	Fred Mann	15,000	7,500	4,500
(20)	Fred Mann, Wilbert Robinson	25,000	12,500	7,500
(21)	Bobby Mathews	15,000	7,500	4,500
(22)	Al Maul	15,000	7,500	4,500
(23)	Chippy McCan (McGarr)	15,000	7,500	4,500
(24)	Deacon McGuire (Fielding)	15,000	7,500	4,500
(25)	Deacon McGuire (Throwing)	15,000	7,500	4,500
(26)	Jocko Milligan, Harry Stowe (Stovey)	15,000	7,500	4,500

(27)	Joseph Mulvey	15,000	7,500	4,500
(28)	Tom Poorman	15,000	7,500	4,500
(29)	Ed Seward	15,000	7,500	4,500
(30)	Harry Stowe (Stovey)	15,000	7,500	4,500
(31)	George Townsend	15,000	7,500	4,500
(32)	George Wood	15,000	7,500	4,500
(33)	Harry Wright	62,500	31,250	18,750
(35)	Athletic Club (Three known, $9,031 paid in 12/04 auction for Good example.)			
(36)	Boston B.B.C. (Believed unique, mount restored, brought $14,434 in 5/05 auction.)			
(37)	Detroit B.B.C. (Believed unique)			
(38)	Philadelphia B.B.C. (Believed unique, VG, brought $9,935 in 12/04 auction.)			
(39)	Pittsburg B.B.C. (Believed unique, sold for $62,299 in Excellent in 12/05 auction.)			

1887 Kalamazoo Bats Team Cards (N693)

The team photos in this set were issued by Charles Gross & Co. of Philadelphia as a promotion for its Kalamazoo Bats brand of cigarettes. The cards, which are similar in design and size (about 4" x 2-1/4") to the related N690 series, are extremely rare. They feature a team photo with the caption in a white box at the bottom of the photo and an ad for Kalamazoo Bats to the left.

		NM	E	VG
Common Team:		12,000	4,200	3,000
(1)	Athletic Club	12,000	4,200	3,000
(2)	Baltimore B.B.C.	38,000	13,300	9,500
(3)	Boston B.B.C.	30,000	10,500	7,500
(4)	Detroit B.B.C.	32,000	11,200	8,000
(5)	Philadelphia B.B.C.	15,000	5,250	3,750
(6)	Pittsburg B.B.C.	38,000	13,300	9,500

1955 Kansas City Athletics Photo Pack

VIC POWER

In the first year following the team's move from Philadelphia to K.C., this set of player pictures was issued, probably sold as a souvenir stand item. The black-and-white photos are in an 8" x 10" format on heavy cardboard. Player poses or portraits are bordered in white with the player name in all-caps at bottom. Backs are blank. This checklist may be incomplete.

		NM	E	VG
Complete Set (29):		200.00	100.00	60.00
Common Player:		9.00	4.50	2.75
(1)	Joe Astroth	9.00	4.50	2.75
(2)	Lou Boudreau	25.00	12.50	7.50
(3)	Cloyd Boyer	9.00	4.50	2.75
(4)	Art Ceccarelli	9.00	4.50	2.75
(5)	Harry Craft	9.00	4.50	2.75
(6)	Joe DeMaestri	9.00	4.50	2.75
(7)	Art Ditmar	9.00	4.50	2.75
(8)	Jim Finigan	9.00	4.50	2.75
(9)	Tom Gorman	9.00	4.50	2.75
(10)	Ray Herbert	9.00	4.50	2.75
(11)	Alex Kellner	9.00	4.50	2.75
(12)	Dick Kryhoski	9.00	4.50	2.75
(13)	Jack Littrell	9.00	4.50	2.75
(14)	Hector Lopez	9.00	4.50	2.75
(15)	Oscar Melillo	9.00	4.50	2.75
(16)	Arnie Portocarrero	9.00	4.50	2.75
(17)	Vic Power	15.00	7.50	4.50
(18)	Vic Raschi	12.00	6.00	3.50

(19)	Bill Renna	9.00	4.50	2.75
(20)	Johnny Sain	12.00	6.00	3.50
(21)	Bobby Shantz	12.00	6.00	3.50
(22)	Wilmer Shantz	9.00	4.50	2.75
(23)	Harry Simpson	15.00	7.50	4.50
(24)	Enos Slaughter	30.00	15.00	9.00
(25)	Lou Sleator	9.00	4.50	2.75
(26)	George Susce	9.00	4.50	2.75
(27)	Elmer Valo	9.00	4.50	2.75
(28)	Bill Wilson	9.00	4.50	2.75
(29)	Gus Zernial	15.00	7.50	4.50

1956-61 Kansas City Athletics Photocards

Issued over a period of several years these black-and-white photocards share an identical format. The cards are 3-1/4" x 5-1/2" with borderless poses and facsimile autographs on front. Backs are blank. The unnumbered cards are checklisted here in alphabetical order, though the list is surely not complete. Gaps have been left in the assigned numbering for future additions.

		NM	E	VG
Common Player:		15.00	7.50	4.50
(1)	Jim Archer	15.00	7.50	4.50
(2)	Mike Baxes	15.00	7.50	4.50
(3)	Zeke Bella	15.00	7.50	4.50
(4)	Lou Boudreau	30.00	15.00	9.00
(5)	Cletis Boyer	20.00	10.00	6.00
(6)	Wally Burnette	15.00	7.50	4.50
(7)	Chico Carrasquel	17.50	8.75	5.25
(8)	Bob Cerv	15.00	7.50	4.50
(9)	Harry Chiti	15.00	7.50	4.50
(10)	Harry Craft	15.00	7.50	4.50
(11)	Jack Crimian	15.00	7.50	4.50
(12)	Bud Daley	15.00	7.50	4.50
(13)	Bob Davis	15.00	7.50	4.50
(14)	Joe DeMaestri	15.00	7.50	4.50
(15)	Art Ditmar	15.00	7.50	4.50
(16)	Jim Ewell (Trainer)	15.00	7.50	4.50
(17)	Jim Finigan	15.00	7.50	4.50
(18)	Hank Foiles	15.00	7.50	4.50
(19)	Ned Garver	17.50	8.75	5.25
(20)	Joe Ginsberg	15.00	7.50	4.50
(21)	Tom Gorman (Cap-to-knees.)	15.00	7.50	4.50
(22)	Tom Gorman (Pitching)	15.00	7.50	4.50
(23)	Bob Grim	15.00	7.50	4.50
(24)	Johnny Groth	15.00	7.50	4.50
(25)	Kent Hadley	15.00	7.50	4.50
(26)	Ray Herbert	15.00	7.50	4.50
(27)	Troy Herriage	15.00	7.50	4.50
(28)	Whitey Herzog	20.00	10.00	6.00
(29)	Frank House	15.00	7.50	4.50
(32)	Alex Kellner	15.00	7.50	4.50
(33)	Lou Kretlow	15.00	7.50	4.50
(34)	Hec Lopez	15.00	7.50	4.50
(35)	Roger Maris	125.00	62.00	37.00
(36)	Oscar Melillo	15.00	7.50	4.50
(37)	Rance Pless	15.00	7.50	4.50
(38)	Vic Power	20.00	10.00	6.00
(39)	Jose Santiago	15.00	7.50	4.50
(40)	Bobby Shantz	25.00	12.50	7.50
(41)	Harry Simpson	17.50	8.75	5.25
(42)	Lou Skizas	15.00	7.50	4.50
(43)	Enos Slaughter	45.00	22.00	13.50
(44)	Hal Smith	15.00	7.50	4.50
(45)	George Susce	15.00	7.50	4.50
(46)	Wayne Terwilliger	15.00	7.50	4.50
(47)	Charles Thompson	15.00	7.50	4.50
(48)	Dick Tomanek	15.00	7.50	4.50
(49)	Bill Tuttle	15.00	7.50	4.50
(52)	Jack Urban	15.00	7.50	4.50
(53)	Preston Ward	15.00	7.50	4.50
(54)	Dick Williams	17.50	8.75	5.25
(55)	Gus Zernial (Batting)	17.50	8.75	5.25
(56)	Gus Zernial (Fielding)	17.50	8.75	5.25

1929 Kashin Publications (R316)

This set of 101 unnumbered cards was issued in 25-card boxed series, with cards measuring 3-1/2" x 4-1/2". The cards feature black-and-white photos with the player's name printed in script near the bottom of the photo. Team and league are designated at bottom in printed letters. The backs of the cards are blank. Four of the cards (Hadley, Haines, Siebold and Todt) are considered to be scarcer than the rest of the set. Some cards have been seen with "MADE IN U.S.A." in one of the picture's lower corners; their significance and value are undetermined.

		NM	E	VG
Complete Set (101):		9,500	4,750	2,750
Common Player:		40.00	20.00	12.00
(1)	Dale Alexander	40.00	20.00	12.00
(2)	Ethan N. Allen	40.00	20.00	12.00
(3)	Larry Benton	40.00	20.00	12.00
(4)	Moe Berg	250.00	125.00	75.00
(5)	Max Bishop	40.00	20.00	12.00
(6)	Del Bissonette	40.00	20.00	12.00
(7)	Lucerne A. Blue	40.00	20.00	12.00
(8)	James Bottomley	100.00	50.00	30.00
(9)	Guy T. Bush	40.00	20.00	12.00
(10)	Harold G. Carlson	40.00	20.00	12.00
(11)	Owen Carroll	40.00	20.00	12.00
(12)	Chalmers W. Cissell (Chalmer)	40.00	20.00	12.00
(13)	Earl Combs	100.00	50.00	30.00
(14)	Hugh M. Critz	40.00	20.00	12.00
(15)	H.J. DeBerry	40.00	20.00	12.00
(16)	Pete Donohue	40.00	20.00	12.00
(17)	Taylor Douthit	40.00	20.00	12.00
(18)	Chas. W. Dressen	40.00	20.00	12.00
(19)	Jimmy Dykes	40.00	20.00	12.00
(20)	Howard Ehmke	40.00	20.00	12.00
(21)	Elwood English	40.00	20.00	12.00
(22)	Urban Faber	100.00	50.00	30.00
(23)	Fred Fitzsimmons	40.00	20.00	12.00
(24)	Lewis A. Fonseca	40.00	20.00	12.00
(25)	Horace H. Ford	40.00	20.00	12.00
(26)	Jimmy Foxx	235.00	115.00	70.00
(27)	Frank Frisch	100.00	50.00	30.00
(28)	Lou Gehrig	1,250	625.00	375.00
(29)	Charles Gehringer	100.00	50.00	30.00
(30)	Leon Goslin	100.00	50.00	30.00
(31)	George Grantham	40.00	20.00	12.00
(32)	Burleigh Grimes	100.00	50.00	30.00
(33)	Robert Grove	200.00	100.00	60.00
(34)	Bump Hadley	150.00	75.00	45.00
(35)	Charlie Hafey	100.00	50.00	30.00
(36)	Jesse J. Haines	250.00	125.00	75.00
(37)	Harvey Hendrick	40.00	20.00	12.00
(38)	Floyd C. Herman	40.00	20.00	12.00
(39)	Andy Hyp	40.00	20.00	12.00
(40)	Urban J. Hodapp	40.00	20.00	12.00
(41)	Frank Hogan	40.00	20.00	12.00
(42)	Rogers Hornsby	175.00	85.00	50.00
(43)	Waite Hoyt	100.00	50.00	30.00
(44)	Willis Hudlin	40.00	20.00	12.00
(45)	Frank O. Hurst	40.00	20.00	12.00
(46)	Charlie Jamieson	40.00	20.00	12.00
(47)	Roy C. Johnson	40.00	20.00	12.00
(48)	Percy Jones	40.00	20.00	12.00
(49)	Sam Jones	40.00	20.00	12.00
(50)	Joseph Judge	40.00	20.00	12.00
(51)	Willie Kamm	40.00	20.00	12.00
(52)	Charles Klein	100.00	50.00	30.00
(53)	Mark Koenig	40.00	20.00	12.00
(54)	Ralph Kress	40.00	20.00	12.00
(55)	Fred M. Leach	40.00	20.00	12.00
(56)	Fred Lindstrom	100.00	50.00	30.00
(57)	Ad Liska	40.00	20.00	12.00
(58)	Fred Lucas (Red)	40.00	20.00	12.00
(59)	Fred Maguire	40.00	20.00	12.00
(60)	Perce L. Malone	40.00	20.00	12.00
(61)	Harry Manush (Henry)	100.00	50.00	30.00
(62)	Walter Maranville	100.00	50.00	30.00
(63)	Douglas McWeeney (McWeeny)	40.00	20.00	12.00
(64)	Oscar Melillo	40.00	20.00	12.00

		NM	E	VG
(65)	Ed "Bing" Miller	40.00	20.00	12.00
(66)	Frank O'Doul	80.00	40.00	24.00
(67)	Melvin Ott	200.00	100.00	60.00
(68)	Herbert Pennock	100.00	50.00	30.00
(69)	William W. Regan	40.00	20.00	12.00
(70)	Harry F. Rice	40.00	20.00	12.00
(71)	Sam Rice	100.00	50.00	30.00
(72)	Lance Richbourgh (Richbourg)	40.00	20.00	12.00
(73)	Eddie Rommel	40.00	20.00	12.00
(74)	Chas. H. Root	40.00	20.00	12.00
(75)	Ed (Edd) Roush	100.00	50.00	30.00
(76)	Harold Ruel (Herold)	40.00	20.00	12.00
(77)	Charles Ruffing	125.00	65.00	35.00
(78)	Jack Russell	40.00	20.00	12.00
(79)	Babe Ruth	1,650	825.00	500.00
(80)	Fred Schulte	40.00	20.00	12.00
(81)	Harry Seibold	150.00	75.00	45.00
(82)	Joe Sewell	100.00	50.00	30.00
(83)	Luke Sewell	40.00	20.00	12.00
(84)	Art Shires	40.00	20.00	12.00
(85)	Al Simmons	100.00	50.00	30.00
(86)	Bob Smith	40.00	20.00	12.00
(87)	Riggs Stephenson	40.00	20.00	12.00
(88)	Wm. H. Terry	100.00	50.00	30.00
(89)	Alphonse Thomas	40.00	20.00	12.00
(90)	Lafayette F. Thompson	40.00	20.00	12.00
(91)	Phil Todt	150.00	75.00	45.00
(92)	Harold J. Traynor	100.00	50.00	30.00
(93)	Dazzy Vance	100.00	50.00	30.00
(94)	Lloyd Waner	100.00	50.00	30.00
(95)	Paul Waner	100.00	50.00	30.00
(96)	Jimmy Welsh	40.00	20.00	12.00
(97)	Earl Whitehill	40.00	20.00	12.00
(98)	A.C. Whitney	40.00	20.00	12.00
(99)	Claude Willoughby	40.00	20.00	12.00
(100)	Hack Wilson	200.00	100.00	60.00
(101)	Tom Zachary	40.00	20.00	12.00

1964 KDKA Pittsburgh Pirates Portraits

Issued prior to the radio/TV stations' much more common color player cards of 1968, this seldom-seen regional issue presents the 1964 Pittsburgh Pirates in a set of 28 large-format (8" x 11-7/8") schedule cards. The cards are printed in sepia tones on blank-backed cardboard. Fronts present a player pose and a '64 Pirates schedule. A redemption offer states that a pair of Bucs' tickets will be given in exchange for a complete set of the portraits, and the pictures will be returned, presumably cancelled in some fashion. The un-numbered cards are checklisted here alphabetically. While the cards advertise the Pirates' broadcasting partners, they were actually issued by Sweet Clean laundry as stiffeners for men's shirts that had been washed. The laundry's name is not mentioned anywhere on the cards.

		NM	E	VG
Complete Set (28):		3,500	1,750	1,000
Common Player:		100.00	50.00	30.00
(1)	Gene Alley	100.00	50.00	30.00
(2)	Bob Bailey	100.00	50.00	30.00
(3)	Frank Bork	100.00	50.00	30.00
(4)	Smoky Burgess	100.00	50.00	30.00
(5)	Tom Butters	100.00	50.00	30.00
(6)	Don Cardwell	100.00	50.00	30.00
(7)	Roberto Clemente	600.00	300.00	180.00
(8)	Donn Clendenon	100.00	50.00	30.00
(9)	Elroy Face	100.00	50.00	30.00
(10)	Gene Freese	100.00	50.00	30.00
(11)	Bob Friend	100.00	50.00	30.00
(12)	Joe Gibbon	100.00	50.00	30.00
(13)	Julio Gotay	100.00	50.00	30.00
(14)	Rex Johnston	100.00	50.00	30.00
(15)	Vernon Law	100.00	50.00	30.00
(16)	Jerry Lynch	100.00	50.00	30.00
(17)	Bill Mazeroski	250.00	125.00	75.00
(18)	Al McBean	100.00	50.00	30.00
(19)	Orlando McFarlane	100.00	50.00	30.00
(20)	Manny Mota	100.00	50.00	30.00
(21)	Danny Murtaugh	100.00	50.00	30.00
(22)	Jim Pagliaroni	100.00	50.00	30.00

(23)	Dick Schofield	100.00	50.00	30.00
(24)	Don Schwall	100.00	50.00	30.00
(25)	Tommie Sisk	100.00	50.00	30.00
(26)	Willie Stargell	250.00	125.00	75.00
(27)	Bob Veale	100.00	50.00	30.00
(28)	Bill Virdon	100.00	50.00	30.00

1968 KDKA Pittsburgh Pirates

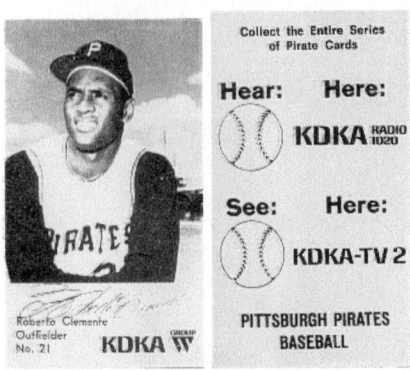

The most common of the many Pirates regional issues of the late 1960s, this 23-card set was sponsored by the Pirates' TV and radio flagship stations, KDKA in Pittsburgh. Cards measure 2-1/2" x 4" and feature at top front a color posed photo of the player, with no top or side borders. In the white panel beneath the photo are a facsimile autograph, the player's name, position and uniform number and the broadcasters' logo. Backs are printed in black on white and feature advertising for the radio and TV station. The checklist is presented here by uniform number.

		NM	E	VG
Complete Set (23):		125.00	65.00	35.00
Common Player:		5.00	2.50	1.50
7	Larry Shepard	5.00	2.50	1.50
8	Willie Stargell	15.00	7.50	4.50
9	Bill Mazeroski	15.00	7.50	4.50
10	Gary Kolb	5.00	2.50	1.50
11	Jose Pagan	5.00	2.50	1.50
12	Gerry May (Jerry)	5.00	2.50	1.50
14	Jim Bunning	10.00	5.00	3.00
15	Manny Mota	5.00	2.50	1.50
17	Donn Clendenon	5.00	2.50	1.50
18	Matty Alou	5.00	2.50	1.50
21	Roberto Clemente	40.00	20.00	12.00
22	Gene Alley	5.00	2.50	1.50
25	Tommy Sisk	5.00	2.50	1.50
26	Roy Face	5.00	2.50	1.50
27	Ron Kline	5.00	2.50	1.50
28	Steve Blass	5.00	2.50	1.50
29	Juan Pizarro	5.00	2.50	1.50
30	Maury Wills	6.50	3.25	2.00
34	Al McBean	5.00	2.50	1.50
35	Manny Sanguillen	5.00	2.50	1.50
38	Bob Moose	5.00	2.50	1.50
39	Bob Veale	5.00	2.50	1.50
40	Dave Wickersham	5.00	2.50	1.50

1922 Keating Candy Co.

To compete with other candy issues featuring baseball cards as premiums, Sacramento, Calif., wholesale candy merchant James P. Keating appears to have purchased un-cut sheets of the blank-back strip cards known as W575-1, overprinted their backs and packaged them with his product. The advertising on back is rubber-stamped. The fact that examples are known that have been cancelled with a hole punch probably indicates there was some sort of prize redemption program attached to the issue. Collectors can expect to pay a premium of about 3X for this version.

	NM	E	VG
Common Player:	85.00	45.00	25.00
Stars: 3X			

(See 1922 W575-1 for checklist and base card values.)

1971 Keds Kedcards

These (usually) 2-1/4" x 2-1/8" cards were printed on the side of Keds athletic shoe boxes. The cards have colorful drawings of various athletes, with dotted lines for cutting. Backs are blank.

		NM	E	VG
Complete Panel Set (3):		150.00	75.00	45.00
Complete Set (10):		120.00	60.00	35.00
Common Player:		8.00	4.00	2.50
	PANEL 1	40.00	20.00	12.00
(1)	Dave Bing (Basketball)	8.00	4.00	2.50
(2)	Clark Graebner (Tennis)	8.00	4.00	2.50
(3)	Jim Maloney	10.00	5.00	3.00
(4)	Bubba Smith (Football)	10.00	5.00	3.00
	PANEL 2	50.00	25.00	15.00
(5)	Johnny Bench (portrait)	30.00	15.00	9.00
(6)	Willis Reed (Basketball)	10.00	5.00	3.00
(7)	Bubba Smith (Football)	10.00	5.00	3.00
(8)	Stan Smith (Tennis)	8.00	4.00	2.50
	PANEL 3	50.00	25.00	15.00
(9)	Willis Reed (Basketball) (5-1/4" x 3-1/2")	15.00	7.50	4.50
(10)	Johnny Bench (5-1/4" x 3-1/2") (batting)	50.00	25.00	15.00

1937 Kellogg's Pep Sports Stamps

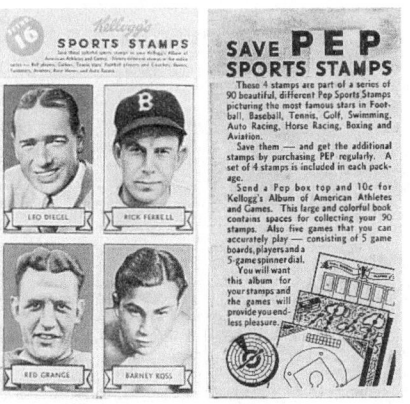

Kellogg's packaged a four-stamp panel of "Sports Stamps" in boxes of Pep cereal. While 24 panels comprise a complete set, six of the stamps were double-printed, creating a set of 90. Backs of the stamp panels gave details for ordering an album and game boards for playing with the stamps. The color-tinted stamps measure 1-1/8" x 2-3/4" individually, and 2-1/4" x 4-1/4" as a panel. Besides the ballplayers checklisted here, the Kellogg's/Pep stamps included football, tennis and golf players, swimmers, boxers, aviaitors and race horses. Baseball player stamps are listed here according to the number of the four-stamp panel on which they appeared. Prices for complete panels would be considerably higher, factoring in the other stamps on the sheet.

		NM	E	VG
Complete Set (18):		900.00	450.00	275.00
Common Player:		60.00	30.00	18.00
Album:		300.00	150.00	100.00
1	Joe Medwick	60.00	30.00	18.00
3	Leo Durocher	60.00	30.00	18.00
5	Gabby Hartnett	60.00	30.00	18.00
6	Billy Herman	60.00	30.00	18.00
7	Luke Appling	60.00	30.00	18.00

		NM	E	VG
8	Arky Vaughan	60.00	30.00	18.00
9	Paul Waner	60.00	30.00	18.00
11	Bill Terry	60.00	30.00	18.00
12	George Selkirk	60.00	30.00	18.00
13	Walter Johnson	120.00	60.00	36.00
15	Lew Fonseca	60.00	30.00	18.00
16	Richard Ferrell	60.00	30.00	18.00
17	Johnny Evers	60.00	30.00	18.00
18	Sam West	60.00	30.00	18.00
19	Buddy Myer	60.00	30.00	18.00
20	Tris Speaker (Double print, also on Panel 23.)	60.00	30.00	18.00
21	Joe Tinker	60.00	30.00	18.00
22	Mordecai Brown	60.00	30.00	18.00
23	Tris Speaker (Double-print, also on Panel 20.)	60.00	30.00	18.00

1948 Kellogg's Corn Flakes Cuban Postcards

These advertising postcards were issued in Cuba. The approximately 3-1/2" x 5-3/8" black-and-white cards have a portrait photo on front. A small logo for the cereal appears in the lower-left corner, while a facsimile autograph is at lower-right. The back is in traditional postcard format, printed in English. This checklist is likely incomplete.

		NM	E	VG
(1)	Tomas de la Cruz	400.00	200.00	120.00
(2)	Salvador Hernandez	400.00	200.00	120.00
(3)	Adolfo Luque	600.00	300.00	180.00
(4)	Roberto Ortiz	400.00	200.00	120.00
(5)	Napoleon Reyes	400.00	200.00	120.00
(6)	Lazaro Salazar	400.00	200.00	120.00

1948 Kellogg's Pep Celebrities

PHIL CAVARETTA

First baseman and outfielder, Chicago Cubs. National league batting champion and most valuable player in 1945. Joined Cubs at age of 17 and has lifetime batting average of .292. Bats and throws left-handed.

Get Complete Series with Kellogg's PEP

Five baseball players are included among the 18 athletes in this set of 1-3/8" x 1-5/8" cards. Fronts have player photos bordered in white. Backs have player name at top, a short career summary and a Kellogg's ad. The baseball players from the unnumbered set are listed here alphabetically.

		NM	E	VG
Complete Set (5):		175.00	90.00	55.00
Common Player:		40.00	20.00	12.00
(1)	Phil Cavaretta	40.00	20.00	12.00
(2)	Orval Grove	40.00	20.00	12.00
(3)	Mike Tresh	40.00	20.00	12.00
(4)	Paul "Dizzy" Trout	40.00	20.00	12.00
(5)	Dick Wakefield	40.00	20.00	12.00

1970 Kellogg's

For 14 years in the 1970s and early 1980s, the Kellogg's cereal company provided Topps with virtually the only meaningful national competition in the baseball card market. Kellogg's kicked off its baseball card program in 1970 with a 75-player set of simulated 3-D cards. Single cards were available in selected brands of the company's cereal, while a mail-in program offered complete sets. The 3-D effect was achieved by the sandwiching of a clear color player photo between a purposely blurred stadium background scene

and a layer of ribbed plastic. The relatively narrow dimension of the card, 2-1/4" x 3-1/2" and the nature of the plastic overlay seem to conspire to cause the cards to curl, often cracking the plastic layer, if not stored properly. Cards with major cracks in the plastic can be considered in Fair condition, at best.

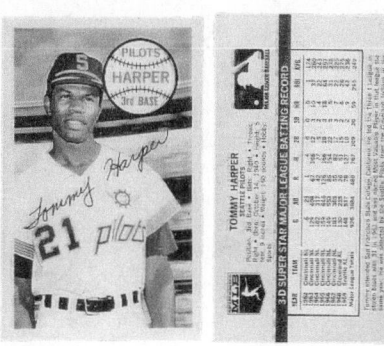

		NM	E	VG
Complete Set (75):		300.00	150.00	90.00
Common Player:		3.50	1.75	1.00
1	Ed Kranepool	3.50	1.75	1.00
2	Pete Rose	20.00	10.00	6.00
3	Cleon Jones	3.50	1.75	1.00
4	Willie McCovey	10.00	5.00	3.00
5	Mel Stottlemyre	3.50	1.75	1.00
6	Frank Howard	3.50	1.75	1.00
7	Tom Seaver	15.00	7.50	4.50
8	Don Sutton	10.00	5.00	3.00
9	Jim Wynn	3.50	1.75	1.00
10	Jim Maloney	3.50	1.75	1.00
11	Tommie Agee	3.50	1.75	1.00
12	Willie Mays	25.00	12.50	7.50
13	Juan Marichal	10.00	5.00	3.00
14	Dave McNally	3.50	1.75	1.00
15	Frank Robinson	15.00	7.50	4.50
16	Carlos May	3.50	1.75	1.00
17	Bill Singer	3.50	1.75	1.00
18	Rick Reichardt	3.50	1.75	1.00
19	Boog Powell	4.50	2.25	1.25
20	Gaylord Perry	10.00	5.00	3.00
21	Brooks Robinson	15.00	7.50	4.50
22	Luis Aparicio	10.00	5.00	3.00
23	Joel Horlen	3.50	1.75	1.00
24	Mike Epstein	3.50	1.75	1.00
25	Tom Haller	3.50	1.75	1.00
26	Willie Crawford	3.50	1.75	1.00
27	Roberto Clemente	35.00	17.50	10.00
28	Matty Alou	3.50	1.75	1.00
29	Willie Stargell	12.50	6.25	3.75
30	Tim Cullen	3.50	1.75	1.00
31	Randy Hundley	3.50	1.75	1.00
32	Reggie Jackson	20.00	10.00	6.00
33	Rich Allen	4.25	2.25	1.25
34	Tim McCarver	3.50	1.75	1.00
35	Ray Culp	3.50	1.75	1.00
36	Jim Fregosi	3.50	1.75	1.00
37	Billy Williams	12.50	6.25	3.75
38	Johnny Odom	3.50	1.75	1.00
39	Bert Campaneris	3.50	1.75	1.00
40	Ernie Banks	20.00	10.00	6.00
41	Chris Short	3.50	1.75	1.00
42	Ron Santo	6.00	3.00	1.75
43	Glenn Beckert	3.50	1.75	1.00
44	Lou Brock	12.50	6.25	3.75
45	Larry Hisle	3.50	1.75	1.00
46	Reggie Smith	3.50	1.75	1.00
47	Rod Carew	15.00	7.50	4.50
48	Curt Flood	3.50	1.75	1.00
49	Jim Lonborg	3.50	1.75	1.00
50	Sam McDowell	3.50	1.75	1.00
51	Sal Bando	3.50	1.75	1.00
52	Al Kaline	15.00	7.50	4.50
53	Gary Nolan	3.50	1.75	1.00
54	Rico Petrocelli	3.50	1.75	1.00
55	Ollie Brown	3.50	1.75	1.00
56	Luis Tiant	3.50	1.75	1.00
57	Bill Freehan	3.50	1.75	1.00
58	Johnny Bench	15.00	7.50	4.50
59	Joe Pepitone	3.50	1.75	1.00
60	Bobby Murcer	3.50	1.75	1.00
61	Harmon Killebrew	15.00	7.50	4.50
62	Don Wilson	3.50	1.75	1.00
63	Tony Oliva	3.50	1.75	1.00
64	Jim Perry	3.50	1.75	1.00
65	Mickey Lolich	3.50	1.75	1.00
66	Coco Laboy	3.50	1.75	1.00
67	Dean Chance	3.50	1.75	1.00
68	Ken Harrelson	3.50	1.75	1.00
69	Willie Horton	3.50	1.75	1.00
70	Wally Bunker	3.50	1.75	1.00

		NM	E	VG
71a	Bob Gibson (1959 IP blank)	12.50	6.25	3.75
71b	Bob Gibson (1959 IP 76)	12.50	6.25	3.75
72	Joe Morgan	12.50	6.25	3.75
73	Denny McLain	3.50	1.75	1.00
74	Tommy Harper	3.50	1.75	1.00
75	Don Mincher	3.50	1.75	1.00

1971 Kellogg's

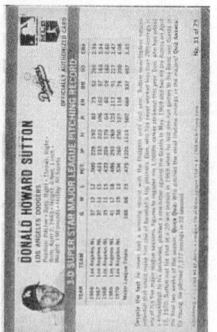

The scarcest and most valuable of the Kellogg's editions, the 75-card 1971 set was the only one not offered by the company on a mail-in basis. The only way to complete it was to buy ... and buy and buy ... boxes of cereal. Kellogg's again used the simulated 3-D effect in the cards' design, with the same result being many of the 2-1/4" x 3-1/2" cards are found today with cracks resulting from the cards' curling. A number of scarcer back variations are checklisted below. All of the base cards can be found with and without the 1970 date before the "Xograph" copyright line on the back. Most, but not all, of the base cards and variations can be found both with and without a 1970 date before the Xograph copyright on back. On most of the cards with statistical variations, only one key sts difference is listed here.

		NM	E	VG
Complete Set (75):		1,000	500.00	300.00
Common Player:		13.50	6.75	4.00
1a	Wayne Simpson (SO 120)	13.50	6.75	4.00
1b	Wayne Simpson (SO 119)	20.00	10.00	6.00
2a	Tom Seaver (IP 1092)	30.00	15.00	9.00
2b	Tom Seaver (IP 1093)	30.00	15.00	9.00
3a	Jim Perry (IP 2238)	13.50	6.75	4.00
3b	Jim Perry (IP 2239)	20.00	10.00	6.00
4a	Bob Robertson (RBI 94)	13.50	6.75	4.00
4b	Bob Robertson (RBI 95)	20.00	10.00	6.00
5	Roberto Clemente	70.00	35.00	20.00
6a	Gaylord Perry (IP 2014)	25.00	12.50	7.50
6b	Gaylord Perry (IP 2015)	30.00	15.00	9.00
7a	Felipe Alou (1970 Oakland NL)	20.00	10.00	6.00
7b	Felipe Alou (1970 Oakland AL)	25.00	12.50	7.50
8	Denis Menke	13.50	6.75	4.00
9a	Don Kessinger (Hits 849)	13.50	6.75	4.00
9b	Don Kessinger (Hits 850)	20.00	10.00	6.00
10	Willie Mays	45.00	22.00	13.50
11	Jim Hickman	13.50	6.75	4.00
12	Tony Oliva	17.50	8.75	5.25
13a	Manny Sanguillen (Hits 324)	13.50	6.75	4.00
13b	Manny Sanguillen (Hits 323)	20.00	6.75	4.00
14a	Frank Howard (1968 Washington NL)	30.00	15.00	9.00
14b	Frank Howard (1968 Washington AL)	20.00	10.00	6.00
15	Frank Robinson	30.00	15.00	9.00
16a	Willie Davis (RBI 620)	13.50	6.75	4.00
16b	Willie Davis (RBI 619)	20.50	6.75	4.00
17	Lou Brock	25.00	12.50	7.50
18	Cesar Tovar	13.50	6.75	4.00
19	Luis Aparicio	25.00	12.50	7.50
20	Boog Powell	17.50	8.75	5.25
21a	Dick Selma (SO 584)	13.50	6.75	4.00
21b	Dick Selma (SO 587)	20.00	10.00	6.00
22	Danny Walton	13.50	6.75	4.00
23a	Carl Morton (SO 167)	13.50	6.75	4.00
23b	Carl Morton (SO 170)	20.00	6.75	4.00
24a	Sonny Siebert (SO 1054)	13.50	6.75	4.00
24b	Sonny Siebert (SO 1055)	20.00	10.00	6.00
25a	Jim Merritt (BB 250)	13.50	6.75	4.00
25b	Jim Merritt (BB 249)	20.00	6.75	4.00
26a	Jose Cardenal (Hits 828)	13.50	6.75	4.00
26b	Jose Cardenal (Hits 829)	20.00	10.00	6.00
27	Don Mincher	13.50	6.75	4.00
28a	Clyde Wright (California state logo, SO 280)	13.50	6.75	4.00
28b	Clyde Wright (California state logo, SO 284)	25.00	10.00	6.00

		NM	E	VG
28c	Clyde Wright (Angels crest logo, SO 280)	20.00	10.00	6.00
29a	Les Cain (SO 166)	13.50	6.75	4.00
29b	Les Cain (SO 169)	20.00	6.75	4.00
30	Danny Cater	13.50	6.75	4.00
31a	Don Sutton (SO 957)	25.00	12.50	7.50
31b	Don Sutton (SO 958)	40.00	12.50	7.50
32a	Chuck Dobson (SO 622)	13.50	6.75	4.00
32b	Chuck Dobson (SO 625)	20.00	6.75	4.00
33a	Willie McCovey (Hits 1399)	25.00	12.50	7.50
33b	Willie McCovey (Hits 1400)	40.00	12.50	7.50
34a	Mike Epstein (Runs 200)	13.50	6.75	4.00
34b	Mike Epstein (Runs 201)	20.00	6.75	4.00
35a	Paul Blair (Runs 386)	13.50	6.75	4.00
35b	Paul Blair (Runs 385)	20.00	10.00	6.00
36a	Gary Nolan (SO 577)	13.50	6.75	4.00
36b	Gary Nolan (SO 581)	20.00	10.00	6.00
37a	Sam McDowell (SO 1966)	13.50	6.75	4.00
37b	Sam McDowell (SO 1967)	20.00	6.75	4.00
38	Amos Otis	13.50	6.75	4.00
39a	Ray Fosse (RBI 69)	13.50	6.75	4.00
39b	Ray Fosse (RBI 70)	20.00	10.00	6.00
40a	Mel Stottlemyre (SO 881)	13.50	6.75	4.00
40b	Mel Stottlemyre (SO 880)	20.00	6.75	4.00
41a	Cito Gaston (Runs 112)	13.50	6.75	4.00
41b	Cito Gaston (Runs 113)	13.50	6.75	4.00
42a	Dick Dietz (RBI 200)	13.50	6.75	4.00
42b	Dick Dietz (RBI 199)	20.00	6.75	4.00
43	Roy White	13.50	6.75	4.00
44	Al Kaline	30.00	15.00	9.00
45a	Carlos May (His 272)	13.50	6.75	4.00
45b	Carlos May (His 273)	20.00	6.75	4.00
46a	Tommie Agee (RBI 313)	13.50	6.75	4.00
46b	Tommie Agee (RBI 314)	20.00	10.00	6.00
47	Tommy Harper	13.50	6.75	4.00
48a	Larry Dierker (SO 875)	13.50	6.75	4.00
48b	Larry Dierker (SO 874)	20.00	6.75	4.00
49a	Mike Cuellar (SO 987)	13.50	6.75	4.00
49b	Mike Cuellar (SO 990)	20.00	6.75	4.00
50	Ernie Banks	30.00	15.00	9.00
51	Bob Gibson	25.00	12.50	7.50
52	Reggie Smith	13.50	6.75	4.00
53a	Matty Alou (RBI 273)	13.50	6.75	4.00
53b	Matty Alou (RBI 274)	20.00	10.00	6.00
54a	Alex Johnson (California state logo.)	13.50	6.75	4.00
54b	Alex Johnson (Angels crest logo.)	20.00	10.00	6.00
55	Harmon Killebrew	30.00	15.00	9.00
56	Billy Grabarkewitz	13.50	6.75	4.00
57	Rich Allen	17.50	8.75	5.25
58	Tony Perez	25.00	12.50	7.50
59a	Dave McNally (SO 1065)	13.50	6.75	4.00
59b	Dave McNally (SO 1067)	20.00	10.00	6.00
60a	Jim Palmer (SO 564)	25.00	12.50	7.50
60b	Jim Palmer (SO 567)	30.00	15.00	9.00
61	Billy Williams	25.00	12.50	7.50
62a	Joe Torre (Hits 1463)	20.00	10.00	6.00
62b	Joe Torre (Hits 1464)	35.00	10.00	6.00
63a	Jim Northrup (AB 2773)	13.50	6.75	4.00
63b	Jim Northrup (AB 2772)	20.00	10.00	6.00
64a	Jim Fregosi (Calif. state logo - Hits 1326)	13.50	6.75	4.00
64b	Jim Fregosi (Calif. state logo - Hits 1327)	20.00	10.00	6.00
64c	Jim Fregosi (Angels crest logo.)	20.00	10.00	6.00
65a	Pete Rose (RBI 486)	60.00	30.00	18.00
65b	Pete Rose (RBI 485)	85.00	30.00	18.00
66a	Bud Harrelson (RBI 112)	13.50	6.75	4.00
66b	Bud Harrelson (RBI 113)	20.00	10.00	6.00
67	Tony Taylor	13.50	6.75	4.00
68	Willie Stargell	25.00	12.50	7.50
69	Tony Horton	25.00	12.50	7.50
70a	Claude Osteen (#70 on back, ERA 3.86)	13.50	6.75	4.00
70b	Claude Osteen (No number on back)	20.00	13.00	6.75
70c	Claude Osteen (#70 on back, ERA 3.82)	25.00	13.00	6.75
71	Glenn Beckert	13.50	6.75	4.00
72	Nate Colbert	13.50	6.75	4.00
73a	Rick Monday (AB 1705)	13.50	6.75	4.00
73b	Rick Monday (AB 1704)	20.00	10.00	6.00
74a	Tommy John (BB 444)	20.00	10.00	6.00
74b	Tommy John (BB 443)	25.00	12.50	7.50
75	Chris Short	13.50	6.75	4.00

1972 Kellogg's

For 1972, Kellogg's reduced both the number of cards in its set and the dimensions of each card, moving to a 2-1/8" x 3-1/4" size and fixing the set at 54 cards. Once again, the cards were produced to simulate a 3-D effect (see description for 1970 Kellogg's). The set was available via a mail-in offer. The checklist includes variations which resulted from the correction of erroneous statistics on the backs of some cards. The complete set values quoted do not include the scarcer variations.

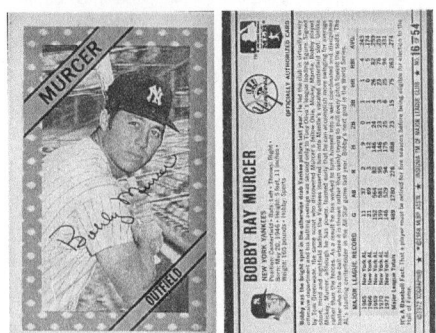

		NM	E	VG
	Complete Set (54):	135.00	65.00	35.00
	Common Player:	1.00	.50	.30
1a	Tom Seaver (1970 ERA 2.85)	10.00	5.00	3.00
1b	Tom Seaver (1970 ERA 2.81)	7.50	3.75	2.25
2	Amos Otis	1.00	.50	.30
3a	Willie Davis (Runs 842)	2.00	1.00	.60
3b	Willie Davis (Runs 841)	1.25	.60	.40
4	Wilbur Wood	1.00	.50	.30
5	Bill Parsons	1.00	.50	.30
6	Pete Rose	15.00	7.50	4.50
7a	Willie McCovey (HR 360)	6.00	3.00	1.75
7b	Willie McCovey (HR 370)	5.00	2.50	1.50
8	Fergie Jenkins	3.50	1.75	1.00
9a	Vida Blue (ERA 2.35)	2.00	1.00	.60
9b	Vida Blue (ERA 2.31)	1.25	.60	.40
10	Joe Torre	2.50	1.25	.70
11	Merv Rettenmund	1.00	.50	.30
12	Bill Melton	1.00	.50	.30
13a	Jim Palmer (Games 170)	6.00	3.00	1.75
13b	Jim Palmer (Games 168)	4.50	2.25	1.25
14	Doug Rader	1.00	.50	.30
15a	Dave Roberts (...Seaver, the NL leader...)	2.00	1.00	.60
15b	Dave Roberts (...Seaver, the league leader...)	1.25	.60	.40
16	Bobby Murcer	1.25	.60	.40
17	Wes Parker	1.00	.50	.30
18a	Joe Coleman (BB 394)	2.00	1.00	.60
18b	Joe Coleman (BB 393)	1.25	.60	.40
19	Manny Sanguillen	1.00	.50	.30
20	Reggie Jackson	10.00	5.00	3.00
21	Ralph Garr	1.00	.50	.30
22	Jim "Catfish" Hunter	3.50	1.75	1.00
23	Rick Wise	1.00	.50	.30
24	Glenn Beckert	1.00	.50	.30
25	Tony Oliva	1.00	.50	.30
26a	Bob Gibson (SO 2577)	6.00	3.00	1.75
26b	Bob Gibson (SO 2578)	4.50	2.25	1.25
27a	Mike Cuellar (1971 ERA 3.80)	2.00	1.00	.60
27b	Mike Cuellar (1971 ERA 3.08)	1.25	.60	.40
28	Chris Speier	1.00	.50	.30
29a	Dave McNally (ERA 3.18)	2.00	1.00	.60
29b	Dave McNally (ERA 3.15)	1.25	.60	.40
30	Chico Cardenas	1.00	.50	.30
31a	Bill Freehan (AVG. .263)	2.00	1.00	.60
31b	Bill Freehan (AVG. .262)	1.25	.60	.40
32a	Bud Harrelson (Hits 634)	2.00	1.00	.60
32b	Bud Harrelson (Hits 624)	1.25	.60	.40
33a	Sam McDowell (...less than 200 innings...)	2.00	1.00	.60
33b	Sam McDowell (...less than 225 innings...)	1.25	.60	.40
34a	Claude Osteen (1971 ERA 3.25)	2.00	1.00	.60
34b	Claude Osteen (1971 ERA 3.51)	1.25	.60	.40
35	Reggie Smith	1.00	.50	.30
36	Sonny Siebert	1.00	.50	.30
37	Lee May	1.00	.50	.30
38	Mickey Lolich	1.00	.50	.30
39a	Cookie Rojas (2B 149)	2.00	1.00	.60
39b	Cookie Rojas (2B 150)	1.25	.60	.40
40	Dick Drago	1.00	.50	.30
41	Nate Colbert	1.00	.50	.30
42	Andy Messersmith	1.00	.50	.30
43a	Dave Johnson (AVG. .262)	2.00	1.00	.60
43b	Dave Johnson (AVG. .264)	1.25	.60	.40
44	Steve Blass	1.00	.50	.30
45	Bob Robertson	1.00	.50	.30

		NM	E	VG
46a	Billy Williams (...missed only one last season...)	6.00	3.00	1.75
46b	Billy Williams (Phrase omitted.)	4.50	2.25	1.25
47	Juan Marichal	4.00	2.00	1.25
48	Lou Brock	4.00	2.00	1.25
49	Roberto Clemente	17.50	8.75	5.25
50	Mel Stottlemyre	1.00	.50	.30
51	Don Wilson	1.00	.50	.30
52a	Sal Bando (RBI 355)	2.00	1.00	.60
52b	Sal Bando (RBI 356)	1.25	.60	.40
53a	Willie Stargell (2B 197)	6.00	3.00	1.75
53b	Willie Stargell (2B 196)	4.50	2.25	1.25
54a	Willie Mays (RBI 1855)	15.00	7.50	4.50
54b	Willie Mays (RBI 1856)	12.00	6.00	3.50

1972 Kellogg's All-Time Baseball Greats

Kellogg's issued a second baseball card set in 1972, inserted into packages of breakfast rolls. The 2-1/4" x 3-1/2" cards also featured a simulated 3-D effect, but the 15 players in the set were "All-Time Baseball Greats," rather than current players. The set is virtually identical to a Rold Gold pretzel issue of 1970; the only difference being the 1972 copyright date on the back of the Kellog's cards, while the pretzel issue bears a 1970 date. The pretzel cards are considerably scarcer than the Kellogg's.

		NM	E	VG
	Complete Set (15):	45.00	22.50	13.50
	Common Player:	2.50	1.25	.70
1	Walter Johnson	3.50	1.75	1.00
2	Rogers Hornsby	2.50	1.25	.70
3	John McGraw	2.50	1.25	.70
4	Mickey Cochrane	2.50	1.25	.70
5	George Sisler	2.50	1.25	.70
6	Babe Ruth (Portrait photo on back.)	15.00	7.50	4.50
7	Robert "Lefty" Grove	2.50	1.25	.70
8	Harold "Pie" Traynor	2.50	1.25	.70
9	Honus Wagner	5.00	2.50	1.50
10	Eddie Collins	2.50	1.25	.70
11	Tris Speaker	2.50	1.25	.70
12	Cy Young	3.50	1.75	1.00
13	Lou Gehrig	10.00	5.00	3.00
14	Babe Ruth (Action photo on back.)	15.00	7.50	4.50
15	Ty Cobb	10.00	5.00	3.00

1973 Kellogg's

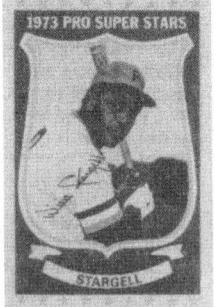 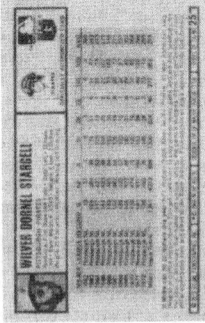

The lone exception to Kellogg's long run of simulated 3-D effect cards came in 1973, when the cereal company's 54-card set was produced by "normal" printing methods. In 2-1/4" x 3-1/2" size, the design was otherwise quite compatible with the issues which preceded and succeeded it. Because it was available via a mail-in offer ($1.25 and two Raisin Bran boxtops), it is not as scarce as the earlier Kellogg's issues.

	NM	E	VG

		NM	E	VG
	Complete Set (54):	65.00	32.50	20.00
	Common Player:	.90	.45	.25
1	Amos Otis	.90	.45	.25
2	Ellie Rodriguez	.90	.45	.25
3	Mickey Lolich	.90	.45	.25
4	Tony Oliva	1.25	.60	.40
5	Don Sutton	3.50	1.75	1.00
6	Pete Rose	12.00	6.00	3.50
7	Steve Carlton	4.50	2.25	1.25
8	Bobby Bonds	.90	.45	.25
9	Wilbur Wood	.90	.45	.25
10	Billy Williams	4.50	2.25	1.25
11	Steve Blass	.90	.45	.25
12	Jon Matlack	.90	.45	.25
13	Cesar Cedeno	.90	.45	.25
14	Bob Gibson	4.50	2.25	1.25
15	Sparky Lyle	.90	.45	.25
16	Nolan Ryan	17.50	8.75	5.25
17	Jim Palmer	4.50	2.25	1.25
18	Ray Fosse	.90	.45	.25
19	Bobby Murcer	.90	.45	.25
20	Jim "Catfish" Hunter	3.50	1.75	1.00
21	Tug McGraw	.90	.45	.25
22	Reggie Jackson	9.00	4.50	2.75
23	Bill Stoneman	.90	.45	.25
24	Lou Piniella	.90	.45	.25
25	Willie Stargell	4.50	2.25	1.25
26	Dick Allen	2.50	1.25	.70
27	Carlton Fisk	4.50	2.25	1.25
28	Fergie Jenkins	3.50	1.75	1.00
29	Phil Niekro	3.50	1.75	1.00
30	Gary Nolan	.90	.45	.25
31	Joe Torre	2.50	1.25	.70
32	Bobby Tolan	.90	.45	.25
33	Nate Colbert	.90	.45	.25
34	Joe Morgan	4.50	2.25	1.25
35	Bert Blyleven	3.50	.45	.25
36	Joe Rudi	.90	.45	.25
37	Ralph Garr	.90	.45	.25
38	Gaylord Perry	3.50	1.75	1.00
39	Bobby Grich	.90	.45	.25
40	Lou Brock	4.00	2.00	1.25
41	Pete Broberg	.90	.45	.25
42	Manny Sanguillen	.90	.45	.25
43	Willie Davis	.90	.45	.25
44	Dave Kingman	.90	.45	.25
45	Carlos May	.90	.45	.25
46	Tom Seaver	6.00	3.00	1.75
47	Mike Cuellar	.90	.45	.25
48	Joe Coleman	.90	.45	.25
49	Claude Osteen	.90	.45	.25
50	Steve Kline	.90	.45	.25
51	Rod Carew	4.50	2.25	1.25
52	Al Kaline	6.00	3.00	1.75
53	Larry Dierker	.90	.45	.25
54	Ron Santo	2.50	1.25	.70

1974 Kellogg's

For 1974, Kellogg's returned to the use of simulated 3-D for its 54-player baseball card issue (see 1970 Kellogg's listing for description). In 2-1/8" x 3-1/4" size, the cards were available as a complete set via a mail-in offer. The complete set price listed here does not include the more expensive variations.

		NM	E	VG
	Complete Set (54):	65.00	32.50	20.00
	Common Player:	.90	.45	.25
1	Bob Gibson	3.50	1.75	1.00
2	Rick Monday	.90	.45	.25
3	Joe Coleman	.90	.45	.25
4	Bert Campaneris	.90	.45	.25
5	Carlton Fisk	4.00	2.00	1.25
6	Jim Palmer	3.50	1.75	1.00
7a	Ron Santo (Chicago Cubs)	2.25	1.25	.70
7b	Ron Santo (Chicago White Sox)	1.25	.60	.40
8	Nolan Ryan	16.00	8.00	4.75
9	Greg Luzinski	.90	.45	.25
10a	Buddy Bell (Runs 134)	2.25	1.25	.70
10b	Buddy Bell (Runs 135)	1.00	.50	.30
11	Bob Watson	.90	.45	.25
12	Bill Singer	.90	.45	.25
13	Dave May	.90	.45	.25
14	Jim Brewer	.90	.45	.25
15	Manny Sanguillen	.90	.45	.25
16	Jeff Burroughs	.90	.45	.25
17	Amos Otis	.90	.45	.25
18	Ed Goodson	.90	.45	.25
19	Nate Colbert	.90	.45	.25
20	Reggie Jackson	6.50	3.25	2.00
21	Ted Simmons	.90	.45	.25
22	Bobby Murcer	1.00	.50	.30
23	Willie Horton	1.00	.50	.30
24	Orlando Cepeda	3.50	1.75	1.00
25	Ron Hunt	.90	.45	.25
26	Wayne Twitchell	.90	.45	.25
27	Ron Fairly	.90	.45	.25
28	Johnny Bench	4.50	2.25	1.25
29	John Mayberry	.90	.45	.25
30	Rod Carew	4.00	2.00	1.25
31	Ken Holtzman	.90	.45	.25
32	Billy Williams	3.50	1.75	1.00
33	Dick Allen	1.50	.70	.45
34a	Wilbur Wood (SO 959)	1.50	.70	.45
34b	Wilbur Wood (SO 960)	1.00	.50	.30
35	Danny Thompson	.90	.45	.25
36	Joe Morgan	3.50	1.75	1.00
37	Willie Stargell	3.50	1.75	1.00
38	Pete Rose	10.00	5.00	3.00
39	Bobby Bonds	.90	.45	.25
40	Chris Speier	.90	.45	.25
41	Sparky Lyle	.90	.45	.25
42	Cookie Rojas	.90	.45	.25
43	Tommy Davis	.90	.45	.25
44	Jim "Catfish" Hunter	3.50	1.75	1.00
45	Willie Davis	.90	.45	.25
46	Bert Blyleven	3.50	.45	.25
47	Pat Kelly	.90	.45	.25
48	Ken Singleton	.90	.45	.25
49	Manny Mota	.90	.45	.25
50	Dave Johnson	.90	.45	.25
51	Sal Bando	.90	.45	.25
52	Tom Seaver	4.50	2.25	1.25
53	Felix Millan	.90	.45	.25
54	Ron Blomberg	.90	.45	.25

1975 Kellogg's

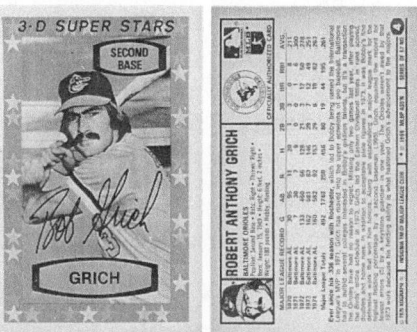

While the card size remained the same at 2-1/8" x 3-1/4", the size of the 1975 Kellogg's "3-D" set was increased by three, to 57 cards. Despite the fact cards could be obtained by a mail-in offer, as well as in cereal boxes, the '75 Kellogg's are noticeably scarcer than the company's other issues, with the exception of the 1971 set. Also helping to raise the value of the cards is the presence of an unusually large number of current and future Hall of Famers.

		NM	E	VG
	Complete Set (57):	175.00	90.00	55.00
	Common Player:	2.00	1.00	.60
1	Roy White	2.00	1.00	.60
2	Ross Grimsley	2.00	1.00	.60
3	Reggie Smith	2.00	1.00	.60
4a	Bob Grich ("...1973 work..." in last line)	3.00	1.50	.90
4b	Bob Grich (no "...1973 work...")	2.00	1.00	.60
5	Greg Gross	2.00	1.00	.60
6	Bob Watson	2.00	1.00	.60
7	Johnny Bench	10.00	5.00	3.00
8	Jeff Burroughs	2.00	1.00	.60
9	Elliott Maddox	2.00	1.00	.60
10	Jon Matlack	2.00	1.00	.60
11	Pete Rose	25.00	12.50	7.50
12	Leroy Stanton	2.00	1.00	.60
13	Bake McBride	2.00	1.00	.60
14	Jorge Orta	2.00	1.00	.60
15	Al Oliver	2.50	1.25	.70
16	John Briggs	2.00	1.00	.60
17	Steve Garvey	4.50	2.25	1.25
18	Brooks Robinson	10.00	5.00	3.00
19	John Hiller	2.00	1.00	.60
20	Lynn McGlothen	2.00	1.00	.60
21	Cleon Jones	2.00	1.00	.60
22	Fergie Jenkins	6.00	3.00	1.75
23	Bill North	2.00	1.00	.60
24	Steve Busby	2.00	1.00	.60
25	Richie Zisk	2.00	1.00	.60
26	Nolan Ryan	35.00	17.50	10.50
27	Joe Morgan	7.50	3.75	2.25
28	Joe Rudi	2.00	1.00	.60
29	Jose Cardenal	2.00	1.00	.60
30	Andy Messersmith	2.00	1.00	.60
31	Willie Montanez	2.00	1.00	.60
32	Bill Buckner	2.00	1.00	.60
33	Rod Carew	7.50	3.75	2.25
34	Lou Piniella	2.50	1.25	.70
35	Ralph Garr	2.00	1.00	.60
36	Mike Marshall	2.00	1.00	.60
37	Garry Maddox	2.00	1.00	.60
38	Dwight Evans	2.00	1.00	.60
39	Lou Brock	7.50	3.75	2.25
40	Ken Singleton	2.00	1.00	.60
41	Steve Braun	2.00	1.00	.60
42	Dick Allen	3.50	1.75	1.00
43	Johnny Grubb	2.00	1.00	.60
44a	Jim Hunter (Oakland)	9.00	4.50	2.75
44b	Jim Hunter (New York)	7.50	3.75	2.25
45	Gaylord Perry	6.00	3.00	1.75
46	George Hendrick	2.00	1.00	.60
47	Sparky Lyle	2.00	1.00	.60
48	Dave Cash	2.00	1.00	.60
49	Luis Tiant	2.00	1.00	.60
50	Cesar Geronimo	2.00	1.00	.60
51	Carl Yastrzemski	12.00	6.00	3.50
52	Ken Brett	2.00	1.00	.60
53	Hal McRae	2.00	1.00	.60
54	Reggie Jackson	15.00	7.50	4.50
55	Rollie Fingers	6.00	3.00	1.75
56	Mike Schmidt	15.00	7.50	4.50
57	Richie Hebner	2.00	1.00	.60

1976 Kellogg's

A sizeable list of corrected errors and other variation cards dots the checklist for the 57-card 1976 Kellogg's 3-D set. Again containing 57 cards, the first three cards in the set are found far less often than cards #4-57, indicating they were short-printed in relation to the rest of the set. The complete set values quoted below do not include the scarcer variation cards. Card size remained at 2-1/8" x 3-1/4". Cards #1-3 were significantly short-printed.

		NM	E	VG
	Complete Set (57):	70.00	35.00	20.00
	Common Player:	1.25	.60	.40
1	Steve Hargan	10.00	5.00	3.00
2	Claudell Washington	10.00	5.00	3.00
3	Don Gullett	10.00	5.00	3.00
4	Randy Jones	1.25	.60	.40
5	Jim "Catfish" Hunter	3.50	1.75	1.00
6a	Clay Carroll (Cincinnati)	2.25	1.25	.70
6b	Clay Carroll (Chicago)	1.25	.60	.40
7	Joe Rudi	1.25	.60	.40
8	Reggie Jackson	9.00	4.50	2.75
9	Felix Millan	1.25	.60	.40
10	Jim Rice	4.00	1.00	.60
11	Bert Blyleven	3.50	.60	.40
12	Ken Singleton	1.25	.60	.40
13	Don Sutton	3.50	1.75	1.00
14	Joe Morgan	4.00	2.00	1.25
15	Dave Parker	1.50	.70	.45
16	Dave Cash	1.25	.60	.40
17	Ron LeFlore	1.25	.60	.40
18	Greg Luzinski	1.25	.60	.40

19	Dennis Eckersley	6.00	3.00	1.75
20	Bill Madlock	1.25	.60	.40
21	George Scott	1.25	.60	.40
22	Willie Stargell	4.00	2.00	1.25
23	Al Hrabosky	1.25	.60	.40
24	Carl Yastrzemski	7.50	3.75	2.25
25a	Jim Kaat (White Sox logo on back.)	3.00	1.50	.90
25b	Jim Kaat (Phillies logo on back.)	1.50	.70	.45
26	Marty Perez	1.25	.60	.40
27	Bob Watson	1.25	.60	.40
28	Eric Soderholm	1.25	.60	.40
29	Bill Lee	1.25	.60	.40
30a	Frank Tanana (1975 ERA 2.63)	2.00	1.00	.60
30b	Frank Tanana (1975 ERA 2.62)	1.25	.60	.40
31	Fred Lynn	1.50	.70	.45
32a	Tom Seaver (1967 PCT. 552)	7.50	3.75	2.25
32b	Tom Seaver (1967 Pct. .552)	6.00	3.00	1.75
33	Steve Busby	1.25	.60	.40
34	Gary Carter	4.00	2.00	1.25
35	Rick Wise	1.25	.60	.40
36	Johnny Bench	5.00	2.50	1.50
37	Jim Palmer	4.00	2.00	1.25
38	Bobby Murcer	1.50	.70	.45
39	Von Joshua	1.25	.60	.40
40	Lou Brock	4.00	2.00	1.25
41a	Mickey Rivers (last line begins "In three...")	2.00	1.00	.60
41b	Mickey Rivers (last line begins "The Yankees...")	1.25	.60	.40
42	Manny Sanguillen	1.25	.60	.40
43	Jerry Reuss	1.25	.60	.40
44	Ken Griffey	1.25	.60	.40
45a	Jorge Orta (AB 1616)	1.75	.90	.50
45b	Jorge Orta (AB 1615)	1.25	.60	.40
46	John Mayberry	1.25	.60	.40
47a	Vida Blue (2nd line reads "...pitched more innings ...")	2.25	1.25	.70
47b	Vida Blue (2nd line reads "...struck out more...")	1.25	.60	.40
48	Rod Carew	4.00	2.00	1.25
49a	Jon Matlack (1975 ER 87)	1.75	.90	.50
49b	Jon Matlack (1975 ER 86)	1.25	.60	.40
50	Boog Powell	2.25	1.25	.70
51a	Mike Hargrove (AB 935)	1.75	.90	.50
51b	Mike Hargrove (AB 934)	1.25	.60	.40
52a	Paul Lindblad (1975 ERA 2.72)	1.75	.90	.50
52b	Paul Lindblad (1975 ERA 2.73)	1.25	.60	.40
53	Thurman Munson	4.00	2.00	1.25
54	Steve Garvey	2.50	1.25	.70
55	Pete Rose	12.50	6.25	3.75
56a	Greg Gross (Games 302)	1.75	.90	.50
56b	Greg Gross (Games 334)	1.25	.60	.40
57	Ted Simmons	1.25	.60	.40

1977 Kellogg's

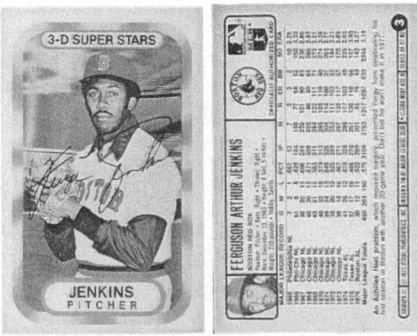

Other than another innovative card design to complement the simulated 3-D effect, there was little change in the 1977 Kellogg's issue. Set size remained at 57 cards, the set remained in the 2-1/8" x 3-1/4" format, and the cards were available either individually in boxes of cereal, or as a complete set via a mail-in box top offer. The 1977 set is the last in which Kellogg's used a player portrait photo on the back of the card.

		NM	E	VG
	Complete Set (57):	60.00	30.00	18.00
	Common Player:	.75	.40	.25
1	George Foster	.75	.40	.25
2	Bert Campaneris	.75	.40	.25
3	Fergie Jenkins	2.50	1.25	.70

4	Dock Ellis	.75	.40	.25
5	John Montefusco	.75	.40	.25
6	George Brett	12.50	6.25	3.75
7	John Candelaria	.75	.40	.25
8	Fred Norman	.75	.40	.25
9	Bill Travers	.75	.40	.25
10	Hal McRae	.75	.40	.25
11	Doug Rau	.75	.40	.25
12	Greg Luzinski	.75	.40	.25
13	Ralph Garr	.75	.40	.25
14	Steve Garvey	1.50	.70	.45
15	Rick Manning	.75	.40	.25
16a	Lyman Bostock (Back photo is N.Y. Yankee Dock Ellis.)	7.50	3.75	2.25
16b	Lyman Bostock (Correct back photo.)	.75	.40	.25
17	Randy Jones	.75	.40	.25
18a	Ron Cey (58 homers in first sentence)	1.00	.50	.30
18b	Ron Cey (48 homers in first sentence)	.75	.40	.25
19	Dave Parker	.75	.40	.25
20	Pete Rose	15.00	7.50	4.50
21a	Wayne Garland (Last line begins "Prior to...")	1.00	.50	.30
21b	Wayne Garland (Last line begins "There he...")	.75	.40	.25
22	Bill North	.75	.40	.25
23	Thurman Munson	4.50	2.25	1.25
24	Tom Poquette	.75	.40	.25
25	Ron LeFlore	.75	.40	.25
26	Mark Fidrych	1.00	.50	.30
27	Sixto Lezcano	.75	.40	.25
28	Dave Winfield	7.50	3.75	2.25
29	Jerry Koosman	.75	.40	.25
30	Mike Hargrove	.75	.40	.25
31	Willie Montanez	.75	.40	.25
32	Don Stanhouse	.75	.40	.25
33	Jay Johnstone	.75	.40	.25
34	Bake McBride	.75	.40	.25
35	Dave Kingman	.75	.40	.25
36	Freddie Patek	.75	.40	.25
37	Garry Maddox	.75	.40	.25
38a	Ken Reitz (Last line begins "The previous...")	1.00	.50	.30
38b	Ken Reitz (Last line begins "In late...")	.75	.40	.25
39	Bobby Grich	.75	.40	.25
40	Cesar Geronimo	.75	.40	.25
41	Jim Lonborg	.75	.40	.25
42	Ed Figueroa	.75	.40	.25
43	Bill Madlock	.75	.40	.25
44	Jerry Remy	.75	.40	.25
45	Frank Tanana	.75	.40	.25
46	Al Oliver	1.00	.50	.30
47	Charlie Hough	.75	.40	.25
48	Lou Piniella	1.00	.50	.30
49	Ken Griffey	.75	.40	.25
50	Jose Cruz	.75	.40	.25
51	Rollie Fingers	2.50	1.25	.70
52	Chris Chambliss	.75	.40	.25
53	Rod Carew	4.50	2.25	1.25
54	Andy Messersmith	.75	.40	.25
55	Mickey Rivers	.75	.40	.25
56	Butch Wynegar	.75	.40	.25
57	Steve Carlton	3.50	1.75	1.00

1978 Kellogg's

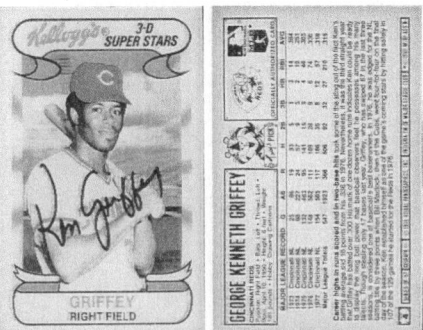

Besides the substitution of a Tony the Tiger drawing for a player portrait photo on the back of the card, the 1978 Kellogg's set offered no major changes from the previous few years issues. Cards were once again in the 2-1/8" x 3-1/4" format, with 57 cards comprising a complete set. Single cards were available in selected brands of the company's cereal, while complete sets could be obtained by a mail-in offer.

		NM	E	VG

	Complete Set (57):	60.00	30.00	18.00
	Common Player:	.90	.45	.25
1	Steve Carlton	4.50	2.25	1.25
2	Bucky Dent	1.25	.60	.40
3	Mike Schmidt	13.50	6.75	4.00
4	Ken Griffey	.90	.45	.25
5	Al Cowens	.90	.45	.25
6	George Brett	13.50	6.75	4.00
7	Lou Brock	4.50	2.25	1.25
8	Rich Gossage	1.25	.60	.40
9	Tom Johnson	.90	.45	.25
10	George Foster	.90	.45	.25
11	Dave Winfield	4.50	2.25	1.25
12	Dan Meyer	.90	.45	.25
13	Chris Chambliss	.90	.45	.25
14	Paul Dade	.90	.45	.25
15	Jeff Burroughs	.90	.45	.25
16	Jose Cruz	.90	.45	.25
17	Mickey Rivers	.90	.45	.25
18	John Candelaria	.90	.45	.25
19	Ellis Valentine	.90	.45	.25
20	Hal McRae	.90	.45	.25
21	Dave Rozema	.90	.45	.25
22	Lenny Randle	.90	.45	.25
23	Willie McCovey	4.50	2.25	1.25
24	Ron Cey	.90	.45	.25
25	Eddie Murray	17.50	8.75	5.25
26	Larry Bowa	.90	.45	.25
27	Tom Seaver	5.00	2.50	1.50
28	Garry Maddox	.90	.45	.25
29	Rod Carew	4.50	2.25	1.25
30	Thurman Munson	4.50	2.25	1.25
31	Garry Templeton	.90	.45	.25
32	Eric Soderholm	.90	.45	.25
33	Greg Luzinski	.90	.45	.25
34	Reggie Smith	.90	.45	.25
35	Dave Goltz	.90	.45	.25
36	Tommy John	1.25	.60	.40
37	Ralph Garr	.90	.45	.25
38	Alan Bannister	.90	.45	.25
39	Bob Bailor	.90	.45	.25
40	Reggie Jackson	12.00	6.00	3.50
41	Cecil Cooper	.90	.45	.25
42	Burt Hooton	.90	.45	.25
43	Sparky Lyle	.90	.45	.25
44	Steve Ontiveros	.90	.45	.25
45	Rick Reuschel	.90	.45	.25
46	Lyman Bostock	.90	.45	.25
47	Mitchell Page	.90	.45	.25
48	Bruce Sutter	3.50	1.75	1.00
49	Jim Rice	4.50	1.25	.70
50	Bob Forsch	.90	.45	.25
51	Nolan Ryan	17.50	8.75	5.25
52	Dave Parker	.90	.45	.25
53	Bert Blyleven	3.50	.45	.25
54	Frank Tanana	.90	.45	.25
55	Ken Singleton	.90	.45	.25
56	Mike Hargrove	.90	.45	.25
57	Don Sutton	3.50	1.75	1.00

1979 Kellogg's

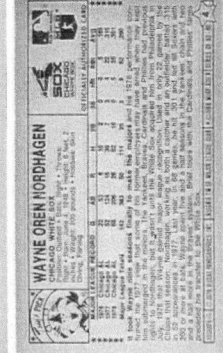

For its 1979 3-D issue, Kellogg's increased the size of the set to 60 cards, but reduced the width of the cards to 1-15/16". Depth stayed the same as in previous years, 3-1/4". The narrower card format seems to have compounded the problem of curling and subsequent cracking of the ribbed plastic surface which helps give the card a 3-D effect. Cards with major cracks can be graded no higher than VG. The complete set price in the checklist that follows does not include the scarcer variations. Numerous minor variations featuring copyright and trademark logos can be found in the set.

		NM	E	VG
	Complete Set (60):	30.00	15.00	9.00
	Common Player:	.60	.30	.20
1	Bruce Sutter	2.50	1.25	.70

		NM	E	VG
2	Ted Simmons	.60	.30	.20
3	Ross Grimsley	.60	.30	.20
4	Wayne Nordhagen	.60	.30	.20
5a	Jim Palmer (PCT. .649)	3.00	1.50	.90
5b	Jim Palmer (PCT. .650)	3.00	1.50	.90
6	John Henry Johnson	.60	.30	.20
7	Jason Thompson	.60	.30	.20
8	Pat Zachry	.60	.30	.20
9	Dennis Eckersley	3.00	1.50	.90
10a	Paul Splittorff (IP 1665)	.60	.30	.20
10b	Paul Splittorff (IP 1666)	.60	.30	.20
11a	Ron Guidry (Hits 397)	.60	.30	.20
11b	Ron Guidry (Hits 396)	.60	.30	.20
12	Jeff Burroughs	.60	.30	.20
13	Rod Carew	3.00	1.50	.90
14a	Buddy Bell (No trade line in bio.)	1.00	.50	.30
14b	Buddy Bell (Trade line in bio.)	.60	.30	.20
15	Jim Rice	1.00	.50	.30
16	Garry Maddox	.60	.30	.20
17	Willie McCovey	3.00	1.50	.90
18	Steve Carlton	3.00	1.50	.90
19a	J. R. Richard (Stats begin with 1972.)	.60	.30	.20
19b	J. R. Richard (Stats begin with 1971.)	.60	.30	.20
20	Paul Molitor	3.00	1.50	.90
21a	Dave Parker (AVG. .281)	.60	.30	.20
21b	Dave Parker (AVG. .318)	.60	.30	.20
22a	Pete Rose (1978 3B 3)	7.50	3.75	2.25
22b	Pete Rose (1978 3B 33)	7.50	3.75	2.25
23a	Vida Blue (Runs 819)	.60	.30	.20
23b	Vida Blue (Runs 818)	.60	.30	.20
24	Richie Zisk	.60	.30	.20
25a	Darrell Porter (2B 101)	.60	.30	.20
25b	Darrell Porter (2B 111)	.60	.30	.20
26a	Dan Driessen (Games 642)	.60	.30	.20
26b	Dan Driessen (Games 742)	.60	.30	.20
27a	Geoff Zahn (1978 Minnessota)	.60	.30	.20
27b	Geoff Zahn (1978 Minnesota)	.60	.30	.20
28	Phil Niekro	2.50	1.25	.70
29	Tom Seaver	3.00	1.50	.90
30	Fred Lynn	.60	.30	.20
31	Bill Bonham	.60	.30	.20
32	George Foster	.60	.30	.20
33a	Terry Puhl (Last line of bio begins "Terry...")	.60	.30	.20
33b	Terry Puhl (Last line of bio begins "His...")	.60	.30	.20
34a	John Candelaria (Age is 24.)	.60	.30	.20
34b	John Candelaria (Age is 25.)	.60	.30	.20
35	Bob Knepper	.60	.30	.20
36	Freddie Patek	.60	.30	.20
37	Chris Chambliss	.60	.30	.20
38a	Bob Forsch (1977 Games 86)	.60	.30	.20
38b	Bob Forsch (1977 Games 35)	.60	.30	.20
39a	Ken Griffey (1978 AB 674)	.60	.30	.20
39b	Ken Griffey (1978 AB 614)	.60	.30	.20
40	Jack Clark	.60	.30	.20
41a	Dwight Evans (1978 Hits 13)	.60	.30	.20
41b	Dwight Evans (1978 Hits 123)	.60	.30	.20
42	Lee Mazzilli	.60	.30	.20
43	Mario Guerrero	.60	.30	.20
44	Larry Bowa	.60	.30	.20
45a	Carl Yastrzemski (Games 9930)	4.00	2.00	1.25
45b	Carl Yastrzemski (Games 9929)	4.00	2.00	1.25
46a	Reggie Jackson (1978 Games 162)	6.00	3.00	1.75
46b	Reggie Jackson (1978 Games 139)	6.00	3.00	1.75
47	Rick Reuschel	.60	.30	.20
48a	Mike Flanagan (1976 SO 57)	.60	.30	.20
48b	Mike Flanagan (1976 SO 56)	.60	.30	.20
49a	Gaylord Perry (1973 Hits 325)	2.50	1.25	.70
49b	Gaylord Perry (1973 Hits 315)	2.50	1.25	.70
50	George Brett	6.00	3.00	1.75
51a	Craig Reynolds (Last line of bio begins "He spent...")	.60	.30	.20
51b	Craig Reynolds (Last line of bio begins "In those...")	.60	.30	.20

52	Davey Lopes	.60	.30	.20
53a	Bill Almon (2B 31)	.60	.30	.20
53b	Bill Almon (2B 41)	.60	.30	.20
54	Roy Howell	.60	.30	.20
55	Frank Tanana	.60	.30	.20
56a	Doug Rau (1978 PCT. .577)	.60	.30	.20
56b	Doug Rau (1978 PCT. .625)	.60	.30	.20
57a	Rick Monday (1976 Runs 197)	.60	.30	.20
57b	Rick Monday (1976 Runs 107)	.60	.30	.20
58	Jon Matlack	.60	.30	.20
59a	Ron Jackson (Last line of bio begins "His best...")	.60	.30	.20
59b	Ron Jackson (Last line of bio begins "The Twins...")	.60	.30	.20
60	Jim Sundberg	.60	.30	.20

1980 Kellogg's

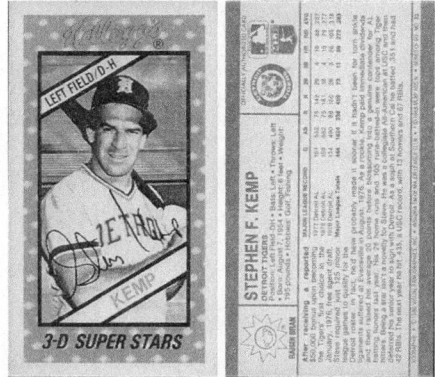

The 1980 cereal company issue featured the narrowest format of any Kellogg's card, 1-7/8" x 3-1/4". For the second straight year, set size remained at 60 cards, available either singly in boxes of cereal, or as complete sets by a mail-in offer.

		NM	E	VG
	Complete Set (60):	25.00	12.50	7.50
	Common Player:	.60	.30	.20
1	Ross Grimsley	.60	.30	.20
2	Mike Schmidt	4.00	2.00	1.25
3	Mike Flanagan	.60	.30	.20
4	Ron Guidry	.60	.30	.20
5	Bert Blyleven	2.50	.30	.20
6	Dave Kingman	.60	.30	.20
7	Jeff Newman	.60	.30	.20
8	Steve Rogers	.60	.30	.20
9	George Brett	4.00	2.00	1.25
10	Bruce Sutter	2.00	1.00	.60
11	Gorman Thomas	.60	.30	.20
12	Darrell Porter	.60	.30	.20
13	Roy Smalley	.60	.30	.20
14	Steve Carlton	2.00	1.00	.60
15	Jim Palmer	2.00	1.00	.60
16	Bob Bailor	.60	.30	.20
17	Jason Thompson	.60	.30	.20
18	Graig Nettles	.60	.30	.20
19	Ron Cey	.60	.30	.20
20	Nolan Ryan	7.50	3.75	2.25
21	Ellis Valentine	.60	.30	.20
22	Larry Hisle	.60	.30	.20
23	Dave Parker	.60	.30	.20
24	Eddie Murray	2.00	1.00	.60
25	Willie Stargell	2.00	1.00	.60
26	Reggie Jackson	4.00	2.00	1.25
27	Carl Yastrzemski	2.50	1.25	.70
28	Andre Thornton	.60	.30	.20
29	Davey Lopes	.60	.30	.20
30	Ken Singleton	.60	.30	.20
31	Steve Garvey	1.00	.50	.30
32	Dave Winfield	2.00	1.00	.60
33	Steve Kemp	.60	.30	.20
34	Claudell Washington	.60	.30	.20
35	Pete Rose	6.00	3.00	1.75
36	Cesar Cedeno	.60	.30	.20
37	John Stearns	.60	.30	.20
38	Lee Mazzilli	.60	.30	.20
39	Larry Bowa	.60	.30	.20
40	Fred Lynn	.60	.30	.20
41	Carlton Fisk	2.00	1.00	.60
42	Vida Blue	.60	.30	.20
43	Keith Hernandez	.60	.30	.20
44	Jim Rice	2.00	.50	.30
45	Ted Simmons	.60	.30	.20
46	Chet Lemon	.60	.30	.20

		NM	E	VG
47	Fergie Jenkins	2.00	1.00	.60
48	Gary Matthews	.60	.30	.20
49	Tom Seaver	2.50	1.25	.70
50	George Foster	.60	.30	.20
51	Phil Niekro	2.00	1.00	.60
52	Johnny Bench	2.50	1.25	.70
53	Buddy Bell	.60	.30	.20
54	Lance Parrish	.60	.30	.20
55	Joaquin Andujar	.60	.30	.20
56	Don Baylor	.60	.30 ·	.20
57	Jack Clark	.60	.30	.20
58	J.R. Richard	.60	.30	.20
59	Bruce Bochte	.60	.30	.20
60	Rod Carew	2.00	1.00	.60

1968 Kelly's Hamburgers Rico Petrocelli

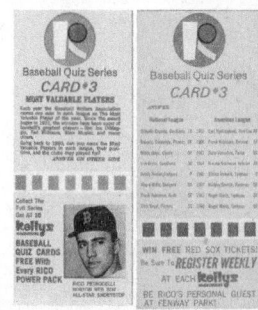

This series of 10 baseball quiz question cards was given away with purchases of Rico Power Pack meals at Boston-area Kelly's Hamburgers restaurants. The cards are 3" x 7" and printed in yellow, red and green, with the color scheme varying on different cards. The portrait of the Red Sox shortstop is the same on each card and printed in black-and-white.

	NM	EX	VG
Complete Set (10):	150.00	75.00	45.00
1-10 Rico Petrocelli	15.00	7.50	4.50

1969 Kelly's Potato Chips Pins

Consisting of 20 pins, each measuring approximately 1-3/16" in diameter, this set was issued by Kelly's Potato Chips in 1969 and has a heavy emphasis on St. Louis Cardinals. The pin has a black-and-white player photo in the center surrounded by either a red border (for A.L. players) or a blue border (for N.L. players) that displays the player's team and name at the top and bottom. "Kelly's" appears to the left while the word "Zip!" is printed to the right. The pins are unnumbered.

		NM	E	VG
	Complete Set (20):	350.00	175.00	100.00
	Common Player:	5.00	2.50	1.50
(1)	Luis Aparicio	25.00	12.50	7.50
(2)	Ernie Banks	45.00	22.00	13.50
(3)	Glenn Beckert	5.00	2.50	1.50
(4)	Lou Brock	25.00	12.50	7.50
(5)	Curt Flood	5.00	2.50	1.50
(6)	Bob Gibson	25.00	12.50	7.50
(7)	Joel Horlen	5.00	2.50	1.50
(8)	Al Kaline	45.00	22.00	13.50
(9)	Don Kessinger	5.00	2.50	1.50
(10)	Mickey Lolich	5.00	2.50	1.50
(11)	Juan Marichal	25.00	12.50	7.50
(12)	Willie Mays	75.00	37.00	22.00
(13)	Tim McCarver	7.50	3.75	2.25
(14)	Denny McLain	6.00	3.00	1.75
(15)	Pete Rose	65.00	32.00	19.50
(16)	Ron Santo	7.50	3.75	2.25
(17)	Joe Torre	15.00	7.50	4.50
(18)	Pete Ward	5.00	2.50	1.50
(19)	Billy Williams	25.00	12.50	7.50
(20)	Carl Yastrzemski	60.00	30.00	18.00

1887 W.S. Kimball Champions (N184)

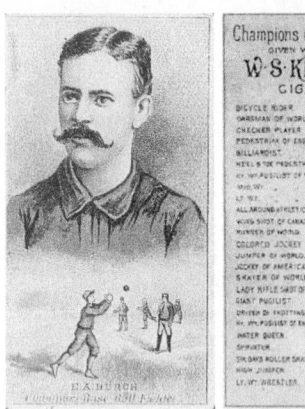

Similar to sets issued by Allen & Ginter and Goodwin, the Kimball tobacco company of Rochester, N.Y., issued its own 50-card set of "Champions of Games and Sport" in 1887, and included four baseball players among the "billiardists, girl riders, tight-rope walkers" and other popular celebrities featured in the series. Measuring 1-1/2" x 2-3/4", the color lithograped artwork on the card features a posed portrait, which occupies the top three-fourths, and a drawing of the player in action at the bottom. The back of the card contains an ad for Kimball Cigarettes along with a list of the various sports and activities depicted in the set. The Kimball promotion also included an album to house the card set.

	NM	E	VG
Complete Set (4):	8,000	4,000	2,400
Common Player:	2,000	1,000	600.00
Album:	4,125	1,650	1,000
(1) E.A. Burch	2,000	1,000	600.00
(2) Dell Darling	2,000	1,000	600.00
(3) Hardie Henderson	2,000	1,000	600.00
(4) James O'Neil (O'Neill)	2,000	1,000	600.00

1957-1959 Kiwanis Orioles Clinic

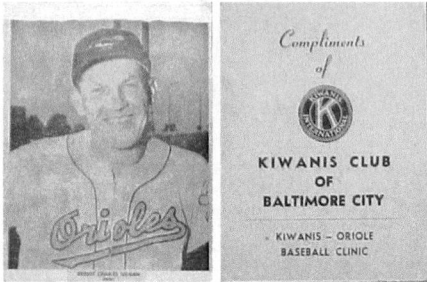

Details are lacking on this card which may or may not have been part of a series. Unless or until further players are checklisted, it is impossible to date the issue any more precisely. The front of the 2-7/8" x 3-1/4" card has a sepia photo that appears to have been copied from a team-issued postcard or picture. On back is the Kiwanis International logo with "Compliments / of" above and "KIWANIS CLUB / OF / BALTIMORE CITY / KIWANIS - ORIOLE / BASEBALL CLINIC" below.

	NM	E	VG
Bob Nieman	40.00	20.00	12.00

1955-1957 Ted Kluszewski Steak House

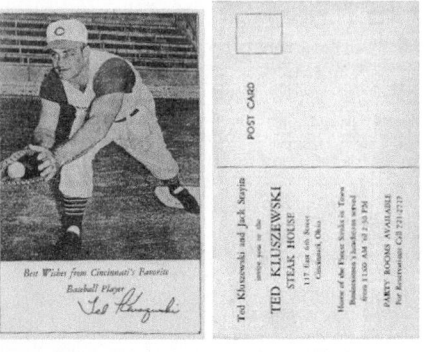

The true scope of this issue combined with the related Charcoal Steak House card (see also) is not known. Based on cards showing Klu in Reds and Angels uniforms, it is possible examples may yet be seen in Pirates and White Sox uniforms. Measuring about 3-1/2" x 5-1/2", the black-and-white cards have a facsimile signature of Kluszewski on front. The back is postcard style and advertises the Cincinnati restaurant he operated with Jack Stayin.

	NM	E	VG
Ted Kluszewski (Reds, fielding, white cap.)	100.00	37.50	22.50
Ted Kluszewski (Reds, portrait, dark cap.)	125.00	50.00	30.00

1930s Knickerbocker Beer Yankees Premium

Jacob Ruppert, who owned both the Yankees and the Knickerbocker Brewing Co., is pictured on this 10" x 8" black-and-white, blank-backed premium photo with a trio of his Italian stars. Facsimile autographs of all are printed on front.

	NM	E	VG
Tony Lazzeri, Jacob Ruppert, Joe DiMaggio, Frank Crosetti	150.00	75.00	45.00

1921 Koester Bread N.Y. Giants/Yankees

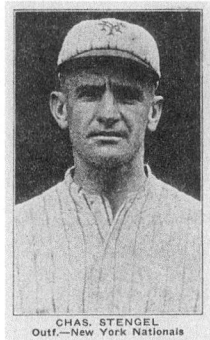

The 1921 World Series was the first of many for the N.Y. Yankees, and it was the first "subway series," as their opponents were the Giants. This special card issue, a blank-backed version of the 1921-22 American Caramel Series of 90/120 (E121), featured the players, managers and coaches of each team. The 2" x about 3-1/4" cards feature black-and-white photos on front. They were distributed in October 1921, by E.H. Koester, a New York bakery. The unnumbered cards are checklisted here alphabetically within team. Several of the players in this issue do not appear in the contemporary American Caramel sets. A rarely seen album was issued to house the cards.

	NM	E	VG
Complete Set (52):	45,000	22,500	13,500
Common Player:	400.00	200.00	120.00
Album:	800.00	400.00	240.00
N.Y. Giants Team Set:	19,000	9,500	5,700
(1) Dave Bancroft	1,200	600.00	350.00
(2) Jesse Barnes	400.00	200.00	120.00
(3) Howard Berry	400.00	200.00	120.00
(4) "Ed." Brown	400.00	200.00	120.00
(5) Jesse Burkett	3,500	1,750	1,050
(6) Geo. J. Burns	400.00	200.00	120.00
(7) Cecil Causey	400.00	200.00	120.00
(8) "Bill" Cunningham	400.00	200.00	120.00
(9) "Phil" Douglas	400.00	200.00	120.00
(10) Frank Frisch	1,200	600.00	350.00

(11) Alexander Gaston	400.00	200.00	120.00
(12) "Mike" Gonzalez	600.00	300.00	180.00
(13) Hugh Jennings	1,200	600.00	350.00
(14) George Kelly	1,200	600.00	350.00
(15) John McGraw	1,200	600.00	350.00
(16) Emil Meusel	400.00	200.00	120.00
(17) Arthur Nehf	400.00	200.00	120.00
(18) John Rawlings	400.00	200.00	120.00
(19) "Bill" Ryan	400.00	200.00	120.00
(20) "Slim" Sallee	400.00	200.00	120.00
(21) "Pat" Shea	400.00	200.00	120.00
(22) Earl Smith	400.00	200.00	120.00
(23) Frank Snyder	400.00	200.00	120.00
(24) Chas. Stengel	1,200	600.00	350.00
(25) Fred Toney	400.00	200.00	120.00
(26) Ross Young (Youngs)	1,200	960.00	350.00
N.Y. Yankees Team Set:	26,000	13,000	7,800
(1) Frank Baker	1,200	600.00	350.00
(2) "Rip" Collins	400.00	200.00	120.00
(3) Lou De Vormer	400.00	200.00	120.00
(4) Alex Ferguson	400.00	200.00	120.00
(5) William Fewster	400.00	200.00	120.00
(6) Harry Harper	400.00	200.00	120.00
(7) "Chicken" Hawks	400.00	200.00	120.00
(8) Fred Hoffmann (Hofmann)	400.00	200.00	120.00
(9) Waite Hoyt	1,200	600.00	350.00
(10) Miller Huggins	1,200	600.00	350.00
(11) Carl Mays	400.00	200.00	120.00
(12) M.J. McNally	400.00	200.00	120.00
(13) R. Meusel	400.00	200.00	120.00
(14) Elmer Miller	400.00	200.00	120.00
(15) John Mitchell	400.00	200.00	120.00
(16) Chas. O'Leary	400.00	200.00	120.00
(17) Roger Peckinpaugh	400.00	200.00	120.00
(18) William Piercy	400.00	200.00	120.00
(19) Walter Pipp	400.00	200.00	120.00
(20) Jack Quinn	400.00	200.00	120.00
(21) Tom Rogers	400.00	200.00	120.00
(22) Robert Roth	400.00	200.00	120.00
(23) George Ruth	15,000	7,500	4,500
(24) Walter Schang	400.00	200.00	120.00
(25) Robert Shawkey	400.00	200.00	120.00
(26) Aaron Ward	400.00	200.00	120.00

1911-16 Kotton Tobacco

The T216 baseball card set, issued with several brands by the People's Tobacco Co., is the last of the Louisiana cigarette sets and the most confusing. Issued over a period of several years between 1911 and 1916, the set employs the same pictures as several contemporary caramel and bakery sets. Cards measure a nominal 1-1/2" x 2-5/8", though reasonable allowance must be made for original cutting variances. Positive identification can be made by the back of the cards. The Peoples Tobacco cards carry advertising for one of three brands of cigarettes: Kotton, Mino or Virginia Extra. The Kotton brand is the most common, with cards found in two types; one has a glossy front finish, while a second scarcer type is printed on a thin paper. The thin paper cards command an additional 15 percent premium. The glossy-front cards can be found with either of two ad styles on back: "KOTTON / TOBACCO" (Factory No. 11) or "KOTTON / CIGARETTES" (Factory No. 4). The cards include players from the American, National and Federal Leagues. The complete set price includes only the least expensive of each variation.

	NM	E	VG
Common Player:	1,000	500.00	300.00
(1) Jack Barry (Batting)	1,000	500.00	300.00
(2) Jack Barry (Fielding)	1,000	500.00	300.00
(3) Harry Bemis	1,000	500.00	300.00
(4a) Chief Bender (Philadelphia, striped cap.)	2,400	1,200	725.00
(4b) Chief Bender (Baltimore, striped cap.)	2,400	1,200	725.00

(5a)	Chief Bender (Philadelphia, white cap.)	2,400	1,200	725.00
(5b)	Chief Bender (Baltimore, white cap.)	2,400	1,200	725.00
(6)	Bill Bergen	1,000	500.00	300.00
(7a)	Bob Bescher (Cincinnati)	1,000	500.00	300.00
(7b)	Bob Bescher (St. Louis)	1,000	500.00	300.00
(8)	Roger Bresnahan	2,400	1,200	725.00
(9)	Al Bridwell (Batting)	1,000	500.00	300.00
(10a)	Al Bridwell (New York, sliding.)	1,000	500.00	300.00
(10b)	Al Bridwell (St. Louis, sliding.)	1,000	500.00	300.00
(11)	Donie Bush	1,000	500.00	300.00
(12)	Doc Casey	1,000	500.00	300.00
(13)	Frank Chance	2,400	1,200	725.00
(14a)	Hal Chase (New York, fielding.)	1,000	500.00	300.00
(14b)	Hal Chase (Buffalo, fielding.)	2,400	1,200	725.00
(15)	Hal Chase (Portrait)	1,600	800.00	475.00
(16a)	Ty Cobb (Detroit Am., standing.)	24,000	12,000	7,200
(16b)	Ty Cobb (Detroit Americans, standing.)	24,000	12,000	7,250
(17)	Ty Cobb (Detroit Americans, batting.)	20,000	10,000	6,000
(18a)	Eddie Collins (Phila. Am.)	2,400	1,200	725.00
(18b)	Eddie Collins (Phila. Amer.)	2,400	1,200	725.00
(19)	Eddie Collins (Chicago)	2,400	1,200	725.00
(20a)	Sam Crawford (Small print.)	2,400	1,200	725.00
(20b)	Sam Crawford (Large print.)	2,400	1,200	725.00
(21)	Harry Davis	1,000	500.00	300.00
(22)	Ray Demmitt	1,000	500.00	300.00
(23)	Art Devlin	1,000	500.00	300.00
(24a)	Wild Bill Donovan (Detroit)	1,000	500.00	300.00
(24b)	Wild Bill Donovan (New York)	1,000	500.00	300.00
(25a)	Red Dooin (Philadelphia)	1,000	500.00	300.00
(25b)	Red Dooin (Cincinnati)	1,000	500.00	300.00
(26a)	Mickey Doolan (Philadelphia)	1,000	500.00	300.00
(26b)	Mickey Doolan (Baltimore)	1,000	500.00	300.00
(27)	Patsy Dougherty	1,000	500.00	300.00
(28a)	Larry Doyle, Larry Doyle (N.Y. Nat'l, batting.)	1,000	500.00	300.00
(28b)	Larry Doyle (New York Nat'l, batting.)	1,000	500.00	300.00
(29)	Larry Doyle (Throwing)	1,000	500.00	300.00
(30)	Clyde Engle	1,000	500.00	300.00
(31a)	Johnny Evers (Chicago)	2,400	1,200	725.00
(31b)	Johnny Evers (Boston)	3,200	1,600	950.00
(32)	Art Fromme	1,000	500.00	300.00
(33a)	George Gibson (Pittsburg Nat'l, back view.)	1,000	500.00	300.00
(33b)	George Gibson (Pittsburgh Nat'l., back view.)	1,000	500.00	300.00
(34a)	George Gibson (Pittsburg Nat'l., front view.)	1,000	500.00	300.00
(34b)	George Gibson (Pittsburgh Nat'l., front view.)	1,000	500.00	300.00
(35a)	Topsy Hartsel (Phila. Am.)	1,000	500.00	300.00
(35b)	Topsy Hartsel (Phila. Amer.)	1,000	500.00	300.00
(36)	Roy Hartzell (Batting)	1,000	500.00	300.00
(37)	Roy Hartzell (Catching)	1,000	500.00	300.00
(38a)	Fred Jacklitsch (Philadelphia)	1,000	500.00	300.00
(38b)	Fred Jacklitsch (Baltimore)	1,000	500.00	300.00
(39a)	Hughie Jennings (Orange background.)	2,400	1,200	725.00
(39b)	Hughie Jennings (Red background.)	2,400	1,200	725.00
(40)	Red Kleinow	1,000	500.00	300.00
(41a)	Otto Knabe (Philadelphia)	1,000	500.00	300.00
(41b)	Otto Knabe (Baltimore)	1,000	500.00	300.00
(42)	Jack Knight	1,000	500.00	300.00
(43a)	Nap Lajoie (Philadelphia, fielding.)	2,400	1,200	725.00
(43b)	Nap Lajoie (Cleveland, fielding.)	2,400	1,200	725.00
(44)	Nap Lajoie (Portrait)	2,400	1,200	725.00
(45a)	Hans Lobert (Cincinnati)	1,000	500.00	300.00
(45b)	Hans Lobert (New York)	1,000	500.00	300.00
(46)	Sherry Magee	1,000	500.00	300.00
(47)	Rube Marquard	2,400	1,200	725.00

(48a)	Christy Matthewson (Mathewson) (Large print.)	8,000	4,000	2,500
(48b)	Christy Matthewson (Mathewson) (Small print.)	8,000	4,000	2,500
(49a)	John McGraw (Large print.)	2,400	1,200	725.00
(49b)	John McGraw (Small print.)	2,400	1,200	725.00
(50)	Larry McLean	1,000	500.00	300.00
(51)	George McQuillan	1,000	500.00	300.00
(52)	Dots Miller (Batting)	1,000	500.00	300.00
(53a)	Dots Miller (Pittsburg, fielding.)	1,000	500.00	300.00
(53b)	Dots Miller (St. Louis, fielding.)	2,000	1,000	600.00
(54a)	Danny Murphy (Philadelphia)	1,000	500.00	300.00
(54b)	Danny Murphy (Brooklyn)	1,000	500.00	300.00
(55)	Rebel Oakes	1,000	500.00	300.00
(56)	Bill O'Hara	1,000	500.00	300.00
(57)	Eddie Plank	4,000	2,000	1,200
(58a)	Germany Schaefer (Washington)	1,000	500.00	300.00
(58b)	Germany Schaefer (Newark)	1,000	500.00	300.00
(59)	Admiral Schlei	1,000	500.00	300.00
(60)	Boss Schmidt	1,000	500.00	300.00
(61)	Johnny Seigle	1,000	500.00	300.00
(62)	Dave Shean	1,000	500.00	300.00
(63)	Boss Smith (Schmidt)	1,000	500.00	300.00
(64)	Tris Speaker	4,000	2,000	1,200
(65)	Oscar Stanage	1,000	500.00	300.00
(66)	George Stovall	1,000	500.00	300.00
(67)	Jeff Sweeney	1,000	500.00	300.00
(68a)	Joe Tinker (Chicago Nat'l, batting.)	2,400	1,200	725.00
(68b)	Joe Tinker (Chicago Feds, batting.)	2,400	1,200	725.00
(69)	Joe Tinker (Portrait)	2,400	1,200	725.00
(70a)	Honus Wagner (Batting, S.S.)	18,000	9,000	5,400
(70b)	Honus Wagner (Batting, 2b.)	18,000	9,000	5,400
(71a)	Honus Wagner (Throwing, S.S.)	18,000	9,000	5,400
(71b)	Honus Wagner (Throwing, 2b.)	18,000	9,000	5,400
(72)	Hooks Wiltse	6,500	3,200	1,950
(73)	Cy Young	4,200	2,100	1,260
(74a)	Heinie Zimmerman (2b.)	1,000	500.00	300.00
(74b)	Heinie Zimmerman (3b.)	1,000	500.00	300.00

1907 Krieg & Co. Chicago Cubs Base Ball Mail Card

Distributed by a shoe retailers' supply firm, this foldout black-and-white postcard features the World Champion Cubs. About 5-1/4" x 3-1/2" closed, the foldout opens to reveal portrait photos of 16 of the players, two per post-card size panel. Manager Frank Chance and the team president each have their own panel. The back cover of the mailer has a composite photo of the team, with a 1907 National League schedule on its flip side.

	NM	E	VG
1907 Chicago Cubs Foldout	2,000	1,000	600.00

1976 Kroger Cincinnati Reds

Blank-backed and unnumbered, they are checklisted here alphabetically. Because the photos were licensed only by the players' union, and not Major League Baseball, photos do not show uniform logos. The grocery store chain gave away these 6 x 9 color photos, four per week, during a span in September and October.

		NM	E	VG
Complete Set (16):		50.00	25.00	15.00
Common Player:		3.00	1.50	.90
Week 1				
Week 2				
(2)	Johnny Bench	15.00	7.50	4.50
(3)	Jack Billingham	3.00	1.50	.90
(4)	Tony Perez	8.00	4.00	2.50
(2)	Ken Griffey Sr.	4.00	2.00	1.25
Week 3				
(3)	Cesar Geronimo	3.00	1.50	.90
(4)	Don Gullett	3.00	1.50	.90
(3)	Cesar Geronimo	3.00	1.50	.90
(3)	Fred Norman	3.00	1.50	.90
Week 2				
(3)	Jack Billingham	3.00	1.50	.90
Week 4				
(3)	Joe Morgan	12.50	6.75	4.00
(3)	Joe Morgan	12.50	6.75	4.00
(4)	Gary Nolan	3.00	1.50	.90
Week 3				
(4)	Don Gullett	3.00	1.50	.90
Week 4				
(4)	Gary Nolan	3.00	1.50	.90
(4)	Pete Rose	25.00	12.50	7.50
Week 2				
(4)	Tony Perez	8.00	4.00	2.50

1977 Kurland Tom Seaver

These large-format (4-3/16" x 5-1/2") black-and-white cards appear to have been produced in conjunction with promotional appearances by Seaver for Kurland Cadillac-Oldsmobile, a metropolitan New York auto dealer. Most of the cards seen are autographed by Seaver. The back is blank.

		NM	E	VG
Complete Set (2):		150.00	75.00	45.00
Common Card:		75.00	37.00	22.00
(1)	Tom Seaver (N.Y. Mets)	75.00	37.00	22.00
(2)	Tom Seaver (Cincinnati Reds)	75.00	37.00	22.00

1926 Kut Outs Giants/Yankees Die-Cuts

These black-and-white, blank-back, die-cut cards were sold as complete sets for 10 cents per team. The size varies with the pose depicted, but the cards are generally about 2" wide and 4-1/2" tall. The player's name is printed at the bottom of his photo. The unnumbered cards are checklisted here in alphabetical order by team. The issue is very similar to the Middy Bread Cardinals/Browns cards of 1927.

	NM	E	VG
Complete Set (20):	16,000	5,800	2,900
Common Player:	350.00	140.00	70.00
N.Y. Giants Team Set:	4,500	1,800	900.00
(1) Ed Farrell	350.00	140.00	70.00
(2) Frank Frisch	1,200	600.00	350.00
(3) George Kelly	1,200	600.00	350.00
(4) Freddie Lindstrom	1,200	600.00	350.00
(5) John McGraw	1,200	600.00	350.00
(6) Emil Meusel	350.00	140.00	70.00
(7) John Scott	350.00	140.00	70.00
(8) Frank Snyder	350.00	140.00	70.00
(9) Billy Southworth	350.00	140.00	70.00
(10) Ross Young (Youngs)	1,200	600.00	350.00
N.Y. Yankees Team Set:	10,000	4,000	2,000
(11) Pat Collins	350.00	140.00	70.00
(12) Earle Combs	1,200	600.00	350.00
(13) Joe Dugan	350.00	140.00	70.00
(14) Lou Gehrig	4,500	1,000	500.00
(15) Miller Huggins	1,200	600.00	350.00
(16) Mark Koenig	350.00	140.00	70.00
(17) Tony Lazzeri	1,200	600.00	350.00
(18) Bob Meusel	350.00	140.00	70.00
(19) Herb Pennock	1,200	600.00	350.00
(20) Babe Ruth	7,250	2,000	1,000

L

1912 L1 Leathers

One of the more unusual baseball collectibles of the tobacco era, the L1 "Leathers" were issued by Helmar Tobacco Co. in 1912 as a premium with its "Turkish Trophies" brand of cigarettes. The set featured 25 of the top baseball players and shared a checklist with the closely-related S81 "Silks," which were another part of the same promotion. The "Leathers," advertised as being 10" x 12", featured drawings of baseball players on horsehide-shaped pieces of leather. The drawings were based on the pictures used for the popular T3 Turkey Red series issued a year earlier. Twenty of the 25 players in the "Leathers" set are from the T3 set. Five pitchers (Rube Marquard, Rube Benton, Marty O'Toole, Grover Alexander and Russ Ford) not pictured in T3 were added to the "Leathers" set, and the Frank Baker error was corrected. According to the promotion, each "Leather" was available in exchange for 50 Helmar coupons. In addition to the 25 baseball stars, the "Leathers" set also included more than 100 other subjects, including female athletes and bathing beauties, famous generals, Indian chiefs, actresses, national flags, college mascots, and others.

	NM	E	VG
Common Player:	2,250	1,150	700.00
86 Rube Marquard	5,750	2,900	1,700
87 Marty O'Toole	2,250	1,150	700.00
88 Rube Benton	2,250	1,150	700.00
89 Grover Alexander	6,400	3,200	2,000
90 Russ Ford	2,250	1,150	700.00
91 John McGraw	5,750	2,900	1,700
92 Nap Rucker	2,250	1,150	700.00
93 Mike Mitchell	2,250	1,150	700.00
94 Chief Bender	7,500	3,750	2,250
95 Home Run Baker	5,750	2,900	1,700
96 Nap Lajoie	5,750	2,900	1,700
97 Joe Tinker	5,750	2,900	1,700

98 Sherry Magee	2,250	1,150	700.00
99 Howie Camnitz	2,250	1,150	700.00
100 Eddie Collins	5,750	2,900	1,700
101 Red Dooin	2,250	1,150	700.00
102 Ty Cobb	45,000	22,500	13,500
103 Hugh Jennings	5,750	2,900	1,700
104 Roger Bresnahan	5,750	2,900	1,700
105 Jake Stahl	2,250	1,150	700.00
106 Tris Speaker	6,400	3,200	2,000
107 Ed Walsh	5,750	2,900	1,700
108 Christy Mathewson	16,000	8,000	4,800
109 Johnny Evers	5,750	2,900	1,700
110 Walter Johnson	16,000	8,000	4,800

1912 La Azora Cigars

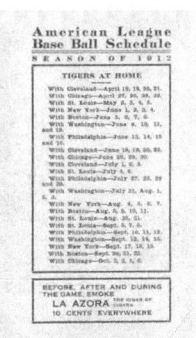

These postcard-size (about 3-3/8" x 5-3/8") ad cards were issued by a Detroit cigar maker. Both cards feature of their front a borderless sepia photo of Ty Cobb, though he is not named. The backs differ somewhat in format and content, but basically provide the Tigers' home and road schedules for the season.

	NM	E	VG
Complete Set (2):	5,000	2,500	1,500
(1) Ty Cobb (Fielding, home schedule.)	3,000	1,500	900.00
(2) Ty Cobb (Sliding, road schedule.)	3,000	1,500	900.00

1958-60 L.A. Dodgers Premium Pictures

Apparently issued over a period of years from 1958 through at least 1960, these black-and-white, 8-1/2" x 11" premium pictures were sold as a set through Dodgers souvenir outlets, though the make-up of a set changed with the comings and goings of players. The blank-backed pictures feature on front a pencil portrait of the player, with his name printed beneath the bottom. The signature of sports artist Nicholas Volpe also appears on front. The unnumbered pictures are checklisted here alphabetically.

	NM	E	VG
Complete Set (16):	300.00	150.00	90.00
Common Player:	15.00	7.50	4.50
(1) Walter Alston	17.50	8.75	5.25
(2) Roy Campanella	30.00	15.00	9.00
(3) Gino Cimoli	15.00	7.50	4.50
(4) Don Drysdale	30.00	15.00	9.00
(5) Carl Erskine	15.00	7.50	4.50
(6) Carl Furillo	20.00	10.00	6.00
(7) Jim Gilliam	17.50	8.75	5.25
(8) Gil Hodges	30.00	15.00	9.00
(9) Clem Labine	15.00	7.50	4.50
(10) Wally Moon	15.00	7.50	4.50
(11) Don Newcombe	17.50	8.75	5.25
(12) Johnny Podres	17.50	8.75	5.25
(13) Pee Wee Reese	30.00	15.00	9.00
(14) Rip Repulski	15.00	7.50	4.50
(15) Vin Scully, Jerry Doggett (Announcers)	15.00	7.50	4.50
(16) Duke Snider	30.00	15.00	9.00

1959 L.A. Dodgers Postcards

In the team's second year in California, the Dodgers began production of an on-going set of color player postcards. Cards were usually sold in 10-card packs in stadium souvenir stands. The makeup of the packs sold varied as players came and went and cards were issued or withdrawn. When supplies of any player's cards were exhausted, he would be included in the current printing. Various photographers and printers were responsible for the issue over the years, but all utilized a similar format of 3-1/2" x 5-1/2" glossy borderless fronts and postcard style backs. The initial effort in 1959 has no player identification on the front. Backs are printed in brown, including player ID, birthdate and place, copyright date and credits to Mirro Krome and Crocker Co. Cards are numbered as shown here, but with an "LA-D-" prefix. The set was also available in the form of an accordian-foldout.

	NM	E	VG
Complete Set (12):	400.00	200.00	125.00
Common Player:	30.00	15.00	9.00
901 Duke Snider	40.00	20.00	12.00
902 Gil Hodges	35.00	17.50	10.00
903 Johnny Podres	30.00	15.00	9.00
904 Carl Furillo	30.00	15.00	9.00
905 Don Drysdale	40.00	20.00	12.00
906 Sandy Koufax	75.00	37.50	22.50
907 Jim Gilliam	30.00	15.00	9.00
908 Don Zimmer	30.00	15.00	9.00
909 Charlie Neal	30.00	15.00	9.00
910 Norm Larker (Photo actually Joe Pignatano.)	30.00	15.00	9.00
911 Clem Labine (Photo actually Stan Williams.)	30.00	15.00	9.00
912 John Roseboro	30.00	15.00	9.00

1960 L.A. Dodgers Postcards

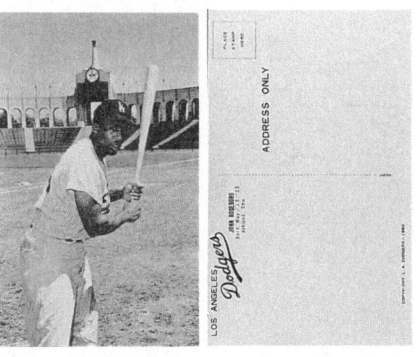

Like many baseball souvenirs, this set of team-issued postcards was "Made in Japan." The 3-1/2" x 5-1/2" cards share the basic format of the 1959 premiere issue with borderless color poses on front and postcard-style back. Backs are printed in blue with player ID and copyright date, but the cards are unnumbered. They are checklisted here alphabetically. The Carl Furillo card is scarce because it was withdrawn when he retired after playing only eight games in 1960.

	NM	E	VG
Complete Set (12):	250.00	125.00	75.00
Common Player:	12.50	6.25	3.75
(1) Walt Alston	12.50	6.25	3.75
(2) Roger Craig	12.50	6.25	3.75
(3) Don Drysdale	15.00	7.50	4.50
(4) Carl Furillo	75.00	37.00	22.00
(5) Gil Hodges	15.00	7.50	4.50
(6) Sandy Koufax	60.00	30.00	18.00
(7) Wally Moon	12.50	6.25	3.75
(8) Charlie Neal	12.50	6.25	3.75
(9) Johnny Podres	12.50	6.25	3.75

		NM	E	VG
(10)	John Roseboro	12.50	6.25	3.75
(11)	Larry Sherry	12.50	6.25	3.75
(12)	Duke Snider	15.00	7.50	4.50

1962 L.A. Dodgers Pins

The attributed date is speculative based on available checklist information. This series of, presumably, stadium souvenir pinback buttons is in an unusually large 3-1/2" format. The pins have black-and-white photos on a white or light blue background. Two styles of name presentation are known, those with names in a white strip at the bottom of the pin and those with the names overprinted on the photo and more towards the center.

	NM	E	VG
Common Player:	75.00	37.50	22.00
NAME IN STRIP			
Don Drysdale	60.00	30.00	18.00
Duke Snider	125.00	62.00	37.00
NAME OVERPRINTED			
Gil Hodges	95.00	47.00	28.00
Sandy Koufax	500.00	250.00	150.00
Maury Wills	75.00	37.50	22.00

1963 L.A. Dodgers Pin-Ups

Borrowing on the concept of the 1938 Goudey Heads-up cards, this set was sold, probably at the stadium souvenir stands, in a white envelope labeled "Los Angeles Dodgers Pin-Ups." The cards feature large full-color head-and-cap photos set atop cartoon ballplayers' bodies. Cards are printed on 7-1/4" x 8-1/2" semi-gloss cardboard with blank backs. The player's name appears in black on the front, along with the instructions, "Push out character carefully. Take scissors and trim white around player's head." Each figure was die-cut to allow its easy removal from the background.

		NM	E	VG
Complete Set (10):		75.00	35.00	25.00
Common Player:		6.00	3.00	1.75
(1)	Tommy Davis	7.50	3.75	2.25
(2)	Willie Davis	7.50	3.75	2.25
(3)	Don Drysdale	10.00	5.00	3.00
(4)	Ron Fairly	6.00	3.00	1.75
(5)	Frank Howard	7.50	3.75	2.25
(6)	Sandy Koufax	25.00	12.50	7.50
(7)	Joe Moeller	6.00	3.00	1.75
(8)	Ron Perranoski	6.00	3.00	1.75
(9)	John Roseboro	6.00	3.00	1.75
(10)	Maury Wills	7.50	3.75	2.25

1965 L.A. Dodgers Motion Pins

These "flasher" pins were issued in conjunction with the Dodgers' World Series appearance and ultimate victory in 1965. The 2-1/2" diameter pins feature player portraits on a seamed blue background resembling a baseball. When the angle of view is changed, the player's name and team logo and the starbursts pop in and out of sight.

	NM	E	VG
Don Drysdale	30.00	7.50	4.50
Sandy Koufax	50.00	12.50	7.50
Dodgers Logo - "Our Champs"	15.00	7.50	4.50

1979 L.A. Dodgers

 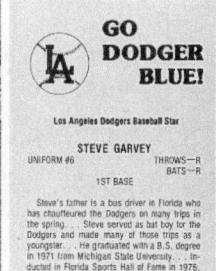

Presumed to be a collectors' issue due to lack of sponsors or licensors logos, this set features the top players of the '79 Dodgers. Fronts of the 2-1/2" x 3-3/8" cards are borderless color photos. Backs are printed in blue and white with career highlights and personal data. Cards are checklisted here in alphabetical order.

		NM	E	VG
Complete Set (15):		15.00	7.50	4.50
Common Player:		2.00	1.00	.60
(1)	Dusty Baker	3.00	1.50	.90
(2)	Ron Cey	2.00	1.00	.60
(3)	Terry Forster	2.00	1.00	.60
(4)	Steve Garvey	4.00	2.00	1.25
(5)	Burt Hooton	2.00	1.00	.60
(6)	Charlie Hough	2.00	1.00	.60
(7)	Tommy Lasorda	3.00	1.50	.90
(8)	Dave Lopes	2.00	1.00	.60
(9)	Rick Monday	2.00	1.00	.60
(10)	Manny Mota	2.00	1.00	.60
(11)	Doug Rau	2.00	1.00	.60
(12)	Bill Russell	2.00	1.00	.60
(13)	Reggie Smith	2.00	1.00	.60
(14)	Don Sutton	4.00	2.00	1.25
(15)	Steve Yeager	2.00	1.00	.60

1980 L.A. Dodgers Police

 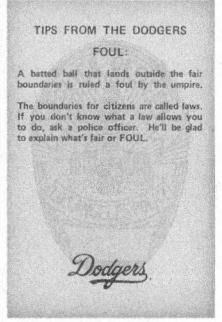

Producers of one of the most popular police and safety sets in the hobby, the Dodgers began this successful promotion in 1980. The 2-13/16" x 4-1/8" cards feature full-color photos on front, along with brief personal statistics. Backs include "Tips from the Dodgers" along with the team and LAPD logos. Cards are numbered by player uniform number, with an unnumbered team card also included in the set.

		NM	E	VG
Complete Set (30):		6.00	3.00	1.75
Common Player:		.50	.25	.15
5	Johnny Oates	.50	.25	.15
6	Steve Garvey	2.00	1.00	.60
7	Steve Yeager	.50	.25	.15
8	Reggie Smith	.50	.25	.15
9	Gary Thomasson	.50	.25	.15
10	Ron Cey	.60	.30	.20
12	Dusty Baker	.60	.30	.20
13	Joe Ferguson	.50	.25	.15

15	Davey Lopes	.50	.25	.15
16	Rick Monday	.50	.25	.15
18	Bill Russell	.50	.25	.15
20	Don Sutton	2.00	1.00	.60
21	Jay Johnstone	.50	.25	.15
23	Teddy Martinez	.50	.25	.15
27	Joe Beckwith	.50	.25	.15
28	Pedro Guerrero	.50	.25	.15
29	Don Stanhouse	.50	.25	.15
30	Derrel Thomas	.50	.25	.15
31	Doug Rau	.50	.25	.15
34	Ken Brett	.50	.25	.15
35	Bob Welch	.50	.25	.15
37	Robert Castillo	.50	.25	.15
38	Dave Goltz	.50	.25	.15
41	Jerry Reuss	.50	.25	.15
43	Rick Sutcliffe	.60	.30	.20
44	Mickey Hatcher	.50	.25	.15
46	Burt Hooton	.50	.25	.15
49	Charlie Hough	.50	.25	.15
51	Terry Forster	.50	.25	.15
---	Team Photo	.50	.25	.15

1913 Napoleon Lajoie Game

Although individual cards are not marked, these cards were produced as part of a Parker Bros. baseball board game called "The National American Baseball Game." Each of the approximately 2-3/8" x 3-1/4", round-cornered cards has a borderless photo on front picturing the Hall of Famer at bat. Backs have a chart of various baseball plays used in the game. Cards can be found with the Lajoie photo tinted either blue or red, the latter being somewhat scarcer.

	NM	E	VG
Complete Game Set:	1,500	750.00	450.00
SINGLE CARD			
Napoleon Lajoie (Blue)	25.00	12.50	7.50
Napoleon Lajoie (Red)	45.00	22.50	13.50

1960 Lake To Lake Dairy Braves

This 28-card set of unnumbered 2-1/2" x 3-1/4" cards offers a special challenge for the condition-conscious collector. Originally issued by being stapled to milk cartons, the cards were redeemable for prizes ranging from pen and pencil sets to Braves tickets. Naturally, collectors most desire cards without the staple and punch holes. Cards are printed in blue ink on front, red ink on back. Because he was traded in May, and his card withdrawn, the Ray Boone card is scarce; the Billy Bruton card is unaccountably scarcer still.

		NM	E	VG
Complete Set (28):		2,250	1,125	650.00
Common Player:		35.00	17.50	10.00
(1)	Henry Aaron	500.00	250.00	150.00
(2)	Joe Adcock	35.00	17.50	10.00
(3)	Ray Boone	250.00	125.00	75.00
(4)	Bill Bruton	500.00	250.00	150.00
(5)	Bob Buhl	35.00	17.50	10.00
(6)	Lou Burdette	35.00	17.50	10.00
(7)	Chuck Cottier	35.00	17.50	10.00
(8)	Wes Covington	35.00	17.50	10.00

(9)	Del Crandall	35.00	17.50	10.00
(10)	Charlie Dressen	35.00	17.50	10.00
(11)	Bob Giggie	35.00	17.50	10.00
(12)	Joey Jay	35.00	17.50	10.00
(13)	Johnny Logan	35.00	17.50	10.00
(14)	Felix Mantilla	35.00	17.50	10.00
(15)	Lee Maye	35.00	17.50	10.00
(16)	Don McMahon	35.00	17.50	10.00
(17)	George Myatt	35.00	17.50	10.00
(18)	Andy Pafko	35.00	17.50	10.00
(19)	Juan Pizarro	35.00	17.50	10.00
(20)	Mel Roach	35.00	17.50	10.00
(21)	Bob Rush	35.00	17.50	10.00
(22)	Bob Scheffing	35.00	17.50	10.00
(23)	Red Schoendienst	75.00	37.50	22.50
(24)	Warren Spahn	150.00	75.00	45.00
(25)	Al Spangler	35.00	17.50	10.00
(26)	Frank Torre	35.00	17.50	10.00
(27)	Carl Willey	35.00	17.50	10.00
(28)	Whitlow Wyatt	35.00	17.50	10.00

1923-24 La Moda

This is appears to be a parallel to the more frequently encountered Cuban cigar cards advertising the Billiken brand. Specialists feel that the La Moda ("The Fashion") branded cards survive at a rate about one per 10 Billikens, though demand is not such that prices follow such a ratio.

	NM	E	VG
Common Player:	1,000	400.00	200.00
Stars: 2X			

(See 1923-24 Billiken for checklist and base card values.)

1970 La Pizza Royale Expos

RUSTY STAUB
Voltigeur

This colorful collectors' issue features only Montreal Expos. Each of the 2-1/2" x 5" cards can be found printed in red, yellow, blue of green duo-tones. "La Pizza Royale" is printed in white above the player photo. Below the photo is the player's name and, in French, his position. Backs are blank and the cards are unnumbered. The checklist is presented here alphabetically. The La Pizza Royale cards are a fantasy issue produced by a collector for sale within the hobby.

	NM	E	VG
Complete Set (14):	25.00	10.00	6.00
Common Player:	2.00	1.00	.60

(1)	Bob Bailey	2.00	1.00	.60
(2)	John Boccabella	2.00	1.00	.60
(3)	Ron Fairly	3.00	1.50	.90
(4)	Jim Gosger	2.00	1.00	.60
(5)	Coco Laboy	2.00	1.00	.60
(6)	Gene Mauch	3.00	1.50	.90
(7)	Rich Nye	2.00	1.00	.60
(8)	John O'Donoghue	2.00	1.00	.60
(9)	Adolfo Phillips	2.00	1.00	.60
(10)	Howie Reed	2.00	1.00	.60
(11)	Marv Staehle	2.00	1.00	.60
(12)	Rusty Staub	4.50	2.25	1.25
(13)	Gary Sutherland	2.00	1.00	.60
(14)	Bobby Wine	2.00	1.00	.60

1967 Laughlin World Series

Apparently a prototype set for subsequent offerings by the sports artist R.G. Laughlin that were produced by Fleer, this set of 64 cards was printed in black-and-white with the cartoon line drawings for which Laughlin was noted. The cards are an odd size, 2-3/4" x 3-1/2", like so many of the Laughlin/Fleer issues of the period. The text on the back is printed in red and offer details of the World Series from that year.

		NM	E	VG
Complete Set (64):		450.00	225.00	135.00
Common Card:		9.00	4.50	2.75
1	1903 Red Sox/Pirates	9.00	4.50	2.75
2	1905 Giants/A's(Christy Mathewson)	20.00	10.00	6.00
3	1906 White Sox/Cubs	9.00	4.50	2.75
4	1907 Cubs/Tigers	9.00	4.50	2.75
5	1908 Cubs/Tigers(Joe Tinker, Evers, Frank Chance)	20.00	10.00	6.00
6	1909 Pirates/Tigers(Honus Wagner, Ty Cobb)	30.00	15.00	9.00
7	1910 A's/Cubs	9.00	4.50	2.75
8	1911 A's/Giants(John McGraw)	9.00	4.50	2.75
9	1912 Red Sox/Giants	9.00	4.50	2.75
10	1913 A's/Giants	9.00	4.50	2.75
11	1914 Braves/A's	9.00	4.50	2.75
12	1915 Red Sox/Phillies(Babe Ruth)	35.00	17.50	10.00
13	1916 White Sox/Dodgers(Babe Ruth)	35.00	17.50	10.00
14	1917 White Sox/Giants	9.00	4.50	2.75
15	1918 Red Sox/Cubs	9.00	4.50	2.75
16	1919 Reds/White Sox	35.00	17.50	10.00
17	1920 Indians/Dodgers(Bill Wambsganss)	9.00	4.50	2.75
18	1921 Giants/Yankees(Waite Hoyt)	9.00	4.50	2.75
19	1922 Giants/Yankees(Frank Frisch, Heinie Groh)	9.00	4.50	2.75
20	1923 Yankees/Giants(Babe Ruth)	35.00	17.50	10.00
21	1924 Senators/Giants(Walter Johnson)	15.00	7.50	4.50
22	1925 Pirates/Senators(Walter Johnson)	15.00	7.50	4.50
23	1926 Cardinals/Yankees(Grover Alexander, Anthony Lazzeri)	15.00	7.50	4.50
24	1927 Yankees/Pirates	9.00	4.50	2.75
25	1928 Yankees/Cardinals(Babe Ruth, Lou Gehrig)	35.00	17.50	10.00
26	1929 A's/Cubs	9.00	4.50	2.75
27	1930 A's/Cardinals	9.00	4.50	2.75
28	1931 Cardinals/A's(Pepper Martin)	9.00	4.50	2.75
29	1932 Yankees/Cubs(Babe Ruth)	35.00	17.50	10.00
30	1933 Giants/Senators(Mel Ott)	12.50	6.25	3.75
31	1934 Cardinals/Tigers(Dizzy Dean, Paul Dean)	20.00	10.00	6.00
32	1935 Tigers/Cubs	9.00	4.50	2.75
33	1936 Yankees/Giants	9.00	4.50	2.75
34a	1937 Yankees/Giants(Carl Hubbell) (#11 on uniform)	12.50	6.25	3.75
34b	1937 Yankees/Giants(Carl Hubbell) (#14 on uniform)	12.50	6.25	3.75
35	1938 Yankees/Cubs	9.00	4.50	2.75
36	1939 Yankees/Reds(Joe DiMaggio)	30.00	15.00	9.00
37	1940 Reds/Tigers	9.00	4.50	2.75
38	1941 Yankees/Dodgers(Mickey Owen)	9.00	4.50	2.75
39	1942 Cardinals/Yankees	9.00	4.50	2.75
40	1943 Yankees/Cardinals(Joe McCarthy)	9.00	4.50	2.75
41	1944 Cardinals/Browns	9.00	4.50	2.75
42	1945 Tigers/Cubs(Hank Greenberg)	15.00	7.50	4.50
43	1946 Cardinals/Red Sox(Enos Slaughter)	9.00	4.50	2.75
44	1947 Yankees/Dodgers(Al Gionfriddo)	9.00	4.50	2.75
45	1948 Indians/Braves(Bob Feller)	12.50	6.25	3.75
46	1949 Yankees/Dodgers(Allie Reynolds, Preacher Roe)	20.00	10.00	6.00
47	1950 Yankees/Phillies	9.00	4.50	2.75
48	1951 Yankees/Giants	9.00	4.50	2.75
49	1952 Yankees/Dodgers(Johnny Mize, Duke Snider)	20.00	10.00	6.00
50	1953 Yankees/Dodgers(Casey Stengel)	20.00	10.00	6.00
51	1954 Giants/Indians(Dusty Rhodes)	9.00	4.50	2.75
52	1955 Dodgers/Yankees(Johnny Podres)	20.00	10.00	6.00
53	1956 Yankees/Dodgers(Don Larsen)	25.00	12.50	7.50
54	1957 Braves/Yankees(Lew Burdette)	9.00	4.50	2.75
55	1958 Yankees/Braves(Hank Bauer)	9.00	4.50	2.75
56	1959 Dodgers/White Sox(Larry Sherry)	9.00	4.50	2.75
57	1960 Pirates/Yankees	25.00	12.50	7.50
58	1961 Yankees/Reds(Whitey Ford)	20.00	10.00	6.00
59	1962 Yankees/Giants	9.00	4.50	2.75
60	1963 Dodgers/Yankees(Sandy Koufax)	20.00	10.00	6.00
61	1964 Cardinals/Yankees(Mickey Mantle)	35.00	17.50	10.00
62	1965 Dodgers/Twins(Sandy Koufax)	9.00	4.50	2.75
63	1966 Orioles/Dodgers	9.00	4.50	2.75
64	1967 Cardinals/Red Sox(Bob Gibson)	9.00	4.50	2.75

1972 Laughlin Great Feats

George Sisler made 257 hits in 1920

Sports artist R.G. Laughlin created this set of 50 numbered cards and one unnumbered title card highlighting top performances by stars over the years. The cards depict the player in pen and ink, with one variation of the set adding flesh tones to the players. One variation of the set has red borders, the other (with the flesh tones) blue. The cards are blank backed and numbered on the front with a brief caption. Cards measure about 2-9/16" x 3-9/16". Sets originally sold for about $3.

	NM	E	VG
Complete Set, Red (51):	45.00	22.50	13.50
Complete Set, Blue (51):	60.00	30.00	18.00
Common Player (Red):	1.50	.70	.45

Common Player (Blue): 1.5-2X

1	Joe DiMaggio	12.00	6.00	3.50
2	Walter Johnson	4.50	2.25	1.25
3	Rudy York	1.50	.70	.45
4	Sandy Koufax	9.00	4.50	2.75
5	George Sisler	1.50	.70	.45
6	Iron Man McGinnity	1.50	.70	.45
7	Johnny VanderMeer	1.50	.70	.45
8	Lou Gehrig	12.00	6.00	3.50
9	Max Carey	1.50	.70	.45
10	Ed Delahanty	1.50	.70	.45
11	Pinky Higgins	1.50	.70	.45
12	Jack Chesbro	1.50	.70	.45
13	Jim Bottomley	1.50	.70	.45
14	Rube Marquard	1.50	.70	.45
15	Rogers Hornsby	1.50	.70	.45
16	Lefty Grove	1.50	.70	.45
17	Johnny Mize	1.50	.70	.45
18	Lefty Gomez	1.50	.70	.45
19	Jimmie Fox (Foxx)	1.50	.70	.45
20	Casey Stengel	1.50	.70	.45
21	Dazzy Vance	1.50	.70	.45
22	Jerry Lynch	1.50	.70	.45
23	Hughie Jennings	1.50	.70	.45
24	Stan Musial	4.50	2.25	1.25
25	Christy Mathewson	4.50	2.25	1.25
26	Elroy Face	1.50	.70	.45
27	Hack Wilson	1.50	.70	.45
28	Smoky Burgess	1.50	.70	.45
29	Cy Young	3.00	1.50	.90
30	Wilbert Robinson	1.50	.70	.45
31	Wee Willie Keeler	1.50	.70	.45
32	Babe Ruth	15.00	7.50	4.50
33	Mickey Mantle	15.00	7.50	4.50
34	Hub Leonard	1.50	.70	.45
35	Ty Cobb	7.50	3.75	2.25
36	Carl Hubbell	1.50	.70	.45
37	Joe Oeschger, Leon Cadore	1.50	.70	.45
38	Don Drysdale	1.50	.70	.45
39	Fred Toney, Hippo Vaughn	1.50	.70	.45
40	Joe Sewell	1.50	.70	.45
41	Grover Cleveland Alexander	1.50	.70	.45
42	Joe Adcock	1.50	.70	.45
43	Eddie Collins	1.50	.70	.45
44	Bob Feller	2.00	1.00	.60
45	Don Larsen	2.00	1.00	.60
46	Dave Philley	1.50	.70	.45
47	Bill Fischer	1.50	.70	.45
48	Dale Long	1.50	.70	.45
49	Bill Wambsganss	1.50	.70	.45
50	Roger Maris	4.50	2.25	1.25
---	**Title Card**	1.50	.70	.45

1973 Laughlin Super Stand-Ups

A dozen Hall of Famers are featured in this collectors' issue of stand-up figures. Printed in color on heavy cardboard, each is die-cut around the player action picture with typical measurements being 7" x 11". The stand-ups are much scarcer than most of the artist's other baseball issues. They are listed here alphabetically. The stand-ups originally retailed for $3.50 apiece.

		NM	E	VG
Complete Set (13):		7,500	3,750	2,250
Common Player:		300.00	150.00	90.00
(1)	Hank Aaron	650.00	325.00	195.00
(2)	Johnny Bench	450.00	225.00	135.00
(3)	Roberto Clemente	750.00	375.00	225.00
(4)	Joe DiMaggio	750.00	375.00	225.00
(5)	Lou Gehrig	750.00	375.00	225.00
(6)	Gil Hodges	450.00	225.00	135.00
(7)	Sandy Koufax	750.00	375.00	225.00
(8)	Mickey Mantle	1,500	750.00	450.00
(9)	Willie Mays	650.00	325.00	195.00
(10)	Stan Musial	500.00	250.00	150.00
(11)	Babe Ruth	1,200	600.00	360.00
(12)	Tom Seaver	450.00	225.00	135.00
(13)	Ted Williams	650.00	325.00	195.00

1974 Laughlin All-Star Games

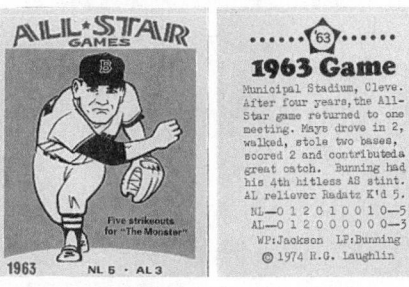

With pen and ink drawings by R.G. Laughlin on the fronts, this set (40 cards) features one card from each year of the game from 1933 to 1973. The 2-3/4" x 3-3/8" cards show a player in black ink in front of a light blue background with a glossy finish, with red printing for the title of the set and the year. The backs are printed in blue, with the year of the All-Star Game serving as the card number. Issue price was $3.50.

		NM	E	VG
Complete Set (40):		60.00	30.00	18.00
Common Player:		3.00	1.50	.90
33	Babe's Homer(Babe Ruth)	25.00	12.50	7.50
34a	Hub Fans Five(Carl Hubbell) (Uniform #11.)	4.50	2.25	1.25
34b	Hub Fans Five(Carl Hubbell) (Uniform #14.)	4.50	2.25	1.25
35	Foxx Smashes HR(Jimmie Foxx)	4.50	2.25	1.25
36	Ol' Diz Fogs 'Em(Dizzy Dean)	4.50	2.25	1.25
37	Four Hits for Ducky(Ducky Medwick)	3.00	1.50	.90
38	No-Hit Vandy(John VanderMeer)	3.00	1.50	.90
39	DiMaggio Homers(Joe DiMaggio)	20.00	10.00	6.00
40	West's 3-Run Shot(Max West)	3.00	1.50	.90
41	Vaughan Busts Two(Arky Vaughan)	3.00	1.50	.90
42	York's 2-Run Smash(Rudy York)	3.00	1.50	.90
43	Doerr's 3-Run Blast(Bobby Doerr)	3.00	1.50	.90
44	Cavarretta Reaches(Phil Cavarretta)	3.00	1.50	.90
46	Field Day for Ted(Ted Williams)	15.00	7.50	4.50
47	Big Cat Plants One(Johnny Mize)	3.00	1.50	.90
48	Raschi Pitches(Vic Raschi)	3.00	1.50	.90
49	Jackie Scores(Jackie Robinson)	12.00	6.00	3.50
50	Schoendienst Breaks(Red Schoendienst)	3.00	1.50	.90
51	Kiner Homers(Ralph Kiner)	3.00	1.50	.90
52	Sauer's Shot(Hank Sauer)	3.00	1.50	.90
53	Slaughter Hustles(Enos Slaughter)	3.00	1.50	.90
54	Rosen Hits(Al Rosen)	3.00	1.50	.90
55	Stan the Man's HR(Stan Musial)	7.50	3.75	2.25
56	Boyer Super(Ken Boyer)	3.00	1.50	.90
57	Kaline's Hits(Al Kaline)	4.50	2.25	1.25
58	Nellie Gets Two(Nellie Fox)	3.00	1.50	.90
59	Robbie Perfect(Frank Robinson)	4.50	2.25	1.25
60	Willie 3-for-4(Willie Mays)	12.00	6.00	3.50
61	Bunning Hitless(Jim Bunning)	3.00	1.50	.90
62	Roberto Perfect(Roberto Clemente)	15.00	7.50	4.50
63	Monster Strikeouts(Dick Radatz)	3.00	1.50	.90
64	Callison's Homer(Johnny Callison)	3.00	1.50	.90
65	Stargell's Big Day(Willie Stargell)	3.00	1.50	.90
66	Brooks Gets Triple(Brooks Robinson)	4.50	2.25	1.25
67	Fergie Fans Six(Fergie Jenkins)	3.00	1.50	.90
68	Tom Terrific(Tom Seaver)	5.00	2.50	1.50
69	Stretch Belts Two(Willie McCovey)	3.00	1.50	.90
70	Yaz' Four Hits(Carl Yastrzemski)	4.50	2.25	1.25
71	Reggie Unloads(Reggie Jackson)	6.00	3.00	1.75
72	Henry Hammers(Hank Aaron)	12.00	6.00	3.50
73	Bonds Perfect(Bobby Bonds)	3.00	1.50	.90

1974 Laughlin Old-Time Black Stars

This set of slightly oversized cards (2-5/8" x 3-1/2") features drawings by R.G. Laughlin. The artwork is printed in brown and a light tan; backs are printed in brown on white stock. The set features many of the greatest players from the Negro Leagues. The cards carry no copyright date and no mention of the prolific Laughlin, but the simple line drawings are obviously his work, and a subsequent issue four years later by Laughlin removes any doubt. Original retail price at time of issue was about $3.25.

		NM	E	VG
Complete Set (36):		100.00	30.00	18.00
Common Player:		2.00	1.00	.60
1	Smokey Joe Williams	5.00	2.50	1.50
2	Rap Dixon	2.00	1.00	.60
3	Oliver Marcelle	2.00	1.00	.60
4	Bingo DeMoss	4.00	2.00	1.25
5	Willie Foster	2.50	1.25	.70
6	John Beckwith	2.00	1.00	.60
7	Floyd (Jelly) Gardner	2.00	1.00	.60
8	Josh Gibson	10.00	5.00	3.00
9	Jose Mendez	5.00	2.50	1.50
10	Pete Hill	5.00	2.50	1.50
11	Buck Leonard	5.00	2.50	1.50
12	Jud Wilson	5.00	2.50	1.50
13	Willie Wells	5.00	2.50	1.50
14	Jimmie Lyons	2.00	1.00	.60
15	Satchel Paige	10.00	5.00	3.00
16	Louis Santop	5.00	2.50	1.50
17	Frank Grant	7.50	3.75	2.25
18	Christobel Torrienti	5.00	2.50	1.50
19	Bullet Rogan	4.00	2.00	1.25
20	Dave Malarcher	2.50	1.25	.70
21	Spot Poles	2.00	1.00	.60
22	Home Run Johnson	2.50	1.25	.70
23	Charlie Grant	4.00	2.00	1.25
24	Cool Papa Bell	5.00	2.50	1.50
25	Cannonball Dick Redding	2.00	1.00	.60
26	Ray Dandridge	5.00	2.50	1.50
27	Biz Mackey	7.50	3.75	2.25
28	Fats Jenkins	2.00	1.00	.60
29	Martin Dihigo	5.00	2.50	1.50
30	Mule Suttles	5.00	2.50	1.50
31	Bill Monroe	2.00	1.00	.60
32	Dan McClellan	2.00	1.00	.60
33	Pop Lloyd	5.00	2.50	1.50
34	Oscar Charleston	5.00	2.50	1.50
35	Andrew "Rube" Foster	5.00	2.50	1.50
36	William (Judy) Johnson	5.00	2.50	1.50

1974 Laughlin Sportslang

Featuring the cartoon artwork of R.G. Laughlin, this 41-card set features 40 cards (plus one unnumbered title card) detailing the history and derivation of slang terms from several sports. The cards are 2-3/4" x 3-1/4", with red and blue printing on the front and red on the back. The cards are numbered on the back.

	NM	E	VG
Complete Set (41):	80.00	40.00	24.00
Common Card:	3.00	1.50	.80

		NM	E	VG
1	Bull Pen	3.00	1.50	.80
2	Charley Horse	3.00	1.50	.80
3	Derby	3.00	1.50	.80
4	Anchor Man	3.00	1.50	.80
5	Mascot	3.00	1.50	.80
6	Annie Oakley	3.00	1.50	.80
7	Taxi Squad	3.00	1.50	.80
8	Dukes	3.00	1.50	.80
9	Rookie	3.00	1.50	.80
10	Jinx	3.00	1.50	.80
11	Dark Horse	3.00	1.50	.80
12	Hat Trick	3.00	1.50	.80
13	Bell Wether	3.00	1.50	.80
14	Love	3.00	1.50	.80
15	Red Dog	3.00	1.50	.80
16	Barnstorm	3.00	1.50	.80
17	Bull's Eye	3.00	1.50	.80
18	Rabbit Punch	3.00	1.50	.80
19	The Upper Hand	3.00	1.50	.80
20	Handi Cap	3.00	1.50	.80
21	Marathon	3.00	1.50	.80
22	Southpaw	3.00	1.50	.80
23	Boner	3.00	1.50	.80
24	Gridiron	3.00	1.50	.80
25	Fan	3.00	1.50	.80
26	Moxie	3.00	1.50	.80
27	Birdie	3.00	1.50	.80
28	Sulky	3.00	1.50	.80
29	Dribble	3.00	1.50	.80
30	Donnybrook	3.00	1.50	.80
31	The Real McCoy	3.00	1.50	.80
32	Even Stephen	3.00	1.50	.80
33	Chinese Homer	3.00	1.50	.80
34	English	3.00	1.50	.80
35	Garrison Finish	3.00	1.50	.80
36	Foot in the Bucket	3.00	1.50	.80
37	Steeple Chase	3.00	1.50	.80
38	Long Shot	3.00	1.50	.80
39	Nip and Tuck	3.00	1.50	.80
40	Battery	3.00	1.50	.80
----	Header Card	3.00	1.50	.80

1975 Laughlin Batty Baseball

This 25-card set depicts one humorous nickname for each of 24 Major League teams, plus one unnumbered title card. The cards are approximately standard size at 2-1/2" x 3-1/2", with simple black and white cartoon drawings on the front with orange back- grounds. The backs are blank and the cards are numbered on front.

		NM	E	VG
Complete Set (25):		60.00	30.00	18.00
Common Card:		3.00	1.50	.90

		NM	E	VG
1	Oakland Daze	3.00	1.50	.90
2	Boston Wet Sox	3.00	1.50	.90
3	Cincinnati Dreads	3.00	1.50	.90
4	Chicago Wide Sox	3.00	1.50	.90
5	Milwaukee Boozers	3.00	1.50	.90
6	Philadelphia Fillies	3.00	1.50	.90
7	Cleveland Engines	3.00	1.50	.90
8	New York Mitts	3.00	1.50	.90
9	Texas Ranchers	3.00	1.50	.90
10	San Francisco Gents	3.00	1.50	.90
11	Houston Disastros	3.00	1.50	.90
12	Chicago Clubs	3.00	1.50	.90

13	Minnesota Wins	3.00	1.50	.90
14	St. Louis Gardeners	3.00	1.50	.90
15	New York Yankers	3.00	1.50	.90
16	California Angles	3.00	1.50	.90
17	Pittsburgh Irates	3.00	1.50	.90
18	Los Angeles Smoggers	3.00	1.50	.90
19	Baltimore Oreos	3.00	1.50	.90
20	Montreal Expose	3.00	1.50	.90
21	San Diego Parties	3.00	1.50	.90
22	Detroit Taggers	3.00	1.50	.90
23	Kansas City Broils	3.00	1.50	.90
24	Atlanta Briefs	3.00	1.50	.90
----	Header Card	3.00	1.50	.90

1976 Laughlin Diamond Jubilee

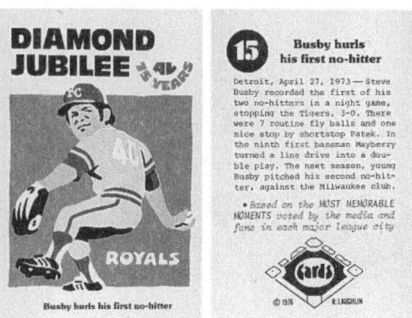

This set of 32 oversized cards (2-3/4" x 4") features Laughlin's drawings of baseball stars highlighting specific events or records. The fronts are printed in black and blue over a red background; the backs are numbered and printed in blue with information about the specific event. Sets originally sold for $3.50.

		NM	E	VG
Complete Set (32):		90.00	45.00	25.00
Common Player:		2.00	1.00	.60

		NM	E	VG
1	Nolan Ryan	30.00	15.00	9.00
2	Ernie Banks	4.50	2.25	1.25
3	Mickey Lolich	2.00	1.00	.60
4	Sandy Koufax	9.00	4.50	2.75
5	Frank Robinson	3.00	1.50	.90
6	Bill Mazeroski	3.00	1.50	.90
7	Catfish Hunter	2.00	1.00	.60
8	Hank Aaron	9.00	4.50	2.75
9	Carl Yastrzemski	3.00	1.50	.90
10	Jim Bunning	2.00	1.00	.60
11	Brooks Robinson	3.00	1.50	.90
12	John VanderMeer	2.00	1.00	.60
13	Harmon Killebrew	3.00	1.50	.90
14	Lou Brock	2.50	1.25	.70
15	Steve Busby	2.00	1.00	.60
16	Nate Colbert	2.00	1.00	.60
17	Don Larsen	2.50	1.25	.70
18	Willie Mays	9.00	4.50	2.75
19	David Clyde	2.00	1.00	.60
20	Mack Jones	2.00	1.00	.60
21	Mike Hegan	2.00	1.00	.60
22	Jerry Koosman	2.00	1.00	.60
23	Early Wynn	2.50	1.25	.70
24	Nellie Fox	2.50	1.25	.70
25	Joe DiMaggio	15.00	7.50	4.50
26	Jackie Robinson	12.00	6.00	3.50
27	Ted Williams	12.00	6.00	3.50
28	Lou Gehrig	12.00	6.00	3.50
29	Bobby Thomson	2.50	1.25	.70
30	Roger Maris	7.50	3.75	2.25
31	Harvey Haddix	2.00	1.00	.60
32	Babe Ruth	20.00	10.00	6.00

1976 Laughlin Indianapolis Clowns

Founder Syd Pollock

Syd Pollock organized the Miami Ethiopian Clowns in 1929. His concept was to create a black club that not only could play pro ball but add laughs and showmanship to the game. The Clowns preceded the Harlem Globetrotters by a year. The national semi-pro champions turned pro in 1942, becoming the Cincinnati Clowns and later the Indianapolis Clowns, as they won numerous Negro AL titles. Also a Braves scout, Pollock retired from traveling baseball in 1964, turning the team over to Ed Hamman. Syd passed away in 1968.

Founder Syd Pollock

In a departure from the style of most Laughlin issues, this 42-card set does not use his artwork but rather black and white photos framed by a light blue border. The cards are oversized at 2-5/8" x 4-1/4", with red printing on front and back. The cards are numbered on the front.

		NM	E	VG
Complete Set (42):		40.00	15.00	9.00
Common Player:		.60	.30	.20

		NM	E	VG
1	Ed Hamman (Ed the Clown)	1.00	.50	.30
2	Dero Austin	.60	.30	.20
3	James Williams (Natureboy)	.60	.30	.20
4	Sam Brison (Birmingham)	.60	.30	.20
5	Richard King (King Tut)	.60	.30	.20
6	Syd Pollock (Founder)	.60	.30	.20
7	Nataniel (Lefty) Small	.60	.30	.20
8	Grant Greene (Double Duty)	.60	.30	.20
9	Nancy Miller (Lady Umpire)	.60	.30	.20
10	Billy Vaughn	.60	.30	.20
11	Sam Brison (Putout for Sam)	.60	.30	.20
12	Ed Hamman	.60	.30	.20
13	Dero Austin (Home Delivery)	.60	.30	.20
14	Steve (Nub) Anderson	.60	.30	.20
15	Joe Cherry	.60	.30	.20
16	Reece (Goose) Tatum	3.00	1.50	.90
17	James Williams (Natureboy)	.60	.30	.20
18	Byron Purnell	.60	.30	.20
19	Bat Boy	.60	.30	.20
20	Spec BeBop	.60	.30	.20
21	Satchel Paige	5.00	2.50	1.50
22	Prince Jo Henry	.60	.30	.20
23	Ed Hamman, Syd Pollock	.60	.30	.20
24	Paul Casanova	.60	.30	.20
25	Steve (Nub) Anderson (Nub Singles)	.60	.30	.20
26	Comiskey Park	.60	.30	.20
27	Toni Stone (Second Basewoman)	1.50	.70	.45
28	Dero Austin (Small Target)	.60	.30	.20
29	Calling Dr. Kildare(Sam Brison, Natureboy Williams)	.60	.30	.20
30	Oscar Charleston	2.00	1.00	.60
31	Richard King (King Tut)	.60	.30	.20
32	Ed and Prospects(Ed Hamman, Joe Cherry, Hal King)	.60	.30	.20
33	Team Bus	.60	.30	.20
34	Hank Aaron	6.00	3.00	1.75
35	The Greta Yogi	1.50	.70	.45
36	W.H. (Chauff) Wilson	.60	.30	.20
37	Doin' Their Thing(Sam Brison, Sonny Jackson)	.60	.30	.20
38	Billy Vaughn (The Hard Way)	.60	.30	.20
39	James Williams (18 the easy way)	.60	.30	.20
40	Casey & Ed(Ed Hamman, Casey Stengel)	1.25	.60	.40
---	Header Card	.60	.30	.20
---	Baseball Laff Book	.60	.30	.20

1978 Laughlin Long Ago Black Stars

2. LARRY BROWN C

LARRY BROWN

This sparkplug came from Birmingham to join the Pitt Keystones in 1921, and became one of the great defensive catchers of black baseball. He caught for the two Chicago teams of '26 and '27 that won the black World Series. After he threw out Ty Cobb five successive times in a '26 game in Havana, Ty asked the light-skinned Brown to join the Tigers as a Cuban—but Larry declined. In '30 "Iron Man" Brown caught 234 games! He never pulled off his mask on a foul. A .300 hitter, Larry played longest for the Memphis Red Sox and also managed. He was voted catcher on many All-Star teams. Died in '72.

© 1978 R.G. Laughlin

In what appears very much like a second series save for slight title alteration, sports artist R.G. Laughlin produced this 36-card set in a format very similar to his 1974 issue highlighting Negro League stars. This set is printed in dark and light green on a non-glossy front, with printing on the back in black. Most of the more widely known Negro League stars appeared in the 1974 issue.

	NM	E	VG
Complete Set (36):	75.00	30.00	18.00
Common Player:	1.50	.70	.45
1 Ted Trent	1.50	.70	.45
2 Larry Brown	1.50	.70	.45
3 Newt Allen	3.00	1.50	.90
4 Norman Stearns	4.50	2.25	1.25
5 Leon Day	6.00	3.00	1.75
6 Dick Lundy	1.50	.70	.45
7 Bruce Petway	1.50	.70	.45
8 Bill Drake	1.50	.70	.45
9 Chaney White	1.50	.70	.45
10 Webster McDonald	2.50	1.25	.70
11 Tommy Butts	1.50	.70	.45
12 Ben Taylor	4.50	2.25	1.25
13 James (Joe) Greene	1.50	.70	.45
14 Dick Seay	1.50	.70	.45
15 Sammy Hughes	1.50	.70	.45
16 Ted Page	3.00	1.50	.90
17 Willie Cornelius	1.50	.70	.45
18 Pat Patterson	1.50	.70	.45
19 Frank Wickware	1.50	.70	.45
20 Albert Haywood	1.50	.70	.45
21 Bill Holland	1.50	.70	.45
22 Sol White	4.50	2.25	1.25
23 Chet Brewer	3.00	1.50	.90
24 Crush Holloway	1.50	.70	.45
25 George Johnson	1.50	.70	.45
26 George Scales	1.50	.70	.45
27 Dave Brown	1.50	.70	.45
28 John Donaldson	1.50	.70	.45
29 William Johnson	3.00	1.50	.90
30 Bill Yancey	3.00	1.50	.90
31 Sam Bankhead	4.00	2.00	1.25
32 Leroy Matlock	1.50	.70	.45
33 Quincy Troupe	2.50	1.25	.70
34 Hilton Smith	3.00	1.50	.90
35 Jim Crutchfield	3.00	1.50	.90
36 Ted Radcliffe	4.00	2.00	1.25

1980 Laughlin 300/400/500

This unusual set features a combination of the line drawings of R.G. Laughlin and a photo head shot of the player depicted. The cards are actually square, 3-1/4" x 3-1/4", with a background in color depicting a baseball diamond. The set is based on 300 wins, batting .400 or better and 500 homers, with a total of 30 cards in the blank backed set. The cards are numbered on the front. This set has been reprinted; the reprints have lighter faces and blurry text.

	NM	E	VG
Complete Set (30):	50.00	25.00	15.00
Common Player:	3.00	1.00	.90
1 Header Card	3.00	1.50	.90
2 Babe Ruth	20.00	10.00	6.00
3 Walter Johnson	6.00	3.00	1.75
4 Ty Cobb	12.00	6.00	3.50
5 Christy Mathewson	6.00	3.00	1.75
6 Ted Williams	8.00	4.00	2.50
7 Bill Terry	3.00	1.50	.90
8 Grover C. Alexander	3.00	1.50	.90
9 Napoleon Lajoie	3.00	1.50	.90
10 Willie Mays	8.00	4.00	2.50
11 Cy Young	6.00	3.00	1.75
12 Mel Ott	3.00	1.50	.90
13 Joe Jackson	20.00	10.00	6.00
14 Harmon Killebrew	3.00	1.50	.90
15 Warren Spahn	3.00	1.50	.90
16 Hank Aaron	8.00	4.00	2.50
17 Rogers Hornsby	3.00	1.50	.90
18 Mickey Mantle	20.00	10.00	6.00
19 Lefty Grove	3.00	1.50	.90
20 Ted Williams	8.00	4.00	2.50
21 Jimmie Fox	3.00	1.50	.90
22 Eddie Plank	3.00	1.50	.90
23 Frank Robinson	3.00	1.50	.90
24 George Sisler	3.00	1.50	.90
25 Eddie Mathews	3.00	1.50	.90
26 Early Wynn	3.00	1.50	.90
27 Ernie Banks	3.00	1.50	.90

28 Harry Heilmann	3.00	1.50	.90
29 Lou Gehrig	15.00	7.50	4.50
30 Willie McCovey	3.00	1.50	.90

1980 Laughlin Famous Feats

A set of 40 cards, this Famous Feats set by sports artist R.G. Laughlin carries a subtitle as the Second Series, apparently a reference to a 1972 issue of the same name by Laughlin that was produced by Fleer. Unlike many of the odd sized Laughlin issues, this one is the standard 2-1/2" x 3-1/2", with full color used with the artist's pen and ink drawings on the front. The cards are numbered on the front and the backs are blank.

	NM	E	VG
Complete Set (40):	15.00	7.50	4.50
Common Player:	.75	.35	.20
1 Honus Wagner	2.50	1.25	.70
2 Herb Pennock	.75	.35	.20
3 Al Simmons	.75	.35	.20
4 Hack Wilson	.75	.35	.20
5 Dizzy Dean	1.50	.70	.45
6 Chuck Klein	.75	.35	.20
7 Nellie Fox	.75	.40	.25
8 Lefty Grove	.75	.35	.20
9 George Sisler	.75	.35	.20
10 Lou Gehrig	3.50	1.75	1.00
11 Rube Waddell	.75	.35	.20
12 Max Carey	.75	.35	.20
13 Thurman Munson	2.00	1.00	.60
14 Mel Ott	.75	.35	.20
15 Doc White	.75	.35	.20
16 Babe Ruth	6.00	3.00	1.75
17 Schoolboy Rowe	.75	.35	.20
18 Jackie Robinson	3.50	1.75	1.00
19 Joe Medwick	.75	.35	.20
20 Casey Stengel	.75	.35	.20
21 Roberto Clemente	4.50	2.25	1.25
22 Christy Mathewson	1.50	.70	.45
23 Jimmie Foxx	1.25	.60	.40
24 Joe Jackson	6.00	3.00	1.75
25 Walter Johnson	1.50	.70	.45
26 Tony Lazzeri	.75	.35	.20
27 Hugh Casey	.75	.35	.20
28 Ty Cobb	3.50	1.75	1.00
29 Stuffy McInnis	.75	.35	.20
30 Cy Young	1.25	.60	.40
31 Lefty O'Doul	.75	.35	.20
32 Eddie Collins	.75	.35	.20
33 Joe McCarty	.75	.35	.20
34 Ed Walsh	.75	.35	.20
35 George Burns	.75	.35	.20
36 Walt Dropo	.75	.35	.20
37 Connie Mack	.75	.35	.20
38 Babe Adams	.75	.35	.20
39 Rogers Hornsby	1.00	.50	.30
40 Grover C. Alexander	.75	.35	.20

1961 Leader Cleaners Chicago White Sox

This series of paper strips appears to have been issued as a wrap-around for dry cleaned shirts by a Chicago dry cleaner (or perhaps a chain of dry cleaners). Printed in red and blue on white, the printed portion of the strip is about 10" x 2-1/2". The entire strip may have been much longer, perhaps 20" or more. The strips were part of a White Sox kids' ticket promotion. The strip mentions 20 players in the series, though only those listed here have been confirmed.

	NM	EX	VG
Common Player:	20.00	10.00	6.00
(9) Juan Pizarro	20.00	10.00	6.00
(10) J.C. Martin	20.00	10.00	6.00

1922 Leader Theatre

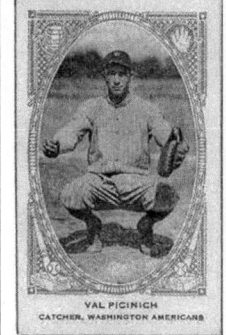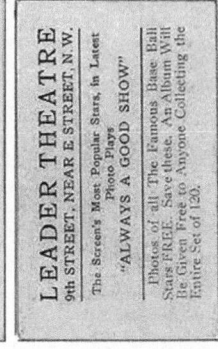

This issue by a Washington, D.C. moviehouse is a version of the W573 and W575-1 strip card sets on which at least two forms of customized advertising were printed on the card backs. The ads state that 120 cards (paralleling W573 and/or W575-1) were originally issued in this version. An album was also offered.

	NM	E	VG
Common Player:	500.00	250.00	150.00

(for non-commons. See 1922 W573 and W575-1 for checklists and base card values. Add 5X premium)

1949 Leaf Premiums

These blank-back, sepia photos were available with the purchase of 1948 Leaf baseball cards. Measuring 5-5/8" x 7-1/4", the pictures have a facsimile autograph and a black box labeled "BASEBALL'S IMMORTALS" at bottom containing a short biography. The unnumbered pictures are checklisted alphabetically.

	NM	E	VG
Complete Set (9):	6,000	3,000	1,800
Common Player:	400.00	200.00	120.00
(1) Grover Alexander	450.00	225.00	135.00
(2) Mickey Cochrane	400.00	200.00	120.00
(3) Lou Gehrig	1,200	600.00	360.00
(4) Walter Johnson	450.00	225.00	135.00
(5) Christy Mathewson	525.00	260.00	155.00
(6) John McGraw	400.00	200.00	120.00
(7) Babe Ruth (Dark background, text boxes.)	1,200	600.00	360.00
(8) Babe Ruth (Light background, no text.)	1,200	600.00	360.00
(9) Ed Walsh	400.00	200.00	120.00

1949 Leaf

The first color baseball cards of the post-World War II era were the 98-card, 2-3/8" x 2-7/8", set produced by Chicago's Leaf Gum Co. for issue in 1949. One of the toughest postwar sets to complete, exactly half of the issue - 49 cards - are significantly harder to find than the others. Probably intended to confound bubblegum buyers of the day, the set is skip-numbered between 1-168. Card backs contain offers of felt pennants, an album for the cards or 5-1/2" x 7-1/2" premium photos of Hall of Famers. While some cards carry a 1948 copyright date on back, it is now believed the issue was not released until 1949. The complete set price does not include the higher value in the variation pairs.

	NM	E	VG
Complete Set (98):	85,000	35,000	17,500
Common Player:	125.00	45.00	22.50
Common Short-print:	750.00	360.00	180.00
Album:	900.00	450.00	275.00
1 Joe DiMaggio	2,450	800.00	975.00
3 Babe Ruth	2,250	1,100	650.00
4 Stan Musial RC	1,600	800.00	480.00
5 Virgil Trucks RC (SP)	1,000	500.00	300.00
8 Satchel Paige RC (SP)	17,000	8,500	5,000
10 Paul Trout	125.00	45.00	22.50
11 Phil Rizzuto RC	325.00	130.00	65.00
13 Casimer Michaels (SP)	750.00	360.00	180.00
14 Billy Johnson	125.00	45.00	22.50
17 Frank Overmire	125.00	45.00	22.50
19 John Wyrostek (SP)	750.00	360.00	180.00
20 Hank Sauer RC (SP)	750.00	400.00	200.00
22 Al Evans	125.00	45.00	22.50
26 Sam Chapman	125.00	45.00	22.50
27 Mickey Harris	125.00	45.00	22.50
28 Jim Hegan RC	125.00	45.00	22.50
29 Elmer Valo RC	125.00	45.00	22.50
30 Bill Goodman RC (SP)	750.00	360.00	180.00
31 Lou Brissie	125.00	45.00	22.50
32 Warren Spahn RC	550.00	180.00	90.00
33 Harry Lowrey (SP)	750.00	360.00	180.00
36 Al Zarilla (SP)	750.00	360.00	180.00
38 Ted Kluszewski RC	300.00	120.00	60.00
39 Ewell Blackwell RC	130.00	50.00	25.00
42a Kent Peterson (Red cap.)	900.00	360.00	180.00
42b Kent Peterson (Black cap.)	125.00	45.00	22.50
43 Eddie Stevens (SP)	750.00	360.00	180.00
45 Ken Keltner (SP)	750.00	360.00	180.00
46 Johnny Mize	250.00	120.00	60.00
47 George Vico	125.00	45.00	22.50
48 Johnny Schmitz (SP)	750.00	360.00	180.00
49 Del Ennis RC	130.00	50.00	25.00
50 Dick Wakefield	125.00	45.00	22.50
51 Alvin Dark RC (SP)	1,750	700.00	350.00
53 John Vandermeer (Vander Meer)	225.00	90.00	45.00
54 Bobby Adams (SP)	750.00	360.00	180.00
55 Tommy Henrich (SP)	1,800	900.00	550.00
56 Larry Jensen RC	130.00	50.00	25.00
57 Bob McCall	125.00	45.00	22.50
59 Luke Appling	200.00	80.00	40.00
61 Jake Early	125.00	45.00	22.50
62 Eddie Joost (SP)	750.00	360.00	180.00
63 Barney McCosky (SP)	750.00	360.00	180.00
65 Bob Elliot (Elliott)	125.00	45.00	22.50
66 Orval Grove (SP)	750.00	360.00	180.00
68 Ed Miller (SP)	750.00	360.00	180.00
70 Honus Wagner	650.00	200.00	100.00
72 Hank Edwards	125.00	45.00	22.50
73 Pat Seerey	125.00	45.00	22.50
75 Dom DiMaggio (SP)	1,100	560.00	280.00
76 Ted Williams	1,475	725.00	425.00
77 Roy Smalley	125.00	45.00	22.50
78 Walter Evers (SP)	750.00	360.00	180.00
79 Jackie Robinson RC	2,300	1,150	645.00
81 George Kurowski (SP)	750.00	360.00	180.00
82 Johnny Lindell	125.00	45.00	22.50
83 Bobby Doerr	225.00	90.00	45.00
84 Sid Hudson	125.00	45.00	22.50
85 Dave Philley RC (SP)	750.00	360.00	180.00
86 Ralph Weigel	125.00	45.00	22.50
88 Frank Gustine (SP)	750.00	360.00	180.00
91 Ralph Kiner RC	225.00	70.00	35.00
93 Bob Feller (SP)	3,800	1,300	650.00
95 George Stirnweiss	125.00	45.00	22.50
97 Martin Marion RC	150.00	60.00	30.00
98a Hal Newhouser RC (SP)	1,800	725.00	360.00
98a Hal Newhouser (Unique prototype, blue/yellow background. Sold in 2/09 auction for $84,000.)			
102a Gene Hermansk (Incorrect spelling.)	2,750	1,100	550.00
102b Gene Hermanski (Correct spelling.)	135.00	55.00	25.00
104 Edward Stewart (SP)	750.00	360.00	180.00
106 Lou Boudreau	200.00	80.00	40.00
108 Matthew Batts (SP)	750.00	360.00	180.00
111 Gerald Priddy	125.00	45.00	22.50
113 Emil Leonard (SP)	750.00	360.00	180.00
117 Joe Gordon	125.00	45.00	22.50
120 George Kell RC (SP)	1,100	440.00	220.00
121 John Pesky RC (SP)	900.00	400.00	200.00
123 Clifford Fannin (SP)	750.00	360.00	180.00
125 Andy Pafko RC	160.00	65.00	30.00
127 Enos Slaughter (SP)	1,750	700.00	350.00

128 Warren Rosar	125.00	45.00	22.50
129 Kirby Higbe (SP)	750.00	360.00	180.00
131 Sid Gordon (SP)	750.00	360.00	180.00
133 Tommy Holmes (SP)	1,000	400.00	200.00
136a Cliff Aberson (Full sleeve.)	125.00	50.00	25.00
136b Cliff Aberson (Short sleeve.)	175.00	70.00	35.00
137 Harry Walker (SP)	750.00	360.00	180.00
138 Larry Doby RC (SP)	4,500	2,200	1,350
139 Johnny Hopp	125.00	45.00	22.50
142 Danny Murtaugh RC (SP)	1,500	750.00	450.00
143 Dick Sisler (SP)	750.00	360.00	180.00
144 Bob Dillinger (SP)	750.00	360.00	180.00
146 Harold Reiser (SP)	900.00	400.00	200.00
149 Henry Majeski (SP)	750.00	360.00	180.00
153 Floyd Baker (SP)	750.00	360.00	180.00
158 Harry Brecheen RC (SP)	750.00	360.00	180.00
159 Mizell Platt	125.00	45.00	22.50
160 Bob Scheffing (SP)	750.00	360.00	180.00
161 Vernon Stephens RC (SP)	900.00	400.00	200.00
163 Freddy Hutchinson RC (SP)	950.00	400.00	200.00
165 Dale Mitchell RC (SP)	900.00	400.00	200.00
168 Phil Cavaretta (SP)	1,650	360.00	180.00

1949 Leaf Prototype

 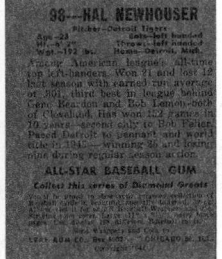

This currently unique card is believed to have been prepared for issue with the first series of 1949 Leaf but for unknown reasons was withdrawn. A Newhouser card with a completely different front and changes to the back was issued with the set's short-printed second series. Graded SGC-Poor, this discovery card was auctioned for $84,000 in 2/09.

98 Hal Newhouser

1960 Leaf Pre-Production

Evidently produced prior to final approval for the design of the 1960 Leaf set, these cards all feature much larger player photos than the issued versions. Generally the issued cards have cap-to-waist photos while the pre-production cards have cap-to-chin shots. Backs of the pre-production cards are virtually identical to the regular cards. The pre-production cards were never publically issued and show evidence of having been hand-cut. The cards of Donovan and Jay appear to be more common than the others.

	NM	E	VG
Complete Set (8):	12,000	7,500	4,500
Common Player:	1,200	750.00	450.00
1 Luis Aparicio	3,200	2,250	1,350
12 Ken Boyer	2,150	1,075	645.00
17 Walt Moryn	1,200	625.00	375.00
23 Joey Jay	1,200	625.00	375.00
35 Jim Coates	1,200	1,125	675.00
58 Hal Smith	1,350	975.00	585.00
61 Vic Rehm	1,200	750.00	450.00
72 Dick Donovan	1,200	625.00	375.00

1960 Leaf

 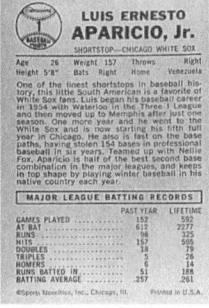

While known to the hobby as "Leaf" cards, this set of 144 carries the copyright of Sports Novelties Inc., Chicago. The 2-1/2" x 3-1/2" cards feature black-and-white player portrait photos, with plain background. Cards were sold in nickel wax packs with a marble, rather than a piece of bubble gum. The second half of the set, #73-144, are quite scarce. Card #25, Jim Grant, is found in two versions, with his own picture (black cap) and with a photo of Brooks Lawrence (white cap). Three back variations of Hal Smith card #58 are also known. Complete set prices do not include variations. In the late 1990s, a large group of high-number (Series 2) boxes - in excess of 4,000 cards - was added to the surviving supply.

	NM	E	VG
Complete Set (144):	2,550	1,000	500.00
Common Player (1-72):	9.00	4.50	2.75
Common Player (73-144):	12.00	6.00	3.50
Wax Pack, Series 1 (5):	120.00		
Wax Box, Series 1 (24):	2,400		
Wax Pack, Series 2 (5):	190.00		
Wax Box, Series 2 (24):	3,000		
1 Luis Aparicio	55.00	15.00	9.00
2 Woody Held	9.00	4.50	2.75
3 Frank Lary	9.00	4.50	2.75
4 Camilo Pascual	9.00	4.50	2.75
5 Frank Herrera	9.00	4.50	2.75
6 Felipe Alou	8.00	4.00	2.50
7 Bennie Daniels	9.00	4.50	2.75
8 Roger Craig	9.00	4.50	2.75
9 Eddie Kasko	9.00	4.50	2.75
10 Bob Grim	9.00	4.50	2.75
11 Jim Busby	9.00	4.50	2.75
12 Ken Boyer	17.50	8.75	5.25
13 Bob Boyd	9.00	4.50	2.75
14 Sam Jones	9.00	4.50	2.75
15 Larry Jackson	9.00	4.50	2.75
16 Roy Face	9.00	4.50	2.75
17 Walt Moryn	9.00	4.50	2.75
18 Jim Gilliam	8.00	4.00	2.50
19 Don Newcombe	8.00	4.00	2.50
20 Glen Hobbie	9.00	4.50	2.75
21 Pedro Ramos	9.00	4.50	2.75
22 Ryne Duren	8.00	4.00	2.50
23 Joe Jay	9.00	4.50	2.75
24 Lou Berberet	9.00	4.50	2.75
25a Jim Grant (White cap, photo actually Brooks Lawrence.)	15.00	7.50	4.50
25b Jim Grant (Dark cap, correct photo.)	22.50	11.00	6.75
26 Tom Borland	9.00	4.50	2.75
27 Brooks Robinson	25.00	12.50	7.50
28 Jerry Adair	9.00	4.50	2.75
29 Ron Jackson	9.00	4.50	2.75
30 George Strickland	9.00	4.50	2.75
31 Rocky Bridges	9.00	4.50	2.75
32 Bill Tuttle	9.00	4.50	2.75
33 Ken Hunt	9.00	4.50	2.75
34 Hal Griggs	9.00	4.50	2.75
35 Jim Coates	9.00	4.50	2.75
36 Brooks Lawrence	9.00	4.50	2.75
37 Duke Snider	30.00	15.00	9.00
38 Al Spangler	9.00	4.50	2.75
39 Jim Owens	9.00	4.50	2.75
40 Bill Virdon	9.00	4.50	2.75
41 Ernie Broglio	9.00	4.50	2.75
42 Andre Rodgers	9.00	4.50	2.75
43 Julio Becquer	9.00	4.50	2.75
44 Tony Taylor	9.00	4.50	2.75
45 Jerry Lynch	9.00	4.50	2.75
46 Clete Boyer	8.00	4.00	2.50
47 Jerry Lumpe	9.00	4.50	2.75
48 Charlie Maxwell	9.00	4.50	2.75
49 Jim Perry	9.00	4.50	2.75
50 Danny McDevitt	9.00	4.50	2.75
51 Juan Pizarro	9.00	4.50	2.75
52 Dallas Green RC	20.00	10.00	6.00
53 Bob Friend	9.00	4.50	2.75
54 Jack Sanford	9.00	4.50	2.75

#	Player			
55	Jim Rivera	9.00	4.50	2.75
56	Ted Wills	9.00	4.50	2.75
57	Milt Pappas	9.00	4.50	2.75
58a	Hal Smith (Team & position on back.)	9.00	4.50	2.75
58b	Hal Smith (Team blackened out on back.)	900.00	375.00	225.00
58c	Hal Smith (Team missing on back.)	75.00	37.50	22.50
59	Bob Avila	9.00	4.50	2.75
60	Clem Labine	9.00	4.50	2.75
61	Vic Rehm	9.00	4.50	2.75
62	John Gabler	9.00	4.50	2.75
63	John Tsitouris	9.00	4.50	2.75
64	Dave Sisler	9.00	4.50	2.75
65	Vic Power	9.00	4.50	2.75
66	Earl Battey	9.00	4.50	2.75
67	Bob Purkey	9.00	4.50	2.75
68	Moe Drabowsky	9.00	4.50	2.75
69	Hoyt Wilhelm	15.00	7.50	4.50
70	Humberto Robinson	9.00	4.50	2.75
71	Whitey Herzog	9.00	4.50	2.75
72	Dick Donovan	9.00	4.50	2.75
73	Gordon Jones	12.00	6.00	3.50
74	Joe Hicks	12.00	6.00	3.50
75	Ray Culp RC	12.00	6.00	3.50
76	Dick Drott	12.00	6.00	3.50
77	Bob Duliba	12.00	6.00	3.50
78	Art Ditmar	12.00	6.00	3.50
79	Steve Korcheck	12.00	6.00	3.50
80	Henry Mason	12.00	6.00	3.50
81	Harry Simpson	12.00	6.00	3.50
82	Gene Green	12.00	6.00	3.50
83	Bob Shaw	12.00	6.00	3.50
84	Howard Reed	12.00	6.00	3.50
85	Dick Stigman	12.00	6.00	3.50
86	Rip Repulski	12.00	6.00	3.50
87	Seth Morehead	12.00	6.00	3.50
88	Camilo Carreon	12.00	6.00	3.50
89	John Blanchard	17.50	8.75	5.25
90	Billy Hoeft	12.00	6.00	3.50
91	Fred Hopke	12.00	6.00	3.50
92	Joe Martin	12.00	6.00	3.50
93	Wally Shannon	12.00	6.00	3.50
94	Baseball's Two Hal Smiths	50.00	25.00	15.00
95	Al Schroll	12.00	6.00	3.50
96	John Kucks	12.00	6.00	3.50
97	Tom Morgan	12.00	6.00	3.50
98	Willie Jones	12.00	6.00	3.50
99	Marshall Renfroe	12.00	6.00	3.50
100	Willie Tasby	12.00	6.00	3.50
101	Irv Noren	12.00	6.00	3.50
102	Russ Snyder	12.00	6.00	3.50
103	Bob Turley	17.50	8.75	5.25
104	Jim Woods	12.00	6.00	3.50
105	Ronnie Kline	12.00	6.00	3.50
106	Steve Bilko	12.00	6.00	3.50
107	Elmer Valo	12.00	6.00	3.50
108	Tom McAvoy	12.00	6.00	3.50
109	Stan Williams	12.00	6.00	3.50
110	Earl Averill	12.00	6.00	3.50
111	Lee Walls	12.00	6.00	3.50
112	Paul Richards	12.00	6.00	3.50
113	Ed Sadowski	12.00	6.00	3.50
114	Stover McIlwain (Photo actually Jim McAnany.)	17.50	8.75	5.25
115	Chuck Tanner (Photo actually Ken Kuhn.)	17.50	8.75	5.25
116	Lou Klimchock	12.00	6.00	3.50
117	Neil Chrisley	12.00	6.00	3.50
118	Johnny Callison	12.00	6.00	3.50
119	Hal Smith	12.00	6.00	3.50
120	Carl Sawatski	12.00	6.00	3.50
121	Frank Leja	12.00	6.00	3.50
122	Earl Torgeson	12.00	6.00	3.50
123	Art Schult	12.00	6.00	3.50
124	Jim Brosnan	12.00	6.00	3.50
125	Sparky Anderson	60.00	30.00	18.00
126	Joe Pignatano	12.00	6.00	3.50
127	Rocky Nelson	12.00	6.00	3.50
128	Orlando Cepeda	45.00	22.50	13.50
129	Daryl Spencer	12.00	6.00	3.50
130	Ralph Lumenti	12.00	6.00	3.50
131	Sam Taylor	12.00	6.00	3.50
132	Harry Brecheen	12.00	6.00	3.50
133	Johnny Groth	12.00	6.00	3.50
134	Wayne Terwilliger	12.00	6.00	3.50
135	Kent Hadley	12.00	6.00	3.50
136	Faye Throneberry	12.00	6.00	3.50
137	Jack Meyer	12.00	6.00	3.50
138	Chuck Cottier RC	12.00	6.00	3.50
139	Joe DeMaestri	12.00	6.00	3.50
140	Gene Freese	12.00	6.00	3.50
141	Curt Flood	30.00	15.00	9.00
142	Gino Cimoli	12.00	6.00	3.50
143	Clay Dalrymple	12.00	6.00	3.50
144	Jim Bunning	50.00	25.00	15.00

1923 Lections

This series of cards was virtually unknown in the hobby until 1997 when 28 cards turned up in Albany, N.Y. The cards measure about 4" x 2-1/2" with rounded corners and are printed on very thick cardboard. At left front is an oval black-and-white player photo with name and team below. At right is green or orange art of a baseball game with the issuer's logo and trademark information. It is unknown with what, if any, product these cards were issued; a candy premium seems the most likely source. Most of the cards seen so far are in grades from Fair-Good, though a few are known in Ex-Mt.

		NM	E	VG
Complete Set (10):		32,500	15,000	9,000
Common Player:		2,000	1,000	600.00
(1)	Frank Chance	3,500	1,750	1,050
(2)	Howard Ehmke	2,000	1,000	600.00
(3)	Frank Frisch	3,500	1,750	1,050
(4)	Roger (Rogers) Hornsby	6,750	2,500	1,500
(5)	Charles Jamieson	2,000	1,000	600.00
(6)	"Bob" Meusel	2,000	1,000	600.00
(7)	Emil Meusel	2,000	1,000	600.00
(8)	"Babe" Ruth	13,250	4,500	2,700
(9)	Charles Schmidt	2,000	1,000	600.00
(10)	"Bob" Shawkey	2,000	1,000	600.00

1975 Lee's Sweets

Professing to be an issue of 68 cards of "Baseball Greats," this collectors' issue first appeared about 1975. Only four players are known. Fronts of the 2-1/2" x 3-3/16" cards have crudely printed black-and-white player photos. Backs describe the series and give the Lee's Sweets address as Camp Hill, Ala.

		NM	E	VG
Complete Set (4):		25.00	12.50	7.50
Common Player:		6.00	3.00	1.75
(1)	Ty Cobb	6.00	3.00	1.75
(2)	Joe DiMaggio	6.00	3.00	1.75
(3)	Lou Gehrig	6.00	3.00	1.75
(4)	Babe Ruth	12.00	6.00	3.50

1909-11 Lenox Cigarettes

Many collectors rank the Lenox back as the third rarest among T206, behind only Ty Cobb and Drum. Lenox cards can be found with the back printing in either black or brown.

PREMIUMS
Black, Common Players: 18-24X
Black, Hall of Famers: 10-15X
Brown, Common Players: 75-100X
Brown, Hall of Famers: 45-65X

(See T206 for checklist and base card values.)

1969 Lincoln-Mercury Sports Panel Postcards

Various celebrity spokesmen on the Lincoln-Mercury Sports Panel can be found on a series of color postcards. In standard 5-1/2" x 3-1/2" format, cards have borderless color photos on front of the spokesman standing with one of the company's new cars; a facsimile autograph also appears. Divided backs identify the player and the automobile.

	NM	E	VG
Al Kaline	80.00	40.00	25.00

1906 Lincoln Publishing Philadelphia A's

Members of the American League Champions (says so right at the top) Philadelphia A's, decked out in their Sunday-best, are featured in this set of black-and-white postcards. The portraits are framed in fancy graphics which include a baseball, the dates 1905 and 1906 and the player's name in a banner beneath the photo. At bottom is a box with "ATHLETIC BASE BALL TEAM." Back of the approximately 3-1/2" x 5-1/2" cards has a box at upper-left enclosing "POST CARD." The unnumbered cards are listed here alphabetically.

		NM	E	VG
Complete Set (20):		50,000	5,000	3,000
Common Player:		1,200	150.00	90.00
(1)	Chief Bender	8,500	750.00	450.00
(2)	Andy Coakley	300.00	150.00	90.00
(3)	Lave Cross	300.00	150.00	90.00
(4)	Monte Cross	300.00	150.00	90.00
(5)	Harry Davis	300.00	150.00	90.00
(6)	Jimmy Dygert	300.00	150.00	90.00
(7)	Topsy Hartsel	300.00	150.00	90.00
(8)	Weldon Henley	300.00	150.00	90.00
(9)	Danny Hoffman	300.00	150.00	90.00
(10)	John Knight	300.00	150.00	90.00
(11)	Bris Lord	300.00	150.00	90.00
(12)	Connie Mack	7,500	750.00	450.00
(13)	Danny Murphy	300.00	150.00	90.00
(14)	Joe Myers	300.00	150.00	90.00
(15)	Rube Oldring	300.00	150.00	90.00
(16)	Eddie Plank	9,500	1,000	600.00
(17)	Mike Powers	300.00	150.00	90.00
(18)	Ossee Schreckengost	300.00	150.00	90.00
(19)	Ralph Seybold	300.00	150.00	90.00
(20)	Rube Waddell	7,500	750.00	450.00

1929 Lindy Theatre Philadelphia A's

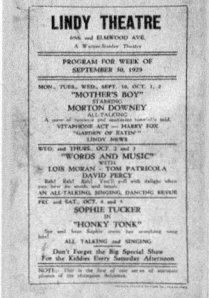

This is one of several theater giveaways of the era capitalizing on the A's consecutive American League Championships of 1929-1931. This series is in a 3-1/2" x 5-5/8" black-and-white format. Fronts have a player photo with his name (in all-capitals) and position (upper- and lower-case) at lower-right. Backs have details of coming attractions at the movie house, generally aimed at youngsters. The extent of the checklist for this set is not yet known.

	NM	EX	VG
Mickey Cochrane	3,500	1,750	1,050
Jimmy Foxx	6,500	3,250	2,300
Bill Shores	3,000	1,500	900.00
Al Simmons	3,500	1,750	1,050

1975 Linnett MLB All-Stars

This series of pencil-portrait prints was done by sports artist Charles Linnett of Walpole, Mass. The black-and-white prints are on 8-1/2" x 11" textured paper, featuring a facsimile autograph of the player. Because the portraits are licensed only by the Players Association, the players are pictured capless with no uniform logos visible. Backs are blank. The 1975 pictures differ from the 1976 issue in that they include a printed player name, besides the facsimile autograph. At least some of the portraits were given away in a ballpark "Portrait Day" promotion at Fenway Park, sponsored by Grant City (W.T. Grant Co.) department stores. A coupon accompanying the SGA portraits offered a discount on a package of three pictures, apparently the standard retail offering that carried a $1.19 price tag. This rudimentary checklist is certainly incomplete.

	NM	E	VG
Common Player:	6.00	3.00	1.75
(25) Fred Lynn	9.00	4.50	2.75
(50) Tom Seaver	9.00	4.50	2.75
(75) Carl Yastrzemski	12.00	6.00	3.50

1976 Linnett Portraits

This series of pencil-portrait prints was done by sports artist Charles Linnett of Walpole, Mass., and includes baseball, football, hockey, NBA and Harlem Globetrotters players (only baseball listed here). The black-and-white prints are on 8-1/2" x 11" textured paper, featuring a facsimile autograph of the player. Because the portraits are licensed only by the Players Association, the players are pictured capless with no uniform logos visible. Backs are blank. The portraits originally sold for 50 cents apiece by mail.

	NM	E	VG
Complete Baseball Set (176):	300.00	150.00	90.00
Common Player:	2.50	1.25	.75
(1) Hank Aaron	10.00	5.00	3.00
(2) Dick Allen	4.00	2.00	1.25
(3) Matty Alou	2.50	1.25	.75
(4) Mike Anderson	2.50	1.25	.75
(5) Luis Aparicio	5.00	2.50	1.50
(6) Sal Bando	2.50	1.25	.75
(7) Mark Belanger	2.50	1.25	.70
(8) Buddy Bell	2.50	1.25	.75
(9) Johnny Bench	6.00	3.00	1.75
(10) Jim Bibby	2.50	1.25	.75
(11) Paul Blair	2.50	1.25	.75
(12) Bert Blyleven	3.00	1.50	.90
(13) Ron Blomberg	2.50	1.25	.75
(14) Bob Bolin	2.50	1.25	.75
(15) Bill Bonham	2.50	1.25	.75
(16) Pedro Borbon	2.50	1.25	.75
(17) Bob Boone	3.00	1.50	.90
(18) Larry Bowa	2.50	1.25	.75
(19) Steve Braun	2.50	1.25	.75
(20) Ken Brett	2.50	1.25	.75
(21) John Briggs	2.50	1.25	.75
(22) Lou Brock	5.00	2.50	1.50
(23) Jack Brohamer	2.50	1.25	.75
(24) Steve Brye	2.50	1.25	.75
(25) Bill Buckner	2.50	1.25	.70
(26) Jeff Burroughs	2.50	1.25	.75
(27) Steve Busby	2.50	1.25	.75
(28) Bert Campaneris	2.50	1.25	.75
(29) Bernie Carbo	2.50	1.25	.75
(30) Jose Cardenal	2.50	1.25	.75
(31) Steve Carlton	5.00	2.50	1.50
(32) Rod Carew	5.00	2.50	1.50
(33) Dave Cash	2.50	1.25	.75
(34) Norm Cash	3.00	1.50	.90
(35) Danny Cater	2.50	1.25	.75
(36) Cesar Cedeno	2.50	1.25	.75
(37) Orlando Cepeda	5.00	2.50	1.50
(38) Ron Cey	2.50	1.25	.70
(39) Chris Chambliss	2.50	1.25	.75
(40) David Clyde	2.50	1.25	.75
(41) Rich Coggins	2.50	1.25	.75
(42) Jim Colborn	2.50	1.25	.75
(43) Dave Concepcion	3.00	1.50	.90
(44) Willie Crawford	2.50	1.25	.75
(45) John Curtis	2.50	1.25	.75
(46) Bobby Darwin	2.50	1.25	.75
(47) Dan Driessen	2.50	1.25	.75
(48) Duffy Dyer	2.50	1.25	.75
(49) John Ellis	2.50	1.25	.75
(50) Darrell Evans	2.50	1.25	.70
(51) Dwight Evans	2.50	1.25	.70
(52) Joe Ferguson	2.50	1.25	.75
(53) Rollie Fingers	4.00	2.00	1.25
(54) Carlton Fisk	5.00	2.50	1.50
(55) Bill Freehan	2.50	1.25	.70
(56) Jim Fregosi	2.50	1.25	.75
(57) Oscar Gamble	2.50	1.25	.75
(58) Pedro Garcia	2.50	1.25	.75
(59) Ralph Garr	2.50	1.25	.75
(60) Wayne Garrett	2.50	1.25	.75
(61) Steve Garvey	2.50	1.25	.70
(62) Cesar Geronimo	2.50	1.25	.75
(63) Bob Gibson	5.00	2.50	1.50
(64) Dave Giusti	2.50	1.25	.75
(65) Bobby Grich	2.50	1.25	.75
(66) Doug Griffin	2.50	1.25	.75
(67) Mario Guerrero	2.50	1.25	.75
(68) Don Gullett	2.50	1.25	.75
(69) Tommy Harper	2.50	1.25	.75
(70) Toby Harrah	2.50	1.25	.75
(71) Bud Harrelson	2.50	1.25	.75
(72) Vic Harris	2.50	1.25	.75
(73) Richie Hebner	2.50	1.25	.75
(74) George Hendrick	2.50	1.25	.75
(75) Ed Hermann	2.50	1.25	.75
(76) John Hiller	2.50	1.25	.75
(77) Willie Horton	2.50	1.25	.75
(78) Jim Hunter	4.00	2.00	1.25
(79) Tommy Hutton	2.50	1.25	.75
(80) Reggie Jackson	7.50	3.75	2.25
(81) Fergie Jenkins	4.00	2.00	1.25
(82) Dave Johnson	2.50	1.25	.75
(83) Cleon Jones	2.50	1.25	.75
(84) Al Kaline	6.00	3.00	1.75
(85) John Kennedy	2.50	1.25	.75
(86) Steve Kline	2.50	1.25	.75
(87) Jerry Koosman	2.50	1.25	.75
(88) Bill Lee	2.50	1.25	.75
(89) Eddie Leon	2.50	1.25	.75
(90) Bob Locker	2.50	1.25	.75
(91) Mickey Lolich	3.00	1.50	.90
(92) Jim Lonborg	2.50	1.25	.75
(93) Davey Lopes	2.50	1.25	.75
(94) Mike Lum	2.50	1.25	.75
(95) Greg Luzinski	2.50	1.25	.75
(96) Sparky Lyle	2.50	1.25	.75
(97) Teddy Martinez	2.50	1.25	.75
(98) Jon Matlack	2.50	1.25	.75
(99) Dave May	2.50	1.25	.75
(100) John Mayberry	2.50	1.25	.75
(101) Willie Mays	10.00	5.00	3.00
(102) Jim McAndrew	2.50	1.25	.75
(103) Dick McAuliffe	2.50	1.25	.75
(104) Sam McDowell	2.50	1.25	.75
(105) Lynn McGlothen	2.50	1.25	.75
(106) Tug McGraw	2.50	1.25	.70
(107) Hal McRae	2.50	1.25	.75
(108) Bill Melton	2.50	1.25	.75
(109) Andy Messersmith	2.50	1.25	.75
(110) Gene Michael	2.50	1.25	.75
(111) Felix Millan	2.50	1.25	.75
(112) Rick Miller	2.50	1.25	.75
(113) John Milner	2.50	1.25	.75
(114) Rick Monday	2.50	1.25	.75
(115) Don Money	2.50	1.25	.75
(116) Bob Montgomery	2.50	1.25	.75
(117) Joe Morgan	5.00	2.50	1.50
(118) Carl Morton	2.50	1.25	.75
(119) Thurman Munson	4.00	2.00	1.25
(120) Bobby Murcer	2.50	1.25	.75
(121) Graig Nettles	3.00	1.50	.90
(122) Jim Northrup	2.50	1.25	.75
(123) Ben Oglivie	2.50	1.25	.75
(124) Al Oliver	3.00	1.50	.90
(125) Bob Oliver	2.50	1.25	.75
(126) Jorge Orta	2.50	1.25	.75
(127) Amos Otis	2.50	1.25	.75
(128) Jim Palmer	5.00	2.50	1.50
(129) Harry Parker	2.50	1.25	.75
(130) Fred Patek	2.50	1.25	.75
(131) Marty Pattin	2.50	1.25	.75
(132) Tony Perez	4.00	2.00	1.25
(133) Gaylord Perry	4.00	2.00	1.25
(134) Jim Perry	2.50	1.25	.75
(135) Rico Petrocelli	2.50	1.25	.75
(136) Rick Reichardt	2.50	1.25	.75
(137) Ken Reitz	2.50	1.25	.75
(138) Jerry Reuss	2.50	1.25	.75
(139) Bill Robinson	2.50	1.25	.75
(140) Brooks Robinson	5.00	2.50	1.50
(141) Frank Robinson	5.00	2.50	1.50
(142) Cookie Rojas	2.50	1.25	.75
(143) Pete Rose	9.00	4.50	2.75
(144) Bill Russell	2.50	1.25	.75
(145) Nolan Ryan	15.00	7.50	4.50
(146) Manny Sanguillen	2.50	1.25	.75
(147) George Scott	2.50	1.25	.75
(148) Mike Schmidt	7.50	3.75	2.25
(149) Tom Seaver	6.00	3.00	1.75
(150) Sonny Siebert	2.50	1.25	.75
(151) Ted Simmons	2.50	1.25	.75
(152) Bill Singer	2.50	1.25	.75
(153) Reggie Smith	2.50	1.25	.75
(154) Chris Speier	2.50	1.25	.75
(155) Charlie Spikes	2.50	1.25	.75
(156) Paul Splittorff	2.50	1.25	.75
(157) Mickey Stanley	2.50	1.25	.75
(158) Lee Stanton	2.50	1.25	.75
(159) Willie Stargell	5.00	2.50	1.50
(160) Rusty Staub	3.00	1.50	.90
(161) Rennie Stennett	2.50	1.25	.75
(162) Steve Stone	3.00	1.50	.90
(163) Mel Stottlemyre	2.50	1.25	.75
(164) Don Sutton	4.00	2.00	1.25
(165) George Theodore	2.50	1.25	.75
(166) Danny Thompson	2.50	1.25	.75
(167) Luis Tiant	3.00	1.50	.90
(168) Joe Torre	3.50	1.75	1.00
(169) Bobby Valentine	2.50	1.25	.75
(170) Bob Veale	2.50	1.25	.75
(171) Billy Williams	5.00	2.50	1.50
(172) Wilbur Wood	2.50	1.25	.75
(173) Jim Wynn	2.50	1.25	.75
(174) Carl Yastrzemski	6.00	3.00	1.75
(175) Robin Yount	5.00	2.50	1.50
(175) Richie Zisk	2.50	1.25	.75

1976 Linnett Superstars

This frequently encountered set of 36 cards has enjoyed little collector interest since its issue in 1976. Officially known as "Pee-Wee Superstars," the cards measure 4" x 5-5/8". Player portraits by artist Charles Linnett are rendered in black-and-white pencil and set against a pale yellow background. Players are shown without caps or uniforms (most appear to be wearing white T-shirts). According to the logos at top the set was fully licensed by both the Players Association and Major League Baseball, and team logos do appear in the lower-left corner. A facsimile autograph in red or purple appears on each card. Front borders are bright purple, red, green, dark brown, or white. Card backs feature either a photo of an antique auto or a drawing of an historic sailing ship. Each of the 12 different back designs appears on one card from each team set. The Linnetts were sold in panels of six perforated cards. An offer on the back of each card makes 8" x 10" premium portraits of each player available for 95 cents. The premium pictures have about the same value as the cards. Inexplicably, the cards are numbered from 90-125. Only the World's Champion Cincinnati Reds, A.L. Champion Boston Red Sox and N.L. runner-up Dodgers are represented in the issue.

		NM	E	VG
Complete Panel Set (6):		15.00	7.50	4.50
Complete Singles Set (36):		15.00	7.50	4.50
Common Player:		.60	.30	.20
Panel 1		7.50	3.75	2.25
90	Don Gullett	.60	.30	.20
91	Johnny Bench	2.50	1.25	.70
92	Tony Perez	1.25	.60	.40
93	Mike Lum	.60	.30	.20
94	Ken Griffey	.60	.30	.20
95	George Foster	.60	.30	.20
Panel 2		9.00	4.50	2.75
96	Joe Morgan	2.50	1.25	.70
97	Pete Rose	6.00	3.00	1.75
98	Dave Concepcion	.60	.30	.20
99	Cesar Geronimo	.60	.30	.20
100	Dan Driessen	.60	.30	.20
101	Pedro Borbon	.60	.30	.20
Panel 3		7.50	3.75	2.25
102	Carl Yastrzemski	2.50	1.25	.70
103	Fred Lynn	.60	.30	.20
104	Dwight Evans	.60	.30	.20
105	Ferguson Jenkins	1.25	.60	.40
106	Rico Petrocelli	.60	.30	.20
107	Denny Doyle	.60	.30	.20
Panel 4		6.00	3.00	1.75
108	Luis Tiant	.60	.30	.20
109	Carlton Fisk	2.50	1.25	.70
110	Rick Burleson	.60	.30	.20
111	Bill Lee	.60	.30	.20
112	Rick Wise	.60	.30	.20
113	Jim Rice	2.50	.50	.30
Panel 5		6.00	3.00	1.75
114	Davey Lopes	.60	.30	.20
115	Steve Garvey	1.25	.60	.40
116	Bill Russell	.60	.30	.20
117	Ron Cey	.60	.30	.20
118	Steve Yeager	.60	.30	.20
119	Doug Rau	.60	.30	.20
Panel 6		6.00	3.00	1.75
120	Don Sutton	1.75	.90	.50
121	Joe Ferguson	.60	.30	.20
122	Mike Marshall	.60	.30	.20
123	Bill Buckner	.60	.30	.20
124	Rick Rhoden	.60	.30	.20
125	Ted Sizemore	.60	.30	.20

1923 Little Wonder Picture Series

Some versions of the W515-2 strip cards are found with part of a line of type in the top border that reads "THE LITTLE WONDER PICTURE SERIES" and includes a Underwood (U&U) logo.

(See W515-2.)

1887 Lone Jack St. Louis Browns (N370)

The Lone Jack set is among the rarest of all 19th Century tobacco issues. Issued by the Lone Jack Cigarette Co. of Lynchburg, Va., the set consists of 13 subjects, all members of the American Association champion St. Louis Browns. Photos for the set are enlarged versions of those used in the more popular N172 Old Judge series. Cards in the set mea-

sure 2-1/2" x 1-1/2" and carry an ad for Lone Jack Cigarettes along the bottom of the front. The set features the Browns' starting lineup for 1886 along with their two top pitchers, backup catcher and owner, Chris Von Der Ahe.

		NM	E	VG
Common Player:		12,000	7,150	4,950
(1)	Doc Bushong	12,000	7,150	4,950
(2)	Bob Caruthers	12,000	7,150	4,950
(3)	Charles Commiskey (Comiskey)	75,000	12,000	8,000
(4)	Dave Foutz	12,000	7,150	4,950
(5)	Will Gleason	12,000	7,150	4,950
(6)	Nat Hudson	12,000	7,150	4,950
(7)	Rudy Kimler (Kemmler)	12,000	7,150	4,950
(8)	Arlie Latham	12,000	7,150	4,950
(9)	Little Nick Nicol	12,000	7,150	4,950
(10)	Tip O'Neil (O'Neill)	12,000	7,150	4,950
(11)	Yank Robinson	11,000	6,500	4,500
(12)	Chris Von Der Ahe	18,000	10,800	7,200
(13)	Curt Welsh (Welch)	12,000	7,150	4,950

1886 Lorillard Team Cards

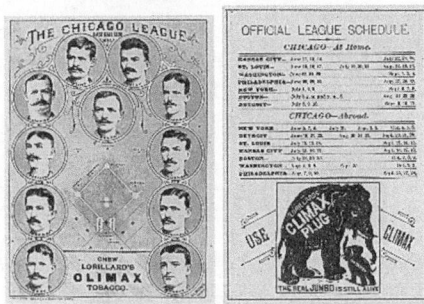

Issued in 1886 by Lorillard Tobacco Co., these 4" x 5-1/2" cards were issued for the Chicago, Detroit and New York baseball clubs. Each card carries the team's schedule (starting with June) on one side and features 11 player portraits enclosed in circles on the other. Each side has advertising for one of Lorillard's tobacco brands - Climax, Rebecca, etc.

		NM	E	VG
Complete Set (4):		45,000	22,500	13,500
Common Team:		10,000	5,000	3,000
(1)	Chicago League Base Ball Club	13,500	7,200	6,000
(2)	Detroit League Base Ball Club	12,000	6,000	3,600
(3)	New York League Base Ball Club	10,000	5,000	3,250
(4)	Philadelphia League Base Ball Club	8,250	3,750	3,000

1949 Lummis Peanut Butter Phillies

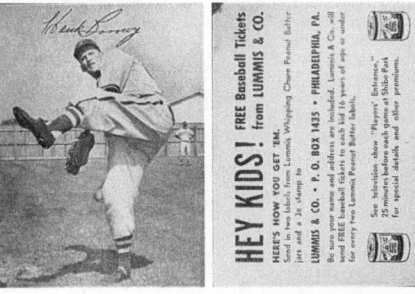

This 12-card regional set featuring the Phillies was issued in the Philadelphia area by Lummis Peanut Butter in 1949. The cards measure 3-1/4" x 4-1/4" and are unnumbered. The fronts feature an action photo with a facsimile autograph, while the backs advertise a game ticket promotion by Lummis Peanut Butter. The same photos and checklist were also used for a regional sticker set issued by Sealtest Dairy the same year.

		NM	E	VG
Complete Set (12):		37,500	11,250	6,750
Common Player:		2,400	675.00	400.00
(1)	Rich Ashburn	7,500	2,250	1,350
(2)	Hank Borowy	1,350	675.00	400.00
(3)	Del Ennis	2,500	750.00	450.00
(4)	Granny Hamner	1,350	675.00	400.00
(5)	Puddinhead Jones	1,350	675.00	400.00
(6)	Russ Meyer	1,350	675.00	400.00
(7)	Bill Nicholson	1,350	675.00	400.00
(8)	Robin Roberts	7,500	2,250	1,350
(9)	"Schoolboy" Rowe	1,350	675.00	400.00
(10)	Andy Seminick	1,350	675.00	400.00
(11)	Curt Simmons	2,500	750.00	450.00
(12)	Eddie Waitkus	1,350	675.00	400.00

1910 Luxello Cigars A's/Phillies Pins (P13)

Players from the two Philadelphia teams are pictured in this series of 7/8" black-and-white pins. The player's last name, team and position are printed below the photo; the Luxello Cigar name at top. On left and right are a horseshoe with monogram inside.

		NM	E	VG
Complete Set (21):		17,500	8,750	5,250
Common Player:		750.00	375.00	225.00
Philadelphia Athletics				
(1)	Franklin Baker	1,600	800.00	400.00
(2)	Jack Barry	900.00	450.00	300.00
(3)	Eddie Collins	1,200	600.00	300.00
(4)	John W. Coombs	900.00	450.00	300.00
(5)	Harry Davis	900.00	450.00	300.00
(6)	James Dygert	900.00	450.00	300.00
(7)	Heinie Heitmuller	900.00	450.00	300.00
(8)	Harry Krause	900.00	450.00	300.00
(9)	Paddy Livingston	900.00	450.00	300.00
(10)	Danny Murphy	900.00	450.00	300.00
(11)	Ed Plank	2,250	1,125	550.00
Philadelphia Phillies				
(12)	John W. Bates	900.00	450.00	300.00
(13)	Chas. S. Dooin	900.00	450.00	300.00
(14)	Mike Doolan	900.00	450.00	300.00
(15)	Eddie Grant	900.00	450.00	300.00
(16)	Otto Knabe	900.00	450.00	300.00
(17)	Geo. McQuillan	900.00	450.00	300.00
(18)	Earl Moore	900.00	450.00	300.00
(19)	Lew Moren	900.00	450.00	300.00
(20)	Louise Schettler	900.00	450.00	300.00
(21)	Tully Sparks	900.00	450.00	300.00
(22)	John Titus	900.00	450.00	300.00

M

1916 M101-4 Blank Backs

The "update" version of this set is nearly identical to the earlier cards. The 200 black-and-white cards once again are printed with player photo, name, position, team and card number on front and blank backs. This version appears to have been sold directly to consumers by the manufacturer, Felix Mendelsohn of Chicago. The same cards can be found with advertising on back from several businesses around the country. Most of the players included on the 1-5/8" x 3" cards also appear in the prior edition. Despite being labeled in the American Card Catalog as M101-4, this version was issued after the M101-5 version, with the first advertising appearing in August 1916. The complete set price does not include variations.

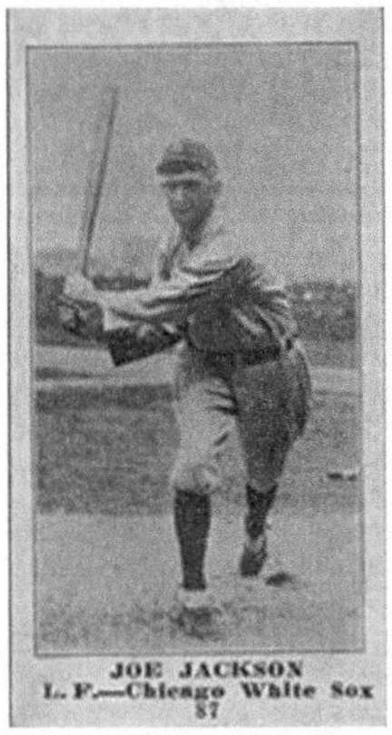
JOE JACKSON
L. F.—Chicago White Sox
87

		NM	E	VG
Complete Set (200):		100,000	50,000	30,000
Common Player:		125.00	30.00	18.00
1	Babe Adams	60.00	30.00	18.00
2	Sam Agnew	60.00	30.00	18.00
3	Eddie Ainsmith	60.00	30.00	18.00
4	Grover Alexander	500.00	250.00	150.00
5	Leon Ames	60.00	30.00	18.00
6	Jimmy Archer	60.00	30.00	18.00
7	Jimmy Austin	60.00	30.00	18.00
8	H.D. Baird	60.00	30.00	18.00
9	J. Franklin Baker	375.00	190.00	115.00
10	Dave Bancroft	375.00	190.00	115.00
11	Jack Barry	60.00	30.00	18.00
12	Zinn Beck	60.00	30.00	18.00
13	"Chief" Bender	375.00	190.00	115.00
14	Joe Benz	60.00	30.00	18.00
15	Bob Bescher	60.00	30.00	18.00
16	Al Betzel	60.00	30.00	18.00
17	Mordecai Brown	375.00	190.00	115.00
18	Eddie Burns	60.00	30.00	18.00
19	George Burns	60.00	30.00	18.00
20	Geo. J. Burns	60.00	30.00	18.00
21	Joe Bush	60.00	30.00	18.00
22	"Donie" Bush	60.00	30.00	18.00
23	Art Butler	60.00	30.00	18.00
24	Bobbie Byrne	60.00	30.00	18.00
25	Forrest Cady	60.00	30.00	18.00
26	Jimmy Callahan	60.00	30.00	18.00
27	Ray Caldwell	60.00	30.00	18.00
28	Max Carey	375.00	190.00	115.00
29	George Chalmers	60.00	30.00	18.00
30	Ray Chapman	90.00	45.00	25.00
31	Larry Cheney	60.00	30.00	18.00
32	Eddie Cicotte	375.00	190.00	115.00
33	Tom Clarke	60.00	30.00	18.00
34	Eddie Collins	375.00	190.00	115.00
35	"Shauno" Collins	60.00	30.00	18.00
36	Charles Comiskey	375.00	190.00	115.00
37	Joe Connolly	60.00	30.00	18.00
38	Ty Cobb	2,500	1,250	750.00
39	Harry Coveleskie (Coveleski)	60.00	30.00	18.00
40	Gavvy Cravath	60.00	30.00	18.00
41	Sam Crawford	375.00	190.00	115.00
42	Jean Dale	60.00	30.00	18.00
43	Jake Daubert	60.00	30.00	18.00
44	Charles Deal	60.00	30.00	18.00
45	Al Demaree	60.00	30.00	18.00
46	Josh Devore	60.00	30.00	18.00
47	William Doak	60.00	30.00	18.00
48	Bill Donovan	60.00	30.00	18.00
49	Charles Dooin	60.00	30.00	18.00
50	Mike Doolan	60.00	30.00	18.00
51	Larry Doyle	60.00	30.00	18.00
52	Jean Dubuc	60.00	30.00	18.00
53	Oscar Dugey	60.00	30.00	18.00
54	Johnny Evers	375.00	190.00	115.00
55	Urban Faber	375.00	190.00	115.00
56	"Hap" Felsch	2,000	375.00	225.00
57	Bill Fischer	60.00	30.00	18.00
58	Ray Fisher	60.00	30.00	18.00
59	Max Flack	60.00	30.00	18.00
60	Art Fletcher	60.00	30.00	18.00
61	Eddie Foster	60.00	30.00	18.00
62	Jacques Fournier	60.00	30.00	18.00
63	Del Gainer (Gainor)	60.00	30.00	18.00
64	"Chic" Gandil	500.00	250.00	150.00
65	Larry Gardner	60.00	30.00	18.00
66	Joe Gedeon	60.00	30.00	18.00
67	Gus Getz	60.00	30.00	18.00
68	Geo. Gibson	60.00	30.00	18.00
69	Wilbur Good	60.00	30.00	18.00
70	Hank Gowdy	60.00	30.00	18.00
71	John Graney	60.00	30.00	18.00
72	Clark Griffith	375.00	190.00	115.00
73	Tom Griffith	60.00	30.00	18.00
74	Heinie Groh	60.00	30.00	18.00
75	Earl Hamilton	60.00	30.00	18.00
76	Bob Harmon	60.00	30.00	18.00
77	Roy Hartzell	60.00	30.00	18.00
78	Claude Hendrix	60.00	30.00	18.00
79	Olaf Henriksen	60.00	30.00	18.00
80	John Henry	60.00	30.00	18.00
81	"Buck" Herzog	60.00	30.00	18.00
82	Hugh High	60.00	30.00	18.00
83	Dick Hoblitzell	60.00	30.00	18.00
84	Harry Hooper	375.00	190.00	115.00
85	Ivan Howard	60.00	30.00	18.00
86	Miller Huggins	375.00	190.00	115.00
87	Joe Jackson	11,500	5,750	3,450
88	William James	60.00	30.00	18.00
89	Harold Janvrin	60.00	30.00	18.00
90	Hugh Jennings	375.00	190.00	115.00
91	Walter Johnson	800.00	400.00	240.00
92	Fielder Jones	60.00	30.00	18.00
93	Joe Judge	60.00	30.00	18.00
94	Bennie Kauff	60.00	30.00	18.00
95	Wm. Killefer Jr.	60.00	30.00	18.00
96	Ed. Konetchy	60.00	30.00	18.00
97	Napoleon Lajoie	550.00	270.00	165.00
98	Jack Lapp	60.00	30.00	18.00
99	John Lavan	60.00	30.00	18.00
100	Jimmy Lavender	60.00	30.00	18.00
101	"Nemo" Leibold	60.00	30.00	18.00
102	H.B. Leonard	60.00	30.00	18.00
103	Duffy Lewis	60.00	30.00	18.00
104	Hans Lobert	60.00	30.00	18.00
105	Tom Long	60.00	30.00	18.00
106	Fred Luderus	60.00	30.00	18.00
107	Connie Mack	375.00	190.00	115.00
108	Lee Magee	60.00	30.00	18.00
109	Sherwood Magee	60.00	30.00	18.00
110	Al. Mamaux	60.00	30.00	18.00
111	Leslie Mann	60.00	30.00	18.00
112	"Rabbit" Maranville	375.00	190.00	115.00
113	Rube Marquard	375.00	190.00	115.00
114	J. Erskine Mayer	125.00	65.00	35.00
115	George McBride	60.00	30.00	18.00
116	John J. McGraw	375.00	190.00	115.00
117	Jack McInnis	60.00	30.00	18.00
118	Fred Merkle	60.00	30.00	18.00
119	Chief Meyers	60.00	30.00	18.00
120	Clyde Milan	60.00	30.00	18.00
121	John Miller	60.00	30.00	18.00
122	Otto Miller	60.00	30.00	18.00
123	Willie Mitchell	60.00	30.00	18.00
124	Fred Mollwitz	60.00	30.00	18.00
125	Pat Moran	60.00	30.00	18.00
126	Ray Morgan	60.00	30.00	18.00
127	Geo. Moriarty	60.00	30.00	18.00
128	Guy Morton	60.00	30.00	18.00
129	Mike Mowrey	60.00	30.00	18.00
130	Ed. Murphy	60.00	30.00	18.00
131	"Hy" Myers	60.00	30.00	18.00
132	J.A. Niehoff	60.00	30.00	18.00
133	Rube Oldring	60.00	30.00	18.00
134	Oliver O'Mara	60.00	30.00	18.00
135	Steve O'Neill	60.00	30.00	18.00
136	"Dode" Paskert	60.00	30.00	18.00
137	Roger Peckinpaugh	60.00	30.00	18.00
138	Walter Pipp	75.00	37.50	22.50
139	Derril Pratt (Derrill)	60.00	30.00	18.00
140	Pat Ragan	60.00	30.00	18.00
141	Bill Rariden	60.00	30.00	18.00
142	Eppa Rixey	375.00	190.00	115.00
143	Davey Robertson	60.00	30.00	18.00
144	Wilbert Robinson	375.00	190.00	115.00
145	Bob Roth	60.00	30.00	18.00
146	Ed. Roush	375.00	190.00	115.00
147	Clarence Rowland	60.00	30.00	18.00
148	"Nap" Rucker	60.00	30.00	18.00
149	Dick Rudolph	60.00	30.00	18.00
150	Reb Russell	60.00	30.00	18.00
151	Babe Ruth	75,000	37,000	22,000
152	Vic Saier	60.00	30.00	18.00
153	"Slim" Sallee	60.00	30.00	18.00
154	Ray Schalk	375.00	190.00	115.00
155	Walter Schang	60.00	30.00	18.00
156	Frank Schulte	60.00	30.00	18.00
157	Everett Scott	60.00	30.00	18.00
158	Jim Scott	60.00	30.00	18.00
159	Tom Seaton	60.00	30.00	18.00
160	Howard Shanks	60.00	30.00	18.00
161	Bob Shawkey	60.00	30.00	18.00
162	Ernie Shore	60.00	30.00	18.00
163	Burt Shotton	60.00	30.00	18.00
164	Geo. Sisler	375.00	190.00	115.00
165	J. Carlisle Smith	60.00	30.00	18.00
166	Fred Snodgrass	60.00	30.00	18.00
167	Geo. Stallings	60.00	30.00	18.00
168a	Oscar Stanage (Catching)	60.00	30.00	24.00
168b	Oscar Stanage (Portrait to thighs.)	750.00	375.00	225.00
169	Charles Stengel	1,100	550.00	325.00
170	Milton Stock	60.00	30.00	18.00
171	Amos Strunk	60.00	30.00	18.00
172	Billy Sullivan	60.00	30.00	18.00
173	"Jeff" Tesreau	60.00	30.00	18.00
174	Joe Tinker	375.00	190.00	115.00
175	Fred Toney	60.00	30.00	18.00
176	Terry Turner	60.00	30.00	18.00
177	George Tyler	60.00	30.00	18.00
178	Jim Vaughn	60.00	30.00	18.00
179	Bob Veach	60.00	30.00	18.00
180	James Viox	60.00	30.00	18.00
181	Oscar Vitt	60.00	30.00	18.00
182	Hans Wagner	2,500	1,250	750.00
183	Clarence Walker	60.00	30.00	18.00
184	Ed. Walsh	375.00	190.00	115.00
185	W. Wambsganss (Photo actually Fritz Coumbe.)	60.00	30.00	18.00
186	Buck Weaver	975.00	490.00	245.00
187	Carl Weilman	60.00	30.00	18.00
188	Zach Wheat	375.00	190.00	115.00
189	Geo. Whitted	60.00	30.00	18.00
190	Fred Williams	60.00	30.00	18.00
191	Art Wilson	60.00	30.00	18.00
192	J. Owen Wilson	60.00	30.00	18.00
193	Ivy Wingo	60.00	30.00	18.00
194	"Mel" Wolfgang	60.00	30.00	18.00
195	Joe Wood	175.00	85.00	50.00
196	Steve Yerkes	60.00	30.00	18.00
197	"Pep" Young	60.00	30.00	18.00
198	Rollie Zeider	60.00	30.00	18.00
199	Heiny Zimmerman	60.00	30.00	18.00
200	Ed. Zwilling	60.00	30.00	18.00

1916 M101-5 Blank Backs

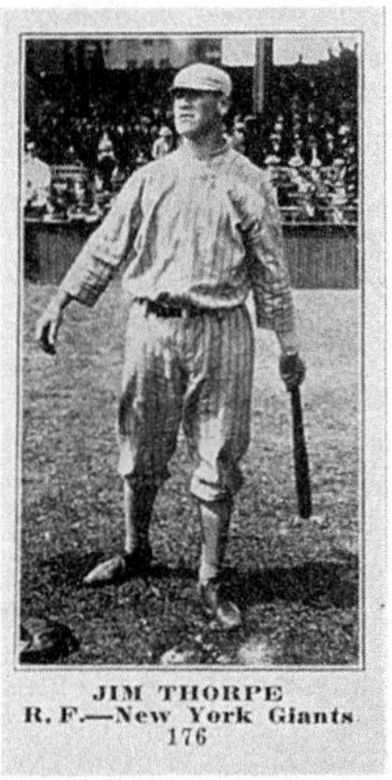
JIM THORPE
R. F.—New York Giants
176

The Chicago printing and publishing firm of Felix Mendelsohn was the originator of this card set, which is often found bearing advertising on back of several businesses from around the country. Mendelsohn is not mentioned on the cards, which are blank-backed. Fronts of the 1-5/8" x 3" black-and-white cards have a player photo, name, position abbreviation, team and card number. The set was prepared in advance of the 1916 season and offered in ads in The Sporting News for $1, or a framed uncut sheet for $2.50. The blank-backs are the most common version of M101-5. There were at least two printings of the set, creating several variations to correct errors or replace players.

		NM	E	VG
Complete Set (200):		130,000	65,000	40,000
Common Player:		125.00	65.00	40.00
1	Babe Adams	125.00	65.00	40.00
2	Sam Agnew	125.00	65.00	40.00
3	Eddie Ainsmith	125.00	65.00	40.00
4	Grover Alexander	750.00	375.00	225.00
5	Leon Ames	125.00	65.00	40.00
6	Jimmy Archer	125.00	65.00	40.00
7	Jimmy Austin	125.00	65.00	40.00
8	J. Franklin Baker	450.00	225.00	135.00
9	Dave Bancroft	450.00	225.00	135.00
10	Jack Barry	125.00	65.00	40.00
11	Zinn Beck	125.00	65.00	40.00
12a	Beals Becker	350.00	175.00	110.00
12b	Lute Boone	125.00	65.00	40.00
13	Joe Benz	125.00	65.00	40.00
14	Bob Bescher	125.00	65.00	40.00

15	Al Betzel	125.00	65.00	40.00
16	Roger Bresnahan	450.00	225.00	135.00
17	Eddie Burns	125.00	65.00	40.00
18	Geo. J. Burns	125.00	65.00	40.00
19	Joe Bush	125.00	65.00	40.00
20	Owen Bush	125.00	65.00	40.00
21	Art Butler	125.00	65.00	40.00
22	Bobbie Byrne	125.00	65.00	40.00
23a	Forrest Cady	1,200	600.00	350.00
23b	Forrest Cady (No number)	1,200	600.00	350.00
23c	Mordecai Brown	1,100	550.00	325.00
24	Jimmy Callahan	125.00	65.00	40.00
25	Ray Caldwell	125.00	65.00	40.00
26	Max Carey	450.00	225.00	135.00
27	George Chalmers	125.00	65.00	40.00
28	Frank Chance	360.00	175.00	105.00
29	Ray Chapman	150.00	75.00	45.00
30	Larry Cheney	125.00	65.00	40.00
31	Eddie Cicotte	450.00	225.00	135.00
32	Tom Clarke	125.00	65.00	40.00
33	Eddie Collins	450.00	225.00	135.00
34	"Shauno" Collins	125.00	65.00	40.00
35	Charles Comisky (Comiskey)	475.00	225.00	135.00
36	Joe Connolly	125.00	65.00	40.00
37	Luther Cook	125.00	65.00	40.00
38	Jack Coombs	125.00	65.00	40.00
39	Dan Costello	125.00	65.00	40.00
40	Harry Coveleskie (Coveleski)	125.00	65.00	40.00
41	Gavvy Cravath	125.00	65.00	40.00
42	Sam Crawford	450.00	225.00	135.00
43	Jean Dale	125.00	65.00	40.00
44	Jake Daubert	125.00	65.00	40.00
45	Geo. A. Davis Jr.	125.00	65.00	40.00
46	Charles Deal	125.00	65.00	40.00
47	Al Demaree	125.00	65.00	40.00
48	William Doak	125.00	65.00	40.00
49	Bill Donovan	125.00	65.00	40.00
50	Charles Dooin	125.00	65.00	40.00
51	Mike Doolan	125.00	65.00	40.00
52	Larry Doyle	125.00	65.00	40.00
53	Jean Dubuc	125.00	60.00	40.00
54	Oscar Dugey	125.00	60.00	40.00
55	Johnny Evers	450.00	225.00	135.00
56	Urban Faber	450.00	225.00	135.00
57	"Hap" Felsch	2,000	415.00	250.00
58	Bill Fischer	125.00	65.00	40.00
59	Ray Fisher	125.00	65.00	40.00
60	Max Flack	125.00	65.00	40.00
61	Art Fletcher	125.00	65.00	40.00
62	Eddie Foster	125.00	60.00	40.00
63	Jacques Fournier	125.00	65.00	40.00
64	Del Gainer (Gainor)	125.00	65.00	40.00
65	Larry Gardner	125.00	65.00	40.00
66	Joe Gedeon	125.00	65.00	40.00
67	Gus Getz	125.00	65.00	40.00
68	Geo. Gibson	125.00	65.00	40.00
69	Wilbur Good	125.00	65.00	40.00
70	Hank Gowdy	125.00	65.00	40.00
71	John Graney	125.00	65.00	40.00
72	Tom Griffith	125.00	65.00	40.00
73	Heinie Groh	125.00	65.00	40.00
74	Earl Hamilton	125.00	65.00	40.00
75	Bob Harmon	125.00	65.00	40.00
76	Roy Hartzell	125.00	65.00	40.00
77	Claude Hendrix	125.00	65.00	40.00
78	Olaf Henriksen	125.00	65.00	40.00
79	John Henry	125.00	65.00	40.00
80	"Buck" Herzog	125.00	65.00	40.00
81	Hugh High	125.00	65.00	40.00
82	Dick Hoblitzell	125.00	65.00	40.00
83	Harry Hooper	450.00	225.00	135.00
84	Ivan Howard	90.00	45.00	30.00
85	Miller Huggins	450.00	225.00	135.00
86	Joe Jackson	15,000	4,950	2,970
87	William James	125.00	65.00	40.00
88	Harold Janvrin	125.00	65.00	40.00
89	Hugh Jennings	450.00	225.00	135.00
90	Walter Johnson	1,500	550.00	330.00
91	Fielder Jones	125.00	65.00	40.00
92	Bennie Kauff	125.00	65.00	40.00
93	Wm. Killefer Jr.	125.00	65.00	40.00
94	Ed. Konetchy	90.00	45.00	30.00
95	Napoleon Lajoie	450.00	225.00	135.00
96	Jack Lapp	125.00	65.00	40.00
97a	John Lavan (Correct spelling.)	125.00	65.00	40.00
97b	John Lavin (Incorrect spelling.)	125.00	65.00	40.00
98	Jimmy Lavender	125.00	65.00	40.00
99	"Nemo" Leibold	125.00	65.00	40.00
100	H.B. Leonard	125.00	65.00	40.00
101	Duffy Lewis	125.00	65.00	40.00
102	Hans Lobert	125.00	65.00	40.00
103	Tom Long	125.00	65.00	40.00
104	Fred Luderus	125.00	65.00	40.00
105	Connie Mack	450.00	225.00	135.00
106	Lee Magee	125.00	65.00	40.00
107	Al. Mamaux	125.00	65.00	40.00
108	Leslie Mann	120.00	65.00	40.00
109	"Rabbit" Maranville	450.00	225.00	135.00
110	Rube Marquard	450.00	225.00	135.00
111	Armando Marsans	150.00	75.00	45.00
112	J. Erskine Mayer	125.00	65.00	40.00
113	George McBride	125.00	65.00	40.00
114	John J. McGraw	450.00	225.00	135.00
115	Jack McInnis	125.00	65.00	40.00
116	Fred Merkle	125.00	65.00	40.00
117	Chief Meyers	125.00	65.00	40.00
118	Clyde Milan	125.00	65.00	40.00
119	Otto Miller	125.00	65.00	40.00
120	Willie Mitchel (Mitchell)	125.00	65.00	40.00
121	Fred Mollwitz	125.00	65.00	40.00
122	J. Herbert Moran	125.00	65.00	40.00
123	Pat Moran	125.00	65.00	40.00
124	Ray Morgan	125.00	65.00	40.00
125	Geo. Moriarty	125.00	65.00	40.00
126	Guy Morton	125.00	65.00	40.00
127	Ed. Murphy (Photo actually Danny Murphy.)	125.00	65.00	40.00
128	John Murray	125.00	65.00	40.00
129	"Hy" Myers	125.00	65.00	40.00
130	J.A. Niehoff	125.00	65.00	40.00
131	Leslie Nunamaker	125.00	65.00	40.00
132	Rube Oldring	125.00	65.00	40.00
133	Oliver O'Mara	125.00	65.00	40.00
134	Steve O'Neill	125.00	65.00	40.00
135	"Dode" Paskert	125.00	65.00	40.00
136	Roger Peckinpaugh (Photo actually Gavvy Cravath.)	125.00	65.00	40.00
137	E.J. Pfeffer (Photo actually Jeff Pfeffer.)	125.00	65.00	40.00
138	Geo. Pierce (Pearce)	125.00	65.00	40.00
139	Walter Pipp	125.00	65.00	40.00
140	Derril Pratt (Derrill)	125.00	65.00	40.00
141	Bill Rariden	125.00	65.00	40.00
142	Eppa Rixey	450.00	225.00	135.00
143	Davey Robertson	125.00	65.00	40.00
144	Wilbert Robinson	3450.00	225.00	135.00
145	Bob Roth	125.00	65.00	40.00
146	Ed. Roush	450.00	225.00	135.00
147	Clarence Rowland	125.00	65.00	40.00
148	"Nap" Rucker	125.00	65.00	40.00
149	Dick Rudolph	125.00	65.00	40.00
150	Reb Russell	125.00	65.00	40.00
151	Babe Ruth	75,000	37,000	22,000
152	Vic Saier	125.00	65.00	40.00
153	"Slim" Sallee	125.00	65.00	40.00
154	"Germany" Schaefer	125.00	65.00	40.00
155	Ray Schalk	450.00	225.00	135.00
156	Walter Schang	125.00	65.00	40.00
157	Chas. Schmidt	125.00	65.00	40.00
158	Frank Schulte	125.00	65.00	40.00
159	Jim Scott	125.00	65.00	40.00
160	Everett Scott	125.00	65.00	40.00
161	Tom Seaton	125.00	65.00	40.00
162	Howard Shanks	125.00	65.00	40.00
163	Bob Shawkey (Photo actually Jack McInnis.)	125.00	65.00	40.00
164	Ernie Shore	125.00	65.00	40.00
165	Burt Shotton	125.00	65.00	40.00
166	George Sisler	450.00	225.00	135.00
167	J. Carlisle Smith	125.00	65.00	40.00
168	Fred Snodgrass	125.00	65.00	40.00
169	Geo. Stallings	125.00	65.00	40.00
170	Oscar Stanage (Photo actually Chas. Schmidt.)	125.00	65.00	40.00
171	Charles Stengel	1,200	600.00	350.00
172	Milton Stock	125.00	65.00	40.00
173	Amos Strunk (Photo actually Olaf Henriksen.)	125.00	65.00	40.00
174	Billy Sullivan	125.00	65.00	40.00
175	Chas. Tesreau	125.00	65.00	40.00
176	Jim Thorpe	22,500	11,250	6,750
177	Joe Tinker	450.00	225.00	135.00
178	Fred Toney	125.00	65.00	40.00
179	Terry Turner	125.00	65.00	40.00
180	Jim Vaughn	125.00	65.00	40.00
181	Bob Veach	125.00	65.00	40.00
182	James Viox	125.00	65.00	40.00
183	Oscar Vitt	125.00	65.00	40.00
184	Hans Wagner	4,500	2,250	1,350
185	Clarence Walker (Photo not Walker.)	125.00	65.00	40.00
186a	Bobby Wallace	5,500	2,750	1,650
186b	Zach Wheat	450.00	225.00	135.00
187	Ed. Walsh	450.00	225.00	135.00
188	Buck Weaver	2,000	360.00	215.00
189	Carl Weilman	125.00	65.00	40.00
190	Geo. Whitted	125.00	65.00	40.00
191	Fred Williams	125.00	65.00	40.00
192	Art Wilson	125.00	65.00	40.00
193	J. Owen Wilson	125.00	65.00	40.00
194	Ivy Wingo	125.00	65.00	40.00
195	"Mel" Wolfgang	125.00	65.00	40.00
196	Joe Wood	500.00	110.00	65.00
197	Steve Yerkes	125.00	65.00	40.00
198	Rollie Zeider	125.00	65.00	40.00
199	Heiny Zimmerman	125.00	65.00	40.00
200	Ed. Zwilling	125.00	65.00	40.00

1947 Mabley & Carew Cincinnati Reds

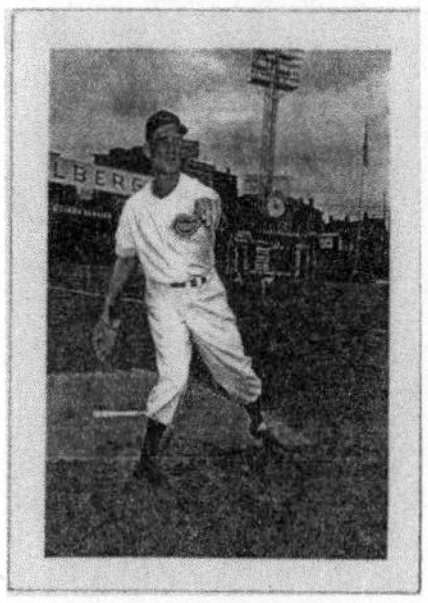

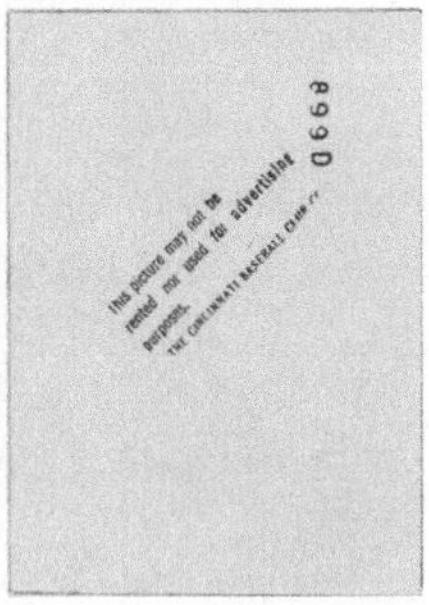

Pictures of Reds players and staff were given away and sold by the boys' shop of the Cincinnati department store. The black-and-white glossy photos measure 3-5/8" x 5-1/16" and have a white border. Backs have a rubber-stamped alpha-numeric identifier and the notice: "This picture may not be rented nor used for advertising purposes. The Cincinnati Baseball Club." The players are not named on the pictures. Small groups of pictures were apparently given away in a tan-and-orange paper folder measuring about 3-7/8" x 5-1/4". The folder pictures the store, has a team roster and schedule and a coupon for purchasing additional photos at a relatively hefty 10 cents apiece. The pictures are listed here alphabetically.

		NM	E	VG
Complete Set (28):		850.00	425.00	250.00
Common Player:		30.00	15.00	9.00
Folder:		30.00	15.00	9.00
(1)	Bob Adams	30.00	15.00	9.00
(2)	Frank Baumholtz	30.00	15.00	9.00
(3)	Ewell Blackwell	40.00	20.00	12.00
(4)	Ed Erautt	30.00	15.00	9.00
(5)	Augie Galan	30.00	15.00	9.00
(6)	Harry Gumbert	30.00	15.00	9.00
(7)	Bert Haas	30.00	15.00	9.00
(8)	Grady Hatton	30.00	15.00	9.00
(9)	John Hetki	30.00	15.00	9.00
(10)	George Kelly	30.00	15.00	9.00
(11)	Ray Lamanno	30.00	15.00	9.00
(12)	Everett Lively	30.00	15.00	9.00
(13)	Ed Lukon	30.00	15.00	9.00
(14)	Eddie Miller	30.00	15.00	9.00
(15)	Ray Mueller	30.00	15.00	9.00
(16)	John Neun	30.00	15.00	9.00
(17)	Phil Page	30.00	15.00	9.00
(18)	Kent Peterson	30.00	15.00	9.00
(19)	Hugh Poland	30.00	15.00	9.00
(20)	Ken Raffensberger	30.00	15.00	9.00
(21)	Elmer Riddle	30.00	15.00	9.00
(22)	Tom Tatum	30.00	15.00	9.00
(23)	Johnny Vander Meer	40.00	20.00	12.00
(24)	Clyde Vollmer	30.00	15.00	9.00
(25)	Kermit Wahl	30.00	15.00	9.00
(26)	Bucky Walters	30.00	15.00	9.00
(27)	Babe Young	30.00	15.00	9.00
(28)	Ben Zientara	30.00	15.00	9.00

1948 Mabley & Carew Cincinnati Reds

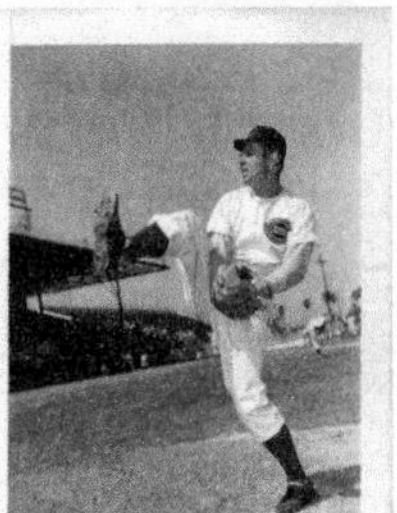

Pictures of the Reds players, manager and coaches were given away and sold by the boys' shops of this Cincinnati department store. The black-and-white glossy photos measure 3-5/8" x 5-1/16" and have a white border. Backs have a rubber-stamped alpha-numeric identification number and the notice, "This picture may not be rented nor used for advertising purposes. / THE CINCINNATI BASEBALL CLUB". The players are not named on the photos, which are sometimes found with player names written on back. The pictures appear to have been given away in pairs in a tan-and-red folder that pictures the department store on front. Inside is a roster of the available pictures and a 1948 Reds schedule that continues on the back, along with a coupon to facilitate the purchase of additional pictures. The pictures are listed here alphabetically.

	NM	EX	VG
Complete Set (34)	650.00	400.00	200.00
Common Player:	20.00	12.00	6.00
(1) Bob Adams	20.00	12.00	6.00
(2) Frank Baumholtz	20.00	12.00	6.00
(3) Ewell Blackwell	40.00	25.00	12.50
(4) Claude Corbitt	20.00	12.00	6.00
(5) Walker Cress	20.00	12.00	6.00
(6) Ed Erautt	20.00	12.00	6.00
(7) Howie Fox	20.00	12.00	6.00
(8) Augie Galan	20.00	12.00	6.00
(9) Harry Gumbert	20.00	12.00	6.00
(10) Grady Hatton	20.00	12.00	6.00
(11) John Hetki	20.00	12.00	6.00
(12) Ken Holcombe	20.00	12.00	6.00
(13) Tommy Hughes	20.00	12.00	6.00
(14) George Kelly	20.00	12.00	6.00
(15) Ted Kluszewski	100.00	60.00	30.00
(16) Ray Lamanno	20.00	12.00	6.00
(17) Everett Lively	20.00	12.00	6.00
(18) Ray Mueller	20.00	12.00	6.00
(19) Johnny Neun	20.00	12.00	6.00
(20) Phil Page	20.00	12.00	6.00
(21) Kent Peterson	20.00	12.00	6.00
(22) Hugh Poland	20.00	12.00	6.00
(23) Ken Raffensberger	20.00	12.00	6.00
(24) Marv Rickert	20.00	12.00	6.00
(25) Hank Sauer	25.00	15.00	7.50
(26) Virgil Stallcup	20.00	12.00	6.00
(27) Johnny Vander Meer	30.00	18.00	9.00
(28) Clyde Vollmer	20.00	12.00	6.00
(29) Kermit Wahl	20.00	12.00	6.00
(30) Herm Wehmeier	20.00	12.00	6.00
(31) Dewey Williams	20.00	12.00	6.00
(32) Johnny Wyrostek	20.00	12.00	6.00
(33) Babe Young	20.00	12.00	6.00
(34) Benny Zientara	20.00	12.00	6.00

1951 Mabley & Carew Cincinnati Reds

Mabley & Carew
Compliments OF
BOYS' SHOPS
SECOND FLOOR

Pictures of the Reds players, manager and coaches were given away and sold by the boys' shops of this Cincinnati department store. The black-and-white glossy photos measure 3-5/8" x 5-1/16" and have a white border. Backs have a rubber-stamped alpha-numeric identification number and the notice, "This picture may not be rented nor used for advertising purposes. / THE CINCINNATI BASEBALL CLUB". The players are not named on the photos, which are sometimes found with player names written on back. The pictures appear to have been given away in pairs in a tan-and-red folder that pictures the department store on front. Inside is a roster of the available pictures and a 1951 Reds schedule that continues on the back, along with a coupon to facilitate the purchase of additional pictures. The pictures are listed here alphabetically.

	NM	EX	VG
Complete Set (27)	600.00	350.00	175.00
Common Player:	20.00	12.00	6.00
(1) Bob Adams	20.00	12.00	6.00
(2) Joe Adcock	45.00	30.00	15.00
(3) Jim Blackburn	20.00	12.00	6.00
(4) Ewell Blackwell	30.00	18.00	9.00
(5) Bud Byerly	20.00	12.00	6.00
(6) Tony Cuccinello	20.00	12.00	6.00
(7) Ed Erautt	20.00	12.00	6.00
(8) Howie Fox	20.00	12.00	6.00
(9) Grady Hatton	20.00	12.00	6.00

(10) Ted Kluszewski	65.00	40.00	20.00
(11) Danny Litwhiler	20.00	12.00	6.00
(12) Roy McMillan	35.00	22.50	12.00
(13) Sammy Meeks	20.00	12.00	6.00
(14) Lloyd Merriman	20.00	12.00	6.00
(15) Phil Page	20.00	12.00	6.00
(16) Harry Perkowski	20.00	12.00	6.00
(17) Kent Peterson	20.00	12.00	6.00
(18) Johnny Pramesa	20.00	12.00	6.00
(19) Ken Raffensberger	20.00	12.00	6.00
(20) Willie Ramsdell	20.00	12.00	6.00
(21) Connie Ryan	20.00	12.00	6.00
(22) Bob Scheffing	20.00	12.00	6.00
(23) Frank Smith	20.00	12.00	6.00
(24) Virgil Stallcup	20.00	12.00	6.00
(25) Bob Usher	20.00	12.00	6.00
(26) Herm Wehmeier	20.00	12.00	6.00
(27) Johnny Wyrostek	20.00	12.00	6.00

1950s-70s MacGregor Advisory Staff Photos

Advisory staff photos were a promotional item which debuted in the early 1950s, flourished in the Sixties and died in the early 1970s. Generally 8" x 10" (sometimes a little larger), these black-and-white (a few later were color) glossy photos picture players who had contracted with a major baseball equipment company to endorse and use their product. Usually the product - most often a glove - was prominently displayed in the photo. The pictures were often displayed in the windows of sporting goods stores or the walls of sports departments and were sometimes made available to customers. Because the companies tended to stick with players over the years, some photos were reissued, sometimes with and sometimes without a change of team, pose or typography. All MacGregor staff photos of the era are checklisted here in alphabetical order. Team designation and pose description is given for each known picture. The photos are checklisted here in alphabetical order. It is unlikely this list is complete. Several arrangements of typography in the bottom border are seen and some photos have a facsimile autograph.

	NM	E	VG
Common Player:	15.00	7.50	4.50
Hank Aaron (Atlanta, batting, color.)	25.00	12.50	7.50
Richie Ashburn (Cubs, full-length, hands on knees.)	25.00	12.50	7.50
Richie Ashburn (Phillies, full-length, hands on knees.)	40.00	20.00	12.00
Gus Bell (Reds, kneeling.)	15.00	7.50	4.50
Ed Bouchee (Phillies, upper body.)	15.00	7.50	4.50
Ed Brinkman (Senators, upper body.)	15.00	7.50	4.50
Roberto Clemente (Full-length.)	125.00	65.00	35.00
Del Crandall (Braves, catching crouch in gear, large.)	15.00	7.50	4.50
Del Crandall (Braves, catching crouch in gear, small.)	15.00	7.50	4.50
Del Crandall (Braves, catching crouch, no gear.)	15.00	7.50	4.50
Del Crandall (Braves, kneeling, glove on knee.)	15.00	7.50	4.50
Al Downing (Dodgers, glove at waist.)	15.00	7.50	4.50
Al Downing (Yankees, upper body.)	15.00	7.50	4.50
Ron Hansen (White Sox, fielding.)	15.00	7.50	4.50
Tommy Helms (Reds, full-length.)	15.00	7.50	4.50
Randy Hundley (Cubs, upper body.)	15.00	7.50	4.50
Jackie Jensen (Red Sox, chest-up.)	15.00	7.50	4.50
Jack Jensen (Red Sox, full-length, batting.)	15.00	7.50	4.50
Jack Jensen (Red Sox, full-length, hands on knees.)	15.00	7.50	4.50
Ralph Kiner (Cubs, hands on knees.)	30.00	15.00	9.00
Ralph Kiner (Pirates, full-length.)	25.00	12.50	7.50
Ted Kluszewski (Reds, batting.)	25.00	12.50	7.50
Ted Kluszewski (White Sox, fielding.)	25.00	12.50	7.50
Ted Kluszewski (Reds, portrait.)	35.00	17.50	10.00

Johnny Kucks (Yankees, pitching.)	15.00	7.50	4.50
Willie Mays (Giants, full-length.)	90.00	45.00	27.00
Bill Mazeroski (Pirates, batting.)	30.00	15.00	9.00
Mike McCormick (Giants, follow-through.)	15.00	7.50	4.50
Gil McDougald (Yankees, throwing.)	15.00	7.50	4.50
Gil McDougald (Yankees, upper-body portrait.)	15.00	7.50	4.50
Tony Oliva (Twins, batting.)	15.00	7.50	4.50
Tony Oliva (Twins, upper body.)	15.00	7.50	4.50
Claude Osteen (Dodgers, pitching.)	15.00	7.50	4.50
Claude Osteen (Dodgers, portrait.)	15.00	7.50	4.50
Juan Pizzaro (White Sox, follow-through.)	15.00	7.50	4.50
Robin Roberts (Phillies, portrait.)	25.00	12.50	7.50
Robin Roberts (Phillies, follow-through.)	25.00	12.50	7.50
Frank Robinson (Orioles, portrait.)	25.00	12.50	7.50
Pete Rose (Reds, kneeling.)	35.00	17.50	10.00
Pete Rose (Reds, leading off, color.)	65.00	32.50	20.00
Pete Rose (Reds, chest-to-cap portrait.)	35.00	17.50	10.00
Al Schoendienst (Cardinals, kneeling.)	25.00	12.50	7.50
Warren Spahn (Boston Braves, follow-through.)	25.00	12.50	7.50
Daryl Spencer (Cardinals, fielding grounder.)	15.00	7.50	4.50
Don Sutton (Dodgers, color, ready to pitch.)	20.00	10.00	6.00
Frank Torre (Braves, ready to throw.)	15.00	7.50	4.50

1960-70s MacGregor Pete Rose

Besides the several series of card issues and Advisory Staff photos issued over the years, MacGregor produced a number of special Pete Rose cards to promote its relationship with one of baseball's top stars of the 1960s and 1970s. All cards in this listing are in black-and-white with blank backs. The 1965-66 cards are 3-1/2" x 5". The later cards are 5" x 7-1/4" to 7-1/2".

	NM	E	VG
1965 Pete Rose (Full-length photo, crouching w/ glove.)	200.00	100.00	60.00
1966 Pete Rose (Half-length photo, crouching w/ glove.)	200.00	100.00	60.00
1969 Pete Rose (Portrait to chest.)	100.00	50.00	30.00
1970 Pete Rose (Fielding, white background.)	75.00	37.50	22.00
1973 Pete Rose (Portrait)	75.00	37.50	22.00
1974 Pete Rose (Portrait to waist, w/glove.)	75.00	37.50	22.00

1960 MacGregor

The MacGregor Sporting Goods Co. was one of the pioneers in celebrity marketing, creating an advisory staff in 1960 to promote its products. The 25-card set features black-and-white photography of several stars and lesser lights, and even a couple of managers. The cards are 3-3/4" x 5" with a thin white border and the words "MacGregor Baseball Advisory Staff of Champions" on the bottom panel. The cards are not numbered and are blank-backed, and include a facsimile autograph in white on the front photo. The checklist is arranged here alphabetically.

		NM	E	VG
	Complete Set (25):	700.00	350.00	210.00
	Common Player:	15.00	7.50	4.50
1	Hank Aaron	110.00	55.00	35.00
2	Richie Ashburn	35.00	17.50	10.00
3	Gus Bell	15.00	7.50	4.50
4	Lou Berberet	15.00	7.50	4.50
5	Jerry Casale	15.00	7.50	4.50
6	Del Crandall	15.00	7.50	4.50
7	Art Ditmar	15.00	7.50	4.50
8	Gene Freese	15.00	7.50	4.50
9	James Gilliam	17.50	8.75	5.25
10	Ted Kluszewski	35.00	17.50	10.00
11	Jim Landis	15.00	7.50	4.50
12	Al Lopez	30.00	15.00	9.00
13	Willie Mays	110.00	55.00	35.00
14	Bill Mazeroski	35.00	17.50	10.00
15	Mike McCormick	15.00	7.50	4.50
16	Gil McDougald	15.00	7.50	4.50
17	Russ Nixon	15.00	7.50	4.50
18	Bill Rigney	15.00	7.50	4.50
19	Robin Roberts	35.00	17.50	10.00
20	Frank Robinson	45.00	22.50	13.50
21	John Roseboro	15.00	7.50	4.50
22	Red Schoendienst	35.00	17.50	10.00
23	Bill Skowron	20.00	10.00	6.00
24	Daryl Spencer	15.00	7.50	4.50
25	Johnny Temple	15.00	7.50	4.50

1965 MacGregor

WILLIE MAYS
MEMBER OF THE MacGregor BRUNSWICK
ADVISORY STAFF

The 1965 MacGregor set is similar to earlier issues, with only a slight change in dimension to 3-1/2" x 5-1/8" and reduced in size to only 10 players. The cards are blank-backed and unnumbered and have a glossy finish. They are checklisted here alphabetically.

		NM	E	VG
	Complete Set (10):	375.00	185.00	110.00
	Common Player:	10.00	5.00	3.00
(1)	Roberto Clemente	150.00	75.00	45.00
(2)	Al Downing	10.00	5.00	3.00
(3)	Johnny Edwards	10.00	5.00	3.00
(4)	Ron Hansen	10.00	5.00	3.00
(5)	Deron Johnson	10.00	5.00	3.00
(6)	Willie Mays	135.00	65.00	40.00
(7)	Tony Oliva	15.00	7.50	4.50
(8)	Claude Osteen	10.00	5.00	3.00
(9)	Bobby Richardson	15.00	7.50	4.50
(10)	Zoilo Versalles	10.00	5.00	3.00

1970s MacGregor Advisory Staff Photos

This advisory staff photo series was among the last in a line of promotional items which debuted in the early 1950s, flourished in the Sixties and died in the 1970s. While earlier advisory staff photos were generally 8" x 10", this later series of black-and-white glossy photos is in a 5" x 7" format. They picture players who had contracted with MacGregor to endorse and use its product. The pictures were often displayed in the windows of sporting goods stores or the walls of sports departments and were sometimes made available to customers. Because the companies tended to stick with players over the years, some photos were reissued, sometimes with a change of team, pose or typography. Known MacGregor staff photos of the era are checklisted here in alphabetical order. Team designation and pose description is given for each picture. It is unlikely this list is complete. Gaps have been left in the assigned numbering to accommodate future additions.

		NM	E	VG
	Common Player:	15.00	7.50	4.50
(1)	Hank Aaron (Braves, chest-to-cap.)	40.00	20.00	12.00
(2)	Rod Carew (Twins, chest-to-cap.)	25.00	12.50	7.50
(3)	Rod Carew (Twins, chin-to-cap.)	25.00	12.50	7.50
(5)	George Foster (Reds, chest-to-cap.)	15.00	7.50	4.50
(8)	Lee May (Orioles, chest-to-cap.)	15.00	7.50	4.50
(10)	Joe Morgan (Reds, neck-to-cap.)	25.00	12.50	7.50
(11)	Joe Morgan (Reds, waist-to-cap.)	25.00	12.50	7.50
(12)	Thurman Munson (Yankees, neck-to-cap.)	27.50	13.50	8.25
(15)	Tony Perez (Reds, neck-to-cap.)	25.00	12.50	7.50
(16)	Tony Perez (Expos, chest-to-cap.)	25.00	12.50	7.50
(20)	Don Sutton (Dodgers, chest-to-cap.)	20.00	10.00	6.00
(21)	Don Sutton (Dodgers, neck-to-cap.)	20.00	10.00	6.00

1975 MacGregor Advisory Staff Poster

The 19-1/2" x 26" color posters feature game-action photos. Two lines of type, "Winners Play MacGregor" and "The Greatest Name In Sports" are above the picture. Back is blank.

	NM	E	VG
Hank Aaron	50.00	25.00	15.00

1975 MacGregor Advisory Staff Poster

This 19-1/2" x 26" color poster features Pete Rose in a game-action photo, leading off at first base. Two lines of type, "Winners Play MacGregor" and "The Greatest Name In Sports" are centered above the picture. Back is blank.

1886 MacIntire Studio Cabinets

The number of baseball players who found themselves in front of the lens at the MacIntire photography studio in Philadelphia is unknown, but all those thus far seen were members of the 1886 Philadelphia National League team. In standard cabinet-card format of about 3-3/4" x 5-3/4", the pieces feature a cream-colored mount with a sepia photo.

		NM	E	VG
	Common Player:	4,500	3,000	2,000
(1)	Tony Cusick	4,500	3,000	2,000
(1)	Tony Cusick	4,500	3,000	2,000
(2)	Edward Dailey	4,500	3,000	2,000
(2)	Edward Dailey	4,500	3,000	2,000
(3)	Jack Farrell	4,500	3,000	2,000
(3)	Jack Farrell	4,500	3,000	2,000
(4)	Charlie Ganzel	4,500	3,000	2,000
(4)	Charlie Ganzel	4,500	3,000	2,000
(5)	Deacon McGuire	4,500	3,000	2,000
(5)	Deacon McGuire	4,500	3,000	2,000
(6)	Cannonball Titcomb	4,500	3,000	2,000
(6)	Cannonball Titcomb	4,500	3,000	2,000
(7)	Harry Wright (Facing his right.)	10,000	4,500	2,800
(7)	Harry Wright (Facing his right.)	10,000	4,500	2,800
(8)	Harry Wright (Pose unrecorded.)	10,000	4,500	2,800
(8)	Harry Wright (Pose unrecorded.)	10,000	4,500	2,800
(9)	Team Photo	6,500	4,500	2,800
(9)	Team Photo	6,500	4,500	2,800

The number of baseball players who found themselves in front of the lens at the MacIntire photography studio in Philadelphia is unknown, but all those thus far seen were members of the 1886 Philadelphia National League team. In standard cabinet-card format of about 3-3/4" x 5-3/4", the

pieces feature a cream-colored mount with a sepia photo.

	NM	E	VG
Common Player:	4,500	3,000	2,000

1951 Connie Mack Book

CONNIE MACK

Washington, N. L., (Buffalo, P. L.,), Pittsb'gh, N. L., (M'waukee, W. L.,) Philadelphia, A. L. 1886-present

Connie Mack has perhaps had more personal friends than any living American. A star catcher, a model of clean sportsmanship, he made his fame as Manager of the Philadelphia A's. His teams have won 9 pennants and 5 World Series.

He did much to shape baseball rules, pioneered in developing the catching art, helped create the big-league baseball bigi, and introduced modern overhand pitching.

His story is an American success saga: the small-town boy starting at 33c a day, building a business property worth millions. More than that, it's the living, breathing, history of America's national sport.

Read all about it in Connie Mack's

My 66 Years in the Big Leagues

In conjunction with the publication of Connie Mack's book "My 66 Years in the Big Leagues," a folder of cards titled, "Four Mighty Heroes" was also issued. The folder contained a quartet of black-and-white player cards. Fronts feature a player photo against a white background. Backs have a bit of player career data and an ad for Mack's book. Cards measure 2-1/4" x 3-1/2".

		NM	E	VG
	Complete Set (4):	3.000	1,500	900.00
	Common Player:	350.00	135.00	80.00
	Book:	60.00	30.00	18.00
(1)	Connie Mack	350.00	135.00	80.00
(2)	Christy Mathewson	750.00	200.00	120.00
(3)	Babe Ruth	2,150	1,075	600.00
(4)	Rube Waddell	350.00	135.00	80.00

1924 Walter Mails Card Game (WG7)

WALTER MAILS
PITCHER—SEALS P. C. L.—FORMERLY CLEVELAND

Fan Out

This set of playing cards features 56 subjects. Card backs are printed in either red or blue, featuring player and umpire figures in each corner. At center is the picture of a pitcher with the name of the game's creator beneath. Walter Mails was a major league pitcher between 1915-26. Fronts feature a black-and-white photo with a facsimile autograph. Printed beneath are the player's name, position and team. At bottom is the designation of a play used in the card game. Both major and minor league players are included in the set. Cards are round-cornered and measure 2-5/16" x 3-1/2". The unnumbered cards are checklisted here alphabetically. It appears as if the blue-back set was issued first and in lesser quantities than those with red backs. Many variations of player personal data between the two colors of backs are reported.

		NM	E	VG
	Complete Set (56):	12,000	6,000	3,500
	Common Player, Major Leaguer:	250.00	100.00	60.00
	Common Player, Minor Leaguer:	200.00	80.00	50.00
	Rules Card:	50.00	20.00	10.00
(1)	Russell "Buzz" Arlett	200.00	80.00	50.00
(2)	J.C. "Jim" Bagby Sr.	200.00	80.00	50.00
(3)	Dave "Beauty" Bancroft	500.00	200.00	125.00
(4)	Johnny Basseler (Bassler)	250.00	100.00	60.00
(5)	Jack Bentley	250.00	100.00	60.00
(6)	J.C. "Rube" Benton	250.00	100.00	60.00
(7)	Geo. Burns	250.00	100.00	60.00
(8)	"Bullet Joe" Bush	250.00	100.00	60.00
(9)	Harold P. Chavezo	200.00	80.00	50.00
(10)	Hugh Critz	200.00	80.00	50.00
(11)	"Jake" E. Daubert	250.00	100.00	60.00
(12)	Wheezer Dell	200.00	80.00	50.00
(13)	Joe Dugan	250.00	100.00	60.00
(14)	Pat Duncan	250.00	100.00	60.00

(15)	Howard J. Ehmke	250.00	100.00	60.00
(16)	Lewis Fonseca	250.00	100.00	60.00
(17)	Ray French	250.00	100.00	60.00
(18)	Ed Gharity (Gharrity)	250.00	100.00	60.00
(19)	Heinie Groh	250.00	100.00	60.00
(20)	George N. Groves	250.00	100.00	60.00
(21)	E.F. "Red" Hargrave	250.00	100.00	60.00
(22)	Elmer Jacobs	250.00	100.00	60.00
(23)	Walter Johnson	1,200	480.00	300.00
(24)	WM. "Duke" Kenworthy	250.00	100.00	60.00
(25)	Harry Krause	200.00	80.00	50.00
(26)	Ray Kremer	250.00	100.00	60.00
(27)	Walter Mails	250.00	100.00	60.00
(28)	Walter "Rabbitt" Maranville	500.00	200.00	125.00
(29)	John "Stuffy" McInnis	250.00	100.00	60.00
(30)	Marty McManus	250.00	100.00	60.00
(31)	Bob Meusel	250.00	100.00	60.00
(32)	Hack Miller	250.00	100.00	60.00
(33)	Pat J. Moran	250.00	100.00	60.00
(34)	Guy Morton	250.00	100.00	60.00
(35)	Johnny Mostil	250.00	100.00	60.00
(36)	Rod Murphy	200.00	80.00	50.00
(37)	Jimmy O'Connell	250.00	100.00	60.00
(38)	Steve O'Neil	250.00	100.00	60.00
(39)	Joe Oeschger	250.00	100.00	60.00
(40)	Roger Peckinpaugh	250.00	100.00	60.00
(41)	Ralph "Babe" Pinelli	250.00	100.00	60.00
(42)	Wally Pipp	250.00	100.00	60.00
(43)	Elmer Ponder	200.00	80.00	50.00
(44)	Sam Rice	500.00	200.00	125.00
(45)	Edwin Rommell (Rommel)	250.00	100.00	60.00
(46)	Walter Schmidt	250.00	100.00	60.00
(47)	Wilford Shupes	200.00	80.00	50.00
(48)	Joe Sewell	500.00	200.00	125.00
(49)	Pat Shea	200.00	80.00	50.00
(50)	W. "Paddy" Siglin	200.00	80.00	50.00
(51)	Geo. H. Sisler	500.00	200.00	125.00
(52)	William "Bill" Skiff	200.00	80.00	50.00
(53)	J. Smith	250.00	100.00	60.00
(54)	Harry "Suds" Sutherland	200.00	80.00	50.00
(55)	James A. Tierney	250.00	100.00	60.00
(56)	Geo. Uhle	250.00	100.00	60.00

1921-1930 Major League Ball Die-Cuts

These die-cut, blank-back player cards were issued over the period 1921-30 for use with a board game called, "Major League Ball - The Indoor Baseball Game Supreme," from The National Game Makers of Washington, D.C. Measuring about 2-1/2" to 2-3/4" tall x 1" to 1-1/4" wide, the cards were originally printed on a sheet of 14 from which they were punched out to play the game. The cards were issued in team sets with on-field roster changes reflected in the player cards over the years. Individual cards are generic, liberally sharing the same poses and portraits with identification possible only by changes to the uniform and the player ID printed in the box below the figure. That player data changed from year to year and the only way to determine exact year of issue is when the player card is found with a complete team set, often in a small pre-printed manila envelope. It is unknown whether all teams were issued in all years. According to information found with the game, stickers could be purchased each year to update the game's figures with new player identification. Beginning in at least 1925 player cards were numbered at bottom within team set.

	NM	E	VG
Typical Team Set:	300.00	150.00	90.00
Common Player:	50.00	25.00	15.00
Typical Hall of Famer:	75.00	37.50	22.50
Ty Cobb	150.00	75.00	45.00
Lou Gehrig	200.00	100.00	60.00
Walter Johnson	125.00	65.00	40.00
Babe Ruth	350.00	175.00	100.00

1969 Major League Baseball Photostamps

This set of 216 player stamps, sponsored by the Major League Baseball Players Association (not authorized by MLB, thus the lack of team uniform insignia) was issued in professional baseball's centennial year of 1969 and was sold in 18 different uncut sheets, with 12 stamps on each sheet. Each individual stamp measured 2" x 3-1/4". There were nine sheets picturing National League players and nine picturing American Leaguers. The full-color stamps display facsimile autographs on the fronts. The backs carry instructions to moisten the stamps and place them in a special album that was also available. Many sheets of these stamps were uncovered by a dealer in the early 1980s and they were available at inexpensive prices.

	NM	E	VG
Complete Sheet Set (18):	60.00	30.00	18.00
Complete Singles Set (216):	60.00	30.00	18.00
A.L. Album and Sheets:	25.00	12.50	7.50
N.L. Album and Sheets:	35.00	17.50	10.00

Common Sheet:		3.50	1.75	1.00
Common Player:		.50	.25	.15
Sheet A.L. 3				
(25)	Danny Cater	.50	.25	.15
Sheet A.L. 4				
(37)	Jim Kaat	.65	.35	.20
Sheet A.L. 5				
(49)	Ed Kirkpatrick	.50	.25	.15
Sheet A.L. 6				
(61)	Ken Berry	.50	.25	.15
Sheet A.L. 8				
(85)	Ed Brinkman	.50	.25	.15
Sheet A.L. 9				
(97)	Joseph Pepitone	.75	.40	.25
Sheet A.L. 1		3.75	2.00	1.00
(2)	Mike Andrews	.50	.25	.15
Sheet A.L. 3				
(26)	Rich Rollins	.50	.25	.15
Sheet A.L. 4				
(38)	Sal Bando	.50	.25	.15
Sheet A.L. 6				
(62)	Wally Bunker	.50	.25	.15
Sheet A.L. 7				
(74)	Duane Josephson	.50	.25	.15
Sheet A.L. 8				
(86)	Vic Davalillo	.50	.25	.15
Sheet A.L. 9				
(98)	Ed Stroud	.50	.25	.15
Sheet N.L. 6				
(170)	Jim Wynn	.50	.25	.15
Sheet N.L. 7				
(182)	Tommy Helms	.50	.25	.15
Sheet N.L. 8				
(194)	Bob Aspromonte	.50	.25	.15
Sheet N.L. 9				
(206)	Lou Brock	2.50	1.25	.70
Sheet A.L. 1				
(3)	Max Alvis	.50	.25	.15
Sheet A.L. 4				
(39)	Ray Oyler	.50	.25	.15
Sheet A.L. 5				
(51)	Mike Hershberger	.50	.25	.15
Sheet A.L. 6				
(63)	Tony Oliva	1.00	.50	.30
Sheet A.L. 7				
(75)	Roger Nelson	.50	.25	.15
Sheet A.L. 8				
(87)	Gary Peters	.50	.25	.15
Sheet A.L. 9				
(99)	Jim McGlothlin	.50	.25	.15
Sheet N.L. 6				
(183)	Denis Menke	.50	.25	.15
Sheet A.L. 3		3.75	2.00	1.00
(27)	Brooks Robinson	3.00	1.50	.90
Sheet A.L. 1				
(4)	Bill Freehan	.50	.25	.15
Sheet A.L. 3				
(28)	Rico Petrocelli	.50	.25	.15
Sheet A.L. 4				
(40)	Dave McNally	.50	.25	.15
Sheet A.L. 5				
(52)	Jack Aker	.50	.25	.15
Sheet A.L. 6				
(64)	Rick Monday	.50	.25	.15
Sheet A.L. 7				
(76)	Ted Uhlaender	.50	.25	.15
Sheet A.L. 8				
(88)	Joe Foy	.50	.25	.15
Sheet A.L. 1				
(5)	Horace Clarke	.50	.25	.15
Sheet A.L. 2				
(17)	Mickey Lolich	.75	.40	.25
Sheet A.L. 3				
(29)	Larry Brown	.50	.25	.15
Sheet A.L. 4				
(41)	George Scott	.50	.25	.15
Sheet A.L. 5				

(53)	Andy Etchebarren	.50	.25	.15
Sheet A.L. 6				
(65)	Chico Salmon	.50	.25	.15
Sheet A.L. 7				
(77)	John Donaldson	.50	.25	.15
Sheet A.L. 8				
(89)	Rod Carew	3.00	1.50	.90
Sheet N.L. 6				
(173)	Mike McCormick	.50	.25	.15
Sheet N.L. 7				
(185)	Al Ferrera	.50	.25	.15
Sheet N.L. 8				
(197)	Claude Osteen	.50	.25	.15
Sheet N.L. 9				
(209)	John Edwards	.50	.25	.15
Sheet A.L. 5		2.50	1.25	.75
(50)	Dean Chance	.50	.25	.15
Sheet A.L. 1				
(6)	Bernie Allen	.50	.25	.15
Sheet A.L. 2				
(18)	Tom Tresh	.75	.40	.25
Sheet A.L. 3				
(30)	Norm Cash	.75	.40	.25
Sheet A.L. 4				
(42)	Joe Azcue	.50	.25	.15
Sheet A.L. 5				
(54)	Ray Culp	.50	.25	.15
Sheet A.L. 6				
(66)	Paul Blair	.50	.25	.15
Sheet A.L. 7				
(78)	Tommy Davis	.50	.25	.15
Sheet A.L. 8				
(90)	Jim "Catfish" Hunter	2.00	1.00	.60
Sheet N.L. 6				
(174)	Ron Santo	.75	.40	.25
Sheet N.L. 8				
(198)	Ed Spiezio	.50	.25	.15
Sheet N.L. 9				
(210)	Len Gabrielson	.50	.25	.15
Sheet A.L. 1				
(7)	Jim Fregosi	.50	.25	.15
Sheet A.L. 2				
(19)	Camilo Pascual	.50	.25	.15
Sheet A.L. 3				
(31)	Jake Gibbs	.50	.25	.15
Sheet A.L. 4				
(43)	Jim Northrup	.50	.25	.15
Sheet A.L. 5				
(55)	Luis Tiant	.65	.35	.20
Sheet A.L. 6				
(67)	Jim Lonborg	.50	.25	.15
Sheet A.L. 7				
(79)	Frank Robinson	3.00	1.50	.90
Sheet A.L. 8				
(91)	Gary Bell	.50	.25	.15
Sheet A.L. 7		2.50	1.25	.75
(73)	Chuck Hinton	.50	.25	.15
Sheet A.L. 1				
(8)	Joe Horlen	.50	.25	.15
Sheet A.L. 2				
(20)	Bob Rodgers	.50	.25	.15
Sheet A.L. 3				
(32)	Mike Epstein	.50	.25	.15
Sheet A.L. 4				
(44)	Fritz Peterson	.50	.25	.15
Sheet A.L. 5				
(56)	Willie Horton	.50	.25	.15
Sheet A.L. 6				
(68)	Zoilo Versalles	.50	.25	.15
Sheet A.L. 7				
(80)	Dick Ellsworth	.50	.25	.15
Sheet A.L. 8				
(92)	Dave Johnson	.50	.25	.15
Sheet N.L. 5				
(164)	Chris Short	.50	.25	.15
Sheet N.L. 6				
(176)	Jerry Koosman	.50	.25	.15

Sheet N.L. 7
| (188) Rusty Staub | .70 | .35 | .20 |

Sheet N.L. 8
| (200) Glenn Beckert | .50 | .25 | .15 |

Sheet N.L. 9
| (212) Gaylord Perry | 2.00 | 1.00 | .60 |

Sheet A.L. 8
| | 5.00 | 2.50 | 1.50 |
| (96) Steve Hamilton | .50 | .25 | .15 |

Sheet A.L. 1
| (9) Jerry Adair | .50 | .25 | .15 |

Sheet A.L. 2
| (21) Pete Ward | .50 | .25 | .15 |

Sheet A.L. 3
| (33) George Brunet | .50 | .25 | .15 |

Sheet A.L. 4
| (45) Paul Casanova | .50 | .25 | .15 |

Sheet A.L. 5
| (57) Roy White | .50 | .25 | .15 |

Sheet A.L. 6
| (69) Denny McLain | .75 | .40 | .25 |

Sheet A.L. 7
| (81) Sam McDowell | .50 | .25 | .15 |

Sheet A.L. 8
| (93) Ken Harrelson | .50 | .25 | .15 |

Sheet N.L. 7
| (189) Bud Harrelson | .50 | .25 | .15 |

Sheet N.L. 8
| (201) Bob Bailey | .50 | .25 | .15 |

Sheet A.L. 2
| (22) Dave Morehead | .50 | .25 | .15 |

Sheet A.L. 3
| (34) Tom McCraw | .50 | .25 | .15 |

Sheet A.L. 4
| (46) Roger Repoz | .50 | .25 | .15 |

Sheet A.L. 5
| (58) Ken McMullen | .50 | .25 | .15 |

Sheet A.L. 6
| (70) Mel Stottlemyre | .50 | .25 | .15 |

Sheet A.L. 7
| (82) Dick McAuliffe | .50 | .25 | .15 |

Sheet A.L. 8
| (94) Tony Horton | .50 | .25 | .15 |

Sheet A.L. 2
| (23) John Roseboro | .50 | .25 | .15 |

Sheet A.L. 3
| (35) Steve Whitaker | .50 | .25 | .15 |

Sheet A.L. 4
| (47) Tommy John | .75 | .40 | .25 |

Sheet A.L. 5
| (59) Rick Reichardt | .50 | .25 | .15 |

Sheet A.L. 6
| (71) Joe Coleman | .50 | .25 | .15 |

Sheet A.L. 7
| (83) Bill Robinson | .50 | .25 | .15 |

Sheet A.L. 8
| (95) Al Kaline | 3.00 | 1.50 | .90 |

Sheet N.L. 5
| (167) Orlando Cepeda | 2.50 | 1.25 | .70 |

Sheet N.L. 6
| (179) Tim McCarver | .75 | .40 | .25 |

Sheet N.L. 7
| (191) Roberto Clemente | 8.00 | 4.00 | 2.50 |

Sheet N.L. 8
| (203) John Briggs | .50 | .25 | .15 |

Sheet N.L. 9
| (215) Ed Charles | .50 | .25 | .15 |

Sheet A.L. 2
| (24) Bert Campaneris | .50 | .25 | .15 |

Sheet A.L. 3
| (36) Bob Allison | .50 | .25 | .15 |

Sheet A.L. 4
| (48) Moe Drabowsky | .50 | .25 | .15 |

Sheet A.L. 5
| (60) Luis Aparicio | 3.00 | 1.50 | .90 |

Sheet A.L. 6
| (72) Bob Knoop | .50 | .25 | .15 |

Sheet A.L. 7

| (84) Frank Howard | .75 | .40 | .25 |

Sheet N.L. 5
| (168) Pete Rose | 8.00 | 4.00 | 2.50 |

Sheet N.L. 6
| (180) Phil Niekro | 2.00 | 1.00 | .60 |

Sheet N.L. 8
| (204) Bill Mazeroski | 2.50 | 1.25 | .70 |

Sheet N.L. 5
	8.00	4.00	2.50
(165) Jim Bunning	2.00	1.00	.60
(166) Nelson Briles	.50	.25	.15

Sheet N.L. 6
	3.00	1.50	.90
(169) Tony Cloninger	.50	.25	.15
(171) Jim Lefebvre	.50	.25	.15
(172) Ron Davis	.50	.25	.15
(175) Ty Cline	.50	.25	.15
(177) Mike Ryan	.50	.25	.15
(178) Jerry May	.50	.25	.15

Sheet N.L. 7
	15.00	7.50	4.50
(181) Hank Aaron	5.00	2.50	1.50
(184) Don Sutton	2.00	1.00	.60
(186) Willie Mays	5.00	2.50	1.50
(187) Bill Hands	.50	.25	.15
(190) Johnny Callison	.50	.25	.15
(192) Julian Javier	.50	.25	.15

Sheet N.L. 8
	2.50	1.25	.75
(193) Joe Torre	1.25	.60	.40
(195) Lee May	.50	.25	.15
(196) Don Wilson	.50	.25	.15
(199) Hal Lanier	.50	.25	.15
(202) Ron Swoboda	.50	.25	.15

Sheet N.L. 9
	3.75	2.00	1.00
(205) Tommie Sisk	.50	.25	.15
(207) Felix Millan	.50	.25	.15
(208) Tony Perez	2.00	1.00	.60
(211) Ollie Brown	.50	.25	.15
(213) Don Kessinger	.50	.25	.15
(214) John Bateman	.50	.25	.15
(216) Woodie Fryman	.50	.25	.15

1969 Major League Baseball Player Pins

ROBERTO CLEMENTE
PITTSBURGH PIRATES

Black-and-white or color player portraits (noted parenthetically) are featured in the center of a red, white and blue design on these 3-1/2" diameter pins. The existing checklist, which may be incomplete, shows a mix of contemporary and retired players. The celluloid pinback buttons were sold at concession stands around the Major Leagues. Production continued at least into 1970, based on some observed player/team combinations.

	NM	E	VG
Common Player:	20.00	12.00	6.00
(1) Hank Aaron (B/W)	60.00	30.00	18.00
(2) Tommie Agee (B/W)	20.00	10.00	6.00
(3) Richie Allen (B/W)	25.00	12.50	7.50
(4) Mike Andrews (B/W)	20.00	10.00	6.00
(5) Mike Andrews (Color)	20.00	10.00	6.00
(6) Luis Aparicio (B/W)	25.00	12.50	7.50
(7) Ernie Banks (B/W)	60.00	30.00	18.00
(8) Ernie Banks (B/W, 2-1/2")	60.00	30.00	18.00
(9) Ernie Banks (Color)	60.00	30.00	18.00
(10) Glenn Beckert (B/W)	20.00	10.00	6.00
(11) Curt Blefary (B/W)	20.00	10.00	6.00
(12) Ken Boswell (B/W)	20.00	10.00	6.00
(13) Lou Brock (B/W)	30.00	15.00	9.00
(14) John Callison (B/W)	20.00	10.00	6.00
(15) Orlando Cepeda (B/W)	25.00	12.50	7.50
(16) Ed Charles (B/W)	20.00	10.00	6.00
(17) Horace Clarke (B/W)	20.00	10.00	6.00
(18) Roberto Clemente (B/W)	75.00	37.00	22.00
(19) Donn Clendenon (B/W)	20.00	10.00	6.00
(20) Billy Conigliaro (B/W)	20.00	10.00	6.00
(21) Tony Conigliaro (B/W)	25.00	12.50	7.50
(22) Tony Conigliaro (Color)	25.00	12.50	7.50
(23) Ray Culp (Color)	20.00	10.00	6.00
(24) Joe DiMaggio (B/W)	50.00	25.00	15.00
(25) Don Drysdale (B/W)	30.00	15.00	9.00
(26) John Ellis (B/W)	20.00	10.00	6.00
(27) Frank Fernandez (Color)	20.00	10.00	6.00
(28) Curt Flood (B/W)	20.00	10.00	6.00
(29) Lou Gehrig (B/W)	50.00	25.00	15.00
(30) Bob Gibson (B/W)	30.00	15.00	9.00
(31) Jerry Grote (B/W)	20.00	10.00	6.00
(32) Jim Hickman (B/W)	20.00	10.00	6.00
(33) Ken Holtzman (B/W)	20.00	10.00	6.00
(34) Frank Howard (B/W)	22.50	11.00	6.75
(35) Randy Hundley (B/W)	20.00	10.00	6.00
(36) Reggie Jackson (Color)	60.00	30.00	18.00
(37) Ferguson Jenkins (B/W)	30.00	15.00	9.00
(38) Cleon Jones (B/W)	20.00	10.00	6.00
(39) Dalton Jones (B/W)	20.00	10.00	6.00
(40) Al Kaline (B/W)	60.00	30.00	18.00
(41) Jerry Kenney (B/W)	20.00	10.00	6.00
(42) Don Kessinger (B/W)	20.00	10.00	6.00
(43) Harmon Killebrew (B/W)	30.00	15.00	9.00
(44) Jerry Koosman (Color)	20.00	10.00	6.00
(45) Sandy Koufax (B/W)	75.00	37.00	22.00
(46) Jim Lonborg (B/W)	20.00	10.00	6.00
(47) Mickey Mantle (B/W)	100.00	50.00	30.00
(48) Carlos May (B/W)	20.00	10.00	6.00
(49) Willie Mays (B/W)	75.00	37.00	22.00
(50) Willie McCovey (B/W)	25.00	12.50	7.50
(51) Denny McLain (B/W)	22.50	11.00	6.75
(52) Gene Michael (B/W)	20.00	10.00	6.00
(53) Gene Michael (Color)	20.00	10.00	6.00
(54) Thurman Munson (B/W)	65.00	32.00	19.00
55) Bobby Murcer (Color)	22.50	11.00	6.75
(56) Joe Pepitone (B/W)	25.00	12.50	7.50
(57) Rico Petrocelli (B/W)	20.00	10.00	6.00
(58) Rico Petrocelli (Color)	20.00	10.00	6.00
(59) Brooks Robinson (B/W)	40.00	20.00	12.00
(60) Frank Robinson (B/W)	35.00	18.00	10.00
(61) Pete Rose (B/W)	75.00	37.00	22.00
(62) Babe Ruth (B/W)	50.00	25.00	15.00
(63) Ron Santo (B/W)	22.50	11.00	6.75
(64) Ron Santo (Color)	22.50	11.00	6.75
(65) Ron Santo (B/W. 2-1/2")	60.00	30.00	18.00
(66) George Scott (B/W)	20.00	10.00	6.00
(67) Tom Seaver (B/W)	45.00	22.00	13.50
(68) Tom Seaver (Color)	45.00	22.00	13.50
(69) Reggie Smith (B/W)	20.00	10.00	6.00
(70) Reggie Smith (Color)	20.00	10.00	6.00
(71) Mel Stottlemyre (B/W)	20.00	10.00	6.00
(72) Mel Stottlemyre (Color)	20.00	10.00	6.00
(73) Ron Swoboda (B/W)	20.00	10.00	6.00
(74) Tony Taylor (B/W, 2-1/2")	20.00	10.00	6.00
(75) Joe Torre (B/W)	22.50	11.00	6.75
(76) Tom Tresh (Color)	20.00	10.00	6.00
(77) Pete Ward (B/W)	20.00	10.00	6.00
(78) Roy White (B/W)	20.00	10.00	6.00
(79) Billy Williams (B/W)	25.00	12.50	7.50
(80) Carl Yastrzemski (B/W)	60.00	30.00	18.00
(81) Carl Yastrzemski (Color)	60.00	30.00	18.00

1969 Major League Baseball Players Association Pins

Issued by the Major League Baseball Players Association in 1969, this unnumbered set consists of 60 pins - 30 players from the N.L. and 30 from the A.L. Each pin measures approximately 7/8" in diameter and features a black-and-white player photo. A.L. players are surrounded by a red border, while N.L. players are framed in blue. The player's name and team appear at the top and bottom. Also along the bottom is a line reading "1969 MLBPA MFG. R.R. Winona, MINN."

	NM	E	VG
Complete Set (60):	250.00	125.00	75.00
Common Player:	6.00	3.00	1.75
(1) Hank Aaron	30.00	15.00	9.00
(2) Richie Allen	10.00	5.00	3.00
(3) Felipe Alou	7.50	3.75	2.25
(4) Max Alvis	6.00	3.00	1.75
(5) Luis Aparicio	12.50	6.25	3.75
(6) Ernie Banks	15.00	7.50	4.50
(7) Johnny Bench	15.00	7.50	4.50
(8) Lou Brock	15.00	7.50	4.50
(9) George Brunet	6.00	3.00	1.75
(10) Johnny Callison	6.00	3.00	1.75
(11) Rod Carew	15.00	7.50	4.50
(12) Orlando Cepeda	12.50	6.25	3.75
(13) Dean Chance	6.00	3.00	1.75
(14) Roberto Clemente	40.00	20.00	12.00
(15) Willie Davis	6.00	3.00	1.75
(16) Don Drysdale	15.00	7.50	4.50
(17) Ron Fairly	6.00	3.00	1.75
(18) Curt Flood	6.00	3.00	1.75
(19) Bill Freehan	6.00	3.00	1.75
(20) Jim Fregosi	6.00	3.00	1.75
(21) Bob Gibson	15.00	7.50	4.50
(22) Ken Harrelson	6.00	3.00	1.75
(23) Bud Harrelson	6.00	3.00	1.75
(24) Jim Ray Hart	6.00	3.00	1.75
(25) Tommy Helms	6.00	3.00	1.75
(26) Joe Horlen	6.00	3.00	1.75
(27) Tony Horton	7.50	3.75	2.25
(28) Willie Horton	6.00	3.00	1.75
(29) Frank Howard	7.50	3.75	2.25

(30)	Al Kaline	15.00	7.50	4.50
(31)	Don Kessinger	6.00	3.00	1.75
(32)	Harmon Killebrew	15.00	7.50	4.50
(33)	Jerry Koosman	6.00	3.00	1.75
(34)	Mickey Lolich	6.00	3.00	1.75
(35)	Jim Lonborg	6.00	3.00	1.75
(36)	Jim Maloney	6.00	3.00	1.75
(37)	Juan Marichal	12.50	6.25	3.75
(38)	Willie Mays	30.00	15.00	9.00
(39)	Tim McCarver	7.50	3.75	2.25
(40)	Willie McCovey	15.00	7.50	4.50
(41)	Sam McDowell	6.00	3.00	1.75
(42)	Denny McLain	7.50	3.75	2.25
(43)	Rick Monday	6.00	3.00	1.75
(44)	Tony Oliva	7.50	3.75	2.25
(45)	Joe Pepitone	7.50	3.75	2.25
(46)	Boog Powell	7.50	3.75	2.25
(47)	Rick Reichardt	6.00	3.00	1.75
(48)	Pete Richert	6.00	3.00	1.75
(49)	Brooks Robinson	15.00	7.50	4.50
(50)	Frank Robinson	15.00	7.50	4.50
(51)	Pete Rose	25.00	12.50	7.50
(52)	Ron Santo	9.00	4.50	2.75
(53)	Mel Stottlemyre	6.00	3.00	1.75
(54)	Ron Swoboda	6.00	3.00	1.75
(55)	Luis Tiant	6.00	3.00	1.75
(56)	Joe Torre	9.00	4.50	2.75
(57)	Pete Ward	6.00	3.00	1.75
(58)	Billy Williams	12.50	6.25	3.75
(59)	Jim Wynn	6.00	3.00	1.75
(60)	Carl Yastrzemski	15.00	7.50	4.50

1970 Major League Baseball Photostamps

For a second year, ballplayer "stamps" were sold in conjunction with team albums. Approximately 1-7/8" x 3", the pieces are printed on glossy paper in full color with a white border and facsimile autograph. Backs, which are not gummed, have gluing instructions and the players name at bottom. The 1970 issue can be differentiated from the 1969 issue in that they have uniform insignia present on the photos whereas the 1969 stamps do not. The unnumbered stamps are checklisted here alphabetically within team.

		NM	E	VG
Complete Set (288):		200.00	100.00	60.00
Common Player:		1.00	.50	.30
	ATLANTA BRAVES			
(1)	Hank Aaron	15.00	7.50	4.50
(2)	Bob Aspromonte	1.00	.50	.30
(3)	Rico Carty	1.00	.50	.30
(4)	Orlando Cepeda	6.00	3.00	1.75
(5)	Bob Didier	1.00	.50	.30
(6)	Tony Gonzalez	1.00	.50	.30
(7)	Pat Jarvis	1.00	.50	.30
(8)	Felix Millan	1.00	.50	.30
(9)	Jim Nash	1.00	.50	.30
(10)	Phil Niekro	4.00	2.00	1.25
(11)	Milt Pappas	1.00	.50	.30
(12)	Ron Reed	1.00	.50	.30
	BALTIMORE ORIOLES			
(1)	Mark Belanger	1.00	.50	.30
(2)	Paul Blair	1.00	.50	.30
(3)	Don Buford	1.00	.50	.30
(4)	Mike Cuellar	1.00	.50	.30
(5)	Andy Etchebarren	1.00	.50	.30
(6)	Dave Johnson	1.00	.50	.30
(7)	Dave McNally	1.00	.50	.30
(8)	Tom Phoebus	1.00	.50	.30
(9)	Boog Powell	2.00	1.00	.60
(10)	Brooks Robinson	6.00	3.00	1.75
(11)	Frank Robinson	6.00	3.00	1.75
(12)	Chico Salmon	1.00	.50	.30
	BOSTON RED SOX			
(1)	Mike Andrews	1.00	.50	.30
(2)	Ray Culp	1.00	.50	.30
(3)	Jim Lonborg	1.00	.50	.30
(4)	Sparky Lyle	1.00	.50	.30
(5)	Gary Peters	1.00	.50	.30
(6)	Rico Petrocelli	1.00	.50	.30
(7)	Vicente Romo	1.00	.50	.30
(8)	Tom Satriano	1.00	.50	.30
(9)	George Scott	1.00	.50	.30
(10)	Sonny Seibert	1.00	.50	.30
(11)	Reggie Smith	1.00	.50	.30
(12)	Carl Yastrzemski	6.00	3.00	1.75
	CALIFORNIA ANGELS			
(1)	Sandy Alomar	1.00	.50	.30
(2)	Jose Azcue	1.00	.50	.30
(3)	Tom Egan	1.00	.50	.30
(4)	Jim Fregosi	1.00	.50	.30
(5)	Alex Johnson	1.00	.50	.30
(6)	Jay Johnstone	1.00	.50	.30
(7)	Rudy May	1.00	.50	.30
(8)	Andy Messersmith	1.00	.50	.30
(9)	Rick Reichardt	1.00	.50	.30
(10)	Roger Repoz	1.00	.50	.30
(11)	Aurelio Rodriguez	1.00	.50	.30
(12)	Ken Tatum	1.00	.50	.30
	CHICAGO CUBS			
(1)	Ernie Banks	7.50	3.75	2.25
(2)	Glenn Beckert	1.00	.50	.30
(3)	Johnny Callison	1.00	.50	.30
(4)	Bill Hands	1.00	.50	.30
(5)	Randy Hundley	1.00	.50	.30
(6)	Ken Holtzman	1.00	.50	.30
(7)	Fergie Jenkins	4.00	2.00	1.25
(8)	Don Kessinger	1.00	.50	.30
(9)	Phil Regan	1.00	.50	.30
(10)	Ron Santo	2.00	1.00	.60
(11)	Dick Selma	1.00	.50	.30
(12)	Billy Williams	5.00	2.50	1.50
	CHICAGO WHITE SOX			
(1)	Luis Aparicio	5.00	2.50	1.50
(2)	Ken Berry	1.00	.50	.30
(3)	Buddy Bradford	1.00	.50	.30
(4)	Ron Hansen	1.00	.50	.30
(5)	Joel Horlen	1.00	.50	.30
(6)	Tommy John	1.50	.70	.45
(7)	Duane Josephson	1.00	.50	.30
(8)	Bobby Knoop	1.00	.50	.30
(9)	Tom McCraw	1.00	.50	.30
(10)	Bill Melton	1.00	.50	.30
(11)	Walt Williams	1.00	.50	.30
(12)	Wilbur Wood	1.00	.50	.30
	CINCINNATI REDS			
(1)	Johnny Bench	7.50	3.75	2.25
(2)	Tony Cloninger	1.00	.50	.30
(3)	Wayne Granger	1.00	.50	.30
(4)	Tommy Helms	1.00	.50	.30
(5)	Jim Maloney	1.00	.50	.30
(6)	Lee May	1.00	.50	.30
(7)	Jim McGlothlin	1.00	.50	.30
(8)	Jim Merritt	1.00	.50	.30
(9)	Gary Nolan	1.00	.50	.30
(10)	Tony Perez	5.00	2.50	1.50
(11)	Pete Rose	12.50	6.25	3.75
(12)	Bobby Tolan	1.00	.50	.30
	CLEVELAND INDIANS			
(1)	Max Alvis	1.00	.50	.30
(2)	Larry Brown	1.00	.50	.30
(3)	Dean Chance	1.00	.50	.30
(4)	Dick Ellsworth	1.00	.50	.30
(5)	Vern Fuller	1.00	.50	.30
(6)	Ken Harrelson	1.00	.50	.30
(7)	Chuck Hinton	1.00	.50	.30
(8)	Tony Horton	1.00	.50	.30
(9)	Sam McDowell	1.00	.50	.30
(10)	Vada Pinson	1.50	.70	.45
(11)	Duke Sims	1.00	.50	.30
(12)	Ted Uhlaender	1.00	.50	.30
	DETROIT TIGERS			
(1)	Norm Cash	1.50	.70	.45
(2)	Bill Freehan	1.00	.50	.30
(3)	Willie Horton	1.00	.50	.30
(4)	Al Kaline	7.50	3.75	2.25
(5)	Mike Kilkenny	1.00	.50	.30
(6)	Mickey Lolich	1.00	.50	.30
(7)	Dick McAuliffe	1.00	.50	.30
(8)	Denny McLain	1.50	.70	.45
(9)	Jim Northrup	1.00	.50	.30
(10)	Mickey Stanley	1.00	.50	.30
(11)	Tom Tresh	1.00	.50	.30
(12)	Earl Wilson	1.00	.50	.30
	HOUSTON ASTROS			
(1)	Jesus Alou	1.00	.50	.30
(2)	Tommy Davis	1.00	.50	.30
(3)	Larry Dierker	1.00	.50	.30
(4)	Johnny Edwards	1.00	.50	.30
(5)	Fred Gladding	1.00	.50	.30
(6)	Denver Lemaster	1.00	.50	.30
(7)	Denis Menke	1.00	.50	.30
(8)	Joe Morgan	6.00	3.00	1.75
(9)	Joe Pepitone	1.50	.70	.45
(10)	Doug Rader	1.00	.50	.30
(11)	Don Wilson	1.00	.50	.30
(12)	Jim Wynn	1.00	.50	.30
	KANSAS CITY ROYALS			
(1)	Jerry Adair	1.00	.50	.30
(2)	Wally Bunker	1.00	.50	.30
(3)	Bill Butler	1.00	.50	.30
(4)	Moe Drabowsky	1.00	.50	.30
(5)	Jackie Hernandez	1.00	.50	.30
(6)	Pat Kelly	1.00	.50	.30
(7)	Ed Kirkpatrick	1.00	.50	.30
(8)	Dave Morehead	1.00	.50	.30
(9)	Roger Nelson	1.00	.50	.30
(10)	Bob Oliver	1.00	.50	.30
(11)	Lou Piniella	1.50	.70	.45
(12)	Paul Schaal	1.00	.50	.30
	LOS ANGELES DODGERS			
(1)	Willie Davis	1.00	.50	.30
(2)	Len Gabrielson	1.00	.50	.30
(3)	Tom Haller	1.00	.50	.30
(4)	Jim Lefebvre	1.00	.50	.30
(5)	Manny Mota	1.00	.50	.30
(6)	Claude Osteen	1.00	.50	.30
(7)	Wes Parker	1.00	.50	.30
(8)	Bill Russell	1.00	.50	.30
(9)	Bill Singer	1.00	.50	.30
(10)	Ted Sizemore	1.00	.50	.30
(11)	Don Sutton	4.00	2.00	1.25
(12)	Maury Wills	1.00	.50	.30
	MINNESOTA TWINS			
(1)	Bob Allison	1.00	.50	.30
(2)	Dave Boswell	1.00	.50	.30
(3)	Leo Cardenas	1.00	.50	.30
(4)	Rod Carew	6.00	3.00	1.75
(5)	Jim Kaat	1.50	.70	.45
(6)	Harmon Killebrew	6.00	3.00	1.75
(7)	Tony Oliva	1.50	.70	.45
(8)	Jim Perry	1.00	.50	.30
(9)	Ron Perranoski	1.00	.50	.30
(10)	Rich Reese	1.00	.50	.30
(11)	Luis Tiant	1.00	.50	.30
(12)	Cesar Tovar	1.00	.50	.30
	MONTREAL EXPOS			
(1)	John Bateman	1.00	.50	.30
(2)	Bob Bailey	1.00	.50	.30
(3)	Ron Brand	1.00	.50	.30
(4)	Ty Cline	1.00	.50	.30
(5)	Ron Fairly	1.00	.50	.30
(6)	Mack Jones	1.00	.50	.30
(7)	Jose Laboy	1.00	.50	.30
(8)	Claude Raymond	1.00	.50	.30
(9)	Joe Sparma	1.00	.50	.30
(10)	Rusty Staub	1.50	.70	.45
(11)	Bill Stoneman	1.00	.50	.30
(12)	Bobby Wine	1.00	.50	.30
	NEW YORK METS			
(1)	Tommie Agee	1.00	.50	.30
(2)	Donn Clendenon	1.00	.50	.30
(3)	Joe Foy	1.00	.50	.30
(4)	Jerry Grote	1.00	.50	.30
(5)	Bud Harrelson	1.00	.50	.30
(6)	Cleon Jones	1.00	.50	.30
(7)	Jerry Koosman	1.00	.50	.30
(8)	Ed Kranepool	1.00	.50	.30
(9)	Nolan Ryan	25.00	12.50	7.50
(10)	Tom Seaver	6.00	3.00	1.75
(11)	Ron Swoboda	1.00	.50	.30
(12)	Al Weis	1.00	.50	.30
	NEW YORK YANKEES			
(1)	Jack Aker	1.00	.50	.30
(2)	Curt Blefary	1.00	.50	.30
(3)	Danny Cater	1.00	.50	.30
(4)	Horace Clarke	1.00	.50	.30
(5)	Jake Gibbs	1.00	.50	.30
(6)	Steve Hamilton	1.00	.50	.30
(7)	Bobby Murcer	1.50	.70	.45
(8)	Fritz Peterson	1.00	.50	.30
(9)	Bill Robinson	1.00	.50	.30
(10)	Mel Stottlemyre	1.00	.50	.30
(11)	Pete Ward	1.00	.50	.30
(12)	Roy White	1.50	.70	.45
	OAKLAND A's			
(1)	Felipe Alou	1.50	.70	.45
(2)	Sal Bando	1.00	.50	.30
(3)	Bert Campaneris	1.00	.50	.30
(4)	Chuck Dobson	1.00	.50	.30
(5)	Tito Francona	1.00	.50	.30
(6)	Dick Green	1.00	.50	.30
(7)	Catfish Hunter	4.00	2.00	1.25
(8)	Reggie Jackson	10.00	5.00	3.00
(9)	Don Mincher	1.00	.50	.30
(10)	Rick Monday	1.00	.50	.30
(11)	John Odom	1.00	.50	.30
(12)	Ray Oyler	1.00	.50	.30
	PHILADELPHIA PHILLIES			
(1)	Johnny Briggs	1.00	.50	.30
(2)	Jim Bunning	4.00	2.00	1.25
(3)	Curt Flood	1.50	.70	.45
(4)	Woodie Fryman	1.00	.50	.30
(5)	Larry Hisle	1.00	.50	.30
(6)	Joe Hoerner	1.00	.50	.30
(7)	Grant Jackson	1.00	.50	.30
(8)	Tim McCarver	1.50	.70	.45
(9)	Mike Ryan	1.00	.50	.30
(10)	Chris Short	1.00	.50	.30
(11)	Tony Taylor	1.00	.50	.30
(12)	Rick Wise	1.00	.50	.30
	PITTSBURGH PIRATES			
(1)	Gene Alley	1.00	.50	.30
(2)	Matty Alou	1.00	.50	.30
(3)	Roberto Clemente	20.00	10.00	6.00
(4)	Ron Davis	1.00	.50	.30
(5)	Richie Hebner	1.00	.50	.30
(6)	Jerry May	1.00	.50	.30
(7)	Bill Mazeroski	6.00	3.00	1.75
(8)	Bob Moose	1.00	.50	.30
(9)	Al Oliver	1.50	.70	.45
(10)	Manny Sanguillen	1.00	.50	.30
(11)	Willie Stargell	5.00	2.50	1.50

(12)	Bob Veale	1.00	.50	.30

SAN DIEGO PADRES

(1)	Ollie Brown	1.00	.50	.30
(2)	Dave Campbell	1.00	.50	.30
(3)	Nate Colbert	1.00	.50	.30
(4)	Pat Dobson	1.00	.50	.30
(5)	Al Ferrera	1.00	.50	.30
(6)	Dick Kelley	1.00	.50	.30
(7)	Clay Kirby	1.00	.50	.30
(8)	Bill McCool	1.00	.50	.30
(9)	Frank Reberger	1.00	.50	.30
(10)	Tommie Sisk	1.00	.50	.30
(11)	Ed Spiezio	1.00	.50	.30
(12)	Larry Stahl	1.00	.50	.30

SAN FRANCISCO GIANTS

(1)	Bobby Bonds	1.50	.70	.45
(2)	Jim Davenport	1.00	.50	.30
(3)	Dick Dietz	1.00	.50	.30
(4)	Jim Ray Hart	1.00	.50	.30
(5)	Ron Hunt	1.00	.50	.30
(6)	Hal Lanier	1.00	.50	.30
(7)	Frank Linzy	1.00	.50	.30
(8)	Juan Marichal	5.00	2.50	1.50
(9)	Willie Mays	15.00	7.50	4.50
(10)	Mike McCormick	1.00	.50	.30
(11)	Willie McCovey	6.00	3.00	1.75
(12)	Gaylord Perry	4.00	2.00	1.25

SEATTLE PILOTS

(1)	Steve Barber	1.00	.50	.30
(2)	Bobby Bolin	1.00	.50	.30
(3)	George Brunet	1.00	.50	.30
(4)	Wayne Comer	1.00	.50	.30
(5)	John Donaldson	1.00	.50	.30
(6)	Tommy Harper	1.00	.50	.30
(7)	Mike Hegan	1.00	.50	.30
(8)	Mike Hershberger	1.00	.50	.30
(9)	Steve Hovley	1.00	.50	.30
(10)	Bob Locker	1.00	.50	.30
(11)	Gerry McNertney	1.00	.50	.30
(12)	Rich Rollins	1.00	.50	.30

ST. LOUIS CARDINALS

(1)	Richie Allen	2.50	1.25	.70
(2)	Nelson Briles	1.00	.50	.30
(3)	Lou Brock	6.00	3.00	1.75
(4)	Jose Cardenal	1.00	.50	.30
(5)	Steve Carlton	6.00	3.00	1.75
(6)	Vic Davalillo	1.00	.50	.30
(7)	Bob Gibson	6.00	3.00	1.75
(8)	Julian Javier	1.00	.50	.30
(9)	Dal Maxvill	1.00	.50	.30
(10)	Cookie Rojas	1.00	.50	.30
(11)	Mike Shannon	1.00	.50	.30
(12)	Joe Torre	3.00	1.50	.90

WASHINGTON SENATORS

(1)	Bernie Allen	1.00	.50	.30
(2)	Dick Bosman	1.00	.50	.30
(3)	Ed Brinkman	1.00	.50	.30
(4)	Paul Casanova	1.00	.50	.30
(5)	Joe Coleman	1.00	.50	.30
(6)	Mike Epstein	1.00	.50	.30
(7)	Frank Howard	1.50	.70	.45
(8)	Ken McMullen	1.00	.50	.30
(9)	John Roseboro	1.00	.50	.30
(10)	Ed Stroud	1.00	.50	.30
(11)	Del Unser	1.00	.50	.30
(12)	Zoilo Versalles	1.00	.50	.30

1983 "1969" MLBPA Pins

Virtually identical in format to the 60-pin 1969 MLBPA issue, these pins were probably not issued prior to 1983 and despite what is printed thereon, are not a licensed issue of the Players Association. The 7/8" diameter pins have a black-and-white player portrait photo on a white background at center. The photo is bordered in red or blue with the player name at top and team at bottom in white. A copyright line on back reads, "1969 MLBPA MFG IN U.S.A." Latter-day pins can be distinguished from the 1969s by the absence of mention of Winona, Minn., on the replicas.

Complete Set (36):

(1)	Hank Aaron
(2)	Bob Allison
(3)	Yogi Berra
(4)	Roy Campanella
(5)	Norm Cash
(6)	Orlando Cepeda
(7)	Roberto Clemente
(8)	Joe DiMaggio
(9)	Bobby Doerr
(10)	Don Drysdale
(11)	Bob Feller
(12)	Whitey Ford
(13)	Nellie Fox
(14)	Frank Howard
(15)	Jim "Catfish" Hunter

(16)	Al Kaline
(17)	Sandy Koufax
(18)	Mickey Mantle
(19)	Juan Marichal
(20)	Eddie Mathews
(21)	Willie Mays
(22)	Willie McCovey
(23)	Stan Musial
(24)	Tony Oliva
(25)	Satchel Paige
(26)	Phil Rizzuto
(27)	Robin Roberts
(28)	Brooks Robinson
(29)	Jackie Robinson
(30)	Ron Santo
(31)	Duke Snider
(32)	Warren Spahn
(33)	Bill Skowron
(34)	Billy Williams
(35)	Ted Williams
(36)	Maury Wills

1910 Makaroff Cigarettes World Series Postcard

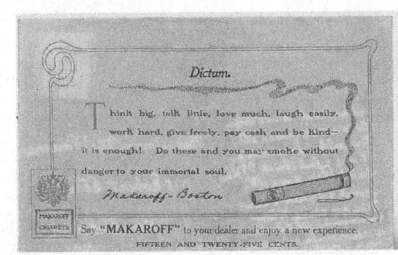

The text on this postcard indicates it may have been given out at World Series games in Philadelphia and Chicago. Two versions are known, one with Connie Mack's portrait at left and the Athletics score listed first, and one with Frank Chance's portrait at left and the Cubs score listed first. On the black-and-white address side are photographic portraits of the A's and Cubs managers with appropriate team pennants. Below is scripted, "Saw the world's championship game to-day." Beneath that are lines to record the score. The front of the card is printed in black, white and red and has a picture of a smoking cigarette and a two-headed Russian eagle logo. At center is this "Dictum. / Think big, talk little, love much, laugh easily, / work hard, give freely, pay cash and be kind - / it is enough! Do these and you may smoke without / danger to your immortal soul."

	NM	E	VG
Frank Chance, Connie Mack	350.00	175.00	100.00
Connie Mack, Frank Chance	350.00	175.00	100.00

1926-1927 Mallorquina Caramels

These tiny (about 3/4" x 1-1/8") cards were distributed with Mallorquina brandcaramels in Cuba. The black-and-white images are printed on hard photographic paper stock. The bordered portrait photos on front have a box at bottom with player identification and card number. Backs are printed in dark blue with the wording "LA MALLORQUINA / CARAMELOS / PELOTEROS" and a few graphic flourishes. The set's first 17 cards feature professional players, including a number of Negro Leagues stars. The last 83 cards in the set are Cuban amateurs. While there was probably some sort of album issued to house the set, none has been reported to date. Because the card of Hall of Famer Willie Foster is his only known career-contemporary issue, and that of Martin Dihigo is his earliest known, "book" values have not been assigned.

	NM	E	VG
Common Player:	200.00	100.00	60.00

		NM	E	VG
1	Adolfo Luque	750.00	375.00	225.00
2	Alfredo Cabrera	250.00	125.00	75.00
3	George Scales	350.00	175.00	105.00
4	Jose Maria Fernandez	250.00	125.00	75.00
5	Oliver Marcelle	3,000	1,500	900.00
6	Oscar Rodriguez	200.00	100.00	60.00
7	Martin Dihigo (VALUE UNDETERMINED)			
8	Cheo Ramos	250.00	125.00	75.00
9	Pop Lloyd	4,500	2,250	1,350
10	Joe Olivares	200.00	100.00	60.00
11	Brujo Rosell	200.00	100.00	60.00
12	Willie Foster (VALUE UNDETERMINED)			
13	Cho Cho Correa	250.00	125.00	75.00
14	Larry Brown	350.00	175.00	105.00
15	Oscar Levis	250.00	125.00	75.00
16	Raul Alvarez	250.00	125.00	75.00
17	Juan Eckelson	250.00	125.00	75.00
18	Quesada	200.00	100.00	60.00
19	J. Rosado	200.00	100.00	60.00
20	A. Unanuo	200.00	100.00	60.00
21	A. Echavarria	200.00	100.00	60.00
22	C. Beltran	200.00	100.00	60.00
23	J. Beltran	200.00	100.00	60.00
24	G. Orama	200.00	100.00	60.00
25	E. Carrillo	200.00	100.00	60.00
26	A. Casuso	200.00	100.00	60.00
27	A. Consuegra	200.00	100.00	60.00
28	R. Gallardo	200.00	100.00	60.00
29	M. Sotolongo	200.00	100.00	60.00
30	M. Llano	200.00	100.00	60.00
31	H. Rocamora	200.00	100.00	60.00
32	Calvo	200.00	100.00	60.00
33	R. Inclan	200.00	100.00	60.00
34	Mendizabal	200.00	100.00	60.00
35	H. Alonso	200.00	100.00	60.00
36	C. Leonard	200.00	100.00	60.00
37	Cap Cordova	200.00	100.00	60.00
38	Cordova	200.00	100.00	60.00
39	Sarasua	200.00	100.00	60.00
40	E. Cubillas	200.00	100.00	60.00
41	B. Wilryc	200.00	100.00	60.00
42	Morera	200.00	100.00	60.00
43	C. Fernandez	200.00	100.00	60.00
44	Milian	200.00	100.00	60.00
45	P. Espinosa	200.00	100.00	60.00
46	Macia	200.00	100.00	60.00
47	J. Lagueruela	200.00	100.00	60.00
48	Bernal	200.00	100.00	60.00
49	J.A. Ruiz	200.00	100.00	60.00
50	**Unknown**			
51	J. Gayoso	200.00	100.00	60.00
52	Castro	200.00	100.00	60.00
53	C. Hernandez	200.00	100.00	60.00
54	Reynolds	200.00	100.00	60.00
55	M. Rodriguez	200.00	100.00	60.00
56	P. Flores	200.00	100.00	60.00
57	A. Collazo	200.00	100.00	60.00
58	R. Gonzalez	200.00	100.00	60.00
59	A. Casas	200.00	100.00	60.00
60	Barcena	200.00	100.00	60.00
61	Quesada	200.00	100.00	60.00
62	Riquerin	200.00	100.00	60.00
63	Carbonere	200.00	100.00	60.00
64	Vega	200.00	100.00	60.00
65	Rodriguez	200.00	100.00	60.00
66	A. Castillo	200.00	100.00	60.00
67	Y. Balleste	200.00	100.00	60.00
68	Fernandez	200.00	100.00	60.00
69	Garros	200.00	100.00	60.00
70	Cabada	200.00	100.00	60.00
71	R.P. Fernandez	200.00	100.00	60.00
72	R. Cejas	200.00	100.00	60.00
73	Gros	200.00	100.00	60.00
74	Mendez	200.00	100.00	60.00
75	M. Sotolongo	200.00	100.00	60.00
76	E. Vela	200.00	100.00	60.00
77	A. Vela	200.00	100.00	60.00
78	F. Pinera	200.00	100.00	60.00
79	M. Valdes	200.00	100.00	60.00
80	L. Romero	200.00	100.00	60.00
81	A. Febles	200.00	100.00	60.00
82	Lugo	200.00	100.00	60.00
83	Polo Calvo	200.00	100.00	60.00
84	Silvio O. Farrill	200.00	100.00	60.00
85	Zalazar	200.00	100.00	60.00
86	Tapia	200.00	100.00	60.00
87	Hernandez	200.00	100.00	60.00
88	Manrrara	200.00	100.00	60.00
89	J. Deschapelle	200.00	100.00	60.00
90	Arguelles	200.00	100.00	60.00
91	E. Arechaede	200.00	100.00	60.00
92	E. Quintanal	200.00	100.00	60.00
93	M. Valdes	200.00	100.00	60.00
94	J. Martinez	200.00	100.00	60.00
95	R. Martinez	200.00	100.00	60.00
96	F. Gali	200.00	100.00	60.00
97	A. Martinez	200.00	100.00	60.00
98	G. Hernandez	200.00	100.00	60.00

		NM	E	VG
99	A. Fernandez	200.00	100.00	60.00
100	Armando Figarola	200.00	100.00	60.00

1916 Mall Theatre

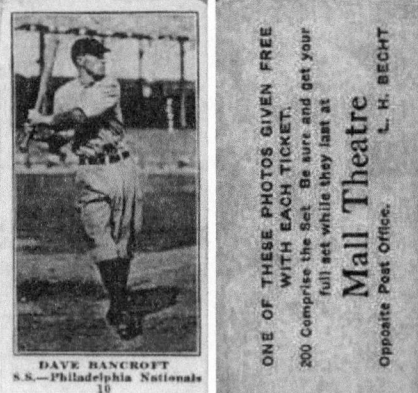

DAVE BANCROFT
S.S.—Philadelphia Nationals
10

Best known for its use as a promotional medium for The Sporting News, this 200-card set can be found with ads on the back for several local and regional businesses. Among them is the Mall Theatre, location unknown. Type-card and superstar collectors can expect to pay a significant premium for individual cards with this advertising over generic 1916 M101-4 Blank Backs values. Cards measure 1-5/8" x 3" and are printed in black-and-white.

PREMIUM: 3-5X

(See 1916 M101-4 Blank Backs for checklist and base card values.)

1961 Manny's Baseball Land 8x10s

In 1961, Manny's Baseball Land issued 18 10-piece 8" x 10" printed black-and-white photo packs, arranged by team. Manny's was a next-door neighbor of Yankee Stadium and the nation's largest purveyor of baseball souvenirs. These photo sets were sold for $1.50 per team. The blank-back photos were printed on semi-gloss paper. Portraits or posed action photos were surrounded by a white border which contains the player's name in all caps at bottom. The unnumbered pictures are checklisted here alphabetically by and within team.

		NM	E	VG
Complete Set (180):		2,500	1,250	750.00
Common Player:		10.00	5.00	3.00
BALTIMORE ORIOLES				
(1)	Jackie Brandt	10.00	5.00	3.00
(2)	Marv Breeding	10.00	5.00	3.00
(3)	Chuck Estrada	10.00	5.00	3.00
(4)	Jack Fisher	10.00	5.00	3.00
(5)	Jim Gentile	10.00	5.00	3.00
(6)	Ron Hansen	10.00	5.00	3.00
(7)	Milt Pappas	10.00	5.00	3.00
(8)	Brooks Robinson	30.00	15.00	9.00
(9)	Gus Triandos	10.00	5.00	3.00
(10)	Jerry Walker	10.00	5.00	3.00
BOSTON RED SOX				
(11)	Tom Brewer	10.00	5.00	3.00
(12)	Don Buddin	10.00	5.00	3.00
(13)	Gene Conley	10.00	5.00	3.00
(14)	Mike Fornieles	10.00	5.00	3.00
(15)	Gary Geiger	10.00	5.00	3.00
(16)	Pumpsie Green	10.00	5.00	3.00
(17)	Jackie Jensen	15.00	7.50	4.50
(18)	Frank Malzone	10.00	5.00	3.00
(19)	Pete Runnels	10.00	5.00	3.00
(20)	Vic Wertz	10.00	5.00	3.00
CHICAGO CUBS				
(21)	George Altman	10.00	5.00	3.00
(22)	Bob Anderson	10.00	5.00	3.00
(23)	Richie Ashburn	30.00	15.00	9.00
(24)	Ernie Banks	35.00	17.50	10.00
(25)	Don Cardwell	10.00	5.00	3.00
(26)	Moe Drabowsky	10.00	5.00	3.00
(27)	Don Elston	10.00	5.00	3.00
(28)	Jerry Kindall	10.00	5.00	3.00
(29)	Ron Santo	15.00	7.50	4.50
(30)	Bob Will	10.00	5.00	3.00
CHICAGO WHITE SOX				
(31)	Luis Aparicio	25.00	12.50	7.50
(32)	Frank Baumann	10.00	5.00	3.00
(33)	Sam Esposito	10.00	5.00	3.00
(34)	Nellie Fox	30.00	15.00	9.00
(35)	Jim Landis	10.00	5.00	3.00
(36)	Sherman Lollar	10.00	5.00	3.00
(37)	Minnie Minoso	20.00	10.00	6.00
(38)	Billy Pierce	10.00	5.00	3.00
(39)	Bob Shaw	10.00	5.00	3.00
(40)	Early Wynn	25.00	12.50	7.50
CINCINNATI REDLEGS				
(41)	Ed Bailey	10.00	5.00	3.00
(42)	Gus Bell	10.00	5.00	3.00
(43)	Gordon Coleman	10.00	5.00	3.00
(44)	Bill Henry	10.00	5.00	3.00
(45)	Jerry Lynch	10.00	5.00	3.00
(46)	Claude Osteen	10.00	5.00	3.00
(47)	Vada Pinson	12.50	6.25	3.75
(48)	Wally Post	10.00	5.00	3.00
(49)	Bob Purkey	10.00	5.00	3.00
(50)	Frank Robinson	35.00	17.50	10.00
CLEVELAND INDIANS				
(51)	Mike de la Hoz	10.00	5.00	3.00
(52)	Tito Francona	10.00	5.00	3.00
(53)	Woody Held	10.00	5.00	3.00
(54)	Barry Latman	10.00	5.00	3.00
(55)	Jim Perry	10.00	5.00	3.00
(56)	Bubba Phillips	10.00	5.00	3.00
(57)	Jim Piersall	12.50	6.25	3.75
(58)	Vic Power	10.00	5.00	3.00
(59)	John Romano	10.00	5.00	3.00
(60)	Johnny Temple	10.00	5.00	3.00
DETROIT TIGERS				
(61)	Hank Aguirre	10.00	5.00	3.00
(62)	Billy Bruton	10.00	5.00	3.00
(63)	Jim Bunning	25.00	12.50	7.50
(64)	Norm Cash	20.00	10.00	6.00
(65)	Rocky Colavito	25.00	12.50	7.50
(66)	Chico Fernandez	10.00	5.00	3.00
(67)	Paul Foytack	10.00	5.00	3.00
(68)	Al Kaline	35.00	17.50	10.00
(69)	Frank Lary	10.00	5.00	3.00
(70)	Don Mossi	10.00	5.00	3.00
KANSAS CITY ATHLETICS				
(71)	Hank Bauer	10.00	5.00	3.00
(72)	Andy Carey	10.00	5.00	3.00
(73)	Leo "Bud" Daley	10.00	5.00	3.00
(74)	Ray Herbert	10.00	5.00	3.00
(75)	John Kucks	10.00	5.00	3.00
(76)	Jerry Lumpe	10.00	5.00	3.00
(77)	Norm Siebern	10.00	5.00	3.00
(78)	Haywood Sullivan	10.00	5.00	3.00
(79)	Marv Throneberry	10.00	5.00	3.00
(80)	Dick Williams	10.00	5.00	3.00
LOS ANGELES ANGELS				
(81)	Ken Aspromonte	10.00	5.00	3.00
(82)	Steve Bilko	10.00	5.00	3.00
(83)	Bob Cerv	10.00	5.00	3.00
(84)	Ned Garver	10.00	5.00	3.00
(85)	Ken Hunt	10.00	5.00	3.00
(86)	Ted Kluszewski	25.00	12.50	7.50
(87)	Jim McAnany	10.00	5.00	3.00
(88)	Duke Maas	10.00	5.00	3.00
(89)	Albie Pearson	10.00	5.00	3.00
(90)	Eddie Yost	10.00	5.00	3.00
LOS ANGELES DODGERS				
(91)	Don Drysdale	30.00	15.00	9.00
(92)	Jim Gilliam	12.50	6.25	3.75
(93)	Frank Howard	12.50	6.25	3.75
(94)	Sandy Koufax	50.00	25.00	15.00
(95)	Norm Larker	10.00	5.00	3.00
(96)	Wally Moon	10.00	5.00	3.00
(97)	Charles Neal	10.00	5.00	3.00
(98)	Johnny Podres	12.50	6.25	3.75
(99)	Larry Sherry	10.00	5.00	3.00
(100)	Maury Wills	12.50	6.25	3.75
MILWAUKEE BRAVES				
(101)	Hank Aaron	50.00	25.00	15.00
(102)	Joe Adcock	10.00	5.00	3.00
(103)	Frank Bolling	10.00	5.00	3.00
(104)	Bob Buhl	10.00	5.00	3.00
(105)	Lew Burdette	10.00	5.00	3.00
(106)	Del Crandall	10.00	5.00	3.00
(107)	Ed Mathews	35.00	17.50	10.00
(108)	Roy McMillan	10.00	5.00	3.00
(109)	Warren Spahn	35.00	17.50	10.00
(110)	Al Spangler	10.00	5.00	3.00
MINNESOTA TWINS				
(111)	Bob Allison	10.00	5.00	3.00
(112)	Earl Battey	10.00	5.00	3.00
(113)	Reno Bertola (Bertoia)	10.00	5.00	3.00
(114)	Billy Consolo	10.00	5.00	3.00
(115)	Billy Gardner	10.00	5.00	3.00
(116)	Harmon Killebrew	35.00	17.50	10.00
(117)	Jim Lemon	10.00	5.00	3.00
(118)	Camilo Pascual	10.00	5.00	3.00
(119)	Pedro Ramos	10.00	5.00	3.00
(120)	Chuck Stobbs	10.00	5.00	3.00
NEW YORK YANKEES				
(121)	Larry "Yogi" Berra	35.00	17.50	10.00
(122)	John Blanchard	10.00	5.00	3.00
(123)	Ed "Whitey" Ford	35.00	17.50	10.00
(124)	Elston Howard	15.00	7.50	4.50
(125)	Tony Kubek	15.00	7.50	4.50
(126)	Mickey Mantle	65.00	32.50	20.00
(127)	Roger Maris	40.00	20.00	12.00
(128)	Bobby Richardson	15.00	7.50	4.50
(129)	Bill Skowron	15.00	7.50	4.50
(130)	Bob Turley	10.00	5.00	3.00
PHILADELPHIA PHILLIES				
(131)	John Callison	10.00	5.00	3.00
(132)	Dick Farrell	10.00	5.00	3.00
(133)	Pancho Herrera	10.00	5.00	3.00
(134)	Joe Koppe	10.00	5.00	3.00
(135)	Art Mahaffey	10.00	5.00	3.00
(136)	Gene Mauch	10.00	5.00	3.00
(137)	Jim Owens	10.00	5.00	3.00
(138)	Robin Roberts	30.00	15.00	9.00
(139)	Frank Sullivan	10.00	5.00	3.00
(140)	Tony Taylor	10.00	5.00	3.00
PITTSBURGH PIRATES				
(141)	Roberto Clemente	60.00	30.00	18.00
(142)	Roy Face	10.00	5.00	3.00
(143)	Bob Friend	10.00	5.00	3.00
(144)	Dick Groat	10.00	5.00	3.00
(145)	Harvey Haddix	10.00	5.00	3.00
(146)	Don Hoak	10.00	5.00	3.00
(147)	Vern Law	10.00	5.00	3.00
(148)	Bill Mazeroski	30.00	15.00	9.00
(149)	Wilmer Mizell	10.00	5.00	3.00
(150)	Bill Virdon	10.00	5.00	3.00
SAN FRANCISCO GIANTS				
(151)	Felipe Alou	12.50	6.25	3.75
(152)	Orlando Cepeda	30.00	15.00	9.00
(153)	Sam Jones	10.00	5.00	3.00
(154)	Harvey Kuenn	10.00	5.00	3.00
(155)	Willie Mays	50.00	25.00	15.00
(156)	Mike McCormick	10.00	5.00	3.00
(157)	Willie McCovey	30.00	15.00	9.00
(158)	Stu Miller	10.00	5.00	3.00
(159)	Billy O'Dell	10.00	5.00	3.00
(160)	Jack Sanford	10.00	5.00	3.00
ST. LOUIS CARDINALS				
(161)	Ernie Broglio	10.00	5.00	3.00
(162)	Ken Boyer	12.50	6.25	3.75
(163)	Joe Cunningham	10.00	5.00	3.00
(164)	Alex Grammas	10.00	5.00	3.00
(165)	Larry Jackson	10.00	5.00	3.00
(166)	Julian Javier	10.00	5.00	3.00
(167)	Lindy McDaniel	10.00	5.00	3.00
(168)	Stan Musial	45.00	22.50	13.50
(169)	Hal Smith	10.00	5.00	3.00
(170)	Daryl Spencer	10.00	5.00	3.00
WASHINGTON SENATORS				
(171)	Pete Daley	10.00	5.00	3.00
(172)	Dick Donovan	10.00	5.00	3.00
(173)	Bob Johnson	10.00	5.00	3.00
(174)	Marty Keough	10.00	5.00	3.00
(175)	Billy Klaus	10.00	5.00	3.00
(176)	Dale Long	10.00	5.00	3.00
(177)	Carl Mathias	10.00	5.00	3.00
(178)	Willie Tasby	10.00	5.00	3.00
(179)	Mickey Vernon	10.00	5.00	3.00
(180)	Gene Woodling	10.00	5.00	3.00

1959 Mickey Mantle's Holiday Inn Postcard

The attributed date is speculative. Much rarer than the more common pose of Mantle in civvies in his Joplin, Mo. motel's lounge, this approximately 3-1/2" x 5-1/2" card features two color poses of the Mick in Yankees uniform on its front. The postcard-style back is printed in blue and gives motel information and features.

	NM	E	VG
Mickey Mantle	100.00	50.00	30.00

1962 Mickey Mantle's Holiday Inn Postcard

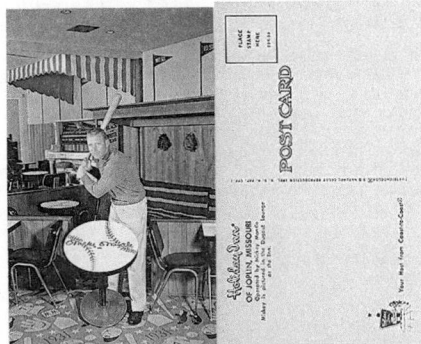

This color postcard pictures Mantle in civilian clothes. On the back of the standard-size (about 3-1/2" x 5-1/2") card it says the Mick is "pictured in the Dugout Lounge at the Inn." The "Inn" is the Joplin, Mo., Holiday Inn which Mantle owned. This was one of the more popular, and thus more common, of the souvenirs issued in conjunction with Mantle's motel.

	NM	E	VG
Mickey Mantle	50.00	25.00	15.00

1962 Mickey Mantle's Holiday Inn Premium Photo

Probably issued in 1962, though not dated, this 8" x 10" photo pictures the M&M Boys in the lounge of Mantle's motel. Back is blank.

	NM	E	VG
Mickey Mantle, Roger Maris	600.00	300.00	180.00

1963 Mickey Mantle Hospital Postcard

With a broken foot in 1963 following hard on a knee injury the previous season, Mantle spent considerable time in the hospital. To assist in answering a mountain of goodwill messages from fans, he had these postcards created. On front of the 3-1/2" x 5-1/2" card is a glossy black-and-white batting-pose photo. The back is printed in blue with a "Dear Friend" message thanking the fan for "the thoughtful attention" and ending optimistically, "Hope to see you all next season," above his facsimile autograph.

	NM	E	VG
Mickey Mantle	450.00	225.00	135.00

1923 Maple Crispette (V117)

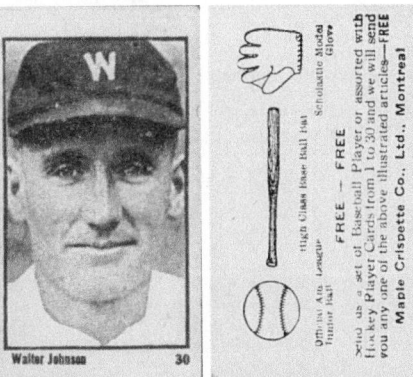

Issued by a Montreal candy company, these small (1-3/8" x 2-1/4") black-and-white cards were redeemable for baseball equipment, accounting for their scarcity today. Card #15, Stengel, was only discovered in 1992 and was obviously short-printed by the issuer to avoid giving away many bats, balls and gloves. Only a single specimen of the Stengel card is currently known; it is not included in the complete set prices. The existence of the card checklisted as 14a Wingo is now in doubt.

		NM	E	VG
	Complete Set, no Stengel (29):	40,000	20,000	12,000
	Common Player:	450.00	220.00	135.00
1	Jesse Barnes	450.00	220.00	135.00
2	Harold Traynor	1,100	550.00	325.00
3	Ray Schalk	1,100	550.00	325.00
4	Eddie Collins	1,100	550.00	325.00
5	Lee Fohl	450.00	220.00	135.00
6	Howard Summa	450.00	220.00	135.00
7	Waite Hoyt	1,100	550.00	325.00
8	Babe Ruth	10,000	5,000	3,000
9	Cozy Dolan	450.00	220.00	135.00
10	Johnny Bassler	450.00	220.00	135.00
11	George Dauss	450.00	220.00	135.00
12	Joe Sewell	1,100	550.00	325.00
13	Syl Johnson	450.00	220.00	135.00
14a	Wingo (Existence questioned)			
14b	Ivy Wingo	450.00	220.00	135.00
15	Casey Stengel	18,000	9,000	4,500
16	Arnold Statz	450.00	220.00	135.00
17	Emil Meusel	450.00	220.00	135.00
18	Bill Jacobson	450.00	220.00	135.00
19	Jim Bottomley	5,000	2,500	1,500
20	Sam Bohne	650.00	320.00	195.00
21	(Bucky) Harris	1,100	550.00	325.00
22	(Ty) Cobb	5,250	2,625	1,575
23	Roger Peckinpaugh	450.00	220.00	135.00
24	Muddy Ruel	450.00	220.00	135.00
25	(Bill) McKechnie	1,100	550.00	325.00
26	Riggs Stephenson	450.00	220.00	135.00
27	Herby Pennock	1,100	550.00	325.00
28	Ed (Edd) Roush	1,100	550.00	325.00
29	Bill Wambsganss	450.00	220.00	135.00
30	Walter Johnson	2,400	960.00	600.00

1962 Roger Maris Action Baseball Game

Baseball's new home run king was featured in this board game by Pressman Toy Co. Besides the colorful metal game board and other pieces, the set contains 88 playing cards. Each 2-1/4" x 3-1/2" card has a black-and-white photo on front of Maris in a batting pose, along with a white facsimile autograph. Backs have two possible game action plays printed, along with a copyright line.

	NM	E	VG
Complete Game:	425.00	210.00	125.00
Single Card:	45.00	22.00	13.50

Roger Maris

1913-14 Martens Bakery

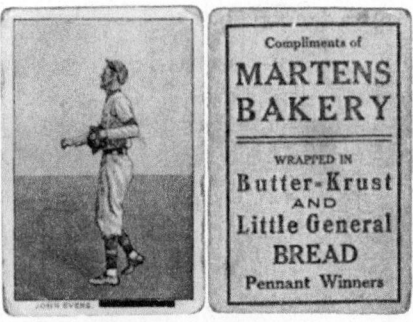

(See 1911-14 General Baking Co. (D304).)

1955 Mascot Dog Food

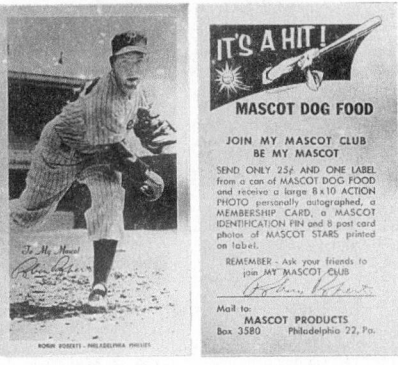

The date of issue shown is approximate. It is likely other players' cards exist, since the back mentions eight stars printed on the label, presumably of the dog food can. In black-and-white, the 3-1/2" x 5-1/2" card has on front a glossy action pose with a facsimile autograph personalized, "To My Mascot" and the player name and position printed in black in the bottom border. The back has an ad for a fan club offering an autographed 8" x 10" membership card and and set of eight postcards for a quarter and a label. label.

(1)   Robin Roberts (value undetermined)

1971 Mattel Instant Replay Records

These 2-3/8" diameter plastic records were produced in conjunction with a hand-held, battery-operated record player. Paper inserts featured illustrations of players in baseball, football and basketball, as well as various racing vehicles and airplanes. The audio recounts career highlights of the depicted player. Additional records were sold in sets of four.

	NM	E	VG
Complete Set (12):	250.00	125.00	75.00
Common Player:	10.00	5.00	3.00
(1) Hank Aaron	30.00	15.00	9.00
(2) Ernie Banks	15.00	7.50	4.50
(3) Roberto Clemente	50.00	25.00	15.00
(4) Al Kaline	15.00	7.50	4.50
(5) Sandy Koufax	40.00	20.00	12.00
(6) Roger Maris	15.00	7.50	4.50
(7) Willie Mays (Plays one side only; came with record player purchase.)	12.00	6.00	3.50
(8) Willie McCovey	12.00	6.00	3.50
(9) Tony Oliva	10.00	5.00	3.00
(10) Frank Robinson	13.50	6.75	4.00
(11) Tom Seaver	15.00	7.50	4.50
(12) Willie Stargell	12.00	6.00	3.50

1895 Mayo's Cut Plug (N300)

These 1-5/8" x 2-7/8" cards were issued by the Mayo Tobacco Works of Richmond, Va. There are 48 cards in the set, with 40 different players pictured. Twenty-eight of the players are pictured in uniform and 12 are shown in street clothes. Eight players appear both ways. Eight of the uniformed players also appear in two variations, creating the 48-card total. Card fronts are black-and-white or sepia portraits on black cardboard, with a Mayo's Cut Plug ad at the bottom of each card. Cards have a blank black back and are unnumbered.

	NM	E	VG
Complete Set (48):	200,000	70,000	30,000
Common Player:	2,000	700.00	300.00
(1) Charlie Abbey	2,000	700.00	300.00
(2) Cap Anson	18,000	6,300	2,700
(3) Jimmy Bannon	2,000	700.00	300.00
(4a) Dan Brouthers (Baltimore on shirt.)	11,500	4,025	1,725
(4b) Dan Brouthers (Louisville on shirt.)	13,000	4,550	1,950
(5) Ed Cartwright	2,000	700.00	300.00
(6) John Clarkson	7,500	2,625	1,125
(7) Tommy Corcoran	2,000	700.00	300.00
(8) Lave Cross	2,000	700.00	300.00
(9) Bill Dahlen	3,000	1,050	450.00
(10) Tom Daly	2,000	700.00	300.00
(11) E.J. Delehanty (Delahanty)	14,500	5,075	2,175
(12) Hugh Duffy	7,500	2,625	1,125
(13a) Buck Ewing (Cleveland on shirt.)	13,000	4,500	1,950
(13b) Buck Ewing (Cincinnati on shirt.)	10,000	3,500	1,500
(14) Dave Foutz	2,000	700.00	300.00
(15) Charlie Ganzel	2,000	700.00	300.00
(16a) Jack Glasscock (Pittsburg on shirt.)	3,000	1,050	450.00
(16b) Jack Glasscock (Louisville on shirt.)	2,000	700.00	300.00
(17) Mike Griffin	2,000	700.00	300.00
(18a) George Haddock (No team on shirt.)	3,300	1,150	500.00
(18b) George Haddock (Philadelphia on shirt.)	2,000	700.00	300.00
(19) Bill Hallman	2,400	850.00	350.00
(20) Billy Hamilton	7,500	2,625	1,250.00
(21) Bill Joyce	2,000	700.00	300.00
(22) Brickyard Kennedy	2,000	700.00	300.00
(23a) Tom Kinslow (No team on shirt.)	3,300	1,150	500.00
(23b) Tom Kinslow (Pittsburg on shirt.)	2,000	700.00	300.00
(24) Arlie Latham	2,000	700.00	300.00

	NM	E	VG
(25) Herman Long	2,000	700.00	300.00
(26) Tom Lovett	2,000	700.00	300.00
(27) Bobby Lowe	2,000	700.00	300.00
(28) Tommy McCarthy	7,900	2,750	1,185
(29) Yale Murphy	2,000	700.00	300.00
(30) Billy Nash	2,000	700.00	300.00
(31) Kid Nichols	13,200	4,625	1,980
(32a) Fred Pfeffer (2nd Base)	2,000	700.00	300.00
(32b) Fred Pfeffer (Retired)	2,000	700.00	300.00
(33) Wilbert Robinson	7,500	2,625	1,125
(34a) Amos Russie (Incorrect spelling.)	16,500	5,775	2,475
(34b) Amos Rusie (Correct)	11,500	4,025	1,725
(35) Jimmy Ryan	2,000	700.00	300.00
(36) Bill Shindle	2,000	700.00	300.00
(37) Germany Smith	2,000	700.00	300.00
(38) Otis Stocksdale (Stockdale)	2,000	700.00	300.00
(39) Tommy Tucker	2,000	700.00	300.00
(40a) Monte Ward (2nd Base)	10,000	3,500	1,500
(40b) Monte Ward (Retired)	8,000	2,800	1,200

1896 Mayo's Die-Cut Game Cards (N301)

Mayo Tobacco Works of Richmond, Va., issued an innovative, if not very popular, series of die-cut baseball player figures in 1896. These tiny (1-1/2" long by just 3/16" wide) cardboard figures were inserted in packages of Mayo's Cut Plug Tobacco and were designed to be used as part of a baseball board game. A "grandstand, base and teetotum" were available free by mail to complete the game pieces. Twenty-eight different die-cut figures were available, representing 26 unspecified New York and Boston players along with two umpires. The players are shown in various action poses - either running, batting, pitching or fielding. The backs carry an ad for Mayo's Tobacco. The players shown do not relate to any actual members of the New York or Boston clubs, diminishing the popularity of this issue, which has an American Card Catalog designation of N301.

	NM	E	VG
Complete Set (28):	4,000	1,600	800.00
Common Player:	150.00	60.00	30.00
(1a) Pitcher (Boston)	150.00	60.00	30.00
(1b) Pitcher (New York)	150.00	60.00	30.00
(2a) 1st Baseman (Boston)	150.00	60.00	30.00
(2b) 1st Baseman (New York)	150.00	60.00	30.00
(3a) 2nd Baseman (Boston)	150.00	60.00	30.00
(3b) 2nd Baseman (New York)	150.00	60.00	30.00
(4a) 3rd Baseman (Boston)	150.00	60.00	30.00
(4b) 3rd Baseman (New York)	150.00	60.00	30.00
(5a) Right Fielder (Boston)	150.00	60.00	30.00
(5b) Right Fielder (New York)	150.00	60.00	30.00
(6a) Center Fielder (Boston)	150.00	60.00	30.00
(6b) Center Fielder (New York)	150.00	60.00	30.00
(7a) Left Fielder (Boston)	150.00	60.00	30.00
(7b) Left Fielder (New York)	150.00	60.00	30.00
(8a) Short Stop (Boston)	150.00	60.00	30.00
(8b) Short Stop (New York)	150.00	60.00	30.00
(9a) Catcher (Boston)	150.00	60.00	30.00
(9b) Catcher (New York)	150.00	60.00	30.00
(10a) Batman (Boston)	150.00	60.00	30.00
(10b) Batman (New York)	150.00	60.00	30.00
(11a) Runner (Boston, standing upright.)	150.00	60.00	30.00
(11b) Runner (New York, standing upright.)	150.00	60.00	30.00
(12a) Runner (Boston, bent slightly forward.)	150.00	60.00	30.00
(12b) Runner (New York, bent slightly forward.)	150.00	60.00	30.00
(13a) Runner (Boston, bent well forward.)	150.00	60.00	30.00
(13b) Runner (New York, bent well forward.)	150.00	60.00	30.00
(14) Umpire (Facing front.)	150.00	60.00	30.00
(15) Field Umpire (Rear view.)	150.00	60.00	30.00

1900 Mayo's Baseball Comics (T203)

As their name implies, the T203 Baseball Comics feature cartoon-like drawings that illustrate various baseball phrases and terminology. Issued with Winner Cut Plug and Mayo Cut Plug tobacco products, the complete set consists of 25 different comics, each measuring approximately 2-1/16" x 3-1/8". Because they do not picture individual players, these cards have never attracted much of a following among serious baseball card collectors. They do, however, hold some interest as a novelty item of the period.

	NM	E	VG
Complete Set (25):	8,750	4,375	1,750
Common Card:	450.00	225.00	90.00
(1) "A Crack Outfielder"	450.00	225.00	90.00
(2) "A Fancy Twirler"	450.00	225.00	90.00
(3) "A Fine Slide"	450.00	225.00	90.00
(4) "A Fowl Bawl"	450.00	225.00	90.00
(5) "A Great Game"	450.00	225.00	90.00
(6) "A Home Run"	450.00	225.00	90.00
(7) "An All Star Battery"	450.00	225.00	90.00
(8) "A Short Stop"	450.00	225.00	90.00
(9) "A Star Catcher"	450.00	225.00	90.00
(10) "A White Wash"	450.00	225.00	90.00
(11) "A Tie Game"	450.00	225.00	90.00
(12) "A Two Bagger"	450.00	225.00	90.00
(13) "A Wild Pitch"	450.00	225.00	90.00
(14) "Caught Napping"	450.00	225.00	90.00
(15) "On To The Curves"	450.00	225.00	90.00
(16) "Out"	450.00	225.00	90.00
(17) "Put Out On 1st"	450.00	225.00	90.00
(18) "Right Over The Plate"	450.00	225.00	90.00
(19) "Rooting For The Home Team"	450.00	225.00	90.00
(20) "Stealing A Base"	450.00	225.00	90.00
(21) "Stealing Home"	450.00	225.00	90.00
(22) "Strike Out"	450.00	225.00	90.00
(23) "The Bleacher"	450.00	225.00	90.00
(24) "The Naps"	450.00	225.00	90.00
(25) "The Red Sox"	450.00	225.00	90.00

1948 Thom McAn Bob Feller Premium

This black-and-white 8" x 10" premium picture has on front a posed action photo and facsimile autograph. On back is a 25-question baseball quiz and advertising for the shoe store chain, along with a copyright for Melville Shoe Co.

	NM	E	VG
Bob Feller	150.00	75.00	45.00

1970 McDonald's Brewers

McDonald's welcomed the American League Brewers to Milwaukee in 1970 by issuing a set of six baseball card panels. Five of the panels picture five players and a team logo, while the sixth panel contains six players, resulting in 31 different players. The panels measure 9" x 9-1/2" and feature full-color paintings of the players. Each sheet displays the heading, "the original milwaukee brewers, 1970." The cards are numbered by uniform number and the backs are blank. Although distributed by McDonald's, their name does not appear on the cards.

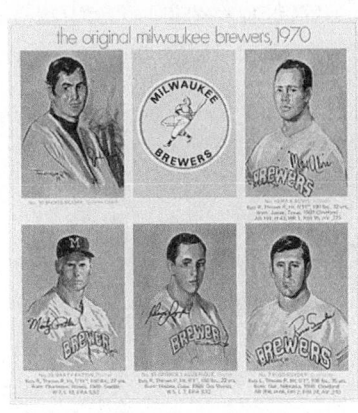

the original milwaukee brewers, 1970

	NM	E	VG
Complete Sheet Set (6):	15.00	7.50	4.50
Complete Singles Set (32):	15.00	7.50	4.50
Common Player:	.50	.25	.15
1 Ted Kubiak	.50	.25	.15
2 Ted Savage	.50	.25	.15
4 Dave Bristol	.50	.25	.15
5 Phil Roof	.50	.25	.15
6 Mike Hershberger	.50	.25	.15
7 Russ Snyder	.50	.25	.15
8 Mike Hegan	.50	.25	.15
9 Rich Rollins	.50	.25	.15
10 Max Alvis	.50	.25	.15
11 John Kennedy	.50	.25	.15
12 Dan Walton	.50	.25	.15
15 Jerry McNertney	.50	.25	.15
18 Wes Stock	.50	.25	.15
20 Wayne Comer	.50	.25	.15
21 Tommy Harper	.50	.25	.15
23 Bob Locker	.50	.25	.15
24 Lew Krausse	.50	.25	.15
25 John Gelnar	.50	.25	.15
26 Roy McMillan	.50	.25	.15
27 Cal Ermer	.50	.25	.15
28 Sandy Valdespino	.50	.25	.15
30 Jackie Moore	.50	.25	.15
32 Gene Brabender	.50	.25	.15
33 Marty Pattin	.50	.25	.15
34 Greg Goossen	.50	.25	.15
35 John Morris	.50	.25	.15
36 Steve Hovley	.50	.25	.15
38 Bob Meyer	.50	.25	.15
39 Bob Bolin	.50	.25	.15
43 John O'Donoghue	.50	.25	.15
49 George Lauzerique	.50	.25	.15
--- Logo Card	.50	.25	.15

1974 McDonald's Gene Michael

GENE "THE STICK" MICHAEL

Though there is no advertising or logo on this one-card "set," this black-and-white card of "The Stick" in his last year as a Yankee was distributed by a Staten Island McDonald's restaurant during an autograph appearance. The card measures 2-5/8" x 4-3/8" and is blank-backed.

	NM	E	VG
Gene "The Stick" Michael	25.00	12.50	7.50

1974 McDonald's Padres Discs

Envisioned as part of a line of sports promotional sets, this concept died following the test with San Diego area McDonalds. At the July 30, 1974, game, Padres fans were given a hinged plastic baseball containing five Padres player photo discs plus a disc with the team's schedule and a

Ronald McDonald disc which listed the dates on which the remaining eight player cards would be distributed at area McDonalds. Only 60,000 of the "starter set" discs were made, while 180,000 of each of the other player discs were printed. The 2-3/8" diameter discs feature a color photo on front and player stats on back. The promotion was the work of Photo Sports, Inc., of Los Angeles.

		NM	E	VG
Complete Set (15):		25.00	12.50	7.50
Common Player:		1.00	.50	.30
(1)	Matty Alou	1.00	.50	.30
(2)	Glenn Beckert	3.00	1.50	.90
(3)	Nate Colbert	1.00	.50	.30
(4)	Bill Grief	1.00	.50	.30
(5)	John Grubb	1.00	.50	.30
(6)	Enzo Hernandez	3.00	1.50	.90
(7)	Randy Jones	3.00	1.50	.90
(8)	Fred Kendall	3.00	1.50	.90
(9)	Willie McCovey	6.00	3.00	1.75
(10)	John McNamara	3.00	1.50	.90
(11)	Dave Roberts	1.00	.50	.30
(12)	Bobby Tolan	1.00	.50	.30
(13)	Dave Winfield	15.00	7.50	4.50
(14)	Padres home game schedule	1.50	.70	.45
(15)	Ronald McDonald	1.50	.70	.45

1978 McDonald's Boston Red Sox

Reportedly because of a production problem, distribtution of these cards was limited to a few Boston-area McDonald's restaurants for a very limited time. The blank-back, approximately 3-1/2" x 6" color cards have borderless portraits on front with the player's facsimile autograph. The cards were reportedly distributed in Treasure Chest meals for kids under 12.

		NM	E	VG
Complete Set (6):		550.00	275.00	165.00
Common Player:		35.00	17.50	10.00
(1)	Rick Burleson	35.00	17.50	10.00
(2)	Carlton Fisk	125.00	60.00	35.00
(3)	Fred Lynn	75.00	37.50	22.50
(4)	Jim Rice	125.00	60.00	35.00
(5)	Luis Tiant	50.00	25.00	15.00
(6)	Carl Yastrzemski	150.00	75.00	45.00

1950-1952 Bill McGowan's School for Umpires

Over a period of at least three years in the early 1950s, Hall of Fame American League umpire Bill McGowan issued a series of black-and-white postcards to promote his umpires' school in Florida. The 3-1/2" x 5-1/2" cards have bordered or borderless photos on front, some of which bear the imprint of Grogan Photo, Danville, Ill.

		NM	E	VG
(1)	1950 - Florida (Students on bleachers.)	60.00	30.00	20.00
(2)	Florida (Students standing on field.)	60.00	30.00	20.00
(3)	Bill McGowan (1951)	500.00	250.00	150.00
(4)	Donatelli Instructs(Augie Donatelli) (1952)	65.00	32.50	20.00
(5)	Guglielmo Instructs(Augie Guglielmo) (1952)	65.00	32.50	20.00

1970s-80s Doug McWilliams Postcards

For more than two decades, California photographer Doug McWilliams (who also worked for Topps for 23 years) produced a series of black-and-white and color postcards for individual use by ballplayers, mostly members of the Oakland A's. Almost uniformly, the 3-1/2" x 5-1/2" cards have no graphics on front (a few have facsimile autographs), just a player pose or portrait. Backs have standard postcard markings, player identification, and McWilliams' credit lines. Backs carry a two-digit year of issue prefix to the card number. Postcards are printed in black-and-white unless noted.

	NM	E	VG
Common Player:	3.00	1.50	.90

(See individual years for checklists and values.)

1970 Doug McWilliams Collectors' Issue Postcards

This set of black-and-white player postcards was produced by San Fransisco art photographer Doug McWilliams as a custom order for an Eastern collector. Fewer than 50 sets were reportedly produced. The 3-1/2" x 5-1/2" cards have glossy photographic fronts and standard postcard backs with player identification. The unnumbered cards are checklisted here in alphabetical order.

		NM	E	VG
Complete Set (22):		400.00	200.00	125.00
Common Player:		20.00	10.00	6.00
(1)	Jerry Adair	20.00	10.00	6.00
(2)	Brant Alyea	20.00	10.00	6.00
(3)	Brant Alyea	20.00	10.00	6.00
(4)	Dwain Anderson	20.00	10.00	6.00
(5)	Curt Blefary	20.00	10.00	6.00
(6)	Bill Daniels	20.00	10.00	6.00
(7)	Mike Epstein	22.50	11.00	6.75
(8)	Adrian Garrett	20.00	10.00	6.00
(9)	Frank Fernandez	20.00	10.00	6.00
(10)	Mike Hegan	20.00	10.00	6.00
(11)	George Hendrick	20.00	10.00	6.00
(12)	Reggie Jackson	125.00	62.00	37.00
(13)	Reggie Jackson	125.00	62.00	37.00
(14)	Ron Klimkowski	20.00	10.00	6.00
(15)	Darold Knowles	20.00	10.00	6.00
(16)	Jerry Lumpe	20.00	10.00	6.00
(17)	Angel Mangual	20.00	10.00	6.00
(18)	Denny McLain	30.00	15.00	9.00

		NM	E	VG
(19)	Denny McLain	30.00	15.00	9.00
(20)	Irv Noren	20.00	10.00	6.00
(21)	Ramon Webster	20.00	10.00	6.00
(22)	Dick Williams	20.00	10.00	6.00

1970 Doug McWilliams Oakland A's Postcards

These 3-1/2" x 5-1/2" black-and-white player postcards were produced by San Francisco photographer Doug McWilliams for sale by Sports Cards for Collectors, a forerunner of TCMA. Each card can be found either with or without borders on front, the latter having a slightly enlarged image. Player identification is on back. The unnumbered cards are check-listed here alphabetically. Fewer than 50 sets were reported produced.

		NM	E	VG
Complete Set (42):		400.00	200.00	125.00
Common Player:		15.00	7.50	4.50
(1)	Felipe Alou	20.00	10.00	6.00
(2)	Sal Bando	20.00	10.00	6.00
(3)	Vida Blue	25.00	12.50	7.50
(4)	Bobby Brooks	15.00	7.50	4.50
(5)	Bert Campaneris	25.00	12.50	7.50
(6)	"Babe" Dahlgren	15.00	7.50	4.50
(7)	Tommy Davis	17.50	8.75	5.25
(8)	Chuck Dobson	15.00	7.50	4.50
(9)	John Donaldson	15.00	7.50	4.50
(10)	Al Downing	15.00	7.50	4.50
(11)	Jim Driscoll	15.00	7.50	4.50
(12)	Dave Duncan	15.00	7.50	4.50
(13)	Frank Fernandez	15.00	7.50	4.50
(14)	Rollie Fingers	45.00	22.00	13.50
(15)	Tito Francona	15.00	7.50	4.50
(16)	Jim Grant	20.00	10.00	6.00
(17)	Dick Green	15.00	7.50	4.50
(18)	Larry Haney	15.00	7.50	4.50
(19)	Bobby Hofman	15.00	7.50	4.50
(20)	Steve Hovley	15.00	7.50	4.50
(21)	Jim Hunter	45.00	22.00	13.50
(22)	Reggie Jackson	125.00	62.00	37.00
(23)	Dave Johnson	15.00	7.50	4.50
(24)	Marcel Lacheman	15.00	7.50	4.50
(25)	Tony LaRussa	40.00	20.00	12.00
(26)	Paul Lindblad	15.00	7.50	4.50
(27)	Bob Locker	15.00	7.50	4.50
(28)	John McNamara	15.00	7.50	4.50
(29)	Don Mincher	15.00	7.50	4.50
(30)	Rick Monday	15.00	7.50	4.50
(31)	"Blue Moon" Odom	17.50	8.75	5.25
(32)	Darrell Osteen	15.00	7.50	4.50
(33)	Ray Oyler	15.00	7.50	4.50
(34)	Roberto Pena	15.00	7.50	4.50
(35)	Bill Posedel	15.00	7.50	4.50
(36)	Roberto Rodriguez	15.00	7.50	4.50
(37)	Jim Roland	15.00	7.50	4.50
(38)	Joe Rudi	20.00	10.00	6.00
(39)	Diego Segui	15.00	7.50	4.50
(40)	Jose Tartabull	15.00	7.50	4.50
(41)	Gene Tenace	15.00	7.50	4.50
(42)	Dooley Womack	15.00	7.50	4.50

1970 Doug McWilliams Postcards

		NM	E	VG
1	Jim Roland	1.00	.50	.30
2a	Mudcat Grant, Mudcat Grant	1.50	.75	.45
2b	Mudcat Grant	1.50	.75	.45
3	Reggie Jackson (Color - only 50 produced.)	150.00	75.00	45.00
4	Darrell Osteen	1.00	.50	.30
5a	Tom Hafey (First printing.)	1.00	.50	.30
5b	Tom Hafey (Second printing.)	1.00	.50	.30
6	Chick Hafey	1.50	.75	.45

1971 Doug McWilliams Postcards

		NM	E	VG
7	Larry Brown	3.00	1.50	.90
8a	Vida Blue (Color - first printing - KV3321.)	6.00	3.00	1.75
8b	Vida Blue (Color - second printing - KV3509.)	6.00	3.00	1.75
8c	Vida Blue (Color - third printing - KV4403.)	6.00	3.00	1.75
9	Dave Duncan	3.00	1.50	.90
10	George Hendrick (Color)	9.00	4.50	2.75
11	Mudcat Grant	3.00	1.50	.90
12	Mudcat Grant	3.00	1.50	.90

1972 Doug McWilliams Postcards

		NM	E	VG
13	John Odom (Color)	6.00	3.00	1.75
14	Reggie Jackson (Color)	20.00	10.00	6.00
15	Sal Bando (Color)	6.00	3.00	1.75
16	Dan Cater	3.00	1.50	.90
17	Bob Locker	3.00	1.50	.90
18a	Joe Rudi (Equal edges to player.)	3.00	1.50	.90
18b	Joe Rudi (Bat close at bottom.)	3.00	1.50	.90
18c	Joe Rudi (Hand close to edge.)	3.00	1.50	.90
19	Larry Brown	3.00	1.50	.90
20a	Dick Green (First printing - glossy.)	3.00	1.50	.90
20b	Dick Green (Second printing - glossy, more contrast.)	3.00	1.50	.90
20c	Dick Green (Third printing - matte.)	3.00	1.50	.90
21	Vida Blue (Color)	6.00	3.00	1.75
22a	Joe Horlen (First printing - bright.)	3.00	1.50	.90
22b	Joe Horlen (Second printing - dark.)	3.00	1.50	.90
23	Gene Tenace (Color)	6.00	3.00	1.75
24a	Ted Kubiak (Glossy)	3.00	1.50	.90
24b	Ted Kubiak (Matte)	3.00	1.50	.90
A	Emeryville Ball Park	3.00	1.50	.90
B	Oakland Coliseum	3.00	1.50	.90

1973 Doug McWilliams Postcards

		NM	E	VG
25	Rene Lachemann	3.00	1.50	.90
26	Tom Greive	3.00	1.50	.90
27	John Odom (Color)	6.00	3.00	1.75
28a	Rollie Fingers (First printing.)	9.00	4.50	2.75
28b	Rollie Fingers (Second printing - thinner stock.)	9.00	4.50	2.75
29	Jim Hunter (Color)	9.00	4.50	2.75
30	Ray Fosse (Color)	6.00	3.00	1.75
31	Charley Pride (Color)	15.00	7.50	4.50
32	Charley Pride (Color)	15.00	7.50	4.50
33	Bill North	3.00	1.50	.90
34	Damasco Blanco	3.00	1.50	.90
35	Paul Lindblad	3.00	1.50	.90
36	Rollie Fingers (Color)	9.00	4.50	2.75
37	Horacio Pina	3.00	1.50	.90
38	Bert Campaneris (Color)	7.50	3.75	2.25
39	Jim Holt (Color)	6.00	3.00	1.75
40	Sal Bando (Color)	6.00	3.00	1.75
41	Joe Rudi (Color)	6.00	3.00	1.75
42	Dick Williams (Color)	6.00	3.00	1.75
43	Jesus Alou	3.00	1.50	.90
44	Joe Niekro	3.75	2.00	1.25
45	Johnny Oates	3.00	1.50	.90

1974 Doug McWilliams Postcards

		NM	E	VG
46a	Ray Fosse (Color - first printing - w/signature.)	6.00	3.00	1.75
46b	Ray Fosse (Color - second printing - no signature.)	6.00	3.00	1.75
46c	Ray Fosse (Color - third printing - no sig., very green grass.)	6.00	3.00	1.75
47	Jesus Alou	3.00	1.50	.90
48	John Summers	3.00	1.50	.90
49	Dal Maxvill	3.00	1.50	.90
50	Joe Rudi (Color)	6.00	3.00	1.75
51	Sal Bando (Color)	6.00	3.00	1.75
52	Reggie Jackson (Color)	20.00	10.00	6.00
53	Ted Kubiak (Color)	6.00	3.00	1.75
54	Dave Hamilton	3.00	1.50	.90
55	Gene Tenace (Color)	6.00	3.00	1.75
56a	Bob Locker (First printing - back foot near edge.)	3.00	1.50	.90
57	Manny Trillo	3.00	1.50	.90

1975 Doug McWilliams Postcards

		NM	E	VG
58a	Dan Godby (First printing.)	3.00	1.50	.90
58b	Dan Godby (Second printing - blank back.)	3.00	1.50	.90
58c	Dan Godby (Third printing - flat contrast.)	3.00	1.50	.90
59	Bob Locker	3.00	1.50	.90
60	Rollie Fingers (Color)	9.00	4.50	2.75
61	Glenn Abbott	3.00	1.50	.90
62	Jim Todd	3.00	1.50	.90
63	Phil Garner	3.00	1.50	.90
64	Paul Lindblad	3.00	1.50	.90
65	Bill North (Color)	6.00	3.00	1.75
66	Dick Sisler	3.00	1.50	.90
67	Angel Mangual	3.00	1.50	.90
68	Claudell Washington	3.00	1.50	.90

1976 Doug McWilliams Postcards

		NM	E	VG
69	Oakland Coliseum (Color)	6.00	3.00	1.75
70	Sal Bando (Color)	6.00	3.00	1.75
71	Mike Torrez (Color)	6.00	3.00	1.75
72	Joe Lonnett	3.00	1.50	.90
73	Chuck Tanner	3.00	1.50	.90
74	Tommy Sandt	3.00	1.50	.90
75	Dick Bosman (Color)	6.00	3.00	1.75
76	Bert Campaneris (Color)	6.00	3.00	1.75
77	Ken Brett	6.00	3.00	1.75
78	Jim Todd (Color)	6.00	3.00	1.75
79	Jeff Newman	3.00	1.50	.90
80	John McCall	3.00	1.50	.90

1977 Doug McWilliams Postcards

		NM	E	VG
81	Don Baylor (Color)	9.00	4.50	2.75
82	Lee Stange	3.00	1.50	.90
83	Rob Picciolo	3.00	1.50	.90
84	Jack Mc Keon (Color)	6.00	3.00	1.75
85	Rollie Fingers (Color)	9.00	4.50	2.75
86	Manny Sanguillen	3.00	1.50	.90
87	Tony Armas	3.00	1.50	.90
88	Jim Tyrone	3.00	1.50	.90
89	Wayne Gross	3.00	1.50	.90
90	Rick Langford	3.00	1.50	.90
91	Rich Gossage	3.00	1.50	.90
92	Phil Garner (Color)	6.00	3.00	1.75

1979 Michigan Sports Collectors

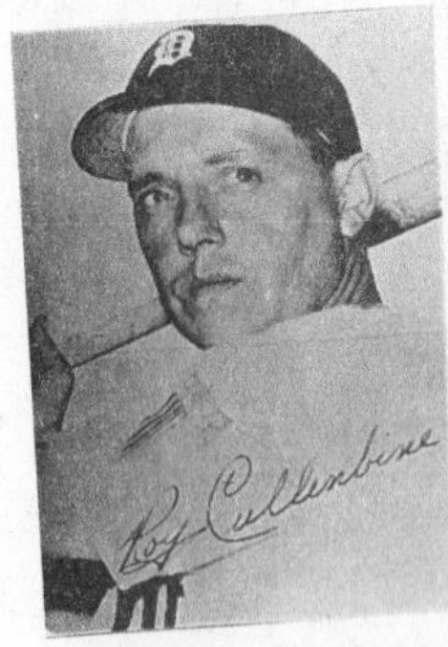
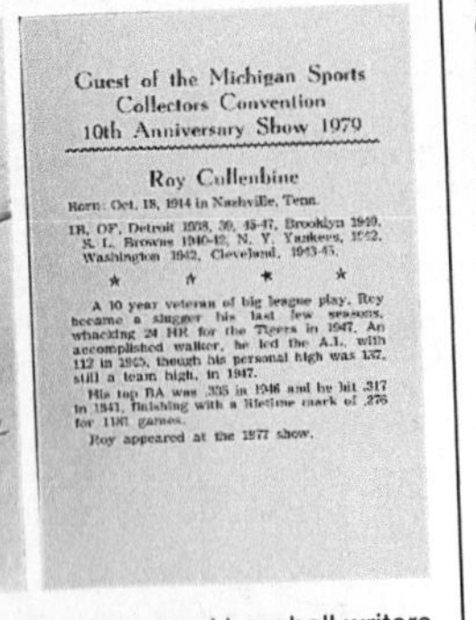

Former Detroit Tigers, along with several baseball writers and announcers, including some who were appearing as autograph guests were featured in this collectors set issued in conjunction with the 1979 Troy, Mich. show. Cards are 3-1/2" x 5-1/16" black-and-white. Backs have personal data and a career summary of the pictured player, along with mention of the show. The unnumbered cards are checklisted here alphabetically.

		NM	E	VG
	Complete Set (20):	20.00	10.00	6.00
	Common Player:	3.00	1.50	.90
(1)	Gates Brown	3.00	1.50	.90
(2)	Norm Cash	5.00	2.50	1.50
(3)	Al Cicotte	3.00	1.50	.90
(4)	Roy Cullenbine	3.00	1.50	.90
(5)	Gene Desautels	3.00	1.50	.90
(6)	Hoot Evers	3.00	1.50	.90
(7)	Joe Falls	3.00	1.50	.90
(8)	Joe Ginsberg	3.00	1.50	.90
(9)	Ernie Harwell	3.00	1.50	.90
(10)	Ray Herbert	3.00	1.50	.90
(11)	John Hiller	3.00	1.50	.90
(12)	Billy Hoeft	4.00	2.00	1.25
(13)	Ralph Houk	3.00	1.50	.90
(14)	Cliff Kachline	5.00	2.50	1.50
(15)	George Kell	4.00	2.00	1.25
(16)	Ron LeFlore	3.00	1.50	.90
(17)	Barney McCosky	3.00	1.50	.90
(18)	Jim Northrup	3.00	1.50	.90
(19)	Dick Radatz	3.00	1.50	.90
(20)	Tom Timmermann	3.00	1.50	.90

194 Michigan Sportservice Detroit Tigers

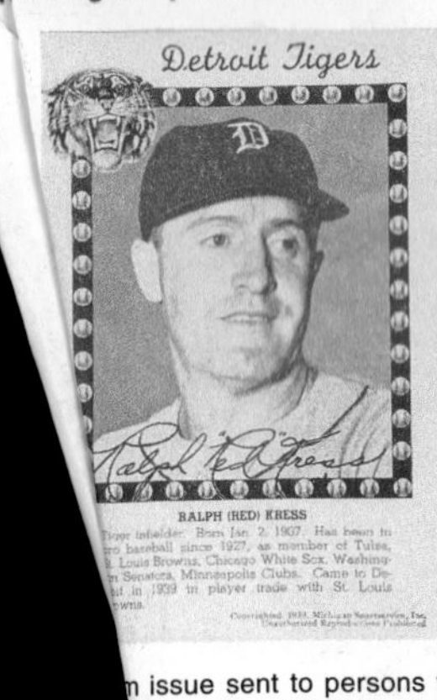

...n issue sent to persons who wrote the ...hotos, these blank-back cards measure ... printed in black-and-white. A facsimile ...over the central portrait, which is sur- ...of baseballs. A few career notes are ...o. At bottom-left is a union printing la- ...printed, "Copyrighted 1939, Michigan ...uthorized Reproduction Prohibited." ...are checklisted here alphabetically.

	NM	E	VG
	5,400	2,700	1,650
	300.00	150.00	90.00
	350.00	175.00	105.00
	300.00	150.00	90.00
	300.00	150.00	90.00
	300.00	150.00	90.00
	300.00	150.00	90.00
	300.00	150.00	90.00
	300.00	150.00	90.00
	400.00	200.00	120.00
	550.00	275.00	165.00
	300.00	150.00	90.00

(11)	Pinky Higgins	300.00	150.00	90.00
(12)	Fred Hutchinson	300.00	150.00	90.00
(13)	Ralph "Red" Kress	300.00	150.00	90.00
(14)	Barney McCosky	300.00	150.00	90.00
(15)	Archie R. McKain	300.00	150.00	90.00
(16)	Hal Newhouser	350.00	175.00	105.00
(17)	Louis "Buck" Newsom	300.00	150.00	90.00
(18)	Schoolboy Rowe	300.00	150.00	90.00
(19)	Birdie Tebbetts	300.00	150.00	90.00
(20)	Dizzy Trout	300.00	150.00	90.00
(21)	Rudy York	300.00	150.00	90.00

1975 Mid-Atlantic Sports Collectors Association

This "Baseball Royalty" collectors' set was issued in conjunction with the 1975 convention of the Mid-Atlantic Sports Collectors Association in Pikesville, Md. The blank-backed, 2-1/2" x 4-3/4" cards are printed in red and blue on white with player photos in blue. Each of the players in the set has a name or nickname pertaining to royalty. The unnumbered cards are checklisted here in alphabetical order.

		NM	E	VG
	Complete Set (8):	20.00	10.00	6.00
	Common Player:	3.00	1.50	.90
(1)	Paul (Duke) Derringer	3.00	1.50	.90
(2)	Elroy (Baron of the Bullpen) Face	3.00	1.50	.90
(3)	Rogers (Rajah) Hornsby	5.00	2.50	1.50
(4)	(King) Carl Hubbell	4.00	2.00	1.25
(5)	Charley (King Kong) Keller	3.00	1.50	.90
(6)	Babe (Sultan of Swat) Ruth	10.00	5.00	3.00
(7)	(Prince) Hal Schumacher	3.00	1.50	.90
(8)	Edwin (Duke) Snider	7.50	3.75	2.25

1927 Middy Bread Browns/Cardinals Die-Cuts

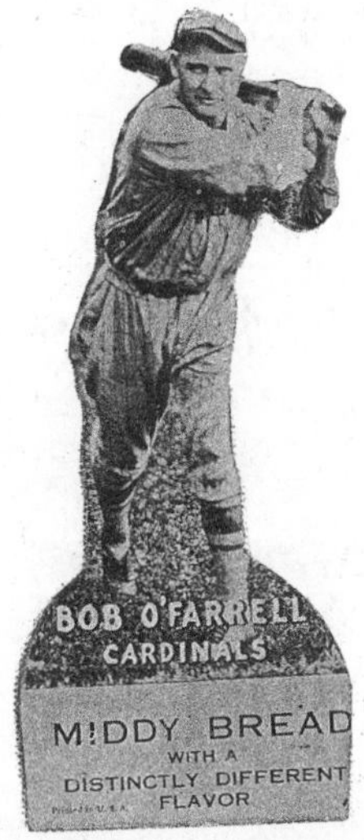

St. Louis Cardinals and St. Louis Browns players comprise this set. Black-and-white, blank-backed and unnumbered, the cards are known only in die-cut form, and vary in size according to the player pose, with a typical card measuring 2-1/4" x 4" or so. The checklist, arranged here alphabetically, consists of 22 players from each team, but may be subject to future additions. Similar to the previous year's issue of Kut Outs Yankees and Giants die-cut cards, this issue features posed action photos with the backgrounds cut away and the player and team name printed at the bottom of the photo. Unlike the earlier New York issue, however, these cards carry an advertisement at bottom for Midday Bread, and were presumably issued in the St. Louis area, though the exact method of their distribution is unknown. Cards are blank-backed and unnumbered. As with all die-cut cards, various appendages and bat ends were easily torn off and cards with such defects suffer severe loss of value.

		NM	E	VG
	Complete Set (44):	13,500	6,750	4,250
	Common Player:	300.00	120.00	60.00
	St. Louis Browns			
	St. Louis Cardinals			
(2)	Herman Bell	300.00	120.00	60.00
(3)	Lester Bell	300.00	120.00	60.00
(4)	Ray Blades	300.00	120.00	60.00
(5)	Jim Bottomley	500.00	200.00	100.00
(6)	Danny Clark	300.00	120.00	60.00
(7)	Taylor Douthit	300.00	120.00	60.00
(8)	Frank Frisch	500.00	200.00	100.00
(9)	Chick Hafey	500.00	200.00	100.00
(16)	Jimmy Ring	300.00	120.00	60.00
(17)	Walter Roettger	300.00	120.00	60.00
(18)	Robert Schang	300.00	120.00	60.00
(19)	Willie Sherdel	300.00	120.00	60.00
(20)	Billy Southworth	300.00	120.00	60.00
(21)	Tommy Thevenow	300.00	120.00	60.00
(22)	George Toporcer	300.00	120.00	60.00
(2)	Herman Bell	300.00	120.00	60.00
(2)	Win Ballou	300.00	120.00	60.00
	St. Louis Cardinals			
(3)	Lester Bell	300.00	120.00	60.00
(3)	Walter Beck	300.00	120.00	60.00
(4)	Herschel Bennett	300.00	120.00	60.00
	St. Louis Cardinals			
(4)	Ray Blades	300.00	120.00	60.00
(5)	Jim Bottomley	500.00	200.00	100.00
(5)	Stewart Bolen	300.00	120.00	60.00
	St. Louis Cardinals			
(6)	Danny Clark	300.00	120.00	60.00
(6)	Leo Dixon	300.00	120.00	60.00
(7)	Chester Falk	300.00	120.00	60.00
	St. Louis Cardinals			
(7)	Taylor Douthit	300.00	120.00	60.00
(8)	Frank Frisch	500.00	200.00	100.00
(8)	Milton Gaston	300.00	120.00	60.00
	St. Louis Cardinals			
(9)	Chick Hafey	500.00	200.00	100.00
(9)	Walter Gerber	300.00	120.00	60.00
(16)	Steve O'Neill	300.00	120.00	60.00
(17)	Harry Rice	300.00	120.00	60.00
	St. Louis Cardinals			
(17)	Walter Roettger	300.00	120.00	60.00
(18)	George Sisler	500.00	200.00	100.00
	St. Louis Cardinals			
(18)	Robert Schang	300.00	120.00	60.00
(19)	Walter Stewart	300.00	120.00	60.00
	St. Louis Cardinals			
(19)	Willie Sherdel	300.00	120.00	60.00
(20)	Billy Southworth	300.00	120.00	60.00
(20)	Elam VanGilder	300.00	120.00	60.00
(21)	Ken Williams	300.00	120.00	60.00
	St. Louis Cardinals			
(21)	Tommy Thevenow	300.00	120.00	60.0
(22)	Ernie Wingard	300.00	120.00	60.0
	St. Louis Cardinals			
(22)	George Toporcer	300.00	120.00	60.0

1976 Midwest Sports Collectors Convention

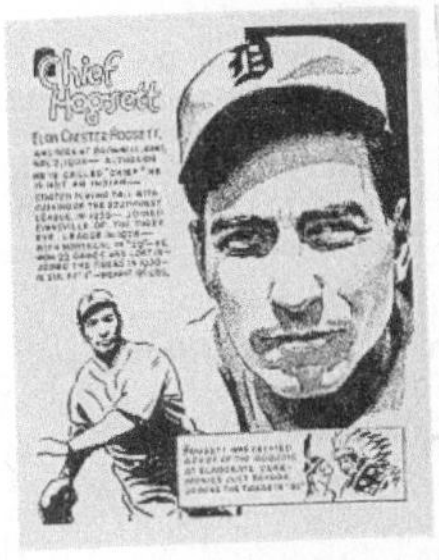
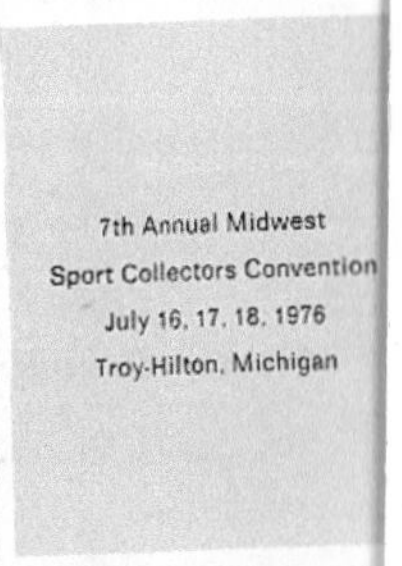

This collectors' issue was produced in conjunction with the 7th annual convention of the Midwest Sports Collec... in Troy, Mich. Former members of the Detroit Tigers, wit... emphasis on the 1930s, are featured on the black-and-w... 2-3/8" x 2-7/8" cards. Players are depicted in portrait... action drawings, with personal data and career highli... added in either written or comic form. Backs advertise... show. The unnumbered cards are checklisted here in al...betical order.

		NM	E
	Complete Set (23):	15.00	7.50
	Common Player:	3.00	1.50
(1)	Eldon Auker	3.00	1.50
(2)	Tommy Bridges	3.00	1.50
(3)	Flea Clifton	3.00	1.50
(4)	Mickey Cochrane	7.50	3.75
(5)	General Crowder	3.00	1.50
(6)	Frank Doljack	3.00	1.50
(7)	Carl Fischer	3.00	1.50
(8)	Pete Fox	3.00	1.50
(9)	Charlie Gehringer	6.00	3.00
(10)	Goose Goslin	4.50	2.25
(11)	Hank Greenberg	9.00	4.50
(12)	Luke Hamlin	3.00	1.50
(13)	Ray Hayworth	3.00	1.50
(14)	Chief Hogsett	3.00	1.50

93	Del Alston	3.00	1.50	.90
94	Bert Blyleven (Color)	7.50	3.75	2.25
95	Willie McCovey (Color)	9.00	4.50	2.75
96	Ken Brett (Color)	6.00	3.00	1.75
97	Doyle Alexander (Color)	6.00	3.00	1.75

1978 Doug McWilliams Postcards

		NM	E	VG
98	Rene Lacheman	3.00	1.50	.90
99	Del Alston	3.00	1.50	.90
100	Lee Stange (Color)	6.00	3.00	1.75
101	Taylor Duncan	3.00	1.50	.90
102	Matt Keough	3.00	1.50	.90
103	Bruce Robinson	3.00	1.50	.90
104	Sal Bando (Color)	6.00	3.00	1.75

1979 Doug McWilliams Postcards

		NM	E	VG
105	Alan Wirth	3.00	1.50	.90
106	Mike Edwards	3.00	1.50	.90
107	Craig Minetto	3.00	1.50	.90
108	Mike Morgan	3.00	1.50	.90
109	Brian Kingman	3.00	1.50	.90

1980 Doug McWilliams Postcards

		NM	E	VG
110	Jim Essian	3.00	1.50	.90
111a	Willie McCovey (Color - first printing - no signature.)	9.00	4.50	2.75
111b	Willie McCovey (Color - second printing - w/ signature, stamp at top.)	9.00	4.50	2.75
111c	Willie McCovey (Color - third printing - w/sig., stamp at bottom.)	9.00	4.50	2.75
112a	Willie McCovey (Color - first printing - no signature.)	9.00	4.50	2.75
112b	Willie McCovey (Color - second printing - w/ signature.)	9.00	4.50	2.75

1964 Meadowgold Dairy

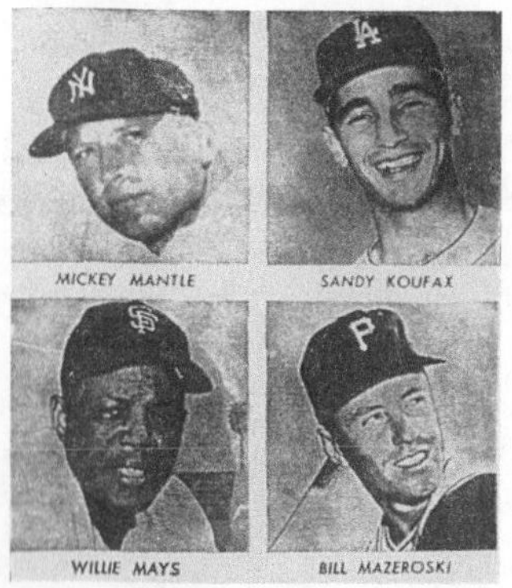

Four of the mid-60s' biggest stars appear as a panel on this milk carton issue. The four-player portion measures about 3-3/4" x 4-1/4" and is printed in shades of blue or green on the white background. Individual cards measure about 1-1/8" x 2-1/16" and are, of course, blank-backed. In 1998, a complete milk carton was sold at auction for $2,475.

		NM	E	VG
	Complete Set, Panel:	3,000	1,500	900.00
	Complete Set, Singles (4):	2,750	1,375	825.00
	Common Player:	600.00	300.00	180.00
(1)	Sandy Koufax	1,200	600.00	350.00
(2)	Mickey Mantle	1,750	875.00	525.00
(3)	Willie Mays	1,000	500.00	300.00
(4)	Bill Mazeroski	600.00	300.00	180.00

1911 Mecca Cigarettes

(See 1911 T201 Double Folders.)

1937 Joe "Ducky" Medwick

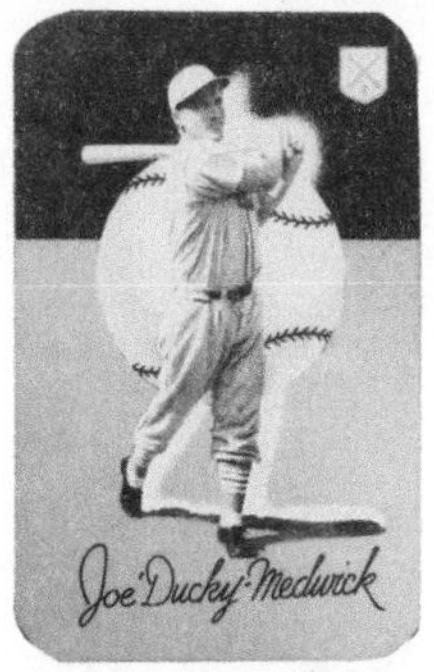

Little is known about these cards featuring the perennial All-Star of the Gashouse Gang. Both styles are in a round-cornered playing card format, about 2-1/4" x 3-1/2". Fronts have black-and-white artwork of Medwick swinging a bat against a large baseball. The background is black-and-orange with a facsimile autograph at bottom. Most cards are found with some sort of card-game baseball scenario on back, while another type has a black-and-white photo of Medwick signing autographs amid a gaggle of children. His name and the date appear at bottom. It is not known whether the two types of cards were distributed together.

	NM	E	VG
Joe "Ducky" Medwick (Game card.)	45.00	22.50	13.50
Joe "Ducky" Medwick (Photo back.)	90.00	45.00	25.00

1910 Mello-Mint (E105)

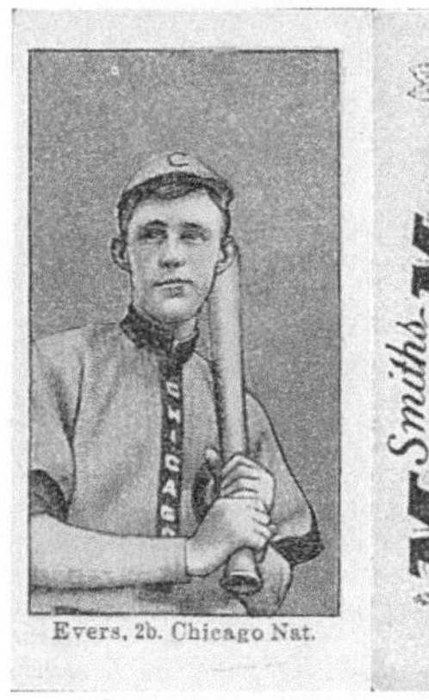

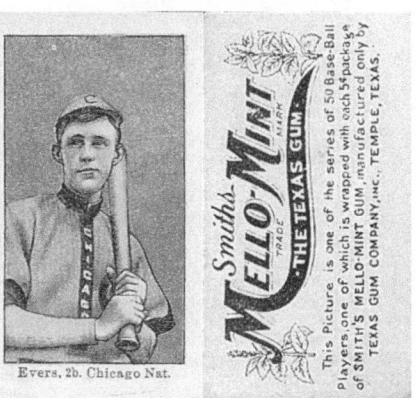

Issued circa 1910 by Smith's Mello-Mint, "The Texas Gum," this set of 50 cards shares the same checklist and artwork as the better known E101 set. Mello-Mint cards are slightly smaller, measuring approximately 1-3/8" x 2-5/8", and are printed on thin paper, making them difficult to find in top condition. Also contributing to condition problems is the fact that many cards were folded vertically to fit the packaging. The backs contain advertising, printed in green, for Mello-Mint Gum. The set carries an ACC designation of E105. Two finds of multiple examples of about eight cards in the 1980s can mislead collectors into thinking the rest of the cards in the set are more common than is actually the case. The cards most heavily over-represented in those finds are indicated with an asterisk.

		NM	E	VG
	Complete Set (50):	195,000	75,000	35,000
	Common Player:	800.00	400.00	250.00
(1)	Jack Barry	3,200	1,300	650.00
(2)	Harry Bemis	3,200	1,300	650.00
(3)	Chief Bender (White hat.)	6,400	2,600	1,300
(4)	Chief Bender (Striped hat.)	5,750	2,300	1,100
(5)	Bill Bergen	3,200	1,300	650.00
(6)	Bob Bescher (*)	800.00	400.00	250.00
(7)	Al Bridwell	3,200	1,300	650.00
(8)	Doc Casey (*)	800.00	400.00	250.00
(9)	Frank Chance	7,200	2,900	1,450
(10)	Hal Chase	4,600	1,850	925.00
(11)	Ty Cobb	25,000	12,500	7,500
(12)	Eddie Collins	7,200	2,900	1,450
(13)	Sam Crawford	7,200	2,900	1,450
(14)	Harry Davis	3,200	1,300	650.00
(15)	Art Devlin	3,200	1,300	650.00
(16)	Wild Bill Donovan	3,200	1,300	650.00
(17)	Red Dooin	3,200	1,300	650.00
(18)	Mickey Doolan	3,200	1,300	650.00
(19)	Patsy Dougherty	3,200	1,300	650.00
(20)	Larry Doyle (With bat.)	3,200	1,300	650.00
(21)	Larry Doyle (Throwing)	3,200	1,300	650.00
(22)	Johnny Evers	7,200	2,900	1,450
(23)	George Gibson	3,200	1,300	650.00
(24)	Topsy Hartsel (*)	800.00	400.00	250.00
(25)	Fred Jacklitsch	3,200	1,300	650.00
(26)	Hugh Jennings	7,200	2,900	1,450
(27)	Red Kleinow	3,200	1,300	650.00
(28)	Otto Knabe	3,200	1,300	650.00
(29)	Jack Knight (*)	800.00	400.00	250.00
(30)	Nap Lajoie (*)	5,000	2,500	1,500
(31)	Hans Lobert	3,200	1,300	650.00
(32)	Sherry Magee	3,200	1,300	650.00
(33)	Christy Matthewson (Mathewson)	21,000	10,500	6,250
(34)	John McGraw	7,200	2,900	1,450
(35)	Larry McLean	3,200	1,300	650.00
(36)	Dots Miller (Batting)	3,200	1,300	650.00
(37)	Dots Miller (Fielding)	3,200	1,300	650.00
(38)	Danny Murphy (*)	800.00	400.00	250.00
(39)	Bill O'Hara	3,200	1,300	650.00
(40)	Germany Schaefer	3,200	1,300	650.00
(41)	Admiral Schlei	3,200	1,300	650.00
(42)	Boss Schmidt	3,200	1,300	650.00
(43)	Johnny Seigle	3,200	1,300	650.00
(44)	Dave Shean (*)	800.00	400.00	250.00
(45)	Boss Smith (Schmidt)	3,200	1,300	650.00
(46)	Joe Tinker	7,200	2,900	1,450
(47)	Honus Wagner (Batting)	24,000	12,000	7,200
(48)	Honus Wagner (Throwing)	24,000	12,000	7,200
(49)	Cy Young (*)	7,500	3,700	2,200
(50)	Heinie Zimmerman	3,200	1,300	650.00

1917-1920 Felix Mendelsohn

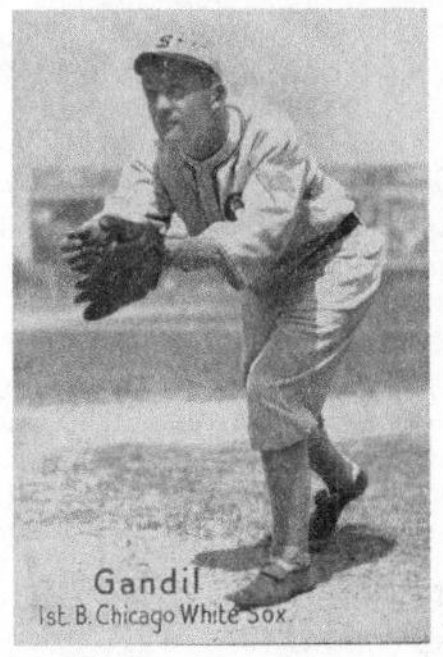

This set of glossy black-and-white player photos was produced by Chicago publisher Felix Mendelsohn, whose initials appear beneath the copyright logo on most pictures. The photos measure about 4-3/8" x 6-3/8" and feature action poses of the player whose name, position and team appear at the bottom of the borderless pictures. Four of the players in the checklist appear with two different teams, indicating the photos were issued over a period of several seasons. The set was offered in ads in The Sporting News at $5 for 100 pictures. This checklist may not be complete. Gaps have been left in the assigned numbering to accommodate future additions.

		NM	E	VG
	Complete Set (119):	56,000	28,000	17,000
	Common Player:	175.00	90.00	50.00
(1)	Grover C. Alexander (Philadelphia)	800.00	425.00	275.00
(2)	Grover C. Alexander (Chicago)	850.00	425.00	275.00
(3)	Jim Bagby Sr.	175.00	90.00	50.00
(4)	Doug Baird	175.00	90.00	50.00
(5)	Franklin Baker	425.00	220.00	125.00
(6)	Dave Bancroft	425.00	220.00	125.00
(7)	Jack Barry	175.00	90.00	50.00
(8)	Johnny Bates	175.00	90.00	50.00
(9)	Carson Bigbee	175.00	90.00	50.00
(10)	"Ping" Bodie	175.00	90.00	50.00
(11)	George Burns	175.00	90.00	50.00
(12)	Joe Bush	175.00	90.00	50.00
(13)	Owen Bush	175.00	90.00	50.00
(14)	Ray Caldwell	175.00	90.00	50.00
(15)	Max Carey	425.00	220.00	125.00
(16)	Ray Chapman	220.00	120.00	75.00
(17)	Hal Chase	350.00	175.00	100.00
(18)	Eddie Cicotte	420.00	220.00	125.00
(19)	Ty Cobb	7,500	3,750	2,250
(20)	Eddie Collins	420.00	220.00	125.00
(21)	Harry Coveleskie (Coveleskie)	175.00	90.00	50.00
(22)	"Gavvy" Cravath	175.00	90.00	50.00
(23)	Sam Crawford	420.00	220.00	125.00

(24)	Walton Cruise	175.00	90.00	50.00
(26)	George Cutshaw	175.00	90.00	50.00
(27)	Jake Daubert	175.00	90.00	50.00
(28)	George Dauss	175.00	90.00	50.00
(29)	Dave Davenport	175.00	90.00	50.00
(30)	Bill Doak	175.00	90.00	50.00
(31)	Larry Doyle	175.00	90.00	50.00
(32)	George Dumont	175.00	90.00	50.00
(33)	Howard Ehmke	175.00	90.00	50.00
(34)	Urban Faber	420.00	220.00	135.00
(35)	Happy Felsch	850.00	425.00	250.00
(36)	Art Fletcher	175.00	90.00	50.00
(37)	Del Gainer (Gainor)	175.00	90.00	50.00
(38)	Chick Gandil	420.00	220.00	135.00
(39)	Larry Gardner	175.00	90.00	50.00
(40)	Mike Gonzales (Gonzalez)	175.00	90.00	50.00
(41)	Jack Graney	175.00	90.00	50.00
(42)	Heinie Groh	175.00	90.00	50.00
(43)	Earl Hamilton	175.00	90.00	50.00
(44)	Harry Heilmann	420.00	220.00	135.00
(45)	Buck Herzog	175.00	90.00	50.00
(46)	Hugh High (New York, photo actually Bob Shawkey.)	175.00	90.00	50.00
(47)	Hugh High (Detroit, correct photo.)	175.00	90.00	50.00
(48)	Bill Hinchman	175.00	90.00	50.00
(49)	Dick Hoblitzell	175.00	90.00	50.00
(51)	Walter Holke (New York)	175.00	90.00	50.00
(52)	Walter Holke (Boston)	175.00	90.00	50.00
(53)	Harry Hooper	420.00	220.00	135.00
(54)	Rogers Hornsby	600.00	300.00	180.00
(55)	Joe Jackson	7,000	3,500	2,200
(56)	Bill Jacobson	175.00	90.00	50.00
(57)	Walter Johnson	1,300	650.00	400.00
(58)	Sam Jones	175.00	90.00	50.00
(59)	Joe Judge	175.00	90.00	50.00
(60)	Benny Kauff	175.00	90.00	50.00
(61)	Bill Killefer	175.00	90.00	50.00
(62)	Ed Konetchy (Boston)	175.00	90.00	50.00
(63)	Ed Konetchy (Brooklyn)	175.00	90.00	50.00
(64)	Nemo Leibold	175.00	90.00	50.00
(65)	Duffy Lewis	175.00	90.00	50.00
(66)	Fred Luderas (Luderus)	175.00	90.00	50.00
(67)	Fred Luderus	175.00	90.00	50.00
(68)	Al Mamaux	175.00	90.00	50.00
(69)	Les Mann	175.00	90.00	50.00
(70)	"Rabbit" Maranville	420.00	220.00	125.00
(71)	Armando Marsans	175.00	90.00	50.00
(72)	John McGraw	420.00	220.00	125.00
(73)	Stuffy McInnis	175.00	90.00	50.00
(74)	Lee Meadows	175.00	90.00	50.00
(76)	Fred Merkle	175.00	90.00	50.00
(77)	Clyde Milan	175.00	90.00	50.00
(78)	Otto Miller	175.00	90.00	50.00
(79)	Guy Morton	175.00	90.00	50.00
(80)	Hy Myers	175.00	90.00	50.00
(81)	Greasy Neale	200.00	100.00	60.00
(82)	Dode Paskert	175.00	90.00	50.00
(83)	Roger Peckinpaugh	175.00	90.00	50.00
(84)	Jeff Pfeffer	175.00	90.00	50.00
(85)	Walter Pipp	175.00	90.00	50.00
(86)	Bill Rariden	175.00	90.00	50.00
(87)	Johnny Rawlings	175.00	90.00	50.00
(88)	Sam Rice	420.00	220.00	125.00
(89)	Dave Robertson	175.00	90.00	50.00
(90)	Bob Roth	175.00	90.00	50.00
(91)	Ed Roush	420.00	220.00	125.00
(92)	Dick Rudolph	175.00	90.00	50.00
(93)	Babe Ruth (Red Sox)	22,500	11,250	6,750
(94)	Babe Ruth (New York)	7,000	3,500	2,200
(95)	Vic Saier	175.00	90.00	50.00
(96)	Ray Schalk	420.00	220.00	125.00
(97)	Hank Severeid	175.00	90.00	50.00
(98)	Ernie Shore	175.00	90.00	50.00
(99)	Burt Shotton	175.00	90.00	50.00
(101)	George Sisler	420.00	220.00	125.00
(102)	Jack Smith	175.00	90.00	50.00
(103)	Frank Snyder	175.00	90.00	50.00
(104)	Tris Speaker	600.00	300.00	180.00
(105)	Oscar Stanage	175.00	90.00	50.00
(106)	Casey Stengel	420.00	220.00	125.00
(107)	Amos Strunk	175.00	90.00	50.00
(108)	Jeff Tesreau	175.00	90.00	50.00
(109)	Fred Toney	175.00	90.00	50.00
(110)	Terry Turner	175.00	90.00	50.00
(111)	Jim Vaughn	175.00	90.00	50.00
(112)	Bobby Veach	175.00	90.00	50.00
(113)	Oscar Vitt	175.00	90.00	50.00
(114)	"Honus" Wagner	4,200	2,100	1,300
(115)	Tilly Walker	175.00	90.00	50.00
(116)	Bill Wambsganss	175.00	90.00	50.00
(117)	"Buck" Weaver	850.00	425.00	250.00
(118)	Zack Wheat	420.00	220.00	125.00
(119)	George Whitted	175.00	90.00	50.00
(120)	Cy Williams	175.00	90.00	50.00
(121)	Ivy Wingo	175.00	90.00	50.00
(122)	Ralph Young	175.00	90.00	50.00
(123)	Heinie Zimmerman	175.00	90.00	50.00

1917 Felix Mendelsohn (M101-UNC)

These 2-1/4" x 4" blank-back, black-and-white cards may have been prototypes for a "Hall of Fame" card set advertised early in 1917 by Felix Mendelsohn in The Sporting News. A set of 200 was offered for $1, but may not have actually been produced. Each example of this set is believed to be unique.

(1) Walter Johnson (VALUE UNDETERMINED)
(2) Christy Mathewson (VALUE UNDETERMINED)
(3) Ray Schalk (Brought $1,464 in 4/05 auction, in Excellent condition.)

1975 Clarence Mengler Baseball's Best

This collectors' issue art set holds the distinction of being one of the first whose distribution was halted by the Major League Baseball Players Association for lack of a license to depict current players. Produced as an autograph medium by Illinois collector Clarence Mengler, the 5" x 3" blank-back cards have portraits drawn by Keith Peterson. Of the original production of 200 sets, fewer than half were sold before the union intervened with threatened legal action. Because of a spelling error, the Ralph Garr card was withdrawn early. Hal McRae's card, also misspelled, was not withdrawn. Originally sold in five series, the unnumbered cards are checklisted alphabetically within series.

		NM	E	VG
Complete Set (125):		150.00	75.00	45.00
Common Player:		1.00	.50	.30
	SERIES A			
(1)	Sal Bando	1.00	.50	.30
(2)	Johnny Bench	4.00	2.00	1.25
(3)	Jack Billingham	1.00	.50	.30
(4)	Paul Blair	1.00	.50	.30
(5)	Bert Blyleven	1.50	.70	.45
(6)	Lou Brock	2.50	1.25	.70
(7)	Jeff Burroughs	1.00	.50	.30
(8)	Nate Colbert	1.00	.50	.30
(9)	Carlton Fisk	2.50	1.25	.70
(10)	Bob Gibson	2.50	1.25	.70
(11)	Ferguson Jenkins	2.00	1.00	.60
(12)	Bob Johnson	1.00	.50	.30
(13)	Dave McNally	1.00	.50	.30
(14)	Bobby Murcer	1.50	.70	.45
(15)	Tony Muser	1.00	.50	.30
(16)	Phil Niekro	2.00	1.00	.60
(17)	Brooks Robinson	3.00	1.50	.90
(18)	Frank Robinson	3.00	1.50	.90
(19)	Nolan Ryan	12.00	6.00	3.50
(20)	Mike Schmidt	6.00	3.00	1.75
(21)	Willie Stargell	2.50	1.25	.70
(22)	Andre Thornton	1.00	.50	.30
(23)	Bobby Tolan	1.00	.50	.30
(24)	Jim Wynn	1.00	.50	.30
(25)	Richie Zisk	1.00	.50	.30
	SERIES B			
(26)	Hank Aaron	9.00	4.50	2.75
(27)	Larry Bowa	1.00	.50	.30
(28)	Steve Carlton	2.50	1.25	.70
(29)	Cesar Cedeno	1.00	.50	.30
(30)	Jim Colborn	1.00	.50	.30
(31)	Tim Foli	1.00	.50	.30
(32)	Steve Garvey	1.50	.70	.45
(33)	Bud Harrelson	1.00	.50	.30
(34)	Willie Horton	1.00	.50	.30
(35)	Jim Hunter	2.00	1.00	.60
(36)	Reggie Jackson	6.00	3.00	1.75
(37)	Billy Martin	1.50	.70	.45
(38)	Bake McBride	1.00	.50	.30
(39)	Andy Messersmith	1.00	.50	.30
(40)	Rick Monday	1.00	.50	.30
(41)	Joe Morgan	2.50	1.25	.70
(42)	Tony Oliva	1.50	.70	.45
(43)	Amos Otis	1.00	.50	.30
(44)	Gaylord Perry	2.00	1.00	.60
(45)	Tom Seaver	5.00	2.50	1.50
(46)	Ken Singleton	1.00	.50	.30
(47)	Chris Speier	1.00	.50	.30
(48)	Gene Tenace	1.00	.50	.30
(49)	Del Unser	1.00	.50	.30
(50)	Carl Yastrzemski	5.00	2.50	1.50
	SERIES C			
(51)	Steve Busby	1.00	.50	.30
(52)	Jose Cardenal	1.00	.50	.30
(53)	Rod Carew	2.50	1.25	.70
(54)	Ron Cey	1.00	.50	.30
(55)	Willie Davis	1.00	.50	.30
(56)	Barry Foote	1.00	.50	.30
(57)	Ken Holtzman	1.00	.50	.30
(58)	Davey Lopes	1.00	.50	.30
(59)	Greg Luzinski	1.00	.50	.30
(60)	Sparky Lyle	1.00	.50	.30
(61)	Dave May	1.00	.50	.30
(62)	Lee May	1.00	.50	.30
(63)	Doc Medich	1.00	.50	.30
(64)	Bill Melton	1.00	.50	.30
(65)	Randy Moffitt	1.00	.50	.30
(66)	Don Money	1.00	.50	.30
(67)	Al Oliver	1.50	.70	.45
(68)	George Scott	1.00	.50	.30
(69)	Ted Simmons	1.00	.50	.30
(70)	Charlie Spikes	1.00	.50	.30
(71)	Rusty Staub	1.25	.60	.40
(72)	Jim Sundberg	1.00	.50	.30
(73)	Bob Watson	1.00	.50	.30
(74)	Dick Williams	1.00	.50	.30
(75)	Dave Winfield	2.50	1.25	.70
	SERIES D			
(76)	Vida Blue	1.00	.50	.30
(77)	Bobby Bonds	1.00	.50	.30
(78)	Jerry Coleman	1.00	.50	.30
(79)	Bob Coluccio	1.00	.50	.30
(80)	Joe Decker	1.00	.50	.30
(81)	Darrell Evans	1.00	.50	.30
(82)	Ralph Gaar (Garr)(SP)	4.00	2.00	1.25
(83)	Richie Hebner	1.00	.50	.30
(84)	Ken Henderson	1.00	.50	.30
(85)	Bill Madlock	1.00	.50	.30
(86)	Jon Matlack	1.00	.50	.30
(87)	Carlos May	1.00	.50	.30
(88)	John Mayberry	1.00	.50	.30
(89)	Willie McCovey	2.50	1.25	.70
(90)	Lynn McGlothen	1.00	.50	.30
(91)	Tug McGraw	1.00	.50	.30
(92)	Roger Metzger	1.00	.50	.30
(93)	Jim Palmer	2.00	1.00	.60
(94)	Rico Petrocelli	1.00	.50	.30
(95)	Ellie Rodriguez	1.00	.50	.30
(96)	Steve Rogers	1.00	.50	.30
(97)	Pete Rose	9.00	4.50	2.75
(98)	Bill Singer	1.00	.50	.30
(99)	Don Sutton	2.00	1.00	.60
(100)	Billy Williams	2.50	1.25	.70
	SERIES E			
(101)	Mark Belanger	1.00	.50	.30
(102)	Buddy Bell	1.00	.50	.30
(103)	Jim Bibby	1.00	.50	.30
(104)	Bob Boone	1.00	.50	.30
(105)	Ken Brett	1.00	.50	.30
(106)	Ron Bryant	1.00	.50	.30
(107)	Bill Buckner	1.00	.50	.30
(108)	Buzz Capra	1.00	.50	.30
(109)	Dave Concepcion	1.00	.50	.30
(110)	Rollie Fingers	2.00	1.00	.60
(111)	Bill Freehan	1.00	.50	.30
(112)	Bobby Grich	1.00	.50	.30
(113)	Fred Kendall	1.00	.50	.30
(114)	Don Kessinger	1.00	.50	.30
(115)	Hal McCrae (McRae)	1.00	.50	.30
(116)	Thurman Munson	2.50	1.25	.70
(117)	Fred Patek	1.00	.50	.30
(118)	Doug Rader	1.00	.50	.30
(119)	A. (Aurelio) Rodriguez	1.00	.50	.30
(120)	Manny Sanguillen	1.00	.50	.30
(121)	Reggie Smith	1.00	.50	.30
(122)	Danny Thompson	1.00	.50	.30
(123)	Luis Tiant	1.00	.50	.30
(124)	Joe Torre	1.50	.70	.45
(125)	Wilbur Wood	1.00	.50	.30

1953-54 Marshall Merrell Milwaukee Braves Portfolio

One of several portfolios of Milwaukee Braves artwork produced during the team's first few years, this issue of 8" x 10" black-and-white lithographs was sold at County Stadium for 25 cents apiece. The player checklist here is believed to be complete, but it is possible other poses may yet be reported. The cards are blank-backed and unnumbered; the checklist here has been arranged alphabetically.

		NM	E	VG
Complete Set (25):		900.00	450.00	275.00
Common Player:		25.00	12.50	7.50
(1)	Henry Aaron	200.00	100.00	60.00
(2)	Joe Adcock	25.00	12.50	7.50
(3)	Johnny Antonelli	25.00	12.50	7.50
(4)	Billy Bruton	25.00	12.50	7.50
(5)	Bob Buhl	25.00	12.50	7.50
(6)	Lou Burdette (Follow-through.)	25.00	12.50	7.50
(7)	Lew Burdette (Wind-up.)	25.00	12.50	7.50
(8)	Gene Conley	25.00	12.50	7.50
(9)	Del Crandall	25.00	12.50	7.50
(10)	Jack Dittmer	25.00	12.50	7.50
(11)	Sid Gordon (Batting)	25.00	12.50	7.50
(12)	Sid Gordon (Standing)	25.00	12.50	7.50
(13)	Charlie Grimm (Tomahawk on jersey.)	25.00	12.50	7.50
(14)	Charlie Grimm (No tomahawk.)	25.00	12.50	7.50
(15)	Don Liddle	25.00	12.50	7.50
(16)	Johnny Logan	25.00	12.50	7.50
(17)	Ed Mathews (Batting)	75.00	37.50	22.50
(18)	Ed Mathews (Standing)	75.00	37.50	22.50
(19)	Danny O'Connell	25.00	12.50	7.50
(20)	Andy Pafko	25.00	12.50	7.50
(21)	Jim Pendleton	25.00	12.50	7.50
(22)	Warren Spahn	75.00	37.50	22.50
(23)	Max Surkont	25.00	12.50	7.50
(24)	Bobby Thomson	45.00	22.50	13.50
(25)	Jim Wilson	25.00	12.50	7.50

1979 Metallic Creations Signature Miniatures

This collectors' issue was created by combining an approximately 3-1/2" tall pewter statue with a 3-5/8" x 5" baseball card. The statues were released in pewter at about $10 apiece and silver-plate at $20. The black-bordered cards feature color portraits in front of a pair of sepia action pictures. The artwork was by J. Payette. Fronts also feature a facsimile autograph. Backs have basic player personal data and career stats. It was reported that 5,000 of each card were printed, though most were never issued due to failure of the venture. The remaining cards and statues were sold into the hobby as remainders. It is unclear whether a Munson card exists, although the Munson statue and the Rose and Ryan cards have been confirmed.

		NM	E	VG
Complete Set, Cards (20):		240.00	120.00	70.00
Common Card:		7.50	3.75	2.25
Complete Set, Pewter Statues (20):		200.00	100.00	60.00
Common Statue:		7.50	3.75	2.25
Silver-plate Statues: 2X				
(1)	Hank Aaron (Card)	12.50	6.25	3.75
(1)	Hank Aaron (Statue)	12.50	6.25	3.75
(2)	Rod Carew (Card)	7.50	3.75	2.25
(2)	Rod Carew (Statue)	7.50	3.75	2.25
(3)	Cesar Cedeno (Card)	7.50	3.75	2.25
(4)	Ty Cobb (Card)	15.00	7.50	4.50
(4)	Ty Cobb (Statue)	12.50	6.25	3.75
(5)	Steve Garvey (Card)	15.00	7.50	4.50
(5)	Steve Garvey (Statue)	15.00	7.50	4.50
(6)	Lou Gehrig (Card)	15.00	7.50	4.50
(6)	Lou Gehrig (Statue)	15.00	7.50	4.50
(7)	Ron Guidry (Card)	7.50	3.75	2.25
(7)	Ron Guidry (Statue)	7.50	3.75	2.25
(8)	Rogers Hornsby (Card)	7.50	3.75	2.25
(8)	Rogers Hornsby (Statue)	7.50	3.75	2.25
(9)	Walter Johnson (Card)	10.00	5.00	3.00
(9)	Walter Johnson (Statue)	10.00	5.00	3.00
(10)	Ralph Kiner (Card)	7.50	3.75	2.25
(10)	Ralph Kiner (Statue)	7.50	3.75	2.25
(11)	Sandy Koufax (Card)	20.00	10.00	6.00
(11)	Sandy Koufax (Statue)	20.00	10.00	6.00
(12)	Davey Lopes (Card)	7.50	3.75	2.25
(12)	Davey Lopes (Statue)	7.50	3.75	2.25
(13)	Christy Mathewson (Card)	10.00	5.00	3.00
(13)	Christy Mathewson (Statue)	10.00	5.00	3.00
(14)	Willie Mays (Card)	15.00	7.50	4.50
(14)	Willie Mays (Statue)	15.00	7.50	4.50
(15)	Willie McCovey (Card)	10.00	5.00	3.00
(15)	Willie McCovey (Statue)	10.00	5.00	3.00
(16)	Thurman Munson (Statue)	10.00	5.00	3.00
(17)	Mel Ott (Card)	7.50	3.75	2.25
(17)	Mel Ott (Statue)	7.50	3.75	2.25
(18)	Pete Rose (Card)	30.00	15.00	9.00
(19)	Babe Ruth (Card)	12.50	6.25	3.75
(19)	Babe Ruth (Statue)	12.50	6.25	3.75
(20)	Nolan Ryan (Card)	30.00	15.00	9.00
(21)	Tris Speaker (Card)	7.50	3.75	2.25
(21)	Tris Speaker (Statue)	7.50	3.75	2.25
(22)	Honus Wagner (Card)	10.00	5.00	3.00
(22)	Honus Wagner (Statue)	10.00	5.00	3.00

1938-39 Metropolitan Clothing Cincinnati Reds Postcards

(See 1937-39 Orcajo Cincinnati Reds postcards for checklist, values.)

-1968 Metropolitan Museum of Art Burdick Collection

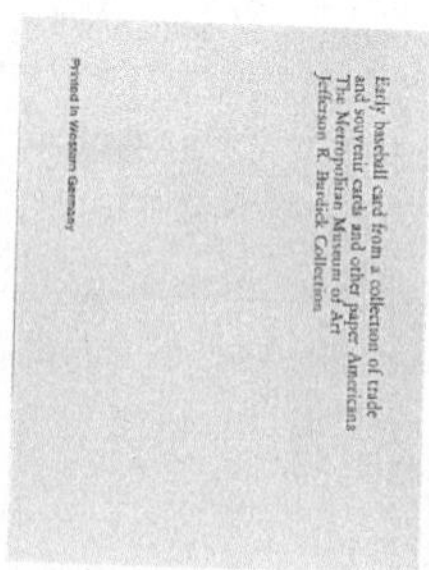

The date of issue is approximate for this set promoting New York's Metropolitan Museum of Art as the repository for the Jefferson Burdick collection, once the world's premier accumulation of trading cards. Burdick, author of the once-standard "American Card Catalog" donated his collection to the Met. The 2-3/4" x 3-5/8" black-and-white glossy card fronts reproduce 1928 R315 cards of major leaguers and earlier Zeenuts cards of minor leaguers. Backs have a few words about the museum and a "Printed in Western Germany" line. The unnumbered cards are checklisted here in alphabetical order.

		NM	E	VG
Complete Set (8):		125.00	65.00	35.00
Common Player:		10.00	5.00	3.00
(1)	Max Bishop	10.00	5.00	3.00
(2)	Lou Gehrig	40.00	20.00	12.00
(3)	Carl Hubbell	15.00	7.50	4.50
(4)	Art Kores	10.00	5.00	3.00
(5)	Bill Leard	10.00	5.00	3.00
(6)	Babe Ruth	50.00	25.00	15.00
(7)	Dazzy Vance	10.00	5.00	3.00
(8)	Elmer Zacher	10.00	5.00	3.00

1931 Metropolitan Studio St. Louis Cardinals

Members of the St. Louis Cardinals are featu[...] 30-card set. The cards were printed on heavy pa[...] ture sepia-toned photos. The player's name ap[...] the bottom white border below the photo. The c[...] 6-1/4" x 9-1/2" and are not numbered. Most ca[...] logo of Metropolitan Studio in a bottom corn[...] have "Sid Whiting St. Louis MO," and a few[...] sor's credit.

		NM
Complete Set (30):		1,80[illegible]
Common Player:		45.[illegible]
(1)	Earl "Sparky" Adams	45[illegible]
(2)	Ray Blades	4[illegible]
(3)	James Bottomley	[illegible]
(4)	Sam Breadon	
(5)	James "Rip" Collins	
(6)	Dizzy Dean	
(7)	Paul Derringer	
(8)	Jake Flowers	
(9)	Frank Frisch	
(10)	Charles Gelbert	
(11)	Miguel Gonzales (Gonzalez)	
(12)	Burleigh Grimes	
(13)	Charles "Chick" Hafe[illegible]	
(14)	William Hallahan	
(15)	Jesse Haines	
(16)	Andrew High	
(17)	Sylvester Johnso[illegible]	
(18)	Tony Kaufmann	
(19)	James Lindsey	
(20)	Gus Mancuso	
(21)	John Leonard Martin	
(22)	Ernest Orsa[illegible]	
(23)	Charles Fli[illegible]	
(24)	Branch Ri[illegible]	
(25)	Walter R[illegible]	
(26)	Allyn St[illegible]	
(27)	"Gabby" [illegible]	
(28)	Clyde [illegible]	
(29)	Geor[illegible]	
(30)	Jam[illegible]	

		NM	E	VG
(15)	Firpo Marberry	3.00	1.50	.90
(16)	Marvin Owen	3.00	1.50	.90
(17)	Cy Perkins	3.00	1.50	.90
(18)	Bill Rogell	3.00	1.50	.90
(19)	Schoolboy Rowe	3.00	1.50	.90
(20)	Heinie Schuble	3.00	1.50	.90
(21)	Vic Sorrell	3.00	1.50	.90
(22)	Gee Walker	3.00	1.50	.90
(23)	Jo Jo White	3.00	1.50	.90

1980 Midwest Sports Collectors Convention

Reprints of a number of the player postcards of J.D. Mc-Carthy were produced in conjunction with the 1980 Detroit show. The blank-backed, black-and-white postcards are 3-1/4" x 5-1/2" and all feature former Detroit Tigers. The unnumbered cards are checklisted here alphabetically.

		NM	E	VG
Complete Set (11):		7.50	3.75	2.25
Common Player:		1.00	.50	.30
(1)	Bob Anderson	1.00	.50	.30
(2)	Babe Birrer	1.00	.50	.30
(3)	Frank Bolling	1.00	.50	.30
(4)	Jim Bunning	2.00	1.00	.60
(5)	Al Cicotte	1.00	.50	.30
(6)	Paul Foytack	1.00	.50	.30
(7)	Joe Ginsberg	1.00	.50	.30
(8)	Steve Gromek	1.00	.50	.30
(9)	Art Houtteman	1.00	.50	.30
(10)	Al Kaline	5.00	2.50	1.50
(11)	Harvey Kuenn	2.00	1.00	.60

1971 Milk Duds

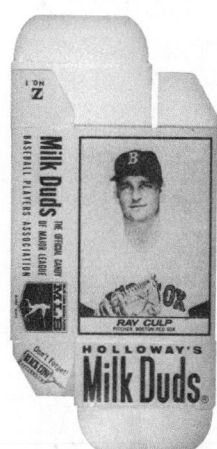

These cards were issued on the backs of five-cent packages of Milk Duds candy. Most collectors prefer complete boxes, rather than cut-out cards, which measure approximately 1-13/16" x 2-5/8" when trimmed tightly. Values quoted below are for complete boxes. Cut cards will bring 50-75 percent of the quoted values. The set includes 37 National League and 32 American League players. Card numbers appear on the box flap, with each number from 1 through 24 being shared by three different players. A suffix (a, b and c) has been added for the collector's convenience. Harmon Killebrew, Brooks Robinson and Pete Rose were double-printed.

		NM	E	VG
Complete Set, Boxes:		1,500	750.00	450.00
Complete Set, Singles (72):		900.00	450.00	275.00
Common Player:		18.00	8.00	5.00
1a	Frank Howard	18.00	8.00	5.00

		NM	E	VG
1b	Fritz Peterson	20.00	10.00	6.00
1c	Pete Rose	100.00	50.00	30.00
2a	Johnny Bench	25.00	12.00	8.00
2b	Rico Carty	18.00	8.00	5.00
2c	Pete Rose	100.00	50.00	30.00
3a	Ken Holtzman	18.00	8.00	5.00
3b	Willie Mays	100.00	50.00	30.00
3c	Cesar Tovar	18.00	8.00	5.00
4a	Willie Davis	18.00	8.00	5.00
4b	Harmon Killebrew	25.00	12.00	8.00
4c	Felix Millan	18.00	8.00	5.00
5a	Billy Grabarkewitz	18.00	8.00	5.00
5b	Andy Messersmith	18.00	8.00	5.00
5c	Thurman Munson	80.00	40.00	25.00
6a	Luis Aparicio	25.00	12.00	8.00
6b	Lou Brock	20.00	10.00	6.00
6c	Bill Melton	18.00	8.00	5.00
7a	Ray Culp	18.00	8.00	5.00
7b	Willie McCovey	35.00	18.00	10.00
7c	Luke Walker	18.00	8.00	5.00
8a	Roberto Clemente	200.00	100.00	60.00
8b	Jim Merritt	18.00	8.00	5.00
8c	Claud Osteen (Claude)	18.00	8.00	5.00
9a	Stan Bahnsen	18.00	8.00	5.00
9b	Sam McDowell	18.00	8.00	5.00
9c	Billy Williams	25.00	15.00	8.00
10a	Jim Hickman	18.00	8.00	5.00
10b	Dave McNally	18.00	8.00	5.00
10c	Tony Perez	35.00	20.00	12.00
11a	Hank Aaron	70.00	35.00	20.00
11b	Glen Beckert (Glenn)	18.00	8.00	5.00
11c	Ray Fosse	18.00	8.00	5.00
12a	Alex Johnson	18.00	8.00	5.00
12b	Gaylord Perry	20.00	10.00	6.00
12c	Wayne Simpson	18.00	8.00	5.00
13a	Dave Johnson	18.00	8.00	5.00
13b	George Scott	18.00	8.00	5.00
13c	Tom Seaver	40.00	20.00	12.00
14a	Bill Freehan	18.00	8.00	5.00
14b	Bud Harrelson	18.00	8.00	5.00
14c	Manny Sanguillen	18.00	8.00	5.00
15a	Bob Gibson	25.00	12.00	8.00
15b	Rusty Staub	20.00	10.00	6.00
15c	Roy White	18.00	8.00	5.00
16a	Jim Fregosi	18.00	8.00	5.00
16b	Catfish Hunter	25.00	12.00	8.00
16c	Mel Stottlemyer (Stottlemyre)	18.00	8.00	5.00
17a	Tommy Harper	18.00	8.00	5.00
17b	Frank Robinson	35.00	20.00	12.00
17c	Reggie Smith	18.00	8.00	5.00
18a	Orlando Cepeda	35.00	20.00	12.00
18b	Rico Petrocelli	18.00	8.00	5.00
18c	Brooks Robinson	35.00	20.00	12.00
19a	Tony Oliva	20.00	10.00	6.00
19b	Milt Pappas	18.00	8.00	5.00
19c	Bobby Tolan	18.00	8.00	5.00
20a	Ernie Banks	55.00	25.00	15.00
20b	Don Kessinger	18.00	8.00	5.00
20c	Joe Torre	20.00	10.00	8.00
21a	Fergie Jenkins	25.00	12.00	8.00
21b	Jim Palmer	25.00	12.00	8.00
21c	Ron Santo	20.00	10.00	6.00
22a	Randy Hundley	18.00	8.00	5.00
22b	Dennis Menke (Denis)	18.00	8.00	5.00
22c	Boog Powell	20.00	10.00	6.00
23a	Dick Dietz	18.00	8.00	5.00
23b	Tommy John	18.00	8.00	5.00
23c	Brooks Robinson	20.00	10.00	6.00
24a	Danny Cater	18.00	8.00	6.00
24b	Harmon Killebrew	25.00	15.00	10.00
24c	Jim Perry	20.00	10.00	6.00

1933 George C. Miller (R300)

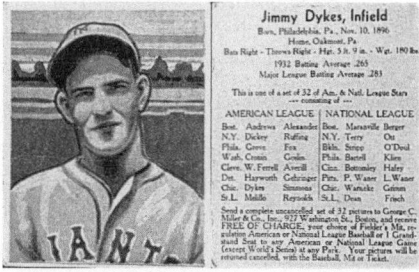

George C. Miller & Co. of Boston, Mass., issued a 32-card set in one-cent packs of toffee in 1933. The set, which received limited distribution, consists of 16 National League and 16 American League players. The cards are color art reproductions of actual photographs and measure 2-3/8" x 2-7/8". Two distinct variations can be found for each card in the set. Type 1 cards have the names "Fox" and "Klien" misspelled on the back, while Type 2 cards have them correctly

as "Foxx" and "Klein." Collectors were advised on the card backs to collect all 32 cards and return them for prizes. (Ivy Andrews' card was short-printed to avoid giving out too many prizes.) The cancelled cards were returned to the collector with the prize. Two forms of cancellation were used; one involved the complete trimming of the bottom one-quarter of the card, the other a diamond-shaped series of punch holes. Cancelled cards have a significantly decreased value.

		NM	E	VG
Complete Set (32):		125,000	62,500	37,500
Common Player:		2,000	1,000	600.00
(1)	Dale Alexander	2,000	1,000	600.00
(2)	"Ivy" Paul Andrews	9,000	4,500	2,700
	Cut-cancelled: 975.00			
	Punch-cancelled: 2,400			
(3)	Earl Averill	4,000	2,000	1,200
(4)	Dick Bartell	2,000	1,000	600.00
(5)	Walter Berger	2,000	1,000	600.00
(6)	Jim Bottomley	4,000	2,000	1,200
(7)	Joe Cronin	4,000	2,000	1,200
(8)	Jerome "Dizzy" Dean	4,750	2,400	1,400
(9)	William Dickey	2,500	1,125	625.00
(10)	Jimmy Dykes	2,000	1,000	600.00
(11)	Wesley Ferrell	2,000	1,000	600.00
(12)	Jimmy Foxx	6,000	3,000	1,800
(13)	Frank Frisch	4,000	2,000	1,200
(14)	Charlie Gehringer	4,000	2,000	1,200
(15)	Leon "Goose" Goslin	4,000	2,000	1,200
(16)	Charlie Grimm	2,000	1,000	600.00
(17)	Bob "Lefty" Grove	4,750	2,400	1,400
(18)	Charles "Chick" Hafey	4,000	2,000	1,200
(19)	Ray Hayworth	2,000	1,000	600.00
(20)	Charles "Chuck" Klein	4,000	2,000	1,200
(21)	Walter "Rabbit" Maranville	4,000	2,000	1,200
(22)	Oscar Melillo	2,000	1,000	600.00
(23)	Frank "Lefty" O'Doul	3,200	1,600	975.00
(24)	Melvin Ott	5,000	2,500	1,500
(25)	Carl Reynolds	2,000	1,000	600.00
(26)	Charles Ruffing	4,000	2,000	1,200
(27)	Al Simmons	4,000	2,000	1,200
(28)	Joe Stripp	2,000	1,000	600.00
(29)	Bill Terry	4,000	2,000	1,200
(30)	Lloyd Waner	4,000	2,000	1,200
(31)	Paul Waner	4,000	2,000	1,200
(32)	Lonnie Warneke	2,000	1,000	600.00

1969 Milton Bradley

The first of three sets issued by Milton Bradley over a four-year period, these cards were part of a baseball board game. The unnumbered cards measure 2" x 3" and have a white border surrounding the black-and-white player photo. The player's name appears above the photo in upper case letters. There are no team designations and the photos are airbrushed to eliminate team logos. Backs display biographical data along the top followed by a list of various game situations used in playing the board game. The cards have square corners. The 1969 and 1972 game cards are virtually identical in format. They can be differentiated by looking at the back at any numeral "1" in a line of red type. If the "1" does not have a base, it is a 1969 card; if there is a base, the card is a 1972. Besides individual player cards, there was a non-photographic team cards for each of the contemporary 24 Major League teams.

		NM	E	VG
Complete Boxed Set:		400.00	200.00	120.00
Complete Set (296):		150.00	75.00	45.00
Common Player:		.50	.25	.15
Team Card:		2.00	1.00	.60
(1)	Hank Aaron	30.00	15.00	9.00
(2)	Ted Abernathy	.50	.25	.15
(3)	Jerry Adair	.50	.25	.15
(4)	Tommy Agee	.50	.25	.15
(5)	Bernie Allen	.50	.25	.15
(6)	Hank Allen	.50	.25	.15
(7)	Richie Allen	5.00	2.50	1.50
(8)	Gene Alley	.50	.25	.15

(9)	Bob Allison	.50	.25	.15
(10)	Felipe Alou	1.00	.50	.30
(11)	Jesus Alou	.50	.25	.15
(12)	Matty Alou	.50	.25	.15
(13)	Max Alvis	.50	.25	.15
(14)	Mike Andrews	.50	.25	.15
(15)	Luis Aparicio	10.00	5.00	3.00
(16)	Jose Arcia	.50	.25	.15
(17)	Bob Aspromonte	.50	.25	.15
(18)	Joe Azcue	.50	.25	.15
(19)	Ernie Banks	20.00	10.00	6.00
(20)	Steve Barber	.50	.25	.15
(21)	John Bateman	.50	.25	.15
(22)	Glen Beckert (Glenn)	.50	.25	.15
(23)	Gary Bell	.50	.25	.15
(24)	John Bench	15.00	7.50	4.50
(25)	Ken Berry	.50	.25	.15
(26)	Frank Bertaina	.50	.25	.15
(27)	Paul Blair	.50	.25	.15
(28)	Wade Blasingame	.50	.25	.15
(29)	Curt Blefary	.50	.25	.15
(30)	John Boccabella	.50	.25	.15
(31)	Bobby Lee Bonds	1.00	.50	.30
(32)	Sam Bowens	.50	.25	.15
(33)	Ken Boyer	1.00	.50	.30
(34)	Charles Bradford	.50	.25	.15
(35)	Darrell Brandon	.50	.25	.15
(36)	Jim Brewer	.50	.25	.15
(37)	John Briggs	.50	.25	.15
(38)	Nelson Briles	.50	.25	.15
(39)	Ed Brinkman	.50	.25	.15
(40)	Lou Brock	10.00	5.00	3.00
(41)	Gates Brown	.50	.25	.15
(42)	Larry Brown	.50	.25	.15
(43)	George Brunet	.50	.25	.15
(44)	Jerry Buchek	.50	.25	.15
(45)	Don Buford	.50	.25	.15
(46)	Jim Bunning	7.50	3.75	2.25
(47)	Johnny Callison	.50	.25	.15
(48)	Campy Campaneris	.50	.25	.15
(49)	Jose Cardenal	.50	.25	.15
(50)	Leo Cardenas	.50	.25	.15
(51)	Don Cardwell	.50	.25	.15
(52)	Rod Carew	12.50	6.25	3.75
(53)	Paul Casanova	.50	.25	.15
(54)	Norm Cash	1.50	.70	.45
(55)	Danny Cater	.50	.25	.15
(56)	Orlando Cepeda	10.00	5.00	3.00
(57)	Dean Chance	.50	.25	.15
(58)	Ed Charles	.50	.25	.15
(59)	Horace Clarke	.50	.25	.15
(60)	Roberto Clemente	45.00	22.00	13.50
(61)	Donn Clendenon	.50	.25	.15
(62)	Ty Cline	.50	.25	.15
(63)	Nate Colbert	.50	.25	.15
(64)	Joe Coleman	.50	.25	.15
(65)	Bob Cox	.50	.25	.15
(66)	Mike Cuellar	.50	.25	.15
(67)	Ray Culp	.50	.25	.15
(68)	Clay Dalrymple	.50	.25	.15
(69)	Vic Davalillo	.50	.25	.15
(70)	Jim Davenport	.50	.25	.15
(71)	Ron Davis	.50	.25	.15
(72)	Tommy Davis	.50	.25	.15
(73)	Willie Davis	.50	.25	.15
(74)	Chuck Dobson	.50	.25	.15
(75)	John Donaldson	.50	.25	.15
(76)	Al Downing	.50	.25	.15
(77)	Moe Drabowsky	.50	.25	.15
(78)	Dick Ellsworth	.50	.25	.15
(79)	Mike Epstein	.50	.25	.15
(80)	Andy Etchebarren	.50	.25	.15
(81)	Ron Fairly	.50	.25	.15
(82)	Dick Farrell	.50	.25	.15
(83)	Curt Flood	1.00	.50	.30
(84)	Joe Foy	.50	.25	.15
(85)	Tito Francona	.50	.25	.15
(86)	Bill Freehan	.75	.40	.25
(87)	Jim Fregosi	.50	.25	.15
(88)	Woodie Fryman	.50	.25	.15
(89)	Len Gabrielson	.50	.25	.15
(90)	Cito Gaston	.50	.25	.15
(91)	Jake Gibbs	.50	.25	.15
(92)	Russ Gibson	.50	.25	.15
(93)	Dave Giusti	.50	.25	.15
(94)	Tony Gonzalez	.50	.25	.15
(95)	Jim Gosger	.50	.25	.15
(96)	Julio Gotay	.50	.25	.15
(97)	Dick Green	.50	.25	.15
(98)	Jerry Grote	.50	.25	.15
(99)	Jimmie Hall	.50	.25	.15
(100)	Tom Haller	.50	.25	.15
(101)	Steve Hamilton	.50	.25	.15
(102)	Ron Hansen	.50	.25	.15
(103)	Jim Hardin	.50	.25	.15
(104)	Tommy Harper	.50	.25	.15
(105)	Bud Harrelson	.50	.25	.15
(106)	Ken Harrelson	.50	.25	.15
(107)	Jim Hart	.50	.25	.15
(108)	Woodie Held	.50	.25	.15
(109)	Tommy Helms	.50	.25	.15
(110)	Elrod Hendricks	.50	.25	.15
(111)	Mike Hershberger	.50	.25	.15
(112)	Jack Hiatt	.50	.25	.15
(113)	Jim Hickman	.50	.25	.15
(114)	John Hiller	.50	.25	.15
(115)	Chuck Hinton	.50	.25	.15
(116)	Ken Holtzman	.50	.25	.15
(117)	Joel Horlen	.50	.25	.15
(118)	Tony Horton	.50	.25	.15
(119)	Willie Horton	.50	.25	.15
(120)	Frank Howard	1.00	.50	.30
(121)	Dick Howser	.50	.25	.15
(122)	Randy Hundley	.50	.25	.15
(123)	Ron Hunt	.50	.25	.15
(124)	Catfish Hunter	7.50	3.75	2.25
(125)	Al Jackson	.50	.25	.15
(126)	Larry Jackson	.50	.25	.15
(127)	Reggie Jackson	30.00	15.00	9.00
(128)	Sonny Jackson	.50	.25	.15
(129)	Pat Jarvis	.50	.25	.15
(130)	Julian Javier	.50	.25	.15
(131)	Ferguson Jenkins	7.50	3.75	2.25
(132)	Manny Jimenez	.50	.25	.15
(133)	Tommy John	1.00	.50	.30
(134)	Bob Johnson	.50	.25	.15
(135)	Dave Johnson	.50	.25	.15
(136)	Deron Johnson	.50	.25	.15
(137)	Lou Johnson	.50	.25	.15
(138)	Jay Johnstone	.50	.25	.15
(139)	Cleon Jones	.50	.25	.15
(140)	Dalton Jones	.50	.25	.15
(141)	Duane Josephson	.50	.25	.15
(142)	Jim Kaat	1.50	.70	.45
(143)	Al Kaline	15.00	7.50	4.50
(144)	Don Kessinger	.50	.25	.15
(145)	Harmon Killebrew	12.50	6.25	3.75
(146)	Harold King	.50	.25	.15
(147)	Ed Kirkpatrick	.50	.25	.15
(148)	Fred Klages	.50	.25	.15
(149)	Ron Kline	.50	.25	.15
(150)	Bobby Knoop	.50	.25	.15
(151)	Gary Kolb	.50	.25	.15
(152)	Andy Kosco	.50	.25	.15
(153)	Ed Kranepool	.50	.25	.15
(154)	Lew Krausse	.50	.25	.15
(155)	Harold Lanier	.50	.25	.15
(156)	Jim Lefebvre	.50	.25	.15
(157)	Denny Lemaster	.50	.25	.15
(158)	Dave Leonhard	.50	.25	.15
(159)	Don Lock	.50	.25	.15
(160)	Mickey Lolich	1.50	.70	.45
(161)	Jim Lonborg	.75	.40	.25
(162)	Mike Lum	.50	.25	.15
(163)	Al Lyle	.50	.25	.15
(164)	Jim Maloney	.50	.25	.15
(165)	Juan Marichal	8.00	4.00	2.50
(166)	J.C. Martin	.50	.25	.15
(167)	Marty Martinez	.50	.25	.15
(168)	Tom Matchick	.50	.25	.15
(169)	Ed Mathews	12.50	6.25	3.75
(170)	Dal Maxvill	.50	.25	.15
(171)	Jerry May	.50	.25	.15
(172)	Lee May	.50	.25	.15
(173)	Lee Maye	.50	.25	.15
(174)	Willie Mays	30.00	15.00	9.00
(175)	Bill Mazeroski	12.50	6.25	3.75
(176)	Richard McAuliffe	.50	.25	.15
(177)	Al McBean	.50	.25	.15
(178)	Tim McCarver	.75	.40	.25
(179)	Bill McCool	.50	.25	.15
(180)	Mike McCormick	.50	.25	.15
(181)	Willie McCovey	12.50	6.25	3.75
(182)	Tom McCraw	.50	.25	.15
(183)	Lindy McDaniel	.50	.25	.15
(184)	Sam McDowell	.75	.40	.25
(185)	Orlando McFarlane	.50	.25	.15
(186)	Jim McGlothlin	.50	.25	.15
(187)	Denny McLain	1.25	.60	.40
(188)	Ken McMullen	.50	.25	.15
(189)	Dave McNally	.50	.25	.15
(190)	Gerry McNertney	.50	.25	.15
(191)	Dennis Menke (Denis)	.50	.25	.15
(192)	Felix Millan	.50	.25	.15
(193)	Don Mincher	.50	.25	.15
(194)	Rick Monday	.50	.25	.15
(195)	Joe Morgan	10.00	5.00	3.00
(196)	Bubba Morton	.50	.25	.15
(197)	Manny Mota	.50	.25	.15
(198)	Jim Nash	.50	.25	.15
(199)	Dave Nelson	.50	.25	.15
(200)	Dick Nen	.50	.25	.15
(201)	Phil Niekro	7.50	3.75	2.25
(202)	Jim Northrup	.50	.25	.15
(203)	Richard Nye	.50	.25	.15
(204)	Johnny Odom	.50	.25	.15
(205)	Tony Oliva	1.00	.50	.30
(206)	Gene Oliver	.50	.25	.15
(207)	Phil Ortega	.50	.25	.15
(208)	Claude Osteen	.50	.25	.15
(209)	Ray Oyler	.50	.25	.15
(210)	Jose Pagan	.50	.25	.15
(211)	Jim Pagliaroni	.50	.25	.15
(212)	Milt Pappas	.50	.25	.15
(213)	Wes Parker	.50	.25	.15
(214)	Camilo Pascual	.50	.25	.15
(215)	Don Pavletich	.50	.25	.15
(216)	Joe Pepitone	.50	.25	.15
(217)	Tony Perez	10.00	5.00	3.00
(218)	Gaylord Perry	7.50	3.75	2.25
(219)	Jim Perry	.50	.25	.15
(220)	Gary Peters	.50	.25	.15
(221)	Rico Petrocelli	.50	.25	.15
(222)	Adolfo Phillips	.50	.25	.15
(223)	Tom Phoebus	.50	.25	.15
(224)	Vada Pinson	2.00	1.00	.60
(225)	Boog Powell	2.00	1.00	.60
(226)	Frank Quilici	.50	.25	.15
(227)	Doug Rader	.50	.25	.15
(228)	Rich Reese	.50	.25	.15
(229)	Phil Regan	.50	.25	.15
(230)	Rick Reichardt	.50	.25	.15
(231)	Rick Renick	.50	.25	.15
(232)	Roger Repoz	.50	.25	.15
(233)	Dave Ricketts	.50	.25	.15
(234)	Bill Robinson	.50	.25	.15
(235)	Brooks Robinson	15.00	7.50	4.50
(236)	Frank Robinson	15.00	7.50	4.50
(237)	Bob Rodgers	.50	.25	.15
(238)	Cookie Rojas	.50	.25	.15
(239)	Rich Rollins	.50	.25	.15
(240)	Phil Roof	.50	.25	.15
(241)	Pete Rose	30.00	15.00	9.00
(242)	John Roseboro	.50	.25	.15
(243)	Chico Ruiz	.50	.25	.15
(244)	Ray Sadecki	.50	.25	.15
(245)	Chico Salmon	.50	.25	.15
(246)	Jose Santiago	.50	.25	.15
(247)	Ron Santo	2.50	1.25	.70
(248)	Tom Satriano	.50	.25	.15
(249)	Paul Schaal	.50	.25	.15
(250)	Tom Seaver	15.00	7.50	4.50
(251)	Art Shamsky	.50	.25	.15
(252)	Mike Shannon	.50	.25	.15
(253)	Chris Short	.50	.25	.15
(254)	Dick Simpson	.50	.25	.15
(255)	Duke Sims	.50	.25	.15
(256)	Reggie Smith	.50	.25	.15
(257)	Willie Smith	.50	.25	.15
(258)	Russ Snyder	.50	.25	.15
(259)	Al Spangler	.50	.25	.15
(260)	Larry Stahl	.50	.25	.15
(261)	Lee Stange	.50	.25	.15
(262)	Mickey Stanley	.50	.25	.15
(263)	Willie Stargell	10.00	5.00	3.00
(264)	Rusty Staub	1.00	.50	.30
(265)	Mel Stottlemyre	.50	.25	.15
(266)	Ed Stroud	.50	.25	.15
(267)	Don Sutton	7.50	3.75	2.25
(268)	Ron Swoboda	.50	.25	.15
(269)	Jose Tartabull	.50	.25	.15
(270)	Tony Taylor	.50	.25	.15
(271)	Luis Tiant	1.00	.50	.30
(272)	Bob Tillman	.50	.25	.15
(273)	Bobby Tolan	.50	.25	.15
(274)	Jeff Torborg	.50	.25	.15
(275)	Joe Torre	2.50	1.25	.70
(276)	Cesar Tovar	.50	.25	.15
(277)	Dick Tracewski	.50	.25	.15
(278)	Tom Tresh	.75	.40	.25
(279)	Ted Uhlaender	.50	.25	.15
(280)	Del Unser	.50	.25	.15
(281)	Hilario Valdespino	.50	.25	.15
(282)	Fred Valentine	.50	.25	.15
(283)	Bob Veale	.50	.25	.15
(284)	Zoilo Versalles	.50	.25	.15
(285)	Pete Ward	.50	.25	.15
(286)	Al Weis	.50	.25	.15
(287)	Don Wert	.50	.25	.15
(288)	Bill White	.50	.25	.15
(289)	Roy White	.50	.25	.15
(290)	Fred Whitfield	.50	.25	.15
(291)	Hoyt Wilhelm	7.50	3.75	2.25
(292)	Billy Williams	10.00	5.00	3.00
(293)	Maury Wills	.75	.40	.25
(294)	Earl Wilson	.50	.25	.15
(295)	Wilbur Wood	.50	.25	.15
(296)	Jerry Zimmerman	.50	.25	.15

1970 Milton Bradley

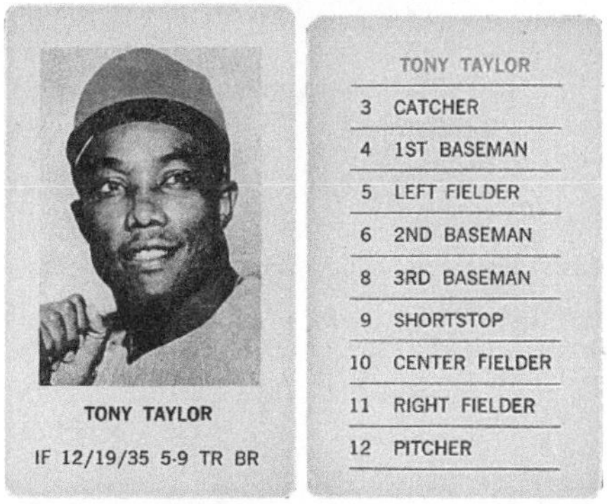
TONY TAYLOR
IF 12/19/35 5-9 TR BR
TONY TAYLOR
3 CATCHER
4 1ST BASEMAN
5 LEFT FIELDER
6 2ND BASEMAN
8 3RD BASEMAN
9 SHORTSTOP
10 CENTER FIELDER
11 RIGHT FIELDER
12 PITCHER

Except for the slightly larger (2-3/8" x 3-1/2") size, the format of the 1970 Milton Bradley set is similar to the 1969 Milton Bradley issue. Again designed for use with a baseball board game, the unnumbered black-and-white cards have rounded corners and wide white borders. The player's name appears in capital letters beneath the photo with his position, birthdate, height and batting and throwing preference on a line below. The back of the card shows the player's name along the top followed by a list of possible game situations used in playing the board game. There are no team designations on the cards and all team insignias have been airbrushed from the photos.

		NM	E	VG
Complete Boxed Set:		175.00	85.00	45.00
Complete Card Set (28):		120.00	55.00	30.00
Common Player:		1.50	.70	.45
(1)	Hank Aaron	15.00	7.50	4.50
(2)	Ernie Banks	10.00	5.00	3.00
(3)	Lou Brock	7.50	3.75	2.25
(4)	Rod Carew	9.00	4.50	2.75
(5)	Roberto Clemente	15.00	7.50	4.50
(6)	Tommy Davis	1.50	.70	.45
(7)	Bill Freehan	1.50	.70	.45
(8)	Jim Fregosi	1.50	.70	.45
(9)	Tom Haller	1.50	.70	.45
(10)	Frank Howard	2.00	1.00	.60
(11)	Reggie Jackson	10.00	5.00	3.00
(12)	Harmon Killebrew	9.00	4.50	2.75
(13)	Mickey S. Lolich	1.50	.70	.45
(14)	Juan Marichal	6.00	3.00	1.75
(15)	Willie Mays	15.00	7.50	4.50
(16)	Willie McCovey	7.50	3.75	2.25
(17)	Sam McDowell	1.50	.70	.45
(18)	Dennis Menke (Denis)	1.50	.70	.45
(19)	Don Mincher	1.50	.70	.45
(20)	Phil Niekro	6.00	3.00	1.75
(21)	Rico Petrocelli	1.50	.70	.45
(22)	Boog Powell	2.00	1.00	.60
(23)	Frank Robinson	9.00	4.50	2.75
(24)	Pete Rose	15.00	7.50	4.50
(25)	Ron Santo	3.00	1.50	.90
(26)	Tom Seaver	9.00	4.50	2.75
(27)	Mel Stottlemyre	1.50	.70	.45
(28)	Tony Taylor	1.50	.70	.45

1972 Milton Bradley

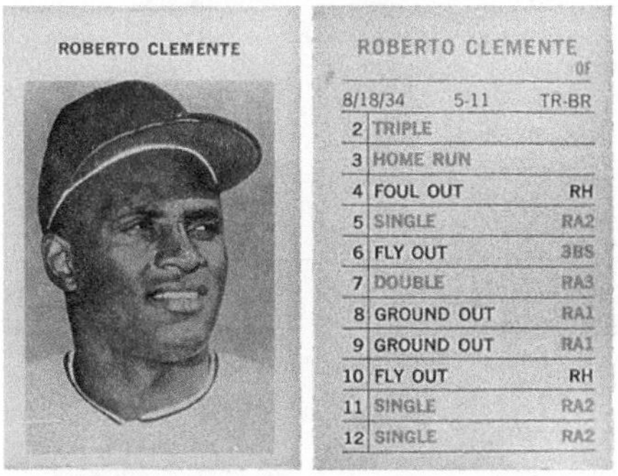
ROBERTO CLEMENTE
ROBERTO CLEMENTE
OF
8/18/34 5-11 TR-BR
2 TRIPLE
3 HOME RUN
4 FOUL OUT RH
5 SINGLE RA2
6 FLY OUT 3BS
7 DOUBLE RA3
8 GROUND OUT RA1
9 GROUND OUT RA1
10 FLY OUT RH
11 SINGLE RA2
12 SINGLE RA2

The 1972 Milton Bradley set was again designed for use with a baseball table game. The 1972 cards are similar to the 1969 and 1970 issues. The unnumbered black-and-white cards measure 2" x 3" and display the player's name along the top of the card. Again, all team insignias have been eliminated by airbrushing, and there are no team designations indicated. Backs carry the player's name and personal data followed by a list of possible game situations used in playing the game. To differentiate a 1972 card from a 1969, look on back for a line of red type which contains the numeral "1." If the digit has a base, the card is a '72; if there is no base to the red "1," it is a 1969. Besides individual player cards, non-photographic team cards were issued for each of the contemporary 24 Major League teams.

		NM	E	VG
Complete Boxed Set:		400.00	200.00	120.00
Complete Card Set (378):		350.00	175.00	110.00
Common Player:		.50	.25	.15
Team Card:		2.00	1.00	.60
(1)	Hank Aaron	25.00	12.50	7.50
(2)	Tommie Aaron	.50	.25	.15
(3)	Ted Abernathy	.50	.25	.15
(4)	Jerry Adair	.50	.25	.15
(5)	Tommy Agee	.50	.25	.15
(6)	Bernie Allen	.50	.25	.15
(7)	Hank Allen	.50	.25	.15
(8)	Richie Allen	1.50	.70	.45
(9)	Gene Alley	.50	.25	.15
(10)	Bob Allison	.50	.25	.15
(11)	Sandy Alomar	.50	.25	.15
(12)	Felipe Alou	.75	.40	.25
(13)	Jesus Alou	.50	.25	.15
(14)	Matty Alou	.50	.25	.15
(15)	Max Alvis	.50	.25	.15
(16)	Brant Alyea	.50	.25	.15
(17)	Mike Andrews	.50	.25	.15
(18)	Luis Aparicio	9.00	4.50	2.75
(19)	Jose Arcia	.50	.25	.15
(20)	Gerald Arrigo	.50	.25	.15
(21)	Bob Aspromonte	.50	.25	.15
(22)	Joe Azcue	.50	.25	.15
(23)	Robert Bailey	.50	.25	.15
(24)	Sal Bando	.50	.25	.15
(25)	Ernie Banks	17.50	8.75	5.25
(26)	Steve Barber	.50	.25	.15
(27)	Robert Barton	.50	.25	.15
(28)	John Bateman	.50	.25	.15
(29)	Glen Beckert (Glenn)	.50	.25	.15
(30)	John Bench	12.50	6.25	3.75
(31)	Ken Berry	.50	.25	.15
(32)	Frank Bertaina	.50	.25	.15
(33)	Paul Blair	.50	.25	.15
(34)	Stephen Blass	.50	.25	.15
(35)	Curt Blefary	.50	.25	.15
(36)	Bobby Bolin	.50	.25	.15
(37)	Bobby Lee Bonds	1.00	.50	.30
(38)	Donald Bosch	.50	.25	.15
(39)	Richard Bosman	.50	.25	.15
(40)	Dave Boswell	.50	.25	.15
(41)	Kenneth Boswell	.50	.25	.15
(42)	Cletis Boyer	.50	.25	.15
(43)	Ken Boyer	1.25	.60	.40
(44)	Charles Bradford	.50	.25	.15
(45)	Ronald Brand	.50	.25	.15
(46)	Ken Brett	.50	.25	.15
(47)	Jim Brewer	.50	.25	.15
(48)	John Briggs	.50	.25	.15
(49)	Nelson Briles	.50	.25	.15
(50)	Ed Brinkman	.50	.25	.15
(51)	James Britton	.50	.25	.15
(52)	Lou Brock	9.00	4.50	2.75
(53)	Gates Brown	.50	.25	.15
(54)	Larry Brown	.50	.25	.15
(55)	Ollie Brown	.50	.25	.15
(56)	George Brunet	.50	.25	.15
(57)	Don Buford	.50	.25	.15
(58)	Wallace Bunker	.50	.25	.15
(59)	Jim Bunning	6.00	3.00	1.75
(60)	William Butler	.50	.25	.15
(61)	Johnny Callison	.50	.25	.15
(62)	Campy Campaneris	.50	.25	.15
(63)	Jose Cardenal	.50	.25	.15
(64)	Leo Cardenas	.50	.25	.15
(65)	Don Cardwell	.50	.25	.15
(66)	Rod Carew	9.00	4.50	2.75
(67)	Cisco Carlos	.50	.25	.15
(68)	Steve Carlton	9.00	4.50	2.75
(69)	Clay Carroll	.50	.25	.15
(70)	Paul Casanova	.50	.25	.15
(71)	Norm Cash	1.50	.70	.45
(72)	Danny Cater	.50	.25	.15
(73)	Orlando Cepeda	9.00	4.50	2.75
(74)	Dean Chance	.50	.25	.15
(75)	Horace Clarke	.50	.25	.15
(76)	Roberto Clemente	30.00	15.00	9.00
(77)	Donn Clendenon	.50	.25	.15
(78)	Ty Cline	.50	.25	.15
(79)	Nate Colbert	.50	.25	.15
(80)	Joe Coleman	.50	.25	.15
(81)	William Conigliaro	.75	.40	.25
(82)	Casey Cox	.50	.25	.15
(83)	Mike Cuellar	.50	.25	.15
(84)	Ray Culp	.50	.25	.15
(85)	George Culver	.50	.25	.15
(86)	Vic Davalillo	.50	.25	.15
(87)	Jim Davenport	.50	.25	.15
(88)	Tommy Davis	.50	.25	.15
(89)	Willie Davis	.50	.25	.15
(90)	Larry Dierker	.50	.25	.15
(91)	Richard Dietz	.50	.25	.15
(92)	Chuck Dobson	.50	.25	.15
(93)	Pat Dobson	.50	.25	.15
(94)	John Donaldson	.50	.25	.15
(95)	Al Downing	.50	.25	.15
(96)	Moe Drabowsky	.50	.25	.15
(97)	John Edwards	.50	.25	.15
(98)	Thomas Egan	.50	.25	.15
(99)	Dick Ellsworth	.50	.25	.15
(100)	Mike Epstein	.50	.25	.15
(101)	Andy Etchebarren	.50	.25	.15
(102)	Ron Fairly	.50	.25	.15
(103)	Frank Fernandez	.50	.25	.15
(104)	Alfred Ferrara	.50	.25	.15
(105)	Michael Fiore	.50	.25	.15
(106)	Curt Flood	1.00	.50	.30
(107)	Vern Fuller	.50	.25	.15
(108)	Joe Foy	.50	.25	.15
(109)	Tito Francona	.50	.25	.15
(110)	Bill Freehan	.50	.25	.15
(111)	Jim Fregosi	.50	.25	.15
(112)	Woodie Fryman	.50	.25	.15
(113)	Len Gabrielson	.50	.25	.15
(114)	Philip Gagliano	.50	.25	.15
(115)	Cito Gaston	.50	.25	.15
(116)	Jake Gibbs	.50	.25	.15
(117)	Russ Gibson	.50	.25	.15
(118)	Dave Giusti	.50	.25	.15
(119)	Fred Gladding	.50	.25	.15
(120)	Tony Gonzalez	.50	.25	.15
(121)	Jim Gosger	.50	.25	.15
(122)	James Grant	.50	.25	.15
(123)	Thomas Griffin	.50	.25	.15
(124)	Dick Green	.50	.25	.15
(125)	Jerry Grote	.50	.25	.15
(126)	Tom Hall	.50	.25	.15
(127)	Tom Haller	.50	.25	.15
(128)	Steve Hamilton	.50	.25	.15
(129)	William Hands	.50	.25	.15
(130)	James Hannan	.50	.25	.15
(131)	Ron Hansen	.50	.25	.15
(132)	Jim Hardin	.50	.25	.15
(133)	Steve Hargan	.50	.25	.15
(134)	Tommy Harper	.50	.25	.15
(135)	Bud Harrelson	.50	.25	.15
(136)	Ken Harrelson	.50	.25	.15
(137)	Jim Hart	.50	.25	.15
(138)	Rich Hebner	.50	.25	.15
(139)	Michael Hedlund	.50	.25	.15
(140)	Tommy Helms	.50	.25	.15
(141)	Elrod Hendricks	.50	.25	.15
(142)	Ronald Herbel	.50	.25	.15
(143)	Jack Hernandez	.50	.25	.15
(144)	Mike Hershberger	.50	.25	.15
(145)	Jack Hiatt	.50	.25	.15
(146)	Jim Hickman	.50	.25	.15
(147)	Dennis Higgins	.50	.25	.15
(148)	John Hiller	.50	.25	.15
(149)	Chuck Hinton	.50	.25	.15
(150)	Larry Hisle	.50	.25	.15
(151)	Ken Holtzman	.50	.25	.15
(152)	Joel Horlen	.50	.25	.15
(153)	Tony Horton	.50	.25	.15
(154)	Willie Horton	.50	.25	.15
(155)	Frank Howard	.75	.40	.25
(156)	Robert Humphreys	.50	.25	.15
(157)	Randy Hundley	.50	.25	.15
(158)	Ron Hunt	.50	.25	.15
(159)	Catfish Hunter	6.00	3.00	1.75
(160)	Grant Jackson	.50	.25	.15
(161)	Reggie Jackson	15.00	7.50	4.50
(162)	Sonny Jackson	.50	.25	.15
(163)	Pat Jarvis	.50	.25	.15
(164)	Larry Jaster	.50	.25	.15
(165)	Julian Javier	.50	.25	.15
(166)	Ferguson Jenkins	6.00	3.00	1.75
(167)	Tommy John	1.00	.50	.30
(168)	Alexander Johnson	.50	.25	.15
(169)	Bob Johnson	.50	.25	.15
(170)	Dave Johnson	.50	.25	.15
(171)	Deron Johnson	.50	.25	.15
(172)	Jay Johnstone	.50	.25	.15
(173)	Cleon Jones	.50	.25	.15
(174)	Dalton Jones	.50	.25	.15
(175)	Mack Jones	.50	.25	.15
(176)	Richard Joseph	.50	.25	.15
(177)	Duane Josephson	.50	.25	.15
(178)	Jim Kaat	2.00	1.00	.60
(179)	Al Kaline	12.50	6.25	3.75
(180)	Richard Kelley	.50	.25	.15
(181)	Harold Kelly	.50	.25	.15
(182)	Gerald Kenney	.50	.25	.15
(183)	Don Kessinger	.50	.25	.15
(184)	Harmon Killebrew	9.00	4.50	2.75
(185)	Ed Kirkpatrick	.50	.25	.15
(186)	Bobby Knoop	.50	.25	.15

(187)	Calvin Koonce	.50	.25	.15
(188)	Jerry Koosman	.50	.25	.15
(189)	Andy Kosco	.50	.25	.15
(190)	Ed Kranepool	.50	.25	.15
(191)	Ted Kubiak	.50	.25	.15
(192)	Jose Laboy	.50	.25	.15
(193)	Joseph Lahoud	.50	.25	.15
(194)	William Landis	.50	.25	.15
(195)	Harold Lanier	.50	.25	.15
(196)	Fred Lasher	.50	.25	.15
(197)	John Lazar	.50	.25	.15
(198)	Jim Lefebvre	.50	.25	.15
(199)	Denny Lemaster	.50	.25	.15
(200)	Dave Leonhard	.50	.25	.15
(201)	Frank Linzy	.50	.25	.15
(202)	Mickey Lolich	.50	.25	.15
(203)	Jim Lonborg	.50	.25	.15
(204)	Mike Lum	.50	.25	.15
(205)	Al Lyle	.50	.25	.15
(206)	Jim Maloney	.50	.25	.15
(207)	Juan Marichal	7.50	3.75	2.25
(208)	David Marshall	.50	.25	.15
(209)	J.C. Martin	.50	.25	.15
(210)	Marty Martinez	.50	.25	.15
(211)	Tom Matchick	.50	.25	.15
(212)	Dal Maxvill	.50	.25	.15
(213)	Carlos May	.50	.25	.15
(214)	Jerry May	.50	.25	.15
(215)	Lee May	.50	.25	.15
(216)	Lee Maye	.50	.25	.15
(217)	Willie Mays	25.00	12.50	7.50
(218)	Bill Mazeroski	9.00	4.50	2.75
(219)	Richard McAuliffe	.50	.25	.15
(220)	Al McBean	.50	.25	.15
(221)	Tim McCarver	.75	.40	.25
(222)	Bill McCool	.50	.25	.15
(223)	Mike McCormick	.50	.25	.15
(224)	Willie McCovey	9.00	4.50	2.75
(225)	Tom McCraw	.50	.25	.15
(226)	Lindy McDaniel	.50	.25	.15
(227)	Sam McDowell	.50	.25	.15
(228)	Leon McFadden	.50	.25	.15
(229)	Daniel McGinn	.50	.25	.15
(230)	Jim McGlothlin	.50	.25	.15
(231)	Fred McGraw	.50	.25	.15
(232)	Denny McLain	.75	.40	.25
(233)	Ken McMullen	.50	.25	.15
(234)	Dave McNally	.50	.25	.15
(235)	Gerry McNertney	.50	.25	.15
(236)	William Melton	.50	.25	.15
(237)	Dennis Menke (Denis)	.50	.25	.15
(238)	John Messersmith	.50	.25	.15
(239)	Felix Millan	.50	.25	.15
(240)	Norman Miller	.50	.25	.15
(241)	Don Mincher	.50	.25	.15
(242)	Rick Monday	.50	.25	.15
(243)	Donald Money	.50	.25	.15
(244)	Barry Moore	.50	.25	.15
(245)	Bob Moose	.50	.25	.15
(246)	David Morehead	.50	.25	.15
(247)	Joe Morgan	9.00	4.50	2.75
(248)	Curt Motton	.50	.25	.15
(249)	Manny Mota	.50	.25	.15
(250)	Bob Murcer	.50	.25	.15
(251)	Thomas Murphy	.50	.25	.15
(252)	Ivan Murrell	.50	.25	.15
(253)	Jim Nash	.50	.25	.15
(254)	Joe Niekro	1.25	.60	.40
(255)	Phil Niekro	6.00	3.00	1.75
(256)	Gary Nolan	.50	.25	.15
(257)	Jim Northrup	.50	.25	.15
(258)	Richard Nye	.50	.25	.15
(259)	Johnny Odom	.50	.25	.15
(260)	John O'Donaghue	.50	.25	.15
(261)	Tony Oliva	1.00	.50	.30
(262)	Al Oliver	1.00	.50	.30
(263)	Robert Oliver	.50	.25	.15
(264)	Claude Osteen	.50	.25	.15
(265)	Ray Oyler	.50	.25	.15
(266)	Jose Pagan	.50	.25	.15
(267)	Jim Palmer	9.00	4.50	2.75
(268)	Milt Pappas	.50	.25	.15
(269)	Wes Parker	.50	.25	.15
(270)	Fred Patek	.50	.25	.15
(271)	Mike Paul	.50	.25	.15
(272)	Joe Pepitone	.50	.25	.15
(273)	Tony Perez	7.50	3.75	2.25
(274)	Gaylord Perry	6.00	3.00	1.75
(275)	Jim Perry	.50	.25	.15
(276)	Gary Peters	.50	.25	.15
(277)	Rico Petrocelli	.50	.25	.15
(278)	Tom Phoebus	.50	.25	.15
(279)	Lou Piniella	1.00	.50	.30
(280)	Vada Pinson	1.50	.70	.45
(281)	Boog Powell	1.50	.70	.45
(282)	Jim Price	.50	.25	.15
(283)	Frank Quilici	.50	.25	.15
(284)	Doug Rader	.50	.25	.15

(285)	Ron Reed	.50	.25	.15
(286)	Rich Reese	.50	.25	.15
(287)	Phil Regan	.50	.25	.15
(288)	Rick Reichardt	.50	.25	.15
(289)	Rick Renick	.50	.25	.15
(290)	Roger Repoz	.50	.25	.15
(291)	Mervin Rettenmund	.50	.25	.15
(292)	Dave Ricketts	.50	.25	.15
(293)	Juan Rios	.50	.25	.15
(294)	Bill Robinson	.50	.25	.15
(295)	Brooks Robinson	12.50	6.25	3.75
(296)	Frank Robinson	12.50	6.25	3.75
(297)	Aurelio Rodriguez	.50	.25	.15
(298)	Ellie Rodriguez	.50	.25	.15
(299)	Cookie Rojas	.50	.25	.15
(300)	Rich Rollins	.50	.25	.15
(301)	Vicente Romo	.50	.25	.15
(302)	Phil Roof	.50	.25	.15
(303)	Pete Rose	25.00	12.50	7.50
(304)	John Roseboro	.50	.25	.15
(305)	Chico Ruiz	.50	.25	.15
(306)	Mike Ryan	.50	.25	.15
(307)	Ray Sadecki	.50	.25	.15
(308)	Chico Salmon	.50	.25	.15
(309)	Manuel Sanguillen	.50	.25	.15
(310)	Ron Santo	3.00	1.50	.90
(311)	Tom Satriano	.50	.25	.15
(312)	Theodore Savage	.50	.25	.15
(313)	Paul Schaal	.50	.25	.15
(314)	Dick Schofield	.50	.25	.15
(315)	George Scott	.50	.25	.15
(316)	Tom Seaver	12.50	6.25	3.75
(317)	Art Shamsky	.50	.25	.15
(318)	Mike Shannon	.50	.25	.15
(319)	Chris Short	.50	.25	.15
(320)	Sonny Siebert	.50	.25	.15
(321)	Duke Sims	.50	.25	.15
(322)	William Singer	.50	.25	.15
(323)	Reggie Smith	.50	.25	.15
(324)	Willie Smith	.50	.25	.15
(325)	Russ Snyder	.50	.25	.15
(326)	Al Spangler	.50	.25	.15
(327)	James Spencer	.50	.25	.15
(328)	Ed Spiezio	.50	.25	.15
(329)	Larry Stahl	.50	.25	.15
(330)	Lee Stange	.50	.25	.15
(331)	Mickey Stanley	.50	.25	.15
(332)	Willie Stargell	9.00	4.50	2.75
(333)	Rusty Staub	2.00	1.00	.60
(334)	James Stewart	.50	.25	.15
(335)	George Stone	.50	.25	.15
(336)	William Stoneman	.50	.25	.15
(337)	Mel Stottlemyre	.50	.25	.15
(338)	Ed Stroud	.50	.25	.15
(339)	Ken Suarez	.50	.25	.15
(340)	Gary Sutherland	.50	.25	.15
(341)	Don Sutton	6.00	3.00	1.75
(342)	Ron Swoboda	.50	.25	.15
(343)	Fred Talbot	.50	.25	.15
(344)	Jose Tartabull	.50	.25	.15
(345)	Kenneth Tatum	.50	.25	.15
(346)	Tony Taylor	.50	.25	.15
(347)	Luis Tiant	.75	.40	.25
(348)	Bob Tillman	.50	.25	.15
(349)	Bobby Tolan	.50	.25	.15
(350)	Jeff Torborg	.50	.25	.15
(351)	Joe Torre	3.00	1.50	.90
(352)	Cesar Tovar	.50	.25	.15
(353)	Tom Tresh	.75	.40	.25
(354)	Ted Uhlaender	.50	.25	.15
(355)	Del Unser	.50	.25	.15
(356)	Bob Veale	.50	.25	.15
(357)	Zoilo Versalles	.50	.25	.15
(358)	Luke Walker	.50	.25	.15
(359)	Pete Ward	.50	.25	.15
(360)	Eddie Watt	.50	.25	.15
(361)	Ramon Webster	.50	.25	.15
(362)	Al Weis	.50	.25	.15
(363)	Don Wert	.50	.25	.15
(364)	Bill White	.50	.25	.15
(365)	Roy White	.50	.25	.15
(366)	Hoyt Wilhelm	6.00	3.00	1.75
(367)	Billy Williams	9.00	4.50	2.75
(368)	Walter Williams	.50	.25	.15
(369)	Maury Wills	.75	.40	.25
(370)	Don Wilson	.50	.25	.15
(371)	Earl Wilson	.50	.25	.15
(372)	Robert Wine	.50	.25	.15
(373)	Richard Wise	.50	.25	.15
(374)	Wilbur Wood	.50	.25	.15
(375)	William Woodward	.50	.25	.15
(376)	Clyde Wright	.50	.25	.15
(377)	James Wynn	.50	.25	.15
(378)	Jerry Zimmerman	.50	.25	.15

1957 Milwaukee Braves Picture Pack

HENRY AARON, Outfielder

Prior to the Jay Publishing Co. photo packs which dominated the market from 1958-62, the Braves issued this souvenir stand picture pack of 5" x 7" black-and-white, blank-back, player pictures. In the wide bottom border player names are printed in all-caps with the position indicated in upper- and lower-case letters. The unnumbered pictures are listed here in alphabetical order.

		NM	E	VG
Complete Set (12):		100.00	50.00	30.00
Common Player:		7.50	3.75	2.25
(1)	Hank Aaron	30.00	15.00	9.00
(2)	Joe Adcock	7.50	3.75	2.25
(3)	Lew Burdette	7.50	3.75	2.25
(4)	Wes Covington	7.50	3.75	2.25
(5)	Del Crandall	7.50	3.75	2.25
(6)	Bob Hazle	7.50	3.75	2.25
(7)	Johnny Logan	7.50	3.75	2.25
(8)	Edwin Mathews	12.50	6.25	3.75
(9)	Don McMahon	7.50	3.75	2.25
(10)	Andy Pafko	7.50	3.75	2.25
(11)	Red Schoendienst	10.00	5.00	3.00
(12)	Warren Spahn	12.50	6.25	3.75

1965 Milwaukee Braves Picture Pack

HANK AARON, Braves

These 4-7/8" x 7-1/8" blank-back, black-and-white pictures were sold in groups of 12 in a white paper window envelope and possibly also as a complete set of 24. Besides the slight size difference, the team-issued pictures differ from the contemporary Jay Publishing pictures in that the city name is not included in the typography in the bottom border.

		NM	E	VG
Complete Set (24):		75.00	37.50	22.50
Common Player:		3.00	1.50	.90
(1)	Hank Aaron	15.00	7.50	4.50
(2)	Sandy Alomar	3.00	1.50	.90
(3)	Felipe Alou	3.00	1.50	.90
(4)	Wade Blasingame	3.00	1.50	.90
(5)	Frank Bolling	3.00	1.50	.90
(6)	Bobby Bragan	3.00	1.50	.90
(7)	Rico Carty	3.00	1.50	.90
(8)	Ty Cline	3.00	1.50	.90
(9)	Tony Cloninger	3.00	1.50	.90
(10)	Mike de la Hoz	3.00	1.50	.90
(11)	Hank Fischer	3.00	1.50	.90
(12)	Mack Jones	3.00	1.50	.90
(13)	Gary Kolb	3.00	1.50	.90
(14)	Denny LeMaster	3.00	1.50	.90
(15)	Eddie Mathews	6.00	3.00	1.75
(16)	Lee Maye	3.00	1.50	.90
(17)	Denis Menke	3.00	1.50	.90
(18)	Billy O'Dell	3.00	1.50	.90
(19)	Gene Oliver	3.00	1.50	.90
(20)	Chi Chi Olivo	3.00	1.50	.90
(21)	Dan Osinski (Osinski)	3.00	1.50	.90
(22)	Bob Sadowski	3.00	1.50	.90
(23)	Bobby Tiefenauer	3.00	1.50	.90
(24)	Joe Torre	4.50	2.25	1.25

1980 Milwaukee Brewers/Pepsi Fan Club

Star Milwaukee infielder Sal Bando is featured on this 2-1/2" x 3-1/2" membership card in a blue-bordered action pose. The back is printed in blue on white with both the team and soda logo.

	NM	E	VG
Sal Bando	6.00	3.00	1.80

1912 Miner's Extra Series of Champions (T227)

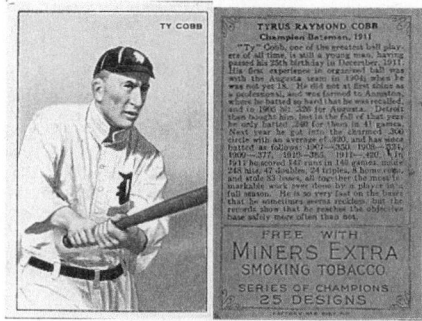

(See 1912 T227 Series of Champions for checklist, price guide.)

1977 Minneapolis Star Twins Scrapbook

Between July 4-August 12, the Star printed one player "Scrapbook" picture each day in the sports section. While sizes vary somewhat, most are about 4-3/16" x 10-3/16". Enclosed in a dotted-line border are a player portrait photo, facsimile autograph, position, uniform number, team logo, career highlights and full stats. Because they are printed on newsprint, the pictures are subject to rapid deterioration.

	NM	E	VG
Complete Set (36):	100.00	50.00	30.00
Common Player:	4.00	2.00	1.25
7/4 Rod Carew	12.00	6.00	3.50
7/5 Geoff Zahn	4.00	2.00	1.25
7/6 Luis Gomez	4.00	2.00	1.25
7/7 Glenn Adams	4.00	2.00	1.25

7/8	Lyman Bostock	6.00	3.00	1.75
7/9	Bob Gorinski	4.00	2.00	1.25
7/11	Butch Wynegar	4.00	2.00	1.25
7/12	Rob Wilfong	4.00	2.00	1.25
7/13	Dave Goltz	4.00	2.00	1.25
7/14	Bill Butler	4.00	2.00	1.25
7/15	Bob Randall	4.00	2.00	1.25
7/16	Jeff Holly	4.00	2.00	1.25
7/18	Gene Mauch	4.00	2.00	1.25
7/19	Walt Terrell	4.00	2.00	1.25
7/20	Rich Chiles	4.00	2.00	1.25
7/21	Paul Thormodsgard	4.00	2.00	1.25
7/22	Dave Johnson	4.00	2.00	1.25
7/23	Mike Cubbage	4.00	2.00	1.25
7/25	Larry Hisle	4.00	2.00	1.25
7/26	Don McMahon	4.00	2.00	1.25
7/27	Glenn Borgmann	4.00	2.00	1.25
7/28	Craig Kusick	4.00	2.00	1.25
7/29	Ron Schueler	4.00	2.00	1.25
7/30	Karl Kuehl	4.00	2.00	1.25
8/1	Roy Smalley	4.00	2.00	1.25
8/2	Tony Oliva	7.50	3.75	2.25
8/3	Jerry Zimmerman	4.00	2.00	1.25
8/4	Dan Ford	4.00	2.00	1.25
8/5	Don Carrithers	4.00	2.00	1.25
8/6	Tom Johnson	4.00	2.00	1.25
8/8	Pete Redfern	4.00	2.00	1.25
8/9	Tom Burgmeier	4.00	2.00	1.25
8/10	Bud Bulling	4.00	2.00	1.25
8/11	Gary Serum	4.00	2.00	1.25
8/12	Calvin Griffith	4.00	2.00	1.25

1977-78 Minnesota Twins Team Issue

Produced by collector Barry Fritz, and sold by the team through its normal concession outlets, this set consists of two 25-card series. Cards 1-25 were issued in 1977; cards 26-50 in 1978. Measuring 2-5/8" x 3-3/4", card fronts feature quality color player poses with no other graphics. Backs are in black-and-white and have all player data, stats with the Twins and overall major league numbers, plus career highlights. Besides being sold as sets, the cards were also offered in uncut sheet form.

		NM	E	VG
Complete Set (50):		35.00	17.50	10.00
Common Player:		1.00	.50	.30
1	Bob Allison	1.00	.50	.30
2	Earl Battey	1.00	.50	.30
3	Dave Boswell	1.00	.50	.30
4	Dean Chance	1.25	.60	.40
5	Jim Grant	1.25	.60	.40
6	Calvin Griffith	1.25	.60	.40
7	Jimmie Hall	1.00	.50	.30
8	Harmon Killebrew	6.00	3.00	1.75
9	Jim Lemon	1.00	.50	.30
10	Billy Martin	3.00	1.50	.90
11	Gene Mauch	1.00	.50	.30
12	Sam Mele	1.00	.50	.30
13	Metropolitan Stadium	1.50	.70	.45
14	Don Mincher	1.00	.50	.30
15	Tony Oliva	3.00	1.50	.90
16	Camilo Pascual	1.00	.50	.30
17	Jim Perry	1.25	.60	.40
18	Frank Quilici	1.00	.50	.30
19	Rich Reese	1.00	.50	.30
20	Bill Rigney	1.00	.50	.30
21	Cesar Tovar	1.00	.50	.30
22	Zoilo Versalles	1.00	.50	.30
23	Al Worthington	1.00	.50	.30
24	Jerry Zimmerman	1.00	.50	.30
25	Checklist / Souvenir List	1.00	.50	.30
26	Bernie Allen	1.00	.50	.30
27	Leo Cardenas	1.00	.50	.30
28	Ray Corbin	1.00	.50	.30
29	Joe Decker	1.00	.50	.30
30	Johnny Goryl	1.00	.50	.30
31	Tom Hall	1.00	.50	.30
32	Bill Hands	1.00	.50	.30

33	Jim Holt	1.00	.50	.30
34	Randy Hundley	1.00	.50	.30
35	Jerry Kindall	1.00	.50	.30
36	Johnny Klippstein	1.00	.50	.30
37	Jack Kralick	1.00	.50	.30
38	Jim Merritt	1.00	.50	.30
39	Joe Nossek	1.00	.50	.30
40	Ron Perranoski	1.00	.50	.30
41	Bill Pleis	1.00	.50	.30
42	Rick Renick	1.00	.50	.30
43	Jim Roland	1.00	.50	.30
44	Lee Stange	1.00	.50	.30
45	Dick Stigman	1.00	.50	.30
46	Danny Thompson	1.00	.50	.30
47	Ted Uhlaender	1.00	.50	.30
48	Sandy Valdespino	1.00	.50	.30
49	Dick Woodson	1.00	.50	.30
50	Checklist #26-50	1.00	.50	.30

1911-16 Mino Cigarettes (T216)

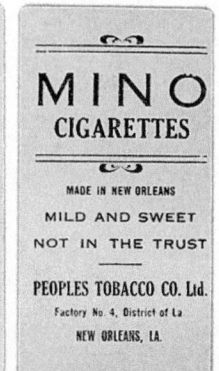

The T216 baseball card set, issued by several brands of the Peoples Tobacco Co., is the last of the Louisiana cigarette sets and the most confusing. Apparently issued over a period of several years between 1911 and 1916, the set employs the same pictures as several contemporary caramel and bakery sets. Positive identification can be made by the back of the cards. The Peoples Tobacco cards carry advertising for one of three brands of cigarettes: Kotton, Mino or Virginia Extra. The Kotton brand is the most common, while the Virginia Extra and Mino backs command a premium. T216 cards are found in two types; one has a glossy front finish, while a second scarcer type is printed on a thin paper. The thin paper cards command an additional 15% premium. The cards represent players from the American, National and Federal leagues. Cards measure a nominal 1-1/2" x 2-5/8", though reasonable allowance for variance must be made on consideration of original standards for cutting.

		NM	E	VG
Common Player:		1,925	870.00	480.00
(1)	Jack Barry (Batting)	1,925	870.00	480.00
(2)	Jack Barry (Fielding)	1,925	870.00	480.00
(3)	Harry Bemis	1,920	870.00	480.00
(4a)	Chief Bender (Philadelphia, striped cap.)	4,200	1,890	1,050
(4b)	Chief Bender (Baltimore, striped cap.)	4,200	1,890	1,050
(5a)	Chief Bender (Philadelphia, white cap.)	4,200	1,890	1,050
(5b)	Chief Bender (Baltimore, white cap.)	4,200	1,890	1,050
(6)	Bill Bergen	1,925	870.00	480.00
(7a)	Bob Bescher (Cincinnati)	1,925	870.00	480.00
(7b)	Bob Bescher (St. Louis)	1,925	870.00	480.00
(8)	Roger Bresnahan	4,200	1,890	1,050
(9)	Al Bridwell (Batting)	1,925	870.00	480.00
(10a)	Al Bridwell (New York, sliding.)	1,925	870.00	480.00
(10b)	Al Bridwell (St. Louis, sliding.)	1,925	870.00	480.00
(11)	Donie Bush	1,925	870.00	480.00
(12)	Doc Casey	1,925	870.00	480.00
(13)	Frank Chance	4,200	1,890	1,050
(14a)	Hal Chase (New York, fielding.)	1,925	870.00	480.00
(14b)	Hal Chase (Buffalo, fielding.)	1,925	870.00	480.00
(15)	Hal Chase (Portrait)	3,000	1,350	800.00
(16a)	Ty Cobb (Detroit Am., standing.)	40,000	20,000	12,000
(16b)	Ty Cobb (Detroit Americans, standing.)	40,000	20,000	12,000
(17)	Ty Cobb (Detroit Americans, batting.)	40,000	20,000	12,000
(18a)	Eddie Collins (Phila. Am.)	4,200	1,890	1,050
(18b)	Eddie Collins (Phila. Amer.)	4,200	1,890	1,050

(19)	Eddie Collins (Chicago)	4,200	1,890	1,050
(20a)	Sam Crawford (Small print.)	4,200	1,890	1,050
(20b)	Sam Crawford (Large print.)	4,200	1,890	1,050
(21)	Harry Davis	1,925	870.00	480.00
(22)	Ray Demmitt	1,925	870.00	480.00
(23)	Art Devlin	1,925	870.00	480.00
(24a)	Wild Bill Donovan (Detroit)	1,925	870.00	480.00
(24b)	Wild Bill Donovan (New York)	1,925	870.00	480.00
(25a)	Red Dooin (Philadelphia)	1,925	870.00	480.00
(25b)	Red Dooin (Cincinnati)	1,925	870.00	480.00
(26a)	Mickey Doolan (Philadelphia)	1,925	870.00	480.00
(26b)	Mickey Doolan (Baltimore)	1,925	870.00	480.00
(27)	Patsy Dougherty	1,925	870.00	480.00
(28a)	Larry Doyle (N.Y. Nat'l,) (W/bat.)	1,925	870.00	480.00
(28b)	Larry Doyle (New York Nat'l)(W/bat.))	1,925	870.00	480.00
(29)	Larry Doyle (Throwing)	1,925	870.00	480.00
(30)	Clyde Engle	1,925	870.00	480.00
(31a)	Johnny Evers (Chicago)	4,200	1,890	1,050
(31b)	Johnny Evers (Boston)	4,200	1,890	1,050
(32)	Art Fromme	1,925	870.00	480.00
(33a)	George Gibson (Pittsburg Nat'l, back view.)	1,925	870.00	480.00
(33b)	George Gibson (Pittsburgh Nat'l., back view.)	1,925	870.00	480.00
(34a)	George Gibson (Pittsburg Nat'l, front view.)	1,925	870.00	480.00
(34b)	George Gibson (Pittsburgh Nat'l., front view.)	1,925	870.00	480.00
(35a)	Topsy Hartsel (Phila. Am.)	1,925	870.00	480.00
(35b)	Topsy Hartsel (Phila. Amer.)	1,925	870.00	480.00
(36)	Roy Hartzell (Batting)	1,925	870.00	480.00
(37)	Roy Hartzell (Catching)	1,925	870.00	480.00
(38a)	Fred Jacklitsch (Philadelphia)	1,925	870.00	480.00
(38b)	Fred Jacklitsch (Baltimore)	1,925	870.00	480.00
(39a)	Hughie Jennings (Orange background.)	4,200	1,890	1,050
(39b)	Hughie Jennings (Red background.)	4,200	1,890	1,050
(40)	Red Kleinow	1,925	870.00	480.00
(41a)	Otto Knabe (Philadelphia)	1,925	870.00	480.00
(41b)	Otto Knabe (Baltimore)	1,925	870.00	480.00
(42)	Jack Knight	1,925	870.00	480.00
(43a)	Nap Lajoie (Philadelphia, fielding.)	4,800	2,160	1,200
(43b)	Nap Lajoie (Cleveland, fielding.)	4,800	2,160	1,200
(44)	Nap Lajoie (Portrait)	4,800	2,160	1,200
(45a)	Hans Lobert (Cincinnati)	1,925	870.00	480.00
(45b)	Hans Lobert (New York)	1,925	870.00	480.00
(46)	Sherry Magee	1,925	870.00	480.00
(47)	Rube Marquard	4,200	1,890	1,050
(48a)	Christy Matthewson (Mathewson) (Large print.)	20,000	10,000	6,000
(48b)	Christy Matthewson (Mathewson) (Small print.)	20,000	10,000	6,000
(49a)	John McGraw (Large print.)	4,200	1,890	1,050
(49b)	John McGraw (Small print.)	5,000	2,250	1,350
(50)	Larry McLean	1,925	870.00	480.00
(51)	George McQuillan	2,750	1,250	750.00
(52)	Dots Miller (Batting)	1,925	870.00	480.00
(53a)	Dots Miller (Pittsburg, fielding.)	2,750	1,250	750.00
(53b)	Dots Miller (St. Louis, fielding.)	1,925	870.00	480.00
(54a)	Danny Murphy (Philadelphia)	1,925	870.00	480.00
(54b)	Danny Murphy (Brooklyn)	2,800	1,250	750.00
(55)	Rebel Oakes	1,925	870.00	480.00
(56)	Bill O'Hara	1,925	870.00	480.00
(57)	Eddie Plank	5,400	2,430	1,350
(58a)	Germany Schaefer (Washington)	1,925	870.00	480.00
(58b)	Germany Schaefer (Newark)	1,925	870.00	480.00
(59)	Admiral Schlei	1,925	870.00	480.00
(60)	Boss Schmidt	1,925	870.00	480.00
(61)	Johnny Seigle	1,925	870.00	480.00
(62)	Dave Shean	1,925	870.00	480.00
(63)	Boss Smith (Schmidt)	1,925	870.00	480.00
(64)	Tris Speaker	9,750	4,500	2,700
(65)	Oscar Stanage	1,925	870.00	480.00
(66)	George Stovall	1,925	870.00	480.00
(67)	Jeff Sweeney	1,925	870.00	480.00
(68a)	Joe Tinker (Chicago Nat'l, batting.)	4,200	1,890	1,050
(68b)	Joe Tinker (Chicago Feds, batting.)	4,200	1,890	1,050
(69)	Joe Tinker (Portrait)	4,200	1,890	1,050

(70a)	Honus Wagner (Batting, S.S.)	35,000	17,500	10,500
(70b)	Honus Wagner (Batting, 2b.)	35,000	17,500	10,500
(71a)	Honus Wagner (Throwing, S.S.)	35,000	17,500	10,500
(71b)	Honus Wagner (Throwing, 2b.)	35,000	17,500	10,500
(72)	Hooks Wiltse	1,925	870.00	480.00
(73)	Cy Young	15,000	6,750	3,750
(74a)	Heinie Zimmerman (2b.)	1,925	870.00	480.00
(74b)	Heinie Zimmerman (3b.)	1,925	870.00	480.00

1962 Molinari's Restaurant Frank Malzone

This black-and-white J.D. McCarthy postcard of the former Red Sox infielder was given to patrons of an Oneonta, N.Y., restaurant in which Malzone was a partner with his brother-in-law. The card measures 3-1/4" x 5-1/2" and has a facsimile autograph on front. A similar promotional postcard is listed under Ticoa Tires.

	NM	E	VG
Frank Malzone	15.00	7.50	4.50

1911 Monarch Typewriter Philadelphia A's

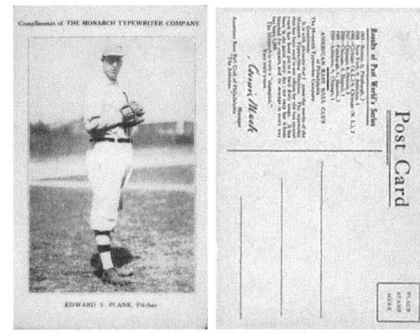

These black-and-white postcards (about 3-1/2" x 5") depict the World Champion 1910 Philadelphia A's. Fronts have posed player photos with a black pin stripe and white borders. The player's name and position are printed in the bottom border. "Compliments of THE MONARCH TYPE-WRITER COMPANY" appears in the top border. Backs are rather standard postcard fare, but include data about the World Series between 1903-1910.

		NM	E	VG
	Complete Set (6):	14,000	7,000	4,200
	Common Player:	2,000	1,000	600.00
(1)	John J. Barry	2,000	1,000	600.00
(2)	Chief Bender	2,750	1,400	850.00
(3)	Eddie Collins	2,750	1,400	850.00
(4)	Rube Oldring	2,000	1,000	600.00
(5)	Eddie Plank	2,750	1,400	850.00
(6)	Ira Thomas	2,000	1,000	600.00

1970 Montreal Expos Player Pins

Produced by "Best in Sports" for sale in the Montreal area for 35¢ apiece, these 1-3/4" diameter pinbacks feature action poses of the players set against a white background. The player's name at top is in black.

		NM	E	VG
	Complete Set (16):	350.00	175.00	100.00
	Common Player:	25.00	12.50	7.50
(1)	John Bateman	25.00	12.50	7.50
(2)	Ron Brand	25.00	12.50	7.50
(3)	Ron Fairly	25.00	12.50	7.50
(4)	Mack Jones	25.00	12.50	7.50
(5)	Coco Laboy	25.00	12.50	7.50
(6)	Gene Mauch	25.00	12.50	7.50
(7)	Dan McGinn	25.00	12.50	7.50
(8)	Adolfo Phillips	25.00	12.50	7.50
(9)	Claude Raymond	25.00	12.50	7.50
(10)	Steve Renko	25.00	12.50	7.50
(11)	Marv Staehle	25.00	12.50	7.50
(12)	Rusty Staub	40.00	20.00	12.00
(13)	Bill Stoneman	25.00	12.50	7.50
(14)	Gary Sutherland	25.00	12.50	7.50
(15)	Bobby Wine	25.00	12.50	7.50
(16)	Expos team logo	10.00	5.00	3.00

1972-76 Montreal Expos Matchbook Covers

In 1972, 1973 and 1976, the Eddy Match Co., Montreal, issued series of seven matchbook covers featuring action photos. Fronts have a red, white and blue team logo on a white background. Backs have a bluetone action photo with the match-striking surface across the lower portion. The player in the photo is not identified on the matchbook. Inside of the 2-1/8" x 4-3/8" cover, printed in blue, is the team home schedule for that season. The unnumbered matchbook covers are checklisted here alphabetically by year. Values shown are for empty matchbooks; full matchbooks would be valued at 2-3X.

		NM	E	VG
	Complete Set (21):	40.00	20.00	12.00
	Common Player:	4.00	2.00	1.25
	1972			
(1)	Boots Day	4.00	2.00	1.25
(2)	Ron Fairly	4.00	2.00	1.25
(3)	Ron Hunt	4.00	2.00	1.25
(4)	Steve Renko	4.00	2.00	1.25
(5)	Rusty Staub	6.00	3.00	1.75
(6)	Bobby Wine	4.00	2.00	1.25
(7)	Hunt's 50th HBP (Scoreboard)	4.00	2.00	1.25
	1973			
(1)	Tim Foli	4.00	2.00	1.25
(2)	Ron Hunt	4.00	2.00	1.25
(3)	Mike Jorgensen	4.00	2.00	1.25
(4)	Gene Mauch	4.00	2.00	1.25
(5)	Balor Moore	4.00	2.00	1.25
(6)	Ken Singleton	4.00	2.00	1.25
(7)	Bill Stoneman	4.00	2.00	1.25
	1976			
(1)	Barry Foote	4.00	2.00	1.25
(2)	Mike Jorgensen	4.00	2.00	1.25
(3)	Pete Mackanin	4.00	2.00	1.25
(4)	Dale Murray	4.00	2.00	1.25
(5)	Larry Parrish	4.00	2.00	1.25
(6)	Steve Rogers	4.00	2.00	1.25
(7)	Dan Warthen	4.00	2.00	1.25

1916 Morehouse Baking Co.

TY COBB
C. F.—Detroit Americans
38

While this 200-card set is most often found with blank

backs or with the advertising of "The Sporting News" on the back, a number of scarcer regional advertisers also can be found. This Massachusetts baker inserted the cards into bread loaves and offered a redemption program. Since cards are known that correspond to both versions of the parent M101 Blank Backs, it not known whether the bakery's version parallels M101-4 and M101-5 or is a hybrid of the two.

	NM	E	VG
PREMIUM: 4-6X			

(See 1916 M101-4 and M101-5 Blank Backs for checklist and price guide.)

1907 Morgan Stationery "Red Belt" Postcards

Only one player is individually identified in this series of postcards, though the identities of others have been discovered over the years. The 3-1/2" x 5-1/2" cards have colorized player and group photos on front with a title printed in white in the lower-left corner. Some photos were taken at the Reds ballpark, then known as the Palace of Fans. Cards include pictures of Reds and Pirates of the National League, and Toledo of the minors. Many of the players have bright red belts, thus the set's nickname. Postcard backs have a credit line: "The Morgan Stationery Co., Cincinnati, O., Publishers." The unnumbered cards are checklisted here alphabetically by title.

		NM	E	VG
Complete Set (12):		3,250	1,625	950.00
Common Card:		275.00	135.00	80.00
(1)	After A High One	275.00	135.00	80.00
(2)	A Home Run	275.00	135.00	80.00
(3)	Hit & Run	275.00	135.00	80.00
(4)	In Consultation	275.00	135.00	80.00
(5)	It's All in the Game - "Noise"	275.00	135.00	80.00
(6)	Huggins Second Baseman Par Excellence(Miller Huggins) (Stadium background.)	325.00	160.00	95.00
(7)	Huggins Second Baseman Par Excellance(Miller Huggins) (Low buildings in background.)	325.00	160.00	95.00
(8)	Opening of the Season 1907	275.00	135.00	80.00
(9)	Out to the Long Green	275.00	135.00	80.00
(10)	Practise (Practice) Makes Perfect(Sam Leever)	275.00	135.00	80.00
(11)	Safe	275.00	135.00	80.00
(12)	Use Two If Necessary(Hans Lobert)	275.00	135.00	80.00

1959 Morrell Meats Dodgers

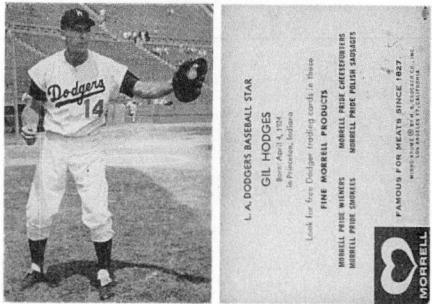

This set of Los Angeles Dodgers was the first issue of a three-year run for the Southern California meat company. The 12 cards in this 2-1/2" x 3-1/2" set are unnumbered and feature full-frame, unbordered color photos. Card backs fea-

ture a company ad and list only the player's name, birthdate and birthplace. Two errors exist in the set; the cards naming Clem Labine and Norm Larker show photos of Stan Williams and Joe Pignatano, respectively.

		NM	E	VG
Complete Set (12):		3,500	1,750	1,000
Common Player:		100.00	50.00	30.00
(1)	Don Drysdale	200.00	100.00	60.00
(2)	Carl Furillo	150.00	75.00	45.00
(3)	Jim Gilliam	125.00	60.00	35.00
(4)	Gil Hodges	200.00	100.00	60.00
(5)	Sandy Koufax	2,400	1,200	725.00
(6)	Clem Labine (Photo actually Stan Williams.)	100.00	50.00	30.00
(7)	Norm Larker (Photo actually Joe Pignatano.)	100.00	50.00	30.00
(8)	Charlie Neal	100.00	50.00	30.00
(9)	Johnny Podres	125.00	60.00	35.00
(10)	John Roseboro	100.00	50.00	30.00
(11)	Duke Snider	200.00	100.00	60.00
(12)	Don Zimmer	125.00	60.00	35.00

1960 Morrell Meats Dodgers

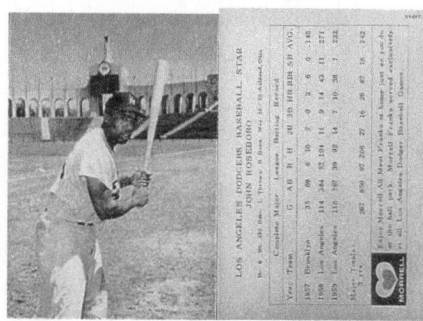

This 12-card set is the same 2-1/2" x 3-1/2" size as the 1959 set, and again features unbordered color card fronts. Five of the players included are new to the Morrell's sets. Card backs in 1960 list player statistics and brief personal data on each player. Cards of Gil Hodges, Carl Furillo and Duke Snider are apparently scarcer than others in the set.

		NM	E	VG
Complete Set (12):		2,200	1,100	650.00
Common Player:		80.00	40.00	24.00
(1)	Walt Alston	90.00	45.00	27.50
(2)	Roger Craig	80.00	40.00	24.00
(3)	Don Drysdale	120.00	60.00	35.00
(4)	Carl Furillo	225.00	110.00	65.00
(5)	Gil Hodges	400.00	200.00	120.00
(6)	Sandy Koufax	500.00	250.00	150.00
(7)	Wally Moon	80.00	40.00	24.00
(8)	Charlie Neal	80.00	40.00	24.00
(9)	Johnny Podres	80.00	40.00	24.00
(10)	John Roseboro	80.00	40.00	24.00
(11)	Larry Sherry	80.00	40.00	24.00
(12)	Duke Snider	450.00	225.00	135.00

1961 Morrell Meats Dodgers

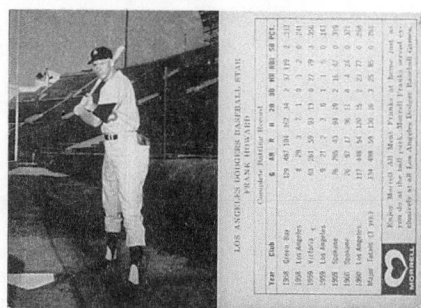

The Morrell set shrunk to just six cards in 1961, with a format almost identical to the 1960 cards. Card fronts are again full-color, unbordered photos. Player statistics appear on the backs. The unnumbered cards measure a slightly smaller 2-1/4" x 3-1/4", and comparison of statistical information can also distinguish the cards from the 1960 version.

		NM	E	VG
Complete Set (6):		900.00	450.00	275.00
Common Player:		90.00	45.00	27.50
(1)	Tommy Davis	90.00	45.00	27.50
(2)	Don Drysdale	120.00	60.00	36.00

(3)	Frank Howard	90.00	45.00	27.50
(4)	Sandy Koufax	450.00	225.00	135.00
(5)	Norm Larker	90.00	45.00	27.50
(6)	Maury Wills	90.00	45.00	27.00

1910 Morton's Buster Brown Bread Tigers Pins (PD2)

Dating of these two issues is arbitrary, since there is no indication on the pins of vintage. Both sets feature members of the Detroit Tigers, American League champions of 1907-09. The Buster Brown Bread pins measure 1-1/4" in diameter and have a small black-and-white player portrait photo surrounded by a yellow border. Artwork to the left depicts Buster Brown with a tiger holding a blue banner with the Morton's name. The player photos carry no identification, which may make the checklist presented here somewhat tentative. Some collectors feel the pin identified as Jimmy Archer is actually Jim Delahanty.

		NM	E	VG
Complete Set (15):		12,000	6,000	3,600
Common Player:		450.00	225.00	135.00
(1)	Jimmy Archer	450.00	225.00	135.00
(2)	Heinie Beckendorf	450.00	225.00	135.00
(3)	Donie Bush	450.00	225.00	135.00
(4)	Ty Cobb	6,500	3,250	1,950
(5)	Sam Crawford	750.00	375.00	225.00
(6)	Wild Bill Donovan	450.00	225.00	135.00
(7)	Hughie Jennings	850.00	425.00	250.00
(8)	Tom Jones	450.00	225.00	135.00
(9)	Red Killefer	450.00	225.00	135.00
(10)	George Moriarty	450.00	225.00	135.00
(11)	George Mullin	450.00	225.00	135.00
(12)	Claude Rossman	450.00	225.00	135.00
(13)	"Germany" Schaefer	450.00	225.00	135.00
(14)	Ed Summers	450.00	225.00	135.00
(15)	Ed Willett	450.00	225.00	135.00

1910 Morton's Pennant Winner Bread Tigers Pins

The American League champion Detroit Tigers (1907-1909) are featured on this set of pins advertising -- appropriately -- Pennant Winner Bread. The 1-1/4" pins have black-and-white player photos surrounded by a yellow border. A Detroit banner with tiger head superimposed is at bottom. The players are not identified anywhere on the pins, which may make this checklist somewhat arbitrary.

		NM	E	VG
Complete Set (16):		12,000	6,000	3,500
Common Player:		500.00	250.00	150.00
(1)	Jimmy Archer	500.00	250.00	150.00
(2)	Heinie Beckendorf	500.00	250.00	150.00
(3)	Donie Bush	500.00	250.00	150.00
(4)	Ty Cobb	4,000	2,000	1,200
(5)	Sam Crawford	900.00	450.00	275.00
(6)	Wild Bill Donovan	500.00	250.00	150.00
(7)	Hughie Jennings	900.00	450.00	275.00
(8)	Davy Jones	500.00	250.00	150.00
(9)	Matty McIntyre	500.00	250.00	150.00
(10)	George Moriarty	500.00	250.00	150.00
(11)	George Mullin	500.00	250.00	150.00
(12)	Claude Rossman	500.00	250.00	150.00
(13)	Herman Schaefer (Schaefer)	500.00	250.00	150.00
(14)	Charles Schmidt	500.00	250.00	150.00
(15)	Ed Summers	500.00	250.00	150.00
(16)	Ed Willett	500.00	250.00	150.00

1916 Mothers' Bread (D303)

Apparently issued in 1916 by the New Orleans branch of the General Baking Co., these unnumbered cards measure 1-1/2" x 2-3/4". The player pictures and format of the cards are identical to the 1915 American Caramel (E106) and 1914 General Baking Co. (D303) sets, but this issue carries an advertisement for Mothers' Bread on back. This version is much scarcer than the General Baking or American Caramel types. It is known that at least one player appears in this set who is not found in E106/D303 and many players are found with team, league and position changes. The checklist here is incomplete and additions are welcome. Gaps have been left in the assigned numbering for future additions.

		NM	E	VG
Common Player:		2,500	1,500	900.00
(1)	Chief Bender (Brooklyn Nat'l.)	6,000	2,700	1,500
(2)	Bob Bescher (St. Louis Nat'l.)	2,500	1,500	900.00
(3)	Rube Bressler (Phila. Am.)	2,500	1,500	900.00
(4)	Donie Bush (Detroit American)	2,500	1,500	900.00
(5)	Hal Chase (Portrait, Cincinnati Nat'l.)	3,900	1,750	950.00
(6)	Bill Donovan ((N.Y. Amer.))	2,500	1,500	900.00
(7)	Larry Doyle (N.Y. Nat'l)	2,500	1,500	900.00
(8)	Happy Felsch (Chicago Am.)(Picture actually Ray Demmitt.))	7,500	3,375	1,875
(9)	George Gibson (Front View)	2,500	1,500	900.00
(11)	Roy Hartzell	2,500	1,500	900.00
(15)	Nap Lajoie (Phila. Americans)	6,000	2,700	1,500
(16)	Hans Lobert (New York Nat'l)	2,500	1,500	900.00
(17)	William Louden (Cincinnati Nat'l) (Picture is Otto Knabe.)	2,500	1,500	900.00
(20)	Rube Marquard (Brooklyn Nat'l)	6,000	2,700	1,500
(21)	Christy Matthewson (Mathewson)	15,000	8,000	5,000
(22)	Billy Meyer (Phila. Am.) (Picture is Fred Jacklitsch.))	2,500	1,500	900.00
(24)	Ray Morgan (Washington Am.)(Picture is Mike Doolan.))	2,500	1,500	900.00
(26)	Eddie Plank (St. Louis Am.)	12,000	6,000	3,500
(28)	Tris Speaker (Cleveland Am.)	8,000	4,000	2,000
(30)	Joe Tinker (Portrait, Mgr. Chicago Am.)	6,000	2,700	1,500
(33)	Honus Wagner (Batting)	45,000	22,000	13,500
(35)	Buck Weaver (Batting, picture is Joe Tinker.)	8,500	4,250	2,550

1920-21 Mother's Bread

Essentially a version of the W514 strip cards with an advertisement on the back, the Mother's Bread cards are much scarcer than the blank-backs with which they share a checklist. The cards are 1-1/2" x 2-1/2" with color drawings of the players on front, along with name, position, team, league and card number.

(See 1920-21 W514 for checklist; cards valued at 2.5X-3X W514 version.)
(Premium: 5-7X.)

1955 Motorola Bob Feller Premium Photo

Dating of this promotional photo is approximate, based on the uniform details. The 8" x 10" glossy black-and-white photo features a facsimile autograph. Feller is described on the picture as "CONSULTANT ON YOUTH ACTIVITIES" for Motorola, Inc. The picture is blank-backed and its method of distribution is unknown.

	NM	E	VG
Bob Feller	60.00	30.00	18.00

1976 Motorola

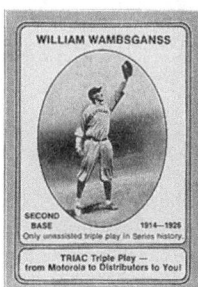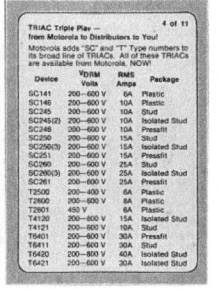

This set of (mostly) Hall of Famers was issued in conjunction with the annual convention of Motorola electronics dealers. Cards were issued singly in a wax wrapper with a piece of bubblegum. Sepia player photos are featured in an oval at center. Player identification and a career highlight are in the white frame around the photo. A sales message appears in a white box at bottom. Overall borders are rust colored. Backs have information about various Motorola products.

		NM	E	VG
Complete Set (11):		25.00	12.50	7.50
Common Player:		2.50	1.25	.70
1	Honus Wagner	4.00	2.00	1.25
2	Nap Lajoie	2.50	1.25	.70
3	Ty Cobb	7.50	3.75	2.25
4	William Wambsganss	2.50	1.25	.70
5	Three Finger Brown	2.50	1.25	.70
6	Ray Schalk	2.50	1.25	.70
7	Frank Frisch	2.50	1.25	.70
8	Pud Galvin	2.50	1.25	.70
9	Babe Ruth	15.00	7.50	4.50
10	Grover Cleveland Alexander	3.00	1.50	.90
11	Frank L. Chance	2.50	1.25	.70

1943 M.P. & Co. (R302-1)

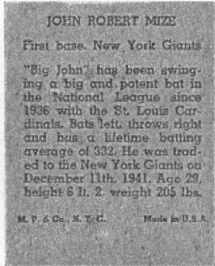

One of the few baseball card sets issued during World War II, this set of unnumbered cards, measuring approximately 2-5/8" x 2-1/4" was produced in two major types and at least five subtypes. The cards feature crude color drawings that have little resemblance to the player named. They were originally produced in strips and sold inexpensively in candy stores. The backs contain brief player write-ups. One major type has the player's full name, team and position on back. The second type has only the player's first and last name and position on back; no team. Variations in ink color and wording

of the biographies on back are also seen. M.P. & Co. stands for Michael Pressner and Co., a New York City novelty and carnival supply firm.

		NM	E	VG
Complete Set (24):		1,750	625.00	275.00
Common Player:		40.00	15.00	5.00
(1)	Ernie Bonham	40.00	15.00	5.00
(2)	Lou Boudreau	60.00	20.00	10.00
(3)	Dolph Camilli	40.00	15.00	5.00
(4)	Mort Cooper	40.00	15.00	5.00
(5)	Walker Cooper	40.00	15.00	5.00
(6)	Joe Cronin	60.00	20.00	10.00
(7)	Hank Danning	40.00	15.00	5.00
(8)	Bill Dickey	75.00	25.00	10.00
(9)	Joe DiMaggio	300.00	100.00	45.00
(10)	Bobby Feller	100.00	35.00	15.00
(11)	Jimmy Foxx	75.00	25.00	10.00
(12)	Hank Greenberg	100.00	35.00	15.00
(13)	Stan Hack	40.00	15.00	5.00
(14)	Tom Henrich	40.00	15.00	5.00
(15)	Carl Hubbell	60.00	20.00	10.00
(16)	Joe Medwick	60.00	20.00	10.00
(17)	John Mize	60.00	20.00	10.00
(18)	Lou Novikoff	40.00	15.00	5.00
(19)	Mel Ott	60.00	20.00	10.00
(20)	Pee Wee Reese	75.00	25.00	10.00
(21)	Pete Reiser	40.00	15.00	5.00
(22)	Charlie Ruffing	60.00	20.00	10.00
(23)	Johnny VanderMeer	40.00	15.00	5.00
(24)	Ted Williams	250.00	85.00	35.00

1948-49 M.P. & Co. Photoprints

One of several 1930s-1940s kits for do-it-yourself production of photos, this issue was produced in New York City by the novelty firm M.P. & Co. A complete outfit consists of a film negative and a piece of light-sensitive paper for producing the photo. The negative and resulting print measure about 2" x 2-1/4". The issue includes 13 subjects, mostly non-sport, but includes Babe Ruth.

	NM	E	VG
Babe Ruth (Negative)	300.00	150.00	90.00
Babe Ruth (Print)	75.00	37.50	22.00

1949 M.P. & Co. (R302-2)

This set appears to be a re-issue of M.P. & Co.'s 1943 cards with several different players (although reusing the same pictures as the '43s). The cards, which measure about 2-11/16" x 2-1/4", feature crude drawings of generic baseball players which have little resemblance to the player named. Most backs include card number and player information. The numbering sequence begins with card 100. Numbers 104, 118, and 120 are unknown, while three of the cards are unnumbered. The set is assigned the American Card Catalog number R302-2.

		NM	E	VG
Complete Set (25):		1,325	425.00	200.00
Common Player:		35.00	12.00	5.00
100	Lou Boudreau	45.00	16.00	7.00
101	Ted Williams	190.00	65.00	27.00
102	Buddy Kerr	35.00	12.00	5.00
103	Bobby Feller	60.00	20.00	7.00
104	Unknown			

105	Joe DiMaggio	250.00	90.00	38.00
106	Pee Wee Reese	60.00	20.00	7.00
107	Ferris Fain	35.00	12.00	5.00
108	Andy Pafko	35.00	12.00	5.00
109	Del Ennis	35.00	12.00	5.00
110	Ralph Kiner	45.00	15.00	7.00
111	Nippy Jones	35.00	12.00	5.00
112	Del Rice	35.00	12.00	5.00
113	Hank Sauer	35.00	12.00	5.00
114	Gil Coan	35.00	12.00	5.00
115	Eddie Joost	35.00	12.00	5.00
116	Alvin Dark	35.00	12.00	5.00
117	Larry Berra	60.00	20.00	8.00
118	Unknown			
119	Bob Lemon	45.00	16.00	7.00
120	Unknown			
121	Johnny Pesky	35.00	12.00	5.00
122	Johnny Sain	35.00	12.00	5.00
123	Hoot Evers	35.00	12.00	5.00
124	Larry Doby	45.00	16.00	7.00
----	Jimmy Foxx	75.00	27.00	12.00
----	Tom Henrich	35.00	12.00	5.00
----	Al Kozar	35.00	12.00	5.00

1977 Mrs. Carter's Bread Sports Illustrated Covers

This two-sport set was issued by Mrs. Carter's Bread. Fronts of the 3-1/2" x 4-3/4" cards reproduce SI covers in full color, surrounded by a white border. Backs have a special offer for SI subscriptions, and are printed in black and blue on white. Despite the higher card numbers, it does not appear any more than five were ever issued.

		NM	E	VG
Complete Set (5):		35.00	17.50	10.00
Common Card:		3.00	1.50	.90
(1)	George Brett	25.00	12.50	7.50
(2)	George Foster	4.00	2.00	1.25
(3)	Bump Wills	4.00	2.00	1.25
(4)	Oakland Wins a Big One (Football)	4.00	2.00	1.25
(5)	Michigan is No. 1 (Football)	6.00	3.00	1.75

1976 Mr. Softee Iron-Ons

Anecdotal evidence connects these iron-on transfers with the Mr. Softee dairy chain. About 4-1/2" x 6" inches, the color transfers have a player portrait on a baseball background, very similar in format to the 1978 Royal Crown Cola iron-ons. Like the RC pieces, the pictures have team logos removed from caps. The Mr. Softees include the team nickname beneath the player picture, along with a Players Association logo and an undated Quaker copyright line. The extent of the checklist is unknown.

		NM	E	VG
Common Player:		4.00	2.00	1.25
(1)	George Brett	10.00	5.00	3.00
(2)	Jim Hunter	6.00	3.00	1.75
(3)	Randy Jones	4.00	2.00	1.25
(4)	Dave Kingman	5.00	2.50	1.50
(5)	Jerry Koosman	4.00	2.00	1.25
(6)	Fred Lynn	5.00	2.50	1.50
(7)	Joe Morgan	6.00	3.00	1.75
(8)	Thurman Munson	10.00	5.00	3.00

(9)	Amos Otis	4.00	2.00	1.25
(10)	Bill Russell	4.00	2.00	1.25
(11)	Nolan Ryan	12.00	6.00	3.60
(12)	Mike Schmidt	10.00	5.00	3.00
(13)	Tom Seaver	10.00	5.00	3.00

1921 Mrs. Sherlock's Bread Pins

The date of issue for these pins is uncertain. The 7/8" diameter pins feature black-and-white player photos with a red border. The player's last name and team are printed beneath the photo; above is "Mrs. Sherlock's Home Made Bread." The set is one of several sponsored by the Toledo bakery. The Babe Ruth pin was reproduced circa 1999 in 1-3/4" size; it has no collectible value.

		NM	E	VG
Complete Set (10):		4,250	2,125	1,275
Common Player:		100.00	50.00	30.00
(1)	Grover Alexander	350.00	175.00	100.00
(2)	Ty Cobb	1,400	700.00	425.00
(3)	Rogers Hornsby	375.00	185.00	110.00
(4)	Walter Johnson	375.00	185.00	110.00
(5)	Rabbit Maranville	300.00	150.00	90.00
(6)	Pat Moran	100.00	50.00	30.00
(7)	"Babe" Ruth	1,900	950.00	575.00
(8)	George Sisler	300.00	150.00	90.00
(9)	Tris Speaker	375.00	185.00	110.00
(10)	Honus Wagner	700.00	350.00	210.00

1975-96 MSA

(See listings under Michael Schechter Associates.)

N

1969 Nabisco Team Flakes

Frank Robinson—OF
Baltimore Orioles

This set of cards is seen in two different sizes: 1-15/16" x 3" and 1-3/4" x 2-15/16". This is explained by the varying widths of the card borders on the backs of Nabisco cereal packages. Cards are action color photos bordered in yellow. Twenty-four of the top players in the game are included in the set, which was issued in three series of eight cards each. No team insignias are visible on any of the cards. Packages described the cards as "Mini Posters."

		NM	E	VG
Complete Set (24):		1,200	600.00	1375.00
Common Player:		20.00	10.00	6.00
(1)	Hank Aaron	120.00	60.00	40.00
(2)	Richie Allen	35.00	20.00	12.00
(3)	Lou Brock	50.00	25.00	15.00
(4)	Paul Casanova	20.00	10.00	6.00
(5)	Roberto Clemente	250.00	125.00	75.00

(6)	Al Ferrara	20.00	10.00	6.00
(7)	Bill Freehan	20.00	10.00	6.00
(8)	Jim Fregosi	20.00	10.00	6.00
(9)	Bob Gibson	50.00	25.00	15.00
(10)	Tony Horton	20.00	10.00	6.00
(11)	Tommy John	20.00	10.00	6.00
(12)	Al Kaline	65.00	35.00	20.00
(13)	Jim Lonborg	20.00	10.00	6.00
(14)	Juan Marichal	50.00	25.00	15.00
(15)	Willie Mays	120.00	60.00	40.00
(16)	Rick Monday	20.00	10.00	6.00
(17)	Tony Oliva	20.00	10.00	6.00
(18)	Brooks Robinson	65.00	35.00	20.00
(19)	Frank Robinson	65.00	35.00	20.00
(20)	Pete Rose	90.00	45.00	25.00
(21)	Ron Santo	35.00	20.00	12.00
(22)	Tom Seaver	65.00	35.00	20.00
(23)	Rusty Staub	20.00	10.00	6.00
(24)	Mel Stottlemyre	20.00	10.00	6.00

1923-1924 Nacionales Cigarros

The baseball players in this mid-20s Cuban issue are part of a larger set which included boxers, actresses, actors, nudes, soccer players and others. The cards measure about 1-5/8" x 2-1/4" and have a distinctive wide black border on front. Backs identify the issue. An album was issued to house the set. The cards are printed on thin cardboard with a glossy finish.

		NM	E	VG
Complete Baseball Set (40):		60,000	24,000	12,000
Common Player:		500.00	200.00	100.00
21	Rafael Almeida	1,500	600.00	300.00
22	Isidro Fabre	1,125	450.00	225.00
23	Eugenio Morin	500.00	200.00	100.00
24	Oscar Rodriguez	500.00	200.00	100.00
25	Joseito Rodriguez	500.00	200.00	100.00
26	Papo Gonzalez	500.00	200.00	100.00
27	Gutierrez	500.00	200.00	100.00
28	Valentin Dreke (Photo actually Lucas Boada.)	1,125	450.00	225.00
29	Jose Maria Fernandez	750.00	300.00	150.00
30	(Cheo) Ramos	500.00	200.00	100.00
31	Paito (Ramon Herrera)	500.00	200.00	100.00
32	Bernardo Baro	1,125	450.00	225.00
33	Manuel Cueto	750.00	300.00	150.00
34	(Oscar) Tuero	500.00	200.00	100.00
35	Kakin Gonzalez	500.00	200.00	100.00
36	Armando Marsans	1,500	600.00	300.00
37	Andy Cooper	9,000	3,600	1,800
38	Dolf Luque	2,500	1,000	500.00
39	Marcelino Guerra	500.00	200.00	100.00
40	Manzanillo (Tatic Campos)	500.00	200.00	100.00
41	Oscar Levis	750.00	300.00	150.00
42	Eufemio Abreu	500.00	200.00	100.00
43	Cristobal Torriente	12,000	4,800	2,400
44	Juanelo Mirabal	750.00	300.00	150.00
45	Merito Acosta	500.00	200.00	100.00
46	Jose Acostica (Acosta)	500.00	200.00	100.00
47	Rogelio Crespo	500.00	200.00	100.00
48	(Jacinto) Calvo	750.00	300.00	150.00
49	(Emilio) Palmero	750.00	300.00	150.00
50	Jose Mendez	9,000	3,600	1,800
51	Alejandro Oms	3,750	1,500	750.00
52	Pedro Dibut	750.00	300.00	150.00
53	Strike (Valentin "Sirique" Gonzalez)	500.00	200.00	100.00
54	Magrinat (Hector Magrinut)	500.00	200.00	100.00
55	Raphael Quintana	500.00	200.00	100.00
56	Bienvenido Jimenez	750.00	300.00	150.00
57	Bartolo Portuando (Portuondo)	1,500	600.00	300.00
58	(Pelayo) Chacon	1,500	600.00	300.00
59	Riant (Red Ryan)	1,500	600.00	300.00
60	Perico El Mano (Mascot)	500.00	200.00	100.00

1909 Nadja Caramels (E92)

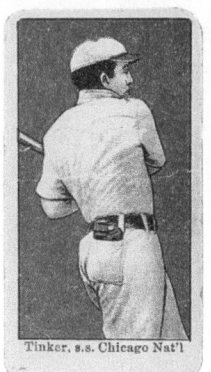 

Tinker, s.s. Chicago Nat'l

One of several 1909-10 issues produced for Nadja Caramels, this set can be distinguished by the players in the checklist (alphabetized here) and the type beneath the color player lithograph. In this set, the player's last name is in upper- and lower-case letters, and his position is given, along with the team. Backs of these 1-1/2" x 2-3/4" cards are identical to later Nadja issues, featuring an ad for the candy brand. Cataloged (along with the cards of Croft's Candy/Cocoa and Dockman Gum) as E92 in the "American Card Catalog," the Nadja set checklist differs from those issues in that it is larger and contains a group of St. Louis players not found in the other sets. Nadja was a brand name of the Blake-Wenneker Candy Co. of St. Louis.

		NM	E	VG
Complete Set (62):		44,000	21,500	13,200
Common Player:		480.00	240.00	145.00
(1)	Bill Bailey	480.00	240.00	145.00
(2)	Jack Barry	480.00	240.00	145.00
(3)	Harry Bemis	480.00	240.00	145.00
(4)	Chief Bender (Striped cap.)	950.00	480.00	275.00
(5)	Chief Bender (White cap.)	950.00	480.00	275.00
(6)	Bill Bergen	480.00	240.00	145.00
(7)	Bob Bescher	480.00	240.00	145.00
(8)	Roger Bresnahan	950.00	480.00	275.00
(9)	Al Bridwell	480.00	240.00	145.00
(10)	Doc Casey	480.00	240.00	145.00
(11)	Frank Chance	950.00	480.00	275.00
(12)	Hal Chase	725.00	360.00	220.00
(13)	Ty Cobb	6,800	3,360	2,000
(14)	Eddie Collins	950.00	480.00	275.00
(15)	Sam Crawford	950.00	480.00	275.00
(16)	Harry Davis	480.00	240.00	145.00
(17)	Art Devlin	480.00	240.00	145.00
(18)	Bill Donovan	480.00	240.00	145.00
(19)	Red Dooin	480.00	240.00	145.00
(20)	Mickey Doolan	480.00	240.00	145.00
(21)	Patsy Dougherty	480.00	240.00	145.00
(22)	Larry Doyle (Throwing)	480.00	240.00	145.00
(23)	Larry Doyle (With bat.)	480.00	240.00	145.00
(24)	Rube Ellis	480.00	240.00	145.00
(25)	Johnny Evers	950.00	480.00	275.00
(26)	George Gibson	480.00	240.00	145.00
(27)	Topsy Hartsel	480.00	240.00	145.00
(28)	Roy Hartzell (Batting)	480.00	240.00	145.00
(29)	Roy Hartzell (Fielding)	480.00	240.00	145.00
(30)	Harry Howell (Ready to pitch.)	480.00	240.00	145.00
(31)	Harry Howell (Follow-through.)	480.00	240.00	145.00
(32)	Fred Jacklitsch	480.00	240.00	145.00
(33)	Hugh Jennings	950.00	480.00	275.00
(34)	Red Kleinow	480.00	240.00	145.00
(35)	Otto Knabe	480.00	240.00	145.00
(36)	Jack Knight	480.00	240.00	145.00
(37)	Nap Lajoie	950.00	480.00	275.00
(38)	Hans Lobert	480.00	240.00	145.00
(39)	Sherry Magee	480.00	240.00	145.00
(40)	Christy Matthewson (Mathewson)	4,400	2,175	1,325
(41)	John McGraw	950.00	480.00	275.00
(42)	Larry McLean	480.00	240.00	145.00
(43)	Dots Miller (Batting)	480.00	240.00	145.00
(44)	Dots Miller (Fielding)	480.00	240.00	145.00
(45)	Danny Murphy	480.00	240.00	145.00
(46)	Rebel Oakes	480.00	240.00	145.00
(47)	Bill O'Hara	480.00	240.00	145.00
(48)	Eddie Phelps	480.00	240.00	145.00
(49)	Germany Schaefer	480.00	240.00	145.00
(50)	Admiral Schlei	480.00	240.00	145.00
(51)	Boss Schmidt	480.00	240.00	145.00
(52)	Johnny Seigle (Siegle)	480.00	240.00	145.00
(53)	Dave Shean	480.00	240.00	145.00
(54)	Boss Smith (Schmidt)	480.00	240.00	145.00
(55)	George Stone (Blue background.)	480.00	240.00	145.00
(56)	George Stone (Green background.)	480.00	240.00	145.00
(57)	Joe Tinker	950.00	480.00	275.00
(58)	Honus Wagner (Batting)	5,600	2,800	1,680
(59)	Honus Wagner (Throwing)	6,000	2,960	1,760
(60)	Bobby Wallace	950.00	480.00	275.00
(61)	Cy Young	2,400	1,200	720.00
(62)	Heinie Zimmerman	480.00	240.00	145.00

1910 Nadja Caramels (E104-3)

 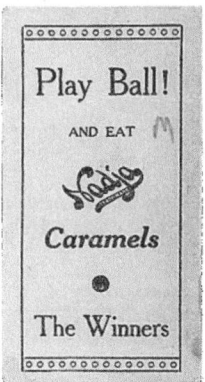

MOORE, Philadelphia

The cards in this issue can each be found with or without a Nadja ad on back; the latter being somewhat scarcer and carrying a premium over the values shown. These 1-1/2" x 2-3/4" cards can be distinguished from the 1909 issue by the line of type beneath the player portrait. On the 1910 cards, the player's last name is in all blue capital letters and there is no position designation given. This checklist is likely incomplete.

		NM	E	VG
Common Player:		2,750	1,350	825.00
Ad Back: 1.25X				
(1)	Bill Abstein	2,750	1,350	825.00
(2)	Red Ames	2,750	1,350	825.00
(3)	Johnny Bates	2,750	1,350	825.00
(4)	Kitty Bransfield	2,750	1,350	825.00
(5)	Al Bridwell	2,750	1,350	825.00
(6)	Hal Chase	5,750	2,875	1,725
(7)	Doc Crandall	2,750	1,350	825.00
(8)	Sam Crawford	7,750	3,875	2,325
(9)	Jim Delehanty (Delahanty)	2,750	1,350	825.00
(10)	Art Devlin	2,750	1,350	825.00
(11)	Red Dooin	2,750	1,350	825.00
(12)	Mickey Doolan	2,750	1,350	825.00
(13)	Larry Doyle	2,750	1,350	825.00
(14)	Eddie Grant	2,750	1,350	825.00
(15)	Fred Jacklitsch	2,750	1,350	825.00
(16)	Hugh Jennings	7,750	3,875	2,325
(17)	Davy Jones	2,750	1,350	825.00
(18)	Tom Jones	2,750	1,350	825.00
(19)	Otto Knabe	2,750	1,350	825.00
(20)	Sherry Magee	2,750	1,350	825.00
(21)	John McGraw	7,750	3,875	2,325
(22)	Matty McIntyre	2,750	1,350	825.00
(23)	Earl Moore	2,750	1,350	825.00
(24)	Pat Moren (Moran)	2,750	1,350	825.00
(25)	George Moriarity	2,750	1,350	825.00
(26)	George Mullin	2,750	1,350	825.00
(27)	Red Murray	2,750	1,350	825.00
(28)	Simon Nicholls	2,750	1,350	825.00
(29)	Charley O'Leary	2,750	1,350	825.00
(30)	Admiral Schlei	2,750	1,350	825.00
(31)	Boss Schmidt	2,750	1,350	825.00
(32)	Cy Seymore (Seymour)	2,750	1,350	825.00
(33)	Tully Sparks	2,750	1,350	825.00
(34)	Ed Summers	2,750	1,350	825.00
(35)	Ed Willetts (Willett)	2,750	1,350	825.00
(36)	Vic Willis	7,750	3,875	2,325
(37)	Hooks Wiltse	2,750	1,350	825.00

1910 Nadja Caramels Philadelphia Athletics (E104-1)

The 18 Philadelphia Athletics players in this set, can each be found in three different variations. Each of the approximately 1-1/2" x 2-3/4" cards can be found with a plain portrait lithograph on front, and either a blank back or a back containing a Nadja ad. Each player can also be found with a black overprint on front, comprised of a white elephant figure on the uniform and the notation "World's Champions 1910" above. The overprinted cards are known only with blank backs, and are somewhat scarcer than the plain cards

of either type. Nadja-back cards should be valued about the same as the overprinted type.

		NM	E	VG
Complete Set, No O/P, Blank Back (18):		36,000	18,000	10,000
Complete Set, With O/P or Ad Back:		45,000	22,500	13,500
Common Player:		1,800	900.00	550.00
(1a)	Home Run Baker	3,200	1,600	1,000
(1b)	Home Run Baker ("World's Champions")	6,500	3,250	2,000
(2a)	Jack Barry	1,800	900.00	550.00
(2b)	Jack Barry ("World's Champions")	6,500	3,250	2,000
(3a)	Chief Bender	3,200	1,600	1,000
(3b)	Chief Bender ("World's Champions")	6,500	3,250	2,000
(4a)	Eddie Collins	3,200	1,600	1,000
(4b)	Eddie Collins ("World's Champions")	6,500	3,250	2,000
(5a)	Harry Davis	1,800	900.00	550.00
(5b)	Harry Davis ("World's Champions")	6,500	3,250	2,000
(6a)	Jimmy Dygert ((1910 above head))	1,800	900.00	550.00
(6b-1)	Jimmy Dygert ("World's Champions")(1910 above head))	6,500	3,250	2,000
(6b-2)	Jimmy Dygert ((1910 at right))	6,500	3,250	2,000
(7a)	Topsy Hartsel	1,800	900.00	550.00
(7b)	Topsy Hartsel ("World's Champions")	6,500	3,2500	2,000
(8a)	Harry Krause	1,800	900.00	550.00
(8b)	Harry Krause ("World's Champions")	6,500	3,250	2,000
(9a)	Jack Lapp	1,800	900.00	550.00
(9b)	Jack Lapp ("World's Champions")	6,500	3,250	2,000
(10a)	Paddy Livingstone (Livingston)	1,800	900.00	550.00
(10b)	Paddy Livingstone (Livingston) ("World's Champions")	6,500	3,250	2,000
(11a)	Bris Lord	1,800	900.00	550.00
(11b)	Bris Lord ("World's Champions")	6,500	3,250	2,000
(12a)	Connie Mack	10,000	5,000	3,000
(12b)	Connie Mack ("World's Champions")	22,000	11,000	7,000
(13a)	Cy Morgan	1,800	900.00	550.00
(13b)	Cy Morgan ("World's Champions")	6,500	3,250	2,000
(14a)	Danny Murphy	1,800	900.00	550.00
(14b)	Danny Murphy ("World's Champions")	6,500	3,250	2,000
(15a)	Rube Oldring	1,800	900.00	550.00
(15b)	Rube Oldring ("World's Champions")	6,500	3,250	2,000
(16a)	Eddie Plank	16,000	8,000	4,750
(16b)	Eddie Plank ("World's Champions")	27,500	13,500	8,250
(17a)	Amos Strunk	1,800	900.00	550.00
(17b)	Amos Strunk ("World's Champions")	6,500	3,250	2,000
(18a)	Ira Thomas	2,350	1,175	725.00
(18b-1)	Ira Thomas ("World's Champions"(1910 above head))	6,500	3,250	2,000
(18b-2)	Ira Thomas ((1910 at right))	6,500	3,250	2,000

1910 Nadja Caramels Pittsburgh Pirates (E104-2)

Similar to the contemporary American Caramel issue, this set of 1-1/2" x 2-3/4" cards features portrait color lithographs of the 1909 World's Champion Pittsburgh (spelled "Pittsburg") Pirates. Each card was issued with both blank back and with a back bearing a Nadja ad. The Nadja-backed cards are scarcer but command little premium.

WAGNER, PITTSBURG

	NM	E	VG
Complete Set (11):	30,000	15,000	9,000
Common Player:	1,325	665.00	400.00
Ad Back: 1.25X			

		NM	E	VG
(1)	Babe Adams	1,325	665.00	400.00
(2)	Fred Clarke	3,000	1,500	900.00
(3)	George Gibson	1,325	665.00	400.00
(4)	Ham Hyatt	1,325	665.00	400.00
(5)	Tommy Leach	1,325	665.00	400.00
(6)	Sam Leever	1,325	665.00	400.00
(7)	Nick Maddox	1,180	665.00	400.00
(8)	Dots Miller	1,325	665.00	400.00
(9)	Deacon Phillippe	1,325	665.00	400.00
(10)	Honus Wagner	20,000	10,000	6,000
(11)	Owen Wilson	1,325	665.00	400.00

1912 Napoleon Little Cigars

While this cigarette brand advertising on the backs of T207 cards is less commonly encountered than Recruit, collectors do not attach a commensurate premium to them, largely because each of the players can be found with more common back ads.

(See T207 for checklist and base card values.)

1963 Nassau County Boy Scouts

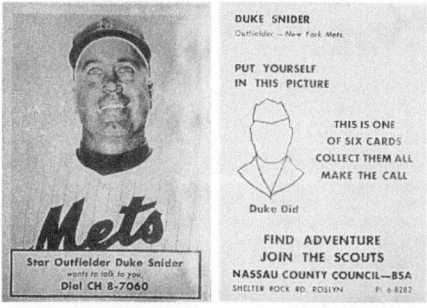

According to the text on the back, six cards were issued in this set. The other subjects are unknown, and may not feature any additional baseball players. The standard-size cards are printed in blue-and-white, both front and back, including a duo-tone photo of Snider in his only season with the Mets.

		NM	E	VG
(1)	Duke Snider	150.00	75.00	45.00

1974 Nassau Tuberculosis and Respiratory Disease Assn.

The date attributed to these cards is arbitrary. The black-and-white 2-1/2" x 3-1/2" cards have a photo of the Yankees pitcher on front and a career summary on back, along with an anti-smoking message.

	NM	E	VG
Whitey Ford (Facing his right.)	45.00	22.50	13.50
Whitey Ford (Follow-through.)	45.00	22.50	13.50

1921-23 National Caramel (E220)

 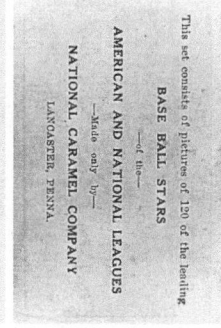

Issued circa 1921 to 1923, this 120-card set is sometimes confused with contemporary American Caramel issues, but is easy to identify because of the words "Made only by National Caramel Company" on the back. With due consideration to normal cutting variances on cards of this era and type, E220s measure about 2" x 3-1/4" and feature black-and-white photos with the player's name, position and team at the bottom. In addition to the line indicating the manufacturer, the backs read "This set consists of pictures of 120 of the leading Base Ball Stars of the American and National Leagues," There are 115 different players included in the set, with five players shown on two cards each. About half of the photos in the set are identical to those used in various American Caramel sets, leading to some confusion regarding the three sets.

		NM	E	VG
Complete Set (120):		27,500	13,500	8,250
Common Player:		100.00	50.00	30.00
(1)	Charles "Babe" Adams	400.00	200.00	120.00
(2)	G.C. Alexander	1,600	800.00	475.00
(3)	James Austin	400.00	200.00	120.00
(4)	Jim Bagbyk Sr. (Bagby)	400.00	200.00	120.00
(5)	Franklin "Home Run" Baker	1,200	600.00	350.00
(6)	Dave Bancroft	1,200	600.00	350.00
(7)	Turner Barber	400.00	200.00	120.00
(8)	George Burns (Cincinnati)	400.00	200.00	120.00
(9)	George Burns (Cleveland)	400.00	200.00	120.00
(10)	Joe Bush	400.00	200.00	120.00
(11)	Leon Cadore	400.00	200.00	120.00
(12)	Max Carey	1,200	600.00	350.00
(13)	Ty Cobb	7,000	3,500	2,100
(14)	Eddie Collins	1,200	600.00	350.00
(15)	John Collins	400.00	200.00	120.00
(16)	Wilbur Cooper	400.00	200.00	120.00
(17)	S. Coveleskie (Coveleski)	1,200	600.00	350.00
(18)	Walton Cruise	400.00	200.00	120.00
(19)	Wm. Cunningham	400.00	200.00	120.00
(20)	George Cutshaw	400.00	200.00	120.00
(21)	Jake Daubert	400.00	200.00	120.00
(22)	Chas. A. Deal	400.00	200.00	120.00
(23)	Bill Doak	400.00	200.00	120.00
(24)	Joe Dugan	400.00	200.00	120.00
(25)	Jimmy Dykes (Batting)	400.00	200.00	120.00
(26)	Jimmy Dykes (Fielding)	400.00	200.00	120.00
(27)	"Red" Faber	1,200	600.00	350.00
(28)	"Chick" Fewster	400.00	200.00	120.00
(29)	Wilson Fewster	400.00	200.00	120.00
(30)	Ira Flagstead	400.00	200.00	120.00
(31)	Arthur Fletcher	400.00	200.00	120.00
(32)	Frank Frisch	1,200	600.00	350.00
(33)	Larry Gardner	400.00	200.00	120.00
(34)	Walter Gerber	400.00	200.00	120.00
(35)	Charles Glazner	400.00	200.00	120.00
(36)	Hank Gowdy	400.00	200.00	120.00
(37)	J.C. Graney (Should be J.G.)	400.00	200.00	120.00
(38)	Tommy Griffith	400.00	200.00	120.00
(39)	Charles Grimm	400.00	200.00	120.00
(40)	Heinie Groh	400.00	200.00	120.00
(41)	Byron Harris	400.00	200.00	120.00

		NM	E	VG
(42)	Sam Harris (Bucky)	1,200	600.00	350.00
(43)	Harry Heilman (Heilmann)	1,200	600.00	350.00
(44)	Claude Hendrix	400.00	200.00	120.00
(45)	Walter Henline	400.00	200.00	120.00
(46)	Chas. Hollocher	400.00	200.00	120.00
(47)	Harry Hooper	1,200	600.00	350.00
(48)	Rogers Hornsby	1,600	800.00	475.00
(49)	Waite Hoyt	1,200	600.00	350.00
(50)	Wilbert Hubbell	400.00	200.00	120.00
(51)	Wm. Jacobson	400.00	200.00	120.00
(52)	Walter Johnson	3,400	1,700	1,00.00
(53)	Jimmy Johnston	400.00	200.00	120.00
(54)	Joe Judge	400.00	200.00	120.00
(55)	Geo. "Bingo" Kelly	1,2000.00	600.00	350.00
(56)	Dick Kerr	400.00	200.00	120.00
(57)	Pete Kilduff (Bending)	400.00	200.00	120.00
(58)	Pete Kilduff (Leaping)	400.00	200.00	120.00
(59)	Larry Kopf	400.00	200.00	120.00
(60)	H.B. Leonard	400.00	200.00	120.00
(61)	Harry Liebold (Leibold)	400.00	200.00	120.00
(62)	Walter "Buster" Mails ("Duster")	400.00	200.00	120.00
(63)	Walter "Rabbit" Maranville	1,200	600.00	350.00
(64)	Carl Mays	400.00	200.00	120.00
(65)	Lee Meadows	400.00	200.00	120.00
(66)	Bob Meusel	400.00	200.00	120.00
(67)	Emil Meusel	400.00	200.00	120.00
(68)	J.C. Milan	400.00	200.00	120.00
(69)	Earl Neale	500.00	250.00	150.00
(70)	Robert Nehf (Arthur)	400.00	200.00	120.00
(71)	Bernie Neis	400.00	200.00	120.00
(72)	Joe Oeschger	400.00	200.00	120.00
(73)	Robert O'Farrell	400.00	200.00	120.00
(74)	Ivan Olson	400.00	200.00	120.00
(75)	Steve O'Neill	400.00	200.00	120.00
(76)	Geo. Paskert	400.00	200.00	120.00
(77)	Roger Peckinpaugh	400.00	200.00	120.00
(78)	Herb Pennock	1,200	600.00	350.00
(79)	Ralph "Cy" Perkins	400.00	200.00	120.00
(80)	Scott Perry (Photo actually Ed Rommel.)	400.00	200.00	120.00
(81)	Jeff Pfeffer	400.00	200.00	120.00
(82)	V.J. Picinich	400.00	200.00	120.00
(83)	Walter Pipp	450.00	230.00	140.00
(84)	Derrill Pratt	400.00	200.00	120.00
(85)	Goldie Rapp	400.00	200.00	120.00
(86)	Edgar Rice	1,200	600.00	350.00
(87)	Jimmy Ring	400.00	200.00	120.00
(88)	Eddie Rousch (Roush)	1,200	600.00	350.00
(89)	Babe Ruth	20,000	10,000	6,000
(90)	Raymond Schmandt	400.00	200.00	120.00
(91)	Everett Scott	400.00	200.00	120.00
(92)	Joe Sewell	1,200	600.00	350.00
(93)	Wally Shang (Schang)	400.00	200.00	120.00
(94)	Maurice Shannon	400.00	200.00	120.00
(95)	Bob Shawkey	400.00	200.00	120.00
(96)	Urban Shocker	400.00	200.00	120.00
(97)	George Sisler	1,200	600.00	350.00
(98)	Earl Smith	400.00	200.00	120.00
(99)	John Smith	400.00	200.00	120.00
(100)	Sherrod Smith	400.00	200.00	120.00
(101)	Frank Snyder (Crouching)	400.00	200.00	120.00
(102)	Frank Snyder (Standing)	400.00	200.00	120.00
(103)	Tris Speaker	1,600	800.00	480.00
(104)	Vernon Spencer	400.00	200.00	120.00
(105)	Chas. "Casey" Stengle (Stengel)	1,400	700.00	425.00
(106)	Milton Stock (Batting)	400.00	200.00	120.00
(107)	Milton Stock (Fielding)	400.00	200.00	120.00
(108)	James Vaughn	400.00	200.00	120.00
(109)	Robert Veach	400.00	200.00	120.00
(110)	Wm. Wambsgauss (Wambsganss)	400.00	200.00	120.00
(111)	Aaron Ward	400.00	200.00	120.00
(112)	Zach Wheat	1,200	600.00	350.00
(113)	George Whitted (Batting)	400.00	200.00	120.00
(114)	George Whitted (Fielding)	400.00	200.00	120.00
(115)	Fred C. Williams	400.00	200.00	120.00
(116)	Arthur Wilson	400.00	200.00	120.00
(117)	Ivy Wingo	400.00	200.00	120.00
(118)	Lawton Witt	400.00	200.00	120.00
(119)	"Pep" Young (Photo actually Ralph Young.)	400.00	200.00	120.00
(120)	Ross Young (Youngs)	1,200	600.00	350.00

1936 National Chicle "Fine Pens" (R313)

Issued in 1936 by the National Chicle Co., this set consists of 120 cards, measuring 3-1/4" x 5-3/8". The black-and-white cards are blank-backed and unnumbered. Although issued by National Chicle, the name of the company does not appear on the cards. The set includes individual player portraits with facsimilie autographs, multi-player cards and action photos. The cards, known in the hobby as "Fine Pen" because of the thin style of writing used for the facsimilie autographs, were originally available as an in-store premium.

	NM	E	VG
Complete Set (120):	6,500	3,250	1,950
Common Player:	50.00	25.00	15.00
(1) Melo Almada	50.00	25.00	15.00
(2) Nick Altrock, Al Schacht	50.00	25.00	15.00
(3) Paul Andrews	50.00	25.00	15.00
(4) Elden Auker (Eldon)	50.00	25.00	15.00
(5) Earl Averill	125.00	65.00	30.00
(6) John Babich, James Bucher	50.00	25.00	15.00
(7) Jim Becher (Bucher)	50.00	25.00	15.00
(8) Moe Berg	250.00	125.00	75.00
(9) Walter Berger	50.00	25.00	15.00
(10) Charles Berry	50.00	25.00	15.00
(11) Ralph Birkhofer (Birkofer)	50.00	25.00	15.00
(12) Cy Blanton	50.00	25.00	15.00
(13) O. Bluege	50.00	25.00	15.00
(14) Cliff Bolton	50.00	25.00	15.00
(15) Zeke Bonura	50.00	25.00	15.00
(16) Stan Bordagaray, George Earnshaw	50.00	25.00	15.00
(17) Jim Bottomley, Charley Gelbert	65.00	33.00	20.00
(18) Thos. Bridges	50.00	25.00	15.00
(19) Sam Byrd	50.00	25.00	15.00
(20) Dolph Camilli	50.00	25.00	15.00
(21) Dolph Camilli, Billy Jurges	50.00	25.00	15.00
(22) Bruce Campbell	50.00	25.00	15.00
(23) Walter "Kit" Carson	50.00	25.00	15.00
(24) Ben Chapman	50.00	25.00	15.00
(25) Harlond Clift, Luke Sewell	50.00	25.00	15.00
(26) Mickey Cochrane, Jimmy Fox (Foxx), Al Simmons	125.00	65.00	30.00
(27) "Rip" Collins	50.00	25.00	15.00
(28) Joe Cronin	125.00	65.00	30.00
(29) Frank Crossetti (Crosetti)	50.00	25.00	15.00
(30) Frank Crosetti, Jimmy Dykes	50.00	25.00	15.00
(31) Kiki Cuyler, Gabby Hartnett	125.00	65.00	30.00
(32) Paul Derringer	50.00	25.00	15.00
(33) Bill Dickey, Hank Greenberg	125.00	65.00	30.00
(34) Bill Dietrich	50.00	25.00	15.00
(35) Joe DiMaggio, Hank Erickson	750.00	375.00	225.00
(36) Carl Doyle	50.00	25.00	15.00
(37) Charles Dressen, Bill Myers	50.00	25.00	15.00
(38) Jimmie Dykes	50.00	25.00	15.00
(39) Rick Ferrell, Wess Ferrell (Wes)	125.00	65.00	30.00
(40) Pete Fox	50.00	25.00	15.00
(41) Frankie Frisch	125.00	65.00	30.00
(42) Milton Galatzer	50.00	25.00	15.00
(43) Chas. Gehringer	125.00	65.00	30.00
(44) Charley Gelbert	50.00	25.00	15.00
(45) Joe Glenn	50.00	25.00	15.00
(46) Jose Gomez	50.00	25.00	15.00
(47) Lefty Gomez, Red Ruffing	125.00	65.00	30.00
(48) Vernon Gomez	125.00	65.00	30.00
(49) Leon Goslin	125.00	65.00	30.00
(50) Hank Gowdy	50.00	25.00	15.00
(51) "Hank" Greenberg	125.00	65.00	30.00
(52) "Lefty" Grove	125.00	65.00	30.00
(53) Stan Hack	50.00	25.00	15.00
(54) Odell Hale	50.00	25.00	15.00
(55) Wild Bill Hallahan	50.00	25.00	15.00
(56) Mel Harder	50.00	25.00	15.00
(57) Stanley Bucky Harriss (Harris)	125.00	65.00	30.00
(58) Gabby Hartnett, Rip Radcliff	50.00	25.00	15.00
(59) Gabby Hartnett, L. Waner	50.00	25.00	15.00
(60) Gabby Hartnett, Lon Warnecke (Warneke)	50.00	25.00	15.00
(61) Buddy Hassett	50.00	25.00	15.00
(62) Babe Herman	50.00	25.00	15.00
(63) Frank Higgins	50.00	25.00	15.00
(64) Oral C. Hildebrand	50.00	25.00	15.00
(65) Myril Hoag	50.00	25.00	15.00
(66) Rogers Hornsby	125.00	65.00	30.00
(67) Waite Hoyt	125.00	65.00	30.00
(68) Willis G. Hudlin	50.00	25.00	15.00
(69) "Woody" Jensen	50.00	25.00	15.00
(70) Woody Jenson (Jensen)	50.00	25.00	15.00
(71) William Knickerbocker	50.00	25.00	15.00
(72) Joseph Kuhel	50.00	25.00	15.00
(73) Cookie Lavagetto	50.00	25.00	15.00
(74) Thornton Lee	50.00	25.00	15.00
(75) Ernie Lombardi	125.00	65.00	30.00
(76) Red Lucas	50.00	25.00	15.00
(77) Connie Mack, John McGraw	125.00	65.00	30.00
(78) Pepper Martin	50.00	25.00	15.00
(79) George McQuinn	50.00	25.00	15.00
(80) George McQuinn, Lee Stine	50.00	25.00	15.00
(81) Joe Medwick	125.00	65.00	30.00
(82) Oscar Melillo	50.00	25.00	15.00
(83) "Buddy" Meyer (Myer)	50.00	25.00	15.00
(84) Randy Moore	50.00	25.00	15.00
(85) T. Moore, Jimmie Wilson	50.00	25.00	15.00
(86) Wallace Moses	50.00	25.00	15.00
(87) V. Mungo	50.00	25.00	15.00
(88) Lamar Newsom (Newsome)	50.00	25.00	15.00
(89) Lewis "Buck" Newsom (Louis)	50.00	25.00	15.00
(90) Steve O'Neill	50.00	25.00	15.00
(91) Tommie Padden	50.00	25.00	15.00
(92) E. Babe Philips (Phelps)	50.00	25.00	15.00
(93) Bill Rogel (Rogell)	50.00	25.00	15.00
(94) Lynn "Schoolboy" Rowe	50.00	25.00	15.00
(95) Luke Sewell	50.00	25.00	15.00
(96) Al Simmons	125.00	65.00	30.00
(97) Casey Stengel	125.00	65.00	30.00
(98) Bill Swift	50.00	25.00	15.00
(99) Cecil Travis	50.00	25.00	15.00
(100) "Pie" Traynor	125.00	65.00	30.00
(101) William Urbansky (Urbanski)	50.00	25.00	15.00
(102) Arky Vaughn (Vaughan)	125.00	65.00	30.00
(103) Joe Vosmik	50.00	25.00	15.00
(104) Honus Wagner	175.00	90.00	55.00
(105) Rube Walberg	50.00	25.00	15.00
(106) Bill Walker	50.00	25.00	15.00
(107) Gerald Walker	50.00	25.00	15.00
(108) L. Waner, P. Waner, Big Jim Weaver	125.00	65.00	30.00
(109) George Washington	50.00	25.00	15.00
(110) Bill Werber	50.00	25.00	15.00
(111) Sam West	50.00	25.00	15.00
(112) Pinkey Whitney	50.00	25.00	15.00
(113) Vernon Wiltshere (Wilshere)	50.00	25.00	15.00
(114) "Pep" Young	50.00	25.00	15.00
(115) Chicago White Sox 1936	50.00	25.00	15.00
(116) Fence Busters	50.00	25.00	15.00
(117) Talking It Over(Leo Durocher)	50.00	25.00	15.00
(118) There She Goes! Chicago City Series	50.00	25.00	15.00
(119) Ump Says No - Cleveland vs. Detroit	50.00	25.00	15.00
(120) World Series 1935(Phil Cavarretta, Goose Goslin, Lon Warneke)	50.00	25.00	15.00

1936 National Chicle Rabbit Maranville 'How To'

Issued by National Chicle in 1936, this 20-card set was a paper issue distributed with Batter-Up Gum. Unfolded, each paper measured 3-5/8" x 6". The numbered set featured a series of baseball tips from Rabbit Maranville and are illustrated with line drawings. American Card Catalog designation was R344.

	NM	E	VG
Complete Set (20):	700.00	350.00	210.00
Common Card:	35.00	17.50	10.00
1 How to Pitch the Out Shoot	35.00	17.50	10.00
2 How to Throw the In Shoot	35.00	17.50	10.00
3 How to Pitch the Drop	35.00	17.50	10.00
4 How to Pitch the Floater	35.00	17.50	10.00
5 How to Run Bases	35.00	17.50	10.00
6 How to Slide	35.00	17.50	10.00
7 How to Catch Flies	35.00	17.50	10.00
8 How to Field Grounders	35.00	17.50	10.00
9 How to Tag A Man Out	35.00	17.50	10.00
10 How to Cover A Base	35.00	17.50	10.00
11 How to Bat	35.00	17.50	10.00
12 How to Steal Bases	35.00	17.50	10.00
13 How to Bunt	35.00	17.50	10.00
14 How to Coach Base Runner	35.00	17.50	10.00
15 How to Catch Behind the Bat	35.00	17.50	10.00
16 How to Throw to Bases	35.00	17.50	10.00
17 How to Signal	35.00	17.50	10.00
18 How to Umpire Balls and Strikes	35.00	17.50	10.00
19 How to Umpire Bases	35.00	17.50	10.00
20 How to Lay Out a Ball Field	35.00	17.50	10.00

1898-99 National Copper Plate Co. Portraits

Besides supplying The Sporting News with the player portrait supplements issued during 1899-1900, this Grand Rapids, Mich., firm also sold nearly identical pieces in portfolios of 50 in a hard-cover, string-bound book. Approximately 10" x 13", the pictures feature the players at the turn of the century in formal portrait poses; some are in uniform, some in civilian clothes. The pictures are vignetted on a white background with the player's full name, team and year of issue printed at bottom. At lower-left on most, but not all, of the pictures is National Copper Plate's credit line. Backs have a player biographies in elaborate scrollwork frames.

	NM	E	VG
Complete Set (50):	60,000	30,000	18,000
Common Player:	1,100	425.00	200.00
(1) M.F. Amole (M.G. "Doc")	1,100	425.00	200.00
(2) A.C. Anson	2,400	950.00	480.00
(3) Robert Becker	1,100	425.00	200.00
(4) Martin Bergen	1,100	425.00	200.00
(5) James J. Collins	2,100	850.00	425.00
(6) Joe Corbett	1,100	425.00	200.00
(7) Louis Criger	1,100	425.00	200.00
(8) Lave Cross	1,100	425.00	200.00
(9) Montford Cross	1,100	425.00	200.00
(10) Eugene DeMontreville	1,100	425.00	200.00
(11) Charlie Dexter	1,100	425.00	200.00
(12) P.J. Donovan	1,100	425.00	200.00
(13) Thomas Dowd	1,100	425.00	200.00
(14) John J. Doyle	1,100	425.00	200.00
(15) Hugh Duffy	1,800	700.00	350.00
(16) Frank Dwyer	1,100	425.00	200.00
(17) Fred Ely ("Bones")	1,100	425.00	200.00
(18) A.F. Esterquest	1,100	425.00	200.00
(19) Wm. Ewing	1,800	700.00	350.00
(20) Elmer Harrison Flick	1,800	700.00	350.00
(21) Daniel Friend	1,100	425.00	200.00
(22) Geo. F. Gilpatrick (Gillpatrick)	1,100	425.00	200.00
(23) J.M. Goar	1,100	425.00	200.00
(24) Mike Griffin	1,100	425.00	200.00
(25) Clark C. Griffith	1,800	700.00	350.00
(26) Wm. Hill	1,100	425.00	200.00
(27) Wm. E. Hoy (Dummy)	2,100	850.00	400.00
(28) James Hughes	1,100	425.00	200.00
(29) William Joyce	1,100	425.00	200.00
(30) William Keeler	1,800	700.00	350.00
(31) Joseph J. Kelley	1,800	700.00	350.00
(32) William Kennedy	1,100	425.00	200.00
(33) William Lange	1,100	425.00	200.00
(34) John J. McGraw	1,800	700.00	350.00
(35) W.B. Mercer (George B. "Win")	1,100	425.00	200.00
(36) Charles A. Nichols	2,100	850.00	400.00
(37) Jerry Nops	1,100	425.00	200.00
(38) John O'Connor	1,100	425.00	200.00
(39) Richard Padden	1,100	425.00	200.00
(40) Wilber Robinson (Wilbert)	1,800	700.00	350.00
(41) William Shindle	1,000	425.00	200.00
(42) Charles Stahl	1,000	425.00	200.00
(43) E.P. Stein	1,100	425.00	200.00
(44) S.L. Thompson	2,100	850.00	400.00

		NM	E	VG
(45)	John Wagner	2,900	1,150	575.00
(46)	R.J. Wallace	1,800	700.00	350.00
(47)	Victor L. Willis	1,800	700.00	350.00
(48)	Parke Wilson	1,100	425.00	200.00
(49)	George Yeager	1,100	425.00	200.00
(50)	C.L. Zimmer	1,100	425.00	200.00

1913 National Game (WG5)

 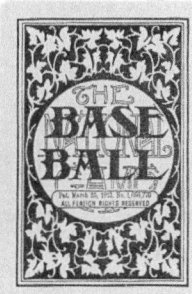

The patent date on the ornate red-and-white backs identify this as a 1913 issue. Fronts of the 2-1/2" x 3-1/2" cards have a black-and-white photo and a pair of baseball play scenarios used to play the card game. Corners are rounded. The set contains 43 identified player cards, a group of nine action photos in which the players are not identified and two header cards. The unnumbered cards are checklisted in alphabetical order. This set carries the ACC designation of WG5.

		NM	E	VG
	Complete Set (54):	5,250	2,625	1,575
	Common Player:	55.00	30.00	20.00
	Action Photo Card:	16.50	8.25	5.00
(1)	Grover Alexander	800.00	100.00	60.00
(2)	Frank Baker	150.00	50.00	30.00
(1A)	Batter swinging, looking forward	15.00	7.50	4.50
(2A)	Batter swinging, looking back	15.00	7.50	4.50
(3A)	Runner sliding, fielder at bag	15.00	7.50	4.50
(4A)	Runner sliding, umpire behind (Some collectors believe the player in the picture is Ty Cobb and are willing to pay a premium for this card.)	75.00	37.50	22.50
(5A)	Runner sliding, hugging base	15.00	7.50	4.50
(6A)	Sliding play at plate, umpire at left	15.00	7.50	4.50
(7A)	Sliding play at plate, umpire at right	15.00	7.50	4.50
(8A)	Play at plate, runner standing	15.00	7.50	4.50
(9A)	Runner looking backwards	15.00	7.50	4.50
(3)	Chief Bender	150.00	50.00	30.00
(4)	Bob Bescher	55.00	30.00	20.00
(5)	Joe Birmingham	55.00	30.00	20.00
(6)	Roger Bresnahan	150.00	50.00	30.00
(7)	Nixey Callahan	55.00	30.00	20.00
(8)	Frank Chance	150.00	50.00	30.00
(9)	Hal Chase	75.00	37.50	22.50
(10)	Fred Clarke	150.00	50.00	30.00
(11)	Ty Cobb	1,000	300.00	180.00
(12)	Sam Crawford	150.00	50.00	30.00
(13)	Bill Dahlen	55.00	30.00	20.00
(14)	Jake Daubert	55.00	30.00	20.00
(15)	Red Dooin	55.00	30.00	20.00
(16)	Johnny Evers	150.00	50.00	30.00
(17)	Vean Gregg	55.00	30.00	20.00
(18)	Clark Griffith	150.00	50.00	30.00
(19)	Dick Hoblitzel	55.00	30.00	20.00
(20)	Miller Huggins	150.00	50.00	30.00
(21)	Joe Jackson	3,500	800.00	480.00
(22)	Hughie Jennings	150.00	50.00	30.00
(23)	Walter Johnson	500.00	125.00	75.00
(24)	Ed Konetchy	55.00	30.00	20.00
(25)	Nap Lajoie	150.00	50.00	30.00
(26)	Connie Mack	150.00	50.00	30.00
(27)	Rube Marquard	150.00	50.00	30.00
(28)	Christy Mathewson	500.00	125.00	75.00
(29)	John McGraw	150.00	50.00	30.00
(30)	Larry McLean	55.00	30.00	20.00
(31)	Clyde Milan	55.00	30.00	20.00
(32)	Marty O'Toole	55.00	30.00	20.00
(33)	Nap Rucker	55.00	30.00	20.00
(34)	Tris Speaker	200.00	75.00	45.00
(35)	Jake Stahl	55.00	30.00	20.00

		NM	E	VG
(36)	George Stallings	55.00	30.00	20.00
(37)	George Stovall	55.00	30.00	20.00
(38)	Bill Sweeney	55.00	30.00	20.00
(39)	Joe Tinker	150.00	50.00	30.00
(40)	Honus Wagner	1,000	200.00	120.00
(41)	Ed Walsh	150.00	50.00	30.00
(42)	Joe Wood	55.00	30.00	20.00
(43)	Cy Young	500.00	125.00	75.00
(---)	Rules Card	55.00	30.00	20.00
(---)	Score Card	55.00	30.00	20.00

1952 National Tea Labels

Another set of bread end-labels, this checklist now comprises 44 players, although there is speculation that others remain to be cataloged. The unnumbered labels measure approximately 2-3/4" x 2-11/16" and are sometimes referred to as "Red Borders" because of their wide, red margins. The player's name and team are printed alongside his photo, and the slogan "Eat More Bread for Health" also appears on some labels.

		NM	E	VG
	Complete Set (44):	10,000	5,000	3,000
	Common Player:	200.00	100.00	60.00
(1)	Gene Bearden	200.00	100.00	60.00
(2)	Yogi Berra	450.00	225.00	135.00
(3)	Lou Brissie	200.00	100.00	60.00
(4)	Sam Chapman	200.00	100.00	60.00
(5)	Chuck Diering	200.00	100.00	60.00
(6)	Dom DiMaggio	250.00	125.00	75.00
(7)	Bruce Edwards	200.00	100.00	60.00
(8)	Del Ennis	200.00	100.00	60.00
(9)	Ferris Fain	200.00	100.00	60.00
(10)	Bob Feller	375.00	185.00	110.00
(11)	Howie Fox	200.00	100.00	60.00
(12)	Sid Gordon	200.00	100.00	60.00
(13)	John Groth	200.00	100.00	60.00
(14)	Granny Hamner	200.00	100.00	60.00
(15)	Jim Hegan	200.00	100.00	60.00
(16)	Sheldon Jones	200.00	100.00	60.00
(17)	Howie Judson	200.00	100.00	60.00
(18)	Sherman Lollar	200.00	100.00	60.00
(19)	Clarence Marshall	200.00	100.00	60.00
(20)	Don Mueller	200.00	100.00	60.00
(21)	Danny Murtaugh	200.00	100.00	60.00
(22)	Dave Philley	200.00	100.00	60.00
(23)	Jerry Priddy	200.00	100.00	60.00
(24)	Bill Rigney	200.00	100.00	60.00
(25)	Robin Roberts	350.00	175.00	100.00
(26)	Eddie Robinson	200.00	100.00	60.00
(27)	Preacher Roe	225.00	110.00	65.00
(28)	Stan Rojek	200.00	100.00	60.00
(29)	Al Rosen	225.00	110.00	65.00
(30)	Bob Rush	200.00	100.00	60.00
(31)	Hank Sauer	200.00	100.00	60.00
(32)	Johnny Schmitz	200.00	100.00	60.00
(33)	Enos Slaughter	350.00	175.00	100.00
(34)	Duke Snider	400.00	200.00	120.00
(35)	Warren Spahn	375.00	185.00	110.00
(36)	Gerry Staley	200.00	100.00	60.00
(37)	Virgil Stallcup	200.00	100.00	60.00
(38)	George Stirnweiss	200.00	100.00	60.00
(39)	Earl Torgeson	200.00	100.00	60.00
(40)	Dizzy Trout	200.00	100.00	60.00
(41)	Mickey Vernon	200.00	100.00	60.00
(42)	Wally Westlake	200.00	100.00	60.00
(43)	Johnny Wyrostek	200.00	100.00	60.00
(44)	Eddie Yost	200.00	100.00	60.00

1922 Neilson's Chocolate Type 1 (V61)

This set is closely related to the popular 1922 American Caramels (E120). The 120-card set was issued in Canada by Neilson's Chocolate Bars and carries the American Card Catalog designation V61. The front of the approximately 2" x 3-1/2" black-and-white cards has oval posed action photos with a decorative border. In the bottom border is the player name, position and team. Backs contain an ad for Neilson's Chocolates. Two types of cards exist. Type 1 is printed on

heavy paper (similar to E120), has a card number in the lower-left corner and features Old English typography of the sponsor's name on back. Type 2 is printed on cardboard, has no card numbers and has no Old English typography on back.

		NM	E	VG
	Complete Set (120):	27,500	11,000	5,500
	Common Player:	225.00	90.00	45.00
1	George Burns	225.00	90.00	45.00
2	John Tobin	225.00	90.00	45.00
3	J.T. Zachary	225.00	90.00	45.00
4	"Bullet" Joe Bush	225.00	90.00	45.00
5	Lu Blue	225.00	90.00	45.00
6	Clarence (Tillie) Walker	225.00	90.00	45.00
7	Carl Mays	225.00	90.00	45.00
8	Leon Goslin	600.00	240.00	120.00
9	Ed Rommel	225.00	90.00	45.00
10	Charles Robertson	225.00	90.00	45.00
11	Ralph (Cy) Perkins	225.00	90.00	45.00
12	Joe Sewell	600.00	240.00	120.00
13	Harry Hooper	600.00	240.00	120.00
14	Urban (Red) Faber	600.00	240.00	120.00
15	Bib Falk (Bibb)	225.00	90.00	45.00
16	George Uhle	225.00	90.00	45.00
17	Emory Rigney	225.00	90.00	45.00
18	George Dauss	225.00	90.00	45.00
19	Herman Pillette	225.00	90.00	45.00
20	Wallie Schang	225.00	90.00	45.00
21	Lawrence Woodall	225.00	90.00	45.00
22	Steve O'Neill	225.00	90.00	45.00
23	Edmund (Bing) Miller	225.00	90.00	45.00
24	Sylvester Johnson	225.00	90.00	45.00
25	Henry Severeid	225.00	90.00	45.00
26	Dave Danforth	225.00	90.00	45.00
27	Harry Heilmann	600.00	240.00	120.00
28	Bert Cole	225.00	90.00	45.00
29	Eddie Collins	600.00	240.00	120.00
30	Ty Cobb	7,000	2,800	1,400
31	Bill Wambsganss	225.00	90.00	45.00
32	George Sisler	600.00	240.00	120.00
33	Bob Veach	225.00	90.00	45.00
34	Earl Sheely	225.00	90.00	45.00
35	T.P. (Pat) Collins	225.00	90.00	45.00
36	Frank (Dixie) Davis	225.00	90.00	45.00
37	Babe Ruth	15,000	7,500	4,400
38	Bryan Harris	225.00	90.00	45.00
39	Bob Shawkey	225.00	90.00	45.00
40	Urban Shocker	225.00	90.00	45.00
41	Martin McManus	225.00	90.00	45.00
42	Clark Pittenger	225.00	90.00	45.00
43	"Deacon" Sam Jones	225.00	90.00	45.00
44	Waite Hoyt	600.00	240.00	120.00
45	Johnny Mostil	225.00	90.00	45.00
46	Mike Menosky	225.00	90.00	45.00
47	Walter Johnson	1,200	480.00	240.00
48	Wallie Pipp (Wally)	225.00	90.00	45.00
49	Walter Gerber	225.00	90.00	45.00
50	Ed Gharrity	225.00	90.00	45.00
51	Frank Ellerbe	225.00	90.00	45.00
52	Kenneth Williams	225.00	90.00	45.00
53	Joe Hauser	350.00	140.00	70.00
54	Carson Bigbee	225.00	90.00	45.00
55	Emil (Irish) Meusel	225.00	90.00	45.00
56	Milton Stock	225.00	90.00	45.00
57	Wilbur Cooper	225.00	90.00	45.00
58	Tom Griffith	225.00	90.00	45.00
59	Walter (Butch) Henline	225.00	90.00	45.00
60	Gene (Bubbles) Hargrave	225.00	90.00	45.00
61	Russell Wrightstone	225.00	90.00	45.00
62	Frank Frisch	600.00	240.00	120.00
63	Frank Parkinson	225.00	90.00	45.00
64	Walter (Dutch) Reuther (Ruether)	225.00	90.00	45.00
65	Bill Doak	225.00	90.00	45.00
66	Marty Callaghan	225.00	90.00	45.00
67	Sammy Bohne	350.00	140.00	70.00
68	Earl Hamilton	225.00	90.00	45.00
69	Grover C. Alexander	650.00	260.00	130.00

70	George Burns	225.00	90.00	45.00
71	Max Carey	600.00	240.00	120.00
72	Adolfo Luque	290.00	120.00	60.00
73	Dave (Beauty) Bancroft	600.00	240.00	120.00
74	Vic Aldridge	225.00	90.00	45.00
75	Jack Smith	225.00	90.00	45.00
76	Bob O'Farrell	225.00	90.00	45.00
77	Pete Donohue	225.00	90.00	45.00
78	Ralph Pinelli	225.00	90.00	45.00
79	Eddie Roush	600.00	240.00	120.00
80	Norman Boeckel	225.00	90.00	45.00
81	Rogers Hornsby	800.00	320.00	160.00
82	George Toporcer	225.00	90.00	45.00
83	Ivy Wingo	225.00	90.00	45.00
84	Virgil Cheeves	225.00	90.00	45.00
85	Vern Clemons	225.00	90.00	45.00
86	Lawrence (Hack) Miller	225.00	90.00	45.00
87	Johnny Kelleher	225.00	90.00	45.00
88	Heinie Groh	225.00	90.00	45.00
89	Burleigh Grimes	600.00	240.00	120.00
90	"Rabbit" Maranville	600.00	240.00	120.00
91	Charles (Babe) Adams	225.00	90.00	45.00
92	Lee King	225.00	90.00	45.00
93	Art Nehf	225.00	90.00	45.00
94	Frank Snyder	225.00	90.00	45.00
95	Raymond Powell	225.00	90.00	45.00
96	Wilbur Hubbell	225.00	90.00	45.00
97	Leon Cadore	225.00	90.00	45.00
98	Joe Oeschger	225.00	90.00	45.00
99	Jake Daubert	225.00	90.00	45.00
100	Will Sherdel	225.00	90.00	45.00
101	Hank DeBerry	225.00	90.00	45.00
102	Johnny Lavan	225.00	90.00	45.00
103	Jesse Haines	600.00	240.00	120.00
104	Joe (Goldie) Rapp	225.00	90.00	45.00
105	Oscar Ray Grimes	225.00	90.00	45.00
106	Ross Young (Youngs)	600.00	240.00	120.00
107	Art Fletcher	225.00	90.00	45.00
108	Clyde Barnhart	225.00	90.00	45.00
109	Louis (Pat) Duncan	225.00	90.00	45.00
110	Charlie Hollocher	225.00	90.00	45.00
111	Horace Ford	225.00	90.00	45.00
112	Bill Cunningham	225.00	90.00	45.00
113	Walter Schmidt	225.00	90.00	45.00
114	Joe Schultz	225.00	90.00	45.00
115	John Morrison	225.00	90.00	45.00
116	Jimmy Caveney	225.00	90.00	45.00
117	Zach Wheat	600.00	240.00	120.00
118	Fred (Cy) Williams	225.00	90.00	45.00
119	George Kelly	600.00	240.00	120.00
120	Jimmy Ring	225.00	90.00	45.00

1922 Neilson's Chocolate Type 2 (V61)

FRANK (DIXIE) DAVIS
PITCHER, ST. LOUIS AMERICANS

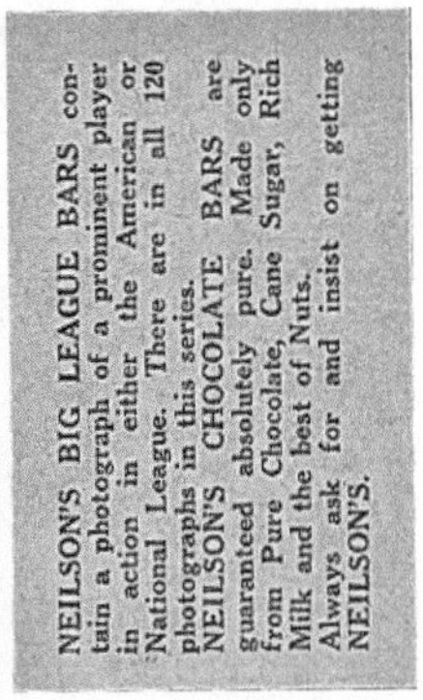

NEILSON'S BIG LEAGUE BARS contain a photograph of a prominent player in action in either the American or National League. There are in all 120 photographs in this series.
NEILSON'S CHOCOLATE BARS are guaranteed absolutely pure. Made only from Pure Chocolate, Cane Sugar, Rich Milk and the best of Nuts.
Always ask for and insist on getting NEILSON'S.

This set is closely related to the popular 1922 American Caramels (E120). The 120-card set was issued in Canada by Neilson's Chocolate Bars and carries the American Card Catalog designation V61. The front of the approximately 2" x 3-1/2" black-and-white cards has oval posed action photos with a decorative border. In the bottom border is the player name, position and team. Backs contain and ad for Neilson's Chocolates. Two types of cards exist. Type 1 is printed on heavy paper (similar to E120), has a card number in the lower-left corner and features Old English typography of the sponsor's name on back. Type 2 is printed on cardboard, has no card numbers and has no Old English typography on back.

		NM	E	VG
Complete Set (120):		53,150	21,250	10,625
Common Player:		250.00	110.00	50.00
(1)	Charles (Babe) Adams	250.00	110.00	50.00
(2)	Vic Aldridge	250.00	110.00	50.00
(3)	Grover C. Alexander	950.00	375.00	190.00
(4)	Dave (Beauty) Bancroft	575.00	225.00	115.00
(5)	Clyde Barnhart	250.00	110.00	50.00
(6)	Carson Bigbee	250.00	110.00	50.00
(7)	Lu Blue	250.00	110.00	50.00
(8)	Norman Boeckel	250.00	110.00	50.00
(9)	Sammy Bohne	325.00	125.00	65.00
(10)	George Burns (Boston)	250.00	110.00	50.00
(11)	George Burns (Cincinnati)	250.00	110.00	50.00
(12)	""Bullet" Joe Bush	250.00	110.00	50.00
(13)	Leon Cadore	250.00	110.00	50.00
(14)	Marty Callaghan	250.00	110.00	50.00
(15)	Max Carey	575.00	225.00	115.00
(16)	Jimmy Caveney	250.00	110.00	50.00
(17)	Virgil Cheeves	250.00	110.00	50.00
(18)	Vern Clemons	250.00	110.00	50.00
(19)	Ty Cobb	6,875	2,750	1,375
(20)	Bert Cole	250.00	110.00	50.00
(21)	Eddie Collins	575.00	225.00	115.00
(22)	T.P. (Pat) Collins	250.00	110.00	50.00
(23)	Wilbur Cooper	250.00	110.00	50.00
(24)	Bill Cunningham	250.00	110.00	50.00
(25)	Dave Danforth	250.00	110.00	50.00
(26)	Jake Daubert	250.00	110.00	50.00
(27)	George Dauss	250.00	110.00	50.00
(28)	Frank (Dixie) Davis	250.00	110.00	50.00
(29)	Hank DeBerry	250.00	110.00	50.00
(30)	Bill Doak	250.00	110.00	50.00
(31)	Pete Donohue	250.00	110.00	50.00
(32)	Louis (Pat) Duncan	250.00	110.00	50.00
(33)	Frank Ellerbe	250.00	110.00	50.00
(34)	Urban (Red) Faber	575.00	225.00	115.00
(35)	Bib (Bibb) Falk	250.00	110.00	50.00
(36)	Art Fletcher	250.00	110.00	50.00
(37)	Horace Ford	250.00	110.00	50.00
(38)	Frank Frisch	575.00	225.00	115.00
(39)	Walter Gerber	250.00	110.00	50.00
(40)	Ed Gharrity	250.00	110.00	50.00
(41)	Leon Goslin	575.00	225.00	115.00
(42)	Tom Griffith	250.00	110.00	50.00
(43)	Burleigh Grimes	575.00	225.00	115.00
(44)	Oscar Ray Grimes	250.00	110.00	50.00
(45)	Heinie Groh	250.00	110.00	50.00
(46)	Jesse Haines	575.00	225.00	115.00
(47)	Earl Hamilton	250.00	110.00	50.00
(48)	Gene (Bubbles) Hargrave	250.00	110.00	50.00
(49)	Bryan Harris	250.00	110.00	50.00
(50)	Joe Hauser	450.00	175.00	90.00
(51)	Harry Heilmann	575.00	225.00	115.00
(52)	Walter (Butch) Henline	250.00	110.00	50.00
(53)	Charlie Hollocher	250.00	110.00	50.00
(54)	Harry Hooper	575.00	225.00	115.00
(55)	Rogers Hornsby	690.00	275.00	140.00
(56)	Waite Hoyt	575.00	225.00	115.00
(57)	Wilbert Hubbell	250.00	110.00	50.00
(58)	Sylvester Johnson	250.00	110.00	50.00
(59)	Walter Johnson	1,000	400.00	200.00
(60)	"Deacon" Sam Jones	250.00	110.00	50.00
(61)	Johnny Kelleher	250.00	110.00	50.00
(62)	George Kelly	575.00	225.00	115.00
(63)	Lee King	250.00	110.00	50.00
(64)	Johnny Lavan	250.00	110.00	50.00
(65)	Adolfo Luque	325.00	125.00	65.00
(66)	"Rabbit" Maranville	575.00	225.00	115.00
(67)	Carl Mays	250.00	110.00	50.00
(68)	Martin McManus	250.00	110.00	50.00
(69)	Mike Menosky	250.00	110.00	50.00
(70)	Emil (Irish) Meusel	250.00	110.00	50.00
(71)	Edmund (Bing) Miller	250.00	110.00	50.00
(72)	Lawrence (Hack) Miller	250.00	110.00	50.00
(73)	John Morrison	250.00	110.00	50.00
(74)	Johnny Mostil	250.00	110.00	50.00
(75)	Art Nehf	250.00	110.00	50.00
(76)	Joe Oeschger	250.00	110.00	50.00
(77)	Bob O'Farrell	250.00	110.00	50.00
(78)	Steve O'Neill	250.00	110.00	50.00
(79)	Frank Parkinson	250.00	110.00	50.00
(80)	Ralph (Cy) Perkins	250.00	110.00	50.00
(81)	Herman Pillette	250.00	110.00	50.00
(82)	Ralph Pinelli	250.00	110.00	50.00
(83)	Wallie (Wally) Pipp	250.00	110.00	50.00
(84)	Clark Pittinger	250.00	110.00	50.00
(85)	Raymond Powell	250.00	110.00	50.00
(86)	Joe (Goldie) Rapp	250.00	110.00	50.00
(87)	Walter (Dutch) Reuther	250.00	110.00	50.00
(88)	Emory Rigney	250.00	110.00	50.00
(89)	Jimmy Ring	250.00	110.00	50.00
(90)	Charles Robertson	250.00	110.00	50.00
(91)	Ed Rommel	250.00	110.00	50.00
(92)	Eddie Roush	575.00	225.00	115.00
(93)	Babe Ruth	12,500	6,250	3,750
(94)	Wallie (Wally) Schang	250.00	110.00	50.00
(95)	Walter Schmidt	250.00	110.00	50.00
(96)	Joe Schultz	250.00	110.00	50.00
(97)	Hank Severeid	250.00	110.00	50.00
(98)	Joe Sewell	575.00	225.00	115.00
(99)	Bob Shawkey	250.00	110.00	50.00
(100)	Earl Sheely	250.00	110.00	50.00
(101)	Will Sherdel	250.00	110.00	50.00
(102)	Urban Shocker	250.00	110.00	50.00
(103)	George Sisler	575.00	225.00	115.00
(104)	Jack Smith	250.00	110.00	50.00
(105)	Frank Snyder	250.00	110.00	50.00
(106)	Milton Stock	250.00	110.00	50.00
(107)	John Tobin	250.00	110.00	50.00
(108)	George Torporcer	250.00	110.00	50.00
(109)	George Uhle	250.00	110.00	50.00
(110)	Bob Veach	250.00	110.00	50.00
(111)	Clarence (Tillie) Walker	250.00	110.00	50.00
(112)	Bill Wambsganss	250.00	110.00	50.00
(113)	Zach Wheat	575.00	225.00	115.00
(114)	Fred (Cy) Williams	250.00	110.00	50.00
(115)	Kenneth Williams	250.00	110.00	50.00
(116)	Ivy Wingo	250.00	110.00	50.00
(117)	Lawrence Woodall	250.00	110.00	50.00
(118)	Russell Wrightstone	250.00	110.00	50.00
(119)	Ross Young (Youngs)	575.00	225.00	115.00
(120)	J.T. Zachary	250.00	110.00	50.00

1923 "Neilson's Chocolates"

This issue, purporting to come from the Canadian candy maker which had produced a 1922 set, was first reported in 1996. The cards appear to be genuine W572 strip cards which have had a Neilson's ad overprinted on the back many years later in an apparent effort to defraud collectors. These altered W572s would have to be significantly downgraded to adjust for the defacing. It can be expected that any card that appears in W572 can be found with the Neilson's back, but the "discovery" contained only 47 different players.

(See W572 for checklist)

1959 Neptune Sardines Jimmy Piersall

Like the earlier advertising postcards he did for various Cain's food products, this 3-1/2" x 5-1/2" black-and-white postcard carries the endorsement of the popular Indians outfielder for Neptune brand sardines. The front has a borderless photo of the player in a batting pose with a facsimile autograph at top. The back has standard postcard indicia along with the ad message and a product picture.

	NM	E	VG
Jimmy Piersall	50.00	25.00	15.00

1976-81 New England Sports Collectors

40th ANNIVERSARY UNIQUE EVENT
NEW YORK
DiMAGGIO BROTHERS - VINCE, JOE & DOM
1940 - EACH PLAY OVER 100 GAMES IN MAJOR LEAGUES

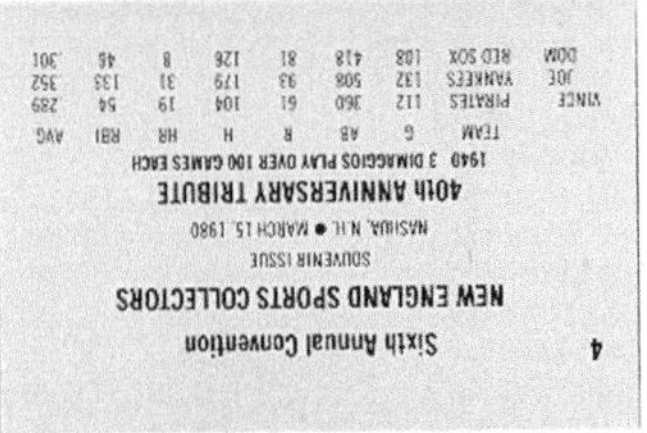

Sixth Annual Convention
NEW ENGLAND SPORTS COLLECTORS
40th ANNIVERSARY TRIBUTE

From the period 1976-81, the New England Sports Collectors club issued a series of postcard-size (3-1/2" x 5-1/4") black-and-white card promoting their annual shows in Nashua, N.H. No card was issued in 1978.

		NM	E	VG
Complete Set (5):		30.00	15.00	9.00
Common Player:		6.00	3.00	1.75
1	Joe DiMaggio (1976)	8.00	4.00	2.50
2	Jackie Robinson (1977)	6.00	3.00	1.75
3	Ted Williams (1979)	7.00	3.50	2.00
4	Vince DiMaggio, Joe DiMaggio, Dom DiMaggio (1980)	6.00	3.00	1.75
5	Mickey Mantle (1981)	9.00	4.50	2.75

1895 Newsboy Cabinets (N566)

Issued in the 1890s by the National Tobacco Works, this massive cabinet card set was distributed as a premium with the Newsboy tobacco brand. Although the set contained over 500 popular actresses, athletes, politicians and other celebrities of the day, only about a dozen cards of baseball players have been found. The cards measure 4-1/4" x 6-1/2" and feature sepia-toned photographs mounted on a backing that usually has "Newsboy New York" printed at bottom. Each portrait photograph is numbered and a few of the photos are round. The ballplayers in the set are mostly members of the 1894 New York Giants with a couple of Brooklyn players. There are two known poses of John Ward. Cards have been seen with advertising on the back for Keystone cigars and Red Indian tobacco, and on front for "Baum & Berstein Clothiers."

		NM	E	VG
	Common Player:	5,000	2,500	1,500
174	W.H. Murphy	5,000	2,500	1,500
175	Amos Rusie	20,000	10,000	6,000
176	Michael Tiernan	5,000	2,500	1,500
177	E.D. Burke	5,000	2,500	1,500
178	J.J. Doyle	5,000	2,500	1,500
179	W.B. Fuller	5,000	2,500	1,500
180	George Van Haltren	5,000	2,500	1,500
181	Dave Foutz	5,000	2,500	1,500
182	Jouett Meekin	5,000	2,500	1,500
183	Michael Griffin	5,000	2,500	1,500
201	W.H. (Dad) Clark (Clarke)	5,000	2,500	1,500
202	Parke Wilson	5,000	2,500	1,500
586	John Ward (Arms folded.)	32,500	16,250	9,750
587	John Ward (Bat at side.)	11,000	6,500	3,900

1886 New York Baseball Club (H812)

This rare 19th Century baseball issue can be classified under the general category of "trade" cards, a popular advertising vehicle of the period. The cards measure 3" x 4-3/4" and feature blue line-drawing portraits of members of the "New York Base Ball Club," which is printed along the top. As was common with this type of trade card, the bottom was left blank to accomodate various messages. The known examples of this set carry ads for local tobacco merchants and other businesses. The portraits are all based on the photographs used in the 1886 Old Judge set. The cards, which have been assigned an ACC designation of H812, are printed on thin paper rather than cardboard.

		NM	E	VG
	Complete Set (8):	84,000	37,200	20,400
	Common Player:	7,200	3,200	1,450
(1)	T. Dealsey	7,200	3,200	1,450
(2)	M. Dorgan	7,200	3,200	1,450
(3)	T. Esterbrook	7,200	3,200	1,450
(4)	W. Ewing	16,200	8,100	4,800
(5)	J. Gerhardt	7,200	3,200	1,450
(6)	J. O'Rourke	16,200	8,100	4,800
(7)	D. Richardson	7,200	3,200	1,450
(8)	M. Welch	16,200	8,100	4,800

1909 Niagara Baking Co.

This is a version of the set known as E101 "Set of 50" which has been rubber-stamped on back with an advertise-

ment for Niagara Baking Co., of Lockport, N.Y. It is unclear whether all 50 cards in E101 can be found with the overprint. Because of the ease with which this regional variation could be faked, collectors must exercise extreme caution. Collectors can expect to pay a considerable premium over E101 prices for this version, especially for common players.

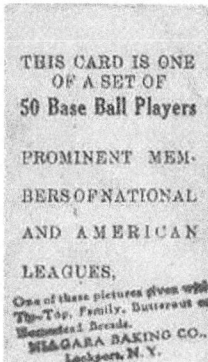

VALUES UNDETERMINED

(See 1909 E101 for checklist.)

1953 Northland Bread Labels

This bread end-label set consists of 32 players - two from each major league team. The unnumbered black and white labels measure approximately 2-11/16" square and include the slogan "Bread for Energy" along the top. An album to house the labels was also part of the promotion. All labels were also issued with "Top Taste" at top in place of the Bread for Energy slogan.

		NM	E	VG
	Complete Set (32):	16,500	8,500	5,000
	Common Player:	400.00	200.00	120.00
(1)	Cal Abrams	400.00	200.00	120.00
(2)	Richie Ashburn	400.00	200.00	120.00
(3)	Gus Bell	400.00	200.00	120.00
(4)	Jim Busby	400.00	200.00	120.00
(5)	Clint Courtney	400.00	200.00	120.00
(6)	Billy Cox	400.00	200.00	120.00
(7)	Jim Dyck	400.00	200.00	120.00
(8)	Nellie Fox	800.00	400.00	240.00
(9)	Sid Gordon	400.00	200.00	120.00
(10)	Warren Hacker	400.00	200.00	120.00
(11)	Jim Hearn	400.00	200.00	120.00
(12)	Fred Hutchinson	400.00	200.00	120.00
(13)	Monte Irvin	800.00	400.00	240.00
(14)	Jackie Jensen	450.00	220.00	130.00
(15)	Ted Kluszewski	700.00	350.00	200.00
(16)	Bob Lemon	800.00	400.00	240.00
(17)	Maury McDermott	400.00	200.00	120.00
(18)	Minny Minoso	700.00	350.00	210.00
(19)	Johnny Mize	800.00	400.00	240.00
(20)	Mel Parnell	400.00	200.00	120.00
(21)	Howie Pollet	400.00	200.00	120.00
(22)	Jerry Priddy	400.00	200.00	120.00
(23)	Allie Reynolds	400.00	200.00	120.00
(24)	Preacher Roe	500.00	250.00	150.00
(25)	Al Rosen	500.00	250.00	150.00
(26)	Connie Ryan	400.00	200.00	120.00
(27a)	Hank Sauer	400.00	200.00	120.00
(28)	Red Schoendienst	800.00	400.00	240.00
(29)	Bobby Shantz	400.00	200.00	120.00
(30)	Enos Slaughter	800.00	400.00	240.00
(31)	Warren Spahn	800.00	400.00	240.00
(32)	Gus Zernial	400.00	200.00	120.00

1978 North Shore Dodge Cecil Cooper

As part of his work as promotional spokesman for a local auto dealership, popular Brewers first baseman Cecil Cooper appears on a one-card set which was given to fans and collectors during public appearances. The card is printed in black-and-white in standard 2-1/2" x 3-1/2" size and is often

found with a genuine autograph on the front.

	NM	E	VG
Cecil Cooper	6.00	3.00	1.75
Cecil Cooper (Autographed)	15.00	7.50	4.50

1980 Nostalgic Enterprises 1903 N.Y. Highlanders

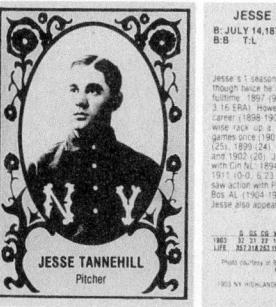

New York City's first team in the American League, the 1903 Highlanders, are featured in this collectors' issue. Fronts of the 2-1/2" x 3-1/2" cards have black-and-white portrait photos with ornate graphics, highlighted in yellow, and a white border. Backs have season and lifetime stats, player data and an extensive career summary. The unnumbered cards are checklisted here in alphabetical order. Sets originally sold for about $2.50.

		NM	E	VG
	Complete Set (17):	15.00	7.50	4.50
	Common Player:	2.00	1.00	.60
(1)	Monte Beville	2.50	1.25	.70
(2)	Jack Chesbro	2.00	1.00	.60
(3)	Wid Conroy	2.00	1.00	.60
(4)	Lefty Davis	2.00	1.00	.60
(5)	John Deering	2.50	1.25	.70
(6)	Kid Elberfeld	2.00	1.00	.60
(7)	Dave Fultz	2.00	1.00	.60
(8)	John Ganzel	2.00	1.00	.60
(9)	Clark Griffith	2.00	1.00	.60
(10)	Harry Howell	2.00	1.00	.60
(11)	Willie Keeler	2.00	1.00	.60
(12)	Herm McFarland	2.00	1.00	.60
(13)	Jack O'Connor	2.00	1.00	.60
(14)	Jesse Tannehill	2.00	1.00	.60
(15)	Jimmy Williams	2.00	1.00	.60
(16)	Jack Zalusky	2.50	1.25	.70
(17)	Header Card/Checklist	2.00	1.00	.60

1907-10 Novelty Cutlery Postcards (PC805)

An ornately bordered black-and-white or sepia portrait or action pose of the day's great players identifies these postcards from a Canton, Ohio, knife company. Cards measure the standard 3-1/2" x 5-1/2" size with postcard indicia on the back. The sponsor is identified in a tiny line of type beneath the lower-right corner of the player photo.

		NM	E	VG
Complete Set (25):		60,000	30,000	18,000
Common Player:		1,000	500.00	300.00
(1)	Roger Bresnahan	2,250	1,125	675.00
(2)	Al Bridwell	1,000	500.00	300.00
(3)	Three Finger Brown	2,250	1,125	675.00
(4)	Frank Chance	2,250	1,125	675.00
(5)	Hal Chase	2,000	1,000	600.00
(6)	Ty Cobb	18,000	7,300	3,600
(7)	Eddie Collins	2,250	1,125	675.00
(8)	Sam Crawford	2,250	1,125	675.00
(9)	Art Devlin	1,000	500.00	300.00
(10)	Red Dooin	1,000	500.00	300.00
(11)	Sam Frock	1,000	500.00	300.00
(12)	George Gibson	1,000	500.00	300.00
(13)	Solly Hofman	1,000	500.00	300.00
(14)	Walter Johnston (Johnson)	6,000	2,400	1,200
(15)	Nap Lajoie	2,250	1,125	675.00
(16)	Bris Lord	1,000	500.00	300.00
(17)	Christy Mathewson	6,000	2,400	1,200
(18)	Orval Overall	1,000	500.00	300.00
(19)	Eddie Plank	2,250	1,125	675.00
(20)	Tris Speaker	4,000	2,000	1,200
(21)	Charley Street	1,000	500.00	300.00
(22)	Honus Wagner	12,000	6,000	3,500
(23)	Ed Walsh	2,250	1,125	675.00
(24)	Ty Cobb, Honus Wagner	13,000	5,200	2,600
(25)	Johnny Evers, Germany Schaefer	2,750	1,375	825.00

1960 Nu-Card Baseball Hi-Lites

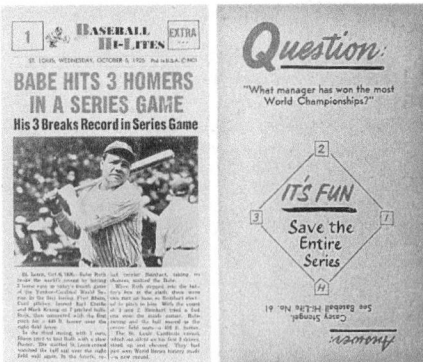

These large, 3-1/4" x 5-3/8" cards are printed in a mock newspaper format, with a headline, picture and story describing one of baseball's greatest moments. Cards are printed in red-and-black on front, and green-and-black on back. Cards #1-18 that are printed only in black and are blank-backed are cataloged under 1960 CVC Baseball Hi-Lites. Each card is numbered in the upper-left corner. Backs offer a quiz question and answer.

		NM	E	VG
Complete Set (72):		750.00	350.00	250.00
Common Player:		8.00	4.00	2.50
1	Babe Hits 3 Homers In A Series Game	60.00	30.00	20.00
2	Podres Pitching Wins Series	12.00	6.00	4.00
3	Bevans Pitches No Hitter, Almost	8.00	4.00	2.50
4	Box Score Devised By Reporter	8.00	4.00	2.50
5	VanderMeer Pitches 2 No Hitters	8.00	4.00	2.50
6	Indians Take Bums	8.00	4.00	2.50
7	DiMag Comes Thru	35.00	20.00	12.00
8	Mathewson Pitches 3 W.S. Shutouts	10.00	5.00	3.00
9	Haddix Pitches 12 Perfect Innings	8.00	4.00	2.50
10	Thomson's Homer Sinks Dodgers	12.00	6.00	4.00
11	Hubbell Strikes Out 5 A.L. Stars	8.00	4.00	2.50
12	Pickoff Ends Series(Marty Marion)	8.00	4.00	2.50
13	Cards Take Series From Yanks(Grover Cleveland Alexander)	8.00	4.00	2.50
14	Dizzy And Daffy Win Series	15.00	8.00	5.00
15	Owen Drops 3rd Strike	8.00	5.00	2.50
16	Ruth Calls His Shot	60.00	30.00	20.00
17	Merkle Pulls Boner	8.00	4.00	2.50
18	Larsen Hurls Perfect World Series Game	15.00	8.00	5.00
19	Bean Ball Ends Career of Mickey Cochrane	8.00	4.00	2.50
20	Banks Belts 47 Homers, Earns MVP Honors	8.00	4.00	2.50
21	Stan Musial Hits 5 Homers In 1 Day	18.00	9.00	5.00
22	Mickey Mantle Hits Longest Homer	80.00	40.00	25.00
23	Sievers Captures Home Run Title	8.00	4.00	2.50
24	Gehrig Consecutive Game Record Ends	35.00	20.00	12.00
25	Red Schoendienst Key Player In Victory	8.00	4.00	2.50
26	Midget Pinch-Hits For St. Louis Browns(Eddie Gaedel)	15.00	8.00	5.00
27	Willie Mays Makes Greatest Catch	35.00	20.00	12.00
28	Homer By Berra Puts Yanks In 1st Place	8.00	4.00	2.50
29	Campy National League's MVP	8.00	4.00	2.50
30	Bob Turley Hurls Yanks To Championship	8.00	4.00	2.50
31	Dodgers Take Series From Sox In Six	8.00	4.00	2.50
32	Furillo Hero As Dodgers Beat Chicago	8.00	4.00	2.50
33	Adcock Gets Four Homers And A Double	8.00	4.00	2.50
34	Dickey Chosen All Star Catcher	8.00	4.00	2.50
35	Burdette Beats Yanks In 3 Series Games	8.00	4.00	2.50
36	Umpires Clear White Sox Bench	8.00	4.00	2.50
37	Reese Honored As Greatest Dodger S.S.	10.00	5.00	3.00
38	Joe DiMaggio Hits In 56 Straight Games	40.00	20.00	12.00
39	Ted Williams Hits .406 For Season	35.00	20.00	12.00
40	Johnson Pitches 56 Scoreless Innings	8.00	4.00	2.50
41	Hodges Hits 4 Home Runs In Nite Game	8.00	4.00	2.50
42	Greenberg Returns To Tigers From Army	15.00	8.00	5.00
43	Ty Cobb Named Best Player Of All Time	20.00	10.00	6.00
44	Robin Roberts Wins 28 Games	8.00	4.00	2.50
45	Rizzuto's 2 Runs Save 1st Place	8.00	4.00	2.50
46	Tigers Beat Out Senators For Pennant(Hal Newhouser)	8.00	4.00	2.50
47	Babe Ruth Hits 60th Home Run	50.00	30.00	20.00
48	Cy Young Honored	8.00	4.00	2.50
49	Killebrew Starts Spring Training	8.00	4.00	2.50
50	Mantle Hits Longest Homer At Stadium	80.00	40.00	25.00
51	Braves Take Pennant(Hank Aaron)	8.00	4.00	2.50
52	Ted Williams Hero Of All Star Game	40.00	20.00	12.00
53	Robinson Saves Dodgers For Playoffs(Jackie Robinson)	18.00	9.00	5.00
54	Snodgrass Muffs A Fly Ball	8.00	4.00	2.50
55	Snider Belts 2 Homers	8.00	4.00	2.50
56	New York Giants Win 26 Straight Games(Christy Mathewson)	8.00	4.00	2.50
57	Ted Kluszewski Stars In 1st Game Win	8.00	4.00	2.50
58	Ott Walks 5 Times In A Single Game(Mel Ott)	8.00	4.00	2.50
59	Harvey Kuenn Takes Batting Title	8.00	4.00	2.50
60	Bob Feller Hurls 3rd No-Hitter Of	8.00	4.00	2.50
61	Yanks Champs Again!(Casey Stengel)	8.00	4.00	2.50
62	Aaron's Bat Beats Yankees In Series	15.00	8.00	5.00
63	Warren Spahn Beats Yanks in World	8.00	4.00	2.50
64	Ump's Wrong Call Helps Dodgers	8.00	4.00	2.50
65	Kaline Hits 3 Homers, 2 In Same Inning	8.00	4.00	2.50
66	Bob Allison Named A.L. Rookie of Year	8.00	4.00	2.50
67	McCovey Blasts Way Into Giant Lineup	8.00	4.00	2.50
68	Colavito Hits Four Homers In One Game	15.00	8.00	5.00
69	Erskine Sets Strike Out Record In W.S.	8.00	4.00	2.50
70	Sal Maglie Pitches No-Hit Game	8.00	4.00	2.50
71	Early Wynn Victory Crushes Yanks	8.00	4.00	2.50
72	Nellie Fox American League's M.V.P.	8.00	4.00	2.50

1961 Nu-Card Baseball Scoops

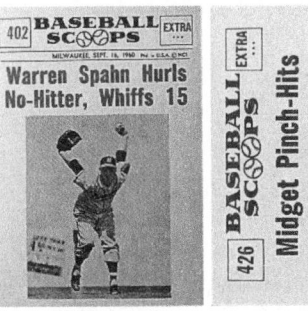

Very similar in style to their set of the year before, the Nu-Card Baseball Scoops were issued in a smaller 2-1/2" x 3-1/2" size, but still featured the mock newspaper card front. This 80-card set is numbered from 401 to 480, with numbers shown on the card front and back. These cards, which commemorate great moments in individual players' careers, included only the headline and black and white photo on the fronts, with the descriptive story on the card backs. Cards are again printed in red and black. It appears the set may have been counterfeited, though when is not known. These reprinted cards can be determined by examining the card photo for unusual blurring and fuzziness.

		NM	E	VG
Complete Set (80):		550.00	275.00	165.00
Common Player:		4.00	2.00	1.25
Wax Pack (7):		135.00		
401	Gentile Powers Birds Into 1st	10.00	6.00	3.00
402	Warren Spahn Hurls No-Hitter, Whiffs 15	7.00	3.50	2.00
403	Mazeroski's Homer Wins Series For Bucs	15.00	8.00	5.00
404	Willie Mays' 3 Triples Paces Giants	20.00	10.00	6.00
405	Woodie Held Slugs 2 Homers, 6 RBIs	4.00	2.00	1.25
406	Vern Law Winner Of Cy Young Award	4.00	2.00	1.25
407	Runnels Makes 9 Hits in Twin-Bill	4.00	2.00	1.25
408	Braves' Lew Burdette Wins No-Hitter	4.00	2.00	1.25
409	Dick Stuart Hits 3 Homers, Single	4.00	2.00	1.25
410	Don Cardwell Of Cubs Pitches No-Hit Game	4.00	2.00	1.25
411	Camilo Pascual Strikes Out 15 Bosox	4.00	2.00	1.25
412	Eddie Mathews Blasts 300th Big League HR	4.00	2.00	1.25
413	Groat, NL Bat King, Named Loop's MVP	4.00	2.00	1.25
414	AL Votes To Expand To 10 Teams(Gene Autry)	4.00	2.00	1.25
415	Bobby Richardson Sets Series Mark	4.00	2.00	1.25
416	Maris Nips Mantle For AL MVP Award	15.00	8.00	5.00
417	Merkle Pulls Boner	4.00	2.00	1.25
418	Larsen Hurls Perfect World Series Game	7.00	3.50	2.00
419	Bean Ball Ends Career Of Mickey Cochrane	4.00	2.00	1.25
420	Banks Belts 47 Homers, Earns MVP Award	10.00	5.00	3.00
421	Stan Musial Hits 5 Homers In 1 Day	12.00	6.00	4.00
422	Mickey Mantle Hits Longest Homer	50.00	25.00	15.00

423	Sievers Captures Home Run Title	4.00	2.00	1.25
424	Gehrig Consecutive Game Record Ends	20.00	10.00	6.00
425	Red Schoendienst Key Player In Victory	4.00	2.00	1.25
426	Midget Pinch-Hits For St. Louis Browns(Eddie Gaedel)	7.00	3.50	2.00
427	Willie Mays Makes Greatest Catch	30.00	15.00	9.00
428	Robinson Saves Dodgers For Playoffs	12.00	6.00	4.00
429	Campy Most Valuable Player	4.00	2.00	1.25
430	Turley Hurls Yanks To Championship	4.00	2.00	1.25
431	Dodgers Take Series From Sox In Six(Larry Sherry)	4.00	2.00	1.25
432	Furillo Hero In 3rd World Series Game	4.00	2.00	1.25
433	Adcock Gets Four Homers, Double	4.00	2.00	1.25
434	Dickey Chosen All Star Catcher	4.00	2.00	1.25
435	Burdette Beats Yanks In 3 Series Games	4.00	2.00	1.25
436	Umpires Clear White Sox Bench	4.00	2.00	1.25
437	Reese Honored As Greatest Dodgers S.S.	4.00	2.00	1.25
438	Joe DiMaggio Hits In 56 Straight Games	30.00	15.00	9.00
439	Ted Williams Hits .406 For Season	30.00	15.00	9.00
440	Johnson Pitches 56 Scoreless Innings	4.00	2.00	1.25
441	Hodges Hits 4 Home Runs In Nite Game	4.00	2.00	1.25
442	Greenberg Returns To Tigers From Army	4.00	2.00	1.25
443	Ty Cobb Named Best Player Of All Time	17.50	9.00	6.00
444	Robin Roberts Wins 28 Games	4.00	2.00	1.25
445	Rizzuto's 2 Runs Save 1st Place	4.00	2.00	1.25
446	Tigers Beat Out Senators For Pennant(Hal Newhouser)	4.00	2.00	1.25
447	Babe Ruth Hits 60th Home Run	30.00	15.00	9.00
448	Cy Young Honored	6.00	3.00	2.00
449	Killebrew Starts Spring Training	4.00	2.00	1.25
450	Mantle Hits Longest Homer At Stadium	50.00	25.00	15.00
451	Braves Take Pennant	4.00	2.00	1.25
452	Ted Williams Hero Of All Star Game	30.00	15.00	9.00
453	Homer By Berra Puts Yanks In 1st Place	4.00	2.00	1.25
454	Snodgrass Muffs A Fly Ball	4.00	2.00	1.25
455	Babe Hits 3 Homers In A Series Game	35.00	20.00	12.00
456	New York Wins 26 Straight Games	4.00	2.00	1.25
457	Ted Kluszewski Stars In 1st Series Win	4.00	2.00	1.25
458	Ott Walks 5 Times In A Single Game	4.00	2.00	1.25
459	Harvey Kuenn Takes Batting Title	4.00	2.00	1.25
460	Bob Feller Hurls 3rd No-Hitter Of Career	4.00	2.00	1.25
461	Yanks Champs Again!(Casey Stengel)	4.00	2.00	1.25
462	Aaron's Bat Beats Yankees In Series	15.00	8.00	5.00
463	Warren Spahn Beats Yanks In World	4.00	2.00	1.25
464	Ump's Wrong Call Helps Dodgers	4.00	2.00	1.25
465	Kaline Hits 3 Homers, 2 In Same Inning	4.00	2.00	1.25
466	Bob Allison Named A.L. Rookie Of Year	4.00	2.00	1.25
467	DiMag Comes Thru	30.00	15.00	9.00
468	Colavito Hits Four Homers In One Game	5.00	2.50	1.50
469	Erskine Sets Strike Out Record In W.S.	4.00	2.00	1.25
470	Sal Maglie Pitches No-Hit Game	4.00	2.00	1.25
471	Early Wynn Victory Crushes Yanks	4.00	2.00	1.25

472	Nellie Fox American League's MVP	4.00	2.00	1.25
473	Pickoff Ends Series(Marty Marion)	4.00	2.00	1.25
474	Podres Pitching Wins Series	4.00	2.00	1.25
475	Owen Drops 3rd Strike	4.00	2.00	1.25
476	Dizzy And Daffy Win Series	12.00	6.00	4.00
477	Mathewson Pitches 3 W.S. Shutouts	15.00	8.00	5.00
478	Haddix Pitches 12 Perfect Innings	4.00	2.00	1.25
479	Hubbell Strike Out 5 A.L. Stars	4.00	2.00	1.25
480	Homer Sinks Dodgers(Bobby Thomson)	8.00	4.00	2.50

1889 Number 7 Cigars (N526)

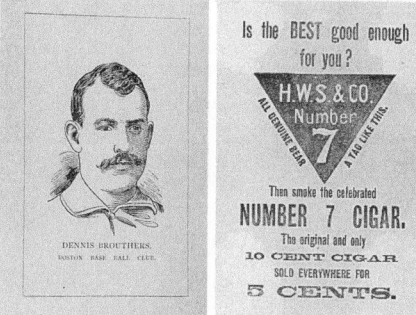

Three versions of this set picturing Boston Beaneaters (N.L.) players were issued in 1889. Number 7 and Diamond S brand cigars are the most commonly encountered advertising printed on the cards' backs. Cards with "C.S. White & Co." at top front are also known. The cards measure approximately 3-1/8" x 4-1/2" and feature black-and-white portrait drawings of the players with their name printed below in capital letters along with the team name. Backs carry ads for either Number 7 Cigars, a product of H.W.S. & Co. Howard W. Spurr & Co.), or Diamond S Cigars, advertised as the "Best 10 cent Cigar in America."

		NM	E	VG
	Complete Set (15):	40,000	20,000	12,000
	Common Player:	2,200	1,100	650.00
(1)	C.W. Bennett	2,200	1,100	650.00
(2)	Dennis Brouthers	5,000	2,500	1,500
(3)	T.T. Brown	2,200	1,100	650.00
(4)	John G. Clarkson	5,000	2,500	1,500
(5)	C.W. Ganzel	1,100	450.00	400.00
(6)	James A. Hart	2,200	1,100	650.00
(7)	R.F. Johnston	2,200	1,100	650.00
(8)	M.J. Kelly	7,000	3,500	2,100
(9)	M.J. Madden	1,100	450.00	400.00
(10)	Wm. Nash	2,200	1,100	650.00
(11)	Jos. Quinn	2,200	1.100.00	650.00
(12)	Chas. Radbourn	5,000	2,500	1,500
(13)	J.B. Ray (Should be I.B.)	2,200	1,100	650.00
(14)	Hardie Richardson	2,200	1,100	650.00
(15)	Wm. Sowders	2,200	1,100	650.00

1949-1950 Num Num Cleveland Indians

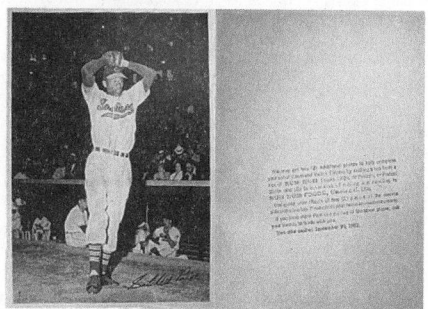

The 6-1/2" x 9" photopack pictures sold at Municipal Stadium in 1949 did double duty when they were also used as a premium for Num Num snack foods. A rubber-stamped notice on the back of the black-and-white photos offered two pictures for 10 cents and a box top, while encouraging trading. The pictures generally feature posed action shots with a facsimile autograph and white border. Backs are blank except for the rubber stamping. The unnumbered cards are checklisted here alphabetically.

		NM	E	VG
	Complete Set (36):	2,000	1,000	600.00
	Common Player:	35.00	17.50	10.00
(1)	Bob Avila	35.00	17.50	10.00
(2)	Gene Bearden	35.00	17.50	10.00
(3)	Al Benton	35.00	17.50	10.00
(4)	John Berardino	45.00	22.50	13.50
(5)	Ray Boone	35.00	17.50	10.00
(6)	Lou Boudreau	65.00	30.00	15.00
(7)	Allie Clark	35.00	17.50	10.00
(8)	Larry Doby	65.00	30.00	15.00
(9)	Luke Easter	35.00	17.50	10.00
(10)	Bob Feller	125.00	60.00	30.00
(11)	Jess Flores	35.00	17.50	10.00
(12)	Mike Garcia	35.00	17.50	10.00
(13)	Joe Gordon	35.00	17.50	10.00
(14)	Hank Greenberg	125.00	65.00	35.00
(15)	Steve Gromek	35.00	17.50	10.00
(16)	Jim Hegan	35.00	17.50	10.00
(17)	Ken Keltner	35.00	17.50	10.00
(18)	Bob Kennedy	35.00	17.50	10.00
(19)	Bob Lemon	65.00	30.00	15.00
(20)	Dale Mitchell	35.00	17.50	10.00
(21)	Ray Murray	35.00	17.50	10.00
(22)	Satchell Paige	200.00	90.00	50.00
(23)	Frank Papish	35.00	17.50	10.00
(24)	Hal Peck	35.00	17.50	10.00
(25)	Chick Pieretti	35.00	17.50	10.00
(26)	Al Rosen	45.00	22.50	13.50
(27)	Dick Rozek (Glove out front.)	35.00	17.50	10.00
(28)	Dick Rozek (Glove under leg.)	35.00	17.50	10.00
(29)	Mike Tresh	35.00	17.50	10.00
(30)	Thurman Tucker	35.00	17.50	10.00
(31)	Bill Veeck	65.00	30.00	15.00
(32)	Mickey Vernon	35.00	17.50	10.00
(33)	Early Wynn	65.00	30.00	15.00
(34)	Sam Zoldak	35.00	17.50	10.00
(35)	Coaches(George Susce, Herold Ruel, Bill McKechnie, Steve O'Neill, Mel Harder)	35.00	17.50	10.00
(36)	Municipal Stadium	35.00	17.50	10.00

1952 Num Num Cleveland Indians

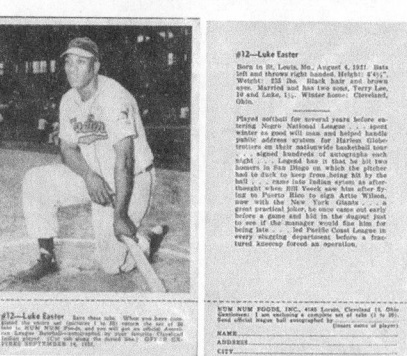

Distributed with packages of Num Num potato chips, pretzels and other snack foods, this black-and-white set, like the 1950 issue, was also issued in a slightly different format directly by the team. The Num Num cards have a 1" tab at the bottom which could be redeemed, when a complete set was collected, for an autographed baseball. The team-issued version of the cards was printed without the tabs. Also like the 1950 Num Nums, Bob Kennedy's card is unaccountably scarce in the 1952 set. The '52 cards measure 3-1/2" x 5-1/2" including the tab, which has the card number on front, along with redemption details. Backs, also printed in black-and-white, repeat the card number in the upper-left corner. There is significant player biographical information and some 1951 season highlights. Cards with no tabs are worth about 1/3 less than the values quoted.

	NM	E	VG
Complete Set, With Tabs (20):	9,500	4,750	2,850
Common Player, With Tab:	200.00	100.00	60.00
Complete Set, No Tabs (20):	4,600	2,300	1,400
Common Player, No Tab:	160.00	80.00	50.00

WITH TABS

		NM	E	VG
1	Lou Brissie	200.00	100.00	60.00
2	Jim Hegan	200.00	100.00	60.00
3	Birdie Tebbetts	200.00	100.00	60.00
4	Bob Lemon	420.00	220.00	125.00
5	Bob Feller	1,300	650.00	400.00
6	Early Wynn	420.00	220.00	125.00
7	Mike Garcia	200.00	100.00	60.00
8	Steve Gromek	200.00	100.00	60.00
9	Bob Chakales	200.00	100.00	60.00

10	Al Rosen	250.00	125.00	75.00
11	Dick Rozek	200.00	100.00	60.00
12	Luke Easter	250.00	125.00	75.00
13	Ray Boone	200.00	100.00	60.00
14	Bobby Avila	200.00	100.00	60.00
15	Dale Mitchell	200.00	100.00	60.00
16	Bob Kennedy (SP)	2,250	1,100	700.00
17	Harry Simpson	200.00	100.00	60.00
18	Larry Doby	420.00	220.00	125.00
19	Sam Jones	200.00	100.00	50.00
20	Al Lopez	420.00	220.00	125.00

NO TABS

1	Lou Brissie	160.00	80.00	50.00
2	Jim Hegan	160.00	80.00	50.00
3	Birdie Tebbetts	160.00	80.00	50.00
4	Bob Lemon	280.00	140.00	85.00
5	Bob Feller	850.00	425.00	250.00
6	Early Wynn	280.00	140.00	85.00
7	Mike Garcia	160.00	80.00	50.00
8	Steve Gromek	160.00	80.00	50.00
9	Bob Chakales	160.00	80.00	50.00
10	Al Rosen	175.00	90.00	50.00
11	Dick Rozek	160.00	80.00	50.00
12	Luke Easter	175.00	90.00	50.00
13	Ray Boone	160.00	80.00	50.00
14	Bobby Avila	160.00	80.00	50.00
15	Dale Mitchell	160.00	80.00	50.00
16	Bob Kennedy (SP)	1,750	875.00	550.00
17	Harry Simpson	160.00	80.00	50.00
18	Larry Doby	280.00	140.00	85.00
19	Sam Jones	160.00	80.00	50.00
20	Al Lopez	280.00	140.00	85.00

1969 N.Y. Boy Scouts

Cards featuring N.Y. Mets and Yankees players were used as a recruitment incentive in 1969. Cards are 2-1/2" x 3-1/2" and printed in black-and-white on thin cardboard. It is unknown, but likely, that players other than those checklisted here were also issued.

		NM	E	VG
	Common Player:	175.00	85.00	50.00
(1)	Tommy Agee	175.00	85.00	50.00
(2)	Bud Harrelson	175.00	85.00	50.00
(3)	Cleon Jones	175.00	85.00	50.00
(4)	Bobby Murcer	260.00	130.00	75.00
(5)	Joe Pepitone	260.00	130.00	75.00
(6)	Art Shamsky	175.00	85.00	50.00
(7)	Tom Seaver	700.00	350.00	210.00
(8)	Mel Stottlemyre	260.00	130.00	75.00
(9)	Ron Swoboda	175.00	85.00	50.00

1879-80 N.Y. Clipper Woodcuts

The N.Y. Clipper was a weekly newspaper devoted to theater and sports (primarily baseball) coverage in New York City between 1853-1923. Like many contemporary papers, the Clipper featured woodcut engravings in its pages in a time before photographic reproduction of pictures was feasible. Between April 1879, and November 1880, the paper printed a series of baseball player portraits. The early pieces were titled "The Clipper Prize Winners." and numbered. All of the woodcuts are about 4-1/2" x 5-3/4" in size featuring portraits within ornate frames with identification and biographical details below. Collectors prefer the woodcuts to be neatly trimmed from the newspaper page, with the biography at bottom intact. Because of the rarity of surviving examples, catalog values are undetermined. Many of these early stars of the game appear on no other contemporary cards or memorabilia issues.

		NM	E	VG

1879

1	M.C. Dorgan (4/12)
2	H.F. McCormick (4/19)
3	Stephen A. Libby (4/26)
4	Roscoe C. Barnes (5/3)
5	David W. Force (5/10)
6	Herman Doescher (Dosher) (5/17)
7a	Joseph Hornung (5/24)
7b	William H. McGunnigle (5/31)
9	Harding Richardson (6/7)
(10)	James L. White (7/14)
(11)	Levi S. Meyerle (6/21)
(12)	Joe Start (6/28)
(13)	T.H. Murnam (Murnane) (7/5)
(14)	Thomas York (7/12)
(15)	Fred Dunlap (7/19)
(16)	A.J. Leonard (7/26)
(17)	J. Lee Richmond (8/2)
(18)	Charles N. Snyder (8/9)
(19)	John Cassidy (8/16)
(20)	Charles Fulmer (8/23)
(21)	Thomas Poorman (8/30)
(22)	John Ward (9/6)
(23)	Larry Corcoran (9/13)
(24)	Douglas Allison (9/20)
(25)	John J. Farrow (9/27)
(26)	E.N. Williamson (10/4)
(27)	George Wright (10/11)
(28)	John J. Burdock (10/18)
(29)	James O'Rourke (10/25)
(30)	Philip Baker (11/1)
(31)	Samuel W. Trott (11/8)
(32)	John Lynch (11/15)
(33)	A.G. Spalding (11/22)
(34)	John C. Chapman (11/29)
(35)	Paul A. Hines (12/6)
(36)	Frank C. Bancroft (12/13)
(37)	John T. O'Conner (12/20)
(38)	Andrew J. Piercy (12/27)

1880

(39)	Harold M. McClure (1/3)
(40)	J.H. Gifford (1/24)
(41)	Sam Wright (5/15)
(42)	T.J. Keefe (5/22)
(43)	M.J. Kelly (5/29)
(44)	John Troy (6/5)
(45)	Joe Quest (6/12)
(46)	Alonzo Knight (6/19)
(47)	Charles E. Mason (6/26)
(48)	F.E. Goldsmith (7/3)
(49)	R.E. McKelvy (7/10)
(50)	Wm. McLean (Umpire)(7/17)
(51)	C.A. McVey (7/24)
(52)	John Manning (7/31)
(53)	Harry D. Stovey (8/7)
(54)	George A. Wood (8/14)
(55)	Robert T. Mathews (8/21)
(56)	D. Brouthers (8/28)
(57)	C.M. Smith (9/4)
(58)	James L. Clinton (9/11)
(59)	A.J. Bushong (9/18)
(60)	William J. Sweeney (9/25)
(61)	Roger Connor (10/2)
(62)	William Hawes (10/9)
(63)	Frank S. Flint (10/16)
(64)	William L. Haug (10/23)
(65)	M. Welch (10/30)
(66)	Aaron B. Clapp (11/6)
(67)	John J. Smith (11/13)
(68)	George Creamer (11/20)

1905 N.Y. Giants Scorecard Postcard

Two versions, black-and-white and color, of this standard size (about 5-1/2" x 3-1/2") postcard were apparently available for several years as it is copyrighted 1905 but postally used examples from years later are often seen. The card has a black background with large cut-out letters "GIANTS" at center featuring action poses of six players. A grid at bottom allows by-inning scores of a game to be posted before mailing. The undivided back has an embellished double-ruled stamp box and a large ornate "Post Card" at top-center.

	NM	E	VG
Black-and-White:	300.00	150.00	90.00
Color:	400.00	200.00	125.00

Frank Bowerman, Red Ames, Sam Mertes, Christy Mathewson, Iron Man McGinnity, Luther Taylor

1932 N.Y. Giants Schedule Postcards

These postcard-size (3-1/2" x 5-1/2") black-and-white cards have an action pose on front with the player's identification and previous season's stats. At bottom is information about ladies' days, directions to the Polo Grounds and an offer to receive a free picture of a favorite player. The divided back has the team's 1932 schedule at left and space for addressing at right. There is also a credit line to Minden Press. The Carl Hubbell card is far more common than all others and can be found on either a thick or thin card stock that is unlike the stock on which the other players are found.

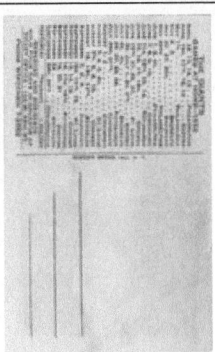

		NM	E	VG
	Common Player:	1,600	800.00	475.00
(1)	Ethan Allen	1,600	800.00	475.00
(2)	Herman Bell	1,600	800.00	475.00
(3)	Hugh Critz	1,600	800.00	475.00
(4)	Freddie Fitzsimmons	1,600	800.00	475.00
(5)	Chick Fullis	1,600	800.00	475.00
(6)	Sam Gibson	1,600	800.00	475.00
(7)	Fran Healey (Healy)	1,600	800.00	475.00
(8)	Frank Hogan	1,600	800.00	475.00
(9a)	Carl Hubbell (Thin stock.)	250.00	125.00	75.00
(9b)	Carl Hubbell (Thick stock.)	3,000	1,500	900.00
(10)	Travis Jackson	2,400	1,200	725.00
(11)	Len Koenecke	1,600	800.00	475.00
(12)	Sam Leslie	1,600	800.00	475.00
(13)	Freddy Lindstrom	2,400	1,200	725.00
(14)	Dolf Luque	1,600	800.00	475.00
(15)	Clarence Mitchell	1,600	800.00	475.00
(16)	Jim Mooney	1,600	800.00	475.00
(17)	Bob O'Farrell	1,600	800.00	475.00
(18)	Mel Ott	3,250	1,600	975.00
(19)	Roy Parmelee	1,600	800.00	475.00
(20)	Bill Terry	2,400	1,200	725.00
(21)	Johnny Vergez	1,600	800.00	475.00
(22)	Bill Walker	1,600	800.00	475.00

1948 N.Y. Giants Photo Pack

This set of player photos was sold at Polo Grounds souvenir stands. Pictures have player portraits in a 6-1/2" x 9" format. The black-and-white photos are blank-backed and have facsimile autographs printed near the bottom on front. A white border surrounds the front. The unnumbered photos are checklisted here in alphabetical order. It is possible the specific lineup of the packs changed over the course of the season to reflect roster moves.

		NM	E	VG
	Complete Set (27):	200.00	100.00	60.00
	Common Player:	5.00	2.50	1.50
(1)	Jack Conway	5.00	2.50	1.50
(2)	Walker Cooper	5.00	2.50	1.50
(3)	Leo Durocher	9.00	4.50	2.75
(4)	Sid Gordon	7.50	3.75	2.25
(5)	Andy Hansen	5.00	2.50	1.50
(6)	Clint Hartung	5.00	2.50	1.50
(7)	Larry Jansen	5.00	2.50	1.50
(8)	Sheldon Jones	5.00	2.50	1.50
(9)	Monte Kennedy	5.00	2.50	1.50
(10)	Buddy Kerr	5.00	2.50	1.50
(11)	Dave Koslo	5.00	2.50	1.50
(12)	Thornton Lee	5.00	2.50	1.50
(13)	Mickey Livingston	5.00	2.50	1.50
(14)	Whitey Lockman	5.00	2.50	1.50
(15)	Jack Lohrke	5.00	2.50	1.50
(16)	Willard Marshall	5.00	2.50	1.50
(17)	Johnnie McCarthy	5.00	2.50	1.50
(18)	Earl McGowan	7.50	3.75	2.25
(19)	Johnny Mize	12.50	6.25	3.75
(20)	Bobo Newsom	5.00	2.50	1.50
(21)	Mel Ott	25.00	12.50	7.50

		NM	E	VG
(22)	Ray Poat	5.00	2.50	1.50
(23)	Bobby Rhawn	5.00	2.50	1.50
(24)	Bill Rigney	5.00	2.50	1.50
(25)	Bobby Thomson	10.00	5.00	3.00
(26)	Ken Trinkle	5.00	2.50	1.50
(27)	Wesley N. Westrum	5.00	2.50	1.50

1949 N.Y. Giants Photo Pack

This set of player photos was sold at Polo Grounds souvenir stands. Pictures have player portraits in a 6-1/2" x 9" format. The black-and-white photos are blank-backed and have facsimile autographs printed near the bottom on front. A white border surrounds the front. The unnumbered photos are checklisted here in alphabetical order.

		NM	E	VG
Complete Set (25):		200.00	100.00	60.00
Common Player:		5.00	2.50	1.50
(1)	Hank Behrman	5.00	2.50	1.50
(2)	Walker Cooper	5.00	2.50	1.50
(3)	Leo Durocher	9.00	4.50	2.75
(4)	Fred Fitzsimmons	5.00	2.50	1.50
(5)	Frank Frisch	12.50	6.25	3.75
(6)	Augie Galan	5.00	2.50	1.50
(7)	Sid Gordon	7.50	3.75	2.25
(8)	Bert Haas	5.00	2.50	1.50
(9)	Andy Hansen	5.00	2.50	1.50
(10)	Clint Hartung	5.00	2.50	1.50
(11)	Bob Hofman	5.00	2.50	1.50
(12)	Larry Jansen	5.00	2.50	1.50
(13)	Sheldon Jones	5.00	2.50	1.50
(14)	Monte Kennedy	5.00	2.50	1.50
(15)	Buddy Kerr	5.00	2.50	1.50
(16)	Dave Koslo	5.00	2.50	1.50
(17)	Mickey Livingston	5.00	2.50	1.50
(18)	Whitey Lockman	5.00	2.50	1.50
(19)	Willard Marshall	5.00	2.50	1.50
(20)	Johnny Mize	12.50	6.25	3.75
(21)	Don Mueller	5.00	2.50	1.50
(22)	Ray Poat	5.00	2.50	1.50
(23)	Bobby Rhawn	5.00	2.50	1.50
(24)	Bill Rigney	5.00	2.50	1.50
(25)	Bobby Thomson	10.00	5.00	3.00

1954 N.Y. Journal-American

Issued during the Golden Age of baseball in New York City, this 59-card set features only players from the Giants, Yankees and Dodgers. The 2" x 4" cards were issued at newsstands with the purchase of the now-extinct newspaper. Card fronts have promotional copy and a contest serial number in addition to the player's name. Cards are printed in black-and-white on colored stock and unnumbered. Backs feature team schedules. It has been theorized that a 60th card should exist, probably a Brooklyn Dodger. Each card

can be found with the word "OFFERS" printed in either red or black, depending on the contest number at bottom. Numbers beginning with "0" have the word in black. Numbers 100000-150000 have the word in red or black, and numbers over 150000 have the word in red.

		NM	E	VG
Complete Set (59):		4,750	2,400	1,400
Common Player:		20.00	10.00	6.00
(1)	Johnny Antonelli	40.00	20.00	12.00
(2)	Hank Bauer	45.00	22.50	13.50
(3)	Yogi Berra	125.00	65.00	35.00
(4)	Joe Black	65.00	32.50	20.00
(5)	Harry Byrd	40.00	20.00	12.00
(6)	Roy Campanella	200.00	100.00	60.00
(7)	Andy Carey	40.00	20.00	12.00
(8)	Jerry Coleman	40.00	20.00	12.00
(9)	Joe Collins	40.00	20.00	12.00
(10)	Billy Cox	65.00	32.50	20.00
(11)	Al Dark	40.00	20.00	12.00
(12)	Carl Erskine	65.00	32.50	20.00
(13)	Whitey Ford	125.00	65.00	35.00
(14)	Carl Furillo	90.00	45.00	27.50
(15)	Junior Gilliam	90.00	45.00	27.50
(16)	Ruben Gomez	40.00	20.00	12.00
(17)	Marv Grissom	40.00	20.00	12.00
(18)	Jim Hearn	40.00	20.00	12.00
(19)	Gil Hodges	125.00	65.00	35.00
(20)	Bobby Hofman	40.00	20.00	12.00
(21)	Jim Hughes	65.00	32.50	20.00
(22)	Monte Irvin	90.00	45.00	27.50
(23)	Larry Jansen	40.00	20.00	12.00
(24)	Ray Katt	40.00	20.00	12.00
(25)	Steve Kraly	40.00	20.00	12.00
(26)	Bob Kuzava	40.00	20.00	12.00
(27)	Clem Labine	65.00	32.50	20.00
(28)	Frank Leja	40.00	20.00	12.00
(29)	Don Liddle	40.00	20.00	12.00
(30)	Whitey Lockman	40.00	20.00	12.00
(31)	Billy Loes	65.00	32.50	20.00
(32)	Eddie Lopat	40.00	20.00	12.00
(33)	Sal Maglie	40.00	20.00	12.00
(34)	Mickey Mantle	975.00	490.00	295.00
(35)	Willie Mays	375.00	185.00	110.00
(36)	Gil McDougald	45.00	22.50	13.50
(37)	Russ Meyer	65.00	32.50	20.00
(38)	Bill Miller	40.00	20.00	12.00
(39)	Tom Morgan	40.00	20.00	12.00
(40)	Don Mueller	40.00	20.00	12.00
(41)	Don Newcombe	75.00	37.50	22.50
(42)	Irv Noren	40.00	20.00	12.00
(43)	Erv Palica	65.00	32.50	20.00
(44)	Pee Wee Reese	130.00	65.00	40.00
(45)	Allie Reynolds	40.00	20.00	12.00
(46)	Dusty Rhodes	40.00	20.00	12.00
(47)	Phil Rizzuto	125.00	65.00	35.00
(48)	Ed Robinson	40.00	20.00	12.00
(49)	Jackie Robinson	250.00	125.00	75.00
(50)	Preacher Roe	65.00	32.50	20.00
(51)	George Shuba	65.00	32.50	20.00
(52)	Duke Snider	200.00	100.00	60.00
(53)	Hank Thompson	40.00	20.00	12.00
(54)	Wes Westrum	40.00	20.00	12.00
(55)	Hoyt Wilhelm	900.00	45.00	27.00
(56)	Davey Williams	40.00	20.00	12.00
(57)	Dick Williams	65.00	32.50	20.00
(58)	Gene Woodling	45.00	22.50	13.50
(59)	Al Worthington	40.00	20.00	12.00

1969 N.Y. News Mets Portfolio of Stars

To commemorate the N.Y. Mets miracle season of 1969, one of the city's daily newspapers, The News, issued a portfolio of player portraits done by editorial cartoonist Bruce Stark. The 9" x 12" pencil drawings are printed on heavy textured paper and were sold as a set in a folder labeled, "The 1969 Mets / A Portfolio of Stars." The black-and-white drawings are on a white background. A facsimile player autograph is printed at lower-left. At lower-right is the signature of the

artist, Stark, along with the paper's logo and a union label. The blank-backed, unnumbered pieces are checklisted here alphabetically.

		NM	E	VG
Complete Set (20):		225.00	110.00	70.00
Common Player:		7.50	3.75	2.25
(1)	Tommie Agee	7.50	3.75	2.25
(2)	Ken Boswell	7.50	3.75	2.25
(3)	Don Cardwell	7.50	3.75	2.25
(4)	Donn Clendenon	10.00	5.00	3.00
(5)	Wayne Garrett	7.50	3.75	2.25
(6)	Gary Gentry	7.50	3.75	2.25
(7)	Jerry Grote	7.50	3.75	2.25
(8)	Bud Harrelson	10.00	5.00	3.00
(9)	Gil Hodges	20.00	10.00	6.00
(10)	Cleon Jones	7.50	3.75	2.25
(11)	Jerry Koosman	7.50	3.75	2.25
(12)	Ed Kranepool	7.50	3.75	2.25
(13)	Jim McAndrew	7.50	3.75	2.25
(14)	Tug McGraw	10.00	5.00	3.00
(15)	Nolan Ryan	150.00	75.00	45.00
(16)	Tom Seaver	40.00	20.00	12.00
(17)	Art Shamsky	7.50	3.75	2.25
(18)	Ron Swoboda	7.50	3.75	2.25
(19)	Ron Taylor	7.50	3.75	2.25
(20)	Al Weis	7.50	3.75	2.25

1973 N.Y. News Mets/Yankees Caricatures

Between June 17 and August 26, the Sunday color comics section of the N.Y. News carried a centerspread picturing one Mets and one Yankees player as caricatured by artist Bruce Stark. Each player picture is printed on newsprint in approximately 10-1/2" x 14-1/2", the pictures have a page of comics or other matter on their backs. Values shown are for single pages. Intact pairs or complete comics section would command a premium.

		NM	E	VG
Complete Set (22):		200.00	100.00	60.00
Common Player:		6.00	3.00	1.75
METS				
(1)	Yogi Berra (6/17)	17.50	8.75	5.25
(2)	Tom Seaver (6/24)	15.00	7.50	4.50
(3)	John Milner (7/1)	6.00	3.00	1.75
(4)	Felix Millan (7/8)	6.00	3.00	1.75
(5)	Bud Harrelson (7/15)	6.00	3.00	1.75
(6)	Jim Fregosi (7/22)	6.00	3.00	1.75
(7)	Jerry Grote (7/29)	6.00	3.00	1.75
(8)	Cleon Jones (8/5)	6.00	3.00	1.75
(9)	Willie Mays (8/12)	25.00	12.50	7.50
(10)	Rusty Staub (8/19)	9.00	4.50	2.75
(11)	Tug McGraw (8/26)	7.50	3.75	2.25
YANKEES				
(12)	Ralph Houk (6/17)	7.50	3.75	2.25
(13)	Mel Stottlemyre (6/24)	7.50	3.75	2.25
(14)	Ron Blomberg (7/1)	6.00	3.00	1.75
(15)	Horace Clarke (7/8)	6.00	3.00	1.75
(16)	Gene Michael (7/15)	6.00	3.00	1.75
(17)	Graig Nettles (7/22)	7.50	3.75	2.25
(18)	Thurman Munson (7/29)	15.00	7.50	4.50
(19)	Roy White (8/5)	9.00	4.50	2.75
(20)	Bobby Murcer (8/12)	9.00	4.50	2.75
(21)	Matty Alou (8/19)	6.00	3.00	1.75
(22)	Sparky Lyle (8/26)	9.00	4.50	2.75

1916 N.Y. World Leaders in Baseball

This set of large-format (about 9" x 4") sepia-tone cards was issued to demonstrate the dominance of the World in New York City's newspaper wars. Each card has a portrait photo of a New York player. Most of the card is devoted to stats to boost the paper's claim as the "Pennant Winner in Advertising and Circulation." A note at left identifies the series as "'Leaders in Baseball' Series II." It is not known whether this checklist is complete.

	NM	E	VG
Common Player:	600.00	300.00	180.00

(1)	Home Run Baker	750.00	375.00	225.00
(2)	Jake Daubert	600.00	300.00	180.00
(3)	Buck Herzog	600.00	300.00	180.00
(4)	Dave Robertson	600.00	300.00	180.00

1944 N.Y. Yankees Stamps

One of the few paper collectibles issued during World War II, this set includes several players who do not appear on any other contemporary baseball card issue. The 1-3/4" x 2-3/8" stamps were issued on a single sheet with an album marking the Yankees 1943 World Series win. Stamps are in full color with the player's name in white on a red strip at bottom. The unnumbered stamps are checklisted here alphabetically. An album, about 6-1/2" x 3-1/2", was issued to display the stamps.

		NM	E	VG
	Complete Set (30):	100.00	50.00	30.00
	Common Player:	12.00	6.00	3.50
	Uncut Sheet:	145.00	75.00	45.00
	Album:	40.00	20.00	12.00
(1)	Ernie Bonham	12.00	6.00	3.50
(2)	Hank Borowy	12.00	6.00	3.50
(3)	Marvin Breuer	12.00	6.00	3.50
(4)	Tommy Byrne	12.00	6.00	3.50
(5)	Spud Chandler	15.00	7.50	4.50
(6)	Earl Combs (Earle)	25.00	12.50	7.50
(7)	Frank Crosetti	20.00	10.00	6.00
(8)	Bill Dickey	35.00	17.50	10.50
(9)	Atley Donald	12.00	6.00	3.50
(10)	Nick Etten	12.00	6.00	3.50
(11)	Art Fletcher	12.00	6.00	3.50
(12)	Joe Gordon	25.00	12.50	7.50
(13)	Oscar Grimes	12.00	6.00	3.50
(14)	Rollie Hemsley	12.00	6.00	3.50
(15)	Bill Johnson	12.00	6.00	3.50
(16)	Charlie Keller	15.00	7.50	4.50
(17)	John Lindell	15.00	7.50	4.50
(18)	Joe McCarthy	25.00	12.50	7.50
(19)	Bud Metheny	12.00	6.00	3.50
(20)	Johnny Murphy	12.00	6.00	3.50
(21)	Pat O'Daugherty	12.00	6.00	3.50
(22)	Marius Russo	12.00	6.00	3.50
(23)	John Schulte	12.00	6.00	3.50
(24)	Ken Sears	12.00	6.00	3.50
(25)	Tuck Stainbeck	12.00	6.00	3.50
(26)	George Stirnweiss	12.00	6.00	3.50
(27)	Jim Turner	12.00	6.00	3.50
(28)	Roy Weatherly	12.00	6.00	3.50
(29)	Charley Wensloff	12.00	6.00	3.50
(30)	Bill Zuber	12.00	6.00	3.50

1947-50 N.Y. Yankees Picture Pack

These team-issued sets offered fans at the souvenir stand more than two dozen pictures of the players and staff. The 6-1/2" x 9" pictures are in black-and-white with a white border and a facsimile autograph. Backs are blank. Players repeated over the years were represented by the same picture. The unnumbered pictures are listed in aphabetical order by year of issue.

		NM	E	VG
	Common Player:	4.00	2.00	1.25
	Complete 1947 Set (25):	100.00	50.00	30.00
(1)	Yogi Berra	20.00	10.00	6.00
(2)	Bill Bevens	4.00	2.00	1.25
(3)	Bobby Brown	4.00	2.00	1.25
(4)	Spud Chandler	4.00	2.00	1.25
(5)	Frank Colman	4.00	2.00	1.25
(6)	John Corriden	4.00	2.00	1.25
(7)	Frank Crosetti	5.00	2.50	1.50
(8)	Joe DiMaggio	40.00	20.00	12.00
(9)	Chuck Dressen	4.00	2.00	1.25
(10)	Randy Gumpert	4.00	2.00	1.25
(11)	Bucky Harris	5.00	2.50	1.50
(12)	Tommy Henrich	4.00	2.00	1.25
(13)	Ralph Houk	5.00	2.50	1.50
(14)	Don Johnson	4.00	2.00	1.25
(15)	Bill Johnson	4.00	2.00	1.25
(16)	Charlie Keller	5.00	2.50	1.50
(17)	John Lindell	4.00	2.00	1.25
(18)	George McQuinn	4.00	2.00	1.25
(19)	Joe Page	4.00	2.00	1.25
(20)	Allie Reynolds	5.00	2.50	1.50
(21)	Phil Rizzuto	12.50	6.25	3.75
(22)	Aaron Robinson	4.00	2.00	1.25
(23)	Frank Shea	4.00	2.00	1.25
(24)	Ken Silvestri	4.00	2.00	1.25
(25)	George Stirnweiss	4.00	2.00	1.25
	Complete 1948 Set (26):	100.00	50.00	30.00
(1)	Yogi Berra	20.00	10.00	6.00
(2)	Bobby Brown	4.00	2.00	1.25
(3)	Red Corriden	4.00	2.00	1.25
(4)	Frank Crosetti	5.00	2.50	1.50
(5)	Joe DiMaggio	40.00	20.00	12.00
(6)	Chuck Dressen	4.00	2.00	1.25
(7)	Karl Drews	4.00	2.00	1.25
(8)	Red Embree	4.00	2.00	1.25
(9)	Randy Gumpert	4.00	2.00	1.25
(10)	Bucky Harris	5.00	2.50	1.50
(11)	Tommy Henrich	4.00	2.00	1.25
(12)	Frank Hiller	4.00	2.00	1.25
(13)	Bill Johnson	4.00	2.00	1.25
(14)	Charlie Keller	5.00	2.50	1.50
(15)	John Lindell	4.00	2.00	1.25
(16)	Eddie Lopat	5.00	2.50	1.50
(17)	Cliff Mapes	4.00	2.00	1.25
(18)	George McQuinn	4.00	2.00	1.25
(19)	Gus Niarhos	4.00	2.00	1.25
(20)	George McQuinn	4.00	2.00	1.25
(21)	Joe Page	4.00	2.00	1.25
(22)	Vic Raschi	5.00	2.50	1.50
(23)	Allie Reynolds	5.00	2.50	1.50
(24)	Phil Rizzuto	12.50	6.25	3.75
(25)	Frank Shea	4.00	2.00	1.25
(26)	Snuffy Stirnweiss	4.00	2.00	1.25
	Complete 1949 Set (25):	100.00	50.00	30.00
(1)	Mel Allen	8.00	4.00	2.50
(2)	Larry Berra	20.00	10.00	6.00
(3)	Bobby Brown	4.00	2.00	1.25
(4)	Tommy Byrne	4.00	2.00	1.25
(5)	Jerry Coleman	4.00	2.00	1.25
(6)	Frank Crosetti	5.00	2.50	1.50
(7)	Bill Dickey	10.00	5.00	3.00
(8)	Joe DiMaggio	40.00	20.00	12.00
(9)	Tommy Henrich	4.00	2.00	1.25
(10)	Bill Johnson	4.00	2.00	1.25
(11)	Charlie Keller	5.00	2.50	1.50
(12)	John Lindell	4.00	2.00	1.25
(13)	Ed Lopat	5.00	2.50	1.50
(14)	Gus Niarhos	4.00	2.00	1.25
(15)	Joe Page	4.00	2.00	1.25
(16)	Bob Porterfield	4.00	2.00	1.25
(17)	Vic Raschi	4.00	2.00	1.25
(18)	Allie Reynolds	5.00	2.50	1.50
(19)	Phil Rizzuto	12.50	6.25	3.75
(20)	Fred Sanford	4.00	2.00	1.25
(21)	Frank Shea	4.00	2.00	1.25
(22)	Casey Stengel	15.00	7.50	4.50
(23)	George Stirnweiss	4.00	2.00	1.25
(24)	Jim Turner	4.00	2.00	1.25
(25)	Gene Woodling	5.00	2.50	1.50
	Complete 1950 Set (25):	100.00	50.00	30.00
(1)	Mel Allen	8.00	4.00	2.50
(2)	Hank Bauer	5.00	2.50	1.50
(3)	Larry Berra	20.00	10.00	6.00
(4)	Bobby Brown	4.00	2.00	1.25
(5)	Tommy Byrne	4.00	2.00	1.25
(6)	Jerry Coleman	4.00	2.00	1.25
(7)	Frank Crosetti	5.00	2.50	1.50
(8)	Bill Dickey	10.00	5.00	3.00
(9)	Joe DiMaggio	40.00	20.00	12.00
(10)	Tommy Henrich	4.00	2.00	1.25
(11)	Jack Jensen	7.50	3.75	2.25
(12)	Bill Johnson	4.00	2.00	1.25
(13)	Ed Lopat	5.00	2.50	1.50
(14)	Cliff Mapes	4.00	2.00	1.25
(15)	Joe Page	4.00	2.00	1.25

		NM	E	VG
(16)	Bob Porterfield	4.00	2.00	1.25
(17)	Vic Raschi	5.00	2.50	1.50
(18)	Allie Reynolds	5.00	2.50	1.50
(19)	Phil Rizzuto	12.50	6.25	3.75
(20)	Fred Sanford	4.00	2.00	1.25
(21)	Charlie Silvera	5.00	2.50	1.50
(22)	Casey Stengel	15.00	7.50	4.50
(23)	George Stirnweiss	4.00	2.00	1.25
(24)	Jim Turner	4.00	2.00	1.25
(25)	Gene Woodling	5.00	2.50	1.50

1955-1957 N.Y. Yankees Picture Pack

The checklist for this set of 5" x 7" black-and-white, blank-back pictures does not allow pinpointing its year of issue more closely. Similar in format to the later Jay Publishing photo packs, this issue differs in that only the team name (in upper- and lower-case letters), and not the city, is presented along with the player name (all-caps) in the identification line in the bottom border. The set was sold for 25 cents in a manila envelope. The unnumbered pictures are listed here alphabetically.

		NM	E	VG
	Complete Set (12):	75.00	37.50	22.50
	Common Player:	4.00	2.00	1.25
(1)	Hank Bauer	5.00	2.50	1.50
(2)	Yogi Berra	7.50	3.75	2.25
(3)	Tommy Byrne	4.00	2.00	1.25
(4)	Andy Carey	4.00	2.00	1.25
(5)	Joe Collins	4.00	2.00	1.25
(6)	Whitey Ford	7.50	3.75	2.25
(7)	Elston Howard	5.00	2.50	1.50
(8)	Mickey Mantle	35.00	17.50	10.00
(9)	Billy Martin	5.00	2.50	1.50
(10)	Gil McDougald	4.00	2.00	1.25
(11)	Casey Stengel	7.50	3.75	2.25
(12)	Bob Turley	4.00	2.00	1.25

1956 N.Y. Yankees "Action Pictures"

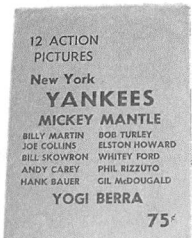

This set of 8" x 10" black-and-white pictures was sold for 75 cents in a paper envelope marked "12 ACTION / PICTURES." The white-bordered pictures have facsimile autographs or printed names on front and are blank-backed.

		NM	E	VG
	Complete Set (12):	125.00	65.00	49.00
	Common Player:	6.00	3.00	1.75
(1)	Hank Bauer	7.50	3.75	2.25
(2)	Yogi Berra	15.00	7.50	4.50
(3)	Andy Carey	6.00	3.00	1.75
(4)	Joe Collins	6.00	3.00	1.75
(5)	Whitey Ford	15.00	7.50	4.50
(6)	Elston Howard	9.00	4.50	2.75
(7)	Mickey Mantle	75.00	37.00	22.00
(8)	Billy Martin	9.00	4.50	2.75
(9)	Gil McDougald	7.50	3.75	2.25
(10)	Phil Rizzuto	15.00	7.50	4.50
(11)	Bill Skowron	9.00	4.50	2.75
(12)	Bob Turley	7.50	3.75	2.25

1956 N.Y. Yankees Picture Pack

This set was issued, probably for sale at Yankee Stadium souvenir stands, in 1956, though some of the photos date as far back as 1951, and a few appear to have been taken during the 1955 World Series at Ebbets Field. Printed in black-and-white on semi-gloss paper, the pictures measure about 6" x 8-7/8". There is a 1/4" white border around the photo and a white strip at the bottom of each photo with the player's name. Backs are blank. The pictures are checklisted in alphabetical order, but the list may not be complete. Some of the photos are familiar from their use on baseball cards, including the 1951 Bowman Mantle.

		NM	E	VG
	Complete Set (22):	275.00	135.00	80.00
	Common Player:	8.00	4.00	2.50
(1)	Hank Bauer	10.00	5.00	3.00
(2)	Larry "Yogi" Berra	20.00	10.00	6.00

(3)	Tommy Byrne	8.00	4.00	2.50
(4)	Andy Carey	8.00	4.00	2.50
(5)	Bob Cerv	8.00	4.00	2.50
(6)	Gerry Coleman	8.00	4.00	2.50
(7)	Joe Collins	8.00	4.00	2.50
(8)	Ed "Whitey" Ford	20.00	10.00	6.00
(9)	Bob Grim	8.00	4.00	2.50
(10)	Elston Howard	10.00	5.00	3.00
(11)	Johnny Kucks	8.00	4.00	2.50
(12)	Don Larsen	12.50	6.25	3.75
(13)	Jerry Lumpe	8.00	4.00	2.50
(14)	Mickey Mantle	130.00	65.00	39.00
(15)	Billy Martin	15.00	7.50	4.50
(16)	Mickey McDermott	8.00	4.00	2.50
(17)	Gil McDougald	10.00	5.00	3.00
(18)	Tom Morgan	8.00	4.00	2.50
(19)	Irv Noren	8.00	4.00	2.50
(20)	Charlie Silvera	8.00	4.00	2.50
(21)	Bill Skowron	10.00	5.00	3.00
(22)	Bob Turley	10.00	5.00	3.00

1957 N.Y. Yankees Picture Pack

Nominally 8" x 10", the actual size on these blank-back, black-and-white pictures varies from about 7-1/2" to 8" wide by 9-7/8" x 10-1/8" tall. The player poses are surrounded with a white border. The player name is printed within the picture. Some of the photos used considerably pre-date the period of issue.

		NM	E	VG
Complete Set (12):		125.00	65.00	40.00
Common Player:		10.00	5.00	3.00
(1)	Hank Bauer	12.50	6.25	3.75
(2)	Larry Berra	20.00	10.00	6.00
(3)	Andy Carey	10.00	5.00	3.00
(4)	Whitey Ford	20.00	10.00	6.00
(5)	Elston Howard	12.50	6.25	3.75
(6)	Tony Kubek	15.00	7.50	4.50
(7)	Don Larsen	12.50	6.25	3.75
(8)	Mickey Mantle	60.00	30.00	18.00
(9)	Gil McDougald	12.50	6.25	3.75
(10)	Bill Skowron	12.50	6.25	3.75
(11)	Bob Turley	12.50	6.25	3.75
(12)	Frank Crosetti, Bill Dickey, Casey Stengel, Jim Turner	10.00	5.00	3.00

1960 N.Y. Yankees "Action Pictures"

This set of 8" x 10" black-and-white pictures was sold for 75 cents in a paper envelope marked "12 ACTION / PICTURES." The white bordered pictures have facsimile autographs or printed names on front and are blank-backed.

		NM	E	VG
Complete Set (12):		200.00	100.00	60.00
Common Player:		10.00	5.00	3.00
(1)	Larry Berra	20.00	10.00	6.00
(2)	Art Ditmar	10.00	5.00	3.00
(3)	Whitey Ford	20.00	10.00	6.00
(4)	Elston Howard	12.50	6.25	3.75
(5)	Tony Kubek	15.00	7.50	4.50
(6)	Hector Lopez	10.00	5.00	3.00
(7)	Mickey Mantle	60.00	30.00	18.00
(8)	Roger Maris	35.00	17.50	10.50
(9)	Bobby Richardson	12.50	6.25	3.75
(10)	Bill Skowron	12.50	6.25	3.75
(11)	Casey Stengel	15.00	7.50	4.50
(12)	Bob Turley	12.50	6.25	3.75

1970 N.Y. Yankees Clinic Schedule Postcards

This series of postcards was issued in conjunction with a series of baseball clinics which the Yankees put on for youngsters prior to selected home games. Fronts of the 3-1/2" x 5-1/2" glossy color cards have player portraits with a facsimile autograph in a white panel at bottom. Backs have player identification and career highlights, a schedule of the clinic days and credit line for Howard Photo Service. White and Murcer cards are scarce because of rainouts on their scheduled clinic appearance days. Cards are checklisted here in alphabetical order.

		NM	E	VG
Complete Set (13):		130.00	65.00	40.00
Common Player:		3.00	1.50	.90
(1)	Stan Bahnsen	3.00	1.50	.90
(2)	Curt Blefary	3.00	1.50	.90
(3)	Danny Cater	3.00	1.50	.90
(4)	Horace Clarke	3.00	1.50	.90
(5)	Joe DiMaggio, Mickey Mantle	25.00	12.50	7.50
(6)	John Ellis	3.00	1.50	.90
(7)	Jerry Kenney	3.00	1.50	.90
(8)	Gene Michael	3.00	1.50	.90
(9)	Thurman Munson	30.00	15.00	9.00
(10)	Bobby Murcer	15.00	7.50	4.50
(11)	Fritz Peterson	3.00	1.50	.90
(12)	Mel Stottlemyre	4.50	2.25	1.25
(13)	Roy White	35.00	17.50	10.50

1971 N.Y. Yankees Clinic Schedule Postcards

These postcards were issued in conjunction with a series of baseball clinics which the Yankees put on for youngsters prior to selected home games. Fronts of the 3-1/2" x 5-1/2" glossy color cards have player portraits with a facsimile autograph in a white panel at bottom. Backs are printed in blue, have player identification and career highlights and a schedule of the clinic days. Cards are checklisted here in alphabetical order.

		NM	E	VG
Complete Set (16):		90.00	45.00	27.00
Common Player:		3.00	1.50	.90
(1)	Felipe Alou, Jim Lyttle	3.00	1.50	.90
(2)	Stan Bahnsen	3.00	1.50	.90
(3)	Frank Baker, Jerry Kenney	3.00	1.50	.90
(4)	Curt Blefary	3.00	1.50	.90
(5)	Danny Cater	3.00	1.50	.90
(6)	Horace Clarke, Gene Michael	3.00	1.50	.90
(7)	John Ellis	3.00	1.50	.90
(8)	Jake Gibbs	3.00	1.50	.90
(9)	Ralph Houk	3.00	1.50	.90
(10)	Mickey Mantle	30.00	15.00	9.00
(11)	Lindy McDaniel	3.00	1.50	.90
(12)	Thurman Munson	15.00	7.50	4.50
(13)	Bobby Murcer	4.50	2.25	1.25
(14)	Fritz Peterson	3.00	1.50	.90
(15)	Mel Stottlemyre	3.00	1.50	.90
(16)	Roy White	3.00	1.50	.90

1971-72 N.Y. Yankees Schedule Cards

These team-issue cards were given to ticket buyers and at pre-season promotional events. Fronts have player photos with a facsimile autograph in the white border at bottom, between a pair of team insignia. Backs have the team schedule.

The unnumbered cards are listed here alphabetically. For unknown reasons, the Mel Stottlemyre card was extremely short-printed.

		NM	E	VG
Complete Set (8):		500.00	250.00	150.00
Common Player:		30.00	15.00	9.00
(1)	Felipe Alou	35.00	17.50	10.50
(2)	Ron Blomberg	30.00	15.00	9.00
(3)	Thurman Munson	225.00	110.00	67.00
(4)	Bobby Murcer	35.00	17.50	10.50
(5)	Mel Stottlemyre SP	200.00	100.00	60.00
(6)	Ron Swoboda	30.00	15.00	9.00
(7)	Roy White	35.00	17.50	10.50
(8)	Frank Messer, Phil Rizzuto, Bill White (Announcers)	30.00	15.00	9.00

O

1969 Oakland A's (Andersen)

5. Joe DiMaggio—coach
OAKLAND A's

Though they are sometimes identified as an issue of Jack in the Box restaurants, there is no identifier of that nature on these cards. In fact, they are a collectors' fantasy issue sold only within the hobby by Boston photographer Mike Andersen. The blank-back black-and-white cards measure 2-1/8" x 3-5/8". Beneath the portrait photo on front is the player's name, position and uniform number. The team name is in gothic script at bottom. Cards are checklisted here by uniform number.

		NM	E	VG
Complete Set (21):		80.00	40.00	24.00
Common Player:		2.50	1.25	.75
1	Dick Green	2.50	1.25	.75
2	Danny Cater	2.50	1.25	.75
3	Mike Hershberger	2.50	1.25	.75
4	Phil Roof	2.50	1.25	.75
5	Joe DiMaggio (Coach)	30.00	15.00	9.00
6	Sal Bando	2.50	1.25	.75
7	Rick Monday	2.50	1.25	.75
9a	Bert Campaneris	5.00	2.50	1.50
9b	Reggie Jackson	45.00	22.00	13.50
13	Blue Moon Odom	3.50	1.75	1.00
17	Jim Pagliaroni	2.50	1.25	.75
19	Bert Campaneris	2.50	1.25	.75
20	Lew Krausse	2.50	1.25	.75
24	Joe Nossek	2.50	1.25	.75
25	Paul Lindblad	2.50	1.25	.75
27	Catfish Hunter	7.50	3.75	2.25
29	Chuck Dobson	2.50	1.25	.75
30	Jim Nash	2.50	1.25	.75
31	Ramon Webster	2.50	1.25	.75
35	Tom Reynolds	2.50	1.25	.75
42	Hank Bauer	2.50	1.25	.70

1969 Oakland A's (Broder)

A second issue of black-and-white collector cards featuring the 1969 A's was produced by West Coast collector/dealer Ed Broder. In larger (2-3/4" x 4") format the Broder issue is considerably scarcer than that produced by Mike Andersen. Availability of the Broders was advertised at 100 sets. The blank-back Broder cards have the player name in the wide white border beneath the photo. At bottom the city name is in gothic script with the A's logo on a baseball flying out of a stadium. The unnumbered cards are checklisted here alphabetically.

Reggie Jackson

OAKLAND A's

	NM	E	VG
Complete Set (14):	130.00	65.00	40.00
Common Player:	4.00	2.00	1.25
(1) Sal Bando	4.00	2.00	1.25
(2) Hank Bauer	4.00	2.00	1.20
(3) Bert Campaneris	5.00	3.00	1.80
(4) Dan Cater	4.00	2.00	1.20
(5) Joe DiMaggio	30.00	15.00	9.00
(6) Chuck Dobson	4.00	2.00	1.20
(7) Dick Green	4.00	2.00	1.20
(8) Mike Hershberger	4.00	2.00	1.20
(9) Jim Hunter	16.00	8.00	5.00
(10) Reggie Jackson	50.00	25.00	15.00
(11) Bob Johnson	4.00	2.00	1.20
(12) Rick Monday	4.00	2.00	1.20
(13) Johnny Moon Odom	8.00	4.00	2.50
(14) Phil Roof	4.00	2.00	1.20

1970 Oakland A's (Andersen)

45 - ROBERTO RODRIQUEZ

Oakland A's

Boston baseball photographer Mike Andersen produced a second collectors' issue of Oakland A's cards in 1970. Nearly identical in format to his 1969 issue, the '70 team set measures 2-1/4" x 3-5/8" with black-and-white player poses at center. Uniform number, name and team are in the bottom border. Backs are blank. Cards are checklisted here by uniform number.

	NM	E	VG
Complete Set (24):	30.00	15.00	9.00
Common Player:	1.50	.75	.45
1 Dick Green	1.50	.75	.45
6 Sal Bando	1.50	.75	.45
7 Rick Monday	1.50	.75	.45
8 Felipe Alou	2.00	1.00	.60
9 Reggie Jackson	15.00	7.50	4.50
10 Dave Duncan	1.50	.75	.45
11 John McNamera (McNamara)	1.50	.75	.45
12 Larry Haney	1.50	.75	.45
13 Blue Moon Odom	2.00	1.00	.60
17 Roberto Pena	1.50	.75	.45
19 Bert Campaneris	2.00	1.00	.60
24 Diego Segui	1.50	.75	.45
25 Paul Lindblad	1.50	.75	.45
27 Catfish Hunter	4.00	2.00	1.25
28 Mudcat Grant	1.50	.75	.45
29 Chuck Dobson	1.50	.75	.45
30 Don Mincher	1.50	.75	.45
31 Jose Tartabull	1.50	.75	.45
33 Jim Roland	1.50	.75	.45
34 Rollie Fingers	4.00	2.00	1.25
36 Tito Francona	1.50	.75	.45
38 Al Downing	1.50	.75	.45
39 Frank Fernandez	1.50	.75	.45
45 Roberto Rodriguez	1.50	.75	.45

1974 Oakley Building and Loan

OAKLEY
building and loan.

This black-and-white, blank-back card was issued in conjunction with an autograph appearance by Joe Morgan at the bank located northeast of Cincinnati. The card measures 3-1/2" x 5-1/2".

	NM	EX	VG
Joe Morgan	75.00	37.50	22.50

1968 Official Major League Players Baseball Marbles

Produced by Creative Creations Inc., though not so identified on the marbles themselves, these approximately 3/4" hard plastic marbles have a player portrait photo (with cap logos removed) on one side and a facsimile autograph on the other, with "JAPAN" beneath. The marbles were issued in series of 20 on colorful cardboard packaging which pictures each player in the series. While the packaging says "Collect All 24 Series" only 120 marbles were actually issued. Suggested retail price at issue was $1.49 per series.

	NM	E	VG
Complete Set (115):	675.00	325.00	200.00
Common Player:	4.00	2.00	1.25
(1) Hank Aaron	40.00	20.00	12.00
(2) Tommie Aaron	4.00	2.00	1.25
(3) Tommy Agee	4.00	2.00	1.25
(4) Richie Allen	7.00	3.50	2.00
(5) Gene Alley	4.00	2.00	1.25
(6) Bob Allison	4.00	2.00	1.25
(7) Felipe Alou	5.00	2.50	1.50
(8) Jesus Alou	4.00	2.00	1.25
(9) Matty Alou	4.00	2.00	1.25
(10) Max Alvis	4.00	2.00	1.25
(11) Mike Andrews	4.00	2.00	1.25
(12) Luis Aparicio	12.50	6.25	3.75
(13) Bob Aspromonte	4.00	2.00	1.25
(14) Stan Bahnsen	4.00	2.00	1.25
(15) Bob Bailey	4.00	2.00	1.25
(16) Ernie Banks	25.00	12.50	7.50
(17) Glenn Beckert	4.00	2.00	1.25
(18) Gary Bell	4.00	2.00	1.25
(19) Johnny Bench	30.00	15.00	9.00
(20) Ken Berry	4.00	2.00	1.25
(21) Paul Blair	4.00	2.00	1.25
(22) Bob Bolin	4.00	2.00	1.25
(23) Dave Boswell	4.00	2.00	1.25
(24) Nelson Briles	4.00	2.00	1.25
(25) Lou Brock	12.50	6.25	3.75
(26) Wally Bunker	4.00	2.00	1.25
(27) Johnny Callison	4.00	2.00	1.25
(28) Norm Cash	5.00	2.50	1.50
(29) Orlando Cepeda	12.50	6.25	3.75
(30) Dean Chance	4.00	2.00	1.25
(31) Roberto Clemente	50.00	25.00	15.00
(32) Donn Clendenon	4.00	2.00	1.25
(33) Tony Cloninger	4.00	2.00	1.25
(34) Tommy Davis	4.00	2.00	1.25
(35) Al Downing	4.00	2.00	1.25
(36) Curt Flood	4.00	2.00	1.25
(37) Bill Freehan	4.00	2.00	1.25
(38) Jim Fregosi	4.00	2.00	1.25
(39) Bob Gibson	12.50	6.25	3.75

(40) Jim "Mudcat" Grant	4.00	2.00	1.25
(41) Jerry Grote	4.00	2.00	1.25
(42) Jimmie Hall	4.00	2.00	1.25
(43) Tom Haller	4.00	2.00	1.25
(44) Ron Hansen	4.00	2.00	1.25
(45) Steve Hargan	4.00	2.00	1.25
(46) Ken Harrelson	4.00	2.00	1.25
(47) Jim Hart	4.00	2.00	1.25
(48) Jimmie Holt	4.00	2.00	1.25
(49) Joe Horlen	4.00	2.00	1.25
(50) Willie Horton	4.00	2.00	1.25
(51) Frank Howard	5.00	2.50	1.50
(52) Dick Hughes	4.00	2.00	1.25
(53) Randy Hundley	4.00	2.00	1.25
(54) Ron Hunt	4.00	2.00	1.25
(55) Jim "Catfish" Hunter	12.50	6.25	3.75
(56) Pat Jarvis	4.00	2.00	1.25
(57) Julian Javier	4.00	2.00	1.25
(58) Tommy John	6.00	3.00	1.75
(59) Deron Johnson	4.00	2.00	1.25
(60) Mack Jones	4.00	2.00	1.25
(61) Jim Kaat	5.00	2.50	1.50
(62) Al Kaline	20.00	10.00	6.00
(63) Don Kessinger	4.00	2.00	1.25
(64) Harmon Killebrew	20.00	10.00	6.00
(65) Jerry Koosman	4.00	2.00	1.25
(66) Jim Lefebvre	4.00	2.00	1.25
(67) Mickey Lolich	4.00	2.00	1.25
(68) Jim Lonborg	4.00	2.00	1.25
(69) Juan Marichal	12.50	6.25	3.75
(70) Roger Maris	30.00	15.00	9.00
(71) Ed Mathews	20.00	10.00	6.00
(72) Jerry May	4.00	2.00	1.25
(73) Willie Mays	40.00	20.00	12.00
(74) Dick McAuliffe	4.00	2.00	1.25
(75) Tim McCarver	5.00	2.50	1.50
(76) Willie McCovey	12.50	6.25	3.75
(77) Sam McDowell	4.00	2.00	1.25
(78) Denny McLain	5.00	2.50	1.50
(79) Dave McNally	4.00	2.00	1.25
(80) Denis Menke	4.00	2.00	1.25
(81) Jim Merritt	4.00	2.00	1.25
(82) Bob Miller	4.00	2.00	1.25
(83) Rick Monday	4.00	2.00	1.25
(84) Joe Morgan	12.50	6.25	3.75
(85) Gary Nolan	4.00	2.00	1.25
(86) Jim Northrup	4.00	2.00	1.25
(87) Rich Nye	4.00	2.00	1.25
(88) Tony Oliva	5.00	2.50	1.50
(89) Milt Pappas	4.00	2.00	1.25
(90) Camilo Pascual	4.00	2.00	1.25
(91) Joe Pepitone	5.00	2.50	1.50
(92) Tony Perez	12.50	6.25	3.75
(93) Jim Perry	4.00	2.00	1.25
(94) Gary Peters	4.00	2.00	1.25
(95) Fritz Peterson	4.00	2.00	1.25
(96) Rico Petrocelli	4.00	2.00	1.25
(97) Vada Pinson	5.00	2.50	1.50
(98) Boog Powell	5.00	2.50	1.50
(99) Rick Reichardt	4.00	2.00	1.25
(100) Brooks Robinson	15.00	7.50	4.50
(101) Frank Robinson	15.00	7.50	4.50
(102) Pete Rose	40.00	20.00	12.00
(103) Chico Salmon	4.00	2.00	1.25
(104) Ron Santo	5.00	2.50	1.50
(105) George Scott	4.00	2.00	1.25
(106) Tom Seaver	15.00	7.50	4.50
(107) Dick Selma	4.00	2.00	1.25
(108) Mike Shannon	4.00	2.00	1.25
(109) Joe Sparma	4.00	2.00	1.25
(110) Willie Stargell	12.50	6.25	3.75
(111) Mel Stottlemyre	4.00	2.00	1.25
(113) Luis Tiant	4.00	2.00	1.25
(114) Cesar Tovar	4.00	2.00	1.25
(115) Tom Tresh	4.50	2.25	1.25
(116) Pete Ward	4.00	2.00	1.25
(117) Billy Williams	12.50	6.25	3.75
(118) Maury Wills	4.00	2.00	1.25
(119) Earl Wilson	4.00	2.00	1.25
(120) Dooley Womack	4.00	2.00	1.25

1974 Oh Henry! Henry Aaron Premium Photo

This 8" x 10" black-and-white photo was prepared as a premium for Oh Henry! candy. It features a full-length pose of Aaron and has a facsimile inscribed autographed on front.

	NM	E	VG
Henry Aaron	20.00	10.00	6.00

1959 Oklahoma Today Major Leaguers

 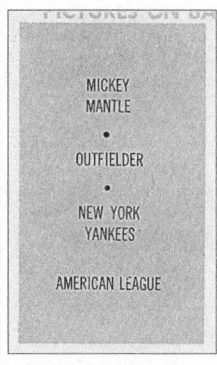

MICKEY MANTLE

•

OUTFIELDER

•

NEW YORK YANKEES

AMERICAN LEAGUE

Contemporary and former ballplayers from the Sooner State were featured in this "card set" which was printed on the back cover of the Summer, 1959, issue of "Oklahoma Today" magazine. If cut from the cover, the cards measure about 1-11/16" x 2-3/4". Fronts have black-and-white photos on green, gold or aqua backgrounds. A white strip at bottom has the player name in red. Gray backs have the player name, position, team and league. The unnumbered cards are checklisted here in alphabetical order.

		NM	E	VG
	Complete Magazine:	1,100	550.00	330.00
	Complete Set, Singles (20):	1,100	550.00	330.00
	Common Player:	45.00	22.50	13.50
(1)	Jerry Adair	45.00	22.00	13.50
(2)	Harry Brecheen	45.00	22.00	13.50
(3)	Johnny Callison	45.00	22.00	13.50
(4)	Alvin Dark	45.00	22.50	13.50
(5)	"Dizzy" Dean	60.00	30.00	18.00
(6)	Paul Dean	45.00	22.00	13.50
(7)	Don Demeter	45.00	22.50	13.50
(8)	Carl Hubbell	50.00	25.00	15.00
(9)	Mickey Mantle	500.00	250.00	150.00
(10)	"Pepper" Martin	45.00	22.00	13.50
(11)	Lindy McDaniel	45.00	22.50	13.50
(12)	Von McDaniel	45.00	22.50	13.50
(13)	Cal McLish	45.00	22.50	13.50
(14)	Dale Mitchel (Mitchell)	45.00	22.50	13.50
(15)	Allie Reynolds	45.00	22.00	13.50
(16)	Warren Spahn	45.00	22.00	13.50
(17)	Tom Sturdivant	45.00	22.50	13.50
(18)	Jerry Walker	45.00	22.50	13.50
(19)	Lloyd Waner	45.00	22.00	13.50
(20)	Paul Waner	45.00	22.00	13.50

1948 Old Gold Jackie Robinson

JACKIE ROBINSON, first baseman of the Brooklyn Dodgers, was born in Cairo, Georgia, 28 years ago. After his family moved to Pasadena, Calif., he entered the University of California, where he distinguished himself as a star athlete in baseball, football, basketball and track.

At 23, Jackie entered the Army, rising to second lieutenant. For 31 months he served overseas, and then joined the Kansas City Monarchs baseball team, for which he fielded so sensationally that he attracted the attention of organized baseball. Impressed with his performance, Branch Rickey, president of the Brooklyn Dodgers, signed him for the Montreal Royals "farm."

So outstanding was Jackie's record with the Montreal Royals that President Rickey signed him to the Dodgers late in 1947. In that way, he became the first Negro to enter the big leagues. He is noted for his speed and batting ability.

A good-looking six-footer, Jackie weighs about 185, and is even-tempered and modest. Off season he lives in Los Angeles with his wife, a former trained nurse, and their young son, Jackie, Jr. His chief ambition is "an earnest desire to contribute to the advancement and recognition of the Negro race."

These postcard-size (3-1/2" x 5-1/2") advertising pieces picture Jackie Robinson and a pack of Old Gold cigarettes on their black-and-white fronts, along with an endorsement from the player and his facsimile autograph. Each back has a different presentation of biography and career summary.

	NM	E	VG
Jackie Robinson (Fielding)	800.00	400.00	240.00
Jackie Robinson (In dugout.)	600.00	300.00	180.00

1886 Old Judge New York Giants (N167)

Produced in 1886, the rare N167 Old Judge tobacco cards were the first to be issued by New York's Goodwin & Co., the parent firm of Old Judge Cigarettes. The 1-1/2" x 2-1/2" sepia-toned cards were printed on thin paper and featured only members of the New York National League club. Twelve subjects are known to exist, six of whom are Hall of Famers. The front of each card lists the player's name, position and team and has the words "Old Judge" at the top. The backs contain another ad for the Old Judge brand and also include a line noting that the player poses were "copied from photo by J. Wood, 208 Bowery, N.Y."

		NM	E	VG
	Common Player:	50,000	25,000	15,000
(1)	Roger Connor	112,500	56,250	33,750
(2)	Larry Corcoran	50,000	25,000	15,000
(3)	Mike Dorgan	50,000	25,000	15,000
(4)	Dude Esterbrook	50,000	25,000	15,000
(5)	Buck Ewing	120,000	60,000	30,000
(6)	Joe Gerhardt	50,000	25,000	15,000
(7)	Pete Gillespie	50,000	25,000	15,000
(8)	Tim Keefe	112,500	56,250	33,750
(9)	Orator Jim O'Rourke	112,500	56,250	33,750
(10)	Danny Richardson	50,000	25,000	15,000
(11)	John Ward	112,500	56,250	33,750
(12)	Mickey Welsh (Welch)	112,500	56,250	33,750

1887-1890 Old Judge (N172)

This is one of the most fascinating of all card sets, being not only one of the first, but also the largest ever. The number of cards issued may never be finally determined. These cards were issued by the Goodwin & Co. tobacco firm in their Old Judge and, to a lesser extent, Gypsy Queen cigarettes. Players from more than 40 major and minor league teams are pictured on the nominally 1-7/16" x 2-1/2" cards (actual size varies), with some 500 different players known to exist. Up to 20 different pose, team and caption variations exist for some players. Cards were issued both with and without dates, numbered and unnumbered, and with both script and machine- printed identification. Known variations number over 3,500. The cards themselves are black-and-white (many now toned sepia or even pink) photographs pasted onto thick cardboard. They are blank-backed. Values shown here are for the most common examples of a specific player's cards, unless otherwise indicated. Demand for various photo, team, league, etc., variations can significantly affect value and, because of the relatively "thin" nature of the market for Old Judge cards, is subject to rapid fluctuations as collectors enter and leave the arena. These listings are presented alphabetically. Few Old Judge cards were issued with the player's first name, or even initial. Where verifiable, the first names have been added to these listings in the form most often encountered at the time of issue. Misspellings were common among the issue. Cases in which all of a player's cards were incorrectly spelled are listed by the misspelling, with the

correct spelling in parentheses following. In cases where the name was sometimes spelled correctly, and sometimes not, the incorrect spellings are provided thus: "(Also: ...)". For each player, the number of different photo/team combinations known is indicated. Minor changes in the player identification caption, such as addition of an initial, presence or absence of period or comma, abbreviation of position, or spelling of team name, are not included in the number of cards listed. Team designations for each player are listed, where known. Pose/designation variations which have historically attracted increased collector interest are specified. These include such subsets as the Brown's Champions and Mets "spotted tie" portrait cards of 1887, the Player's League designations of 1890 and some other popularly collected subsets, such as the dual-player cards. Cards which depict and name both players are listed here under each player's name and are numbered with a "DP" prefix. League designations found in the listings include: AA - American Association; NL - National League; PL - Player's League; WA - Western Association. Gaps have been left in the assigned numbering to accommodate future additions.

		NM	EX	VG
	Common Card:	725.00	325.00	180.00
(1)	Gus Albert (Alberts) 7			
1 (a)	(Cleveland)	1.100	495.00	275.00
1 (b)	(Milwaukee)	725.00	325.00	180.00
(2)	Charles Alcott 6			
2 (a)	(Mansfield)	1,500	675.00	375.00
2 (b)	(St. Louis Whites WA)	975.00	435.00	250.00
(3)	Daniel Alexander 4			
3 (a)	(Des Moines)	950.00	435.00	225.00
(4)	Bob Allen 7			
4 (a)	(Philadelphia NL)	725.00	325.00	180.00
4 (a)	(Pittsburgh)	725.00	325.00	180.00
(5)	Myron Allen 6			
5 (a)	(Kansas City)	1,650	745.00	415.00
(6)	Billy Alvord 3			
6 (a)	(Des Moines)	725.00	325.00	180.00
6 (b)	(Toledo)	975.00	425.00	250.00
(7)	Varney Anderson 3			
7 (a)	(St. Paul)	11,500	5,175	2,1875
(8)	Ed Andrews 6			
8 (a)	(Philadelphia NL)	725.00	325.00	180.00
DP 1	(Being tagged by Buster Hoover.)	1,000	450.00	250.00
(9)	Wally Andrews 3			
9 (a)	(Omaha)	850.00	375.00	180.00
(10)	Bill Annis 4			
10 (a)	(Omaha)	900.00	400.00	230.00
10 (b)	(Worcester)	725.00	325.00	180.00
(11)	Cap Anson			
	See Hall of Fame Section Following			
(12)	Joe Ardner 4			
12 (a)	(Kansas City)	725.00	325.00	180.00
12 (b)	(St. Joseph)	1,150	500.00	275.00
(13)	Tug Arundel 5			
13 (a)	(Indianapolis)	725.00	325.00	180.00
(14)	Jersey Bakley (Bakely) 5			
14 (a)	(Cleveland)	1,100	500.00	275.00
(15)	Kid Baldwin 5			
15 (a)	(Cincinnati)	725.00	325.00	180.00
(16)	Lady Baldwin 4			
16 (a)	(Detroit)	2,200	990.00	550.00
(17)	Mark Baldwin 10			
17 (a)	(Chicago NL)	850.00	375.00	180.00
17 (b)	(Chicago NL)(Portrait)	1,750	800.00	450.00
17 (c)	(Chicago PL)	2,250	1,000	550.00
17 (d)	(Columbus)	725.00	325.00	180.00
(18)	Jim Banning 5			
18 (a)	(Washington)	725.00	325.00	180.00
(19)	Sam Barkley 8			
19 (a)	(Kansas City)	975.00	425.00	250.00
19 (b)	(Pittsburgh)	920.00	400.00	230.00
DP 6	(Watching Jocko Fields field.)	1,250	575.00	300.00
DP 7	(Tagged by Jocko Fields.)	1,250	575.00	300.00

(20)	John Barnes (Also: Barns) 2			
20 (a)	(St. Paul)	1,400	600.00	350.00
(21)	Billy Barnie 1	2,700	1,215	675.00
21 (a)	(Baltimore)	920.00	400.00	250.00
(22)	Charley Bassett 3			
22 (a)	(Indianapolis)	725.00	325.00	180.00
22 (b)	(New York NL)	725.00	325.00	180.00
(23)	Charlie Bastian 6			
23 (a)	(Chicago NL)	725.00	325.00	180.00
23 (b)	(Chicago PL)	2,700	1,200	600.00
23 (c)	(Philadelphia NL)	600.00	275.00	150.00
DP 2	(Being tagged by Pop Schriver.)	1,150	500.00	275.00
(24)	Ed Beatin (Also: Beattin) 3			
24 (a)	(Cleveland)	725.00	325.00	180.00
(25)	Jake Beckley			

See Hall of Fame Section Following

(26)	Stephen Behel 1			
26 (a)	(New York AA "dotted tie")	16,000	7,200	4,000
(27)	Charlie Bennett 1			
27 (a)	(Boston NL)	725.00	325.00	180.00
(28)	Lou Bierbauer (Also: Bierbaur) 5			
28 (a)	(Philadelphia AA)	1,250	625.00	375.00
DP 3	(Tagging Bob Gamble.)	1,800	850.00	450.00
(29)	Bill Bishop 4			
29 (a)	(Pittsburgh)	725.00	325.00	180.00
29 (b)	(Syracuse)	725.00	325.00	180.00
(30)	Bill Blair 5			
30 (a)	(Hamilton)	1,025	500.00	400.00
30 (b)	(Philadelphia AA)	725.00	325.00	180.00
(31)	Ned Bligh 6			
31 (a)	(Columbus)	725.00	325.00	180.00
(32)	Walter Bogart 5			
32 (a)	(Indianapolis)	725.00	325.00	180.00
(33)	Abner Boyce 4			
33 (a)	(Washington) (Never played for Wash.)	950.00	470.00	280.00
(34)	Boyd 2			
34 (a)	(Chicago Maroons WA)	2,000	900.00	500.00
(35)	Henry Boyle 6			
35 (a)	(Indianapolis)	725.00	325.00	180.00
35 (b)	(New York NL) (Never played for N.Y.)	725.00	325.00	180.00
(36)	Jack Boyle 6			
36 (a)	(Chicago PL)	6,000	2,700	1,500
36 (b)	(St. Louis AA)	875.00	325.00	180.00
(37)	George Bradley 5			
37 (a)	(Sioux City)	725.00	325.00	180.00
(38)	Nick Bradley 4			
38 (a)	(Kansas City)	725.00	325.00	180.00
38 (b)	(Worcester)	725.00	325.00	180.00
(39)	Steve Brady 1			
39 (a)	(New York AA "dotted tie")	3,375	1,525	850.00
(40)	E.L. Breckenridge 1			
40 (a)	(Sacramento) (Value Undetermined)			

Willie Breslin - See Mascot

(41)	Timothy Brosnan (Also: Brosman) 8			
41 (a)	(Minneapolis)	725.00	325.00	180.00
41 (b)	(Sioux City)	725.00	325.00	180.00
(42)	Cal Broughton 5			
42 (a)	(St. Paul)	725.00	325.00	180.00
(43)	Dan Brouthers			

See Hall of Fame Section Following

(44)	Tom Brown 7			
44 (a)	(Boston NL)	725.00	325.00	180.00
44 (b)	(Boston PL)	2,700	1,200	700.00
44 (c)	(Pittsburgh)	600.00	275.00	150.00
(45)	Willard (California) Brown 6			
45 1	(New York NL)	725.00	325.00	180.00
45 1	(New York PL)	2,250	1,000	550.00
(46)	Pete Browning 5			
46 (a)	(Louisville)	7,000	3,500	2,100
(47)	Charlie Brynan (Also: Bryn) 6			
47 (a)	(Chicago NL)	725.00	325.00	180.00
47 (b)	(Des Moines)	725.00	325.00	180.00
(48)	Al Buckenberger 2			
48 (a)	(Columbus)	3,000	1,200	725.00
(49)	Dick Buckley 7			
49 (a)	(Indianapolis)	725.00	325.00	180.00
49 (b)	(New York NL)	725.00	325.00	180.00
(50)	Charlie Buffinton (Also: Buffington) 4			
50 (a)	(Philadelphia NL)	1.100	500.00	285.00
50 (b)	(Philadelphia PL)	2,700	1,200	600.00
(51)	Ernie Burch 8			
51 (a)	(Brooklyn)	2,300	1,025	575.00
51 (b)	(St. Louis Whites WA)	725.00	325.00	180.00
(52)	Bill Burdick 4			
52 (a)	(Indianapolis)	725.00	325.00	180.00
52 (b)	(Omaha)	850.00	375.00	180.00
(53)	Jack Burdock 5			
53 (a)	(Boston NL)	1,500	675.00	375.00
(54)	Bob Burks (Burk) 3			
54 (a)	(Sioux City)	1,100	500.00	285.00
(55)	Watch Burnham 1			
55 (a)	(Indianapolis)	1,350	600.00	335.00
(56)	Jim Burns 8			
56 (a)	(Kansas City)	1,100	500.00	285.00
56 (b)	(Omaha)	725.00	325.00	180.00
(58)	Oyster Burns 5			
58 (a)	(Baltimore)	725.00	325.00	180.00
58 (b)	(Brooklyn)	850.00	375.00	180.00
DP 22	(Being tagged by Sam Trott.)	1,150	500.00	285.00
(59)	Tom Burns (Also: "E. Burns") 4			
59 (a)	(Chicago NL)	725.00	325.00	180.00
(60)	Doc Bushong 6			
60 (a)	(Brooklyn)	850.00	375.00	180.00
60 2	(St. Louis AA "Brown's Champions")	1,000	450.00	300.00
(61)	John (Patsy) Cahill 2			
61 (a)	(Indianapolis)	725.00	325.00	180.00
(62)	Count Campau 7			
62 (a)	(Detroit)	725.00	325.00	180.00
62 (b)	(Kansas City)	725.00	325.00	180.00
(63)	Jimmy Canavan 3			
63 (a)	(Omaha)	725.00	325.00	180.00
(64)	Bart Cantz (Also: McCantz) 5			
64 (a)	(Baltimore)	725.00	325.00	180.00
64 (b)	(St. Louis Whites WA)	725.00	325.00	180.00
(65)	Jack Carney 5			
65 (a)	(Washington)	725.00	325.00	180.00
(66)	Hick Carpenter 5			
66 (a)	(Cincinnati)	725.00	325.00	180.00
66 (b)	(Tagging player.)	1,150	575.00	345.00
(67)	Cliff Carroll 2			
67 (a)	(Washington)	725.00	325.00	180.00
(68)	Fred Carroll 3			
68 (a)	(Pittsburgh)	725.00	325.00	180.00
(69)	Scrappy Carroll 8			
69 (a)	(Chicago NL)	725.00	325.00	180.00
69 (b)	(St. Paul)	725.00	325.00	180.00
(70)	Ed Cartwright 5			
70 (a)	(Kansas City)	725.00	325.00	180.00
70 (b)	(St. Joseph)	725.00	325.00	180.00
(71)	Bob Caruthers 7			
71 (a)	(Brooklyn)	725.00	400.00	240.00
71 (b)	(St. Louis AA "Brown's Champions")	1,875	850.00	450.00
(72)	Dan Casey 3			
72 (a)	(Philadelphia NL)	1,100	500.00	285.00
(73)	Elton Chamberlain 6			
73 (a)	(St. Louis)	725.00	325.00	180.00
(74)	Cupid Childs 5			
74 (a)	(Philadelphia NL)	1,150	500.00	275.00
74 (b)	(Syracuse)	950.00	475.00	285.00

Chreve - See Shreve

(75)	Bob Clark 6			
75 (a)	(Brooklyn)	725.00	325.00	180.00
DP 4	(Tagging Mickey Hughes.)	2,300	1,025	575.00
(76)	Spider Clark 4			
76 (a)	(Washington)	1,100	550.00	325.00
(77)	Dad Clarke (Also: Clark) 11			
77 (a)	(Chicago NL)	725.00	325.00	180.00
77 (b)	(Omaha)	950.00	275.00	235.00
(78)	John Clarkson			

See Hall of Fame Section Following

(79)	Jack Clements 3			
79 (a)	(Philadelphia NL)	900.00	425.00	225.00
(80)	Elmer Cleveland 6			
80 (a)	(New York NL)	725.00	325.00	180.00
(81)	Monk Cline 5			
81 (a)	(Sioux City)	725.00	325.00	180.00
(82)	Mike Cody 4			
82 (a)	(Des Moines)	950.00	470.00	280.00
(83)	John Coleman 5			
83 (a)	(Pittsburgh)	725.00	325.00	180.00
(84)	Bill Collins 13			
84 (a)	(Lowell)	725.00	325.00	180.00
84 (b)	(Newark)	950.00	470.00	280.00
84 (c)	(New York) (Never played for N.Y.)	900.00	400.00	230.00
(85)	Hub Collins 6			
85 (a)	(Brooklyn)	725.00	325.00	180.00
85 (b)	(Louisville)	975.00	425.00	250.00
(86)	Charlie Comiskey (Also: Commiskey)			
86 (a)	See Hall of Fame Section Following			
(87)	Pete Connell 2			
87 (a)	(Des Moines, 3B, dark uniform.)	725.00	325.00	180.00
87 (b)	(Des Moines, 1B, light uniform. Photo actually P.J. O'Connell.)	725.00	325.00	180.00
(88)	Roger Connor (Also: Conner)			

See Hall of Fame Section Following

(89)	Dick Conway 6			
89 (a)	(Boston NL)	1,025	450.00	250.00
89 (b)	(Worcester)	725.00	325.00	180.00
(90)	Jim Conway 5			
90 (a)	(Kansas City)	725.00	325.00	180.00
(91)	Pete Conway 10			
91 (a)	(Detroit)	725.00	325.00	180.00
91 (b)	(Pittsburgh)	725.00	325.00	180.00
91 (c)	(Indianapolis)	725.00	325.00	180.00
(92)	Paul Cook 4			
92 (a)	(Louisville)	725.00	325.00	180.00
(93)	Jimmy Cooney 5			
93 (a)	(Chicago NL)	725.00	325.00	180.00
93 (b)	(Omaha)	850.00	375.00	180.00
(94)	Larry Corcoran 4			
94 (a)	(Indianapolis)	850.00	375.00	180.00
94 (b)	(London)	850.00	375.00	180.00
(95)	Pop Corkhill 7			
95 (a)	(Brooklyn)	725.00	325.00	180.00
95 (b)	(Cincinnati)	725.00	325.00	180.00
(96)	Cannonball Crane 7			
96 (a)	(New York NL)	725.00	325.00	180.00
96 (b)	(New York PL)	2,700	1,200	600.00
(97)	Sam Crane 3			
97 (a)	(Washington)	725.00	325.00	180.00
(98)	Jack Crogan (Croghan) 5			
98 (a)	(Chicago Maroons WA)	2,000	900.00	500.00
(99)	John Crooks 7			
99 (a)	(Omaha)	850.00	375.00	180.00

99 (b) (St. Louis Whites WA)   725.00   325.00   180.00

(100)   Lave Cross 6
100 (a) (Louisville)   725.00   325.00   180.00
100 (b) (Philadelphia AA)   950.00   470.00   280.00
100 (c) (Philadelphia PL)   2,700   1,200   600.00

(101)   William Crossley 5
101 (a) (Milwaukee)   750.00   325.00   180.00

(102)   Joe Crotty 5
102 (a) (New York AA "dotted tie")   2,800   1,250   700.00
102 (b) (Sioux City)   1,400   650.00   350.00

(103)   Billy Crowell 9
103 (a) (Cleveland)   725.00   325.00   180.00
103 (b) (St. Joseph)   725.00   325.00   180.00

(104)   Jim Cudworth 4
104 (a) (Worcester)   725.00   325.00   180.00

(105)   Bert Cunningham 6
105 (a) (Baltimore)   850.00   375.00   180.00
105 (b) (Philadelphia PL)   2,700   1,200   600.00

(106)   Tacks Curtis 5
106 (a) (St. Joseph)   950.00   470.00   280.00

(107)   Ed Cushman 3
107 (a) (New York AA "dotted tie")   2,800   1,250   600.00
107 (b) (New York AA)   2,300   300.00   175.00
107 (c) (Toledo)   4,250   2,100   1,250

(108)   Tony Cusick 2
108 (a) (Milwaukee)   5,750   300.00   175.00

(109)   Edward Dailey (Also: Daley) 7
109 (a) (Columbus)   725.00   325.00   180.00
109 (b) (Philadelphia NL)   725.00   325.00   180.00
109 (c) (Washington)   725.00   325.00   180.00

(110)   Vincent Dailey 1
110 (a) (Oakland)(SGC-graded Poor auctioned for $101,100 12/05.)

(111)   Bill Daley 2
111 (a) (Boston NL)   725.00   400.00   240.00
111 (b) (Boston PL)   2,400   1,100   600.00

(112)   Con Daley (Daily) 9
112 (a) (Boston NL)   900.00   405.00   225.00
112 (b) (No name, team, etc.)   2,600   1,150   650.00
112 (c) (Indianapolis)   725.00   325.00   180.00

(113)   Abner Dalrymple 7
113 (a) (Denver)   1,050   475.00   250.00
113 (b) (Pittsburgh)   725.00   325.00   180.00
113 (c) (Pittsburgh) ("Dolrynicle")   3,500   1,750   1,050

(114)   Sun Daly 5
114 (a) (Minneapolis)   900.00   405.00   225.00

(115)   Tom Daly 7
115 (a) (Chicago NL)   900.00   325.00   180.00
115 (b) (Chicago NL)(Portrait)   1,200   600.00   350.00
115 (c) (Cleveland)   725.00   325.00   180.00

(Never played with Cleveland.)

(116)   Law Daniels 5
116 (a) (Kansas City)   725.00   325.00   180.00

(117)   Dell Darling 6
117 (a) (Chicago NL)   1,100   500.00   285.00
117 (b) (Portrait)   2,000   900.00   500.00
117 (c) (Chicago PL)   2,700   1,215   675.00

(118)   William Darnbrough 2
118 (a) (Denver)   850.00   375.00   180.00

(119)   D.J. Davin 2
119 (a) (Milwaukee)   5,750   300.00   175.00

(120)   Jumbo Davis 5
120 (a) (Kansas City)   725.00   325.00   180.00

(121)   Pat Dealey (Also: Dealy) 6
121 (a) (Washington)   725.00   400.00   240.00

(122)   Tom Deasley 20
122 (a) (New York NL)   725.00   325.00   180.00
122 (b) (Washington)   725.00   325.00   180.00

(123)   Harry Decker 5
123 (a) (Philadelphia NL)   725.00   400.00   240.00

(124)   Ed Delahanty

See Hall of Fame Section Following

(125)   Jerry Denny 4
125 (a) (Indianapolis)   725.00   325.00   180.00
125 (b) (New York NL)   725.00   325.00   180.00

(126)   Jim Devlin (Also: Delvin) 5
126 (a) (St. Louis AA)   725.00   325.00   180.00

(127)   Tom Dolan 5
127 (a) (Denver)   725.00   325.00   180.00
127 (b) (St. Louis AA)   725.00   325.00   180.00

(128)   Jack Donahue 1
128 (a) (San Francisco) (SGC-certified Poor, $52,240, 12/04 auction.)

(129)   Jim Donahue (Also: Donohue) 7
129 (a) (New York AA "dotted tie")   3,375   1,525   850.00
129 (b) (Kansas City)   725.00   325.00   180.00

(130)   Jim Donnelly 3
130 (a) (Washington)   850.00   375.00   180.00

(131)   Charlie Dooley 1
131 (a) (Oakland) (SGC-certified Poor, $52,240, 12/04 auction.)

(132)   John Doran 2
132 (a) (Omaha)   4,500   2,200   1,350

(133)   Mike Dorgan 17
133 (a) (New York NL)   725.00   325.00   180.00
     (Sliding)   1,100   500.00   250.00

(134)   Con Doyle 1
134 (a) (San Francisco) (Unique. Sold for $129,500 in June, 2010 auction)

(135)   Charlie Duffe (Duffee) 5
135 (a) (St. Louis AA)   1,150   575.00   345.00

(136)   Hugh Duffy

See Hall of Fame Section Following

(137)   Dan Dugdale 7
137 (a) (Chicago Maroons WA)   2,000   900.00   500.00
137 (b) (Minneapolis)   725.00   400.00   240.00

(138)   Martin Duke 5
138 (a) (Minneapolis)   725.00   325.00   180.00

(139)   Fred Dunlap 9
139 (b) (Pittsburgh)   825.00   375.00   180.00

(140)   J.E. Dunn 5
140 (a) (Chicago Maroons WA)   2,300   1,100   600.00

(141)   Jesse Duryea 4
141 (a) (Cincinnati)   725.00   325.00   180.00
141 (b) (St. Paul)   725.00   325.00   180.00

(142)   Frank Dwyer 5
142 (a) (Chicago NL)   725.00   325.00   180.00
142 (b) (Chicago Maroons WA)   2,300   1,100   600.00

(143)   Billy Earle (Also: Earl) 4
143 (a) (Cincinnati)   725.00   325.00   180.00
143 (b) (St. Paul)   725.00   325.00   180.00

(144)   Hi Ebright 2
144 (a) (Washington)   725.00   325.00   180.00

(145)   Red Ehret 4
145 (a) (Louisville)   725.00   325.00   180.00

Eidner - See Weidner

(146)   R. Emmerke 5
146 (a) (Des Moines)   725.00   325.00   180.00

(147)   Dude Esterbrook 11
147 (a) (Indianapolis)   725.00   325.00   180.00
147 (b) (Louisville)   725.00   325.00   180.00
147 (c) (New York AA)   1,300   575.00   325.00
147 (d) (New York NL)   725.00   325.00   180.00

(148)   Henry Esterday (Easterday) 6
148 (a) (Columbus)   1,400   700.00   425.00
148 (b) (Kansas City)   1,150   575.00   345.00

(149)   Buck Ewing

See Hall of Fame Section Following

(150)   John Ewing 4
150 (a) (Louisville)   725.00   325.00   180.00

(151)   Jay Faatz 3

(151)   (a) (Cleveland)   725.00   325.00   180.00

(152)   Bill Fagan 5
152 (a) (Denver)   950.00   470.00   280.00
152 (b) (Kansas City)   950.00   470.00   280.00

(153)   Bill Farmer 7
153 (a) (Pittsburgh)   950.00   425.00   235.00
153 (b) (St. Paul)   1,100   500.00   275.00

(154)   Sid Farrar (Also: Farrer, Faraer) 8
154 (a) (Philadelphia NL)   950.00   425.00   235.00
154 (b) (Philadelphia PL)   3,250   1,465   815.00

(155)   Duke Farrell (Also: Farrel) 5
155 (a) (Chicago NL)   900.00   450.00   270.00
155 (b) (Chicago PL)   2,700   1,200   6750.00

(156)   Jack Farrell 12
156 (a) (Baltimore)   725.00   325.00   180.00
156 (b) (Washington)   725.00   325.00   180.00
156 (c) (Washington)
     (Tagging Paul Hines.)   875.00   400.00   230.00

(157)   Frank Fennelly 5
157 (a) (Cincinnati)   725.00   325.00   180.00
157 (b) (Philadelphia AA)   725.00   325.00   180.00

(158)   Charlie Ferguson 4
158 (a) (Philadelphia NL)   950.00   470.00   280.00

(159)   Alex Ferson 5
159 (a) (Washington)   850.00   375.00   180.00

(160)   Wallace Fessenden 4
160 1   (Umpire)   1,850   825.00   450.00

(161)   Jocko Fields (Also: Field) 6
161 (a) (Pittsburgh)   725.00   325.00   180.00
DP 6   (Fielding, Sam Barkley
     looking on.)   1,250   575.00   300.00
DP 7   (Tagging Sam Barkley.)   1,250   575.00   300.00

(162)   Fischer 3
162 (a) (Chicago Maroons WA)   25,875   11,500   6,475

(163)   Thomas Flanigan (Flanagan) 4
163 (a) (Cleveland)   950.00   470.00   280.00
     (Never played for Cleveland.)
163 (b) (Sioux City)   725.00   325.00   180.00

(164)   Silver Flint 5
164 (a) (Chicago NL)   950.00   470.00   280.00
164 (b) (Chicago NL) (Portrait, street clothes)   1,500   700.00   450.00

(165)   Thomas Flood 5
165 (a) (St. Joseph)   725.00   325.00   180.00

(166)   Jocko Flynn 2
166 (a) (Omaha)(Two known.)   11,500

(167)   Jim Fogarty (Also: Fogerty) 5
167 (a) (Philadelphia NL)   950.00   425.00   225.00

(168)   Frank Foreman 6
168 (a) (Baltimore)   725.00   325.00   180.00
168 (b) (Cincinnati)   1,250   575.00   300.00

(169)   Tom Forster (Also: "F.W. Foster") 3
169 (a) (Hartford)   725.00   325.00   180.00
169 (b) (Milwaukee, squatting.)   850.00   375.00   180.00
169 (c) (New York AA "dotted tie")   3,375   1,525   850.00
169 (d) Tom Forester
     (Milwaukee, standing.)   725.00   400.00   240.00

(170)   Elmer Foster 7
170 (a) (New York AA "dotted tie")   4,500   2,025   1,125
170 (b) (New York NL)   950.00   425.00   235.00
170 (c) (Minneapolis)   725.00   325.00   180.00

(171)   Dave Foutz 5
171 (a) (Brooklyn)   950.00   425.00   235.00
171 (b) (St. Louis AA "Brown's Champions")   1,700   765.00   425.00

(172)   Julie Freeman 5
172 (a) (Milwaukee)   850.00   375.00   180.00

(173)   Will Fry 4
173 (a) (St. Joseph)   850.00   375.00   250.00

(174)   Frank Fudger 1
174 (a) (Oakland) (Value Undetermined)

(175)   Shorty Fuller 5
175 (a) (St. Louis AA)   850.00   375.00   180.00

(176) William Fuller 5
176 (a) (Milwaukee) 725.00 400.00 240.00

(177) Chris Fulmer (Also: Fullmer) 6
177 (a) (Baltimore) 725.00 325.00 180.00
DP 8 (Tagging Tom Tucker.) 3,000 1,500 900.00

(178) John Gaffney 1
178 (a) (Washington) 1,100 500.00 285.00
DP 21 (Behind George Shoch.) 1,150 500.00 300.00

(179) Pud Galvin

See Hall of Fame Section Following

(180) Bob Gamble 3
180 (a) (Philadelphia AA) 950.00 425.00 235.00
DP 3 (Being tagged by Lou
Bierbauer.) (Bierbauer.) 1,800 850.00 450.00

(181) Charlie Ganzel (Also: Gauzel) 5
181 (a) (Boston) 725.00 325.00 180.00
181 (b) (Detroit) 725.00 325.00 180.00

(182) Gid Gardner 5
182 (a) (Philadelphia NL) 725.00 325.00 180.00
182 (b) (Washington) 1,025 450.00 250.00
DP 9 (Tagging Miah Murray.) 2,875 1,300 700.00

(183) Hank Gastreich (Gastright) 5
183 (a) (Columbus) 725.00 325.00 180.00

(184) Emil Geiss 6
184 (a) (Chicago NL) 725.00 325.00 180.00
184 (b) (Chicago NL) (Portrait) 1,100 500.00 280.00

(185) Frank Genins (Also: Genius) 5
185 (a) (Sioux City) 725.00 400.00 240.00

(186) Bill George 5
186 (a) (New York NL) 725.00 325.00 180.00

(187) Joe Gerhardt 4
187 (a) (Jersey City) 725.00 325.00 180.00
187 (b) (New York NL) 1,400 625.00 350.00

(188) Charlie Getzein (Getzien) 6
188 (a) (Detroit) 725.00 325.00 180.00
188 (b) (Indianapolis) 725.00 325.00 180.00

(189) Whitey Gibson 1
189 (a) (Philadelphia AA, two
known.) 11,500 5.175 3,800

(190) Bob Gilks 6
190 (a) (Cleveland) 725.00 325.00 180.00

(191) Pete Gillespie 5
191 (a) (New York NL) 850.00 375.00 180.00

(192) Barney Gilligan 3
192 (a) (Detroit) 725.00 325.00 180.00
192 (b) (Washington) 725.00 400.00 240.00

(193) Frank Gilmore 5
193 (a) (Washington) 1,025 450.00 250.00

(194) Jack Glasscock (Also: Glassock, Glass, Cock) 5
194 (a) (Indianapolis) 950.00 425.00 240.00
194 (b) (New York NL) 725.00 325.00 180.00

(195) Bill Gleason 5
195 (a) (Louisville) 725.00 325.00 180.00
195 (b) (Philadelphia AA) 725.00 325.00 180.00
195 (c) (St. Louis AA "Brown's
Champions") 2,200 1,000 525.00
DP 23 (W/ Curt Welch.) 2,300 1,100 550.00

(196) Kid Gleason 5
196 (a) (Philadelphia NL) 725.00 325.00 180.00

(197) Ed Glenn 5
197 (a) (Sioux City) 850.00 375.00 180.00

(198) Mike Goodfellow 9
198 (a) (Cleveland) 950.00 425.00 235.00
198 (b) (Detroit) 900.00 405.00 225.00

(199) George Gore 10
199 (a) (New York NL) 1,025 450.00 250.00
199 (b) (New York PL) 2,700 1,200 600.00

(200) Frank Graves 6
200 (a) (Minneapolis) 725.00 325.00 180.00

(201) Bill Greenwood 8
201 (a) (Baltimore) 1,500 675.00 375.00

201 (b) (Columbus) 725.00 325.00 180.00

(202) Ed Greer 3
202 (a) (Brooklyn) 850.00 375.00 180.00
DP 10 (Catching, Hardie
Henderson batting.) 1,150 500.00 300.00

(203) Mike Griffin 6
203 (a) (Baltimore) 1,150 500.00 300.00
203 (b) (Philadelphia PL) 2,700 1,200 675.00

(204) Clark Griffith

See Hall of Fame Section Following

(205) Henry Gruber 4
205 (a) (Cleveland) 1,650 900.00 415.00

(206) Ad Gumbert 5
206 (a) (Chicago NL) 725.00 325.00 180.00
206 (b) (Boston PL) 2,700 1,200 600.00

(207) Tom Gunning 4
207 (a) (Philadelphia AA) 725.00 325.00 180.00
207 (b) (Philadelphia NL) 725.00 325.00 180.00

(208) Joe Gunson 4
208 (a) (Kansas City) 725.00 400.00 240.00

(209) George Haddock 5
209 (a) (Washington) 725.00 325.00 180.00

(210) Frank Hafner 5
210 (a) (Kansas City) 725.00 400.00 240.00

(211) Willie Hahn (Mascot)
211 (a) (Chicago NL) 850.00 375.00 180.00
DP 24 (W/ Ned Williamson.) 4,000 2,250 1,000

Halliday - See Holliday

(212) Bill Hallman 6
212 (a) (Philadelphia NL) 850.00 375.00 180.00
212 (b) (Philadelphia PL) 2,700 1,200 675.00

(213) Billy Hamilton

See Hall of Fame Section Following

(214) Frank Hankinson 1
214 (a) (New York AA "dotted tie") 27,000 12,150 6,750

(215) Ned Hanlon 6

See Hall of Fame Section Following

Hannon - See Shannon

(216) Bill Hanrahan 9
216 (a) (Chicago Maroons WA) 1,025 450.00 250.00
216 (b) (Minneapolis) 725.00 325.00 180.00

(217) Al Hapeman 1
217 (a) (Sacramento) (Value Undetermined)

(218) John Harkins (Also: Harkens) 9
218 (a) (Baltimore) 1.300 675.00 325.00
218 (b) (Brooklyn) 725.00 325.00 180.00

(219) Bill Hart 5
219 (a) (Cincinnati) 725.00 325.00 180.00
(Never played for Cincinnati.)
219 (b) (Des Moines) 850.00 375.00 180.00

(220) Bill Hasamdear (Hassamaer) 3
220 (a) (Kansas City) 725.00 325.00 180.00

(221) Gil Hatfield 5
221 (a) (New York NL) 725.00 325.00 180.00
221 (b) (New York PL) 2,700 1,200 675.00

(222) Bill Hawes (Also Howes) 5
222 (a) (Minneapolis) 725.00 325.00 180.00
222 (b) (St. Paul) 875.00 400.00 225.00

(223) John J. "Egyptian" Healey (Healy) 5
223 (a) (Indianapolis) 725.00 400.00 240.00
223 (b) (Washington) 950.00 470.00 280.00
223 (c) (Washington, portrait,
w/ moustache, no cap,
possibly unique.) 34,500 15,300 8,625

(224) John C. "Jack" Healy (Also: Healey) 8
224 (a) (Denver) 1,050 475.00 275.00
224 (b) (Omaha) 850.00 375.00 180.00

(225) Guy Hecker 5
225 (a) (Louisville) 2,200 975.00 550.00

(226) Tony Hellman 5
226 (a) (Sioux City) 1,000 500.00 300.00

(227) Hardie Henderson 13
227 (a) (Brooklyn) 725.00 325.00 180.00
227 (b) (Pittsburgh) 725.00 325.00 180.00
DP 10 (Batting, Ed Greer
catching.) 1,150 500.00 300.00
DP 11 (Tagging Jimmy Peoples.) 1,600 725.00 400.00

(228) Moxie Hengle 10
228 (a) (Chicago Maroons WA) 950.00 470.00 280.00
228 (b) (Minneapolis) 950.00 470.00 280.00

(229) John Henry 5
229 (a) (Philadelphia) 725.00 325.00 180.00
(Never actually played for Philadelphia.)

(230) Ed Herr 7
230 (a) (Milwaukee) 950.00 470.00 280.00
230 (b) (St. Louis Whites WA) 1,300 650.00 400.00

(231) Hunkey Hines 4
231 (a) (St. Louis Whites WA) 1,400 775.00 350.00

(232) Paul Hines 7
232 (a) (Indianapolis) 950.00 470.00 280.00
232 (b) (Washington) 1,500 800.00 375.00

(233) Frank Hoffman 4
233 (a) (Denver) 975.00 425.00 250.00

(234) Eddie Hogan 5
234 (a) (Cleveland) 975.00 450.00 275.00

(235) Bill Holbert 10
235 (a) (Brooklyn) 1,200 450.00 250.00
235 (b) (Jersey City) 1,025 450.00 250.00
235 (c) (New York AA "dotted tie") 10,700 4,800 2,650
235 (d) (New York AA) 2,250 1,125 675.00

(236) Bug Holliday (Also: Halliday) 7
236 (a) (Cincinnati) 725.00 325.00 180.00
236 (b) (Des Moines) 1,450 325.00 180.00

(238) Buster Hoover 3
238 (a) (Philadelphia) 725.00 325.00 180.00
238 (b) (Toronto) 725.00 400.00 240.00
(Never played for Phila. in N172 era.)
DP 1 (Hoover tagging Ed
Andrews.) 1,000 500.00 300.00

(239) Charlie Hoover 7
239 (a) (Chicago) 1,100 325.00 180.00
(Never played for Chicago.)
239 (b) (Kansas City) 725.00 325.00 180.00

(240) Jack Horner (Also: Hodner) 6
240 (a) (Milwaukee) 725.00 325.00 180.00
240 (b) (New Haven) 725.00 325.00 180.00
240 (c) (Photo actually E.H.
Warner.) 725.00 325.00 180.00
DP 5 (W/ Ed Warner.) 1,150 500.00 300.00

(241) Joe Hornung (Also: Horning) 6
241 (a) (Baltimore) 725.00 325.00 180.00
241 (b) (Boston) 1,000 500.00 300.00
241 (c) (New York NL) 725.00 325.00 180.00

(242) Pete Hotaling (Also: Hotoling) 4
242 (a) (Cleveland) 725.00 325.00 180.00

Howes - See Hawes

(243) Dummy Hoy 5
243 (a) (Washington) 8,750 3,900 2,150

(244) Nat Hudson 6
244 (a) (St. Louis AA "Brown's
Champions") 2,250 1,125 675.00
244 (b) (St. Louis AA) 1,100 550.00 325.00

(245) Mickey Hughes 7
245 (a) (Brooklyn) 725.00 325.00 180.00
DP 4 (Being tagged by Bob
Clark.) 2,300 1,100 600.00

(246) Al Hungler 4
246 (a) (Sioux City) 725.00 325.00 180.00

(247) Bill Hutchinson 4
247 (a) (Chicago NL) 1,400 600.00 350.00

(248) Arthur Irwin 13
248 (a) (Boston PL) 1,200 550.00 300.00
248 (b) (Philadelphia NL) 875.00 400.00 225.00
(Portrait, cap off.) 2,300 1,100 600.00
248 (c) (Washington) 725.00 325.00 180.00

(249)   John Irwin 5
249 (a) (Washington)   725.00   325.00   180.00
249 (b) (Wilkes-Barre)   875.00   400.00   225.00

(250)   A.C. Jantzen 5
250 (a) (Minneapolis)   1,350   675.00   405.00

(251)   Frederick Jevne 5
251 (a) (Minneapolis)   900.00   450.00   270.00

(252)   Spud Johnson 6
252 (a) (Columbus)   725.00   325.00   180.00
252 (b) (Kansas City)   950.00   470.00   280.00

(253)   Dick Johnston 7
253 (a) (Boston NL)   1,300   650.00   400.00
253 (b) (Boston PL)   2,700   1,200   600.00

(254)   W.T. Jordan 5
254 (a) (Minneapolis)   950.00   470.00   280.00

(255)   Heinie Kappell (Kappel) 8
255 (a) (Cincinnati)   725.00   325.00   180.00
255 (b) (Columbus)   725.00   325.00   180.00

(256)   Tim (Also: Jim) Keefe, (Also: Keef, Keefep)

See Hall of Fame Section Following

(257)   George Keefe 5
257 (a) (Washington)   725.00   325.00   180.00

(258)   Jim Keenan 5
258 (a) (Cincinnati)   725.00   325.00   180.00

(259)   Charlie Kelly 5
259 (a) (Philadelphia AA)   1,850   825.00   450.00

(260)   Honest John Kelly 4
260 (a) (Louisville)   725.00   325.00   180.00
260 (b) (Umpire WA)   1,800   800.00   450.00
DP 14 (W/ Jim Powell.)   1,150   500.00   275.00

(261)   King Kelly

See Hall of Fame Section Following

(262)   Rudy Kemmler (Also: Kemler) 2
262 (a) (St. Louis AA "Brown's
          Champions")   1,425   650.00   350.00
262 (b) (St. Paul)   725.00   325.00   180.00

(263)   Ted Kennedy 9
263 (a) (Des Moines)   850.00   375.00   180.00
263 (b) (Omaha)   1,150   500.00   275.00

(264)   J.J. Kenyon 7
264 (a) (Des Moines)   1,000   450.00   250.00
264 (b) (St. Louis Whites WA)   950.00   405.00   225.00

(265)   John Kerins 6
265 (a) (Louisville)   850.00   375.00   180.00

(266)   Matt Kilroy 7
266 (a) (Baltimore)   1,500   600.00   350.00
266 (b) (Boston PL)   2,700   1,200   600.00

(267)   Silver King 3
267 (a) (Chicago PL)   2,700   1,200   600.00
267 (b) (St. Louis AA)   725.00   325.00   180.00

(268)   Gus Kloff (Klopf) 7
268 (a) (Minneapolis)   725.00   325.00   180.00
268 (b) (St. Joseph)   725.00   325.00   180.00
DP 15 (W/ Bill Krieg.)   1,150   500.00   275.00

(269)   Billy Klusman 7
269 (a) (Denver)   1,100   500.00   250.00
269 (b) (Milwaukee)   725.00   325.00   180.00

(270)   Phil Knell 5
270 (a) (St. Joseph)   850.00   475.00   250.00

(271)   Ed Knouff 5
271 (a) (St. Louis AA)   725.00   325.00   180.00

(272)   Charles Kremmeyer (Krehmeyer) 1
272 (a) (Sacramento)(SGC-certified Fair, $50,233 12/04
          auction.)

(273)   Bill Krieg (Also: Kreig) 14
273 (a) (Minneapolis)   950.00   425.00   225.00
273 (b) (St. Joseph)   725.00   325.00   180.00
273 (c) (Washington)   725.00   325.00   180.00
DP 15 (W/ Gus Kloff.) (Klopf)   1,150   500.00   300.00

(274)   Gus Krock 5
274 (a) (Chicago NL)   725.00   325.00   180.00

(275)   Willie Kuehne (Also: Kuchne) 5
275 (a) (Pittsburgh)   725.00   325.00   180.00

(276)   Fred Lange 5
276 (a) (Chicago Maroons WA)   2,100   900.00   500.00
(277)   Henry Larkin 4
277 (a) (Philadelphia AA)   725.00   325.00   180.00

(278)   Arlie Latham 7
278 (a) (St. Louis AA "Brown's
          Champions")   2,800   1,400   850.00
278 (b) (St. Louis AA)   725.00   325.00   180.00
278 (c) (Chicago PL)   2,700   1,200   600.00

(279)   Chuck Lauer 4
279 (a) (Pittsburgh)   725.00   325.00   180.00

(280)   John Leighton 5
280 (a) (Omaha)   850.00   375.00   180.00

(281)   Levy 1
281 (a) (San Francisco) (Value Undetermined)

(282)   Tom Loftus 2
282 (a) (Cleveland)   725.00   325.00   180.00
282 (b) (St. Louis Whites WA)   1,200.   600.00   375.00

(283)   Danny Long 1
283 (a) (Oakland) (Value Undetermined)

(284)   Herman Long 7
284 (a) (Chicago Maroons WA)   3,100   1,400   775.00
284 (b) (Kansas City)   900.00   400.00   250.00

(285)   Tom Lovett 6
285 (a) (Brooklyn)   900.00   400.00   250.00
285 (b) (Omaha)   850.00   375.00   180.00

(286)   Bobby Lowe 6
286 (a) (Milwaukee)   1,300   650.00   400.00
DP 18 (About to be tagged by Pat
          Pettee.)   1,400   600.00   350.00

(287)   Jack Lynch 5
287 (a) (New York AA "dotted tie")   3,375   1,500   850.00
287 (b) (New York AA)   725.00   325.00   180.00

(288)   Denny Lyons 4
288 (a) (Philadelphia AA)   725.00   325.00   180.00

(289)   Harry Lyons 6
289 (a) (St. Louis AA)   725.00   325.00   180.00
289 (b) (Jersey City)   725.00   325.00   180.00

(290)   Connie Mack 3

See Hall of Fame Section Following

(291)   Reddy Mack 6
291 (a) (Baltimore)   725.00   325.00   180.00
291 (b) (Louisville)   2,100   1,100   650.00

(292)   Jimmy Macullar 7
292 (a) (Des Moines)   1,400   600.00   350.00
292 (b) (Milwaukee)   725.00   325.00   180.00

(293)   Kid Madden 9
293 (a) (Boston NL)   725.00   325.00   180.00
293 (b) (Boston NL)(Portrait)   2,875   1,300   700.00
293 (c) (Boston PL)   2,700   1,200   600.00

(294)   Danny Mahoney 1
294 (a) (St. Joseph)   2,525   1,125   600.00

(295)   Willard Maines (Mains) 5
295 (a) (St. Paul)   725.00   325.00   180.00

(296)   Fred Mann 5
296 (a) (Hartford)   725.00   325.00   180.00
296 (b) (St. Louis AA)   1,350   675.00   400.00
          (Never played for St. Louis.)

(297)   Jimmy Manning 6
297 (a) (Kansas City)   850.00   375.00   180.00

(298)   Lefty Marr 7
298 (a) (Cincinnati)   725.00   325.00   180.00
298 (b) (Columbus)   900.00   450.00   275.00

(299)   Mascot (Willie Breslin 1)
299 (a) New York NL (Caption reads
          "New York Mascot.")   2,400   1,080   600.00

(300)   Leech Maskrey 5
300 (a) (Des Moines)   725.00   325.00   180.00
300 (b) (Milwaukee)   725.00   325.00   180.00
300 (c) (Photo actually Jimmy
          Macullar.)   725.00   325.00   180.00

Massitt - See Messitt

(301)   Bobby Mathews 3
301 (a) (Philadelphia AA)   900.00   400.00   250.00

(302)   Mike Mattimore (Also: Mattemore) 19
302 (a) (New York NL)   725.00   325.00   180.00
302 (b) (Philadelphia AA)   725.00   400.00   250.00

(303)   Al Maul 7
303 (a) (Pittsburgh)   1,100   500.00   325.00

(304)   Al Mays 5
304 (a) (New York AA "dotted tie")   4,250   2,150   1,275
304 (b) (Columbus)   725.00   325.00   180.00

(305)   Jimmy McAleer 4
305 (a) (Cleveland)   725.00   325.00   180.00

(306)   John McCarthy (McCarty) 3
306 (a) (Kansas City)   900.00   400.00   250.00

(307)   Tommy McCarthy

See Hall of Fame Section Following

(308)   Jim McCauley 3
308 (a) (Chicago Maroons WA)   2,100   900.00   500.00

(309)   Bill McClellan (Also: McClennan) 3
309 (a) (Brooklyn)   725.00   325.00   180.00
309 (b) (Denver)   1,400   600.00   350.00

(310)   Jim McCormack 4
310 (a) (St. Louis Whites WA)   725.00   325.00   180.00

(311)   Jim McCormick 10
311 (a) (Chicago)   2,000   900.00   500.00
311 (b) (Portrait)   7,500   3,750   2,250
311 (c) (Pittsburgh)   850.00   375.00   180.00

(312)   McCreachery 1
312 (a) (Indianapolis) (Value Undetermined)

(Nobody named McCreachery ever managed Indianapolis.

Photo actually Deacon White.)

(313)   Tom McCullum (McCallum) 4
313 (a) (Minneapolis)   1,100   525.00   325.00

(314)   Jim McDonald 1
314 (a) (Oakland) (Value Undetermined)

(315)   Chippy McGarr 5
315 (a) (Kansas City)   725.00   325.00   180.00
315 (b) (St. Louis AA)   725.00   325.00   180.00
315 (c) (St. Louis AA, batting,
          umpire behind.)   875.00   400.00   225.00

(316)   Jack McGeachy 4
316 (a) (Indianapolis)   850.00   375.00   180.00

(317)   John McGlone 7
317 (a) (Cleveland)   1,100   500.00   285.00
317 (b) (Detroit)   725.00   325.00   180.00

(318)   Deacon McGuire 5
318 (a) (Philadelphia NL)   725.00   400.00   250.00
318 (b) (Toronto)   900.00   450.00   300.00

(319)   Bill McGunnigle 1
319 (a) (Brooklyn)   1,800   775.00   425.00

(320)   Ed McKean 5
320 (a) (Cleveland)   725.00   325.00   180.00

(321)   Alex McKinnon 4
321 (a) (Pittsburgh)   725.00   325.00   180.00

(322)   Tom McLaughlin 1
322 (a) (New York AA "dotted tie")   7,875   3,550   1,975

(323)   Bid McPhee

See Hall of Fame Section Following

(324)   Jack McQuaid 1
324 (a) (Umpire)   2,300   1,025   575.00

(325)   James McQuaid 3
325 (a) (Denver)   1,800   775.00   425.00

(326)   Jim McTamany (Also: McTammany) 6
326 (a) (Brooklyn)   1,800   775.00   425.00
326 (b) (Columbus)   1,800   775.00   425.00
326 (c) (Kansas City)   1,800   775.00   425.00

(327) George McVey 9
327 (a) (Denver) 725.00 325.00 180.00
327 (b) (Milwaukee) 725.00 325.00 180.00
327 (c) (St. Joseph) 750.00 325.00 180.00

(328) Pete Meegan 1
328 (a) (San Francisco) (Value Undetermined)

(329) John Messitt (Also: Massitt, Wassitt) 3
329 (a) (Omaha) 1,600 720.00 400.00

Micholson - See Nicholson

(330) Doggie Miller 5
330 (a) (Pittsburgh) 725.00 325.00 180.00

(331) Joe Miller 4
331 (a) (Minneapolis) 725.00 325.00 180.00
331 (b) (Omaha) 850.00 425.00 250.00

(332) Jocko Milligan 6
332 (a) (Philadelphia PL) 2,700 1,200 600.00
332 (b) (St. Louis AA) 725.00 325.00 180.00

(333) E.L. Mills 5
333 (a) (Milwaukee) 725.00 325.00 180.00

(334) Daniel Minnehan (Minahan) 4
334 (a) (Minneapolis) 725.00 325.00 180.00

(335) Sam Moffet 3
335 (a) (Indianapolis) 725.00 325.00 180.00

(336) John Morrill (Also: Morrell) 4
336 (a) (Boston NL) 1,250 550.00 300.00
336 (b) (Boston NL)(Portrait) 2,100 900.00 500.00
336 (c) (Washington) 2,100 1,050. 650.00

(337) Ed Morris 6
337 (a) (Pittsburgh) 725.00 325.00 180.00

(338) Tony Mullane 7
338 (a) (Cincinnati) 1,250 625.00 400.00

(339) Joe Mulvey 4
339 (a) (Philadelphia NL) 725.00 325.00 180.00
339 (b) (Philadelphia PL) 2,700 1,200 600.00

(340) Pat Murphy 3
340 (a) (New York NL) 725.00 325.00 180.00

(341) P.L. Murphy 5
341 (a) (St. Paul) 1,200. 600.00 400.00

(342) Miah Murray 5
342 (a) (Washington) 725.00 325.00 180.00
DP 9 (Being tagged by
Gid Gardner.) 2,875 1,300 700.00

(343) Jim Mutrie 3
343 (a) (New York NL) 1,100 500.00 285.00

(344) Al Myers 6
344 (a) (Philadelphia NL) 725.00 325.00 180.00
344 (b) (Washington) 725.00 400.00 250.00

(345) George Myers 3
345 (a) (Indianapolis) 1,000 450.00 250.00

(346) Tom Nagle 6
346 (a) (Chicago NL) 725.00 325.00 180.00
346 (b) (Omaha) 850.00 425.00 275.00

(347) Billy Nash 7
347 (a) (Boston NL) 1,375 700.00 425.00
347 (b) (Tagging (unnamed)
Old Hoss Radbourn.) 2,000 1,000 600.00
347 (c) (Boston PL) 2,700 1,200 600.00

(348) Jack Nelson 1
348 (a) (New York AA "dotted tie") 8,500 3,825 2,125

(349) Kid Nichols
SEE HALL OF FAME SECTION FOLLOWING

(350) Samuel Nichols (Nichol) 4
350 (a) (Pittsburgh) 725.00 325.00 180.00

(351) J.W. Nicholson 6
351 (a) (Chicago Maroons WA) 4,000 2,000 1,200

(352) Parson Nicholson (Also: Micholson) 7
352 (a) (Cleveland) 725.00 325.00 180.00
(Never played for
Cleveland.)
352 (b) (St. Louis Whites WA) 725.00 325.00 180.00

(353) Hugh Nicol (Also: Nicoll) 8

(353) (a) (St. Louis AA "Brown's
Champions") 1,600 800.00 480.00
353 (b) (Cincinnati) 825.00 375.00 180.00
DP 16 (Side by side w/ John
Reilly.) 2,400 1,025 575.00
DP 17 (Facing John Reilly.) 2,525 1,125 625.00

(354) Frederick Nyce 4
354 (a) (Burlington) 725.00 325.00 180.00
354 (b) (St. Louis Whites WA) 725.00 325.00 180.00

(355) Doc Oberlander 8
355 (a) (Cleveland) 950.00 325.00 180.00
355 (b) (Syracuse) 725.00 325.00 180.00

(356) Billy O'Brien 5
356 (a) (Washington) 900.00 400.00 250.00

(357) Darby O'Brien 5
357 (a) (Brooklyns or "Bk'ns") 725.00 325.00 180.00

(358) Jack O'Brien 8
358 (a) (Baltimore) 725.00 325.00 180.00
358 (b) ("Brooklyn") 725.00 325.00 180.00
358 (c) ("Mini" photo.) 5,750 2,600 1,425

(359) John O'Brien 4
359 (a) (Cleveland) 900.00 400.00 250.00

(360) P.J. O'Connell 5
360 (a) (Des Moines) 725.00 400.00 250.00
360 (b) (Omaha) 725.00 325.00 180.00

(361) Jack O'Connor 8
361 (a) (Cincinnati) 725.00 325.00 180.00
361 (b) (Columbus) 725.00 325.00 180.00

(362) Hank O'Day 3
362 (a) (Washington) 1,250 625.00 375.00

(363) Harry O'Day 1
363 (a) (Sacramento)(VALUE UNDETERMINED)

(364) Norris O'Neill 1
364 (a) (Oakland)(VALUE UNDETERMINED)

(365) Tip O'Neill (Also: O'Neil) 11
365 (a) (Chicago PL) 2,500 1,100 625.00
365 (b) (St. Louis AA "Brown's
Champions") 1,875 850.00 475.00
365 (c) (St. Louis AA) 725.00 325.00 180.00
365 (d) (Photo actually Bill White.)
(W/moustasche,
stooping to field
grounder.) 975.00 425.00 250.00

(366) Orator Jim O'Rourke
SEE HALL OF FAME SECTION FOLLOWING

(367) Tom O'Rourke (Also: Rourke) 8
367 (a) (Boston NL) 1,100 375.00 180.00
367 (b) (Jersey City) 725.00 325.00 180.00

(368) Dave Orr 10
368 (a) (Brooklyn) 900.00 400.00 250.00
368 (b) (Columbus) 3,500 1,750 1,050
368 (c) (New York AA "dotted tie") 15,750 7,100 3,925
368 (d) (New York AA) 725.00 325.00 180.00

(369) Charlie Parsons 4
369 (a) (Minneapolis) 725.00 325.00 180.00

(370) Owen Patton 8
370 (a) (Des Moines) 1,325 600.00 335.00
370 (b) (Minneapolis) 850.00 375.00 180.00

(371) Jimmy Peeples (Peoples) 4
371 (a) (Brooklyn) 725.00 325.00 180.00
371 (b) (Columbus) 725.00 325.00 180.00
DP 11 (Being tagged by Hardie
Henderson.) 1,600 725.00 400.00

(372) Hip Perrier 1
372 (a) (San Francisco)(VALUE UNDETERMINED)

(373) Pat Pettee 4
373 (a) (London) 3,000 1,500 600.00
373 (b) (Milwaukee) 725.00 325.00 180.00
DP 18 (About to tag Bobby Lowe.) 1,400 600.00 350.00

(374) Fred Pfeffer 5
374 (a) (Chicago NL) 1,100 650.00 400.00

(375) Dick Phelan 5
375 (a) (Des Moines) 725.00 325.00 180.00

(376) Bill Phillips 7
376 (a) (Brooklyn, large photo.) 2,000 600.00 350.00

376 (b) (Brooklyn, mini photo.) 5,175 2,325 1,300
376 (c) (Kansas City) 725.00 325.00 180.00

(377) John Pickett 12
377 (a) (Kansas City) 725.00 325.00 180.00
377 (b) (Philadelphia PL) 1,300 400.00 225.00
377 (c) (St. Paul) 725.00 325.00 180.00

(378) George Pinkney (Pinckney) 5
378 (a) (Brooklyn) 725.00 325.00 180.00

(379) Tom Poorman (Also: Poor Man, Porrman) 7
379 (a) (Milwaukee) 725.00 325.00 180.00
379 (b) (Philadelphia AA) 725.00 325.00 180.00

(380) Henry Porter 7
380 (a) (Brooklyn) 1,100 550.00 350.00
380 (b) (Kansas City) 1,125 500.00 275.00

(381) Jim Powell 5
381 (a) (Sioux City) 1,450 650.00 365.00
DP 14 (w/ Honest John Kelly.) 1,600 725.00 400.00

(382) Thomas Powers (Power) 1
382 (a) (San Francisco)(VALUE UNDETERMINED)

(383) Blondie Purcell 7
383 (b) (Baltimore) 725.00 325.00 180.00
383 (b) (Philadelphia AA) 725.00 325.00 180.00

(384) Tom Quinn 5
384 (a) (Baltimore) 950.00 475.00 300.00

(385) Joe Quinn 3
385 (a) (Boston NL) 1,400 600.00 350.00
385 (b) (Des Moines) 725.00 325.00 180.00

(386) Old Hoss Radbourn

SEE HALL OF FAME SECTION FOLLOWING

(387) Paul Radford 8
387 (a) (Brooklyn) 725.00 325.00 180.00
387 (b) (Cleveland) 725.00 325.00 180.00

(388) Tom Ramsey 3
388 (a) (Louisville) 1,050 450.00 300.00

(389) Rehse 5
389 (a) (Minneapolis) 725.00 325.00 180.00

(390) Charlie Reilly (Also: Riley) 4
390 (a) (St. Paul) 725.00 325.00 180.00

(391) Long John Reilly 3
391 (a) (Cincinnati) 1,050 450.00 250.00
DP 16 (Side by side w/ Hugh
Nicol.) 2,300 1,125 575.00
DP 17 (Facing Hugh Nicol.) 2,600 1,150 625.00

(392) Charlie Reynolds 4
392 (a) (Kansas City) 725.00 325.00 180.00

(393) Danny Richardson (Also: Richards) 5
393 (a) (New York NL) 725.00 325.00 180.00
393 (b) (New York PL) 2,700 1,200 600.00
DP 12 (Being tagged by Tim
Keefe.) 2,600 1,150 625.00
DP 13 (Sliding, Tim Keefe fielding
ball.) 4,250 2,150 1,300

(394) Hardy Richardson 5
394 (a) (Boston NL) 725.00 325.00 180.00
394 (b) (Detroit) 725.00 325.00 180.00

(395) Charlie Ripslager (Reipschlager) 1
395 (a) (New York AA "dotted tie") 9,000 4,050 2,250

(396) John Roach 6
396 (a) (New York NL) 725.00 400.00 250.00

(397) M.C. Robinson 6
397 (a) (Minneapolis) 725.00 325.00 180.00

(398) Wilbert Robinson
SEE HALL OF FAME SECTION FOLLOWING

(399) Yank Robinson 6
399 (a) (St. Louis AA "Brown's
Champions") 1,500 675.00 375.00
399 (b) (St. Louis AA) 725.00 325.00 180.00

(400) George Rooks 6
400 (a) (Chicago Maroons WA) 1,200 540.00 300.00
400 (b) (Detroit) 725.00 325.00 180.00
(Never played for Detroit.)

(401) Chief Roseman 1

401 (a) (New York AA "dotted tie") 7,850 3,525 1,950

Rourke - See Tom O'Rourke

(402) Dave Rowe 8
402 (a) (Denver)   1,600 725.00 400.00
402 (b) (Kansas City, portrait.) 6,325 2,850 1,600
402 (c) (Kansas City)   1,050 450.00 250.00

(403) Jack Rowe 3
403 (a) (Detroit)   875.00 400.00 225.00

(404) Amos Rusie (Also: Russie)
    SEE HALL OF FAME SECTION FOLLOWING

(405) Jimmy Ryan 8
405 (a) (Chicago NL)   1,000 500.00 300.00
405 (b) (Chicago PL)   2,700 1,200 600.00
405 (c) (Philadelphia)(Never player
    for Phila.)   725.00 325.00 180.00

(406) Harry Sage 6
406 (a) (Des Moines)   725.00 325.00 180.00
406 (b) (Toledo)   1,750 800.00 425.00
DP 19 (W/ Bill Van Dyke.)
    (Des Moines)   1,150 500.00 300.00
DP 20 (W/ Bill Van Dyke.) (Toledo) 1,150 500.00 300.00

(407) Ben Sanders 5
407 (a) (Philadelphia NL) 725.00 325.00 180.00
407 (b) (Philadelphia PL) 2,700 1,200 600.00

(408) Frank Scheibeck 4
408 (a) (Detroit)   850.00 375.00 180.00

(409) Al Schellhase 5
409 (a) (St. Joseph)   900.00 400.00 250.00

(410) Bill Schenkel (Also: Schenkle) 4
410 (a) (Milwaukee)   725.00 325.00 180.00

(411) L. Schildknecht 4
411 (a) (Des Moines)   725.00 325.00 180.00
411 (b) (Milwaukee)   725.00 325.00 180.00

(412) Gus Schmelz 2
412 (a) (Cincinnati)   1,800 775.00 425.00

Schoch - See Shoch

(413) Jumbo Schoeneck 8
413 (a) (Chicago Maroons WA) 1,300 650.00 400.00
413 (b) (Indianapolis)   725.00 325.00 180.00

(414) Pop Schriver 5
414 (a) (Philadelphia NL) 725.00 325.00 180.00
DP 2 (Tagging Charlie Bastian.) 1,150 500.00 300.00

Schwartwood - See Swartwood

(415) Emmett Seery 4
415 (a) (Indianapolis)   825.00 325.00 180.00

(416) Billy Serad 5
416 (a) (Cincinnati)   725.00 325.00 180.00
416 (b) (Toronto)   850.00 375.00 180.00

(417) Ed Seward 3
417 (a) (Philadelphia AA) 1,600 800.00 450.00

(418) Orator Shafer (Shaffer) 5
418 (a) (Des Moines)   725.00 325.00 180.00

(419) Taylor Shafer (Shaffer) 3
419 (a) (St. Louis Whites WA) 725.00 325.00 180.00
419 (b) (St. Paul)   725.00 325.00 180.00

(420) Daniel Shannon (Also: Hannon) 6
420 (a) (Louisville)   725.00 325.00 180.00
420 (b) (Omaha)   725.00 325.00 180.00
420 (c) (Philadelphia PL) 2,700 1,200 600.00

(421) Bill Sharsig 1
421 (a) (Philadelphia AA) 725.00 325.00 180.00

(422) John Shaw 5
422 (a) (Minneapolis)   725.00 325.00 180.00

(423) Samuel Shaw 4
423 (a) (Baltimore)   1,050 450.00 250.00
423 (b) (Newark)   1,150 500.00 300.00

(424) Bill Shindle (Also: Shindel) 7
424 (a) (Baltimore)   850.00 375.00 180.00
424 (b) (Philadelphia PL)
    ("PL" not on card.)   3,300 1,500 825.00

(425) George Shoch (Also: Schoch) 4

(425) (a) (Washington)   725.00 325.00 180.00
DP 21 (Batting, John Gaffney
    behind.)   1,150 500.00 300.00

(426) Otto Shomberg (Schomberg) 3
426 (a) (Indianapolis)   725.00 325.00 180.00

(427) Lev Shreve 7
427 (a) (Indianapolis)   950.00 425.00 225.00

(428) Ed Silch 8
428 (a) (Brooklyn)   725.00 325.00 180.00
428 (b) (Denver)   900.00 450.00 250.00

(429) Mike Slattery 6
429 (a) (New York NL)   1,100 550.00 350.00
429 (b) (New York PL)   2,700 1,200 600.00

(430) Elmer Smith 5
430 (a) (Cincinnati)   725.00 325.00 180.00

(431) Fred Smith 5
431 (a) (Des Moines)   725.00 325.00 180.00

(432) Germany (Geo.) Smith 5
432 (a) (Brooklyn)   925.00 415.00 215.00

(433) Nick Smith 5
433 (a) (St. Joseph)   900.00 405.00 225.00

(434) Phenomenal Smith 10
434 (a) (Baltimore)   1,400 625.00 350.00
434 (b) (Baltimore, portrait.)
    (No team designation.) 9,775 4,400 2,450
434 (c) (Philadelphia AA) 1,750 875.00 550.00

(435) Pop Smith 5
435 (a) (Boston NL)   775.00 325.00 180.00
435 (b) (Pittsburgh)   1,100 550.00 350.00

(436) Skyrocket (Sam) Smith 4
436 (a) (Louisville)   725.00 325.00 180.00

(437) Pete Somers 5
437 (a) (St. Louis AA)   725.00 325.00 180.00
    (Never played for St. Louis.)

(438) Joe Sommer (Also: Sommers) 5
438 (a) (Baltimore)   1,450 650.00 350.00

(439) Pete Sommers 7
439 (a) (Chicago NL)   725.00 325.00 180.00
439 (b) (New York NL)   725.00 325.00 180.00

(440) Bill Sowders 7
440 (a) (Boston NL)   725.00 325.00 180.00

(441) John Sowders 4
441 (a) (Kansas City)   1,4000 625.00 325.00
441 (b) (St. Paul)   725.00 325.00 180.00

(442) Charlie Sprague 9
442 (a) (Chicago NL)   850.00 425.00 250.00
442 (b) (Chicago Maroons WA) 1,050 450.00 250.00
442 (c) (Cleveland)   725.00 400.00 250.00

(443) Ed Sproat 5
443 (a) (St. Louis Whites WA) 975.00 425.00 250.00

(444) Harry Staley (Also: Stoley) 7
444 (a) (Pittsburgh)   725.00 325.00 180.00
444 (b) (St. Louis Whites WA) 900.00 450.00 300.00

(445) Dan Stearns (Also: Tearns) 4
445 (a) (Des Moines)   725.00 325.00 180.00
445 (b) (Kansas City)   1,000 500.00 300.00

(446) Bill Stemmeyer (Also: Stemmyer) 6
446 (a) (Boston NL)   725.00 325.00 180.00
446 (b) (Cleveland)   1,050 450.00 250.00

(447) B.F. Stephens 3
447 (a) (Milwaukee)   725.00 325.00 180.00

(448) John Sterling 4
448 (a) (Minneapolis)   725.00 325.00 180.00

(449) Len Stockwell 1
449 (a) (San Francisco) (Value Undetermined)

Stoley - See Staley

(450) Harry Stovey 9
450 (a) (Boston PL)   2,700 1,200 600.00
450 (b) (Philadelphia AA) 1,600 725.00 400.00

(451) Scott Stratton 5
451 (a) (Louisville)   725.00 325.00 180.00

(452) Joe Strauss (Also: Straus) 8
452 (a) (Milwaukee)   725.00 325.00 180.00
452 (b) (Omaha)   1,600 800.00 500.00

(453) Cub Stricker 3
453 (a) (Cleveland)   725.00 325.00 180.00

(454) Marty Sullivan 7
454 (a) (Chicago NL)   950.00 450.00 230.00
454 (b) (Indianapolis)   725.00 325.00 180.00

(455) Mike Sullivan 3
455 (a) (Philadelphia AA) 950.00 450.00 230.00

(457) Billy Sunday 10
457 (a) (Chicago NL)   2,350 1,200 585.00
457 (b) (Pittsburgh)   2,250 1,175 575.00

(458) Sy Sutcliffe 5
458 (a) (Cleveland)   900.00 400.00 250.00

(459) Ezra Sutton 8
459 (a) (Boston NL)   950.00 450.00 2380.00
459 (b) (Milwaukee)   850.00 425.00 275.00

(460) Ed Swartwood (Also: Schwartwood) 7
460 (a) (Brooklyn)   725.00 325.00 180.00
460 (b) (Des Moines)   725.00 325.00 180.00
460 (c) (Hamilton)   950.00 475.00 325.00

(461) Park Swartzel 6
461 (a) (Kansas City)   900.00 425.00 225.00

(462) Pete Sweeney (Also: Sweeny) 5
462 (a) (Washington)   1,050 450.00 250.00

(463) Louis Sylvester 1
463 (a) (Sacramento) (Value Undetermined)

(464) Pop Tate 6
464 (a) (Baltimore)   725.00 325.00 180.00
464 (b) (Boston NL)   725.00 325.00 180.00

(465) Patsy (Oliver) Tebeau 8
465 (a) (Chicago NL)   725.00 325.00 180.00
465 (b) (Cleveland)   950.00 475.00 325.00

Tearns - See Stearns

(466) John Tener 5
466 (a) (Chicago NL)   1,425 650.00 350.00

(467) Adonis Terry 5
467 (a) (Brooklyn)   900.00 450.00 300.00

(468) Sam Thompson

See Hall of Fame Section Following

(469) Mike Tiernan 6
469 (a) (New York NL)   725.00 325.00 180.00

(470) Cannonball Titcomb 5
470 (a) (New York NL)   725.00 325.00 180.00

(471) Phil Tomney 4
471 (a) (Louisville)   725.00 325.00 180.00

(472) Steve Toole 7
472 (a) (Brooklyn)   850.00 375.00 225.00
472 (b) (Kansas City)   725.00 325.00 180.00
472 (c) (Rochester)   900.00 450.00 300.00

(473) George Townsend 3
473 (a) (Philadelphia AA) 1,500 675.00 375.00
(474) Bill Traffley 4
474 (a) (Des Moines)   725.00 325.00 180.00

(475) George Treadway (Also: Tredway) 6
475 (a) (Denver)   1,000 500.00 300.00
475 (b) (St. Paul)   850.00 450.00 275.00

(476) Sam Trott 10
476 (a) (Baltimore)   725.00 325.00 180.00
476 (b) (Newark)   725.00 325.00 180.00
DP 22 (Tagging Oyster Burns.) 1,150 500.00 300.00

(477) Tommy Tucker 5
477 (a) (Baltimore)   1,400 600.00 350.00
DP 8 (Being tagged by Chris
    Fulmer.)   3,000 1,500 1,000

(478) A.M. Tuckerman 5
478 (a) (St. Paul)   725.00 325.00 180.00

(479) George Turner 5
479 (a) (Minneapolis)   725.00 325.00 180.00

(480) Larry Twitchell 6			
480 (a) (Cleveland)	925.00	425.00	225.00
480 (b) (Detroit)	725.00	325.00	180.00

(481) Jim Tyng 4			
481 (a) (Philadelphia NL)	725.00	325.00	180.00

(482) Bill Van Dyke 3			
482 (a) (Des Moines)	725.00	325.00	180.00
482 (b) (Toledo)	725.00	325.00	180.00
DP 19 (W/ Harry Sage.) (Des Moines)	1,150	500.00	300.00
DP 20 (W/ Harry Sage.) (Toledo)	1,150	500.00	300.00

(483) George Van Haltren 4			
483 (a) (Chicago NL)	1,725	875.00	525.00

(484) Farmer Vaughn 7			
484 (a) (Louisville)	725.00	325.00	180.00
484 (b) (New York PL)	4,500	2,025	1,125

(485) Peek-A-Boo Veach 4			
485 (a) (Sacramento) (Value Undetermined)			
485 (b) (St. Paul)	725.00	325.00	180.00

(486) Leon Viau 5			
486 (a) (Cincinnati)	725.00	400.00	275.00

(487) Bill Vinton 4			
487 (a) (Minneapolis)	825.00	325.00	180.00

(488) Joe Visner 5			
488 (a) (Brooklyn)	725.00	325.00	180.00

(489) Chris Von Der Ahe 1			
489 (a) (St. Louis AA "Brown's Champions")	4,325	1,950	1,075

(490) Reddy Walsh 5			
490 (a) (Omaha)	850.00	375.00	225.00

(491) John Ward

See Hall of Fame Section Following

(492) Ed Warner 2			
492 (a) (Milwaukee)	725.00	325.00	180.00
DP 5 (W/ Jack Horner.)	1,150	500.00	300.00

Wassitt - See Messitt

(493) Bill Watkins 2			
493 (a) (Detroit)	725.00	325.00	180.00
493 (b) (Kansas City)	900.00	400.00	250.00

(494) Farmer Weaver 4			
494 (a) (Louisville)	1,800	900.00	450.00

(495) Charlie Weber 5			
495 (a) (Sioux City)	900.00	400.00	250.00

(496) Stump Weidman (Wiedman) 4			
496 (a) (Detroit)	725.00	325.00	180.00

(497) Wild Bill Weidner (Widner) 5			
497 (a) (Columbus)	900.00	400.00	250.00

(498) Curt Welch (Also: Welsh) 7			
498 (a) (St. Louis AA "Brown's Champions")	1,875	850.00	475.00
498 (b) (Philadelphia AA)	725.00	325.00	180.00
DP 23 (W/ Bill Gleason.)	2,300	1,050	575.00

(499) Mickey Welch (Also: Welsh)

See Hall of Fame Section Following

(500) Jake Wells 2			
500 (a) (Kansas City)	1,325	600.00	325.00

(501) Frank Wells 1			
501 (a) (Milwaukee)	850.00	375.00	225.00

(502) Joe Werrick 5			
502 (a) (Louisville)	725.00	325.00	180.00
502 (b) (St. Paul)	975.00	450.00	250.00

(503) Buck West 5			
503 (a) (Minneapolis)	850.00	375.00	225.00

(504) Gus Weyhing 3			
504 (a) (Philadelphia AA)	725.00	325.00	180.00

(505) John Weyhing 4			
505 (a) (Columbus)	725.00	325.00	180.00
505 (b) (Philadelphia AA) (Never played for Phila.)	1,100	500.00	300.00

(506) Bobby Wheelock 9			
506 (a) (Boston NL)	900.00	425.00	225.00
506 (b) (Detroit) (Never played for Detroit.)	725.00	325.00	180.00
506 (c) (Photo actually Con Daily.)	725.00	325.00	180.00

(508) Pat Whitaker (Also: Whitacre) 7			
508 (a) (Baltimore)	725.00	325.00	180.00
508 (b) (Philadelphia AA) (Never played for Philadelphia.)	725.00	325.00	180.00

(509) Bill White 5			
509 (a) (Louisville)	3,000	1,350	750.00

(510) Deacon White 10			
510 (a) (Detroit)	1,550	700.00	375.00
510 (b) (Pittsburgh)	725.00	325.00	180.00

(511) Art Whitney 7			
511 (a) (New York NL)	725.00	325.00	180.00
511 (b) (New York PL)	2,700	1,200	600.00
511 (c) (Pittsburgh)	725.00	325.00	180.00
511 (d) (W/dog.)	4,800	2,150	1,200

(512) G. Whitney 5			
512 (a) (St. Joseph)	850.00	375.00	225.00

(513) Jim Whitney 4			
513 (a) (Indianapolis)	725.00	325.00	180.00
513 (b) (Washington)	950.00	475.00	300.00

E. Williams, W. Williams - See Ned Williamson

(514) Jimmy Williams 2			
514 (a) (Cleveland)	1,050	450.00	250.00

(515) Ned Williamson 8			
515 (a) (Chicago NL)	1,250	625.00	400.00
515 (c) (in dress clothes)	5,175	2,325	1,300
515 (c) (Chicago PL)	3,000	1,350	750.00
DP 24 (W/ Willie Hahn. (Mascot)	4,000	1,800	1,200

(516) Tit Willis 5			
516 (a) (Omaha)	725.00	325.00	180.00

(517) Walt Wilmot 8			
517 (a) (Chicago NL)	725.00	325.00	180.00
517 (b) (Washington)	725.00	400.00	250.00

(518) George Winkleman (Winkelman) 4			
518 (a) (Hartford)	2,500	400.00	225.00
518 (b) (Minneapolis)	2,500	400.00	225.00

(519) Sam Wise 5			
519 (a) (Boston NL)	1,350	600.00	335.00
519 (b) (Washington)	725.00	325.00	180.00

(520) Chicken Wolf 5			
520 (a) (Louisville)	1,200	550.00	300.00

(521) George Wood 5 (L.F.)			
521 (a) (Philadelphia NL)	725.00	325.00	180.00
521 (b) (Philadelphia PL)	2,700	1,200	600.00

(522) Pete Wood 5 (P)			
522 (a) (Philadelphia NL)	875.00	400.00	225.00

(523) Harry Wright

See Hall of Fame Section Following

(524) Chief Zimmer 4			
524 (a) (Cleveland)	925.00	425.00	225.00

(525) Frank Zinn 3			
525 (a) (Philadelphia AA)	725.00	325.00	180.00

1888-1889 Old Judge Cabinets (N173)

These cabinet cards were issued by Goodwin & Co. in 1888-89 as a premium available by exchanging coupons found in Old Judge or Dogs Head brand cigarettes. The cabinet cards consist of approximately 3-3/4" x 5-3/4" photographs affixed to a cardboard backing that measures approximately 4-1/4" x 6-1/2". The mounting is usually pale yellow with gold-leaf trimmings, but backings have also been found in red, blue or black. An ad for Old Judge Cigarettes appears along the bottom of the cabinet. Cabinets obtained by exchanging coupons from Dogs Head cigarettes include an ad for both Old Judge and Dogs Head, and are scarcer. According to an advertising sheet, cabinets were available of "every prominent player in the National League, Western League and American Association." There will continue to be additions to this checklist. This list includes all confirmed photo and team variations; minor differences in spelling of team name, position abbreviations or punctuation are not recorded, except in the case of Hall of Famers. Several Old Judge cabinets are not known to exist in the standard N172 format.

OLD JUDGE CIGARETTES Goodwin & Co., New York.

	NM	EX	VG
Common Player:	2,500	1,500	1,000
Black or Colored Mount: 3-5X			
Unlisted Dogs Head: 2-3X			
(4) Bob Allen			
4 (a) Pittsburgh, hands clasped at waist	2,500	1,500	1,000
4 (b) Pittsburgh, batting, Dogs Head	4,500	2,250	1,350
(5) Myron Allen			
5 (a) Kansas City, fielding	2,500	1,500	1,000
(7) Varney Anderson			
7 (a) pitching, right hand head-high	2,500	1,500	1,000
(8) Ed Andrews			
8 (a) Philadelphia, both hands shoulder-high	2,500	1,500	1,000
8 (b) Philadelphia, one hand above head	2,500	1,500	1,000
DP 1 being tagged by Buster Hoover	3,750	2,250	1,625
(9) Wally Andrews			
9 (a) Omaha, hands shoulder-high	2,500	1,500	1,000
(11) Cap Anson			
11 (a) portrait	18,550	10,150	6,700
11 (b) portrait, Dogs Head	45,000	27,000	18,750
(15) Kid Baldwin			
15 (a) ball in hands, head-high	2,500	1,500	1,000
(16) Lady Baldwin			
16 (a) Detroit, pitching, left hand head-high	2,500	1,500	1,000
(17) Mark Baldwin			
17 (a) Chicago, batting, heels together	2,750	1,400	1,000
17 (b) Chicago, pitching, right hand above head	2,750	1,400	1,000
17 (c) Chicago, pitching, right hand waist-high	2,750	1,400	1,000
17 (d) Columbus, ball in hands, neck-high	2,500	1,500	1,000
(20) John Barnes			
20 (a) portrait	5,500	2,250	1,650
(21) Billy Barnie			
21 (a) portrait	3,000	1,800	1,300
(22) Charley Bassett			
22 (a) Indianapolis, bat at ready	2,500	1,500	1,000
(23) Charlie Bastian			
23 (a) Chicago, bat over shoulder	2,500	1,500	1,000
23 (b) Chicago, fielding, hands chest-high	2,500	1,500	1,000
23 (c) Philadelphia, stooping to field low ball	2,500	1,500	1,000
DP 2 Philadelphia, tagging Pop Schriver	3,750	2,250	1,625
(24) Ed Beatin			
24 (a) pitching, right arm forward	2,500	1,500	1,000
(27) Charlie Bennett			
27 (a) batting	2,500	1,500	1,000
27 (b) batting, Dogs Head	5,250	3,150	2,250
(28) Lou Bierbauer			
28 (a) fielding grounder	2,500	1,500	1,000
28 (b) fielding, hands chest-high	3,375	2,000	1,450
28 (c) throwing	3,750	2,250	1,650

(31) Ned Bligh				
31 (a) fielding, hands head-high	2,500	1,500	1,000	
	2,500	1,500	1,000	
(32) Bogart	2,500	1,500	1,000	
32 (a) fielding, hands chest-high	2,500	1,500	1,000	
(33) Abner Boyce				
33 (a) Washington, fielding	3,500	2,000	1,250	
(35) Henry Boyle	2,500	1,500	1,000	
35 (a) Indianapolis, pitch., right arm extended	2,500	1,500	1,000	
(36) Jack Boyle				
36 (a) St. Louis, bat at side	2,500	1,500	1,000	
36 (b) St. Louis, bat at ready	2,500	1,500	1,000	
36 (c) St. Louis, catching, hands knee-high	2,500	1,500	1,000	
(37) George Bradley				
37 (a) Sioux City, fielding, looking up at ball	2,500	1,500	1,000	
(43) Dan Brouthers				
43 (a) Boston, batting	6,750	3,375	2,400	
43 (b) Boston, batting, Dogs Head	9,750	5,850	4,200	
43 (c) Boston, fielding, hands at waist	6,750	3,400	2,400	
43 (d) Boston, throwing, horizontal format	6,000	3,600	2,600	
43 (e) Detroit, batting	5,625	3,375	2,400	
(44) Tom Brown				
44 (a) Boston, bat at ready	2,500	1,500	1,000	
44 (b) Boston, bat at side	2,500	1,500	1,000	
44 (c) Boston, bat at side, Dogs Head	4,500	2,300	1,350	
44 (d) Boston, fielding	2,500	1,500	1,000	
(45) Willard (California) Brown				
45 (a) New York, bat at side	2,500	1,500	1,000	
45 (b) New York, batting	2,500	1,500	1,000	
45 (c) New York, throwing, mask in left hand	2,500	1,500	1,000	
(46) Pete Browning				
46 (a) batting, feet together	5,625	3,375	2,400	
(47) Charlie Brynan				
47 (a) Chicago, pitching, right arm neck-high	2,500	1,500	1,000	
47 (b) Des Moines, pitching, right arm forward	2,500	1,500	1,000	
(48) Al Buckenberger				
48 (a) portrait, looking right	2,500	1,500	1,000	
(49) Dick Buckley				
49 (a) Indianapolis, fielding, hands chest-high	2,500	1,500	1,000	
(50) Charlie Buffinton				
50 (a) fielding, hands chest-high	2,500	1,500	1,000	
50 (b) pitch., right hand above head, Dogs Head	9,000	5,400	3,850	
(52) Jack Burdock				
52 (a) fielding grounder	2,500	1,500	1,000	
(56) Jim Burns				
56 (a) Kansas City, fielding grounder	2,500	1,500	1,000	
(58) Oyster Burns				
58 (a) Brooklyn, bat at ready vertically	3,000	1,500	1,000	
58 (b) Brooklyn, throwing, right hand head-high	2,500	1,500	1,000	
(59) Tom Burns				
59 (a) Chicago, bat at side	2,500	1,500	1,000	
59 (a) Chicago, bat at ready	2,500	1,500	1,000	
59 (b) Chicago, fielding	2,500	1,500	1,000	
59 (c) Chicago, tagging player	2,850	1,725	1,225	
(60) Doc Bushong				
60 (a) stooping, hands waist-high	2,500	1,500	1,000	
60 (b) throwing	3,750	2,250	1,625	
(63) Jimmy Canavan				
63 (a) batting	2,500	1,500	1,000	
(66) Hick Carpenter				
66 (a) batting	2,500	1,500	1,000	
(68) Fred Carroll				
68 (a) Pittsburgh, throwing	2,500	1,500	1,000	

(69) Scrappy Carroll			
69 (a) St. Paul, fielding, hands chest-high	3,375	2,000	1,450
(70) Ed Cartwright			
70 (a) St. Joseph, throwing	2,500	1,500	1,000
(71) Bob Caruthers			
71 (a) batting, feet apart	2,500	1,500	1,000
71 (b) holding ball in left hand, neck-high	3,500	2,000	1,500
(72) Daniel Casey			
72 (a) pitching, left hand shoulder-high	2,500	1,500	1,000
(73) Elton Chamberlain			
73 (a) batting, looking at camera	2,500	1,500	1,000
73 (b) pitching, hands chest-high	2,500	1,500	1,000
73 (c) pitching, right hand head-high	2,500	1,500	1,000
(74) Cupid Childs			
74 (a) fielding	2,500	1,500	1,000
(75) Bob Clark			
75 (a) Brookyln, fielding, hands shoulder-high	2,500	1,500	1,000
75 (b) Brooklyn, throwing	2,500	1,500	1,000
DP 4 Brooklyn, tagging Mickey Hughes	6,750	4,050	2,875
DP 4 Brooklyn, tagging M. Hughes, Dogs Head	8,250	4,950	3,550
Clark, Chicago - See Dad Clarke	2,500	1,500	1,000
(76) Spider Clark			
76 (a) Washington, pose unrecorded	2,500	1,500	1,000
(77) Dad Clark (Clarke)			
77 (a) Chicago, right arm extended forward	2,500	1,500	1,000
77 (b) Omaha, batting	2,500	1,500	1,000
(78) John Clarkson			
78 (a) Boston, batting	5,250	3,150	2,250
78 (b) Boston, right arm forward, left on thigh	7,125	4,275	3,075
78 (c) Boston, pitching, right arm back	5,250	3,150	2,250
78 (d) Boston, pitching, arm back, Dogs Head	10,500	6,300	4,500
(79) Jack Clements			
79 (a) batting	2,500	1,500	1,000
79 (b) fielding	3,225	1,950	1,375
79 (c) hands on knees	2,500	1,500	1,000
(80) Elmer Cleveland			
80 (a) pose unrecorded	2,500	1,500	1,000
(81) Monk Cline			
81 (a) bat nearly vertical	2,500	1,500	1,000
(83) John Coleman			
83 (a) ball in hands at waist	2,500	1,500	1,000
83 (b) bat in hands below waist	2,500	1,500	1,000
(85) Hub Collins			
85 (a) Brooklyn, batting	2,500	1,500	1,000
85 (b) Brooklyn, fielding, hands chest-high	2,500	1,500	1,000
(86) Charlie Comiskey			
86 (a) arms folded	7,500	4,500	3,225
86 (b) fielding, hands neck-high, ball visible	7,500	4,500	3,225
86 (c) fielding, hands shoulder-high, no ball	11,250	6,750	4,825
86 (d) sliding	14,250	8,550	6,100
(88) Roger Connor			
88 (a) batting, home plate, batter's boxes on floor	11,250	6,750	4,825
88 (b) batting, outdoors scene on backdrop	9,750	6,000	4,200
88 (c) fielding, hands at waist	7,500	4,500	3,225
88 (d) hands on knees	9,000	4,500	3,225
(89) Dick Conway			
89 (a) Boston, bat in hand at side	4,500	2,700	1,950
(90) Jim Conway			
90 (a) Kansas City, pitching, left ear visible	3,600	1,800	1,100

90 (b) K.C., pitching, left ear not visible	3,600	1,800	1,100
(91) Pete Conway			
91 (a) Detroit, pitching, right hand extended	2,500	1,500	1,000
91 (b) Detroit, pitching, hands at chest	2,500	1,500	1,000
(92) Paul Cook			
92 (a) fielding in mask	2,500	1,500	1,000
92 (b) tagging baserunner	2,500	1,500	1,000
(93) Jimmy Cooney			
93 (a) batting, Omaha, Dogs Head	5,250	3,150	2,250
(95) Pop Corkhill			
95 (a) Brooklyn, batting	2,500	1,500	1,000
95 (b) Brooklyn, fielding, hands neck-high	2,500	1,500	1,000
(96) Cannonball Crane			
96 (a) New York, pitching, right hand head-high	2,500	1,500	1,000
(99) John Crooks			
99 (a) Omaha, pose unrecorded	2,500	1,500	1,000
(100) Lave Cross			
100 (a) Louisville, hands on thighs	2,500	1,500	1,000
100 (b) Athletics, right arm head high	2,500	1,500	1,000
100 (c) Philadelphia, fielding grounder	2,500	1,500	1,000
(105) Bert Cunningham			
105 (a) both arms waist level	2,500	1,500	1,000
(109) Edward Dailey			
109 (a) Columbus, pitching, right hand head-high	2,500	1,500	1,000
109 (b) Washington, pitch., right hand head-high	2,500	1,500	1,000
(111) Bill Daley			
111 (a) Boston, ball in hands above waist	3,000	1,500	1,000
(112) Con Daley (Daily)			
112 (a) Indianapolis, right hand on hip	2,500	1,500	1,000
(113) Abner Dalrymple			
113 (a) Pittsburgh, hands on hips, feet apart	2,500	1,500	1,000
(114) Sun Daly			
114 (a) Minneapolis, fielding, hands chest-high	2,500	1,500	1,000
(115) Tom Daly			
115 (a) Chicago, fielding, hands chest-high	3,000	1,500	1,000
115 (b) Chicago, hands on knees	3,000	1,500	1,000
115 (c) Washington, fielding, hands chest-high	3,000	1,500	1,000
(117) Dell Darling			
117 (a) fielding, hands waist-high	2,500	1,500	1,000
117 (b) standing, arms crossed	2,500	1,500	1,000
(118) William Darnbrough			
118 (a) pitching	2,500	1,500	1,000
(122) Tom Deasley			
122 (a) New York, fielding	2,500	1,500	1,000
(123) Harry Decker			
123 (a) bat nearly horizontal	2,500	1,500	1,000
(124) Ed Delehanty			
124 (a) bat by shoulder	31,250	5,400	3,875
124 (b) bat horizontal	9,000	5,400	3,875
124 (c) fielding	22,500	13,500	9,675
(125) Jerry Denny			
125 (a) Indianapolis, batting	2,500	1,500	1,000
125 (b) Indianapolis, fielding	2,500	1,500	1,000
(126) Jim Devlin			
126 (a) pitching, left hand shoulder-high	2,500	1,500	1,000
126 (b) sliding	2,500	1,500	1,000
(130) Jim Donnelly			
130 (a) batting	2,500	1,500	1,000
(132) John Doran			

132 (a) fielding	24,000	12,000	7,200
(133) Mike Dorgan			
133 (a) sliding, horizontal format	3,375	2,000	1,450
(135) Charlie Duffe (Duffee)			
135 (a) batting	2,500	1,500	1,000
135 (b) fielding, bending to left	2,500	1,500	1,000
135 (c) fielding grounder	2,500	1,500	1,000
135 (d) fielding, standing upright	2,500	1,500	1,000
(136) Hugh Duffy			
136 (a) batting	4,875	2,925	2,100
136 (b) fielding, hands chin-high	4,875	2,925	2,100
136 (c) fielding grounder	6,000	3,600	2,600
(138) Martin Duke			
138 (a) ball in hands, chest-high	3,750	2,250	1,625
(139) Fred Dunlap			
139 (a) arms at side	2,500	1,500	1,000
139 (b) holding ball aloft	2,500	1,500	1,000
139 (c) holding ball aloft, Dogs Head	4,500	2,700	1,950
139 (d) sliding, right arm up	4,000	2,000	1,200
(141) Jesse Duryea			
141 (a) batting	2,500	1,500	1,000
(142) Frank Dwyer			
142 (a) bat at side	3,750	2,250	1,625
142 (b) bat in air	2,500	1,500	1,000
142 (c) fielding	2,500	1,500	1,000
(143) Billy Earle			
143 (a) Cincinnati, fielding, hands over head	2,500	1,500	1,000
(145) Red Ehret			
145 (a) batting	2,500	1,500	1,000
(147) Dude Esterbrook			
147 (a) Indianapolis, fielding grounder	2,500	1,500	1,000
147 (b) Indianapolis, fielding, hands chest-high	2,500	1,500	1,000
147 (c) Louisville, fielding, hands chest high	2,500	1,500	1,000
(149) Buck Ewing			
149 (a) New York, bat at side	12,500	6,000	3,200
149 (b) New York, bat in air	12,500	6,000	3,200
149 (c) New York, fielding, hands head-high	12,500	6,000	3,200
149 (d) New York, hands on knees	12,500	6,000	3,200
149 (e) New York, throwing, right arm extended forward	12,500	6,000	3,200
149 (f) New York, with mascot Willie Breslin	22,500	11,500	5,500
149 (g) New York, w/ mascot, Dogs Head	26,250	15,750	11,275
(150) John Ewing			
150 (a) Louisville, bat almost vertical	2,500	1,500	1,000
(151) Jay Faatz			
151 (a) throwing	2,500	1,500	1,000
151 (b) batting	2,500	1,500	1,000
(152) Bill Farmer			
152 (a) Pittsburgh, hands on knees	2,500	1,500	1,000
(154) Sid Farrar			
154 (a) fielding grounder	2,500	1,500	1,000
154 (b) fielding, hands head-high	2,500	1,500	1,000
(155) Duke Farrell			
155 (a) Chicago, fielding grounder	3,000	1,500	1,000
155 (b) Chicago, hands on knees	3,000	1,500	1,000
(157) Frank Fennelly			
157 (a) Cincinnati, fielding grounder	2,500	1,500	1,000
(158) Charlie Ferguson			
158 (a) pitching, hands at chest	2,500	1,500	1,000
(159) Alex Ferson			
159 (a) pitching, hands neck-high, looking front	2,500	1,500	1,000
(161) Jocko Fields			
161 (a) hands on thighs	2,500	1,500	1,000
(164) Silver Flint			
164 (a) batting	2,500	1,500	1,000
164 (b) catching, with mask, hands waist-high	3,000	1,800	1,300

(167) Jim Fogarty			
167 (a) batting	2,500	1,500	1,000
167 (b) fielding, hands neck-high	2,500	1,500	1,000
167 (c) running to left	2,500	1,500	1,000
167 (d) sliding	2,500	1,500	1,000
(168) Frank Foreman			
168 (a) Baltimore, ball in hands by right thigh	3,375	2,000	1,450
(170) Elmer Foster			
170 (a) Minneapolis, batting	2,500	1,500	1,000
170 (b) New York, fielding	2,500	1,500	1,000
(171) Dave Foutz			
171 (a) bat at 45 degrees	2,500	1,500	1,000
171 (b) throwing	2,500	1,500	1,000
(175) Shorty Fuller			
175 (a) bat on shoulder	2,500	1,500	1,000
175 (b) fielding	2,500	1,500	1,000
175 (c) hands on knees	2,500	1,500	1,000
175 (d) swinging bat	2,500	1,500	1,000
(177) Chris Fulmer			
DP 8 tagging Tom Tucker, Dogs Head	6,750	4,050	2,875
(178) John Gaffney			
178 (a) Washington, leaning to right	2,500	1,500	1,000
(179) Pud Galvin			
179 (a) batting	5,625	3,375	2,400
(181) Charlie Ganzel			
181 (a) Boston, batting	2,500	1,500	1,000
181 (b) Boston, fielding, hands shoulder-high	3,750	2,250	1,625
181 (c) Boston, fielding, hands thigh-high	2,500	1,500	1,000
(182) Gid Gardner			
182 (a) Philadelphia, fielding low ball	2,500	1,500	1,000
(183) Hank Gastreich			
183 (a) pitching, left hand by thigh	2,500	1,500	1,000
(185) Frank Genins			
185 (a) batting, looking at ball	2,500	1,500	1,000
185 (b) batting, looking at camera	2,500	1,500	1,000
(186) Bill George			
186 (a) bat at side	2,500	1,500	1,000
(187) Joe Gearhardt			
187 (a) Jersey City, throwing	2,500	1,500	1,000
(188) Charlie Getzein (Getzien)			
188 (a) pitching, hands above waist	2,500	1,500	1,000
(190) Bobby Gilks			
190 (a) batting	2,500	1,500	1,000
(192) Barney Gilligan			
192 (a) Washington, fielding	2,500	1,500	1,000
(193) Frank Gilmore			
193 (a) pitching, hands neck-high	2,500	1,500	1,000
(194) Jack Glasscock			
194 (a) Indianapolis, bat at side, Dogs Head	5,250	3,150	2,250
194 (b) Indianapolis, hands on knees	2,500	1,500	1,000
194 (c) Indianapolis, throwing	2,500	1,500	1,000
(195) Bill Gleason			
195 (a) Louisville, batting	2,500	1,500	1,000
195 (b) Louisville, stooping, hands clasped	2,500	1,500	1,000
DP 23 with Curt Welch	3,375	2,025	1,450
(196) Kid Gleason			
196 (a) Philadelphia, fielding grounder	3,375	2,025	1,450
196 (b) Philadelphia, ball in hands at chin	3,375	2,025	1,450
(197) Ed Glenn			
197 (a) fielding, hands neck-high	2,500	1,500	1,000
(199) George Gore			
199 (a) bat nearly horizontal	2,500	1,500	1,000
199 (b) bat at ready over left shoulder	2,500	1,500	1,000
199 (c) fielding grounder	2,500	1,500	1,000

(205) Henry Gruber			
205 (a) pitching, right hand chin-high	2,500	1,500	1,000
(206) Ad Gumbert			
206 (a) pitching, right hand eye-high	3,150	1,875	1,350
206 (b) pitching, right hand waist-high	2,500	1,500	1,000
(207) Tom Gunning			
207 (a) bending forward, hands by right knee	2,500	1,500	1,000
(208) Joe Gunson			
208 (a) wearing jacket	2,500	1,500	1,000
(212) Bill Hallman			
212 (a) leaning left to catch ball chest-high	2,500	1,500	1,000
(213) Billy Hamilton			
213 (a) Kansas City, batting: looking at camera	9,000	5,400	3,875
213 (b) Kansas City, fielding, hands neck-high	9,000	5,400	3,875
213 (c) Kansas City, fielding grounder	9,000	5,400	3,875
(215) Ned Hanlon			
215 (a) Detroit, batting	4,500	2,700	1,950
215 (b) Pittsburgh, fielding	4,875	2,925	2,100
(216) Bill Hanrahan			
216 (a) bat at side	2,500	1,500	1,000
(221) Gil Hatfield			
221 (a) bat at waist	2,500	1,500	1,000
221 (b) bat over shoulder	2,500	1,500	1,000
221 (c) fielding, hands chest-high	2,500	1,500	1,000
(223) Egyptian Healey (Healy)			
223 (a) Indianapolis, pitching, hands at chest	2,500	1,500	1,000
(227) Hardie Henderson			
227 (a) Brooklyn, outdoors, throwing, right hand head-high	7,500	4,000	2,500
(228) Moxie Hengle			
228 (a) Minneapolis, hands on knees	2,500	1,500	1,000
(229) John Henry			
229 (a) throwing, right hand neck-high	2,500	1,500	1,000
(231) Hunkey Hines			
231 (a) St. Louis Whites, fielding	2,500	1,500	1,000
(232) Paul Hines			
232 (a) Washington, arms at side	2,500	1,500	1,000
(233) Frank Hoffman			
233 (a) pitching, right hand head-high	2,500	1,500	1,000
(235) Bill Holbert			
235 (a) throwing	2,500	1,500	1,000
(236) Bug Holliday			
236 (a) Cincinnati, arms at side	2,500	1,500	1,000
236 (b) Cincinnati, ball in hands at shoulder	2,500	1,500	1,000
(238) Buster Hoover			
238 (a) Philadelphia, fielding, hands head-high	2,500	1,500	1,000
DP 1 being tagged by Ed Andrews	3,750	2,250	1,625
(239) Charlie Hoover			
239 (a) Chicago, fielding grounder (Never played for Chicago)	2,500	1,500	1,000
239 (b) Kansas City, pose unrecorded	2,500	1,500	1,000
(241) Joe Hornung			
241 (a) Boston, batting	2,500	1,500	1,000
(243) Dummy Hoy			
243 (a) fielding grounder	6,750	4,050	2,875
(244) Nat Hudson			
244 (a) ball in hands waist-high	2,500	1,500	1,000

244 (b) pitching, right hand head-high	2,500	1,500	1,000
244 (c) pitching, right hand waist-high	2,500	1,500	1,000
(245) Mickey Hughes	2,500	1,500	1,000
245 (a) holding ball at chest	2,500	1,500	1,000
245 (b) holding ball at side	2,500	1,500	1,000
245 (c) right hand extended	2,500	1,500	1,000
DP 4 being tagged by Bob Clark	5,625	3,375	2,400
(247) Bill Hutchinson			
247 (a) ball in hand, right heel hidden	2,500	1,500	1,000
247 (b) ball in hand, right heel visible	2,500	1,500	1,000
247 (c) batting	2,500	1,500	1,000
(248) Arthur Irwin			
248 (a) Philadelphia, fielding, hands chest-high	2,500	1,500	1,000
248 (b) Phila., throwing, right hand head-high	2,500	1,500	1,000
(249) John Irwin			
249 (a) Washington, hands on knees	2,500	1,500	1,000
249 (b) Washington, throwing	2,500	1,500	1,000
(250) A.C. Jantzen			
250 (a) batting, looking at camera	2,500	1,500	1,000
(252) Spud Johnson			
252 (a) Columbus, pose unrecorded	2,500	1,500	1,000
(253) Dick Johnston			
253 (a) batting, looking at ball	2,500	1,500	1,000
253 (b) batting, looking at camera	2,500	1,500	1,000
253 (c) hands on hips	2,500	1,500	1,000
253 (d) throwing right hand head high	2,500	1,500	1,000
(256) Tim Keefe			
256 (a) bat nearly horizontal, Old Judge	8,500	4,700	2,950
256 (b) bat nearly horizontal, Dogs Head	18,750	11,250	8,100
256 (c) ball in hands at chest	7,750	4,250	2,625
256 (d) pitching, right hand head-high	8,000	4,500	2,550
256 (e) pitching, right hand waist-high	8,000	4,500	2,550
(258) Jim Keenan			
258 (a) Cincinnati, fielding	4,000	2,000	1,200
(259) Charlie Kelly			
259 (a) Philadelphia, fielding, hands head-high	2,500	1,500	1,000
(261) King Kelly			
261 (a) "Kelly, Boston.", bat at 45-degree angle	15,000	7,500	4,500
261 (b) "Kelly, Boston.", bat at 45-degree angle, Dogs Head	17,500	8,750	5,300
261 (c) "Mike Kelly, C, Bostons", bat at 45-degree angle	12,000	5,400	3,875
261 (d) "Kelly, Capt.", bat at 45-degree angle	12,000	5,400	3,875
(262) Rudy Kemmler			
262 (a) fielding, hands chest-high	2,500	1,500	1,000
(263) Ted Kennedy			
263 (a) Omaha, pose unrecorded	2,500	1,500	1,000
(264) J.J. Kenyon			
264 (a) Des Moines, right hand in glove, head-high	2,500	1,500	1,000
(265) John Kerins			
265 (a) hands on thighs	2,500	1,500	1,000
(266) Matt Kilroy			
266 (a) pitching, hands waist-high to left	2,500	1,500	1,000
(267) Silver King			
267 (a) St. Louis, pitching, hands chest-high	2,500	1,500	1,000
267 (b) St. Louis, pitching, hands chin-high	2,500	1,500	1,000
(269) Billy Klusman			
269 (a) fielding grounder	2,500	1,500	1,000
(274) Gus Krock			

274 (a) ball in hands above waist	2,650	1,400	1,000
274 (b) batting	2,650	1,400	1,000
274 (c) pitching, right hand chin-high	2,650	1,400	1,000
(275) Willie Kuehne			
275 (a) fielding grounder	2,500	1,500	1,000
(277) Henry Larkin			
277 (a) fielding, hands thigh-high	2,500	1,500	1,000
277 (b) right hand shoulder-high	2,500	1,500	1,000
(278) Arlie Latham			
278 (a) batting	2,500	1,500	1,000
278 (b) throwing	3,950	2,000	1,250
278 (c) sliding	2,500	1,500	1,000
(279) Chuck Lauer			
279 (a) fielding, hands chest-high	2,500	1,500	1,000
(280) John Leighton			
280 (a) batting	2,500	1,500	1,000
280 (b) fielding	2,500	1,500	1,000
(284) Herman Long			
284 (a) Kansas City, bat at side	2,500	1,500	1,000
284 (b) Kansas City, fielding, hands chest-high	2,500	1,500	1,000
(285) Tom Lovett			
285 (a) Brooklyn, bat on shoulder	2,500	1,500	1,000
285 (b) Brooklyn, pitching, hands over head	2,500	1,500	1,000
285 (c) Brooklyn, right hand extended	2,500	1,500	1,000
(288) Denny Lyons			
288 (a) Philadelphia AA, bat at ready	2,500	1,500	1,000
288 (b) Phila. AA, fielding, left hand over head	2,500	1,500	1,000
(289) Harry Lyons			
289 (a) St. Louis, at first base	2,500	1,500	1,000
(290) Connie Mack			
290 (a) Washington, batting	31,250	11,250	8,100
290 (b) Washington, squatting, hands on knees	31,250	13,500	9,675
(292) Jimmy Macullar			
292 (a) Des Moines, fielding, hands head-high	2,500	1,500	1,000
(293) Kid Madden			
293 (a) ball in hand over head	2,500	1,500	1,000
293 (b) ball in hands, neck-high	2,500	1,500	1,000
293 (c) ball in left hand, eye-high	2,500	1,500	1,000
(297) Jimmy Manning			
297 (a) bat at side	2,500	1,500	1,000
297 (b) fielding grounder	2,500	1,500	1,000
(298) Lefty Marr			
298 (a) Columbus, left hand neck-high	2,500	1,500	1,000
(299) Mascot (Willie Breslin)			
299 (a) New York	3,500	1,750	1,050
(300) Leech Maskrey			
300 (a) Des Moines, ball in hands chin-high	2,500	1,500	1,000
(302) Mike Mattimore			
302 (a) Phila. AA, sliding, left hand raised	2,500	1,500	1,000
(303) Al Maul			
303 (a) pitching, hands at chest	2,500	1,500	1,000
(304) Al Mays			
304 (a) pitching, hands chest-high	2,500	1,500	1,000
(305) Jimmy McAleer			
305 (a) batting, looking at ball	2,500	1,500	1,000
(307) Tommy McCarthy			
307 (a) St. Louis, batting, indoors	5,250	3,150	2,250
307 (b) St. Louis, right hand head-high, indoors	5,250	3,150	2,250
307 (c) tagging player	6,900	4,125	2,950
(318) Deacon McGuire			
318 (a) Phila., fielding, hands shoulder-high	2,500	1,500	1,000
(319) Bill McGunnigle			

319 (a) looking to right	2,900	1,500	1,000
(320) Ed McKean			
320 (a) batting, looking at camera	2,500	1,500	1,000
320 (b) fielding, hands over head	2,500	1,500	1,000
(325) James McQuaid			
325 (a) fielding, hands near chin	2,500	1,500	1,000
(330) Doggie Miller			
330 (a) Pittsburgh, ball in hands, Dogs Head	8,250	4,950	3,550
330 (b) Pittsburgh, bat at side	2,500	1,500	1,000
330 (c) fielding, hands chest-high	2,500	1,500	1,000
(331) Joe Miller			
331 (a) Minneapolis, bat at side	2,500	1,500	1,000
331 (b) Minneapolis, fielding	2,500	1,500	1,000
(332) Jocko Milligan			
332 (a) bat at side	2,500	1,500	1,000
332 (b) bat in air	2,500	1,500	1,000
332 (c) fielding	2,500	1,500	1,000
332 (d) throwing	2,500	1,500	1,000
(334) Daniel Minnehan (Minahan)			
334 (a) batting, looking at camera	2,500	1,500	1,000
(335) Sam Moffet			
335 (a) pose unrecorded	2,500	1,500	1,000
(336) John Morrill			
336 (a) Boston, batting	2,500	1,500	1,000
(338) Tony Mullane			
338 (a) ball in hands above waist	4,125	2,475	1,750
(339) Joe Mulvey			
339 (a) batting	2,500	1,500	1,000
339 (b) fielding	2,500	1,500	1,000
(340) Pat Murphy			
340 (a) New York, fielding, hands head-high	3,000	1,500	1,000
(341) P.L. Murphy			
341 (a) St. Paul, batting	3,000	1,800	1,300
(342) Miah Murray			
342 (a) on knee, hands at shoulder	2,500	1,500	1,000
(343) Jim Mutrie			
343 (a) seated	3,000	1,500	1,000
343 (b) standing	3,500	1,700	1,200
(344) Al Myers			
344 (a) Wash., right hand at side, left at back	2,500	1,500	1,000
(345) George Myers			
345 (a) Indianpolis, batting	2,500	1,500	1,000
(346) Tom Nagle			
346 (a) Omaha, batting	2,500	1,500	1,000
346 (b) fielding, Dogs Head	9,000	5,400	3,875
(347) Billy Nash			
347 (a) hands atop vertical bat	2,500	1,500	1,000
347 (b) hands atop vertical, Dogs Head	7,500	3,750	2,250
347 (c) hands on knees	3,375	2,025	1,450
347 (d) throwing	2,500	1,500	1,000
(349) Kid Nichols			
349 (a) Omaha, batting, looking at ball	6,375	3,825	2,750
349 (b) Omaha, pitching, right hand forward	6,375	3,825	2,750
(353) Hugh Nicol			
DP 16 side by side with Reilly, "Long & Short"	3,200	2,025	1,450
(357) Darby O'Brien			
357 (a) Brooklyn, batting, looking at camera	2,500	1,500	1,000
(359) John O'Brien			
359 (a) Cleveland, batting	2,500	1,500	1,000
359 (b) Cleveland, pose unrecorded, Dogs Head	7,125	4,275	3,075
(361) Jack O'Connor			
361 (a) Columbus, throwing	2,500	1,500	1,000
(362) Hank O'Day			
362 (a) ball in right hand, head-high	2,500	1,500	1,000

(365) Tip O'Neill

365 (a) bat held horizontally	3,600	1,650	1,000
365 (b) bat over shoulder	3,600	1,650	1,000
365 (c) batting, facing camera	6,000	3,000	1,800
365 (d) fielding grounder	3,600	1,650	1,000
365 (e) throwing	6,000	3,000	1,800

(366) Orator Jim O'Rourke

366 (a) New York, bat in hand at side	6,000	3,600	2,600
366 (b) New York, batting	7,125	4,275	3,075
366 (c) New York, throwing, hand head-high	5,250	3,150	2,250

(367) Tom O'Rourke

367 (a) Boston, fielding, hands thigh-high	3,375	2,025	1,450

(368) Dave Orr

368 (a) Columbus, bat at ready, nearly vertical	2,500	1,500	1,000

(370) Owen Patton

370 (a) Des Moines, bat at head	2,500	1,500	1,000

(374) Fred Pfeffer

374 (a) batting, looking at ball	2,500	1,500	1,000
374 (b) tagging player	2,850	1,725	1,225
374 (c) throwing, right-hand neck-high	2,500	1,500	1,000

(375) Dick Phelan

375 (a) batting, looking at ball	2,500	1,500	1,000

(377) Jack Pickett

377 (a) St. Paul, bat over shoulder	2,500	1,500	1,000
377 (b) St. Paul, fielding grounder	2,500	1,500	1,000
377 (c) St. Paul, throwing, right hand head-high	2,500	1,500	1,000

(378) George Pinkney (Pinckny)

378 (a) bat in air, nearly vertical	2,500	1,500	1,000
378 (b) bat over shoulder	2,500	1,500	1,000
378 (c) fielding	5,250	2,650	1,600
DP 25 (w/ Steve Toole)	6,750	4,050	2,875

(381) Jim Powell

381 (a) batting, looking at camera	2,500	1,500	1,000

(383) Blondie Purcell

383 (a) throwing	2,500	1,500	1,000

(385) Joe Quinn

385 (a) ball in hands by chin	2,500	1,500	1,000
385 (b) ready to run	2,500	1,500	1,000
385 (c) ready to run, Dogs Head	4,500	2,250	1,400

(386) Old Hoss Radbourn

386 (a) hands at waist, Dogs Head	9,750	5,850	4,200
386 (b) hands on hips, bat on left	4,500	2,700	1,950
386 (c) tagging player	5,250	3,150	2,250

(388) Tom Ramsey

388 (a) bat at ready, nearly vertical	2,500	1,500	1,000
388 (b) bat over right shoulder, Dogs Head	6,000	3,600	2,600

(390) Charlie Reilly

390 (a) St. Paul, throwing	2,500	1,500	1,000

(391) Long John Reilly

391 (a) Cincinnati, fielding	2,500	1,500	1,000
DP 16 side by side w/Nicol, "Long & Short"	3,375	2,025	1,450

(393) Danny Richardson

393 (a) New York, moving left, arms at side	2,500	1,500	1,000
393 (b) New York, throwing	2,500	1,500	1,000
393 (c) New york, bat on shoulder	2,500	1,500	1,000

(394) Hardy Richardson

394 (a) Boston, bat over shoulder	2,500	1,500	1,000
394 (b) Detroit, bat over shoulder	2,500	1,500	1,000
394 (c) Boston, fielding, hands head-high	2,500	1,500	1,000

(398) Wilbert Robinson

398 (a) Philadelphia AA, batting	5,625	3,375	2,475
398 (b) Phila. AA, catching, hands neck-high	5,625	3,375	2,475
398 (c) Philadelphia AA, throwing	5,625	3,375	2,475

(399) Yank Robinson

399 (a) St. Louis, batting	3,150	1,875	1,350
399 (b) St. Louis, fielding grounder	3,150	1,875	1,350
399 (c) St. Louis, hands at chest	3,150	1,875	1,350

(402) Dave Rowe

402 (a) Kansas City, fielding, Dogs Head	5,250	3,150	2,250

(403) Jack Rowe

403 (a) Detroit, batting, looking at camera	2,500	1,500	1,000
403 (b) Detroit, bat on shoulder, looking at ball	2,500	1,500	1,000

(404) Amos Rusie

404 (a) Indianapolis, ball in right hand, thigh-high	11,250	6,750	4,875

(405) Jimmy Ryan

405 (a) bat at side	4,500	2,150	1,400
405 (b) batting	4,500	2,150	1,400
405 (c) stooping for knee-high catch	4,250	2,150	1,400
405 (d) throwing, left hand head-high	4,250	2,150	1,400

(407) Ben Sanders

407 (a) batting	2,500	1,500	1,000
407 (b) fielding	2,500	1,500	1,000
407 (c) right hand head-high	2,500	1,500	1,000

(408) Frank Scheibeck

408 (a) fielding, hand over head	2,500	1,500	1,000

(412) Gus Schmelz

412 (a) portrait	2,500	1,500	1,000

(413) Jumbo Schoeneck

413 (a) fielding, hands chin-high	2,500	1,500	1,000

(414) Pop Schriver

414 (a) fielding, hands ankle-high	2,500	1,500	1,000
414 (b) hands cupped chest-high	1,750	1,050	750.00
DP 2 being tagged by Charlie Bastian	3,750	2,250	1,750

(415) Emmett Seery

415 (a) arms folded	2,500	1,500	1,000

(417) Ed Seward

417 (a) ball in hands neck-high	2,500	1,500	1,000

(420) Daniel Shannon

420 (a) Louisville, leaning to tag player	2,500	1,500	1,000

(421) Bill Sharsig

421 (a) full length in bowler hat	2,500	1,500	1,000

(425) George Shoch

425 (a) fielding grounder	2,500	1,500	1,000

(426) Otto Shomberg (Schomberg)

426 (a) fielding, hands head-high	2,500	1,500	1,000

(427) Lev Shreve

427 (a) right hand eye-high, looking at camera	2,500	1,500	1,000

(429) Mike Slattery

429 (a) fielding, hands chest-high	2,500	1,500	1,000

(431) Germany Smith

431 (a) Cincinnati, pitching, left hand head-high, looking at camera	2,500	1,500	1,000
431 (a) Brooklyn, batting, looking at ball	2,500	1,500	1,000
431 (b) Brooklyn, hands on knees	2,500	1,500	1,000
431 (c) Brooklyn, right hand head-high	2,500	1,500	1,000

(435) Pop Smith

435 (a) Boston, batting	2,500	1,500	1,000
435 (b) Pittsburgh, batting	2,500	1,500	1,000
435 (c) hands on knees	2,500	1,500	1,000

(439) Pete Sommers

439 (a) portrait	3,375	2,025	1,450

(440) Bill Sowders

440 (a) Boston, pitching, hands at throat	2,500	1,500	1,000
440 (b) Boston, pitching, right hand cap-high, left hand waist-high	3,000	1,800	1,300

(442) Charlie Sprague

442 (a) Chicago, left hand at back head-high	2,500	1,500	1,000
442 (b) Cleveland, left hand at back head-high	2,500	1,500	1,000

(444) Harry Staley

444 (a) pitching, right hand chest-high	2,500	1,500	1,000

(445) Dan Stearns

445 (a) Kansas City, fielding, hands neck-high	3,750	2,250	1,750

(450) Harry Stovey

450 (a) bat at ready by head	3,375	2,025	1,450
450 (b) Bat at ready by head, Dogs Head	7,250	3,700	2,500
450 (c) batting, hands chest-high, Dogs Head	18,000	10,800	7,725
450 (d) hands on knees	2,500	1,500	1,000

(451) Scott Stratton

451 (a) batting	2,500	1,500	1,000

(452) Joe Straus (Strauss)

452 (a) Milwaukee, kneeling, looking to right	2,500	1,500	1,000
452 (b) Omaha, batting	3,500	1,750	1,100
452 (c) Omaha, throwing	3,000	1,500	1,000

(453) Cub Stricker

453 (a) fielding, hands over head	2,500	1,500	1,000

(454) Marty Sullivan

454 (a) Chicago, batting, looking at ball	2,500	1,500	1,000
454 (b) Indianapolis, hands chest-high	2,500	1,500	1,000

(457) Billy Sunday

457 (a) Pittsburgh, bat at side	5,250	3,150	2,250
457 (b) Pittsburgh, batting	7,500	4,500	3,225
457 (c) Pittsburgh, fielding, hands thigh-high	5,250	3,150	2,250

(459) Ezra Sutton

459 (a) batting, looking down at ball	2,500	1,500	1,000
459 (b) fielding, hands shoulder-high	2,500	1,500	1,000

(461) Park Swartzel

461 (a) arms at side	2,500	1,500	1,000

(464) Pop Tate

464 (a) Boston, batting	2,500	1,500	1,000

(465) Patsy Tebeau

465 (a) Chicago, fielding grounder	3,000	1,500	1,000

(466) John Tener

466 (a) ball in right hand chin-high	3,750	2,250	1,750
466 (b) batting	3,250	2,250	1,750

(467) Adonis Terry

467 (a) arms extended horizontally	2,500	1,500	1,000
467 (b) bat on shoulder	2,500	1,500	1,000

(468) Sam Thompson

468 (a) Detroit, bat ready at 45 degree angle	9,750	5,850	4,200
468 (b) Philadelphia, batting, ball above head	12,500	6,850	5,200

(469) Mike Tiernan

469 (a) batting	2,500	1,500	1,000
469 (b) sliding	3,375	2,025	1,450
469 (c) throwing, left hand chin-high	2,500	1,500	1,000

(470) Cannonball Titcomb

470 (a) pitching, hands chin-high	2,500	1,500	1,000

(471) Phil Tomney

471 (a) fielding, hands over head	2,500	1,500	1,000

(472) Steve Toole

DP 25 (w/ George Pinkney (Pinckney))	6,750	4,050	2,875

(473) George Townsend

473 (a) bat at ready by head	2,500	1,500	1,000
473 (b) fielding. hands chest-high	2,500	1,500	1,000

(474) Bill Traffley

474 (a) hands on thighs	2,500	1,500	1,000

(477) Tommy Tucker

477 (a) ball in hands at chest	2,500	1,500	1,000
DP 8 being tagged by Chris Fulmer	6,750	4,050	2,875

(479) George Turner

	NM	EX	VG
479 (a) fielding, hands head-high	2,500	1,500	1,000

(480) Larry Twitchell

480 (a) Cleveland, pitching, hands at chest	2,500	1,500	1,000
480 (b) Detroit, pitching, hands at chest	2,500	1,500	1,000

(481) Jim Tyng

481 (a) pitching	2,500	1,500	1,000

(483) George Van Haltren

483 (a) batting	5,250	2,700	1,950
483 (b) ball in hands at waist	5,250	2,700	1,950
482 (c) right hand at thigh	5,250	2,700	1,950

(484) Farmer Vaughn

484 (a) bat at ready, looking at camera	2,500	1,500	1,000

486 Leon Viau

486 (a) right hand cap-high	2,500	1,500	1,000

(488) Joe Visner

488 (a) arms at side	2,500	1,500	1,000
488 (b) batting	2,500	1,500	1,000
488 (c) throwing	2,500	1,500	1,000

(490) Reddy Walsh

490 (a) batting	2,500	1,500	1,000

(491) John Ward

491 (a) hands behind back	6,000	3,600	2,600
491 (b) hands on hips	10,500	6,300	4,500
491 (c) portrait in dress clothes) (Value Undetermine)	2,500	1,500	1,000
491 (d) sliding, left arm in air	6,000	3,600	2,600
491 (e) throwing, right profile	6,000	3,600	2,600
491 (f) cap in right hand at side	6,000	3,600	2,600
491 (g) cap in right hand at side, Dogs Head	9,000	5,400	3,875

(493) Bill Watkins

493 (a) Detroit, portrait	2,500	1,500	1,000
493 (b) Kansas City, portrait	2,500	1,500	1,000

(494) Farmer Weaver

494 (a) fielding, left hand over head	2,500	1,500	1,000

(496) Stump Weidman (Wiedman)

496 (a) New York, batting	2,500	1,500	1,000

(497) Wild Bill Weidner (Widner)

497 (a) batting	2,500	1,500	1,000

(498) Curt Welch

498 (a) Philadelphia AA, fielding grounder	2,500	1,500	1,000
DP 23 with Will Gleason	3,375	2,025	1,450

(499) Mickey Welch

499 (a) N.Y., pitching, right arm extended forward, name incorrect (Welsh)	4,500	2,700	1,950
499 (b) N.Y., pitching, right arm extended forward, name correct	4,500	2,700	1,950
499 (c) N.Y., pitching, right arm behind head, Dogs Head	22,500	13,500	9,675

(504) A.C. (Gus) Weyhing

504 (a) right hand cap-high	2,500	1,500	1,000
504 (b) Philadelphia AA, right hand chest-high	2,500	1,500	1,000

(505) John Weyhing

505 (a) Philadelphia AA, left hand chest-high (Never played for Philadelphia)	2,500	1,500	1,000

(510) Deacon White

510 (a) Detroit, hands above head	2,500	1,500	1,000
510 (b) looking down at ball	2,500	1,500	1,000

(511) Art Whitney

511 (a) New York, with dog	18,750	11,250	8,100
511 (b) New York, fielding, hands thigh-high	2,500	1,500	1,000
511 (c) Pittsburgh, fielding, hands thigh-high	2,500	1,500	1,000

(512) G. Whitney

512 (a) St. Joseph, batting, looking at ball	2,500	1,500	1,000

(513) Jim Whitney

513 (a) Wash., pitching, right hand waist-high	2,500	1,500	1,000

(515) Ned Williamson

515 (a) arms folded	3,000	1,500	1,000
515 (b) batting, looking at ball	3,000	1,500	1,000
515 (c) fielding	3,000	1,500	1,000
515 (d) throwing	3,000	1,500	1,000

(516) Tit Willis

516 (a) pitching, arms head-high	2,500	1,500	1,000

(517) Walt Wilmot

517 (a) Washington, fielding, hands at chest	2,500	1,500	1,000

(519) Sam Wise

519 (a) Boston, bat at side	2,500	1,500	1,000
519 (b) Boston, hands on knees	3,000	1,800	1,300

(520) Chicken Wolf

520 (a) bat at ready, team name visible on shirt	2,500	1,500	1,000

(521) George Wood (L.F.)

521 (a) both hands neck-high	2,500	1,500	1,000
521 (b) right hand head-high	2,500	1,500	1,000

(522) Pete Wood (P.)

522 (a) bat on shoulder	2,500	1,500	1,000

(523) Harry Wright

523 (a) portrait, looking to his left	30,000	18,000	13,000

(524) Chief Zimmer

524 (a) fielding, hands at chest	2,500	1,500	1,000
524 (b) throwing	2,500	1,500	1,000

1887-1890 Old Judge Hall of Famers Pose Variations

Because of the popularity of collecting Old Judge cards of Hall of Famers, and the sometimes widely varying market values of different poses for those players, this appendix lists each known pose and/or caption variation. These listings disregard the presence, absence or placement of Old Judge advertising within the photo area. Caption variations consider only those machine-printed captions outside of the photo area.

	NM	EX	VG
(11) Cap Anson			
11 (a) Street Clothes			
(A.C. ANSON, Chicago's)	11,000	5,500	3,300
(Chicago's)	10,200	4,600	2,550
(ANSON, CAPT., Chicagos (N L)	15,000	6,750	3,750
(CAPT. Anson,Chicago's)	12,000	6,000	3,000
11 (b) In Uniform			
(Chicago N L)	250,000	75,000	40,000
(25) Jake Beckley			
25 (a) Pittsburgh			
(Batting, "O" just visible on jersey, Pittsburghs.)	5,400	2,430	1,350
(Batting, "O" just visible on jersey, Pittsburgs.)	5,400	2,425	1,350
(Fielding, ball knee-high, "BECKLEY, 1st B., Pittsburgs.")	5,400	2,430	1,350
(Fielding, hands neck-high, Pittsburgh.)	5,400	2,430	1,350
(Fielding, hands neck-high, "J. BECKLEY, 1st B., Pittsburghs.")	7,800	3,500	1,950
(Fielding, hands neck-high, Pittsburgs.)	5,400	2,430	1,350
25 (b) St. Louis Whites			
(Batting, "O" just visible on jersey.)	7,800	3,500	1,950
(Batting, "TLO" visible on jersey.)	7,800	3,500	1,950
(Fielding, ball knee-high, "J. BECKLEY, 1st B., St. Louis Whites.")	10,200	4,600	2,550
(Fielding, hands neck-high, "J. BECKLEY.")	6,000	2,700	1,500
(43) Dan Brouthers			
43 (a) Boston, N.L.			
(Bat at ready, looking to right, "1st B., Bostons.")	3,300	1,620	900.00
(Fielding, Brouthers on front, Bostons.)	3,120	1,400	780.00
43 (b) Boston, P.L.			
(Pose unrecorded.)	7,200	3,240	1,800
43 (c) Detroit			
(Bat at ready, looking down at ball.)	4,800	2,160	1,200
(Bat at ready, looking to right, "1st B., Detroits.")	4,500	2,000	1,125
(Fielding, "BROUTHERS, 1st B. Detroits.")	5,100	2,280	1,260
(Fielding, "D. BROUTHERS.")	4,800	2,160	1,200
(78) John Clarkson			
78 (a) Boston			
(Batting, Bostons.)	2,275	1,025	570.00
(Right arm forward, left hand on thigh, Boston.)	2,275	1,025	570.00
(Right arm forward, left hand on thigh, "P., Bostons.")	2,280	1,025	570.00
(Right arm back, left hand clear of thigh, "P., Bostons.")	2,700	1,470	825.00
(Right hand hip-high, Bostons.)	1,500	725.00	400.00
78 (b) Chicago			
(Ball in hands at chest, "P. Chicago.")	3,000	1,350	750.00
(Batting, "P. Chicago.")	3,600	1,620	900.00
(Fielding, hands head-high, "P. Chicago.")	3,600	1,620	900.00
(Right arm forward, left hand on thigh, "P. Chicago.")	3,600	1,800	1,020
(Right arm back, left hand clear of thigh, "P. Chicago.")	3,000	1,350	750.00
(Right arm back, left hand on thigh, "P. Chicago.")	3,000	1,350	750.00
(Right hand hip-high, "P. Chicago.")	3,000	1,350	750.00
(86) Charlie Comiskey			
86 (a) St. Louis Browns ("Brown's Champions")	7,500	3,750	1,875
86 (b) St. Louis Browns (Arms folded.)	5,100	2,300	1,275
(Batting, "COMISKEY, Capt. St. Louis Browns.")	8,000	4,000	2,400
(Fielding, hands head-high, "CHAS. COMISKEY, 1st B., Capt. St. Louis Browns.")	4,800	2,280	1,260
(Fielding, hands shoulder-high, "COMISKEY, Capt. St. Louis.")	5,100	2,280	1,260
(Fielding, hands shoulder-high, "C. COMMISKEY, 1st B., St. L. B's.")	4,800	2,160	1,200
(Sliding, "CHAS. COMISKEY, 1st B., Capt. St. Louis Brown.")	4,800	2,160	1,200
(Sliding, "COMISKEY, Capt., St. Louis.")	4,800	2,160	1,200
86 (c) Chicago, P.L. (Arms folded, "COMMISKEY, 1st B., Chicagos.")	24,000	10,800	6,000
(88) Roger Connor			
88 (a) New York, N.L.			
(Batter's box on floor, script name.)	6,900	3,100	1,700
(Bat on shoulder, name in script.)	6,900	3,100	1,700
(Bat on shoulder, N Y's.)	5,100	2,400	1,200
(Fielding, "B. CONNOR," New Yorks.)	4,800	2,400	1,200
(Fielding, hands at waist, "CONNER, 1st B., New Yorks.")	5,100	2,400	1,200
(Hands on knees, name in script.)	6,900	3,100	1,700
(Hands on knees, New York.)	4,800	2,160	1,200
(Hands on knees, New Yorks.)	4,800	2,160	1,200
(Hands on knees, N Y's.)	4,800	2,160	1,200
(124) Ed Delahanty			
124 (a) Philadelphia			
(Bat on right shoulder, "2d B., Phila.")	14,000	10,000	6,000
(Bat on right shoulder, "2d B., Phila's")	14,000	10,000	6,000
(Bat nearly horizontal, "2d B., Phila.")	14,000	10,000	6,000
(Fielding grounder, Phila.)	14,000	9,000	4,800

(Fielding, hands at waist, "2d B., Phila.") 14,000 7,600 4,200
(Fielding, hands at waist, Phila's.) 14,000 7,600 4,200
(Throwing, "2d B., Phila.") 15,000 10,500 5,900
(Throwing, Phila's.) 15,000 10,500 5,900

(136) Hugh Duffy
136 (a) Chicago, N.L.
(Batting, S.S. Chicago.) 4,500 2,250 1,350
(Batting, "H. DUFFY, S.S., Chicagos.") 4,500 2,250 1,350
(Batting, "DUFFY, S.S., Chicago's.") 4,500 2,250 1,350
(Fielding grounder, "H. DUFFY, S.S., Chicago.") 4,500 2,250 1,350
(Fielding grounder, Chicagos.) 4,500 2,250 1,350
(Fielding, hands chin-high, right heel behind left leg, Chicago.) 4,500 2,250 1,350
(Fielding, hands chin-high, right heel behind left leg, Chicagos.) 4,500 2,250 1,350
(Fielding, hands chin-high, right heel behind left leg, Chicago's.) 4,500 2,250 1,350
(Fielding, hands neck-high, feet apart, Chicago.) 4,500 2,250 1,350
(Throwing, right hand head-high, Chicago.) 4,500 2,250 1,350
(Throwing, right hand head-high, Chicago's.) 4,500 2,250 1,350
136 (b) Chicago, P.L.
(Pose unrecorded.) (Value Undetermined)

(149) Buck Ewing
149 (a) New York, N.L.
(Bat at 45 degrees, New Yorks.) 3,600 1,800 1,100
(Bat at 45 degrees, N Y's.) 3,600 1,800 1,100
(Bat in hand at side, New Yorks.) 3,600 1,800 1,100
(Bat nearly horizontal, Capt. New Yorks.) 3,600 1,800 1,100
(Bat nearly horizontal, Captain, New Yorks.) 3,600 1,800 1,100
(Fielding grounder, "BUCK EWING, Capt., New Yorks.") 3,600 1,800 1,100
(Fielding grounder, "EWING, C., New Yorks.") 3,600 1,800 1,100
(Fielding, hands head-high, New Yorks.) 3,600 1,800 1,100
(Fielding, hands head-high, N Y's.) 3,600 1,800 1,100
(Hands on knees, C. New Yorks.) 3,600 1,800 900.00
(Hands on knees, Captain, New Yorks.) 3,600 1,800 900.00
(Hands on knees, Capt. N Y's.) 3,600 1,800 900.00
(Running to left, C., New Yorks.) 3,600 1,620 900.00
(Running to left, Captain, New Yorks.) 3,600 1,620 900.00
(Sliding, C., New York.) 3,600 1,620 900.00
(Sliding, C., New Yorks.) 3,600 1,620 900.00
(Sliding, Capt., New York.) 3,600 1,620 900.00
(Throwing, right arm forward, C., New Yorks.) 4,200 1,900 1,050
(Throwing, right arm forward, Captain, New Yorks.) 4,200 1,900 1,050
(Throwing, right hand waist-high at side, "EWING, Captain, New Yorks.") 4,800 2,160 1,200
149 (b) New York, P.L.
(Hands on knees, C. New York.(PL) 7,800 3,500 1,950
149 (c) With mascot Willie Breslin.
("EWING & MASCOT, New Yorks") 5,750 2,875 1,450
(N. Y's) 5,750 2,875 1,450
149 (c) "EWING, MASCOT New York P L" (A Fair-Good example sold at auction 5/05 for $7,475.)

(179) Pud Galvin
179 (a) Pittsburgh
(Arms at sides, P. Pittsburg.) 5,400 2,430 1,350
(Arms at sides, P. Pittsburgs.) 5,400 2,430 1,350

(Arms at sides, P. Pittsburgh.) 5,400 2,430 1,350
(Arms at sides, Pitcher.) 5,400 2,430 1,350
(Ball in hands above waist, P.) 5,000 2,000 1,125
(Ball in hands above waist, Pitcher.) 5,000 2,000 1,125
(Bat at ready, P.) 5,000 2,500 1,500
(Bat at ready, Pitcher.) 5,000 2,500 1,500
(Bat in hand at side, "GALVIN, P. Pittsburg.") 11,000 5,500 3,300
(Bat in hand at side, "GALVIN, Pitcher Pittsburg.") 10,000 5,000 2,800
(Bat in hand at side "GALVIN, P., Pittsburgs.") 10,000 5,000 2,800
(Bat in hand at side, "J. GALVIN, P., Pittsburghs.") 10,000 5,000 2,800
(Bat in hand at side, "JIM GALVIN.") 10,000 5,000 2,800

(204) Clark Griffith
204 (a) Milwaukee
(Ball in hands at chest.) 5,500 2,750 1,650
(Batting, looking at ball.) 5,500 2,750 1,650
(Batting, looking at camera, Milwaukee.) 5,500 2,750 1,650
(Batting, looking at camera, Milwaukees.) 6,000 3,000 1,800
(Pitching, hands at neck, Milwaukees.) 5,500 2,750 1,650
(Pitching, right hand head-high, Milwaukees.) 5,500 2,750 1,650

(213) Billy Hamilton
213 (a) Kansas City
(Batting, looking at camera, Kansas Citys.) 4,500 2,250 1,350
(Batting, looking up at ball, "L.F. KANSAS CITYS.") 4,500 2,250 1,350
(Batting, looking up at ball, K.C.s.) 4,500 2,250 1,350
(Fielding grounder.) 4,500 2,250 1,350
(Fielding, hands above waist, "L.F. Kansas Citys.") 4,500 2,250 1,350
(Fielding, hands neck-high, "L.F. Kansas Citys.") 4,500 2,250 1,350
213 (b) Philadelphia, N.L.
(Fielding, hands above waist, Philadelphia N.L.) 3,250 1,650 975.00
(Fielding, hands neck-high, Philadelphia N.L.) 3,250 1,650 975.00

(215) Ned Hanlon
215 (a) Boston
(Never played for Boston.)
(Bat in hand at sides, Bostons.) 3,900 1,620 900.00
215 (b) Detroit
(Bat in hand at side, C.F. Detroits.) 3,900 1,620 900.00
(Batting, Detroits.) 3,900 1,620 900.00
(Fielding, Detroits.) 3,900 1,620 900.00
215 (c) Pittsburgh
(Batting, Pittsburgs.) 3,900 1,620 975.00
(Fielding, C.F., Pittsburghs.) 3,900 1,620 975.00

(256) Tim Keefe
256 (a) New York, N.L.
(Ball in hands, front view, "KEEFE, P., New Yorks.") 3,600 1,500 840.00
(Ball in hands, front view, TIM KEEFE, P. N.Y's.") 3,600 1,500 840.00
(Ball in hands, side view, "JIM KEEFE," New Yorks.") 3,360 1,500 840.00
(Ball in hands, side view, "TIM KEEFE," New Yorks.") 3,360 1,500 840.00
(Ball in hands, side view, "TIM KEEFE, P. N.Y's.") 3,360 1,500 840.00
(Bat nearly horizontal, "KEEFE, P., New Yorks.") 3,360 1,500 840.00
(Bat nearly horizontal, "TIM KEEF," New Yorks.") 3,360 1,500 840.00
(Bat nearly horizontal, "TIM KEEFE," New Yorks.") 3,360 1,500 840.00
(Bat nearly horizontal, "TIM KEEFE," N. Y's.") 3,360 1,500 840.00

(Bat nearly vertical, JIM KEEFE, P., New Yorks) 3,500 1,750 1,000
(Bat nearly vertical, "TIM KEEFE, P. New Yorks.") 3,500 1,750 1,000
(Bat nearly vertical, "TIM...) 3,500 1,750 1,000
(Pitching, right hand at back, "JIM KEEFE," New Yorks.) 3,350 1,620 900.00
(Pitching, right hand at back, "TIM KEEF," New Yorks.) 3,350 1,620 900.00
(Pitching, right hand at back, "TIM KEEFE," New Yorks.) 3,350 1,620 900.00
(Pitching, right hand at back, "TIM KEEFE," N. Y's.) 3,350 1,620 900.00
(Pitching, right hand head-high, "KEEFE P., New Yorks.") 3,350 1,620 900.00
(Pitching, right hand head-high, "TIM KEEFE, P. N. Y's.") 3,350 1,620 900.00
(Pitching, right hand waist-high, "KEEFE, P., New Yorks.") 2,880 1,300 720.00
(Pitching, right hand waist-high, "TIM KEEFE, P. N.Y's.") 3,500 1,750 850.00
256 (b) New York, P.L.
(Pose unrecorded.) (VALUE UNDETERMINED)
DP 12 Tagging Danny Richardson.
("KEEFE, P., New Yorks") 2,700 1,225 675.00
("Keefe & Richardson") 2,700 1,200 675.00
("Keefe and Richardson Stealing 2d, N.Y's") 2,700 1,200 675.00
DP 13 Fielding Ball, Danny Richardson Sliding.
("Keefe and Richardson Stealing 2d, N.Y's") 4,250 2,100 1,300

(261) King Kelly
261 (a) Chicago
(Bat at 45 degrees, left-handed, "$10,000 KELLY" Chicago on jersey.) 8,750 4,400 2,600
(Portrait, bare head, "$10,000 KELLY," Chicago on jersey.) 9,300 3,970 2,300
(Portrait in cap, "$10,000 KELLY," Chicago on jersey.) 8,250 4,125 1,950
261 (b) Boston, N.L.
(Bat at 45 degrees, "$10,000 KELLY.") 9,000 4,500 2,700
(Bat at 45 degrees, no position, Boston.) 6,000 2,700 1,500
(Bat at 45 degrees, "Kelly, C., Boston.") 5,250 2,160 1,200
(Bat at 45 degrees, "Kelly, C., Bostons.") 5,250 2,160 1,200
(Bat horizontal, "$10,000 KELLY.") 7,250 3,600 2,200
(Bat in left hand at side, "$10,000 KELLY.") 8,500 4,250 2,100
(Bat on right shoulder, "$10,000 KELLY.") 7,200 3,240 1,800
(Fielding, hands chest-high, "$10,000 KELLY.") 8,500 4,250 2,100
(Fielding, hands head-high, "$10,000 KELLY.") 8,500 4,250 2,100
(Portrait, bare head, "$10,000 KELLY," Boston on jersey.) 11,400 5,130 2,850
261 (c) Boston, P.L.
(Bat at 45 degrees, no position, Boston. (PL) (Value Undetermined)

(290) Connie Mack
290 (a) Washington
(Batting, C.) 12,500 6,250 3,100
(Batting, Catcher.) 12,500 6,250 3,100
(Stooping, hands on knees, C. Washington.) 12,500 6,250 3,100
(Stooping, hands on knees, Catcher.) 12,500 6,250 3,100
(Throwing, C.) 10,800 6,250 3,100
(Throwing, Catcher, "C. MACK.") 12,500 6,250 3,100
(Throwing, Catcher, "MACK.") 12,500 6,250 3,100

(307) Tommy McCarthy
307 (a) Philadelphia, N.L.

(Batting, indoor
background, "2d B.
Phila.") 4,000 1,900 1,050
(Batting, indoor
background,
"McCARTHY, Second
Base, Philadelphia.") 4,000 1,900 1,050
(Fielding, hands chest-
high, "McCARTHY, 2d
B. Phila.") 5,400 2,430 1,350
(Fielding, hands chest-
high, Philadelphia.) 5,400 2,430 1,350
(Sliding, indoor
background, 2d B.
Phila.) 4,800 2,160 1,200
(Sliding, Philadelphia.) 4,800 2,160 1,200
(Tagging player, Phila.) 4,000 1,900 1,050
(Tagging player,
Philadelphia.) 4,000 1,900 1,050
(Throwing, 2d B. Phila.) 4,000 1,900 1,050
(Throwing, Philadelphia.) 4,000 1,900 1,050

307 (b) St. Louis Browns
(Batting, indoor
background, St. Louis
Browns.) 4,000 2,100 1,300
(Batting, outdoor
background, St. Louis.) 4,000 2,100 1,300
(Batting, outdoor
background, St. Louis
Browns.) 4,000 2,100 1,300
(Fielding, hands chest-
high, 2d B. St. Louis.) 4,000 2,100 1,300
(Fielding, hands chest-
high, C.F.) 4,000 2,100 1,300
(Fielding, hands
head-high, "TOMMY
CARTHY," St. Louis
Brown.) 4,000 2,100 1,300
(Fielding, hands
head-high, "TOMMY
McCARTHY," St. Louis
Brown.) 4,000 2,100 1,300
(Fielding, hands head-
high, "cCARTHY, C. F.
St. Louis Brown.") 4,000 2,100 1,300
(Fielding, hands
head-high, "TOMMY
McCARTHY" St. Louis
Browns.) 4,000 2,100 1,300
(Fielding, hands head-
high, "T. McCARTHY,
C.F., St. Louis Browns.) 4,000 2,100 1,300
(Sliding, indoor
background,
"McCARTHY, 2d B. St.
Louis.") 4,000 2,100 1,300
(Sliding, indoor
background, C.F., St.
Louis.) 4,000 2,100 1,300
(Sliding, outdoor
background, St. Louis.) 4,000 2,100 1,300
(Sliding, outdoor
background, C.F. St.
Louis Browns.) 4,000 2,100 1,300
(Tagging player, 2d B.) 4,000 2,100 1,300
(Tagging player, C.F.) 4,000 2,100 1,300
(Throwing, "T.
McCARTHY," St. Louis.) 4,500 2,250 1,350
(Throwing, "T.
McCARTHY," St. Louis
Browns.) 4,500 2,250 1,350
(Throwing, "McCARTHY,"
St. Louis Browns.) 4,500 2,250 1,350
(Throwing, "McCARTHY,"
C.F., St. Louis.") 4,500 2,250 1,350

(323) Bid McPhee
323 (a) Cincinnati
(Batting, looking at ball,
"McPHEE.") 18,500 9,300 5,550
(Batting, looking at ball,
"JOHN McPHEE.") 18,500 9,300 5,550
(Batting, looking at
camera, Cincinnati.) 18,500 9,300 5,550
(Batting, looking at camera,
Cincinnati. (NL) 18,500 9,300 5,550
(Batting, looking at
camera, Cincinnatti.) 18,500 9,300 5,550
(Fielding, hands ankle-
high, "McPHEE, 2d B.,
Cincinnat.) 18,500 9,300 5,550
(Fielding, hands ankle-
high, "JOHN McPHEE,
2d B., Cincinnatis.") 18,500 9,300 5,550
(Fielding, hands head-
high, "McPHEE, 2d B.,
Cincinnatti.") 18,500 9,300 5,550

(Fielding, hands head-
high, "JOHN McPHEE,
2d B. Cincinnati.") 18,500 9,300 5,550
(Fielding, hands head-
high, "McPHEE, 2d B.,
Cincinnatis.") 18,500 9,300 5,550
(Fielding, hands head-
high, Cincinnatti.) 18,500 9,300 5,550
(Throwing, Cincinnati.) 18,500 9,300 5,550
(Throwing, Cincinnatti.) 18,500 9,300 5,550

(349) Kid Nichols
349 (a) Omaha
(Batting, looking at ball,
Omaha.) 10,500 5,000 2,250
(Batting, looking at
camera, Omaha.) 10,500 5,000 2,250
(Batting, looking at
camera, "NICHOLS, P.,
Omahas.") 10,500 5,000 2,250
(Pitching, hands at chest,
Omaha.) 10,500 5,000 2,250
(Pitching, right hand
behind back, Omaha.) 10,500 5,000 2,250
(Pitching, right hand
behind back,
"NICHOLS, P.,
Omahas.") 10,500 5,000 2,250
(Pitching, right hand
forward, P., Omaha.) 10,500 5,000 2,250
(Pitching, right hand
forward, P., Omahas.) 10,500 5,000 2,250

(366) Orator Jim O'Rourke
366 (a) New York, N.L.
(Bat in hand at side, C.,
New Yorks.) 4,800 2,400 1,200
(Bat in hand at side, 3d B.,
New Yorks.) 6,000 2,700 1,500
(Bat in hand at side, 3d B.
N.Y's.) 6,000 2,700 1,500
(Bat in hand at side, 3d B.,
N. Y's.) 6,000 2,700 1,500
(Batting, 3d B., New
Yorks.) 6,000 2,700 1,500
(Batting, 3d B., N. Y's.) 6,000 2,700 1,500
(Fielding, "JIM
O'ROURKE, 3d B. N.
Y's.") 4,200 1,900 1,050
(Throwing, 3d B., N. Y's.) 4,800 2,160 1,200

(386) Old Hoss Radbourn
386 (a) Boston, N.L.
(Bat on shoulder, P.,
Boston.) 4,250 1,740 975.00
(Bat on shoulder, P.,
Bostons.) 4,250 1,750 975.00
(Bat on shoulder, Pitcher,
Boston.) 4,250 1,740 975.00
(Bat on shoulder, Pitcher,
Bostons.) 4,250 1,740 975.00
(Hands at waist, no space
visible between hands
and belt, P.) 4,250 1,620 900.00
(Hands at waist, no space
visible between hands
and belt, Pitcher.) 4,250 1,620 900.00
(Hands at waist, white
uniform visible between
hands and belt, P.) 5,500 2,160 1,200
(Hands at waist, white
uniform visible between
hands and belt,
Pitcher.) 4,800 2,160 1,200
(Hands on hips, P.) 9,750 4,860 2,700
(Hands on hips, Pitcher.) 9,750 4,860 2,700
(Portrait, P., Boston.) 9,750 4,320 2,400
(Portrait, Pitcher, Boston.) 9,750 4,440 2,430
(Tagging Billy Nash, P.,
Boston.) 5,400 2,430 1,350
(Tagging Billy Nash,
Pitcher.) 5,400 2,430 1,350
386 (b) Boston, P.L.
(Hands on hips, Pitcher, Boston.(PL) (VALUE
UNDETERMINED)

(398) Wilbert Robinson
398 (a) Philadelphia Athletics
(Batting) 5,500 2,150 1,200
(Fielding, hands above
head, C. Athletics.) 5,500 2,160 1,200
(Fielding, hands above
head, C., Athletics.) 5,500 2,160 1,200
(Fielding, hands neck-
high, C. Athletics.) 5,500 2,160 1,200
(Fielding, hands thigh-
high.) 5,500 2,160 1,200
(Throwing) 5,500 2,160 1,200

(404) Amos Rusie
404 (a) Indianapolis
(Batting, P., Indianapolis.) 4,200 1,900 1,050
(Pitching, hands at neck.) 4,200 1,900 1,050
(Pitching, right hand
forward chin-high.) 4,200 1,900 1,050
(Pitching, right hand head-
high to side, "RUSIE, P.,
Indianapolis.") 7,000 3,500 2,100
(Pitching, right hand head-
high to side, "RUSSIE.") 7,000 3,500 2,100
(Ball in right hand, thigh-
high "P., Indianapolis.") 9,000 4,500 2,700
404 (b) New York, N.L.
(Pitching, hands at neck,
New Yorks.(NL) 24,000 10,800 6,000
(Pitching, right hand
forward chin-high, New
Yorks.(NL) 24,000 10,800 6,000

(468) Sam Thompson
468 (a) Detroit
(Arms folded, R.F.
Detroits.) 4,200 2,000 1,200
(Bat at 45 degrees,
Detroits.) 5,000 2,500 1,500
(Bat in hand at side,
Detroits.) 4,200 1,900 1,050
(Batting, ball above head,
Detroits.) 3,000 1,350 750.00
(Batting, ball chest-high,
R.F. Detroits.) 3,000 1,350 750.00
468 (b) Philadelphia, N.L.
(Arms folded, Phil'a.(NL) 3,000 1,500 900.00
(Bat in hand at side,
Philadelphia.) 3,000 1,500 900.00
(Bat in hand at side, R.F.,
Philadelphias.) 3,000 1,500 900.00
(Bat in hand at side,
Phila's.) 3,000 1,500 900.00

(491) John Ward
491 (a) New York, N.L.
(Batting, New Yorks.) 3,000 1,300 720.00
(Batting, "Capt. JOHN
WARD, S.S. N Y's.") 3,000 1,300 720.00
(Cap in hand at side,
"Capt. JOHN WARD.") 4,200 1,900 1,050
(Cap in hand at side,
"J. WARD, S.S., New
Yorks.") 4,200 1,900 1,050
(Cap in hand at side,
"JOHN WARD.") 4,200 1,900 1,050
(Hands behind back, New
Yorks.) 3,000 1,350 750.00
(Hands behind back,
"Capt. JOHN WARD,
S.S. N. Y's.") 3,000 1,350 750.00
(Hands on hips, "J.M.
WARD, S.S. New
Yorks.") 4,500 2,000 1,125
(Hands on hips, "Capt.
JOHN WARD, S.S. N.
Y's.") 6,600 2,970 1,650
(Portrait, "Capt. JOHN
WARD.") 5,600 2,430 1,350
(Portrait, "J. WARD, S.S.,
New Yorks.") 5,600 2,430 1,350
(Portrait, "J.M. WARD,
S.S., New Yorks.") 5,600 2,430 1,350
(Sliding, left hand raised,
"Capt. JOHN WARD,
S.S. N Y's.") 2,640 1,190 660.00
(Sliding, left hand raised,
"J.M. WARD, S.S., New
Yorks.") 2,640 1,190 660.00
(Sliding, left hand raised,
"WARD.") 2,640 1,190 660.00
(Sliding, right hand raised,
New Yorks.) 3,000 1,350 750.00
(Sliding, right hand raised,
"Capt. JOHN WARD,
S.S. N Y's.") 3,000 1,350 750.00
(Throwing, left profile, New
Yorks.) 4,200 1,900 1,050
(Throwing, left profile,
"Capt. JOHN WARD,
S.S. N. Y's.") 4,200 1,900 1,050
(Throwing, right profile,
"Capt. JOHN WARD,
S.S. N. Y's.") 4,200 1,900 1,050
(Throwing, right profile,
"JOHN WARD.") 4,200 1,900 1,050

(499) Mickey Welch
499 (a) New York, N.L.

(Ball in hands above waist, "SMILING MICKEY.")	6,000	3,000	1,800
(Ball in hands above waist, "WELSH.")	6,000	3,000	1,800
(Right arm extended forward, "SMILING MICKEY.")	6,000	3,000	1,800
(Right hand at right thigh, "WELCH," New Yorks.)	6,000	3,000	1,800
(Right hand at right thigh, "WELCH," New Yorks. (NL))	6,000	3,000	1,800
(Right hand at right thigh, "WELSH," New Yorks.)	6,000	3,000	1,800
(Right hand head-high, "WELCH," New York.)	6,000	3,000	1,800
(Right hand head-high, "WELCH," N.Y's.)	6,000	3,000	1,800
(Right hand head-high, "WELSH," New Yorks.)	6,000	3,000	1,800

(523) Harry Wright
523 (a) Philadelphia, N.L.

(Portrait, looking to his right, beard clear of right side of collar, "HARRY WRIGHT, Man'g. Philas.")	18,000	8,100	4,500
(Portrait, looking to his right, beard just over right side of collar, "Mgr., Phila. N L.")	18,000	8,100	4,500
(Portrait, looking to his right, beard just over right side of collar, "Man'g. Phila.")	18,000	8,100	4,500
(Portrait, looking to his right, beard just over right side of collar, "Mgr. Phila's.")	18,000	8,100	4,500
(Portrait, looking to his left, "Man'g. Phila.")	18,000	8,100	4,500
(Portrait, looking to his left, "Man'g. Philas.")	18,000	8,100	4,500
(Portrait, looking to his left, Phila. (NL))	19,200	8,640	4,800
(Portrait, looking to his left, "Mgr. Phila's.")	18,000	8,100	5,400

1965 Old London Coins

These 1-1/2" diameter metal coins were included in Old London snack food packages. The 40 coins in this set feature two players from each of the major leagues' 20 teams, except St. Louis (3) and the New York Mets (1). Coin fronts have color photos and player names, while the silver-colored backs give a brief biography. An Old London logo is also displayed on each coin back. Space Magic Ltd. produced the coins. This is the same company which produced similar sets for Topps in 1964 and 1971.

		NM	E	VG
Complete Set (40):		475.00	240.00	140.00
Common Player:		3.00	1.50	.90
Unopened Set:		1,800	900.00	525.00
Unopened Coin: 3-4X				
(1)	Henry Aaron	35.00	17.50	10.50
(2)	Richie Allen	7.50	3.75	2.25
(3)	Bob Allison	3.00	1.50	.90
(4)	Ernie Banks	25.00	12.50	7.50
(5)	Ken Boyer	4.50	2.25	1.25
(6)	Jim Bunning	15.00	7.50	4.50
(7)	Orlando Cepeda	12.50	6.25	3.75
(8)	Dean Chance	3.00	1.50	.90
(9)	Rocky Colavito	10.00	5.00	3.00
(10)	Vic Davalillo	3.00	1.50	.90
(11)	Tommy Davis	3.00	1.50	.90
(12)	Ron Fairly	3.00	1.50	.90
(13)	Dick Farrell	3.00	1.50	.90
(14)	Jim Fregosi	3.00	1.50	.90
(15)	Bob Friend	3.00	1.50	.90
(16)	Dick Groat	3.00	1.50	.90
(17)	Ron Hunt	3.00	1.50	.90
(18)	Chuck Hinton	3.00	1.50	.90

(19)	Ken Johnson	3.00	1.50	.90
(20)	Al Kaline	20.00	10.00	6.00
(21)	Harmon Killebrew	20.00	10.00	6.00
(22)	Don Lock	3.00	1.50	.90
(23)	Mickey Mantle	100.00	50.00	30.00
(24)	Roger Maris	30.00	15.00	9.00
(25)	Willie Mays	35.00	17.50	10.50
(26)	Bill Mazeroski	12.50	6.25	3.75
(27)	Gary Peters	3.00	1.50	.90
(28)	Vada Pinson	3.50	1.75	1.00
(29)	Boog Powell	4.50	2.25	1.25
(30)	Dick Radatz	3.00	1.50	.90
(31)	Brooks Robinson	20.00	10.00	6.00
(32)	Frank Robinson	20.00	10.00	6.00
(33)	Tracy Stallard	3.00	1.50	.90
(34)	Joe Torre	7.50	3.75	2.25
(35)	Leon Wagner	3.00	1.50	.90
(36)	Pete Ward	3.00	1.50	.90
(37)	Dave Wickersham	3.00	1.50	.90
(38)	Billy Williams	15.00	7.50	4.50
(39)	John Wyatt	3.00	1.50	.90
(40)	Carl Yastrzemski	25.00	12.50	7.50

1909-11 Old Mill Cigarettes

T206 cards bearing the Old Mill advertising are, with a major exception, among the most common of the set's back variations. Two styles of Old Mill T206 backs are found. One, which appears on cards of major league players and minor leaguers other than those from the Southern leagues, mentions a "BASE BALL / SUBJECTS / LARGE ASSORTMENT." The other specifies the four Southern leagues from which the players depicted originate. In recent years advanced T206 specialists have become aware of a brown-ink version of the Southern leagues back, much rarer than the black-ink version usually found on both types of Old Mill backs. All of the confirmed brown-ink cards appear to have been hand-cut from a sheet, leading to speculation as to whether they represent an actual issued variation or were salvaged from a scrapped printing. Some brown-ink Southern League cards are found with a red overprint on back, "Factory 649 - District 1 - State N.Y." Cards showing a similar overprint in black have been fraudulently altered. Contemporary with the T206 issues, Old Mill also produced a lengthy series of red-bordered minor league player cards in 1910. Those are listed in the minor league section of this book.

PREMIUMS
Common: 2-2.5X
Stars/So. Leagues: 1X
Red overprint: 20X
Brown-ink So. Leagues:15-25X

(See T206. A common-player card with red factory 649 New York overprint sold for $19,975 in May 2010.)

1910 Old Put Cigar

This is a version of the anonymous E98 "Set of 30" on which an advertisement for "OLD PUT / 5 ct. CIGAR" has been rubber-stamped in purple. Cards can be found with either red or blue backgrounds on front. Because of the ease with which these could be faked, collectors must exercise extreme caution.

		NM	E	VG
Common Player:		3,750	1,875	1,125
(1)	Christy Matthewson (Mathewson)	13,500	6,750	4,050
(2)	John McGraw	6,000	3,000	1,800
(3)	Johnny Kling	3,750	1,875	1,025
(4)	Frank Chance	6,000	3,000	1,800
(5)	Hans Wagner	16,500	8,250	4,950

(6)	Fred Clarke	3,750	1,875	1,025
(7)	Roger Bresnahan	3,750	1,875	1,025
(8)	Hal Chase	6,000	3,000	1,800
(9)	Russ Ford	3,750	1,875	1,025
(10)	"Ty" Cobb	20,000	10,000	6,000
(11)	Hughey Jennings	3,750	1,875	1,025
(12)	Chief Bender	6,000	3,000	1,800
(13)	Ed Walsh	3,750	1,875	1,025
(14)	Cy Young	12,000	6,000	3,600
(15)	Al Bridwell	3,750	1,875	1,025
(16)	Miner Brown	3,750	1,875	1,025
(17)	George Mullin	3,750	1,875	1,025
(18)	Chief Meyers	3,750	1,875	1,025
(19)	Hippo Vaughn	3,750	1,875	1,025
(20)	Red Dooin	3,750	1,875	1,025
(21)	Fred Tenny (Tenney)	3,750	1,875	1,025
(22)	Larry McLean	3,750	1,875	1,025
(23)	Nap Lajoie	6,000	3,000	1,800
(24)	Joe Tinker	6,000	3,000	1,800
(25)	Johnny Evers	6,000	3,000	1,800
(26)	Harry Davis	3,750	1,875	1,025
(27)	Eddie Collins	6,000	3,000	1,800
(28)	Bill Dahlen	3,750	1,875	1,025
(29)	Connie Mack	6,000	3,000	1,800
(30)	Jack Coombs	3,750	1,875	1,025

1951 Olmes Studio Postcards

This line of Philadelphia player postcards (all but one from the A's) was produced by a local photographer, probably for player use in satisfying fans' autograph requests. The 3-1/2" x 5-1/2" cards have a glossy black-and-white player photo on front. Backs have only standard postcard indicia and the Olmes credit line. Other players may remain to be checklisted. The unnumbered cards are listed here alphabetically.

		NM	E	VG
Common Player:		75.00	37.50	22.50
(1)	Sam Chapman	75.00	37.50	22.50
(2)	Ferris Fain (Ready to hit, on grass.)	100.00	50.00	30.00
(3)	Ferris Fain (Batting, choking up.)	100.00	50.00	30.00
(4)	Ferris Fain (Batting, follow-through.)	100.00	50.00	30.00
(5)	Ferris Fain (Kneeling)	100.00	50.00	30.00
(6)	Dick Fowler	75.00	37.50	22.50
(7)	Bob Hooper	75.00	37.50	22.50
(8)	Skeeter Kell	75.00	37.50	22.50
(9)	Paul Lehner	75.00	37.50	22.50
(10)	Lou Limmer	75.00	37.50	22.50
(11)	Barney McCosky	75.00	37.50	22.50
(12)	Robin Roberts	275.00	135.00	80.00
(13)	Carl Scheib	75.00	37.50	22.50
(14)	Bobby Shantz	75.00	37.50	22.50
(15)	Joe Tipton	75.00	37.50	22.50
(16)	Gus Zernial (Batting)	100.00	50.00	30.00
(17)	Gus Zernial (Kneeling)	100.00	50.00	30.00

1937 O-Pee-Chee

Kind of a combination of 1934 Goudeys and 1934-36 Batter Ups, the '37 OPC "Baseball Stars" set features black-and-white action photos against a stylized ballpark. About halfway up the 2-5/8" x 2-15/16" cards, the background was die-cut to allow it to be folded back to create a stand-up card. Backs are printed in English and French. The 40 cards in "Series A" are all American Leaguers, leading to speculation that a Series B of National League players was to have been issued at a later date. The set carries the American Card Catalog designation of V300.

		NM	E	VG
	Complete Set (40):	24,000	12,000	7,250
	Common Player:	450.00	225.00	135.00
101	John Lewis	450.00	225.00	135.00
102	"Jack" Hayes	450.00	225.00	135.00
103	Earl Averill	650.00	320.00	195.00
104	Harland Clift (Harland)	450.00	225.00	135.00
105	"Beau" Bell	450.00	225.00	135.00
106	Jimmy Foxx (Jimmie)	1,200	600.00	350.00
107	Hank Greenberg	1,325	660.00	400.00
108	George Selkirk	450.00	225.00	135.00
109	Wally Moses	450.00	135.00	225.00
110	"Gerry" Walker	450.00	225.00	135.00
111	"Goose" Goslin	650.00	320.00	195.00
112	Charlie Gehringer	425.00	210.00	125.00
113	Hal Trosky	450.00	225.00	135.00
114	"Buddy" Myer	450.00	225.00	135.00
115	Luke Appling	650.00	320.00	195.00
116	"Zeke" Bonura	450.00	225.00	135.00
117	Tony Lazzeri	425.00	210.00	125.00
118	Joe DiMaggio	7,500	3,700	2,200
119	Bill Dickey	600.00	300.00	180.00
120	Bob Feller	1,600	800.00	480.00
121	Harry Kelley	450.00	225.00	135.00
122	Johnny Allen	450.00	225.00	135.00
123	Bob Johnson	450.00	225.00	135.00
124	Joe Cronin	650.00	320.00	195.00
125	"Rip" Radcliff	450.00	225.00	135.00
126	Cecil Travis	450.00	225.00	135.00
127	Joe Kuhel	450.00	225.00	135.00
128	Odell Hale	450.00	225.00	135.00
129	Sam West	450.00	225.00	135.00
130	Ben Chapman	450.00	225.00	135.00
131	Monte Pearson	450.00	225.00	135.00
132	"Rick" Ferrell	650.00	325.00	195.00
133	Tommy Bridges	450.00	225.00	135.00
134	"Schoolboy" Rowe	450.00	225.00	135.00
135	Vernon Kennedy	450.00	225.00	135.00
136	"Red" Ruffing	650.00	320.00	195.00
137	"Lefty" Grove	500.00	250.00	150.00
138	Wes Farrell	450.00	225.00	135.00
139	"Buck" Newsom	450.00	225.00	135.00
140	Rogers Hornsby	750.00	375.00	225.00

1960 O-Pee-Chee Tattoos

Though much scarcer than the contemporary Topps version, this Canadian specialty bubblegum issue does not currently enjoy any price premium. The OPC type is identifiable by its imprint on the outside of the wrapper.

(See 1960 Topps Tattoos for description, checklist and price guide.)

1965 O-Pee-Chee

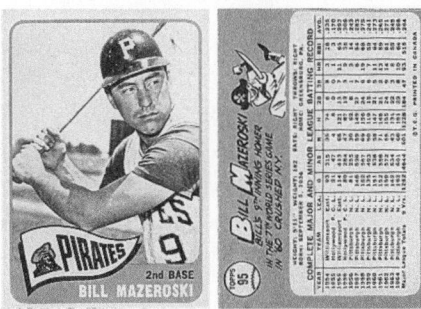

Identical in design to the 1965 Topps set, the Canadian-issued 1965 O-Pee-Chee set was printed on gray stock and consists of 283 cards, each measuring the standard 2-1/2" x 3-1/2". The words "Printed in Canada" appear along the bottom of the back of the cards. The checklist for '65 OPC parallels the first 283 cards in 1965 Topps.

	NM	E	VG
Complete Set (283):	3,150	1,575	950.00
Common Player (1-196):	3.00	1.50	9.00
Common Player (197-283):	6.00	3.00	1.80
Stars: 2-3X Topps			

(See 1965 Topps #1-283 for checklist and star card values.)

1966 O-Pee-Chee

Utilizing the same design as the 1966 Topps set, the 1966 O-Pee-Chee set consists of 196 cards, measuring 2-1/2" x 3-1/2". The words "Ptd. in Canada" appear along the bottom on the back of the cards. The '66 OPC checklist parallels the first 196 cards in the Topps version.

	NM	E	VG
Complete Set (196):	1,600	800.00	475.00
Common Player (1-196):	2.50	1.25	.75
Stars: 2-3X Topps			

(See 1966 Topps #1-196 for checklist and base star card values.)

1967 O-Pee-Chee

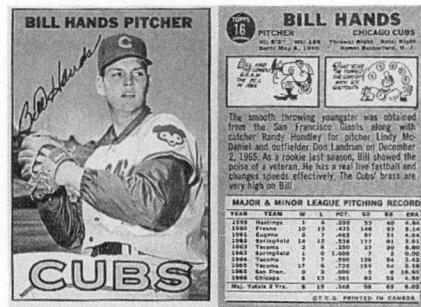

Cards in the 196-card Canadian set are nearly identical in design to the 1967 Topps set, except the words "Printed in Canada" are found on the back in the lower-right corner. Cards measure 2-1/2" x 3-1/2". The '67 OPC set parallels the first 196 cards on the Topps checklist, including "corrected" versions of the checklists and McCormick card.

	NM	E	VG
Complete Set (196):	1,100	550.00	330.00
Common Player (1-109):	2.00	1.00	.60
Common Player (110-196):	2.50	1.25	.75
Wax Pack: 275.00			
Stars: 2-3X Topps			

(See 1967 Topps #1-196 for checklist and base star card values.)

1968 O-Pee-Chee

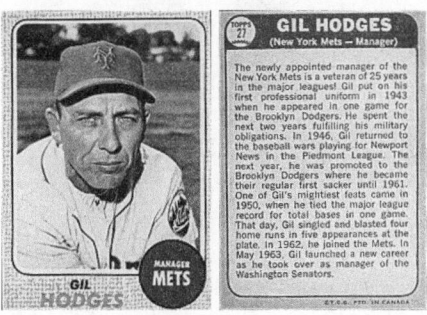

The O-Pee-Chee set for 1968 again consists of 196 cards, in the standard 2-1/2" x 3-1/2". The design is identical to the 1968 Topps set, except the color of the backs is slightly different and the words "Prd. in Canada" appear in the lower-right corner of the back. The checklist parallels the first 196 cards in '68 Topps, though only the "b" versions of the checklists and name-color variations are found in OPC.

	NM	E	VG
Complete Set (196):	3,000	1,500	900.00
Common Player:	2.00	1.00	.60

Stars: 2-3X Topps

(See 1968 Topps #1-196 for checklist and base star card values.)

		NM	E	VG
177	Mets Rookies(Jerry Koosman, Nolan Ryan)	1600.00	800.00	475.00

1968 O-Pee-Chee Posters

The 5" x 7" "All Star Pin-ups" were inserts to 1968 OPC wax packs, but are virtually identical to the Topps version issued in 1967. The OPC posters have a small "Ptd. in Canada" line at bottom. They feature a full- color picture with the player's name, position and team in a circle in the lower-right corner on front. The numbered set consists of 32 players (generally big names). Because the large paper pin-ups had to be folded several times to fit into the wax packs, they are almost never found in technical Mint or NM condition.

		NM	E	VG
	Complete Set (32):	300.00	150.00	90.00
	Common Player:	3.00	1.50	.90
1	Brooks Robinson	25.00	12.50	7.50
2	Bert Campaneris	3.00	1.50	.90
3	Carl Yastrzemski	25.00	12.50	7.50
4	Roberto Clemente	50.00	25.00	15.00
5	Cleon Jones	3.00	1.50	.90
6	Don Drysdale	25.00	12.50	7.50
7	Orlando Cepeda	15.00	7.50	4.50
8	Hank Aaron	50.00	25.00	15.00
9	Tommie Agee	6.00	3.00	1.75
10	Boog Powell	4.50	2.25	1.25
11	Mickey Mantle	75.00	38.00	23.00
12	Chico Cardenas	3.00	1.50	.90
13	John Callison	3.00	1.50	.90
14	Frank Howard	3.75	2.00	1.25
15	Willie Mays	50.00	25.00	13.00
16	Sam McDowell	4.50	2.25	1.25
17	Al Kaline	25.00	12.50	7.50
18	Juan Marichal	15.00	7.50	4.50
19	Denny McLain	4.50	2.25	1.25
20	Matty Alou	3.00	1.50	.90
21	Felipe Alou	4.50	2.25	1.25
22	Joe Pepitone	4.50	2.25	1.25
23	Leon Wagner	3.00	1.50	.90
24	Bobby Knoop	3.00	1.50	.90
25	Tony Oliva	4.50	2.25	1.25
26	Joe Torre	4.50	2.25	1.25
27	Ron Santo	6.00	3.00	1.75
28	Willie McCovey	25.00	12.50	7.50
29	Frank Robinson	25.00	12.50	7.50
30	Ron Hunt	3.00	1.50	.90
31	Harmon Killebrew	25.00	12.50	7.50
32	Joe Morgan	25.00	12.50	7.50

1969 O-Pee-Chee

O-Pee-Chee increased the number of cards in its 1969 set to 218, maintaining the standard 2-1/2" x 3-1/2" size. The card design is identical to the 1969 Topps set, except for the appearance of an OPC logo on back, a slightly different color on the back and the words "Ptd. in Canada," which appear along the bottom. The checklist for '69 OPC parallels the Topps version, but includes only the later-printed "b" versions of the variation cards. This was the first year for the N.L. expansion Montreal Expos, and the Canadian versions of their cards generally sell for a modest premium.

	NM	E	VG
Complete Set (218):	775.00	375.00	225.00
Common Player:	2.50	1.25	.75
Stars: 1-2X Topps			
Expos: 1.5X Topps			

(See 1969 Topps #1-218 for checklist and base star card values.)

1969 O-Pee-Chee Deckle

Very similar in design to the Topps Deckle Edge set of the same year, the 1969 O-Pee-Chee set consists of 24 (rather than Topps' 33) unnumbered black-and-white cards. The Canadian version measures 2-1/8" x 3-1/8", slightly smaller than the Topps set, but features the same "deckle cut" borders. The OPC set is blank-backed and has the facsimile autographs in black ink, rather than blue.

		NM	E	VG
Complete Set (24):		225.00	115.00	70.00
Common Player:		2.50	1.25	.75
(1)	Rich Allen	3.00	1.50	.90
(2)	Luis Aparicio	7.50	3.75	2.25
(3)	Rodney Carew	20.00	10.00	6.00
(4)	Roberto Clemente	45.00	25.00	15.00
(5)	Curt Flood	2.50	1.25	.75
(6)	Bill Freehan	2.50	1.25	.75
(7)	Robert Gibson	7.50	3.75	2.25
(8)	Ken Harrelson	2.50	1.25	.75
(9)	Tommy Helms	2.50	1.25	.75
(10)	Tom Haller	2.50	1.25	.75
(11)	Willie Horton	2.50	1.25	.70
(12)	Frank Howard	2.50	1.25	.75
(13)	Willie McCovey	10.00	5.00	3.00
(14)	Denny McLain	2.50	1.25	.75
(15)	Juan Marichal	7.50	3.75	2.25
(16)	Willie Mays	45.00	25.00	15.00
(17)	John "Boog" Powell	3.00	1.50	.90
(18)	Brooks Robinson	20.00	10.00	6.00
(19)	Ronald Santo	3.00	1.50	.90
(20)	Rusty Staub	3.00	1.50	.90
(21)	Mel Stottlemyre	2.50	1.25	.75
(22)	Luis Tiant	2.50	1.25	.75
(23)	Maurie Wills	2.50	1.25	.75
(24)	Carl Yastrzemski	20.00	10.00	6.00

1970 O-Pee-Chee

The 1970 O-Pee-Chee set, identical in design to the 1970 Topps set, expanded to 546 cards, measuring 2-1/2" x 3-1/2". The Canadian-issued O-Pee-Chee set is easy to distinguish because the backs are printed in both French and English and include the words "Printed in Canada." The '70 OPC checklist parallels the Topps versions. Besides the star cards generally bringing a premium over the Topps version due to scarcity, collectors pay a modest premium for OPC cards of Expos players.

	NM	E	VG
Complete Set (546):	1,750	875.00	525.00
Common Player (1-459):	1.50	.75	.45
Common Player (460-546):	2.50	1.25	.75
Stars: 1-2X Topps			
Expos: 1.5X Topps			

(See 1970 Topps #1-546 for checklist and base card values.)

1971 O-Pee-Chee

For 1971 O-Pee-Chee increased the number of cards in its set to 752, the same as the 1971 Topps set, which shares the same black-bordered design. The backs of the OPC are printed in yellow, rather than green, in a slightly different format and (except card numbers 524-752) are printed in both French and English. The words "Printed in Canada" appear on the back. Fourteen of the OPC cards have different photos from their corresponding Topps' cards or list the player with a different team. The '71 OPC checklist parallels the Topps version. Because of relative scarcity, superstars in the OPC set command a premium, as do cards of the "local" Expos players.

	NM	E	VG
Complete Set (752):	4,000	2,000	1,200
Common Player (1-523):	2.75	1.50	.80
Common Player (524-643):	4.50	2.25	1.25
Common Player (644-752):	6.50	3.25	2.00
Stars: 1-2X Topps			
Expos: 1.5X Topps			

(See 1971 Topps for checklist and base card values.)

1972 O-Pee-Chee

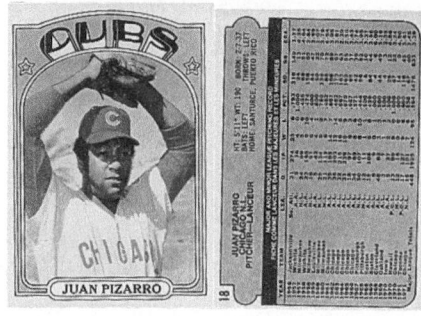

Identical in design to the Topps cards of the same year, the Canadian-issued 1972 O-Pee-Chee set numbers 525 cards, measuring 2-1/2" x 3-1/2". The backs state "Printed in Canada" and are written in both French and English. The O-Pee-Chee card of Gil Hodges notes the Mets' manager's death. The '72 OPC set parallels the first 525 cards on the '72 Topps checklist, though without any of the scarcer "a" variations. Because of relative scarcity, superstars in the OPC brand bring a premium over Topps cards, while increased demand for Expos players causes their cards to bring a similar modest premium.

	NM	E	VG
Complete Set (525):	875.00	425.00	250.00
Common Player (1-263):	.60	.30	.20
Common Player (264-394):	.90	.45	.25
Common Player (395-525):	1.00	.50	.30
Stars: 1-2X Topps			
Expos: 1.5X Topps			

(See 1972 Topps #1-525 for checklist and base card values.)

1973 O-Pee-Chee

The 1973 Canadian-issued O-Pee-Chee set numbers 660 cards and is identical in design and checklist (including only the later-printed "b" variations) to the 1973 Topps set. The backs of the OPC cards are written in both French and English and contain the line "Printed in Canada" along the bottom. The cards measure 2-1/2" x 3-1/2". Unlike the '73 Topps set, which was issued in series of increasing scarcity throughout the summer, the '73 OPC cards were issued in a single series, with cards #529-660 being somewhat short-printed. OPC star cards generally sell for more than the Topps version due to relative scarcity, while Expos players in OPC rate a similar premium due to increased "local" demand.

	NM	E	VG
Complete Set (660):	500.00	250.00	150.00
Common Player (1-528):	.75	.35	.20
Common Player (529-660):	1.25	.60	.40
Stars/Expos: 1.5X Topps			
Wax Pack (10):	55.00		
Wax Box (36):	1,900		

(See 1973 Topps for checklist and base card values.)

1973 O-Pee-Chee Team Checklists

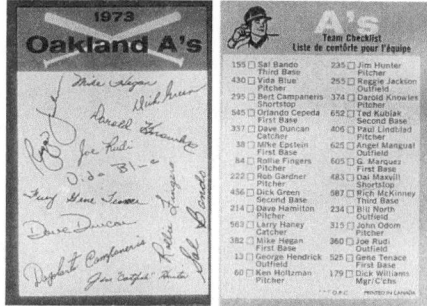

Similar to the 1973 Topps team checklist cards, this set was produced in Canada. The set consists of 24 unnumbered cards (2-1/2" x 3-1/2") with blue borders. The card fronts contain facsimile autographs of players from the same team. The backs contain team checklists of players found in the 1973 O-Pee-Chee regular issue set. The card backs contain the French translation for Team Checklist plus a copyright line "O.P.C. Printed in Canada."

	NM	E	VG
Complete Set (24):	60.00	30.00	18.00
Common Card:	3.00	1.50	.90

(1)	Atlanta Braves	3.00	1.50	.90
(2)	Baltimore Orioles	3.00	1.50	.90
(3)	Boston Red Sox	3.00	1.50	.90
(4)	California Angels	3.00	1.50	.90
(5)	Chicago Cubs	3.00	1.50	.90
(6)	Chicago White Sox	3.00	1.50	.90
(7)	Cincinnati Reds	4.00	2.00	1.25
(8)	Cleveland Indians	3.00	1.50	.90
(9)	Detroit Tigers	4.00	2.00	1.25
(10)	Houston Astros	3.00	1.50	.90
(11)	Kansas City Royals	3.00	1.50	.90
(12)	Los Angeles Dodgers	3.00	1.50	.90
(13)	Milwaukee Brewers	3.00	1.50	.90
(14)	Minnesota Twins	3.00	1.50	.90
(15)	Montreal Expos	6.00	3.00	1.75
(16)	New York Mets	4.00	2.00	1.25
(17)	New York Yankees	3.00	1.50	.90
(18)	Oakland A's	4.50	2.25	1.25
(19)	Philadelphia Phillies	3.00	1.50	.90
(20)	Pittsburgh Pirates	3.00	1.50	.90
(21)	St. Louis Cardinals	3.00	1.50	.90
(22)	San Diego Padres	3.00	1.50	.90
(23)	San Francisco Giants	3.00	1.50	.90
(24)	Texas Rangers	3.00	1.50	.90

1974 O-Pee-Chee

Again numbering 660 cards, the 1974 O-Pee-Chee set borrows its design and, except for 10 of the cards, shares its checklist with the Topps set of the same year. The cards measure the standard 2-1/2" x 3-1/2" and the backs are printed in both French and English and state "Printed in Canada." Because the OPC cards were printed later than Topps, there are no "Washington, Nat'l. League" variations in the Canadian set. Superstar cards and Expos players in OPC command a modest premium over the Topps version due to relative scarcity and increased local demand, respectively. Those OPC cards which differ from Topps are listed below, with the Topps version of each card number shown parenthetically.

		NM	E	VG
Complete Set (660):		950.00	475.00	275.00
Common Player:		.50	.25	.15
Stars/Expos: 1.5X Topps				
Wax Pack (8):		65.00		
Wax Box (36):		2,150		
3	Aaron Special 1958-1959 (Aaron Special 1958-1961)	7.00	3.50	2.00
4	Aaron Special 1960-1961 (Aaron Special 1962-1965)	7.00	3.50	2.00
5	Aaron Special 1962-1963 (Aaron Special 1966-1969)	7.00	3.50	2.00
6	Aaron Special 1964-1965 (Aaron Special 1970-1973)	7.00	3.50	2.00
7	Aaron Special 1966-1967 (Jim Hunter)	7.00	3.50	2.00
8	Aaron Special 1968-1969 (George Theodore)	7.00	3.50	2.00
9	Aaron Special 1970-1973 (Mickey Lolich)	7.00	3.50	2.00
99	George Theodore (Brewers Mgr./ Coaches)	1.50	.70	.45
166	Mickey Lolich (Royals Mgr./Coaches)	2.00	1.00	.60
196	Jim Hunter (Jim Fregosi) (See 1974 Topps for checklist and base card values.)	7.50	3.75	2.25

1974 O-Pee-Chee Team Checklists

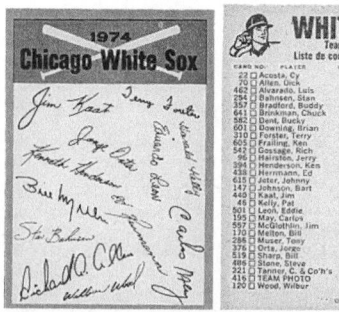

The 1974 O-Pee-Chee Team Checklists set is nearly identical to its Topps counterpart of the same year. Twenty-four unnumbered cards that measure 2-1/2" x 3-1/2" make up the set. The card fronts contain facsimile autographs while the backs carry a team checklist of players found in the regular issue O-Pee-Chee set of 1974. The cards have red borders and can be differentiated from the U.S. version by the "O.P.C. Printed in Canada" line on the back.

	NM	E	VG
Complete Set (24):	25.00	12.50	7.50
Common Checklist:	1.50	.70	.40
(1) Atlanta Braves	1.50	.70	.45
(2) Baltimore Orioles	1.50	.70	.45
(3) Boston Red Sox	1.50	.70	.45
(4) California Angels	1.50	.70	.45
(5) Chicago Cubs	1.50	.70	.45
(6) Chicago White Sox	1.50	.70	.45
(7) Cincinnati Reds	1.50	.70	.45
(8) Cleveland Indians	1.50	.70	.45
(9) Detroit Tigers	1.50	.70	.45
(10) Houston Astros	1.50	.70	.45
(11) Kansas City Royals	1.50	.70	.45
(12) Los Angeles Dodgers	1.50	.70	.45
(13) Milwaukee Brewers	1.50	.70	.45
(14) Minnesota Twins	1.50	.70	.45
(15) Montreal Expos	3.00	1.50	.90
(16) New York Mets	1.50	.70	.45
(17) New York Yankees	1.50	.70	.45
(18) Oakland A's	1.50	.70	.45
(19) Philadelphia Phillies	1.50	.70	.45
(20) Pittsburgh Pirates	1.50	.70	.45
(21) St. Louis Cardinals	1.50	.70	.45
(22) San Diego Padres	1.50	.70	.45
(23) San Francisco Giants	1.50	.70	.45
(24) Texas Rangers	1.50	.70	.45

1975 O-Pee-Chee

The 1975 O-Pee-Chee set was again complete at 660 cards, each measuring 2-1/2" x 3-1/2", and using the same design as the 1975 Topps set. The backs of the O-Pee-Chee cards are written in both French and English and state that the cards were printed in Canada. The checklist for OPC and Topps are identical in '75. Because they are relatively scarcer, OPC superstars sell for a premium over Topps. Expos players also enjoy a premium due to increased local demand.

	NM	E	VG
Complete Set (660):	725.00	365.00	225.00
Common Player:	.45	.25	.15
Stars: 2X Topps			
Expos: 1.5X Topps			
Wax Pack (8):	30.00		
Wax Box (48):	1,200		

(See 1975 Topps for checklist and base card values.)

1976 O-Pee-Chee

Identical in design to, and sharing a checklist with, the 1976 Topps set, the Canadian-issued 1976 O-Pee-Chees comprise 660 cards, each 2-1/2" x 3-1/2". The backs are printed in both French and English and state "Ptd. in Canada." Stars and Expos players enjoy a modest premium over the Topps versions due to relative scarcity and increased local demand, respectively.

	NM	E	VG
Complete Set (660):	700.00	350.00	210.00
Common Player:	.20	.10	.05
Stars/Expos 2X Topps			
Wax Pack (8):	30.00		
Wax Box (48):	750.00		

(See 1976 Topps for checklist and base card values.)

1977 O-Pee-Chee

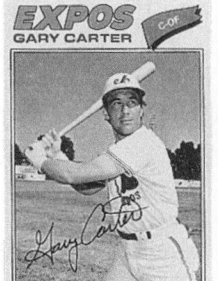 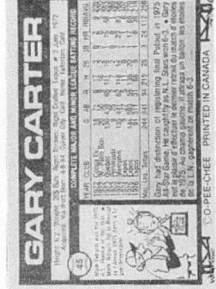

The 1977 O-Pee-Chee set represents a change in philosophy for the Canadian company. The design of the set is still identical to the Topps set of the same year, but the number of cards was reduced to 264 with more emphasis on players from the two Canadian teams. The backs are printed in both French and English and state "O-Pee-Chee Printed in Canada." About 1/3 of the photos in the OPC set differ from the corresponding Topps cards either with entirely different photos, airbrushed uniform changes, the removal of All-Star and Rookie Team designations, or significant photo cropping variations. Cards measure the standard 2-1/2" x 3-1/2".

		NM	E	VG
	Complete Set (264):	200.00	100.00	60.00
	Common Player:	.25	.13	.08
	Wax Pack (8):	12.00		
	Wax Box (48):	285.00		
1	Batting Leaders(George Brett, Bill Madlock)	4.00	2.00	1.25
2	Home Run Leaders(Graig Nettles, Mike Schmidt)	2.75	1.50	.80
3	Runs Batted In Leaders(George Foster, Lee May)	.25	.13	.08
4	Stolen Base Leaders(Dave Lopes, Bill North)	.25	.13	.08
5	Victory Leaders(Randy Jones, Jim Palmer)	1.00	.50	.30
6	Strikeout Leaders(Nolan Ryan, Tom Seaver)	12.50	6.25	3.75
7	Earned Run Avg. Leaders(John Denny, Mark Fidrych)	.25	.13	.08
8	Leading Firemen(Bill Campbell, Rawly Eastwick)	.25	.13	.08
9	Mike Jorgensen	.25	.13	.08
10	Jim Hunter	4.00	2.00	1.25
11	Ken Griffey	.25	.13	.08
12	Bill Campbell	.25	.13	.08
13	Otto Velez	.25	.13	.08
14	Milt May	.25	.13	.08
15	Dennis Eckersley	4.00	2.00	1.25
16	John Mayberry	.25	.13	.08
17	Larry Bowa	.25	.13	.08
18	Don Carrithers	.25	.13	.08
19	Ken Singleton	.25	.13	.08
20	Bill Stein	.25	.13	.08
21	Ken Brett	.25	.13	.08
22	Gary Woods	.25	.13	.08
23	Steve Swisher	.25	.13	.08
24	Don Sutton	4.00	2.00	1.25
25	Willie Stargell	4.00	2.00	1.25
26	Jerry Koosman	.25	.13	.08
27	Del Unser	.25	.13	.08
28	Bob Grich	.25	.13	.08
29	Jim Slaton	.25	.13	.08
30	Thurman Munson	4.00	2.00	1.25
31	Dan Driessen	.25	.13	.08
32	Tom Bruno (Not in Topps.)	.25	.13	.08
33	Larry Hisle	.25	.13	.08
34	Phil Garner	.25	.13	.08
35	Mike Hargrove	.25	.13	.08
36	Jackie Brown	.25	.13	.08
37	Carl Yastrzemski	7.50	3.75	2.25
38	Dave Roberts	.25	.13	.08
39	Ray Fosse	.25	.13	.08
40	Dave McKay	.25	.13	.08
41	Paul Splittorff	.25	.13	.08
42	Garry Maddox	.25	.13	.08
43	Phil Niekro	4.00	2.00	1.25
44	Roger Metzger	.25	.13	.08
45	Gary Carter	7.50	3.75	2.25
46	Jim Spencer	.25	.13	.08
47	Ross Grimsley	.25	.13	.08
48	Bob Bailor	.25	.13	.08
49	Chris Chambliss	.25	.13	.08
50	Will McEnaney	.25	.13	.08
51	Lou Brock	4.50	2.25	1.25
52	Rollie Fingers	4.00	2.00	1.25
53	Chris Speier	.25	.13	.08
54	Bombo Rivera	.25	.13	.08
55	Pete Broberg	.25	.13	.08
56	Bill Madlock	.25	.13	.08
57	Rick Rhoden	.25	.13	.08
58	Blue Jay Coaches(Don Leppert, Bob Miller, Jackie Moore, Harry Warner)	.50	.25	.15
59	John Candelaria	.25	.13	.08
60	Ed Kranepool	.25	.13	.08
61	Dave LaRoche	.25	.13	.08
62	Jim Rice	4.50	2.25	1.25
63	Don Stanhouse	.25	.13	.08
64	Jason Thompson	.25	.13	.08
65	Nolan Ryan	25.00	12.50	7.50
66	Tom Poquette	.25	.13	.08
67	Leon Hooten	.25	.13	.08
68	Bob Boone	.25	.13	.08
69	Mickey Rivers	.25	.13	.08
70	Gary Nolan	.25	.13	.08
71	Sixto Lezcano	.25	.13	.08
72	Larry Parrish	.25	.13	.08
73	Dave Goltz	.25	.13	.08
74	Bert Campaneris	.25	.13	.08
75	Vida Blue	.25	.13	.08
76	Rick Cerone	.25	.13	.08
77	Ralph Garr	.25	.13	.08
78	Ken Forsch	.25	.13	.08
79	Willie Montanez	.25	.13	.08
80	Jim Palmer	4.50	2.25	1.25
81	Jerry White	.25	.13	.08
82	Gene Tenace	.25	.13	.08
83	Bobby Murcer	.25	.13	.08
84	Garry Templeton	.25	.13	.08
85	Bill Singer	.25	.13	.08
86	Buddy Bell	.25	.13	.08
87	Luis Tiant	.25	.13	.08
88	Rusty Staub	.25	.13	.08
89	Sparky Lyle	.25	.13	.08
90	Jose Morales	.25	.13	.08
91	Dennis Leonard	.25	.13	.08
92	Tommy Smith	.25	.13	.08
93	Steve Carlton	5.50	2.75	1.75
94	John Scott	.25	.13	.08
95	Bill Bonham	.25	.13	.08
96	Dave Lopes	.25	.13	.08
97	Jerry Reuss	.25	.13	.08
98	Dave Kingman	.35	.20	.11
99	Dan Warthen	.25	.13	.08
100	Johnny Bench	7.50	3.75	2.25
101	Bert Blyleven	4.00	2.00	1.25
102	Cecil Cooper	.25	.13	.08
103	Mike Willis	.25	.13	.08
104	Dan Ford	.25	.13	.08
105	Frank Tanana	.25	.13	.08
106	Bill North	.25	.13	.08
107	Joe Ferguson	.25	.13	.08
108	Dick Williams	.25	.13	.08
109	John Denny	.25	.13	.08
110	Willie Randolph	.25	.13	.08
111	Reggie Cleveland	.25	.13	.08
112	Doug Howard	.25	.13	.08
113	Randy Jones	.25	.13	.08
114	Rico Carty	.25	.13	.08
115	Mark Fidrych	2.75	1.50	.80
116	Darrell Porter	.25	.13	.08
117	Wayne Garrett	.25	.13	.08
118	Greg Luzinski	.25	.13	.08
119	Jim Barr	.25	.13	.08
120	George Foster	.25	.13	.08
121	Phil Roof	.25	.13	.08
122	Bucky Dent	.25	.13	.08
123	Steve Braun	.25	.13	.08
124	**Checklist 1-132**	.40	.20	.12
125	Lee May	.25	.13	.08
126	Woodie Fryman	.25	.13	.08
127	Jose Cardenal	.25	.13	.08
128	Doug Rau	.25	.13	.08
129	Rennie Stennett	.25	.13	.08
130	Pete Vuckovich	.25	.13	.08
131	Cesar Cedeno	.25	.13	.08
132	Jon Matlack	.25	.13	.08
133	Don Baylor	.30	.15	.09
134	Darrel Chaney	.25	.13	.08
135	Tony Perez	4.00	2.00	1.25
136	Aurelio Rodriguez	.25	.13	.08
137	Carlton Fisk	4.00	2.00	1.25
138	Wayne Garland	.25	.13	.08
139	Dave Hilton	.25	.13	.08
140	Rawly Eastwick	.25	.13	.08
141	Amos Otis	.25	.13	.08
142	Tug McGraw	.25	.13	.08
143	Rod Carew	5.50	2.75	1.75
144	Mike Torrez	.25	.13	.08
145	Sal Bando	.25	.13	.08
146	Dock Ellis	.25	.13	.08
147	Jose Cruz	.25	.13	.08
148	Alan Ashby	.25	.13	.08
149	Gaylord Perry	4.00	2.00	1.25
150	Keith Hernandez	.25	.13	.08
151	Dave Pagan	.25	.13	.08
152	Richie Zisk	.25	.13	.08
153	Steve Rogers	.25	.13	.08
154	Mark Belanger	.25	.13	.08
155	Andy Messersmith	.25	.13	.08
156	Dave Winfield	6.00	3.00	1.75
157	Chuck Hartenstein	.25	.13	.08
158	Manny Trillo	.25	.13	.08
159	Steve Yeager	.25	.13	.08
160	Cesar Geronimo	.25	.13	.08
161	Jim Rooker	.25	.13	.08
162	Tim Foli	.25	.13	.08
163	Fred Lynn	.25	.13	.08
164	Ed Figueroa	.25	.13	.08
165	Johnny Grubb	.25	.13	.08
166	Pedro Garcia	.25	.13	.08
167	Ron LeFlore	.25	.13	.08
168	Rich Hebner	.25	.13	.08

		NM	E	VG
169	Larry Herndon	.25	.13	.08
170	George Brett	15.00	7.50	4.50
171	Joe Kerrigan	.25	.13	.08
172	Bud Harrelson	.25	.13	.08
173	Bobby Bonds	.25	.13	.08
174	Bill Travers	.25	.13	.08
175	John Lowenstein	.25	.13	.08
176	Butch Wynegar	.25	.13	.08
177	Pete Falcone	.25	.13	.08
178	Claudell Washington	.25	.13	.08
179	Checklist 133-264	.40	.20	.12
180	Dave Cash	.25	.13	.08
181	Fred Norman	.25	.13	.08
182	Roy White	.25	.13	.08
183	Marty Perez	.25	.13	.08
184	Jesse Jefferson	.25	.13	.08
185	Jim Sundberg	.25	.13	.08
186	Dan Meyer	.25	.13	.08
187	Fergie Jenkins	6.00	3.00	1.75
188	Tom Veryzer	.25	.13	.08
189	Dennis Blair	.25	.13	.08
190	Rick Manning	.25	.13	.08
191	Doug Bird	.25	.13	.08
192	Al Bumbry	.25	.13	.08
193	Dave Roberts	.25	.13	.08
194	Larry Christenson	.25	.13	.08
195	Chet Lemon	.25	.13	.08
196	Ted Simmons	.25	.13	.08
197	Ray Burris	.25	.13	.08
198	Expos Coaches(Jim Brewer, Billy Gardner, Mickey Vernon, Ozzie Virgil)	.25	.13	.08
199	Ron Cey	.25	.13	.08
200	Reggie Jackson	12.50	6.25	3.75
201	Pat Zachry	.25	.13	.08
202	Doug Ault	.25	.13	.08
203	Al Oliver	.25	.13	.08
204	Robin Yount	5.50	2.75	1.75
205	Tom Seaver	7.50	3.75	2.25
206	Joe Rudi	.25	.13	.08
207	Barry Foote	.25	.13	.08
208	Toby Harrah	.25	.13	.08
209	Jeff Burroughs	.25	.13	.08
210	George Scott	.25	.13	.08
211	Jim Mason	.25	.13	.08
212	Vern Ruhle	.25	.13	.08
213	Fred Kendall	.25	.13	.08
214	Rick Reuschel	.25	.13	.08
215	Hal McRae	.25	.13	.08
216	Chip Lang	.25	.13	.08
217	Graig Nettles	.30	.15	.09
218	George Hendrick	.25	.13	.08
219	Glenn Abbott	.25	.13	.08
220	Joe Morgan	4.50	2.25	1.25
221	Sam Ewing	.25	.13	.08
222	George Medich	.25	.13	.08
223	Reggie Smith	.25	.13	.08
224	Dave Hamilton	.25	.13	.08
225	Pepe Frias	.25	.13	.08
226	Jay Johnstone	.25	.13	.08
227	J.R. Richard	.25	.13	.08
228	Doug DeCinces	.25	.13	.08
229	Dave Lemanczyk	.25	.13	.08
230	Rick Monday	.25	.13	.08
231	Manny Sanguillen	.25	.13	.08
232	John Montefusco	.25	.13	.08
233	Duane Kuiper	.25	.13	.08
234	Ellis Valentine	.25	.13	.08
235	Dick Tidrow	.25	.13	.08
236	Ben Oglivie	.25	.13	.08
237	Rick Burleson	.25	.13	.08
238	Roy Hartsfield	.25	.13	.08
239	Lyman Bostock	.25	.13	.08
240	Pete Rose	13.50	6.75	4.00
241	Mike Ivie	.25	.13	.08
242	Dave Parker	.35	.20	.11
243	Bill Greif	.25	.13	.08
244	Freddie Patek	.25	.13	.08
245	Mike Schmidt	15.00	7.50	4.50
246	Brian Downing	.25	.13	.08
247	Steve Hargan	.25	.13	.08
248	Dave Collins	.25	.13	.08
249	Felix Millan	.25	.13	.08
250	Don Gullett	.25	.13	.08
251	Jerry Royster	.25	.13	.08
252	Earl Williams	.25	.13	.08
253	Frank Duffy	.25	.13	.08
254	Tippy Martinez	.25	.13	.08
255	Steve Garvey	2.75	1.50	.80
256	Alvis Woods	.25	.13	.08
257	John Hiller	.25	.13	.08
258	Dave Concepcion	.25	.13	.08
259	Dwight Evans	.25	.13	.08
260	Pete MacKanin	.25	.13	.08
261	George Brett (Record Breaker)	5.00	2.50	1.50
262	Minnie Minoso (Record Breaker)	.25	.13	.08
263	Jose Morales (Record Breaker)	.25	.13	.08
264	Nolan Ryan (Record Breaker)	12.50	6.25	3.75

1978 O-Pee-Chee

STEVE ROGERS

The 1978 O-Pee-Chee set was further reduced to 242 cards and again had heavy representation from the two Canadian teams. The cards measure the standard 2-1/2" x 3-1/2" and the backs are printed in both French and English. The cards use the same design as the 1978 Topps set. Some of the cards contain an extra line on the front indicating a team change.

		NM	E	VG
	Complete Set (242):	120.00	60.00	35.00
	Common Player:	.25	.13	.08
	Wax Pack (10):	8.00		
	Wax Box (36):	275.00		
1	Batting Leaders(Rod Carew, Dave Parker)	.75	.40	.25
2	Home Run Leaders(George Foster, Jim Rice)	.50	.25	.15
3	Runs Batted In Leaders(George Foster, Larry Hisle)	.25	.13	.08
4	Stolen Base Leaders(Freddie Patek, Frank Taveras)	.25	.13	.08
5	Victory Leaders(Steve Carlton, Dave Goltz, Dennis Leonard, Jim Palmer)	.45	.25	.14
6	Strikeout Leaders(Phil Niekro, Nolan Ryan)	1.50	.70	.45
7	Earned Run Avg. Ldrs. (John Candelaria, Frank Tanana)	.25	.13	.08
8	Leading Firemen(Bill Campbell, Rollie Fingers)	.45	.25	.14
9	Steve Rogers	.25	.13	.08
10	Graig Nettles	.25	.13	.08
11	Doug Capilla	.25	.13	.08
12	George Scott	.25	.13	.08
13	Gary Woods	.25	.13	.08
14	Tom Veryzer	.25	.13	.08
15	Wayne Garland	.25	.13	.08
16	Amos Otis	.25	.13	.08
17	Larry Christenson	.25	.13	.08
18	Dave Cash	.25	.13	.08
19	Jim Barr	.25	.13	.08
20	Ruppert Jones	.25	.13	.08
21	Eric Soderholm	.25	.13	.08
22	Jesse Jefferson	.25	.13	.08
23	Jerry Morales	.25	.13	.08
24	Doug Rau	.25	.13	.08
25	Rennie Stennett	.25	.13	.08
26	Lee Mazzilli	.25	.13	.08
27	Dick Williams	.25	.13	.08
28	Joe Rudi	.25	.13	.08
29	Robin Yount	2.00	1.00	.60
30	Don Gullett	.25	.13	.08
31	Roy Howell	.25	.13	.08
32	Cesar Geronimo	.25	.13	.08
33	Rick Langford	.25	.13	.08
34	Dan Ford	.25	.13	.08
35	Gene Tenace	.25	.13	.08
36	Santo Alcala	.25	.13	.08
37	Rick Burleson	.25	.13	.08
38	Dave Rozema	.25	.13	.08
39	Duane Kulper	.25	.13	.08
40	Ron Fairly	.25	.13	.08
41	Dennis Leonard	.25	.13	.08
42	Greg Luzinski	.25	.13	.08
43	Willie Montanez	.25	.13	.08

		NM	E	VG
44	Enos Cabell	.25	.13	.08
45	Ellis Valentine	.25	.13	.08
46	Steve Stone	.25	.13	.08
47	Lee May	.25	.13	.08
48	Roy White	.25	.13	.08
49	Jerry Garvin	.25	.13	.08
50	Johnny Bench	2.00	1.00	.60
51	Garry Templeton	.25	.13	.08
52	Doyle Alexander	.25	.13	.08
53	Steve Henderson	.25	.13	.08
54	Stan Bahnsen	.25	.13	.08
55	Dan Meyer	.25	.13	.08
56	Rick Reuschel	.25	.13	.08
57	Reggie Smith	.25	.13	.08
58	Blue Jays Team	.50	.25	.15
59	John Montefusco	.25	.13	.08
60	Dave Parker	.25	.13	.08
61	Jim Bibby	.25	.13	.08
62	Fred Lynn	.25	.13	.08
63	Jose Morales	.25	.13	.08
64	Aurelio Rodriguez	.25	.13	.08
65	Frank Tanana	.25	.13	.08
66	Darrell Porter	.25	.13	.08
67	Otto Velez	.25	.13	.08
68	Larry Bowa	.25	.13	.08
69	Jim Hunter	1.50	.70	.45
70	George Foster	.25	.13	.08
71	Cecil Cooper	.25	.13	.08
72	Gary Alexander	.25	.13	.08
73	Paul Thormodsgard	.25	.13	.08
74	Toby Harrah	.25	.13	.08
75	Mitchell Page	.25	.13	.08
76	Alan Ashby	.25	.13	.08
77	Jorge Orta	.25	.13	.08
78	Dave Winfield	3.00	1.50	.90
79	Andy Messersmith	.25	.13	.08
80	Ken Singleton	.25	.13	.08
81	Will McEnaney	.25	.13	.08
82	Lou Piniella	.25	.13	.08
83	Bob Forsch	.25	.13	.08
84	Dan Driessen	.25	.13	.08
85	Dave Lemanczyk	.25	.13	.08
86	Paul Dade	.25	.13	.08
87	Bill Campbell	.25	.13	.08
88	Ron LeFlore	.25	.13	.08
89	Bill Madlock	.25	.13	.08
90	Tony Perez	.25	.13	.08
91	Freddie Patek	.25	.13	.08
92	Glenn Abbott	.25	.13	.08
93	Garry Maddox	.25	.13	.08
94	Steve Staggs	.25	.13	.08
95	Bobby Murcer	.25	.13	.08
96	Don Sutton	1.50	.70	.45
97	Al Oliver	.25	.13	.08
98	Jon Matlack	.25	.13	.08
99	Sam Mejias	.25	.13	.08
100	Pete Rose	6.00	3.00	1.75
101	Randy Jones	.25	.13	.08
102	Sixto Lezcano	.25	.13	.08
103	Jim Clancy	.25	.13	.08
104	Butch Wynegar	.25	.13	.08
105	Nolan Ryan	15.00	7.50	4.50
106	Wayne Gross	.25	.13	.08
107	Bob Watson	.25	.13	.08
108	Joe Kerrigan	.25	.13	.08
109	Keith Hernandez	.25	.13	.08
110	Reggie Jackson	5.00	2.50	1.50
111	Denny Doyle	.25	.13	.08
112	Sam Ewing	.25	.13	.08
113	Bert Blyleven	1.50	.75	.45
114	Andre Thornton	.25	.13	.08
115	Milt May	.25	.13	.08
116	Jim Colborn	.25	.13	.08
117	Warren Cromartie	.25	.13	.08
118	Ted Sizemore	.25	.13	.08
119	Checklist 1-121	.35	.20	.11
120	Tom Seaver	2.50	1.25	.70
121	Luis Gomez	.25	.13	.08
122	Jim Spencer	.25	.13	.08
123	Leroy Stanton	.25	.13	.08
124	Luis Tiant	.25	.13	.08
125	Mark Belanger	.25	.13	.08
126	Jackie Brown	.25	.13	.08
127	Bill Buckner	.25	.13	.08
128	Bill Robinson	.25	.13	.08
129	Rick Cerone	.25	.13	.08
130	Ron Cey	.25	.13	.08
131	Jose Cruz	.25	.13	.08
132	Len Randle	.25	.13	.08
133	Bob Grich	.25	.13	.08
134	Jeff Burroughs	.25	.13	.08
135	Gary Carter	6.00	3.00	1.75
136	Milt Wilcox	.25	.13	.08
137	Carl Yastrzemski	2.50	1.25	.70
138	Dennis Eckersley	1.50	.70	.45
139	Tim Nordbrook	.25	.13	.08
140	Ken Griffey	.25	.13	.08
141	Bob Boone	.25	.13	.08

142	Dave Goltz	.25	.13	.08
143	Al Cowens	.25	.13	.08
144	Bill Atkinson	.25	.13	.08
145	Chris Chambliss	.25	.13	.08
146	Jim Slaton	.25	.13	.08
147	Bill Stein	.25	.13	.08
148	Bob Bailor	.25	.13	.08
149	J.R. Richard	.25	.13	.08
150	Ted Simmons	.25	.13	.08
151	Rick Manning	.25	.13	.08
152	Lerrin LaGrow	.25	.13	.08
153	Larry Parrish	.25	.13	.08
154	Eddie Murray	15.00	7.50	4.50
155	Phil Niekro	1.50	.70	.45
156	Bake McBride	.25	.13	.08
157	Pete Vuckovich	.25	.13	.08
158	Ivan DeJesus	.25	.13	.08
159	Rick Rhoden	.25	.13	.08
160	Joe Morgan	2.00	1.00	.60
161	Ed Ott	.25	.13	.08
162	Don Stanhouse	.25	.13	.08
163	Jim Rice	2.00	1.00	.60
164	Bucky Dent	.25	.13	.08
165	Jim Kern	.25	.13	.08
166	Doug Rader	.25	.13	.08
167	Steve Kemp	.25	.13	.08
168	John Mayberry	.25	.13	.08
169	Tim Foli	.25	.13	.08
170	Steve Carlton	2.00	1.00	.60
171	Pepe Frias	.25	.13	.08
172	Pat Zachry	.25	.13	.08
173	Don Baylor	.25	.13	.08
174	Sal Bando	.25	.13	.08
175	Alvis Woods	.25	.13	.08
176	Mike Hargrove	.25	.13	.08
177	Vida Blue	.25	.13	.08
178	George Hendrick	.25	.13	.08
179	Jim Palmer	2.00	1.00	.60
180	Andre Dawson	10.00	5.00	3.00
181	Paul Moskau	.25	.13	.08
182	Mickey Rivers	.25	.13	.08
183	Checklist 122-242	.35	.20	.11
184	Jerry Johnson	.25	.13	.08
185	Willie McCovey	2.00	1.00	.60
186	Enrique Romo	.25	.13	.08
187	Butch Hobson	.25	.13	.08
188	Rusty Staub	.45	.25	.14
189	Wayne Twitchell	.25	.13	.08
190	Steve Garvey	1.00	.50	.30
191	Rick Waits	.25	.13	.08
192	Doug DeCinces	.25	.13	.08
193	Tom Murphy	.25	.13	.08
194	Rich Hebner	.25	.13	.08
195	Ralph Garr	.25	.13	.08
196	Bruce Sutter	1.50	.70	.45
197	Tom Poquette	.25	.13	.08
198	Wayne Garrett	.25	.13	.08
199	Pedro Borbon	.25	.13	.08
200	Thurman Munson	2.00	1.00	.60
201	Rollie Fingers	1.50	.70	.45
202	Doug Ault	.25	.13	.08
203	Phil Garner	.25	.13	.08
204	Lou Brock	2.00	1.00	.60
205	Ed Kranepool	.25	.13	.08
206	Bobby Bonds	.25	.13	.08
207	Expos Team	.25	.13	.08
208	Bump Wills	.25	.13	.08
209	Gary Matthews	.25	.13	.08
210	Carlton Fisk	2.00	1.00	.60
211	Jeff Byrd	.25	.13	.08
212	Jason Thompson	.25	.13	.08
213	Larvell Blanks	.25	.13	.08
214	Sparky Lyle	.25	.13	.08
215	George Brett	6.00	3.00	1.75
216	Del Unser	.25	.13	.08
217	Manny Trillo	.25	.13	.08
218	Roy Hartsfield	.25	.13	.08
219	Carlos Lopez	.25	.13	.08
220	Dave Concepcion	.25	.13	.08
221	John Candelaria	.25	.13	.08
222	Dave Lopes	.25	.13	.08
223	Tim Blackwell	.25	.13	.08
224	Chet Lemon	.25	.13	.08
225	Mike Schmidt	6.00	3.00	1.75
226	Cesar Cedeno	.25	.13	.08
227	Mike Willis	.25	.13	.08
228	Willie Randolph	.25	.13	.08
229	Doug Bair	.25	.13	.08
230	Rod Carew	2.00	1.00	.60
231	Mike Flanagan	.25	.13	.08
232	Chris Speier	.25	.13	.08
233	Don Aase	.25	.13	.08
234	Buddy Bell	.25	.13	.08
235	Mark Fidrych	.30	.15	.09
236	Lou Brock (Record Breaker)	.75	.40	.25
237	Sparky Lyle (Record Breaker)	.25	.13	.08

238	Willie McCovey (Record Breaker)	.45	.25	.14
239	Brooks Robinson (Record Breaker)	.90	.45	.25
240	Pete Rose (Record Breaker)	2.00	1.00	.60
241	Nolan Ryan (Record Breaker)	10.00	5.00	3.00
242	Reggie Jackson (Record Breaker)	1.50	.70	.45

1979 O-Pee-Chee

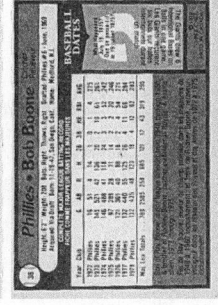

The 1979 O-Pee-Chee cards are nearly identical in design to the Topps set of the same year, but display the O-Pee-Chee logo inside the baseball in the lower-left corner of the front. The number of cards in the set was increased to 374, each measuring 2-1/2" x 3-1/2".

	NM	E	VG
Complete Set (374):	80.00	40.00	24.00
Common Player:	.25	.13	.08
Wax Pack (10):	10.00		
Wax Box (36):	200.00		

1	Lee May	.25	.13	.08
2	Dick Drago	.25	.13	.08
3	Paul Dade	.25	.13	.08
4	Ross Grimsley	.25	.13	.08
5	Joe Morgan	2.00	1.00	.60
6	Kevin Kobel	.25	.13	.08
7	Terry Forster	.25	.13	.08
8	Paul Molitor	12.00	6.00	3.50
9	Steve Carlton	2.00	1.00	.60
10	Dave Goltz	.25	.13	.08
11	Dave Winfield	3.00	1.50	.90
12	Dave Rozema	.25	.13	.08
13	Ed Figueroa	.25	.13	.08
14	Alan Ashby	.25	.13	.08
15	Dale Murphy	2.50	1.25	.70
16	Dennis Eckersley	1.50	.70	.45
17	Ron Blomberg	.25	.13	.08
18	Wayne Twitchell	.25	.13	.08
19	Al Hrabosky	.25	.13	.08
20	Fred Norman	.25	.13	.08
21	Steve Garvey	1.00	.50	.30
22	Willie Stargell	2.00	1.00	.60
23	John Hale	.25	.13	.08
24	Mickey Rivers	.25	.13	.08
25	Jack Brohamer	.25	.13	.08
26	Tom Underwood	.25	.13	.08
27	Mark Belanger	.25	.13	.08
28	Elliott Maddox	.25	.13	.08
29	John Candelaria	.25	.13	.08
30	Shane Rawley	.25	.13	.08
31	Steve Yeager	.25	.13	.08
32	Warren Cromartie	.25	.13	.08
33	Jason Thompson	.25	.13	.08
34	Roger Erickson	.25	.13	.08
35	Gary Matthews	.25	.13	.08
36	Pete Falcone	.25	.13	.08
37	Dick Tidrow	.25	.13	.08
38	Bob Boone	.25	.13	.08
39	Jim Bibby	.25	.13	.08
40	Len Barker	.25	.13	.08
41	Robin Yount	2.00	1.00	.60
42	Sam Mejias	.25	.13	.08
43	Ray Burris	.25	.13	.08
44	Tom Seaver	2.50	1.25	.70
45	Roy Howell	.25	.13	.08
46	Jim Todd	.25	.13	.08
47	Frank Duffy	.25	.13	.08
48	Joel Youngblood	.25	.13	.08
49	Vida Blue	.25	.13	.08
50	Cliff Johnson	.25	.13	.08
51	Nolan Ryan	15.00	7.50	4.50
52	Ozzie Smith	20.00	10.00	6.00
53	Jim Sundberg	.25	.13	.08
54	Mike Paxton	.25	.13	.08
55	Lou Whitaker	1.00	.50	.30
56	Dan Schatzeder	.25	.13	.08
57	Rick Burleson	.25	.13	.08

58	Doug Bair	.25	.13	.08
59	Ted Martinez	.25	.13	.08
60	Bob Watson	.25	.13	.08
61	Jim Clancy	.25	.13	.08
62	Rowland Office	.25	.13	.08
63	Bobby Murcer	.25	.13	.08
64	Don Gullett	.25	.13	.08
65	Tom Paciorek	.25	.13	.08
66	Rick Rhoden	.25	.13	.08
67	Duane Kuiper	.25	.13	.08
68	Bruce Boisclair	.25	.13	.08
69	Manny Sarmiento	.25	.13	.08
70	Wayne Cage	.25	.13	.08
71	John Hiller	.25	.13	.08
72	Rick Cerone	.25	.13	.08
73	Dwight Evans	.25	.13	.08
74	Buddy Solomon	.25	.13	.08
75	Roy White	.25	.13	.08
76	Mike Flanagan	.25	.13	.08
77	Tom Johnson	.25	.13	.08
78	Glenn Burke	.25	.13	.08
79	Frank Taveras	.25	.13	.08
80	Don Sutton	1.50	.70	.45
81	Leon Roberts	.25	.13	.08
82	George Hendrick	.25	.13	.08
83	Aurelio Rodriguez	.25	.13	.08
84	Ron Reed	.25	.13	.08
85	Alvis Woods	.25	.13	.08
86	Jim Beattie	.25	.13	.08
87	Larry Hisle	.25	.13	.08
88	Mike Garman	.25	.13	.08
89	Tim Johnson	.25	.13	.08
90	Paul Splittorff	.25	.13	.08
91	Darrel Chaney	.25	.13	.08
92	Mike Torrez	.25	.13	.08
93	Eric Soderholm	.25	.13	.08
94	Ron Cey	.25	.13	.08
95	Randy Jones	.25	.13	.08
96	Bill Madlock	.25	.13	.08
97	Steve Kemp	.25	.13	.08
98	Bob Apodaca	.25	.13	.08
99	Johnny Grubb	.25	.13	.08
100	Larry Milbourne	.25	.13	.08
101	Johnny Bench	2.00	1.00	.60
102	Dave Lemanczyk	.25	.13	.08
103	Reggie Cleveland	.25	.13	.08
104	Larry Bowa	.25	.13	.08
105	Denny Martinez	1.00	.50	.30
106	Bill Travers	.25	.13	.08
107	Willie McCovey	2.00	1.00	.60
108	Wilbur Wood	.25	.13	.08
109	Dennis Leonard	.25	.13	.08
110	Roy Smalley	.25	.13	.08
111	Cesar Geronimo	.25	.13	.08
112	Jesse Jefferson	.25	.13	.08
113	Dave Revering	.25	.13	.08
114	Rich Gossage	.30	.15	.09
115	Steve Stone	.25	.13	.08
116	Doug Flynn	.25	.13	.08
117	Bob Forsch	.25	.13	.08
118	Paul Mitchell	.25	.13	.08
119	Toby Harrah	.25	.13	.08
120	Steve Rogers	.25	.13	.08
121	**Checklist 1-125**	.25	.13	.08
122	Balor Moore	.25	.13	.08
123	Rick Reuschel	.25	.13	.08
124	Jeff Burroughs	.25	.13	.08
125	Willie Randolph	.25	.13	.08
126	Bob Stinson	.25	.13	.08
127	Rick Wise	.25	.13	.08
128	Luis Gomez	.25	.13	.08
129	Tommy John	.25	.13	.08
130	Richie Zisk	.25	.13	.08
131	Mario Guerrero	.25	.13	.08
132	Oscar Gamble	.25	.13	.08
133	Don Money	.25	.13	.08
134	Joe Rudi	.25	.13	.08
135	Woodie Fryman	.25	.13	.08
136	Butch Hobson	.25	.13	.08
137	Jim Colborn	.25	.13	.08
138	Tom Grieve	.25	.13	.08
139	Andy Messersmith	.25	.13	.08
140	Andre Thornton	.25	.13	.08
141	Kevin Kravec	.25	.13	.08
142	Bobby Bonds	.25	.13	.08
143	Jose Cruz	.25	.13	.08
144	Dave Lopes	.25	.13	.08
145	Jerry Garvin	.25	.13	.08
146	Pepe Frias	.25	.13	.08
147	Mitchell Page	.25	.13	.08
148	Ted Sizemore	.25	.13	.08
149	Rich Gale	.25	.13	.08
150	Steve Ontiveros	.25	.13	.08
151	Rod Carew	2.00	1.00	.60
152	Lary Sorensen	.25	.13	.08
153	Willie Montanez	.25	.13	.08
154	Floyd Bannister	.25	.13	.08
155	Bert Blyleven	1.50	.75	.45

156	Ralph Garr	.25	.13	.08
157	Thurman Munson	1.50	.75	.45
158	Bob Robertson	.25	.13	.08
159	Jon Matlack	.25	.13	.08
160	Carl Yastrzemski	2.50	1.25	.70
161	Gaylord Perry	1.50	.70	.45
162	Mike Tyson	.25	.13	.08
163	Cecil Cooper	.25	.13	.08
164	Pedro Borbon	.25	.13	.08
165	Art Howe	.25	.13	.08
166	Joe Coleman	.25	.13	.08
167	George Brett	6.00	3.00	1.75
168	Gary Alexander	.25	.13	.08
169	Chet Lemon	.25	.13	.08
170	Craig Swan	.25	.13	.08
171	Chris Chambliss	.25	.13	.08
172	John Montague	.25	.13	.08
173	Ron Jackson	.25	.13	.08
174	Jim Palmer	2.00	1.00	.60
175	Willie Upshaw	.75	.40	.25
176	Tug McGraw	.25	.13	.08
177	Bill Buckner	.25	.13	.08
178	Doug Rau	.25	.13	.08
179	Andre Dawson	3.50	1.75	1.00
180	Jim Wright	.25	.13	.08
181	Garry Templeton	.25	.13	.08
182	Bill Bonham	.25	.13	.08
183	Lee Mazzilli	.25	.13	.08
184	Alan Trammell	2.00	1.00	.60
185	Amos Otis	.25	.13	.08
186	Tom Dixon	.25	.13	.08
187	Mike Cubbage	.25	.13	.08
188	Sparky Lyle	.25	.13	.08
189	Juan Bernhardt	.25	.13	.08
190	Bump Wills	.25	.13	.08
191	Dave Kingman	.25	.13	.08
192	Lamar Johnson	.25	.13	.08
193	Lance Rautzhan	.25	.13	.08
194	Ed Herrmann	.25	.13	.08
195	Bill Campbell	.25	.13	.08
196	Gorman Thomas	.25	.13	.08
197	Paul Moskau	.25	.13	.08
198	Dale Murray	.25	.13	.08
199	John Mayberry	.25	.13	.08
200	Phil Garner	.25	.13	.08
201	Dan Ford	.25	.13	.08
202	Gary Thomasson	.25	.13	.08
203	Rollie Fingers	1.50	.70	.45
204	Al Oliver	.25	.13	.08
205	Doug Ault	.25	.13	.08
206	Scott McGregor	.25	.13	.08
207	Dave Cash	.25	.13	.08
208	Bill Plummer	.25	.13	.08
209	Ivan DeJesus	.25	.13	.08
210	Jim Rice	2.00	1.00	.60
211	Ray Knight	.25	.13	.08
212	Paul Hartzell	.25	.13	.08
213	Tim Foli	.25	.13	.08
214	Butch Wynegar	.25	.13	.08
215	Darrell Evans	.25	.13	.08
216	Ken Griffey	.25	.13	.08
217	Doug DeCinces	.25	.13	.08
218	Ruppert Jones	.25	.13	.08
219	Bob Montgomery	.25	.13	.08
220	Rick Manning	.25	.13	.08
221	Chris Speier	.25	.13	.08
222	Bobby Valentine	.25	.13	.08
223	Dave Parker	.25	.13	.08
224	Larry Biittner	.25	.13	.08
225	Ken Clay	.25	.13	.08
226	Gene Tenace	.25	.13	.08
227	Frank White	.25	.13	.08
228	Rusty Staub	.35	.20	.11
229	Lee Lacy	.25	.13	.08
230	Doyle Alexander	.25	.13	.08
231	Bruce Bochte	.25	.13	.08
232	Steve Henderson	.25	.13	.08
233	Jim Lonborg	.25	.13	.08
234	Dave Concepcion	.25	.13	.08
235	Jerry Morales	.25	.13	.08
236	Len Randle	.25	.13	.08
237	Bill Lee	.25	.13	.08
238	Bruce Sutter	1.50	.70	.45
239	Jim Essian	.25	.13	.08
240	Graig Nettles	.25	.13	.08
241	Otto Velez	.25	.13	.08
242	Checklist 126-250	.25	.13	.08
243	Reggie Smith	.25	.13	.08
244	Stan Bahnsen	.25	.13	.08
245	Garry Maddox	.25	.13	.08
246	Joaquin Andujar	.25	.13	.08
247	Dan Driessen	.25	.13	.08
248	Bob Grich	.25	.13	.08
249	Fred Lynn	.25	.13	.08
250	Skip Lockwood	.25	.13	.08
251	Craig Reynolds	.25	.13	.08
252	Willie Horton	.25	.13	.08
253	Rick Waits	.25	.13	.08

254	Bucky Dent	.25	.13	.08
255	Bob Knepper	.25	.13	.08
256	Miguel Dilone	.25	.13	.08
257	Bob Owchinko	.25	.13	.08
258	Al Cowens	.25	.13	.08
259	Bob Bailor	.25	.13	.08
260	Larry Christenson	.25	.13	.08
261	Tony Perez	1.50	.70	.45
262	Blue Jays Team	.25	.13	.08
263	Glenn Abbott	.25	.13	.08
264	Ron Guidry	.50	.25	.15
265	Ed Kranepool	.25	.13	.08
266	Charlie Hough	.25	.13	.08
267	Ted Simmons	.25	.13	.08
268	Jack Clark	.25	.13	.08
269	Enos Cabell	.25	.13	.08
270	Gary Carter	6.00	3.00	1.75
271	Sam Ewing	.25	.13	.08
272	Tom Burgmeier	.25	.13	.08
273	Freddie Patek	.25	.13	.08
274	Frank Tanana	.25	.13	.08
275	Leroy Stanton	.25	.13	.08
276	Ken Forsch	.25	.13	.08
277	Ellis Valentine	.25	.13	.08
278	Greg Luzinski	.25	.13	.08
279	Rick Bosetti	.25	.13	.08
280	John Stearns	.25	.13	.08
281	Enrique Romo	.25	.13	.08
282	Bob Bailey	.25	.13	.08
283	Sal Bando	.25	.13	.08
284	Matt Keough	.25	.13	.08
285	Biff Pocoroba	.25	.13	.08
286	Mike Lum	.25	.13	.08
287	Jay Johnstone	.25	.13	.08
288	John Montefusco	.25	.13	.08
289	Ed Ott	.25	.13	.08
290	Dusty Baker	.25	.13	.08
291	Rico Carty	.25	.13	.08
292	Nino Espinosa	.25	.13	.08
293	Rich Hebner	.25	.13	.08
294	Cesar Cedeno	.25	.13	.08
295	Darrell Porter	.25	.13	.08
296	Rod Gilbreath	.25	.13	.08
297	Jim Kern	.25	.13	.08
298	Claudell Washington	.25	.13	.08
299	Luis Tiant	.25	.13	.08
300	Mike Parrott	.25	.13	.08
301	Pete Broberg	.25	.13	.08
302	Greg Gross	.25	.13	.08
303	Darold Knowles	.25	.13	.08
304	Paul Blair	.25	.13	.08
305	Julio Cruz	.25	.13	.08
306	Hal McRae	.25	.13	.08
307	Ken Reitz	.25	.13	.08
308	Tom Murphy	.25	.13	.08
309	Terry Whitfield	.25	.13	.08
310	J.R. Richard	.25	.13	.08
311	Mike Hargrove	.25	.13	.08
312	Rick Dempsey	.25	.13	.08
313	Phil Niekro	1.50	.70	.45
314	Bob Stanley	.25	.13	.08
315	Jim Spencer	.25	.13	.08
316	George Foster	.25	.13	.08
317	Dave LaRoche	.25	.13	.08
318	Rudy May	.25	.13	.08
319	Jeff Newman	.25	.13	.08
320	Rick Monday	.25	.13	.08
321	Omar Moreno	.25	.13	.08
322	Dave McKay	.25	.13	.08
323	Mike Schmidt	6.00	3.00	1.75
324	Ken Singleton	.25	.13	.08
325	Jerry Remy	.25	.13	.08
326	Bert Campaneris	.25	.13	.08
327	Pat Zachry	.25	.13	.08
328	Larry Herndon	.25	.13	.08
329	Mark Fidrych	.25	.13	.08
330	Del Unser	.25	.13	.08
331	Gene Garber	.25	.13	.08
332	Bake McBride	.25	.13	.08
333	Jorge Orta	.25	.13	.08
334	Don Kirkwood	.25	.13	.08
335	Don Baylor	.25	.13	.08
336	Bill Robinson	.25	.13	.08
337	Manny Trillo	.25	.13	.08
338	Eddie Murray	3.00	1.50	.90
339	Tom Hausman	.25	.13	.08
340	George Scott	.25	.13	.08
341	Rick Sweet	.25	.13	.08
342	Lou Piniella	.25	.13	.08
343	Pete Rose	15.00	7.50	4.50
344	Stan Papi	.25	.13	.08
345	Jerry Koosman	.25	.13	.08
346	Hosken Powell	.25	.13	.08
347	George Medich	.25	.13	.08
348	Ron LeFlore	.25	.13	.08
349	Expos Team	.75	.40	.25
350	Lou Brock	2.00	1.00	.60
351	Bill North	.25	.13	.08

352	Jim Hunter	1.50	.70	.45
353	Checklist 251-374	.25	.13	.08
354	Ed Halicki	.25	.13	.08
355	Tom Hutton	.25	.13	.08
356	Mike Caldwell	.25	.13	.08
357	Larry Parrish	.25	.13	.08
358	Geoff Zahn	.25	.13	.08
359	Derrel Thomas	.25	.13	.08
360	Carlton Fisk	2.00	1.00	.60
361	John Henry Johnson	.25	.13	.08
362	Dave Chalk	.25	.13	.08
363	Dan Meyer	.25	.13	.08
364	Sixto Lezcano	.25	.13	.08
365	Rennie Stennett	.25	.13	.08
366	Mike Willis	.25	.13	.08
367	Buddy Bell	.25	.13	.08
368	Mickey Stanley	.25	.13	.08
369	Dave Rader	.25	.13	.08
370	Burt Hooton	.25	.13	.08
371	Keith Hernandez	.25	.13	.08
372	Bill Stein	.25	.13	.08
373	Hal Dues	.25	.13	.08
374	Reggie Jackson	3.00	1.50	.90

1980 O-Pee-Chee

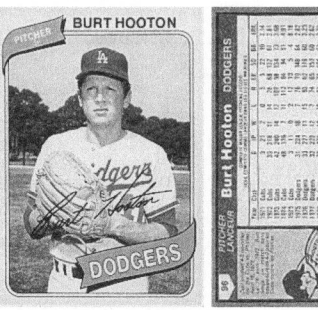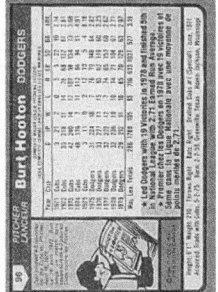

The 1980 Canadian-issued O-Pee-Chee set was again complete at 374 cards, which measure 2-1/2" x 3-1/2" and share the same design as the 1980 Topps set. The OPC cards are printed on a white stock, rather than the traditional gray stock used by Topps, and their backs are written in both French and English. Some of the cards include an extra line on the front indicating a new team designation.

		NM	E	VG
Complete Set (374):		110.00	55.00	32.50
Common Player:		.15	.08	.05
Wax Pack (10):		10.00		
Wax Box (36):		290.00		

1	Craig Swan	.15	.08	.05
2	Denny Martinez	.15	.08	.05
3	Dave Cash	.15	.08	.05
4	Bruce Sutter	1.50	.70	.45
5	Ron Jackson	.15	.08	.05
6	Balor Moore	.15	.08	.05
7	Dan Ford	.15	.08	.05
8	Pat Putnam	.15	.08	.05
9	Derrel Thomas	.15	.08	.05
10	Jim Slaton	.15	.08	.05
11	Lee Mazzilli	.15	.08	.05
12	Del Unser	.15	.08	.05
13	Mark Wagner	.15	.08	.05
14	Vida Blue	.15	.08	.05
15	Jay Johnstone	.15	.08	.05
16	Julio Cruz	.15	.08	.05
17	Tony Scott	.15	.08	.05
18	Jeff Newman	.15	.08	.05
19	Luis Tiant	.15	.08	.05
20	Carlton Fisk	1.50	.70	.45
21	Dave Palmer	.15	.08	.05
22	Bombo Rivera	.15	.08	.05
23	Bill Fahey	.15	.08	.05
24	Frank White	.15	.08	.05
25	Rico Carty	.15	.08	.05
26	Bill Bonham	.15	.08	.05
27	Rick Miller	.15	.08	.05
28	J.R. Richard	.15	.08	.05
29	Joe Ferguson	.15	.08	.05
30	Bill Madlock	.15	.08	.05
31	Pete Vuckovich	.15	.08	.05
32	Doug Flynn	.15	.08	.05
33	Bucky Dent	.15	.08	.05
34	Mike Ivie	.15	.08	.05
35	Bob Stanley	.15	.08	.05
36	Al Bumbry	.15	.08	.05
37	Gary Carter	5.00	2.50	1.50
38	John Milner	.15	.08	.05
39	Sid Monge	.15	.08	.05
40	Bill Russell	.15	.08	.05
41	John Stearns	.15	.08	.05
42	Dave Stieb	1.25	.60	.40

43	Ruppert Jones	.15	.08	.05
44	Bob Owchinko	.15	.08	.05
45	Ron LeFlore	.15	.08	.05
46	Ted Sizemore	.15	.08	.05
47	Ted Simmons	.15	.08	.05
48	Pepe Frias	.15	.08	.05
49	Ken Landreaux	.15	.08	.05
50	Manny Trillo	.15	.08	.05
51	Rick Dempsey	.15	.08	.05
52	Cecil Cooper	.15	.08	.05
53	Bill Lee	.15	.08	.05
54	Victor Cruz	.15	.08	.05
55	Johnny Bench	1.50	.70	.45
56	Rich Dauer	.15	.08	.05
57	Frank Tanana	.15	.08	.05
58	Francisco Barrios	.15	.08	.05
59	Bob Horner	.30	.15	.09
60	Fred Lynn	.15	.08	.05
61	Bob Knepper	.15	.08	.05
62	Sparky Lyle	.15	.08	.05
63	Larry Cox	.15	.08	.05
64	Dock Ellis	.15	.08	.05
65	Phil Garner	.15	.08	.05
66	Greg Luzinski	.15	.08	.05
67	Checklist 1-125	.25	.13	.08
68	Dave Lemanczyk	.15	.08	.05
69	Tony Perez	1.50	.70	.45
70	Gary Thomasson	.15	.08	.05
71	Craig Reynolds	.15	.08	.05
72	Amos Otis	.15	.08	.05
73	Biff Pocoroba	.15	.08	.05
74	Matt Keough	.15	.08	.05
75	Bill Buckner	.15	.08	.05
76	John Castino	.15	.08	.05
77	Rich Gossage	.25	.13	.08
78	Gary Alexander	.15	.08	.05
79	Phil Huffman	.15	.08	.05
80	Bruce Bochte	.15	.08	.05
81	Darrell Evans	.15	.08	.05
82	Terry Puhl	.15	.08	.05
83	Jason Thompson	.15	.08	.05
84	Lary Sorenson	.15	.08	.05
85	Jerry Remy	.15	.08	.05
86	Tony Brizzolara	.15	.08	.05
87	Willie Wilson	.15	.08	.05
88	Eddie Murray	3.00	1.50	.90
89	Larry Christenson	.15	.08	.05
90	Bob Randall	.15	.08	.05
91	Greg Pryor	.15	.08	.05
92	Glenn Abbott	.15	.08	.05
93	Jack Clark	.15	.08	.05
94	Rick Waits	.15	.08	.05
95	Luis Gomez	.15	.08	.05
96	Burt Hooton	.15	.08	.05
97	John Henry Johnson	.15	.08	.05
98	Ray Knight	.15	.08	.05
99	Rick Reuschel	.15	.08	.05
100	Champ Summers	.15	.08	.05
101	Ron Davis	.15	.08	.05
102	Warren Cromartie	.15	.08	.05
103	Ken Reitz	.15	.08	.05
104	Hal McRae	.15	.08	.05
105	Alan Ashby	.15	.08	.05
106	Kevin Kobel	.15	.08	.05
107	Buddy Bell	.15	.08	.05
108	Dave Goltz	.15	.08	.05
109	John Montefusco	.15	.08	.05
110	Lance Parrish	.65	.35	.20
111	Mike LaCoss	.15	.08	.05
112	Jim Rice	2.00	1.00	.60
113	Steve Carlton	1.50	.70	.45
114	Sixto Lezcano	.15	.08	.05
115	Ed Halicki	.15	.08	.05
116	Jose Morales	.15	.08	.05
117	Dave Concepcion	.15	.08	.05
118	Joe Cannon	.15	.08	.05
119	Willie Montanez	.15	.08	.05
120	Lou Piniella	.15	.08	.05
121	Bill Stein	.15	.08	.05
122	Dave Winfield	3.00	1.50	.90
123	Alan Trammell	.30	.15	.09
124	Andre Dawson	4.00	2.00	1.25
125	Marc Hill	.15	.08	.05
126	Don Aase	.15	.08	.05
127	Dave Kingman	.15	.08	.05
128	Checklist 126-250	.25	.13	.08
129	Dennis Lamp	.15	.08	.05
130	Phil Niekro	1.00	.50	.30
131	Tim Foli	.15	.08	.05
132	Jim Clancy	.15	.08	.05
133	Bill Atkinson	.15	.08	.05
134	Paul Dade	.15	.08	.05
135	Dusty Baker	.15	.08	.05
136	Al Oliver	.15	.08	.05
137	Dave Chalk	.15	.08	.05
138	Bill Robinson	.15	.08	.05
139	Robin Yount	1.50	.70	.45
140	Dan Schatzeder	.15	.08	.05
141	Mike Schmidt	5.00	2.50	1.50
142	Ralph Garr	.15	.08	.05
143	Dale Murphy	1.00	.50	.30
144	Jerry Koosman	.15	.08	.05
145	Tom Veryzer	.15	.08	.05
146	Rick Bosetti	.15	.08	.05
147	Jim Spencer	.15	.08	.05
148	Gaylord Perry	1.00	.50	.30
149	Paul Blair	.15	.08	.05
150	Don Baylor	.15	.08	.05
151	Dave Rozema	.15	.08	.05
152	Steve Garvey	.50	.25	.15
153	Elias Sosa	.15	.08	.05
154	Larry Gura	.15	.08	.05
155	Tim Johnson	.15	.08	.05
156	Steve Henderson	.15	.08	.05
157	Ron Guidry	.20	.10	.06
158	Mike Edwards	.15	.08	.05
159	Butch Wynegar	.15	.08	.05
160	Randy Jones	.15	.08	.05
161	Denny Walling	.15	.08	.05
162	Mike Hargrove	.15	.08	.05
163	Dave Parker	.15	.08	.05
164	Roger Metzger	.15	.08	.05
165	Johnny Grubb	.15	.08	.05
166	Steve Kemp	.15	.08	.05
167	Bob Lacey	.15	.08	.05
168	Chris Speier	.15	.08	.05
169	Dennis Eckersley	1.00	.50	.30
170	Keith Hernandez	.15	.08	.05
171	Claudell Washington	.15	.08	.05
172	Tom Underwood	.15	.08	.05
173	Dan Driessen	.15	.08	.05
174	Al Cowens	.15	.08	.05
175	Rich Hebner	.15	.08	.05
176	Willie McCovey	1.50	.70	.45
177	Carney Lansford	.15	.08	.05
178	Ken Singleton	.15	.08	.05
179	Jim Essian	.15	.08	.05
180	Mike Vail	.15	.08	.05
181	Randy Lerch	.15	.08	.05
182	Larry Parrish	.15	.08	.05
183	Checklist 251-374	.25	.13	.08
184	George Hendrick	.15	.08	.05
185	Bob Davis	.15	.08	.05
186	Gary Matthews	.15	.08	.05
187	Lou Whitaker	.15	.08	.05
188	Darrell Porter	.15	.08	.05
189	Wayne Gross	.15	.08	.05
190	Bobby Murcer	.15	.08	.05
191	Willie Aikens	.15	.08	.05
192	Jim Kern	.15	.08	.05
193	Cesar Cedeno	.15	.08	.05
194	Joel Youngblood	.15	.08	.05
195	Ross Grimsley	.15	.08	.05
196	Jerry Mumphrey	.15	.08	.05
197	Kevin Bell	.15	.08	.05
198	Garry Maddox	.15	.08	.05
199	Dave Freisleben	.15	.08	.05
200	Ed Ott	.15	.08	.05
201	Enos Cabell	.15	.08	.05
202	Pete LaCock	.15	.08	.05
203	Fergie Jenkins	1.50	.70	.45
204	Milt Wilcox	.15	.08	.05
205	Ozzie Smith	5.00	2.50	1.50
206	Ellis Valentine	.15	.08	.05
207	Dan Meyer	.15	.08	.05
208	Barry Foote	.15	.08	.05
209	George Foster	.15	.08	.05
210	Dwight Evans	.15	.08	.05
211	Paul Molitor	5.00	2.50	1.50
212	Tony Solaita	.15	.08	.05
213	Bill North	.15	.08	.05
214	Paul Splittorff	.15	.08	.05
215	Bobby Bonds	.15	.08	.05
216	Butch Hobson	.15	.08	.05
217	Mark Belanger	.15	.08	.05
218	Grant Jackson	.15	.08	.05
219	Tom Hutton	.15	.08	.05
220	Pat Zachry	.15	.08	.05
221	Duane Kuiper	.15	.08	.05
222	Larry Hisle	.15	.08	.05
223	Mike Krukow	.15	.08	.05
224	Johnnie LeMaster	.15	.08	.05
225	Billy Almon	.15	.08	.05
226	Joe Niekro	.15	.08	.05
227	Dave Revering	.15	.08	.05
228	Don Sutton	1.00	.50	.30
229	John Hiller	.15	.08	.05
230	Alvis Woods	.15	.08	.05
231	Mark Fidrych	.15	.08	.05
232	Duffy Dyer	.15	.08	.05
233	Nino Espinosa	.15	.08	.05
234	Doug Bair	.15	.08	.05
235	George Brett	5.00	2.50	1.50
236	Mike Torrez	.15	.08	.05
237	Frank Taveras	.15	.08	.05
238	Bert Blyleven	1.50	.75	.45
239	Willie Randolph	.15	.08	.05
240	Mike Sadek	.15	.08	.05
241	Jerry Royster	.15	.08	.05
242	John Denny	.15	.08	.05
243	Rick Monday	.15	.08	.05
244	Jesse Jefferson	.15	.08	.05
245	Aurelio Rodriguez	.15	.08	.05
246	Bob Boone	.15	.08	.05
247	Cesar Geronimo	.15	.08	.05
248	Bob Shirley	.15	.08	.05
249	Expos Team	.25	.13	.08
250	Bob Watson	.15	.08	.05
251	Mickey Rivers	.15	.08	.05
252	Mike Tyson	.15	.08	.05
253	Wayne Nordhagen	.15	.08	.05
254	Roy Howell	.15	.08	.05
255	Lee May	.15	.08	.05
256	Jerry Martin	.15	.08	.05
257	Bake McBride	.15	.08	.05
258	Silvio Martinez	.15	.08	.05
259	Jim Mason	.15	.08	.05
260	Tom Seaver	2.00	1.00	.60
261	Rick Wortham	.15	.08	.05
262	Mike Cubbage	.15	.08	.05
263	Gene Garber	.15	.08	.05
264	Bert Campaneris	.15	.08	.05
265	Tom Buskey	.15	.08	.05
266	Leon Roberts	.15	.08	.05
267	Ron Cey	.15	.08	.05
268	Steve Ontiveros	.15	.08	.05
269	Mike Caldwell	.15	.08	.05
270	Nelson Norman	.15	.08	.05
271	Steve Rogers	.15	.08	.05
272	Jim Morrison	.15	.08	.05
273	Clint Hurdle	.15	.08	.05
274	Dale Murray	.15	.08	.05
275	Jim Barr	.15	.08	.05
276	Jim Sundberg	.15	.08	.05
277	Willie Horton	.15	.08	.05
278	Andre Thornton	.15	.08	.05
279	Bob Forsch	.15	.08	.05
280	Joe Strain	.15	.08	.05
281	Rudy May	.15	.08	.05
282	Pete Rose	9.00	4.50	2.75
283	Jeff Burroughs	.15	.08	.05
284	Rick Langford	.15	.08	.05
285	Ken Griffey	.15	.08	.05
286	Bill Nahorodny	.15	.08	.05
287	Art Howe	.15	.08	.05
288	Ed Figueroa	.15	.08	.05
289	Joe Rudi	.15	.08	.05
290	Alfredo Griffin	.15	.08	.05
291	Dave Lopes	.15	.08	.05
292	Rick Manning	.15	.08	.05
293	Dennis Leonard	.15	.08	.05
294	Bud Harrelson	.15	.08	.05
295	Skip Lockwood	.15	.08	.05
296	Roy Smalley	.15	.08	.05
297	Kent Tekulve	.15	.08	.05
298	Scot Thompson	.15	.08	.05
299	Ken Kravec	.15	.08	.05
300	Blue Jays Team	.25	.13	.08
301	Scott Sanderson	.15	.08	.05
302	Charlie Moore	.15	.08	.05
303	Nolan Ryan	20.00	10.00	6.00
304	Bob Bailor	.15	.08	.05
305	Bob Stinson	.15	.08	.05
306	Al Hrabosky	.15	.08	.05
307	Mitchell Page	.15	.08	.05
308	Garry Templeton	.15	.08	.05
309	Chet Lemon	.15	.08	.05
310	Jim Palmer	1.50	.70	.45
311	Rick Cerone	.15	.08	.05
312	Jon Matlack	.15	.08	.05
313	Don Money	.15	.08	.05
314	Reggie Jackson	5.00	2.50	1.50
315	Brian Downing	.15	.08	.05
316	Woodie Fryman	.15	.08	.05
317	Alan Bannister	.15	.08	.05
318	Ron Reed	.15	.08	.05
319	Willie Stargell	1.50	.70	.45
320	Jerry Garvin	.15	.08	.05
321	Cliff Johnson	.15	.08	.05
322	Doug DeCinces	.15	.08	.05
323	Gene Richards	.15	.08	.05
324	Joaquin Andujar	.15	.08	.05
325	Richie Zisk	.15	.08	.05
326	Bob Grich	.15	.08	.05
327	Gorman Thomas	.15	.08	.05
328	Chris Chambliss	.15	.08	.05
329	Blue Jays Future Stars(Butch Edge, Pat Kelly, Ted Wilborn)	.25	.13	.08
330	Larry Bowa	.15	.08	.05
331	Barry Bonnell	.15	.08	.05
332	John Candelaria	.15	.08	.05
333	Toby Harrah	.15	.08	.05
334	Larry Biittner	.15	.08	.05

335	Mike Flanagan	.15	.08	.05
336	Ed Kranepool	.15	.08	.05
337	Ken Forsch	.15	.08	.05
338	John Mayberry	.15	.08	.05
339	Rick Burleson	.15	.08	.05
340	Milt May	.15	.08	.05
341	Roy White	.15	.08	.05
342	Joe Morgan	1.50	.70	.45
343	Rollie Fingers	1.00	.50	.30
344	Mario Mendoza	.15	.08	.05
345	Stan Bahnsen	.15	.08	.05
346	Tug McGraw	.15	.08	.05
347	Rusty Staub	.15	.08	.05
348	Tommy John	.15	.08	.05
349	Ivan DeJesus	.15	.08	.05
350	Reggie Smith	.15	.08	.05
351	Expos Future Stars(Tony Bernazard, Randy Miller, John Tamargo)	.40	.20	.12
352	Floyd Bannister	.15	.08	.05
353	Rod Carew	1.50	.70	.45
354	Otto Velez	.15	.08	.05
355	Gene Tenace	.15	.08	.05
356	Freddie Patek	.15	.08	.05
357	Elliott Maddox	.15	.08	.05
358	Pat Underwood	.15	.08	.05
359	Graig Nettles	.15	.08	.05
360	Rodney Scott	.15	.08	.05
361	Terry Whitfield	.15	.08	.05
362	Fred Norman	.15	.08	.05
363	Sal Bando	.15	.08	.05
364	Greg Gross	.15	.08	.05
365	Carl Yastrzemski	2.00	1.00	.60
366	Paul Hartzell	.15	.08	.05
367	Jose Cruz	.15	.08	.05
368	Shane Rawley	.15	.08	.05
369	Jerry White	.15	.08	.05
370	Rick Wise	.15	.08	.05
371	Steve Yeager	.15	.08	.05
372	Omar Moreno	.15	.08	.05
373	Bump Wills	.15	.08	.05
374	Craig Kusick	.15	.08	.05

1979 Open Pantry/Lake to Lake MACC

To benefit Milwaukee Athletes Against Childhood Cancer the Open Pantry convenience stores in Wisconsin teamed with Lake to Lake Dairy to produce this card set. Red, white and black fronts of the 5" x 6" cards have a player photo, facsimile autograph and team logo. Backs are printed in red with a message from the player about the MACC fund. Besides members of the Milwaukee Brewers listed here, the set features Green Bay Packers and Milwaukee Bucks players. The unnumbered cards are checklisted here alphabetically.

	NM	E	VG
Complete Set (12):	10.00	5.00	3.00
Common (Baseball) Player:	2.00	1.00	.60
(1) Jerry Augustine	3.00	1.50	.90
(2) Sal Bando	3.00	1.50	.90
(3) Cecil Cooper	4.00	2.00	1.25
(4) Larry Hisle	3.00	1.50	.90
(5) Lary Sorensen	3.00	1.50	.90

1910 "Orange Borders"

Known in the hobby as "Orange Borders," these 1-1/2" x 2-7/16" cards were issued in 1910 and were printed on candy boxes that displayed the words "American Sports and Candy and Jewelry." The end flaps indicate the producers as the "Geo. Davis Co., Inc." and the "P.R. Warren Co., Warrenville Lowell, Mass." According to the box, the complete set includes "144 leading ballplayers," but to date just over two dozen different subjects are known. When found today, these black and white photos are often surrounded by orange borders which, in reality, were part of the candy box. One of the team cards was found on each box, with a player card on the other side. Similar in format to the "Baseball Bats" cards, Orange Borders have player names which are hand-lettered, rather than typeset. Gaps have been left in the assigned numbering to accomodate future additions to the checklist.

		NM	E	VG
Common Player:		725.00	375.00	220.00
(1)	Jack Berry	725.00	375.00	220.00
(2)	Bill Bergen	725.00	375.00	220.00
(3)	Bill Bradley	725.00	375.00	220.00
(4)	Bill Carrigan	725.00	375.00	220.00
(5)	Hal Chase	900.00	450.00	240.00
(6)	Fred Clark (Clarke)	1,100	575.00	300.00
(7)	Ty Cobb	9,000	4,500	2,400
(8)	Sam Crawford	900.00	450.00	240.00
(9)	Lou Criger	725.00	375.00	220.00
(10)	Harry Davis	725.00	375.00	220.00
(11)	Art Devlin	725.00	375.00	220.00
(12)	Mickey Doolan	725.00	375.00	220.00
(13)	Larry Doyle	725.00	375.00	220.00
(14)	George Gibson	725.00	375.00	220.00
(15)	Addie Joss	1,200	600.00	300.00
(16)	Nap Lajoie	1,100	575.00	300.00
(17)	Frank LaPorte	725.00	375.00	220.00
(18)	Harry Lord	725.00	375.00	220.00
(19)	Christy Mathewson	4,100	2,100	1,250
(20)	Amby McConnell	725.00	375.00	220.00
(21)	John McGraw	1,100	575.00	300.00
(22)	Dots Miller	725.00	375.00	220.00
(23)	George Mullin	725.00	375.00	220.00
(24)	Harry Niles	725.00	375.00	220.00
(25)	Eddie Plank	1,110	575.00	300.00
(26)	Tris Speaker	1,680	675.00	335.00
(27)	Jake Stahl	725.00	375.00	220.00
(28)	Harry Steinfeldt	725.00	375.00	220.00
(29)	Honus Wagner (Batting)	6,750	3,400	2,000
(30)	Honus Wagner (Portrait)	6,750	3,400	2,000
(31)	Jack Warhop	725.00	375.00	220.00
(32)	American League Champions, 1909 (Detroit)	900.00	450.00	270.00
(33)	National League Champions, 1909 (Pittsburgh)	900.00	450.00	270.00

1976 Orbaker's Discs

One of several regional sponsors of player disc sets in 1976 was the Orbaker's restaurant chain. The discs are 3-3/8" diameter with a black-and-white player portrait photo in the center of the baseball design. A line of red stars is above, while the left and right panels feature one of several bright colors. Produced by Michael Schecter Associates under license from the Major League Baseball Players Association, the player photos have had uniform and cap logos removed. Backs are printed in red and purple. The unnumbered checklist here is presented in alphabetical order.

	NM	E	VG
Complete Set (70):	30.00	15.00	9.00
Common Player:	1.00	.50	.30
(1) Henry Aaron	10.00	5.00	3.00
(2) Johnny Bench	6.00	3.00	1.75
(3) Vida Blue	1.00	.50	.30
(4) Larry Bowa	1.00	.50	.30
(5) Lou Brock	4.00	2.00	1.25
(6) Jeff Burroughs	1.00	.50	.30
(7) John Candelaria	1.00	.50	.30
(8) Jose Cardenal	1.00	.50	.30
(9) Rod Carew	4.00	2.00	1.25
(10) Steve Carlton	4.00	2.00	1.25

		NM	E	VG
(11)	Dave Cash	1.00	.50	.30
(12)	Cesar Cedeno	1.00	.50	.30
(13)	Ron Cey	1.00	.50	.30
(14)	Carlton Fisk	4.00	2.00	1.25
(15)	Tito Fuentes	1.00	.50	.30
(16)	Steve Garvey	2.00	1.00	.60
(17)	Ken Griffey	1.00	.50	.30
(18)	Don Gullett	1.00	.50	.30
(19)	Willie Horton	1.00	.50	.30
(20)	Al Hrabosky	1.00	.50	.30
(21)	Catfish Hunter	3.00	1.50	.90
(22)	Reggie Jackson (A's)	9.00	4.50	2.75
(23)	Randy Jones	1.00	.50	.30
(24)	Jim Kaat	1.00	.50	.30
(25)	Don Kessinger	1.00	.50	.30
(26)	Dave Kingman	1.00	.50	.30
(27)	Jerry Koosman	1.00	.50	.30
(28)	Mickey Lolich	1.00	.50	.30
(29)	Greg Luzinski	1.00	.50	.30
(30)	Fred Lynn	1.00	.50	.30
(31)	Bill Madlock	1.00	.50	.30
(32)	Carlos May	1.00	.50	.30
(33)	John Mayberry	1.00	.50	.30
(34)	Bake McBride	1.00	.50	.30
(35)	Doc Medich	1.00	.50	.30
(36)	Andy Messersmith	1.00	.50	.30
(37)	Rick Monday	1.00	.50	.30
(38)	John Montefusco	1.00	.50	.30
(39)	Jerry Morales	1.00	.50	.30
(40)	Joe Morgan	4.00	2.00	1.25
(41)	Thurman Munson	3.00	1.50	.90
(42)	Bobby Murcer	1.00	.50	.30
(43)	Al Oliver	1.00	.50	.30
(44)	Jim Palmer	4.00	2.00	1.25
(45)	Dave Parker	1.00	.50	.30
(46)	Tony Perez	3.00	1.50	.90
(47)	Jerry Reuss	1.00	.50	.30
(48)	Brooks Robinson	6.00	3.00	1.75
(49)	Frank Robinson	6.00	3.00	1.75
(50)	Steve Rogers	1.00	.50	.30
(51)	Pete Rose	12.50	6.25	3.75
(52)	Nolan Ryan	12.50	6.25	3.75
(53)	Manny Sanguillen	1.00	.50	.30
(54)	Mike Schmidt	9.00	4.50	2.75
(55)	Tom Seaver	6.00	3.00	1.75
(56)	Ted Simmons	1.00	.50	.30
(57)	Reggie Smith	1.00	.50	.30
(58)	Willie Stargell	4.00	2.00	1.25
(59)	Rusty Staub	1.50	.70	.45
(60)	Rennie Stennett	1.00	.50	.30
(61)	Don Sutton	3.00	1.50	.90
(62)	Andy Thornton	1.00	.50	.30
(63)	Luis Tiant	1.00	.50	.30
(64)	Joe Torre	1.00	.50	.30
(65)	Mike Tyson	1.00	.50	.30
(66)	Bob Watson	1.00	.50	.30
(67)	Wilbur Wood	1.00	.50	.30
(68)	Jimmy Wynn	1.00	.50	.30
(69)	Carl Yastrzemski	6.00	3.00	1.75
(70)	Richie Zisk	1.00	.50	.30

1932 Orbit Gum Pins - Numbered (PR2)

Issued circa 1932, this skip-numbered set of small (13/16" diameter) pins was produced by Orbit Gum and carries the Amerian Card Catalog designation of PR2. A color player lithograph is set against a green background with the player's name and team printed on a strip of yellow below. The pin number is at the very bottom; pins after #40 are skip-numbered.

		NM	E	VG
Complete Set (53):		2,500	1,250	750.00
Common Player:		30.00	15.00	9.00
1	Ivy Andrews	30.00	15.00	9.00
2	Carl Reynolds	30.00	15.00	9.00
3	Riggs Stephenson	30.00	15.00	9.00
4	Lon Warneke	30.00	15.00	9.00
5	Frank Grube	30.00	15.00	9.00
6	"Kiki" Cuyler	60.00	30.00	18.00
7	Marty McManus	30.00	15.00	9.00
8	Lefty Clark	30.00	15.00	9.00
9	George Blaeholder	30.00	15.00	9.00
10	Willie Kamm	30.00	15.00	9.00
11	Jimmy Dykes	30.00	15.00	9.00

		NM	E	VG
12	Earl Averill	60.00	30.00	18.00
13	Pat Malone	30.00	15.00	9.00
14	Dizzy Dean	110.00	55.00	35.00
15	Dick Bartell	30.00	15.00	9.00
16	Guy Bush	30.00	15.00	9.00
17	Bud Tinning	30.00	15.00	9.00
18	Jimmy Foxx	150.00	75.00	45.00
19	Mule Haas	30.00	15.00	9.00
20	Lew Fonseca	30.00	15.00	9.00
21	Pepper Martin	40.00	20.00	12.00
22	Phil Collins	30.00	15.00	9.00
23	Bill Cissell	30.00	15.00	9.00
24	Bump Hadley	30.00	15.00	9.00
25	Smead Jolley	30.00	15.00	9.00
26	Burleigh Grimes	60.00	30.00	18.00
27	Dale Alexander	30.00	15.00	9.00
28	Mickey Cochrane	60.00	30.00	18.00
29	Mel Harder	30.00	15.00	9.00
30	Mark Koenig	30.00	15.00	9.00
31a	Lefty O'Doul (Dodgers)	50.00	25.00	15.00
31b	Lefty O'Doul (Giants)	90.00	45.00	27.00
32a	Woody English (With bat.)	30.00	15.00	9.00
32b	Woody English (Without bat.)	80.00	40.00	24.00
33a	Billy Jurges (With bat.)	30.00	15.00	9.00
33b	Billy Jurges (Without bat.)	80.00	40.00	24.00
34	Bruce Campbell	30.00	15.00	9.00
35	Joe Vosmik	30.00	15.00	9.00
36	Dick Porter	30.00	15.00	9.00
37	Charlie Grimm	30.00	15.00	9.00
38	George Earnshaw	30.00	15.00	9.00
39	Al Simmons	60.00	30.00	18.00
40	Red Lucas	30.00	15.00	9.00
51	Wally Berger	30.00	15.00	9.00
55	Jim Levey	30.00	15.00	9.00
58	Ernie Lombardi	60.00	30.00	18.00
64	Jack Burns	30.00	15.00	9.00
67	Billy Herman	60.00	30.00	18.00
72	Bill Hallahan	30.00	15.00	9.00
92	Don Brennan	30.00	15.00	9.00
96	Sam Byrd	30.00	15.00	9.00
99	Ben Chapman	30.00	15.00	9.00
103	John Allen	30.00	15.00	9.00
107	Tony Lazzeri	60.00	30.00	18.00
111	Earl Combs (Earle)	60.00	30.00	18.00
116	Joe Sewell	60.00	30.00	18.00
120	Vernon Gomez	60.00	30.00	18.00

1932 Orbit Gum Pins - Unnumbered (PR3)

This set, issued by Orbit Gum circa 1932, has the American Card Catalog designation PR3. The pins are identical to the PR2 set, except they are unnumbered.

		NM	E	VG
Complete Set (60):		3,750	1,850	1,100
Common Player:		60.00	30.00	18.00
(1)	Dale Alexander	60.00	30.00	18.00
(2)	Ivy Andrews	60.00	30.00	18.00
(3)	Earl Averill	100.00	50.00	30.00
(4)	Dick Bartell	60.00	30.00	18.00
(5)	Wally Berger	60.00	30.00	18.00
(6)	George Blaeholder	60.00	30.00	18.00
(7)	Jack Burns	60.00	30.00	18.00
(8)	Guy Bush	60.00	30.00	18.00
(9)	Bruce Campbell	60.00	30.00	18.00
(10)	Bill Cissell	60.00	30.00	18.00
(11)	Lefty Clark	60.00	30.00	18.00
(12)	Mickey Cochrane	100.00	50.00	30.00
(13)	Phil Collins	60.00	30.00	18.00
(14)	"Kiki" Cuyler	100.00	50.00	30.00
(15)	Dizzy Dean	175.00	87.00	52.00
(16)	Jimmy Dykes	60.00	30.00	18.00
(17)	George Earnshaw	60.00	30.00	18.00
(18)	Woody English	60.00	30.00	18.00
(19)	Lew Fonseca	60.00	30.00	18.00
(20)	Jimmy (Jimmie) Foxx	175.00	87.00	52.00
(21)	Burleigh Grimes	100.00	50.00	30.00
(22)	Charlie Grimm	60.00	30.00	18.00
(23)	Lefty Grove	100.00	50.00	30.00
(24)	Frank Grube	60.00	30.00	18.00
(25)	Mule Haas	60.00	30.00	18.00
(26)	Bump Hadley	60.00	30.00	18.00
(27)	Chick Hafey	100.00	50.00	30.00
(28)	Jesse Haines	100.00	50.00	30.00

		NM	E	VG
(29)	Bill Hallahan	60.00	30.00	18.00
(30)	Mel Harder	60.00	30.00	18.00
(31)	Gabby Hartnett	100.00	50.00	30.00
(32)	Babe Herman	65.00	32.00	19.50
(33)	Billy Herman	100.00	50.00	30.00
(34)	Rogers Hornsby	135.00	67.00	40.00
(35)	Roy Johnson	60.00	30.00	18.00
(36)	Smead Jolley	60.00	30.00	18.00
(37)	Billy Jurges	60.00	30.00	18.00
(38)	Willie Kamm	60.00	30.00	18.00
(39)	Mark Koenig	60.00	30.00	18.00
(40)	Jim Levey	60.00	30.00	18.00
(41)	Ernie Lombardi	100.00	50.00	30.00
(42)	Red Lucas	60.00	30.00	18.00
(43)	Ted Lyons	100.00	50.00	30.00
(44)	Connie Mack	100.00	50.00	30.00
(45)	Pat Malone	60.00	30.00	18.00
(46)	Pepper Martin	75.00	37.00	22.00
(47)	Marty McManus	60.00	30.00	18.00
(48)	Lefty O'Doul	80.00	40.00	24.00
(49)	Dick Porter	60.00	30.00	18.00
(50)	Carl Reynolds	60.00	30.00	18.00
(51)	Charlie Root	60.00	30.00	18.00
(52)	Bob Seeds	60.00	30.00	18.00
(53)	Al Simmons	100.00	50.00	30.00
(54)	Riggs Stephenson	60.00	30.00	18.00
(55)	Bud Tinning	60.00	30.00	18.00
(56)	Joe Vosmik	60.00	30.00	18.00
(57)	Rube Walberg	60.00	30.00	18.00
(58)	Paul Waner	100.00	50.00	30.00
(59)	Lon Warneke	60.00	30.00	18.00
(60)	Pinky Whitney	60.00	30.00	18.00

1937-39 Orcajo Cincinnati Reds Postcards (PC786)

Orcajo, a Dayton, Ohio, photo firm, issued a series of Reds player postcards (plus, inexplicably, Joe DiMaggio) from 1937-39. Besides those found with just the issuer's imprint on the back, some or all of the players' cards can be found with the advertising on front of the Val Decker Packing Co., a meat dealer, Metropolitan Clothing Co., and an inset photo of WHIO radio announcer Si Burick (the latter are the 1937 cards and have no Orcajo imprint on back, utilizing different photos than the 1938-39 cards). The 3-1/2" x 5-1/2" cards have glossy black-and-white player poses on front with the player's name overprinted. Backs have standard postcard indicia. A number of spelling errors and several variations exist. The unnumbered cards are checklisted here alphabetically; those with ads for the meat company, men's store or radio station are appropriately noted.

		NM	E	VG
Complete Set (37):		3,775	1,700	945.00
Common Player:		100.00	45.00	25.00
(1)	Wally Berger	100.00	45.00	25.00
(2)	Bongiovanni (First name Nino.)	100.00	45.00	25.00
(3)	Frenchy Bordagaray	100.00	45.00	25.00
(4)	Joe Cascarella, Gene Schott (Val Decker only.)	100.00	45.00	25.00
(5)	Allan Cooke (Allen)(Val Decker only.))	100.00	45.00	25.00
(6)	Harry Craft (Also Val Decker.)	100.00	45.00	25.00
(7)	Kiki Cuyler (WHIO only.)	160.00	72.00	40.00
(8)	Ray Davis	100.00	45.00	25.00
(9)	Virgil Davis (Val Decker only.)	100.00	45.00	25.00
(10)	Paul Derringer (Also Val Decker.)	100.00	45.00	25.00
(11)	Joe DiMaggio	825.00	370.00	205.00
(12a)	Linus Frey (Also Val Decker.) (No right foot, large caption.))	100.00	45.00	25.00

		NM	E	VG
(12b)	Linus Frey (Also Val Decker.) (Right foot shows, small caption.))	100.00	45.00	25.00
(13)	Lee Gamble	100.00	45.00	25.00
(14)	Ivan Goodman (Ival)(Also Val Decker.))	100.00	45.00	25.00
(15)	Hank Gowdy	100.00	45.00	25.00
(16)	Lee Grissom	100.00	45.00	25.00
(17a)	Willard Hershberger (Hershberger, name in white.) (Also Val Decker.))	100.00	45.00	25.00
(17b)	Willard Hershberger (Name in black.)	100.00	45.00	25.00
(18a)	Al Hollingsworth	100.00	45.00	25.00
(18b)	Al Hollingsworth (WHIO)	100.00	45.00	25.00
(18c)	Al Hollingsworth (Val Decker.)	100.00	45.00	25.00
(19)	Hank Johnson	100.00	45.00	25.00
(20)	Edwin Joost	100.00	45.00	25.00
(21a)	Ernie Lombardi (Plain letters.) (Also Val Decker, Metro.))	160.00	72.00	40.00
(21b)	Ernie Lombardi (Fancy letters.) (Also Val Decker, Metro.))	160.00	72.00	40.00
(22)	Frank McCormick (Also Val Decker, Metro.)	100.00	45.00	25.00
(23)	Bill McKecknie (McKechnie)	145.00	65.00	36.00
(24)	Billy Meyers (Myers)(Also Val Decker.))	100.00	45.00	25.00
(25a)	Whitey Moore (Photo actually Bucky Walters.)	100.00	45.00	25.00
(25b)	Whitey Moore (Correct photo.)	100.00	45.00	25.00
(26)	Lew Riggs	100.00	45.00	25.00
(27)	Edd Roush (Val Decker only.)	145.00	65.00	36.00
(28a)	Leo Scarsella (Les)	160.00	72.00	40.00
(28b)	Les Scarcella (WHIO)	100.00	45.00	25.00
(29)	Gene Schott (WHIO)	100.00	45.00	25.00
(30)	Milburn Shoffner	100.00	45.00	25.00
(31)	Junior Thompson	100.00	45.00	25.00
(32a)	Johnny VanderMeer (Throwing)(Also Metro, Val Decker.))	175.00	79.00	44.00
(32b)	Johnny VanderMeer (Fielding)(Also Metro.))	175.00	79.00	44.00
(33)	Bucky Walters	100.00	45.00	25.00
(34)	Bill Werber	100.00	45.00	25.00
(35)	Dick West	100.00	45.00	25.00
(36)	Jimmie Wilson	100.00	45.00	25.00
(37)	Cincinnati Reds composite team card.	100.00	45.00	25.00

1929 Orient Theatre Philadelphia A's

This is one of several theater giveaways of the era capitalizing on the A's consecutive American League Championships of 1929-1931. This series is in a 3-1/2" x 5-5/8" black-and-white format. Fronts have a player photo with his name (in all-capitals) at center. Backs have details of coming attractions at the movie house, generally aimed at youngsters. The extent of the checklist for this set is not yet known.

	NM	EX	VG
Jimmy Dykes	1,000	500.00	300.00

1933 Oriental Theatre

To advertise its movie schedule for the week of June 17-23, as well as a Father's Day prize drawing, the Oriental Theatre (location unknown, possibly Dorchester, Mass., or Chicago) printed its message on the back of a 1929 Kashin Publications (R316) card or cards. The extent to which this overprinting was undertaken is unknown.

	NM	E	VG
Ed "Bing" Miller	125.00	62.50	37.50

1963 Otto Milk

The attributed issue date of this commemorative milk carton is approximate. A 4" x 8" panel on the front of the milk carton has a picture and history of Honus Wagner printed in red and blue. Wagner is the only ballplayer in the milk carton series honoring Western Pennsylvania celebrities.

		NM	E	VG
(1)	Honus Wagner (Complete carton.)	250.00	125.00	75.00
(1)	Honus Wagner (Cut panel.)	60.00	30.00	18.00

1938 Our National Game Pins

This unnumbered 30-pin set issued circa 1938 carries the American Card Catalog designation of PM8. The pins, which measure 7/8" in diameter, have a bendable "tab" rather than a pin back. The player photo is printed in blue-and-white. The player's name and team are printed at bottom. The pins were originally sold on a square of cardboard decorated with stars and stripes and imprinted "OUR NATIONAL GAME" above the pin, and "A BASEBALL HERO" below. A large number of the pins, complete with their cardboard backing, were found in a hoard in Oklahoma in the early 1990s.

		NM	E	VG
Complete Set (30):		1,200	600.00	350.00
Common Player:		20.00	10.00	6.00
(1)	Wally Berger	20.00	10.00	6.00
(2)	Lou Chiozza	20.00	10.00	6.00
(3)	Joe Cronin	40.00	20.00	12.00
(4)	Frank Crosetti	25.00	12.50	7.50
(5)	Jerome (Dizzy) Dean	75.00	37.00	22.00
(6)	Frank DeMaree (Demaree)	20.00	10.00	6.00

		NM	E	VG
(7)	Joe DiMaggio	100.00	50.00	30.00
(8)	Bob Feller	65.00	32.00	19.50
(9)	Jimmy Foxx (Jimmie)	75.00	37.00	22.00
(10)	Lou Gehrig	100.00	50.00	30.00
(11)	Charles Gehringer	50.00	25.00	15.00
(12)	Lefty Gomez	40.00	20.00	12.00
(13)	Hank Greenberg	65.00	32.00	19.50
(14)	Irving (Bump) Hadley	20.00	10.00	6.00
(15)	Leo Hartnett	40.00	20.00	12.00
(16)	Carl Hubbell	50.00	25.00	15.00
(17)	John (Buddy) Lewis	20.00	10.00	6.00
(18)	Gus Mancuso	20.00	10.00	6.00
(19)	Joe McCarthy	40.00	20.00	12.00
(20)	Joe Medwick	40.00	20.00	12.00
(21)	Joe Moore	20.00	10.00	6.00
(22)	Mel Ott	50.00	25.00	15.00
(23)	Jake Powell	20.00	10.00	6.00
(24)	Jimmy Ripple	20.00	10.00	6.00
(25)	Red Ruffing	40.00	20.00	12.00
(26)	Hal Schumacher	20.00	10.00	6.00
(27)	George Selkirk	20.00	10.00	6.00
(28)	"Al" Simmons	40.00	20.00	12.00
(29)	Bill Terry	40.00	20.00	12.00
(30)	Harold Trosky	20.00	10.00	6.00

1936 Overland Candy Co. (R301)

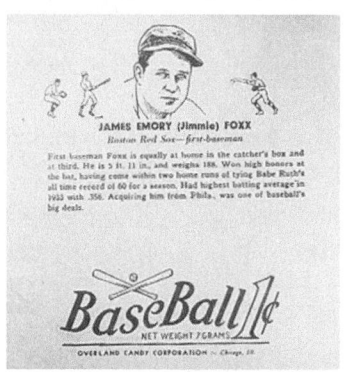

Used as wrappers for a piece of penny candy, these 5" x 5-1/4" waxed papers are usually found with resultant folds and creases, though unfolded examples are known. Printed in dark blue, the top of the wrapper features a line drawing portrait of the player, his formal name and nickname, team, position and career summary. The unnumbered wrappers are checklisted here alphabetically.

		NM	E	VG
Complete Set (60):		45,000	20,000	9,000
Common Player:		650.00	300.00	130.00
(1)	Melo (Mel) Almada	650.00	300.00	130.00
(2)	Lucius B. (Luke) Appling	900.00	400.00	180.00
(3)	Howard Earl Averill	900.00	400.00	180.00
(4)	Walter Antone (Wally) Berger	650.00	300.00	130.00
(5)	Henry John (Zeke) Bonura	650.00	300.00	130.00
(6)	Dolph Camilli	650.00	300.00	130.00
(7)	Philip Joseph (Phil) Cavarretta	650.00	300.00	130.00
(8)	William Ben (Chappy) Chapman	650.00	300.00	130.00
(9)	Harland Clift (First name Harlond.)	650.00	300.00	130.00
(10a)	John Walter (Johnny) Cooney (Bees)	650.00	300.00	130.00
(10b)	John Walter (Johnny) Cooney (Dodgers)	650.00	300.00	130.00
(11)	Harry Danning	650.00	300.00	130.00
(12)	William N. (Bill) Dickey (Middle initial is N.)	950.00	425.00	190.00
(13a)	William J. (Bill) Dietrich (Athletics)	650.00	300.00	130.00
(13b)	William J. (Bill) Dietrich (White Sox)	650.00	300.00	130.00
(14)	Joseph (Deadpan Joe) DiMaggio	3,000	1,350	600.00
(15)	Wesley Cheek Ferrell	650.00	300.00	130.00
(16)	James Emory (Jimmie) Foxx	1,200	540.00	240.00
(17)	Henry Louis (Lou) Gehrig	4,000	1,800	1,075
(18)	Charles Leonard (Charley) Gehringer	900.00	400.00	180.00
(19)	Jose Luis (Chile) Gomez	650.00	300.00	130.00
(20)	Vernon (Lefty) Gomez	900.00	400.00	180.00
(21)	Joe Gordon	650.00	300.00	130.00
(22)	Henry (Hank) Greenberg	1,200	540.00	240.00
(23)	Robert Moses (Lefty) Grove	950.00	425.00	190.00
(24)	George W. (Mule) Haas	650.00	300.00	130.00

		NM	E	VG
(25)	Ralston Burdett (Rollie) Hemsley	650.00	300.00	130.00
(26)	Michael Francis (Pinky) Higgins (Middle name Franklin.)	650.00	300.00	130.00
(27)	Oral Clyde (Hildy) Hildebrand	650.00	300.00	130.00
(28)	Robert Lee (Cherokee) Johnson	650.00	300.00	130.00
(29)	Baxter Byerly (Buck) Jordan	650.00	300.00	130.00
(30)	Ken Keltner	650.00	300.00	130.00
(31)	Fabian Kowalik	650.00	300.00	130.00
(32)	Harry A. Lavagetto	650.00	300.00	130.00
(33)	Anthony Michael (Poosh 'em Up) Lazzeri	900.00	400.00	180.00
(34)	Samuel A. Leslie	650.00	300.00	130.00
(35)	Dan (Slug) Lithwhiler (Last name Litwhiler.)	650.00	300.00	130.00
(36)	Theodore A. (Ted) Lyons	900.00	400.00	180.00
(37)	George McQuinn	650.00	300.00	130.00
(38)	John Robert (Skippy) Mize	900.00	400.00	180.00
(39)	Terry Moore	650.00	300.00	130.00
(40)	Charles Solomon (Buddy) Myer	650.00	300.00	130.00
(41)	Louis Norman (Buck) Newsom	650.00	300.00	130.00
(42)	Bill Nicholson	650.00	300.00	130.00
(43)	Raymond Pepper	650.00	300.00	130.00
(44)	Frank A. (Pity) Pytlak	650.00	300.00	130.00
(45)	Raymond Allen (Rip) Radcliff	650.00	300.00	130.00
(46)	Peter (Pete) Reiser (Correct name Harold Patrick.)	650.00	300.00	130.00
(47)	Carl Nettles (Sheeps) Reynolds	650.00	300.00	130.00
(48)	Robert Abial (Red) Rolfe	650.00	300.00	130.00
(49)	Lynwood Thomas (Schoolboy) Rowe	650.00	300.00	130.00
(50)	Aloysius Harry (Al) Simmons	900.00	400.00	180.00
(51)	Cecil Howard Travis (Middle name is Howell.)	650.00	300.00	130.00
(52)	Harold Arthus (Hal) Trosky	650.00	300.00	130.00
(53)	Joseph Franklin (Joe) Vosmik	650.00	300.00	130.00
(54)	Harold Burton (Rabbit) Warstler	650.00	300.00	130.00
(55)	William M. (Bill) Werber	650.00	300.00	130.00
(56)	Max West	650.00	300.00	130.00
(57)	Samuel F. (Sam) West	650.00	300.00	130.00
(58)	Whitlow (Whit) Wyatt	650.00	300.00	130.00

1921 Oxford Confectionery (E253)

Issued in 1921 by Oxford Confectionery of Oxford, Pa., this 20-card set was printed on thin paper and distributed with caramels. Each card measures 1-5/8" x 2-3/4" and features a black-and-white player photo with the player's name and team printed in a white band along the bottom. The back carries a checklist of the players in the set, 14 of whom are now in the Hall of Fame. The set is designated as E253 in the ACC.

		NM	E	VG
Complete Set (20):		43,750	19,750	8,750
Common Player:		1,250	575.00	350.00
(1)	Grover Alexander	2,250	1,025	625.00
(2)	Dave Bancroft	1,500	675.00	435.00
(3)	Max Carey	1,500	675.00	425.00
(4)	Ty Cobb	7,500	3,375	2,025
(5)	Eddie Collins	1,500	675.00	425.00
(6)	Frankie Frisch	1,500	675.00	425.00

		NM	E	VG
(7)	Burleigh Grimes	1,500	675.00	425.00
(8)	"Bill" Holke (Walter)	1,250	575.00	350.00
(9)	Rogers Hornsby	2,250	1,025	625.00
(10)	Walter Johnson	3,750	1,675	1,025
(11)	Lee Meadows	1,250	575.00	350.00
(12)	Cy Perkins	1,250	575.00	350.00
(13)	Derrill Pratt	1,250	575.00	350.00
(14)	Ed Rousch (Roush)	1,500	675.00	425.00
(15)	"Babe" Ruth	15,000	6,750	4,050
(16)	Ray Schalk	1,500	675.00	425.00
(17)	George Sisler	1,500	675.00	425.00
(18)	Tris Speaker	2,250	1,025	625.00
(19)	Cy Williams	1,250	575.00	350.00
(20)	Whitey Witt	1,250	575.00	350.00

P

1958 Packard-Bell

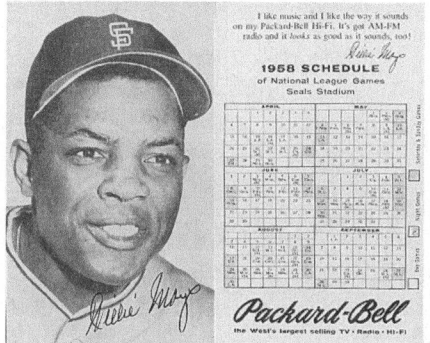

Issued by the "world's largest seller of TVs, radios and hi-fis," this set was distributed in California and features members of the newly arrived Los Angeles Dodgers and San Francisco Giants. The 3-1/2" x 5-1/2" black-and-white cards are unnumbered, checklisted here alphabetically.

		NM	E	VG
Complete Set (7):		1,500	750.00	450.00
Common Player:		100.00	50.00	30.00
(1)	Walter Alston	125.00	65.00	35.00
(2)	John A. Antonelli	100.00	50.00	30.00
(3)	Jim Gilliam	125.00	65.00	35.00
(4)	Gil Hodges	200.00	100.00	60.00
(5)	Willie Mays	800.00	400.00	240.00
(6)	Bill Rigney	100.00	50.00	30.00
(7)	Hank Sauer	100.00	50.00	30.00

1978 Papa Gino's Discs

This promotion was largely confined to the Boston area, as 25 of the 40 players represented are Red Sox, the other 15 are all from American League teams. The 3-3/8" discs were given away with the purchase of soft drinks at the restaurant chain. Fronts have player portraits at center with name in the dark blue border at top and team below. Photos have the uniform logos airbrushed away because the discs were licensed only by the players' union, not MLB. Backs retain the color scheme with player data, previous season's stats, uniform and card numbers, sponsor's ad, etc.

		NM	E	VG
Complete Set (40):		20.00	10.00	6.00
Common Player:		2.00	1.00	.60
1	Allen Ripley	2.00	1.00	.60
2	Jerry Remy	2.00	1.00	.60
3	Jack Brohamer	2.00	1.00	.60
4	Butch Hobson	2.00	1.00	.60
5	Dennis Eckersley	3.50	1.75	1.00
6	Sam Bowen	2.00	1.00	.60
7	Rick Burleson	2.00	1.00	.60
8	Carl Yastrzemski	5.00	2.50	1.50
9	Bill Lee	2.00	1.00	.60
10	Bob Montgomery	2.00	1.00	.60
11	Dick Drago	2.00	1.00	.60
12	Bob Stanley	2.00	1.00	.60
13	Fred Kendall	2.00	1.00	.60
14	Jim Rice	4.00	2.00	1.25
15	George Scott	2.00	1.00	.60
16	Tom Burgmeier	2.00	1.00	.60
17	Frank Duffy	2.00	1.00	.60
18	Jim Wright	2.00	1.00	.60
19	Fred Lynn	2.00	1.00	.60
20	Bob Bailey	2.00	1.00	.60
21	Mike Torrez	2.00	1.00	.60
22	Bill Campbell	2.00	1.00	.60
23	Luis Tiant	2.00	1.00	.60
24	Dwight Evans	2.00	1.00	.60
25	Carlton Fisk	4.00	2.00	1.25
26	Reggie Jackson	5.00	2.50	1.50
27	Thurman Munson	3.50	1.75	1.00
28	Ron Guidry	2.00	1.00	.60
29	Bruce Bochte	2.00	1.00	.60
30	Richie Zisk	2.00	1.00	.60
31	Jim Palmer	4.00	2.00	1.25
32	Mark Fidrych	2.50	1.25	.70
33	Frank Tanana	2.00	1.00	.60
34	Buddy Bell	2.00	1.00	.60
35	Rod Carew	4.00	2.00	1.25
36	George Brett	7.50	3.75	2.25
37	Ralph Garr	2.00	1.00	.60
38	Larry Hisle	2.00	1.00	.60
39	Mitchell Page	2.00	1.00	.60
40	John Mayberry	2.00	1.00	.60

1974 Bob Parker 2nd Best

Star players who came in second, often to lesser-known players, in various statistical categories between 1899-1955 are featured in this collectors issue from Bob Parker. The blank-backed, black-and-white cards measure an unusual 3" x 8" and feature the story of the 1-2 finish in cartoon form. The unnumbered cards are listed here in chronological order.

		NM	E	VG
Complete Set (25):		55.00	25.00	15.00
Common Player:		3.00	1.50	.90
(1)	Jesse Burkett, Ed Delahanty (1899)	3.00	1.50	.90
(2)	Hans Wagner, Cy Seymour (1905)	4.00	2.00	1.25
(3)	Gavvy Cravath, Jake Daubert (1913)	3.00	1.50	.90
(4)	Joe Jackson, Ty Cobb (1913)	10.00	5.00	3.00
(5)	Eddie Collins, Ty Cobb (1914)	4.00	2.00	1.25
(6)	Babe Ruth, Heinie Manush (1926)	7.50	3.75	2.25
(7)	Chick Hafey, Jim Bottomley, Hack Wilson (1928)	3.00	1.50	.90
(8)	Paul Waner, Rogers Hornsby (1928)	3.00	1.50	.90
(9)	Babe Herman, Lefty O'Doul (1929)	3.00	1.50	.90
(10)	Al Simmons, Lew Fonseca (1929)	3.00	1.50	.90
(11)	Lou Gehrig, Babe Ruth (1930)	10.00	5.00	3.00
(12)	Babe Herman, Bill Terry (1930)	3.00	1.50	.90
(13)	Chuck Klein, Hack Wilson (1930)	3.00	1.50	.90
(14)	Jim Bottomley, Bill Terry, Chick Hafey (1931)	3.00	1.50	.90
(15)	Jimmy (Jimmie) Foxx, Dale Alexander (1932)	3.00	1.50	.90
(16)	Spud Davis, Chuck Klein (1933)	3.00	1.50	.90
(17)	Heinie Manush, Jimmy Foxx (1933)	3.00	1.50	.90
(18)	Mel Ott, Wally Berger (1935)	3.00	1.50	.90
(19)	Joe Vosmik, Buddy Myer (1935)	3.00	1.50	.90
(20)	Blimp Phelps, Paul Waner (1936)	3.00	1.50	.90
(21)	Bobby Doerr, Lou Boudreau (1944)	3.00	1.50	.90
(22)	Stan Musial, Dixie Walker (1944)	4.00	2.00	1.25
(23)	George Kell, Billy Goodman (1950)	3.00	1.50	.90
(24)	Al Rosen, Mickey Vernon (1953)	3.00	1.50	.90
(25)	Vic Power, Al Kaline (1955)	3.00	1.50	.90

1976 Bob Parker More Baseball Cartoons

This collectors' issue showcased the pen and ink artwork of Ohio cartoonist Bob Parker on cards featuring current and former ballplayers from the great to the obscure. Cards are in 3-1/2" x 5" format with black-and-white fronts and blank backs.

		NM	E	VG
Complete Set (24):		65.00	32.50	20.00
Common Card:		3.00	1.50	.90
1	Hank Aaron, Babe Ruth (All-Time HR Specialists)	7.50	3.75	2.25
2	Ernie Banks	4.00	2.00	1.25
3	Rod Carew	3.00	1.50	.90
4	Joe DiMaggio	15.00	7.50	4.50
5	Doug Flynn	3.00	1.50	.90
6	Mike Garcia	3.00	1.50	.90
7	Steve Garvey, Greg Luzinski (All-Stars)	3.00	1.50	.90
8	Lou Gehrig	15.00	7.50	4.50
9	Chuck Klein, Hack Wilson (Hall of Famers?)	3.00	1.50	.90
10	Don Larsen	3.00	1.50	.90
11	Fred Lynn	3.00	1.50	.90
12	Roy Majtyka	3.00	1.50	.90
13	Pepper Martin	3.00	1.50	.90
14	Christy Mathewson	5.00	2.50	1.50
15	Cal McVey	3.00	1.50	.90
16	Tony Perez	3.00	1.50	.90
17	Lou Gehrig, Babe Ruth (Great Moments)	15.00	7.50	4.50
18	Everett Scott	3.00	1.50	.90
19	Bobby Thomson	3.00	1.50	.90
20	Ted Williams (1939)	7.50	3.75	2.25
21	Ted Williams (Great Moments)	7.50	3.75	2.25
22	Bill Madlock	3.00	1.50	.90
23	Henry Chadwick, Buck Ewing, Albert Spalding, Honus Wagner (Hall of Famers)	3.00	1.50	.90
---	Checklist	3.00	1.50	.90

1977 Bob Parker Cincinnati Reds

In the late 1970s, Ohio cartoonist Bob Parker drew a series of Reds feature cartoons for the weekly "Reds Alert." Later, he assembled two groups of those cartoons into collectors' issue card sets. The cards are black-and-white with blank backs. Fronts have portraits and/or action main drawings, usually with some cartoon figures included to draw attention to the player's career highlights. Size is 3-1/2" x 5". The unnumbered series is listed in alphabetical order.

		NM	E	VG
	Complete Set (48):	110.00	55.00	32.50
	Common Player:	3.00	1.50	.90
	UNNUMBERED SERIES (24):	55.00	25.00	15.00
(1)	Sparky Anderson	4.00	2.00	1.25
(2)	Wally Berger	3.00	1.50	.90
(3)	Pedro Borbon	3.00	1.50	.90
(4)	Rube Bressler	3.00	1.50	.90
(5)	Gordy Coleman	3.00	1.50	.90
(6)	Dave Concepcion	3.00	1.50	.90
(7)	Harry Craft	3.00	1.50	.90
(8)	Hugh Critz	3.00	1.50	.90
(9)	Dan Driessen	3.00	1.50	.90
(10)	Pat Duncan	3.00	1.50	.90
(11)	Lonnie Frey	3.00	1.50	.90
(12)	Ival Goodman	3.00	1.50	.90
(13)	Heinie Groh	3.00	1.50	.90
(14)	Noodles Hahn	3.00	1.50	.90
(15)	Mike Lum	3.00	1.50	.90
(16)	Bill McKechnie	3.00	1.50	.90
(17)	Pat Moran	3.00	1.50	.90
(18)	Billy Myers	3.00	1.50	.90
(19)	Gary Nolan	3.00	1.50	.90
(20)	Fred Norman	3.00	1.50	.90
(21)	Jim O'Toole	3.00	1.50	.90
(22)	Vada Pinson	4.00	2.00	1.25
(23)	Bucky Walters	3.00	1.50	.90
(24)	**Checklist**	3.00	1.50	.90
	NUMBERED SERIES (24):	60.00	30.00	18.00
1	Ted Kluszewski	6.00	3.00	1.75
2	Johnny Bench	10.00	5.00	3.00
3	Jim Maloney	3.00	1.50	.90
4	Bubbles Hargrave	3.00	1.50	.90
5	Don Gullett	3.00	1.50	.90
6	Joe Nuxhall	4.00	2.00	1.25
7	Edd Roush	3.00	1.50	.90
8	Wally Post	3.00	1.50	.90
9	George Wright	3.00	1.50	.90
10	George Foster	3.00	1.50	.90
11	Pete Rose	15.00	7.50	4.50
12	Red Lucas	3.00	1.50	.90
13	Joe Morgan	4.00	2.00	1.25
14	Eppa Rixey	3.00	1.50	.90
15	Bill Werber	3.00	1.50	.90
16	Frank Robinson	6.00	3.00	1.75
17	Dolf Luque	4.00	2.00	1.25
18	Paul Derringer	3.00	1.50	.90
19	Frank McCormick	3.00	1.50	.90
20	Ken Griffey	3.00	1.50	.90
21	Jack Billingham	3.00	1.50	.90
22	Larry Kopf	3.00	1.50	.90
23	Ernie Lombardi	3.00	1.50	.90
24	Johnny Vander Meer	3.00	1.50	.90

1977-81 Bob Parker Hall of Fame

This is one of many collectors issues produced in the mid to late 1970s by midwestern sports artist Bob Parker. The 3-3/8" x 5-1/2" cards are printed in sepia on tan cardboard; they are blank-backed. Fronts have a portrait drawing of the player, with career highlights in cartoon form. Three series were issued: #1-54 in 1977; #55-77 in 1980 and #78-100 in 1981. A header card was issued with each series.

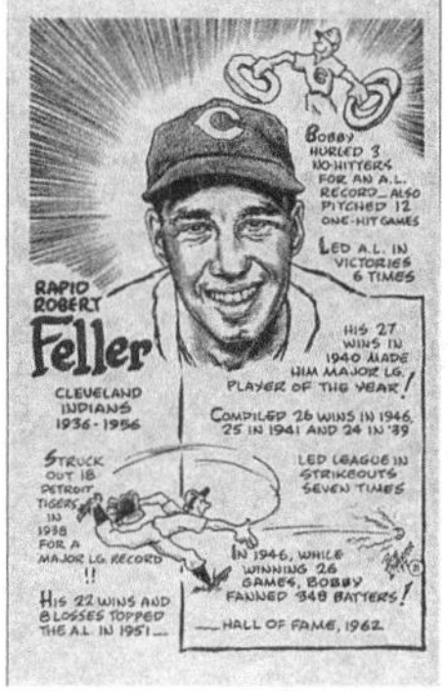

		NM	E	VG
	Complete Set (103):	125.00	65.00	35.00
	Common Player:	3.00	1.50	.90
	First Series Set (55):	50.00	25.00	15.00
---	**First Series Header**	1.00	.50	.30
1	Grover Alexander	3.00	1.50	.90
2	Cap Anson	3.00	1.50	.90
3	Luke Appling	3.00	1.50	.90
4	Ernie Banks	4.00	2.00	1.25
5	Chief Bender	3.00	1.50	.90
6	Jim Bottomley	3.00	1.50	.90
7	Dan Brouthers	3.00	1.50	.90
8	Morgan Bulkeley	3.00	1.50	.90
9	Roy Campanella	7.50	3.75	2.25
10	Alexander Cartwright	3.00	1.50	.90
11	Henry Chadwick	3.00	1.50	.90
12	John Clarkson	3.00	1.50	.90
13	Ty Cobb	10.00	5.00	3.00
14	Eddie Collins	3.00	1.50	.90
16	Charles Comiskey	3.00	1.50	.90
17	Sam Crawford	3.00	1.50	.90
18	Dizzy Dean	4.00	2.00	1.25
19	Joe DiMaggio	16.00	8.00	4.75
20	Buck Ewing	3.00	1.50	.90
21	Bob Feller	4.00	2.00	1.25
22	Lou Gehrig	16.00	8.00	4.75
23	Goose Goslin	3.00	1.50	.90
24	Burleigh Grimes	3.00	1.50	.90
25	Chick Hafey	3.00	1.50	.90
26	Rogers Hornsby	3.00	1.50	.90
27	Carl Hubbell	3.00	1.50	.90
28	Miller Huggins	3.00	1.50	.90
29	Tim Keefe	3.00	1.50	.90
30	Mike Kelly	3.00	1.50	.90
31	Nap Lajoie	3.00	1.50	.90
32	Freddie Lindstrom	3.00	1.50	.90
33	Connie Mack	3.00	1.50	.90
34	Mickey Mantle	25.00	12.50	7.50
35	Heinie Manush	3.00	1.50	.90
36	Joe McGinnity	3.00	1.50	.90
37	John McGraw	3.00	1.50	.90
38	Ed Plank	3.00	1.50	.90
39	Eppa Rixey	3.00	1.50	.90
40	Jackie Robinson	12.00	6.00	3.50
41	Edd Roush	3.00	1.50	.90
42	Babe Ruth	20.00	10.00	6.00
43	Al Simmons	3.00	1.50	.90
44	Al Spalding	3.00	1.50	.90
45	Tris Speaker	3.00	1.50	.90
46	Casey Stengel	3.00	1.50	.90
47	Bill Terry	3.00	1.50	.90
48	Rube Waddell	3.00	1.50	.90
49	Honus Wagner	5.00	2.50	1.50
50	Paul Waner	3.00	1.50	.90
51	John Montgomery Ward	3.00	1.50	.90
52	Ted Williams	10.00	5.00	3.00
53	George Wright	3.00	1.50	.90
54	Harry Wright	3.00	1.50	.90
	Second Series Set (24):	40.00	20.00	12.00
---	**Second Series Header**	1.00	.50	.30
55	Mordecai Brown	3.00	1.50	.90
56	Frank Chance	3.00	1.50	.90
57	Candy Cummings	3.00	1.50	.90
58	Frank Frisch	3.00	1.50	.90
59	Gabby Hartnett	3.00	1.50	.90
60	Billy Herman	3.00	1.50	.90
61	Waite Hoyt	3.00	1.50	.90
62	Walter Johnson	5.00	2.50	1.50
63	Kenesaw Landis	3.00	1.50	.90
64	Rube Marquard	3.00	1.50	.90
65	Christy Mathewson	6.00	3.00	1.75
66	Eddie Mathews	3.00	1.50	.90
67	Willie Mays	10.00	5.00	3.00
68	Bill McKechnie	3.00	1.50	.90
69	Stan Musial	7.50	3.75	2.25
70	Mel Ott	3.00	1.50	.90
71	Satchel Paige	7.50	3.75	2.25
72	Robin Roberts	3.00	1.50	.90
73	George Sisler	3.00	1.50	.90
74	Warren Spahn	3.00	1.50	.90
75	Joe Tinker	3.00	1.50	.90
76	Dazzy Vance	3.00	1.50	.90
77	Cy Young	6.00	3.00	1.75
	Third Series Set (24):	40.00	20.00	12.00
---	**Third Series Header**	1.00	.50	.30
78	Home Run Baker	3.00	1.50	.90
79	Yogi Berra	4.00	2.00	1.25
80	Max Carey	3.00	1.50	.90
81	Roberto Clemente	16.00	8.00	4.75
82	Mickey Cochrane	3.00	1.50	.90
83	Roger Connor	3.00	1.50	.90
84	Joe Cronin	3.00	1.50	.90
85	Kiki Cuyler	3.00	1.50	.90
86	Johnny Evers	3.00	1.50	.90
87	Jimmie Foxx	3.00	1.50	.90
88	Charlie Gehringer	3.00	1.50	.90
89	Lefty Gomez	3.00	1.50	.90
90	Jesse Haines	3.00	1.50	.90
91	Will Harridge	3.00	1.50	.90
92	Monte Irvin	3.00	1.50	.90
93	Addie Joss	3.00	1.50	.90
94	Al Kaline	3.00	1.50	.90
95	Sandy Koufax	10.00	5.00	3.00
96	Rabbit Maranville	3.00	1.50	.90
97	Jim O'Rourke	3.00	1.50	.90
98	Wilbert Robinson	3.00	1.50	.90
99	Pie Traynor	3.00	1.50	.90
100	Zack Wheat	3.00	1.50	.90

1968-70 Partridge Meats Reds

These cards were produced in conjunction with Reds' autograph appearances at Kroger food stores in the Cincinnati area. Players' service with the Reds indicates this set was issued over a period of several years. Similar cards are known for other Cincinnati pro sports teams. The 1968 cards measure 4" x 5" and feature a black-and-white player photo set against a borderless white background. The player's name and team and the word "Likes" are printed in black, the ad for the issuing meat company at bottom is printed in red. Cards have a blank back. The 1969-70 cards are in the same format but in 3-3/4" x 5-1/2" format. The unnumbered cards are checklisted here in alphabetical order.

		NM	E	VG
	Complete Set (11):	1,000	500.00	300.00
	Common Player:	40.00	20.00	12.00
(1)	Ted Abernathy	80.00	40.00	25.00
(2)	John Bench	100.00	50.00	30.00
(3)	Jimmy Bragan	40.00	20.00	12.00
(4)	Dave Bristol	80.00	40.00	25.00
(5)	Tommy Helms	80.00	40.00	25.00
(6)	Gary Nolan	40.00	20.00	12.00
(7)	Milt Pappas	80.00	40.00	25.00
(8)	Don Pavletich	80.00	40.00	25.00
(9)	Mel Queen	80.00	40.00	25.00
(10)	Pete Rose	300.00	150.00	90.00
(11)	Jim Stewart	80.00	40.00	25.00

1972 Partridge Meats Reds

Similar in format to the meat company's 1968-70 issue, these later cards are in a slightly different size - 3-3/4" x 5-1/2". The ad on the '72 cards reads "Photo courtesy of Partridge Meats."

		NM	E	VG
Complete Set (7):		225.00	110.00	65.00
Common Player:		30.00	15.00	9.00
(1)	Don Gullett	30.00	15.00	9.00
(2)	Lee May	30.00	15.00	9.00
(3)	Denis Menke	30.00	15.00	9.00
(4)	Jim Merritt	30.00	15.00	9.00
(5)	Joe Morgan	60.00	30.00	18.00
(6)	Gary Nolan	30.00	15.00	9.00
(7)	Tony Perez	120.00	60.00	36.00
(8)	Bob Tolan	30.00	15.00	9.00

1922 Wm. Paterson

Believed to have been a Canadian candy premium, this 50-card set of 2" x 3-1/4" cards features portrait or posed action photos with wide white borders. Beneath the photo is a card number, player name, team, and in two lines, "Wm. Paterson, Limited / Brantford, Canada." Backs are blank. Two distinct types are seen, black-and-white and sepia, though the reason for the variations is unknown.

		NM	E	VG
Complete Set (50):		120,000	50,000	25,000
Common Player:		950.00	400.00	200.00
1	Eddie Roush	2,000	800.00	400.00
2	Rube Marquard	2,000	800.00	400.00
3	Del Gainor	950.00	400.00	200.00
4	George Sisler	2,000	800.00	400.00
5	Joe Bush	950.00	400.00	200.00
6	Joe Oeschger	950.00	400.00	200.00
7	Willie Kamm	950.00	400.00	200.00
8	John Watson	950.00	400.00	200.00
9	Dolf Luque	1,100	450.00	225.00
10	Miller Huggins	2,000	800.00	400.00
11	Wally Schang	950.00	400.00	200.00
12	Bob Shawkey	950.00	400.00	200.00
13	Tris Speaker	3,500	1,400	700.00
14	Hugh McQuillan	950.00	400.00	200.00
15	"Long George" Kelly	2,000	800.00	400.00
16	Ray Schalk	2,000	800.00	400.00
17	Sam Jones	950.00	400.00	200.00
18	Grover Alexander	3,500	1,400	700.00
19	Bob Meusel	950.00	400.00	200.00
20	"Irish" Emil Meusel	950.00	400.00	200.00
21	Rogers Hornsby	3,500	1,400	700.00
22	Harry Heilmann	2,000	800.00	400.00
23	Heinie Groh	950.00	400.00	200.00
24	Frank Frisch	2,000	800.00	400.00
25	Babe Ruth	30,000	12,000	6,000
26	Jack Bentley	950.00	400.00	200.00
27	Everett Scott	950.00	400.00	200.00
28	Max Carey	2,000	800.00	400.00
29	Chick Fewster	950.00	400.00	200.00
30	Cy Williams	950.00	400.00	200.00
31	Burleigh Grimes	2,000	800.00	400.00
32	Waite Hoyt	2,000	800.00	400.00
33	Frank Snyder	950.00	400.00	200.00
34	Clyde Milan	950.00	400.00	200.00
35	Eddie Collins	2,000	800.00	400.00
36	Travis Jackson	2,000	800.00	400.00
37	Ken Williams	950.00	400.00	200.00
38	Dave Bancroft	2,000	800.00	400.00
39	Mike McNally	950.00	800.00	400.00
40	John J. McGraw	2,000	800.00	400.00
41	Art Nehf	950.00	400.00	200.00
42	"Rabbit" Maranville	2,000	800.00	400.00
43	Chas. Grimm	950.00	400.00	200.00
44	Joe Judge	950.00	400.00	200.00
45	Wally Pipp	950.00	400.00	200.00
46	Ty Cobb	20,000	8,000	4,000
47	Walter Johnson	6,000	2,500	1,200
48	Jake Daubert	950.00	400.00	200.00
49	Zack Wheat	2,000	800.00	400.00
50	Herb Pennock	2,000	800.00	400.00

1921 Pathe Freres Phonograph Co.

One of the rarest early-1920s Babe Ruth items is this premium photo issued by Pathe Freres Phonograph Co. of Brooklyn. Ruth is pictured bare-headed in a pinstriped uniform on the front of this approximately 7" x 9-1/4" card, printed in green and gray tones with a white border. A photo credit to White Studios of New York is given on the front and there is a facsimile autograph at bottom front. The black-and-white back has a listing of Ruth's 1920 homers in a box at left, and a Pathe ad at bottom-right.

	NM	E	VG
Babe Ruth	7,000	3,500	2,100

1947 Van Patrick Cleveland Indians Postcards

Fans could obtain these black-and-white postcard-size (3-1/2" x 5-1/2") photos of their favorite Indians players by writing to radio broadcaster Van Patrick. Backs do not have postcard markings, and carry a message from Patrick. The unnumbered cards are checklisted here alphabetically, though the listing may not be complete.

		NM	E	VG
Common Player:		100.00	50.00	30.00
(1)	Don Black	100.00	50.00	30.00
	(See listings alphabetically under Patrick, Van.)			
(2)	Eddie Bockman	100.00	50.00	30.00
(3)	Lou Boudreau	200.00	100.00	60.00
(4)	Jack Conway	100.00	50.00	30.00
(5)	Hank Edwards	100.00	50.00	30.00
(6)	Red Embree	100.00	50.00	30.00
(7)	Bob Feller (Pitching)	300.00	150.00	90.00
(8)	Bob Feller (Pitching, leg in air.)	300.00	150.00	90.00
(9)	Les Fleming	100.00	50.00	30.00
(10)	Allen Gettel	100.00	50.00	30.00
(11)	Joe Gordon	200.00	100.00	60.00
(12)	Steve Gromek	100.00	50.00	30.00
(13)	Mel Harder	125.00	62.00	37.00
(14)	Jim Hegan	110.00	55.00	33.00
(15)	Ken Keltner	110.00	55.00	33.00
(16)	Ed Klieman	100.00	50.00	30.00
(17)	Bob Lemon	200.00	100.00	60.00
(18)	Al Lopez	200.00	100.00	60.00
(19)	George Metkovich	100.00	50.00	30.00
(20)	Dale Mitchell	100.00	50.00	30.00
(21)	Hal Peck	100.00	50.00	30.00
(22)	Eddie Robinson	100.00	50.00	30.00
(23)	Hank Ruszkowski	100.00	50.00	30.00
(24)	Pat Seerey	100.00	50.00	30.00
(25)	Bryan Stephens	100.00	50.00	30.00
(26)	Les Willis	100.00	50.00	30.00

1910 PC796 Sepia Postcards

The manufacturer of these sepia-toned 3-1/2" x 5-1/2" postcards is unknown, but most of the photos utilized are familiar from other card issues of the era. Fronts have the player name at bottom in fancy capital letters. Backs have a standard divided postcard indicia. The set was given the PC796 designation in the "American Card Catalog." The unnumbered cards are checklisted here alphabetically.

		NM	E	VG
Complete Set (25):		68,000	27,000	14,500
Common Player:		900.00	360.00	180.00
(1)	Roger Bresnahan	1,800	700.00	360.00
(2)	Al Bridwell	900.00	360.00	180.00
(3)	Mordecai Brown	1,800	720.00	360.00
(4)	Frank Chance	1,800	720.00	360.00
(5)	Hal Chase	1,350	550.00	270.00
(6)	Ty Cobb	10,000	5,000	3,000
(7)	Ty Cobb, Hanus Wagner	9,000	4,500	2,250
(8)	Eddie Collins	1,800	720.00	360.00
(9)	Sam Crawford	1,800	720.00	360.00
(10)	Art Devlin	900.00	360.00	180.00
(11)	Red Dooin	900.00	360.00	180.00
(12)	Johnny Evers, Germany Schaefer	1,200	480.00	240.00
(13)	Sam Frock	900.00	360.00	180.00
(14)	George Gibson	900.00	360.00	180.00
(15)	Artie Hoffman (Hofman)	900.00	360.00	180.00
(16)	Walter Johnson	3,600	1,500	720.00
(17)	Nap Lajoie	1,800	720.00	360.00
(18)	Harry Lord	900.00	360.00	180.00
(19)	Christy Mathewson	5,000	2,400	1,200
(20)	Orval Overall	900.00	360.00	180.00
(21)	Eddie Plank	1,800	600.00	360.00
(22)	Tris Speaker	2,250	1,000	450.00
(23)	Gabby Street	900.00	360.00	180.00
(24)	Honus Wagner	8,000	4,000	1,800
(25)	Ed Walsh	1,800	720.00	360.00

1869 Peck & Snyder Cincinnati Red Stockings - Large

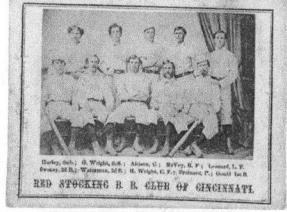

Many consider this to be the first true baseball card in that it was produced in large quantities (relative to the cabinets and carte de visites of the era) and offered to firms wishing to place their advertising on the back. The 4-3/16" x 3-5/16" card features a sepia team photo on front of baseball's first real professional team, including Hall of Famers George and Harry Wright. On this larger format, the players are identified on front with the team name in ornate black or red (slightly scarcer) type at bottom. Backs have been seen with ads for New York "Sportsman's Emporium" along with a caricature of a bearded ballplayer, and for "The New York City Base Ball & Skate Emporium," with a large illsutration of an ice skate.

	E	VG
Cincinnati Red Stocking Team	45,000	27,500

1869 Peck & Snyder Cincinnati Red Stockings - Small

Many consider this to be the first true baseball card in that it was produced in large quantities (relative to the cabinets and carte de visites of the era) and offered to firms wishing to place their advertising on the back. The 3-15/16" x 2-3/8" card features a sepia team photo on front of baseball's first real professional team, including Hall of Famers George and Harry Wright. The Peck & Snyder ad back is the most commonly found, but others are known, including a back which lists only the team's line-up.

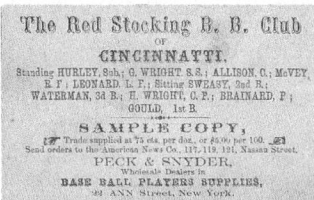

	E	VG
Cincinnati Red Stocking Team	30,000	18,000

1870 Peck & Snyder Chicago White Stockings

Using popular baseball teams of the day as an advertising medium, this apporoximately 4" x 2-3/4" black-and-white card pictures and identifies on front the 1870 Chicago White Stockings of pre-National Association days. On back is an ad for Peck & Snyder of New York City.

	E	VG
Chicago White Stockings	35,000	21,000

1870 Peck & Snyder New York Mutuals

Using popular baseball teams of the day as an advertising medium, this apporoximately 4" x 2-3/4" black-and-white card pictures and identifies on front the 1870 New York Mutuals of pre-National Association days. On back is a cartoon ad for Peck & Snyder of New York City.

	E	VG
New York Mutuals James Creighton	35,000	21,000

1870 Peck & Snyder Philadelphia Athletics

A composite photo of the players in street clothes is featured on this promotional card for the New York City sporting goods dealer whose advertising appears on back.

Philadelphia Athletics (Sold for $2,780 in 10/01 auction in Poor condition.)

1963 Pepsi-Cola Colt .45's

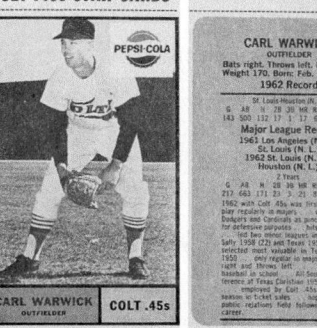

This issue was distributed regionally in Texas in bottled six-packs of Pepsi. The cards were issued on 2-3/8" x 9-1/8" panels. A 2-3/8" x 3-3/4" card was printed on each panel, which also included promos for Pepsi and the Colt .45's, as well as a team schedule. Card fronts are black-and-white posed action photos with blue and red trim. Backs offer player statistics and career highlights. The John Bateman card was apparently never distributed publicly and is among the rarest baseball cards of the 1960s. The unnumbered cards are checklisted here alphabetically. Values shown are for complete panels with top and bottom tabs; those without are valued about 25 percent.

		NM	E	VG
	Common Player:	10.00	5.00	3.00
(1)	Bob Aspromonte	10.00	5.00	3.00
(2)	John Bateman (SP) (Value undetermined)			
(3)	Bob Bruce	10.00	5.00	3.00
(4)	Jim Campbell	10.00	5.00	3.00
(5)	Dick Farrell	10.00	5.00	3.00
(6)	Ernie Fazio	10.00	5.00	3.00
(7)	Carroll Hardy	10.00	5.00	3.00
(8)	J.C. Hartman	10.00	5.00	3.00
(9)	Ken Johnson	10.00	5.00	3.00
(10)	Bob Lillis (SP)	1,200	600.00	350.00
(11)	Don McMahon	10.00	5.00	3.00
(12)	Pete Runnels	10.00	5.00	3.00
(13)	Al Spangler	10.00	5.00	3.00
(14)	Rusty Staub	35.00	17.50	10.00
(15)	Johnny Temple	10.00	5.00	3.00
(16)	Carl Warwick (SP)	1,000	500.00	300.00

1977 Pepsi-Cola Baseball Stars

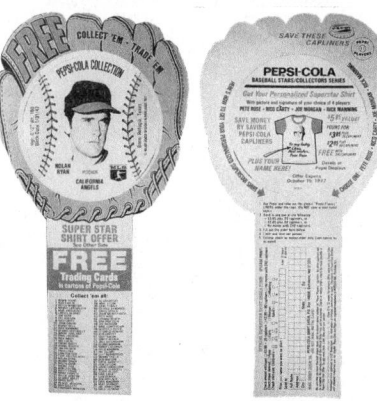

An Ohio regional promotion (the checklist is extra heavy with Indians and Reds players), large numbers of these cards found their way into hobby dealers' hands. Designed to be inserted into cartons of soda, the cards have a 3-3/8" diameter central disc attached with perforations to a baseball glove design. A tab beneath the glove contains the checklist (the card discs themselves are unnumbered) and a coupon on back for ordering a player t-shirt, the offer for which is made on the back of the player disc. The Players Association logo appears on front, but the producer, Mike Schechter Associates, did not seek licensing by Major League Baseball, with the result that uniform logos have been removed from the black-and-white player photos. Prices shown are for complete glove/disc/tab cards. Values for unattached player discs will be no more than one-half of those shown. The discs of Reggie Jackson and Mike Schmidt can be found with either orange, green, purple, light blue or sky blue side panels; the other player discs are known in only one color each.

		NM	E	VG
Complete Set (72):		35.00	17.50	10.00
W/Color Variations (80):		75.00	37.50	22.50
Common Player:		1.00	.50	.30
1	Robin Yount	4.00	2.00	1.25
2	Rod Carew	4.00	2.00	1.25
3	Butch Wynegar	1.00	.50	.30
4	Manny Sanguillen	1.00	.50	.30
5	Mike Hargrove	1.00	.50	.30
6	Larvel (Larvell) Blanks	1.00	.50	.30
7	Jim Kern	1.00	.50	.30
8	Pat Dobson	1.00	.50	.30
9	Rico Carty	1.00	.50	.30
10	John Grubb	1.00	.50	.30
11	Buddy Bell	1.00	.50	.30
12	Rick Manning	1.00	.50	.30
13	Dennis Eckersley	4.00	2.00	1.25
14	Wayne Garland	1.00	.50	.30
15	Dave LaRoche	1.00	.50	.30
16	Rick Waits	1.00	.50	.30
17	Ray Fosse	1.00	.50	.30
18	Frank Duffy	1.00	.50	.30
19	Duane Kuiper	1.00	.50	.30
20	Jim Palmer	4.00	2.00	1.25
21	Fred Lynn	1.00	.50	.30
22	Carlton Fisk	4.00	2.00	1.25
23	Carl Yastrzemski	6.00	3.00	1.75
24	Nolan Ryan	17.50	8.75	5.25
25	Bobby Grich	1.00	.50	.30
26	Ralph Garr	1.00	.50	.30
27	Richie Zisk	1.00	.50	.30
28	Ron LeFlore	1.00	.50	.30
29	Rusty Staub	1.00	.50	.30
30	Mark Fidrych	1.50	.70	.45
31	Willie Horton	1.00	.50	.30
32	George Brett	10.00	5.00	3.00
33	Amos Otis	1.00	.50	.30
34a	Reggie Jackson (Green)	7.50	3.75	2.25
34b	Reggie Jackson (Light blue.)	7.50	3.75	2.25
34c	Reggie Jackson (Orange)	7.50	3.75	2.25
34d	Reggie Jackson (Purple)	7.50	3.75	2.25
34e	Reggie Jackson (Sky blue.)	7.50	3.75	2.25
35	Don Gullett	1.00	.50	.30
36	Thurman Munson	3.00	1.50	.90
37	Al Hrabosky	1.00	.50	.30
38	Mike Tyson	1.00	.50	.30
39	Gene Tenace	1.00	.50	.30

		NM	E	VG
40	George Hendrick	1.00	.50	.30
41	Chris Speier	1.00	.50	.30
42	John Montefusco	1.00	.50	.30
43	Pete Rose	10.00	5.00	3.00
44	Johnny Bench	5.00	2.50	1.50
45	Dan Driessen	1.00	.50	.30
46	Joe Morgan	4.00	2.00	1.25
47	Dave Concepcion	1.00	.50	.30
48	George Foster	1.00	.50	.30
49	Cesar Geronimo	1.00	.50	.30
50	Ken Griffey	1.00	.50	.30
51	Gary Nolan	1.00	.50	.30
52	Santo Alcala	1.00	.50	.30
53	Jack Billingham	1.00	.50	.30
54	Pedro Borbon	1.00	.50	.30
55	Rawly Eastwick	1.00	.50	.30
56	Fred Norman	1.00	.50	.30
57	Pat Zachary (Zachry)	1.00	.50	.30
58	Jeff Burroughs	1.00	.50	.30
59	Manny Trillo	1.00	.50	.30
60	Bob Watson	1.00	.50	.30
61	Steve Garvey	1.50	.70	.45
62	Don Sutton	4.00	2.00	1.25
63	John Candelaria	1.00	.50	.30
64	Willie Stargell	4.00	2.00	1.25
65	Jerry Reuss	1.00	.50	.30
66	Dave Cash	1.00	.50	.30
67	Tom Seaver	5.00	2.50	1.50
68	Jon Matlock	1.00	.50	.30
69	Dave Kingman	1.00	.50	.30
70a	Mike Schmidt (Green)	7.50	3.75	2.25
70b	Mike Schmidt (Light blue.)	7.50	3.75	2.25
70c	Mike Schmidt (Orange)	7.50	3.75	2.25
70d	Mike Schmidt (Purple)	7.50	3.75	2.25
70e	Mike Schmidt (Sky blue.)	7.50	3.75	2.25
71	Jay Johnstone	1.00	.50	.30
72	Greg Luzinski	1.00	.50	.30

1977 Pepsi-Cola Cincinnati Reds Playing Cards

Similar to a multi-sport series produced by Cubic Corp. (see also), these playing cards sets feature on back the pencil drawings of Al Landsman. Each boxed deck featured one Reds star player within a red border. Also on each card back are a facsimile autograph and Pepsi logo. Cards are standard bridge size (2-1/4" x 3-1/2") with rounded corners. Decks were available by sending in 250 16-oz. Pepsi cap liners or a combination of cash and cap liners.

		NM	E	VG
(1)	Johnny Bench (Boxed deck.)	35.00	17.50	10.00
(1)	Johnny Bench (Single card.)	1.50	.70	.45
(2)	Joe Morgan (Boxed deck.)	20.00	10.00	6.00
(2)	Joe Morgan (Single card.)	1.00	.50	.30
(3)	Pete Rose (Boxed deck.)	55.00	27.50	16.50
(3)	Pete Rose (Single card.)	4.00	2.00	1.25

1978 Pepsi-Cola Superstars

In its second year of producing carton-stuffer baseball cards, Cincinnati area Pepsi bottlers issued a 40-card set featuring 25 Reds players and 15 other major league stars. The entire carton insert measures 2-1/8" x 9-1/2". Besides the baseball card at top, there is a checklist and mail-in offer for playing cards featuring Johnny Bench, Joe Morgan and Pete Rose. The card element at the top measures 2-1/8" x 2-1/2". A player portrait, with uniform logos airbrushed off, is featured in black-and-white in a white star on a red background. The Major League Baseball Players Association logo appears in dark blue in the upper-left. Printed in black below are the player's name, team, position, birthdate and place and a few 1977 stats. In back, printed in red, white and blue, is part of the offer for the playing cards. Large quantities of this set found their way into hobby hands and they remain common today.

		NM	E	VG
	Complete Set (40):	30.00	15.00	9.00
	Common Player:	.75	.35	.20
(1)	Sparky Anderson	2.00	1.00	.60
(2)	Rick Auerbach	.75	.35	.20
(3)	Doug Bair	.75	.35	.20
(4)	Buddy Bell	.75	.35	.20
(5)	Johnny Bench	4.00	2.00	1.25
(6)	Bill Bonham	.75	.35	.20
(7)	Pedro Borbon	.75	.35	.20
(8)	Larry Bowa	.75	.35	.20
(9)	George Brett	7.50	3.75	2.25
(10)	Jeff Burroughs	.75	.35	.20
(11)	Rod Carew	3.00	1.50	.90
(12)	Dave Collins	.75	.35	.20
(13)	Dave Concepcion	.75	.35	.20
(14)	Dan Driessen	.75	.35	.20
(15)	George Foster	.75	.35	.20
(16)	Steve Garvey	1.50	.70	.45
(17)	Cesar Geronimo	.75	.35	.20
(18)	Ken Griffey	.75	.35	.20
(19)	Ken Henderson	.75	.35	.20
(20)	Tom Hume	.75	.35	.20
(21)	Reggie Jackson	7.50	3.75	2.25
(22)	Junior Kennedy	.75	.35	.20
(23)	Dave Kingman	.75	.40	.25
(24)	Ray Knight	.75	.35	.20
(25)	Jerry Koosman	.75	.35	.20
(26)	Mike Lum	.75	.35	.20
(27)	Bill Madlock	.75	.35	.20
(28)	Joe Morgan	3.00	1.50	.90
(29)	Paul Moskau	.75	.35	.20
(30)	Fred Norman	.75	.35	.20
(31)	Jim Palmer	3.00	1.50	.90
(32)	Pete Rose	10.00	5.00	3.00
(33)	Nolan Ryan	12.50	6.25	3.75
(34)	Manny Sarmiento	.75	.35	.20
(35)	Tom Seaver	4.00	2.00	1.25
(36)	Ted Simmons	.75	.35	.20
(37)	Dave Tomlin	.75	.35	.20
(38)	Don Werner	.75	.35	.20
(39)	Carl Yastrzemski	4.00	2.00	1.25
(40)	Richie Zisk	.75	.35	.20

1980 Pepsi-Cola All-Stars Prototypes

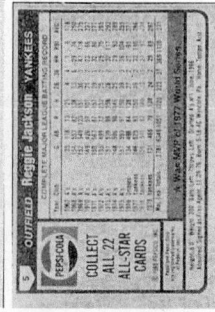

These prototype cards were prepared by Topps and Mike Schechter Associates for a proposed Pepsi promotion. Three sets of the cards were given to Pepsi officials for consideration but only two were returned when the deal fell through. The third sheet was cut up and sold into the hobby. The Pepsi cards share the format of Topps' regular 1980 issue, although Pepsi logos have been added on front and back, name and banner colors changed on front and a position circle added. In 2005, a number of the individual cards were offered on eBay by Topps.

		NM	E	VG
	Common Player:	250.00	125.00	75.00
1	Rod Carew	1,000	500.00	300.00
2	Paul Molitor	1,000	500.00	300.00
3	George Brett	1,500	750.00	450.00
4	Robin Yount	1,000	500.00	300.00
5	Reggie Jackson	1,500	750.00	450.00
6	Fred Lynn	250.00	125.00	75.00
7	Ken Landreaux	250.00	125.00	75.00
8	Jim Sundberg	250.00	125.00	75.00
9	Ron Guidry (One known, other two cut from sheets and destroyed; negatives reversed.)	1,450	725.00	435.00
10	Jim Palmer	1,000	500.00	300.00
11	Goose Gossage	250.00	125.00	75.00
12	Keith Hernandez	250.00	125.00	75.00
13	Dave Lopes	250.00	125.00	75.00
14	Mike Schmidt	1,500	750.00	450.00
15	Garry Templeton	250.00	125.00	75.00
16	Dave Parker	250.00	125.00	75.00
17	George Foster	250.00	125.00	75.00
18	Dave Winfield	1,000	500.00	300.00
19	Ted Simmons	250.00	125.00	75.00
20	Steve Carlton	1,000	500.00	300.00
21	J.R. Richard	400.00	200.00	120.00
22	Bruce Sutter	1,000	500.00	300.00

1966 Gaylord Perry Insurance

The attributed date is arbitrary, near the middle of his stay with the S.F. Giants in whose uniform he is pictured on this approximately 3-1/2" x 5-1/2", blank-backed, black-and-white "business" card for his insurance agency.

	NM	E	VG
Gaylord Perry	40.00	20.00	12.00

1971 Pete Rose & Johnny Bench Lincoln-Mercury Postcards

This series of promotional postcards was issued in 1970-71 in conjunction with a Dayton, Ohio, Lincoln-Mercury auto dealership owned by Reds teammates Rose and Bench. Fronts of the 5-1/2" x 3-1/2" postcards feature color photos of new cars. Black-and-white backs have portraits of the players, a description of the auto, the address of the dealership and a credit line for the postcard's printer. Besides those listed here, other auto fronts may exist.

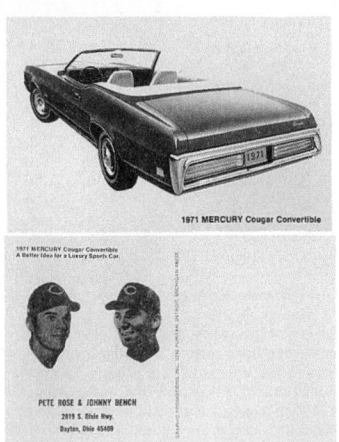

1971 MERCURY Cougar Convertible

		NM	E	VG
	Common Card:	50.00	25.00	15.00
(1)	Johnny Bench, Pete Rose (1971 Lincoln Continental Sedan)	25.00	12.50	7.50
(2)	Johnny Bench, Pete Rose (1971 Mercury Cougar Convertible)	25.00	12.50	7.50
(3)	Johnny Bench, Pete Rose (1971 Mercury Montego)	25.00	12.50	7.50
(3)	Johnny Bench, Pete Rose (1971 Mercury Monterrey)	50.00	25.00	15.00

1972 Pete Rose & Johnny Bench Lincoln-Mercury Postcards

This series of promotional postcards was issued in 1971-72 in conjunction with a Dayton, Ohio, Lincoln-Mercury auto dealership owned by Reds teammates Rose and Bench. Fronts of the 5-1/2" x 3-1/2" postcards feature color photos of new cars. Black, white and backs have portraits of the players, a description of the auto, the address of the dealership and a credit line for the postcard's printer. Besides those listed here, other auto fronts may exist.

		NM	E	VG
(1)	Pete Rose, Johnny Bench (1972 Mercury Marquis Brougham Colony Park Station Wagon)	50.00	25.00	15.00

1961 Peters Meats Twins

This set, featuring the first-year 1961 Minnesota Twins, is in a large, 4-5/8" x 3-1/2", format. Cards are on thick cardboard and heavily waxed, as they were used as partial packaging for the company's meat products. Card fronts feature full-color photos, team and Peters logos, and biographical information. The cards are blank-backed. Prices shown are for cards with the surrounding packaging panel. Cut cards are worth about 50-75 percent of the prices shown.

		NM	E	VG
	Complete Set, Panels (26):	1,925	975.00	575.00
	Complete Set, Cards (26):	1,500	750.00	450.00
	Common Player, Panel:	80.00	40.00	24.00
	Common Player, Card:	50.00	25.00	15.00
1	Zoilo Versalles	160.00	80.00	48.00
2	Eddie Lopat	80.00	40.00	24.00
3	Pedro Ramos	160.00	80.00	48.00
4	Charles "Chuck" Stobbs	80.00	40.00	24.00
5	Don Mincher	80.00	40.00	24.00
6	Jack Kralick	80.00	40.00	24.00
7	Jim Kaat	125.00	65.00	35.00
8	Hal Naragon	80.00	40.00	24.00
9	Don Lee	80.00	40.00	24.00
10	Harry "Cookie" Lavagetto	80.00	40.00	24.00
11	Tom "Pete" Whisenant	80.00	40.00	24.00
12	Elmer Valo	80.00	40.00	24.00
13	Ray Moore	80.00	40.00	24.00
14	Billy Gardner	80.00	40.00	24.00
15	Lenny Green	80.00	40.00	24.00
16	Sam Mele	80.00	40.00	24.00
17	Jim Lemon	80.00	40.00	24.00
18	Harmon "Killer" Killebrew	450.00	220.00	135.00
19	Paul Giel	80.00	40.00	24.00
20	Reno Bertoia	80.00	40.00	24.00
21	Clyde McCullough	80.00	40.00	24.00
22	Earl Battey	80.00	40.00	24.00
23	Camilo Pascual	160.00	80.00	48.00
24	Dan Dobbek	80.00	40.00	24.00
25	Joe "Valvy" Valdivielso	80.00	40.00	24.00
26	Billy Consolo	80.00	40.00	24.00

1952 Philadelphia A's/Phillies Player Pins

Only players on the Philadelphia A's and Phillies are found in this series of player pinbacks. The 1-3/4" diameter celluloid pins have black-and-white player portraits on front. The player name is printed in block letters across his shoulders, while the team name is printed in script across the chest. It is possible other player pins may exist. The unnumbered pieces are checklisted here in alphabetical order.

		NM	E	VG
	Common Player:	150.00	75.00	45.00
	Philadelphia Athletics			
(1)	Ferris Fain	200.00	100.00	60.00
(2)	Bobby Shantz	200.00	100.00	60.00
(3)	Gus Zernial	200.00	100.00	60.00
	Philadelphia Phillies			
(1)	Richie Ashburn	300.00	150.00	90.00
(2)	Del Ennis	150.00	75.00	45.00
(3)	Granny Hamner	150.00	75.00	45.00
(4)	Willie Jones	150.00	75.00	45.00
(5)	Jim Konstanty	150.00	75.00	45.00
(6)	Robin Roberts	300.00	150.00	90.00
(7)	Andy Seminick	150.00	75.00	45.00
(8)	Curt Simmons	150.00	75.00	45.00
(9)	Dick Sisler	150.00	75.00	45.00
(10)	Eddie Waitkus	150.00	75.00	45.00

1938-53 Philadelphia A's Team-Issue Photos

For a decade and a half the Philadelphia A's issued souvenir sets of black-and-white player photos. All are in a 7" x 10" format but the size of picture, the use of posed action and portrait photos and the type style of the name printed in the bottom border differ among the years. In many cases, pictures were re-issued year after year making it impossible 50 years later to reconstruct the composition of any particular year's issue. The unnumbered pictures are checklisted here alphabetically. Multiple player listings are the result of known pose variations. Gaps have been left in the assigned numbering for future additions.

		NM	E	VG
	Common Player:	12.00	6.00	3.50
(1)	Joe Astroth	12.00	6.00	3.50
(2)	Loren Babe	12.00	6.00	3.50
(3)	Johnny Babich	12.00	6.00	3.50
(4)	Bill Beckman	12.00	6.00	3.50
(5)	Joe Berry	12.00	6.00	3.50
(6)	Herman Besse	12.00	6.00	3.50
(7)	Hal Bevan	12.00	6.00	3.50
(8)	Henry Biasatti	12.00	6.00	3.50
(9)	Don Black	12.00	6.00	3.50
(10)	Lena Blackburne	12.00	6.00	3.50
(11)	Buddy Blair	12.00	6.00	3.50
(12)	Don Bollweg	12.00	6.00	3.50
(13)	Al Brancato	12.00	6.00	3.50
(14)	Lou Brissie	12.00	6.00	3.50
(15)	Earle Brucker	12.00	6.00	3.50
(16)	Earle Brucker	12.00	6.00	3.50
(17)	Earle Brucker	12.00	6.00	3.50
(18)	William Burgo	15.00	7.50	4.50
(19)	Joe Burns	12.00	6.00	3.50
(20)	Ed Burtschy	12.00	6.00	3.50
(21)	Edgar Busch	12.00	6.00	3.50
(22)	Harry Byrd	12.00	6.00	3.50
(23)	Fred Caligiuri	18.00	9.00	5.50
(24)	George Caster	12.00	6.00	3.50
(25)	Jim Castiglia	12.00	6.00	3.50
(27)	Sam Chapman	12.00	6.00	3.50
(28)	Sam Chapman	12.00	6.00	3.50
(29)	Sam Chapman	12.00	6.00	3.50
(30)	Russ Christopher	12.00	6.00	3.50
(31)	Joe Coleman	12.00	6.00	3.50
(32)	Eddie Collins Jr.	15.00	7.50	4.50
(33)	Lawrence Davis	12.00	6.00	3.50
(34)	Tom Davis	12.00	6.00	3.50
(35)	Chubby Dean	12.00	6.00	3.50
(36)	Joe DeMaestri	12.00	6.00	3.50
(37)	Russ Derry	12.00	6.00	3.50
(38)	Gene Desautels	12.00	6.00	3.50
(39)	Art Ditmar	12.00	6.00	3.50
(40)	Jimmy Dykes	12.00	6.00	3.50
(41)	Bob Estalella	12.00	6.00	3.50
(42)	Nick Etten	12.00	6.00	3.50
(43)	Ferris Fain	18.00	9.00	5.50
(44)	Tom Ferrick	12.00	6.00	3.50
(45)	Jim Finigan	12.00	6.00	3.50
(46)	Lewis Flick	12.00	6.00	3.50
(47)	Jesse Flores	12.00	6.00	3.50
(48)	Richard Fowler	12.00	6.00	3.50
(49)	Nelson Fox	30.00	15.00	9.00
(51)	Marion Fricano	12.00	6.00	3.50
(52)	Joe Gantenbein	12.00	6.00	3.50
(53)	Ford Garrison	12.00	6.00	3.50
(54)	Mike Guerra	12.00	6.00	3.50
(55)	Irv Hadley	12.00	6.00	3.50
(56)	Irv Hall	12.00	6.00	3.50
(57)	Luke Hamlin	12.00	6.00	3.50
(58)	Gene Handley	12.00	6.00	3.50
(59)	Bob Harris	12.00	6.00	3.50
(60)	Charlie Harris	12.00	6.00	3.50
(61)	Luman C. Harris (Full-length.)	12.00	6.00	3.50
(62)	Luman Harris	12.00	6.00	3.50
(63)	Frank Hayes	12.00	6.00	3.50
(64)	Bob Johnson	15.00	7.50	4.50
(65)	Bob Johnson	15.00	7.50	4.50
(66)	Eddie Joost	12.00	6.00	3.50
(67)	David Keefe	12.00	6.00	3.50
(68)	George Kell	20.00	10.00	6.00
(69)	Everett Kell	15.00	7.50	4.50
(70)	Alex Kellner	12.00	6.00	3.50
(71)	Alex Kellner	12.00	6.00	3.50
(72)	Lou Klein	12.00	6.00	3.50
(73)	Bill Knickerbocker	12.00	6.00	3.50
(74)	Jack Knott	12.00	6.00	3.50
(75)	Mike Kreevich	12.00	6.00	3.50
(76)	John Kucab	12.00	6.00	3.50
(77)	Paul Lehner	12.00	6.00	3.50

(78)	Bill Lillard	12.00	6.00	3.50
(79)	Lou Limmer	12.00	6.00	3.50
(80)	Lou Limmer	12.00	6.00	3.50
(81)	Dario Lodigiani	12.00	6.00	3.50
(82)	Connie Mack	20.00	10.00	6.00
(83)	Connie Mack	20.00	10.00	6.00
(84)	Connie Mack	20.00	10.00	6.00
(85)	Connie Mack	20.00	10.00	6.00
(86)	Earle Mack	15.00	7.50	4.50
(87)	Earle Mack	15.00	7.50	4.50
(88)	Felix Mackiewicz	12.00	6.00	3.50
(89)	Hank Majeski	12.00	6.00	3.50
(90)	Hank Majeski	12.00	6.00	3.50
(91)	Phil Marchildon	12.00	6.00	3.50
(92)	Phil Marchildon	12.00	6.00	3.50
(93)	Phil Marchildon	12.00	6.00	3.50
(94)	Morris Martin	12.00	6.00	3.50
(95)	Barney McCosky	12.00	6.00	3.50
(96)	Bennie McCoy	12.00	6.00	3.50
(97)	Les McCrabb	12.00	6.00	3.50
(98)	Bill McGhee	18.00	9.00	5.50
(99)	George McQuinn	12.00	6.00	3.50
(101)	Charlie Metro	12.00	6.00	3.50
(102)	Cass Michaels	12.00	6.00	3.50
(103)	Dee Miles	12.00	6.00	3.50
(104)	Wally Moses	12.00	6.00	3.50
(105)	Wally Moses	12.00	6.00	3.50
(106)	Ray Murray	12.00	6.00	3.50
(107)	Bill Nagel	12.00	6.00	3.50
(108)	Bobo Newsom	12.00	6.00	3.50
(109)	Skeeter Newsome	12.00	6.00	3.50
(110)	Hal Peck	12.00	6.00	3.50
(111)	Dave Philley	12.00	6.00	3.50
(112)	Cotton Pippen	12.00	6.00	3.50
(113)	Arnie Portocarrero	12.00	6.00	3.50
(114)	Nelson Potter	12.00	6.00	3.50
(115)	Vic Power	15.00	7.50	4.50
(116)	Jim Pruett	12.00	6.00	3.50
(117)	Bill Renna	12.00	6.00	3.50
(118)	Al Robertson	12.00	6.00	3.50
(119)	Ed Robinson	12.00	6.00	3.50
(120)	Buddy Rosar	12.00	6.00	3.50
(121)	Buddy Rosar	12.00	6.00	3.50
(122)	Al Rubeling	12.00	6.00	3.50
(123)	Joseph Rullo	18.00	9.00	5.50
(124)	Carl Scheib	12.00	6.00	3.50
(125)	Bill Shantz	15.00	7.50	4.50
(126)	Bob Shantz	18.00	9.00	5.50
(127)	Newman Shirley	12.00	6.00	3.50
(128)	Dick Siebert (Thigh-to-cap.)	12.00	6.00	3.50
(129)	Dick Siebert	12.00	6.00	3.50
(130)	Al Simmons	25.00	12.50	7.50
(131)	Al Simmons	25.00	12.50	7.50
(132)	Tuck Stainback	12.00	6.00	3.50
(133)	Pete Suder (Waist-to-cap.)	12.00	6.00	3.50
(134)	Pete Suder	12.00	6.00	3.50
(135)	Bob Swift	12.00	6.00	3.50
(136)	Keith Thomas	12.00	6.00	3.50
(137)	Eric Tipton	12.00	6.00	3.50
(138)	Bob Trice	12.00	6.00	3.50
(139)	Elmer Valo (Portrait to waist.)	12.00	6.00	3.50
(140)	Elmer Valo	12.00	6.00	3.50
(141)	Ozzie Van Brabant	18.00	9.00	5.50
(142)	Porter Vaughan	12.00	6.00	3.50
(143)	Harold Wagner	12.00	6.00	3.50
(144)	Harold Wagner	12.00	6.00	3.50
(145)	Jack Wallaesa	12.00	6.00	3.50
(146)	Johnny Welaj	12.00	6.00	3.50
(147)	Elwood Wheaton	15.00	7.50	4.50
(148)	Don White	12.00	6.00	3.50
(149)	Jo Jo White	12.00	6.00	3.50
(151)	Roger Wolff	12.00	6.00	3.50
(152)	Tom Wright	12.00	6.00	3.50
(153)	Gus Zernial	17.50	8.75	5.25
(154)	1938 A's Team	30.00	15.00	9.00
(155)	1939 A's Team	30.00	15.00	9.00
(156)	1940 A's Team	30.00	15.00	9.00
(157)	1941 A's Team	30.00	15.00	9.00
(158)	1942 A's Team	30.00	15.00	9.00
(159)	1943 A's Team	30.00	15.00	9.00
(160)	1944 A's Team	30.00	15.00	9.00
(161)	1945 A's Team	30.00	15.00	9.00
(162)	1946 A's Team	24.00	12.00	7.25
(163)	1948 A's Team	24.00	12.00	7.25
(164)	1949 A's Team	24.00	12.00	7.25
(165)	Shibe Park	30.00	15.00	9.00

1954 Philadelphia A's Stickers

The issuer of this novelty set and the exact scope of its checklist are currently unknown. The pieces are printed in black-and-white on 4-1/2" x 6-1/2" to 8-1/4," depending on pose gummed-back paper. Instructions on front say, "(Moisten back. Paste on Cardboard and cut out.)" Only the player name is printed beneath the photo.

JOE ASTROTH

		NM	E	VG
Common Player:		25.00	12.50	7.50
(1)	Joe Astroth	25.00	12.50	7.50
(2)	Charlie Bishop	25.00	12.50	7.50
(3)	Don Bollweg	25.00	12.50	7.50
(4)	Bob Cain	25.00	12.50	7.50
(5)	Joe DeMaestri	25.00	12.50	7.50
(6)	Marion Fricano	25.00	12.50	7.50
(7)	Tom Giordano	25.00	12.50	7.50
(8)	Forrest Jacobs	25.00	12.50	7.50
(9)	Eddie Joost	25.00	12.50	7.50
(10)	Alex Kellner	25.00	12.50	7.50
(11)	Morrie Martin	25.00	12.50	7.50
(12)	Ed McGhee	25.00	12.50	7.50
(13)	Arnold Portocarrero	25.00	12.50	7.50
(14)	Vic Power	35.00	17.50	10.50
(15)	Bill Renna	25.00	12.50	7.50
(16)	Jim Robertson	25.00	12.50	7.50
(17)	Carl Scheib	25.00	12.50	7.50
(18)	Bob Shantz	35.00	17.50	10.50
(19)	Pete Suder	25.00	12.50	7.50
(20)	Bob Trice	25.00	12.50	7.50
(21)	Bill Upton	25.00	12.50	7.50
(22)	Elmer Valo	25.00	12.50	7.50
(23)	Leroy Wheat	25.00	12.50	7.50
(24)	Gus Zernial	25.00	12.50	7.50

1948 Philadelphia Bulletin Stand-Ups

These player pictures were printed in the "Fun Book" color section of the Sunday paper. The full-body pose cutouts carry facsimile autographs and were printed four per week on a page of about 9-1/2" x 14". While the individual pictures vary is size according to the pose, most are about 3" to 4" x 6-1/2" to 7". The player pictures are in black-and-white with a blue background and red base. They were intended to be cut out around the heavy black line, pasted to cardboard and folded at their base to create a stand-up figure. Values shown here are for well trimmed pieces without evidence of mounting. Complete pages carry a premium somewhat greater than the sum of the players present.

		NM	E	VG
Common Player:		15.00	7.50	4.50
	PHILADELPHIA A's			
	June 13	75.00	37.00	22.00
(1)	Ferris Fain	15.00	7.50	4.50
(2)	Eddie Joost	15.00	7.50	4.50
(3)	Hank Majeski	15.00	7.50	4.50
(4)	Pete Suder	15.00	7.50	4.50
	June 20	75.00	37.00	22.00
(5)	Sam Chapman	15.00	7.50	4.50
(6)	Barney McCosky	15.00	7.50	4.50
(7)	Buddy Rosar	15.00	7.50	4.50
(8)	Elmer Valo	15.00	7.50	4.50
	June 27	75.00	37.00	22.00
(9)	Mike Guerra	15.00	7.50	4.50
(10)	Dick Fowler	15.00	7.50	4.50
(11)	Phil Marchildon	15.00	7.50	4.50
(12)	Carl Sheib	15.00	7.50	4.50

	July 4	75.00	37.00	22.00
(13)	Joe Coleman	15.00	7.50	4.50
(14)	Bob Savage	15.00	7.50	4.50
(15)	Don White	15.00	7.50	4.50
(16)	Rudy York	15.00	7.50	4.50
	July 11	75.00	37.00	22.00
(17)	Herman Franks	15.00	7.50	4.50
(18)	Charlie Harris	15.00	7.50	4.50
(19)	Bill McCahan	15.00	7.50	4.50
(20)	Skeeter Webb	15.00	7.50	4.50
	July 18	75.00	37.00	22.00
(21)	Lou Brissie	15.00	7.50	4.50
(22)	Ray Coleman	15.00	7.50	4.50
(23)	Billy DeMars	15.00	7.50	4.50
(24)	Skeeter Webb (Photo not Webb)	15.00	7.50	4.50
	PHILADELPHIA PHILLIES			
	July 25	90.00	45.00	27.00
(1)	Don Padgett	15.00	7.50	4.50
(2)	Schoolboy Rowe	15.00	7.50	4.50
(3)	Andy Seminick	15.00	7.50	4.50
(4)	Curt Simmons	20.00	10.00	6.00
	August 1	225.00	110.00	67.00
(5)	Richie Ashburn	150.00	75.00	45.00
(6)	Johnny Blatnik	15.00	7.50	4.50
(7)	Del Ennis	20.00	10.00	6.00
(8)	Harry Walker	15.00	7.50	4.50
	August 8	75.00	37.00	22.00
(9)	Bert Haas	15.00	7.50	4.50
(10)	Granny Hamner	15.00	7.50	4.50
(11)	Eddie Miller	15.00	7.50	4.50
(12)	Dick Sisler	15.00	7.50	4.50
	August 15	200.00	100.00	60.00
(13)	Ralph Caballero	15.00	7.50	4.50
(14)	Ed Heusser	15.00	7.50	4.50
(15)	Robin Roberts	125.00	62.00	37.00
(16)	Emil Verban	15.00	7.50	4.50
	August 22	75.00	37.00	22.00
(17)	Blix Donnelly	15.00	7.50	4.50
(18)	Walt Dubiel	15.00	7.50	4.50
(19)	Ken Heintzelman	15.00	7.50	4.50
(20)	Dutch Leonard	15.00	7.50	4.50
	August 29	75.00	37.00	22.00
(21)	Charlie Bicknell	15.00	7.50	4.50
(22)	Al Lakeman	15.00	7.50	4.50
(23)	Sam Nahem	15.00	7.50	4.50
(24)	Carvel "Bama" Rowell	15.00	7.50	4.50

1949 Philadelphia Bulletin A's/Phillies

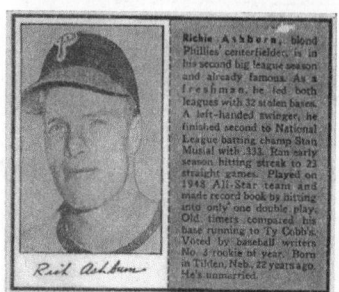

Each Sunday between May 22 and July 24, 1949, the "Fun Book" rotogravure section of the Bulletin included a page of (usually) six baseball "cards" of the hometeam A's and Phillies which could be cut out and pasted to cardboard. The left side (front) of each card has a sepia portrait of the player, while a colored box at right (back) has biographical and career information. Uncut and unfolded, each card measures about 4-1/2" x 3-5/8". If cut out and pasted onto cardboard, the created cards would measure about 2-1/4" x 3-5/8". Complete pages measure about 9-1/2" x 13-3/8". Values shown are for single "cards" which have been cut off the page, but not pasted onto a backing.

		NM	E	VG
Complete Set (60):		1,600	800.00	480.00
Common Player:		25.00	12.50	7.50
	MAY 22			
(1)	Richie Ashburn	265.00	130.00	79.00
(2)	Granny Hamner	25.00	12.50	7.50
(3)	Eddie Joost	25.00	12.50	7.50
(4)	Bill Nicholson	25.00	12.50	7.50
(5)	Buddy Rosar	25.00	12.50	7.50
(6)	Pete Suder	25.00	12.50	7.50
	MAY 29			
(7)	Hank Borowy	25.00	12.50	7.50
(8)	Del Ennis	35.00	17.50	10.50
(9)	Ferris Fain	35.00	17.50	10.50
(10)	Phil Marchildon	25.00	12.50	7.50
(11)	Wally Moses	25.00	12.50	7.50
(12)	Eddie Waitkus	25.00	12.50	7.50
	JUNE 5			

(13)	Dick Fowler	25.00	12.50	7.50
(14)	Willie Jones	25.00	12.50	7.50
(15)	Stan Lopata	25.00	12.50	7.50
(16)	Hank Majeski	25.00	12.50	7.50
(17)	Schoolboy Rowe	25.00	12.50	7.50
(18)	Elmer Valo	25.00	12.50	7.50
JUNE 12				
(19)	Joe Coleman	25.00	12.50	7.50
(20)	Charley Harris	25.00	12.50	7.50
(21)	Russ Meyer	25.00	12.50	7.50
(22)	Eddie Miller	25.00	12.50	7.50
(23)	Robin Roberts	265.00	130.00	79.00
(24)	Taft Wright	25.00	12.50	7.50
JUNE 19				
(25)	Lou Brissie	25.00	12.50	7.50
(26)	Ralph Caballero	25.00	12.50	7.50
(27)	Sam Chapman	25.00	12.50	7.50
(28)	Fermin (Mike) Guerra	25.00	12.50	7.50
(29)	Jim Konstanty	35.00	17.50	10.50
(30)	Curt Simmons	35.00	17.50	10.50
JUNE 26				
(31)	Charles Bicknell	25.00	12.50	7.50
(32)	Ken Heintzelman	25.00	12.50	7.50
(33)	Alex Kellner	25.00	12.50	7.50
(34)	Barney McCosky	25.00	12.50	7.50
(35)	Bobby Shantz	35.00	17.50	10.50
(36)	Ken Trinkle	25.00	12.50	7.50
JULY 3				
(37)	Blix Donnelly	25.00	12.50	7.50
(38)	Bill McCahan	25.00	12.50	7.50
(39)	Carl Scheib	25.00	12.50	7.50
(40)	Andy Seminick	25.00	12.50	7.50
(41)	Dick Sisler	25.00	12.50	7.50
(42)	Don White	25.00	12.50	7.50
JULY 10				
(43)	Joe Astroth	25.00	12.50	7.50
(44)	Henry Biasetti	25.00	12.50	7.50
(45)	Buddy Blattner	25.00	12.50	7.50
(46)	Thomas O. Davis	25.00	12.50	7.50
(47)	Stan Hollmig	25.00	12.50	7.50
(48)	Jackie Mayo	25.00	12.50	7.50
JULY 17				
(49)	Benny Bengough	25.00	12.50	7.50
(50)	Earle Brucker	25.00	12.50	7.50
(51)	Dusty Cooke	25.00	12.50	7.50
(52)	Jimmy Dykes	25.00	12.50	7.50
(53)	Cy Perkins	25.00	12.50	7.50
(54)	Al Simmons	40.00	20.00	12.00
JULY 24				
(55)	Nellie Fox	265.00	130.00	79.00
(56)	Connie Mack	200.00	100.00	60.00
(57)	Earle Mack	25.00	12.50	7.50
(58)	Eddie Sawyer	25.00	12.50	7.50
(59)	Ken Silvestri	25.00	12.50	7.50
(59)	Phillies / A's Pennants	25.00	12.50	7.50

1950 Philadelphia Bulletin Pin-Ups

This series of 8" x 10" black-and-white portraits of Phillies players, coaches, and manager was produced in two versions. A (mostly) numbered newsprint version was issued one per day in the paper, between September 13-30. A premium version, printed on heavy paper with a semi-gloss finish and blank back, was made available to fans for a nickel at the newspaper's office or a dime by mail. Each of the pictures is a cap-less portrait with facsimile autograph on front. A number of players in the premium version were not issued in the newsprint style.

		NM	E	VG
Complete Set (26):		900.00	450.00	275.00
Common Player:		40.00	20.00	12.00
(1)	Rich Ashburn	75.00	37.00	22.00
(2)	Jimmy Bloodworth	40.00	20.00	12.00
(3)	Ralph Caballero	40.00	20.00	12.00
(4)	Milo Candini	40.00	20.00	12.00
(5)	Emory Church	40.00	20.00	12.00
(6)	Sylvester (Blix) Donnelly	40.00	20.00	12.00
(7)	Del Ennis	50.00	25.00	15.00
(8)	Mike Goliat	40.00	20.00	12.00

(9)	Gran Hamner	40.00	20.00	12.00
(10)	Ken Heintzelman	40.00	20.00	12.00
(11)	Stan Hollmig	40.00	20.00	12.00
(12)	Ken Johnson	40.00	20.00	12.00
(13)	Willie Jones	40.00	20.00	12.00
(14)	Jim Konstanty	40.00	20.00	12.00
(15)	Stan Lopata	40.00	20.00	12.00
(16)	Russ Meyer	40.00	20.00	12.00
(17)	Bob Miller	40.00	20.00	12.00
(18)	Bill Nicholson	40.00	20.00	12.00
(19)	Robin Roberts	65.00	32.00	19.50
(20)	Eddie Sawyer	40.00	20.00	12.00
(21)	Andy Seminick	40.00	20.00	12.00
(22)	Ken Silvestri	40.00	20.00	12.00
(23)	Curtis T. Simmons	50.00	25.00	15.00
(24)	Dick Sisler	40.00	20.00	12.00
(25)	Eddie Waitkus	40.00	20.00	12.00
(26)	Dick Whitman	40.00	20.00	12.00

1964 Philadelphia Bulletin Phillies Album (Paper)

This series of newspaper features was the basis for the more often-encountered mail-in premiums. About 5-1/2" x 9", these pieces were printed in black-and-white in the sports section of the daily paper. The artwork is by staff artist Jim Porter. While the newspaper pieces are numbered, they are checklisted here in alphabetical order due to uncertainty about the original issue sequence.

		NM	E	VG
Complete Set (27):		400.00	200.00	120.00
Common Player:		15.00	7.50	4.50
(1)	Richie Allen	40.00	20.00	12.00
(2)	Ruben Amaro	15.00	7.50	4.50
(3)	Jack Baldschun	15.00	7.50	4.50
(4)	Dennis Bennett	15.00	7.50	4.50
(5)	John Boozer	15.00	7.50	4.50
(6)	Johnny Briggs	15.00	7.50	4.50
(7)	Jim Bunning	50.00	25.00	15.00
(8)	Johnny Callison	15.00	7.50	4.50
(9)	Danny Cater	15.00	7.50	4.50
(10)	Wes Covington	15.00	7.50	4.50
(11)	Ray Culp	15.00	7.50	4.50
(12)	Clay Dalrymple	15.00	7.50	4.50
(13)	Tony Gonzalez	15.00	7.50	4.50
(14)	John Herrnstein	15.00	7.50	4.50
(15)	Alex Johnson	15.00	7.50	4.50
(16)	Art Mahaffey	15.00	7.50	4.50
(17)	Gene Mauch	15.00	7.50	4.50
(18)	Vic Power	15.00	7.50	4.50
(19)	Ed Roebuck	15.00	7.50	4.50
(20)	Cookie Rojas	15.00	7.50	4.50
(21)	Bobby Shantz	15.00	7.50	4.50
(22)	Chris Short	15.00	7.50	4.50
(23)	Tony Taylor	15.00	7.50	4.50
(24)	Frank Thomas	15.00	7.50	4.50
(25)	Gus Triandos	15.00	7.50	4.50
(26)	Bobby Wine	15.00	7.50	4.50
(27)	Rick Wise	15.00	7.50	4.50

1909 Philadelphia Caramel (E95)

Similar in style to several other early candy and caramel cards, the set designated as E95 by the American Card Catalog is a 25-card issue produced by the Philadelphia Caramel Co., Camden, N.J., in 1909. The cards measure approximately 1-1/2" x 2-5/8" and contain a full-color player drawing. The back, which differentiates the set from other similar issues, checklists the 25 players in black ink at the bottom. The Philadelphia Caramel Co. name at the bottom. Blank-back cards printed on thinner stock exist; these are not proofs, but were cut off a "Base Ball Series" notebook cover, they are valued about 25-50 percent of a corresponding regular-issue card. This set has been widely counterfeited.

MORGAN, ATHLETICS AMER.

		NM	E	VG
Complete Set (25):		50,000	20,000	10,000
Common Player:		1,000	400.00	140.00
1	Honus Wagner	10,000	5,000	3,000
2	Nick Maddox	1,000	400.00	140.00
3	Fred Merkle	1,000	400.00	140.00
4	Cy Morgan	1,000	400.00	140.00
5	Chief Bender	2,000	1,000	600.00
6	Harry Krause	1,000	400.00	140.00
7	Art Devlin	1,000	400.00	140.00
8	Matty McIntyre	1,000	400.00	140.00
9	Ty Cobb	10,000	5,000	3,000
10	Ed Willetts (Willett)	1,000	400.00	140.00
11	Sam Crawford	2,000	1,000	600.00
12	Christy Matthewson (Mathewson)	8,750	4,375	2,625
13	Hooks Wiltse	1,000	400.00	140.00
14	Larry Doyle	1,000	400.00	140.00
15	Tommy Leach	1,000	400.00	140.00
16	Harry Lord	1,000	400.00	140.00
17	Ed Cicotte	3,375	1,500	700.00
18	Bill Carrigan	1,000	400.00	140.00
19	Vic Willis	2,500	1,250	750.00
20	Johnny Evers	2,500	1,250	750.00
21	Frank Chance	2,000	1,000	600.00
22	Solly Hoffman (Hofman)	1,000	400.00	140.00
23	Eddie Plank	4,500	2,200	1,350
24	Eddie Collins	2,000	1,000	600.00
25	Ed Reulbach	1,000	400.00	140.00

1910 Philadelphia Caramel (E96)

This set of 30 subjects, known by the ACC designation E96, was issued in 1910 by the Philadelphia Caramel Co. The approximately 1-1/2" x 2-5/8" size and front design remained the same, but the two issues can be identified by the backs. The backs of E96 cards are printed in red and carry a checklist of 30 players. There is also a line at the bottom advising "Previous series 25, making total issue 55 cards." Just below that appears "Philadelphia Caramel Co./Camden, N.J." Blank-back cards printed on thinner stock are not proofs, but rather were cut off a "Base Ball Series" notebook cover. They are valued about 25-50 percent of a corresponding regular-issue card.

		NM	E	VG
Complete Set (30):		38,500	15,500	7,700
Common Player:		2,000	800.00	400.00
1	Harry Davis	2,000	800.00	400.00
2	Connie Mack	3,000	1,200	600.00
3	Ira Thomas	2,000	800.00	400.00
4	Home Run Baker	3,000	1,200	600.00
5	Red Dooin	2,000	800.00	400.00
6	George McQuillan	2,000	800.00	400.00

7	Ed Konetchy	2,000	800.00	400.00
8	Ed Karger	2,000	800.00	400.00
9	Mike Mowrey	2,000	800.00	400.00
10	Red Murray	2,000	800.00	400.00
11	Nap Lajoie	3,250	1,300	650.00
12	Claude Rossman	2,000	800.00	400.00
13	Nap Rucker	2,000	800.00	400.00
14	Hugh Jennings	3,000	1,200	600.00
15	Wild Bill Donovan	3,000	1,200	600.00
16	Jim Delahanty	2,000	800.00	400.00
17	George Mullin	2,000	800.00	400.00
18	Frank Arrelanes (Arellanes)	2,000	800.00	400.00
19	Tubby Spencer	2,000	800.00	400.00
20	Johnny Kling	2,000	800.00	400.00
21	Jack Pfister (Pfiester)	2,000	800.00	400.00
22	Mordecai Brown	3,000	1,200	600.00
23	Joe Tinker	3,000	1,200	600.00
24	Fred Clark (Clarke)	3,000	1,200	600.00
25	George Gibson	2,000	800.00	400.00
26	Babe Adams	2,000	800.00	400.00
27	Red Ames	2,000	800.00	400.00
28	Rube Marquard	3,000	1,200	600.00
29	Buck Herzog	2,000	800.00	400.00
30	Chief Myers (Meyers)	2,000	800.00	400.00

1913 Philadelphia Caramel Proofs

CHANCE, NEW YORK, A. L.

The attribution of these cards to Philadelphia Caramel is speculative, since no advertising is found on their blank backs. The three known pieces, however, have pictures and color identical to the players' cards in the 1910 E96 Philadelphia Caramel issue. These proofs differ only in the team designations. Nominally 1-1/2" x 2-5/8", the known examples were hand-cut from a sheet and are, at present, each unique. The Kling card was offered at auction in 2003 without meeting a $500 reserve.

Frank Chance (New York, A.L.)
Harry Davis (Cleveland)
Johnny Kling (Boston, A.L.)

1913 Philadelphia Evening Times Supplements

The checklist comprised almost entirely of Connie Mack's A's and John McGraw's Giants suggests this series of newspaper supplements was issued around World Series time. The blank-backed, sepia-toned pictures have posed action photos, are printed on light cardboard stock and measure about 7-1/2" x 9-1/2". This checklist may be incomplete.

		NM	E	VG
	Common Player:	200.00	100.00	60.00
(1)	Frank Baker	400.00	200.00	120.00
(2)	Jack Barry	200.00	100.00	60.00
(3)	Chief Bender	400.00	200.00	120.00
(4)	George Burns	200.00	100.00	60.00
(5)	Ty Cobb	1,200	600.00	360.00
(6)	Eddie Collins	400.00	200.00	120.00
(7)	Al Demaree	200.00	100.00	60.00
(8)	Larry Doyle	200.00	100.00	60.00
(9)	Walter Johnson	800.00	400.00	240.00

(10)	Rube Marquard	400.00	200.00	120.00
(11)	Christy Mathewson	800.00	400.00	240.00
(12)	Stuffy McInnis	200.00	100.00	60.00
(13)	Chief Meyers	200.00	100.00	60.00
(14)	Rube Oldring	200.00	100.00	60.00
(15)	Eddie Plank	400.00	200.00	120.00
(16)	Jeff Tesreau	200.00	100.00	60.00

1950 Philadelphia Inquirer Fightin' Phillies

RALPH JOSEPH CABALLERO, Infielder
Richmond "Putsy" Born Nov. 3, 1927, at New Orleans. Signed with Phils in 1944 as a 16-year-old. Threw, bats right-handed. Married, has one son. Can fill in at second base, third base or shortstop. Sees considerable service as pinch-runner. Batting .236 through Aug. 20.
Stephen Rights Phillies Album

As the Whiz Kids battled to a National League pennant the "Philadelphia Inquirer" instituted a set of cut-out baseball cards in the Sunday rotogravure editions during September. The 4-7/8" x 6-7/8" cards have colored portrait photos surrounded with a white border. A facsimile autograph is printed across the chest. In the bottom border are the player's formal name, position, career summary and the line, "Inquirer Fightin' Phillies Album." Backs have whatever articles or ads were on the next page. The unnumbered cards are printed here in alphabetical order.

		NM	E	VG
	Complete Set (24):	350.00	175.00	105.00
	Common Player:	15.00	7.50	4.50
(1)	Richie Ashburn	35.00	17.50	10.50
(2)	James Henry Bloodworth	15.00	7.50	4.50
(3)	Ralph Joseph Caballero	15.00	7.50	4.50
(4)	Milo Candini	15.00	7.50	4.50
(5)	Emory Church	15.00	7.50	4.50
(6)	Sylvester Urban Donnelly	15.00	7.50	4.50
(7)	Delmer Ennis	15.00	7.50	4.50
(8)	Mike Mitchel Goliat (Mitchell)	15.00	7.50	4.50
(9)	Granville Wilbur Hamner	15.00	7.50	4.50
(10)	Kenneth Alphonse Heintzelman	15.00	7.50	4.50
(11)	Stanley Ernst Hollmig	15.00	7.50	4.50
(12)	Kenneth W. Johnson	15.00	7.50	4.50
(13)	Willie Edward Jones	15.00	7.50	4.50
(14)	Stanley Edward Lopata	15.00	7.50	4.50
(15)	Russell Charles Meyer	15.00	7.50	4.50
(16)	Robert Miller	15.00	7.50	4.50
(17)	William Beck Nicholson	15.00	7.50	4.50
(18)	Robin Evan Roberts	35.00	17.50	10.50
(19)	Andrew Wasal Seminick	15.00	7.50	4.50
(20)	Kenneth Joseph Silvestri	15.00	7.50	4.50
(21)	Curtis Thomas Simmons	15.00	7.50	4.50
(22)	Richard Alan Sisler	15.00	7.50	4.50
(23)	Edward Stephen Waitkus	15.00	7.50	4.50
(24)	Dick Whitman	15.00	7.50	4.50

1954 Philadelphia Inquirer Album of Baseball Stars

Stanley Margata
[caption text illegible]

A series of four baseball players from each of Philadelphia's teams appeared on a pair of pages in the Colorama color rotogravure section of the Sunday. Philadelphia Inquirer. Each picture is about 6-3/4" x 9-3/4" and was separated from the other three on its "ALBUM OF SPORTS" page by a black dotted line, indicative of an intention for them to be cut out and saved. Under the portrait is a brief career summary. Backs have other newspaper content as printed each

Sunday.

		NM	E	VG
	Complete Set (8):	75.00	37.50	22.50
	Common Player:	8.00	4.00	2.50
	JULY 25			
(1)	Richie Ashburn	25.00	12.50	7.50
(2)	Jim Finigan	8.00	4.00	2.50
(3)	Gran Hamner	8.00	4.00	2.50
(4)	Bill Shantz	8.00	4.00	2.50
	SEPT. 12			
(1)	Smoky Burgess	10.00	5.00	3.00
(2)	Arnold Portocarrero	8.00	4.00	2.50
(3)	Robin Roberts	16.00	8.00	4.75
(4)	Curt Simmons	10.00	5.00	3.00

1940 Philadelphia Phillies Photo Pack

This set of 25 photos show players in poses on the field with the Quaker figure and "PHILADELPHIA NATIONAL LEAGUE BASE BALL CLUB" around it in a circular logo in the upper right hand corner. Size is 6" x 8-1/2".

		NM	E	VG
	Complete Set (25):	150.00	75.00	30.00
	Common Player:	7.50	3.75	2.25
(1)	Morrie Arnovich	7.50	3.75	2.25
(2)	Bill Atwood	7.50	3.75	2.25
(3)	Walter Beck	7.50	3.75	2.25
(4)	Stan Benjamin	7.50	3.75	2.25
(5)	Bob Bragan	7.50	3.75	2.25
(6)	Roy Bruner	7.50	3.75	2.25
(7)	Kirby Higbie	7.50	3.75	2.25
(8)	Si Johnson	7.50	3.75	2.25
(9)	Syl Johnson	7.50	3.75	2.25
(10)	Chuck Klein	7.50	3.75	2.25
(11)	Ed Levy	7.50	3.75	2.25
(12)	Dan Litwhiler	7.50	3.75	2.25
(13)	Hans Lobert	7.50	3.75	2.25
(14)	Herschel Martin	7.50	3.75	2.25
(15)	Joe Marty	7.50	3.75	2.25
(16)	Maerrill May	7.50	3.75	2.25
(17)	Walk Millies	7.50	3.75	2.25
(18)	Hugh Mulcahy	7.50	3.75	2.25
(19)	Ike Pearson	7.50	3.75	2.25
(20)	Doc Prothro	7.50	3.75	2.25
(21)	George Scharen	7.50	3.75	2.25
(22)	Clyde Smoll	7.50	3.75	2.25
(23)	Gus Suhr	7.50	3.75	2.25
(24)	Ben Warren	7.50	3.75	2.25
(25)	Del Young	7.50	3.75	2.25

1941 Philadelphia Phillies Photo Pack

This set features 26 player photos in black-and-white with facsimile autographs on a 6" x 8-1/2" format. They appear to have been issued as a concession stand souvenir item. Backs are blanks. The unnumbered cards are checklisted here in alphabetical order.

		NM	EX	VG
	Complete Set (26):	200.00	100.00	60.00
	Common Player:	8.00	4.00	2.50
(1)	Morrie Arnovich	8.00	4.00	2.50
(2)	Bill Atwood	8.00	4.00	2.50
(3)	Walter Beck	8.00	4.00	2.50
(4)	Stan Benjamin	8.00	4.00	2.50
(5)	Bob Bragan	8.00	4.00	2.50
(6)	Roy Bruner	8.00	4.00	2.50
(7)	Kirby Higbe	8.00	4.00	2.50
(8)	Frank Hoerst	8.00	4.00	2.50
(9)	Si Johnson	8.00	4.00	2.50
(10)	Syl Johnson	8.00	4.00	2.50
(11)	Chuck Klein	30.00	15.00	9.00
(12)	Ed Levy	8.00	4.00	2.50
(13)	Dan Litwhiler	8.00	4.00	2.50
(14)	Hans lobert	8.00	4.00	2.50
(15)	Hershel Martin	8.00	4.00	2.50
(16)	Joe Marty	8.00	4.00	2.50
(17)	Merrill May	8.00	4.00	2.50
(18)	Walt Millies	8.00	4.00	2.50
(19)	Hugh Mulcahy	8.00	4.00	2.50
(20)	Ike Pearson	8.00	4.00	2.50
(21)	Doc Prothro	8.00	4.00	2.50
(22)	George Scharein	8.00	4.00	2.50
(23)	Clyde Smoll	8.00	4.00	2.50
(24)	Gus Suh	8.00	4.00	2.50
(25)	Ben Warren	8.00	4.00	2.50
(26)	Del Young	8.00	4.00	2.50

1943 Philadelphia Phillies Photo Pack

Like many teams in that era, the Phillies issued souvenir photo packs for sale at the stadium and by mail-order. This team issue is in a 6" x 8-1/2", blank-back, black-and-white format. The player picture is bordered in white with the player name in all-caps in the bottom border. From the large number of players known, it is evident that the composition of the photo packs was changed from time to time as the team roster changed. It is possible this checklist is not complete. The unnumbered pictures have been listed here alphabetically.

"BUCKY" HARRIS

	NM	E	VG
Complete Set (42):	300.00	150.00	90.00
Common Player:	8.00	4.00	2.50
(1) Buster Adams	8.00	4.00	2.50
(2) Walter Beck	8.00	4.00	2.50
(3) Stan Benjamin	8.00	4.00	2.50
(4) Cy Blanton	8.00	4.00	2.50
(5) Bobby Bragan	8.00	4.00	2.50
(6) Charlie Brewster	8.00	4.00	2.50
(7) Paul Busby	8.00	4.00	2.50
(8) Ben Culp	8.00	4.00	2.50
(9) Babe Dahlgren	8.00	4.00	2.50
(10) Lloyd Dietz	8.00	4.00	2.50
(11) Nick Etten	8.00	4.00	2.50
(12) George Eyrich	8.00	4.00	2.50
(13) Charlie Fuchs	8.00	4.00	2.50
(14) Al Glossop	8.00	4.00	2.50
(15) Al Gerheauser	8.00	4.00	2.50
(16) "Bucky" Harris	12.00	6.00	3.50
(17) Frank Hoerst	8.00	4.00	2.50
(18) Si Johnson	8.00	4.00	2.50
(19) Bill Killefer	8.00	4.00	2.50
(20) Newell Kimball	8.00	4.00	2.50
(21) Chuck Klein	15.00	7.50	4.50
(22) Ernie Koy	8.00	4.00	2.50
(23) Tex Kraus	8.00	4.00	2.50
(24) Danny Litwhiler	8.00	4.00	2.50
(25) Mickey Livingston	8.00	4.00	2.50
(26) Hans Lobert	8.00	4.00	2.50
(27) Henry Marnie	8.00	4.00	2.50
(28) Merrill May	8.00	4.00	2.50
(29) Rube Melton	8.00	4.00	2.50
(30) Danny Murtaugh	10.00	5.00	3.00
(31) Sam Nahem	8.00	4.00	2.50
(32) Earl Naylor	8.00	4.00	2.50
(33) Ron Northey	8.00	4.00	2.50
(34) Tommy Padden	8.00	4.00	2.50
(35) Ike Pearson	8.00	4.00	2.50
(36) Johnny Podgajny	8.00	4.00	2.50
(37) Schoolboy Rowe	10.00	5.00	3.00
(38) Glen Stewart	8.00	4.00	2.50
(39) Coaker Triplett	8.00	4.00	2.50
(40) Lloyd Waner	15.00	7.50	4.50
(41) Ben Warren	8.00	4.00	2.50
(42) Jimmy Wasdell	8.00	4.00	2.50

1958 Philadelphia Phillies Picture Pack

This set of 5" x 7" blank-backed, black-and-white player pictures was most likely issued in 1958, though it is also possible the set was issued in 1957 (or both). This team-issue set differs from the contemporary Jay Publishing picture packs in that it does not have the city name in the identication line, only the player name in all-caps and "Phillies." The unnumbered pictures are listed here alphabetically.

	NM	E	VG
Complete Set (12):	75.00	40.00	22.50
Common Player:	7.50	3.75	2.25
(1) Harry Anderson	7.50	3.75	2.25
(2) Richie Ashburn	15.00	7.50	4.50
(3) Bob Bowman	7.50	3.75	2.25
(4) Turk Farrell	7.50	3.75	2.25
(5) Chico Fernandez	7.50	3.75	2.25
(6) Granny Hamner	7.50	3.75	2.25
(7) Stan Lopata	7.50	3.75	2.25
(8) Rip Repulski	7.50	3.75	2.25
(9) Robin Roberts	15.00	7.50	4.50
(10) Jack Sanford	7.50	3.75	2.25
(11) Curt Simmons	7.50	3.75	2.25
(12) Mayo Smith	7.50	3.75	2.25

1958-60 Philadelphia Phillies Team Issue

Thus far 22 different cards have been discovered in this format; it is likely the checklist here is not yet complete. Like many teams, the Phillies issued these cards to players and staff to honor fan requests for photos and autographs. The cards are 3-1/4" x 5-1/2" and have black-and-white portrait photos with white borders. Backs are blank. The unnumbered cards are listed here alphabetically.

	NM	E	VG
Common Player:	6.00	3.00	1.75
(1) Harry Anderson	6.00	3.00	1.75
(2) Richie Ashburn	12.00	6.00	3.50
(3) Ed Bouchee	6.00	3.00	1.75
(4) Smoky Burgess	7.50	3.75	2.25
(5) Johnny Callison	8.00	4.00	2.50
(6) Jim Coker	6.00	3.00	1.75
(7) Clay Dalrymple	6.00	3.00	1.75
(8) Del Ennis	7.50	3.75	2.25
(9) Tony Gonzalez	6.00	3.00	1.75
(10) Granny Hamner	6.00	3.00	1.75
(11) Willie Jones	6.00	3.00	1.75
(12) Stan Lopata	6.00	3.00	1.75
(13) Art Mahaffey	6.00	3.00	1.75
(14) Gene Mauch	6.00	3.00	1.75
(15) Bob Morgan	6.00	3.00	1.75
(16) Wally Post	6.00	3.00	1.75
(17) Robin Roberts	12.00	6.00	3.50
(18) Eddie Sawyer	6.00	3.00	1.75
(19) Andy Seminick	6.00	3.00	1.50
(20) Ray Semproch	6.00	3.00	1.75
(21) Chris Short	6.00	3.00	1.75
(22) Curt Simmons	8.00	4.00	2.50
(23) Earl Torgeson	6.00	3.00	1.75

1964 Philadelphia Phillies Player Pins

Only four players are checklisted in this series, but it is expected more will be added in the future. These pinbacks are 2-3/16" in diameter and have black-and-white player portraits on front, on a white background. The player's name is printed at bottom in block letters.

	NM	E	VG
Common Player:	45.00	22.50	13.50
(1) Dick Allen	90.00	45.00	27.50
(2) Jim Bunning	90.00	45.00	27.50
(3) Chris Short	45.00	22.50	13.50
(4) Roy Sievers	45.00	22.50	13.50

1965 Philadelphia Phillies Tiles

These decorative heavy ceramic tiles feature color portraits and facsimile autographs on a white background. In 6" x 6" format the tiles were made in England, but decorated in the U.S. They appear to have been originally issued with cork backing and some have been seen with a hangar attached on back.

	NM	E	VG
Complete Set (12):	600.00	300.00	180.00
Common Player:	40.00	20.00	12.00
(1) Richie Allen	100.00	50.00	30.00
(2) Bo Belinsky	60.00	30.00	18.00
(3) Jim Bunning	125.00	65.00	35.00
(4) Johnny Callison	60.00	30.00	18.00
(5) Wes Covington	40.00	20.00	12.00
(6) Clay Dalrymple	40.00	20.00	12.00
(7) Gene Mauch	40.00	20.00	12.00
(8) Cookie Rojas	40.00	20.00	12.00
(9) Tony Taylor	40.00	20.00	12.00
(10) Chris Short	40.00	20.00	12.00
(11) Dick Stuart	40.00	20.00	12.00
(12) Bobby Wine	40.00	20.00	12.00

1965 Go! Phillies Go! Pins

These large (3-1/2" diameter) pinback buttons feature a dozen members of the '65 Phils. Player portraits are on a white background and have had the cap and pinstripes colored in red. At top, the title is printed in red and blue. The facsimile autograph at bottom is printed in blue.

	NM	E	VG
Complete Set (12):	750.00	375.00	225.00
Common Player:	50.00	25.00	15.00
(1) Rich Allen	100.00	50.00	30.00
(2) Ruben Amaro	50.00	25.00	15.00
(3) Bo Belinsky	65.00	32.50	20.00
(4) Jim Bunning	100.00	50.00	30.00
(5) Johnny Callison	65.00	32.50	20.00
(6) Wes Covington	50.00	25.00	15.00
(7) Ray Culp	50.00	25.00	15.00
(8) Cookie Rojas	50.00	25.00	15.00
(9) Chris Short	50.00	25.00	15.00
(10) Dick Stuart	50.00	25.00	15.00
(11) Tony Taylor	50.00	25.00	15.00
(12) Bobby Wine	50.00	25.00	15.00

1967 Philadelphia Phillies Safe Driving

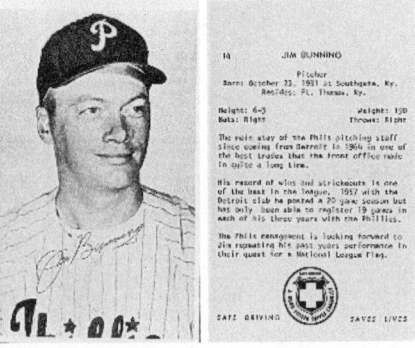

The honor of producing the only safety set of the 1960s goes to the Phillies for this traffic safety set. Measuring 2-3/4" x 4-1/2", the cards have a black-and-white front featuring the standard publicity photo of the player, with a facsimile autograph superimposed. Backs are printed in blue and include a few career and biographical details, along with the player's uniform number, by which the set is checklisted here. At bottom is a circle and shield design with the safety message.

	NM	E	VG
Complete Set (13):	75.00	35.00	20.00
Common Player:	8.00	4.00	2.50
4 Gene Mauch	8.00	4.00	2.50
6 Johnny Callison	10.00	5.00	3.00
10 Bill White	10.00	5.00	3.00
11 Clay Dalrymple	8.00	4.00	2.50
12 Johnny Briggs	8.00	4.00	2.50
14 Jim Bunning	20.00	10.00	6.00
15 Dick Allen	18.00	9.00	5.50
16 Cookie Rojas	8.00	4.00	2.50
24 Dick Groat	10.00	5.00	3.00
25 Tony Gonzalez	8.00	4.00	2.50
37 Dick Ellsworth	8.00	4.00	2.50
41 Chris Short	8.00	4.00	2.50
46 Larry Jackson	8.00	4.00	2.50

1975 Philadelphia Phillies Photocards

JOE HOERNER

These 3-1/4" x 5-1/2" blank-back, black-and-white cards feature player portrait photos with only the player name in the white border at bottom. Fronts have a semi-gloss finish. It is likely the checklist, presented here alphabetically, is incomplete.

	NM	E	VG
Common Player:	3.00	1.50	.90
(1) Tom Hilgendorf	3.00	1.50	.90
(2) Terry Harmon	3.00	1.50	.90
(3) Joe Hoerner	3.00	1.50	.90
(4) Tommy Hutton	3.00	1.50	.90
(5) Jim Lonborg	4.00	2.00	1.25
(6) John Oates	3.00	1.50	.90

1913 Philadelphia Evening Telegraph Postcards

THE PHILLIES' LEADER

Manager Charles Dooin
Compliments of "The Evening Telegraph"

The attributed date of issue is speculative, about midway through Phillies manager Red Dooin's tenure. Issued by one of the city's daily newspapers, these 3-1/2" x 5-1/2" black-and-white postcards picture the managers of the Phils and A's in large portrait photos. The postcard-style back has ornate typography and embellishments.

	NM	E	VG
Complete Set (2):	1,100	550.00	325.00
Common Card:	500.00	250.00	150.00
(1) Charles Dooin	500.00	250.00	150.00
(2) Connie Mack	650.00	325.00	200.00

1961 Phillies Cigar Mickey Mantle

This 6-1/2" x 9" blank-back color photo card of Mickey Mantle was part of a redemption program for Phillies cigars. For $3.39 and 20 cigar bands, a person could receive a Mickey Mantle model baseball glove and this "autographed" (facsimile) photo.

	NM	E	VG
Mickey Mantle	225.00	112.50	67.50

1912 Photo Art Shop Boston Red Sox

JOE WOOD AND WALTER JOHNSON
Boston Am. Wash. Am.
WORLDS RECORD PITCHERS
Season 1912

Two postcards are currently known to have been produced, according to the legend on the back, by The Photo Art Shop of Swampscott, Mass. The standard-size (about 3-1/2" x 5-1/2") cards are printed in black-and-white. A vertically formatted card shows opposing World Series aces Joe Wood and Walter Johnson. A horizontal team-photo card has each player's last name printed over his picture and describes the team as "Champions of the American League". The Red Sox went on to defeat the Giants in the World Series.

	NM	E	VG
Joe Wood, Walter Johnson	1,800	900.00	540.00
1912 Boston Red Sox	900.00	450.00	275.00

1964 Photo Linen Emblems

The attributed date of issue is only approximate. About 3-1/2" x 4-1/2", these sew-on patches feature black-and-white photos with an embroidered red border. The patches

were sold in a cello-wrapped package. The checklist presented here in alphabetical order is not complete.

	NM	E	VG
Complete Set (10):	625.00	300.00	180.00
Common Player:	30.00	15.00	9.00
(1) Yogi Berra	50.00	25.00	15.00
(2) Clete Boyer	30.00	15.00	9.00
(3) Elston Howard	30.00	15.00	9.00
(4) Sandy Koufax	175.00	87.00	52.00
(5) Tony Kubek	30.00	15.00	9.00
(6) Mickey Mantle	250.00	125.00	75.00
(7) Roger Maris	90.00	45.00	27.00
(8) Joe Pepitone	30.00	15.00	9.00
(9) Bobby Richardson	30.00	15.00	9.00
(10) Tom Tresh	30.00	15.00	9.00

1972 Photo Sports Co. L.A. Dodgers

This is the first known issue of a sports novelty marketed by Photo Sports Co., Los Angeles. The company is best known to collectors for its 1974 McDonald's promotional "Foto Balls" with player discs. The Dodgers set is similar in concept with a hinged plastic baseball which opens to reveal player discs. A "keyhole" punched at the bottom of the discs keeps them in place within the ball. The Dodgers never rolled out the project and surviving sets are extremely rare. Discs are 2-5/8" diameter with borderless color photos on front. Backs have player stats and the team logo. The unnumbered discs are checklisted here in alphabetical order.

	NM	E	VG
Complete Set (Ball and Discs):	300.00	150.00	90.00
Common Player:	16.00	8.00	4.75
(1) Red Adams	16.00	8.00	4.75
(2) Walt Alston	35.00	17.50	10.50
(3) Willie Crawford	16.00	8.00	4.75
(4) Willie Davis	24.00	12.00	7.25
(5) Al Downing	16.00	8.00	4.75
(6) Jim Gilliam	24.00	12.00	7.25
(7) Bill Grabarkewitz	16.00	8.00	4.75
(8) Jim Lefebvre	16.00	8.00	4.75
(9) Pete Mikkelsen	16.00	8.00	4.75
(10) Manny Mota	18.00	9.00	5.50
(11) Claude Osteen	16.00	8.00	4.75
(12) Wes Parker	16.00	8.00	4.75
(13) Duke Sims	16.00	8.00	4.75
(14) Bill Singer	16.00	8.00	4.75
(15) Bill Sudakis	16.00	8.00	4.75
(16) Don Sutton	30.00	15.00	9.00
(17) Bob Valentine	18.00	9.00	5.50
(18) Maury Wills	22.00	11.00	6.50

1953 Pictsweet Milwaukee Braves

STAR CATCHER
OF THE MILWAUKEE BRAVES
WALKER COOPER

This black-and-white mini-poster (8-1/2" x 11-1/4") depicts a player holding a package of frozen vegetables. They were probably intended for grocery store window or aisle display. Backs are blank. It's unknown how many players are in the set. See also, Top Taste Bread.

	NM	E	VG
Common Player:	150.00	75.00	45.00
(1) "Bullet Bill" Bruton	150.00	75.00	45.00
(2) Walker Cooper	150.00	75.00	45.00
(3) Sid Gordon	150.00	75.00	45.00
(4) Charlie Grimm	150.00	75.00	45.00
(5) Sibby Sisti	150.00	75.00	45.00
(6) Max Surkont	150.00	75.00	45.00

1970 Pictures of Champions Baltimore Orioles

12
DAVE MAY

Pictures of Champions

Issued in 1970 in the Baltimore area, this 16-card set pictures members of the Baltimore Orioles. The 2-1/8" x 2-3/4" cards feature black and white player photos on orange card stock. The method of distribution is unknown.

		NM	E	VG
Complete Set (16):		80.00	40.00	25.00
Common Player:		2.00	1.00	.60
4	Earl Weaver	7.50	3.75	2.25
5	Brooks Robinson	25.00	12.50	7.50
7	Mark Belanger	2.00	1.00	.60
8	Andy Etchebarren	2.00	1.00	.60
9	Don Buford	2.00	1.00	.60
10	Ellie Hendricks	2.00	1.00	.60
12	Dave May	2.00	1.00	.60
15	Dave Johnson	2.00	1.00	.60
16	Dave McNally	2.00	1.00	.60
20	Frank Robinson	20.00	10.00	6.00
22	Jim Palmer	20.00	10.00	6.00
24	Pete Richert	2.00	1.00	.60
29	Dick Hall	2.00	1.00	.60
35	Mike Cuellar	2.00	1.00	.60
39	Eddie Watt	2.00	1.00	.60
40	Dave Leonhard	2.00	1.00	.60

1909-11 Piedmont Cigarettes

In both T205 and T206, Piedmont is the brand found most often on the cards' backs. In T205, Piedmonts backs are printed in blue with either Factory 25 and 42 designation, the latter of which is much scarcer but commands little premium, more due to collector indifference than relative scarcity. In T206, the familiar blue Piedmont logo is found in all three series. In the "150 Subjects" and "350 Subjects" series, only Factory 25 (Va.) is seen. In the "350-460 Subjects" series, both Factory 25 and Factory 42 (N.C.) are seen. The latter is much scarcer and commands a premium over the more common Factory 25 version.

FACTORY 42 OVERPRINTS PREMIUM:
Common Players: 7-12X
Hall of Famers: 2X

(See T205, T206)

1914 Piedmont Art Stamps (T330-2)

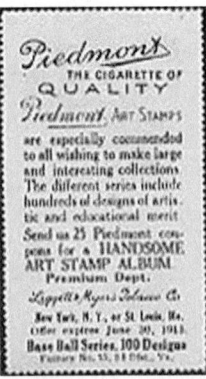 

This series of "Piedmont Art Stamps" looks like a fragile version of the more popular T205 Gold Border tobacco cards of 1911, employing the same basic design on front. The Piedmont stamps measure 1-1/2" x 2-5/8". Though the backs advertise "100 designs," more than 110 different players are known. And, because some of the players are pictured in two separate poses, there are actually 118 different stamps known, with new discoveries still being made. All but three of the subjects in the Piedmont set were taken from the T205 set; the exceptions being Joe Wood, Walt Blair and Bill Killifer. Because of their fragile composition, and since they are stamps that were frequently stuck to album pages, examples of Piedmont Art Stamps in Near Mint or better condition are

very scarce. The back of the stamps offered a "handsome" album in exchange for 25 Piedmont coupons. The set has an American Card Catalog designation of T330-2. Gaps have been left in the assigned numbering to accommodate future additions.

		NM	E	VG
Common Player:		150.00	60.00	30.00
(1)	Leon K. Ames	150.00	60.00	30.00
(2)	Jimmy Archer	150.00	60.00	30.00
(3)	Jimmy Austin	150.00	60.00	30.00
(4)	Home Run Baker	450.00	180.00	90.00
(5)	Cy Barger (Full "B" on cap.)	150.00	60.00	30.00
(6)	Cy Barger (Partial "B" on cap.)	150.00	60.00	30.00
(7)	Jack Barry	150.00	60.00	30.00
(8)	Johnny Bates	150.00	60.00	30.00
(9)	Fred Beck	150.00	60.00	30.00
(10)	Beals Becker	150.00	60.00	30.00
(11)	Chief Bender	450.00	180.00	90.00
(12)	Bob Bescher	150.00	60.00	30.00
(13)	Joe Birmingham	150.00	60.00	30.00
(14)	Walt Blair	150.00	60.00	30.00
(15)	Roger Bresnahan	450.00	180.00	90.00
(16)	Al Bridwell	150.00	60.00	30.00
(17)	Mordecai Brown	450.00	180.00	90.00
(18)	Bobby Byrne	150.00	60.00	30.00
(19)	Howie Camnitz	150.00	60.00	30.00
(20)	Bill Carrigan	150.00	60.00	30.00
(21)	Frank Chance	450.00	180.00	90.00
(22)	Hal Chase ("Chase" on front.)	250.00	100.00	50.00
(23)	Hal Chase ("Hal Chase" on front.)	300.00	120.00	60.00
(24)	Ed Cicotte	375.00	150.00	75.00
(25)	Fred Clarke	450.00	180.00	90.00
(26)	Ty Cobb	5,500	2,200	1,100
(27)	Eddie Collins (Mouth closed.)	450.00	180.00	90.00
(28)	Eddie Collins (Mouth open.)	450.00	180.00	90.00
(29)	Otis "Doc" Crandall	150.00	60.00	30.00
(30)	Bill Dahlen	150.00	60.00	30.00
(31)	Jake Daubert	150.00	60.00	30.00
(32)	Jim Delahanty	150.00	60.00	30.00
(33)	Josh Devore	150.00	60.00	30.00
(34)	Red Dooin	150.00	60.00	30.00
(35)	Mickey Doolan	150.00	60.00	30.00
(36)	Tom Downey	150.00	60.00	30.00
(37)	Larry Doyle	150.00	60.00	30.00
(38)	Dick Egan	150.00	60.00	30.00
(39)	Kid Elberfield (Elberfeld)	150.00	60.00	30.00
(40)	Clyde Engle	150.00	60.00	30.00
(41)	Louis Evans	150.00	60.00	30.00
(42)	Johnny Evers	450.00	180.00	90.00
(43)	Ray Fisher	150.00	60.00	30.00
(44)	Art Fletcher	150.00	60.00	30.00
(45)	Russ Ford (Dark cap.)	150.00	60.00	30.00
(46)	Russ Ford (White cap.)	150.00	60.00	30.00
(47)	Art Fromme	150.00	60.00	30.00
(48)	George Gibson	150.00	60.00	30.00
(49)	William Goode (Wilbur Good)	150.00	60.00	30.00
(51)	Eddie Grant	225.00	90.00	45.00
(52)	Clark Griffith	450.00	180.00	90.00
(53)	Bob Groom	150.00	60.00	30.00
(54)	Bob Harmon	150.00	60.00	30.00
(55)	Arnold Hauser	150.00	60.00	30.00
(56)	Buck Herzog	150.00	60.00	30.00
(57)	Dick Hoblitzell	150.00	60.00	30.00
(58)	Miller Huggins	450.00	180.00	90.00
(59)	John Hummel	150.00	60.00	30.00
(60)	Hughie Jennings	450.00	180.00	90.00
(61)	Walter Johnson	750.00	300.00	150.00
(62)	Davy Jones	150.00	60.00	30.00
(63)	Bill Killifer (Killefer)	150.00	60.00	30.00
(64)	Jack Knight	150.00	60.00	30.00
(65)	Ed Konetchy	150.00	60.00	30.00
(66)	Frank LaPorte	150.00	60.00	30.00
(67)	Thomas Leach	150.00	60.00	30.00
(68)	Edgar Lennox	150.00	60.00	30.00
(69)	Hans Lobert	150.00	60.00	30.00
(70)	Harry Lord	150.00	60.00	30.00
(71)	Sherry Magee	150.00	60.00	30.00
(72)	Rube Marquard	450.00	180.00	90.00
(73)	Christy Mathewson	1,250	500.00	250.00
(74)	George McBride	150.00	60.00	30.00
(76)	J.J. McGraw	450.00	180.00	90.00
(77)	Larry McLean	150.00	60.00	30.00
(78)	Fred Merkle	150.00	60.00	30.00
(79)	Chief Meyers	150.00	60.00	30.00
(80)	Clyde Milan	150.00	60.00	30.00
(81)	Dots Miller	150.00	60.00	30.00
(82)	Mike Mitchell	150.00	60.00	30.00
(83)	Pat Moran	150.00	60.00	30.00
(84)	George Moriarity (Moriarty)	150.00	60.00	30.00
(85)	George Mullin	150.00	60.00	30.00
(86)	Danny Murphy	150.00	60.00	30.00
(87)	Jack "Red" Murray	150.00	60.00	30.00
(88)	Tom Needham	150.00	60.00	30.00
(89)	Rebel Oakes	150.00	60.00	30.00
(90)	Rube Oldring	150.00	60.00	30.00
(91)	Fred Parent	325.00	160.00	97.50
(92)	Dode Paskert	150.00	60.00	30.00
(93)	Jack Quinn	150.00	60.00	30.00
(94)	Ed Reulbach	150.00	60.00	30.00
(95)	Lewis Ritchie	150.00	60.00	30.00
(96)	Jack Rowan	150.00	60.00	30.00
(97)	Nap Rucker	150.00	60.00	30.00
(98)	Germany Schaefer	150.00	60.00	30.00
(99)	Wildfire Schulte	150.00	60.00	30.00
(101)	Jim Scott	150.00	60.00	30.00
(102)	Fred Snodgrass	150.00	60.00	30.00
(103)	Tris Speaker	600.00	240.00	120.00
(104)	Oscar Stamage (Stanage)	150.00	60.00	30.00
(105)	George Stovall	150.00	60.00	30.00
(106)	George Suggs	150.00	60.00	30.00
(107)	Jeff Sweeney	150.00	60.00	30.00
(108)	Ira Thomas	150.00	60.00	30.00
(109)	Joe Tinker	450.00	180.00	90.00
(110)	Terry Turner	150.00	60.00	30.00
(111)	Hippo Vaughn	150.00	60.00	30.00
(112)	Heinie Wagner	150.00	60.00	30.00
(113)	Bobby Wallace (No cap.)	450.00	180.00	90.00
(114)	Bobby Wallace (With cap.)	450.00	180.00	90.00
(115)	Ed Walsh	450.00	180.00	90.00
(116)	Zach Wheat	450.00	180.00	90.00
(117)	Irwin "Kaiser" Wilhelm	150.00	60.00	30.00
(118)	Ed Willett	150.00	60.00	30.00
(119)	Owen Wilson	150.00	60.00	30.00
(120)	Hooks Wiltse	150.00	60.00	30.00
(121)	Joe Wood	150.00	60.00	30.00

1939 Piel's Beer Coasters

New York Giants manager Bill Terry was the only baseball player among a trio of local celebrities endoring the beer brand in this series of approximately 4" diameter bar coasters. The printing is in black-and-red.

	NM	E	VG
Bill Terry	30.00	15.00	9.00

1913-1915 Pinkerton Score/Photo/Post Cards

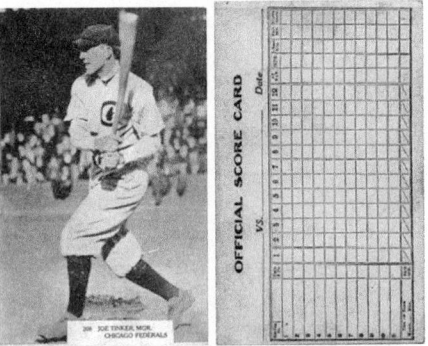

The picture portions of the T5 Pinkerton cabinets have also been seen in other formats, in printed rather than photographic presentation. The most desirable of these have backs printed for use as baseball scorecards. These measure a nominal 3-1/2" x 5-1/2", give or take 1/4". They are believed to have been printed some years after the cabinet cards. It is unknown to what extent the checklist of T5 can be found in this format. Postcard-style backs have also been seen for some Pinkerton pictures, as well as blank-backed versions; they are considerably discounted from the scorecard type. Confirmed examples are listed here.

	NM	E	VG
Common Player:	250.00	125.00	75.00

SCORECARD BACKS

153	Hughie Jennings	7,500	3,700	2,200
159	Ty Cobb	3,500	1,750	1,050
203	King Cole	500.00	250.00	150.00
205	Heinie Zimmerman	500.00	250.00	150.00
206	Wildfire Schulte	500.00	250.00	150.00
208	Joe Tinker	500.00	250.00	150.00
251	Christy Mathewson	6,000	3,000	1,800
252	Fred Merkle	500.00	250.00	150.00
260	Larry Doyle	500.00	250.00	150.00
303	Red Dooin	500.00	250.00	150.00
420	R.C. Hoblitzell	500.00	250.00	150.00
424	Mike Mitchell	500.00	250.00	150.00
505	Connie Mack	1,000	500.00	300.00
511	Eddie Collins	1,000	500.00	300.00
512	Frank Baker	500.00	250.00	150.00
872	Hans Wagner	5,500	2,700	1,650

POSTCARD OR BLANK BACKS

159	Ty Cobb	1,500	750.00	450.00
203	King Cole	300.00	150.00	90.00
205	Heinie Zimmerman	300.00	150.00	90.00
206	Frank Schulte	300.00	150.00	90.00
208	Joe Tinker	500.00	250.00	150.00
251	Christy Mathewson	1,800	900.00	550.00
252	Fred Merkle	300.00	150.00	90.00
260	Larry Doyle	300.00	150.00	90.00
264	Chief Myers (Meyers)	300.00	150.00	90.00
419	Clark Griffith	500.00	250.00	150.00
424	Mike Mitchell	300.00	150.00	90.00
501	Chas. Bender	500.00	250.00	150.00
511	Eddie Collins	500.00	250.00	150.00
512	Frank Baker	500.00	250.00	150.00
627	Napoleon Lajoie	650.00	325.00	195.00
855	Fred Clarke	500.00	250.00	150.00
865	Babe Adams	300.00	150.00	90.00
872	Hans Wagner	3,250	1,600	975.00

1912 Pirate Cigarettes (T215)

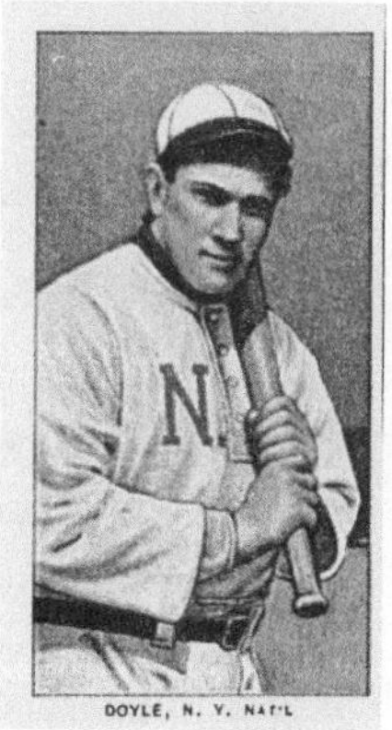

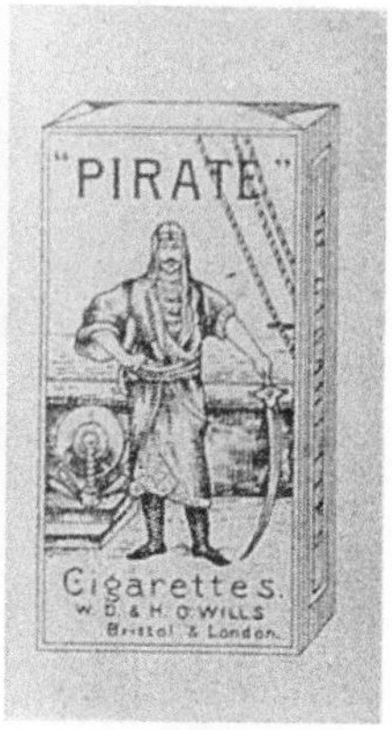

This set can be considerd a British version of the T215 Red Cross Type 1 set. Distributed by Pirate brand cigarettes of Bristol and London, England, the fronts of the cards are identical to the Red Cross cards, but the green backs carry advertising for Pirate Cigarettes. It is believed that the Pirate cards were printed for distribution to U.S. servicemen in the South Seas. There is reason to believe the "standard" tobacco card length of 2-5/8" (width 1-7/16") may not be universally applicable to the Pirate cards, possibly because of packaging considerations.

		NM	E	VG
	Common Player:	11,000	5,500	3,300
(1)	Red Ames	11,000	5,500	3,300
(2)	Home Run Baker	16,000	8,000	4,800
(3)	Neal Ball	11,000	5,500	3,300
(4)	Chief Bender	16,000	8,000	4,800
(5)	Al Bridwell	11,000	5,500	3,300
(6)	Bobby Byrne ((St. Louis))	11,000	5,500	3,300
(7)	Mordecai Brown (Chicago on shirt.)	16,000	8,000	4,800
(8)	Howie Camnitz	11,000	5,500	3,300
(9)	Frank Chance	9,800	4,900	2,950
(10)	Hal Chase	14,500	7,250	4,350
(11)	Eddie Collins	16,000	8,000	4,800
(12)	Doc Crandall	11,000	5,500	3,300
(13)	Sam Crawford	16,000	8,000	4,800
(14)	Birdie Cree	11,000	5,500	3,300
(15)	Harry Davis	11,000	5,500	3,300
(16)	Josh Devore	11,000	5,500	3,300
(17)	Mike Donlin	11,000	5,500	3,300
(18)	Mickey Doolan (Batting)	11,000	5,500	3,300
(19)	Mickey Doolan (Fielding)	11,000	5,500	3,300
(20)	Patsy Dougherty	11,000	5,500	3,300
(21)	Larry Doyle (Batting)	11,000	5,500	3,300
(22)	Larry Doyle (Portrait)	11,000	5,500	3,300
(23)	Jean Dubuc	11,000	5,500	3,300
(24)	Kid Elberfeld	11,000	5,500	3,300
(25)	Steve Evans	11,000	5,500	3,300
(26)	Johnny Evers	16,000	8,000	4,800
(27)	Russ Ford	11,000	5,500	3,300
(28)	Art Fromme	11,000	5,500	3,300
(29)	Clark Griffith	16,000	8,000	4,800
(30)	Bob Groom	11,000	5,500	3,300
(31)	Topsy Hartsel	11,000	5,500	3,300
(32)	Buck Herzog	11,000	5,500	3,300
(33)	Dick Hoblitzell	11,000	5,500	3,300
(34)	Solly Hofman	11,000	5,500	3,300
(35)	Del Howard	11,000	5,500	3,300
(36)	Miller Huggins (Hands at mouth.)	16,000	8,000	4,800
(37)	Miller Huggins (Portrait)	16,000	8,000	4,800
(38)	John Hummel	11,000	5,500	3,300
(39)	Hughie Jennings (Both hands showing.)	16,000	8,000	4,800
(40)	Hughie Jennings (One hand showing.)	16,000	8,000	4,800
(41)	Walter Johnson	35,000	17,500	10,500
(42)	Joe Kelley	16,000	8,000	4,800
(43)	Ed Konetchy	11,000	5,500	3,300
(44)	Harry Krause	11,000	5,500	3,300
(45)	Nap Lajoie	16,000	8,000	4,800
(46)	Joe Lake	11,000	5,500	3,300
(47)	Lefty Leifield	11,000	5,500	3,300
(48)	Harry Lord	11,000	5,500	3,300
(49)	Sherry Magee	11,000	5,500	3,300
(50)	Rube Marquard (Pitching)	16,000	8,000	4,800
(51)	Rube Marquard (Portrait)	16,000	8,000	4,800
(52)	Christy Mathewson ((Black cap.))	20,000	10,000	5,000
(53)	Joe McGinnity	16,000	8,000	4,800
(54)	John McGraw (Glove at side.)	16,000	8,000	4,800
(55)	John McGraw (Portrait)	16,000	8,000	4,800
(56)	Harry McIntyre (Chicago)	11,000	5,500	3,300
(57)	Harry McIntyre (Brooklyn & Chicago)	11,000	5,500	3,300
(58)	Matty McIntyre ((Detroit))	11,000	5,500	3,300
(59)	Larry McLean	11,000	5,500	3,300
(60)	Fred Merkle	11,000	5,500	3,300
(61)	Chief Meyers	11,000	5,500	3,300
(62)	Mike Mitchell	11,000	5,500	3,300
(63)	Dots Miller	11,000	5,500	3,300
(64)	Mike Mowrey	11,000	5,500	3,300
(65)	George Mullin	11,000	5,500	3,300
(66)	Danny Murphy	11,000	5,500	3,300
(67)	Red Murray	11,000	5,500	3,300
(68)	Rebel Oakes	11,000	5,500	3,300
(69)	Rube Oldring	11,000	5,500	3,300
(70)	Charley O'Leary	11,000	5,500	3,300
(71)	Dode Paskert	11,000	5,500	3,300
(72)	Barney Pelty	11,000	5,500	3,300
(73)	Billy Purtell	11,000	5,500	3,300
(74)	Jack Quinn	11,000	5,500	3,300
(75)	Ed Reulbach	11,000	5,500	3,300
(76)	Nap Rucker	11,000	5,500	3,300
(77)	Germany Schaefer	11,000	5,500	3,300
(78)	Wildfire Schulte	11,000	5,500	3,300
(79)	Jimmy Sheckard	11,000	5,500	3,300
(80)	Frank Smith	11,000	5,500	3,300
(81)	Tris Speaker	18,000	9,000	5,400
(82)	Jake Stahl	11,000	5,500	3,300
(83)	Harry Steinfeldt	11,000	5,500	3,300
(84)	Gabby Street	11,000	5,500	3,300
(85)	Ed Summers	11,000	5,500	3,300
(86)	Jeff Sweeney	11,000	5,500	3,300
(87)	Lee Tannehill	11,000	5,500	3,300
(88)	Ira Thomas	11,000	5,500	3,300
(89)	Joe Tinker	16,000	8,000	4,800
(90)	Heinie Wagner	11,000	5,500	3,300
(91)	Jack Warhop	11,000	5,500	3,300
(92)	Zack Wheat	16,000	8,000	4,800
(93)	Ed Willetts (Willett)	11,000	5,500	3,300
(94)	Owen Wilson	11,000	5,500	3,300
(95)	Hooks Wiltse (Pitching)	11,000	5,500	3,300
(96)	Hooks Wiltse (Portrait)	11,000	5,500	3,300

1962 Pittsburgh Exhibits

The attributed date is approximate since none is shown on the cards; nor is a credit line to the manufacturer. Player content suggests Pittsburgh was the center of distribution and veteran collectors report having received the cards in penny arcade vending machines at Kennywood Amusement Park near there. It has also been reported that the cards were given over the counter as prizes for getting a winning gumball from a machine. The 3-1/4" x 5-1/4" cards are printed in black-and-white, or red, black and white. They are usually blank-backed, but examples have been seen with apprarent prize references printed on back. Most of the card "denominations" can be found with more than one subject. Besides the ballplayers listed here, the set contained TV and movie cowboys, rock-and-roll stars, boxers, wrestlers and cartoon characters.

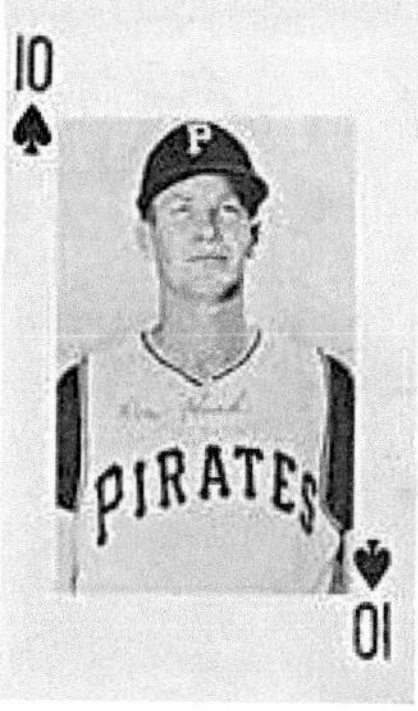

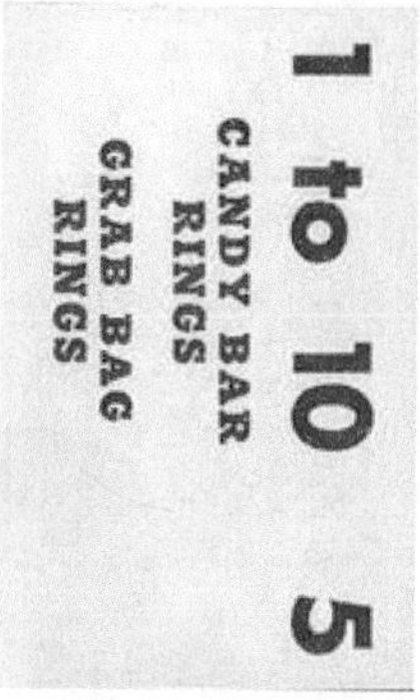

		NM	E	VG
	Complete Set (81):	2,500	1,250	750.00
	Common Player:	7.50	3.75	2.25
AC	Bill Mazeroski	25.00	12.50	7.50
2C	Whitey Ford	30.00	15.00	9.00
2C	Al Kaline	20.00	10.00	6.00
2C	Pirates logo cartoon	7.50	3.75	2.25
4C	Frank Robinson	20.00	10.00	6.00
4C	Babe Ruth	125.00	65.00	35.00
5C	Wilmer Mizell	7.50	3.75	2.25
5C	Mickey Mantle	175.00	85.00	50.00
5C	Honus Wagner	35.00	17.50	10.00
6C	Eddie Mathews	20.00	10.00	6.00
6C	Willie Mays	90.00	45.00	27.00
7C	**Dodgers' "Bum" cartoon logo**	7.50	2.25	3.75
7C	Eddie Mathews	20.00	10.00	6.00
7C	Willie Mays	90.00	45.00	27.00
8C	Walter Johnson	20.00	10.00	6.00
8C	Mickey Mantle	175.00	85.00	50.00
8C	Wilmer Mizell	7.50	3.75	2.25
9C	Hank Aaron	90.00	45.00	27.00
9C	Frank Robinson	40.00	20.00	12.00
10C	Lew Burdette	7.50	3.75	2.25
JC	Harvey Haddix	7.50	3.75	2.25
JC	Bill Mazeroski	25.00	12.50	7.50
JC	Al McBean	7.50	3.75	2.25
QC	Ty Cobb	60.00	30.00	18.00
QC	Whitey Ford	30.00	15.00	9.00
QC	Don Leppert	7.50	3.75	2.25
KC	Al Kaline	20.00	10.00	6.00
KC	Honus Wagner	35.00	17.50	10.00
AS	Lew Burdette	7.50	3.75	2.25
AS	Ty Cobb	60.00	30.00	18.00
2S	Smoky Burgess	7.50	3.75	2.25
3S	Don Hoak	7.50	3.75	2.25
4S	Roy Face	7.50	3.75	2.25
5S	Roberto Clemente	125.00	65.00	35.00
5S	Danny Murtaugh	7.50	3.75	2.25
6S	Christy Mathewson	25.00	12.50	7.50
6S	Dick Stuart	7.50	3.75	2.25
7S	Christy Mathewson	25.00	12.50	7.50
7S	Dick Stuart	7.50	3.75	2.25
8S	Danny Murtaugh	7.50	3.75	2.25
9S	Roy Face	7.50	3.75	2.25
10S	Don Hoak	7.50	3.75	2.25
JS	Smoky Burgess	7.50	3.75	2.25
QS	Walter Johnson	20.00	10.00	6.00
QS	Babe Ruth	125.00	65.00	35.00
KS	Hank Aaron	90.00	45.00	27.00
KS	Harvey Haddix	7.50	3.75	2.25
AH	Don Drysdale	20.00	10.00	6.00
AH	Ken Boyer	7.50	3.75	2.25
2H	Satchel Paige	60.00	30.00	18.00
3H	Rocky Colavito	20.00	10.00	6.00
4H	Stan Musial	50.00	25.00	15.00
4H	Bobby Richardson	15.00	7.50	4.50
5H	Ken Boyer	7.50	3.75	2.25
5H	Harmon Killebrew	20.00	10.00	6.00
6H	Luis Aparicio	20.00	10.00	6.00
6H	Ralph Kiner	20.00	10.00	6.00
7H	Sandy Koufax	75.00	37.50	22.00
8H	Warren Spahn	20.00	10.00	6.00
9H	Jimmy Piersall	7.50	3.75	2.25
10H	Yogi Berra	30.00	15.00	9.00
10H	Ralph Kiner	20.00	10.00	6.00
JH	Orlando Cepeda	20.00	10.00	6.00
JH	Ken Boyer	7.50	3.75	2.25
QH	Roger Maris	75.00	37.50	22.00
QH	Stan Musial	50.00	25.00	15.00
KH	Bob Purkey	7.50	3.75	2.25
AD	Don Drysdale	20.00	10.00	6.00
AD	Don Hoak	7.50	3.75	2.25
2D	Satchel Paige	60.00	30.00	18.00
6D	Luis Aparicio	20.00	10.00	6.00
6D	Ernie Banks	25.00	12.50	7.50
7D	Bill Virdon	7.50	3.75	2.25
7D	Sandy Koufax	75.00	37.50	22.00
8D	Bob Skinner	7.50	3.75	2.25

9D	Dick Groat	7.50	3.75	2.25
10D	Vernon Law	7.50	3.75	2.25
JD	Joe Adcock	7.50	3.75	2.25
JD	Orlando Cepeda	20.00	10.00	6.00
QD	Roger Maris	75.00	37.50	22.00
KD	Bob Friend	7.50	3.75	2.25

1910 Pittsburgh Gazette Times Honus Wagner Postcard

Describing him as "The Worlds' Greatest Base Ball Player," the local newspaper published this black-and-white standard size, typically marked, photographic postcard picturing the Flying Dutchman and landmarks from his Carnegie, Pa., hometown.

	NM	E	VG
Honus Wagner	750.00	370.00	220.00

1908 Pittsburgh Pirates Vignette Postcards

It has been reliably reported that 15 postcards and an album were produced for this souvenir issue sold at Pittsburgh's Exhibition Field. Only Pirates are pictured in this series of black-and-white standard-format postcards published locally by J.B. Coyle. Cards have an irregularly shaped posed photo of the player at center with his last name (or nickname), position and "PGH-08" crudely printed in white. Divided postcard backs have a stamp box and publisher's credit line. The incomplete checklist presented here is alphabetically arranged. Later editions of the American Card Catalog listed this set as PC800.

	NM	E	VG
Common Player:	250.00	125.00	75.00
(1) Abby (Ed Abbaticchio)	250.00	125.00	75.00
(2) Howie Camnitz	250.00	125.00	75.00
(3) Fred Clarke	350.00	175.00	105.00
(4) George Gibson	250.00	125.00	75.00
(5) Tommy Leach	250.00	125.00	75.00
(6) Dan Moeller	250.00	125.00	75.00
(10) Allen Storke	250.00	125.00	75.00
(14) Honus Wagner	3,000	1,5500.00	900.00
(15) Owen Wilson	250.00	125.00	75.00

1909 Pittsburgh Pirates Extension Postcard

One of many novelty souvenirs commemorating the Bucs' World Championship season of 1909 was this uniquely formatted postcard. Picturing manager Fred Clarke on front, the 3-1/4" x 5-1/2" postcard opens up accordian fashion to a length of 14", revealing small action photos of 17 players each on a white background and identified by last name and position. The card was produced by W.M. Dick Co., Pittsburgh.

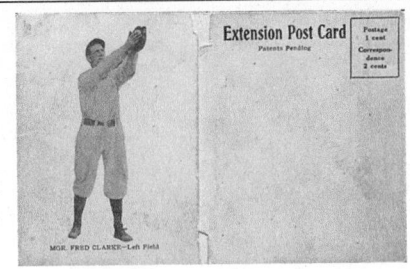

	NM	E	VG
1909 Pittsburgh Pirates	2,750	1,375	825.00

1950 Pittsburgh Pirates Photo Pack

The player photos in this picture pack that was sold at Forbes Field measure 6-1/2" x 9" and are printed in black-and-white on heavy, blank-backed paper. A facsimile "autograph" is printed on front of each picture, though all were written in the same hand. Several of the photos from this set were the basis for the color paintings found on 1951 Bowman cards. The unnumbered pictures are checklisted here alphabetically.

	NM	E	VG
Complete Set (26):	250.00	125.00	75.00
Common Player:	12.00	6.00	3.50
(1) Ted Beard	12.00	6.00	3.50
(2) Gus Bell	20.00	10.00	6.00
(3) Pete Castiglione	12.00	6.00	3.50
(4) Cliff Chambers	12.00	6.00	3.50
(5) Dale Coogan	12.00	6.00	3.50
(6) Murry Dickson	12.00	6.00	3.50
(7) Bob Dillinger	12.00	6.00	3.50
(8) Froilan Fernandez	12.00	6.00	3.50
(9) Johnny Hopp	12.00	6.00	3.50
(10) Ralph Kiner	30.00	15.00	9.00
(11) Vernon Law	20.00	10.00	6.00
(12) Vic Lombardi	12.00	6.00	3.50
(13) Bill MacDonald	12.00	6.00	3.50
(14) Clyde McCullough	12.00	6.00	3.50
(15) Bill Meyer	12.00	6.00	3.50
(16) Ray Mueller	12.00	6.00	3.50
(17) Danny Murtaugh	12.00	6.00	3.50
(18) Jack Phillips	12.00	6.00	3.50
(19) Mel Queen	12.00	6.00	3.50
(20) Stan Rojek	12.00	6.00	3.50
(21) Henry Schenz	12.00	6.00	3.50
(22) George Strickland	12.00	6.00	3.50
(23) Earl Turner	12.00	6.00	3.50
(24) Jim Walsh	12.00	6.00	3.50
(25) Bill Werle	12.00	6.00	3.50
(26) Wally Westlake	12.00	6.00	3.50

1950-60s Pittsburgh Pirates Postcards

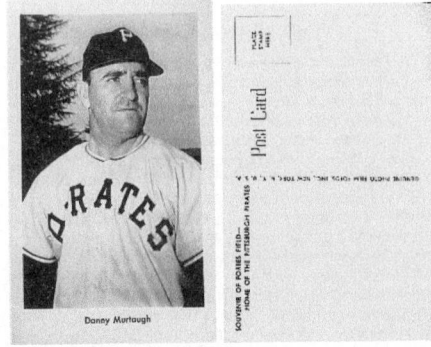

This listing encompasses the issues of several different postcard publishers who supplied black-and-white cards to the players for use in answering fan mail. Several different types of card stock are found, both matte and glossy. Some cards have postcard markings on back, others do not, especially those picturing players in the 1960s style sleeveless style uniforms. Because it is likely other players and poses will be reported, a description of each pose is included.

		NM	E	VG
Common Player:		15.00	7.50	4.50
(1)	Gair Allie (Ready to hit.)	15.00	7.50	4.50
(2)	Toby Atwell (Squatting w/ glove.)	15.00	7.50	4.50
(3)	Tony Bartirome (Stretching at 1B.)	15.00	7.50	4.50
(4)	Carlos Bernier (Batting)	15.00	7.50	4.50
(5)	Ron Blackburn (Pitching, left leg up.)	15.00	7.50	4.50
(6)	Ron Brand (Kneeling w/ glove.)	15.00	7.50	4.50
(7)	Jim Bunning (Pitching, to letters.)	25.00	12.50	7.50
(8)	Don (Swede) Carlson (Pitching, by wall.)	15.00	7.50	4.50
(9)	Pete Castiglione (Ready to hit.)	15.00	7.50	4.50
(10)	Pete Castiglione (Kneeling w/bat.)	15.00	7.50	4.50
(12)	Cliff Chambers (Pitching, leg up.)	15.00	7.50	4.50
(13)	Bob Chesnes (Follow-through.)	15.00	7.50	4.50
(14)	Roberto Clemente (Kneeling w/bat.)	125.00	65.00	35.00
(15)	Dick Cole (Fielding)	15.00	7.50	4.50
(16)	Dale Coogan (Ready to hit.)	15.00	7.50	4.50
(18)	Bobby Del Greco (Batting follow-through.)	15.00	7.50	4.50
(20)	Elroy Face (Follow-through, cloth cap, sleeves.)	17.50	8.75	5.25
(21)	Elroy Face (Follow-through, cloth cap, no sleeves.)	17.50	8.75	5.25
(22)	Elroy Face (Follow-through, helmet, sleeves.)	17.50	8.75	5.25
(23)	Elroy Face (Follow-through, helmet, no sleeves.)	17.50	8.75	5.25
(24)	Hank Foiles (Squatting)	15.00	7.50	4.50
(25)	Gene Freese (Ready to hit.)	15.00	7.50	4.50
(26)	Bob Friend (Follow-through.)	15.00	7.50	4.50
(27)	Bob Friend (Pitching, leg up.)	15.00	7.50	4.50
(28)	Bob Friend (Standing in dugout.)	15.00	7.50	4.50
(29)	Dick Groat (Ready to hit.)	17.50	8.75	5.25
(30)	Fred Haney (Arms folded.)	15.00	7.50	4.50
(31)	John Hetki (Follow-through.)	15.00	7.50	4.50
(32)	Johnny Hopp (Stretching at 1B.)	15.00	7.50	4.50
(34)	Ralph Kiner (Batting, two decks.)	25.00	12.50	7.50
(35)	Nellie King (Follow-through.)	15.00	7.50	4.50
(36)	Ron Kline (Follow-through.)	15.00	7.50	4.50
(37)	Ron Kline (Pitching, leg up.)	15.00	7.50	4.50
(38)	Ted Kluszewski (Kneeling with bat.)	20.00	10.00	6.00
(39)	Ted Kluszewski (Pose to chest.)	20.00	10.00	6.00
(41)	Nick Koback (Kneeling)	15.00	7.50	4.50
(42)	Clem Koshorek (Fielding)	15.00	7.50	4.50
(43)	Danny Kravitz (Ready to hit.)	15.00	7.50	4.50
(44)	Vern Law (Follow-through, bleachers.)	17.50	8.75	5.25
(45)	Vern Law (Follow-through, trees.)	17.50	8.75	5.25
(46)	Vern Law (Follow-through, right foot cut off.)	17.50	8.75	5.25
(47)	Vern Law (Kneeling)	17.50	8.75	5.25
(48)	Vern Law (Pitching, leg up.)	17.50	8.75	5.25
(49)	Lenny Levy (Catching)	15.00	7.50	4.50
(50)	Lenny Levy (Standing in dugout.)	15.00	7.50	4.50
(51)	Dale Long (Batting)	15.00	7.50	4.50

(52)	Dale Long (Kneeling w/ bat.)	15.00	7.50	4.50
(53)	Jerry Lynch (Batting, sleeves.)	15.00	7.50	4.50
(54)	Jerry Lynch (Batting, no sleeves.)	15.00	7.50	4.50
(55)	Bill MacDonald (Pitching, leg up.)	15.00	7.50	4.50
(56)	Bill Mazeroski (Fielding, ball in glove, horizontal.)	25.00	12.50	7.50
(57)	Bill Mazeroski (Fielding, ball in hand.)	25.00	12.50	7.50
(58)	Danny Murtaugh (Fielding)	15.00	7.50	4.50
(59)	Danny Murtaugh (Portrait, helmet.)	15.00	7.50	4.50
(60)	George "Red" Munger (Pitching)	15.00	7.50	4.50
(61)	Johnny O'Brien (Jumping)	15.00	7.50	4.50
(63)	Danny O'Connell (Batting)	15.00	7.50	4.50
(64)	Bob Oldis (Portrait to belt.)	15.00	7.50	4.50
(65)	Laurin Pepper (Follow-through.)	15.00	7.50	4.50
(66)	Pete Peterson (Catching)	15.00	7.50	4.50
(68)	Buddy Pritchard (Batting)	15.00	7.50	4.50
(69)	Bob Purkey (Follow-through.)	15.00	7.50	4.50
(70)	Bob Purkey (Portrait)	15.00	7.50	4.50
(71)	Mel Queen (Pitching, leg up.)	15.00	7.50	4.50
(72)	Curt Raydon (Follow-through, horizontal.)	15.00	7.50	4.50
(74)	Dino Restelli (Batting)	15.00	7.50	4.50
(75)	Stan Rojek (Batting)	15.00	7.50	4.50
(76)	Stan Rojek (Standing in dugout.)	15.00	7.50	4.50
(78)	Tom Saffell (Batting)	15.00	7.50	4.50
(80)	Don Schwall (Pitching, no cap.)	15.00	7.50	4.50
(81)	Bob Skinner (Batting)	15.00	7.50	4.50
(82)	Bob Smith (Follow-through.)	15.00	7.50	4.50
(83)	Paul Smith (Batting)	15.00	7.50	4.50
(84)	Art Swanson (Hands on hips.)	15.00	7.50	4.50
(86)	Frank Thomas (Batting, cap.)	17.50	8.75	5.25
(87)	Frank Thomas (Batting, helmet.)	17.50	8.75	5.25
(90)	Bill Virdon (Batting, matte.)	17.50	8.75	5.25
(91)	Bill Virdon (Batting, glossy.)	17.50	8.75	5.25
(92)	Bill Virdon (Kneeling)	17.50	8.75	5.25
(93)	Harry Walker (Portrait)	15.00	7.50	4.50
(94)	Lee Walls (Batting, glove in pocket.)	15.00	7.50	4.50
(95)	Lee Walls (Batting, trees.)	15.00	7.50	4.50
(96)	Jim Walsh (Follow-through, horizontal.)	15.00	7.50	4.50
(97)	Preston Ward (Batting, #44 in background.)	15.00	7.50	4.50
(98)	Preston Ward (Batting, no #44.)	15.00	7.50	4.50
(99)	Fred Waters (Pitching, leg up.)	15.00	7.50	4.50
(100)	Bill Werle (Pitching)	15.00	7.50	4.50

1967 Pittsburgh Pirates Autograph Cards

A souvenir stand item introduced by the Pirates in 1967 was a series of color player cards bearing facsimile autographs. The 3-1/4" x 4-1/4" cards identify the player with a line of type beneath the photo giving name, position and uniform number. Backs are blank. The cards are checklisted here in alphabetical order.

	NM	E	VG
Complete Set (24):	100.00	50.00	30.00

Common Player:	4.00	2.00	1.25
SERIES A			
(1) Gene Alley	8.00	4.00	2.40
(2) Steve Blass	8.00	4.00	2.40
(3) Roberto Clemente	70.00	35.00	21.00
(4) Donn Clendenon	10.00	5.00	3.00
(5) Roy Face	10.00	5.00	3.00
(6) Jesse Gonder	8.00	4.00	2.40
(7) Jerry May	8.00	4.00	2.40
(8) Manny Mota	10.00	5.00	3.00
(9) Jose Pagan	8.00	4.00	2.40
(10) Dennis Ribant	8.00	4.00	2.40
(11) Tommie Sisk	8.00	4.00	2.40
(12) Bob Veale	8.00	4.00	2.40
SERIES B			
(13) Matty Alou	8.00	4.00	2.40
(14) Woody Fryman	8.00	4.00	2.40
(15) Vernon Law	10.00	5.00	3.00
(16) Bill Mazeroski	35.00	17.50	10.50
(17) Al McBean	8.00	4.00	2.40
(18) Pete Mikkelsen	8.00	4.00	2.40
(19) Jim Pagliaroni	8.00	4.00	2.40
(20) Juan Pizarro	8.00	4.00	2.40
(21) Andy Rodgers	8.00	4.00	2.40
(22) Willie Stargell	30.00	15.00	9.00
(23) Harry Walker	8.00	4.00	2.40
(24) Maury Wills	13.00	6.50	4.00

1968 Pittsburgh Pirates Autograph Cards

These team-issued autograph cards were sold in packages at Forbes Field. The 3-1/4" x 4-1/4" cards feature a color player photo and facsimile autograph. They are blank-backed. Cards were issued in Series A and Series B, with header cards in each series providing a checklist. Cards are listed here by series according to the uniform number found on the card.

	NM	E	VG
Complete Set (26):	45.00	22.00	13.50
Common Player:	2.00	1.00	.60
SERIES A			
7 Larry Shepard	4.00	2.00	1.25
11 Jose Pagan	4.00	2.00	1.25
12 Jerry May	4.00	2.00	1.25
14 Jim Bunning	15.00	7.50	4.50
15 Manny Mota	4.00	2.00	1.25
17 Donn Clendenon	6.00	3.00	1.75
21 Roberto Clemente	15.00	7.50	4.50
22 Gene Alley	4.00	2.00	1.20
25 Tommie Sisk	4.00	2.00	1.20
26 Roy Face	4.00	2.00	1.20
28 Steve Blass	4.00	2.00	1.20
39 Bob Veale	4.00	2.00	1.20
-- Checklist Card, Series A	2.00	1.00	.60
SERIES B			
8 Willie Stargell	16.00	8.00	4.75
9 Bill Mazeroski	18.00	9.00	5.50
10 Gary Kolb	4.00	2.00	1.25
18 Matty Alou	5.00	2.50	1.50
27 Ronnie Kline	4.00	2.00	1.20
29 Juan Pizzaro	4.00	2.00	1.20
30 Maury Wills	4.00	2.00	1.25
34 Al McBean	4.00	2.00	1.20
35 Manny Sanguillen	4.00	2.00	1.20
38 Bob Moose	4.00	2.00	1.20
40 Dave Wickersham	4.00	2.00	1.20
-- Jim Shellenback	2.00	1.00	.60
-- Checklist Card, Series B	2.00	1.00	.60

1969 Pittsburgh Pirates Autograph Cards

Sold in Series A with a blue header card/checklist and Series B with a pink header card/checklist, these team-issue autograph cards were available at Forbes Field. Identical in format to the previous year's issue, the 3-1/4" x 4-1/4" cards are blank-backed and feature a color player photo on front with a facsimile autograph in the wide white bottom border. Cards are checklisted here by series and uniform number (found on card fronts) within series.

	NM	E	VG
Complete Set:	50.00	25.00	15.00
Common Player:	2.00	1.00	.60

Series A

		NM	E	VG
7	Bill Virdon	5.00	2.50	1.50
11	Jose Pagan	4.00	2.00	1.20
12	Jerry May	4.00	2.00	1.20
14	Jim Bunning	15.00	7.50	4.50
18	Matty Alou	5.00	2.50	1.00
20	Richie Hebner	6.00	3.00	1.75
21	Roberto Clemente	30.00	15.00	9.00
22	Gene Alley	4.00	2.00	1.20
32	Vernon Law	2.50	1.25	.70
36	Carl Taylor	2.00	1.00	.60
40	Dock Ellis	2.50	1.25	.70
43	Bruce Dal Canton	4.00	2.00	1.20

Series B

		NM	E	VG
2	Fred Patek	4.00	2.00	1.20
4	Larry Shepard	4.00	2.00	1.20
8	Willie Stargell	12.00	6.00	3.50
9	Bill Mazeroski	18.00	9.00	5.50
10	Gary Kolb	4.00	2.00	1.20
23	Luke Walker	2.00	1.00	.60
28	Steve Blass	2.00	1.00	.60
29	Al Oliver	4.00	2.00	1.25
35	Manny Sanguillen	2.50	1.25	.70
38	Bob Moose	2.00	1.00	.60
39	Bob Veale	2.00	1.00	.60
42	Chuck Hartenstein	2.00	1.00	.60

1970 Pittsburgh Pirates (Andersen)

Boston baseball photographer Mike Andersen is believed to have produced this collectors' issue of Pirates cards. Nearly identical in format to his 1969-70 Oakland A's issues, the '70 Pirates measures 2-1/4" x 3-5/8" with black-and-white player poses at center. Player identification and 1969 stats are in the bottom border. Backs are blank. Cards are checklisted here alphabetically.

		NM	E	VG
Complete Set (12):		40.00	20.00	12.00
Common Player:		2.00	1.00	.60
(1)	Gene Alley	2.00	1.00	.60
(2)	Dave Cash	2.00	1.00	.60
(3)	Dock Ellis	2.00	1.00	.60
(4)	Dave Giusti	2.00	1.00	.60
(5)	Jerry May	2.00	1.00	.60
(6)	Bill Mazeroski	12.00	6.00	3.50
(7)	Al Oliver	4.00	2.00	1.25
(8)	Jose Pagan	2.00	1.00	.60
(9)	Fred Patek	2.00	1.00	.60
(10)	Bob Robertson	2.00	1.00	.60
(11)	Manny Sanguillen	2.00	1.00	.60
(12)	Willie Stargell	12.00	6.00	3.50

1970 Pittsburgh Pirates Autograph Cards

Retaining the 3-1/4" x 4-1/4" format from previous years, these team-issued autograph cards can be distinguished from the 1968-69 issues by the Three Rivers Stadium photo background on each card. The Pirates moved from Forbes Field in June, 1970. The set is checklisted here by uniform number without regard to Series A and B.

		NM	E	VG
	Complete Set (25):	90.00	45.00	27.50
	Common Player:	3.00	1.50	.80
2	Fred Patek	6.00	3.00	1.75
5	Dave Ricketts	6.00	3.00	1.75
8	Willie Stargell	24.00	12.00	7.25
9	Bill Mazeroski	24.00	12.00	7.25
10	Richie Hebner	6.00	3.00	1.75
11	Jose Pagan	6.00	3.00	1.75
12	Jerry May	6.00	3.00	1.75
16	Al Oliver	10.00	5.00	3.00
17	Dock Ellis	6.00	3.00	1.75
18	Matty Alou	6.00	3.00	1.75
19	Joe Gibbon	6.00	3.00	1.75
21	Roberto Clemente	25.00	12.50	7.50
22	Gene Alley	6.00	3.00	1.75
22	Orlando Pena	6.00	3.00	1.75
23	Luke Walker	6.00	3.00	1.75
25	John Jeter	6.00	3.00	1.75
25	Bob Robertson	6.00	3.00	1.75
30	Dave Cash	6.00	3.00	1.75
31	Dave Giusti	6.00	3.00	1.75
35	Manny Sanguillen	6.00	3.00	1.75
36	Dick Calpaert (Colpaert)	6.00	3.00	1.75
38	Bob Moose	6.00	3.00	1.75
39	Bob Veale	6.00	3.00	1.75
40	Danny Murtaugh	6.00	3.00	1.75
50	Jim Nelson	6.00	3.00	1.75

1971 Pittsburgh Pirates Autograph Cards

DAVE GIUSTI (Pitcher) #31

The '71 team-issued Pirates autograph cards are distinguished by the appearance of mustard-yellow caps on the players' portraits. Otherwise the blank-back 3-1/4" x 4-1/2" photocards are identical in format to those of earlier seasons. Players are checklisted here alphabetically within series.

		NM	E	VG
	Complete Set (20):	45.00	22.50	13.50
	Common Player:	2.00	1.00	.60
	Series A			
(1)	Gene Alley	4.00	2.00	1.25
(2)	Nelson Briles	4.00	2.00	1.25
(3)	Dave Cash	4.00	2.00	1.25
(4)	Dock Ellis	4.00	2.00	1.25
(5)	Mudcat Grant	5.00	2.50	1.50
(6)	Bill Mazeroski	18.00	9.00	5.50
(7)	Jim Nelson	4.00	2.00	1.25
(8)	Al Oliver	8.00	4.00	2.50
(9)	Manny Sanguillen	5.00	2.50	1.50
(10)	Luke Walker	4.00	2.00	1.25
	Series B			
(11)	Steve Blass	4.00	2.00	1.25
(12)	Bob Clemente	30.00	15.00	9.00
(13)	Dave Giusti	4.00	2.00	1.25
(14)	Richie Hebner	5.00	2.50	1.50
(15)	Bob Johnson	4.00	2.00	1.25
(16)	Bob Moose	4.00	2.00	1.25
(17)	Jose Pagan	4.00	2.00	1.25
(18)	Bob Robertson	4.00	2.00	1.25
(19)	Willie Stargell	16.00	8.00	4.75
(20)	Bob Veale	4.00	2.00	1.25

1963-64 Pittsburgh Pirates Picture Pack

ROBERTO CLEMENTE, Pirates

This set of 5" x 7" black-and-white blank-back player pictures was created for sale at stadium concession stands and other souvenir outlets. The players are pictured in portraits or posed action photos, bordered in white. In the wide bottom border, the player's name is printed in all capital letters, with the team nickname in upper- and lower-case letters. The set was sold in a white picture envelope.

		NM	EX	VG
	Complete Set (12):			
	Common Player:			
(1)	Bob Bailey	4.00	2.00	1.25
(2)	Smoky Burgess	4.00	2.00	1.25
(3)	Roberto Clemente	40.00	20.00	12.50
(4)	Roy Face	4.00	2.00	1.25
(5)	Bob Friend	4.00	2.00	1.25
(6)	Joe Gibbon	4.00	2.00	1.25
(7)	Jerry Lynch	4.00	2.00	1.25
(8)	Bill Mazeroski	12.00	6.00	3.75
(9)	Danny Murtaugh	4.00	2.00	1.25
(10)	Jim Pagliaroni	4.00	2.00	1.25
(11)	Dick Schofield	4.00	2.00	1.25
(12)	Bill Virdon	4.00	2.00	1.25

1973 Pittsburgh Post-Gazette Pirates

This set of Pirates pictures was printed on newspaper stock one per day in the sports section of the daily paper. The black-bordered black-and-white photos are 5-1/4" x 9-1/4". At top is "'73 Pirate Album" and a short career summary. At bottom are 1972 and career stats. The first six pictures are unnumbered, the others are numbered alphabetically.

		NM	E	VG
	Complete Set (25):	125.00	60.00	35.00
	Common Player:	6.00	3.00	1.75
	Gene Alley	6.00	3.00	1.75
	Steve Blass	6.00	3.00	1.75
	Nellie Briles	6.00	3.00	1.75
	Dave Cash	6.00	3.00	1.75
	Roberto Clemente	40.00	20.00	12.00
	Gene Clines	6.00	3.00	1.75
6	Vic Davalillo	6.00	3.00	1.75
7	Dock Ellis	6.00	3.00	1.75
8	Dave Giusti	6.00	3.00	1.75
9	Richie Hebner	6.00	3.00	1.75
10	Jackie Hernandez	6.00	3.00	1.75
11	Ramon Hernandez	6.00	3.00	1.75
12	Bob Johnson	6.00	3.00	1.75
13	Bruce Kison	6.00	3.00	1.75
14	Milt May	6.00	3.00	1.75
15	Bob Miller	6.00	3.00	1.75
16	Bob Moose	6.00	3.00	1.75
17	Al Oliver	7.50	3.75	2.25
18	Bob Robertson	6.00	3.00	1.75
19	Charlie Sands	6.00	3.00	1.75
20	Manny Sanguillen	6.00	3.00	1.75
21	Willie Stargell	12.00	6.00	3.50
22	Rennie Stennett	6.00	3.00	1.75
23	Luke Walker	6.00	3.00	1.75
24	Bill Virdon	7.50	3.75	2.25

1972 Pittsburgh Press "Buc-A-Day" Pirates

BUC-A-DAY . . . No. 6

Bill Mazeroski

WILLIAM STANLEY MAZEROSKI (28)

Through the month of March 1972, the daily Pittsburgh Press carried a "Buc-A-Day" feature highlighting members of the team. The feature was intended to be cut out of the

paper and saved. Individual pieces measure 3-3/8" wide and vary in length from 9-1/4" to 11-1/16" depending on the length of the biographical information provided. Each player is pictured in a black-and-white photo in street clothes. Some are pictured with golf clubs, fishing poles, with their children, etc. Because of the nature of their distribution and their fragile nature, complete sets are very scarce.

		NM	E	VG
	Complete Set (25):	100.00	50.00	30.00
	Common Player:	2.50	1.25	.70
1	Willie Stargell	7.50	3.75	2.25
2	Steve Blass	2.50	1.25	.70
3	Al Oliver	3.00	1.50	.90
4	Bob Moose	2.50	1.25	.70
5	Dave Cash	2.50	1.25	.70
6	Bill Mazeroski	7.50	3.75	2.25
7	Bob Johnson	2.50	1.25	.70
8	Nellie Briles	2.50	1.25	.70
9	Manny Sanguillen	3.00	1.50	.90
10	Vic Davalillo	2.50	1.25	.70
11	Dave Giusti	2.50	1.25	.70
12	Luke Walker	2.50	1.25	.70
13	Gene Clines	2.50	1.25	.70
14	Milt May	2.50	1.25	.70
15	Bob Robertson	2.50	1.25	.70
16	Roberto Clemente	15.00	7.50	4.50
17	Gene Alley	2.50	1.25	.70
18	Bruce Kison	2.50	1.25	.70
19	Jose Pagan	2.50	1.25	.70
20	Dock Ellis	2.50	1.25	.70
21	Richie Hebner	2.50	1.25	.70
22	Bob Miller	2.50	1.25	.70
23	Jackie Hernandez	2.50	1.25	.70
24	Rennie Stennett	2.50	1.25	.70
25	Bob Veale	2.50	1.25	.70

1948 Pittsburgh Provision & Packing Co.

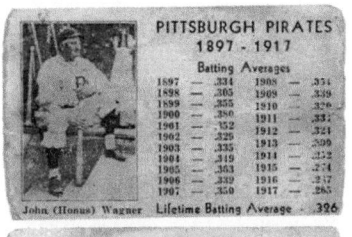

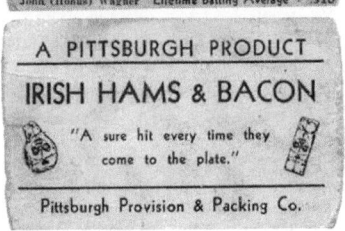

The attributed date is totally arbitrary, based on the photo shown. Also unknown are the scope of the issue and its manner of distribution. Hobby history would suggest the card was created to promote Wagner's ties to the meat company as a spokesman, or perhaps the card was created for Wagner to distribute at appearances on behalf of the packing company. The dark green-printed card measures about 4" x 2-1/2" and is printed on rather thin cardboard. It is not known whether similar cards exist for other players.

	NM	E	VG
Honus Wagner	400.00	200.00	120.00

1936 Pittsburgh Sun-Telegraph Sport Stamps

Ralph Birkofer, p., Pirates

Similar to several contemporary issues, the Sport Stamps were printed in a single edition of the daily newspaper. Thirteen players were printed for each of the 16 Major League teams. About 2" x 3", depending on the length of the biography and how well they were cut off the paper, they are printed in black-and-white. A tightly cropped player portrait is centered on a 1-3/4" x 2-1/4" stamp design with the paper's name above and the player's name, position and team below. This checklist is incomplete.

		NM	E	VG
Complete Set (208):				
Common Player:		12.00	6.00	3.50
(1)	Ralph Birkofer	12.00	6.00	3.50
(2)	Cy Blanton	12.00	6.00	3.50
(3)	Bill Brubaker	12.00	6.00	3.50
(4)	Guy Bush	12.00	6.00	3.50
(5)	Ty Cobb	25.00	12.50	7.50
(6)	Jerome "Dizzy" Dean	25.00	12.50	7.50
(7)	Joe DiMaggio	75.00	37.00	22.00
(8)	Hank Greenberg	25.00	12.50	7.50
(9)	Waite Hoyt	20.00	10.00	6.00
(10)	Carl Hubbell	20.00	10.00	6.00
(11)	Woody Jensen	12.00	6.00	3.50
(12)	Red Lucas	12.00	6.00	3.50
(13)	Joe Medwick	20.00	10.00	6.00
(13)	Tommy Padden	12.00	6.00	3.50
(14)	Casey Stengel	20.00	10.00	6.00
(15)	Clarence Strass	12.00	6.00	3.50
(16)	Gus Suhr	12.00	6.00	3.50
(17)	Bill Swift	12.00	6.00	3.50
(18)	John Tising	12.00	6.00	3.50
(19)	Al Todd	12.00	6.00	3.50
(20)	Pie Traynor	20.00	10.00	6.00
(21)	Honus Wagner	25.00	12.50	7.50
(22)	Lloyd Waner	20.00	10.00	6.00
(23)	Paul Waner	20.00	10.00	6.00
(24)	Jim Weaver	12.00	6.00	3.50
(25)	Floyd Young	12.00	6.00	3.50

1954 Plankinton Milwaukee Braves Playing Tips

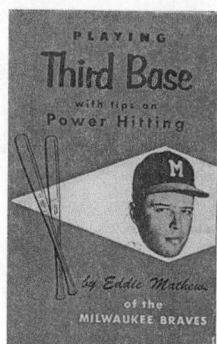

This set of "How to Play Better Baseball" poster booklets was apparently distributed in packages of hot dogs on a regional basis. Folded, the booklet measures 2-7/8" x 4-3/8" and has a black-and-white player portrait photo with a red background. When opened, the booklet forms an 11" x 17" poster offering big league tips from Braves players. The tips are well illustrated with many photos. There is a booklet for each position as well as one for right- and left-handed pitchers, a coach and even a team trainer.

		NM	E	VG
Complete Set (12):		800.00	400.00	240.00
Common Player:		75.00	37.50	22.50
1	Joe Adcock	90.00	45.00	27.50
2	Danny O'Connell	75.00	37.50	22.50
3	Eddie Mathews	150.00	75.00	45.00
4	Johnny Logan	75.00	37.50	22.50
5	Bobby Thomson	90.00	45.00	27.50
6	Bill Bruton	75.00	37.50	22.50
7	Andy Pafko	75.00	37.50	22.50
8	Del Crandall	75.00	37.50	22.50
9	Warren Spahn	150.00	75.00	45.00
10	Gene Conley	75.00	37.50	22.50
11	Charlie Grimm	75.00	37.50	22.50
12	Joe Taylor	75.00	37.50	22.50

1939 Play Ball (R334)

With the issue of this card set by Gum Inc., a new era of baseball cards was born. Although the cards are black-and-white, the photos on front are of better quality than previously seen, and the 2-1/2" x 3-1/8" size was larger than virtually all of the tobacco and caramel cards of the early 20th Century. Card backs feature full player names, "Joseph Paul DiMaggio" instead of "Joe DiMaggio" and extensive biographies. Players are listed here by their most commonly used name. There are 161 cards in the set; card #126 was never issued.

The complete set price does not include all back variations found in the low-numbered series. Many of the cards between #2-115 (indicated with an asterisk) can be found with the player name either in all capital letters, or in both upper- and lower-case letters. Minor differences in typography, along with variations in details of the biographical data, or within the wording of the career summary may be found on those cards that exist in two versions. No premium currently attaches to either version, though the cards with name in upper- and lower-case are somewhat scarcer.

		NM	E	VG
Complete Set (161):		10,000	4,750	2,750
Common Player (1-115):		35.00	17.50	10.50
Common Player (116-162):		65.00	32.50	19.50
1	Jake Powell	135.00	15.00	7.50
2	Lee Grissom	35.00	17.50	10.50
3	Red Ruffing (*)	100.00	50.00	30.00
4	Eldon Auker (*)	35.00	17.50	10.50
5	Luke Sewell (*)	35.00	17.50	10.50
6	Leo Durocher (*)	100.00	50.00	30.00
7	Bobby Doerr (*)	100.00	50.00	30.00
8	Cotton Pippen	35.00	17.50	10.50
9	Jim Tobin (*)	35.00	17.50	10.50
10	Jimmie DeShong	35.00	17.50	10.50
11	Johnny Rizzo	35.00	17.50	10.50
12	Hersh Martin	35.00	17.50	10.50
13	Luke Hamlin (*)	35.00	17.50	10.50
14	Jim Tabor (*)	35.00	17.50	10.50
15	Paul Derringer (*)	35.00	17.50	10.50
16	Johnny Peacock	35.00	17.50	10.50
17	Emerson Dickman	35.00	17.50	10.50
18	Harry Danning (*)	35.00	17.50	10.50
19	Paul Dean	50.00	25.00	15.00
20	Joe Heving	35.00	17.50	10.50
21	Dutch Leonard (*)	35.00	17.50	10.50
22	Bucky Walters (*)	35.00	17.50	10.50
23	Burgess Whitehead	35.00	17.50	10.50
24	Dick Coffman (*)	35.00	17.50	10.50
25	George Selkirk (*)	35.00	17.50	10.50
26	Joe DiMaggio (*)	1,275	625.00	425.00
27	Fritz Ostermueller (*)	35.00	17.50	10.50
28	Syl Johnson	35.00	17.50	10.50
29	Jack Wilson (*)	35.00	17.50	10.50
30	Bill Dickey (*)	175.00	85.00	55.00
31	Sammy West (*)	35.00	17.50	10.50
32	Bob Seeds	35.00	17.50	10.50
33	Del Young	35.00	17.50	10.50
34	Frank Demaree (*)	35.00	17.50	10.50
35	Bill Jurges (*)	35.00	17.50	10.50
36	Frank McCormick (*)	35.00	17.50	10.50
37	Spud Davis	35.00	17.50	10.50
38	Billy Myers (*)	35.00	17.50	10.50
39	Rick Ferrell (*)	100.00	50.00	30.00
40	Jim Bagby Jr.	35.00	17.50	10.50
41	Lon Warneke (*)	35.00	17.50	10.50
42	Arndt Jorgens	35.00	17.50	10.50
43	Mel Almada	35.00	17.50	10.00
44	Don Heffner	35.00	17.50	10.50
45	Pinky May (*)	35.00	17.50	10.50
46	Morrie Arnovich (*)	40.00	20.00	12.00
47	Buddy Lewis (*)	35.00	17.50	10.50
48	Lefty Gomez (*)	100.00	50.00	30.00
49	Eddie Miller	35.00	17.50	10.50
50	Charlie Gehringer (*)	100.00	50.00	30.00
51	Mel Ott (*)	135.00	65.00	40.00
52	Tommy Henrich (*)	60.00	30.00	18.00
53	Carl Hubbell (*)	125.00	65.00	35.00
54	Harry Gumbert (*)	35.00	17.50	10.50
55	Arky Vaughan (*)	100.00	50.00	30.00
56	Hank Greenberg (*)	250.00	125.00	75.00
57	Buddy Hassett (*)	35.00	17.50	10.50
58	Lou Chiozza	35.00	17.50	10.50
59	Ken Chase	35.00	17.50	10.50
60	Schoolboy Rowe (*)	35.00	17.50	10.50
61	Tony Cuccinello (*)	35.00	17.50	10.50
62	Tom Carey	35.00	17.50	10.50
63	Heinie Mueller	35.00	17.50	10.50
64	Wally Moses (*)	35.00	17.50	10.50
65	Harry Craft (*)	35.00	17.50	10.50
66	Jimmy Ripple	35.00	17.50	10.50
67	Eddie Joost	35.00	17.50	10.50
68	Fred Sington	35.00	17.50	10.50
69	Elbie Fletcher	35.00	17.50	10.50
70	Fred Frankhouse	35.00	17.50	10.50
71	Monte Pearson (*)	35.00	17.50	10.50
72	Debs Garms (*)	35.00	17.50	10.50
73	Hal Schumacher (*)	35.00	17.50	10.50
74	Cookie Lavagetto (*)	35.00	17.50	10.50
75	Frenchy Bordagaray (*)	35.00	17.50	10.50
76	Goody Rosen	40.00	20.00	12.00
77	Lew Riggs	35.00	17.50	10.50
78	Moose Solters (*)	35.00	17.50	10.50
79	Joe Moore (*)	35.00	17.50	10.50
80	Pete Fox (*)	35.00	17.50	10.50
81	Babe Dahlgren (*)	35.00	17.50	10.50
82	Chuck Klein (*)	100.00	50.00	30.00
83	Gus Suhr (*)	35.00	17.50	10.50
84	Skeeter Newsome	35.00	17.50	10.50
85	Johnny Cooney	35.00	17.50	10.50
86	Dolph Camilli (*)	35.00	17.50	10.50
87	Milt Shoffner	35.00	17.50	10.50
88	Charlie Keller	35.00	17.50	10.00
89	Lloyd Waner (*)	100.00	50.00	30.00
90	Bob Klinger (*)	35.00	17.50	10.50
91	Jack Knott (*)	35.00	17.50	10.50
92	Ted Williams (*)	2,250	1,000	625.00
93	Charley Gelbert	35.00	17.50	10.50
94	Heinie Manush	100.00	50.00	30.00
95	Whit Wyatt (*)	35.00	17.50	10.50
96	Babe Phelps (*)	35.00	17.50	10.50
97	Bob Johnson (*)	35.00	17.50	10.50
98	Pinky Whitney	35.00	17.50	10.50
99	Wally Berger (*)	35.00	17.50	10.50
100	Buddy Myer (*)	35.00	17.50	10.50
101	Doc Cramer (*)	35.00	17.50	10.50
102	Pep Young (*)	35.00	17.50	10.50
103	Moe Berg	140.00	75.00	45.00
104	Tommy Bridges (*)	35.00	17.50	10.50
105	Eric McNair (*)	35.00	17.50	10.50
106	Dolly Stark	50.00	25.00	15.00
107	Joe Vosmik	35.00	17.50	10.50
108	Frankie Hayes (*)	35.00	17.50	10.50
109	Myril Hoag (*)	35.00	17.50	10.50
110	Freddie Fitzsimmons	35.00	17.50	10.50
111	Van Lingle Mungo (*)	35.00	17.50	10.00
112	Paul Waner (*)	100.00	50.00	30.00
113	Al Schacht	50.00	25.00	15.00
114	Cecil Travis (*)	35.00	17.50	10.50
115	Red Kress (*)	35.00	17.50	10.50
116	Gene Desautels	65.00	32.50	19.50
117	Wayne Ambler	65.00	32.50	19.50
118	Lynn Nelson	65.00	32.50	19.50
119	Will Hershberger	65.00	32.50	19.50
120	Rabbit Warstler	65.00	32.50	19.50
121	Bill Posedel	65.00	32.50	19.50
122	George McQuinn	65.00	32.50	19.50
123	Peaches Davis	65.00	32.50	19.50
124	Jumbo Brown	65.00	32.50	19.50
125	Cliff Melton	65.00	32.50	19.50
126	Not issued			
127	Gil Brack	65.00	32.50	19.50
128	Joe Bowman	65.00	32.50	19.50
129	Bill Swift	65.00	32.50	19.50
130	Bill Brubaker	65.00	32.50	19.50
131	Mort Cooper	65.00	32.50	19.50
132	Jimmy Brown	65.00	32.50	19.50
133	Lynn Myers	65.00	32.50	19.50
134	Tot Pressnell	65.00	32.50	19.50
135	Mickey Owen	65.00	32.50	19.50
136	Roy Bell	65.00	32.50	19.50
137	Pete Appleton	65.00	32.50	19.50
138	George Case	65.00	32.50	19.50
139	Vito Tamulis	65.00	32.50	19.50
140	Ray Hayworth	65.00	32.50	19.50
141	Pete Coscarart	65.00	32.50	19.50
142	Ira Hutchinson	65.00	32.50	19.50
143	Earl Averill	175.00	90.00	55.00
144	Zeke Bonura	65.00	32.50	19.50
145	Hugh Mulcahy	65.00	32.50	19.50
146	Tom Sunkel	65.00	32.50	19.50
147	George Coffman	65.00	32.50	19.50
148	Bill Trotter	65.00	32.50	19.50
149	Max West	65.00	32.50	19.50
150	Jim Walkup	65.00	32.50	19.50
151	Hugh Casey	65.00	32.50	19.50
152	Roy Weatherly	65.00	32.50	19.50
153	Dizzy Trout	65.00	32.50	19.50
154	Johnny Hudson	65.00	32.50	19.50
155	Jimmy Outlaw	65.00	32.50	19.50
156	Ray Berres	65.00	32.50	19.50
157	Don Padgett	65.00	32.50	19.50
158	Bud Thomas	65.00	32.50	19.50
159	Red Evans	65.00	32.50	19.50
160	Gene Moore Jr.	65.00	32.50	19.50
161	Lonny Frey	65.00	32.50	19.50
162	Whitey Moore	200.00	30.00	17.50

1939 Play Ball Samples

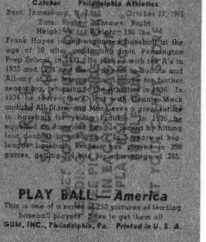

Each of the first 115 cards in the 1939 Play Ball set can be found with red overprinting on the back indicating sample card status. The overprint reads: FREE / SAMPLE CARD / GET YOUR PICTURES OF / LEADING BASEBALL PLAYERS. / THREE PICTURE CARDS PACKED / IN EACH PACKAGE OF / "PLAY BALL AMERICA" / BUBBLE GUM. / AT YOUR CANDY STORE / 1c." Collectors will pay a small premium for a type card of a common player. Sample cards of most star players sell for about double the price of the regular-issue cards, while DiMaggio and Williams samples sell for about the same price as their regular-issue cards.

		NM	E	VG
Common Player:		35.00	17.50	10.00
26	Joe DiMaggio	1,750	875.00	525.00
92	Ted Williams	2,225	1,115	675.00

1940 Play Ball (R335)

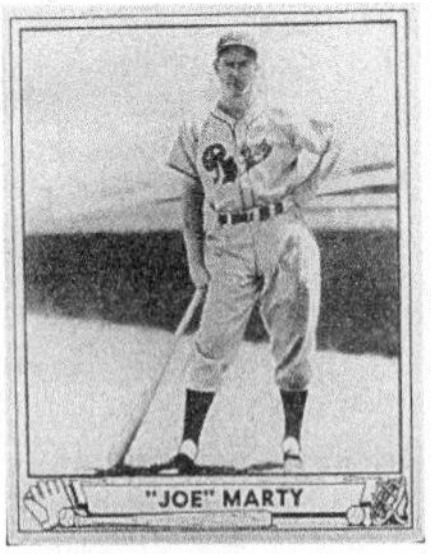

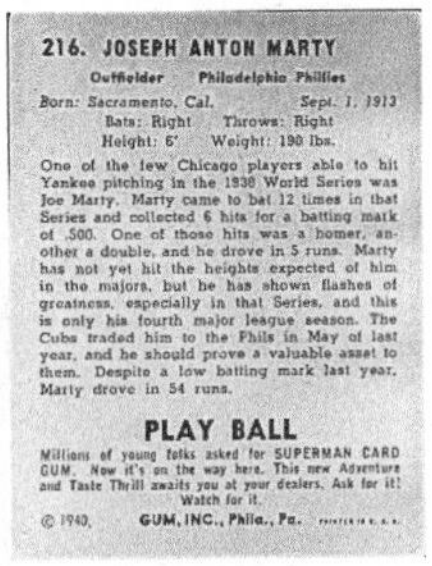
216. JOSEPH ANTON MARTY

Outfielder Philadelphia Phillies

Born: Sacramento, Cal. Sept. 1, 1913

Bats: Right Throws: Right

Height: 6' Weight: 190 lbs.

One of the few Chicago players able to hit Yankee pitching in the 1938 World Series was Joe Marty. Marty came to bat 12 times in that Series and collected 6 hits for a batting mark of .500. One of those hits was a homer, another a double, and he drove in 5 runs. Marty has not yet hit the heights expected of him in the majors, but he has shown flashes of greatness, especially in that Series, and this is only his fourth major league season. The Cubs traded him to the Phils in May of last year, and he should prove a valuable asset to them. Despite a low batting mark last year, Marty drove in 54 runs.

PLAY BALL

Millions of young folks asked for SUPERMAN CARD GUM. Now it's on the way here. This new Adventure and Taste Thrill awaits you at your dealers. Ask for it! Watch for it.

© 1940. GUM, INC., Phila., Pa.

Following the success of its initial effort in 1939, Gum Inc. issued a bigger and better set in 1940. The 240 black-and-white cards are once again in 2-1/2" x 3-1/8" size, but the front photos are enclosed by a frame with the player's name. Backs again offer extensive biographies and are dated. A number of former stars were issued along with contemporary players, and many Hall of Famers are included. The final 60 cards of the set are more difficult to obtain.

		NM	E	VG
Complete Set (240):		22,500	11,000	6,500
Common Player (1-180):		40.00	20.00	12.00
Common Player (181-240):		90.00	45.00	27.00
1	Joe DiMaggio	3,500	1,750	1,050
2	"Art" Jorgens	40.00	20.00	12.00
3	"Babe" Dahlgren	40.00	20.00	12.00
4	"Tommy" Henrich	60.00	30.00	18.00
5	"Monte" Pearson	40.00	20.00	12.00
6	"Lefty" Gomez	130.00	65.00	40.00
7	"Bill" Dickey	175.00	85.00	50.00
8	"Twinkletoes" Selkirk	40.00	20.00	12.00
9	"Charley" Keller	40.00	20.00	12.00
10	"Red" Ruffing	130.00	65.00	40.00
11	"Jake" Powell	40.00	20.00	12.00
12	"Johnny" Schulte	40.00	20.00	12.00
13	"Jack" Knott	40.00	20.00	12.00
14	"Rabbit" McNair	40.00	20.00	12.00
15	George Case	40.00	20.00	12.00
16	Cecil Travis	40.00	20.00	12.00
17	"Buddy" Myer	40.00	20.00	12.00
18	"Charley" Gelbert	40.00	20.00	12.00
19	Ken Chase	40.00	20.00	12.00
20	"Buddy" Lewis	40.00	20.00	12.00
21	"Rick" Ferrell	130.00	65.00	40.00
22	"Sammy" West	40.00	20.00	12.00
23	"Dutch" Leonard	40.00	20.00	12.00
24	Frank "Blimp" Hayes	40.00	20.00	12.00
25	"Cherokee" Bob Johnson	40.00	20.00	12.00
26	"Wally" Moses	40.00	20.00	12.00
27	"Ted" Williams	1,750	600.00	360.00
28	"Gene" Desautels	40.00	20.00	12.00
29	"Doc" Cramer	40.00	20.00	12.00
30	"Moe" Berg	160.00	80.00	45.00
31	Jack Wilson	40.00	20.00	12.00
32	"Jim" Bagby Jr.	40.00	20.00	12.00
33	"Fritz" Ostermueller	40.00	20.00	12.00
34	John Peacock	40.00	20.00	12.00
35	"Joe" Heving	40.00	20.00	12.00
36	"Jim" Tabor	40.00	20.00	12.00
37	Emerson Dickman	40.00	20.00	12.00
38	"Bobby" Doerr	130.00	65.00	40.00
39	"Tom" Carey	40.00	20.00	12.00
40	"Hank" Greenberg	350.00	175.00	105.00
41	"Charley" Gehringer	150.00	75.00	45.00
42	"Bud" Thomas	40.00	20.00	12.00
43	Pete Fox	40.00	20.00	12.00
44	"Dizzy" Trout	40.00	20.00	12.00
45	"Red" Kress	40.00	20.00	12.00
46	Earl Averill	130.00	65.00	40.00
47	"Old Os" Vitt	40.00	20.00	12.00
48	"Luke" Sewell	40.00	20.00	12.00
49	"Stormy Weather" Weatherly	40.00	20.00	12.00
50	"Hal" Trosky	40.00	20.00	12.00
51	"Don" Heffner	40.00	20.00	12.00
52	Myril Hoag	40.00	20.00	12.00
53	"Mac" McQuinn	40.00	20.00	12.00
54	"Bill" Trotter	40.00	20.00	12.00
55	"Slick" Coffman	40.00	20.00	12.00
56	"Eddie" Miller	40.00	20.00	12.00
57	Max West	40.00	20.00	12.00
58	"Bill" Posedel	40.00	20.00	12.00
59	"Rabbit" Warstler	40.00	20.00	12.00
60	John Cooney	40.00	20.00	12.00
61	"Tony" Cuccinello	40.00	20.00	12.00
62	"Buddy" Hassett	40.00	20.00	12.00
63	"Pete" Cascarart (Coscarart)	40.00	20.00	12.00
64	"Van" Mungo	40.00	20.00	12.00
65	"Fitz" Fitzsimmons	40.00	20.00	12.00
66	"Babe" Phelps	40.00	20.00	12.00
67	"Whit" Wyatt	40.00	20.00	12.00
68	"Dolph" Camilli	40.00	20.00	12.00
69	"Cookie" Lavagetto	40.00	20.00	12.00
70	"Hot Potato" Hamlin	40.00	20.00	12.00
71	Mel Almada	40.00	20.00	12.00
72	"Chuck" Dressen	40.00	20.00	12.00
73	"Bucky" Walters	40.00	20.00	12.00
74	"Duke" Derringer	40.00	20.00	12.00
75	"Buck" McCormick	40.00	20.00	12.00
76	"Lonny" Frey	40.00	20.00	12.00
77	"Bill" Hershberger	60.00	30.00	18.00
78	"Lew" Riggs	40.00	20.00	12.00
79	"Wildfire" Craft	40.00	20.00	12.00
80	"Bill" Myers	40.00	20.00	12.00
81	"Wally" Berger	40.00	20.00	12.00
82	"Hank" Gowdy	40.00	20.00	12.00
83	"Clif" Melton (Cliff)	40.00	20.00	12.00
84	"Jo-Jo" Moore	40.00	20.00	12.00
85	"Hal" Schumacher	40.00	20.00	12.00
86	Harry Gumbert	40.00	20.00	12.00
87	Carl Hubbell	160.00	80.00	45.00
88	"Mel" Ott	200.00	100.00	60.00
89	"Bill" Jurges	40.00	20.00	12.00
90	Frank Demaree	40.00	20.00	12.00
91	Bob "Suitcase" Seeds	40.00	20.00	12.00
92	"Whitey" Whitehead	40.00	20.00	12.00
93	Harry "The Horse" Danning	40.00	20.00	12.00
94	"Gus" Suhr	40.00	20.00	12.00
95	"Mul" Mulcahy	40.00	20.00	12.00
96	"Heinie" Mueller	40.00	20.00	12.00
97	"Morry" Arnovich	40.00	20.00	12.00
98	"Pinky" May	40.00	20.00	12.00
99	"Syl" Johnson	40.00	20.00	12.00
100	"Hersh" Martin	40.00	20.00	12.00
101	"Del" Young	40.00	20.00	12.00
102	"Chuck" Klein	130.00	65.00	40.00
103	"Elbie" Fletcher	40.00	20.00	12.00
104	"Big Poison" Waner	130.00	65.00	40.00
105	"Little Poison" Waner	130.00	65.00	40.00
106	"Pep" Young	40.00	20.00	12.00
107	"Arky" Vaughan	130.00	65.00	40.00
108	"Johnny" Rizzo	40.00	20.00	12.00
109	Don Padgett	40.00	20.00	12.00
110	"Tom" Sunkel	40.00	20.00	12.00
111	"Mickey" Owen	40.00	20.00	12.00
112	"Jimmy" Brown	40.00	20.00	12.00
113	"Mort" Cooper	40.00	20.00	12.00
114	"Lon" Warneke	40.00	20.00	12.00
115	"Mike" Gonzales (Gonzalez)	40.00	20.00	12.00
116	"Al" Schacht	60.00	30.00	18.00
117	"Dolly" Stark	75.00	37.50	22.50
118	"Schoolboy" Hoyt	130.00	65.00	40.00
119	"Ol Pete" Alexander	175.00	85.00	50.00
120	Walter "Big Train" Johnson	275.00	135.00	80.00
121	Atley Donald	40.00	20.00	12.00
122	"Sandy" Sundra	40.00	20.00	12.00
123	"Hildy" Hildebrand	40.00	20.00	12.00
124	"Colonel" Combs	120.00	60.00	35.00
125	"Art" Fletcher	40.00	20.00	12.00
126	"Jake" Solters	40.00	20.00	12.00
127	"Muddy" Ruel	40.00	20.00	12.00
128	"Pete" Appleton	40.00	20.00	12.00
129	"Bucky" Harris	120.00	60.00	35.00
130	"Deerfoot" Milan	40.00	20.00	12.00
131	"Zeke" Bonura	40.00	20.00	12.00
132	Connie Mack	120.00	60.00	35.00
133	"Jimmie" Foxx	300.00	150.00	90.00
134	"Joe" Cronin	130.00	65.00	40.00
135	"Line Drive" Nelson	40.00	20.00	12.00
136	"Cotton" Pippen	40.00	20.00	12.00
137	"Bing" Miller	40.00	20.00	12.00
138	"Beau" Bell	40.00	20.00	12.00
139	Elden Auker (Eldon)	40.00	20.00	12.00
140	"Dick" Coffman	40.00	20.00	12.00
141	"Casey" Stengel	200.00	100.00	60.00
142	"Highpockets" Kelly	120.00	60.00	35.00
143	"Gene" Moore	40.00	20.00	12.00
144	"Joe" Vosmik	40.00	20.00	12.00
145	"Vito" Tamulis	40.00	20.00	12.00
146	"Tot" Pressnell	40.00	20.00	12.00
147	"Johnny" Hudson	40.00	20.00	12.00
148	"Hugh" Casey	40.00	20.00	12.00
149	"Pinky" Shoffner	40.00	20.00	12.00
150	"Whitey" Moore	40.00	20.00	12.00
151	Edwin Joost	40.00	20.00	12.00
152	Jimmy Wilson	40.00	20.00	12.00
153	"Bill" McKechnie	120.00	60.00	35.00
154	"Jumbo" Brown	40.00	20.00	12.00
155	"Ray" Hayworth	40.00	20.00	12.00
156	"Daffy" Dean	65.00	32.50	20.00
157	"Lou" Chiozza	40.00	20.00	12.00
158	"Stonewall" Jackson	120.00	60.00	35.00
159	"Pancho" Snyder	40.00	20.00	12.00
160	"Hans" Lobert	40.00	20.00	12.00
161	"Debs" Garms	40.00	20.00	12.00
162	Joe Bowman	40.00	20.00	12.00
163	"Spud" Davis	40.00	20.00	12.00
164	"Ray" Berres	40.00	20.00	12.00
165	"Bob" Klinger	40.00	20.00	12.00
166	"Bill" Brubaker	40.00	20.00	12.00
167	"Frankie" Frisch	130.00	65.00	40.00
168	"Honus" Wagner	250.00	125.00	75.00
169	"Gabby" Street	40.00	20.00	12.00
170	"Tris" Speaker	135.00	70.00	40.00
171	Harry Heilmann	120.00	60.00	35.00
172	"Chief" Bender	120.00	60.00	35.00
173	"Larry" Lajoie	120.00	60.00	35.00
174	"Johnny" Evers	120.00	60.00	35.00
175	"Christy" Mathewson	250.00	125.00	75.00
176	"Heinie" Manush	130.00	65.00	40.00
177	Frank "Homerun" Baker	120.00	60.00	35.00
178	Max Carey	120.00	60.00	35.00
179	George Sisler	120.00	60.00	35.00
180	"Mickey" Cochrane	175.00	87.50	52.50
181	"Spud" Chandler	90.00	45.00	27.00
182	"Knick" Knickerbocker	90.00	45.00	27.00
183	Marvin Breuer	90.00	45.00	27.00
184	"Mule" Haas	90.00	45.00	27.00
185	"Joe" Kuhel	90.00	45.00	27.00
186	Taft Wright	90.00	45.00	27.00
187	"Jimmy" Dykes	90.00	45.00	27.00
188	"Joe" Krakauskas	90.00	45.00	27.00
189	"Jim" Bloodworth	90.00	45.00	27.00
190	"Charley" Berry	90.00	45.00	27.00
191	John Babich	90.00	45.00	27.00
192	"Dick" Siebert	90.00	45.00	27.00
193	"Chubby" Dean	90.00	45.00	27.00
194	Sam Chapman	90.00	45.00	27.00
195	"Dee" Miles	90.00	45.00	27.00
196	"Nonny" Nonnenkamp	90.00	45.00	27.00
197	"Lou" Finney	90.00	45.00	27.00
198	"Denny" Galehouse	90.00	45.00	27.00
199	"Pinky" Higgins	90.00	45.00	27.00
200	"Soupy" Campbell	90.00	45.00	27.00
201	Barney McCosky	90.00	45.00	27.00
202	Al Milnar	90.00	45.00	27.00
203	"Bad News" Hale	90.00	45.00	27.00
204	Harry Eisenstat	90.00	45.00	27.00
205	"Rollie" Hemsley	90.00	45.00	27.00
206	"Chet" Laabs	90.00	45.00	27.00
207	"Gus" Mancuso	90.00	45.00	27.00
208	Lee Gamble	90.00	45.00	27.00
209	"Hy" Vandenberg	90.00	45.00	27.00
210	"Bill" Lohrman	90.00	45.00	27.00
211	"Pop" Joiner	90.00	45.00	27.00
212	"Babe" Young	90.00	45.00	27.00
213	John Rucker	90.00	45.00	27.00
214	"Ken" O'Dea	90.00	45.00	27.00
215	"Johnnie" McCarthy	90.00	45.00	27.00
216	"Joe" Marty	90.00	45.00	27.00
217	Walter Beck	90.00	45.00	27.00
218	"Wally" Millies	90.00	45.00	27.00
219	Russ Bauers	90.00	45.00	27.00
220	Mace Brown	90.00	45.00	27.00
221	Lee Handley	90.00	45.00	27.00
222	"Max" Butcher	90.00	45.00	27.00
223	Hugh "Ee-Yah" Jennings	140.00	70.00	40.00
224	"Pie" Traynor	140.00	70.00	40.00
225	"Shoeless Joe" Jackson	2,500	1,250	700.00
226	Harry Hooper	140.00	70.00	40.00
227	"Pop" Haines	140.00	70.00	40.00
228	"Charley" Grimm	90.00	45.00	27.00
229	"Buck" Herzog	90.00	45.00	27.00
230	"Red" Faber	140.00	70.00	40.00
231	"Dolf" Luque	90.00	45.00	27.00
232	"Goose" Goslin	140.00	70.00	40.00
233	"Moose" Earnshaw	90.00	45.00	27.00
234	Frank "Husk" Chance	140.00	70.00	40.00
235	John J. McGraw	140.00	70.00	40.00
236	"Sunny Jim" Bottomley	140.00	70.00	40.00
237	"Wee Willie" Keeler	140.00	70.00	40.00
238	"Poosh 'Em Up Tony" Lazzeri	175.00	85.00	50.00
239	George Uhle	90.00	45.00	27.00
240	"Bill" Atwood	120.00	40.00	20.00

1940 Play Ball Colorized Proofs

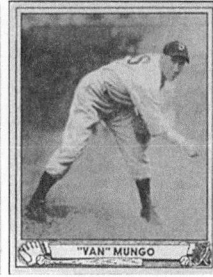

Probably created as part of the process which resulted in the introduction of color cards in 1941, these 1940 Play Balls have very muted color tones. It is unknown how many other players' cards from 1940 PB were created or survive in this form. The Mungo and Dean cards, authenticated and graded Excellent by SGC, sold in a 12/04 auction for $2,221.

	NM	E	VG
Common Player:	1,000	500.00	300.00

64	"Van" Mungo	
66	"Babe" Phelps	
76	"Lonny" Frey	
76	Harry Gumbert	
90	Frank Demaree	
90	"Whitey" Whitehead	
141	"Casey" Stengel	
141	"Whitey" Moore	
156	"Daffy" Dean	

1941 Play Ball (R336)

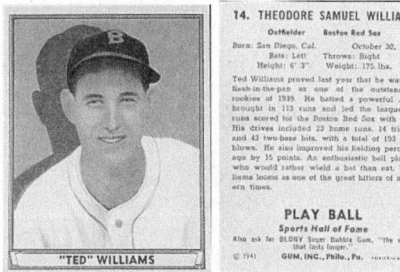

While the backs are quite similar to the black-and-white cards Gum Inc. issued in 1940, the card fronts in the 1941 set are printed in color. Many of the card photos, however, are just colorized versions of the player's 1940 card. The cards are still in the 2-1/2" x 3-1/8" size, but only 72 cards are included in the set. Card numbers 49-72 are rarer than the lower-numbered cards. The cards were printed in sheets of 12, and can still be found that way. Cards #1-48 can be found with or without the 1941 copyright date at lower-left; cards 49-72 are not found with the 1941 date. Some believe this indicates that a revised (no copyright) version of the low numbers and all of the high numbers were issued in 1942.

	NM	E	VG
Complete Set (72):	15,000	7,500	4,500
Common Player (1-48):	75.00	37.50	22.50
Common Player (49-72):	100.00	50.00	30.00

1	"Eddie" Miller	340.00	60.00	25.00
2	Max West	110.00	37.50	22.50
3	"Bucky" Walters	75.00	37.50	22.50
4	"Duke" Derringer	75.00	37.50	22.50
5	"Buck" McCormick	75.00	37.50	22.50
6	Carl Hubbell	225.00	115.00	70.00
7	"The Horse" Danning	75.00	37.50	22.50
8	"Mel" Ott	340.00	170.00	100.00
9	"Pinky" May	75.00	37.50	22.50
10	"Arky" Vaughan	190.00	95.00	55.00
11	Debs Garms	75.00	37.50	22.50
12	"Jimmy" Brown	75.00	37.50	22.50
13	"Jimmie" Foxx	500.00	250.00	150.00
14	"Ted" Williams	1,550	750.00	450.00
15	"Joe" Cronin	190.00	95.00	55.00
16	"Hal" Trosky	75.00	37.50	22.50
17	"Stormy" Weatherly	75.00	37.50	22.50
18	"Hank" Greenberg	500.00	250.00	150.00
19	"Charley" Gehringer	275.00	135.00	82.50
20	"Red" Ruffing	190.00	95.00	55.00
21	"Charlie" Keller	125.00	65.00	40.00
22	"Indian Bob" Johnson	75.00	37.50	22.50
23	"Mac" McQuinn	75.00	37.50	22.50
24	"Dutch" Leonard	75.00	37.50	22.50
25	"Gene" Moore	75.00	37.50	22.50
26	Harry "Gunboat" Gumbert	75.00	37.50	22.50
27	"Babe" Young	75.00	37.50	22.50
28	"Joe" Marty	75.00	37.50	22.50
29	Jack Wilson	75.00	37.50	22.50
30	"Lou" Finney	75.00	37.50	22.50
31	"Joe" Kuhel	75.00	37.50	22.50
32	Taft Wright	75.00	37.50	22.50
33	"Happy" Milnar	75.00	37.50	22.50
34	"Rollie" Hemsley	75.00	37.50	22.50
35	"Pinky" Higgins	75.00	37.50	22.50
36	Barney McCosky	75.00	37.50	22.50
37	"Soupy" Campbell	75.00	37.50	22.50
38	Atley Donald	75.00	37.50	22.50
39	"Tommy" Henrich	150.00	75.00	45.00
40	"Johnny" Babich	75.00	37.50	22.50
41	Frank "Blimp" Hayes	75.00	37.50	22.50
42	"Wally" Moses	75.00	37.50	22.50
43	Albert "Bronk" Brancato	75.00	37.50	22.50
44	Sam Chapman	75.00	37.50	22.50
45	Elden Auker (Eldon)	75.00	37.50	22.50
46	"Sid" Hudson	75.00	37.50	22.50
47	"Buddy" Lewis	75.00	37.50	22.50
48	Cecil Travis	75.00	37.50	22.50
49	"Babe" Dahlgren	100.00	50.00	30.00
50	"Johnny" Cooney	100.00	50.00	30.00
51	"Dolph" Camilli	100.00	50.00	30.00
52	Kirby Higbe	100.00	50.00	30.00
53	Luke "Hot Potato" Hamlin	100.00	50.00	30.00
54	"Pee Wee" Reese	900.00	450.00	270.00
55	"Whit" Wyatt	100.00	50.00	30.00
56	"Vandy" Vander Meer	100.00	50.00	30.00
57	"Moe" Arnovich	125.00	65.00	35.00
58	"Frank" Demaree	100.00	50.00	30.00
59	"Bill" Jurges	100.00	50.00	30.00
60	"Chuck" Klein	225.00	115.00	70.00
61	"Vince" DiMaggio	225.00	115.00	70.00
62	"Elbie" Fletcher	100.00	50.00	30.00
63	"Dom" DiMaggio	400.00	200.00	120.00
64	"Bobby" Doerr	300.00	150.00	90.00
65	"Tommy" Bridges	100.00	50.00	30.00
66	Harland Clift (Harland)	100.00	50.00	30.00
67	"Walt" Judnich	100.00	50.00	30.00
68	"Jack" Knott	100.00	50.00	30.00
69	George Case	100.00	50.00	30.00
70	"Bill" Dickey	350.00	175.00	100.00
71	"Joe" DiMaggio	3,000	1,500	700.00
72	"Lefty" Gomez	425.00	180.00	60.00

1941 Play Ball Paper Version

As cardboard became a critical commodity during the months prior to the United States' entry into WWII, Play Ball experimented by issuing a version of the first 24 cards in the 1941 set on paper sheets of 12, comprising the color-printed layer of the regular cards and the backs. These paper versions, understandably, did not stand up to handling as well as the cardboard cards and survivors are much scarcer today.

	NM	E	VG
Complete Set (24):	10,000	5,000	3,000
Common Player:	160.00	55.00	30.00
Complete Sheet 1-12:	3,000	700.00	325.00
Complete Sheet 13-24:	5,000	2,500	1,500

1	Eddie Miller	160.00	55.00	30.00
2	Max West	160.00	55.00	30.00
3	Bucky Walters	160.00	55.00	30.00
4	"Duke" Derringer	160.00	55.00	30.00
5	"Buck" McCormick	160.00	55.00	30.00
6	Carl Hubbell	600.00	210.00	120.00
7	"The Horse" Danning	160.00	55.00	30.00
8	Mel Ott	650.00	225.00	130.00
9	"Pinky" May	160.00	55.00	30.00
10	"Arky" Vaughan	400.00	140.00	80.00
11	Debs Garms	160.00	55.00	30.00
12	"Jimmy" Brown	160.00	55.00	30.00
13	Jimmie Foxx	1,100	385.00	220.00
14	Ted Williams	3,200	1,125	640.00
15	Joe Cronin	400.00	140.00	80.00
16	Hal Trosky	160.00	55.00	30.00
17	Roy Weatherly	160.00	55.00	30.00
18	Hank Greenberg	1,100	385.00	220.00
19	Charley Gehringer	600.00	210.00	120.00
20	"Red" Ruffing	400.00	140.00	80.00
21	Charlie Keller	180.00	65.00	35.00
22	Bob Johnson	160.00	55.00	30.00
23	"Mac" McQuinn	160.00	55.00	30.00
24	Dutch Leonard	160.00	55.00	30.00

1976 Playboy Press Who Was Harry Steinfeldt?

(Babe Ruth)

This 12-card set was issued in 1976 by Playboy Press to promote author Bert Randolph Sugar's book "Who Was Harry Steinfeldt? & Other Baseball Trivia Questions." (Steinfeldt was the third baseman in the Cubs' famous infield that featured Hall of Famers Tinker, Evers and Chance). The black and white cards measure the standard 2-1/2" x 3-1/2" with a player photo on the front and a trivia question and ad for the book on the back.

	NM	E	VG
Complete Set (12):	150.00	75.00	45.00
Common Player:	9.00	4.50	2.75

(1)	Frankie Baumholtz	9.00	4.50	2.75
(2)	Jim Bouton	12.00	6.00	3.50
(3)	Tony Conigliaro	9.00	4.50	2.75
(4)	Don Drysdale	17.50	8.75	5.25
(5)	Hank Greenberg	15.00	7.50	4.50
(6)	Walter Johnson	25.00	12.50	7.50
(7)	Billy Loes	9.00	4.50	2.75
(8)	Johnny Mize	15.00	7.50	4.50
(9)	Frank "Lefty" O'Doul	12.00	6.00	3.50
(10)	Babe Ruth	50.00	25.00	15.00
(11)	Johnny Sain	12.00	6.00	3.50
(12)	Jim Thorpe	40.00	20.00	12.00

1947 Pleetwood Slacks Jackie Robinson

The date of issue cited is conjectural. This card, about 5" x 8", depicts Jackie Robinson in a coat and tie in a black-and-white photo on front, along with a facsimile autograph. In a strip at bottom is his name and an endorsement for "Pleetwood Slacks." The back is blank. The card was probably used as an autograph vehicle for personal appearances by Robinson at clothing stores.

	NM	E	VG
Jackie Robinson	600.00	300.00	180.00

1910-12 Plow Boy Tobacco

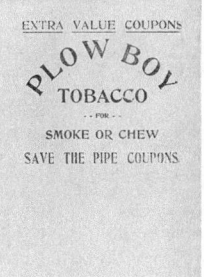

1910-12 Plow Boy Tobacco

Plowboy Tobacco, a product of the Spaulding & Merrick Co., issued a set of cabinet-size cards in the Chicago area featuring members of the Cubs and White Sox. From the checklist, it appears the bulk of the set was originally issued in 1910 with a few additional cards appearing over the next several years. Measuring approximately 5-3/4" x 8", the Plow Boys feature sepia-toned player photos in poses not found on other tobacco issues. The player's name appears in the lower-left corner, while the team name appears in the lower-right. Two different backs are known. One consists of a simple advertisement for Plow Boy Tobacco, while a second, more difficult, variety includes a list of premiums available in exchange for coupons. The set is among the rarest of all 20th Century tobacco issues.

	NM	E	VG
Common Player:	3,650	1,450	725.00
Premium Back: 1.5X			

		NM	E	VG
(1)	Jimmy Archer	3,650	1,450	725.00
(2)	Ginger Beaumont	3,650	1,450	725.00
(3)	Lena Blackburne	3,650	1,450	725.00
(4)	Bruno Block	3,650	1,450	725.00
(5)	Ping Bodie	3,650	1,450	725.00
(6)	Mordecai Brown	5,500	2,200	1,100
(7)	Al Carson	3,650	1,450	725.00
(8)	Frank Chance	5,500	2,200	1,100
(9)	Ed Cicotte	5,250	2,100	1,050
(10)	King Cole	3,650	1,450	725.00
(11)	Shano Collins	3,650	1,450	725.00
(12)	George Davis	5,500	2,200	1,100
(13)	Patsy Dougherty	3,650	1,450	725.00
(14)	Johnny Evers	5,500	2,200	1,100
(15)	Chick Gandel (Gandil)	5,250	2,100	1,050
(16)	Ed Hahn	3,650	1,450	725.00
(17)	Solly Hoffman (Hofman)	3,650	1,450	725.00
(18)	Del Howard	3,650	1,450	725.00
(19)	Bill Jones	3,650	1,450	725.00
(20)	Johnny Kling	3,650	1,450	725.00
(21)	Rube Kroh	3,650	1,450	725.00
(22)	Frank Lange	3,650	1,450	725.00
(23)	Fred Luderus	3,650	1,450	725.00
(24)	Harry McIntyre (McIntire)	3,650	1,450	725.00
(25)	Ward Miller	3,650	1,450	725.00
(26)	Charlie Mullen	3,650	1,450	725.00
(27)	Tom Needham	3,650	1,450	725.00
(28)	Fred Olmstead	3,650	1,450	725.00
(29)	Orval Overall	3,650	1,450	725.00
(30)	Fred Parent	3,650	1,450	725.00
(31)	Fred Payne	3,650	1,450	725.00
(32)	Francis "Big Jeff" Pfeffer	3,650	1,450	725.00
(33)	Jake Pfeister	3,650	1,450	725.00
(34)	Billy Purtell	3,650	1,450	725.00
(35)	Ed Reulbach	3,650	1,450	725.00
(36)	Lew Richie	3,650	1,450	725.00
(37)	Jimmy Scheckard (Sheckard)	3,650	1,450	725.00
(38)	Wildfire Schulte	3,650	1,450	725.00
(39a)	Jim Scot (Name incorrect.)	3,650	1,450	725.00
(39b)	Jim Scott (Name correct.)	3,650	1,450	725.00
(40)	Frank Smith	3,650	1,450	725.00
(41)	Harry Steinfeldt	3,650	1,450	725.00
(42)	Billy Sullivan	3,650	1,450	725.00
(43)	Lee Tannehill	3,650	1,450	725.00
(44)	Joe Tinker	5,500	2,200	1,100
(45)	Ed Walsh	5,500	2,200	1,100
(46)	Doc White	3,650	1,450	725.00
(47)	Irv Young	3,650	1,450	725.00
(48)	Rollie Zeider	3,650	1,450	725.00
(49)	Heinie Zimmerman	3,650	1,450	725.00

1912 Plow's Candy (E300)

PLOW'S CANDY COLLECTION

DELEHANTY
DETROIT AMERICANS

An extremely rare candy issue, cards in this 1912 set measure 3" x 4" and feature sepia-toned photos surrounded by a wide border. The player's name and team appear in the border below the photo, while the words "Plow's Candy Collection" appear at the top. The backs are blank. Not even known to exist until the late 1960s, this set has been assigned the designation of E300 and additions to the checklist continue

to appear every few years.

	NM	E	VG
Common Player:	3,000	1,500	900.00

		NM	E	VG
(1)	Babe Adams	3,000	1,500	900.00
(2)	Home Run Baker	4,800	2,400	1,440
(3)	Cy Barger	3,000	1,500	900.00
(4)	Jack Barry	3,000	1,150	900.00
(5)	Johnny Bates	3,000	1,500	900.00
(7)	Joe Benz	3,000	1,150	900.00
(8)	Bill Berger (Bergen)	3,000	1,500	900.00
(9)	Roger Bresnahan	4,800	2,400	1,440
(10)	Mordecai Brown	4,800	2,400	1,440
(11)	Donie Bush	3,000	1,500	900.00
(12)	Bobby Byrne	3,000	1,500	900.00
(13)	Nixey Callahan	3,000	1,500	900.00
(14)	Bill Carrigan	3,000	1,500	900.00
(15)	Hal Chase	4,500	2,250	1,350
(16)	Fred Clarke	4,800	2,400	1,440
(17)	Ty Cobb	42,000	16,500	9,900
(18)	King Cole	3,000	1,500	900.00
(19)	Eddie Collins	5,500	2,750	1,650
(20)	Jack Coombs	3,000	1,500	900.00
(21)	Bill Dahlen	3,000	1,500	900.00
(22)	Bert Daniels	3,000	1,500	900.00
(23)	Harry Davis	3,000	1,500	900.00
(24)	Jim Delehanty	3,000	1,500	900.00
(25)	Josh Devore	3,000	1,500	900.00
(26)	Wild Bill Donovan	3,000	1,500	900.00
(27)	Red Dooin	3,000	1,500	900.00
(28)	Larry Doyle	3,000	1,500	900.00
(29)	Johnny Evers	4,800	2,400	1,440
(30)	Russ Ford	3,000	1,500	900.00
(31)	Del Gainor	3,000	1,500	900.00
(32)	Vean Gregg	3,000	1,500	900.00
(33)	Bob Harmon	3,000	1,500	900.00
(34)	Arnold Hauser	3,000	1,500	900.00
(35)	Dick Hoblitzelle (Hoblitzell)	3,000	1,500	900.00
(36)	Solly Hofman	3,000	1,500	900.00
(37)	Miller Huggins	4,800	2,400	1,440
(38)	John Hummel	3,000	1,500	900.00
(39)	Walter Johnson	7,200	3,600	2,160
(40)	Johnny Kling	3,000	1,500	900.00
(41)	Nap Lajoie	5,400	2,700	1,620
(42)	Jack Lapp	3,000	1,500	900.00
(43)	Fred Luderus	3,000	1,500	900.00
(44)	Sherry Magee	3,000	1,500	900.00
(45)	Rube Marquard	4,800	2,400	1,440
(46)	Christy Mathewson	25,000	10,000	5,000
(47)	Stuffy McInnes (McInnis)	3,000	1,500	900.00
(48)	Larry McLean	3,000	1,500	900.00
(49)	Fred Merkle	3,000	1,500	900.00
(50)	Cy Morgan	3,000	1,500	900.00
(51)	George Moriarty	3,000	1,500	900.00
(52)	Mike Mowrey	3,000	1,500	900.00
(53)	Chief Myers (Meyers)	3,000	1,500	900.00
(54)	Rube Oldring	3,000	1,500	900.00
(55)	Marty O'Toole	3,000	1,500	900.00
(56)	Eddie Plank	5,400	2,700	1,620
(57)	Nap Rucker	3,000	1,500	900.00
(58)	Slim Sallee	3,000	1,500	900.00
(59)	Boss Schmidt	3,000	1,500	900.00
(60)	Jimmy Sheckard	3,000	1,500	900.00
(61)	Tris Speaker	5,400	2,700	1,620
(62)	Billy Sullivan	3,000	1,500	900.00
(63)	Ira Thomas	3,000	1,500	900.00
(64)	Joe Tinker	4,800	2,400	1,440
(65)	John Titus	3,000	1,500	900.00
(66)	Hippo Vaughan (Vaughn)	3,000	1,500	900.00
(67)	Honus Wagner	50,000	15,000	9,000
(68)	Ed Walsh	4,800	2,400	1,440
(69)	Bob Williams	3,000	1,500	900.00

1915 PM1 Ornate-Frame Pins

ARCHER

Little is known about these tiny (approximately 1-1/16" x 1") pins, such as who issued them, when and how they were distributed and how many are in the set. The pins feature a sepia-tone player photo surrounded by an ornate gilded metal frame. The player's name is usually printed in a black

strip at the bottom of the photo. The pins were originally sold for 19 cents. Gaps have been left in the assigned numbering for future additions to the checklist. A few examples are known in stick-pin format,

	NM	E	VG
Common Pin:	600.00	300.00	170.00

		NM	E	VG
(1a)	Jimmy Archer	600.00	300.00	170.00
(1b)	Jimmy Archer (No name.)	775.00	380.00	235.00
(2)	Frank Baker	1,500	750.00	500.00
(3)	Jack Barry	600.00	300.00	170.00
(4a)	Chief Bender (No name.)	1,500	750.00	500.00
(4b)	Chief Bender ((With name.))	1,500	750.00	500.00
(5)	Frank Chance	1,500	750.00	500.00
(6)	Ty Cobb	7,400	3,700	2,220
(7)	Jake Daubert	600.00	300.00	170.00
(8)	Al Demaree	600.00	300.00	170.00
(9a)	Johnny Evers (Name only.)	1,500	750.00	500.00
(9b)	Johnny Evers (Name and city.)	1,500	750.00	500.00
(10)	Rube Foster	600.00	300.00	170.00
(11)	Dick Hoblitzell	600.00	300.00	170.00
(12)	Walter Johnson	2,700	1,350	800.00
(13)	Benny Kauff	600.00	300.00	170.00
(14)	Johnny Kling (No name.)	600.00	300.00	170.00
(15)	Ed Konetchy	600.00	300.00	170.00
(16)	Nap Lajoie	1,500	750.00	500.00
(17)	Sherry Magee	600.00	300.00	170.00
(18)	Rube Marquard	1,500	750.00	500.00
(19)	Christy Mathewson	2,750	1,375	800.00
(21)	John McGraw	1,500	750.00	500.00
(22)	Ed Reulbach	600.00	300.00	170.00
(23)	Eppa Rixey	1,500	750.00	500.00
(24)	Babe Ruth	19,500	10,000	5,850
(25)	Tris Speaker (Batting, facing forward.)	1,500	750.00	500.00
(26)	Tris Speaker (Batting, side view.)	1,500	750.00	500.00
(27)	Jeff Tesreau	600.00	300.00	170.00
(28)	Joe Tinker	1,500	750.00	500.00
(29)	Honus Wagner	3,600	1,800	1,075

1928 PM6 Baseball Player Pins

TY COBB

The method of distribution for these small (3/8" diameter) pin-backs is unknown, but it has been reported they were given away in cereal boxes. The black-and-white photographic pins have the player name in a black arc at bottom. The extent of the checklist is unknown.

	NM	E	VG
Common Player:	450.00	225.00	135.00

		NM	E	VG
(1)	Grover Alexander	600.00	300.00	180.00
(2)	Ty Cobb	1,400	700.00	420.00
(3)	Bucky Harris	450.00	225.00	135.00
(4)	Rogers Hornsby	700.00	350.00	210.00
(5)	Walter Johnson	900.00	450.00	275.00
(6)	Babe Ruth	1,600	800.00	475.00
(7)	Geo. Sisler	450.00	225.00	135.00
(8)	Tris Speaker	600.00	300.00	175.00

1940 PM10 Baseball Player Pins

DODGERS

PETE REISER

This was the first of two issues that share a nearly identical format. The 1-3/4" celluloid pin-back buttons feature a black-and-white player photo surrounded by a white border. The player's name is in black capital letters at bottom, and his team nickname in the same type size and style at top. These pins were originally sold at ballparks and other souvenir outlets. The checklist, arranged here in alphabetical order, is not complete.

Common Player:	NM	E	VG
	30.00	15.00	9.00
Dick Bartell	30.00	15.00	9.00
Dolph Camilli	30.00	15.00	9.00
Bill Dickey	50.00	25.00	15.00
Joe DiMaggio	275.00	135.00	85.00
Lou Gehrig	675.00	335.00	200.00
Lou Gehrig (Black border, "NEVER FORGOTTEN" at top.)	650.00	325.00	195.00
Lefty Gomez	50.00	25.00	15.00
Carl Hubbell	100.00	50.00	30.00
Cliff Melton	30.00	15.00	9.00
Pete Reiser	30.00	15.00	9.00
Dixie Walker	30.00	15.00	9.00
Whitlow Wyatt	30.00	15.00	9.00

1951 PM10 Baseball Player Pins

This was the second of two issues that share a nearly identical format. The 1-3/4" celluloid pin-back buttons feature a black-and-white player photo surrounded by a white border. The player's name is in black capital letters at bottom, and full team name in the same type size and style at top. These pins were originally sold at ballparks and other souvenir outlets. The checklist, arranged here in alphabetical order, is likely not complete. Note that the woeful Pittsburgh Pirates represent more than half the known players in this issue.

Common Player:	NM	E	VG
	50.00	25.00	15.00
Luke Easter	225.00	115.00	70.00
Ned Garver	50.00	25.00	15.00
Monte Irvin	100.00	50.00	30.00
Ralph Kiner	100.00	50.00	30.00
Bob Lemon	100.00	50.00	30.00
Willie Mays	175.00	87.00	52.00
Clyde McCullouhg (McCullough)	50.00	25.00	15.00
Billy Meyer	50.00	25.00	15.00
Danny Murtaugh	50.00	25.00	15.00
Don Newcombe	50.00	25.00	15.00
Saul Rogovin	50.00	25.00	15.00
Stan Rojek	50.00	25.00	15.00
Hank Thompson	50.00	25.00	15.00
Bill Werle	50.00	25.00	15.00

1950s-60s PM10 Baseball Player Pins - Name at Bottom

Issued over a period of years in a variety of styles, these celluloid pinback buttons have in common their approximately 1-3/4" diameter and the appearance of the player name at bottom. Black-and-white player portrait photos are found on a variety of backgrounds. In this checklist, the color of the background is listed, where known, immediately after the team name (where known). Other distinguishing characteristics may also be noted. The pins were usually originally sold with a red, white and blue swallow-tailed silk pennant attached and a brass chain with a baseball, bat or glove charms, or similar plastic toys. Values shown are for pins alone. The checklist here is incomplete.

Common Player:	NM	E	VG
	20.00	10.00	6.00
Hank Aaron (Blue, script name, team above.)	100.00	50.00	30.00
Sandy Amoros (Brooklyn, blue.)	60.00	30.00	18.00
Harry Anderson (Phillies, photo.)	125.00	65.00	35.00
John Antonelli (NY cap, "floating head.")	20.00	10.00	6.00
John Antonelli (SF cap, ring around photo.)	20.00	10.00	6.00
Luis Aparicio (White Sox, white.)	75.00	37.00	22.00
Ernest Banks (Cubs, white, no cap logo.)	350.00	175.00	105.00
Bo Belinsky (Phillies, white.)	40.00	20.00	12.00
Gus Bell (White)	20.00	10.00	6.00
Gus Bell ("CINCINNATI REDLEGS" beneath name.)	100.00	50.00	30.00
Larry Berra (White)	90.00	45.00	27.00
Larry Berra (Blue)	100.00	50.00	30.00
Yogi Berra	80.00	40.00	24.00
Joe Black (Brooklyn, photo.)	40.00	20.00	12.00
Joe Black (Brooklyn, white, facing front.)	40.00	20.00	12.00
Joe Black (Brooklyn, white, facing his left.)	25.00	12.50	7.50
Don Bollweg (A's, photo.)	20.00	10.00	6.00
Lou Boudreau (Photo, script name.)	60.00	30.00	18.00
Lou Boudreau (Red Sox, white.)	50.00	25.00	15.00
Jackie Brandt (Orioles, photo.)	40.00	20.00	12.00
Eddie Bressoud	20.00	10.00	6.00
Bill Bruton (Braves, white.)	100.00	50.00	30.00
Jim Bunning (Phillies)	40.00	20.00	12.00
Roy Campanella (Brooklyn, blue.)	90.00	45.00	27.50
Roy Campanella (Brooklyn, yellow.)	80.00	40.00	24.00
Roy Campanella (Brooklyn, white, cap backwards.)	75.00	37.50	22.50
Roy Campanella (Brooklyn, white, name across photo.)	60.00	30.00	18.00
Roy Campanella (Brooklyn, white, name under photo.)	60.00	30.00	18.00
Roy Campanella (Brooklyn, white, name in strip.)	100.00	50.00	30.00
Roy Campanella (Brooklyn, white circle border, team at top.)	250.00	125.00	75.00
Chico Carrasquel (Name in script, team at top.)	50.00	25.00	15.00
Phil Cavarretta (Cubs, script name, stars above.)	150.00	75.00	45.00
Orlando Cepeda (Gray)	30.00	15.00	9.00
Orlando Cepeda (S.F. name in strip, photo.)	30.00	15.00	9.00
Gerry Coleman (Dark)	40.00	20.00	12.00
Gerry Coleman (Light)	40.00	20.00	12.00
Tony Conigliaro (Red Sox, gray.)	40.00	20.00	12.00
Morton Cooper (Cardinals, white/black background.)	40.00	20.00	12.00
Billy Cox (Brooklyn, white, neck-to-cap.)	95.00	47.50	28.00
Billy Cox (Brooklyn, white, chest-to-cap.)	60.00	30.00	18.00
Alvin Dark (NY cap, "floating head.")	20.00	10.00	6.00
Jerome (Dizzy) Dean (Black)	90.00	45.00	27.50
Dom DiMaggio (White)	40.00	20.00	12.00
Dom DiMaggio (Dark)	40.00	20.00	12.00
Joe DiMaggio (Black)	475.00	235.00	140.00
Joe DiMaggio (Dark blue, name beyond shoulders.)	250.00	125.00	75.00
Joe DiMaggio (Light blue, name within shoulders.)	150.00	75.00	45.00

Common Player:	NM	E	VG
Joe DiMaggio (Light blue, name "ear to ear" - modern fantasy, no collectible value.)			
Joe DiMaggio (Green border.)	200.00	100.00	60.00
Joe DiMaggio (White, name in strip.)	200.00	100.00	60.00
Joe DiMaggio (White, name not in strip.)	215.00	100.00	65.00
Joe DiMaggio (Yellow, "YANKEES" under name.)	350.00	175.00	100.00
Larry Doby (Dark)	60.00	30.00	18.00
Larry Doby (Indians, white.)	90.00	45.00	27.50
Carl Erskine (Brooklyn, white.)	75.00	37.50	22.50
Bob Feller (Indians, white.)	80.00	40.00	24.00
Bob Feller (Brown, name in script.)	325.00	160.00	100.00
Whitey Ford	80.00	40.00	24.00
Nelson Fox (White Sox, fox figures at top.)	350.00	175.00	100.00
Carl Furillo (Brooklyn, blue.)	75.00	37.50	22.50
Carl Furillo (Brooklyn, gray.)	65.00	32.50	20.00
Carl Furillo (Brooklyn, photo, dark sleeves.)	100.00	50.00	30.00
Carl Furillo (Brooklyn, photo, no sleeves.)	115.00	60.00	35.00
Ned Garver (Browns, white, belly-to-cap.)	30.00	15.00	9.00
Ned Garver (Browns, white, chest-to-cap.)	30.00	15.00	9.00
Junior Gilliam (Brooklyn, white.)	100.00	50.00	30.00
Junior Gilliam (Broklyn, photo.)	100.00	50.00	30.00
Ruben Gomez (SF cap, ring around photo.)	30.00	15.00	9.00
Billy Goodman (White)	100.00	50.00	30.00
Ron Hansen (Orioles, photo.)	40.00	20.00	12.00
Gabby Hartnett (Cubs, black.)	40.00	20.00	12.00
Mike Hegan (Indians, white border, script name.)	450.00	225.00	135.00
Tom Henrich (Gray)	40.00	20.00	12.00
Mike Higgins (Red Sox, dark.)	45.00	22.50	13.50
Gil Hodges (Brooklyn, blue.)	100.00	50.00	30.00
Gil Hodges (Brooklyn, red/orange.)	50.00	25.00	15.00
Gil Hodges (Brooklyn, photo.)	40.00	20.00	12.00
Gil Hodges (Brooklyn, white, name across photo.)	60.00	30.00	18.00
Gil Hodges (Brooklyn, white, name in strip.)	200.00	100.00	60.00
Gil Hodges (Brooklyn, white, name under photo.)	40.00	20.00	12.00
Roger Hornsby (Rogers) (Browns, white circle border.)	150.00	75.00	45.00
Monte Irvin (Giants, dark.)	80.00	40.00	24.00
Ransom Jackson (Cubs, stars above.)	150.00	75.00	45.00
Forrest "Spook" Jacobs (Gray)	20.00	10.00	6.00
Forrest "Spook" Jacobs (A's, photo.)	20.00	10.00	6.00
Jackie Jensen (Dark)	50.00	25.00	15.00
Jackie Jensen (White)	50.00	25.00	15.00
Ed Joost (A's, photo.)	20.00	10.00	6.00
Harmon Killebrew ("W" on cap, photo.)	375.00	185.00	110.00
Harmon Killebrew (Twins, name in black script)	250.00	125.00	75.00
Ralph Kiner (Color, facsimile autograph.)	125.00	65.00	40.00
Ralph Kiner (Cubs, hearts above.)	800.00	400.00	240.00
Ted Kluszewski (Dark, name overprinted horizontally.)	200.00	100.00	60.00
Ted Kluszewski (Reds, white, name in strip.)	40.00	20.00	12.00
Ed Kranepool (White)	50.00	25.00	15.00
Big Bill Lee (Cubs, black/gray.)	20.00	10.00	6.00

Bob Lemon (Light)	40.00	20.00	12.00
Whitey Lockman (NY cap, gray.)	25.00	12.50	7.50
Peanuts Lowrey (Cardinals, white.)	25.00	12.50	7.50
Sal Maglie (Brooklyn, photo.)	50.00	25.00	15.00
Frank Malzone	40.00	20.00	12.00
Mickey Mantle (White, batting to waist, name from elbow to armpit.)	275.00	135.00	80.00
Mickey Mantle (White, batting to waist, name from wrist to shoulder.)	300.00	150.00	90.00
Mickey Mantle (Baseball background, name in strip.)	200.00	100.00	60.00
Mickey Mantle (Blue, name in strip.) (Modern replicas are commonly encountered.)	250.00	125.00	75.00
Mickey Mantle (White, portrait.)	300.00	150.00	90.00
Juan Marichal (SF cap, uncentered black border.)	60.00	30.00	18.00
Marty Marion (Browns, white circle border.)	300.00	150.00	90.00
Roger Maris (no cap insignia. White, looking over shoulder.)	125.00	60.00	35.00
Willie Mays (S.F. Giants, gray.)	325.00	160.00	97.00
Willie Mays (Photo, N.Y. cap.)	300.00	150.00	90.00
Willie Mays (Photo, grass background, S.F. cap.)	300.00	150.00	90.00
Willie Mays (Photo, stadium background, S.F. cap.)	300.00	150.00	90.00
Willie Mays (White, N.Y. cap.)	230.00	115.00	70.00
Willie Mays (White, S.F. cap.)	150.00	75.00	45.00
Willie McCovey (Pats on shoulder, no cap logo.)	200.00	100.00	60.00
Willie McCovey (SF cap, name in ear-to-ear white stripe.)	40.00	20.00	12.00
Gil McDougald (Yankees, gray.)	45.00	22.50	13.50
"Vinegar Bend" Mizell (Cardinals, white.)	30.00	15.00	9.00
Bill Monbouquette	40.00	20.00	12.00
Don Mueller (White, "floating head.")	40.00	20.00	12.00
Bobby Murcer (White)	30.00	15.00	9.00
Stan Musial (Cardinals, white, MUSIAL at bottom, "STAN" THE MAN at top.)	125.00	65.00	40.00
Stan Musial (Cardinals, white, piping shows.)	100.00	50.00	30.00
Stan Musial (Cardinals, white, no piping.)	100.00	50.00	30.00
Stan Musial (White, team name above photo, facsimile autograph.)	100.00	50.00	30.00
Stan Musial (Yellow)	125.00	65.00	35.00
Don Newcombe (Brooklyn, blue.)	450.00	225.00	135.00
Don Newcombe (Brooklyn, white, name in strip.)	30.00	15.00	9.00
Don Newcombe (Brooklyn, white, name under photo.)	30.00	20.00	12.00
Don Newcombe (Brooklyn, white circle border, team at top.)	60.00	30.00	18.00
Don Newcombe (Yellow)	50.00	25.00	15.00
Dan O'Connell (SF cap, ring around photo.)	40.00	20.00	12.00
Andy Pafko (Brooklyn, black.)	30.00	15.00	9.00
Joe Page (White)	50.00	25.00	15.00
Leroy (Satchel) Paige (White)	175.00	85.00	50.00
Mel Parnell (Red Sox, white.)	45.00	22.50	13.50
Joe Pepitone (White)	30.00	15.00	9.00
Johnny Pesky (Red Sox, white.)	100.00	50.00	30.00
Billy Pierce (Name in serif type.)	40.00	20.00	12.00
Jimmy Piersall (Light)	50.00	25.00	15.00

Johnny Podres (Brooklyn, white.)	45.00	22.00	13.50
Wally Post ("CINCINNATI REDLEGS" beneath name.)	50.00	25.00	15.00
Vic Power (A's, photo.)	25.00	12.50	7.50
Bob Purkey (A's, photo.)	200.00	100.00	60.00
Dick Radatz (Red Sox, gray.)	30.00	15.00	9.00
Vic Raschi (Yankees, white.)	60.00	30.00	18.00
PeeWee Reese (Brooklyn, gray, name in strip.)	200.00	100.00	60.00
"Pee Wee" Reese (Brooklyn, gray, name across photo.)	60.00	30.00	18.00
"Pee Wee" Reese (Brooklyn, white, large photo.)	125.00	65.00	35.00
"Pee Wee" Reese (Brooklyn, white, small photo.)	100.00	50.00	30.00
"Pee Wee" Reese (Brooklyn, photo, name in strip.)	60.00	30.00	18.00
Bill Rigney (NY cap, dark background.)	20.00	10.00	6.00
Phil Rizzuto (White)	80.00	40.00	24.00
Robin Roberts (Phillies, photo.)	50.00	25.00	15.00
Frank Robinson ("Cincinnati Redlegs" at bottom.)	250.00	125.00	75.00
Jackie Robinson (Brooklyn, blue.)	175.00	90.00	55.00
Jackie Robinson (Brooklyn, yellow.)	275.00	135.00	80.00
Jackie Robinson (Brooklyn, white, chest-to-cap.)	200.00	100.00	60.00
Jackie Robinson (Brooklyn, white, neck-to-cap.)	250.00	125.00	75.00
Jackie Robinson (Brooklyn, white, name across bottom, facing his left.)	200.00	100.00	60.00
Jackie Robinson (Brooklyn, gray, name across photo, facing his left.)	200.00	100.00	60.00
Jackie Robinson (Brooklyn, white, name in strip, cap logo not visible.)	600.00	300.00	180.00
Jackie Robinson (Brooklyn, photo.)	275.00	135.00	80.00
Preacher Roe (Brooklyn, wind-up pose.)	90.00	45.00	27.50
Al Rosen (Light background.)	40.00	20.00	12.00
Charles Herbert Ruffing (Yankees, gray.)	40.00	20.00	12.00
Pete Runnels	40.00	20.00	12.00
Ron Santo (Cubs, white.)	40.00	20.00	12.00
Hank Sauer (Cubs, script name, stars above.)	150.00	75.00	45.00
Chuck Schilling	40.00	20.00	12.00
George Scott (White, "floating head.")	20.00	10.00	6.00
Bobby Shantz (A's, white.)	30.00	15.00	9.00
Frank Shea (Yankees, gray.)	50.00	25.00	15.00
Harry Simpson (Indians, white, team name at top, script name at bottom.)	650.00	325.00	195.00
Enos Slaughter (Cardinals, white.)	50.00	25.00	15.00
Enos Slaughter (Cardinals, black.)	50.00	25.00	15.00
Roy Smalley (Cubs, script name, stars above.)	150.00	75.00	45.00
Duke Snider (Brooklyn, white.)	80.00	40.00	24.00
Duke Snider (Brooklyn, blue.)	65.00	35.00	20.00
Duke Snider (Brooklyn, gray.)	75.00	37.50	22.50
Duke Snider (Brooklyn, photo.)	150.00	75.00	45.00
Gerald Staley (Cardinals, white.)	20.00	10.00	6.00
Bobby Thomson (NY cap, white, uniform shows.)	40.00	20.00	12.00

Bobby Thomson (NY cap, white, "floating head.")	30.00	15.00	9.00
Gus Triandos (Orioles, photo.)	40.00	20.00	12.00
Robt. Lee Trice (A's, photo.)	25.00	12.50	7.50
Sam White (Red Sox, white.)	30.00	15.00	9.00
James Hoyt Wilhelm (Orioles)	200.00	100.00	60.00
Ted Williams (Name beneath bust, white.)	200.00	100.00	60.00
Ted Williams (Name in strip, black.)	450.00	225.00	135.00
Ted Williams (Name in strip, white.)	400.00	200.00	120.00
Ted Williams (Name in strip, photo, belt-up.)	90.00	45.00	27.50
Ted Williams (Belt-up photo, name in strip at top, team in strip at bottom) (1-1/4")	50.00	25.00	15.00
Ted Williams (Belt-up photo, name in strip at top, team in strip at bottom) (1-3/4")	100.00	50.00	30.00
Ted Williams (Name in strip, photo, close-up.)	150.00	75.00	45.00
Carl Yastrzemski	100.00	50.00	30.00

1950s-60s PM10 Baseball Player Pins - Name at Top

This series of baseball player pins is similar to contemporary issues in its 1-3/4" (unless otherwise noted) black-and-white celluloid format, but differs in that the player name appears at top. Players known in the series indicate the buttons were issued over a period of several years, probably for sale in stadium concession stands and other souvenir outlets. The alphabetical checklist here is not complete.

	NM	E	VG
Common Player:	60.00	30.00	18.00
Felipe Alou (Script name.)	40.00	20.00	12.00
Luis Arroyo	20.00	10.00	6.00
Hank Bauer	60.00	30.00	18.00
Yogi Berra	135.00	67.00	40.00
Johnny Blanchard	60.00	30.00	18.00
Cletis Boyer	75.00	37.00	22.00
Joe Collins	60.00	30.00	18.00
Junior Gilliam	75.00	37.00	22.00
Ruben Gomez	40.00	20.00	12.00
Ken Harrelson (Red Sox, white.)	50.00	25.00	15.00
Don Hoak (Brooklyn, white.)	60.00	30.00	18.00
Elston Howard	75.00	37.00	22.00
Jackie Jensen (Red Sox, white.)	75.00	37.00	22.00
Clem Labine (Brooklyn, white.)	60.00	30.00	18.00
Ed Lopat	60.00	30.00	18.00
Hector Lopez	40.00	20.00	12.00
Frank Malzone (Red Sox, white.)	50.00	25.00	15.00
Billy Martin	75.00	37.00	22.00
Bill Monbouquette (Red Sox, white.)	50.00	25.00	15.00
Irv Noren	60.00	30.00	18.00
Allie Reynolds	60.00	30.00	18.00
Preacher Roe (Brooklyn, white.)	60.00	30.00	18.00
Pete Runnels (Red Sox, white.)	50.00	25.00	15.00
Chuck Schilling (Red Sox, white.)	50.00	25.00	15.00
Bill Skowron	60.00	30.00	18.00
Enos Slaughter	60.00	30.00	18.00
Warren Spahn	120.00	60.00	36.00
Bob Turley	60.00	30.00	18.00
Gene Woodling	60.00	30.00	18.00
Carl Yastrzemski	200.00	100.00	60.00
Don Zimmer (Brooklyn, white.)	75.00	37.50	22.50

1956 PM15 Yellow Basepath Pins

These pins were issued circa 1956; the sponsor of this 32-pin set is not indicated. The set, which has been assigned the American Card Catalog designation PM15, is commonly called "Yellow Basepaths" because of the design of the pin, which features a black-and-white player photo set inside a green infield with yellow basepaths. The unnumbered pins measure 7/8" in diameter.

		NM	E	VG
	Complete Set (32):	4,500	2,250	1,350
	Common Player:	85.00	40.00	25.00
(1)	Hank Aaron	400.00	200.00	120.00
(2)	Joe Adcock	85.00	40.00	25.00
(3)	Luis Aparicio	140.00	70.00	40.00
(4)	Richie Ashburn	150.00	75.00	45.00
(5)	Gene Baker	85.00	40.00	25.00
(6)	Ernie Banks	225.00	110.00	65.00
(7)	Yogi Berra	245.00	120.00	75.00
(8)	Bill Bruton	85.00	40.00	25.00
(9)	Larry Doby	140.00	70.00	40.00
(10)	Bob Friend	85.00	40.00	25.00
(11)	Nellie Fox	140.00	70.00	40.00
(12)	Ted Greengrass (Jim)	85.00	40.00	25.00
(13)	Steve Gromek	85.00	40.00	25.00
(14)	Johnny Groth	85.00	40.00	25.00
(15)	Gil Hodges	200.00	100.00	60.00
(16)	Al Kaline	150.00	75.00	45.00
(17)	Ted Kluzewski			
	(Kluszewski)	140.00	70.00	40.00
(18)	Johnny Logan	85.00	40.00	25.00
(19)	Dale Long	85.00	40.00	25.00
(20)	Mickey Mantle	600.00	300.00	180.00
(21)	Ed Matthews (Mathews)	150.00	75.00	45.00
(22)	Minnie Minoso	100.00	50.00	30.00
(23)	Stan Musial	350.00	175.00	100.00
(24)	Don Newcombe	140.00	70.00	40.00
(25)	Bob Porterfield	85.00	40.00	25.00
(26)	Pee Wee Reese	200.00	100.00	60.00
(27)	Robin Roberts	140.00	70.00	40.00
(28)	Red Schoendienst	140.00	70.00	40.00
(29)	Duke Snider	225.00	110.00	65.00
(30)	Vern Stephens	85.00	40.00	25.00
(31)	Gene Woodling	100.00	50.00	30.00
(32)	Gus Zernial	85.00	40.00	25.00

1909-11 Polar Bear Tobacco

The most distinctive advertising-back found on 1909-11 T206 is that of Polar Bear with its dark blue background and white topography. A more conventional style of ad was used on 1911 T205 cards, also printed in blue. Because the cards were packaged loose among the tobacco leaves in Polar Bear pouches, stains on surviving cards are frequently seen. Polar Bear is among the most common brands found in both series.

PREMIUMS:
T205: 1X
T206: 1-1.5X

(See T205, T206 for checklists and card values.)

1973 Pogue's Photocards

This 3-1/2" x 5-1/2" semi-glossy, blank-back photocard

was issued by Pogue's department store in Cincinnati, presumably in conjunction with a player autograph appearance. Whether there were other players issued is unknown. The card is virtually identical to the team-issued photocard of 1973, with the exception of the red store logo at bottom.

		NM	EX	VG
(1)	Joe Morgan	40.00	20.00	12.00

1889 Police Gazette Cabinets

Issued in the late 1880s through early 1890s as a premium by Police Gazette, a popular newspaper of the day, these cabinet cards are very rare. They originally sold for 10 cents each. The 4-1/4" x 6-1/2" cards consist of sepia-toned photographs mounted on cardboard of various colors. Only about two dozen players are currently known. Some photographs correspond to those used in the S.F. Hess card series and many players are depicted in suit and tie, rather than baseball uniform. Each card displays the name of the player beneath his portrait, along with the signature of "Richard K. Fox" and a line identifying him as "Editor and Proprietor / Police Gazette / Franklin Square, New York."

	NM	E	VG
Common Player:	8,800	4,400	2,650
Hick Carpenter	8,800	4,400	2,650
Fred Carroll	8,800	4,400	2,650
Bob Clark	8,800	4,400	2,650
John Coleman	8,800	4,400	2,650
Roger Conner (Connor)	11,000	5,500	3,500
Pete Conway	8,800	4,400	2,650
John Corkhill	8,800	4,400	2,650
Jerry Denny	8,800	4,400	2,650
Jas. A. Donohue			
(Donahue)	8,800	4,400	2,650
Buck Ewing	11,000	5,500	3,500
Bob Ferguson	8,800	4,400	2,650
Jocko Fields	8,800	4,400	2,650
Elmer Foster	8,800	4,400	2,650
Charlie Getzein (Getzien)	8,800	4,400	2,650
Pebbly Jack Glasscock	8,800	4,400	2,650
Bill Gleason	8,800	4,400	2,650
George Gore	8,800	4,400	2,650
Tim Keefe	11,000	5,500	3,500
Gus Krock	8,800	4,400	2,650
A.J. Maul	8,800	4,400	2,650
Ed Morris	8,800	4,400	2,650
Tip O'Neil (O'Neill)	8,800	4,400	2,650
N. (Fred) Pfeffer	8,800	4,400	2,650
Danny Richardson	8,800	4,400	2,650
A.B. Sanders	8,800	4,400	2,650
Charley (Pop) Smith	8,800	4,400	2,650
Elmer Smith	8,800	4,400	2,650
Harry Staley	8,800	4,400	2,650
William Swett (San			
Francisco)	11,000	5,500	3,500
George Tebeau	8,800	4,400	2,650
John Tener	9,900	5,000	3,000
Billy Terry (Adonis)	8,800	4,400	2,650
Sam Thompson	11,000	5,500	3,500
John M. Ward	12,000	6,000	3,600
Curt Welch	8,800	4,400	2,650
Mickey Welsh	11,000	5,500	3,500
Wheeler C. Wikoff			
(Wykoff) (Pres.			
American Association)	8,800	4,400	2,650

1895 Police Gazette Supplement

The 12 captains of the National League's teams, collectively termed "Our Baseball Heroes," are pictured in sepia lithographic portraits surrounding a colorful baseball action scene on this supplement issued with the June 1 edition of the men's newspaper. Overall the supplement measures about 21-1/2" x 15-1/2" and is the most impressive of the baseball items issued by the paper prior to the turn of the 20th Century.

	NM	E	VG
Supplement:	15,000	7,000	4,000

Cap Anson
Jack Boyle
Ed Cartwright
George Davis
Buck Ewing
Jack Glasscock
Mike Griffin
Connie Mack
Doggie Miller
Billy Nash
Patsy Tebeau
Wilbert Robinson

1901-1917 Police Gazette Supplements

Each issue of the weekly men's magazine included a large-format (about 11-1/4" x 16-1/4") blank-backed, black-and-white supplement. In keeping with the publication's editorial focus at the time, the pictures featured baseball players, boxers, other atheletes, actresses and female models. The photos appear in a frame design and measure about 8-1/2" x 12-1/2". The supplements are designated as such by a line of type at top or bottom that names the publication, issue number and issue date. The subject is identified in capital letters beneath the photo and there are a few lines of information at bottom. The magazine sometimes printed the same pictures in nearly identical format within its regular pages. These can be differentiated from the supplements in that they are on pink paper, have advertising or other editorial material on back and are not marked as supplements. Such pages do not enjoy the same popularity and value as the supplements. In this possibly incomplete checklist, the card number shown is the issue number in which the supplement was inserted. The player name or title may not always exactly correspond to that printed on the piece. Because of their large size, the supplements are often found trimmed to remove evidence of corner creases and edge damage. This checklist includes only the baseball subjects.

		NM	E	VG
	Common Player:	100.00	50.00	30.00
	1901			
	George Davis (Issue date			
	unknown.)	200.00	100.00	60.00
1251	Christy Mathewson	2,000	1,000	600.00
	1903			
1351	Roy Thomas	100.00	50.00	30.00
1353	Red Dooin	100.00	50.00	30.00
1357	Tommy Leach	100.00	50.00	30.00
1359	John McGraw	200.00	100.00	60.00
1361	Cy Seymour	100.00	50.00	30.00
1363	Joe McGinnity	200.00	100.00	60.00
1365	Jack Cronin	100.00	50.00	30.00
	1904			
1400	Dan McGann	100.00	50.00	30.00
1403	Red Ames	100.00	50.00	30.00
1407	Jack Warner	100.00	50.00	30.00
1411	Frank Bowerman	100.00	50.00	30.00
1413	Roger Bresnahan	200.00	100.00	60.00
	1905			

		NM	E	VG
1450	Joe McGinnity	200.00	100.00	60.00
1451	Napoleon Lajoie	250.00	125.00	75.00
1452	Hans Wagner	1,250	625.00	375.00
1453	Malachi Kittredge	100.00	50.00	30.00
1457	Jack Chesbro	200.00	100.00	60.00
1459	Roger Bresnahan	200.00	100.00	60.00
1461	**1905 Pittsburg Team**	900.00	450.00	275.00
1463	Willie Keeler	200.00	100.00	60.00
1465	Sam Mertes	100.00	50.00	30.00
1466	Dave Fultz	100.00	50.00	30.00
1467	**Carlisle University Team**	150.00	75.00	45.00
1468	Bill Hogg	100.00	50.00	30.00
	1906			
1502	Aleck Smith	100.00	50.00	30.00
1504	Jack Kleinow	100.00	50.00	30.00
1505	Rube Waddell	200.00	100.00	60.00
1507	Clark Griffith	200.00	100.00	60.00
1510	Nap Shea	100.00	50.00	30.00
1516	Jimmy Casey	100.00	50.00	30.00
1518	Hal Chase	200.00	100.00	60.00
	1907			
1548	Harry Davis	100.00	50.00	30.00
1549	Mike Powers	100.00	50.00	30.00
1551	Willie Keeler, Jack Kleinow	150.00	75.00	45.00
1554	Eddie Plank	250.00	125.00	75.00
1557	George Moriarty	100.00	50.00	30.00
1559	Bill Dahlen	100.00	50.00	30.00
1562	Cecil Ferguson	100.00	50.00	30.00
1564	Sammy Strang	100.00	50.00	30.00
1567	Hal Chase, Charlie Armbruster	150.00	75.00	45.00
1571	Mordecai Brown	200.00	100.00	60.00
1572	Danny Hoffman	100.00	50.00	30.00
	1908			
1607	Harry Bay	100.00	50.00	30.00
1613	Harry Lunn	100.00	50.00	30.00
1615	Charley Hemphill	100.00	50.00	30.00
	1909			
1655	Buck Herzog	100.00	50.00	30.00
1657	Al Bridwell	100.00	50.00	30.00
1660	Hans Lobert	100.00	50.00	30.00
1663	Bugs Raymond	100.00	50.00	30.00
1664	Harry Coveleski	100.00	50.00	30.00
1665	Chief Meyers	100.00	50.00	30.00
1667	Orval Overall	100.00	50.00	30.00
1673	Al Burch	100.00	50.00	30.00
1674	Mike Donlin	100.00	50.00	30.00
1676	Del Howard	100.00	50.00	30.00
1678	Dick Morris (Amateur)	100.00	50.00	30.00
	1910			
1716	Jack Warhop	100.00	50.00	30.00
1717	George Mullen (Mullin)	100.00	50.00	30.00
1720	Russ Ford	100.00	50.00	30.00
1721	Owen Bush	100.00	50.00	30.00
1722	Sherry Magee	100.00	50.00	30.00
1724	Jack Dalton	100.00	50.00	30.00
1726	Bert Daniels	100.00	50.00	30.00
1727	Birdie Cree	100.00	50.00	30.00
1729	Josh Devore	100.00	50.00	30.00
1730	Louis Drucke	100.00	50.00	30.00
	1911			
1771	Christy Mathewson	750.00	375.00	225.00
1779	Arthur Wilson	100.00	50.00	30.00
1782	Hans Wagner, Roger Bresnahan	750.00	375.00	225.00
1791	Home Run Baker	200.00	100.00	60.00
	1912			
1812	Zach Wheat	200.00	100.00	60.00
1814	Rube Marquard	200.00	100.00	60.00
1821	Tex Erwin	100.00	50.00	30.00
1823	Heinie Zimmerman	100.00	50.00	30.00
1825	Jake Stahl	100.00	50.00	30.00
	1913			
1856	Frank Chance	200.00	100.00	60.00
1861	Joe Wood	125.00	62.50	37.50
1867	Jim Thorpe	4,000	2,000	1,200
1872	Jake Daubert	100.00	50.00	30.00
1877	Nap Rucker	100.00	50.00	30.00
1883	Joe Jackson	4,000	2,000	1,200
1888	Walter Johnson	750.00	375.00	225.00
	1914			
1920	Ty Cobb	1,500	750.00	450.00
1926	Sam Crawford	200.00	100.00	60.00
1932	Dave Robertson	100.00	50.00	30.00
1938	Fritz Maisel	100.00	50.00	30.00
1942	Boston N.L. Team	200.00	100.00	60.00
1943	Philadelphia A.L. Team	200.00	100.00	60.00
	1915			
1961	Ray Caldwell	100.00	50.00	30.00
1966	Rabbit Maranville	200.00	100.00	60.00
1970	Sherry Magee	100.00	50.00	30.00
1975	Hans Lobert	100.00	50.00	30.00
1982	Eddie Collins	200.00	100.00	60.00
1985	Dick Hoblitzell	100.00	50.00	30.00
1989	Grover Alexander	500.00	250.00	150.00
	1916			
2011	Larry Doyle	100.00	50.00	30.00

2018	Fred Luderus	100.00	50.00	30.00
2020	Jimmy Archer	100.00	50.00	30.00
2023	Dick Rudolph	100.00	50.00	30.00
2026	Benny Kauff	100.00	50.00	30.00
2029	Sam Crawford	200.00	100.00	60.00
2035	Nick Cullop	100.00	50.00	30.00
2040	Clarence Mitchell	100.00	50.00	30.00
2042	George Sisler	200.00	100.00	60.00
2046	Pol Perritt	100.00	50.00	30.00
	1917			
2064	Ping Bodie	100.00	50.00	30.00
2070	Benny Kauff	100.00	50.00	30.00
2074	Hans Lobert	100.00	50.00	30.00
2078	Harry Coveleskie (Coveleski)	100.00	50.00	30.00
2081	Jack Coombs	100.00	50.00	30.00

1914 Polo Grounds Game (WG4)

 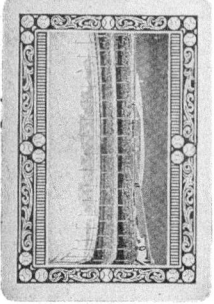

Called the "Polo Grounds Game" for the green-and-white photo of that stadium on each card's back, this set was officially issued as "All Star Card Base Ball" by The Card Baseball Co. of Norfolk, Va. Fronts of the round-cornered 2-1/2" x 3-1/2" cards have a black-and-white player photo and a baseball play scenario that is used to play the game. The set as issued includes 30 different players cards and 24 duplicate cards on which different game plays are displayed. The unnumbered cards are checklisted here alphabetically.

		NM	E	VG
	Complete Boxed Set (54):	6,650	3,325	2,000
	Complete Set (30):	3,000	1,500	900.00
	Common Player:	40.00	20.00	12.00
(1)	Jimmy Archer	40.00	20.00	12.00
(2)	Frank Baker	125.00	50.00	30.00
(3)	Frank Chance	125.00	50.00	30.00
(4)	Larry Cheney	40.00	20.00	12.00
(5)	Ty Cobb	800.00	250.00	150.00
(6)	Eddie Collins	100.00	50.00	30.00
(7)	Larry Doyle	40.00	20.00	12.00
(8)	Art Fletcher	40.00	20.00	12.00
(9)	Claude Hendrix	40.00	20.00	12.00
(10)	Joe Jackson	1,500	385.00	230.00
(11)	Hughie Jennings	125.00	50.00	30.00
(12)	Nap Lajoie	125.00	50.00	30.00
(13)	Jimmy Lavender	40.00	20.00	12.00
(14)	Fritz Maisel	40.00	20.00	12.00
(15)	Rabbit Maranville	125.00	50.00	30.00
(16)	Rube Marquard	125.00	50.00	30.00
(17)	Matty (Christy Mathewson)	500.00	100.00	60.00
(18)	John McGraw	125.00	50.00	30.00
(19)	Stuffy McInnis	40.00	20.00	12.00
(20)	Chief Meyers	40.00	20.00	12.00
(21)	Red Murray	40.00	20.00	12.00
(22)	Ed Plank	150.00	50.00	30.00
(23)	Nap Rucker	40.00	20.00	12.00
(24)	Reb Russell	40.00	20.00	12.00
(25)	Wildfire Schulte	40.00	20.00	12.00
(26)	Jim Scott	40.00	20.00	12.00
(27)	Tris Speaker	175.00	62.00	37.00
(28)	Honus Wagner	750.00	450.00	250.00
(29)	Ed Walsh	125.00	50.00	30.00
(30)	Joe Wood	100.00	30.00	18.00

1915 Postaco Stamps

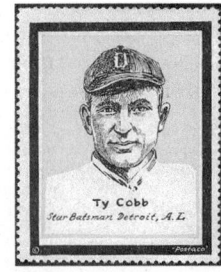

A small find of these early stamps in complete sheets of 12 in the mid-1990s made the issue collectible, rather than impossibly rare. Individual stamps are 1-3/4" x 2-1/8" and feature black-and-white player portraits set against a bright background of either yellow or red-orange. The player name, position (in most cases), team and league are designated at the bottom of the picture. In the black frame between the picture and the perforated white border is a copyright symbol and "Postaco." Backs are, of course, blank. Stamps are checklisted here in alphabetical order within color group.

		NM	E	VG
	Complete Set, Sheets (3):	3,000	1,500	900.00
	Complete Set, Singles (36):	2,500	1,250	750.00
	Common Player:	30.00	15.00	9.00
	Red-Orange Background			
(1)	Home Run Baker	100.00	50.00	30.00
(2)	Chief Bender	100.00	50.00	30.00
(3)	George Burns	40.00	20.00	12.00
(4)	John Evers	100.00	50.00	30.00
(5)	Max Flack	40.00	20.00	12.00
(6)	Hank Gawdy (Gowdy)	40.00	20.00	12.00
(7)	Claude Ray Hendrix	40.00	20.00	12.00
(8)	Walter Johnson	200.00	100.00	60.00
(9)	Nap Lajoie	100.00	50.00	30.00
(10)	Hans Lobert	40.00	20.00	12.00
(11)	Sherwood Magee	40.00	20.00	12.00
(12)	Rabbit Maranville	100.00	50.00	30.00
(13)	Christy Mathewson	250.00	125.00	75.00
(14)	George McBride	40.00	20.00	12.00
(15)	John McGraw	100.00	50.00	30.00
(16)	Fred Merkle	40.00	20.00	12.00
(17)	Jack Miller	40.00	20.00	12.00
(18)	Emiliano Palmero	40.00	20.00	12.00
(19)	Pol Perritt	40.00	20.00	12.00
(20)	Derrill Pratt	40.00	20.00	12.00
(21)	Richard Rudolph	40.00	20.00	12.00
(22)	Butch Schmidt	40.00	20.00	12.00
(23)	Joe Tinker	100.00	50.00	30.00
(24)	Honus Wagner	300.00	150.00	90.00
	Yellow Background			
(25)	G.C. Alexander	100.00	50.00	30.00
(26)	J.P. Archer	30.00	15.00	9.00
(27)	Ty Cobb	300.00	150.00	90.00
(28)	Eugene Cocreham	30.00	15.00	9.00
(29)	E.S. Cottrell	30.00	15.00	9.00
(30)	Josh Devore	30.00	15.00	9.00
(31)	A. Hartzell (Roy)	30.00	15.00	9.00
(32)	Wm. H. James (middle initial actually L)	30.00	15.00	9.00
(33)	Connie Mack	75.00	37.50	22.50
(34)	M. McHale	30.00	15.00	9.00
(35)	Geo. T. Stallings	30.00	15.00	9.00
(36)	Ed. Sweeney	30.00	15.00	9.00

1930 Post Cereal Famous North Americans

CHRISTY MATHEWSON (1880-1925)—Greatest of all baseball pitchers.

The year of issue is unconfirmed. Mathewson is the only baseball player from a group of cereal-box cards printed in panels of four and featuring presidents, generals, Indian chiefs, explorers, etc. The front is printed in red and blue, the back is blank. The card measures about 2-5/8" x 3-1/2".

	NM	E	VG
Christy Mathewson	600.00	300.00	180.00

1960 Post Cereal

These cards were issued on the backs of Grape Nuts

Flakes cereal and measure an oversized 7" x 8-3/4". The nine cards in the set include five baseball players two football (Frank Gifford and John Unitas) and two basketball players (Bob Cousy and Bob Pettit). The full-color photos are bordered by a wood frame design. The cards covered the entire back of the cereal box and are blank backed. Card fronts include the player's name, team and a facsimile autograph. A panel on the side of the box has biographical information.

	NM	E	VG
Common Player:	400.00	200.00	120.00
(1) Don Drysdale	400.00	200.00	120.00
(2) Al Kaline	400.00	200.00	120.00
(3) Harmon Killebrew	400.00	200.00	120.00
(4) Ed Mathews	400.00	200.00	120.00
(5) Mickey Mantle	2,000	1,000	600.00

1961 Post Cereal

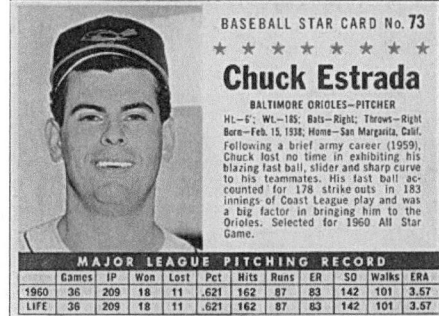

Two hundred different players are included in this set, but with variations the number of different cards exceeds 350. Cards were issued singly and in various panel configurations on the backs of cereal boxes, as well as on thinner stock in 10-card team sheets available from Post via a mail-in offer. Because of placement on less popular sizes and brands of cereal, or because they were issued only on box backs or company sheets, some cards were issued in significantly smaller quantities, making their prices much higher than other comparable players in the set. Well-cut individual cards measure about 3-1/2" x 2-1/2". All cards are numbered in the upper-right corner. Card fronts have full-color portait photos of the player, along with biographical information and 1960 and career statistics. Backs are blank. The complete set price includes only the most common variation of each player.

	NM	E	VG
Complete Set (200):	2,000	1,000	600.00
Common Player:	4.00	2.00	1.25
1a Yogi Berra (Box)	40.00	16.00	10.00
1b Yogi Berra (Company)	25.00	10.00	6.00
2a Elston Howard (Box)	7.50	3.00	2.00
2b Elston Howard (Company)	7.50	3.00	2.00
3a Bill Skowron (Box)	7.50	3.00	2.00
3b Bill Skowron (Company)	7.50	3.00	2.00
4a Mickey Mantle (Box)	160.00	65.00	40.00
4b Mickey Mantle (Company)	125.00	65.00	40.00
5 Bob Turley (Company)	40.00	16.00	10.00
6a Whitey Ford (Box)	20.00	8.00	5.00
6b Whitey Ford (Company)	12.50	5.00	3.00
7a Roger Maris (Box)	35.00	15.00	9.00
7b Roger Maris (Company)	35.00	15.00	9.00
8a Bobby Richardson (Box)	15.00	6.00	4.00
8b Bobby Richardson (Company)	10.00	4.00	2.50
9a Tony Kubek (Box)	25.00	10.00	6.25
9b Tony Kubek (Company)	35.00	15.00	9.00
10 Gil McDougald (Box)	60.00	25.00	15.00
11 Cletis Boyer (Box)	6.00	2.50	1.50
12a Hector Lopez (Box)	12.50	5.00	3.00
12b Hector Lopez (Company)	7.50	3.00	2.00
13 Bob Cerv (Box)	4.00	1.50	1.00
14 Ryne Duren (Box)	4.00	1.50	1.00
15 Bobby Shantz (Box)	4.00	1.50	1.00
16 Art Ditmar (Box)	4.00	1.50	1.00
17 Jim Coates (Box)	4.00	1.50	1.00
18 John Blanchard (Box)	4.00	1.50	1.00
19a Luis Aparicio (Box)	7.50	3.00	2.00
19b Luis Aparicio (Company)	15.00	6.00	4.00
20a Nelson Fox (Box)	22.50	9.00	5.75
20b Nelson Fox (Company)	20.00	8.00	5.00
21a Bill Pierce (Box)	20.00	8.00	5.00
21b Bill Pierce (Company)	9.00	3.50	2.25
22a Early Wynn (Box)	17.50	7.00	4.50
22b Early Wynn (Company)	25.00	10.00	6.25
23 Bob Shaw (Box)	125.00	50.00	30.00
24a Al Smith (Box)	20.00	8.00	5.00
24b Al Smith (Company)	17.50	7.00	4.50
25a Minnie Minoso (Box)	15.00	6.00	4.00

	NM	E	VG
25b Minnie Minoso (Company)	10.00	4.00	2.50
26a Roy Sievers (Box)	4.00	1.50	1.00
26b Roy Sievers (Company)	7.50	3.00	2.00
27a Jim Landis (Box)	15.00	6.00	3.75
27b Jim Landis (Company)	7.50	3.00	2.00
28a Sherman Lollar (Box)	4.00	1.50	1.00
28b Sherman Lollar (Company)	7.50	3.00	2.00
29 Gerry Staley (Box)	4.00	1.50	1.00
30a Gene Freese (Box, White Sox.)	4.00	1.50	1.00
30b Gene Freese (Company, Reds.)	9.00	3.50	2.25
31 Ted Kluszewski (Box)	15.00	6.00	4.00
32 Turk Lown (Box)	4.00	1.50	1.00
33a Jim Rivera (Box)	4.00	1.50	1.00
33b Jim Rivera (Company)	7.50	3.00	2.00
34 Frank Baumann (Box)	4.00	1.50	1.00
35a Al Kaline (Box)	25.00	10.00	6.25
35b Al Kaline (Company)	30.00	12.00	7.50
36a Rocky Colavito (Box)	30.00	12.00	7.50
36b Rocky Colavito (Company)	22.50	9.00	5.75
37a Charley Maxwell (Box)	20.00	8.00	5.00
37b Charley Maxwell (Company)	15.00	6.00	3.75
38a Frank Lary (Box)	4.00	1.50	1.00
38b Frank Lary (Company)	9.00	3.50	2.00
39a Jim Bunning (Box)	20.00	8.00	5.00
39b Jim Bunning (Company)	15.00	6.00	4.00
40a Norm Cash (Box)	4.00	1.50	1.00
40b Norm Cash (Company)	12.50	5.00	3.00
41a Frank Bolling (Box, Tigers.)	15.00	6.00	3.75
41b Frank Bolling (Company, Braves.)	9.00	3.50	2.00
42a Don Mossi (Box)	10.00	4.00	2.50
42b Don Mossi (Company)	9.00	3.50	2.00
43a Lou Berberet (Box)	10.00	4.00	2.50
43b Lou Berberet (Company)	9.00	3.50	2.00
44 Dave Sisler (Box)	4.00	1.50	1.00
45 Ed Yost (Box)	4.00	1.50	1.00
46 Pete Burnside (Box)	4.00	1.50	1.00
47a Pete Runnels (Box)	20.00	8.00	5.00
47b Pete Runnels (Company)	17.50	7.00	4.50
48a Frank Malzone (Box)	12.50	5.00	3.00
48b Frank Malzone (Company)	7.50	3.00	2.00
49a Vic Wertz (Box)	15.00	6.00	3.75
49b Vic Wertz (Company)	20.00	8.00	5.00
50a Tom Brewer (Box)	4.00	1.50	1.00
50b Tom Brewer (Company)	7.50	3.00	2.00
51a Willie Tasby (Box, no sold line.)	7.50	3.00	2.00
51b Willie Tasby (Company, sold line.)	15.00	6.00	4.00
52a Russ Nixon (Box)	4.00	1.50	1.00
52b Russ Nixon (Company)	7.50	3.00	2.00
53a Don Buddin (Box)	4.00	1.50	1.00
53b Don Buddin (Company)	7.50	3.00	2.00
54a Bill Monbouquette (Box)	4.00	1.50	1.00
54b Bill Monbouquette (Company)	7.50	3.00	2.00
55a Frank Sullivan (Box, Red Sox.)	4.00	1.50	1.00
55b Frank Sullivan (Company, Phillies.)	25.00	10.00	6.25
56a Haywood Sullivan (Box)	4.00	1.50	1.00
56b Haywood Sullivan (Company)	7.50	3.00	2.00
57a Harvey Kuenn (Box, Indians.)	25.00	10.00	6.25
57b Harvey Kuenn (Company, Giants.)	9.00	3.50	2.00
58a Gary Bell (Box)	7.50	3.00	2.00
58b Gary Bell (Company)	7.50	3.00	2.00
59a Jim Perry (Box)	4.00	1.50	1.00
59b Jim Perry (Company)	7.50	3.00	2.00
60a Jim Grant (Box)	4.00	1.50	1.00
60b Jim Grant (Company)	20.00	8.00	5.00
61a Johnny Temple (Box)	4.00	1.50	1.00
61b Johnny Temple (Company)	7.50	3.00	2.00
62a Paul Foytack (Box)	4.00	1.50	1.00
62b Paul Foytack (Company)	7.50	3.00	2.00
63a Vic Power (Box)	15.00	6.00	3.75
63b Vic Power (Company)	7.50	3.00	2.00
64a Tito Francona (Box)	4.00	1.50	1.00
64b Tito Francona (Company)	7.50	3.00	2.00
65a Ken Aspromonte (Box, no sold line.)	9.00	3.50	2.00
65b Ken Aspromonte (Company, sold line.)	9.00	3.50	2.00
66 Bob Wilson (Box)	4.00	1.50	1.00
67a John Romano (Box)	4.00	1.50	1.00
67b John Romano (Company)	7.50	3.00	2.00
68a Jim Gentile (Box)	4.00	1.50	1.00

	NM	E	VG
68b Jim Gentile (Company)	9.00	3.50	2.00
69a Gus Triandos (Box)	4.00	1.50	1.00
69b Gus Triandos (Company)	9.00	3.50	2.00
70 Gene Woodling (Box)	30.00	12.00	7.50
71a Milt Pappas (Box)	4.00	1.50	1.00
71b Milt Pappas (Company)	17.50	7.00	4.50
72a Ron Hansen (Box)	4.00	1.50	1.00
72b Ron Hansen (Company)	9.00	3.50	2.00
73 Chuck Estrada (Company)	110.00	45.00	27.50
74a Steve Barber (Box)	12.00	4.75	3.00
74b Steve Barber (Company)	9.00	3.50	2.00
75a Brooks Robinson (Box)	35.00	15.00	9.00
75b Brooks Robinson (Company)	35.00	15.00	9.00
76a Jackie Brandt (Box)	4.00	1.50	1.00
76b Jackie Brandt (Company)	9.00	3.50	2.00
77a Marv Breeding (Box)	4.00	1.50	1.00
77b Marv Breedding (Company)	9.00	3.50	2.00
78 Hal Brown (Box)	4.00	1.50	1.00
79 Billy Klaus (Box)	4.00	1.50	1.00
80a Hoyt Wilhelm (Box)	7.50	3.00	2.00
80b Hoyt Wilhelm (Company)	12.50	5.00	3.00
81a Jerry Lumpe (Box)	9.00	3.50	2.00
81b Jerry Lumpe (Company)	7.50	3.00	2.00
82a Norm Siebern (Box)	4.00	1.50	1.00
82b Norm Siebern (Company)	7.50	3.00	2.00
83a Bud Daley (Box)	15.00	6.00	4.00
83b Bud Daley (Company)	25.00	10.00	6.25
84a Bill Tuttle (Box)	4.00	1.50	1.00
84b Bill Tuttle (Company)	7.50	3.00	2.00
85a Marv Throneberry (Box)	4.00	1.50	1.00
85b Marv Throneberry (Company)	7.50	3.00	2.00
86a Dick Williams (Box)	15.00	6.00	3.75
86b Dick Williams (Company)	7.50	3.00	2.00
87a Ray Herbert (Box)	4.00	1.50	1.00
87b Ray Herbert (Company)	7.50	3.00	2.00
88a Whitey Herzog (Box)	4.00	1.50	1.00
88b Whitey Herzog (Company)	7.50	3.00	2.00
89a Ken Hamlin (Box, no sold line.)	4.00	1.50	1.00
89b Ken Hamlin (Company, sold line.)	9.00	3.50	2.00
90a Hank Bauer (Box)	15.00	6.00	3.75
90b Hank Bauer (Company)	9.00	3.50	2.00
91a Bob Allison (Box, Minneapolis.)	9.00	3.50	2.00
91b Bob Allison (Company, Minnesota.)	20.00	8.00	5.00
92a Harmon Killebrew (Box, Minneapolis.)	50.00	20.00	12.50
92b Harmon Killebrew (Company, Minnesota.)	75.00	35.00	20.00
93a Jim Lemon (Box, Minneapolis.)	50.00	20.00	10.00
93b Jim Lemon (Company, Minnesota.)	30.00	12.00	7.50
94 Chuck Stobbs (Company)	150.00	60.00	35.00
95a Reno Bertoia (Box, Minneapolis.)	4.00	1.50	1.00
95b Reno Bertoia (Company, Minnesota.)	20.00	8.00	5.00
96a Billy Gardner (Box, Minneapolis.)	4.00	1.50	1.00
96b Billy Gardner (Company, Minnesota.)	20.00	8.00	5.00
97a Earl Battey (Box, Minneapolis.)	6.00	2.50	1.50
97b Earl Battey (Company, Minnesota.)	20.00	8.00	5.00
98a Pedro Ramos (Box, Minneapolis.)	4.00	1.50	1.00
98b Pedro Ramos (Company, Minnesota.)	20.00	8.00	5.00
99a Camilio Pascual (Camilo) (Box, Minneapolis.)	4.00	1.50	1.00
99b Camilio Pascual (Camilo) (Company, Minnesota.)	20.00	8.00	5.00
100a Billy Consolo (Box, Minneapolis.)	4.00	1.50	1.00
100b Billy Consolo (Company, Minnesota.)	22.50	9.00	5.75
101a Warren Spahn (Box)	35.00	14.00	9.00
101b Warren Spahn (Company)	25.00	10.00	6.00
102a Lew Burdette (Box)	4.00	1.50	1.00
102b Lew Burdette (Company)	7.50	3.00	2.00
103a Bob Buhl (Box)	4.00	1.50	1.00
103b Bob Buhl (Company)	12.50	5.00	3.25
104a Joe Adcock (Box)	12.50	5.00	3.25
104b Joe Adcock (Company)	7.50	3.00	2.00
105a John Logan (Box)	6.00	2.50	1.50
105b John Logan (Company)	15.00	6.00	4.00
106 Ed Mathews (Box)	40.00	16.00	10.00
107a Hank Aaron (Box)	30.00	12.00	7.50
107b Hank Aaron (Company)	30.00	12.00	7.50

108a	Wes Covington (Box)	4.00	1.50	1.00
108b	Wes Covington (Company)	7.50	3.00	2.00
109a	Bill Bruton (Box, Braves.)	25.00	10.00	6.25
109b	Bill Bruton (Company, Tigers.)	12.50	5.00	3.00
110a	Del Crandall (Box)	6.00	2.50	1.50
110b	Del Crandall (Company)	7.50	3.00	2.00
111	Red Schoendienst (Box)	12.50	5.00	3.00
112	Juan Pizarro (Box)	4.00	1.50	1.00
113	Chuck Cottier (Box)	15.00	6.00	4.00
114	Al Spangler (Cox)	4.00	1.50	1.00
115a	Dick Farrell (Box)	25.00	10.00	6.25
115b	Dick Farrell (Company)	7.50	3.00	2.00
116a	Jim Owens (Box)	15.00	6.00	3.75
116b	Jim Owens (Company)	7.50	3.00	2.00
117a	Robin Roberts (Box)	12.50	5.00	3.00
117b	Robin Roberts (Company)	12.50	5.00	3.00
118a	Tony Taylor (Box)	4.00	1.50	1.00
118b	Tony Taylor (Company)	7.50	3.00	2.00
119a	Lee Walls (Box)	4.00	1.50	1.00
119b	Lee Walls (Company)	7.50	3.00	2.00
120a	Tony Curry (Box)	4.00	1.50	1.00
120b	Tony Curry (Company)	7.50	3.00	2.00
121a	Pancho Herrera (Box)	4.00	1.50	1.00
121b	Pancho Herrera (Company)	7.50	3.00	2.00
122a	Ken Walters (Box)	4.00	1.50	1.00
122b	Ken Walters (Company)	7.50	3.00	2.00
123a	John Callison (Box)	4.00	1.50	1.00
123b	John Callison (Company)	7.50	3.00	2.00
124a	Gene Conley (Box, Phillies.)	4.00	1.50	1.00
124b	Gene Conley (Company, Red Sox.)	20.00	8.00	5.00
125a	Bob Friend (Box)	5.00	2.00	1.25
125b	Bob Friend (Company)	7.50	3.00	2.00
126a	Vernon Law (Box)	5.00	2.00	1.25
126b	Vernon Law (Company)	7.50	3.00	2.00
127a	Dick Stuart (Box)	4.00	1.50	1.00
127b	Dick Stuart (Company)	7.50	3.00	2.00
128a	Bill Mazeroski (Box)	20.00	8.00	5.00
128b	Bill Mazeroski (Company)	12.50	5.00	3.00
129a	Dick Groat (Box)	4.00	1.50	1.00
129b	Dick Groat (Company)	10.00	4.00	2.50
130a	Don Hoak (Box)	4.00	1.50	1.00
130b	Don Hoak (Company)	7.50	3.00	2.00
131a	Bob Skinner (Box)	4.00	1.50	1.00
131b	Bob Skinner (Company)	7.50	3.00	2.00
132a	Bob Clemente (Box)	50.00	20.00	12.50
132b	Bob Clemente (Company)	90.00	35.00	25.00
133	Roy Face (Box)	15.00	6.00	4.00
134	Harvey Haddix (Box)	10.00	4.00	2.50
135	Bill Virdon (Box)	40.00	16.00	10.00
136a	Gino Cimoli (Box)	4.00	1.50	1.00
136b	Gino Cimoli (Company)	7.50	3.00	2.00
137	Rocky Nelson (Box)	6.00	2.50	1.50
138a	Smoky Burgess (Box)	4.00	1.50	1.00
138b	Smoky Burgess (Company)	7.50	3.00	2.00
139	Hal Smith (Box)	6.00	2.50	1.50
140	Wilmer Mizell (Box)	12.00	4.75	3.00
141a	Mike McCormick (Box)	4.00	1.50	1.00
141b	Mike McCormick (Company)	7.50	3.00	2.00
142a	John Antonelli (Box, Giants.)	4.00	1.50	1.00
142b	John Antonelli (Company, Indians.)	9.00	3.50	2.00
143a	Sam Jones (Box)	5.00	2.00	1.25
143b	Sam Jones (Company)	7.50	3.00	2.00
144a	Orlando Cepeda (Box)	22.50	9.00	5.75
144b	Orlando Cepeda (Company)	12.50	5.00	3.00
145a	Willie Mays (Box)	55.00	22.50	13.50
145b	Willie Mays (Company)	45.00	18.00	10.00
146a	Willie Kirkland (Box, Giants.)	60.00	24.00	15.00
146b	Willie Kirkland (Company, Indians.)	25.00	10.00	6.25
147a	Willie McCovey (Box)	20.00	8.00	5.00
147b	Willie McCovey (Company)	25.00	10.00	6.00
148a	Don Blasingame (Box)	4.00	1.50	1.00
148b	Don Blasingame (Company)	7.50	3.00	2.00
149a	Jim Davenport (Box)	4.00	1.50	1.00
149b	Jim Davenport (Company)	7.50	3.00	2.00
150a	Hobie Landrith (Box)	4.00	1.50	1.00
150b	Hobie Landrith (Company)	7.50	3.00	2.00
151	Bob Schmidt (Box)	9.00	3.50	2.00
152a	Ed Bressoud (Box)	4.00	1.50	1.00
152b	Ed Bressoud (Company)	7.50	3.00	2.00
153a	Andre Rodgers (Box, no traded line.)	9.00	3.50	2.00

153b	Andre Rodgers (Box, traded line.)	4.00	1.50	1.00
154	Jack Sanford (Box)	20.00	8.00	5.00
155	Billy O'Dell (Box)	4.00	1.50	1.00
156a	Norm Larker (Box)	7.50	3.00	2.00
156b	Norm Larker (Company)	7.50	3.00	2.00
157a	Charlie Neal (Box)	4.00	1.50	1.00
157b	Charlie Neal (Company)	7.50	3.00	2.00
158a	Jim Gilliam (Box)	7.50	3.00	2.00
158b	Jim Gilliam (Company)	7.50	3.00	2.00
159a	Wally Moon (Box)	20.00	8.00	5.00
159b	Wally Moon (Company)	12.00	4.75	3.00
160a	Don Drysdale (Box)	20.00	8.00	5.00
160b	Don Drysdale (Company)	20.00	8.00	5.00
161a	Larry Sherry (Box)	4.00	1.50	1.00
161b	Larry Sherry (Company)	7.50	3.00	2.00
162	Stan Williams (Box)	7.50	3.00	2.00
163	Mel Roach (Box)	65.00	25.00	15.00
164a	Maury Wills (Box)	20.00	8.00	5.00
164b	Maury Wills (Company)	35.00	14.00	9.00
165	Tom Davis (Box)	4.00	1.50	1.00
166a	John Roseboro (Box)	4.00	1.50	1.00
166b	John Roseboro (Company)	7.50	3.00	2.00
167a	Duke Snider (Box)	15.00	6.00	3.75
167b	Duke Snider (Company)	20.00	8.00	5.00
168a	Gil Hodges (Box)	7.50	3.00	2.00
168b	Gil Hodges (Company)	12.50	5.00	3.00
169	John Podres (Box)	4.00	1.50	1.00
170	Ed Roebuck (Box)	4.00	1.50	1.00
171a	Ken Boyer (Box)	15.00	6.00	3.75
171b	Ken Boyer (Company)	7.50	3.00	2.00
172a	Joe Cunningham (Box)	12.50	5.00	3.00
172b	Joe Cunningham (Company)	9.00	3.50	2.00
173a	Daryl Spencer (Box)	4.00	1.50	1.00
173b	Daryl Spencer (Company)	7.50	3.00	2.00
174a	Larry Jackson (Box)	12.50	5.00	3.00
174b	Larry Jackson (Company)	7.50	3.00	2.00
175a	Lindy McDaniel (Box)	7.50	3.00	2.00
175b	Lindy McDaniel (Company)	7.50	3.00	2.00
176a	Bill White (Box)	4.00	1.50	1.00
176b	Bill White (Company)	7.50	3.00	2.00
177a	Alex Grammas (Box)	20.00	8.00	5.00
177b	Alex Grammas (Company)	7.50	3.00	2.00
178a	Curt Flood (Box)	4.00	1.50	1.00
178b	Curt Flood (Company)	12.50	5.00	3.00
179a	Ernie Broglio (Box)	4.00	1.50	1.00
179b	Ernie Broglio (Company)	8.00	3.25	2.00
180a	Hal Smith (Box)	8.00	3.25	2.00
180b	Hal Smith (Company)	12.50	5.00	3.00
181a	Vada Pinson (Box)	20.00	8.00	5.00
181b	Vada Pinson (Company)	7.50	3.00	2.00
182a	Frank Robinson (Box)	30.00	12.00	7.50
182b	Frank Robinson (Company)	35.00	15.00	9.00
183	Roy McMillan (Box)	80.00	30.00	15.00
184a	Bob Purkey (Box)	4.00	1.50	1.00
184b	Bob Purkey (Company)	7.50	3.00	2.00
185a	Ed Kasko (Box)	7.50	3.00	2.00
185b	Ed Kasko (Company)	7.50	3.00	2.00
186a	Gus Bell (Box)	4.00	1.50	1.00
186b	Gus Bell (Company)	7.50	3.00	2.00
187a	Jerry Lynch (Box)	4.00	1.50	1.00
187b	Jerry Lynch (Company)	7.50	3.00	2.00
188a	Ed Bailey (Box)	4.00	1.50	1.00
188b	Ed Bailey (Company)	7.50	3.00	2.00
189a	Jim O'Toole (Box)	4.00	1.50	1.00
189b	Jim O'Toole (Company)	7.50	3.00	2.00
190a	Billy Martin (Box, no sold line.)	6.00	2.50	1.50
190b	Billy Martin (Company, sold line.)	12.50	5.00	3.00
191a	Ernie Banks (Box)	35.00	15.00	9.00
191b	Ernie Banks (Company)	20.00	8.00	5.00
192a	Richie Ashburn (Box)	12.50	5.00	3.00
192b	Richie Ashburn (Company)	22.50	9.00	5.75
193a	Frank Thomas (Box)	100.00	40.00	25.00
193b	Frank Thomas (Company)	40.00	16.00	10.00
194a	Don Cardwell (Box)	6.00	2.50	1.50
194b	Don Cardwell (Company)	7.50	3.00	2.00
195a	George Altman (Box)	15.00	6.00	3.75
195b	George Altman (Company)	7.50	3.00	2.00
196a	Ron Santo (Box)	6.00	2.50	1.50
196b	Ron Santo (Company)	30.00	12.00	7.50
197a	Glen Hobbie (Box)	4.00	1.50	1.00
197b	Glen Hobbie (Company)	7.50	3.00	2.00
198a	Sam Taylor (Box)	4.00	1.50	1.00
198b	Sam Taylor (Company)	7.50	3.00	2.00
199a	Jerry Kindall (Box)	8.00	3.25	2.00
199b	Jerry Kindall (Company)	7.50	3.00	2.00
200a	Don Elston (Box)	12.00	4.75	3.00
200b	Don Elston (Company)	7.50	3.00	2.00

1961 Post Cereal Company Sheets

Via a mail-in offer, sheets of 10 cards from each team could be ordered from the cereal company. Known to collectors as "company" cards, the sheets were issued in a perforated format on cardboard that is somewhat thinner than box-back cards. Sheet cards have perforations on one, two, or three sides, depending on their original placement on the sheet. Because of player movements between the time the box-back cards and sheet cards were printed, some cards are only found on the mail-in sheets, while others could not be obtained via the mail-in offer, and some are shown on the sheets of the "wrong" team.

		NM	E	VG
	Complete Set (16):	6,500	3,250	1,950
	Common Team:	300.00	150.00	90.00
(1)	Baltimore Orioles	300.00	150.00	90.00
(2)	Boston Red Sox	300.00	150.00	90.00
(3)	Chicago Cubs	300.00	150.00	90.00
(4)	Chicago White Sox	300.00	150.00	90.00
(5)	Cincinnati Reds	300.00	150.00	90.00
(6)	Cleveland Indians	300.00	150.00	90.00
(7)	Detroit Tigers	300.00	150.00	90.00
(8)	Kansas City Athletics	300.00	150.00	90.00
(9)	Los Angeles Dodgers	375.00	185.00	110.00
(10)	Milwaukee Braves	375.00	185.00	110.00
(11)	Minnesota Twins	475.00	235.00	140.00
(12)	New York Yankees	600.00	300.00	180.00
(13)	Philadelphia Phillies	300.00	150.00	90.00
(14)	Pittsburgh Pirates	375.00	185.00	110.00
(15)	San Francisco Giants	375.00	185.00	110.00
(16)	St. Louis Cardinals	300.00	150.00	90.00

1961 Post Cereal Display Pinwheel

Designed for use in grocery stores to promote sales of Post cereal with baseball cards on the back, this display features double-sided, oversize (about 8-1/2" x 6") examples of nine of the cards arranged in a circle. At center was a cardboard cutout of a youngster and accommodation for an electric motor.

	NM	E	VG
Complete Display:	6,500	3,750	2,000

Ken Boyer, Lew Burdette, Roy Face, Whitey
Ford, Nellie Fox, Jim Gentile, Jim Lemon,
Willie Mays, Pete Runnels

1962 Post Cereal

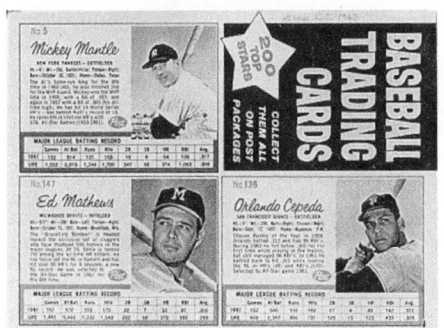

Like the 1961 Post set, there are 200 players pictured in
this set of 3-1/2" x 2-1/2" cards. Differences include a Post
logo on the card fronts and the player's name in script lettering. Cards are again blank backed and were issued in panels
of three to seven cards on cereal boxes. American League
players are numbered 1-100 and National League players
101-200. With variations there are 210 cards known. Some
of the '62 cards, usually those printed on the backs of less
popular brands or sizes, were issued in smaller quantities
and sell for more than players of star caliber. The cards of
Mickey Mantle and Roger Maris were reproduced in a special
two-card panel for a Life magazine insert. The card stock
for this insert is slightly thinner, with white margins. The
1962 Post Canadian and Jell-O sets have virtually the same
checklist as this set. The complete set price does not include
the scarcer variations. The #5 Mickey Mantle card has been
extensively counterfeited in recent years by pasting a reproduction of the Life magazine promo card (no lines in the stats
area) to a piece of blank cardboard. All genuine cereal-box
Mantle cards have a grid of lines in the stats area.

	NM	E	VG
Complete Set (200):	1,000	500.00	250.00
Common Player:	4.00	1.50	1.00
April 13 Life magazine w/ad panel:	100.00	50.00	25.00
1 Bill Skowron	10.00	4.00	2.50
2 Bobby Richardson	12.50	5.00	3.00
3 Cletis Boyer	7.50	3.00	2.00
4 Tony Kubek	9.00	3.50	2.00
5a Mickey Mantle (From box, no printing on back.)	70.00	35.00	17.50
5b Mickey Mantle (From ad, printing on back.)	50.00	25.00	12.50
6a Roger Maris (From box, no printing on back.)	35.00	14.00	9.00
6b Roger Maris (From ad, printing on back.)	30.00	12.00	7.50
7 Yogi Berra	27.50	11.00	7.00
8 Elston Howard	20.00	8.00	5.00
9 Whitey Ford	22.50	9.00	6.00
10 Ralph Terry	10.00	4.00	2.50
11 John Blanchard	4.00	1.50	1.00
12 Luis Arroyo	20.00	8.00	5.00
13 Bill Stafford	4.00	1.50	1.00
14a Norm Cash (Throws: Right)	30.00	12.00	7.50
14b Norm Cash (Throws: Left)	10.00	4.00	2.50
15 Jake Wood	7.50	3.00	2.00
16 Steve Boros	10.00	4.00	2.50
17 Chico Fernandez	4.00	1.50	1.00
18 Bill Bruton	4.00	1.50	1.00
19 Rocky Colavito	16.00	6.50	4.00
20 Al Kaline	20.00	8.00	5.00
21 Dick Brown	4.00	1.50	1.00
22 Frank Lary	4.00	1.50	1.00
23 Don Mossi	4.00	1.50	1.00
24 Phil Regan	4.00	1.50	1.00
25 Charley Maxwell	7.50	3.00	2.00
26 Jim Bunning	30.00	12.00	7.50
27a Jim Gentile (Home: Baltimore)	4.00	1.50	1.00
27b Jim Gentile (Home: San Lorenzo)	6.00	2.50	1.50
28 Marv Breeding	4.00	1.50	1.00
29 Brooks Robinson	17.50	7.00	4.50
30 Ron Hansen	4.00	1.50	1.00
31 Jackie Brandt	4.00	1.50	1.00
32 Dick Williams	4.00	1.50	1.00
33 Gus Triandos	4.00	1.50	1.00
34 Milt Pappas	7.50	3.00	2.00

35 Hoyt Wilhelm	15.00	6.00	3.50
36 Chuck Estrada	12.50	5.00	3.00
37 Vic Power	4.00	1.50	1.00
38 Johnny Temple	4.00	1.50	1.00
39 Bubba Phillips	4.00	1.50	1.00
40 Tito Francona	9.00	3.50	2.00
41 Willie Kirkland	4.00	1.50	1.00
42 John Romano	4.00	1.50	1.00
43 Jim Perry	4.00	1.50	1.00
44 Woodie Held	4.00	1.50	1.00
45 Chuck Essegian	4.00	1.50	1.00
46 Roy Sievers	4.00	1.50	1.00
47 Nellie Fox	7.50	3.00	2.00
48 Al Smith	4.00	1.50	1.00
49 Luis Aparicio	12.50	5.00	3.25
50 Jim Landis	7.50	3.00	2.00
51 Minnie Minoso	10.00	4.00	2.50
52 Andy Carey	7.50	3.00	2.00
53 Sherman Lollar	4.00	1.50	1.00
54 Bill Pierce	7.50	3.00	2.00
55 Early Wynn	50.00	20.00	12.50
56 Chuck Schilling	7.50	3.00	2.00
57 Pete Runnels	15.00	6.00	3.75
58 Frank Malzone	4.00	1.50	1.00
59 Don Buddin	4.00	1.50	1.00
60 Gary Geiger	25.00	10.00	6.25
61 Carl Yastrzemski	40.00	20.00	10.00
62 Jackie Jensen	7.50	3.00	2.00
63 Jim Pagliaroni	4.00	1.50	1.00
64 Don Schwall	4.00	1.50	1.00
65 Dale Long	4.00	1.50	1.00
66 Chuck Cottier	4.00	1.50	1.00
67 Billy Klaus	9.00	3.50	2.00
68 Coot Veal	9.00	3.50	2.00
69 Marty Keough	60.00	30.00	15.00
70 Willie Tasby	9.00	3.50	2.00
71 Gene Woodling	4.00	1.50	1.00
72 Gene Green	4.00	1.50	1.00
73 Dick Donovan	4.00	1.50	1.00
74 Steve Bilko	4.00	1.50	1.00
75 Rocky Bridges	4.00	1.50	1.00
76 Eddie Yost	4.00	1.50	1.00
77 Leon Wagner	4.00	1.50	1.00
78 Albie Pearson	7.50	3.00	2.00
79 Ken Hunt	4.00	1.50	1.00
80 Earl Averill	4.00	1.50	1.00
81 Ryne Duren	4.00	1.50	1.00
82 Ted Kluszewski	6.00	2.50	1.50
83 Bob Allison	90.00	35.00	20.00
84 Billy Martin	9.00	3.50	2.00
85 Harmon Killebrew	40.00	16.00	10.00
86 Zoilo Versalles	20.00	8.00	5.00
87 Lenny Green	10.00	4.00	2.50
88 Bill Tuttle	4.00	1.50	1.00
89 Jim Lemon	4.00	1.50	1.00
90 Earl Battey	4.00	1.50	1.00
91 Camilo Pascual	4.00	1.50	1.00
92 Norm Siebern	55.00	27.50	13.75
93 Jerry Lumpe	4.00	1.50	1.00
94 Dick Howser	4.00	1.50	1.00
95a Gene Stephens (Born: Jan. 5)	4.00	1.50	1.00
95b Gene Stephens (Born: Jan. 20)	20.00	8.00	5.00
96 Leo Posada	4.00	1.50	1.00
97 Joe Pignatano	7.50	3.00	2.00
98 Jim Archer	4.00	1.50	1.00
99 Haywood Sullivan	4.00	1.50	1.00
100 Art Ditmar	6.00	2.50	1.50
101 Gil Hodges	50.00	25.00	12.50
102 Charlie Neal	4.00	1.50	1.00
103 Daryl Spencer	25.00	10.00	6.00
104 Maury Wills	4.00	1.50	1.00
105 Tommy Davis	4.00	1.50	1.00
106 Willie Davis	4.00	1.50	1.00
107 John Roseboro	7.50	3.00	2.00
108 John Podres	4.00	1.50	1.00
109a Sandy Koufax (Blue lines around stats.)	2,250	1,125	675.00
109b Sandy Koufax (Red lines around stats.)	40.00	20.00	12.00
110 Don Drysdale	20.00	8.00	5.00
111 Larry Sherry	4.00	1.50	1.00
112 Jim Gilliam	7.50	3.00	2.00
113 Norm Larker	65.00	32.50	16.25
114 Duke Snider	20.00	8.00	5.00
115 Stan Williams	4.00	1.50	1.00
116 Gordy Coleman	55.00	27.50	13.75
117 Don Blasingame	12.50	5.00	3.00
118 Gene Freese	4.00	1.50	1.00
119 Ed Kasko	4.00	1.50	1.00
120 Gus Bell	4.00	1.50	1.00
121 Vada Pinson	7.50	3.00	2.00
122 Frank Robinson	50.00	20.00	12.50
123 Bob Purkey	4.00	1.50	1.00
124a Joey Jay (Blue lines around stats.)	300.00	150.00	90.00

124b Joey Jay (Red lines around stats.)	6.00	2.50	1.50
125 Jim Brosnan	45.00	22.50	11.25
126 Jim O'Toole	4.00	1.50	1.00
127 Jerry Lynch	55.00	27.50	13.75
128 Wally Post	4.00	1.50	1.00
129 Ken Hunt	4.00	1.50	1.00
130 Jerry Zimmerman	4.00	1.50	1.00
131 Willie McCovey	55.00	27.50	13.75
132 Jose Pagan	4.00	1.50	1.00
133 Felipe Alou	4.00	1.50	1.00
134 Jim Davenport	4.00	1.50	1.00
135 Harvey Kuenn	4.00	1.50	1.00
136 Orlando Cepeda	15.00	6.00	3.75
137 Ed Bailey	4.00	1.50	1.00
138 Sam Jones	4.00	1.50	1.00
139 Mike McCormick	4.00	1.50	1.00
140 Juan Marichal	55.00	27.50	13.75
141 Jack Sanford	4.00	1.50	1.00
142 Willie Mays	35.00	17.50	8.75
143 Stu Miller (Photo actually Chuck Hiller.)	5.00	2.00	1.25
144 Joe Amalfitano	35.00	14.00	9.00
145a Joe Adock (Name incorrect.)	75.00	40.00	25.00
145b Joe Adcock (Name correct.)	4.00	1.50	1.00
146 Frank Bolling	4.00	1.50	1.00
147 Ed Mathews	17.50	7.00	4.50
148 Roy McMillan	4.00	1.50	1.00
149 Hank Aaron	40.00	20.00	10.00
150 Gino Cimoli	4.00	1.50	1.00
151 Frank Thomas	4.00	1.50	1.00
152 Joe Torre	25.00	10.00	6.25
153 Lou Burdette	4.00	1.50	1.00
154 Bob Buhl	10.00	4.00	2.50
155 Carlton Willey	20.00	8.00	5.00
156 Lee Maye	20.00	8.00	5.00
157 Al Spangler	7.50	3.00	2.00
158 Bill White	30.00	15.00	7.50
159 Ken Boyer	6.00	2.50	1.50
160 Joe Cunningham	4.00	1.50	1.00
161 Carl Warwick	4.00	1.50	1.00
162 Carl Sawatski	4.00	1.50	1.00
163 Lindy McDaniel	4.00	1.50	1.00
164 Ernie Broglio	4.00	1.50	1.00
165 Larry Jackson	4.00	1.50	1.00
166 Curt Flood	4.00	1.50	1.00
167 Curt Simmons	4.00	1.50	1.00
168 Alex Grammas	4.00	1.50	1.00
169 Dick Stuart	10.00	4.00	2.50
170 Bill Mazeroski	20.00	8.00	5.00
171 Don Hoak	20.00	8.00	5.00
172 Dick Groat	4.00	1.50	1.00
173a Roberto Clemente (Blue lines around stats.)	1,500	750.00	450.00
173b Roberto Clemente (Red lines around stats.)	40.00	20.00	12.00
174 Bob Skinner	4.00	1.50	1.00
175 Bill Virdon	4.00	1.50	1.00
176 Smoky Burgess	9.00	3.50	2.25
177 Elroy Face	4.00	1.50	1.00
178 Bob Friend	4.00	1.50	1.00
179 Vernon Law	4.00	1.50	1.00
180 Harvey Haddix	4.00	1.50	1.00
181 Hal Smith	7.50	3.00	2.00
182 Ed Bouchee	4.00	1.50	1.00
183 Don Zimmer	4.00	1.50	1.00
184 Ron Santo	7.50	3.00	2.00
185 Andre Rodgers	4.00	1.50	1.00
186 Richie Ashburn	12.50	5.00	3.00
187a George Altman (Last line is "...1955.")")	6.00	2.50	1.50
187b George Altman (Last line is "...1955.")	7.50	3.00	2.00
188 Ernie Banks	17.50	7.00	4.50
189 Sam Taylor	25.00	10.00	6.25
190 Don Elston	7.50	3.00	2.00
191 Jerry Kindall	4.00	1.50	1.00
192 Pancho Herrera	4.00	1.50	1.00
193 Tony Taylor	4.00	1.50	1.00
194 Ruben Amaro	9.00	3.50	2.00
195 Don Demeter	4.00	1.50	1.00
196 Bobby Gene Smith	4.00	1.50	1.00
197 Clay Dalrymple	4.00	1.50	1.00
198 Robin Roberts	10.00	4.00	2.50
199 Art Mahaffey	4.00	1.50	1.00
200 John Buzhardt	4.00	1.50	1.00

1962 Post Cereal - Canadian

This Post set is scarce due to the much more limited distribution in Canada. Most cards were printed on the back of
the cereal boxes and contain a full-color player photo with
biography and statistics given in both French and English.
Card backs are blank. Cards measure 3-1/2" x 2-1/2". This
200-card set is very similar to the Post Cereal cards printed
in the United States. The Post logo appears at the upper-

left corner in the Canadian issue. Several cards are scarce because of limited distribution and there are two Whitey Ford cards, the corrected version being the most scarce. The complete set price does not include the scarcer variations. Certain cereal brands had the cards packaged inside the box on perforated panels, and will be found with perforated edges on one side or other.

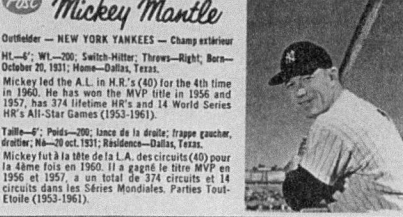

		NM	E	VG
	Complete Set (200):	5,000	2,005	1,250
	Common Player:	8.00	3.25	2.00
1	Bill Skowron	35.00	15.00	9.00
2	Bobby Richardson	12.00	4.75	3.00
3	Cletis Boyer	10.00	4.00	2.50
4	Tony Kubek	12.00	4.75	3.00
5a	Mickey Mantle (Stats list 153 hits.)	215.00	85.00	55.00
5b	Mickey Mantle (163 hits; first line of bio ends: "4th time in")	120.00	50.00	30.00
5c	Mickey Mantle (163 hits; first line of bio ends: "4th time")	125.00	50.00	30.00
6a	Roger Maris (First line of French bio has large "P" in "Pour les circuits.")	65.00	25.00	15.00
6b	Roger Maris (French text reads, "Residence." Small "p" in "pour.")	55.00	22.50	13.50
6c	Roger Maris (French text reads, "a," not "Residence." Small "p" in "pour.")	55.00	22.50	13.50
7	Yogi Berra	40.00	16.00	10.00
8	Elston Howard	12.00	4.75	3.00
9a	Whitey Ford (Dodgers)	55.00	22.50	13.50
9b	Whitey Ford (Yankees)	80.00	32.00	20.00
10	Ralph Terry	95.00	38.00	24.00
11	John Blanchard	8.00	3.25	2.00
12	Luis Arroyo	8.00	3.25	2.00
13	Bill Stafford	8.00	3.25	2.00
14	Norm Cash	10.00	4.00	2.50
15	Jake Wood	8.00	3.25	2.00
16	Steve Boros	8.00	3.25	2.00
17	Chico Fernandez	8.00	3.25	2.00
18	Bill Bruton	8.00	3.25	2.00
19a	Rocky Colavito (Script name large.)	17.50	7.00	4.50
19b	Rocky Colavito (Script name small.)	17.50	7.00	4.50
20	Al Kaline	85.00	35.00	20.00
21	Dick Brown	12.00	4.75	3.00
22a	Frank Lary ("Residence-Northport, Alabama.")	17.50	7.00	4.50
22b	Frank Lary ("a Northport, Alabama.")	65.00	25.00	15.00
23	Don Mossi	8.00	3.25	2.00
24	Phil Regan	8.00	3.25	2.00
25	Charley Maxwell	8.00	3.25	2.00
26	Jim Bunning	25.00	10.00	6.25
27a	Jim Gentile (French bio begins "Le 8 mai, Jim ...")	13.50	5.50	3.50
27b	Jim Gentile (Begins, "Le 8 mai 1961, Jim ...")	13.50	5.50	3.50
28	Marv Breeding	17.50	7.00	4.50
29	Brooks Robinson	50.00	20.00	12.50
30	Ron Hansen	8.00	3.25	2.00
31	Jackie Brandt	8.00	3.25	2.00
32	Dick Williams	55.00	22.50	13.50
33	Gus Triandos	10.00	4.00	2.50
34	Milt Pappas	10.00	4.00	2.50
35	Hoyt Wilhelm	95.00	38.00	24.00
36	Chuck Estrada	8.00	3.25	2.00
37	Vic Power	8.00	3.25	2.00
38	Johnny Temple	8.00	3.25	2.00
39	Bubba Phillips	55.00	22.50	13.50
40	Tito Francona	55.00	22.50	13.50
41	Willie Kirkland	13.50	5.50	3.50
42	John Romano	13.50	5.50	3.50
43	Jim Perry	10.00	4.00	2.50
44	Woodie Held	8.00	3.25	2.00
45	Chuck Essegian	8.00	3.25	2.00
46	Roy Sievers	40.00	16.00	10.00
47	Nellie Fox	25.00	10.00	6.25
48	Al Smith	8.00	3.25	2.00
49	Luis Aparicio	100.00	40.00	25.00
50	Jim Landis	13.50	5.50	3.50
51	Minnie Minoso	55.00	22.50	13.50
52	Andy Carey	12.00	4.75	3.00
53	Sherman Lollar	8.00	3.25	2.00
54	Bill Pierce	10.00	4.00	2.50
55	Early Wynn	30.00	12.00	7.50
56	Chuck Schilling	10.00	4.00	2.50
57	Pete Runnels	10.00	4.00	2.50
58	Frank Malzone	8.00	3.25	2.00
59	Don Buddin	12.00	4.75	3.00
60	Gary Geiger	8.00	3.25	2.00
61	Carl Yastrzemski	60.00	25.00	15.00
62	Jackie Jensen	40.00	16.00	10.00
63	Jim Pagliaroni	8.00	3.25	2.00
64	Don Schwall	25.00	10.00	6.25
65	Dale Long	20.00	8.00	5.00
66	Chuck Cottier	8.00	3.25	2.00
67	Billy Klaus	8.00	3.25	2.00
68	Coot Veal	8.00	3.25	2.00
69	Marty Keough	8.00	3.25	2.00
70	Willie Tasby	125.00	50.00	30.00
71	Gene Woodling (Photo reversed.)	10.00	4.00	2.50
72	Gene Green	12.00	4.75	3.00
73	Dick Donovan	8.00	3.25	2.00
74	Steve Bilko	13.50	5.50	3.50
75	Rocky Bridges	12.00	4.75	3.00
76	Eddie Yost	8.00	3.25	2.00
77	Leon Wagner	65.00	25.00	15.00
78	Albie Pearson	13.50	5.50	3.50
79	Ken Hunt	8.00	3.25	2.00
80	Earl Averill	8.00	3.25	2.00
81	Ryne Duren	10.00	4.00	2.50
82	Ted Kluszewski	30.00	12.00	7.50
83	Bob Allison	13.50	5.50	3.50
84	Billy Martin	17.50	7.00	4.50
85	Harmon Killebrew	125.00	50.00	30.00
86	Zoilo Versalles	8.00	3.25	2.00
87	Lenny Green	95.00	38.00	24.00
88	Bill Tuttle	8.00	3.25	2.00
89	Jim Lemon	8.00	3.25	2.00
90	Earl Battey	13.50	5.50	3.50
91	Camilo Pascual	10.00	4.00	2.50
92	Norm Siebern	8.00	3.25	2.00
93	Jerry Lumpe	8.00	3.25	2.00
94	Dick Howser	80.00	32.00	20.00
95	Gene Stephens	8.00	3.25	2.00
96	Leo Posada	8.00	3.25	2.00
97	Joe Pignatano	8.00	3.25	2.00
98	Jim Archer	8.00	3.25	2.00
99	Haywood Sullivan	80.00	35.00	20.00
100	Art Ditmar	25.00	10.00	6.25
101	Gil Hodges	35.00	15.00	9.00
102	Charlie Neal	8.00	3.25	2.00
103	Daryl Spencer	8.00	3.25	2.00
104	Maury Wills	17.50	7.00	4.50
105	Tommy Davis	65.00	25.00	15.00
106	Willie Davis	12.00	4.75	3.00
107	John Rosboro (Roseboro)	10.00	4.00	2.50
108	John Podres	10.00	4.00	2.50
109	Sandy Koufax	135.00	55.00	35.00
110	Don Drysdale	35.00	15.00	9.00
111	Larry Sherry	75.00	30.00	18.00
112	Jim Gilliam	75.00	30.00	18.00
113	Norm Larker	8.00	3.25	2.00
114	Duke Snider	30.00	12.00	7.50
115	Stan Williams	13.50	5.50	3.50
116	Gordy Coleman	8.00	3.25	2.00
117	Don Blasingame	160.00	65.00	40.00
118	Gene Freese	40.00	16.00	10.00
119	Ed Kasko	13.50	5.50	3.50
120	Gus Bell	8.00	3.25	2.00
121	Vada Pinson	10.00	4.00	2.50
122	Frank Robinson	50.00	20.00	12.50
123	Bob Purkey	55.00	22.50	13.50
124	Joey Jay	8.00	3.25	2.00
125	Jim Brosnan	17.50	7.00	4.50
126	Jim O'Toole	8.00	3.25	2.00
127	Jerry Lynch	15.00	6.00	3.75
128	Wally Post	135.00	55.00	35.00
129	Ken Hunt	8.00	3.25	2.00
130	Jerry Zimmerman	8.00	3.25	2.00
131	Willie McCovey	40.00	16.00	10.00
132	Jose Pagan	12.00	4.75	3.00
133	Felipe Alou	10.00	4.00	2.50
134	Jim Davenport	8.00	3.25	2.00
135	Harvey Kuenn	10.00	4.00	2.50
136	Orlando Cepeda	25.00	10.00	6.25
137	Ed Bailey	75.00	30.00	18.50
138	Sam Jones	55.00	22.50	13.50
139	Mike McCormick	8.00	3.25	2.00
140	Juan Marichal	35.00	15.00	9.00
141	Jack Sanford	8.00	3.25	2.00
142a	Willie Mays (Big head.)	90.00	35.00	18.00
142b	Willie Mays (Small head.)	60.00	24.00	15.00
143	Stu Miller	8.00	3.25	2.00
144	Joe Amalfitano	100.00	40.00	25.00
145	Joe Adcock	13.50	5.50	3.50
146	Frank Bolling	13.50	5.50	3.50
147	Ed Mathews	30.00	12.00	7.50
148	Roy McMillan	24.00	9.50	6.00
149a	Hank Aaron (Script name large.)	80.00	32.00	20.00
149b	Hank Aaron (Script name small.)	60.00	24.00	15.00
150	Gino Cimoli	8.00	3.25	2.00
151	Frank Thomas	8.00	3.25	2.00
152	Joe Torre	25.00	10.00	6.25
153	Lou Burdette	25.00	10.00	6.25
154	Bob Buhl	10.00	4.00	2.50
155	Carlton Willey	12.00	4.75	3.00
156	Lee Maye	8.00	3.25	2.00
157	Al Spangler	8.00	3.25	2.00
158	Bill White	10.00	4.00	2.50
159	Ken Boyer	40.00	16.00	10.00
160	Joe Cunningham	8.00	3.25	2.00
161	Carl Warwick	55.00	22.50	13.50
162	Carl Sawatski	8.00	3.25	2.00
163	Lindy McDaniel	8.00	3.25	2.00
164	Ernie Broglio	8.00	3.25	2.00
165	Larry Jackson	8.00	3.25	2.00
166	Curt Flood	25.00	10.00	6.25
167	Curt Simmons	17.50	7.00	4.50
168	Alex Grammas	8.00	3.25	2.00
169	Dick Stuart	25.00	10.00	6.25
170	Bill Mazeroski	40.00	16.00	10.00
171	Don Hoak	8.00	3.25	2.00
172	Dick Groat	17.50	7.00	4.50
173	Roberto Clemente	100.00	40.00	25.00
174	Bob Skinner	8.00	3.25	2.00
175	Bill Virdon	10.00	4.00	2.50
176	Smoky Burgess	40.00	16.00	10.00
177	Elroy Face	17.50	7.00	4.50
178	Bob Friend	10.00	4.00	2.50
179	Vernon Law	10.00	4.00	2.50
180	Harvey Haddix	10.00	4.00	2.50
181	Hal Smith	85.00	35.00	20.00
182	Ed Bouchee	100.00	40.00	25.00
183	Don Zimmer	10.00	4.00	2.50
184	Ron Santo	13.50	5.50	3.50
185	Andre Rogers (Rodgers)	8.00	3.25	2.00
186	Richie Ashburn	30.00	12.00	7.50
187	George Altman	8.00	3.25	2.00
188	Ernie Banks	40.00	16.00	10.00
189	Sam Taylor	30.00	12.00	7.50
190	Don Elston	8.00	3.25	2.00
191	Jerry Kindall	8.00	3.25	2.00
192	Pancho Herrera	8.00	3.25	2.00
193	Tony Taylor	8.00	3.25	2.00
194	Ruben Amaro	8.00	3.25	2.00
195	Don Demeter	55.00	22.50	13.50
196	Bobby Gene Smith	8.00	3.25	2.00
197	Clay Dalrymple	8.00	3.25	2.00
198	Robin Roberts	45.00	18.00	11.00
199	Art Mahaffey	8.00	3.25	2.00
200	John Buzhardt	8.00	3.25	2.50

1963 Post Cereal

Another 200-player, 3-1/2" x 2-1/2" set that, with variations, totals more than 205 cards. Numerous color variations also exist due to the different cereal boxes on which the cards were printed. More than any of the other 1960s Post baseball issues, the set is rife with short-prints and other scarcities which make it more difficult to complete than earlier years' sets. The 1963 Post cards are almost identical to the '63 Jell-O set, which is a slight 1/4" narrower. Cards are blank-backed, with a color player photo, biographies and statistics on the numbered card fronts. No Post logo appears on the '63 cards. The complete set price does not include the scarcer variations. An album to hold the cards was given away at grocery stores in a display featuring Mickey Mantle.

		NM	E	VG
	Complete Set (200):	3,300	1,650	825.00
	Common Player:	5.00	2.00	1.25
1	Vic Power	9.00	3.50	2.00
2	Bernie Allen	6.00	2.50	1.50
3	Zoilo Versalles	7.50	3.00	2.00
4	Rich Rollins	5.00	2.00	1.25
5	Harmon Killebrew	25.00	10.00	6.00
6	Lenny Green	30.00	15.00	7.50
7	Bob Allison	9.00	3.50	2.00
8	Earl Battey	12.50	5.00	3.00
9	Camilo Pascual	15.00	6.00	3.50
10a	Jim Kaat (Light pole in background.)	15.00	6.00	3.50
10b	Jim Kaat (No light pole.)	10.00	4.00	2.50
11	Jack Kralick	7.50	3.00	2.00
12	Bill Skowron	15.00	6.00	3.50
13	Bobby Richardson	15.00	6.00	3.50
14	Cletis Boyer	15.00	6.00	3.50
15	Mickey Mantle	300.00	120.00	75.00
16	Roger Maris	115.00	45.00	30.00
17	Yogi Berra	30.00	12.00	7.50
18	Elston Howard	13.50	5.50	3.50
19	Whitey Ford	15.00	6.00	3.50
20	Ralph Terry	6.00	2.50	1.50
21	John Blanchard	10.00	4.00	2.50
22	Bill Stafford	5.00	2.00	1.25
23	Tom Tresh	9.00	3.50	2.00
24	Steve Bilko	15.00	6.00	3.50
25	Bill Moran	5.00	2.00	1.25
26a	Joe Koppe (1962 Avg. is .277)	17.50	7.00	4.50
26b	Joe Koppe (1962 Avg. is .227)	45.00	22.50	11.25
27	Felix Torres	7.50	3.00	2.00
28a	Leon Wagner (Lifetime Avg. is .278.)	15.00	6.00	3.50
28b	Leon Wagner (Lifetime Avg. is .272.)	25.00	10.00	6.00
29	Albie Pearson	5.00	2.00	1.25
30	Lee Thomas (Photo actually George Thomas.)	90.00	45.00	27.00
31	Bob Rodgers	5.00	2.00	1.25
32	Dean Chance	5.00	2.00	1.25
33	Ken McBride	7.50	3.00	2.00
34	George Thomas (Photo actually Lee Thomas.)	9.00	3.50	2.00
35	Joe Cunningham	5.00	2.00	1.25
36a	Nelson Fox (No bat showing.)	30.00	12.00	7.50
36b	Nelson Fox (Part of bat showing.)	25.00	10.00	6.00
37	Luis Aparicio	15.00	6.00	3.75
38	Al Smith	40.00	20.00	10.00
39	Floyd Robinson	175.00	87.50	52.50
40	Jim Landis	5.00	2.00	1.25
41	Charlie Maxwell	5.00	2.00	1.25
42	Sherman Lollar	5.00	2.00	1.25
43	Early Wynn	9.00	3.50	2.00
44	Juan Pizarro	5.00	2.00	1.25
45	Ray Herbert	5.00	2.00	1.25
46	Norm Cash	25.00	10.00	6.25
47	Steve Boros	5.00	2.00	1.25
48	Dick McAuliffe	35.00	15.00	9.00
49	Bill Bruton	25.00	8.00	5.00
50	Rocky Colavito	25.00	10.00	6.25
51	Al Kaline	25.00	10.00	6.25
52	Dick Brown	5.00	2.00	1.25
53	Jim Bunning	95.00	42.50	21.25
54	Hank Aguirre	5.00	2.00	1.25
55	Frank Lary	5.00	2.00	1.25
56	Don Mossi	7.50	3.00	2.00
57	Jim Gentile	9.00	3.50	2.00
58	Jackie Brandt	7.50	3.00	2.00
59	Brooks Robinson	25.00	10.00	6.00
60	Ron Hansen	5.00	2.00	1.25
61	Jerry Adair	275.00	137.50	82.50
62	John (Boog) Powell	15.00	6.00	3.75
63	Russ Snyder	5.00	2.00	1.25
64	Steve Barber	10.00	4.00	2.50
65	Milt Pappas	5.00	2.00	1.25
66	Robin Roberts	10.00	4.00	2.50
67	Tito Francona	5.00	2.00	1.25
68	Jerry Kindall	12.50	5.00	3.00
69	Woodie Held	5.00	2.00	1.25

70	Bubba Phillips	35.00	15.00	9.00
71	Chuck Essegian	5.00	2.00	1.25
72	Willie Kirkland	5.00	2.00	1.25
73	Al Luplow	5.00	2.00	1.25
74	Ty Cline	5.00	2.00	1.25
75	Dick Donovan	5.00	2.00	1.25
76	John Romano	5.00	2.00	1.25
77	Pete Runnels	6.00	2.50	1.50
78	Ed Bressoud	5.00	2.00	1.25
79	Frank Malzone	10.00	4.00	2.50
80	Carl Yastrzemski	200.00	80.00	50.00
81	Gary Geiger	5.00	2.00	1.25
82	Lou Clinton	5.00	2.00	1.25
83	Earl Wilson	7.50	3.00	2.00
84	Bill Monbouquette	5.00	2.00	1.25
85	Norm Siebern	5.00	2.00	1.25
86	Jerry Lumpe	95.00	40.00	25.00
87	Manny Jimenez	75.00	37.50	18.75
88	Gino Cimoli	9.00	3.50	2.00
89	Ed Charles	5.00	2.00	1.25
90	Ed Rakow	5.00	2.00	1.25
91	Bob Del Greco	5.00	2.00	1.25
92	Haywood Sullivan	5.00	2.00	1.25
93	Chuck Hinton	5.00	2.00	1.25
94	Ken Retzer	12.50	5.00	3.00
95	Harry Bright	5.00	2.00	1.25
96	Bob Johnson	7.50	3.00	2.00
97	Dave Stenhouse	20.00	8.00	5.00
98	Chuck Cottier	25.00	10.00	6.25
99	Tom Cheney	7.50	3.00	2.00
100	Claude Osteen	35.00	15.00	9.00
101	Orlando Cepeda	7.50	3.00	2.00
102	Charley Hiller	7.50	3.00	2.00
103	Jose Pagan	5.00	2.00	1.25
104	Jim Davenport	5.00	2.00	1.25
105	Harvey Kuenn	15.00	6.00	3.50
106	Willie Mays	35.00	17.50	8.75
107	Felipe Alou	7.50	3.00	2.00
108	Tom Haller	75.00	37.50	18.75
109	Juan Marichal	10.00	4.00	2.50
110	Jack Sanford	5.00	2.00	1.25
111	Bill O'Dell	5.00	2.00	1.25
112	Willie McCovey	12.50	5.00	3.00
113	Lee Walls	10.00	4.00	2.50
114	Jim Gilliam	15.00	6.00	3.50
115	Maury Wills	17.50	7.00	4.50
116	Ron Fairly	5.00	2.00	1.25
117	Tommy Davis	5.00	2.00	1.25
118	Duke Snider	25.00	10.00	6.25
119	Willie Davis	200.00	80.00	50.00
120	John Roseboro	5.00	2.00	1.25
121	Sandy Koufax	35.00	17.50	8.75
122	Stan Williams	9.00	3.50	2.00
123	Don Drysdale	20.00	8.00	5.00
124a	Daryl Spencer (No arm showing.)	7.50	3.00	2.00
124b	Daryl Spencer (Part of arm showing.)	15.00	6.00	3.50
125	Gordy Coleman	7.50	3.00	2.00
126	Don Blasingame	5.00	2.00	1.25
127	Leo Cardenas	5.00	2.00	1.25
128	Eddie Kasko	165.00	65.00	40.00
129	Jerry Lynch	35.00	15.00	9.75
130	Vada Pinson	15.00	6.00	3.50
131a	Frank Robinson (No stripes on cap.)	30.00	12.00	7.50
131b	Frank Robinson (Stripes on cap.)	115.00	57.50	34.50
132	John Edwards	15.00	6.00	3.50
133	Joey Jay	5.00	2.00	1.25
134	Bob Purkey	5.00	2.00	1.25
135	Marty Keough	15.00	6.00	3.50
136	Jim O'Toole	5.00	2.00	1.25
137	Dick Stuart	7.50	3.00	2.00
138	Bill Mazeroski	12.50	5.00	3.00
139	Dick Groat	6.00	2.50	1.50
140	Don Hoak	25.00	10.00	6.00
141	Bob Skinner	25.00	10.00	6.25
142	Bill Virdon	40.00	16.00	10.00
143	Roberto Clemente	125.00	62.50	37.50
144	Smoky Burgess	15.00	6.00	3.50
145	Bob Friend	5.00	2.00	1.25
146	Al McBean	5.00	2.00	1.25
147	El Roy Face (Elroy)	20.00	8.00	5.00
148	Joe Adcock	13.50	5.50	3.50
149	Frank Bolling	5.00	2.00	1.25
150	Roy McMillan	7.50	3.00	2.00
151	Eddie Mathews	25.00	10.00	6.00
152	Hank Aaron	65.00	32.00	19.50
153	Del Crandall	25.00	10.00	6.25
154a	Bob Shaw (Third sentence has "In 1959" twice.)	10.00	4.00	2.50
154b	Bob Shaw (Third sentence has "In 1959" once.)	9.00	3.50	2.00
155	Lew Burdette	20.00	8.00	5.00
156	Joe Torre	7.50	3.00	2.00

157	Tony Cloninger	5.00	2.00	1.25
158a	Bill White (Ht. 6')	6.00	2.50	1.50
159	Julian Javier	5.00	2.00	1.25
160	Ken Boyer	7.50	3.00	2.00
161	Julio Gotay	5.00	2.00	1.25
162	Curt Flood	85.00	42.50	21.25
163	Charlie James	9.00	3.50	2.00
164	Gene Oliver	5.00	2.00	1.25
165	Ernie Broglio	15.00	6.00	3.50
166	Bob Gibson	45.00	18.00	11.00
167a	Lindy McDaniel (Asterisk before trade line.)	10.00	4.00	2.50
167b	Lindy McDaniel (No asterisk before trade line.)	12.50	5.00	3.25
168	Ray Washburn	5.00	2.00	1.25
169	Ernie Banks	17.50	7.00	4.50
170	Ron Santo	25.00	10.00	6.25
171	George Altman	7.50	3.00	2.00
172	Billy Williams	235.00	117.50	70.50
173	Andre Rodgers	10.00	4.00	2.50
174	Ken Hubbs	25.00	10.00	6.00
175	Don Landrum	5.00	2.00	1.25
176	Dick Bertell	20.00	8.00	5.00
177	Roy Sievers	7.50	3.00	2.00
178	Tony Taylor	12.50	5.00	3.50
179	John Callison	5.00	2.00	1.25
180	Don Demeter	5.00	2.00	1.25
181	Tony Gonzalez	25.00	10.00	6.25
182	Wes Covington	35.00	15.00	9.00
183	Art Mahaffey	5.00	2.00	1.25
184	Clay Dalrymple	7.50	3.00	2.00
185	Al Spangler	6.00	2.50	1.50
186	Roman Mejias	7.50	3.00	2.00
187	Bob Aspromonte	350.00	175.00	87.50
188	Norm Larker	25.00	10.00	6.00
189	Johnny Temple	7.50	3.00	2.00
190	Carl Warwick	15.00	6.00	3.50
191	Bob Lillis	9.00	3.50	2.00
192	Dick Farrell	5.00	2.00	1.25
193	Gil Hodges	35.00	15.00	9.00
194	Marv Throneberry	7.50	3.00	2.00
195	Charlie Neal	30.00	12.00	7.50
196	Frank Thomas	175.00	87.50	43.75
197	Richie Ashburn	35.00	15.00	9.00
198	Felix Mantilla	10.00	4.00	2.50
199	Rod Kanehl	45.00	22.50	11.25
200	Roger Craig	20.00	8.00	5.00

1963 Post/Jell-O Album

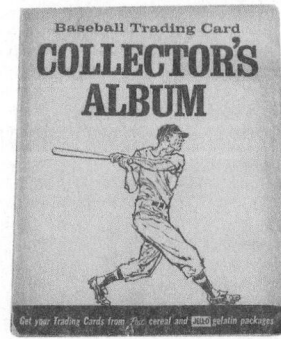

The baseball history and other printed matter in this 26-page 8-1/2" x 11" album seems to point to 1963 as the issue date, though 1962 would not be impossible. Each major league team has a page on which the box-back cards from Post cereals and Jell-O could be pasted. The front cover is printed in red-and-white while the interior pages are in black-and-white.

	NM	E	VG
Post/Jell-O Album	90.00	45.00	25.00

1978 Post Cereal Steve Garvey Baseball Tips

These 7-1/8" x 2-5/8" cut-out panels bordered in red "baseball" stitching were printed on the backs of 15-oz. (#1-6) and 20-oz. (#7-12) packages of Post Raisin Brand cereal. The panels have a green background with black-and-white artwork of a generic player illustrating the tip and a color portrait of Garvey.

		NM	E	VG
Complete Set (12):		30.00	15.00	9.00
Common Panel:		3.00	1.50	.90
1	The Batting Stance	3.00	1.50	.90
2	Bunting	3.00	1.50	.90
3	Rounding First Base	3.00	1.50	.90
4	The Grip in Throwing	3.00	1.50	.90
5	Fielding a Pop-Up	3.00	1.50	.90
6	Proper Fielding Stances	3.00	1.50	.90
7	On-Deck Observation	3.00	1.50	.90
8	Sliding	3.00	1.50	.90
9	Hitting to the Opposite Field	3.00	1.50	.90
10	Throwing From the Outfield	3.00	1.50	.90
11	Mental Preparation for Each Play	3.00	1.50	.90
12	Total Conditioning	3.00	1.50	.90

1978 Post-Intelligencer 1969 Pilot Profiles

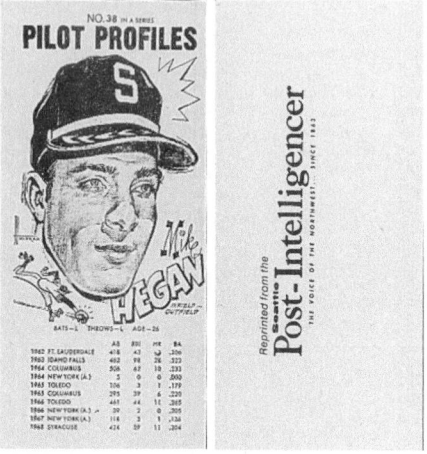

This series of cards of the one-year American League team states on its back they are reprinted from the Seattle Post-Intelligencer newspaper. The 2-3/8" x 5" cards are printed in black-and-white on semi-gloss cardboard. Fronts feature a pencil caricature of the player and include major and minor league stats. A card number is at top. Backs have the newspaper's ad. The cards were a collectors' issue produced by long-time minor league card maker Frank Caruso, with the paper's permission. The cartoons originally ran in a 3" x 6-3/8" format within the pages of the newspaper and are themselves highly collectible, with values about 2X-3X those of the reprints listed here. Reprint sets were originally sold for $6.

		NM	E	VG
Complete Set (39):		100.00	50.00	30.00
Common Player:		4.00	3.00	1.50
1	Don Mincher	4.00	3.00	1.50
2	Tommy Harper	5.00	2.50	1.50
3	Ray Oyler	4.00	3.00	1.50
4	Jerry McNertney	4.00	3.00	1.50
5	Not issued	4.00	3.00	1.50
6	Tommy Davis	5.00	2.50	1.50
7	Gary Bell	4.00	3.00	1.50
8	Chico Salmon	4.00	3.00	1.50
9	Jack Aker	4.00	3.00	1.50
10	Rich Rollins	4.00	3.00	1.50
11	Diego Segui	4.00	3.00	1.50
12	Steve Barber	5.00	2.50	1.50
13	Wayne Comer	4.00	3.00	1.50
14	John Kennedy	4.00	3.00	1.50
15	Buzz Stephen	4.00	3.00	1.50
16	Jim Gosger	4.00	3.00	1.50
17	Mike Ferraro	4.00	3.00	1.50
18	Marty Pattin	4.00	3.00	1.50
19	Gerry Schoen	4.00	3.00	1.50
20	Steve Hovely	4.00	3.00	1.50
21	Frank Crosetti	5.00	2.50	1.50
22	Charles Bates	4.00	3.00	1.50
23	Jose Vidal	4.00	3.00	1.50
24	Bob Richmond	4.00	3.00	1.50
25	Lou Piniella	6.00	3.00	1.75
26	John Miklos	4.00	3.00	1.50
27	John Morris	4.00	3.00	1.50
28	Larry Haney	4.00	3.00	1.50
29	Mike Marshall	5.00	2.50	1.50
30	Marv Staehle	4.00	3.00	1.50
31	Gus Gil	4.00	3.00	1.50
32	Sal Maglie	5.00	2.50	1.50
33	Ron Plaza	4.00	3.00	1.50
34	Ed O'Brien	4.00	3.00	1.50
35	Jim Bouton	6.00	3.00	1.75
36	Bill Stafford	4.00	3.00	1.50
37	Darrell Brandon	4.00	3.00	1.50
38	Mike Hegan	4.00	3.00	1.50
39	Dick Baney	4.00	3.00	1.50

1910 Doc Powers Day Postcard

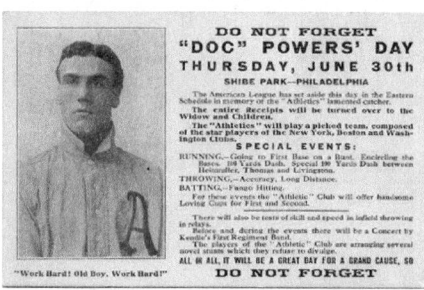

To announce to fans the forthcoming "'Doc' Powers' Day" benefit game, the Philadelphia A's produced this standard-sized (about 5-1/2" x 3-1/2") black-and-white postcard. Front has a photo of the late A's catcher and information about the special events to be held June 30. On back is a message over the facsimile autograph of Connie Mack asking fans to remember the widow and children of their fallen star.

	NM	E	VG
Doc Powers	750.00	375.00	225.00

1975 Praeger Publishers Ty Cobb

 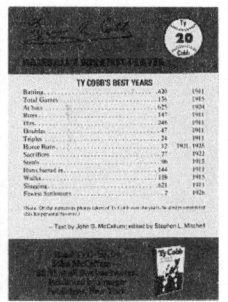

This set was produced by Washington state collector Stephen Mitchell in conjunction with Praeger Publishers of New York to promote the book "Ty Cobb" by John McCallum. Slightly larger than the current 2-1/2" x 3-1/2" standard, the cards featured black-and-white photos on front surrounded by a woodgrain-effect frame and with a plaque at bottom bearing the card title. Backs have an excerpt from the book, an ad for the book and a facsimile autograph. Cards are numbered in a baseball at upper-right. Sets originally sold for $3.25.

		NM	E	VG
Complete Set (20):		25.00	12.50	7.50
Common Card:		2.00	1.00	.60
1	Ty Breaks In	3.00	1.50	.90
2	Four Inches of the Plate	2.00	1.00	.60
3	Slashing into Third	2.00	1.00	.60
4	Inking Another Contract	2.00	1.00	.60
5	Captain Tyrus R. Cobb	2.00	1.00	.60
6	Ty with "The Big Train" (With Walter Johnson.)	4.00	2.00	1.25
7	The End of an Era (With Babe Ruth.)	6.00	3.00	1.75
8	All-Time Centerfielder	2.00	1.00	.60
9	Ty Could "Walk 'em down"	2.00	1.00	.60
10	Menacing Batsman	2.00	1.00	.60
11	With Brother Paul	2.00	1.00	.60
12	Thomas Edison, Cobb Fan	3.00	1.50	.90
13	Ty Tangles with Muggsy McGraw	2.50	1.25	.70
14	Author McCallum with Cy Young	2.00	1.00	.60
15	Speaker - DiMaggio - Cobb	5.00	2.50	1.50
16	Ted Gets a Lesson (With Ted Williams.)	5.00	2.50	1.50
17	Five for Fivel	2.00	1.00	.60
18	"I have but one regret ..."	2.00	1.00	.60
19	Excellence: The Cobb Standard	2.00	1.00	.60
20	His Favorite Photo	3.00	1.50	.90

1954 Preferred Products Milwaukee Braves

Sold as a 12-piece set in an envelope marked "Braves Team Autographed Portraits," this portfolio was one of several issued in the team's early years in Milwaukee. The artwork is apparently by Scott Douglas, whose copyright appears on the outer envelope. The same pictures can be found on Preferred Product felt patches and t-shirts. These 8" x 10" portraits are printed in sepia on cream-colored heavy textured paper and feature facsimile autographs. Backs are blank. The unnumbered portraits are checklisted here alphabetically.

		NM	E	VG
Complete Set (12):		300.00	150.00	90.00
Common Player:		25.00	12.50	7.50
(1)	Joe Adcock	25.00	12.50	7.50
(2)	Bill Bruton	25.00	12.50	7.50
(3)	Bob Buhl	25.00	12.50	7.50
(4)	Lew Burdette	25.00	12.50	7.50
(5)	Del Crandall	25.00	12.50	7.50
(6)	Johnny Logan	25.00	12.50	7.50
(7)	Ed Mathews	40.00	20.00	12.00
(8)	Danny O'Connell	25.00	12.50	7.50
(9)	Andy Pafko	25.00	12.50	7.50
(10)	Jim Pendleton	25.00	12.50	7.50
(11)	Warren Spahn	40.00	20.00	12.00
(12)	Bob Thomson	25.00	12.50	7.50

1954 Preferred Products Milwaukee Braves Patches

While they are not so identified, the use of the same portraits and facsimile autographs found on the company's player pictures pinpoint this as a Preferred Products issue, as does a paper tag enclosed in the cellophane wrapper in which the patch was sold. The patches are of heavy felt, with blue or sepia pictures and red "stitching" on the baseball background. At 4-7/8" in diameter, they were intended to be sewn to jackets, etc. While only a handful of players have been confirmed to date, it is possible, even likely, that all 12 of the players from the picture set were also issued in this format.

		NM	E	VG
Common Player:		175.00	85.00	50.00
(1)	Joe Adcock	175.00	85.00	50.00
(2)	Bill Bruton	175.00	85.00	50.00
(2)	Bob Buhl	175.00	85.00	50.00
(4)	Lew Burdette	175.00	85.00	50.00
(5)	Del Crandall	175.00	85.00	50.00
(6)	Johnny Logan	175.00	85.00	50.00
(7)	Eddie Mathews	225.00	112.50	67.50
(8)	Danny O'Connell	175.00	85.00	50.00
(9)	Andy Pafko	175.00	85.00	50.00
(11)	Warren Spahn	225.00	112.50	67.50

1957-60 Preferred Products Milwaukee Braves

Similar in format to the company's 1954 issue, these 8" x 10" portraits are printed in sepia on cream-colored heavy textured paper with player names printed beneath. Backs are blank. The unnumbered portraits are checklisted here alphabetically, but the list may not be complete.

CARL SAWATSKI

	NM	E	VG
Common Player:	25.00	12.50	7.50
(1) Hank Aaron	100.00	50.00	30.00
(2) Joe Adcock	25.00	12.50	7.50
(3) Bill Bruton	25.00	12.50	7.50
(4) Bob Buhl	25.00	12.50	7.50
(5) Lew Burdette	25.00	12.50	7.50
(6) Wes Covington	25.00	12.50	7.50
(7) Johnny Logan	25.00	12.50	7.50
(8) Johnny Logan	25.00	12.50	7.50
(9) Carl Sawatski	25.00	12.50	7.50
(10) Red Schoendienst	35.00	17.50	10.50
(11) Red Schoendienst	50.00	25.00	15.00
(12) Frank Torre	25.00	12.50	7.50

1950 Prest-O-lite

The attributed date of issue is approximate for this multi-sport promotional postcard issue. Besides the two baseball players, football stars Doak Walker and Leon Hart also exist. The black-and-white, approximately 3-1/2" x 5-1/2" cards on front have a borderless action pose with a salutation and facsimile autograph. The postcard-style divided back has a pre-printed message over the player's facsimile autograph, asking the recipient to view ads for the battery manufacturer in various magazines.

	NM	E	VG
Tommy Henrich	200.00	100.00	60.00
Ted Williams	400.00	200.00	120.00

1914 Pritchard Publishing Giants/ Yankees Stamps

These colorful large-format (about 1-7/8" x 2-5/8") stamps are copyrighted 1914 by Pritchard Publishing Co., New York. All players are N.Y. Giants or Yankees. A similar issue of Yale baseball players is listed in the minor league section. The unnumbered stamps are listed alphabetically by team.

	NM	E	VG
Common Player:	200.00	100.00	60.00
N.Y. GIANTS			
(1) Bob Bescher	200.00	100.00	60.00
(2) George Burns	200.00	100.00	60.00

		NM	E	VG
(3)	Josh Devore	200.00	100.00	60.00
(4)	Larry Doyle	200.00	100.00	60.00
(5)	Art Fletcher	200.00	100.00	60.00
(6)	Christy Mathewson	900.00	450.00	270.00
(7)	Fred Merkle	200.00	100.00	60.00
(8)	Chief Meyers	200.00	100.00	60.00
(9)	Red Murray	200.00	100.00	60.00
(10)	Fred Snodgrass	200.00	100.00	60.00
	N.Y. YANKEES			
(1)	Ray Caldwell	200.00	100.00	60.00
(2)	Les Channell	200.00	100.00	60.00
(3)	Roy Hartzell	200.00	100.00	60.00
(4)	Bill Holden	200.00	100.00	60.00
(5)	Fritz Maisel	200.00	100.00	60.00
(6)	Roger Peckinpaugh	200.00	100.00	60.00
(7)	Jeff Sweeney	200.00	100.00	60.00
(8)	Jimmy Walsh	200.00	100.00	60.00
(9)	Harry Williams	200.00	100.00	60.00

1956 Prize Frankies Cleveland Indians

VIC WERTZ - 10

ANY PERSON who collects a complete set of these pictures is entitled to TWO BOX SEATS for a future Indian game. One FREE picture is in each package of PRIZE BRAND FRANKIES. There are 24 different pictures. A complete set is 24 different pictures.

Complete sets should be sent to John Liber & Co., R. D. #3, Alliance, Ohio. Your tickets and this card will be mailed to you.

Though the back of the cards says 24 Indians' cards were issued, only one player has ever been seen - and precious few of him. The 2-1/4" x 3-3/8" cards have a black-and-white photo on front with the player's name and number in black in the white border at bottom. Backs have an Indian logo and instructions to redeem complete sets of the cards for a pair of box seats. It is unlikely this alone accounts for the scarcity of the cards. More likely this card was made as a prototype for a promotion that never materialized.

		NM	E	VG
10	Vic Wertz	600.00	300.00	180.00

1924 Proctor's Theatre Babe Ruth

COMPLIMENTS OF Mr. F. F. Proctor TO BABE RUTH'S MANY MT. VERNON FRIENDS

APPEARING AT PROCTOR'S MOUNT VERNON Nov. 3rd-4th-5th

This 1-5/8" x 2-7/8" black-and-white card was issued to promote a vaudeville appearance by Babe Ruth in upstate New York during November 1924. The front has a photo with a facsimile autograph inscribed, "To My Mount Vernon Admirers." Back has details of his appearance.

	NM	E	VG
Babe Ruth	16,000	8,000	4,750

1946-47 Propagandas Montiel Los Reyes del Deporte

The 180 athletes in this issue of "Sporting Kings" cards are featured in a couple of different styles. Most cards from #1-101 have only the athlete's photo on front, surrounded by a yellow or orange border. Most cards #100-180 also have the card number and player ID on front, with a chest-to-cap photo set a colored frame. All are roughly 2-1/8" x 3-1/8". Backs have biographical data, the issuer's name and, sometimes, an ad for a Cuban novelty store or radio program. Most examples in the hobby today were once pasted in the colorful album accompanying the issue and it is rare to find cards in

better than VG condition. The set opens with a run of boxers, then a group of Cuban baseball stars of the past and present, former big league greats and contemporary major leaguers, plus a few wrestlers. Cards #100-180 (except 101) feature players from the Florida International League, a Class B circuit within Organized Baseball with teams in Havana, Miami, Miami Beach, Lakeland and Tampa included. Curiously, the West Palm Beach team is not represented.

Propagandas MONTIEL presenta
LOS REYES DEL DEPORTE
29
ADOLFO LUQUE
(Papá Montero)

Nació en la Habana, el 4 de Agosto de 1890. Bateá y tira a la derecha. Debutó en las Grandes Ligas en 1914. En 1915 las zo para el Toronto y en 1916, 1917 y parte de 1918 estuvo en el Louisville. A fines de 1918 pasó al Cincinnati. En 1922 al New York Gigantes. En las Grandes Ligas ganó 194 juegos y perdió 179. En 1923 fue Champion Pitcher de la Liga Nacional. Participó en las Series Mundiales de 1919 y 1933. Recientemente firmó con su muy querido Almendares.

		NM	E	VG
Complete Set (180):		20,000	8,800	4,000
Common Baseball Player:		45.00	20.00	9.00
Album:		300.00	135.00	60.00
1	John L. Sullivan (Boxer)	135.00	60.00	27.50
2	James J. Corbett (Boxer)	85.00	37.50	17.50
3	Bob Fitzsimmons (Boxer)	70.00	30.00	15.00
4	James J. Jeffries (Boxer)	85.00	37.50	17.50
5	Tommy Burns (Boxer)	70.00	30.00	15.00
6	Jack Johnson (Boxer)	90.00	40.00	18.00
7	Jess Willard (Boxer)	75.00	35.00	15.00
8	Jack Dempsey (Boxer)	135.00	60.00	27.50
9	Gene Tunney (Boxer)	75.00	35.00	15.00
10	Max Schmeling (Boxer)	75.00	35.00	15.00
11	Jack Sharkey (Boxer)	70.00	30.00	15.00
12	Primo Carnera (Boxer)	70.00	30.00	15.00
13	Max Baer (Boxer)	70.00	30.00	15.00
14	James J. Braddock (Boxer)	70.00	30.00	15.00
15	Joe Louis (Boxer)	135.00	60.00	27.50
16	Georges Carpentier (Boxer)	70.00	30.00	15.00
17	Tommy Loughran (Boxer)	70.00	30.00	15.00
18	Tony Zale (Boxer)	70.00	30.00	15.00
19	Johnny Dundee (Boxer)	55.00	25.00	10.00
20	Billy Conn (Boxer)	70.00	30.00	15.00
21	Holman Williams (Boxer)	55.00	25.00	10.00
22	Kid Tuncro (Tunero) (Boxer)	55.00	25.00	10.00
23	Lazaro Salazar	300.00	135.00	60.00
24	Napoleon Reyes	120.00	55.00	25.00
25	Roberto Estalella	110.00	50.00	22.50
26	Juan Oliva (Boxer)	55.00	25.00	10.00
27	Gilberto Torres	75.00	35.00	15.00
28	Heberto Blanco	75.00	35.00	15.00
29	Adolfo Luque	375.00	175.00	75.00
30	Luis Galvani (Boxer)	55.00	25.00	10.00
31	Miguel Angel Gonzalez	195.00	90.00	40.00
32	Chuck Klein	110.00	50.00	22.50
33	Joe Legon (Boxer)	55.00	25.00	10.00
34	Carlos Blanco	75.00	35.00	15.00
35	Santos Amaro	225.00	100.00	45.00
36	Kid Chocolate (Boxer)	85.00	37.50	17.50
37	Henry Armstrong (Boxer)	55.00	25.00	10.00
38	Silvio Garcia	300.00	135.00	60.00
39	Martin Dihigo	3,750	1,850	1,100
40	Fermin Guerra	120.00	55.00	25.00
41	Babe Ruth	1,250	560.00	250.00
42	Ty Cobb	1,000	500.00	300.00
43	Alejandro Crespo	75.00	35.00	15.00
44	Ted Williams	2,000	1,000	600.00
45	Jose Maria Fernandez	85.00	37.50	17.50
46	Dom DiMaggio	110.00	50.00	22.50
47	Julio Rojo	75.00	35.00	15.00
48	Armando Marsans	110.00	50.00	22.50
49	Dick Sisler	75.00	35.00	15.00
50	Antonio Rodriguez	75.00	35.00	15.00
51	Joscito Rodriguez	75.00	35.00	15.00
52	Antonio Ordenana	80.00	35.00	15.00
53	Armandito Pi (Boxer)	55.00	25.00	10.00
54	Paul Derringer	75.00	35.00	15.00
55	Bob Feller	185.00	85.00	37.50
56a	Bill Dickey (Photo is Gabby Hartnett.) (Light cap.))	150.00	65.00	30.00
56b	Bill Dickey (Corrected photo.) (Dark cap.))	225.00	100.00	45.00
57	Lou Gehrig	750.00	335.00	150.00
58	Joe DiMaggio	2,250	1,125	675.00
59	Hank Greenberg	165.00	75.00	35.00
60	Red Ruffing	110.00	50.00	22.50

		NM	E	VG
61	Tex Hughson	75.00	35.00	15.00
62	Bucky Walters	75.00	35.00	15.00
63	Stanley Hack	75.00	35.00	15.00
64	Stanley Musial	1,900	950.00	575.00
65	Melvin Ott	135.00	60.00	27.50
66	Dutch Leonard	75.00	35.00	15.00
67	Frank Overmire	75.00	35.00	15.00
68	Mort Cooper	75.00	35.00	15.00
69	Edward Miller	75.00	35.00	15.00
70	Jimmie Foxx	165.00	75.00	35.00
71	Joseph Cronin	110.00	50.00	22.50
72	James Vernon	75.00	35.00	15.00
73	Carl Hubbell	165.00	75.00	35.00
74	Andrew Pafko	75.00	35.00	15.00
75	David Ferris	75.00	35.00	15.00
76	John Mize	110.00	50.00	22.50
77	Spud Chandler	75.00	35.00	15.00
78	Joseph Medwick	110.00	50.00	22.50
79	Christy Mathewson	450.00	200.00	90.00
80	Nelson Potter	75.00	35.00	15.00
81	James Tabor	75.00	35.00	15.00
82	Martin Marion	75.00	35.00	15.00
83	Rip Sewell	75.00	35.00	15.00
84	Philip Cavaretta (Cavarretta)	75.00	35.00	15.00
85	Al Lopez	110.00	50.00	22.50
86	Rudy York	75.00	35.00	15.00
87	Walter Masterson	75.00	35.00	15.00
88	Roger Wolff	75.00	35.00	15.00
89	Jacob Early	75.00	35.00	15.00
90	Oswald Bluege	75.00	35.00	15.00
91	Zoco Godoy (Wrestler)	45.00	20.00	9.00
92	John Kelly Lewis	75.00	35.00	15.00
93	Well Stewart (Wrestler)	45.00	20.00	9.00
94	Bruce Campbell	75.00	35.00	15.00
95	Sherrod Robertson	75.00	35.00	15.00
96	Rose Evans (Wrestler)	45.00	20.00	9.00
97	Maurice "El Angel" Tillet (Wrestler)	45.00	20.00	9.00
98	Nicholas Altrock	75.00	35.00	15.00
99	Helen Willis (Tennis)	70.00	30.00	15.00
100	Borrest Smith	45.00	20.00	9.00
101	Merito Acosta	80.00	35.00	15.00
102	Oscar Rodriguez	45.00	20.00	9.00
103	Octavio Rubert	45.00	20.00	9.00
104	Antonio Lorenzo	45.00	20.00	9.00
105	Agustin del Toro	45.00	20.00	9.00
106	Hector Arago	45.00	20.00	9.00
107	Agustin de la Ville	45.00	20.00	9.00
108	Valeriano (Lilo) Fano	45.00	20.00	9.00
109	Orlando Moreno	45.00	20.00	9.00
110	"Bicho" Dunabeitia	45.00	20.00	9.00
111	Rafael Rivas	45.00	20.00	9.00
112	Jose Traspuestro	45.00	20.00	9.00
113	Mario Diaz	45.00	20.00	9.00
114	Armando Valdes	45.00	20.00	9.00
115	Alberto Matos	45.00	20.00	9.00
116	Humberto Baez	45.00	20.00	9.00
117	Orlando (Tango) Suarez	45.00	20.00	9.00
118	Manuel (Chino) Hidalgo	45.00	20.00	9.00
119	Fernando Rodriguez	45.00	20.00	9.00
120	Jose Cendan	45.00	20.00	9.00
121	Francisco Gallardo	45.00	20.00	9.00
122	Orlando Mejido	45.00	20.00	9.00
123	Julio (Jiqui) Moreno	45.00	20.00	9.00
124	Efrain Vinajcras	45.00	20.00	9.00
125	Luis Suarez	45.00	20.00	9.00
126	Oscar del Calvo	45.00	20.00	9.00
127	Julio Gomez	45.00	20.00	9.00
128	Ernesto Morillas	45.00	20.00	9.00
129	Leonardo Goicochea	45.00	20.00	9.00
130	Max Rosenfeld	300.00	135.00	60.00
131	Oscar Garmendia	45.00	20.00	9.00
132	Fernando Solis	45.00	20.00	9.00
133	Oliverio Ortiz	55.00	25.00	10.00
134	Osmaro Blanco	45.00	20.00	9.00
135	Oral Ratliff	45.00	20.00	9.00
136	Deo Grose	45.00	20.00	9.00
137	Homer Daugherty	45.00	20.00	9.00
138	Frank Matthews	45.00	20.00	9.00
139	Roger LaFrance	45.00	20.00	9.00
140	Harold Cowan	45.00	20.00	9.00
141	Richard Henton	45.00	20.00	9.00
142	Banks McDowell	45.00	20.00	9.00
143	Harold Graham	45.00	20.00	9.00
144	Jack Sweeting	45.00	20.00	9.00
145	Bill Wixted	45.00	20.00	9.00
146	Larry Graham	45.00	20.00	9.00
147	Ralph Brown	45.00	20.00	9.00
148	Felipe Jimenez	45.00	20.00	9.00
149	John Ippolito	45.00	20.00	9.00
150	Joe Benito	45.00	20.00	9.00
151	Bernardo Fernandez	45.00	20.00	9.00
152	Buckey Winkler	45.00	20.00	9.00
153	Carl Armstrong	45.00	20.00	9.00
154	Jack Bearden	45.00	20.00	9.00
155	George Bucci	45.00	20.00	9.00
156	John Pere (Pare)	45.00	20.00	9.00

		NM	E	VG
157	Mickey O'Brien	45.00	20.00	9.00
158	Lamar Murphy	45.00	20.00	9.00
159	Devon Chaptman (Choptman)	45.00	20.00	9.00
160	Hal Johnson	45.00	20.00	9.00
161	"Bitsy" Mott	45.00	20.00	9.00
162	Charles Cuellar	45.00	20.00	9.00
163	Chester Covington	45.00	20.00	9.00
164	Howard Ermisch	45.00	20.00	9.00
165	Bill Lewis	45.00	20.00	9.00
166	Roy Knepper	45.00	20.00	9.00
167	Bull Enos	45.00	20.00	9.00
168	Joe Wilder	45.00	20.00	9.00
169	Jake Baker	45.00	20.00	9.00
170	Joe Bodner	45.00	20.00	9.00
171	Jackie Myer	45.00	20.00	9.00
172	Mel Fisher	45.00	20.00	9.00
173	Larry Baldwin	45.00	20.00	9.00
174	Richard Farkas	45.00	20.00	9.00
175	Alston McGahgin	45.00	20.00	9.00
176	Ray Weiss	45.00	20.00	9.00
177	Paul Waner	400.00	180.00	80.00
178	Frank Miller	45.00	20.00	9.00
179	John Sabatie	45.00	20.00	9.00
180	John Maire	45.00	20.00	9.00

1966 Pro's Pizza Chicago Cubs

These black-and-white player cards were printed on boxes in which individual-serving pizzas were sold, reportedly only at Wrigley Field. The panel measures 6" x 6" and has a black-and-white player photo at left, with his name in a white strip at bottom. At right are drawn sports action scenes and toward the top is a black box with "the pro's PIZZA" in white. The backs are blank. The unnumbered pieces are listed here alphabetically. The example pictured was autographed by the player, no facsimile signature was printed originally.

		NM	E	VG
	Complete Set (15):	3,250	1,600	975.00
	Common Player:	160.00	80.00	50.00
(1)	Ted Abernathy	160.00	80.00	50.00
(2)	Joe Amalfitano	160.00	80.00	50.00
(3)	George Altman	160.00	80.00	50.00
(4)	Ernie Banks	650.00	325.00	200.00
(5)	Ernie Broglio	160.00	80.00	50.00
(6)	Billy Connors	160.00	80.00	50.00
(7)	Dick Ellsworth	160.00	80.00	50.00
(8)	Bill Faul	160.00	80.00	50.00
(9)	Bill Hoeft	160.00	80.00	50.00
(10)	Ken Holtzman	160.00	80.00	50.00
(11)	Randy Hundley	160.00	80.00	50.00
(12)	Ferguson Jenkins	325.00	160.00	100.00
(13)	Chris Krug	160.00	80.00	50.00
(14)	Ron Santo	245.00	120.00	75.00
(15)	Carl Warwick	160.00	80.00	50.00
(16)	Billy Williams	400.00	200.00	120.00

1967 Pro's Pizza - B & W

For a second year, Chicago players - Cubs and White Sox - were featured on boxes of individual-serving pizza reportedly sold only at the ballparks. The panel on which the player photos (black-and-white) are printed measures 4-3/4" x 5-3/4" and is similar in design to the 1966 issue, except there is a vertical perforation allowing most of the player photo to be torn away in a 3-1/16" x 5-3/4" size. Cards are unnumbered and listed here alphabetically. Values are for unseparated panels. Those separated at the perforation line

are worth 60-75%.

		NM	E	VG
	Complete Set (10):	1,500	750.00	450.00
	Common Player:	125.00	65.00	35.00
(1)	Ernie Banks	425.00	225.00	130.00
(2)	Glenn Beckert	125.00	65.00	35.00
(3)	Byron Browne	125.00	65.00	35.00
(4)	Don Buford	125.00	65.00	35.00
(5)	Joel Horlen	125.00	65.00	35.00
(6)	Randy Hundley	125.00	65.00	35.00
(7)	Don Kessinger	125.00	65.00	35.00
(8)	Gary Peters	125.00	65.00	35.00
(9)	Ron Santo	175.00	85.00	50.00
(10)	Billy Williams	200.00	100.00	60.00

1967 Pro's Pizza - Color

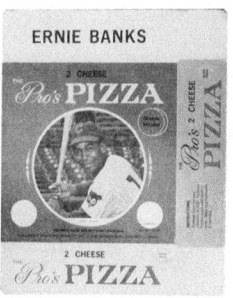

Only Chicago Cubs are included in this set of cards printed on the top of individual serving pizza boxes, reportedly sold only at Wrigley Field. The color player poses are printed in a 4-3/4" diameter circle on top of the box, with the player's name in a white panel at bottom. The player's name was also printed in large black letters on one side of the box. Values shown here for the unnumbered cards are for the complete box top. A similar issue of Chicago Bears players was also produced.

		NM	E	VG
	Complete Set (12):	5,000	2,500	1,500
	Common Player:	400.00	200.00	120.00
(1)	Joe Amalfitano	400.00	200.00	120.00
(2)	Ernie Banks	1,500	750.00	450.00
(3)	Glenn Beckert	400.00	200.00	120.00
(4)	John Boccabella	400.00	200.00	120.00
(5)	Bill Hands	400.00	200.00	120.00
(6)	Ken Holtzman	400.00	200.00	120.00
(7)	Randy Hundley	400.00	200.00	120.00
(8)	Ferguson Jenkins	675.00	335.00	200.00
(9)	Don Kessinger	400.00	200.00	120.00
(10)	Adolfo Phillips	400.00	200.00	120.00
(11)	Ron Santo	750.00	375.00	225.00
(12)	Billy Williams	850.00	425.00	255.00

1972 Pro Star Promotions

This set of postcard-sized (3-1/2" x 5-1/2") color photocards features players from 14 major league teams, with a heavy emphasis on Montreal Expos. Uniforms in the photos have had team logos removed. Cards have a facsimile autograph on front. In the white border at bottom is the player name, league, copyright notice and "Printed in Canada." The unnumbered cards are checklisted here in alphabetical order.

		NM	E	VG
	Complete Set (40):	275.00	135.00	85.00
	Common Player:	3.00	1.50	.90
(1)	Hank Aaron	17.50	8.75	5.25
(2)	Bob Bailey	3.00	1.50	.90
(3)	Johnny Bench	12.50	6.25	3.75
(4)	Vida Blue	3.00	1.50	.90
(5)	John Boccabella	3.00	1.50	.90

		NM	E	VG
(6)	Roberto Clemente	20.00	10.00	6.00
(7)	Boots Day	3.00	1.50	.90
(8)	Jim Fairey	3.00	1.50	.90
(9)	Tim Foli	3.00	1.50	.90
(10)	Ron Hunt	3.00	1.50	.90
(11)	Catfish Hunter	7.50	3.75	2.25
(12)	Reggie Jackson	15.00	7.50	4.50
(13)	Fergy Jenkins	10.00	5.00	3.00
(14)	Mike Jorgensen	3.00	1.50	.90
(15)	Al Kaline	12.50	6.25	3.75
(16)	Harmon Killebrew	12.50	6.25	3.75
(17)	Mickey Lolich	3.00	1.50	.90
(18)	Juan Marichal	7.50	3.75	2.25
(19)	Willie Mays	17.50	8.75	5.25
(20)	Willie McCovey	10.00	5.00	3.00
(21)	Ernie McAnally	3.00	1.50	.90
(22)	Dave McNally	3.00	1.50	.90
(23)	Bill Melton	3.00	1.50	.90
(24)	Carl Morton	3.00	1.50	.90
(25)	Bobby Murcer	3.00	1.50	.90
(26)	Fritz Peterson	3.00	1.50	.90
(27)	Boog Powell	6.00	3.00	1.75
(28)	Steve Renko	3.00	1.50	.90
(29)	Merv Rettenmund	3.00	1.50	.90
(30)	Brooks Robinson	12.50	6.25	3.75
(31)	Frank Robinson	12.50	6.25	3.75
(32)	Pete Rose	17.50	8.75	5.25
(33)	Tom Seaver	12.50	6.25	3.75
(34)	Ken Singleton	3.00	1.50	.90
(35)	Willie Stargell	10.00	5.00	3.00
(36)	Bill Stoneman	3.00	1.50	.90
(37)	Joe Torre	6.00	3.00	1.75
(38)	Checklist - American League	1.50	.70	.45
(39)	Checklist - National League	1.50	.70	.45
(40)	Checklist - Montreal Expos	1.50	.70	.45

1971 Pro Stars Publications Montreal Expos

Posed action photos of the Expos are featured on this postcard-size (3-1/2" x 5-1/2") issue. The color photos are surrounded by a white border and have a facsimile autograph. Printed in the bottom border is, "Copyright Pro Stars Publications 1971 Printed in Canada." Backs are blank. The unnumbered cards are checklisted here in alphabetical order.

		NM	E	VG
Complete Set (28):		175.00	85.00	50.00
Common Player:		6.00	3.00	1.80
(1)	Bob Bailey	6.00	3.00	1.80
(2)	John Bateman	6.00	3.00	1.80
(3)	John Boccabella	6.00	3.00	1.80
(4)	Ron Brand	6.00	3.00	1.80
(5)	Boots Day	6.00	3.00	1.80
(6)	Jim Fairey	6.00	3.00	1.80
(7)	Ron Fairly	7.50	3.75	2.25
(8)	Jim Gosger	6.00	3.00	1.80
(9)	Don Hahn	6.00	3.00	1.80
(10)	Ron Hunt	6.00	3.00	1.80
(11)	Mack Jones	6.00	3.00	1.80
(12)	Coco Laboy	6.00	3.00	1.80
(13)	Mike Marshall	7.50	3.75	2.25
(14)	Clyde Mashore	6.00	3.00	1.80
(15)	Gene Mauch	7.50	3.75	2.25
(16)	Dan McGinn	6.00	3.00	1.80
(17)	Carl Morton	6.00	3.00	1.80
(18)	John O'Donoghue	6.00	3.00	1.80
(19)	Adolfo Phillips	6.00	3.00	1.80
(20)	Claude Raymond	6.00	3.00	1.80
(21)	Howie Reed	6.00	3.00	1.80
(22)	Steve Renko	6.00	3.00	1.80
(23)	Rusty Staub	10.00	5.00	3.00
(24)	Bill Stoneman	6.00	3.00	1.80
(25)	John Strohmayer	6.00	3.00	1.80
(26)	Gary Sutherland	6.00	3.00	1.80
(27)	Mike Wegener	6.00	3.00	1.80
(28)	Bobby Wine	6.00	3.00	1.80

1950s Publix Markets

It is not known whether this is a one-card set or whether similar cards exist for other players. Without information on other subjects it is impossible to date the issue more precisely. The black-and-white card is printed on thin, semi-gloss cardboard in 4" x 4-3/4" format. The front has a facsimile autograph. The back has a message to Little Leaguers from the Red Sox pitcher and a list of sponsors, along with the Publix logo.

	NM	E	VG
Tom Brewer	150.00	75.00	45.00

1972 Puerto Rican League Stickers

Often mistakenly called "minor league" cards, this issue consists of 231 ungummed stickers pertinent to the Puerto Rican winter baseball league. A colorful album was available in which to paste the stickers, though obviously stickers that have evidence of glue or torn paper have little collector value. Besides individual player photos, there are stickers of "old-timers" and groups of stickers which make up composite photos of all-star teams and of the island's god of baseball, Roberto Clemente. Team emblem stickers are also included. Many big league stars who were either beginning or ending their pro careers can be found in the set, including some current and future Hall of Famers. Stickers have color photos on the front, with backs printed in Spanish. They measure 2-1/4" x 3".

	NM	E	VG
Complete Set (231):	1,000	500.00	300.00
Complete Set in Album:	1,200	600.00	350.00
Common Player:	5.00	2.50	1.50
Album:	200.00	100.00	60.00
Unopened Pack:	50.00		

		NM	E	VG
1	Santurce All-Star Team Composite Photo	10.00	5.00	3.00
2	Santurce All-Star Team Composite Photo	10.00	5.00	3.00
3	Santurce All-Star Team Composite Photo	10.00	5.00	3.00
4	Santurce All-Star Team Composite Photo	10.00	5.00	3.00
5	Santurce All-Star Team Composite Photo	10.00	5.00	3.00
6	Santurce All-Star Team Composite Photo	10.00	5.00	3.00
7	Santurce All-Star Team Composite Photo	10.00	5.00	3.00
8	Santurce All-Star Team Composite Photo	10.00	5.00	3.00
9	Santurce All-Star Team Composite Photo	10.00	5.00	3.00
10	Ponce All-Star Team Composite Photo	10.00	5.00	3.00
11	Ponce All-Star Team Composite Photo	10.00	5.00	3.00
12	Ponce All-Star Team Composite Photo	10.00	5.00	3.00
13	Ponce All-Star Team Composite Photo	10.00	5.00	3.00
14	Ponce All-Star Team Composite Photo	10.00	5.00	3.00
15	Ponce All-Star Team Composite Photo	10.00	5.00	3.00
16	Ponce All-Star Team Composite Photo	10.00	5.00	3.00
17	Ponce All-Star Team Composite Photo	10.00	5.00	3.00
18	Ponce All-Star Team Composite Photo	10.00	5.00	3.00
19	Arecibo Team Emblem	5.00	2.50	1.50
20	Caguas-Guayana Team Emblem	5.00	2.50	1.50
21	Mayaguez Team Emblem	5.00	2.50	1.50
22	Ponce Team Emblem	5.00	2.50	1.50
23	San Juan Team Emblem	5.00	2.50	1.50
24	Santurce Team Emblem	5.00	2.50	1.50
25	Steve Boros	5.00	2.50	1.50
26	Luis Isaac	5.00	2.50	1.50
27	Emmanuel Toledo	5.00	2.50	1.50
28	Gregorio Perez	5.00	2.50	1.50
29	Rosario Llanos	5.00	2.50	1.50
30	Jose Geigel	5.00	2.50	1.50
31	Eduardo Figueroa	5.00	2.50	1.50
32	Julian Muniz	5.00	2.50	1.50
33	Fernando Gonzalez	5.00	2.50	1.50
34	Bennie Ayala	5.00	2.50	1.50
35	Miguel Villaran	5.00	2.50	1.50
36	Efrain Vazquez	5.00	2.50	1.50
37	Ramon Ariles	5.00	2.50	1.50
38	Angel Alcaraz	5.00	2.50	1.50
39	Henry Cruz	5.00	2.50	1.50
40	Jose Silva	5.00	2.50	1.50
41	Jose Alcaide	5.00	2.50	1.50
42	Pepe Mangual	5.00	2.50	1.50
43	Mike Jackson	5.00	2.50	1.50
44	Lynn McGlothen	5.00	2.50	1.50
45	Frank Ortenzio	5.00	2.50	1.50
46	Norm Angelini	5.00	2.50	1.50
47	Richard Coggins	5.00	2.50	1.50
48	Lance Clemons	5.00	2.50	1.50
49	Mike Kelleher	5.00	2.50	1.50
50	Ken Wright	5.00	2.50	1.50
51	Buck Martinez	5.00	2.50	1.50
52	Billy De Mars	5.00	2.50	1.50
53	Elwood Huyke	5.00	2.50	1.50
54	Pedro Garcia	5.00	2.50	1.50
55	Bob Boone	15.00	7.50	4.50
56	Jose Laboy	5.00	2.50	1.50
57	Eduardo Rodriguez	5.00	2.50	1.50
58	Jesus Hernaiz	5.00	2.50	1.50
59	Joaquin Quintana	5.00	2.50	1.50
60	Domingo Figueroa	5.00	2.50	1.50
61	Juan Lopez	5.00	2.50	1.50
62	Luis Alvarado	5.00	2.50	1.50
63	Otoniel Velez	5.00	2.50	1.50
64	Mike Schmidt	500.00	250.00	150.00
65	Felix Millan	5.00	2.50	1.50
66	Guillermo Montanez	5.00	2.50	1.50
67	Ivan de Jesus	7.50	3.75	2.25
68	Sixto Lezcano	5.00	2.50	1.50
69	Jerry Morales	5.00	2.50	1.50
70	Bombo Rivera	5.00	2.50	1.50
71	Mike Ondina	5.00	2.50	1.50
72	Grant Jackson	5.00	2.50	1.50
73	Roger Freed	5.00	2.50	1.50
74	Steve Rogers	5.00	2.50	1.50
75	Mac Scarce	5.00	2.50	1.50
76	Mike Jorgensen	5.00	2.50	1.50
77	Jerry Crider	5.00	2.50	1.50
78	Fred Beene	5.00	2.50	1.50
79	Carl Ermer	5.00	2.50	1.50
80	Luis Marquez	5.00	2.50	1.50
81	Hector Valle	5.00	2.50	1.50
82	Ramon Vega	5.00	2.50	1.50
83	Cirito Cruz	5.00	2.50	1.50
84	Fernando Vega	5.00	2.50	1.50
85	Porfiro Sanchez	5.00	2.50	1.50
86	Jose Sevillano	5.00	2.50	1.50
87	Felix Roque	5.00	2.50	1.50
88	Enrique Rivera	5.00	2.50	1.50
89	Wildredo Rios	5.00	2.50	1.50
90	Javier Andino	5.00	2.50	1.50
91	Milton Ramirez	5.00	2.50	1.50
92	Max Oliveras	5.00	2.50	1.50
93	Jose Calero	5.00	2.50	1.50
94	Esteban Vazquez	5.00	2.50	1.50
95	Hector Cruz	5.00	2.50	1.50
96	Felix Arce	5.00	2.50	1.50
97	Gilberto Rivera	5.00	2.50	1.50
98	Rafael Rodriguez	5.00	2.50	1.50
99	Julio Gonzalez	5.00	2.50	1.50
100	Rosendo Cedeno	5.00	2.50	1.50
101	Pedro Cintron	5.00	2.50	1.50
102	Osvaldo Ortiz	5.00	2.50	1.50
103	Frank Verdi	5.00	2.50	1.50
104	Carlos Santiago	5.00	2.50	1.50
105	Ramon Conde	5.00	2.50	1.50
106	Pat Corrales	5.00	2.50	1.50
107	Jose Morales	5.00	2.50	1.50

108	Jack Whillock	5.00	2.50	1.50
109	Raul Mercado	5.00	2.50	1.50
110	Bonifacio Aponte	5.00	2.50	1.50
111	Angel Alicea	5.00	2.50	1.50
112	Santos Alomar	10.00	5.00	3.00
113	Francisco Libran	5.00	2.50	1.50
114	Edwin Pacheco	5.00	2.50	1.50
115	Luis Gonzalez	5.00	2.50	1.50
116	Juan Rios	5.00	2.50	1.50
117	Jorge Roque	5.00	2.50	1.50
118	Carlos Velez	5.00	2.50	1.50
119	David Gonzalez	5.00	2.50	1.50
120	Jose Cruz	7.50	3.75	2.25
121	Luis Melendez	5.00	2.50	1.50
122	Jose Ortiz	5.00	2.50	1.50
123	David Rosello	5.00	2.50	1.50
124	Juan Veintidos	5.00	2.50	1.50
125	Arnaldo Nazario	5.00	2.50	1.50
126	Dave Lemonds	5.00	2.50	1.50
127	Jim Magnuson	5.00	2.50	1.50
128	Tom Kelley	7.50	3.75	2.25
129	Chris Zachary	5.00	2.50	1.50
130	Hal Breeden	5.00	2.50	1.50
131	Jackie Hernandez	5.00	2.50	1.50
132	Rick Gossage	30.00	15.00	9.00
133	Frank Luchessi	5.00	2.50	1.50
134	Nino Escalera	5.00	2.50	1.50
135	Julio Navarro	5.00	2.50	1.50
136	Manny Sanguillen	15.00	7.50	4.50
137	Bob Johnson	5.00	2.50	1.50
138	Chuck Coggins	5.00	2.50	1.50
139	Orlando Gomez	5.00	2.50	1.50
140	William Melendez	5.00	2.50	1.50
141	Jose Del Moral	5.00	2.50	1.50
142	Jacinto Camacho	5.00	2.50	1.50
143	Emiliano Rivera	5.00	2.50	1.50
144	Luis Peraza	5.00	2.50	1.50
145	Carlos Velazquez	5.00	2.50	1.50
146	Luis Raul Garcia	5.00	2.50	1.50
147	Eliseo Rodriguez	5.00	2.50	1.50
148	Santiago Rosario	5.00	2.50	1.50
149	Ruben Castillo	5.00	2.50	1.50
150	Sergio Ferrer	5.00	2.50	1.50
151	Jose Pagan	5.00	2.50	1.50
152	Raul Colon	5.00	2.50	1.50
153	Robert Rauch	5.00	2.50	1.50
154	Luis Rosado	5.00	2.50	1.50
155	Francisco Lopez	5.00	2.50	1.50
156	Richard Zisk	5.00	2.50	1.50
157	Orlando Alvarez	5.00	2.50	1.50
158	Jaime Rosario	5.00	2.50	1.50
159	Rosendo Torres	5.00	2.50	1.50
160	Jim McKee	5.00	2.50	1.50
161	Mike Nagy	5.00	2.50	1.50
162	Brent Strom	5.00	2.50	1.50
163	Tom Walker	5.00	2.50	1.50
164	Angel Davila	5.00	2.50	1.50
165	Jose Cruz	5.00	2.50	1.50
166	Frank Robinson	25.00	12.50	7.50
167	German Rivera	5.00	2.50	1.50
168	Reinaldo Oliver	5.00	2.50	1.50
169	Geraldo Rodriguez	5.00	2.50	1.50
170	Elrod Hendricks	5.00	2.50	1.50
171	Gilberto Flores	5.00	2.50	1.50
172	Ruben Gomez	5.00	2.50	1.50
173	Juan Pizarro	5.00	2.50	1.50
174	William De Jesus	5.00	2.50	1.50
175	Rogelio Morel	5.00	2.50	1.50
176	Victor Agosto	5.00	2.50	1.50
177	Esteban Texidor	5.00	2.50	1.50
178	Ramon Hernandez	5.00	2.50	1.50
179	Gilberto Rondon Olivo	5.00	2.50	1.50
180	Juan Beniquez	5.00	2.50	1.50
181	Arturo Miranda	5.00	2.50	1.50
182	Manuel Ruiz	5.00	2.50	1.50
183	Julio Gotay	5.00	2.50	1.50
184	Arsenio Rodriguez	5.00	2.50	1.50
185	Luis Delgado	5.00	2.50	1.50
186	Jorge Rivera	5.00	2.50	1.50
187	Willie Crawford	5.00	2.50	1.50
188	Angel Mangual	5.00	2.50	1.50
189	Mike Strahler	5.00	2.50	1.50
190	Doyle Alexander	5.00	2.50	1.50
191	Bob Reynolds	5.00	2.50	1.50
192	Ron Cey	7.50	3.75	2.25
193	Jerr Da Vanon	5.00	2.50	1.50
194	Don Baylor	12.50	6.25	3.75
195	Tony Perez	25.00	12.50	7.50
196	Lloyd Allen	5.00	2.50	1.50
197	Orlando Cepeda	20.00	10.00	6.00
198	Roberto Clemente			
	Composite Photo	15.00	7.50	4.50
199	Roberto Clemente			
	Composite Photo	15.00	7.50	4.50
200	Roberto Clemente			
	Composite Photo	15.00	7.50	4.50
201	Roberto Clemente			
	Composite Photo	15.00	7.50	4.50

202	Roberto Clemente			
	Composite Photo	15.00	7.50	4.50
203	Roberto Clemente			
	Composite Photo	15.00	7.50	4.50
204	Roberto Clemente			
	Composite Photo	15.00	7.50	4.50
205	Roberto Clemente			
	Composite Photo	15.00	7.50	4.50
206	Roberto Clemente			
	Composite Photo	15.00	7.50	4.50
207	Jaime Almendro	5.00	2.50	1.50
208	Jose R. Santiago	5.00	2.50	1.50
209	Luis Cabrera	5.00	2.50	1.50
210	Jorge Tirado	5.00	2.50	1.50
211	Radames Lopez	5.00	2.50	1.50
212	Juan Vargas	5.00	2.50	1.50
213	Francisco Coimbre	5.00	2.50	1.50
214	Freddie Thon	5.00	2.50	1.50
215	Manuel Alvarez	5.00	2.50	1.50
216	Luis Olmo	5.00	2.50	1.50
217	Jose Santiago	7.50	3.75	2.25
218	Hiram Bithorn	12.50	6.25	3.75
219	Willard Brown	30.00	15.00	9.00
220	Robert Thurman	10.00	5.00	3.00
221	Buster Clarkson	7.50	3.75	2.25
222	Satchel Paige	40.00	20.00	12.00
223	Raymond Brown	30.00	15.00	9.00
224	Alonso Perry	7.50	3.75	2.25
225	Quincy Trouppe	12.50	6.25	3.75
226	Santiago Muratti	5.00	2.50	1.50
227	Johnny Davis	5.00	2.50	1.50
228	Lino Suarez	5.00	2.50	1.50
229	Demetrio Pesante	5.00	2.50	1.50
230	Luis Arroyo	5.00	2.50	1.50
231	Jose Garcia	5.00	2.50	1.50

1905 Harry Pulliam Cigar Label

The attributed dated is speculative. Pulliam was the first president of the modern National League. These colorful gold-leaf highlighted lithographed cigar box labels measure 4-1/4" square with clipped corners. Since all examples seen appear to be unused it is believed that the cigar brand never materialized, possibly having been aborted when Pulliam commited suicide in 1909.

	NM	E	VG
Harry Pulliam	150.00	75.00	45.00

1910 Punch Cigars

By virtue of its age, scarcity and checklist, this is among the most popular of the Cuban card sets. Issued contemporary with a visit by the Detroit Tigers and Philadelphia A's for an exhibition series in Cuba, these cards feature an approximately 1-1/4" x 1-7/8" black-and-white portrait photo attached to a decorative cardboard backing of about 1-3/4" x 2-1/4". Known cards include a dozen each of the Major League teams and, it is speculated, an equal number from Cuba's professional Almendares and Havana clubs; though the complete checklist remains unknown. The scarcity of surviving specimens may be traced to the copy on the original cardboard backing that offers an album for anybody turning in a complete set. Only a tiny percentage of Punch cards are known with their cardboard backing attached. Because most cards seen to date have been in wretched condition, no values are quoted above VG condition. Cards with backing should command a 3X premium.

	NM
Common Cuban Player:	750.00
Common Major Leaguer:	1,125

ALMENDARES

(1)	Armando Cabanas	1,125
(2)	Alfredo Cabrera	750.00
(3)	Gervasio Gonzalez	1,500
(4)	Eleadoro Hidalgo	1,500
(5)	Armando Marzans (Marsans)	2,250
(6)	Jose Mendez	30,000
(7)	Evaristo Pia (Trainer)	750.00
(8)	Carlos Roggers (Royer)	1,125
(9)	Rogelio Valdes	750.00
(9)	Rogelio Valdes	1,125

HAVANA

(1)	P. (Pete) Hill	5,250
(2)	Carlos Moran	2,250
(3)	Agustin Molina	4,500
(4)	Luis Padron	2,250
(5)	Agustin Parpetti	1,500
(6)	Bruce Petway	5,500

DETROIT TIGERS

(1)	Joe Casey	1,125
(2)	Ty Cobb	11,250
(3)	Sam Crawford	5,250
(4)	Tom Jones	1,125
(5)	Matty McIntyre	1,125
(6)	George Moriarty	1,125
(7)	George Mullin	1,125
(8)	Charley O'Leary	1,125
(9)	Germany Schaefer	1,125
(10)	Oscar Stanage	1,125
(11)	Ed Summers	1,125
(12)	Ed Willetts (Willett)	1,125

PHILADELPHIA A'S

(1)	Jack Barry	1,125
(2)	Chief Bender	5,250
(3)	Jack Coombs	1,125
(4)	Harry Davis	1,125
(5)	Claude Derrick	1,125
(6)	Topsy Hartsel	1,125
(7)	Jack Lapp	1,125
(8)	Bris Lord	1,125
(9)	Stuffy McInnis	1,125
(10)	Danny Murphy	1,125
(11)	Eddie Plank	6,000
(12)	Ira Thomas	1,125

1966 Pure Oil Atlanta Braves

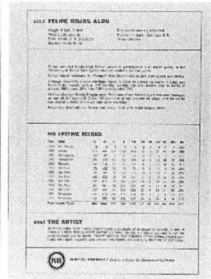

In their first year in Atlanta a set of Braves premium pictures done by noted portrait artist Nicholas Volpe was sponsored by Pure Oil. The 8-1/2" x 11" pictures were given away with gas purchases. Fronts featured a large pastel portrait and smaller full-figure action picture of the player set against a black background. A facsimile player autograph was penciled at the bottom, along with the artist's signature. The player's name was printed in black in the white bottom border. Backs are printed in black-and-white and include biographical and career notes, full major and minor league stats, a short biography of the artist and the sponsoring company's logo. The unnumbered cards are checklisted here alphabetically.

		NM	E	VG
Complete Set (12):		75.00	37.50	22.00
Common Player:		5.00	2.50	1.50
(1)	Hank Aaron	25.00	12.50	7.50
(2)	Felipe Alou	6.00	3.00	1.75
(3)	Frank Bolling	5.00	2.50	1.50
(4)	Bobby Bragan	5.00	2.50	1.50
(5)	Rico Carty	5.00	2.50	1.50
(6)	Tony Cloninger	5.00	2.50	1.50
(7)	Mack Jones	5.00	2.50	1.50
(8)	Denny LeMaster	5.00	2.50	1.50
(9)	Eddie Mathews	15.00	7.50	4.50
(10)	Denis Menke	5.00	2.50	1.50
(11)	Lee Thomas	5.00	2.50	1.50
(12)	Joe Torre	7.50	3.75	2.25

1933 PX3 Double Header Coins

Issued by Gum Inc. circa 1933, this unnumbered set consists of 43 metal discs approximately 1-1/4" in diameter. The front lists the player's name and team beneath his picture. The numbers "1" or "2" also appear inside a small circle at the bottom of the disc, and the wrapper advised collectors to "put 1 and 2 together and make a double header." Some players are found in more than one color. The set is designated as PX3 in the American Card Catalog.

		NM	E	VG
Complete Set (43):		1,750	875.00	525.00
Common Player:		40.00	20.00	12.00
(1)	Sparky Adams	40.00	20.00	12.00
(2)	Dale Alexander	40.00	20.00	12.00
(3)	Earl Averill	75.00	37.00	22.00
(4)	Dick Bartell	40.00	20.00	12.00
(5)	Walter Berger	40.00	20.00	12.00
(6)	Jim Bottomley	75.00	37.00	22.00
(7)	Lefty Brandt	40.00	20.00	12.00
(8)	Owen Carroll	40.00	20.00	12.00
(9)	Lefty Clark	40.00	20.00	12.00
(10)	Mickey Cochrane	75.00	37.00	22.00
(11)	Joe Cronin	75.00	37.00	22.00
(12)	Jimmy Dykes	40.00	20.00	12.00
(13)	George Earnshaw	40.00	20.00	12.00
(14)	Wes Ferrell	40.00	20.00	12.00
(15)	Neal Finn	40.00	20.00	12.00
(16)	Lew Fonseca	40.00	20.00	12.00
(17)	Jimmy Foxx	100.00	50.00	30.00
(18)	Frankie Frisch	75.00	37.00	22.00
(19)	Chick Fullis	40.00	20.00	12.00
(20)	Charley Gehringer	75.00	37.00	22.00
(21)	Goose Goslin	75.00	37.00	22.00
(22)	Johnny Hodapp	40.00	20.00	12.00
(23)	Frank Hogan	40.00	20.00	12.00
(24)	Si Johnson	40.00	20.00	12.00
(25)	Joe Judge	40.00	20.00	12.00
(26)	Chuck Klein	75.00	37.00	22.00
(27)	Al Lopez	75.00	37.00	22.00
(28)	Ray Lucas	40.00	20.00	12.00
(29)	Red Lucas	40.00	20.00	12.00
(30)	Ted Lyons	75.00	37.00	22.00
(31)	Firpo Marberry	40.00	20.00	12.00
(32)	Oscar Melillo	40.00	20.00	12.00
(33)	Lefty O'Doul	50.00	25.00	15.00
(34)	George Pipgras	40.00	20.00	12.00
(35)	Flint Rhem	40.00	20.00	12.00
(36)	Sam Rice	75.00	37.00	22.00
(37)	Muddy Ruel	40.00	20.00	12.00
(38)	Harry Seibold	40.00	20.00	12.00
(39)	Al Simmons	75.00	37.00	22.00
(40)	Joe Vosmik	40.00	20.00	12.00
(41)	Gerald Walker	40.00	20.00	12.00
(42)	Pinky Whitney	40.00	20.00	12.00
(43)	Hack Wilson	75.00	37.00	22.00

Q

1934 Quaker Oats Babe Ruth Premium Photo (8x10)

Members of the cereal company's Babe Ruth Baseball Club could obtain this souvenir photo among many other promotional items endorsed by the slugger. This 8" x 10" black-and-white photo has a facsimile autograph and is inscribed, "To My Pal." Advertising for Quaker Oats appears in the white border at bottom.

	NM	E	VG
Babe Ruth	450.00	275.00	125.00

1954 Quaker Sports Oddities

Available both as cereal-box premiums and a mail-away set, this issue of horizontal-format 3-1/2" x 2-1/2", round-corner cards depicts "Odd but True" moments in sports. Fronts of the multi-sports set feature portrait and action color art. Backs describe the sports oddity.

		NM	E	VG
Complete Set (27):		200.00	100.00	60.00
Common Card:		3.00	1.50	.90
1	Johnny Miller (Football)	4.00	2.00	1.25
2	Fred Snite Jr. (Golf)	3.00	1.50	.90
3	George Quam (Handball)	3.00	1.50	.90
4	John B. Maypole (Speed boating.)	3.00	1.50	.90
5	Harold (Bunny) Leavitt (Basketball)	5.00	2.50	1.50
6	Wake Forest College (Football)	5.00	2.50	1.50
7	Amos Alonzo Stagg (Football)	20.00	10.00	6.00
8	Catherine Fellmuth (Bowling)	3.00	1.50	.90
9	Bill Wilson (Golf)	3.00	1.50	.90
10	Chicago Blackhawks (Hockey)	20.00	10.00	6.00
11	Betty Robinson (Track)	3.00	1.50	.90
12	Dartmouth College/ University of Utah (Basketball)	5.00	2.50	1.50
13	Ab Jenkins (Auto racing.)	3.00	1.50	.90
14	Capt. Eddie Rickenbacker (Auto racing.)	5.00	2.50	1.50
15	Jackie LaVine (Swimming)	3.00	1.50	.90
16	Jack Riley (Wrestling)	3.00	1.50	.90
17	Carl Stockton (Biking)	3.00	1.50	.90
18	Jimmy Smilgoff (Baseball)	3.00	1.50	.90
19	George Halas (Football)	20.00	10.00	6.00
20	Joyce Rosenbom (Basketball)	5.00	2.50	1.50
21	Squatters Rights (Baseball)	3.00	1.50	.90
22	Richard Dwyer (Skating)	3.00	1.50	.90
23	Harlem Globetrotters (Basketball)	25.00	12.50	7.50
24	Everett Dean (Basketball)	3.00	1.50	.90
25	Texas U./Northwestern U. (football)	5.00	2.50	1.50
26	Bronko Nagurski (Football)	25.00	12.50	7.50
27	Yankee Stadium (Baseball)	20.00	10.00	6.00

R

1936 R311 Glossy Finish

The cards in this 28-card set, which was available as a premium in 1936, measure 6" x 8" and were printed on a glossy cardboard. The photos are either black and white or sepia-toned and include a facsimile autograph. The unnumbered set includes individual players and team photos. The Boston Red Sox team card can be found in two varieties; one shows the sky above the building on the card's right side, while the other does not. Some of the cards are scarcer than others in the set and command a premium. Babe Ruth is featured on the Boston Braves team card.

		NM	E	VG
Complete Set (27):		3,750	1,850	1,100
Common Player:		60.00	30.00	18.00
(1)	Earl Averill	100.00	50.00	30.00
(2)	James L. "Jim" Bottomley	100.00	50.00	30.00
(3)	Gordon S. "Mickey" Cochrane	100.00	50.00	30.00
(4)	Joe Cronin	100.00	50.00	30.00
(5)	Jerome "Dizzy" Dean	150.00	75.00	45.00
(6)	Jimmy Dykes	60.00	30.00	18.00
(7)	Jimmy Foxx	125.00	65.00	35.00
(8)	Frankie Frisch	100.00	50.00	30.00
(9)	Henry "Hank" Greenberg	120.00	60.00	35.00
(10)	Mel Harder (SP)	120.00	60.00	35.00
(11)	Pepper Martin (SP)	225.00	110.00	65.00
(12)	Lynwood "Schoolboy" Rowe (SP)	120.00	60.00	35.00
(13)	William "Bill" Terry	100.00	50.00	30.00
(14)	Harold "Pie" Traynor	100.00	50.00	30.00
(15)	American League All-Stars - 1935	275.00	135.00	80.00
(16)	American League Pennant Winners - 1934 (Detroit Tigers)	125.00	65.00	35.00
(17)	Boston Braves - 1935	300.00	150.00	90.00
(18a)	Boston Red Sox (Sky visible above building at right.)	100.00	50.00	30.00
(18b)	Boston Red Sox (No sky visible.)	180.00	90.00	55.00
(19)	Brooklyn Dodgers - 1935 (SP)	225.00	110.00	65.00
(20)	Chicago White Sox - 1935	100.00	50.00	30.00
(21)	Columbus Red Birds (1934 Pennant Winners of American Association)(SP)	150.00	75.00	45.00
(22)	National League All-Stars - 1935	180.00	90.00	55.00
(23)	National League Champions - 1935 (Chicago Cubs)	100.00	50.00	30.00
(24)	New York Yankees - 1935	180.00	90.00	55.00
(25)	Pittsburgh Pirates - 1935 (SP)	200.00	100.00	60.00
(26)	St. Louis Browns - 1935	100.00	50.00	30.00
(27)	The World Champions, 1934 (St. Louis Cardinals)	100.00	50.00	30.00

1936 R311 Leather Finish

This set of 15 unnumbered cards, issued as a premium in 1936, is distinctive because of its uneven, leather-like surface. The cards measure 6" x 8" and display a facsimile autograph on the black and white photo surrounded by a plain border. The cards are unnumbered and include individual player photos, multi-player photos and team photos of the 1935 pennant winners.

		NM	E	VG
Complete Set (15):		2,750	1,325	825.00
Common Player:		90.00	45.00	25.00
(1)	Frank Crosetti, Joe DiMaggio, Tony Lazzeri	825.00	410.00	245.00
(2)	Paul Derringer	90.00	45.00	25.00
(3)	Wes Ferrell	90.00	45.00	25.00
(4)	Jimmy (Jimmie) Foxx	180.00	90.00	55.00
(5)	Charlie Gehringer	165.00	80.00	50.00
(6)	Mel Harder	90.00	45.00	25.00
(7)	Gabby Hartnett	165.00	80.00	50.00
(8)	Rogers Hornsby	190.00	95.00	55.00
(9)	Connie Mack	165.00	80.00	50.00
(10)	Van Mungo	90.00	45.00	25.00
(11)	Steve O'Neill	90.00	45.00	25.00
(12)	Charles Ruffing	165.00	80.00	50.00
(13)	Arky Vaughan, Honus Wagner	245.00	120.00	75.00
(14)	American League Pennant Winners - 1935 (Detroit Tigers)	165.00	80.00	50.00
(15)	National League Pennant Winners - 1935 (Chicago Cubs)	165.00	80.00	50.00

1936 R312

The 50 cards in this set of 4" x 5-3/8" point-of-purchase premiums are black-and-white photos that have been tinted in soft pastel colors. The set includes 25 individual player portraits, 14 multi-player cards and 11 action photos. Six of the action photos include facsimilie autographs, while the other five have printed legends. The Allen card is scarcer than the others in the set.

		NM	E	VG
Complete Set (50):		8,500	4,250	2,500
Common Player:		90.00	45.00	20.00
(1)	John Thomas Allen	90.00	35.00	20.00
(2)	Nick Altrock, Al Schact	140.00	55.00	35.00
(3)	Ollie Bejma, Rolly Hemsley	90.00	35.00	20.00
(4)	Les Bell, Zeke Bonura	90.00	35.00	20.00
(5)	Cy Blanton	90.00	35.00	20.00
(6)	Cliff Bolton, Earl Whitehill	90.00	35.00	20.00
(7)	Frenchy Bordagaray, George Earnshaw	90.00	35.00	20.00
(8)	Mace Brown	90.00	35.00	20.00
(9)	Dolph Camilli	90.00	35.00	20.00
(10)	Phil Cavaretta (Cavarretta), Frank Demaree, Augie Galan, Stan Hack, Gabby Hartnett, Billy Herman, Billy Jurges, Chuck Klein, Fred Lindstrom	185.00	75.00	45.00
(11)	Phil Cavaretta (Cavarretta), Stan Hack, Billy Herman, Billy Jurges	185.00	75.00	45.00
(12)	Gordon Cochrane	185.00	75.00	45.00
(13)	Jim Collins, Stan Hack	90.00	35.00	20.00
(14)	Rip Collins	90.00	35.00	20.00
(15)	Joe Cronin, Buckey Harris (Bucky)	125.00	50.00	30.00
(16)	Alvin Crowder	90.00	35.00	20.00
(17)	Kiki Cuyler	185.00	75.00	45.00
(18)	Kiki Cuyler, Tris Speaker, Danny Taylor	225.00	90.00	55.00
(19)	"Bill" Dickey	185.00	75.00	45.00
(20)	Joe DiMagio (DiMaggio)	2,200	850.00	550.00
(21)	"Chas." Dressen	90.00	35.00	20.00
(22)	Rick Ferrell, Russ Van Atta	125.00	50.00	30.00
(23)	Pete Fox, Goose Goslin, "Jo Jo" White	165.00	65.00	40.00
(24)	Jimmey Foxx, Luke Sewell	215.00	85.00	55.00
(25)	Benny Frey	90.00	35.00	20.00
(26)	Augie Galan, "Pie" Traynor	165.00	65.00	40.00
(27)	Lefty Gomez, Myril Hoag	165.00	65.00	40.00
(28)	"Hank" Greenberg	185.00	75.00	45.00
(29)	Lefty Grove, Connie Mack	250.00	100.00	65.00
(30)	Muel Haas (Mule), Mike Kreevich, Dixie Walker	90.00	35.00	20.00
(31)	Mel Harder	90.00	35.00	20.00
(32)	Gabby Hartnett (Mickey Cochrane, Frank Demaree, Ernie Quigley (ump) in photo)	165.00	65.00	40.00
(33)	Gabby Hartnett, Lonnie Warnecke (Warneke)	135.00	55.00	35.00
(34)	Roger Hornsby (Rogers)	250.00	100.00	65.00
(35)	Rogers Hornsby, Allen Sothoren (Sothoron)	185.00	75.00	45.00
(36)	Ernie Lombardi	185.00	75.00	45.00
(37)	Al Lopez	185.00	75.00	45.00
(38)	Pepper Martin	110.00	45.00	25.00
(39)	"Johnny" Mize	185.00	75.00	45.00
(40)	Van L. Mungo	100.00	40.00	20.00
(41)	Bud Parmelee	90.00	35.00	20.00
(42)	Schoolboy Rowe	90.00	35.00	20.00
(43)	Chas. Ruffing	185.00	75.00	45.00
(44)	Eugene Schott	90.00	35.00	20.00
(45)	Casey Stengel	185.00	75.00	45.00
(46)	Bill Sullivan	90.00	35.00	20.00
(47)	Bill Swift	90.00	35.00	20.00
(48)	Floyd Vaughan, Hans Wagner	225.00	90.00	55.00
(49)	L. Waner, P. Waner, Big Jim Weaver	215.00	85.00	55.00
(50)	Ralph Winegarner	90.00	35.00	20.00

1936 R314

(See 1936 Goudey "Wide Pen" Premiums.)

1929-1930 R315

Apparently issued over a period of at least two years, based on observed player/team combinations, the 58 cards in this set can be found in either black-and-white or yellow-and-black. The unnumbered, blank-backed cards measure a nominal 3-1/4" x 5-1/4" though original cutting variances abound. The cards feature either portraits or posed action photos. The set includes several different types of cards, depending on the caption. Cards can be found with the player's name and team inside a white box in a lower corner; other cards add the position and team in small type in the bottom border; a third type has the player's name in hand lettering near the bottom; and the final type includes the position and team printed in small type along the bottom border.

		NM	E	VG
Complete Set (46):		6,000	2,400	1,200
Common Player:		45.00	20.00	10.00
(1)	Earl Averill	90.00	35.00	25.00
(2)	"Benny" Bengough	45.00	20.00	10.00
(3)	Laurence Benton (Lawrence)	45.00	20.00	10.00
(4)	"Max" Bishop	45.00	20.00	10.00
(5)	"Sunny Jim" Bottomley	90.00	35.00	20.00
(6)	Bill Cissell	45.00	20.00	10.00
(7)	Bud Clancey (Clancy)	45.00	20.00	10.00
(8)	"Freddy" Fitzsimmons	45.00	20.00	10.00
(9)	"Jimmy" Foxx	300.00	120.00	75.00
(10)	"Johnny" Fredericks (Frederick)	45.00	20.00	10.00
(11)	Frank Frisch	150.00	60.00	35.00
(12)	"Lou" Gehrig	3,000	1,500	900.00
(13)	"Goose" Goslin	90.00	35.00	20.00
(14)	Burleigh Grimes	90.00	35.00	20.00
(15)	"Lefty" Grove	125.00	50.00	30.00
(16)	"Mule" Haas	45.00	20.00	10.00
(17)	Harvey Hendricks (Hendrick)	45.00	20.00	10.00
(18)	"Babe" Herman	60.00	25.00	15.00
(19)	"Roger" Hornsby (Rogers)	175.00	70.00	40.00
(20)	Karl Hubbell (Carl)	90.00	35.00	20.00
(21)	"Stonewall" Jackson	90.00	35.00	20.00
(22)	Smead Jolley	45.00	20.00	10.00
(23)	"Chuck" Klein	90.00	35.00	20.00
(24)	Mark Koenig	45.00	20.00	10.00
(25)	"Tony" Lazerri (Lazzeri)	90.00	35.00	20.00
(26)	Fred Leach	45.00	20.00	10.00
(27)	"Freddy" Lindstrom	90.00	35.00	20.00
(28)	Fred Marberry	45.00	20.00	10.00
(29)	"Bing" Miller	45.00	20.00	10.00
(30)	"Bob" O'Farrell	45.00	20.00	10.00
(31)	Frank O'Doul	75.00	30.00	18.50
(32)	"Herbie" Pennock	90.00	35.00	20.00
(33)	George Pipgras	45.00	20.00	10.00
(34)	Andrew Reese	45.00	20.00	10.00
(35)	Carl Reynolds	45.00	20.00	10.00
(36)	"Babe" Ruth	3,200	1,600	960.00
(37)	"Bob" Shawkey	45.00	20.00	10.00
(38)	Art Shires	45.00	20.00	10.00
(39)	"Al" Simmons	90.00	35.00	20.00
(40)	"Riggs" Stephenson	45.00	20.00	10.00
(41)	"Bill" Terry	90.00	35.00	20.00
(42)	"Pie" Traynor	90.00	35.00	20.00
(43)	"Dazzy" Vance	90.00	35.00	20.00
(44)	Paul Waner	90.00	35.00	20.00
(45)	Hack Wilson	90.00	35.00	20.00
(46)	"Tom" Zachary	45.00	20.00	10.00

1929 R316

(See Kashin Publications.)

1929 R316 5x7 Photos

There is nothing concrete to connect this set of player photos with the Kashin Publications card set which carried the R316 designation in the American Card Catalog except that these 4-7/8" x 6-3/4" heavy-paper pictures use the same photos and graphics as the smaller cards. It is thought that the photos are the work of Charles M. Conlon and that the 5x7s may have some connection to the Spalding sporting goods company for whom he worked. Pictures feature white borders and facsimile autographs on front, along with the player's city and league on two lines of type at bottom. While the photos are all the same as seen on R316, the city/league designation on some of the photos is sometimes in black instead of white as on the card, or vice versa. Because almost every card from R316 is known in the 5x7 series, it is reasonable to expect that pictures of Frank Hogan and Jimmy Welsh may also exist. A number of players in the 5x7 set do not appear in the Kashin Publications set, and are noted here with an asterisk.

		NM	E	VG
Complete Set (111):		7,000	3,500	2,100
Common Player:		50.00	25.00	15.00
(1)	Dale Alexander	50.00	25.00	15.00
(2)	Ethan N. Allen	50.00	25.00	15.00
(3)	Ray Benge (*)	50.00	25.00	15.00
(4)	Larry Benton	50.00	25.00	15.00

(5)	Moe Berg	65.00	32.50	20.00
(6)	Max Bishop	50.00	25.00	15.00
(7)	Del Bissonette	50.00	25.00	15.00
(8)	Lucerne A. Blue	50.00	25.00	15.00
(9)	James Bottomley	75.00	37.50	22.50
(10)	Raymond B. Bressler (*)	50.00	25.00	15.00
(11)	Fred Brickell (*)	50.00	25.00	15.00
(12)	Guy T. Bush	50.00	25.00	15.00
(13)	Harold G. Carlson	50.00	25.00	15.00
(14)	Owen Carroll	50.00	25.00	15.00
(15)	Chalmers W. Cissell (Chalmer)	50.00	25.00	15.00
(16)	Mickey Cochrane (*)	85.00	45.00	25.00
(17)	Earl (Earle) Combs	75.00	37.50	22.50
(18)	Hugh M. Critz	50.00	25.00	15.00
(19)	H.J. DeBerry	50.00	25.00	15.00
(20)	Pete Donohue	50.00	25.00	15.00
(21)	Taylor Douthit	50.00	25.00	15.00
(22)	Chas. W. Dressen	50.00	25.00	15.00
(23)	Clise Dudley (*)	50.00	25.00	15.00
(24)	Jimmy Dykes	50.00	25.00	15.00
(25)	Howard Ehmke	50.00	25.00	15.00
(26)	Elwood English	50.00	25.00	15.00
(27)	Urban Faber	75.00	37.50	22.50
(28)	Fred Fitzsimmons	50.00	25.00	15.00
(29)	Lewis A. Fonseca	50.00	25.00	15.00
(30)	Horace H. Ford	50.00	25.00	15.00
(31)	Jimmy Foxx	85.00	45.00	25.00
(32)	Frank Frisch	75.00	37.50	22.50
(33)	Lou Gehrig	335.00	165.00	100.00
(34)	Charles Gehringer	75.00	37.50	22.50
(35)	Walter Gilbert (*)	50.00	25.00	15.00
(36)	Leon Goslin	75.00	37.50	22.50
(37)	George Grantham	50.00	25.00	15.00
(38)	Burleigh Grimes	75.00	37.50	22.50
(39)	Robert Grove	85.00	45.00	25.00
(40)	Bump Hadley	50.00	25.00	15.00
(41)	Charlie Hafey	75.00	37.50	22.50
(42)	Jesse J. Haines	75.00	37.50	22.50
(43)	Harvey Hendrick	50.00	25.00	15.00
(44)	Floyd C. Herman	50.00	25.00	15.00
(45)	Andy High	50.00	25.00	15.00
(46)	Urban J. Hodapp	50.00	25.00	15.00
(47)	Frank Hogan (Existence unconfirmed)			
(48)	Rogers Hornsby	90.00	45.00	25.00
(49)	Waite Hoyt	75.00	37.50	22.50
(50)	Willis Hudlin	50.00	25.00	15.00
(51)	Frank O. Hurst	50.00	25.00	15.00
(52)	Charlie Jamieson	50.00	25.00	15.00
(53)	Roy C. Johnson	50.00	25.00	15.00
(54)	Percy Jones	50.00	25.00	15.00
(55)	Sam Jones	50.00	25.00	15.00
(56)	Joseph Judge	50.00	25.00	15.00
(57)	Willie Kamm	50.00	25.00	15.00
(58)	Charles Klein	75.00	37.50	22.50
(59)	Mark Koenig	50.00	25.00	15.00
(60)	Ralph Kress	50.00	25.00	15.00
(61)	Fred M. Leach	50.00	25.00	15.00
(62)	Carl Lind (*)	50.00	25.00	15.00
(63)	Fred Lindstrom	75.00	37.50	22.50
(64)	Ad Liska	50.00	25.00	15.00
(65)	Fred Lucas (Red)	50.00	25.00	15.00
(66)	Fred Maguire	50.00	25.00	15.00
(67)	Perce L. Malone	50.00	25.00	15.00
(68)	Harry Manush (Henry)	75.00	37.50	22.50
(69)	Walter Maranville	75.00	37.50	22.50
(70)	Earl McNeely (*)	50.00	25.00	15.00
(71)	Douglas McWeeney (McWeeny)	50.00	25.00	15.00
(72)	Oscar Melillo	50.00	25.00	15.00
(73)	Alex Metzler (*)	50.00	25.00	15.00
(74)	Ed "Bing" Miller	50.00	25.00	15.00
(75)	Clarence Mitchell (*)	50.00	25.00	15.00
(76)	Ed Morgan (*)	50.00	25.00	15.00
(77)	Chas. S. Myer (*)	50.00	25.00	15.00
(78)	Frank O'Doul	65.00	32.50	20.00
(79)	Melvin Ott	85.00	45.00	25.00
(80)	Herbert Pennock	75.00	37.50	22.50
(81)	William W. Regan	50.00	25.00	15.00
(82)	Harry F. Rice	50.00	25.00	15.00
(83)	Sam Rice	75.00	37.50	22.50
(84)	Lance Richbourgh (Richbourg)	50.00	25.00	15.00
(85)	Eddie Rommel	50.00	25.00	15.00
(86)	Chas. H. Root	50.00	25.00	15.00
(87)	Ed Roush	75.00	37.50	22.50
(88)	Harold Ruel (Herold)	50.00	25.00	15.00
(89)	Charles Ruffing	75.00	37.50	22.50
(90)	Jack Russell	50.00	25.00	15.00
(91)	Babe Ruth	750.00	375.00	225.00
(92)	Fred Schulte	50.00	25.00	15.00
(93)	Harry Seibold	50.00	25.00	15.00
(94)	Joe Sewell	75.00	37.50	22.50
(95)	Luke Sewell	50.00	25.00	15.00
(96)	Art Shires	50.00	25.00	15.00
(97)	Al Simmons	75.00	37.50	22.50
(98)	Bob Smith	50.00	25.00	15.00
(99)	Riggs Stephenson	50.00	25.00	15.00
(100)	Wm. H. Terry	75.00	37.50	22.50
(101)	Alphonse Thomas	50.00	25.00	15.00
(102)	Lafayette F. Thompson	50.00	25.00	15.00
(103)	Phil Todt	50.00	25.00	15.00
(104)	Harold J. Traynor	75.00	37.50	22.50
(105)	Dazzy Vance	75.00	37.50	22.50
(106)	Lloyd Waner	75.00	37.50	22.50
(107)	Paul Waner	75.00	37.50	22.50
(108)	Jimmy Welsh (Existence unconfirmed.)			
(109)	Earl Whitehill	50.00	25.00	15.00
(110)	A.C. Whitney	50.00	25.00	15.00
(111)	Claude Willoughby	50.00	25.00	15.00
(112)	Hack Wilson	75.00	37.50	22.50
(113)	Tom Zachary	50.00	25.00	15.00

1933 R337

(See 1933 Eclipse Import.)

1948 R346 Blue Tint

Issued circa 1948-49, the cards in this set derive their name from the distinctive blue coloring used to tint the black-and-white photos. The cards have blank backs and measure 2" x 2-5/8". The set has a high percentage of New York players and was originally issued in strips of six or eight cards each and therefore would have been more appropriately cataloged as a "W" strip card set. The set includes several variations of team desginations. It appears that all cards #25-48, along with possibly some of the team variations can also be found in black-and-white, rather than blue printing. The complete set price does not include the variations. Proof cards have been found with printing on the back indicating they were photographed by Al Weinstein of Brooklyn.

	NM	E	VG
Complete Set (48):	1,300	650.00	375.00
Common Player:	15.00	7.50	4.50
Black-and-White: 1.5-3X			

1	Bill Johnson	15.00	7.50	4.50
2a	Leo Durocher (Brooklyn)	30.00	15.00	9.00
2b	Leo Durocher (New York)	30.00	15.00	9.00
3	Marty Marion	20.00	10.00	6.00
4	Ewell Blackwell	15.00	7.50	4.50
5	John Lindell	15.00	7.50	4.50
6	Larry Jansen	15.00	7.50	4.50
7	Ralph Kiner	30.00	15.00	9.00
8	Chuck Dressen	15.00	7.50	4.50
9	Bobby Brown	15.00	7.50	4.50
10	Luke Appling	30.00	15.00	9.00
11	Bill Nicholson	15.00	7.50	4.50
12	Phil Masi	15.00	7.50	4.50
13	Frank Shea	15.00	7.50	4.50
14	Bob Dillinger	15.00	7.50	4.50
15	Pete Suder	15.00	7.50	4.50
16	Joe DiMaggio	385.00	192.50	115.50
17	John Corriden	15.00	7.50	4.50
18a	Mel Ott (New York)	40.00	20.00	12.00
18b	Mel Ott (No team.)	40.00	20.00	12.00
19	Warren Rosar	15.00	7.50	4.50
20	Warren Spahn	35.00	17.50	10.00
21	Allie Reynolds	20.00	10.00	6.00
22	Lou Boudreau	30.00	15.00	9.00
23	Harry Majeski (Hank) (Photo actually Randy Gumpert.))	15.00	7.50	4.50
24	Frank Crosetti	15.00	7.50	4.50
25	Gus Niarhos	15.00	7.50	4.50
26	Bruce Edwards	15.00	7.50	4.50
27	Rudy York	15.00	7.50	4.50
28	Don Black	15.00	7.50	4.50
29	Lou Gehrig	225.00	110.00	65.00
30	Johnny Mize	30.00	15.00	9.00
31	Ed Stanky	15.00	7.50	4.50
32	Vic Raschi	20.00	10.00	6.00
33	Cliff Mapes	15.00	7.50	4.50
34	Enos Slaughter	30.00	15.00	9.00
35	Hank Greenberg	35.00	17.50	10.00
36	Jackie Robinson	225.00	112.50	67.50
37	Frank Hiller	15.00	7.50	4.50
38	Bob Elliot (Elliott)	15.00	7.50	4.50
39	Harry Walker	15.00	7.50	4.50
40	Ed Lopat	15.00	7.50	4.50
41	Bobby Thomson	20.00	10.00	6.00
42	Tommy Henrich	20.00	10.00	6.00
43	Bobby Feller	35.00	17.50	10.00
44	Ted Williams	125.00	62.50	37.50
45	Dixie Walker	15.00	7.50	4.50
46	Johnnie Vander Meer	20.00	10.00	6.00
47	Clint Hartung	15.00	7.50	4.50
(48)	Charlie Keller	20.00	10.00	6.00

1950 R423

These tiny (5/8" x 7/8") cards are numbered roughly in alphabetical order from 1 through 120. They were issued in 13-card perforated strips from vending machines. The black-and-white cards are printed on thin stock and include the player's name beneath his photo. The backs - most commonly printed in orange, but sometimes purple or green - display a rough drawing of a baseball infield with tiny figures at the various positions. It appears the cards were intended to be used to play a game of baseball. Many of the cards were printed on more than one strip, creating varying levels of scarcity not necessarily reflected in pricing.

	NM	E	VG
Complete Set (119):	850.00	425.00	250.00
Common Player:	6.00	3.00	1.75

1	Richie Ashburn	12.50	6.25	3.75
2	Grover Alexander	10.00	5.00	3.00
3	Frank Baumholtz	6.00	3.00	1.75
4	Ralph Branca	6.00	3.00	1.75
5	Yogi Berra	15.00	7.50	4.50
6	Ewell Blackwell	7.50	3.75	2.25
7	Lou Boudreau	7.50	3.75	2.25
8	Harry Brecheen	6.00	3.00	1.75
9	Chico Carrasquel	6.00	3.00	1.75
10	Jerry Coleman	6.00	3.00	1.75
11	Walker Cooper	6.00	3.00	1.75
12	Roy Campanella	17.50	8.75	5.25
13	Phil Cavaretta (Cavarretta)	6.00	3.00	1.75
14a	Ty Cobb (W/ facsimile autograph.)	30.00	15.00	9.00
14b	Ty Cobb (No facsimile autograph.)	40.00	20.00	12.00
15	Mickey Cochrane	7.50	3.75	2.25
16	Ed Collins	7.50	3.75	2.25
17	Frank Crosetti	7.50	3.75	2.25
18	Larry Doby	7.50	3.75	2.25
19	Walter Dropo	6.00	3.00	1.75
20	Alvin Dark	6.00	3.00	1.75
21	Dizzy Dean	17.50	8.75	5.25
22	Bill Dickey	15.00	7.50	4.50
23	Murray Dickson (Murry)	6.00	3.00	1.75
24	Dom DiMaggio	7.50	3.75	2.25
25	Joe DiMaggio	50.00	25.00	15.00
26	Leo Durocher	7.50	3.75	2.25
27	Luke Easter	6.00	3.00	1.75
28	Bob Elliott	6.00	3.00	1.75
29	Del Ennis	6.00	3.00	1.75
30	Ferris Fain	6.00	3.00	1.75
31	Bob Feller	15.00	7.50	4.50
32	Frank Frisch	7.50	3.75	2.25
33	Billy Goodman	6.00	3.00	1.75
34	Lefty Gomez	7.50	3.75	2.25
35	Lou Gehrig	40.00	20.00	12.00
36	Joe Gordon	6.00	3.00	1.75
37	Sid Gordon	6.00	3.00	1.75
38	Hank Greenberg	15.00	7.50	4.50
39	Lefty Grove	10.00	5.00	3.00
40	Art Houtteman	6.00	3.00	1.75
41	Sid Hudson	6.00	3.00	1.75
42	Ken Heintzelman	6.00	3.00	1.75
43	Gene Hermanski	6.00	3.00	1.75
44	Jim Hearn	6.00	3.00	1.75
45	Gil Hodges	12.50	6.25	3.75
46	Harry Heilman (Heilmann)	7.50	3.75	2.25
47	Tommy Henrich	7.50	3.75	2.25
48	Roger Hornsby (Rogers)	10.00	5.00	3.00

49	Carl Hubbell	10.00	5.00	3.00
50	Edwin Joost	6.00	3.00	1.75
51	John Jorgensen	6.00	3.00	1.75
52	Larry Jansen	6.00	3.00	1.75
53	Nippy Jones	6.00	3.00	1.75
54	Walter Johnson	12.50	6.25	3.75
55	Ellis Kinder	6.00	3.00	1.75
56	Jim Konstanty	6.00	3.00	1.75
57	George Kell	7.50	3.75	2.25
58	Ralph Kiner	7.50	3.75	2.25
59	Bob Lemon	7.50	3.75	2.25
60	Whitey Lockman	6.00	3.00	1.75
61	Ed Lopat	7.50	3.75	2.25
62	Tony Lazzeri	7.50	3.75	2.25
63	Cass Michaels	6.00	3.00	1.75
64	Cliff Mapes	6.00	3.00	1.75
65	Willard Marshall	6.00	3.00	1.75
66	Clyde McCullough	6.00	3.00	1.75
67	Connie Mack	7.50	3.75	2.25
68	Christy Mathewson	17.50	8.75	5.25
69	Joe Medwick	7.50	3.75	2.25
70	Johnny Mize	7.50	3.75	2.25
71	Terry Moore	6.00	3.00	1.75
72	Stan Musial	20.00	10.00	6.00
73	Hal Newhouser	7.50	3.75	2.25
74	Don Newcombe	7.50	3.75	2.25
75	Lefty O'Doul	7.50	3.75	2.25
76	Mel Ott	10.00	5.00	3.00
77	Mel Parnell	6.00	3.00	1.75
78	Johnny Pesky	6.00	3.00	1.75
79	Gerald Priddy	6.00	3.00	1.75
80	Dave Philley	6.00	3.00	1.75
81	Bob Porterfield	6.00	3.00	1.75
82	Andy Pafko	6.00	3.00	1.75
83	Howie Pollet	6.00	3.00	1.75
84	Herb Pennock	7.50	3.75	2.25
85	Al Rosen	7.50	3.75	2.25
86	Pee Wee Reese	15.00	7.50	4.50
87	Del Rice	6.00	3.00	1.75
88	Vic Raschi	7.50	3.75	2.25
89	Allie Reynolds	7.50	3.75	2.25
90	Phil Rizzuto	15.00	7.50	4.50
91	Jackie Robinson	35.00	17.50	10.50
92	Babe Ruth	40.00	20.00	12.00
93	Casey Stengel	15.00	7.50	4.50
94	Vern Stephens	6.00	3.00	1.75
95	Duke Snider	15.00	7.50	4.50
96	Enos Slaughter	7.50	3.75	2.25
97	Al Schoendienst	7.50	3.75	2.25
98	Gerald Staley	6.00	3.00	1.75
99	Clyde Shoun	6.00	3.00	1.75
100	Unknown			
101	Hank Sauer	6.00	3.00	1.75
102	Al Simmons	7.50	3.75	2.25
103	George Sisler	7.50	3.75	2.25
104	Tris Speaker	12.50	6.25	3.75
105	Ed Stanky	6.00	3.00	1.75
106	Virgil Trucks	6.00	3.00	1.75
107	Henry Thompson	6.00	3.00	1.75
108	Bobby Thomson	7.50	3.75	2.25
109	Dazzy Vance	7.50	3.75	2.25
110	Lloyd Waner	7.50	3.75	2.25
111	Paul Waner	7.50	3.75	2.25
112	Gene Woodling	7.50	3.75	2.25
113	Ted Williams	35.00	17.50	10.50
114	Vic Wertz	6.00	3.00	1.75
115	Wes Westrom (Westrum)	6.00	3.00	1.75
116	Johnny Wyrostek	6.00	3.00	1.75
117	Eddie Yost	6.00	3.00	1.75
118	Allen Zarilla	6.00	3.00	1.75
119	Gus Zernial	6.00	3.00	1.75
120	Sam Zoldack (Zoldak)	6.00	3.00	1.75

1909 Ramly Cigarettes (T204)

While issued with both Ramly and T.T.T. brand Turkish tobacco cigarettes, the cards in this set take their name from the more common of the two brands. By whatever name, the set is one of the more interesting and attractive of the early 20th Century. The 2" x 2-1/2" cards carry black-and-white photographic portraits with impressive gold embossed frames and borders on the front. Toward the bottom appears the player's last name, position, team and league. The backs carry only the most basic information on the cigarette company. The complete set price does not include the scarce variations of some players' cards on which the photos are square and surrounded by a heavy gold frame with white borders.

		NM	E	VG
Complete Set (121):		125,000	37,500	18,750
Common Player:		1,750	525.00	265.00
T.T.T.: 4-6X				
(1)	Whitey Alperman	1,750	525.00	265.00
(2a)	John Anderson (Photo inside oval frame.)	1,750	525.00	265.00
(2b)	John Anderson (Photo inside square frame.)	22,500	6,750	3,375
(3)	Jimmy Archer	1,750	525.00	265.00
(4)	Frank Arrelanes (Arellanes)	1,750	525.00	265.00
(5)	Jim Ball	1,750	525.00	265.00
(6)	Neal Ball	1,750	525.00	265.00
(7a)	Frank C. Bancroft (Photo inside oval frame.)	1,750	525.00	265.00
(7b)	Frank C. Bancroft (Photo inside square frame.)	30,000	10,000	5,000
(8)	Johnny Bates	1,750	525.00	265.00
(9)	Fred Beebe	1,750	525.00	265.00
(10)	George Bell	1,750	525.00	265.00
(11)	Chief Bender	5,500	1,650	825.00
(12)	Walter Blair	1,750	525.00	265.00
(13)	Cliff Blankenship	1,750	525.00	265.00
(14)	Frank Bowerman	1,750	525.00	265.00
(15a)	Wm. Bransfield (Photo inside oval frame.)	1,750	525.00	265.00
(15b)	Wm. Bransfield (Photo inside square frame.)	22,500	6,750	3,375
(16)	Roger Bresnahan	5,500	1,650	825.00
(17)	Al Bridwell	1,750	525.00	265.00
(18)	Mordecai Brown	5,500	1,650	825.00
(19)	Fred Burchell	1,750	525.00	265.00
(20a)	Jesse C. Burkett (Photo inside oval frame.)	20,000	6,000	3,000
(20b)	Jesse C. Burkett (Photo inside square frame.)	25,000	7,500	3,750
(21)	Bobby Byrnes (Byrne)	1,750	525.00	265.00
(22)	Bill Carrigan	1,750	525.00	265.00
(23)	Frank Chance	5,500	1,650	825.00
(24)	Charlie Chech	1,750	525.00	265.00
(25)	Ed Cicolte (Cicotte)	3,000	1,000	500.00
(26)	Otis Clymer	1,750	525.00	265.00
(27)	Andy Coakley	1,750	525.00	265.00
(28)	Jimmy Collins	5,500	1,650	825.00
(29)	Ed. Collins	5,500	1,650	825.00
(30)	Wid Conroy	1,750	525.00	265.00
(31)	Jack Coombs	1,750	525.00	265.00
(32)	Doc Crandall	1,750	525.00	265.00
(33)	Lou Criger	1,750	525.00	265.00
(34)	Harry Davis	1,750	525.00	265.00
(35)	Art Devlin	1,750	525.00	265.00
(36a)	Wm. H. Dineen (Dinneen) (Photo inside oval frame.)	1,750	525.00	265.00
(36b)	Wm. H. Dineen (Dinneen) (Photo inside square frame.)	22,500	6,500	3.375.00
(37)	Pat Donahue	1,750	525.00	265.00
(38)	Mike Donlin	1,750	525.00	265.00
(39)	Wild Bill Donovan	1,750	525.00	265.00
(40)	Gus Dorner	1,750	525.00	265.00
(41)	Joe Dunn	1,750	525.00	265.00
(42)	Kid Elberfield (Elberfeld)	1,750	525.00	265.00
(43)	Johnny Evers	5,500	1,650	825.00
(44)	Bob Ewing	1,750	525.00	265.00
(45)	Cecil Ferguson	1,750	525.00	265.00
(46)	Hobe Ferris	1,750	525.00	265.00
(47)	Jerry Freeman	1,750	525.00	265.00
(48)	Art Fromme	1,750	525.00	265.00
(49)	Bob Ganley	1,750	525.00	265.00
(50)	Doc Gessler	1,750	525.00	265.00
(51)	Peaches Graham	1,750	525.00	265.00
(52)	Clark Griffith	5,5000.00	1,650	825.00
(53)	Roy Hartzell (Photo is Topsy Hartsel)	1,750	525.00	265.00
(54)	Charlie Hemphill	1,750	525.00	265.00
(55)	Dick Hoblitzel (Hoblitzell)	1,750	525.00	265.00
(56a)	Geo. Howard (Photo inside oval frame.)	1,750	525.00	265.00
(56b)	Geo. Howard (Photo inside square frame.)	22,500	6,500	3,250
(57)	Harry Howell (Photo is Jack Powell)	1,750	525.00	265.00
(58)	Miller Huggins	5,500	1,650	825.00
(59)	John Hummell (Hummel)	1,750	525.00	265.00
(60)	Walter Johnson	35,000	10,500	5,250
(61)	Thos. Jones	1,750	525.00	265.00
(62)	Mike Kahoe	1,750	525.00	265.00
(63)	Ed Kargar	1,750	525.00	265.00
(64)	Wee Willie Keeler	5,500	1,650	825.00
(65)	Red Kleinon (Kleinow)	1,750	525.00	265.00
(66)	Jack Knight	1,750	525.00	265.00
(67)	Ed Konetchey	1,750	525.00	265.00
(68)	Vive Lindaman	1,750	525.00	265.00
(69)	Hans Loebert (Lobert)	1,750	525.00	265.00
(70)	Harry Lord	1,750	525.00	265.00
(71)	Harry Lumley	1,750	525.00	265.00
(72)	Johnny Lush	1,750	525.00	265.00
(73)	Rube Manning	1,750	525.00	265.00
(74)	Jimmy McAleer	1,750	875.00	525.00
(75)	Amby McConnell	1,750	525.00	265.00
(76)	Moose McCormick	1,750	525.00	265.00
(77)	Harry McIntyre	1,750	525.00	265.00
(78)	Larry McLean	1,750	525.00	265.00
(79)	Fred Merkle	1,750	525.00	265.00
(80)	Clyde Milan	1,750	525.00	265.00
(81)	Mike Mitchell	1,750	525.00	265.00
(82a)	Pat Moran (Photo inside oval frame.)	1,750	525.00	265.00
(82b)	Pat Moran (Photo inside square frame.)	22,500	6,500	3,250
(83)	Cy Morgan	1,750	525.00	265.00
(84)	Tim Murname (Murnane)	1,750	525.00	265.00
(85)	Danny Murphy	1,750	525.00	265.00
(86)	Red Murray	1,750	525.00	265.00
(87)	Doc Newton	1,750	525.00	265.00
(88)	Simon Nichols (Nicholls)	1,750	525.00	265.00
(89)	Harry Niles	1,750	525.00	265.00
(90)	Bill O'Hare (Photo is Tom O'Hara)	1,750	525.00	265.00
(91)	Charley O'Leary	1,750	525.00	265.00
(92)	Dode Paskert	1,750	525.00	265.00
(93)	Barney Pelty	1,750	525.00	265.00
(94)	Jake Pfeister	1,750	525.00	265.00
(95)	Ed Plank	17,250	5,175	2,575
(96)	Jack Powell (Photo is Harry Howell)	1,750	525.00	265.00
(97)	Bugs Raymond	1,750	525.00	265.00
(98)	Tom Reilly	1,750	525.00	265.00
(99)	Claude Ritchey	1,750	525.00	265.00
(100)	Nap Rucker	1,750	525.00	265.00
(101)	Ed Ruelbach (Reulbach)	1,750	525.00	265.00
(102)	Slim Sallee	1,750	525.00	265.00
(103)	Germany Schaefer	1,750	525.00	265.00
(104)	Jimmy Schekard (Sheckard)	1,750	525.00	265.00
(105)	Admiral Schlei	1,750	525.00	265.00
(106)	Wildfire Schulte	1,750	525.00	265.00
(107)	Jimmy Sebring	1,750	525.00	265.00
(108)	Bill Shipke	1,750	525.00	265.00
(109)	Charlie Smith	1,750	525.00	265.00
(110)	Tubby Spencer	1,750	525.00	265.00
(111)	Jake Stahl	1,750	525.00	265.00
(112)	Jim Stephens	1,750	525.00	265.00
(113)	Harry Stienfeldt (Steinfeldt)	1,750	525.00	265.00
(114)	Gabby Street	1,750	525.00	265.00
(115)	Bill Sweeney	1,750	525.00	265.00
(116)	Fred Tenney	1,750	525.00	265.00
(117)	Ira Thomas	1,750	525.00	265.00
(118)	Joe Tinker	5,500	1,650	825.00
(119)	Bob Unglane (Unglaub)	1,750	525.00	265.00
(120)	Heinie Wagner	1,750	525.00	265.00
(121)	Bobby Wallace	5,500	1,650	825.00

1910 Ramly Team Composite Premiums

At least two versions of coupons found in boxes of Ramly (and possibly T.T.T.) cigarettes offered a large-format (about 23" x 18-1/2") black-and-white photogravure premium featuring a composite of player portraits for five, or six, popular teams of the era. Players are identified in the bottom border, which also has a credit line for the tobacco company. To date, only the 1909 pennant winners' premiums have been confirmed as surviving.

		NM	E	VG
(1)	Boston Red Sox (Unconfirmed)			
(2)	Boston Rustlers			
(3)	Detroit Tigers			
(4)	New York Giants (Unconfirmed)			
(5)	Philadelphia A's (unconfirmed)			
(6)	Pittsburgh Pirates (5/04 auction, trimmed, $3,163)			

1881 Randall Studio Cabinets

What the players of the 1881 Boston Beaneaters were doing posing in their Sunday best suits at the Detroit studio of Randall the photographer is open to speculation, as is the question of whether other teams' players were also photographed there. These cabinets are about 4-1/4" x 6-1/2" and blank-backed. On most of them the player name and city and in small type on the portrait.

		NM	E	VG
Common Player:		2,000	1,000	600.00
(1)	Tommy Bond	2,000	1,000	600.00
(2)	Tom Deasley	2,000	1,000	600.00
(3)	John Morrill	2,000	1,000	600.00
(4)	John Richmond	2,000	1,000	600.00
(5)	Ezra Sutton	2,000	1,000	600.00
(6)	Jim Whitney	2,000	1,000	600.00
(7)	Harry Wright	8,000	4,000	2,400

1950s-70s Rawlings Advisory Staff Photos

Advisory staff photos were a promtional item which debuted in the early 1950s, flourished in the Sixties and died in the early 1970s. Generally 8" x 10" (sometimes a little larger), these black-and-white (a few later were color) glossy photos picture players who had contracted with a major baseball equipment company to endorse and use their product. Usually the product - most often a glove - was prominently displayed in the photo. The pictures were often displayed in the windows of sporting goods stores or the walls of sports departments and were sometimes made available to customers. Because the companies tended to stick with players over the years, some photos were reissued, sometimes with and sometimes without a change of team, pose or style. All advisory staff photos of the era are checklisted here in alphabetical order. A pose description is given for each known picture. The photos are checklisted here in alphabetical order. It is unlikely this list is complete. In general, Rawlings advisory staff photos feature a white box within the photo which contains the glove-company logo and a facsimile autograph of the player. Gaps have been left in the checklist numbering to accommodate possible additions.

		NM	E	VG
Common Player:		25.00	12.50	7.50
(1)	Joe Adcock (Braves, kneeling.)	35.00	17.50	10.50
(2)	Joe Adcock (Braves, locker room.)	25.00	12.50	7.50
(3)	Joe Adcock (Braves, upper body.)	25.00	12.50	7.50
(4)	Hank Aguirre (Tigers, glove on knee.)	25.00	12.50	7.50
(5)	Bobby Avila (Indians, upper body.)	25.00	12.50	7.50
(6)	Bob Bailey (Pirates, kneeling.)	25.00	12.50	7.50
(7)	Ed Bailey (Reds, gearing up in dugout.)	25.00	12.50	7.50
(8)	Ed Bailey (Giants, catching crouch.)	25.00	12.50	7.50
(9)	Earl Battey (Twins, catching crouch.)	25.00	12.50	7.50
(10)	Earl Battey (Twins, kneeling w/bat.)	25.00	12.50	7.50
(11)	Johnny Bench (Crouching, no catcher's gear.)	45.00	22.00	13.50
(12)	Dick Bertell (Cubs, catching crouch.)	25.00	12.50	7.50

		NM	E	VG
(13)	John Blanchard (Yankees, catching crouch.)	25.00	12.50	7.50
(14)	John Blanchard (Yankees, dugout step.)	25.00	12.50	7.50
(15)	"Clete" Boyer (Yankees, fielding.)	25.00	12.50	7.50
(16)	Ken Boyer (Cardinals, in front of locker.)	25.00	12.50	7.50
(17)	Ken Boyer (Cardinals, b/w, kneeling.)	25.00	12.50	7.50
(18)	Ken Boyer (Mets, b/w, full-length.)	25.00	12.50	7.50
(19)	Ken Boyer (Mets, color, leaning on bat.)	25.00	12.50	7.50
(20)	Ken Boyer (White Sox, upper body.)	30.00	15.00	9.00
(21)	Lew Burdette (Braves, beginning wind-up.)	25.00	12.50	7.50
(22)	Lew Burdette (Braves, upper body w/ball.)	35.00	17.50	10.50
(23)	Bob Cerv (A's, at bat rack.)	25.00	12.50	7.50
(24)	Gordon Coleman (Reds, kneeling w/bat.)	25.00	12.50	7.50
(25)	Tony Conigliaro (Red Sox, glove at chest.)	45.00	22.00	13.50
(26)	Wes Covington (Braves, upper body.)	25.00	12.50	7.50
(27)	Joe Cunningham (White Sox, glove at knee.)	25.00	12.50	7.50
(28)	Joe Cunningham (Cardinals, chest-up.)	25.00	12.50	7.50
(29)	Tommy Davis (Dodgers, dugout step.)	25.00	12.50	7.50
(30)	Don Demeter (Dodgers, upper body.)	25.00	12.50	7.50
(31)	Don Demeter (Phillies, hands on knees.)	25.00	12.50	7.50
(32)	Dick Dietz (Giants, catching pose.)	25.00	12.50	7.50
(33)	Tito Francona (Indians, sitting w/glove.)	25.00	12.50	7.50
(34)	Steve Garvey (Dodgers, horizontal, pose and action.)	25.00	12.50	7.50
(35)	Mudcat Grant (Indians, horizontal, upper body.)	25.00	12.50	7.50
(36)	Dick Groat (Pirates, b/w, full-length.)	25.00	12.50	7.50
(37)	Dick Groat (Pirates, b/w, upper body.)	25.00	12.50	7.50
(38)	Dick Groat (Cardinals, b/w, kneeling w/bat.)	25.00	12.50	7.50
(39)	Dick Groat (Cardinals, b/w, kneeling.)	25.00	12.50	7.50
(40)	Harvey Haddix (Pirates, kneeling.)	25.00	12.50	7.50
(41)	Harvey Haddix (Pirates, locker room.)	25.00	12.50	7.50
(42)	Ken Holtzman (Cubs, hands on knees.)	25.00	12.50	7.50
(43)	Ken Holtzman (A's, horizontal, two poses.)	25.00	12.50	7.50
(44)	Elston Howard (Yankees, catching crouch.)	30.00	15.00	9.00
(45)	Al Hrabosky (Cardinals, upper body.)	25.00	12.50	7.50
(46)	Larry Jackson (Cubs, kneeling.)	25.00	12.50	7.50
(47)	Larry Jackson (Cardinals, fielding.)	25.00	12.50	7.50
(48)	Larry Jackson (Cardinals, full-length on mound.)	25.00	12.00	7.50
(49)	Reggie Jackson (A's, full-length.)	40.00	20.00	12.00
(50)	Joey Jay (Reds, dugout step, glove on rail.)	25.00	12.50	7.50
(51)	Fergie Jenkins (Cubs, hands on knees.)	25.00	12.50	7.50
(52)	Ed Kranepool (Mets, color, batting.)	25.00	12.50	7.50
(53)	Tony Kubek (Full-length, fielding.)	25.00	12.50	7.50
(54)	Tony Kubek (Kneeling, no bat.)	25.00	12.50	7.50
(55)	Tony Kubek (Kneeling w/bat.)	25.00	12.50	7.50
(56)	Tony Kubek (Horizontal, upper body.)	25.00	12.50	7.50
(57)	Vern Law (Locker room.)	25.00	12.50	7.50
(58)	Jim Lefebvre (Dodgers, kneeling, bat on shoulder.)	25.00	12.50	7.50

		NM	E	VG
(59)	Sherman Lollar (White Sox, throwing from crouch.)	25.00	12.50	7.50
(60)	Art Mahaffey (Phillies, upper body.)	25.00	12.50	7.50
(61)	Mickey Mantle (Upper body, road uniform.)	150.00	75.00	45.00
(62)	Mickey Mantle (Leaning, hands on knees.)	100.00	50.00	30.00
(63)	Mickey Mantle (Seated w/ bat, glove on knee.)	130.00	65.00	40.00
(64)	Mickey Mantle (Kneeling)	150.00	75.00	45.00
(65)	Mickey Mantle (Seated at locker, pointing to glove.)	150.00	75.00	45.00
(66)	Eddie Mathews (Braves, full-length.)	45.00	22.00	13.50
(67)	Eddie Mathews (Braves, sepia, upper body.)	45.00	22.00	13.50
(68)	Eddie Mathews (Braves, upper body, glove in front.)	45.00	22.00	13.50
(69)	Eddie Mathews (Braves, upper body, looking at glove.)	45.00	22.00	13.50
(70)	Dal Maxvill (Cardinals, bat on shoulder.)	25.00	12.50	7.50
(71)	Dal Maxvill (Cardinals, fielding.)	25.00	12.50	7.50
(72)	Charlie Maxwell (Tigers, horizontal, upper body.)	25.00	12.50	7.50
(73)	Tim McCarver (Cardinals, catching crouch.)	25.00	12.50	7.50
(74)	Lindy McDaniel (Cardinals, b/w, on dugout steps.)	25.00	12.50	7.50
(75)	Dave McNally (Orioles, upper body.)	25.00	12.50	7.50
(76)	Wilmer Mizell (Cardinals, upper body.)	25.00	12.50	7.50
(77)	Wally Moon (Dodgers, kneeling.)	25.00	12.50	7.50
(78)	Wally Moon (Dodgers, standing.)	25.00	12.50	7.50
(79)	Stan Musial (Upper body.)	50.00	25.00	15.00
(80)	Stan Musial (Horizontal, batting.)	50.00	25.00	15.00
(81)	Stan Musial (Full-length holding glove and bat.)	50.00	25.00	15.00
(82)	Stan Musial (Kneeling on bat.)	50.00	25.00	15.00
(83)	Stan Musial (Kneeling on bat, glove on ground.)	50.00	25.00	15.00
(84)	Stan Musial (Kneeling, glove in front, Busch Stadium.)	50.00	25.00	15.00
(85)	Stan Musial (Full-length, hands on knees.)	80.00	40.00	24.00
(86)	Stan Musial (Socks to cap, white background, in proposed '56 road uniform.)	125.00	62.00	37.00
(87)	Charlie Neal (Dodgers, kneeling.)	25.00	12.50	7.50
(88)	Charlie Neal (Dodgers, looking into glove.)	25.00	12.50	7.50
(89)	Rocky Nelson (Pirates, kneeling.)	25.00	12.50	7.50
(90)	Rocky Nelson (Pirates, fielding.)	25.00	12.50	7.50
(91)	Amos Otis (Royals, upper body.)	25.00	12.50	7.50
(92)	Jim Perry (Indians, pitching.)	25.00	12.50	7.50
(93)	Boog Powell (Orioles, full-length.)	25.00	12.50	7.50
(94)	Rick Reichardt (Angels, full-length.)	25.00	12.50	7.50
(95)	Brooks Robinson (Dugout step.)	45.00	22.00	13.50
(96)	Brooks Robinson (Throwing)	45.00	22.00	13.50
(97)	Brooks Robinson (Standing w/glove.)	45.00	22.00	13.50
(98)	Brooks Robinson (Tying shoe.)	45.00	22.00	13.50
(99)	John Romano (Indians, adjusting shinguard.)	25.00	12.50	7.50
(101)	Manny Sanguillen (Pirates, catching crouch.)	25.00	12.50	7.50
(102)	Chuck Schilling (Full-length.)	25.00	12.50	7.50
(103)	Herb Score (Indians, pitching.)	25.00	12.50	7.50
(104)	Norm Siebern (A's, vest.)	25.00	12.50	7.50

(105)	Norm Siebern (A's, jersey.)	25.00	12.50	7.50
(106)	Roy Sievers (Senators, full-length.)	25.00	12.50	7.50
(107)	Roy Sievers (White Sox, drinking fountain.)	25.00	12.50	7.50
(108)	Roy Sievers (Phillies, kneeling.)	25.00	12.50	7.50
(109)	Bob Skinner (Pirates, upper body.)	25.00	12.50	7.50
(110)	Duke Snider (Brooklyn Dodgers, full-length.)	45.00	22.00	13.50
(111)	Duke Snider (L.A. Dodgers, upper body.)	45.00	22.00	13.50
(112)	Warren Spahn (Braves, b/w, wind-up.)	45.00	22.00	13.50
(114)	Willie Stargell (Upper body.)	35.00	17.50	10.50
(115)	Willie Stargell (Full-length.)	35.00	17.50	10.50
(116)	Tom Tresh (Yankees, fielding.)	25.00	12.50	7.50
(117)	Tom Tresh (Yankees, full-length.)	25.00	12.50	7.50
(119)	Bob Turley (Yankees, upper body.)	25.00	12.50	7.50
(120)	Bob Turley (At water fountain.)	25.00	12.50	7.50
(121)	Bill White (Cardinals, glove over rail.)	25.00	12.50	7.50
(122)	Bill White (Phillies, b/w, full-length.)	25.00	12.50	7.50
(123)	Bill White (Phillies, color, full-length.)	25.00	12.50	7.50
(124)	Billy Williams (Cubs, full-length.)	35.00	17.50	10.50
(126)	Steve Yeager (Dodgers, upper body.)	25.00	12.50	7.50

1952 Rawlings Stan Musial Premium Photo

In this black-and-white, blank-backed premium photo, Musial is shown in a batting stance superimposed over a game-action photo at Sportsman's Park. A white facsimile autograph is at lower-right. The wide bottom border of the 5" x 7" picture has the Rawlings logoscript and address.

	NM	E	VG
Stan Musial	40.00	20.00	12.00

1954 Rawlings Stan Musial

The date of issue is speculation although the picture is certainly from 1955 or earlier. This 5-1/2" x 7-1/2" colorized photo is actually part of a cardboard Rawlings glove box. The panel at lower-right of the card identifies it as "A GENUINE RAWLINGS FACSIMILE AUTOGRAPH PICTURE." Back is blank.

	NM	E	VG
Stan Musial	300.00	150.00	90.00

1955 Rawlings Stan Musial

Though missing from Topps and Bowman card sets from 1954-57, Cardinals superstar Stan Musial wasn't entirely unavailable on baseball cards. About 1955 he appeared on a series of six cards found on boxes of Rawlings baseball gloves carrying Musial's endorsement. The cards feature black-and-white photos of Musial set against a blue background. Because the cards were part of a display box, they are blank-backed. Depending on the position on the box, the cards measure approximately 2" x 3" (#1A and 2A) or 2-1/2" x 3-3/4" (#1-4). Cards are numbered in a yellow star at upper left.

		NM	E	VG
	Complete Set (6):	2,500	1,250	750.00
	Complete Box:	3,000	1,500	900.00
	Common Card:	450.00	225.00	125.00
1	Stan Musial (Portrait)	450.00	225.00	125.00
1A	Stan Musial (Portrait with bat.)	450.00	225.00	125.00
2	Stan Musial (Kneeling)	450.00	225.00	125.00
2A	Stan Musial (Portrait)	450.00	225.00	125.00
3	Stan Musial (Swinging, horizontal.)	450.00	225.00	125.00
4	Stan Musial (Batting pose.)	450.00	225.00	125.00

1963 Rawlings Stan Musial Premium

This premium was available by mail and commemorates the career of long-time Rawlings spokesman Stan Musial upon his retirement. The package contains an approximately 9" x 10" color portrait photo of Musial with a facsimile autograph, a sheet illustrated with four portraits of Musial during his career and listing his many records, and a note from the company indicating future availability of Musial gloves.

	NM	E	VG
Stan Musial	60.00	30.00	18.00

1964 Rawlings Glove Box

Measuring about 2-3/8" x 4" when properly cut off the glove boxes on which they were printed, these full-color cards show stars of the day posing with their Rawlings glove prominently displayed. The blank-backed unnumbered cards are checklisted here alphabetically. The quality of cutting should be considered in grading these cards. In actuality, the cards were not meant to be cut from the boxes, but rather to show which premium photo was packed inside the glove box. Two cards of each player appear on the box.

		NM	E	VG
	Complete Set (8):	450.00	225.00	135.00
	Common Player:	25.00	12.50	7.50
	Complete Box:	750.00	375.00	225.00
(1)	Ken Boyer	35.00	17.50	10.50
(2)	Tommy Davis	25.00	12.50	7.50
(3)	Dick Groat	25.00	12.50	7.50
(4)	Mickey Mantle	200.00	100.00	60.00
(5)	Brooks Robinson	60.00	30.00	18.00
(6)	Warren Spahn	50.00	25.00	15.00
(7)	Tom Tresh	25.00	12.50	7.50
(8)	Billy Williams	45.00	22.00	13.50

1964-66 Rawlings Premium Photos

One premium photo was inserted into each baseball glove box sold by Rawlings beginning in 1964 and continuing at least into 1966, when some changes in players and pictures were added. The 8" x 9-1/2" full-color photos were advertised on the outside of the boxes in miniature form. Each of the photos pictures a player posed with his Rawlings leather prominently displayed. A black facsimile autograph is printed on the front.

		NM	E	VG
	Complete Set (12):	600.00	300.00	180.00
	Common Player:	20.00	10.00	6.00
(1a)	Ken Boyer (Cardinals, 1964.)	25.00	12.50	7.50
(1b)	Ken Boyer (Mets, 1966.)	25.00	12.50	7.50
(2)	Tommy Davis	20.00	10.00	6.00
(3)	Dick Groat	20.00	10.00	6.00
(4a)	Mickey Mantle (No undershirt, 1964.)	150.00	75.00	45.00
(4b)	Mickey Mantle (Black undershirt, 1966.)	150.00	75.00	45.00
(5a)	Brooks Robinson (Full-bird cap, 1964.)	70.00	35.00	21.00
(5b)	Brooks Robinson (Bird's-head cap, 1966.)	85.00	42.00	25.00
(6)	Warren Spahn	75.00	37.00	22.00
(7)	Tom Tresh	20.00	10.00	6.00
(8)	Bill White (1966)	20.00	10.00	6.00
(9)	Billy Williams	50.00	25.00	15.00

1965 Rawlings MVP Premiums

The American and National League MVPs are featured in this pair of 8-1/8" x 10-1/4" premium pictures sponsored by the sporting goods manufacturer. The manner of their distribution is unknown. Printed on thin card stock, the premiums feature the artwork of Amadee Wohlschlaeger.

		NM	E	VG
	Complete Set (2):	125.00	65.00	40.00
(1)	Ken Boyer	65.00	35.00	20.00
(2)	Brooks Robinson	75.00	40.00	25.00

1969 Rawlings

How these cards were distributed is not certain today, nor is the extent of the series known. The approximately 3" x 5" black-and-white cards feature a portrait photo on front, with a wide white border at bottom that holds a facsimile autograph. The back has complete major and minor league stats, career highlights and a Rawlings ad.

	NM	E	VG
Reggie Jackson	900.00	450.00	275.00
Mickey Mantle	2,500	1,250	750.00

1930 Ray-O-Print Photo Kits

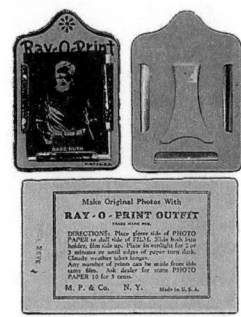

This was one of several contemporary kits for do-it-your-self production of photo prints. The outfits were produced by M.P. & Co., of New York. The novelty kit consists of a 4-1/8" x 2-1/2" kraft paper envelope with production instructions printed on the outside and the name of the subject rubber-stamped on one end. Inside was a film negative, a piece of light-sensitive photo paper (each 1-7/8" x 2-15/16") and a tin stand for exposing and displaying the photo. Values shown are for complete kits. Individual components would be pro-rated, with the negative being the most valuable of the pieces. Anyone with a negative could make unlimited prints today, and even make them look old; collectors should use caution in purchasing prints alone.

	NM	E	VG
Complete Set (8):	1,000	500.00	300.00
Common Kit:	125.00	67.00	38.00
Card: 20 Percent			
(1) Lou Gehrig	250.00	125.00	75.00
(2) Babe Ruth	400.00	200.00	120.00
(3) Jack Dempsey (Boxer)	100.00	50.00	30.00
(4) Herbert Hoover (President)	75.00	37.00	22.00
(5) "Lindy"(Charles Lindbergh) (Aviator)	150.00	75.00	45.00
(6) Mary Pickford (Actress)	50.00	25.00	15.00
(7) Will Rogers (Humorist)	50.00	25.00	15.00
(8) We(Charles Lindbergh) (W/ plane, Spirit of St. Louis.)	150.00	75.00	45.00

1899 Henry Reccius Cigars Honus Wagner

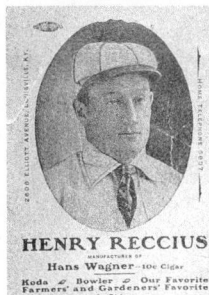

The date of this card's issue is probable, though it could have been issued anytime between 1897-99 during Wagner's stay in Louisville. The 3-3/8" x 4-11/16" card is printed in black-on-orange with an oval photograph of Wagner at center. Advertising for the company that marketed cigars under his name is around the border. The back has a lengthy pro-trade union poem. Only one example of the card is known. It was graded by PSA sometime after 1998 and given a Poor-Fair designation. The card was auctioned in November, 2001, for $21,850, and again in April, 2006, for $52,040.

1912 Recruit Little Cigars

This is the most common of the back advertisements found in T207. Factory 606 (Maryland) backs are much scarcer than those with Factory 240 (Pennsylvania), but currently carry little premium on that basis. Back printing is usually found in black, but several examples have been authenticated with brown ink printing on back. Their value is undetermined.

(See 1912 T207.)

1976 Red Barn Discs

The scarcest among the several regional sponsors of player disc sets issued in 1976 are those of the Red Barn family restaurant chain in Southeastern Wisconsin. The discs are 3-3/8" diameter with a black-and-white player portrait photo in the center of the baseball design. A line of red stars is above, while the left and right panels feature one of several bright colors. Produced by Michael Schecter Associates under license from the Major League Baseball Players Association, the player photos have had uniform and cap logos removed. Backs are printed in red and purple. The unnumbered checklist here is presented in alphabetical order.

		NM	E	VG
Complete Set (70):		500.00	250.00	150.00
Common Player:		8.00	4.00	2.50
(1)	Henry Aaron	65.00	32.00	19.50
(2)	Johnny Bench	25.00	12.50	7.50
(3)	Vida Blue	8.00	4.00	2.50
(4)	Larry Bowa	8.00	4.00	2.50
(5)	Lou Brock	20.00	10.00	6.00
(6)	Jeff Burroughs	8.00	4.00	2.50
(7)	John Candelaria	8.00	4.00	2.50
(8)	Jose Cardenal	8.00	4.00	2.50
(9)	Rod Carew	20.00	10.00	6.00
(10)	Steve Carlton	25.00	12.50	7.50
(11)	Dave Cash	8.00	4.00	2.50
(12)	Cesar Cedeno	8.00	4.00	2.50
(13)	Ron Cey	8.00	4.00	2.50
(14)	Carlton Fisk	20.00	10.00	6.00
(15)	Tito Fuentes	8.00	4.00	2.50
(16)	Steve Garvey	12.00	6.00	3.50
(17)	Ken Griffey	8.00	4.00	2.50
(18)	Don Gullett	8.00	4.00	2.50
(19)	Willie Horton	8.00	4.00	2.50
(20)	Al Hrabosky	8.00	4.00	2.50
(21)	Catfish Hunter	20.00	10.00	6.00
(22)	Reggie Jackson	40.00	20.00	12.00
(23)	Randy Jones	8.00	4.00	2.50
(24)	Jim Kaat	8.00	4.00	2.50
(25)	Don Kessinger	8.00	4.00	2.50
(26)	Dave Kingman	8.00	4.00	2.50
(27)	Jerry Koosman	8.00	4.00	2.50
(28)	Mickey Lolich	8.00	4.00	2.50
(29)	Greg Luzinski	8.00	4.00	2.50
(30)	Fred Lynn	10.00	5.00	3.00
(31)	Bill Madlock	8.00	4.00	2.50
(32)	Carlos May	8.00	4.00	2.50
(33)	John Mayberry	8.00	4.00	2.50
(34)	Bake McBride	8.00	4.00	2.50
(35)	Doc Medich	8.00	4.00	2.50
(36)	Andy Messersmith	8.00	4.00	2.50
(37)	Rick Monday	8.00	4.00	2.50
(38)	John Montefusco	8.00	4.00	2.50
(39)	Jerry Morales	8.00	4.00	2.50
(40)	Joe Morgan	20.00	10.00	6.00
(41)	Thurman Munson	15.00	7.50	4.50
(42)	Bobby Murcer	8.00	4.00	2.50
(43)	Al Oliver	8.00	4.00	2.50
(44)	Jim Palmer	20.00	10.00	6.00
(45)	Dave Parker	8.00	4.00	2.50
(46)	Tony Perez	20.00	10.00	6.00
(47)	Jerry Reuss	8.00	4.00	2.50
(48)	Brooks Robinson	25.00	12.50	7.50
(49)	Frank Robinson	25.00	12.50	7.50
(50)	Steve Rogers	8.00	4.00	2.50
(51)	Pete Rose	65.00	32.00	19.50
(52)	Nolan Ryan	100.00	50.00	30.00
(53)	Manny Sanguillen	8.00	4.00	2.50
(54)	Mike Schmidt	45.00	22.00	13.50
(55)	Tom Seaver	25.00	12.50	7.50
(56)	Ted Simmons	8.00	4.00	2.50
(57)	Reggie Smith	8.00	4.00	2.50
(58)	Willie Stargell	20.00	10.00	6.00
(59)	Rusty Staub	12.00	6.00	3.50
(60)	Rennie Stennett	8.00	4.00	2.50
(61)	Don Sutton	20.00	10.00	6.00
(62)	Andy Thornton	8.00	4.00	2.50
(63)	Luis Tiant	8.00	4.00	2.50
(64)	Joe Torre	12.00	6.00	3.50
(65)	Mike Tyson	8.00	4.00	2.50
(66)	Bob Watson	8.00	4.00	2.50
(67)	Wilbur Wood	8.00	4.00	2.50
(68)	Jimmy Wynn	8.00	4.00	2.50
(69)	Carl Yastrzemski	25.00	12.50	7.50
(70)	Richie Zisk	8.00	4.00	2.50

1912 Red Cross Tobacco (T207)

Among the rarest back variations known in the tobacco card series is the Red Cross back on T207. Only a handful of examples have ever been seen. Determination of values is an inexact science.

(See 1912 T207 for potential checklist. A small group of specimens new to the market was discovered in mid-2010.

Russell Blackburne (Sold for $9,400 in G-VG in 5/10 auction)
George Weaver (Sold for $10,187 in Fair in 9/02 auction)

1910-12 Red Cross Tobacco Type 1 (T215)

The T215 set issued by Red Cross Tobacco is another of the Louisiana regional sets closely related to the T206 "White Border" tobacco cards. Very similar to the T213 Coupon cards, the Red Cross Tobacco cards are found in two distinct types, both featuring color player lithographs and measuring approximately 1-1/2" x 2-5/8", the standard tobacco card size. Type 1 Red Cross cards, issued from 1910 to 1912, have brown captions; while Type 2 cards, most of which appear to be from 1912-13, have blue printing. The backs of both types are identical, displaying the Red Cross name and emblem, which can be used to positively identify the set and differentiate it from the other Louisiana sets of the same period. Several variations have been found, most of them involving caption changes. Gaps have been left in the assigned numbering to accommodate future additions to these checklists.

		NM	E	VG
Common Player:		825.00	330.00	165.00
(1)	Red Ames	825.00	330.00	165.00
(2)	Home Run Baker	3,000	1,500	900.00
(3)	Neal Ball	825.00	330.00	165.00

(4)	Chief Bender (No trees in background.)	3,000	1,500	900.00
(5)	Chief Bender (Trees in background.)	3,000	1,500	900.00
(6)	Al Bridwell	825.00	330.00	165.00
(7)	Bobby Byrne	825.00	330.00	165.00
(8)	Howie Camnitz	825.00	330.00	165.00
(9)	Frank Chance	3,000	1,500	900.00
(10)	Hal Chase (Holding trophy.)	3,500	1,750	1,050
(11)	Ty Cobb	12,500	6,250	3,750
(12)	Eddie Collins	3,000	1,500	900.00
(13)	Wid Conroy	825.00	330.00	165.00
(14)	Doc Crandall	825.00	330.00	165.00
(15)	Sam Crawford	3,000	1,500	900.00
(16)	Birdie Cree	825.00	330.00	165.00
(17)	Harry Davis	825.00	330.00	165.00
(18)	Josh Devore	825.00	330.00	165.00
(19)	Mike Donlin	825.00	330.00	165.00
(20)	Mickey Doolan	825.00	330.00	165.00
(21)	Patsy Dougherty	825.00	330.00	165.00
(22)	Larry Doyle (Batting)	825.00	330.00	165.00
(23)	Larry Doyle (Portrait)	825.00	330.00	165.00
(24)	Kid Elberfeld	825.00	330.00	165.00
(25)	Russ Ford	825.00	330.00	165.00
(26)	Art Fromme	825.00	330.00	165.00
(27)	Clark Griffith	3,000	1,500	900.00
(28)	Topsy Hartsel	825.00	330.00	165.00
(29)	Dick Hoblitzell	825.00	330.00	165.00
(30)	Solly Hofman	825.00	330.00	165.00
(31)	Del Howard	825.00	330.00	165.00
(32)	Miller Huggins (Hands at mouth.)	3,000	1,500	900.00
(33)	Miller Huggins (Portrait)	3,000	1,500	900.00
(34)	John Hummel	825.00	330.00	165.00
(35)	Hughie Jennings (Both hands showing.)	3,000	1,500	900.00
(36)	Hughie Jennings (One hand showing.)	3,000	1,500	900.00
(37)	Walter Johnson	4,500	2,250	1,350
(38)	Ed Konetchy	825.00	330.00	165.00
(39)	Harry Krause	825.00	330.00	165.00
(41)	Nap Lajoie	3,000	1,500	900.00
(42)	Joe Lake	825.00	330.00	165.00
(43)	Arlie Latham	825.00	330.00	165.00
(44)	Tommy Leach	825.00	330.00	165.00
(45)	Lefty Leifield	825.00	330.00	165.00
(46)	Harry Lord	825.00	330.00	165.00
(47)	Sherry Magee	825.00	330.00	165.00
(48)	Rube Marquard (Pitching)	3,000	1,500	900.00
(49)	Rube Marquard (Portrait)	3,000	1,500	900.00
(51)	Christy Mathewson (Dark cap.)	7,500	3,700	2,200
(52)	Christy Mathewson (White cap.)	9,000	4,500	2,700
(53)	Joe McGinnity	3,000	1,500	900.00
(54)	John McGraw (Glove at hip.)	3,000	1,500	900.00
(55)	John McGraw (Portrait)	3,000	1,500	900.00
(56)	Harry McIntyre	825.00	330.00	165.00
(57)	Fred Merkle	825.00	330.00	165.00
(58)	Chief Meyers	825.00	330.00	165.00
(59)	Dots Miller	825.00	330.00	165.00
(61)	Mike Mowrey	825.00	330.00	165.00
(62)	Danny Murphy	825.00	330.00	165.00
(63)	Red Murray	825.00	330.00	165.00
(64)	Rebel Oakes	825.00	330.00	165.00
(65)	Charley O'Leary	825.00	330.00	165.00
(66)	Dode Paskert	825.00	330.00	165.00
(67)	Barney Pelty	825.00	330.00	165.00
(68)	Jack Quinn	825.00	330.00	165.00
(69)	Ed Reulbach	825.00	330.00	165.00
(71)	Nap Rucker	825.00	330.00	165.00
(72)	Germany Schaefer	825.00	330.00	165.00
(73)	Wildfire Schulte	825.00	330.00	165.00
(74)	Jimmy Sheckard	825.00	330.00	165.00
(75)	Frank Smith	825.00	330.00	165.00
(76)	Frank Smither (Smith)	825.00	330.00	165.00
(77)	Tris Speaker	3,500	1,750	1,050
(78)	Jake Stahl	825.00	330.00	165.00
(79)	Harry Steinfeldt	825.00	330.00	165.00
(81)	Gabby Street (Catching)	825.00	330.00	165.00
(82)	Gabby Street (Portrait)	825.00	330.00	165.00
(83)	Jeff Sweeney	825.00	330.00	165.00
(84)	Lee Tannehill	825.00	330.00	165.00
(85)	Joe Tinker (Bat off shoulder.)	3,000	1,500	900.00
(86)	Joe Tinker (Bat on shoulder.)	3,000	1,500	900.00
(87)	Heinie Wagner	825.00	330.00	165.00
(88)	Jack Warhop	825.00	330.00	165.00
(89)	Zach Wheat	3,000	1,500	900.00
(91)	Doc White	825.00	330.00	165.00
(92)	Ed Willetts (Willett)	825.00	330.00	165.00
(93)	Owen Wilson	825.00	330.00	165.00
(94)	Hooks Wiltse (pitching)	825.00	330.00	165.00
(95)	Hooks Wiltse (portrait)	825.00	330.00	165.00
(96)	Cy Young	8,500	4,200	2,500

1912-13 Red Cross Tobacco Type 2 (T215)

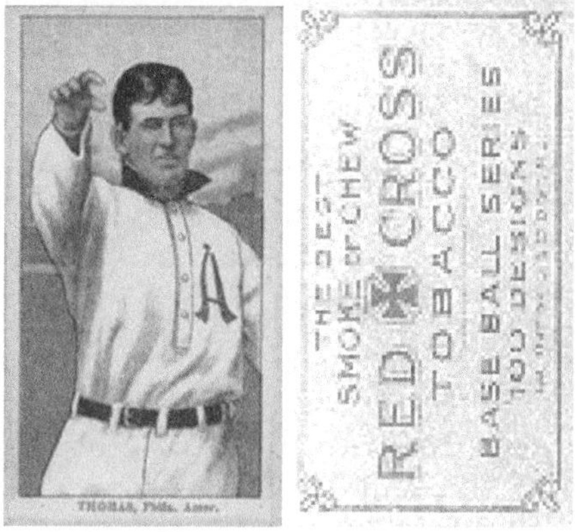

		NM	E	VG
	Common Player:	1,250	500.00	250.00
(1)	Red Ames	1,250	500.00	250.00
(2)	Neal Ball	1,250	500.00	250.00
(3)	Home Run Baker	3,600	1,450	725.00
(4)	Chief Bender (No trees in background.)	3,600	1,450	725.00
(5)	Chief Bender (Trees in background.)	3,600	1,450	725.00
(6)	Roger Bresnahan	3,600	1.450.00	725.00
(7)	Al Bridwell	1,250	500.00	250.00
(8)	Mordecai Brown	3,600	1,450	725.00
(9)	Bobby Byrne	1,250	500.00	250.00
(10)	Howie Camnitz	1,250	500.00	250.00
(11)	Frank Chance	3,600	1,450	725.00
(12)	Hal Chase	2,250	900.00	450.00
(13)	Ty Cobb	14,000	7,000	3,000
(14)	Eddie Collins	3,600	1,450	725.00
(15)	Doc Crandall	1,250	500.00	250.00
(16)	Sam Crawford	3,600	1,450	725.00
(17)	Birdie Cree	1,250	500.00	250.00
(18)	Harry Davis	1,250	500.00	250.00
(19)	Josh Devore	1,250	500.00	250.00
(21)	Mike Donlin	1,250	500.00	250.00
(22)	Mickey Doolan (Batting)	1,250	500.00	250.00
(23)	Mickey Doolan (Fielding)	1,250	500.00	250.00
(24)	Patsy Dougherty	1,250	500.00	250.00
(25)	Larry Doyle (Batting)	1,250	500.00	250.00
(26)	Larry Doyle (Portrait)	1,250	500.00	250.00
(27)	Jean Dubuc	1,250	500.00	250.00
(28)	Kid Elberfeld	1,250	500.00	250.00
(29)	Johnny Evers	3,600	1,450	725.00
(30)	Russ Ford	1,250	500.00	250.00
(31)	Art Fromme	1,250	500.00	250.00
(32)	Clark Griffith	3,600	1,450	725.00
(33)	Bob Groom	1,250	500.00	250.00
(34)	Topsy Hartsel	1,250	500.00	250.00
(35)	Buck Herzog	1,250	500.00	250.00
(36)	Dick Hoblitzell	1,250	500.00	250.00
(37)	Solly Hofman	1,250	500.00	250.00
(38)	Miller Huggins (Hands at mouth.)	3,600	1,450	725.00
(39)	Miller Huggins (Portrait)	3,600	1,450	725.00
(41)	John Hummel	1,250	500.00	250.00
(42)	Hughie Jennings	3,600	1,450	725.00
(43)	Walter Johnson	4,700	1,900	950.00
(44)	Joe Kelley	3,600	1,450	725.00
(45)	Ed Konetchy	1,250	500.00	250.00
(46)	Harry Krause	1,250	500.00	250.00
(47)	Nap Lajoie	3,600	1,450	725.00
(48)	Joe Lake	1,250	500.00	250.00
(49)	Tommy Leach	1,250	500.00	250.00
(50)	Lefty Leifield	1,250	500.00	250.00
(51)	Harry Lord	1,250	500.00	250.00
(52)	Sherry Magee	1,250	500.00	250.00
(53)	Rube Marquard (Pitching)	3,600	1,450	725.00
(54)	Rube Marquard (Portrait)	3,600	1,450	725.00
(55)	Christy Mathewson	5,200	2,100	1,100
(56)	John McGraw (Glove at side.)	3,600	1,450	725.00
(57)	John McGraw (Portrait)	3,600	1,450	725.00
(58)	Harry McIntire	1,250	500.00	250.00
(59)	Larry McLean	1,250	500.00	250.00
(61)	Fred Merkle	1,250	500.00	250.00
(62)	Chief Meyers	1,500	600.00	300.00
(63)	Dots Miller	1,250	500.00	250.00
(64)	Mike Mitchell	1,250	500.00	250.00
(65)	Mike Mowrey	1,250	500.00	250.00
(66)	George Mullin	1,250	500.00	250.00
(67)	Danny Murphy	1,250	500.00	250.00
(68)	Red Murray	1,250	500.00	250.00
(69)	Rebel Oakes	1,250	500.00	250.00
(70)	Rube Oldring	1,250	500.00	250.00
(71)	Charley O'Leary	1,250	500.00	250.00
(72)	Dode Paskert	1,250	500.00	250.00
(73)	Barney Pelty	1,250	500.00	250.00
(74)	Billy Purtell	1,250	500.00	250.00
(75)	Ed Reulbach	1,250	500.00	250.00
(76)	Nap Rucker	1,250	500.00	250.00
(77)	Germany Schaefer (Chicago)	1,250	500.00	250.00
(78)	Germany Schaefer (Washington)	1,250	500.00	250.00
(79)	Wildfire Schulte	1,250	500.00	250.00
(80)	Frank Smith	1,250	500.00	250.00
(81)	Frank Smither (Smith)	1,250	500.00	250.00
(83)	Tris Speaker	3,600	1,450	725.00
(84)	Jake Stahl	1,250	500.00	250.00
(85)	Harry Steinfeldt	1,250	500.00	250.00
(86)	Ed Summers	1,250	500.00	250.00
(87)	Jeff Sweeney	1,250	500.00	250.00
(88)	Ira Thomas	1,250	500.00	250.00
(89)	Joe Tinker (Bat off shoulder.)	3,600	1,450	725.00
(90)	Joe Tinker (Bat on shoulder.)	2,375	950.00	475.00
(91)	Heinie Wagner	825.00	330.00	165.00
(92)	Jack Warhop	825.00	330.00	165.00
(93)	Doc White	825.00	330.00	165.00
(94)	Hooks Wiltse (Pitching)	825.00	330.00	165.00
(95)	Hooks Wiltse (Portrait)	825.00	330.00	165.00

1954 Red Heart Dog Food

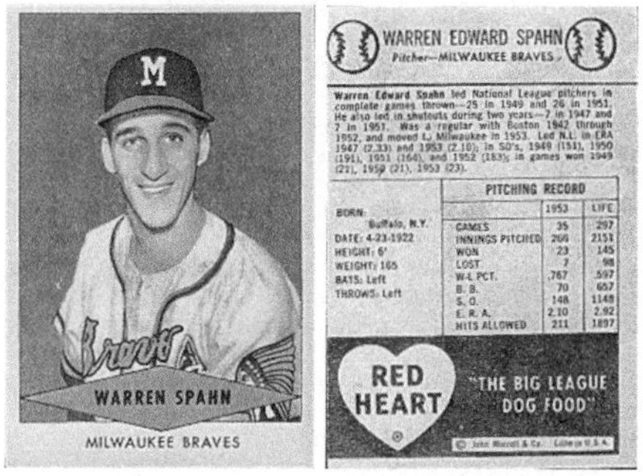

This set of 33 cards was issued in three color-coded series by the Red Heart Dog Food Co. Card fronts feature hand-colored photos on either a blue, green or red background. The 11 red-background cards are scarcer than the 11-card blue or green series. Backs of the 2-5/8" x 3-3/4" cards contain biographical and statistical information along with a Red Heart ad. Each 11-card series was available via a mail-in offer. As late as the early 1970s, the company was still sending cards to collectors who requested them.

		NM	E	VG
	Complete Set (33):	3,300	1,650	990.00
	Common Player:	45.00	25.00	15.00
(1)	Richie Ashburn	150.00	60.00	30.00
(2)	Frankie Baumholtz	60.00	25.00	12.00
(3)	Gus Bell	45.00	25.00	15.00
(4)	Billy Cox	60.00	25.00	12.00
(5)	Alvin Dark	45.00	25.00	15.00
(6)	Carl Erskine	125.00	50.00	30.00
(7)	Ferris Fain	60.00	25.00	12.00
(8)	Dee Fondy	45.00	25.00	15.00
(9)	Nelson Fox	125.00	60.00	35.00
(10)	Jim Gilliam	75.00	30.00	15.00
(11)	Jim Hegan	60.00	25.00	12.00
(12)	George Kell	125.00	65.00	30.00
(13)	Ted Kluszewski	100.00	50.00	30.00
(14)	Ralph Kiner	90.00	45.00	25.00
(15)	Harvey Kuenn	45.00	25.00	15.00
(16)	Bob Lemon	80.00	35.00	20.00
(17)	Sherman Lollar	45.00	25.00	15.00
(18)	Mickey Mantle	600.00	310.00	190.00
(19)	Billy Martin	100.00	50.00	30.00
(20)	Gil McDougald	80.00	40.00	20.00
(21)	Roy McMillan	45.00	25.00	15.00
(22)	Minnie Minoso	75.00	30.00	15.00
(23)	Stan Musial	425.00	210.00	125.00
(24)	Billy Pierce	60.00	25.00	12.00
(25)	Al Rosen	65.00	30.00	15.00
(26)	Hank Sauer	45.00	25.00	15.00
(27)	Red Schoendienst	115.00	50.00	25.00
(28)	Enos Slaughter	100.00	50.00	30.00
(29)	Duke Snider	300.00	150.00	75.00
(30)	Warren Spahn	100.00	50.00	30.00
(31)	Sammy White	45.00	25.00	15.00
(32)	Eddie Yost	45.00	25.00	15.00
(33)	Gus Zernial	45.00	25.00	15.00

1952-1954 Red Man Posters

These colorful lithographed paper posters, 11" x 15-1/2", were intended as point-of-purchase displays to encourage sales of the chewing tobacco and offer a baseball cap in exchange for the tabs found on the bottom of each card. The posters were reproduced in 11" x 16" format on cardboard in the 1980s.

	NM	E	VG
1952 Ralph Kiner (11" x 15")	200.00	100.00	60.00
1953 Enos Slaughter (11" x 15")	300.00	150.00	90.00
1954 Johnny Mize (12" x 15-1/2")	325.00	160.00	95.00

1952 Red Man Tobacco

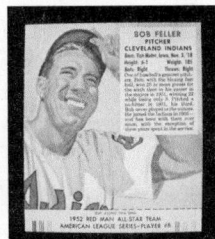

This was the first national set of tobacco cards produced since the golden days of tobacco sets in the early part of the century. There are 52 cards in the set, with 25 top players and one manager from each league. Player selection was made by editor J.G. Taylor Spink of The Sporting News. Cards measure 3-1/2" x 4", including a 1/2" tab at the bottom of each card. These tabs were redeemable for a free baseball cap from Red Man. Cards are harder to find with tabs intact, and thus more valuable in that form. Values quoted here are for cards with tabs. Cards with the tabs removed would be valued about 25-35 percent of the quoted figures. Card fronts are full color paintings of each player with biographical information inset in the portrait area. Card backs contain company advertising. Cards are numbered and dated only on the tabs. The 1952 Red Man cards can be found with either of two expiration dates on back, March 31 or June 1, 1953; neither commands a premium.

	NM	E	VG
Complete Set, W/Tab (52):	10,000	4,000	2,000
Common Player, W/Tab:	100.00	40.00	20.00
Complete Set, No Tab (52):	2,250	550.00	275.00
Common Player, No Tab:	20.00	8.00	4.00
WITH TAB			
1A Casey Stengel	250.00	100.00	50.00
1N Leo Durocher	200.00	80.00	40.00
2A Roberto Avila	100.00	40.00	20.00
2N Richie Ashburn	240.00	95.00	45.00
3A Larry "Yogi" Berra	375.00	150.00	75.00
3N Ewell Blackwell	120.00	45.00	25.00
4A Gil Coan	100.00	40.00	20.00
4N Cliff Chambers	100.00	40.00	20.00
5A Dom DiMaggio	140.00	55.00	27.50
5N Murry Dickson	100.00	40.00	20.00
6A Larry Doby	215.00	85.00	45.00
6N Sid Gordon	100.00	40.00	20.00
7A Ferris Fain	100.00	40.00	20.00
7N Granny Hamner	100.00	40.00	20.00
8A Bob Feller	325.00	130.00	65.00
8N Jim Hearn	100.00	40.00	20.00
9A Nelson Fox	215.00	85.00	45.00
9N Monte Irvin	215.00	85.00	45.00
10A Johnny Groth	100.00	40.00	20.00
10N Larry Jansen	100.00	40.00	20.00
11A Jim Hegan	100.00	40.00	20.00
11N Willie Jones	100.00	40.00	20.00
12A Eddie Joost	100.00	40.00	20.00
12N Ralph Kiner	215.00	85.00	45.00
13A George Kell	215.00	85.00	45.00
13N Whitey Lockman	100.00	40.00	20.00

	NM	E	VG
14A Gil McDougald	100.00	40.00	20.00
14N Sal Maglie	100.00	40.00	20.00
15A Orestes Minoso	100.00	40.00	20.00
15N Willie Mays	600.00	240.00	120.00
16A Bill Pierce	100.00	40.00	20.00
16N Stan Musial	575.00	230.00	115.00
17A Bob Porterfield	100.00	40.00	20.00
17N Pee Wee Reese	340.00	135.00	65.00
18A Eddie Robinson	100.00	40.00	20.00
18N Robin Roberts	215.00	85.00	45.00
19A Saul Rogovin	100.00	40.00	20.00
19N Al Schoendienst	215.00	85.00	45.00
20A Bobby Shantz	100.00	40.00	20.00
20N Enos Slaughter	215.00	85.00	45.00
21A Vern Stephens	100.00	40.00	20.00
21N Duke Snider	275.00	110.00	55.00
22A Vic Wertz	100.00	40.00	20.00
22N Warren Spahn	215.00	85.00	45.00
23A Ted Williams	1,800	725.00	360.00
23N Eddie Stanky	100.00	40.00	20.00
24A Early Wynn	215.00	85.00	45.00
24N Bobby Thomson	100.00	40.00	20.00
25A Eddie Yost	100.00	40.00	20.00
25N Earl Torgeson	100.00	40.00	20.00
26A Gus Zernial	100.00	40.00	20.00
26N Wes Westrum	100.00	40.00	20.00
NO TAB			
1A Casey Stengel	45.00	18.00	9.00
1N Leo Durocher	35.00	14.00	7.00
2A Roberto Avila	20.00	8.00	4.00
2N Richie Ashburn	55.00	22.00	11.00
3A Larry "Yogi" Berra	85.00	35.00	17.50
3N Ewell Blackwell	25.00	10.00	5.00
4A Gil Coan	20.00	8.00	4.00
4N Cliff Chambers	20.00	8.00	4.00
5A Dom DiMaggio	30.00	12.00	6.00
5N Murry Dickson	20.00	8.00	4.00
6A Larry Doby	45.00	18.00	9.00
6N Sid Gordon	20.00	8.00	4.00
7A Ferris Fain	20.00	8.00	4.00
7N Granny Hamner	20.00	8.00	4.00
8A Bob Feller	80.00	32.00	16.00
8N Jim Hearn	20.00	8.00	4.00
9A Nelson Fox	50.00	20.00	10.00
9N Monte Irvin	45.00	18.00	9.00
10A Johnny Groth	20.00	8.00	4.00
10N Larry Jansen	20.00	8.00	4.00
11A Jim Hegan	20.00	8.00	4.00
11N Willie Jones	20.00	8.00	4.00
12A Eddie Joost	20.00	8.00	4.00
12N Ralph Kiner	45.00	18.00	9.00
13A George Kell	45.00	18.00	9.00
13N Whitey Lockman	20.00	8.00	4.00
14A Gil McDougald	25.00	10.00	5.00
14N Sal Maglie	20.00	8.00	4.00
15A Orestes Minoso	30.00	12.00	6.00
15N Willie Mays	200.00	80.00	40.00
16A Bill Pierce	20.00	8.00	4.00
16N Stan Musial	175.00	70.00	35.00
17A Bob Porterfield	20.00	8.00	4.00
17N Pee Wee Reese	70.00	28.00	14.00
18A Eddie Robinson	20.00	8.00	4.00
18N Robin Roberts	45.00	18.00	9.00
19A Saul Rogovin	20.00	8.00	4.00
19N Al Schoendienst	45.00	18.00	9.00
20A Bobby Shantz	20.00	8.00	4.00
20N Enos Slaughter	45.00	18.00	9.00
21A Vern Stephens	20.00	8.00	4.00
21N Duke Snider	85.00	35.00	17.50
22A Vic Wertz	20.00	8.00	4.00
22N Warren Spahn	45.00	18.00	9.00
23A Ted Williams	375.00	150.00	75.00
23N Eddie Stanky	20.00	8.00	4.00
24A Early Wynn	45.00	18.00	9.00
24N Bobby Thomson	20.00	8.00	4.00
25A Eddie Yost	20.00	8.00	4.00
25N Earl Torgeson	20.00	8.00	4.00
26A Gus Zernial	20.00	8.00	4.00
26N Wes Westrum	20.00	8.00	4.00

1953 Red Man Tobacco

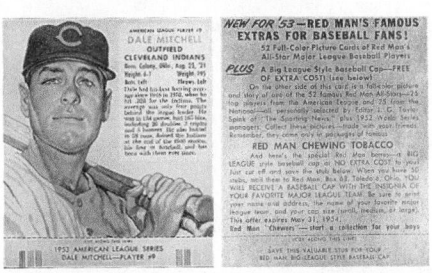

This was the chewing tobacco company's second annual

set of 3-1/2" x 4" cards, including the tabs at the bottom of the cards. Formats for front and back are similar to the '52 edition. The 1953 Red Man cards, however, include card numbers within the player biographical section, and the card backs are headlined "New for '53." Once again, cards with intact tabs (which were redeemable for a free cap) are more valuable. Prices below are for cards with tabs. Cards with tabs removed are worth about 25-35 percent of the stated values. Each league is represented by 25 players and a manager on the full-color cards, a total of 52. Values quoted here are for cards with tabs. Cards with the tabs removed would be valued about 35-40 percent of the quoted figures. The 1953 Red Man cards can be found with either of two expiration dates on back, March 31 or May 31, 1954; neither commands a premium.

	NM	E	VG
Complete Set, W/Tab (52):	5,500	2,200	1,100
Common Player:	60.00	24.00	12.00
Complete Set, No Tab (52):	1,400	550.00	275.00
Common Player, No Tab:	12.50	5.00	2.50
WITH TAB			
1A Casey Stengel	150.00	60.00	30.00
1N Charlie Dressen	75.00	30.00	15.00
2A Hank Bauer	75.00	30.00	15.00
2N Bobby Adams	60.00	24.00	12.00
3A Larry "Yogi" Berra	300.00	120.00	60.00
3N Richie Ashburn	125.00	50.00	25.00
4A Walt Dropo	60.00	24.00	12.00
4N Joe Black	100.00	40.00	20.00
5A Nelson Fox	125.00	50.00	25.00
5N Roy Campanella	300.00	120.00	60.00
6A Jackie Jensen	75.00	30.00	15.00
6N Ted Kluszewski	95.00	40.00	20.00
7A Eddie Joost	60.00	24.00	12.00
7N Whitey Lockman	60.00	24.00	12.00
8A George Kell	125.00	50.00	25.00
8N Sal Maglie	60.00	24.00	12.00
9A Dale Mitchell	60.00	24.00	12.00
9N Andy Pafko	60.00	24.00	12.00
10A Phil Rizzuto	225.00	90.00	45.00
10N Pee Wee Reese	250.00	100.00	50.00
11A Eddie Robinson	60.00	24.00	12.00
11N Robin Roberts	125.00	50.00	25.00
12A Gene Woodling	70.00	28.00	14.00
12N Red Schoendienst	125.00	50.00	25.00
13A Gus Zernial	60.00	24.00	12.00
13N Enos Slaughter	125.00	50.00	25.00
14A Early Wynn	125.00	50.00	25.00
14N Edwin "Duke" Snider	300.00	120.00	60.00
15A Joe Dobson	60.00	24.00	12.00
15N Ralph Kiner	125.00	50.00	25.00
16A Billy Pierce	60.00	24.00	12.00
16N Hank Sauer	60.00	24.00	12.00
17A Bob Lemon	125.00	50.00	25.00
17N Del Ennis	60.00	24.00	12.00
18A Johnny Mize	145.00	60.00	30.00
18N Granny Hamner	60.00	24.00	12.00
19A Bob Porterfield	60.00	24.00	12.00
19N Warren Spahn	145.00	60.00	30.00
20A Bobby Shantz	60.00	24.00	12.00
20N Wes Westrum	60.00	24.00	12.00
21A "Mickey" Vernon	60.00	24.00	12.00
21N Hoyt Wilhelm	125.00	50.00	25.00
22A Dom DiMaggio	75.00	30.00	15.00
22N Murry Dickson	60.00	24.00	12.00
23A Gil McDougald	70.00	28.00	14.00
23N Warren Hacker	60.00	24.00	12.00
24A Al Rosen	70.00	28.00	14.00
24N Gerry Staley	60.00	24.00	12.00
25A Mel Parnell	60.00	24.00	12.00
25N Bobby Thomson	60.00	24.00	12.00
26A Roberto Avila	60.00	24.00	12.00
26N Stan Musial	700.00	280.00	140.00
NO TAB			
1A Casey Stengel	35.00	14.00	7.00
1N Charlie Dressen	17.50	7.00	3.50
2A Hank Bauer	17.50	7.00	3.50
2N Bobby Adams	12.50	5.00	2.50
3A Larry "Yogi" Berra	65.00	26.00	13.00
3N Richie Ashburn	40.00	16.00	8.00
4A Walt Dropo	12.50	5.00	2.50
4N Joe Black	20.00	8.00	4.00
5A Nelson Fox	40.00	16.00	8.00
5N Roy Campanella	65.00	26.00	13.00
6A Jackie Jensen	20.00	8.00	4.00
6N Ted Kluszewski	25.00	10.00	5.00
7A Eddie Joost	12.50	5.00	2.50
7N Whitey Lockman	12.50	5.00	2.50
8A George Kell	40.00	16.00	8.00
8N Sal Maglie	15.00	6.00	3.00
9A Dale Mitchell	12.50	5.00	2.50
9N Andy Pafko	12.50	5.00	2.50
10A Phil Rizzuto	50.00	20.00	10.00
10N Pee Wee Reese	60.00	24.00	12.00
11A Eddie Robinson	12.50	5.00	2.50
11N Robin Roberts	40.00	16.00	8.00
12A Gene Woodling	15.00	6.00	3.00

12N	Red Schoendienst	40.00	16.00	8.00
13A	Gus Zernial	12.50	5.00	2.50
13N	Enos Slaughter	40.00	16.00	8.00
14A	Early Wynn	40.00	16.00	8.00
14N	Edwin "Duke" Snider	75.00	30.00	15.00
15A	Joe Dobson	12.50	5.00	2.50
15N	Ralph Kiner	40.00	16.00	8.00
16A	Billy Pierce	15.00	6.00	3.00
16N	Hank Sauer	12.50	5.00	2.50
17A	Bob Lemon	40.00	16.00	8.00
17N	Del Ennis	12.50	5.00	2.50
18A	Johnny Mize	40.00	16.00	8.00
18N	Granny Hamner	12.50	5.00	2.50
19A	Bob Porterfield	12.50	5.00	2.50
19N	Warren Spahn	45.00	18.00	9.00
20A	Bobby Shantz	12.50	5.00	2.50
20N	Wes Westrum	12.50	5.00	2.50
21A	"Mickey" Vernon	12.50	5.00	2.50
21N	Hoyt Wilhelm	35.00	14.00	7.00
22A	Dom DiMaggio	25.00	10.00	5.00
22N	Murry Dickson	12.50	5.00	2.50
23A	Gil McDougald	15.00	6.00	3.00
23N	Warren Hacker	12.50	5.00	2.50
24A	Al Rosen	17.50	7.00	3.50
24N	Gerry Staley	12.50	5.00	2.50
25A	Mel Parnell	12.50	5.00	2.50
25N	Bobby Thomson	12.50	5.00	2.50
26A	Roberto Avila	12.50	5.00	2.50
26N	Stan Musial	125.00	50.00	25.00

1954 Red Man Tobacco

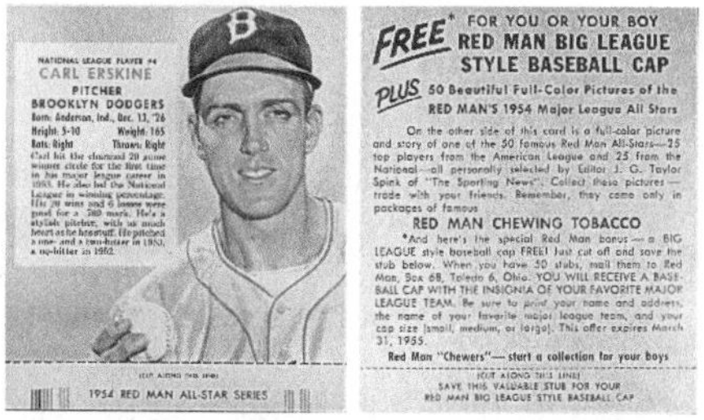

In 1954, the Red Man set eliminated managers from the set, and issued only 25 player cards for each league. There are, however, four variations which bring the total set size to 54 full-color cards. Two cards exist for Gus Bell and Enos Slaughter, while American Leaguers George Kell, Sam Mele and Dave Philley are each shown with two different teams. Complete set prices quoted below do not include the scarcer of the variation pairs. Cards measure 3-1/2" x 4" with tabs intact. Cards without tabs are worth about 25-35 percent of the values quoted below. Formats for the cards remain virtually unchanged, with card numbers included within the player information boxes as well as on the tabs. Cards can be found with either of two expiration dates on back, March 31 or May 31, 1955; neither commands a premium.

	NM	E	VG
Complete Set, W/Tab (50):	4,000	1,600	800.00
Common Player, W/Tab:	45.00	18.00	9.00
Complete Set, No Tab (50):	1,400	550.00	275.00
Common Player, No Tab:	15.00	6.00	3.00

	WITH TAB			
1A	Bobby Avila	45.00	18.00	9.00
1N	Richie Ashburn	90.00	36.00	18.00
2A	Jim Busby	45.00	18.00	9.00
2N	Billy Cox	55.00	22.00	11.00
3A	Nelson Fox	90.00	36.00	18.00
3N	Del Crandall	45.00	18.00	9.00
4Aa	George Kell (Boston)	125.00	50.00	25.00
4Ab	George Kell (Chicago)	180.00	70.00	35.00
4N	Carl Erskine	60.00	24.00	12.00
5A	Sherman Lollar	45.00	18.00	9.00
5N	Monte Irvin	90.00	36.00	18.00
6Aa	Sam Mele (Baltimore)	90.00	36.00	18.00
6Ab	Sam Mele (Chicago)	110.00	44.00	22.00
6N	Ted Kluszewski	100.00	40.00	20.00
7A	Orestes Minoso	65.00	26.00	13.00
7N	Don Mueller	45.00	18.00	9.00
8A	Mel Parnell	45.00	18.00	9.00
8N	Andy Pafko	45.00	18.00	9.00
9Aa	Dave Philley (Cleveland)	75.00	30.00	15.00
9Ab	Dave Philley (Philadelphia)	145.00	60.00	30.00
9N	Del Rice	45.00	18.00	9.00
10A	Billy Pierce	45.00	18.00	9.00
10N	Al Schoendienst	90.00	36.00	18.00
11A	Jim Piersall	60.00	24.00	12.00
11N	Warren Spahn	100.00	40.00	20.00
12A	Al Rosen	50.00	20.00	10.00
12N	Curt Simmons	45.00	18.00	9.00
13A	"Mickey" Vernon	45.00	18.00	9.00
13N	Roy Campanella	215.00	85.00	45.00
14A	Sammy White	45.00	18.00	9.00
14N	Jim Gilliam	60.00	24.00	12.00
15A	Gene Woodling	60.00	24.00	12.00
15N	"Pee Wee" Reese	160.00	64.00	32.00
16A	Ed "Whitey" Ford	140.00	56.00	28.00
16N	Edwin "Duke" Snider	215.00	85.00	45.00
17A	Phil Rizzuto	140.00	56.00	28.00
17N	Rip Repulski	45.00	18.00	9.00
18A	Bob Porterfield	45.00	18.00	9.00
18N	Robin Roberts	90.00	36.00	18.00
19A	Al "Chico" Carrasquel	45.00	18.00	9.00
19Na	Enos Slaughter	215.00	85.00	45.00
19Nb	Gus Bell	190.00	75.00	35.00
20A	Larry "Yogi" Berra	200.00	80.00	40.00
20N	Johnny Logan	45.00	18.00	9.00
21A	Bob Lemon	90.00	36.00	18.00
21N	Johnny Antonelli	45.00	18.00	9.00
22A	Ferris Fain	45.00	18.00	9.00
22N	Gil Hodges	90.00	36.00	18.00
23A	Hank Bauer	50.00	20.00	10.00
23N	Eddie Mathews	100.00	40.00	20.00
24A	Jim Delsing	45.00	18.00	9.00
24N	Lew Burdette	45.00	18.00	9.00
25A	Gil McDougald	55.00	22.00	11.00
25N	Willie Mays	425.00	170.00	85.00
	NO TAB			
1A	Bobby Avila	15.00	6.00	3.00
1N	Richie Ashburn	35.00	14.00	7.00
2A	Jim Busby	15.00	6.00	3.00
2N	Billy Cox	20.00	8.00	4.00
3A	Nelson Fox	35.00	14.00	7.00
3N	Del Crandall	15.00	6.00	3.00
4Aa	George Kell (Boston)	50.00	20.00	10.00
4Ab	George Kell (Chicago)	65.00	26.00	13.00
4N	Carl Erskine	22.50	9.00	4.50
5A	Sherman Lollar	15.00	6.00	3.00
5N	Monte Irvin	35.00	14.00	7.00
6Aa	Sam Mele (Baltimore)	30.00	12.00	6.00
6Ab	Sam Mele (Chicago)	55.00	22.00	11.00
6N	Ted Kluszewski	30.00	12.00	6.00
7A	Orestes Minoso	25.00	10.00	5.00
7N	Don Mueller	15.00	6.00	3.00
8A	Mel Parnell	15.00	6.00	3.00
8N	Andy Pafko	15.00	6.00	3.00
9Aa	Dave Philley (Cleveland)	30.00	12.00	6.00
9Ab	Dave Philley (Philadelphia)	65.00	26.00	13.00
9N	Del Rice	15.00	6.00	3.00
10A	Billy Pierce	15.00	6.00	3.00
10N	Al Schoendienst	35.00	14.00	7.00
11A	Jim Piersall	20.00	8.00	4.00
11N	Warren Spahn	35.00	14.00	7.00
12A	Al Rosen	20.00	8.00	4.00
12N	Curt Simmons	15.00	6.00	3.00
13A	"Mickey" Vernon	15.00	6.00	3.00
13N	Roy Campanella	65.00	26.00	13.00
14A	Sammy White	15.00	6.00	3.00
14N	Jim Gilliam	22.50	9.00	4.50
15A	Gene Woodling	22.50	9.00	4.50
15N	"Pee Wee" Reese	55.00	22.00	11.00
16A	Ed "Whitey" Ford	45.00	18.00	9.00
16N	Edwin "Duke" Snider	65.00	26.00	13.00
17A	Phil Rizzuto	50.00	20.00	10.00
17N	Rip Repulski	15.00	6.00	3.00
18A	Bob Porterfield	15.00	6.00	3.00
18N	Robin Roberts	35.00	14.00	7.00
19A	Al "Chico" Carrasquel	20.00	8.00	4.00
19Na	Enos Slaughter	70.00	28.00	14.00
19Nb	Gus Bell	70.00	28.00	14.00
20A	Larry "Yogi" Berra	65.00	26.00	13.00
20N	Johnny Logan	15.00	6.00	3.00
21A	Bob Lemon	35.00	14.00	7.00
21N	Johnny Antonelli	15.00	6.00	3.00
22A	Ferris Fain	15.00	6.00	3.00
22N	Gil Hodges	35.00	14.00	7.00
23A	Hank Bauer	20.00	8.00	4.00
23N	Eddie Mathews	35.00	14.00	7.00
24A	Jim Delsing	15.00	6.00	3.00
24N	Lew Burdette	15.00	6.00	3.00
25A	Gil McDougald	20.00	8.00	4.00
25N	Willie Mays	130.00	55.00	25.00

1955 Red Man Tobacco

These 50 cards are quite similar to the 1954 edition, with card fronts virtually unchanged except for the data in the biographical box on the color picture area. This set of the 3-1/2" x 4" cards includes 25 players from each league, with no known variations. As with all Red Man sets, those cards complete with the redeemable tabs are more valuable. Values quoted below are for cards with tabs. Cards with the tabs removed are worth about 25-35 percent of those figures. Each card can be found with two different expiration dates on back, April 15 or June 15, 1956; neither version commands a premium.

	NM	E	VG
Complete Set, W/Tab (50):	3,750	1,500	750.00
Common Player, W/Tab:	60.00	24.00	12.00
Complete Set, No Tab (50):	900.00	360.00	180.00
Common Player, No Tab:	10.00	4.00	2.00

	WITH TAB			
1A	Ray Boone	60.00	24.00	12.00
1N	Richie Ashburn	95.00	38.00	19.00
2A	Jim Busby	60.00	24.00	12.00
2N	Del Crandall	60.00	24.00	12.00
3A	Ed "Whitey" Ford	125.00	50.00	25.00
3N	Gil Hodges	90.00	36.00	18.00
4A	Nelson Fox	90.00	36.00	18.00
4N	Brooks Lawrence	60.00	24.00	12.00
5A	Bob Grim	60.00	24.00	12.00
5N	Johnny Logan	60.00	24.00	12.00
6A	Jack Harshman	60.00	24.00	12.00
6N	Sal Maglie	60.00	24.00	12.00
7A	Jim Hegan	60.00	24.00	12.00
7N	Willie Mays	250.00	100.00	50.00
8A	Bob Lemon	90.00	36.00	18.00
8N	Don Mueller	60.00	24.00	12.00
9A	Irv Noren	60.00	24.00	12.00
9N	Bill Sarni	60.00	24.00	12.00
10A	Bob Porterfield	60.00	24.00	12.00
10N	Warren Spahn	90.00	36.00	18.00
11A	Al Rosen	75.00	30.00	15.00
11N	Henry Thompson	60.00	24.00	12.00
12A	"Mickey" Vernon	60.00	24.00	12.00
12N	Hoyt Wilhelm	90.00	36.00	18.00
13A	Vic Wertz	60.00	24.00	12.00
13N	Johnny Antonelli	60.00	24.00	12.00
14A	Early Wynn	90.00	36.00	18.00
14N	Carl Erskine	75.00	30.00	15.00
15A	Bobby Avila	60.00	24.00	12.00
15N	Granny Hamner	60.00	24.00	12.00
16A	Larry "Yogi" Berra	165.00	65.00	35.00
16N	Ted Kluszewski	75.00	30.00	15.00
17A	Joe Coleman	60.00	24.00	12.00
17N	Pee Wee Reese	125.00	50.00	25.00
18A	Larry Doby	90.00	36.00	18.00
18N	Al Schoendienst	90.00	36.00	18.00
19A	Jackie Jensen	65.00	26.00	13.00
19N	Duke Snider	165.00	65.00	35.00
20A	Pete Runnels	60.00	24.00	12.00
20N	Frank Thomas	60.00	24.00	12.00
21A	Jim Piersall	60.00	24.00	12.00
21N	Ray Jablonski	60.00	24.00	12.00
22A	Hank Bauer	65.00	26.00	13.00
22N	James "Dusty" Rhodes	60.00	24.00	12.00
23A	"Chico" Carrasquel	60.00	24.00	12.00
23N	Gus Bell	60.00	24.00	12.00
24A	Orestes Minoso	75.00	30.00	15.00
24N	Curt Simmons	60.00	24.00	12.00
25A	Sandy Consuegra	60.00	24.00	12.00
25N	Marvin Grissom	60.00	24.00	12.00
	NO TAB			
1A	Ray Boone	10.00	4.00	2.00
1N	Richie Ashburn	30.00	12.00	6.00
2A	Jim Busby	10.00	4.00	2.00
2N	Del Crandall	10.00	4.00	2.00
3A	Ed "Whitey" Ford	35.00	14.00	7.00
3N	Gil Hodges	30.00	12.00	6.00
4A	Nelson Fox	30.00	12.00	6.00
4N	Brooks Lawrence	10.00	4.00	2.00
5A	Bob Grim	10.00	4.00	2.00
5N	Johnny Logan	10.00	4.00	2.00
6A	Jack Harshman	10.00	4.00	2.00
6N	Sal Maglie	10.00	4.00	2.00
7A	Jim Hegan	10.00	4.00	2.00
7N	Willie Mays	100.00	40.00	20.00
8A	Bob Lemon	30.00	12.00	6.00
8N	Don Mueller	10.00	4.00	2.00
9A	Irv Noren	10.00	4.00	2.00
9N	Bill Sarni	10.00	4.00	2.00
10A	Bob Porterfield	10.00	4.00	2.00
10N	Warren Spahn	30.00	12.00	6.00
11A	Al Rosen	13.50	5.50	2.75
11N	Henry Thompson	10.00	4.00	2.00
12A	"Mickey" Vernon	10.00	4.00	2.00
12N	Hoyt Wilhelm	30.00	12.00	6.00
13A	Vic Wertz	10.00	4.00	2.00
13N	Johnny Antonelli	10.00	4.00	2.00
14A	Early Wynn	30.00	12.00	6.00
14N	Carl Erskine	15.00	6.00	3.00
15A	Bobby Avila	10.00	4.00	2.00

15N	Granny Hamner	10.00	4.00	2.00
16A	Larry "Yogi" Berra	50.00	20.00	10.00
16N	Ted Kluszewski	20.00	8.00	4.00
17A	Joe Coleman	10.00	4.00	2.00
17N	Pee Wee Reese	50.00	20.00	10.00
18A	Larry Doby	30.00	12.00	6.00
18N	Al Schoendienst	30.00	12.00	6.00
19A	Jackie Jensen	13.50	5.50	2.75
19N	Duke Snider	55.00	22.00	11.00
20A	Pete Runnels	10.00	4.00	2.00
20N	Frank Thomas	10.00	4.00	2.00
21A	Jim Piersall	13.50	5.50	2.75
21N	Ray Jablonski	10.00	4.00	2.00
22A	Hank Bauer	13.50	5.50	2.75
22N	James "Dusty" Rhodes	10.00	4.00	2.00
23A	"Chico" Carrasquel	10.00	4.00	2.00
23N	Gus Bell	10.00	4.00	2.00
24A	Orestes Minoso	15.00	6.00	3.00
24N	Curt Simmons	10.00	4.00	2.00
25A	Sandy Consuegra	10.00	4.00	2.00
25N	Marvin Grissom	10.00	4.00	2.00

"1952-54" Red Man Posters

Some 30 years after the original 11" x 15-1/2" paper posters were used to advertise Red Man chewing tobacco and the baseball cards and caps available as premiums, three of the pieces were reproduced. Posters which are printed on cardboard and in a 11" x 16" size are modern reproductions with only decorative, rather than collectible, value.

NO COLLECTOR VALUE

1952	Ralph Kiner
1953	Enos Slaughter
1954	Johnny Mize

1976 Redpath Sugar Expos

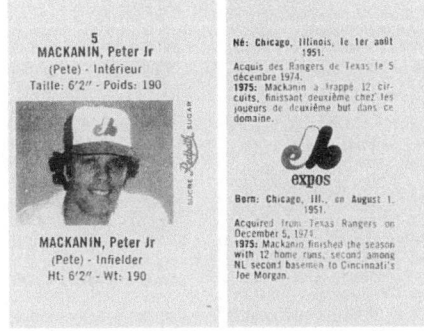

Among the more unusual baseball collectibles of the late 1970s are the Montreal Expos sugar packs produced by Redpath Sugar for distribution in Quebec. About 1-1/2" x 2-3/4" in size, the sugar packs feature color portraits of the players on front, along with bi-lingual personal information and a uniform number. Backs have a color team logo and career highlights. Uncut sheets or the packaging are known which indicate several players were double- or triple-printed. The checklist here is arranged by uniform number.

		NM	E	VG
	Complete Set (36):	75.00	37.00	22.00
	Common Player:	2.00	1.00	.60
1	Osvaldo Jose Virgil	2.00	1.00	.60
5	Peter Mackanin, Jr.	2.00	1.00	.60
8	Karl Otto Kuehl	2.00	1.00	.60
8	Gary Edmund Carter	15.00	7.50	4.50
9	Barry Clifton Foote	2.00	1.00	.60
11	Jose Manuel Mangual	2.00	1.00	.60
14	Lawrence Eugene Doby	6.00	3.00	1.75
15	Larry Alton Parrish	2.00	1.00	.60
16	Michael Jorgensen	2.00	1.00	.60
17	Andre Thornton	4.00	2.00	1.25

18	Joseph Thomas Kerrigan	2.00	1.00	.60
19	Timothy John Foli (DP)	2.00	1.00	.60
20	James Lawrence Lyttle, Jr.	2.00	1.00	.60
21	Frederick John Scherman, Jr.	2.00	1.00	.60
22	Ellis Clarence Valentine	2.00	1.00	.60
26	Donald Joseph Stanhouse	2.00	1.00	.60
27	Dale Albert Murray	2.00	1.00	.60
31	Clayton Laws Kirby, Jr.	2.00	1.00	.60
33	Robert David Lang	2.00	1.00	.60
34	Jose Manuel Morales	2.00	1.00	.60
35	Woodrow Thompson Fryman	3.00	1.50	.90
36	Steven John Dunning	2.00	1.00	.60
37	Jerome Cardell White	2.00	1.00	.60
38	Jesus Maria Frias (Andujar)	2.00	1.00	.60
39	Daniel Dean Warthen	2.00	1.00	.60
40	Donald George Carrithers (3P)	2.00	1.00	.60
41	Ronald Jacques Piche	2.00	1.00	.60
43	James Edward Dwyer	2.00	1.00	.60
44	Jesus Rivera (Torres), Jr.	2.00	1.00	.60
45	Stephen Douglas Rogers (DP)	2.00	1.00	.60
46	Marion Danne Adair	2.00	1.00	.60
47	Wayne Allen Granger	2.00	1.00	.60
48	Lawrence Donald Bearnarth	2.00	1.00	.60
---	Roland Wayne Garrett	2.00	1.00	.60
---	Charles Gilbert Taylor	2.00	1.00	.60
---	Delbert Bernard Unser	2.00	1.00	.60

1977 Redpath Sugar Expos

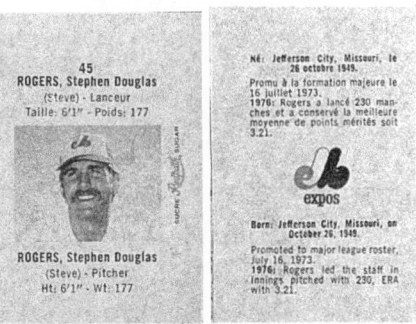

One of the more obscure regional Canadian issues, this 30-player set features members of the Expos and was printed on sugar packets distributed in the Montreal area in 1977. The front of the packet features a color photo of the player with his name, uniform number, position, height and weight listed in both English and French. A line identifying Redpath Sugar appears alongside the photo. The backs display the Expos logo and brief player highlights (again printed in both French and English). The set has been seen in uncut sheets, revealing that the packets of Steve Rogers and David Cash, Jr. were double printed.

		NM	E	VG
	Complete Set (30):	75.00	37.00	22.00
	Common Player:	1.50	.70	.45
1	Osvaldo Jose Virgil	1.50	.70	.45
2	James Thomas Brewer	1.50	.70	.45
3	James Barton Vernon	1.50	.70	.45
4	Chris Edward Speier	1.50	.70	.45
5	Peter Mackanin Jr.	1.50	.70	.45
6	William Frederick Gardner	1.50	.70	.45
8	Gary Edmund Carter	15.00	7.50	4.50
9	Barry Clifton Foote	1.50	.70	.45
10	Andre Dawson	6.00	3.00	1.75
11	Ronald Wayne Garrett	1.50	.70	.45
14	Samuel Elias Mejias	1.50	.70	.45
15	Larry Alton Parrish	2.00	1.00	.60
16	Michael Jorgensen	1.50	.70	.45
17	Ellis Clarence Valentine	1.50	.70	.45
18	Joseph Thomas Kerrigan	1.50	.70	.45
20	William Henry McEnaney	1.50	.70	.45
23	Richard Hirshfield Williams	2.00	1.00	.60
24	Atanasio Rigal Perez	3.00	1.50	.90
25	Delbert Bernard Unser	1.50	.70	.45
26	Donald Joseph Stanhouse	1.50	.70	.45
30	David Cash, Jr.	1.50	.70	.45
31	Jackie Gene Brown	1.50	.70	.45
34	Jose Manual Morales	1.50	.70	.45
35	Gerald Ellis Hannahs	1.50	.70	.45

38	Jesus Maria Frias (Andujar)	1.50	.70	.45
39	Daniel Dean Warthen	1.50	.70	.45
42	William Cecil Glenn Atkinson	1.50	.70	.45
45	Stephen Douglas Rogers	2.25	1.25	.70
48	Jeffrey Michael Terpko	1.50	.70	.45
49	Warren Livingston Cromartie	1.50	.70	.45

1886 Red Stocking Cigars

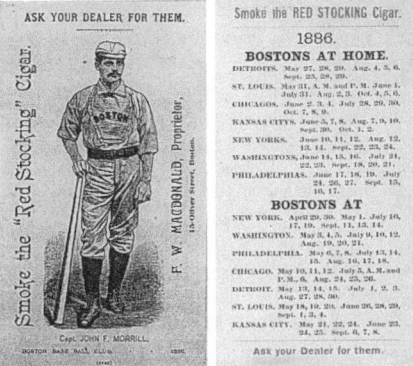

This set of Boston Red Stockings schedule cards was issued in 1886, and the three known cards measure 6-1/2" x 3-3/4". The cards were printed in black and red. One side carries the 1886 Boston schedule, while the other side features a full-length player drawing. Both sides include advertising for "Red Stocking" cigars. Only three different players are known.

	NM	E	VG
Complete Set (3):	175,000	70,000	25,000
Common Player:	45,000	18,000	9,000
(1) C.G. Buffington	45,000	18,000	9,000
(2) Capt. John F. Morrill	45,000	18,000	9,000
(3) Charles Radbourn	85,000	34,000	17,000

1972 Regent Glove Hang Tag

This 2-1/4" x 3" card was distributed as an attachment to baseball gloves sold at retail outlets. A hole punched at top allowed the card to be strung to the glove. Front has a blue background and black-and-white portrait photo of 1971 MVP Vida Blue. His facsimile autograph is on back.

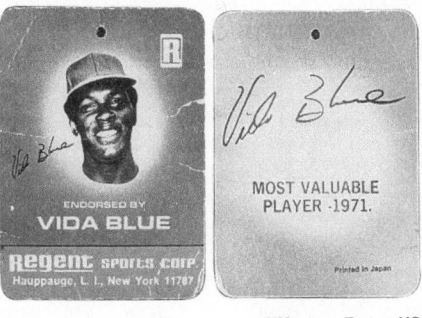

	NM	E	VG
Vida Blue	15.00	7.50	4.50

1964-66 Requena N.Y. Yankees 8x10s

Many of the same Yankees players and poses which appear in the standard (3-1/2" x 5-1/2") Requena postcard series can also be found, along with additional subjects, in an 8" x 10" blank-back format. The large format cards are listed here in alphabetical order.

	NM	E	VG
Complete Set (21):	300.00	150.00	90.00
Common Player:	9.00	4.50	2.75
(1) Yogi Berra	20.00	10.00	6.00
(2) John Blanchard	9.00	4.50	2.75
(3) Jim Bouton	12.50	6.25	3.75
(4) Clete Boyer	9.00	4.50	2.75
(5) Al Downing	9.00	4.50	2.75
(6) Whitey Ford	20.00	10.00	6.00
(7) Ralph Houk	9.00	4.50	2.75
(8) Elston Howard	12.50	6.25	3.75
(9) Tony Kubek	12.50	6.25	3.75
(10) Phil Linz	9.00	4.50	2.75
(11) Mickey Mantle	35.00	17.50	10.00
(12) Mickey Mantle, Roger Maris	30.00	15.00	9.00
(13a) Roger Maris (Facsimile autograph.)	25.00	12.50	7.50
(13b) Roger Maris (No facsimile autograph.)	25.00	12.50	7.50
(14) Joe Pepitone	12.50	6.25	3.75
(15) Pedro Ramos	9.00	4.50	2.75
(16) Bobby Richardson	12.50	6.25	3.75
(17) Bill Stafford	9.00	4.50	2.75
(18) Mel Stottlemyre	9.00	4.50	2.75
(19) Ralph Terry	9.00	4.50	2.75
(20) Tom Tresh	12.50	6.25	3.75

1964-68 Requena N.Y. Yankees Postcards

Over a period of several years in the 1960s a series of Yankee color player postcards was issued with the identifier "Photo by Requena." Similar in format, the 3-1/2" x 5-1/2" cards have borderless color photos on front. Except for facsimile autographs on some players' cards, there are no other front graphics. Backs are printed in dark green with player ID at upper-left, a "K"-within-diamond Kodachrome logo at bottom-left, a card number centered at bottom, the Requena line vertically at center and standard postcard markings at right.

	NM	E	VG
Complete Set (17):	300.00	150.00	90.00
Common Player:	15.00	7.50	4.50
66443 Phil Linz	15.00	7.50	4.50
66880 Clete Boyer	15.00	7.50	4.50
66881 Jim Bouton	20.00	10.00	6.00
66882 Tom Tresh	20.00	10.00	6.00
66883 Joe Pepitone	20.00	10.00	6.00
66884 Tony Kubek	20.00	10.00	6.00
66885 Elston Howard	20.00	10.00	6.00
66886 Ralph Terry	15.00	7.50	4.50
66887 Bill Stafford	15.00	7.50	4.50
66888 Whitey Ford	30.00	15.00	9.00
66889 Bob Richardson	20.00	10.00	6.00
69891 Yogi Berra (Signature at top.)	30.00	15.00	9.00
69891 Yogi Berra (Signature at bottom.)	30.00	15.00	9.00
74284 John Blanchard	15.00	7.50	4.50
78909 Pedro Ramos	15.00	7.50	4.50
78910 Mel Stottlemyre	15.00	7.50	4.50
98553 Fritz Peterson	15.00	7.50	4.50
101461 Steve Barber	15.00	7.50	4.50

1953 R.G. Dun Cigars Milwaukee Braves

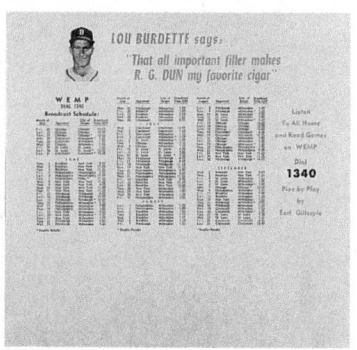

This series of counter cards was issued by a cigar company and features the radio schedule for the 1953 Braves. The cards are printed in red and black on cream cardboard and measure 10" x 9-1/2". They are unnumbered and blank-backed. The cards have vertical slits from bottom to about 1/3 the height of the cards, probably so they could be inserted into some type of counter display for Dun cigars. It's unknown how many players were represented in the series.

	NM	E	VG
Common Player:	35.00	17.50	10.00
(1) Lew Burdette	35.00	17.50	10.00
(2) Jim Wilson	35.00	17.50	10.00

1935 Rice-Stix (UM7)

 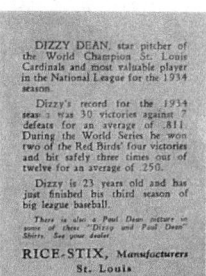

This two-card set was distributed in packages of shirts from a St. Louis firm. Measuring about 2-1/4" x 3", the cards feature color painting of the pitchers on front, along with a facsimile autograph and photo credits. Backs have a short career summary and an ad for the issuer.

	NM	E	VG
Complete Set (2):	3,250	1,600	975.00
(1) Dizzy Dean	2,500	1,250	750.00
(2) Paul Dean	950.00	470.00	280.00

1972 Richmond Square Mall

This black-and-white, blank-back card was issued in conjunction with an autograph appearance by the Reds' pitcher at the mall located in Richmond, Ind., north of Cincinnati. The card measures 3-3/4" x 5-1/2". The date attributed is speculative.

	NM	EX	VG
Don Gullett	20.00	10.00	6.00

1927 Rinkeydink Stamps

These 1-1/4" x 1-1/2" pieces are not actually stamps, but rather are printed on newsprint with unrelated matter on back. The printing is in red, green and black and each stamp has a "denomination" of 2 in a baseball design at top. The "stamps" were featured in the heading of the "Winnie Winkle" comic strip in the Sunday funnies section of newspapers.

	NM	E	VG
Complete Set (10):	650.00	325.00	195.00
Common Player:	30.00	15.00	9.00

(1) Grover C. Alexander	40.00	20.00	12.00
(2) Ty Cobb	150.00	75.00	45.00
(3) Eddie Collins	30.00	15.00	9.00
(4) Bucky Harris	30.00	15.00	9.00
(5) Rogers Hornsby	40.00	20.00	12.00
(6) Walter Johnson	50.00	25.00	15.00
(7) George Kelly	30.00	15.00	9.00
(8) Herb Pennock	30.00	15.00	9.00
(9) Babe Ruth	200.00	100.00	60.00
(10) Tris Speaker	40.00	20.00	12.00

1933 Rittenhouse Candy (E285)

Designed to resemble a set of playing cards, this set, issued circa 1933 by the Rittenhouse Candy Company of Philadelphia, carries the ACC designation E285 and is generally considered to be the last of the E-card issues. Each card measures 1-7/16" x 2-1/4" and features a small player photo in the center of the playing card design. Cards are known printed in red, orange, blue and green. The backs of the cards usually consist of just one large letter and were part of a promotion in which collectors were instructed to find enough different letters to spell "Rittenhouse Candy Co." Other backs explaining the contest and the prizes available were also issued, as were backs with numbers. Because it was designed as a deck of playing cards, the set is complete at 52 cards, featuring 46 different players (six are pictured on two cards each).

	NM	E	VG
Complete Set (52):	16,000	8,000	4,800
Common Player:	175.00	90.00	55.00
(1) Dick Bartell	175.00	90.00	55.00
(2) Walter Berger	175.00	90.00	55.00
(3) Max Bishop	175.00	90.00	55.00
(4) James Bottomley	350.00	175.00	100.00
(5) Fred Brickell	175.00	90.00	55.00
(6) Sugar Cain	175.00	90.00	55.00
(7) Ed. Cihocki	175.00	90.00	55.00
(8) Phil Collins	175.00	90.00	55.00
(9) Roger Cramer	175.00	90.00	55.00
(10) Hughie Critz	175.00	90.00	55.00
(11) Joe Cronin	350.00	175.00	100.00
(12) Hazen (Kiki) Cuyler	350.00	175.00	100.00
(13) Geo. Davis	175.00	90.00	55.00
(14) Spud Davis	175.00	90.00	55.00
(15) Jimmy Dykes	175.00	90.00	55.00
(16) George Earnshaw	175.00	90.00	55.00
(17) Jumbo Elliot	175.00	90.00	55.00
(18) Lou Finney	175.00	90.00	55.00
(19) Jimmy Foxx	500.00	250.00	150.00
(20) Frankie Frisch (3 of Spades)	350.00	175.00	100.00
(21) Frankie Frisch (7 of Spades)	350.00	175.00	100.00
(22) Robert (Lefty) Grove	360.00	180.00	110.00
(23) Mule Haas	175.00	90.00	55.00
(24) Chick Hafey	350.00	175.00	100.00
(25) Chas. Leo Hartnett	350.00	175.00	100.00
(26) Babe Herman	185.00	90.00	55.00
(27) Wm. Herman	350.00	175.00	100.00
(28) Kid Higgins	175.00	90.00	55.00
(29) Rogers Hornsby	425.00	200.00	125.00
(30) Don Hurst (Jack of Diamonds)	175.00	90.00	55.00
(31) Don Hurst (6 of Spades)	175.00	90.00	55.00
(32) Chuck Klein	350.00	175.00	100.00
(33) Leroy Mahaffey	175.00	90.00	55.00
(34) Gus Mancuso	175.00	90.00	55.00
(35) Rabbit McNair	175.00	90.00	55.00
(36) Bing Miller	175.00	90.00	55.00
(37) Frank (Lefty) O'Doul	185.00	90.00	55.00
(38) Mel Ott	350.00	175.00	100.00
(39) Babe Ruth (Ace of Spades)	1,750	875.00	525.00
(40) Babe Ruth (King of Clubs)	1,750	875.00	525.00
(41) Al Simmons	350.00	175.00	100.00
(42) Bill Terry	350.00	175.00	100.00
(43) Pie Traynor	350.00	175.00	100.00

(44)	Rube Wallberg (Walberg)	175.00	90.00	55.00
(45)	Lloyd Waner	350.00	175.00	100.00
(46)	Paul Waner	350.00	175.00	100.00
(47)	Lloyd Warner (Waner)	350.00	175.00	100.00
(48)	Paul Warner (Waner)	350.00	175.00	100.00
(49)	Pinkey Whitney	175.00	90.00	55.00
(50)	Dib Williams	175.00	90.00	55.00
(51)	Hack Wilson (9 of Spades)	350.00	175.00	100.00
(52)	Hack Wilson (9 of Clubs)	350.00	175.00	100.00

1948 R.K.O. Theaters Babe Ruth Premium

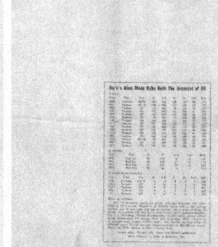

The attributed date is speculative, based on the similarity of the back copy to the 1948 American Association Babe Ruth memorial card. Apparently issued as a premium at moviehouses, this 8" x 9-1/2" picture is printed on thin cardboard. On front is a sepia action photo of Ruth in the 1932 World Series. In the bottom border is the R.K.O. attribution. Back has biographical details, career highlights and complete major league stats.

	NM	E	VG
Babe Ruth	800.00	400.00	240.00

1949 Roadmaster Photos

Black-and-white glossy photos of at least two major league stars were available as a premium from Roadmaster bicycles. Contemporary ads said that for a dime, an 8" x 10" photo could be obtained. The photos show the uniformed players seated on Roadmaster bikes inside a ballpark. There is a facsimile autograph on each. Backs may be found either blank, or with advertising from the sponsor. It's possible other player photos may yet be seen.

		NM	E	VG
(1)	Bob Feller ("C" on jersey.)	300.00	150.00	90.00
(2)	Bob Feller ("Indians" on jersey.)	300.00	150.00	90.00
(3)	Pee Wee Reese	400.00	200.00	120.00

1947 Jackie Robinson Pins

In his historic debut season with the Brooklyn Dodgers, a number of celluloid pinback buttons featuring Jackie Robinson were issued. Ranging in size from about 1-1/4" to 1-3/4", the pins usually feature a black-and-white portrait photo at center and were originally sold with a silk pennant and plastic or potmetal baseball charms attached.

		NM	E	VG
(1)	"Jackie" (1-1/4" white background)	600.00	300.00	180.00
(2)	HI TEAMMATES (1-3/8", batting, blue background)	250.00	125.00	75.00
(3)	I'M FOR JACKIE (Blue type on white ball, no photo.)	200.00	100.00	60.00
(4)	I'm Rooting for Jackie Robinson (1-3/4", red border)	275.00	135.00	80.00
(5)	I'm Rooting for Jackie Robinson (1-1/4", white background)	350.00	175.00	100.00
(6)	I'm Rooting for Jackie Robinson (1-3/4", gray background)	500.00	250.00	150.00
(7)	JACKIE ROBINSON / DODGERS (1-3/4", b/w photo batting in pinstripes and plain cap)	400.00	200.00	125.00
(8)	JACKIE ROBINSON / DODGERS (1-1/4", white background)	200.00	100.00	60.00
(9)	Jackie Robinson Outstanding Rookie (3-3/8" white border)	200.00	100.00	60.00
(10)	19 Rookie of the Year 47 (exist.) 1-3/4" red border)(Modern reproductions)	325.00	160.00	100.00

1950s Jackie Robinson WNBC Photocard

This black-and-white 5-3/4" x 7-1/2" photocard pictures Robinson in his post-playing days career as a broadcaster for the NBC radio network's flagship station in New York.

	NM	E	VG
Jackie Robinson	35.00	17.50	10.50

1911 Rochester Baking Philadelphia A's (D359)

The 1911 Rochester Baking set, an 18-card Philadelphia Athletics set, is among the scarcest of early 20th Century bakery issues. The set commemorates the Athletics' 1910 Championship season, and, except for pitcher Jack Coombs, the checklist includes nearly all key members of the club, including manager Connie Mack. The cards are the standard size for the era, 1-1/2" x 2-5/8". The front of each card features a player portrait set against a colored background. The player's name and the word "Athletics" appear at the bottom, while "World's Champions 1910" is printed along the top. The backs of the cards advertise the set as the "Athletics Series." Collectors should be aware that the same checklist was used for a similar Athletics set issued by Williams Baking and Cullivan's Firesdie tobacco (T208), and also that blank-backed

versions are also known to exist, but these are classified as E104 cards in the American Card Catalog.

		NM	E	VG
Complete Set (18):		70,000	35,000	21,000
Common Player:		2,000	1,000	600.00
(1)	Home Run Baker	9,000	4,500	2,225
(2)	Jack Barry	2,000	1,000	600.00
(3)	Chief Bender	9,000	4,500	2,225
(4)	Eddie Collins	9,000	4,500	2,225
(5)	Harry Davis	2,000	1,000	600.00
(6)	Jimmy Dygert	2,000	1,000	600.00
(7)	Topsy Hartsel	2,000	1,000	600.00
(8)	Harry Krause	2,000	1,000	600.00
(9)	Jack Lapp	2,000	1,000	600.00
(10)	Paddy Livingston	2,000	1,000	600.00
(11)	Bris Lord	2,000	1,000	600.00
(12)	Connie Mack	14,000	7,900	4,575
(13)	Cy Morgan	2,000	1,000	600.00
(14)	Danny Murphy	2,000	1,000	600.00
(15)	Rube Oldring	2,000	1,000	600.00
(16)	Eddie Plank	14,000	7,900	4,575
(17)	Amos Strunk	2,000	1,000	600.00
(18)	Ira Thomas	2,000	1,000	600.00

1955 Rodeo Meats Athletics

Don Bollweg

This set of 2-1/2" x 3-1/2" color cards was issued by a local meat company to commemorate the first year of the Athletics in Kansas City. There are 38 different players included in the set, with nine players known to apppear in two different variations for a total of 47 cards in the set. Most variations are in background colors, although Bobby Shantz is also listed incorrectly as "Schantz" on one variation. The cards are unnumbered, with the Rodeo logo and player name on the fronts, and an ad for a scrapbook album listed on the backs.

		NM	E	VG
Complete Set (47):		12,500	6,250	3,750
Common Player:		225.00	110.00	45.00
Album:		550.00	275.00	125.00
(1)	Joe Astroth	225.00	110.00	45.00
(2)	Harold Bevan	275.00	135.00	55.00
(3)	Charles Bishop	275.00	135.00	55.00
(4)	Don Bollweg	275.00	135.00	55.00
(5)	Lou Boudreau	600.00	300.00	120.00
(6)	Cloyd Boyer (Blue background)	375.00	185.00	75.00
(7)	Cloyd Boyer (Pink background.)	275.00	135.00	55.00
(8)	Ed Burtschy	275.00	135.00	55.00
(9)	Art Ceccarelli	225.00	110.00	45.00
(10)	Joe DeMaestri (Pea green background.)	275.00	135.00	55.00
(11)	Joe DeMaestri (Light green background.)	225.00	110.00	45.00
(12)	Art Ditmar	225.00	110.00	45.00
(13)	John Dixon	275.00	135.00	55.00
(14)	Jim Finigan	225.00	110.00	45.00
(15)	Marion Fricano	275.00	135.00	55.00
(16)	Tom Gorman	275.00	135.00	55.00
(17)	John Gray	225.00	110.00	45.00
(18)	Ray Herbert	225.00	110.00	45.00
(19)	Forest "Spook" Jacobs (Forrest)	275.00	135.00	55.00
(20)	Alex Kellner	275.00	135.00	55.00
(21)	Harry Kraft (Craft)	225.00	110.00	45.00
(22)	Jack Littrell	225.00	110.00	45.00
(23)	Hector Lopez	275.00	135.00	55.00
(24)	Oscar Melillo	225.00	110.00	45.00
(25)	Arnold Portocarrero (Purple background.)	275.00	135.00	55.00
(26)	Arnold Portocarrero (Gray background.)	225.00	110.00	45.00
(27)	Vic Power (Pink background.)	325.00	160.00	65.00
(28)	Vic Power (Yellow background.)	275.00	135.00	55.00
(29)	Vic Raschi	275.00	135.00	55.00
(30)	Bill Renna (Dark pink background.)	275.00	135.00	55.00

(31)	Bill Renna (Light pink background.)	225.00	110.00	45.00
(32)	Al Robertson	275.00	135.00	55.00
(33)	Johnny Sain	300.00	150.00	60.00
(34a)	Bobby Schantz (Incorrect spelling.)	900.00	450.00	180.00
(34b)	Bobby Shantz (Correct spelling.)	300.00	150.00	60.00
(35)	Wilmer Shantz (Orange background.)	300.00	150.00	60.00
(36)	Wilmer Shantz (Purple background.)	275.00	135.00	55.00
(37)	Harry Simpson	225.00	110.00	45.00
(38)	Enos Slaughter	650.00	325.00	130.00
(39)	Lou Sleater	225.00	110.00	45.00
(40)	George Susce	225.00	110.00	45.00
(41)	Bob Trice	275.00	135.00	55.00
(42)	Elmer Valo (Yellow background.)	275.00	135.00	55.00
(43)	Elmer Valo (Green background.)	225.00	110.00	45.00
(44)	Bill Wilson (Yellow background.)	300.00	150.00	60.00
(45)	Bill Wilson (Purple background.)	250.00	125.00	50.00
(46)	Gus Zernial	250.00	125.00	50.00

1956 Rodeo Meats Athletics

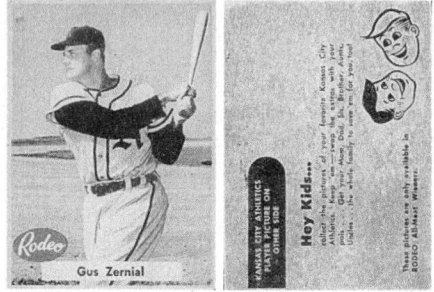

Gus Zernial

Hey Kids...

Rodeo Meats issued another Kansas City Athletics set in 1956, but this one was a much smaller 13-card set. The 2-1/2" x 3-1/2" cards are again unnumbered, with the player name and Rodeo logo on the fronts. Card backs feature some of the same graphics and copy as the 1955 cards, but the album offer is omitted. The full-color cards were only available in packages of Rodeo hot dogs.

		NM	E	VG
Complete Set (12):		6,500	2,600	1,300
Common Player:		550.00	220.00	110.00
(1)	Joe Astroth	550.00	220.00	110.00
(2)	Lou Boudreau	650.00	260.00	130.00
(3)	Joe DeMaestri	550.00	220.00	110.00
(4)	Art Ditmar	550.00	220.00	110.00
(5)	Jim Finigan	550.00	220.00	110.00
(6)	Hector Lopez	550.00	220.00	110.00
(7)	Vic Power	550.00	220.00	110.00
(8)	Bobby Shantz	550.00	220.00	110.00
(9)	Harry Simpson	550.00	220.00	110.00
(10)	Enos Slaughter	700.00	280.00	140.00
(11)	Elmer Valo	550.00	220.00	110.00
(12)	Gus Zernial	550.00	220.00	110.00

1976 Rodeo Meats Athletics Commemorative

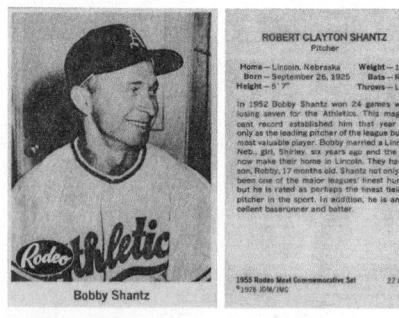

Bobby Shantz

This collectors' issue essentially reprints many of the 1955-56 Rodeo Meats cards in a 2-1/2" x 3-1/2" black-and-white format. Fronts have player photos, the Rodeo logo and the player name in the white border at bottom. Backs, instead of the original Rodeo ads, have player identification, biographical information and career summary, along with a reprint notice.

	NM	E	VG
Complete Set (30):	20.00	10.00	6.00

Common Player:		2.00	1.00	.60
1	Header Card	.50	.25	.15
2	Checklist Card	.50	.25	.15
3	Joe Astroth	2.00	1.00	.60
4	Lou Boudreau	3.00	1.50	.90
5	Cloyd Boyer	2.00	1.00	.60
6	Art Ceccarelli	2.00	1.00	.60
7	Harry Craft	2.00	1.00	.60
8	Joe DeMaestri	2.00	1.00	.60
9	Art Ditmar	2.00	1.00	.60
10	Jim Finigan	2.00	1.00	.60
11	Ray Herbert	2.00	1.00	.60
12	Tom Gorman	2.00	1.00	.60
13	Alex Kellner	2.00	1.00	.60
14	Jack Littrell	2.00	1.00	.60
15	Hector Lopez	2.00	1.00	.60
16	Oscar Melillo	2.00	1.00	.60
17	Arnie Portocarrero	2.00	1.00	.60
18	Vic Power	2.50	1.25	.70
19	Vic Raschi	2.50	1.25	.70
20	Bill Renna	2.00	1.00	.60
21	Johnny Sain	2.50	1.25	.70
22	Bobby Shantz	2.50	1.25	.70
23	Wilmer Shantz	2.00	1.00	.60
24	Harry Simpson	2.50	1.25	.70
25	Enos Slaughter	4.00	2.00	1.25
26	Lou Sleator	2.00	1.00	.60
27	George Susce	2.00	1.00	.60
28	Elmer Valo	2.00	1.00	.60
29	Bill Wilson	2.00	1.00	.60
30	Gus Zernial	2.50	1.25	.70

1930s Rogers Peet Sport Album

18.— HERB PENNOCK

This is one of the scarcest multi-sport issues of the 1930s. It was the promotion of a New York-Boston chain of stores (boys' clothing) in the form of a frequent customer program. Boys visiting the store with a parent could receive a set of four cards to be placed in a 14-page 4-1/2" x 7-1/4" album. Individual cards are about 1-7/8" x 2-1/2" and feature black-and-white photos with a white border. The athlete's name and card number are printed in the bottom border. Numbers correspond to spaces in the album. Only the "Baseball Stars" from the issue are checklisted here. Others include hockey, football, track, swimming, golf, tennis, aviation, etc.

		NM	E	VG
Complete Set (44):		7,500	3,750	2,250
Complete Set in Album:		5,000	2,500	1,500
Common Sticker:		30.00	15.00	9.00
Album:		500.00	250.00	150.00
5	Dazzy Vance	225.00	110.00	65.00
13	Walter Johnson	650.00	325.00	195.00
16	Rogers Hornsby	450.00	225.00	135.00
18	Herb Pennock	225.00	110.00	65.00
28	Lou Gehrig	1,600	800.00	475.00
34	Ty Cobb	1,500	750.00	450.00
38	Tris Speaker	450.00	225.00	135.00
48	Babe Ruth	1,750	875.00	525.00

1960s Rogers Printing Co. Postcards

The extent to which this Columbus, Ohio, firm may have provided baseball players with postcards to answer fan mail requests is unknown. At present, only a single card is known, that of Bob Wills, who played his entire major league career (1957-63) with the Cubs. The card is printed in black-and-white on glossy stock in a 3-1/2" x 5-1/2" format. A facsimile autograph message is printed on front. Postcard-style backs have the imprint of the printer.

	NM	E	VG
Bob Will	3.00	1.50	.90

1970 Rold Gold Pretzels

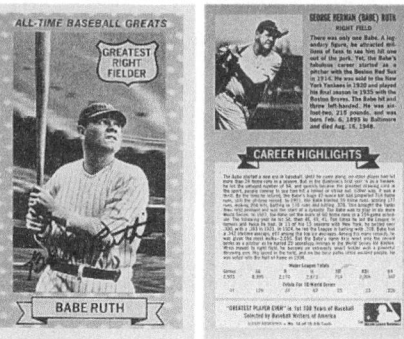

The 1970 Rold Gold Pretzels set of 15 cards honors the "Greatest Players Ever" in the first 100 years of baseball as chosen by the Baseball Writers of America. The cards, which measure 2-1/4" x 3-1/2" in size, feature a simulated 3-D effect. The set was re-released in 1972 by Kellogg's in packages of Danish-Go-Rounds. Rold Gold cards can be differentiated from the Kellogg's cards of 1972 by the 1970 copyright date found on the card reverse.

		NM	E	VG
Complete Set (15):		50.00	25.00	15.00
Common Player:		2.00	1.00	.60
1	Walter Johnson	6.00	3.00	1.75
2	Rogers Hornsby	3.00	1.50	.90
3	John McGraw	2.00	1.00	.60
4	Mickey Cochrane	2.00	1.00	.60
5	George Sisler	2.00	1.00	.60
6	Babe Ruth ("Greatest Ever")	15.00	7.50	4.50
7	Robert "Lefty" Grove	2.00	1.00	.60
8	Harold "Pie" Traynor	2.00	1.00	.60
9	Honus Wagner	7.50	3.75	2.25
10	Eddie Collins	2.00	1.00	.60
11	Tris Speaker	3.00	1.50	.90
12	Cy Young	5.00	2.50	1.50
13	Lou Gehrig	10.00	5.00	3.00
14	Babe Ruth ("Greatest Right Fielder")	15.00	7.50	4.50
15	Ty Cobb	9.00	4.50	2.75

1908-1909 Rose Company Postcards

Among the most ornate and attractive baseball cards of the pre-1910 period is the set of postcards produced by The Rose Co., between 1908-09. The 3-1/2" x 5-1/2" cards feature a black-and-white player portrait photo at center, surrounded by an embossed round gold frame. The player's surname and (usually) team are in a white panel under the photo. The background of the card's front is in green and includes crossed bats and a baseball, a diamond diagram and pictures of a fielder and batter. The postcard-format back is printed in black-and-white with a TRC logo at bottom-center. The unnumbered postcards are checklisted here alphabetically; including 11 minor league players from Scranton in the New York State League. It is possible future discoveries will be added to this checklist; gaps have been left in the numbering to accommodate them.

		NM	E	VG
Common Player:		2,400	720.00	360.00
(1)	Ed Abbaticchio	2,400	720.00	360.00
(2)	Bill Abstein	2,400	720.00	360.00
(3)	Whitey Alperman	2,400	720.00	360.00
(4)	Nick Altrock	2,400	720.00	360.00
(5)	John Anderson	2,400	720.00	360.00
(6)	Shad Barry	2,400	720.00	360.00
(7)	Ginger Beaumont	2,400	720.00	360.00
(8)	Heinie Beckendorf	2,400	720.00	360.00
(9)	Fred Beebe	2,400	720.00	360.00
(10)	Harry Bemis	2,400	720.00	360.00
(11)	Chief Bender	6,000	1,800	900.00
(12)	Bills	2,400	720.00	360.00
(13)	Joe Birmingham	2,400	720.00	360.00
(14)	Frank Bowerman	2,400	720.00	360.00
(15)	Bill Bradley	2,400	720.00	360.00
(16)	Kitty Bransfield	2,400	720.00	360.00

(17)	Roger Bresnahan	6,000	1,800	900.00
(18)	Al Bridwell	2,400	720.00	360.00
(19)	Buster Brown (Brown.) Philadelphia)(Photo actually Mordecai)	3,750	1,125	565.00
(20)	Samuel Brown (Boston)	2,400	720.00	360.00
(21)	Mordecai Brown (Chicago)	6,000	1,800	900.00
(22)	Bobby Byrne	2,400	720.00	360.00
(23)	Howie Camnitz	2,400	720.00	360.00
(24)	Billy Campbell	2,400	720.00	360.00
(26)	Frank Chance	6,000	1,800	900.00
(27)	Hal Chase	2,400	720.00	360.00
(28)	Charlie Chech	2,400	720.00	360.00
(29)	Jack Chesbro	6,000	1,800	900.00
(30)	Fred Clarke (Pittsburg)	6,000	1,800	900.00
(31)	Nig Clarke (Cleveland)	2,400	720.00	360.00
(32)	Otis Clymer	2,400	720.00	360.00
(33a)	Andy Coakley (Cincinnati)	2,400	800.00	400.00
(33b)	Andy Coakley (No team name.)	2,400	800.00	400.00
(34)	Ty Cobb	24,000	7,200	3,6000.00
(35)	Jimmy Collins	6,000	1,800	900.00
(36)	Wid Conroy	2,400	720.00	360.00
(37)	Jack Coombs	2,400	720.00	360.00
(38)	Frank Corridon	2,400	720.00	360.00
(39)	Bill Coughlin	2,400	720.00	360.00
(40)	Sam Crawford	6,000	1,800	900.00
(41a)	Lou Criger (Boston)	2,400	720.00	360.00
(41b)	Lou Criger (No team.)	2,400	720.00	360.00
(42)	Bill Dahlen	2,400	720.00	360.00
(43)	Harry Davis	2,400	720.00	360.00
(44)	Joe Delahanty (St. Louis)	2,400	720.00	360.00
(45)	Frank Delehanty (N.Y., A.L.) Delahanty) (Washington; team actually)	2,400	720.00	360.00
(46)	Art Devlin	2,400	720.00	360.00
(47)	Mike Donlin	2,400	800.00	400.00
(48)	Jiggs Donohue (Donahue)	2,400	720.00	360.00
(49)	Wild Bill Donovan	2,400	720.00	360.00
(51)	Red Dooin	2,400	720.00	360.00
(52)	Mickey Doolan	2,400	720.00	360.00
(53)	Larry Doyle	2,400	720.00	360.00
(54)	Jimmy Dygert	2,400	720.00	360.00
(55)	Kid Elberfeld	2,400	720.00	360.00
(56)	Eley	2,400	720.00	360.00
(57)	Johnny Evers	6,000	1,800	900.00
(58)	Bob Ewing	2,400	720.00	360.00
(59)	George Ferguson	2,400	720.00	360.00
(60)	Hobe Ferris	2,400	720.00	360.00
(61)	Jerry Freeman	2,400	720.00	360.00
(62)	Bob Ganley	2,400	720.00	360.00
(63)	John Ganzel	2,400	720.00	360.00
(64)	Doc Gessler	2,400	720.00	360.00
(65)	George Gibson	2,400	720.00	360.00
(66)	Billy Gilbert	2,400	720.00	360.00
(67)	Fred Glade	2,400	720.00	360.00
(68)	Ralph Glaze	2,400	720.00	360.00
(69)	Graham	2,400	720.00	360.00
(70)	Eddie Grant	2,400	720.00	360.00
(71)	Groh	2,400	720.00	360.00
(72)	Charley Hale (Hall)	2,400	720.00	360.00
(73)	Halligan	2,400	720.00	360.00
(74)	Topsy Hartsel	2,400	720.00	360.00
(75)	Charlie Hemphill	2,400	720.00	360.00
(76)	Bill Hinchman	2,400	720.00	360.00
(77)	Art Hoelskoetter	2,400	720.00	360.00
(78)	Danny Hoffman	2,400	720.00	360.00
(79)	Solly Hofmann	2,400	720.00	360.00
(80)	Houser	2,400	720.00	360.00
(81)	Harry Howell	2,400	720.00	360.00
(82)	Miller Huggins	6,000	1,800	900.00
(83)	Rudy Hulswitt	2,400	720.00	360.00
(84)	John Hummel	2,400	720.00	360.00
(85a)	Frank Isbel (Isbell) (Chicago)	2,400	720.00	360.00
(85b)	Frank Isbel (Isbell)(No team.))	2,400	720.00	360.00
(86)	Walter Johnson	12,000	3,600	1,800
(87)	Fielder Jones (Chicago)	2,400	720.00	360.00
(88)	Tom Jones (St. Louis)	2,400	720.00	360.00
(89)	Tim Jordan	2,400	720.00	360.00
(90)	Addie Joss	12,000	3,600	1,800
(91)	Johnny Kane	2,400	720.00	360.00
(92)	Ed Karger	2,400	720.00	360.00
(93)	Wee Willie Keeler	6,000	1,800	900.00
(94)	Kellogg	2,400	720.00	360.00
(95)	Ed Killian	2,400	720.00	360.00
(96)	Malachi Kittredge (Kittridge)	2,400	720.00	360.00
(97)	Red Kleinow	2,400	720.00	360.00
(98)	Johnny Kling	2,400	720.00	36.00
(99)	Otto Knabe	2,400	720.00	360.00
(101)	John Knight	2,400	720.00	360.00
(102)	Ed Konetchy	2,400	720.00	360.00
(103)	Nap Lajoie	12,000	3,600	1,800
(104)	Frank LaPorte	2,400	720.00	360.00
(105)	Tommy Leach	2,400	720.00	360.00
(106)	Glenn Leibhardt (Liebhardt)	2,400	720.00	360.00
(107)	Phil Lewis	2,400	720.00	360.00
(108)	Vive Lindamann (Lindaman)	2,400	720.00	360.00
(109)	Hans Lobert	2,400	720.00	360.00
(110)	Harry Lord	2,400	720.00	360.00
(111)	Harry Lumley	2,400	720.00	360.00
(112)	Johnny Lush	2,400	720.00	360.00
(113)	Nick Maddox	2,400	720.00	360.00
(114)	Sherry Magee	2,400	720.00	360.00
(115)	Billy Maloney	2,400	720.00	360.00
(116)	Christy Mathewson	12,000	3,600	1,800
(117)	George McBride	2,400	720.00	360.00
(118)	Joe McGinnity	6,000	1,800	900.00
(119)	Stoney McGlynn	2,400	720.00	360.00
(120)	Harry McIntyre (McIntire)(Brooklyn)	2,400	720.00	360.00
(121)	Matty McIntyre (Detroit)	2,400	720.00	360.00
(122)	Larry McLean	2,400	720.00	360.00
(123)	George McQuillen (McQuillan)	2,400	720.00	360.00
(124)	Clyde Milan	2,400	720.00	360.00
(126)	Mike Mitchell	2,400	720.00	360.00
(127)	Moran	2,400	720.00	360.00
(128)	Mike Mowrey	2,400	720.00	360.00
(129)	George Mullin	2,400	720.00	360.00
(130)	Danny Murphy	2,400	720.00	360.00
(131)	J.J. Murray	2,400	720.00	360.00
(132)	Doc Newton	2,400	720.00	360.00
(133)	Simon Nicholls	2,400	720.00	360.00
(134)	Harry Niles	2,400	720.00	360.00
(135)	Rebel Oakes	2,400	720.00	360.00
(136)	Rube Oldring	2,400	720.00	360.00
(137)	Charley O'Leary	2,400	720.00	360.00
(138)	Patsy O'Rourke	2,400	720.00	360.00
(139)	Al Orth	2,400	720.00	360.00
(140)	Fred Osborne (Osborn)	2,400	720.00	360.00
(141)	Orval Overall	2,400	720.00	360.00
(142)	Freddy Parent	2,400	1,000	500.00
(143)	George Paskert	2,400	720.00	360.00
(144)	Case Patten	2,400	720.00	360.00
(145)	Jeff Pfeffer	2,400	720.00	360.00
(146)	Deacon Phillippi (Phillippe)	2,400	720.00	360.00
(147)	Eddie Plank	12,000	3,600	1,800
(148)	Jack Powell	2,400	720.00	360.00
(149)	Tex Pruiett	2,400	720.00	360.00
(150)	Ed Reulbach	2,400	720.00	360.00
(151)	Bob Rhoades (Rhoads)	2,400	720.00	360.00
(152)	Claude Ritchey	2,400	720.00	360.00
(153)	Claude Rossman	2,400	720.00	360.00
(154)	Nap Rucker	2,400	720.00	360.00
(155)	Germany Schaefer	2,400	720.00	360.00
(156)	George Schlei	2,400	720.00	360.00
(157)	Boss Schmidt	2,400	720.00	360.00
(158)	Ossie Schreck	2,400	720.00	360.00
(159)	Wildfire Schulte	2,400	720.00	360.00
(160)	Schultz	2,400	720.00	360.00
(161)	Socks Seybold	2,400	720.00	360.00
(162)	Cy Seymour	2,400	720.00	360.00
(163)	Spike Shannon	2,400	720.00	360.00
(164)	Jimmy Sheckard	2,400	720.00	360.00
(165)	Tommy Sheehan	2,400	720.00	360.00
(166)	Bill Shipke	2,400	720.00	360.00
(167)	Jimmy Slagle	2,400	720.00	360.00
(168)	Charlie Smith (Chicago)	2,400	720.00	360.00
(169)	Frank Smith (Washington)	2,400	720.00	360.00
(170)	Bob Spade	2,400	720.00	360.00
(171)	Tully Sparks	2,400	720.00	360.00
(172)	Tris Speaker	6,000	1,800	900.00
(173)	Tubby Spencer	2,400	720.00	360.00
(174)	Jake Stahl	2,400	720.00	360.00
(175)	Steele	2,400	720.00	360.00
(176)	Harry Steinfeldt	2,400	720.00	360.00
(177)	George Stone	2,400	720.00	360.00
(178)	George Stovall	2,400	720.00	360.00
(179)	Billy Sullivan	2,400	720.00	360.00
(180)	Ed Summers	2,400	720.00	360.00
(181)	Bill Sweeney	2,400	720.00	360.00
(182)	Lee Tannehill	2,400	720.00	360.00
(183)	Dummy Taylor	2,400	720.00	360.00
(184)	Fred Tenney	2,400	720.00	360.00
(185)	Ira Thomas (No team.)	2,400	720.00	360.00
(186)	Roy Thomas (Pittsburg)	2,400	720.00	360.00
(187)	Jack Thoney	2,400	720.00	360.00
(188)	Joe Tinker	6,000	1,800	900.00
(189)	John Titus	2,400	720.00	360.00
(190)	Terry Turner	2,400	720.00	360.00
(191)	Bob Unglaub	2,400	720.00	360.00
(192)	Rube Waddell	6,000	1,800	900.00
(193)	Heinie Wagner (Boston)	2,400	720.00	360.00
(194)	Honus Wagner (Pittsburg)	24,000	7,200	3,600
(195)	Ed Walsh	6,000	1,800	900.00
(196)	Jack Warner	2,400	720.00	360.00
(197a)	Jake Weimer (Cincinnati)	2,400	720.00	360.00
(197b)	Jake Weimer (No team.)	2,400	720.00	360.00
(198)	Doc White	2,400	720.00	360.00
(199)	Jimmy Williams	2,400	720.00	360.00
(200)	Chief Wilson	2,400	720.00	360.00
(201)	Hooks Wiltse	2,400	720.00	360.00
(202)	George Winter	2,400	720.00	360.00
(203)	Cy Young (Boston)	12,000	3,600	1,800
(204)	Harley Young (Pittsburg)	2,400	720.00	360.00

1905 Rotograph Postcards

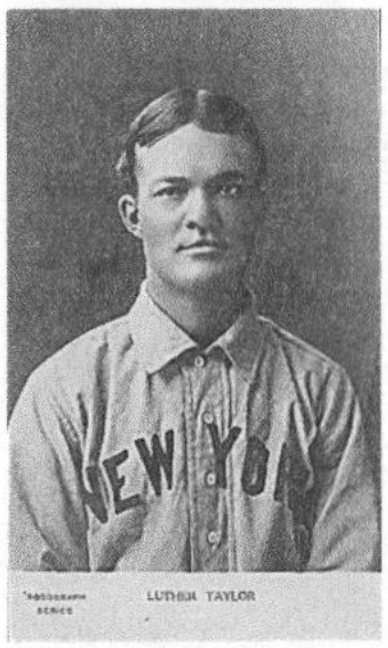

Only New York players have been seen on this series of 3-1/4" x 5-3/8" black-and-white or blue-and-white duotone postcards. Cards have player portrait photos with a white strip at bottom identifying the player; a "Rotograph / Series" notation is at left. Backs have typical postcard markings. This checklist may not be complete. The set was listed in the American Card Catalog under the number PC782.

		NM	E	VG
Common Player:		800.00	400.00	250.00
(1)	Geo. Brown (Browne)	800.00	400.00	250.00
(2)	J.D. Chesbro	1,000	500.00	300.00
(3)	Wm. F. Dahlen	800.00	400.00	250.00
(4)	Clark Griffill (Griffith)	1,350	675.00	405.00
(5)	Joseph McGinnity	1,000	500.00	300.00
(6)	John McGraw	1,500	750.00	450.00
(7)	A. Puttmann	800.00	400.00	250.00
(8)	Luther Taylor	1,250	625.00	375.00
(9)	Team Composite	3,500	1,750	1,050

1977 Jim Rowe 1929 Cubs Postcards

Originally retailed for $3 per set, these collector-issue postcards feature on front borderless black-and-white photos in 3-1/2" x 5-7/16" format. Backs are standard Kodak postcard style, with no mention of the issuer. The player name is usually found penned at top.

		NM	E	VG
Complete Set (13):		30.00	20.00	12.00
Common Player:		3.00	1.50	.90
(1)	Guy Bush	3.00	1.50	.90
(2)	Kiki Cuyler	3.00	1.50	.90
(3)	Woody English	3.00	1.50	.90
(4)	Charlie Grimm	3.00	1.50	.90
(5)	Gabby Hartnett	3.00	1.50	.90
(6)	Rogers Hornsby	3.00	1.50	.90
(7)	Pat Malone	3.00	1.50	.90
(8)	Norman McMillan	3.00	1.50	.90
(9)	Charlie Root	3.00	1.50	.90
(10)	Riggs Stephenson	3.00	1.50	.90
(11)	Zach Taylor	3.00	1.50	.90
(12)	Hack Wilson	3.00	1.50	.90
(13)	**Team photo**	3.00	1.50	.90

1977 Jim Rowe 1956 Braves Postcards

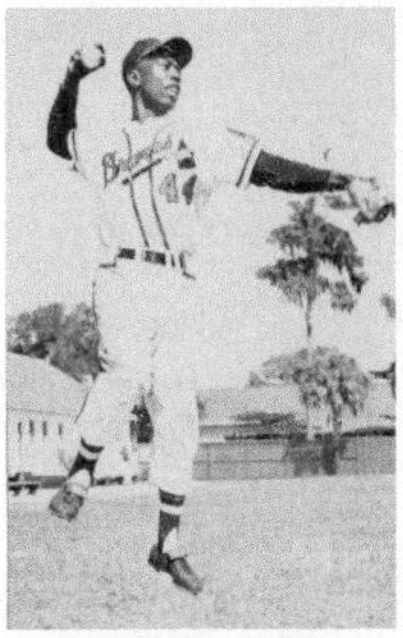

Originally retailed for $4 per set, these collector-issue postcards feature on front borderless black-and-white photos in 3-1/2" x 5-7/16" format. Backs are standard Kodak postcard style, with no mention of the issuer. The player name is usually found penned at top.

		NM	E	VG
	Complete Set (16):	35.00	17.50	10.50
	Common Player:	3.00	1.50	.90
(1)	Hank Aaron	4.00	2.00	1.25
(2)	Joe Adcock	3.00	1.50	.90
(3)	Bill Bruton	3.00	1.50	.90
(4)	Bob Buhl	3.00	1.50	.90
(5)	Lew Burdette	3.00	1.50	.90
(6)	Gene Conley	3.00	1.50	.90
(7)	Del Crandall	3.00	1.50	.90
(8)	Charlie Grimm	3.00	1.50	.90
(9)	Fred Haney	3.00	1.50	.90
(10)	Joey Jay	3.00	1.50	.90
(11)	Johnny Logan	3.00	1.50	.90
(12)	Chet Nichols	3.00	1.50	.90
(13)	Danny O'Connell	3.00	1.50	.90
(14)	Andy Pafko	3.00	1.50	.90
(15)	Warren Spahn	3.00	1.50	.90
(16)	Bobby Thomson	3.00	1.50	.90

1977 Jim Rowe 4-on-1 Exhibits

PIE TRAYNOR
PITTSBURGH N.L.

LLOYD WANER
PITTSBURGH N.L.

HONUS WAGNER
PITTSBURGH N.L.

PAUL WANER
PITTSBURGH N.L.

This collectors' edition set harkens back to the four-player cards issued in the 1930s by Exhibit Supply Co. The 1977 version is printed in black on yellow in a 3-1/4" x 5-1/2" format. Backs are blank. Each of the four player photos on front is identified by name. The cards are checklisted here in order of team name.

		NM	E	VG
	Complete Set (16):	90.00	45.00	27.00
	Common Card:	5.00	2.50	1.50
(1)	Boston Braves(Al Lopez, Rabbit Maranville, Warren Spahn, Casey Stengel)	5.00	2.50	1.50
(2)	Boston Red Sox(Joe Cronin, Herb Pennock, Babe Ruth, Ted Williams)	15.00	7.50	4.50
(3)	Brooklyn Dodgers(Max Carey, Burleigh Grimes, Joe Medwick, Dazzy Vance)	5.00	2.50	1.50
(4)	Chicago Cubs(Kiki Cuyler, Gabby Hartnett, Billy Herman, Freddy Lindstrom)	5.00	2.50	1.50
(5)	Chicago White Sox(Luke Appling, Red Faber, Ted Lyons, Red Ruffing)	5.00	2.50	1.50
(6)	Cincinnati Reds(Chick Hafey, George Kelly, Bill McKechnie, Edd Roush)	5.00	2.50	1.50
(7)	Cleveland Indians(Earl Averill, Lou Boudreau, Bob Feller, Bob Lemon)	5.00	2.50	1.50

		NM	E	VG
(8)	Detroit Tigers(Ty Cobb, Charlie Gehringer, Goose Goslin, Hank Greenberg)	11.00	5.50	3.25
(9)	New York Giants(Dave Bancroft, Carl Hubbell, Mel Ott, Bill Terry)	5.00	2.50	1.50
(10)	New York Yankees(Bill Dickey, Joe DiMaggio, Lou Gehrig, Lefty Gomez)	12.00	6.00	3.50
(11)	Philadelphia Athletics(Mickey Cochrane, Eddie Collins, Lefty Grove, Al Simmons)	5.00	2.50	1.50
(12)	Philadelphia Phillies(Grover Alexander, Jimmie Foxx, Eppa Rixey, Robin Roberts)	5.00	2.50	1.50
(13)	Pittsburgh Pirates(Pie Traynor, Honus Wagner, Lloyd Waner, Paul Waner)	6.00	3.00	1.75
(14)	St. Louis Browns(Jim Bottomley, Earle Combs, Rogers Hornsby, George Sisler)	5.00	2.50	1.50
(15)	St. Louis Cardinals(Dizzy Dean, Frankie Frisch, Jesse Haines, Stan Musial)	5.00	2.50	1.50
(16)	Washington Senators(Bucky Harris, Walter Johnson, Heinie Manush, Sam Rice)	6.00	3.00	1.75

1955 Royal Castle /Vic Wertz Premium

This premium picture is 8" x 10," blank-backed and printed on rather heavy textured paper. It features a posed dugout photo of Cleveland Indians first baseman Vic Wertz and long-time Indians radio play-by-play announcer Jimmy Dudley. The picture can't be reliably dated any more specifically than Wertz's entire stint with the Tribe, 1954-57. Facsimile autographs and endorsements by the pair appear across the front. A pennant at bottom has the Royal Castle logo and slogan "Hamburgers fit for a king".

	NM	EX	VG
Vic Wertz	150.00	75.00	
45.00			

1978 Royal Crown Cola Iron-Ons

These iron-on color transfers were available in team strips of five players for 50 cents and six bottle cap liners. Because they were licensed only by the Players' Association, and not MLB, the approximately 4-1/4" x 6-1/4" transfers do not show team logos or nicknames.

		NM	E	VG
	Complete Set (130):	750.00	375.00	225.00
	Common Player:	6.00	3.00	1.75
	Atlanta Strip	25.00	12.50	7.50
(1)	Jeff Burroughs	6.00	3.00	1.75
(2)	Gary Matthews	6.00	3.00	1.75
(3)	Phil Niekro	7.50	3.75	2.25
(4)	Biff Pocoroba	6.00	3.00	1.75
(5)	Dick Ruthven	6.00	3.00	1.75
	Baltimore Strip	50.00	25.00	15.00
(6)	Al Bumbry	6.00	3.00	1.75
(7)	Lee May	6.00	3.00	1.75
(8)	Eddie Murray	30.00	15.00	9.00
(9)	Jim Palmer	15.00	7.50	4.50
(10)	Ken Singleton	6.00	3.00	1.75
	Boston Strip	40.00	20.00	12.00
(11)	Bill Campbell	6.00	3.00	1.75
(12)	Fred Lynn	6.00	3.00	1.75
(13)	Jim Rice	7.50	3.75	2.25
(14)	George Scott	6.00	3.00	1.75
(15)	Carl Yastrzemski	25.00	12.50	7.50
	California Strip	75.00	37.50	22.50
(16)	Dave Chalk	6.00	3.00	1.75
(17)	Bobby Grich	6.00	3.00	1.75
(18)	Joe Rudi	6.00	3.00	1.75
(19)	Nolan Ryan	60.00	30.00	18.00
(20)	Frank Tanana	6.00	3.00	1.75
	Chicago (Cubs) Strip	30.00	15.00	9.00
(21)	Bill Buckner	6.00	3.00	1.75
(22)	Dave Kingman	6.00	3.00	1.75
(23)	Steve Ontiveros	6.00	3.00	1.75
(24)	Bruce Sutter	7.50	3.75	2.25
(25)	Manny Trillo	6.00	3.00	1.75
	Chicago (White Sox) Strip	25.00	12.50	7.50
(26)	Ron Blomberg	6.00	3.00	1.75
(27)	Bobby Bonds	6.00	3.00	1.75
(28)	Ralph Garr	6.00	3.00	1.75
(29)	Jorge Orta	6.00	3.00	1.75
(30)	Eric Soderholm	6.00	3.00	1.75
	Cincinnati Strip	15.00	7.50	4.50
(31)	Johnny Bench	6.00	3.00	1.75
(32)	George Foster	9.00	4.50	2.70
(33)	Joe Morgan	15.00	7.50	4.50
(34)	Tom Seaver	15.00	7.50	4.50
(35)	Pete Rose	40.00	20.00	12.00
	Cleveland Strip	25.00	12.50	7.50
(36)	Buddy Bell	6.00	3.00	1.75
(37)	Wayne Garland	6.00	3.00	1.75
(38)	Johnny Grubb	6.00	3.00	1.75
(39)	Rick Manning	6.00	3.00	1.75
(40)	Andre Thornton	6.00	3.00	1.75
	Detroit Strip	25.00	12.50	7.50
(41)	Mark Fidrych	6.00	3.00	1.75
(42)	John Hiller	6.00	3.00	1.75
(43)	Ron LeFlore	6.00	3.00	1.75
(44)	Milt May	6.00	3.00	1.75
(45)	Jason Thompson	6.00	3.00	1.75
	Houston Strip	25.00	12.50	7.50
(46)	Enos Cabell	6.00	3.00	1.75
(47)	Cesar Cedeno	6.00	3.00	1.75
(48)	Joe Ferguson	6.00	3.00	1.75
(49)	J.R. Richard	6.00	3.00	1.75
(50)	Bobby Watson	6.00	3.00	1.75
	Kansas City Strip	45.00	22.50	13.50
(51)	George Brett	30.00	15.00	9.00
(52)	Al Cowens	6.00	3.00	1.75
(53)	Hal McRae	6.00	3.00	1.75
(54)	Amos Otis	6.00	3.00	1.75
(55)	Fred Patek	6.00	3.00	1.75
	Los Angeles Strip	30.00	15.00	9.00
(56)	Ron Cey	6.00	3.00	1.75
(57)	Steve Garvey	7.50	3.75	2.25
(58)	Tommy John	6.00	3.00	1.75
(59)	Bill Russell	6.00	3.00	1.75
(60)	Don Sutton	7.50	3.75	2.25
	Milwaukee Strip	30.00	15.00	9.00
(61)	Sal Bando	6.00	3.00	1.75
(62)	Ray Fosse	6.00	3.00	1.75
(63)	Larry Hisle	6.00	3.00	1.75
(64)	Sixto Lezcano	6.00	3.00	1.75
(65)	Robin Yount	15.00	7.50	4.50
	Minnesota Strip	30.00	15.00	9.00
(66)	Rod Carew	15.00	7.50	4.50
(67)	Dan Ford	6.00	3.00	1.75
(68)	Dave Goltz	6.00	3.00	1.75
(69)	Roy Smalley	6.00	3.00	1.75
(70)	Butch Wynegar	6.00	3.00	1.75
	Montreal Strip	30.00	15.00	9.00
(71)	Dave Cash	6.00	3.00	1.75
(72)	Andre Dawson	7.50	3.75	2.25
(73)	Tony Perez	7.50	3.75	2.25
(74)	Steve Rogers	6.00	3.00	1.75
(75)	Ellis Valentine	6.00	3.00	1.75
	New York (Mets) Strip	25.00	12.50	7.50
(76)	Steve Henderson	6.00	3.00	1.75

		NM	E	VG
(77)	Jerry Koosman	6.00	3.00	1.75
(78)	Elliott Maddox	6.00	3.00	1.75
(79)	Willie Montanez	6.00	3.00	1.75
(80)	Lenny Randle	6.00	3.00	1.75
	New York (Yankees) Strip	30.00	15.00	9.00
(81)	Sparky Lyle	6.00	3.00	1.75
(82)	Thurman Munson	7.50	3.75	2.25
(83)	Lou Piniella	6.00	3.00	1.75
(84)	Willie Randolph	6.00	3.00	1.75
(85)	Mickey Rivers	6.00	3.00	1.75
	Oakland Strip	25.00	12.50	7.50
(86)	Wayne Gross	6.00	3.00	1.75
(87)	Rick Langford	6.00	3.00	1.75
(88)	Bill North	6.00	3.00	1.75
(89)	Mitchell Page	6.00	3.00	1.75
(90)	Gary Thomasson	6.00	3.00	1.75
	Philadelphia Strip	60.00	30.00	18.00
(91)	Larry Bowa	6.00	3.00	1.75
(92)	Steve Carlton	15.00	7.50	4.50
(93)	Greg Luzinski	6.00	3.00	1.75
(94)	Garry Maddox	6.00	3.00	1.75
(95)	Mike Schmidt	35.00	17.50	10.50
	Pittsburgh Strip	30.00	15.00	9.00
(96)	John Candelaria	6.00	3.00	1.75
(97)	Dave Parker	6.00	3.00	1.75
(98)	Bill Robinson	6.00	3.00	1.75
(99)	Willie Stargell	15.00	7.50	4.50
(100)	Rennie Stennett	6.00	3.00	1.75
	San Diego Strip	35.00	17.50	10.00
(101)	Rollie Fingers	7.50	3.75	2.25
(102)	Oscar Gamble	6.00	3.00	1.75
(103)	Randy Jones	6.00	3.00	1.75
(104)	Gene Tenace	6.00	3.00	1.75
(105)	Dave Winfield	15.00	7.50	4.50
	San Francisco Strip	30.00	15.00	9.00
(106)	Vida Blue	6.00	3.00	1.75
(107)	Gary Lavelle	6.00	3.00	1.75
(108)	Bill Madlock	6.00	3.00	1.75
(109)	Willie McCovey	15.00	7.50	4.50
(110)	John Montefusco	6.00	3.00	1.75
	Seattle Strip	25.00	12.50	7.50
(111)	Bruce Bochte	6.00	3.00	1.75
(112)	Ruppert Jones	6.00	3.00	1.75
(113)	Dan Meyer	6.00	3.00	1.75
(114)	Lee Stanton	6.00	3.00	1.75
(115)	Bill Stein	6.00	3.00	1.75
	St. Louis Strip	30.00	15.00	9.00
(116)	Lou Brock	15.00	7.50	4.50
(117)	Bob Forsch	6.00	3.00	1.75
(118)	Ken Reitz	6.00	3.00	1.75
(119)	Ted Simmons	6.00	3.00	1.75
(120)	Garry Templeton	6.00	3.00	1.75
	Texas Strip	25.00	12.50	7.50
(121)	Mike Hargrove	6.00	3.00	1.75
(122)	Toby Harrah	6.00	3.00	1.75
(123)	Jon Matlack	6.00	3.00	1.75
(124)	Jim Sundberg	6.00	3.00	1.75
(125)	Richie Zisk	6.00	3.00	1.75
	Toronto Strip	25.00	12.50	7.50
(126)	Doug Ault	6.00	3.00	1.75
(127)	Bob Bailor	6.00	3.00	1.75
(128)	Jerry Garvin	6.00	3.00	1.75
(129)	Roy Howell	6.00	3.00	1.75
(130)	Al Woods	6.00	3.00	1.75

1950-52 Royal Desserts

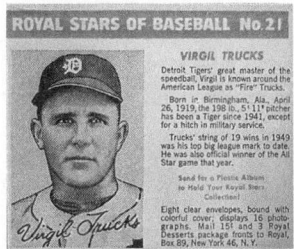

This set was issued one per box on the backs of various Royal Dessert products over a period of three years. The basic set contains 24 players, however a number of variations create the much higher total for the set. In 1950, Royal issued cards with two different tints - black and white with red, or blue and white with red. Over the next two years, various sentences of the cards' biographies were updated; up to three times in some cases. Some players from the set left the majors after 1950 and others were apparently never updated, but the 23 biography updates that do exist, added to the original 24 cards issued in 1950, give the set a total of 47 cards. The 2-5/8" x 3-1/4" cards are blank-backed with personal and playing biographies alongside the card front photos. Some sample cards can be found with advertising for the desserts on back; they are valued at about double regular card prices. A comb-bound album with seven pages to hold 14 cards was

also issued in a 3-1/4" x 3-3/8" format with "Royal Stars" and a crown logo printed in red on white.

		NM	E	VG
Common Player:		125.00	55.00	25.00
Album:		200.00	90.00	40.00
1a	Stan Musial (2nd paragraph begins "Musial's 207...")	525.00	235.00	100.00
1b	Stan Musial (2nd paragraph begins "Musial batted...")	525.00	235.00	100.00
2a	Pee Wee Reese (2nd paragraph begins "Pee Wee's...")	330.00	150.00	65.00
2b	Pee Wee Reese (2nd paragraph begins "Captain...")	330.00	150.00	65.00
3a	George Kell (2nd paragraph ends "...in 1945, '46.")	200.00	90.00	40.00
3b	George Kell (2nd paragraph ends "...two base hits, 56.")	200.00	90.00	40.00
4a	Dom DiMaggio (2nd paragraph ends "...during 1947.")	165.00	75.00	35.00
4b	Dom DiMaggio (2nd paragraph ends "...with 11.")	165.00	75.00	35.00
5a	Warren Spahn (2nd paragraph ends "...shutouts 7.")	265.00	120.00	55.00
5b	Warren Spahn (2nd paragraph ends "...with 191.")	265.00	120.00	55.00
6a	Andy Pafko (2nd paragraph ends "...7 games.")	125.00	56.00	25.00
6b	Andy Pafko (2nd paragraph ends "...National League.")	125.00	55.00	25.00
6c	Andy Pafko (2nd paragraph ends "...weighs 190.")	125.00	55.00	25.00
7a	Andy Seminick (2nd paragraph ends "...as outfield.")	125.00	55.00	25.00
7b	Andy Seminick (2nd paragraph ends "...since 1916.")	125.00	55.00	25.00
7c	Andy Seminick (2nd paragraph ends "...in the outfield. ")	125.00	55.00	25.00
7d	Andy Seminick (2nd paragraph ends "...right handed.")	125.00	55.00	25.00
8a	Lou Brissie (2nd paragraph ends "...when pitching.")	125.00	55.00	25.00
8b	Lou Brissie (2nd paragraph ends "...weighs 215.")	125.00	55.00	25.00
9a	Ewell Blackwell (2nd paragraph begins "Despite recent illness...")	145.00	65.00	30.00
9b	Ewell Blackwell (2nd paragraph begins "Blackwell's...")	145.00	65.00	30.00
10a	Bobby Thomson (2nd paragraph begins "In 1949...")	165.00	75.00	35.00
10b	Bobby Thomson (2nd paragraph begins "Thomson is...")	165.00	75.00	35.00
11a	Phil Rizzuto (2nd paragraph ends "...one 1942 game.")	330.00	150.00	65.00
11b	Phil Rizzuto (2nd paragraph ends "...Most Valuable Player.")	330.00	150.00	65.00
12	Tommy Henrich	155.00	70.00	30.00
13	Joe Gordon	200.00	100.00	60.00
14a	Ray Scarborough (Senators)	125.00	55.00	25.00
14b	Ray Scarborough (White Sox, 2nd paragraph ends "...military service.")	125.00	55.00	25.00
14c	Ray Scarborough (White Sox, 2nd paragraph ends "...the season.")	125.00	55.00	25.00
14d	Ray Scarborough (Red Sox)	125.00	55.00	25.00
15a	Stan Rojek (Pirates)	125.00	55.00	25.00
15b	Stan Rojek (Browns)	125.00	55.00	25.00
16	Luke Appling	180.00	80.00	35.00
17	Willard Marshall	125.00	55.00	25.00
18	Alvin Dark	125.00	55.00	25.00
19a	Dick Sisler (2nd paragraph ends "...service record.")	125.00	55.00	25.00
19b	Dick Sisler (2nd paragraph ends "...National League flag.")	125.00	55.00	25.00
19c	Dick Sisler (2nd paragraph ends "...Nov. 2, 1920.")	125.00	55.00	25.00
19d	Dick Sisler (2nd paragraph ends "...from '46 to '48. ")	125.00	55.00	25.00
20a	Johnny Ostrowski (White Sox)	125.00	55.00	25.00
20b	Johnny Ostrowski (Senators)	125.00	55.00	25.00
21a	Virgil Trucks (2nd paragraph ends "...in military service.")	125.00	55.00	25.00
21b	Virgil Trucks (2nd paragraph ends "...that year.")	125.00	55.00	25.00
21c	Virgil Trucks (2nd paragraph ends "...for military service.")	125.00	55.00	25.00
22	Eddie Robinson	125.00	55.00	25.00
23	Nanny Fernandez	125.00	55.00	25.00
24	Ferris Fain	125.00	55.00	25.00

1952 Royal Desserts

This set, issued as a premium by Royal Desserts in 1952, consists of 16 unnumbered black and white cards, each measuring 5" x 7". The cards include the inscription "To A Royal Fan" along with the player's facsimile autograph. Backs are blank.

		NM	E	VG
Complete Set (16):		1,400	625.00	275.00
Common Player:		55.00	25.00	10.00
(1)	Ewell Blackwell	55.00	25.00	10.00
(2)	Leland V. Brissie Jr.	55.00	25.00	10.00
(3)	Alvin Dark	55.00	25.00	10.00
(4)	Dom DiMaggio	100.00	45.00	20.00
(5)	Ferris Fain	55.00	25.00	10.00
(6)	George Kell	100.00	45.00	20.00
(7)	Stan Musial	280.00	125.00	55.00
(8)	Andy Pafko	55.00	25.00	10.00
(9)	Pee Wee Reese	175.00	80.00	35.00
(10)	Phil Rizzuto	160.00	70.00	30.00
(11)	Eddie Robinson	55.00	25.00	10.00
(12)	Ray Scarborough	55.00	25.00	10.00
(13)	Andy Seminick	55.00	25.00	10.00
(14)	Dick Sisler	55.00	25.00	10.00
(15)	Warren Spahn	140.00	65.00	25.00
(16)	Bobby Thomson	80.00	35.00	15.00

1920 Babe Ruth "Headin' Home"

This was one of several series of promotional cards issued to advertise the Bambino's starring role in the 1920 silent film, "Headin' Home." The black-and-white cards measure about 1-1/2" x 2-7/16". They feature borderless photos with the three-line caption: BABE RUTH / IN / "HEADIN' HOME." The cards are frequently found miscut with a portion of another card showing at one or more of the edges. Backs may be blank or carry the advertising of a local theater.

		NM	E	VG
Complete Set (6):		16,000	8,000	4,750
Common Card:		3,000	1,500	900.00
(1)	Babe Ruth (Bat at shoulder, crotch-to-cap.)	3,000	1,500	900.00
(2)	Babe Ruth (Bat extended to his right.)	3,000	1,500	900.00
(3)	Babe Ruth (Bat on shoulder, full-length.)	3,000	1,500	900.00
(4)	Babe Ruth (Follow-through, bat head-high.)	3,000	1,500	900.00
(5)	Babe Ruth (Follow-through, bat below waist.)	3,000	1,500	900.00
(6)	Babe Ruth (Horizontal card, holding bat.)	3,000	1,500	900.00

1920 Babe Ruth "Headin' Home" (Tex Rickard)

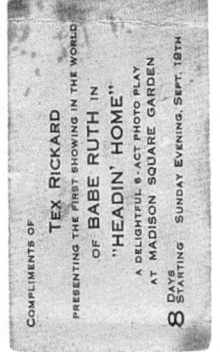

Taking advantage of the Babe's enormous popularity in the pinstripes of his new team, he was given a starring role in a 1920 silent movie titled "Headin Home." To promote the flick, a small set of cards was issued. The 1-7/8" x 3-1/4" black-and-white cards have posed photos of Ruth on front. Dropped out in white in the lower portion of the photo is his name and movie title. Backs have an ad for the movie (some cards are known with blank backs, as well). Tex Rickard was the Ebbets Field announcer for the Brooklyn Dodgers for over 30 years.

		NM	E	VG
Common Card:		5,000	2,500	1,500
(1)	Babe Ruth (Bat on shoulder, crotch to cap.)	5,000	2,500	1,500
(2)	Babe Ruth (Bat on shoulder, full-length.)	5,000	2,500	1,500
(3)	Babe Ruth (Batting follow-through.)	5,000	2,500	1,500

1920 Babe Ruth "Headin' Home" Theater Cards

To promote the showing of "Headin' Home," a silent movie starring Babe Ruth, theaters had these cards printed up with details of show dates. Fronts of the 1-3/4" x 3-1/4" cards have a sepia photo of Ruth swinging the bat. On back is an advertisement from a local theater. This is one of the first cards ever to picture Ruth as a N.Y. Yankee.

	NM	E	VG
Babe Ruth (Both hands on bat.)	2,750	1,375	825.00
Babe Ruth (One hand on bat.)	2,750	1,375	825.00

1920s Babe Ruth Postcard

There is no indication of publisher or specific date of issue on this standard-size, typically marked black-and-white photo postcard which pictures the Babe in street clothes informally posed with a cane chair. The number "210" near the bottom of the photo indicates it was part of a series. The horizontal divided back has typical postcard markings.

	NM	E	VG
210 Babe Ruth	750.00	375.00	225.00

1920s Babe Ruth Underwear Premium Photo

While the product itself and the boxes and display pieces are collectibles in their own right, among the scarcest pieces associated with the Babe Ruth brand underwear is this approximately 8" x 10" premium photo which was apparently only included in some forms of packaging. The blank-back photo shows a buff Babe in the product and has a facsimile autograph on his right bicep.

	NM	E	VG
Babe Ruth	500.00	250.00	150.00

1927 "Babe Comes Home" Strip Cards (R94)

This strip card set of unknown scope (at least 75 known) was cataloged as "Movie Stars and Scenes (R94)" in the American Card Catalog. At least two of the cards depict Babe Ruth as "Babe Dugan" in scenes from his silent film. Cards are nominally about 2-7/8" x 2-5/16" and can be found printed in black-and-white or as red, blue or green duotones. The name of the movie is printed in white at bottom. Backs and blank.

	NM	E	VG
Babe Ruth (In suit w/ police.)	1,350	675.00	400.00
Babe Ruth (In uniform, locker room.)	1,350	675.00	400.00

1928 Babe Ruth Home Run Candy Club Membership Card

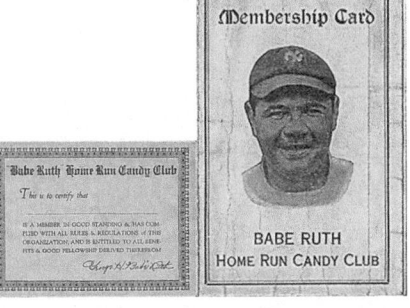

In conjunction with his candy bar, Ruth created the "Babe Ruth Home Run Candy Club," and issued this membership card. Front has a black-and-white portrait photo. Back of the 2-3/4" x 4" card has 10 rules of sportsmanship for members. The card folds open to reveal a membership certificate with a facsimile autograph.

	NM	E	VG
Babe Ruth	2,500	1,250	750.00

1928 George Ruth Candy Co.

This circa 1928 issue features sepia-toned photos of Babe Ruth. According to the back of the cards, it was issued by the Geo. H. Ruth Candy Co. Cards measure 1-7/8" x 4" and picture Ruth during a 1924 promotional West Coast tour and in scenes from the movie "Babe Comes Home." The cards are numbered and include photo captions at the bottom. The backs of most cards contain an offer to exchange the six cards for an autographed baseball, which may explain their scarcity today. Cards have been seen with the address to mail for exchange as Cleveland and as San Francisco. Cards can also be found with blank backs. This issue was deceptively counterfeited in the early 21st Century.

		NM	E	VG
Complete Set (6):		9,500	4,000	1,620
Common Card:		1,600	800.00	425.00
Wrapper:		3,500	2,000	1,250
1	"Babe" Ruth ("King of them all...")	1,600	800.00	425.00
2	"Babe" Ruth ("Knocked out 60 Home Runs...")	1,600	800.00	425.00
3	"Babe" Ruth ("The only player...")	1,600	800.00	425.00
4	"Babe" Ruth ("The Popular Bambino...")	1,600	800.00	425.00
5	"Babe" Ruth ("A favorite with the Kiddies...")	1,600	800.00	425.00
6	"Babe" Ruth ("The King of Swat...")	1,600	800.00	425.00

S

1910-11 S74 Silks - White

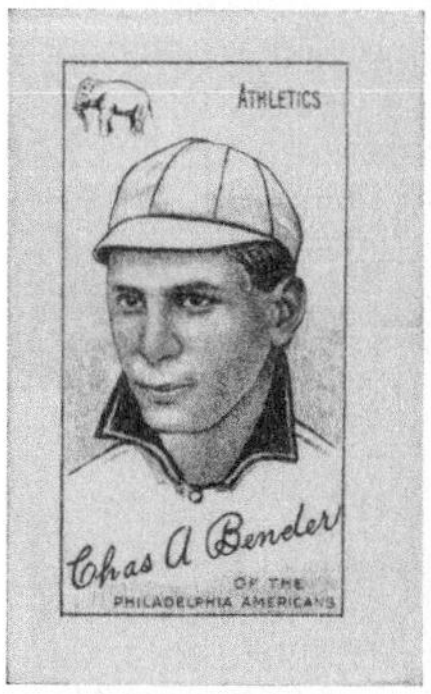

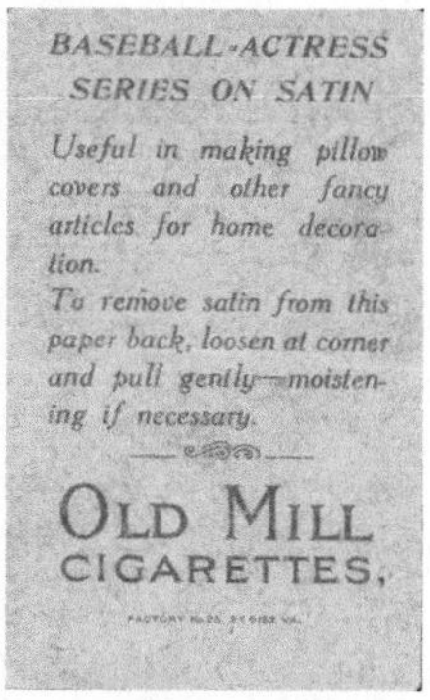

Designated as S74 in the "American Card Catalog," these delicate fabric collectibles are popular with advanced collectors. The silks were issued as premiums with several different brands of cigarettes: Turkey Red (with or without border around type), Old Mill, Red Sun, and, rarely, Helmar. The satin-like silks can be found in two different styles, either "white" or "colored." The white silks measure 1-7/8" x 3" and were originally issued with a brown paper backing that carried an advertisement for one of the cigarette brands. The backing also advised that the silks were "useful in making pillow covers and other fancy articles for home decoration." Many undoubtedly were used for such purposes, making silks with the paper backing still intact more difficult to find. White silks must have the backing intact to command top values shown here. Ninety-two subjects are known in the "white" silks. The silks feature the player pictures found in the popular T205 Gold Border tobacco card set.

		NM	E	VG
Complete Set (87):		24,000	8,600	6,300
Common Player:		300.00	150.00	90.00
No Paper Backing: 50 Percent				
(1)	Home Run Baker	675.00	220.00	135.00
(2)	Cy Barger	300.00	150.00	90.00
(3)	Jack Barry	300.00	150.00	90.00
(4)	Johnny Bates	300.00	150.00	90.00
(5)	Fred Beck	300.00	150.00	90.00
(6)	Beals Becker	300.00	150.00	90.00
(7)	George Bell	300.00	150.00	90.00
(8)	Chief Bender	675.00	220.00	135.00
(9)	Roger Bresnahan	675.00	220.00	135.00
(10)	Al Bridwell	675.00	220.00	135.00
(11)	Mordecai Brown	675.00	220.00	135.00
(12)	Bobby Byrne	300.00	150.00	90.00
(13)	Howie Camnitz	300.00	150.00	90.00
(14)	Bill Carrigan	300.00	150.00	90.00
(15)	Frank Chance	675.00	220.00	135.00
(16)	Hal Chase	400.00	200.00	120.00
(17)	Fred Clarke	675.00	220.00	135.00
(18)	Ty Cobb	6,750	3,300	2,025
(19)	Eddie Collins	675.00	220.00	135.00
(20)	Doc Crandall	300.00	150.00	90.00
(21)	Lou Criger	300.00	150.00	90.00
(22)	Jim Delahanty	300.00	150.00	90.00
(23)	Art Devlin	300.00	150.00	90.00
(24)	Red Dooin	300.00	150.00	90.00
(25)	Mickey Doolan	300.00	150.00	90.00
(26)	Larry Doyle	300.00	150.00	90.00
(27)	Jimmy Dygert	300.00	150.00	90.00
(28)	Kid Elberfield (Elberfeld)	300.00	150.00	90.00
(29)	Steve Evans	300.00	150.00	90.00
(30)	Johnny Evers	675.00	220.00	135.00
(31)	Bob Ewing	300.00	150.00	90.00
(32)	Art Fletcher	300.00	150.00	90.00
(33)	John Flynn	300.00	150.00	90.00
(34)	Bill Foxen	300.00	150.00	90.00
(35)	George Gibson	300.00	150.00	90.00
(36)	Peaches Graham (Cubs) (Existence now questioned.)			
(37)	Peaches Graham (Rustlers)	300.00	150.00	90.00
(38)	Clark Griffith	675.00	220.00	135.00
(39)	Topsy Hartsel	300.00	150.00	90.00
(40)	Arnold Hauser	300.00	150.00	90.00
(41)	Charlie Hemphill	300.00	150.00	90.00
(42)	Davy Jones	300.00	150.00	90.00
(43)	Jack Knight	300.00	150.00	90.00
(44)	Ed Konetchy	300.00	150.00	90.00
(45)	Harry Krause	300.00	150.00	90.00
(46)	Tommy Leach (Existence now questioned.)			
(47)	Rube Marquard	675.00	220.00	135.00
(48)	Christy Mathewson	1,500	750.00	450.00
(49)	Al Mattern	300.00	150.00	90.00
(50)	Amby McConnell	300.00	150.00	90.00
(51)	John McGraw	675.00	220.00	135.00
(52)	Harry McIntire (McIntyre)	300.00	150.00	90.00
(53)	Fred Merkle	300.00	150.00	90.00
(54)	Chief Meyers	300.00	150.00	90.00
(55)	Dots Miller	300.00	150.00	90.00
(56)	Danny Murphy	300.00	150.00	90.00
(57)	Red Murray	300.00	150.00	90.00
(58)	Tom Needham	300.00	150.00	90.00
(59)	Rebel Oakes	300.00	150.00	90.00
(60)	Rube Oldring	300.00	150.00	90.00
(61)	Orval Overall	300.00	150.00	90.00
(62)	Fred Parent	300.00	150.00	90.00
(63)	Fred Payne	300.00	150.00	90.00
(64)	Barney Pelty	300.00	150.00	90.00
(65)	Deacon Phillippe	300.00	150.00	90.00
(66)	Jack Quinn	300.00	150.00	90.00
(67)	Bugs Raymond (Existence now questioned.)			
(68)	Ed Reulbach	300.00	150.00	90.00
(69)	Doc Scanlon (Scanlan) (Existence now questioned.)			
(70)	Germany Schaefer	300.00	150.00	90.00
(71)	Geo. Schlei	300.00	150.00	90.00
(72)	Wildfire Schulte	300.00	150.00	90.00
(73)	Dave Shean	300.00	150.00	90.00
(74)	Jimmy Sheckard	300.00	150.00	90.00
(75)	Tony Smith (Superbas)	300.00	150.00	90.00
(76)	Harry Smith (Rustlers)	500.00	200.00	125.00
(77)	Fred Snodgrass	300.00	150.00	90.00
(78)	Tris Speaker	775.00	400.00	240.00
(79)	Harry Steinfeldt (Cubs)	300.00	150.00	90.00
(80)	Harry Steinfeldt (Rustlers) (Existence now questioned.)			
(81)	George Stone	300.00	150.00	90.00
(82)	Gabby Street	300.00	150.00	90.00
(83)	Ed Summers	300.00	150.00	90.00
(84)	Lee Tannehill	300.00	150.00	90.00
(85)	Joe Tinker	675.00	220.00	135.00
(86)	John Titus	300.00	150.00	90.00
(87)	Terry Turner	300.00	150.00	90.00
(88)	Bobby Wallace	675.00	220.00	135.00
(89)	Doc White	300.00	150.00	90.00
(90)	Ed Willett	300.00	150.00	90.00
(91)	Art Wilson	300.00	150.00	90.00
(92)	Harry Wolter	300.00	150.00	90.00

1911 S74 Silks - Colored

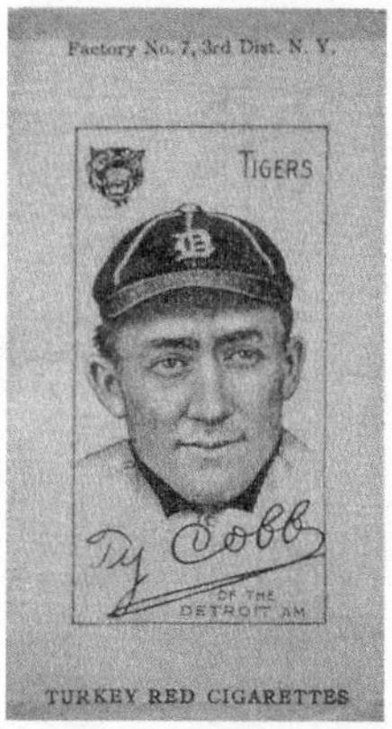

Designated as S74 in the "American Card Catalog," these delicate fabric collectibles are popular with advanced collectors. The silks were issued as premiums with several different brands of cigarettes: Turkey Red, Old Mill, Helmar, and, rarely, Red Sun. The satin-like silks can be found in two different styles, either "white" or "colored." The S74 "colored" silks, as their name indicates, were issued in a variety of colors. They are slightly larger than the white version, measuring 1-7/8" x 3-1/2", and were issued without a paper backing, carrying the cigarette brand name on the lower front of the fabric. (No color silks advertising the Helmar brand are known to exist.) In the colored silks, 120 subjects are known. The silks feature the same player pictures found in the popular T205 Gold Border tobacco card set.

		NM	E	VG
Complete Set (120):		20,000	8,000	5,000
Common Player:		150.00	60.00	35.00
(1)	Red Ames	150.00	60.00	35.00
(2)	Jimmy Archer	150.00	60.00	35.00
(3)	Home Run Baker	300.00	120.00	70.00
(4)	Cy Barger	150.00	60.00	35.00
(5)	Jack Barry	150.00	60.00	35.00
(6)	Johnny Bates	150.00	60.00	35.00
(7)	Beals Becker	150.00	60.00	35.00
(8)	George Bell	150.00	60.00	35.00
(9)	Chief Bender	300.00	120.00	70.00
(10)	Bill Bergen	150.00	60.00	35.00
(11)	Bob Bescher	150.00	60.00	35.00
(12)	Roger Bresnahan (Mouth closed.)	300.00	120.00	70.00
(13)	Roger Bresnahan (Mouth open.)	300.00	120.00	70.00
(14)	Al Bridwell	150.00	60.00	35.00
(15)	Mordecai Brown	300.00	120.00	70.00
(16)	Bobby Byrne	150.00	60.00	35.00
(17)	Howie Camnitz	150.00	60.00	35.00
(18)	Bill Carrigan	150.00	60.00	35.00
(19)	Frank Chance	300.00	120.00	70.00
(20)	Hal Chase	225.00	90.00	55.00
(21)	Ed Cicotte	300.00	120.00	70.00
(22)	Fred Clarke	300.00	120.00	70.00
(23)	Ty Cobb	1,200	480.00	290.00
(24)	Eddie Collins	300.00	120.00	70.00
(25)	Doc Crandall	150.00	60.00	35.00
(26)	Bill Dahlen	150.00	60.00	35.00
(27)	Jake Daubert	150.00	60.00	35.00
(28)	Jim Delahanty	150.00	60.00	35.00
(29)	Art Devlin	150.00	60.00	35.00
(30)	Josh Devore	150.00	60.00	35.00
(31)	Red Dooin	150.00	60.00	35.00
(32)	Mickey Doolan	150.00	60.00	35.00
(33)	Tom Downey	150.00	60.00	35.00
(34)	Larry Doyle	150.00	60.00	35.00
(35)	Hugh Duffy	300.00	120.00	70.00
(36)	Jimmy Dygert	150.00	60.00	35.00
(37)	Kid Elberfield (Elberfeld)	150.00	60.00	35.00
(38)	Steve Evans	150.00	60.00	35.00
(39)	Johnny Evers	300.00	120.00	70.00
(40)	Bob Ewing	150.00	60.00	35.00
(41)	Art Fletcher	150.00	60.00	35.00
(42)	John Flynn	150.00	60.00	35.00
(43)	Russ Ford	150.00	60.00	35.00
(44)	Bill Foxen	150.00	60.00	35.00
(45)	Art Fromme	150.00	60.00	35.00
(46)	George Gibson	150.00	60.00	35.00
(47)	Peaches Graham	150.00	60.00	35.00
(48)	Eddie Grant	150.00	60.00	35.00
(49)	Clark Griffith	300.00	120.00	70.00
(50)	Topsy Hartsel	150.00	60.00	35.00
(51)	Arnold Hauser	150.00	60.00	35.00
(52)	Charlie Hemphill	150.00	60.00	35.00
(53)	Dick Hoblitzell	150.00	60.00	35.00
(54)	Miller Huggins	300.00	120.00	70.00
(55)	John Hummel	150.00	60.00	35.00
(56)	Walter Johnson	600.00	240.00	145.00
(57)	Davy Jones	150.00	60.00	35.00
(58)	Johnny Kling	150.00	60.00	35.00
(59)	Jack Knight	150.00	60.00	35.00
(60)	Ed Konetchy	150.00	60.00	35.00
(61)	Harry Krause	150.00	60.00	35.00
(62)	Tommy Leach	150.00	60.00	35.00
(63)	Lefty Leifield	150.00	60.00	35.00
(64)	Hans Lobert	150.00	60.00	35.00
(65)	Rube Marquard	300.00	120.00	70.00
(66)	Christy Mathewson	750.00	300.00	180.00
(67)	Al Mattern	150.00	60.00	35.00
(68)	Amby McConnell	150.00	60.00	35.00
(69)	John McGraw	300.00	120.00	70.00
(70)	Harry McIntire (McIntyre)	150.00	60.00	35.00
(71)	Fred Merkle	150.00	60.00	35.00
(72)	Chief Meyers	150.00	60.00	35.00
(73)	Dots Miller	150.00	60.00	35.00
(74)	Mike Mitchell	150.00	60.00	35.00
(75)	Pat Moran	150.00	60.00	35.00
(76)	George Moriarty	150.00	60.00	35.00
(77)	George Mullin	150.00	60.00	35.00
(78)	Danny Murphy	150.00	60.00	35.00
(79)	Red Murray	150.00	60.00	35.00
(80)	Tom Needham	150.00	60.00	35.00
(81)	Rebel Oakes	150.00	60.00	35.00
(82)	Rube Oldring	150.00	60.00	35.00
(83)	Orval Overall	150.00	60.00	35.00
(84)	Fred Parent	150.00	60.00	35.00
(85)	Dode Paskert	150.00	60.00	35.00
(86)	Fred Payne	150.00	60.00	35.00
(87)	Barney Pelty	150.00	60.00	35.00
(88)	Deacon Phillippe	150.00	60.00	35.00
(89)	Jack Quinn	150.00	60.00	35.00
(90)	Bugs Raymond	150.00	60.00	35.00
(91)	Ed Reulbach	150.00	60.00	35.00
(92)	Jack Rowan	150.00	60.00	35.00
(93)	Nap Rucker	150.00	60.00	35.00
(94)	Doc Scanlon (Scanlan)	150.00	60.00	35.00
(95)	Germany Schaefer	150.00	60.00	35.00
(96)	Geo. Schlei	150.00	60.00	35.00
(97)	Wildfire Schulte	150.00	60.00	35.00
(98)	Dave Shean	150.00	60.00	35.00
(99)	Jimmy Sheckard	150.00	60.00	35.00
(100)	Happy Smith	150.00	60.00	35.00

		NM	E	VG
(101)	Fred Snodgrass	150.00	60.00	35.00
(102)	Tris Speaker	400.00	160.00	95.00
(103)	Jake Stahl	150.00	60.00	35.00
(104)	Harry Steinfeldt	150.00	60.00	35.00
(105)	George Stone	150.00	60.00	35.00
(106)	Gabby Street	150.00	60.00	35.00
(107)	Ed Summers	150.00	60.00	35.00
(108)	Lee Tannehill	150.00	60.00	35.00
(109)	Joe Tinker	300.00	120.00	70.00
(110)	John Titus	150.00	60.00	35.00
(111)	Terry Turner	150.00	60.00	35.00
(112)	Bobby Wallace	300.00	120.00	70.00
(113)	Zack Wheat	300.00	120.00	70.00
(114)	Doc White (White Sox)	150.00	60.00	35.00
(115)	Kirby White (Pirates)	150.00	60.00	35.00
(116)	Ed Willett	150.00	60.00	35.00
(117)	Owen Wilson	150.00	60.00	35.00
(118)	Hooks Wiltse	150.00	60.00	35.00
(119)	Harry Wolter	150.00	60.00	35.00
(120)	Cy Young	750.00	300.00	180.00

1912 S110 Baseball Player Silks Pillow Case

Closely related to the S81 silks, and issued as a premium for 100 coupons, this approximately 23" x 23" pillow case shares the same designs as the individual silks of the players thereon. Cross-stich borders for the player images on the cloth pillow case would indicate the silks were meant to be sewn on as they were acquired. Besides the baseball players pillow cases, similar premiums are known for the other Turkey Red/Helmar silks -- Indians, generals, etc.

		NM	E	VG
(1)	Home Run Baker, Ty Cobb, Walter Johnson, Christy Mathewson, Tris Speaker	7,500	4,250	2,550
(2)	Home Run Baker, Ty Cobb, Christy Mathewson, Marty O'Toole, Tris Speaker	7,250	3,625	2,175

1912 S81 Silks

The 1912 S81 "Silks," so-called because they featured pictures of baseball players on a satin-like fabric rather than paper or cardboard, are closely related to the better-known T3 Turkey Red cabinet cards of the same era. The silks, which featured 25 of the day's top baseball players among its other various subjects, were available as a premium with Helmar "Turkish Trophies" cigarettes. According to an advertising sheet, one silk could be obtained for 25 Helmar coupons. The silks measure about 6-3/4" x 8-3/4" and, with a few exceptions, used the same pictures featured on the popular Turkey Red cards. Five players (Rube Marquard, Rube Benton, Marty O'Toole, Grover Alexander and Russ Ford) appear in the "Silks" set that were not included in the T3 set. In addition, an error involving the Frank Baker card was corrected for the "Silks" set. (In the T3 set, Baker's card actually pictured Jack Barry.) Several years ago a pair of New England collectors found a small stack of Christy Mathewson "Silks," making his, by far, the most common. Otherwise, the "Silks" are generally so rare that it is difficult to determine the relative scarcity of the others. Baseball enthusiasts are usually

only attracted to the 25 baseball players in the "Silks" premium set, but it is interesting to note that the promotion also offered dozens of other subjects, including "beautiful women in bathing and athletic costumes, charming dancers in gorgeous attire, national flags and generals on horseback."

		NM	E	VG
Complete Set (25):		145,000	50,000	27,500
Common Player:		3,000	1,000	575.00
86	Rube Marquard	6,500	2,275	1,225
87	Marty O'Toole	3,000	1,000	575.00
88	Rube Benton	3,000	1,000	575.00
89	Grover Alexander	12,000	6,000	3,600
90	Russ Ford	3,000	1,000	575.00
91	John McGraw	6,500	2,275	1,225
92	Nap Rucker	3,000	1,000	575.00
93	Mike Mitchell	3,000	1,000	575.00
94	Chief Bender	6,500	2,275	1,225
95	Home Run Baker	6,500	2,275	1,225
96	Nap Lajoie	9,000	4,500	2,700
97	Joe Tinker	6,500	2,275	1,225
98	Sherry Magee	3,000	1,000	575.00
99	Howie Camnitz	3,000	1,000	575.00
100	Eddie Collins	6,500	2,275	1,225
101	Red Dooin	3,000	1,000	575.00
102	Ty Cobb	15,000	5,250	2,850
103	Hugh Jennings	6,500	2,275	1,225
104	Roger Bresnahan	6,500	2,275	1,225
105	Jake Stahl	3,000	1,000	575.00
106	Tris Speaker	10,000	5,000	3,000
107	Ed Walsh	6,500	2,275	1,225
108	Christy Mathewson	6,000	2,100	1,150
109	Johnny Evers	6,500	2,275	1,225
110	Walter Johnson	12,000	4,200	2,275

1976 Safelon Discs

One of several regional sponsors of player disc sets in 1976, Safelon, of New York, advertised its "Super Star Lunch Bags" in red and purple on the backs of its discs. The discs are 3-3/8" diameter with a black-and-white player portrait photo in the center of the baseball design. A line of red stars is above, while the left and right panels feature one of several bright colors. Produced by Michael Schechter Associates under license from the Major League Baseball Players Association, the player photos have had uniform and cap logos removed. The unnumbered checklist here is presented in alphabetical order.

		NM	E	VG
Complete Set (70):		100.00	50.00	30.00
Common Player:		3.00	1.50	.90
(1)	Henry Aaron	20.00	10.00	6.00
(2)	Johnny Bench	8.00	4.00	2.50
(3)	Vida Blue	3.00	1.50	.90
(4)	Larry Bowa	3.00	1.50	.90
(5)	Lou Brock	6.00	3.00	1.75
(6)	Jeff Burroughs	3.00	1.50	.90
(7)	John Candelaria	3.00	1.50	.90
(8)	Jose Cardenal	3.00	1.50	.90
(9)	Rod Carew	6.00	3.00	1.75
(10)	Steve Carlton	6.00	3.00	1.75
(11)	Dave Cash	3.00	1.50	.90
(12)	Cesar Cedeno	3.00	1.50	.90
(13)	Ron Cey	3.00	1.50	.90
(14)	Carlton Fisk	6.00	3.00	1.75
(15)	Tito Fuentes	3.00	1.50	.90
(16)	Steve Garvey	4.00	2.00	1.25
(17)	Ken Griffey	3.00	1.50	.90
(18)	Don Gullett	3.00	1.50	.90
(19)	Willie Horton	3.00	1.50	.90
(20)	Al Hrabosky	3.00	1.50	.90
(21)	Catfish Hunter	6.00	3.00	1.75
(22)	Reggie Jackson (A's)	12.00	6.00	3.50
(23)	Randy Jones	3.00	1.50	.90
(24)	Jim Kaat	3.00	1.50	.90
(25)	Don Kessinger	3.00	1.50	.90
(26)	Dave Kingman	3.00	1.50	.90
(27)	Jerry Koosman	3.00	1.50	.90
(28)	Mickey Lolich	3.00	1.50	.90
(29)	Greg Luzinski	3.00	1.50	.90
(30)	Fred Lynn	3.00	1.50	.90
(31)	Bill Madlock	3.00	1.50	.90
(32)	Carlos May (White Sox)	3.00	1.50	.90
(33)	John Mayberry	3.00	1.50	.90
(34)	Bake McBride	3.00	1.50	.90
(35)	Doc Medich	3.00	1.50	.90
(36)	Andy Messersmith	3.00	1.50	.90
(37)	Rick Monday	3.00	1.50	.90
(38)	John Montefusco	3.00	1.50	.90
(39)	Jerry Morales	3.00	1.50	.90
(40)	Joe Morgan	6.00	3.00	1.75
(41)	Thurman Munson	5.00	2.50	1.50
(42)	Bobby Murcer	3.00	1.50	.90
(43)	Al Oliver	3.00	1.50	.90
(44)	Jim Palmer	6.00	3.00	1.75
(45)	Dave Parker	3.00	1.50	.90
(46)	Tony Perez	6.00	3.00	1.75
(47)	Jerry Reuss	3.00	1.50	.90
(48)	Brooks Robinson	9.00	4.50	2.75
(49)	Frank Robinson	9.00	4.50	2.75
(50)	Steve Rogers	3.00	1.50	.90
(51)	Pete Rose	15.00	7.50	4.50
(52)	Nolan Ryan	40.00	20.00	12.00
(53)	Manny Sanguillen	3.00	1.50	.90
(54)	Mike Schmidt	12.00	6.00	3.50
(55)	Tom Seaver	9.00	4.50	2.75
(56)	Ted Simmons	3.00	1.50	.90
(57)	Reggie Smith	3.00	1.50	.90
(58)	Willie Stargell	6.00	3.00	1.75
(59)	Rusty Staub	3.00	1.50	.90
(60)	Rennie Stennett	3.00	1.50	.90
(61)	Don Sutton	6.00	3.00	1.75
(62)	Andy Thornton (Cubs)	3.00	1.50	.90
(63)	Luis Tiant	3.00	1.50	.90
(64)	Joe Torre	3.00	1.50	.90
(65)	Mike Tyson	3.00	1.50	.90
(66)	Bob Watson	3.00	1.50	.90
(67)	Wilbur Wood	3.00	1.50	.90
(68)	Jimmy Wynn	3.00	1.50	.90
(69)	Carl Yastrzemski	9.00	4.50	2.75
(70)	Richie Zisk	3.00	1.50	.90

1948-50 Safe-T-Card

The earliest known safety issue is this series sponsored by a children's television show which was in turn sponsored by a Washington, D.C. auto dealer. Player selection and team indications on the cards point to a three-year (1948-50) range of issue dates for the cards. Minor differences in typography and information printed on the front probably differentiate the years of issue. All cards are about 2-1/2" x 3-1/2" with rounded corners. Fronts feature rather crude black-and-white drawings of the players with a facsimile autograph superimposed. A safety message is at top and, on most cards, the player's position and team are printed at bottom. Backs are printed in one of several colors and have a picture of the TV host and an ad for the program and its sponsors. The set is checklisted here alphabetically, though it's possible other cards may be added in the future. Only the baseball players from the set are listed here. Cards featuring football, basketball and other sports figures were also produced, along with cards for team executives, sports reporters and broadcasters.

		NM	E	VG
Complete (Baseball) Set (21):		2,925	1,450	875.00
Common Player:		125.00	65.00	35.00
(1)	Ossie Bluege	125.00	65.00	35.00
(2)	Gil Coan	125.00	65.00	35.00
(3)	Sam Dente	125.00	65.00	35.00
(4)	Jake Early	125.00	65.00	35.00
(5)	Al Evans	125.00	65.00	35.00
(6)	Calvin Griffith	250.00	125.00	75.00
(7)	Clark Griffith	150.00	75.00	45.00
(8)	Bucky Harris	150.00	75.00	45.00
(9)	Sid Hudson	125.00	65.00	35.00
(10)	Joe Kuhel	125.00	65.00	35.00
(11)	Bob Lemon	150.00	75.00	45.00
(12)	Bill McGowan	400.00	200.00	120.00
(13)	George McQuinn	125.00	65.00	35.00
(14)	Don Newcombe	250.00	125.00	75.00
(15)	Joe Ostrowski	125.00	65.00	35.00
(16)	Sam Rice	150.00	75.00	45.00
(17)	Bert Shepard	150.00	75.00	45.00
(18)	Ray Scarborough	125.00	65.00	35.00

		NM	E	VG
(19)	Mickey Vernon	125.00	65.00	35.00
(20)	Early Wynn	150.00	75.00	45.00
(21)	Eddie Yost	125.00	65.00	35.00

1977 Saga Discs

Virtually identical in format to the several locally sponsored disc sets of the previous year, these 3-3/8" diameter player discs were given away with the purchase of school lunches in the Philadelphia area. They are the scarcest of the 1977 disc sets. Discs once again feature black-and-white player portrait photos in the center of a baseball design. The left and right panels are in one of several bright colors. Licensed by the Players Association through Mike Schechter Associates, the player photos carry no uniform logos. Backs are printed in orange with background art of a sunrise over the mountains. The unnumbered discs are checklisted here alphabetically.

		NM	E	VG
Complete Set (70):		850.00	425.00	250.00
Common Player:		12.50	6.25	3.75
(1)	Sal Bando	12.50	6.25	3.75
(2)	Buddy Bell	12.50	6.25	3.75
(3)	Johnny Bench	40.00	20.00	12.00
(4)	Larry Bowa	12.50	6.25	3.75
(5)	Steve Braun	12.50	6.25	3.75
(6)	George Brett	125.00	62.00	37.00
(7)	Lou Brock	35.00	17.50	10.50
(8)	Jeff Burroughs	12.50	6.25	3.75
(9)	Bert Campaneris	12.50	6.25	3.75
(10)	John Candelaria	12.50	6.25	3.75
(11)	Jose Cardenal	12.50	6.25	3.75
(12)	Rod Carew	35.00	17.50	10.50
(13)	Steve Carlton	35.00	17.50	10.50
(14)	Dave Cash	12.50	6.25	3.75
(15)	Cesar Cedeno	12.50	6.25	3.75
(16)	Ron Cey	12.50	6.25	3.75
(17)	Dave Concepcion	12.50	6.25	3.75
(18)	Dennis Eckersley	35.00	17.50	10.50
(19)	Mark Fidrych	17.50	8.75	5.25
(20)	Rollie Fingers	35.00	17.50	10.50
(21)	Carlton Fisk	35.00	17.50	10.50
(22)	George Foster	12.50	6.25	3.75
(23)	Wayne Garland	12.50	6.25	3.75
(24)	Ralph Garr	12.50	6.25	3.75
(25)	Steve Garvey	25.00	12.50	7.50
(26)	Cesar Geronimo	12.50	6.25	3.75
(27)	Bobby Grich	12.50	6.25	3.75
(28)	Ken Griffey Sr.	12.50	6.25	3.75
(29)	Don Gullett	12.50	6.25	3.75
(30)	Mike Hargrove	12.50	6.25	3.75
(31)	Al Hrabosky	12.50	6.25	3.75
(32)	Jim Hunter	35.00	17.50	10.50
(33)	Reggie Jackson	50.00	25.00	15.00
(34)	Randy Jones	12.50	6.25	3.75
(35)	Dave Kingman	15.00	7.50	4.50
(36)	Jerry Koosman	12.50	6.25	3.75
(37)	Dave LaRoche	12.50	6.25	3.75
(38)	Greg Luzinski	12.50	6.25	3.75
(39)	Fred Lynn	12.50	6.25	3.75
(40)	Bill Madlock	12.50	6.25	3.75
(41)	Rick Manning	12.50	6.25	3.75
(42)	Jon Matlock	12.50	6.25	3.75
(43)	John Mayberry	12.50	6.25	3.75
(44)	Hal McRae	12.50	6.25	3.75
(45)	Andy Messersmith	12.50	6.25	3.75
(46)	Rick Monday	12.50	6.25	3.75
(47)	John Montefusco	12.50	6.25	3.75
(48)	Joe Morgan	35.00	17.50	10.50
(49)	Thurman Munson	30.00	15.00	9.00
(50)	Bobby Murcer	12.50	6.25	3.75
(51)	Bill North	12.50	6.25	3.75
(52)	Jim Palmer	35.00	17.50	10.50
(53)	Tony Perez	35.00	17.50	10.50
(54)	Jerry Reuss	12.50	6.25	3.75
(55)	Brooks Robinson	40.00	20.00	12.00
(56)	Pete Rose	110.00	55.00	33.00
(57)	Joe Rudi	12.50	6.25	3.75
(58)	Nolan Ryan	135.00	67.00	40.00
(59)	Manny Sanguillen	12.50	6.25	3.75
(60)	Mike Schmidt	75.00	37.00	22.00
(61)	Tom Seaver	40.00	20.00	12.00
(62)	Bill Singer	12.50	6.25	3.75
(63)	Willie Stargell	35.00	17.50	10.50
(64)	Rusty Staub	15.00	7.50	4.50
(65)	Luis Tiant	12.50	6.25	3.75
(66)	Bob Watson	12.50	6.25	3.75
(67)	Butch Wynegar	12.50	6.25	3.75
(68)	Carl Yastrzemski	40.00	20.00	12.00
(69)	Robin Yount	35.00	17.50	10.50
(70)	Richie Zisk	12.50	6.25	3.75

1978 Saga Discs

One player from each major league team was selected for inclusion in this disc set distributed by Saga, a provider of school lunches; discs were given one per lunch purchase at selected schools. The 3-3/8" diameter discs have a sepia-toned player portrait photo at center within a white diamond and surrounded by a brightly colored border with four colored stars at top. Licensed by the Players Association through Michael Schechter Associates, the photos have had uniform logos removed. Backs are nearly identical to the previous year, but printed in red. The unnumbered Saga discs are checklisted here according to the numbers found on the Big T/Tastee Freeze versions.

		NM	E	VG
Complete Set (26):		130.00	65.00	40.00
Common Player:		6.00	3.00	1.75
(1)	Buddy Bell	6.00	3.00	1.75
(2)	Jim Palmer	12.50	6.25	3.75
(3)	Steve Garvey	7.50	3.75	2.25
(4)	Jeff Burroughs	6.00	3.00	1.75
(5)	Greg Luzinski	6.00	3.00	1.75
(6)	Lou Brock	12.50	6.25	3.75
(7)	Thurman Munson	10.00	5.00	3.00
(8)	Rod Carew	12.50	6.25	3.75
(9)	George Brett	50.00	25.00	15.00
(10)	Tom Seaver	15.00	7.50	4.50
(11)	Willie Stargell	12.50	6.25	3.75
(12)	Jerry Koosman	6.00	3.00	1.75
(13)	Bill North	6.00	3.00	1.75
(14)	Richie Zisk	6.00	3.00	1.75
(15)	Bill Madlock	6.00	3.00	1.75
(16)	Carl Yastrzemski	15.00	7.50	4.50
(17)	Dave Cash	6.00	3.00	1.75
(18)	Bob Watson	6.00	3.00	1.75
(19)	Dave Kingman	6.50	3.25	2.00
(20)	Gene Tenance (Tenace)	6.00	3.00	1.75
(21)	Ralph Garr	6.00	3.00	1.75
(22)	Mark Fidrych	6.50	3.25	2.00
(23)	Frank Tanana	6.00	3.00	1.75
(24)	Larry Hisle	6.00	3.00	1.75
(25)	Bruce Bochte	6.00	3.00	1.75
(26)	Bob Bailor	6.00	3.00	1.75

1962 John Sain Spinner Promotional Postcard

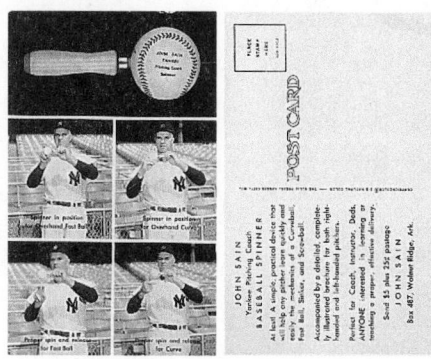

The attributed date of issue is approximate. This 3-7/16" x 5-7/16" color postcard was issued to promote the John Sain Spinner, a device to teach pitching mechanics. The front pictures the Yankees pitching coach in four views demonstrating the device, which is itself pictured at top. Black-and-white back is in traditional postcard divided-back format with information on the spinner and ordering information.

	NM	E	VG
John Sain	15.00	7.50	4.50

1962 Salada-Junket Coins

These 1-3/8" diameter plastic coins were issued in packages of Salada Tea and Junket Pudding mix. There are 221 different players available, with variations bringing the total of different coins to 265. Each coin has a paper color photo inserted in the front which contains the player's name and position plus the coin number. The plastic rims come in six different colors, coded by team. Production began with 180 coins, but the addition of the New York Mets and Houston Colt .45's to the National League allowed the company to expand the set's size. Twenty expansion players were added along with 21 other players. Several players' coins were dropped after the initial 180 run, causing some scarcities. Embossed green plastic shields into which 10 coins could be placed were available via a mail-in offer. About 9" x 10-1/2", the shields have a banner near the top with the team name. Many of the players in the 180 series can be found with variations in the placement of the front typography relative to the colored portrait. Though these variations seem to affect a tiny percentage of some players' 180 coins, they are in most cases too difficult to distinguish except by direct comparison between specimens and are of interest only to the most dedicated Salada collectors.

		NM	E	VG
Complete Set, no variations (221):		3,000	1,500	900.00
Complete Set, w/ variations (267):		7,500	3,700	2,200
Complete Boxed Presentation Set (180):		1,900	950.00	575.00
Complete Boxed Presentation Set (200):		2,600	1,300	800.00
Uncut Sheet (180):		1,800	900.00	550.00
Common Player (1-180):		4.00	2.00	1.25
Common Player (181-221):		10.00	5.00	3.00
Team Shield (Empty):		60.00	30.00	18.00
1	Jim Gentile	5.00	2.50	1.50
2	Bill Pierce	65.00	32.50	20.00
3a	Chico Fernandez (Light blue jersey piping.)	4.00	2.00	1.25
3b	Chico Fernandez (Dark blue jersey piping.)	12.00	6.00	3.50
4	Tom Brewer	15.00	7.50	4.50
5	Woody Held	4.00	2.00	1.25
6	Ray Herbert	22.50	11.00	7.00
7a	Ken Aspromonte (Angels)	10.00	5.00	3.00
7b	Ken Aspromonte (Indians)	10.00	5.00	3.00
8	Whitey Ford	20.00	10.00	6.00
9a	Jim Lemon (Jim at center of ear. Value undetermined.)			
9b	Jim Lemon (Jim at bottom of ear.)	4.00	2.00	1.25
10	Billy Klaus	4.00	2.00	1.25
11	Steve Barber	27.50	13.50	8.25
12	Nellie Fox	17.50	8.75	5.25
13	Jim Bunning	15.00	7.50	4.50
14	Frank Malzone	5.00	2.50	1.50
15	Tito Francona	4.00	2.00	1.25
16	Bobby Del Greco	4.00	2.00	1.25
17a	Steve Bilko (Red shirt buttons.)	9.00	4.50	2.75
17b	Steve Bilko (White shirt buttons.)	9.00	4.50	2.75
18	Tony Kubek	35.00	17.50	10.00
19	Earl Battey	4.00	2.00	1.25
20	Chuck Cottier	4.00	2.00	1.25
21	Willie Tasby	4.00	2.00	1.25
22	Bob Allison	6.00	3.00	1.75
23	Roger Maris	25.00	12.50	7.50
24a	Earl Averill (Red shirt buttons.)	9.00	4.50	2.75
24b	Earl Averill (White shirt buttons.)	5.00	2.50	1.50
25	Jerry Lumpe	4.00	2.00	1.25
26	Jim Grant	17.50	8.75	5.25
27	Carl Yastrzemski	30.00	15.00	9.00
28a	Rocky Colavito (Light blue jersey piping.)	20.00	10.00	6.00
28b	Rocky Colavito (Dark blue jersey piping.)	12.50	6.25	3.75
29	Al Smith	4.00	2.00	1.25
30	Jim Busby	30.00	15.00	9.00

#	Player			
31	Dick Howser	4.00	2.00	1.25
32	Jim Perry	4.00	2.00	1.25
33	Yogi Berra	25.00	12.50	7.50
34a	Ken Hamlin (Red shirt buttons.)	7.00	3.50	2.00
34b	Ken Hamlin (White shirt buttons.)	4.00	2.00	1.25
35	Dale Long	4.00	2.00	1.25
36a	Harmon Killebrew (Typography horizontal. Value undetermined.)			
36b	Harmon Killebrew (Typography at angle.)	20.00	10.00	6.00
37a	Dick Brown (Light blue jersey piping.)	12.00	6.00	3.50
37b	Dick Brown (Dark blue jersey piping.)	4.00	2.00	1.25
38	Gary Geiger	4.00	2.00	1.25
39a	Minnie Minoso (White Sox)	20.00	10.00	6.00
39b	Minnie Minoso (Cardinals)	9.00	4.50	2.75
40	Brooks Robinson	20.00	10.00	6.00
41	Mickey Mantle	70.00	35.00	20.00
42	Bennie Daniels	4.00	2.00	1.25
43	Billy Martin	12.00	6.00	3.50
44	Vic Power	5.00	2.50	1.50
45	Joe Pignatano	4.00	2.00	1.25
46a	Ryne Duren (Red shirt buttons, name far from ear. Value undetermined.)			
46b	Ryne Duren (White shirt buttons, name close to ear.)	9.00	4.50	2.75
46c	Ryne Duren (White shirt buttons, name close to ear.)	8.00	4.00	2.50
47a	Pete Runnels (2B)	12.00	6.00	3.50
47b	Pete Runnels (1B)	7.50	3.75	2.25
48a	Dick Williams (Name on right.)	1,800	900.00	550.00
48b	Dick Williams (Name on left.)	4.00	2.00	1.25
49	Jim Landis	4.00	2.00	1.25
50	Steve Boros	4.00	2.00	1.25
51a	Zoilo Versalles (Red shirt buttons.)	7.00	3.50	2.00
51b	Zoilo Versalles (White shirt buttons.)	7.00	3.50	2.00
52a	Johnny Temple (Indians)	12.50	6.25	3.75
52b	Johnny Temple (Orioles)	21.50	10.75	6.50
53a	Jackie Brandt (Oriole)	15.00	7.50	4.50
53b	Jackie Brandt (Orioles)	1,600	800.00	475.00
54	Joe McClain	4.00	2.00	1.25
55	Sherman Lollar	5.00	2.50	1.50
56	Gene Stephens	4.00	2.00	1.25
57a	Leon Wagner (Red shirt buttons.)	7.00	3.50	2.00
57b	Leon Wagner (White shirt buttons.)	5.00	2.50	1.50
58	Frank Lary	6.00	3.00	1.75
59	Bill Skowron	10.00	5.00	3.00
60	Vic Wertz	20.00	10.00	6.00
61	Willie Kirkland	4.00	2.00	1.25
62	Leo Posada	4.00	2.00	1.25
63a	Albie Pearson (Red shirt buttons.)	9.00	4.50	2.75
63b	Albie Pearson (White shirt buttons.)	8.00	4.00	2.50
64	Bobby Richardson	15.00	7.50	4.50
65a	Marv Breeding (SS)	9.00	4.50	2.75
65b	Marv Breeding (2B)	12.00	6.00	3.50
66	Roy Sievers	70.00	35.00	20.00
67	Al Kaline	25.00	12.50	7.50
68a	Don Buddin (Red Sox)	15.00	7.50	4.50
68b	Don Buddin (Colts)	5.00	2.50	1.50
69a	Lenny Green (Red shirt buttons.)	8.00	4.00	2.50
69b	Lenny Green (White shirt buttons.)	6.00	3.00	1.75
70	Gene Green	40.00	20.00	12.00
71	Luis Aparicio	12.00	6.00	3.50
72	Norm Cash	16.00	8.00	4.75
73	Jackie Jensen	20.00	10.00	6.00
74	Bubba Phillips	6.00	3.00	1.75
75	Jim Archer	4.00	2.00	1.25
76a	Ken Hunt (Red shirt buttons.)	9.00	4.50	2.75
76b	Ken Hunt (White shirt buttons.)	4.00	2.00	1.25
77	Ralph Terry	4.00	2.00	1.25
78	Camilo Pascual	4.00	2.00	1.25
79	Marty Keough	27.50	13.50	8.25
80	Cletis Boyer	10.00	5.00	3.00
81	Jim Pagliaroni	4.00	2.00	1.25
82a	Gene Leek (Red shirt buttons.)	9.00	4.50	2.75
82b	Gene Leek (White shirt buttons.)	4.00	2.00	1.25
83	Jake Wood	5.00	2.50	1.50
84	Coot Veal	25.00	12.50	7.50
85	Norm Siebern	5.00	2.50	1.50
86a	Andy Carey (White Sox)	25.00	12.50	7.50
86b	Andy Carey (Phillies)	9.00	4.50	2.75
87a	Bill Tuttle (Red shirt buttons.)	9.00	4.50	2.75
87b	Bill Tuttle (White shirt buttons.)	25.00	12.50	7.50
88a	Jimmy Piersall (Indians)	20.00	10.00	6.00
88b	Jimmy Piersall (Senators)	20.00	10.00	6.00
89	Ron Hansen	25.00	12.50	7.50
90a	Chuck Stobbs (Red shirt buttons.)	8.00	4.00	2.50
90b	Chuck Stobbs (White shirt buttons.)	4.00	2.00	1.25
91a	Ken McBride (Red shirt buttons.)	9.00	4.50	2.75
91b	Ken McBride (White shirt buttons.)	7.50	3.75	2.25
92	Bill Bruton	4.00	2.00	1.25
93	Gus Triandos	4.00	2.00	1.25
94	John Romano	4.00	2.00	1.25
95	Elston Howard	10.00	5.00	3.00
96	Gene Woodling	6.00	3.00	1.75
97a	Early Wynn (Pitching pose.)	45.00	22.00	13.50
97b	Early Wynn (Portrait)	15.00	7.50	4.50
98	Milt Pappas	4.00	2.00	1.25
99	Bill Monbouquette	4.00	2.00	1.25
100	Wayne Causey	4.00	2.00	1.25
101	Don Elston	4.00	2.00	1.25
102a	Charlie Neal (Dodgers)	12.00	6.00	3.50
102b	Charlie Neal (Mets)	4.00	2.00	1.25
103	Don Blasingame	4.00	2.00	1.25
104	Frank Thomas	30.00	15.00	9.00
105	Wes Covington	4.00	2.00	1.25
106	Chuck Hiller	5.00	2.50	1.50
107	Don Hoak	4.00	2.00	1.25
108a	Bob Lillis (Cardinals)	27.50	13.50	8.25
108b	Bob Lillis (Colts)	4.00	2.00	1.25
109	Sandy Koufax	30.00	15.00	9.00
110	Gordy Coleman	4.00	2.00	1.25
111	Ed Matthews (Mathews)	20.00	10.00	6.00
112	Art Mahaffey	4.00	2.00	1.25
113a	Ed Bailey (Partial left shoulder; "C" level w/ ear.)	1,750	875.00	525.00
113b	Ed Bailey (Full left shoulder; second button red.)	10.00	5.00	3.00
113c	Ed Bailey (Full left shoulder; second button white.)	4.00	2.00	1.25
114	Smoky Burgess	7.00	3.50	2.00
115	Bill White	6.00	3.00	1.75
116	Ed Bouchee	25.00	12.50	7.50
117	Bob Buhl	8.00	4.00	2.50
118	Vada Pinson	4.00	2.00	1.25
119	Carl Sawatski	4.00	2.00	1.25
120	Dick Stuart	6.00	3.00	1.75
121	Harvey Kuenn	40.00	20.00	12.00
122	Pancho Herrera	4.00	2.00	1.25
123a	Don Zimmer (Cubs)	12.50	6.25	3.75
123b	Don Zimmer (Mets)	5.00	2.50	1.50
124	Wally Moon	6.00	3.00	1.75
125	Joe Adcock	9.00	4.50	2.75
126	Joey Jay	4.00	2.00	1.25
127a	Maury Wills (Blue "3" on shirt.)	10.00	5.00	3.00
127b	Maury Wills (Red "3" on shirt.)	10.00	5.00	3.00
128	George Altman	4.00	2.00	1.25
129a	John Buzhardt (Phillies)	30.00	15.00	9.00
129b	John Buzhardt (White Sox)	10.00	5.00	3.00
130	Felipe Alou	4.00	2.00	1.25
131	Bill Mazeroski	15.00	7.50	4.50
132	Ernie Broglio	4.00	2.00	1.25
133	John Roseboro	4.00	2.00	1.25
134	Mike McCormick	4.00	2.00	1.25
135a	Chuck Smith (Phillies)	15.00	7.50	4.50
135b	Chuck Smith (White Sox)	10.00	5.00	3.00
136	Ron Santo	12.00	6.00	3.50
137	Gene Freese	4.00	2.00	1.25
138	Dick Groat	5.00	2.50	1.50
139	Curt Flood	4.00	2.00	1.25
140	Frank Bolling	4.00	2.00	1.25
141	Clay Dalrymple	4.00	2.00	1.25
142	Willie McCovey	16.00	8.00	4.75
143	Bob Skinner	4.00	2.00	1.25
144	Lindy McDaniel	4.00	2.00	1.25
145	Glen Hobbie	4.00	2.00	1.25
146a	Gil Hodges (Dodgers)	30.00	15.00	9.00
146b	Gil Hodges (Mets)	22.50	11.00	6.75
147	Eddie Kasko	4.00	2.00	1.25
148	Gino Cimoli	25.00	12.50	7.50
149	Willie Mays	30.00	15.00	9.00
150	Roberto Clemente	65.00	32.00	18.00
151	Red Schoendienst	15.00	7.50	4.50
152	Joe Torre	5.00	2.50	1.50
153	Bob Purkey	4.00	2.00	1.25
154a	Tommy Davis (3B)	7.50	3.75	2.25
154b	Tommy Davis (OF)	12.00	6.00	3.50
155a	Andre Rogers (Incorrect spelling, 1B.)	7.50	3.75	2.25
155b	Andre Rodgers (Correct spelling, SS.)	12.00	6.00	3.50
156	Tony Taylor	4.00	2.00	1.25
157	Bob Friend	4.00	2.00	1.25
158a	Gus Bell (Redlegs)	20.00	10.00	6.00
158b	Gus Bell (Mets)	4.00	2.00	1.25
159	Roy McMillan	4.00	2.00	1.25
160	Carl Warwick	4.00	2.00	1.25
161	Willie Davis	4.00	2.00	1.25
162	Sam Jones	60.00	30.00	18.00
163	Ruben Amaro	6.00	3.00	1.75
164	Sam Taylor	4.00	2.00	1.25
165	Frank Robinson	15.00	7.50	4.50
166	Lou Burdette	5.00	2.50	1.50
167	Ken Boyer	13.50	6.75	4.00
168	Bill Virdon	4.00	2.00	1.25
169	Jim Davenport	4.00	2.00	1.25
170	Don Demeter	4.00	2.00	1.25
171	Richie Ashburn	40.00	20.00	12.00
172	John Podres	8.00	4.00	2.50
173a	Joe Cunningham (Cardinals)	30.00	15.00	9.00
173b	Joe Cunningham (White Sox)	12.50	6.25	3.75
174	ElRoy Face	5.00	2.50	1.50
175	Orlando Cepeda	12.00	6.00	3.50
176a	Bobby Gene Smith (Phillies)	15.00	7.50	4.50
176b	Bobby Gene Smith (Mets)	6.00	3.00	1.75
177a	Ernie Banks (OF)	25.00	12.50	7.50
177b	Ernie Banks (SS)	20.00	10.00	6.00
178a	Daryl Spencer (3B)	20.00	10.00	6.00
178b	Daryl Spencer (1B)	12.00	6.00	3.50
179	Bob Schmidt	25.00	12.50	7.50
180	Hank Aaron	35.00	17.50	10.50
181	Hobie Landrith	10.00	5.00	3.00
182a	Ed Broussard (Bressoud)	425.00	210.00	125.00
182b	Ed Bressoud	25.00	12.50	7.50
183	Felix Mantilla	10.00	5.00	3.00
184	Dick Farrell	10.00	5.00	3.00
185	Bob Miller	10.00	5.00	3.00
186	Don Taussig	15.00	7.50	4.50
187	Pumpsie Green	10.00	5.00	3.00
188	Bobby Shantz	10.00	5.00	3.00
189	Roger Craig	10.00	5.00	3.00
190	Hal Smith	10.00	5.00	3.00
191	John Edwards	10.00	5.00	3.00
192	John DeMerit	10.00	5.00	3.00
193	Joe Amalfitano	10.00	5.00	3.00
194	Norm Larker	10.00	5.00	3.00
195	Al Heist	10.00	5.00	3.00
196	Al Spangler	10.00	5.00	3.00
197	Alex Grammas	10.00	5.00	3.00
198	Gerry Lynch	10.00	5.00	3.00
199	Jim McKnight	15.00	7.50	4.50
200	Jose Pagen (Pagan)	10.00	5.00	3.00
201	Junior Gilliam	20.00	10.00	6.00
202	Art Ditmar	10.00	5.00	3.00
203	Pete Daley	10.00	5.00	3.00
204	Johnny Callison	20.00	10.00	6.00
205	Stu Miller	10.00	5.00	3.00
206	Russ Snyder	10.00	5.00	3.00
207	Billy Williams	25.00	12.50	7.50
208	Walter Bond	10.00	5.00	3.00
209	Joe Koppe	10.00	5.00	3.00
210	Don Schwall	16.00	8.00	4.75
211	Billy Gardner	15.00	7.50	4.50
212	Chuck Estrada	10.00	5.00	3.00
213	Gary Bell	15.00	7.50	4.50
214	Floyd Robinson	10.00	5.00	3.00
215	Duke Snider	25.00	12.50	7.50
216	Lee Maye	10.00	5.00	3.00
217	Howie Bedell	10.00	5.00	3.00
218	Bob Will	10.00	5.00	3.00
219	Dallas Green	15.00	7.50	4.50
220	Carroll Hardy	15.00	7.50	4.50
221	Danny O'Connell	10.00	5.00	3.00

1962 Salada-Junket Coins - Clip Back

A very rare version of the Salada Tea/Junket Dessert plastic coins exists in a clip-back format. An extruded tab at back center would allow the coin to be slid onto a cap bill or shirt flap as a decoration. With the exception of Averill (Angels), all clip-back Saladas confirmed thus far depict Boston Red Sox players. It has been reported that the clip-back coins were created for use in Opening Day stadium promotions by the Red Sox, Yankees and Mets.

		NM	E	VG
	Common Player:	450.00	225.00	135.00
14	Frank Malzone	450.00	225.00	135.00
24	Earl Averill	450.00	225.00	135.00
27	Carl Yastrzemski	600.00	300.00	180.00
38	Gary Geiger	450.00	225.00	135.00
47	Pete Runnels	450.00	225.00	135.00
73	Jackie Jensen	450.00	225.00	135.00
81	Jim Pagliaroni	450.00	225.00	135.00
99	Bill Monbouquette	450.00	225.00	135.00
182	Ed Broussard (Bressoud)	450.00	225.00	135.00
187	Pumpsie Green	450.00	225.00	135.00
210	Don Schwall	450.00	225.00	135.00
220	Carroll Hardy	450.00	225.00	135.00

1963 Salada-Junket Coins

A much smaller set of baseball coins was issued by Salada/Junket in 1963. The 63 coins issued were called "All-Star Baseball Coins" and included most of the top players of the day. Unlike 1962, the coins were made of metal and measured a slightly larger 1-1/2" diameter. American League players have blue rims on their coins, while National Leaguers are rimmed in red. Coin fronts contain no printing on the full-color player photos, while backs list coin number, player name, team and position, along with brief statistics and the sponsors' logos.

		NM	E	VG
	Complete Set (63):	1,000	500.00	300.00
	Common Player:	9.00	4.50	3.00
1	Don Drysdale	20.00	10.00	6.00
2	Dick Farrell	9.00	4.50	3.00
3	Bob Gibson	20.00	10.00	6.00
4	Sandy Koufax	55.00	30.00	15.00
5a	Juan Marichal (No buttons.)	20.00	10.00	6.00
5b	Juan Marichal (Jersey buttons.)	15.00	8.00	5.00
6	Bob Purkey	9.00	4.50	3.00
7	Bob Shaw	9.00	4.50	3.00
8	Warren Spahn	20.00	10.00	6.00
9	Johnny Podres	12.00	6.00	4.00
10	Art Mahaffey	9.00	4.50	3.00
11	Del Crandall	9.00	4.50	3.00
12	John Roseboro	9.00	4.50	3.00
13	Orlando Cepeda	15.00	8.00	5.00
14	Bill Mazeroski	15.00	8.00	5.00
15	Ken Boyer	12.00	6.00	4.00
16	Dick Groat	9.00	4.50	3.00
17	Ernie Banks	25.00	12.00	8.00
18	Frank Bolling	9.00	4.50	3.00
19	Jim Davenport	9.00	4.50	3.00
20	Maury Wills	12.00	6.00	4.00
21	Tommy Davis	9.00	4.50	3.00
22	Willie Mays	55.00	30.00	15.00
23	Roberto Clemente	70.00	35.00	20.00
24	Henry Aaron	45.00	25.00	15.00
25	Felipe Alou	9.00	4.50	3.00
26	Johnny Callison	9.00	4.50	3.00
27	Richie Ashburn	20.00	10.00	6.00
28	Eddie Mathews	20.00	10.00	6.00

29	Frank Robinson	15.00	8.00	5.00
30	Billy Williams	15.00	8.00	5.00
31	George Altman	9.00	4.50	3.00
32	Hank Aguirre	9.00	4.50	3.00
33	Jim Bunning	15.00	8.00	5.00
34	Dick Donovan	9.00	4.50	3.00
35	Bill Monbouquette	9.00	4.50	3.00
36	Camilo Pascual	9.00	4.50	3.00
37	David Stenhouse	9.00	4.50	3.00
38	Ralph Terry	9.00	4.50	3.00
39	Hoyt Wilhelm	15.00	8.00	5.00
40	Jim Kaat	12.00	6.00	4.00
41	Ken McBride	9.00	4.50	3.00
42	Ray Herbert	9.00	4.50	3.00
43	Milt Pappas	9.00	4.50	3.00
44	Earl Battey	9.00	4.50	3.00
45	Elston Howard	12.00	6.00	4.00
46	John Romano	9.00	4.50	3.00
47	Jim Gentile	9.00	4.50	3.00
48	Billy Moran	9.00	4.50	3.00
49	Rich Rollins	9.00	4.50	3.00
50	Luis Aparicio	15.00	8.00	5.00
51	Norm Siebern	9.00	4.50	3.00
52	Bobby Richardson	12.00	6.00	4.00
53	Brooks Robinson	25.00	12.00	8.00
54	Tom Tresh	12.00	6.00	4.00
55	Leon Wagner	9.00	4.50	3.00
56	Mickey Mantle	125.00	65.00	40.00
57	Roger Maris	35.00	18.00	10.00
58	Rocky Colavito	30.00	15.00	9.00
59	Lee Thomas	9.00	4.50	3.00
60	Jim Landis	9.00	4.50	3.00
61	Pete Runnels	9.00	4.50	3.00
62	Yogi Berra	35.00	18.00	10.50
63	Al Kaline	30.00	15.00	9.00

1961 Sam's Family Restaurants Roger Maris

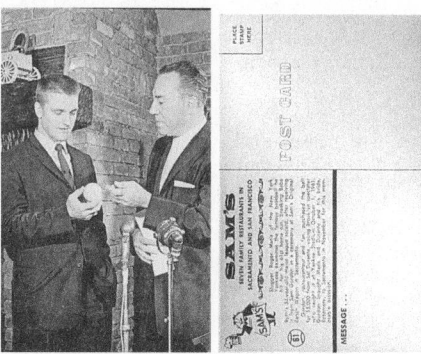

This postcard was issued to commemorate the presentation of Roger Maris' historic 61st home run ball back to the slugger. Pictured with Maris on this color 3-1/2" x 5-1/2" postcard is Sam Gordon, owner of a chain of family restaurants in northern California. Gordon purchased the ball from the fan who caught it, Sal Durante, and flew Durante and his wife, and Maris to Sacramento where he paid $5,000 for the ball and presented it to Maris, who later donated it to the Hall of Fame. On front is a borderless color photo of the presentation. Back has the historical details and the traditional postcard indicia.

		NM	E	VG
61	Roger Maris, Sam Gordon	50.00	25.00	15.00

1886 W.H. Sanders New York Baseball Club (H812)

This rare 19th Century baseball issue can be classified under the general category of "trade" cards, a popular advertising vehicle of the period. The cards measure 3" x 4-3/4" and feature blue line-drawing portraits of members of the "New York Base Ball Club," which is printed along the top. As was common with this type of trade card, the bottom was left blank to accomodate various messages. The known examples of this set carry ads for local tobacco merchants and other businesses. The portraits are all based on the photographs used in the 1886 Old Judge set. The cards, which have been assigned an ACC designation of H812, are printed on thin paper rather than cardboard.

(See 1889 New York Baseball Club for checklist and values.)

1969 San Diego Padres Premium Pictures

Unlike most of the contemporary large-format (8-1/2" x 11") premium pictures, this issue carries no advertising and appears to have been a team-issue in the Padres inaugural year. Fronts feature large portraits and smaller action pictures of the player against a dark background with a facsimile autograph at the bottom and the player's name printed in the white bottom border. The signature of the artist appears in the lower-left corner. The artwork was done by Nicholas Volpe, who produced many similar items for teams in all sports in the '60s, '70s and '80s. Backs have a large team logo at center and a sketch of the artist at bottom. There is evidence to suggest that the picture of Cito Gaston is scarcer than the other seven.

		NM	E	VG
	Complete Set (8):	60.00	30.00	18.00
	Common Player:	7.50	3.75	2.25
(1)	Ollie Brown	7.50	3.75	2.25
(2)	Tommy Dean	7.50	3.75	2.25
(3)	Al Ferrara	7.50	3.75	2.25
(4)	Clarence Gaston	10.00	5.00	3.00
(5)	Preston Gomez	7.50	3.75	2.25
(6)	Johnny Podres	9.00	4.50	2.75
(7)	Al Santorini	7.50	3.75	2.25
(8)	Ed Spiezio	7.50	3.75	2.25

1977 San Diego Padres Schedule Cards

Members of the 1977 San Diego Padres, players and management, are featured in this set. The 2-1/4" x 3-3/8" cards are printed in brown on thin white stock. Fronts have a player photo with a pinstripe around and the team and player name at bottom. Backs have the team logo at top, a list of promotional dates in the center and ticket information at bottom. While some card backs state "One in a Series of 40 Player Photos," more than 80 variations are known, including some poses with blank backs. The unnumbered cards are checklisted here in alphabetical order, within three types differentiated by back printing.

		NM	E	VG
	Complete Set (89):	60.00	30.00	18.00
	Common Player:	1.00	.50	.30
Type 1 - "Series of 40"				
(3)	Buzzy Bavasi (General Manager)	1.00	.50	.30

(4)	Vic Bernal	1.00	.50	.30
(5)	Mike Champion	1.00	.50	.30
(6)	Billy Champion, Bill Almon	1.00	.50	.30
(7)	Roger Craig	1.00	.50	.30
(8)	John D'Acquisto	1.00	.50	.30
(9)	Bob Davis	1.00	.50	.30
(29)	Dan Spillner	1.00	.50	.30
(30)	Brent Strom	1.00	.50	.30
(31)	Gary Sutherland	1.00	.50	.30
(32)	Gene Tenace	1.00	.50	.30
(33)	Dave Tomlin	1.00	.50	.30
(34)	Jerry Turner	1.00	.50	.30
(35)	Bobby Valentine	1.00	.50	.30
(36)	Dan Wehrmeister	1.00	.50	.30
(37)	Whitey Wietelmann	1.00	.50	.30
(38)	Don Williams	1.00	.50	.30
(39)	Dave Winfield (One bat.)	10.00	5.00	3.00
(40)	Dave Winfield (Two bats.)	5.00	2.50	1.50

Type 2 - No "Series of 40"

(3)	Steve Arlin (Glove to chest.)	1.00	.50	.30
(4)	Steve Arlin (Follow-through.)	1.00	.50	.30
(5)	Bob Barton	1.00	.50	.30
(6)	Glenn Beckert	1.50	.75	.45
(7)	Ollie Brown	1.00	.50	.30
(8)	Dave Campbell (Bat on shoulder.)	1.00	.50	.30
(9)	Dave Campbell (Kneeling)	1.00	.50	.30
(29)	Bob Miller	1.00	.50	.30
(30)	Fred Norman (Arms above head.)	1.00	.50	.30
(31)	Fred Norman (Kneeling)	1.00	.50	.30
(32)	Gene Richards	1.00	.50	.30
(33)	Ballard Smith (General Manager)	1.00	.50	.30
(34)	Ed Spiezio	1.00	.50	.30
(35)	Derrell (Darrel) Thomas (Glasses)	1.00	.50	.30
(36)	Derrel Thomas (No glasses.)	1.00	.50	.30
(37)	Bobby Tolan (Batting)	1.00	.50	.30
(38)	Bobby Tolan (Kneeling)	1.00	.50	.30
(39)	Jerry Turner	1.00	.50	.30
(40)	Dave Winfield	5.00	2.50	1.50

Type 1 - "Series of 40"

(3)	Buzzy Bavasi (General Manager)	1.00	.50	.30

Type 3 - Blank back

(3)	Mike Ivie	1.00	.50	.30

Type 2 - No "Series of 40"

(3)	Steve Arlin (Glove to chest.)	1.00	.50	.30

Type 3 - Blank back

(3)	Mike Ivie	1.00	.50	.30
(4)	Randy Jones and Bowie Kuhn	1.00	.50	.30
(5)	Mike Kilkenny	1.00	.50	.30
(6)	Ray Kroc (Owner)	1.00	.50	.30
(7)	Willie McCovey	5.00	2.50	1.50
(8)	John McNamara (Facing his right.)	1.00	.50	.30
(9)	Dave Winfield	7.50	3.75	2.25
(4)	Randy Jones and Bowie Kuhn	1.00	.50	.30

Type 2 - No "Series of 40"

(4)	Steve Arlin (Follow-through.)	1.00	.50	.30

Type 1 - "Series of 40"

(4)	Vic Bernal	1.00	.50	.30

Type 2 - No "Series of 40"

(5)	Bob Barton	1.00	.50	.30

Type 1 - "Series of 40"

(5)	Mike Champion	1.00	.50	.30

Type 3 - Blank back

(5)	Mike Kilkenny	1.00	.50	.30

Type 1 - "Series of 40"

(6)	Billy Champion, Bill Almon	1.00	.50	.30

Type 2 - No "Series of 40"

(6)	Glenn Beckert	1.50	.75	.45

Type 3 - Blank back

(6)	Ray Kroc (Owner)	1.00	.50	.30

Type 2 - No "Series of 40"

(7)	Ollie Brown	1.00	.50	.30

Type 1 - "Series of 40"

(7)	Roger Craig	1.00	.50	.30

Type 3 - Blank back

---

(7)	Willie McCovey	5.00	2.50	1.50

Type 2 - No "Series of 40"

(8)	Dave Campbell (Bat on shoulder.)	1.00	.50	.30

Type 1 - "Series of 40"

(8)	John D'Acquisto	1.00	.50	.30

Type 3 - Blank back

(8)	John McNamara (Facing his right.)	1.00	.50	.30

Type 1 - "Series of 40"

(9)	Bob Davis	1.00	.50	.30

Type 2 - No "Series of 40"

(9)	Dave Campbell (Kneeling)	1.00	.50	.30

Type 3 - Blank back

(9)	Dave Winfield	7.50	3.75	2.25

Type 1 - "Series of 40"

(29)	Dan Spillner	1.00	.50	.30
(30)	Brent Strom	1.00	.50	.30

Type 2 - No "Series of 40"

(30)	Fred Norman (Arms above head.)	1.00	.50	.30
(31)	Fred Norman (Kneeling)	1.00	.50	.30

Type 1 - "Series of 40"

(31)	Gary Sutherland	1.00	.50	.30

Type 2 - No "Series of 40"

(32)	Gene Richards	1.00	.50	.30

Type 1 - "Series of 40"

(32)	Gene Tenace	1.00	.50	.30

Type 2 - No "Series of 40"

(33)	Ballard Smith (General Manager)	1.00	.50	.30

Type 1 - "Series of 40"

(33)	Dave Tomlin	1.00	.50	.30

Type 2 - No "Series of 40"

(34)	Ed Spiezio	1.00	.50	.30

Type 1 - "Series of 40"

(34)	Jerry Turner	1.00	.50	.30
(35)	Bobby Valentine	1.00	.50	.30

Type 2 - No "Series of 40"

(35)	Derrell (Darrel) Thomas (Glasses)	1.00	.50	.30

Type 1 - "Series of 40"

(36)	Dan Wehrmeister	1.00	.50	.30

Type 2 - No "Series of 40"

(36)	Derrel Thomas (No glasses.)	1.00	.50	.30
(37)	Bobby Tolan (Batting)	1.00	.50	.30

Type 1 - "Series of 40"

(37)	Whitey Wietelmann	1.00	.50	.30

Type 2 - No "Series of 40"

(38)	Bobby Tolan (Kneeling)	1.00	.50	.30

Type 1 - "Series of 40"

(38)	Don Williams	1.00	.50	.30
(39)	Dave Winfield (One bat.)	10.00	5.00	3.00

Type 2 - No "Series of 40"

(39)	Jerry Turner	1.00	.50	.30
(40)	Dave Winfield	5.00	2.50	1.50

Type 1 - "Series of 40"

(40)	Dave Winfield (Two bats.)	5.00	2.50	1.50

1972 San Diego Padres Team Issue

It is uncertain whether this 12-player checklist represents the entirety of this set of team-issued pictures. The black-

---

and-white portraits are presented in a 3-3/8" x 5-3/8" blank-back format.

		NM	EX	VG
Complete Set (12):		30.00	15.00	9.00
Common Player:		3.00	1.50	.90
(1)	Steve Arlin	3.00	1.50	.90
(2)	Nate Colbert	3.00	1.50	.90
(3)	Pat Corrales	4.50	2.25	1.35
(4)	Clarence Gaston	4.50	2.25	1.35
(5)	Bill Grief	3.00	1.50	.90
(6)	Enzo Hernandez	3.00	1.50	.90
(7)	Clay Kirby	3.00	1.50	.90
(8)	Leron Lee	3.00	1.50	.90
(9)	Jerry Morales	3.00	1.50	.90
(10)	Dave Roberts	3.00	1.50	.90
(11)	Darrel (Derrel) Thomas	3.00	1.50	.90
(12)	Don Zimmer	4.50	2.25	1.35

1936 S and S Game

Small black-and-white player photos are featured on the fronts of this 52-card game set. Measuring about 2-1/4" x 3-1/2", with rounded corners, the cards feature plain green or cream-colored backs. Besides the player photo on front, there are a few biographical details and stats, and a pair of game scenarios. The cards are unnumbered and are check-listed here alphabetically. The complete game included a special scoreboard, at least two "directions" cards and a contest card.

		NM	E	VG
Complete Set (52):		750.00	370.00	220.00
Complete Boxed Set:		1,325	665.00	400.00
Common Player:		12.50	6.25	3.75
(1)	Luke Appling	30.00	15.00	9.00
(2)	Earl Averill	30.00	15.00	9.00
(3)	Zeke Bonura	12.50	6.25	3.75
(4)	Dolph Camilli	12.50	6.25	3.75
(5)	Ben Cantwell	12.50	6.25	3.75
(6)	Phil Cavaretta (Cavarretta)	12.50	6.25	3.75
(7)	Rip Collins	12.50	6.25	3.75
(8)	Joe Cronin	30.00	15.00	9.00
(9)	Frank Crosetti	20.00	10.00	6.00
(10)	Kiki Cuyler	30.00	15.00	9.00
(11)	Virgil Davis	12.50	6.25	3.75
(12)	Frank Demaree	12.50	6.25	3.75
(13)	Paul Derringer	12.50	6.25	3.75
(14)	Bill Dickey	50.00	25.00	15.00
(15)	Woody English	12.50	6.25	3.75
(16)	Fred Fitzsimmons	12.50	6.25	3.75
(17)	Richard Ferrell	30.00	15.00	9.00
(18)	Pete Fox	12.50	6.25	3.75
(19)	Jimmy (Jimmie) Foxx	60.00	30.00	18.00
(20)	Larry French	12.50	6.25	3.75
(21)	Frank Frisch	30.00	15.00	9.00
(22)	August Galan	12.50	6.25	3.75
(23)	Chas. Gehringer	30.00	15.00	9.00
(24)	John Gill	12.50	6.25	3.75
(25)	Charles Grimm	12.50	6.25	3.75
(26)	Mule Haas	12.50	6.25	3.75
(27)	Stanley Hack	12.50	6.25	3.75
(28)	Bill Hallahan	12.50	6.25	3.75
(29)	Melvin Harder	12.50	6.25	3.75
(30)	Gabby Hartnett	30.00	15.00	9.00
(31)	Ray Hayworth	12.50	6.25	3.75
(32)	Ralston Hemsley	12.50	6.25	3.75
(33)	Bill Herman	30.00	15.00	9.00
(34)	Frank Higgins	12.50	6.25	3.75
(35)	Carl Hubbell	40.00	20.00	12.00
(36)	Bill Jurges	12.50	6.25	3.75
(37)	Vernon Kennedy	12.50	6.25	3.75
(38)	Chuck Klein	30.00	15.00	9.00
(39)	Mike Kreevich	12.50	6.25	3.75
(40)	Bill Lee	12.50	6.25	3.75
(41)	Jos. Medwick	30.00	15.00	9.00
(42)	Van Mungo	12.50	6.25	3.75
(43)	James O'Dea	12.50	6.25	3.75
(44)	Mel Ott	50.00	25.00	15.00
(45)	Rip Radcliff	12.50	6.25	3.75
(46)	Pie Traynor	30.00	15.00	9.00
(47)	Arky Vaughan (Vaughn)	30.00	15.00	9.00

		NM	E	VG
(48)	Joe Vosmik	12.50	6.25	3.75
(49)	Lloyd Waner	30.00	15.00	9.00
(50)	Paul Waner	30.00	15.00	9.00
(51)	Lon Warneke	12.50	6.25	3.75
(52)	Floyd Young	12.50	6.25	3.75

1932 Sanella Margarine

One of several "foreign" Babe Ruth cards issued during his prime was included in a 112-card set produced as premiums for Sanella margarine in Germany. Ruth is the only major league ballplayer in the issue. Cards are in full color, measuring 2-3/4" x 4-1/8". Backs of the unnumbered cards are printed in German. Three types of backs can be found on the Ruth card. Type 1 has the Sanella name nearly centered. The Type 2 back has the brand name printed closer to the bottom of the card, with only four lines of type under it. Type 3 is a variation of Type 2 on which the appropriate page number (83) of the accompanying album is mentioned on the line immediately above "Handbuch des Sports" near the top. Type 1 cards also mention the page number; current hobby data suggests that no Sanellas with centered logos do not mention the page. One card was given with the purchase of each 1/2 pound of margarine and the album could be ordered by mail. See also Astra Margarine.

		NM	E	VG
Type 1	Babe Ruth (Centered w/83)	200.00	100.00	60.00
Type 2	Babe Ruth (At bottom.)	140.00	70.00	42.00
Type 3	Babe Ruth (At bottom w/83.)	200.00	100.00	60.00

1958 San Francisco Call-Bulletin Giants

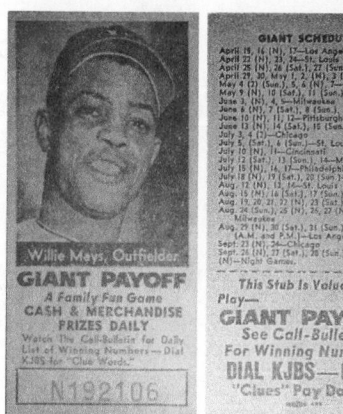

These unnumbered cards, picturing members of the San Francisco Giants, were inserted in copies of the San Francisco Call-Bulletin newspaper as part of a promotional contest. The 25 cards in the set measure 2" x 4" and were printed on orange paper. The top of the card contains a black and white player photo, while the bottom contains a perforated stub with a serial number used to win prizes. (Cards without the stub intact are approximately 50 percent of the prices listed.) The contest name, "Giant Payoff," appears prominently on both sides of the stub. The back of the card contains a 1958 Giants schedule.

		NM	E	VG
Complete Set (25):		1,800	900.00	550.00
Common Player:		25.00	12.50	7.50
(1)	Johnny Antonelli	25.00	12.50	7.50
(2)	Curt Barclay	25.00	12.50	7.50
(3)	Tom Bowers (SP)	400.00	200.00	120.00
(4)	Ed Bressoud (SP)	150.00	75.00	45.00
(5)	Orlando Cepeda	250.00	125.00	75.00
(6)	Ray Crone	25.00	12.50	7.50
(7)	Jim Davenport	25.00	12.50	7.50

		NM	E	VG
(8)	Paul Giel	25.00	12.50	7.50
(9)	Ruben Gomez	25.00	12.50	7.50
(10)	Marv Grissom	25.00	12.50	7.50
(11)	Ray Jablonski (SP)	150.00	75.00	45.00
(12)	Willie Kirkland (SP)	150.00	75.00	45.00
(13)	Whitey Lockman	25.00	12.50	7.50
(14)	Willie Mays	250.00	125.00	75.00
(15)	Mike McCormick	25.00	12.50	7.50
(16)	Stu Miller	25.00	12.50	7.50
(17)	Ramon Monzant	25.00	12.50	7.50
(18)	Danny O'Connell	25.00	12.50	7.50
(19)	Bill Rigney	25.00	12.50	7.50
(20)	Hank Sauer	25.00	12.50	7.50
(21)	Bob Schmidt	25.00	12.50	7.50
(22)	Daryl Spencer	25.00	12.50	7.50
(23)	Valmy Thomas	25.00	12.50	7.50
(24)	Bobby Thomson	45.00	22.50	13.50
(25)	Allan Worthington	25.00	12.50	7.50

1971-1982 San Francisco Giants Autograph Cards

For more than 10 years the Giants issued a number of different types of cards bearing facsimile autographs that the players could use to respond to fan mail. The cards vary in size from 3" x 5" to 3" x 6" and have a black-and-white photo (usually a portrait). The cards are blank-backed. Besides the cards with pre-printed autographs, a number of special cards in similar format were issued without facsimile signature. The listings are presented here in two major styles, those with player name in all-capital letters and those with names in upper and lower case.

		NM	E	VG
Common Player:		6.00	3.00	1.75
	NAME IN ALL-CAPITAL LETTERS			
(1)	Doyle Alexander	6.00	3.00	1.75
(2)	Gary Alexander	6.00	3.00	1.75
(3)	Joe Altobelli	6.00	3.00	1.75
(4)	Rob Andrews (Portrait)	6.00	3.00	1.75
(5)	Rob Andrews (Fielding)	6.00	3.00	1.75
(6)	Jim Barr (Pitching)	6.00	3.00	1.75
(7)	Dave Bergman	6.00	3.00	1.75
(8)	Vida Blue (Portrait)	8.00	4.00	2.50
(9)	Vida Blue (Pitching)	8.00	4.00	2.50
(10)	Bill Bordley	6.00	3.00	1.75
(11)	Fred Breining	6.00	3.00	1.75
(12)	Dave Bristol	6.00	3.00	1.75
(13)	Enos Cabell	6.00	3.00	1.75
(14)	Jack Clark (Ready to bat.)	8.00	4.00	2.50
(15)	Jack Clark (Swinging bat.)	8.00	4.00	2.50
(16)	Terry Cornutt	6.00	3.00	1.75
(17)	Heity Cruz	6.00	3.00	1.75
(18)	John Curtis	6.00	3.00	1.75
(19)	Jim Dwyer	6.00	3.00	1.75
(20)	Randy Elliott	6.00	3.00	1.75
(21)	Darrell Evans (Portrait)	8.00	4.00	2.50
(22)	Darrell Evans (Batting)	8.00	4.00	2.50
(23)	Tim Foli (Fielding)	6.00	3.00	1.75
(24)	Tom Griffin	6.00	3.00	1.75
(25)	Ed Halicki (Portrait)	6.00	3.00	1.75
(26)	Ed Halicki (Pitching)	6.00	3.00	1.75
(27)	Vic Harris	6.00	3.00	1.75
(28)	Dave Heaverlo (Action)	6.00	3.00	1.75
(29)	Tom Heintzelman	6.00	3.00	1.75
(30)	Larry Herndon	6.00	3.00	1.75
(31)	Marc Hill	6.00	3.00	1.75
(32)	Al Holland	6.00	3.00	1.75
(33)	Mike Ivie (Looks to side.)	6.00	3.00	1.75
(34)	Mike Ivie (Looks to front.)	6.00	3.00	1.75
(35)	Skip James	6.00	3.00	1.75
(36)	Bob Knepper	6.00	3.00	1.75
(37)	Gary Lavelle (Portrait)	6.00	3.00	1.75
(38)	Gary Lavelle (Pitching)	6.00	3.00	1.75

		NM	E	VG
(39)	Johnnie Lemaster (Fielding)	6.00	3.00	1.75
(40)	Dennis Littlejohn	6.00	3.00	1.75
(41)	Bill Madlock (Picture reversed.)	8.00	4.00	2.50
(42)	Bill Madlock (Corrected)	8.00	4.00	2.50
(43)	Jerry Martin	6.00	3.00	1.75
(44)	Milt May	6.00	3.00	1.75
(45)	Willie McCovey (Portrait)	15.00	7.50	4.50
(46)	Willie McCovey (Batting)	15.00	7.50	4.50
(47)	Lynn McGlothen (Pitching)	6.00	3.00	1.75
(48)	Roger Metzger	6.00	3.00	1.75
(49)	Greg Minton	6.00	3.00	1.75
(50)	Randy Moffitt (Portrait)	6.00	3.00	1.75
(51)	Randy Moffitt (Pitching)	6.00	3.00	1.75
(52)	John Montefusco (To neck.)	6.00	3.00	1.75
(53)	John Montefusco (To letters.)	6.00	3.00	1.75
(54)	Joe Morgan	15.00	7.50	4.50
(55)	Rich Murray	6.00	3.00	1.75
(56)	Phil Nastu	6.00	3.00	1.75
(57)	Bill North	6.00	3.00	1.75
(58)	Joe Pettini	6.00	3.00	1.75
(59)	Allen Ripley	6.00	3.00	1.75
(60)	Dave Roberts	6.00	3.00	1.75
(61)	Frank Robinson	20.00	10.00	6.00
(62)	Mike Sadek (To neck.)	6.00	3.00	1.75
(63)	Mike Sadek (To letters.)	6.00	3.00	1.75
(64)	Billy Smith	6.00	3.00	1.75
(65)	Rennie Stennett	6.00	3.00	1.75
(66)	Joe Strain	6.00	3.00	1.75
(67)	John Tamargo	6.00	3.00	1.75
(68)	Derrel Thomas (Throwing)	6.00	3.00	1.75
(69)	Gary Thomasson	6.00	3.00	1.75
(70)	Max Venable	6.00	3.00	1.75
(71)	Terry Whitfield	6.00	3.00	1.75
(72)	Ed Whitson	6.00	3.00	1.75
(73)	Charlie Williams	6.00	3.00	1.75
(74)	Jim Wohlford	6.00	3.00	1.75
(1)	Jim Barr (Mouth closed.)	6.00	3.00	1.75
(2)	Jim Barr (Mouth open, fence.)	6.00	3.00	1.75
(3)	Jim Barr (Mouth open, no fence.)	6.00	3.00	1.75
(4)	Bobby Bonds	9.00	4.50	2.75
(5)	Tom Bradley	6.00	3.00	1.75
(6)	Ron Bryant	6.00	3.00	1.75
(7)	Don Carrithers (To neck.)	6.00	3.00	1.75
(8)	Don Carrithers (To letters.)	6.00	3.00	1.75
(9)	Pete Falcone	6.00	3.00	1.75
(10)	Charlie Fox	6.00	3.00	1.75
(11)	Tito Fuentes (To neck.)	6.00	3.00	1.75
(12)	Tito Fuentes (To letters.)	6.00	3.00	1.75
(13)	Alan Gallagher	6.00	3.00	1.75
(14)	Russ Gibson	6.00	3.00	1.75
(15)	Ed Goodson	6.00	3.00	1.75
(16)	Ed Halicki (Pitching)	6.00	3.00	1.75
(17)	Marc Hill	6.00	3.00	1.75
(18)	Jim Howarth	6.00	3.00	1.75
(19)	Jerry Johnson	6.00	3.00	1.75
(20)	Von Joshua	6.00	3.00	1.75
(21)	Gary Lavelle (Pitching)	6.00	3.00	1.75
(22)	Garry Maddox	6.00	3.00	1.75
(23)	Juan Marichal	15.00	7.50	4.50
(24)	Gary Matthews	8.00	4.00	2.50
(25)	Randy Moffitt	6.00	3.00	1.75
(26)	Willie McCovey	15.00	7.50	4.50
(27)	Willie Montanez	6.00	3.00	1.75
(28)	John Montefusco (Pitching)	6.00	3.00	1.75
(29)	Bobby Murcer (Batting)	8.00	4.00	2.50
(30)	Dave Rader	6.00	3.00	1.75
(31)	Ken Reitz (Batting)	6.00	3.00	1.75
(32)	Bill Rigney	6.00	3.00	1.75
(33)	Mike Sadek	6.00	3.00	1.75
(34)	Elias Sosa	6.00	3.00	1.75
(35)	Chris Speier (To neck.)	6.00	3.00	1.75
(36)	Chris Speier (To shoulders.)	6.00	3.00	1.75
(37)	Steve Stone	8.00	4.00	2.50
(38)	Derrel Thomas	6.00	3.00	1.75
(39)	Gary Thomasson	6.00	3.00	1.75
(40)	Jim Willoughby	6.00	3.00	1.75
	TYPE 3 - 25th Anniversary Logo			
(1)	Jim Barr	6.00	3.00	1.75
(2)	Bob Brenly	6.00	3.00	1.75
(5)	Jim Davenport	6.00	3.00	1.75
(6)	Chili Davis	8.00	4.00	2.50
(7)	Alan Fowlkes	6.00	3.00	1.75
(8)	Rich Gale	6.00	3.00	1.75
(9)	Atlee Hammaker	6.00	3.00	1.75
(10)	Al Holland	6.00	3.00	1.75
(11)	Duane Kuiper	6.00	3.00	1.75
(12)	Bill Laskey	6.00	3.00	1.75

Caption (under image 3): RANDY MOFFITT — Randy Moffitt — Chris Arnold - infielder — Giants autograph card courtesy of Redwood City Tribune

(13)	Jim Lefebvre	6.00	3.00	1.75
(14)	Johnnie Lemaster	6.00	3.00	1.75
(15)	Jeff Leonard (Chain in background.)	8.00	4.00	2.50
(16)	Jeff Leonard (No chain.)	8.00	4.00	2.50
(17)	Renie Martin	6.00	3.00	1.75
(18)	Willie McCovey	15.00	7.50	4.50
(21)	Greg Minton	6.00	3.00	1.75
(22)	Joe Morgan	15.00	7.50	4.50
(23)	Tom O'Malley	6.00	3.00	1.75
(24)	Frank Robinson	20.00	10.00	6.00
(25)	Mike Sadek	6.00	3.00	1.75
(26)	Reggie Smith	6.00	3.00	1.75
(27)	Guy Sularz	6.00	3.00	1.75
(28)	Champ Summers	6.00	3.00	1.75
(31)	Jim Wohlford	6.00	3.00	1.75
	autograph			
(1)	Chris Speier	6.00	3.00	1.75
	autograph			
(1)	Bobby Bonds	9.00	4.50	2.75
(2)	Dick Dietz	6.00	3.00	1.75
(3)	Tito Fuentes	6.00	3.00	1.75
(4)	Ken Henderson	6.00	3.00	1.75
	Valley Bicycles, no autograph			
(1)	Alan Gallagher	6.00	3.00	1.75
	TYPE 7 - Best Chevrolet, no autograph			
(1)	Tito Fuentes	6.00	3.00	1.75
(2)	Chris Speier	6.00	3.00	1.75
	autograph			
(1)	Jim Barr	6.00	3.00	1.75
	NAME IN UPPER- AND LOWER CASE LETTERS			
	TYPE A - Name only			
(1)	John D'Acquisto	6.00	3.00	1.75
(2)	Mike Caldwell	6.00	3.00	1.75
(3)	Ed Goodson	6.00	3.00	1.75
(4)	Dave Kingman	8.00	4.00	2.50
(5)	Steve Ontiveros	6.00	3.00	1.75
(6)	Mike Phillips	6.00	3.00	1.75
(7)	"Wes" Westrum	6.00	3.00	1.75
(8)	Charlie Williams	6.00	3.00	1.75
	TYPE B - Team after name, no autograph			
(1)	Rich Robertson	6.00	3.00	1.75
	autograph			
(1)	Rich Robertson	6.00	3.00	1.75
	TYPE D - Position after name			
(1)	Garry Maddox	6.00	3.00	1.75
	no autograph			
(1)	Chris Arnold	6.00	3.00	1.75
(2)	Jim Barr	6.00	3.00	1.75
(3)	Jim Howarth	6.00	3.00	1.75
(4)	Garry Maddox	6.00	3.00	1.75
(5)	Dave Rader	6.00	3.00	1.75
(6)	Chris Speier	6.00	3.00	1.75
	newspaper logo, no autograph			
(1)	Chris Arnold	6.00	3.00	1.75
(2)	Jim Barr	6.00	3.00	1.75
(3)	Ed Goodson	6.00	3.00	1.75
	TYPE G - Name only, old Giants logo			
(1)	Dave Kingman	8.00	4.00	2.50
(2)	Juan Marichal	15.00	7.50	4.50

1977 San Francisco Giants Team Issue

These 3-1/2" x 5" blank-back cards feature black-and-white player photos surrounded by an orange frame with black borders. The manager, coaches and instructors are featured along with players in the issue. The unnumbered cards are checklisted here in alphabetical order.

		NM	E	VG
Complete Set (25):		15.00	7.50	4.50
Common Player:		1.50	.75	.45
(1)	Joe Altobelli	1.50	.75	.45
(2)	Jim Barr	1.50	.75	.45
(3)	Jack Clark	2.50	1.25	.70
(4)	Terry Cornutt	1.50	.75	.45
(5)	Rob Dressler	1.50	.75	.45
(6)	Darrell Evans	2.50	1.25	.70
(7)	Frank Funk	1.50	.75	.45
(8)	Ed Halicki	1.50	.75	.45
(9)	Tom Haller	1.50	.75	.45
(10)	Marc Hill	1.50	.75	.45

(11)	Skip James	1.50	.75	.45
(12)	Bob Knepper	1.50	.75	.45
(13)	Gary Lavelle	1.50	.75	.45
(14)	Bill Madlock	1.75	.90	.50
(15)	Willie McCovey	6.00	3.00	1.75
(16)	Randy Moffitt	1.50	.75	.45
(17)	John Montefusco	1.50	.75	.45
(18)	Marty Perez	1.50	.75	.45
(19)	Frank Riccelli	1.50	.75	.45
(20)	Mike Sadek	1.50	.75	.45
(21)	Hank Sauer	1.50	.75	.45
(22)	Chris Speier	1.50	.75	.45
(23)	Gary Thomasson	1.50	.75	.45
(24)	Tommy Toms	1.50	.75	.45
(25)	Bobby Winkles	1.50	.75	.45

1979 San Francisco Giants Police

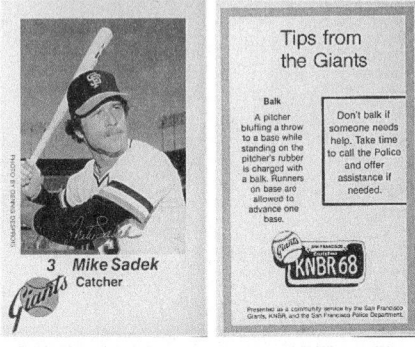

Each of the full-color cards measures 2-5/8" x 4-1/8" and is numbered by player uniform number. The set includes players and coaches. The player's name, position and facsimile autograph are on front, along with the Giants logo. Backs have a "Tip from the Giants" and sponsor logos for the Giants and radio station KNBR, all printed in orange and black. Half of the set was distributed as a ballpark promotion, while the other cards were available from police agencies in several San Francisco Bay area counties.

		NM	E	VG
Complete Set (29):		10.00	5.00	3.00
Common Player:		.50	.25	.15
1	Dave Bristol	.50	.25	.15
2	Marc Hill	.50	.25	.15
3	Mike Sadek	.50	.25	.15
5	Tom Haller	.50	.25	.15
6	Joe Altobelli	.50	.25	.15
8	Larry Shepard	.50	.25	.15
9	Heity Cruz	.50	.25	.15
10	Johnnie LeMaster	.50	.25	.15
12	Jim Davenport	.50	.25	.15
14	Vida Blue	.75	.40	.25
15	Mike Ivie	.50	.25	.15
16	Roger Metzger	.50	.25	.15
17	Randy Moffitt	.50	.25	.15
18	Bill Madlock	.60	.30	.20
21	Rob Andrews	.50	.25	.15
22	Jack Clark	.75	.40	.25
25	Dave Roberts	.50	.25	.15
26	John Montefusco	.50	.25	.15
28	Ed Halicki	.50	.25	.15
30	John Tamargo	.50	.25	.15
31	Larry Herndon	.50	.25	.15
36	Bill North	.50	.25	.15
39	Bob Knepper	.50	.25	.15
40	John Curtis	.50	.25	.15
41	Darrell Evans	.75	.40	.25
43	Tom Griffin	.50	.25	.15
44	Willie McCovey	5.00	2.50	1.50
46	Gary Lavelle	.50	.25	.15
49	Max Venable	.50	.25	.15

1980 San Francisco Giants Police

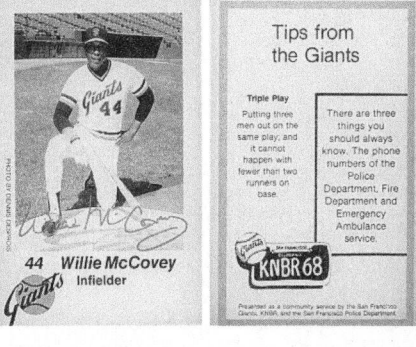

The 1980 Giants police set is virtually identical in format to its 1979 forerunner, with radio station KNBR and the San Francisco Police Department once again co-sponsors. The 2-5/8" x 4-1/8" cards feature full-color photos and facsimile autographs. Backs are in the team's orange and black colors. The set includes players and coaches, with each card numbered by uniform number. As in 1979, half the cards were distributed as a stadium promotion, with the remainder available only from police officers.

		NM	E	VG
Complete Set (31):		9.00	4.50	2.75
Common Player:		.50	.25	.15
1	Dave Bristol	.50	.25	.15
2	Marc Hill	.50	.25	.15
3	Mike Sadek	.50	.25	.15
5	Jim Lefebvre	.50	.25	.15
6	Rennie Stennett	.50	.25	.15
7	Milt May	.50	.25	.15
8	Vern Benson	.50	.25	.15
9	Jim Wohlford	.50	.25	.15
10	Johnnie LeMaster	.50	.25	.15
12	Jim Davenport	.50	.25	.15
14	Vida Blue	.75	.40	.25
15	Mike Ivie	.50	.25	.15
16	Roger Metzger	.50	.25	.15
17	Randy Moffitt	.50	.25	.15
19	Al Holland	.50	.25	.15
20	Joe Strain	.50	.25	.15
22	Jack Clark	.50	.25	.15
26	John Montefusco	.50	.25	.15
28	Ed Halicki	.50	.25	.15
31	Larry Herndon	.50	.25	.15
32	Ed Whitson	.50	.25	.15
36	Bill North	.50	.25	.15
38	Greg Minton	.50	.25	.15
39	Bob Knepper	.50	.25	.15
41	Darrell Evans	.60	.30	.20
42	John Van Ornum	.50	.25	.15
43	Tom Griffin	.50	.25	.15
44	Willie McCovey	4.00	2.00	1.25
45	Terry Whitfield	.50	.25	.15
46	Gary Lavelle	.50	.25	.15
47	Don McMahon	.50	.25	.15

1940s Sarra Trade Cards

While the cards are undated, one of the uniforms shown places its issue between 1940-1950. These ad cards are about 3-1/2" x 5-3/8" and printed in sepia on thick cream-colored paper stock. The backs picture examples of the company's personal care products, including cologne, available in sizes up to one quart!

	NM	E	VG
Ralph Kiner	250.00	125.00	75.00
Stan Musial	350.00	175.00	100.00
Babe Ruth	550.00	275.00	165.00

1938 Sawyer Biscuit Cubs/White Sox

In the late 1930s, a local baker ran a promotion by which fans could redeem a coupon found in its product along with a dime for a matted black-and-white portrait photo of a favorite Chicago ballplayer. The photo was delivered in a thick textured maroon frame about 4-3/4" x 5-3/4" in size that had a punch-out stand on back. The Sawyer company name is not found on the actual photo, but is seen on the envelope and cover letter which are sometimes found with the pictures. It is unknown whether the list presented here is complete.

		NM	E	VG
Common Player:		600.00	300.00	180.00
	CHICAGO CUBS			
(1)	Jim Asbell	600.00	300.00	180.00
(2)	Clay Bryant	600.00	300.00	180.00
(3)	Tex Carleton	600.00	300.00	180.00
(4)	Phil Cavarretta	600.00	300.00	180.00
(5)	Rip Collins	600.00	300.00	180.00
(6)	Jerome "Dizzy" Dean	1,200	600.00	360.00
(7)	Frank Demaree	600.00	300.00	180.00
(8)	Al Epperly	600.00	300.00	180.00
(9)	Larry French	600.00	300.00	180.00
(10)	Augie Galan	600.00	300.00	180.00
(11)	Bob Garbark	600.00	300.00	180.00
(12)	Charlie Grimm	600.00	300.00	180.00
(13)	Stan Hack	650.00	325.00	195.00
(14)	Gabby Hartnett	750.00	375.00	225.00
(15)	Billy Herman	750.00	375.00	225.00
(16)	Bill Jurges	600.00	300.00	180.00
(17)	Tony Lazzeri	750.00	375.00	225.00
(18)	Bill Lee	600.00	300.00	180.00
(19)	Bob Logan	600.00	300.00	180.00
(20)	Joe Marty	600.00	300.00	180.00
(21)	Ken O'Dea	600.00	300.00	180.00
(22)	Carl Reynolds	600.00	300.00	180.00
(23)	Charlie Root	600.00	300.00	180.00
(24)	Jack Russell	600.00	300.00	180.00
	CHICAGO WHITE SOX			
(1)	Luke Appling	750.00	375.00	225.00
(2)	Boze Berger	600.00	300.00	180.00
(3)	Clint Brown	600.00	300.00	180.00
(4)	Frog Dietrich	600.00	300.00	180.00
(5)	Jimmie Dykes	600.00	300.00	180.00
(6)	Frank Gabler	600.00	300.00	180.00
(7)	Jackie Hayes	600.00	300.00	180.00
(8)	Jack Knott	600.00	300.00	180.00
(9)	Mike Kreevich	600.00	300.00	180.00
(10)	Joe Kuhel	600.00	300.00	180.00
(11)	Thornton Lee	600.00	300.00	180.00
(12)	Ted Lyons	750.00	375.00	225.00
(13)	Marv Owen	600.00	300.00	180.00
(14)	Tony Rensa	600.00	300.00	180.00
(15)	Dunc Rigney	600.00	300.00	180.00
(16)	Larry Rosenthal	600.00	300.00	180.00
(17)	Norm Schlueter	600.00	300.00	180.00
(18)	Luke Sewell	600.00	300.00	180.00
(19)	Henk Steinbacher	600.00	300.00	180.00
(20)	Monty Stratton	625.00	310.00	185.00
(21)	Gee Gee Walker	600.00	300.00	180.00
(22)	Porkshops Whitehead	600.00	300.00	180.00
	BROADCASTER			
	Bob Elson	600.00	300.00	180.00

1921-22 Schapira Bros. Big Show Candy

The players known, with the teams on which they are pictured, can pinpoint the issue date no closer than 1921-22. Nominally about 1-3/4" or 1-7/8" x 2-3/8" (size varies because the cards were printed without borders in sheet form, and are often found crudely cut), the cards were one of several types of insert cards and toys found in boxes of Schapira's "Big Show" candy. The cards have black-and-white borderless photos on which the player name is (usually) printed diagonally in script at lower right. Most cards have an Underwood & Underwood credit line on front, as well. Backs are blank. The unnumbered cards are listed here alphabetically, though the checklist may not be complete. Most cards are found with a horizontal crease at center, possibly to get them into the tight-fitting candy box.

		NM	E	VG
Common Player:		600.00	300.00	180.00
(1)	George J. Burns	600.00	300.00	180.00

		NM	E	VG
(2)	Ty Cobb	2,700	1,350	800.00
(3)	Stan Coveleski	750.00	375.00	225.00
(4)	(Jake) Daubert	600.00	300.00	180.00
(5)	Joe Dugan	600.00	300.00	180.00
(6)	Jimmy Dykes	600.00	300.00	180.00
(7)	Walter Holke	600.00	300.00	180.00
(8)	Walter Johnson	1,200	600.00	360.00
(9)	Joe Judge	600.00	300.00	180.00
(10)	Geo. Kelly	750.00	375.00	225.00
(11)	Dick Kerr	600.00	300.00	180.00
(12)	Rabbit Maranville	750.00	375.00	225.00
(13)	Carl Mays	600.00	300.00	180.00
(14)	(Bob) Meusel	600.00	300.00	180.00
(15)	Hy Meyers (Myers)	600.00	300.00	180.00
(16)	O'Neil (Mickey?)	600.00	300.00	180.00
(17)	Roger Peckinpaugh	600.00	300.00	180.00
(18)	Cy Perkins	600.00	300.00	180.00
(19)	Edd Rousch (Roush)	750.00	375.00	225.00
(20)	Ray Schalk	600.00	300.00	180.00
(21)	Everett Scott	600.00	300.00	180.00
(22)	Aaron Ward	600.00	300.00	180.00

1921 Schapira Bros. Candy Babe Ruth

The date assigned to this rare candy issue is a best guess based on the uniform in which the Babe is shown on the various cards. The blank-back cards measure between 1-5/8" and 1-3/4" in width, and are 2-1/2" tall. Printed in red, white and blue the cards were printed on a candy box and come in two types. Apparently each box contained a portrait card of Ruth which offered "a base ball autographed by Babe Ruth" for 250 of the pictures, plus one of five action photos. The portrait card would thus be much more common than any particular action pose, unless great numbers of them were redeemed. The cards illustrated here are not front and back, but show a typical action card and the portrait card. The unnumbered cards are checklisted here in alphabetical order based on the card's caption.

		NM	E	VG
Complete Set (6):		11,000	5,500	3,250
(1)	Cleared the Bags(Babe Ruth)	2,000	1,000	600.00
(2)	Home Run(Babe Ruth)	2,000	1,000	600.00
(3)	Over the Fence(Babe Ruth)	2,000	1,000	600.00
(4)	They Passed Him(Babe Ruth)	2,000	1,000	600.00
(5)	Waiting for a High One(Babe Ruth)	2,000	1,000	600.00
(6a)	Babe Ruth (Portrait (Arrows point to top of ball.))	1,550	775.00	465.00
(6b)	Babe Ruth ((No arrows.))	1,550	775.00	465.00

1975 Michael Schechter Associates Test Discs

Prior to rolling out its 70-disc set in 1976, Michael Schechter Associates issued this sample set of discs the previous year. Slightly larger, at 3-9/16" diameter, than the '76 issues, the '75 sample discs share a similar format. Fronts have a black-and-white player photo from which uniform logo details have been removed due to lack of licensing by Major League Baseball. Backs are blank. The Seaver and Bench discs are considerably scarcer than the other four players in the set.

	NM	E	VG
Complete Set (6):	175.00	90.00	55.00

		NM	E	VG
Common Player:		6.00	3.00	1.75
(1)	Hank Aaron	15.00	7.50	4.50
(2)	Johnny Bench	60.00	30.00	18.00
(3)	Catfish Hunter	6.00	3.00	1.75
(4)	Fred Lynn	6.00	3.00	1.75
(5)	Pete Rose	10.00	5.00	3.00
(6)	Tom Seaver	100.00	50.00	30.00

1976 Michael Schechter Associates Discs

Following its test issue of 1975, Michael Schechter Associates ran out its baseball player disc issues on a large scale in 1976. While most were sold with specific sponsor advertising on back, they were also made available with blank backs. The discs are 3-3/8" diameter with a black-and-white player portrait photo in the center of the baseball design. A line of red stars is above, while the left and right panels feature one of several bright colors. Produced by MSA under license from the Major League Players Association, the player photos have had uniform and cap logos removed. The unnumbered discs are presented in alphabetical order.

		NM	E	VG
Complete Set (70):		60.00	30.00	18.00
Common Player:		.50	.25	.15
(1)	Henry Aaron	12.50	6.25	3.75
(2)	Johnny Bench	6.00	3.00	1.75
(3)	Vida Blue	.50	.25	.15
(4)	Larry Bowa	.50	.25	.15
(5)	Lou Brock	4.50	2.25	1.25
(6)	Jeff Burroughs	.50	.25	.15
(7)	John Candelaria	.50	.25	.15
(8)	Jose Cardenal	.50	.25	.15
(9)	Rod Carew	6.00	3.00	1.75
(10)	Steve Carlton	4.50	2.25	1.25
(11)	Dave Cash	.50	.25	.15
(12)	Cesar Cedeno	.50	.25	.15
(13)	Ron Cey	.50	.25	.15
(14)	Carlton Fisk	4.50	2.25	1.25
(15)	Tito Fuentes	.50	.25	.15
(16)	Steve Garvey	3.00	1.50	.90
(17)	Ken Griffey	.50	.25	.15
(18)	Don Gullett	.50	.25	.15
(19)	Willie Horton	.50	.25	.15
(20)	Al Hrabosky	.50	.25	.15
(21)	Catfish Hunter	4.50	2.25	1.25
(22)	Reggie Jackson (A's)	9.00	4.50	2.75
(23)	Randy Jones	.50	.25	.15
(24)	Jim Kaat	.50	.25	.15
(25)	Don Kessinger	.50	.25	.15
(26)	Dave Kingman	.50	.25	.15
(27)	Jerry Koosman	.50	.25	.15
(28)	Mickey Lolich	.60	.30	.20
(29)	Greg Luzinski	.50	.25	.15
(30)	Fred Lynn	.50	.25	.15
(31)	Bill Madlock	.50	.25	.15
(32)	Carlos May (White Sox)	.50	.25	.15
(33)	John Mayberry	.50	.25	.15
(34)	Bake McBride	.50	.25	.15
(35)	Doc Medich	.50	.25	.15
(36)	Andy Messersmith	.50	.25	.15
(37)	Rick Monday	.50	.25	.15
(38)	John Montefusco	.50	.25	.15
(39)	Jerry Morales	.50	.25	.15
(40)	Joe Morgan	4.50	2.25	1.25
(41)	Thurman Munson	4.50	2.25	1.25
(42)	Bobby Murcer	.50	.25	.15
(43)	Al Oliver	.50	.25	.15
(44)	Jim Palmer	4.50	2.25	1.25
(45)	Dave Parker	.50	.25	.15
(46)	Tony Perez	4.50	2.25	1.25
(47)	Jerry Reuss	.50	.25	.15
(48)	Brooks Robinson	6.00	3.00	1.75
(49)	Frank Robinson	6.00	3.00	1.75
(50)	Steve Rogers	.50	.25	.15
(51)	Pete Rose	10.00	5.00	3.00
(52)	Nolan Ryan	15.00	7.50	4.50
(53)	Manny Sanguillen	.50	.25	.15
(54)	Mike Schmidt	10.00	5.00	3.00
(55)	Tom Seaver	6.00	3.00	1.75
(56)	Ted Simmons	.50	.25	.15
(57)	Reggie Smith	.50	.25	.15
(58)	Willie Stargell	4.50	2.25	1.25
(59)	Rusty Staub	.75	.40	.25

		NM	E	VG
(60)	Rennie Stennett	.50	.25	.15
(61)	Don Sutton	4.50	2.25	1.25
(62)	Andy Thornton	.50	.25	.15
(63)	Luis Tiant	.50	.25	.15
(64)	Joe Torre	.50	.25	.15
(65)	Mike Tyson	.50	.25	.15
(66)	Bob Watson	.50	.25	.15
(67)	Wilbur Wood	.50	.25	.15
(68)	Jimmy Wynn	.50	.25	.15
(69)	Carl Yastrzemski	6.00	3.00	1.75
(70)	Richie Zisk	.50	.25	.15

1977 Michael Schechter Associates Cup Lids

One of MSA's early baseball novelty issues was a set of drink-cup lids. The 3-1/2" diameter pieces are made of pressed and waxed cardboard. They are 3/16" thick and have a 3/8" die-cut hole for inserting a straw. Design is similar to other MSA issues of the era, with a black-and-white player portrait photo at center of a simulated baseball design. Personal data is printed in colored panels at left and right, and there is a row of colored stars above the photo. Player caps do not show team insignia because the issue was licensed only by the players' union, and not the owners. The unnumbered lids are checklisted here in alphabetical order.

		NM	E	VG
Complete Set (49):		700.00	350.00	225.00
Common Player:		10.00	5.00	3.00
(1)	Sal Bando	10.00	5.00	3.00
(2)	Johnny Bench	30.00	15.00	9.00
(3)	Larry Bowa	10.00	5.00	3.00
(4)	Steve Braun	10.00	5.00	3.00
(5)	George Brett	100.00	50.00	30.00
(6)	Lou Brock	30.00	15.00	9.00
(7)	Bert Campaneris	10.00	5.00	3.00
(8)	Bill Campbell	10.00	5.00	3.00
(9)	Jose Cardenal	10.00	5.00	3.00
(10)	Rod Carew	30.00	15.00	9.00
(11)	Dave Cash	10.00	5.00	3.00
(12)	Cesar Cedeno	10.00	5.00	3.00
(13)	Chris Chambliss	10.00	5.00	3.00
(14)	Dave Concepcion	10.00	5.00	3.00
(15)	Mark Fidrych	10.00	5.00	3.00
(16)	Rollie Fingers	20.00	10.00	6.00
(17)	George Foster	10.00	5.00	3.00
(18)	Wayne Garland	10.00	5.00	3.00
(19)	Steve Garvey	20.00	10.00	6.00
(20)	Cesar Geronimo	10.00	5.00	3.00
(21)	Bobby Grich	10.00	5.00	3.00
(22)	Don Gullett	10.00	5.00	3.00
(23)	Mike Hargrove	10.00	5.00	3.00
(24)	Catfish Hunter	20.00	10.00	6.00
(25)	Randy Jones	10.00	5.00	3.00
(26)	Dave Kingman	15.00	7.50	4.50
(27)	Dave LaRoche	10.00	5.00	3.00
(28)	Greg Luzinski	10.00	5.00	3.00
(29)	Fred Lynn	10.00	5.00	3.00
(30)	Jon Matlack	10.00	5.00	3.00
(31)	Bake McBride	10.00	5.00	3.00
(32)	Joe Morgan	25.00	12.50	7.50
(33)	Phil Niekro	20.00	10.00	6.00
(34)	Jim Palmer	25.00	12.50	7.50
(35)	Dave Parker	10.00	5.00	3.00
(36)	Fred Patek	10.00	5.00	3.00
(37)	Mickey Rivers	10.00	5.00	3.00
(38)	Brooks Robinson	30.00	15.00	9.00
(39)	Pete Rose	75.00	37.00	22.00
(40)	Nolan Ryan	100.00	50.00	30.00
(41)	Tom Seaver (1976)	60.00	30.00	18.00
(42)	Mike Schmidt	50.00	25.00	15.00
(43)	Bill Singer	10.00	5.00	3.00
(44)	Chris Speier	10.00	5.00	3.00
(45)	Willie Stargell	25.00	12.50	7.50
(46)	Luis Tiant	12.50	6.25	3.75
(47)	Butch Wynegar	10.00	5.00	3.00
(48)	Robin Yount	20.00	10.00	6.00
(49)	Richie Zisk	10.00	5.00	3.00

1977 Mike Schechter Associates Customized Sports Discs

Virtually identical in format to the several locally sponsored disc sets of the previous year, these 3-3/8" diameter player discs once again feature black-and-white player portrait photos in the center of a baseball design. The left and right panels are in one of several bright colors. Licensed by the Players' Association, the photos carry no uniform logos. Backs of the discs are printed in dark blue and carry an ad from MSA for "Customized Sports Discs" and novelties for which Schechter held the licenses. The unnumbered discs are checklisted here alphabetically.

		NM	E	VG
Complete Set (70):		350.00	175.00	100.00
Common Player:		3.00	1.50	.90
(1)	Sal Bando	3.00	1.50	.90
(2)	Buddy Bell	3.00	1.50	.90
(3)	Johnny Bench	20.00	10.00	6.00
(4)	Larry Bowa	3.00	1.50	.90
(5)	Steve Braun	3.00	1.50	.90
(6)	George Brett	125.00	62.00	37.00
(7)	Lou Brock	15.00	7.50	4.50
(8)	Jeff Burroughs	3.00	1.50	.90
(9)	Bert Campaneris	3.00	1.50	.90
(10)	John Candelaria	3.00	1.50	.90
(11)	Jose Cardenal	3.00	1.50	.90
(12)	Rod Carew	20.00	10.00	6.00
(13)	Steve Carlton	20.00	10.00	6.00
(14)	Dave Cash	3.00	1.50	.90
(15)	Cesar Cedeno	3.00	1.50	.90
(16)	Ron Cey	3.00	1.50	.90
(17)	Dave Concepcion	3.00	1.50	.90
(18)	Dennis Eckersley	15.00	7.50	4.50
(19)	Mark Fidrych	6.00	3.00	1.75
(20)	Rollie Fingers	15.00	7.50	4.50
(21)	Carlton Fisk	15.00	7.50	4.50
(22)	George Foster	3.00	1.50	.90
(23)	Wayne Garland	3.00	1.50	.90
(24)	Ralph Garr	3.00	1.50	.90
(25)	Steve Garvey	12.50	6.25	3.75
(26)	Cesar Geronimo	3.00	1.50	.90
(27)	Bobby Grich	3.00	1.50	.90
(28)	Ken Griffey Sr.	3.00	1.50	.90
(29)	Don Gullett	3.00	1.50	.90
(30)	Mike Hargrove	3.00	1.50	.90
(31)	Al Hrabosky	3.00	1.50	.90
(32)	Jim Hunter	15.00	7.50	4.50
(33)	Reggie Jackson	30.00	15.00	9.00
(34)	Randy Jones	3.00	1.50	.90
(35)	Dave Kingman	5.00	2.50	1.50
(36)	Jerry Koosman	3.00	1.50	.90
(37)	Dave LaRoche	3.00	1.50	.90
(38)	Greg Luzinski	3.00	1.50	.90
(39)	Fred Lynn	3.00	1.50	.90
(40)	Bill Madlock	3.00	1.50	.90
(41)	Rick Manning	3.00	1.50	.90
(42)	Jon Matlack	3.00	1.50	.90
(43)	John Mayberry	3.00	1.50	.90
(44)	Hal McRae	3.00	1.50	.90
(45)	Andy Messersmith	3.00	1.50	.90
(46)	Rick Monday	3.00	1.50	.90
(47)	John Montefusco	3.00	1.50	.90
(48)	Joe Morgan	15.00	7.50	4.50
(49)	Thurman Munson	12.50	6.25	3.75
(50)	Bobby Murcer	3.00	1.50	.90
(51)	Bill North	3.00	1.50	.90
(52)	Jim Palmer	15.00	7.50	4.50
(53)	Tony Perez	15.00	7.50	4.50
(54)	Jerry Reuss	3.00	1.50	.90
(55)	Brooks Robinson	20.00	10.00	6.00
(56)	Pete Rose	75.00	37.00	22.00
(57)	Joe Rudi	3.00	1.50	.90
(58)	Nolan Ryan	125.00	62.00	37.00
(59)	Manny Sanguillen	3.00	1.50	.90
(60)	Mike Schmidt	100.00	50.00	30.00
(61)	Tom Seaver	20.00	10.00	6.00
(62)	Bill Singer	3.00	1.50	.90
(63)	Willie Stargell	15.00	7.50	4.50
(64)	Rusty Staub	5.00	2.50	1.50
(65)	Luis Tiant	3.00	1.50	.90
(66)	Bob Watson	3.00	1.50	.90
(67)	Butch Wynegar	3.00	1.50	.90
(68)	Carl Yastrzemski	20.00	10.00	6.00
(69)	Robin Yount	15.00	7.50	4.50
(70)	Richie Zisk	3.00	1.50	.90

1915 Schmelzer's Sporting Goods Pins

The date of issue attributed is speculative, based on the limited checklist currently available. These pin-back celluloid buttons measure about 1-1/4" in diameter. A color lithographed figure of a generic ballplayer shares the front with a smaller inset black-and-white photo of an actual player and a fancy script position designation. The player's last name appears at the bottom of the photo. Issuer identification is on back. It is presumed at least one pinback was issued for each of the nine positions.

		NM	E	VG
Common Player:		3,000	1,500	900.00
RF	"Ty" Cobb	17,500	8,750	5,250
3B	Charlie Deal	3,000	1,500	900.00
C	Hank Gowdy	3,000	1,500	900.00
LF	Hoffman	3,000	1,500	900.00
CF	Joe Jackson	12,000	6,000	3,600
P	Christy Mathewson	6,750	3,375	2,025
SS	Rabbit Maranville	3,000	1,500	900.00
1B	Butch Schmidt	3,000	1,500	900.00

1949 Schumacher Service Station

Because some of these cards have been found with the advertising of Schumacher Service Station (location unknown) printed in red on the back, the issue is so designated for cataloging purposes. Given that the (living) players from this set were with their respective teams in 1949-1950, the issue date could be either year. Measuring 2-5/8" x 3-9/16", the cards are black-and-white on the front. It is unknown whether other players were issued in this series.

		NM	E	VG
Complete Set (9):		2,200	1,100	650.00
Common Player:		200.00	100.00	60.00
(1)	Joe Garagiola	250.00	125.00	75.00
(2)	Marty Marion	225.00	110.00	65.00
(3)	Les Moss	200.00	100.00	60.00
(4)	George (Red) Munger	200.00	100.00	60.00
(5)	Don Newcomb (Newcombe)	250.00	125.00	75.00
(6)	Howard Pollet	200.00	100.00	60.00
(7)	George Herman (Babe) Ruth	600.00	300.00	180.00
(8)	Red Schoendienst	250.00	125.00	75.00
(9)	Vernon Stephens	200.00	100.00	60.00

1935 Schutter-Johnson (R332)

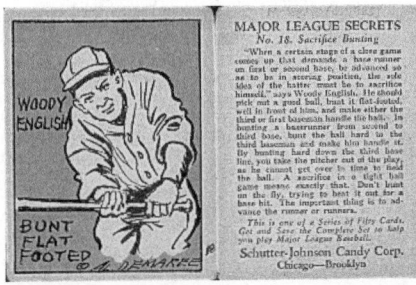

This 50-card set was issued by the Schutter-Johnson Candy Corp. of Chicago and Brooklyn circa 1930 and features drawings of major league players offering baseball playing tips. The cards measure 2-1/4" x 2-7/8". The drawings on the front are set against a red background while the backs are titled "Major League Secrets" and give the player's advice on some aspect of the game. The Scutter-Johnson name appears at the bottom.

	NM	E	VG
Complete Set (50):	17,500	7,000	3,500
Common Player:	200.00	100.00	50.00
1 Al Simmons	350.00	140.00	70.00
2 Lloyd Waner	275.00	110.00	55.00
3 Kiki Cuyler	275.00	110.00	55.00
4 Frank Frisch	275.00	110.00	55.00
5 Chick Hafey	275.00	110.00	55.00
6 Bill Klem (Umpire)	450.00	180.00	90.00
7 Rogers Hornsby	300.00	120.00	60.00
8 Carl Mays	200.00	100.00	50.00
9 Chas. Rigler (Umpire)	275.00	110.00	55.00
10 Christy Mathewson	900.00	360.00	180.00
11 Bill Dickey	275.00	110.00	55.00
12 Walter Berger	200.00	100.00	50.00
13 George Earnshaw	200.00	100.00	50.00
14 Hack Wilson	275.00	110.00	55.00
15 Charley Grimm	200.00	100.00	50.00
16 Lloyd Waner, Paul Waner	275.00	110.00	55.00
17 Chuck Klein	275.00	110.00	55.00
18 Woody English	200.00	100.00	50.00
19 Grover Alexander	350.00	175.00	105.00
20 Lou Gehrig	3,000	1,500	900.00
21 Wes Ferrell	200.00	100.00	50.00
22 Carl Hubbell	300.00	120.00	60.00
23 Pie Traynor	275.00	110.00	55.00
24 Gus Mancuso	200.00	100.00	50.00
25 Ben Cantwell	200.00	100.00	50.00
26 Babe Ruth	4,750	2,400	1,400
27 "Goose" Goslin	275.00	110.00	55.00
28 Earle Combs	275.00	110.00	55.00
29 "Kiki" Cuyler	275.00	110.00	55.00
30 Jimmy Wilson	200.00	100.00	50.00
31 Dizzy Dean	450.00	180.00	90.00
32 Mickey Cochrane	275.00	110.00	55.00
33 Ted Lyons	275.00	110.00	55.00
34 Si Johnson	200.00	100.00	50.00
35 Dizzy Dean	475.00	240.00	140.00
36 Pepper Martin	225.00	90.00	45.00
37 Joe Cronin	275.00	110.00	55.00
38 Gabby Hartnett	275.00	110.00	55.00
39 Oscar Melillo	200.00	100.00	50.00
40 Ben Chapman	200.00	100.00	50.00
41 John McGraw	275.00	110.00	55.00
42 Babe Ruth	2,350	940.00	470.00
43 "Red" Lucas	200.00	100.00	50.00
44 Charley Root	200.00	100.00	50.00
45 Dazzy Vance	275.00	110.00	55.00
46 Hugh Critz	200.00	100.00	50.00
47 "Firpo" Marberry	200.00	100.00	50.00
48 Grover Alexander	300.00	120.00	60.00
49 Lefty Grove	325.00	130.00	65.00
50 Heinie Meine	200.00	100.00	50.00

1888 "Scrapps Tobacco" Die-Cuts

The origin of these die-cut, embossed player busts is not known, but they were apparently part of a book of "punchouts" issued in the late 1880s. When out of their original album, they apparently resembled scraps of paper, presumably leading to their unusual name. An earlier theory that they were issued by "Scrapps Tobacco" has since been disocunted after research indicated there never was such a company. The die-cuts include 18 different players - nine members of the American Association St. Louis Browns and nine from the National League Detroit Wolverines. Although they vary slightly in size, the player busts are generally about 2" wide and 3" high. The drawings for the St. Louis player busts were taken from the Old Judge "Brown's Champions" set. The player's name appears along the bottom.

	NM	E	VG
Complete Set (18):	35,000	14,000	7,000
Common Player:	1,500	600.00	300.00

(1)	C.W. Bennett	1,500	600.00	300.00
(2)	D. Brouthers	2,400	960.00	480.00
(3)	A.J. Bushong	1,500	600.00	300.00
(4)	Robert L. Caruthers	1,500	600.00	300.00
(5)	Charles Comiskey	2,400	960.00	480.00
(6)	F. Dunlap	1,500	600.00	300.00
(7)	David L. Foutz	1,500	600.00	300.00
(8)	C.H. Getzen (Getzien)	1,500	600.00	300.00
(9)	Wm. Gleason	1,500	600.00	300.00
(10)	E. Hanlon	2,400	960.00	500.00
(11)	Walter A. Latham	1,500	600.00	300.00
(12)	James O'Neill	1,500	600.00	300.00
(13)	H. Richardson	1,500	600.00	300.00
(14)	Wm. Robinson	2,400	960.00	480.00
(15)	J.C. Rowe	1,500	600.00	300.00
(16)	S. Thompson	2,400	960.00	480.00
(17)	Curtis Welch	1,500	600.00	300.00
(18)	J.L. White	1,500	600.00	325.00

1949 Sealtest Phillies Stickers

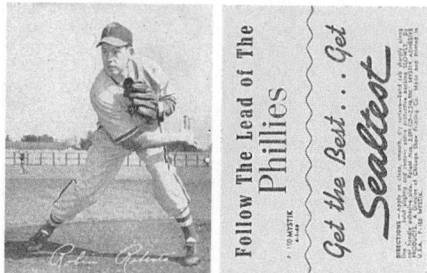

This regional Phillies set was issued in the Philadelphia area in 1949 by Sealtest Dairy. It consisted of 12 large (3-1/2" by 4-1/4") sticker cards with peel-off backs. The front of the unnumbered cards featured an action photo with facsimilie autograph, while the back has an advertisement for Sealtest products. The same format, photos and checklist were also used for the Lummis Peanut Butter card set issued in Philadelphia the same year.

	NM	E	VG
Complete Set (12):	8,000	4,000	2,400
Common Player:	700.00	350.00	210.00
(1) Rich Ashburn	1,900	950.00	560.00
(2) Hank Borowy	700.00	350.00	210.00
(3) Del Ennis	700.00	350.00	210.00
(4) Granny Hamner	700.00	350.00	210.00
(5) Puddinhead Jones	700.00	350.00	210.00
(6) Russ Meyer	700.00	350.00	210.00
(7) Bill Nicholson	700.00	350.00	210.00
(8) Robin Roberts	1,900	950.00	560.00
(9) "Schoolboy" Rowe	700.00	350.00	210.00
(10) Andy Seminick	700.00	350.00	210.00
(11) Curt Simmons	600.00	300.00	180.00
(12) Eddie Waitkus	700.00	350.00	210.00

1946 Sears St. Louis Browns/Cardinals Postcards

One of the more popular issues of the immediate post-war period are the black-and-white postcards of St. Louis Browns and Cardinals players issued by Sears in East St. Louis. The 3-1/2" x 5-3/8" postcards have posed player portraits on front with the player's name and Sears "Compliments of" line in the white border beneath. Backs are stamped "POST CARD / ACTUAL PHOTOGRAPH." The cards were reported to have been issued in groups of five on a bi-weekly basis, sold both at the Sears store and through the mail. The unnumbered cards are checklisted here alphabetically within team.

	NM	E	VG
Complete Set (69):	16,000	8,000	4,750
Common Player:	200.00	100.00	60.00

St. Louis Browns Set

(33):	6,000	3,000	1,800
(1) John Berardino	200.00	100.00	60.00
(2) Frank Biscan	400.00	200.00	120.00
(3) Mark Christman	200.00	100.00	60.00
(4) Babe Dahlgren	200.00	100.00	60.00
(5) Bob Dillinger	200.00	100.00	60.00
(6) Stanley Ferens	200.00	100.00	3600.00
(7) Denny Galehouse	200.00	100.00	60.00
(8) Joe Grace	200.00	100.00	60.00
(9) Jeff Heath	200.00	100.00	60.00
(10) Henry Helf	200.00	100.00	60.00
(11) Fred Hoffman	200.00	100.00	60.00
(12) Walt Judnich	200.00	100.00	60.00
(13) Ellis Kinder	200.00	100.00	60.00
(14) Jack Kramer	200.00	100.00	60.00
(15) Chet Laabs	200.00	100.00	60.00
(16) Al LaMacchia	250.00	125.00	75.00
(17) John Lucadello	200.00	100.00	60.00
(18) Frank Mancuso	200.00	100.00	60.00
(19) Glenn McQuillen	200.00	100.00	60.00
(20) John Miller	200.00	100.00	60.00
(21) Al Milnar	300.00	150.00	90.00
(22) Bob Muncrief	200.00	100.00	60.00
(23) Nelson Potter	200.00	100.00	60.00
(24) Ken Sears	200.00	100.00	60.00
(25) Len Schulte	200.00	100.00	60.00
(26) Luke Sewell	200.00	100.00	60.00
(27) Joe Schultz	200.00	100.00	60.00
(28) Tex Shirley	200.00	100.00	60.00
(29) Vern Stephens	200.00	100.00	60.00
(30) Chuck Stevens	200.00	100.00	60.00
(31) Zack Taylor	200.00	100.00	60.00
(32) Al Zarilla	200.00	100.00	60.00
(33) Sam Zoldak	200.00	100.00	60.00

St. Louis Cardinals Set

(36):	10,000	5,000	3,000
(1) Buster Adams	200.00	100.00	60.00
(2) Red Barrett	200.00	100.00	60.00
(3) Johnny Beazley	200.00	100.00	60.00
(4) Al Brazle	200.00	100.00	60.00
(5) Harry Brecheen	200.00	100.00	60.00
(6) Ken Burkhart	200.00	100.00	60.00
(7) Joffre Cross	200.00	100.00	60.00
(8) Murray Dickson	200.00	100.00	60.00
(9) George Dockins	200.00	100.00	60.00
(10) Blix Donnelly	300.00	150.00	90.00
(11) Erv Dusak	200.00	100.00	60.00
(12) Eddie Dyer	200.00	100.00	60.00
(13) Bill Endicott	200.00	100.00	60.00
(14) Joe Garagiola	800.00	400.00	240.00
(15) Mike Gonzales (Gonzalez)	250.00	125.00	75.00
(16) Lou Klein	200.00	100.00	60.00
(17) Clyde Kluttz	200.00	100.00	60.00
(18) Howard Krist	200.00	100.00	60.00
(19) George Kurowski	200.00	100.00	60.00
(20) Danny Litwhiler	200.00	100.00	60.00
(21) Marty Marion	300.00	150.00	90.00
(22) Fred Martin	200.00	100.00	60.00
(23) Terry Moore	250.00	125.00	75.00
(24) Stan Musial	2,000	1,000	600.00
(25) Ken O'Dea	200.00	100.00	60.00
(26) Howard Pollet	200.00	100.00	60.00
(27) Del Rice	200.00	100.00	60.00
(28) Red Schoendienst	600.00	300.00	180.00
(29) Walt Sessi	200.00	100.00	60.00
(30) Dick Sisler	200.00	100.00	60.00
(31) Enos Slaughter	600.00	300.00	180.00
(32) Max Surkont	200.00	100.00	60.00
(33) Harry Walker	200.00	100.00	60.00
(34) Buzzy Wares	200.00	100.00	60.00
(35) Ernie White	200.00	100.00	60.00
(36) Ted Wilks	200.00	100.00	60.00

1969 Seattle Pilots Premium Pictures

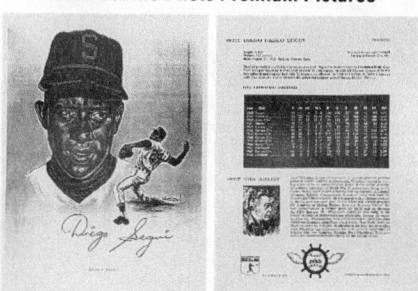

This set of 8-1/2" x 11" premium pictures is based on the artwork of John Wheeldon, who did contemporary issues for the Mets, Twins and Red Sox, as well. The pastels feature large portraits and smaller action pictures with a large facsimile autograph at bottom. Backs are in black-and-white and feature biographical data, comprehensive career summary and complete minor and major league stats. There is a self-portrait and biographical sketch of the artist on back, as well. The premiums were given away at selected Pilots home games during their lone season in Seattle. They were later sold for 25 cents each in the concession stand. The unnumbered pictures are checklisted here in alphabetical order.

	NM	E	VG
Complete Set (8):	75.00	37.00	22.00
Common Player:	8.00	4.00	2.50
(1) Wayne Comer	8.00	4.00	2.50
(2) Tommy Harper	10.00	5.00	3.00
(3) Mike Hegan	8.00	4.00	2.50
(4) Jerry McNertney	8.00	4.00	2.50
(5) Don Mincher	8.00	4.00	2.50
(6) Ray Oyler	8.00	4.00	2.50
(7) Marty Pattin	8.00	4.00	2.50
(8) Diego Segui	8.00	4.00	2.50

1914 Lawrence Semon Postcards

Seven players are currently known in this series, but it's possible others remain to be reported. The approximately 3-1/2" x 5-1/2" postcards feature on their fronts either portrait or action drawings of star players by Lawrence Semon. A few biographical and career details are printed at bottom, which have allowed the assignment of 1914 as the year of issue. Backs are standard postcard style. The unnumbered cards are checklisted here alphabetically. Some cards have overprinted in red, "SKETCHED FROM LIFE BY LAWRENCE SEMON Cartoonist of the EVENING SUN."

	NM	E	VG
Common Player:	1,000	500.00	300.00
(1) George Burns	1,000	500.00	300.00
(2) Frank Chance	2,000	1,000	600.00
(3) Ty Cobb	19,000	9,000	5,600
(4) Walter Johnson	9,000	4,500	2,700
(5) Cornelius McGillicuddy (Connie Mack)	1,600	800.00	500.00
(6) Richard (Rube) Marquard	1,600	800.00	500.00
(7) John J. McGraw	1,600	800.00	500.00

1946-1947 Sensacion Premiums

 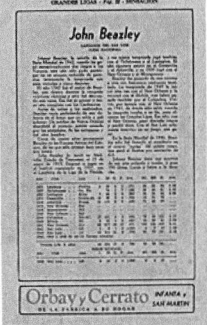

Two types of baseball premium pictures were issued by the magazine "Sensacion" during the winter league season of 1946-47. One series of 27 features Cuban stars (some of whom played in the Major Leagues), while a series of 11 Major League stars was also issued. Printed in color on newspaper stock, the pictures measure about 7-3/4" x 11". Fronts have large portraits or posed action photos with the player name in a fancy bottom border. Backs have lengthy career summaries and full stats, along with a small ad. The premiums were issued in magazines as well as in a complete album of each type. They are numbered according to the apparent order of their appearance.

	NM	E	VG
Complete Set, Cubans (27):	1,500	750.00	450.00
Complete Set, Major Leaguers (11):	600.00	300.00	175.00

	NM	E	VG
Common Cuban Player:	30.00	15.00	9.00
Common Major Leaguer:	45.00	22.50	13.50

Estrellas del Base Ball Cubano

	NM	E	VG
(1) Napoleon Reyes	45.00	22.50	13.50
(2) Fermin Guerra	30.00	15.00	9.00
(3) Gilberto Torres	30.00	15.00	9.00
(4) Martin Dihigo	750.00	375.00	225.00
(5) Lazaro Salazar	100.00	50.00	30.00
(6) Silvio Garcia	100.00	50.00	30.00
(7) Pollo Rodriguez	30.00	15.00	9.00
(8) Herberto Blanco	30.00	15.00	9.00
(9) Andres Fleitas	30.00	15.00	9.00
(10) Jorge J. Torres	30.00	15.00	9.00
(11) Salvador Hernandez	30.00	15.00	9.00
(12) Agapito Mayor	30.00	15.00	9.00
(13) Tomas de la Cruz	30.00	15.00	9.00
(14) Gilberto Valdivia	30.00	15.00	9.00
(15) Julio Moreno	30.00	15.00	9.00
(16) Regino Otero	30.00	15.00	9.00
(17) Claro Duany	50.00	25.00	15.00
(18) Pedro Jimenez	30.00	15.00	9.00
(19) Tony Castanos	30.00	15.00	9.00
(20) Alberto Hernandez	30.00	15.00	9.00
(21) Hector Rodriguez	40.00	20.00	12.00
(22) Carlos Blanco	30.00	15.00	9.00
(23) Roberto Ortiz	50.00	25.00	15.00
(24) Rene Monteagudo	30.00	15.00	9.00
(25) Pedro Pages	30.00	15.00	9.00
(26) Conrado Marrero	40.00	20.00	12.00
(27) Chino Hidalgo	30.00	15.00	9.00

Estrellas de las Grandes Ligas

	NM	E	VG
(1) Stan Musial	150.00	75.00	45.00
(2) Jim (Mickey) Vernon	50.00	25.00	15.00
(3) Dave Ferris	45.00	22.50	13.50
(4) Johnny Pesky	45.00	22.50	13.50
(5) Howie Pollett	45.00	22.50	13.50
(6) Ted Williams	200.00	100.00	60.00
(7) Johnny Hopp	45.00	22.50	13.50
(8) Dom DiMaggio	75.00	37.00	22.00
(9) Tex Hughson	45.00	22.50	13.50
(10) Johnny Beazley	45.00	22.00	13.50
(11) Tommy Holmes	45.00	22.50	13.50

1977 Sertoma Stars

This collectors' issue was produced by an Indianapolis service club. The 3" x 4" cards are printed in black on a textured yellow stock. Fronts have borderless player poses, many of which were lifted from earlier-issued cards. Backs have the Sertoma logo, set name and player name at top. Beneath a squiggly line is a business-card size ad for different members of the organization.

	NM	E	VG
Complete Set (24):	45.00	22.50	13.50
Common Player:	2.00	1.00	.60
(1) Hank Aaron	10.00	5.00	3.00
(2) Bob Allison	2.00	.75	.60
(3) Clete Boyer	2.00	.75	.60
(4) Don Buford	2.00	.75	.60
(5) Rod Carew	3.00	1.50	.90
(6) Rico Carty	2.00	.75	.60
(7) Roberto Clemente	15.00	7.50	4.50
(8) Jim Ray Hart	2.00	.75	.60
(9) Dave Johnson	2.00	.75	.60
(10) Harmon Killebrew	3.00	1.50	.90
(11) Mickey Mantle	20.00	10.00	6.00
(12) Juan Marichal	3.00	1.50	.90
(13) Bill Mazeroski	3.00	1.50	.90
(14) Joe Morgan	3.00	1.50	.90
(15) Phil Niekro	2.50	1.25	.70
(16) Tony Oliva	2.00	1.00	.60
(17) Gaylord Perry	2.50	1.25	.70
(18) Boog Powell	2.00	1.00	.60
(19) Brooks Robinson	3.50	1.75	1.00
(20) Frank Robinson	3.50	1.75	1.00
(21) John Roseboro	2.00	.75	.60
(22) Rusty Staub	2.00	.75	.60
(23) Joe Torre	2.00	1.00	.60
(24) Jim Wynn	2.00	.75	.60

1977 Sertoma Stars - Puzzle Backs

This collectors set was issued in conjunction with the Indianapolis Sports Collectors Convention in 1977. The set was sold for $3 with proceeds benefiting the local Sertoma (Service to Mankind) Club's charity works. Cards measure 2-3/4" x 4-1/8". A 2-1/2" black circle at center contains a black-and-white player photo. The background on front is yellow, with red and black printing. Backs are borderless and form an old Pittsburgh Pirates team photo puzzle. Sets were originally sold for $3.50.

	NM	E	VG
Complete Set (25):	75.00	37.50	22.50
Common Player:	2.00	1.00	.60
(1) Bernie Allen	2.00	1.00	.60
(2) Home Run Baker	2.00	1.00	.60
(3) Ted Beard	2.00	1.00	.60
(4) Don Buford	2.00	1.00	.60
(5) Eddie Cicotte	4.00	2.00	1.25
(6) Roberto Clemente	20.00	10.00	6.00
(7) Dom Dallessandro	2.00	1.00	.60
(8) Carl Erskine	2.00	1.00	.60
(9) Nellie Fox	6.00	3.00	1.75
(10) Lou Gehrig	20.00	10.00	6.00
(11) Joe Jackson	20.00	10.00	6.00
(12) Len Johnston	2.00	1.00	.60
(13) Benny Kauff	2.00	1.00	.60
(14) Dick Kenworthy	2.00	1.00	.60
(15) Harmon Killebrew	6.00	3.00	1.75
(16) "Lefty Bob" Logan	2.00	1.00	.60
(17) Willie Mays	15.00	7.50	4.50
(18) Satchel Paige	9.00	4.50	2.75
(19) Edd Roush	2.00	1.00	.60
(20) Chico Ruiz	2.00	1.00	.60
(21) Babe Ruth	20.00	10.00	6.00
(22) Herb Score	2.00	1.00	.60
(23) George Sisler	2.00	1.00	.60
(24) Buck Weaver	5.00	2.50	1.50
(25) Early Wynn	2.00	1.00	.60

1961 7-11

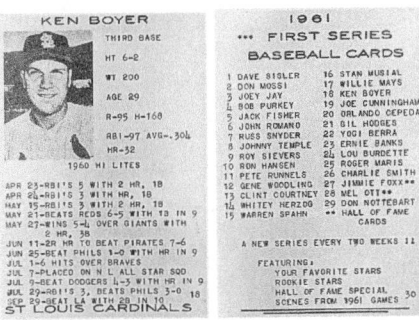

The first of 7-11's baseball card issues was a crude attempt which was abruptly halted. The checklist for the 30-card set indicated that it was the first of planned series to be issued two weeks apart. No follow-up to the first series was ever distributed. The 2-7/16" x 3-3/8" cards are printed on pink cardboard stock, with blank backs. Small black-and-white player portraits appear in the upper-left, with the player name at top, team name at bottom and card number in the lower-right corner. There are a few biographical bits and stats to the right of the photo, and several lines of 1960 season highlights below. The cards were sold seven for a nickel in vending machines.

	NM	E	VG
Complete Set (30):	3,000	1,500	900.00
Common Player:	75.00	35.00	20.00
1 Dave Sisler	75.00	35.00	20.00
2 Don Mossi	75.00	35.00	20.00
3 Joey Jay	75.00	35.00	20.00

4	Bob Purkey	75.00	35.00	20.00
5	Jack Fisher	75.00	35.00	20.00
6	John Romano	75.00	35.00	20.00
7	Russ Snyder	75.00	35.00	20.00
8	Johnny Temple	75.00	35.00	20.00
9	Roy Sievers	75.00	35.00	20.00
10	Ron Hansen	75.00	35.00	20.00
11	Pete Runnels	75.00	35.00	25.00
12	Gene Woodling	75.00	35.00	25.00
13	Clint Courtney	75.00	35.00	25.00
14	Whitey Herzog	75.00	35.00	25.00
15	Warren Spahn	150.00	75.00	45.00
16	Stan Musial	300.00	150.00	90.00
17	Willie Mays	500.00	250.00	150.00
18	Ken Boyer	75.00	35.00	20.00
19	Joe Cunningham	75.00	35.00	20.00
20	Orlando Cepeda	125.00	65.00	40.00
21	Gil Hodges	175.00	85.00	50.00
22	Yogi Berra	250.00	125.00	75.00
23	Ernie Banks	350.00	175.00	105.00
24	Lou Burdette	75.00	35.00	20.00
25	Roger Maris	350.00	175.00	105.00
26	Charlie Smith	75.00	35.00	20.00
27	Jimmie Foxx	75.00	35.00	20.00
28	Mel Ott	75.00	35.00	20.00
29	Don Nottebart	75.00	35.00	20.00
----	Checklist	75.00	35.00	20.00

1975 Shakey's Pizza West Coast Greats

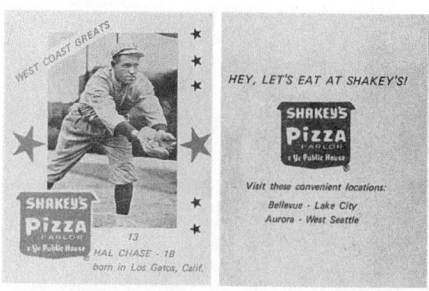

This collectors' issue was sponsored by Seattle area Shakey's Pizza restaurants in conjunction with the 1975 convention of the Washington State Sports Collectors Assn. Two thousand sets were produced featuring players who were born and/or played on the West Coast. The first 1,000 attendees at the convention were given a free sample of card #1, DiMaggio. Cards are 2-3/4" x about 3-5/8". Fronts have a black-and-white photo at center with black and red graphics. A large Shakey's logo is at lower-left. The card number, player name, position and connection to the West Coast are printed at lower-right. Backs are in red and white with the pizza chain's logo and a list of four Seattle-area locations.

		NM	E	VG
Complete Set (18):		30.00	15.00	9.00
Common Player:		4.00	2.00	1.25
1	Joe DiMaggio	15.00	7.50	4.50
2	Paul Waner	4.00	2.00	1.25
3	Lefty Gomez	4.00	2.00	1.25
4	Earl Averill	4.00	2.00	1.25
5	Ernie Lombardi	4.00	2.00	1.25
6	Joe Cronin	4.00	2.00	1.25
7	George Burns	4.00	2.00	1.25
8	Casey Stengel	5.00	2.50	1.50
9	Wahoo Sam Crawford	4.00	2.00	1.25
10	Ted Williams	12.50	6.25	3.75
11	Fred Hutchinson	4.00	2.00	1.25
12	Duke Snider	7.50	3.75	2.25
13	Hal Chase	4.00	2.00	1.25
14	Bobby Doerr	4.00	2.00	1.25
15	Arky Vaughan	4.00	2.00	1.25
16	Tony Lazzeri	4.00	2.00	1.25
17	Lefty O'Doul	4.00	2.00	1.25
18	Stan Hack	4.00	2.00	1.25

1976 Shakey's Pizza Hall of Fame

Between 1975-77 the Washington State Sports Collectors Assn. worked with the Shakey's pizza chain in the Seattle area to produce and distribute several sets of "old timers" cards. Generally one card from the set was given away to hobbyists attending the club's annual convention, with other cards available at the pizza places. Complete sets were also widely sold within the hobby. Interpretation of whether these are "legitimate" cards or a collector issue is up to each collector. The 1976 cards were issued in four series: Hall of Fame, Greatest Players, Immortals and All-Time Greats. The format was identical, with the (approximately) 2-1/2" x 3-1/2" cards featuring black-and-white player photos on front, surrounded by a red frame and bright blue border. Backs are in red, black and white with large Shakey ads at top and bottom. Also on

back are player biographies and career stats. The cards were issued in order of the players' induction into the Hall of Fame. All four series are skip-numbered. Cards of Sam Thompson and Robin Roberts were re-issued in Series 2 to correct errors.

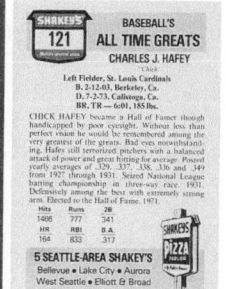

		NM	E	VG
Complete Set (160):		100.00	50.00	30.00
Complete Set, no coupons (158):		75.00	37.50	22.00
Common Player:		2.00	1.00	.60
Series 1 - Baseball's Hall of Fame		35.00	17.50	10.50
A	Earl Averill ($1 off pizza coupon on back; card show giveaway)	4.00	2.00	1.25
1	Ty Cobb	7.50	3.75	2.25
3	Walter Johnson	3.00	1.50	.90
12	Connie Mack	2.00	1.00	.60
18	Lou Gehrig	9.00	4.50	2.75
20	George Sisler	2.00	1.00	.60
21	Cap Anson	2.00	1.00	.60
36	Mike "King" Kelly	2.00	1.00	.60
41	Jack Chesbro	2.00	1.00	.60
50	Mickey Cochrane	2.00	1.00	.60
52	Lefty Grove	2.00	1.00	.60
54	Herb Pennock	2.00	1.00	.60
55	Pie Traynor	2.00	1.00	.60
56	Charlie Gehringer	2.00	1.00	.60
57	Three-Finger Brown	2.00	1.00	.60
58	Kid Nichols	2.00	1.00	.60
59	Jimmie Foxx	2.00	1.00	.60
64	Al Simmons	2.00	1.00	.60
72	Rabbit Maranville	2.00	1.00	.60
73	Bill Terry	2.00	1.00	.60
80	Joe Cronin	2.00	1.00	.60
83	Joe McCarthy	2.00	1.00	.60
86	Bill Hamilton	2.00	1.00	.60
88	Jackie Robinson	7.50	3.75	2.25
89	Bill McKechnie	2.00	1.00	.60
93	Sam Rice	2.00	1.00	.60
95	Luke Appling	2.00	1.00	.60
103	Ted Williams	7.50	3.75	2.25
104	Casey Stengel	2.00	1.00	.60
107	Lloyd Waner	2.00	1.00	.60
108	Joe Medwick	2.00	1.00	.60
115	Lou Boudreau	2.00	1.00	.60
122	Harry Hooper	2.00	1.00	.60
127	Yogi Berra	3.00	1.50	.90
129	Lefty Gomez	2.00	1.00	.60
131	Sandy Koufax	7.50	3.75	2.25
143	Jocko Conlan	2.00	1.00	.60
144	Whitey Ford	2.00	1.00	.60
146	Sam Thompson	2.00	1.00	.60
147	Earl Averill	2.00	1.00	.60
149	Billy Herman	2.00	1.00	.60
154	Cal Hubbard	2.00	1.00	.60
156	Fred Lindstrom	2.00	1.00	.60
157	Robin Roberts	2.00	1.00	.60
Series 2 - Baseball's Greatest Players		35.00	17.50	10.50
A	Earl Averill (Card show giveaway; coupon on back.)	2.00	1.00	.60
4	Christy Mathewson	3.00	1.50	.90
6	Nap Lajoie	2.00	1.00	.60
7	Tris Speaker	2.00	1.00	.60
9	Morgan Bulkeley	2.00	1.00	.60
10	Ban Johnson	2.00	1.00	.60
11	John McGraw	2.00	1.00	.60
14	Grover Alexander	2.00	1.00	.60
17	Eddie Collins	2.00	1.00	.60
19	Willie Keeler	2.00	1.00	.60
22	Charles Comiskey	2.00	1.00	.60
24	Buck Ewing	2.00	1.00	.60
31	Fred Clarke	2.00	1.00	.60
32	Jimmy Collins	2.00	1.00	.60
34	Hugh Duffy	2.00	1.00	.60
35	Hugh Jennings	2.00	1.00	.60
38	Wilbert Robinson	2.00	1.00	.60
40	Frank Chance	2.00	1.00	.60

42	John Evers	2.00	1.00	.60
43	Clark Griffith	2.00	1.00	.60
47	Joe Tinker	2.00	1.00	.60
51	Frank Frisch	2.00	1.00	.60
53	Carl Hubbell	2.00	1.00	.60
65	Ed Barrow	2.00	1.00	.60
66	Chief Bender	2.00	1.00	.60
67	Tommy Connolly	2.00	1.00	.60
74	Joe DiMaggio	12.50	6.25	3.75
75	Gabby Hartnett	2.00	1.00	.60
78	Home Run Baker	2.00	1.00	.60
81	Hank Greenberg	3.00	1.50	.90
87	Bob Feller	2.00	1.00	.60
90	Edd Roush	2.00	1.00	.60
109	Kiki Cuyler	2.00	1.00	.60
111	Roy Campanella	4.00	2.00	1.25
113	Stan Coveleski	2.00	1.00	.60
116	Earle Combs	2.00	1.00	.60
120	Jake Beckley	2.00	1.00	.60
125	Satchel Paige	4.00	2.00	1.25
128	Josh Gibson	3.00	1.50	.90
135	Roberto Clemente	10.00	5.00	3.00
141	Cool Papa Bell	2.00	1.00	.60
142	Jim Bottomley	2.00	1.00	.60
146	Sam Thompson	2.00	1.00	.60
150	Judy Johnson	2.00	1.00	.60
152	Oscar Charleston	2.00	1.00	.60
158	Robin Roberts	2.00	1.00	.60
Series 3 - Baseball's Immortals		25.00	12.50	7.50
5	Honus Wagner	3.50	1.75	1.00
13	George Wright	2.00	1.00	.60
15	Alexander Cartwright	2.00	1.00	.60
16	Henry Chadwick	2.00	1.00	.60
23	Candy Cummings	2.00	1.00	.60
25	Old Hoss Radbourne	2.00	1.00	.60
26	Al Spalding	2.00	1.00	.60
28	Judge Landis	2.00	1.00	.60
29	Roger Bresnahan	2.00	1.00	.60
30	Dan Brouthers	2.00	1.00	.60
33	Ed Delahanty	2.00	1.00	.60
37	Jim O'Rourke	2.00	1.00	.60
39	Jesse Burkett	2.00	1.00	.60
44	Tommy McCarthy	2.00	1.00	.60
45	Joe McGinnity	2.00	1.00	.60
46	Eddie Plank	2.00	1.00	.60
49	Ed Walsh	2.00	1.00	.60
61	Harry Heilmann	2.00	1.00	.60
68	Bill Klem	2.00	1.00	.60
70	Harry Wright	2.00	1.00	.60
85	Max Carey	2.00	1.00	.60
91	John Clarkson	2.00	1.00	.60
92	Elmer Flick	2.00	1.00	.60
96	Red Faber	2.00	1.00	.60
97	Burleigh Grimes	2.00	1.00	.60
98	Miller Huggins	2.00	1.00	.60
99	Tim Keefe	2.00	1.00	.60
101	Monte Ward	2.00	1.00	.60
102	Pud Galvin	2.00	1.00	.60
110	Goose Goslin	2.00	1.00	.60
114	Waite Hoyt	2.00	1.00	.60
117	Ford Frick	2.00	1.00	.60
118	Jesse Haines	2.00	1.00	.60
126	George Weiss	2.00	1.00	.60
130	William Harridge	2.00	1.00	.60
132	Buck Leonard	2.00	1.00	.60
133	Early Wynn	2.00	1.00	.60
136	Billy Evans	2.00	1.00	.60
137	Monte Irvin	2.00	1.00	.60
138	George Kelly	2.00	1.00	.60
140	Mickey Welch	2.00	1.00	.60
148	Bucky Harris	2.00	1.00	.60
151	Ralph Kiner	2.00	1.00	.60
153	Roger Connor	2.00	1.00	.60
Series 4 - Ball's All-Time Greats		20.00	10.00	6.00
2	Babe Ruth	12.50	6.25	3.75
8	Cy Young	2.50	1.25	.70
27	Rogers Hornsby	2.00	1.00	.60
48	Rube Waddell	2.00	1.00	.60
62	Paul Waner	2.00	1.00	.60
63	Dizzy Dean	2.50	1.25	.70
69	Bobby Wallace	2.00	1.00	.60
71	Bill Dickey	2.00	1.00	.60
77	Dazzy Vance	2.00	1.00	.60
79	Ray Schalk	2.00	1.00	.60
82	Sam Crawford	2.00	1.00	.60
84	Zack Wheat	2.00	1.00	.60
94	Eppa Rixey	2.00	1.00	.60
100	Heinie Manush	2.00	1.00	.60
105	Red Ruffing	2.00	1.00	.60
106	Branch Rickey	2.00	1.00	.60
112	Stan Musial	5.00	2.50	1.50
119	Dave Bancroft	2.00	1.00	.60
121	Chick Hafey	2.00	1.00	.60
123	Joe Kelley	2.00	1.00	.60
124	Rube Marquard	2.00	1.00	.60
134	Ross Youngs	2.00	1.00	.60

139	Warren Spahn	2.00	1.00	.60
145	Mickey Mantle	16.00	8.00	4.75
155	Bob Lemon	2.00	1.00	.60

1977 Shakey's All-Time Superstars

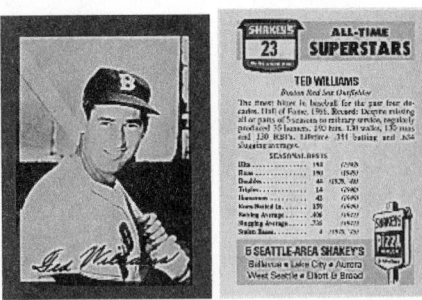

This set of baseball's all-time greatest (at least through the 1950s) was the final production of the Washington State Sports Collectors Assn. and local Shakey's restaurants. About 2-3/8" x 3", the cards feature black-and-white player photos at center with a red border around. A facsimile autograph appears in blue on the photo. Backs are similar to earlier Shakey's issues, with large logos for the pizza chain, player information and "Seasonal Bests" stats, all printed in red and black on white. Several special cards were produced for distribution at the 1977 annual convention and other venues.

		NM	E	VG
	Complete Set (28):	35.00	17.50	10.00
	Complete Set (25):	25.00	12.50	7.50
	Common Player:	2.00	1.00	.60
	Welcome to WSSCA Show Card (Collectibles collage.)	3.00	1.50	.90
A	Earl Averill	3.00	1.50	.90
B	John Mize ($1 coupon on back)	3.00	1.50	.90
C	Robert Lee Johnson	3.00	1.50	.90
1	Connie Mack	2.00	1.00	.60
2	John J. McGraw	2.00	1.00	.60
3	Denton T. (Cy) Young	4.00	2.00	1.25
4	Walter Johnson	4.00	2.00	1.25
5	G.C. Alexander	2.00	1.00	.60
6	Christy Mathewson	4.00	2.00	1.25
7	Lefty Grove	2.00	1.00	.60
8	Mickey Cochrane	2.00	1.00	.60
9	Bill Dickey	2.00	1.00	.60
10	Lou Gehrig	7.50	3.75	2.25
11	George Sisler	2.00	1.00	.60
12	Cap Anson	2.00	1.00	.60
13	Jimmie Foxx	2.00	1.00	.60
14	Rogers Hornsby	2.00	1.00	.60
15	Nap Lajoie	2.00	1.00	.60
16	Eddie Collins	2.00	1.00	.60
17	Pie Traynor	2.00	1.00	.60
18	Honus Wagner	4.00	2.00	1.25
19	Ty Cobb	7.50	3.75	2.25
20	Babe Ruth	10.00	5.00	3.00
21	Joe Jackson	10.00	5.00	3.00
22	Tris Speaker	2.00	1.00	.60
23	Ted Williams	6.00	3.00	1.75
24	Joe DiMaggio	7.50	3.75	2.25
25	Stan Musial	5.00	2.50	1.50
---	WSSCA Club Information Card	4.00	2.00	1.25

1952 Shelby Bicycles

The year of issue stated is conjectural, based on the familiar picture of Berra used for this promotional photo. The photo shows Yogi kneeling in full catcher's gear, except mask, ready to throw the ball; it is seen on his '50 Bowman card, among others. The blank-back, black-and-white photos

are 5" x 7" with a white border all around. Scripted at bottom is, "Ride Shelby / The Winner's Bike / Sincerely / Yogi Berra."

	NM	E	VG
Yogi Berra	150.00	75.00	45.00

1958-1959 Shillito's Boys' Shop Cincinnati Reds

This rare regional set was issued by a Cincinnati-area chain department store. The 2-1/2" x 3-1/2" black-and-white glossy cards are essentially a version of contemporary team-issued photos except for the presence (usually) on the otherwise blank back of a purple "SHILLITO'S / BOYS' SHOPS" rubber-stamp. Some cards have been seen wuthout the ad on back. The unnumbered pictures are listed here in alphabetical order.

		NM	E	VG
	Complete Set (23):	3,500	1,750	1,050
	Common Player:	200.00	100.00	60.00
(1)	Tom Acker	200.00	100.00	60.00
(2)	Ed Bailey	200.00	100.00	60.00
(3)	Gus Bell	200.00	100.00	60.00
(4)	John "Dutch" Dotterer	200.00	100.00	60.00
(5)	Walt Dropo	200.00	100.00	60.00
(6)	Del Ennis	200.00	100.00	60.00
(7)	Jay Hook	200.00	100.00	60.00
(8)	Hal Jeffcoat	200.00	100.00	60.00
(9)	Eddie Kasko	200.00	100.00	60.00
(10)	Brooks Lawrence	200.00	100.00	60.00
(11)	Jerry Lynch	200.00	100.00	60.00
(12)	Roy McMillan	200.00	100.00	60.00
(13)	Eddie Miksis	200.00	100.00	60.00
(14)	Don Newcombe	230.00	115.00	69.00
(15)	Joe Nuxhall	250.00	125.00	75.00
(16)	Jim O'Toole	200.00	100.00	60.00
(17)	Vada Pinson	250.00	125.00	75.00
(18)	Bob Purkey	200.00	100.00	60.00
(19)	Frank Robinson	500.00	250.00	150.00
(20)	Frank Thomas	200.00	100.00	60.00
(21)	Johnny Temple	200.00	100.00	60.00
(22)	Bob Thurman	200.00	100.00	60.00
(23)	Pete Whisenant	200.00	100.00	60.00

1974 Shillito's Pete Rose

Probably issued in conjunction with an autograph-signing appearance at the Cincinnati department store, this glossy black-and-white, blank-back photo measures 5-1/2" x 8". The autograph on the example shown is genuine, the photo does not have a facsimile signature.

	NM	E	VG
Pete Rose	150.00	75.00	45.00

1976 Shillito's Kahn's Reds Clubhouse

Though the format for each photo differs, this series of Reds player photos was issued under the sponsorship of the Shillito's department store and Kahn's meats. In about 5" x 7-3/16" format, the blank-back photos are black-and-white with at least one (Bench) having red highlights. The pictures

were given out at player autograph appearances at various Shillito's locations between June 21 and August 18. Youngsters enrolled in the club received a membership card, probably entitling them to an autograph at each event.

		NM	E	VG
	Common Player:			
(1)	Johnny Bench (Kenwood Plaza)	100.00	50.00	30.00
(2)	Dave Concepcion (No sponsor.)	30.00	15.00	9.00
(3)	Doug Flynn ((Kahn's - WLW Radio))	12.00	6.00	3.50
(4)	George Foster (Three sponsors listed.)	25.00	12.50	7.50
(5)	Mike Lum (four sponsors.)	12.00	6.00	3.50
(6)	Pete Rose (Shillito's)	100.00	50.00	30.00
---	Membership Card	10.00	5.00	3.00

1962 Shirriff Coins

This is a Canadian version of the better-known Salada-Junket plastic player coins issued in the U.S. Backs specify an issue of 200; 21 of the players from the Salada set were not issued by Shirriff. Because the Canadian coins were produced after the U.S. version they are not found with all the variations known in Salada, nor the differing levels of scarcity. Shirriff coins were packed in bags of potato chips, with each coin sealed in a clear cellophane wrapper. Although the Canadian coins are much scarcer than the U.S., significantly less demand keeps prices lower, as well.

		NM	E	VG
	Complete Set (200):	1,600	800.00	525.00
	Common Player:	6.00	3.00	1.75
1	Jim Gentile	7.00	3.50	2.00
2	NOT ISSUED(Bill Pierce)			
3	Chico Fernandez (Light blue piping.)	6.00	3.00	1.75
4	NOT ISSUED(Tom Brewer)			
5	Woody Held	6.00	3.00	1.75
6	NOT ISSUED(Ray Herbert)			
7	Ken Aspromonte	6.00	3.00	1.75
8	Whitey Ford	40.00	20.00	12.00
9	Jim Lemon	6.00	3.00	1.75
10	Billy Klaus	6.00	3.00	1.75
11	NOT ISSUED(Steve Barber)			
12	Nellie Fox	25.00	12.50	7.50
13	Jim Bunning	25.00	12.50	7.50
14	Frank Malzone	6.00	3.00	1.75
15	Tito Francona	6.00	3.00	1.75
16	Bobby Del Greco	6.00	3.00	1.75
17	Steve Bilko	6.00	3.00	1.75
18	NOT ISSUED(Tony Kubek)			
19	Earl Battey	6.00	3.00	1.75
20	Chuck Cottier	6.00	3.00	1.75
21	Willie Tasby	6.00	3.00	1.75
22	Bob Allison	7.00	3.50	2.00
23	Roger Maris	40.00	20.00	12.00
24	Earl Averill	6.00	3.00	1.75
25	Jerry Lumpe	6.00	3.00	1.75
26	NOT ISSUED(Jim Grant)			
27	Carl Yastrzemski	50.00	25.00	15.00
28	Rocky Colavito	20.00	10.00	6.00
29	Al Smith	6.00	3.00	1.75
30	NOT ISSUED(Jim Busby)			
31	Dick Howser	6.00	3.00	1.75
32	Jim Perry	6.00	3.00	1.75
33	Yogi Berra	50.00	25.00	15.00
34	Ken Hamlin	6.00	3.00	1.75
35	Dale Long	6.00	3.00	1.75

#	Player	NM	EX	VG
36	Harmon Killebrew	35.00	17.50	10.50
37	Dick Brown	6.00	3.00	1.75
38	Gary Geiger	6.00	3.00	1.75
39	Minnie Minoso	9.00	4.50	2.75
40	Brooks Robinson	35.00	17.50	10.50
41	Mickey Mantle	180.00	90.00	54.00
42	Bennie Daniels	6.00	3.00	1.75
43	Billy Martin	15.00	7.50	4.50
44	Vic Power	7.00	3.50	2.00
45	Joe Pignatano	6.00	3.00	1.75
46	Ryne Duren	7.00	3.50	2.00
47	Pete Runnels	6.00	3.00	1.75
48	Dick Williams	6.00	3.00	1.75
49	Jim Landis	6.00	3.00	1.75
50	Steve Boros	6.00	3.00	1.75
51	Zoilo Versalles	7.00	3.50	2.00
52	Johnny Temple	6.00	3.00	1.75
53	Jackie Brandt	6.00	3.00	1.75
54	Joe McClain	6.00	3.00	1.75
55	Sherman Lollar	6.00	3.00	1.75
56	Gene Stephens	6.00	3.00	1.75
57	Leon Wagner	6.00	3.00	1.75
58	Frank Lary	6.00	3.00	1.75
59	Bill Skowron	12.00	6.00	3.50
60	NOT ISSUED(Vic Wertz)			
61	Willie Kirkland	6.00	3.00	1.75
62	Leo Posada	6.00	3.00	1.75
63	Albie Pearson	7.00	3.50	2.00
64	Bobby Richardson	15.00	7.50	4.50
65	Marv Breeding	6.00	3.00	1.75
66	NOT ISSUED(Roy Sievers)			
67	Al Kaline	35.00	17.50	10.50
68	Don Buddin	6.00	3.00	1.75
69	Lenny Green	6.00	3.00	1.75
70	NOT ISSUED(Gene Green)			
71	Luis Aparicio	25.00	12.50	7.50
72	Norm Cash	12.00	6.00	3.50
73	NOT ISSUED(Jackie Jensen)			
74	Bubba Phillips	6.00	3.00	1.75
75	Jim Archer	6.00	3.00	1.75
76	Ken Hunt	6.00	3.00	1.75
77	Ralph Terry	6.00	3.00	1.75
78	Camilo Pascual	6.00	3.00	1.75
79	NOT ISSUED(Marty Keough)			
80	Cletis Boyer	9.00	4.50	2.75
81	Jim Pagliaroni	6.00	3.00	1.75
82	Gene Leek	6.00	3.00	1.75
83	Jake Wood	6.00	3.00	1.75
84	NOT ISSUED(Coot Veal)			
85	Norm Siebern	6.00	3.00	1.75
86	Andy Carey	6.00	3.00	1.75
87	Bill Tuttle	6.00	3.00	1.75
88	Jimmy Piersall	6.00	3.00	1.75
89	NOT ISSUED(Ron Hansen)			
90	Chuck Stobbs	6.00	3.00	1.75
91	Ken McBride	6.00	3.00	1.75
92	Bill Bruton	6.00	3.00	1.75
93	Gus Triandos	6.00	3.00	1.75
94	John Romano	6.00	3.00	1.75
95	Elston Howard	12.00	6.00	3.50
96	Gene Woodling	6.00	3.00	1.75
97	Early Wynn	20.00	10.00	6.00
98	Milt Pappas	6.00	3.00	1.75
99	Bill Monbouquette	6.00	3.00	1.75
100	Wayne Causey	6.00	3.00	1.75
101	Don Elston	6.00	3.00	1.75
102	Charlie Neal	6.00	3.00	1.75
103	Don Blasingame	6.00	3.00	1.75
104	NOT ISSUED(Frank Thomas)			
105	Wes Covington	6.00	3.00	1.75
106	Chuck Hiller	6.00	3.00	1.75
107	Don Hoak	6.00	3.00	1.75
108	Bob Lillis	6.00	3.00	1.75
109	Sandy Koufax	65.00	32.00	19.50
110	Gordy Coleman	6.00	3.00	1.75
111	Ed Matthews (Mathews)	30.00	15.00	9.00
112	Art Mahaffey	6.00	3.00	1.75
113	Ed Bailey	6.00	3.00	1.75
114	Smoky Burgess	7.00	3.50	2.00
115	Bill White	7.00	3.50	2.00
116	NOT ISSUED(Ed Bouchee)			
117	Bob Buhl	6.00	3.00	1.75
118	Vada Pinson	7.00	3.50	2.00
119	Carl Sawatski	6.00	3.00	1.75
120	Dick Stuart	7.00	3.50	2.00
121	NOT ISSUED(Harvey Kuenn)			
122	Pancho Herrera	6.00	3.00	1.75
123	Don Zimmer	7.00	3.50	2.00
124	Wally Moon	7.00	3.50	2.00
125	Joe Adcock	6.00	3.00	1.75
126	Joey Jay	6.00	3.00	1.75
127	Maury Wills	12.00	6.00	3.50
128	George Altman	6.00	3.00	1.75
129	John Buzhardt	6.00	3.00	1.75
130	Felipe Alou	7.00	3.50	2.00
131	Bill Mazeroski	25.00	12.50	7.50
132	Ernie Broglio	6.00	3.00	1.75
133	John Roseboro	7.00	3.50	2.00
134	Mike McCormick	6.00	3.00	1.75
135	Chuck Smith	6.00	3.00	1.75
136	Ron Santo	12.00	6.00	3.50
137	Gene Freese	6.00	3.00	1.75
138	Dick Groat	7.00	3.50	2.00
139	Curt Flood	7.00	3.50	2.00
140	Frank Bolling	6.00	3.00	1.75
141	Clay Dalrymple	6.00	3.00	1.75
142	Willie McCovey	30.00	15.00	9.00
143	Bob Skinner	6.00	3.00	1.75
144	Lindy McDaniel	6.00	3.00	1.75
145	Glen Hobbie	6.00	3.00	1.75
146	Gil Hodges	20.00	10.00	6.00
147	Eddie Kasko	6.00	3.00	1.75
148	NOT ISSUED(Gino Cimoli)			
149	Willie Mays	75.00	37.00	22.00
150	Roberto Clemente	90.00	45.00	27.00
151	Red Schoendienst	25.00	12.50	7.50
152	Joe Torre	9.00	4.50	2.75
153	Bob Purkey	6.00	3.00	1.75
154	Tommy Davis	7.50	3.75	2.25
155	Andre Rogers	6.00	3.00	1.75
156	Tony Taylor	6.00	3.00	1.75
157	Bob Friend	6.00	3.00	1.75
158	Gus Bell	6.00	3.00	1.75
159	Roy McMillan	6.00	3.00	1.75
160	Carl Warwick	6.00	3.00	1.75
161	Willie Davis	6.00	3.00	1.75
162	NOT ISSUED(Sam Jones)			
163	Ruben Amaro	6.00	3.00	1.75
164	Sam Taylor	6.00	3.00	1.75
165	Frank Robinson	35.00	17.50	10.50
166	Lou Burdette	6.00	3.00	1.75
167	Ken Boyer	10.00	5.00	3.00
168	Bill Virdon	6.00	3.00	1.75
169	Jim Davenport	6.00	3.00	1.75
170	Don Demeter	6.00	3.00	1.75
171	NOT ISSUED(Richie Ashburn)			
172	John Podres	7.50	3.75	2.25
173	Joe Cunningham	6.00	3.00	1.75
174	ElRoy Face	6.00	3.00	1.75
175	Orlando Cepeda	25.00	12.50	7.50
176	Bobby Gene Smith	6.00	3.00	1.75
177	Ernie Banks	50.00	25.00	15.00
178	Daryl Spencer	6.00	3.00	1.75
179	NOT ISSUED(Bob Schmidt)			
180	Hank Aaron	75.00	37.00	22.00
181	Hobie Landrith	6.00	3.00	1.75
182	Ed Bressoud	6.00	3.00	1.75
183	Felix Mantilla	6.00	3.00	1.75
184	Dick Farrell	6.00	3.00	1.75
185	Bob Miller	6.00	3.00	1.75
186	Don Taussig	6.00	3.00	1.75
187	Pumpsie Green	6.00	3.00	1.75
188	Bobby Shantz	7.50	3.75	2.25
189	Roger Craig	6.00	3.00	1.75
190	Hal Smith	6.00	3.00	1.75
191	John Edwards	6.00	3.00	1.75
192	John DeMerit	6.00	3.00	1.75
193	Joe Amalfitano	6.00	3.00	1.75
194	Norm Larker	6.00	3.00	1.75
195	Al Heist	6.00	3.00	1.75
196	Al Spangler	6.00	3.00	1.75
197	Alex Grammas	6.00	3.00	1.75
198	Gerry Lynch	6.00	3.00	1.75
199	Jim McKnight	6.00	3.00	1.75
200	Jose Pagen (Pagan)	6.00	3.00	1.75
201	Junior Gilliam	7.50	3.75	2.25
202	Art Ditmar	6.00	3.00	1.75
203	Pete Daley	6.00	3.00	1.75
204	Johnny Callison	6.00	3.00	1.75
205	Stu Miller	6.00	3.00	1.75
206	Russ Snyder	6.00	3.00	1.75
207	Billy Williams	25.00	12.50	7.50
208	Walter Bond	6.00	3.00	1.75
209	Joe Koppe	6.00	3.00	1.75
210	Don Schwall	6.00	3.00	1.75
211	Billy Gardner	6.00	3.00	1.75
212	Chuck Estrada	6.00	3.00	1.75
213	Gary Bell	6.00	3.00	1.75
214	Floyd Robinson	6.00	3.00	1.75
215	Duke Snider	35.00	17.50	10.50
216	Lee Maye	6.00	3.00	1.75
217	Howie Bedell	6.00	3.00	1.75
218	Bob Will	6.00	3.00	1.75
219	Dallas Green	7.50	3.75	2.25
220	Carroll Hardy	6.00	3.00	1.75
221	Danny O'Connell	6.00	3.00	1.75

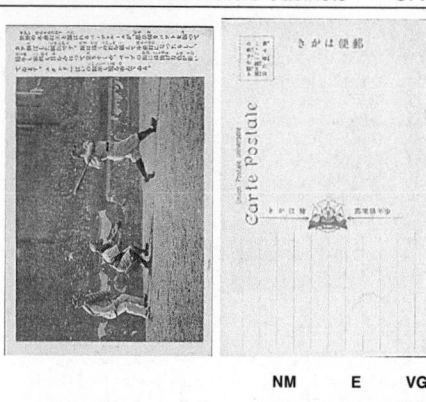

	NM	E	VG
Babe Ruth	800.00	400.00	240.00

1921 Shotwell

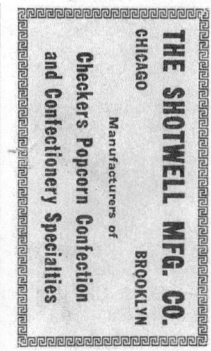

It is not known to what extent this issue actually parallels the 1921 American Caramel Co. Series of 80 (E121), with which it shares a format. The cards are printed in black-and-white, approximately 2" x 3-1/4". Since only two cards with this back advertising are known, each currently unique, it is possible they were part of a prototype printing intended to sell the concept of baseball card inserts to Shotwell Mfg. Co., a Chicago-based confectionery company that competed with Cracker Jack. Cards are listed here in conformity with the numbering assigned to 1921 American Caramel Series of 80.

	NM	EX	VG
Common Player:	2,000	1,000	600.00
(48) Wm. C. Jacobson	2,000	1,000	600.00

(86a) Babe Ruth PSA-graded Fair, auctioned for $6,143 in 8/09

1889 G. Waldon Smith Boston Beaneaters Cabinets

Boston photographer G. Waldon Smith immortalized the players of the 1889 Nation League club ("Beaneaters") in this series of 4-1/4" x 6-1/2" cabinet cards. Each sepia toned photo is a capless, chest-up portrait. The studio's name and location are printed in red in the bottom border. The players are not identified on the cards, though most examples have the name added by hand on either front or back. The cards from the 1889 N.L. series can be distinguished from the studio's 1890 issue of Players League subjects by the plain typography used for the studio address in the lower-right; the 1890 cards have a more ornate presentation of that information. It is not known if the checklist here is complete; gaps have been left in the assigned numbering for possible future additions.

1929 Shonen Club Babe Ruth Postcard

This card, which the Japanese inscription describes as picturing Babe Ruth hitting his first home run of 1926, was part of a multi-sport premium issue by the Japanese magazine Shonen Kubulu ("Youth Club"). The front has a colorized black-and-white photo, with blue inscriptions at right. Back is in blue with standard international postcard indicia.

		NM	E	VG
Common Player:		4,000	2,000	1,200
(1)	Charlie Bennett	3,600	1,800	1,080
(2)	Tom Brown	4,000	2,000	1,200
(3)	John Clarkson	8,000	4,000	2,400
(5)	Harry Ganzel	4,000	2,000	1,200
(7)	Kid Madden	3,600	1,800	1,080
(8)	Billy Nash	4,000	2,000	1,200
(10)	Old Hoss Radbourn	8,000	4,000	2,400
(11)	Pop Smith	4,000	2,000	1,200
(13)	The Boston Base Ball Club (Team photo, 21" x 18")	15,000	7,500	4,500

1890 G. Waldon Smith Players League Cabinets

Boston photographer G. Waldon Smith immortalized the players of the 1890 Players League Boston Red Stockings and Brooklyn Wonders in this series of 4-1/4" x 6-1/2" cabinet cards. Each sepia toned photo is a (usually) capless and mustachioed chest-up portrait. The studio's name and location are printed in the bottom border. The players are not identified on the cards, though most examples have the name added by hand on either front or back. The cards from the 1890 P.L. series can be distinguished from the studio's 1889 issue of Boston national League subjects by the ornate typography used for the studio address in the lower-right; the 1889 cards have a more austere presentation of that information. It is not known if the checklist here is complete; gaps have been left in the assigned numbering for possible future additions.

		NM	E	VG
Common Player:		4,500	2,250	1,350
BOSTON RED STOCKINGS				
BROOKLYN WONDERS				
(2)	Ben Conroy	4,500	2,250	1,350
(2)	Tom Brown	4,500	2,250	1,350
BROOKLYN WONDERS				
(2)	Ben Conroy	4,500	2,250	1,350
(3)	Paul Cook	4,500	2,250	1,350
(4)	Con Dailey	4,500	2,250	1,350
(6)	Jackie Hayes	4,500	2,250	1,350
(7)	Bill Joyce	4,500	2,250	1,350
(8)	Tom Kinslow	4,500	2,250	1,350
(16)	Gus Weyhing	4,500	2,250	1,350
(3)	Dan Brouthers	7,500	3,750	2,250
BROOKLYN WONDERS				
(3)	Paul Cook	4,500	2,250	1,350
(4)	Con Dailey	4,500	2,250	1,350
(5)	Bill Daley	4,500	2,250	1,350
BROOKLYN WONDERS				
(6)	Jackie Hayes	4,500	2,250	1,350
(7)	Ad Gumbert	4,500	2,250	1,350
BROOKLYN WONDERS				
(7)	Bill Joyce	4,500	2,250	1,350
(8)	Arthur Irwin	4,500	2,250	1,350
BROOKLYN WONDERS				
(8)	Tom Kinslow	4,500	2,250	1,350
(9)	Dick Johnston	4,500	2,250	1,350
(15)	Joe Quinn	4,500	2,250	1,350
BROOKLYN WONDERS				
(16)	Gus Weyhing	4,500	2,250	1,350
(16)	Irv Ray	4,500	2,250	1,350
(17)	Hardy Richardson	4,500	2,250	1,350
(19)	Harry Stovey	4,500	2,250	1,350
(20)	Boston Base Ball Club / Players League (Team photo, 22" x 18")	20,000	10,000	6,000

1904 G. Waldon Smith Cabinets

Following a move down Tremont St. to No. 164A, this Boston photographer was still producing baseball player cabinet photos. Like his earlier photos, the circa 1904 pieces have black-and-white photographs mounted on stiff 4-1/4" x 6-1/2" cardboard backings. The only currently known picture in this series is a full-length portrait of Kip Selbach. Others almost certainly exist.

	NM	E	VG
	NM	E	VG
Kip Selbach	2,500	1,250	750.00

1909 W.W. Smith Postcards

Only two subjects are known in this series of postcards issued contemporary with the 1909 World Series between the Tigers and Pirates, though it is possible a card of Ty Cobb might have also been issued. The 3-1/2" x 5-1/2" black-and-white cards have pencil portraits by W.W. Smith. Backs have standard postcard markings.

THE MIGHTY HONUS

		NM	E	VG
Complete Set (2):		7,500	3,750	2,250
(1)	The Mighty Honus(Honus Wagner)	3,000	1,500	900.00
(2)	Two of a Kind(Ty Cobb, Honus Wagner)	6,000	3,000	1,800

1957 Sohio Gas Indians/Reds

In 1957 Sohio (Standard Oil of Ohio) gas stations in Ohio issued sets of Cleveland Indians and Cincinnati Reds photocards and team albums. The blank-backed cards are 5" x 7" and printed in black-and-white with one or more perforated edges. The cards have a facsimile autograph as the only identification. The unnumbered cards are checklisted here alphabetically within team.

		NM	E	VG
Complete Set (36):		450.00	225.00	135.00
Common Player:		10.00	5.00	3.00
Cleveland Indians				
Complete Set (18):		250.00	125.00	75.00
CLEVELAND INDIANS				
(2)	Jim Busby	10.00	5.00	3.00
(3)	Chico Carrasquel	10.00	5.00	3.00
(4)	Rocky Colavito	75.00	37.00	22.00
(5)	Mike Garcia	10.00	5.00	3.00
(6)	Jim Hegan	10.00	5.00	3.00
(7)	Bob Lemon	20.00	10.00	6.00
(8)	Roger Maris	150.00	75.00	45.00
(9)	Don Mossi	10.00	5.00	3.00
(18)	Early Wynn	20.00	10.00	6.00
----	Cleveland Indians Album	60.00	30.00	18.00
CINCINNATI REDS				
Complete Set (18):		225.00	115.00	70.00
(2)	Gus Bell	10.00	5.00	3.00
(3)	Rocky Bridges	10.00	5.00	3.00
(4)	Smoky Burgess	10.00	5.00	3.00
(5)	Hersh Freeman	10.00	5.00	3.00
(6)	Alex Grammas	10.00	5.00	3.00
(7)	Don Gross	10.00	5.00	3.00
(8)	Warren Hacker	10.00	5.00	3.00
(9)	Don Hoak	10.00	5.00	3.00
(18)	Johnny Temple	10.00	5.00	3.00
----	Cincinnati Redlegs Album	60.00	30.00	18.00
(2)	Gus Bell	10.00	5.00	3.00
CLEVELAND INDIANS				
(2)	Jim Busby	10.00	5.00	3.00
(3)	Chico Carrasquel	10.00	5.00	3.00
CINCINNATI REDS				
(3)	Rocky Bridges	10.00	5.00	3.00
CLEVELAND INDIANS				
(4)	Rocky Colavito	75.00	37.00	22.00
CINCINNATI REDS				
(4)	Smoky Burgess	10.00	5.00	3.00
(5)	Hersh Freeman	10.00	5.00	3.00
CLEVELAND INDIANS				

		NM	E	VG
(5)	Mike Garcia	10.00	5.00	3.00
CINCINNATI REDS				
(6)	Alex Grammas	10.00	5.00	3.00
CLEVELAND INDIANS				
(6)	Jim Hegan	10.00	5.00	3.00
(7)	Bob Lemon	20.00	10.00	6.00
CINCINNATI REDS				
(7)	Don Gross	10.00	5.00	3.00
CLEVELAND INDIANS				
(8)	Roger Maris	150.00	75.00	45.00
CINCINNATI REDS				
(8)	Warren Hacker	10.00	5.00	3.00
(9)	Don Hoak	10.00	5.00	3.00
CLEVELAND INDIANS				
(9)	Don Mossi	10.00	5.00	3.00
(18)	Early Wynn	20.00	10.00	6.00
CINCINNATI REDS				
(18)	Johnny Temple	10.00	5.00	3.00

1969 Solon Kansas City Royals

LOU PINIELLA
Outfielder

This collectors' issue is believed to have originated with Illinois hobbyist Bob Solon. The black-and-white, blank-back cards feature members of the expansion Royals. The border beneath the posed photos features a team logo and player identification at bottom. Cards measure 2-1/8" x 3-5/8". The checklist here is arranged alphabetically, as the cards are unnumbered.

		NM	E	VG
Complete Set (15):		16.00	8.00	4.75
Common Player:		2.00	1.00	.60
(1)	Jerry Adair	2.00	1.00	.60
(2)	Wally Bunker	2.00	1.00	.60
(3)	Moe Drabowsky	3.00	1.50	.90
(4)	Dick Drago	2.00	1.00	.60
(5)	Joe Foy	2.00	1.00	.60
(6)	Joe Gordon	2.00	1.00	.60
(7)	Chuck Harrison	2.00	1.00	.60
(8)	Mike Hedlund	2.00	1.00	.60
(9)	Jack Hernandez	2.00	1.00	.60
(10)	Pat Kelly	2.00	1.00	.60
(11)	Roger Nelson	2.00	1.00	.60
(12)	Bob Oliver	2.00	1.00	.60
(13)	Lou Piniella	6.00	3.00	1.75
(14)	Ellie Rodriguez	2.00	1.00	.60
(15)	Dave Wickersham	2.00	1.00	.60

1905 Souvenir Post Card Shop of Cleveland

Formal portraits of the 1905 Cleveland Naps are featured in this set of black-and-white postcards. The 3-1/4" x 5-1/2"

cards have a wide white border at bottom which carries the legend, "SOUVENIR POST CARD SHOP OF CLEVELAND." The player name is in white at the bottom of the photo. Backs have postage rate information and a notice, "NOTHING BUT ADDRESS ON THIS SIDE."

		NM	E	VG
Complete Set (19):		16,500	8,250	5,000
Common Player:		950.00	475.00	285.00
(1)	Harry Bay	950.00	475.00	285.00
(2)	Harry Bemis	950.00	475.00	285.00
(3)	Bill Bernhard	950.00	475.00	285.00
(4)	Bill Bradley	950.00	475.00	285.00
(5)	Fred Buelow	950.00	475.00	285.00
(6)	Charles C. Carr	950.00	475.00	285.00
(7)	Frank Donahue	950.00	475.00	285.00
(8)	Elmer Flick	1,425	710.00	425.00
(9)	Otto Hess	950.00	475.00	285.00
(10)	Jay Jackson	950.00	475.00	285.00
(11)	Addie Joss	2,750	1,375	825.00
(12)	Nick Kahl	950.00	475.00	285.00
(13)	Napoleon Lajoie	2,000	1,000	600.00
(14)	Earl Moore	950.00	475.00	285.00
(15)	Robert Rhoads	950.00	475.00	285.00
(16)	George Stovall	950.00	475.00	285.00
(17)	Terry Turner	950.00	475.00	285.00
(18)	Ernest Vinson	950.00	475.00	285.00
(19)	Team Portraits Composite	1,500	750.00	450.00

1909-11 Sovereign Cigarettes

Premiums shown are for common-player cards. Hall of Famers or other high-demand cards generally realize little or no premium with Sovereign back. On T205s, the backs are printed in green.

PREMIUMS
T205: 1.5-2X
T206 150 Subjects: 1-1.5X
T206 350 Subjects: 1.5X
T206 460 Subjects: 1.5-2X

(See T205, T206 for checklists and base card values.)

1949 Spalding Joe DiMaggio Glove Premium Photos

The attributed date is only approximate. Lucky youngsters who received a Spalding Joe DiMaggio fielder's glove also got a pair of 8" x 10" black-and-white posed action photos of the Yankee Clipper. Each blank-back, borderless photo has a facsimile autograph.

		NM	E	VG
(1)	Joe DiMaggio (No ball in photo.)	125.00	65.00	40.00
(2)	Joe DiMaggio (Ball in photo.)	125.00	65.00	40.00

1950s-70s Spalding Advisory Staff Photos

Advisory staff photos were a promotional item which debuted in the early 1950s, flourished in the 1960s and died in the early 1970s. Generally 8" x 10" (sometimes a little larger), these black-and-white (a few later were color) glossy photos picture players who had contracted with a major baseball equipment company to endorse and use their product. Usually the product - most often a glove - was prominently displayed in the photo. The pictures were often displayed in the windows of sporting goods stores or the walls of sports departments and were sometimes made available to customers. Because the companies tended to stick with players over the years, some photos were reissued, sometimes with and sometimes without a change of team, pose or typography. Spalding staff photos of the era are checklisted here in alphabetical order. Team designation and pose description is given for each known picture. The photos are checklisted here in alphabetical order. It is unlikely this list is complete. Several arrangements of typography in the bottom border are seen for Spalding advisory staff pictures.

		NM	E	VG
Common Player:		12.00	6.00	3.50
(1)	Richie Allen (Phillies, batting helmet.)	20.00	10.00	6.00
(2)	Gene Alley (Pirates, upper body.)	12.00	6.00	3.50
(3)	Mike Andrews (Red Sox, upper body.)	12.00	6.00	3.50
(4)	Bob Aspromonte (Dodgers, upper body.)	12.00	6.00	3.50
(5)	Sal Bando (A's, upper body.)	12.00	6.00	3.50
(7)	Steve Barber (Orioles, chest-to-cap.)	12.00	6.00	3.50
(8)	John Bateman (Colt .45s, upper body.)	12.00	6.00	3.50
(9)	Yogi Berra (Yankees, batting.)	30.00	15.00	9.00
(10)	Yogi Berra (Mets, upper body.)	30.00	15.00	9.00
(11)	Don Bessent (Brooklyn, follow-through.)	20.00	10.00	6.00
(12a)	Frank Bolling (Tigers, fielding.)	15.00	7.50	4.50
(12b)	Frank Bolling (Braves, chest up.)	15.00	7.50	4.50
(13)	Jim Bouton (Yankees, upper body.)	15.00	7.50	4.50
(14)	Jim Bunning (Phillies, upper body.)	20.00	10.00	6.00
(16)	John Callison (Phillies, batson shoulder.)	12.00	6.00	3.50
(17)	Rocky Colavito (Tigers, batting.)	25.00	12.50	7.50
(18)	Roger Craig (Brooklyn, follow-through.)	15.00	7.50	4.50
(19)	Clay Dalrymple (Phillies, upper body.)	12.00	6.00	3.50
(20)	Alvin Dark (Cardinals, batting follow-through.)	20.00	10.00	6.00
(21)	Don Drysdale (Dodgers, pitching follow-through.)	25.00	12.50	7.50
(22)	Sam Esposito (White Sox, hands on knees.)	12.00	6.00	3.50
(23)	Ron Fairly (Dodgers, upper body.)	12.00	6.00	3.50
(24)	Dick Farrell (Phillies, follow-through.)	25.00	12.50	7.50
(25)	Whitey Ford (Yankees, hands over head. Picture frame.)	30.00	15.00	9.00
(26)	Jim Fregosi (L.A. Angels, upper body.)	15.00	7.50	4.50
(27)	Jim Fregosi (California Angels, upper body, looking front.)	15.00	7.50	4.50
(28)	Jim Fregosi (California Angels, upper body, looking right.)	15.00	7.50	4.50
(29)	Jim Fregosi (Angels, green borders, b/w portrait.)	15.00	7.50	4.50
(30)	Bob Gibson (Color, stretch position.)	25.00	12.50	7.50
(33)	Tom Haller (Giants, catching crouch.)	12.00	6.00	3.50
(34)	Richie Hebner (Pirates, full-length.)	12.00	6.00	3.50
(35)	Mike Hegan (Brewers, upper body.)	12.00	6.00	3.50
(36)	Jim Hickman (Mets, upper body.)	12.00	6.00	3.50
(37)	Ken Hunt (Reds, follow-through.)	20.00	10.00	6.00
(38)	Jerry Koosman (Mets, ready to pitch.)	15.00	7.50	4.50

		NM	E	VG
(39)	Jerry Koosman (Mets, upper body.)	15.00	7.50	4.50
(40)	Don Larsen (Yankees, follow-through.)	25.00	12.50	7.50
(41)	Charlie Lau (Braves, upper body.)	15.00	7.50	4.50
(42)	Mickey Lolich (Tigers, upper body, ready to pitch.)	15.00	7.50	4.50
(43)	Jerry Lumpe (Tigers, belt-up.)	12.00	6.00	3.50
(45)	Roger Maris (Yankees, batting.)	30.00	15.00	9.00
(46)	Roger Maris (Yankees, full-length.)	30.00	15.00	9.00
(47)	Roger Maris (Cardinals, "picture-frame," b/w photo.)	30.00	15.00	9.00
(49)	Dick McAuliffe (Tigers, portrait.)	12.00	6.00	3.50
(50)	Bill Monbouquette (Red Sox, wind-up.)	12.00	6.00	3.50
(51)	Bobby Murcer (Yankees, upper body.)	12.00	6.00	3.50
(53)	Jim Northrup (Tigers, batting.)	12.00	6.00	3.50
(56)	Jim Pagliaroni (Pirates, batting.)	12.00	6.00	3.50
(58)	Jim Palmer (Upper body.)	25.00	12.50	7.50
(60)	Joe Pepitone (Yankees, batting.)	15.00	7.50	4.50
(61)	Gary Peters (White Sox, green borders, b/w portrait.)	12.00	6.00	3.50
(62)	Rico Petrocelli (Red Sox, upper body.)	12.00	6.00	3.50
(64)	Joe Pignatano (A's, hands on hips.)	12.00	6.00	3.50
(66)	Bob Rodgers (Angels, portrait.)	12.00	6.00	3.50
(67)	Rich Rollins (Twins, arms crossed.)	12.00	6.00	3.50
(69)	Nolan Ryan (Angels, color, pitching.)	75.00	37.00	22.00
(72)	Tom Seaver (Mets, waist-to-cap.)	30.00	15.00	9.00
(73)	Tom Seaver (Mets, color, pitching.)	30.00	15.00	9.00
(75)	Mel Stottlemyre (Yankees, rust borders, b/w pitching pose.)	12.00	6.00	3.50
(76)	Dick Stuart (Pirates, batting.)	15.00	7.50	4.50
(78)	Joe Torre (Braves, upper body.)	15.00	7.50	4.50
(79)	Joe Torre (Cardinals, red borders, b/w portrait.)	15.00	7.50	4.50
(85)	Pete Ward (White Sox, portrait.)	12.00	6.00	3.50
(86)	Carlton Willey (Braves, full-length.)	12.00	6.00	3.50
(88)	Maury Wills (Dodgers, chest-to-cap.)	15.00	7.50	4.50
(89)	Maury Wills (No team, full-length batting.)	12.00	6.00	3.50
(90)	Carl Yastrzemski (Kneeling w/ bats.)	30.00	15.00	9.00
(91)	Carl Yastrzemski (Picture-frame border, b/w portrait.)	30.00	15.00	9.00

1969 Spare-Time Products Minnesota Twins Discs

The intended use and manner of distribution of these 8" uniface color discs is unknown. The hard composition discs have a baseball design on which is centered a player portrait. A facsimile autograph is at bottom and there is a hole at top for hanging. Copyright information appears at lower-right.

		NM	E	VG
Complete Set (8):		400.00	200.00	125.00
Common Player:		30.00	15.00	9.00
(1)	Dave Boswell	30.00	22.00	9.00
(2)	Leo Cardenas	30.00	15.00	9.00

(3)	Dean Chance	30.00	15.00	9.00
(4)	Jim Kaat	45.00	22.00	13.50
(5)	Tony Oliva (SP)	150.00	75.00	45.00
(6)	Ron Perranoski	30.00	22.00	9.00
(7)	Jim Perry	30.00	15.00	9.00
(8)	John Roseboro	30.00	15.00	9.00

1948 Speedway 79 Tiger of the Week Photos

This set of blank-back, black-and-white 8" x 10" photos was issued by one of the Tigers radio sponsors. One photo, bearing a facsimile autograph on front, was given away each week to honor the outstanding Tigers performer. The photos have no markings identifying the issuer and they are unnumbered. They are checklisted here alphabetically.

		NM	E	VG
Complete Set (14):		350.00	175.00	100.00
Common Player:		30.00	15.00	9.00
(1)	Neil Berry	30.00	15.00	9.00
(2)	"Hoot" Evers	30.00	15.00	9.00
(3)	Ted Gray	30.00	15.00	9.00
(4)	Art Houtteman	30.00	15.00	9.00
(5)	Fred Hutchinson	30.00	15.00	9.00
(6)	George Kell	50.00	25.00	15.00
(7)	Eddie Lake	30.00	15.00	9.00
(8)	Johnny Lipon	30.00	15.00	9.00
(9)	Hal Newhouser	50.00	25.00	15.00
(10)	Dizzy Trout	30.00	15.00	9.00
(11)	Virgil Trucks	30.00	15.00	9.00
(12)	George Vico	30.00	15.00	9.00
(13)	Dick Wakefield	30.00	15.00	9.00
(14)	Bill Wertz	30.00	15.00	9.00

1936 Spencer Shoes Jimmie Foxx Premium Photo

The attributed date is speculative, based on the uniform in which the player is pictured on this 7" x 9", blank-back, black-and-white premium photo. The picture has a facsimile autograph at left. At bottom-right in script is, "Courtesy of Spencer Shoes."

	NM	E	VG
Jimmie Foxx	350.00	175.00	105.00

1953-55 Spic and Span Braves

The first of several regional issues from a Milwaukee dry cleaner, the 1953-55 Spic and Span Braves set consists of black-and-white cards, 3-1/4" x 5-1/2". The fronts of the card have a facsimile autograph beneath the player photo. Cards are found with blank backs or with a Spic and Span advertising message on the back. Blank-backed cards are believed to have been issued by Wisco gas stations.

 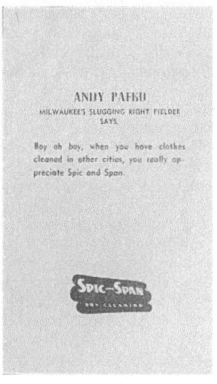

		NM	E	VG
Complete Set (29):		1,800	900.00	540.00
Common Player:		50.00	25.00	15.00
(1)	Hank Aaron	600.00	300.00	180.00
(2)	Joe Adcock	50.00	25.00	15.00
(3)	John Antonelli	50.00	25.00	15.00
(4)	Vern Bickford	50.00	25.00	15.00
(5)	Bill Bruton	50.00	25.00	15.00
(6)	Bob Buhl	50.00	25.00	15.00
(7)	Lew Burdette	50.00	25.00	15.00
(8)	Dick Cole	50.00	25.00	15.00
(9)	Walker Cooper	50.00	25.00	15.00
(10)	Del Crandall	50.00	25.00	15.00
(11)	George Crowe	50.00	25.00	15.00
(12)	Jack Dittmer	50.00	25.00	15.00
(13)	Sid Gordon	50.00	25.00	15.00
(14)	Ernie Johnson	50.00	25.00	15.00
(15)	Dave Jolly	50.00	25.00	15.00
(16)	Don Liddle	50.00	25.00	15.00
(17)	John Logan	50.00	25.00	15.00
(18)	Ed Mathews	200.00	100.00	60.00
(19)	Chet Nichols	50.00	25.00	15.00
(20)	Dan O'Connell	50.00	25.00	15.00
(21)	Andy Pafko	50.00	25.00	15.00
(22)	Jim Pendleton	50.00	25.00	15.00
(23)	Ebba St. Claire	50.00	25.00	15.00
(24)	Warren Spahn	200.00	100.00	60.00
(25)	Max Surkont	50.00	25.00	15.00
(26)	Bob Thomson	75.00	37.50	22.00
(27)	Bob Thorpe	50.00	25.00	15.00
(28)	Roberto Vargas	50.00	25.00	15.00
(29)	Jim Wilson	50.00	25.00	15.00

1953-57 Spic and Span Braves 7x10 Photos

This regional set was issued by Spic and Span Dry Cleaners of Milwaukee over a four-year period and consists of large (7" x 10") photos of Braves players. Of all the various Spic and Span sets, this one seems to be the easiest to find. The fronts feature a player photo with a facsimile autograph below. The Spic and Span logo also appears on the fronts, while the backs are blank. A header card picturing Milwaukee County Stadium also exists.

		NM	E	VG
Complete Set (14):		335.00	165.00	100.00
Common Player:		25.00	12.50	7.50
(1)	Joe Adcock	25.00	12.50	7.50
(2)	William H. Bruton	25.00	12.50	7.50
(3)	Robert Buhl	25.00	12.50	7.50
(4)	Lou Burdette	25.00	12.50	7.50
(5)	Del Crandall	25.00	12.50	7.50
(6)	Jack Dittmer	25.00	12.50	7.50
(7)	Johnny Logan	25.00	12.50	7.50
(8)	Edwin L. Mathews, Jr.	75.00	37.50	22.00
(9)	Chet Nichols	25.00	12.50	7.50
(10)	Danny O'Connell	25.00	12.50	7.50
(11)	Andy Pafko	25.00	12.50	7.50
(12)	Warren E. Spahn	75.00	37.50	22.00
(13)	Bob Thomson	35.00	17.50	10.00
(14)	Milwaukee County Stadium	35.00	17.50	10.00

1954 Spic and Span Braves

Player selection points to 1954 as the date of this issue, making it contemporary with several other card sets produced by the chain of Wisconsin dry cleaners. These cards are printed in blue on 5-1/2" x 8-1/2" yellow cardstock. Fronts have player portraits by an artist signed as "Warmuth," facsimile autographs, a promotional quote from the player and the sponsor's logo. Backs are blank. It is not known whether the set is complete at 13.

		NM	E	VG
Complete Set (13):		1,200	600.00	350.00
Common Player:		75.00	37.50	22.50
(1)	Joe Adcock	90.00	45.00	27.50
(2)	William H. Bruton	75.00	37.50	22.50
(3)	Robert Buhl	75.00	37.50	22.50
(4)	Lou Burdette	75.00	37.50	22.50
(5)	Del Crandall	75.00	37.50	22.50
(6)	Jack Dittmer	75.00	37.50	22.50
(7)	Johnny Logan	75.00	37.50	22.50
(8)	Edwin L. Mathews Jr.	225.00	110.00	70.00
(9)	Chet Nichols	75.00	37.50	22.50
(10)	Danny O'Connell	75.00	37.50	22.50
(11)	Andy Pafko	75.00	37.50	22.50
(12)	Warren E. Spahn	225.00	110.00	70.00
(13)	Bob Thomson	90.00	45.00	27.50

1954-56 Spic and Span Braves

Issued during the three-year period from 1954-1956, this Spic and Span set consists of 18 postcard-size (4" x 6") cards. The front of the cards include a facsimile autograph printed in white and the Spic and Span logo.

		NM	E	VG
Complete Set (18):		1,350	675.00	400.00
Common Player:		35.00	17.50	10.00
(1)	Hank Aaron	400.00	200.00	120.00
(2)	Joe Adcock	35.00	17.50	10.00
(3)	William H. Bruton	35.00	17.50	10.00
(4)	Robert Buhl	35.00	17.50	10.00
(5)	Lou Burdette	35.00	17.50	10.00
(6)	Gene Conley	35.00	17.50	10.00
(7)	Del Crandall	35.00	17.50	10.00
(8)	Ray Crone	35.00	17.50	10.00
(9)	Jack Dittmer	35.00	17.50	10.00
(10)	Ernie Johnson	35.00	17.50	10.00
(11)	Dave Jolly	35.00	17.50	10.00
(12)	Johnny Logan	35.00	17.50	10.00
(13)	Edwin L. Mathews, Jr.	225.00	110.00	70.00
(14)	Chet Nichols	35.00	17.50	10.00
(15)	Danny O'Connell	35.00	17.50	10.00
(16)	Andy Pafko	35.00	17.50	10.00
(17)	Warren E. Spahn	220.00	110.00	70.00
(18)	Bob Thomson	60.00	30.00	18.00

1955 Spic and Span Braves Die-Cuts

This 17-card, die-cut set is the rarest of all the Spic and Span issues. The stand-ups, which measure approximately 7-1/2" x 7", picture the players in action poses and were designed to be punched out, allowing them to stand up. Most cards were used in this fashion, making better-condition cards very rare today. The front of the card includes a facsimile autograph and the Spic and Span logo.

		NM	E	VG
Complete Set (18):		4,400	2,200	1,250
Common Player:		175.00	90.00	55.00
(1)	Hank Aaron	900.00	450.00	275.00
(2)	Joe Adcock	175.00	90.00	55.00
(3)	Bill Bruton	175.00	90.00	55.00
(4)	Bob Buhl	175.00	90.00	55.00
(5)	Lew Burdette	175.00	90.00	55.00
(6)	Gene Conley	175.00	90.00	55.00
(7)	Del Crandall	175.00	90.00	55.00
(8)	Jack Dittmer	175.00	90.00	55.00
(9)	Ernie Johnson	175.00	90.00	55.00
(10)	Dave Jolly	175.00	90.00	55.00
(11)	John Logan	175.00	90.00	55.00
(12)	Ed Mathews	450.00	225.00	135.00
(13)	Chet Nichols	175.00	90.00	55.00
(14)	Dan O'Connell	175.00	90.00	55.00
(15)	Andy Pafko	175.00	90.00	55.00
(16)	Warren Spahn	450.00	225.00	135.00
(17)	Bob Thomson	225.00	110.00	65.00
(18)	Jim Wilson	175.00	90.00	55.00

1957 Spic and Span Braves

This 20-card set was issued in 1957, the year the Braves were World Champions and is a highly desirable set. The cards measure 4" x 5" and have a wide white border surrounding the player photo. A blue Spic and Span logo appears in the lower-right corner and the card includes a salutation and facsimile autograph, also in blue.

		NM	E	VG
Complete Set (20):		1,250	625.00	375.00
Common Player:		25.00	12.50	7.50
(1)	Hank Aaron	400.00	200.00	120.00
(2)	Joe Adcock	25.00	12.50	7.50
(3)	Bill Bruton	25.00	12.50	7.50
(4)	Bob Buhl	25.00	12.50	7.50
(5)	Lew Burdette	25.00	12.50	7.50
(6)	Gene Conley	25.00	12.50	7.50
(7)	Wes Covington (SP)	50.00	25.00	15.00
(8)	Del Crandall	25.00	12.50	7.50
(9)	Ray Crone	25.00	12.50	7.50
(10)	Fred Haney	25.00	12.50	7.50
(11)	Ernie Johnson	25.00	12.50	7.50
(12)	John Logan	25.00	12.50	7.50
(13)	Felix Mantilla (SP)	50.00	25.00	15.00
(14)	Ed Mathews	85.00	45.00	25.00
(15)	Dan O'Connell	25.00	12.50	7.50
(16)	Andy Pafko	25.00	12.50	7.50
(17)	Red Schoendienst (SP)	110.00	55.00	35.00
(18)	Warren Spahn	85.00	45.00	25.00
(19)	Bob Thomson	45.00	22.50	13.50
(20)	Bob Trowbridge (SP)	50.00	25.00	15.00

1960 Spic and Span Braves

Spic and Span's final Milwaukee Braves issue consists of 26 cards, each measuring 2-3/4" x 3-1/8". The fronts contain a white-bordered photo with no printing, while the backs include a facsimile autograph and the words "Photographed

and Autographed Exclusively for Spic and Span." The 1960 set includes the only known variation in the Spic and Span sets; a "flopped" negative error showing catcher Del Crandall batting left-handed was later corrected.

 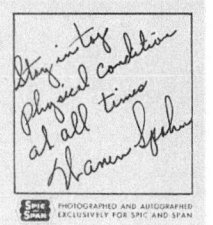

		NM	E	VG
Complete Set (26):		1,650	825.00	500.00
Common Player:		35.00	17.50	10.00
(1)	Hank Aaron	650.00	325.00	200.00
(2)	Joe Adcock	35.00	17.50	10.00
(3)	Bill Bruton	35.00	17.50	10.00
(4)	Bob Buhl	35.00	17.50	10.00
(5)	Lew Burdette	35.00	17.50	10.00
(6)	Chuck Cottier	35.00	17.50	10.00
(7a)	Del Crandall (Photo reversed.)	60.00	30.00	18.00
(7b)	Del Crandall (Correct photo.)	35.00	17.50	10.00
(8)	Chuck Dressen	35.00	17.50	10.00
(9)	Joey Jay	35.00	17.50	10.00
(10)	John Logan	35.00	17.50	10.00
(11)	Felix Mantilla	35.00	17.50	10.00
(12)	Ed Mathews	125.00	65.00	35.00
(13)	Lee Maye	35.00	17.50	10.00
(14)	Don McMahon	35.00	17.50	10.00
(15)	George Myatt	35.00	17.50	10.00
(16)	Andy Pafko	35.00	17.50	10.00
(17)	Juan Pizarro	35.00	17.50	10.00
(18)	Mel Roach	35.00	17.50	10.00
(19)	Bob Rush	35.00	17.50	10.00
(20)	Bob Scheffing	35.00	17.50	10.00
(21)	Red Schoendienst	90.00	45.00	27.50
(22)	Warren Spahn	125.00	65.00	35.00
(23)	Al Spangler	35.00	17.50	10.00
(24)	Frank Torre	35.00	17.50	10.00
(25)	Carl Willey	35.00	17.50	10.00
(26)	Whit Wyatt	35.00	17.50	10.00

1964-67 Sport Hobbyist Famous Card Series

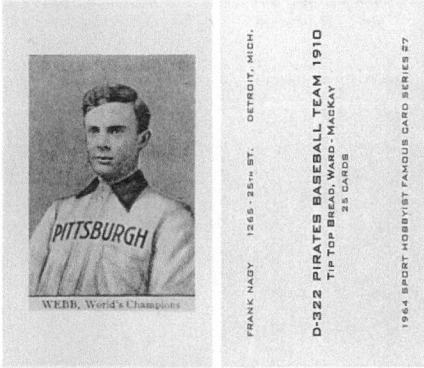

These very early collectors issues were produced over a period of several years in the mid-1960s during Frank Nagy's ownership of the "Sport Hobbyist" magazine. The 2-1/4" x 3-3/4" black-and-white cards picture on their fronts reproductions of rare and famous baseball cards from Nagy's unequaled collection, including eight of the very rare Tarzan Bread issue of the mid-1930s which few collectors even today have ever seen. Backs have identification of the pictured card, utilizing the then-standard "American Card Catalog" set designations.

		NM	E	VG
Complete Set (30):		90.00	45.00	27.50
Common Player:		5.00	2.50	1.50
1	T206 Honus Wagner	12.50	6.25	3.75
2	T212 Henley	5.00	2.50	1.50
3	C46 Simmons	5.00	2.50	1.50
4	M116 Christy Mathewson	5.00	2.50	1.50
5	M101-5 Jack Barry	5.00	2.50	1.50
6	T204 Mordecai Brown	5.00	2.50	1.50
7	D322 Tip Top Bread Webb	5.00	2.50	1.50
8	S74 Lou Criger	5.00	2.50	1.50
9	R333 DeLong Kiki Cuyler	5.00	2.50	1.50
10	R319 Nap Lajoie	7.50	3.75	2.25
11	T205 John McGraw	5.00	2.50	1.50
12	E107 Addie Joss	5.00	2.50	1.50
13	W502 George Sisler	5.00	2.50	1.50
14	Allen & Ginter N29 Buck Ewing	5.00	2.50	1.50
15	E90 Chief Bender	5.00	2.50	1.50
16	E104 George Mullin	5.00	2.50	1.50
17	E95 Fred Merkle	5.00	2.50	1.50
18	E121 Walter Schang	5.00	2.50	1.50
19	Allen & Ginter N28 Tim Keefe	5.00	2.50	1.50
20	E120 Harold (Muddy) Ruel	5.00	2.50	1.50
21	D382 Irving (Jack) Burns	5.00	2.50	1.50
22	D382 George Connally	5.00	2.50	1.50
23	D382 Myril Hoag	5.00	2.50	1.50
24	D382 Willie Kamm	5.00	2.50	1.50
25	D382 Dutch Leonard	5.00	2.50	1.50
26	D382 Clyde Manion	5.00	2.50	1.50
27	D382 Johnny Vergez	5.00	2.50	1.50
28	D382 Tom Zachary	5.00	2.50	1.50
29	E145 Ty Cobb	7.50	3.75	2.25
30	Playing Card, Richardson	5.00	2.50	1.50

1971 Sport Hobbyist Famous Card Series

 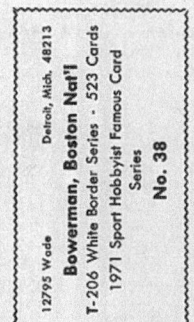

A new series of collector cards, designed as the first-ever attempt to reproduce the T206 tobacco set, was begun under the hobby paper's new ownership but quickly abandoned. The 2" x 3" cards have a black-and-white picture of a card at center, surrounded by a red frame (except Bescher, which has a black frame). Backs identify the card and include a card number.

		NM	E	VG
Complete Set (21):		90.00	45.00	27.50
Common Card:		5.00	2.50	1.50
31	T206 Abbaticchio	5.00	2.50	1.50
32	T206 Barbeau	5.00	2.50	1.50
33	T206 Burch	5.00	2.50	1.50
34	T206 M. Brown	5.00	2.50	1.50
35	T206 Chase	5.00	2.50	1.50
36	T206 Ball	5.00	2.50	1.50
37	T206 Abstein	5.00	2.50	1.50
38	T206 Bowerman	5.00	2.50	1.50
39	T206 Chase	5.00	2.50	1.50
40	T206 Criss	5.00	2.50	1.50
41	T206 Beck	5.00	2.50	1.50
42	T206 Bresnahan	5.00	2.50	1.50
43	T206 Bradley	5.00	2.50	1.50
44	T206 Berger	5.00	2.50	1.50
45	T206 Bransfield	5.00	2.50	1.50
46	T206 Bescher	5.00	2.50	1.50
47	T206 Bell	5.00	2.50	1.50
48	T206 Bergen	5.00	2.50	1.50
49	T206 Bender	5.00	2.50	1.50
50	T206 Bush	5.00	2.50	1.50
51	T206 Chesbro	5.00	2.50	1.50

1975 Sport Hobbyist

This was one of several series of collectors issues produced in the 1960s and 1970s by the Sport Hobbyist, one of the card hobby's earliest periodicals. This series features the past greats of the game in postcard size (3-1/2" x 5-1/2"). Cards are found either blank-backed or with an ad offering various new-card products. Fronts of cards numbered through 115 have watercolor portraits in an oval frame. A box below offers a career summary. Higher number cards feature photos and/or artwork, sometimes with a caption, and sometimes with no identification. Cards are numbered with an SH prefix. Each series of 18 were originally sold for $1.50.

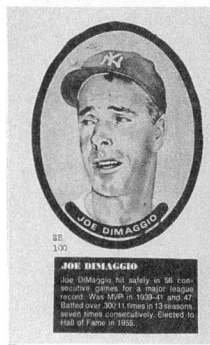

		NM	E	VG
	Complete Set (48):	150.00	75.00	45.00
	Common Player:	5.00	2.50	1.50
98	Lou Gehrig	15.00	7.50	4.50
99	Ty Cobb	12.50	6.25	3.75
100	Joe DiMaggio	15.00	7.50	4.50
101	Mel Ott	5.00	2.50	1.50
102	Carl Hubbell	5.00	2.50	1.50
103	Babe Ruth	20.00	10.00	6.00
104	Rogers Hornsby	7.50	3.75	2.25
105	Tris Speaker	7.50	3.75	2.25
106	Hank Greenberg	7.50	3.75	2.25
107	Jimmy (Jimmie) Foxx	7.50	3.75	2.25
108	Ted Williams	15.00	7.50	4.50
109	Mickey Cochrane	5.00	2.50	1.50
110	Bob Feller	7.50	3.75	2.25
111	Cy Young	9.00	4.50	2.75
112	George Sissler (Sisler)	5.00	2.50	1.50
113	Honus Wagner	9.00	4.50	2.75
114	Lefty Grove	5.00	2.50	1.50
115	Dizzy Dean	7.50	3.75	2.25
116	Babe Ruth (Farewell address.)	9.00	4.50	2.75
117	Jackie Robinson	7.50	3.75	2.25
118	Mike Kelly (Woodcut)	5.00	2.50	1.50
119	Honus Wagner (Portrait and action.)	5.00	2.50	1.50
120	Babe Ruth (W/mascot Ray Kelly.)	9.00	4.50	2.75
121	Babe Ruth (Photos/ artwork.)	5.00	2.50	1.50
122	John M. Ward (Newsboy cabinet.)	5.00	2.50	1.50
123	Babe Ruth (Photos/ artwork.)	5.00	2.50	1.50
124	Babe Ruth (Artwork)	5.00	2.50	1.50
125	Hall of Fame Dedication, 1939	5.00	2.50	1.50
126	Babe Ruth (At microphone.)	5.00	2.50	1.50
127	Babe Ruth, Jacob Ruppert	7.50	3.75	2.25
128	Stan Musial	7.50	3.75	2.25
129	Babe Ruth (W/others.)	5.00	2.50	1.50
130	George Kell	5.00	2.50	1.50
131	Luke Appling	5.00	2.50	1.50
132	Cecil Travis	5.00	2.50	1.50
133	Larry "Yogi" Berra	7.50	3.75	2.25
134	Harry Heilman (Heilmann)	5.00	2.50	1.50
135	Johnny Mize	5.00	2.50	1.50
136	Christy Mathewson	7.50	3.75	2.25
137	Ralph Kiner	5.00	2.50	1.50
138	Bill Dickey	5.00	2.50	1.50
139	Hank Sauer	5.00	2.50	1.50
140	Hank Greenberg	7.50	3.75	2.25
141	Charlie Gehringer	5.00	2.50	1.50
142	Walter Evers	5.00	2.50	1.50
143	John Pepper Martin	5.00	2.50	1.50
144	Vern Stephens	5.00	2.50	1.50
145	Bobbie (Bobby) Doerr	5.00	2.50	1.50

1975 Sport Hobbyist Team Composites

This was one of several series of collectors issues produced in the 1960s and 1970s by the Sport Hobbyist, one of the card hobby's earliest periodicals. This series features black-and-white postcard size (about 3-1/2" x 5-1/4") reproductions of team composite photos from the 1931 Spalding Guide. Cards are blank-backed. Most of the cards are numbered, with an SH prefix, though some are not.

		NM	E	VG
	Common Card:	6.00	3.00	1.80
70	Chicago Cubs	6.00	3.00	1.80
71	Philadelphia Athletics	6.00	3.00	1.80
72	N.Y. Giants	6.00	3.00	1.80
73				
74	Pittsburgh Pirates	6.00	3.00	1.80
75	Chicago Cubs	6.00	3.00	1.80
76				
77	Boston Braves	6.00	3.00	1.80
78	Cincinnati Reds	6.00	3.00	1.80
79	Brooklyn Dodgers	6.00	3.00	1.80
80				
81	Philadelphia A's	6.00	3.00	1.80
82	Cleveland Indians	6.00	3.00	1.80
83	Detroit Tigers	6.00	3.00	1.80
84	Chicago White Sox	6.00	3.00	1.80
85	Chicago White Sox	6.00	3.00	1.80
86	Boston Red Sox	6.00	3.00	1.80
87	Boston Red Sox	6.00	3.00	1.80
88	N.Y. Yankees	10.00	5.00	3.00
89	Cleveland Indians	6.00	3.00	1.80
90	St. Louis Browns	6.00	3.00	1.80
91	Washington Senators	6.00	3.00	1.80
92	Boston Braves	6.00	3.00	1.80
93	St. Louis Browns	6.00	3.00	1.80
94	Washington Senators	6.00	3.00	1.80
95	Philadelphia Phillies	6.00	3.00	1.80
96	Cincinnati Reds	6.00	3.00	1.80
97	Philadelphia Phillies	6.00	3.00	1.80
	UNNUMBERED			
---	Brooklyn Dodgers	6.00	3.00	1.80
---	Detroit Tigers	6.00	3.00	1.80
---	N.Y. Yankees	10.00	5.00	3.00
---	Pittsburgh Pirates	6.00	3.00	1.80

1888-1889 Sporting Extra World Tour Imperial Cabinets

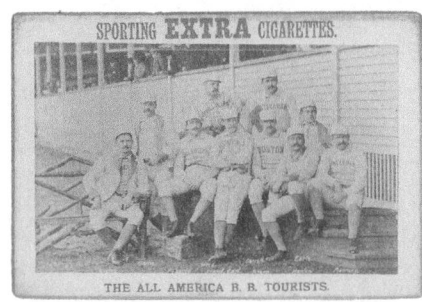

These large-format (about 9-3/4" x 6-1/2") imperial cabinet cards were issued in conjunction with "Spalding's World Base Ball Tour" of 1888-1889, though their method of distribution is unknown. The cards feature team portraits on a heavy cardboard, gilt-edge mount. At top is the name of the sponsoring cigarette brand, at bottom is the team name, printed in red. Backs are blank. Each of the cards that appeared in a 12/05 auction is believed unique.

(1)	THE ALL AMERICA B.B. TOURISTS
(2)	THE CHICAGO B.B. TOURISTS
	Pair sold in 12/05 auction for $27,709.

1902-11 Sporting Life Cabinets (W600)

From 1902 through 1911, Sporting Life, a weekly newspaper published in Philadelphia, produced and sold a lengthy run of 5" x 7-1/2" "Cabinet Phototypes of Well-known Baseball Players." They were collectively given the catalog number of W600 in "The American Card Catalog." Because many players were issued with different team designations as they moved about over the years, and because there are new discoveries from this issue being made even today, it is likely this checklist will remain in flux for some time to come. For that reason, gaps in the assigned card numbers in this checklist have been left to accommodate additions. Several different styles and colors of mattes were used over the years, with many players issued in more than one of them. Many of the earliest cabinets picture the players in suit-and-tie, while later issues show them in uniform. Where verified, cabinets showing players in street clothes are noted. The black-and-white player portraits are mounted on heavy cardboard mattes. The player's name, position, team and league are printed beneath the photo. Backs are blank. Each cabinet was issued in a transparent envelope. They were originally given away for three two-cents stamps and a coupon found in the paper; later they were offered for sale for 10 cents apiece; 12 for a dollar. The checklist here is presented in alphabetical order. Most of the names are as presented in contemporary ads from the newspaper; rife with misspellings and misidentifications, and may or may not represent the actual spelling shown on the cards. The year shown in parentheses indicates the first year the player was issued with that team. Because these cards were sold individually upon fan request, this is an issue in which the superstars of the day are more common than the benchwarmers. It is also likely that some of the cards on this list were never issued or do not survive.

		NM	E	VG
	Common Player:	2,100	1,050	630.00
(1)	Edward Abbatichio (Abbaticchio)(Boston NL, 1903.))	3,600	1,800	1,100
(2)	Edward Abbaticchio (Pittsburg, 1907.)	2,100	1,050	630.00
(3)	William Abstein (St. Louis AL, 1910.)	2,100	1,050	630.00
(4)	Charles B. Adams (Pittsburg, 1909.)	2,100	1,050	630.00
(5)	C.A. Alperman (Brooklyn, 1906.)	2,100	1,050	630.00
(6)	David Altizer (Washington, 1907.)	2,100	1,050	630.00
(7)	Nick Altrock (Chicago AL, 1903.)	4,300	2,150	1,300
(8)	Leon Ames (New York, NL, 1904.)	2,100	1,050	630.00
(9)	John Anderson (St. Louis AL, 1902, street.)	3,600	1,800	1,100
(10)	John Anderson (New York AL, 1904.)	2,100	1,050	630.00
(11)	John Anderson (Washington, 1905.)	2,100	1,050	630.00
(12)	Frank Arelanes (Arellanes)(Boston AL, 1910.))	2,100	1,050	630.00
(13)	Charles Armbruster (Boston AL, 1906.)	2,100	1,050	630.00
(14)	William R. Armour (Detroit, 1906.)	2,100	1,050	630.00
(15)	Harry Arndt (St. Louis NL, 1906.)	2,100	1,050	630.00
(16)	Harry J. Aubrey (Boston NL, 1903.)	3,600	1,800	1,100
(17)	James Austin (New York AL, 1910.)	2,100	1,050	630.00
(18)	Charles Babb (New York NL, 1903.)	3,600	1,800	1,100
(19)	Charles Babb (Brooklyn, 1904.)	2,100	1,050	630.00
(20)	William Bailey (St. Louis AL, 1910.)	2,100	1,050	630.00
(21)	Frank Baker (Philadelphia AL, 1910.)	6,500	3,250	1,950

(22)	J. Barbeau (Cleveland, 1906.)	2,100	1,050	630.00
(23)	G.O. Barclay (Boston NL, 1904.)	2,100	1,050	630.00
(24)	Edward Barger (First name Eros.) (Brooklyn, 1910.))	2,100	1,050	630.00
(25)	James Barrett (Detroit, 1902, street.)	3,600	1,800	1,100
(26)	James Barrett (Boston AL, 1906.)	2,100	1,050	630.00
(27)	John C. Barry (Philadelphia NL, 1902.)	3,600	1,800	1,100
(28)	John C. Barry (Chicago NL, 1904.)	2,100	1,050	630.00
(29)	John C. Barry (Cincinnati, 1905.)	2,100	1,050	630.00
(30)	John C. Barry (St. Louis NL, 1906.)	2,100	1,050	630.00
(31)	John J. Barry (Philadelphia AL, 1910.)	2,100	1,050	630.00
(32)	Harry L. Barton (Philadelphia AL, 1905.)	2,100	1,050	630.00
(33)	Henry Batch (Brooklyn, 1906.)	2,100	1,050	630.00
(34)	Joseph Bates (Johnny) (Boston NL, 1907.))	2,100	1,050	630.00
(35)	Harry Bay (Cleveland, 1903.)	3,600	1,800	1,100
(36)	Clarence H. Beaumont (Pittsburg, 1902, street.)	3,600	1,800	1,100
(37)	Clarence H. Beaumont (Pittsburg, 1902, uniform.)	3,600	1,800	1,100
(38)	Clarence H. Beaumont (Boston NL, 1907.)	2,100	1,050	630.00
(39)	Fred Beck (Boston NL, 1910.)	2,100	1,050	630.00
(40)	Harry Beckendorf (Detroit, 1910.)	2,100	1,050	630.00
(41)	Jacob Beckley (Cincinnati, 1902.)	7,900	4,000	2,375
(42)	Jacob Beckley (St. Louis NL, 1904.)	6,500	3,250	1,950
(43)	Fred L. Beebe (St. Louis NL, 1906.)	2,100	1,050	630.00
(44)	George C. Bell (Brooklyn, 1910.)	2,100	1,050	630.00
(45)	Harry Bemis (Cleveland, 1903.)	3,600	1,800	1,100
(46)	Charles Bender (Philadelphia AL, 1903, street.)	7,900	4,000	2,375
(47)	Charles Bender (Philadelphia AL, 1903, uniform.)	7,900	4,000	2,375
(48)	Justin J. Bennett (St. Louis NL, 1907.)	2,100	1,050	630.00
(49)	William Bergen (Brooklyn, 1904.)	2,100	1,050	630.00
(50)	Charles Berger (Cleveland, 1907.)	2,100	1,050	630.00
(51)	William Bernhardt (Bernhard) (Cleveland, 1902, street.))	3,000	1,500	900.00
(52)	Robert Bescher (Cincinnati, 1910.)	2,100	1,050	630.00
(53)	Walter Beville (Henry "Monte") (New York, AL 1903.)	3,600	1,800	1,100
(54)	Walter Beville (Henry "Monte") (Detroit, 1904.))	2,100	1,050	630.00
(55)	Russell Blackburne (Chicago AL, 1910.)	2,100	1,050	630.00
(56)	Elmer Bliss (St. Louis NL, 1910.)	2,100	1,050	630.00
(57)	Frank Bowerman (New York NL, 1903.)	3,600	1,800	1,100
(58)	Frank (William J.) Bradley (Cleveland, 1903.)	3,600	1,800	1,100
(59)	William J. Bradley (Cleveland, 1903.)	3,600	1,800	1,100
(60)	David L. Brain (St. Louis NL, 1903.)	3,600	1,800	1,100
(61)	David L. Brain (Pittsburg, 1905.)	2,100	1,050	630.00
(62)	David L. Brain (Boston NL, 1906.)	2,100	1,050	630.00
(63)	William Bransfield (Pittsburg, 1902, street.)	3,600	1,800	1,100
(64)	William Bransfield (Pittsburg, 1902, uniform.)	3,600	1,800	1,100
(65)	William Bransfield (Philadelphia NL, 1905.)	2,100	1,050	630.00
(66)	Roger Bresnahan (New York NL, 1903.)	7,900	4,000	2,375
(67)	Roger Bresnahan (St. Louis NL, 1909.)	6,750	3,375	2,025
(68)	Albert Bridwell (Boston NL, 1906.)	2,100	1,050	630.00
(69)	Herbert Briggs (Chicago NL, 1905.)	2,100	1,050	630.00
(70)	Herbert Briggs (Brooklyn, 1906.)	2,100	1,050	630.00
(71)	Charles E. Brown (St. Louis NL, 1906.)	2,100	1,050	630.00
(72)	Charles E. Brown (Philadelphia NL, 1907.)	2,100	1,050	630.00
(73)	Mordecai Brown (Chicago NL, 1904.)	6,750	3,250	1,950
(74)	Samuel Brown (Boston NL, 1907.)	2,100	1,050	630.00
(75)	George Browne (New York NL, 1903.)	3,600	1,800	1,100
(76)	Fred Buelow (Detroit, 1903.)	3,600	1,800	1,100
(77)	Fred Buelow (Cleveland, 1904.)	2,100	1,050	630.00
(78)	James T. Burke (St. Louis NL, 1903.)	3,600	1,800	1,100
(79)	James T. Burke (Philadelphia AL, 1906.)	2,100	1,050	630.00
(80)	Jesse Burkett (St. Louis AL, 1903.)	53,500	26,750	16,050
(81)	Jesse Burkett (Boston AL, 1905.)	6,500	3,250	1,950
(82)	James J. Callahan (Chicago AL, 1903.)	3,000	1,500	900.00
(83)	Howard Camnitz (Pittsburg, 1910.)	2,100	1,050	630.00
(84)	Wirt V. Cannell (Virgin Wirt) (Boston NL, 1903.))	3,600	1,800	1,100
(85)	Joseph Cantillion (Washington, 1907.)	2,100	1,050	630.00
(86)	George Carey (Washington, 1903.)	3,600	1,800	1,100
(87)	P.J. Carney (Boston NL, 1903.)	3,600	1,800	1,100
(88)	Charles C. Carr (Cleveland, 1904.)	2,100	1,050	630.00
(89)	Charles C. Carr (Cincinnati, 1906.)	2,100	1,050	630.00
(90)	William Carrigan (Boston AL, 1910.)	2,100	1,050	630.00
(91)	James P. Casey (Chicago NL, 1902, street.)	3,600	1,800	1,100
(92)	James P. Casey (Brooklyn, 1906.)	2,100	1,050	630.00
(93)	Joseph Cassidy (Washington, 1904.)	2,100	1,050	630.00
(94)	Luis Castro (Philadelphia AL, 1902, street.)	2,100	1,050	630.00
(95)	Frank Chance (Chicago NL, 1902, street.)	7,900	4,000	2,375
(96)	Frank Chance (Chicago NL, 1902, uniform.)	7,900	4,000	2,375
(97)	Harold Chase (New York AL, 1906.)	5,000	2,600	1,400
(98)	John Chesbro (Pittsburg, 1902, street.)	6,750	3,375	2,025
(99)	John Chesbro (New York AL, 1903, uniform.)	7,900	4,000	2,375
(100)	Edw. V. Cicotte (Boston AL, 1910.)	6,500	3,250	1,950
(101)	William Clark (Clarke) (Washington, 1903.))	3,000	1,500	900.00
(102)	William Clark (Clarke) (New York NL, 1905.))	2,100	1,050	630.00
(103)	Fred Clarke (Pittsburg, 1902, street.)	7,900	4,000	2,375
(104)	Fred Clarke (Pittsburg, 1902, uniform.)	7,900	4,000	2,375
(104)	Justin J. Clarke (Cleveland, 1906.)	2,100	1,050	630.00
(105)	Thomas Clarke (Cincinnati, 1910.)	2,100	1,050	630.00
(106)	Walter Clarkson (New York AL, 1906.)	2,100	1,050	630.00
(107)	Walter Clarkson (Cleveland, 1907.)	2,100	1,050	630.00
(108)	Otis Clymer (Pittsburg, 1905.)	2,100	1,050	630.00
(109)	Otis Clymer (Washington, 1907.)	2,100	1,050	630.00
(110)	Andrew Coakley (Philadelphia AL, 1905.)	2,100	1,050	630.00
(111)	Andrew Coakley (Cincinnati, 1907.)	2,100	1,050	630.00
(112)	Tyrus R. Cobb (Detroit, 1907.)	35,000	17,500	10,500
(115)	Edward Collins (Philadelphia AL, 1907.)	6,500	3,250	1,950
(116)	James Collins (Boston AL, 1902, uniform.)	6,250	3,125	1,875
(117)	W.M. Congalton (Cleveland, 1906.)	2,100	1,050	630.00
(118)	W.A. Congalton (Boston AL, 1907.)	2,100	1,050	630.00
(119)	William Conroy (New York AL, 1903.)	3,600	1,800	1,100
(120)	Richard Cooley (Boston NL, 1902, street.)	3,600	1,800	1,100
(121)	Richard Cooley (Detroit, 1905.)	2,100	1,050	630.00
(122)	John W. Coombs (Philadelphia AL, 1910.)	2,100	1,050	630.00
(123)	T.W. Corcoran (Cincinnati, 1904.)	2,100	1,050	630.00
(124)	T.W. Corcoran (New York NL, 1907.)	2,100	1,050	630.00
(125)	Frank J. Corridon (Philadelphia NL, 1907.)	2,100	1,050	630.00
(126)	William Coughlin (Washington, 1903.)	3,000	1,500	900.00
(127)	William Coughlin (Detroit, 1904.)	2,100	1,050	630.00
(128)	Ernest Courtney (Philadelphia NL, 1905.)	2,100	1,050	630.00
(129)	Otis Crandall (New York NL, 1910.)	2,100	1,050	630.00
(130)	Samuel Crawford (Cincinnati, 1902, street.)	7,900	4,000	2,375
(131)	Samuel Crawford (Detroit, 1903.)	7,900	4,000	2,375
(132)	Burde Cree (Birdie) (New York AL, 1911.))	2,100	1,050	630.00
(134)	Louis Criger (Boston AL, 1903.)	3,600	1,800	1,100
(135)	Dode Criss (St. Louis AL, 1910.)	2,100	1,050	630.00
(136)	John Cronin (New York NL, 1903.)	3,600	1,800	1,100
(137)	John Cronin (Brooklyn, 1904.)	2,400	1,200	720.00
(138)	Lafayette Cross (Philadelphia AL, 1902, street.)	3,600	1,800	1,100
(139)	Lafayette Cross (Washington, 1906.)	2,100	1,050	630.00
(140)	Monte Cross (Philadelphia AL, 1902.)	3,600	1,800	1,100
(142)	Clarence Currie (St. Louis NL, 1903.)	3,600	1,800	1,100
(143)	Clarence Currie (Chicago NL, 1903.)	3,600	1,800	1,100
(145)	William Dahlen (Brooklyn, 1902, street.)	4,300	2,150	1,300
(146)	William Dahlen (New York NL, 1904.)	2,100	1,050	630.00
(147)	Thomas Daly (Chicago AL, 1903, street.)	3,600	1,800	1,100
(148)	Thomas Daly (Cincinnati, 1903.)	3,600	1,800	1,100
(148)	George Davis (Chicago AL, 1902.)	7,900	4,000	2,375
(150)	Harry Davis (Philadelphia AL, 1902, street.)	3,000	1,500	900.00
(152)	Edward J. Delahanty (Washington, 1902, street.)	19,400	9,700	5,825
(153)	James Delahanty (Boston NL, 1904.)	2,100	1,050	630.00
(154)	James Delahanty (Cincinnati, 1906.)	2,100	1,050	630.00
(155)	James Delahanty (St. Louis AL, 1907.)	2,100	1,050	630.00
(156)	James Delahanty (Washington, 1907.)	2,100	1,050	630.00
(158)	Arthur Devlin (New York NL, 1905.)	2,100	1,050	630.00
(159)	Joshua Devore (New York NL, 1911.)	2,100	1,050	630.00

(160)	Charles Dexter (Boston NL, 1903.)	3,600	1,800	1,100
(161)	Frank Dillon (Brooklyn, 1903.)	3,600	1,800	1,100
(162)	William Dinneen (Boston AL, 1903.)	3,000	1,500	900.00
(163)	William Dineen (St. Louis AL, 1907.)	2,100	1,050	630.00
(164)	John Dobbs (Brooklyn, 1903.)	3,600	1,800	1,100
(164)	Edward Doheny (Pittsburg, 1903.)	3,600	1,800	1,100
(165)	Harry Dolan (Patrick Henry "Cozy") (Cincinnati, 1904.))	2,100	1,050	630.00
(166)	Harry Dolan (Patrick Henry "Cozy")(Boston NL, 1905.))	2,100	1,050	630.00
(167)	Frank Donahue (St. Louis AL, 1903.)	3,600	1,800	1,100
(168)	Frank Donahue (Cleveland, 1903.)	3,600	1,800	1,100
(169)	Frank Donahue (Detroit, 1906.)	2,100	1,050	630.00
(170)	J. "Jiggs" Donahue (Chicago AL, 1903.)	3,600	1,800	1,100
(171)	Michael Donlin (Cincinnati, 1902, street.)	3,600	1,800	1,100
(172)	Michael Donlin (New York NL, 1904.)	2,100	1,050	630.00
(173)	P.J. (Patrick) Donovan (St. Louis NL, 1902, street.)	3,600	1,800	1,100
(174)	Patrick J. Donovan (Washington, 1904.)	2,100	1,050	630.00
(175)	Patrick J. Donovan (Brooklyn, 1906, street.)	2,400	1,200	720.00
(176)	William Donovan (Detroit, 1903.)	3,000	1,500	900.00
(177)	Charles Dooin (Philadelphia NL, 1903.)	3,600	1,800	1,100
(178)	Michael Doolin (Doolan) (Philadelphia NL, 1906.))	2,100	1,050	630.00
(180)	Thomas Doran (Boston AL, 1904.)	2,100	1,050	630.00
(181)	Thomas Doran (Detroit, 1905.)	2,100	1,050	630.00
(182)	August Dorner (Boston NL, 1907.)	2,100	1,050	630.00
(183)	Patrick Dougherty (Boston AL, 1903.)	3,600	1,800	1,100
(184)	Patrick Dougherty (New York AL, 1904.)	2,100	1,050	630.00
(185)	Patrick Dougherty (Chicago AL, 1906.)	2,100	1,050	630.00
(186)	William Douglas (Douglass) (Philadelphia NL, 1902.))	3,600	1,800	1,100
(187)	Thomas Downey (Cincinnati, 1910.)	2,100	1,050	630.00
(188)	J.W. Downs (Detroit, 1907.)	2,100	1,050	630.00
(189)	Joe Doyle (New York AL, 1907.)	2,100	1,050	630.00
(190)	John Doyle (Brooklyn, 1903.)	3,600	1,800	1,100
(191)	John Doyle (Philadelphia NL, 1904.)	2,400	1,200	720.00
(192)	Larry J. Doyle (New York NL, 1908.)	2,100	1,050	630.00
(194)	Louis Drill (Washington, 1903.)	3,600	1,800	1,100
(195)	Louis Drill (Detroit, 1904.)	2,400	1,200	720.00
(196)	Hugh Duffy (Philadelphia NL, 1905.)	6,500	3,250	1,950
(197)	William Duggleby (Philadelphia NL, 1903.)	3,600	1,800	1,100
(198)	William Duggleby (Pittsburg, 1907.)	2,100	1050.00	630.00
(199)	August Dundon (Chicago AL, 1904.)	2,100	1,050	630.00
(200)	Edward Dunkle (Washington, 1903.)	3,600	1,800	1,100
(201)	James Dunleavy (John) (St. Louis NL, 1904.))	2,100	1,050	630.00
(202)	John Dunn (New York NL, 1903.)	3,600	1,800	1,100
(203)	James H. Dygert (Philadelphia AL, 1905.)	2,100	1,050	630.00
(204)	Malcolm Eason (Brooklyn, 1906.)	2,100	1,050	630.00
(205)	Harry Eells (Cleveland, 1906.)	2,100	1,050	630.00
(206)	Richard J. Egan (Cincinnati, 1910.)	2,100	1,050	630.00
(207)	Norman Elberfeld (Detroit, 1903.)	3,600	1,800	1,100
(208)	Norman Elberfeld (New York AL, 1903.)	3,600	1,800	1,100
(209)	Claude Elliott (New York NL, 1904.)	2,100	1,050	630.00
(210)	George W. Ellis (St. Louis NL, 1910.)	2,100	1,050	630.00
(212)	John Eubank (Detroit, 1906.)	2,100	1,050	630.00
(213)	John Evers (Chicago NL, 1903.)	7,900	4,000	2,375
(214)	Robert Ewing (George L.) (Cincinnati, 1904.))	2,100	1,050	630.00
(216)	Fred Falkenberg (Washington, 1906.)	2,100	1,050	630.00
(217)	Charles Farrell (Brooklyn, 1902, street.)	3,600	1,800	1,100
(218)	Charles Farrell (Boston AL, 1903.)	3,600	1,800	1,100
(219)	John S. Farrell (St. Louis NL, 1903.)	3,600	1,800	1,100
(220)	Cecil Ferguson (George) (New York NL, 1906.))	2,100	1,050	630.00
(221)	Hobe Ferris (Boston AL, 1903.)	3,600	1,800	1,100
(222)	Thomas S. Fisher (Middle initial C.)(Boston NL, 1903.))	2,100	1,050	630.00
(223)	Patrick Flaherty (Chicago AL, 1903.)	3,600	1,800	1,100
(224)	Patrick Flaherty (Pittsburg, 1904.)	2,100	1,050	630.00
(225)	Patrick Flaherty (Boston NL, 1907.)	2,100	1,050	630.00
(226)	Elmer Flick (Cleveland, 1903.)	5,750	2,875	1,725
(227)	John Flynn (Pittsburg, 1910.)	2,100	1,050	630.00
(229)	William Foxen (Chicago NL, 1910.)	2,100	1,050	630.00
(231)	Charles Fraser (Philadelphia NL, 1903, street.)	3,600	1,800	1,100
(232)	Charles Fraser (Boston NL, 1905.)	2,100	1,050	630.00
(233)	Charles Fraser (Chicago NL, 1907.)	2,100	1,050	630.00
(234)	John ("Buck") Freeman (Boston AL, 1902.)	4,300	2,150	1,300
(235)	William Friel (St. Louis AL, 1903.)	3,600	1,800	1,100
(236)	Arthur Fromme (Cincinnati, 1910.)	2,100	1,050	630.00
(237)	David L. Fultz (Philadelphia AL, 1902, street.)	3,600	1,800	1,100
(238)	David L. Fultz (New York AL, 1903.)	3,600	1,800	1,100
(240)	Robert S. Ganley (Pittsburg, 1906.)	2,100	1,050	630.00
(241)	Robert S. Ganley (Washington, 1907.)	2,100	1,050	630.00
(242)	John Ganzel (Ganzel) (New York AL, 1903.))	3,600	1,800	1,100
(243)	John Ganzel (Ganzell) (Cincinnati, 1907.))	2,100	1,050	630.00
(244)	Virgil Garvin (Brooklyn, 1903.)	3,000	1,500	900.00
(245)	Harry L. Gaspar (Cincinnati, 1910.)	2,100	1,050	630.00
(246)	Philip Geier (Boston NL, 1904.)	2,100	1,050	630.00
(247)	Harry Gessler (Brooklyn, 1903.)	3,600	1,800	1,100
(248)	Harry Gessler (Chicago NL, 1906.)	2,100	1,050	630.00
(250)	George Gibson (Pittsburg, 1905.)	2,100	1,050	630.00
(251)	Norwood Gibson (Boston AL, 1903.)	3,600	1,800	1,100
(252)	William Gilbert (New York NL, 1903.)	3,600	1,800	1,100
(253)	Frederick Glade (St. Louis AL, 1904.)	2,100	1,050	630.00
(254)	Harry Gleason (Boston AL, 1903.)	3,600	1,800	1,100
(255)	Harry Gleason (St. Louis AL, 1904.)	2,100	1,050	630.00
(256)	William Gleason (Philadelphia NL, 1903.)	3,600	1,800	1,100
(258)	William Gochnauer (John Gochnaur)(Cleveland, 1903.))	3,600	1,800	1,100
(259)	Michael Grady (St. Louis NL, 1904.)	2,100	1,050	630.00
(260)	Edward L. Grant (Philadelphia NL, 1910.)	3,450	1,725	1,050
(262)	Daniel Green (Chicago AL, 1903.)	3,600	1,800	1,100
(263)	E.W. Greminger (Boston NL, 1903.)	3,600	1,800	1,100
(264)	E.W. Greminger (Detroit, 1904.)	2,100	1,050	630.00
(265)	Clarke Griffith (Clark) (Chicago AL, 1902.))	7,900	4,000	2,375
(266)	Clarke Griffith (Clark) (New York AL, 1903.))	7,900	4,000	2,375
(267)	Myron Grimshaw (Boston AL, 1906.)	2,100	1,050	630.00
(269)	James Hackett (St. Louis NL, 1903.)	3,600	1,800	1,100
(270)	Edgar Hahn (Chicago AL, 1906.)	2,100	1,050	630.00
(271)	Frank Hahn (Cincinnati, 1902, street.)	2,100	1,050	630.00
(272)	Frank Hahn (New York AL, 1905.)	2,100	1,050	630.00
(273)	Charles Hall (Cincinnati, 1907.)	2,100	1,050	630.00
(274)	William H. Hallman (Philadelphia NL, 1903.)	3,600	1,800	1,100
(275)	William H. Hallman (Pittsburg, 1906.)	2,100	1,050	630.00
(276)	Edward Hanlon (Brooklyn, 1905, street.)	6,500	3,250	1,950
(277)	Edward Hanlon (Cincinnati, 1906.)	6,500	3,250	1,950
(278)	Richard Harley (Chicago NL, 1903.)	3,600	1,800	1,100
(279)	Robert Harmon (St. Louis NL, 1910.)	2,100	1,050	630.00
(280)	Charles Harper (Cincinnati, 1903.)	3,600	1,800	1,100
(281)	Charles Harper (Chicago NL, 1906.)	2,100	1,050	630.00
(282)	Joseph Harris (Boston AL, 1906.)	2,100	1,050	630.00
(283)	Harry Hart (Chicago AL, 1906.)	2,100	1,050	630.00
(284)	Frederick L. Hartzell (Hartsel)(Philadelphia AL, 1902.)	3,600	1,800	1,100
(285)	Roy A. Hartzell (St. Louis AL, 1906.)	2,100	1,050	630.00
(287)	J.E. Heidrick (St. Louis AL, 1903.)	3,600	1,800	1,100
(288)	Charles Hemphill (St. Louis AL, 1903.)	3,600	1,800	1,100
(289)	Weldon Henley (Philadelphia AL, 1903, street.)	3,600	1,800	1,100
(290)	Otto Hess (Cleveland, 1904.)	2,100	1,050	630.00
(291)	Edward Heydon (Mike) (Washington, 1906.))	2,100	1,050	630.00
(292)	Charles Hickman (Cleveland, 1903.)	3,600	1,800	1,100
(293)	Charles Hickman (Detroit, 1904.)	2,100	1,050	630.00
(294)	Charles Hickman (Washington, 1905.)	2,100	1,050	630.00
(295)	Charles Hickman (Chicago AL, 1907.)	2,100	1,050	630.00
(296)	Hunter Hill (St. Louis AL, 1903.)	3,600	1,800	1,100
(297)	Hunter Hill (Washington, 1904.)	2,100	1,050	630.00
(298)	Homer Hillebrand (Pittsburg, 1905.)	2,100	1,050	630.00
(299)	Harry Hinchman (Cleveland, 1907.)	2,100	1,050	630.00
(300)	William Hinchman (Cleveland, 1907.)	2,100	1,050	630.00
(303)	R. C. Hoblitzel (Cincinnati, 1910.)	2,100	1,050	630.00
(304)	Daniel Hoffman (Philadelphia AL, 1903.)	3,600	1,800	1,100
(305)	Daniel Hoffman (New York AL, 1906.)	2,100	1,050	630.00
(306)	Arthur Hofman (Chicago NL, 1906.)	2,100	1,050	630.00
(307)	William Hogg (New York AL, 1906.)	2,100	1,050	630.00

(308)	A. Holesketter (St. Louis NL, 1907.)	2,100	1,050	630.00
(309)	William Holmes (James Wm. "Ducky")(Chicago AL, 1903.))	3,600	1,800	1,100
(310)	George Howard (Pittsburg, 1905.)	2,100	1,050	630.00
(311)	George Howard (Boston NL, 1906.)	2,100	1,050	630.00
(312)	Harry Howell (Baltimore, 1902, street.)	3,600	1,800	1,100
(313)	Harry Howell (New York AL, 1903, street.)	3,600	1,800	1,100
(314)	Harry Howell (St. Louis AL, 1904.)	2,100	1,050	630.00
(315)	Miller Huggins (Cincinnati, 1906.)	6,500	3,250	1,950
(316)	James Hughes (Brooklyn, 1902, street.)	3,600	1,800	1,100
(317)	Thomas Hughes (Boston AL, 1902.)	3,600	1,800	1,100
(318)	Thomas Hughes (New York AL, 1904.)	2,100	1,050	630.00
(319)	Thomas Hughes (Washington, 1904.)	2,100	1,050	630.00
(320)	John Hulseman (Frank Huelsman) (Washington, 1904.))	2,100	1,050	630.00
(321)	Rudolph Hulswitt (Philadelphia NL, 1903.)	3,600	1,800	1,100
(322)	John Hummell (Hummel) (Brooklyn, 1906.))	2,100	1,050	630.00
(323)	Berthold J. Husting (Philadelphia AL, 1902, street.)	3,600	1,800	1,100
(324)	Hamilton Hyatt (Pittsburg, 1909.)	2,100	1,050	630.00
(325)	Frank Isbell (Chicago AL, 1903.)	3,600	1,800	1,100
(326)	Fred Jacklitsch (Brooklyn, 1903, street.)	3,600	1,800	1,100
(327)	Fred Jacklitsch (Philadelphia NL, 1907.)	2,100	1,050	630.00
(328)	James Jackson (Cleveland, 1906.)	2,100	1,050	630.00
(329)	Harry Jacobson (Albert "Beany")(Washington, 1904.))	2,100	1,050	630.00
(330)	Harry Jacobson (Albert "Beany")(St. Louis AL, 1906.))	2,100	1,050	630.00
(331)	Harry Jacobson (Albert "Beany")(Boston AL, 1907.))	2,100	1,050	630.00
(333)	Hugh Jennings (Philadelphia NL, 1902.)	7,900	4,000	2,375
(334)	Hugh Jennings (Detroit, 1907.)	6,500	3,250	1,950
(335)	Charles Jones (Washington, 1905.)	2,100	1,050	630.00
(336)	David Jones (Chicago NL, 1904.)	2,100	1,050	630.00
(337)	David Jones (Detroit, 1906.)	2,100	1,050	630.00
(338)	Fielder Jones (Chicago AL, 1902.)	3,600	1,800	1,100
(339)	Oscar Jones (Brooklyn, 1903.)	3,600	1,800	1,100
(340)	Thomas Jones (St. Louis AL, 1904.)	2,100	1,050	630.00
(341)	Otto Jordan ("Dutch") (Brooklyn, 1903.))	3,600	1,800	1,100
(342)	Otto Jordan ("Dutch") (Cleveland, 1905.))	2,100	1,050	630.00
(343)	Tim Jordan (Brooklyn, 1906.)	2,100	1,050	630.00
(344)	Adrian Joss (Cleveland, 1903.)	8,600	4,300	2,600
(345)	Michael Kahoe (St. Louis AL, 1903.)	3,600	1,800	1,100
(346)	Michael Kahoe (Philadelphia NL, 1905.)	2,100	1,050	630.00
(347)	Michael Kahoe (Chicago NL, 1907.)	2,100	1,050	630.00
(348)	Michael Kahoe (Washington, 1907.)	2,100	1,050	630.00
(349)	Edward Karger (Edwin) (Boston AL, 1910.))	2,100	1,050	630.00
(350)	Robert Keefe (New York AL, 1906.)	2,100	1,050	630.00
(351)	William Keeler (Brooklyn, 1902, street.)	7,900	4,000	2,375
(352)	William Keeler (New York, AL 1903, street.)	8,350	4,175	2,500

(353)	William Keister (Philadelphia NL, 1903.)	8,750	4,375	2,625
(355)	Joseph J. Kelley (Cincinnati, 1902, street.)	11,000	5,500	3,300
(356)	William Kennedy (Pittsburg, 1903, street.)	3,600	1,800	1,100
(357)	Edward Killian (Detroit, 1907.)	2,100	1,050	630.00
(358)	James Kissinger (Chas. "Rube" Kisinger) (Detroit, 1903.))	3,600	1,800	1,100
(359)	Frank Kitson (Brooklyn, 1902, street.)	3,600	1,800	1,100
(360)	Frank Kitson (Detroit, 1903.)	3,600	1,800	1,100
(361)	Frank Kitson (Washington, 1906.)	2,400	1,200	720.00
(362)	Frank Kitson (New York AL, 1907.)	2,100	1,050	630.00
(363)	Malachi Kittridge (Washington, 1903.)	3,600	1,800	1,100
(365)	John Kleinow (New York AL, 1905, street.)	2,100	1,050	630.00
(366)	John Kleinow (New York AL, 1905, uniform.)	2,100	1,050	630.00
(367)	John Kling (Chicago NL, 1903.)	3,600	1,800	1,100
(368)	F. Otto Knabe (Philadelphia NL, 1910.)	2,100	1,050	630.00
(369)	John Knight (Philadelphia AL, 1905.)	2,100	1,050	630.00
(370)	John Knight (Boston AL, 1907.)	2,100	1,050	630.00
(371)	Bernard Koehler (St. Louis AL, 1906.)	2,100	1,050	630.00
(372)	Edward Konetchy (St. Louis NL, 1907.)	2,100	1,050	630.00
(373)	Harry Krause (Philadelphia AL, 1910.)	2,100	1,050	630.00
(374)	Otto Krueger (Pittsburg, 1903.)	3,600	1,800	1,100
(375)	Otto Krueger (Philadelphia NL, 1905.)	2,100	1,050	630.00
(376)	George LaChance (Boston AL, 1903.)	3,600	1,800	1,100
(377)	Napoleon Lajoie (Cleveland, 1902, street.)	7,900	4,000	2,375
(378)	Napoleon Lajoie (Cleveland, 1902, uniform.)	9,500	4,750	2,850
(379)	Joseph Lake (St. Louis AL, 1910.)	2,100	1,050	630.00
(380)	Frank Laporte (LaPorte) (New York AL, 1906.))	2,100	1,050	630.00
(381)	Louis Laroy (LeRoy)	2,100	1,050	630.00
(382)	William Lauder (New York NL, 1903.)	3,600	1,800	1,100
(383)	Thomas Leach (Pittsburg, 1902.)	3,600	1,800	1,100
(384)	Wyatt Lee (Washington, 1903.)	3,600	1,800	1,100
(385)	Wyatt Lee (Pittsburg, 1904.)	2,100	1,050	630.00
(386)	Samuel Leever (Pittsburg, 1902, street.)	3,600	1,800	1,100
(387)	Samuel Leever (Pittsburg, 1902, uniform.)	2,100	1,050	630.00
(388)	Philip Lewis (Brooklyn, 1908.)	2,100	1,050	630.00
(389)	Vive A. Lindaman (Boston NL, 1906.)	2,100	1,050	630.00
(390)	Paddy Livingstone (Livingston) (Philadelphia AL, 1910.))	2,100	1,050	630.00
(391)	John Lobert (Cincinnati, 1907.)	2,100	1,050	630.00
(392)	Herman Long (Boston NL, 1902.)	3,600	1,800	1,100
(393)	Herman Long (Detroit, 1903.)	3,600	1,800	1,100
(394)	Herman Long (New York AL, 1903.)	3,600	1,800	1,100
(395)	Briscoe Lord (Philadelphia AL, 1905.)	2,100	1,050	630.00
(396)	Harry D. Lord (Chicago AL, 1910.)	2,100	1,050	630.00
(397)	Robert H. Lowe (Detroit, 1907.)	2,100	1,050	630.00

(398)	Harry Lumley (Brooklyn, 1904.)	2,100	1,050	630.00
(399)	Carl Lundgren (Chicago NL, 1903.)	3,600	1,800	1,100
(400)	John Lush	2,100	1,050	630.00
(401)	William L. Lush (Detroit, 1903.)	3,600	1,800	1,100
(402)	William L. Lush (Cleveland, 1904.)	2,100	1,050	630.00
(403)	Michael M. Lynch (Pittsburg, 1906.)	2,100	1,050	630.00
(404)	Michael M. Lynch (New York NL, 1907.)	2,100	1,050	630.00
(405)	Connie Mack (Philadelphia AL, 1902, street.)	7,900	4,000	2,375
(406)	Nick Maddox (Pittsburg, 1909.)	2,100	1,050	630.00
(407)	Sherwood Magee (Philadelphia NL, 1905.)	2,100	1,050	630.00
(408)	George H. Magoon (Chicago AL, 1903.)	3,600	1,800	1,100
(409)	John Malarkey (Boston NL, 1903.)	3,600	1,800	1,100
(410)	William Maloney (Chicago NL, 1905.)	2,100	1,050	630.00
(411)	William Maloney (Brooklyn, 1906.)	2,100	1,050	630.00
(412)	William R. Marshall (New York NL, 1905.)	2,100	1,050	630.00
(413)	William R. Marshall (St. Louis NL, 1906.)	2,100	1,050	630.00
(414)	William R. Marshall (Brooklyn, 1909.)	2,100	1,050	630.00
(415)	Christopher Matthewson (Mathewson) (New York NL, 1902, street.)	30,000	15,000	9,000
(416a)	Christopher Matthewson (Mathewson) (New York NL, 1902, uniform.)	20,000	10,000	6,000
(416b)	Christopher Mathewson (New York, NL, uniform, corrected.)	17,500	8,750	5,250
(417)	James A. McAleer (St. Louis AL, 1906.)	2,100	1,050	630.00
(418)	Louis McAllister (Lewis) (Detroit, 1903.))	3,600	1,800	1,100
(419)	John McCarthy (Cleveland, 1903.)	3,600	1,800	1,100
(420)	John McCarthy (Chicago NL, 1903.)	3,600	1,800	1,100
(421)	John McCarthy (Brooklyn, 1906.)	2,100	1,050	630.00
(422)	John J. McCloskey (St. Louis NL, 1906.)	2,100	1,050	630.00
(423)	Ambrose McConnell (Boston AL, 1910.)	2,100	1,050	630.00
(424)	George W. McQuillan (Philadelphia NL, 1907.)	2,100	1,050	630.00
(425)	Barry McCormick (St. Louis AL, 1903.)	3,600	1,800	1,100
(426)	Barry McCormick (Washington, 1903.)	3,600	1,800	1,100
(427)	Michael McCormick (Brooklyn, 1904.)	2,100	1,050	630.00
(428)	Charles McFarland (St. Louis NL, 1903.)	3,600	1,800	1,100
(429)	Charles McFarland (Pittsburg, 1906.)	2,100	1,050	630.00
(430)	Edward McFarland (Chicago AL, 1902, street.)	3,600	1,800	1,100
(431)	Herm McFarland (Hermas)(New York AL, 1903.))	3,600	1,800	1,100
(432)	John McFetridge (Philadelphia NL, 1903.)	3,600	1,800	1,100
(433)	Dan McGann (New York NL, 1903.)	3,600	1,800	1,100
(434)	Joseph McGinnity (New York NL, 1902, street.)	8,000	4,000	2,375
(435)	Joseph McGinnity (New York NL, 1902, uniform.)	8,000	4,000	2,375
(436)	John J. McGraw (Infielder, New York NL, 1902, street.)	8,000	4,000	2,375
(437)	John J. McGraw (Manager, New York NL, 1902, street.)	9,500	4,750	2,850
(438)	James McGuire (Detroit, 1903.)	2,100	1,050	630.00
(439)	James McGuire (New York AL, 1904.)	2,100	1,050	630.00

(440) James McGuire (Boston AL, 1907.)	2,100	1,050	630.00
(441) Harry McIntyre (McIntire) (Brooklyn, 1905.))	2,100	1,050	630.00
(442) Matty McIntyre (Detroit, 1904, street.)	2,100	1,050	630.00
(443) John B. McLean (Cincinnati, 1910.)	2,100	1,050	630.00
(444) John Menefee (Chicago NL, 1903.)	3,600	1,800	1,100
(445) Fred Merkle (New York NL, 1908.)	2,100	1,050	630.00
(446) Samuel Mertes (New York NL, 1903.)	3,600	1,800	1,100
(447) Samuel Mertes (St. Louis NL, 1906.)	2,100	1,050	630.00
(448) Samuel Mertes (Boston NL, 1907.)	2,100	1,050	630.00
(451) Clyde Milan (Washington, 1910.)	2,100	1,050	630.00
(452) John B. Miller (Pittsburg, 1909.)	2,100	1,050	630.00
(453) Roscoe Miller (Photo actually George Mullin. New York NL, 1903.)	3,600	1,800	1,100
(454) Roscoe Miller (Pittsburg, 1903.)	3,600	1,800	1,100
(455) William Milligan (New York NL, 1904.)	2,100	1,050	630.00
(456) Frederick Mitchell (Philadelphia NL, 1903, street.)	3,000	1,500	900.00
(457) Frederick Mitchell (Brooklyn, 1904.)	2,100	1,050	630.00
(458) M.F. Mitchell (Cincinnati, 1910.)	2,100	1,050	630.00
(461) Earl Moore (Cleveland, 1903.)	2,100	1,050	630.00
(462) Earl Moore (New York AL, 1907.)	2,100	1,050	630.00
(463) Charles P. Moran (Middle initial V.) (Washington, 1904.))	2,100	1,050	630.00
(464) Charles P. Moran (Middle initial V.) (St. Louis AL, 1904.))	2,100	1,050	630.00
(465) Patrick J. Moran (Boston NL, 1902, street.)	3,600	1,800	1,100
(466) Patrick J. Moran (Chicago NL, 1906.)	2,100	1,050	630.00
(467) Lewis Moren (Philadelphia NL, 1910.)	2,100	1,050	630.00
(468) Harry R. Morgan (Philadelphia AL, 1910.)	2,100	1,050	630.00
(469) Eugene Moriarty (George)(New York AL, 1906.))	2,100	1,050	630.00
(470) John Morrissey (Cincinnati, 1903.)	3,600	1,800	1,100
(471) Michael Mowery (Cincinnati, 1907.)	2,100	1,050	630.00
(472) George Mullin (Detroit, 1903.)	3,600	1,800	1,100
(473) Daniel Murphy (Philadelphia AL, 1902, street.)	3,600	1,800	1,100
(474) John J. Murray (St. Louis NL, 1907.)	2,100	1,050	630.00
(475) William Murray (Boston NL, 1907.)	2,100	1,050	630.00
(477) Joseph Nealon (Jim) (Pittsburg, 1906.))	2,100	1,050	630.00
(478) Daniel Needham (Thomas)(Boston NL, 1904.))	2,100	1,050	630.00
(479) Eustace J. Newton (New York AL, 1906.)	2,100	1,050	630.00
(481) Simon Nicholls (Philadelphia AL, 1907.)	2,100	1,050	630.00
(482) Harry Niles (St. Louis AL, 1906.)	2,100	1,050	630.00
(483) George Nill (Washington, 1906.)	2,100	1,050	630.00
(484) George Nill (Cleveland, 1907.)	2,100	1,050	630.00
(485) Pete Noonan (St. Louis NL, 1906.)	2,100	1,050	630.00
(486) John O'Brien (Boston AL, 1903.)	3,600	1,800	1,100
(487) Peter O'Brien (St. Louis AL, 1906.)	2,100	1,050	630.00
(488) Peter O'Brien (Cleveland, 1907.)	2,400	1,200	720.00
(489) Peter O'Brien (Washington, 1907.)	2,100	1,050	630.00
(490) John O'Connor (Pittsburg, 1902.)	3,600	1,800	1,100
(491) John O'Connor (New York AL, 1903.)	3,600	1,800	1,100
(492) John O'Connor (St. Louis AL, 1904.)	2,400	1,200	720.00
(493) Reuben Oldring (Philadelphia AL, 1906.)	2,100	1,050	630.00
(494) Charles O'Leary (Detroit, 1904.)	2,100	1,050	630.00
(495) John J. O'Neil (O'Neill) (St. Louis NL, 1903.))	3,000	1,500	900.00
(496) John J. O'Neil (O'Neill) (Chicago NL, 1904.))	2,100	1,050	630.00
(497) John O'Neil (O'Neill) (Boston NL, 1906.))	2,100	1,050	630.00
(498) Michael J. O'Neil (O'Neill) (St. Louis NL, 1903.))	3,600	1,800	1,100
(499) Michael J. O'Neil (O'Neill) (Brooklyn, 1906.))	2,100	1,050	630.00
(500) Albert Orth (Washington, 1903.)	3,000	1,500	900.00
(501) Albert Orth (New York AL, 1904.)	2,100	1,050	630.00
(502) Orville Overall (Orval) (Chicago NL, 1906.))	2,100	1,050	630.00
(503) Frank Owen (Chicago AL, 1903.)	3,600	1,800	1,100
(504) Richard Padden (St. Louis AL, 1903.)	3,600	1,800	1,100
(505) Frederick Parent (Boston AL, 1902.)	3,600	1,800	1,100
(508) George Paskert (Cincinnati, 1910.)	2,100	1,050	630.00
(509) James Pastorious (Brooklyn, 1906.)	2,100	1,050	630.00
(510) Case Patten (Washington, 1903.)	3,600	1,800	1,100
(511) Roy Patterson (Chicago AL, 1903.)	3,600	1,800	1,100
(512) Frederick Payne (Detroit, 1906.)	2,100	1,050	630.00
(513) Henry Peitz (Cincinnati, 1904.)	2,100	1,050	630.00
(514) Henry Peitz (Pittsburg, 1905.)	2,100	1,050	630.00
(515) Barney Pelty (St. Louis AL, 1904.)	2,100	1,050	630.00
(516) Frank Pfeiffer ("Big Jeff" Pfeffer)(Chicago NL, 1905.))	2,100	1,050	630.00
(517) Frank Pfeiffer ("Big Jeff" Pfeffer)(Boston NL, 1906.))	2,100	1,050	630.00
(518) John Pfiester (Chicago NL, 1907.)	2,100	1,050	630.00
(519) Edward Phelps (Pittsburg, 1903.)	3,000	1,500	900.00
(520) Edward Phelps (Cincinnati, 1905.)	2,100	1,050	630.00
(521) Charles Phillippe (Pittsburg, 1903.)	3,600	1,800	1,100
(522) William Phillips (Cincinnati, 1902, street.)	3,600	1,800	1,100
(523) Wiley Piatt (Boston NL, 1903.)	3,600	1,800	1,100
(524) Oliver Pickering (Philadelphia AL, 1903.)	3,600	1,800	1,100
(525) Oliver Pickering (St. Louis AL, 1906.)	2,100	1,050	630.00
(526) Charles Pittinger (Boston NL, 1903.)	3,600	1,800	1,100
(527) Charles Pittinger (Philadelphia NL, 1905.)	2,100	1,050	630.00
(528) Edward S. Plank (Philadelphia AL, 1902 street.)	12,250	6,125	3,675
(529) Edward S. Plank (Philadelphia AL, 1902, uniform.)	12,250	6,125	3,675
(530) Edward Poole (Cincinnati, 1903.)	3,600	1,800	1,100
(531) Edward Poole (Brooklyn, 1904.)	2,100	1,050	630.00
(532) John Powell (St. Louis AL, 1903.)	3,600	1,800	1,100
(533) John Powell (New York AL, 1904.)	2,100	1,050	630.00
(534) Maurice R. Powers (Michael)(Philadelphia AL, 1902, street.))	3,600	1,800	1,100
(535) William Purtell (Boston AL, 1910.)	2,100	1,050	630.00
(536) Ambrose Puttmann (New York AL, 1905.)	2,100	1,050	630.00
(539) Thomas Raub (Chicago NL, 1903.)	3,600	1,800	1,100
(540) Frederick Raymer (Boston NL, 1904.)	2,100	1,050	630.00
(541) William Reidy (Brooklyn, 1903.)	3,600	1,800	1,100
(542) Ed Reulbach (Chicago NL, 1907.)	2,100	1,050	630.00
(543) R.B. Rhoades (Rhoads) (Cleveland, 1903.))	3,600	1,800	1,100
(544) Lewis Richie (Chicago NL, 1910.)	2,100	1,050	630.00
(545) Branch Rickey (New York AL, 1907.)	6,500	3,250	1,950
(546) Claude Ritchey (Pittsburg, 1902, street.)	3,600	1,800	1,100
(547) Claude Ritchey (Boston NL, 1907.)	2,100	1,050	630.00
(548) Louis Ritter (Lewis) (Brooklyn, 1903.))	3,600	1,800	1,100
(549) Clyde Robinson (Detroit, 1904.)	2,100	1,050	630.00
(550) George Rohe (Chicago AL, 1906.)	2,100	1,050	630.00
(553) Claude Rossman (Cleveland, 1906.)	2,100	1,050	630.00
(554) Claude Rossman (Detroit, 1907.)	2,100	1,050	630.00
(555) Frank Roth (Philadelphia NL, 1903.)	3,600	1,800	1,100
(556) Frank Roth (St. Louis AL, 1905.)	2,100	1,050	630.00
(557) Frank Roth (Chicago AL, 1906.)	2,100	1,050	630.00
(558) John A. Rowan (Cincinnati, 1910.)	2,100	1,050	630.00
(559) James Ryan (Washington, 1902, street.)	3,600	1,800	1,100
(562) Harry Sallee (St. Louis NL, 1910.)	2,100	1,050	630.00
(563) Herman Schaefer (Detroit, 1907.)	2,100	1,050	630.00
(564) George Schlei (Cincinnati, 1906.)	2,100	1,050	630.00
(565) Charles Schmidt (Detroit, 1906.)	2,100	1,050	630.00
(566) Harry S. Schmidt ((Brooklyn, 1903.))	3,600	1,800	1,100
(567) Osee F. Schreckengost (Ossee)(Philadelphia AL, 1902, street.))	3,600	1,800	1,100
(568) Osee F. Schreckengost (Ossee)(Philadelphia AL, 1902, uniform.))	3,600	1,800	1,100
(569) Frank Schulte (Chicago NL, 1905.)	2,100	1,050	630.00
(570) Al Schweitzer (St. Louis AL, 1910.)	2,100	1,050	630.00
(571) James Sebring (Pittsburg, 1903.)	3,600	1,800	1,100
(572) James Sebring (Cincinnati, 1904.)	2,100	1,050	630.00
(573) James Sebring (Chicago NL, 1905.)	2,100	1,050	630.00
(575) Albert Selbach (Washington, 1903.)	3,600	1,800	1,100
(576) Albert Selbach (Boston AL, 1904.)	2,100	1,050	630.00
(577) Ralph O. "Socks" Seybold (Philadelphia AL, 1902, street.)	3,600	1,800	1,100
(578) J. Bentley Seymour (Cincinnati, 1903.)	3,600	1,800	1,100
(579) J. Bentley Seymour (New York NL, 1906.)	2,100	1,050	630.00
(580) Arthur Shafer (New York NL, 1910.)	2,100	1,050	630.00
(581) W.P. Shannon (St. Louis NL, 1904.)	2,100	1,050	630.00
(582) W.P. Shannon (New York NL, 1906.)	2,100	1,050	630.00
(583) Daniel Shay (St. Louis NL, 1904.)	2,100	1,050	630.00
(586) David Shean (Boston NL, 1910.)	2,100	1,050	630.00
(587) James Sheckard (Brooklyn, 1902, street.)	3,600	1,800	1,100
(588) James Sheckard (Chicago NL, 1906.)	2,100	1,050	630.00
(589) Edward Siever (Detroit, 1903.)	3,600	1,800	1,100
(590) Edward Siever (St. Louis AL, 1903.)	3,600	1,800	1,100

(591)	James Slagle (Chicago NL, 1903.)	3,600	1,800	1,100
(592)	John Slattery (Chicago AL, 1903.)	3,600	1,800	1,100
(593)	Alexander Smith ("Broadway Aleck") (Boston AL, 1903.))	3,600	1,800	1,100
(594)	Alexander Smith ("Broadway Aleck") (Chicago NL, 1904.))	2,100	1,050	630.00
(595)	Alexander Smith ("Broadway Aleck") (New York NL, 1906.))	2,100	1,050	630.00
(596)	Charles Smith (Boston AL, 1910.)	2,100	1,050	630.00
(597)	Edward Smith (St. Louis AL, 1906.)	2,100	1,050	630.00
(598)	Frank Smith (Chicago AL, 1904.)	2,100	1,050	630.00
(599)	Harry Smith (Pittsburg, 1902, street.)	3,600	1,800	1,100
(600)	Heinie Smith (Detroit, 1903, street.)	3,600	1,800	1,100
(602)	Homer Smoot (St. Louis NL, 1903.)	3,600	1,800	1,100
(603)	Homer Smoot (Cincinnati, 1906.)	2,100	1,050	630.00
(604)	Frank Sparks (.) T. Frank "Tully")(Philadelphia, NL, 1903)	3,600	1,800	1,100
(605)	Charles ("Chic") Stahl (Boston AL, 1902.)	4,000	1,950	1,200
(606)	Jacob G. Stahl (Washington, 1904.)	2,100	1,050	630.00
(607)	Jacob G. Stahl (Washington)	2,100	1,050	630.00
(609)	J.B. Stanley (Boston NL, 1903.)	3,600	1,800	1,100
(610)	J.B. Stanley (Washington, 1905.)	2,100	1,050	630.00
(611)	Harry Steinfeldt (Cincinnati, 1902, street.)	3,600	1,800	1,100
(612)	Harry Steinfeldt (Chicago NL, 1905.)	2,100	1,050	630.00
(615)	James Stephens (St. Louis AL, 1910.)	2,100	1,050	630.00
(616)	George Stone (St. Louis AL, 1905.)	2,100	1,050	630.00
(617)	George Stovall (Cleveland, 1904.)	2,100	1,050	630.00
(618)	Jesse Stovall (Detroit, 1904.)	2,100	1,050	630.00
(619)	Samuel Strang (Brooklyn, 1903.)	3,600	1,800	1,100
(620)	Samuel Strang (New York NL, 1905.)	2,100	1,050	630.00
(621)	Elmer Stricklett (Brooklyn, 1906.)	2,100	1,050	630.00
(622)	Willie Sudhoff (St. Louis AL, 1903.)	3,600	1,800	1,100
(623)	Willie Sudhoff (Washington, 1906.)	2,100	1,050	630.00
(624)	Joseph Sugden (St. Louis AL, 1903.)	3,600	1,800	1,100
(625)	George Suggs (Cincinnati, 1910.)	2,100	1,050	630.00
(628)	William D. Sullivan (Middle initial J.) (Chicago AL, 1902.))	3,600	1,800	1,100
(629)	Edgar Summers (Detroit, 1909.)	2,100	1,050	630.00
(630)	William J. Sweeney (Boston NL, 1910.)	2,100	1,050	630.00
(632)	Jesse Tannehill (New York AL, 1903.)	3,600	1,800	1,100
(633)	Jesse Tannehill (Boston AL, 1904.)	2,100	1,050	630.00
(634)	Lee Tannehill (Chicago AL, 1903.)	3,600	1,800	1,100
(636)	John Taylor (Chicago NL, 1902.)	3,600	1,800	1,100
(637)	John Taylor (St. Louis NL, 1904.)	2,100	1,050	630.00
(638)	Luther H. Taylor (New York NL, 1903.)	7,900	4,000	2,375
(639)	Fred Tenney (Boston NL, 1903.)	3,600	1,800	1,100
(640)	Ira Thomas (New York AL, 1906.)	2,100	1,050	630.00
(641)	Roy Thomas (Philadelphia NL, 1903.)	3,600	1,800	1,100
(642)	John Thoney (Cleveland, 1903.)	3,600	1,800	1,100
(643)	John Thoney (Washington, 1904.)	2,100	1,050	630.00

(644)	John Thoney (New York AL, 1904.)	2,100	1,050	630.00
(645)	Joseph B. Tinker (Chicago NL, 1903.)	6,600	3,300	1,980
(646)	John Townsend (Washington, 1903.)	3,600	1,800	1,100
(647)	John Townsend (Cleveland, 1906.)	2,100	1,050	630.00
(648)	Terrence Turner (Cleveland, 1904.)	2,100	1,050	630.00
(650)	Robert Unglaub (Boston AL, 1905.)	2,100	1,050	630.00
(652)	George Van Haltren (New York NL, 1902, street.)	4,300	2,150	1,300
(653)	George Van Haltren (New York NL, 1902, uniform.)	3,250	1,625	975.00
(654)	Fred Veil (Pittsburg, 1903.)	3,250	1,625	975.00
(655)	Ernest Vinson (Cleveland, 1905.)	2,100	1,050	630.00
(656)	Ernest Vinson (Chicago AL, 1905.)	2,100	1,050	630.00
(660)	George Edward "Rube" Waddell (Philadelphia AL, 1902, street.)	8,000	4,000	2,375
(661)	George Edward Waddell (St. Louis AL, 1908.)	6,500	3,250	1,950
(663)	Charles Wagner (Boston AL, 1910.)	2,100	1,050	630.00
(664)	John ("Hans") Wagner (Pittsburg, 1902, street.)	20,000	10,000	6,000
(665)	John ("Hans") Wagner (Pittsburg, 1905, uniform.)	27,500	13,750	8,250
(666)	Robert Wallace (St. Louis AL, 1902.)	8,000	4,000	2,375
(668)	Edward A. Walsh (Chicago AL, 1904.)	6,500	3,250	1,950
(670)	John Warner (New York NL, 1903.)	3,600	1,800	1,100
(671)	John Warner (St. Louis NL, 1905.)	2,100	1,050	630.00
(672)	John Warner (Detroit, 1905.)	2,100	1,050	630.00
(673)	John Warner (Washington, 1906.)	2,400	1,200	720.00
(674)	Arthur Weaver (Pittsburg, 1903.)	3,600	1,800	1,100
(675)	Arthur Weaver (St. Louis AL, 1905.)	2,100	1,050	630.00
(676)	Jacob Weimer (Chicago NL, 1903.)	3,600	1,800	1,100
(677)	Jacob Weimer (Cincinnati, 1906.)	2,100	1,050	630.00
(678)	G. Harry White (G. Harris "Doc")(Chicago AL, 1903.)	3,600	1,800	1,100
(679)	Robert Wicker (Chicago NL, 1903.)	3,600	1,800	1,100
(680)	Robert Wicker (Cincinnati, 1906.)	2,100	1,050	630.00
(681)	Fredrick Wilhelm (Irvin "Kaiser")(Pittsburg, 1903.))	3,600	1,800	1,100
(682)	Fredrick Wilhelm (Irvin "Kaiser")(Boston NL, 1904.))	2,100	1,050	630.00
(683)	Edgar Willett (Detroit, 1907.)	2,100	1,050	630.00
(684)	James Williams (Baltimore, 1902, street.)	3,600	1,800	1,100
(685)	James Williams (New York AL, 1903, street.)	3,600	1,800	1,100
(686)	James Williams (New York AL, 1903, uniform.)	3,600	1,800	1,100
(687)	Otto G. Williams (Chicago NL, 1904.)	2,100	1,050	630.00
(688)	Otto G. Williams (Philadelphia AL, 1905.)	2,100	1,050	630.00
(689)	Otto G. Williams (Washington, 1906.)	2,100	1,050	630.00
(692)	Victor J. Willis (Boston NL, 1903.)	8,000	4,000	2,375
(693)	Victor J. Willis (Pittsburg, 1906.)	6,500	2,350	1,950
(694)	Howard P. Wilson (Philadelphia AL, 1902, street.)	3,600	1,800	1,100
(695)	Howard P. Wilson (Washington, 1903.)	3,600	1,800	1,100
(696)	Howard P. Wilson (Cleveland, 1906.)	2,100	1,050	630.00

(698)	J. Owen Wilson (Pittsburg, 1910.)	2,100	1,050	630.00
(699)	George Wiltse (New York NL, 1904.)	2,100	1,050	630.00
(700)	Louis Wiltse (Lewis) (Baltimore, 1902.))	3,600	1,800	1,100
(701)	Louis Wiltse (Lewis)(New York AL, 1903.))	3,600	1,800	1,100
(702)	George Winters (Winter) (Boston AL, 1902, street.))	3,000	1,500	900.00
(705)	William Wolfe (Wilbert) (Washington, 1904.))	2,100	1,050	630.00
(706)	Harry Wolverton (Philadelphia NL, 1902, street.)	3,600	1,800	1,100
(707)	Harry Wolverton (Boston NL, 1905.)	2,100	1,050	630.00
(708)	Robert Wood (Detroit, 1904.)	2,100	1,050	630.00
(710)	Eugene Wright (Clarence Eugene)(Cleveland, 1903.))	3,600	1,800	1,100
(711)	Eugene Wright (Clarence Eugene)(St. Louis AL, 1903.))	3,600	1,800	1,100
(712)	Joseph Yeager (Detroit, 1902, street.)	3,600	1,800	1,100
(713)	Joseph Yeager (New York AL, 1905.)	2,100	1,050	630.00
(714)	Joseph Yeager (St. Louis AL, 1907.)	2,100	1,050	630.00
(715)	Denton ("Cy") Young (Boston AL, 1902.)	22,250	11,125	6,675
(716)	Irving Young (Boston NL, 1905.)	2,100	1,050	630.00
(717)	David Zearfoss (St. Louis NL, 1904.)	2,100	1,050	630.00
(718)	Charles Zimmer (Pittsburg, 1902.)	3,600	1,800	1,100
(719)	Charles Zimmer (Philadelphia NL, 1903.)	3,600	1,800	1,100
(720)	H. Zimmerman (Chicago NL, 1910.)	2,100	1,050	630.00

TRAP SHOOTERS

(T1)	Neas Apgar	950.00	500.00	300.00
(T2)	Chas. W. Budd	950.00	500.00	300.00
(T3)	W.R. Crosby	950.00	500.00	300.00
(T4)	J.A.R. Elliott	950.00	500.00	300.00
(T5)	J.S. Fanning	950.00	500.00	300.00
(T6)	Fred Gilbert	950.00	500.00	300.00
(T7)	Rolla O. Heikes	950.00	500.00	300.00
(T8)	H.C. Hirschy	950.00	500.00	300.00
(T9)	Tom A. Marshall	950.00	500.00	300.00
(T10)	Harvey McMurchy	950.00	500.00	300.00
(T11)	Ralph Trimble	950.00	500.00	300.00

1902 Sporting Life Team Composites (W601)

Printed on heavy 13" x 14" paper and featuring a composite of player photos arranged around that of the manager and a notice of league championship status, these prints were offered to readers of the weekly sports paper for six cents in postage stamps or 50 cents per dozen. The art was often found on the covers of "Sporting Life." While the prints were issued in 1902, they specify the teams as champions "for 1903." The Buck Weaver shown on the Butte composite is not the future Black Sox shortstop.

	NM	E	VG
Complete Set:	4,500	2,200	1,350
Common Team:	300.00	150.00	90.00
(1) Philadelphia, American League	500.00	250.00	150.00
(2) Pittsburg, National League	500.00	250.00	150.00
(3) Albany, New York State League	300.00	150.00	90.00

		NM	E	VG
(4)	Butte, Pacific Northwest League	400.00	200.00	120.00
(5)	Indianapolis, American Association	400.00	200.00	120.00
(6)	Kansas City, Western League	400.00	200.00	120.00
(7)	Manchester, New England League	300.00	150.00	90.00
(8)	Nashville, Southern League	350.00	175.00	105.00
(9)	New Haven, Connecticut League	300.00	150.00	90.00
(10)	Rockford, Illinois-Indiana-Iowa League	300.00	150.00	90.00
(11)	Toronto, Eastern League	400.00	200.00	120.00

1903 Sporting Life Team Composites (W601)

Portraits of the individual players, usually identified by name and position, surround the manager's portrait in this series of team composites sold by Sporting Life newspaper. The 1903 series is the first in which all major league team composites were available. The 13" x 14" pictures are printed on heavy enamel paper and were sold for six cents in postage stamps, 50 cents per dozen. In some years bound portfolio complete sets were also offered, as were some of the more popular minor league teams. Notations of league and World Championships were incorporated into the design where appropriate. While issued in 1903, the pictures of league championship teams carry the notation "For 1904."

		NM	E	VG
Complete Set (25):		5,550	2,700	1,650
Common (Major League) Team:		400.00	200.00	120.00
(1)	Boston, National League	400.00	200.00	120.00
(2)	Brooklyn, National League	400.00	200.00	120.00
(3)	Chicago, National League	600.00	300.00	180.00
(4)	Cincinnati, National League	400.00	200.00	120.00
(5)	New York, National League	500.00	250.00	150.00
(6)	Philadelphia, National League	400.00	200.00	120.00
(7)	Pittsburg, National League	500.00	250.00	150.00
(8)	St. Louis, National League	400.00	200.00	120.00
(9)	Boston, American League	450.00	225.00	135.00
(10)	Chicago, American League	400.00	200.00	120.00
(11)	Cleveland, American League	400.00	200.00	120.00
(12)	Detroit, American League	400.00	200.00	120.00
(13)	New York, American League	450.00	225.00	135.00
(14)	Philadelphia, American League	450.00	225.00	135.00
(15)	St. Louis, American League	400.00	200.00	120.00
(16)	Washington, American League	400.00	200.00	120.00
(17)	Ft. Wayne, Central League	250.00	125.00	75.00
(18)	Holyoke, Connecticut League	250.00	125.00	75.00
(19)	Jersey City, Eastern League	300.00	150.00	90.00
(20)	Los Angeles, Pacific Coast League	300.00	150.00	90.00
(21)	Lowell, New England League	250.00	125.00	75.00
(22)	Memphis, Southern League	250.00	125.00	75.00
(23)	Schenectady, New York State League	250.00	125.00	75.00
(24)	Sedalia, Missouri Valley League	250.00	125.00	75.00
(25)	St. Paul, American Association	300.00	150.00	90.00

1904 Sporting Life Team Composites (W601)

Portraits of the individual players, usually identified by name and position, surround the manager's portrait in this series of team composites sold by Sporting Life newspaper. The 13" x 14" pictures are printed on heavy enamel paper and were sold for a dime apiece postpaid. In some years bound portfolio complete sets were also offered, as were some of the more popular minor league teams. Notations of league and World Championships were incorporated into the design where appropriate.

		NM	E	VG
Complete Set (24):		5,550	2,700	1,650
Common (Major League) Team:		400.00	200.00	120.00
(1)	Boston, National League	400.00	200.00	120.00
(2)	Brooklyn, National League	400.00	200.00	120.00
(3)	Chicago, National League	600.00	300.00	180.00
(4)	Cincinnati, National League	400.00	200.00	120.00
(5)	New York, National League	500.00	250.00	150.00
(6)	Philadelphia, National League	400.00	200.00	120.00
(7)	Pittsburg, National League	550.00	275.00	165.00
(8)	St. Louis, National League	400.00	200.00	120.00
(9)	Boston, American League	450.00	225.00	135.00
(10)	Chicago, American League	400.00	200.00	120.00
(11)	Cleveland, American League	400.00	200.00	120.00
(12)	Detroit, American League	400.00	200.00	120.00
(13)	New York, American League	450.00	225.00	135.00
(14)	Philadelphia, American League	550.00	275.00	165.00
(15)	St. Louis, American League	400.00	200.00	120.00
(16)	Washington, American League	400.00	200.00	120.00
(17)	Buffalo, Eastern League	300.00	150.00	90.00
(18)	Ft. Wayne, Central League	200.00	100.00	60.00
(19)	Haverhill, New England League	200.00	100.00	60.00
(20)	Macon, South Atlantic League	200.00	100.00	60.00
(21)	Memphis, Southern League	200.00	100.00	60.00
(22)	League	200.00	100.00	60.00
(23)	St. Paul, American Association	250.00	125.00	75.00
(24)	Syracuse, New York League (1903 Indiana-Illinois-Iowa League Champs)	200.00	100.00	60.00

1905 Sporting Life Team Composites (W601)

Portraits of the individual players, usually identified by name and position, surround the manager's portrait in this series of team composites sold by Sporting Life newspaper. The 13" x 14" pictures are printed on heavy enamel paper and were sold for a dime apiece postpaid. In some years bound portfolio complete sets were also offered, as were some of the more popular minor league teams. Notations of league and World Championships were incorporated into the

design where appropriate.

		NM	E	VG
Complete Set (23):		5,500	2,700	1,650
Common (Major League) Team:		400.00	200.00	120.00
(1)	Boston, National League	400.00	200.00	120.00
(2)	Brooklyn, National League	400.00	200.00	120.00
(3)	Chicago, National League	600.00	300.00	180.00
(4)	Cincinnati, National League	400.00	200.00	120.00
(5)	New York, National League	450.00	225.00	135.00
(6)	Philadelphia, National League	400.00	200.00	120.00
(7)	Pittsburgh, National League	750.00	375.00	225.00
(8)	St. Louis, National League	400.00	200.00	120.00
(9)	Boston, American League	400.00	200.00	120.00
(10)	Chicago, American League	400.00	200.00	120.00
(11)	Cleveland, American League	400.00	200.00	120.00
(12)	Detroit, American League	400.00	200.00	120.00
(13)	New York, American League	600.00	300.00	180.00
(14)	Philadelphia, American League	600.00	300.00	180.00
(15)	St. Louis, American League	400.00	200.00	120.00
(16)	Washington, American League	400.00	200.00	120.00
(17)	A., J. & G., New York League	200.00	100.00	60.00
(18)	Columbus, American Association	250.00	125.00	75.00
(19)	Concord, New England League	200.00	100.00	60.00
(20)	Des Moines, Western League	200.00	100.00	60.00
(21)	Macon, South Atlantic League	200.00	100.00	60.00
(22)	New Orleans, Southern League	250.00	125.00	75.00
(23)	Providence, Eastern League	250.00	125.00	75.00

1906-07 Sporting Life Team Composite Postcards

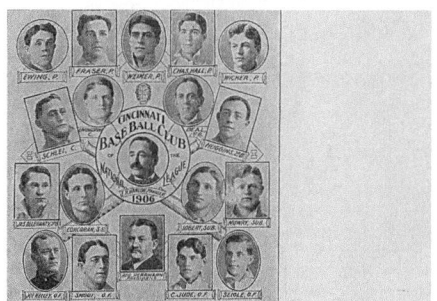

A miniature version of the Sporting Life's team composite lithographs was utilized to create a postcard set. In 3-5/8" x 5-7/16" format, the postcards have a composite of player portraits surrounding that of the manager, with a wide white right margin. Backs have standard postcard indicia. Some cards have been found with backs containing an ad offering either league's set for 10 cents in stamps.

		NM	E	VG
Complete Set (16):		13,500	6,750	4,150
Common Team:		675.00	335.00	200.00
(1)	Boston, National League	675.00	335.00	200.00

		NM	E	VG
(2)	Brooklyn, National League	900.00	450.00	270.00
(3)	Chicago, National League	1,400	700.00	420.00
(4)	Cincinnati, National League	850.00	425.00	255.00
(5)	New York, National League	850.00	425.00	255.00
(6)	Philadelphia, National League	675.00	335.00	200.00
(7)	Pittsburg, National League	1,000	500.00	300.00
(8)	St. Louis, National League	675.00	335.00	200.00
(9)	Boston, American League	700.00	350.00	210.00
(10)	Chicago, American League	700.00	350.00	210.00
(11)	Cleveland, American League	1,100	550.00	330.00
(12)	Detroit, American League	7,000	3,500	2,100
(13)	New York, American League	1,100	550.00	330.00
(14)	Philadelphia, American League	900.00	450.00	270.00
(15)	St. Louis, American League	900.00	450.00	270.00
(16)	Washington, American League	800.00	400.00	240.00

1906 Sporting Life Team Composites (W601)

Originally sold as a string-bound "Premier Art Portfolio" containing 24 major and minor league team composite pictures, single pieces from this premium issue are not uncommonly found as they were later offered individually for 10 cents apiece. The individual pieces measure 13" x 14" and are printed in black-and-white on heavy enameled paper. Individual player pictures are arranged around a baseball containing the manager's picture. Each player is identified beneath his photo by name and position. By 1906 the year printed on the pictures corresponds to the year of issue.

		NM	E	VG
Complete Set (24):		12,000	6,000	3,500
Common Major League Team:		550.00	275.00	165.00
Common Minor League Team:		300.00	150.00	90.00
(1)	Boston, National League	750.00	375.00	225.00
(2)	Brooklyn, National League	550.00	275.00	165.00
(3)	Chicago, National League	800.00	400.00	240.00
(4)	Cincinnati, National League	550.00	275.00	165.00
(5)	New York, National League	650.00	325.00	195.00
(6)	Philadelphia, National League	675.00	335.00	200.00
(7)	Pittsburg, National League	650.00	325.00	195.00
(8)	St. Louis, National League	550.00	275.00	165.00
(9)	Boston, American League	800.00	400.00	240.00
(10)	Chicago, American League	650.00	325.00	195.00
(11)	Cleveland, American League	1,200	600.00	360.00
(12)	Detroit, American League	1,200	600.00	360.00
(13)	New York, American League	800.00	400.00	240.00
(14)	Philadelphia, American League	800.00	400.00	240.00
(15)	St. Louis, American League	550.00	275.00	165.00
(16)	Washington, American League	550.00	275.00	165.00
(17)	National League president, managers	600.00	300.00	180.00
(18)	American League president, managers	600.00	300.00	180.00
(19)	Birmingham, Southern League	300.00	150.00	90.00
(20)	Buffalo, Eastern League	300.00	150.00	90.00
(21)	Columbus, American Association	300.00	150.00	90.00
(22)	Grand Rapids, Central League	300.00	150.00	90.00
(23)	Norwich, Connecticut League	300.00	150.00	90.00
(24)	Scranton, New York League	300.00	150.00	90.00

1907 Sporting Life Team Composites (W601)

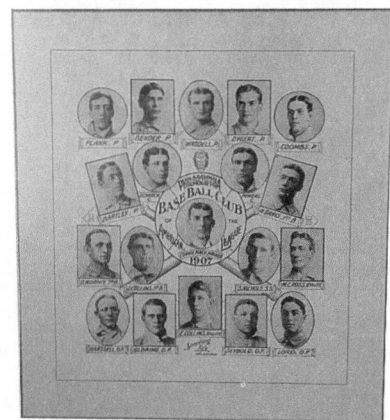

Portraits of the individual players, usually identified by name and position, surround the manager's portrait in this series of team composites sold by Sporting Life newspaper. The 13" x 14" pictures are printed on heavy enamel paper and were sold for a dime apiece postpaid. In some years bound portfolio complete sets were also offered, as were some of the more popular minor league teams. Notations of league and World Championships were incorporated into the design where appropriate.

		NM	E	VG
Complete Set (23):		5,500	2,700	1,600
Common (Major League) Team:		400.00	200.00	120.00
(1)	Boston, National League	400.00	200.00	120.00
(2)	Brooklyn, National League	400.00	200.00	120.00
(3)	Chicago, National League	500.00	250.00	150.00
(4)	Cincinnati, National League	400.00	200.00	120.00
(5)	New York, National League	500.00	250.00	150.00
(6)	Philadelphia, National League	400.00	200.00	120.00
(7)	Pittsburg, National League	450.00	225.00	135.00
(8)	St. Louis, National League	400.00	200.00	120.00
(9)	Boston, American League	400.00	200.00	120.00
(10)	Chicago, American League	400.00	200.00	120.00
(11)	Cleveland, American League	400.00	200.00	120.00
(12)	Detroit, American League	600.00	300.00	180.00
(13)	New York, American League	450.00	225.00	135.00
(14)	Philadelphia, American League	400.00	200.00	120.00
(15)	St. Louis, American League	400.00	200.00	120.00
(16)	Washington, American League	500.00	250.00	150.00
(17)	Toronto, Eastern League	300.00	150.00	90.00
(18)	Columbus, American Association	300.00	150.00	90.00
(19)	Williamsport, Tri-State League	200.00	100.00	60.00
(20)	Albany, New York League	200.00	100.00	60.00
(21)	Atlanta, Southern League	200.00	100.00	60.00
(22)	Holyoke, Connecticut League	200.00	100.00	60.00
(23)	Norfolk, Virginia League	200.00	100.00	60.00

1908 Sporting Life Team Composites (W601)

Portraits of the individual players, usually identified by name and position, surround the manager's portrait in this series of team composites sold by Sporting Life newspaper. The 13" x 14" pictures are printed on heavy enamel paper and were sold for a dime apiece postpaid. In some years bound portfolio complete sets were also offered, as were some of the more popular minor league teams. Notations of league and World Championships were incorporated into the design where appropriate.

		NM	E	VG
Complete Set (16):		4,500	2,250	1,350
Common Team:		400.00	200.00	120.00
(1)	Boston, National League	400.00	200.00	120.00
(2)	Brooklyn, National League	400.00	200.00	120.00
(3)	Chicago, National League	500.00	250.00	150.00
(4)	Cincinnati, National League	400.00	200.00	120.00
(5)	New York, National League	425.00	210.00	125.00
(6)	Philadelphia, National League	400.00	200.00	120.00
(7)	Pittsburgh, National League	450.00	225.00	135.00
(8)	St. Louis, National League	400.00	200.00	120.00
(9)	Boston, American League	400.00	200.00	120.00
(10)	Chicago, American League	400.00	200.00	120.00
(11)	Cleveland, American League	400.00	200.00	120.00
(12)	Detroit, American League	600.00	300.00	180.00
(13)	New York, American League	450.00	225.00	135.00
(14)	Philadelphia, American League	400.00	200.00	120.00
(15)	St. Louis, American League	400.00	200.00	120.00
(16)	Washington, American League	450.00	225.00	135.00

1909 Sporting Life Team Composites (W601)

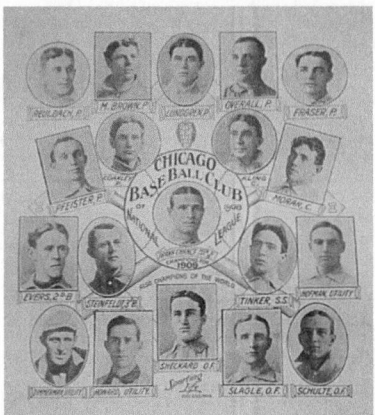

Portraits of the individual players, usually identified by name and position, surround the manager's portrait in this series of team composites sold by Sporting Life newspaper. The 13" x 14" pictures are printed on heavy enamel paper and were sold for a dime apiece postpaid. In some years bound portfolio complete sets were also offered, as were some of the more popular minor league teams. Notations of league and World Championships were incorporated into the design where appropriate.

		NM	E	VG
Complete Set (16):		6,500	3,250	1,850
Common Team:		600.00	300.00	180.00
(1)	Boston, National League	600.00	300.00	180.00
(2)	Brooklyn, National League	600.00	300.00	180.00
(3)	Chicago, National League	750.00	375.00	225.00
(4)	Cincinnati, National League	600.00	300.00	180.00
(5)	New York, National League	675.00	335.00	200.00
(6)	Philadelphia, National League	600.00	300.00	180.00
(7)	Pittsburgh, National League	1,125	560.00	335.00
(8)	St. Louis, National League	1,000	500.00	300.00
(9)	Boston, American League	600.00	300.00	180.00
(10)	Chicago, American League	600.00	300.00	180.00
(11)	Cleveland, American League	600.00	300.00	180.00
(12)	Detroit, American League	900.00	450.00	270.00
(13)	New York, American League	675.00	335.00	200.00

(14)	Philadelphia, American League	600.00	300.00	180.00
(15)	St. Louis, American League	600.00	300.00	180.00
(16)	Washington, American League	675.00	335.00	200.00

1910-11 Sporting Life (M116)

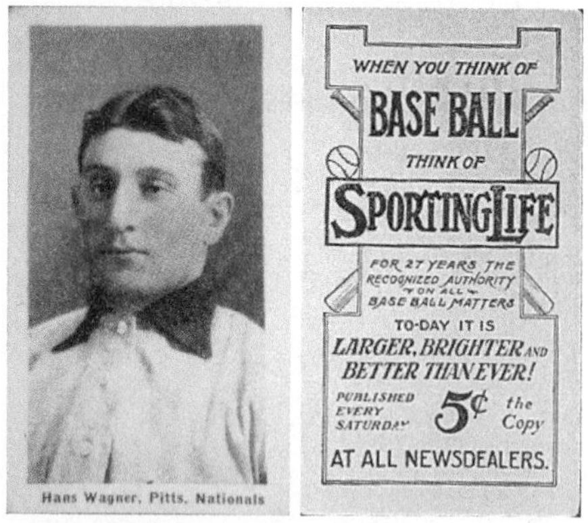
Hans Wagner, Pitts. Nationals
WHEN YOU THINK OF
BASE BALL
THINK OF
SPORTING LIFE
FOR 27 YEARS THE RECOGNIZED AUTHORITY ON ALL BASE BALL MATTERS
TO-DAY IT IS
LARGER, BRIGHTER AND BETTER THAN EVER!
PUBLISHED EVERY SATURDAY
5¢ the Copy
AT ALL NEWSDEALERS.

This set of nominally 1-1/2" x 2-5/8" (individual card sizes vary even moreso than typically found on early 20th Century cards, notably with the "high numbers" often found somewhat larger) cards was offered to subscribers to "Sporting Life," a major competitor of "The Sporting News" in the early part of the century. The cards were issued in 24 series of 12 cards each, sold by mail for four cents per series. Card fronts feature color-tinted black-and-white portrait photos with the name and team printed below. Backs have various ads for the weekly paper. The last three 24-card series are scarcer than the earlier cards. These 72 cards have "Over 300 subjects" printed on back. Values in this checklist are adjusted according to that scarcity. The scarce blue-background cards appear to have been a second printing of the first two 12-card series which no doubt sold out quickly in the original pastel-background version due to the popularity of the players included. The 12 players in the Third Series can be found in an original printing with the ad on back printed in black, and a later version with a blue back. Each of the Third Series cards also exhibits on front subtle differences in the size and coloring of the player portrait. The complete set price does not include variations. Early series cards with over 300 subjects back should have 30% premium.

		NM	E	VG
	Common Player:	225.00	115.00	65.00
(1)	Ed Abbaticchio	225.00	115.00	65.00
(2a)	Babe Adams (Black back.)	225.00	115.00	65.00
(2b)	Babe Adams (Blue back.)	325.00	160.00	95.00
(3)	Red Ames	625.00	315.00	190.00
(4)	Jimmy Archer	625.00	315.00	190.00
(5)	Frank Arrelanes (Arellanes)	225.00	115.00	65.00
(6)	Tommy Atkins	625.00	315.00	190.00
(7)	Jimmy Austin	625.00	315.00	190.00
(8)	Les Bachman (Backman)	225.00	115.00	65.00
(9)	Bill Bailey	360.00	180.00	110.00
(10a)	Home Run Baker (Black back.)	1,000	500.00	300.00
(10b)	Home Run Baker (Blue back.)	1,500	750.00	450.00
(11)	Cy Barger	225.00	115.00	65.00
(12)	Jack Barry	225.00	115.00	65.00
(13a)	Johnny Bates (Philadelphia)	225.00	115.00	65.00
(13b)	Johnny Bates (Cincinnati) (A G-VG example sold at auction 4/06 for $22,987.)			
(14)	Ginger Beaumont	225.00	115.00	65.00
(15)	Fred Beck	225.00	115.00	65.00
(16)	Heinie Beckendorf	225.00	115.00	65.00
(17)	Fred Beebe	225.00	115.00	65.00
(18)	George Bell	225.00	115.00	65.00
(19)	Harry Bemis	225.00	115.00	65.00
(20a)	Chief Bender (Blue background.)	1,500	750.00	450.00
(20b)	Chief Bender (Pastel background.)	1,000	500.00	300.00
(21)	Bill Bergen	225.00	115.00	65.00
(22)	Heinie Berger	225.00	115.00	65.00
(23)	Bob Bescher	225.00	115.00	65.00
(24)	Joe Birmingham	225.00	115.00	65.00
(25)	Lena Blackburn (Blackburne)	225.00	115.00	65.00
(26)	John Bliss	625.00	315.00	190.00
(27)	Bruno Block	625.00	315.00	190.00
(28)	Bill Bradley	225.00	115.00	65.00
(29)	Kitty Bransfield	225.00	115.00	65.00
(30a)	Roger Bresnahan (Blue)	1,500	750.00	450.00
(30b)	Roger Bresnahan (Pastel)	1,000	500.00	300.00
(31)	Al Bridwell	225.00	115.00	65.00
(32)	Buster Brown (Boston)	225.00	115.00	65.00
(33a)	Mordecai Brown (Blue, Chicago.)	1,500	750.00	450.00
(33b)	Mordecai Brown (Pastel, Chicago.)	1,000	500.00	300.00
(34)	Al Burch	225.00	115.00	65.00
(35)	Donie Bush	225.00	115.00	65.00
(36)	Bobby Byrne	225.00	115.00	65.00
(37)	Howie Camnitz	225.00	115.00	65.00
(38)	Vin Campbell	625.00	315.00	190.00
(39)	Bill Carrigan	225.00	115.00	65.00
(40a)	Frank Chance (Blue)	1,500	750.00	450.00
(40b)	Frank Chance (Pastel)	1,000	500.00	300.00
(41)	Chappy Charles	225.00	115.00	65.00
(42a)	Hal Chase (Blue)	1,000	500.00	300.00
(42b)	Hal Chase (Pastel)	700.00	350.00	210.00
(43)	Ed Cicotte	1,125	565.00	335.00
(44a)	Fred Clarke (Pittsburgh, black back.)	1,000	500.00	300.00
(44b)	Fred Clarke (Pittsburgh, blue back.)	1,500	750.00	450.00
(45)	Nig Clarke (Cleveland)	225.00	115.00	65.00
(46)	Tommy Clarke (Cincinnati)	625.00	315.00	190.00
(47a)	Ty Cobb (Blue)	8,250	4,125	2,475
(47b)	Ty Cobb (Pastel)	5,250	2,6001.550.00	
(48a)	Eddie Collins (Blue)	1,500	750.00	450.00
(48b)	Eddie Collins (Pastel)	1,000	500.00	300.00
(49)	Ray Collins	625.00	315.00	190.00
(50)	Wid Conroy	225.00	115.00	65.00
(51)	Jack Coombs	225.00	115.00	65.00
(52)	Frank Corridon	225.00	115.00	65.00
(53)	Harry Coveleskie (Coveleski)	1,250	625.00	375.00
(54)	Doc Crandall	225.00	115.00	65.00
(55a)	Sam Crawford (Blue)	1,500	750.00	450.00
(55b)	Sam Crawford (Pastel)	1,000	500.00	300.00
(56)	Birdie Cree	220.00	115.00	65.00
(57)	Lou Criger	225.00	115.00	65.00
(58)	Dode Criss	625.00	315.00	190.00
(59)	Cliff Curtis	625.00	315.00	190.00
(60)	Bill Dahlen	225.00	115.00	65.00
(62)	Bill Davidson	625.00	315.00	190.00
(62a)	Harry Davis (Blue)	625.00	315.00	190.00
(62b)	Harry Davis (Pastel)	225.00	115.00	65.00
(63)	Jim Delehanty (Delahanty)	225.00	115.00	65.00
(64)	Ray Demmitt	625.00	315.00	190.00
(65)	Rube Dessau	625.00	315.00	190.00
(66a)	Art Devlin (Black back.)	225.00	115.00	65.00
(66b)	Art Devlin (Blue back.)	325.00	160.00	95.00
(67)	Josh Devore	625.00	315.00	190.00
(68)	Pat Donahue	225.00	115.00	65.00
(69)	Patsy Donovan	625.00	315.00	190.00
(70a)	Wild Bill Donovan (Blue)	625.00	315.00	190.00
(70b)	Wild Bill Donovan (Pastel)	225.00	115.00	65.00
(71a)	Red Dooin (Blue)	625.00	315.00	190.00
(71b)	Red Dooin (Pastel)	225.00	115.00	65.00
(72)	Mickey Doolan	225.00	115.00	65.00
(73)	Patsy Dougherty	225.00	115.00	65.00
(74)	Tom Downey	225.00	115.00	65.00
(75)	Jim Doyle	225.00	115.00	65.00
(76a)	Larry Doyle (Blue)	625.00	315.00	190.00
(76b)	Larry Doyle (Pastel)	225.00	115.00	65.00
(77)	Hugh Duffy	1,000	500.00	300.00
(78)	Jimmy Dygert	225.00	115.00	65.00
(79)	Dick Eagan (Egan)	225.00	115.00	65.00
(80)	Kid Elberfeld	225.00	115.00	65.00
(81)	Rube Ellis	225.00	115.00	65.00
(82)	Clyde Engle	225.00	115.00	65.00
(83)	Tex Erwin	625.00	315.00	190.00
(84)	Steve Evans	625.00	315.00	190.00
(85a)	Johnny Evers (Black back.)	1,000	500.00	300.00
(85b)	Johnny Evers (Blue back.)	1,500	750.00	450.00
(86)	Bob Ewing	225.00	115.00	65.00
(87)	Cy Falkenberg	225.00	115.00	65.00
(88)	George Ferguson	225.00	115.00	65.00
(89)	Art Fletcher	1,000	500.00	300.00
(90)	Elmer Flick	1,000	500.00	300.00
(91)	John Flynn	625.00	315.00	190.00
(92)	Russ Ford	625.00	315.00	190.00
(93)	Eddie Foster	625.00	315.00	190.00
(94)	Bill Foxen	225.00	115.00	90.00
(95)	John Frill	625.00	315.00	190.00
(96)	Sam Frock	625.00	315.00	190.00
(97)	Art Fromme	225.00	115.00	65.00
(98)	Earl Gardner (New York)	625.00	315.00	190.00
(99)	Larry Gardner (Boston)	625.00	315.00	190.00
(100)	Harry Gaspar	625.00	315.00	190.00
(101)	Doc Gessler	225.00	115.00	65.00
(102a)	George Gibson (Blue)	625.00	315.00	190.00
(102b)	George Gibson (Pastel)	225.00	115.00	65.00
(103)	Bill Graham (St. Louis)	225.00	115.00	65.00
(104)	Peaches Graham (Boston)	225.00	115.00	65.00
(105)	Eddie Grant	225.00	115.00	65.00
(106)	Clark Griffith	1,000	500.00	300.00
(107)	Ed Hahn	225.00	115.00	65.00
(108)	Charley Hall	225.00	115.00	65.00
(109)	Bob Harmon	625.00	315.00	90.00
(110)	Topsy Hartsel	225.00	115.00	65.00
(111)	Roy Hartzell	225.00	115.00	65.00
(112)	Heinie Heitmuller	225.00	115.00	65.00
(113)	Buck Herzog	225.00	115.00	65.00
(114)	Dick Hoblitzel (Hoblitzell)	225.00	115.00	65.00
(115)	Danny Hoffman	225.00	115.00	65.00
(116)	Solly Hofman	225.00	115.00	65.00
(117)	Harry Hooper	1,000	500.00	300.00
(118)	Harry Howell	225.00	115.00	65.00
(119)	Miller Huggins	1,000	500.00	300.00
(120)	Long Tom Hughes	625.00	315.00	190.00
(121)	Rudy Hulswitt	225.00	115.00	65.00
(122)	John Hummel	225.00	115.00	65.00
(123)	George Hunter	225.00	115.00	65.00
(124)	Ham Hyatt	225.00	115.00	65.00
(125)	Fred Jacklitsch	225.00	115.00	65.00
(126a)	Hughie Jennings (Blue)	1,500	750.00	450.00
(126b)	Hughie Jennings (Pastel)	1,000	500.00	300.00
(127)	Walter Johnson	3,500	1,750	1,050
(128a)	Davy Jones (Blue)	625.00	315.00	190.00
(128b)	Davy Jones (Pastel)	225.00	115.00	65.00
(129)	Tom Jones	225.00	115.00	65.00
(130a)	Tim Jordan (Blue)	625.00	315.00	190.00
(130b)	Tim Jordan (Pastel)	225.00	115.00	65.00
(131)	Addie Joss	1,200	600.00	360.00
(132)	Johnny Kane	225.00	115.00	65.00
(133)	Ed Karger	225.00	115.00	65.00
(134)	Red Killifer (Killefer)	625.00	315.00	190.00
(135)	Johnny Kling	225.00	115.00	65.00
(136)	Otto Knabe	225.00	115.00	65.00
(137)	John Knight	625.00	315.00	190.00
(138)	Ed Konetchy	225.00	115.00	65.00
(139)	Harry Krause	225.00	115.00	65.00
(140)	Rube Kroh	225.00	115.00	65.00
(141)	Art Krueger	1,000	500.00	300.00
(142a)	Nap Lajoie (Blue)	1,500	750.00	450.00
(142b)	Nap Lajoie (Pastel)	1,000	500.00	300.00
(143)	Fred Lake (Boston)	225.00	115.00	65.00
(144)	Joe Lake (St. Louis)	625.00	315.00	190.00
(145)	Frank LaPorte	225.00	115.00	65.00
(146)	Jack Lapp	625.00	315.00	190.00
(147)	Chick Lathers	625.00	315.00	190.00
(148a)	Tommy Leach (Blue)	625.00	315.00	190.00
(148b)	Tommy Leach (Pastel)	225.00	115.00	65.00
(149)	Sam Leever	225.00	115.00	65.00
(150)	Lefty Leifeld	225.00	115.00	65.00
(151)	Ed Lennox	225.00	115.00	65.00
(152)	Fred Linke (Link)	625.00	315.00	190.00
(153)	Paddy Livingstone (Livingston)	225.00	115.00	65.00
(154)	Hans Lobert	225.00	115.00	65.00
(155)	Bris Lord	225.00	115.00	65.00
(156a)	Harry Lord (Blue)	625.00	315.00	190.00
(156b)	Harry Lord (Pastel)	225.00	115.00	65.00
(157)	Johnny Lush	225.00	115.00	65.00
(158)	Connie Mack	1,000	500.00	300.00
(159)	Tom Madden	625.00	315.00	190.00
(160)	Nick Maddox	225.00	115.00	65.00
(161)	Sherry Magee	225.00	115.00	65.00
(162a)	Christy Mathewson (Blue)	4,600	2,300	1,375
(162b)	Christy Mathewson (Pastel)	2,450	1,225	750.00
(163)	Al Mattern	225.00	115.00	65.00
(164)	Jimmy McAleer	225.00	115.00	65.00
(165)	George McBride	625.00	315.00	190.00
(166a)	Amby McConnell (Boston)	225.00	115.00	65.00
(166b)	Amby McConnell (Chicago)	6,250	3,125	1,875
(167)	Pryor McElveen	225.00	115.00	65.00
(168)	John McGraw	1,000	500.00	300.00
(169)	Deacon McGuire	225.00	115.00	65.00
(170)	Stuffy McInnes (McInnis)	625.00	315.00	190.00
(171)	Harry McIntire (McIntyre)	225.00	115.00	65.00
(172)	Matty McIntyre	225.00	115.00	65.00
(173)	Larry McLean	225.00	115.00	65.00
(174)	Tommy McMillan	225.00	115.00	65.00
(175a)	George McQuillan (Blue, Philadelphia.)	625.00	315.00	190.00
(175b)	George McQuillan (Pastel, Philadelphia.)	225.00	115.00	65.00
(175c)	George McQuillan (Cincinnati)	3,125	1,565	950.00
(176)	Paul Meloan	625.00	315.00	190.00
(177)	Fred Merkle	225.00	115.00	65.00
(178)	Clyde Milan	225.00	115.00	65.00
(179)	Dots Miller (Pittsburgh)	225.00	115.00	65.00

(180)	Warren Miller (Washington)	625.00	315.00	190.00
(181)	Fred Mitchell	625.00	315.00	190.00
(182)	Mike Mitchell	225.00	115.00	65.00
(183)	Earl Moore	225.00	115.00	65.00
(184)	Pat Moran	225.00	115.00	65.00
(185a)	Lew Moren (Black back.)	325.00	160.00	95.00
(185b)	Lew Moren (Blue back.)	225.00	115.00	65.00
(186)	Cy Morgan	225.00	115.00	65.00
(187)	George Moriarty	225.00	115.00	65.00
(188)	Mike Mowery (Mowrey)	625.00	315.00	190.00
(189a)	George Mullin (Black back.)	225.00	115.00	65.00
(189b)	George Mullin (Blue back.)	325.00	160.00	95.00
(190)	Danny Murphy	225.00	115.00	65.00
(191)	Red Murray	225.00	115.00	65.00
(192)	Chief Myers (Meyers)	625.00	315.00	190.00
(193)	Tom Needham	225.00	115.00	65.00
(194)	Harry Niles	225.00	115.00	65.00
(195)	Rebel Oakes	625.00	315.00	190.00
(196)	Jack O'Connor	225.00	115.00	65.00
(197)	Paddy O'Connor	225.00	115.00	65.00
(198)	Bill O'Hara	625.00	315.00	190.00
(199)	Rube Oldring	225.00	115.00	65.00
(200)	Charley O'Leary	225.00	115.00	65.00
(201)	Orval Overall	225.00	115.00	65.00
(202)	Freddy Parent	225.00	115.00	65.00
(203)	Dode Paskert	625.00	315.00	190.00
(204)	Fred Payne	625.00	315.00	190.00
(205)	Barney Pelty	225.00	115.00	65.00
(206)	Hub Pernoll	625.00	315.00	190.00
(207)	George Perring	625.00	315.00	190.00
(208)	Big Jeff Pfeffer	625.00	315.00	190.00
(209)	Jack Pfiester	225.00	115.00	65.00
(210)	Art Phelan	625.00	315.00	190.00
(211)	Ed Phelps	225.00	115.00	65.00
(212)	Deacon Phillippe	225.00	115.00	65.00
(213)	Eddie Plank	2,225	1,100	650.00
(214)	Jack Powell	225.00	115.00	65.00
(215)	Billy Purtell	225.00	115.00	65.00
(216)	Farmer Ray	625.00	315.00	190.00
(217)	Bugs Raymond	225.00	115.00	65.00
(218)	Doc Reisling	225.00	115.00	65.00
(219)	Ed Reulbach	225.00	115.00	65.00
(220)	Lew Richie	225.00	115.00	65.00
(221)	Jack Rowan	225.00	115.00	65.00
(222a)	Nap Rucker (Black back.)	225.00	115.00	65.00
(222b)	Nap Rucker (Blue back.)	325.00	160.00	95.00
(223)	Slim Sallee	225.00	115.00	65.00
(224)	Doc Scanlon	225.00	115.00	65.00
(225)	Germany Schaefer	225.00	115.00	65.00
(226)	Lou Schettler	625.00	315.00	190.00
(227)	Admiral Schlei	225.00	115.00	65.00
(228)	Boss Schmidt	225.00	115.00	65.00
(229)	Wildfire Schulte	225.00	115.00	65.00
(230)	Al Schweitzer	225.00	115.00	65.00
(231)	Jim Scott	625.00	315.00	190.00
(232a)	Cy Seymour (N.Y.)	225.00	115.00	65.00
(232b)	Cy Seymour (Baltimore)(Two known; 4/04 auction $18,000+ Fair-Good.))			
(233)	Tillie Shafer	225.00	115.00	65.00
(234)	Bud Sharpe	625.00	315.00	190.00
(235)	Dave Shean	625.00	315.00	190.00
(236)	Jimmy Sheckard	225.00	115.00	65.00
(237)	Mike Simon	625.00	315.00	190.00
(238)	Charlie Smith (Boston)	625.00	315.00	190.00
(239)	Frank Smith (Chicago)	225.00	115.00	65.00
(240)	Harry Smith (Boston)	225.00	115.00	65.00
(241)	Fred Snodgrass	225.00	115.00	65.00
(242)	Bob Spade	225.00	115.00	65.00
(243)	Tully Sparks	225.00	115.00	65.00
(244)	Tris Speaker	2,125	1,050	625.00
(245)	Jake Stahl	225.00	115.00	65.00
(246)	George Stallings	225.00	115.00	65.00
(247)	Oscar Stanage	225.00	115.00	65.00
(248)	Harry Steinfeldt	225.00	115.00	65.00
(249)	Jim Stephens	225.00	115.00	65.00
(250)	George Stone	225.00	115.00	65.00
(251)	George Stovall	225.00	115.00	65.00
(252)	Gabby Street	225.00	115.00	65.00
(253)	Sailor Stroud	625.00	315.00	190.00
(254)	Amos Strunk	625.00	315.00	190.00
(255)	George Suggs	625.00	315.00	190.00
(256)	Billy Sullivan	225.00	115.00	65.00
(257a)	Ed Summers (Black back.)	225.00	115.00	65.00
(257b)	Ed Summers (Blue back.)	325.00	160.00	95.00
(258)	Bill Sweeney (Boston)	225.00	115.00	65.00
(259)	Jeff Sweeney (New York)	625.00	315.00	190.00
(260)	Lee Tannehill	225.00	115.00	65.00
(261a)	Fred Tenney (Blue)	625.00	315.00	190.00
(261b)	Fred Tenney (Pastel)	225.00	115.00	65.00
(262a)	Ira Thomas (Blue)	625.00	315.00	190.00
(262b)	Ira Thomas (Pastel)	225.00	115.00	65.00
(263)	Jack Thoney	225.00	115.00	65.00
(264a)	Joe Tinker (Black back.)	1,000	500.00	300.00
(264b)	Joe Tinker (Blue back.)	1,500	750.00	450.00

(265)	John Titus	625.00	315.00	190.00
(266)	Terry Turner	225.00	115.00	65.00
(267)	Bob Unglaub	225.00	115.00	65.00
(268a)	Rube Waddell (Black back.)	1,000	500.00	300.00
(268b)	Rube Waddell (Blue back.)	1,500	750.00	450.00
(269a)	Hans Wagner (Pittsburgh, blue.)	7,250	3,600	2,150
(269b)	Hans Wagner (Pittsburgh, pastel.)	5,000	2,500	1,500
(270)	Heinie Wagner (Boston)	225.00	115.00	65.00
(271)	Bobby Wallace	1,000	500.00	300.00
(272)	Ed Walsh (Chicago)	1,000	500.00	300.00
(273a)	Jimmy Walsh (Gray background, Philadelphia.)	900.00	450.00	270.00
(273b)	Jimmy Walsh (White background, Philadelphia.)	900.00	450.00	270.00
(274)	Doc White	225.00	115.00	65.00
(275)	Kaiser Wilhelm	225.00	115.00	65.00
(276)	Ed Willett	225.00	115.00	65.00
(277)	Vic Willis	1,000	500.00	300.00
(278)	Art Wilson (New York)	625.00	315.00	190.00
(279)	Owen Wilson (Pittsburgh)	225.00	115.00	65.00
(280)	Hooks Wiltse	225.00	115.00	65.00
(281)	Harry Wolter	225.00	115.00	65.00
(282)	Smokey Joe Wood	1,675	800.00	475.00
(283)	Ralph Works	225.00	115.00	65.00
(284a)	Cy Young (Black back.)	1,450	725.00	425.00
(284b)	Cy Young (Blue back.)	2,000	1,000	600.00
(285)	Irv Young	225.00	115.00	65.00
(286)	Heinie Zimmerman	625.00	315.00	190.00
(287)	Dutch Zwilling	225.00	115.00	65.00

1910 Sporting Life Team Composites (W601)

After several years of issuing composite team photos for all major league teams (and some minor league teams), Sporting Life in 1910 began issuing them only for the league and World's Champions. Like the others, they are 13" x 14", printed on heavy enamel paper with individual player portrait photos surrounding the manager at center.

		NM	E	VG
Complete Set (2):		1,200	600.00	350.00
Common Team:		300.00	150.00	90.00
(1)	Chicago Cubs (N.L. Champs)	450.00	225.00	135.00
(2)	Philadelphia Athletics (World's Champions)	750.00	375.00	225.00

1911 Sporting Life Cabinets (M110)

This set of 5-5/8" x 7-1/2" premium photos is similar to, but much scarcer than, the contemporary T3 Turkey Red cabinets. Like those, the Sporting Life cabinets feature a pastel player picture surrounded by a gray frame with a "gold"

nameplate at bottom. Backs have advertising for the weekly sports paper printed in blue.

		NM	E	VG
Complete Set (6):		200,000	100,000	60,000
Common Player:		15,000	7,500	4,500
(1)	Frank Chance	20,000	10,000	6,000
(2)	Hal Chase	15,000	7,500	4,500
(3)	Ty Cobb	75,000	37,500	22,500
(4)	Napoleon Lajoie	25,000	12,500	7,500
(5)	Christy Mathewson	50,000	25,000	15,000
(6)	Honus Wagner	65,000	32,500	19,500

1911 Sporting Life Team Composites (W601)

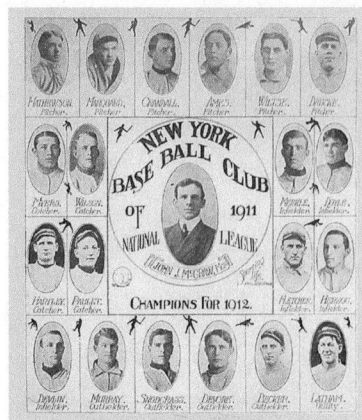

After several years of issuing composite team photos for all major league teams (and some minor league teams), Sporting Life in 1910 began issuing them only for the league and World's Champions. Like the others, they are 13" x 14", printed on heavy enamel paper with individual player portrait photos surrounding the manager at center.

		NM	E	VG
Complete Set (2):		1,200	600.00	350.00
Common Team:		300.00	150.00	90.00
(1)	New York Giants (N.L. Champs)	600.00	300.00	180.00
(2)	Philadelphia Athletics (World's Champions)	750.00	375.00	225.00

1899-1900 Sporting News Supplements (M101-1)

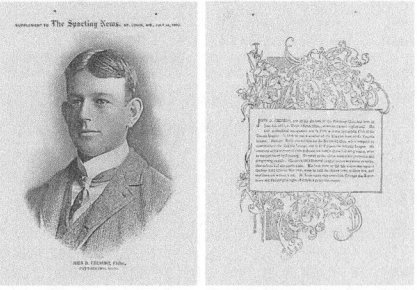

For much of 1899 and 1900, the weekly issues of The Sporting News included a baseball player portrait supplement. About 8-3/4" x 11", the pictures offered vignetted photos of the era's stars on a glossy paper stock. Virtually all pictures were formal head-and-shoulders portraits; some in uniform, some in civilian clothes. A handful of players are depicted in full-length poses. The pictures were produced for the sports paper by National Copper Plate Co., (which issued its own set of prints listed elsewhere in this catalog). The TSN supplements have a logotype above the photo and the date in which it was included in the paper. Full player name and team/year are printed at bottom. Backs have a small box offering career information. Besides offering the pictures with weekly issues, portfolios of 50 could be had by starting or renewing a subscription for $2 a year.

		NM	E	VG
Complete Set (62):		90,000	36,000	18,000
Common Player:		1,125	450.00	225.00
1899				
(1)	William Lange (Apr. 22)	1,125	450.00	225.00
(2)	Hugh Duffy (Apr. 29)	1,875	750.00	375.00
(3)	Charles A. Nichols (May 6)	1,875	750.00	375.00
(4)	Martin Bergen (May 13)	1,125	450.00	225.00
(5)	Michael Griffin (May 20)	1,125	450.00	225.00

(6)	Wilbert Robinson (May 27)	1,875	750.00	375.00
(7)	Clark C. Griffith (June 3)	1,875	750.00	375.00
(8)	John J. Doyle (June 10)	1,125	450.00	225.00
(9)	R.J. Wallace (June 17)	1,875	750.00	375.00
(10)	John O'Connor (June 24)	1,125	450.00	225.00
(11)	Louis Criger (July 1)	1,125	450.00	225.00
(12)	Jerry H. Nops (July 8)	1,125	450.00	225.00
(13)	William Kennedy (July 15)	1,125	450.00	225.00
(14)	P.J. Donovan (July 22)	1,125	450.00	225.00
(15)	William H. Keeler (July 29)	1,875	750.00	375.00
(16)	John J. McGraw (Aug. 5)	1,875	750.00	375.00
(17)	James Hughes (Aug. 12)	1,125	450.00	225.00
(18)	John Wagner (Aug. 19)	11,250	4,500	2,250
(19)	Victor G. Willis (Aug. 26)	1,875	750.00	375.00
(20)	James J. Collins (Sept. 2)	1,875	750.00	375.00
(21)	Eugene DeMontreville (Sept. 9)	1,125	450.00	225.00
(22)	Joseph J. Kelley (Sept. 16)	1,875	750.00	375.00
(23)	Frank L. Donahue (Francis R. "Red") (Sept. 23)	1,125	450.00	225.00
(24)	Edward J. Delehanty (Delahanty)(Sept. 30)	1,125	450.00	225.00
(25)	Fred C. Clark (Clarke) (Oct. 7)	1,875	750.00	375.00
(26)	Napoleon Lajoie (Oct. 14)	1,875	750.00	375.00
(27)	Edward Hanlon (Oct. 21)	1,875	750.00	375.00
(28)	Charles Stahl (Oct. 28)	1,125	450.00	225.00
(29)	Lave N. Cross (Nov. 4)	1,125	450.00	225.00
(30)	Elmer H. Flick (Nov. 11)	1,875	750.00	375.00
(31)	Frank LeRoy Chance (Nov. 18)	1,875	750.00	375.00
(32)	George S. Davis (Nov. 25)	1,875	750.00	375.00
(33)	Hugh J. Jennings (Dec. 2)	1,875	750.00	375.00
(34)	Denton T. Young (Dec. 9)	3,750	1,500	750.00
	1900			
(35)	George E. Waddell (Apr. 14)	1,875	750.00	375.00
(36)	John Dunn (Apr. 21)	1,125	450.00	225.00
(37)	Clarence Beaumont (Apr. 28)	1,125	450.00	225.00
(38)	James T. McGuire (May 5)	1,125	450.00	225.00
(39)	William H. Dineen (May 12)	1,125	450.00	225.00
(40)	James T. Williams (May 19)	1,125	450.00	225.00
(41)	Thomas W. Corcoran (May 26)	1,125	450.00	225.00
(42)	John Freeman (June 2)	1,125	450.00	225.00
(43)	Henry Peitz (June 9)	1,125	450.00	225.00
(44)	Charles Phillippe (June 16)	1,125	450.00	225.00
(45)	Frank Hahn (June 23)	1,125	450.00	225.00
(46)	J. Emmet Heidrick (June 30)	1,125	450.00	225.00
(47)	Joseph McGinnity (July 7)	1,875	750.00	375.00
(48)	John D. Chesbro (July 14)	1,875	750.00	375.00
(49)	William R. Hamilton (July 21)	1,125	450.00	225.00
(50)	Samuel Leever (July 28)	1,125	450.00	225.00
(51)	Mike Donlin (Aug. 4)	1,125	450.00	225.00
(52)	William F. Dahlen (Aug. 11)	1,125	450.00	225.00
(53)	Frederick Tenney (Aug. 18)	1,125	450.00	225.00
(54)	Edward P. Scott (Aug. 25)	1,125	450.00	225.00
(55)	Edward M. Lewis (Sept. 1)	1,125	450.00	225.00
(56)	Theodore Breitenstein (Sept. 8)	1,125	450.00	225.00
(57)	Herman C. Long (Sept. 15)	1,125	450.00	225.00
(58)	Jesse Tannehill (Sept. 22)	1,125	450.00	225.00
(59)	Burt E. Jones (Sept. 29)	1,125	450.00	225.00
(60)	J. Callahan (Nixey) (Oct. 6)	1,125	450.00	225.00
(61)	Claude Ritchey (Oct. 13)	1,125	450.00	225.00
(62)	Roy Thomas (Oct. 20)	1,125	450.00	225.00

1909-1913 Sporting News Supplements (M101-2)

Among the finest large-format baseball collectibles published in the early part of the 20th Century was the 100-piece series of sepia-toned supplements issued by The Sporting News. Initially issued in a size of about 7-1/2" x 10", by late 1909 the size evolved to about 8-1/2" x 10" with the team photos issued in a 16" x 10" format. The series was begun with the insertion of a supplement in the July 22, 1909, issue of TSN. One supplement was issued with each week's paper through April 7, 1910. There were several gaps over the course of the next several years, until the final piece was issued with the TSN dated Dec. 11, 1913. Most of the supplements feature full-length poses of the players. Each is labeled "Supplement to The Sporting News" with the issue date at top. At bottom is a box with the player's name and team. Backs are usually blank, but some supplements are found with colored advertising on back for various other collectibles from the newspaper. The TSN supplements were printed on heavy paper and are usually found with corner creases or other signs of wear.

		NM	E	VG
	Complete Set (100):	25,000	12,500	7,500
	Common Player:	80.00	40.00	25.00
	Ad backs: 3X			
	1909			
(1)	Roger Bresnahan (7/22)	600.00	300.00	180.00
(2)	Denton Young, Louis Criger (7/29)	450.00	225.00	135.00
(3)	Christopher Mathewson (8/5)	1,000	500.00	300.00
(4)	Tyrus R. Cobb (8/12)	1,200	600.00	360.00
(5)	Napoleon Lajoie (8/19)	550.00	275.00	165.00
(6)	Sherwood N. Magee (8/26)	80.00	40.00	25.00
(7)	Frank L. Chance (9/2)	500.00	250.00	150.00
(8)	Edward Walsh (9/9)	500.00	250.00	150.00
(9)	Nap Rucker (9/16)	80.00	40.00	25.00
(10)	Honus Wagner (9/23)	1,000	500.00	300.00
(11)	Hugh Jennings (9/30)	550.00	275.00	165.00
(12)	Fred C. Clarke (10/7)	550.00	275.00	165.00
(13)	Byron Bancroft Johnson (10/14)	550.00	275.00	165.00
(14)	Charles A. Comiskey (10/21)	550.00	275.00	165.00
(15)	Edward Collins (10/28)	550.00	275.00	165.00
(16)	James A. McAleer (11/4)	160.00	80.00	50.00
(17)	Pittsburgh Team (11/11)	350.00	175.00	100.00
(18)	Detroit Team (11/18)	350.00	175.00	100.00
(19)	George Bell (11/25)	160.00	80.00	50.00
(20)	Tris Speaker (12/2)	650.00	325.00	195.00
(21)	Mordecai Brown (12/9)	550.00	275.00	165.00
(22)	Hal Chase (12/16)	550.00	275.00	165.00
(23)	Thomas W. Leach (12/23)	160.00	80.00	50.00
(24)	Owen Bush (12/30)	160.00	80.00	50.00
	1910			
(25)	John J. Evers (1/6)	400.00	200.00	120.00
(26)	Harry Krause (1/13)	80.00	40.00	25.00
(27)	Chas. B. Adams (1/20)	80.00	40.00	25.00
(28)	Addie Joss (1/27)	400.00	200.00	120.00
(29)	Orval Overall (2/3)	80.00	40.00	25.00
(30)	Samuel E. Crawford (2/10)	400.00	200.00	120.00
(31)	Fred Merkle (2/17)	90.00	45.00	25.00
(32)	George Mullin (2/24)	80.00	40.00	25.00
(33)	Edward Konetchy (3/3)	80.00	40.00	25.00
(34)	George Gibson, Arthur Raymond (3/10)	80.00	40.00	25.00
(35)	Ty Cobb, Hans Wagner (3/17)	2,250	1,125	625.00
(36)	Connie Mack (3/24)	400.00	200.00	120.00
(37)	Wm. Evans, "Silk" O'Loughlin, William Klem, Wm. Johnston (3/31)	550.00	275.00	165.00
(38)	Edward Plank (4/7)	325.00	160.00	95.00
(39)	Walter Johnson, Charles E. Street (9/1)	500.00	250.00	150.00
(40)	John C. Kling (9/8)	80.00	40.00	25.00
(41)	Frank Baker (9/15)	400.00	200.00	120.00
(42)	Charles S. Dooin (9/22)	80.00	40.00	25.00
(43)	Wm. F. Carrigan (9/29)	80.00	40.00	25.00
(44)	John B. McLean (10/6)	80.00	40.00	25.00
(45)	John W. Coombs (10/13)	80.00	40.00	25.00
(46)	Jos. B. Tinker (10/20)	350.00	175.00	100.00
(47)	John I. Taylor (10/27)	80.00	40.00	25.00
(48)	Russell Ford (11/3)	80.00	40.00	25.00
(49)	Leonard L. Cole (11/10)	80.00	40.00	25.00
(50)	Harry Lord (11/17)	80.00	40.00	25.00
(51)	Philadelphia-A Team (11/24)	130.00	65.00	40.00
(52)	Chicago-N Team (12/1)	130.00	65.00	40.00
(53)	Charles A. Bender (12/8)	400.00	200.00	120.00
(54)	Arthur Hofman (12/15)	80.00	40.00	25.00
(55)	Bobby Wallace (12/21)	325.00	160.00	95.00
(56)	Jno. J. McGraw (12/28)	325.00	160.00	95.00
	1911			
(57)	Harry H. Davis (1/5)	80.00	40.00	25.00
(58)	James P. Archer (1/12)	80.00	40.00	25.00
(59)	Ira Thomas (1/19)	80.00	40.00	25.00
(60)	Robert Byrnes (1/26)	80.00	40.00	25.00
(61)	Clyde Milan (2/2)	80.00	40.00	25.00
(62)	John T. Meyer (2/9) (Meyers)	80.00	40.00	25.00
(63)	Robert Bescher (2/16)	80.00	40.00	25.00
(64)	John J. Barry (2/23)	80.00	40.00	25.00
(65)	Frank Schulte (3/2)	80.00	40.00	25.00
(66)	C. Harris White (3/9)	80.00	40.00	25.00
(67)	Lawrence Doyle (3/16)	80.00	40.00	25.00
(68)	Joe Jackson (3/23)	2,500	1,250	750.00
(69)	Martin O'Toole, William Kelly (10/26)	80.00	40.00	25.00
(70)	Vean Gregg (11/2)	80.00	40.00	25.00
(71)	Richard W. Marquard (11/9)	325.00	160.00	95.00
(72)	John E. McInnis (11/16)	80.00	40.00	25.00
(73)	Grover C. Alexander (11/23)	350.00	175.00	100.00
(74)	Del Gainor (11/30)	80.00	40.00	25.00
(75)	Fred Snodgrass (12/7)	80.00	40.00	25.00
(76)	James J. Callahan (12/14)	80.00	40.00	25.00
(77)	Robert Harmon (12/21)	80.00	40.00	25.00
(78)	George Stovall (12/28)	80.00	40.00	25.00
	1912			
(79)	Zack D. Wheat (1/4)	325.00	160.00	95.00
(80)	Frank "Ping" Bodie (1/11)	80.00	40.00	25.00
(81)	Boston-A Team (10/10)	130.00	65.00	40.00
(82)	New York-N Team (10/17)	130.00	65.00	40.00
(83)	Jake Stahl (10/24)	80.00	40.00	25.00
(84)	Joe Wood (10/31)	275.00	135.00	80.00
(85)	Charles Wagner (11/7)	80.00	40.00	25.00
(86)	Lew Ritchie (11/14)	80.00	40.00	25.00
(87)	Clark Griffith (11/21)	325.00	160.00	95.00
(88)	Arnold Hauser (11/28)	80.00	40.00	25.00
(89)	Charles Herzog (12/5)	80.00	40.00	25.00
(90)	James Lavender (12/12)	80.00	40.00	25.00
(91)	Jeff Tesreau (12/19)	80.00	40.00	25.00
(92)	August Herrmann (12/26)	110.00	55.00	30.00
	1913			
(93)	Jake Daubert (10/23)	80.00	40.00	25.00
(94)	Heinie Zimmerman (10/30)	80.00	40.00	25.00
(95)	Ray Schalk (11/6)	325.00	160.00	95.00
(96)	Hans Lobert (11/13)	80.00	40.00	25.00
(97)	Albert W. Demaree (11/20)	80.00	40.00	25.00
(98)	Arthur Fletcher (11/27)	80.00	40.00	25.00
(99)	Charles A. Somers (12/4)	80.00	40.00	25.00
(100)	Joe Birmingham (12/11)	80.00	40.00	25.00

1913 Sporting News Postcards (M101-3)

This six-card set was issued as a premium by the weekly sports newspaper. The 3-1/2" x 5-1/2" cards have borderless front photos printed in duotone color. Along with the player and team names at bottom is a "Published by The Sporting News" tag line. Postcard-format backs are in black-and-white. The unnumbered cards are checklisted here alphabetically.

		NM	E	VG
	Complete Set (6):	4,250	2,125	1,275
	Common Player:	275.00	135.00	80.00
(1)	Roger Bresnahan	900.00	450.00	270.00
(2)	Ty Cobb	4,000	2,000	1,200
(3)	Eddie Collins	900.00	450.00	270.00
(4)	Vean Gregg	550.00	275.00	165.00
(5)	Walter Johnson, Gabby Street	1,500	750.00	450.00
(6)	Rube Marquard	900.00	450.00	270.00

1916 The Sporting News (M101-4)

JIMMY ARCHER
C.—Chicago Cubs
6

The "update" version of the promotional premium issued by The Sporting News is nearly identical to the earlier cards. The 200 black-and-white cards once again are printed with player photo, name, position, team and card number on front and advertising on the backs. The set checklist, and, generally, values are the same for sets issued by several other businesses around the country. Most of the players included on the 1-5/8" x 3" cards also appear in the prior edition. Despite being labeled in the American Card Catalog as M101-4, this version was issued after the M101-5 version, with the first advertising appearing in August 1916. Cards could be ordered in series of 20 for a dime, or the complete set was free with a $2 subscription. The complete set price does not include variations.

		NM	E	VG
	Complete Set (200):	65,000	32,000	19,500
	Common Player:	95.00	50.00	30.00
1	Babe Adams	110.00	50.00	30.00
2	Sam Agnew	95.00	50.00	30.00
3	Eddie Ainsmith	95.00	50.00	30.00
4	Grover Alexander	1,250	375.00	180.00
5	Leon Ames	95.00	50.00	30.00
6	Jimmy Archer	95.00	50.00	30.00
7	Jimmy Austin	95.00	50.00	30.00
8	H.D. Baird	95.00	50.00	30.00
9	J. Franklin Baker	450.00	225.00	135.00
10	Dave Bancroft	450.00	225.00	135.00
11	Jack Barry	95.00	50.00	30.00
12	Zinn Beck	95.00	50.00	30.00
13	"Chief" Bender	450.00	225.00	135.00
14	Joe Benz	95.00	50.00	30.00
15	Bob Bescher	95.00	50.00	30.00
16	Al Betzel	95.00	50.00	30.00
17	Mordecai Brown	450.00	225.00	135.00
18	Eddie Burns	95.00	50.00	30.00
19	George Burns	95.00	50.00	30.00
20	Geo. J. Burns	95.00	50.00	30.00
21	Joe Bush	95.00	50.00	30.00
22	"Donie" Bush	95.00	50.00	30.00
23	Art Butler	95.00	50.00	30.00
24	Bobbie Byrne	95.00	50.00	30.00
25	Forrest Cady	95.00	50.00	30.00
26	Jimmy Callahan	95.00	50.00	30.00
27	Ray Caldwell	95.00	50.00	30.00
28	Max Carey	450.00	225.00	135.00
29	George Chalmers	95.00	50.00	30.00
30	Ray Chapman	95.00	50.00	30.00
31	Larry Cheney	95.00	50.00	30.00
32	Eddie Cicotte	600.00	300.00	180.00
33	Tom Clarke	95.00	50.00	30.00
34	Eddie Collins	450.00	225.00	135.00
35	"Shauno" Collins	95.00	50.00	30.00
36	Charles Comiskey	450.00	225.00	135.00
37	Joe Connolly	95.00	50.00	30.00
38	Ty Cobb	5,500	2,700	1,650
39	Harry Coveleskie (Coveleski)	95.00	50.00	30.00
40	Gavvy Cravath	95.00	50.00	30.00
41	Sam Crawford	450.00	225.00	135.00
42	Jean Dale	95.00	50.00	30.00
43	Jake Daubert	95.00	50.00	30.00
44	Charles Deal	95.00	50.00	30.00
45	Al Demaree	95.00	50.00	30.00
46	Josh Devore	95.00	50.00	30.00
47	William Doak	95.00	50.00	30.00
48	Bill Donovan	95.00	50.00	30.00
49	Charles Dooin	95.00	50.00	30.00
50	Mike Doolan	95.00	50.00	30.00
51	Larry Doyle	95.00	50.00	30.00
52	Jean Dubuc	95.00	50.00	30.00
53	Oscar Dugey	95.00	50.00	30.00
54	Johnny Evers	450.00	225.00	135.00
55	Urban Faber	450.00	225.00	135.00
56	"Hap" Felsch	1,000	285.00	170.00
57	Bill Fischer	95.00	50.00	30.00
58	Ray Fisher	95.00	50.00	30.00
59	Max Flack	95.00	50.00	30.00
60	Art Fletcher	95.00	50.00	30.00
61	Eddie Foster	95.00	50.00	30.00
62	Jacques Fournier	95.00	50.00	30.00
63	Del Gainer (Gainor)	95.00	50.00	30.00
64	"Chic" Gandil	1,000	190.00	115.00
65	Larry Gardner	95.00	50.00	30.00
66	Joe Gedeon	95.00	50.00	30.00
67	Gus Getz	95.00	50.00	30.00
68	Geo. Gibson	95.00	50.00	30.00
69	Wilbur Good	95.00	50.00	30.00
70	Hank Gowdy	95.00	50.00	30.00
71	John Graney	95.00	50.00	30.00
72	Clark Griffith	450.00	225.00	135.00
73	Tom Griffith	95.00	50.00	30.00
74	Heinie Groh	95.00	50.00	30.00
75	Earl Hamilton	95.00	50.00	30.00
76	Bob Harmon	95.00	50.00	30.00
77	Roy Hartzell	95.00	50.00	30.00
78	Claude Hendrix	95.00	50.00	30.00
79	Olaf Henriksen	95.00	50.00	30.00
80	John Henry	95.00	50.00	30.00
81	"Buck" Herzog	95.00	50.00	30.00
82	Hugh High	95.00	50.00	30.00
83	Dick Hoblitzell	95.00	50.00	30.00
84	Harry Hooper	450.00	225.00	135.00
85	Ivan Howard	95.00	50.00	30.00
86	Miller Huggins	390.00	190.00	115.00
87	Joe Jackson	17,500	8,750	5,250
88	William James	95.00	50.00	30.00
89	Harold Janvrin	95.00	50.00	30.00
90	Hugh Jennings	450.00	225.00	135.00
91	Walter Johnson	1,140	570.00	345.00
92	Fielder Jones	95.00	50.00	30.00
93	Joe Judge	95.00	50.00	30.00
94	Bennie Kauff	95.00	50.00	30.00
95	Wm. Killefer Jr.	95.00	50.00	30.00
96	Ed. Konetchy	95.00	50.00	30.00
97	Napoleon Lajoie	650.00	325.00	195.00
98	Jack Lapp	95.00	50.00	30.00
99	John Lavan	95.00	50.00	30.00
100	Jimmy Lavender	95.00	50.00	30.00
101	"Nemo" Leibold	95.00	50.00	30.00
102	H.B. Leonard	95.00	50.00	30.00
103	Duffy Lewis	95.00	50.00	30.00
104	Hans Lobert	95.00	50.00	30.00
105	Tom Long	95.00	50.00	30.00
106	Fred Luderus	95.00	50.00	30.00
107	Connie Mack	450.00	225.00	135.00
108	Lee Magee	95.00	50.00	30.00
109	Sherwood Magee	95.00	50.00	30.00
110	Al. Mamaux	95.00	50.00	30.00
111	Leslie Mann	95.00	50.00	30.00
112	"Rabbit" Maranville	450.00	225.00	135.00
113	Rube Marquard	450.00	225.00	135.00
114	J. Erskine Mayer	150.00	80.00	45.00
115	George McBride	95.00	50.00	30.00
116	John J. McGraw	450.00	225.00	135.00
117	Jack McInnis	95.00	50.00	30.00
118	Fred Merkle	95.00	50.00	30.00
119	Chief Meyers	95.00	50.00	30.00
120	Clyde Milan	95.00	50.00	30.00
121	John Miller	95.00	50.00	30.00
122	Otto Miller	95.00	50.00	30.00
123	Willie Mitchell	95.00	50.00	30.00
124	Fred Mollwitz	95.00	50.00	30.00
125	Pat Moran	95.00	50.00	30.00
126	Ray Morgan	95.00	50.00	30.00
127	Geo. Moriarty	95.00	50.00	30.00
128	Guy Morton	95.00	50.00	30.00
129	Mike Mowrey	95.00	50.00	30.00
130	Ed. Murphy	95.00	50.00	30.00
131	"Hy" Myers	95.00	50.00	30.00
132	J.A. Niehoff	95.00	50.00	30.00
133	Rube Oldring	95.00	50.00	30.00
134	Oliver O'Mara	95.00	50.00	30.00
135	Steve O'Neill	95.00	50.00	30.00
136	"Dode" Paskert	95.00	50.00	30.00
137	Roger Peckinpaugh	95.00	50.00	30.00
138	Walter Pipp	95.00	50.00	30.00
139	Derril Pratt (Derrill)	95.00	50.00	30.00
140	Pat Ragan	95.00	50.00	30.00
141	Bill Rariden	95.00	50.00	30.00
142	Eppa Rixey	450.00	225.00	135.00
143	Davey Robertson	95.00	50.00	30.00
144	Wilbert Robinson	450.00	225.00	135.00
145	Bob Roth	95.00	50.00	30.00
146	Ed. Roush	450.00	225.00	135.00
147	Clarence Rowland	95.00	50.00	30.00
148	"Nap" Rucker	95.00	50.00	30.00
149	Dick Rudolph	95.00	50.00	30.00
150	Reb Russell	95.00	50.00	30.00
151	Babe Ruth	37,500	18,500	11,000
152	Vic Saier	95.00	50.00	30.00
153	"Slim" Sallee	95.00	50.00	30.00
154	Ray Schalk	450.00	225.00	135.00
155	Walter Schang	95.00	50.00	30.00
156	Frank Schulte	95.00	50.00	30.00
157	Everett Scott	95.00	50.00	30.00
158	Jim Scott	95.00	50.00	30.00
159	Tom Seaton	95.00	50.00	30.00
160	Howard Shanks	95.00	50.00	30.00
161	Bob Shawkey	95.00	50.00	30.00
162	Ernie Shore	95.00	50.00	30.00
163	Burt Shotton	95.00	50.00	30.00
164	Geo. Sisler	450.00	225.00	135.00
165	J. Carlisle Smith	95.00	50.00	30.00
166	Fred Snodgrass	95.00	50.00	30.00
167	Geo. Stallings	95.00	50.00	30.00
168a	Oscar Stanage (Catching)	95.00	50.00	30.00
168b	Oscar Stanage (Portrait to thighs.)	900.00	450.00	270.00
169	Charles Stengel	650.00	325.00	195.00
170	Milton Stock	95.00	50.00	30.00
171	Amos Strunk	95.00	50.00	30.00
172	Billy Sullivan	95.00	50.00	30.00
173	"Jeff" Tesreau	95.00	50.00	30.00
174	Joe Tinker	450.00	225.00	135.00
175	Fred Toney	95.00	50.00	30.00
176	Terry Turner	95.00	50.00	30.00
177	George Tyler	95.00	50.00	30.00
178	Jim Vaughn	95.00	50.00	30.00
179	Bob Veach	95.00	50.00	30.00
180	James Viox	95.00	50.00	30.00
181	Oscar Vitt	95.00	50.00	30.00
182	Hans Wagner	4,500	2,250	1,350
183	Clarence Walker	95.00	50.00	30.00
184	Ed. Walsh	450.00	225.00	135.00
185	W. Wambsganss (Photo actually Fritz Coumbe.)	95.00	50.00	30.00
186	Buck Weaver	1,200	600.00	360.00
187	Carl Weilman	95.00	50.00	30.00
188	Zach Wheat	450.00	225.00	135.00
189	Geo. Whitted	95.00	50.00	30.00
190	Fred Williams	95.00	50.00	30.00
191	Art Wilson	95.00	50.00	30.00
192	J. Owen Wilson	95.00	50.00	30.00
193	Ivy Wingo	95.00	50.00	30.00
194	"Mel" Wolfgang	95.00	50.00	30.00
195	Joe Wood	500.00	120.00	75.00
196	Steve Yerkes	95.00	50.00	30.00
197	"Pep" Young	95.00	50.00	30.00
198	Rollie Zeider	95.00	50.00	30.00
199	Heiny Zimmerman	95.00	50.00	30.00
200	Ed. Zwilling	95.00	50.00	30.00

1916 The Sporting News (M101-5)

CHARLES STENGEL
R. F.—Brooklyn Nationals
171

(Though listed in catalogs for more than 25 years, it is now believed M101-5 cards with Sporting News backs do not exist.)

1919 Sporting News (M101-6)

(The issue listed in previous editions as 1919 Sporting News Supplements (M101-6) is now listed as 1917-1920 Felix Mendelsohn.)

1926 Sporting News Supplements (M101-7)

This set of 11 player photos was issued as a post-World Series weekly supplement by The Sporting News in 1926. Sepia-toned portrait or posed photos are featured on the 7" x 10" supplements. The player's name and team are printed at the bottom, while a line identifying The Sporting News and the date appear in the upper left corner. The unnumbered set includes a half-dozen Hall of Famers. Large-format (10" x 14-1/4") team photos of the 1926 Yankees (October 28) and Cardinals were also issued in the weeks preceding the start of issue for the weekly player supplements.

		NM	E	VG
Complete Set (13):		2,000	800.00	400.00
Common Player:		40.00	16.00	8.00
(1)	Hazen "Kiki" Cuyler	100.00	40.00	20.00
(2)	Rogers Hornsby	125.00	50.00	25.00
(3)	Tony Lazzeri	100.00	40.00	20.00
(4)	Harry E. Manush (Henry)	100.00	40.00	20.00
(5)	John Mostil	40.00	16.00	8.00
(6)	Harry Rice	40.00	16.00	8.00
(7)	George Herman "Babe" Ruth	1,200	480.00	240.00
(8)	Al Simmons	100.00	40.00	20.00
(9)	Harold "Pie" Traynor	100.00	40.00	20.00
(10)	George Uhle	40.00	16.00	8.00
(11)	Glenn Wright	40.00	16.00	8.00
(12)	1926 Cardinals Team Photo	100.00	40.00	20.00
(13)	1926 Yankees Team Photo	200.00	80.00	40.00

1927-1928 Sporting News Ad-Back Supplements (M101-7)

Evidently faced with a surplus of player supplements from its 1926 issue, The Sporting News recycled at least some of them in subsequent years as subscription sales advertising. Fronts of the supplements differ in that the sports paper's logo and the original issue date from 1926 have been removed from the upper-left border. Instead of blank backs, however, the re-issues have color (blue or red seen to date) advertising on back. Respond-by dates in 1927 have been seen rubber-stamped on the back of some pieces, while that of Kiki Cuyler mentions his team as being the Cubs, who he joined in 1928.

	NM	E	VG
Kiki Cuyler	300.00	125.00	65.00
Babe Ruth	1,500	600.00	300.00

1932 Sporting News Supplements (M101-8)

 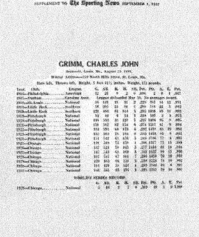

This issue of player-picture supplements from TSN is unusual not only in its brevity - only four were issued - but also in that the pictures have printed matter on back, consisting of player personal data and complete major/minor league stats. Only the Grimm piece has an issue date: Sept. 1, 1932. The pictures are on thin card stock in an 8-1/4 x 10-1/2" format. Fronts have a black-and-white photo with the player named in the wide bottom border.

		NM	E	VG
Complete Set (4):		2,000	1,000	600.00
Common Player:		240.00	120.00	72.00
(1)	Jerome H. (Dizzy) Dean	900.00	450.00	270.00
(2)	Vernon Gomez	600.00	300.00	180.00
(3)	Charles John Grimm	250.00	125.00	75.00
(4)	Lonnie Warneke	250.00	125.00	75.00

1939 Sporting News Supplements (M101-9)

These dated supplements feature a trio of team photos and two star players as individuals. The team pictures are about 15" x 10-1/2" and comprise double-page spreads; the single players are 7-1/2" x 10".

		NM	E	VG
Complete Set (5):		800.00	400.00	240.00
Common:		150.00	75.00	45.00
(1)	Joseph DiMaggio (Oct. 26)	200.00	100.00	60.00
(2)	Robert Feller (Nov. 9)	150.00	75.00	45.00
(3)	Cincinnati Reds Team (Nov. 2)	150.00	75.00	45.00
(4)	N.Y. Yankees Team (Oct. 19)	200.00	100.00	60.00
(5)	St. Louis Cardinals Team (Nov. 16)	150.00	75.00	45.00

1888 Sporting Times (M117)

Examples of these cards, issued in 1888 and 1889 by the Sporting Times weekly newspaper, are very rare. The complete set price includes all variations. The cabinet-size cards (7-1/4" x 4-1/2") feature line drawings of players in action poses on soft cardboard stock. The cards came in a variety of pastel colors surrounded by a 1/4" white border. The player's last name is printed on each drawing, as are the words "Courtesy Sporting Times New York." A pair of crossed bats and a baseball appear along the bottom of the card. Twenty-seven different players are known to exist. The drawing of Cap Anson is the same one used in the N28 Allen & Ginter series, and some of the other drawings are based on photos used in the popular Old Judge series.

		NM	E	VG
Common Player:		15,000	10,000	6,000
(1)	Cap Anson	35,000	17,500	10,000
(2)	Jersey Bakely	15,000	10,000	6,000
(3)	Dan Brouthers	25,000	12,500	7,500
(4)	Doc Bushong	15,000	10,000	6,000
(5)	Jack Clements	15,000	10,000	6,000
(6)	Charlie Comiskey	25,000	12,500	7,500
(7)	Jerry Denny	15,000	10,000	6,000
(8)	Buck Ewing	25,000	12,500	7,500
(9)	Dude Esterbrook	15,000	10,000	6,000
(10)	Jay Faatz	15,000	10,000	6,000
(11)	Pud Galvin	25,000	12,500	7,500
(12)	Jack Glasscock	15,000	10,000	6,000
(13)	Tim Keefe	25,000	12,500	7,500
(14)	King Kelly	30,000	15,000	9,000
(15)	Matt Kilroy	15,000	10,000	6,000
(16)	Arlie Latham	15,000	10,000	6,000
(17)	Doggie Miller	15,000	10,000	6,000
(18)	Hank O'Day	15,000	10,000	6,000
(19)	Fred Pfeffer	15,000	10,000	6,000
(20)	Henry Porter	15,000	10,000	6,000
(21)	Toad Ramsey	15,000	10,000	6,000
(22)	Long John Reilly	15,000	10,000	6,000
(23)	Mike Smith	15,000	10,000	6,000
(24)	Harry Stovey	15,000	10,000	6,000
(25)	Sam Thompson	25,000	12,500	7,500
(26)	John Ward	25,000	12,500	7,500
(27)	Mickey Welch	25,000	12,500	7,500

1933 Sport Kings (R338)

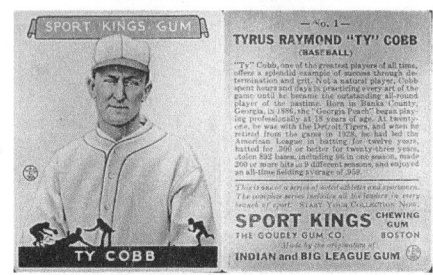

This 48-card set features athletes at the top of several sports such as boxing, football, skiing, dogsled racing, and swimming, as well as three hall-of-fame baseball players. the cards measure 2-3/8" x 2-7/8" and feature waist-up portrait artwork.

		NM	E	VG
Complete Set (48):		30,000	15,000	9,000
Common Player (1-24):		200.00	100.00	60.00
Common Player (25-48):		250.00	125.00	75.00
1	Ty Cobb	2,500	1,250	750.00
2	Babe Ruth	7,500	3,750	2,250
3	Nat Holman	200.00	100.00	60.00
4	Harold "Red" Grange	1,500	750.00	450.00
5	Ed Wachter	600.00	300.00	150.00
6	Jim Thorpe	1,600	800.00	480.00
7	Bobby Walthour, Jr.	200.00	100.00	60.00
8	Walter Hagen	500.00	250.00	150.00
9	Ed Blood	200.00	100.00	60.00
10	Anton Lekang	200.00	100.00	60.00
11	Charles Jewtraw	200.00	100.00	60.00
12	Bobby McLean	200.00	100.00	60.00
13	LaVerne Fatour	200.00	100.00	60.00
14	Jim Londos	200.00	100.00	60.00
15	Reggie McNamara	200.00	100.00	60.00
16	William Tilden	200.00	100.00	60.00
17	Jack Dempsey	600.00	300.00	180.00
18	Gene Tunney	200.00	100.00	60.00
19	Eddie Shore	500.00	250.00	150.00
20	Duke Kahanamoku	200.00	100.00	60.00
21	Johnny Weissmuller	500.00	250.00	150.00
22	Gene Sarazen	500.00	250.00	150.00
23	Vincent Richards	200.00	100.00	60.00
24	Howie Morenz	500.00	250.00	150.00
25	Ralph Snoddy	250.00	125.00	75.00
26	James R. Wedell	250.00	125.00	75.00
27	Roscoe Turner	250.00	125.00	75.00
28	Jimmy Doolittle	250.00	125.00	75.00
29	Ace Bailey	600.00	300.00	180.00
30	Ching Johnson	400.00	200.00	120.00
31	Bobby Walthour, Jr.	250.00	125.00	75.00
32	Joe Lopchick	250.00	125.00	75.00
33	Eddie Burke	250.00	125.00	75.00
34	Irving Jaffee	250.00	125.00	75.00
35	Knute Rockne	1,000	500.00	300.00
36	Willie Hoppe	250.00	125.00	75.00
37	Helene Madison	250.00	125.00	75.00
38	Bobby Jones	2,250	1,125	675.00
39	Jack Westrope	250.00	125.00	75.00
40	Don George	250.00	125.00	75.00
41	Jim Browning	250.00	125.00	75.00
42	Carl Hubbell	500.00	250.00	150.00
43	Primo Carnera	250.00	125.00	75.00
44	Max Baer	250.00	125.00	75.00
45	Babe Didrickson	500.00	250.00	150.00
46	Ellsworth Vines	250.00	125.00	75.00
47	J. Hubert Stevens	250.00	125.00	75.00
48	Leonhard Seppala	375.00	185.00	110.00

1947 Sport Magazine Premium

This 8-1/2" x 11", blank-back, paper-stock picture appears to have been a premium issued in conjunction with Sport magazine's premiere issue in March 1947, perhaps as a send-away offer. The picture has a black-and-white portrait photo on a bright orange background, surrounded with a white border. In the lower-left corner is "March '47." "15 Sport" appears at lower-right.

		NM	E	VG
15	Joe DiMaggio	35.00	17.50	10.50

1953 Sport Magazine All-Star Portfolio

This set of 5-3/8" x 7" glossy color pictures was used by Sport Magazine as a subscription premium. Featuring the outstanding photography of Ozzie Sweet, all but the Bob Mathias pictures are portraits, surrounded with a white border and the player name at bottom. Backs are blank. The heavy cardboard mailing envelope contains short athlete biographies.

		NM	E	VG
	Complete Set (10):	350.00	175.00	100.00
	Common Player:	30.00	15.00	9.00
(1)	Joe Black	40.00	20.00	12.00
(2)	Robert Cousy (Basketball)	30.00	15.00	9.00
(3)	Elroy Hirsch (Football)	30.00	15.00	9.00
(4)	Rocky Marciano (Boxing)	45.00	25.00	15.00
(5)	Robert Bruce Mathias (Track and field.)	30.00	15.00	9.00
(6)	Stanley Frank Musial	70.00	35.00	22.00
(7)	John Olszewski (Football)	30.00	15.00	9.00
(8)	Allie Pierce Reynolds	30.00	15.00	9.00
(9)	Robin Evan Roberts	45.00	25.00	15.00
(10)	Robert Clayton Shantz	30.00	15.00	9.00

1963 Sports "Hall of Fame" Busts

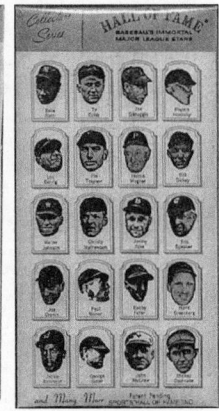

Licensed by the National Baseball Hall of Fame, this set of 20 plastic player busts was produced by Sports "Hall of Fame," Inc., of New York. Each six-inch statue has a white player figure atop a wood-look pedestal with a plaque providing career details. The busts were sold in a red, white and gold display box with photos of the players on the back. Though the box back promised "Many More," only the 20 players pictured were ever issued. Retail price at issue was $1-1.25. The first 12 busts are more common than the final eight, with Foxx and Greenberg especially scarce. Values quoted are for busts alone, add $25 for accompanying box and $50 or more for unopened box with cellophane.

		NM	E	VG
	Complete Set (20):	3,000	1,500	900.00
	Common Player:	75.00	35.00	20.00
(1)	Babe Ruth	135.00	65.00	40.00
(2)	Ty Cobb	90.00	45.00	25.00
(3)	Joe DiMaggio	110.00	55.00	30.00
(4)	Rogers Hornsby	80.00	40.00	24.00
(5)	Lou Gehrig	100.00	50.00	30.00
(6)	Pie Traynor	75.00	35.00	20.00
(7)	Honus Wagner	150.00	75.00	45.00
(8)	Bill Dickey	110.00	55.00	30.00
(9)	Walter Johnson	135.00	65.00	40.00
(10)	Christy Mathewson	110.00	55.00	30.00
(11)	Jimmie Foxx	335.00	165.00	100.00
(12)	Tris Speaker	75.00	35.00	20.00
(13)	Joe Cronin	180.00	90.00	50.00
(14)	Paul Waner	165.00	80.00	45.00
(15)	Bobby Feller	225.00	110.00	65.00
(16)	Hank Greenberg	350.00	175.00	105.00
(17)	Jackie Robinson	260.00	130.00	75.00
(18)	George Sisler	225.00	112.50	67.50
(19)	John McGraw	225.00	112.50	67.50
(20)	Mickey Cochrane	250.00	125.00	75.00

1968-69 Sports Cards for Collectors

These Myron Aronstein-drawn 3-1/2" x 4-1/4" postcards feature 78 pre-1950 players. Cards 1-36 feature blank backs, and 37-78 have brief biographical and statistical data. The last four are checklists.

		NM	E	VG
	Complete Set (82):	100.00	50.00	30.00
	Common Player:	2.00	1.00	.60
1	Babe Ruth	15.00	7.50	5.00
2	Rube Marquard	2.00	1.00	.60
3	Zack Wheat	2.00	1.00	.60
4	John Clarkson	2.00	1.00	.60
5	Honus Wagner	2.00	1.00	.60
6	Johnny Evers	2.00	1.00	.60
7	Bill Dickey	2.00	1.00	.60
8	Elmer Smith	2.00	1.00	.60
9	Ty Cobb	10.00	5.00	3.00
10	Jack Chesbro	2.00	1.00	.60
11	George Gibson	2.00	1.00	.60
12	Bullet Joe Bush	2.00	1.00	.60
13	George Mullin	2.00	1.00	.60
14	Buddy Meyer	2.00	1.00	.60
15	Jimmy Collins	2.00	1.00	.60
16	Bill Wambsganss	2.00	1.00	.60
17	Jack Barry	2.00	1.00	.60
18	Dickie Kerr	2.00	1.00	.60
19	Connie Mack	2.00	1.00	.60
20	Rabbit Maranville	2.00	1.00	.60
21	Roger Peckinpaugh	2.00	1.00	.60
22	Mickey Cochrane	2.00	1.00	.60
23	George Kelly	2.00	1.00	.60
24	Frank "Home Rune" Baker	2.00	1.00	.60
25	Wally Schang	2.00	1.00	.60
26	Eddie Plank	2.00	1.00	.60
27	Bill Donovan	2.00	1.00	.60
28	Red Faber	2.00	1.00	.60
29	Hack Wilson	2.00	1.00	.60
30	Mordecai "3 Finger" Brown	2.00	1.00	.60
31	Fred Merkle	2.00	1.00	.60
32	Heinie Groh	2.00	1.00	.60
33	Stuffy McInnis	2.00	1.00	.60
34	Hal Chase	2.00	1.00	.60
35	Judge Kenesaw Mountain Landis	2.00	1.00	.60
36	Chief Bender	2.00	1.00	.60
37	Fred Snodgrass	2.00	1.00	.60
38	Tony Lazzeri	2.00	1.00	.60
39	John McGraw	2.00	1.00	.60
40	Mel Ott	10.00	5.00	3.00
41	Grover Alexander	2.00	1.00	.60
42	Rube Waddell	2.00	1.00	.60
43	Wilbert Robinson	2.00	1.00	.60
44	Cap Anson	2.00	1.00	.60
45	Eddie Cicotte	2.00	1.00	.60
46	Hank Gowdy	2.00	1.00	.60
47	Frankie Frisch	2.00	1.00	.60
48	Charles Comiskey	2.00	1.00	.60
49	Clyde Milan	2.00	1.00	.60
50	Jimmy Wilson	2.00	1.00	.60
51	Christy Mathewson	10.00	5.00	3.00
52	Tim Keefe	2.00	1.00	.60
53	Abner Doubleday	2.00	1.00	.60
54	Ed Walsh	2.00	1.00	.60
55	Jim Thorpe	10.00	5.00	3.00
56	Roger Bresnahan	2.00	1.00	.60
57	Frank Chance	2.00	1.00	.60
58	Heinie Manush	2.00	1.00	.60
59	Max Carey	2.00	1.00	.60
60	Joe Tinker	2.00	1.00	.60
61	Benny Kauff	2.00	1.00	.60
62	Fred Clarke	2.00	1.00	.60
63	Smokey Joe Wood	2.00	1.00	.60
64	George Burns	2.00	1.00	.60
65	Walter Johnson	10.00	5.00	3.00
66	Ferdie Schupp	2.00	1.00	.60
67	Jimmy McAleer	2.00	1.00	.60
68	Larry Gardner	2.00	1.00	.60
69	Buck Ewing	2.00	1.00	.60
70	George Sisler	2.00	1.00	.60
71	Charley Robertson	2.00	1.00	.60
72	Bill Dineen	2.00	1.00	.60
73	Kid Gleason	2.00	1.00	.60
74	Jim Bottomley	2.00	1.00	.60
75	Sam Crawford	2.00	1.00	.60
76	Kid Nichols	2.00	1.00	.60
77	Dick Rudolph	2.00	1.00	.60
78	Bill Klem	2.00	1.00	.60
79	Checklist			
80	Checklist			
81	Checklist			
82	Checklist			

1970 Sports Cards for Collectors Old Timer Postcards

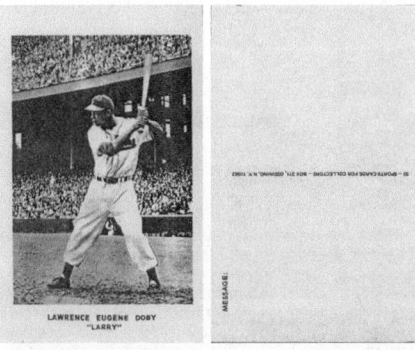

The date of issue given here is approximate. This collectors issue "Old Timer Postcard Series" features black-and-white photos bordered in white in a 3-1/2" x 5-1/2" format. Player identification in the bottom border usually offers his complete name on one line and his nickname below. Backs are divided by a card number and the name and address of the issuer. At left is a space for "MESSAGE:."

		NM	E	VG
	Complete Set (32):	75.00	37.50	22.00
	Common Player:	4.00	2.00	1.25
1	Babe Ruth, Lou Gehrig	12.00	6.00	3.50
2	Larry Doby	6.00	3.00	1.75
3	Mike Garcia	4.00	2.00	1.25
4	Bob Feller	10.00	5.00	3.00
5	Early Wynn	4.00	2.00	1.25
6	Burleigh Grimes	4.00	2.00	1.25
7	Rabbit Maranville	4.00	2.00	1.25
8	Babe Ruth	15.00	7.50	4.50
9	Lou Gehrig	12.00	6.00	3.50
10	Joe DiMaggio	12.00	6.00	3.50
11	Ty Cobb	10.00	5.00	3.00
12	Lou Boudreau	4.00	2.00	1.25
13	Jimmie Foxx	4.00	2.00	1.25
14	Casey Stengel	6.00	3.00	1.75
15	Kenesaw M. Landis	4.00	2.00	1.25
16	Max Carey	4.00	2.00	1.25
17	Wilbert Robinson	4.00	2.00	1.25
18	Paul Richards	4.00	2.00	1.25
19	Zack Wheat	4.00	2.00	1.25
20	Rube Marquard	4.00	2.00	1.25
21	Dave Bancroft	4.00	2.00	1.25
22	Bobby Thomson	4.00	2.00	1.25
23	Mel Ott	4.00	2.00	1.25
24	Bobo Newsom	4.00	2.00	1.25
25	Johnny Mize	4.00	2.00	1.25
26	Walker Cooper	4.00	2.00	1.25
27	Fred "Dixie" Walker	4.00	2.00	1.25
28	Augie Galan	4.00	2.00	1.25
29	"Snuffy" Sturnweiss (Stirnweiss)	4.00	2.00	1.25
30	Floyd Caves "Babe" Herman	4.00	2.00	1.25
31	Babe Ruth	15.00	7.50	4.50
32	Babe Ruth	15.00	7.50	4.50

1970 Sports Cards for Collectors Sports Stuff

This set includes 10 Myron Aronsten-drawn 3-1/2" x 4-1/4" postcards depicting pre-1920 baseball luminaries, trivia, and legends.

	NM	E	VG
Complete Set (10):	20.00	10.00	6.00
Common Player:	2.00	1.00	.60
1 Manager Trivia	2.00	1.00	.60
2 1914 Miracle Braves	2.00	1.00	.60
3 1919 Black Sox	2.00	1.00	.60
4 Eddie Plank, Fred Clarke, Roger Bresnahan, Babe Ruth	5.00	2.50	1.50
5 Bobby Lowe	2.00	1.00	.60
6 $100,000 Athletics Infield	2.00	1.00	.60
7 Joe Bush, Eddie Plank, Chief Bender	2.00	1.00	.60
8 Joe Tinker, Johnny Evers, Frank Chance	2.00	1.00	.60
9 Wilbert Robinson, John McGraw, Roger Peckinpaugh	2.00	1.00	.60
10 Ty Cobb	5.00	2.50	1.50

1977-79 Sportscaster

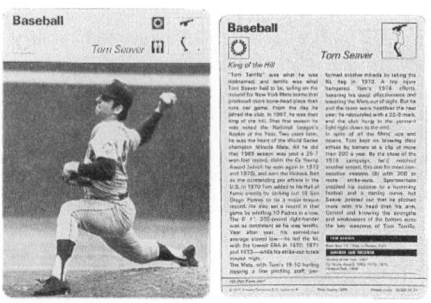

This massive set of full-color cards includes players from dozens of different sports - some of them very obscure - among more than 2,000 different subjects, making it one of the biggest sets of trading cards ever issued. Available by mail subscription from 1977 through 1979, the Sportscaster cards are large, measuring 4-3/4" x 6-1/4". Subscribers were mailed one series of 24 cards for $1.89 plus postage every month or so. The set has an international flavor to it, including such sports as rugby, soccer, lawn bowling, fencing, karate, bicycling, curling, skiing, bullfighting, auto racing, mountain climbing, hang gliding, yachting, sailing, badminton, bobsledding, etc. Each card has a series of icons in the upper-right corner to assist collectors in the various methods of sorting. Most popular among American collectors are the baseball, football and basketball stars in the set, which includes the 140 baseball subjects listed here. The checklist includes many Hall of Famers. Backs contain detailed write-ups of the player featured. Because the set was issued in series, and many collectors dropped out of the program before the end, cards in the higher series are especially scarce. This accounts for prices on some of the superstar cards, issued in early series, being lower than for some of the lesser-known players. The cards of Aaron and Bench are quite common because they were mailed to large numbers of persons as samples to introduce the program. The cards were also sold in several European countries and can be found with backs printed in French, Swedish and other languages.

	NM	E	VG
Complete (Baseball) Set (140):	350.00	175.00	100.00
Common Player:	1.00	.50	.30
Beyond Sports (Baseball) Set: (6):			
(2) Clowns(Al Schacht, Nick Altrock)	4.00	2.00	1.25
(3) Fellowship of Christian Athletes(Don Kessinger)	4.00	2.00	1.25
(4) High School Record Book(David Clyde)	2.50	1.25	.70
(5) Hutchinson Award(Al Kaline)	40.00	20.00	12.00
(6) Walkie-Talkie(Yogi Berra)	5.00	2.50	1.50
(2) Clowns(Al Schacht, Nick Altrock)	4.00	2.00	1.25
(2) Danny Ainge	30.00	15.00	9.00
Beyond Sports (Baseball) Set: (6):			
(3) Fellowship of Christian Athletes(Don Kessinger)	4.00	2.00	1.25
(3) Emmett Ashford (Umpire)	2.50	1.25	.70
Beyond Sports (Baseball) Set: (6):			
(4) High School Record Book(David Clyde)	2.50	1.25	.70
(4) Ernie Banks	2.75	1.50	.80
Beyond Sports (Baseball) Set: (6):			
(5) Hutchinson Award(Al Kaline)	40.00	20.00	12.00
(5) Johnny Bench	7.50	3.75	2.25

(6) Vida Blue	1.75	.90	.50
Beyond Sports (Baseball) Set: (6):			
(6) Walkie-Talkie(Yogi Berra)	5.00	2.50	1.50
(7) Bert Blyleven	1.25	.60	.40
(8) Bobby Bonds	3.25	1.75	1.00
(9) Lyman Bostock	1.25	.60	.40
(11) Lou Brock	3.25	1.75	1.00
(12) Jeff Burroughs	1.25	.60	.40
(13) Roy Campanella	8.00	4.00	2.50
(14) John Candelaria	1.25	.60	.40
(15) Rod Carew	3.25	1.75	1.00
(16) Steve Carlton	4.00	2.00	1.25
(17) Ron Cey	1.00	.50	.30
(18) Roberto Clemente	10.00	5.00	3.00
(19) Steve Dembowski	2.25	1.25	.70
(20) Joe DiMaggio	5.00	2.50	1.50
(21) Dennis Eckersley	4.00	2.00	1.25
(22) Mark Fidrych	1.75	.90	.50
(23) Carlton Fisk	6.00	3.00	1.75
(24) Mike Flanagan	3.00	1.50	.90
(25) Steve Garvey	5.00	2.50	1.50
(26) Ron Guidry	3.00	1.50	.90
(27) Gil Hodges	4.00	2.00	1.25
(28) Catfish Hunter	4.00	2.00	1.25
(29) Tommy John	1.25	.60	.40
(30) Randy Jones	1.00	.50	.30
(31) Dave Kingman	1.75	.90	.50
(32) Sandy Koufax	6.00	3.00	1.75
(33) Tommy Lasorda	6.50	3.25	2.00
(34) Ron LeFlore	1.25	.60	.40
(35) Greg Luzinski	1.00	.50	.30
(36) Billy Martin	3.25	1.75	1.00
(37) Willie Mays	4.00	2.00	1.25
(38) Lee Mazzilli	5.00	2.50	1.50
(39) Willie McCovey	3.75	2.00	1.25
(40) Joe Morgan	2.75	1.50	.80
(41) Thurman Munson	4.00	2.00	1.25
(42) Stan Musial	5.00	2.50	1.50
(43) Phil Niekro	4.00	2.00	1.25
(44) Jim Palmer	3.00	1.50	.90
(45) Dave Parker	1.75	.90	.50
(46) Freddie Patek	1.25	.60	.40
(47) Gaylord Perry	2.25	1.25	.70
(48) Jim Piersall	2.75	1.50	.80
(49) Vada Pinson	1.25	.60	.40
(50) Rick Reuschel	1.25	.60	.40
(51) Jim Rice	6.00	3.00	1.75
(52) J.R. Richard	2.25	1.25	.70
(53) Brooks Robinson	3.75	2.00	1.25
(54) Frank Robinson	5.00	2.50	1.50
(55) Jackie Robinson	5.00	2.50	1.50
(56) Pete Rose	6.00	3.00	1.75
(57) Joe Rudi	1.00	.50	.30
(58) Babe Ruth	6.00	3.00	1.75
(59) Nolan Ryan	7.00	3.50	2.00
(60) Tom Seaver	3.75	2.00	1.25
(61) Warren Spahn	3.75	2.00	1.25
(62) Monty Stratton	2.25	1.25	.70
(63) Craig Swan	1.75	.90	.50
(64) Frank Tanana	1.00	.50	.30
(65) Ron Taylor	2.25	1.25	.70
(66) Garry Templeton	1.00	.50	.30
(67) Gene Tenace	1.00	.50	.30
(68) Bobby Thomson	1.75	.90	.50
(69) Andre Thornton	1.25	.60	.40
(70) Johnny VanderMeer	1.75	.90	.50
(71) Ted Williams	7.00	3.50	2.00
(72) Maury Wills	1.00	.50	.30
(73) Hack Wilson	3.25	1.75	1.00
(74) Dave Winfield (Hitting)	8.00	4.00	2.50
(75) Dave Winfield (Portrait)	4.00	2.00	1.25
(76) Cy Young	2.75	1.50	.80
(77) The 1927 Yankees	2.75	1.50	.80
(78) 1969 Mets	6.50	3.25	2.00
(79) All-Star Game(Steve Garvey, Joe Morgan)	2.75	1.50	.80
(80) Amateur Draft(Rick Monday)	1.25	.60	.40
(81) At-A-Glance Reference(Tom Seaver)	5.00	2.50	1.50
(82) Babe Ruth Baseball(Ed Figueroa)	6.50	3.25	2.00
(83) Baltimore Memorial Stadium	3.00	1.50	.90
(84) Boston's Fenway Park	5.00	2.50	1.50
(85) Brother vs. Brother(Joe Niekro)	2.75	1.50	.80
(86) Busch Memorial Stadium	2.50	1.25	.70
(87) Candlestick Park	2.00	1.00	.60
(88) Cape Cod League(Jim Beattie)	6.00	3.00	1.75
(89) A Century and a Half of Baseball(Johnny Bench)	1.75	.90	.50
(90) Cy Young Award(Tom Seaver)	2.75	1.50	.80

(91) The Dean Brothers(Dizzy Dean, Paul Dean)	5.00	2.50	1.50
(92) Designated Hitter(Rusty Staub)	2.25	1.25	.70
(93) Dodger Stadium	2.75	1.50	.80
(94) Perfect Game(Don Larsen)	3.25	1.75	1.00
(95) The Double Steal(Davey Lopes)	5.00	2.50	1.50
(96) Fenway Park	4.00	2.00	1.25
(97) The Firemen(Goose Gossage)	4.00	2.00	1.25
(98) Forever Blowing Bubbles(Davey Lopes)	2.00	1.00	.60
(99) The Forsch Brothers(Bob Forsch, Ken Forsch)	5.00	2.50	1.50
(102) Great Moments(Bob Gibson)	3.25	1.75	1.00
(103) Great Moments(Ferguson Jenkins)	2.25	1.25	.70
(104) Great Moments(Mickey Lolich)	1.75	.90	.50
(105) Great Moments(Carl Yastrzemski)	3.25	1.75	1.00
(106) Hidden Ball Trick(Carl Yastrzemski)	2.75	1.50	.80
(107) Hit And Run(George Foster)	1.25	.60	.40
(108) Hitting The Cutoff Man	1.00	.50	.30
(109) Hitting Pitchers(Don Drysdale)	3.25	1.75	1.00
(110) Infield Fly Rule(Bobby Grich)	1.25	.60	.40
(111) Instruction(Rod Carew)	2.75	1.50	.80
(112) Interference(Johnny Bench)	2.75	1.50	.80
(113) Iron Mike (Pitching Machine)	2.75	1.50	.80
(114) Keeping Score	1.75	.90	.50
(115) Like Father, Like Son(Roy Smalley)	3.75	2.00	1.25
(116) Lingo I(Gary Carter)	1.75	.90	.50
(117) Lingo II(Earl Weaver)	2.75	1.50	.80
(118) Little Leagues To Big Leagues(Hector Torres)	1.75	.90	.50
(119) Maris and Mantle(Mickey Mantle, Roger Maris)	4.00	2.00	1.25
(120) Measurements (Memorial Stadium)	1.00	.50	.30
(121) The Money Game(Dennis Eckersley)	6.00	3.00	1.75
(122) NCAA Tournament (Aggies-Longhorns)	1.75	.90	.50
(123) The Oakland A's, 1971-75	3.00	1.50	.90
(124) The Perfect Game(Sandy Koufax)	3.50	1.75	1.00
(125) Pickoff(Luis Tiant)	1.25	.60	.40
(126) The Presidential Ball (William Howard Taft)	1.75	.90	.50
(127) Relief Pitching(Mike Marshall)	1.25	.60	.40
(128) The Rules(Hank Aaron)	2.75	1.50	.80
(129) Rundown (Mets vs. Astros)	1.75	.90	.50
(130) 7th Game of the World Series(Bert Campaneris)	2.25	1.25	.70
(131) Shea Stadium	2.50	1.25	.70
(132) The 3000 Hit Club(Roberto Clemente)	8.00	4.00	2.50
(133) Training Camps (Orioles)	2.75	1.50	.80
(134) Triple Crown(Carl Yastrzemski)	16.00	8.00	4.75
(135) Triple Play(Rick Burleson)	2.75	1.50	.80
(136) Triple Play(Bill Wambsganss)	1.75	.90	.50
(137) Umpires Strike	1.75	.90	.50
(138) Veterans Stadium	2.50	1.25	.70
(139) Wrigley Marathon (Mike Schmidt)	8.00	4.00	2.50
(140) Yankee Stadium	1.00	.50	.30

1977 Sports Challenge Records

Taped highlights and an interview with the player are featured on this series of 33-1/3 RPM records. The 6" diameter records have a centerhole to be punched out to play the record. Fronts have a stylized picture of the player, his name and a title. Backs describe the highlight and give other career details.

	NM	E	VG
Complete Set (12):	250.00	125.00	75.00
Common Player:	20.00	10.00	6.00
(1) Henry Aaron (Hits 715th Homer)	45.00	22.50	13.50
(2) Johnny Bench (Beats Pirates in '72 Playoff)	30.00	15.00	9.00
(3) Jerry Koosman, Donn Clendenon (1969 Miracle Mets)	20.00	10.00	6.00
(4) Don Larsen ('56 World Series Perfect Game)	20.00	10.00	6.00
(5) Fred Lynn (Has Incredible Day in Detroit)	20.00	10.00	6.00
(6) Willie Mays (Hits 1st Met Homer)	35.00	17.50	10.50
(7) Bill Mazeroski (Wins 1960 World Series)	25.00	12.50	7.50
(8) Frank Robinson (Homers 1st Time as Indian)	20.00	10.00	6.00
(9) Nolan Ryan (4th No Hitter)	45.00	22.50	13.50
(10) Tom Seaver (Cubs Ruin Perfect Game)	25.00	12.50	7.50
(11) Bobby Thomson (Shot Heard 'Round the World)	20.00	10.00	6.00
(12) Ted Williams (Last Time at Bat in Boston)	35.00	17.50	10.50

1926 Sports Co. of America Champions

Little was known of these small (1-1/2" x 2-1/4") black-and-white cards until an original store display was discovered in the late 1980s. Carrying a copyright date of November 1926, from Sports Co. of America, a San Francisco publishing firm, these cards were produced for A. G. Spalding & Bros., the sporting goods firm. Each card was issued in a wax paper baggie with a like-sized red, white and blue "Sport-Scrip" which was serial numbered for use in a candy prize drawing at the store or could be redeemed for 10 cents on Spalding equipment. The cards themselves feature ornately framed photos at center, with "CHAMPIONS" in a cartouche at top and the player's name and sport in a second ornate frame at bottom. Most backs have biographical and career notes, but some are seen with advertising offering an album for the pieces. Nearly 50 baseball players are known from a list of over 175 male and female athletes from sports as diverse as fishing, chess and balloon racing. The unnumbered baseball players from the set are checklisted here in alphabetical order.

	NM	E	VG
Common Baseball Player:	45.00	20.00	10.00
Ad Back: 2X			
(1) "Babe" Adams	45.00	20.00	10.00
(2) Grover Alexander	275.00	110.00	55.00
(3) Nick Altrock	45.00	20.00	10.00
(4) Dave Bancroft	220.00	90.00	45.00
(5) Jesse Barnes	45.00	20.00	10.00
(6) Oswald Bluege	45.00	20.00	10.00
(7) Jim Bottomley	220.00	90.00	45.00
(8) Max Carey	220.00	90.00	45.00
(9) Ty Cobb (Possibly unique)			
(10) Mickey Cochrane	220.00	90.00	45.00
(11) Eddie Collins	220.00	90.00	45.00
(12) Stan Coveleskie (Coveleski)	220.00	90.00	45.00
(13) Kiki Cuyler	220.00	90.00	45.00
(14) Hank DeBerry	45.00	20.00	10.00
(15) Jack Fournier	45.00	20.00	10.00
(16) Goose Goslin	220.00	90.00	45.00
(17) Charlie Grimm	45.00	20.00	10.00

(18) Bucky Harris	220.00	90.00	45.00
(19) Gabby Hartnett	220.00	90.00	45.00
(20) Fred Hofmann	45.00	20.00	10.00
(21) Rogers Hornsby	275.00	110.00	55.00
(22) Waite Hoyt	220.00	90.00	45.00
(23) Walter Johnson	715.00	290.00	145.00
(24) Joe Judge	45.00	20.00	10.00
(25) Willie Kamm	45.00	20.00	10.00
(26) Tony Lazzeri	220.00	90.00	45.00
(27) Rabbit Maranville	220.00	90.00	45.00
(28) Fred Marberry	45.00	20.00	10.00
(29) Rube Marquard	220.00	90.00	45.00
(30) "Stuffy" McInnis	45.00	20.00	10.00
(31) "Babe" Pinelli	45.00	20.00	10.00
(32) Wally Pipp	45.00	20.00	10.00
(33) Sam Rice	220.00	90.00	45.00
(34) Emory Rigney	45.00	20.00	10.00
(35) Dutch Ruether	45.00	20.00	10.00
(36a) Babe Ruth (1926 Copyright)	1,675	850.00	510.00
(36b) Babe Ruth (1927 Copyright)	7,500	3,750	2,200
(37) Ray Schalk	220.00	90.00	45.00
(38) Joey Sewell	220.00	90.00	45.00
(39) Urban Shocker	45.00	20.00	10.00
(40) Al Simmons	220.00	90.00	45.00
(41) George Sisler	220.00	90.00	45.00
(42) Tris Speaker	275.00	110.00	55.00
(43) Pie Traynor	220.00	90.00	45.00
(44) George Uhle	45.00	20.00	10.00
(45) Paul Waner	220.00	90.00	45.00
(46) Aaron L. Ward	45.00	20.00	10.00
(47) Ken Williams	45.00	20.00	10.00
(48) Glenn Wright	45.00	20.00	10.00
(49) Emil Yde	45.00	20.00	10.00

1946-49 Sports Exchange All-Star Picture File

Produced and sold (originally at 50 cents per series) by "The Trading Post," one of the first card collectors' publications, over a period which spanned several years in the late 1940s, this 113-card set was issued in 12 series. Most of the series were nine cards each, printed in black-and-white, unnumbered and blank-backed in a 7" x 10" format. The first 27 cards carry no series designation but were advertised as Series 1A and 1B and Series 2. Series 3 features 11 cards and is printed in sepia tones rather than black-and-white. The fourth series is also unmarked. The final two series consist of 12 cards each, printed two per sheet in smaller format. The photos are labeled as originating with the International News Service. Most of the same players and photos appearing in this set are also found in the Sports Exchange Baseball Miniatures set. Because this was one of the first baseball card sets issued after World War II, it contains cards of several players not found in other issues. The set carries a W603 designation in the "American Card Catalog." Cards are listed alphabetically within series in the checklist which follows. Cards of Series 4 are found with or without "Set Number 4" at lower left.

	NM	E	VG
Complete Set (113):	2,750	1,350	825.00
Common Card:	15.00	7.50	4.50
SERIES 5			
(48) Eddie Dyer	15.00	7.50	4.50
SERIES 6			
(57) Ewell Blackwell	25.00	12.50	7.50
SERIES 7			
(66) Floyd Bevens	15.00	7.50	4.50
SERIES 8			
(75) Nick Altrock	20.00	10.00	6.00
SERIES 9			
(84) George Case	15.00	7.50	4.50
SERIES 10			
(93) Lu Blue	15.00	7.50	4.50
SERIES 1A			
(5) Whitey Kurowski	15.00	7.50	4.50

(6) Marty Marion	20.00	10.00	6.00
(7) Rip Sewell	15.00	7.50	4.50
(8) Eddie Stanky	20.00	10.00	6.00
(9) Dixie Walker	15.00	7.50	4.50
SERIES 5			
(49) Charlie Grimm	15.00	7.50	4.50
SERIES 6			
(58) Jimmy Outlaw	15.00	7.50	4.50
SERIES 7			
(67) Hugh Casey	15.00	7.50	4.50
SERIES 8			
(76) Mark Christman	15.00	7.50	4.50
SERIES 9			
(85) Jake Early	15.00	7.50	4.50
SERIES 5			
(50) Billy Herman	30.00	15.00	9.00
SERIES 6			
(59) Andy Pafko	15.00	7.50	4.50
SERIES 7			
(68) Sam Chapman	15.00	7.50	4.50
SERIES 8			
(77) Earle Combs	30.00	15.00	9.00
SERIES 9			
(86) Carl Furillo	30.00	15.00	9.00
SERIES 10			
(95) Elbie Fletcher	15.00	7.50	4.50
SERIES 5			
(51) Ted Lyons	30.00	15.00	9.00
SERIES 6			
(60) Pee Wee Reese	75.00	37.00	22.00
SERIES 7			
(69) Joe DiMaggio	150.00	75.00	45.00
SERIES 8			
(78) Travis Jackson	30.00	15.00	9.00
SERIES 9			
(87) Augie Galan	15.00	7.50	4.50
SERIES 10			
(96) Joe Gordon	15.00	7.50	4.50
SERIES 1A			
(5) Whitey Kurowski	15.00	7.50	4.50
SERIES 5			
(52) Lefty O'Doul	25.00	12.50	7.50
SERIES 6			
(61) Phil Rizzuto	60.00	30.00	18.00
SERIES 7			
(70) Tommy Henrich	25.00	12.50	7.50
SERIES 8			
(79) Bob Muncrief	15.00	7.50	4.50
SERIES 9			
(88) Bert Haas	15.00	7.50	4.50
SERIES 10			
(97) Tommy Holmes	15.00	7.50	4.50
SERIES 1A			
(6) Marty Marion	20.00	10.00	6.00
SERIES 5			
(53) Steve O'Neill	15.00	7.50	4.50
SERIES 6			
(62) Buddy Rosar	15.00	7.50	4.50
SERIES 7			
(71) Ralph Kiner	30.00	15.00	9.00
SERIES 8			
(80) Earl Neale	25.00	12.50	7.50
SERIES 9			
(89) Johnny Hopp	15.00	7.50	4.50
SERIES 10			
(98) Billy Johnson	15.00	7.50	4.50
SERIES 5			
(48) Eddie Dyer	15.00	7.50	4.50
(49) Charlie Grimm	15.00	7.50	4.50
(50) Billy Herman	30.00	15.00	9.00
(51) Ted Lyons	30.00	15.00	9.00
(52) Lefty O'Doul	25.00	12.50	7.50
(53) Steve O'Neill	15.00	7.50	4.50
(54) Herb Pennock	30.00	15.00	9.00
(55) Luke Sewell	15.00	7.50	4.50
(56) Billy Southworth	15.00	7.50	4.50
SERIES 1A			
(7) Rip Sewell	15.00	7.50	4.50
SERIES 5			

(54)	Herb Pennock	30.00	15.00	9.00

SERIES 6

(63)	Johnny Sain	25.00	12.50	7.50

SERIES 7

(72)	Cookie Lavagetto	15.00	7.50	4.50

SERIES 8

(81)	Joe Page	15.00	7.50	4.50

SERIES 9

(90)	Ray Lamanno	15.00	7.50	4.50

SERIES 10

(99)	Phil Masi	15.00	7.50	4.50

SERIES 6

(57)	Ewell Blackwell	25.00	12.50	7.50
(58)	Jimmy Outlaw	15.00	7.50	4.50
(59)	Andy Pafko	15.00	7.50	4.50
(60)	Pee Wee Reese	75.00	37.00	22.00
(61)	Phil Rizzuto	60.00	30.00	18.00
(62)	Buddy Rosar	15.00	7.50	4.50
(63)	Johnny Sain	25.00	12.50	7.50
(64)	Dizzy Trout	15.00	7.50	4.50
(65)	Harry Walker	15.00	7.50	4.50

SERIES 1A

(8)	Eddie Stanky	20.00	10.00	6.00

SERIES 5

(55)	Luke Sewell	15.00	7.50	4.50

SERIES 6

(64)	Dizzy Trout	15.00	7.50	4.50

SERIES 7

(73)	Vic Lombardi	15.00	7.50	4.50

SERIES 8

(82)	Honus Wagner	75.00	37.00	22.00

SERIES 9

(91)	Buddy Lewis	15.00	7.50	4.50

SERIES 7

(66)	Floyd Bevens	15.00	7.50	4.50
(67)	Hugh Casey	15.00	7.50	4.50
(68)	Sam Chapman	15.00	7.50	4.50
(69)	Joe DiMaggio	150.00	75.00	45.00
(70)	Tommy Henrich	25.00	12.50	7.50
(71)	Ralph Kiner	30.00	15.00	9.00
(72)	Cookie Lavagetto	15.00	7.50	4.50
(73)	Vic Lombardi	15.00	7.50	4.50
(74)	Cecil Travis	15.00	7.50	4.50

SERIES 1A

(9)	Dixie Walker	15.00	7.50	4.50

SERIES 5

(56)	Billy Southworth	15.00	7.50	4.50

SERIES 6

(65)	Harry Walker	15.00	7.50	4.50

SERIES 7

(74)	Cecil Travis	15.00	7.50	4.50

SERIES 8

(83)	Mickey Witek	15.00	7.50	4.50

SERIES 9

(92)	Warren Spahn	40.00	20.00	12.00

SERIES 8

(75)	Nick Altrock	20.00	10.00	6.00
(76)	Mark Christman	15.00	7.50	4.50
(77)	Earle Combs	30.00	15.00	9.00
(78)	Travis Jackson	30.00	15.00	9.00
(79)	Bob Muncrief	15.00	7.50	4.50
(80)	Earl Neale	25.00	12.50	7.50
(81)	Joe Page	15.00	7.50	4.50
(82)	Honus Wagner	75.00	37.00	22.00
(83)	Mickey Witek	15.00	7.50	4.50

SERIES 9

(84)	George Case	15.00	7.50	4.50
(85)	Jake Early	15.00	7.50	4.50
(86)	Carl Furillo	30.00	15.00	9.00
(87)	Augie Galan	15.00	7.50	4.50
(88)	Bert Haas	15.00	7.50	4.50
(89)	Johnny Hopp	15.00	7.50	4.50
(90)	Ray Lamanno	15.00	7.50	4.50
(91)	Buddy Lewis	15.00	7.50	4.50
(92)	Warren Spahn	40.00	20.00	12.00

SERIES 10

(93)	Lu Blue	15.00	7.50	4.50
q94)	Bruce Edwards	15.00	7.50	4.50
(95)	Elbie Fletcher	15.00	7.50	4.50
(96)	Joe Gordon	15.00	7.50	4.50
(97)	Tommy Holmes	15.00	7.50	4.50
(98)	Billy Johnson	15.00	7.50	4.50
(99)	Phil Masi	15.00	7.50	4.50

SERIES 12

(113)	Sibbi Sisti, Zach Taylor	45.00	22.00	13.50

1947 Sports Exchange Baseball Miniatures

Heinie Manush

Produced and sold (originally at $1 per series) by one of the hobby's first periodicals, "The Trading Post," this 108-card set was released in three series, designated by red, green and gold borders. The blank-back, unnumbered cards are printed in black-and-white and were sold in sheets of six. When cut from the sheets, individual cards in the red- and green-bordered series measure 2-1/2" x 3," while the gold-bordered cards measure 2-1/2" x 3-1/8". The set is check-listed here alphabetically within series. The set carries an American Card Catalog designation of W602.

		NM	E	VG
Complete Set (108):		4,750	2,400	1,400
Common Player:		15.00	7.50	4.50

GOLD BORDER SERIES

(73)	Al Benton	30.00	15.00	9.00

GREEN BORDER SERIES

(6)	Hugh Casey	15.00	7.50	4.50
(7)	Phil Cavaretta	15.00	7.50	4.50
(8)	Sam Chapman	15.00	7.50	4.50
(9)	Mark Christman	15.00	7.50	4.50

GOLD BORDER SERIES

(74)	Ralph Branca	25.00	12.50	7.50

RED BORDER SERIES

(50)	Rogers Hornsby	50.00	25.00	15.00
(51)	Carl Hubbell	45.00	22.00	13.50
(52)	Travis Jackson	35.00	17.50	10.50
(53)	Bill Johnson	15.00	7.50	4.50
(54)	Ken Keltner	15.00	7.50	4.50
(55)	Whitey Kurowski	15.00	7.50	4.50
(56)	Ray Lamanno	15.00	7.50	4.50
(57)	Johnny Lindell	15.00	7.50	4.50
(58)	Peanuts Lowrey	15.00	7.50	4.50
(59)	Phil Masi	15.00	7.50	4.50
(60)	Earl Neale	20.00	10.00	6.00
(61)	Hal Newhouser	35.00	17.50	10.50
(62)	Lefty O'Doul	25.00	12.50	7.50
(63)	Herb Pennock	35.00	17.50	10.50
(64)	Red Rolfe	35.00	17.50	10.50
(65)	Babe Ruth	450.00	225.00	135.00
(66)	Luke Sewell	15.00	7.50	4.50
(67)	Rip Sewell	15.00	7.50	4.50
(68)	Warren Spahn	60.00	30.00	18.00
(69)	Vern Stephens	15.00	7.50	4.50
(70)	Dizzy Trout	15.00	7.50	4.50
(71)	Wally Westlake	15.00	7.50	4.50
(72)	Hack Wilson	50.00	25.00	15.00

GOLD BORDER SERIES

(75)	George Case	30.00	15.00	9.00
(73)	Al Benton	30.00	15.00	9.00
(74)	Ralph Branca	25.00	12.50	7.50
(75)	George Case	30.00	15.00	9.00
(76)	Spud Chandler	30.00	15.00	9.00
(77)	Jake Early	30.00	15.00	9.00
(78)	Bruce Edwards	30.00	15.00	9.00
(79)	Del Ennis	30.00	15.00	9.00
(80)	Bob Feller	80.00	40.00	24.00
(81)	Dave Ferriss	30.00	15.00	9.00
(82)	Les Fleming	30.00	15.00	9.00
(83)	Carl Furillo	150.00	75.00	45.00
(84)	Augie Galan	30.00	15.00	9.00
(85)	Hank Greenberg	100.00	50.00	30.00
(86)	Bert Haas	30.00	15.00	9.00
(87)	Jeff Heath	30.00	15.00	9.00
(88)	Billy Herman	60.00	30.00	18.00
(89)	Kirby Higbe	30.00	15.00	9.00
(90)	Tex Hughson	30.00	15.00	9.00
(91)	Johnny Hopp	30.00	15.00	9.00
(92)	Joe Jackson	650.00	325.00	195.00
(93)	Larry Jansen	30.00	15.00	9.00
(94)	Eddie Joost	30.00	15.00	9.00
(95)	Buddy Lewis	30.00	15.00	9.00
(96)	Heinie Manush	60.00	30.00	18.00
(97)	Marty Marion	30.00	15.00	9.00
(98)	George McQuinn	30.00	15.00	9.00
(99)	Johnny Mize	60.00	30.00	18.00
(108)	Ted Williams (Photo actually Bobby Doerr.)	200.00	100.00	60.00
(76)	Spud Chandler	30.00	15.00	9.00

(77)	Jake Early	30.00	15.00	9.00

GREEN BORDER SERIES

(6)	Hugh Casey	15.00	7.50	4.50

GOLD BORDER SERIES

(78)	Bruce Edwards	30.00	15.00	9.00

GREEN BORDER SERIES

(7)	Phil Cavaretta	15.00	7.50	4.50

GOLD BORDER SERIES

(79)	Del Ennis	30.00	15.00	9.00

GREEN BORDER SERIES

(8)	Sam Chapman	15.00	7.50	4.50

GOLD BORDER SERIES

(80)	Bob Feller	80.00	40.00	24.00

GREEN BORDER SERIES

(9)	Mark Christman	15.00	7.50	4.50

GOLD BORDER SERIES

(81)	Dave Ferriss	30.00	15.00	9.00
(82)	Les Fleming	30.00	15.00	9.00
(83)	Carl Furillo	150.00	75.00	45.00
(84)	Augie Galan	30.00	15.00	9.00
(85)	Hank Greenberg	100.00	50.00	30.00
(86)	Bert Haas	30.00	15.00	9.00

RED BORDER SERIES

(51)	Carl Hubbell	45.00	22.00	13.50

GOLD BORDER SERIES

(87)	Jeff Heath	30.00	15.00	9.00

RED BORDER SERIES

(52)	Travis Jackson	35.00	17.50	10.50

GOLD BORDER SERIES

(88)	Billy Herman	60.00	30.00	18.00

RED BORDER SERIES

(53)	Bill Johnson	15.00	7.50	4.50

GOLD BORDER SERIES

(89)	Kirby Higbe	30.00	15.00	9.00

RED BORDER SERIES

(54)	Ken Keltner	15.00	7.50	4.50

GOLD BORDER SERIES

(90)	Tex Hughson	30.00	15.00	9.00

RED BORDER SERIES

(55)	Whitey Kurowski	15.00	7.50	4.50

GOLD BORDER SERIES

(91)	Johnny Hopp	30.00	15.00	9.00

RED BORDER SERIES

(56)	Ray Lamanno	15.00	7.50	4.50

GOLD BORDER SERIES

(92)	Joe Jackson	650.00	325.00	195.00

RED BORDER SERIES

(57)	Johnny Lindell	15.00	7.50	4.50

GOLD BORDER SERIES

(93)	Larry Jansen	30.00	15.00	9.00

RED BORDER SERIES

(58)	Peanuts Lowrey	15.00	7.50	4.50

GOLD BORDER SERIES

(94)	Eddie Joost	30.00	15.00	9.00

RED BORDER SERIES

(59)	Phil Masi	15.00	7.50	4.50

GOLD BORDER SERIES

(95)	Buddy Lewis	30.00	15.00	9.00

RED BORDER SERIES

(60)	Earl Neale	20.00	10.00	6.00

GOLD BORDER SERIES

(96)	Heinie Manush	60.00	30.00	18.00

RED BORDER SERIES

(61)	Hal Newhouser	35.00	17.50	10.50

GOLD BORDER SERIES

(97)	Marty Marion	30.00	15.00	9.00

RED BORDER SERIES

(62)	Lefty O'Doul	25.00	12.50	7.50

GOLD BORDER SERIES

(98)	George McQuinn	30.00	15.00	9.00

RED BORDER SERIES

(63)	Herb Pennock	35.00	17.50	10.50

GOLD BORDER SERIES

(99)	Johnny Mize	60.00	30.00	18.00

RED BORDER SERIES

(64)	Red Rolfe	35.00	17.50	10.50
(65)	Babe Ruth	450.00	225.00	135.00
(66)	Luke Sewell	15.00	7.50	4.50
(67)	Rip Sewell	15.00	7.50	4.50

(68)	Warren Spahn	60.00	30.00	18.00
(69)	Vern Stephens	15.00	7.50	4.50
(70)	Dizzy Trout	15.00	7.50	4.50
(71)	Wally Westlake	15.00	7.50	4.50
(72)	Hack Wilson	50.00	25.00	15.00

1964 Sports Heroes Stickers

These red, white and blue 2-3/4" diameter were issued circa 1964 by Hunter Publishing Co., Winston-Salem, N.C. Besides their suitability to be used as wall, notebook, locker, etc., decorations, there were cardboard display pages issued on which the stickers could be placed. Currently only four teams are known to be represented, with the likelihood that four players were issued for each team. The teams represented in the issue are: Cardinals, Tigers, Pirates and Yankees. Gaps have been left in the assigned numbering to accommodate future additions to the checklist.

		NM	EX	VG
Common Player:		75.00	40.00	25.00
(1)	Ernie Broglio	75.00	40.00	25.00
(2)	Roberto Clemente	400.00	200.00	125.00
(3)	Donn Clendenon	100.00	50.00	30.00
(4)	Don Demeter	75.00	40.00	25.00
(6)	Curt Flood	100.00	50.00	30.00
(7)	Bill Freehan	100.00	50.00	30.00
(8)	Bob Friend	75.00	40.00	25.00
(10)	Elston Howard	100.00	50.00	30.00
(11)	Al Kaline	200.00	100.00	60.00
(13)	Mickey Mantle	600.00	300.00	180.00
(14)	Roger Maris	200.00	100.00	60.00
(15)	Bill Mazeroski	150.00	75.00	45.00
(16)	Tom Tresh	100.00	50.00	30.00

1954 Sports Illustrated Topps Foldouts

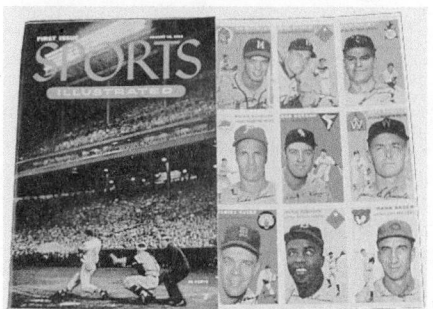

		NM	E	VG
Aug. 16, 1954 Issue				
(Original)		250.00	125.00	75.00
Aug. 16, 1954 Issue (2001				
Reprint)		30.00	15.00	9.00
1	Ted Williams			
2	Gus Zernial			
4	Hank Sauer			
6	Pete Runnels			
7	Ted Kluszewski			
9	Harvey Haddix			
10	Jackie Robinson			
15	Al Rosen			
24	Granny Hamner			
25	Harvey Kuenn			
26	Ray Jablonski			
27	Ferris Fain			
29	Jim Hegan			
30	Ed Mathews			
32	Duke Snider			
34	Jim Rivera			
40	Mel Parnell			
45	Richie Ashburn			
70	Larry Doby			
77	Ray Boone			
85	Bob Turley			
90	Willie Mays			
100	Bob Keegan			
102	Gil Hodges			
119	Johnny Antonelli			
137	Wally Moon			
235	Vern Law			
Aug. 23, 1954 Issue		225.00	112.50	67.50
5	Ed Lopat			
17	Phil Rizzuto			
37	Whitey Ford			
50	Yogi Berra			
56	Willie Miranda			
62	Eddie Robinson			
83	Joe Collins			
96	Charlie Silvera			
101	Gene Woodling			

105	Andy Carey			
130	Hank Bauer			
175	Frank Leja			
205	Johnny Sain			
230	Bob Kuzava			
239	Bill Skowron			
	Harry Byrd			
	Bob Cerv			
	Jerry Coleman			
	Tom Gorman			
	Bob Grim			
	Mickey Mantle			
	Jim McDonald			
	Gil McDougald			
	Tom Morgan			
	Irv Noren			
	Allie Reynolds			
	Enos Slaughter			

1955 Sports Illustrated Topps Foldouts

SI kicked off the 1955 baseball season by including a page of 1955 Topps card reproductions in its April 11 and April 18 issues. Unlike the tri-fold panels of 1954, the 1955 issues contain only eight reproductions per magazine. Printed in full size in full color on glossy magazine paper, the pages are exact front and back replicas of regular-issue 1955 Topps cards. The April 11 issue features on its cover Willie Mays, Leo Durocher and Lorraine Day (Mrs. D.); the April 18 issue has Al Rosen at bat. Surviving examples of these 1955 SI issues are scarce and the paper cards are seldom seen as singles.

		NM	E	VG
April 11, 1955 Issue		200.00	100.00	60.00
1	Dusty Rhodes			
26	Dick Groat			
28	Ernie Banks			
31	Warren Spahn			
56	Ray Jablonski			
67	Wally Moon			
79	Danny Schell			
90	Karl Spooner			
April 18, 1955 Issue		60.00	30.00	18.00
8	Hal Smith			
10	Bob Keegan			
11	Ferris Fain			
16	Roy Sievers			
38	Bob Turley			
70	Al Rosen			
77	Arnie Portocarrero			
106	Frank Sullivan			

1968-70 Sports Illustrated Posters

Between 1968-70, Sports Illustrated issued a series of baseball player posters. The 2' x 3' blank-back posters have borderless color action or posed photos. In an upper corner are the player identification, copyright, poster number, etc., in small type. Values for the posters issued in 1969 and 1970 are higher than those produced in 1968. Current market values reflect the fact that many superstars' posters were sold in larger quantities than those of journeyman players and survive in greater numbers. The posters are listed here alphabetically within year of issue. Original selling price of the posters was $1.50 each, plus postage.

		NM	E	VG
Complete Set (86):		2,500	1,250	750.00
Common Player:		10.00	5.00	3.00
1968				
(1)	Hank Aaron	45.00	22.50	13.50
(2)	Rich Allen	30.00	15.00	9.00
(3)	Gene Alley	15.00	7.50	4.50
(4)	Felipe Alou	15.00	7.50	4.50
(5)	Max Alvis	10.00	5.00	3.00
(6)	Bob Aspromonte	10.00	5.00	3.00

(7)	Ernie Banks (Photo actually Billy Williams.)	35.00	17.50	10.50
(8)	Clete Boyer	12.50	6.25	3.75
(9)	Lou Brock	15.00	7.50	4.50
(10)	John Callison	15.00	7.50	4.50
(11)	Campy Campaneris	12.50	6.25	3.75
(12)	Leo Cardenas	12.50	6.25	3.75
(13)	Paul Casanova	17.50	8.75	5.25
(14)	Orlando Cepeda	17.50	8.75	5.25
(15)	Roberto Clemente	185.00	95.00	55.00
(16)	Tony Conigliaro	20.00	10.00	6.00
(17)	Willie Davis	15.00	7.50	4.50
(18)	Don Drysdale	17.50	8.75	5.25
(19)	Al Ferrara	12.50	6.25	3.75
(20)	Curt Flood	15.00	7.50	4.50
(21)	Bill Freehan	30.00	15.00	9.00
(22)	Jim Fregosi	10.00	5.00	3.00
(23)	Bob Gibson	15.00	7.50	4.50
(24)	Bud Harrelson (Photo actually Ken Harrelson.)	20.00	10.00	6.00
(25)	Joe Horlen	10.00	5.00	3.00
(26)	Tony Horton	15.00	7.50	4.50
(27)	Tommy John	12.50	6.25	3.75
(28)	Al Kaline	40.00	20.00	12.00
(29)	Harmon Killebrew	17.50	8.75	5.25
(30)	Jim Lonborg	17.50	8.75	5.25
(31)	Jim Maloney	12.50	6.25	3.75
(32)	Mickey Mantle	185.00	92.00	55.00
(33)	Juan Marichal	17.50	8.75	5.25
(34)	Willie Mays	110.00	55.00	35.00
(35)	Bill Mazeroski	25.00	12.50	7.50
(36)	Tim McCarver	17.50	8.75	5.25
(37)	Mike McCormick	15.00	7.50	4.50
(38)	Willie McCovey	45.00	22.50	13.50
(39a)	Don Mincher (Angels)	15.00	7.50	4.50
(39b)	Don Mincher (Pilots)	20.00	10.00	6.00
(40)	Rick Monday	12.50	6.25	3.75
(41)	Tony Oliva	15.00	7.50	4.50
(42)	Rick Reichardt	10.00	5.00	3.00
(43)	Brooks Robinson	175.00	90.00	50.00
(44)	Frank Robinson	75.00	37.50	22.00
(45)	Pete Rose	100.00	50.00	30.00
(46)	Ron Santo	17.50	8.75	5.25
(47)	Tom Seaver	130.00	65.00	39.00
(48)	Chris Short	15.00	7.50	4.50
(49)	Reggie Smith	12.50	6.25	3.75
(50)	Rusty Staub	17.50	8.75	5.25
(51)	Mel Stottlemyre	20.00	10.00	6.00
(52)	Ron Swoboda	25.00	12.50	7.50
(53)	Cesar Tovar	15.00	7.50	4.50
(54)	Earl Wilson	17.50	8.75	5.25
(55)	Jim Wynn	10.00	5.00	3.00
(56)	Carl Yastrzemski	25.00	12.50	7.50
1969				
(1)	Tommie Agee	17.50	8.75	5.25
(2)	Mike Andrews	12.50	6.25	3.75
(3)	Ernie Banks (Batting)	15.00	7.50	4.50
(4a)	Gary Bell (Indians)	20.00	10.00	6.00
(4b)	Gary Bell (Pilots)	20.00	10.00	6.00
(5a)	Tommy Davis (White Sox)	17.50	8.75	5.25
(5b)	Tommy Davis (Pilots)	20.00	10.00	6.00
(6)	Frank Howard	20.00	10.00	6.00
(7)	Reggie Jackson	95.00	47.00	28.00
(8)	Fergie Jenkins	45.00	22.00	13.50
(9)	Let's Go Mets (Tommie Agee, Jerry Grote, Cleon Jones, Jerry Koosman, Ed Kranepool, Tom Seaver, Ron Swoboda)	20.00	10.00	6.00
(10)	Denny McLain	15.00	7.50	4.50
(11)	Bobby Murcer	45.00	22.00	13.50
(12)	John Odom	17.50	8.75	5.25
(13)	Rico Petrocelli	17.50	8.75	5.25
(14)	Boog Powell	20.00	10.00	6.00
(15)	Roy White	25.00	12.50	7.50
1970				
(1)	Glenn Beckert	17.50	8.75	5.25
(2)	Bobby Bonds	20.00	10.00	6.00
(3)	Rod Carew	17.50	8.75	5.25
(4)	Mike Cuellar	17.50	8.75	5.25
(5)	Mike Epstein	15.00	7.50	4.50
(6)	Ken Holtzman	15.00	7.50	4.50
(7)	Cleon Jones	15.00	7.50	4.50
(8)	Mickey Lolich	15.00	7.50	4.50
(9)	Sam McDowell	20.00	10.00	6.00
(10)	Phil Niekro	35.00	17.50	10.50
(11)	Wes Parker	17.50	8.75	5.25
(12)	Tony Perez	25.00	12.50	7.50
(13)	Bill Singer	10.00	5.00	3.00
(14)	Walt Williams	20.00	10.00	6.00

1968 Sports Memorabilia All Time Baseball Team

This is one of the earliest collectors' issue baseball card sets created for distribution solely within the hobby. The 2-1/2" x 3-1/2" cards feature the artwork of Art Oulette done in sepia tones on a white background and surrounded by a yellow border. Backs have career information, copyright and player identification. Issue price was $2.50.

 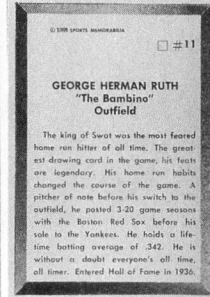

	NM	E	VG
Complete Set (15):	35.00	17.50	10.00
Common Player:	2.00	1.00	.60

		NM	E	VG
1	Checklist	.50	.25	.15
2	"Connie" Mack	2.00	1.00	.60
3	Walter Johnson	4.00	2.00	1.25
4	Warren Spahn	2.00	1.00	.60
5	Christy Mathewson	4.00	2.00	1.25
6	Lefty Grove	2.00	1.00	.60
7	Mickey Cochrane	2.00	1.00	.60
8	Bill Dickey	2.00	1.00	.60
9	"Tris" Speaker	2.50	1.25	.75
10	"Ty" Cobb	6.00	3.00	2.00
11	"Babe" Ruth	10.00	5.00	3.00
12	"Lou" Gehrig	7.50	3.75	2.25
13	Rogers Hornsby	2.50	1.25	.75
14	"Honus" Wagner	5.00	2.50	1.50
15	"Pie" Traynor	2.00	1.00	.60

1960 Sports Novelties Inc. Genuine Baseball Photos

 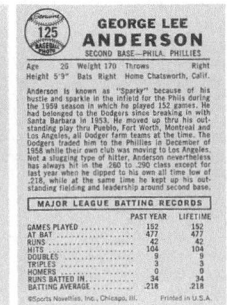

(See 1960 Leaf for checklist and price guide.)

1960s Sports Pix Premiums

These black-and-white blank-back pictures were distributed as a premium for Sports Pix magazine in the early 1960s. Two sizes are known: A smaller (about 8" x 10") style was issued in the early 1960s, while a larger (about 8-1/2" x 10-1/2") format was produced after 1963. Both styles have the photo bordered in white, with the player name centered at bottom. In the bottom-right corner is a three-line credit to the magazine and its Washington, D.C. address. Gaps have been left in the assigned numbering to accommodate future additions.

		NM	E	VG
Common Player:		10.00	5.00	3.00
(1)	Ty Cobb (Large)	7.50	3.75	2.25
(2)	Mickey Cochrane (Large)	3.00	1.50	.90
(3)	Rocky Colavito (Large)	5.00	2.50	1.50

(3)	Joe Cronin (Large)	3.00	1.50	.90
(4)	Bill Dickey (Large)	3.00	2.00	1.00
(5)	Joe DiMaggio (Large, glossy, w/caption.)	7.50	3.75	2.25
(7)	Bob Feller (Large)	3.00	2.00	1.00
(8)	Lou Gehrig (Large)	7.50	3.75	2.25
(9)	Charlie Gehringer (Large)	3.00	2.00	1.00
(11)	"Lefty" Grove (Large)	2.00	1.00	
(12)	Rogers Hornsby (Large)	3.00	2.00	1.00
(13)	Walter Johnson (Large)	5.00	2.50	1.50
(14)	Sandy Koufax (Small)	5.00	2.50	1.50
(15)	Sandy Koufax (Large)	5.00	2.50	1.50
(16)	Mickey Mantle (Large)	15.00	7.50	4.50
(17)	Mickey Mantle (Small)	15.00	7.50	4.50
(18)	Roger Maris (Large)	4.50	2.25	1.25
(19)	Willie Mays (Large)	7.50	3.75	2.25
(20)	Willie Mays (Small)	7.50	3.75	2.25
(21)	John McGraw (Large)	3.00	2.00	1.00
(22)	Stan Musial (Large)	5.00	2.50	1.50
(24)	Babe Ruth (Large)	7.50	3.75	2.25
(25)	George Sisler (Large)	3.00	2.00	1.00
(26)	Warren Spahn (Large)	3.00	2.00	1.00
(27)	"Casey" Stengel (Large)	3.00	2.00	1.00
(28)	"Pie" Traynor (Large)	3.00	2.00	1.00
(30)	"Honus" Wagner (Large)	4.50	2.25	1.25
(32)	Ted Williams (Large)	7.50	3.75	2.25

1979 Sports Reading Series

This set of large-format (about 8-1/2" x 14") was designed to encourage youthful readers. The black-and-white cards have one or more photos and lengthy text describing the player and/or action depicted.

		NM	E	VG
Complete Set (50):		250.00	125.00	75.00
Common Player:		5.00	2.50	1.50
1	Carlos May	5.00	2.50	1.50
2	Babe Ruth	10.00	5.00	3.00
3	Eddie Gaedel	6.00	3.00	1.75
4	Cesar Gutierrez	5.00	2.50	1.50
5	Ted Williams	7.50	3.75	2.25
6	Pete Gray	6.00	3.00	1.75
7	Hank Aaron	7.50	3.75	2.25
8	Lou Brock	5.00	2.50	1.50
9	Virgil Trucks	5.00	2.50	1.50
10	Cesar Tovar	5.00	2.50	1.50
11	Wrigley Field	5.00	2.50	1.50
12	Ron Guidry	5.00	2.50	1.50
13	Bill Davis	5.00	2.50	1.50
14	Jimmy Piersall	5.00	2.50	1.50
15	Eddie Gaedel	6.00	3.00	1.75
16	Reggie Jackson	7.50	3.75	2.25
17	Mark Fidrych	5.00	2.50	1.50
18	Sandy Koufax	7.50	3.75	2.25
19	Dale Long	5.00	2.50	1.50
20	Herb Score	5.00	2.50	1.50
21	Dizzy Dean, Daffy Dean	5.00	2.50	1.50
22	Stan Musial	7.50	3.75	2.25
23	1903 N.Y. Giants	5.00	2.50	1.50
24	Pete Rose	7.50	3.75	2.25
25	Cy Young	5.00	2.50	1.50
26	Ferguson Jenkins	5.00	2.50	1.50
27	Minnie Minoso	5.00	2.50	1.50
28	Mort Cooper, Walker Cooper	5.00	2.50	1.50
29	Jim Thorpe	7.50	3.75	2.25
30	Lefty Grove	5.00	2.50	1.50
31	Roberto Clemente	9.00	4.50	2.75
32	Pres. Coolidge Throws Out First Ball	5.00	2.50	1.50
33	Lou Gehrig	7.50	3.75	2.25
34	Nolan Ryan	10.00	5.00	3.00
35	1969 N.Y. Mets	5.00	2.50	1.50
36	Yankee Stadium	5.00	2.50	1.50
37	Jackie Robinson	7.50	3.75	2.25
38	Carl Hubbell	5.00	2.50	1.50
39	Willie Mays	7.50	3.75	2.25
40	Mike Schmidt	6.00	3.00	1.75
41	Harvey Haddix	5.00	2.50	1.50
42	Pete Reiser	5.00	2.50	1.50
43	Gary Cooper (Pride of the Yankees)	5.00	2.50	1.50
44	Jackie Robinson	7.50	3.75	2.25
45	Walter Johnson	5.00	2.50	1.50
46	Hall of Fame	5.00	2.50	1.50
47	Jose Morales	5.00	2.50	1.50
48	Rod Carew	5.00	2.50	1.50
49	Lou Boudreau	5.00	2.50	1.50
50	Hank Greenberg	5.00	2.50	1.50

1950 Sport Stars Luckee Key Charms

This series of 1-3/8" square, diamond-format aluminum tags depicts on front an action picture of a player along with his facsimile autograph. A good luck and sportsmanship message appears on back. The charms are holed at the top to accomodate a beaded chain. While the charms

themselves are not so marked, they were produced by Ralpat Co., of Cleveland, and sold on an approximately 3" x 5" cardboard backing card which has a line-art portrait of the player, his name, "Sport Stars" and "Luckee Key Charm." Values shown are for complete card/charm combinations. The metal charms themselves would be valued at about 35-50 percent.

		NM	E	VG
Complete Set (5):		150.00	75.00	45.00
Common Player:		15.00	7.50	4.50
(1)	Ewell Blackwell	15.00	7.50	4.50
(2)	Bob Feller	30.00	15.00	9.00
(3)	Ralph Kiner	20.00	10.00	6.00
(4)	Hal Newhouser	17.50	8.75	5.25
(5)	Ted Williams	100.00	50.00	30.00

1976 Sportstix

These peel-off player stickers were sold in five-piece plastic packs, with specific contents noted on the header. Stickers are found in three formats: 3-1/2" square, 3-1/2" square with clipped corners and 3" diameter round. The set includes 10 numbered current players and three retired baseball superstars identified as A, B and D. Stickers have full-color player pictures on front with no border. The player's name and sticker number are printed in black. Backs are blank. Besides the baseball players, there were stickers for football and basketball players, in a total issue of 30.

		NM	E	VG
Complete Baseball Set (13):		40.00	20.00	12.00
Common Player:		1.00	.50	.30
A	Willie Mays	10.00	5.00	3.00
C	Roberto Clemente	12.50	6.25	3.75
D	Mickey Mantle	15.00	7.50	4.50
1	Dave Kingman	1.00	.50	.30
2	Steve Busby	1.00	.50	.30
3	Bill Madlock	1.00	.50	.30
4	Jeff Burroughs	1.00	.50	.30
5	Ted Simmons	1.00	.50	.30
6	Randy Jones	1.00	.50	.30
7	Buddy Bell	1.00	.50	.30
8	Dave Cash	1.00	.50	.30
9	Jerry Grote	1.00	.50	.30
10	Davey Lopes	1.00	.50	.30

1975 SSPC

This set, produced by the Sport Star Publishing Company in 1975 as a collectors' issue (though not actually issued until 1976), was withdrawn from the market because of legal entanglements. Because SSPC agreed never to reprint the issue, some collectors feel it has an air of legitimacy. The complete set contains 630 full-color cards, each 2-1/2" x 3-1/2" in size. The cards look similar to 1953 Bowmans, with only the player picture (no identification) on the fronts. Card backs are in a vertical format, with personal stats, brief biographies, uniform and card numbers printed in a variety of colors. Sets originally sold for $9.99.

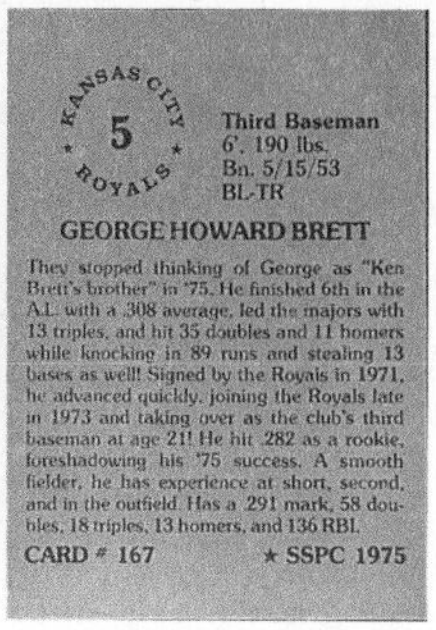
KANSAS CITY
5
ROYALS
Third Baseman
6', 190 lbs.
Bn. 5/15/53
BL-TR
GEORGE HOWARD BRETT
They stopped thinking of George as "Ken Brett's brother" in '75. He finished 6th in the A.L. with a .308 average, led the majors with 13 triples, and hit 35 doubles and 11 homers while knocking in 89 runs and stealing 13 bases as well! Signed by the Royals in 1971, he advanced quickly, joining the Royals late in 1973 and taking over as the club's third baseman at age 21! He hit .282 as a rookie, foreshadowing his '75 success. A smooth fielder, he has experience at short, second, and in the outfield. Has a .291 mark, 58 doubles, 18 triples, 13 homers, and 136 RBI.
CARD # 167
★ SSPC 1975

		NM	E	VG
Complete Set (630):		75.00	37.50	22.50
Common Player:		.10	.05	.03
1	Lee William (Buzz) Capra	.10	.05	.03
2	Thomas Ross House	.10	.05	.03
3	Maximino Leon	.10	.05	.03
4	Carl Wendle Morton	.10	.05	.03
5	Philip Henry Niekro	1.50	.70	.45
6	Michael Wayne Thompson	.10	.05	.03
7	Elias Sosa (Martinez)	.10	.05	.03
8	Larvell Blanks	.10	.05	.03
9	Darrell Wayne Evans	.10	.05	.03
10	Rodney Joe Gilbreath	.10	.05	.03
11	Michael Ken-Wai Lum	.10	.05	.03
12	Craig George Robinson	.10	.05	.03
13	Earl Craig Williams, Jr.	.10	.05	.03
14	Victor Crosby Correll	.10	.05	.03
15	Biff Pocoroba	.10	.05	.03
16	Johnny B. (Dusty) Baker, Jr.	.35	.20	.11
17	Ralph Allen Garr	.10	.05	.03
18	Clarence Edward (Cito) Gaston	.10	.05	.03
19	David LaFrance May	.10	.05	.03
20	Rowland Johnnie Office	.10	.05	.03
21	Robert Brooks Beall	.10	.05	.03
22	George Lee (Sparky) Anderson	1.00	.50	.30
23	John Eugene Billingham	.10	.05	.03
24	Pedro Rodriguez Borbon	.10	.05	.03
25	Clay Palmer Carroll	.10	.05	.03
26	Patrick Leonard Darcy	.10	.05	.03
27	Donald Edward Gullett	.10	.05	.03
28	Clayton Laws Kirby	.10	.05	.03
29	Gary Lynn Nolan	.10	.05	.03
30	Fredie Hubert Norman	.10	.05	.03
31	Johnny Lee Bench	2.50	1.25	.70
32	William Francis Plummer	.10	.05	.03
33	Darrel Lee Chaney	.10	.05	.03
34	David Ismael Concepcion	.10	.05	.03
35	Terrence Michael Crowley	.10	.05	.03
36	Daniel Driessen	.10	.05	.03
37	Robert Douglas Flynn, Jr.	.10	.05	.03
38	Joe Leonard Morgan	2.00	1.00	.60
39	Atanasio Rigal (Tony) Perez	1.50	.70	.45
40	George Kenneth (Ken) Griffey	.35	.20	.11
41	Peter Edward Rose	5.00	2.50	1.50
42	Edison Rosanda Armbrister	.10	.05	.03
43	John Christopher Vukovich	.10	.05	.03
44	George Arthur Foster	.10	.05	.03
45	Cesar Francisco Geronimo	.10	.05	.03
46	Mervin Weldon Rettenmund	.10	.05	.03
47	James Frederick Crawford	.10	.05	.03
48	Kenneth Roth Forsch	.10	.05	.03
49	Douglas James Konieczny	.10	.05	.03
50	Joseph Franklin Niekro	.10	.05	.03
51	Clifford Johnson	.10	.05	.03
52	Alfred Henry (Skip) Jutze	.10	.05	.03
53	Milton Scott May	.10	.05	.03
54	Robert Patrick Andrews	.10	.05	.03
55	Kenneth George Boswell	.10	.05	.03
56	Tommy Vann Helms	.10	.05	.03
57	Roger Henry Metzger	.10	.05	.03
58	Lawrence William Milbourne	.10	.05	.03
59	Douglas Lee Rader	.10	.05	.03
60	Robert Jose Watson	.10	.05	.03
61	Enos Milton Cabell, Jr.	.10	.05	.03
62	Jose Delan Cruz	.10	.05	.03
63	Cesar Cedeno	.10	.05	.03
64	Gregory Eugene Gross	.10	.05	.03
65	Wilbur Leon Howard	.10	.05	.03
66	Alphonso Erwin Downing	.10	.05	.03
67	Burt Carlton Hooton	.10	.05	.03
68	Charles Oliver Hough	.10	.05	.03
69	Thomas Edward John	.25	.13	.08
70	John Alexander Messersmith	.10	.05	.03
71	Douglas James Rau	.10	.05	.03
72	Richard Alan Rhoden	.10	.05	.03
73	Donald Howard Sutton	1.50	.70	.45
74	Frederick Steven Auerbach	.10	.05	.03
75	Ronald Charles Cey	.10	.05	.03
76	Ivan De Jesus	.10	.05	.03
77	Steven Patrick Garvey	1.00	.50	.30
78	Leonadus Lacy	.10	.05	.03
79	David Earl Lopes	.10	.05	.03
80	Kenneth Lee McMullen	.10	.05	.03
81	Joseph Vance Ferguson	.10	.05	.03
82	Paul Ray Powell	.10	.05	.03
83	Stephen Wayne Yeager	.10	.05	.03
84	Willie Murphy Crawford	.10	.05	.03
85	Henry Cruz	.10	.05	.03
86	Charles Fuqua Manuel	.10	.05	.03
87	Manuel Mota	.10	.05	.03
88	Thomas Marian Paciorek	.10	.05	.03
89	James Sherman Wynn	.10	.05	.03
90	Walter Emmons Alston	1.00	.50	.30
91	William Joseph Buckner	.10	.05	.03
92	James Leland Barr	.10	.05	.03
93	Ralph Michael (Mike) Caldwell	.10	.05	.03
94	John Francis D'Acquisto	.10	.05	.03
95	David Wallace Heaverlo	.10	.05	.03
96	Gary Robert Lavelle	.10	.05	.03
97	John Joseph Montefusco, Jr.	.10	.05	.03
98	Charles Prosek Williams	.10	.05	.03
99	Christopher Paul Arnold	.10	.05	.03
100	Mark Kevin Hill (Marc)	.10	.05	.03
101	David Martin Rader	.10	.05	.03
102	Charles Bruce Miller	.10	.05	.03
103	Guillermo Naranjo (Willie) Montanez	.10	.05	.03
104	Steven Robert Ontiveros	.10	.05	.03
105	Chris Edward Speier	.10	.05	.03
106	Derrel Osbon Thomas	.10	.05	.03
107	Gary Leah Thomasson	.10	.05	.03
108	Glenn Charles Adams	.10	.05	.03
109	Von Everett Joshua	.10	.05	.03
110	Gary Nathaniel Matthews	.10	.05	.03
111	Bobby Ray Murcer	.10	.05	.03
112	Horace Arthur Speed III	.10	.05	.03
113	Wesley Noreen Westrum	.10	.05	.03
114	Richard Nevin Folkers	.10	.05	.03
115	Alan Benton Foster	.10	.05	.03
116	David James Freisleben	.10	.05	.03
117	Daniel Vincent Frisella	.10	.05	.03
118	Randall Leo Jones	.10	.05	.03
119	Daniel Ray Spillner	.10	.05	.03
120	Howard Lawrence (Larry) Hardy	.10	.05	.03
121	Cecil Randolph (Randy) Hundley	.10	.05	.03
122	Fred Lyn Kendall	.10	.05	.03
123	John Francis McNamara	.10	.05	.03
124	Rigoberto (Tito) Fuentes	.10	.05	.03
125	Enzo Octavio Hernandez	.10	.05	.03
126	Stephen Michael Huntz	.10	.05	.03
127	Michael Wilson Ivie	.10	.05	.03
128	Hector Epitacio Torres	.10	.05	.03
129	Theodore Rodger Kubiak	.10	.05	.03
130	John Maywood Grubb, Jr.	.10	.05	.03
131	John Henry Scott	.10	.05	.03
132	Robert Tolan	.10	.05	.03
133	David Mark Winfield	2.50	1.25	.70
134	William Joseph Gogolewski	.10	.05	.03
135	Danny L. Osborn	.10	.05	.03
136	James Lee Kaat	.25	.13	.08
137	Claude Wilson Osteen	.10	.05	.03
138	Cecil Lee Upshaw, Jr.	.10	.05	.03
139	Wilbur Forrester Wood, Jr.	.10	.05	.03
140	Lloyd Cecil Allen	.10	.05	.03
141	Brian Jay Downing	.10	.05	.03
142	James Sarkis Essian, Jr.	.10	.05	.03
143	Russell Earl (Bucky) Dent	.50	.25	.15
144	Jorge Orta	.10	.05	.03
145	Lee Edward Richard	.10	.05	.03
146	William Allen Stein	.10	.05	.03
147	Kenneth Joseph Henderson	.10	.05	.03
148	Carlos May	.10	.05	.03
149	Nyls Wallace Rex Nyman	.10	.05	.03
150	Robert Pasquali Coluccio, Jr.	.10	.05	.03
151	Charles William Tanner, Jr.	.10	.05	.03
152	Harold Patrick (Pat) Kelly	.10	.05	.03
153	Jerry Wayne Hairston Sr.	.10	.05	.03
154	Richard Fred (Pete) Varney, Jr.	.10	.05	.03
155	William Edwin Melton	.10	.05	.03
156	Richard Michael Gossage	.50	.25	.15
157	Terry Jay Forster	.10	.05	.03
158	Richard Michael Hinton	.10	.05	.03
159	Nelson Kelley Briles	.10	.05	.03
160	Alan James Fitzmorris	.10	.05	.03
161	Stephen Bernard Mingori	.10	.05	.03
162	Martin William Pattin	.10	.05	.03
163	Paul William Splittorff, Jr.	.10	.05	.03
164	Dennis Patrick Leonard	.10	.05	.03
165	John Albert (Buck) Martinez	.10	.05	.03
166	Gorrell Robert (Bob) Stinson III	.10	.05	.03
167	George Howard Brett	7.50	3.75	2.25
168	Harmon Clayton Killebrew, Jr.	2.50	1.25	.70
169	John Claiborn Mayberry	.10	.05	.03
170	Freddie Joe Patek	.10	.05	.03
171	Octavio (Cookie) Rojas	.10	.05	.03
172	Rodney Darrell Scott	.10	.05	.03
173	Tolia (Tony) Solaita	.10	.05	.03
174	Frank White, Jr.	.10	.05	.03
175	Alfred Edward Cowens, Jr.	.10	.05	.03
176	Harold Abraham McRae	.10	.05	.03
177	Amos Joseph Otis	.10	.05	.03
178	Vada Edward Pinson, Jr.	.50	.25	.15
179	James Eugene Wohlford	.10	.05	.03
180	James Douglas Bird	.10	.05	.03
181	Mark Alan Littell	.10	.05	.03
182	Robert McClure	.10	.05	.03
183	Steven Lee Busby	.10	.05	.03
184	Francis Xavier Healy	.10	.05	.03
185	Dorrel Norman Elvert (Whitey) Herzog	.10	.05	.03
186	Andrew Earl Hassler	.10	.05	.03
187	Lynn Nolan Ryan, Jr.	7.50	3.75	2.25
188	William Robert Singer	.10	.05	.03
189	Frank Daryl Tanana	.10	.05	.03
190	Eduardo Figueroa	.10	.05	.03
191	David S. Collins	.10	.05	.03
192	Richard Hirshfeld Williams	.10	.05	.03
193	Eliseo Rodriguez	.10	.05	.03
194	David Lee Chalk	.10	.05	.03
195	Winston Enriquillo Llenas	.10	.05	.03
196	Rudolph Bart Meoli	.10	.05	.03
197	Orlando Ramirez	.10	.05	.03
198	Gerald Peter Remy	.10	.05	.03
199	Billy Edward Smith	.10	.05	.03
200	Bruce Anton Bochte	.10	.05	.03
201	Joseph Michael Lahoud, Jr.	.10	.05	.03
202	Morris Nettles, Jr.	.10	.05	.03
203	John Milton (Mickey) Rivers	.10	.05	.03
204	Leroy Bobby Stanton	.10	.05	.03
205	Victor Albury	.10	.05	.03
206	Thomas Henry Burgmeier	.10	.05	.03
207	William Franklin Butler	.10	.05	.03
208	William Richard Campbell	.10	.05	.03
209	Alton Ray Corbin	.10	.05	.03
210	George Henry (Joe) Decker, Jr.	.10	.05	.03
211	James Michael Hughes	.10	.05	.03
212	Edward Norman Bane (Photo actually Mike Pazik.)	.10	.05	.03
213	Glenn Dennis Borgmann	.10	.05	.03
214	Rodney Cline Carew	2.50	1.25	.70
215	Stephen Robert Brye	.10	.05	.03
216	Darnell Glenn (Dan) Ford	.10	.05	.03
217	Antonio Oliva	.35	.20	.11
218	David Allan Goltz	.10	.05	.03
219	Rikalbert Blyleven	2.00	1.00	.60
220	Larry Eugene Hisle	.10	.05	.03
221	Stephen Russell Braun, III	.10	.05	.03
222	Jerry Wayne Terrell	.10	.05	.03
223	Eric Thane Soderholm	.10	.05	.03
224	Philip Anthony Roof	.10	.05	.03
225	Danny Leon Thompson	.10	.05	.03
226	James William Colborn	.10	.05	.03
227	Thomas Andrew Murphy	.10	.05	.03
228	Eduardo Rodriguez	.10	.05	.03
229	James Michael Slaton	.10	.05	.03
230	Edward Nelson Sprague	.10	.05	.03
231	Charles William Moore, Jr.	.10	.05	.03
232	Darrell Ray Porter	.10	.05	.03
233	Kurt Anthony Bevacqua	.10	.05	.03
234	Pedro Garcia	.10	.05	.03
235	James Michael (Mike) Hegan	.10	.05	.03
236	Donald Wayne Money	.10	.05	.03
237	George C. Scott, Jr.	.10	.05	.03
238	Robin R. Yount	5.00	2.50	1.50
239	Henry Louis Aaron	5.00	2.50	1.50
240	Robert Walker Ellis	.10	.05	.03
241	Sixto Lezcano	.10	.05	.03
242	Robert Vance Mitchell	.10	.05	.03
243	James Gorman Thomas, III	.10	.05	.03
244	William Edward Travers	.10	.05	.03
245	Peter Sven Broberg	.10	.05	.03
246	William Howard Sharp	.10	.05	.03
247	Arthur Bobby Lee Darwin	.10	.05	.03
248	Rick Gerald Austin (Photo actually Larry Anderson.)	.10	.05	.03
249	Lawrence Dennis Anderson (Photo actually Rick Austin.)	.10	.05	.03
250	Thomas Antony Bianco	.10	.05	.03
251	DeLancy LaFayette Currence	.10	.05	.03
252	Steven Raymond Foucault	.10	.05	.03
253	William Alfred Hands, Jr.	.10	.05	.03
254	Steven Lowell Hargan	.10	.05	.03
255	Ferguson Arthur Jenkins	1.50	.70	.45
256	Bob Mitchell Sheldon	.10	.05	.03
257	James Umbarger	.10	.05	.03
258	Clyde Wright	.10	.05	.03

259	William Roger Fahey	.10	.05	.03
260	James Howard Sundberg	.10	.05	.03
261	Leonardo Alfonso Cardenas	.10	.05	.03
262	James Louis Fregosi	.10	.05	.03
263	Dudley Michael (Mike) Hargrove	.10	.05	.03
264	Colbert Dale (Toby) Harrah	.10	.05	.03
265	Roy Lee Howell	.10	.05	.03
266	Leonard Shenoff Randle	.10	.05	.03
267	Roy Frederick Smalley III	.10	.05	.03
268	James Lloyd Spencer	.10	.05	.03
269	Jeffrey Alan Burroughs	.10	.05	.03
270	Thomas Alan Grieve	.10	.05	.03
271	Joseph Lovitto, Jr.	.10	.05	.03
272	Frank Joseph Lucchesi	.10	.05	.03
273	David Earl Nelson	.10	.05	.03
274	Ted Lyle Simmons	.10	.05	.03
275	Louis Clark Brock	2.00	1.00	.60
276	Ronald Ray Fairly	.10	.05	.03
277	Arnold Ray (Bake) McBride	.10	.05	.03
278	Carl Reginald (Reggie) Smith	.10	.05	.03
279	William Henry Davis	.10	.05	.03
280	Kenneth John Reitz	.10	.05	.03
281	Charles William (Buddy) Bradford	.10	.05	.03
282	Luis Antonio Melendez	.10	.05	.03
283	Michael Ray Tyson	.10	.05	.03
284	Ted Crawford Sizemore	.10	.05	.03
285	Mario Miguel Guerrero	.10	.05	.03
286	Larry Lintz	.10	.05	.03
287	Kenneth Victor Rudolph	.10	.05	.03
288	Richard Arlin Billings	.10	.05	.03
289	Jerry Wayne Mumphrey	.10	.05	.03
290	Michael Sherman Wallace	.10	.05	.03
291	Alan Thomas Hrabosky	.10	.05	.03
292	Kenneth Lee Reynolds	.10	.05	.03
293	Michael Douglas Garman	.10	.05	.03
294	Robert Herbert Forsch	.10	.05	.03
295	John Allen Denny	.10	.05	.03
296	Harold R. Rasmussen	.10	.05	.03
297	Lynn Everratt McGlothen (Everett)	.10	.05	.03
298	Michael Roswell Barlow	.10	.05	.03
299	Gregory John Terlecky	.10	.05	.03
300	Albert Fred (Red) Schoendienst	1.00	.50	.30
301	Ricky Eugene Reuschel	.10	.05	.03
302	Steven Michael Stone	.10	.05	.03
303	William Gordon Bonham	.10	.05	.03
304	Oscar Joseph Zamora	.10	.05	.03
305	Kenneth Douglas Frailing	.10	.05	.03
306	Milton Edward Wilcox	.10	.05	.03
307	Darold Duane Knowles	.10	.05	.03
308	Rufus James (Jim) Marshall	.10	.05	.03
309	Bill Madlock, Jr.	.10	.05	.03
310	Jose Domec Cardenal	.10	.05	.03
311	Robert James (Rick) Monday, Jr.	.10	.05	.03
312	Julio Ruben (Jerry) Morales	.10	.05	.03
313	Timothy Kenneth Hosley	.10	.05	.03
314	Gene Taylor Hiser	.10	.05	.03
315	Donald Eulon Kessinger	.10	.05	.03
316	Jesus Manuel (Manny) Trillo	.10	.05	.03
317	Ralph Pierre (Pete) LaCock, Jr.	.10	.05	.03
318	George Eugene Mitterwald	.10	.05	.03
319	Steven Eugene Swisher	.10	.05	.03
320	Robert Walter Sperring	.10	.05	.03
321	Victor Lanier Harris	.10	.05	.03
322	Ronald Ray Dunn	.10	.05	.03
323	Jose Manuel Morales	.10	.05	.03
324	Peter MacKanin, Jr.	.10	.05	.03
325	James Charles Cox	.10	.05	.03
326	Larry Alton Parrish	.10	.05	.03
327	Michael Jorgensen	.10	.05	.03
328	Timothy John Foli	.10	.05	.03
329	Harold Noel Breeden	.10	.05	.03
330	Nathan Colbert, Jr.	.10	.05	.03
331	Jesus Maria (Pepe) Frias	.10	.05	.03
332	James Patrick (Pat) Scanlon	.10	.05	.03
333	Robert Sherwood Bailey	.10	.05	.03
334	Gary Edmund Carter	2.00	1.00	.60
335	Jose Mauel (Pepe) Mangual	.10	.05	.03
336	Lawrence David Biittner	.10	.05	.03
337	James Lawrence Lyttle, Jr.	.10	.05	.03
338	Gary Roenicke	.10	.05	.03
339	Anthony Scott	.10	.05	.03
340	Jerome Cardell White	.10	.05	.03
341	James Edward Dwyer	.10	.05	.03
342	Ellis Clarence Valentine	.10	.05	.03
343	Frederick John Scherman, Jr.	.10	.05	.03
344	Dennis Herman Blair	.10	.05	.03
345	Woodrow Thompson Fryman	.10	.05	.03
346	Charles Gilbert Taylor	.10	.05	.03
347	Daniel Dean Warthen	.10	.05	.03
348	Donald George Carrithers	.10	.05	.03
349	Stephen Douglas Rogers	.10	.05	.03
350	Dale Albert Murray	.10	.05	.03
351	Edwin Donald (Duke) Snider	3.00	1.50	.90
352	Ralph George Houk	.10	.05	.03
353	John Frederick Hiller	.10	.05	.03
354	Michael Stephen Lolich	.10	.05	.03
355	David Lawrence Lemancyzk	.10	.05	.03
356	Lerrin Harris LaGrow	.10	.05	.03
357	Fred Arroyo	.10	.05	.03
358	Joseph Howard Coleman	.10	.05	.03
359	Benjamin A. Oglivie	.10	.05	.03
360	Willie Wattison Horton	.10	.05	.03
361	John Clinton Knox	.10	.05	.03
362	Leon Kauffman Roberts	.10	.05	.03
363	Ronald LeFlore	.10	.05	.03
364	Gary Lynn Sutherland	.10	.05	.03
365	Daniel Thomas Meyer	.10	.05	.03
366	Aurelio Rodriguez	.10	.05	.03
367	Thomas Martin Veryzer	.10	.05	.03
368	Lavern Jack Pierce	.10	.05	.03
369	Eugene Richard Michael	.10	.05	.03
370	Robert (Billy) Baldwin	.10	.05	.03
371	William James Gates Brown	.10	.05	.03
372	Mitchell Jack (Mickey) Stanley	.10	.05	.03
373	Terryal Gene Humphrey	.10	.05	.03
374	Doyle Lafayette Alexander	.10	.05	.03
375	Miguel Angel (Mike) Cuellar	.10	.05	.03
376	Marcus Wayne Garland	.10	.05	.03
377	Ross Albert Grimsley III	.10	.05	.03
378	Grant Dwight Jackson	.10	.05	.03
379	Dyar K. Miller	.10	.05	.03
380	James Alvin Palmer	2.00	1.00	.60
381	Michael Augustine Torrez	.10	.05	.03
382	Michael Henry Willis	.10	.05	.03
383	David Edwin Duncan	.10	.05	.03
384	Elrod Jerome Hendricks	.10	.05	.03
385	James Neamon Hutto Jr.	.10	.05	.03
386	Robert Michael Bailor	.10	.05	.03
387	Douglas Vernon DeCinces	.10	.05	.03
388	Robert Anthony Grich	.10	.05	.03
389	Lee Andrew May	.10	.05	.03
390	Anthony Joseph Muser	.10	.05	.03
391	Timothy C. Nordbrook	.10	.05	.03
392	Brooks Calbert Robinson, Jr.	2.50	1.25	.70
393	Royle Stillman	.10	.05	.03
394	Don Edward Baylor	.10	.05	.03
395	Paul L.D. Blair	.10	.05	.03
396	Alonza Benjamin Bumbry	.10	.05	.03
397	Larry Duane Harlow	.10	.05	.03
398	Herman Thomas (Tommy) Davis, Jr.	.10	.05	.03
399	James Thomas Northrup	.10	.05	.03
400	Kenneth Wayne Singleton	.10	.05	.03
401	Thomas Michael Shopay	.10	.05	.03
402	Fredrick Michael Lynn	.75	.40	.25
403	Carlton Ernest Fisk	2.00	1.00	.60
404	Cecil Celester Cooper	.10	.05	.03
405	James Edward Rice	2.00	1.00	.60
406	Juan Jose Beniquez	.10	.05	.03
407	Robert Dennis Doyle	.10	.05	.03
408	Dwight Michael Evans	.10	.05	.03
409	Carl Michael Yastrzemski	3.00	1.50	.90
410	Richard Paul Burleson	.10	.05	.03
411	Bernardo Carbo	.10	.05	.03
412	Douglas Lee Griffin, Jr.	.10	.05	.03
413	Americo P. Petrocelli	.10	.05	.03
414	Robert Edward Montgomery	.10	.05	.03
415	Timothy P. Blackwell	.10	.05	.03
416	Richard Alan Miller	.10	.05	.03
417	Darrell Dean Johnson	.10	.05	.03
418	Jim Scott Burton	.10	.05	.03
419	James Arthur Willoughby	.10	.05	.03
420	Rogelio (Roger) Moret	.10	.05	.03
421	William Francis Lee, III	.10	.05	.03
422	Richard Anthony Drago	.10	.05	.03
423	Diego Pablo Segui	.10	.05	.03
424	Luis Clemente Tiant	.10	.05	.03
425	James Augustus (Catfish) Hunter	1.50	.70	.45
426	Richard Clyde Sawyer	.10	.05	.03
427	Rudolph May Jr.	.10	.05	.03
428	Richard William Tidrow	.10	.05	.03
429	Albert Walter (Sparky) Lyle	.10	.05	.03
430	George Francis (Doc) Medich	.10	.05	.03
431	Patrick Edward Dobson, Jr.	.10	.05	.03
432	David Percy Pagan	.10	.05	.03
433	Thurman Lee Munson	2.00	1.00	.60
434	Carroll Christopher Chambliss	.10	.05	.03
435	Roy Hilton White	.10	.05	.03
436	Walter Allen Williams	.10	.05	.03
437	Graig Nettles	.10	.05	.03
438	John Rikard (Rick) Dempsey	.10	.05	.03
439	Bobby Lee Bonds	.25	.13	.08
440	Edward Martin Hermann (Herrmann)	.10	.05	.03
441	Santos Alomar	.10	.05	.03
442	Frederick Blair Stanley	.10	.05	.03
443	Terry Bertland Whitfield	.10	.05	.03
444	Richard Alan Bladt	.10	.05	.03
445	Louis Victor Piniella	.50	.25	.15
446	Richard Allen Coggins	.10	.05	.03
447	Edwin Albert Brinkman	.10	.05	.03
448	James Percy Mason	.10	.05	.03
449	Larry Murray	.10	.05	.03
450	Ronald Mark Blomberg	.10	.05	.03
451	Elliott Maddox	.10	.05	.03
452	Kerry Dineen	.10	.05	.03
453	Alfred Manuel (Billy) Martin	.50	.25	.15
454	Dave Bergman	.10	.05	.03
455	Otoniel Velez	.10	.05	.03
456	Joseph Walter Hoerner	.10	.05	.03
457	Frank Edwin (Tug) McGraw, Jr.	.10	.05	.03
458	Henry Eugene (Gene) Garber	.10	.05	.03
459	Steven Norman Carlton	2.00	1.00	.60
460	Larry Richard Christenson	.10	.05	.03
461	Thomas Gerald Underwood	.10	.05	.03
462	James Reynold Lonborg	.10	.05	.03
463	John William (Jay) Johnstone, Jr.	.10	.05	.03
464	Lawrence Robert Bowa	.10	.05	.03
465	David Cash, Jr.	.10	.05	.03
466	Ollie Lee Brown	.10	.05	.03
467	Gregory Michael Luzinski	.10	.05	.03
468	Johnny Lane Oates	.10	.05	.03
469	Michael Allen Anderson	.10	.05	.03
470	Michael Jack Schmidt	4.00	2.00	1.25
471	Robert Raymond Boone	.10	.05	.03
472	Thomas George Hutton	.10	.05	.03
473	Richard Anthony Allen	.50	.25	.15
474	Antonio Taylor	.10	.05	.03
475	Jerry Lindsey Martin	.10	.05	.03
476	Daniel Leonard Ozark	.10	.05	.03
477	Richard David Ruthven	.10	.05	.03
478	James Richard Todd, Jr.	.10	.05	.03
479	Paul Aaron Lindblad	.10	.05	.03
480	Roland Glen Fingers	1.50	.70	.45
481	Vida Blue, Jr.	.10	.05	.03
482	Kenneth Dale Holtzman	.10	.05	.03
483	Richard Allen Bosman	.10	.05	.03
484	Wilfred Charles (Sonny) Siebert	.10	.05	.03
485	William Glenn Abbott	.10	.05	.03
486	Stanley Raymond Bahnsen	.10	.05	.03
487	Michael Norris	.10	.05	.03
488	Alvin Ralph Dark	.10	.05	.03
489	Claudell Washington	.10	.05	.03
490	Joseph Oden Rudi	.10	.05	.03
491	William Alex North	.10	.05	.03
492	Dagoberto Blanco (Bert) Campaneris	.10	.05	.03
493	Fury Gene Tenace	.10	.05	.03
494	Reginald Martinez Jackson	4.00	2.00	1.25
495	Philip Mason Garner	.10	.05	.03
496	Billy Leo Williams	2.00	1.00	.60
497	Salvatore Leonard Bando	.10	.05	.03
498	James William Holt	.10	.05	.03
499	Teodoro Noel Martinez	.10	.05	.03
500	Raymond Earl Fosse	.10	.05	.03
501	Matthew Alexander	.10	.05	.03
502	Wallace Larry Haney	.10	.05	.03
503	Angel Luis Mangual	.10	.05	.03
504	Fred Ray Beene	.10	.05	.03
505	Thomas William Buskey	.10	.05	.03
506	Dennis Lee Eckersley	2.00	1.00	.60
507	Roric Edward Harrison	.10	.05	.03
508	Donald Harris Hood	.10	.05	.03
509	James Lester Kern	.10	.05	.03
510	David Eugene LaRoche	.10	.05	.03
511	Fred Ingels (Fritz) Peterson	.10	.05	.03
512	James Michael Strickland	.10	.05	.03
513	Michael Richard (Rick) Waits	.10	.05	.03
514	Alan Dean Ashby	.10	.05	.03
515	John Charles Ellis	.10	.05	.03
516	Rick Cerone	.10	.05	.03
517	David Gus (Buddy) Bell	.10	.05	.03
518	John Anthony Brohamer, Jr.	.10	.05	.03
519	Ricardo Adolfo Jacobo Carty	.10	.05	.03
520	Edward Carlton Crosby	.10	.05	.03
521	Frank Thomas Duffy	.10	.05	.03
522	Duane Eugene Kuiper (Photo actually Rick Manning.)	.10	.05	.03
523	Joseph Anthony Lis	.10	.05	.03
524	John Wesley (Boog) Powell	.50	.25	.15
525	Frank Robinson	2.50	1.25	.70
526	Oscar Charles Gamble	.10	.05	.03
527	George Andrew Hendrick	.10	.05	.03
528	John Lee Lowenstein	.10	.05	.03
529	Richard Eugene Manning (photo actually Duane Kuiper)	.10	.05	.03
530	Tommy Alexander Smith	.10	.05	.03

531	Leslie Charles (Charlie)			
	Spikes	.10	.05	.03
532	Steve Jack Kline	.10	.05	.03
533	Edward Emil Kranepool	.10	.05	.03
534	Michael Vail	.10	.05	.03
535	Delbert Bernard Unser	.10	.05	.03
536	Felix Bernardo Martinez			
	Millan	.10	.05	.03
537	Daniel Joseph (Rusty) Staub	.25	.13	.08
538	Jesus Maria Rojas Alou	.10	.05	.03
539	Ronald Wayne Garrett	.10	.05	.03
540	Michael Dwaine Phillips	.10	.05	.03
541	Joseph Paul Torre	.10	.05	.03
542	David Arthur Kingman	.10	.05	.03
543	Eugene Anthony Clines	.10	.05	.03
544	Jack Seale Heidemann	.10	.05	.03
545	Derrel McKinley (Bud)			
	Harrelson	.10	.05	.03
546	John Hardin Stearns	.10	.05	.03
547	John David Milner	.10	.05	.03
548	Robert John Apodaca	.10	.05	.03
549	Claude Edward (Skip)			
	Lockwood Jr.	.10	.05	.03
550	Kenneth George Sanders	.10	.05	.03
551	George Thomas (Tom)			
	Seaver	3.00	1.50	.90
552	Ricky Alan Baldwin	.10	.05	.03
553	Jonathan Trumpbour Matlack	.10	.05	.03
554	Henry Gaylon Webb	.10	.05	.03
555	Randall Lee Tate	.10	.05	.03
556	Tom Edward Hall	.10	.05	.03
557	George Heard Stone Jr.	.10	.05	.03
558	Craig Steven Swan	.10	.05	.03
559	Gerald Allen Cram	.10	.05	.03
560	Roy J. Staiger	.10	.05	.03
561	Kenton C. Tekulve	.10	.05	.03
562	Jerry Reuss	.10	.05	.03
563	John R. Candelaria	.10	.05	.03
564	Lawrence C. Demery	.10	.05	.03
565	David John Giusti Jr.	.10	.05	.03
566	James Phillip Rooker	.10	.05	.03
567	Ramon Gonzalez Hernandez	.10	.05	.03
568	Bruce Eugene Kison	.10	.05	.03
569	Kenneth Alven Brett (Alvin)	.10	.05	.03
570	Robert Ralph Moose Jr.	.10	.05	.03
571	Manuel Jesus Sanguillen	.10	.05	.03
572	David Gene Parker	.10	.05	.03
573	Wilver Dornel Stargell	2.00	1.00	.60
574	Richard Walter Zisk	.10	.05	.03
575	Renaldo Antonio Stennett	.10	.05	.03
576	Albert Oliver Jr.	.25	.13	.08
577	William Henry Robinson Jr.	.10	.05	.03
578	Robert Eugene Robertson	.10	.05	.03
579	Richard Joseph Hebner	.10	.05	.03
580	Edgar Leon Kirkpatrick	.10	.05	.03
581	Don Robert (Duffy) Dyer	.10	.05	.03
582	Craig Reynolds	.10	.05	.03
583	Franklin Fabian Taveras	.10	.05	.03
584	William Larry Randolph	.10	.05	.03
585	Arthur H. Howe	.10	.05	.03
586	Daniel Edward Murtaugh	.10	.05	.03
587	Charles Richard (Rich)			
	McKinney	.10	.05	.03
588	James Edward Goodson	.10	.05	.03
589	George Brett, Al Cowans/			
	Checklist	1.50	.70	.45
590	Keith Hernandez, Lou Brock/			
	Checklist	.15	.08	.05
591	Jerry Koosman, Duke			
	Snider/Checklist	.25	.13	.08
592	John Knox, Maury Wills/			
	Checklist	.10	.05	.03
593a	Catfish Hunter, Noland			
	Ryan/Checklist	4.00	2.00	1.25
593b	Catfish Hunter, Nolan Ryan/			
	Checklist	3.00	1.50	.90
594	Pee Wee Reese, Ralph			
	Branca, Carl Erskine	1.00	.50	.30
595	Willie Mays, Herb Score/			
	Checklist	1.00	.50	.30
596	Larry Eugene Cox	.10	.05	.03
597	Eugene William Mauch	.10	.05	.03
598	William Frederick (Whitey)			
	Wietelmann	.10	.05	.03
599	Wayne Kirby Simpson	.10	.05	.03
600	Melvin Erskine Thomason	.10	.05	.03
601	Issac Bernard (Ike) Hampton	.10	.05	.03
602	Kenneth S. Crosby	.10	.05	.03
603	Ralph Emanuel Rowe	.10	.05	.03
604	James Vernon Tyrone	.10	.05	.03
605	Michael Dennis Kelleher	.10	.05	.03
606	Mario Mendoza	.10	.05	.03
607	Michael George Rogodzinski	.10	.05	.03
608	Robert Collins Gallagher	.10	.05	.03
609	Jerry Martin Koosman	.10	.05	.03
610	Joseph Filmore Frazier	.10	.05	.03
611	Karl Kuehl	.10	.05	.03
612	Frank J. LaCorte	.10	.05	.03

613	Raymond Douglas Bare	.10	.05	.03
614	Billy Arnold Muffett	.10	.05	.03
615	William Harry Laxton	.10	.05	.03
616	Willie Howard Mays	5.00	2.50	1.50
617	Philip Joseph Cavaretta			
	(Cavarretta)	.10	.05	.03
618	Theodore Bernard			
	Kluszewski	.50	.25	.15
619	Elston Gene Howard	.10	.05	.03
620	Alexander Peter Grammas	.10	.05	.03
621	James Barton (Mickey)			
	Vernon	.10	.05	.03
622	Richard Allan Sisler	.10	.05	.03
623	Harvey Haddix, Jr.	.10	.05	.03
624	Bobby Brooks Winkles	.10	.05	.03
625	John Michael Pesky	.10	.05	.03
626	James Houston Davenport	.10	.05	.03
627	David Allen Tomlin	.10	.05	.03
628	Roger Lee Craig	.10	.05	.03
629	John Joseph Amalfitano	.10	.05	.03
630	James Harrison Reese	.25	.13	.08

1975 SSPC Mets/Yankees

Team sets of the New York clubs were issued by SSPC bearing a 1975 copyright date and in the same "pure card" format as most of the company's other issues. The 2-1/2" x 3-1/2" cards have a posed color photo on front with a thin white border and no extraneous graphics - not even the player's name. Backs are printed in red and blue with personal data and a career summary, along with the player's full formal name. The checklist lists the player as he is best known. Issue price was $1.25 per team set.

		NM	E	VG
Complete Set (45):		15.00	7.50	4.50
Common Player:		.25	.13	.08
New York Mets Team				
Set:		9.00	4.50	2.75
1	John Milner	.25	.13	.08
2	Henry Webb	.25	.13	.08
3	Tom Hall	.25	.13	.08
4	Del Unser	.25	.13	.08
5	Wayne Garrett	.25	.13	.08
6	Jesus Alou	.25	.13	.08
7	Rusty Staub	.40	.20	.12
8	John Stearns	.25	.13	.08
9	Dave Kingman	.75	.40	.25
10	Ed Kranepool	.35	.20	.11
11	Cleon Jones	.40	.20	.12
12	Tom Seaver	4.00	2.00	1.25
13	George Stone	.25	.13	.08
14	Jerry Koosman	.35	.20	.11
15	Bob Apodaca	.25	.13	.08
16	Felix Millan	.25	.13	.08
17	Gene Clines	.25	.13	.08
18	Mike Phillips	.25	.13	.08
19	Yogi Berra	3.00	1.50	.90
20	Joe Torre	1.50	.70	.45
21	Jon Matlack	.25	.13	.08
22	Ricky Baldwin	.25	.13	.08
New York Yankees Team				
Set:		9.00	4.50	2.75
1	Catfish Hunter	1.00	.50	.30
2	Bobby Bonds	.35	.20	.11
3	Ed Brinkman	.25	.13	.08
4	Ron Blomberg	.25	.13	.08
5	Thurman Munson	3.50	1.75	1.00
6	Roy White	.35	.20	.11
7	Larry Gura	.25	.13	.08
8	Ed Hermann	.25	.13	.08
9	Bill Virdon	.25	.13	.08
10	Elliott Maddox	.25	.13	.08
11	Lou Piniella	.50	.25	.15
12	Rick Dempsey	.25	.13	.08
13	Fred Stanley	.25	.13	.08
14	Chris Chambliss	.25	.13	.08
15	Doc Medich	.25	.13	.08
16	Pat Dobson	.25	.13	.08
17	Alex Johnson	.25	.13	.08
18	Jim Mason	.25	.13	.08
19	Sandy Alomar	.25	.13	.08

20	Graig Nettles	.50	.25	.15
21	Walt Williams	.25	.13	.08
22	Sparky Lyle	.35	.20	.11
23	Dick Tidrow	.25	.13	.08

1975 SSPC Promo Cards

The six players in this sample set can each be found with three different backs. Some backs are similar to the cards issued in 1976, with player data and career summary. Some cards will have an ad message on back offering the complete 1976 SSPC set and team sets. Still others have blank backs. All cards are in 2-1/2" x 3-1/2" format with color photos on front surrounded by a white border and no extraneous graphics. Blank-back versions are worth 2-4X the values quoted here.

		NM	E	VG
Complete Set (6):		15.00	7.50	4.50
Common Player:		1.50	.75	.45
(1)	Hank Aaron	4.00	2.00	1.25
(2)	Catfish Hunter	2.00	1.00	.60
(3)	Dave Kingman	1.50	.75	.45
(4)	Mickey Mantle	7.50	3.75	2.25
(5)	Willie Mays	4.00	2.00	1.25
(6)	Tom Seaver	3.00	1.50	.90

1975 SSPC Puzzle Backs

A large black-and-white puzzle picture of Nolan Ryan and Catfish Hunter can be assembled with the backs of these cards. Fronts of the 3-9/16" x 4-1/4" cards have a color player pose with a white border. The player's name, position and team are printed at bottom. Fronts have a glossy surface. The SSPC identification only appears around the border of the puzzle. The unnumbered cards are checklisted here alphabetically. Issue price was $2.

		NM	E	VG
Complete Set, Uncut Sheet:		40.00	20.00	12.00
Complete Set (24):		20.00	10.00	6.00
Common Player:		.30	.15	.09
(1)	Hank Aaron	4.00	2.00	1.25
(2)	Johnny Bench	1.75	.90	.50
(3)	Bobby Bonds	.35	.20	.11
(4)	Jeff Burroughs	.30	.15	.09
(5)	Rod Carew	1.75	.90	.50
(6)	Dave Cash	.30	.15	.09
(7)	Cesar Cedeno	.30	.15	.09
(8)	Bucky Dent	.30	.15	.09
(9)	Rollie Fingers	1.25	.60	.40
(10)	Steve Garvey	1.00	.50	.30
(11)	John Grubb	.30	.15	.09
(12)	Reggie Jackson	2.00	1.00	.60
(13)	Jim Kaat	.30	.15	.09
(14)	Greg Luzinski	.30	.15	.09
(15)	Fred Lynn	.50	.25	.15
(16)	Bill Madlock	.30	.15	.09
(17)	Andy Messersmith	.30	.15	.09
(18)	Thurman Munson	2.00	1.00	.60
(19)	Jim Palmer	1.25	.60	.40
(20)	Dave Parker	.30	.15	.09
(21)	Jim Rice	1.50	.75	.45
(22)	Pete Rose	4.00	2.00	1.25
(23)	Tom Seaver	1.75	.90	.50
(24)	Chris Speier	.30	.15	.09

1975 SSPC Sample Cards

 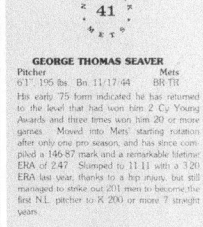

The Winter 1975 issue of "Collector's Quarterly" magazine (an advertising vehicle for Mike Aronstein, SSPC's principal) contained a two-page cardboard insert previewing the 1976 SSPC set. The cards could be cut apart into singles and represented something of a traded set, as each player or manager changed teams between the end of the 1975 season and the start of 1976. The cards have the players pictured on front in their old uniforms, with their new teams identified on back. Backs of the 2-1/2" x 3-1/2" cards are printed in red and black with a player biography and uniform number. "SAMPLE CARD 1975" is printed around the uniform number. A card number is in the lower-left corner, with 1975 copyright at bottom-right.

	NM	E	VG
Complete Set, Uncut Sheet:	25.00	12.50	7.50
Complete Set, Singles (18):	20.00	10.00	6.00
Common Card:	1.50	.75	.45
1 Harry Parker	1.50	.75	.45
2 Jim Bibby	1.50	.75	.45
3 Mike Wallace	1.50	.75	.45
4 Tony Muser	1.50	.75	.45
5 Yogi Berra	7.50	3.75	2.25
6 Preston Gomez	1.50	.75	.45
7 Jack McKeon	1.50	.75	.45
8 Sam McDowell	1.50	.70	.45
9 Gaylord Perry	4.00	2.00	1.25
10 Fred Stanley	1.50	.75	.45
11 Willie Davis	1.50	.70	.45
12 Don Hopkins	1.50	.75	.45
13 Whitey Herzog	1.50	.70	.45
14 Ray Sadecki	1.50	.75	.45
15 Stan Bahnsen	1.50	.75	.45
16 Bob Oliver	1.50	.75	.45
17 Denny Doyle	1.50	.75	.45
18 Deron Johnson	1.50	.70	.45

1975 SSPC Superstars

Nearly four dozen of the game's contemporary and former stars are featured in this set. Like other SSPC issues of 1975, fronts of the 2-1/2" x 3-1/2" cards have posed color photos with a white border. There are no other graphics, not even the player's name. The horizontal backs feature the player's full formal name (checklist here uses popular name) along with personal data, career summary and stats. Issue price was $4.

	NM	E	VG
Complete Set (42):	25.00	12.50	7.50
Common Player:	.25	.13	.08
1 Wilbur Wood	.25	.13	.08
2 Johnny Sain	.25	.13	.08
3 Bill Melton	.25	.13	.08
4 Dick Allen	.50	.25	.15
5 Jim Palmer	1.00	.50	.30
6 Brooks Robinson	1.50	.70	.45
7 Tommy Davis	.25	.13	.08
8 Frank Robinson	1.50	.70	.45
9 Vada Pinson (Nolan Ryan in background of photo.)	1.00	.50	.30
10 Nolan Ryan	4.00	2.00	1.25

11	Reggie Jackson	3.00	1.50	.90
12	Vida Blue	.25	.13	.08
13	Sal Bando	.25	.13	.08
14	Bert Campaneris	.25	.13	.08
15	Tom Seaver	2.00	1.00	.60
16	Bud Harrelson	.25	.13	.08
17	Jerry Koosman	.25	.13	.08
18	Dave Nelson	.25	.13	.08
19	Ted Williams	3.50	1.75	1.00
20	Tony Oliva	.35	.20	.11
21	Mickey Lolich	.25	.13	.08
22	Amos Otis	.25	.13	.08
23	Carl Yastrzemski	2.00	1.00	.60
24	Mike Cuellar	.25	.13	.08
25	Doc Medich	.25	.13	.08
26	Cesar Cedeno	.25	.13	.08
27	Jeff Burroughs	.25	.13	.08
28	Ted Williams, Sparky Lyle	.75	.40	.25
29	Johnny Bench	2.00	1.00	.60
30	Gaylord Perry	1.00	.50	.30
31	John Mayberry	.25	.13	.08
32	Rod Carew	1.00	.50	.30
33	Whitey Ford	2.00	1.00	.60
34	Al Kaline	2.00	1.00	.60
35	Willie Mays	3.50	1.75	1.00
36	Warren Spahn	1.00	.50	.30
37	Mickey Mantle	5.00	2.50	1.50
38	Norm Cash	.35	.20	.11
39	Steve Busby	.25	.13	.08
40	Yogi Berra	2.00	1.00	.60
41	Harvey Kuenn	.25	.13	.08
42	Felipe Alou, Jesus Alou, Matty Alou	.60	.30	.20

1976 SSPC 1887 World Series

The history of the 1887 "World Series" between the Detroit Wolverines of the National League and the St. Louis Browns of the American Association is told on the backs of this collector's issue. The 2-1/2" x 3-1/2" cards were printed on a pair of uncut sheets inserted in the Fall 1976 issue of "Collectors Quarterly" magazine. Fronts of the cards reproduce in full color the Scrapps tobacco die-cut cards originally issued in 1888. Backs recount the individual players' performances in the series as well as giving a career summary; they are printed in red and black. Detroit won the Series, a best-of-15 contest.

	NM	E	VG
Complete Magazine:	15.00	7.50	4.50
Complete Set, Singles:	12.00	6.00	3.50
Common Player:	.75	.40	.25
1 Bob Caruthers	.75	.40	.25
2 David Foutz	.75	.40	.25
3 W.A. Latham	.75	.40	.25
4 Charles H. Getzin (Getzien)	.75	.40	.25
5 J.C. Rowe	.75	.40	.25
6 Fred Dunlap	.75	.40	.25
7 James O'Neill	.75	.40	.25
8 Curtis Welch	.75	.40	.25
9 William Gleason	.75	.40	.25
10 Sam Thompson	.75	.40	.25
11 Ned Hanlon	.75	.40	.25
12 Dan Brothers (Brouthers)	.75	.40	.25
13 Albert Bushong	.75	.40	.25
14 Charles Comiskey	.75	.40	.25
15 Wm. Robinson	.75	.40	.25
16 Charles Bennett	.75	.40	.25
17 Hardy Richardson	.75	.40	.25
18 Deacon White	.75	.40	.25

1976 SSPC 1963 New York Mets

Issued in the Summer 1976 issue of "Collectors Quarterly" magazine as a two-page uncut sheet, this 18-card issue features the 1963 Mets. Like contemporary collectors' issues from SSPC, the cards feature white-bordered color photos on front with no other graphics or player identification. Backs are printed in black-and-white, contain player biographical data, a career summary and uniform number, by which the checklist is arranged. Size is standard 2-1/2" x 3-1/2".

 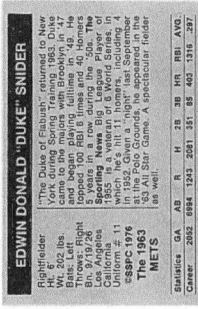

	NM	E	VG
Complete Magazine:	25.00	12.50	7.50
Complete Set, Singles (18):	15.00	7.50	4.50
Common Player:	1.00	.50	.30
1 Duke Carmel	1.00	.50	.30
5 Norman Burt Sherry	1.00	.50	.30
7 Casey Stengel	5.00	2.50	1.50
9 Jim Hickman	1.00	.50	.30
10 Rod Kanehl	1.00	.50	.30
11 Duke Snider	7.50	3.75	2.25
12 Jesse Gonder	1.00	.50	.30
16 Dick Smith	1.00	.50	.30
17 Clarence Coleman	1.00	.50	.30
18 Pumpsie Green	1.00	.50	.30
23 Joe Christopher	1.00	.50	.30
36 Tracy Stallard	1.00	.50	.30
39 Steve Dillon	1.00	.50	.30
40 Rich Moran	1.00	.50	.30
41 Grover Powell	1.00	.50	.30
43 Ted Schreiber	1.00	.50	.30
53 Ernest White	1.00	.50	.30
56 Ed Bauta	1.00	.50	.30

1976 SSPC Yankees Old Timers Day

JOE DIMAGGIO

The Spring 1976 edition of "Collectors Quarterly" magazine contained a nine-card sheet of players who had appeared at an old timers' games in Yankees Stadium. The sheet could be cut into individual 2-1/2" x 3-1/2" cards with a color player photo and name on front. Backs form a black-and-white puzzle picture of Joe DiMaggio, Mickey Mantle, Whitey Ford, and Billy Martin. Cards are checklisted here alphabetically.

	NM	E	VG
Complete Magazine:	25.00	12.50	7.50
Complete Set, Singles:	15.00	7.50	4.50
Common Player:	.35	.20	.11
(1) Earl Averill	.35	.20	.11
(2) Joe DiMaggio	6.00	3.00	1.75
(3) Tommy Henrich	.35	.20	.11
(4) Billy Herman	.35	.20	.11
(5) Monte Irvin	.35	.20	.11
(6) Jim Konstanty	.35	.20	.11
(7) Mickey Mantle	7.50	3.75	2.25
(8) Pee Wee Reese	3.00	1.50	.90
(9) Bobby Thompson (Thomson)	.50	.25	.15

1978 SSPC All Star Gallery

A series of team "Photo Fact Cards" was produced by Sports Stars Publishing Co., for insertion in its 48-page "All Star Gallery" magazine, sold for $2. Fully licensed by MLB and the Players Union, the 27 cards in each team set are printed on a triple-fold 24" x 10-7/8" cardboard sheet stapled into the center of the magazine. Cards are not perforated, though the back of each nine-card panel has dotted lines to guide the cutting of 2-1/2" x 3-1/2" single cards from the sheet. Fronts are full-color poses with no extraneous graphics. Backs are in black-and-white with a few vital data, a career summary, uniform number and a card number from within the overall issue of 270. Only eight teams are represented in the All-Star Gallery magazine series. The Yankees

(#001-027) and Phillies cards (#028-054) issued with other magazines that year may be considered part of the All-Star Gallery issue.

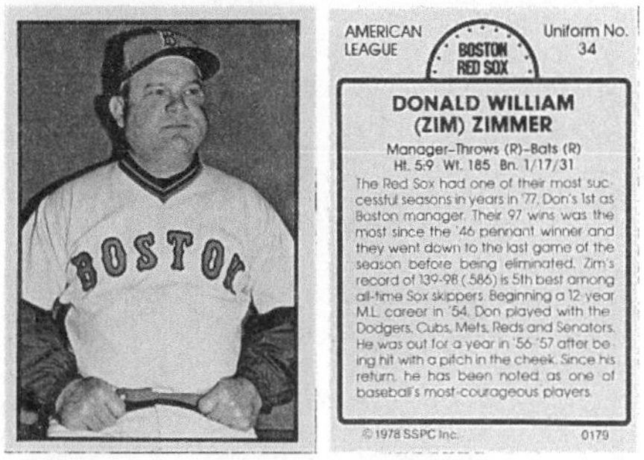
AMERICAN LEAGUE
BOSTON RED SOX
Uniform No. 34
DONALD WILLIAM (ZIM) ZIMMER
Manager-Throws (R)-Bats (R)
Ht. 5-9 Wt. 185 Bn. 1/17/31
The Red Sox had one of their most successful seasons in years in '77, Don's 1st as Boston manager. Their 97 wins was the most since the '46 pennant winner and they went down to the last game of the season before being eliminated. Zim's record of 139-98 (.586) is 5th best among all-time Sox skippers. Beginning a 12-year M.L. career in '54, Don played with the Dodgers, Cubs, Mets, Reds and Senators. He was out for a year in '56-'57 after being hit with a pitch in the cheek. Since his return, he has been noted as one of baseball's most-courageous players.
©1978 SSPC Inc.
0179

	NM	E	VG
Complete Set, Magazines (8):	135.00	65.00	40.00
Complete Set, Singles (216):	125.00	60.00	35.00
Common Player:	.50	.25	.15

		NM	E	VG
	Los Angeles Dodgers			
	Magazine:	15.00	7.50	4.50
0055	Burt Hooton	.50	.25	.15
0056	Bill Russell	.50	.25	.15
0057	Dusty Baker	.60	.30	.20
0058	Reggie Smith	.50	.25	.15
0059	Dick Rhoden	.50	.25	.15
0060	Jerry Grote	.50	.25	.15
0061	Bill Butler	.50	.25	.15
0062	Ron Cey	.50	.25	.15
0063	Ron Cey	.50	.25	.15
0064	Ted Martinez	.50	.25	.15
0065	Ed Goodson	.50	.25	.15
0066	Vic Davalillo	.50	.25	.15
0067	Davey Lopes	.50	.25	.15
0068	Terry Forster	.50	.25	.15
0069	Lee Lacy	.50	.25	.15
0070	Mike Garman	.50	.25	.15
0071	Steve Garvey	1.50	.70	.45
0072	Johnny Oates	.50	.25	.15
0073	Steve Yaeger	.50	.25	.15
0074	Rafael Landestoy	.50	.25	.15
0075	Tommy John	.60	.30	.20
0076	Glenn Burke	.50	.25	.15
0077	Rick Monday	.50	.25	.15
0078	Doug Rau	.50	.25	.15
0079	Manny Mota	.50	.25	.15
0080	Don Sutton	2.00	1.00	.60
0081	Charlie Hough	.50	.25	.15
	Texas Rangers			
	Magazine:	12.50	6.25	3.75
0082	Mike Hargrove	.50	.25	.15
0083	Jim Sundberg	.50	.25	.15
0084	Fergie Jenkins	2.00	1.00	.60
0085	Paul Lindblad	.50	.25	.15
0086	Sandy Alomar	.50	.25	.15
0087	John Lowenstein	.50	.25	.15
0088	Claudell Washington	.50	.25	.15
0089	Toby Harrah	.50	.25	.15
0090	Jim Umbarger	.50	.25	.15
0091	Len Barker	.50	.25	.15
0092	Dave May	.50	.25	.15
0093	Kurt Bevacqua	.50	.25	.15
0094	Jim Mason	.50	.25	.15
0095	Bump Wills	.50	.25	.15
0096	Dock Ellis	.50	.25	.15
0097	Bill Fahey	.50	.25	.15
0098	Richie Zisk	.50	.25	.15
0099	Jon Matlack	.50	.25	.15
0100	John Ellis	.50	.25	.15
0101	Bert Campaneris	.50	.25	.15
0102	Doc Medich	.50	.25	.15
0103	Juan Beniquez	.50	.25	.15
0104	Bill Hunter	.50	.25	.15
0105	Doyle Alexander	.50	.25	.15
0106	Roger Moret	.50	.25	.15
0107	Mike Jorgensen	.50	.25	.15
0108	Al Oliver	.60	.30	.20
	Cincinnati Reds			
	Magazine:	15.00	7.50	4.50
0109	Fred Norman	.50	.25	.15
0110	Ray Knight	.50	.25	.15
0111	Pedro Borbon	.50	.25	.15
0112	Bill Bonham	.50	.25	.15
0113	George Foster	.60	.30	.20
0114	Doug Bair	.50	.25	.15
0115	Cesar Geronimo	.50	.25	.15
0116	Tom Seaver	3.50	1.75	1.00
0117	Mario Soto	.50	.25	.15
0118	Ken Griffey	.50	.25	.15
0119	Mike Lum	.50	.25	.15
0120	Tom Hume	.50	.25	.15
0121	Joe Morgan	2.50	1.25	.70
0122	Manny Sarmiento	.50	.25	.15
0123	Dan Driessen	.50	.25	.15
0124	Ed Armbrister	.50	.25	.15
0125	John Summers	.50	.25	.15
0126	Fred Auerbach	.50	.25	.15
0127	Doug Capilla	.50	.25	.15
0128	Johnny Bench	3.50	1.75	1.00
0129	Sparky Anderson	1.50	.70	.45
0130	Raul Ferreyra	.50	.25	.15
0131	Dale Murray	.50	.25	.15
0132	Pete Rose	7.50	3.75	2.25
0133	Dave Concepcion	.50	.25	.15
0134	Junior Kennedy	.50	.25	.15
0135	Dave Collins	.50	.25	.15
	Chicago White Sox			
	Magazine:	12.50	6.25	3.75
0136	Mike Eden	.50	.25	.15
0137	Lamar Johnson	.50	.25	.15
0138	Ron Schueler	.50	.25	.15
0139	Bob Lemon	.75	.40	.25
0140	Thad Bosley	.50	.25	.15
0141	Bobby Bonds	.60	.30	.20
0142	Wilbur Wood	.50	.25	.15
0143	Jorge Orta	.50	.25	.15
0144	Francisco Barrios	.50	.25	.15
0145	Greg Pryor	.50	.25	.15
0146	Chet Lemon	.50	.25	.15
0147	Mike Squires	.50	.25	.15
0148	Eric Soderholm	.50	.25	.15
0149	Reggie Sanders	.50	.25	.15
0150	Kevin Bell	.50	.25	.15
0151	Alan Bannister	.50	.25	.15
0152	Henry Cruz	.50	.25	.15
0153	Larry Doby	2.00	1.00	.60
0154	Don Kessinger	.50	.25	.15
0155	Ralph Garr	.50	.25	.15
0156	Bill Nahorodny	.50	.25	.15
0157	Ron Blomberg	.50	.25	.15
0158	Bob Molinaro	.50	.25	.15
0159	Junior Moore	.50	.25	.15
0160	Minnie Minoso	1.50	.70	.45
0161	Lerrin LaGrow	.50	.25	.15
0162	Wayne Nordhagen	.50	.25	.15
	Boston Red Sox			
	Magazine:	20.00	10.00	6.00
0163	Ramon Aviles	.50	.25	.15
0164	Bob Stanley	.50	.25	.15
0165	Reggie Cleveland	.50	.25	.15
0166	John Brohamer	.50	.25	.15
0167	Bill Lee	.50	.25	.15
0168	Jim Burton	.50	.25	.15
0169	Bill Campbell	.50	.25	.15
0170	Mike Torrez	.50	.25	.15
0171	Dick Drago	.50	.25	.15
0172	Butch Hobson	.50	.25	.15
0173	Bob Bailey	.50	.25	.15
0174	Fred Lynn	.50	.25	.15
0175	Rick Burleson	.50	.25	.15
0176	Luis Tiant	.50	.25	.15
0177	Ted Williams	6.00	3.00	1.75
0178	Dennis Eckersley	2.00	1.00	.60
0179	Don Zimmer	.50	.25	.15
0180	Carlton Fisk	2.50	1.25	.70
0181	Dwight Evans	.50	.25	.15
0182	Fred Kendall	.50	.25	.15
0183	George Scott	.50	.25	.15
0184	Frank Duffy	.50	.25	.15
0185	Bernie Carbo	.50	.25	.15
0186	Jerry Remy	.50	.25	.15
0187	Carl Yastrzemski	4.00	2.00	1.25
0188	Allen Ripley	.50	.25	.15
0189	Jim Rice	2.50	1.25	.75
	California Angels			
	Magazine:	20.00	10.00	6.00
0190	Ken Landreaux	.50	.25	.15
0191	Paul Hartzell	.50	.25	.15
0192	Ken Brett	.50	.25	.15
0193	Dave Garcia	.50	.25	.15
0194	Bobby Grich	.50	.25	.15
0195	Lyman Bostock	.50	.25	.15
0196	Isaac Hampton	.50	.25	.15
0197	Dave LaRoche	.50	.25	.15
0198	Dave Chalk	.50	.25	.15
0199	Rick Miller	.50	.25	.15
0200	Floyd Rayford	.50	.25	.15
0201	Willie Aikens	.50	.25	.15
0202	Balor Moore	.50	.25	.15
0203	Nolan Ryan	10.00	5.00	3.00
0204	Dan Goodwin	.50	.25	.15
0205	Ron Fairly	.50	.25	.15
0206	Dyar Miller	.50	.25	.15
0207	Carney Lansford	.50	.25	.15
0208	Don Baylor	.60	.30	.20
0209	Gil Flores	.50	.25	.15
0210	Terry Humphrey	.50	.25	.15
0211	Frank Tanana	.50	.25	.15
0212	Chris Knapp	.50	.25	.15
0213	Ron Jackson	.50	.25	.15
0214	Joe Rudi	.50	.25	.15
0215	Tony Solaita	.50	.25	.15
0216	Steve Mulliniks	.50	.25	.15
	Kansas City Royals			
	Magazine:	20.00	10.00	6.00
0217	George Brett	6.00	3.00	1.75
0218	Doug Bird	.50	.25	.15
0219	Hal McRae	.50	.25	.15
0220	Dennis Leonard	.50	.25	.15
0221	Darrell Porter	.50	.25	.15
0222	Randy McGilberry	.50	.25	.15
0223	Pete LaCock	.50	.25	.15
0224	Whitey Herzog	.50	.25	.15
0225	Andy Hassler	.50	.25	.15
0226	Joe Lahoud	.50	.25	.15
0227	Amos Otis	.50	.25	.15
0228	Al Hrabosky	.50	.25	.15
0229	Clint Hurdle	.50	.25	.15
0230	Paul Splittorff	.50	.25	.15
0231	Marty Pattin	.50	.25	.15
0232	Frank White	.50	.25	.15
0233	John Wathan	.50	.25	.15
0234	Freddie Patek	.50	.25	.15
0235	Rich Gale	.50	.25	.15
0236	U.L. Washington	.50	.25	.15
0237	Larry Gura	.50	.25	.15
0238	Jim Colburn	.50	.25	.15
0239	Tom Poquette	.50	.25	.15
0240	Al Cowens	.50	.25	.15
0241	Willie Wilson	.50	.25	.15
0242	Steve Mingori	.50	.25	.15
0243	Jerry Terrell	.50	.25	.15
	Chicago Cubs			
	Magazine:	12.50	6.25	3.75
0244	Larry Biitner	.50	.25	.15
0245	Rick Reuschel	.50	.25	.15
0246	Dave Rader	.50	.25	.15
0247	Paul Reuschel	.50	.25	.15
0248	Hector Cruz	.50	.25	.15
0249	Woody Fryman	.50	.25	.15
0250	Steve Ontiveros	.50	.25	.15
0251	Mike Gordon	.50	.25	.15
0252	Dave Kingman	.50	.25	.15
0253	Gene Clines	.50	.25	.15
0254	Bruce Sutter	2.00	1.00	.60
0255	Guillermo Hernandez	.50	.25	.15
0256	Ivan DeJesus	.50	.25	.15
0257	Greg Gross	.50	.25	.15
0258	Larry Cox	.50	.25	.15
0259	Joe Wallis	.50	.25	.15
0260	Dennis Lamp	.50	.25	.15
0261	Ray Burris	.50	.25	.15
0262	Bill Caudill	.50	.25	.15
0263	Donnie Moore	.50	.25	.15
0264	Bill Buckner	.60	.30	.20
0265	Bobby Murcer	.60	.30	.20
0266	Dave Roberts	.50	.25	.15
0267	Mike Krukow	.50	.25	.15
0268	Herman Franks	.50	.25	.15
0269	Mike Kelleher	.50	.25	.15
0270	Rudy Meoli	.50	.25	.15

1978 SSPC Baseball the Phillies Way

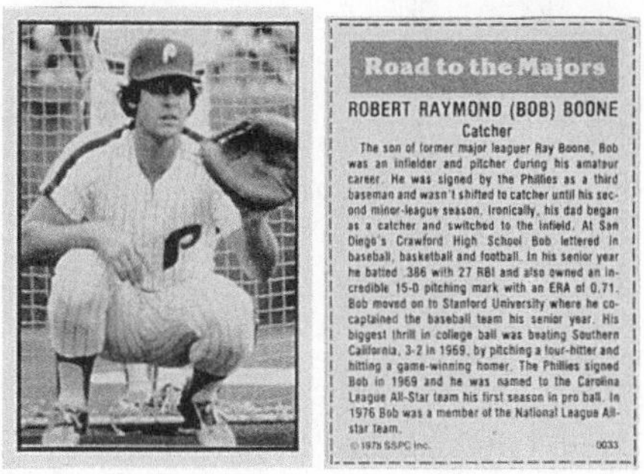
Road to the Majors
ROBERT RAYMOND (BOB) BOONE
Catcher
The son of former major leaguer Ray Boone, Bob was an infielder and pitcher during his amateur career. He was signed by the Phillies as a third baseman and wasn't shifted to catcher until his second minor-league season. Ironically, his dad began as a catcher and switched to the infield. At San Diego's Crawford High School Bob lettered in baseball, basketball and football. In his senior year he batted .386 with 27 RBI and also owned an incredible 15-0 pitching mark with an ERA of 0.71. Bob moved on to Stanford University where he co-captained the baseball team his senior year. His biggest thrill in college ball was beating Southern California, 3-2 in 1969, by pitching a four-hitter and hitting a game-winning homer. The Phillies signed Bob in 1969 and he was named to the Carolina League All-Star team his first season in pro ball. In 1976 Bob was a member of the National League All-Star team.
©1978 SSPC Inc.
0033

This team set was produced on a tri-fold insert in an SSPC magazine titled, "Baseball the Phillies Way." The magazine offered playing tips. Cards are in the contemporary SSPC format of a posed front photo with a white border and no other graphics. Backs are printed in red, white and black with player ID, career data and card numbers between 0028-0054, continuing the sequence begun with the Yankees yearbook team set which continues with the All-Star Gallery set. Cards could be cut from the sheets into 2-1/2" x 3-1/2" singles.

	NM	E	VG
Complete Magazine:	15.00	7.50	4.50
Complete Set, Singles (27):	12.00	6.00	3.50
Common Player:	.50	.25	.15

		NM	E	VG
0028	Garry Maddox	.50	.25	.15
0029	Steve Carlton	2.50	1.25	.70
0030	Ron Reed	.50	.25	.15

0031	Greg Luzinski	.50	.25	.15
0032	Bobby Wine	.50	.25	.15
0033	Bob Boone	1.50	.70	.45
0034	Carroll Beringer	.50	.25	.15
0035	Dick Hebner	.50	.25	.15
0036	Ray Ripplemeyer	.50	.25	.15
0037	Terry Harmon	.50	.25	.15
0038	Gene Garber	.50	.25	.15
0039	Ted Sizemore	.50	.25	.15
0040	Barry Foote	.50	.25	.15
0041	Tony Taylor	.50	.25	.15
0042	Tug McGraw	.75	.40	.25
0043	Jay Johnstone	.65	.35	.20
0044	Randy Lerch	.50	.25	.15
0045	Billy DeMars	.50	.25	.15
0046	Mike Schmidt	5.00	2.50	1.50
0047	Larry Christenson	.50	.25	.15
0048	Tim McCarver	1.00	.50	.30
0049	Larry Bowa	.65	.35	.20
0050	Danny Ozark	.50	.25	.15
0051	Jerry Martin	.50	.25	.15
0052	Jim Lonborg	.50	.25	.15
0053	Bake McBride	.50	.25	.15
0054	Warren Brusstar	.50	.25	.15

1978 SSPC Yankees Yearbook

This team set was printed on a tri-fold insert found both in the 1978 Yankees yearbook and a magazine titled "Diary of a Champion Yankee," produced by SSPC. The nine cards on each sheet could be cut apart into 2-1/2" x 3-1/2" singles. Cards follow the basic SSPC format of a posed color photo on front with a white border and no graphic elements. Backs have player identification, career summary and "CHAMPIONSHIP SEASON" highlights, printed in black and blue on white. Cards are numbered from 0001-0027, and may be considered part of the larger All-Star Gallery issue.

		NM	E	VG
Complete Magazine:		12.50	6.25	3.75
Complete Set, Singles (27):		10.00	5.00	3.00
Common Player:		.50	.25	.15
0001	Thurman Munson	3.00	1.50	.90
0002	Cliff Johnson	.50	.25	.15
0003	Lou Piniella	.75	.40	.25
0004	Dell Alston	.50	.25	.15
0005	Yankee Stadium	1.00	.50	.30
0006	Ken Holtzman	.50	.25	.15
0007	Chris Chambliss	.50	.25	.15
0008	Roy White	.60	.30	.20
0009	Ed Figueroa	.50	.25	.15
0010	Dick Tidrow	.50	.25	.15
0011	Sparky Lyle	.60	.30	.20
0012	Fred Stanley	.50	.25	.15
0013	Mickey Rivers	.50	.25	.15
0014	Billy Martin	.75	.40	.25
0015	George Zeber	.50	.25	.15
0016	Ken Clay	.50	.25	.15
0017	Ron Guidry	.75	.40	.25
0018	Don Gullett	.50	.25	.15
0019	Fran Healy	.50	.25	.15
0020	Paul Blair	.50	.25	.15
0021	Mickey Klutts	.50	.25	.15
0022	Yankee team	.50	.25	.15
0023	Catfish Hunter	1.50	.70	.45
0024	Bucky Dent	.75	.40	.25
0025	Graig Nettles	.75	.40	.25
0026	Reggie Jackson	3.00	1.50	.90
0027	Willie Randolph	.60	.30	.20

1889 "The Stage" Stars of the Diamond

Titled "Stars of the Diamond" and issued weekly between May 25-Aug. 31, 1889, these numbered supplements were printed in "The Stage" newspaper, a Philadelphia-based publication. Two types of supplements are found, those picturing New York players in uniforms (from Joseph Hall photos), and those picturing members of the Philadelphia National League and American Association teams in street clothes. The black-and-white portraits are printed in a 9" x

12" format on newsprint, making surviving examples very rare today.

		NM	E	VG
Common Player:		250.00	125.00	75.00
1	Charles Buffington	250.00	125.00	75.00
2	John Clements	250.00	125.00	75.00
3	Harry D. Stovey	250.00	125.00	75.00
4	"Gus" Weyhing	250.00	125.00	75.00
5	L.M. Cross	250.00	125.00	75.00
6	Edward Seward	250.00	125.00	75.00
7	Wm. Robinson (Wilbert)	375.00	185.00	110.00
8	Denny Lyons	375.00	185.00	110.00
9	A.B. Sanders	250.00	125.00	75.00
10	William Schriver	250.00	125.00	75.00
11	Daniel M. Casey	250.00	125.00	75.00
12	"Tim" Keefe	375.00	185.00	110.00
13	"Buck" Ewing	375.00	185.00	110.00
14	John Ward	375.00	185.00	110.00

1953 Stahl-Meyer Franks

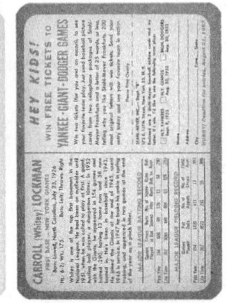

These nine cards, issued in packages of hot dogs by a New York area meat company, feature three players from each of the New York teams of the day - Dodgers Giants and Yankees. Cards in the set measure 3-1/4" x 4-1/2". The card fronts in this unnumbered set feature color photos with player name and facsimile autograph. The backs list both biographical and statistical information on half the card and a ticket offer promotion on the other half. The card corners are cut diagonally, although some cards (apparently cut from sheets) with square corners have been seen. Cards are white-bordered.

		NM	E	VG
Complete Set (9):		20,000	9,000	4,000
Common Player:		500.00	225.00	100.00
(1)	Hank Bauer	550.00	245.00	110.00
(2)	Roy Campanella	2,000	900.00	400.00
(3)	Gil Hodges	1,250	560.00	250.00
(4)	Monte Irvin	750.00	335.00	150.00
(5)	Whitey Lockman	500.00	225.00	100.00
(6)	Mickey Mantle	15,000	6,100	2,750
(7)	Phil Rizzuto	1,250	560.00	250.00
(8)	Duke Snider	2,000	900.00	400.00
(9)	Bobby Thomson	650.00	290.00	130.00

1954 Stahl-Meyer Franks

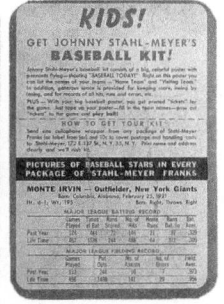

The 1954 set of Stahl-Meyer Franks was increased to 12 cards which retained the 3-1/4" x 4-1/2" size. The most prominent addition to the '54 set was New York Giants slugger Willie Mays. The card fronts are identical in format to the previous year's set. However, the backs are different as they are designed on a vertical format. The backs also contain an advertisement for a "Johnny Stahl-Meyer Baseball Kit." The cards in the set are unnumbered.

		NM	E	VG
Complete Set (12):		30,000	13,500	6,000
Common Player:		650.00	290.00	130.00
(1)	Hank Bauer	750.00	335.00	150.00
(2)	Carl Erskine	750.00	335.00	150.00
(3)	Gil Hodges	2,000	900.00	400.00
(4)	Monte Irvin	1,000	450.00	200.00
(5)	Whitey Lockman	650.00	290.00	130.00
(6)	Gil McDougald	750.00	335.00	150.00
(7)	Mickey Mantle	17,500	5,750	2,500
(8)	Willie Mays	9,000	3,050	1,825
(9)	Don Mueller	650.00	290.00	130.00
(10)	Don Newcombe	750.00	335.00	150.00
(11)	Phil Rizzuto	2,000	900.00	400.00
(12)	Duke Snider	2,000	900.00	400.00

1955 Stahl-Meyer Franks

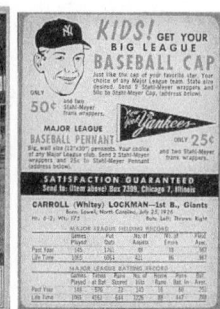

Eleven of the 12 players in the 1955 set are the same as those featured in 1954. The exception is the New York Giants Dusty Rhodes, who replaced Willie Mays on the 3-1/4" x 4-1/2" cards. The card fronts are again full-color photos bordered in yellow with diagonal corners, and four players from each of the three New York teams are featured. The backs offer a new promotion, with a drawing of Mickey Mantle and advertisements selling pennants and caps. Player statistics are still included on the vertical card backs. The cards in the set are unnumbered.

		NM	E	VG
Complete Set (12):		30,000	13,500	6,000
Common Player:		650.00	290.00	130.00
(1)	Hank Bauer	750.00	335.00	150.00
(2)	Carl Erskine	750.00	335.00	150.00
(3)	Gil Hodges	2,000	900.00	400.00
(4)	Monte Irvin	1,000	450.00	200.00
(5)	Whitey Lockman	650.00	290.00	130.00
(6)	Mickey Mantle	13,000	5,500	2,400
(7)	Gil McDougald	750.00	335.00	150.00
(8)	Don Mueller	650.00	290.00	130.00
(9)	Don Newcombe	750.00	335.00	150.00
(10)	Jim Rhodes	500.00	225.00	100.00
(11)	Phil Rizzuto	2,000	900.00	400.00
(12)	Duke Snider	2,000	900.00	400.00

1916 Standard Biscuit (D350-1)

The range of cards in this issue is uncertain as examples can be found corresponding to the checklists of both of the 1916 sets known as M101-5 and M101-4 Blank Backs. Standard Biscuit cards in this format are also known that correspond to neither M101-5 nor M101-4. The approximately 1-5/8" x 3" black-and-white cards usually command a modest premium from collectors seeking to enhance a type collection or superstar collection. A trial checklist is begun herewith. Since D350-1 can be found corresponding to both M101-4 and M101-5, they have two different numerical checklists and should be split into D350-1a & D350-1b.

		NM	E	VG
Common Player:		90.00	45.00	30.00
1	Babe Adams	90.00	45.00	30.00
3	Ed Ainsmith	90.00	45.00	30.00

6	Jimmy Archer	90.00	45.00	30.00
12a	Beals Becker	90.00	45.00	30.00
12b	Zinn Beck (May be unique) (Value undetermined)			
13	Joe Benz	90.00	45.00	30.00
14	Bob Bescher	90.00	45.00	30.00
15	Al Betzel	90.00	45.00	30.00
18	Eddie Burns	90.00	45.00	30.00
25	Forest Cady	90.00	45.00	30.00
27	George Chalmers	90.00	45.00	30.00
35	Charles Comiskey	400.00	200.00	130.00
37	Joe Connolly	90.00	45.00	30.00
39	Harry Coveleskie (Coveleski)	90.00	45.00	30.00
42	Sam Crawford	400.00	200.00	130.00
48	William Doak	90.00	45.00	30.00
50	Charles Dooin	90.00	45.00	30.00
54	Johnny Evers	500.00	250.00	150.00
56	Urban Faber	400.00	200.00	120.00
60	Max Flack	90.00	45.00	30.00
61	Art Fletcher	90.00	45.00	30.00
63	Jacques Fournier	90.00	45.00	30.00
64	"Chic" Gandil	900.00	450.00	300.00
66	Joe Gedeon	90.00	45.00	30.00
68	George Gibson	90.00	45.00	30.00
69	Wilbur Good	90.00	45.00	30.00
71	John Graney	90.00	45.00	30.00
72	Tom Griffith	90.00	45.00	30.00
73	Heinie Groh	90.00	45.00	30.00
75	Bob Harmon	90.00	45.00	30.00
77	Claude Hendrix	90.00	45.00	30.00
79	John Henry	90.00	45.00	30.00
80	Buck Herzog	90.00	45.00	30.00
82	Dick Hoblitzell	90.00	45.00	30.00
84	Ivan Howard	90.00	45.00	30.00
86	Joe Jackson	15,000	7,500	4,500
87	Joe Jackson	15,000	7,500	4,500
89	Hugh Jennings	400.00	200.00	130.00
116	John McGraw	750.00	375.00	225.00
131	Les Nunamaker	90.00	45.00	30.00
137	E.J. Pfeffer	90.00	45.00	30.00
151	Babe Ruth	30,000	15,000	9,000
164	Ernie Shore	90.00	45.00	30.00
170	Milton Stock	90.00	45.00	30.00
172a	Milton Stock	90.00	45.00	30.00
172b	Billy Sullivan	90.00	45.00	30.00
176	Jim Thorpe	26,250	13,125	7,875
184	Honus Wagner	2,700	1,350	510.00
186	Bobby Wallace	600.00	300.00	200.00
191	Fred Williams	90.00	45.00	30.00
195	Joe Wood	600.00	300.00	180.00
196	Joe Wood	600.00	300.00	180.00
199	Heiny Zimmerman	90.00	45.00	30.00

1917 Standard Biscuit (D350-2)

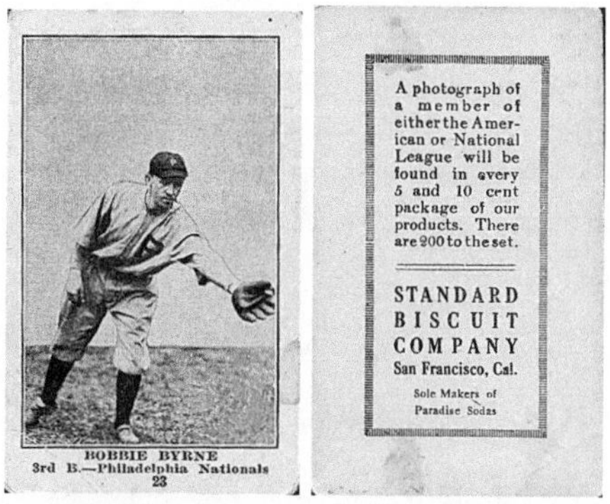
BOBBIE BYRNE
3rd B.—Philadelphia Nationals
23
A photograph of a member of either the American or National League will be found in every 5 and 10 cent package of our products. There are 200 to the set.
STANDARD BISCUIT COMPANY
San Francisco, Cal.
Sole Makers of Paradise Sodas

The 200 cards in this set are more commonly found with the advertising of Collins-McCarthy Candy Co. on the back. The cards measure about 2" x 3-1/4" and are printed in black-and-white. Though the Standard Biscuit cards are scarcer than the Collins-McCarthy version, collectors do not attach much premium to them.

		NM	E	VG
Complete Set (200):		70,000	35,000	21,000
Common Player:		150.00	75.00	45.00
1	Sam Agnew	150.00	75.00	45.00
2	Grover Alexander	1,000	700.00	300.00
3	W.S. Alexander (W.E.)	150.00	75.00	45.00
4	Leon Ames	150.00	75.00	45.00
5	Fred Anderson	150.00	75.00	45.00
6	Ed Appleton	150.00	75.00	45.00
7	Jimmy Archer	150.00	75.00	45.00
8	Jimmy Austin	150.00	75.00	45.00
9	Jim Bagby Sr.	150.00	75.00	45.00
10	H.D. Baird	150.00	75.00	45.00
11	J. Franklin Baker	1,000	700.00	300.00
12	Dave Bancroft	1,000	700.00	300.00
13	Jack Barry	150.00	75.00	45.00
14	Joe Benz	150.00	75.00	45.00
15	Al Betzel	150.00	75.00	45.00
16	Ping Bodie	150.00	75.00	45.00
17	Joe Boehling	150.00	75.00	45.00
18	Eddie Burns	150.00	75.00	45.00
19	George Burns	150.00	75.00	45.00
20	Geo. J. Burns	150.00	75.00	45.00
21	Joe Bush	150.00	75.00	45.00
22	Owen Bush	150.00	75.00	45.00
23	Bobby Byrne	150.00	75.00	45.00
24	Forrest Cady	150.00	75.00	45.00
25	Max Carey	1,000	700.00	300.00
26	Ray Chapman	200.00	100.00	60.00
27	Larry Cheney	150.00	75.00	45.00
28	Eddie Cicotte	1,000	700.00	300.00
29	Tom Clarke	150.00	75.00	45.00
30	Ty Cobb	5,000	3,000	2,000
31	Eddie Collins	1,000	700.00	300.00
32	"Shauno" Collins (Shano)	150.00	75.00	45.00
33	Fred Coumbe	150.00	75.00	45.00
34	Harry Coveleskie (Coveleski)	150.00	75.00	45.00
35	Gavvy Cravath	150.00	75.00	45.00
36	Sam Crawford	1,000	700.00	300.00
37	Geo. Cutshaw	150.00	75.00	45.00
38	Jake Daubert	150.00	75.00	45.00
39	Geo. Dauss	150.00	75.00	45.00
40	Charles Deal	150.00	75.00	45.00
41	"Wheezer" Dell	150.00	75.00	45.00
42	William Doak	150.00	75.00	45.00
43	Bill Donovan	150.00	75.00	45.00
44	Larry Doyle	150.00	75.00	45.00
45	Johnny Evers	1,000	700.00	300.00
46	Urban Faber	1,000	700.00	300.00
47	"Hap" Felsch	1,000	700.00	300.00
48	Bill Fischer	150.00	75.00	45.00
49	Ray Fisher	150.00	75.00	45.00
50	Art Fletcher	150.00	75.00	45.00
51	Eddie Foster	150.00	75.00	45.00
52	Jacques Fournier	150.00	75.00	45.00
53	Del Gainer (Gainor)	150.00	75.00	45.00
54	Bert Gallia	150.00	75.00	45.00
55	"Chic" Gandil (Chick)	1,000	700.00	300.00
56	Larry Gardner	150.00	75.00	45.00
57	Joe Gedeon	150.00	75.00	45.00
58	Gus Getz	150.00	75.00	45.00
59	Frank Gilhooley	150.00	75.00	45.00
60	Wm. Gleason	150.00	75.00	45.00
61	M.A. Gonzales (Gonzalez)	165.00	80.00	50.00
62	Hank Gowdy	150.00	75.00	45.00
63	John Graney	150.00	75.00	45.00
64	Tom Griffith	150.00	75.00	45.00
65	Heinie Groh	150.00	75.00	45.00
66	Bob Groom	150.00	75.00	45.00
67	Louis Guisto	150.00	75.00	45.00
68	Earl Hamilton	150.00	75.00	45.00
69	Harry Harper	150.00	75.00	45.00
70	Grover Hartley	150.00	75.00	45.00
71	Harry Heilmann	5,000	4,000	2,000
72	Claude Hendrix	150.00	75.00	45.00
73	Olaf Henriksen	150.00	75.00	45.00
74	John Henry	150.00	75.00	45.00
75	"Buck" Herzog	150.00	75.00	45.00
76	Hugh High	150.00	75.00	45.00
77	Dick Hoblitzell	150.00	75.00	45.00
78	Walter Holke	150.00	75.00	45.00
79	Harry Hooper	1,000	700.00	300.00
80	Rogers Hornsby	20,000	12,500	7,000
81	Ivan Howard	150.00	75.00	45.00
82	Joe Jackson	16,500	8,500	5,000
83	Harold Janvrin	150.00	75.00	45.00
84	William James	150.00	75.00	45.00
85	C. Jamieson	150.00	75.00	45.00
86	Hugh Jennings	1,000	700.00	300.00
87	Walter Johnson	3,000	2,000	1,000
88	James Johnston	150.00	75.00	45.00
89	Fielder Jones	150.00	75.00	45.00
90	Joe Judge	150.00	75.00	45.00
91	Hans Lobert	150.00	75.00	45.00
92	Benny Kauff	150.00	75.00	45.00
93	Wm. Killefer Jr.	150.00	75.00	45.00
94	Ed. Konetchy	150.00	75.00	45.00
95	John Lavan	150.00	75.00	45.00
96	Jimmy Lavender	150.00	75.00	45.00
97	"Nemo" Leibold	150.00	75.00	45.00
98	H.B. Leonard	150.00	75.00	45.00
99	Duffy Lewis	150.00	75.00	45.00
100	Tom Long	150.00	75.00	45.00
101	Wm. Louden	150.00	75.00	45.00
102	Fred Luderus	150.00	75.00	45.00
103	Lee Magee	150.00	75.00	45.00
104	Sherwood Magee	150.00	75.00	45.00
105	Al Mamaux	150.00	75.00	45.00
106	Leslie Mann	150.00	75.00	45.00
107	"Rabbit" Maranville	1,000	700.00	300.00
108	Rube Marquard	1,000	700.00	300.00
109	Armando Marsans	165.00	85.00	50.00
110	J. Erskine Mayer	175.00	85.00	50.00
111	George McBride	150.00	75.00	45.00
112	Lew McCarty	150.00	75.00	45.00
113	John J. McGraw	1,000	700.00	300.00
114	Jack McInnis	150.00	75.00	45.00
115	Lee Meadows	150.00	75.00	45.00
116	Fred Merkle	150.00	75.00	45.00
117	"Chief" Meyers	150.00	75.00	45.00
118	Clyde Milan	150.00	75.00	45.00
119	Otto Miller	150.00	75.00	45.00
120	Clarence Mitchell	150.00	75.00	45.00
121	Ray Morgan	150.00	75.00	45.00
122	Guy Morton	150.00	75.00	45.00
123	"Mike" Mowrey	150.00	75.00	45.00
124	Elmer Myers	150.00	75.00	45.00
125	"Hy" Myers	150.00	75.00	45.00
126	A.E. Neale	175.00	85.00	50.00
127	Arthur Nehf	150.00	75.00	45.00
128	J.A. Niehoff	150.00	75.00	45.00
129	Steve O'Neill	150.00	75.00	45.00
130	"Dode" Paskert	150.00	75.00	45.00
131	Roger Peckinpaugh	150.00	75.00	45.00
132	"Pol" Perritt	150.00	75.00	45.00
133	"Jeff" Pfeffer	150.00	75.00	45.00
134	Walter Pipp	150.00	75.00	45.00
135	Derril Pratt (Derrill)	150.00	75.00	45.00
136	Bill Rariden	150.00	75.00	45.00
137	E.C. Rice	350.00	175.00	100.00
138	Wm. A. Ritter (Wm. H.)	150.00	75.00	45.00
139	Eppa Rixey	1,000	700.00	300.00
140	Davey Robertson	150.00	75.00	45.00
141	"Bob" Roth	150.00	75.00	45.00
142	Ed. Roush	1,000	700.00	300.00
143	Clarence Rowland	150.00	75.00	45.00
144	Dick Rudolph	150.00	75.00	45.00
145	William Rumler	150.00	75.00	45.00
146	Reb Russell	150.00	75.00	45.00
147	"Babe" Ruth	12,500	6,250	3,750
148	Vic Saier	150.00	75.00	45.00
149	"Slim" Sallee	150.00	75.00	45.00
150	Ray Schalk	1,000	700.00	300.00
151	Walter Schang	150.00	75.00	45.00
152	Frank Schulte	150.00	75.00	45.00
153	Ferd Schupp	150.00	75.00	45.00
154	Everett Scott	150.00	75.00	45.00
155	Hank Severeid	150.00	75.00	45.00
156	Howard Shanks	150.00	75.00	45.00
157	Bob Shawkey	150.00	75.00	45.00
158	Jas. Sheckard	150.00	75.00	45.00
159	Ernie Shore	150.00	75.00	45.00
160	C.H. Shorten	150.00	75.00	45.00
161	Burt Shotton	150.00	75.00	45.00
162	Geo. Sisler	1,000	700.00	300.00
163	Elmer Smith	150.00	75.00	45.00
164	J. Carlisle Smith	150.00	75.00	45.00
165	Fred Snodgrass	150.00	75.00	45.00
166	Tris Speaker	2,000	1,500	1,000
167	Oscar Stanage	150.00	75.00	45.00
168	Charles Stengel	1,000	700.00	500.00
169	Milton Stock	150.00	75.00	45.00
170	Amos Strunk	150.00	75.00	45.00
171	"Zeb" Terry	150.00	75.00	45.00
172	"Jeff" Tesreau	150.00	75.00	45.00
173	Chester Thomas	150.00	75.00	45.00
174	Fred Toney	150.00	75.00	45.00
175	Terry Turner	150.00	75.00	45.00
176	George Tyler	150.00	75.00	45.00
177	Jim Vaughn	150.00	75.00	45.00
178	Bob Veach	150.00	75.00	45.00
179	Oscar Vitt	150.00	75.00	45.00
180	Hans Wagner	3,500	1,750	1,050
181	Clarence Walker	150.00	75.00	45.00
182	Jim Walsh	150.00	75.00	45.00
183	Al Walters	150.00	75.00	45.00
184	W. Wambsganss	150.00	75.00	45.00
185	Buck Weaver	1,000	500.00	300.00
186	Carl Weilman	150.00	75.00	45.00
187	Zack Wheat	1,000	700.00	300.00
188	Geo. Whitted	150.00	75.00	45.00
189	Joe Wilhoit	150.00	75.00	45.00
190	Claude Williams	750.00	375.00	225.00
191	Fred Williams	150.00	75.00	45.00
192	Art Wilson	150.00	75.00	45.00
193	Lawton Witt	150.00	75.00	45.00
194	Joe Wood	150.00	75.00	45.00
195	William Wortman	150.00	75.00	45.00
196	Steve Yerkes	150.00	75.00	45.00
197	Earl Yingling	150.00	75.00	45.00
198	"Pep" (Ralph) Young	150.00	75.00	45.00
199	Rollie Zeider	150.00	75.00	45.00
200	Henry Zimmerman	150.00	75.00	45.00

1921 Standard Biscuit (D350-3)

It is unknown to what extent this scarcest of the three Standard Biscuit advertising issues actually parallels the E121 Series of 80, on which American Caramel Co. backs are more commonly found. This uncertainty contributes to the relatively low premium value (about 2X) attached to the Standard Biscuit versions. Backs have been seen in two styles; one mentions "80 to the set," the other mentions "contains 80 photographs." Cards are printed in black-and-white in a size of about 2" x 3-1/4". A checklist has been started here in an effort to better understand the issue.

A photograph of a member of either the American or National League will be found in every 5 and 10 cent package of our products. There are 80 to the set.

STANDARD BISCUIT COMPANY
San Francisco, Cal.

Sole Makers of Paradise Sodas

CHESTER THOMAS
C.—Cleveland Americans

PREMIUM: 2-4X

(3)	Jim Bagby
(4a)	J. Franklin Baker
(12)	Max Carey (Hands at hips.)
(14)	Ty Cobb (Throwing, looking front.)
(15b)	Ty Cobb (Throwing, looking right, manager on front.)
(16)	Eddie Collins
(19)	Dave Davenport
(37)	Tom Griffith
(40)	John Henry
(41)	Clarence Hodge
(45)	Rogers Hornsby
(52)	James Johnston
(61)	Al Mamaux
(62)	"Rabbit" Maranville
	Jeff Pfeffer
(83)	Eppa Rixey, Jr.
(86)	Babe Ruth
(90)	Ray Schalk
(103)	Chester Thomas
(109)	Jim Vaughn (Dark cap.)
(113)	Oscar Vitt
(116)	Zach Wheat
(120)	Joe Wood

1910 Standard Caramel Co. (E93)

WILTSE, N. Y. NAT'L

BASE BALL STARS
This card is one of a set of 30 stars from original photographs
1. AMES, New York National
2. BENDER, Phila. American
3. BROWN, Chicago National
4. COLLINS, Phila. American
5. CHANCE, Chicago National
6. COVELESKIE, Cincinnati Nat'l
7. CHASE, New York American
8. COBB, Detroit American
9. CLARKE, Pittsburg National
10. DELEHANTY, Detroit American
11. DONOVAN, Detroit American
12. DOOIN, Philadelphia National
13. EVERS, Chicago National
14. GIBSON, Pittsburg National
15. GRIFFITH, Cincinnati National
16. JENNINGS, Detroit American
17. JONES, Detroit American
18. JOSS, Cleveland American
19. LAJOIE, Cleveland National
20. LEACH, Pittsburg National
21. MATHEWSON, N. Y. National
22. McGRAW, New York National
23. PHILLIPPI, Pittsburg National
24. PLANK, Philadelphia American
25. PASTORIOUS, Brooklyn Nat'l
26. TINKER, Chicago National
27. WADDELL, St. Louis American
28. WAGNER, Pittsburg National
29. WILTSE, New York National
30. CY, YOUNG, Cleveland Amer.
Manufactured only by
Standard Caramel Co., Lancaster, Pa.

This 30-card set issued in 1910 by Standard Caramel Co. of Lancaster, Pa., is closely related to several other candy sets from this period which share the same format and, in many cases, the same player poses. The cards measure 1-1/2" x 2-3/4" and utilize tinted black-and-white player photos. The back of each card contains an alphabetical checklist of the set plus a line indicating it was manufactured by Standard Caramel Co., Lancaster, Pa. The set carries the ACC designation of E93.

		NM	E	VG
Complete Set (30):		80,000	24,000	12,000
Common Player:		1,200	360.00	180.00
(1)	Red Ames	1,200	360.00	180.00
(2)	Chief Bender	4,000	1,200	600.00
(3)	Mordecai Brown	4,000	1,200	600.00
(4)	Frank Chance	4,000	1,200	600.00
(5)	Hal Chase	3,750	1,125	565.00
(6)	Fred Clarke	4,000	1,200	600.00
(7)	Ty Cobb	12,000	3,600	1,800

(8)	Eddie Collins	2,400	720.00	360.00
(9)	Harry Coveleskie (Coveleski)	1,200	360.00	180.00
(10)	Jim Delehanty	1,600	480.00	240.00
(11)	Wild Bill Donovan	1,200	360.00	180.00
(12)	Red Dooin	1,200	360.00	180.00
(13)	Johnny Evers	4,000	1,200	600.00
(14)	George Gibson	1,200	360.00	180.00
(15)	Clark Griffith	4,000	1,200	600.00
(16)	Hugh Jennings	4,000	1,200	600.00
(17)	Davy Jones	1,200	360.00	180.00
(18)	Addie Joss	4,500	1,350	675.00
(19)	Nap Lajoie	4,500	1,350	675.00
(20)	Tommy Leach	1,200	360.00	180.00
(21)	Christy Mathewson	7,000	2,100	1,050
(22)	John McGraw	4,000	1,200	600.00
(23)	Jim Pastorious	1,200	360.00	180.00
(24)	Deacon Phillippi (Phillippe)	1,200	360.00	180.00
(25)	Eddie Plank	4,000	1,200	600.00
(26)	Joe Tinker	4,000	1,200	600.00
(27)	Rube Waddell	4,000	1,200	600.00
(28)	Honus Wagner	9,600	2,880	1,440
(29)	Hooks Wiltse	1,200	360.00	180.00
(30)	Cy Young	6,400	1,925	965.00

1952 Star-Cal Decals Type 1

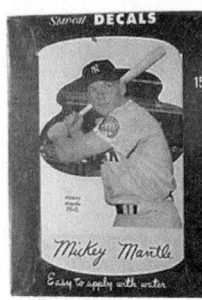

The Meyercord Co., of Chicago issued two sets of base-ball player decals in 1952. The Type I Star-Cal Decal set consists of 68 different major leaguers, each pictured on a large (4-1/8" x 6-1/8") decal. The player's name and facsimile autograph appear on the decal, along with the decal number listed on the checklist here. Values shown are for decals complete with outer directions envelope.

		NM	E	VG
Complete Set (68):		11,250	5,625	3,375
Common Player:		68.00	34.00	20.00
70A	Allie Reynolds	75.00	38.00	23.00
70B	Ed Lopat	75.00	38.00	23.00
70C	Yogi Berra	300.00	150.00	90.00
70D	Vic Raschi	75.00	38.00	23.00
70E	Jerry Coleman	68.00	34.00	20.00
70F	Phil Rizzuto	165.00	83.00	50.00
70G	Mickey Mantle	2,265	1,315	785.00
71A	Mel Parnell	68.00	34.00	20.00
71B	Ted Williams	600.00	300.00	180.00
71C	Ted Williams	600.00	300.00	180.00
71D	Vern Stephens	68.00	34.00	20.00
71E	Billy Goodman	68.00	34.00	20.00
71F	Dom DiMaggio	75.00	38.00	23.00
71G	Dick Gernert	68.00	34.00	20.00
71H	Hoot Evers	68.00	34.00	20.00
72A	George Kell	75.00	38.00	23.00
72B	Hal Newhouser	75.00	38.00	23.00
72C	Hoot Evers	68.00	34.00	20.00
72D	Vic Wertz	68.00	34.00	20.00
72E	Fred Hutchinson	68.00	34.00	20.00
72F	Johnny Groth	68.00	34.00	20.00
73A	Al Zarilla	68.00	34.00	20.00
73B	Billy Pierce	68.00	34.00	20.00
73C	Eddie Robinson	68.00	34.00	20.00
73D	Chico Carrasquel	75.00	38.00	23.00
73E	Minnie Minoso	75.00	38.00	23.00
73F	Jim Busby	68.00	34.00	20.00
73G	Nellie Fox	83.00	42.00	25.00
73H	Sam Mele	68.00	34.00	20.00
74A	Larry Doby	83.00	42.00	25.00
74B	Al Rosen	75.00	38.00	23.00
74C	Bob Lemon	83.00	42.00	25.00
74D	Jim Hegan	68.00	34.00	20.00
74E	Bob Feller	135.00	68.00	41.00
74F	Dale Mitchell	68.00	34.00	20.00
75A	Ned Garver	68.00	34.00	20.00
76A	Gus Zernial	68.00	34.00	20.00
76B	Ferris Fain	68.00	34.00	20.00
76C	Bobby Shantz	68.00	34.00	20.00
77A	Richie Ashburn	90.00	45.00	27.00
77B	Ralph Kiner	83.00	42.00	25.00
77C	Curt Simmons	68.00	34.00	20.00
78A	Bobby Thomson	83.00	42.00	25.00

78B	Alvin Dark	68.00	34.00	20.00
78C	Sal Maglie	68.00	34.00	20.00
78D	Larry Jansen	68.00	34.00	20.00
78E	Willie Mays	635.00	315.00	190.00
78F	Monte Irvin	83.00	42.00	25.00
78G	Whitey Lockman	68.00	34.00	20.00
79A	Gil Hodges	135.00	68.00	40.00
79B	Pee Wee Reese	165.00	83.00	50.00
79C	Roy Campanella	165.00	83.00	50.00
79D	Don Newcombe	83.00	42.00	25.00
79E	Duke Snider	165.00	83.00	50.00
79F	Preacher Roe	75.00	38.00	23.00
79G	Jackie Robinson	525.00	260.00	155.00
80A	Eddie Miksis	68.00	34.00	20.00
80B	Dutch Leonard	68.00	34.00	20.00
80C	Randy Jackson	68.00	34.00	20.00
80D	Bob Rush	68.00	34.00	20.00
80E	Hank Sauer	68.00	34.00	20.00
80F	Phil Cavarretta	68.00	34.00	20.00
80G	Warren Hacker	68.00	34.00	20.00
81A	Red Schoendienst	83.00	42.00	25.00
81B	Wally Westlake	68.00	34.00	20.00
81C	Cliff Chambers	68.00	34.00	20.00
81D	Enos Slaughter	83.00	42.00	25.00
81E	Stan Musial	415.00	210.00	125.00
81F	Stan Musial	415.00	210.00	125.00
81G	Jerry Staley	68.00	34.00	20.00

1952 Star-Cal Decals Type 2

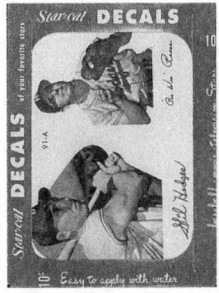
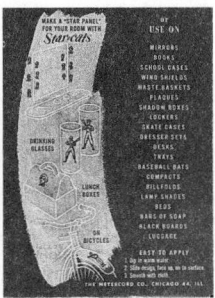

Also produced by Chicago's Meyercord Co. in 1952, these Star-Cal Decals are similar to the Type I variety, except the decal sheets are smaller, measuring 4-1/8" x 3-1/16", and each sheet features two players instead of one.

		NM	E	VG
Complete Set (32):		4,500	2,250	1,350
Common Player:		68.00	34.00	20.00
84A	Vic Raschi, Allie Reynolds	120.00	60.00	35.00
84B	Yogi Berra, Ed Lopat	250.00	125.00	75.00
84C	Jerry Coleman, Phil Rizzuto	205.00	102.00	60.00
85A	Ted Williams, Ted Williams	675.00	335.00	200.00
85B	Dom DiMaggio, Mel Parnell	90.00	45.00	27.00
85C	Billy Goodman, Vern Stephens	68.00	34.00	20.00
86A	George Kell, Hal Newhouser	120.00	60.00	35.00
86B	Hoot Evers, Vic Wertz	68.00	34.00	20.00
86C	Johnny Groth, Fred Hutchinson	68.00	34.00	20.00
87A	Eddie Robinson, Eddie Robinson	68.00	34.00	20.00
87B	Chico Carrasquel, Minnie Minoso	90.00	45.00	25.00
87C	Nellie Fox, Billy Pierce	100.00	50.00	30.00
87D	Jim Busby, Al Zarilla	68.00	34.00	20.00
88A	Jim Hegan, Bob Lemon	100.00	50.00	30.00
88B	Larry Doby, Bob Feller	250.00	125.00	75.00
88C	Dale Mitchell, Al Rosen	68.00	34.00	20.00
89A	Ned Garver, Ned Garver	68.00	34.00	20.00
89B	Ferris Fain, Gus Zernial	68.00	34.00	20.00
89C	Richie Ashburn, Richie Ashburn	115.00	55.00	35.00
89D	Ralph Kiner, Ralph Kiner	115.00	55.00	35.00
90A	Monty Irvin, Willie Mays (Monte)	450.00	225.00	135.00
90B	Larry Jansen, Sal Maglie	68.00	34.00	20.00
90C	Al Dark, Bobby Thomson	83.00	42.00	25.00
91A	Gil Hodges, Pee Wee Reese	335.00	170.00	100.00
91B	Roy Campanella, Jackie Robinson	450.00	225.00	135.00
91C	Preacher Roe, Duke Snider	300.00	150.00	90.00
92A	Phil Cavarretta, Dutch Leonard	68.00	34.00	20.00
92B	Randy Jackson, Eddie Miksis	68.00	34.00	20.00

		NM	E	VG
92C	Bob Rush, Hank Sauer	68.00	34.00	20.00
93A	Stan Musial, Stan Musial	525.00	260.00	160.00
93B	Red Schoendienst, Enos Slaughter	135.00	68.00	40.00
93C	Cliff Chambers, Wally Westlake	68.00	34.00	20.00

1976 Star Market Red Sox

Only Red Sox are featured in this set issued by the Star Market chain in the Boston area. Players are photographed hatless in jerseys which feature the Massachusetts Bicentennial logo. Pictures measure 5-7/8" x 9" and have a 3/16" white border all around. A facsimile autograph is printed on the front in black. Backs are blank. The unnumbered pictures are checklisted here alphabetically.

		NM	E	VG
Complete Set (16):		35.00	17.50	10.00
Common Player:		1.50	.75	.45
(1)	Rick Burleson	1.50	.75	.45
(2)	Reggie Cleveland	1.50	.75	.45
(3)	Cecil Cooper	2.50	1.25	.70
(4)	Denny Doyle	1.50	.75	.45
(5)	Dwight Evans	2.50	1.25	.70
(6)	Carlton Fisk	6.00	3.00	1.80
(7)	Tom House	1.50	.75	.45
(8)	Fergie Jenkins	4.00	2.00	1.25
(9)	Bill Lee	1.50	.75	.45
(10)	Fred Lynn	2.50	1.25	.70
(11)	Rick Miller	1.50	.75	.45
(12)	Rico Petrocelli	2.50	1.25	.70
(13)	Jim Rice	6.00	3.00	1.80
(14)	Luis Tiant	2.50	1.25	.70
(15)	Rick Wise	1.50	.75	.45
(16)	Carl Yastrzemski	10.00	5.00	3.00

1928 Star Player Candy

WALLY SCHANG

Little is known about the origin of this set. The producer is not identified, but experienced collectors generally refer to it as the Star Player Candy set, possibly because it was distributed with a product of that name. The cards measure 1-7/8" x 2-7/8", are sepia-toned, blank-backed and printed on thin paper. The player's name (but no team designation) appears in the border below the photo in brown capital letters. To date the checklist of baseball players numbers 73, but more may exist, and cards of football players have also been found.

		NM	E	VG
Common Player:		900.00	360.00	180.00
(1)	Dave Bancroft	4,000	2,000	1,200
(2)	Emile Barnes	1,800	900.00	550.00
(3)	L.A. Blue	1,800	900.00	550.00
(4)	Garland Buckeye	1,800	900.00	550.00
(5)	George Burns	1,800	900.00	550.00
(6)	Guy T. Bush	1,800	900.00	550.00
(7)	Owen T. Carroll	1,800	900.00	550.00
(8)	Chalmer Cissell	1,800	900.00	550.00
(9)	Ty Cobb	20,000	8,000	4,000

		NM	E	VG
(10)	Gordon Cochrane	4,000	2,000	1,200
(11)	Richard Coffman	1,800	900.00	550.00
(12)	Eddie Collins	4,000	2,000	1,200
(13)	Stanley Coveleskie (Coveleski)	4,000	2,000	1,200
(14)	Hugh Critz	1,800	900.00	550.00
(15)	Hazen Cuyler	4,000	2,000	1,200
(16)	Charles Dressen	1,800	900.00	550.00
(17)	Joe Dugan	1,800	900.00	550.00
(18)	Elwood English	1,800	900.00	550.00
(19)	Bib Falk (Bibb)	1,800	900.00	550.00
(20)	Ira Flagstead	1,800	900.00	550.00
(21)	Bob Fothergill	1,800	900.00	550.00
(22)	Frank T. Frisch	4,000	2,000	1,200
(23)	Foster Ganzel	1,800	900.00	550.00
(24)	Lou Gehrig	22,500	9,000	4,500
(25)	Chas. Gihringer (Gehringer)	4,000	2,000	1,200
(26)	George Gerken	1,800	900.00	550.00
(27)	Grant Gillis	1,800	900.00	550.00
(28)	Miguel Gonzales (Gonzalez)	1,800	900.00	550.00
(29)	Sam Gray	1,800	900.00	550.00
(30)	Chas. J. Grimm	1,800	900.00	550.00
(31)	Robert M. Grove	4,500	2,250	1,350
(32)	Chas. J. Hafey	4,000	2,000	1,200
(33)	Jesse Haines	4,000	2,000	1,200
(34)	Chas. L. Hartnett	4,000	2,000	1,200
(35)	Clifton Heathcote	1,800	900.00	550.00
(36)	Harry Heilmann	4,000	2,000	1,200
(37)	John Heving	1,800	900.00	550.00
(38)	Waite Hoyt	4,000	2,000	1,200
(39)	Chas. Jamieson	1,800	900.00	550.00
(40)	Joe Judge	1,800	900.00	550.00
(41)	Willie Kamm	1,800	900.00	550.00
(42)	George Kelly	4,000	2,000	1,200
(43)	Tony Lazzeri	4,000	2,000	1,200
(44)	Adolfo Luque	1,800	900.00	550.00
(45)	Ted Lyons	4,000	2,000	1,200
(46)	Hugh McMullen	1,800	900.00	550.00
(47)	Bob Meusel	1,800	900.00	550.00
(48)	Wilcey Moore (Wilcy)	1,800	900.00	550.00
(49)	Ed C. Morgan	1,800	900.00	550.00
(50)	Buddy Myer	1,800	900.00	550.00
(51)	Herb Pennock	4,000	2,000	1,200
(52)	Everett Purdy	1,800	900.00	550.00
(53)	William Regan	1,800	900.00	550.00
(54)	Eppa Rixey	4,000	2,000	1,200
(55)	Charles Root	1,800	900.00	550.00
(56)	Jack Rothrock	1,800	900.00	550.00
(57)	Harold Ruel (Herold)	1,800	900.00	550.00
(58)	Babe Ruth	32,500	13,000	6,500
(59)	Wally Schang	1,800	900.00	550.00
(60)	Joe Sewell	4,000	2,000	1,200
(61)	Luke Sewell	1,800	900.00	550.00
(62)	Joe Shaute	1,800	900.00	550.00
(63)	George Sisler	4,000	2,000	1,200
(64)	Tris Speaker	5,000	2,500	1,500
(65)	Riggs Stephenson	1,800	900.00	550.00
(66)	Jack Tavener	1,800	900.00	550.00
(67)	Al Thomas	1,800	900.00	550.00
(68)	Harold J. Traynor	4,000	2,000	1,200
(69)	George Uhle	1,800	900.00	550.00
(70)	Dazzy Vance	4,000	2,000	1,200
(71)	Cy Williams	1,800	900.00	550.00
(72)	Ken Williams	1,800	900.00	550.00
(73)	Lewis R. Wilson	4,000	2,000	1,200

1929 Star Player Candy

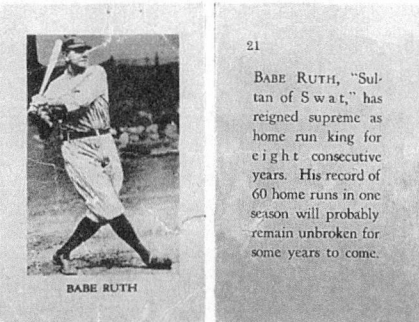

21

BABE RUTH, "Sultan of Swat," has reigned supreme as home run king for eight consecutive years. His record of 60 home runs in one season will probably remain unbroken for some years to come.

BABE RUTH

Three baseball players are included in this multi-subject set of cards that were sold in one-cent glassine envelopes with several dozen tiny pellets of bubblegum under the title "Dockman's 'Headliners & Gum'". Cards are about 1-7/8" x 2-7/8", printed in sepia on this cardboard. Backs have a few words about the subject pictured on front and a card number.

		NM	E	VG
21	Babe Ruth	12,000	6,000	3,600

		NM	E	VG
32	Lou Gehrig	7,000	3,500	2,100
(# Ukn.)	Walter Johnson	6,000	3,000	1,800

1892 J.U. Stead Studio Cabinets

J.U. STEAD   363 6th Ave., N.Y.

Only members of the N.Y. Giants are thus far known in this series of cabinet cards from New York City photographer J.U. Stead. About standard cabinet size (4-1/2" x 6-1/2") the cards have black-and-white portraits. On the thick cardboard mount's bottom border is the name and address of the studio. Backs repeat that information and have three lines of type at bottom extolling "Instantaneous Photographs." Unless the player name was pencilled on the card by a previous owner, the players are not otherwise identified. Fortunately, the plethora of contemporary issues from other sources makes matching names and photos fairly easy. The issue date attributed is speculative.

	NM	E	VG
Common Player:	3,000	1,500	900.00
Roger Connor	6,000	2,000	1,200
Willie Keeler	10,000	3,750	2,250
Mike Tiernan	3,000	1,500	900.00

1909-16 Max Stein Postcards (PC758)

Issued over a period of several years these sepia-toned photo postcards depict most of the stars of the day. In standard 3-1/2" x 5-1/2" format they have typical postcard indicia on the back. Some cards have been seen with a "United States Pub." legend on the back. Most of the subjects played in Stein's Chicago location. Besides the baseball players listed here, the series also included "Statesmen, etc., Aeroplanes and Flyers, Fighters, etc.," and, "Dancing Girls," according to advertising found on the back of some cards. Wholesale prices when issued were 35 cents per hundred, $2.75 per thousand.

		NM	E	VG
Common Player:		200.00	80.00	40.00
Advertising Back: 1.5X				
(1)	Ping Bodie	400.00	200.00	120.00
(2)	Frank Chance	800.00	400.00	240.00
(3)	Ty Cobb	3,750	1,875	1,125
(4)	Johnny Evers	800.00	400.00	240.00
(5)	Rube Marquard	800.00	400.00	240.00
(6)	Christy Mathewson	2,400	1,200	725.00
(7)	John McGraw	800.00	400.00	240.00
(8)	Chief Meyers	400.00	200.00	120.00
(9)	Marty O'Toole	400.00	200.00	120.00
(10)	Wildfire Schulte	400.00	200.00	120.00
(11)	Tris Speaker	900.00	450.00	270.00
(12)	Jake Stahl	400.00	200.00	120.00
(13)	Jim Thorpe	5,000	2,500	1,500
(14)	Joe Tinker	800.00	400.00	240.00
(15)	Honus Wagner	3,500	1,750	1,050
(16)	Ed Walsh	800.00	400.00	240.00
(17)	Buck Weaver	3,500	1,750	1,050
(18)	Joe Wood	400.00	200.00	120.00
(19)	Heinie Zimmerman	400.00	200.00	120.00

		NM	E	VG
(20)	Chicago Cubs(Jimmy Archer, Roger Bresnahan, Johnny Evers, Mike Hechinger, Tom Needham)	400.00	200.00	120.00
(21)	Chicago Cubs(Bill Clymer, Wilbur Good, Ward Miller, Mike Mitchell, Wildfire Schulte)	400.00	200.00	120.00
(22)	Boston Americans Team Photo	400.00	200.00	120.00
(23)	1916 Chicago Cubs Team Photo	600.00	300.00	180.00
(24)	1916 Cincinnati Reds Team Photo	400.00	200.00	120.00
(25)	New York Nationals Team Photo	400.00	200.00	120.00
(26)	Johnny Coulon, Jess Willard (Boxers)	400.00	200.00	120.00

1904 Stenzel's Rooter Buttons

The extent of the checklist for this rare Cincinnati 1-1/4" pinback celluloid button issue is unknown. According to a paper label found in the back of well-preserved examples, the buttons are the issue of "Jake Stenzel B.B. Exchange located opposite Ball Park." Fronts have "STENZEL'S ROOTER BUTTON" at top and a player portrait photo at center with last name and position below.

		NM	E	VG
(1)	Mike Donlin	750.00	375.00	225.00
(2)	Bob Ewing	600.00	300.00	180.00
(3)	Jack Harper	600.00	300.00	180.00
(4)	Joe Kelley	1,750	875.00	525.00
(5)	Win Kellum	600.00	300.00	180.00
(6)	Peaches O'Neil (O'Neill)	900.00	450.00	275.00
(7)	Heinie Pietz (Peitz)	600.00	300.00	180.00
(8)	Admiral Schlei	600.00	300.00	180.00
(9)	Cy Seymour	600.00	300.00	180.00
(10)	Jack Sutthoff	600.00	300.00	180.00
(11)	Sam Woodruff	600.00	300.00	180.00

1911 Stevens Firearms Philadelphia Athletics

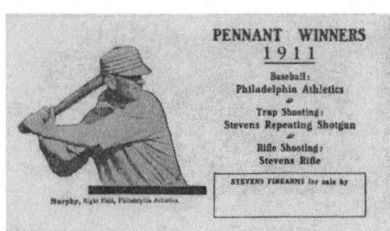

Riding on the coattails of the A's American League pennant (and eventual World Series) win, Stevens Firearms created this set of cards to promote its rifles and shotguns. About 6-3/16" x 3-7/16", the blank-back, medium-weight cards have a black-and-white posed action photo at left with the player identified by name, position and team. At top right is advertising, at bottom-right is a box where local retailers' addresses could be stamped or printed. Cards have been seen printed on several different colors of stock. In actuality, these are really ink blotters from the old fountain pen days as opposed to "cards." Other players are likely to have been issued.

		NM	E	VG
Common Player:		1,000	500.00	300.00
(1)	Frank Baker	3,000	1,500	900.00
(2)	Chief Bender	3,000	1,500	900.00
(3)	Bris Lord	1,000	500.00	300.00
(4)	Connie Mack	3,000	1,500	900.00
(5)	Danny Murphy	1,000	500.00	300.00
(6)	Rube Oldring	1,000	500.00	300.00
(7)	Harry Davis	1,000	500.00	300.00
(8)	Ira Thomas	1,000	500.00	300.00

1888-1889 Stevens Studio Australian Tour

Cabinets

After the 1888 season, Albert Spalding toured to Australia with a group of major league players to increase interest in baseball Down Under (as well as to increase demand for the baseball equipment his firm sold). Prior to departure, many of the players gathered at Stevens Studio in Chicago for portrait photos to be made into cabinet cards, presumably for sale as souvenirs on the junket. Vignetted portraits present the players in their Sunday best. Below a decorative dividing line is "Spalding's Australian Base Ball Tour / Stevens 1888-89 Chicago." Back has a large ornate ad for the photographer. The full extent of the checklist is unknown.

	NM	E	VG
Common Player:	3,500	1,750	1,000
Cap Anson	10,000	5,000	3,000
Jim Donnelly	3,500	1,750	1,000
Jim Fogarty	3,500	1,750	1,000
Egyptian Healey	3,500	1,750	1,000
Ned Williamson	3,500	1,750	1,000

1890 Stevens Studio Chicago Pirates Cabinets

The single-season players' revolution that spawned the Players League is marked with this issue of cabinet cards from the Stevens studio of Chicago. Only members of the Chicago Pirates P.L. team have been seen in this issue, all in street clothes and identified by a name penned on the front. A composite-photo card is also known, providing reasonable expectations that more individual player cabinets will be discovered. The studio advertising on back is ornately printed in maroon.

		NM	E	VG
Common Player:		1,800	900.00	550.00
(1)	Charles Comiskey	3,850	1,925	1,100
(2)	Hugh Duffy	3,850	1,925	1,100
(3)	Silver Flint	1,800	900.00	550.00
(4)	Jimmy Ryan	1,800	900.00	550.00
(5)	Team Composite	10,000	5,000	3,000

1890 Stevens Studio Chicago White Stockings Cabinets

Cabinet cards in the standard 4-1/4" x 6-1/2" format of at least five of the 1890 Chicago National Leaguers, as well as a team composite picture are known to have been produced by the Stevens Art Studio. Fronts have vignetted portraits of the players in dress clothes. Backs have an ornate ad for the photographer, which includes the note, "DUPLICATES OF THIS PICTURE CAN BE HAD AT ANY TIME, AT REDUCED RATES." Player names are often found penned on the cards, as the photos are otherwise unidentified. At least two styles of cardboard mounts are seen with the White Stockings cabinets. The extent of the checklist is also unknown.

		NM	E	VG
Common Player:		1,800	900.00	550.00
(1)	Cap Anson	8,250	4,125	2,475

		NM	E	VG
(2)	Duke Farrell	1,800	900.00	550.00
(3)	John Luby	1,800	900.00	550.00
(4)	Mike Sullivan	1,800	900.00	550.00
(5)	1890 Chicago White	4,400	2,200	1,325
(6)	Stockings	1,800	900.00	550.00

 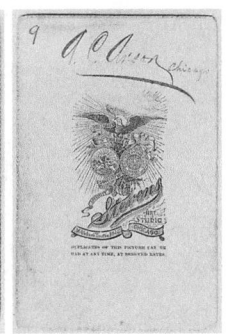

		NM	E	VG
Common Player:		2,400	1,200	720.00
(1)	Cap Anson	8,250	4,125	2,475
(2)	Mark Baldwin	2,400	1,200	720.00
(3)	Jack Boyle	2,400	1,200	720.00
(4)	Charles Comiskey	7,500	3,750	2,250
(5)	Del Darling	2,400	1,200	720.00
(6)	Hugh Duffy	7,500	3,750	2,250
(7)	Frank Dwyer	2,400	1,200	720.00
(8)	Steve Flint	2,400	1,200	720.00
(9)	Arlie Latham	2,400	1,200	720.00
(10)	Pat Luby	2,400	1,200	720.00
(11)	Jimmy Ryan	2,400	1,200	720.00
(12)	Mike Sullivan	1,800	900.00	550.00
(13)	Pat Wright	1,800	900.00	550.00
(14)	1890 Chicago White Stockings	4,400	2,200	1,325

1941 St. Louis Browns team issue (W753)

Measuring 2-1/8" x 2-5/8", this unnumbered boxed set of cards features the St. Louis Browns in black-and-white portrait photos on front. Backs have player name, position and personal and statistical information. There are also cards for coaches and one of the the club's two managers that season (Luke Sewell). As the Browns weren't much of a team in 1941 (or in most seasons for that matter) there are no major stars in the set. The issue was cataloged as W753 in the ACC.

		NM	E	VG
Complete Set (30):		850.00	425.00	250.00
Common Player:		35.00	17.50	10.00
Box:		75.00	35.00	25.00
(1)	Johnny Allen	35.00	17.50	10.00
(2)	Elden Auker (Eldon)	35.00	17.50	10.00
(3)	Donald L Barnes	35.00	17.50	10.00
(4)	Johnny Berardino	50.00	25.00	15.00
(5)	George Caster	35.00	17.50	10.00
(6)	Harlond Benton (Darky) Clift	35.00	17.50	10.00
(7)	Roy J. Cullenbine	35.00	17.50	10.00
(8)	William O. DeWitt (Vice-President)	35.00	17.50	10.00
(9)	Roberto Estalella	35.00	17.50	10.00
(10)	Richard Benjamin (Rick) Ferrell	60.00	30.00	18.00
(11)	Dennis W. Galehouse	35.00	17.50	10.00
(12)	Joseph L. Grace	35.00	17.50	10.00
(13)	Frank Grube	35.00	17.50	10.00
(14)	Robert A. Harris	35.00	17.50	10.00
(15)	Donald Henry Heffner	35.00	17.50	10.00
(16)	Fred Hofmann	35.00	17.50	10.00
(17)	Walter Franklin Judnich	35.00	17.50	10.00
(18)	John Henry (Jack) Kramer	35.00	17.50	10.00
(19)	Chester (Chet) Laabs	35.00	17.50	10.00
(20)	John Lucadello	35.00	17.50	10.00

(21)	George Hartley McQuinn	35.00	17.50	10.00
(22)	Robert Cleveland Muncrief, Jr.	35.00	17.50	10.00
(23)	John Niggeling	35.00	17.50	10.00
(24)	Fred Raymond (Fritz) Ostermueller	35.00	17.50	10.00
(25)	James Luther (Luke) Sewell	35.00	17.50	10.00
(26)	Alan Cochran Strange (Cochrane)	35.00	17.50	10.00
(27)	Robert Virgil (Bob) Swift	35.00	17.50	10.00
(28)	James W. (Zack) Taylor	35.00	17.50	10.00
(29)	William Felix (Bill) Trotter	35.00	17.50	10.00
(30)	Presentation Card/Order Form	10.00	5.00	3.00

1952 St. Louis Browns Postcards

This series of player postcards features black-and-white glossy photos on front with a white border. The cards bear no player identification and were evidently intended for use in honoring fan requests for autographs. The 1952 issue can be differentiated from that of 1953 by the absence of a stamp box on back. The unnumbered cards are checklisted here alphabetically, though the list may be incomplete. Multiple player names indicate known different poses.

		NM	E	VG
Common Player:		50.00	25.00	15.00
(1)	Tommy Byrne	50.00	25.00	15.00
(2)	Bob Cain	50.00	25.00	15.00
(3)	Bob Cain	50.00	25.00	15.00
(4)	Clint Courtney	50.00	25.00	15.00
(5)	Jim Delsing	50.00	25.00	15.00
(6)	Jim Dyck	50.00	25.00	15.00
(7)	Jim Dyck	50.00	25.00	15.00
(8)	Ned Garver	50.00	25.00	15.00
(9)	Marty Marion	60.00	30.00	18.00
(10)	Cass Michaels	50.00	25.00	15.00
(11)	Bob Nieman	50.00	25.00	15.00
(12)	Satchel Paige	200.00	100.00	60.00
(13)	Duane Pillette	50.00	25.00	15.00
(14)	Jim Rivera	50.00	25.00	15.00
(15)	Bill Veeck	75.00	37.00	22.00
(16)	Bobby Young	50.00	25.00	15.00

1953 St. Louis Browns Postcards

This series of player postcards from the team's final year in St. Louis features black-and-white glossy photos on front with a white border. The cards bear no player identification and were evidently intended for use in honoring fan requests for autographs. The 1953 issue can be differentiated from that of 1952 by the presence of a stamp box on back identifying the issuer as Deorite Peerless. The unnumbered cards are checklisted here alphabetically though the list is likely incomplete.

		NM	E	VG
Common Player:		50.00	25.00	15.00

(1)	Connie Berry	50.00	25.00	15.00
(2)	Mike Blyzka	50.00	25.00	15.00
(3)	Harry Brecheen	50.00	25.00	15.00
(4)	Bob Cain	50.00	25.00	15.00
(5)	Clint Courtney	50.00	25.00	15.00
(6)	Jim Dyck	50.00	25.00	15.00
(7)	Hank Edwards	50.00	25.00	15.00
(8)	Ned Garver	50.00	25.00	15.00
(9)	Johnny Groth	50.00	25.00	15.00
(11)	Bobo Holloman	50.00	25.00	15.00
(12)	Billy Hunter	50.00	25.00	15.00
(13)	Dick Kokos	50.00	25.00	15.00
(14)	Dick Kryhoski	50.00	25.00	15.00
(15)	Max Lanier	50.00	25.00	15.00
(16)	Don Larsen	75.00	37.50	22.00
(17)	Don Lenhardt	50.00	25.00	15.00
(18)	Dick Littlefield	50.00	25.00	15.00
(19)	Marty Marion	60.00	30.00	18.00
(21)	Babe Martin	50.00	25.00	15.00
(22)	Willy Miranda	50.00	25.00	15.00
(23)	Les Moss	50.00	25.00	15.00
(24)	Bill Norman	50.00	25.00	15.00
(25)	Satchel Paige (Kneeling)	200.00	100.00	60.00
(26)	Satchel Paige (Pitching)	200.00	100.00	60.00
(27)	Duane Pillette	50.00	25.00	15.00
(28)	Bob Scheffing	50.00	25.00	15.00
(29)	Roy Sievers	60.00	30.00	18.00
(31)	Marlin Stuart	50.00	25.00	15.00
(32)	Virgil Trucks	65.00	32.00	19.50
(33)	Bill Veeck	75.00	37.00	22.00
(34)	Vic Wertz	50.00	25.00	15.00
(35)	Bobby Young	50.00	25.00	12.00

1941 St. Louis Cardinals Team Issue (W754)

A companion set to W753, this time featuring the National League team in St. Louis. Cards measure 2-1/8" x 2-5/8" and are unnumbered. Like the Browns set, this issue features black-and-white portrait photos on front and the individual's name, position and personal and statistical information on back. One interesting addition to the set is a card of Branch Rickey which, coupled with cards of Enos Slaughter and Johnny Mize, gives the set a bit more appeal than the Browns set. ACC designation is W754.

		NM	E	VG
Complete Set (30):		1,000	500.00	300.00
Common Player:		35.00	17.50	10.00
Box:		75.00	35.00	25.00
(1)	Sam Breadon	35.00	17.50	10.00
(2)	James Brown	35.00	17.50	10.00
(3)	Morton Cooper	35.00	17.50	10.00
(4)	William Walker Cooper	35.00	17.50	10.00
(5)	Estel Crabtree	35.00	17.50	10.00
(6)	Frank Crespi	35.00	17.50	10.00
(7)	William Crouch	35.00	17.50	10.00
(8)	Miguel Mike Gonzalez	50.00	25.00	15.00
(9)	Harry Gumbert	35.00	17.50	10.00
(10)	John Hopp	35.00	17.50	10.00
(11)	Ira Hutchinson	35.00	17.50	10.00
(12)	Howard Krist	35.00	17.50	10.00
(13)	Edward E. Lake	35.00	17.50	10.00
(14)	Hubert Max Lanier	35.00	17.50	10.00
(15)	Gus Mancuso	35.00	17.50	10.00
(16)	Martin Marion	55.00	27.50	16.50
(17)	Steve Mesner	35.00	17.50	10.00
(18)	John Mize	100.00	50.00	30.00
(19)	Capt. Terry Moore	50.00	25.00	15.00
(20)	Sam Nahem	75.00	38.50	23.00
(21)	Don Padgett	35.00	17.50	10.00
(22)	Branch Rickey (Vice-President)	60.00	30.00	18.00
(23)	Clyde Shoun	35.00	17.50	10.00
(24)	Enos Slaughter	100.00	50.00	30.00
(25)	William H. (Billy) Southworth	35.00	17.50	10.00
(26)	Herman Coaker Triplett	35.00	17.50	10.00
(27)	Clyde Buzzy Wares	35.00	17.50	10.00
(28)	Lon Warneke	35.00	17.50	10.00
(29)	Ernest White	35.00	17.50	10.00
(30)	**Presentation Card/ Order Form**	10.00	5.00	3.00

1966 St. Louis Cardinals Busch Stadium Immortals Coins

A dozen all-time great Cardinals are included in this set of commemorative medallions. Each 1-1/2" bright bronze "coin" has a portrait and career summary. The coins were issued in a 9" x 10-1/2" cardinal-red cardboard holder with gold logo and graphics.

		NM	E	VG
Complete Board/Coin Set:		75.00	37.50	22.50
Common Player:		7.50	3.75	2.25
(1)	Dizzy Dean	10.00	5.00	3.00
(2)	Frank Frisch	7.50	3.75	2.25
(3)	Chick Hafey	7.50	3.75	2.25
(4)	Jesse Haines	7.50	3.75	2.25
(5)	Marty Marion	7.50	3.75	2.25
(6)	Joe Medwick	7.50	3.75	2.25
(7)	Johnny Mize	7.50	3.75	2.25
(8)	Terry Moore	7.50	3.75	2.25
(9)	Stan Musial	15.00	7.50	4.50
(10)	Red Schoendienst	7.50	3.75	2.25
(11)	George Sisler	7.50	3.75	2.25
(12)	Enos Slaughter	7.50	3.75	2.25

1953 Stop & Shop Boston Red Sox

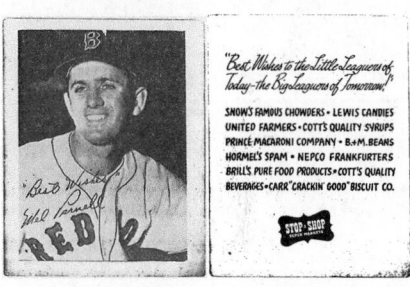

Four of the early 1950s Red Sox appear in this series issued by a Boston grocery chain. The cards may have been distributed in conjunction with players' in-store appearances. The cards measure 3-3/4" x 5" and are printed in black-and-white. A facsimile autograph appears on the front. Backs have the sponsor's advertising. The unnumbered cards are checklisted here alphabetically. See also 1953 First National Super Market Boston Red Sox.

		NM	E	VG
Complete Set (4):		3,000	1,500	900.00
Common Player:		750.00	375.00	225.00
(1)	Billy Goodman	750.00	375.00	225.00
(2)	Ellis Kinder	750.00	375.00	225.00
(3)	Mel Parnell	750.00	375.00	225.00
(4)	Sammy White	750.00	375.00	225.00

1888 Sub Rosa Cigarettes Girl Baseball Players (N508)

(See 1888 Allen & Ginter Girl Baseball Players.)

1916 Successful Farming

Best known for its use as a promotional medium for The Sporting News (M101-5), this 200-card set can be found with ads on the back for several local and regional businesses. Among them is Successful Farming magazine of Des Moines, Iowa. Some collectors believe that cards with the magazine's advertising on back were promotional cards, and that the cards actually delivered with the subscription offer were blank-back M101-5s. This would account for the scarcity of the ad-back versions.

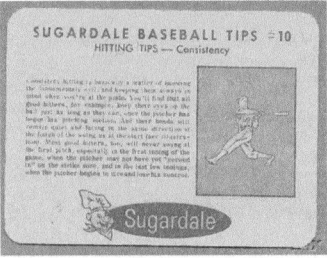

PREMIUM: 6-8X

(See 1916 Sporting News M101-5 for checklist and base
card values.)

1976 Sugar Daddy Sports World

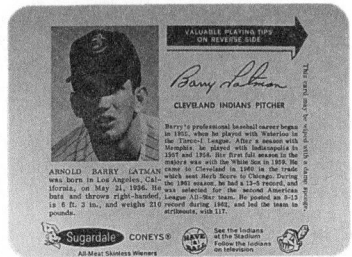

Two baseball related cards were issued as part of this
multi-sport candy insert set. Each card is titled "BASEBALL"
and they detail the 1974 and 1975 World Series and depict a
player - though not naming him - in action. The cards are 1" x
2-3/4" and have a white-bordered color photo on front. Backs
include various advertising details.

		NM	E	VG
	Complete Set (25):	75.00	37.50	22.50
12	Pete Rose (Series 1, 1974 World Series)	40.00	20.00	12.00
25	Bobby Murcer (Series 2, 1975 World Series)	25.00	12.50	7.50

1962 Sugardale Weiners

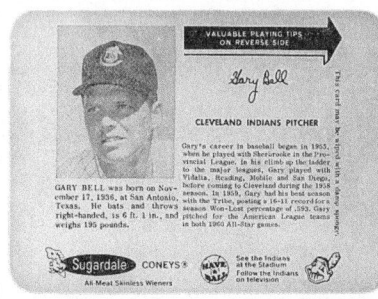

The Sugardale Meats set of black and white cards measure 5-1/8" x 3-3/4". The 22-card set includes 18 Cleveland
Indians and four Pittsburgh Pirates players. The Indians
cards are numbered from 1-19 with card number 6 not issued. The Pirates cards are lettered from A to D. The card
fronts contain a relatively small player photo, with biographical information and Sugardale logo. The backs are printed in
red and offer playing tips and another company logo. Card
number 10 (Bob Nieman) is considerably more scarce than
other cards in the set.

		NM	E	VG
	Complete Set (22):	12,500	5,000	2,500
	Common Player:	450.00	180.00	90.00
A	Dick Groat	450.00	180.00	90.00
B	Roberto Clemente	5,500	2,200	1,100
C	Don Hoak	450.00	180.00	90.00
D	Dick Stuart	450.00	180.00	90.00
1	Barry Latman	450.00	180.00	90.00
2	Gary Bell	450.00	180.00	90.00
3	Dick Donovan	450.00	180.00	90.00
4	Frank Funk	450.00	180.00	90.00
5	Jim Perry	450.00	180.00	90.00
6	Not Issued			
7	Johnny Romano	450.00	180.00	90.00
8	Ty Cline	450.00	180.00	90.00
9	Tito Francona	450.00	180.00	90.00
10	Bob Nieman (SP)	1,725	690.00	345.00
11	Willie Kirkland	450.00	180.00	90.00
12	Woodie Held	450.00	180.00	90.00
13	Jerry Kindall	450.00	180.00	90.00
14	Bubba Phillips	450.00	180.00	90.00
15	Mel Harder	450.00	180.00	90.00
16	Salty Parker	450.00	180.00	90.00
17	Ray Katt	450.00	180.00	90.00
18	Mel McGaha	450.00	180.00	90.00
19	Pedro Ramos	45000	180.00	90.00

1963 Sugardale Weiners

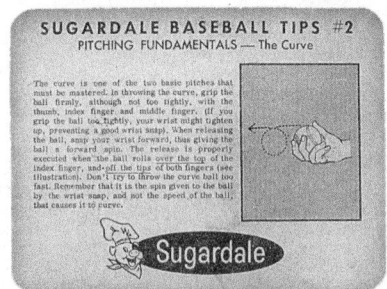

Sugardale Meats again featured Cleveland and Pittsburgh
players in its 1963 set, which grew to 31 cards. The black and
white cards again measure 5-1/8" x 3-3/4", and consist of 28
Indians and five Pirates players. Card formats are virtually
identical to the 1962 cards, with the only real difference being the information included in the player biographies. The
cards are numbered 1-38, with numbers 6, 21, 22 and 29-32
not issued. Cards for Bob Skinner (#35) and Jim Perry (#5)
are scarce as these two players were traded during the season and their cards withdrawn from distribution. The red card
backs again offer playing tips.

		NM	E	VG
	Complete Set (31):	10,000	4,000	2,000
	Common Player:	450.00	180.00	90.00
A	Don Cardwell	450.00	180.00	90.00
B	Robert R. Skinner (SP)	650.00	260.00	130.00
C	Donald B. Schwall	450.00	180.00	90.00
D	Jim Pagliaroni	450.00	180.00	90.00
E	Dick Schofield	450.00	180.00	90.00
1	Barry Latman	450.00	180.00	90.00
2	Gary Bell	450.00	180.00	90.00
3	Dick Donovan	450.00	180.00	90.00
4	Joe Adcock	500.00	200.00	100.00
5	Jim Perry (SP)	650.00	260.00	130.00
6	Not Issued			
7	Johnny Romano	450.00	180.00	90.00
8	Mike de la Hoz	450.00	180.00	90.00
9	Tito Francona	450.00	180.00	90.00
10	Gene Green	450.00	180.00	90.00
11	Willie Kirkland	450.00	180.00	90.00
12	Woodie Held	450.00	180.00	90.00
13	Jerry Kindall	450.00	180.00	90.00
14	Max Alvis	450.00	180.00	90.00
15	Mel Harder	450.00	180.00	90.00
16	George Strickland	450.00	180.00	90.00
17	Elmer Valo	450.00	180.00	90.00
18	Birdie Tebbetts	450.00	180.00	90.00
19	Pedro Ramos	450.00	180.00	90.00
20	Al Luplow	450.00	180.00	90.00
21	Not Issued			
22	Not Issued			
23	Jim Grant	450.00	180.00	90.00
24	Victor Davalillo	450.00	180.00	90.00
25	Jerry Walker	450.00	180.00	90.00
26	Sam McDowell	500.00	200.00	100.00
27	Fred Whitfield	450.00	180.00	90.00
28	Jack Kralick	450.00	180.00	90.00
29	Not Issued			
30	Not Issued			
31	Not Issued			
32	Not Issued			
33	Bob Allen	450.00	180.00	90.00

1933 Sulima Cigarettes

This is one of several early 1930s German cigarette cards
to picture Babe Ruth. In this case he is pictured on the 1-5/8"
x 2-3/8" black-and-white card with American comedic actor Harold Lloyd. The card is part of a numbered set of 272
movie star cards. Backs are printed in German. The card
is identical in format to the Josetti cigarette cards.

		NM	E	VG
151	Babe Ruth, Harold Lloyd	1,100	550.00	330.00

1936 Sunday Advertiser Sport Stamps

(See 1936 Boston American Sport Stamps.)

1974 Sun-Glo Pop Al Kaline

This 2-1/4" x 4-1/2" card was issued as an attachment to bottles of soda pop. The blank-back card features a modishly dressed portrait of the former Tigers great and his endorsement for the soda. Cards are printed in black on various brightly colored backgrounds.

	NM	E	VG
Al Kaline	6.00	3.00	1.75

1960s Sunny Ayr Farms Johnny Callison

In the absence of other player cardsm, it is impossible to date this issue any more precisely than Callison's tenure with the Phillies which encompassed the 1960s. The 3-1/2" x 5-1/2" black-and-white card had a facsimile autograph on front. The divided back is printed in red.

	NM	E	VG
Johnny Callison	100.00	50.00	30.00

1969 Sunoco Cubs/Brewers Pins

Fans in Southern Wisconsin and Northern Illinois could acquire 1-1/8" lithographed steel baseball player pins of the Cubs and Brewers at participating Sunoco gas stations. The blue-and-white (Cubs) or red-and-white (Brewers) pins have black-and-white player portrait photos at center on which cap logos have been removed. The Brewers pins are somewhat scarcer than those of the Cubs.

	NM	E	VG
Complete Set (18):	100.00	50.00	30.00
Common Player:	4.00	2.00	1.25
Chicago Cubs Team Set:	65.00	32.50	20.00
(1) Ernie Banks	25.00	12.50	7.50
(2) Glenn Beckert	4.00	2.00	1.25
(3) Jim Hickman	4.00	2.00	1.25
(4) Randy Hundley	4.00	2.00	1.25

		NM	E	VG
(5)	Ferguson Jenkins	7.50	3.75	2.25
(6)	Don Kessinger	6.00	3.00	1.75
(7)	Joe Pepitone	6.00	3.00	1.75
(8)	Ron Santo	12.00	6.00	4.00
(9)	Billy Williams	12.50	6.25	3.75
	Milwaukee Brewers Team Set:	50.00	25.00	15.00
(1)	Tommy Harper	6.00	3.00	1.75
(2)	Mike Hegan	6.00	3.00	1.75
(3)	Lew Krausse	6.00	3.00	1.75
(4)	Ted Kubiak	6.00	3.00	1.75
(5)	Marty Pattin	6.00	3.00	1.75
(6)	Phil Roof	6.00	3.00	1.75
(7)	Ken Sanders	6.00	3.00	1.75
(8)	Ted Savage	6.00	3.00	1.75
(9)	Danny Walton	6.00	3.00	1.75

1931 Sun Pictures Photo Kits

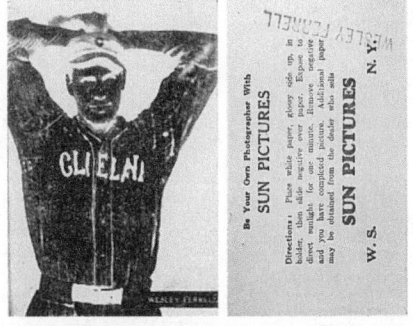

One of several contemporary kits for do-it-yourself production of photos, this issue was produced in New York City by a firm identified only as "W.S." A complete outfit consists of a 4-1/4" x 2-1/2" pink or kraft paper envelope with the name of the subject inside rubber-stamped on one end, a film negative, a piece of photo paper and a stand for producing/displaying the photo. The negative and resulting print measure 2-5/16" x 3-1/4". The set is listed in the American Card Catalog as W626. Prices shown are for complete kits; individual pieces would be pro-rated, with the negative the most valuable component. Because individual prints can be easily made even today, they have little collectible value. Only the baseball players are listed here.

		NM	E	VG
Common Player Kit:		100.00	50.00	30.00
(1)	George Earnshaw	100.00	50.00	30.00
(2)	Wesley Ferrell	100.00	50.00	30.00
(3)	Lefty Grove	225.00	112.50	67.50
(4)	Leo Hartnett	200.00	100.00	60.00
(5)	Tony Lazzeri	225.00	112.50	67.50
(6)	Herb Pennock	200.00	100.00	60.00
(7)	Babe Ruth	2,000	1,000	600.00
(8)	Al Simmons	200.00	100.00	60.00
(9)	Dazzy Vance	200.00	100.00	60.00
(10)	Hack Wilson	225.00	112.50	67.50

1970 Superballs

Manufactured by Chemtoy (though not credited on the balls), these high-bouncing hard rubber balls are composed of see-through material in which is imbedded a disc with a baseball player's portrait and identification. About 1-1/8" in diameter, the balls identify the player by name, team and position and include a four-digit number. In this checklist, the balls are listed alphabetically for lack of access to a complete list of the actual numbers. It is also possible the checklist in incomplete.

		NM	E	VG
Complete Set (286):		1,650	825.00	500.00
Common Player:		5.00	2.50	1.50
(1)	Hank Aaron	60.00	30.00	18.00
(2)	Jerry Adair	5.00	2.50	1.50
(3)	Tommie Agee	5.00	2.50	1.50
(4)	Bernie Allen	5.00	2.50	1.50
(5)	Lloyd Allen	5.00	2.50	1.50

		NM	E	VG
(6)	Gene Alley	5.00	2.50	1.50
(7)	Bob Allison	5.00	2.50	1.50
(8)	Sandy Alomar	5.00	2.50	1.50
(9)	Jesus Alou	5.00	2.50	1.50
(10)	Matty Alou	5.00	2.50	1.50
(11)	Max Alvis	5.00	2.50	1.50
(12)	Mike Andrews	5.00	2.50	1.50
(13)	Luis Aparicio	25.00	12.50	7.50
(14)	Jose Arcia	5.00	2.50	1.50
(15)	Bob Aspromonte	5.00	2.50	1.50
(16)	Jose Azcue	5.00	2.50	1.50
(17)	Bob Bailey	5.00	2.50	1.50
(18)	Jack Baldschun	5.00	2.50	1.50
(19)	Sal Bando	5.00	2.50	1.50
(20)	Ernie Banks	40.00	20.00	12.00
(21)	John Bateman	5.00	2.50	1.50
(22)	Glenn Beckert	5.00	2.50	1.50
(23)	Mark Belanger	5.00	2.50	1.50
(24)	Ken Berry	5.00	2.50	1.50
(25)	Paul Blair	5.00	2.50	1.50
(26)	Curt Blefary	5.00	2.50	1.50
(27)	John Boccabella	5.00	2.50	1.50
(28)	Bobby Bonds	5.00	2.50	1.50
(29)	John Boozer	5.00	2.50	1.50
(30)	Ken Boswell	5.00	2.50	1.50
(31)	Clete Boyer	5.00	2.50	1.50
(32)	Gene Brabender	5.00	2.50	1.50
(33)	Ron Brand	5.00	2.50	1.50
(34)	Jim Brewer	5.00	2.50	1.50
(35)	Johnny Briggs	5.00	2.50	1.50
(36)	Nelson Briles	5.00	2.50	1.50
(37)	Ed Brinkman	5.00	2.50	1.50
(38)	Lou Brock	25.00	12.50	7.50
(39)	Don Buford	5.00	2.50	1.50
(40)	Tom Burgmeier	5.00	2.50	1.50
(41)	Bill Butler	5.00	2.50	1.50
(42)	Johnny Callison	5.00	2.50	1.50
(43)	Bert Campaneris	5.00	2.50	1.50
(44)	Jim Campanis	5.00	2.50	1.50
(45)	Chris Cannizzaro	5.00	2.50	1.50
(46)	Jose Cardenal	5.00	2.50	1.50
(47)	Leo Cardenas	5.00	2.50	1.50
(48)	Rod Carew	40.00	20.00	12.00
(49)	Clay Carroll	5.00	2.50	1.50
(50)	Rico Carty	5.00	2.50	1.50
(51)	Paul Casanova	5.00	2.50	1.50
(52)	Norm Cash	15.00	7.50	4.50
(53)	Orlando Cepeda	25.00	12.50	7.50
(54)	Billy Champion	5.00	2.50	1.50
(55)	Dean Chance	5.00	2.50	1.50
(56a)	Roberto Clemente (Red insert.)	100.00	50.00	30.00
(56b)	Roberto Clemente (Blue insert.)	75.00	38.00	23.00
(57)	Tony Cloninger	5.00	2.50	1.50
(58)	Nate Colbert	5.00	2.50	1.50
(59)	Joe Coleman	5.00	2.50	1.50
(60)	Kevin Collins	5.00	2.50	1.50
(61)	Wayne Comer	5.00	2.50	1.50
(62)	Tony Conigliaro	15.00	7.50	4.50
(63)	Billy Cowan	5.00	2.50	1.50
(64)	Casey Cox	5.00	2.50	1.50
(65)	Willie Crawford	5.00	2.50	1.50
(66)	Mike Cuellar	5.00	2.50	1.50
(67)	Al Dark	5.00	2.50	1.50
(68)	Vic Davalillo	5.00	2.50	1.50
(69)	Jim Davenport	5.00	2.50	1.50
(70)	Willie Davis	5.00	2.50	1.50
(71)	Tommy Dean	5.00	2.50	1.50
(72)	Larry Dierker	5.00	2.50	1.50
(73)	Dick Dietz	5.00	2.50	1.50
(74)	Moe Drabowsky	5.00	2.50	1.50
(75)	Leo Durocher	20.00	10.00	6.00
(76)	Johnny Edwards	5.00	2.50	1.50
(77)	Dock Ellis	5.00	2.50	1.50
(78)	Dick Ellsworth	5.00	2.50	1.50
(79)	Mike Epstein	5.00	2.50	1.50
(80)	Andy Etchebarren	5.00	2.50	1.50
(81)	Ron Fairly	5.00	2.50	1.50
(82)	Al Ferrera	5.00	2.50	1.50
(83)	Rollie Fingers	20.00	10.00	6.00
(84)	Mike Fiore	5.00	2.50	1.50
(85)	Eddie Fisher	5.00	2.50	1.50
(86)	Jack Fisher	5.00	2.50	1.50
(87)	Ray Fosse	5.00	2.50	1.50
(88)	Bill Freehan	5.00	2.50	1.50
(89)	Jim Fregosi	5.00	2.50	1.50
(90)	Tito Fuentes	5.00	2.50	1.50
(91)	Vern Fuller	5.00	2.50	1.50
(92)	Woody Fryman	5.00	2.50	1.50
(93)	Len Gabrielson	5.00	2.50	1.50
(94)	Gary Gentry	5.00	2.50	1.50
(95)	Jake Gibbs	5.00	2.50	1.50
(96)	Russ Gibson	5.00	2.50	1.50
(97)	Billy Grabarkewitz	5.00	2.50	1.50
(98)	Dick Green	5.00	2.50	1.50
(99)	Tom Griffin	5.00	2.50	1.50
(100)	Jerry Grote	5.00	2.50	1.50

(101)	Tom Haller	5.00	2.50	1.50
(102)	Steve Hamilton	5.00	2.50	1.50
(103)	Ron Hansen	5.00	2.50	1.50
(104)	Tommy Harmon	5.00	2.50	1.50
(105)	Tommy Harper	5.00	2.50	1.50
(106)	Bud Harrelson	5.00	2.50	1.50
(107)	Jim Ray Hart	5.00	2.50	1.50
(108)	Richie Hebner	5.00	2.50	1.50
(109)	Mike Hedlund	5.00	2.50	1.50
(110)	Mike Hegan	5.00	2.50	1.50
(111)	Tommy Helms	5.00	2.50	1.50
(112)	Angel Hermoso	5.00	2.50	1.50
(113)	Ed Herrmann	5.00	2.50	1.50
(114)	Mike Hershberger	5.00	2.50	1.50
(115)	Jim Hickman	5.00	2.50	1.50
(116)	Jim Hicks	5.00	2.50	1.50
(117)	Chuck Hinton	5.00	2.50	1.50
(118)	Larry Hisle	5.00	2.50	1.50
(119)	Gil Hodges	20.00	10.00	6.00
(120)	Ken Holtzman	5.00	2.50	1.50
(121)	Joel Horlen	5.00	2.50	1.50
(122)	Willie Horton	5.00	2.50	1.50
(123)	Ralph Houk	5.00	2.50	1.50
(124)	Frank Howard	7.50	3.75	2.25
(125)	Randy Hundley	5.00	2.50	1.50
(126)	Ron Hunt	5.00	2.50	1.50
(127)	Jim Hunter	20.00	10.00	6.00
(128)	Steve Huntz	5.00	2.50	1.50
(129)	Al Jackson	5.00	2.50	1.50
(130)	Reggie Jackson	45.00	23.00	12.00
(131)	Pat Jarvis	5.00	2.50	1.50
(132)	Julian Javier	5.00	2.50	1.50
(133)	Tommy John	15.00	7,50	4.50
(134)	Dave Johnson	5.00	2.50	1.50
(135)	Jerry Johnson	5.00	2.50	1.50
(136)	Jay Johnstone	5.00	2.50	1.50
(137)	Cleon Jones	5.00	2.50	1.50
(138)	Dalton Jones	5.00	2.50	1.50
(139)	Jim Kaat	7.50	3.75	2.25
(140)	Al Kaline	30.00	15.00	9.00
(141)	Dick Kelley	5.00	2.50	1.50
(142)	Pat Kelly	5.00	2.50	1.50
(143)	John Kennedy	5.00	2.50	1.50
(144)	Joe Keough	5.00	2.50	1.50
(145)	Don Kessinger	5.00	2.50	1.50
(146)	Harmon Killebrew	30.00	15.00	9.00
(147)	Clay Kirby	5.00	2.50	1.50
(148)	Darold Knowles	5.00	2.50	1.50
(149)	Jerry Koosman	5.00	2.50	1.50
(150)	Andy Kosco	5.00	2.50	1.50
(151)	Ed Kranepool	5.00	2.50	1.50
(152)	Lew Krausse	5.00	2.50	1.50
(153)	Coco Laboy	5.00	2.50	1.50
(154)	Hal Lanier	5.00	2.50	1.50
(155)	George Lauzerique	5.00	2.50	1.50
(156)	Denny Lemaster	5.00	2.50	1.50
(157)	Bob Locker	5.00	2.50	1.50
(158)	Mickey Lolich	5.00	2.50	1.50
(159)	Jim Lonborg	5.00	2.50	1.50
(160)	Mike Lum	5.00	2.50	1.50
(161)	Jim Maloney	5.00	2.50	1.50
(162)	Juan Marichal	25.00	12.50	7.50
(163)	Dal Maxvill	5.00	2.50	1.50
(164)	Carlos May	5.00	2.50	1.50
(165)	Lee May	5.00	2.50	1.50
(166)	Willie Mays	60.00	30.00	18.00
(167)	Bill Mazeroski	25.00	12.50	7.50
(168)	Dick McAuliffe	5.00	2.50	1.50
(169)	Mike McCormick	5.00	2.50	1.50
(170)	Willie McCovey	30.00	15.00	9.00
(171)	Denny McLain	5.00	2.50	1.50
(172)	Jerry McNertney	5.00	2.50	1.50
(173)	Bill Melton	5.00	2.50	1.50
(174)	Denis Menke	5.00	2.50	1.50
(175)	Jim Merritt	5.00	2.50	1.50
(176)	Gene Michael	5.00	2.50	1.50
(177)	Pete Mikkelsen	5.00	2.50	1.50
(178)	Felix Millan	5.00	2.50	1.50
(179)	Norm Miller	5.00	2.50	1.50
(180)	Don Mincher	5.00	2.50	1.50
(181)	George Mitterwald	5.00	2.50	1.50
(182)	Rick Monday	5.00	2.50	1.50
(183)	Don Money	5.00	2.50	1.50
(184)	Bob Moose	5.00	2.50	1.50
(185)	Dave Morehead	5.00	2.50	1.50
(186)	Joe Morgan	25.00	12.50	7.50
(187)	Bobby Mercer (Murcer)	7.50	3.75	2.25
(188)	Ivan Murrell	5.00	2.50	1.50
(189)	Phil Niekro	20.00	10.00	6.00
(190)	Jim Northrup	5.00	2.50	1.50
(191)	Tony Oliva	15.00	7.50	4.50
(192)	Al Oliver	5.00	2.50	1.50
(193)	Claude Osteen	5.00	2.50	1.50
(194)	Jose Pagan	5.00	2.50	1.50
(195)	Jim Pagliaroni	5.00	2.50	1.50
(196)	Jim Palmer	20.00	10.00	6.00
(197)	Lowell Palmer	5.00	2.50	1.50
(198)	Milt Pappas	5.00	2.50	1.50
(199)	Marty Pattin	5.00	2.50	1.50
(200)	Roberto Pena	5.00	2.50	1.50
(201)	Joe Pepitone	7.50	3.75	2.25
(202)	Tony Perez	25.00	12.50	7.50
(203)	Gaylord Perry	20.00	10.00	6.00
(204)	Jim Perry	5.00	2.50	1.50
(205)	Fritz Peterson	5.00	2.50	1.50
(206)	Rico Petroceli (Petrocelli)	5.00	2.50	1.50
(207)	Lefty Phillips	5.00	2.50	1.50
(208)	Tom Phoebus	5.00	2.50	1.50
(209)	Lou Piniella	7.50	3.75	2.25
(210)	Vada Pinson	7.50	3.75	2.25
(211)	Boog Powell	10.00	5.00	3.00
(212)	Frank Quillici	5.00	2.50	1.50
(213)	Doug Rader	5.00	2.50	1.50
(214)	Ron Reed	5.00	2.50	1.50
(215)	Rich Reese	5.00	2.50	1.50
(216)	Rick Reichardt	5.00	2.50	1.50
(217)	Phil Regan	5.00	2.50	1.50
(218)	Roger Repoz	5.00	2.50	1.50
(219)	Juan Rios	5.00	2.50	1.50
(220)	Brooks Robinson	30.00	15.00	9.00
(221)	Frank Robinson	30.00	15.00	9.00
(222)	Cookie Rojas	5.00	2.50	1.50
(223)	Rich Rollins	5.00	2.50	1.50
(224)	Pete Rose	60.00	30.00	18.00
(225)	Gary Ross	5.00	2.50	1.50
(226)	Joe Rudi	5.00	2.50	1.50
(227)	Manny Sanguillen	5.00	2.50	1.50
(228)	Jose Santiago	5.00	2.50	1.50
(229)	Ron Santo	15.00	7.50	4.50
(230)	Tom Satriano	5.00	2.50	1.50
(231)	Richie Scheinblum	5.00	2.50	1.50
(232)	Red Schoendienst	20.00	10.00	6.00
(233)	George Scott	5.00	2.50	1.50
(234)	Tom Seaver	30.00	15.00	9.00
(235)	Norm Siebern	5.00	2.50	1.50
(236)	Sonny Siebert	5.00	2.50	1.50
(237)	Duke Sims	5.00	2.50	1.50
(238)	Tommie Sisk	5.00	2.50	1.50
(239)	Ted Sizemore	5.00	2.50	1.50
(240)	Mayo Smith	5.00	2.50	1.50
(241)	Reggie Smith	5.00	2.50	1.50
(242)	Willie Smith	5.00	2.50	1.50
(243)	Russ Snyder	5.00	2.50	1.50
(244)	Joe Sparma	5.00	2.50	1.50
(245)	Lee Stange	5.00	2.50	1.50
(246)	Mickey Stanley	5.00	2.50	1.50
(247)	Willie Stargell	25.00	12.50	7.50
(248)	Rusty Staub	7.50	3.75	2.25
(249)	Ron Stone	5.00	2.50	1.50
(250)	Bill Stoneman	5.00	2.50	1.50
(251)	Mel Stottlemyre	5.00	2.50	1.50
(252)	Ed Stroud	5.00	2.50	1.50
(253)	Bill Sudakis	5.00	2.50	1.50
(254)	Gary Sutherland	5.00	2.50	1.50
(255)	Ron Swoboda	5.00	2.50	1.50
(256)	Carl Taylor	5.00	2.50	1.50
(257)	Tony Taylor	5.00	2.50	1.50
(258)	Bob Tillman	5.00	2.50	1.50
(259)	Bobby Tolan	5.00	2.50	1.50
(260)	Cesar Tovar	5.00	2.50	1.50
(261)	Jeff Torborg	5.00	2.50	1.50
(262)	Joe Torre	10.00	5.00	3.00
(263)	Hector Torres	5.00	2.50	1.50
(264)	Tom Tresh	7.50	3.75	2.25
(265)	Ted Uhlaender	5.00	2.50	1.50
(266)	Del Unser	5.00	2.50	1.50
(267)	Bob Veale	5.00	2.50	1.50
(268)	Zoilo Versalles	5.00	2.50	1.50
(269)	Bill Voss	5.00	2.50	1.50
(270)	Pete Ward	5.00	2.50	1.50
(271)	Greg Washburn	5.00	2.50	1.50
(272)	Eddie Watt	5.00	2.50	1.50
(273)	Ramon Webster	5.00	2.50	1.50
(274)	Al Weis	5.00	2.50	1.50
(275)	Roy White	5.00	2.50	1.50
(276)	Billy Williams	25.00	12.50	7.50
(277)	Ted Williams	50.00	25.00	15.00
(278)	Walt Williams	5.00	2.50	1.50
(279)	Billy Wilson	5.00	2.50	1.50
(280)	Don Wilson	5.00	2.50	1.50
(281)	Earl Wilson	5.00	2.50	1.50
(282)	Rick Wise	5.00	2.50	1.50
(283)	Bobby Wine	5.00	2.50	1.50
(284)	Wilbur Wood	5.00	2.50	1.50
(285)	Woody Woodward	5.00	2.50	1.50
(286)	Billy Wynne	5.00	2.50	1.50

1980 Superstar

This collectors' issue, probably produced by Card Collectors Closet in Springfield, Mass., included up to five cards each of the most famous former players. The 2-1/2" x 3-1/2" cards have black-and-white photos on front, with yellow, white and blue graphics. Backs are in black-and-white with career narrative. The set sold originally for $3.50.

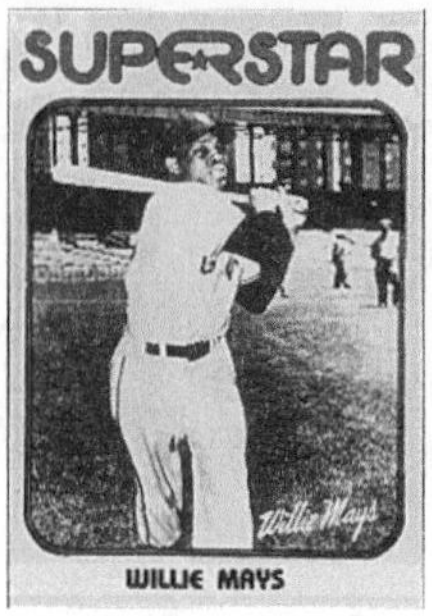

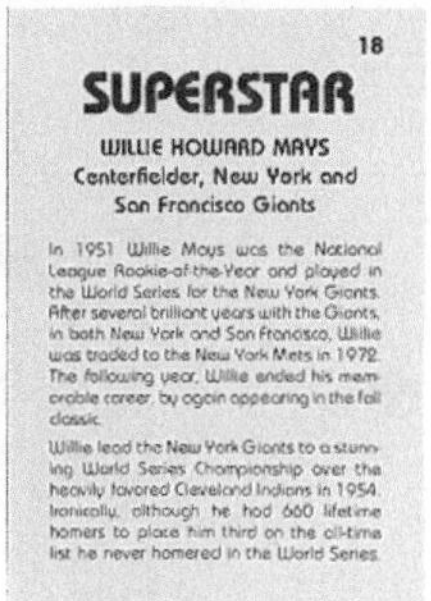

		NM	E	VG
Complete Set (45):		20.00	10.00	6.00
Common Player:		.75	.35	.20
1	Babe Ruth	1.25	.60	.40
2	Roberto Clemente	1.00	.50	.30
3	Roberto Clemente	1.00	.50	.30
4	Roberto Clemente	1.00	.50	.30
5	Lou Gehrig, Joe DiMaggio	.75	.35	.20
6	Mickey Mantle, Roger Maris	1.75	.90	.50
7	Roger Maris, Yogi Berra, Mickey Mantle	1.25	.60	.40
8	Whitey Ford, Sandy Koufax	.75	.35	.20
9	Babe Ruth	1.25	.60	.40
10	Roger Maris, Mickey Mantle	1.75	.90	.50
11	Ted Williams, Stan Musial, Willie Mays	.75	.35	.20
12	Mickey Mantle, Hank Aaron	1.25	.60	.40
13	Sandy Koufax	.75	.35	.20
14	Sandy Koufax	.75	.35	.20
15	Thurman Munson	.75	.35	.20
16	Sandy Koufax	.75	.35	.20
17	Sandy Koufax	.75	.35	.20
18	Willie Mays	.75	.35	.20
19	Willie Mays	.75	.35	.20
20	Willie Mays	.75	.35	.20
21	Willie Mays	.75	.35	.20
22	Ted Williams	.75	.35	.20
23	Ted Williams	.75	.35	.20
24	Ted Williams	.75	.35	.20
25	Ted Williams	.75	.35	.20
26	Lou Gehrig	.75	.35	.20
27	Lou Gehrig	.75	.35	.20
28	Lou Gehrig	.75	.35	.20
29	Lou Gehrig	.75	.35	.20
30	Mickey Mantle	2.00	1.00	.60
31	Mickey Mantle	2.00	1.00	.60
32	Mickey Mantle	2.00	1.00	.60
33	Mickey Mantle	2.00	1.00	.60
34	Hank Aaron	.75	.35	.20
35	Joe DiMaggio	.75	.35	.20
36	Joe DiMaggio	.75	.35	.20
37	Joe DiMaggio	.75	.35	.20
38	Joe DiMaggio	.75	.35	.20
39	Roberto Clemente	1.00	.50	.30
40	Babe Ruth	1.25	.60	.40
41	Babe Ruth	1.25	.60	.40
42	Babe Ruth	1.25	.60	.40
43	Hank Aaron	.75	.35	.20
44	Hank Aaron	.75	.35	.20
45	Hank Aaron	.75	.35	.20

1970 Super Valu Minnesota Twins

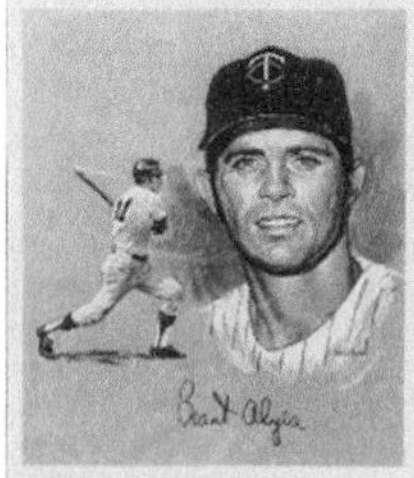

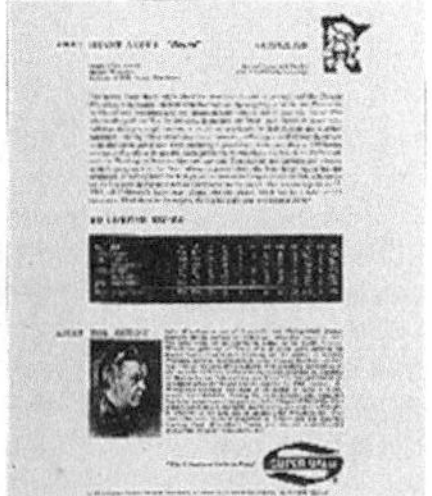

One of many Minnesota Twins regional issues from the team's first decade, this set of player portraits was painted by noted celebrity artist John Wheeldon. Individual player pictures were given away at Super Valu grocery stores. The premiums feature large portraits and smaller action pictures, painted in pastels, against a pastel background. A facsimile autograph is printed below the pictures and the player's name is printed in the bottom border. At 7-3/4" x 9-3/8", the Twins portraits are somewhat smaller than similar contemporary issues. Backs are printed in black-and-white and include a self-portrait and biography of the artist. Player information includes biographical bits, a lengthy career summary and complete major and minor league stats. Team and sponsor logo are also included on the unnumbered card backs. The set is checklisted here alphabetically.

	NM	E	VG
Complete Set (12):	90.00	45.00	27.50
Common Player:	6.00	3.00	1.75
(1) Brant Alyea	6.00	3.00	1.75
(2) Leo Cardenas	6.00	3.00	1.75
(3) Rod Carew	30.00	10.00	6.00
(4) Jim Kaat	9.00	4.50	2.75
(5) Harmon Killebrew	30.00	10.00	6.00
(6) George Mitterwald	6.00	3.00	1.75
(7) Tony Oliva	10.00	4.50	2.75
(8) Ron Perranoski	6.00	3.00	1.75
(9) Jim Perry	6.00	3.00	1.75
(10) Rich Reese	6.00	3.00	1.75
(11) Luis Tiant	7.50	3.75	2.25
(12) Cesar Tovar	6.00	3.00	1.75

1874 Suppards & Fennemore Cabinets

Only members of the hometown 1874 Athletics (National Association) have been reported in this issue of cabinet cards from the Philadelphia studio. The 4-1/4" x 6-1/2" cards have full-length poses on front. Backs carry an ornate ad for the photographer. The players are not identified on the cards, unless an earlier owner has written the name. Thus far the team's most famous player, Cap Anson, has not been reported.

	NM	E	VG
Common Player:	3,750	1,875	1,125
(1) Joe Battin (Bat on shoulder.)	3,750	1,875	1,125
(2) John Clapp (Cap on floor to his right.)	3,750	1,875	1,125
(3) Wes Fisler (Bat at right side, no cap on floor.)	3,750	1,875	1,125
(4) Dick McBride (Ball in hands at waist.)	3,750	1,875	1,125
(5) Mike McGeary (Bat in crook of arm.)	3,750	1,875	1,125
(6) John McMullin (Bat at his left, cap on floor at left.)	3,750	1,875	1,125
(7) Tim Murnane (Bat at his right, cap on floor at left.)	4,050	2,025	1,200

1966 Swap-N-Save Album

While this 4" x 9" album pictures 1965 and 1966 Topps cards in full color on front and back, it is not connected with Topps. The album's interior pages feature die-cuts which allow the central panel to be removed so both front and back of each card can be viewed. Informational pages include team rosters.

	NM	E	VG
Album:	80.00	40.00	20.00

1909-11 Sweet Caporal

Among the most common of the American Tobacco Co. brands advertising on the backs of 1909-11 T206 and 1911 T205 is Sweet Caporal. T206s can be found with factory designations of No. 25, No. 30, No. 42 (overprinted), No. 649 and No. 649 (overprinted). In T205, Sweet Cap backs can be found printed in red (no factory number, or No. 42) or black, No. 25, No. 42.

(See T205, T206.)

1909-12 Sweet Caporal Domino Discs (PX7)

Domino Discs, distributed by Sweet Caporal Cigarettes from 1909 to 1912, are among the more obscure 20th Century tobacco issues. Although the disc set contains many of the same players - some even pictured in the same poses - as the later Sweet Caporal pin set, the discs have always

lagged behind the pins in collector appeal. The Domino Discs, so called because each disc has a large, white domino printed on the back, measure approximately 1-1/8" in diameter and are made of thin cardboard surrounded by a metal rim. The fronts of the discs contain a player portrait against a background of either red, green or blue. The words "Sweet Caporal Cigarettes" appear on the front along with the player's last name and team. There are 129 different major leaguers featured in the set. Each player can be found with two picture variations involving uniform or cap details, or just the size of the portrait. Also known to exist as part of the set is a disc which pictures a generic player and contains the words "Home Team" against a red background on one side and "Visiting Team" with a green background on the reverse. Because each of the players can theoretically be found in two pictures, with three different background colors and with varying numbers of dots on the dominoes, there is almost an impossible number of variations available. Collectors, however, generally collect the discs without regard to background color or domino arrangement. The Domino Disc set was assigned the designation PX7 in the American Card Catalog.

	NM	E	VG
Complete Set (129):	13,500	6,750	4,100
Common Player:	80.00	40.00	25.00
(1) Red Ames	80.00	40.00	25.00
(2) Jimmy Archer	80.00	40.00	25.00
(3) Jimmy Austin	80.00	40.00	25.00
(4) Home Run Baker	175.00	85.00	60.00
(5) Neal Ball	80.00	40.00	25.00
(6) Cy Barger	80.00	40.00	25.00
(7) Jack Barry	80.00	40.00	25.00
(8) Johnny Bates	80.00	40.00	25.00
(9) Beals Becker	80.00	40.00	25.00
(10) George Bell	80.00	40.00	25.00
(11) Chief Bender	175.00	85.00	60.00
(12) Bill Bergen	80.00	40.00	25.00
(13) Bob Bescher	80.00	40.00	25.00
(14) Joe Birmingham	80.00	40.00	25.00
(15) Roger Bresnahan	175.00	85.00	60.00
(16) Al Bridwell	80.00	40.00	25.00
(17) Mordecai Brown	175.00	85.00	60.00
(18) Bobby Byrne	80.00	40.00	25.00
(19) Nixey Callahan	80.00	40.00	25.00
(20) Howie Camnitz	80.00	40.00	25.00
(21) Bill Carrigan	80.00	40.00	25.00
(22) Frank Chance	175.00	85.00	60.00
(23) Hal Chase	80.00	40.00	25.00
(24) Ed Cicotte	80.00	40.00	25.00
(25) Fred Clarke	170.00	85.00	60.00
(26a) Ty Cobb ("D" on cap.)	800.00	400.00	250.00
(26b) Ty Cobb (No "D" on cap.)	800.00	400.00	250.00
(27) Eddie Collins	175.00	85.00	60.00
(28) Doc Crandall	80.00	40.00	25.00
(29) Birdie Cree	80.00	40.00	25.00
(30) Bill Dahlen	80.00	40.00	25.00
(31) Jim Delahanty	80.00	40.00	25.00
(32) Art Devlin	80.00	40.00	25.00
(33) Josh Devore	80.00	40.00	25.00
(34) Red Dooin	80.00	40.00	25.00
(35) Mickey Doolan	80.00	40.00	25.00
(36) Patsy Dougherty	80.00	40.00	25.00
(37) Tom Downey	80.00	40.00	25.00
(38) Larry Doyle	80.00	40.00	25.00
(39) Louis Drucke	80.00	40.00	25.00
(40) Clyde Engle	80.00	40.00	25.00
(41) Tex Erwin	80.00	40.00	25.00
(42) Steve Evans	80.00	40.00	25.00
(43) Johnny Evers	175.00	85.00	60.00
(44) Cecil Ferguson	80.00	40.00	25.00
(45) Russ Ford	80.00	40.00	25.00
(46) Art Fromme	80.00	40.00	25.00
(47) Harry Gaspar	80.00	40.00	25.00
(48) George Gibson	80.00	40.00	25.00
(49) Eddie Grant	90.00	45.00	25.00
(50) Clark Griffith	175.00	85.00	60.00
(51) Bob Groom	80.00	40.00	25.00
(52) Bob Harmon	80.00	40.00	25.00
(53) Topsy Hartsel	80.00	40.00	25.00
(54) Arnold Hauser	80.00	40.00	25.00
(55) Dick Hoblitzell	80.00	40.00	25.00
(56) Danny Hoffman	80.00	40.00	25.00
(57) Miller Huggins	175.00	85.00	60.00
(58) John Hummel	80.00	40.00	25.00
(59) Hugh Jennings	175.00	85.00	60.00

(60) Walter Johnson	475.00	240.00	160.00
(61) Ed Karger	80.00	40.00	25.00
(62a) Jack Knight (Yankees)	80.00	40.00	25.00
(62b) Jack Knight (Senators)	80.00	40.00	25.00
(63) Ed Konetchy	80.00	40.00	25.00
(64) Harry Krause	80.00	40.00	25.00
(65) Frank LaPorte	80.00	40.00	25.00
(66) Nap Lajoie	175.00	85.00	60.00
(67) Tommy Leach	80.00	40.00	25.00
(68) Sam Leever	80.00	40.00	25.00
(69) Lefty Leifield	80.00	40.00	25.00
(70) Paddy Livingston	80.00	40.00	25.00
(71) Hans Lobert	80.00	40.00	25.00
(72) Harry Lord	80.00	40.00	25.00
(73) Nick Maddox	80.00	40.00	25.00
(74) Sherry Magee	80.00	40.00	25.00
(75) Rube Marquard	175.00	85.00	60.00
(76) Christy Mathewson	550.00	275.00	185.00
(77) Al Mattern	80.00	40.00	25.00
(78) George McBride	80.00	40.00	25.00
(79) John McGraw	175.00	85.00	60.00
(80) Harry McIntire	80.00	40.00	25.00
(81) Matty McIntyre	80.00	40.00	25.00
(82) Larry McLean	80.00	40.00	25.00
(83) Fred Merkle	80.00	40.00	25.00
(84) Chief Meyers	80.00	40.00	25.00
(85) Clyde Milan	80.00	40.00	25.00
(86) Dots Miller	80.00	40.00	25.00
(87) Mike Mitchell	80.00	40.00	25.00
(88a) Pat Moran (Cubs)	80.00	40.00	25.00
(88b) Pat Moran (Phillies)	80.00	40.00	25.00
(89) George Mullen (Mullin)	80.00	40.00	25.00
(90) Danny Murphy	80.00	40.00	25.00
(91) Red Murray	80.00	40.00	25.00
(92) Tom Needham	80.00	40.00	25.00
(93) Rebel Oakes	80.00	40.00	25.00
(94) Rube Oldring	80.00	40.00	25.00
(95) Fred Parent	80.00	40.00	25.00
(96) Dode Paskert	80.00	40.00	25.00
(97) Barney Pelty	80.00	40.00	25.00
(98) Eddie Phelps	80.00	40.00	25.00
(99) Deacon Phillippe	80.00	40.00	25.00
(100) Jack Quinn	80.00	40.00	25.00
(101) Ed Reulbach	80.00	40.00	25.00
(102) Lew Richie	80.00	40.00	25.00
(103) Jack Rowan	80.00	40.00	25.00
(104) Nap Rucker	80.00	40.00	25.00
(105a) Doc Scanlon (Scanlan) (Superbas)	80.00	40.00	25.00
(105b) Doc Scanlon (Scanlan) (Phillies)	80.00	40.00	25.00
(106) Germany Schaefer	80.00	40.00	25.00
(107) Boss Schmidt	80.00	40.00	25.00
(108) Wildfire Schulte	80.00	40.00	25.00
(109) Jimmy Sheckard	80.00	40.00	25.00
(110) Hap Smith	80.00	40.00	25.00
(111) Tris Speaker	200.00	100.00	60.00
(112) Harry Stovall	80.00	40.00	25.00
(113a) Gabby Street (Senators)	80.00	40.00	25.00
(113b) Gabby Street (Yankees)	80.00	40.00	25.00
(114) George Suggs	80.00	40.00	25.00
(115) Ira Thomas	80.00	40.00	25.00
(116) Joe Tinker	175.00	85.00	60.00
(117) John Titus	80.00	40.00	25.00
(118) Terry Turner	85.00	40.00	25.00
(119) Heinie Wagner	80.00	40.00	25.00
(120) Bobby Wallace	175.00	85.00	60.00
(121) Ed Walsh	175.00	85.00	60.00
(122) Jack Warhop	80.00	40.00	25.00
(123) Zach Wheat	175.00	85.00	60.00
(124) Doc White	80.00	40.00	25.00
(125a) Art Wilson (Dark cap, Pirates.)	80.00	40.00	25.00
(125b) Art Wilson (Dark cap, Giants.)	85.00	40.00	25.00
(126a) Owen Wilson (White cap, Giants.)	85.00	40.00	25.00
(126b) Owen Wilson (White cap, Pirates.)	80.00	40.00	25.00
(127) Hooks Wiltse	80.00	40.00	25.00
(128) Harry Wolter	80.00	40.00	25.00
(129) Cy Young	550.00	275.00	165.00

1910-12 Sweet Caporal Pins (P2)

Expanding its premiums to include more than just trading cards, the American Tobacco Co. issued a series of baseball pins circa 1910-12. The sepia-colored pins measure 7/8" in diameter. The set includes 152 different players, but because of numerous "large letter" and "small letter" variations, collectors generally consider the set complete at 205 different pins. Fifty of the players are pictured on a second pin that usually displays the same photo but has the player's name and team designation printed in larger letters. Three players (Bresnahan, Mullin and Wallace) have three pins each. It is now generally accepted that there are 153 pins with "small letters" and another 52 "large letter" variations in a complete set. Research among advanced collectors has shown that 19 of the pins, including six of the "large letter" variations, are considered more difficult to find. The back of each pin has a variously colored paper insert advertising Sweet Caporal Cigarettes. The red backings are generally less common. The Sweet Caporal pins are closely related to the popular T205 Gold Border tobacco cards, also issued by the American Tobacco Co. about the same time. All but nine of the players featured in the pin set were also pictured on T205 cards, and in nearly all cases the photos are identical. The Sweet Caporal pins are designated as P2 in the American Card Catalog. The complete set price includes all variations.

		NM	E	VG
Complete Set (204):		10,000	5,000	3,000
Common Player:		40.00	20.00	12.00
(1)	Ed Abbaticchio	40.00	20.00	12.00
(2)	Red Ames	40.00	20.00	12.00
(3a)	Jimmy Archer (Small letters.)	40.00	20.00	12.00
(3b)	Jimmy Archer (Large letters.)	45.00	17.50	10.00
(4a)	Jimmy Austin (Small letters.)	40.00	20.00	12.00
(4b)	Jimmy Austin (Large letters.)	45.00	17.50	10.00
(5)	Home Run Baker	90.00	45.00	27.00
(6)	Neal Ball	40.00	20.00	12.00
(7)	Cy Barger	40.00	20.00	12.00
(8)	Jack Barry	40.00	20.00	12.00
(9)	Johnny Bates	40.00	20.00	12.00
(10)	Beals Becker	40.00	20.00	12.00
(11)	Fred Beebe	40.00	20.00	12.00
(12a)	George Bell (Small letters.)	40.00	20.00	12.00
(12b)	George Bell (Large letters.)	45.00	17.50	10.00
(13a)	"Chief" Bender (Small letters.)	90.00	45.00	27.00
(13b)	"Chief" Bender (Large letters.)	100.00	50.00	30.00
(14)	Bill Bergen	40.00	20.00	12.00
(15)	Bob Bescher	40.00	20.00	12.00
(16)	Joe Birmingham	40.00	20.00	12.00
(17)	Kitty Bransfield	65.00	32.50	20.00
(18a)	Roger Bresnahan (Mouth closed, small letters.)	125.00	65.00	37.00
(18b)	Roger Bresnahan (Mouth closed, large letters.)	100.00	50.00	30.00
(19)	Roger Bresnahan (Mouth open.)	90.00	45.00	27.00
(20)	Al Bridwell	40.00	20.00	12.00
(21a)	Mordecai Brown (Small letters.)	90.00	45.00	27.00
(21b)	Mordecai Brown (Large letters.)	100.00	50.00	30.00
(22)	Bobby Byrne	40.00	20.00	12.00
(23)	Nixey Callahan	40.00	20.00	12.00
(24a)	Howie Camnitz (Small letters.)	40.00	20.00	12.00
(24b)	Howie Camnitz (Large letters.)	45.00	17.50	10.00
(25a)	Bill Carrigan (Small letters.)	40.00	20.00	12.00
(25b)	Bill Carrigan (Large letters.)	45.00	17.50	10.00
(26a)	Frank Chance (Small letters.)	90.00	45.00	27.00
(26b)	Frank Chance (Large letters.)	100.00	50.00	30.00
(27)	Hal Chase (Small letters.)	50.00	25.00	15.00
(28)	Hal Chase (Large letters.)	125.00	65.00	39.00
(29)	Ed Cicotte	125.00	65.00	39.00
(30a)	Fred Clarke (Small letters.)	90.00	45.00	27.00
(30b)	Fred Clarke (Large letters.)	100.00	50.00	30.00
(31a)	Ty Cobb (Small letters, "D" on cap.)	600.00	300.00	180.00
(31b)	Ty Cobb (Large letters, no "D" on cap.)	675.00	335.00	200.00
(32a)	Eddie Collins (Small letters.)	90.00	45.00	27.00
(32b)	Eddie Collins (Large letters.)	100.00	50.00	30.00
(33)	Doc Crandall	40.00	20.00	12.00

(34)	Birdie Cree	65.00	32.50	20.00
(35)	Bill Dahlen	40.00	20.00	12.00
(36)	Jim Delahanty	40.00	20.00	12.00
(37)	Art Devlin	40.00	20.00	12.00
(38)	Josh Devore	40.00	20.00	12.00
(39)	Wild Bill Donovan	65.00	32.50	20.00
(40a)	Red Dooin (Small letters)	40.00	20.00	12.00
(40b)	Red Dooin (Large letters)	45.00	17.50	10.00
(41a)	Mickey Doolan (Small letters.)	40.00	20.00	12.00
(41b)	Mickey Doolan (Large letters.)	45.00	17.50	10.00
(42)	Patsy Dougherty	40.00	20.00	12.00
(43a)	Tom Downey (Small letters.)	40.00	20.00	12.00
(43b)	Tom Downey (Large letters.)	45.00	17.50	10.00
(44a)	Larry Doyle (Small letters.)	40.00	20.00	12.00
(44b)	Larry Doyle (Large letters.)	45.00	17.50	10.00
(45)	Louis Drucke	40.00	20.00	12.00
(46a)	Hugh Duffy (Small letters.)	90.00	45.00	27.00
(46b)	Hugh Duffy (Large letters.)	100.00	50.00	30.00
(47)	Jimmy Dygert	40.00	20.00	12.00
(48a)	Kid Elberfeld (Small letters.)	40.00	20.00	12.00
(48b)	Kid Elberfeld (Large letters.)	45.00	17.50	10.00
(49a)	Clyde Engle (Small letters.)	40.00	20.00	12.00
(49b)	Clyde Engle (Large letters.)	45.00	17.50	10.00
(50)	Tex Erwin	40.00	20.00	12.00
(51)	Steve Evans	40.00	20.00	12.00
(52)	Johnny Evers	100.00	60.00	36.00
(53)	Cecil Ferguson	40.00	20.00	12.00
(54)	John Flynn	40.00	20.00	12.00
(55a)	Russ Ford (Small letters)	40.00	20.00	12.00
(55b)	Russ Ford (Large letters)	45.00	17.50	10.00
(56)	Art Fromme	40.00	20.00	12.00
(57)	Harry Gaspar	40.00	20.00	12.00
(58a)	George Gibson (Small letters.)	40.00	20.00	12.00
(58b)	George Gibson (Large letters.)	45.00	17.50	10.00
(59)	Eddie Grant	65.00	32.50	20.00
(60)	Dolly Gray	40.00	20.00	12.00
(61a)	Clark Griffith (Small letters.)	90.00	45.00	27.00
(61b)	Clark Griffith (Large letters.)	100.00	50.00	30.00
(62)	Bob Groom	40.00	20.00	12.00
(63)	Bob Harmon	40.00	20.00	12.00
(64)	Topsy Hartsel	40.00	20.00	12.00
(65)	Arnold Hauser	65.00	32.50	20.00
(66)	Ira Hemphill	40.00	20.00	12.00
(67a)	Buck Herzog (Small letters.)	40.00	20.00	12.00
(67b)	Buck Herzog (Large letters.)	45.00	17.50	10.00
(68)	Dick Hoblitzell	40.00	20.00	12.00
(69)	Danny Hoffman	40.00	20.00	12.00
(70)	Harry Hooper	90.00	45.00	27.00
(71a)	Miller Huggins (Small letters.)	90.00	45.00	27.00
(71b)	Miller Huggins (Large letters.)	100.00	50.00	30.00
(72)	John Hummel	40.00	20.00	12.00
(73)	Hugh Jennings (Small letters.)	90.00	45.00	27.00
(74)	Hugh Jennings (Large letters.)	100.00	50.00	30.00
(75a)	Walter Johnson (Small letters.)	200.00	100.00	60.00
(75b)	Walter Johnson (Large letters.)	275.00	135.00	85.00
(76)	Tom Jones	65.00	32.50	20.00
(77)	Ed Karger	40.00	20.00	12.00
(78)	Ed Killian	65.00	32.50	20.00
(79a)	Jack Knight (Small letters.)	40.00	20.00	12.00
(79b)	Jack Knight (Large letters.)	45.00	17.50	10.00
(80)	Ed Konetchy	40.00	20.00	12.00
(81)	Harry Krause	40.00	20.00	12.00
(82)	Rube Kroh	40.00	20.00	12.00
(83)	Nap Lajoie	90.00	45.00	27.00
(84a)	Frank LaPorte (Small letters.)	40.00	20.00	12.00
(84b)	Frank LaPorte (Large letters.)	45.00	17.50	10.00
(85)	Arlie Latham	40.00	20.00	12.00
(86a)	Tommy Leach (Small letters.)	40.00	20.00	12.00

(86b)	Tommy Leach (Large letters.)	45.00	17.50	10.00
(87)	Sam Leever	40.00	20.00	12.00
(88)	Lefty Leifield	40.00	20.00	12.00
(89)	Hans Lobert	40.00	20.00	12.00
(90a)	Harry Lord (Small letters.)	40.00	20.00	12.00
(90b)	Harry Lord (Large letters.)	45.00	17.50	10.00
(91)	Paddy Livingston	40.00	20.00	12.00
(92)	Nick Maddox	40.00	20.00	12.00
(93)	Sherry Magee	40.00	20.00	12.00
(94)	Rube Marquard	90.00	45.00	27.00
(95a)	Christy Mathewson (Small letters.)	225.00	110.00	65.00
(95b)	Christy Mathewson (Large letters.)	275.00	135.00	80.00
(96a)	Al Mattern (Small letters.)	40.00	20.00	12.00
(96b)	Al Mattern (Large letters.)	45.00	17.50	10.00
(97)	George McBride	40.00	20.00	12.00
(98a)	John McGraw (Small letters.)	90.00	45.00	27.00
(98b)	John McGraw (Large letters.)	100.00	50.00	30.00
(99)	Harry McIntire (Cubs)	40.00	20.00	12.00
(100a)	Matty McIntyre (White Sox, small letters.)	40.00	20.00	12.00
(100b)	Matty McIntyre (White Sox, large letters.)	45.00	17.50	10.00
(101a)	John McLean (Small letters.)	40.00	20.00	12.00
(101b)	John McLean (Large letters.)	45.00	17.50	10.00
(102)	Fred Merkle	40.00	20.00	12.00
(103)	Chief Meyers	40.00	20.00	12.00
(104)	Clyde Milan	40.00	20.00	12.00
(105)	Dots Miller	40.00	20.00	12.00
(106)	Mike Mitchell	40.00	20.00	12.00
(107)	Pat Moran	40.00	20.00	12.00
(108a)	George Mullen (Mullin) (Small letters.)	40.00	20.00	12.00
(108b)	George Mullin (Large letters, white cap.)	90.00	45.00	27.00
(109)	Danny Murphy	40.00	20.00	12.00
(110a)	Red Murray (Small letters.)	45.00	17.50	10.00
(110b)	Red Murray (Large letters.)	40.00	20.00	12.00
(111)	Tom Needham	65.00	32.50	20.00
(112a)	Rebel Oakes (Small letters.)	40.00	20.00	12.00
(112b)	Rebel Oakes (Large letters.)	45.00	17.50	10.00
(113)	Rube Oldring	40.00	20.00	12.00
(114)	Charley O'Leary	40.00	20.00	12.00
(115)	Orval Overall	65.00	32.50	20.00
(116)	Fred Parent	40.00	20.00	12.00
(117a)	Dode Paskert (Small letters.)	40.00	20.00	12.00
(117b)	Dode Paskert (Large letters.)	45.00	17.50	10.00
(118)	Barney Pelty	40.00	20.00	12.00
(119)	Jake Pfeister	40.00	20.00	12.00
(120)	Eddie Phelps	40.00	20.00	12.00
(121)	Deacon Phillippe	40.00	20.00	12.00
(122)	Jack Quinn	40.00	20.00	12.00
(123)	Ed Reulbach	40.00	20.00	12.00
(124)	Lew Richie	40.00	20.00	12.00
(125)	Jack Rowan	40.00	20.00	12.00
(126a)	Nap Rucker (Small letters.)	40.00	20.00	12.00
(126b)	Nap Rucker (Large letters.)	45.00	17.50	10.00
(127)	Doc Scanlon (Scanlan)	65.00	32.50	20.00
(128)	Germany Schaefer	40.00	20.00	12.00
(129)	Jimmy Scheckard (Sheckard)	40.00	20.00	12.00
(130a)	Boss Schmidt (Small letters.)	40.00	20.00	12.00
(130b)	Boss Schmidt (Large letters.)	45.00	17.50	10.00
(131)	Wildfire Schulte	40.00	20.00	12.00
(132)	Hap Smith	40.00	20.00	12.00
(133a)	Tris Speaker (Small letters.)	150.00	75.00	45.00
(133b)	Tris Speaker (Large letters.)	175.00	85.00	50.00
(134)	Oscar Stanage	40.00	20.00	12.00
(135)	Harry Steinfeldt	40.00	20.00	12.00
(136)	George Stone	40.00	20.00	12.00
(137a)	George Stoval (Stovall) (Small letters.))	40.00	20.00	12.00
(137b)	George Stoval (Stovall) (Large letters.)	45.00	17.50	10.00
(138a)	Gabby Street (Small letters.)	40.00	20.00	12.00
(138b)	Gabby Street (Large letters.)	45.00	17.50	10.00
(139)	George Suggs	40.00	20.00	12.00

		NM	E	VG
(140a)	Ira Thomas (Small letters.)	40.00	20.00	12.00
(140b)	Ira Thomas (Large letters.)	45.00	17.50	10.00
(141a)	Joe Tinker (Small letters.)	90.00	45.00	27.00
(141b)	Joe Tinker (Large letters.)	100.00	50.00	30.00
(142a)	John Titus (Small letters.)	40.00	20.00	12.00
(142b)	John Titus (Large letters.)	45.00	17.50	10.00
(143)	Terry Turner	40.00	20.00	12.00
(144)	Heinie Wagner	40.00	20.00	12.00
(145a)	Bobby Wallace (With cap, small letters.)	90.00	45.00	27.00
(145b)	Bobby Wallace (With cap, large letters.)	100.00	50.00	30.00
(146)	Bobby Wallace (Without cap.)	90.00	45.00	27.00
(147)	Ed Walsh	90.00	45.00	27.00
(148)	Jack Warhop	40.00	20.00	12.00
(149a)	Zach Wheat (Small letters.)	90.00	45.00	27.00
(149b)	Zach Wheat (Large letters.)	100.00	50.00	30.00
(150)	Doc White	40.00	20.00	12.00
(151)	Art Wilson (Giants)	40.00	20.00	12.00
(152)	Owen Wilson (Pirates)	40.00	20.00	12.00
(153)	Hooks Wiltse	40.00	20.00	12.00
(154)	Harry Wolter	40.00	20.00	12.00
(155a)	"Cy" Young ("C" on cap.)	200.00	100.00	60.00
(155b)	Old Cy Young (Plain cap.)	225.00	110.00	65.00

1928 Sweetman

(27) TY COBB

This set consists of 60 of the most prominent Baseball players in the big Leagues. We have made up an album which will hold the complete set. On receipt of 15 cents in stamps we will send an album to any address in the United States.

Manufactured only by the
SWEETMAN CO. INC.
1611 Cass Ave.   St. Louis, Mo.

The cards of this St. Louis firm share the format - about 1-3/8" x 2-1/2", black-and-white with card number in parentheses to the left of player name on front - and checklist with the 1928 York Caramels Type 2 issue, but are less frequently encountered. Backs of the Sweetman cards offer an album for 15 cents in stamps. The type of business in which Sweetman Co., Inc., was engaged is unknown.

		NM	E	VG
Complete Set (60):		25,000	12,500	7,500
Common Player:		250.00	125.00	75.00
1	Burleigh Grimes	400.00	200.00	120.00
2	Walter Reuther (Ruether)	250.00	125.00	75.00
3	Joe Dugan	250.00	125.00	75.00
4	Red Faber	400.00	200.00	120.00
5	Gabby Hartnett	400.00	200.00	120.00
6	Babe Ruth	6,000	3,000	1,800
7	Bob Meusel	250.00	125.00	75.00
8	Herb Pennock	400.00	200.00	120.00
9	George Burns	250.00	125.00	75.00
10	Joe Sewell	400.00	200.00	120.00
11	George Uhle	250.00	125.00	75.00
12	Bob O'Farrell	250.00	125.00	75.00
13	Rogers Hornsby	500.00	250.00	150.00
14	"Pie" Traynor	400.00	200.00	120.00
15	Clarence Mitchell	250.00	125.00	75.00
16	Eppa Jepha Rixey	400.00	200.00	120.00
17	Carl Mays	300.00	150.00	90.00
18	Adolfo Luque	250.00	125.00	75.00
19	Dave Bancroft	400.00	200.00	120.00
20	George Kelly	400.00	200.00	120.00
21	Earl (Earle) Combs	400.00	200.00	120.00
22	Harry Heilmann	400.00	200.00	120.00
23	Ray W. Schalk	400.00	200.00	120.00
24	Johnny Mostil	250.00	125.00	75.00
25	Hack Wilson	400.00	200.00	120.00
26	Lou Gehrig	4,000	2,000	1,200
27	Ty Cobb	4,000	2,000	1,200
28	Tris Speaker	500.00	250.00	150.00
29	Tony Lazzeri	400.00	200.00	120.00
30	Waite Hoyt	400.00	200.00	120.00
31	Sherwood Smith	250.00	125.00	75.00
32	Max Carey	400.00	200.00	120.00
33	Eugene Hargrave	250.00	125.00	75.00
34	Miguel L. Gonzales (Miguel A. Gonzalez)	250.00	125.00	75.00
35	Joe Judge	250.00	125.00	75.00
36	E.C. (Sam) Rice	400.00	200.00	120.00
37	Earl Sheely	250.00	125.00	75.00
38	Sam Jones	250.00	125.00	75.00
39	Bib (Bibb) A. Falk	250.00	125.00	75.00
40	Willie Kamm	250.00	125.00	75.00
41	Stanley Harris	400.00	200.00	120.00
42	John J. McGraw	400.00	200.00	120.00
43	Artie Nehf	250.00	125.00	75.00
44	Grover Alexander	500.00	250.00	150.00
45	Paul Waner	400.00	200.00	120.00
46	William H. Terry	400.00	200.00	120.00
47	Glenn Wright	250.00	125.00	75.00
48	Earl Smith	250.00	125.00	75.00
49	Leon (Goose) Goslin	400.00	200.00	120.00
50	Frank Frisch	400.00	200.00	120.00
51	Joe Harris	250.00	125.00	75.00
52	Fred (Cy) Williams	250.00	125.00	75.00
53	Eddie Roush	400.00	200.00	120.00
54	George Sisler	400.00	200.00	120.00
55	Ed. Rommel	250.00	125.00	75.00
56	Rogers Peckinpaugh (Roger)	250.00	125.00	75.00
57	Stanley Coveleskie (Coveleski)	400.00	200.00	120.00
58	Lester Bell	250.00	125.00	75.00
59	Clyde Barnhart	250.00	125.00	75.00
60	John P. McInnis	250.00	125.00	75.00

1948 Swell Babe Ruth Story

No. 1
"THE BABE RUTH STORY"
IN THE MAKING

Babe Ruth gives William Bendix some fine pointers in the art of hitting home runs.

Bendix enacts the part of the Bambino in the film's glorification of Ruth's dramatic life, an Allied Artists picture produced by Roy Del Ruth.

As bat boy for the Yankees Ruth was Bendix's idol years ago. Little did he think that more than 20 years later he would be selected to play the Sultan of Swat in the motion picture "The Babe Ruth Story".

Send on 5 Swell Bubble Gum wrappers and 5¢ for a large autographed picture of William Bendix, starring as Babe Ruth.

SWELL BUBBLE GUM
Philadelphia Chewing Gum Corporation
Havertown, Pa.

The Philadelphia Gum Co., in 1948, created a card set about the movie "The Babe Ruth Story," which starred William Bendix and Claire Trevor. The set, whose American Card Catalog designation is R421, contains 28 black and white, numbered cards which measure 2" x 2-1/2". The Babe Ruth Story set was originally intended to consist of sixteen cards. Twelve additional cards (#'s 17-28) were added when Ruth died before the release of the film. The card backs include an offer for an autographed photo of William Bendix, starring as the Babe, for five Swell Bubble Gum wrappers and five cents.

		NM	E	VG
Complete Set (28):		2,750	1,100	550.00
Common Card (1-16):		45.00	20.00	10.00
Common Card (17-28):		125.00	55.00	30.00
1	"The Babe Ruth Story" in the Making	150.00	65.00	35.00
2	Batboy Becomes the Babe(William Bendix)	45.00	20.00	10.00
3	Claire Hodgson(Claire Trevor)	45.00	20.00	10.00
4	Babe Ruth and Claire Hodgson	45.00	20.00	10.00
5	Brother Mathias(Charles Bickford)	45.00	20.00	10.00
6	Phil Conrad(Sam Levene)	45.00	20.00	10.00
7	Nightclub Singer(Gertrude Niesen)	45.00	20.00	10.00
8	Baseball's Famous Deal, Jack Dunn(William Frawley)	45.00	20.00	10.00
9	Mr. and Mrs. Babe Ruth	45.00	20.00	10.00
10	Mathias	45.00	20.00	10.00
11	Babe Ruth and Miller Huggins(Fred Lightner)	45.00	20.00	10.00
12	Babe at Bed of Ill Boy Johnny Sylvester(Gregory Marshall)	45.00	20.00	10.00
13	Sylvester Family Listening to Game	45.00	20.00	10.00
14	"When a Feller Needs a Friend" (With dog at police station)	45.00	20.00	10.00
15	Dramatic Home Run	45.00	20.00	10.00
16	The Homer That Set the Record - #60 (#60)	75.00	34.00	18.50
17	Career"	125.00	55.00	30.00
18	The Babe Plays Santa Claus	125.00	55.00	30.00
19	Meeting of Owner and Manager	125.00	55.00	30.00
20	"Broken Window Paid Off"	125.00	55.00	30.00
21	Babe in a Crowd of Autograph Collectors	200.00	90.00	50.00
22	Charley Grimm, William Bendix	125.00	55.00	30.00
23	Ted Lyons, William Bendix	125.00	55.00	30.00
24	Lefty Gomez, William Bendix, Bucky Harris	150.00	65.00	35.00
25	Babe Ruth, William Bendix	400.00	180.00	100.00
26	Babe Ruth, William Bendix	400.00	180.00	100.00
27	Babe Ruth, Claire Trevor	400.00	180.00	100.00
28	William Bendix, Babe Ruth, Claire Trevor	400.00	180.00	100.00

1948 Swell Sport Thrills

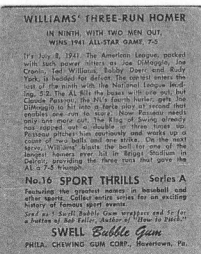

This is a set of black-and-white cards which depicts memorable events in baseball history. The cards measure 2-1/2" x 3" and have a picture frame border and event title on the card fronts. The card backs describe the event in detail. Twenty cards were produced in this set by the Swell Gum Co. of Philadelphia. Each card is numbered, and card numbers 9, 11, 16 and 20 are considered more difficult to obtain.

		NM	E	VG
Complete Set (20):		2,400	1,200	720.00
Common Player:		50.00	25.00	15.00
1	Greatest Single Inning(Mickey Cochrane, Jimmy (Jimmie) Foxx, George Haas, Bing Miller, Al Simmons)	140.00	70.00	45.00
2	Amazing Record(Pete Reiser)	50.00	25.00	15.00
3	Dramatic Debut(Jackie Robinson)	280.00	140.00	85.00
4	Greatest Pitcher(Walter Johnson)	120.00	60.00	35.00
5	Three Strikes Not Out!(Tommy Henrich, Mickey Owen)	50.00	25.00	15.00
6	Home Run Wins Series(Bill Dickey)	55.00	25.00	15.00
7	Never Say Die Pitcher(Hal Schumacher)	50.00	25.00	15.00
8	Five Strikeouts!(Carl Hubbell)	65.00	35.00	20.00
9	Greatest Catch!(Al Gionfriddo)	90.00	45.00	30.00
10	No Hits! No Runs!(Johnny VanderMeer)	50.00	25.00	15.00
11	Bases Loaded!(Tony Lazzeri, Bob O'Farrell)	50.00	25.00	15.00
12	Most Dramatic Home Run(Lou Gehrig, Babe Ruth)	500.00	250.00	150.00
13	Winning Run(Tommy Bridges, Mickey Cochrane, Goose Goslin)	50.00	25.00	15.00
14	Great Slugging(Lou Gehrig)	600.00	300.00	180.00
15	Four Men to Stop Him!(Jim Bagby Sr., Al Smith)	80.00	40.00	25.00
16	Three Run Homer in Ninth!(Joe DiMaggio, Joe Gordon, Ted Williams)	600.00	300.00	180.00
17	Football Block!(Whitey Kurowski, Johnny Lindell)	50.00	25.00	15.00

18	Home Run to Fame(Pee			
	Wee Reese)	140.00	70.00	45.00
19	Strikout Record!(Bob			
	Feller)	100.00	50.00	30.00
20	Rifle Arm!(Carl Furillo)	80.00	40.00	25.00

1957 Swift Meats

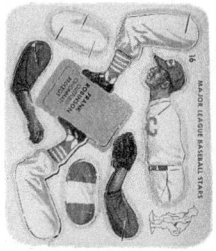 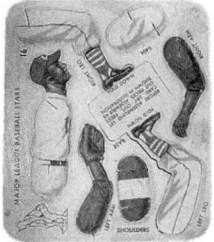

One of the really different baseball card issues of the 50s was the set of 18 3-D baseball player figures which could be punched out and assembled from cards included in packages of hot dogs. The unpunched cards measure approximately 3-1/2" x 4". Prices below are for unpunched cards. Values for assembled figures are problematical.

		NM	E	VG
Complete Set, Singles (18):		1,500	750.00	450.00
Complete Set w/ Mailer, Playing				
Board:		3,000	1,500	900.00
Common Player:		60.00	30.00	18.00
1	John Podres	75.00	37.50	22.50
2	Gus Triandos	60.00	30.00	18.00
3	Dale Long	60.00	30.00	18.00
4	Billy Pierce	60.00	30.00	18.00
5	Ed Bailey	60.00	30.00	18.00
6	Vic Wertz	60.00	30.00	18.00
7	Nelson Fox	130.00	65.00	40.00
8	Ken Boyer	75.00	37.50	22.50
9	Gil McDougald	75.00	37.50	22.50
10	Junior Gilliam	75.00	37.50	22.50
11	Eddie Yost	60.00	30.00	18.00
12	Johnny Logan	60.00	30.00	18.00
13	Hank Aaron	200.00	100.00	60.00
14	Bill Tuttle	60.00	30.00	18.00
15	Jackie Jensen	60.00	30.00	18.00
16	Frank Robinson	200.00	100.00	60.00
17	Richie Ashburn	130.00	65.00	40.00
18	Rocky Colavito	200.00	100.00	60.00

1951 Sylvania Leo Durocher Postcard

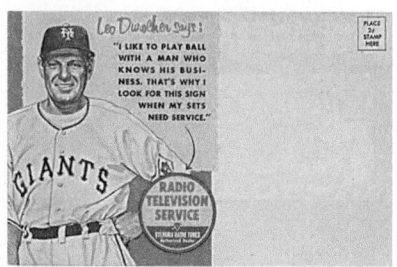

The N.Y. Giants manager endorses Sylvania radio/television service on this large-format (8-1/2" x 5-1/2") postcard. Color artwork features Durocher with a quotation endorsing Sylvania parts and service.

	NM	E	VG
Leo Durocher	50.00	25.00	15.00

T

1910-1911 T3 Turkey Red Cabinets

Turkey Red cabinet cards were obtained by mailing in coupons found in Turkey Red, Fez and Old Mill brand cigarettes. Turkey Reds measure 5-3/4" x 8", and feature full-color lithograph fronts with wide gray frames. Backs are known in three styles: 1) checklist with no ordering information, 2) checklist with ordering information, and, 3) with an illustrated ad for Turkey Red cigarettes. The checklist backs are found with both low- and high-number cards, the ad backs are only on cards #77-126. The series consists of 25 boxers and 100 baseball players. Coupons issued in the cigarette boxes indicate the first 50 baseball player cards were produced for spring, 1910, delivery, with the 25 boxers produced later that year and the final 50 baseball players issued in 1911.

		NM	E	VG
Complete Set (130):		250,000	125,000	50,000
Common Player:		1,500	600.00	300.00
Turkey Red Ad Back: 1.5-2X				
1	Mordecai Brown	3,300	1,650	660.00
2	Bill Bergen	1,500	750.00	300.00
3	Tommy Leach	1,500	600.00	300.00
4	Roger Bresnahan	2,750	1,275	550.00
5	Sam Crawford	2,750	1,275	550.00
6	Hal Chase	1,700	850.00	340.00
7	Howie Camnitz	1,500	600.00	300.00
8	Fred Clarke	2,750	1,275	550.00
9	Ty Cobb	40,000	20,000	8,000
10	Art Devlin	1,500	600.00	300.00
11	Bill Dahlen	1,500	600.00	300.00
12	Wild Bill Donovan	1,500	600.00	300.00
13	Larry Doyle	1,500	600.00	300.00
14	Red Dooin	1,500	600.00	300.00
15	Kid Elberfeld	1,500	600.00	300.00
16	Johnny Evers	3,250	1,650	650.00
17	Clark Griffith	2,750	1,250	550.00
18	Hughie Jennings	2,750	1,250	550.00
19	Addie Joss	4,000	1,800	800.00
20	Tim Jordan	1,500	600.00	300.00
21	Red Kleinow	1,500	600.00	300.00
22	Harry Krause	1,500	600.00	300.00
23	Nap Lajoie	5,250	2,625	1,050
24	Mike Mitchell	1,500	600.00	300.00
25	Matty McIntyre	1,500	600.00	300.00
26	John McGraw	3,000	1,500	600.00
27	Christy Mathewson	17,500	8,750	3,500
28a	Harry McIntyre (Brooklyn)	1,500	600.00	300.00
28b	Harry McIntyre (Brooklyn			
	and Chicago)	1,500	600.00	300.00
29	Amby McConnell	2,000	1,000	400.00
30	George Mullin	1,500	600.00	300.00
31	Sherry Magee	1,500	600.00	300.00
32	Orval Overall	1,500	600.00	300.00
33	Jake Pfeister	1,500	600.00	300.00
34	Nap Rucker	1,500	600.00	300.00
35	Joe Tinker	4,000	1,800	800.00
36	Tris Speaker	7,000	3,000	1,400
37	Slim Sallee	1,500	600.00	300.00
38	Jake Stahl	1,500	600.00	300.00
39	Rube Waddell	2,750	1,275	550.00
40	Vic Willis	2,750	1,275	550.00
41	Hooks Wiltse	1,500	600.00	300.00
42	Cy Young	15,000	7,500	3,000
43	Out At Third	1,750	800.00	350.00
44	Trying To Catch Him			
	Napping	1,600	700.00	425.00
45	Jordan & Herzog At First	1,600	700.00	425.00
46	Safe At Third	1,600	700.00	425.00
47	Frank Chance	3,250	1,650	650.00
48	Jack Murray	1,500	600.00	300.00
49	A Close Play At Second	1,750	800.00	350.00
50	Chief Myers	1,500	600.00	300.00
77	Red Ames	1,500	600.00	300.00

78	Home Run Baker	2,750	1,275	550.00
79	George Bell	1,500	600.00	300.00
80	Chief Bender	2,750	1,275	550.00
81	Bob Bescher	1,500	600.00	300.00
82	Kitty Bransfield	1,500	600.00	300.00
83	Al Bridwell	1,500	600.00	300.00
84	George Browne	1,500	600.00	300.00
85	Bill Burns	1,500	600.00	300.00
86	Bill Carrigan	1,500	600.00	300.00
87	Eddie Collins	2,750	1,275	550.00
88	Harry Coveleski	1,500	600.00	300.00
89	Lou Criger	1,500	600.00	300.00
90a	Mickey Doolin (Doolan)	1,600	700.00	400.00
90b	Mickey Doolan (Name			
	correct.)	2,500	1,250	500.00
91	Tom Downey	1,500	600.00	300.00
92	Jimmy Dygert	1,500	600.00	300.00
93	Art Fromme	1,500	600.00	300.00
94	George Gibson	1,500	600.00	300.00
95	Peaches Graham	1,500	600.00	300.00
96	Bob Groom	1,500	600.00	300.00
97	Dick Hoblitzell	1,500	600.00	300.00
98	Solly Hofman	1,500	600.00	300.00
99	Walter Johnson	17,500	8,750	3,500
100	Davy Jones	1,500	600.00	300.00
101	Wee Willie Keeler	2,750	1,200	550.00
102	Johnny Kling	1,500	600.00	300.00
103	Ed Konetchy	1,500	600.00	300.00
104	Ed Lennox	1,500	600.00	300.00
105	Hans Lobert	1,500	600.00	300.00
106	Harry Lord	1,500	600.00	300.00
107	Rube Manning	2,000	1,000	400.00
108	Fred Merkle	1,500	600.00	300.00
109	Pat Moran	1,500	600.00	300.00
110	George McBride	1,500	600.00	300.00
111	Harry Niles	1,500	600.00	300.00
112a	Dode Paskert (Cincinnati)	1,500	600.00	300.00
112b	Dode Paskert (Cincinnati			
	and Philadelphia)	1,500	600.00	300.00
113	Bugs Raymond	1,500	600.00	300.00
114	Bob Rhoades (Rhoads)	9,000	4,500	1,800
115	Admiral Schlei	1,500	600.00	300.00
116	Boss Schmidt	1,750	800.00	350.00
117	Wildfire Schulte	1,500	600.00	300.00
118	Frank Smith	1,500	600.00	300.00
119	George Stone	1,500	600.00	300.00
120	Gabby Street	1,500	600.00	300.00
121	Billy Sullivan	1,500	600.00	300.00
122a	Fred Tenney (New York)	2,500	1,100	500.00
122b	Fred Tenney (New York			
	and Boston)	4,500	2,250	900.00
123	Ira Thomas	1,500	600.00	300.00
124	Bobby Wallace	2,750	1,250	550.00
125	Ed Walsh	2,750	1,250	550.00
126	Owen Wilson	1,500	600.00	300.00

1911 T5 Pinkerton Cabinets

Because they are photographs affixed to a cardboard backing, the cards in the 1911 Pinkerton set are considered "true" cabinet cards. The Pinkerton cabinets are a rather obscure issue, and because of their original method of distribution, it would be virtually impossible to assemble a complete set today. It remains uncertain how many subjects exist in the set. Pinkerton, the parent of Red Man and other tobacco products, offered the cabinets in exchange for coupons found in cigarette packages. According to an original advertising sheet, some 376 different photos were available. A consumer could exchange 10 coupons for the card of his choice. The photos available included players from the 16 major league teams plus teams from the minor league American Association, Southern Michigan Association, and, probably, others. Pinkertons vary in both size and type of mount. The most desirable combination is a 3-3/8" x 5-1/2" photograph affixed to a thick cardboard mount measuring approximately 4-3/4" x 7-3/4". But original Pinkerton cabinets have also been found in different sizes and with less substantial backings. The most attractive mounts are embossed around the picture, but some Pinkertons have a white border surrounding the photograph. Prices listed are for cards with cardboard mounts.

Cards with paper mounts are worth about 50-75 percent of listed prices. Some of the Pinkerton photos were reproduced in postcard size printed issues in later years; some with post-card style backs, some with scorecard backs and others are blank-backed (See 1911 Pinkerton).

	NM	E	VG
Common Player:	1,000	500.00	315.00
Checklist Brochure:	625.00	315.00	190.00
Redemption Coupon:	500.00	250.00	150.00
Blank-Back Card: 5-10 Percent			
Postcard-Back: 10-15 Percent			

101	Jim Stephens	1,000	500.00	315.00
102	Bobby Wallace	3,500	1,750	1,050
103	Joe Lake	1,000	500.00	315.00
104	George Stone	1,000	500.00	315.00
105	Jack O'Connor	1,000	500.00	315.00
106	Bill Abstein	1,000	500.00	315.00
107	Rube Waddell	3,500	1,095	655.00
108	Roy Hartzell	1,000	500.00	315.00
109	Danny Hoffman	1,000	500.00	315.00
110	Dode Cris	1,000	500.00	315.00
111	Al Schweitzer	1,000	500.00	315.00
112	Art Griggs	1,000	500.00	315.00
113	Bill Bailey	1,000	500.00	315.00
114	Pat Newman	1,000	500.00	315.00
115	Harry Howell	1,000	500.00	315.00
117	Hobe Ferris	1,000	500.00	315.00
118	John McAleese	1,000	500.00	315.00
119	Ray Demmitt	1,000	500.00	315.00
120	Red Fisher	1,000	500.00	315.00
121	Frank Truesdale	1,000	500.00	315.00
122	Barney Pelty	1,000	500.00	315.00
123	Ed Killifer (Killefer)	1,000	500.00	315.00
151	Matty McIntyre	1,000	500.00	315.00
152	Jim Delahanty	1,000	500.00	315.00
153	Hughey Jennings	3,500	1,095	655.00
154	Ralph Works	1,000	500.00	315.00
155	George Moriarity (Moriarty)	1,000	500.00	315.00
156	Sam Crawford	3,500	1,095	655.00
157	Charley Schmidt	1,000	500.00	315.00
158	Owen Bush	1,000	500.00	315.00
159	Ty Cobb	8,750	4,375	2,625
160	Bill Donovan	1,000	500.00	315.00
161	Oscar Stanage	1,000	500.00	315.00
162	George Mullen (Mullin)	1,000	500.00	315.00
163	Davy Jones	1,000	500.00	315.00
164	Charley O'Leary	1,000	500.00	315.00
165	Tom Jones	1,000	500.00	315.00
166	Joe Casey	1,000	500.00	315.00
167	Ed Willetts (Willett)	1,000	500.00	315.00
168	Ed Lafeite (Lafitte)	1,000	500.00	315.00
169	Ty Cobb	20,000	10,000	6,0000
170	Ty Cobb	20,000	10,000	6,000
201	John Evers	3,500	1,095	655.00
202	Mordecai Brown	3,500	1,095	655.00
203	King Cole	1,000	500.00	315.00
204	Johnny Cane	1,000	500.00	315.00
205	Heinie Zimmerman	1,000	500.00	315.00
206	Frank Schulte	1,000	500.00	315.00
207	Frank Chance	3,500	1,095	655.00
208	Joe Tinker	3,500	1,095	655.00
209	Orvall Overall	1,000	500.00	315.00
210	Jimmy Archer	1,000	500.00	315.00
211	Johnny Kling	1,000	500.00	315.00
212	Jimmy Sheckard	1,000	500.00	315.00
213	Harry McIntyre	1,000	500.00	315.00
214	Lew Richie	1,000	500.00	315.00
215	Ed Ruelbach	1,000	500.00	315.00
216	Artie Hoffman (Hofman)	1,000	500.00	315.00
217	Jake Pfeister	1,000	500.00	315.00
218	Harry Steinfeldt	1,000	500.00	315.00
219	Tom Needham	1,000	500.00	315.00
220	Ginger Beaumont	1,000	500.00	315.00
251	Christy Mathewson	10,000	5,000	3,000
252	Fred Merkle	1,000	500.00	315.00
253	Hooks Wiltsie	1,000	500.00	315.00
254	Art Devlin	1,000	500.00	315.00
255	Fred Snodgrass	1,000	500.00	315.00
256	Josh Devore	1,000	500.00	315.00
257	Red Murray	1,000	500.00	315.00
258	Cy Seymour	1,000	500.00	315.00
259	Rube Marquard	3,500	1,095	655.00
260	Larry Doyle	1,000	500.00	315.00
261	Bugs Raymond	1,000	500.00	315.00
262	Doc Crandall	1,000	500.00	315.00
263	Admiral Schlei	1,000	500.00	315.00
264	Chief Myers (Meyers)	1,000	500.00	315.00
265	Bill Dahlen	1,000	500.00	315.00
266	Beals Becker	1,000	500.00	315.00
267	Louis Drucke	1,000	500.00	315.00
301	Fred Luderus	1,000	500.00	315.00
302	John Titus	1,000	500.00	315.00
303	Red Dooin	1,000	500.00	315.00
304	Eddie Stack	1,000	500.00	315.00
305	Kitty Bransfield	1,000	500.00	315.00
306	Sherry Magee	1,000	500.00	315.00
307	Otto Knabe	1,000	500.00	315.00
308	Jimmy "Runt" Walsh	1,000	500.00	315.00
309	Earl Moore	1,000	500.00	315.00
310	Mickey Doolan	1,000	500.00	315.00
311	Ad Brennan	1,000	500.00	315.00
312	Bob Ewing	1,000	500.00	315.00
313	Lou Schettler	1,000	500.00	315.00
351	Joe Willis	1,000	500.00	315.00
352	Rube Ellis	1,000	500.00	315.00
353	Steve Evans	1,000	500.00	315.00
354	Miller Huggins	3,500	1,095	655.00
355	Arnold Hauser	1,000	500.00	315.00
356	Frank Corridon	1,000	500.00	315.00
357	Roger Bresnahan	3,500	1,095	655.00
358	Slim Sallee	1,000	500.00	315.00
359	Mike Mowrey	1,000	500.00	315.00
360	Ed Konetchy	1,000	500.00	315.00
361	Beckman	1,000	500.00	315.00
362	Rebel Oakes	1,000	500.00	315.00
363	Johnny Lush	1,000	500.00	315.00
364	Eddie Phelps	1,000	500.00	315.00
365	Robert Harmon	1,000	500.00	315.00
401	Lou (Pat) Moran	1,000	500.00	315.00
402	George McQuillian (McQuillan)	1,000	500.00	315.00
403	Johnny Bates	1,000	500.00	315.00
404	Eddie Grant	1,000	500.00	315.00
405	Tommy McMillan	1,000	500.00	315.00
406	Tommy Clark (Clarke)	1,000	500.00	315.00
407	Jack Rowan	1,000	500.00	315.00
408	Bob Bescher	1,000	500.00	315.00
409	Fred Beebe	1,000	500.00	315.00
410	Tom Downey	1,000	500.00	315.00
411	George Suggs	1,000	500.00	315.00
412	Hans Lobert	1,000	500.00	315.00
413	Jimmy Phelan	1,000	500.00	315.00
414	Dode Paskert	1,000	500.00	315.00
415	Ward Miller	1,000	500.00	315.00
416	Richard J. Egan	1,000	500.00	315.00
417	Art Fromme	1,000	500.00	315.00
418	Bill Burns	1,000	500.00	315.00
419	Clark Griffith	3,500	1,095	655.00
420	Dick Hoblitzell	1,000	500.00	315.00
421	Harry Gasper	1,000	500.00	315.00
422	Dave Altizer	1,000	500.00	315.00
423	Larry McLean	1,000	500.00	315.00
424	Mike Mitchell	1,000	500.00	315.00
451	John Hummel	1,000	500.00	315.00
452	Tony Smith	1,000	500.00	315.00
453	Bill Davidson	1,000	500.00	315.00
454	Ed Lennox	1,000	500.00	315.00
455	Zach Wheat	3,500	1,095	655.00
457	Elmer Knetzer	1,000	500.00	315.00
458	Rube Dessau	1,000	500.00	315.00
459	George Bell	1,000	500.00	315.00
460	Jake Daubert	1,000	500.00	315.00
461	Doc Scanlan	1,000	500.00	315.00
462	Nap Rucker	1,000	500.00	315.00
463	Cy Barger	1,000	500.00	315.00
464	Kaiser Wilhelm	1,000	500.00	315.00
465	Bill Bergen	1,000	500.00	315.00
466	Tex Erwin	1,000	500.00	315.00
501	Chas. Bender	3,500	1,095	655.00
502	John Coombs	1,000	500.00	315.00
503	Ed Plank	4,500	2,250	1,350
504	Amos Strunk	1,000	500.00	315.00
505	Connie Mack	3,500	1,095	655.00
506	Ira Thomas	1,000	500.00	315.00
507	Biscoe Lord (Briscoe)	1,000	500.00	315.00
508	Stuffy McInnis	1,000	500.00	315.00
509	Jimmy Dygert	1,000	500.00	315.00
510	Rube Oldring	1,000	500.00	315.00
511	Eddie Collins	3,500	1,095	655.00
512	Home Run Baker	3,500	1,095	655.00
513	Harry Krause	1,000	500.00	315.00
514	Harry Davis	1,000	500.00	315.00
515	Jack Barry	1,000	500.00	315.00
516	Jack Lapp	1,000	500.00	315.00
517	Cy Morgan	1,000	500.00	315.00
518	Danny Murphy	1,000	500.00	315.00
519	Topsy Hartsell	1,000	500.00	315.00
520	Paddy Livingston	1,000	500.00	315.00
521	P. Adkins	1,000	500.00	315.00
522	Eddie Collins	3,500	1,095	655.00
523	Paddy Livingston	1,000	500.00	315.00
551	Doc Gessler	1,000	500.00	315.00
552	Bill Cunningham	1,000	500.00	315.00
554	John Henry	1,000	500.00	315.00
555	Jack Lelivelt	1,000	500.00	315.00
556	Bobby Groome	1,000	500.00	315.00
557	Doc Ralston	1,000	500.00	315.00
558	Kid Elberfelt (Elberfeld)	1,000	500.00	315.00
559	Doc Reisling	1,000	500.00	315.00
560	Herman Schaefer	1,000	500.00	315.00
561	Walter Johnson	6,000	3,000	1,800
562	Dolly Gray	1,000	500.00	315.00
563	Wid Conroy	1,000	500.00	315.00
564	Charley Street	1,000	500.00	315.00
565	Bob Unglaub	1,000	500.00	315.00
566	Clyde Milan	1,000	500.00	315.00
567	George Browne	1,000	500.00	315.00
568	George McBride	1,000	500.00	315.00
569	Red Killifer (Killefer)	1,000	500.00	315.00
601	Addie Joss	3,500	1,095	655.00
602	Addie Joss	3,500	1,095	655.00
603	Napoleon Lajoie	7,500	3,750	2,250
604	Nig Clark (Clarke)	1,000	500.00	315.00
605	Cy Falkenberg	1,000	500.00	315.00
606	Harry Bemis	1,000	500.00	315.00
607	George Stovall	1,000	500.00	315.00
608	Fred Blanding	1,000	500.00	315.00
609	Elmer Koestner	1,000	500.00	315.00
610	Ted Easterly	1,000	500.00	315.00
611	Willie Mitchell	1,000	500.00	315.00
612	Hornhorst	1,000	500.00	315.00
613	Elmer Flick	3,500	1,095	655.00
614	Speck Harkness	1,000	500.00	315.00
615	Tuck Turner	1,000	500.00	315.00
616	Joe Jackson	60,000	20,000	12,000
617	Grover Land	1,000	500.00	315.00
618	Gladstone Graney	1,000	500.00	315.00
619	Dave Callahan	1,000	500.00	315.00
620	Ben DeMott	1,000	500.00	315.00
621	Neill Ball (Neal)	1,000	500.00	315.00
622	Dode Birmingham	1,000	500.00	315.00
623	George Kaler (Kahler)	1,000	500.00	315.00
624	Sid Smith	1,000	500.00	315.00
625	Bert Adams	1,000	500.00	315.00
626	Bill Bradley	1,000	500.00	315.00
627	Napoleon Lajoie	7,500	3,750	2,250
651	Bill Corrigan (Carrigan)	1,000	500.00	315.00
652	Joe Woods (Wood)	1,000	500.00	315.00
653	Heinie Wagner	1,000	500.00	315.00
654	Billy Purtell	1,000	500.00	315.00
655	Frank Smith	1,000	500.00	315.00
656	Harry Lord	1,000	500.00	315.00
657	Patsy Donovan	1,000	500.00	315.00
658	Duffy Lewis	1,000	500.00	315.00
659	Jack Kleinow	1,000	500.00	315.00
660	Ed Karger	1,000	500.00	315.00
661	Clyde Engle	1,000	500.00	315.00
662	Ben Hunt	1,000	500.00	315.00
663	Charlie Smith	1,000	500.00	315.00
664	Tris Speaker	4,500	2,250	1,350
665	Tom Madden	1,000	500.00	315.00
666	Larry Gardner	1,000	500.00	315.00
667	Harry Hooper	3,500	1,095	655.00
668	Marty McHale	1,000	500.00	315.00
669	Ray Collins	1,000	500.00	315.00
670	Jake Stahl	1,000	500.00	315.00
701	Dave Shean	1,000	500.00	315.00
702	Roy Miller	1,000	500.00	315.00
703	Fred Beck	1,000	500.00	315.00
704	Bill Collings (Collins)	1,000	500.00	315.00
705	Bill Sweeney	1,000	500.00	315.00
706	Buck Herzog	1,000	500.00	315.00
707	Bud Sharp (Sharpe)	1,000	500.00	315.00
708	Cliff Curtis	1,000	500.00	315.00
709	Al Mattern	1,000	500.00	315.00
710	Buster Brown	1,000	500.00	315.00
711	Bill Rariden	1,000	500.00	315.00
712	Grant	1,000	500.00	315.00
713	Ed Abbaticchio	1,000	500.00	315.00
714	Cecil Ferguson	1,000	500.00	315.00
715	Billy Burke	1,000	500.00	315.00
716	Sam Frock	1,000	500.00	315.00
717	Wilbur Goode (Good)	1,000	500.00	315.00
751	Charlie French	1,000	500.00	315.00
752	Patsy Dougherty	1,000	500.00	315.00
753	Shano Collins	1,000	500.00	315.00
754	Fred Parent	1,000	500.00	315.00
755	Willis Cole	1,000	500.00	315.00
756	Billy Sullivan	1,000	500.00	315.00
757	Rube Sutor (Suter)	1,000	500.00	315.00
758	Chick Gandil	2,400	1,155	695.00
759	Jim Scott	1,000	500.00	315.00
760	Ed Walsh	3,500	1,095	655.00
761	Gavvy Cravath	1,000	500.00	315.00
762	Bobby Messenger	1,000	500.00	315.00
763	Doc White	1,000	500.00	315.00
764	Rollie Zeider	1,000	500.00	315.00
765	Fred Payne	1,000	500.00	315.00
766	Lee Tannehill	1,000	500.00	315.00
767	Eddie Hahn	1,000	500.00	315.00
768	Hugh Duffy	3,500	1,095	655.00
769	Fred Olmstead	1,000	500.00	315.00
770	Lena Blackbourne (Blackburne)	1,000	500.00	315.00
771	Young "Cy" Young	1,000	500.00	315.00
801	Lew Brockett	1,000	500.00	315.00
802	Frank Laporte (LaPorte)	1,000	500.00	315.00
803	Bert Daniels	1,000	500.00	315.00
804	Walter Blair	1,000	500.00	315.00
805	Jack Knight	1,000	500.00	315.00
806	Jimmy Austin	1,000	500.00	315.00
807	Hal Chase	2,000	1,000	600.00

808	Birdie Cree	1,000	500.00	315.00
809	Jack Quinn	1,000	500.00	315.00
810	Walter Manning	1,000	500.00	315.00
811	Jack Warhop	1,000	500.00	315.00
812	Jeff Sweeney	1,000	500.00	315.00
813	Charley Hemphill	1,000	500.00	315.00
814	Harry Wolters	1,000	500.00	315.00
815	Tom Hughes	1,000	500.00	315.00
816	Earl Gardiner (Gardner)	1,000	500.00	315.00
851	John Flynn	1,000	500.00	315.00
852	Bill Powell	1,000	500.00	315.00
853	Honus Wagner	15,000	3,750	2,250
854	Bill Powell	1,000	500.00	315.00
855	Fred Clarke	3,500	1,095	655.00
856	Owen Wilson	1,000	500.00	315.00
857	George Gibson	1,000	500.00	315.00
858	Mike Simon	1,000	500.00	315.00
859	Tommy Leach	1,000	500.00	315.00
860	Lefty Leifeld (Leifield)	1,000	500.00	315.00
861	Nick Maddox	1,000	500.00	315.00
862	Dots Miller	1,000	500.00	315.00
863	Howard Camnitz	1,000	500.00	315.00
864	Deacon Phillippi (Phillippe)	1,000	500.00	315.00
865	Babe Adams	1,000	500.00	315.00
866	Ed Abbaticchio	1,000	500.00	315.00
867	Paddy O'Connor	1,000	500.00	315.00
868	Bobby Byrne	1,000	500.00	315.00
869	Vin Campbell	1,000	500.00	315.00
870	Ham Hyatt	1,000	500.00	315.00
871	Sam Leever	1,000	500.00	315.00
872	Hans Wagner	15,000	3,750	2,250
873	Hans Wagner	15,000	3,750	2,250
874	Bill McKecknie (McKechnie)	3,500	1,095	655.00
875	Kirby White	1,000	500.00	315.00
901	Jimmie Burke	1,000	500.00	315.00
902	Charlie Carr	1,000	500.00	315.00
903	Larry Cheney	1,000	500.00	315.00
904	Chet Chadbourne	1,000	500.00	315.00
905	Dan Howley	1,000	500.00	315.00
906	Jimmie Burke	1,000	500.00	315.00
907	Ray Mowe	1,000	500.00	315.00
908	Billy Milligan	1,000	500.00	315.00
909	Frank Oberlin	1,000	500.00	315.00
910	Ralph Glaze	1,000	500.00	315.00
911	O'Day	1,000	500.00	315.00
912	Kerns	1,000	500.00	315.00
913	Jim Duggan	1,000	500.00	315.00
914	Simmy Murch	1,000	500.00	315.00
915	Frank Delehanty	1,000	500.00	315.00
916	Craig	1,000	500.00	315.00
917	Jack Coffee (Coffey)	1,000	500.00	315.00
918	Lefty George	1,000	500.00	315.00
919	Otto Williams	1,000	500.00	315.00
920	M. Hayden	1,000	500.00	315.00
951	Joe Cantillion	1,000	500.00	315.00
952	Smith	1,000	500.00	315.00
953	Claud Rossman (Claude)	1,000	500.00	315.00
1001	Tony James	1,000	500.00	315.00
1002	Jack Powell	1,000	500.00	315.00
1003	Wm. J. Harbeau	1,000	500.00	315.00
1004	Homer Smoot	1,000	500.00	315.00
1051	Bill Friel	1,000	500.00	315.00
1052	Bill Friel	1,000	500.00	315.00
1053	Fred Odwell	1,000	500.00	315.00
1054	Alex Reilley	1,000	500.00	315.00
1055	Eugene Packard	1,000	500.00	315.00
1056	Irve Wrattan	1,000	500.00	315.00
1057	"Red" Nelson	1,000	500.00	315.00
1058	George Perring	1,000	500.00	315.00
1059	Glen Liebhardt	1,000	500.00	315.00
1060	Jimmie O'Rourke	1,000	500.00	315.00
1061	Fred Cook	1,000	500.00	315.00
1062	Charles Arbogast	1,000	500.00	315.00
1063	Jerry Downs	1,000	500.00	315.00
1064	"Bunk" Congalton	1,000	500.00	315.00
1065	Fred Carisch	1,000	500.00	315.00
1066	"Red" Sitton	1,000	500.00	315.00
1067	George Kaler (Kahler)	1,000	500.00	315.00
1068	Arthur Kruger	1,000	500.00	315.00
1102	Earl Yingling	1,000	500.00	315.00
1103	Jerry Freeman	1,800	500.00	315.00
1104	Harry Hinchman	1,000	500.00	315.00
1105	Jim Baskette (Toledo)	1,000	500.00	315.00
1106	Denny Sullivan	1,000	500.00	315.00
1107	Carl Robinson	1,000	500.00	315.00
1108	Bill Rodgers	1,000	500.00	315.00
1109	Hi West	1,000	500.00	315.00
1110	Billy Hallman	1,000	500.00	315.00
1111	Wm. Elwert	1,000	500.00	315.00
1112	Piano Legs Hickman	1,000	500.00	315.00
1113	Joe McCarthy	3,500	1,095	655.00
1114	Fred Abbott	1,000	500.00	315.00
1115	Jack Guilligan (Gilligan)	1,000	500.00	315.00
1510	Musser	1,000	500.00	315.00
1613	C. Winger	1,000	500.00	315.00

1911 T201 Mecca Double Folders

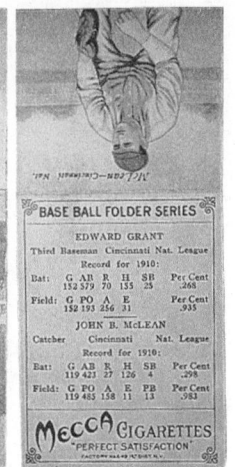

These cards found in packages of Mecca cigarettes feature one player when the card is open, and another when the card is folded; two players sharing the same pair of legs. Mecca Double Folders measure about 2-1/8" to 2-3/16" x 4-11/16". The pictures are color lithographs, the text is printed in black. The cards contain an innovation in the form of the first use of player statistics. The 50-card set contains 100 different players including a number of Hall of Famers. Examples authenticated and graded by major certification firms carry a much larger premium than most other cards of the era.

		NM	E	VG
Complete Set (50):		25,000	7,000	2,650
Common Player:		315.00	65.00	25.00
(1)	William Abstein, John Butler	315.00	65.00	25.00
(2)	Frank Baker, Edward Collins	700.00	315.00	190.00
(3)	Harry Baker, Thomas Downie (Downey)	315.00	65.00	25.00
(4)	James Barrett, Grant McGlynn	315.00	65.00	25.00
(5)	John Barry, John Lapp	315.00	65.00	25.00
(6)	Charles Bender, Reuben Oldring	435.00	135.00	55.00
(7)	William Bergen, Zack Wheat	425.00	130.00	50.00
(8)	Walter Blair, Roy Hartzell	315.00	65.00	25.00
(9)	Roger Bresnahan, Miller Huggins	650.00	200.00	80.00
(10)	Albert Bridwell, Christy Matthewson (Mathewson)	1,350	720.00	425.00
(11)	Mordecai Brown, Arthur Hofman	425.00	140.00	55.00
(12)	Robert Byrne, Fred Clarke	425.00	115.00	45.00
(13)	Frank Chance, John Evers	700.00	200.00	80.00
(14)	Harold Chase, Edward Sweeney	425.00	100.00	40.00
(15)	Edward Cicotte, John Thoney	450.00	140.00	55.00
(16)	Thomas Clarke, Harry Gaspar	315.00	65.00	25.00
(17)	Ty Cobb, Sam Crawford	3,100	1,100	400.00
(18)	Leonard Cole, John Kling	315.00	65.00	25.00
(19)	John Coombs, Ira Thomas	315.00	65.00	25.00
(20)	Jake Daubert, Nap Rucker	315.00	65.00	25.00
(21)	Bill Donovan, Ralph Stroud	315.00	65.00	25.00
(22)	Charles Dooin, John Titus	315.00	65.00	25.00
(23)	Patsy Dougherty, Harry Lord	500.00	165.00	65.00
(24)	Jerry Downs, Fred Odwell	315.00	65.00	25.00
(25)	Larry Doyle, Chief Meyers	315.00	65.00	25.00
(26)	James Dygert, Cy Seymour	315.00	65.00	25.00
(27)	Norman Elberfeld, George McBride	315.00	65.00	25.00
(28)	Fred Falkenberg, Napoleon Lajoie	800.00	200.00	75.00
(29)	Edward Fitzpatrick, Ed Killian	315.00	65.00	25.00
(30)	Russell Ford, Otis Johnson	315.00	65.00	25.00
(31)	Edward Foster, Joseph Ward	315.00	65.00	25.00
(32)	Earl Gardner, Tris Speaker	650.00	290.00	175.00
(33)	George Gibson, Thomas Leach	315.00	65.00	25.00
(34)	George Graham, Al Mattern	315.00	65.00	25.00
(35)	Edward Grant, John McLean	315.00	65.00	25.00
(36)	Arnold Hauser, Ernest Lush	315.00	65.00	25.00
(37)	Charles Herzog, Roy Miller	315.00	65.00	25.00
(38)	Charles Hickman, Harry Hinchman	315.00	65.00	25.00
(39)	Hugh Jennings, Edgar Summers	425.00	140.00	55.00
(40)	Walter Johnson, Charles Street	900.00	250.00	100.00
(41)	Frank LaPorte, James Stephens	315.00	65.00	25.00
(42)	Joseph Lake, Robert Wallace	425.00	130.00	50.00
(43)	Albert Leifield, Mike Simon	315.00	65.00	25.00
(44)	John Lobert, Earl Moore	315.00	65.00	25.00
(45)	Arthur McCabe, Charles Starr	315.00	65.00	25.00
(46)	Lewis McCarty, Joseph McGinnity	425.00	130.00	60.00
(47)	Fred Merkle, George Wiltse	315.00	65.00	25.00
(48)	Frederick Payne, Edward Walsh	425.00	130.00	60.00
(49)	George Stovall, Terrence Turner	315.00	65.00	25.00
(50)	Otto Williams, Orville Woodruff	315.00	65.00	25.00

1912 T202 Hassan Triple Folders

Measuring about 5-1/4" x 2-1/4", Hassan cigarette cards carried the concept of multiple-player cards even further than the double-fold Mecca set of the previous year. Scored so that the player pictures on each end - which are full-color and very close to exact duplicates of T205 "Gold Borders" cards - can fold over the black-and-white action-photo center panel, the Hassan Triple Folder appears like a booklet when closed. The individual player panels are not necessarily related to the action scene. The Hassan Triple Folders feature player biographies on the back of the two individual cards with a description of the action on the back of the center panel. Values depend on the player featured in the center panel, as well as the players featured on the end cards. Moreso than most contemporary cards, the value of NM or better T202s that have been graded by a major certification company well as the players featured on the end cards. Moreso than most contemporary issues, T202s that have been graded NM or better by a reputable certification company carry a larger premium over ungraded examples.

		NM	E	VG
Complete Set (132):		175,000	57,000	26,250
Common Player:		650.00	215.00	95.00
(1)	A Close Play At The Home Plate(LaPorte, Wallace)	650.00	215.00	95.00
(2)	A Close Play At The Home Plate(Pelty, Wallace)	650.00	215.00	95.00
(3)	A Desperate Slide For Third(Cobb, O'Leary)	5,000	1,650	750.00
(4)	A Great Batsman(Barger, Bergen)	650.00	215.00	95.00
(5)	A Great Batsman(Bergen, Rucker)	650.00	215.00	95.00
(6)	Ambrose McConnell At Bat(Blair, Quinn)	650.00	215.00	95.00

(7)	A Wide Throw Saves Crawford(Mullin, Stanage)	650.00	215.00	95.00
(8)	Baker Gets His Man(Baker, Collins)	1,200	400.00	180.00
(9)	Birmingham Gets To Third(Johnson, Street)	1,250	450.00	185.00
(10)	Birmingham's Home Run(Birmingham, Turner)	1,200	400.00	180.00
(11)	Bush Just Misses Austin(Magee, Moran)	650.00	215.00	95.00
(12)	Carrigan Blocks His Man(Gaspar, McLean)	650.00	215.00	95.00
(13)	Carrigan Blocks His Man(Carrigan, Wagner)	650.00	215.00	95.00
(14)	Catching Him Napping(Bresnahan, Oakes)	650.00	215.00	95.00
(15)	Caught Asleep Off First(Bresnahan, Harmon)	650.00	215.00	95.00
(16)	Chance Beats Out A Hit(Chance, Foxen)	1,200	400.00	180.00
(17)	Chance Beats Out A Hit(Archer, McIntyre)	650.00	215.00	95.00
(18)	Chance Beats Out A Hit(Archer, Overall)	650.00	215.00	95.00
(19)	Chance Beats Out A Hit(Archer, Rowan)	650.00	215.00	95.00
(20)	Chance Beats Out A Hit(Chance, Shean)	1,100	365.00	165.00
(21)	Chase Dives Into Third(Chase, Wolter)	650.00	215.00	95.00
(22)	Chase Dives Into Third(Clarke, Gibson)	650.00	215.00	95.00
(23)	Chase Dives Into Third(Gibson, Phillippe)	650.00	215.00	95.00
(24)	Chase Gets Ball Too Late(Egan, Mitchell)	650.00	215.00	95.00
(25)	Chase Gets Ball Too Late(Chase, Wolter)	650.00	215.00	95.00
(26)	Chase Guarding First(Chase, Wolter)	650.00	215.00	95.00
(27)	Chase Guarding First(Clarke, Gibson)	650.00	215.00	95.00
(28)	Chase Guarding First(Gibson, Leifield)	650.00	215.00	95.00
(29)	Chase Ready For The Squeeze Play(Magee, Paskert)	650.00	215.00	95.00
(30)	Chase Safe At Third(Baker, Barry)	650.00	215.00	95.00
(31)	Chief Bender Waiting For A Good One(Bender, Thomas)	650.00	215.00	95.00
(32)	Clarke Hikes For Home(Bridwell, Kling)	650.00	215.00	95.00
(33)	Close At First(Ball, Stovall)	650.00	215.00	95.00
(34)	Close At The Plate(Payne, Walsh)	650.00	215.00	95.00
(35)	Close At The Plate(Payne, White)	650.00	215.00	95.00
(36)	Close At Third - Speaker(Speaker, Wood)	1,400	500.00	200.00
(37)	Close At Third - Wagner(Carrigan, Wagner)	650.00	215.00	95.00
(38)	Collins Easily Safe(Byrne, Clarke)	650.00	215.00	95.00
(39)	Collins Easily Safe(Baker, Collins)	1,100	365.00	165.00
(40)	Collins Easily Safe(Collins, Murphy)	800.00	265.00	120.00
(41)	Crawford About To Smash One(Stanage, Summers)	650.00	215.00	95.00
(42)	Cree Rolls Home(Daubert, Hummel)	650.00	215.00	95.00
(43)	Davy Jones' Great Slide(Delahanty, Jones)	650.00	215.00	95.00
(44)	Devlin Gets His Man(Devlin (Giants), Mathewson)	1,600	525.00	240.00
(45)	Devlin Gets His Man(Devlin (Rustlers), Mathewson)	3,000	1,000	450.00
(46)	Devlin Gets His Man(Fletcher, Mathewson)	1,900	600.00	285.00
(47)	Devlin Gets His Man (Mathewson, Meyers)	2,000	700.00	300.00
(48)	Donlin Out At First (Camnitz, Gibson)	650.00	215.00	95.00
(49)	Donlin Out At First(Doyle, Merkle)	650.00	215.00	95.00
(50)	Donlin Out At First(Leach, Wilson)	650.00	215.00	95.00
(51)	Donlin Out At First(Dooin, Magee)	650.00	215.00	95.00
(52)	Donlin Out At First(Gibson, Phillippe)	650.00	215.00	95.00
(53)	Dooin Gets His Man(Dooin, Doolan)	650.00	215.00	95.00
(54)	Dooin Gets His Man(Dooin, Lobert)	650.00	215.00	95.00
(55)	Dooin Gets His Man(Dooin, Titus)	650.00	215.00	95.00
(56)	Easy For Larry(Doyle, Merkle)	650.00	215.00	95.00
(57)	Elberfeld Beats The Throw(Elberfeld, Milan)	650.00	215.00	95.00
(58)	Elberfeld Gets His Man(Elberfeld, Milan)	650.00	215.00	95.00
(59)	Engle In A Close Play(Engle, Speaker)	1,300	400.00	200.00
(60)	Evers Makes A Safe Slide(Archer, Evers)	650.00	215.00	95.00
(61)	Evers Makes A Safe Slide(Chance, Evers)	1,700	600.00	300.00
(62)	Evers Makes A Safe Slide(Archer, Overall)	650.00	215.00	95.00
(63)	Evers Makes A Safe Slide(Archer, Reulbach)	650.00	215.00	95.00
(64)	Evers Makes A Safe Slide(Chance, Tinker)	2,650	875.00	395.00
(65)	Fast Work At Third(Cobb, O'Leary)	3,750	1,200	675.00
(66)	Ford Putting Over A Spitter(Ford, Vaughn)	650.00	215.00	95.00
(67)	Ford Putting Over A Spitter(Sweeney, Ford)	650.00	215.00	95.00
(68)	Good Play At Third(Cobb, Moriarity (Moriarty))	3,800	1,300	570.00
(69)	Grant Gets His Man(Grant, Hoblitzell)	650.00	215.00	95.00
(70)	Hal Chase Too Late(McConnell, McIntyre)	650.00	215.00	95.00
(71)	Hal Chase Too Late(McLean, Suggs)	650.00	215.00	95.00
(72)	Harry Lord At Third(Lennox, Tinker)	650.00	215.00	95.00
(73)	Hartzell Covering Third(Dahlen, Scanlan)	650.00	215.00	95.00
(74)	Hartsel Strikes Out(Gray, Groom)	650.00	215.00	95.00
(75)	Held At Third(Lord, Tannehill)	650.00	215.00	95.00
(76)	Jake Stahl Guarding First(Cicotte, Stahl)	1,300	450.00	200.00
(77)	Jim Delahanty At Bat(Delahanty, Jones)	650.00	215.00	95.00
(78)	Just Before The Battle(Ames, Meyers)	650.00	215.00	95.00
(79)	Just Before The Battle(Bresnahan, McGraw)	750.00	215.00	95.00
(80)	Just Before The Battle(Crandall, Meyers)	650.00	215.00	95.00
(81)	Just Before The Battle(Becker, Devore)	650.00	215.00	95.00
(82)	Just Before The Battle(Fletcher, Mathewson)	1,900	700.00	300.00
(83)	Just Before The Battle(Marquard, Meyers)	650.00	215.00	95.00
(84)	Just Before The Battle(Jennings, McGraw)	1,350	440.00	200.00
(85)	Just Before The Battle(Mathewson, Meyers)	1,300	430.00	200.00
(86)	Just Before The Battle(Murray, Snodgrass)	650.00	215.00	95.00
(87)	Just Before The Battle(Meyers, Wiltse)	650.00	215.00	95.00
(88)	Knight Catches A Runner(Johnson, Knight)	1,200	400.00	180.00
(89)	Lobert Almost Caught(Bridwell, Kling)	650.00	215.00	95.00
(90)	Lobert Almost Caught(Kling, Young)	1,950	450.00	225.00
(91)	Lobert Almost Caught (Kling, Mattern)	650.00	215.00	95.00
(92)	Lobert Almost Caught (Kling, Steinfeldt)	650.00	215.00	95.00
(93)	Lobert Gets Tenney(Dooin, Lobert)	650.00	215.00	95.00
(94)	Lord Catches His Man(Lord, Tannehil)	650.00	215.00	95.00
(95)	McConnell Caught(Needham, Richie)	1,300	400.00	200.00
(96)	McIntyre At Bat(McConnell, McIntyre)	650.00	215.00	95.00
(97)	Moriarty Spiked(Stanage, Willett)	650.00	215.00	95.00
(98)	Nearly Caught(Bates, Bescher)	650.00	215.00	95.00
(99)	Oldring Almost Home(Lord, Oldring)	650.00	215.00	95.00
(100)	Schaefer On First(McBride, Milan)	650.00	215.00	95.00
(101)	Schaefer Steals Second(Griffith, McBride)	650.00	215.00	95.00
(102)	Scoring From Second(Lord, Oldring)	650.00	215.00	95.00
(103)	Scrambling Back To First(Barger, Bergen)	650.00	215.00	95.00
(104)	Scrambling Back To First(Chase, Wolter)	650.00	215.00	95.00
(105)	Speaker Almost Caught(Clarke, Miller)	850.00	325.00	125.00
(106)	Speaker Rounding Third(Speaker, Wood)	1,800	600.00	270.00
(107)	Speaker Scores(Engle, Speaker)	1,100	240.00	99.00
(108)	Stahl Safe(Austin, Stovall)	650.00	215.00	95.00
(109)	Stone About To Swing(Schulte, Sheckard)	650.00	215.00	95.00
(110)	Sullivan Puts Up A High One(Evans, Huggins)	650.00	215.00	95.00
(111)	Sullivan Puts Up A High One(Gray, Groom)	650.00	215.00	95.00
(112)	Sweeney Gets Stahl(Ford, Vaughn)	650.00	215.00	95.00
(113)	Sweeney Gets Stahl(Ford, Sweeney)	650.00	215.00	95.00
(114)	Tenney Lands Safely(Latham, Raymond)	650.00	215.00	95.00
(115)	The Athletic Infield(Baker, Barry)	750.00	250.00	115.00
(116)	The Athletic Infield(Brown, Graham)	750.00	250.00	115.00
(117)	The Athletic Infield(Hauser, Konetchy)	750.00	250.00	115.00
(118)	The Athletic Infield(Krause, Thomas)	750.00	250.00	115.00
(119)	The Pinch Hitter(Egan, Hoblitzell)	650.00	215.00	95.00
(120)	The Scissors Slide(Birmingham, Turner)	650.00	215.00	95.00
(121)	Tom Jones At Bat(Fromme, McLean)	650.00	215.00	95.00
(122)	Tom Jones At Bat(Gaspar, McLean)	650.00	215.00	95.00
(123)	Too Late For Devlin(Ames, Meyers)	650.00	215.00	95.00
(124)	Too Late For Devlin(Crandall, Meyers)	650.00	215.00	95.00
(125)	Too Late For Devlin(Devlin (Giants), Mathewson)	3,000	1,000	450.00
(126)	Too Late For Devlin(Devlin (Rustlers), Mathewson)	3,900	1,300	585.00
(127)	Too Late For Devlin(Marquard, Meyers)	650.00	215.00	95.00
(128)	Too Late For Devlin(Meyers, Wiltse)	650.00	215.00	95.00
(129)	Ty Cobb Steals Third(Cobb, Jennings)	5,500	1,800	825,00
(130)	Ty Cobb Steals Third(Cobb, Moriarty)	5,100	1,685	765.00
(131)	Ty Cobb Steals Third(Austin, Stovall)	2,500	900.00	400.00
(132)	Wheat Strikes Out(Dahlen, Wheat)	1,000	333.00	150.00

1909 T204

(See 1909 Ramly Cigarettes, 1909 T.T.T. Cigarettes.)

1911 T205 Gold Border

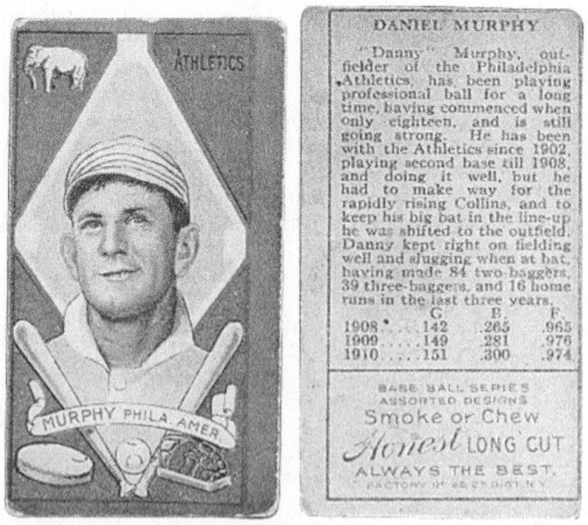

Featuring distinctive gold-leaf borders, these cards were issued in a number of different cigarette brands. The cards nominally measure 1-7/16" x 2-5/8" although many cards, even though untrimmed or unaltered, measure somewhat less than those dimensions in length and/or width. American League cards feature a color lithograph of the player inside a stylized baseball diamond. National League cards have head-and-shoulders portraits on a plain background, plus the first-ever use of a facsimile autograph in a major card set. The 12 minor league players in the set feature three-quarter length portraits or action pictures in an elaborate frame of columns and other devices. Card backs of the major leaguers carry the player's full name (another first) and statistics. Card backs of the minor leaguers lack the statistics. The complete set price does not include the scarcer of the letter-suffixed variations. Values shown are for cards with the most common cigarette advertising on back: Piedmont and Sweet Caporal. Cards of other brands may carry a premium (see listings under brand name). The condition of the fragile gold leaf on the borders is an important grading consideration.

		NM	E	VG
Common Player:		600.00	100.00	42.00
(1)	Edward J. Abbaticchio	600.00	100.00	42.00
(2)	Doc Adkins	1,650	245.00	95.00
(3)	Leon K. Ames	600.00	100.00	42.00
(4)	Jas. P. Archer	600.00	100.00	42.00
(5)	Jimmy Austin	600.00	100.00	42.00
(6)	Bill Bailey	600.00	100.00	42.00
(7)	Home Run Baker	2,100	365.00	145.00
(8)	Neal Ball	600.00	100.00	42.00
(9)	E.B. Barger (Full "B" on cap.)	1,500	220.00	90.00
(10)	E.B. Barger (Partial "B" on cap.)	2,400	360.00	145.00
(11)	Jack Barry	600.00	100.00	42.00
(12)	Emil Batch	1,650	245.00	95.00
(13)	John W. Bates	600.00	100.00	42.00
(14)	Fred Beck	600.00	100.00	42.00
(15)	B. Becker	600.00	100.00	42.00
(16)	George G. Bell	600.00	100.00	42.00
(17)	Chas. Bender	2,100	315.00	120.00
(18)	William Bergen	600.00	100.00	42.00
(19)	Bob Bescher	600.00	100.00	42.00
(20)	Joe Birmingham	600.00	100.00	42.00
(21)	Lena Blackburne	600.00	100.00	42.00
(22)	William E. Bransfield	600.00	100.00	42.00
(23)	Roger P. Bresnahan (Mouth closed.)	1,650	250.00	100.00
(24)	Roger P. Bresnahan (Mouth open.)	3,425	515.00	205.00
(25)	A.H. Bridwell	600.00	100.00	42.00
(26)	Mordecai Brown	2,000	375.00	150.00
(27)	Robert Byrne	600.00	100.00	42.00
(28)	Hick Cady	1,650	240.00	95.00
(29)	H. Camnitz	600.00	100.00	42.00
(30)	Bill Carrigan	600.00	100.00	42.00
(31)	Frank J. Chance	2,100	240.00	96.00
(32a)	Hal Chase (Both ears show, gold diamond frame extends below shoulders.)	1,100	165.00	66.00
(32b)	Hal Chase (Both ears show, gold diamond frame ends at shoulders.)	1,625	245.00	95.00
(33)	Hal Chase (Only left ear shows.)	3,250	485.00	195.00
(34)	Ed Cicotte	2,400	360.00	145.00
(35)	Fred C. Clarke	1,650	215.00	90.00
(36)	Ty Cobb	17,500	3,250	1,100
(37)	Eddie Collins (Mouth closed.)	2,100	315.00	120.00
(38)	Eddie Collins (Mouth open.)	4,675	675.00	270.00
(39)	Jimmy Collins	2,600	390.00	155.00
(40)	Frank J. Corridon	600.00	100.00	42.00
(41a)	Otis Crandall ("t" not crossed in name)	900.00	150.00	60.00
(41b)	Otis Crandall ("t" crossed in name)	1,325	200.00	80.00
(42)	Lou Criger	600.00	100.00	42.00
(43)	W.F. Dahlen	2,200	400.00	175.00
(44)	Jake Daubert	600.00	10.00	42.00
(45)	Jim Delahanty	600.00	100.00	42.00
(46)	Arthur Devlin	600.00	100.00	42.00
(47)	Josh Devore	600.00	100.00	42.00
(48)	W.R. Dickson	600.00	100.00	42.00
(49)	Jiggs Donohue (Donahue)	2,875	410.00	165.00
(50)	Chas. S. Dooin	600.00	100.00	42.00
(51)	Michael J. Doolan	600.00	100.00	42.00
(52a)	Patsy Dougherty (Red sock for team emblem.)	2,500	500.00	200.00
(52b)	Patsy Dougherty (White sock for team emblem.)	1,600	240.00	96.00
(53)	Thomas Downey	600.00	100.00	42.00
(54)	Larry Doyle	600.00	100.00	42.00
(55)	Hugh Duffy	2,300	410.00	165.00
(56)	Jack Dunn	2,650	425.00	180.00
(57)	Jimmy Dygert	600.00	100.00	42.00
(58)	R. Egan	600.00	100.00	42.00
(59)	Kid Elberfeld	600.00	100.00	42.00
(60)	Clyde Engle	600.00	100.00	42.00
(61)	Louis Evans	600.00	100.00	42.00
(62)	John J. Evers	2,750	410.00	165.00
(63)	Robert Ewing	600.00	100.00	42.00
(64)	G.C. Ferguson	600.00	100.00	42.00
(65)	Ray Fisher	2,950	440.00	175.00
(66)	Arthur Fletcher	600.00	100.00	42.00
(67)	John A. Flynn	600.00	100.00	42.00
(68)	Russ Ford (Black cap.)	700.00	100.00	50.00
(69)	Russ Ford (White cap.)	2,200	330.00	135.00
(70)	Wm. A. Foxen	600.00	100.00	42.00
(71)	Jimmy Frick	1,625	240.00	100.00
(72)	Arthur Fromme	600.00	100.00	42.00
(73)	Earl Gardner	700.00	100.00	50.00
(74)	H.L. Gaspar	600.00	100.00	42.00
(75)	George Gibson	600.00	100.00	42.00
(76)	Wilbur Goode	600.00	100.00	42.00
(77)	George F. Graham (Rustlers)	600.00	100.00	42.00
(78)	George F. Graham (Cubs)	2,150	255.00	105.00
(79)	Edward L. Grant	2,400	360.00	145.00
(80a)	Dolly Gray (No stats on back.)	1,350	200.00	50.00
(80b)	Dolly Gray (Stats on back.)	7,250	1,000	500.00
(81)	Clark Griffith	1,800	270.00	110.00
(82)	Bob Groom	600.00	100.00	55.00
(83)	Charlie Hanford	1,900	285.00	115.00
(84)	Bob Harmon (Both ears show.)	1,000	135.00	45.00
(85)	Bob Harmon (Only left ear shows.)	2,525	380.00	150.00
(86)	Topsy Hartsel	600.00	100.00	42.00
(87)	Arnold J. Hauser	600.00	100.00	42.00
(88)	Charlie Hemphill	600.00	100.00	42.00
(89)	C.L. Herzog	600.00	100.00	42.00
(90a)	R. Hoblitzell (No stats on back.)		18,500	10,500
(90b)	R. Hoblitzell ("Cin." after 2nd 1908 in stats.)	1,550	230.00	95.00
(90c)	R. Hoblitzel (Name incorrect, no "Cin." after 1908 in stats.)	3,420	510.00	210.00
(90d)	R. Hoblitzell (Name correct, no "Cin." after 1908 in stats.)	8,500	1,200	510.00
(91)	Danny Hoffman	600.00	100.00	42.00
(92)	Miller J. Huggins	1,920	290.00	115.00
(93)	John E. Hummel	600.00	100.00	42.00
(94)	Fred Jacklitsch	600.00	100.00	42.00
(95)	Hughie Jennings	1,450	215.00	90.00
(96)	Walter Johnson	8,400	1,320	510.00
(97)	D. Jones	600.00	100.00	42.00
(98)	Tom Jones	600.00	100.00	42.00
(99)	Addie Joss	9,000	1,500	700.00
(100)	Ed Karger	1,600	300.00	100.00
(101)	Ed Killian	600.00	100.00	42.00
(102)	Red Kleinow	1,560	235.00	90.00
(103)	John G. Kling	600.00	100.00	42.00
(104)	Jack Knight	600.00	100.00	42.00
(105)	Ed Konetchy	600.00	100.00	42.00
(106)	Harry Krause	600.00	100.00	42.00
(107)	Floyd M. Kroh	600.00	100.00	42.00
(108)	Frank LaPorte	600.00	100.00	42.00
(109)	Frank Lang (Lange)	600.00	100.00	42.00
(110a)	A. Latham (A. Latham on back.)	700.00	100.00	50.00
(110b)	A. Latham (W.A. Latham on back.)	1,600	300.00	50.00
(111)	Thomas W. Leach	600.00	100.00	42.00
(112)	Watty Lee	1,620	240.00	100.00
(113)	Sam Leever	600.00	100.00	42.00
(114a)	A. Leifield (Initial "A." on front.)	700.00	100.00	50.00
(114b)	A.P. Leifield (Initials "A.P." on front.)	1,600	300.00	50.00
(115)	Edgar Lennox	600.00	100.00	42.00
(116)	Paddy Livingston	600.00	100.00	42.00
(117)	John B. Lobert	600.00	100.00	42.00
(118)	Bris Lord (Athletics)	600.00	100.00	42.00
(119)	Harry Lord (White Sox)	600.00	100.00	42.00
(120)	Jno. C. Lush	600.00	100.00	42.00
(121)	Nick Maddox	600.00	100.00	42.00
(122)	Sherwood R. Magee	850.00	125.00	50.00
(123)	R.W. Marquard	2,280	345.00	140.00
(124)	C. Mathewson	8,500	1,250	510.00
(124a)	Christy Mathewson (1 loss variation (only on Cycle backs).)		10,000	4,000
(125)	A.A. Mattern	600.00	100.00	42.00
(126)	Sport McAllister	1,620	240.00	100.00
(127)	George McBride	870.00	135.00	55.00
(128)	Amby McConnell	600.00	100.00	42.00
(129)	P.M. McElveen	600.00	100.00	42.00
(130)	J.J. McGraw	2,100	315.00	125.00
(131)	Harry McIntire (Cubs)	600.00	100.00	42.00
(132)	Matty McIntyre (White Sox)	600.00	100.00	42.00
(133)	M.A. McLean (Initials actually J.B.)	600.00	100.00	435.00
(134)	Fred Merkle	600.00	100.00	42.00
(135)	George Merritt	1,620	240.00	100.00
(136)	J.T. Meyers	600.00	100.00	42.00
(137)	Clyde Milan	600.00	100.00	42.00
(138a)	J.D. Miller (bio begins 'John B. Miller"	600.00	100.00	42.00
(138b)	J.D. Miller (bio begins "John D. Miller")	625.00	115.00	40.00
(139)	M.F. Mitchell	600.00	100.00	42.00
(140a)	P.J. Moran (Stray line of type below stats.)	12,000	1,800	720.00
(140b)	P.J. Moran (No stray line.)	600.00	100.00	42.00
(141)	George Moriarty	600.00	100.00	42.00
(142)	George Mullin	600.00	100.00	42.00
(143)	Danny Murphy	600.00	100.00	42.00
(144)	Jack Murray	600.00	100.00	42.00
(145)	John Nee	1,620	240.00	100.00
(146)	Thomas J. Needham	600.00	100.00	42.00
(147)	Rebel Oakes	600.00	100.00	42.00
(148)	Rube Oldring	600.00	100.00	42.00
(149)	Charley O'Leary	600.00	100.00	42.00
(150)	Fred Olmstead	600.00	100.00	42.00
(151)	Orval Overall	600.00	100.00	42.00
(152)	Freddy Parent	600.00	100.00	42.00
(153)	George Paskert	600.00	100.00	42.00
(154)	Fred Payne	600.00	100.00	42.00
(155)	Barney Pelty	840.00	135.00	55.00
(156)	John Pfeister	600.00	100.00	42.00
(157)	Jimmy Phelan	1,300	195.00	80.00
(158)	E.J. Phelps	600.00	100.00	42.00
(159)	C. Phillippe	600.00	100.00	42.00
(160)	Jack Quinn	600.00	100.00	42.00
(161)	A.L. Raymond	1,600	400.00	200.00
(162)	E.M. Reulbach	600.00	100.00	42.00
(163)	Lewis Richie	600.00	100.00	42.00
(164)	John A. Rowan	3,000	500.00	200.00
(165)	George N. Rucker	600.00	100.00	42.00
(166)	W.D. Scanlan	2,900	435.00	175.00
(167)	Germany Schaefer	600.00	100.00	42.00
(168)	George Schlei	600.00	100.00	42.00
(169)	Boss Schmidt	600.00	100.00	42.00
(170)	F.M. Schulte	600.00	100.00	42.00
(171)	Jim Scott	600.00	100.00	42.00
(172)	B.H. Sharpe	600.00	100.00	42.00
(173)	David Shean (Rustlers)	600.00	100.00	42.00
(174)	David Shean (Cubs)	2,520	380.00	150.00
(175)	Jas. T. Sheckard	600.00	100.00	42.00
(176)	Hack Simmons	600.00	100.00	42.00
(177)	Tony Smith	600.00	100.00	42.00
(178)	Fred C. Snodgrass	600.00	100.00	42.00
(179)	Tris Speaker	5,000	750.00	300.00
(180)	Jake Stahl	1,100	165.00	70.00
(181)	Oscar Stanage	600.00	100.00	42.00
(182)	Harry Steinfeldt	600.00	100.00	42.00
(183)	George Stone	600.00	100.00	42.00
(184)	George Stovall	600.00	100.00	42.00
(185)	Gabby Street	600.00	100.00	42.00
(186)	George F. Suggs	3,000	500.00	200.00
(187)	Ed Summers	600.00	100.00	42.00
(188)	Jeff Sweeney	2,700	405.00	165.00
(189)	Lee Tannehill	600.00	100.00	42.00
(190)	Ira Thomas	600.00	100.00	42.00
(191)	Joe Tinker	2,160	330.00	135.00

(192)	John Titus	600.00	100.00	42.00
(193)	Terry Turner	3,100	395.00	155.00
(194)	James Vaughn	2,880	435.00	175.00
(195)	Charles Wagner	3,180	475.00	195.00
(196)	Bobby Wallace (With cap.)	1,770	270.00	110.00
(197a)	Bobby Wallace (No cap, one line of 1910 stats.)	15,000	3,300	1,500
(197b)	Bobby Wallace (No cap, two lines of 1910 stats.)	8,000	1,500	600.00
(198)	Ed Walsh	4,000	600.00	240.00
(199)	Z.D. Wheat	2,280	345.00	140.00
(200)	Doc White (White Sox)	750.00	110.00	45.00
(201)	Kirb. White (Pirates)	1,600	300.00	100.00
(202a)	Irvin K. Wilhelm ("suffered" in 18th line of bio. Very scarce, only found with Hassan back.)	9,000	5,000	2,000
(202b)	Irvin K. Wilhelm ("suffe ed" in 18th line of bio)	4,800	600.00	240.00
(203)	Ed Willett	600.00	100.00	42.00
(204)	J. Owen Wilson	600.00	100.00	42.00
(205)	George R. Wiltse (Both ears show.)	600.00	100.00	42.00
(206)	George R. Wiltse (Only right ear shows.)	3,500	395.00	160.00
(207)	Harry Wolter	600.00	100.00	42.00
(208)	Cy Young	11,250	1,650	660.00

1909-11 T206 White Border

The nearly 525 cards which make up the T206 set are the most popular of the early tobacco card issues. Players are depicted in color lithographs surrounded by a white border. The player's last name on the 1-7/16" x 2-5/8" cards appears at the bottom with the city and league, when a city had more than one team. Backs contain an ad for one of 16 brands of cigarettes. There are 389 major leaguer cards and 134 minor leaguer cards in the set, but with front/back varieties the number of potentially different cards runs into the thousands. The set features many expensive cards including a number of pose and/or team variations. Values shown are for cards with the most common advertising on back: Piedmont and Sweet Caporal. Other backs carry a premium depending on scarcity (see listings under brand names). Several popularly collected printing errors have been included in a separate listing.

		NM	E	VG
	Common Player:	550.00	135.00	55.00
(1)	Ed Abbaticchio (Blue sleeves.)	550.00	135.00	55.00
(2)	Ed Abbaticchio (Brown sleeves.)	550.00	135.00	55.00
(3)	Fred Abbott	550.00	135.00	55.00
(4)	Bill Abstein	550.00	135.00	55.00
(5)	Doc Adkins	550.00	135.00	55.00
(6)	Whitey Alperman	550.00	135.00	55.00
(7)	Red Ames (Hands at chest.)	800.00	200.00	100.00
(8)	Red Ames (Hands above head.)	550.00	135.00	55.00
(9)	Red Ames (Portrait)	550.00	135.00	55.00
(10)	John Anderson	550.00	135.00	55.00
(11)	Frank Arellanes	550.00	135.00	55.00
(12)	Herman Armbruster	550.00	135.00	55.00
(13)	Harry Arndt	550.00	135.00	55.00
(14)	Jake Atz	550.00	135.00	55.00
(15)	Home Run Baker	1,675	837.50	502.50
(16)	Neal Ball (New York)	550.00	135.00	55.00
(17)	Neal Ball (Cleveland)	550.00	135.00	55.00
(18)	Jap Barbeau	550.00	135.00	55.00
(19)	Cy Barger	550.00	135.00	55.00
(20)	Jack Barry (Philadelphia)	550.00	135.00	55.00
(21)	Shad Barry (Milwaukee)	550.00	135.00	55.00
(22)	Jack Bastian	1,500	400.00	340.00
(23)	Emil Batch	550.00	135.00	55.00
(24)	Johnny Bates	550.00	135.00	55.00
(25)	Harry Bay	1,500	400.00	340.00
(26)	Ginger Beaumont	600.00	150.00	75.00
(27)	Fred Beck	550.00	135.00	55.00
(28)	Beals Becker	550.00	135.00	55.00
(29)	Jake Beckley	1,400	350.00	140.00
(30)	George Bell (Hands above head.)	550.00	135.00	55.00
(31)	George Bell (Pitching follow through.)	550.00	135.00	55.00
(32)	Chief Bender (Pitching, no trees in background.)	1,650	400.00	165.00
(33)	Chief Bender (Pitching, trees in background.)	2,025	500.00	200.00
(34)	Chief Bender (Portrait)	2,000	500.00	200.00
(35)	Bill Bergen (Batting)	550.00	135.00	55.00
(36)	Bill Bergen (Catching)	550.00	135.00	55.00
(37)	Heinie Berger	550.00	135.00	55.00
(38)	Bill Bernhard	1,500	375.00	150.00
(39)	Bob Bescher (Hands in air.)	550.00	135.00	55.00
(40)	Bob Bescher (Portrait)	550.00	135.00	55.00
(41)	Joe Birmingham	900.00	225.00	110.00
(42)	Lena Blackburne	550.00	135.00	55.00
(43)	Jack Bliss	550.00	135.00	55.00
(44)	Frank Bowerman	550.00	135.00	55.00
(45)	Bill Bradley (Portrait)	550.00	135.00	55.00
(46)	Bill Bradley (With bat.)	550.00	125.00	60.00
(47)	Dave Brain	550.00	135.00	55.00
(48)	Kitty Bransfield	550.00	135.00	55.00
(49)	Roy Brashear	550.00	135.00	55.00
(50)	Ted Breitenstein	1,550	385.00	155.00
(51)	Roger Bresnahan (Portrait)	1,500	385.00	150.00
(52)	Roger Bresnahan (With bat.)	1,600	400.00	160.00
(53)	Al Bridwell (Portrait, no cap.)	550.00	135.00	55.00
(54)	Al Bridwell (Portrait, with cap.)	550.00	135.00	55.00
(55a)	George Brown (Browne) (Chicago)	550.00	135.00	55.00
(55b)	George Brown (Browne) (Washington)	1,800	450.00	180.00
(56)	Mordecai Brown (Chicago on shirt.)	1,525	385.00	150.00
(57)	Mordecai Brown (Cubs on shirt.)	3,250	800.00	325.00
(58)	Mordecai Brown (Portrait)	1,900	475.00	190.00
(59)	Al Burch (Batting)	1,000	250.00	100.00
(60)	Al Burch (Fielding)	550.00	135.00	55.00
(61)	Fred Burchell	550.00	135.00	55.00
(62)	Jimmy Burke	550.00	135.00	55.00
(63)	Bill Burns	550.00	135.00	55.00
(64)	Donie Bush	550.00	135.00	55.00
(65)	John Butler	550.00	135.00	55.00
(66)	Bobby Byrne	550.00	135.00	55.00
(67)	Howie Camnitz (Arm at side.)	550.00	135.00	55.00
(68)	Howie Camnitz (Arms folded.)	550.00	135.00	55.00
(69)	Howie Camnitz (Hands above head.)	550.00	135.00	55.00
(70)	Billy Campbell	550.00	135.00	55.00
(71)	Scoops Carey	1,125	565.00	340.00
(72)	Charley Carr	550.00	135.00	55.00
(73)	Bill Carrigan	550.00	135.00	55.00
(74)	Doc Casey	550.00	135.00	55.00
(75)	Peter Cassidy	550.00	135.00	55.00
(76)	Frank Chance (Batting)	1,950	350.00	195.00
(77)	Frank Chance (Portrait, red background.)	2,000	500.00	200.00
(78)	Frank Chance (Portrait, yellow background.)	1,325	425.00	135.00
(79)	Bill Chappelle	550.00	135.00	55.00
(80)	Chappie Charles	550.00	135.00	55.00
(81)	Hal Chase (Holding trophy.)	825.00	200.00	100.00
(82)	Hal Chase (Portrait, blue background.)	875.00	420.00	255.00
(83)	Hal Chase (Portrait, pink background.)	1,300	425.00	130.00
(84)	Hal Chase (Throwing, dark cap.)	875.00	240.00	85.00
(85)	Hal Chase (Throwing, white cap.)	1,000	250.00	100.00
(86)	Jack Chesbro	2,550	600.00	255.00
(87)	Ed Cicotte	1,250	300.00	125.00
(88)	Bill Clancy (Clancey)	550.00	135.00	55.00
(89)	Josh Clark (Columbus) (Clarke)	550.00	135.00	55.00
(90)	Fred Clarke (Pittsburgh, holding bat.)	1,300	400.00	130.00
(91)	Fred Clarke (Pittsburgh, portrait.)	1,425	425.00	145.00
(92)	J.J. Clarke (Nig) (Cleveland)	550.00	135.00	55.00
(93)	Bill Clymer	550.00	135.00	55.00
(94)	Ty Cobb (Portrait, green background.)	12,000	3,100	1,450
(95a)	Ty Cobb (Portrait, red background.)	7,750	2,300	875.00
(95b)	Ty Cobb (Portrait, red background, Ty Cobb brand back. See 1909-11 Ty Cobb Tobacco. In 2010 a PSA Fair sold for $135,4032, a PSA Good brought $111,625)			
(96)	Ty Cobb (Bat off shoulder.)	7,500	1,965	975.00
(97)	Ty Cobb (Bat on shoulder.)	9,300	2,675	1,000
(98)	Cad Coles	1,550	400.00	155.00
(99)	Eddie Collins (Philadelphia)	1,825	450.00	185.00
(100)	Jimmy Collins (Minneapolis)	1,300	325.00	130.00
(101)	Bunk Congalton	550.00	135.00	55.00
(102)	Wid Conroy (Fielding)	575.00	290.00	175.00
(103)	Wid Conroy (With bat.)	550.00	135.00	55.00
(104)	Harry Covaleski (Coveleski)	550.00	135.00	55.00
(105)	Doc Crandall (Portrait, no cap.)	550.00	135.00	55.00
(106)	Doc Crandall (Portrait, with cap.)	550.00	135.00	55.00
(107)	Bill Cranston	1,550	385.00	155.00
(108)	Gavvy Cravath	550.00	135.00	55.00
(109)	Sam Crawford (Throwing)	1,825	450.00	185.00
(110)	Sam Crawford (With bat.)	1,625	400.00	165.00
(111)	Birdie Cree	550.00	135.00	55.00
(112)	Lou Criger	550.00	135.00	55.00
(113)	Dode Criss	550.00	135.00	55.00
(114)	Monte Cross	550.00	135.00	55.00
(115a)	Bill Dahlen (Boston)	1,000	135.00	100.00
(115b)	Bill Dahlen (Brooklyn)	2,400	600.00	240.00
(116)	Paul Davidson	550.00	135.00	55.00
(117)	George Davis (Chicago)	1,400	350.00	140.00
(118)	Harry Davis (Philadelphia, Davis on front.)	550.00	135.00	55.00
(119)	Harry Davis (Philadelphia, H. Davis on front.)	550.00	135.00	55.00
(120)	Frank Delehanty (Delahanty) (Louisville)	550.00	135.00	55.00
(121)	Jim Delehanty (Delahanty) (Washington)	550.00	135.00	55.00
(122a)	Ray Demmitt (New York)	550.00	135.00	55.00
(122b)	Ray Demmitt (St. Louis)	32,600	10,000	5,000
(123)	Rube Dessau	550.00	135.00	55.00
(124)	Art Devlin	550.00	135.00	55.00
(125)	Josh Devore	550.00	135.00	55.00
(126)	Bill Dineen (Dinneen)	550.00	135.00	55.00
(127)	Mike Donlin (Fielding)	900.00	225.00	90.00
(128)	Mike Donlin (Seated)	750.00	185.00	75.00
(129)	Mike Donlin (With bat.)	550.00	135.00	55.00
(130)	Jiggs Donohue (Donahue)	550.00	135.00	55.00
(131)	Wild Bill Donovan (Portrait)	550.00	135.00	70.00
(132)	Wild Bill Donovan (Throwing)	550.00	135.00	55.00
(133)	Red Dooin	550.00	135.00	55.00
(134)	Mickey Doolan (Batting)	550.00	135.00	55.00
(135)	Mickey Doolan (Fielding)	550.00	135.00	55.00
(136)	Mickey Doolin (Doolan)	550.00	135.00	55.00
(137)	Gus Dorner	550.00	135.00	55.00
(138)	Patsy Dougherty (Arm in air.)	550.00	135.00	55.00
(139)	Patsy Dougherty (Portrait)	550.00	135.00	55.00
(140)	Tom Downey (Batting)	550.00	135.00	55.00
(141)	Tom Downey (Fielding)	550.00	135.00	55.00
(142)	Jerry Downs	550.00	135.00	55.00
(143a)	Joe Doyle (N.Y. Nat'l., hands above head. An SGc Authentic was auctioned for $186,155)			
(143b)	Joe Doyle (N.Y., hands above head.)	2,500	625.00	250.00
(144)	Larry Doyle (N.Y. Nat'l., portrait.)	550.00	135.00	55.00
(145)	Larry Doyle (N.Y. Nat'l., throwing.)	550.00	135.00	55.00
(146)	Larry Doyle (N.Y. Nat'l., with bat.)	550.00	135.00	55.00
(147)	Jean Dubuc	550.00	135.00	55.00
(148)	Hugh Duffy	1,700	425.00	175.00
(149)	Jack Dunn (Baltimore)	550.00	135.00	55.00
(150)	Joe Dunn (Brooklyn)	550.00	135.00	55.00
(151)	Bull Durham	550.00	135.00	55.00
(152)	Jimmy Dygert	550.00	135.00	55.00
(153)	Ted Easterly	550.00	135.00	55.00
(154)	Dick Egan	550.00	135.00	55.00
(155a)	Kid Elberfeld (New York)	600.00	150.00	60.00
(155b)	Kid Elberfeld (Washington, portrait.)	7,150	1,785	715.00
(156)	Kid Elberfeld (Washington, fielding.)	550.00	135.00	55.00
(157)	Roy Ellam	1,500	375.00	150.00
(158)	Clyde Engle	550.00	135.00	55.00
(159)	Steve Evans	550.00	135.00	55.00
(160)	Johnny Evers (Portrait)	3,750	935.00	375.00
(161)	Johnny Evers (With bat, Chicago on shirt.)	1,525	375.00	150.00
(162)	Johnny Evers (With bat, Cubs on shirt.)	2,150	500.00	215.00
(163)	Bob Ewing	550.00	135.00	55.00

(164) Cecil Ferguson	550.00	135.00	55.00
(165) Hobe Ferris	550.00	135.00	55.00
(166) Lou Fiene (Portrait)	550.00	135.00	55.00
(167) Lou Fiene (Throwing)	550.00	135.00	55.00
(168) Steamer Flanagan	550.00	135.00	55.00
(169) Art Fletcher	550.00	135.00	55.00
(170) Elmer Flick	1,650	400.00	165.00
(171) Russ Ford	550.00	135.00	55.00
(172) Ed Foster	1,650	400.00	165.00
(173) Jerry Freeman	550.00	135.00	55.00
(174) John Frill	550.00	135.00	55.00
(175) Charlie Fritz	1,550	375.00	155.00
(176) Art Fromme	550.00	135.00	55.00
(177) Chick Gandil	1,075	250.00	105.00
(178) Bob Ganley	550.00	135.00	55.00
(179) John Ganzel	550.00	135.00	55.00
(180) Harry Gasper	550.00	135.00	55.00
(181) Rube Geyer	550.00	135.00	55.00
(182) George Gibson	550.00	135.00	55.00
(183) Billy Gilbert	550.00	135.00	55.00
(184) Wilbur Goode (Good)	550.00	135.00	55.00
(185) Bill Graham (St. Louis)	550.00	135.00	55.00
(186) Peaches Graham (Boston)	550.00	135.00	55.00
(187) Dolly Gray	550.00	135.00	55.00
(188) Ed Greminger	1,550	375.00	155.00
(189) Clark Griffith (Batting)	1,650	400.00	165.00
(190) Clark Griffith (Portrait)	1,550	375.00	166.00
(191) Moose Grimshaw	550.00	135.00	55.00
(192) Bob Groom	550.00	135.00	55.00
(193) Tom Guiheen	1,550	375.00	155.00
(194) Ed Hahn	550.00	135.00	55.00
(195) Bob Hall	550.00	135.00	55.00
(196) Bill Hallman	550.00	135.00	55.00
(197) Jack Hannifan (Hannifin)	550.00	135.00	55.00
(198) Bill Hart (Little Rock)	1,300	325.00	160.00
(199) Jimmy Hart (Montgomery)	1,300	325.00	160.00
(200) Topsy Hartsel	550.00	135.00	55.00
(201) Jack Hayden	550.00	135.00	55.00
(202) J. Ross Helm	1,300	325.00	160.00
(203) Charlie Hemphill	550.00	135.00	55.00
(204) Buck Herzog (Boston)	800.00	200.00	100.00
(205) Buck Herzog (New York)	550.00	135.00	55.00
(206) Gordon Hickman	1,550	375.00	160.00
(207) Bill Hinchman (Cleveland)	550.00	135.00	55.00
(208) Harry Hinchman (Toledo)	550.00	135.00	55.00
(209) Dick Hoblitzell	550.00	135.00	55.00
(210) Danny Hoffman (St. Louis)	550.00	135.00	55.00
(211) Izzy Hoffman (Providence)	550.00	135.00	55.00
(212) Solly Hofman	550.00	135.00	55.00
(213) Bock Hooker	1,550	325.00	160.00
(214) Del Howard (Chicago)	550.00	135.00	55.00
(215) Ernie Howard (Savannah)	1,550	325.00	160.00
(216) Harry Howell (Hand at waist.)	550.00	135.00	55.00
(217) Harry Howell (Portrait)	550.00	135.00	55.00
(218) Miller Huggins (Hands at mouth.)	1,550	325.00	160.00
(219) Miller Huggins (Portrait)	1,200	300.00	55.00
(220) Rudy Hulswitt	550.00	135.00	55.00
(221) John Hummel	550.00	135.00	55.00
(222) George Hunter	550.00	135.00	55.00
(223) Frank Isbell	550.00	135.00	55.00
(224) Fred Jacklitsch	550.00	135.00	55.00
(225) Jimmy Jackson	550.00	135.00	55.00
(226) Hughie Jennings (One hand showing.)	1,450	360.00	180.00
(227) Hughie Jennings (Both hands showing.)	1,400	350.00	140.00
(228) Hughie Jennings (Portrait)	1,550	325.00	160.00
(229) Walter Johnson (Hands at chest.)	5,750	1,350	650.00
(230) Walter Johnson (Portrait)	5,050	1,475	475.00
(231) Fielder Jones (Chicago, hands at hips.)	550.00	135.00	55.00
(232) Fielder Jones (Chicago, portrait.)	550.00	135.00	55.00
(233) Davy Jones (Detroit)	550.00	135.00	55.00
(234) Tom Jones (St. Louis)	550.00	135.00	55.00
(235) Dutch Jordan (Atlanta)	1,550	325.00	160.00
(236) Tim Jordan (Brooklyn, batting.)	550.00	135.00	55.00
(237) Tim Jordan (Brooklyn, portrait.)	550.00	135.00	55.00
(238) Addie Joss (Pitching)	2,000	500.00	200.00
(239) Addie Joss (Portrait)	1,650	410.00	205.00
(240) Ed Karger	550.00	135.00	55.00
(241) Willie Keeler (Portrait)	2,750	685.00	345.00
(242) Willie Keeler (W/bat.)	2,200	500.00	220.00
(243) Joe Kelley	1,550	325.00	160.00
(244) J.F. Kiernan	1,550	325.00	160.00
(245) Ed Killian (Pitching)	550.00	135.00	55.00
(246) Ed Killian (Portrait)	550.00	135.00	55.00
(247) Frank King	1,550	325.00	160.00
(248) Rube Kisinger	550.00	135.00	55.00
(249a) Red Kleinow (Boston)	2,100	525.00	210.00
(249b) Red Kleinow (New York, catching.)	550.00	135.00	55.00
(250) Red Kleinow (New York, with bat.)	550.00	135.00	55.00
(251) Johnny Kling	550.00	135.00	55.00
(252) Otto Knabe	550.00	135.00	55.00
(253) Jack Knight (Portrait)	550.00	135.00	55.00
(254) Jack Knight (With bat.)	550.00	135.00	55.00
(255) Ed Konetchy (Glove above head.)	550.00	135.00	55.00
(256) Ed Konetchy (Glove near ground.)	475.00	120.00	60.00
(257) Harry Krause (Pitching)	550.00	135.00	55.00
(258) Harry Krause (Portrait)	550.00	135.00	55.00
(259) Rube Kroh	550.00	135.00	55.00
(260) Art Kruger (Krueger)	550.00	135.00	55.00
(261) James Lafitte	1,550	325.00	160.00
(262) Nap Lajoie (Portrait)	3,275	800.00	325.00
(263) Nap Lajoie (Throwing)	3,000	750.00	300.00
(264) Nap Lajoie (With bat.)	4,400	1,100	440.00
(265) Joe Lake (New York)	550.00	135.00	55.00
(266) Joe Lake (St. Louis, ball in hand.)	550.00	135.00	55.00
(267) Joe Lake (St. Louis, no ball in hand.)	550.00	135.00	55.00
(268) Frank LaPorte	550.00	135.00	55.00
(269) Arlie Latham	550.00	135.00	55.00
(270) Bill Lattimore	550.00	135.00	55.00
(271) Jimmy Lavender	550.00	135.00	55.00
(272) Tommy Leach (Bending over.)	550.00	135.00	55.00
(273) Tommy Leach (Portrait)	550.00	135.00	55.00
(274) Lefty Leifield (Batting)	550.00	135.00	55.00
(275) Lefty Leifield (Pitching)	550.00	135.00	55.00
(276) Ed Lennox	550.00	135.00	55.00
(277) Harry Lentz (Sentz)	1,550	325.00	160.00
(278) Glenn Liebhardt	550.00	135.00	55.00
(279) Vive Lindaman	550.00	135.00	55.00
(280) Perry Lipe	1,550	325.00	160.00
(281) Paddy Livingstone (Livingston)	550.00	135.00	55.00
(282) Hans Lobert	550.00	135.00	55.00
(283) Harry Lord	550.00	135.00	55.00
(284) Harry Lumley	550.00	135.00	55.00
(285a) Carl Lundgren (Chicago)	5,150	1,285	515.00
(285b) Carl Lundgren (Kansas City)	550.00	135.00	55.00
(286) Nick Maddox	550.00	135.00	55.00
(287a) Sherry Magie (Magee) Values shown represent auction prices realized of graded examples only VG-EX - 26,438 VG - 16,855 GOOD - 9,400 FAIR - 7,625 POOR - 5,500			
(287b) Sherry Magee (Portrait)	900.00	225.00	90.00
(288) Sherry Magee (With bat.)	550.00	135.00	55.00
(289) Bill Malarkey	550.00	135.00	55.00
(290) Billy Maloney	550.00	135.00	55.00
(291) George Manion	1,550	325.00	160.00
(292) Rube Manning (Batting)	550.00	135.00	55.00
(293) Rube Manning (Pitching)	550.00	135.00	55.00
(294) Rube Marquard (Hands at thighs.)	1,600	400.00	200.00
(295) Rube Marquard (Follow-through.)	1,600	400.00	200.00
(296) Rube Marquard (Portrait)	2,575	600.00	255.00
(297) Doc Marshall	550.00	135.00	55.00
(298) Christy Mathewson (Dark cap.)	5,800	1,450	575.00
(299) Christy Mathewson (Portrait)	5,800	1,450	575.00
(300) Christy Mathewson (White cap.)	5,000	1,250	625.00
(301) Al Mattern	550.00	135.00	55.00
(302) John McAleese	550.00	135.00	55.00
(303) George McBride	550.00	135.00	55.00
(304) Pat McCauley	1,550	325.00	160.00
(305) Moose McCormick	550.00	135.00	55.00
(306) Pryor McElveen	550.00	135.00	55.00
(307) Dan McGann	550.00	135.00	55.00
(308) Jim McGinley	550.00	135.00	55.00
(309) Iron Man McGinnity	1,500	375.00	190.00
(310) Stoney McGlynn	550.00	135.00	55.00
(311) John McGraw (Finger in air.)	1,800	450.00	180.00
(312) John McGraw (Glove at hip.)	1,800	450.00	180.00
(313) John McGraw (Portrait, no cap.)	1,900	475.00	190.00
(314) John McGraw (Portrait, with cap.)	1,450	365.00	145.00
(315) Harry McIntyre (Brooklyn)	550.00	135.00	55.00
(316) Harry McIntyre (Brooklyn & Chicago)	550.00	135.00	55.00
(317) Matty McIntyre (Detroit)	550.00	135.00	55.00
(318) Larry McLean	550.00	135.00	55.00
(319) George McQuillan (Ball in hand.)	550.00	135.00	55.00
(320) George McQuillan (With bat.)	550.00	135.00	55.00
(321) Fred Merkle (Portrait)	550.00	135.00	55.00
(322) Fred Merkle (Throwing)	550.00	135.00	55.00
(323) George Merritt	550.00	135.00	55.00
(324) Chief Meyers	550.00	135.00	55.00
(325) Clyde Milan	550.00	135.00	55.00
(326) Dots Miller (Pittsburgh)	550.00	135.00	55.00
(327) Molly Miller (Dallas)	1,550	325.00	160.00
(328) Bill Milligan	550.00	135.00	55.00
(329) Fred Mitchell (Toronto)	550.00	135.00	55.00
(330) Mike Mitchell (Cincinnati)	550.00	135.00	55.00
(331) Dan Moeller	550.00	135.00	55.00
(332) Carlton Molesworth	1,550	325.00	160.00
(333) Herbie Moran (Providence)	550.00	135.00	55.00
(334) Pat Moran (Chicago)	550.00	135.00	55.00
(335) George Moriarty	550.00	135.00	55.00
(336) Mike Mowrey	550.00	135.00	55.00
(337) Dom Mullaney	1,550	325.00	160.00
(338) George Mullen (Mullin)	550.00	135.00	55.00
(339) George Mullin (Throwing)	900.00	225.00	110.00
(340) George Mullin (With bat.)	550.00	135.00	55.00
(341) Danny Murphy (Batting)	550.00	135.00	55.00
(342) Danny Murphy (Throwing)	675.00	170.00	65.00
(343) Red Murray (Batting)	550.00	135.00	55.00
(344) Red Murray (Portrait)	550.00	135.00	55.00
(345) Chief Myers (Meyers) (Batting)	550.00	135.00	55.00
(346) Chief Myers (Meyers) (Fielding)	550.00	135.00	55.00
(347) Billy Nattress	550.00	135.00	55.00
(348) Tom Needham	550.00	135.00	55.00
(349) Simon Nicholls (Hands on knees.)	550.00	135.00	55.00
(350) Simon Nichols (Nicholls) (Batting)	550.00	135.00	55.00
(351) Harry Niles	550.00	135.00	55.00
(352) Rebel Oakes	550.00	135.00	55.00
(353) Frank Oberlin	550.00	135.00	55.00
(354) Peter O'Brien	550.00	135.00	55.00
(355a) Bill O'Hara (New York)	550.00	135.00	55.00
(355b) Bill O'Hara (St. Louis)		18,000	4,100
(356) Rube Oldring (Batting)	550.00	135.00	55.00
(357) Rube Oldring (Fielding)	550.00	135.00	55.00
(358) Charley O'Leary (Hands on knees.)	550.00	135.00	55.00
(359) Charley O'Leary (Portrait)	550.00	135.00	55.00
(360) William J. O'Neil	550.00	135.00	55.00
(361) Al Orth	1,550	325.00	160.00
(362) William Otey	1,550	325.00	160.00
(363) Orval Overall (Hand face level.)	550.00	135.00	55.00
(364) Orval Overall (Hands waist level.)	550.00	135.00	55.00
(365) Orval Overall (Portrait)	550.00	135.00	55.00
(366) Frank Owen	550.00	135.00	55.00
(367) George Paige	1,550	325.00	160.00
(368) Fred Parent	550.00	135.00	55.00
(369) Dode Paskert	550.00	135.00	55.00
(370) Jim Pastorius	550.00	135.00	55.00
(371) Harry Pattee	850.00	225.00	85.00
(372) Fred Payne	550.00	135.00	55.00
(373) Barney Pelty (Horizontal photo.)	900.00	225.00	110.00
(374) Barney Pelty (Vertical photo.)	550.00	135.00	55.00
(375) Hub Perdue	1,550	325.00	160.00
(376) George Perring	550.00	135.00	55.00
(377) Arch Persons	1,450	360.00	180.00
(378) Francis (Big Jeff) Pfeffer	550.00	125.00	60.00
(379) Jake Pfeister (Pfiester) (Seated)	550.00	135.00	55.00
(380) Jake Pfeister (Pfiester) (Throwing)	550.00	135.00	55.00
(381) Jimmy Phelan	550.00	135.00	55.00
(382) Eddie Phelps	550.00	135.00	55.00
(383) Deacon Phillippe	550.00	135.00	55.00
(384) Ollie Pickering	550.00	135.00	55.00
(385) Eddie Plank Values shown are for graded examples only at auction EX-MT - 100,000 VG - 66,500 GOOD - 35,775 POOR - 20,000			
(386) Phil Poland	550.00	135.00	55.00
(387) Jack Powell	900.00	225.00	110.00
(388) Mike Powers	550.00	135.00	55.00
(389) Billy Purtell	550.00	135.00	55.00

(390)	Ambrose Puttman (Puttmann)	550.00	135.00	55.00
(391)	Lee Quillen (Quillin)	550.00	135.00	55.00
(392)	Jack Quinn	550.00	135.00	55.00
(393)	Newt Randall	550.00	135.00	55.00
(394)	Bugs Raymond	550.00	135.00	55.00
(395)	Ed Reagan	1,550	325.00	160.00
(396)	Ed Reulbach (Glove showing.)	1,100	275.00	135.00
(397)	Ed Reulbach (No glove showing.)	550.00	135.00	55.00
(398)	Dutch Revelle	1,550	325.00	160.00
(399)	Bob Rhoades (Rhoads) (Hands at chest.)	550.00	135.00	55.00
(400)	Bob Rhoades (Rhoads) (Right arm extended.)	800.00	200.00	80.00
(401)	Charlie Rhodes	550.00	135.00	55.00
(402)	Claude Ritchey	550.00	135.00	55.00
(403)	Lou Ritter	550.00	135.00	55.00
(404)	Ike Rockenfeld	1,550	325.00	160.00
(405)	Claude Rossman	550.00	135.00	55.00
(406)	Nap Rucker (Portrait)	550.00	135.00	55.00
(407)	Nap Rucker (Throwing)	550.00	135.00	55.00
(408)	Dick Rudolph	550.00	135.00	55.00
(409)	Ray Ryan	1,550	325.00	160.00
(410)	Germany Schaefer (Detroit)	550.00	135.00	55.00
(411)	Germany Schaefer (Washington)	550.00	135.00	55.00
(412)	George Schirm	600.00	150.00	75.00
(413)	Larry Schlafly	550.00	135.00	55.00
(414)	Admiral Schlei (Batting)	550.00	135.00	55.00
(415)	Admiral Schlei (Catching)	550.00	135.00	55.00
(416)	Admiral Schlei (Portrait)	550.00	135.00	55.00
(417)	Boss Schmidt (Portrait)	550.00	135.00	55.00
(418)	Boss Schmidt (Throwing)	550.00	135.00	55.00
(419)	Ossee Schreck (Schreckengost)	780.00	195.00	100.00
(420)	Wildfire Schulte (Front view.)	1,000	135.00	125.00
(421)	Wildfire Schulte (Back view.)	550.00	135.00	55.00
(422)	Jim Scott	550.00	135.00	55.00
(423)	Charles Seitz	1,550	325.00	160.00
(424)	Cy Seymour (Batting)	550.00	135.00	55.00
(425)	Cy Seymour (Portrait)	450.00	110.00	55.00
(426)	Cy Seymour (Throwing)	550.00	135.00	55.00
(427)	Spike Shannon	600.00	150.00	75.00
(428)	Bud Sharpe	550.00	135.00	55.00
(429)	Shag Shaughnessy	1,550	325.00	160.00
(430)	Al Shaw (St. Louis)	550.00	135.00	55.00
(431)	Hunky Shaw (Providence)	550.00	135.00	55.00
(432)	Jimmy Sheckard (Glove showing.)	550.00	135.00	55.00
(433)	Jimmy Sheckard (No glove showing.)	550.00	135.00	55.00
(434)	Bill Shipke	550.00	135.00	55.00
(435)	Jimmy Slagle	550.00	135.00	55.00
(436)	Carlos Smith (Shreveport)	1,550	325.00	160.00
(437)	Frank Smith (Chicago, F. Smith on front.)	550.00	135.00	55.00
(438a)	Frank Smith (Chicago, white cap.)	550.00	135.00	55.00
(438b)	Frank Smith (Chicago & Boston)	2,425	600.00	245.00
(439)	Happy Smith (Brooklyn)	550.00	135.00	55.00
(440)	Heinie Smith (Buffalo)	550.00	135.00	55.00
(441)	Sid Smith (Atlanta)	1,550	325.00	160.00
(442)	Fred Snodgrass (Batting)	550.00	135.00	55.00
(443)	Fred Snodgrass (Catching)	550.00	135.00	55.00
(444)	Bob Spade	550.00	135.00	55.00
(445)	Tris Speaker	4,150	1,025	520.00
(446)	Tubby Spencer	550.00	135.00	55.00
(447)	Jake Stahl (Glove shows.)	550.00	135.00	55.00
(448)	Jake Stahl (No glove shows.)	550.00	135.00	55.00
(449)	Oscar Stanage	550.00	135.00	55.00
(450)	Dolly Stark	1,550	325.00	160.00
(451)	Charlie Starr	550.00	135.00	55.00
(452)	Harry Steinfeldt (Portrait)	550.00	135.00	55.00
(453)	Harry Steinfeldt (With bat.)	550.00	135.00	55.00
(454)	Jim Stephens	550.00	135.00	55.00
(455)	George Stone	550.00	135.00	55.00
(456)	George Stovall (Batting)	550.00	135.00	55.00
(457)	George Stovall (Portrait)	550.00	135.00	55.00
(458)	Sam Strang	550.00	135.00	55.00
(459)	Gabby Street (Catching)	550.00	135.00	55.00
(460)	Gabby Street (Portrait)	550.00	135.00	55.00
(461)	Billy Sullivan	550.00	135.00	55.00
(462)	Ed Summers	550.00	135.00	55.00
(463)	Bill Sweeney (Boston)	550.00	135.00	55.00
(464)	Jeff Sweeney (New York)	550.00	135.00	55.00

(465)	Jesse Tannehill (Washington)	550.00	135.00	55.00
(466)	Lee Tannehill (Chicago, L. Tannehill on front.)	450.00	110.00	55.00
(467)	Lee Tannehill (Chicago, Tannehill on front.)	550.00	135.00	55.00
(468)	Dummy Taylor	550.00	135.00	55.00
(469)	Fred Tenney	550.00	135.00	55.00
(470)	Tony Thebo	1,550	325.00	160.00
(471)	Jake Thielman	550.00	135.00	55.00
(472)	Ira Thomas	550.00	135.00	55.00
(473)	Woodie Thornton	1,750	425.00	175.00
(474)	Joe Tinker (Bat off shoulder.)	1,800	450.00	180.00
(475)	Joe Tinker (Bat on shoulder.)	1,775	430.00	175.00
(476)	Joe Tinker (Hands on knees.)	1,975	485.00	195.00
(477)	Joe Tinker (Portrait)	2,000	500.00	200.00
(478)	John Titus	550.00	135.00	55.00
(479)	Terry Turner	550.00	135.00	55.00
(480)	Bob Unglaub	550.00	135.00	55.00
(481)	Juan Violat (Viola)	1,550	325.00	160.00
(482)	Rube Waddell (Portrait)	1,900	475.00	190.00
(483)	Rube Waddell (Throwing)	2,075	500.00	210.00
(484)	Heinie Wagner (Bat on left shoulder.)	550.00	135.00	55.00
(485)	Heinie Wagner (Bat on right shoulder.)	550.00	135.00	55.00
(486)	Honus Wagner Values shown reflect auction prices for graded examples only NM-MT - 2,800,000 VG+ - 1,200,000 VG - 800,500 GOOD - 350,000 FAIR - 300,000 POOR - 270,000 Authentic - 225,000			
(487)	Bobby Wallace	1,350	335.00	170.00
(488)	Ed Walsh	2,100	525.00	255.00
(489)	Jack Warhop	550.00	135.00	55.00
(490)	Jake Weimer	550.00	135.00	55.00
(491)	James Westlake	1,550	325.00	160.00
(492)	Zack Wheat	1,600	400.00	200.00
(493)	Doc White (Chicago, pitching.)	550.00	135.00	55.00
(494)	Doc White (Chicago, portrait.)	550.00	135.00	55.00
(495)	Foley White (Houston)	1,550	325.00	160.00
(496)	Jack White (Buffalo)	550.00	135.00	55.00
(497)	Kaiser Wilhelm (Hands at chest.)	550.00	135.00	55.00
(498)	Kaiser Wilhelm (With bat.)	550.00	135.00	55.00
(499)	Ed Willett	550.00	135.00	55.00
(500)	Ed Willetts (Willett)	550.00	135.00	55.00
(501)	Jimmy Williams	550.00	135.00	55.00
(502)	Vic Willis (Portrait)	1,625	405.00	165.00
(503)	Vic Willis (Throwing)	1,325	330.00	165.00
(504)	Vic Willis (With bat.)	1,400	350.00	140.00
(505)	Owen Wilson	550.00	135.00	55.00
(506)	Hooks Wiltse (Pitching)	550.00	135.00	55.00
(507)	Hooks Wiltse (Portrait, no cap.)	550.00	135.00	55.00
(508)	Hooks Wiltse (Portrait, with cap.)	550.00	135.00	55.00
(509)	Lucky Wright	550.00	135.00	55.00
(510)	Cy Young (Cleveland, glove shows.)	4,500	1,125	450.00
(511)	Cy Young (Cleveland, bare hand shows.)	5,750	1,435	575.00
(512)	Cy Young (Cleveland, portrait.)	10,000	2,500	1,000
(513)	Irv Young (Minneapolis)	550.00	135.00	55.00
(514)	Heinie Zimmerman	550.00	135.00	55.00

1909-11 T206 Errors

Because of the complexity of the lithographic process by which T206 cards were printed, a number of significant printing errors - missing colors, broken or missing type, etc. - are known. Early in hobby history some of these errors were collected alongside such true design variations as the "Magie" misspelling and Joe Doyle "N.Y. Nat'l." Because of the continued popularity of T206, some of these errors remain in demand today and can command significant premium values. It should be noted, however, that not all similar errors within T206 bring such high prices; value seems dependent on the length of time the errors have been known in the hobby. Because of the ease with which various typographic elements - "S" in Snodgrass, "o" in Toronto, can be erased, many fakes of this type of error are known; collectors should be wary and consider having the cards professionally authenticated.

SWEENEY, BOSTON NAT'L.

		NM	E	VG
(27)	Beck, no "B"s (Missing red ink.)	1,500	750.00	450.00
(28)	Becker, no "B" (Missing red ink.)	1,500	750.00	450.00
(95a)	Cobb, orange background (Missing red ink.)	4,000	1,500	900.00
(137)	Dopner (Three have been recently found, & authenticated: pricing pending sales)			
(164)	Ferguson, no "B" (Missing red ink.)	2,300	1,150	700.00
(279)	Lindaman, no "B" (Missing red ink.)	1,500	750.00	450.00
(286)	Maddox, Pittsburg (No team, name, city.)	6,000	3,000	1,800
(297)	Marshall, no "B" (Missing blue ink.)	2,000	1,000	600.00
(329)	Mitchell, "TORONT" (No last "O.")	2,000	1,000	600.00
(343)	Murray (Yellow background.)	1,500	750.00	450.00
(428)	Shappe, Newark (Should be Sharpe.)	3,100	1,600	700.00
(442)	nodgrass - batting ("S" missing. Should be Snodgrass; most of initial)	4,000	2,000	1,000
(443)	nodgrass - catching (All known examples, even those in grading company holders, are altered specimens with no collectible value.)			
(463)	Sweeney, no "B" (Missing magenta ink.)	6,000	3,000	1,800
(484)	Wagner, no "B" (Bat on left shoulder, missing magenta.)	2,500	1,250	750.00
	Common Player (Missing one or more colors.)	500.00	250.00	150.00
	Common Player (Blank Back)	350.00	175.00	100.00

1912 T207 Brown Background

LORD-CHICAGO-AMER.

Harry Lord

Harry Lord, the brilliant White Sox third baseman, came to Chicago in one of the queerest baseball deals ever recorded. Lord first achieved success in the New England League, where, in 1908, he was lifted to the Boston Americans. Although rated as a wonderful ball player, he fell out with the club management and was traded to Comiskey, who secured a star. Lord played wonderful ball in 1911 and is rated by many as the greatest third baseman now playing—a worthy successor to Bradley and Collins. Last season he batted .321, fielded .941 and led his club with stolen bases.

RECRUIT LITTLE CIGARS

FACTORY No 930 1st DIST. PA.

Less popular and even less understood than their T205 and T206 antecedents from American Tobacco, the T207 "Brown Background" series shares the same approximately 1-7/16" x 2-5/8" format with the earlier T-cards. A chocolate background frames the rather drab player drawings, which rely on occasional bit of color on the uniform to break up the predominant earth tones. The cards have beige borders. A white strip below the picture has the player's last name, city and league. Unlike most other cards of its time, T207 has a glossy coating on front which over the years tends to crack and/or "craze" exacerbating the appaearance of creases and other signs of wear. Card backs have the player's full name, career summary and (usually) an ad for one of several brands of cigarettes. Red Cross brand backs are virtually impossible to find, while red Cycle advertising is noticeably scarcer than more common Broadleaf or "anonymous" (no-advertising) versions. Cards with Recruit Little Cigars advertising on back are the most common. There are a number of unaccountably scarce cards in the set, including a higher than usual number of obscure players. The Davis card with blue "C" on cap carried in earlier catalogs has been removed for lack of evidence of its existence. The previously listed Carrigan-Wagner wrongbacks have also been de-listed due to their nature as wrong-back printing errors rather than true variations.

	NM	E	VG
Common Player:	225.00	75.00	45.00
Red Cycle Backs: 1.5X anonymous or broadleaf backs.			
(1) John B. Adams	1,760	615.00	355.00
(2) Edward Ainsmith	225.00	75.00	45.00
(3) Rafael Almeida	1,250	625.00	300.00
(4a) James Austin (Insignia on shirt.)	450.00	155.00	90.00
(4b) James Austin (No insignia on shirt.)	225.00	75.00	45.00
(5) Neal Ball	250.00	90.00	50.00
(6) Eros Barger	225.00	75.00	45.00
(7) Jack Barry	250.00	90.00	50.00
(8) Charles Bauman ((Baumann))	1,250	625.00	300.00
(9) Beals Becker	350.00	120.00	70.00
(10) Chief (Albert) Bender	800.00	280.00	160.00
(11) Joseph Benz	1,250	625.00	300.00
(12) Robert Bescher	225.00	75.00	45.00
(13) Joe Birmingham	1,250	625.00	300.00
(14) Russell Blackburne	1,250	625.00	300.00
(15) Fred Blanding	1,250	625.00	300.00
(16) Jimmy Block	500.00	175.00	100.00
(17) Ping Bodie	225.00	75.00	45.00
(18) Hugh Bradley	225.00	75.00	45.00
(19) Roger Bresnaham (Bresnahan)	700.00	245.00	140.00
(20) J.F. Bushelman	1,250	625.00	300.00
(21) Henry (Hank) Butcher	1,250	625.00	300.00
(22) Robert M. Byrne	225.00	75.00	45.00
(23) John James Callahan	225.00	75.00	45.00
(24) Howard Camnitz	225.00	75.00	45.00
(25) Max Carey	850.00	295.00	170.00
(26) Bill Carrigan	225.00	75.00	45.00
(27) George Chalmers	225.00	75.00	45.00
(28) Frank Leroy Chance	725.00	255.00	145.00
(29) Edward Cicotte	1,100	385.00	220.00
(30) Tom Clarke	225.00	75.00	45.00
(31) Leonard Cole	225.00	75.00	45.00
(32) John Collins	300.00	105.00	60.00
(33) Robert Coulson	225.00	75.00	45.00
(34) Tex Covington	225.00	75.00	45.00
(35) Otis Crandall	225.00	75.00	45.00
(36) William Cunningham	1,250	625.00	300.00
(37) Dave Danforth	250.00	95.00	50.00
(38) Bert Daniels	450.00	155.00	90.00
(39) John Daubert (Jake)	225.00	75.00	45.00
(40) Harry Davis	250.00	90.00	50.00
(41) Jim Delehanty	225.00	75.00	45.00
(42) Claude Derrick	225.00	75.00	45.00
(43) Arthur Devlin	250.00	95.00	50.00
(44) Joshua Devore	225.00	75.00	45.00
(45) Mike Donlin	2,750	960.00	550.00
(46) Edward Donnelly	1,250	625.00	300.00
(47) Charles Dooin	225.00	75.00	45.00
(48) Tom Downey	875.00	305.00	175.00
(49) Lawrence Doyle	450.00	155.00	90.00
(50) Del Drake	400.00	140.00	80.00
(51) Ted Easterly	225.00	75.00	45.00
(52) George Ellis	675.00	235.00	135.00
(53) Clyde Engle	375.00	130.00	75.00
(54) R.E. Erwin	675.00	235.00	135.00
(55) Louis Evans	225.00	75.00	45.00
(56) John Ferry	225.00	75.00	45.00
(57a) Ray Fisher (Blue cap.)	225.00	75.00	45.00
(57b) Ray Fisher (White cap.)	300.00	150.00	75.00
(58) Arthur Fletcher	225.00	75.00	45.00
(59) Jacques Fournier	1,250	625.00	300.00
(60) Arthur Fromme	250.00	90.00	50.00
(61) Del Gainor	225.00	75.00	45.00
(62) William Lawrence Gardner	350.00	120.00	70.00
(63) Lefty George	450.00	155.00	90.00
(64) Roy Golden	225.00	75.00	45.00
(65) Harry Gowdy	225.00	75.00	45.00
(66) George Graham	675.00	235.00	135.00
(67) J.G. Graney	825.00	285.00	165.00
(68) Vean Gregg	1,250	625.00	300.00
(69) Casey Hageman	450.00	155.00	90.00
(70) Charlie Hall	450.00	155.00	90.00
(71) E.S. Hallinan	225.00	75.00	45.00
(72) Earl Hamilton	225.00	75.00	45.00
(73) Robert Harmon	225.00	75.00	45.00
(74) Grover Hartley	450.00	155.00	90.00
(75) Olaf Henriksen	225.00	79.00	45.00
(76) John Henry	450.00	155.00	90.00
(77) Charles Herzog	1,250	625.00	300.00
(78) Robert Higgins	300.00	105.00	60.00
(79) Chester Hoff	1,250	625.00	300.00
(80) William Hogan	300.00	105.00	60.00
(81) Harry Hooper	1,320	470.00	265.00
(82) Ben Houser	1,250	625.00	300.00
(83) Hamilton Hyatt	1,250	625.00	300.00
(84) Walter Johnson	2,100	735.00	420.00
(85) George Kaler	225.00	75.00	45.00
(86) William Kelly	1,250	625.00	300.00
(87) Jay Kirke	450.00	155.00	90.00
(88) John Kling	725.00	255.00	145.00
(89) Otto Knabe	225.00	75.00	45.00
(90) Elmer Knetzer	225.00	75.00	45.00
(91) Edward Konetchy	225.00	75.00	45.00
(92) Harry Krause	225.00	75.00	45.00
(93) "Red" Kuhn	1,250	625.00	300.00
(94) Joseph Kutina	1,250	625.00	300.00
(95) F.H. (Bill) Lange	1,250	625.00	300.00
(96) Jack Lapp	225.00	75.00	45.00
(97) W. Arlington Latham	225.00	75.00	45.00
(98) Thomas W. Leach	225.00	75.00	45.00
(99) Albert Leifield	225.00	75.00	45.00
(100) Edgar Lennox	225.00	75.00	45.00
(101) Duffy Lewis	500.00	175.00	100.00
(102a) Irving Lewis (No emblem on sleeve.)	30,000	10,500	6,000
(102b) Irving Lewis (Emblem on sleeve.)	12,500	4,500	2,500
(103) Jack Lively	225.00	75.00	45.00
(104a) Paddy Livingston ("A" on shirt.)	1,200	425.00	245.00
(104b) Paddy Livingston (Big "C" on shirt.)	1,265	440.00	255.00
(104c) Paddy Livingston (Small "C" on shirt.)	350.00	120.00	70.00
(105) Briscoe Lord (Philadelphia)	450.00	155.00	90.00
(106) Harry Lord (Chicago)	450.00	155.00	90.00
(107) Louis Lowdermilk	8,000	2,800	1,600
(108) Richard Marquard	550.00	190.00	110.00
(109) Armando Marsans	775.00	270.00	155.00
(110) George McBride	300.00	105.00	60.00
(111) Alexander McCarthy	1,650	575.00	330.00
(112) Edward McDonald	325.00	115.00	65.00
(113) John J. McGraw	650.00	225.00	130.00
(114) Harry McIntire	225.00	75.00	45.00
(115) Matthew McIntyre	225.00	75.00	45.00
(116) William McKechnie	2,000	1,000	500.00
(117) Larry McLean	225.00	75.00	45.00
(118) Clyde Milan	225.00	75.00	45.00
(119) John B. Miller (Pittsburg)	225.00	75.00	45.00
(120) Otto Miller (Brooklyn)	450.00	155.00	90.00
(121) Roy Miller (Boston)	1,000	350.00	200.00
(122) Ward Miller (Chicago)	8,000	4,000	2,000
(123) Mike Mitchell (Cleveland, picture is Willie Mitchell.)	225.00	75.00	45.00
(124) Mike Mitchell (Cincinnati)	350.00	120.00	70.00
(125) Geo. Mogridge	1,500	750.00	375.00
(126) Earl Moore	1,250	625.00	300.00
(127) Patrick J. Moran	225.00	75.00	45.00
(128) Cy Morgan (Philadelphia)	225.00	75.00	45.00
(129) Ray Morgan (Washington)	225.00	75.00	45.00
(130) George Moriarty	1,250	625.00	300.00
(131a) George Mullin ("D" on cap.)	250.00	90.00	50.00
(131b) George Mullin (No "D" on cap.)	750.00	260.00	150.00
(132) Thomas Needham	350.00	120.00	70.00
(133) Red Nelson	1,250	625.00	300.00
(134) Herbert Northen (Hubbard)	325.00	115.00	65.00
(135) Leslie Nunamaker	225.00	75.00	45.00
(136) Rebel Oakes	225.00	75.00	45.00
(137) Buck O'Brien	350.00	120.00	70.00
(138) Rube Oldring	225.00	75.00	45.00
(139) Ivan Olson	225.00	75.00	45.00
(140) Martin J. O'Toole	225.00	75.00	45.00
(141) George Paskart (Paskert)	225.00	75.00	45.00
(142) Barney Pelty	2,000	1,250	500.00
(143) Herbert Perdue	300.00	105.00	60.00
(144) O.C. Peters	1,250	625.00	300.00
(145) Arthur Phelan	1,250	625.00	300.00
(146) Jack Quinn	450.00	155.00	90.00
(147) Don Carlos Ragan	1,500	750.00	400.00
(148) Arthur Rasmussen	1,500	750.00	400.00
(149) Morris Rath	1,500	750.00	400.00
(150) Edward Reulbach	350.00	120.00	70.00
(151) Napoleon Rucker	450.00	155.00	90.00
(152) J.B. Ryan	1,250	625.00	300.00
(153) Victor Saier	2,300	810.00	470.00
(154) William Scanlon	225.00	75.00	45.00
(155) Germany Schaefer	225.00	75.00	45.00
(156) Wilbur Schardt	225.00	75.00	45.00
(157) Frank Schulte	225.00	75.00	45.00
(158) Jim Scott	500.00	175.00	100.00
(159) Henry Severoid (Severeid)	225.00	75.00	45.00
(160) Mike Simon	225.00	75.00	45.00
(161) Frank E. Smith (Cincinnati)	225.00	75.00	45.00
(162) Wallace Smith (St. Louis)	225.00	75.00	45.00
(163) Fred Snodgrass	225.00	75.00	45.00
(164) Tristam Speaker	4,000	2,000	750.00
(165) Harry Lee Spratt	225.00	75.00	45.00
(166) Edward Stack	550.00	195.00	110.00
(167) Oscar Stanage	225.00	75.00	45.00
(168) William Steele	675.00	235.00	135.00
(169) Harry Steinfeldt	450.00	155.00	90.00
(170) George Stovall	225.00	75.00	45.00
(171) Charles (Gabby) Street	275.00	96.00	55.00
(172) Amos Strunk	225.00	75.00	45.00
(173) William Sullivan	325.00	115.00	65.00
(174) William J. Sweeney	1,250	625.00	300.00
(175) Leeford Tannehill	225.00	75.00	45.00
(176) C.D. Thomas	725.00	255.00	145.00
(177) Joseph Tinker	900.00	315.00	180.00
(178) Bert Tooley	225.00	75.00	45.00
(179) Terence Turner (Terrence)	225.00	75.00	45.00
(180) George Tyler	2,000	1,000	500.00
(181) Jim Vaughn	400.00	140.00	80.00
(182) Chas. (Heinie) Wagner	225.00	75.00	45.00
(183) Ed (Dixie) Walker	225.00	75.00	45.00
(184) Robert Wallace	1,250	625.00	300.00
(185) John Warhop	225.00	75.00	45.00
(186) George Weaver	5,225	1,900	1,100
(187) Zach Wheat	900.00	315.00	180.00
(188) G. Harris White	325.00	115.00	65.00
(189) Ernest Wilie	275.00	95.00	55.00
(190) Bob Williams	225.00	75.00	45.00
(191) Arthur Wilson (New York)	250.00	90.00	50.00
(192) Owen Wilson (Pittsburg)	1,250	625.00	300.00
(193) George Wiltse	225.00	75.00	45.00
(194) Ivey Wingo	400.00	140.00	80.00
(195) Harry Wolverton	225.00	75.00	45.00
(196) Joe Wood	2,640	925.00	530.00
(197) Eugene Woodburn	900.00	315.00	180.00
(198) Ralph Works	1,250	625.00	300.00
(199) Stanley Yerkes	225.00	75.00	45.00
(200) Rollie Zeider	350.00	120.00	70.00

1912 T227 Series Of Champions

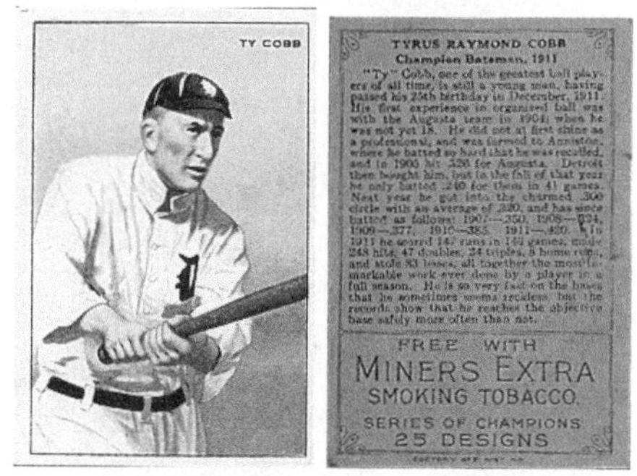

The 1912 "Series of Champions" card set issued by the "Honest Long Cut" and "Miners Extra" tobacco brands features several baseball stars among its 25 famous athletes of the day. Larger than a standard-size tobacco issue, each card in the "Champions" series measures 3-3/8" x 2-5/16". The back includes a relatively lengthy player biography, while the front features a lithograph of the player in action. Although the set includes only four baseball players, these attractive cards are popular among collectors because of the stature of the four players selected. The "Champions" series holds additional significance because it includes the only known baseball cards issued under the "Miners Extra" brand name. The set carries the American Card Catalog designation of T227.

	NM	E	VG
Complete Set (4):	22,500	10,000	5,500
Common Player:	3,600	1,620	900.00
(1) "Home Run" Baker	3,600	1,620	900.00
(2) "Chief" Bender	3,600	1,620	900.00
(3) Ty Cobb	16,200	7,200	4,200
(4) Rube Marquard	3,600	1,620	900.00

1928 Tabacalera la Morena

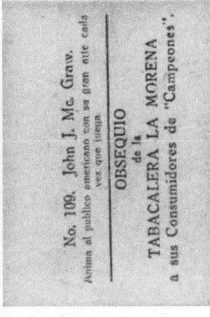

Believed to have been issued in El Salvador in the late 1920s, the extent of this card issue is not yet known. It is possible other American baseball players are included in the issue. Approximately 1-7/8" x 2-5/8", the cards are printed in black-and-white with some color tints added. The borderless front that includes the card number at bottom. Backs are printed in Spanish and repeat the card number along with player identification and a few words about the pictured players. An ad at bottom attributes the card (roughly): "Courtesy of Rich Brown Tobacco, the Champion among Consumers."

		NM	E	VG
96	St. Louis Cardinals Team	100.00	50.00	30.00
97	Everett Scott	50.00	25.00	15.00
98	Babe Ruth	1,500	750.00	450.00
100	Lou Gehrig, Babe Ruth	2,000	1,000	600.00
101	George Kelly	100.00	50.00	30.00
103	Earl Webb	50.00	25.00	15.00
105	Ty Cobb, Babe Ruth	300.00	150.00	90.00
106	Jim Bottomley	100.00	50.00	30.00
107	Christy Mathewson, John McGraw	150.00	75.00	45.00
109	John J. Mc Graw	100.00	50.00	30.00
110	Ullmann	50.00	25.00	15.00
111	Lee Todd, P Todd	50.00	25.00	15.00
114	St. Louis Cardinals/ Brooklyn Robins	50.00	25.00	15.00
120	St. Louis Cardinals/ Brooklyn Robins	50.00	25.00	15.00

1916 Tango Eggs

Unknown until the discovery of a hoard of "fewer than 500" cards in 1991, this 18-card set was produced for L. Frank & Co. of New Orleans to be distributed in an as-yet unknown manner in connection with its Tango brand eggs. Similar in size (1-7/16" x 2-3/4") and format to contemporary caramel cards, the Tango set features familiar player pictures from those issues. In fact, several of the Tango cards have player designations which differ from the same pictures used in the E106 American Caramel issue of 1915. The Tango cards feature a glossy front surface, and are brightly colored. The hoard varied greatly in the number of each player's card. Some were found in quantities as low as one, while some were represented by more than 50 specimens. Because several of the cards exist in only a single specimen, no price for a complete set is quoted.

		NM	E	VG
(1)	Bob Bescher	200.00	100.00	60.00
(2)	Roger Bresnahan (Four known.)	2,400	960.00	480.00
(3)	Al Bridwell (Fewer than 10 known.)	870.00	350.00	175.00
(4)	Hal Chase	1,080	430.00	215.00

		NM	E	VG
(5)	Ty Cobb (One known, VG, value undetermined.)			
(6)	Eddie Collins	2,250	1,125	675.00
(7)	Sam Crawford (Fewer than five known.)	2,400	960.00	480.00
(8)	Red Dooin	850.00	425.00	250.00
(9)	Johnny Evers (One known, G/VG, value undetermined.)			
(10)	Happy Felsch (Picture actually Ray Demmitt.) (2-3 known))	2,880	1,150	575.00
(11)	Hughie Jennings (100+ known)	660.00	265.00	135.00
(12)	George McQuillen	600.00	300.00	180.00
(13)	Billy Meyer (Picture actually Fred Jacklitsch.)	400.00	200.00	100.00
(14)	Ray Morgan (Picture actually Mike Doolan.) (2-3 known))	1,920	770.00	385.00
(15)	Danny Murphy	485.00	242.50	145.50
(16)	Germany Schaefer (1-2 known)	2,400	960.00	480.00
(17)	Buck Weaver (Picture actually Joe Tinker.)	2,400	1,200	720.00
(18)	Heinie Zimmerman (Fewer than 10 known.)	870.00	350.00	175.00

1934 Tarzan Bread (D382)

Among the rarest issues of the 1930s is this set sponsored by an unusually named brand of bread from a bakery whose location is unknown. The cards are printed in black-and-white in 2-1/4" x 3-1/4" format. Borderless front photos have the player name in capital letters. Backs have the sponsor's name and a short career summary. Some cards have a red "TROPHY" sticker at top on back, covering the "TARZAN." The checklist here, almost certainly incomplete, is arranged alphabetically; the cards are unnumbered.

		NM	E	VG
	Common Player:	2,750	1,375	825.00
(1)	Sparky Adams	2,750	1,375	825.00
(2)	Walter Betts	2,750	1,375	825.00
(3)	George Blaeholder	2,750	1,375	825.00
(4)	Ed Brandt	2,750	1,375	825.00
(5)	Tommy Bridges	2,750	1,375	825.00
(6)	Irving "Jack" Burns	2,750	1,375	825.00
(7)	Bruce Campbell	2,750	1,375	825.00
(8)	Tex Carleton	2,750	1,375	825.00
(9)	Dick Coffman	2,750	1,375	825.00
(10)	George Connally	2,750	1,375	825.00
(11)	Tony Cuccinello	2,750	1,375	825.00
(12)	Debs Garms	2,750	1,375	825.00
(13)	Milt Gaston	2,750	1,375	825.00
(14)	Bill Hallahan	2,750	1,375	825.00
(15)	Myril Hoag	2,750	1,375	825.00
(16)	Chief Hogsett	2,750	1,375	825.00
(17)	Arndt Jorgens	2,750	1,375	825.00
(18)	Willie Kamm	2,750	1,375	825.00
(19)	Dutch Leonard	2,750	1,375	825.00
(20)	Clyde Manion	2,750	1,375	825.00
(21)	Eric McNair	2,750	1,375	825.00
(22)	Oscar Melillo	2,750	1,375	825.00
(23)	Oscar Melillo	2,750	1,375	825.00
(24)	Bob O'Farrell	2,750	1,375	825.00
(25)	Gus Suhr	2,750	1,375	825.00
(26)	Evar Swanson	2,750	1,375	825.00
(27)	Billy Urbanski	2,750	1,375	825.00
(28)	Johnny Vergez	2,750	1,375	825.00
(29)	Robert Worthington	2,750	1,375	825.00
(30)	Tom Zachary	2,750	1,375	825.00

1969 Tasco All-Star Collection Caricatures

This set of large - 11-1/2" x 16" - player posters features colorful caricatures with an emphasis on Tigers players, befitting the Detroit address of the publisher. Licensed by MLBPA, the pictures are listed here alphabetically. They were originally sold for less than $1 apiece.

	NM	E	VG
Complete Set (46):	450.00	225.00	135.00
Common Player:	7.50	3.75	2.25
(1) Hank Aaron	35.00	17.50	10.50
(2) Richie Allen	12.50	6.25	3.75
(3) Luis Aparicio	17.50	8.75	5.25
(4) Ernie Banks	25.00	12.50	7.50
(5) Glenn Beckert	7.50	3.75	2.25
(6) Johnny Bench	20.00	10.00	6.00
(7) Norm Cash	10.00	5.00	3.00
(8) Danny Cater	7.50	3.75	2.25
(9) Pat Dobson	7.50	3.75	2.25
(10) Don Drysdale	17.50	8.75	5.25
(11) Bill Freehan	7.50	3.75	2.25
(12) Jim Fregosi	7.50	3.75	2.25
(13) Bob Gibson	17.50	8.75	5.25
(14) Bill Hands	7.50	3.75	2.25
(15) Ken Holtzman	7.50	3.75	2.25
(16) Willie Horton	7.50	3.75	2.25
(17) Frank Howard	9.00	4.50	2.75
(18) Randy Hundley	7.50	3.75	2.25
(19) Ferguson Jenkins	17.50	8.75	5.25
(20) Al Kaline	25.00	12.50	7.50
(21) Don Kessinger	7.50	3.75	2.25
(22) Jerry Koosman	7.50	3.75	2.25
(23) Mickey Lolich	7.50	3.75	2.25
(24) Juan Marichal	17.50	8.75	5.25
(25) Willie Mays	35.00	17.50	10.50
(26) Bill Mazeroski	17.50	8.75	5.25
(27) Dick McAuliffe	7.50	3.75	2.25
(28) Denny McLain	7.50	3.75	2.25
(29) Dave McNally	7.50	3.75	2.25
(30) Jim Northrup	7.50	3.75	2.25
(31) Tony Oliva	9.00	4.50	2.75
(32) Adolfo Phillips	7.50	3.75	2.25
(33) Jim Price	7.50	3.75	2.25
(34) Brooks Robinson	20.00	10.00	6.00
(35) Pete Rose	35.00	17.50	10.50
(36) Ron Santo	15.00	7.50	4.50
(37) Joe Sparma	7.50	3.75	2.25
(38) Mickey Stanley	7.50	3.75	2.25
(39) Mel Stottlemyre	7.50	3.75	2.25
(40) Luis Tiant	7.50	3.75	2.25
(41) Joe Torre	9.00	4.50	2.75
(42) Dick Tracewski	7.50	3.75	2.25
(43) Don Wert	7.50	3.75	2.25
(44) Billy Williams	17.50	8.75	5.25
(45) Earl Wilson	7.50	3.75	2.25
(46) Carl Yastrzemski	25.00	12.50	7.50

1970 Tasco Caricatures

This group of colorful player caricatures was sold in a four-pack featuring two each baseball and football players. The 8-1/2" x 10-7/8" blank-back pictures have central images surrounded by colorful borders.

	NM	E	VG
Complete Set (4):	150.00	75.00	45.00
Common Player:	40.00	20.00	12.00
(1) Jim "Catfish" Hunter	40.00	20.00	12.00
(2) Al Kaline	50.00	25.00	15.00
(3) Joe Namath	75.00	37.00	22.00
(4) O.J. Simpson	50.00	25.00	15.00

1933 Tattoo Orbit (R305)

 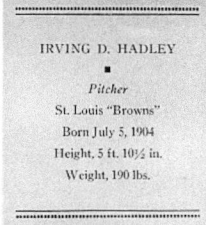

IRVING D. HADLEY

■

Pitcher
St. Louis "Browns"
Born July 5, 1904
Height, 5 ft. 10½ in.
Weight, 190 lbs.

Found in 1¢ packages of Tattoo gum, these 2" x 2-1/4" cards were produced by the Orbit Gum Co., of Chicago, a subsidiary of Wrigley's. Fronts feature a black-and-white photo which is tinted to give the skin some color. Stylized ballpark backgrounds are separated from the photograph by a black line. The rest of the background is printed in vivid red, yellow and green. Backs have player identification and vitals. Cards of Bump Hadley and George Blaeholder are the most elusive, followed by those of Ivy Andrews and Rogers Hornsby.

	NM	E	VG
Complete Set (60):	24,000	12,000	7,200
Common Player:	300.00	150.00	100.00
(1) Dale Alexander	300.00	150.00	100.00
(2) Ivy Paul Andrews	1,100	550.00	330.00
(3) Earl Averill	480.00	240.00	150.00
(4) Richard Bartell	300.00	150.00	100.00
(5) Walter Berger	300.00	150.00	100.00
(6) George F. Blaeholder	1,200	600.00	360.00
(7) Irving J. Burns	300.00	150.00	100.00
(8) Guy T. Bush	300.00	150.00	100.00
(9) Bruce D. Campbell	300.00	150.00	100.00
(10) William Cissell	300.00	150.00	100.00
(11) Lefty Clark	300.00	150.00	100.00
(12) Mickey Cochrane	480.00	240.00	150.00
(13) Phil Collins	300.00	150.00	100.00
(14) Hazen Kiki Cuyler	480.00	240.00	150.00
(15) Dizzy Dean	700.00	350.00	225.00
(16) Jimmy Dykes	300.00	150.00	100.00
(17) George L. Earnshaw	300.00	150.00	100.00
(18) Woody English	300.00	150.00	100.00
(19) Lewis A. Fonseca	300.00	150.00	100.00
(20) Jimmy Foxx	900.00	450.00	270.00
(21) Burleigh A. Grimes	480.00	240.00	150.00
(22) Charles John Grimm	300.00	150.00	100.00
(23) Robert M. Grove	600.00	300.00	180.00
(24) Frank Grube	300.00	150.00	100.00
(25) George W. Haas	300.00	150.00	100.00
(26) Irving D. Hadley	1,200	600.00	360.00
(27) Chick Hafey	480.00	240.00	150.00
(28) Jesse Joseph Haines	480.00	240.00	150.00
(29) William Hallahan	300.00	150.00	100.00
(30) Melvin Harder	300.00	150.00	100.00
(31) Gabby Hartnett	480.00	240.00	150.00
(32) Babe Herman	300.00	150.00	100.00
(33) William Herman	480.00	240.00	150.00
(34) Rogers Hornsby	1,450	720.00	450.00
(35) Roy C. Johnson	300.00	150.00	100.00
(36) J. Smead Jolley	300.00	150.00	100.00
(37) William Jurges	300.00	150.00	100.00
(38) William Kamm	300.00	150.00	100.00
(39) Mark A. Koenig	300.00	150.00	100.00
(40) James J. Levey	550.00	275.00	200.00
(41) Ernie Lombardi	480.00	240.00	150.00
(42) Red Lucas	300.00	150.00	100.00
(43) Ted Lyons	480.00	240.00	150.00
(44) Connie Mack	480.00	150.00	240.00
(45) Pat Malone	300.00	150.00	100.00
(46) Pepper Martin	400.00	200.00	120.00
(47) Marty McManus	300.00	150.00	100.00
(48) Frank J. O'Doul	420.00	210.00	140.00
(49) Richard Porter	300.00	150.00	100.00
(50) Carl N. Reynolds	300.00	150.00	100.00
(51) Charles Henry Root	300.00	150.00	100.00
(52) Robert Seeds	300.00	150.00	100.00
(53) Al H. Simmons	480.00	240.00	150.00
(54) Jackson Riggs Stephenson	300.00	150.00	100.00
(55) Bud Tinning	300.00	150.00	100.00
(56) Joe Vosmik	300.00	150.00	100.00
(57) Rube Walberg	300.00	150.00	100.00
(58) Paul Waner	480.00	240.00	150.00
(59) Lonnie Warneke	300.00	150.00	100.00
(60) Arthur C. Whitney	300.00	150.00	100.00

1933 Tattoo Orbit (R308)

This obscure set of cards, issued with Tattoo Orbit gum, is numbered from 151 through 207, with a few of the numbers still unknown. Most surviving examples measure 1-7/8" x 1-1/4," but larger pieces (2-1/2" x 3-7/8") are also known with the same players and numbers. The player pictures on the cards "developed" when moistened and rubbed with a piece of blotting paper. Besides the baseball players, there were also pictures of movie stars and other celebrities.

	NM	E	VG
Common Player:	200.00	90.00	50.00
Large-Format: 4X			
151 Vernon Gomez	500.00	225.00	125.00
152 Kiki Cuyler	500.00	225.00	125.00
153 Jimmy Foxx	850.00	380.00	210.00
154 Al Simmons	500.00	225.00	125.00
155 Chas. J. Grimm	200.00	90.00	50.00
156 William Jurges	200.00	90.00	50.00
157 Chuck Klein	500.00	225.00	125.00
158 Richard Bartell	200.00	90.00	50.00
159 Pepper Martin	275.00	125.00	69.00
160 Earl Averill	500.00	225.00	125.00
161 William Dickey	500.00	225.00	125.00
162 Wesley Ferrell	200.00	90.00	50.00
163 Oral Hildebrand	200.00	90.00	50.00
164 Wm. Kamm	200.00	90.00	50.00
165 Earl Whitehill	200.00	90.00	50.00
166 Charles Fullis	200.00	90.00	50.00
167 Jimmy Dykes	200.00	90.00	50.00
168 Ben Cantwell	200.00	90.00	50.00
169 George Earnshaw	200.00	90.00	50.00
170 Jackson Stephenson	200.00	90.00	50.00
171 Randolph Moore	200.00	90.00	50.00
172 Ted Lyons	500.00	225.00	125.00
173 Goose Goslin	500.00	225.00	125.00
174 E. Swanson	200.00	90.00	50.00
175 Lee Roy Mahaffey	200.00	90.00	50.00
176 Joe Cronin	500.00	225.00	125.00
177 Tom Bridges	200.00	90.00	50.00
178 Henry Manush	500.00	225.00	125.00
179 Walter Stewart	200.00	90.00	50.00
180 Frank Pytlak	200.00	90.00	50.00
181 Dale Alexander	200.00	90.00	50.00
182 Robert Grove	600.00	270.00	150.00
183 Charles Gehringer	500.00	225.00	125.00
184 Lewis Fonseca	200.00	90.00	50.00
185 Alvin Crowder	200.00	90.00	50.00
186 Mickey Cochrane	500.00	225.00	125.00
187 Max Bishop	200.00	90.00	50.00
188 Connie Mack	500.00	225.00	125.00
189 Guy Bush	200.00	90.00	50.00
190 Charlie Root	200.00	90.00	50.00
191a Burleigh Grimes	500.00	225.00	125.00
191b Gabby Hartnett	500.00	225.00	125.00
192 Pat Malone	200.00	90.00	50.00
193 Woody English	200.00	90.00	50.00
194 Lonnie Warneke	200.00	90.00	50.00
195 Babe Herman	275.00	125.00	69.00
196 Unknown			
197 Unknown			
198 Unknown			
199 Unknown			
200 Gabby Hartnett	500.00	225.00	125.00
201 Paul Waner	500.00	225.00	125.00
202 Dizzy Dean	750.00	335.00	185.00
203 Unknown			
204 Unknown			
205 Jim Bottomley	500.00	225.00	125.00
206 Unknown			
207 Charles Hafey	500.00	225.00	125.00
208 Unknown			
209 Unknown			
210 Unknown			

1907-09 H.M. Taylor Detroit Tigers Postcards

Various players and groups of players are featured in this issue of hometown heroes from H. M. Taylor in Detroit. The 5-1/2" x 3-1/2" black-and-white cards have white borders on front. Undivided backs have a gothic "Post Card" at top, a one-cent stamp box and, at bottom-left, "Rights reserved by H. M. Taylor, Detroit."

	NM	E	VG
Complete Set (7):	7,000	3,500	2,100
Common Card:	525.00	260.00	150.00
(1) Tyrus Cobb (At bat.)	3,600	1,800	1,080
(2) Bill Coughlin (Batting)	525.00	260.00	150.00
(3) Sam Crawford (Ready for the Ball.)	900.00	450.00	270.00
(4) Detroit Club (Team photo.)	850.00	425.00	250.00
(5) Wild Bill Donovan (Floral horseshoe presented at Philadelphia.)	525.00	260.00	150.00
(6) Hughie Jennings ("WEE'AH")	750.00	450.00	270.00
(7) Hughie Jennings, Wild Bill Donovan, Frank Chance (In dugout.)	525.00	260.00	150.00

1972 TCMA The 1930's

 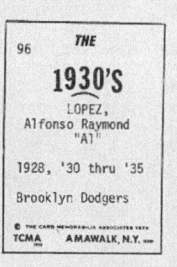

Extending to over 500 cards, this was one of TCMA's first ventures into the business of creating collectors' edition card sets of former players. Over the length of the series there were a number of style differences. The set was issued in 21 series of 24 cards each. All cards were printed in black-and-white (except for Series 18-19 printed in blue) and feature player photos on usually borderless fronts. Dimensions were about 2" x 2-3/4" for most series, with Series 15-16 in a 2-1/2" x 3-1/2" format. Except for a TCMA copyright line on some of the earlier cards, there is no other printing on front. Backs have player identification, team affiliations, TCMA copyright and, after #72, a card number. Production is reported as 1,000 sets. Blank-bank versions and uncut panels of 12 exist.

	NM	E	VG
Complete Set (504):	400.00	200.00	120.00
Common Player:	3.00	1.50	.90
(1) Roy Bell	3.00	1.50	.90
(2) Max Bishop	3.00	1.50	.90
(3) Bob Boken	3.00	1.50	.90
(4) Cliff Bolton	3.00	1.50	.90
(5) John Broaca	3.00	1.50	.90
(6) Bill Brubaker	3.00	1.50	.90
(7) Slick Castleman	3.00	1.50	.90
(8) Dick Coffman	3.00	1.50	.90
(9) Phil Collins	3.00	1.50	.90
(10) Earle Combs	3.00	1.50	.90
(11) Doc Cramer	3.00	1.50	.90
(12) Joe Cronin	3.00	1.50	.90
(13) Jack Crouch	3.00	1.50	.90
(14) Tony Cuccinello	3.00	1.50	.90
(15) Babe Dahlgren	3.00	1.50	.90
(16) Spud Davis	3.00	1.50	.90
(17) Dizzy Dean	6.00	3.00	1.75
(18) Paul Dean	3.00	1.50	.90
(19) Bill Dickey	3.00	1.50	.90
(20) Joe DiMaggio	10.00	5.00	3.00
(21) George Earnshaw	3.00	1.50	.90
(22) Woody English	3.00	1.50	.90
(23) Woody English	3.00	1.50	.90
(24) Hal Finney	3.00	1.50	.90

(25)	Freddie Fitzsimmons, Bump Hadley	3.00	1.50	.90
(26)	Tony Freitas	3.00	1.50	.90
(27)	Frank Frisch	3.00	1.50	.90
(28)	Milt Gaston	3.00	1.50	.90
(29)	Sid Gautreaux	3.00	1.50	.90
(30)	Charlie Gehringer	3.00	1.50	.90
(31)	Charley Gelbert	3.00	1.50	.90
(32)	Lefty Gomez	3.00	1.50	.90
(33)	Lefty Grove	5.00	2.50	1.50
(34)	Chick Hafey	3.00	1.50	.90
(35)	Jesse Haines	3.00	1.50	.90
(36)	Bill Hallahan	3.00	1.50	.90
(37)	Bucky Harris	3.00	1.50	.90
(38)	Ed Heusser	3.00	1.50	.90
(39)	Carl Hubbell	3.00	1.50	.90
(40)	Carl Hubbell	3.00	1.50	.90
(41)	Jimmy Jordan	3.00	1.50	.90
(42)	Joe Judge	3.00	1.50	.90
(43)	Len Koenecke	3.00	1.50	.90
(44)	Mark Koenig	3.00	1.50	.90
(45)	Cookie Lavagetto	3.00	1.50	.90
(46)	Roxie Lawson	3.00	1.50	.90
(47)	Tony Lazzeri	3.00	1.50	.90
(48)	Gus Mancuso	3.00	1.50	.90
(49)	John McCarthy	3.00	1.50	.90
(50)	Joe Medwick	3.00	1.50	.90
(51)	Cliff Melton	3.00	1.50	.90
(52)	Terry Moore	3.00	1.50	.90
(53)	John Murphy	3.00	1.50	.90
(54)	Ken O'Dea	3.00	1.50	.90
(55)	Bob O'Farrell	3.00	1.50	.90
(56)	Manuel Onis	3.00	1.50	.90
(57)	Monte Pearson	3.00	1.50	.90
(58)	Paul Richards	3.00	1.50	.90
(59)	Max Rosenfeld	6.00	3.00	1.75
(60)	Red Ruffing	3.00	1.50	.90
(61)	Red Ruffing	3.00	1.50	.90
(62)	Hal Schumacher	3.00	1.50	.90
(63)	George Selkirk	3.00	1.50	.90
(64)	Joe Shaute	3.00	1.50	.90
(65)	Gordon Slade	3.00	1.50	.90
(66)	Lindo Storti	3.00	1.50	.90
(67)	Smokey Sundra	3.00	1.50	.90
(68)	Bill Terry	3.00	1.50	.90
(69)	Jack Tising	3.00	1.50	.90
(70)	Sandy Vance	3.00	1.50	.90
(71)	Rube Walberg	3.00	1.50	.90
(72)	Sammy West	3.00	1.50	.90
73	Vito Tamulis	3.00	1.50	.90
74	Kemp Wicker	3.00	1.50	.90
75	Bob Seeds	3.00	1.50	.90
76	Jack Saltzgaver	3.00	1.50	.90
77	Walter Brown	3.00	1.50	.90
78	Spud Chandler	3.00	1.50	.90
79	Myril Hoag	3.00	1.50	.90
80	Joe Glenn	3.00	1.50	.90
81	Lefty Gomez	3.00	1.50	.90
82	Arndt Jorgens	3.00	1.50	.90
83	Jesse Hill	3.00	1.50	.90
84	Red Rolfe	3.00	1.50	.90
85	Wes Ferrell	3.00	1.50	.90
86	Joe Morrissey	3.00	1.50	.90
87	Tony Piet	3.00	1.50	.90
88	Fred Walker	3.00	1.50	.90
89	Bill Dietrich	3.00	1.50	.90
90	Lyn Lary	3.00	1.50	.90
91	Lyn Lary	3.00	1.50	.90
92	Lyn Lary	3.00	1.50	.90
93	Lyn Lary	3.00	1.50	.90
94	Buzz Boyle	3.00	1.50	.90
95	Tony Malinosky	3.00	1.50	.90
96	Al Lopez	3.00	1.50	.90
97	Linus Frey	3.00	1.50	.90
98	Tony Malinosky	3.00	1.50	.90
99	Owen Carroll	3.00	1.50	.90
100	Buddy Hassett	3.00	1.50	.90
101	Gib Brack	3.00	1.50	.90
102	Sam Leslie	3.00	1.50	.90
103	Fred Heimach	3.00	1.50	.90
104	Burleigh Grimes	3.00	1.50	.90
105	Ray Benge	3.00	1.50	.90
106	Joe Stripp	3.00	1.50	.90
107	Joe Becker	3.00	1.50	.90
108	Oscar Melillo	3.00	1.50	.90
109	Charley O'Leary, Rogers Hornsby	3.00	1.50	.90
110	Luke Appling	3.00	1.50	.90
111	Stan Hack	3.00	1.50	.90
112	Ray Hayworth	3.00	1.50	.90
113	Charles Wilson	3.00	1.50	.90
114	Hal Trosky	3.00	1.50	.90
115	Wes Ferrell	3.00	1.50	.90
116	Lyn Lary	3.00	1.50	.90
117	Milt Gaston	3.00	1.50	.90
118	Eldon Auker	3.00	1.50	.90
119	Heinie Manush	3.00	1.50	.90
120	Jimmie Foxx	6.00	3.00	1.75
121	Don Heffner	3.00	1.50	.90
122	George Pipgras	3.00	1.50	.90
123	Bump Hadley	3.00	1.50	.90
124	Tommy Henrich	3.00	1.50	.90
125	Joe McCarthy	3.00	1.50	.90
126	Joe Sewell	3.00	1.50	.90
127	Frank Crosetti	3.00	1.50	.90
128	Fred Walker	3.00	1.50	.90
129	Ted Kleinhans	3.00	1.50	.90
130	Jake Powell	3.00	1.50	.90
131	Ben Chapman	3.00	1.50	.90
132	John Murphy	3.00	1.50	.90
133	Lon Warneke	3.00	1.50	.90
134	Augie Galan	3.00	1.50	.90
135	Gene Lillard	3.00	1.50	.90
136	Stan Hack	3.00	1.50	.90
137	Frank Demaree	3.00	1.50	.90
138	Tony Piet	3.00	1.50	.90
139	Tony Piet	3.00	1.50	.90
140	Don Brennan	3.00	1.50	.90
141	Hal Schumacher, Lefty Gomez	3.00	1.50	.90
142	Bump Hadley	3.00	1.50	.90
143	Ollie Bejma	3.00	1.50	.90
144	Jim Bottomley	3.00	1.50	.90
145	Clay Bryant	3.00	1.50	.90
146	Charlie Grimm	3.00	1.50	.90
147	Flea Clifton	3.00	1.50	.90
148	Rollie Stiles	3.00	1.50	.90
149	Al Simmons	3.00	1.50	.90
150	Al Simmons	3.00	1.50	.90
151	Lyn Lary	3.00	1.50	.90
152	Roy Weatherly	3.00	1.50	.90
153	Whit Wyatt	3.00	1.50	.90
154	Oscar Vitt	3.00	1.50	.90
155	Jack Kroner	3.00	1.50	.90
156	Ted Lyons	3.00	1.50	.90
157	Joe Malay	3.00	1.50	.90
158	John McCarthy	3.00	1.50	.90
159	Hy Vandenberg	3.00	1.50	.90
160	Hank Leiber	3.00	1.50	.90
161	Joe Moore	3.00	1.50	.90
162	Cliff Melton	3.00	1.50	.90
163	Harry Danning	3.00	1.50	.90
164	Ray Harrell	3.00	1.50	.90
165	Bruce Ogrodowski	3.00	1.50	.90
166	Leo Durocher	3.00	1.50	.90
167	Leo Durocher	3.00	1.50	.90
168	William Walker	3.00	1.50	.90
169	Alvin Crowder	3.00	1.50	.90
170	Gus Suhr	3.00	1.50	.90
171	Monty Stratton	4.50	2.25	1.25
172	Boze Berger	3.00	1.50	.90
173	John Whitehead	3.00	1.50	.90
174	Joe Heving	3.00	1.50	.90
175	Merv Shea	3.00	1.50	.90
176	Ed Durham	3.00	1.50	.90
177	Buddy Myer	3.00	1.50	.90
178	Earl Whitehill	3.00	1.50	.90
179	Joe Cronin	3.00	1.50	.90
180	Zeke Bonura	3.00	1.50	.90
181	John Knott	3.00	1.50	.90
182	John Allen	3.00	1.50	.90
183	William Knickerbocker	3.00	1.50	.90
184	Earl Averill	3.00	1.50	.90
185	Bob Feller	4.50	2.25	1.25
186	Steve O'Neill	3.00	1.50	.90
187	Bruce Campbell	3.00	1.50	.90
188	Ivy Andrews	3.00	1.50	.90
189	Ivy Andrews	3.00	1.50	.90
190	Muddy Ruel	3.00	1.50	.90
191	Art Scharein	3.00	1.50	.90
192	Merv Shea	3.00	1.50	.90
193	George Myatt	3.00	1.50	.90
194	Bill Werber	3.00	1.50	.90
195	Red Lucas	3.00	1.50	.90
196	Hugh Luby	3.00	1.50	.90
197	Vic Sorrell	3.00	1.50	.90
198	Mickey Cochrane	3.00	1.50	.90
199	Rudy York	3.00	1.50	.90
200	Ray Mack	3.00	1.50	.90
201	Vince DiMaggio	4.50	2.25	1.25
202	Mel Ott	4.50	2.25	1.25
203	John Lucadello	3.00	1.50	.90
204	Debs Garms	3.00	1.50	.90
205	John Murphy, Pat Malone, Bump Hadley, Kemp Wicker, John Broaca	3.00	1.50	.90
206	Stan Sperry	3.00	1.50	.90
207	Hal Schumacher	3.00	1.50	.90
208	Blondy Ryan	3.00	1.50	.90
209	Bob Seeds	3.00	1.50	.90
210	Danny MacFayden	3.00	1.50	.90
211	Fran Healy	3.00	1.50	.90
212	Al Spohrer	3.00	1.50	.90
213	Ed Linke	3.00	1.50	.90
214	Joe Schultz	3.00	1.50	.90
215	Casey Stengel	3.00	1.50	.90
216	Casey Stengel	3.00	1.50	.90
217	Phil Hensick	3.00	1.50	.90
218	Rollie Hemsley	3.00	1.50	.90
219	Ace Parker	4.50	2.25	1.25
220	Henry Helf	3.00	1.50	.90
221	Bill Schuster	3.00	1.50	.90
222	Heinie Schuble	3.00	1.50	.90
223	John Salveson	3.00	1.50	.90
224	Robert Grace	3.00	1.50	.90
225	Sig Gryska	3.00	1.50	.90
226	Mickey Haslin	3.00	1.50	.90
227	Randy Gumpert	3.00	1.50	.90
228	Frank Gustine	3.00	1.50	.90
229	Marv Gudat	3.00	1.50	.90
230	Bob Logan	3.00	1.50	.90
231	Marvin Owen	3.00	1.50	.90
232	Bucky Walters	3.00	1.50	.90
233	Marty Hopkins	3.00	1.50	.90
234	Jimmy Dykes	3.00	1.50	.90
235	Lefty O'Doul	3.00	1.50	.90
236	Larry Rosenthal	3.00	1.50	.90
237	Mickey Haslin	3.00	1.50	.90
238	Eugene Schott	3.00	1.50	.90
239	Sad Sam Jones	3.00	1.50	.90
240	Edwin Rommel	3.00	1.50	.90
241	Rip Collins	3.00	1.50	.90
242	Rosy Ryan	3.00	1.50	.90
243	James Bucher	3.00	1.50	.90
244	Ethan Allen	3.00	1.50	.90
245	Dick Bartell	3.00	1.50	.90
246	Henry Leiber	3.00	1.50	.90
247	Lou Chiozza	3.00	1.50	.90
248	Babe Herman	3.00	1.50	.90
249	Tommy Henrich	3.00	1.50	.90
250	Thornton Lee	3.00	1.50	.90
251	Joe Kuhel	3.00	1.50	.90
252	George Pipgras	3.00	1.50	.90
253	Luke Sewell	3.00	1.50	.90
254	Tony Lazzeri	3.00	1.50	.90
255	Ival Goodman	3.00	1.50	.90
256	George Rensa	3.00	1.50	.90
257	Hal Newhouser	3.00	1.50	.90
258	Rogers Hornsby	5.00	2.50	1.50
259	Tuck Stainback	3.00	1.50	.90
260	Vance Page	3.00	1.50	.90
261	Art Scharein	3.00	1.50	.90
262	Mike Ryba	3.00	1.50	.90
263	James Lindsey	3.00	1.50	.90
264	Ed Parsons	3.00	1.50	.90
265	Elon Hogsett	3.00	1.50	.90
266	Bud Hafey	3.00	1.50	.90
267	John Gill	3.00	1.50	.90
268	Owen Bush	3.00	1.50	.90
269	Ethan Allen	3.00	1.50	.90
270	Jim Bagby Sr.	3.00	1.50	.90
271	Bill Atwood	3.00	1.50	.90
272	Phil Cavarretta	3.00	1.50	.90
273	Travis Jackson	3.00	1.50	.90
274	Ted Olson	3.00	1.50	.90
275	Boze Berger	3.00	1.50	.90
276	Norb Kleinke	3.00	1.50	.90
277	Rip Radcliff	3.00	1.50	.90
278	Mule Haas	3.00	1.50	.90
279	Julius Solters	3.00	1.50	.90
280	Ivey Shiver	3.00	1.50	.90
281	Wes Schulmerich	3.00	1.50	.90
282	Ray Kolp	3.00	1.50	.90
283	Si Johnson	3.00	1.50	.90
284	Al Hollingsworth	3.00	1.50	.90
285	D'Arcy Flowers	3.00	1.50	.90
286	Adam Comorosky	3.00	1.50	.90
287	Allen Cooke	3.00	1.50	.90
288	Clyde Kimsey	3.00	1.50	.90
289	Fred Ostermueller	3.00	1.50	.90
290	Angelo Giuliani	3.00	1.50	.90
291	John Wilson	3.00	1.50	.90
292	George Dickman	3.00	1.50	.90
293	Jim DeShong	3.00	1.50	.90
294	Red Evans	3.00	1.50	.90
295	Curtis Davis	3.00	1.50	.90
296	Charlie Berry	3.00	1.50	.90
297	George Gibson	3.00	1.50	.90
298	Fern Bell	3.00	1.50	.90
299	Irv Bartling	3.00	1.50	.90
300	Babe Barna	3.00	1.50	.90
301	Henry Johnson	3.00	1.50	.90
302	Harlond Clift	3.00	1.50	.90
303	Lu Blue	3.00	1.50	.90
304	George Hockette	3.00	1.50	.90
305	Walt Bashore	3.00	1.50	.90
306	Walter Beck	3.00	1.50	.90
307	Jewel Ens	3.00	1.50	.90
308	Doc Prothro	3.00	1.50	.90
309	Morrie Arnovich	3.00	1.50	.90
310	Bill Killefer	3.00	1.50	.90
311	Pete Appleton	3.00	1.50	.90
312	Fred Archer	3.00	1.50	.90
313	Bill Lohrman	3.00	1.50	.90

314	Fred Haney	3.00	1.50	.90
315	Jimmy Ripple	3.00	1.50	.90
316	Johnny Kerr	3.00	1.50	.90
317	Harry Gumbert	3.00	1.50	.90
318	Samuel Derringer	3.00	1.50	.90
319	Firpo Marberry	3.00	1.50	.90
320	Waite Hoyt	3.00	1.50	.90
321	Rick Ferrell	3.00	1.50	.90
322	Hank Greenberg	6.00	3.00	1.75
323	Carl Reynolds	3.00	1.50	.90
324	Roy Johnson	3.00	1.50	.90
325	Gil English	3.00	1.50	.90
326	Al Smith	3.00	1.50	.90
327	Dolph Camilli	3.00	1.50	.90
328	Oscar Grimes	3.00	1.50	.90
329	Ray Berres	3.00	1.50	.90
330	Norm Schlueter	3.00	1.50	.90
331	Joe Vosmik	3.00	1.50	.90
332	Jimmy Dykes	3.00	1.50	.90
333	Vern Washington	3.00	1.50	.90
334	"Bad News" Hale	3.00	1.50	.90
335	Lew Fonseca	3.00	1.50	.90
336	Mike Kreevich	3.00	1.50	.90
337	Bob Johnson	3.00	1.50	.90
338	"Jeep" Handley	3.00	1.50	.90
339	Gabby Hartnett	3.00	1.50	.90
340	Freddie Lindstrom	3.00	1.50	.90
341	Bert Haas	3.00	1.50	.90
342	Elbie Fletcher	3.00	1.50	.90
343	Tom Hafey	3.00	1.50	.90
344	Rip Collins	3.00	1.50	.90
345	John Babich	3.00	1.50	.90
346	Joe Beggs	3.00	1.50	.90
347	Bobo Newsom	3.00	1.50	.90
348	Wally Berger	3.00	1.50	.90
349	Bud Thomas	3.00	1.50	.90
350	Tom Heath	3.00	1.50	.90
351	Cecil Travis	3.00	1.50	.90
352	Jack Redmond	3.00	1.50	.90
353	Fred Schulte	3.00	1.50	.90
354	Pat Malone	3.00	1.50	.90
355	Hugh Critz	3.00	1.50	.90
356	Frank Pytlak	3.00	1.50	.90
357	Glenn Liebhardt	3.00	1.50	.90
358	Al Milnar	3.00	1.50	.90
359	Al Benton	3.00	1.50	.90
360	Moe Berg	6.00	3.00	1.75
361	Al Brancato	3.00	1.50	.90
362	Mark Christman	3.00	1.50	.90
363	Fabian Gaffke	3.00	1.50	.90
364	George Gill	3.00	1.50	.90
365	Oral Hildebrand	3.00	1.50	.90
366	Lou Fette	3.00	1.50	.90
367	Tex Carleton	3.00	1.50	.90
368	Don Gutteridge	3.00	1.50	.90
369	Pete Fox	3.00	1.50	.90
370	George Blaeholder	3.00	1.50	.90
371	George Caster	3.00	1.50	.90
372	Joe Cascarella	3.00	1.50	.90
373	Jimmy Hitchcock	3.00	1.50	.90
374	Frank Croucher	3.00	1.50	.90
375	LeRoy Parmelee	3.00	1.50	.90
376	Joe Mulligan	3.00	1.50	.90
377	John Welch	3.00	1.50	.90
378	Donald McNair	3.00	1.50	.90
379	Frenchy Bordagaray	3.00	1.50	.90
380	Denny Galehouse	3.00	1.50	.90
381	Robert Harris	3.00	1.50	.90
382	Max Butcher	3.00	1.50	.90
383	Sam Byrd	3.00	1.50	.90
384	Pete Coscarart	3.00	1.50	.90
385	George Case	3.00	1.50	.90
386	John Hudson	3.00	1.50	.90
387	Frank Crespi	3.00	1.50	.90
388	Gene Desautels	3.00	1.50	.90
389	Bill Cissell	3.00	1.50	.90
390	John Burns	3.00	1.50	.90
391	Larry Benton	3.00	1.50	.90
392	James Holbrook	3.00	1.50	.90
393	Ernie Koy	3.00	1.50	.90
394	Bobby Doerr	3.00	1.50	.90
395	Harry Boyles	3.00	1.50	.90
396	Pinky Higgins	3.00	1.50	.90
397	Mel Almada	3.00	1.50	.90
398	Carl Fischer	3.00	1.50	.90
399	Rabbit Maranville, Johnny Evers, Hank Gowdy	3.00	1.50	.90
400	Lou Gehrig	10.00	5.00	3.00
401	Lincoln Blakely	3.00	1.50	.90
402	James Henry	3.00	1.50	.90
403	Ed Holley	3.00	1.50	.90
404	Elmer Hodgin	3.00	1.50	.90
405	Bob Garbark	3.00	1.50	.90
406	John Burnett	3.00	1.50	.90
407	David Harris	3.00	1.50	.90
408	Johnny Dickshot	3.00	1.50	.90
409	Ray Mueller	3.00	1.50	.90
410	John Welaj	3.00	1.50	.90

411	Les McCrabb	3.00	1.50	.90
412	George Uhle	3.00	1.50	.90
413	Leo Mangum	3.00	1.50	.90
414	Howard Maple	3.00	1.50	.90
415	Syl Johnson	3.00	1.50	.90
416	Hershel Martin	3.00	1.50	.90
417	Joe Martin	3.00	1.50	.90
418	Phil Masi	3.00	1.50	.90
419	Bobby Mattick	3.00	1.50	.90
420	Marshall Mauldin	3.00	1.50	.90
421	Frank May	3.00	1.50	.90
422	Merrill May	3.00	1.50	.90
423	Bill McAfee	3.00	1.50	.90
424	Benny McCoy	3.00	1.50	.90
425	Charlie George	3.00	1.50	.90
426	Roy Hughes	3.00	1.50	.90
427	Bill Kerksieck	3.00	1.50	.90
428	Wes Kingdon	3.00	1.50	.90
429	Lynn King	3.00	1.50	.90
430	Harry Kinzy	3.00	1.50	.90
431	Harry Kimberlin	3.00	1.50	.90
432	Bob Klinger	3.00	1.50	.90
433	Wilfred Knothe	3.00	1.50	.90
434	Lou Finney	3.00	1.50	.90
435	Roy Johnson	3.00	1.50	.90
436	Woody Jensen	3.00	1.50	.90
437	George Jeffcoat	3.00	1.50	.90
438	Roy Joiner	3.00	1.50	.90
439	Baxter Jordan	3.00	1.50	.90
440	Edwin Joost	3.00	1.50	.90
441	Bubber Jonnard	3.00	1.50	.90
442	Bucky Jacobs	3.00	1.50	.90
443	Art Jacobs	3.00	1.50	.90
444	Orville Jorgens	3.00	1.50	.90
445	Hal Kelleher	3.00	1.50	.90
446	Harry Kelley	3.00	1.50	.90
447	Ken Keltner	3.00	1.50	.90
448	Paul Kardon	3.00	1.50	.90
449	Alex Kampouris	3.00	1.50	.90
450	Willie Kamm	3.00	1.50	.90
451	Bob Kahle	3.00	1.50	.90
452	Billy Jurges	3.00	1.50	.90
453	Ken Jungels	3.00	1.50	.90
454	John Juelich	3.00	1.50	.90
455	John Marcum	3.00	1.50	.90
456	Walt Masterson	3.00	1.50	.90
457	Clint Brown	3.00	1.50	.90
458	Buddy Lewis	3.00	1.50	.90
459	Watty Clark	3.00	1.50	.90
460	Johnny Cooney	3.00	1.50	.90
461	Mel Harder	3.00	1.50	.90
462	Justin McLaughlin	3.00	1.50	.90
463	Frank Grube	3.00	1.50	.90
464	Jeff Heath	3.00	1.50	.90
465	Cliff Heathcote	3.00	1.50	.90
466	Harvey Hendrick	3.00	1.50	.90
467	Johnny Hodapp	3.00	1.50	.90
468	Bob Holland	3.00	1.50	.90
469	Otto Huber	3.00	1.50	.90
470	Rudy Hulswitt	3.00	1.50	.90
471	Roy Johnson	3.00	1.50	.90
472	Smead Jolley	3.00	1.50	.90
473	Rollie Hemsley, Bob Smith, John Moore	3.00	1.50	.90
474	John Jones	3.00	1.50	.90
475	Harry Kelley	3.00	1.50	.90
476	George Kelly	3.00	1.50	.90
477	Chuck Klein	3.00	1.50	.90
478	Joe Krakauskas	3.00	1.50	.90
479	Mike Kreevich	3.00	1.50	.90
480	Dick Lanahan	3.00	1.50	.90
481	Emil "Dutch" Leonard	3.00	1.50	.90
482	Harl Maggert	3.00	1.50	.90
483	Cyrus Malis	3.00	1.50	.90
484	Dario Lodigiani	3.00	1.50	.90
485	Walt Masterson	3.00	1.50	.90
486	Rabbit Maranville	3.00	1.50	.90
487	Ed Marshall	3.00	1.50	.90
488	Tim McKeithan	3.00	1.50	.90
489	Patrick McLaughlin	3.00	1.50	.90
490	Bob McNamara	3.00	1.50	.90
491	Steve Mesner	3.00	1.50	.90
492	Clarence Mitchell	3.00	1.50	.90
493	Mal Moss	3.00	1.50	.90
494	Joe Murray	3.00	1.50	.90
495	Pete Naktenis	3.00	1.50	.90
496	Bill Nicholson	3.00	1.50	.90
497	John Rigney	3.00	1.50	.90
498	Clyde Sukeforth	3.00	1.50	.90
499	Evar Swanson	3.00	1.50	.90
500	Dan Taylor	3.00	1.50	.90
501	Sloppy Thurston	3.00	1.50	.90
502	Forrest Wright	3.00	1.50	.90
503	Ray Lucas	3.00	1.50	.90
504	Nig Lipscomb	3.00	1.50	.90

1973 TCMA "Bobo"

The major league travels of Bobo Newsom are chronicled in this set of 3-1/2" x 5-1/2" black-and-white cards depicting the pitcher in the uniforms of the nine teams for whom he played between 1929-53.

		NM	E	VG
Complete Set (10):		25.00	12.50	7.50
Common Card:		4.00	2.00	1.25
(1)	Bobo Newsom (A's)	4.00	2.00	1.25
(2)	Bobo Newsom (A's, with Bobby Shantz.)	4.00	2.00	1.25
(3)	Bobo Newsom (Browns)	4.00	2.00	1.25
(4)	Bobo Newsom (Cubs)	4.00	2.00	1.25
(5)	Bobo Newsom (Dodgers, with Leo Durocher.)	4.00	2.00	1.25
(6)	Bobo Newsom (Giants)	4.00	2.00	1.25
(7)	Bobo Newsom (Red Sox)	4.00	2.00	1.25
(8)	Bobo Newsom (Senators, with Ossie Bluege.)	4.00	2.00	1.25
(9)	Bobo Newsom (Tigers, with Paul Derringer.)	4.00	2.00	1.25
(10)	Bobo Newsom (Yankees, with Vic Rashi, Bucky Harris.)	4.00	2.00	1.25

1973 TCMA 1874 Philadelphia Athletics

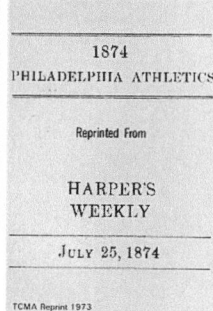

This early collectors' issue reproduces woodcuts of the A's as they appeared in the July 25, 1874, edition of Harper's Weekly. The 3-1/16" x 4-1/2" cards are printed in black-and-white with the player name and position in the white border at bottom. Identical backs credit the pictures' original source and state "TCMA Reprint 1973." The unnumbered cards are checklisted here alphabetically.

		NM	E	VG
Complete Set (9):		25.00	12.50	7.50
Common Player:		3.00	1.50	.90
(1)	Cap Anson	10.00	5.00	3.00
(2)	Joseph Battin	3.00	1.50	.90
(3)	John Clapp	3.00	1.50	.90
(4)	Wes Fisler	3.00	1.50	.90
(5)	Count Gedney	3.00	1.50	.90
(6)	Dick McBride	3.00	1.50	.90
(7)	Mike McGeary	3.00	1.50	.90
(8)	J.F. McMullen	3.00	1.50	.90
(9)	Ezra Sutton	3.00	1.50	.90

1973 TCMA 1890 Base-ball Season

This set commemorates the baseball "war" of 1890 when many National League players - stars and journeymen alike - defected to a new player-owned league called, appropriately enough, the Players League. Fronts of these 3-1/8" x 4-1/2" black-and-white cards feature reproductions of woodcuts originally printed in Harper's Weekly. Backs have information about the teams in each league. The unnumbered cards are checklisted here in alphabetical order. Original issue price of the set was $3.

1890
BASE-BALL SEASON
HARPER'S
WEEKLY
MAY 3, 1890.

M. J. Kelly,   C. A. Radbourne,
C. Sweet,   Boston (16 Men)
M. E. Murphy,   Adison Gumbert,
M. Kilroy,   M. Madden,
D. Brouthers,   W. Daley,
Arthur Irwin,   J. Quinn,
H. Richardson,   William Nash,
H. Storey,   R. F. Johnson,
                                Thomas Brown.

TCMA Reprint 1973

	NM	E	VG
Complete Set (30):	48.00	24.00	14.50
Common Player:	2.00	1.00	.60

(1)	Cap Anson	2.00	1.00	.60
(2)	Dan Brouthers	2.00	1.00	.60
(3)	Thomas E. Burns	2.00	1.00	.60
(4)	John Clarkson	2.00	1.00	.60
(5)	C.A. Comiskey	2.00	1.00	.60
(6)	Roger Connor	2.00	1.00	.60
(7)	E.N. Crane	2.00	1.00	.60
(8)	Jeremiah Denny	2.00	1.00	.60
(9)	William B. Ewing	2.00	1.00	.60
(10)	D.L. Foutz	2.00	1.00	.60
(11)	John W. Glasscock	2.00	1.00	.60
(12)	W. Hallman	2.00	1.00	.60
(13)	Edward Hanlon	2.00	1.00	.60
(14)	Timothy J. Keefe	2.00	1.00	.60
(15)	M.J. Kelly	2.00	1.00	.60
(16)	M. Kilroy	2.00	1.00	.60
(17)	W.A. Latham	2.00	1.00	.60
(18)	J.A. McPhee	2.00	1.00	.60
(19)	Joseph Mulvey	2.00	1.00	.60
(20)	W.D. O'Brien	2.00	1.00	.60
(21)	David Orr	2.00	1.00	.60
(22)	John G. Reilly	2.00	1.00	.60
(23)	S.L. Thompson	2.00	1.00	.60
(24)	M. Tiernan	2.00	1.00	.60
(25)	John M. Ward	2.00	1.00	.60
(26)	M. Welsh (Welch)	2.00	1.00	.60
(27)	A. Weyhing	2.00	1.00	.60
(28)	Charles Zimmer	2.00	1.00	.60
(29)	**A dive for second base**	1.00	.50	.30
(30)	**Brotherhood Players Header Card**	1.00	.50	.30

1973 TCMA 1930's No Hit Pitchers and 6 for 6 Hitters

These large-format (3-1/2" x 5-1/2") cards feature the no-hit pitchers and 6-for-6 hitters of the 1930s. Borderless front photos are in black-and-white. On back of the pitchers' cards is a list of the decade's no-hitters, the date, score and opposing team. A similar list of the 6-for-6 hitters is on the back of their cards. The cards are unnumbered.

	NM	E	VG
Complete Set (12):	40.00	20.00	12.00
Common Player:	4.00	2.00	1.25

	PITCHERS			
(1)	Paul Dean	6.00	3.00	1.75
(2)	Bill Dietrich	4.00	2.00	1.25
(3)	Vern Kennedy	4.00	2.00	1.25
(4)	Monte Pearson	4.00	2.00	1.25
(5)	Johnny Vander Meer	5.00	2.50	1.50
	HITTERS			
(6)	Jim Bottomley	6.00	3.00	1.75
(7)	Bruce Campbell	4.00	2.00	1.25
(8)	Doc Cramer	4.00	2.00	1.25
(9)	Myril Hoag	4.00	2.00	1.25
(10)	Cookie Lavagetto	4.00	2.00	1.25
(11)	Terry Moore	5.00	2.50	1.50
(12)	Henry Steinbacher	4.00	2.00	1.25

1973 TCMA 1941 Brooklyn Dodgers

These 3-3/8" x 2-1/2" cards are printed in blue-and-white. The unnumbered cards do not have player names on front.

	NM	E	VG
Complete Set (32):	50.00	25.00	15.00
Common Player	2.00	1.00	.60

(1)	**Title Card**	1.00	.50	.30
(2)	John Allen	2.00	1.00	.60
(3)	Mace Brown	2.00	1.00	.60
(4)	Dolph Camilli	2.00	1.00	.60
(5)	Hugh Casey	2.00	1.00	.60
(6)	Curt Davis	2.00	1.00	.60
(7)	Tom Drake	2.00	1.00	.60
(8)	Leo Durocher	4.00	2.00	1.25
(9)	Fred Fitzsimmons	2.00	1.00	.60

(10)	Herman Franks	2.00	1.00	.60
(11)	Augie Galan	2.00	1.00	.60
(12)	Tony Giuliani	2.00	1.00	.60
(13)	Luke Hamlin	2.00	1.00	.60
(14)	Billy Herman	4.00	2.00	1.25
(15)	Kirby Higbe	2.00	1.00	.60
(16)	Alex Kampouris	2.00	1.00	.60
(17)	Newt Kimball	2.00	1.00	.60
(18)	Cookie Lavagetto	2.00	1.00	.60
(19)	Ducky Medwick	4.00	2.00	1.25
(20)	Van Mungo	2.00	1.00	.60
(21)	Mickey Owen	2.00	1.00	.60
(22)	Babe Phelps	2.00	1.00	.60
(23)	Pee Wee Reese	8.00	4.00	2.50
(24)	Pete Reiser	2.00	1.00	.60
(25)	Lew Riggs	2.00	1.00	.60
(26)	Bill Swift	2.00	1.00	.60
(27)	Vito Tamulis	2.00	1.00	.60
(28)	Joe Vosmik	2.00	1.00	.60
(29)	Dixie Walker	2.00	1.00	.60
(30)	Paul Waner	4.00	2.00	1.25
(31)	Jimmy Wasdell	2.00	1.00	.60
(32)	Whit Wyatt	2.00	1.00	.60

1973 TCMA All Time New York Yankees Team

Outfield-Mickey Mantle

Printed in black-and-white in 3-1/2" x 5-1/2" format, these cards have borderless photos on front with a white strip at bottom in which the player's position and name appear. Backs list the all-time roster but are not numbered or dated. Production was 1,000 sets.

	NM	E	VG
Complete Set (12):	25.00	12.50	7.50
Common Player:	3.50	1.75	1.00

(1)	Bill Dickey	3.50	1.75	1.00
(2)	Joe DiMaggio	10.00	5.00	3.00
(3)	Whitey Ford	5.00	2.50	1.50
(4)	Lou Gehrig	10.00	5.00	3.00
(5)	Tony Lazzeri	3.50	1.75	1.00
(6)	Mickey Mantle	15.00	7.50	4.50
(7)	Johnny Murphy	3.50	1.75	1.00
(8)	Phil Rizzuto	5.00	2.50	1.50
(9)	Red Rolfe	3.50	1.75	1.00
(10)	Red Ruffing	3.50	1.75	1.00
(11)	Babe Ruth	10.00	5.00	3.00
(12)	Casey Stengel	3.50	1.75	1.00

1973-80 TCMA All-Time Greats Postcards

ALL-TIME Greats

HANK GREENBERG

1973 TCMA Ltd.

One of the longest collectors' series issued by TCMA in the 1970s was this set of player postcards. Measuring 3-1/2" x 5-1/2" the black-and-white cards have large photos on front, bordered in black and highlighted with banners and baseball equipment. Backs have postcard markings. Six series of cards were issued between 1973-80 and the un-numbered cards are checklisted here in alphabetical order within series.

	NM	E	VG
Complete Set (156):	150.00	75.00	45.00
Common Player:	3.00	1.50	.90

	SERIES 1			
(1)	Luke Appling	3.00	1.50	.90
(2)	Mickey Cochrane	3.00	1.50	.90
(3)	Eddie Collins	3.00	1.50	.90
(4)	Kiki Cuyler	3.00	1.50	.90
(5)	Bill Dickey	3.00	1.50	.90
(6)	Joe DiMaggio	7.50	3.75	2.25
(7)	Bob Feller	3.00	1.50	.90
(8)	Frank Frisch	3.00	1.50	.90
(9)	Lou Gehrig	7.50	3.75	2.25
(10)	Goose Goslin	3.00	1.50	.90
(11)	Chick Hafey	3.00	1.50	.90
(12)	Gabby Hartnett	3.00	1.50	.90
(13)	Rogers Hornsby	4.00	2.00	1.25
(14)	Ted Lyons	3.00	1.50	.90
(15)	Connie Mack	3.00	1.50	.90
(16)	Heinie Manush	3.00	1.50	.90
(17)	Rabbit Maranville	3.00	1.50	.90
(18)	Ducky Medwick	3.00	1.50	.90
(19)	Al Simmons	3.00	1.50	.90
(20)	Bill Terry	3.00	1.50	.90
(21)	Pie Traynor	3.00	1.50	.90
(22)	Dazzy Vance	3.00	1.50	.90
(23)	Cy Young	5.00	2.50	1.50
(24)	Gabby Hartnett, Babe Ruth	6.00	3.00	1.75
	SERIES 2			
(1)	Roger Bresnahan	3.00	1.50	.90
(2)	Dizzy Dean	4.00	2.00	1.25
(3)	Buck Ewing & mascot	3.00	1.50	.90
(4)	Jimmie Foxx	4.50	2.25	1.25
(5)	Hank Greenberg	4.50	2.25	1.25
(6)	Burleigh Grimes	3.00	1.50	.90
(7)	Harry Heilmann	3.00	1.50	.90
(8)	Waite Hoyt	3.00	1.50	.90
(9)	Walter Johnson	5.00	2.50	1.50
(10)	George Kelly	3.00	1.50	.90
(11)	Christy Mathewson	5.00	2.50	1.50
(12)	John McGraw	3.00	1.50	.90
(13)	Stan Musial	4.00	2.00	1.25
(14)	Mel Ott	3.00	1.50	.90
(15)	Satchel Paige	6.00	3.00	1.75
(16)	Sam Rice	3.00	1.50	.90
(17)	Edd Roush	3.00	1.50	.90
(18)	Red Ruffing	3.00	1.50	.90
(19)	Casey Stengel	3.00	1.50	.90
(20)	Honus Wagner	6.00	3.00	1.75
(21)	Lloyd Waner	3.00	1.50	.90
(22)	Paul Waner	3.00	1.50	.90
(23)	Harry Wright	3.00	1.50	.90
(24)	Ross Youngs	3.00	1.50	.90
	SERIES 3			
(1)	Home Run Baker	3.00	1.50	.90
(2)	Chief Bender	3.00	1.50	.90
(3)	Jim Bottomley	3.00	1.50	.90
(4)	Lou Boudreau	3.00	1.50	.90
(5)	Mordecai Brown	3.00	1.50	.90
(6)	Roy Campanella	3.50	1.75	1.00
(7)	Max Carey	3.00	1.50	.90
(8)	Ty Cobb	7.50	3.75	2.25
(9)	Earle Combs	3.00	1.50	.90
(10)	Jocko Conlan	3.00	1.50	.90
(11)	Hugh Duffy	3.00	1.50	.90
(12)	Red Faber	3.00	1.50	.90
(13)	Lefty Grove	3.00	1.50	.90
(14)	Judge K.M. Landis	3.00	1.50	.90
(15)	Eddie Plank	3.00	1.50	.90
(16)	Hoss Radbourne	3.00	1.50	.90
(17)	Eppa Rixey	3.00	1.50	.90
(18)	Jackie Robinson	6.00	3.00	1.75
(19)	Babe Ruth	7.50	3.75	2.25
(20)	George Sisler	3.00	1.50	.90
(21)	Zack Wheat	3.00	1.50	.90
(22)	Ted Williams	6.00	3.00	1.75
(23)	Mel Ott, Babe Ruth	6.00	3.00	1.75
(24)	Tris Speaker, Wilbert Robinson	3.00	1.50	.90
	SERIES 4			
(1)	Grover C. Alexander	3.50	1.75	1.00
(2)	Cap Anson	3.00	1.50	.90
(3)	Earl Averill	3.00	1.50	.90
(4)	Ed Barrow	3.00	1.50	.90
(5)	Yogi Berra	3.50	1.75	1.00
(6)	Roberto Clemente	6.00	3.00	1.75
(7)	Jimmy Collins	3.00	1.50	.90
(8)	Whitey Ford	3.50	1.75	1.00
(9)	Ford Frick	3.00	1.50	.90
(10)	Vernon Gomez	3.00	1.50	.90
(11)	Bucky Harris	3.00	1.50	.90
(12)	Billy Herman	3.00	1.50	.90
(13)	Carl Hubbell	3.00	1.50	.90
(14)	Miller Huggins	3.00	1.50	.90
(15)	Monte Irvin	3.00	1.50	.90
(16)	Ralph Kiner	3.00	1.50	.90
(17)	Bill Klem	3.00	1.50	.90

(18)	Sandy Koufax	6.00	3.00	1.75
(19)	Napoleon Lajoie	3.00	1.50	.90
(20)	Bob Lemon	3.00	1.50	.90
(21)	Mickey Mantle	7.50	3.75	2.25
(22)	Rube Marquard	3.00	1.50	.90
(23)	Joe McCarthy	3.00	1.50	.90
(24)	Bill McKechnie	3.00	1.50	.90
(25)	Herb Pennock	3.00	1.50	.90
(26)	Warren Spahn	3.00	1.50	.90
(27)	Joe Tinker	3.00	1.50	.90
(28)	Early Wynn	3.00	1.50	.90
(29)	Joe Cronin, Honus Wagner, Bill Terry	3.00	1.50	.90
(30)	Jimmie Foxx, Lou Gehrig	6.00	3.00	1.75
(31)	Hank Greenberg, Ralph Kiner	3.00	1.50	.90
(32)	Walter Johnson, Connie Mack	3.00	1.50	.90
(33)	Connie Mack, Bob Feller	3.00	1.50	.90
(34)	Mel Ott, Lou Gehrig	6.00	3.00	1.75
(35)	Al Simmons, Tris Speaker, Ty Cobb	3.00	1.50	.90
(36)	Ted Williams, Lou Boudreau	3.00	1.50	.90

SERIES 5

(1)	Dave Bancroft	3.00	1.50	.90
(2)	Ernie Banks	3.50	1.75	1.00
(3)	Frank Chance	3.00	1.50	.90
(4)	Stan Coveleski	3.00	1.50	.90
(5)	Billy Evans	3.00	1.50	.90
(6)	Clark Griffith	3.00	1.50	.90
(7)	Jesse Haines	3.00	1.50	.90
(8)	Will Harridge	3.00	1.50	.90
(9)	Harry Hooper	3.00	1.50	.90
(10)	Cal Hubbard	3.00	1.50	.90
(11)	Hugh Jennings	3.00	1.50	.90
(12)	Wee Willie Keeler	3.00	1.50	.90
(13)	Fred Lindstrom	3.00	1.50	.90
(14)	Pop Lloyd	3.00	1.50	.90
(15)	Al Lopez	3.00	1.50	.90
(16)	Robin Roberts	3.00	1.50	.90
(17)	Amos Rusie	3.00	1.50	.90
(18)	Ray Schalk	3.00	1.50	.90
(19)	Joe Sewell	3.00	1.50	.90
(20)	Rube Waddell	3.00	1.50	.90
(21)	George Weiss	3.00	1.50	.90
(22)	Dizzy Dean, Gabby Hartnett	3.00	1.50	.90
(23)	Joe DiMaggio, Mickey Mantle	7.50	3.75	2.25
(24)	Ted Williams, Joe DiMaggio	6.00	3.00	1.75

SERIES 6

(1)	Jack Chesbro	3.00	1.50	.90
(2)	Tom Connolly	3.00	1.50	.90
(3)	Sam Crawford	3.00	1.50	.90
(4)	Elmer Flick	3.00	1.50	.90
(5)	Charlie Gehringer	3.00	1.50	.90
(6)	Warren Giles	3.00	1.50	.90
(7)	Ban Johnson	3.00	1.50	.90
(8)	Addie Joss	3.00	1.50	.90
(9)	Al Kaline	3.00	1.50	.90
(10)	Willie Mays	6.00	3.00	1.75
(11)	Joe McGinnity	3.00	1.50	.90
(12)	Larry McPhail (MacPhail)	3.00	1.50	.90
(13)	Branch Rickey	3.00	1.50	.90
(14)	Wilbert Robinson	3.00	1.50	.90
(15)	Duke Snider	3.00	1.50	.90
(16)	Tris Speaker	4.00	2.00	1.25
(17)	Bobby Wallace	3.00	1.50	.90
(18)	Hack Wilson	.45	.25	.14
(19)	Yogi Berra, Casey Stengel	4.00	2.00	1.25
(20)	Warren Giles, Roberto Clemente	4.50	2.25	1.25
(21)	Mickey Mantle, Willie Mays	6.00	3.00	1.75
(22)	John McGraw, Babe Ruth	6.00	3.00	1.75
(23)	Satchel Paige, Bob Feller	2.50	2.50	1.50
(24)	Paul Waner, Lloyd Waner	4.00	2.00	1.25

1973-1974 TCMA Autograph Series

These postcard-size black-and-white cards have border-less front photos with a wide white strip at bottom to accommodate an autograph. They are blank-backed.

		NM	E	VG
Complete Set (36):		125.00	65.00	35.00
Common Player:		4.00	2.00	1.20
1	Satchel Paige	7.50	3.75	2.25
2	Phil Rizzuto	6.00	3.00	1.75
3	Sid Gordon	4.00	2.00	1.20
4	Ernie Lombardi	4.00	2.00	1.20
5	Jesse Haines	4.00	2.00	1.20
6	Joe Gordon	4.00	2.00	1.20
7	Bill Terry	4.00	2.00	1.20
8	Bill Dickey	6.00	3.00	1.75
9	Joe DiMaggio	12.00	6.00	3.50
10	Carl Hubbell	5.00	2.50	1.50
11	Fred Lindstrom	4.00	2.00	1.20
12	Ted Lyons	4.00	2.00	1.20
13	Red Ruffing	4.00	2.00	1.20
14	Joe Gordon	4.00	2.00	1.20
15	Bob Feller	6.00	3.00	1.75
16	Yogi Berra	7.50	3.75	2.25
17	Ford Frick, Whitey Ford	5.00	2.50	1.50
18	Sandy Koufax	12.00	6.00	3.50
19	Ted Williams	10.00	5.00	3.00
20	Warren Spahn	5.00	2.50	1.50
21	Al Rosen	4.00	2.00	1.20
22	Luke Appling	4.00	2.00	1.20
23	Joe Bush	4.00	2.00	1.20
24	Joe Medwick	4.00	2.00	1.20
25	Lou Boudreau	4.00	2.00	1.20
26	Ralph Kiner	4.00	2.00	1.20
27	Lloyd Waner	4.00	2.00	1.20
28	Pee Wee Reese	7.50	3.75	2.25
29	Duke Snider	7.50	3.75	2.25
30	Sal Maglie	4.00	2.00	1.20
31	Monte Irvin	4.00	2.00	1.20
32	Lefty Gomez	4.00	2.00	1.20
33	George Kelly	4.00	2.00	1.20
34	Joe Adcock	4.00	2.00	1.20
35	Max Carey	4.00	2.00	1.20
36	Rube Marquard	4.00	2.00	1.20

1973 TCMA Autographs & Drawings Postcards

These black-and-white postcards feature drawings of the players, along with facsimile autographs.

		NM	E	VG
Complete Set (12):		50.00	25.00	15.00
Common Player:		5.00	2.50	1.50
1	Mickey Cockran (Cochrane)	5.00	2.50	1.50
2	Christy Mathewson	5.00	2.50	1.50
3	Roberto Clemente	10.00	5.00	3.00
4	Rogers Hornsby	5.00	2.50	1.50
5	Pie Traynor	5.00	2.50	1.50
6	Frankie Frisch	5.00	2.50	1.50
7	Ty Cobb	7.50	3.75	2.25
8	Connie Mack	5.00	2.50	1.50
9	Babe Ruth	10.00	5.00	3.00
10	Lou Gehrig	8.00	4.00	2.50
11	Gil Hodges	5.00	2.50	1.50
12	Jackie Robinson	8.00	4.00	2.50

1973 TCMA Giants 1886

		NM	E	VG
Complete Set (15):		40.00	20.00	12.00
Common Player:		2.00	1.00	.60
1	Roger Connor	2.00	1.00	.60
2	Larry Corcoran	2.00	1.00	.60
3	Tom Deasley	2.00	1.00	.60
4	Mike Dorgan	2.00	1.00	.60
5	Dude Esterbrook	2.00	1.00	.60
6	Buck Ewing	2.00	1.00	.60
7	Joe Gerhardt	2.00	1.00	.60
8	Pete Gillespie	2.00	1.00	.60
9	Tim Keefe	2.00	1.00	.60
10	Jim Mutrie	2.00	1.00	.60
11	Jim O'Rourke	2.00	1.00	.60
12	Daniel Richardson	2.00	1.00	.60
13	John M. Ward	2.00	1.00	.60
14	Mickey Welch	2.00	1.00	.60
15	**Bat Boy**	2.00	1.00	.60

1973-78 TCMA League Leaders

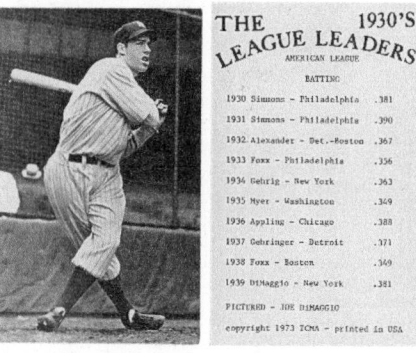

One of TCMA's earliest major series of collectors cards was this run of postcard-size (3-1/2" x 5-1/2") black-and-whites honoring various statistical leaders in each league from the 1920s through the 1950s. Backs have a list of the leaders by year within decade, with one of them pictured on the front. The unnumbered cards are checklisted here in alphabetical order within decade, as they were issued.

		NM	E	VG
Complete Set (96):		190.00	95.00	55.00
Common Player:		5.00	2.50	1.50
Complete Set, The 1920s		50.00	25.00	15.00
(1)	Grover C. Alexander	5.00	2.50	1.50
(2)	Jim Bagby Sr.	5.00	2.50	1.50
(3)	Jim Bottomley	5.00	2.50	1.50
(4)	Eddie Collins	5.00	2.50	1.50
(5)	Earle Combs	5.00	2.50	1.50
(6)	Kiki Cuyler	5.00	2.50	1.50
(7)	Urban "Red" Faber	5.00	2.50	1.50
(8)	Johnny Frederick	5.00	2.50	1.50
(9)	Charlie Gehringer	5.00	2.50	1.50
(10)	Goose Goslin	5.00	2.50	1.50
(11)	Rogers Hornsby	5.00	2.50	1.50
(12)	Walter Johnson	6.00	3.00	1.75
(13)	Freddie Lindstrom	5.00	2.50	1.50
(14)	Bob Meusel	5.00	2.50	1.50
(15)	Charlie Root	5.00	2.50	1.50
(16)	Babe Ruth, Rogers Hornsby	7.50	3.75	2.25
(17)	Al Simmons, Babe Ruth	7.50	3.75	2.25
(18)	Tris Speaker	5.00	2.50	1.50
(19)	Dazzy Vance	5.00	2.50	1.50
(20)	Lloyd Waner	5.00	2.50	1.50
(21)	Cy Williams	5.00	2.50	1.50
(22)	Ken Williams	5.00	2.50	1.50
(23)	Hack Wilson	5.00	2.50	1.50
(24)	Ross Youngs	5.00	2.50	1.50
Complete Set, The 1930s		50.00	25.00	15.00
(1)	Johnny Allen	5.00	2.50	1.50
(2)	Beau Bell	5.00	2.50	1.50
(3)	Cy Blanton	5.00	2.50	1.50
(4)	Ben Chapman	5.00	2.50	1.50
(5)	Joe Cronin	5.00	2.50	1.50
(6)	Dizzy Dean	6.50	3.25	2.00
(7)	Joe DiMaggio	20.00	10.00	6.00
(8)	Jimmie Foxx	5.00	2.50	1.50
(9)	Lou Gehrig	15.00	7.50	4.50
(10)	Charlie Gehringer	5.00	2.50	1.50
(11)	Lefty Gomez	5.00	2.50	1.50
(12)	Ival Goodman	5.00	2.50	1.50
(13)	Lefty Grove	5.00	2.50	1.50
(14)	Billy Herman	5.00	2.50	1.50
(15)	Ernie Lombardi	5.00	2.50	1.50
(16)	Chuck Klein	5.00	2.50	1.50
(17)	Heinie Manush	5.00	2.50	1.50
(18)	Pepper Martin	5.00	2.50	1.50
(19)	Joe Medwick	5.00	2.50	1.50
(20)	Van Mungo	5.00	2.50	1.50
(21)	Mel Ott	5.00	2.50	1.50
(22)	Bill Terry	5.00	2.50	1.50
(23)	Hal Trosky	5.00	2.50	1.50
(24)	Arky Vaughan	5.00	2.50	1.50
Complete Set, The 1940s		50.00	25.00	15.00
(1)	Gene Bearden	5.00	2.50	1.50

		NM	E	VG
(2)	Lou Boudreau	5.00	2.50	1.50
(3)	George Case	5.00	2.50	1.50
(4)	Phil Cavarretta	5.00	2.50	1.50
(5)	Bob Feller	6.00	3.00	1.75
(6)	Boo Ferriss	5.00	2.50	1.50
(7)	Hank Greenberg	9.00	4.50	2.75
(8)	Jeff Heath	5.00	2.50	1.50
(9)	Tommy Holmes	5.00	2.50	1.50
(10)	Larry Jansen	5.00	2.50	1.50
(11)	George Kell	5.00	2.50	1.50
(12)	Ralph Kiner	5.00	2.50	1.50
(13)	Marty Marion	5.00	2.50	1.50
(14)	Johnny Mize	5.00	2.50	1.50
(15)	Stan Musial	10.00	5.00	3.00
(16)	Bill Nicholson	5.00	2.50	1.50
(17)	Johnny Pesky	5.00	2.50	1.50
(18)	Jackie Robinson	10.00	5.00	3.00
(19)	Enos Slaughter	5.00	2.50	1.50
(20)	Snuffy Stirnweiss	5.00	2.50	1.50
(21)	Bill Voiselle	5.00	2.50	1.50
(22)	Bucky Walters	5.00	2.50	1.50
(23)	Ted Williams	10.00	5.00	3.00
(24)	Ted Williams, Joe DiMaggio	10.00	5.00	3.00
	Complete Set, The 1950s	50.00	25.00	15.00
(1)	Luis Aparicio	5.00	2.50	1.50
(2)	Ernie Banks	5.00	2.50	1.50
(3)	Bill Bruton	5.00	2.50	1.50
(4)	Lew Burdette	5.00	2.50	1.50
(5)	Rocky Colavito	5.00	2.50	1.50
(6)	Dom DiMaggio	5.00	2.50	1.50
(7)	Ferris Fain	5.00	2.50	1.50
(8)	Whitey Ford	5.00	2.50	1.50
(9)	Don Hoak	5.00	2.50	1.50
(10)	Sam Jethroe	5.00	2.50	1.50
(11)	Ted Kluszewski	5.00	2.50	1.50
(12)	Harvey Kuenn	5.00	2.50	1.50
(13)	Bob Lemon	5.00	2.50	1.50
(14)	Mickey Mantle	30.00	15.00	9.00
(15)	Willie Mays	15.00	7.50	4.50
(16)	Willie Mays, Bobby Avila	5.00	2.50	1.50
(17)	Minnie Minoso	5.00	2.50	1.50
(18)	Don Newcombe	5.00	2.50	1.50
(19)	Robin Roberts	5.00	2.50	1.50
(20)	Hank Sauer	5.00	2.50	1.50
(21)	Bobby Shantz	5.00	2.50	1.50
(22)	Roy Sievers	5.00	2.50	1.50
(23)	Duke Snider	6.00	3.00	1.75
(24)	Mickey Vernon	5.00	2.50	1.50

1973 TCMA Pudge Gautreaux

This custom-published postcard of the Brooklyn Dodgers catcher (1936-37) was printed in black-and-white in a 3-1/2" x 6" format. The issue date is approximate.

	NM	E	VG
Sid "Pudge" Gautreaux	4.00	2.00	1.25

1973 TCMA Sports Scoop Hall of Fame

This set of large-format (3-1/2" x 5-1/2") black-and-white cards was produced by TCMA for the collectors' magazine Sports Scoop, which was promoting the players to be inducted into the Hall of Fame. Backs have information about the player's career and HoF credentials.

		NM	E	VG
Complete Set (12):		20.00	10.00	6.00
Common Player:		2.00	1.00	.60
(1)	Earl Averill	2.50	1.25	.70
(2)	Ben Chapman	2.00	1.00	.60
(3)	Doc Cramer	2.00	1.00	.60
(4)	Spud Davis	2.00	1.00	.60

		NM	E	VG
(5)	Babe Herman	2.00	1.00	.60
(6)	Billy Herman	2.50	1.25	.70
(7)	Chuck Klein	2.50	1.25	.70
(8)	Bob Meusel	2.00	1.00	.60
(9)	Johnny Mize	3.00	1.50	.90
(10)	Joe Sewell	2.50	1.25	.70
(11)	Enos Slaughter	3.00	1.50	.90
(12)	Hal Trosky	2.00	1.00	.60

1973 TCMA Stan Martucci Postcards

This set of postcards was custom-produced by TCMA for card dealer Stan Martucci who apparently used them as "ride alongs" when filling orders. Approximately 3-1/2" x 5-1/2", the fronts have borderless, unidentified black-and-white photos of popular former stars. The back is in standard postcard format and had the player identified at top-left and a note from Martucci in the message area.

		NM	E	VG
Complete Set (16):		15.00	7.50	4.50
Common Player:		1.00	.50	.30
(1)	Joe Cronin	1.00	.50	.30
(2)	Dizzy Dean	2.00	1.00	.60
(3)	Joe DiMaggio	5.00	2.50	1.50
(4)	Jimmie Foxx	2.00	1.00	.60
(5)	Lou Gehrig	5.00	2.50	1.50
(6)	Charlie Gehringer	1.00	.50	.30
(7)	Lefty Gomez	1.00	.50	.30
(8)	Lefty Grove	1.00	.50	.30
(9)	Carl Hubbell	1.00	.50	.30
(10)	Ted Lyons	1.00	.50	.30
(11)	Heinie Manush	1.00	.50	.30
(12)	Joe Medwick	1.00	.50	.30
(13)	Mel Ott	1.00	.50	.30
(14)	Red Ruffing	1.00	.50	.30
(15)	Bill Terry	1.00	.50	.30
(16)	Paul Waner	1.00	.50	.30

1974 TCMA 1890 Brooklyn Club

The National League champion Brooklyn Bridegrooms are featured in this collectors issue. Fronts of the 3-1/2" x 3-3/4" black-and-white cards picture the players in dress suits with ornate designs around the border. The design was copied from an 1890 Brooklyn scorecard/yearbook. Backs have biographical information and career highlights, also copied from the earlier publication. The back also includes a 1974 TCMA reprint notice. The unnumbered cards are checklisted here in alphabetical order.

		NM	E	VG
Complete Set (16):		30.00	15.00	9.00
Common Player:		3.00	1.50	.90
(1)	Thomas P. Burns	3.00	1.50	.90
(2)	Albert J. Bushong	3.00	1.50	.90
(3)	Robert Lee Caruthers	3.00	1.50	.90
(4)	Robert H. Clark	3.00	1.50	.90
(5)	Hubbert Collins	3.00	1.50	.90
(6)	John S. Corkhill	3.00	1.50	.90
(7)	Thomas P. Daly	3.00	1.50	.90
(8)	D.L. Foutz	3.00	1.50	.90
(9)	Michael F. Hughes	3.00	1.50	.90
(10)	Thomas J. Lovett	3.00	1.50	.90
(11)	W.H. McGunnigle	3.00	1.50	.90
(12)	Wm. D. O'Brien	3.00	1.50	.90
(13)	George Burton Pinkney	3.00	1.50	.90
(14)	George J. Smith	3.00	1.50	.90
(15)	George T. Stallings	3.00	1.50	.90
(16)	Wm. H. Terry	3.00	1.50	.90

1974 TCMA 1910-14 Philadelphia Athletics Postcards

This series of collectors' issue postcards (about 3-1/2" x 5-3/4") was issued in two forms; printed front and back in black-and-white or in blue-and-white. While numbered between 501 and 518, only 12 cards were issued. The cards are reproductions of the images from the 1911 Pinkerton cabinets (T5). The postcard-format backs have a "1974 TCMA Reprint" notice along with the list of the dynasty's league and world championships.

		NM	E	VG
Complete Set (12):		10.00	5.00	3.00
Common Player:		1.00	.50	.30
501	Chas. Bender	1.50	.70	.45
502	John Coombs	1.00	.50	.30
503	Eddie Plank	1.50	.70	.45
504	Amos Strunk	1.00	.50	.30
506	Ira Thomas	1.00	.50	.30
508	Stuffy McInnis	1.00	.50	.30
510	Rube Oldring	1.00	.50	.30
511	Eddie Collins	1.50	.70	.45
512	Frank Baker	1.50	.70	.45
515	Jack Barry	1.00	.50	.30
516	Jack Lapp	1.00	.50	.30
518	Danny Murphy	1.00	.50	.30

1974 TCMA 1929-31 Athletics

Stars of the Philadelphia A's dynasty which won two World Series and an A.L. pennant from 1929-31 are featured in this collectors issue. The 2-5/8" x 4" cards have black-and-white player photos at center. Printed in green in the white border at top is "1929-31 Athletics." At bottom, printed in black, is the player's name and position. Backs are in black-and-white with stats for 1929, 1930 and 1931, as appropriate. The unnumbered cards are checklisted here in alphabetical order.

		NM	E	VG
Complete Set (29):		30.00	15.00	9.00
Common Player:		2.00	1.00	.60
(1)	Max Bishop	2.00	1.00	.60
(2)	Joe Boley	2.00	1.00	.60
(3)	George Burns	2.00	1.00	.60
(4)	Mickey Cochrane	3.00	1.50	.90
(5)	Eddie Collins, Lew Krausse	2.00	1.00	.60
(6)	"Doc" Cramer	2.00	1.00	.60
(7)	Jimmy Dykes	2.00	1.00	.60
(8)	George Earnshaw	2.00	1.00	.60
(9)	Howard Ehmke	2.00	1.00	.60
(10)	Lou Finney, John Heving	2.00	1.00	.60
(11)	Jimmie Foxx	4.00	2.00	1.25
(12)	Walt French, Waite Hoyt	2.00	1.00	.60
(13)	"Lefty" Grove	3.00	1.50	.90
(14)	"Mule" Haas	2.00	1.00	.60
(15)	Sammy Hale	2.00	1.00	.60
(16)	"Pinky" Higgins, Phil Todt	2.00	1.00	.60
(17)	Earle Mack, Connie Mack	2.00	1.00	.60
(18)	Roy Mahaffey	2.00	1.00	.60
(19)	Eric McNair	2.00	1.00	.60
(20)	Bing Miller	2.00	1.00	.60
(21)	Jim Moore, Jim Peterson	2.00	1.00	.60
(22)	Jack Quinn	2.00	1.00	.60
(23)	Eddie Rommel	2.00	1.00	.60
(24)	Wally Schang	2.50	1.25	.70
(25)	Al Simmons	2.50	1.25	.70
(26)	Homer Summa	2.00	1.00	.60
(27)	Rube Walberg	2.00	1.00	.60
(28)	"Dib" Williams	2.00	1.00	.60
(29)	Team Photo Card (10" x 5")			
		10.00	5.00	3.00

1974 TCMA 1934 St. Louis Cardinals

The Gas House Gang

DeLancey,
William Pinkney

Games	93
At Bats	253
Hits	80
Home Runs	13
Runs	41
RBI's	40
Bat. Ave.	.316

1974 TCMA, Ltd.

Bill DeLancey   C

		NM	E	VG
	Complete Set (31):	50.00	25.00	15.00
	Common Player:	2.00	1.00	.60
(1)	"Tex" Carleton	2.00	1.00	.60
(2)	"Ripper" Collins	2.00	1.00	.60
(3)	"Pat" Crawford	2.00	1.00	.60
(4)	"Spud" Davis	2.00	1.00	.60
(5)	"Daffy" Dean	2.50	1.25	.70
(6)	"Dizzy" Dean	4.00	2.00	1.25
(7)	Bill DeLancey	2.00	1.00	.60
(8)	Leo Durocher	2.50	1.25	.70
(9)	Frank Frisch	2.50	1.25	.70
(10)	"Chick" Fullis	2.00	1.00	.60
(11)	"Mike" Gonzalez	2.50	1.25	.70
(12)	"Pop" Haines	2.50	1.25	.70
(13)	Bill Hallahan	2.00	1.00	.60
(14)	Francis Healey (Healy)	2.00	1.00	.60
(15)	Jim Lindsey	2.00	1.00	.60
(16)	"Pepper" Martin	2.50	1.25	.70
(17)	"Ducky" Medwick	2.50	1.25	.70
(18)	Jim Mooney	2.00	1.00	.60
(19)	Ernie Orsatti	2.00	1.00	.60
(20)	Flint Rhem	2.00	1.00	.60
(21)	John Rothrock	2.00	1.00	.60
(22)	"Dazzy" Vance	2.50	1.25	.70
(23)	Bill Walker	2.00	1.00	.60
(24)	"Buzzy" Wares	2.00	1.00	.60
(25)	"Whitey" Whitehead	2.00	1.00	.60
(26)	Jim Winford	2.00	1.00	.60
(27)	"Daffy" & "Dizzy"(Daffy Dean, Dizzy Dean)	6.00	3.00	1.75
(28)	Dizzy & Leo Celebrate(Dizzy Dean, Leo Durocher)	4.00	2.00	1.25
(29)	Durocher Scores(Leo Durocher) (1934 World Series)	4.00	2.00	1.25
(30)	Medwick Out Cochrane Catcher(Mickey Cochrane, Ducky Medwick) (1934 World Series)	4.00	2.00	1.25
(31)	1934 St. Louis Cardinals World Champions	4.00	2.00	1.25

1974 TCMA 1934-5 Detroit Tigers

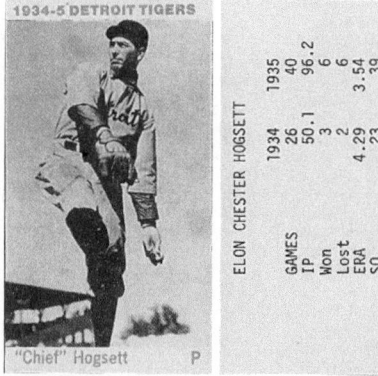

1934-5 DETROIT TIGERS

ELON CHESTER HOGSETT

	1934	1935
GAMES	26	40
IP	50.1	96.2
Won	3	6
Lost	2	6
ERA	4.29	3.54
SO	23	39
BB	19	49

1974 TCMA LTD

"Chief" Hogsett   P

Members of the 1934 A.L. Champion and 1935 World's Champion teams are featured in this collectors issue team set. Except for a pair of large-format (4-1/4" x 3-3/4") cards, the cards measure about 2-1/8" x 3-5/8". Fronts have black-and-white photos. Above and below the photo are white stripes with the set title, player name and position. Backs are in black-and-white with 1934 and/or 1935 stats. The unnumbered cards are checklisted here alphabetically.

		NM	E	VG
	Complete Set (36):	35.00	17.50	10.00
	Common Player:	2.00	1.00	.60
(1)	Eldon Auker	2.00	1.00	.60
(2)	Del Baker	2.00	1.00	.60
(3)	Tommy Bridges	2.00	1.00	.60
(4)	"Flea" Clifton	2.00	1.00	.60
(5)	Mickey Cochrane	4.00	2.00	1.25
(6)	"General" Crowder	2.00	1.00	.60
(7)	Frank Doljack	2.00	1.00	.60
(8)	Carl Fischer	2.00	1.00	.60
(9)	Pete Fox	2.00	1.00	.60
(10)	Vic Frasier	2.00	1.00	.60
(11)	Charlie Gehringer	4.00	2.00	1.25
(12)	Goose Goslin	2.00	1.00	.60
(13)	Hank Greenberg	5.00	2.50	1.50
(14)	Luke Hamlin	2.00	1.00	.60
(15)	Clyde Hatter	2.00	1.00	.60
(16)	Ray Hayworth	2.00	1.00	.60
(17)	"Chief" Hogsett	2.00	1.00	.60
(18)	Roxie Lawson	2.00	1.00	.60
(19)	"Firpo" Marberry	2.00	1.00	.60
(20)	Chet Morgan	2.00	1.00	.60
(21)	Marv Owen	2.00	1.00	.60
(22)	"Cy" Perkins	2.00	1.00	.60
(23)	"Red" Phillips	2.00	1.00	.60
(24)	Frank Reiber	2.00	1.00	.60
(25)	Billy Rogell	2.00	1.00	.60
(26)	"Schoolboy" Rowe	2.00	1.00	.60
(27)	"Heinie" Schuble	2.00	1.00	.60
(28)	Hugh Shelley	2.00	1.00	.60
(29)	Vic Sorrell	2.00	1.00	.60
(30)	Joe Sullivan	2.00	1.00	.60
(31)	"Gee" Walker	2.00	1.00	.60
(32)	"Hub" Walker	2.00	1.00	.60
(33)	"Jo-Jo" White	2.00	1.00	.60
(34)	Rudy York	2.00	1.00	.60
(35)	1934 Pitchers(Eldon Auker, Firpo Marberry, Tommy Bridges, Schoolboy Rowe) (4-1/4" x 3-3/4")	5.00	2.50	1.50
(36)	1935 Outfield(Goose Goslin, Jo-Jo White, Pete Fox) (4-1/4" x 3-3/4")	5.00	2.50	1.50

1974 TCMA 1936-1939 Yankee Dynasty

1936 - 1939 Yankee Dynasty

JOHN JOSEPH MURPHY

	1936	1937	1938	1939
Games	27	39	32	38
Won	9	13	8	3
Lost	3	4	2	6
Pct.	.750	.765	.800	.333
BB	41	56	42	28
SO	34	46	43	30
ERA	3.38	4.17	4.24	4.40

T.C.M.A. Ltd.

Johnny Murphy   P

Many of the players who participated in one or more of the Yankees' four consecutive World Champion seasons in the late 1930s are included in this collectors' edition. Cards are 2-3/4" x 4" and feature black-and-white photos on front. In the white borders at top and bottom, the set name and player identification are printed in blue. Backs have stats for each season and are printed in black-and-white on a white background. A virtual reprint of this set was made circa 1983 with two player cards added and a brown background on back. The unnumbered cards are checklisted here alphabetically.

		NM	E	VG
	Complete Set (56):	75.00	37.50	22.50
	Complete Set (51):	45.00	22.50	13.50
	Common Player:	2.00	1.00	.60
(1)	"Poison Ivy" Andrews	2.00	1.00	.60
(2)	Joe Beggs	2.00	1.00	.60
(3)	Marv Breuer	2.00	1.00	.60
(4)	Johnny Broaca	2.00	1.00	.60
(5)	"Jumbo" Brown	2.00	1.00	.60
(6)	"Spud" Chandler	2.00	1.00	.60
(7)	Ben Chapman	2.00	1.00	.60
(8)	Earle Combs	2.00	1.00	.60
(9)	Frankie Crosetti	2.00	1.00	.60
(10)	"Babe" Dahlgren	2.00	1.00	.60
(11)	Bill Dickey	2.50	1.25	.70
(12)	Joe DiMaggio	10.00	5.00	3.00
(13)	Atley Donald	2.00	1.00	.60
(14)	Wes Ferrell	2.00	1.00	.60
(15)	Artie Fletcher	2.00	1.00	.60
(16)	Joe Gallagher	2.00	1.00	.60
(17)	Lou Gehrig	10.00	5.00	3.00
(18)	Joe Glenn	2.00	1.00	.60
(19)	"Lefty" Gomez	2.00	1.00	.60
(20)	Joe Gordon	2.00	1.00	.60
(21)	"Bump" Hadley	2.00	1.00	.60
(22)	Don Heffner	2.00	1.00	.60
(23)	Tommy Henrich	2.00	1.00	.60
(24)	Oral Hildebrand	2.00	1.00	.60
(25)	Myril Hoag	2.00	1.00	.60
(26)	Roy Johnson	2.00	1.00	.60
(27)	Arndt Jorgens	2.00	1.00	.60
(28)	Charlie Keller	2.00	1.00	.60
(29)	Ted Kleinhans	2.00	1.00	.60
(30)	Billy Knickerbocker	2.00	1.00	.60
(31)	Tony Lazzeri	2.50	1.25	.70
(32)	Frank Makosky	2.00	1.00	.60
(33)	"Pat" Malone	2.00	1.00	.60
(34)	Johnny Murphy	2.00	1.00	.60
(35)	"Monty" Pearson	2.00	1.00	.60
(36)	"Jake" Powell	2.00	1.00	.60
(37)	"Red" Rolfe	2.00	1.00	.60
(38)	"Buddy" Rosar	2.00	1.00	.60
(39)	"Red" Ruffing	2.50	1.25	.70
(40)	Marius Russo	2.00	1.00	.60
(41)	"Jack" Saltzgaver	2.00	1.00	.60
(42)	Paul Schreiber	2.00	1.00	.60
(43)	Johnny Schulte	2.00	1.00	.60
(44)	Bob Seeds	2.00	1.00	.60
(45)	"Twinkletoes" Selkirk	2.00	1.00	.60
(46)	Lee Stine	2.00	1.00	.60
(47)	Steve Sundra	2.00	1.00	.60
(48)	"Sandy" Vance	2.00	1.00	.60
(49)	Dixie Walker	2.00	1.00	.60
(50)	Kemp Wicker	2.00	1.00	.60
(51)	Joe McCarthy, Jacob Ruppert	2.00	1.00	.60

5-1/2" x 4" FEATURE CARDS

		NM	E	VG
(52)	Joe DiMaggio, Frank Crosetti, Tony Lazzeri, Bill Dickey, Lou Gehrig, Jake Powell, George Selkirk	5.00	2.50	1.50
(53)	Lou Gehrig, Joe DiMaggio	7.50	3.75	2.25
(54)	Gehrig Hits Another	6.00	3.00	1.75
(55)	Red Rolfe, Tony Lazzeri, Lou Gehrig, Frank Crosetti	5.00	2.50	1.50
(56)	World Champions - 1936	6.00	3.00	1.75

1974 TCMA 1936-37 New York Giants

This is the rarest of the TCMA Great Teams sets. Fewer than half of the 1,000 sets got into the hands of customers before legal action by Dick Bartell forced the company to halt sales and destroy more than 500 sets. The 2-5/8" x 3-3/8" cards are printed in black-and-orange. They are unnumbered and checklisted here in alphabetical order.

		NM	E	VG
	Complete Set (36):	90.00	45.00	27.50
	Common Player:	2.50	1.25	.75
(1)	**Title card**	1.00	.50	.30
(2)	Tom Baker	2.50	1.25	.75
(3)	Dick Bartell	2.50	1.25	.75
(4)	Wally Berger	2.50	1.25	.75
(5)	Don Brennan	2.50	1.25	.75
(6)	Walter Brown	2.50	1.25	.75
(7)	Clyde Castleman	2.50	1.25	.75
(8)	Lou Chiozza	2.50	1.25	.70
(9)	Dick Coffman	2.50	1.25	.75
(10)	Harry Danning	2.50	1.25	.75
(11)	George Davis	2.50	1.25	.75
(12)	Charlie English	2.50	1.25	.75
(13)	Freddie Fitzsimmons	2.50	1.25	.75
(14)	Frank Gabler	2.50	1.25	.75
(15)	Harry Gumbert	2.50	1.25	.75
(16)	Mickey Haslin	2.50	1.25	.75
(17)	Carl Hubbell	6.00	3.00	1.75
(18)	Travis Jackson	4.00	2.00	1.25
(19)	Mark Koenig	2.50	1.25	.75
(20)	Hank Leiber	2.50	1.25	.75
(21)	Sam Leslie	2.50	1.25	.75
(22)	Bill Lohrman	2.50	1.25	.75
(23)	Eddie Mayo	2.50	1.25	.75
(24)	John McCarthy	2.50	1.25	.75
(25)	Cliff Melton	2.50	1.25	.75
(26)	Jo Jo Moore	2.50	1.25	.75
(27)	Mel Ott	6.00	3.00	1.75
(28)	Jimmy Ripple	2.50	1.25	.75
(29)	Hal Schumacher	2.50	1.25	.75
(30)	Al Smith	2.50	1.25	.75
(31)	Roy Spencer	2.50	1.25	.75
(32)	Bill Terry	5.00	2.50	1.50
(33)	Hy Vandenberg	2.50	1.25	.75
(34)	Phil Weintraub	2.50	1.25	.75
(35)	Burgess Whitehead	2.50	1.25	.75
(36)	Babe Young	2.50	1.25	.75

1974 TCMA 1952 Brooklyn Dodgers

1952
BROOKLYN
DODGERS

ALBERT BLUFORD WALKER

Catcher   #10

Games	46
AB	139
Hits	36
Runs	9
HR	1
RBI	19
BA	.259

Rube

T.C.M.A. 1974

The National League champion '52 Dodgers are featured in this collectors issue. Nominally 2-3/4" x 3-3/8", the cards are often found with minor variations in size. Fronts are printed in red and blue with a white border. The only identification on front is the player's first name or nickname. Backs are in black-and-white with the player's full name, position, uniform number, 1952 stats and TCMA copyright. Cards are checklisted here in alphabetical order.

		NM	E	VG
	Complete Set (40):	25.00	15.00	7.50
	Common Player:	2.00	1.00	.60
(1)	Header/Team History Card (Jackie Robinson, Gil Hodges, Roy Campanella, Billy Cox, Pee Wee Reese)	2.00	1.00	.60
(2)	Cal Abrams	2.00	1.00	.60
(3)	Sandy Amoros	2.00	1.00	.60
(4)	Joe Black	2.00	1.00	.60
(5)	Ralph Branca	2.00	1.00	.60
(6)	Rocky Bridges	2.00	1.00	.60
(7)	Roy Campanella	4.00	2.00	1.25
(8)	Billy Cox	2.00	1.00	.60
(9)	Chuck Dressen	2.00	1.00	.60
(10)	Carl Erskine	2.00	1.00	.60
(11)	Carl Furillo	3.00	1.50	.90
(12)	Billy Herman	2.00	1.00	.60
(13)	Gil Hodges	4.00	2.00	1.25
(14)	Tommy Holmes	2.00	1.00	.60
(15)	Jim Hughes	2.00	1.00	.60
(16)	Clyde King	2.00	1.00	.60
(17)	Clem Labine	2.00	1.00	.60
(18)	Joe Landrum	2.00	1.00	.60
(19)	Cookie Lavagetto	2.00	1.00	.60
(20)	Ken Lehman	2.00	1.00	.60
(21)	Steve Lembo	2.00	1.00	.60
(22)	Billy Loes	2.00	1.00	.60
(23)	Ray Moore	2.00	1.00	.60
(24)	Bobby Morgan	2.00	1.00	.60
(25)	Ron Negray	2.00	1.00	.60
(26)	Rocky Nelson	2.00	1.00	.60
(27)	Andy Pafko	2.00	1.00	.60
(28)	Jake Pitler	2.00	1.00	.60
(29)	Bud Podbielan	2.00	1.00	.60
(30)	Pee Wee Reese	4.00	2.00	1.25
(31)	Jackie Robinson	7.50	3.75	2.25
(32)	Preacher Roe	2.00	1.00	.60
(33)	Johnny Rutherford	2.00	1.00	.60
(34)	Johnny Schmitz	2.00	1.00	.60
(35)	George Shuba	2.00	1.00	.60
(36)	Duke Snider	4.00	2.00	1.25
(37)	Chris Van Cuyk	2.00	1.00	.60
(38)	Ben Wade	2.00	1.00	.60
(39)	Rube Walker	2.00	1.00	.60
(40)	Dick Williams	2.00	1.00	.60

1974 TCMA Nicknames

"Nicknames"

WILD BILL

Nicknames of notable ballplayers of the 1930s-40s are featured in this early collectors' set. Fronts of the 2-5/16" x 3-1/2" cards have a black-and-white photo with the player's nickname in the bottom border and "Nicknames" in the top border, both printed in red. Backs have a card number, the player's full name, position and the teams and years he played in the major leagues. The set originally sold for $3.

		NM	E	VG
	Complete Set (28):	40.00	20.00	12.00
	Common Player:	3.00	1.50	.90
1	Rapid Robert Feller	4.50	2.25	1.25
2	Babe Dahlgren	3.00	1.50	.90
3	Spud Chandler	3.00	1.50	.90
4	Ducky Medwick	3.00	1.50	.90
5	Silent Cal Benge	3.00	1.50	.90
6	Goose Goslin	3.00	1.50	.90
7	Mule Haas	3.00	1.50	.90
8	Dizzy Dean	6.00	3.00	1.75
9	Cowboy Harrell	3.00	1.50	.90
10	Buzz Boyle	3.00	1.50	.90
11	Coonskin Davis	3.00	1.50	.90
12	Moose Solters	3.00	1.50	.90
13	Sad Sam Jones	3.00	1.50	.90
14	Bad News Hale	3.00	1.50	.90
15	Bucky Harris	3.00	1.50	.90
16	Lord Jim Jordan	3.00	1.50	.90
17	Zeke Bonura	3.00	1.50	.90
18	Heave-o Hafey	3.00	1.50	.90
19	Spud Davis	3.00	1.50	.90
20	Bing Miller	3.00	1.50	.90
21	Preacher Roe	3.00	1.50	.90
22	Wild Bill Hallahan	3.00	1.50	.90
23	Indian Bob Johnson	3.00	1.50	.90
24	Flash Gordon	3.00	1.50	.90
25	Tot Pressnell	3.00	1.50	.90
26	Hot Potato Hamlin	3.00	1.50	.90
27	Old Reliable Henrich	3.00	1.50	.90
28	Tom Hafey	3.00	1.50	.90

1974 TCMA Sports Nostalgia Store Postcards

To celebrate the opening of one of the first, if not the first, sports collectors' retail stores, TCMA issued a set of four 3-1/2" x 5-1/2" black-and-white postcards. The set includes one current N.Y. Yankees player and three former boxers. The set was issued in an edition of 1,000.

		NM	E	VG
	Complete Set (4):	20.00	10.00	6.00
	Common Card:	5.00	2.50	1.50
(1)	Gene Michael	7.50	3.75	2.25
(2)	Emile Griffith	5.00	2.50	1.50
(3)	Floyd Patterson	5.00	2.50	1.50
(4)	Willie Pep	5.00	2.50	1.50

1974-75 TCMA St. Louis Browns

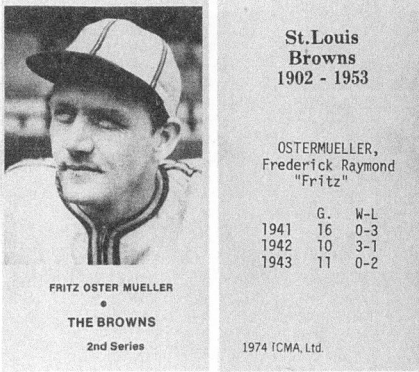

St. Louis
Browns
1902 - 1953

OSTERMUELLER,
Frederick Raymond
"Fritz"

	G.	W-L
1941	16	0-3
1942	10	3-1
1943	11	0-2

FRITZ OSTER MUELLER

THE BROWNS

2nd Series

1974 TCMA, Ltd.

Some of baseball's most loveable losers from about the 1930s through the team's flight to Baltimore in 1953 are pre-sented in this multi-series collectors' issue. Cards are printed in a 2-1/4" x 3-7/8" format, with brown ink used on front and on back of Series 1 and 2; Series 3 cards have black ink on back. Some cards have player identification on front, some only on back. All cards have a TCMA copyright date line and a few player stats for his years with the Brownies. The unnumbered cards are checklisted here alphabetically by series.

		NM	E	VG
	Complete Set (108):	80.00	40.00	20.00
	Common Player:	1.50	.75	.45
	Series 1 - 1974	25.00	12.50	7.50
(1)	Ethan Allen	1.50	.75	.45
(2)	Mel Almada	2.00	1.00	.60
(3)	Ed Baecht	1.50	.75	.45
(4)	John Berardino	4.00	2.00	1.25
(5)	Emil Bildilli	1.50	.75	.45
(6)	John Blake	1.50	.75	.45
(7)	Julio Bonetti	1.50	.75	.45
(8)	Earl Caldwell	1.50	.75	.45
(9)	Scoops Carey	1.50	.75	.45
(10)	Stinky Davis	1.50	.75	.45
(11)	Fred Haney	1.50	.75	.45
(12)	Jeff Heath	1.50	.75	.45
(13)	Don Heffner	1.50	.75	.45
(14)	Rollie Hemsley	1.50	.75	.45
(15)	Oral Hildebrand	1.50	.75	.45
(16)	Elon Hogsett	1.50	.75	.45
(17)	Ben Huffman	1.50	.75	.45
(18)	Sig Jakucki	1.50	.75	.45
(19)	Billy Knickerbocker	1.50	.75	.45
(20)	John Knott	1.50	.75	.45
(21)	Jack Kramer	1.50	.75	.45
(22)	Red Kress	1.50	.75	.45
(23)	Chet Laabs	1.50	.75	.45
(24)	Gerard "Nig" Lipscomb	1.50	.75	.45
(25)	John Lucadello	1.50	.75	.45
(26)	Mel Mazzera	1.50	.75	.45
(27)	Red McQuillen	1.50	.75	.45
(28)	George McQuinn	1.50	.75	.45
(29)	Oscar Melillo	1.50	.75	.45
(30)	Howard Mills	1.50	.75	.45
(31)	Bob Muncrief	1.50	.75	.45
(32)	Hank Thompson	1.50	.75	.45
(33)	Russell "Sheriff" Van Atta	1.50	.75	.45
(34)	Joe Vosmik	1.50	.75	.45
(35)	Jim Walkup	1.50	.75	.45
(36)	Sam West	1.50	.75	.45
	Series 2 - 1974	30.00	15.00	9.00
(37)	Floyd Baker	1.50	.75	.45
(38)	John Bassler	1.50	.75	.45
(39)	Ollie Bejma	1.50	.75	.45
(40)	Jim Bottomley	2.00	1.00	.60
(41)	Willard Brown	4.50	2.25	1.25
(42)	Bob Dillinger	1.50	.75	.45
(43)	Owen "Red" Friend	1.50	.75	.45
(44)	Eddie Gaedel	5.00	2.50	1.50
(45)	Dennis Galehouse	1.50	.75	.45
(46)	Joseph Gallagher	1.50	.75	.45
(47)	Ned Garver	1.50	.75	.45
(48)	Robert Harris	1.50	.75	.45
(49)	Al Hollingsworth	1.50	.75	.45
(50)	Walter Judnich	1.50	.75	.45
(51)	William "Lefty" Kennedy	1.50	.75	.45
(52)	Lou Kretlow	1.50	.75	.45
(53)	Martin Marion	1.50	.70	.45
(54)	Les Moss	1.50	.75	.45
(55)	Louis "Bobo" Newsom	1.50	.75	.45
(56)	Fritz Ostermueller	1.50	.75	.45
(57)	Joe Ostrowski	1.50	.75	.45
(58)	Edward Pellagrini	1.50	.75	.45
(59)	Duane Pillette	1.50	.75	.45
(60)	Nelson Potter	1.50	.75	.45
(61)	Raymond "Rip" Radcliff	1.50	.75	.45
(62)	Harry Rice	1.50	.75	.45
(63)	Jim Rivera	1.50	.75	.45
(64)	John "Fred" Sanford	1.50	.75	.45
(65)	Luke Sewell	1.50	.75	.45
(66)	Al Shirley	1.50	.75	.45
(67)	Junior Stephens	1.50	.75	.45
(68)	Thomas Turner	1.50	.75	.45
(69)	Ken Wood	1.50	.75	.45
(70)	Allen "Zeke" Zarilla	1.50	.75	.45
(71)	Samuel "Sad Sam" Zoldak	1.50	.75	.45
(72)	1944 Infield	1.50	.75	.45
	Series 3 - 1975	30.00	15.00	9.00
(73)	Bow-Wow Arft	1.50	.75	.45
(74)	Matthew Batts	1.50	.75	.45
(75)	Tommy Byrne	1.50	.75	.45
(76)	Skippy Byrnes	1.50	.75	.45
(77)	Raymond Coleman	1.50	.75	.45
(78)	Scrap Iron Courtney	1.50	.75	.45
(79)	James Delsing	1.50	.75	.45
(80)	William "Kid" DeMars	1.50	.75	.45
(81)	Clifford "Mule" Fannin	1.50	.75	.45
(82)	Tom Fine	1.50	.75	.45

		NM	E	VG
(83)	Pete Gray	5.00	2.50	1.50
(84)	Red Hayworth	1.50	.75	.45
(85)	Procopio Herrera	1.50	.70	.45
(86)	Fred Hoffman	1.50	.75	.45
(87)	Walter "Union Man" Holke	1.50	.75	.45
(88)	Hal Hudson	1.50	.70	.45
(89)	Richard Kokos	1.50	.75	.45
(90)	Michael Kreevich	1.50	.75	.45
(91)	Richard Kryhoski	1.50	.75	.45
(92)	Paul "Peanuts" Lehner	1.50	.75	.45
(93)	Footsie Lenhardt	1.50	.75	.45
(94)	Joe Lutz	1.50	.75	.45
(95)	Robert Mahoney	1.50	.75	.45
(96)	Frank Mancuso	1.50	.75	.45
(97)	Clifford Mapes	1.50	.75	.45
(98)	Cass Michaels	1.50	.75	.45
(99)	Frank "Stubby" Overmire	1.50	.75	.45
(100)	Satchel Paige	5.00	2.50	1.50
(101)	Roy Sievers	1.50	.75	.45
(102)	Louis Sleator	1.50	.75	.45
(103)	Richard Starr	1.50	.75	.45
(104)	Thomas "Muscles" Upton	1.50	.75	.45
(105)	Jerome Witte	1.50	.75	.45
(106)	Robert Young	1.50	.75	.45
(107)	1951 Browns	1.50	.75	.45
(108)	1952 Browns	1.50	.75	.45

1974 TCMA Stadium Postcards

These 5" x 3-1/2" black-and-white postcards are not numbered and are listed here alphabetically.

		NM	E	VG
	Complete Set (12):	35.00	17.50	10.50
	Common Card:	4.00	2.00	1.20
(1)	Baltimore Stadium	4.00	2.00	1.20
(2)	Boston Braves Field	4.00	2.00	1.20
(3)	Crosley Field	4.00	2.00	1.20
(4)	Ebbett's (Ebbets) Field	6.00	3.00	1.75
(5)	Forbes Field	4.00	2.00	1.20
(6)	Griffith Field	4.00	2.00	1.20
(7)	Milwaukee County Stadium	4.00	2.00	1.20
(8)	Narvin (Navin) Field	4.00	2.00	1.20
(9)	Polo Grounds	4.00	2.00	1.20
(10)	Shea Stadium	4.00	2.00	1.20
(11)	Wrigley Field	5.00	2.50	1.50
(12)	Yankee Stadium	7.50	3.75	2.25

1974 TCMA The Babe Postcards

This set of black-and-white postcards features photos of Ruth with contemporary players and managers. Cards measure 5-1/2" x 3-1/2" and have standard postcard indicia on the backs, along with a short photo caption.

		NM	E	VG
	Complete Set (6):	20.00	10.00	6.00
	Common Card:	5.00	2.50	1.50
1	Babe Ruth, Bill Terry	5.00	2.50	1.50
2	Babe Ruth, Walter Johnson	5.00	2.50	1.50
3	Babe Ruth, Lou Gehrig, Joe McCarthy	5.00	2.50	1.50
4	Babe Ruth, Miller Huggins	5.00	2.50	1.50
5	Babe Ruth, Tony Lazzeri	5.00	2.50	1.50
6	Babe Ruth and 1934 All-Stars	5.00	2.50	1.50

1975 TCMA 1913 Philadelphia Athletics

Members of the World Champion A's of 1913 are featured in this collectors' edition card set. In an unusual 3-1/8" x 5-11/16" format, the cards have black-and-white photos on front, with white borders and player identification at bottom. Backs feature season statistics. The unnumbered cards are checklisted here alphabetically.

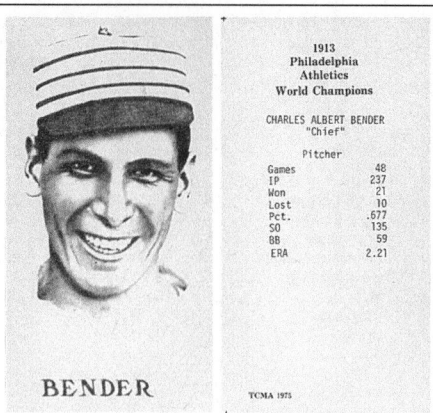

		NM	E	VG
	Complete Set (16):	20.00	10.00	6.00
	Common Player:	3.00	1.50	.90
(1)	Home Run Baker	3.00	1.50	.90
(2)	Jack Barry	3.00	1.50	.90
(3)	Chief Bender	3.00	1.50	.90
(4)	Joe Bush	3.00	1.50	.90
(5)	Eddie Collins	3.00	1.50	.90
(6)	Jack Coombs	3.00	1.50	.90
(7)	Jack Lapp	3.00	1.50	.90
(8)	Connie Mack	3.00	1.50	.90
(9)	Stuffy McInnis	3.00	1.50	.90
(10)	Dan Murphy	3.00	1.50	.90
(11)	Eddie Murphy	3.00	1.50	.90
(12)	Rube Oldring	3.00	1.50	.90
(13)	William Orr	3.00	1.50	.90
(14)	Ed Plank	3.00	1.50	.90
(15)	Walter Schang	3.00	1.50	.90
(16)	Amos Strunk	3.00	1.50	.90

1975 TCMA 1919 Chicago White Sox

The infamous Black Sox who threw the 1919 World Series, and their teammates, are featured in this collectors' edition. The 2-1/2" x 3-1/2" cards are printed in black-and-white. Fronts have player photos with identification in the white border at bottom. Backs have 1919 season stats. The unnumbered cards are checklisted here alphabetically.

		NM	E	VG
	Complete Set (28):	35.00	17.50	10.00
	Common Player:	1.00	.50	.30
(1)	Joe Benz	1.00	.50	.30
(2)	Eddie Cicotte	3.50	1.75	1.00
(3)	Eddie Collins	2.50	1.25	.70
(4)	Shano Collins	1.00	.50	.30
(5)	Dave Danforth	1.00	.50	.30
(6)	Red Faber	1.00	.40	.25
(7)	Happy Felsch	3.50	1.75	1.00
(8)	Chick Gandil	5.00	2.50	1.50
(9)	Kid Gleason	1.00	.50	.30
(10)	Joe Jackson	10.00	5.00	3.00
(11)	Bill James	1.00	.50	.30
(12)	Dickie Kerr	1.00	.50	.30
(13)	Nemo Leibold	1.00	.50	.30
(14)	Byrd Lynn	1.00	.50	.30
(15)	Erskine Mayer	2.00	1.00	.60
(16)	Harvey McClellan	1.00	.50	.30
(17)	Fred McMullin	4.00	2.00	1.25
(18)	Eddie Murphy	1.00	.50	.30
(19)	Pat Ragan	1.00	.50	.30
(20)	Swede Risberg	4.00	2.00	1.25
(21)	Charlie Robertson	1.00	.50	.30
(22)	Reb Russell	1.00	.50	.30
(23)	Ray Schalk	1.00	.40	.25
(24)	Buck Weaver	6.00	3.00	1.75
(25)	Roy Wilkinson	1.00	.50	.30
(26)	Lefty Williams	4.00	2.00	1.25

		NM	E	VG
(27)	Frank Shellenback, Grover Lowdermilk, Joe Jenkins, Dickie Kerr, Ray Schalk	1.00	.50	.30
(28)	Team Photo (4-3/4" x 3-1/2")	7.50	3.75	2.25

1975 TCMA 1924-1925 Washington Senators

The back-to-back American League champion Senators of 1924-25 are featured in this collectors' edition card set. Cards measure 2-3/8" x 3-7/16". Fronts have black-and-white photos with blue captions and white borders. Backs have player stats for the two seasons. The unnumbered cards are checklisted here in alphabetical order.

		NM	E	VG
	Complete Set (42):	30.00	15.00	9.00
	Common Player:	1.50	.75	.45
(1)	Spencer Adams	1.50	.75	.45
(2)	Nick Altrock	1.50	.75	.45
(3)	Ossie Bluege	1.50	.75	.45
(4)	Stan Coveleski	1.50	.75	.45
(5)	Alex Ferguson	1.50	.75	.45
(6)	Showboat Fisher	1.50	.75	.45
(7)	Goose Goslin	1.50	.75	.45
(8)	Bart Griffith	1.50	.75	.45
(9)	Pinky Hargrave	1.50	.75	.45
(10)	Bucky Harris	1.50	.75	.45
(11)	Joe Harris	1.50	.75	.45
(12)	Tex Jeanes	1.50	.75	.45
(13)	Walter Johnson	4.00	2.00	1.25
(14)	Joe Judge	1.50	.75	.45
(15)	Wade Lefler	1.50	.75	.45
(16)	Nemo Leibold	1.50	.75	.45
(17)	Firpo Marberry	1.50	.75	.45
(18)	Joe Martina	1.50	.75	.45
(19)	Wid Matthews	1.50	.75	.45
(20)	Mike McNally	1.50	.75	.45
(21)	Earl McNeely	1.50	.75	.45
(22)	Ralph Miller	1.50	.75	.45
(23)	George Mogridge	1.50	.75	.45
(24)	Buddy Myer	1.50	.75	.45
(25)	Curly Ogden	1.50	.75	.45
(26)	Roger Peckinpaugh	1.50	.75	.45
(27)	Spencer Pumpelly	1.50	.75	.45
(28)	Sam Rice	1.50	.75	.45
(29)	Muddy Ruel	1.50	.75	.45
(30)	Dutch Ruether	1.50	.75	.45
(31)	Allen Russell	1.50	.75	.45
(32)	Everett Scott	1.50	.75	.45
(33)	Hank Severeid	1.50	.75	.45
(34)	Mule Shirley	1.50	.75	.45
(35)	Byron Speece	1.50	.75	.45
(36)	Benny Tate	1.50	.75	.45
(37)	Bobby Veach	1.50	.75	.45
(38)	Tom Zachary	1.50	.75	.45
(39)	Paul Zahniser	1.50	.75	.45
	5" x 3-1/2" FEATURE CARDS	1.50	.75	.45
(40)	Bucky Harris, Bill McKechnie	2.00	1.00	.60
(41)	Ossie Bluege, Roger Peckinpaugh, Bucky Harris, Joe Judge	2.00	1.00	.60
(42)	Tom Zachary, Firpo Marberry, Alex Ferguson, Walter Johnson	2.50	1.25	.70

1975 TCMA 1927 New York Yankees

One of the greatest teams in baseball history is featured in this set of collectors' cards. The 2-1/2" x 3-1/2" cards have black-and-white photos with a white border. At top is the team identification, at bottom is player name and position. The back has the player's 1927 season stats. The unnumbered cards are checklisted here alphabetically.

1927 NEW YORK YANKEES

URBAN JAMES SHOCKER	
Games	31
IP	200
Won	18
Lost	6
Pct.	.750
BB	41
SO	35
ERA	2.84

T.C.M.A. 1975

Urban Shocker   P

		NM	E	VG
	Complete Set (30):	40.00	20.00	12.00
	Common Player:	2.00	1.00	.60
(1)	Walter Beall	2.00	1.00	.60
(2)	Benny Bengough	2.00	1.00	.60
(3)	Pat Collins	2.00	1.00	.60
(4)	Earle Combs	2.00	1.00	.60
(5)	Joe Dugan	2.00	1.00	.60
(6)	Cedric Durst	2.00	1.00	.60
(7)	Mike Gazella	2.00	1.00	.60
(8)	Lou Gehrig	7.50	3.75	2.25
(9)	Joe Giard	2.00	1.00	.60
(10)	Johnny Grabowski	2.00	1.00	.60
(11)	Waite Hoyt	2.00	1.00	.60
(12)	Miller Huggins	2.00	1.00	.60
(13)	Mark Koenig	2.00	1.00	.60
(14)	Tony Lazzeri	2.00	1.00	.60
(15)	Bob Meusel	2.00	1.00	.60
(16)	Wilcy Moore	2.00	1.00	.60
(17)	Ray Morehart	2.00	1.00	.60
(18)	Ben Paschal	2.00	1.00	.60
(19)	Herb Pennock	2.00	1.00	.60
(20)	George Pipgras	2.00	1.00	.60
(21)	Dutch Ruether	2.00	1.00	.60
(22)	Jacob Ruppert	2.00	1.00	.60
(23)	Babe Ruth	12.00	6.00	3.50
(24)	Bob Shawkey	2.00	1.00	.60
(25)	Urban Shocker	2.00	1.00	.60
(26)	Myles Thomas	2.00	1.00	.60
(27)	Julie Wera	2.00	1.00	.60
(28)	Yankee Coaches and Manager(Charlie O'Leary, Miller Huggins, Artie Fletcher)	2.00	1.00	.60
(29)	Yankee Stadium	3.00	1.50	.90
(30)	Yankees infield(Lou Gehrig, Tony Lazzeri, Mark Koenig, Joe Dugan) (5" x 3-5/8")	9.00	4.50	2.75

1975 TCMA 1942-46 St. Louis Cardinals

1942 St. Louis Cardinals

This collectors' issue set features players and staff from the Cards' war-years dynasty. In 2-1/2" x 3-5/8" format, the cards have black-and-white photos with red printing on front. The unnumbered cards have statistics on back.

		NM	E	VG
	Complete Set (66):	40.00	20.00	12.00
	Common Player:	1.00	.50	.30
(1)	Buster Adams	1.00	.50	.30
(2)	Red Barrett	1.00	.50	.30
(3)	John Beazley	1.00	.50	.30
(4)	Al Brazle	1.00	.50	.30
(5)	Harry Brecheen	1.00	.50	.30
(6)	Jimmy Brown	1.00	.50	.30
(7)	Ken Burkhart	1.00	.50	.30
(8)	Bud Byerly	1.00	.50	.30
(9)	Mort Cooper	1.00	.50	.30
(10)	Walker Cooper	1.00	.50	.30
(11)	Estel Crabtree	1.00	.50	.30
(12)	Creepy Crespi	1.00	.50	.30

		NM	E	VG
(13)	Jeff Cross	1.00	.50	.30
(14)	Frank Demaree	1.00	.50	.30
(15)	Murrey Dickson (Murry)	1.00	.50	.30
(16)	Blix Donnelly	1.00	.50	.30
(17)	Erv Dusak	1.00	.50	.30
(18)	Eddie Dyer	1.00	.50	.30
(19)	Bill Endicott	1.00	.50	.30
(20)	George Fallon	1.00	.50	.30
(21)	Joe Garagiola	3.00	1.50	.90
(22)	Debs Garms	1.00	.50	.30
(23)	Mike Gonzalez	1.25	.60	.40
(24)	Johnny Grodzicki	1.00	.50	.30
(25)	Harry Gumbert	1.00	.50	.30
(26)	Johnny Hopp	1.00	.50	.30
(27)	Nippy Jones	1.00	.50	.30
(28)	Lou Klein	1.00	.50	.30
(29)	Clyde Kluttz	1.00	.50	.30
(30)	Howie Krist	1.00	.50	.30
(31)	Whitey Kurowski	1.00	.50	.30
(32)	Max Lanier	1.00	.50	.30
(33)	Danny Litwhiler	1.00	.50	.30
(34)	Bill Lohrman	1.00	.50	.30
(35)	Marty Marion	1.50	.70	.45
(36)	Freddie Martin	1.00	.50	.30
(37)	Pepper Martin	2.00	1.00	.60
(38)	Terry Moore	1.00	.50	.30
(39)	Red Munger	1.00	.50	.30
(40)	Stan Musial	5.00	2.50	1.50
(41)	Sam Narron	1.00	.50	.30
(42)	Ken O'Dea	1.00	.50	.30
(43)	Howie Pollet	1.00	.50	.30
(44)	Del Rice	1.00	.50	.30
(45)	Ray Sanders	1.00	.50	.30
(46)	Fred Schmidt	1.00	.50	.30
(47)	Red Schoendienst	3.00	1.50	.90
(48)	Walt Sessi	1.00	.50	.30
(49)	Clyde Shoun	1.00	.50	.30
(50)	Dick Sisler	1.00	.50	.30
(51)	Enos Slaughter	3.00	1.50	.90
(52)	Billy Southworth	1.00	.50	.30
(53)	Coaker Triplett	1.00	.50	.30
(54)	Emil Verban	1.00	.50	.30
(55)	Harry Walker	1.00	.50	.30
(56)	Buzzy Wares	1.00	.50	.30
(57)	Lon Warneke	1.00	.50	.30
(58)	Ernie White	1.00	.50	.30
(59)	Del Wilber	1.00	.50	.30
(60)	Ted Wilks	1.00	.50	.30
(61)	Leo Durocher, Eddie Dyer	1.00	.50	.30
(62)	Stan Musial, Billy Southworth, Johnny Hopp	1.00		.30
(63)	Stan Musial, Billy Southworth, Ray Sanders	1.00	.50	.30
(64)	Red Ruffing, Johnny Beazley	1.00	.50	.30
(65)	1942 St. Louis Cardinals (5" x 3-1/2")	3.00	1.50	.90
(66)	Sportsman's Park (5" x 3-1/2")	2.50	1.25	.70

1975 TCMA 1946 Boston Red Sox

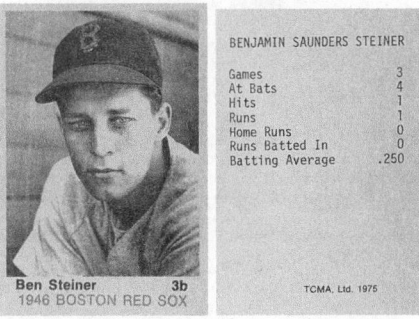

BENJAMIN SAUNDERS STEINER	
Games	3
At Bats	4
Hits	1
Runs	1
Home Runs	0
Runs Batted In	0
Batting Average	.250

Ben Steiner   3b
1946 BOSTON RED SOX

TCMA, Ltd. 1975

The Red Sox American League champions of 1946 are featured in this collectors' issue. Blue-and-white player photos appear on front, with the player's name and position in black below. At bottom-front is the team name in red. Backs of the 2-1/2" x 3-1/2" cards have the player's 1946 stats. The unnumbered cards are checklisted here in alphabetical order.

		NM	E	VG
	Complete Set (43):	45.00	22.50	13.50
	Common Player:	1.50	.75	.45
(1)	Jim Bagby Sr.	1.50	.75	.45
(2)	Del Baker	1.50	.75	.45
(3)	Mace Brown	1.50	.75	.45
(4)	Bill Butland	1.50	.75	.45
(5)	Paul Campbell	1.50	.75	.45
(6)	Tom Carey	1.50	.75	.45
(7)	Joe Cronin	2.00	1.00	.60
(8)	Leon Culberson	1.50	.75	.45
(9)	Tom Daly	1.50	.75	.45
(10)	Dom DiMaggio	2.50	1.25	.70
(11)	Joe Dobson	1.50	.75	.45
(12)	Bobby Doerr	1.50	.75	.45
(13)	Clem Dreisewerd	1.50	.75	.45
(14)	"Boo" Ferriss	1.50	.75	.45
(15)	Andy Gilbert	1.50	.75	.45
(16)	Don Gutteridge	1.50	.75	.45
(17)	Mickey Harris	1.50	.75	.45
(18)	Randy Heflin	1.50	.75	.45
(19)	"Pinky" Higgins	1.50	.75	.45
(20)	"Tex" Hughson	1.50	.75	.45
(21)	Earl Johnson	1.50	.75	.45
(22)	Bob Klinger	1.50	.75	.45
(23)	Johnny Lazor	1.50	.75	.45
(24)	Tom McBride	1.50	.75	.45
(25)	Ed McGah	1.50	.75	.45
(26)	"Catfish" Metkovich	1.50	.75	.45
(27)	Wally Moses	1.50	.75	.45
(28)	Roy Partee	1.50	.75	.45
(29)	Eddie Pellagrini	1.50	.75	.45
(30)	Johnny Pesky	1.50	.75	.45
(31)	Frank Pytlak	1.50	.75	.45
(32)	"Rip" Russell	1.50	.75	.45
(33)	Mike Ryba	1.50	.75	.45
(34)	Ben Steiner	1.50	.70	.45
(35)	Charlie Wagner	1.50	.75	.45
(36)	Hal Wagner	1.50	.75	.45
(37)	Ted Williams	7.50	3.75	2.25
(38)	Larry Woodall	1.50	.75	.45
(39)	Rudy York	1.50	.75	.45
(40)	Bill Zuber	1.50	.75	.45
(41)	Team Photo	2.00	1.00	.60
(42)	Larry Woodall, Hal Wagner, Del Baker	1.50	.75	.45
(43)	Rudy York, Wally Moses, Dom DiMaggio, Bobby Doerr, Charlie Wagner (5" x 3-1/2")	4.00	2.00	1.25

1975 TCMA 1950 Philadelphia Phillies/Whiz Kids

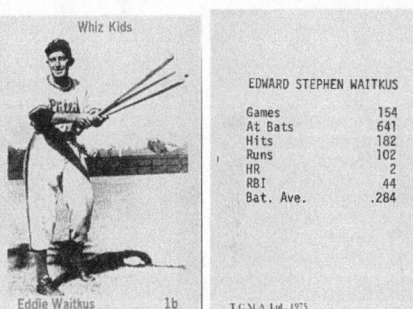

Whiz Kids

EDWARD STEPHEN WAITKUS	
Games	154
At Bats	641
Hits	182
Runs	102
HR	2
RBI	44
Bat. Ave.	.284

Eddie Waitkus   1b   T.C.M.A. Ltd. 1975

The National League Champion "Whiz Kids" are featured in this collectors' issue. The 2-1/2" x 3-1/2" cards have black-and-white photos on front with the player's name and position in red at bottom and either "Whiz Kids" or "1950 Philadelphia Phillies" in red at top. Black-and-white backs have 1950 season stats. The unnumbered cards are checklisted here alphabetically. The large-format multiple-player card was issued coincidentally with the set.

		NM	E	VG
	Complete Set (32):	45.00	22.50	13.50
	Common Player:	2.00	1.00	.60
(1)	Richie Ashburn	11.00	5.50	3.25
(2)	Benny Bengough	2.00	1.00	.60
(3)	Jimmy Bloodworth	2.00	1.00	.60
(4)	Hank Borowy	2.00	1.00	.60
(5)	"Putsy" Caballero	2.00	1.00	.60
(6)	"Bubba" Church	2.00	1.00	.60
(7)	Dusty Cooke	2.00	1.00	.60
(8)	Blix Donnelly	2.00	1.00	.60
(9)	Del Ennis	2.00	1.00	.60
(10)	Mike Goliat	2.00	1.00	.60
(11)	Granny Hamner	2.00	1.00	.60
(12)	Ken Heintzelman	2.00	1.00	.60
(13)	Stan Hollmig	2.00	1.00	.60
(14)	Ken Johnson	2.00	1.00	.60
(15)	"Puddin-Head" Jones	2.00	1.00	.60
(16)	Jim Konstanty	2.00	1.00	.60
(17)	Stan Lopata	2.00	1.00	.60
(18)	Jackie Mayo	2.00	1.00	.60
(19)	Russ Meyer	2.00	1.00	.60
(20)	Bob Miller	2.00	1.00	.60
(21)	Bill Nicholson	2.00	1.00	.60
(22)	Cy Perkins	2.00	1.00	.60
(23)	Robin Roberts	11.00	5.50	3.25
(24)	Eddie Sawyer	2.00	1.00	.60

(25)	Andy Seminick	2.00	1.00	.60
(26)	Ken Silvestri	2.00	1.00	.60
(27)	Curt Simmons	2.00	1.00	.60
(28)	Dick Sisler	2.00	1.00	.60
(29)	"Jocko" Thompson	2.00	1.00	.60
(30)	Eddie Waitkus	2.00	1.00	.60
(31)	Dick Whitman	2.00	1.00	.60
(32)	Russ Meyer, Hank Borowy, Bill Nicholson, Willie Jones (4-7/8" x 3-1/2")	15.00	7.50	4.50

1975 TCMA 1951 New York Giants

Artie Wilson OF
1951 NEW YORK GIANTS

ARTHUR LEE WILSON

Infielder

Games	19
At Bats	44
Hits	4
Runs	2
HR	0
RBI	1
Bat Ave.	.182

TCMA, Ltd. 1975

The National League Champion Giants of 1951 are honored in this collectors' issue card set. The 2-1/2" x 3-1/2" cards have black-and-white photos on front, with player name, team and position in the bottom border in red-orange ink. Backs are black-and-white with 1951 stats. The unnumbered cards are listed here in alphabetical order.

		NM	E	VG
	Complete Set (34):	35.00	17.50	10.00
	Common Player:	1.50	.75	.45
(1)	George Bamberger	1.50	.75	.45
(2)	Roger Bowman	1.50	.75	.45
(3)	Al Corwin	1.50	.75	.45
(4)	Alvin Dark	2.00	1.00	.60
(5)	Allen Gettel	1.50	.75	.45
(6)	Clint Hartung	1.50	.75	.45
(7)	Jim Hearn	1.50	.75	.45
(8)	Monte Irvin	2.00	1.00	.60
(9)	Larry Jansen	1.50	.75	.45
(10)	Sheldon Jones	1.50	.75	.45
(11)	"Spider" Jorgensen	1.50	.75	.45
(12)	Monte Kennedy	1.50	.75	.45
(13)	Alex Konikowski	1.50	.70	.45
(14)	Dave Koslo	1.50	.75	.45
(15)	Jack Kramer	1.50	.75	.45
(16)	Whitey Lockman	1.50	.75	.45
(17)	"Lucky" Lohrke	1.50	.75	.45
(18)	Sal Maglie	1.50	.70	.45
(19)	Jack Maguire	1.50	.70	.45
(20)	Willie Mays	10.00	5.00	3.00
(21)	Don Mueller	1.50	.75	.45
(22)	Ray Noble	1.50	.75	.45
(23)	Earl Rapp	1.50	.75	.45
(24)	Bill Rigney	1.50	.75	.45
(25)	George Spencer	1.50	.75	.45
(26)	Eddie Stanky	1.50	.70	.45
(27)	Hank Thompson	1.50	.75	.45
(28)	Bobby Thomson	2.50	1.20	.70
(29)	Wes Westrum	1.50	.75	.45
(30)	Davey Williams	1.50	.75	.45
(31)	Artie Wilson	1.50	.75	.45
(32)	Sal Yvars	1.50	.75	.45
(33)	Leo Durocher, Willie Mays (3-5/8" x 5")	7.00	3.50	2.00
(34)	Durocher and coaches (3-5/8" x 5")	3.00	1.50	.90

1975 TCMA 1954 Cleveland Indians

Art Houtteman P

1954 CLEVELAND INDIANS

ARTHUR JOSEPH HOUTTEMAN

Games	32
IP	188
Won	15
Lost	7
Pct.	6.82
BB	59
SO	68
ERA	3.35

T.C.M.A. 1975

The American League Champions of 1954 are featured in this collectors issue. Individual player cards are 2-1/2" x 3-1/2" printed in black-and-white. Backs have 1954 season stats. Three large-format (3-3/4" x 5-1/8") multi-player cards were issued with the complete set. The unnumbered cards are checklisted here alphabetically.

		NM	E	VG
	Complete Set (39):	35.00	17.50	10.00
	Common Player:	1.50	.75	.45
(1)	Bobby Avila	2.00	1.00	.60
(2)	Bob Chakales	1.50	.75	.45
(3)	Tony Cuccinello	1.50	.75	.45
(4)	Sam Dente	1.50	.75	.45
(5)	Larry Doby	3.50	1.75	1.00
(6)	Luke Easter	2.00	1.00	.60
(7)	Bob Feller	5.00	2.50	1.50
(8)	Mike Garcia	2.00	1.00	.60
(9)	Joe Ginsberg	1.50	.75	.45
(10)	Bill Glynn	1.50	.75	.45
(11)	Mickey Grasso	1.50	.75	.45
(12)	Mel Harder	1.50	.75	.45
(13)	Jim Hegan	1.50	.75	.45
(14)	Bob Hooper	1.50	.75	.45
(15)	Dave Hoskins	1.50	.75	.45
(16)	Art Houtteman	1.50	.75	.45
(17)	Bob Kennedy	1.50	.75	.45
(18)	Bob Lemon	2.50	1.25	.70
(19)	Al Lopez	2.50	1.25	.70
(20)	Hank Majeski	1.50	.75	.45
(21)	Dale Mitchell	1.50	.75	.45
(22)	Don Mossi	1.50	.75	.45
(23)	Hal Naragon	1.50	.75	.45
(24)	Ray Narleski	1.50	.75	.45
(25)	Rocky Nelson	1.50	.75	.45
(26)	Hal Newhouser	2.50	1.25	.70
(27)	Dave Philley	1.50	.75	.45
(28)	Dave Pope	1.50	.75	.45
(29)	Rudy Regalado	1.50	.75	.45
(30)	Al Rosen	2.00	1.00	.60
(31)	Jose Santiago	1.50	.75	.45
(32)	Al Smith	1.50	.75	.45
(33)	George Strickland	1.50	.75	.45
(34)	Vic Wertz	1.50	.75	.45
(35)	Wally Westlake	1.50	.75	.45
(36)	Early Wynn	2.50	1.25	.70
	Large Format Cards	1.50	.75	.45
(37)	Al Lopez and Coaches	5.00	2.50	1.50
(38)	Al Lopez and Pitchers	5.00	2.50	1.50
(39)	Indians Outfielders	5.00	2.50	1.50

1975 TCMA All Time Brooklyn/Los Angeles Dodgers

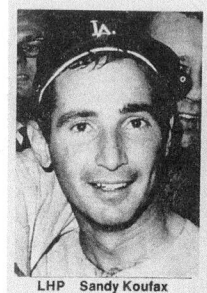

LHP Sandy Koufax

ALL TIME
BROOKLYN/LOS ANGELES
DODGERS

1b	Gil Hodges
2b	Jackie Robinson
ss	Pee Wee Reese
3b	Junior Gilliam
OF	Duke Snider
OF	Dixie Walker
OF	Zack Wheat
C	Roy Campanella
RHP	Don Drysdale
LHP	Sandy Koufax
RP	Hugh Casey
Mgr	Walter Alston

T.C.M.A. Ltd. 1975

A picked team of former Dodgers stars is featured in this collectors issue team set. Cards are in black-and-white in the standard 2-1/2" x 3-1/2" format. Fronts have player identification in the border beneath the photo. Backs have a checklist by position and a TCMA copyright line. The unnumbered cards are checklisted here in the order presented on back.

		NM	E	VG
	Complete Set (12):	25.00	12.50	7.50
	Common Player:	2.25	1.25	.70
(1)	Gil Hodges	3.00	1.50	.90
(2)	Jackie Robinson	10.00	5.00	3.00
(3)	Pee Wee Reese	3.00	1.50	.90
(4)	Junior Gilliam	2.25	1.25	.70
(5)	Duke Snider	3.00	1.50	.90
(6)	Dixie Walker	2.25	1.25	.70
(7)	Zack Wheat	2.25	1.25	.70
(8)	Roy Campanella	4.00	2.00	1.25
(9)	Don Drysdale	3.00	1.50	.90
(10)	Sandy Koufax	8.00	4.00	2.50
(11)	Hugh Casey	2.25	1.25	.70
(12)	Walter Alston	2.25	1.25	.70

1975 TCMA All Time New York Giants

ss Alvin Dark

ALL TIME
NEW YORK GIANTS

1b	Bill Terry
2b	Frankie Frisch
ss	Alvin Dark
3b	Fred Lindstrom
LF	Bobby Thomson
CF	Willie Mays
RF	Mel Ott
C	Wes Westrum
LHP	Carl Hubbell
RHP	Christy Mathewson
RP	Hoyt Wilhelm
Mgr	John McGraw

TCMA Ltd. 1975

An all-time line-up of Giants is presented in this collector issue. Fronts of the 2-1/2" x 3-1/2" cards have black-and-white player photos with the player's name and position printed in red in the white bottom border. Backs are in black-and-white and present the all-time roster. The unnumbered cards are checklisted here alphabetically.

		NM	E	VG
	Complete Set (12):	30.00	15.00	9.00
	Common Player:	2.00	1.00	.60
(1)	Alvin Dark	2.00	1.00	.60
(2)	Frankie Frisch	2.00	1.00	.60
(3)	Carl Hubbell	2.00	1.00	.60
(4)	Freddie Lindstrom	2.00	1.00	.60
(5)	Christy Mathewson	4.00	2.00	1.25
(6)	Willie Mays	15.00	7.50	4.50
(7)	John McGraw	2.00	1.00	.60
(8)	Mel Ott	2.00	1.00	.60
(9)	Bill Terry	2.00	1.00	.60
(10)	Bobby Thomson	2.00	1.00	.60
(11)	Wes Westrum	2.00	1.00	.60
(12)	Hoyt Wilhelm	2.00	1.00	.60

1975 TCMA All Time New York Yankees

SS Phil Rizzuto

ALL TIME
NEW YORK
YANKEE TEAM

1B	Lou Gehrig
2B	Tony Lazzeri
3B	Red Rolfe
SS	Phil Rizzuto
OF	Babe Ruth
OF	Mickey Mantle
OF	Joe DiMaggio
C	Bill Dickey
P	Red Ruffing
P	Whitey Ford
RP	Johnny Murphy
Mgr	Casey Stengel

T.C.M.A. LTD 1975

The best players on the best team in baseball history are featured in this collectors' edition. Cards measure 2-1/2" x 3-3/4" and feature black-and-white photos on front, with white borders. Player name and position are printed in a white strip toward the bottom of the picture. Backs have a list of the all-time team. The unnumbered cards are listed here in that order.

		NM	E	VG
	Complete Set (12):	15.00	7.50	4.50
	Common Player:	2.00	1.00	.60
(1)	Lou Gehrig	4.00	2.00	1.25
(2)	Tony Lazzeri	2.00	1.00	.60
(3)	Red Rolfe	2.00	1.00	.60
(4)	Phil Rizzuto	2.50	1.25	.70
(5)	Babe Ruth	5.00	2.50	1.50
(6)	Mickey Mantle	6.00	3.00	1.75
(7)	Joe DiMaggio	4.00	2.00	1.25
(8)	Bill Dickey	2.00	1.00	.60
(9)	Red Ruffing	2.00	1.00	.60
(10)	Whitey Ford	2.50	1.25	.70
(11)	Johnny Murphy	2.00	1.00	.60
(12)	Casey Stengel	2.00	1.00	.60

1975 TCMA All-Time Greats

This is a smaller - both in size and number - version of TCMA's Hall of Famer postcard set issued between 1973-80. These collectors' edition cards measure 2-3/8" x 3-3/4" and were issued in strips of six. Two printings were done, the first with blue-and-white fronts and red backs, the second in black-and-white, blank-backed. Surrounding the photo on front is a blue or black border with baseball equipment ornamentation. The unnumbered cards are checklisted here in alphabetical order.

LOUIS BOUDREAU

Shortstop

| Indians | Red Sox |
| 1938 | – 1952 |

Games	1646
At Bats	6030
Hits	1779
Home Runs	68
Batting Ave.	.295
Hall of Fame	1970

LOU BOUDREAU

		NM	E	VG
Complete Set (39):		40.00	20.00	12.00
Common Player:		2.00	1.00	.60
(1)	"Luke" Appling	2.00	1.00	.60
(2)	Roger Bresnahan	2.00	1.00	.60
(3)	Ty Cobb	8.00	4.00	2.50
(4)	Mickey Cochrane	2.00	1.00	.60
(5)	Eddie Collins	2.00	1.00	.60
(6)	Kiki Cuyler	2.00	1.00	.60
(7)	Dizzy Dean	4.00	2.00	1.25
(8)	Bill Dickey	2.00	1.00	.60
(9)	Joe DiMaggio	8.00	4.00	2.50
(10)	Bob Feller	2.00	1.00	.60
(11)	Elmer Flick	2.00	1.00	.60
(12)	Frank Frisch	2.00	1.00	.60
(13)	Lou Gehrig	8.00	4.00	2.50
(14)	Hank Greenberg	4.00	2.00	1.25
(15)	Goose Goslin	2.00	1.00	.60
(16)	Chick Hafey	2.00	1.00	.60
(17)	Gabby Hartnett	2.00	1.00	.60
(18)	Harry Heilmann	2.00	1.00	.60
(19)	Rogers Hornsby	2.00	1.00	.60
(20)	Waite Hoyt	2.00	1.00	.60
(21)	Walter Johnson	4.00	2.00	1.25
(22)	George Kelly	2.00	1.00	.60
(23)	Ted Lyons	2.00	1.00	.60
(24)	Connie Mack	2.00	1.00	.60
(25)	Mickey Mantle	10.00	5.00	3.00
(26)	Rabbit Maranville	2.00	1.00	.60
(27)	Mel Ott	2.00	1.00	.60
(28)	Edd Roush	2.00	1.00	.60
(29)	Red Ruffing	2.00	1.00	.60
(30)	Babe Ruth	10.00	5.00	3.00
(31)	Al Simmons	2.00	1.00	.60
(32)	Casey Stengel	2.00	1.00	.60
(33)	Pie Traynor	2.00	1.00	.60
(34)	Dazzy Vance	2.00	1.00	.60
(35)	Honus Wagner	4.00	2.00	1.25
(36)	Lloyd Waner	2.00	1.00	.60
(37)	Paul Waner	2.00	1.00	.60
(38)	Ted Williams	6.00	3.00	1.75
(39)	Harry Wright	2.00	1.00	.60

1975 TCMA Guam WW2

This set of 3-1/2" x 5-1/2" black-and-white cards details the connection between Major League Baseball and the Pacific island of Guam during WWII. Some cards picture players in the their military uniforms, others shown them in baseball uniforms. Backs contain a narrative of the series.

		NM	E	VG
Complete Set (18):		25.00	12.50	7.50
Common Card:		1.00	.50	.30
1	Phil Rizzuto, Terry Moore	5.00	2.50	1.50
2	Gab Gab Guam 1945	1.00	.50	.30
3	Team Photo	1.00	.50	.30
4	Merrill May, Pee Wee Reese, Johnny Vander Meer	2.50	1.25	.70
5	Team Photo	1.00	.50	.30
6	Team Photo	1.00	.50	.30
7	Del Ennis	2.00	1.00	.60
8	Mace Brown	2.00	1.00	.60

		NM	E	VG
9	Pee Wee Reese, Joe Gordon, Bill Dickey	3.50	1.75	1.00
10	Glenn McQuillen	2.00	1.00	.60
11	Mike Budnick	2.00	1.00	.60
12	Team Photo	1.00	.50	.30
13	"Skeets" Dickey	2.00	1.00	.60
14	Connie Ryan	2.00	1.00	.60
15	Hal White	2.00	1.00	.60
16	Mickey Cochrane	7.50	3.75	2.25
17	Barney McCosky	2.00	1.00	.60
18	Ben Huffman	2.00	1.00	.60

1975 TCMA Larry French Postcards

The career of National League pitcher Larry French is recounted in this set of 3-1/2" x 5-1/2" black-and-white postcard-size cards. Fronts have photos of him with the Pirates, Cubs and Dodgers. Backs have a continuing biography.

		NM	E	VG
Complete Set (6):		15.00	7.50	4.50
Common Card:		3.00	1.50	.90
1	Larry French (Pittsburgh Pirates)	3.00	1.50	.90
2	Larry French (Chicago Cubs)	3.00	1.50	.90
3	Larry French (W/Bill Lee, Charlie Root, Tuck Stainback.)	3.00	1.50	.90
4	Larry French (W/ Charlie Grimm, Fred Lindstrom.)	3.00	1.50	.90
5	Larry French (Brooklyn Dodgers)	3.00	1.50	.90
6	Larry French (W/Mickey Owen.)	3.00	1.50	.90

1975 TCMA/ASCCA Ad Card

To promote the American Sports Card Collectors Association Show in New York City, this 3-1/2" x 5-1/2" black-and-white card done in the format of the All-Time Greats postcards was issued. The front pictures two of the game's greatest pitchers and offers a discount on show admission. The back provides a detailed description of the show.

	NM	E	VG
Dizzy Dean, Lefty Grove	6.00	3.00	1.80

1976 TCMA 1911 N.Y. Highlanders Postcard

This black-and-white postcard was issued singly circa the mid-1970s. It measures approximately 6" x 3-1/2".

	NM	E	VG
1911 N.Y. Highlanders Team Photo	12.00	6.00	3.50

1976 TCMA 1938 Chicago Cubs

AUGUST JOHN GALAN

Games	110
At Bats	395
Hits	113
Runs	52
Home Runs	6
RBI	69
Bat. Ave.	.286

1938 CHICAGO CUBS
NATIONAL LEAGUE CHAMPIONS
1976 TCMA LTD.

Augie Galan   OF

The National League Champion Chicago Cubs of 1938 are featured in this collectors issue. The 2-1/2" x 3-1/2" cards have black-and-white player photos on front with the player's name and position in blue at bottom. Backs are in black-and-white with season stats. The unnumbered cards are checklisted here alphabetically.

		NM	E	VG
Complete Set (33):		40.00	20.00	12.00
Common Player:		2.00	1.00	.60
(1)	Jim Asbell	2.00	1.00	.60
(2)	Clay Bryant	2.00	1.00	.60
(3)	Tex Carleton	2.00	1.00	.60
(4)	Phil Cavarretta	2.00	1.00	.60
(5)	Ripper Collins	2.00	1.00	.60
(6)	"Red" Corriden	2.00	1.00	.60
(7)	Dizzy Dean	7.50	3.75	2.25
(8)	Frank Demaree	2.00	1.00	.60
(9)	Al Epperly	2.00	1.00	.60
(10)	Larry French	2.00	1.00	.60
(11)	Augie Galan	2.00	1.00	.60
(12)	Bob Garbark	2.00	1.00	.60
(13)	Charlie Grimm	2.00	1.00	.60
(14)	Stan Hack	2.00	1.00	.60
(15)	Gabby Hartnett	3.00	1.50	.90
(16)	Billy Herman	3.00	1.50	.90
(17)	Kirby Higbe	2.00	1.00	.60
(18)	Hardrock Johnson	2.00	1.00	.60
(19)	Billy Jurges	2.00	1.00	.60
(20)	Newt Kimball	2.00	1.00	.60
(21)	Tony Lazzeri	3.00	1.50	.90
(22)	Bill Lee	2.00	1.00	.60
(23)	Bob Logan	2.00	1.00	.60
(24)	Joe Marty	2.00	1.00	.60
(25)	Bobby Mattick	2.00	1.00	.60
(26)	Steve Mesner	2.00	1.00	.60
(27)	Ken O'Dea	2.00	1.00	.60
(28)	Vance Page	2.00	1.00	.60
(29)	Carl Reynolds	2.00	1.00	.60
(30)	Charlie Root	2.00	1.00	.60
(31)	Jack Russell	2.00	1.00	.60
(32)	Coaker Triplett	2.00	1.00	.60
(33)	Team History Card	.70	.35	.20

1976 TCMA DiMaggio Brothers Postcard

This black-and-white postcard was issued singly circa the mid-1970s. It measures approximately 3-1/2" x 5-1/2".

	NM	E	VG
Dom DiMaggio, Joe DiMaggio, Vince DiMaggio	12.00	6.00	3.50

1976 TCMA Larry Rosenthal

This custom-published card of the long-time American League outfielder (1936-1945) was printed in red, black and white in a 2-5/8" x 4-5/8" format. The issue date is approximate.

	NM	E	VG
Larry Rosenthal	6.00	3.00	2.00

1976 TCMA Umpires

American League

Don Denkinger   Umpire

Eight of the better-known umpires of the era apparently commissioned TCMA to produce cards for them. The cards are black-and-white in the standard 2-1/2" x 3-1/2" format.

		NM	E	VG
Complete Set (8):		25.00	12.50	7.50
Common Card:		4.00	2.00	1.25
(1)	Larry Barnett	4.00	2.00	1.25
(2)	Al Clark	4.00	2.00	1.25
(3)	Nick Colosi	4.00	2.00	1.25
(4)	Don Denkinger	4.00	2.00	1.25
(5)	Art Frantz	4.00	2.00	1.25

		NM	E	VG
(6)	Marty Springstead	4.00	2.00	1.25
(7)	Ed Sudol	4.00	2.00	1.25
(8)	Bill Williams	4.00	2.00	1.25

1976 Quaker Iron-Ons

(See 1976 Mr. Softee Iron-Ons.)

1977 TCMA 1920 Cleveland Indians

The World Champion Indians are pictured on this collectors' issue team set. In standard 2-1/2" x 3-1/2" size with black-and-white photos, the cards are unnumbered. Some of the players are pictured in their 1921 uniforms with the "World Champions" lettering.

		NM	E	VG
	Complete Set (22):	25.00	12.50	7.50
	Common Player:	2.00	1.00	.60
(1)	Jim Bagby Sr.	2.00	1.00	.60
(2)	George Burns	2.00	1.00	.60
(3)	Ray Caldwell	2.00	1.00	.60
(4)	Ray Chapman	3.00	1.50	.90
(5)	Stan Coveleski	2.50	1.25	.70
(6)	Joe Evans	2.00	1.00	.60
(7)	Larry Gardner	2.00	1.00	.60
(8)	Jack Graney	2.00	1.00	.60
(9)	Charlie Jamieson	2.00	1.00	.60
(10)	Doc Johnston	2.00	1.00	.60
(11)	Harry Lunte	2.00	1.00	.60
(12)	Duster Mails	2.00	1.00	.60
(13)	Guy Morton	2.00	1.00	.60
(14)	Les Nunamaker	2.00	1.00	.60
(15)	Steve O'Neill	2.00	1.00	.60
(16)	Joe Sewell	2.50	1.25	.70
(17)	Elmer Smith	2.00	1.00	.60
(18)	Tris Speaker	4.00	2.00	1.25
(19)	George Uhle	2.00	1.00	.60
(20)	Bill Wambsganss	2.50	1.25	.70
(21)	Joe Wood	2.50	1.25	.70
(22)	World Series Foes (Wilbert Robinson, Tris Speaker) (5-1/2" x 3")	4.00	2.00	1.25

1977 TCMA 1927 Yankees 50th Anniversary

As an insert in its inaugural issue of "Baseball Quarterly" magazine dated Winter, 1977, TCMA included a 16-3/4" x 11" cardboard panel with 18 black-and-white cards featuring members of the 1927 N.Y. Yankees. Measuring about 2-1/2" x 3-3/8" if cut apart, the individual cards have unadorned photos on front framed in black with a white border. Backs have player identification, a 50th anniversary logo, career summary and 1927 and career stats. The unnumbered cards are listed here in alphabetical order.

		NM	E	VG
	Complete Panel:	35.00	17.50	10.50
	Complete Set (18):	25.00	12.50	7.50
	Common Player:	2.00	1.00	.60
(1)	Bernard Oliver Bengough	2.00	1.00	.60
(2)	Tharon Patrick Collins	2.00	1.00	.60
(3)	Earle Bryan Combs	2.00	1.00	.60
(4)	Joseph Anthony Dugan	2.00	1.00	.60
(5)	Henry Louis Gehrig	6.00	3.00	1.75
(6)	John Patrick Grabowski	2.00	1.00	.60
(7)	Waite Charles Hoyt	2.00	1.00	.60
(8)	Miller James Huggins	2.00	1.00	.60
(9)	Mark Anthony Koenig	2.00	1.00	.60
(10)	Anthony Michael Lazzeri	2.00	1.00	.60
(11)	Robert Williams Meusel	2.00	1.00	.60
(12)	William Wilcy Moore	2.00	1.00	.60
(13)	Herbert Jeffries Pennock	2.00	1.00	.60
(14)	George William Pipgras	2.00	1.00	.60
(15)	Walter Henry Ruether	2.00	1.00	.60
(16)	George Herman Ruth	8.00	4.00	2.50
(17)	James Robert Shawkey	2.00	1.00	.60
(18)	Urban James Shocker	2.00	1.00	.60

1977 TCMA 1939-40 Cincinnati Reds

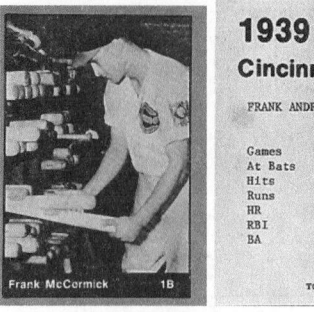

The National League Champion Reds of 1939 and the World's Champion team of 1940 are featured in this collectors' issue. The 2-1/2" x 3-1/2" cards have black-and-white photos on front surrounded by red borders. Backs, also in black-and white, have 1939 and/or 1940 season stats.

		NM	E	VG
	Complete Set (45):	35.00	17.50	10.00
	Common Player:	1.50	.75	.45
1	Vince DiMaggio	2.50	1.25	.70
2	Wally Berger	1.50	.75	.45
3	Nolan Richardson (Nolen)	1.50	.75	.45
4	Ernie Lombardi	2.50	1.25	.70
5	Ival Goodman	1.50	.75	.45
6	Jim Turner	1.50	.75	.45
7	Bucky Walters	1.50	.75	.45
8	Jimmy Ripple	1.50	.75	.45
9	Hank Johnson	1.50	.75	.45
10	Bill Baker	1.50	.75	.45
11	Al Simmons	2.00	1.00	.60
12	Johnny Hutchings	1.50	.75	.45
13	Peaches Davis	1.50	.75	.45
14	Willard Hershberger	2.50	1.25	.70
15	Bill Werber	1.50	.75	.45
16	Harry Craft	1.50	.75	.45
17	Milt Galatzer	1.50	.75	.45
18	Dick West	1.50	.75	.45
19	Art Jacobs	1.50	.75	.45
20	Joe Beggs	1.50	.75	.45
21	Frenchy Bordagaray	1.50	.75	.45
22	Lee Gamble	1.50	.75	.45
23	Lee Grissom	1.50	.75	.45
24	Eddie Joost	1.50	.75	.45
25	Milt Shofner	1.50	.75	.45
26	Morrie Arnovich	1.50	.75	.45
27	Pete Naktenis	1.50	.75	.45
28	Jim Weaver	1.50	.75	.45
29	Mike McCormick	1.50	.75	.45
30	John Niggeling	1.50	.75	.45
31	Les Scarsella	1.50	.75	.45
32	Lonny Frey	1.50	.75	.45
33	Bill Myers	1.50	.75	.45
34	Frank McCormick	1.50	.75	.45
35	Lew Riggs	1.50	.75	.45
36	Nino Bongiovanni	1.50	.75	.45
37	Johnny Rizzo	1.50	.75	.45
38	Wes Livengood	1.50	.75	.45
39	Junior Thompson	1.50	.75	.45
40	Mike Dejan	1.50	.75	.45
41	Jimmy Wilson	1.50	.75	.45
42	Paul Derringer	1.50	.75	.45
43	Johnny Vander Meer	2.00	1.00	.60
44	Whitey Moore	1.50	.75	.45
45	Bill McKechnie	2.00	1.00	.60

1977 TCMA 1960 Pittsburgh Pirates

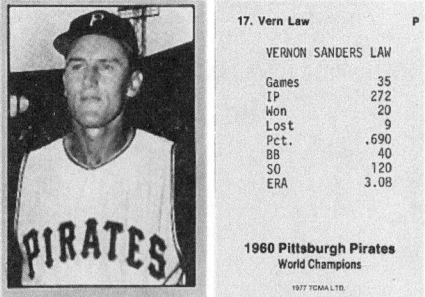

The World's Champions Pirates are featured on this collector issue. The 2-1/2" x 3-1/2" cards have black-and-white photos on front surrounded by orange borders. Backs, also in black-and-white, have a card number, player name and position at top and season stats.

		NM	E	VG
	Complete Set (42):	100.00	50.00	30.00
	Common Player:	3.00	1.50	.90
1	Danny Murtaugh	3.00	1.50	.90
2	Dick Stuart	4.00	2.00	1.25
3	Bill Mazeroski	10.00	5.00	3.00
4	Dick Groat	4.00	2.00	1.25
5	Don Hoak	3.00	1.50	.90
6	Roberto Clemente	20.00	10.00	6.00
7	Bill Virdon	3.00	1.50	.90
8	Bob Skinner	3.00	1.50	.90
9	Smoky Burgess	3.00	1.50	.90
10	Gino Cimoli	3.00	1.50	.90
11	Rocky Nelson	3.00	1.50	.90
12	Hal Smith	3.00	1.50	.90
13	Dick Schofield	3.00	1.50	.90
14	Joe Christopher	3.00	1.50	.90
15	Gene Baker	3.00	1.50	.90
16	Bob Oldis	3.00	1.50	.90
17	Vern Law	3.00	1.50	.90
18	Bob Friend	3.00	1.50	.90
19	Wilmer Mizell	3.00	1.50	.90
20	Harvey Haddix	3.00	1.50	.90
21	Roy Face	3.00	1.50	.90
22	Fred Green	3.00	1.50	.90
23	Joe Gibbon	3.00	1.50	.90
24	Clem Labine	3.00	1.50	.90
25	Paul Giel	3.00	1.50	.90
26	Tom Cheney	3.00	1.50	.90
27	Earl Francis	3.00	1.50	.90
28	Jim Umbricht	3.00	1.50	.90
29	George Witt	3.00	1.50	.90
30	Bennie Daniels	3.00	1.50	.90
31	Don Gross	3.00	1.50	.90
32	Diomedes Olivo	4.00	2.00	1.25
33	Roman Mejias	3.00	1.50	.90
34	R.C. Stevens	3.00	1.50	.90
35	Mickey Vernon	3.00	1.50	.90
36	Danny Kravitz	3.00	1.50	.90
37	Harry Bright	3.00	1.50	.90
38	Dick Barone	3.00	1.50	.90
39	Bill Burwell	3.00	1.50	.90
40	Lenny Levy	4.00	2.00	1.25
41	Sam Narron	3.00	1.50	.90
42	Team Card (Bob Friend)	3.00	1.50	.90

1977 TCMA All-Time White Sox

All-Time Chicago White Sox	
Eddie Robinson	1B
Eddie Collins	2B
Willie Kamm	3B
Luke Appling	SS
Ray Schalk	C
Al Simmons	LF
Johnny Mostil	CF
Harry Hooper	RF
Ted Lyons	RHP
Billy Pierce	LHP
Gerry Staley	RP
Al Lopez	Mgr

Because this is one of the few early TCMA issues not to have a date printed on the back, the quoted year of issue is approximate. Fronts of the 2-1/2" x 3-1/2" cards have black-and-white player photos with name and position printed in red in the bottom border. Black-and-white backs have an all-time team roster of position players, pitchers and manager. The unnumbered cards are checklisted here in alphabetical order.

		NM	E	VG
	Complete Set (12):	24.00	12.00	7.25
	Common Player:	2.00	1.00	.60
(1)	Luke Appling	2.50	1.25	.70
(2)	Eddie Collins	2.50	1.25	.70
(3)	Harry Hooper	2.00	1.00	.60
(4)	Willie Kamm	2.00	1.00	.60
(5)	Al Lopez	2.00	1.00	.60
(6)	Ted Lyons	2.00	1.00	.60
(7)	Johnny Mostil	2.00	1.00	.60
(8)	Billy Pierce	2.00	1.00	.60
(9)	Eddie Robinson	2.00	1.00	.60
(10)	Ray Schalk	2.00	1.00	.60
(11)	Al Simmons	2.00	1.00	.60
(12)	Gerry Staley	2.00	1.00	.60

1977 TCMA Chicago Cubs All Time Team

The best of the Cubs are presented in this collectors issue. An all-time great at each position is featured on the 2-1/2" x 3-1/2" card. Fronts have black-and-white photos with orange graphics. Backs are in black-and-white and list the team by position. The unnumbered cards are checklisted here in that order.

Chicago Cubs
All Time Team

1B - Charlie Grimm
2B - Rogers Hornsby
SS - Ernie Banks
3B - Ron Santo
C - Gabby Hartnett
LF - Billy Williams
RF - Kiki Cuyler
CF - Hack Wilson
RHP - Charlie Root
LHR - Larry French
RP - Emil Kush
MGR - Charlie Grimm
INF - Billy Herman

	NM	E	VG
Complete Set (12):	30.00	15.00	9.00
Common Player:	3.00	1.50	.90
(1) Charlie Grimm	3.00	1.50	.90
(2) Rogers Hornsby	4.00	2.00	1.25
(3) Ernie Banks	4.00	2.00	1.25
(4) Ron Santo	3.00	1.50	.90
(5) Gabby Hartnett	3.00	1.50	.90
(6) Billy Williams	3.00	1.50	.90
(7) Kiki Cuyler	3.00	1.50	.90
(8) Hack Wilson	4.00	2.00	1.25
(9) Charlie Root	3.00	1.50	.90
(10) Larry French	3.00	1.50	.90
(11) Emil Kush	3.00	1.50	.90
(12) Billy Herman	3.00	1.50	.90

1977 TCMA Stars of the Twenties

Six players are featured on this 22" x 11" triple-folder which was glued into issues of the Summer, 1977, "Baseball Quarterly" magazine from TCMA. The pictures feature artwork by John Anderson in sepia tones on heavy cream-colored textured paper stock. The pictures are back-to-back in pairs as listed here, with individual pictures varying in width from 7-1/4" to 7-1/2".

	NM	E	VG
Complete Foldout:	10.00	5.00	3.00
Common Pair:	3.00	1.50	.90
(1/2) Joe Bush, Gabby Hartnett	3.00	1.50	.90
(3/4) Jim Bottomley, "Mule" Haas	3.00	1.50	.90
(5/6) Sam Rice, Buddy Myer	3.00	1.50	.90

1977-80 TCMA The War Years

 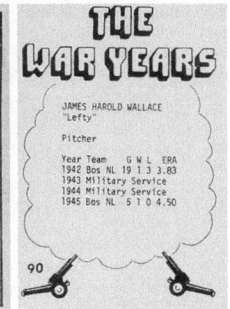

The decimated major league rosters circa 1942-46 are reflected in this collectors' card set. The 2-1/2" x 3-1/2" cards have black-and-white player photos on front, with a white border around. There is no typography on front. Backs have player identification, stats and the set title. Series 1, cards #1-45 was issued in 1977 and is much scarcer than Series 2, #46-90, which was issued in 1980.

	NM	E	VG
Complete Set (90):	140.00	70.00	42.50
Common Player:	2.00	1.00	.60

1	Samuel Narron	3.00	1.50	.90
2	Raymond Mack	3.00	1.50	.90
3	Arnold (Mickey) Owen	3.00	1.50	.90
4	John Peacock	3.00	1.50	.90
5	Paul (Dizzy) Trout	3.00	1.50	.90
6	George (Birdie) Tebbetts	3.00	1.50	.90
7	Alfred Todd	3.00	1.50	.90
8	Harlond Clift	3.00	1.50	.90
9	Don G.N. (Gil) Torres	3.00	1.50	.90
10	Alfonso Lopez	4.00	2.00	1.25
11	Ulysses (Tony) Lupien	3.00	1.50	.90
12	Lucius Appling	4.00	2.00	1.25
13	James (Pat) Seery	3.00	1.50	.90
14	Phil Masi	3.00	1.50	.90
15	Thomas Turner	3.00	1.50	.90
16	Nicholas Piccuito	3.00	1.50	.90
17	Mel Ott	7.50	3.75	2.25
18	Thadford Treadway	3.00	1.50	.90
19	Sam Naham (Neham)	3.00	1.50	.90
20	Truett (Rip) Sewell	3.00	1.50	.90
21	Roy Partee	3.00	1.50	.90
22	Richard Siebert	3.00	1.50	.90
23	Francis (Red) Barrett	3.00	1.50	.90
24	Paul O'Dea	3.00	1.50	.90
25	Lou Parisse	3.00	1.50	.90
26	Martin Marion	4.00	2.00	1.25
27	Eugene Moore	3.00	1.50	.90
28	Walter Beck	3.00	1.50	.90
29	Donald Manno	3.00	1.50	.90
30	Harold Newhouser	4.00	2.00	1.25
31	August Mancuso	3.00	1.50	.90
32	Merrill May	3.00	1.50	.90
33	Gerald Priddy	3.00	1.50	.90
34	Herman Besse	3.00	1.50	.90
35	Luis Olmo	3.00	1.50	.90
36	Robert O'Neill	3.00	1.50	.90
37	John Barrett	3.00	1.50	.90
38	Gordon Maltzberger	3.00	1.50	.90
39	William Nicholson	3.00	1.50	.90
40	Ron Northey	3.00	1.50	.90
41	Howard Pollet	3.00	1.50	.90
42	Aloysius Piechota	3.00	1.50	.90
43	Albert Shepard	7.50	3.75	2.25
44	Alfred Anderson	3.00	1.50	.90
45	Damon Phillips	3.00	1.50	.90
46	Herman Franks	2.00	1.00	.60
47	Aldon Wilke	2.00	1.00	.60
48	Max Macon	2.00	1.00	.60
49	Lester Webber	2.00	1.00	.60
50	Robert Swift	2.00	1.00	.60
51	Philip Weintraub	2.00	1.00	.60
52	Nicholas Strincevich	2.00	1.00	.60
53	Michael Tresh	2.00	1.00	.60
54	William Trotter	2.00	1.00	.60
55	1943 Yankees(Spud Chandler, Frank Crosetti, Bill Dickey, Nick Etten, Joe Gordon, Billy Johnson, Charlie Keller, John Lindell, Bud Metheny)	4.00	2.00	1.25
56	John Sturm	2.00	1.00	.60
57	Silas Johnson	2.00	1.00	.60
58	Donald Kolloway	2.00	1.00	.60
59	Cecil Vaughn (Vaughan)	2.00	1.00	.60
60	St. Louis Browns Bombers(Harlond Clift, Walt Judnich, Chet Laabs)	3.00	1.50	.90
61	Harold Wagner	2.00	1.00	.60
62	Alva Javery	2.00	1.00	.60
63	1941 Boston Bees Pitchers(George Barnicle, Ed Carnett, Art Johnson, Frank LaManna, Casey Stengel, Bob Williams)	3.00	1.50	.90
64	Adolph Camilli	2.00	1.00	.60
65	Myron McCormick	2.00	1.00	.60
66	Richard Wakefield	2.00	1.00	.60
67	James (Mickey) Vernon	3.00	1.50	.90
68	John Vander Meer	3.00	1.50	.90
69	James McDonnell	4.00	2.00	1.25
70	Thomas Jordan	2.00	1.00	.60
71	Maurice Van Robays	2.00	1.00	.60
72	Charles Stanceau	2.00	1.00	.60
73	Samuel Zoldak	2.00	1.00	.60
74	Raymond Starr	2.00	1.00	.60
75	Roger Wolff	2.00	1.00	.60
76	Cecil Travis	2.00	1.00	.60
77	Arthur Johnson	2.00	1.00	.60
78	Louis (Lewis) Riggs	2.00	1.00	.60
79	Peter Suder	2.00	1.00	.60
80	Thomas Warren	2.00	1.00	.60
81	John Welaj	2.00	1.00	.60
82	Gerald Walker	2.00	1.00	.60
83	Dewey Williams	2.00	1.00	.60
84	Leonard Merullo	2.00	1.00	.60
85	John Johnson	2.00	1.00	.60
86	Eugene Thompson	2.00	1.00	.60
87	William Zuber	2.00	1.00	.60
88	Earl Johnson	2.00	1.00	.60
89	Norman Young	2.00	1.00	.60
90	James Wallace	2.00	1.00	.60

1977 TCMA/ASCCA Ad Card

To promote the American Sports Card Collectors Association Show in New York City, this 2-1/2" x 3-1/2" black-and-white, gold highlighted card was issued. The front pictures Babe Ruth and offers a 25-cent discount on show admission. The back provides a detailed description of the show.

	NM	E	VG
Babe Ruth	6.00	3.00	1.80

1977-84 TCMA/Renata Galasso

MICKEY MANTLE
CENTER FIELDER-NEW YORK YANKEES

This issue of six 45-card series is in similar format but with different players, checklists and copyright dates produced by TCMA and marketed by Renata Galasso. In 2-1/2" x 3-1/2" format the cards have black-and-white photos on front. Backs are printed in red and blue and include a career summary, large Galasso ad and TCMA dateline.

	NM	E	VG
Complete Set (270):	45.00	22.00	13.50
Common Player:	.25	.13	.08
SERIES 1 - 1977	12.50	6.25	3.75
1 Joe DiMaggio	4.00	2.00	1.25
2 Ralph Kiner	.25	.13	.08
3 Don Larsen	.25	.13	.08
4 Robin Roberts	.25	.13	.08
5 Roy Campanella	.50	.25	.15
6 Smoky Burgess	.25	.13	.08
7 Mickey Mantle	6.00	3.00	1.75
8 Willie Mays	3.00	1.50	.90
9 George Kell	.25	.13	.08
10 Ted Williams	3.00	1.50	.90
11 Carl Furillo	.25	.13	.08
12 Bob Feller	.25	.13	.08
13 Casey Stengel	.25	.13	.08
14 Richie Ashburn	.25	.13	.08
15 Gil Hodges	.25	.13	.08
16 Stan Musial	.75	.40	.25
17 Don Newcombe	.25	.13	.08
18 Jackie Jensen	.25	.13	.08
19 Lou Boudreau	.25	.13	.08
20 Jackie Robinson	2.00	1.00	.60
21 Billy Goodman	.25	.13	.08
22 Satchel Paige	1.00	.50	.30
23 Hoyt Wilhelm	.25	.13	.08
24 Duke Snider	.25	.13	.08
25 Whitey Ford	.25	.13	.08
26 Monte Irvin	.25	.13	.08
27 Hank Sauer	.25	.13	.08
28 Sal Maglie	.25	.13	.08
29 Ernie Banks	.25	.13	.08
30 Billy Pierce	.25	.13	.08
31 Pee Wee Reese	.25	.13	.08
32 Al Lopez	.25	.13	.08
33 Allie Reynolds	.25	.13	.08
34 Eddie Mathews	.25	.13	.08
35 Al Rosen	.25	.13	.08
36 Early Wynn	.25	.13	.08
37 Phil Rizzuto	.25	.13	.08
38 Warren Spahn	.25	.13	.08
39 Bobby Thomson	.25	.13	.08
40 Enos Slaughter	.25	.13	.08
41 Roberto Clemente	4.00	2.00	1.25
42 Luis Aparicio	.25	.13	.08
43 Roy Sievers	.25	.13	.08
44 Hank Aaron	4.00	2.00	1.25
45 Mickey Vernon	.25	.13	.08
SERIES 2 - 1979	10.00	5.00	3.00
46 Lou Gehrig	3.00	1.50	.90
47 Lefty O'Doul	.25	.13	.08

#	Player	NM	E	VG
48	Chuck Klein	.25	.13	.08
49	Paul Waner	.25	.13	.08
50	Mel Ott	.25	.13	.08
51	Riggs Stephenson	.25	.13	.08
52	Dizzy Dean	.50	.25	.15
53	Frankie Frisch	.25	.13	.08
54	Red Ruffing	.25	.13	.08
55	Lefty Grove	.25	.13	.08
56	Heinie Manush	.25	.13	.08
57	Jimmie Foxx	.25	.13	.08
58	Al Simmons	.25	.13	.08
59	Charlie Root	.25	.13	.08
60	Goose Goslin	.25	.13	.08
61	Mickey Cochrane	.25	.13	.08
62	Gabby Hartnett	.25	.13	.08
63	Ducky Medwick	.25	.13	.08
64	Ernie Lombardi	.25	.13	.08
65	Joe Cronin	.25	.13	.08
66	Pepper Martin	.25	.13	.08
67	Jim Bottomley	.25	.13	.08
68	Bill Dickey	.25	.13	.08
69	Babe Ruth	5.00	2.50	1.50
70	Joe McCarthy	.25	.13	.08
71	Doc Cramer	.25	.13	.08
72	Kiki Cuyler	.25	.13	.08
73	Johnny Vander Meer	.25	.13	.08
74	Paul Derringer	.25	.13	.08
75	Freddie Fitzsimmons	.25	.13	.08
76	Lefty Gomez	.25	.13	.08
77	Arky Vaughan	.25	.13	.08
78	Stan Hack	.25	.13	.08
79	Earl Averill	.25	.13	.08
80	Luke Appling	.25	.13	.08
81	Mel Harder	.25	.13	.08
82	Hank Greenberg	.25	.13	.08
83	Schoolboy Rowe	.25	.13	.08
84	Billy Herman	.25	.13	.08
85	Gabby Street	.25	.13	.08
86	Lloyd Waner	.25	.13	.08
87	Jocko Conlan	.25	.13	.08
88	Carl Hubbell	.25	.13	.08
89	Series 1 checklist	.25	.13	.08
90	Series 2 checklist	.25	.13	.08
	SERIES 3 - 1980	7.50	3.75	2.25
91	Babe Ruth	3.00	1.50	.90
92	Rogers Hornsby	.25	.13	.08
93	Edd Roush	.25	.13	.08
94	George Sisler	.25	.13	.08
95	Harry Heilmann	.25	.13	.08
96	Tris Speaker	.25	.13	.08
97	Burleigh Grimes	.25	.13	.08
98	John McGraw	.25	.13	.08
99	Eppa Rixey	.25	.13	.08
100	Ty Cobb	1.00	.50	.30
101	Zack Wheat	.25	.13	.08
102	Pie Traynor	.25	.13	.08
103	Max Carey	.25	.13	.08
104	Dazzy Vance	.25	.13	.08
105	Walter Johnson	.50	.25	.15
106	Herb Pennock	.25	.13	.08
107	Joe Sewell	.25	.13	.08
108	Sam Rice	.25	.13	.08
109	Earle Combs	.25	.13	.08
110	Ted Lyons	.25	.13	.08
111	Eddie Collins	.25	.13	.08
112	Bill Terry	.25	.13	.08
113	Hack Wilson	.25	.13	.08
114	Rabbit Maranville	.25	.13	.08
115	Charlie Grimm	.25	.13	.08
116	Tony Lazzeri	.25	.13	.08
117	Waite Hoyt	.25	.13	.08
118	Stan Coveleski	.25	.13	.08
119	George Kelly	.25	.13	.08
120	Jimmy Dykes	.25	.13	.08
121	Red Faber	.25	.13	.08
122	Dave Bancroft	.25	.13	.08
123	Judge Landis	.25	.13	.08
124	Branch Rickey	.25	.13	.08
125	Jesse Haines	.25	.13	.08
126	Carl Mays	.25	.13	.08
127	Fred Lindstrom	.25	.13	.08
128	Miller Huggins	.25	.13	.08
129	Sad Sam Jones	.25	.13	.08
130	Joe Judge	.25	.13	.08
131	Ross Young (Youngs)	.25	.13	.08
132	Bucky Harris	.25	.13	.08
133	Bob Meusel	.25	.13	.08
134	Billy Evans	.25	.13	.08
135	1927 N.Y. Yankees Team Photo/Checklist	.50	.25	.15
	SERIES 4 - 1981	7.50	3.75	2.25
136	Ty Cobb	1.00	.50	.30
137	Nap Lajoie	.25	.13	.08
138	Tris Speaker	.25	.13	.08
139	Heinie Groh	.25	.13	.08
140	Sam Crawford	.25	.13	.08
141	Clyde Milan	.25	.13	.08
142	Chief Bender	.25	.13	.08

#	Player	NM	E	VG
143	Big Ed Walsh	.25	.13	.08
144	Walter Johnson	.50	.25	.15
145	Connie Mack	.25	.13	.08
146	Hal Chase	.25	.13	.08
147	Hugh Duffy	.25	.13	.08
148	Honus Wagner	.50	.25	.15
149	Tom Connolly	.25	.13	.08
150	Clark Griffith	.25	.13	.08
151	Zack Wheat	.25	.13	.08
152	Christy Mathewson	.50	.25	.15
153	Grover C. Alexander	.25	.13	.08
154	Joe Jackson	3.00	1.50	.90
155	Home Run Baker	.25	.13	.08
156	Ed Plank	.25	.13	.08
157	Larry Doyle	.25	.13	.08
158	Rube Marquard	.25	.13	.08
159	Johnny Evers	.25	.13	.08
160	Joe Tinker	.25	.13	.08
161	Frank Chance	.25	.13	.08
162	Wilbert Robinson	.25	.13	.08
163	Roger Peckinpaugh	.25	.13	.08
164	Fred Clarke	.25	.13	.08
165	Babe Ruth	3.00	1.50	.90
166	Wilbur Cooper	.25	.13	.08
167	Germany Schaefer	.25	.13	.08
168	Addie Joss	.25	.13	.08
169	Cy Young	.50	.25	.15
170	Ban Johnson	.25	.13	.08
171	Joe Judge	.25	.13	.08
172	Harry Hooper	.25	.13	.08
173	Bill Klem	.25	.13	.08
174	Ed Barrow	.25	.13	.08
175	Ed Cicotte	.25	.13	.08
176	Hughie Jennings	.25	.13	.08
177	Ray Schalk	.25	.13	.08
178	Nick Altrock	.25	.13	.08
179	Roger Bresnahan	.25	.13	.08
180	$100,000 Infield	.25	.13	.08
	SERIES 5 - 1983	7.50	3.75	2.25
181	Lou Gehrig	3.00	1.50	.90
182	Eddie Collins	.25	.13	.08
183	Art Fletcher	.25	.13	.08
184	Jimmie Foxx	.25	.13	.08
185	Lefty Gomez	.25	.13	.08
186	Oral Hildebrand	.25	.13	.08
187	General Crowder	.25	.13	.08
188	Bill Dickey	.25	.13	.08
189	Wes Ferrell	.25	.13	.08
190	Al Simmons	.25	.13	.08
191	Tony Lazzeri	.25	.13	.08
192	Sam West	.25	.13	.08
193	Babe Ruth	3.00	1.50	.90
194	Connie Mack	.25	.13	.08
195	Lefty Grove	.25	.13	.08
196	Eddie Rommel	.25	.13	.08
197	Ben Chapman	.25	.13	.08
198	Joe Cronin	.25	.13	.08
199	Rich Ferrell (Rick)	.25	.13	.08
200	Charlie Gehringer	.25	.13	.08
201	Jimmy Dykes	.25	.13	.08
202	Earl Averill	.25	.13	.08
203	Pepper Martin	.25	.13	.08
204	Bill Terry	.25	.13	.08
205	Pie Traynor	.25	.13	.08
206	Gabby Hartnett	.25	.13	.08
207	Frank Frisch	.25	.13	.08
208	Carl Hubbell	.25	.13	.08
209	Paul Waner	.25	.13	.08
210	Woody English	.25	.13	.08
211	Bill Hallahan	.25	.13	.08
212	Dick Bartell	.25	.13	.08
213	Bill McKechnie	.25	.13	.08
214	Max Carey	.25	.13	.08
215	John McGraw	.25	.13	.08
216	Jimmie Wilson	.25	.13	.08
217	Chick Hafey	.25	.13	.08
218	Chuck Klein	.25	.13	.08
219	Lefty O'Doul	.25	.13	.08
220	Wally Berger	.25	.13	.08
221	Hal Schumacher	.25	.13	.08
222	Lon Warneke	.25	.13	.08
223	Tony Cuccinello	.25	.13	.08
(224)	1933 A.L. All-Stars	.50	.25	.15
(225)	1933 N.L. All-Stars	.50	.25	.15
	SERIES 6 - 1984	15.00	7.50	4.50
226	Roger Maris	.75	.40	.25
227	Babe Ruth	3.00	1.50	.90
228	Jackie Robinson	2.00	1.00	.60
229	Pete Gray	.75	.40	.25
230	Ted Williams	3.00	1.50	.90
231	Hank Aaron	3.00	1.50	.90
232	Mickey Mantle	5.00	2.50	1.50
233	Gil Hodges	.25	.13	.08
234	Walter Johnson	.50	.25	.15
235	Joe DiMaggio	3.00	1.50	.90
236	Lou Gehrig	3.00	1.50	.90
237	Stan Musial	.75	.40	.25
238	Mickey Cochrane	.25	.13	.08

#	Player	NM	E	VG
239	Denny McLain	.25	.13	.08
240	Carl Hubbell	.25	.13	.08
241	Harvey Haddix	.25	.13	.08
242	Christy Mathewson	.50	.25	.15
243	Johnny VanderMeer	.25	.13	.08
244	Sandy Koufax	3.00	1.50	.90
245	Willie Mays	3.00	1.50	.90
246	Don Drysdale	.25	.13	.08
247	Bobby Richardson	.25	.13	.08
248	Hoyt Wilhelm	.25	.13	.08
249	Yankee Stadium	.25	.13	.08
250	Bill Terry	.25	.13	.08
251	Roy Campanella	.50	.25	.15
252	Roberto Clemente	3.00	1.50	.90
253	Casey Stengel	.25	.13	.08
254	Ernie Banks	.50	.25	.15
255	Bobby Thomson	.25	.13	.08
256	Mel Ott	.25	.13	.08
257	Tony Oliva	.25	.13	.08
258	Satchel Paige	1.00	.50	.30
259	Joe Jackson	3.00	1.50	.90
260	Larry Lajoie	.25	.13	.08
261	Bill Mazeroski	.25	.13	.08
262	Bill Wambsganss	.25	.13	.08
263	Willie McCovey	.25	.13	.08
264	Warren Spahn	.25	.13	.08
265	Lefty Gomez	.25	.13	.08
266	Dazzy Vance	.25	.13	.08
267	Sam Crawford	.25	.13	.08
268	Tris Speaker	.25	.13	.08
269	Lou Brock	.25	.13	.08
270	Cy Young	.25	.13	.08

1978 TCMA 1941 Brooklyn Dodgers

 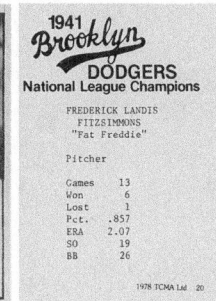

The National League Champion Brooklyn Dodgers are featured in the collectors' edition card set. Measuring 2-1/2" x 3-1/2", the cards have blue duotone player photos on front with the name and position overprinted in black at bottom. A white border surrounds the photo. Backs are in black-and-white with a large championship logo and a few stats from the 1941 season.

#	Player	NM	E	VG
	Complete Set (43):	25.00	12.50	7.50
	Common Player:	1.50	.75	.45
1	Mickey Owen	2.50	1.25	.70
2	Pee Wee Reese	7.50	3.75	2.25
3	Hugh Casey	1.50	.75	.45
4	Larry French	1.50	.75	.45
5	Tom Drake	1.50	.75	.45
6	Ed Albosta	1.50	.75	.45
7	Tommy Tatum	1.50	.75	.45
8	Paul Waner	3.50	1.75	1.00
9	Van Lingle Mungo	2.50	1.25	.70
10	Bill Swift	1.50	.75	.45
11	Dolph Camilli	2.50	1.25	.70
12	Pete Coscarart	1.50	.75	.45
13	Vito Tamulis	1.50	.75	.45
14	John Allen	1.50	.75	.45
15	Lee Grissom	1.50	.75	.45
16	Billy Herman	2.50	1.25	.70
17	Joe Vosmik	1.50	.75	.45
18	Babe Phelps	1.50	.75	.45
19	Mace Brown	1.50	.75	.45
20	Freddie Fitzsimmons	1.50	.75	.45
21	Angelo Guiliani	1.50	.75	.45
22	Lewis Riggs	1.50	.75	.45
23	Jimmy Wasdell	1.50	.75	.45
24	Herman Franks	1.50	.75	.45
25	Alex Kampouris	1.50	.75	.45
26	Kirby Higbe	1.50	.75	.45
27	Joe Medwick	2.50	1.25	.70
28	Newt Kimball	1.50	.75	.45
29	Curt Davis	1.50	.75	.45
30	Augie Galan	1.50	.75	.45
31	Luke Hamlin	1.50	.75	.45
32	Cookie Lavagetto	1.50	.75	.45
33	Joe Gallagher	1.50	.75	.45
34	Whitlow Wyatt	1.50	.75	.45

35	Dixie Walker	1.50	.75	.45
36	Pete Reiser	1.50	.75	.45
37	Leo Durocher	2.50	1.25	.70
38	Pee Wee Reese, Joe Medwick (3" x 5")	4.50	2.25	1.25
39	Dixie Walker, Joe Medwick, Dolph Camilli, Pete Reiser (3" x 5")	4.50	2.25	1.25
40	Team photo	3.00	1.50	.90
41	Kemp Wicker	1.50	.75	.45
42	George Pfister	2.00	1.00	.60
43	Chuck Dressen	1.50	.75	.45

1978 TCMA Baseball Nostalgia Postcard

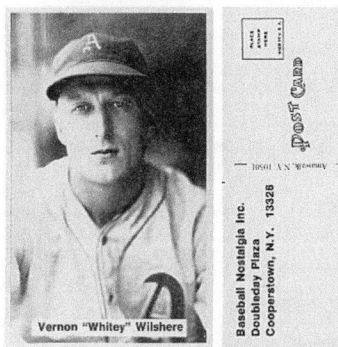

Vernon "Whitey" Wilshere

TCMA produced this card for Baseball Nostalgia, Inc., a Cooperstown, N.Y., hobby shop, in an edition of 500. The card pictures a Cooperstown resident who taught at the local high school following a short (1934-36) major league pitching career. The 3-1/2" x 5-1/2" black-and-white card has standard postcard markings on back.

	NM	E	VG
Vernon "Whitey" Wilshere	6.00	3.00	1.80

1978 TCMA The 1960's

Nearly 300 players of the 1960s are featured in this collectors issue. Fronts of the 2-1/2" x 3-1/2" cards have a color photo with a black frameline and white border. There are no other graphics. Backs are printed in green and include a lengthy career summary. On some cards the set's title, "The 1960's" is printed at top. Several mistakes in card numbering are noted in the accompanying checklist.

		NM	E	VG
Complete Set (293):		32.50	16.00	9.75
Common Player:		.25	.13	.08
1	Smoky Burgess	.25	.13	.08
2	Juan Marichal	1.00	.50	.30
3	Don Drysdale	1.00	.50	.30
4	Jim Gentile	.25	.13	.08
5	Roy Face	.25	.13	.08
6	Joe Pepitone	.25	.13	.08
7	Joe Christopher	.25	.13	.08
8	Wayne Causey	.25	.13	.08
9	Frank Bolling	.25	.13	.08
10	Jim Maloney	.25	.13	.08
11	Roger Maris	2.50	1.25	.70
12	Bill White	.25	.13	.08
13	Roberto Clemente	7.50	3.75	2.25
14	Bob Saverine	.25	.13	.08
15	Barney Schultz	.25	.13	.08
16	Albie Pearson	.25	.13	.08
17	Denny Lemaster	.25	.13	.08
18	Ernie Broglio	.25	.13	.08
19	Bobby Klaus	.25	.13	.08
20	Tony Cloninger	.25	.13	.08
21	Whitey Ford	1.50	.70	.45
22	Ron Santo	.60	.30	.20

23	Jim Duckworth	.25	.13	.08
24	Willie Davis	.25	.13	.08
25	Ed Charles	.25	.13	.08
26	Bob Allison	.25	.13	.08
27	Fritz Ackley	.25	.13	.08
28	Ruben Amaro	.25	.13	.08
29	Johnny Callison	.25	.13	.08
30	Greg Bollo	.25	.13	.08
31	Felix Millan	.25	.13	.08
32	Camilo Pascual	.25	.13	.08
33	Jackie Brandt	.25	.13	.08
34	Don Lock	.25	.13	.08
35	Chico Ruiz	.25	.13	.08
36	Joe Azcue	.25	.13	.08
37	Ed Bailey	.25	.13	.08
38	Pete Ramos	.25	.13	.08
39	Eddie Bressoud	.25	.13	.08
40	Al Kaline	1.50	.70	.45
41	Ron Brand	.25	.13	.08
42	Bob Lillis	.25	.13	.08
43	Not Issued (See #125.)	.25	.13	.08
44	Buster Narum	.25	.13	.08
45	Jim Gilliam	.25	.13	.08
46	Claude Raymond	.25	.13	.08
47	Billy Bryan	.25	.13	.08
48	Marshall Bridges	.25	.13	.08
49	Norm Cash	.45	.25	.14
50	Orlando Cepeda	1.00	.50	.30
51	Lee Maye	.25	.13	.08
52	Andre Rodgers	.25	.13	.08
53	Ken Berry	.25	.13	.08
54	Don Mincher	.25	.13	.08
55	Jerry Lumpe	.25	.13	.08
56	Milt Pappas	.25	.13	.08
57	Steve Barber	.25	.13	.08
58	Denis Menke	.25	.13	.08
59	Larry Maxie	.25	.13	.08
60	Bob Gibson	1.00	.50	.30
61	Larry Bearnarth	.25	.13	.08
62	Bill Mazeroski	1.00	.50	.30
63	Bob Rodgers	.25	.13	.08
64	Jerry Arrigo	.25	.13	.08
65	Joe Nuxhall	.25	.13	.08
66	Dean Chance	.25	.13	.08
67	Ken Boyer	.60	.30	.20
68	John Odom	.25	.13	.08
69	Chico Cardenas	.25	.13	.08
70	Maury Wills	.35	.20	.11
71	Tony Oliva	.45	.25	.14
72	Don Nottebart	.25	.13	.08
73	Joe Adcock	.25	.13	.08
74	Felipe Alou	.25	.13	.08
75	Matty Alou	.25	.13	.08
76	Dick Radatz	.25	.13	.08
77	Jim Bouton	.25	.13	.08
78	John Blanchard	.25	.13	.08
79	Juan Pizarro	.25	.13	.08
80	Boog Powell	.45	.25	.14
81	Earl Robinson	.25	.13	.08
82	Bob Chance	.25	.13	.08
83	Max Alvis	.25	.13	.08
84	Don Blasingame	.25	.13	.08
85	Tom Cheney	.25	.13	.08
86	Jerry Arrigo	.25	.13	.08
87	Tommy Davis	.25	.13	.08
88	Steve Boros	.25	.13	.08
89	Don Cardwell	.25	.13	.08
90	Harmon Killebrew	1.50	.70	.45
91	Jim Pagliaroni	.25	.13	.08
92	Jim O'Toole	.25	.13	.08
93	Dennis Bennett	.25	.13	.08
94	Dick McAuliffe	.25	.13	.08
95	Dick Brown	.25	.13	.08
96	Joe Amalfitano	.25	.13	.08
97	Phil Linz	.25	.13	.08
98	Not Issued (See #165.)	.25	.13	.08
99	Dave Nicholson	.25	.13	.08
100	Hoyt Wilhelm	1.00	.50	.30
101	Don Leppert	.25	.13	.08
102	Jose Pagan	.25	.13	.08
103	Sam McDowell	.25	.13	.08
104	Jack Baldschun	.25	.13	.08
105	Jim Perry	.25	.13	.08
106	Hal Reniff	.25	.13	.08
107	Lee Maye	.25	.13	.08
108	Joe Adcock	.25	.13	.08
109	Bob Bolin	.25	.13	.08
110	Don Leppert	.25	.13	.08
111	Bill Monbouquette	.25	.13	.08
112	Bobby Richardson	.45	.25	.14
113	Earl Battey	.25	.13	.08
114	Bob Veale	.25	.13	.08
115	Lou Jackson	.25	.13	.08
116	Frank Kreutzer	.25	.13	.08
117	Jerry Zimmerman	.25	.13	.08
118	Don Schwall	.25	.13	.08
119	Rich Rollins	.25	.13	.08
120	Pete Ward	.25	.13	.08

121	Moe Drabowsky	.25	.13	.08
122	Jesse Gonder	.25	.13	.08
123	Hal Woodeshick	.25	.13	.08
124	John Herrnstein	.25	.13	.08
125a	Gary Peters (Should be #43.)	.25	.13	.08
125b	Leon Wagner	.25	.13	.08
126	Dwight Siebler	.25	.13	.08
027	Gary Kroll	.25	.13	.08
128	Tony Horton	.25	.13	.08
129	John DeMerit	.25	.13	.08
130	Sandy Koufax	6.00	3.00	1.75
131	Jim Davenport	.25	.13	.08
132	Wes Covington	.25	.13	.08
133	Tony Taylor	.25	.13	.08
134	Jack Kralick	.25	.13	.08
135	Bill Pleis	.25	.13	.08
136	Russ Snyder	.25	.13	.08
137	Joe Torre	.75	.40	.25
138	Ted Wills	.25	.13	.08
139	Wes Stock	.25	.13	.08
140	Frank Robinson	1.50	.70	.45
141	Dave Stenhouse	.25	.13	.08
142	Ron Hansen	.25	.13	.08
143	Don Elston	.25	.13	.08
144	Del Crandall	.25	.13	.08
145	Bennie Daniels	.25	.13	.08
146	Vada Pinson	.45	.25	.14
147	Bill Spanswick	.25	.13	.08
148	Earl Wilson	.25	.13	.08
149	Ty Cline	.25	.13	.08
150	Dick Groat	.25	.13	.08
151	Jim Duckworth	.25	.13	.08
152	Jimmie Schaffer	.25	.13	.08
153	George Thomas	.25	.13	.08
154	Wes Stock	.25	.13	.08
155	Mike White	.25	.13	.08
156	John Podres	.25	.13	.08
157	Willie Crawford	.25	.13	.08
158	Fred Gladding	.25	.13	.08
159	John Wyatt	.25	.13	.08
160	Bob Friend	.25	.13	.08
161	Ted Uhlaender	.25	.13	.08
162	Dick Stigman	.25	.13	.08
163	Don Wert	.25	.13	.08
164	Eddie Bressoud	.25	.13	.08
165a	Ed Roebuck (Should be #98.)	.25	.13	.08
165b	Leon Wagner	.25	.13	.08
166	Al Spangler	.25	.13	.08
167	Bob Sadowski	.25	.13	.08
168	Ralph Terry	.25	.13	.08
169	Jimmie Schaffer	.25	.13	.08
170a	Jim Fregosi (Should be #180.)	.25	.13	.08
170b	Dick Hall	.25	.13	.08
171	Al Spangler	.25	.13	.08
172	Bob Tillman	.25	.13	.08
173	Ed Bailey	.25	.13	.08
174	Cesar Tovar	.25	.13	.08
175	Morrie Stevens	.25	.13	.08
176	Floyd Weaver	.25	.13	.08
177	Frank Malzone	.25	.13	.08
178	Norm Siebern	.25	.13	.08
179	Dick Phillips	.25	.13	.08
180	Not Issued (See #170.)	.25	.13	.08
181	Bobby Wine	.25	.13	.08
182	Masanori Murakami	.75	.40	.25
183	Chuck Schilling	.25	.13	.08
184	Jimmie Schaffer	.25	.13	.08
185	John Roseboro	.25	.13	.08
186	Jake Wood	.25	.13	.08
187	Dallas Green	.25	.13	.08
188	Tom Haller	.25	.13	.08
189	Chuck Cottier	.25	.13	.08
190	Brooks Robinson	1.50	.70	.45
191	Ty Cline	.25	.13	.08
192	Bubba Phillips	.25	.13	.08
193	Al Jackson	.25	.13	.08
194	Herm Starrette	.25	.13	.08
195	Dave Wickersham	.25	.13	.08
196	Vic Power	.25	.13	.08
197	Ray Culp	.25	.13	.08
198	Don Demeter	.25	.13	.08
199	Dick Schofield	.25	.13	.08
200	Stephen Grant	.25	.13	.08
201	Roger Craig	.25	.13	.08
202	Dick Farrell	.25	.13	.08
203	Clay Dalrymple	.25	.13	.08
204	Jim Duffalo	.25	.13	.08
205	Tito Francona	.25	.13	.08
206	Tony Conigliaro	.45	.25	.14
207	Jim King	.25	.13	.08
208	Joe Gibbon	.25	.13	.08
209	Arnold Earley	.25	.13	.08
210	Denny McLain	.25	.13	.08
211	Don Larsen	.25	.13	.08
212	Ron Hunt	.25	.13	.08

213	Deron Johnson	.25	.13	.08
214	Harry Bright	.25	.13	.08
215	Ernie Fazio	.25	.13	.08
216	Joey Jay	.25	.13	.08
217	Jim Coates	.25	.13	.08
218	Jerry Kindall	.25	.13	.08
219	Joe Gibbon	.25	.13	.08
220	Frank Howard	.35	.20	.11
221	Howie Koplitz	.25	.13	.08
222	Larry Jackson	.25	.13	.08
223	Dale Long	.25	.13	.08
224	Jimmy Dykes	.25	.13	.08
225	Hank Aguirre	.25	.13	.08
226	Earl Francis	.25	.13	.08
227	Vic Wertz	.25	.13	.08
228	Larry Haney	.25	.13	.08
229	Tony LaRussa	.45	.25	.14
230	Moose Skowron	.35	.20	.11
231a	Tito Francona (Should be #235.)	.25	.13	.08
231b	Lee Thomas	.25	.13	.08
232	Ken Johnson	.25	.13	.08
233	Dick Howser	.25	.13	.08
234	Bobby Knoop	.25	.13	.08
235	Not Issued (See #231.)	.25	.13	.08
236	Elston Howard	.35	.20	.11
237	Donn Clendenon	.25	.13	.08
238	Jesse Gonder	.25	.13	.08
239	Vern Law	.25	.13	.08
240	Curt Flood	.25	.13	.08
241	Dal Maxvill	.25	.13	.08
242	Roy Sievers	.25	.13	.08
243	Jim Brewer	.25	.13	.08
244	Harry Craft	.25	.13	.08
245	Dave Eilers	.25	.13	.08
246	Dave DeBusschere	.25	.13	.08
247	Ken Harrelson	.25	.13	.08
248	Not Issued (See #249.)	.25	.13	.08
249a	Jim Duffalo	.25	.13	.08
249b	Eddie Kasko (Should be #248.)	.25	.13	.08
250	Luis Aparicio	1.00	.50	.30
251	Ron Kline	.25	.13	.08
252	Chuck Hinton	.25	.13	.08
253	Frank Lary	.25	.13	.08
254	Stu Miller	.25	.13	.08
255	Ernie Banks	2.00	1.00	.60
256	Dick Farrell	.25	.13	.08
257	Bud Daley	.25	.13	.08
258	Luis Arroyo	.25	.13	.08
259	Bob Del Greco	.25	.13	.08
260	Ted Williams	6.00	3.00	1.75
261	Mike Epstein	.25	.13	.08
262	Mickey Mantle	10.00	5.00	3.00
263	Jim LeFebvre	.25	.13	.08
264	Pat Jarvis	.25	.13	.08
265	Chuck Hinton	.25	.13	.08
266	Don Larsen	.25	.13	.08
267	Jim Coates	.25	.13	.08
268	Gary Kolb	.25	.13	.08
269	Jim Ray Hart	.25	.13	.08
270	Dave McNally	.25	.13	.08
271	Jerry Kindall	.25	.13	.08
272	Hector Lopez	.25	.13	.08
273	Claude Osteen	.25	.13	.08
274	Jack Aker	.25	.13	.08
275	Mike Shannon	.25	.13	.08
276	Lew Burdette	.25	.13	.08
277	Mack Jones	.25	.13	.08
278	Art Shamsky	.25	.13	.08
279	Bob Johnson	.25	.13	.08
280	Willie Mays	6.00	3.00	1.75
281	Rich Nye	.25	.13	.08
282	Bill Cowan	.25	.13	.08
283	Gary Kolb	.25	.13	.08
284	Woody Held	.25	.13	.08
285	Bill Freehan	.25	.13	.08
286	Larry Jackson	.25	.13	.08
287	Mike Hershberger	.25	.13	.08
288	Julian Javier	.25	.13	.08
289	Charley Smith	.25	.13	.08
290	Hank Aaron	6.00	3.00	1.75
291	John Boccabella	.25	.13	.08
292	Charley James	.25	.13	.08
293	Sammy Ellis	.25	.13	.08

1979 TCMA 1927 New York Yankees

Perhaps the finest baseball team of all time is featured in this collectors' set. The sepia oval photos at center are surrounded by black-and-white graphics of baseball equipment and other ornamentation. Player name and position are in a strip beneath the photo. Backs have personal data and a career summary. The cards are in standard 2-1/2" x 3-1/2".

1927 NEW YORK YANKEES
ARTHUR FLETCHER
COACH

Ht. 5-10 Wt. 170 Ba. R Th. R
Bn. 1/5/85 Dd. 2/6/50

Art coached for the Yankees from '27 to '45 and managed the team for the last 11 games in '29 when Miller Huggins died. Prior to his coaching career with the Yankees, he was a shortstop for the New York Giants and Philadelphia Phillies in a 13-year big league career. '09-'22. He was the Giants' regular shortstop from '12 to '20 when he was shipped to the Phillies and became their regular shortstop for two seasons. Art was a .277 lifetime hitter and played in four World Series, all with the Giants. He also managed the Phillies from '23 to '26, but finished no higher than sixth place.

© TCMA 1979   7

		NM	E	VG
	Complete Set (32):	20.00	10.00	6.00
	Common Player:	1.00	.50	.30
1	Babe Ruth	6.00	3.00	1.75
2	Lou Gehrig	4.00	2.00	1.25
3	Tony Lazzeri	1.00	.50	.30
4	Mark Koenig	1.00	.50	.30
5	Julie Wera	1.00	.50	.30
6	Ray Morehart	1.00	.50	.30
7	Art Fletcher	1.00	.50	.30
8	Joe Dugan	1.00	.50	.30
9	Charley O'Leary	1.00	.50	.30
10	Bob Meusel	1.00	.50	.30
11	Earle Combs	1.00	.50	.30
12	Cedric Durst	1.00	.50	.30
13	Johnny Grabowski	1.00	.50	.30
14	Mike Gazella	1.00	.50	.30
15	Pat Collins	1.00	.50	.30
16	Waite Hoyt	1.00	.50	.30
17	Myles Thomas	1.00	.50	.30
18	Benny Bengough	1.00	.50	.30
19	Herb Pennock	1.00	.50	.30
20	Wilcy Moore	1.00	.50	.30
21	Urban Shocker	1.00	.50	.30
22	Dutch Ruether	1.00	.50	.30
23	George Pipgras	1.00	.50	.30
24	Jacob Ruppert	1.00	.50	.30
25	Eddie Bennett	1.00	.50	.30
26	Ed Barrow	1.00	.50	.30
27	Ben Paschal	1.00	.50	.30
28	Miller Huggins	1.00	.50	.30
29	Joe Giard	1.00	.50	.30
30	Bob Shawkey	1.00	.50	.30
31	Walter Beall	1.00	.50	.30
32	Don Miller	1.00	.50	.30

1979 TCMA All Time Tigers

ALL TIME
DETROIT TIGER
TEAM

Hank Greenberg	1B
Charlie Gehringer	2B
George Kell	3B
Billy Rogell	SS
Ty Cobb	OF
Harry Heilmann	OF
Al Kaline	OF
Mickey Cochrane	C
Denny McLain	RHP
Hal Newhouser	LHP
Terry Fox	RP
Steve O'Neil	Mgr

T.C.M.A. Ltd. 1979

Utilizing a format similar to its several minor league team sets of the same year, this collectors' issue from TCMA features an "All Time" Tigers team selection of position players, pitchers and manager. The 2-1/2" x 3-1/2" cards have black-and-white photos on front with the player's name and position in an orange "wave" at bottom; the whole is surrounded by a white border. Backs are in black-and-white and detail the all-time line-up. The unnumbered cards are checklisted here alphabetically.

		NM	E	VG
	Complete Set (12):	20.00	10.00	6.00
	Common Player:	1.50	.70	.45
(1)	Ty Cobb	6.00	3.00	1.75
(2)	Mickey Cochrane	1.50	.70	.45
(3)	Terry Fox	1.50	.70	.45
(4)	Charlie Gehringer	2.50	1.25	.70
(5)	Hank Greenberg	5.00	2.50	1.50
(6)	Harry Heilmann	1.50	.70	.45
(7)	Al Kaline	5.00	2.50	1.50
(8)	George Kell	1.50	.70	.45
(9)	Denny McLain	1.50	.70	.45
(10)	Hal Newhouser	1.50	.70	.45
(11)	Steve O'Neil (O'Neill)	1.50	.70	.45
(12)	Billy Rogell	1.50	.70	.45

1979 TCMA Baseball History Series: The Fifties

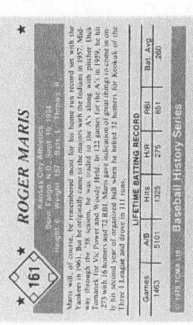

The "pure" format of the 1953 Bowman set was borrowed in this collectors' issue featuring the stars and journeymen of baseball in the 1950s. The 2-1/2" x 3-1/2" cards have color photos on front with white borders. Backs are in red and black with personal data and career summary and stats. Each set originally sold by TCMA came with two large-format (5" x 3-1/2") team-photo cards.

		NM	E	VG
	Complete Set (291):	27.50	13.50	8.25
	Common Player:	.25	.13	.08
1	Joe DiMaggio	7.50	3.75	2.25
2	Yogi Berra	1.50	.70	.45
3	Warren Spahn	.75	.40	.25
4	Robin Roberts	.60	.30	.20
5	Ernie Banks	1.50	.70	.45
6	Willie Mays	5.00	2.50	1.50
7	Mickey Mantle	10.00	5.00	3.00
8	Roy Campanella	1.50	.70	.45
9	Stan Musial	4.00	2.00	1.25
10	Ted Williams	5.00	2.50	1.50
11	Ed Bailey	.25	.13	.08
12	Ted Kluszewski	.60	.30	.20
13	Ralph Kiner	.60	.30	.20
14	Dick Littlefield	.25	.13	.08
15	Nellie Fox	.60	.30	.20
16	Billy Pierce	.25	.13	.08
17	Richie Ashburn	.60	.30	.20
18	Del Ennis	.25	.13	.08
19	Bob Lemon	.50	.25	.15
20	Early Wynn	.50	.25	.15
21	Joe Collins	.25	.13	.08
22	Hank Bauer	.25	.13	.08
23	Roberto Clemente	6.00	3.00	1.75
24	Frank Thomas	.25	.13	.08
25	Alvin Dark	.25	.13	.08
26	Whitey Lockman	.25	.13	.08
27	Larry Doby	.60	.30	.20
28	Bob Feller	.75	.40	.25
29	Willie Jones	.25	.13	.08
30	Granny Hamner	.25	.13	.08
31	Clem Labine	.25	.13	.08
32	Ralph Branca	.25	.13	.08
33	Jack Harshman	.25	.13	.08
34	Dick Donovan	.25	.13	.08
35	Tommy Henrich	.25	.13	.08
36	Jerry Coleman	.25	.13	.08
37	Billy Hoeft	.25	.13	.08
38	Johnny Groth	.25	.13	.08
39	Harvey Haddix	.25	.13	.08
40	Gerry Staley	.25	.13	.08
41	Dale Long	.25	.13	.08
42	Vern Law	.25	.13	.08
43	Dodger Power	1.50	.70	.45
44	Sam Jethroe	.25	.13	.08
45	Vic Wertz	.25	.13	.08
46	Wes Westrum	.25	.13	.08
47	Dee Fondy	.25	.13	.08
48	Gene Baker	.25	.13	.08
49	Sandy Koufax	5.00	2.50	1.50
50	Billy Loes	.25	.13	.08
51	Chuck Diering	.25	.13	.08
52	Joe Ginsberg	.25	.13	.08
53	Jim Konstanty	.25	.13	.08
54	Curt Simmons	.25	.13	.08
55	Alex Kellner	.25	.13	.08
56	Charlie Dressen	.25	.13	.08
57	Frank Sullivan	.25	.13	.08
58	Mel Parnell	.25	.13	.08
59	Bobby Hofman	.25	.13	.08
60	Bill Connelly	.25	.13	.08
61	Corky Valentine	.25	.13	.08
62	Johnny Klippstein	.25	.13	.08
63	Chuck Tanner	.25	.13	.08
64	Dick Drott	.25	.13	.08
65	Dean Stone	.25	.13	.08
66	Jim Busby	.25	.13	.08
67	Sid Gordon	.25	.13	.08
68	Del Crandall	.25	.13	.08

69	Walker Cooper	.25	.13	.08
70	Hank Sauer	.25	.13	.08
71	Gil Hodges	.75	.40	.25
72	Duke Snider	1.00	.50	.30
73	Sherman Lollar	.25	.13	.08
74	Chico Carrasquel	.25	.13	.08
75	Gus Triandos	.25	.13	.08
76	Bob Harrison	.25	.13	.08
77	Eddie Waitkus	.25	.13	.08
78	Ken Heintzelman	.25	.13	.08
79	Harry Simpson	.25	.13	.08
80	Luke Easter	.25	.13	.08
81	Ed Dick	.25	.13	.08
82	Jim DePaola	.25	.13	.08
83	Billy Cox	.25	.13	.08
84	Pee Wee Reese	1.00	.50	.30
85	Virgil Trucks	.25	.13	.08
86	George Kell	.50	.25	.15
87	Mickey Vernon	.25	.13	.08
88	Eddie Yost	.25	.13	.08
89	Gus Bell	.25	.13	.08
90	Wally Post	.25	.13	.08
91	Ed Lopat	.25	.13	.08
92	Dick Wakefield	.25	.13	.08
93	Solly Hemus	.25	.13	.08
94	Al "Red" Schoendienst	.60	.30	.20
95	Sammy White	.25	.13	.08
96	Billy Goodman	.25	.13	.08
97	Jim Hearn	.25	.13	.08
98	Ruben Gomez	.25	.13	.08
99	Marty Marion	.25	.13	.08
100	Bill Virdon	.25	.13	.08
101	Chuck Stobbs	.25	.13	.08
102	Ron Samford	.25	.13	.08
103	Bill Tuttle	.25	.13	.08
104	Harvey Kuenn	.25	.13	.08
105	Joe Cunningham	.25	.13	.08
106	Bill Sarni	.25	.13	.08
107	Jack Kramer	.25	.13	.08
108	Eddie Stanky	.25	.13	.08
109	Carmen Mauro	.25	.13	.08
110	Wayne Belardi	.25	.13	.08
111	Preston Ward	.25	.13	.08
112	Jack Shepard	.25	.13	.08
113	Buddy Kerr	.25	.13	.08
114	Vern Bickford	.25	.13	.08
115	Ellis Kinder	.25	.13	.08
116	Walt Dropo	.25	.13	.08
117	Duke Maas	.25	.13	.08
118	Billy Hunter	.25	.13	.08
119	Ewell Blackwell	.25	.13	.08
120	Hershell Freeman	.25	.13	.08
121	Freddie Martin	.25	.13	.08
122	Erv Dusak	.25	.13	.08
123	Roy Hartsfield	.25	.13	.08
124	Willard Marshall	.25	.13	.08
125	Jack Sanford	.25	.13	.08
126	Herm Wehmeier	.25	.13	.08
127	Hal Smith	.25	.13	.08
128	Jim Finigan	.25	.13	.08
129	Bob Hale	.25	.13	.08
130	Jim Wilson	.25	.13	.08
131	Bill Wight	.25	.13	.08
132	Mike Fornieles	.25	.13	.08
133	Steve Gromek	.25	.13	.08
134	Herb Score	.35	.20	.11
135	Ryne Duren	.25	.13	.08
136	Bob Turley	.25	.13	.08
137	Wally Moon	.25	.13	.08
138	Fred Hutchinson	.25	.13	.08
139	Jim Hegan	.25	.13	.08
140	Dale Mitchell	.25	.13	.08
141	Walt Moryn	.25	.13	.08
142	Cal Neeman	.25	.13	.08
143	Billy Martin	.50	.25	.15
144	Phil Rizzuto	1.00	.50	.30
145	Preacher Roe	.25	.13	.08
146	Carl Erskine	.25	.13	.08
147	Vic Power	.25	.13	.08
148	Elmer Valo	.25	.13	.08
149	Don Mueller	.25	.13	.08
150	Hank Thompson	.25	.13	.08
151	Stan Lopata	.25	.13	.08
152	Dick Sisler	.25	.13	.08
153	Willard Schmidt	.25	.13	.08
154	Roy McMillan	.25	.13	.08
155	Gil McDougald	.25	.13	.08
156	Gene Woodling	.25	.13	.08
157	Eddie Mathews	.75	.40	.25
158	Johnny Logan	.25	.13	.08
159	Dan Bankhead	.25	.13	.08
160	Joe Black	.25	.13	.08
161	Roger Maris	1.50	.70	.45
162	Bob Cerv	.25	.13	.08
163	Paul Minner	.25	.13	.08
164	Bob Rush	.25	.13	.08
165	Gene Hermanski	.25	.13	.08
166	Harry Brecheen	.25	.13	.08
167	Davey Williams	.25	.13	.08
168	Monte Irvin	.60	.30	.20
169	Clint Courtney	.25	.13	.08
170	Sandy Consuegra	.25	.13	.08
171	Bobby Shantz	.25	.13	.08
172	Harry Byrd	.25	.13	.08
173	Marv Throneberry	.25	.13	.08
174	Woody Held	.25	.13	.08
175	Al Rosen	.25	.13	.08
176	Rance Pless	.25	.13	.08
177	Steve Bilko	.25	.13	.08
178	Joe Presko	.25	.13	.08
179	Ray Boone	.25	.13	.08
180	Jim Lemon	.25	.13	.08
181	Andy Pafko	.25	.13	.08
182	Don Newcombe	.35	.20	.11
183	Frank Lary	.25	.13	.08
184	Al Kaline	.75	.40	.25
185	Allie Reynolds	.25	.13	.08
186	Vic Raschi	.25	.13	.08
187	**Dodger Braintrust**	.50	.25	.15
188	Jim Piersall	.25	.13	.08
189	George Wilson	.25	.13	.08
190	Jim "Dusty" Rhodes	.25	.13	.08
191	Duane Pillette	.25	.13	.08
192	Dave Philley	.25	.13	.08
193	Bobby Morgan	.25	.13	.08
194	Russ Meyer	.25	.13	.08
195	Hector Lopez	.25	.13	.08
196	Arnie Portocarrero	.25	.13	.08
197	Joe Page	.25	.13	.08
198	Tommy Byrne	.25	.13	.08
199	Ray Monzant	.25	.13	.08
200	John "Windy" McCall	.25	.13	.08
201	Leo Durocher	.50	.25	.15
202	Bobby Thomson	.35	.20	.11
203	Jack Banta	.25	.13	.08
204	Joe Pignatano	.25	.13	.08
205	Carlos Paula	.25	.13	.08
206	Roy Sievers	.25	.13	.08
207	Mickey McDermott	.25	.13	.08
208	Ray Scarborough	.25	.13	.08
209	Bill Miller	.25	.13	.08
210	Bill Skowron	.25	.13	.08
211	Bob Nieman	.25	.13	.08
212	Al Pilarcik	.25	.13	.08
213	Jerry Priddy	.25	.13	.08
214	Frank House	.25	.13	.08
215	Don Mossi	.25	.13	.08
216	Rocky Colavito	.60	.30	.20
217	Brooks Lawrence	.25	.13	.08
218	Ted Wilks	.25	.13	.08
219	Zack Monroe	.25	.13	.08
220	Art Ditmar	.25	.13	.08
221	Cal McLish	.25	.13	.08
222	Gene Bearden	.25	.13	.08
223	Norm Siebern	.25	.13	.08
224	Bob Wiesler	.25	.13	.08
225	Foster Castleman	.25	.13	.08
226	Daryl Spencer	.25	.13	.08
227	Dick Williams	.25	.13	.08
228	Don Zimmer	.25	.13	.08
229	Jackie Jensen	.25	.13	.08
230	Billy Johnson	.25	.13	.08
231	Dave Koslo	.25	.13	.08
232	Al Corwin	.25	.13	.08
233	Erv Palica	.25	.13	.08
234	Bob Milliken	.25	.13	.08
235	Ray Katt	.25	.13	.08
236	Sammy Calderone	.25	.13	.08
237	Don Demeter	.25	.13	.08
238	Karl Spooner	.25	.13	.08
239	The Veteran and The Rookie	.50	.25	.15
240	Enos Slaughter	.50	.25	.15
241	Dick Kryhoski	.25	.13	.08
242	Art Houtteman	.25	.13	.08
243	Andy Carey	.25	.13	.08
244	Tony Kubek	.35	.20	.11
245	Mike McCormick	.25	.13	.08
246	Bob Schmidt	.25	.13	.08
247	Nelson King	.25	.13	.08
248	Bob Skinner	.25	.13	.08
249	Dick Bokelmann	.25	.13	.08
250	Eddie Kazak	.25	.13	.08
251	Billy Klaus	.25	.13	.08
252	Norm Zauchin	.25	.13	.08
253	Art Schult	.25	.13	.08
254	Bob Martyn	.25	.13	.08
255	Larry Jansen	.25	.13	.08
256	Sal Maglie	.25	.13	.08
257	Bob Darnell	.25	.13	.08
258	Ken Lehman	.25	.13	.08
259	Jim Blackburn	.25	.13	.08
260	Bob Purkey	.25	.13	.08
261	Harry Walker	.25	.13	.08
262	Joe Garagiola	.35	.20	.11
263	Gus Zernial	.25	.13	.08
264	Walter "Hoot" Evers	.25	.13	.08
265	Mark Freeman	.25	.13	.08
266	Charlie Silvera	.25	.13	.08
267	Johnny Podres	.25	.13	.08
268	Jim Hughes	.25	.13	.08
269	Al Worthington	.25	.13	.08
270	Hoyt Wilhelm	.50	.25	.15
271	Elston Howard	.25	.13	.08
272	Don Larsen	.40	.20	.12
273	Don Hoak	.25	.13	.08
274	Chico Fernandez	.25	.13	.08
275	Gail Harris	.25	.13	.08
276	Valmy Thomas	.25	.13	.08
277	George Shuba	.25	.13	.08
278	Al "Rube" Walker	.25	.13	.08
279	Willard Ramsdell	.25	.13	.08
280	Lindy McDaniel	.25	.13	.08
281	Bob Wilson	.25	.13	.08
282	Chuck Templeton	.25	.13	.08
283	Eddie Robinson	.25	.13	.08
284	Bob Porterfield	.25	.13	.08
285	Larry Miggins	.25	.13	.08
286	Minnie Minoso	.25	.13	.08
287	Lou Boudreau	.50	.25	.15
288	Jim Davenport	.25	.13	.08
289	Bob Miller	.25	.13	.08
290	Jim Gilliam	.25	.13	.08
291	Jackie Robinson	4.00	2.00	1.25

Bonus 1955 Brooklyn Dodgers

1	Team Card	10.00	5.00	3.00

Bonus 1957 Milwaukee Braves

2	Team	10.00	5.00	3.00

1979 TCMA Japan Pro Baseball

 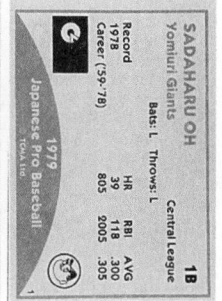

Stars of Japan's Pacific and Central "major" leagues are featured in this collectors' issue. More than a dozen Americans playing or managing in Japan at the time are included in the set, as well as several Japanese Hall of Famers including home-run king Sadaharu Oh. Cards feature a color posed portrait with a light blue semi-circle at bottom containing the team and player name in royal blue. Backs are printed in red and black on white and have a few personal data, 1978 and career stats, plus league and team logos and TCMA copyright. Cards are nominally standard 2-1/2" x 3-1/2" in size, but actual size varies a bit due to cutting discrepancies.

		NM	E	VG
	Complete Set (90):	40.00	20.00	12.00
	Common Player:	.50	.25	.15
1	Sadaharu Oh	15.00	7.50	4.50
2	Jinten Haku	.50	.25	.15
3	Toshizo Sakamoto	.50	.25	.15
4	Tony Muser	1.00	.50	.30
5	Makoto Matsubara	.50	.25	.15
6	Masayuki Nakaysuka	.50	.25	.15
7	Daisuke Yamashita	.50	.25	.15
8	Koji Yamamoto	.50	.25	.15
9	Sachio Kinugasa	4.00	2.00	1.25
10	Bernie Williams	.60	.30	.20
11	Bobby Marcano	.60	.30	.20
12	Koichi Tabuchi	.50	.25	.15
13	Katsuya Nomura	3.00	1.50	.90
14	Jack Maloof	.60	.30	.20
15	Masahiro Doi	.50	.25	.15
16	Hiroyuki Yamazaki	.50	.25	.15
17	Vernon Law	2.00	1.00	.60
18	Dave Hilton	.60	.30	.20
19	Katsuo Osugi	.50	.25	.15
20	Tsutomu Wakamatsu	.50	.25	.15
21	John Scott	.60	.30	.20
22	Toru Sugiura	.50	.25	.15
23	Akihiko Kondo	.50	.25	.15
24	Shintaro Mizutani	.50	.25	.15
25	Tatsuro Hirooka	.50	.25	.15
26	Kojiro Ikegaya	.50	.25	.15
27	Yutaka Enatsu	1.50	.70	.45
28	Tomehiro Kaneda	.50	.25	.15
29	Yoshihiko Takahashi	.50	.25	.15
30	Jitsuo Mizutani	.50	.25	.15
31	Adrian Garrett	.60	.30	.20

32	Jim Lyttle	.60	.30	.20
33	Takeshi Koba	.50	.25	.15
34	Sam Ewing	.60	.30	.20
35	Kazumi Takahashi	.50	.25	.15
36	Kazushi Saeki	.50	.25	.15
37	Masanori Murakami	7.50	3.75	2.25
38	Toshiro Kato	.50	.25	.15
39	Junichi Kashiwabara	.50	.25	.15
40	Masaru Tomita	.50	.25	.15
41	Bobby Mitchell	.60	.30	.20
42	Mikio Sendoh	.50	.25	.15
43	Chris Arnold	.60	.30	.20
44	Charlie Manuel	.60	.30	.20
45	Keiji Suzuki	.50	.25	.15
46	Toru Ogawa	.50	.25	.15
47	Shigeru Ishiwata	.50	.25	.15
48	Kyosuke Sasaki	.50	.25	.15
49	Iwao Ikebe	.50	.25	.15
50	Kaoru Betto	.50	.25	.15
51	Gene Martin	.60	.30	.20
52	Felix Millan	1.00	.50	.30
53	Mitsuo Motoi	.50	.25	.15
54	Tomio Tashiro	.50	.25	.15
55	Shigeo Nagashima	7.50	3.75	2.25
56	Yoshikazu Takagi	.50	.25	.15
57	Keiichi Nagasaki	.50	.25	.15
58	Rick Krueger	.60	.30	.20
59	John Sipin	.60	.30	.20
60	Osao Shibata	.50	.25	.15
61	Isao Harimoto	.50	.25	.15
62	Shigeru Takada	.50	.25	.15
63	Michiyo Arito	.50	.25	.15
64	Hisao Niura	.50	.25	.15
65	Teruhide Sakurai	.50	.25	.15
66	Yoshito Oda	.50	.25	.15
67	Leron Lee	.60	.30	.20
68	Carlos May	.60	.30	.20
69	Frank Ortenzio	.60	.30	.20
70	Leon Lee	.60	.30	.20
71	Mitsuru Fujiwara	.50	.25	.15
72	Senichi Hoshino	.50	.25	.15
73	Tatsuhiko Kimata	.50	.25	.15
74	Morimichi Takagi	.50	.25	.15
75	Yasunori Oshima	.50	.25	.15
76	Yasushi Tao	.50	.25	.15
77	Wayne Garrett	.60	.30	.20
78	Bob Jones	.60	.30	.20
79	Toshiro Naka	.50	.25	.15
80	Don Blasingame	3.00	1.50	.90
81	Mike Reinbach	.60	.30	.20
82	Masashi Takenouchi	.50	.25	.15
83	Masayuki Kakefu	.50	.25	.15
84	Katsuhiro Nakamura	.50	.25	.15
85	Shigeru Kobayashi	.50	.25	.15
86	Lee Stanton	.60	.30	.20
87	Takenori Emoto	.50	.25	.15
88	Sohachi Aniya	.50	.25	.15
89	Wally Yonamine	4.00	2.00	1.25
90	Kazuhiro Yamauchi	.50	.25	.15

1980 TCMA 1914 Miracle (Boston) Braves

The 1914 Boston Braves team which went from dead last in the National League in mid-July to winning the pennant by 10-1/2 games and sweeping the Philadelphia A's in the World Series is featured on this collectors' issue. In standard 2-1/2" x 3-1/2" format, the cards feature sepia photos in fancy borders. Backs have details of the person's contribution to the "Miracle," along with stats and biographical data.

		NM	E	VG
	Complete Set (32):	30.00	15.00	9.00
	Common Player:	1.00	.50	.30
1	Joe Connolly	1.00	.50	.30
2	Lefty Tyler	1.00	.50	.30
3	Tom Hughes	1.00	.50	.30
4	Hank Gowdy	1.00	.50	.30
5	Gene Cochreham			
	(Cocreham)	1.25	.60	.40
6	Larry Gilbert	1.00	.50	.30
7	George Davis	1.00	.50	.30
8	Hub Perdue	1.00	.50	.30
9	Otto Hess	1.00	.50	.30
10	Clarence Kraft	1.25	.60	.40
11	Tommy Griffith	1.00	.50	.30
12	1914 World Series	1.00	.50	.30
13	Oscar Dugey	1.00	.50	.30
14	Josh Devore	1.00	.50	.30
15	George Stallings	1.00	.50	.30
16	Rabbit Maranville	1.50	.70	.45
17	Paul Strand	1.00	.50	.30
18	Charlie Deal	1.00	.50	.30
19	Dick Rudolph	1.00	.50	.30
20	Butch Schmidt	1.00	.50	.30
21	Johnny Evers	2.00	1.00	.60
22	Dick Crutcher	1.25	.60	.40
23	Possum Whitted	1.00	.50	.30
24	Fred Mitchell	1.00	.50	.30

25	Herbie Moran	1.00	.50	.30
26	Bill James	1.00	.50	.30
27	Ted Cather	1.00	.50	.30
28	Red Smith	1.00	.50	.30
29	Les Mann	1.00	.50	.30
30	Herbie Moran, Wally Schrang (Schang)	1.00	.50	.30
31	NOT ISSUED			
32	Johnny Evers (1914 MVP)	1.00	.50	.30
33	Jim Gaffney	1.25	.60	.40

1980 TCMA 1950 Philadelphia Phillies/Whiz Kids

The National League Champions of 1950 are featured in this collectors' issue team-set. The 2-1/2" x 3-1/2" cards have black-and-white player photo surrounded by red borders. Backs are in black-and-white with player personal data, career summary and 1950 and lifetime stats.

		NM	E	VG
	Complete Set (31):	20.00	10.00	6.00
	Common Player:	.60	.30	.20
1	Ken Silvestri	.50	.25	.15
2	Hank Borowy	.50	.25	.15
3	Bob Miller	.50	.25	.15
4	Jocko Thompson	.50	.25	.15
5	Curt Simmons	.50	.25	.15
6	Dick Sisler	.50	.25	.15
7	Eddie Waitkus	.50	.25	.15
8	Dick Whitman	.50	.25	.15
9	Andy Seminick	.50	.25	.15
10	Richie Ashburn	5.00	2.50	1.50
11	Bubba Church	.50	.25	.15
12	Jackie Mayo	.50	.25	.15
13	Eddie Sawyer	.50	.25	.15
14	Benny Bengough	.50	.25	.15
15	Jim Konstanty	.50	.25	.15
16	Robin Roberts	5.00	2.50	1.50
17	Del Ennis	.50	.25	.15
18	Dusty Cooke	.50	.25	.15
19	Mike Goliat	.50	.25	.15
20	Russ Meyer	.50	.25	.15
21	Granny Hamner	.50	.25	.15
22	Stan Lopata	.50	.25	.15
23	Willie Jones	.50	.25	.15
24	Stan Hollmig	.50	.25	.15
25	Jimmy Bloodworth	.50	.25	.15
26	Ken Johnson	.50	.25	.15
27	Bill Nicholson	.50	.25	.15
28	Ken Heintzelman	.50	.25	.15
29	Blix Donnelly	.50	.25	.15
30	Putsy Caballero	.50	.25	.15
31	Cy Perkins	.50	.25	.15

1980 TCMA 1957 Milwaukee Braves

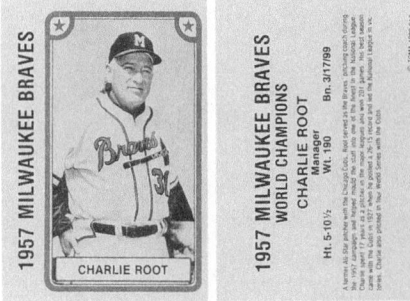

The World Champion Milwaukee Braves are featured in this collectors' issue. The 2-1/2" x 3-1/2" cards have blue-and-white player photos with white borders, blue typography and red graphics. Backs are in blue-and-white with a few bits of player data, career information and stats, along with a TCMA copyright line.

		NM	E	VG
	Complete Set (42):	30.00	15.00	9.00
	Common Player:	.50	.25	.15
1	Don McMahon	.50	.25	.15
2	Joey Jay	.75	.40	.25
3	Phil Paine	.50	.25	.15
4	Bob Trowbridge	.50	.25	.15
5	Bob Buhl	.50	.25	.15
6	Lew Burdette	.75	.40	.25
7	Ernie Johnson	.50	.25	.15
8	Ray Crone	.50	.25	.15
9	Taylor Phillips	.50	.25	.15
10	Johnny Logan	.50	.25	.15
11	Frank Torre	.50	.25	.15
12	John DeMerit	.50	.25	.15
13	Red Murff	.50	.25	.15
14	Nippy Jones	.50	.25	.15
15	Bobby Thomson	.75	.40	.25
16	Chuck Tanner	.50	.25	.15
17	Charlie Root	.50	.25	.15
18	Juan Pizarro	.50	.25	.15
19	Hawk Taylor	.50	.25	.15
20	Mel Roach	.50	.25	.15
21	Bob Hazle	.75	.40	.25
22	Del Rice	.50	.25	.15
23	Felix Mantilla	.50	.25	.15
24	Andy Pafko	.50	.25	.15
25	Del Crandall	.75	.40	.25
26	Wes Covington	.50	.25	.15
27	Eddie Mathews	5.00	2.50	1.50
28	Joe Adcock	.75	.40	.25
29	Dick Cole	.50	.25	.15
30	Carl Sawatski	.50	.25	.15
31	Warren Spahn	5.00	2.50	1.50
32	Hank Aaron	10.00	5.00	3.00
33	Bob Keely	.50	.25	.15
34	Johnny Riddle	.50	.25	.15
35	Connie Ryan	.50	.25	.15
36	Harry Hanebrink	.50	.25	.15
37	Danny O'Connell	.50	.25	.15
38	Fred Haney	.50	.25	.15
39	Dave Jolly	.50	.25	.15
40	Red Schoendienst	3.50	1.75	1.00
41	Gene Conley	.50	.25	.15
42	Bill Bruton	.50	.25	.15

1980 TCMA 1959 L.A. Dodgers

This collectors' issue features the members of the 1959 World Champion L.A. Dodgers. The 2-1/2" x 3-1/2" cards can be found printed in either black-and-white or blue-and-white on front and back. Fronts have player photos with white borders. Backs have personal data, 1959 and career stats and a few sentences about the player's performance in the championship season.

		NM	E	VG
	Complete Set (40):	40.00	20.00	12.00
	Common Player:	1.00	.50	.30
1	Joe Pignatano	1.00	.50	.30
2	Carl Furillo	1.50	.70	.45
3	Bob Lillis	1.00	.50	.30
4	Chuck Essegian	1.00	.50	.30
5	Dick Gray	1.00	.50	.30
6	Rip Repulski	1.00	.50	.30
7	Jim Baxes	1.00	.50	.30
8	Frank Howard	2.50	1.25	.70
9	Solly Drake	1.00	.50	.30
10	Sandy Amoros	1.50	.70	.45
11	Norm Sherry	1.50	.70	.45
12	Tommy Davis	1.50	.70	.45
13	Jim Gilliam	1.50	.70	.45
14	Duke Snider	5.00	2.50	1.50
15	Maury Wills	2.50	1.25	.70
16	Don Demeter	1.00	.50	.30
17	Wally Moon	1.50	.70	.45
18	John Roseboro	1.50	.70	.45
19	Ron Fairly	1.50	.70	.45
20	Norm Larker	1.50	.70	.45
21	Charlie Neal	1.50	.70	.45

22	Don Zimmer	1.50	.70	.45
23	Chuck Dressen	1.00	.50	.30
24	Gil Hodges	4.00	2.00	1.25
25	Joe Becker	1.00	.50	.30
26	Walter Alston	1.50	.70	.45
27	Greg Mulleavy	1.00	.50	.30
28	Don Drysdale	4.00	2.00	1.25
29	Johnny Podres	1.50	.70	.45
30	Sandy Koufax	7.50	3.75	2.25
31	Roger Craig	1.50	.70	.45
32	Danny McDevitt	1.00	.50	.30
33	Bill Harris	1.00	.50	.30
34	Larry Sherry	1.00	.50	.30
35	Stan Williams	1.50	.70	.45
36	Clem Labine	1.50	.70	.45
37	Chuck Churn	1.00	.50	.30
38	Johnny Klippstein	1.00	.50	.30
39	Carl Erskine	1.50	.70	.45
40	Fred Kipp	1.00	.50	.30

1980 TCMA 1960 Pittsburgh Pirates

The World Champion 1960 Pirates are featured in this collectors issue team-set. Black-and-white player photos are bordered in gold on the fronts of the 2-1/2" x 3-1/2" cards. Backs are in black-and-white with personal data, career summary and stats for the 1960 season and career. The Cimoli error card #39 was pulled from distribution and replaced with the unnumbered corrected version.

		NM	E	VG
	Complete Set (41):	30.00	15.00	9.00
	(No #39 Cimoli error.)			
	Common Player:	.50	.25	.15
1	Clem Labine	.50	.25	.15
2	Bob Friend	.75	.40	.25
3	Roy Face	.75	.40	.25
4	Vern Law	.75	.40	.25
5	Harvey Haddix	.75	.40	.25
6	Vinegar Bend Mizell	.50	.25	.15
7	Bill Burwell	.50	.25	.15
8	Diomedes Olivo	.50	.25	.15
9	Don Gross	.50	.25	.15
10	Fred Green	.50	.25	.15
11	Jim Umbricht	.50	.25	.15
12	George Witt	.50	.25	.15
13	Tom Cheney	.50	.25	.15
14	Bennie Daniels	.50	.25	.15
15	Earl Francis	.50	.25	.15
16	Joe Gibbon	.50	.25	.15
17	Paul Giel	.50	.25	.15
18	Danny Kravitz	.50	.25	.15
19	R.C. Stevens	.50	.25	.15
20	Roman Mejias	.50	.25	.15
21	Dick Barone	.50	.25	.15
22	Sam Narron	.50	.25	.15
23	Harry Bright	.50	.25	.15
24	Mickey Vernon	.50	.25	.15
25	Bob Skinner	.60	.30	.20
26	Smoky Burgess	.60	.30	.20
27	Bill Virdon	.60	.30	.20
28	NOT ISSUED			
29	Don Hoak	.60	.30	.20
30	Bill Mazeroski	6.00	3.00	1.75
31	Dick Stuart	1.50	.70	.45
32	Dick Groat	1.50	.70	.45
33	Bob Oldis	.50	.25	.15
34	Gene Baker	.50	.25	.15
35	Joe Christopher	.50	.25	.15
36	Dick Schofield	.60	.30	.20
37	Hal Smith	.50	.25	.15
38	Rocky Nelson	.50	.25	.15
39	Gino Cimoli (Photo actually Dick Schofield.)	6.00	3.00	1.75
40	Danny Murtaugh	.50	.25	.15
41	Lenny Levy	.50	.25	.15
---	Gino Cimoli	.50	.25	.15
---	Roberto Clemente	12.00	6.00	3.50

1980 TCMA 1961 Cincinnati Reds

Virtually every member of the World Champion Cincinnati Reds team of 1961 is included in this collectors issue. Fronts of the 2-1/2" x 3-1/2" cards feature black-and-white player poses with red graphics. Backs are in black-and-white with personal data, 1961 and career stats and a short career summary.

		NM	E	VG
	Complete Set (41):	30.00	15.00	9.00
	Common Player:	1.00	.50	.30
1	Eddie Kasko	1.00	.50	.30
2	Wally Post	1.00	.50	.30
3	Vada Pinson	2.50	1.25	.70
4	Frank Robinson	7.50	3.75	2.25
5	Pete Whisenant	1.00	.50	.30
6	Reggie Otero	1.00	.50	.30
7	Dick Sisler	1.00	.50	.30
8	Jim Turner	1.00	.50	.30
9	Fred Hutchinson	1.00	.50	.30
10	Gene Freese	1.00	.50	.30
11	Gordy Coleman	1.00	.50	.30
12	Don Blasingame	1.00	.50	.30
13	Gus Bell	1.00	.50	.30
14	Leo Cardenas	1.00	.50	.30
15	Elio Chacon	1.00	.50	.30
16	Dick Gernert	1.00	.50	.30
17	Jim Baumer	1.00	.50	.30
18	Willie Jones	1.00	.50	.30
19	Joe Gaines	1.00	.50	.30
20	Cliff Cook	1.00	.50	.30
21	Harry Anderson	1.00	.50	.30
22	Jerry Zimmerman	1.00	.50	.30
23	Johnny Edwards	1.00	.50	.30
24	Bob Schmidt	1.00	.50	.30
25	Darrell Johnson	1.00	.50	.30
26	Ed Bailey	1.00	.50	.30
27	Joey Jay	1.00	.50	.30
28	Jim O'Toole	1.00	.50	.30
29	Bob Purkey	1.00	.50	.30
30	Jim Brosnan	1.00	.50	.30
31	Ken Hunt	1.00	.50	.30
32	Ken Johnson	1.00	.50	.30
33	Jim Mahoney	1.00	.50	.30
34	Bill Henry	1.00	.50	.30
35	Jerry Lynch	1.00	.50	.30
36	Hal Bevan	1.00	.50	.30
37	Howie Nunn	1.00	.50	.30
38	Sherman Jones	1.00	.50	.30
39	Jay Hook	1.00	.50	.30
40	Claude Osteen	1.00	.50	.30
41	Marshall Bridges	1.00	.50	.30

1980 TCMA All Time Brooklyn Dodgers

		NM	E	VG
	Complete Set (12):	6.00	3.00	1.80
	Common Player:	.50	.25	.15
1	Gil Hodges	1.00	.50	.30
2	Jim Gilliam	.50	.25	.15
3	Pee Wee Reese	1.00	.50	.30
4	Jackie Robinson	3.00	1.50	.90
5	Sandy Koufax	3.00	1.50	.90
6	Zach Wheat	.50	.25	.15

7	Dixie Walker	.50	.25	.15
8	Hugh Casey	.50	.25	.15
9	Dazzy Vance	.50	.25	.15
10	Duke Snider	1.00	.50	.30
11	Roy Campanella	1.50	.70	.45
12	Walter Alston	.50	.25	.15

1980 TCMA All Time Cubs

		NM	E	VG
	Complete Set (12):	6.00	3.00	1.80
	Common Player:	.50	.25	.15
1	Billy Williams	1.50	.70	.45
2	Charlie Root	.50	.25	.15
3	Ron Santo	1.50	.70	.45
4	Larry French	.50	.25	.15
5	Gabby Hartnett	.50	.25	.15
6	Emil Kush	.50	.25	.15
7	Charlie Grimm	.50	.25	.15
8	Kiki Cuyler	.50	.25	.15
9	Billy Herman	.50	.25	.15
10	Hack Wilson	1.00	.50	.30
11	Rogers Hornsby	1.00	.50	.30
12	Ernie Banks	4.00	2.00	1.25

1980 TCMA All Time N.Y. Giants

		NM	E	VG
	Complete Set (12):	6.00	3.00	1.80
	Common Player:	.50	.25	.15
1	Willie Mays	4.00	2.00	1.25
2	Wes Westrum	.50	.25	.15
3	Carl Hubbell	.50	.25	.15
4	Hoyt Wilhelm	.50	.25	.15
5	Bobby Thomson	1.00	.50	.30
6	Frankie Frisch	.50	.25	.15
7	Bill Terry	.50	.25	.15
8	Alvin Dark	.50	.25	.15
9	Mel Ott	1.00	.50	.30
10	Christy Mathewson	2.50	1.25	.70
11	Freddie Lindstrom	.50	.25	.15
12	John McGraw	.50	.25	.15

1980 TCMA All Time Tigers

Sets printed with blue or red borders.

	NM	E	VG
Complete Set (12):	6.00	3.00	1.80
Common Player:	.50	.25	.15
1	George Kell	.50	.25	.15
2	Billy Rogell	.50	.25	.15
3	Ty Cobb	4.00	2.00	1.25
4	Hank Greenberg	2.50	1.25	.70
5	Al Kaline	1.50	.70	.45
6	Charlie Gehringer	.75	.40	.25
7	Harry Heilmann	.50	.25	.15
8	Hal Newhouser	.50	.25	.15
9	Steve O'Neill	.50	.25	.15
10	Denny McLain	.50	.25	.15
11	Mickey Cochrane	.50	.25	.15
12	John Hiller	.50	.25	.15

1980 TCMA All Time White Sox

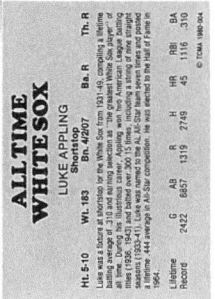

	NM	E	VG
Complete Set (12):	6.00	3.00	1.80
Common Player:	.50	.25	.15
1	Ted Lyons	.50	.25	.15
2	Eddie Collins	2.00	1.00	.60
3	Al Lopez	.75	.40	.25
4	Luke Appling	2.00	1.00	.60
5	Billy Pierce	.75	.40	.25
6	Willie Kamm	.50	.25	.15
7	Johnny Mostil	.50	.25	.15
8	Al Simmons	.75	.40	.25
9	Ray Schalk	.50	.25	.15
10	Gerry Staley	.50	.25	.15
11	Harry Hooper	.50	.25	.15
12	Eddie Robinson	.50	.25	.15

1980 TCMA All Time Yankees

	NM	E	VG
Complete Set (12):	16.00	8.00	4.75
Common Player:	.50	.25	.15
1	Lou Gehrig	4.00	2.00	1.25
2	Tony Lazzeri	.50	.25	.15
3	Red Rolfe	.50	.25	.15
4	Phil Rizzuto	1.00	.50	.30
5	Babe Ruth	4.00	2.00	1.25
6	Mickey Mantle	5.00	2.50	1.50
7	Joe DiMaggio	4.00	2.00	1.25
8	Bill Dickey	.75	.40	.25
9	Red Ruffing	.50	.25	.15
10	Whitey Ford	1.00	.50	.30
11	Johnny Murphy	.50	.25	.15
12	Casey Stengel	.75	.40	.25

1980 TCMA All-Time Teams

In 1980, TCMA began a new series of sets featuring 11 all-time great players and a manager from several of the 26 teams. In standard 2-1/2" x 3-1/2" format, most of the cards utilize black-and-white player photos, though some more recent stars are pictured in color. Several decorative borders, varying by team, surround the front photos. On most team sets there is an "All Time" designation at top, with the player name and (usually) position at bottom. Backs are fairly uniform, printed in blue or black, and offering a few biographical details and career highlights or a checklist. Besides hobby sales, these old-timers' sets were also sold in several major retail chains.

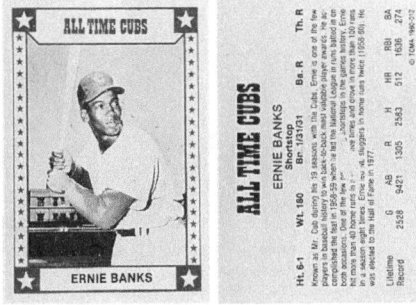

(Team sets listed individually.)

1980 TCMA/Sports Nostalgia Store Babe Ruth

The same photo on the Babe Ruth card which appeared in TCMA's 1927 N.Y. Yankees set from 1979 was utilized by Sports Nostalgia as an advertising medium. On the back of the ad card is store information and an offer to redeem the card there for a free picture of Ruth. Production was 500 cards.

	NM	E	VG
Babe Ruth	7.50	3.75	2.25

1978 Allen P. Terach Immortals of Baseball

These souvenir cards were issued as the first of what was intended to be a series honoring baseball's greatest players. No succeeding issues were forthcoming. The images on the 9" x 6-1/2" blank-back cards are printed in black-and-white and sepia. Fine print at the bottom states the card is part of an edition of 3,500. Issue price was just under $5 apiece.

		NM	E	VG
Souvenir Card:				
1	Babe Ruth, Joe DiMaggio	9.00	4.50	2.75
2	Ty Cobb, Stan Musial	6.00	3.00	1.75

1914 Texas Tommy Type 1 (E224)

Designated as E224 in the American Card Catalog these cards measure about 2-3/8" x 3-1/2". Fronts feature sepia-toned action photos with the player's name in capital letters and his team below in parenthesis. The back carries a lengthy player biography and most cards, although not all, include year-by-year statistics at the bottom. The words "Texas Tommy" appear at the top. Texas Tommy was a candy bar brand from the Cardinet Candy Co., Oakland, Calif. The candy bar took its name from a popular dance of the era. Most examples of this set have been found in northern California. There is also a second variety of the set, smaller in size (1-7/8" x 3"), which have borderless pictures and a glossy finish. Gaps have been left in the assigned numbers on this checklist to accomodate future additions.

		NM	E	VG
Common Player:		5,850	2,925	1,755
(1)	Jimmy Archer	5,850	2,925	1,755
(2)	Jimmy Austin	5,850	2,925	1,755
(3)	Home Run Baker	9,750	4,875	2,925
(4)	Chief Bender	9,750	4,875	2,925
(5)	Bob Bescher	5,850	2,925	1,755
(6)	Ping Bodie	5,850	2,925	1,755
(7)	Donie Bush	5,850	2,925	1,755
(8)	Bobby Byrne	5,850	2,925	1,755
(9)	Nixey Callanan (Callahan)	5,850	2,925	1,755
(10)	Howie Camnitz	5,850	2,925	1,755
(11)	Frank Chance	9,750	4,875	2,925
(12)	Hal Chase	8,450	4,225	2,535
(13)	Ty Cobb	45,500	22,750	13,000
(14)	Jack Coombs	5,850	2,925	1,755
(15)	Sam Crawford	9,750	4,875	2,925
(16)	Birdie Cree	5,850	2,925	1,755
(17)	Al Demaree	5,850	2,925	1,755
(18)	Red Dooin	5,850	2,925	1,755
(19)	Larry Doyle	5,850	2,925	1,755
(20)	Johnny Evers	9,750	4,875	2,925
(21)	Vean Gregg	5,850	2,925	1,755
(22)	Bob Harmon	5,850	2,925	1,755
(23)	Joe Jackson	58,500	29,250	17,550
(24)	Walter Johnson	19,500	9,750	5,850
(25)	Otto Knabe	5,850	2,925	1,755
(26)	Nap Lajoie	9,750	4,875	2,925
(27)	Harry Lord	5,850	2,925	1,755
(28)	Connie Mack	9,750	4,875	2,925
(29)	Armando Marsans	5,850	2,925	1,755
(30)	Christy Mathewson	20,000	10,000	6,000
(31)	George McBride	5,850	2,925	1,755
(32)	John McGraw	9,750	4,875	2,925
(33)	Stuffy McInnis	5,850	2,925	1,755
(34)	Chief Meyers	5,850	2,925	1,755
(35)	Earl Moore	5,850	2,925	1,755
(36)	Mike Mowrey	5,850	2,925	1,755
(37)	Rebel Oakes	5,850	2,925	1,755
(38)	Marty O'Toole	5,850	2,925	1,755
(39)	Eddie Plank	13,000	6,500	3,900
(41)	Bud Ryan	5,850	2,925	1,755
(42)	Tris Speaker	16,250	8,125	4,875
(43)	Jake Stahl	5,850	2,925	1,755
(44)	Oscar Strange (Stanage)	5,850	2,925	1,755
(45)	Bill Sweeney	5,850	2,925	1,755
(46)	Honus Wagner	42,500	21,000	12,500
(47)	Ed Walsh	9,750	4,875	2,925
(48)	Zach Wheat	9,750	4,875	2,925
(49)	Harry Wolter	5,850	2,925	1,755
(50)	Joe Wood	7,150	3,575	2,145
(51)	Steve Yerkes	5,850	2,925	1,755
(52)	Heinie Zimmerman	5,850	2,925	1,755

1914 Texas Tommy Type 2 (E224)

Type 2 Texas Tommy cards are smaller in size, at about 1-7/8" x 3" to 3-1/16", have a glossy front surface and are blank-backed. Their only real link to the Type 1 Texas Tommy cards is the shared front on those players who appear in both checklists.

		NM	E	VG
Common Player:		6,000	3,000	1,800
(1)	Ping Bodie	6,000	3,000	1,800
(2)	Larry Doyle	6,000	3,000	1,800
(3)	Vean Gregg	6,000	3,000	1,800
(4)	Harry Hooper	7,800	3,900	2,340
(5)	Walter Johnson	12,000	6,000	3,600
(6)	Connie Mack	7,800	3,900	2,340
(7)	Rube Marquard	7,800	3,900	2,340
(8)	Christy Mathewson	14,400	7,200	4,320
(9)	John McGraw	7,800	3,900	2,340
(10)	Chief Meyers	6,000	3,000	1,800
(11)	Fred Snodgrass	6,000	3,000	1,800

(12)	Jake Stahl	6,000	3,000	1,800
(13)	Honus Wagner	16,200	8,100	4,860
(14)	Joe Wood	6,600	3,300	1,980
(15)	Steve Yerkes	6,000	3,000	1,800

1928 Tharp's Ice Cream

(6) BABE RUTH

SAVE THESE PICTURES
One ice cream bar will be given free for each picture of Babe Ruth.

ALSO
One gallon of Tharp's ice cream will be delivered free to the holder of a complete set of sixty different Baseball Stars, upon surrender of same to any Tharp dealer.

Sharing the same format and checklist with several other contemporary ice cream sets this 60-card set includes all of the top stars of the day. Cards are printed in black-and-white on a 1-3/8" x 2-1/2" format. There appears to have been two different types issued, but the extent of each version is unknown. The variations are found in the player's name and card number which can appear either in a strip within the frame of the photo, or printed in the border beneath the photo. Card backs have a redemption offer that includes an ice cream bar in exchange for a Babe Ruth card, or a gallon of ice cream for a complete set of 60. Tharp's was located in Shamokin, Pa.

		NM	E	VG
	Complete Set (60):	20,000	8,000	4,000
	Common Player:	115.00	45.00	20.00
1	Burleigh Grimes	225.00	90.00	45.00
2	Walter Reuther (Ruether)	115.00	45.00	20.00
3	Joe Dugan	115.00	45.00	20.00
4	Red Faber	225.00	90.00	45.00
5	Gabby Hartnett	225.00	90.00	45.00
6a	Babe Ruth (Portrait)	7,500	3,000	1,500
6b	Babe Ruth (Throwing)	7,500	3,000	1,500
7	Bob Meusel	115.00	45.00	20.00
8	Herb Pennock	225.00	90.00	45.00
9	George Burns	115.00	45.00	20.00
10	Joe Sewell	225.00	90.00	45.00
11	George Uhle	115.00	45.00	20.00
12	Bob O'Farrell	115.00	45.00	20.00
13	Rogers Hornsby	350.00	140.00	70.00
14	"Pie" Traynor	225.00	90.00	45.00
15	Clarence Mitchell	115.00	45.00	20.00
16a	Eppa Jepha Rixey	225.00	90.00	45.00
16b	Eppa Rixey	225.00	90.00	45.00
17	Carl Mays	115.00	45.00	20.00
18	Adolfo Luque	125.00	50.00	25.00
19	Dave Bancroft	225.00	90.00	45.00
20	George Kelly	225.00	90.00	45.00
21	Earl (Earle) Combs	225.00	90.00	45.00
22	Harry Heilmann	225.00	90.00	45.00
23a	Ray W. Schalk	225.00	90.00	45.00
23b	Ray Schalk	225.00	90.00	45.00
24	Johnny Mostil	115.00	45.00	20.00
25	Hack Wilson	225.00	90.00	45.00
26	Lou Gehrig	2,500	1,000	500.00
27	Ty Cobb	1,500	600.00	300.00
28	Tris Speaker	350.00	140.00	70.00
29	Tony Lazzeri	225.00	90.00	45.00
30	Waite Hoyt	225.00	90.00	45.00
31	Sherwood Smith	115.00	45.00	20.00
32	Max Carey	225.00	90.00	45.00
33	Eugene Hargrave	115.00	45.00	20.00
34	Miguel L. Gonzalez (Middle initial A.)	125.00	50.00	25.00
35	Joe Judge	115.00	45.00	20.00
36	E.C. (Sam) Rice	225.00	90.00	45.00
37	Earl Sheely	115.00	45.00	20.00
38	Sam Jones	115.00	45.00	20.00
39	Bib (Bibb) A. Falk	115.00	45.00	20.00
40	Willie Kamm	115.00	45.00	20.00
41	Stanley Harris	225.00	90.00	45.00
42	John J. McGraw	225.00	90.00	45.00
43	Artie Nehf	115.00	45.00	20.00
44	Grover Alexander	700.00	280.00	140.00
45	Paul Waner	225.00	90.00	45.00
46	William H. Terry (Photo actually Zeb Terry.)	225.00	90.00	45.00
47	Glenn Wright	115.00	45.00	20.00
48	Earl Smith	115.00	45.00	20.00
49	Leon (Goose) Goslin	225.00	90.00	45.00

50	Frank Frisch	225.00	90.00	45.00
51	Joe Harris	115.00	45.00	20.00
52	Fred (Cy) Williams	115.00	45.00	20.00
53	Eddie Roush	225.00	90.00	45.00
54	George Sisler	225.00	90.00	45.00
55	Ed. Rommel	115.00	45.00	20.00
56	Rogers Peckinpaugh (Roger)	115.00	45.00	20.00
57	Stanley Coveleskie (Coveleski)	225.00	90.00	45.00
58	Lester Bell	115.00	45.00	20.00
59	L. Waner	225.00	90.00	45.00
60	John P. McInnis	115.00	45.00	20.00

1978 The Card Coach Milwaukee Braves Greats

MILWAUKEE BRAVES GREATS

9 JOE ADCOCK
FIRST BASEMAN

Throws: Right   Height: 6' 4"
Bats: Right   Weight: 210 lbs.
Born: October 30, 1927, Coushatta, La.

A favorite with the fans, Joe Adcock seldom was a disappointment at the plate. The big hit was his specialty -- Joe could hit the ball harder than anyone in the League. Adcock's best year was 1954 when he batted .308. He swatted 38 round-trippers in 1956, his personal high.

MAJOR LEAGUE RECORD (1950-1966)

Games 1959   Doubles 295
At Bats 6606   Triples 35
Hits 1832   H.R. 336
Batting Ave. .. .277   RBI's 1122

Years as a Milwaukee Brave -- 1953-1962
© 1978, T.C.C.

JOE ADCOCK

Stars of the Milwaukee Braves from the early 1950s through the early 1960s are featured in this collectors' issue. The 2-1/2" x 3-1/2" cards have black-and-white player photos on front with the player name in the white border at bottom. Backs are also in black-and-white with personal data, career summary and stats. Cards are numbered by uniform number.

		NM	E	VG
	Complete Set (15):	10.00	5.00	3.00
	Common Player:	2.00	1.00	.60
1	Del Crandall	2.00	1.00	.60
4	Red Schoendienst	2.00	1.00	.60
8	Bob Uecker	2.50	1.25	.70
9	Joe Adcock	2.00	1.00	.60
10	Bob Buhl	2.00	1.00	.60
15	Joe Torre	2.50	1.25	.70
16	Carlton Willey	2.00	1.00	.60
21	Warren Spahn	3.00	1.50	.90
22	Johnny Logan	2.00	1.00	.60
33	Lew Burdette	2.00	1.00	.60
34	Billy Bruton	2.00	1.00	.60
41	Eddie Mathews	3.00	1.50	.90
43	Wes Covington	2.00	1.00	.60
44	Hank Aaron	7.50	3.75	2.25
48	Andy Pafko (Checklist)	2.00	1.00	.60

1971 Ticketron L.A. Dodgers/S.F. Giants

Essentially large team schedule cards with promotional dates noted and an ad for the ticket service, the Ticketron Dodgers/Giants cards of 1971 are similar in format. Each has a color photo on front with facsimile autograph. The Dodgers cards are 4" x 6" with no borders on fronts; the 3-3/4" x 5-3/4" Giants cards have a white border. Backs are white with red and blue printing. The unnumbered cards are checklisted here alphabetically within team.

		NM	E	VG
	Complete Dodgers Set (20):	75.00	37.00	22.00
	Complete Giants Set (10):	150.00	75.00	45.00
	Common Dodger Player:	3.00	1.50	.90
	Common Giant Player:	6.00	3.00	1.75
	LOS ANGELES DODGERS			
(1)	Richie Allen	15.00	7.50	4.50
(2)	Walter Alston	6.00	3.00	1.75
(3)	Jim Brewer	3.00	1.50	.90
(4)	Willie Crawford	3.00	1.50	.90
(5)	Willie Davis	4.50	2.25	1.25
(6)	Steve Garvey	20.00	10.00	6.00
(7)	Bill Grabarkewitz	3.00	1.50	.90
(8)	Jim Lefebvre	3.00	1.50	.90
(9)	Pete Mikkelsen	3.00	1.50	.90
(10)	Joe Moeller	3.00	1.50	.90
(11)	Manny Mota	4.50	2.25	1.25
(12)	Claude Osteen	3.00	1.50	.90
(13)	Wes Parker	3.00	1.50	.90
(14)	Bill Russell	4.50	2.25	1.25
(15)	Duke Sims	3.00	1.50	.90
(16)	Bill Singer	3.00	1.50	.90
(17)	Bill Sudakis	3.00	1.50	.90
(18)	Don Sutton	20.00	10.00	6.00
(19)	Maury Wills	7.50	3.75	2.25
(20)	Jerry Doggett, Vin Scully	3.00	1.50	.90
	SAN FRANSICO GIANTS			
(1)	Bobby Bonds	9.00	4.50	2.75
(2)	Dick Dietz	6.00	3.00	1.75
(3)	Charles Fox	6.00	3.00	1.75
(4)	Tito Fuentes	6.00	3.00	1.75
(5)	Ken Henderson	6.00	3.00	1.75
(6)	Juan Marichal	20.00	10.00	6.00
(7)	Willie Mays	60.00	30.00	18.00
(8)	Willie McCovey	25.00	12.50	7.50
(9)	Don McMahon	3.00	1.50	.90
(10)	Gaylord Perry	15.00	7.50	4.50

1972 Ticketron Phillies

DON MONEY

How to see the Phillies Player of the Week

TICKETRON

The Phillies' main off-site ticket outlet produced this set of schedule cards. Fronts are in horizontal 6" x 3-7/8" format with a color player photo at center. Backs are in black-and-white and include a Phillies home schedule and sponsor advertising. Because he was traded to the Expos in mid-season, the card of Tim McCarver is scarcer than the others.

		NM	E	VG
	Complete Set (10):	95.00	47.00	28.00
	Common Player:	8.00	4.00	2.50
(1)	Mike Anderson	8.00	4.00	2.50
(2)	Larry Bowa	8.00	4.00	2.50
(3)	Steve Carlton	15.00	7.50	4.50
(4)	Deron Johnson	8.00	4.00	2.50
(5)	Frank Lucchesi	8.00	4.00	2.50
(6)	Greg Luzinski	10.00	5.00	3.00
(7)	Tim McCarver	35.00	17.50	10.50
(8)	Don Money	8.00	4.00	2.50
(9)	Willie Montanez	8.00	4.00	2.50
(10)	Dick Selma	8.00	4.00	2.50

1959 Ticoa Tires Frank Malzone

TICOA TIRES
BOSTON
SOUTHBRIDGE   QUINCY
WORCESTER   FRAMINGHAM
FITCHBURG   BURLINGTON

This black-and-white J.D. McCarthy postcard of the former Red Sox infielder was issued in conjunction with Malzone's endorsement of the Boston area tire store chain. The card measures 3-1/4" x 5-1/2" and has a blue facsimile autograph on front. A similar promotional postcard is listed under Molinari's Restaurant.

	NM	E	VG
Frank Malzone	25.00	12.50	7.50

1910 Tip-Top Bread Pittsburgh Pirates (D322)

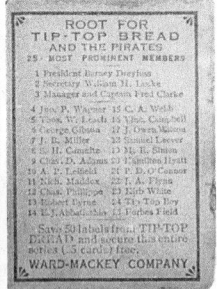

The previous season's World Champion Pittsburgh Pirates are featured in this issue. The cards have an unusual - for the era - nearly square (1-13/16" x 2-3/8") format. Fronts have pastel paintings of the subjects with identification in the white border below as "World's Champions." Backs have a checklist, ad for the bakery and offer to send the complete set of cards for 50 bread labels.

	NM	E	VG
Complete Set (25):	120,000	60,000	36,000
Common Player:	2,650	1,325	800.00
1 Barney Dreyfuss (President)	15,000	7,500	4,500
2 William H. Locke (Secretary)	2,650	1,325	800.00
3 Fred Clarke	6,000	3,000	1,800
4 Honus Wagner	60,000	30,000	18,000
5 Tom Leach	2,650	1,325	800.00
6 George Gibson	2,650	1,325	800.00
7 Dots Miller	2,650	1,325	800.00
8 Howie Camnitz	2,650	1,325	800.00
9 Babe Adams	2,650	1,325	725.00
10 Lefty Leifield	2,650	1,325	800.00
11 Nick Maddox	2,650	1,325	800.00
12 Deacon Philippe	2,650	1,325	800.00
13 Bobby Byrne	2,650	1,325	800.00
14 Ed Abbaticchio	2,650	1,325	800.00
15 Lefty Webb	2,650	1,325	800.00
16 Vin Campbell	2,650	1,325	800.00
17 Owen Wilson	2,650	1,325	800.00
18 Sam Leever	2,650	1,325	800.00
19 Mike Simon	2,650	1,325	800.00
20 Ham Hyatt	2,650	1,325	800.00
21 Paddy O'Connor	2,650	1,325	800.00
22 John Flynn	2,650	1,325	800.00
23 Kirby White	2,650	1,325	800.00
24 Tip Top Boy Mascot	7,000	3,500	2,100
25 Forbes Field	4,000	2,000	1,200

1939 Tip-Top Bread Joe DiMaggio Pin

This 1-1/4" black-and-white photo portrait pin has a white background and printed endorsement for the Ward's brand. Similar pins were issued of boxer Billy Conn and hockey star Eddie Shore.

	NM	E	VG
Joe DiMaggio	500.00	250.00	150.00

1947 Tip Top Bread

This 163-card set actually consists of a group of regional issues, some of which are scarcer than others. The 2-1/4" x 3" cards are borderless at top and sides, with a black-and-white player photo below which is a white strip containing the player identification. Backs carry an illustrated advertisement. The set is known for a quantity of obscure players, many of whom played during the talent-lean World War II seasons.

	NM	E	VG
Complete Set (163):	20,000	10,000	6,000
Common Player:	75.00	30.00	15.00
(1) Bill Ayers	75.00	30.00	15.00
(2) Floyd Baker	125.00	50.00	25.00
(3) Charles Barrett	125.00	50.00	25.00
(4) Eddie Basinski	75.00	30.00	15.00
(5) John Berardino	125.00	50.00	25.00
(6) Larry Berra	625.00	250.00	125.00
(7) Bill Bevens	125.00	50.00	25.00
(8) Robert Blattner	75.00	30.00	15.00
(9) Ernie Bonham	75.00	30.00	15.00
(10) Bob Bragan	80.00	32.00	16.00
(11) Ralph Branca	125.00	50.00	25.00
(12) Alpha Brazle	75.00	30.00	15.00
(13) Bobbie Brown (Bobby)	125.00	50.00	25.00
(14) Mike Budnick	75.00	30.00	15.00
(15) Ken Burkhart	75.00	30.00	15.00
(16) Thomas Byrne	125.00	50.00	25.00
(17) Earl Caldwell	125.00	50.00	25.00
(18) "Hank" Camelli	125.00	50.00	25.00
(19) Hugh Casey	100.00	40.00	20.00
(20) Phil Cavarretta	125.00	50.00	25.00
(21) Bob Chipman	125.00	50.00	25.00
(22) Lloyd Christopher	125.00	50.00	25.00
(23) Bill Cox	75.00	30.00	15.00
(24) Bernard Creger	75.00	30.00	15.00
(25) Frank Crosetti	125.00	50.00	25.00
(26) Joffre Cross	75.00	30.00	15.00
(27) Leon Culberson	125.00	50.00	25.00
(28) Dick Culler	125.00	50.00	25.00
(29) Dom DiMaggio	250.00	100.00	50.00
(30) George Dickey	125.00	50.00	25.00
(31) Chas. E. Diering	75.00	30.00	15.00
(32) Joseph Dobson	125.00	50.00	25.00
(33) Bob Doerr	345.00	125.00	60.00
(34) Ervin Dusak	75.00	30.00	15.00
(35) Bruce Edwards	75.00	24.00	12.00
(36) Walter "Hoot" Evers	160.00	60.00	35.00
(37) Clifford Fannin	75.00	30.00	15.00
(38) "Nanny" Fernandez	125.00	50.00	25.00
(39) Dave "Boo" Ferriss	125.00	50.00	25.00
(40) Elbie Fletcher	75.00	30.00	15.00
(41) Dennis Galehouse	75.00	30.00	15.00
(42) Joe Garagiola	280.00	105.00	55.00
(43) Sid Gordon	75.00	30.00	15.00
(44) John Gorsica	125.00	50.00	25.00
(45) Hal Gregg	75.00	24.00	12.00
(46) Frank Gustine	75.00	30.00	15.00
(47) Stanley Hack	125.00	50.00	25.00
(48) Mickey Harris	125.00	50.00	25.00
(49) Clinton Hartung	75.00	30.00	15.00
(50) Joe Hatten	75.00	24.00	12.00
(51) Frank Hayes	125.00	50.00	25.00
(52) "Jeff" Heath	75.00	30.00	15.00
(53) Tom Henrich	130.00	52.00	26.00
(54) Gene Hermanski	75.00	24.00	12.00
(55) Kirby Higbe	75.00	30.00	15.00
(56) Ralph Hodgin	125.00	50.00	25.00
(57) Tex Hughson	125.00	50.00	25.00
(58) Fred Hutchinson	150.00	60.00	30.00
(59) LeRoy Jarvis	75.00	30.00	15.00
(60) "Si" Johnson	125.00	50.00	25.00
(61) Don Johnson	125.00	50.00	25.00
(62) Earl Johnson	80.00	32.00	16.00
(63) John Jorgensen	75.00	24.00	12.00
(64) Walter Judnick (Judnich)	75.00	30.00	15.00
(65) Tony Kaufmann	75.00	30.00	15.00
(66) George Kell	345.00	125.00	65.00
(67) Charlie Keller	125.00	50.00	25.00
(68) Bob Kennedy	125.00	50.00	25.00
(69) Montia Kennedy	75.00	30.00	15.00
(70) Ralph Kiner	175.00	70.00	35.00
(71) Dave Koslo	75.00	30.00	15.00
(72) Jack Kramer	75.00	30.00	15.00
(73) Joe Kuhel	125.00	50.00	25.00
(74) George Kurowski	75.00	30.00	15.00
(75) Emil Kush	125.00	50.00	25.00
(76) "Eddie" Lake	125.00	50.00	25.00
(77) Harry Lavagetto	100.00	40.00	20.00
(78) Bill Lee	125.00	50.00	25.00
(79) Thornton Lee	125.00	50.00	25.00
(80) Paul Lehner	75.00	30.00	15.00
(81) John Lindell	125.00	50.00	25.00
(82) Danny Litwhiler	125.00	50.00	25.00
(83) "Mickey" Livingston	125.00	50.00	25.00
(84) Carroll Lockman	75.00	30.00	15.00
(85) Jack Lohrke	75.00	30.00	15.00
(86) Ernie Lombardi	175.00	70.00	32.00
(87) Vic Lombardi	75.00	24.00	12.00
(88) Edmund Lopat	130.00	52.00	26.00
(89) Harry Lowrey	125.00	50.00	25.00
(90) Marty Marion	100.00	40.00	20.00
(91) Willard Marshall	75.00	30.00	15.00
(92) Phil Masi	125.00	50.00	25.00
(93) Edward J. Mayo	125.00	50.00	25.00
(94) Clyde McCullough	125.00	50.00	25.00
(95) Frank Melton	125.00	50.00	25.00
(96) Cass Michaels	125.00	50.00	25.00
(97) Ed Miksis	125.00	50.00	25.00
(98) Arthur Mills	125.00	50.00	25.00
(99) Johnny Mize	175.00	70.00	35.00
(100) Lester Moss	75.00	30.00	15.00
(101) "Pat" Mullin	125.00	50.00	25.00
(102) "Bob" Muncrief	75.00	30.00	15.00
(103) George Munger	75.00	30.00	15.00
(104) Fritz Ostermueller	75.00	30.00	15.00
(105) James P. Outlaw	125.00	50.00	25.00
(106) Frank "Stub" Overmire	125.00	50.00	25.00
(107) Andy Pafko	125.00	50.00	25.00
(108) Joe Page	125.00	50.00	25.00
(109) Roy Partee	125.00	50.00	25.00
(110) Johnny Pesky	125.00	50.00	25.00
(111) Nelson Potter	75.00	30.00	15.00
(112) Mel Queen	125.00	50.00	25.00
(113) Marion Rackley	75.00	24.00	12.00
(114) Al Reynolds	125.00	50.00	25.00
(115) Del Rice	75.00	30.00	15.00
(116) Marv Rickert	125.00	50.00	25.00
(117) John Rigney	125.00	50.00	25.00
(118) Phil Rizzuto	475.00	190.00	90.00
(119) Aaron Robinson	125.00	50.00	25.00
(120) "Preacher" Roe	80.00	32.00	16.00
(121) Carvel Rowell	125.00	50.00	25.00
(122) Jim Russell	75.00	30.00	15.00
(123) Rip Russell	125.00	50.00	25.00
(124) Connie Ryan	125.00	50.00	25.00
(125) John Sain	125.00	50.00	25.00
(126) Ray Sanders	125.00	50.00	25.00
(127) Fred Sanford	75.00	30.00	15.00
(128) Johnny Schmitz	125.00	50.00	25.00
(129) Joe Schultz	75.00	30.00	15.00
(130) "Rip" Sewell	75.00	30.00	15.00
(131) Dick Sisler	75.00	30.00	15.00
(132) "Sibby" Sisti	125.00	50.00	25.00
(133) Enos Slaughter	130.00	52.00	26.00
(134) "Billy" Southworth	125.00	50.00	25.00
(135) Warren Spahn	595.00	230.00	115.00
(136) Verne Stephens (Vern)	75.00	30.00	15.00
(137) George Sternweiss (Stirnweiss)	125.00	50.00	25.00
(138) Ed Stevens	75.00	24.00	12.00
(139) Nick Strincevich	75.00	30.00	15.00
(140) "Bobby" Sturgeon	125.00	50.00	25.00
(141) Robt. "Bob" Swift	125.00	50.00	25.00
(142) Geo. "Birdie" Tibbetts (Tebbetts)	125.00	50.00	25.00
(143) "Mike" Tresh	125.00	50.00	25.00
(144) Ken Trinkle	75.00	30.00	15.00
(145) Paul "Diz" Trout	125.00	50.00	25.00
(146) Virgil "Fire" Trucks	125.00	50.00	25.00
(147) Thurman Tucker	125.00	50.00	25.00
(148) Bill Voiselle	75.00	30.00	15.00
(149) Hal Wagner	125.00	50.00	25.00
(150) Honus Wagner	595.00	235.00	140.00
(151) Eddy Waitkus	125.00	50.00	25.00
(152) Richard "Dick" Wakefield	125.00	50.00	25.00
(153) Jack Wallaesa	125.00	50.00	25.00
(154) Charles Wensloff	125.00	50.00	25.00
(155) Ted Wilks	75.00	30.00	15.00
(156) Mickey Witek	75.00	30.00	15.00
(157) "Jerry" Witte	75.00	30.00	15.00
(158) Ed Wright	125.00	50.00	25.00
(159) Taft Wright	125.00	50.00	25.00
(160) Henry Wyse	125.00	50.00	25.00
(161) "Rudy" York	125.00	50.00	25.00
(162) Al Zarilla	75.00	30.00	15.00
(163) Bill Zuber	125.00	50.00	25.00

1952 Tip Top Bread Labels

This unnumbered set of bread end-labels consists of 48 different labels, including two of Phil Rizzuto. The player's photo, name and team appear inside a star, with the words "Tip Top" printed above. The labels measure approximately 2-1/2" x 2-3/4". An advertising message appears in red on back. A large fold-out sheet to collect and display the labels was also issued. Each space is labeled with a player name and basic information, and is die-cut to allow the label to be slid in.

		NM	E	VG
	Complete Set (48):	27,500	13,750	9,200
	Common Player:	550.00	275.00	185.00
	Display Sheet:	350.00	175.00	120.00
(1)	Hank Bauer	625.00	300.00	200.00
(2)	Yogi Berra	975.00	500.00	300.00
(3)	Ralph Branca	625.00	300.00	200.00
(4)	Lou Brissie	550.00	275.00	185.00
(5)	Roy Campanella	975.00	500.00	300.00
(6)	Phil Cavarretta (Cavarretta)	550.00	275.00	185.00
(7)	Murray Dickson (Murry)	550.00	275.00	185.00
(8)	Ferris Fain	550.00	275.00	185.00
(9)	Carl Furillo	625.00	300.00	200.00
(10)	Ned Garver	550.00	275.00	185.00
(11)	Sid Gordon	550.00	275.00	185.00
(12)	John Groth	550.00	275.00	185.00
(13)	Gran Hamner	550.00	275.00	185.00
(14)	Jim Hearn	550.00	275.00	185.00
(15)	Gene Hermanski	550.00	275.00	185.00
(16)	Gil Hodges	775.00	400.00	240.00
(17)	Larry Jansen	550.00	275.00	185.00
(18)	Eddie Joost	550.00	275.00	185.00
(19)	George Kell	700.00	350.00	240.00
(20)	Dutch Leonard	550.00	275.00	185.00
(21)	Whitey Lockman	550.00	275.00	185.00
(22)	Ed Lopat	625.00	300.00	200.00
(23)	Sal Maglie	550.00	275.00	185.00
(24)	Mickey Mantle	6,200	3,100	2,100
(25)	Gil McDougald	625.00	300.00	200.00
(26)	Dale Mitchell	550.00	275.00	185.00
(27)	Don Mueller	550.00	275.00	185.00
(28)	Andy Pafko	550.00	275.00	185.00
(29)	Bob Porterfield	550.00	275.00	185.00
(30)	Ken Raffensberger	550.00	275.00	185.00
(31)	Allie Reynolds	625.00	300.00	200.00
(32a)	Phil Rizzuto (Rizzuto) ("NY" shows on shirt.)	825.00	425.00	275.00
(32b)	Phil Rizzuto (Rizzuto) (No "NY" visible on shirt.)	825.00	400.00	275.00
(33)	Robin Roberts	775.00	400.00	250.00
(34)	Saul Rogovin	550.00	275.00	185.00
(35)	Ray Scarborough	550.00	275.00	185.00
(36)	Red Schoendienst	700.00	350.00	225.00
(37)	Dick Sisler	550.00	275.00	185.00
(38)	Enos Slaughter	700.00	350.00	225.00
(39)	Duke Snider	825.00	400.00	225.00
(40)	Warren Spahn	825.00	400.00	225.00
(41)	Vern Stephens	550.00	275.00	185.00
(42)	Earl Torgeson	550.00	275.00	185.00
(43)	Mickey Vernon	550.00	275.00	185.00
(44)	Ed Waitkus	550.00	275.00	185.00
(45)	Wes Westrum	550.00	275.00	185.00
(46)	Eddie Yost	550.00	275.00	185.00
(47)	Al Zarilla	550.00	275.00	185.00

1887 Tobin Lithographs B/W

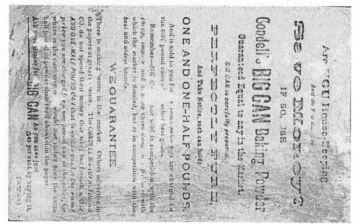

The black-and-white Tobin Lithographs were likely created to offer 19th Century advertisers a lower-cost venue than the lavishly colored version of the same cards. It appears, however, that most advertisers opted for the color type and/or that the color cards were saved more often because the black-and-white cards are today many times scarcer than their color counterparts. Despite the disparity in rarity, the black-and-whites carry only a modest premium value over the color, again probably attributable to the grander overall appearance of the colored cards.

		NM	E	VG
	Complete Set (10):	19,000	9,500	6,350
	Common Player:	1,900	950.00	650.00
(1)	"Go It Old Boy"(Ed Andrews)	1,900	950.00	650.00
(2)	"Oh, Come Off!"(Cap Anson)	3,750	1,875	1,250
(3)	"Watch Me Soak it"(Dan Brouthers)	2,250	1,150	750.00
(4)	"Not Onto It"(Charlie Ferguson)	1,900	950.00	650.00
(5)	"Struck By A Cyclone"(Pebbly Jack Glasscock)	1,900	950.00	650.00
(6)	"An Anxious Moment"(Paul Hines)	1,900	950.00	650.00
(7)	"Where'l You Have It?"(Tim Keefe)	2,250	1,150	750.00
(8)	"The Flower Of The Flock"(Our Own Kelly)	2,850	1,425	950.00
(9)	"A Slide For Home"(Jim M'Cormick) (McCormick)	1,900	950.00	650.00
(10)	"Ain't It A Daisy?"(Smiling Mickey Welch)	2,250	1,150	750.00

1887 Tobin Lithographs Color

The Tobin lithographs, measuring about 3" x 4-1/2", are typical of the "trade" cards that were popular advertising vehicles in the late 19th Century. Found in both black-and-white and color, the lithos include 10 cards depicting caricature action drawings of popular baseball players of the era. Each cartoon-like drawing is accompanied by a colorful caption along with the player's name in parenthesis below. The team affiliation is printed in the upper-left corner, while a large space in the upper-right corner was left blank to accomodate advertising messages. As a result, Tobin cards can be found with ads for various products and services or left blank. Similarly the backs of the cards are also found either blank or with advertising. The set takes its name from the manufacturer, whose name ("Tobin N.Y.") appears in the lower-right corner of each card.

		NM	E	VG
	Complete Set (10):	10,000	5,000	3,000
	Common Player:	1,000	500.00	300.00
(1)	"Go It Old Boy"(Ed Andrews)	1,000	500.00	300.00
(2)	"Oh, Come Off!"(Cap Anson)	2,000	1,000	600.00
(3)	"Watch Me Soak it"(Dan Brouthers)	1,200	600.00	400.00
(4)	"Not Onto It"(Charlie Ferguson)	1,000	500.00	300.00
(5)	"Struck By A Cyclone"(Pebbly Jack Glasscock)	1,000	500.00	300.00
(6)	"An Anxious Moment"(Paul Hines)	1,000	500.00	300.00
(7)	"Where'l You Have It?"(Tim Keefe)	1,200	600.00	400.00
(8)	"The Flower Of The Flock"(Our Own Kelly)	1,500	750.00	500.00
(9)	"A Slide For Home"(Jim M'Cormick) (McCormick)	1,000	500.00	300.00
(10)	"Ain't It A Daisy?"(Smiling Mickey Welch)	1,200	600.00	400.00

1889 Tobin Lithograph Baby Talk Trade Cards

The "Baby Talk Series" that was cataloged as H804-1B in the American Card Catalog is a specific subset of a larger body of similar issues issued between 1887-1889. The principal distinguishing feature of this set is the appearance at lower-right of a name associated with the ball-playing baby pictured. Even within this series, there are variations, such as some cards having a copyright notice in the bottom-right border, while some do not. All have the number "5" in the lower-left border. The 3" x 4-5/8" color lithographed cards were originally sold with blank backs. Some advertisers chose to print messages on the backs, others overprinted their sales pitch on the fronts. Dozens of different advertisers are known to have used these cards as a medium. Those cards that have name references to well-known players of the era King Kelly and Cap Anson, are more highly sought than the others.

		NM	EX	VG
	Complete Set (9):	5,000	2,500	1,500
	Common Card:	600.00	300.00	175.00
(1)	Fee stykes, out. (Lord Fauntleroy)	600.00	300.00	175.00
(2)	I'se a do'en home. (Baby Bunting)	600.00	300.00	175.00
(3)	Oh, I dot it. (Kingdon Gould)	600.00	300.00	175.00
(4)	Oh, I'se all'lite (Little Mascot)	600.00	300.00	175.00
(5)	Oh, Mamma! (Baby Anson)	900.00	450.00	275.00
(6)	Tan "oo" Tetch. (Baby McKee)	600.00	300.00	175.00
(7)	Tum an Pay. (Mull Tobin)	600.00	300.00	175.00
(8)	Tee-he-he! (Dixey, Jr.)	600.00	300.00	175.00
(9)	Wow-ow! (Baby Kelly)	900.00	450.00	275.00

1948-1949 Toleteros

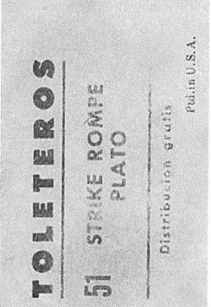

This was the first of three annual issues during the Puerto Rican League winter seasons. Cards are about 1-1/2" x 2-1/4", printed in sepia on thin cardboard. Backs are printed in black-and-white and have a "play" designation for use in a card game. They are numbered, but the numbers are not unique to specific players. Several of the cards were issued in photographic format, rather than printed. It is believed these are scarcer than the regular cards and may account for most of the seven cards which are not currently checklisted. They are designated here with a (P) notation. This checklist is presented alphabetically. An album was issued with the set, and like most contemporary Caribbean issues, cards are usually found in well-used condition with evidence of past mounting. Toleteros is roughly translated as "sluggers."

	NM	E	VG
Complete Set (168): VALUE UNDETERMINED			
Common Player:	150.00	75.00	45.00
Album:			
(1) Yuyo Acosta	150.00	75.00	45.00
(2) Hector Agosto	150.00	75.00	45.00
(3) Alberto Alberdeston	150.00	75.00	45.00
(4) Alberto Alicea	150.00	75.00	45.00
(5) Jaime Almendro	150.00	75.00	45.00
(6) Guinea Alomar	150.00	75.00	45.00
(7) Pedro Alomar	150.00	75.00	45.00
(8) Alfredo Alonso	150.00	75.00	45.00
(9) Yiyo Alonso	150.00	75.00	45.00
(10) Pablo Andino	150.00	75.00	45.00
(11) Jueyito Andrade	150.00	75.00	45.00
(12) Paday Anglero	150.00	75.00	45.00
(13) Luis Arroyo	200.00	100.00	60.00
(14) Pedro J. Arroyo	150.00	75.00	45.00
(15) Joe Atkins (P)	300.00	150.00	90.00
(16) Eugene Baker	300.00	150.00	90.00
(17) Dan Bankhead	300.00	150.00	90.00
(18) Bennett	150.00	75.00	45.00
(19) Carlos Bernier	200.00	100.00	60.00
(20) Hiram Bithorn	250.00	125.00	75.00
(21) Efrain Blasini	150.00	75.00	45.00
(22) Oswaldo Brau	150.00	75.00	45.00
(23) Johnny Britton	150.00	75.00	45.00
(25) George Brown	150.00	75.00	45.00
(26) Willard Brown	4,500	2,250	1,350
(27) Jose Burgos	150.00	75.00	45.00
(28) Tommy Butts	1,200	600.00	360.00
(29) Joe Buzas	150.00	75.00	45.00
(30) Luis R. Cabrera	150.00	75.00	45.00
(31) Marzo Cabrera	150.00	75.00	45.00
(32) Eugenio Camara	150.00	75.00	45.00
(33) Juan Carrero	150.00	75.00	45.00
(34) Medina Chapman	150.00	75.00	45.00
(35) Fernando Clara	150.00	75.00	45.00
(36) Buster Clarkson (P)	800.00	400.00	240.00
(37) Francisco Coimbre	1,000	500.00	300.00
(38) Eugene Collins	400.00	200.00	120.00
(39) Cefo Conde	150.00	75.00	45.00
(40) Johnny Cox	150.00	75.00	45.00
(41) Vitin Cruz	150.00	75.00	45.00
(42) Johnny Davis	500.00	250.00	150.00
(43) Piper Davis	500.00	250.00	150.00
(44) Felle Delgado	150.00	75.00	45.00
(45) Luke Easter	500.00	250.00	150.00
(46) Howard Easterling	600.00	300.00	180.00
(47) Saturnino Escalera	150.00	75.00	45.00
(49) Teggy Espinosa	150.00	75.00	45.00
(50) Coco Ferrer	150.00	75.00	45.00
(51) Wilmer Fields	400.00	200.00	120.00
(52) Tite Figueroa	150.00	75.00	45.00
(53) Oscar Mir Flores	150.00	75.00	45.00
(54) Jesus M. Freyre	150.00	75.00	45.00
(55) Cinque Garcia	150.00	75.00	45.00
(56) Alfonso Gerard	150.00	75.00	45.00
(57) Jim Gilliam (P)	800.00	400.00	240.00
(58) Charlie Glock	150.00	75.00	45.00
(59) Ruben Gomez	250.00	125.00	75.00
(60) David Gonzalez	150.00	75.00	45.00
(61) Gely Goyco	150.00	75.00	45.00
(62) Jack Graham	150.00	75.00	45.00
(63) Roberto Griffith	600.00	300.00	180.00
(64) Jesus Guilbe	150.00	75.00	45.00
(65) Juan Guilbe	150.00	75.00	45.00
(66) Hector Haddock	150.00	75.00	45.00
(67) Sam Hairston	200.00	100.00	60.00
(68) Van Harrington	150.00	75.00	45.00
(69) Luman Harris	150.00	75.00	45.00
(70) Manuel Hernandez	150.00	75.00	45.00
(71) Efrain Hidalgo	150.00	75.00	45.00
(73) Dixie Howell	150.00	75.00	45.00
(74) Jim Lamarque (P)	800.00	400.00	240.00
(75) Carlos Lanauze	150.00	75.00	45.00
(76) Ramon Lasa	150.00	75.00	45.00
(77) Lee Layton	150.00	75.00	45.00
(78) Liebould	150.00	75.00	45.00
(79) Royce Lint	150.00	75.00	45.00
(80) Radames Lopez	150.00	75.00	45.00
(81) Louis Louden	250.00	125.00	75.00
(82) Robert Lynn	150.00	75.00	45.00
(83) Caro Maldonado	150.00	75.00	45.00
(84) Canena Marquez	500.00	250.00	150.00
(85) Antonio Marrero	150.00	75.00	45.00
(86) Gilberto Marrero	150.00	75.00	45.00
(87) Humberto Marti	150.00	75.00	45.00
(88) Millito Martinez	150.00	75.00	45.00
(89) Jose E. Montalvo	150.00	75.00	45.00
(90) Luis Morales	150.00	75.00	45.00
(91) Willie Morales	150.00	75.00	45.00
(92) Howard Moss	150.00	75.00	45.00
(93) Chaguin Muratti	150.00	75.00	45.00
(94) Domingo Navarro	150.00	75.00	45.00
(95) Millito Navarro	200.00	100.00	60.00
(97) Alfredo Olivencia	150.00	75.00	45.00
(98) Guayubin Olivo	200.00	100.00	60.00
(99) Noel Oquendo	150.00	75.00	45.00
(100) Otoniel Ortiz	150.00	75.00	45.00
(101) Rafaelito Ortiz	150.00	75.00	45.00
(102) Alberto Padilla	150.00	75.00	45.00
(103) Fernando Diaz Pedroso	200.00	100.00	60.00
(104) Victor Pellot (Power)	250.00	125.00	75.00
(105) Pedro Pena	150.00	75.00	45.00
(106) Pepin Pereira	150.00	75.00	45.00
(107) Ismael Perez	150.00	75.00	45.00
(108) Juan Perez	150.00	75.00	45.00
(109) Palomo Perez	150.00	75.00	45.00
(110) Villodas Perez	150.00	75.00	45.00
(111) Alonso Perry	500.00	250.00	150.00
(112) Jose Polanco	150.00	75.00	45.00
(113) Bill Powell	200.00	100.00	60.00
(114) Tomas Quinones	200.00	100.00	60.00
(115) R. Cuebas Quintana	150.00	75.00	45.00
(116) Milton Ralat	150.00	75.00	45.00
(117) Otto Ralat	150.00	75.00	45.00
(118) Fernando Ramos	150.00	75.00	45.00
(119) Xavier Rescigno	150.00	75.00	45.00
(121) Miguel L. Rivera	150.00	75.00	45.00
(122) Charlie Rivero	150.00	75.00	45.00
(123) Bienvenido Rodriguez	150.00	75.00	45.00
(124) Pedro Rodriguez	150.00	75.00	45.00
(125) Anastasio Rosario	150.00	75.00	45.00
(126) Jorge Rosas	150.00	75.00	45.00
(127) Cafe Salaberrios	150.00	75.00	45.00
(128) Wilfredo Salas	150.00	75.00	45.00
(129) Juan Sanchez	150.00	75.00	45.00
(130) Carlos M. Santiago	150.00	75.00	45.00
(131) Jose G. Santiago (P)	400.00	200.00	120.00
(132) Ed Sauer	150.00	75.00	45.00
(133) George Scales	1,200	600.00	360.00
(134) Kermit Schmidt	150.00	75.00	45.00
(135) Ken Sears (P)	400.00	200.00	120.00
(136) Herbert Sewell (Souell)	250.00	125.00	75.00
(137) Dwain Sloat	150.00	75.00	45.00
(138) Eugene Smith	200.00	100.00	60.00
(139) Hilton Smith	20,000	10,000	6,000
(140) John Ford Smith	400.00	200.00	120.00
(141) Fernando Sola	150.00	75.00	45.00
(142) Ismael Solla	150.00	75.00	45.00
(143) Francisco Sostre	150.00	75.00	45.00
(144) Earl Taborn	200.00	100.00	60.00
(145) Freddie Thon	150.00	75.00	45.00
(146) Bob Thurman	400.00	200.00	120.00
(147) Griffin Tirado	150.00	75.00	45.00
(148) Leon Tirado	150.00	75.00	45.00
(149) Pedro J. Toro	150.00	75.00	45.00
(150) Bin Torres	150.00	75.00	45.00
(151) Carmelo Torres	150.00	75.00	45.00
(152) Onofre Torres	150.00	75.00	45.00
(153) Penpen Torres	150.00	75.00	45.00
(154) Quincy Trouppe	1,000	500.00	300.00
(155) Foca Valentin	150.00	75.00	45.00
(156) Roberto Vargas	150.00	75.00	45.00
(157) Tetelo Vargas	1,000	500.00	300.00
(158) Rafael Vasquez	150.00	75.00	45.00
(159) Guillermo Vega	150.00	75.00	45.00
(160) Jose L. Velazquez	150.00	75.00	45.00
(161) Laru Velazquez	150.00	75.00	45.00
(162) Vicente Villafane	150.00	75.00	45.00
(165) Luis Villodas	200.00	100.00	60.00
(166) Jesse Williams	200.00	100.00	60.00
(167) Artie Wilson	500.00	250.00	150.00
(168) Rogelio Wiscovich	150.00	75.00	45.00

1949-1950 Toleteros

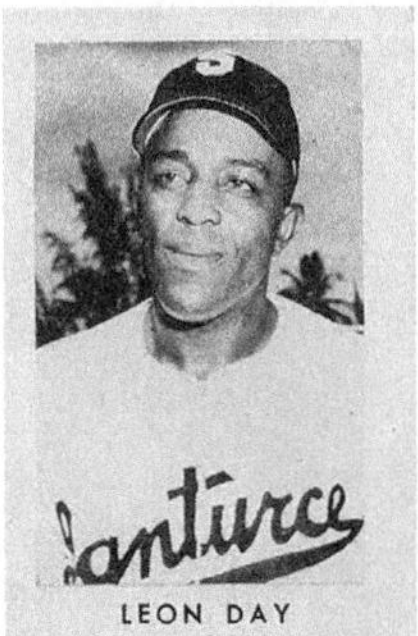
Santurce
LEON DAY

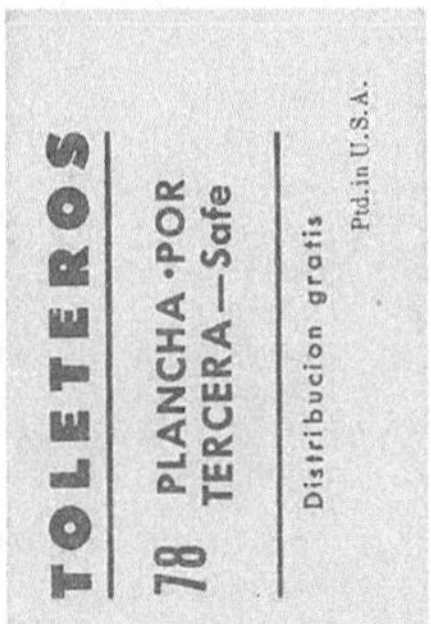
TOLETEROS
78
PLANCHA - POR
TERCERA—Safe
Distribucion gratis
Ptd. in U.S.A.

The second of three annual issues during the Puerto Rican League winter seasons, these cards are similar in format to the previous year's set. Front photos are printed in black-and-white, and the backs are printed in red. Cards are about 1-1/2" x 2-1/4", printed on thin cardboard with a light gloss. Backs have a "play" designation for use in a card game and are numbered, though the numbers are not unique to specific players. This checklist is presented alphabetically. Some players can be found in two different poses. Where the variations are known, they are described parenthetically; where the poses are not known, an asterisk is shown. Players with a (P) designation were produced on photographic, rather than printed stock and are scarcer than the regular cards. An album was issued with the set, and like most contemporary Caribbean issues, cards are usually found in well-used condition with evidence of past mounting. Toleteros is roughly translated as "sluggers."

	NM	E	VG
Complete Set (216): VALUE UNDETERMINED			
Common Player:	100.00	50.00	30.00
Album:	600.00	300.00	180.00
(1) Hector Agosto	100.00	50.00	30.00
(2) Alberto Alberdeston	100.00	50.00	30.00
(3) Alberto Alicea	100.00	50.00	30.00
(4) Jaime Almendro (*)	100.00	50.00	30.00
(5) Guinea Alomar	100.00	50.00	30.00
(6) Pedro Alomar	100.00	50.00	30.00
(7) Alfredo Alonso	100.00	50.00	30.00
(8) Yiyo Alonso	100.00	50.00	30.00
(9) Ismael Alvarado	100.00	50.00	30.00
(10) Manuel Alvarez (*)	100.00	50.00	30.00
(11) Pablo Andino	100.00	50.00	30.00
(12) Jueyito Andrade	100.00	50.00	30.00
(13) Paday Anglero	100.00	50.00	30.00
(14) Luis Arroyo (*)	125.00	65.00	40.00
(15) Pedro J. Arroyo	100.00	50.00	30.00
(16) Eugene Baker	150.00	75.00	45.00
(17) Dan Bankhead	150.00	75.00	45.00
(18) Sammy Bankhead	475.00	240.00	140.00
(19) Ramon Bayron	100.00	50.00	30.00
(20) Carlos Bernier	160.00	80.00	480.00
(21) Hiram Bithorn	275.00	135.00	82.50
(22) Efrain Blasini	100.00	50.00	30.00
(23) Anil Bonilla (*)	100.00	50.00	30.00
(24) Stan Bread (Breard)	100.00	50.00	30.00
(25) Chester Brewer	1,000	500.00	300.00
(26) Johnny Britton	100.00	50.00	30.00
(27) George Brown	100.00	50.00	30.00
(28) Willard Brown (*)	3,750	1,850	1,100
(29) J.A. Burgos (*)	100.00	50.00	30.00
(30) Tommy Butts	225.00	112.50	67.50
(31) Joe Buzas	100.00	50.00	30.00
(32) Rafael Cabezudo	100.00	50.00	30.00
(33) Luis R. Cabrera	100.00	50.00	30.00
(34) Marzo Cabrera	100.00	50.00	30.00
(35) Manolete Caceres (*)	100.00	50.00	30.00
(36) Eugenio Camara	100.00	50.00	30.00
(37) Maximo Casals	100.00	50.00	30.00
(38) Rafael Casanovas	100.00	50.00	30.00
(39) Nino Zurdo Castro	100.00	50.00	30.00
(40) Perucho Cepeda (*)	500.00	250.00	150.00
(41) Medina Chapman	100.00	50.00	30.00
(42) T. Gomez Checo	100.00	50.00	30.00
(43) Buster Clarkson	300.00	150.00	90.00
(44) Francisco Coimbre	400.00	200.00	120.00
(45a) Eugene Collins (Chest-up.)	200.00	100.00	60.00
(45b) Eugene Collins (Waist-up.)	200.00	100.00	60.00
(46) Luis Colmenero	100.00	50.00	30.00
(47) Luis Colon	100.00	50.00	30.00
(48) M. Concepcion (*)	125.00	65.00	40.00
(49) Cefo Conde	100.00	50.00	30.00
(50) Omar Cordero	100.00	50.00	30.00
(51) Johnny Cox	100.00	50.00	30.00
(52) Vitin Cruz	100.00	50.00	30.00
(53) Johnny Davis	400.00	200.00	120.00
(54) Lomax Davis	150.00	75.00	45.00
(55) Piper Davis	200.00	100.00	60.00
(56) Leon Day	12,000	6,000	3,600
(57) Felle Delgado	100.00	50.00	30.00
(58) Carmelo Delpin	100.00	50.00	30.00
(59) Ruben Diaz	100.00	50.00	30.00
(60) Lucius Easter	300.00	150.00	90.00
(61) Howard Easterling	160.00	80.00	48.00
(62) Saturnino Escalera	125.00	62.50	37.50
(63) Teggy Espinosa	100.00	50.00	30.00
(64) George Fallon	100.00	50.00	30.00
(65) Coco Ferrer (*)	100.00	50.00	30.00
(66) Walter Fialla (Fiala)	100.00	50.00	30.00
(67) Wilmer Fields (*)	300.00	150.00	90.00
(68) Tite Figueroa	100.00	50.00	30.00
(69) Oscar Mir Flores	100.00	50.00	30.00
(70) Jesus M. Freyre	100.00	50.00	30.00
(71) (Les) Fusselmann (Fusselman)	100.00	50.00	30.00
(72) Cinque Garcia	100.00	50.00	30.00

(73)	Alfonso Gerard	100.00	50.00	30.00
(74)	Alban Glossopp (Glossop)	100.00	50.00	30.00
(75)	Ruben Gomez (*)	160.00	80.00	48.00
(76)	Faelo Gonzalez (P)	200.00	100.00	60.00
(77)	Rafael Gonzalez	100.00	50.00	30.00
(78)	Gely Goyco	100.00	50.00	30.00
(79)	Jack Graham	100.00	50.00	30.00
(80)	Bill Greason	125.00	65.00	40.00
(81)	Felo Guilbe	100.00	50.00	30.00
(82)	Jesus Guilbe	100.00	50.00	30.00
(83)	Juan Guilbe	100.00	50.00	30.00
(84)	Hector Haddock	100.00	50.00	30.00
(85)	Sam Hairston	150.00	75.00	45.00
(86)	Luman Harris	100.00	50.00	30.00
(87a)	Vic Harris (Black background.)	1,000	500.00	300.00
(87b)	Vic Harris (Outdoors background.)	1,000	500.00	300.00
(88)	Angel Hernaiz (P)	200.00	100.00	60.00
(89)	Manuel Hernandez	100.00	50.00	30.00
(90)	Efrain Hidalgo	100.00	50.00	30.00
(91)	Dixie Howell	100.00	50.00	30.00
(92)	Roy Hughes (*)	100.00	50.00	30.00
(93)	Natalio Irizarry	100.00	50.00	30.00
(94)	Walter James	100.00	50.00	30.00
(95)	Cecyl Kayser (P)	300.00	150.00	90.00
(96)	Jack Krauss	100.00	50.00	30.00
(97)	Jim Lamarque	160.00	80.00	48.00
(98)	Carlos Lanauze	100.00	50.00	30.00
(99)	Ramon Lasa	100.00	50.00	30.00
(100)	Rafael Lastra	100.00	50.00	30.00
(101)	Lee Layton	100.00	50.00	30.00
(102)	Lettish	100.00	50.00	30.00
(103)	Johnny Logan	100.00	50.00	30.00
(104)	Radames Lopez	100.00	50.00	30.00
(105)	Louis Louden	150.00	75.00	45.00
(106)	Robert Lynn	100.00	50.00	30.00
(107)	Al Lyons	100.00	50.00	30.00
(108)	Cirico Machuca	100.00	50.00	30.00
(109)	Caro Maldonado	100.00	50.00	30.00
(110)	Clifford Mapes	100.00	50.00	30.00
(111)	Jim Markland (P)	200.00	100.00	60.00
(112)	Canena Marquez	200.00	100.00	60.00
(113)	Leo Marquez	100.00	50.00	30.00
(114)	Antonio Marrero (*)	100.00	50.00	30.00
(115)	Gilberto Marrero	100.00	50.00	30.00
(116)	Humberto Marti	100.00	50.00	30.00
(117)	Achin Matos	100.00	50.00	30.00
(118)	Booker McDaniels	150.00	75.00	45.00
(119)	George McQuillen	100.00	50.00	30.00
(120)	Agustin Medina	100.00	50.00	30.00
(121)	John Medina	100.00	50.00	30.00
(122)	Vicente Medina	100.00	50.00	30.00
(123)	Henry Miller (P)	300.00	150.00	90.00
(124)	Jose E. Montalvo	100.00	50.00	30.00
(125a)	Luis A. Morales (*)	100.00	50.00	30.00
(125b)	Luis A. Morales (*)	100.00	50.00	30.00
(126)	Pedroso Morales	100.00	50.00	30.00
(127)	Willie Morales	100.00	50.00	30.00
(128)	Howard Moss	100.00	50.00	30.00
(129)	Gallego Munoz	100.00	50.00	30.00
(130)	Digno Navarro	100.00	50.00	30.00
(131)	Domingo Navarro	100.00	50.00	30.00
(132)	Millito Navarro	160.00	80.00	48.00
(133)	Earl Naylor (P)	200.00	100.00	60.00
(134)	Alfredo Olivencia	100.00	50.00	30.00
(135)	Guayubin Olivo	125.00	65.00	40.00
(136)	Noel Oquendo	100.00	50.00	30.00
(137)	Otoniel Ortiz	100.00	50.00	30.00
(138)	Rafaelito Ortiz	100.00	50.00	30.00
(139)	Alberto Padilla	100.00	50.00	30.00
(140)	Miguel Payano (P)	200.00	100.00	60.00
(141)	Fernando Diaz Pedroso (*)	125.00	65.00	40.00
(142)	Victor Pellot (Power)	150.00	75.00	45.00
(143)	Pedro Pena	100.00	50.00	30.00
(144)	Pepin Pereira (*)	100.00	50.00	30.00
(145)	Ismael Perez	100.00	50.00	30.00
(146)	Juan Perez	100.00	50.00	30.00
(147)	Palomo Perez	100.00	50.00	30.00
(148)	Rogelio Perez	100.00	50.00	30.00
(149)	Villodas Perez	100.00	50.00	30.00
(150)	Alonso Perry	200.00	100.00	60.00
(151)	Russ Peters	100.00	50.00	30.00
(152)	Jose Polanco	100.00	50.00	30.00
(153)	(Bill) Powell	100.00	50.00	30.00
(154)	Thomas Quinones (*)	125.00	65.00	40.00
(155)	Milton Ralat	100.00	50.00	30.00
(156)	Otto Ralat	100.00	50.00	30.00
(157)	Fernando Ramos	100.00	50.00	30.00
(158)	Lionel Richards	100.00	50.00	30.00
(159)	Enrique Reinoso	100.00	50.00	30.00
(160)	Xavier Rescigno	100.00	50.00	30.00
(161)	Miguel A. Rivera	100.00	50.00	30.00
(162)	Bienvenido Rodriguez	100.00	50.00	30.00
(163)	Pedro Rodriguez	100.00	50.00	30.00
(164)	Jose M. Roque	100.00	50.00	30.00
(165)	Fachy Rosado	100.00	50.00	30.00
(166)	Jorge Rosas	100.00	50.00	30.00
(167)	Ramon Salgado (*)	100.00	50.00	30.00
(168)	Juan Sanchez	100.00	50.00	30.00
(169)	Carlos M. Santiago	100.00	50.00	30.00
(170)	Jose G. Santiago	100.00	50.00	30.00
(171)	Ed Sauer (*)	100.00	50.00	30.00
(172)	George Scales	800.00	400.00	240.00
(173)	Kermit Schmidt (*)	100.00	50.00	30.00
(174)	Ken Sears	100.00	50.00	30.00
(175)	Dick Seay	700.00	350.00	210.00
(176)	Jose Seda	100.00	50.00	30.00
(177)	Barney Serrell	200.00	100.00	60.00
(178)	McDuffie Sevilla (*)	100.00	50.00	30.00
(179)	Dwain Sloat	100.00	50.00	30.00
(180)	Eugene Smith	125.00	65.00	40.00
(181)	Hilton Smith	12,000	6,000	3,600
(182)	John F. Smith	150.00	75.00	45.00
(183)	Jerome Snider	100.00	50.00	30.00
(184)	Ismael Solla	100.00	50.00	30.00
(185)	Francisco Sostre	100.00	50.00	30.00
(186)	Herb Souell	100.00	50.00	30.00
(187)	Luis St. Clair	100.00	50.00	30.00
(188)	Tetelo Sterling	100.00	50.00	30.00
(189)	Lonnie Summers	125.00	65.00	40.00
(190)	Jim Tabor (*)	100.00	50.00	30.00
(191)	Earl Taborn	100.00	50.00	30.00
(192)	Israel Ten (*)	100.00	50.00	30.00
(193)	Leo Thomas	100.00	50.00	30.00
(194)	Freddie Thon	100.00	50.00	30.00
(195)	Bob Thurman (*)	200.00	100.00	60.00
(196)	Griffin Tirado (*)	100.00	50.00	30.00
(197)	Leon Tirado	100.00	50.00	30.00
(198)	Bin Torres	100.00	50.00	30.00
(199)	Carmelo Torres	100.00	50.00	30.00
(200)	Indian Torres	100.00	50.00	30.00
(201)	Quincy Trouppe	700.00	350.00	210.00
(202)	Hector Trussa	100.00	50.00	30.00
(203)	Foca Valentin	100.00	50.00	30.00
(204)	Roberto Vargas	100.00	50.00	30.00
(205)	Tetelo Vargas	300.00	150.00	90.00
(206)	Rafael Vazquez	100.00	50.00	30.00
(207)	Guillermo Vega	100.00	50.00	30.00
(208)	Jose L. Velazquez	100.00	50.00	30.00
(209)	Vicente Villafane (*)	100.00	50.00	30.00
(210)	Luis Villodas	100.00	50.00	30.00
(211)	Curley Williams (P)	300.00	150.00	90.00
(212)	Marvin Williams (P)	300.00	150.00	90.00
(213)	Artie Wilson	300.00	150.00	90.00
(214)	Robert Wilson (*)	100.00	50.00	30.00
(215)	Rogelio Wiscovich	100.00	50.00	30.00
(216)	Rafael Zavala	100.00	50.00	30.00

1950-1951 Toleteros

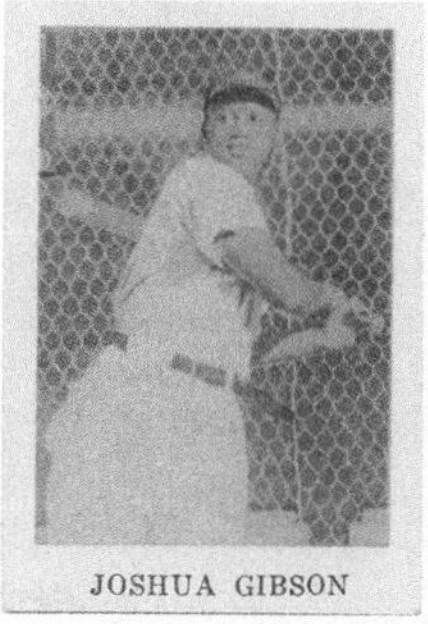

The last of three annual issues during the Puerto Rican League winter seasons, these cards are similar in format to the previous years' sets, with the principal difference being that the approximately 1-3/4" x 2-1/2" cards are printed in color rather than black-and-white. Most are printed on thin cardboard, but some are produced on photographic stock and believed to be scarcer than the others. Those are designated with a (P) in the checklist. Unlike the previous years' issues, backs are blank. This checklist is presented alphabetically. An album was issued with the set, and like most contemporary Caribbean issues, cards are usually found in well-used condition with evidence of past mounting. Toleteros is roughly translated as "sluggers."

		NM	E	VG
Complete Set (192): VALUE UNDETERMINED				
Common Player:		60.00	30.00	18.00
Album:		300.00	150.00	90.00
(1)	Hector Agosto	60.00	30.00	18.00
(2)	Robert Alexander	60.00	30.00	18.00
(3)	Alberto Alicea	60.00	30.00	18.00
(4)	Jaime Almendro (Blue Senadores.)	75.00	37.00	22.00
(5)	Jaime Almendro (Red Senadores.)	60.00	30.00	18.00
(6)	Pedro Alomar	60.00	30.00	18.00
(7)	Ismael Alvarado (Ponce)	60.00	30.00	18.00
(8)	Ismael Alvarado (Aguadilla)	60.00	30.00	18.00
(9)	Jueyito Andrade	60.00	30.00	18.00
(10)	Nick Andromidas	60.00	30.00	18.00
(11)	Pacay Anglero	60.00	30.00	18.00
(12)	Luis (Tite) Arroyo	75.00	37.50	22.50
(13)	Pedro J. Arroyo	60.00	30.00	18.00
(14)	Dan Bankhead	100.00	50.00	30.00
(15)	Babe Barna	60.00	30.00	18.00
(16)	Carlos Bernier	75.00	37.50	22.50
(17)	John Bero	60.00	30.00	18.00
(18)	Wayne Blackburn	60.00	30.00	18.00
(19)	Efrain Blasini	60.00	30.00	18.00
(20)	Bill Boyd	75.00	37.50	22.50
(21)	Stan Breard	60.00	30.00	18.00
(22)	Willard Brown	4,250	2,125	1,275
(23)	Lou Burdette (P)	125.00	65.00	35.00
(24)	Jose A. Burgos	60.00	30.00	18.00
(25)	Rafael Cabezudo	60.00	30.00	18.00
(26)	Luis R. Cabrera	60.00	30.00	18.00
(27)	Marzo Cabrera	60.00	30.00	18.00
(28)	Manolete Caceres	60.00	30.00	18.00
(29)	Rafael Casanova	60.00	30.00	18.00
(30)	Medina Chapman	60.00	30.00	18.00
(31)	Al Cihosky (P)	125.00	65.00	35.00
(32)	Mike Clark	75.00	37.00	22.00
(33)	Buster Clarkson (Santurce)	250.00	125.00	75.00
(34)	Buster Clarkson (Ponce)	250.00	125.00	75.00
(35)	Francisco Coimbre	300.00	150.00	90.00
(36)	Rafael Colmenero	60.00	30.00	18.00
(37)	Luis Colon	60.00	30.00	18.00
(38)	Monchile Concepcion	75.00	37.50	22.50
(39)	Cefo Conde	60.00	30.00	18.00
(40)	Omar Cordero	60.00	30.00	18.00
(41)	William Costa	60.00	30.00	18.00
(42)	Clinton Courtney	75.00	37.50	22.50
(43)	George Crowe	75.00	37.50	22.50
(44)	Johnny Davis (Mayaguez)	150.00	75.00	45.00
(45)	Johnny Davis (San Juan)	150.00	75.00	45.00
(46)	Piper Davis	200.00	100.00	60.00
(47)	Ellis Deal	100.00	50.00	30.00
(48)	Felle Delgado	60.00	30.00	18.00
(49)	Luke Easter	175.00	85.00	50.00
(50)	Jaime A. Escalera	60.00	30.00	18.00
(51)	Saturnino Escalera	85.00	42.00	25.00
(52)	Luis Ferbe	60.00	30.00	18.00
(53)	L.E. Fernandez	60.00	30.00	18.00
(54)	Coco Ferrer	60.00	30.00	18.00
(55)	Walter Fialla (Fiala)	60.00	30.00	18.00
(56)	Wilmer Fields	150.00	75.00	45.00
(57)	Jose A. Figueroa	75.00	37.50	22.50
(58)	Oscar Mir Flores	60.00	30.00	18.00
(59)	Jesus M. Freyre	60.00	30.00	18.00
(60)	Dominic Galata	60.00	30.00	18.00
(61)	Felipe Garcia	60.00	30.00	18.00
(62)	Alfonso Gerard	60.00	30.00	18.00
(63)	Al Gerheauser (P)	225.00	112.50	67.50
(64)	Joshua Gibson	25,000	12,500	7,500
(65)	James Gilliam	325.00	162.50	97.50
(66)	Ruben Gomez	125.00	62.50	37.50
(67)	Rafael Gonzalez	60.00	30.00	18.00
(68)	Felo Guilbe (Ponce)	60.00	30.00	18.00
(69)	Felo Guilbe (San Juan)	60.00	30.00	18.00
(70)	Juan Guilbe	60.00	30.00	18.00
(71)	Hector Haddock	60.00	30.00	18.00
(72)	Red Hardy (P)	125.00	60.00	35.00
(73)	Van Harrington (P)	200.00	100.00	60.00
(74)	Ray Hathaway	60.00	30.00	18.00
(75)	Ralston Hemsley	75.00	37.50	22.50
(76)	Angel Hernaiz	60.00	30.00	18.00
(77)	Rudy Hernandez	125.00	62.50	37.50
(78)	Don Hoak	100.00	50.00	30.00
(79)	Rogers Hornsby	700.00	350.00	210.00
(80)	Dixie Howell	60.00	30.00	18.00
(81)	Natalio Irizarry (P)	125.00	60.00	35.00
(82)	Walter James	60.00	30.00	18.00
(83)	Stan Karpinsky (P)	125.00	60.00	35.00
(84)	Cecyl Kayser	100.00	50.00	30.00
(85)	Carlos Lanauze	60.00	30.00	18.00
(86)	Rafael Lastra	60.00	30.00	18.00
(87)	Quique Leon	60.00	30.00	18.00
(88)	George Lerchen (P)	125.00	60.00	35.00
(89)	Lou Limmer	150.00	75.00	45.00
(90)	Royce Lint	60.00	30.00	18.00
(91)	Al Lyons	60.00	30.00	18.00
(92)	Glenn MacQuillen	60.00	30.00	18.00
(93)	Jim Markland	60.00	30.00	18.00
(94)	Luis A. Marquez	225.00	110.00	65.00
(95)	Bob Marquis	60.00	30.00	18.00
(96)	Antonio Marrero	60.00	30.00	18.00
(97)	Humberto Marti	60.00	30.00	18.00
(98)	Vicente Medina	60.00	30.00	18.00
(99)	M. Monserrate Jr.	60.00	30.00	18.00
(100)	Jose E. Montalvo (Blue Senadores.)	60.00	30.00	18.00
(101)	Jose E. Montalvo (Red Senadores.)	90.00	45.00	27.00

(102)	Luis Morales	100.00	50.00	30.00
(103)	Pedroso Morales	60.00	30.00	18.00
(104)	Willie Morales	60.00	30.00	18.00
(105)	Luis M. Munoz (Blue Senadores.)	60.00	30.00	18.00
(106)	Luis M. Munoz (Red Senadores.)	60.00	30.00	18.00
(107)	Napier	75.00	37.00	22.00
(108)	Digno Navarro	60.00	30.00	18.00
(109)	Ernest Nevel	60.00	30.00	18.00
(110)	Alfredo Olivencia	60.00	30.00	18.00
(111)	L. Rodriguez Olmo	135.00	67.50	40.50
(112)	Noel Oquendo	60.00	30.00	18.00
(113)	Otoniel Ortiz	60.00	30.00	18.00
(114)	Rafaelito Ortiz	60.00	30.00	18.00
(115)	Roy Partlow	175.00	85.00	50.00
(116)	Miguel Payano (Red Senadores.)	60.00	30.00	18.00
(117)	Miguel Payano (Mayaguez)	60.00	30.00	18.00
(118)	Fernando Pedroso	75.00	37.50	22.50
(119)	Victor Pellot (Power)	100.00	50.00	30.00
(120)	Pedro Pena	60.00	30.00	18.00
(121)	Jose Pereira	60.00	30.00	18.00
(122)	Ismael Perez	60.00	30.00	18.00
(123)	Juan Perez	60.00	30.00	18.00
(124)	Villodas Perez	60.00	30.00	18.00
(125)	Alonso Perry	300.00	150.00	90.00
(126)	Alonso Perry	300.00	150.00	90.00
(127)	Jose D. Polanco	60.00	30.00	18.00
(128)	A. Portocarrero	125.00	62.50	37.50
(129)	Bill Powell	75.00	37.50	22.50
(130)	Tomas Quinones	75.00	37.50	22.50
(131)	Milton Ralat	60.00	30.00	18.00
(132)	Fernando Ramos	60.00	30.00	18.00
(133)	Henry Rementeria	60.00	30.00	18.00
(134)	Luis Renta	60.00	30.00	18.00
(135)	Herminio Reyes	60.00	30.00	18.00
(136)	Lionel Richards	60.00	30.00	18.00
(137)	Gene Richardson	75.00	37.50	22.50
(138)	Jim Rivera	125.00	62.50	37.50
(139)	Miguel A. Rivera	60.00	30.00	18.00
(140)	Roberto Rivera	60.00	30.00	18.00
(141)	Jack Robinson	60.00	30.00	18.00
(142)	Ministro Rodriguez	60.00	30.00	18.00
(143)	Pedro Rodriguez	60.00	30.00	18.00
(144)	Jorge Rosas	60.00	30.00	18.00
(145)	Miguel Ruiz	60.00	30.00	18.00
(146)	Ramon Salgado	60.00	30.00	18.00
(147)	Juan Sanchez	60.00	30.00	18.00
(148)	Carlos M. Santiago	60.00	30.00	18.00
(149)	Jose G. Santiago	150.00	75.00	45.00
(150)	George Scales	250.00	125.00	75.00
(151)	Scarpatte	60.00	30.00	18.00
(152)	Kermit Schmidt (Ponce)	60.00	30.00	18.00
(153)	Kermit Schmidt (Red Senadores.)	60.00	30.00	18.00
(154)	Ken Sears	60.00	30.00	18.00
(155)	Dick Seay	300.00	150.00	90.00
(156)	Pedro Seda	60.00	30.00	18.00
(157)	McDuffie Sevilla	60.00	30.00	18.00
(158)	Vincent Shuppe	60.00	30.00	18.00
(159)	William Skowron	150.00	75.00	45.00
(160)	Dwain Sloat	60.00	30.00	18.00
(161)	John Ford Smith	175.00	85.00	50.00
(162)	Francisco Sostre	60.00	30.00	18.00
(163)	Jose St. Clair (Looking forward.)	60.00	30.00	18.00
(164)	Jose St. Clair (Looking left.)	60.00	30.00	18.00
(165)	Luis St. Clair	60.00	30.00	18.00
(166)	Jimmy Starks	75.00	37.50	22.50
(167)	Israel Ten	60.00	30.00	18.00
(168)	Leo Thomas	60.00	30.00	18.00
(169)	Valmy Thomas (P)	375.00	187.50	112.50
(170)	Freddie Thon	60.00	30.00	18.00
(171)	Bob Thurman	200.00	100.00	60.00
(172)	Miguel A. Tineo	60.00	30.00	18.00
(173)	Griffin Tirado (Blue background.)	60.00	30.00	18.00
(174)	Griffin Tirado (Trees in background.)	160.00	80.00	48.00
(175)	Bin Torres	60.00	30.00	18.00
(176)	Clarkson Torres	60.00	30.00	18.00
(177)	Manuel Traboux	60.00	30.00	18.00
(178)	Gilberto Valentin	60.00	30.00	18.00
(179)	Roberto Vargas	60.00	30.00	18.00
(180)	Tetelo Vargas	425.00	212.50	127.50
(181)	Rafael Vazquez	60.00	30.00	18.00
(182)	Guillermo Vega	60.00	30.00	18.00
(183)	Jose L. Velazquez	60.00	30.00	18.00
(184)	Vicente Villafane	60.00	30.00	18.00
(185)	Luis Villodas	75.00	37.50	22.50
(186)	Curley Williams (P)	150.00	75.00	45.00
(187)	Artie Wilson	225.00	110.00	65.00
(188)	Robert Wilson (P)	150.00	75.00	45.00
(189)	Jerry Witte (P)	125.00	60.00	35.00
(190)	Pete Wojey	60.00	30.00	18.00

(191)	Andres Zabala	60.00	30.00	18.00
(192)	Rafael Zavala	60.00	30.00	18.00

1950-1951 Toleteros In Action

90. Piper intenta sacar a Tetelo- SAFE

		NM	E	VG
	Complete Set (178):	6,500	3,250	2,000
	Common Card:	50.00	25.00	15.00
1	Pellot fildea con elegencia.(Victor Pellot (Power))	60.00	30.00	18.00
2	Burgos conecta hit de piernas.(Jose Burgos)	50.00	25.00	15.00
3	OUT por medio paso.	50.00	25.00	15.00
4	Te gusta el mamabo, Canena?(Canena Marquez)	65.00	32.50	20.00
5	OUT!!	50.00	25.00	15.00
6	Lanauze se eleva tras la bola.(Carlos Lanauze)	50.00	25.00	15.00
7	Simpson se escurre en tercera. . .	50.00	25.00	15.00
8	Si no se la cae la bola. . .	50.00	25.00	15.00
9	Escalera realiza brillante cogida.(Saturnino Escalera)	50.00	25.00	15.00
10	Lucha Grecoromana?	50.00	25.00	15.00
11	Gallego a punto deslizarse. . .(Gallego Munoz)	50.00	25.00	15.00
12	Parece. . .pero no lo empuja. . .	50.00	25.00	15.00
13	Ramos da out a Felo en primera.(Fernando Ramos)	50.00	25.00	15.00
14	El Chiquitin y El Magnifico.	50.00	25.00	15.00
15	Limmer llege de pie tras triple.(Lou Limmer)	50.00	25.00	15.00
16	Arroyo toca a Costa. . .OUT.(Luis Arroyo)	50.00	25.00	15.00
17	Thon a salvo en tercera.(Freddie Thon)	50.00	25.00	15.00
18	Thurman hacia home Scales lo felicita.(Bob Thurman, George Scales)	65.00	32.50	20.00
19	NOT ISSUED			
20	NOT ISSUED			
21	Coca trata de escurrirse - OUT.(Coco Ferrer)	50.00	25.00	15.00
22	Thurman out a manos de Lanauze(Bob Thurman, Carlos Lanauzue)	65.00	32.50	20.00
23	Santiago felicita a Atkins(Carlos M. Santiago, Joe Atkins)	50.00	25.00	15.00
24	Griffin captura a Miller en home.(Griffin Tirado, Henry Miller)	50.00	25.00	15.00
25	"Detente Villodas": Escalera.(Luis Villodas, Saturnino Escalera)	50.00	25.00	15.00
26	Felo se desliza. . .SAFE.(Felo Guilbe)	50.00	25.00	15.00
27	Gallego llega safe a Home.(Gallego Munoz)	50.00	25.00	15.00
28	Que pena! Se cayo la bola. . .	50.00	25.00	15.00
29	Easterling esperando la bola - OUT.(Howard Easterling)	80.00	40.00	24.00
30	Pitcher McDuffie anotando.(McDuffie Sevilla)	50.00	25.00	15.00
31	El raudo Roberto se desliza - SAFE.(Roberto Vargas)	50.00	25.00	15.00
32	Harris felicita Brown tras homerun(Willard Brown)	275.00	137.50	82.50

33	Burgos intenta sacar Easter - SAFE.(Jose Burgos, Luke Easter)	80.00	40.00	24.00
34	Los Leones felicitan a Clarkson.(Buster Clarkson)	65.00	32.50	20.00
35	Otoniel realiza dificil cogida. . .(Otoniel Ortiz)	65.00	32.00	19.50
36	Thurman safe en tercera. . .(Bob Thurman)	65.00	32.50	20.00
37	Bernier safe en home.(Carlos Bernier)	50.00	25.00	15.00
38	Chifflan Clark se va de homerun.(Chiflan Clark)	50.00	25.00	15.00
39	El gran Easter llega tras homerun.(Luke Easter)	65.00	32.50	20.00
40	Se cae bola a Fields; Graham safe.(Wilmer Fields, Jack Graham)	60.00	30.00	18.00
41	Otoniel trata sacar Taborn - SAFE.(Otoniel Ortiz, Earl Taborn)	50.00	25.00	15.00
42	McQuillen se desliza tercera - SAFE.(George McQuillen)	50.00	25.00	15.00
43	Uno, dos y tres. . .Y anota Coimbre(Francisco Coimbre)	90.00	45.00	27.50
44	Carlos Manuel llega trade. . .OUT.(Carlos M. Santiago)	50.00	25.00	15.00
45	Aprieta el paso, Griffin. . .(Griffin Tirado)	50.00	25.00	15.00
46	Pepe Lucas saca out a Resbaloso.(Pepe Lucas)	50.00	25.00	15.00
47	"No hay quien pase", dice Howell(Dixie Howell)	50.00	25.00	15.00
48	Y que dice el Umpiere?	50.00	25.00	15.00
49	Pedroso intenta robo home - OUT.(Fernando Pedroso)	50.00	25.00	15.00
50	Se formo el nudo. . .	50.00	25.00	15.00
51	Cogelo con calma, Leo. . .(Leo Thomas)	50.00	25.00	15.00
52	Tetelo galopando hacia primera. . .(Tetelo Vargas)	90.00	45.00	27.50
53	Haciendose burla?	50.00	25.00	15.00
54	Los tiburones felicitan. . .	50.00	25.00	15.00
55	La No. 29 de Bernier.(Carlos Bernier)	50.00	25.00	15.00
56	Jockey entra facilmente a primera.	50.00	25.00	15.00
57	Buzas felicita a Collins.(Joe Buzas, Eugene Collins)	50.00	25.00	15.00
58	Ya es tarde, Jose Enrique. . .	50.00	25.00	15.00
59	Lomax Davis entra tras homerun(Lomax Davis)	50.00	25.00	15.00
60	Haddock no puede sacar Villafane.(Hector Haddock)	50.00	25.00	15.00
61	Otoniel Ortiz se va de hom,erun. . .(Otoniel Ortiz)	50.00	25.00	15.00
62	Otra mas para Bernier(Carlos Bernier)	50.00	25.00	15.00
63	Montalvo se desliza en tercera (?)(Jose E. Montalvo)	50.00	25.00	15.00
64	Willie es todo ojos. .(Willie Morales)	50.00	25.00	15.00
65	La Mucura esta llegando. . .(Johnny Davis)	60.00	30.00	18.00
66	Chapman da out espectacular.(Medina Chapman)	50.00	25.00	15.00
67	McQuillen pisa plato tras homerun(George McQuillen)	50.00	25.00	15.00
68	"Coimbre, Safe". .dice el Umpire.(Francisco Coimbre)	90.00	45.00	27.50
69	Llega Perry despues de Homerun. . .(Alonso Perry)	65.00	32.50	20.00
70	Griffin, ya es tuyo. . .(Griffin Tirado)	50.00	25.00	15.00
71	Fields pisa plato tras Homerun. . .(Wilmer Fields)	50.00	25.00	15.00
72	EL HOMBRE ESE. . .(Willard Brown)	200.00	100.00	60.00

#	Description	NM	E	VG
73	Jockey se desliza violentamente...	50.00	25.00	15.00
74	Montalvo esperando a Tite - OUT.(Jose E. Montalvo)	50.00	25.00	15.00
75	Perry anota transqueando...(Alonso Perry)	65.00	32.50	20.00
76	Fields pivotea para double-play.(Wilmer Fields)	60.00	30.00	18.00
77	Andando en la cuerda, Piper?(Piper Davis)	65.00	32.50	20.00
78	Montalvo en pie de combate...(Jose E. Montalvo)	50.00	25.00	15.00
79	EN GRAN EXPECTATIVA...	50.00	25.00	15.00
80	Indios reciben Gachito tras homer	50.00	25.00	15.00
81	Butts esquiva la bola - SAFE.(Pee Wee Butts)	50.00	25.00	15.00
82	Otro para el Gaucho Davis...(Johnny Davis)	60.00	30.00	18.00
83	Los leones se alborotan...(Piper Davis)	60.00	30.00	18.00
84	Lanauze safe en home...(Carlos Lanauze)	50.00	25.00	15.00
85	Lanauze se alarga - OUT.(Carlos Lanauze)	50.00	25.00	15.00
86	Thurman llega tras homerun.(Bob Thurman)	65.00	32.50	20.00
87	Sauer roba home espectacularmente(Ed Sauer)	50.00	25.00	15.00
88	PERRY SE ESTIRA...OUT.(Alonso Perry)	65.00	32.50	20.00
89	Clarkson conecta otro homerun.(Buster Clarkson)	80.00	40.00	24.00
90	Piper intenta sacar a Tetelo - SAFE(Tetelo Vargas, Piper Davis)	90.00	45.00	27.50
91	QUE QUE USTED DICE...?	50.00	25.00	15.00
92	Bernier se roba el home...(Carlos Bernier)	50.00	25.00	15.00
93	UNA ESCENA DE RUTINA...(Willard Brown)	400.00	200.00	120.00
94	Taborn trata de esquvarse - OUT.(Earl Taborn)	50.00	25.00	15.00
95	Pita Marti safe en tercera.(Humberto Marti)	50.00	25.00	15.00
96	PIE CONTRA PIE...(?)	50.00	25.00	15.00
97	NO QUIERE NI VERLO...	50.00	25.00	15.00
98	SUDOR Y ARENA...	50.00	25.00	15.00
99	Jueyito safe en primera.(Jueyito Andrade)	50.00	25.00	15.00
100	QUIEN LLEGO PRIMERO?	50.00	25.00	15.00
101	LLEGO TARDE EL TIRO..SAFE.	50.00	25.00	15.00
102	Escalera se estira...pero es SAFE.(Saturnino Escalera)	50.00	25.00	15.00
103	Howell aspera...Almendro observa.(Dixie Howell)	50.00	25.00	15.00
104	A todo vapor hacia tercera...	50.00	25.00	15.00
105	Buena cogida, pero es SAFE.	50.00	25.00	15.00
106	El arbitro observa...SAFE.	50.00	25.00	15.00
107	SAFE EN HOME.	50.00	25.00	15.00
108	Regreso a tiempo...SAFE.	50.00	25.00	15.00
109	Canena es felicitados tras Homer.(Canena Marquez)	65.00	32.50	20.00
110	"COC SAFE", canta el umpiere.(Coco Ferrer)	50.00	25.00	15.00
111	Taft Wright jonronen...(Taft Wright)	50.00	25.00	15.00
112	Esta solo...pero siempre gana.	50.00	25.00	15.00
113	????????, CANTE!	50.00	25.00	15.00
114	Casanovas quieto en tercera...(Rafael Casanovas)	50.00	25.00	15.00
115	Wilson espera pero no llega...SAFE.(Artie Wilson)	65.00	32.50	20.00
116	FELLE FELICITA MONTALVO(Felle Delgado, Jose E. Montalvo)	50.00	25.00	15.00
117	El tigre tambien se desliza...Safe.	50.00	25.00	15.00
118	Limmer se adelanta...Montalvo out.(Lou Limmer, Jose E. Montalvo)	50.00	25.00	15.00
119	TIRO MALO...BUTTS SAFE.(Pee Wee Butts)	50.00	25.00	15.00
120	SAFE EN TERCERA.	50.00	25.00	15.00
121	EL JIBARO CONECTA HIT...	50.00	25.00	15.00
122	Chapman no puede alcanzarla...(Medina Chapman)	50.00	25.00	15.00
123	Guinea Alomar da OUT en Home.(Guinea Alomar)	50.00	25.00	15.00
124	INDIO ANOTA EN SLIDE...	50.00	25.00	15.00
125	Miller saca a Serrel en primera.(Henry Miller, Barney Serrell)	50.00	25.00	15.00
126	El gran COIMBRE llega SAFE.(Francisco Coimbre)	90.00	45.00	27.50
127	El arbitro tome impulsa...OUT!	50.00	25.00	15.00
128	TROUPPE DA OUT EN HOME.(Quincy Trouppe)	90.00	45.00	27.50
129	BANKHEAD OUT EN PRIMERA.(Bankhead)	60.00	30.00	18.00
130	Tiene que pensarlo bien...	50.00	25.00	15.00
131	Escalera a salvo en tercera...(Saturnino Escalera)	50.00	25.00	15.00
132	DOS MANOS QUE BUSCAN...	50.00	25.00	15.00
133	FIGUEROA SE DESLIZA - SAFE(Tite Figueroa)	50.00	25.00	15.00
134	VIENE LA BOLA...OUT.	50.00	25.00	15.00
135	Esperando el tiro...OUT.	50.00	25.00	15.00
136	KAYSER SAFE EN PRIMERA.(Cecyl Kayser)	65.00	32.00	19.50
137	COCO FERRER DA OUT.(Coco Ferrer)	50.00	25.00	15.00
138	Lo atajaron a tiempo...OUT.	50.00	25.00	15.00
139	Limmer da su primer homer.(Lou Limmer)	50.00	25.00	15.00
140	Starks y Blasini alegan...(Jimmy Starks, Efrain Blasini)	50.00	25.00	15.00
141	BARNA SE VA DE HOMERUN.(Babe Barna)	65.00	32.00	19.50
142	"La antesala del gran choque...(George Scales)	60.00	30.00	18.00
143	"QUIETO". DICE EL UMPIRE.	50.00	25.00	15.00
144	LO SACARON POR UN PELO...	50.00	25.00	15.00
145	Un recibimiento poco agradable.	50.00	25.00	15.00
146	Montalvo se desliza...OUT.(Jose E. Montalvo)	50.00	25.00	15.00
147	ALOMAR OUT EN HOME...(Alomar)	50.00	25.00	15.00
148	EASTER SAFE EN HOME...(Luke Easter)	65.00	32.50	20.00
149	Grillo se anota hit de piernas...	50.00	25.00	15.00
150	BARNA SAFE EN TERCERA.(Babe Barna)	50.00	25.00	15.00
151	Esta en la base pero es OUT.	50.00	25.00	15.00
152	TYBOR DA OUT A TABORN.(Jim Tabor, Earl Taborn)	50.00	25.00	15.00
153	BUTTS OUT EN PRIMERA.(Pee Wee Butts)	50.00	25.00	15.00
154	Viene la bola...Hernaiz SAFE.(Angel Hernaiz)	50.00	25.00	15.00
155	VILLODAS LO ESPERA...OUT.(Luis Villodas)	50.00	25.00	15.00
156	TYBOR SACA A COCA FERRER.(Jim Tabor, Coco Ferrer)	50.00	25.00	15.00
157	LO FUSILAN EN TERCERA.	50.00	25.00	15.00
158	B L O Q U E A D O...	50.00	25.00	15.00
159	"Estoy firme en base", dice Coco.(Coco Ferrer)	50.00	25.00	15.00
160	Ruben Gomez se tira slide...SAFE.(Ruben Gomez)	50.00	25.00	15.00
161	HOWELL OUT EN PRIMERA.(Dixie Howell)	50.00	25.00	15.00
162	SAFE EN HOME.	50.00	25.00	15.00
163	PERRY ES ESCURRE...SAFE.(Alonso Perry)	65.00	32.50	20.00
164	PEDROSO SE LESIONA.(Fernando Pedroso)	50.00	25.00	15.00
165	LA APOTEOSIS DEL TRIUNFO.	50.00	25.00	15.00
166	Ruben jonroneo ganar su juego.(Ruben Gomez)	50.00	25.00	15.00
167	Primer homerun CANENA 1950-51(Canena Marquez)	65.00	32.50	20.00
168	GOLPE DE IZQUIRDA? SAFE.	50.00	25.00	15.00
169	PELLOT OUT EN HOME.(Victor Pellot (Power))	65.00	32.50	20.00
170	Muchos ojos tras Scales y Mullens.(George Scales)	60.00	30.00	18.00
171	Nube de polvo en el Castillo...	50.00	25.00	15.00
172	Bero participa carnaval jonrones.(John Bero)	50.00	25.00	15.00
173	Lanauze completa out a Butts.(Carlos Lanauze, Pee Wee Butts)	50.00	25.00	15.00
174	SE LE ESCAPO LA PILDORA.	50.00	25.00	15.00
175	EL UMPIRE DECIDIRA...	50.00	25.00	15.00
176	Llego tarde el HOMBRE ESE.(Willard Brown)	200.00	100.00	60.00
177	THON SE DESLIZA...SAFE.(Freddie Thon)	50.00	25.00	15.00
178	AL REVES, PERO SAFE...	50.00	25.00	15.00
179	Hughes no puede sacar al corredor.(Roy Hughes)	50.00	25.00	15.00
180	"Chiflan Safe"...dice el Umpiere.(Chiflan Clark)	50.00	25.00	15.00

1909-11 Tolstoi Cigarettes

PREMIUMS:
Commons: 1.5-2X
Hall of Famers: 1.5-2X

(See T206 for checklist and base values.)

1887 Tomlinson Studios Cabinets

The extent to which this Detroit photographer promulgated individual player cabinet cards of the 1887 Wolverines is unknown. However, since the portrait on the known Bennett card is the same as that found on a team-composite cabinet card, it is not unreasonable to expect that each of the other 13 players pictured on the team card may have been issued individually. The cabinet is in the typical 4-1/4" x 6-1/2" format, with blank back.

	NM	E	VG
C.W. Bennett ((Portrait))	5,000	2,500	1,500
C.W. Bennett ((Batting))	5,000	2,500	1,500
Dan Bouthers ((Batting))	8,000	4,000	2,400

Charles Getzien			
((Batting))	5,000	2,500	1,500
Jimmy Manning	5,000	2,500	1,500
Deacon White	5,000	2,500	1,500

1909 Topping & Co. Detroit Tigers Postcards

This set of postcards features the members of the 1909 American League Champion Detroit Tigers. About 3-1/2" x 5-1/2" in size, vertically formatted fronts with black-and-white player portraits at center within a yellow six-pointed star. "Tiger Stars" appears in script in a yellow stripe at top, while the player name and position are in a similar strip at bottom. Black trim surrounds the design elements. Backs are black-and-white with standard postcard markings and a credit line for Topping and Publishers Co., Detroit. The un-numbered cards are listed here alphabetically.

	NM	E	VG
Complete Set (21):	18,000	9,000	5,400
Common Player:	750.00	375.00	225.00
(1) Henry Beckendorf	750.00	375.00	225.00
(2) Donie Bush	750.00	375.00	225.00
(3) Ty Cobb	6,500	3,250	1,950
(4) Sam Crawford	2,100	1,050	630.00
(5) Jim Delehanty	750.00	375.00	225.00
(6) Bill Donovan	750.00	375.00	225.00
(7) Hughie Jennings	2,100	1,050	630.00
(8) Davy Jones	750.00	375.00	225.00
(9) Tom Jones	750.00	375.00	225.00
(10) Ed Killian	750.00	375.00	225.00
(11) Matty McIntyre	750.00	375.00	225.00
(12) George Moriarty	750.00	375.00	225.00
(13) George Mullin	750.00	375.00	225.00
(14) Charley O'Leary	750.00	375.00	225.00
(15) Germany Schaefer (existence now doubted)			
(16) Charlie Schmidt	750.00	375.00	225.00
(17) George Speer	750.00	375.00	225.00
(18) Oscar Stanage	750.00	375.00	225.00
(19) Eddie Summers	750.00	375.00	225.00
(20) Ed Willett	750.00	375.00	225.00
(21) Ralph Works	750.00	375.00	225.00

1948 Topps Magic Photos

The first Topps baseball cards appeared as a subset of 19 cards from an issue of 252 "Magic Photos." The set takes its name from the self-developing nature of the cards. The cards were blank on the front when first taken from the wrapper. By spitting on the wrapper and holding it to the card while exposing it to light the black-and-white photo appeared. Measuring 7/8" x 1-1/2", the cards are very similar to Topps 1955 and 1956 "Hocus Focus" issues.

	NM	E	VG
Complete Set (19):	2,400	1,200	725.00

Common Card:	60.00	30.00	18.00
1 Lou Boudreau	125.00	65.00	38.00
2 Cleveland Indians	60.00	30.00	18.00
3 Bob Eliott	90.00	45.00	27.00
4 Cleveland Indians 4-3	60.00	30.00	18.00
5 Cleveland Indians 4-1	60.00	30.00	18.00
6 Babe Ruth	450.00	225.00	135.00
7 Tris Speaker	90.00	45.00	27.00
8 Rogers Hornsby	90.00	45.00	27.50
9 Connie Mack	75.00	37.50	22.50
10 Christy Mathewson	150.00	75.00	45.00
11 Hans Wagner	100.00	50.00	30.00
12 Grover Alexander	90.00	45.00	27.50
13 Ty Cobb	275.00	135.00	80.00
14 Lou Gehrig	275.00	135.00	80.00
15 Walter Johnson	125.00	65.00	35.00
16 Cy Young	125.00	65.00	35.00
17 George Sisler	75.00	37.50	22.50
18 Tinker and Evers	125.00	65.00	35.00
19 Third Base Cleveland Indians	75.00	37.50	22.50

1951 Topps Blue Backs

Sold two cards in a package with a piece of candy for 1¢, the Topps Blue Backs are considerably scarcer than their Red Back counterparts. The 2" x 2-5/8" cards carry a black-and-white player photograph on a red, white, yellow and green background along with the player's name and other information including their 1950 record on the front. The back is printed in blue on a white background. The 52-card set has varied baseball situations on them, making the playing of a rather elementary game of baseball possible. Although scarce, Blue Backs were printed on thick cardboard and have survived quite well over the years. There are, however, few stars in the set.

	NM	E	VG
Complete Set (52):	2,000	1,000	600.00
Common Player:	35.00	17.50	10.50
Wax Pack (2):	200.00		
1 Eddie Yost	40.00	20.00	10.00
2 Henry (Hank) Majeski	35.00	17.50	10.50
3 Richie Ashburn	175.00	90.00	54.00
4 Del Ennis	35.00	17.50	10.50
5 Johnny Pesky	35.00	17.50	10.50
6 Albert (Red) Schoendienst	100.00	50.00	25.00
7 Gerald Staley	35.00	17.50	10.50
8 Dick Sisler	35.00	17.50	10.50
9 Johnny Sain	40.00	20.00	10.00
10 Joe Page	35.00	17.50	10.50
11 Johnny Groth	35.00	17.50	10.50
12 Sam Jethroe	35.00	17.50	10.50
13 James (Mickey) Vernon	35.00	17.50	10.50
14 George Munger	35.00	17.50	10.50
15 Eddie Joost	35.00	17.50	10.50
16 Murry Dickson	35.00	17.50	10.50
17 Roy Smalley	35.00	17.50	10.50
18 Ned Garver	35.00	17.50	10.50
19 Phil Masi	35.00	17.50	10.50
20 Ralph Branca	40.00	20.00	10.00
21 Billy Johnson	35.00	17.50	10.50
22 Bob Kuzava	35.00	17.50	10.50
23 Paul (Dizzy) Trout	35.00	17.50	10.50
24 Sherman Lollar	35.00	17.50	10.50
25 Sam Mele	35.00	17.50	10.50
26 Chico Carrasquel	35.00	17.50	10.50
27 Andy Pafko	35.00	17.50	10.50
28 Harry (The Cat) Brecheen	35.00	17.50	10.50
29 Granville Hamner	35.00	17.50	10.50
30 Enos (Country) Slaughter	100.00	50.00	25.00
31 Lou Brissie	35.00	17.50	10.50
32 Bob Elliott	35.00	17.50	10.50
33 Don Lenhardt	35.00	17.50	10.50
34 Earl Torgeson	35.00	17.50	10.50
35 Tommy Byrne	35.00	17.50	10.50
36 Cliff Fannin	35.00	17.50	10.50
37 Bobby Doerr	80.00	40.00	24.00
38 Irv Noren	35.00	17.50	10.50
39 Ed Lopat	40.00	20.00	10.00
40 Vic Wertz	35.00	17.50	10.50
41 Johnny Schmitz	35.00	17.50	10.50
42 Bruce Edwards	35.00	17.50	10.50
43 Willie (Puddin' Head) Jones	35.00	17.50	10.50
44 Johnny Wyrostek	35.00	17.50	10.50
45 Bill Pierce	35.00	17.50	10.50
46 Gerry Priddy	35.00	17.50	10.50
47 Herman Wehmeier	35.00	17.50	10.50
48 Billy Cox	35.00	17.50	10.50
49 Henry (Hank) Sauer	35.00	17.50	10.50
50 Johnny Mize	100.00	50.00	25.00
51 Eddie Waitkus	35.00	17.50	10.50
52 Sam Chapman	35.00	17.50	10.50

1951 Topps Connie Mack's All-Stars

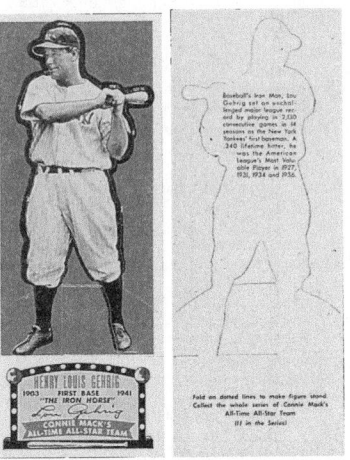

A set of die-cut, 2-1/16" x 5-1/4" cards, all 11 players are Hall of Famers. The cards feature a black-and-white action player photograph printed on a red background with a col-ored name plaque underneath. Like the "Current All-Stars," with which they were issued, the background could be fold-ed, making it possible for the card to stand up. This practice, however, resulted in the card's mutilation and lowers its con-dition in the eyes of today's collectors. Connie Mack All-Stars are scarce today and, despite being relatively expensive, re-tain a certain popularity as one of Topps first issues.

	NM	E	VG
Complete Set (11):	18,000	5,400	2,700
Common Player:	750.00	225.00	110.00
(1) Grover Cleveland Alexander	900.00	300.00	150.00
(2) Gordon Stanley Cochrane	600.00	200.00	100.00
(3) Edward Trowbridge Collins	600.00	200.00	100.00
(4) James J. Collins	600.00	200.00	100.00
(5) Lou Gehrig	6,000	2,000	1,0000
(6) Walter Johnson	1,000	300.00	150.00
(7) Connie Mack	600.00	200.00	100.00
(8) Christopher Mathewson	1,125	335.00	165.00
(9) George Herman Ruth	4,500	1,350	675.00
(10) Tris Speaker	600.00	200.00	100.00
(11) Honus Wagner	1,800	600.00	300.00

1951 Topps Major League All-Stars

 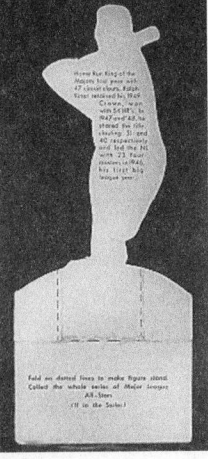

The Topps Major League All-Stars are very similar to the Connie Mack All-Stars of the same year. The 2-1/16" x 5-1/4"

cards have a black-and-white photograph on a red die-cut background. Most of the background could be folded over so that the card would stand up. A plaque at the base carries brief biographical information. The set was to contain 11 cards, but only eight were actually issued in gum packs. Those of Konstanty, Roberts and Stanky were not issued and are very rare, with only a handful of each known. A big problem with the set is that if the card was used as it was intended it was folded and, thus, damaged from a collector's viewpoint. That makes top quality examples of any players difficult to find and quite expensive.

	NM	E	VG
Complete Set (11):	30,000	10,000	5,000
Common Player:	2,000	600.00	300.00
(1) Yogi Berra	7,000	2,100	1,050
(2) Larry Doby	4,500	1,350	675.00
(3) Walt Dropo	900.00	270.00	135.00
(4) "Hoot" Evers	900.00	270.00	135.00
(5) George Clyde Kell	3,500	1,025	515.00
(6) Ralph Kiner	3,500	1,025	515.00
(7) Jim Konstanty			45,000
(8) Bob Lemon	3,500	1,025	515.00
(9) Phil Rizzuto	5,000	1,500	750.00
(10) Robin Roberts			60,000
(11) Ed Stanky			45,000

1951 Topps Red Backs

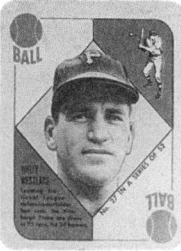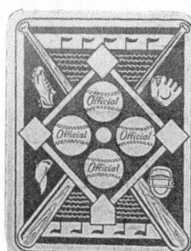

Like the Blue Backs, the Topps Red Backs which were sold at the same time came two to a package for 1¢. Their black-and-white photographs appear on a red, white, blue and yellow background. The back printing is red on white. Their 2" x 2-5/8" size is the same as Blue Backs. Also identical is the set size (52 cards) and the game situations to be found on the fronts of the cards, for use in playing a card game of baseball. Red Backs are more common than the Blue Backs by virtue of a 1980s discovery of a large hoard of unopened boxes. Red Backs are also known to have been sold in a plastic-bagged set along with a foldout paper game board for 29 cents.

	NM	E	VG
Complete Set (52):	1,200	600.00	360.00
Common Player:	15.00	7.50	4.50
Wax Pack (2):	150.00		
1 Larry (Yogi) Berra	125.00	65.00	39.00
2 Sid Gordon	15.00	7.50	4.50
3 Ferris Fain	15.00	7.50	4.50
4 Verne Stephens	15.00	7.50	4.50
5 Phil Rizzuto	60.00	30.00	15.00
6 Allie Reynolds	30.00	15.00	7.50
7 Howie Pollet	15.00	7.50	4.50
8 Early Wynn	35.00	17.50	8.75
9 Roy Sievers	15.00	7.50	4.50
10 Mel Parnell	15.00	7.50	4.50
11 Gene Hermanski	15.00	7.50	4.50
12 Jim Hegan	15.00	7.50	4.50
13 Dale Mitchell	15.00	7.50	4.50
14 Wayne Terwilliger	15.00	7.50	4.50
15 Ralph Kiner	35.00	17.50	8.75
16 Preacher Roe	25.00	15.00	7.50
17 Dave Bell	15.00	7.50	4.50
18 Gerry Coleman	20.00	10.00	5.00
19 Dick Kokos	15.00	7.50	4.50
20 Dominick DiMaggio	40.00	20.00	12.00
21 Larry Jansen	15.00	7.50	4.50
22 Bob Feller	60.00	30.00	18.00
23 Ray Boone	15.00	7.50	4.50
24 Hank Bauer	20.00	10.00	5.00
25 Cliff Chambers	15.00	7.50	4.50
26 Luke Easter	20.00	10.00	5.00
27 Wally Westlake	15.00	7.50	4.50
28 Elmer Valo	15.00	7.50	4.50
29 Bob Kennedy	15.00	7.50	4.50
30 Warren Spahn	50.00	25.00	14.00
31 Gil Hodges	40.00	20.00	11.00
32 Henry Thompson	15.00	7.50	4.50
33 William Werle	15.00	7.50	4.50
34 Grady Hatton	15.00	7.50	4.50
35 Al Rosen	20.00	10.00	5.00
36a Gus Zernial (Chicago in bio.)	50.00	25.00	15.00
36b Gus Zernial (Philadelphia in bio.)	25.00	12.50	8.00
37 Wes Westrum	15.00	7.50	4.50
38 Ed (Duke) Snider	60.00	30.00	18.00
39 Ted Kluszewski	30.00	15.00	7.50
40 Mike Garcia	15.00	7.50	4.50
41 Whitey Lockman	15.00	7.50	4.50
42 Ray Scarborough	15.00	7.50	4.50
43 Maurice McDermott	15.00	7.50	4.50
44 Sid Hudson	15.00	7.50	4.50
45 Andy Seminick	15.00	7.50	4.50
46 Billy Goodman	15.00	7.50	4.50
47 Tommy Glaviano	15.00	7.50	4.50
48 Eddie Stanky	15.00	7.50	4.50
49 Al Zarilla	15.00	7.50	4.50
50 Monte Irvin	40.00	20.00	10.00
51 Eddie Robinson	15.00	7.50	4.50
52a Tommy Holmes (Boston in bio.)	50.00	25.00	15.00
52b Tommy Holmes (Hartford in bio.)	25.00	12.50	8.00

1951 Topps Teams

An innovative issue for 1951, the Topps team cards were a nine-card set, 5-1/4" x 2-1/16," which carry a black-and-white picture of a major league team surrounded by a yellow border on the front. The back identifies team members with red printing on white cardboard. There are two versions of each card, with and without the date "1950" in the banner that carries the team name. Undated versions are valued slightly higher than the cards with dates. Strangely only nine teams were issued. Scarcity varies, with the Cardinals and Red Sox being the most difficult to obtain.

	NM	E	VG
(1a) Boston Red Sox (1950)	475.00	235.00	140.00
(1b) Boston Red Sox (Undated)	500.00	250.00	150.00
(2a) Brooklyn Dodgers (1950)	375.00	185.00	110.00
(2b) Brooklyn Dodgers (Undated)	400.00	200.00	120.00
(3a) Chicago White Sox (1950)	275.00	135.00	80.00
(3b) Chicago White Sox (Undated)	250.00	125.00	75.00
(4a) Cincinnati Reds (1950)	300.00	150.00	90.00
(4b) Cincinnati Reds (Undated)	325.00	160.00	95.00
(5a) New York Giants (1950)	300.00	150.00	90.00
(5b) New York Giants (Undated)	325.00	160.00	95.00
(6a) Philadelphia Athletics (1950)	225.00	110.00	65.00
(6b) Philadelphia Athletics (Undated)	250.00	125.00	75.00
(7a) Philadelphia Phillies (1950)	225.00	110.00	65.00
(7b) Philadelphia Phillies (Undated)	400.00	200.00	120.00
(8a) St. Louis Cardinals (1950)	400.00	200.00	120.00
(8b) St. Louis Cardinals (Undated)	425.00	210.00	125.00
(9a) Washington Senators (1950)	250.00	125.00	75.00
(9b) Washington Senators (Undated)	300.00	150.00	90.00

1952 Topps

At 407 cards, the 1952 Topps set was the largest set of its day, both in number of cards and physical dimensions of the cards. Cards are 2-5/8" x 3-3/4" with a colorized black-and-white photo on front. Major baseball card innovations presented in the set include the first-ever use of color team logos as part of the design, and the inclusion of stats for the previous season and career on the backs. The first 80 cards in the set can be found with backs printed entirely in black

or black and red. While "Black Backs" used to command a significant premium over the "Red Back" version, that differential has diminished in recent years to the point of insignificance. Several cards in the #1-80 range can be found with noticeable color differences on front depending on whether they are Red Back or Black Back. Cards #311-407, known as the "high numbers," were distributed in limited areas and are extremely rare.

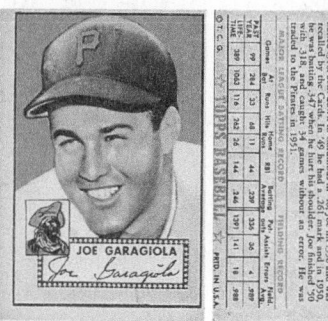

	NM	E	VG
Complete Set (407):	120,000	55,000	30,000
Common Player (1-250):	50.00	25.00	15.00
Common Player (251-310):	65.00	32.00	20.00
Common Player (311-407):	400.00	200.00	120.00
1 Andy Pafko	9,000	1,000.00	225.00
2 James E. Runnels RC	3,000	200.00	30.00
3 Hank Thompson	200.00	32.00	15.00
4 Don Lenhardt	50.00	25.00	15.00
5 Larry Jansen	75.00	38.00	23.00
6 Grady Hatton	50.00	25.00	15.00
7 Wayne Terwilliger	55.00	27.50	16.50
8 Fred Marsh	50.00	25.00	15.00
9 Bobby Hogue	75.00	38.00	23.00
10 Al Rosen	325.00	163.00	98.00
11 Phil Rizzuto	750.00	375.00	187.00
12 Monty Basgall	50.00	25.00	15.00
13 Johnny Wyrostek	50.00	25.00	15.00
14 Bob Elliott	50.00	25.00	15.00
15 Johnny Pesky	50.00	25.00	15.00
16 Gene Hermanski	50.00	25.00	15.00
17 Jim Hegan	50.00	25.00	15.00
18 Merrill Combs	50.00	25.00	15.00
19 Johnny Bucha	50.00	25.00	15.00
20 Billy Loes RC	350.00	175.00	105.00
21 Ferris Fain	65.00	32.00	20.00
22 Dom DiMaggio	125.00	75.00	50.00
23 Billy Goodman	50.00	25.00	15.00
24 Luke Easter	65.00	32.00	20.00
25 Johnny Groth	50.00	25.00	15.00
26 Monty Irvin	200.00	100.00	60.00
27 Sam Jethroe	50.00	25.00	15.00
28 Jerry Priddy	50.00	25.00	15.00
29 Ted Kluszewski	150.00	75.00	37.50
30 Mel Parnell	50.00	25.00	15.00
31 Gus Zernial	100.00	50.00	25.00
32 Eddie Robinson	50.00	25.00	15.00
33 Warren Spahn	300.00	150.00	75.00
34 Elmer Valo	50.00	25.00	15.00
35 Hank Sauer	50.00	25.00	15.00
36 Gil Hodges	475.00	235.00	140.00
37 Duke Snider	500.00	250.00	150.00
38 Wally Westlake	50.00	25.00	15.00
39 "Dizzy" Trout	50.00	25.00	15.00
40 Irv Noren	50.00	25.00	15.00
41 Bob Wellman	50.00	25.00	15.00
42 Lou Kretlow	50.00	25.00	15.00
43 Ray Scarborough	50.00	25.00	15.00
44 Con Dempsey	50.00	25.00	15.00
45 Eddie Joost	50.00	25.00	15.00
46 Gordon Goldsberry	50.00	25.00	15.00
47 Willie Jones	50.00	25.00	15.00
48a Joe Page (Wrong (Sain) back.)	1,350	675.00	405.00
48b Joe Page (Correct back.)	350.00	175.00	105.00
49a Johnny Sain (Wrong (Page) back.)	1,600	800.00	480.00
49b Johnny Sain (Correct back.)	350.00	175.00	105.00
50 Marv Rickert	50.00	25.00	15.00
51 Jim Russell	55.00	27.50	16.50
52 Don Mueller	50.00	25.00	15.00
53 Chris Van Cuyk	55.00	27.50	16.50
54 Leo Kiely	50.00	25.00	15.00
55 Ray Boone	50.00	25.00	15.00
56 Tommy Glaviano	50.00	25.00	15.00
57 Ed Lopat	90.00	50.00	25.00
58 Bob Mahoney	50.00	25.00	15.00
59 Robin Roberts	200.00	100.00	65.00
60 Sid Hudson	50.00	25.00	15.00
61 "Tookie" Gilbert	50.00	25.00	15.00
62 Chuck Stobbs	50.00	25.00	15.00

63	Howie Pollet	50.00	25.00	15.00
64	Roy Sievers	75.00	38.00	23.00
65	Enos Slaughter	250.00	125.00	75.00
66	"Preacher" Roe	100.00	50.00	35.00
67	Allie Reynolds	120.00	65.00	35.00
68	Cliff Chambers	50.00	25.00	15.00
69	Virgil Stallcup	50.00	25.00	15.00
70	Al Zarilla	50.00	25.00	15.00
71	Tom Upton	50.00	25.00	15.00
72	Karl Olson	50.00	25.00	15.00
73	William Werle	50.00	25.00	15.00
74	Andy Hansen	50.00	25.00	15.00
75	Wes Westrum	50.00	25.00	15.00
76	Eddie Stanky	50.00	25.00	15.00
77	Bob Kennedy	50.00	25.00	15.00
78	Ellis Kinder	50.00	25.00	15.00
79	Gerald Staley	50.00	25.00	15.00
80	Herman Wehmeier	50.00	25.00	15.00
81	Vernon Law	75.00	38.00	23.00
82	Duane Pillette	50.00	25.00	15.00
83	Billy Johnson	50.00	25.00	15.00
84	Vern Stephens	50.00	25.00	15.00
85	Bob Kuzava	55.00	27.50	16.50
86	Ted Gray	50.00	25.00	15.00
87	Dale Coogan	50.00	25.00	15.00
88	Bob Feller	285.00	140.00	85.00
89	Johnny Lipon	50.00	25.00	15.00
90	Mickey Grasso	50.00	25.00	15.00
91	Al Schoendienst	140.00	70.00	40.00
92	Dale Mitchell	50.00	25.00	15.00
93	Al Sima	50.00	25.00	15.00
94	Sam Mele	50.00	25.00	15.00
95	Ken Holcombe	50.00	25.00	15.00
96	Willard Marshall	50.00	25.00	15.00
97	Earl Torgeson	50.00	25.00	15.00
98	Bill Pierce	55.00	27.50	16.50
99	Gene Woodling	80.00	40.00	24.00
100	Del Rice	50.00	25.00	15.00
101	Max Lanier	50.00	25.00	15.00
102	Bill Kennedy	50.00	25.00	15.00
103	Cliff Mapes	50.00	25.00	15.00
104	Don Kolloway	50.00	25.00	15.00
105	John Pramesa	50.00	25.00	15.00
106	Mickey Vernon	50.00	25.00	15.00
107	Connie Ryan	50.00	25.00	15.00
108	Jim Konstanty	50.00	25.00	15.00
109	Ted Wilks	50.00	25.00	15.00
110	Dutch Leonard	50.00	25.00	15.00
111	Harry Lowrey	50.00	25.00	15.00
112	Henry Majeski	50.00	25.00	15.00
113	Dick Sisler	50.00	25.00	15.00
114	Willard Ramsdell	50.00	25.00	15.00
115	George Munger	50.00	25.00	15.00
116	Carl Scheib	50.00	25.00	15.00
117	Sherman Lollar	50.00	25.00	15.00
118	Ken Raffensberger	50.00	25.00	15.00
119	Maurice McDermott	50.00	25.00	15.00
120	Bob Chakales	50.00	25.00	15.00
121	Gus Niarhos	50.00	25.00	15.00
122	Jack Jensen	115.00	58.00	35.00
123	Eddie Yost	50.00	25.00	15.00
124	Monte Kennedy	50.00	25.00	15.00
125	Bill Rigney	50.00	25.00	15.00
126	Fred Hutchinson	50.00	25.00	15.00
127	Paul Minner	50.00	25.00	15.00
128	Don Bollweg	55.00	27.50	16.50
129	Johnny Mize	140.00	70.00	35.00
130	Sheldon Jones	50.00	25.00	15.00
131	Morrie Martin	50.00	25.00	15.00
132	Clyde Kluttz	50.00	25.00	15.00
133	Al Widmar	50.00	25.00	15.00
134	Joe Tipton	50.00	25.00	15.00
135	Dixie Howell	50.00	25.00	15.00
136	Johnny Schmitz	50.00	25.00	15.00
137	Roy McMillan **RC**	50.00	25.00	15.00
138	Bill MacDonald	50.00	25.00	15.00
139	Ken Wood	50.00	25.00	15.00
140	John Antonelli	50.00	25.00	15.00
141	Clint Hartung	50.00	25.00	15.00
142	Harry Perkowski	50.00	25.00	15.00
143	Les Moss	50.00	25.00	15.00
144	Ed Blake	50.00	25.00	15.00
145	Joe Haynes	50.00	25.00	15.00
146	Frank House	50.00	25.00	15.00
147	Bob Young	50.00	25.00	15.00
148	Johnny Klippstein	50.00	25.00	15.00
149	Dick Kryhoski	50.00	25.00	15.00
150	Ted Beard	50.00	25.00	15.00
151	Wally Post **RC**	55.00	27.50	16.50
152	Al Evans	50.00	25.00	15.00
153	Bob Rush	50.00	25.00	15.00
154	Joe Muir	50.00	25.00	15.00
155	Frank Overmire	55.00	27.50	16.50
156	Frank Hiller	50.00	25.00	15.00
157	Bob Usher	50.00	25.00	15.00
158	Eddie Waitkus	50.00	25.00	15.00
159	Saul Rogovin	50.00	25.00	15.00
160	Owen Friend	50.00	25.00	15.00
161	Bud Byerly	50.00	25.00	15.00
162	Del Crandall	50.00	25.00	15.00
163	Stan Rojek	50.00	25.00	15.00
164	Walt Dubiel	50.00	25.00	15.00
165	Eddie Kazak	50.00	25.00	15.00
166	Paul LaPalme	50.00	25.00	15.00
167	Bill Howerton	50.00	25.00	15.00
168	Charlie Silvera **RC**	75.00	37.50	25.00
169	Howie Judson	50.00	25.00	15.00
170	Gus Bell	65.00	32.50	20.00
171	Ed Erautt	50.00	25.00	15.00
172	Eddie Miksis	50.00	25.00	15.00
173	Roy Smalley	50.00	25.00	15.00
174	Clarence Marshall	50.00	25.00	15.00
175	Billy Martin **RC**	750.00	375.00	225.00
176	Hank Edwards	50.00	25.00	15.00
177	Bill Wight	50.00	25.00	15.00
178	Cass Michaels	50.00	25.00	15.00
179	Frank Smith	50.00	25.00	15.00
180	Charley Maxwell **RC**	65.00	32.00	20.00
181	Bob Swift	50.00	25.00	15.00
182	Billy Hitchcock	50.00	25.00	15.00
183	Erv Dusak	50.00	25.00	15.00
184	Bob Ramazzotti	50.00	25.00	15.00
185	Bill Nicholson	50.00	25.00	15.00
186	Walt Masterson	50.00	25.00	15.00
187	Bob Miller	50.00	25.00	15.00
188	Clarence Podbielan	50.00	25.00	15.00
189	Pete Reiser	50.00	25.00	15.00
190	Don Johnson	50.00	25.00	15.00
191	Yogi Berra	1,300.00	650.00	390.00
192	Myron Ginsberg	50.00	25.00	15.00
193	Harry Simpson	50.00	25.00	15.00
194	Joe Hatten	50.00	25.00	15.00
195	Orestes Minoso **RC**	190.00	95.00	57.00
196	Solly Hemus	50.00	25.00	15.00
197	George Strickland	50.00	25.00	15.00
198	Phil Haugstad	50.00	25.00	15.00
199	George Zuverink	50.00	25.00	15.00
200	Ralph Houk	125.00	65.00	40.00
201	Alex Kellner	50.00	25.00	15.00
202	Joe Collins	65.00	32.00	20.00
203	Curt Simmons	50.00	25.00	15.00
204	Ron Northey	50.00	25.00	15.00
205	Clyde King	50.00	25.00	15.00
206	Joe Ostrowski	55.00	27.50	16.50
207	Mickey Harris	50.00	25.00	15.00
208	Marlin Stuart	50.00	25.00	15.00
209	Howie Fox	50.00	25.00	15.00
210	Dick Fowler	50.00	25.00	15.00
211	Ray Coleman	50.00	25.00	15.00
212	Ned Garver	50.00	25.00	15.00
213	Nippy Jones	50.00	25.00	15.00
214	Johnny Hopp	55.00	27.50	16.50
215	Hank Bauer	95.00	50.00	25.00
216	Richie Ashburn	260.00	130.00	65.00
217	George Stirnweiss	50.00	25.00	15.00
218	Clyde McCullough	50.00	25.00	15.00
219	Bobby Shantz	55.00	27.50	16.50
220	Joe Presko	50.00	25.00	15.00
221	Granny Hamner	50.00	25.00	15.00
222	"Hoot" Evers	50.00	25.00	15.00
223	Del Ennis	50.00	25.00	15.00
224	Bruce Edwards	50.00	25.00	15.00
225	Frank Baumholtz	50.00	25.00	15.00
226	Dave Philley	50.00	25.00	15.00
227	Joe Garagiola	100.00	50.00	25.00
228	Al Brazle	50.00	25.00	15.00
229	Gene Bearden	50.00	25.00	15.00
230	Matt Batts	50.00	25.00	15.00
231	Sam Zoldak	50.00	25.00	15.00
232	Billy Cox	90.00	50.00	25.00
233	Bob Friend **RC**	100.00	50.00	30.00
234	Steve Souchock	50.00	25.00	15.00
235	Walt Dropo	50.00	25.00	15.00
236	Ed Fitz Gerald	50.00	25.00	15.00
237	Jerry Coleman	100.00	50.00	30.00
238	Art Houtteman	50.00	25.00	15.00
239	Rocky Bridges **RC**	50.00	25.00	15.00
240	Jack Phillips	50.00	25.00	15.00
241	Tommy Byrne	50.00	25.00	15.00
242	Tom Poholsky	50.00	25.00	15.00
243	Larry Doby	100.00	50.00	25.00
244	Vic Wertz	50.00	25.00	15.00
245	Sherry Robertson	50.00	25.00	15.00
246	George Kell	100.00	50.00	25.00
247	Randy Gumpert	50.00	25.00	15.00
248	Frank Shea	50.00	25.00	15.00
249	Bobby Adams	50.00	25.00	15.00
250	Carl Erskine	100.00	50.00	25.00
251	Chico Carrasquel	95.00	47.50	27.50
252	Vern Bickford	65.00	32.00	20.00
253	Johnny Berardino	75.00	37.50	25.00
254	Joe Dobson	65.00	32.00	20.00
255	Clyde Vollmer	65.00	32.00	20.00
256	Pete Suder	65.00	32.00	20.00
257	Bobby Avila	65.00	32.00	20.00
258	Steve Gromek	65.00	32.00	20.00
259	Bob Addis	65.00	32.00	20.00
260	Pete Castiglione	65.00	32.00	20.00
261	Willie Mays	2,650	1,325	575.00
262	Virgil Trucks	65.00	32.00	20.00
263	Harry Brecheen	65.00	32.00	20.00
264	Roy Hartsfield	65.00	32.00	20.00
265	Chuck Diering	65.00	32.00	20.00
266	Murry Dickson	65.00	32.00	20.00
267	Sid Gordon	65.00	32.00	20.00
268	Bob Lemon	125.00	62.50	31.25
269	Willard Nixon	65.00	32.00	20.00
270	Lou Brissie	65.00	32.00	20.00
271	Jim Delsing	65.00	32.00	20.00
272	Mike Garcia	65.00	32.00	20.00
273	Erv Palica	70.00	35.00	20.00
274	Ralph Branca	125.00	62.50	31.25
275	Pat Mullin	65.00	32.00	20.00
276	Jim Wilson	65.00	32.00	20.00
277	Early Wynn	175.00	85.00	50.00
278	Al Clark	65.00	32.00	20.00
279	Ed Stewart	65.00	32.00	20.00
280	Cloyd Boyer	65.00	32.00	20.00
281	Tommy Brown	65.00	32.00	20.00
282	Birdie Tebbetts	65.00	32.00	20.00
283	Phil Masi	65.00	32.00	20.00
284	Hank Arft	65.00	32.00	20.00
285	Cliff Fannin	65.00	32.00	20.00
286	Joe De Maestri	65.00	32.00	20.00
287	Steve Bilko	65.00	32.00	20.00
288	Chet Nichols	65.00	32.00	20.00
289	Tommy Holmes	65.00	32.00	20.00
290	Joe Astroth	65.00	32.00	20.00
291	Gil Coan	65.00	32.00	20.00
292	Floyd Baker	65.00	32.00	20.00
293	Sibby Sisti	65.00	32.00	20.00
294	Walker Cooper	65.00	32.00	20.00
295	Phil Cavarretta	65.00	32.00	20.00
296	"Red" Rolfe	65.00	32.00	20.00
297	Andy Seminick	65.00	32.00	20.00
298	Bob Ross	65.00	32.00	20.00
299	Ray Murray	65.00	32.00	20.00
300	Barney McCosky	65.00	32.00	20.00
301	Bob Porterfield	65.00	32.00	20.00
302	Max Surkont	65.00	32.00	20.00
303	Harry Dorish	65.00	32.00	20.00
304	Sam Dente	65.00	32.00	20.00
305	Paul Richards	65.00	32.00	20.00
306	Lou Sleator	65.00	32.00	20.00
307b	Frank Campos (Red star on back to right of "TOPPS BASEBALL."))	65.00	32.00	20.00
308	Luis Aloma	65.00	32.00	20.00
309	Jim Busby	65.00	32.00	20.00
310	George Metkovich	225.00	115.00	69.00
311a	Mickey Mantle (DP) (Stitching on ball on back points clockwise)	36,000	14,000	7,300
311b	Mickey Mantle (DP) (Stitching countr-clockwise)	36,000	14,000	7,300
312a	Jackie Robinson (DP) (Stitching on bacll on back points clockwise)	2,400	1,200	725.00
312b	Jackie Robinson (DP) (Sticthing counter-clockwise)	2,400	1,200	725.00
313a	Bobby Thomson (DP) (Stitching on ball on back points clockwise)	450.00	225.00	135.00
313b	Bobby Thomson (DP) (Stitching counter-clockwise)	450.00	225.00	135.00
314	Roy Campanella	2,500	1,250	625.00
315	Leo Durocher	600.00	300.00	150.00
316	Davey Williams	400.00	200.00	120.00
317	Connie Marrero	400.00	200.00	120.00
318	Hal Gregg	400.00	200.00	120.00
319	Al Walker	600.00	150.00	90.00
320	John Rutherford	600.00	150.00	90.00
321	Joe Black **RC**	400.00	200.00	120.00
322	Randy Jackson	400.00	200.00	120.00
323	Bubba Church	400.00	200.00	120.00
324	Warren Hacker	400.00	200.00	120.00
325	Bill Serena	400.00	200.00	120.00
326	George Shuba	600.00	200.00	120.00
327	Archie Wilson	400.00	200.00	120.00
328	Bob Borkowski	400.00	200.00	120.00
329	Ivan Delock	400.00	200.00	120.00
330	Turk Lown	400.00	200.00	120.00
331	Tom Morgan	400.00	200.00	120.00
332	Tony Bartirome	400.00	200.00	120.00
333	Pee Wee Reese	1,700	900.00	450.00
334	Wilmer Mizell	400.00	200.00	120.00
335	Ted Lepcio	400.00	200.00	120.00
336	Dave Koslo	400.00	200.00	120.00
337	Jim Hearn	400.00	200.00	120.00
338	Sal Yvars	400.00	200.00	120.00
339	Russ Meyer	400.00	200.00	120.00

340	Bob Hooper	400.00	200.00	120.00
341	Hal Jeffcoat	400.00	200.00	120.00
342	Clem Labine **RC**	600.00	250.00	125.00
343	Dick Gernert	400.00	200.00	120.00
344	Ewell Blackwell	400.00	200.00	120.00
345	Sam White	400.00	200.00	120.00
346	George Spencer	400.00	200.00	120.00
347	Joe Adcock	450.00	225.00	100.00
348	Bob Kelly	400.00	200.00	120.00
349	Bob Cain	400.00	200.00	120.00
350	Cal Abrams	400.00	200.00	120.00
351	Al Dark	450.00	150.00	90.00
352	Karl Drews	400.00	200.00	120.00
353	Bob Del Greco	400.00	200.00	120.00
354	Fred Hatfield	400.00	200.00	120.00
355	Bobby Morgan	600.00	150.00	90.00
356	Toby Atwell	400.00	200.00	120.00
357	Smoky Burgess	450.00	175.00	100.00
358	John Kucab	400.00	200.00	120.00
359	Dee Fondy	400.00	200.00	120.00
360	George Crowe	400.00	200.00	120.00
361	Bill Posedel	400.00	200.00	120.00
362	Ken Heintzelman	400.00	200.00	120.00
363	Dick Rozek	400.00	200.00	120.00
364	Clyde Sukeforth	400.00	200.00	120.00
365	"Cookie" Lavagetto	400.00	200.00	120.00
366	Dave Madison	400.00	200.00	120.00
367	Bob Thorpe	400.00	200.00	120.00
368	Ed Wright	400.00	200.00	120.00
369	Dick Groat **RC**	600.00	200.00	120.00
370	Billy Hoeft	400.00	200.00	120.00
371	Bob Hofman	400.00	200.00	120.00
372	Gil McDougald **RC**	650.00	250.00	150.00
373	Jim Turner	650.00	187.50	100.00
374	Al Benton	400.00	200.00	120.00
375	Jack Merson	400.00	200.00	120.00
376	Faye Throneberry	400.00	200.00	120.00
377	Chuck Dressen	400.00	200.00	120.00
378	Les Fusselman	400.00	200.00	120.00
379	Joe Rossi	400.00	200.00	120.00
380	Clem Koshorek	400.00	200.00	120.00
381	Milton Stock	400.00	200.00	120.00
382	Sam Jones	400.00	200.00	120.00
383	Del Wilber	400.00	200.00	120.00
384	Frank Crosetti	500.00	250.00	125.00
385	Herman Franks	400.00	200.00	120.00
386	Eddie Yuhas	400.00	200.00	120.00
387	Billy Meyer	400.00	200.00	120.00
388	Bob Chipman	400.00	200.00	120.00
389	Ben Wade	550.00	150.00	90.00
390	Glenn Nelson	550.00	150.00	90.00
391	Ben Chapman (Photo actually Sam Chapman.)	400.00	200.00	120.00
392	Hoyt Wilhelm **RC**	925.00	450.00	225.00
393	Ebba St. Claire	600.00	200.00	120.00
394	Billy Herman	800.00	225.00	120.00
395	Jake Pitler	600.00	150.00	90.00
396	Dick Williams **RC**	900.00	225.00	120.00
397	Forrest Main	400.00	200.00	120.00
398	Hal Rice	400.00	200.00	120.00
399	Jim Fridley	400.00	200.00	120.00
400	Bill Dickey	1,100	550.00	332.00
401	Bob Schultz	400.00	200.00	120.00
402	Earl Harrist	400.00	200.00	120.00
403	Bill Miller	750.00	150.00	90.00
404	Dick Brodowski	400.00	200.00	120.00
405	Eddie Pellagrini	400.00	200.00	120.00
406	Joe Nuxhall **RC**	900.00	225.00	120.00
407	Eddie Mathews **RC**	10,000	3,000	1,350

1952 Topps "Canadian"

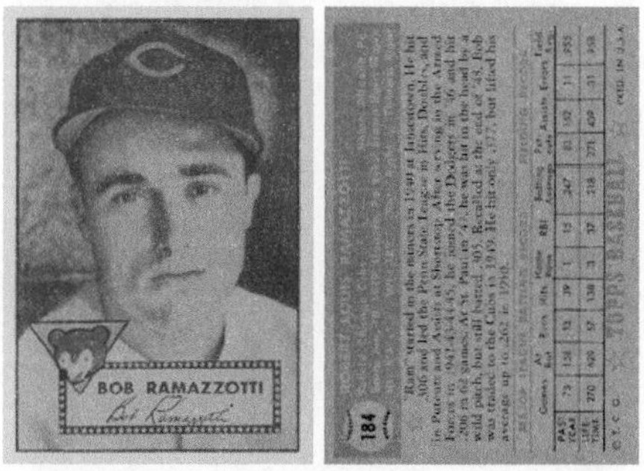
BOB RAMAZZOTTI
184

Perhaps because the "gray back" 1954 Topps cards have long been known as the "Canadian" issue, there is growing hobby support for the belief that a similar abbreviated set was printed in Canada for distribution there. The cards differ from the regular 1952 Topps of the same numerical range in that they are printed on a gray-backed cardboard stock, distinctly different from the cream-colored stock found on most '52 Topps #131-190. Additionally, the fronts of most, but not all, of the "Canadian" cards have colors which are subjectively darker or more muted than the the "U.S.A." versions. The market is just beginning to differentiate values between the two types, though the gray-backs are considered scarcer.

		NM	E	VG
Complete Set (60):		7,000	3,500	2,100
Common Player:		125.00	60.00	36.00
131	Morrie Martin	125.00	60.00	36.00
132	Clyde Kluttz	125.00	60.00	36.00
133	Al Widmar	125.00	60.00	36.00
134	Joe Tipton	125.00	60.00	36.00
135	Dixie Howell	125.00	60.00	36.00
136	Johnny Schmitz	85.00	42.50	25.00
137	Roy McMillan	125.00	60.00	36.00
138	Bill MacDonald	125.00	60.00	36.00
139	Ken Wood	125.00	60.00	36.00
140	John Antonelli	125.00	60.00	36.00
141	Clint Hartung	125.00	60.00	36.00
142	Harry Perkowski	125.00	60.00	36.00
143	Les Moss	125.00	60.00	36.00
144	Ed Blake	125.00	60.00	36.00
145	Joe Haynes	125.00	60.00	36.00
146	Frank House	125.00	60.00	36.00
147	Bob Young	125.00	60.00	36.00
148	Johnny Klippstein	125.00	60.00	36.00
149	Dick Kryhoski	125.00	60.00	36.00
150	Ted Beard	125.00	60.00	36.00
151	Wally Post	125.00	60.00	36.00
152	Al Evans	125.00	60.00	36.00
153	Bob Rush	125.00	60.00	36.00
154	Joe Muir	125.00	60.00	36.00
155	Frank Overmire	85.00	42.50	25.00
156	Frank Hiller	125.00	60.00	36.00
157	Bob Usher	125.00	60.00	36.00
158	Eddie Waitkus	125.00	60.00	36.00
159	Saul Rogovin	125.00	60.00	36.00
160	Owen Friend	125.00	60.00	36.00
161	Bud Byerly	125.00	60.00	36.00
162	Del Crandall	125.00	60.00	36.00
163	Stan Rojek	125.00	60.00	36.00
164	Walt Dubiel	125.00	60.00	36.00
165	Eddie Kazak	125.00	60.00	36.00
166	Paul LaPalme	125.00	60.00	36.00
167	Bill Howerton	125.00	60.00	36.00
168	Charlie Silvera	150.00	75.00	45.00
169	Howie Judson	125.00	60.00	36.00
170	Gus Bell	175.00	90.00	60.00
171	Ed Erautt	125.00	60.00	36.00
172	Eddie Miksis	125.00	60.00	36.00
173	Roy Smalley	125.00	60.00	36.00
174	Clarence Marshall	125.00	60.00	36.00
175	Billy Martin	500.00	250.00	150.00
176	Hank Edwards	125.00	60.00	36.00
177	Bill Wight	125.00	60.00	36.00
178	Cass Michaels	125.00	60.00	36.00
179	Frank Smith	125.00	60.00	36.00
180	Charley Maxwell	125.00	60.00	36.00
181	Bob Swift	125.00	60.00	36.00
182	Billy Hitchcock	125.00	60.00	36.00
183	Erv Dusak	125.00	60.00	36.00
184	Bob Ramazzotti	125.00	60.00	36.00
185	Bill Nicholson	125.00	60.00	36.00
186	Walt Masterson	125.00	60.00	36.00
187	Bob Miller	125.00	60.00	36.00
188	Clarence Podbielan	125.00	60.00	36.00
189	Pete Reiser	125.00	60.00	36.00
190	Don Johnson	125.00	60.00	36.00

1953 Topps

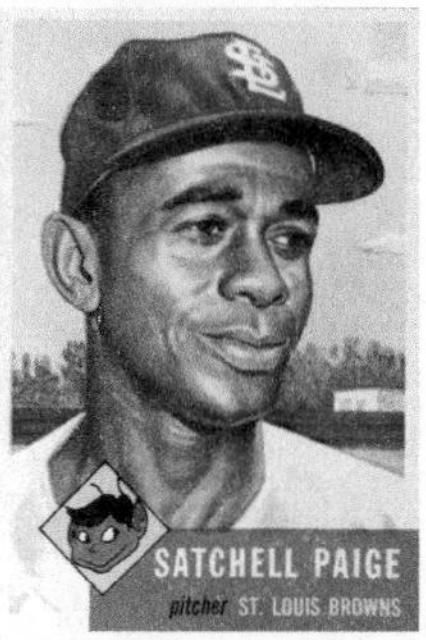
SATCHELL PAIGE
pitcher ST. LOUIS BROWNS

The 1953 Topps set reflects the company's continuing legal battles with Bowman. The set, originally intended to consist of 280 cards, is lacking six numbers (253, 261, 267, 268, 271 and 275) that represent players whose contracts were lost to the competition. The 2-5/8" x 3-3/4" cards feature painted player pictures. A color team logo appears at a bottom panel (red for American League and black for National). Card backs contain the first baseball-card trivia questions along with brief statistics and player biographies. In the red panel at the top, which lists the player's personal data, cards from the 2nd Series (#86-165 plus 10, 44, 61, 72 and 81) can be found with that data printed in either black or white, black being the marginally scarcer variety. Eighty-five cards between #1-165 were printed in noticeably larger quantities than the others, and are indicated in these listings with a double-print (DP) notation. Cards #221-280, the high numbers, were printed late in the season, in smaller quantities than the earlier series. Among the high numbers, even scarcer short-printed (SP) cards are interspersed in the series.

		NM	E	VG
Complete Set (274):		30,000	15,000	9,000
Common Player (1-165):		30.00	15.00	9.00
Common Player (166-220):		35.00	17.50	10.00
Common Player (221-280):		60.00	30.00	18.00
Short-print Player (221-280):		90.00	45.00	27.50
1	Jackie Robinson (DP)	1,000	300.00	125.00
2	Luke Easter (DP)	40.00	20.00	12.00
3	George Crowe	40.00	20.00	12.00
4	Ben Wade	45.00	22.50	13.50
5	Joe Dobson	40.00	20.00	12.00
6	Sam Jones	40.00	20.00	12.00
7	Bob Borkowski (DP)	30.00	15.00	9.00
8	Clem Koshorek (DP)	30.00	15.00	9.00
9	Joe Collins	45.00	22.50	13.50
10	Smoky Burgess (SP)	70.00	35.00	20.00
11	Sal Yvars	40.00	20.00	12.00
12	Howie Judson (DP)	30.00	15.00	9.00
13	Connie Marrero (DP)	30.00	15.00	9.00
14	Clem Labine (DP)	60.00	30.00	18.00
15	Bobo Newsom (DP)	30.00	15.00	9.00
16	Harry Lowrey (DP)	30.00	15.00	9.00
17	Billy Hitchcock	40.00	20.00	12.00
18	Ted Lepcio (DP)	30.00	15.00	9.00
19	Mel Parnell (DP)	30.00	15.00	9.00
20	Hank Thompson	40.00	20.00	12.00
21	Billy Johnson	40.00	20.00	12.00
22	Howie Fox	40.00	20.00	12.00
23	Toby Atwell (DP)	30.00	15.00	9.00
24	Ferris Fain	40.00	20.00	12.00
25	Ray Boone	40.00	20.00	12.00
26	Dale Mitchell (DP)	30.00	15.00	9.00
27	Roy Campanella (DP)	300.00	150.00	75.00
28	Eddie Pellagrini	40.00	20.00	12.00
29	Hal Jeffcoat	40.00	20.00	12.00
30	Willard Nixon	40.00	20.00	12.00
31	Ewell Blackwell	60.00	30.00	16.50
32	Clyde Vollmer	40.00	20.00	12.00
33	Bob Kennedy (DP)	30.00	15.00	9.00
34	George Shuba	60.00	30.00	18.00
35	Irv Noren (DP)	35.00	17.50	10.00
36	Johnny Groth (DP)	30.00	15.00	9.00
37	Ed Mathews (DP)	275.00	187.50	100.00
38	Jim Hearn (DP)	30.00	15.00	9.00
39	Eddie Miksis	40.00	20.00	12.00
40	John Lipon	40.00	20.00	12.00
41	Enos Slaughter	80.00	40.00	24.00
42	Gus Zernial (DP)	30.00	15.00	9.00
43	Gil McDougald	75.00	37.50	22.50
44	Ellis Kinder (SP)	75.00	37.50	22.50
45	Grady Hatton (DP)	30.00	15.00	9.00
46	Johnny Klippstein (DP)	30.00	15.00	9.00
47	Bubba Church (DP)	30.00	15.00	9.00
48	Bob Del Greco (DP)	30.00	15.00	9.00
49	Faye Throneberry (DP)	30.00	15.00	9.00
50	Chuck Dressen (DP)	40.00	20.00	12.00
51	Frank Campos (DP)	30.00	15.00	9.00
52	Ted Gray (DP)	30.00	15.00	9.00
53	Sherman Lollar (DP)	30.00	15.00	9.00
54	Bob Feller (DP)	165.00	82.50	45.00
55	Maurice McDermott (DP)	30.00	15.00	9.00
56	Gerald Staley (DP)	30.00	15.00	9.00
57	Carl Scheib	40.00	20.00	12.00
58	George Metkovich	40.00	20.00	12.00
59	Karl Drews (DP)	30.00	15.00	9.00
60	Cloyd Boyer (DP)	30.00	15.00	9.00
61	Early Wynn (SP)	125.00	62.50	31.25
62	Monte Irvin (DP)	110.00	55.00	33.00
63	Gus Niarhos (DP)	30.00	15.00	9.00
64	Dave Philley	40.00	20.00	12.00
65	Earl Harrist	40.00	20.00	12.00
66	Orestes Minoso	75.00	35.00	20.00
67	Roy Sievers (DP)	30.00	15.00	9.00
68	Del Rice	40.00	20.00	12.00
69	Dick Brodowski	40.00	20.00	12.00
70	Ed Yuhas	40.00	20.00	12.00
71	Tony Bartirome	40.00	20.00	12.00
72	Fred Hutchinson (SP)	75.00	37.50	22.50
73	Eddie Robinson	40.00	20.00	12.00
74	Joe Rossi	40.00	20.00	12.00
75	Mike Garcia	40.00	20.00	12.00
76	Pee Wee Reese	200.00	100.00	60.00
77	Johnny Mize (DP)	75.00	37.50	22.50
78	Al Schoendienst	100.00	50.00	30.00
79	Johnny Wyrostek	40.00	20.00	12.00
80	Jim Hegan	40.00	20.00	12.00
81	Joe Black (SP)	80.00	40.00	20.00
82	Mickey Mantle	3,175	1,400	750.00

83	Howie Pollet	40.00	20.00	12.00
84	Bob Hooper (DP)	30.00	15.00	9.00
85	Bobby Morgan (DP)	40.00	20.00	12.00
86	Billy Martin	175.00	87.50	43.75
87	Ed Lopat	65.00	32.00	18.00
88	Willie Jones (DP)	30.00	15.00	9.00
89	Chuck Stobbs (DP)	30.00	15.00	9.00
90	Hank Edwards (DP)	30.00	15.00	9.00
91	Ebba St. Claire (DP)	30.00	15.00	9.00
92	Paul Minner (DP)	30.00	15.00	9.00
93	Hal Rice (DP)	30.00	15.00	9.00
94	William Kennedy (DP)	30.00	15.00	9.00
95	Willard Marshall (DP)	30.00	15.00	9.00
96	Virgil Trucks	40.00	20.00	12.00
97	Don Kolloway (DP)	30.00	15.00	9.00
98	Cal Abrams (DP)	30.00	15.00	9.00
99	Dave Madison	40.00	20.00	12.00
100	Bill Miller	40.00	20.00	12.00
101	Ted Wilks	40.00	20.00	12.00
102	Connie Ryan (DP)	30.00	15.00	9.00
103	Joe Astroth (DP)	30.00	15.00	9.00
104	Yogi Berra	415.00	200.00	100.00
105	Joe Nuxhall (DP)	35.00	17.50	10.00
106	John Antonelli	40.00	20.00	12.00
107	Danny O'Connell (DP)	30.00	15.00	9.00
108	Bob Porterfield (DP)	30.00	15.00	9.00
109	Alvin Dark	40.00	20.00	12.00
110	Herman Wehmeier (DP)	30.00	15.00	9.00
111	Hank Sauer (DP)	30.00	15.00	9.00
112	Ned Garver (DP)	30.00	15.00	9.00
113	Jerry Priddy	40.00	20.00	12.00
114	Phil Rizzuto	225.00	125.00	62.50
115	George Spencer	40.00	20.00	12.00
116	Frank Smith (DP)	30.00	15.00	9.00
117	Sid Gordon (DP)	30.00	15.00	9.00
118	Gus Bell (DP)	30.00	15.00	9.00
119	John Sain	75.00	37.50	22.50
120	Davey Williams	40.00	20.00	12.00
121	Walt Dropo	40.00	20.00	12.00
122	Elmer Valo	40.00	20.00	12.00
123	Tommy Byrne (DP)	30.00	15.00	9.00
124	Sibby Sisti (DP)	30.00	15.00	9.00
125	Dick Williams (DP)	35.00	17.50	10.00
126	Bill Connelly (DP)	30.00	15.00	9.00
127	Clint Courtney (DP)	30.00	15.00	9.00
128	Wilmer Mizell (DP)	30.00	15.00	9.00
129	Keith Thomas	40.00	20.00	12.00
130	Turk Lown (DP)	30.00	15.00	9.00
131	Harry Byrd (DP)	30.00	15.00	9.00
132	Tom Morgan	45.00	22.50	13.50
133	Gil Coan	40.00	20.00	12.00
134	Rube Walker	45.00	22.50	13.50
135	Al Rosen (DP)	45.00	22.50	13.50
136	Ken Heintzelman (DP)	30.00	15.00	9.00
137	John Rutherford (DP)	35.00	17.50	10.00
138	George Kell	55.00	27.50	16.50
139	Sammy White	40.00	20.00	12.00
140	Tommy Glaviano	40.00	20.00	12.00
141	Allie Reynolds (DP)	75.00	37.50	22.50
142	Vic Wertz	40.00	20.00	12.00
143	Billy Pierce	40.00	20.00	12.00
144	Bob Schultz (DP)	30.00	15.00	9.00
145	Harry Dorish (DP)	30.00	15.00	9.00
146	Granville Hamner	40.00	20.00	12.00
147	Warren Spahn	200.00	100.00	50.00
148	Mickey Grasso	40.00	20.00	12.00
149	Dom DiMaggio (DP)	65.00	32.50	20.00
150	Harry Simpson (DP)	30.00	15.00	9.00
151	Hoyt Wilhelm	100.00	50.00	25.00
152	Bob Adams (DP)	30.00	15.00	9.00
153	Andy Seminick (DP)	30.00	15.00	9.00
154	Dick Groat	40.00	20.00	12.00
155	Dutch Leonard	40.00	20.00	12.00
156	Jim Rivera (DP)	30.00	15.00	9.00
157	Bob Addis (DP)	30.00	15.00	9.00
158	John Logan **RC**	40.00	20.00	12.00
159	Wayne Terwilliger (DP)	30.00	15.00	9.00
160	Bob Young	40.00	20.00	12.00
161	Vern Bickford (DP)	30.00	15.00	9.00
162	Ted Kluszewski	80.00	40.00	24.00
163	Fred Hatfield (DP)	30.00	15.00	9.00
164	Frank Shea (DP)	30.00	15.00	9.00
165	Billy Hoeft	40.00	20.00	12.00
166	Bill Hunter	35.00	17.50	10.00
167	Art Schult	35.00	17.50	10.00
168	Willard Schmidt	35.00	17.50	10.00
169	Dizzy Trout	35.00	17.50	10.00
170	Bill Werle	35.00	17.50	10.00
171	Bill Glynn	35.00	17.50	10.00
172	Rip Repulski	35.00	17.50	10.00
173	Preston Ward	35.00	17.50	10.00
174	Billy Loes	45.00	22.50	13.50
175	Ron Kline	35.00	17.50	10.00
176	Don Hoak **RC**	40.00	20.00	12.00
177	Jim Dyck	35.00	17.50	10.00
178	Jim Waugh	35.00	17.50	10.00
179	Gene Hermanski	35.00	17.50	10.00
180	Virgil Stallcup	35.00	17.50	10.00
181	Al Zarilla	35.00	17.50	10.00
182	Bob Hofman	35.00	17.50	10.00
183	Stu Miller **RC**	35.00	17.50	10.00
184	Hal Brown **RC**	35.00	17.50	10.00
185	Jim Pendleton **RC**	35.00	17.50	10.00
186	Charlie Bishop	35.00	17.50	10.00
187	Jim Fridley	35.00	17.50	10.00
188	Andy Carey **RC**	60.00	30.00	18.00
189	Ray Jablonski	35.00	17.50	10.00
190	Dixie Walker	35.00	17.50	10.00
191	Ralph Kiner	85.00	37.50	18.75
192	Wally Westlake	35.00	17.50	10.00
193	Mike Clark	35.00	17.50	10.00
194	Eddie Kazak	35.00	17.50	10.00
195	Ed McGhee	35.00	17.50	10.00
196	Bob Keegan	35.00	17.50	10.00
197	Del Crandall	35.00	17.50	10.00
198	Forrest Main	35.00	17.50	10.00
199	Marion Fricano	35.00	17.50	10.00
200	Gordon Goldsberry	35.00	17.50	10.00
201	Paul La Palme	35.00	17.50	10.00
202	Carl Sawatski	35.00	17.50	10.00
203	Cliff Fannin	35.00	17.50	10.00
204	Dick Bokelmann	35.00	17.50	10.00
205	Vern Benson	35.00	17.50	10.00
206	Ed Bailey **RC**	35.00	17.50	10.00
207	Whitey Ford	310.00	150.00	75.00
208	Jim Wilson	35.00	17.50	10.00
209	Jim Greengrass	35.00	17.50	10.00
210	Bob Cerv **RC**	45.00	22.20	13.50
211	J.W. Porter	35.00	17.50	10.00
212	Jack Dittmer	35.00	17.50	10.00
213	Ray Scarborough	35.00	17.50	10.00
214	Bill Bruton **RC**	35.00	17.50	10.00
215	Gene Conley **RC**	35.00	17.50	10.00
216	Jim Hughes	40.00	20.00	12.00
217	Murray Wall	35.00	17.50	10.00
218	Les Fusselman	35.00	17.50	10.00
219	Pete Runnels (Picture actually Don Johnson.)	35.00	17.50	10.00
220	Satchell Paige	800.00	350.00	210.00
221	Bob Milliken (SP)	100.00	50.00	30.00
222	Vic Janowicz	100.00	50.00	30.00
223	John O'Brien	60.00	30.00	18.00
224	Lou Sleater	60.00	30.00	18.00
225	Bobby Shantz (SP)	90.00	45.00	27.50
226	Ed Erautt (SP)	90.00	45.00	27.50
227	Morris Martin (SP)	90.00	45.00	27.50
228	Hal Newhouser (SP)	150.00	75.00	37.50
229	Rocky Krsnich (SP)	90.00	45.00	27.50
230	Johnny Lindell	60.00	30.00	18.00
231	Solly Hemus	60.00	30.00	18.00
232	Dick Kokos (SP)	90.00	45.00	27.50
233	Al Aber (SP)	90.00	45.00	27.50
234	Ray Murray	60.00	30.00	18.00
235	John Hetki	60.00	30.00	18.00
236	Harry Perkowski	60.00	30.00	18.00
237	Clarence Podbielan	60.00	30.00	18.00
238	Cal Hogue	60.00	30.00	18.00
239	Jim Delsing (SP)	90.00	45.00	27.50
240	Freddie Marsh (SP)	90.00	45.00	27.50
241	Al Sima	60.00	30.00	18.00
242	Charlie Silvera (SP)	100.00	50.00	30.00
243	Carlos Bernier	60.00	30.00	18.00
244	Willie Mays (SP)	2,400	850.00	380.00
245	Bill Norman	90.00	45.00	27.50
246	Roy Face **RC**	75.00	37.50	22.50
247	Mike Sandlock	60.00	30.00	18.00
248	Gene Stephens	60.00	30.00	18.00
249	Ed O'Brien (SP)	90.00	45.00	27.50
250	Bob Wilson (SP)	90.00	45.00	27.50
251	Sid Hudson (SP)	90.00	45.00	27.50
252	Henry Foiles (SP)	90.00	45.00	27.50
253	Not Issued			
254	Preacher Roe	100.00	50.00	25.00
255	Dixie Howell (SP)	100.00	50.00	25.00
256	Les Peden (SP)	90.00	45.00	27.50
257	Bob Boyd (SP)	90.00	45.00	27.50
258	Jim Gilliam **RC** (SP)	400.00	200.00	100.00
259	Roy McMillan	60.00	30.00	18.00
260	Sam Calderone (SP)	90.00	45.00	27.50
261	Not Issued			
262	Bob Oldis (SP)	90.00	45.00	27.50
263	Johnny Podres **RC** (SP)	310.00	150.00	90.00
264	Gene Woodling	95.00	47.50	27.50
265	Jackie Jensen (SP)	125.00	62.50	31.25
266	Bob Cain (SP)	90.00	45.00	27.50
267	Not Issued			
268	Not Issued			
269	Duane Pillette (SP)	90.00	45.00	27.50
270	Vern Stephens (SP)	90.00	45.00	27.50
271	Not Issued			
272	Bill Antonello (SP)	100.00	50.00	30.00
273	Harvey Haddix **RC** (SP)	125.00	62.50	31.25
274	John Riddle (SP)	90.00	45.00	27.50
275	Not Issued			
276	Ken Raffensberger (SP)	90.00	45.00	27.50
277	Don Lund (SP)	90.00	45.00	27.50
278	Willie Miranda (SP)	90.00	45.00	27.50
279	Joe Coleman	60.00	30.00	18.00
280	Milt Bolling **RC** (SP)	475.00	60.00	30.00

1954 Topps

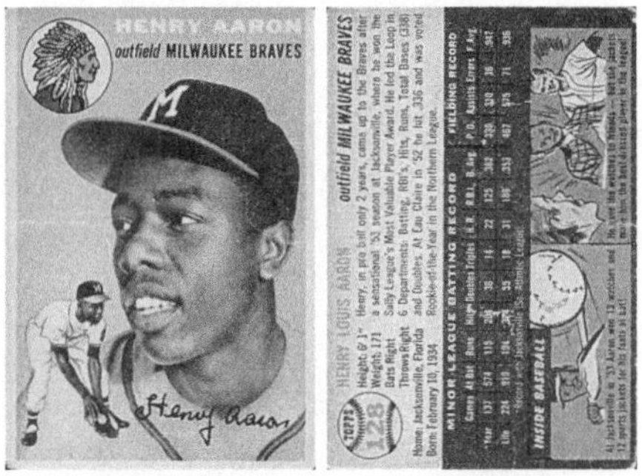

The first issue to use two player pictures on the front, the 1954 Topps set remains popular today. Solid color backgrounds frame both color portraits and black-and-white action pictures of the player. The player's name, position, team and team logo appear at the top. Backs include an "Inside Baseball" cartoon regarding the player as well as statistics and biography. The 250-card, 2-5/8" x 3-3/4", set includes manager and coaches cards. A gray-back version of cards #1-50 is known, distinguished by the use of dark gray cardboard on back. These are often attributed to Canadian issue and carry a modest premium.

	NM	E	VG
Complete Set (250):	11,000	5,500	3,250
Common Player (1-50):	20.00	10.00	6.00
Common Player (51-75):	35.00	17.50	10.00
Common Player (76-250):	20.00	10.00	6.00

1	Ted Williams	850.00	220.00	100.00
2	Gus Zernial	35.00	10.00	6.00
3	Monte Irvin	60.00	30.00	18.00
4	Hank Sauer	20.00	10.00	6.00
5	Ed Lopat	25.00	12.50	7.50
6	Pete Runnels	20.00	10.00	6.00
7	Ted Kluszewski	35.00	17.50	10.00
8	Bobby Young	20.00	10.00	6.00
9	Harvey Haddix	20.00	10.00	6.00
10	Jackie Robinson	290.00	150.00	90.00
11	Paul Smith	20.00	10.00	6.00
12	Del Crandall	20.00	10.00	6.00
13	Billy Martin	100.00	50.00	25.00
14	Preacher Roe	35.00	17.50	10.00
15	Al Rosen	30.00	15.00	9.00
16	Vic Janowicz	25.00	12.50	7.50
17	Phil Rizzuto	125.00	62.50	31.25
18	Walt Dropo	20.00	10.00	6.00
19	Johnny Lipon	20.00	10.00	6.00
20	Warren Spahn	150.00	75.00	37.50
21	Bobby Shantz	20.00	10.00	6.00
22	Jim Greengrass	20.00	10.00	6.00
23	Luke Easter	25.00	12.50	7.50
24	Granny Hamner	20.00	10.00	6.00
25	Harvey Kuenn **RC**	40.00	17.50	10.00
26	Ray Jablonski	20.00	10.00	6.00
27	Ferris Fain	20.00	10.00	6.00
28	Paul Minner	20.00	10.00	6.00
29	Jim Hegan	20.00	10.00	6.00
30	Ed Mathews	90.00	45.00	27.00
31	Johnny Klippstein	20.00	10.00	6.00
32	Duke Snider	140.00	70.00	42.00
33	Johnny Schmitz	20.00	10.00	6.00
34	Jim Rivera	20.00	10.00	6.00
35	Junior Gilliam	35.00	17.50	10.00
36	Hoyt Wilhelm	40.00	20.00	12.00
37	Whitey Ford	200.00	100.00	50.00
38	Eddie Stanky	20.00	10.00	6.00
39	Sherm Lollar	20.00	10.00	6.00
40	Mel Parnell	20.00	10.00	6.00
41	Willie Jones	20.00	10.00	6.00
42	Don Mueller	20.00	10.00	6.00
43	Dick Groat	20.00	10.00	6.00
44	Ned Garver	20.00	10.00	6.00
45	Richie Ashburn	80.00	40.00	20.00
46	Ken Raffensberger	20.00	10.00	6.00
47	Ellis Kinder	20.00	10.00	6.00
48	Billy Hunter	20.00	10.00	6.00
49	Ray Murray	20.00	10.00	6.00
50	Yogi Berra	250.00	125.00	75.00
51	Johnny Lindell	35.00	17.50	10.00
52	Vic Power **RC**	40.00	20.00	12.00
53	Jack Dittmer	35.00	17.50	10.00
54	Vern Stephens	35.00	17.50	10.00
55	Phil Cavarretta	35.00	17.50	10.00
56	Willie Miranda	35.00	17.50	10.00
57	Luis Aloma	35.00	17.50	10.00
58	Bob Wilson	35.00	17.50	10.00

59	Gene Conley	35.00	17.50	10.00
60	Frank Baumholtz	35.00	17.50	10.00
61	Bob Cain	35.00	17.50	10.00
62	Eddie Robinson	40.00	20.00	12.00
63	Johnny Pesky	35.00	17.50	10.00
64	Hank Thompson	35.00	17.50	10.00
65	Bob Swift	35.00	17.50	10.00
66	Ted Lepcio	35.00	17.50	10.00
67	Jim Willis	35.00	17.50	10.00
68	Sammy Calderone	35.00	17.50	10.00
69	Bud Podbielan	35.00	17.50	10.00
70	Larry Doby	75.00	37.50	18.75
71	Frank Smith	35.00	17.50	10.00
72	Preston Ward	35.00	17.50	10.00
73	Wayne Terwilliger	35.00	17.50	10.00
74	Bill Taylor	35.00	17.50	10.00
75	Fred Haney	35.00	17.50	10.00
76	Bob Scheffing	20.00	10.00	6.00
77	Ray Boone	20.00	10.00	6.00
78	Ted Kazanski	20.00	10.00	6.00
79	Andy Pafko	20.00	10.00	6.00
80	Jackie Jensen	30.00	15.00	9.00
81	Dave Hoskins	20.00	10.00	6.00
82	Milt Bolling	20.00	10.00	6.00
83	Joe Collins	25.00	12.50	7.50
84	Dick Cole	20.00	10.00	6.00
85	Bob Turley **RC**	35.00	17.50	10.00
86	Billy Herman	45.00	22.50	13.50
87	Roy Face	20.00	10.00	6.00
88	Matt Batts	20.00	10.00	6.00
89	Howie Pollet	20.00	10.00	6.00
90	Willie Mays	525.00	215.00	135.00
91	Bob Oldis	20.00	10.00	6.00
92	Wally Westlake	20.00	10.00	6.00
93	Sid Hudson	20.00	10.00	6.00
94	Ernie Banks **RC**	1,100	575.00	300.00
95	Hal Rice	20.00	10.00	6.00
96	Charlie Silvera	25.00	12.50	7.50
97	Jerry Lane	20.00	10.00	6.00
98	Joe Black	60.00	30.00	20.00
99	Bob Hofman	20.00	10.00	6.00
100	Bob Keegan	20.00	10.00	6.00
101	Gene Woodling	50.00	25.00	15.00
102	Gil Hodges	95.00	45.00	22.50
103	Jim Lemon **RC**	25.00	12.50	7.50
104	Mike Sandlock	20.00	10.00	6.00
105	Andy Carey	25.00	12.50	7.50
106	Dick Kokos	20.00	10.00	6.00
107	Duane Pillette	20.00	10.00	6.00
108	Thornton Kipper	20.00	10.00	6.00
109	Bill Bruton	20.00	10.00	6.00
110	Harry Dorish	20.00	10.00	6.00
111	Jim Delsing	20.00	10.00	6.00
112	Bill Renna	20.00	10.00	6.00
113	Bob Boyd	20.00	10.00	6.00
114	Dean Stone	20.00	10.00	6.00
115	"Rip" Repulski	20.00	10.00	6.00
116	Steve Bilko	20.00	10.00	6.00
117	Solly Hemus	20.00	10.00	6.00
118	Carl Scheib	20.00	10.00	6.00
119	Johnny Antonelli	20.00	10.00	6.00
120	Roy McMillan	20.00	10.00	6.00
121	Clem Labine	45.00	22.50	13.50
122	Johnny Logan	20.00	10.00	6.00
123	Bobby Adams	20.00	10.00	6.00
124	Marion Fricano	20.00	10.00	6.00
125	Harry Perkowski	20.00	10.00	6.00
126	Ben Wade	25.00	12.50	7.50
127	Steve O'Neill	20.00	10.00	6.00
128	Hank Aaron **RC**	1,925	850.00	450.00
129	Forrest Jacobs	20.00	10.00	6.00
130	Hank Bauer	40.00	20.00	10.00
131	Reno Bertoia	20.00	10.00	6.00
132	Tom Lasorda **RC**	250.00	125.00	62.50
133	Del Baker	20.00	10.00	6.00
134	Cal Hogue	20.00	10.00	6.00
135	Joe Presko	20.00	10.00	6.00
136	Connie Ryan	20.00	10.00	6.00
137	Wally Moon **RC**	35.00	17.50	10.00
138	Bob Borkowski	20.00	10.00	6.00
139	Ed O'Brien, Johnny O'Brien	60.00	30.00	15.00
140	Tom Wright	20.00	10.00	6.00
141	Joe Jay **RC**	40.00	20.00	12.00
142	Tom Poholsky	20.00	10.00	6.00
143	Rollie Hemsley	20.00	10.00	6.00
144	Bill Werle	20.00	10.00	6.00
145	Elmer Valo	20.00	10.00	6.00
146	Don Johnson	20.00	10.00	6.00
147	John Riddle	20.00	10.00	6.00
148	Bob Trice	20.00	10.00	6.00
149	Jim Robertson	20.00	10.00	6.00
150	Dick Kryhoski	20.00	10.00	6.00
151	Alex Grammas	20.00	10.00	6.00
152	Mike Blyzka	20.00	10.00	6.00
153	Rube Walker	25.00	12.50	7.50
154	Mike Fornieles	20.00	10.00	6.00
155	Bob Kennedy	20.00	10.00	6.00
156	Joe Coleman	20.00	10.00	6.00
157	Don Lenhardt	20.00	10.00	6.00
158	"Peanuts" Lowrey	20.00	10.00	6.00
159	Dave Philley	20.00	10.00	6.00
160	"Red" Kress	20.00	10.00	6.00
161	John Hetki	20.00	10.00	6.00
162	Herman Wehmeier	20.00	10.00	6.00
163	Frank House	20.00	10.00	6.00
164	Stu Miller	20.00	10.00	6.00
165	Jim Pendleton	20.00	10.00	6.00
166	Johnny Podres	45.00	22.50	13.50
167	Don Lund	20.00	10.00	6.00
168	Morrie Martin	20.00	10.00	6.00
169	Jim Hughes	25.00	12.50	7.50
170	Jim Rhodes **RC**	40.00	20.00	12.00
171	Leo Kiely	20.00	10.00	6.00
172	Hal Brown	20.00	10.00	6.00
173	Jack Harshman	20.00	10.00	6.00
174	Tom Qualters	20.00	10.00	6.00
175	Frank Leja **RC**	25.00	12.50	7.50
176	Bob Keely	20.00	10.00	6.00
177	Bob Milliken	25.00	12.50	7.50
178	Bill Gylnn (Glynn)	20.00	10.00	6.00
179	Gair Allie	20.00	10.00	6.00
180	Wes Westrum	20.00	10.00	6.00
181	Mel Roach	20.00	10.00	6.00
182	Chuck Harmon	20.00	10.00	6.00
183	Earle Combs	25.00	12.50	7.50
184	Ed Bailey	20.00	10.00	6.00
185	Chuck Stobbs	20.00	10.00	6.00
186	Karl Olson	20.00	10.00	6.00
187	"Heinie" Manush	25.00	12.50	7.50
188	Dave Jolly	20.00	10.00	6.00
189	Bob Ross	20.00	10.00	6.00
190	Ray Herbert	20.00	10.00	6.00
191	Dick Schofield **RC**	25.00	12.50	7.50
192	"Cot" Deal	20.00	10.00	6.00
193	Johnny Hopp	20.00	10.00	6.00
194	Bill Sarni	20.00	10.00	6.00
195	Bill Consolo	20.00	10.00	6.00
196	Stan Jok	20.00	10.00	6.00
197	"Schoolboy" Rowe	20.00	10.00	6.00
198	Carl Sawatski	20.00	10.00	6.00
199	"Rocky" Nelson	20.00	10.00	6.00
200	Larry Jansen	20.00	10.00	6.00
201	Al Kaline **RC**	625.00	315.00	160.00
202	Bob Purkey **RC**	20.00	10.00	6.00
203	Harry Brecheen	20.00	10.00	6.00
204	Angel Scull	20.00	10.00	6.00
205	Johnny Sain	40.00	20.00	10.00
206	Ray Crone	20.00	10.00	6.00
207	Tom Oliver	20.00	10.00	6.00
208	Grady Hatton	20.00	10.00	6.00
209	Charlie Thompson	25.00	12.50	7.50
210	Bob Buhl **RC**	20.00	10.00	6.00
211	Don Hoak	25.00	12.50	7.50
212	Mickey Micelotta	20.00	10.00	6.00
213	John Fitzpatrick	20.00	10.00	6.00
214	Arnold Portocarrero	20.00	10.00	6.00
215	Ed McGhee	20.00	10.00	6.00
216	Al Sima	20.00	10.00	6.00
217	Paul Schreiber	20.00	10.00	6.00
218	Fred Marsh	20.00	10.00	6.00
219	Charlie Kress	20.00	10.00	6.00
220	Ruben Gomez	20.00	10.00	6.00
221	Dick Brodowski	20.00	10.00	6.00
222	Bill Wilson	20.00	10.00	6.00
223	Joe Haynes	20.00	10.00	6.00
224	Dick Weik	20.00	10.00	6.00
225	Don Liddle	20.00	10.00	6.00
226	Jehosie Heard	20.00	10.00	6.00
227	Buster Mills	20.00	10.00	6.00
228	Gene Hermanski	20.00	10.00	6.00
229	Bob Talbot	20.00	10.00	6.00
230	Bob Kuzava	25.00	12.50	7.50
231	Roy Smalley	20.00	10.00	6.00
232	Lou Limmer	20.00	10.00	6.00
233	Augie Galan	20.00	10.00	6.00
234	Jerry Lynch **RC**	20.00	10.00	6.00
235	Vern Law	20.00	10.00	6.00
236	Paul Penson	20.00	10.00	6.00
237	Mike Ryba	20.00	10.00	6.00
238	Al Aber	20.00	10.00	6.00
239	Bill Skowron **RC**	90.00	45.00	22.50
240	Sam Mele	20.00	10.00	6.00
241	Bob Miller	20.00	10.00	6.00
242	Curt Roberts	20.00	10.00	6.00
243	Ray Blades	20.00	10.00	6.00
244	Leroy Wheat	20.00	10.00	6.00
245	Roy Sievers	20.00	10.00	6.00
246	Howie Fox	20.00	10.00	6.00
247	Eddie Mayo	20.00	10.00	6.00
248	Al Smith **RC**	20.00	10.00	6.00
249	Wilmer Mizell	20.00	10.00	6.00
250	Ted Williams	850.00	225.00	130.00

1954 Topps "Canadian"

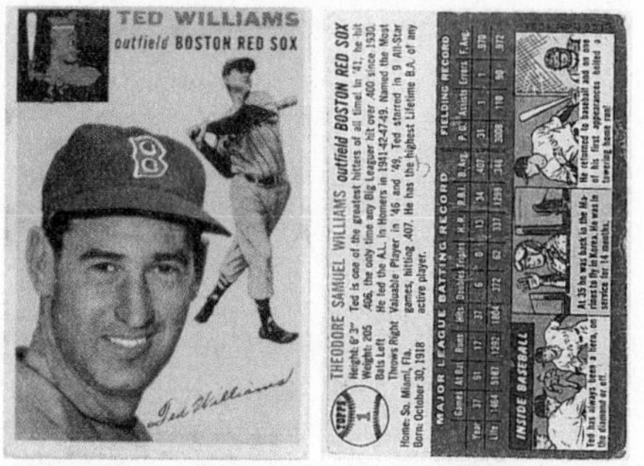

This version of the first 50 cards from 1954 Topps has long been known as the "Canadian" issue. It is widely believed that the abbreviated set was intended solely for Canadian distribution. The cards differ from the regular 1954 Topps in that they are printed on a gray-backed cardboard stock, distinctly different from the white stock found on most '54 Topps. Later series white-back Topps cards were sold in Canada in O-Pee-Chee marked wrappers at four for a nickel as opposed to six for five cents in the U.S.

		NM	E	VG
Complete Set (50):		5,500	2,750	1,750
Common Player:		40.00	20.00	12.00
1	Ted Williams	1,500	700.00	450.00
2	Gus Zernial	60.00	20.00	12.00
3	Monte Irvin	115.00	55.00	35.00
4	Hank Sauer	40.00	20.00	12.00
5	Ed Lopat	50.00	25.00	15.00
6	Pete Runnels	40.00	20.00	12.00
7	Ted Kluszewski	75.00	35.00	22.50
8	Bobby Young	40.00	20.00	12.00
9	Harvey Haddix	40.00	20.00	12.00
10	Jackie Robinson	525.00	250.00	150.00
11	Paul Smith	40.00	20.00	12.00
12	Del Crandall	40.00	20.00	12.00
13	Billy Martin	225.00	100.00	65.00
14	Preacher Roe	75.00	35.00	22.50
15	Al Rosen	85.00	40.00	25.00
16	Vic Janowicz	45.00	22.00	13.50
17	Phil Rizzuto	225.00	110.00	65.00
18	Walt Dropo	40.00	20.00	12.00
19	Johnny Lipon	40.00	20.00	12.00
20	Warren Spahn	215.00	100.00	60.00
21	Bobby Shantz	45.00	22.50	13.50
22	Jim Greengrass	40.00	20.00	12.00
23	Luke Easter	40.00	20.00	12.00
24	Granny Hamner	40.00	20.00	12.00
25	Harvey Kuenn	75.00	35.00	22.50
26	Ray Jablonski	40.00	20.00	12.00
27	Ferris Fain	40.00	20.00	12.00
28	Paul Minner	40.00	20.00	12.00
29	Jim Hegan	40.00	20.00	12.00
30	Ed Mathews	165.00	80.00	47.50
31	Johnny Klippstein	40.00	20.00	12.00
32	Duke Snider	315.00	150.00	90.00
33	Johnny Schmitz	40.00	20.00	12.00
34	Jim Rivera	40.00	20.00	12.00
35	Junior Gilliam	85.00	40.00	25.00
36	Hoyt Wilhelm	115.00	55.00	32.50
37	Whitey Ford	215.00	100.00	60.00
38	Eddie Stanky	45.00	22.50	13.50
39	Sherm Lollar	40.00	20.00	12.00
40	Mel Parnell	40.00	20.00	12.00
41	Willie Jones	40.00	20.00	12.00
42	Don Mueller	40.00	20.00	12.00
43	Dick Groat	40.00	20.00	12.00
44	Ned Garver	40.00	20.00	12.00
45	Richie Ashburn	140.00	70.00	40.00
46	Ken Raffensberger	40.00	20.00	12.00
47	Ellis Kinder	40.00	20.00	12.00
48	Billy Hunter	40.00	20.00	12.00
49	Ray Murray	40.00	20.00	12.00
50	Yogi Berra	365.00	175.00	100.00

1954 Topps Look 'N See

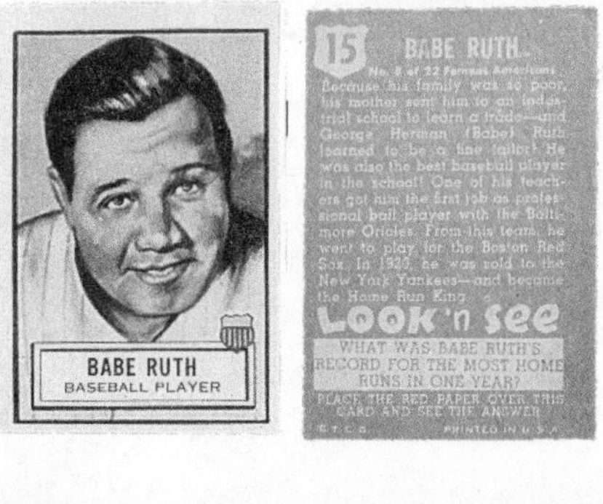

Among the 135 historical figures in this set is only one baseball player - Babe Ruth. These 2-1/16" x 2-15/16" cards feature colorful portrait paintings on the front and biographies on the back. The answer to a trivia question on back can be discovered by laying a piece of red cellophane over the question box.

	NM	E	VG
Complete Set (135):	3,000	1,500	900.00
Common Card:	4.00	2.00	1.25
15 Babe Ruth	150.00	75.00	45.00

1954 Topps Scoops

World - and sports - history from the mid-18th Century through October 1953, is chronicled in this 156-card set. Four baseball subjects are presented in the set. Cards are 2-1/16" x 2-15/16" and feature on the front a color painting with a dated caption box at bottom. Originally a black scratch-off ink covered the caption box (cards with the black ink removed can still be considered Mint as those with the ink currently command little premium value). Backs feature a simulated newspaper front page with banner headline and picture, along with a description of the event.

	NM	E	VG
Complete Set (156):	3,500	1,750	1,050
Common Card:	6.00	3.00	1.75
27 Bob Feller Strikeout King, Oct. 2, 1938 (Bob Feller)	60.00	30.00	18.00
41 Babe Ruth Sets Record, Sept. 30, 1927 (Babe Ruth)	250.00	125.00	75.00
130 Braves Go to Milwaukee	40.00	20.00	12.00
154 26-Inning Tie Game May 1, 1920	60.00	30.00	18.00

1955 Topps

The 1955 Topps set is numerically the smallest of the regular annual issues. The 3-3/4" x 2-5/8" cards mark the first time that Topps used a horizontal format for the entire set. While that format was new, the design was not; they are very similar to the 1954 cards to the point many pictures appeared in both years. Although it was slated for a 210-card set, the 1955 Topps set turned out to be only 206 cards with numbers 175, 186, 203 and 209 never being released. The scarce high numbers in this set begin with #161.

	NM	E	VG
Complete Set (206):	8,000	3,750	2,250
Common Player (1-150):	20.00	10.00	6.00
Common Player (151-160):	25.00	12.50	7.50
Common Player (161-210):	45.00	22.50	13.50

		NM	E	VG
1	"Dusty" Rhodes	110.00	20.00	12.00
2	Ted Williams	525.00	225.00	135.00
3	Art Fowler	20.00	10.00	6.00
4	Al Kaline	150.00	75.00	45.00
5	Jim Gilliam	60.00	30.00	15.00
6	Stan Hack	25.00	12.50	7.50
7	Jim Hegan	20.00	10.00	6.00
8	Hal Smith	20.00	10.00	6.00
9	Bob Miller	20.00	10.00	6.00
10	Bob Keegan	20.00	10.00	6.00
11	Ferris Fain	20.00	10.00	6.00
12	"Jake" Thies	20.00	10.00	6.00
13	Fred Marsh	20.00	10.00	6.00
14	Jim Finigan	20.00	10.00	6.00
15	Jim Pendleton	20.00	10.00	6.00
16	Roy Sievers	20.00	10.00	6.00
17	Bobby Hofman	20.00	10.00	6.00
18	Russ Kemmerer	20.00	10.00	6.00
19	Billy Herman	40.00	20.00	10.00
20	Andy Carey	25.00	12.50	7.50
21	Alex Grammas	20.00	10.00	6.00
22	Bill Skowron	45.00	22.00	13.00
23	Jack Parks	20.00	10.00	6.00
24	Hal Newhouser	45.00	22.00	13.00
25	Johnny Podres	45.00	22.00	13.00
26	Dick Groat	20.00	10.00	6.00
27	Billy Gardner **RC**	20.00	10.00	6.00
28	Ernie Banks	250.00	125.00	62.50
29	Herman Wehmeier	20.00	10.00	6.00
30	Vic Power	20.00	10.00	6.00
31	Warren Spahn	150.00	75.00	37.50
32	Ed McGhee	20.00	10.00	6.00
33	Tom Qualters	20.00	10.00	6.00
34	Wayne Terwilliger	20.00	10.00	6.00
35	Dave Jolly	20.00	10.00	6.00
36	Leo Kiely	20.00	10.00	6.00
37	Joe Cunningham **RC**	20.00	10.00	6.00
38	Bob Turley	27.50	13.50	8.25
39	Bill Glynn	20.00	10.00	6.00
40	Don Hoak	25.00	12.50	7.50
41	Chuck Stobbs	20.00	10.00	6.00
42	"Windy" McCall	20.00	10.00	6.00
43	Harvey Haddix	20.00	10.00	6.00
44	"Corky" Valentine	20.00	10.00	6.00
45	Hank Sauer	20.00	10.00	6.00
46	Ted Kazanski	20.00	10.00	6.00
47	Hank Aaron	300.00	150.00	95.00
48	Bob Kennedy	20.00	10.00	6.00
49	J.W. Porter	20.00	10.00	6.00
50	Jackie Robinson	375.00	175.00	100.00
51	Jim Hughes	25.00	12.50	7.50
52	Bill Tremel	20.00	10.00	6.00
53	Bill Taylor	20.00	10.00	6.00
54	Lou Limmer	20.00	10.00	6.00
55	"Rip" Repulski	20.00	10.00	6.00
56	Ray Jablonski	20.00	10.00	6.00
57	Billy O'Dell **RC**	20.00	10.00	6.00
58	Jim Rivera	20.00	10.00	6.00
59	Gair Allie	20.00	10.00	6.00
60	Dean Stone	20.00	10.00	6.00
61	"Spook" Jacobs	20.00	10.00	6.00
62	Thornton Kipper	20.00	10.00	6.00
63	Joe Collins	25.00	12.50	7.50
64	Gus Triandos **RC**	25.00	12.50	7.50
65	Ray Boone	20.00	10.00	6.00
66	Ron Jackson	20.00	10.00	6.00
67	Wally Moon	20.00	10.00	6.00
68	Jim Davis	20.00	10.00	6.00
69	Ed Bailey	20.00	10.00	6.00
70	Al Rosen	40.00	20.00	12.00
71	Ruben Gomez	20.00	10.00	6.00
72	Karl Olson	20.00	10.00	6.00
73	Jack Shepard	20.00	10.00	6.00
74	Bob Borkowski	20.00	10.00	6.00
75	Sandy Amoros **RC**	50.00	25.00	12.50
76	Howie Pollet	20.00	10.00	6.00
77	Arnold Portocarrero	20.00	10.00	6.00
78	Gordon Jones	20.00	10.00	6.00
79	Danny Schell	20.00	10.00	6.00
80	Bob Grim	25.00	12.50	7.50
81	Gene Conley	20.00	10.00	6.00
82	Chuck Harmon	20.00	10.00	6.00
83	Tom Brewer	20.00	10.00	6.00
84	Camilo Pascual **RC**	35.00	17.50	10.00
85	Don Mossi **RC**	35.00	17.50	10.00
86	Bill Wilson	20.00	10.00	6.00
87	Frank House	20.00	10.00	6.00
88	Bob Skinner **RC**	20.00	10.00	6.00
89	Joe Frazier **RC**	20.00	10.00	6.00
90	Karl Spooner **RC**	25.00	12.50	7.50
91	Milt Bolling	20.00	10.00	6.00
92	Don Zimmer **RC**	70.00	35.00	21.00
93	Steve Bilko	20.00	10.00	6.00
94	Reno Bertoia	20.00	10.00	6.00
95	Preston Ward	20.00	10.00	6.00
96	Charlie Bishop	20.00	10.00	6.00
97	Carlos Paula	20.00	10.00	6.00
98	Johnny Riddle	20.00	10.00	6.00
99	Frank Leja	25.00	12.50	7.50
100	Monte Irvin	40.00	20.00	12.00
101	Johnny Gray	20.00	10.00	6.00
102	Wally Westlake	20.00	10.00	6.00
103	Charlie White	20.00	10.00	6.00
104	Jack Harshman	20.00	10.00	6.00
105	Chuck Diering	20.00	10.00	6.00
106	Frank Sullivan **RC** (Several variations exist in the size, shape and density of the dot over the "i" in the facsimile autograph.)	20.00	10.00	6.00
107	Curt Roberts	20.00	10.00	6.00
108	"Rube" Walker	25.00	12.50	7.50
109	Ed Lopat	30.00	15.00	9.00
110	Gus Zernial	20.00	10.00	6.00
111	Bob Milliken	25.00	12.50	7.50
112	Nelson King	20.00	10.00	6.00
113	Harry Brecheen	20.00	10.00	6.00
114	Lou Ortiz	20.00	10.00	6.00
115	Ellis Kinder	20.00	10.00	6.00
116	Tom Hurd	20.00	10.00	6.00
117	Mel Roach	20.00	10.00	6.00
118	Bob Purkey	20.00	10.00	6.00
119	Bob Lennon	20.00	10.00	6.00
120	Ted Kluszewski	55.00	25.50	15.50
121	Bill Renna	20.00	10.00	6.00
122	Carl Sawatski	20.00	10.00	6.00
123	"Sandy" Koufax **RC**	885.00	375.00	225.00
124	Harmon Killebrew **RC**	300.00	130.00	80.00
125	Ken Boyer **RC**	80.00	40.00	24.00
126	Dick Hall **RC**	20.00	10.00	6.00
127	Dale Long **RC**	20.00	10.00	6.00
128	Ted Lepcio	20.00	10.00	6.00
129	Elvin Tappe	20.00	10.00	6.00
130	Mayo Smith	20.00	10.00	6.00
131	Grady Hatton	20.00	10.00	6.00
132	Bob Trice	20.00	10.00	6.00
133	Dave Hoskins	20.00	10.00	6.00
134	Joe Jay	20.00	10.00	6.00
135	Johnny O'Brien	20.00	10.00	6.00
136	"Bunky" Stewart	20.00	10.00	6.00
137a	Harry Elliott (Last line in bio is, "the Cards in '53.")	20.00	10.00	6.00
137b	Harry Elliott (Last line in bio ends, "the Cards in (crescent mark).")	20.00	10.00	6.00
137c	Harry Elliott (Last line in bio ends, "the Cards in.")	20.00	10.00	6.00
138	Ray Herbert	20.00	10.00	6.00
139	Steve Kraly	25.00	12.50	7.50
140	Mel Parnell	20.00	10.00	6.00
141	Tom Wright	20.00	10.00	6.00
142	Jerry Lynch	20.00	10.00	6.00
143	Dick Schofield	20.00	10.00	6.00
144	Joe Amalfitano **RC**	20.00	10.00	6.00
145	Elmer Valo	20.00	10.00	6.00
146	Dick Donovan **RC**	20.00	10.00	6.00
147	Laurin Pepper	20.00	10.00	6.00
148	Hal Brown	20.00	10.00	6.00
149	Ray Crone	20.00	10.00	6.00
150	Mike Higgins	20.00	10.00	6.00
151	"Red" Kress	25.00	12.50	7.50
152	Harry Agganis **RC**	115.00	60.00	30.00
153	"Bud" Podbielan	25.00	12.50	7.50
154	Willie Miranda	25.00	12.50	7.50
155	Ed Mathews	150.00	75.00	45.00
156	Joe Black	60.00	30.00	18.00
157	Bob Miller	25.00	12.50	7.50
158	Tom Carroll	35.00	17.50	10.50
159	Johnny Schmitz	25.00	12.50	7.50
160	Ray Narleski	25.00	12.50	7.50
161	Chuck Tanner **RC**	60.00	30.00	18.00
162	Joe Coleman	45.00	22.50	13.50
163	Faye Throneberry	45.00	22.50	13.50
164	Roberto Clemente **RC**	2,150	975.00	535.00
165	Don Johnson	45.00	22.50	13.50
166	Hank Bauer	85.00	37.50	18.75
167	Tom Casagrande	45.00	22.50	13.50
168	Duane Pillette	45.00	22.50	13.50
169	Bob Oldis	45.00	22.50	13.50
170	Jim Pearce	45.00	22.50	13.50
171	Dick Brodowski	45.00	22.50	13.50
172	Frank Baumholtz	45.00	22.50	13.50
173	Bob Kline	45.00	22.50	13.50
174	Rudy Minarcin	45.00	22.50	13.50
175	Not Issued			
176	Norm Zauchin	45.00	22.50	13.50
177a	Jim Robertson (incomplete stat boxes at Life B. Avg. and Life P.O.)	45.00	22.50	13.50

177b	Jim Robertson (complete stat boxes)	45.00	22.50	13.50
178	Bobby Adams	45.00	22.50	13.50
179	Jim Bolger	45.00	22.50	13.50
180	Clem Labine	65.00	30.00	18.00
181	Roy McMillan	45.00	22.50	13.50
182	Humberto Robinson	45.00	22.50	13.50
183	Tony Jacobs	45.00	22.50	13.50
184	Harry Perkowski	45.00	22.50	13.50
185	Don Ferrarese	45.00	22.50	13.50
186	Not Issued			
187	Gil Hodges	165.00	87.50	43.75
188	Charlie Silvera	50.00	25.00	15.00
189	Phil Rizzuto	170.00	87.50	43.75
190	Gene Woodling	40.00	20.00	10.00
191	Ed Stanky	45.00	22.50	13.50
192	Jim Delsing	45.00	22.50	13.50
193	Johnny Sain	50.00	25.00	12.50
194	Willie Mays	650.00	280.00	170.00
195	Ed Roebuck	50.00	25.00	15.00
196	Gale Wade	45.00	22.50	13.50
197	Al Smith	45.00	22.50	13.50
198	Yogi Berra	250.00	130.00	65.00
199	Bert Hamric	50.00	25.00	15.00
200	Jack Jensen	70.00	30.00	18.00
201	Sherm Lollar	45.00	22.50	13.50
202	Jim Owens	45.00	22.50	13.50
203	Not Issued			
204	Frank Smith	60.00	30.00	18.00
205	Gene Freese	90.00	45.00	27.00
206	Pete Daley	55.00	22.50	13.50
207	Bill Consolo	45.00	22.50	13.50
208	Ray Moore	45.00	22.50	13.50
209	Not Issued			
210	Duke Snider	625.00	140.00	90.00

1955 Topps Doubleheaders

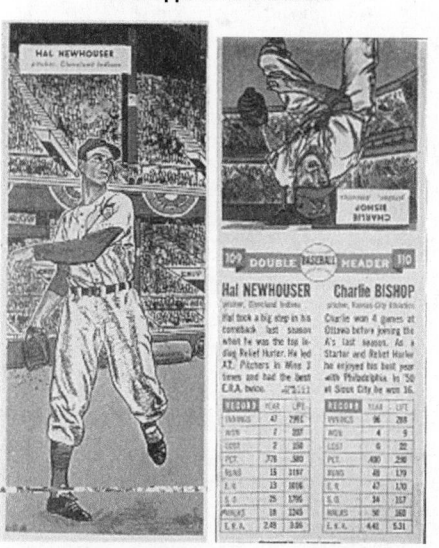

This set is a throwback to the 1911 T201 Mecca Double Folders. The cards are perforated through the middle, allowing them to be folded. Open, there is a color painting of a player set against a stadium background. When folded, a different player and stadium appears; both players share the same lower legs and feet. Backs have abbreviated career histories and stats. Placed side by side in reverse numerical order, the backgrounds form a continuous stadium scene. When open the cards measure 2-1/16" x 4-7/8". The 66 cards in the set mean 132 total players, all of whom also appeared in the lower numbers of the regular 1955 Topps set.

		NM	E	VG
Complete Set (66):		4,000	2,000	1,200
Common Card:		45.00	22.50	13.50
Wax Pack:		240.00		
1-2	Al Rosen, Chuck Diering	60.00	25.00	15.00
3-4	Monte Irvin, Russ Kemmerer	60.00	30.00	18.00
5-6	Ted Kazanski, Gordon Jones	45.00	22.50	13.50
7-8	Bill Taylor, Billy O'Dell	45.00	22.50	13.50
9-10	J.W. Porter, Thornton Kipper	45.00	22.50	13.50
11-12	Curt Roberts, Arnie Portocarrero	45.00	22.50	13.50
13-14	Wally Westlake, Frank House	45.00	22.50	13.50
15-16	Rube Walker, Lou Limmer	45.00	22.50	13.50

17-18	Dean Stone, Charlie White	45.00	22.50	13.50
19-20	Karl Spooner, Jim Hughes	50.00	25.00	15.00
21-22	Bill Skowron, Frank Sullivan	60.00	30.00	18.00
23-24	Jack Shepard, Stan Hack	45.00	22.50	13.50
25-26	Jackie Robinson, Don Hoak	325.00	160.00	100.00
27-28	Dusty Rhodes, Jim Davis	45.00	22.50	13.50
29-30	Vic Power, Ed Bailey	45.00	22.50	13.50
31-32	Howie Pollet, Ernie Banks	200.00	100.00	60.00
33-34	Jim Pendleton, Gene Conley	45.00	22.50	13.50
35-36	Karl Olson, Andy Carey	45.00	22.50	13.50
37-38	Wally Moon, Joe Cunningham	45.00	22.50	13.50
39-40	Fred Marsh, "Jake" Thies	45.00	22.50	13.50
41-42	Ed Lopat, Harvey Haddix	45.00	22.50	13.50
43-44	Leo Kiely, Chuck Stobbs	45.00	22.50	13.50
45-46	Al Kaline, "Corky" Valentine	225.00	110.00	65.00
47-48	"Spook" Jacobs, Johnny Gray	45.00	22.50	13.50
49-50	Ron Jackson, Jim Finigan	45.00	22.50	13.50
51-52	Ray Jablonski, Bob Keegan	45.00	22.50	13.50
53-54	Billy Herman, Sandy Amoros	60.00	30.00	18.00
55-56	Chuck Harmon, Bob Skinner	45.00	22.50	13.50
57-58	Dick Hall, Bob Grim	45.00	22.50	13.50
59-60	Bill Glynn, Bob Miller	45.00	22.50	13.50
61-62	Billy Gardner, John Hetki	45.00	22.50	13.50
63-64	Bob Borkowski, Bob Turley	45.00	22.50	13.50
65-66	Joe Collins, Jack Harshman	45.00	22.50	13.50
67-68	Jim Hegan, Jack Parks	45.00	22.50	13.50
69-70	Ted Williams, Hal Smith	400.00	200.00	120.00
71-72	Gair Allie, Grady Hatton	45.00	22.50	13.50
73-74	Jerry Lynch, Harry Brecheen	45.00	22.50	13.50
75-76	Tom Wright, "Bunky" Stewart	45.00	22.50	13.50
77-78	Dave Hoskins, Ed McGhee	45.00	22.50	13.50
79-80	Roy Sievers, Art Fowler	45.00	22.50	13.50
81-82	Danny Schell, Gus Triandos	45.00	22.50	13.50
83-84	Joe Frazier, Don Mossi	45.00	22.50	13.50
85-86	Elmer Valo, Hal Brown	45.00	22.50	13.50
87-88	Bob Kennedy, "Windy" McCall	45.00	22.50	13.50
89-90	Ruben Gomez, Jim Rivera	45.00	22.50	13.50
91-92	Lou Ortiz, Milt Bolling	45.00	22.50	13.50
93-94	Carl Sawatski, Elvin Tappe	45.00	22.50	13.50
95-96	Dave Jolly, Bobby Hofman	45.00	22.50	13.50
97-98	Preston Ward, Don Zimmer	45.00	22.50	13.50
99-100	Bill Renna, Dick Groat	45.00	22.50	13.50
101-102	Bill Wilson, Bill Tremel	45.00	22.50	13.50
103-104	Hank Sauer, Camilo Pascual	45.00	22.50	13.50
105-106	Hank Aaron, Ray Herbert	400.00	200.00	120.00
107-108	Alex Grammas, Tom Qualters	45.00	22.50	13.50
109-110	Hal Newhouser, Charlie Bishop	60.00	30.00	18.00
111-112	Harmon Killebrew, John Podres	225.00	110.00	65.00
113-114	Ray Boone, Bob Purkey	45.00	22.50	13.50
115-116	Dale Long, Ferris Fain	45.00	22.50	13.50
117-118	Steve Bilko, Bob Milliken	45.00	22.50	13.50
119-120	Mel Parnell, Tom Hurd	45.00	22.50	13.50
121-122	Ted Kluszewski, Jim Owens	60.00	30.00	18.00
123-124	Gus Zernial, Bob Trice	45.00	22.50	13.50
125-126	"Rip" Repulski, Ted Lepcio	45.00	22.50	13.50

127-128	Warren Spahn, Tom Brewer	150.00	75.00	45.00
129-130	Jim Gilliam, Ellis Kinder	60.00	30.00	18.00
131-132	Herm Wehmeier, Wayne Terwilliger	45.00	22.50	13.50

1955 Topps Hocus Focus

This set is a direct descendant of the 1948 "Topps Magic Photo" issue. Again, the baseball players were part of a larger overall series covering several topical areas. The cards, 7/8 x 1-3/8", state on the back that they are a series of 23. The photos on these cards were developed by wetting the card's surface and exposing to light. Prices below are for cards with well-developed pictures. Cards with poorly developed photos are worth significantly less.

		NM	E	VG
Complete Set (23):		20,000	10,000	6,000
Common Player:		250.00	125.00	75.00
1	Babe Ruth	3,500	1,750	1,000
2	Lou Gehrig	3,500	1,750	1,000
3	Dick Groat	650.00	325.00	160.00
4	Ed Lopat	450.00	225.00	110.00
5	Hank Sauer	400.00	200.00	100.00
6	"Dusty" Rhodes	400.00	200.00	100.00
7	Ted Williams	2,750	1,375	700.00
8	Harvey Haddix	400.00	200.00	100.00
9	Ray Boone	400.00	200.00	100.00
10	Al Rosen	600.00	300.00	150.00
11	Mayo Smith	400.00	200.00	100.00
12	Warren Spahn	1,200	600.00	300.00
13	Jim Rivera	400.00	200.00	100.00
14	Ted Kluszewski	900.00	450.00	225.00
15	Gus Zernial	400.00	200.00	100.00
16	Jackie Robinson	2,750	1,375	700.00
17	Hal Smith	400.00	200.00	100.00
18	Johnny Schmitz	400.00	200.00	100.00
19	Wally Moon	400.00	200.00	100.00
20	Karl Spooner	400.00	200.00	100.00
21	Ed Mathews	1,200	600.00	300.00
22	"Spool" Jacobs	400.00	200.00	100.00
23	Mel Parnell	400.00	200.00	100.00

1955 Topps Stamps

An extremely rare and enigmatic test issue, these stamps are the same size as Topps' 1955 card issue and have a blank, gummed back. Most of the specimens currently known are imperforate along one of the sides. All of the known examples have counterparts in the regular set which range from card #6 through 108. The unnumbered stamps are checklisted here alphabetically, with gaps left in the numbering to accommodate future discoveries.

		NM	E	VG
Common Player:		750.00	375.00	225.00
(1)	Ray Boone	750.00	375.00	225.00
(2)	Joe Cunningham	750.00	375.00	225.00
(3)	Jim Davis	750.00	375.00	225.00
(4)	Chuck Diering	750.00	375.00	225.00
(5)	Ruben Gomez	750.00	375.00	225.00
(6)	Alex Grammas	750.00	375.00	225.00

(7)	Stan Hack	750.00	375.00	225.00
(8)	Harvey Haddix	750.00	375.00	225.00
(9)	Bobby Hofman	750.00	375.00	225.00
(11)	Ray Jablonski	750.00	375.00	225.00
(12)	Dave Jolly	750.00	375.00	225.00
(13)	Ted Kazanski	750.00	375.00	225.00
(14)	Don Mossi	775.00	385.00	230.00
(15)	Jim Pendleton	750.00	375.00	225.00
(16)	Howie Pollet	750.00	375.00	225.00
(17)	Jack Shepard	750.00	375.00	225.00
(18)	Bob Skinner	750.00	375.00	225.00
(19)	Bill Skowron	975.00	485.00	290.00
(20)	Karl Spooner	775.00	385.00	230.00
(21)	Bill Tremel	750.00	375.00	225.00
(22)	Corky Valentine	750.00	375.00	225.00
(23)	Rube Walker	775.00	385.00	230.00
(24)	Charlie White	750.00	375.00	225.00

1956 Topps

This set is similar in format to the 1955 Topps set, again using both a portrait and an "action" picture. Some portraits are the same as those used in 1955 (and even 1954). Innovations found in the 1956 Topps set of 2-5/8" x 3-3/4" cards include team cards introduced as part of a regular set. Additionally, there are two unnumbered checklist cards (the complete set price quoted below does not include the checklist cards). Finally, there are cards of the two league presidents, William Harridge and Warren Giles. On the backs, a three-panel cartoon depicts big moments from the player's career while biographical information appears above the cartoon and the statistics below. Card backs for numbers 1-180 can be found with either white or gray cardboard. Some hobbyists feel a premium is warranted for gray backs between #1-100 and white backs from #101-180.

	NM	E	VG
Complete Set (340):	9,000	4,250	2,550
Common Player (1-180):	15.00	7.50	4.50
Common Player (181-340):	20.00	10.00	6.00

1	William Harridge	125.00	25.00	15.00
2	Warren Giles	65.00	12.00	6.00
3	Elmer Valo	15.00	7.50	4.50
4	Carlos Paula	15.00	7.50	4.50
5	Ted Williams	425.00	220.00	135.00
6	Ray Boone	15.00	7.50	4.50
7	Ron Negray	15.00	7.50	4.50
8	Walter Alston	45.00	22.50	13.50
9	Ruben Gomez	15.00	7.50	4.50
10	Warren Spahn	125.00	62.50	31.25
11a	Chicago Cubs - 1955	80.00	40.00	20.00
11b	Chicago Cubs (No date, name centered.)	60.00	30.00	18.00
11c	Chicago Cubs (No date, name at left.)	70.00	35.00	20.00
12	Andy Carey	20.00	10.00	6.00
13	Roy Face	15.00	7.50	4.50
14	Ken Boyer	25.00	12.50	7.50
15	Ernie Banks	125.00	62.50	31.25
16	Hector Lopez **RC**	20.00	10.00	6.00
17	Gene Conley	15.00	7.50	4.50
18	Dick Donovan	15.00	7.50	4.50
19	Chuck Diering	15.00	7.50	4.50
20	Al Kaline	125.00	62.50	31.25
21	Joe Collins	20.00	10.00	6.00
22	Jim Finigan	15.00	7.50	4.50
23	Freddie Marsh	20.00	10.00	6.00
24	Dick Groat	20.00	10.00	6.00
25	Ted Kluszewski	35.00	17.50	10.00
26	Grady Hatton	15.00	7.50	4.50
27	Nelson Burbrink	15.00	7.50	4.50
28	Bobby Hofman	15.00	7.50	4.50
29	Jack Harshman	15.00	7.50	4.50
30	Jackie Robinson	300.00	150.00	75.00
31	Hank Aaron	300.00	150.00	90.00
32	Frank House	15.00	7.50	4.50
33	Roberto Clemente	400.00	200.00	120.00
34	Tom Brewer	15.00	7.50	4.50
35	Al Rosen	20.00	10.00	6.00
36	Rudy Minarcin	15.00	7.50	4.50
37	Alex Grammas	15.00	7.50	4.50
38	Bob Kennedy	15.00	7.50	4.50
39	Don Mossi	15.00	7.50	4.50
40	Bob Turley	25.00	12.50	7.50
41	Hank Sauer	15.00	7.50	4.50
42	Sandy Amoros	25.00	12.50	7.50
43	Ray Moore	15.00	7.50	4.50
44	"Windy" McCall	15.00	7.50	4.50
45	Gus Zernial	15.00	7.50	4.50
46	Gene Freese	15.00	7.50	4.50
47	Art Fowler	15.00	7.50	4.50
48	Jim Hegan	15.00	7.50	4.50
49	Pedro Ramos **RC**	20.00	10.00	6.00
50	"Dusty" Rhodes	15.00	7.50	4.50
51	Ernie Oravetz	15.00	7.50	4.50
52	Bob Grim	20.00	10.00	6.00
53	Arnold Portocarrero	15.00	7.50	4.50
54	Bob Keegan	15.00	7.50	4.50
55	Wally Moon	15.00	7.50	4.50
56	Dale Long	15.00	7.50	4.50
57	"Duke" Maas	15.00	7.50	4.50
58	Ed Roebuck	20.00	10.00	6.00
59	Jose Santiago	15.00	7.50	4.50
60	Mayo Smith	15.00	7.50	4.50
61	Bill Skowron	35.00	17.50	10.00
62	Hal Smith	15.00	7.50	4.50
63	Roger Craig **RC**	27.50	13.50	8.00
64	Luis Arroyo	15.00	7.50	4.50
65	Johnny O'Brien	15.00	7.50	4.50
66	Bob Speake	15.00	7.50	4.50
67	Vic Power	15.00	7.50	4.50
68	Chuck Stobbs	15.00	7.50	4.50
69	Chuck Tanner	15.00	7.50	4.50
70	Jim Rivera	15.00	7.50	4.50
71	Frank Sullivan	15.00	7.50	4.50
72a	Philadelphia Phillies - 1955	125.00	60.00	30.00
72b	Philadelphia Phillies (No date, name centered.)	45.00	20.00	12.00
72c	Philadelphia Phillies (No date, name at left.)	60.00	30.00	18.00
73	Wayne Terwilliger	15.00	7.50	4.50
74	Jim King	15.00	7.50	4.50
75	Roy Sievers	15.00	7.50	4.50
76	Ray Crone	15.00	7.50	4.50
77	Harvey Haddix	15.00	7.50	4.50
78	Herman Wehmeier	15.00	7.50	4.50
79	Sandy Koufax	290.00	145.00	87.00
80	Gus Triandos	15.00	7.50	4.50
81	Wally Westlake	15.00	7.50	4.50
82	Bill Renna	15.00	7.50	4.50
83	Karl Spooner	20.00	10.00	6.00
84	"Babe" Birrer	15.00	7.50	4.50
85a	Cleveland Indians - 1955	125.00	60.00	30.00
85b	Cleveland Indians (No date, name centered.)	60.00	30.00	18.00
85c	Cleveland Indians (No date, name at left.)	80.00	40.00	20.00
86	Ray Jablonski	15.00	7.50	4.50
87	Dean Stone	15.00	7.50	4.50
88	Johnny Kucks	20.00	10.00	6.00
89	Norm Zauchin	15.00	7.50	4.50
90a	Cincinnati Redlegs - 1955	100.00	50.00	30.00
90b	Cincinnati Redlegs (No date, name centered.)	45.00	22.50	13.50
90c	Cincinnati Redlegs (No date, name at left.)	90.00	45.00	27.50
91	Gail Harris	15.00	7.50	4.50
92	"Red" Wilson	15.00	7.50	4.50
93	George Susce, Jr.	15.00	7.50	4.50
94	Ronnie Kline	15.00	7.50	4.50
95a	Milwaukee Braves - 1955	125.00	60.00	30.00
95b	Milwaukee Braves (No date, name centered.)	70.00	35.00	18.00
95c	Milwaukee Braves (No date, name at left.)	55.00	27.50	16.50
96	Bill Tremel	15.00	7.50	4.50
97	Jerry Lynch	15.00	7.50	4.50
98	Camilo Pascual	15.00	7.50	4.50
99	Don Zimmer	30.00	15.00	9.00
100a	Baltimore Orioles - 1955	100.00	50.00	25.00
100b	Baltimore Orioles (No date, name centered.)	100.00	50.00	25.00
100c	Baltimore Orioles (No date, name at left.)	100.00	50.00	25.00
101	Roy Campanella	140.00	75.00	37.50
102	Jim Davis	15.00	7.50	4.50
103	Willie Miranda	15.00	7.50	4.50
104	Bob Lennon	15.00	7.50	4.50
105	Al Smith	15.00	7.50	4.50
106	Joe Astroth	15.00	7.50	4.50
107	Ed Mathews	95.00	50.00	25.00
108	Laurin Pepper	15.00	7.50	4.50
109	Enos Slaughter	32.50	16.00	10.00
110	Yogi Berra	175.00	90.00	45.00
111	Boston Red Sox	45.00	17.50	10.00
112	Dee Fondy	15.00	7.50	4.50
113	Phil Rizzuto	120.00	60.00	35.00
114	Jim Owens	15.00	7.50	4.50
115	Jackie Jensen	20.00	10.00	6.00
116	Eddie O'Brien	15.00	7.50	4.50
117	Virgil Trucks	15.00	7.50	4.50
118	"Nellie" Fox	50.00	25.00	15.00
119	Larry Jackson **RC**	15.00	7.50	4.50
120	Richie Ashburn	50.00	25.00	15.00
121	Pittsburgh Pirates	65.00	32.50	20.00
122	Willard Nixon	15.00	7.50	4.50
123	Roy McMillan	15.00	7.50	4.50
124	Don Kaiser	15.00	7.50	4.50
125	"Minnie" Minoso	30.00	15.00	9.00
126	Jim Brady	15.00	7.50	4.50
127	Willie Jones	15.00	7.50	4.50
128	Eddie Yost	15.00	7.50	4.50
129	"Jake" Martin	15.00	7.50	4.50
130	Willie Mays	300.00	110.00	70.00
131	Bob Roselli	15.00	7.50	4.50
132	Bobby Avila	15.00	7.50	4.50
133	Ray Narleski	15.00	7.50	4.50
134	St. Louis Cardinals	25.00	12.50	7.50
135	Mickey Mantle	1,200	550.00	335.00
136	Johnny Logan	15.00	7.50	4.50
137	Al Silvera	15.00	7.50	4.50
138	Johnny Antonelli	15.00	7.50	4.50
139	Tommy Carroll	20.00	10.00	6.00
140	Herb Score **RC**	35.00	17.50	10.00
141	Joe Frazier	15.00	7.50	4.50
142	Gene Baker	15.00	7.50	4.50
143	Jim Piersall	20.00	10.00	6.00
144	Leroy Powell	15.00	7.50	4.50
145	Gil Hodges	55.00	27.50	16.50
146	Washington Nationals	50.00	25.00	15.00
147	Earl Torgeson	15.00	7.50	4.50
148	Alvin Dark	15.00	7.50	4.50
149	"Dixie" Howell	15.00	7.50	4.50
150	"Duke" Snider	150.00	75.00	37.50
151	"Spook" Jacobs	15.00	7.50	4.50
152	Billy Hoeft	15.00	7.50	4.50
153	Frank Thomas	15.00	7.50	4.50
154	Dave Pope	15.00	7.50	4.50
155	Harvey Kuenn	15.00	7.50	4.50
156	Wes Westrum	15.00	7.50	4.50
157	Dick Brodowski	15.00	7.50	4.50
158	Wally Post	15.00	7.50	4.50
159	Clint Courtney	15.00	7.50	4.50
160	Billy Pierce	15.00	7.50	4.50
161	Joe De Maestri	15.00	7.50	4.50
162	"Gus" Bell	15.00	7.50	4.50
163	Gene Woodling	15.00	7.50	4.50
164	Harmon Killebrew	175.00	80.00	45.00
165	"Red" Schoendienst	35.00	17.50	10.00
166	Brooklyn Dodgers	200.00	100.00	50.00
167	Harry Dorish	15.00	7.50	4.50
168	Sammy White	15.00	7.50	4.50
169	Bob Nelson	15.00	7.50	4.50
170	Bill Virdon	15.00	7.50	4.50
171	Jim Wilson	15.00	7.50	4.50
172	Frank Torre **RC**	20.00	10.00	6.00
173	Johnny Podres	30.00	15.00	9.00
174	Glen Gorbous	15.00	7.50	4.50
175	Del Crandall	15.00	7.50	4.50
176	Alex Kellner	15.00	7.50	4.50
177	Hank Bauer	30.00	15.00	9.00
178	Joe Black	20.00	10.00	6.00
179	Harry Chiti	15.00	7.50	4.50
180	Robin Roberts	50.00	20.00	12.00
181	Billy Martin	95.00	50.00	25.00
182	Paul Minner	20.00	10.00	6.00
183	Stan Lopata	20.00	10.00	6.00
184	Don Bessent	25.00	12.50	7.50
185	Bill Bruton	20.00	10.00	6.00
186	Ron Jackson	20.00	10.00	6.00
187	Early Wynn	55.00	27.50	16.50
188	Chicago White Sox	60.00	30.00	15.00
189	Ned Garver	20.00	10.00	6.00
190	Carl Furillo	50.00	22.50	13.50
191	Frank Lary	20.00	10.00	6.00
192	"Smoky" Burgess	20.00	10.00	6.00
193	Wilmer Mizell	20.00	10.00	6.00
194	Monte Irvin	55.00	27.50	16.50
195	George Kell	45.00	22.50	13.50
196	Tom Poholsky	20.00	10.00	6.00
197	Granny Hamner	20.00	10.00	6.00
198	Ed Fitzgerald	20.00	10.00	6.00
199	Hank Thompson	20.00	10.00	6.00
200	Bob Feller	120.00	60.00	30.00
201	"Rip" Repulski	20.00	10.00	6.00
202	Jim Hearn	20.00	10.00	6.00
203	Bill Tuttle	20.00	10.00	6.00
204	Art Swanson	20.00	10.00	6.00
205	"Whitey" Lockman	20.00	10.00	6.00
206	Erv Palica	20.00	10.00	6.00
207	Jim Small	20.00	10.00	6.00
208	Elston Howard	55.00	25.00	15.00
209	Max Surkont	20.00	10.00	6.00
210	Mike Garcia	20.00	10.00	6.00
211	Murry Dickson	20.00	10.00	6.00
212	Johnny Temple	20.00	10.00	6.00
213	Detroit Tigers	60.00	30.00	18.00
214	Bob Rush	20.00	10.00	6.00

215	Tommy Byrne	25.00	12.50	7.50
216	Jerry Schoonmaker	20.00	10.00	6.00
217	Billy Klaus	20.00	10.00	6.00
218	Joe Nuxall (Nuxhall)	25.00	12.50	7.50
219	Lew Burdette	20.00	10.00	6.00
220	Del Ennis	20.00	10.00	6.00
221	Bob Friend	20.00	10.00	6.00
222	Dave Philley	20.00	10.00	6.00
223	Randy Jackson	25.00	12.50	7.50
224	"Bud" Podbielan	20.00	10.00	6.00
225	Gil McDougald	35.00	17.50	10.00
226	New York Giants	50.00	25.00	15.00
227	Russ Meyer	20.00	10.00	6.00
228	"Mickey" Vernon	20.00	10.00	6.00
229	Harry Brecheen	20.00	10.00	6.00
230	"Chico" Carrasquel	20.00	10.00	6.00
231	Bob Hale	20.00	10.00	6.00
232	"Toby" Atwell	20.00	10.00	6.00
233	Carl Erskine	30.00	15.00	9.00
234	"Pete" Runnels	20.00	10.00	6.00
235	Don Newcombe	55.00	27.50	16.50
236	Kansas City Athletics	35.00	17.50	10.00
237	Jose Valdivielso	20.00	10.00	6.00
238	Walt Dropo	20.00	10.00	6.00
239	Harry Simpson	20.00	10.00	6.00
240	"Whitey" Ford	110.00	55.00	30.00
241	Don Mueller	20.00	10.00	6.00
242	Hershell Freeman	20.00	10.00	6.00
243	Sherm Lollar	20.00	10.00	6.00
244	Bob Buhl	20.00	10.00	6.00
245	Billy Goodman	20.00	10.00	6.00
246	Tom Gorman	20.00	10.00	6.00
247	Bill Sarni	20.00	10.00	6.00
248	Bob Porterfield	20.00	10.00	6.00
249	Johnny Klippstein	20.00	10.00	6.00
250	Larry Doby	45.00	22.50	13.50
251	New York Yankees	250.00	125.00	75.00
252	Vernon Law	20.00	10.00	6.00
253	Irv Noren	25.00	12.50	7.50
254	George Crowe	20.00	10.00	6.00
255	Bob Lemon	35.00	17.50	10.00
256	Tom Hurd	20.00	10.00	6.00
257	Bobby Thomson	25.00	12.50	7.50
258	Art Ditmar	20.00	10.00	6.00
259	Sam Jones	20.00	10.00	6.00
260	"Pee Wee" Reese	150.00	75.00	37.50
261	Bobby Shantz	20.00	10.00	6.00
262	Howie Pollet	20.00	10.00	6.00
263	Bob Miller	20.00	10.00	6.00
264	Ray Monzant	20.00	10.00	6.00
265	Sandy Consuegra	20.00	10.00	6.00
266	Don Ferrarese	20.00	10.00	6.00
267	Bob Nieman	20.00	10.00	6.00
268	Dale Mitchell	20.00	10.00	6.00
269	Jack Meyer	20.00	10.00	6.00
270	Billy Loes	25.00	12.50	7.50
271	Foster Castleman	20.00	10.00	6.00
272	Danny O'Connell	20.00	10.00	6.00
273	Walker Cooper	20.00	10.00	6.00
274	Frank Baumholtz	20.00	10.00	6.00
275	Jim Greengrass	20.00	10.00	6.00
276	George Zuverink	20.00	10.00	6.00
277	Daryl Spencer	20.00	10.00	6.00
278	Chet Nichols	20.00	10.00	6.00
279	Johnny Groth	20.00	10.00	6.00
280	Jim Gilliam	45.00	22.50	13.50
281	Art Houtteman	20.00	10.00	6.00
282	Warren Hacker	20.00	10.00	6.00
283	Hal Smith	20.00	10.00	6.00
284	Ike Delock	20.00	10.00	6.00
285	Eddie Miksis	20.00	10.00	6.00
286	Bill Wight	20.00	10.00	6.00
287	Bobby Adams	20.00	10.00	6.00
288	Bob Cerv (SP)	55.00	25.00	15.00
289	Hal Jeffcoat	20.00	10.00	6.00
290	Curt Simmons	20.00	10.00	6.00
291	Frank Kellert	20.00	10.00	6.00
292	Luis Aparicio RC	150.00	75.00	37.50
293	Stu Miller	20.00	10.00	6.00
294	Ernie Johnson	20.00	10.00	6.00
295	Clem Labine	30.00	15.00	9.00
296	Andy Seminick	20.00	10.00	6.00
297	Bob Skinner	20.00	10.00	6.00
298	Johnny Schmitz	20.00	10.00	6.00
299	Charley Neal (SP)	40.00	20.00	12.00
300	Vic Wertz	20.00	10.00	6.00
301	Marv Grissom	20.00	10.00	6.00
302	Eddie Robinson	25.00	12.50	7.50
303	Jim Dyck	20.00	10.00	6.00
304	Frank Malzone	20.00	10.00	6.00
305	Brooks Lawrence	20.00	10.00	6.00
306	Curt Roberts	20.00	10.00	6.00
307	Hoyt Wilhelm	45.00	20.00	12.00
308	"Chuck" Harmon	20.00	10.00	6.00
309	Don Blasingame RC	25.00	12.50	7.50
310	Steve Gromek	20.00	10.00	6.00
311	Hal Naragon	20.00	10.00	6.00
312	Andy Pafko	20.00	10.00	6.00

313	Gene Stephens	20.00	10.00	6.00
314	Hobie Landrith	20.00	10.00	6.00
315	Milt Bolling	20.00	10.00	6.00
316	Jerry Coleman	25.00	12.50	7.50
317	Al Aber	20.00	10.00	6.00
318	Fred Hatfield	20.00	10.00	6.00
319	Jack Crimian	20.00	10.00	6.00
320	Joe Adcock	20.00	10.00	6.00
321	Jim Konstanty	25.00	12.50	7.50
322	Karl Olson	20.00	10.00	6.00
323	Willard Schmidt	20.00	10.00	6.00
324	"Rocky" Bridges	20.00	10.00	6.00
325	Don Liddle	20.00	10.00	6.00
326	Connie Johnson	20.00	10.00	6.00
327	Bob Wiesler	20.00	10.00	6.00
328	Preston Ward	20.00	10.00	6.00
329	Lou Berberet	20.00	10.00	6.00
330	Jim Busby	20.00	10.00	6.00
331	Dick Hall	20.00	10.00	6.00
332	Don Larsen	55.00	27.50	16.50
333	"Rube" Walker	25.00	12.50	7.50
334	Bob Miller	20.00	10.00	6.00
335	Don Hoak	20.00	10.00	6.00
336	Ellis Kinder	20.00	10.00	6.00
337	Bobby Morgan	20.00	10.00	6.00
338	Jim Delsing	20.00	10.00	6.00
339	Rance Pless	20.00	10.00	6.00
340	Mickey McDermott	85.00	15.00	8.00
----	Checklist 1/3	250.00	125.00	62.50
----	Checklist 2/4	250.00	125.00	62.50

1956 Topps Hocus Focus

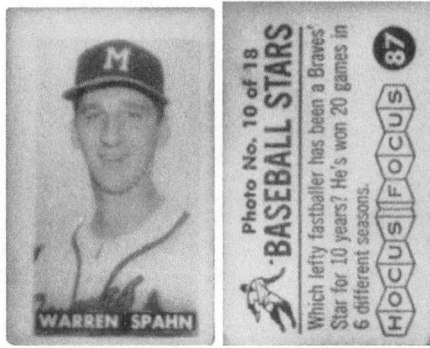

Following its 1955 issue with a somewhat larger format (1" x 1-5/8") the following year, the baseball players in this set are part of a larger overall series covering several topical areas. Cards backs specify an issue of 18 baseball stars. The black-and-white photos on these cards were developed by wetting the card's surface and exposing to light. Prices below are for cards with well-developed pictures. Cards with poorly developed photos are worth significantly less.

		NM	E	VG
Complete Set (18):		7,000	3,500	2,100
Common Player:		220.00	110.00	66.00
1	Dick Groat	225.00	110.00	65.00
2	Ed Lopat	425.00	210.00	125.00
3	Hank Sauer	225.00	110.00	65.00
4	"Dusty" Rhodes	225.00	110.00	65.00
5	Ted Williams	1,600	800.00	480.00
6	Harvey Haddix	225.00	110.00	65.00
7	Ray Boone	225.00	110.00	65.00
8	Al Rosen	250.00	125.00	75.00
9	Mayo Smith	225.00	110.00	65.00
10	Warren Spahn	550.00	275.00	165.00
11	Jim Rivera	225.00	110.00	65.00
12	Ted Kluszewski	450.00	225.00	135.00
13	Gus Zernial	225.00	110.00	65.00
14	Jackie Robinson	1,350	675.00	400.00
15	Hal Smith	225.00	110.00	65.00
16	Johnny Schmitz	225.00	110.00	65.00
17	"Spook" Jacobs	225.00	110.00	65.00
18	Mel Parnell	225.00	110.00	65.00

1956 Topps Pins

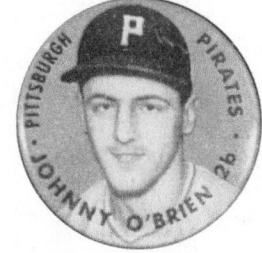

One of Topps first specialty issues, the 60-pin set of ballplayers issued in 1956 contains a high percentage of big-name stars which, combined with the scarcity of the pins, makes collecting a complete set extremely challenging. Compounding the situation is the fact that some pins are seen far less often than others, though the reason is unknown. Chuck Stobbs, Hector Lopez and Chuck Diering are unaccountably scarce. Measuring 1-1/8" in diameter, the pins utilize the same portraits found on 1956 Topps baseball cards. The photos are set against a solid color background. The pins were sold in a box picturing the Ted Williams pin, with a piece of bubblegum for five cents.

		NM	E	VG
Complete Set (60):		4,250	2,125	1,050
Common Player:		50.00	25.00	15.00
Box:		700.00	350.00	210.00
(1)	Hank Aaron	200.00	100.00	60.00
(2)	Sandy Amoros	60.00	30.00	20.00
(3)	Luis Arroyo	50.00	25.00	15.00
(4)	Ernie Banks	150.00	75.00	45.00
(5)	Yogi Berra	150.00	75.00	45.00
(6)	Joe Black	60.00	30.00	18.00
(7)	Ray Boone	50.00	25.00	15.00
(8)	Ken Boyer	60.00	30.00	20.00
(9)	Joe Collins	50.00	25.00	15.00
(10)	Gene Conley	50.00	25.00	15.00
(11)	Chuck Diering	275.00	135.00	85.00
(12)	Dick Donovan	50.00	25.00	15.00
(13)	Jim Finigan	50.00	25.00	15.00
(14)	Art Fowler	50.00	25.00	15.00
(15)	Ruben Gomez	50.00	25.00	15.00
(16)	Dick Groat	50.00	25.00	15.00
(17)	Harvey Haddix	50.00	25.00	15.00
(18)	Jack Harshman	50.00	25.00	15.00
(19)	Grady Hatton	50.00	25.00	15.00
(20)	Jim Hegan	50.00	25.00	15.00
(21)	Gil Hodges	100.00	50.00	30.00
(22)	Bobby Hofman	50.00	25.00	15.00
(23)	Frank House	50.00	25.00	15.00
(24)	Jackie Jensen	60.00	30.00	20.00
(25)	Al Kaline	100.00	50.00	30.00
(26)	Bob Kennedy	50.00	25.00	15.00
(27)	Ted Kluszewski	85.00	42.50	25.00
(28)	Dale Long	50.00	25.00	15.00
(29)	Hector Lopez/SP	335.00	170.00	90.00
(30)	Ed Mathews	100.00	50.00	30.00
(31)	Willie Mays	200.00	100.00	60.00
(32)	Roy McMillan	50.00	25.00	15.00
(33)	Willie Miranda	50.00	25.00	15.00
(34)	Wally Moon	50.00	25.00	15.00
(35)	Don Mossi	50.00	25.00	15.00
(36)	Ron Negray	50.00	25.00	15.00
(37)	Johnny O'Brien	50.00	25.00	15.00
(38)	Carlos Paula	50.00	25.00	15.00
(39)	Vic Power	50.00	25.00	15.00
(40)	Jim Rivera	50.00	25.00	15.00
(41)	Phil Rizzuto	150.00	75.00	45.00
(42)	Jackie Robinson	180.00	90.00	55.00
(43)	Al Rosen	55.00	25.00	15.00
(44)	Hank Sauer	50.00	25.00	15.00
(45)	Roy Sievers	50.00	25.00	15.00
(46)	Bill Skowron	60.00	30.00	20.00
(47)	Al Smith	50.00	25.00	15.00
(48)	Hal Smith	50.00	25.00	15.00
(49)	Mayo Smith	50.00	25.00	15.00
(50)	Duke Snider	125.00	65.00	35.00
(51)	Warren Spahn	100.00	50.00	30.00
(52)	Karl Spooner	55.00	22.50	13.50
(53)	Chuck Stobbs/SP	225.00	110.00	65.00
(54)	Frank Sullivan	50.00	25.00	15.00
(55)	Bill Tremel	50.00	25.00	15.00
(56)	Gus Triandos	50.00	25.00	15.00
(57)	Bob Turley	60.00	30.00	20.00
(58)	Herman Wehmeier	50.00	25.00	15.00
(59)	Ted Williams	225.00	110.00	65.00
(60)	Gus Zernial	50.00	25.00	15.00

1957 Topps

For 1957, Topps reduced the size of its cards to the now-standard 2-1/2" x 3-1/2." Set size was increased to 407 cards.

Another change came in the form of the use of real color photographs as opposed to the hand-colored black and whites of previous years. For the first time since 1954, there were also cards with more than one player. The two, "Dodger Sluggers" and "Yankees' Power Hitters" began a trend toward the increased use of multiple-player cards. Another first-time innovation, found on the backs, is complete players statistics. The scarce cards in the set are not the highest numbers, but rather numbers 265-352. Four unnumbered checklist cards were issued along with the set. They are quite expensive and are not included in the complete set prices quoted below.

	NM	E	VG
Complete Set (407):	13,500	6,750	4,050
Common Player (1-264):	12.00	6.00	3.50
Common Player (265-352):	25.00	12.50	7.50
Common Player (353-407):	12.00	6.00	3.50

1	Ted Williams	450.00	185.00	115.00
2	Yogi Berra	200.00	100.00	50.00
3	Dale Long	12.00	6.00	3.50
4	Johnny Logan	12.00	6.00	3.50
5	Sal Maglie	20.00	10.00	6.00
6	Hector Lopez	12.00	6.00	3.50
7	Luis Aparicio	40.00	20.00	12.00
8	Don Mossi	12.00	6.00	3.50
9	Johnny Temple	12.00	6.00	3.50
10	Willie Mays	300.00	150.00	90.00
11	George Zuverink	12.00	6.00	3.50
12	Dick Groat	12.00	6.00	3.50
13	Wally Burnette	12.00	6.00	3.50
14	Bob Nieman	12.00	6.00	3.50
15	Robin Roberts	60.00	30.00	15.00
16	Walt Moryn	12.00	6.00	3.50
17	Billy Gardner	12.00	6.00	3.50
18	Don Drysdale **RC**	250.00	125.00	62.50
19	Bob Wilson	12.00	6.00	3.50
20	Hank Aaron (Photo reversed.)	275.00	140.00	80.00
21	Frank Sullivan	12.00	6.00	3.50
22	Jerry Snyder (Photo actually Ed Fitz Gerald.)	12.00	6.00	3.50
23	Sherman Lollar	12.00	6.00	3.50
24	Bill Mazeroski **RC**	75.00	40.00	20.00
25	Whitey Ford	135.00	70.00	35.00
26	Bob Boyd	12.00	6.00	3.50
27	Ted Kazanski	12.00	6.00	3.50
28	Gene Conley	12.00	6.00	3.50
29	Whitey Herzog **RC**	30.00	15.00	7.50
30	Pee Wee Reese	75.00	37.50	22.50
31	Ron Northey	12.00	6.00	3.50
32	Hersh Freeman	12.00	6.00	3.50
33	Jim Small	12.00	6.00	3.50
34	Tom Sturdivant	15.00	7.50	4.50
35	Frank Robinson **RC**	285.00	115.00	70.00
36	Bob Grim	15.00	7.50	4.50
37	Frank Torre	12.00	6.00	3.50
38	Nellie Fox	40.00	20.00	12.00
39	Al Worthington	12.00	6.00	3.50
40	Early Wynn	35.00	15.00	9.00
41	Hal Smith	12.00	6.00	3.50
42	Dee Fondy	12.00	6.00	3.50
43	Connie Johnson	12.00	6.00	3.50
44	Joe DeMaestri	12.00	6.00	3.50
45	Carl Furillo	45.00	20.00	12.00
46	Bob Miller	12.00	6.00	3.50
47	Don Blasingame	12.00	6.00	3.50
48	Bill Bruton	12.00	6.00	3.50
49	Daryl Spencer	12.00	6.00	3.50
50	Herb Score	25.00	12.50	7.50
51	Clint Courtney	12.00	6.00	3.50
52	Lee Walls	12.00	6.00	3.50
53	Clem Labine	20.00	10.00	6.00
54	Elmer Valo	12.00	6.00	3.50
55	Ernie Banks	125.00	65.00	32.50
56	Dave Sisler	12.00	6.00	3.50
57	Jim Lemon	12.00	6.00	3.50
58	Ruben Gomez	12.00	6.00	3.50
59	Dick Williams	12.00	6.00	3.50
60	Billy Hoeft	12.00	6.00	3.50
61	Dusty Rhodes	12.00	6.00	3.50
62	Billy Martin	50.00	25.00	15.00
63	Ike Delock	12.00	6.00	3.50
64	Pete Runnels	12.00	6.00	3.50
65	Wally Moon	12.00	6.00	3.50
66	Brooks Lawrence	12.00	6.00	3.50
67	Chico Carrasquel	12.00	6.00	3.50
68	Ray Crone	12.00	6.00	3.50
69	Roy McMillan	12.00	6.00	3.50
70	Richie Ashburn	55.00	22.50	13.50
71	Murry Dickson	12.00	6.00	3.50
72	Bill Tuttle	12.00	6.00	3.50
73	George Crowe	12.00	6.00	3.50
74	Vito Valentinetti	12.00	6.00	3.50
75	Jim Piersall	15.00	7.50	4.50
76	Bob Clemente	225.00	120.00	70.00
77	Paul Foytack	12.00	6.00	3.50
78	Vic Wertz	12.00	6.00	3.50
79	Lindy McDaniel **RC**	15.00	7.50	4.50
80	Gil Hodges	50.00	22.50	13.50
81	Herm Wehmeier	12.00	6.00	3.50
82	Elston Howard	30.00	15.00	9.00
83	Lou Skizas	12.00	6.00	3.50
84	Moe Drabowsky	12.00	6.00	3.50
85	Larry Doby	50.00	25.00	15.00
86	Bill Sarni	12.00	6.00	3.50
87	Tom Gorman	12.00	6.00	3.50
88	Harvey Kuenn	12.00	6.00	3.50
89	Roy Sievers	12.00	6.00	3.50
90	Warren Spahn	85.00	40.00	24.00
91	Mack Burk	12.00	6.00	3.50
92	Mickey Vernon	12.00	6.00	3.50
93	Hal Jeffcoat	12.00	6.00	3.50
94	Bobby Del Greco	12.00	6.00	3.50
95	Mickey Mantle	800.00	350.00	210.00
96	Hank Aguirre **RC**	12.00	6.00	3.50
97	New York Yankees Team	100.00	50.00	25.00
98	Al Dark	12.00	6.00	3.50
99	Bob Keegan	12.00	6.00	3.50
100	League Presidents (Warren Giles, William Harridge)	55.00	30.00	18.00
101	Chuck Stobbs	12.00	6.00	3.50
102	Ray Boone	12.00	6.00	3.50
103	Joe Nuxhall	12.00	6.00	3.50
104	Hank Foiles	12.00	6.00	3.50
105	Johnny Antonelli	12.00	6.00	3.50
106	Ray Moore	12.00	6.00	3.50
107	Jim Rivera	12.00	6.00	3.50
108	Tommy Byrne	15.00	7.50	4.50
109	Hank Thompson	12.00	6.00	3.50
110	Bill Virdon	12.00	6.00	3.50
111	Hal Smith	12.00	6.00	3.50
112	Tom Brewer	12.00	6.00	3.50
113	Wilmer Mizell	12.00	6.00	3.50
114	Milwaukee Braves Team	40.00	20.00	12.00
115	Jim Gilliam	35.00	18.00	11.00
116	Mike Fornieles	12.00	6.00	3.50
117	Joe Adcock	12.00	6.00	3.50
118	Bob Porterfield	12.00	6.00	3.50
119	Stan Lopata	12.00	6.00	3.50
120	Bob Lemon	35.00	17.50	10.00
121	Cletis Boyer **RC**	35.00	15.00	9.00
122	Ken Boyer	20.00	10.00	6.00
123	Steve Ridzik	12.00	6.00	3.50
124	Dave Philley	12.00	6.00	3.50
125	Al Kaline	85.00	40.00	24.00
126	Bob Wiesler	12.00	6.00	3.50
127	Bob Buhl	12.00	6.00	3.50
128	Ed Bailey	12.00	6.00	3.50
129	Saul Rogovin	12.00	6.00	3.50
130	Don Newcombe	30.00	15.00	9.00
131	Milt Bolling	12.00	6.00	3.50
132	Art Ditmar	12.00	6.00	3.50
133	Del Crandall	12.00	6.00	3.50
134	Don Kaiser	12.00	6.00	3.50
135	Bill Skowron	30.00	15.00	9.00
136	Jim Hegan	12.00	6.00	3.50
137	Bob Rush	12.00	6.00	3.50
138	Minnie Minoso	25.00	12.50	7.50
139	Lou Kretlow	12.00	6.00	3.50
140	Frank Thomas	12.00	6.00	3.50
141	Al Aber	12.00	6.00	3.50
142	Charley Thompson	12.00	6.00	3.50
143	Andy Pafko	12.00	6.00	3.50
144	Ray Narleski	12.00	6.00	3.50
145	Al Smith	12.00	6.00	3.50
146	Don Ferrarese	12.00	6.00	3.50
147	Al Walker	15.00	7.50	4.50
148	Don Mueller	12.00	6.00	3.50
149	Bob Kennedy	12.00	6.00	3.50
150	Bob Friend	12.00	6.00	3.50
151	Willie Miranda	12.00	6.00	3.50
152	Jack Harshman	12.00	6.00	3.50
153	Karl Olson	12.00	6.00	3.50
154	Red Schoendienst	30.00	15.00	9.00
155	Jim Brosnan	12.00	6.00	3.50
156	Gus Triandos	12.00	6.00	3.50
157	Wally Post	12.00	6.00	3.50
158	Curt Simmons	12.00	6.00	3.50
159	Solly Drake	12.00	6.00	3.50
160	Billy Pierce	12.00	6.00	3.50
161	Pitsburgh Pirates Team	20.00	10.00	6.00
162	Jack Meyer	12.00	6.00	3.50
163	Sammy White	12.00	6.00	3.50
164	Tommy Carroll	15.00	7.50	4.50
165	Ted Kluszewski	80.00	40.00	20.00
166	Roy Face	12.00	6.00	3.50
167	Vic Power	12.00	6.00	3.50
168	Frank Lary	12.00	6.00	3.50
169	Herb Plews	12.00	6.00	3.50
170	Duke Snider	130.00	65.00	30.00
171	Boston Red Sox Team	45.00	23.00	10.00
172	Gene Woodling	12.00	6.00	3.50
173	Roger Craig	15.00	7.50	4.50
174	Willie Jones	12.00	6.00	3.50
175	Don Larsen	35.00	17.50	10.00
176a	Gene Baker	12.00	6.00	3.50
176b	Gene Baker (Error on back, "EUGENF W. BAKEP.")	850.00	420.00	250.00
177	Eddie Yost	12.00	6.00	3.50
178	Don Bessent	15.00	7.50	4.50
179	Ernie Oravetz	12.00	6.00	3.50
180	Gus Bell	12.00	6.00	3.50
181	Dick Donovan	12.00	6.00	3.50
182	Hobie Landrith	12.00	6.00	3.50
183	Chicago Cubs Team	25.00	12.50	7.50
184	Tito Francona **RC**	12.00	6.00	3.50
185	Johnny Kucks	15.00	7.50	4.50
186	Jim King	12.00	6.00	3.50
187	Virgil Trucks	12.00	6.00	3.50
188	Felix Mantilla	12.00	6.00	3.50
189	Willard Nixon	12.00	6.00	3.50
190	Randy Jackson	15.00	7.50	4.50
191	Joe Margoneri	12.00	6.00	3.50
192	Jerry Coleman	15.00	7.50	4.50
193	Del Rice	12.00	6.00	3.50
194	Hal Brown	12.00	6.00	3.50
195	Bobby Avila	12.00	6.00	3.50
196	Larry Jackson	12.00	6.00	3.50
197	Hank Sauer	12.00	6.00	3.50
198	Detroit Tigers Team	20.00	10.00	6.00
199	Vernon Law	12.00	6.00	3.50
200	Gil McDougald	25.00	12.50	7.50
201	Sandy Amoros	25.00	12.50	7.50
202	Dick Gernert	12.00	6.00	3.50
203	Hoyt Wilhelm	25.00	12.50	7.50
204	Kansas City A's Team	20.00	10.00	6.00
205	Charley Maxwell	12.00	6.00	3.50
206	Willard Schmidt	12.00	6.00	3.50
207	Billy Hunter	12.00	6.00	3.50
208	Lew Burdette	12.00	6.00	3.50
209	Bob Skinner	12.00	6.00	3.50
210	Roy Campanella	120.00	60.00	34.00
211	Camilo Pascual	12.00	6.00	3.50
212	Rocky Colavito **RC**	100.00	50.00	30.00
213	Les Moss	12.00	6.00	3.50
214	Philadelphia Phillies Team	35.00	12.50	7.50
215	Enos Slaughter	35.00	17.50	10.00
216	Marv Grissom	12.00	6.00	3.50
217	Gene Stephens	12.00	6.00	3.50
218	Ray Jablonski	12.00	6.00	3.50
219	Tom Acker	12.00	6.00	3.50
220	Jackie Jensen	17.50	8.75	5.25
221	Dixie Howell	12.00	6.00	3.50
222	Alex Grammas	12.00	6.00	3.50
223	Frank House	12.00	6.00	3.50
224	Marv Blaylock	12.00	6.00	3.50
225	Harry Simpson	12.00	6.00	3.50
226	Preston Ward	12.00	6.00	3.50
227	Jerry Staley	12.00	6.00	3.50
228	Smoky Burgess	12.00	6.00	3.50
229	George Susce	12.00	6.00	3.50
230	George Kell	25.00	12.50	7.50
231	Solly Hemus	12.00	6.00	3.50
232	Whitey Lockman	12.00	6.00	3.50
233	Art Fowler	12.00	6.00	3.50
234	Dick Cole	12.00	6.00	3.50
235	Tom Poholsky	12.00	6.00	3.50
236	Joe Ginsberg	12.00	6.00	3.50
237	Foster Castleman	12.00	6.00	3.50
238	Eddie Robinson	12.00	6.00	3.50
239	Tom Morgan	12.00	6.00	3.50
240	Hank Bauer	35.00	15.00	9.00
241	Joe Lonnett	12.00	6.00	3.50
242	Charley Neal	15.00	7.50	4.50
243	St. Louis Cardinals Team	20.00	10.00	6.00
244	Billy Loes	12.00	6.00	3.50
245	Rip Repulski	12.00	6.00	3.50
246	Jose Valdivielso	12.00	6.00	3.50
247	Turk Lown	12.00	6.00	3.50
248	Jim Finigan	12.00	6.00	3.50
249	Dave Pope	12.00	6.00	3.50
250	Ed Mathews	55.00	27.50	16.50
251	Baltimore Orioles Team	20.00	10.00	6.00
252	Carl Erskine	20.00	10.00	6.00
253	Gus Zernial	12.00	6.00	3.50
254	Ron Negray	12.00	6.00	3.50
255	Charlie Silvera	12.00	6.00	3.50
256	Ronnie Kline	12.00	6.00	3.50
257	Walt Dropo	12.00	6.00	3.50
258	Steve Gromek	12.00	6.00	3.50
259	Eddie O'Brien	12.00	6.00	3.50
260	Del Ennis	12.00	6.00	3.50
261	Bob Chakales	12.00	6.00	3.50
262	Bobby Thomson	15.00	7.50	4.50
263	George Strickland	12.00	6.00	3.50
264	Bob Turley	25.00	12.50	7.50
265	Harvey Haddix	25.00	12.50	7.50
266	Ken Kuhn	25.00	12.50	7.50
267	Danny Kravitz	25.00	12.50	7.50
268	Jackie Collum	25.00	12.50	7.50

269	Bob Cerv	25.00	12.50	7.50
270	Washington Senators Team	45.00	22.50	13.50
271	Danny O'Connell	25.00	12.50	7.50
272	Bobby Shantz	40.00	20.00	12.00
273	Jim Davis	25.00	12.50	7.50
274	Don Hoak	25.00	12.50	7.50
275	Cleveland Indians Team	50.00	20.00	12.00
276	Jim Pyburn	25.00	12.50	7.50
277	Johnny Podres	50.00	20.00	12.00
278	Fred Hatfield	25.00	12.50	7.50
279	Bob Thurman	25.00	12.50	7.50
280	Alex Kellner	25.00	12.50	7.50
281	Gail Harris	25.00	12.50	7.50
282	Jack Dittmer	25.00	12.50	7.50
283	Wes Covington RC	25.00	12.50	7.50
284	Don Zimmer	40.00	20.00	12.00
285	Ned Garver	25.00	12.50	7.50
286	Bobby Richardson RC	120.00	60.00	30.00
287	Sam Jones	25.00	12.50	7.50
288	Ted Lepcio	25.00	12.50	7.50
289	Jim Bolger	25.00	12.50	7.50
290	Andy Carey	35.00	17.50	10.00
291	Windy McCall	20.00	10.00	6.00
292	Billy Klaus	25.00	12.50	7.50
293	Ted Abernathy	25.00	12.50	7.50
294	Rocky Bridges	25.00	12.50	7.50
295	Joe Collins	45.00	20.00	12.00
296	Johnny Klippstein	25.00	12.50	7.50
297	Jack Crimian	25.00	12.50	7.50
298	Irv Noren	25.00	12.50	7.50
299	Chuck Harmon	25.00	12.50	7.50
300	Mike Garcia	25.00	12.50	7.50
301	Sam Esposito	25.00	12.50	7.50
302	Sandy Koufax	380.00	190.00	115.00
303	Billy Goodman	25.00	12.50	7.50
304	Joe Cunningham	25.00	12.50	7.50
305	Chico Fernandez	25.00	12.50	7.50
306	Darrell Johnson RC	35.00	17.50	10.00
307	Jack Phillips	25.00	12.50	7.50
308	Dick Hall	25.00	12.50	7.50
309	Jim Busby	25.00	12.50	7.50
310	Max Surkont	25.00	12.50	7.50
311	Al Pilarcik	25.00	12.50	7.50
312	Tony Kubek RC	90.00	45.00	22.50
313	Mel Parnell	25.00	12.50	7.50
314	Ed Bouchee	25.00	12.50	7.50
315	Lou Berberet	25.00	12.50	7.50
316	Billy O'Dell	25.00	12.50	7.50
317	New York Giants Team	55.00	30.00	15.00
318	Mickey McDermott	25.00	12.50	7.50
319	Gino Cimoli RC	35.00	15.00	9.00
320	Neil Chrisley	25.00	12.50	7.50
321	Red Murff	25.00	12.50	7.50
322	Cincinnati Redlegs Team	50.00	22.50	13.50
323	Wes Westrum	25.00	12.50	7.50
324	Brooklyn Dodgers Team	130.00	62.50	31.25
325	Frank Bolling	25.00	12.50	7.50
326	Pedro Ramos	25.00	12.50	7.50
327	Jim Pendleton	25.00	12.50	7.50
328	Brooks Robinson RC	400.00	200.00	100.00
329	Chicago White Sox Team	45.00	22.50	13.50
330	Jim Wilson	25.00	12.50	7.50
331	Ray Katt	25.00	12.50	7.50
332	Bob Bowman	25.00	12.50	7.50
333	Ernie Johnson	25.00	12.50	7.50
334	Jerry Schoonmaker	25.00	12.50	7.50
335	Granny Hamner	25.00	12.50	7.50
336	Haywood Sullivan RC	25.00	12.50	7.50
337	Rene Valdes (Valdez)	30.00	15.00	9.00
338	Jim Bunning RC	150.00	75.00	37.50
339	Bob Speake	25.00	12.50	7.50
340	Bill Wight	25.00	12.50	7.50
341	Don Gross	25.00	12.50	7.50
342	Gene Mauch	25.00	12.50	7.50
343	Taylor Phillips	25.00	12.50	7.50
344	Paul LaPalme	25.00	12.50	7.50
345	Paul Smith	25.00	12.50	7.50
346	Dick Littlefield	25.00	12.50	7.50
347	Hal Naragon	25.00	12.50	7.50
348	Jim Hearn	25.00	12.50	7.50
349	Nelson King	25.00	12.50	7.50
350	Eddie Miksis	25.00	12.50	7.50
351	Dave Hillman	25.00	12.50	7.50
352	Ellis Kinder	25.00	12.50	7.50
353	Cal Neeman	12.00	6.00	3.50
354	Rip Coleman	12.00	6.00	3.50
355	Frank Malzone	12.00	6.00	3.50
356	Faye Throneberry	12.00	6.00	3.50
357	Earl Torgeson	12.00	6.00	3.50
358	Jerry Lynch	12.00	6.00	3.50
359	Tom Cheney	12.00	6.00	3.50
360	Johnny Groth	12.00	6.00	3.50
361	Curt Barclay	12.00	6.00	3.50
362	Roman Mejias	12.00	6.00	3.50
363	Eddie Kasko	12.00	6.00	3.50
364	Cal McLish RC	12.00	6.00	3.50
365	Ossie Virgil	12.00	6.00	3.50
366	Ken Lehman	15.00	7.50	4.50
367	Ed FitzGerald	12.00	6.00	3.50
368	Bob Purkey	12.00	6.00	3.50
369	Milt Graff	12.00	6.00	3.50
370	Warren Hacker	12.00	6.00	3.50
371	Bob Lennon	12.00	6.00	3.50
372	Norm Zauchin	12.00	6.00	3.50
373	Pete Whisenant	12.00	6.00	3.50
374	Don Cardwell	12.00	6.00	3.50
375	Jim Landis RC	12.00	6.00	3.50
376	Don Elston	15.00	7.50	4.50
377	Andre Rodgers	12.00	6.00	3.50
378	Elmer Singleton	12.00	6.00	3.50
379	Don Lee	12.00	6.00	3.50
380	Walker Cooper	12.00	6.00	3.50
381	Dean Stone	12.00	6.00	3.50
382	Jim Brideweser	12.00	6.00	3.50
383	Juan Pizarro RC	12.00	6.00	3.50
384	Bobby Gene Smith	12.00	6.00	3.50
385	Art Houtteman	12.00	6.00	3.50
386	Lyle Luttrell	12.00	6.00	3.50
387	Jack Sanford RC	12.00	6.00	3.50
388	Pete Daley	12.00	6.00	3.50
389	Dave Jolly	12.00	6.00	3.50
390	Reno Bertoia	12.00	6.00	3.50
391	Ralph Terry RC	15.00	7.50	4.50
392	Chuck Tanner	12.00	6.00	3.50
393	Raul Sanchez	12.00	6.00	3.50
394	Luis Arroyo	12.00	6.00	3.50
395	Bubba Phillips	12.00	6.00	3.50
396	Casey Wise	12.00	6.00	3.50
397	Roy Smalley	12.00	6.00	3.50
398	Al Cicotte	15.00	7.50	4.50
399	Billy Consolo	12.00	6.00	3.50
400	Dodgers' Sluggers (Roy Campanella, Carl Furillo, Gil Hodges, Duke Snider)	150.00	75.00	45.00
401	Earl Battey RC	15.00	7.50	4.50
402	Jim Pisoni	12.00	6.00	3.50
403	Dick Hyde	12.00	6.00	3.50
404	Harry Anderson	12.00	6.00	3.50
405	Duke Maas	12.00	6.00	3.50
406	Bob Hale	12.00	6.00	3.50
407	Yankees' Power Hitters (Mickey Mantle, Yogi Berra)	465.00	230.00	115.00
----	Checklist Series 1-2 (Big Blony ad on back)	550.00	275.00	165.00
----	Checklist Series 1-2 (Bazooka ad on back)	550.00	275.00	165.00
----	Checklist Series 2-3 (Big Blony)	600.00	300.00	180.00
----	Checklist Series 2-3 (Bazooka)	600.00	300.00	180.00
----	Checklist Series 3-4 (Twin Blony)	900.00	450.00	270.00
----	Checklist Series 3-4 (Bazooka)	900.00	450.00	270.00
----	Checklist Series 4-5 (Twin Blony)	1,500	750.00	450.00
----	Checklist Series 4-5 (Bazooka)	1,500	750.00	450.00
----	Contest May 4	100.00	50.00	25.00
----	Contest May 25	135.00	65.00	40.00
----	Contest June 22	145.00	75.00	45.00
----	Contest July 19	200.00	100.00	60.00
----	Lucky Penny insert card	250.00	125.00	75.00

1957 Topps Paper Proofs

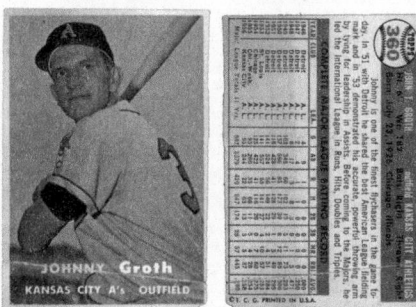

A 1979 advertisement in a hobby magazine revealed the existence of more than 30 fully printed (front and back) glossy paper-stock proofs of 1957 Topps high-numbers. The full extent of the issue is unknown, specifically, whether all 55 cards in the high-number series were preserved in paper proof format. The checklist here corresponds to the individual proofs offered in that ad, as well as a few others reported by collectors. Each proof card is believed to be unique and thus is not priced here.

353	Cal Neeman			
354	Rip Coleman			
356	Faye Throneberry			
358	Jerry Lynch			
359	Tom Cheney			
360	Johnny Groth			
361	Curt Barclay			
363	Eddie Kasko			
366	Ken Lehman			
367	Ed FitzGerald			
368	Bob Purkey			
369	Milt Graff			
370	Warren Hacker			
371	Bob Lennon			
372	Norm Zauchin			
373	Pete Whisenant			
374	Don Cardwell			
376	Don Elston			
378	Elmer Singleton			
380	Walker Cooper			
383	Juan Pizarro			
384	Bobby Gene Smith			
386	Lyle Luttrell			
387	Jack Sanford			
388	Pete Daley			
389	Dave Jolly			
392	Chuck Tanner			
393	Raul Sanchez			
394	Luis Arroyo			
396	Casey Wise			
397	Roy Smalley			
399	Billy Consolo			
400	Dodgers' Sluggers			
401	Earl Battey			
404	Harry Anderson			

1958 Topps

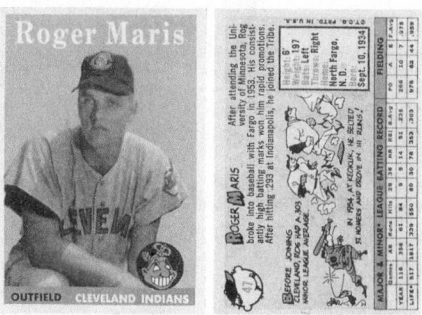

Topps continued to expand its set size in 1958 with the release of a 494-card set. One card (#145) was not issued after Ed Bouchee was suspended from baseball. Cards retained the 2-1/2" x 3-1/2" size. There are a number of variations, including player or team names found in either yellow or white lettering on 33 cards between numbers 2-108 (higher priced yellow-letter variations checklisted below are not included in the complete set prices). The number of multiple-player cards was increased. A major innovation is the addition of 20 "All-Star" cards. For the first time, checklists were incorporated into the numbered series, on the backs of team cards.

	NM	E	VG
Complete Set (494):	8,500	4,250	2,500
Common Player (1-495):	9.00	4.50	2.57

1	Ted Williams	550.00	150.00	90.00
2a	Bob Lemon (Yellow team.)	125.00	60.00	36.00
2b	Bob Lemon (White team.)	30.00	15.00	9.00
3	Alex Kellner	9.00	4.50	2.57
4	Hank Foiles	9.00	4.50	2.57
5	Willie Mays	250.00	125.00	75.00
6	George Zuverink	9.00	4.50	2.57
7	Dale Long	9.00	4.50	2.57
8a	Eddie Kasko (Yellow name.)	90.00	45.00	27.00
8b	Eddie Kasko (White name.)	9.00	4.50	2.57
9	Hank Bauer	20.00	10.00	6.00
10	Lou Burdette	9.00	4.50	2.57
11a	Jim Rivera (Yellow team.)	90.00	45.00	27.00
11b	Jim Rivera (White team.)	9.00	4.50	2.57
12	George Crowe	9.00	4.50	2.57
13a	Billy Hoeft (Yellow name.)	90.00	45.00	27.00
13b	Billy Hoeft (White name, orange triangle by foot.)	9.00	4.50	2.57
13c	Billy Hoeft (White name, red triangle by foot.)	9.00	4.50	2.57
14	Rip Repulski	9.00	4.50	2.57
15	Jim Lemon	9.00	4.50	2.57
16	Charley Neal	9.00	4.50	2.57
17	Felix Mantilla	9.00	4.50	2.57
18	Frank Sullivan	9.00	4.50	2.57
19	1957 Giants Team	40.00	20.00	12.00

20a	Gil McDougald (Yellow name.)	110.00	55.00	33.00
20b	Gil McDougald (White name.)	20.00	10.00	6.00
21	Curt Barclay	9.00	4.50	2.57
22	Hal Naragon	9.00	4.50	2.57
23a	Bill Tuttle (Yellow name.)	90.00	45.00	27.00
23b	Bill Tuttle (White name.)	9.00	4.50	2.57
24a	Hobie Landrith (Yellow name.)	90.00	45.00	27.00
24b	Hobie Landrith (White name.)	9.00	4.50	2.57
25	Don Drysdale	100.00	50.00	25.00
26	Ron Jackson	9.00	4.50	2.57
27	Bud Freeman	9.00	4.50	2.57
28	Jim Busby	9.00	4.50	2.57
29	Ted Lepcio	9.00	4.50	2.57
30a	Hank Aaron (Yellow name.)	490.00	245.00	140.00
30b	Hank Aaron (White name.)	200.00	100.00	55.00
31	Tex Clevenger	9.00	4.50	2.57
32a	J.W. Porter (Yellow name.)	90.00	45.00	27.00
32b	J.W. Porter (White name.)	9.00	4.50	2.57
33a	Cal Neeman (Yellow team.)	90.00	45.00	27.00
33b	Cal Neeman (White team.)	9.00	4.50	2.57
34	Bob Thurman	9.00	4.50	2.57
35a	Don Mossi (Yellow team.)	90.00	45.00	27.00
35b	Don Mossi (White team.)	9.00	4.50	2.57
36	Ted Kazanski	9.00	4.50	2.57
37	Mike McCormick **RC** (Photo actually Ray Monzant.)	9.00	4.50	2.57
38	Dick Gernert	9.00	4.50	2.57
39	Bob Martyn	9.00	4.50	2.57
40	George Kell	20.00	10.00	6.00
41	Dave Hillman	9.00	4.50	2.57
42	John Roseboro **RC**	35.00	12.50	7.50
43	Sal Maglie	12.50	6.25	3.75
44	Wash. Senators Team	20.00	10.00	6.00
45	Dick Groat	9.00	4.50	2.57
46a	Lou Sleater (Yellow name.)	90.00	45.00	27.00
46b	Lou Sleater (White name.)	9.00	4.50	2.57
47	Roger Maris **RC**	425.00	210.00	125.00
48	Chuck Harmon	9.00	4.50	2.57
49	Smoky Burgess	9.00	4.50	2.57
50a	Billy Pierce (Yellow team.)	90.00	45.00	27.00
50b	Billy Pierce (White team.)	9.00	4.50	2.57
51	Del Rice	9.00	4.50	2.57
52a	Bob Clemente (Yellow team.)	400.00	200.00	120.00
52b	Bob Clemente (White team.)	300.00	150.00	75.00
53a	Morrie Martin (Yellow name.)	90.00	45.00	27.00
53b	Morrie Martin (White name.)	9.00	4.50	2.57
54	Norm Siebern **RC**	12.50	6.25	3.75
55	Chico Carrasquel	9.00	4.50	2.57
56	Bill Fischer	9.00	4.50	2.57
57a	Tim Thompson (Yellow name.)	90.00	45.00	27.00
57b	Tim Thompson (White name.)	9.00	4.50	2.57
58a	Art Schult (Yellow team.)	90.00	45.00	27.00
58b	Art Schult (White team.)	9.00	4.50	2.57
59	Dave Sisler	9.00	4.50	2.57
60a	Del Ennis (Yellow name.)	90.00	45.00	27.00
60b	Del Ennis (White name.)	9.00	4.50	2.57
61a	Darrell Johnson (Yellow name.)	100.00	50.00	30.00
61b	Darrell Johnson (White name.)	15.00	7.50	4.50
62	Joe DeMaestri	9.00	4.50	2.57
63	Joe Nuxhall	9.00	4.50	2.57
64	Joe Lonnett	9.00	4.50	2.57
65a	Von McDaniel (Yellow name.)	90.00	45.00	27.00
65b	Von McDaniel (White name.)	9.00	4.50	2.57
66	Lee Walls	9.00	4.50	2.57
67	Joe Ginsberg	9.00	4.50	2.57
68	Daryl Spencer	9.00	4.50	2.57
69	Wally Burnette	9.00	4.50	2.57
70a	Al Kaline (Yellow name.)	300.00	150.00	90.00
70b	Al Kaline (White name.)	100.00	50.00	25.00
71	1957 Dodgers Team	80.00	40.00	20.00
72	Bud Byerly (Photo actually Hal Griggs.)	9.00	4.50	2.57
73	Pete Daley	9.00	4.50	2.57
74	Roy Face	9.00	4.50	2.57
75	Gus Bell	9.00	4.50	2.57
76a	Dick Farrell (Yellow team.)	90.00	45.00	27.00
76b	Dick Farrell (White team.)	9.00	4.50	2.57
77a	Don Zimmer (Yellow team.)	100.00	50.00	30.00
77b	Don Zimmer (White team.)	15.00	7.50	4.50
78a	Ernie Johnson (Yellow name.)	90.00	45.00	27.00
78b	Ernie Johnson (White name.)	9.00	4.50	2.57
79a	Dick Williams (Yellow team.)	90.00	45.00	27.00
79b	Dick Williams (White team.)	9.00	4.50	2.57
80	Dick Drott	9.00	4.50	2.57
81a	Steve Boros **RC** (Yellow team.)	90.00	45.00	27.00
81b	Steve Boros **RC** (White team.)	9.00	4.50	2.57
82	Ronnie Kline	9.00	4.50	2.57
83	Bob Hazle **RC**	9.00	4.50	2.57
84	Billy O'Dell	9.00	4.50	2.57
85a	Luis Aparicio (Yellow team.)	140.00	70.00	40.00
85b	Luis Aparicio (White team.)	30.00	15.00	9.00
86	Valmy Thomas	9.00	4.50	2.57
87	Johnny Kucks	10.00	5.00	3.00
88	Duke Snider	45.00	22.50	13.50
89	Billy Klaus	9.00	4.50	2.57
90	Robin Roberts	30.00	15.00	9.00
91	Chuck Tanner	9.00	4.50	2.57
92a	Clint Courtney (Yellow name.)	90.00	45.00	27.00
92b	Clint Courtney (White name.)	9.00	4.50	2.57
93	Sandy Amoros	12.00	6.00	3.50
94	Bob Skinner	9.00	4.50	2.57
95	Frank Bolling	9.00	4.50	2.57
96	Joe Durham	9.00	4.50	2.57
97a	Larry Jackson (Yellow name.)	90.00	45.00	27.00
97b	Larry Jackson (White name.)	9.00	4.50	2.57
98a	Billy Hunter (Yellow name.)	90.00	45.00	27.00
98b	Billy Hunter (White name.)	9.00	4.50	2.57
99	Bobby Adams	9.00	4.50	2.57
100a	Early Wynn (Yellow team.)	110.00	55.00	30.00
100b	Early Wynn (White team.)	20.00	10.00	6.00
101a	Bobby Richardson (Yellow name.)	100.00	50.00	30.00
101b	Bobby Richardson (White name.)	30.00	15.00	9.00
102	George Strickland	9.00	4.50	2.57
103	Jerry Lynch	9.00	4.50	2.57
104	Jim Pendleton	9.00	4.50	2.57
105	Billy Gardner	9.00	4.50	2.57
106	Dick Schofield	9.00	4.50	2.57
107	Ossie Virgil	9.00	4.50	2.57
108a	Jim Landis (Yellow team.)	90.00	45.00	27.00
108b	Jim Landis (White team.)	9.00	4.50	2.57
109	Herb Plews	9.00	4.50	2.57
110	Johnny Logan	9.00	4.50	2.57
111	Stu Miller	9.00	4.50	2.57
112	Gus Zernial	9.00	4.50	2.57
113	Jerry Walker	9.00	4.50	2.57
114	Irv Noren	9.00	4.50	2.57
115	Jim Bunning	20.00	10.00	6.00
116	Dave Philley	9.00	4.50	2.57
117	Frank Torre	9.00	4.50	2.57
118	Harvey Haddix	9.00	4.50	2.57
119	Harry Chiti	9.00	4.50	2.57
120	Johnny Podres	12.00	6.00	3.50
121	Eddie Miksis	9.00	4.50	2.57
122	Walt Moryn	9.00	4.50	2.57
123	Dick Tomanek	9.00	4.50	2.57
124	Bobby Usher	9.00	4.50	2.57
125	Al Dark	9.00	4.50	2.57
126	Stan Palys	9.00	4.50	2.57
127	Tom Sturdivant	10.00	5.00	3.00
128	Willie Kirkland **RC**	9.00	4.50	2.57
129	Jim Derrington	9.00	4.50	2.57
130	Jackie Jensen	10.00	5.00	3.00
131	Bob Henrich	9.00	4.50	2.57
132	Vernon Law	9.00	4.50	2.57
133	Russ Nixon	9.00	4.50	2.57
134	Phila. Phillies Team	16.00	8.00	4.75
135	Mike Drabowsky	9.00	4.50	2.57
136	Jim Finingan	9.00	4.50	2.57
137	Russ Kemmerer	9.00	4.50	2.57
138	Earl Torgeson	9.00	4.50	2.57
139	George Brunet	9.00	4.50	2.57
140	Wes Covington	9.00	4.50	2.57
141	Ken Lehman	9.00	4.50	2.57
142	Enos Slaughter	30.00	15.00	9.00
143	Billy Muffett	9.00	4.50	2.57
144	Bobby Morgan	9.00	4.50	2.57
145	Not Issued			
146	Dick Gray	9.00	4.50	2.57
147	Don McMahon **RC**	9.00	4.50	2.57
148	Billy Consolo	9.00	4.50	2.57
149	Tom Acker	9.00	4.50	2.57
150	Mickey Mantle	775.00	350.00	215.00
151	Buddy Pritchard	9.00	4.50	2.57
152	Johnny Antonelli	9.00	4.50	2.57
153	Les Moss	9.00	4.50	2.57
154	Harry Byrd	9.00	4.50	2.57
155	Hector Lopez	9.00	4.50	2.57
156	Dick Hyde	9.00	4.50	2.57
157	Dee Fondy	9.00	4.50	2.57
158	Cleve. Indians Team	25.00	12.50	7.50
159	Taylor Phillips	10.00	5.00	3.00
160	Don Hoak	9.00	4.50	2.57
161	Don Larsen	25.00	12.50	7.50
162	Gil Hodges	30.00	15.00	9.00
163	Jim Wilson	9.00	4.50	2.57
164	Bob Taylor	9.00	4.50	2.57
165	Bob Nieman	9.00	4.50	2.57
166	Danny O'Connell	9.00	4.50	2.57
167	Frank Baumann	9.00	4.50	2.57
168	Joe Cunningham	9.00	4.50	2.57
169	Ralph Terry	9.00	4.50	2.57
170	Vic Wertz	9.00	4.50	2.57
171	Harry Anderson	9.00	4.50	2.57
172	Don Gross	9.00	4.50	2.57
173	Eddie Yost	9.00	4.50	2.57
174	K.C. Athletics Team	20.00	10.00	6.00
175	Marv Throneberry **RC**	25.00	12.50	7.50
176	Bob Buhl	9.00	4.50	2.57
177	Al Smith	9.00	4.50	2.57
178	Ted Kluszewski	20.00	10.00	6.00
179	Willy Miranda	9.00	4.50	2.57
180	Lindy McDaniel	9.00	4.50	2.57
181	Willie Jones	9.00	4.50	2.57
182	Joe Caffie	9.00	4.50	2.57
183	Dave Jolly	9.00	4.50	2.57
184	Elvin Tappe	9.00	4.50	2.57
185	Ray Boone	9.00	4.50	2.57
186	Jack Meyer	9.00	4.50	2.57
187	Sandy Koufax	225.00	137.50	68.75
188	Milt Bolling (Photo actually Lou Berberet.)	9.00	4.50	2.57
189	George Susce	9.00	4.50	2.57
190	Red Schoendienst	25.00	10.00	6.00
191	Art Ceccarelli	9.00	4.50	2.57
192	Milt Graff	9.00	4.50	2.57
193	Jerry Lumpe **RC**	12.50	6.25	3.75
194	Roger Craig	9.00	4.50	2.57
195	Whitey Lockman	9.00	4.50	2.57
196	Mike Garcia	9.00	4.50	2.57
197	Haywood Sullivan	9.00	4.50	2.57
198	Bill Virdon	9.00	4.50	2.57
199	Don Blasingame	9.00	4.50	2.57
200	Bob Keegan	9.00	4.50	2.57
201	Jim Bolger	9.00	4.50	2.57
202	Woody Held **RC**	9.00	4.50	2.57
203	Al Walker	9.00	4.50	2.57
204	Leo Kiely	9.00	4.50	2.57
205	Johnny Temple	9.00	4.50	2.57
206	Bob Shaw	9.00	4.50	2.57
207	Solly Hemus	9.00	4.50	2.57
208	Cal McLish	9.00	4.50	2.57
209	Bob Anderson	9.00	4.50	2.57
210	Wally Moon	9.00	4.50	2.57
211	Pete Burnside	9.00	4.50	2.57
212	Bubba Phillips	9.00	4.50	2.57
213	Red Wilson	9.00	4.50	2.57
214	Willard Schmidt	9.00	4.50	2.57
215	Jim Gilliam	12.50	6.25	3.75
216	St. Louis Cards Team	25.00	12.50	7.50
217	Jack Harshman	9.00	4.50	2.57
218	Dick Rand	9.00	4.50	2.57
219	Camilo Pascual	9.00	4.50	2.57
220	Tom Brewer	9.00	4.50	2.57
221	Jerry Kindall	9.00	4.50	2.57
222	Bud Daley	9.00	4.50	2.57
223	Andy Pafko	9.00	4.50	2.57
224	Bob Grim	10.00	5.00	3.00
225	Billy Goodman	9.00	4.50	2.57
226	Bob Smith (Photo actually Bobby Gene Smith.)	9.00	4.50	2.57
227	Gene Stephens	9.00	4.50	2.57
228	Duke Maas	9.00	4.50	2.57
229	Frank Zupo	9.00	4.50	2.57
230	Richie Ashburn	30.00	15.00	9.00
231	Lloyd Merritt	9.00	4.50	2.57
232	Reno Bertoia	9.00	4.50	2.57
233	Mickey Vernon	9.00	4.50	2.57
234	Carl Sawatski	9.00	4.50	2.57
235	Tom Gorman	9.00	4.50	2.57
236	Ed FitzGerald	9.00	4.50	2.57
237	Bill Wight	9.00	4.50	2.57
238	Bill Mazeroski	30.00	15.00	9.00
239	Chuck Stobbs	9.00	4.50	2.57
240	Moose Skowron	20.00	10.00	6.00
241	Dick Littlefield	9.00	4.50	2.57
242	Johnny Klippstein	9.00	4.50	2.57
243	Larry Raines	9.00	4.50	2.57
244	Don Demeter **RC**	9.00	4.50	2.57
245	Frank Lary **RC**	9.00	4.50	2.57
246	New York Yankees Team	100.00	50.00	25.00
247	Casey Wise	9.00	4.50	2.57
248	Herm Wehmeier	9.00	4.50	2.57
249	Ray Moore	9.00	4.50	2.57
250	Roy Sievers	9.00	4.50	2.57

251	Warren Hacker	9.00	4.50	2.57
252	Bob Trowbridge	9.00	4.50	2.57
253	Don Mueller	9.00	4.50	2.57
254	Alex Grammas	9.00	4.50	2.57
255	Bob Turley	25.00	12.50	7.50
256	Chicago White Sox Team	20.00	10.00	6.00
257	Hal Smith	9.00	4.50	2.57
258	Carl Erskine	17.50	8.75	5.25
259	Al Pilarcik	9.00	4.50	2.57
260	Frank Malzone	9.00	4.50	2.57
261	Turk Lown	9.00	4.50	2.57
262	Johnny Groth	9.00	4.50	2.57
263	Eddie Bressoud	9.00	4.50	2.57
264	Jack Sanford	9.00	4.50	2.57
265	Pete Runnels	9.00	4.50	2.57
266	Connie Johnson	9.00	4.50	2.57
267	Sherm Lollar	9.00	4.50	2.57
268	Granny Hamner	9.00	4.50	2.57
269	Paul Smith	9.00	4.50	2.57
270	Warren Spahn	80.00	40.00	20.00
271	Billy Martin	20.00	10.00	6.00
272	Ray Crone	9.00	4.50	2.57
273	Hal Smith	9.00	4.50	2.57
274	Rocky Bridges	9.00	4.50	2.57
275	Elston Howard	20.00	10.00	6.00
276	Bobby Avila	9.00	4.50	2.57
277	Virgil Trucks	9.00	4.50	2.57
278	Mack Burk	9.00	4.50	2.57
279	Bob Boyd	9.00	4.50	2.57
280	Jim Piersall	9.00	4.50	2.57
281	Sam Taylor	9.00	4.50	2.57
282	Paul Foytack	9.00	4.50	2.57
283	Ray Shearer	9.00	4.50	2.57
284	Ray Katt	9.00	4.50	2.57
285	Frank Robinson	100.00	50.00	25.00
286	Gino Cimoli	9.00	4.50	2.57
287	Sam Jones	9.00	4.50	2.57
288	Harmon Killebrew	100.00	50.00	25.00
289	Series Hurling Rivals(Lou Burdette, Bobby Shantz)	25.00	12.50	7.50
290	Dick Donovan	9.00	4.50	2.57
291	Don Landrum	9.00	4.50	2.57
292	Ned Garver	9.00	4.50	2.57
293	Gene Freese	9.00	4.50	2.57
294	Hal Jeffcoat	9.00	4.50	2.57
295	Minnie Minoso	20.00	10.00	6.00
296	Ryne Duren **RC**	50.00	25.00	15.00
297	Don Buddin	9.00	4.50	2.57
298	Jim Hearn	9.00	4.50	2.57
299	Harry Simpson	9.00	4.50	2.57
300	League Presidents(Warren Giles, William Harridge)	35.00	17.50	10.00
301	Randy Jackson	9.00	4.50	2.57
302	Mike Baxes	9.00	4.50	2.57
303	Neil Chrisley	9.00	4.50	2.57
304	Tigers' Big Bats(Al Kaline, Harvey Kuenn)	35.00	17.50	10.00
305	Clem Labine	12.50	6.25	3.75
306	Whammy Douglas	9.00	4.50	2.57
307	Brooks Robinson	100.00	50.00	25.00
308	Paul Giel	9.00	4.50	2.57
309	Gail Harris	9.00	4.50	2.57
310	Ernie Banks	100.00	50.00	30.00
311	Bob Purkey	9.00	4.50	2.57
312	Boston Red Sox Team	25.00	12.50	7.50
313	Bob Rush	9.00	4.50	2.57
314	Dodgers' Boss & Power(Duke Snider, Walter Alston)	35.00	17.50	10.00
315	Bob Friend	9.00	4.50	2.57
316	Tito Francona	9.00	4.50	2.57
317	Albie Pearson **RC**	10.00	5.00	3.00
318	Frank House	9.00	4.50	2.57
319	Lou Skizas	9.00	4.50	2.57
320	Whitey Ford	80.00	40.00	20.00
321	Sluggers Supreme(Ted Kluszewski, Ted Williams)	100.00	50.00	25.00
322	Harding Peterson	9.00	4.50	2.57
323	Elmer Valo	9.00	4.50	2.57
324	Hoyt Wilhelm	20.00	10.00	6.00
325	Joe Adcock	9.00	4.50	2.57
326	Bob Miller	9.00	4.50	2.57
327	Chicago Cubs Team	20.00	10.00	6.00
328	Ike Delock	9.00	4.50	2.57
329	Bob Cerv	9.00	4.50	2.57
330	Ed Bailey	9.00	4.50	2.57
331	Pedro Ramos	9.00	4.50	2.57
332	Jim King	9.00	4.50	2.57
333	Andy Carey	10.00	5.00	3.00
334	Mound Aces(Bob Friend, Billy Pierce)	12.00	6.00	3.50
335	Ruben Gomez	9.00	4.50	2.57
336	Bert Hamric	9.00	4.50	2.57
337	Hank Aguirre	9.00	4.50	2.57
338	Walt Dropo	9.00	4.50	2.57
339	Fred Hatfield	9.00	4.50	2.57
340	Don Newcombe	25.00	12.50	7.50

341	Pittsburgh Pirates Team	30.00	15.00	9.00
342	Jim Brosnan	9.00	4.50	2.57
343	Orlando Cepeda **RC**	100.00	50.00	25.00
344	Bob Porterfield	9.00	4.50	2.57
345	Jim Hegan	9.00	4.50	2.57
346	Steve Bilko	9.00	4.50	2.57
347	Don Rudolph	9.00	4.50	2.57
348	Chico Fernandez	9.00	4.50	2.57
349	Murry Dickson	9.00	4.50	2.57
350	Ken Boyer	12.50	6.25	3.75
351	Braves' Fence Busters(Hank Aaron, Joe Adcock, Del Crandall, Eddie Mathews)	90.00	45.00	27.00
352	Herb Score	12.50	6.25	3.75
353	Stan Lopata	9.00	4.50	2.57
354	Art Ditmar	10.00	5.00	3.00
355	Bill Bruton	9.00	4.50	2.57
356	Bob Malkmus	9.00	4.50	2.57
357	Danny McDevitt	9.00	4.50	2.57
358	Gene Baker	9.00	4.50	2.57
359	Billy Loes	9.00	4.50	2.57
360	Roy McMillan	9.00	4.50	2.57
361	Mike Fornieles	9.00	4.50	2.57
362	Ray Jablonski	9.00	4.50	2.57
363	Don Elston	9.00	4.50	2.57
364	Earl Battey	9.00	4.50	2.57
365	Tom Morgan	9.00	4.50	2.57
366	Gene Green	9.00	4.50	2.57
367	Jack Urban	9.00	4.50	2.57
368	Rocky Colavito	50.00	25.00	15.00
369	Ralph Lumenti	9.00	4.50	2.57
370	Yogi Berra	150.00	75.00	45.00
371	Marty Keough	9.00	4.50	2.57
372	Don Cardwell	9.00	4.50	2.57
373	Joe Pignatano	9.00	4.50	2.57
374	Brooks Lawrence	9.00	4.50	2.57
375	Pee Wee Reese	45.00	22.50	13.50
376	Charley Rabe	9.00	4.50	2.57
377a	Milwaukee Braves Team (Alphabetical checklist.)	20.00	10.00	6.00
377b	Milwaukee Braves Team (Numerical checklist.)	140.00	70.00	40.00
378	Hank Sauer	9.00	4.50	2.57
379	Ray Herbert	9.00	4.50	2.57
380	Charley Maxwell	9.00	4.50	2.57
381	Hal Brown	9.00	4.50	2.57
382	Al Cicotte	10.00	5.00	3.00
383	Lou Berberet	9.00	4.50	2.57
384	John Goryl	9.00	4.50	2.57
385	Wilmer Mizell	9.00	4.50	2.57
386	Birdie's Young Sluggers (Ed Bailey, Frank Robinson, Birdie Tebbetts)	20.00	10.00	6.00
387	Wally Post	9.00	4.50	2.57
388	Billy Moran	9.00	4.50	2.57
389	Bill Taylor	9.00	4.50	2.57
390	Del Crandall	9.00	4.50	2.57
391	Dave Melton	9.00	4.50	2.57
392	Bennie Daniels	9.00	4.50	2.57
393	Tony Kubek	24.00	12.00	7.00
394	Jim Grant **RC**	10.00	5.00	3.00
395	Willard Nixon	9.00	4.50	2.57
396	Dutch Dotterer	9.00	4.50	2.57
397a	Detroit Tigers Team (Alphabetical checklist.)	15.00	7.50	4.50
397b	Detroit Tigers Team (Numerical checklist.)	140.00	70.00	40.00
398	Gene Woodling	9.00	4.50	2.57
399	Marv Grissom	9.00	4.50	2.57
400	Nellie Fox	25.00	12.50	7.50
401	Don Bessent	9.00	4.50	2.57
402	Bobby Gene Smith	9.00	4.50	2.57
403	Steve Korcheck	9.00	4.50	2.57
404	Curt Simmons	9.00	4.50	2.57
405	Ken Aspromonte	9.00	4.50	2.57
406	Vic Power	9.00	4.50	2.57
407	Carlton Willey	9.00	4.50	2.57
408a	Baltimore Orioles Team (Alphabetical checklist.)	15.00	7.50	4.50
408b	Baltimore Orioles Team (Numerical checklist.)	140.00	70.00	40.00
409	Frank Thomas	9.00	4.50	2.57
410	Murray Wall	9.00	4.50	2.57
411	Tony Taylor **RC**	9.00	4.50	2.57
412	Jerry Staley	9.00	4.50	2.57
413	Jim Davenport **RC**	9.00	4.50	2.57
414	Sammy White	9.00	4.50	2.57
415	Bob Bowman	9.00	4.50	2.57
416	Foster Castleman	9.00	4.50	2.57
417	Carl Furillo	15.00	7.50	4.50
418	World Series Foes(Hank Aaron, Mickey Mantle)	400.00	200.00	100.00
419	Bobby Shantz	15.00	7.50	4.50
420	Vada Pinson **RC**	20.00	10.00	6.00
421	Dixie Howell	9.00	4.50	2.57

422	Norm Zauchin	9.00	4.50	2.57
423	Phil Clark	9.00	4.50	2.57
424	Larry Doby	20.00	10.00	6.00
425	Sam Esposito	9.00	4.50	2.57
426	Johnny O'Brien	9.00	4.50	2.57
427	Al Worthington	9.00	4.50	2.57
428a	Cincinnati Redlegs Team (Alphabetical checklist.)	15.00	7.50	4.50
428b	Cincinnati Redlegs Team (Numerical checklist.)	125.00	65.00	35.00
429	Gus Triandos	9.00	4.50	2.57
430	Bobby Thomson	12.00	6.00	3.50
431	Gene Conley	9.00	4.50	2.57
432	John Powers	9.00	4.50	2.57
433	Pancho Herrera	9.00	4.50	2.57
433a	Pancho Herrera (Printing error, no "a" in Herrera.)	6,000	3,000	1,800
434	Harvey Kuenn	9.00	4.50	2.57
435	Ed Roebuck	9.00	4.50	2.57
436	Rival Fence Busters(Willie Mays, Duke Snider)	80.00	40.00	20.00
437	Bob Speake	9.00	4.50	2.57
438	Whitey Herzog	9.00	4.50	2.57
439	Ray Narleski	9.00	4.50	2.57
440	Ed Mathews	80.00	40.00	20.00
441	Jim Marshall	9.00	4.50	2.57
442	Phil Paine	9.00	4.50	2.57
443	Billy Harrell (SP)	20.00	7.50	4.50
444	Danny Kravitz	9.00	4.50	2.57
445	Bob Smith	9.00	4.50	2.57
446	Carroll Hardy (SP)	20.00	7.50	4.50
447	Ray Monzant	9.00	4.50	2.57
448	Charlie Lau **RC**	13.50	7.00	4.00
449	Gene Fodge	9.00	4.50	2.57
450	Preston Ward (SP)	20.00	7.50	4.50
451	Joe Taylor	9.00	4.50	2.57
452	Roman Mejias	9.00	4.50	2.57
453	Tom Qualters	9.00	4.50	2.57
454	Harry Hanebrink	9.00	4.50	2.57
455	Hal Griggs (Photo actually Bud Byerly.)	9.00	4.50	2.57
456	Dick Brown	9.00	4.50	2.57
457	Milt Pappas **RC**	10.00	5.00	3.00
458	Julio Becquer	9.00	4.50	2.57
459	Ron Blackburn	9.00	4.50	2.57
460	Chuck Essegian	9.00	4.50	2.57
461	Ed Mayer	9.00	4.50	2.57
462	Gary Geiger (SP)	20.00	7.50	4.50
463	Vito Valentinetti	9.00	4.50	2.57
464	Curt Flood **RC**	30.00	15.00	9.00
465	Arnie Portocarrero	9.00	4.50	2.57
466	Pete Whisenant	9.00	4.50	2.57
467	Glen Hobbie	9.00	4.50	2.57
468	Bob Schmidt	9.00	4.50	2.57
469	Don Ferrarese	9.00	4.50	2.57
470	R.C. Stevens	9.00	4.50	2.57
471	Lenny Green	9.00	4.50	2.57
472	Joe Jay	9.00	4.50	2.57
473	Bill Renna	9.00	4.50	2.57
474	Roman Semproch	9.00	4.50	2.57
475	All-Star Managers(Fred Haney, Casey Stengel)	35.00	15.00	9.00
476	Stan Musial (All-Star)	36.00	17.50	10.00
477	Bill Skowron (All-Star)	15.00	7.50	4.50
478	Johnny Temple (All-Star)	10.00	5.00	3.00
479	Nellie Fox (All-Star)	20.00	7.50	4.50
480	Eddie Mathews (All-Star)	30.00	12.50	7.50
481	Frank Malzone (All-Star)	10.00	5.00	3.00
482	Ernie Banks (All-Star)	30.00	15.00	9.00
483	Luis Aparicio (All-Star)	22.50	10.00	6.00
484	Frank Robinson (All-Star)	30.00	15.00	9.00
485	Ted Williams (All-Star)	125.00	60.00	36.00
486	Willie Mays (All-Star)	75.00	37.50	18.75
487	Mickey Mantle (All-Star) (Triple Print)	150.00	75.00	45.00
488	Hank Aaron (All-Star)	60.00	27.50	16.50
489	Jackie Jensen (All-Star)	12.00	6.00	3.50
490	Ed Bailey (All-Star)	10.00	5.00	3.00
491	Sherman Lollar (All-Star)	10.00	5.00	3.00
492	Bob Friend (All-Star)	10.00	5.00	3.00
493	Bob Turley (All-Star)	15.00	7.50	4.50
494	Warren Spahn (All-Star)	30.00	15.00	9.00
495	Herb Score (All-Star)	15.00	7.50	4.50
----	Contest Card (All-Star Game, July 8)	70.00	35.00	20.00
----	Felt Emblems Insert Card	45.00	22.50	13.50

1959 Topps

These 2-1/2" x 3-1/2" cards have a round photograph on front with a solid-color background above and below and a white border. A facsimile autograph is found across the photo. The 572-card set marks the largest set issued to that time. Card numbers below 507 have red and green printing on back with the card number in white in a green box. On high number cards beginning with #507, the printing is black and red and the card number is in a black box. Specialty cards include multiple-player cards, team cards with checklists on back, "All-Star" cards, "Baseball Thrills," and 31 "Rookie Stars." There is also a card of the commissioner, Ford Frick, and one of Roy Campanella in a wheelchair. A handful of cards can be found with and without lines added to the biographies on back indicating trades or demotions; those without the added lines are scarcer and more valuable and are not included in the complete set price. Card numbers 199-286 can be found with either white or gray backs, with the gray stock being the less common.

		NM	E	VG
	Complete Set (572):	12,000	6,000	3,600
	Common Player (1-506):	7.00	3.50	2.00
	Common Player (507-572):	15.00	7.50	4.50
1	Ford Frick	80.00	40.00	20.00
2	Eddie Yost	12.00	3.50	2.00
3	Don McMahon	7.00	3.50	2.00
4	Albie Pearson	7.00	3.50	2.00
5	Dick Donovan	7.00	3.50	2.00
6	Alex Grammas	7.00	3.50	2.00
7	Al Pilarcik	7.00	3.50	2.00
8	Philadelphia Phillies Team (SP)	90.00	45.00	27.50
9	Paul Giel	7.00	3.50	2.00
10	Mickey Mantle	800.00	400.00	240.00
11	Billy Hunter	7.00	3.50	2.00
12	Vern Law	7.00	3.50	2.00
13	Dick Gernert	7.00	3.50	2.00
14	Pete Whisenant	7.00	3.50	2.00
15	Dick Drott	7.00	3.50	2.00
16	Joe Pignatano	7.00	3.50	2.00
17	Danny's All-Stars (Ted Kluszewski, Danny Murtaugh, Frank J. Thomas)	13.50	7.00	4.00
18	Jack Urban	7.00	3.50	2.00
19	Ed Bressoud	7.00	3.50	2.00
20	Duke Snider	45.00	20.00	12.00
21	Connie Johnson	7.00	3.50	2.00
22	Al Smith	7.00	3.50	2.00
23	Murry Dickson	7.00	3.50	2.00
24	Red Wilson	7.00	3.50	2.00
25	Don Hoak	7.00	3.50	2.00
26	Chuck Stobbs	7.00	3.50	2.00
27	Andy Pafko	7.00	3.50	2.00
28	Red Worthington	7.00	3.50	2.00
29	Jim Bolger	7.00	3.50	2.00
30	Nellie Fox	30.00	15.00	9.00
31	Ken Lehman	7.00	3.50	2.00
32	Don Buddin	7.00	3.50	2.00
33	Ed Fitz Gerald	7.00	3.50	2.00
34	Pitchers Beware (Al Kaline, Charlie Maxwell)	25.00	12.50	7.50
35	Ted Kluszewski	17.50	8.75	5.25
36	Hank Aguirre	7.00	3.50	2.00
37	Gene Green	7.00	3.50	2.00
38	Morrie Martin	7.00	3.50	2.00
39	Ed Bouchee	7.00	3.50	2.00
40a	Warren Spahn (Born 1931.)	100.00	50.00	25.00
40b	Warren Spahn (Born 1931, "3" partially obscured.)	100.00	50.00	25.00
40c	Warren Spahn (Born 1921.)	60.00	30.00	18.00
41	Bob Martyn	7.00	3.50	2.00
42	Murray Wall	7.00	3.50	2.00
43	Steve Bilko	7.00	3.50	2.00
44	Vito Valentinetti	7.00	3.50	2.00
45	Andy Carey	9.00	4.50	2.75
46	Bill Henry	7.00	3.50	2.00
47	Jim Finigan	7.00	3.50	2.00
48	Baltimore Orioles Team	17.50	8.75	5.25
49	Bill Hall	7.00	3.50	2.00
50	Willie Mays	150.00	75.00	45.00
51	Rip Coleman	7.00	3.50	2.00
52	Coot Veal	7.00	3.50	2.00
53	Stan Williams **RC**	20.00	10.00	6.00
54	Mel Roach	7.00	3.50	2.00
55	Tom Brewer	7.00	3.50	2.00
56	Carl Sawatski	7.00	3.50	2.00
57	Al Cicotte	7.00	3.50	2.00
58	Eddie Miksis	7.00	3.50	2.00
59	Irv Noren	7.00	3.50	2.00
60	Bob Turley	15.00	7.50	4.50
61	Dick Brown	7.00	3.50	2.00
62	Tony Taylor	7.00	3.50	2.00
63	Jim Hearn	7.00	3.50	2.00
64	Joe DeMaestri	7.00	3.50	2.00
65	Frank Torre	7.00	3.50	2.00
66	Joe Ginsberg	7.00	3.50	2.00
67	Brooks Lawrence	7.00	3.50	2.00
68	Dick Schofield	7.00	3.50	2.00
69	San Francisco Giants Team	27.50	14.00	8.00
70	Harvey Kuenn	7.00	3.50	2.00
71	Don Bessent	7.00	3.50	2.00
72	Bill Renna	7.00	3.50	2.00
73	Ron Jackson	7.00	3.50	2.00
74	Directing the Power (Cookie Lavagetto, Jim Lemon, Roy Sievers)	9.00	4.50	2.75
75	Sam Jones	7.00	3.50	2.00
76	Bobby Richardson	25.00	12.50	7.50
77	John Goryl	7.00	3.50	2.00
78	Pedro Ramos	7.00	3.50	2.00
79	Harry Chiti	7.00	3.50	2.00
80	Minnie Minoso	15.00	7.50	4.50
81	Hal Jeffcoat	7.00	3.50	2.00
82	Bob Boyd	7.00	3.50	2.00
83	Bob Smith	7.00	3.50	2.00
84	Reno Bertoia	7.00	3.50	2.00
85	Harry Anderson	7.00	3.50	2.00
86	Bob Keegan	7.00	3.50	2.00
87	Danny O'Connell	7.00	3.50	2.00
88	Herb Score	15.00	7.50	4.50
89	Billy Gardner	7.00	3.50	2.00
90	Bill Skowron (SP)	55.00	30.00	18.00
91	Herb Moford	7.00	3.50	2.00
92	Dave Philley	7.00	3.50	2.00
93	Julio Becquer	7.00	3.50	2.00
94	Chicago White Sox Team	30.00	15.00	9.00
95	Carl Willey	7.00	3.50	2.00
96	Lou Berberet	7.00	3.50	2.00
97	Jerry Lynch	7.00	3.50	2.00
98	Arnie Portocarrero	7.00	3.50	2.00
99	Ted Kazanski	7.00	3.50	2.00
100	Bob Cerv	7.00	3.50	2.00
101	Alex Kellner	7.00	3.50	2.00
102	Felipe Alou **RC**	25.00	12.50	7.50
103	Billy Goodman	7.00	3.50	2.00
104	Del Rice	7.00	3.50	2.00
105	Lee Walls	7.00	3.50	2.00
106	Hal Woodeshick	7.00	3.50	2.00
107	Norm Larker **RC**	10.00	5.00	3.00
108	Zack Monroe	9.00	4.50	2.75
109	Bob Schmidt	7.00	3.50	2.00
110	George Witt	7.00	3.50	2.00
111	Cincinnati Red Legs Team	16.00	8.00	4.75
112	Billy Consolo	7.00	3.50	2.00
113	Taylor Phillips	7.00	3.50	2.00
114	Earl Battey	7.00	3.50	2.00
115	Mickey Vernon	7.00	3.50	2.00
116	Bob Allison **RC**	13.50	7.00	4.00
117	John Blanchard **RC**	15.00	7.50	4.50
118	John Buzhardt	7.00	3.50	2.00
119	John Callison **RC**	12.50	6.25	3.75
120	Chuck Coles	7.00	3.50	2.00
121	Bob Conley	7.00	3.50	2.00
122	Bennie Daniels	7.00	3.50	2.00
123	Don Dillard	7.00	3.50	2.00
124	Dan Dobbek	7.00	3.50	2.00
125	Ron Fairly **RC**	13.50	6.75	4.00
126	Eddie Haas	7.00	3.50	2.00
127	Kent Hadley	7.00	3.50	2.00
128	Bob Hartman	7.00	3.50	2.00
129	Frank Herrera	7.00	3.50	2.00
130	Lou Jackson	7.00	3.50	2.00
131	Deron Johnson **RC**	10.00	5.00	3.00
132	Don Lee	7.00	3.50	2.00
133	Bob Lillis **RC**	7.00	3.50	2.00
134	Jim McDaniel	7.00	3.50	2.00
135	Gene Oliver	7.00	3.50	2.00
136	Jim O'Toole **RC**	7.50	3.75	2.25
137	Dick Ricketts	7.00	3.50	2.00
138	John Romano	7.00	3.50	2.00
139	Ed Sadowski	7.00	3.50	2.00
140	Charlie Secrest	7.00	3.50	2.00
141	Joe Shipley	7.00	3.50	2.00
142	Dick Stigman	7.00	3.50	2.00
143	Willie Tasby	7.00	3.50	2.00
144	Jerry Walker	7.00	3.50	2.00
145	Dom Zanni	7.00	3.50	2.00
146	Jerry Zimmerman	7.00	3.50	2.00
147	Cubs' Clubbers (Ernie Banks, Dale Long, Walt Moryn)	20.00	10.00	6.00
148	Mike McCormick	7.00	3.50	2.00
149	Jim Bunning	20.00	10.00	6.00
150	Stan Musial	115.00	60.00	35.00
151	Bob Malkmus	7.00	3.50	2.00
152	Johnny Klippstein	7.00	3.50	2.00
153	Jim Marshall	7.00	3.50	2.00
154	Ray Herbert	7.00	3.50	2.00
155	Enos Slaughter	20.00	10.00	6.00
156	Ace Hurlers (Billy Pierce, Robin Roberts)	12.50	6.25	3.75
157	Felix Mantilla	7.00	3.50	2.00
158	Walt Dropo	7.00	3.50	2.00
159	Bob Shaw	7.00	3.50	2.00
160	Dick Groat	7.00	3.50	2.00
161	Frank Baumann	7.00	3.50	2.00
162	Bobby G. Smith	7.00	3.50	2.00
163	Sandy Koufax	160.00	80.00	40.00
164	Johnny Groth	7.00	3.50	2.00
165	Bill Bruton	7.00	3.50	2.00
166	Destruction Crew (Rocky Colavito, Larry Doby, Minnie Minoso)	20.00	10.00	6.00
167	Duke Maas	7.00	3.50	2.00
168	Carroll Hardy	7.00	3.50	2.00
169	Ted Abernathy	7.00	3.50	2.00
170	Gene Woodling	7.00	3.50	2.00
171	Willard Schmidt	7.00	3.50	2.00
172	Kansas City Athletics Team	16.00	8.00	4.75
173	Bill Monbouquette **RC**	7.00	3.50	2.00
174	Jim Pendleton	7.00	3.50	2.00
175	Dick Farrell	7.00	3.50	2.00
176	Preston Ward	7.00	3.50	2.00
177	Johnny Briggs	7.00	3.50	2.00
178	Ruben Amaro	7.00	3.50	2.00
179	Don Rudolph	7.00	3.50	2.00
180	Yogi Berra	90.00	45.00	20.00
181	Bob Porterfield	7.00	3.50	2.00
182	Milt Graff	7.00	3.50	2.00
183	Stu Miller	7.00	3.50	2.00
184	Harvey Haddix	7.00	3.50	2.00
185	Jim Busby	7.00	3.50	2.00
186	Mudcat Grant	7.00	3.50	2.00
187	Bubba Phillips	7.00	3.50	2.00
188	Juan Pizarro	7.00	3.50	2.00
189	Neil Chrisley	7.00	3.50	2.00
190	Bill Virdon	7.00	3.50	2.00
191	Russ Kemmerer	7.00	3.50	2.00
192	Charley Beamon	7.00	3.50	2.00
193	Sammy Taylor	7.00	3.50	2.00
194	Jim Brosnan	7.00	3.50	2.00
195	Rip Repulski	7.00	3.50	2.00
196	Billy Moran	7.00	3.50	2.00
197	Ray Semproch	7.00	3.50	2.00
198	Jim Davenport	7.00	3.50	2.00
199	Leo Kiely	7.00	3.50	2.00
200	Warren Giles	20.00	10.00	6.00
201	Tom Acker	7.00	3.50	2.00
202	Roger Maris	120.00	60.00	30.00
203	Ozzie Virgil	7.00	3.50	2.00
204	Casey Wise	7.00	3.50	2.00
205	Don Larsen	20.00	10.00	6.00
206	Carl Furillo	20.00	10.00	6.00
207	George Strickland	7.00	3.50	2.00
208	Willie Jones	7.00	3.50	2.00
209	Lenny Green	7.00	3.50	2.00
210	Ed Bailey	7.00	3.50	2.00
211	Bob Blaylock	7.00	3.50	2.00
212	Fence Busters (Hank Aaron, Eddie Mathews)	65.00	32.00	17.00
213	Jim Rivera	7.00	3.50	2.00
214	Marcelino Solis	7.00	3.50	2.00
215	Jim Lemon	7.00	3.50	2.00
216	Andre Rodgers	7.00	3.50	2.00
217	Carl Erskine	12.50	6.25	3.75
218	Roman Mejias	7.00	3.50	2.00
219	George Zuverink	7.00	3.50	2.00
220	Frank Malzone	7.00	3.50	2.00
221	Bob Bowman	7.00	3.50	2.00
222	Bobby Shantz	15.00	7.50	4.50
223	St. Louis Cardinals Team	20.00	10.00	6.00
224	Claude Osteen **RC**	7.50	3.75	2.25
225	Johnny Logan	7.00	3.50	2.00
226	Art Ceccarelli	7.00	3.50	2.00
227	Hal Smith	7.00	3.50	2.00
228	Don Gross	7.00	3.50	2.00
229	Vic Power	7.00	3.50	2.00
230	Bill Fischer	7.00	3.50	2.00
231	Ellis Burton	7.00	3.50	2.00
232	Eddie Kasko	7.00	3.50	2.00
233	Paul Foytack	7.00	3.50	2.00
234	Chuck Tanner	7.00	3.50	2.00
235	Valmy Thomas	7.00	3.50	2.00
236	Ted Bowsfield	7.00	3.50	2.00

Num	Name			
237	Run Preventers(Gil McDougald, Bobby Richardson, Bob Turley)	20.00	10.00	6.00
238	Gene Baker	7.00	3.50	2.00
239	Bob Trowbridge	7.00	3.50	2.00
240	Hank Bauer	13.50	7.00	4.00
241	Billy Muffett	7.00	3.50	2.00
242	Ron Samford	7.00	3.50	2.00
243	Marv Grissom	7.00	3.50	2.00
244	Dick Gray	7.00	3.50	2.00
245	Ned Garver	7.00	3.50	2.00
246	J.W. Porter	7.00	3.50	2.00
247	Don Ferrarese	7.00	3.50	2.00
248	Boston Red Sox Team	16.00	8.00	4.75
249	Bobby Adams	7.00	3.50	2.00
250	Billy O'Dell	7.00	3.50	2.00
251	Cletis Boyer	15.00	7.50	4.50
252	Ray Boone	7.00	3.50	2.00
253	Seth Morehead	7.00	3.50	2.00
254	Zeke Bella	7.00	3.50	2.00
255	Del Ennis	7.00	3.50	2.00
256	Jerry Davie	7.00	3.50	2.00
257	Leon Wagner **RC**	9.00	4.50	2.75
258	Fred Kipp	7.00	3.50	2.00
259	Jim Pisoni	7.00	3.50	2.00
260	Early Wynn	20.00	10.00	6.00
261	Gene Stephens	7.00	3.50	2.00
262	Hitters' Foes(Don Drysdale, Clem Labine, Johnny Podres)	20.00	10.00	6.00
263	Buddy Daley	7.00	3.50	2.00
264	Chico Carrasquel	7.00	3.50	2.00
265	Ron Kline	7.00	3.50	2.00
266	Woody Held	7.00	3.50	2.00
267	John Romonosky	7.00	3.50	2.00
268	Tito Francona	7.00	3.50	2.00
269	Jack Meyer	7.00	3.50	2.00
270	Gil Hodges	20.00	10.00	6.00
271	Orlando Pena **RC**	7.00	3.50	2.00
272	Jerry Lumpe	9.00	4.50	2.75
273	Joe Jay	7.00	3.50	2.00
274	Jerry Kindall	7.00	3.50	2.00
275	Jack Sanford	7.00	3.50	2.00
276	Pete Daley	7.00	3.50	2.00
277	Turk Lown	7.00	3.50	2.00
278	Chuck Essegian	7.00	3.50	2.00
279	Ernie Johnson	7.00	3.50	2.00
280	Frank Bolling	7.00	3.50	2.00
281	Walt Craddock	7.00	3.50	2.00
282	R.C. Stevens	7.00	3.50	2.00
283	Russ Heman	7.00	3.50	2.00
284	Steve Korcheck	7.00	3.50	2.00
285	Joe Cunningham	7.00	3.50	2.00
286	Dean Stone	7.00	3.50	2.00
287	Don Zimmer	12.50	6.25	3.75
288	Dutch Dotterer	7.00	3.50	2.00
289	Johnny Kucks	9.00	4.50	2.75
290	Wes Covington	7.00	3.50	2.00
291	Pitching Partners(Camilo Pascual, Pedro Ramos)	9.00	4.50	2.75
292	Dick Williams	7.00	3.50	2.00
293	Ray Moore	7.00	3.50	2.00
294	Hank Foiles	7.00	3.50	2.00
295	Billy Martin	17.50	8.75	5.25
296	Ernie Broglio **RC**	7.00	3.50	2.00
297	Jackie Brandt **RC**	7.00	3.50	2.00
298	Tex Clevenger	7.00	3.50	2.00
299	Billy Klaus	7.00	3.50	2.00
300	Richie Ashburn	25.00	12.50	7.50
301	Earl Averill	7.00	3.50	2.00
302	Don Mossi	7.00	3.50	2.00
303	Marty Keough	7.00	3.50	2.00
304	Chicago Cubs Team	16.00	8.00	4.75
305	Curt Raydon	7.00	3.50	2.00
306	Jim Gilliam	12.00	6.00	3.50
307	Curt Barclay	7.00	3.50	2.00
308	Norm Siebern	9.00	4.50	2.75
309	Sal Maglie	7.00	3.50	2.00
310	Luis Aparicio	25.00	12.50	7.50
311	Norm Zauchin	7.00	3.50	2.00
312	Don Newcombe	9.00	4.50	2.75
313	Frank House	7.00	3.50	2.00
314	Don Cardwell	7.00	3.50	2.00
315	Joe Adcock	7.00	3.50	2.00
316a	Ralph Lumenti (No optioned statement.)	100.00	50.00	30.00
316b	Ralph Lumenti (Optioned statement.)	7.00	3.50	2.00
317	N.L. Hitting Kings(Richie Ashburn, Willie Mays)	40.00	22.50	13.50
318	Rocky Bridges	7.00	3.50	2.00
319	Dave Hillman	7.00	3.50	2.00
320	Bob Skinner	7.00	3.50	2.00
321a	Bob Giallombardo (No optioned statement.)	100.00	50.00	30.00
321b	Bob Giallombardo (Optioned statement.)	7.00	3.50	2.00
322a	Harry Hanebrink (No trade statement.)	100.00	45.00	27.50
322b	Harry Hanebrink (Trade statement.)	7.00	3.50	2.00
323	Frank Sullivan	7.00	3.50	2.00
324	Don Demeter	7.00	3.50	2.00
325	Ken Boyer	13.50	7.00	4.00
326	Marv Throneberry	10.00	5.00	3.00
327	Gary Bell **RC**	7.00	3.50	2.00
328	Lou Skizas	7.00	3.50	2.00
329	Detroit Tigers Team	17.50	8.75	5.25
330	Gus Triandos	7.00	3.50	2.00
331	Steve Boros	7.00	3.50	2.00
332	Ray Monzant	7.00	3.50	2.00
333	Harry Simpson	7.00	3.50	2.00
334	Glen Hobbie	7.00	3.50	2.00
335	Johnny Temple	7.00	3.50	2.00
336a	Billy Loes (No trade statement.)	100.00	50.00	30.00
336b	Billy Loes (Trade statement.)	7.00	3.50	2.00
337	George Crowe	7.00	3.50	2.00
338	George Anderson **RC** (Sparky)	30.00	15.00	9.00
339	Roy Face	7.00	3.50	2.00
340	Roy Sievers	7.00	3.50	2.00
341	Tom Qualters	7.00	3.50	2.00
342	Ray Jablonski	7.00	3.50	2.00
343	Billy Hoeft	7.00	3.50	2.00
344	Russ Nixon	7.00	3.50	2.00
345	Gil McDougald	12.50	6.25	3.75
346	Batter Bafflers(Tom Brewer, Dave Sisler)	9.00	4.50	2.75
347	Bob Buhl	7.00	3.50	2.00
348	Ted Lepcio	7.00	3.50	2.00
349	Hoyt Wilhelm	15.00	7.50	4.50
350	Ernie Banks	75.00	40.00	20.00
351	Earl Torgeson	7.00	3.50	2.00
352	Robin Roberts	20.00	10.00	6.00
353	Curt Flood	12.00	6.00	3.50
354	Pete Burnside	7.00	3.50	2.00
355	Jim Piersall	9.00	4.50	2.75
356	Bob Mabe	7.00	3.50	2.00
357	Dick Stuart **RC**	10.00	5.00	3.00
358	Ralph Terry	7.00	3.50	2.00
359	Bill White **RC**	12.50	6.25	3.75
360	Al Kaline	40.00	17.50	10.00
361	Willard Nixon	7.00	3.50	2.00
362a	Dolan Nichols (No optioned statement.)	100.00	50.00	30.00
362b	Dolan Nichols (Optioned statement.)	7.00	3.50	2.00
363	Bobby Avila	7.00	3.50	2.00
364	Danny McDevitt	7.00	3.50	2.00
365	Gus Bell	7.00	3.50	2.00
366	Humberto Robinson	7.00	3.50	2.00
367	Cal Neeman	7.00	3.50	2.00
368	Don Mueller	7.00	3.50	2.00
369	Dick Tomanek	7.00	3.50	2.00
370	Pete Runnels	7.00	3.50	2.00
371	Dick Brodowski	7.00	3.50	2.00
372	Jim Hegan	7.00	3.50	2.00
373	Herb Plews	7.00	3.50	2.00
374	Art Ditmar	9.00	4.50	2.75
375	Bob Nieman	7.00	3.50	2.00
376	Hal Naragon	7.00	3.50	2.00
377	Johnny Antonelli	7.00	3.50	2.00
378	Gail Harris	7.00	3.50	2.00
379	Bob Miller	7.00	3.50	2.00
380	Hank Aaron	150.00	70.00	42.50
381	Mike Baxes	7.00	3.50	2.00
382	Curt Simmons	7.00	3.50	2.00
383	Words of Wisdom(Don Larsen, Casey Stengel)	16.00	8.00	4.75
384	Dave Sisler	7.00	3.50	2.00
385	Sherm Lollar	7.00	3.50	2.00
386	Jim Delsing	7.00	3.50	2.00
387	Don Drysdale	25.00	12.50	7.50
388	Bob Will	7.00	3.50	2.00
389	Joe Nuxhall	7.00	3.50	2.00
390	Orlando Cepeda	25.00	12.50	7.50
391	Milt Pappas	7.00	3.50	2.00
392	Whitey Herzog	7.00	3.50	2.00
393	Frank Lary	7.00	3.50	2.00
394	Randy Jackson	7.00	3.50	2.00
395	Elston Howard	15.00	7.50	4.50
396	Bob Rush	7.00	3.50	2.00
397	Washington Senators Team	16.00	8.00	4.75
398	Wally Post	7.00	3.50	2.00
399	Larry Jackson	7.00	3.50	2.00
400	Jackie Jensen	10.00	5.00	3.00
401	Ron Blackburn	7.00	3.50	2.00
402	Hector Lopez	7.00	3.50	2.00
403	Clem Labine	12.50	6.25	3.75
404	Hank Sauer	7.00	3.50	2.00
405	Roy McMillan	7.00	3.50	2.00
406	Solly Drake	7.00	3.50	2.00
407	Moe Drabowsky	7.00	3.50	2.00
408	Keystone Combo(Luis Aparicio, Nellie Fox)	20.00	10.00	6.00
409	Gus Zernial	7.00	3.50	2.00
410	Billy Pierce	7.00	3.50	2.00
411	Whitey Lockman	7.00	3.50	2.00
412	Stan Lopata	7.00	3.50	2.00
413	Camillo (Camilo) Pascual	7.00	3.50	2.00
414	Dale Long	7.00	3.50	2.00
415	Bill Mazeroski	20.00	10.00	6.00
416a	Haywood Sullivan (No circle around copyright symbol, no period after "A" in "U.S.A.")	15.00	7.50	4.50
416b	Haywood Sullivan (No circle around copyright symbol, period added after "A" in "U.S.A.")	7.00	3.50	2.00
416c	Haywood Sullivan (Circle around copyright symbol, period after "A" in "U.S.A.")	7.00	3.50	2.00
417	Virgil Trucks	7.00	3.50	2.00
418	Gino Cimoli	7.00	3.50	2.00
419	Milwaukee Braves Team	16.00	8.00	4.75
420	Rocky Colavito	20.00	10.00	6.00
421	Herm Wehmeier	7.00	3.50	2.00
422	Hobie Landrith	7.00	3.50	2.00
423	Bob Grim	7.00	3.50	2.00
424	Ken Aspromonte	7.00	3.50	2.00
425	Del Crandall	7.00	3.50	2.00
426	Jerry Staley	7.00	3.50	2.00
427	Charlie Neal	7.00	3.50	2.00
428	Buc Hill Aces(Roy Face, Bob Friend, Ron Kline, Vern Law)	9.00	4.50	2.75
429	Bobby Thomson	9.00	4.50	2.75
430	Whitey Ford	40.00	20.00	12.00
431	Whammy Douglas	7.00	3.50	2.00
432	Smoky Burgess	7.00	3.50	2.00
433	Billy Harrell	7.00	3.50	2.00
434	Hal Griggs	7.00	3.50	2.00
435	Frank Robinson	30.00	15.00	9.00
436	Granny Hamner	7.00	3.50	2.00
437	Ike Delock	7.00	3.50	2.00
438	Sam Esposito	7.00	3.50	2.00
439	Brooks Robinson	30.00	15.00	9.00
440	Lou Burdette	7.00	3.50	2.00
441	John Roseboro	7.00	3.50	2.00
442	Ray Narleski	7.00	3.50	2.00
443	Daryl Spencer	7.00	3.50	2.00
444	Ronnie Hansen **RC**	7.00	3.50	2.00
445	Cal McLish	7.00	3.50	2.00
446	Rocky Nelson	7.00	3.50	2.00
447	Bob Anderson	7.00	3.50	2.00
448	Vada Pinson	12.00	6.00	2.40
449	Tom Gorman	7.00	3.50	2.00
450	Ed Mathews	45.00	22.50	13.50
451	Jimmy Constable	7.00	3.50	2.00
452	Chico Fernandez	7.00	3.50	2.00
453	Les Moss	7.00	3.50	2.00
454	Phil Clark	7.00	3.50	2.00
455	Larry Doby	15.00	7.50	4.50
456	Jerry Casale	7.00	3.50	2.00
457	Los Angeles Dodgers Team	20.00	10.00	6.00
458	Gordon Jones	7.00	3.50	2.00
459	Bill Tuttle	7.00	3.50	2.00
460	Bob Friend	7.00	3.50	2.00
461	Mantle Hits 42nd Homer For Crown(Mickey Mantle)	115.00	57.50	34.50
462	Colavito's Great Catch Saves Game(Rocky Colavito)	12.50	6.25	3.75
463	Kaline Becomes Youngest Batting Champ(Al Kaline)	15.00	7.50	4.50
464	Mays' Catch Makes Series History(Willie Mays)	30.00	17.50	10.00
465	Sievers Sets Homer Mark(Roy Sievers)	7.00	3.50	2.00
466	Pierce All-Star Starter(Billy Pierce)	7.00	3.50	2.00
467	Aaron Clubs World Series Homer(Hank Aaron)	35.00	15.00	9.00
468	Snider's Play Brings L.A. Victory(Duke Snider)	15.00	7.50	4.50
469	Hustler Banks Wins M.V.P. Award(Ernie Banks)	16.00	8.00	5.00
470	Musial Raps Out 3,000th Hit(Stan Musial)	25.00	12.50	7.50
471	Tom Sturdivant	9.00	4.50	2.75

472	Gene Freese	7.00	3.50	2.00
473	Mike Fornieles	7.00	3.50	2.00
474	Moe Thacker	7.00	3.50	2.00
475	Jack Harshman	7.00	3.50	2.00
476	Cleveland Indians Team	16.00	8.00	4.75
477	Barry Latman	7.00	3.50	2.00
478	Bob Clemente	165.00	80.00	40.00
479	Lindy McDaniel	7.00	3.50	2.00
480	Red Schoendienst	20.00	10.00	6.00
481	Charley Maxwell	7.00	3.50	2.00
482	Russ Meyer	7.00	3.50	2.00
483	Clint Courtney	7.00	3.50	2.00
484	Willie Kirkland	7.00	3.50	2.00
485	Ryne Duren	10.00	5.00	3.00
486	Sammy White	7.00	3.50	2.00
487	Hal Brown	7.00	3.50	2.00
488	Walt Moryn	7.00	3.50	2.00
489	John C. Powers	7.00	3.50	2.00
490	Frank Thomas	7.00	3.50	2.00
491	Don Blasingame	7.00	3.50	2.00
492	Gene Conley	7.00	3.50	2.00
493	Jim Landis	7.00	3.50	2.00
494	Don Pavletich	7.00	3.50	2.00
495	Johnny Podres	11.00	5.50	3.25
496	Wayne Terwilliger	7.00	3.50	2.00
497	Hal R. Smith	7.00	3.50	2.00
498	Dick Hyde	7.00	3.50	2.00
499	Johnny O'Brien	7.00	3.50	2.00
500	Vic Wertz	7.00	3.50	2.00
501	Bobby Tiefenauer	7.00	3.50	2.00
502	Al Dark	7.00	3.50	2.00
503	Jim Owens	7.00	3.50	2.00
504	Ossie Alvarez	7.00	3.50	2.00
505	Tony Kubek	20.00	10.00	6.00
506	Bob Purkey	7.00	3.50	2.00
507	Bob Hale	15.00	7.50	4.50
508	Art Fowler	15.00	7.50	4.50
509	Norm Cash RC	90.00	40.00	20.00
510	New York Yankees Team	125.00	62.50	31.25
511	George Susce	15.00	7.50	4.50
512	George Altman	15.00	7.50	4.50
513	Tom Carroll	15.00	7.50	4.50
514	Bob Gibson RC	325.00	160.00	90.00
515	Harmon Killebrew	100.00	50.00	30.00
516	Mike Garcia	15.00	7.50	4.50
517	Joe Koppe	15.00	7.50	4.50
518	Mike Cuellar RC	20.00	10.00	6.00
519	Infield Power(Dick			
	Gernert, Frank			
	Malzone, Pete			
	Runnels)	17.50	8.75	5.25
520	Don Elston	15.00	7.50	4.50
521	Gary Geiger	15.00	7.50	4.50
522	Gene Snyder	15.00	7.50	4.50
523	Harry Bright	15.00	7.50	4.50
524	Larry Osborne	15.00	7.50	4.50
525	Jim Coates	17.50	8.75	5.25
526	Bob Speake	15.00	7.50	4.50
527	Solly Hemus	15.00	7.50	4.50
528	Pittsburgh Pirates Team	40.00	20.00	12.00
529	George Bamberger RC	15.00	7.50	4.50
530	Wally Moon	15.00	7.50	4.50
531	Ray Webster	15.00	7.50	4.50
532	Mark Freeman	15.00	7.50	4.50
533	Darrell Johnson	17.50	8.75	5.25
534	Faye Throneberry	15.00	7.50	4.50
535	Ruben Gomez	15.00	7.50	4.50
536	Dan Kravitz	15.00	7.50	4.50
537	Rodolfo Arias	15.00	7.50	4.50
538	Chick King	15.00	7.50	4.50
539	Gary Blaylock	15.00	7.50	4.50
540	Willy Miranda	15.00	7.50	4.50
541	Bob Thurman	15.00	7.50	4.50
542	Jim Perry RC	30.00	15.00	9.00
543	Corsair Outfield			
	Trio(Roberto			
	Clemente, Bob			
	Skinner, Bill Virdon)	75.00	40.00	20.00
544	Lee Tate	15.00	7.50	4.50
545	Tom Morgan	15.00	7.50	4.50
546	Al Schroll	15.00	7.50	4.50
547	Jim Baxes	15.00	7.50	4.50
548	Elmer Singleton	15.00	7.50	4.50
549	Howie Nunn	15.00	7.50	4.50
550	Roy Campanella (Symbol			
	of Courage)	100.00	50.00	30.00
551	Fred Haney (All-Star)	15.00	7.50	4.50
552	Casey Stengel (All-Star)	25.00	12.50	7.50
553	Orlando Cepeda (All-Star)	25.00	12.50	7.50
554	Bill Skowron (All-Star)	22.50	11.00	6.75
555	Bill Mazeroski (All-Star)	25.00	12.50	7.50
556	Nellie Fox (All-Star)	27.50	13.50	8.25
557	Ken Boyer (All-Star)	20.00	10.00	6.00
558	Frank Malzone (All-Star)	15.00	7.50	4.50
559	Ernie Banks (All-Star)	45.00	22.50	13.50
560	Luis Aparicio (All-Star)	24.00	10.00	6.00
561	Hank Aaron (All-Star)	120.00	60.00	36.00

562	Al Kaline (All-Star)	30.00	15.00	9.00
563	Willie Mays (All-Star)	125.00	62.50	31.25
564	Mickey Mantle (All-Star)	215.00	100.00	60.00
565	Wes Covington (All-Star)	15.00	7.50	4.50
566	Roy Sievers (All-Star)	15.00	7.50	4.50
567	Del Crandall (All-Star)	15.00	7.50	4.50
568	Gus Triandos (All-Star)	15.00	7.50	4.50
569	Bob Friend (All-Star)	15.00	7.50	4.50
570	Bob Turley (All-Star)	17.50	8.75	5.25
571	Warren Spahn (All-Star)	27.50	13.50	8.25
572	Billy Pierce (All-Star)	200.00	15.00	9.00
----	Elect Your Favorite			
	Rookie Insert (Paper			
	stock, September 29			
	date on back.)	200.00	100.00	60.00
----	Felt Pennants Insert			
	(paper stock)	30.00	15.00	9.00

1960 Topps

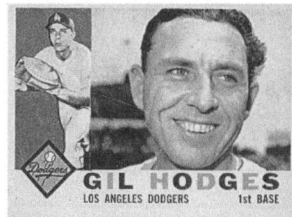

In 1960, Topps opted for a horizontal format in standard 3-1/2" x 2-1/2" size. Basic fronts have a large color portrait or pose at right and black-and-white action photograph at left. After a one-year hiatus, backs returned to the use of lifetime statistics along with a cartoon and short career summary or previous season highlights. Specialty cards in the 572-card set are multi-player cards, managers and coaches cards, and highlights of the 1959 World Series. Two groups of rookie cards are included. The first are numbers 117-148, which are the Sport Magazine rookies. The second group is called "Topps All-Star Rookies." Finally, there is a run of All-Star cards to close out the set in the scarcer high numbers. Cards #375-440 can be found with backs printed on either white or grey cardboard, with the white stock being the less common. Team cards have checklists on the back.

	NM	E	VG
Complete Set (572):	6,500	3,250	2,000
Common Player (1-440):	6.00	3.00	1.75
Common Player (441-506):	9.00	4.50	2.75
Common Player (507-572):	15.00	7.50	4.50

1	Early Wynn	45.00	10.00	6.00
2	Roman Mejias	20.00	4.00	1.75
3	Joe Adcock	6.00	3.00	1.75
4	Bob Purkey	6.00	3.00	1.75
5	Wally Moon	6.00	3.00	1.75
6	Lou Berberet	6.00	3.00	1.75
7	Master and Mentor(Willie			
	Mays, Bill Rigney)	20.00	10.00	6.00
8	Bud Daley	6.00	3.00	1.75
9	Faye Throneberry	6.00	3.00	1.75
10	Ernie Banks	70.00	35.00	17.50
11	Norm Siebern	6.00	3.00	1.75
12	Milt Pappas	6.00	3.00	1.75
13	Wally Post	6.00	3.00	1.75
14	Jim Grant	6.00	3.00	1.75
15	Pete Runnels	6.00	3.00	1.75
16	Ernie Broglio	6.00	3.00	1.75
17	Johnny Callison	6.00	3.00	1.75
18	Los Angeles Dodgers			
	Team	35.00	17.50	10.00
19	Felix Mantilla	6.00	3.00	1.75
20	Roy Face	6.00	3.00	1.75
21	Dutch Dotterer	6.00	3.00	1.75
22	Rocky Bridges	6.00	3.00	1.75
23	Eddie Fisher	6.00	3.00	1.75
24	Dick Gray	6.00	3.00	1.75
25	Roy Sievers	6.00	3.00	1.75
26	Wayne Terwilliger	6.00	3.00	1.75
27	Dick Drott	6.00	3.00	1.75
28	Brooks Robinson	40.00	20.00	12.00
29	Clem Labine	8.00	4.00	2.50
30	Tito Francona	6.00	3.00	1.75
31	Sammy Esposito	6.00	3.00	1.75

32	Sophomore Stalwarts(Jim			
	O'Toole, Vada Pinson)	9.00	4.50	2.75
33	Tom Morgan	6.00	3.00	1.75
34	George Anderson			
	(Sparky)	20.00	10.00	6.00
35	Whitey Ford	40.00	17.50	10.00
36	Russ Nixon	6.00	3.00	1.75
37	Bill Bruton	6.00	3.00	1.75
38	Jerry Casale	6.00	3.00	1.75
39	Earl Averill	6.00	3.00	1.75
40	Joe Cunningham	6.00	3.00	1.75
41	Barry Latman	6.00	3.00	1.75
42	Hobie Landrith	6.00	3.00	1.75
43	Washington Senators			
	Team	15.00	7.50	4.50
44	Bobby Locke	6.00	3.00	1.75
45	Roy McMillan	6.00	3.00	1.75
46	Jack Fisher	6.00	3.00	1.75
47	Don Zimmer	12.00	6.00	3.50
48	Hal Smith	6.00	3.00	1.75
49	Curt Raydon	6.00	3.00	1.75
50	Al Kaline	50.00	25.00	12.50
51	Jim Coates	6.00	3.00	1.75
52	Dave Philley	6.00	3.00	1.75
53	Jackie Brandt	6.00	3.00	1.75
54	Mike Fornieles	6.00	3.00	1.75
55	Bill Mazeroski	20.00	10.00	6.00
56	Steve Korcheck	6.00	3.00	1.75
57	Win-Savers(Turk Lown,			
	Gerry Staley)	6.00	3.00	1.75
58	Gino Cimoli	6.00	3.00	1.75
59	Juan Pizarro	6.00	3.00	1.75
60	Gus Triandos	6.00	3.00	1.75
61	Eddie Kasko	6.00	3.00	1.75
62	Roger Craig	6.00	3.00	1.75
63	George Strickland	6.00	3.00	1.75
64	Jack Meyer	6.00	3.00	1.75
65	Elston Howard	15.00	7.50	4.50
66	Bob Trowbridge	6.00	3.00	1.75
67	Jose Pagan RC	6.00	3.00	1.75
68	Dave Hillman	6.00	3.00	1.75
69	Billy Goodman	6.00	3.00	1.75
70	Lou Burdette	6.00	3.00	1.75
71	Marty Keough	6.00	3.00	1.75
72	Detroit Tigers Team	15.00	7.50	4.50
73	Bob Gibson	50.00	25.00	15.00
74	Walt Moryn	6.00	3.00	1.75
75	Vic Power	6.00	3.00	1.75
76	Bill Fischer	6.00	3.00	1.75
77	Hank Foiles	6.00	3.00	1.75
78	Bob Grim	6.00	3.00	1.75
79	Walt Dropo	6.00	3.00	1.75
80	Johnny Antonelli	6.00	3.00	1.75
81	Russ Snyder	6.00	3.00	1.75
82	Ruben Gomez	6.00	3.00	1.75
83	Tony Kubek	25.00	12.50	7.50
84	Hal Smith	6.00	3.00	1.75
85	Frank Lary	6.00	3.00	1.75
86	Dick Gernert	6.00	3.00	1.75
87	John Romonosky	6.00	3.00	1.75
88	John Roseboro	6.00	3.00	1.75
89	Hal Brown	6.00	3.00	1.75
90	Bobby Avila	6.00	3.00	1.75
91	Bennie Daniels	6.00	3.00	1.75
92	Whitey Herzog	6.00	3.00	1.75
93	Art Schult	6.00	3.00	1.75
94	Leo Kiely	6.00	3.00	1.75
95	Frank Thomas	6.00	3.00	1.75
96	Ralph Terry	7.50	3.75	2.25
97	Ted Lepcio	6.00	3.00	1.75
98	Gordon Jones	6.00	3.00	1.75
99	Lenny Green	6.00	3.00	1.75
100	Nellie Fox	20.00	10.00	6.00
101	Bob Miller	6.00	3.00	1.75
102	Kent Hadley	6.00	3.00	1.75
103	Dick Farrell	6.00	3.00	1.75
104	Dick Schofield	6.00	3.00	1.75
105	Larry Sherry RC	12.00	6.00	3.50
106	Billy Gardner	6.00	3.00	1.75
107	Carl Willey	6.00	3.00	1.75
108	Pete Daley	6.00	3.00	1.75
109	Cletis Boyer	13.50	6.75	4.00
110	Cal McLish	6.00	3.00	1.75
111	Vic Wertz	6.00	3.00	1.75
112	Jack Harshman	6.00	3.00	1.75
113	Bob Skinner	6.00	3.00	1.75
114	Ken Aspromonte	6.00	3.00	1.75
115	Fork and Knuckler(Roy			
	Face, Hoyt Wilhelm)	9.00	4.50	2.75
116	Jim Rivera	6.00	3.00	1.75
117	Tom Borland	6.00	3.00	1.75
118	Bob Bruce	6.00	3.00	1.75
119	Chico Cardenas RC	6.00	3.00	1.75
120	Duke Carmel	6.00	3.00	1.75
121	Camilo Carreon	6.00	3.00	1.75
122	Don Dillard	6.00	3.00	1.75
123	Dan Dobbek	6.00	3.00	1.75
124	Jim Donohue	6.00	3.00	1.75

125	Dick Ellsworth **RC**	6.00	3.00	1.75
126	Chuck Estrada **RC**	6.00	3.00	1.75
127	Ronnie Hansen	6.00	3.00	1.75
128	Bill Harris	6.00	3.00	1.75
129	Bob Hartman	6.00	3.00	1.75
130	Frank Herrera	6.00	3.00	1.75
131	Ed Hobaugh	6.00	3.00	1.75
132	Frank Howard **RC**	20.00	10.00	6.00
133	Manuel Javier **RC**	6.00	3.00	1.75
134	Deron Johnson	7.50	3.75	2.25
135	Ken Johnson	6.00	3.00	1.75
136	Jim Kaat **RC**	20.00	10.00	6.00
137	Lou Klimchock	6.00	3.00	1.75
138	Art Mahaffey **RC**	6.00	3.00	1.75
139	Carl Mathias	6.00	3.00	1.75
140	Julio Navarro	6.00	3.00	1.75
141	Jim Proctor	6.00	3.00	1.75
142	Bill Short	6.00	3.00	1.75
143	Al Spangler	6.00	3.00	1.75
144	Al Stieglitz	6.00	3.00	1.75
145	Jim Umbricht	6.00	3.00	1.75
146	Ted Wieand	6.00	3.00	1.75
147	Bob Will	6.00	3.00	1.75
148	Carl Yastrzemski **RC**	200.00	100.00	50.00
149	Bob Nieman	6.00	3.00	1.75
150	Billy Pierce	6.00	3.00	1.75
151	San Francisco Giants Team	15.00	7.50	4.50
152	Gail Harris	6.00	3.00	1.75
153	Bobby Thomson	7.50	3.75	2.25
154	Jim Davenport	6.00	3.00	1.75
155	Charlie Neal	6.00	3.00	1.75
156	Art Ceccarelli	6.00	3.00	1.75
157	Rocky Nelson	6.00	3.00	1.75
158	Wes Covington	6.00	3.00	1.75
159	Jim Piersall	8.00	4.00	2.50
160	Rival All-Stars(Ken Boyer, Mickey Mantle)	110.00	55.00	30.00
161	Ray Narleski	6.00	3.00	1.75
162	Sammy Taylor	6.00	3.00	1.75
163	Hector Lopez	6.00	3.00	1.75
164	Cincinnati Reds Team	15.00	7.50	4.50
165	Jack Sanford	6.00	3.00	1.75
166	Chuck Essegian	6.00	3.00	1.75
167	Valmy Thomas	6.00	3.00	1.75
168	Alex Grammas	6.00	3.00	1.75
169	Jake Striker	6.00	3.00	1.75
170	Del Crandall	6.00	3.00	1.75
171	Johnny Groth	6.00	3.00	1.75
172	Willie Kirkland	6.00	3.00	1.75
173	Billy Martin	10.00	5.00	3.00
174	Cleveland Indians Team	15.00	7.50	4.50
175	Pedro Ramos	6.00	3.00	1.75
176	Vada Pinson	10.00	5.00	3.00
177	Johnny Kucks	6.00	3.00	1.75
178	Woody Held	6.00	3.00	1.75
179	Rip Coleman	6.00	3.00	1.75
180	Harry Simpson	6.00	3.00	1.75
181	Billy Loes	6.00	3.00	1.75
182	Glen Hobbie	6.00	3.00	1.75
183	Eli Grba	6.00	3.00	1.75
184	Gary Geiger	6.00	3.00	1.75
185	Jim Owens	6.00	3.00	1.75
186	Dave Sisler	6.00	3.00	1.75
187	Jay Hook	6.00	3.00	1.75
188	Dick Williams	6.00	3.00	1.75
189	Don McMahon	6.00	3.00	1.75
190	Gene Woodling	6.00	3.00	1.75
191	Johnny Klippstein	6.00	3.00	1.75
192	Danny O'Connell	6.00	3.00	1.75
193	Dick Hyde	6.00	3.00	1.75
194	Bobby Gene Smith	6.00	3.00	1.75
195	Lindy McDaniel	6.00	3.00	1.75
196	Andy Carey	6.00	3.00	1.75
197	Ron Kline	6.00	3.00	1.75
198	Jerry Lynch	6.00	3.00	1.75
199	Dick Donovan	6.00	3.00	1.75
200	Willie Mays	150.00	75.00	40.00
201	Larry Osborne	6.00	3.00	1.75
202	Fred Kipp	6.00	3.00	1.75
203	Sammy White	6.00	3.00	1.75
204	Ryne Duren	7.50	3.75	2.25
205	Johnny Logan	6.00	3.00	1.75
206	Claude Osteen	6.00	3.00	1.75
207	Bob Boyd	6.00	3.00	1.75
208	Chicago White Sox Team	15.00	7.50	4.50
209	Ron Blackburn	6.00	3.00	1.75
210	Harmon Killebrew	30.00	15.00	9.00
211	Taylor Phillips	6.00	3.00	1.75
212	Walt Alston	12.00	6.00	3.50
213	Chuck Dressen	6.00	3.00	1.75
214	Jimmie Dykes	6.00	3.00	1.75
215	Bob Elliott	6.00	3.00	1.75
216	Joe Gordon	6.00	3.00	1.75
217	Charley Grimm	6.00	3.00	1.75
218	Solly Hemus	6.00	3.00	1.75
219	Fred Hutchinson	6.00	3.00	1.75
220	Billy Jurges	6.00	3.00	1.75
221	Cookie Lavagetto	6.00	3.00	1.75
222	Al Lopez	10.00	5.00	3.00
223	Danny Murtaugh	6.00	3.00	1.75
224	Paul Richards	6.00	3.00	1.75
225	Bill Rigney	6.00	3.00	1.75
226	Eddie Sawyer	6.00	3.00	1.75
227	Casey Stengel	17.50	8.75	5.25
228	Ernie Johnson	6.00	3.00	1.75
229	Joe Morgan	6.00	3.00	1.75
230	Mound Magicians(Bob Buhl, Lou Burdette, Warren Spahn)	17.50	8.75	5.25
231	Hal Naragon	6.00	3.00	1.75
232	Jim Busby	6.00	3.00	1.75
233	Don Elston	6.00	3.00	1.75
234	Don Demeter	6.00	3.00	1.75
235	Gus Bell	6.00	3.00	1.75
236	Dick Ricketts	6.00	3.00	1.75
237	Elmer Valo	6.00	3.00	1.75
238	Danny Kravitz	6.00	3.00	1.75
239	Joe Shipley	6.00	3.00	1.75
240	Luis Aparicio	17.50	8.75	5.25
241	Albie Pearson	6.00	3.00	1.75
242	St. Louis Cardinals Team	15.00	7.50	4.50
243	Bubba Phillips	6.00	3.00	1.75
244	Hal Griggs	6.00	3.00	1.75
245	Eddie Yost	6.00	3.00	1.75
246	Lee Maye	6.00	3.00	1.75
247	Gil McDougald	12.00	6.00	3.50
248	Del Rice	6.00	3.00	1.75
249	Earl Wilson **RC**	6.00	3.00	1.75
250	Stan Musial	100.00	50.00	25.00
251	Bobby Malkmus	6.00	3.00	1.75
252	Ray Herbert	6.00	3.00	1.75
253	Eddie Bressoud	6.00	3.00	1.75
254	Arnie Portocarrero	6.00	3.00	1.75
255	Jim Gilliam	10.00	5.00	3.00
256	Dick Brown	6.00	3.00	1.75
257	Gordy Coleman	6.00	3.00	1.75
258	Dick Groat	6.00	3.00	1.75
259	George Altman	6.00	3.00	1.75
260	Power Plus(Rocky Colavito, Tito Francona)	11.00	5.50	3.25
261	Pete Burnside	6.00	3.00	1.75
262	Hank Bauer	7.50	3.75	2.25
263	Darrell Johnson	6.00	3.00	1.75
264	Robin Roberts	12.50	6.25	3.75
265	Rip Repulski	6.00	3.00	1.75
266	Joe Jay	6.00	3.00	1.75
267	Jim Marshall	6.00	3.00	1.75
268	Al Worthington	6.00	3.00	1.75
269	Gene Green	6.00	3.00	1.75
270	Bob Turley	10.00	5.00	3.00
271	Julio Becquer	6.00	3.00	1.75
272	Fred Green	6.00	3.00	1.75
273	Neil Chrisley	6.00	3.00	1.75
274	Tom Acker	6.00	3.00	1.75
275	Curt Flood	9.00	4.50	2.75
276	Ken McBride	6.00	3.00	1.75
277	Harry Bright	6.00	3.00	1.75
278	Stan Williams	6.00	3.00	1.75
279	Chuck Tanner	6.00	3.00	1.75
280	Frank Sullivan	6.00	3.00	1.75
281	Ray Boone	6.00	3.00	1.75
282	Joe Nuxhall	6.00	3.00	1.75
283	John Blanchard	7.50	3.75	2.25
284	Don Gross	6.00	3.00	1.75
285	Harry Anderson	6.00	3.00	1.75
286	Ray Semproch	6.00	3.00	1.75
287	Felipe Alou	7.50	3.75	2.25
288	Bob Mabe	6.00	3.00	1.75
289	Willie Jones	6.00	3.00	1.75
290	Jerry Lumpe	6.00	3.00	1.75
291	Bob Keegan	6.00	3.00	1.75
292	Dodger Backstops(Joe Pignatano, John Roseboro)	7.50	3.75	2.25
293	Gene Conley	6.00	3.00	1.75
294	Tony Taylor	6.00	3.00	1.75
295	Gil Hodges	15.00	7.50	4.50
296	Nelson Chittum	6.00	3.00	1.75
297	Reno Bertoia	6.00	3.00	1.75
298	George Witt	6.00	3.00	1.75
299	Earl Torgeson	6.00	3.00	1.75
300	Hank Aaron	125.00	60.00	32.00
301	Jerry Davie	6.00	3.00	1.75
302	Philadelphia Phillies Team	15.00	7.50	4.50
303	Billy O'Dell	6.00	3.00	1.75
304	Joe Ginsberg	6.00	3.00	1.75
305	Richie Ashburn	15.00	7.50	4.50
306	Frank Baumann	6.00	3.00	1.75
307	Gene Oliver	6.00	3.00	1.75
308	Dick Hall	6.00	3.00	1.75
309	Bob Hale	6.00	3.00	1.75
310	Frank Malzone	6.00	3.00	1.75
311	Raul Sanchez	6.00	3.00	1.75
312	Charlie Lau	6.00	3.00	1.75
313	Turk Lown	6.00	3.00	1.75
314	Chico Fernandez	6.00	3.00	1.75
315	Bobby Shantz	11.00	5.50	3.25
316	Willie McCovey **RC**	145.00	75.00	37.50
317	Pumpsie Green	7.50	3.75	2.25
318	Jim Baxes	6.00	3.00	1.75
319	Joe Koppe	6.00	3.00	1.75
320	Bob Allison	6.00	3.00	1.75
321	Ron Fairly	6.00	3.00	1.75
322	Willie Tasby	6.00	3.00	1.75
323	Johnny Romano	6.00	3.00	1.75
324	Jim Perry	7.50	3.75	2.25
325	Jim O'Toole	6.00	3.00	1.75
326	Bob Clemente	130.00	65.00	39.00
327	Ray Sadecki **RC**	6.00	3.00	1.75
328	Earl Battey	6.00	3.00	1.75
329	Zack Monroe	6.00	3.00	1.75
330	Harvey Kuenn	6.00	3.00	1.75
331	Henry Mason	6.00	3.00	1.75
332	New York Yankees Team	45.00	22.00	13.00
333	Danny McDevitt	6.00	3.00	1.75
334	Ted Abernathy	6.00	3.00	1.75
335	Red Schoendienst	12.50	6.25	3.75
336	Ike Delock	6.00	3.00	1.75
337	Cal Neeman	6.00	3.00	1.75
338	Ray Monzant	6.00	3.00	1.75
339	Harry Chiti	6.00	3.00	1.75
340	Harvey Haddix	6.00	3.00	1.75
341	Carroll Hardy	6.00	3.00	1.75
342	Casey Wise	6.00	3.00	1.75
343	Sandy Koufax	110.00	55.00	30.00
344	Clint Courtney	6.00	3.00	1.75
345	Don Newcombe	7.50	3.75	2.25
346	J.C. Martin (Photo actually Gary Peters.)	6.00	3.00	1.75
347	Ed Bouchee	6.00	3.00	1.75
348	Barry Shetrone	6.00	3.00	1.75
349	Moe Drabowsky	6.00	3.00	1.75
350	Mickey Mantle	445.00	225.00	125.00
351	Don Nottebart	6.00	3.00	1.75
352	Cincy Clouters(Gus Bell, Jerry Lynch, Frank Robinson)	12.00	6.00	3.50
353	Don Larsen	8.00	4.00	2.50
354	Bob Lillis	6.00	3.00	1.75
355	Bill White	6.00	3.00	1.75
356	Joe Amalfitano	6.00	3.00	1.75
357	Al Schroll	6.00	3.00	1.75
358	Joe De Maestri	6.00	3.00	1.75
359	Buddy Gilbert	6.00	3.00	1.75
360	Herb Score	7.50	3.75	2.25
361	Bob Oldis	6.00	3.00	1.75
362	Russ Kemmerer	6.00	3.00	1.75
363	Gene Stephens	6.00	3.00	1.75
364	Paul Foytack	6.00	3.00	1.75
365	Minnie Minoso	12.50	6.25	3.75
366	Dallas Green **RC**	9.00	4.50	2.75
367	Bill Tuttle	6.00	3.00	1.75
368	Daryl Spencer	6.00	3.00	1.75
369	Billy Hoeft	6.00	3.00	1.75
370	Bill Skowron	17.50	8.75	5.25
371	Bud Byerly	6.00	3.00	1.75
372	Frank House	6.00	3.00	1.75
373	Don Hoak	6.00	3.00	1.75
374	Bob Buhl	6.00	3.00	1.75
375	Dale Long	6.00	3.00	1.75
376	Johnny Briggs	6.00	3.00	1.75
377	Roger Maris	100.00	50.00	25.00
378	Stu Miller	6.00	3.00	1.75
379	Red Wilson	6.00	3.00	1.75
380	Bob Shaw	6.00	3.00	1.75
381	Milwaukee Braves Team	16.00	8.00	4.75
382	Ted Bowsfield	6.00	3.00	1.75
383	Leon Wagner	6.00	3.00	1.75
384	Don Cardwell	6.00	3.00	1.75
385	World Series Game 1 (Neal Steals Second)	10.00	5.00	3.00
386	World Series Game 2 (Neal Belts 2nd Homer)	10.00	5.00	3.00
387	World Series Game 3 (Furillo Breaks Up Game)	10.00	5.00	3.00
388	World Series Game 4 (Hodges' Winning Homer)	10.00	5.00	3.00
389	World Series Game 5 (Luis Swipes Base)	12.00	6.00	3.50
390	World Series Game 6 (Scrambling After Ball)	10.00	5.00	3.00
391	World Series Summary (The Champs Celebrate)	10.00	5.00	3.00
392	Tex Clevenger	6.00	3.00	1.75
393	Smoky Burgess	6.00	3.00	1.75
394	Norm Larker	6.00	3.00	1.75
395	Hoyt Wilhelm	13.50	6.75	4.00
396	Steve Bilko	6.00	3.00	1.75

397	Don Blasingame	6.00	3.00	1.75
398	Mike Cuellar	6.00	3.00	1.75
399	Young Hill Stars(Jack Fisher, Milt Pappas, Jerry Walker)	6.00	3.00	1.75
400	Rocky Colavito	20.00	10.00	6.00
401	Bob Duliba	6.00	3.00	1.75
402	Dick Stuart	6.00	3.00	1.75
403	Ed Sadowski	6.00	3.00	1.75
404	Bob Rush	6.00	3.00	1.75
405	Bobby Richardson	25.00	12.50	7.50
406	Billy Klaus	6.00	3.00	1.75
407	Gary Peters RC (Photo actually J.C. Martin.)	6.00	3.00	1.75
408	Carl Furillo	11.00	5.50	3.25
409	Ron Samford	6.00	3.00	1.75
410	Sam Jones	6.00	3.00	1.75
411	Ed Bailey	6.00	3.00	1.75
412	Bob Anderson	6.00	3.00	1.75
413	Kansas City Athletics Team	15.00	7.50	4.50
414	Don Williams	6.00	3.00	1.75
415	Bob Cerv	6.00	3.00	1.75
416	Humberto Robinson	6.00	3.00	1.75
417	Chuck Cottier	6.00	3.00	1.75
418	Don Mossi	6.00	3.00	1.75
419	George Crowe	6.00	3.00	1.75
420	Ed Mathews	25.00	12.50	7.50
421	Duke Maas	6.00	3.00	1.75
422	Johnny Powers	6.00	3.00	1.75
423	Ed Fitz Gerald	6.00	3.00	1.75
424	Pete Whisenant	6.00	3.00	1.75
425	Johnny Podres	10.00	5.00	3.00
426	Ron Jackson	6.00	3.00	1.75
427	Al Grunwald	6.00	3.00	1.75
428	Al Smith	6.00	3.00	1.75
429	American League Kings(Nellie Fox, Harvey Kuenn)	12.50	6.25	3.75
430	Art Ditmar	6.00	3.00	1.75
431	Andre Rodgers	6.00	3.00	1.75
432	Chuck Stobbs	6.00	3.00	1.75
433	Irv Noren	6.00	3.00	1.75
434	Brooks Lawrence	6.00	3.00	1.75
435	Gene Freese	6.00	3.00	1.75
436	Marv Throneberry	6.00	3.00	1.75
437	Bob Friend	6.00	3.00	1.75
438	Jim Coker	6.00	3.00	1.75
439	Tom Brewer	6.00	3.00	1.75
440	Jim Lemon	6.00	3.00	1.75
441	Gary Bell	9.00	4.50	2.75
442	Joe Pignatano	9.00	4.50	2.75
443	Charlie Maxwell	9.00	4.50	2.75
444	Jerry Kindall	9.00	4.50	2.75
445	Warren Spahn	40.00	17.50	10.00
446	Ellis Burton	9.00	4.50	2.75
447	Ray Moore	9.00	4.50	2.75
448	Jim Gentile RC	15.00	7.50	4.50
449	Jim Brosnan	9.00	4.50	2.75
450	Orlando Cepeda	30.00	15.00	9.00
451	Curt Simmons	9.00	4.50	2.75
452	Ray Webster	9.00	4.50	2.75
453	Vern Law	9.00	4.50	2.75
454	Hal Woodeshick	9.00	4.50	2.75
455	Baltimomre Orioles Coaches(Harry Brecheen, Lum Harris, Eddie Robinson)	9.00	4.50	2.75
456	Boston Red Sox Coaches(Del Baker, Billy Herman, Sal Maglie, Rudy York)	15.00	7.50	4.50
457	Chicago Cubs Coaches(Lou Klein, Charlie Root, Elvin Tappe)	9.00	4.50	2.75
458	Chicago White Sox Coaches(Ray Berres, Johnny Cooney, Tony Cuccinello, Don Gutteridge)	9.00	4.50	2.75
459	Cincinnati Reds Coaches(Cot Deal, Wally Moses, Reggie Otero)	9.00	4.50	2.75
460	Cleveland Indians Coaches(Mel Harder, Red Kress, Bob Lemon, Jo-Jo White)	10.00	5.00	3.00
461	Detroit Tigers Coaches(Luke Appling, Tom Ferrick, Billy Hitchcock)	10.00	5.00	3.00
462	Kansas City A's Coaches(Walker Cooper, Fred Fitzsimmons, Don Heffner)	9.00	4.50	2.75

463	L.A. Dodgers Coaches(Joe Becker, Bobby Bragan, Greg Mulleavy, Pete Reiser)	9.00	4.50	2.75
464	Milwaukee Braves Coaches(George Myatt, Andy Pafko, Bob Scheffing, Whitlow Wyatt)	9.00	4.50	2.75
465	N.Y. Yankees Coaches(Frank Crosetti, Bill Dickey, Ralph Houk, Ed Lopat)	20.00	10.00	6.00
466	Phila. Phillies Coaches(Dick Carter, Andy Cohen, Ken Silvestri)	9.00	4.50	2.75
467	Pitts. Pirates Coaches(Bill Burwell, Sam Narron, Frank Oceak, Mickey Vernon)	9.00	4.50	2.75
468	St. Louis Cards Coaches(Ray Katt, Johnny Keane, Howie Pollet, Harry Walker)	9.00	4.50	2.75
469	San Fran. Giants Coaches(Salty Parker, Bill Posedel, Wes Westrum)	9.00	4.50	2.75
470	Wash. Senators Coaches(Ellis Clary, Sam Mele, Bob Swift)	9.00	4.50	2.75
471	Ned Garver	9.00	4.50	2.75
472	Al Dark	9.00	4.50	2.75
473	Al Cicotte	9.00	4.50	2.75
474	Haywood Sullivan	9.00	4.50	2.75
475	Don Drysdale	38.00	17.50	10.00
476	Lou Johnson	9.00	4.50	2.75
477	Don Ferrarese	9.00	4.50	2.75
478	Frank Torre	9.00	4.50	2.75
479	Georges Maranda	9.00	4.50	2.75
480	Yogi Berra	85.00	45.00	22.50
481	Wes Stock	9.00	4.50	2.75
482	Frank Bolling	9.00	4.50	2.75
483	Camilo Pascual	9.00	4.50	2.75
484	Pittsburgh Pirates Team	25.00	12.50	7.50
485	Ken Boyer	15.00	7.50	4.50
486	Bobby Del Greco	9.00	4.50	2.75
487	Tom Sturdivant	9.00	4.50	2.75
488	Norm Cash	15.00	7.50	4.50
489	Steve Ridzik	9.00	4.50	2.75
490	Frank Robinson	40.00	20.00	12.00
491	Mel Roach	9.00	4.50	2.75
492	Larry Jackson	9.00	4.50	2.75
493	Duke Snider	50.00	25.00	12.50
494	Baltimore Orioles Team	20.00	10.00	6.00
495	Sherm Lollar	9.00	4.50	2.75
496	Bill Virdon	9.00	4.50	2.75
497	John Tsitouris	9.00	4.50	2.75
498	Al Pilarcik	9.00	4.50	2.75
499	Johnny James	9.00	4.50	2.75
500	Johnny Temple	9.00	4.50	2.75
501	Bob Schmidt	9.00	4.50	2.75
502	Jim Bunning	20.00	10.00	6.00
503	Don Lee	9.00	4.50	2.75
504	Seth Morehead	9.00	4.50	2.75
505	Ted Kluszewski	15.00	7.50	4.50
506	Lee Walls	9.00	4.50	2.75
507	Dick Stigman	15.00	7.50	4.50
508	Billy Consolo	15.00	7.50	4.50
509	Tommy Davis RC	20.00	10.00	6.00
510	Jerry Staley	15.00	7.50	4.50
511	Ken Walters	15.00	7.50	4.50
512	Joe Gibbon	15.00	7.50	4.50
513	Chicago Cubs Team	20.00	10.00	6.00
514	Steve Barber RC	17.50	8.75	5.25
515	Stan Lopata	15.00	7.50	4.50
516	Marty Kutyna	15.00	7.50	4.50
517	Charley James	15.00	7.50	4.50
518	Tony Gonzalez RC	15.00	7.50	4.50
519	Ed Roebuck	15.00	7.50	4.50
520	Don Buddin	15.00	7.50	4.50
521	Mike Lee	15.00	7.50	4.50
522	Ken Hunt	15.00	7.50	4.50
523	Clay Dalrymple RC	15.00	7.50	4.50
524	Bill Henry	15.00	7.50	4.50
525	Marv Breeding	15.00	7.50	4.50
526	Paul Giel	15.00	7.50	4.50
527	Jose Valdivielso	15.00	7.50	4.50
528	Ben Johnson	15.00	7.50	4.50
529	Norm Sherry	17.50	8.75	5.25
530	Mike McCormick	15.00	7.50	4.50
531	Sandy Amoros	15.00	7.50	4.50
532	Mike Garcia	15.00	7.50	4.50
533	Lu Clinton	15.00	7.50	4.50
534	Ken MacKenzie	15.00	7.50	4.50
535	Whitey Lockman	15.00	7.50	4.50
536	Wynn Hawkins	15.00	7.50	4.50

537	Boston Red Sox Team	25.00	12.50	7.50
538	Frank Barnes	15.00	7.50	4.50
539	Gene Baker	15.00	7.50	4.50
540	Jerry Walker	15.00	7.50	4.50
541	Tony Curry	15.00	7.50	4.50
542	Ken Hamlin	15.00	7.50	4.50
543	Elio Chacon	15.00	7.50	4.50
544	Bill Monbouquette	15.00	7.50	4.50
545	Carl Sawatski	15.00	7.50	4.50
546	Hank Aguirre	15.00	7.50	4.50
547	Bob Aspromonte RC	17.50	8.75	5.25
548	Don Mincher RC	15.00	7.50	4.50
549	John Buzhardt	15.00	7.50	4.50
550	Jim Landis	15.00	7.50	4.50
551	Ed Rakow	15.00	7.50	4.50
552	Walt Bond	15.00	7.50	4.50
553	Bill Skowron (All-Star)	20.00	10.00	6.00
554	Willie McCovey (All-Star)	35.00	17.50	10.00
555	Nellie Fox (All-Star)	20.00	10.00	6.00
556	Charlie Neal (All-Star)	17.50	8.75	5.25
557	Frank Malzone (All-Star)	17.50	8.75	5.25
558	Eddie Mathews (All-Star)	25.00	12.50	7.50
559	Luis Aparicio (All-Star)	20.00	10.00	6.00
560	Ernie Banks (All-Star)	35.00	17.50	10.00
561	Al Kaline (All-Star)	30.00	15.00	9.00
562	Joe Cunningham (All-Star)	17.50	8.75	5.25
563	Mickey Mantle (All-Star)	275.00	137.50	68.75
564	Willie Mays (All-Star)	90.00	45.00	22.00
565	Roger Maris (All-Star)	90.00	45.00	22.00
566	Hank Aaron (All-Star)	90.00	45.00	22.00
567	Sherm Lollar (All-Star)	17.50	8.75	5.25
568	Del Crandall (All-Star)	17.50	8.75	5.25
569	Camilo Pascual (All-Star)	17.50	8.75	5.25
570	Don Drysdale (All-Star)	25.00	12.50	7.50
571	Billy Pierce (All-Star)	17.50	8.75	5.25
572	Johnny Antonelli (All-Star)	25.00	9.00	5.25
----	Elect Your Favorite Rookie Insert (Paper stock, no date on back.)	30.00	15.00	9.00
----	Hot Iron Transfer Insert (Paper stock.)	30.00	15.00	9.00

1950s-60s Topps "PROMOTIONAL SAMPLES"

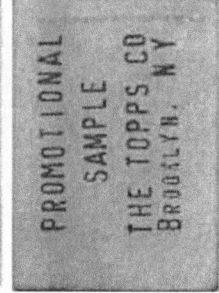

These mini sample cards are fantasy items created in the late 1990s to defraud collectors. Often sold grouped in an older frame or otherwise made to look old, they are pictures which have been cut out of the "Topps Baseball Cards" books or the team-issued Surf books which reproduced Topps cards in about 1-1/4" x 1-3/4" format. The color glossy pictures were then glued to a cardboard back which has been rubber-stamped "PROMOTIONAL / SAMPLE / THE TOPPS CO / BROOKLYN, N Y." There were no legitimate miniature Topps promotional or sample cards produced.

(No Collectible Value.)

1960 Topps Proofs

Subsequent to a pair of December 1959 trades, the 1960 Topps cards of three players were significantly changed. Whether the change occurred prior to regular production printing and packaging or while the cards were still in the proofing stage is unknown. The changes affect the cards of Gino Cimoli, Kent Hadley and Faye Throneberry. In the very rare versions each player's card has at bottom left the logo of his team prior to the trade. The common regular-issue version has the new team logo. The front of Hadley's rare card names his team as the Yankees, while Cimoli's rare version says Cardinals.

		NM
9	Faye Throneberry (Yankees logo.)	
58	Gino Cimoli (Cardinals logo.) (No recent sales.))	
102	Kent Hadley (A's logo.) (Nov., 1999 auction record.))	13,500

1960 Topps Tattoos

Probably the least popular of all Topps products among parents and teachers, the Tattoos were printed on the reverse of the wrappers of Topps "Tattoo Bubble Gum." The entire wrapper was 1-9/16" x 3-1/2." The owner moistened their skin and applied the back of the wrapper to the wet spot, producing a colorful "tattoo" (although often blurred by running colors). The set offered 96 tattoo possibilities of which 55 were players, 16 teams, 15 action pictures and 10 autographed balls. Because the packaged gum slides easily in and out of the "sealed" wrapper, allowing the tattoo to be easily seen, unopened packs command little premium.

		NM	E	VG
Complete Set (96):		2,750	1,350	825.00
Common Player:		20.00	10.00	6.00
Common Non-player:		12.00	6.00	3.50
(1)	Hank Aaron	150.00	75.00	45.00
(2)	Bob Allison	20.00	10.00	6.00
(3)	John Antonelli	20.00	10.00	6.00
(4)	Richie Ashburn	40.00	20.00	12.00
(5)	Ernie Banks	65.00	32.00	19.50
(6)	Yogi Berra	60.00	30.00	18.00
(7)	Lew Burdette	20.00	10.00	6.00
(8)	Orlando Cepeda	35.00	17.50	10.50
(9)	Rocky Colavito	35.00	17.50	10.50
(10)	Joe Cunningham	20.00	10.00	6.00
(11)	Buddy Daley	20.00	10.00	6.00
(12)	Don Drysdale	40.00	20.00	12.00
(13)	Ryne Duren	20.00	10.00	6.00
(14)	Roy Face	20.00	10.00	6.00
(15)	Whitey Ford	60.00	30.00	18.00
(16)	Nellie Fox	35.00	17.50	10.50
(17)	Tito Francona	20.00	10.00	6.00
(18)	Gene Freese	20.00	10.00	6.00
(19)	Jim Gilliam	20.00	10.00	6.00
(20)	Dick Groat	20.00	10.00	6.00
(21)	Ray Herbert	20.00	10.00	6.00
(22)	Glen Hobbie	20.00	10.00	6.00
(23)	Jackie Jensen	20.00	10.00	6.00
(24)	Sam Jones	20.00	10.00	6.00
(25)	Al Kaline	60.00	30.00	18.00
(26)	Harmon Killebrew	40.00	20.00	12.00
(27)	Harvey Kuenn	20.00	10.00	6.00
(28)	Frank Lary	20.00	10.00	6.00
(29)	Vernon Law	20.00	10.00	6.00
(30)	Frank Malzone	20.00	10.00	6.00
(31)	Mickey Mantle	300.00	150.00	90.00
(32)	Roger Maris	75.00	37.00	22.00
(33)	Ed Mathews	40.00	20.00	12.00
(34)	Willie Mays	150.00	75.00	45.00
(35)	Cal Mclish	20.00	10.00	6.00
(36)	Wally Moon	20.00	10.00	6.00
(37)	Walt Moryn	20.00	10.00	6.00
(38)	Don Mossi	20.00	10.00	6.00

(39)	Stan Musial	100.00	50.00	30.00
(40)	Charlie Neal	20.00	10.00	6.00
(41)	Don Newcombe	20.00	10.00	6.00
(42)	Milt Pappas	20.00	10.00	6.00
(43)	Camilo Pascual	20.00	10.00	6.00
(44)	Billie (Billy) Pierce	20.00	10.00	6.00
(45)	Robin Roberts	35.00	17.50	10.50
(46)	Frank Robinson	40.00	20.00	12.00
(47)	Pete Runnels	20.00	10.00	6.00
(48)	Herb Score	20.00	10.00	6.00
(49)	Warren Spahn	35.00	17.50	10.50
(50)	Johnny Temple	20.00	10.00	6.00
(51)	Gus Triandos	20.00	10.00	6.00
(52)	Jerry Walker	20.00	10.00	6.00
(53)	Bill White	20.00	10.00	6.00
(54)	Gene Woodling	20.00	10.00	6.00
(55)	Early Wynn	35.00	17.50	10.50
(56)	Chicago Cubs Logo	15.00	7.50	4.50
(57)	Cincinnati Reds Logo	15.00	7.50	4.50
(58)	Los Angeles Dodgers Logo	15.00	7.50	4.50
(59)	Milwaukee Braves Logo	15.00	7.50	4.50
(60)	Philadelphia Phillies Logo	15.00	7.50	4.50
(61)	Pittsburgh Pirates Logo	20.00	10.00	6.00
(62)	San Francisco Giants Logo	15.00	7.50	4.50
(63)	St. Louis Cardinals Logo	15.00	7.50	4.50
(64)	Baltimore Orioles Logo	15.00	7.50	4.50
(65)	Boston Red Sox Logo	15.00	7.50	4.50
(66)	Chicago White Sox Logo	15.00	7.50	4.50
(67)	Cleveland Indians Logo	15.00	7.50	4.50
(68)	Detroit Tigers Logo	15.00	7.50	4.50
(69)	Kansas City Athletics Logo	15.00	7.50	4.50
(70)	New York Yankees Logo	20.00	10.00	6.00
(71)	Washington Senators Logo	15.00	7.50	4.50
(72)	Autograph(Richie Ashburn)	20.00	10.00	6.00
(73)	Autograph(Rocky Colavito)	25.00	12.50	7.50
(74)	Autograph(Roy Face)	15.00	7.50	4.50
(75)	Autograph(Jackie Jensen)	15.00	7.50	4.50
(76)	Autograph(Harmon Killebrew)	25.00	12.50	7.50
(77)	Autograph(Mickey Mantle)	100.00	50.00	30.00
(78)	Autograph(Willie Mays)	50.00	25.00	15.00
(79)	Autograph(Stan Musial)	50.00	25.00	15.00
(80)	Autograph(Billy Pierce)	15.00	7.50	4.50
(81)	Autograph(Jerry Walker)	15.00	7.50	4.50
(82)	Run-Down	12.00	6.00	3.50
(83)	Out At First	12.00	6.00	3.50
(84)	The Final Word	12.00	6.00	3.50
(85)	Twisting Foul	12.00	6.00	3.50
(86)	Out At Home	12.00	6.00	3.50
(87)	Circus Catch	12.00	6.00	3.50
(88)	Great Catch	12.00	6.00	3.50
(89)	Stolen Base	12.00	6.00	3.50
(90)	Grand Slam Homer	12.00	6.00	3.50
(91)	Double Play	12.00	6.00	3.50
(92)	Left-Handed Follow Thru	12.00	6.00	3.50
(93)	Left-Handed High Leg Kick	12.00	6.00	3.50
(94)	Right-handed pitcher	12.00	6.00	3.50
(95)	Right-handed batter	12.00	6.00	3.50
(96)	Left-handed batter	12.00	6.00	3.50

1961 Topps

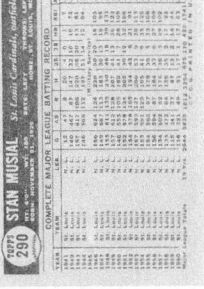

Except for some of the specialty cards, Topps returned to a vertical format with their 1961 cards. The set is numbered through 589, however, only 587 cards were printed. No numbers 426, 587 and 588 were issued. Two cards numbered 463 exist (one a Braves team card and one a player card of Jack Fisher). Actually, the Braves team card is checklisted as #426. Designs for 1961 are basically large color portraits; the backs return to extensive statistics. A three-panel cartoon highlighting the player's career appears on the card backs.

Innovations include numbered checklists, cards for statistical leaders, and 10 "Baseball Thrills" cards. The scarce high numbers are card numbers 523-589.

		NM	E	VG
Complete Set (587):		7,500	3,750	2,250
Common Player (1-522):		6.00	3.00	1.75
Common Player (523-589):		20.00	10.00	6.00
1	Dick Groat	25.00	6.00	2.00
2	Roger Maris	180.00	90.00	54.00
3	John Buzhardt	6.00	3.00	1.75
4	Lenny Green	6.00	3.00	1.75
5	Johnny Romano	6.00	3.00	1.75
6	Ed Roebuck	6.00	3.00	1.75
7	Chicago White Sox Team	15.00	7.50	4.50
8	Dick Williams	6.00	3.00	1.75
9	Bob Purkey	6.00	3.00	1.75
10	Brooks Robinson	40.00	20.00	12.00
11	Curt Simmons	6.00	3.00	1.75
12	Moe Thacker	6.00	3.00	1.75
13	Chuck Cottier	6.00	3.00	1.75
14	Don Mossi	6.00	3.00	1.75
15	Willie Kirkland	6.00	3.00	1.75
16	Billy Muffett	6.00	3.00	1.75
17	1st Series Checklist (1-88)	12.00	6.00	3.50
18	Jim Grant	6.00	3.00	1.75
19	Cletis Boyer	10.00	5.00	3.00
20	Robin Roberts	15.00	7.50	4.50
21	Zoilo Versalles **RC**	12.50	6.25	3.75
22	Clem Labine	6.00	3.00	1.75
23	Don Demeter	6.00	3.00	1.75
24	Ken Johnson	6.00	3.00	1.75
25	Reds' Heavy Artillery(Gus Bell, Vada Pinson, Frank Robinson)	15.00	7.50	4.50
26	Wes Stock	6.00	3.00	1.75
27	Jerry Kindall	6.00	3.00	1.75
28	Hector Lopez	6.00	3.00	1.75
29	Don Nottebart	6.00	3.00	1.75
30	Nellie Fox	20.00	10.00	6.00
31	Bob Schmidt	6.00	3.00	1.75
32	Ray Sadecki	6.00	3.00	1.75
33	Gary Geiger	6.00	3.00	1.75
34	Wynn Hawkins	6.00	3.00	1.75
35	Ron Santo **RC**	60.00	30.00	18.00
36	Jack Kralick	6.00	3.00	1.75
37	Charlie Maxwell	6.00	3.00	1.75
38	Bob Lillis	6.00	3.00	1.75
39	Leo Posada	6.00	3.00	1.75
40	Bob Turley	10.00	5.00	3.00
41	N.L. Batting Leaders (Roberto Clemente, Dick Groat, Norm Larker, Willie Mays)	21.00	10.00	6.00
42	A.L. Batting Leaders (Minnie Minoso, Pete Runnels, Bill Skowron, Al Smith)	9.00	4.50	2.75
43	N.L. Home Run Leaders (Hank Aaron, Ernie Banks, Ken Boyer, Eddie Mathews)	20.00	10.00	6.200
44	A.L. Home Run Leaders (Rocky Colavito, Jim Lemon, Mickey Mantle, Roger Maris)	60.00	30.00	18.00
45	N.L. E.R.A. Leaders (Ernie Broglio, Don Drysdale, Bob Friend, Mike McCormick, Stan Williams)	10.00	5.00	3.00
46	A.L. E.R.A. Leaders (Frank Baumann, Hal Brown, Jim Bunning, Art Ditmar)	9.00	4.50	2.75
47a	N.L. Pitching Leaders (Ernie Broglio, Lou Burdette, Vern Law, Warren Spahn) (Vertical black bar to right of 19.)	12.00	6.00	3.50
47b	N.L. Pitching Leaders (Ernie Broglio, Lew Burdette, Vern Law, Warren Spahn) (No black bar.)	12.00	6.00	3.50
48	A.L. Pitching Leaders (Bud Daley, Art Ditmar, Chuck Estrada, Frank Lary, Milt Pappas, Jim Perry)	7.00	3.50	2.00
49	N.L. Strikeout Leaders (Ernie Broglio, Don Drysdale, Sam Jones, Sandy Koufax)	15.00	7.50	4.50

50	A.L. Strikeout Leaders (Jim Bunning, Frank Lary, Pedro Ramos, Early Wynn)	12.00	6.00	3.50
51	Detroit Tigers Team	10.00	5.00	3.00
52	George Crowe	6.00	3.00	1.75
53	Russ Nixon	6.00	3.00	1.75
54	Earl Francis	6.00	3.00	1.75
55	Jim Davenport	6.00	3.00	1.75
56	Russ Kemmerer	6.00	3.00	1.75
57	Marv Throneberry	6.00	3.00	1.75
58	Joe Schaffernoth	6.00	3.00	1.75
59	Jim Woods	6.00	3.00	1.75
60	Woodie Held	6.00	3.00	1.75
61	Ron Piche	6.00	3.00	1.75
62	Al Pilarcik	6.00	3.00	1.75
63	Jim Kaat	9.00	4.50	2.75
64	Alex Grammas	6.00	3.00	1.75
65	Ted Kluszewski	13.00	6.00	3.50
66	Bill Henry	6.00	3.00	1.75
67	Ossie Virgil	6.00	3.00	1.75
68	Deron Johnson	6.00	3.00	1.75
69	Earl Wilson	6.00	3.00	1.75
70	Bill Virdon	6.00	3.00	1.75
71	Jerry Adair	6.00	3.00	1.75
72	Stu Miller	6.00	3.00	1.75
73	Al Spangler	6.00	3.00	1.75
74	Joe Pignatano	6.00	3.00	1.75
75	Lindy Shows Larry (Larry Jackson, Lindy McDaniel)	6.00	3.00	1.75
76	Harry Anderson	6.00	3.00	1.75
77	Dick Stigman	6.00	3.00	1.75
78	Lee Walls	6.00	3.00	1.75
79	Joe Ginsberg	6.00	3.00	1.75
80	Harmon Killebrew	25.00	12.50	7.50
81	Tracy Stallard	6.00	3.00	1.75
82	Joe Christopher	6.00	3.00	1.75
83	Bob Bruce	6.00	3.00	1.75
84	Lee Maye	6.00	3.00	1.75
85	Jerry Walker	6.00	3.00	1.75
86	Los Angeles Dodgers Team	15.00	7.50	4.50
87	Joe Amalfitano	6.00	3.00	1.75
88	Richie Ashburn	15.00	7.50	4.50
89	Billy Martin	9.00	4.50	2.75
90	Jerry Staley	6.00	3.00	1.75
91	Walt Moryn	6.00	3.00	1.75
92	Hal Naragon	6.00	3.00	1.75
93	Tony Gonzalez	6.00	3.00	1.75
94	Johnny Kucks	6.00	3.00	1.75
95	Norm Cash	12.50	6.25	3.75
96	Billy O'Dell	6.00	3.00	1.75
97	Jerry Lynch	6.00	3.00	1.75
98a	2nd Series Checklist (9-176) ("Checklist" in red on front.)	12.00	6.00	3.50
98b	2nd Series Checklist (89-176) ("Checklist" in yellow, 98 on back in black.)	12.00	6.00	3.50
98c	2nd Series Checklist (89-176) ("Checklist" in yellow, 98 on back in white.)	12.00	6.00	3.50
99	Don Buddin	6.00	3.00	1.75
100	Harvey Haddix	6.00	3.00	1.75
101	Bubba Phillips	6.00	3.00	1.75
102	Gene Stephens	6.00	3.00	1.75
103	Ruben Amaro	6.00	3.00	1.75
104	John Blanchard	7.50	3.75	2.25
105	Carl Willey	6.00	3.00	1.75
106	Whitey Herzog	6.00	3.00	1.75
107	Seth Morehead	6.00	3.00	1.75
108	Dan Dobbek	6.00	3.00	1.75
109	Johnny Podres	7.50	3.75	2.25
110	Vada Pinson	9.00	4.50	2.75
111	Jack Meyer	6.00	3.00	1.75
112	Chico Fernandez	6.00	3.00	1.75
113	Mike Fornieles	6.00	3.00	1.75
114	Hobie Landrith	6.00	3.00	1.75
115	Johnny Antonelli	6.00	3.00	1.75
116	Joe DeMaestri	6.00	3.00	1.75
117	Dale Long	6.00	3.00	1.75
118	Chris Cannizzaro	6.00	3.00	1.75
119	A's Big Armor(Hank Bauer, Jerry Lumpe, Norm Siebern)	9.00	4.50	2.75
120	Ed Mathews	25.00	15.00	9.00
121	Eli Grba	6.00	3.00	1.75
122	Chicago Cubs Team	13.00	6.00	3.50
123	Billy Gardner	6.00	3.00	1.75
124	J.C. Martin	6.00	3.00	1.75
125	Steve Barber	6.00	3.00	1.75
126	Dick Stuart	6.00	3.00	1.75
127	Ron Kline	6.00	3.00	1.75
128	Rip Repulski	6.00	3.00	1.75
129	Ed Hobaugh	6.00	3.00	1.75

130	Norm Larker	6.00	3.00	1.75
131	Paul Richards	6.00	3.00	1.75
132	Al Lopez	12.50	6.25	3.75
133	Ralph Houk	25.00	12.50	7.50
134	Mickey Vernon	6.00	3.00	1.75
135	Fred Hutchinson	6.00	3.00	1.75
136	Walt Alston	12.50	6.25	3.75
137	Chuck Dressen	6.00	3.00	1.75
138	Danny Murtaugh	6.00	3.00	1.75
139	Solly Hemus	6.00	3.00	1.75
140	Gus Triandos	6.00	3.00	1.75
141	Billy Williams **RC**	60.00	30.00	15.00
142	Luis Arroyo	6.00	3.00	1.75
143	Russ Snyder	6.00	3.00	1.75
144	Jim Coker	6.00	3.00	1.75
145	Bob Buhl	6.00	3.00	1.75
146	Marty Keough	6.00	3.00	1.75
147	Ed Rakow	6.00	3.00	1.75
148	Julian Javier	6.00	3.00	1.75
149	Bob Oldis	6.00	3.00	1.75
150	Willie Mays	100.00	50.00	30.00
151	Jim Donohue	6.00	3.00	1.75
152	Earl Torgeson	6.00	3.00	1.75
153	Don Lee	6.00	3.00	1.75
154	Bobby Del Greco	6.00	3.00	1.75
155	Johnny Temple	6.00	3.00	1.75
156	Ken Hunt	6.00	3.00	1.75
157	Cal McLish	6.00	3.00	1.75
158	Pete Daley	6.00	3.00	1.75
159	Baltimore Orioles Team	13.00	6.00	3.50
160	Whitey Ford	50.00	25.00	12.50
161	Sherman Jones	6.00	3.00	1.75
162	Jay Hook	6.00	3.00	1.75
163	Ed Sadowski	6.00	3.00	1.75
164	Felix Mantilla	6.00	3.00	1.75
165	Gino Cimoli	6.00	3.00	1.75
166	Danny Kravitz	6.00	3.00	1.75
167	San Francisco Giants Team	12.00	6.00	3.50
168	Tommy Davis	6.00	3.00	1.75
169	Don Elston	6.00	3.00	1.75
170	Al Smith	6.00	3.00	1.75
171	Paul Foytack	6.00	3.00	1.75
172	Don Dillard	6.00	3.00	1.75
173	Beantown Bombers(Jackie Jensen, Frank Malzone, Vic Wertz)	14.00	7.00	4.00
174	Ray Semproch	6.00	3.00	1.75
175	Gene Freese	6.00	3.00	1.75
176	Ken Aspromonte	6.00	3.00	1.75
177	Don Larsen	7.50	3.75	2.25
178	Bob Nieman	6.00	3.00	1.75
179	Joe Koppe	6.00	3.00	1.75
180	Bobby Richardson	15.00	7.50	4.50
181	Fred Green	6.00	3.00	1.75
182	Dave Nicholson **RC**	6.00	3.00	1.75
183	Andre Rodgers	6.00	3.00	1.75
184	Steve Bilko	6.00	3.00	1.75
185	Herb Score	6.00	3.00	1.75
186	Elmer Valo	6.00	3.00	1.75
187	Billy Klaus	6.00	3.00	1.75
188	Jim Marshall	6.00	3.00	1.75
189a	3rd Series Checklist (177-264) (No "4" on player at left.)	10.00	5.00	3.00
189b	3rd Series Checklist (177-264) ("4" shows on player on left)	10.00	5.00	3.00
190	Stan Williams	6.00	3.00	1.75
191	Mike de la Hoz	6.00	3.00	1.75
192	Dick Brown	6.00	3.00	1.75
193	Gene Conley	6.00	3.00	1.75
194	Gordy Coleman	6.00	3.00	1.75
195	Jerry Casale	6.00	3.00	1.75
196	Ed Bouchee	6.00	3.00	1.75
197	Dick Hall	6.00	3.00	1.75
198	Carl Sawatski	6.00	3.00	1.75
199	Bob Boyd	6.00	3.00	1.75
200	Warren Spahn	40.00	20.00	10.00
201	Pete Whisenant	6.00	3.00	1.75
202	Al Neiger	6.00	3.00	1.75
203	Eddie Bressoud	6.00	3.00	1.75
204	Bob Skinner	6.00	3.00	1.75
205	Bill Pierce	6.00	3.00	1.75
206	Gene Green	6.00	3.00	1.75
207	Dodger Southpaws (Sandy Koufax, Johnny Podres)	20.00	10.00	6.00
208	Larry Osborne	6.00	3.00	1.75
209	Ken McBride	6.00	3.00	1.75
210	Pete Runnels	6.00	3.00	1.75
211	Bob Gibson	30.00	12.50	7.50
212	Haywood Sullivan	6.00	3.00	1.75
213	Bill Stafford **RC**	6.00	3.00	1.75
214	Danny Murphy	6.00	3.00	1.75
215	Gus Bell	6.00	3.00	1.75
216	Ted Bowsfield	6.00	3.00	1.75
217	Mel Roach	6.00	3.00	1.75

218	Hal Brown	6.00	3.00	1.75
219	Gene Mauch	6.00	3.00	1.75
220	Al Dark	6.00	3.00	1.75
221	Mike Higgins	6.00	3.00	1.75
222	Jimmie Dykes	6.00	3.00	1.75
223	Bob Scheffing	6.00	3.00	1.75
224	Joe Gordon	6.00	3.00	1.75
225	Bill Rigney	6.00	3.00	1.75
226	Harry Lavagetto	6.00	3.00	1.75
227	Juan Pizarro	6.00	3.00	1.75
228	New York Yankees Team	45.00	23.00	11.00
229	Rudy Hernandez	6.00	3.00	1.75
230	Don Hoak	6.00	3.00	1.75
231	Dick Drott	6.00	3.00	1.75
232	Bill White	6.00	3.00	1.75
233	Joe Jay	6.00	3.00	1.75
234	Ted Lepcio	6.00	3.00	1.75
235	Camilo Pascual	6.00	3.00	1.75
236	Don Gile	6.00	3.00	1.75
237	Billy Loes	6.00	3.00	1.75
238	Jim Gilliam	7.50	3.75	2.25
239	Dave Sisler	6.00	3.00	1.75
240	Ron Hansen	6.00	3.00	1.75
241	Al Cicotte	6.00	3.00	1.75
242	Hal W. Smith	6.00	3.00	1.75
243	Frank Lary	6.00	3.00	1.75
244	Chico Cardenas	6.00	3.00	1.75
245	Joe Adcock	6.00	3.00	1.75
246	Bob Davis	6.00	3.00	1.75
247	Billy Goodman	6.00	3.00	1.75
248	Ed Keegan	6.00	3.00	1.75
249	Cincinnati Reds Team	13.00	6.00	3.50
250	Buc Hill Aces(Roy Face, Vern Law)	9.00	4.50	2.75
251	Bill Bruton	6.00	3.00	1.75
252	Bill Short	6.00	3.00	1.75
253	Sammy Taylor	6.00	3.00	1.75
254	Ted Sadowski	6.00	3.00	1.75
255	Vic Power	6.00	3.00	1.75
256	Billy Hoeft	6.00	3.00	1.75
257	Carroll Hardy	6.00	3.00	1.75
258	Jack Sanford	6.00	3.00	1.75
259	John Schaive	6.00	3.00	1.75
260	Don Drysdale	20.00	10.00	6.00
261	Charlie Lau	6.00	3.00	1.75
262	Tony Curry	6.00	3.00	1.75
263	Ken Hamlin	6.00	3.00	1.75
264	Glen Hobbie	6.00	3.00	1.75
265	Tony Kubek	15.00	7.50	4.50
266	Lindy McDaniel	6.00	3.00	1.75
267	Norm Siebern	6.00	3.00	1.75
268	Ike DeLock (Delock)	6.00	3.00	1.75
269	Harry Chiti	6.00	3.00	1.75
270	Bob Friend	6.00	3.00	1.75
271	Jim Landis	6.00	3.00	1.75
272	Tom Morgan	6.00	3.00	1.75
273a	4th Series Checklist (265-352) (Copyright ends opposite fifth name.)	12.00	6.00	3.50
273b	4th Series Checklist (265-352) (Copyright ends opposite top name.)	12.00	6.00	3.50
274	Gary Bell	6.00	3.00	1.75
275	Gene Woodling	6.00	3.00	1.75
276	Ray Rippelmeyer	6.00	3.00	1.75
277	Hank Foiles	6.00	3.00	1.75
278	Don McMahon	6.00	3.00	1.75
279	Jose Pagan	6.00	3.00	1.75
280	Frank Howard	9.00	4.50	2.75
281	Frank Sullivan	6.00	3.00	1.75
282	Faye Throneberry	6.00	3.00	1.75
283	Bob Anderson	6.00	3.00	1.75
284	Dick Gernert	6.00	3.00	1.75
285	Sherm Lollar	6.00	3.00	1.75
286	George Witt	6.00	3.00	1.75
287	Carl Yastrzemski	60.00	30.00	18.00
288	Albie Pearson	6.00	3.00	1.75
289	Ray Moore	6.00	3.00	1.75
290	Stan Musial	75.00	40.00	24.00
291	Tex Clevenger	6.00	3.00	1.75
292	Jim Baumer	6.00	3.00	1.75
293	Tom Sturdivant	6.00	3.00	1.75
294	Don Blasingame	6.00	3.00	1.75
295	Milt Pappas	6.00	3.00	1.75
296	Wes Covington	6.00	3.00	1.75
297	Kansas City Athletics Team	13.00	6.00	3.50
298	Jim Golden	6.00	3.00	1.75
299	Clay Dalrymple	6.00	3.00	1.75
300	Mickey Mantle	415.00	210.00	125.00
301	Chet Nichols	6.00	3.00	1.75
302	Al Heist	6.00	3.00	1.75
303	Gary Peters	6.00	3.00	1.75
304	Rocky Nelson	6.00	3.00	1.75
305	Mike McCormick	6.00	3.00	1.75
306	World Series Game 1 (Virdon Saves Game)	9.00	4.50	2.75

307	World Series Game 2 (Mantle Slams 2 Homers)	60.00	30.00	18.00
308	World Series Game 3 (Richardson Is Hero)	15.00	7.50	4.50
309	World Series Game 4 (Cimoli Safe In Crucial Play)	9.00	4.50	2.75
310	World Series Game 5 (Face Saves The Day)	10.00	5.00	3.00
311	World Series Game 6 (Ford Pitches Second Shutout)	15.00	7.50	4.50
312	World Series Game 7 (Mazeroski's Homer Wins It!)	25.00	12.50	7.50
313	World Series (The Winners Celebrate)	20.00	10.00	6.00
314	Bob Miller	6.00	3.00	1.75
315	Earl Battey	6.00	3.00	1.75
316	Bobby Gene Smith	6.00	3.00	1.75
317	Jim Brewer **RC**	6.00	3.00	1.75
318	Danny O'Connell	6.00	3.00	1.75
319	Valmy Thomas	6.00	3.00	1.75
320	Lou Burdette	6.00	3.00	1.75
321	Marv Breeding	6.00	3.00	1.75
322	Bill Kunkel	6.00	3.00	1.75
323	Sammy Esposito	6.00	3.00	1.75
324	Hank Aguirre	6.00	3.00	1.75
325	Wally Moon	6.00	3.00	1.75
326	Dave Hillman	6.00	3.00	1.75
327	Matty Alou **RC**	17.50	9.00	5.50
328	Jim O'Toole	6.00	3.00	1.75
329	Julio Becquer	6.00	3.00	1.75
330	Rocky Colavito	15.00	7.50	4.50
331	Ned Garver	6.00	3.00	1.75
332	Dutch Dotterer (Photo actually Tommy Dotterer.)	6.00	3.00	1.75
333	Fritz Brickell	6.00	3.00	1.75
334	Walt Bond	6.00	3.00	1.75
335	Frank Bolling	6.00	3.00	1.75
336	Don Mincher	6.00	3.00	1.75
337	Al's Aces(Al Lopez, Herb Score, Early Wynn)	13.00	6.00	3.75
338	Don Landrum	6.00	3.00	1.75
339	Gene Baker	6.00	3.00	1.75
340	Vic Wertz	6.00	3.00	1.75
341	Jim Owens	6.00	3.00	1.75
342	Clint Courtney	6.00	3.00	1.75
343	Earl Robinson	6.00	3.00	1.75
344	Sandy Koufax	85.00	40.00	24.00
345	Jim Piersall	7.50	3.75	2.25
346	Howie Nunn	6.00	3.00	1.75
347	St. Louis Cardinals Team	13.00	6.00	3.50
348	Steve Boros	6.00	3.00	1.75
349	Danny McDevitt	6.00	3.00	1.75
350	Ernie Banks	45.00	25.00	12.50
351	Jim King	6.00	3.00	1.75
352	Bob Shaw	6.00	3.00	1.75
353	Howie Bedell	6.00	3.00	1.75
354	Billy Harrell	6.00	3.00	1.75
355	Bob Allison	6.00	3.00	1.75
356	Ryne Duren	7.50	3.75	2.25
357	Daryl Spencer	6.00	3.00	1.75
358	Earl Averill	6.00	3.00	1.75
359	Dallas Green	7.50	3.75	2.25
360	Frank Robinson	25.00	12.50	7.50
361a	5th Series Checklist (353-429) ("Topps Baseball" in black on front.)	13.00	6.00	3.50
361b	5th Series Checklist (353-429) ("Topps Baseball" in yellow.)	15.00	7.50	4.50
362	Frank Funk	6.00	3.00	1.75
363	John Roseboro	6.00	3.00	1.75
364	Moe Drabowsky	6.00	3.00	1.75
365	Jerry Lumpe	6.00	3.00	1.75
366	Eddie Fisher	6.00	3.00	1.75
367	Jim Rivera	6.00	3.00	1.75
368	Bennie Daniels	6.00	3.00	1.75
369	Dave Philley	6.00	3.00	1.75
370	Roy Face	6.00	3.00	1.75
371	Bill Skowron (SP)	45.00	25.00	12.50
372	Bob Hendley	6.00	3.00	1.75
373	Boston Red Sox Team	13.00	6.00	3.50
374	Paul Giel	6.00	3.00	1.75
375	Ken Boyer	13.50	6.75	4.00
376	Mike Roarke	6.00	3.00	1.75
377	Ruben Gomez	6.00	3.00	1.75
378	Wally Post	6.00	3.00	1.75
379	Bobby Shantz	6.00	3.00	1.75
380	Minnie Minoso	9.00	4.50	2.75
381	Dave Wickersham	6.00	3.00	1.75
382	Frank Thomas	6.00	3.00	1.75
383	Frisco First Liners(Mike McCormick, Billy O'Dell, Jack Sanford)	7.50	3.75	2.25

384	Chuck Essegian	6.00	3.00	1.75
385	Jim Perry	6.00	3.00	1.75
386	Joe Hicks	6.00	3.00	1.75
387	Duke Maas	6.00	3.00	1.75
388	Bob Clemente	125.00	70.00	35.00
389	Ralph Terry	6.00	3.00	1.75
390	Del Crandall	6.00	3.00	1.75
391	Winston Brown	6.00	3.00	1.75
392	Reno Bertoia	6.00	3.00	1.75
393	Batter Bafflers(Don Cardwell, Glen Hobbie)	7.50	3.75	2.25
394	Ken Walters	6.00	3.00	1.75
395	Chuck Estrada	6.00	3.00	1.75
396	Bob Aspromonte	6.00	3.00	1.75
397	Hal Woodeshick	6.00	3.00	1.75
398	Hank Bauer	7.50	3.75	2.25
399	Cliff Cook	6.00	3.00	1.75
400	Vern Law	6.00	3.00	1.75
401	Babe Ruth Hits 60th Homer	50.00	25.00	15.00
402	Larsen Pitches Perfect Game (SP)	25.00	12.50	7.50
403	Brooklyn-Boston Play 26-Inning Tie	6.00	3.00	1.75
404	Hornsby Tops N.L. with .424 Average	9.00	4.50	2.75
405	Gehrig Benched After 2,130 Games	75.00	37.50	18.75
406	Mantle Blasts 565 ft. Home Run	100.00	50.00	25.00
407	Jack Chesbro Wins 41st Game	6.00	3.00	1.75
408	Mathewson Strikes Out 267 Batters (SP)	17.50	8.75	5.25
409	Johnson Hurls 3rd Shutout In 4 Days	9.00	4.50	2.75
410	Haddix Pitches 12 Perfect Innings	9.00	4.50	2.70
411	Tony Taylor	6.00	3.00	1.75
412	Larry Sherry	6.00	3.00	1.75
413	Eddie Yost	6.00	3.00	1.75
414	Dick Donovan	6.00	3.00	1.75
415	Hank Aaron	100.00	50.00	30.00
416	Dick Howser **RC** (SP)	12.50	6.25	3.75
417	Juan Marichal **RC**	95.00	50.00	25.00
418	Ed Bailey	6.00	3.00	1.75
419	Tom Borland	6.00	3.00	1.75
420	Ernie Broglio	6.00	3.00	1.75
421	Ty Cline (SP)	12.50	6.25	3.75
422	Bud Daley	6.00	3.00	1.75
423	Charlie Neal (SP)	12.50	6.25	3.75
424	Turk Lown	6.00	3.00	1.75
425	Yogi Berra	80.00	42.50	21.25
426	Not Issued (See #463.)			
427	Dick Ellsworth	6.00	3.00	1.75
428	Ray Barker (SP)	12.50	6.25	3.75
429	Al Kaline	45.00	25.00	12.50
430	Bill Mazeroski (SP)	45.00	25.00	12.50
431	Chuck Stobbs	6.00	3.00	1.75
432	Coot Veal	6.00	3.00	1.75
433	Art Mahaffey	6.00	3.00	1.75
434	Tom Brewer	6.00	3.00	1.75
435	Orlando Cepeda	15.00	7.50	4.50
436	Jim Maloney **RC** (SP)	25.00	10.00	6.00
437a	6th Series Checklist (430-506) (#440 is Louis Aparicio)	12.00	6.00	3.50
437b	6th Series Checklist (430-506) (#440 is Luis Aparicio)	10.00	5.00	3.00
438	Curt Flood	7.50	3.75	2.25
439	Phil Regan **RC**	6.00	3.00	1.75
440	Luis Aparicio	15.00	7.50	4.50
441	Dick Bertell	6.00	3.00	1.75
442	Gordon Jones	6.00	3.00	1.75
443	Duke Snider	30.00	15.00	9.00
444	Joe Nuxhall	6.00	3.00	1.75
445	Frank Malzone	6.00	3.00	1.75
446	Bob "Hawk" Taylor	6.00	3.00	1.75
447a	Harry Bright (clear blue sky on right)	6.00	3.00	1.75
447b	Harry Bright (blue "swoosh" in sky, right)	6.00	3.00	1.75
448	Del Rice	6.00	3.00	1.75
449	Bobby Bolin **RC**	6.00	3.00	1.75
450	Jim Lemon	6.00	3.00	1.75
451	Power For Ernie(Ernie Broglio, Daryl Spencer, Bill White)	7.50	3.75	2.25
452	Bob Allen	6.00	3.00	1.75
453	Dick Schofield	6.00	3.00	1.75
454	Pumpsie Green	6.00	3.00	1.75
455	Early Wynn	15.00	7.50	4.50
456	Hal Bevan	6.00	3.00	1.75
457	Johnny James	6.00	3.00	1.75
458	Willie Tasby	6.00	3.00	1.75
459	Terry Fox	6.00	3.00	1.75
460	Gil Hodges	12.50	6.25	3.75

461	Smoky Burgess	6.00	3.00	1.75
462	Lou Klimchock	6.00	3.00	1.75
463a	Milwaukee Braves Team (Should be card #426.)	10.00	5.00	3.00
463b	Jack Fisher	6.00	3.00	1.75
464	Leroy Thomas **RC**	6.00	3.00	1.75
465	Roy McMillan	6.00	3.00	1.75
466	Ron Moeller	6.00	3.00	1.75
467	Cleveland Indians Team	13.00	6.00	3.50
468	Johnny Callison	6.00	3.00	1.75
469	Ralph Lumenti	6.00	3.00	1.75
470	Roy Sievers	6.00	3.00	1.75
471	Phil Rizzuto (MVP)	30.00	15.00	7.50
472	Yogi Berra (MVP)	55.00	25.00	12.50
473	Bobby Shantz (MVP)	7.50	3.75	2.25
474	Al Rosen (MVP)	7.50	3.75	2.25
475	Mickey Mantle (MVP)	200.00	100.00	50.00
476	Jackie Jensen (MVP)	7.50	3.75	2.25
477	Nellie Fox (MVP)	17.50	8.75	5.25
478	Roger Maris (MVP)	60.00	30.00	15.00
479	Jim Konstanty (MVP)	6.00	3.00	1.75
480	Roy Campanella (MVP)	40.00	20.00	10.00
481	Hank Sauer (MVP)	6.00	3.00	1.75
482	Willie Mays (MVP)	50.00	25.00	12.50
483	Don Newcombe (MVP)	7.50	3.75	2.25
484	Hank Aaron (MVP)	50.00	25.00	12.50
485	Ernie Banks (MVP)	20.00	10.00	6.00
486	Dick Groat (MVP)	7.50	3.75	2.25
487	Gene Oliver	6.00	3.00	1.75
488	Joe McClain	6.00	3.00	1.75
489	Walt Dropo	6.00	3.00	1.75
490	Jim Bunning	17.50	6.25	3.75
491	Philadelphia Phillies Team	13.00	6.00	3.50
492	Ron Fairly	6.00	3.00	1.75
493	Don Zimmer	7.50	3.75	2.25
494	Tom Cheney	6.00	3.00	1.75
495	Elston Howard	15.00	7.50	4.50
496	Ken MacKenzie	6.00	3.00	1.75
497	Willie Jones	6.00	3.00	1.75
498	Ray Herbert	6.00	3.00	1.75
499	Chuck Schilling **RC**	6.00	3.00	1.75
500	Harvey Kuenn	6.00	3.00	1.75
501	John DeMerit	6.00	3.00	1.75
502	Clarence Coleman	6.00	3.00	1.75
503	Tito Francona	6.00	3.00	1.75
504	Billy Consolo	6.00	3.00	1.75
505	Red Schoendienst	12.50	6.25	3.75
506	Willie Davis **RC**	13.50	6.75	4.00
507	Pete Burnside	6.00	3.00	1.75
508	Rocky Bridges	6.00	3.00	1.75
509	Camilo Carreon	6.00	3.00	1.75
510	Art Ditmar	6.00	3.00	1.75
511	Joe Morgan	6.00	3.00	1.75
512	Bob Will	6.00	3.00	1.75
513	Jim Brosnan	6.00	3.00	1.75
514	Jake Wood	6.00	3.00	1.75
515	Jackie Brandt	6.00	3.00	1.75
516a	7th Series Checklist (507-587) (Second "C" of "CHECK" above #13's cap.)	16.00	8.00	4.50
516b	7th Series Checklist (506-587) (Second "C" of "CHECK" covers top of #13's cap.)	18.00	9.00	5.50
517	Willie McCovey	35.00	20.00	10.00
518	Andy Carey	6.00	3.00	1.75
519	Jim Pagliaroni	6.00	3.00	1.75
520	Joe Cunningham	6.00	3.00	1.75
521	Brother Battery(Larry Sherry, Norm Sherry)	13.00	6.00	3.50
522	Dick Farrell	6.00	3.00	1.75
523	Joe Gibbon	20.00	10.00	6.00
524	Johnny Logan	20.00	10.00	6.00
525	Ron Perranoski **RC**	45.00	25.00	15.00
526	R.C. Stevens	20.00	10.00	6.00
527	Gene Leek	20.00	10.00	6.00
528	Pedro Ramos	20.00	10.00	6.00
529	Bob Roselli	20.00	10.00	6.00
530	Bobby Malkmus	20.00	10.00	6.00
531	Jim Coates	20.00	10.00	6.00
532	Bob Hale	20.00	10.00	6.00
533	Jack Curtis	20.00	10.00	6.00
534	Eddie Kasko	20.00	10.00	6.00
535	Larry Jackson	20.00	10.00	6.00
536	Bill Tuttle	20.00	10.00	6.00
537	Bobby Locke	20.00	10.00	6.00
538	Chuck Hiller	20.00	10.00	6.00
539	Johnny Klippstein	20.00	10.00	6.00
540	Jackie Jensen	27.50	11.00	7.00
541	Roland Sheldon	20.00	10.00	6.00
542	Minnesota Twins Team	45.00	20.00	10.00
543	Roger Craig	20.00	10.00	6.00
544	George Thomas	20.00	10.00	6.00
545	Hoyt Wilhelm	50.00	25.00	15.00
546	Marty Kutyna	20.00	10.00	6.00
547	Leon Wagner	20.00	10.00	6.00
548	Ted Wills	20.00	10.00	6.00

			NM	E	VG
549	Hal R. Smith		20.00	10.00	6.00
550	Frank Baumann		20.00	10.00	6.00
551	George Altman		20.00	10.00	6.00
552	Jim Archer		20.00	10.00	6.00
553	Bill Fischer		20.00	10.00	6.00
554	Pittsburgh Pirates Team		80.00	37.50	18.75
555	Sam Jones		20.00	10.00	6.00
556	Ken R. Hunt		20.00	10.00	6.00
557	Jose Valdivielso		20.00	10.00	6.00
558	Don Ferrarese		20.00	10.00	6.00
559	Jim Gentile		60.00	30.00	15.00
560	Barry Latman		20.00	10.00	6.00
561	Charley James		20.00	10.00	6.00
562	Bill Monbouquette		20.00	10.00	6.00
563	Bob Cerv		20.00	10.00	6.00
564	Don Cardwell		20.00	10.00	6.00
565	Felipe Alou		25.00	12.50	6.25
566	Paul Richards (All-Star)		25.00	10.00	6.00
567	Danny Murtaugh (All-Star)		25.00	10.00	6.00
568	Bill Skowron (All-Star)		25.00	12.50	7.50
569	Frank Herrera (All-Star)		20.00	10.00	6.00
570	Nellie Fox (All-Star)		45.00	25.00	12.50
571	Bill Mazeroski (All-Star)		45.00	25.00	12.50
572	Brooks Robinson (All-Star)		55.00	30.00	15.00
573	Ken Boyer (All-Star)		25.00	12.00	7.00
574	Luis Aparicio (All-Star)		50.00	25.00	12.50
575	Ernie Banks (All-Star)		100.00	50.00	25.00
576	Roger Maris (All-Star)		140.00	70.00	40.00
577	Hank Aaron (All-Star)		160.00	80.00	40.00
578	Mickey Mantle (All-Star)		400.00	200.00	120.00
579	Willie Mays (All-Star)		160.00	80.00	40.00
580	Al Kaline (All-Star)		80.00	40.00	20.00
581	Frank Robinson (All-Star)		75.00	40.00	20.00
582	Earl Battey (All-Star)		20.00	10.00	6.00
583	Del Crandall (All-Star)		20.00	10.00	6.00
584	Jim Perry (All-Star)		20.00	10.00	6.00
585	Bob Friend (All-Star)		20.00	10.00	6.00
586	Whitey Ford (All-Star)		90.00	45.00	27.00
587	Not Issued				
588	Not Issued				
589	Warren Spahn (All-Star)		80.00	40.00	24.00

1961 Topps Dice Game

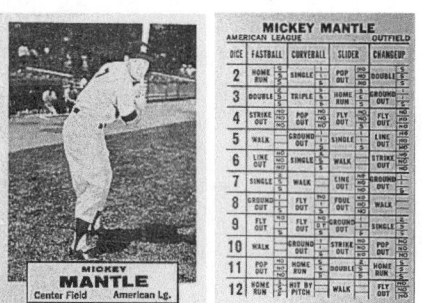

One of the more obscure Topps test issues that may have never actually been issued is the 1961 Topps Dice Game. Eighteen black and white cards, each measuring 2-1/2" x 3-1/2" in size, comprise the set. Interestingly, there are no identifying marks, such as copyrights or trademarks, to indicate the set was produced by Topps. The card backs contain various baseball plays that occur when a certain pitch is called and a specific number of the dice is rolled.

		NM	E	VG
Common Player:		3.000	1.500	750.00
(1)	Earl Battey	3,000	1,500	750.00
(2)	Del Crandall	3,000	1,500	750.00
(3)	Jim Davenport	3,000	1,500	750.00
(4)	Don Drysdale	9,000	4,500	2,250
(5)	Dick Groat	3,000	1,500	750.00
(6)	Al Kaline	20,000	10,000	5,000
(7)	Tony Kubek	3,250	1,625	975.00
(8)	Mickey Mantle	60,000	30,000	15,000
(9)	Willie Mays	40,000	10,000	5,00
(10)	Bill Mazeroski	4,500	2,250	1,350
(11)	Stan Musial	40,000	20,000	10,000
(12)	Camilo Pascual	3,000	1,500	750.00
(13)	Bobby Richardson	7,500	3,750	1,875
(14)	Brooks Robinson	20,000	10,000	5,000
(15)	Frank Robinson	20,000	10,000	5,000
(16)	Norm Siebern	3,000	1,500	750.00
(17)	Leon Wagner	3,000	1,500	750.00
(18)	Bill White	3,000	1,500	750.00

1961 Topps Magic Rub-Offs

Not too different in concept from the tattoos of the previous year, the Topps Magic Rub-Off was designed to leave impressions of team themes or individual players when properly applied. Measuring 2-1/16" x 3-1/16", the Magic Rub-Off was not designed specifically for application to the owner's

skin. The set features team themes that are a far cry from official logos, and the players (one per team) seem to have been included for their nicknames.

		NM	E	VG
Complete Set (36):		300.00	150.00	90.00
Common Player:		9.00	4.50	2.50
(1)	Baltimore Orioles Pennant	9.00	4.50	2.50
(2)	Ernie "Bingo" Banks	22.50	11.25	4.50
(3)	Yogi Berra	22.50	11.25	4.50
(4)	Boston Red Sox Pennant	9.00	4.50	2.50
(5)	Jackie "Ozark" Brandt	9.00	4.50	2.50
(6)	Jim "Professor" Brosnan	9.00	4.50	2.50
(7)	Chicago Cubs Pennant	9.00	4.50	2.50
(8)	Chicago White Sox Pennant	9.00	4.50	2.50
(9)	Cincinnati Red Legs Pennant	9.00	4.50	2.50
(10)	Cleveland Indians Pennant	9.00	4.50	2.50
(11)	Detroit Tigers Pennant	9.00	4.50	2.50
(12)	Henry "Dutch" Dotterer	9.00	4.50	2.50
(13)	Joe "Flash" Gordon	9.00	4.50	2.50
(14)	Harvey "The Kitten" Haddix	9.00	4.50	2.50
(15)	Frank "Pancho" Hererra	9.00	4.50	2.50
(16)	Frank "Tower" Howard	11.25	5.50	2.25
(17)	"Sad" Sam Jones	9.00	4.50	2.50
(18)	Kansas City Athletics Pennant	9.00	4.50	2.50
(19)	Los Angeles Angels Pennant	11.25	5.50	2.25
(20)	Los Angeles Dodgers Pennant	11.25	5.50	2.25
(21)	Omar "Turk" Lown	9.00	4.50	2.50
(22)	Billy "The Kid" Martin	11.25	5.50	2.25
(23)	Duane "Duke" Mass (Maas)	9.00	4.50	2.50
(24)	Charlie "Paw Paw" Maxwell	9.00	4.50	2.50
(25)	Milwaukee Braves Pennant	9.00	4.50	2.50
(26)	Minnesota Twins Pennant	11.25	5.50	2.25
(27)	"Farmer" Ray Moore	9.00	4.50	2.50
(28)	Walt "Moose" Moryn	9.00	4.50	2.50
(29)	New York Yankees Pennant	20.25	6.75	2.75
(30)	Philadelphia Phillies Pennant	9.00	4.50	2.50
(31)	Pittsburgh Pirates Pennant	9.00	4.50	2.50
(32)	John "Honey" Romano	9.00	4.50	2.50
(33)	"Pistol Pete" Runnels	9.00	4.50	2.50
(34)	St. Louis Cardinals Pennant	9.00	4.50	2.50
(35)	San Francisco Giants Pennant	9.00	4.50	2.50
(36)	Washington Senators Pennant	20.25	6.75	2.75

1961 Topps Stamps

Issued as an added insert to 1961 Topps wax packs these 1-3/8" x 1-3/16" stamps were desigend to be collected and

placed in an album which could be bought for an additional 10¢. Packs of cards contained two stamps. There are 208 stamps in a complete set which depict 207 different players (Al Kaline appears twice). There are 104 players on brown stamps and 104 on green. While there are many Hall of Famers on the stamps, prices remain low because there is relatively little interest in what is a non-card set.

		NM	E	VG
Complete Set (208):		750.00	375.00	225.00
Common Player:		2.00	1.00	.60
Stamp Album (Green):		65.00	30.00	20.00
(1)	Hank Aaron	20.00	10.00	6.00
(2)	Joe Adcock	2.00	1.00	.60
(3)	Hank Aguirre	2.00	1.00	.60
(4)	Bob Allison	2.00	1.00	.60
(5)	George Altman	2.00	1.00	.60
(6)	Bob Anderson	2.00	1.00	.60
(7)	Johnny Antonelli	2.00	1.00	.60
(8)	Luis Aparicio	12.00	6.00	3.50
(9)	Luis Arroyo	2.00	1.00	.60
(10)	Richie Ashburn	13.50	6.75	4.00
(11)	Ken Aspromonte	2.00	1.00	.60
(12)	Ed Bailey	2.00	1.00	.60
(13)	Ernie Banks	13.50	6.75	4.00
(14)	Steve Barber	2.00	1.00	.60
(15)	Earl Battey	2.00	1.00	.60
(16)	Hank Bauer	2.00	1.00	.60
(17)	Gus Bell	2.00	1.00	.60
(18)	Yogi Berra	13.50	6.75	4.00
(19)	Reno Bertoia	2.00	1.00	.60
(20)	John Blanchard	2.00	1.00	.60
(21)	Don Blasingame	2.00	1.00	.60
(22)	Frank Bolling	2.00	1.00	.60
(23)	Steve Boros	2.00	1.00	.60
(24)	Ed Bouchee	2.00	1.00	.60
(25)	Bob Boyd	2.00	1.00	.60
(26)	Cletis Boyer	2.00	1.00	.60
(27)	Ken Boyer	3.00	1.50	.90
(28)	Jackie Brandt	2.00	1.00	.60
(29)	Marv Breeding	2.00	1.00	.60
(30)	Eddie Bressoud	2.00	1.00	.60
(31)	Jim Brewer	2.00	1.00	.60
(32)	Tom Brewer	2.00	1.00	.60
(33)	Jim Brosnan	2.00	1.00	.60
(34)	Bill Bruton	2.00	1.00	.60
(35)	Bob Buhl	2.00	1.00	.60
(36)	Jim Bunning	10.00	5.00	3.00
(37)	Smoky Burgess	2.00	1.00	.60
(38)	John Buzhardt	2.00	1.00	.60
(39)	Johnny Callison	2.00	1.00	.60
(40)	Chico Cardenas	2.00	1.00	.60
(41)	Andy Carey	2.00	1.00	.60
(42)	Jerry Casale	2.00	1.00	.60
(43)	Norm Cash	4.00	2.00	1.25
(44)	Orlando Cepeda	10.00	5.00	3.00
(45)	Bob Cerv	2.00	1.00	.60
(46)	Harry Chiti	2.00	1.00	.60
(47)	Gene Conley	2.00	1.00	.60
(48)	Wes Covington	2.00	1.00	.60
(49)	Del Crandall	2.00	1.00	.60
(50)	Tony Curry	2.00	1.00	.60
(51)	Bud Daley	2.00	1.00	.60
(52)	Pete Daley	2.00	1.00	.60
(53)	Clay Dalrymple	2.00	1.00	.60
(54)	Jim Davenport	2.00	1.00	.60
(55)	Tommy Davis	2.00	1.00	.60
(56)	Bobby Del Greco	2.00	1.00	.60
(57)	Ike Delock	2.00	1.00	.60
(58)	Art Ditmar	2.00	1.00	.60
(59)	Dick Donovan	2.00	1.00	.60
(60)	Don Drysdale	13.50	6.75	4.00
(61)	Dick Ellsworth	2.00	1.00	.60
(62)	Don Elston	2.00	1.00	.60
(63)	Chuck Estrada	2.00	1.00	.60
(64)	Roy Face	2.00	1.00	.60
(65)	Dick Farrell	2.00	1.00	.60
(66)	Chico Fernandez	2.00	1.00	.60
(67)	Curt Flood	2.00	1.00	.60
(68)	Whitey Ford	13.50	6.75	4.00
(69)	Tito Francona	2.00	1.00	.60
(70)	Gene Freese	2.00	1.00	.60
(71)	Bob Friend	2.00	1.00	.60
(72)	Billy Gardner	2.00	1.00	.60
(73)	Ned Garver	2.00	1.00	.60
(74)	Gary Geiger	2.00	1.00	.60
(75)	Jim Gentile	2.00	1.00	.60
(76)	Dick Gernert	2.00	1.00	.60
(77)	Tony Gonzalez	2.00	1.00	.60
(78)	Alex Grammas	2.00	1.00	.60
(79)	Jim Grant	2.00	1.00	.60
(80)	Dick Groat	2.00	1.00	.60
(81)	Dick Hall	2.00	1.00	.60
(82)	Ron Hansen	2.00	1.00	.60
(83)	Bob Hartman	2.00	1.00	.60
(84)	Woodie Held	2.00	1.00	.60
(85)	Ray Herbert	2.00	1.00	.60
(86)	Frank Herrera	2.00	1.00	.60

(87)	Whitey Herzog	2.00	1.00	.60
(88)	Don Hoak	2.00	1.00	.60
(89)	Elston Howard	5.00	2.50	1.50
(90)	Frank Howard	4.00	2.00	1.25
(91)	Ken Hunt	2.00	1.00	.60
(92)	Larry Jackson	2.00	1.00	.60
(93)	Julian Javier	2.00	1.00	.60
(94)	Joe Jay	2.00	1.00	.60
(95)	Jackie Jensen	2.00	1.00	.60
(96)	Jim Kaat	2.50	1.25	.70
(97)	Al Kaline (Green)	25.00	12.50	7.50
(98)	Al Kaline (Brown)	15.00	7.50	4.50
(99)	Eddie Kasko	2.00	1.00	.60
(100)	Russ Kemmerer	2.00	1.00	.60
(101)	Harmon Killebrew	13.50	6.75	4.00
(102)	Billy Klaus	2.00	1.00	.60
(103)	Ron Kline	2.00	1.00	.60
(104)	Johnny Klippstein	2.00	1.00	.60
(105)	Ted Kluszewski	10.00	5.00	3.00
(106)	Tony Kubek	5.00	2.50	1.50
(107)	Harvey Kuenn	2.00	1.00	.60
(108)	Jim Landis	2.00	1.00	.60
(109)	Hobie Landrith	2.00	1.00	.60
(110)	Norm Larker	2.00	1.00	.60
(111)	Frank Lary	2.00	1.00	.60
(112)	Barry Latman	2.00	1.00	.60
(113)	Vern Law	2.00	1.00	.60
(114)	Jim Lemon	2.00	1.00	.60
(115)	Sherman Lollar	2.00	1.00	.60
(116)	Dale Long	2.00	1.00	.60
(117)	Jerry Lumpe	2.00	1.00	.60
(118)	Jerry Lynch	2.00	1.00	.60
(119)	Art Mahaffey	2.00	1.00	.60
(120)	Frank Malzone	2.00	1.00	.60
(121)	Felix Mantilla	2.00	1.00	.60
(122)	Mickey Mantle	75.00	30.00	18.00
(123)	Juan Marichal	13.50	6.75	4.00
(124)	Roger Maris	25.00	12.50	7.50
(125)	Billy Martin	5.00	2.50	1.50
(126)	J.C. Martin	2.00	1.00	.60
(127)	Ed Mathews	13.50	6.75	4.00
(128)	Charlie Maxwell	2.00	1.00	.60
(129)	Willie Mays	20.00	10.00	6.00
(130)	Bill Mazeroski	12.00	6.00	3.50
(131)	Mike McCormick	2.00	1.00	.60
(132)	Willie McCovey	13.50	6.75	4.00
(133)	Lindy McDaniel	2.00	1.00	.60
(134)	Roy McMillan	2.00	1.00	.60
(135)	Minnie Minoso	3.00	1.50	.90
(136)	Bill Monbouquette	2.00	1.00	.60
(137)	Wally Moon	2.00	1.00	.60
(138)	Stan Musial	20.00	10.00	6.00
(139)	Charlie Neal	2.00	1.00	.60
(140)	Rocky Nelson	2.00	1.00	.60
(141)	Russ Nixon	2.00	1.00	.60
(142)	Billy O'Dell	2.00	1.00	.60
(143)	Jim O'Toole	2.00	1.00	.60
(144)	Milt Pappas	2.00	1.00	.60
(145)	Camilo Pascual	2.00	1.00	.60
(146)	Jim Perry	2.00	1.00	.60
(147)	Bubba Phillips	2.00	1.00	.60
(148)	Bill Pierce	2.00	1.00	.60
(149)	Jim Piersall	2.00	1.00	.60
(150)	Vada Pinson	3.00	1.50	.90
(151)	Johnny Podres	2.50	1.25	.70
(152)	Wally Post	2.00	1.00	.60
(153)	Vic Powers (Power)	2.00	1.00	.60
(154)	Pedro Ramos	2.00	1.00	.60
(155)	Robin Roberts	10.00	5.00	3.00
(156)	Brooks Robinson	13.50	6.75	4.00
(157)	Frank Robinson	13.50	6.75	4.00
(158)	Ed Roebuck	2.00	1.00	.60
(159)	John Romano	2.00	1.00	.60
(160)	John Roseboro	2.00	1.00	.60
(161)	Pete Runnels	2.00	1.00	.60
(162)	Ed Sadowski	2.00	1.00	.60
(163)	Jack Sanford	2.00	1.00	.60
(164)	Ron Santo	3.00	1.50	.90
(165)	Ray Semproch	2.00	1.00	.60
(166)	Bobby Shantz	2.00	1.00	.60
(167)	Bob Shaw	2.00	1.00	.60
(168)	Larry Sherry	2.00	1.00	.60
(169)	Norm Siebern	2.00	1.00	.60
(170)	Roy Sievers	2.00	1.00	.60
(171)	Curt Simmons	2.00	1.00	.60
(172)	Dave Sisler	2.00	1.00	.60
(173)	Bob Skinner	2.00	1.00	.60
(174)	Al Smith	2.00	1.00	.60
(175)	Hal Smith	2.00	1.00	.60
(176)	Hal Smith	2.00	1.00	.60
(177)	Duke Snider	13.50	6.75	4.00
(178)	Warren Spahn	13.50	6.75	4.00
(179)	Daryl Spencer	2.00	1.00	.60
(180)	Bill Stafford	2.00	1.00	.60
(181)	Jerry Staley	2.00	1.00	.60
(182)	Gene Stephens	2.00	1.00	.60
(183)	Chuck Stobbs	2.00	1.00	.60
(184)	Dick Stuart	2.00	1.00	.60
(185)	Willie Tasby	2.00	1.00	.60
(186)	Sammy Taylor	2.00	1.00	.60
(187)	Tony Taylor	2.00	1.00	.60
(188)	Johnny Temple	2.00	1.00	.60
(189)	Marv Throneberry	2.00	1.00	.60
(190)	Gus Triandos	2.00	1.00	.60
(191)	Bob Turley	2.00	1.00	.60
(192)	Bill Tuttle	2.00	1.00	.60
(193)	Zoilo Versalles	2.00	1.00	.60
(194)	Bill Virdon	2.00	1.00	.60
(195)	Lee Walls	2.00	1.00	.60
(196)	Vic Wertz	2.00	1.00	.60
(197)	Pete Whisenant	2.00	1.00	.60
(198)	Bill White	2.00	1.00	.60
(199)	Hoyt Wilhelm	10.00	5.00	3.00
(200)	Bob Will	2.00	1.00	.60
(201)	Carl Willey	2.00	1.00	.60
(202)	Billy Williams	12.00	6.00	3.50
(203)	Dick Williams	2.00	1.00	.60
(204)	Stan Williams	2.00	1.00	.60
(205)	Gene Woodling	2.00	1.00	.60
(206)	Early Wynn	10.00	5.00	3.00
(207)	Carl Yastrzemski	13.50	6.75	4.00
(208)	Eddie Yost	2.00	1.00	.60

1961 Topps Stamps Panels

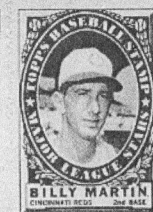

Some advanced collectors pursue the 1961 Topps stamps in the form of the two-stamp panels in which they were issued. The 208 different stamps which make up the issue can be found on 182 different two-stamp panels. The unnumbered stamps are listed here alphabetically according to the name of the player which appears on the left end of the panel. Values shown are for complete panels of two players stamps plus the attached tab at left.

		NM	E	VG
Complete Panel Set (182):		3,000	1,500	900.00
Common Panel:		9.00	4.50	2.75
(1)	Hank Aguirre/Bob Boyd	9.00	4.50	2.75
(2)	Bob Allison/Orlando Cepeda	20.00	10.00	6.00
(3)	Bob Allison/Early Wynn	20.00	10.00	6.00
(4)	George Altman/Andy Carey	9.00	4.50	2.75
(5)	George Altman/Lindy McDaniel	9.00	4.50	2.75
(6)	Johnny Antonelli/Ken Hunt	9.00	4.50	2.75
(7)	Richie Ashburn/Don Drysdale	30.00	15.00	9.00
(8)	Richie Ashburn/Joe Jay	25.00	12.50	7.50
(9)	Ken Aspromonte/Chuck Estrada	9.00	4.50	2.75
(10)	Ken Aspromonte/Jerry Lynch	9.00	4.50	2.75
(11)	Ed Bailey/Marv Breeding	9.00	4.50	2.75
(12)	Ed Bailey/Smoky Burgess	9.00	4.50	2.75
(13)	Ernie Banks/Chico Fernandez	30.00	15.00	9.00
(14)	Ernie Banks/Pedro Ramos	30.00	15.00	9.00
(15)	Steve Barber/Eddie Kasko	9.00	4.50	2.75
(16)	Steve Barber/Roy Sievers	9.00	4.50	2.75
(17)	Earl Battey/Art Ditmar	9.00	4.50	2.75
(18)	Earl Battey/Bill White	9.00	4.50	2.75
(19)	Gus Bell/Gary Geiger	9.00	4.50	2.75
(20)	Gus Bell/Early Wynn	20.00	10.00	6.00
(21)	John Blanchard/Dick Donovan	9.00	4.50	2.75
(22)	John Blanchard/Ray Semproch	9.00	4.50	2.75
(23)	Don Blasingame/Elston Howard	12.00	6.00	3.50
(24)	Don Blasingame/Charlie Maxwell	9.00	4.50	2.75
(25)	Frank Bolling/Luis Aparicio	20.00	10.00	6.00
(26)	Frank Bolling/Whitey Herzog	9.00	4.50	2.75
(27)	Steve Boros/Ike Delock	9.00	4.50	2.75
(28)	Steve Boros/Russ Nixon	9.00	4.50	2.75
(29)	Ed Bouchee/Larry Sherry	9.00	4.50	2.75
(30)	Ed Bouchee/Willie Tasby	9.00	4.50	2.75

(31)	Cletis Boyer/Johnny Klippstein	9.00	4.50	2.75
(32)	Jim Brewer/Vern Law	9.00	4.50	2.75
(33)	Jim Brewer/Camilo Pascual	9.00	4.50	2.75
(34)	Tom Brewer/Tommy Davis	9.00	4.50	2.75
(35)	Tom Brewer/Larry Sherry	9.00	4.50	2.75
(36)	Jim Brosnan/Roy McMillan	9.00	4.50	2.75
(37)	Jim Brosnan/Calr Willey	9.00	4.50	2.75
(38)	Bill Bruton/Ken Boyer	12.00	6.00	3.50
(39)	Bill Bruton/Mickey Mantle	200.00	100.00	60.00
(40)	Bob Buhl/Willie Mays	60.00	30.00	18.00
(41)	Bob Buhl/Roy Sievers	9.00	4.50	2.75
(42)	Jim Bunning/Bob Boyd	20.00	10.00	6.00
(43)	Jim Bunning/Ron Hansen	20.00	10.00	6.00
(44)	John Buzhardt/Brooks Robinson	30.00	15.00	9.00
(45)	John Buzhardt/Dick Williams	9.00	4.50	2.75
(46)	Johnny Callison/Jim Landis	9.00	4.50	2.75
(47)	Johnny Callison/Ed Roebuck	9.00	4.50	2.75
(48)	Harry Chiti/Jackie Brandt	9.00	4.50	2.75
(49)	Harry Chiti/Gene Conley	9.00	4.50	2.75
(50)	Del Crandall/Billy Gardner	9.00	4.50	2.75
(51)	Bud Daley/Al Kaline	30.00	15.00	9.00
(52)	Bud Daley/Dave Sisler	9.00	4.50	2.75
(53)	Pete Daley/Dick Ellsworth	9.00	4.50	2.75
(54)	Pete Daley/Hal (R.) Smith	9.00	4.50	2.75
(55)	Clay Dalrymple/Norm Larker	9.00	4.50	2.75
(56)	CLay Dalrymple/Stan Williams	9.00	4.50	2.75
(57)	Jim Davenport/Reno Bertoia	9.00	4.50	2.75
(58)	Jim Davenport/Jerry Lynch	9.00	4.50	2.75
(59)	Bobby Del Greco/Roy Face	9.00	4.50	2.75
(60)	Bobby Del Greco/Frank Howard	12.00	6.00	3.50
(61)	Gene Freese/Wes Covington	9.00	4.50	2.75
(62)	Gene Freese/Vada Pinson	9.00	4.50	2.75
(63)	Bob Friend/Hank Aaron	60.00	30.00	18.00
(64)	Bob Friend/Lee Walls	9.00	4.50	2.75
(65)	Jim Gentile/Chuck Estrada	9.00	4.50	2.75
(66)	Jim Gentile/Billy O'Dell	9.00	4.50	2.75
(67)	Dick Gernert/Russ Nixon	9.00	4.50	2.75
(68)	Alex Grammas/Eddie Bressoud	9.00	4.50	2.75
(69)	Frank Herrera/Joe Jay	9.00	4.50	2.75
(70)	Frank Herrera/Jim Landis	9.00	4.50	2.75
(71)	Julian Javier/Eddie Kasko	9.00	4.50	2.75
(72)	Jackie Jensen/Hank Bauer	15.00	7.50	4.50
(73)	Jackie Jensen/Mickey Mantle	200.00	100.00	60.00
(74)	Al Kaline/Dick Hall	30.00	15.00	9.00
(75)	Al Kaline/Ray Herbert	30.00	15.00	9.00
(76)	Russ Kemmerer/Ed Sadowski	9.00	4.50	2.75
(77)	Harmon Killebrew/Bill Stafford	30.00	15.00	9.00
(78)	Harmon Killebrew/Bill White	30.00	15.00	9.00
(79)	Billy Klaus/Bob Anderson	9.00	4.50	2.75
(80)	Ron Kline/Juan Marichal	20.00	10.00	6.00
(81)	Ron Kline/Curt Simmons	9.00	4.50	2.75
(82)	Tony Kubek/Reno Bertoia	12.00	6.00	3.50
(83)	Frank Lary/Andy Carey	9.00	4.50	2.75
(84)	Barry Latman/Hank Bauer	9.00	4.50	2.75
(85)	Jim Lemon/Tony Curry	9.00	4.50	2.75
(86)	Jim Lemon/Dick Williams	9.00	4.50	2.75
(87)	Sherm Lollar/Willie Mays	60.00	30.00	18.00
(88)	Sherm Lollar/Duke Snider	30.00	15.00	9.00
(89)	Dale Long/Bob Anderson	9.00	4.50	2.75
(90)	Dale Long/Don Elston	9.00	4.50	2.7
(91)	Art Mahaffey/Vada Pinson	9.00	4.50	
(92)	Art Mahaffey/Robin Roberts	20.00	10.00	
(93)	Frank Malzone/Dick Hall	9.00	4.50	
(94)	Frank Malzone/Bob Hartman	9.00	4	
(95)	Felix Mantilla/Billy Gardner	9.00		
(96)	Felix Mantilla/Gary Geiger	9.00		
(97)	Roger Maris/Johnny Klippstein	45		

		NM	E	VG
(98)	Roger Maris/Ray Semproch	45.00	22.00	13.50
(99)	Billy Martin/Hank Aaron	60.00	30.00	18.00
(100)	Billy Martin/Whitey Herzog	15.00	7.50	4.50
(101)	J.C. Martin/Bob Cerv	9.00	4.50	2.75
(102)	J.C. Martin/Eddie Yost	9.00	4.50	2.75
(103)	Ed Mathews/Chico Cardenas	30.00	15.00	9.00
(104)	Bill Mazeroski/Joe Adcock	20.00	10.00	6.00
(105)	Bill Mazeroski/Elston Howard	20.00	10.00	6.00
(106)	Mike McCormick/Rocky Nelson	9.00	4.50	2.75
(107)	Mike McCormick/Curt Simmons	9.00	4.50	2.75
(108)	Wille McCovey/Smoky Burgess	30.00	15.00	9.00
(109)	Minnie Minoso/Ted Kluszewski	15.00	7.50	4.50
(110)	Minnie Minoso/Eddie Yost	12.00	6.00	3.50
(111)	Bikll Monbouquette/Tony Curry	9.00	4.50	2.75
(112)	Bill Monbouquette/ Sammy Taylor	9.00	4.50	2.75
(113)	Wally Moon/Roy Face	9.00	4.50	2.75
(114)	Stan Musial/Rocky Nelson	60.00	30.00	18.00
(115)	Charlie Neal/Marv Breeding	9.00	4.50	2.75
(116)	Charlie Neal/Jim Grant	9.00	4.50	2.75
(117)	Jim O'Toole/Chico Cardenas	9.00	4.50	2.75
(118)	Jim O'Toole/Roy McMillan	9.00	4.50	2.75
(119)	Milt Pappas/Tito Francona	9.00	4.50	2.75
(120)	Milt Pappas/Jim Piersall	9.00	4.50	2.75
(121)	Jim Perry/Bob Cerv	9.00	4.50	2.75
(122)	Jim Perry/Ken Hunt	9.00	4.50	2.75
(123)	Bubba Phillips/Art Ditmar	9.00	4.50	2.75
(124)	Bubba Phillips/Jim Kaat	15.00	7.50	4.50
(125)	Johnny Podres/Dick Farrell	9.00	4.50	2.75
(126)	Wally Post/Dick Farrell	9.00	4.50	2.75
(127)	Wally Post/Robin Roberts	20.00	10.00	6.00
(128)	Frank Robinson/Jim Grant	30.00	15.00	9.00
(129)	Frank Robinson/Don Hoak	30.00	15.00	9.00
(130)	John Romano/Al Kaline	30.00	15.00	9.00
(131)	John Roseboro/Dick Groat	9.00	4.50	2.75
(132)	Pete Runnels/Larry Jackson	9.00	4.50	2.75
(133)	Jack Sanford/Whitey Ford	30.00	15.00	9.00
(134)	Jack Sanford/Pedro Ramos	9.00	4.50	2.75
(135)	Ron Santo/Harvey Kuenn	15.00	7.50	4.50
(136)	Ron Santo/Vern Law	15.00	7.50	4.50
(137)	Bobby Shantz/Joe Adcock	9.00	4.50	2.75
(138)	Bobby Shantz/Dick Groat	9.00	4.50	2.75
(139)	Bob Shaw/Jerry Casale	9.00	4.50	2.75
(140)	Bob Shaw/Ned Garver	9.00	4.50	2.75
(141)	Norm Siebern/Tony Gonzalez	9.00	4.50	2.75
(142)	Norm Siebern/Woodie Held	9.00	4.50	2.75
(143)	Bob Skinner/Hobie Landrith	9.00	4.50	2.75
(144)	Bob Skinner/Juan Marichal	20.00	10.00	6.00
(145)	Al Smith/Don Drysdale	25.00	12.50	7.50
(146)	Hal (W.) Smith/Eddie Bressoud	9.00	4.50	2.75
(147)	Hal (W.) Smith/Harvey Kuenn	9.00	4.50	2.75
(148)	Daryl Spencer/Norm Cash	9.00	4.50	2.75
(149)	Daryl Spencer/Vic Powers	9.00	4.50	2.75
(150)	Jerry Staley/Ned Garver	9.00	4.50	2.75
(151)	Jerry Staley/Ed Sadowski	9.00	4.50	2.75
(152)	Gene Stephens/Gene Conley	9.00	4.50	2.75
(153)	Gene Stephens/Ike Delock	9.00	4.50	2.75
(154)	Chuck Stobbs/Ken Boyer	12.00	6.00	3.50
(155)	Chuck Stobbs/Curt Flood	9.00	4.50	2.75
56)	Dick Stuart/Whitey Ford	30.00	15.00	9.00
'57)	Dick Stuart/Larry Jackson	9.00	4.50	2.75
58)	Tony Taylor/Frank Howard	12.00	6.00	3.50
9)	Tony Taylor/Norm Larker	9.00	4.50	2.75
)	Johnny Temple/Norm Cash	9.00	4.50	2.75

		NM	E	VG
(161)	Johnny Temple/Dave Sisler	9.00	4.50	2.75
(162)	Marv Throneberry/Yogi Berra	45.00	22.00	13.50
(163)	Marv Throneberry/ Tommy Davis	9.00	4.50	2.75
(164)	Gus Triandos/Sammy Taylor	9.00	4.50	2.75
(165)	Bob Turley/Luis Aparicio	20.00	10.00	6.00
(166)	Bill Tuttle/Jerry Casale	9.00	4.50	2.75
(167)	Bill Tuttle/Bill Pierce	9.00	4.50	2.75
(168)	Zoilo Versalles/Bill Stafford	9.00	4.50	2.75
(169)	Bill Virdon/Yogi Berra	30.00	15.00	9.00
(170)	Vic Wertz/Bob Hartman	9.00	4.50	2.75
(171)	Vic Wertz/Jerry Lumpe	9.00	4.50	2.75
(172)	Pete Whisenant/Luis Arroyo	9.00	4.50	2.75
(173)	Pete Whisenant/Dick Donovan	9.00	4.50	2.75
(174)	Hoyt Wilhelm/Ron Hansen	20.00	10.00	6.00
(175)	Hoyt Wilhelm/Jim Piersall	20.00	10.00	6.00
(176)	Bob Will/Tony Gonzalez	9.00	4.50	2.75
(177)	Bob Will/Lindy McDaniel	9.00	4.50	2.75
(178)	Billy Williams/Warren Spahn	30.00	15.00	9.00
(179)	Billy Williams/Carl Willey	25.00	12.50	7.50
(180)	Gene Woodling/Don Elston	9.00	4.50	2.75
(181)	Gene Woodling/Hal (R.) Smith	9.00	4.50	2.75
(182)	Carl Yastrzemski/Jerry Lumpe	60.00	30.00	18.00

1962 Topps

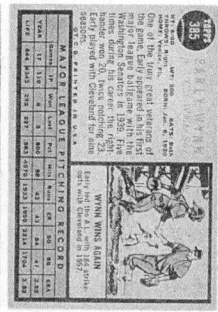

The 1962 Topps set established another plateau for set size with 598 cards. The 2-1/2" x 3-1/2" cards feature a photograph set against a woodgrain background. The lower-right corner has been made to look like it is curling away. Many established specialty cards dot the set including statistical leaders, multi-player cards, team cards, checklists, World Series cards and All-Stars. Of note is that 1962 was the first year of the multi-player rookie card. There is a nine-card "In Action" subset and a 10-card run of special Babe Ruth cards. Photo variations of several cards in the 2nd Series (#110-196) exist. All cards in the 2nd Series can be found with two distinct printing variations, an early printing with the cards containing a very noticeable greenish tint, having been corrected to clear photos in subsequent print runs. The complete set price in the checklist that follows does not include the higher-priced variations. Among the high numbers (#523-598) certain cards were "short-printed," produced in lesser quantities. These cards carry a higher value and are indicated in the checklist by the notation (SP) after the player name.

		NM	E	VG
Complete Set (598):		7,000	3,500	2,100
Common Player (1-446):		4.00	2.00	1.25
Common Player (447-522):		7.00	3.50	2.00
Common Player (523-598):		10.00	5.00	3.00
1	Roger Maris	450.00	100.00	60.00
2	Jim Brosnan	4.00	2.00	1.25
3	Pete Runnels	4.00	2.00	1.25
4	John DeMerit	4.00	2.00	1.25
5	Sandy Koufax	150.00	75.00	37.50
6	Marv Breeding	4.00	2.00	1.25
7	Frank Thomas	4.00	2.00	1.25
8	Ray Herbert	4.00	2.00	1.25
9	Jim Davenport	4.00	2.00	1.25
10	Bob Clemente	200.00	100.00	50.00
11	Tom Morgan	4.00	2.00	1.25
12	Harry Craft	4.00	2.00	1.25
13	Dick Howser	4.00	2.00	1.25
14	Bill White	4.00	2.00	1.25
15	Dick Donovan	4.00	2.00	1.25
16	Darrell Johnson	4.00	2.00	1.25
17	Johnny Callison	4.00	2.00	1.25

		NM	E	VG
18	Managers' Dream (Mickey Mantle, Willie Mays)	185.00	90.00	50.00
19	Ray Washburn RC	4.00	2.00	1.25
20	Rocky Colavito	20.00	10.00	6.00
21	Jim Kaat	6.00	3.00	1.75
22a	1st Series Checklist (1-88) (Numbers 121-176 on back.)	6.00	3.00	1.75
22b	1st Series Checklist (1-88) (Numbers 33-88 on back.)	9.00	4.50	2.75
23	Norm Larker	4.00	2.00	1.25
24	Detroit Tigers Team	7.00	3.50	2.00
25	Ernie Banks	60.00	30.00	16.00
26	Chris Cannizzaro	4.00	2.00	1.25
27	Chuck Cottier	4.00	2.00	1.25
28	Minnie Minoso	9.00	4.50	2.75
29	Casey Stengel	17.50	6.75	4.00
30	Ed Mathews	27.50	12.50	7.50
31	Tom Tresh RC	16.00	8.00	4.00
32	John Roseboro	4.00	2.00	1.25
33	Don Larsen	4.00	2.00	1.25
34	Johnny Temple	4.00	2.00	1.25
35	Don Schwall RC	4.00	2.00	1.25
36	Don Leppert	4.00	2.00	1.25
37	Tribe Hill Trio (Barry Latman, Jim Perry, Dick Stigman)	6.00	3.00	1.75
38	Gene Stephens	4.00	2.00	1.25
39	Joe Koppe	4.00	2.00	1.25
40	Orlando Cepeda	20.00	8.00	4.75
41	Cliff Cook	4.00	2.00	1.25
42	Jim King	4.00	2.00	1.25
43	Los Angeles Dodgers Team	10.00	5.00	3.00
44	Don Taussig	4.00	2.00	1.25
45	Brooks Robinson	35.00	15.00	9.00
46	Jack Baldschun RC	4.00	2.00	1.25
47	Bob Will	4.00	2.00	1.25
48	Ralph Terry	4.00	2.00	1.25
49	Hal Jones	4.00	2.00	1.25
50	Stan Musial	90.00	50.00	25.00
51	A.L. Batting Leaders (Norm Cash, Elston Howard, Al Kaline, Jim Piersall)	12.50	6.25	3.75
52	N.L. Batting Leaders (Ken Boyer, Roberto Clemente, Wally Moon, Vada Pinson)	17.50	7.50	4.50
53	A.L. Home Run Leaders (Jim Gentile, Harmon Killebrew, Mickey Mantle, Roger Maris)	80.00	40.00	24.00
54	N.L. Home Run Leaders (Orlando Cepeda, Willie Mays, Frank Robinson)	12.50	6.25	3.75
55	A.L. E.R.A. Leaders (Dick Donovan, Don Mossi, Milt Pappas, Bill Stafford)	6.00	3.00	1.75
56	N.L. E.R.A. Leaders (Mike McCormick, Jim O'Toole, Curt Simmons, Warren Spahn)	7.00	3.50	2.00
57	A.L. Win Leaders (Steve Barber, Jim Bunning, Whitey Ford, Frank Lary)	15.00	7.50	4.50
58	N.L. Win Leaders (Joe Jay, Jim O'Toole, Warren Spahn)	7.00	3.50	2.00
59	A.L. Strikeout Leaders (Jim Bunning, Whitey Ford, Camilo Pascual, Juan Pizarro)	7.50	3.75	2.25
60	N.L. Strikeout Leaders (Don Drysdale, Sandy Koufax, Jim O'Toole, Stan Williams)	17.50	8.00	4.75
61	St. Louis Cardinals Team	7.00	3.50	2.00
62	Steve Boros	4.00	2.00	1.25
63	Tony Cloninger RC	7.00	3.50	2.00
64	Russ Snyder	4.00	2.00	1.25
65	Bobby Richardson	21.00	10.00	6.00
66	Cuno Barragon (Barragan)	4.00	2.00	1.25
67	Harvey Haddix	4.00	2.00	1.25
68	Ken L. Hunt	4.00	2.00	1.25
69	Phil Ortega	4.00	2.00	1.25
70	Harmon Killebrew	30.00	12.50	7.50
71	Dick LeMay	4.00	2.00	1.25
72	Bob's Pupils (Steve Boros, Bob Scheffing, Jake Wood)	4.50	2.25	1.25
73	Nellie Fox	23.00	10.00	6.00

74	Bob Lillis	4.00	2.00	1.25
75	Milt Pappas	4.00	2.00	1.25
76	Howie Bedell	4.00	2.00	1.25
77	Tony Taylor	4.00	2.00	1.25
78	Gene Green	4.00	2.00	1.25
79	Ed Hobaugh	4.00	2.00	1.25
80	Vada Pinson	7.00	3.50	2.00
81	Jim Pagliaroni	4.00	2.00	1.25
82	Deron Johnson	4.00	2.00	1.25
83	Larry Jackson	4.00	2.00	1.25
84	Lenny Green	4.00	2.00	1.25
85	Gil Hodges	20.00	7.50	4.50
86	Donn Clendenon **RC**	6.00	3.00	1.75
87	Mike Roarke	4.00	2.00	1.25
88	Ralph Houk	10.00	5.00	3.00
89	Barney Schultz	4.00	2.00	1.25
90	Jim Piersall	6.00	3.00	1.75
91	J.C. Martin	4.00	2.00	1.25
92	Sam Jones	4.00	2.00	1.25
93	John Blanchard	5.00	2.50	1.50
94	Jay Hook	4.00	2.00	1.25
95	Don Hoak	4.00	2.00	1.25
96	Eli Grba	4.00	2.00	1.25
97	Tito Francona	4.00	2.00	1.25
98	2nd Series Checklist (89-176)	6.00	3.00	1.75
99	John Powell **RC** (Boog)	24.00	10.00	6.00
100	Warren Spahn	45.00	25.00	12.50
101	Carroll Hardy	4.00	2.00	1.25
102	Al Schroll	4.00	2.00	1.25
103	Don Blasingame	4.00	2.00	1.25
104	Ted Savage	4.00	2.00	1.25
105	Don Mossi	4.00	2.00	1.25
106	Carl Sawatski	4.00	2.00	1.25
107	Mike McCormick	4.00	2.00	1.25
108	Willie Davis	5.00	2.50	1.50
109	Bob Shaw	4.00	2.00	1.25
110	Bill Skowron	22.50	11.00	7.00
111	Dallas Green	4.00	2.00	1.25
112	Hank Foiles	4.00	2.00	1.25
113	Chicago White Sox Team	7.00	3.50	2.00
114	Howie Koplitz	4.00	2.00	1.25
115	Bob Skinner	4.00	2.00	1.25
116	Herb Score	4.00	2.00	1.25
117	Gary Geiger	4.00	2.00	1.25
118	Julian Javier	4.00	2.00	1.25
119	Danny Murphy	4.00	2.00	1.25
120	Bob Purkey	4.00	2.00	1.25
121	Billy Hitchcock	4.00	2.00	1.25
122	Norm Bass	4.00	2.00	1.25
123	Mike de la Hoz	4.00	2.00	1.25
124	Bill Pleis	4.00	2.00	1.25
125	Gene Woodling	4.00	2.00	1.25
126	Al Cicotte	4.00	2.00	1.25
127	Pride of the A's(Hank Bauer, Jerry Lumpe, Norm Siebern)	4.50	2.25	1.25
128	Art Fowler	4.00	2.00	1.25
129a	Lee Walls (Pinstriped jersey.)	20.00	10.00	6.00
129b	Lee Walls (Plain jersey.)	6.00	3.00	1.75
130	Frank Bolling	4.00	2.00	1.25
131	Pete Richert **RC**	4.00	2.00	1.25
132a	Los Angeles Angels Team (With inset photos.)	20.00	10.00	6.00
132b	Los Angeles Angels Team (No inset photos.)	13.50	7.00	4.00
133	Felipe Alou	9.00	4.50	2.75
134a	Billy Hoeft (Green sky.)	22.50	10.00	6.00
134b	Billy Hoeft (Blue sky.)	12.00	6.00	3.50
135	Babe as a Boy(Babe Ruth)	20.00	10.00	6.00
136	Babe Joins Yanks(Babe Ruth)	20.00	10.00	6.00
137	Babe and Mgr. Huggins(Babe Ruth)	20.00	10.00	6.00
138	The Famous Slugger(Babe Ruth)	30.00	15.00	7.50
139a	Hal Reniff (Pitching)	30.00	15.00	7.50
139b	Hal Reniff (Portrait)	15.00	7.50	4.50
139c	Babe Hits 60(Babe Ruth) (Pole in background at left.)	50.00	25.00	12.50
139d	Babe Hits 60(Babe Ruth) (No pole.)	60.00	30.00	18.00
140	Gehrig and Ruth(Babe Ruth)	35.00	17.50	10.00
141	Twilight Years(Babe Ruth)	20.00	10.00	6.00
142	Coaching for the Dodgers(Babe Ruth)	20.00	10.00	6.00
143	Greatest Sports Hero(Babe Ruth)	20.00	10.00	6.00
144	Farewell Speech(Babe Ruth)	20.00	10.00	6.00
145	Barry Latman	4.00	2.00	1.25
146	Don Demeter	4.00	2.00	1.25
147a	Bill Kunkel (Ball in hand.)	17.50	8.75	5.25
147b	Bill Kunkel (Portrait)	16.00	6.00	3.50
148	Wally Post	4.00	2.00	1.25
149	Bob Duliba	4.00	2.00	1.25
150	Al Kaline	50.00	25.00	12.50
151	Johnny Klippstein	4.00	2.00	1.25
152	Mickey Vernon	4.00	2.00	1.25
153	Pumpsie Green	4.00	2.00	1.25
154	Lee Thomas	4.00	2.00	1.25
155	Stu Miller	4.00	2.00	1.25
156	Merritt Ranew	4.00	2.00	1.25
157	Wes Covington	4.00	2.00	1.25
158	Milwaukee Braves Team	7.00	3.50	2.00
159	Hal Reniff	4.00	2.00	1.25
160	Dick Stuart	4.00	2.00	1.25
161	Frank Baumann	4.00	2.00	1.25
162	Sammy Drake	4.00	2.00	1.25
163	Hot Corner Guardians(Cletis Boyer, Billy Gardner)	15.00	7.00	4.00
164	Hal Naragon	4.00	2.00	1.25
165	Jackie Brandt	4.00	2.00	1.25
166	Don Lee	4.00	2.00	1.25
167	Tim McCarver **RC**	25.00	12.00	7.00
168	Leo Posada	4.00	2.00	1.25
169	Bob Cerv	4.00	2.00	1.25
170	Ron Santo	12.50	6.25	3.75
171	Dave Sisler	4.00	2.00	1.25
172	Fred Hutchinson	4.00	2.00	1.25
173	Chico Fernandez	4.00	2.00	1.25
174a	Carl Willey (With cap.)	20.00	10.00	6.00
174b	Carl Willey (No cap.)	8.00	4.00	2.50
175	Frank Howard	5.00	2.50	1.50
176a	Eddie Yost (Batting)	20.00	10.00	6.00
176b	Eddie Yost (Portrait)	4.00	2.00	1.25
177	Bobby Shantz	4.00	2.00	1.25
178	Camilo Carreon	4.00	2.00	1.25
179	Tom Sturdivant	4.00	2.00	1.25
180	Bob Allison	4.00	2.00	1.25
181	Paul Brown	4.00	2.00	1.25
182	Bob Nieman	4.00	2.00	1.25
183	Roger Craig	4.00	2.00	1.25
184	Haywood Sullivan	4.00	2.00	1.25
185	Roland Sheldon	4.00	2.00	1.25
186	Mack Jones **RC**	4.00	2.00	1.25
187	Gene Conley	4.00	2.00	1.25
188	Chuck Hiller	4.00	2.00	1.25
189	Dick Hall	4.00	2.00	1.25
190a	Wally Moon (With cap.)	22.50	10.00	6.00
190b	Wally Moon (No cap.)	6.00	3.00	1.75
191	Jim Brewer	4.00	2.00	1.25
192a	3rd Series Checklist (177-264) (192 is Check List, 3)	7.00	3.50	2.00
192b	3rd Series Checklist (177-264) (192 is Check List 3)	8.00	4.00	2.50
193	Eddie Kasko	4.00	2.00	1.25
194	Dean Chance **RC**	12.50	6.25	3.75
195	Joe Cunningham	4.00	2.00	1.25
196	Terry Fox	4.00	2.00	1.25
197	Daryl Spencer	4.00	2.00	1.25
198	Johnny Keane	4.00	2.00	1.25
199	Gaylord Perry **RC**	80.00	40.00	20.00
200	Mickey Mantle	525.00	225.00	135.00
201	Ike Delock	4.00	2.00	1.25
202	Carl Warwick	4.00	2.00	1.25
203	Jack Fisher	4.00	2.00	1.25
204	Johnny Weekly	4.00	2.00	1.25
205	Gene Freese	4.00	2.00	1.25
206	Washington Senators Team	7.00	3.50	2.00
207	Pete Burnside	4.00	2.00	1.25
208	Billy Martin	12.00	6.00	3.50
209	Jim Fregosi **RC**	15.00	7.50	4.50
210	Roy Face	4.00	2.00	1.25
211	Midway Masters(Frank Bolling, Roy McMillan)	4.50	2.25	1.25
212	Jim Owens	4.00	2.00	1.25
213	Richie Ashburn	21.00	10.00	6.00
214	Dom Zanni	4.00	2.00	1.25
215	Woody Held	4.00	2.00	1.25
216	Ron Kline	4.00	2.00	1.25
217	Walt Alston	10.00	5.00	3.00
218	Joe Torre **RC**	65.00	30.00	18.00
219	Al Downing **RC**	12.00	6.00	3.50
220	Roy Sievers	4.00	2.00	1.25
221	Bill Short	4.00	2.00	1.25
222	Jerry Zimmerman	4.00	2.00	1.25
223	Alex Grammas	4.00	2.00	1.25
224	Don Rudolph	4.00	2.00	1.25
225	Frank Malzone	4.00	2.00	1.25
226	San Francisco Giants Team	7.00	3.50	2.00
227	Bobby Tiefenauer	4.00	2.00	1.25
228	Dale Long	4.00	2.00	1.25
229	Jesus McFarlane	4.00	2.00	1.25
230	Camlio Pascual	4.00	2.00	1.25
231	Ernie Bowman	4.00	2.00	1.25
232	World Series Game 1 (Yanks Win Opener)	8.00	4.00	2.50
233	World Series Game 2 (Jay Ties It Up)	10.00	5.00	3.00
234	World Series Game 3 (Maris Wins It In the 9th)	25.00	11.00	7.00
235	World Series Game 4 (Ford Sets New Mark)	20.00	8.75	5.25
236	World Series Game 5 (Yanks Crush Reds in Finale)	7.00	3.50	2.00
237	World Series (The Winners Celebrate)	14.00	7.00	4.00
238	Norm Sherry	4.00	2.00	1.25
239	Cecil Butler	4.00	2.00	1.25
240	George Altman	4.00	2.00	1.25
241	Johnny Kucks	4.00	2.00	1.25
242	Mel McGaha	4.00	2.00	1.25
243	Robin Roberts	15.00	7.50	4.50
244	Don Gile	4.00	2.00	1.25
245	Ron Hansen	4.00	2.00	1.25
246	Art Ditmar	4.00	2.00	1.25
247	Joe Pignatano	4.00	2.00	1.25
248	Bob Aspromonte	4.00	2.00	1.25
249	Ed Keegan	4.00	2.00	1.25
250	Norm Cash	20.00	10.00	6.00
251	New York Yankees Team	50.00	25.00	12.50
252	Earl Francis	4.00	2.00	1.25
253	Harry Chiti	4.00	2.00	1.25
254	Gordon Windhorn	4.00	2.00	1.25
255	Juan Pizarro	4.00	2.00	1.25
256	Elio Chacon	4.00	2.00	1.25
257	Jack Spring	4.00	2.00	1.25
258	Marty Keough	4.00	2.00	1.25
259	Lou Klimchock	4.00	2.00	1.25
260	Bill Pierce	4.00	2.00	1.25
261	George Alusik	4.00	2.00	1.25
262	Bob Schmidt	4.00	2.00	1.25
263	The Right Pitch(Joe Jay, Bob Purkey, Jim Turner)	4.50	2.25	1.25
264	Dick Ellsworth	4.00	2.00	1.25
265	Joe Adcock	4.00	2.00	1.25
266	John Anderson	4.00	2.00	1.25
267	Dan Dobbek	4.00	2.00	1.25
268	Ken McBride	4.00	2.00	1.25
269	Bob Oldis	4.00	2.00	1.25
270	Dick Groat	4.00	2.00	1.25
271	Ray Rippelmeyer	4.00	2.00	1.25
272	Earl Robinson	4.00	2.00	1.25
273	Gary Bell	4.00	2.00	1.25
274	Sammy Taylor	4.00	2.00	1.25
275	Norm Siebern	4.00	2.00	1.25
276	Hal Kostad	4.00	2.00	1.25
277	4th Series Checklist (265-352)	7.00	3.50	2.00
278	Ken Johnson	4.00	2.00	1.25
279	Hobie Landrith	4.00	2.00	1.25
280	Johnny Podres	7.50	3.75	2.25
281	Jake Gibbs **RC**	7.50	3.75	2.25
282	Dave Hillman	4.00	2.00	1.25
283	Charlie Smith	4.00	2.00	1.25
284	Ruben Amaro	4.00	2.00	1.25
285	Curt Simmons	4.00	2.00	1.25
286	Al Lopez	14.00	7.00	4.00
287	George Witt	4.00	2.00	1.25
288	Billy Williams	30.00	17.50	8.75
289	Mike Krsnich	4.00	2.00	1.25
290	Jim Gentile	6.00	3.00	1.75
291	Hal Stowe	4.00	2.00	1.25
292	Jerry Kindall	4.00	2.00	1.25
293	Bob Miller	4.00	2.00	1.25
294	Philadelphia Phillies Team	7.50	3.75	2.25
295	Vern Law	4.00	2.00	1.25
296	Ken Hamlin	4.00	2.00	1.25
297	Ron Perranoski	4.00	2.00	1.25
298	Bill Tuttle	4.00	2.00	1.25
299	Don Wert **RC**	4.00	2.00	1.25
300	Willie Mays	200.00	100.00	60.00
301	Galen Cisco	4.00	2.00	1.25
302	John Edwards **RC**	4.00	2.00	1.25
303	Frank Torre	4.00	2.00	1.25
304	Dick Farrell	4.00	2.00	1.25
305	Jerry Lumpe	4.00	2.00	1.25
306	Redbird Rippers(Larry Jackson, Lindy McDaniel)	5.00	2.50	1.50
307	Jim Grant	4.00	2.00	1.25
308	Neil Chrisley	4.00	2.00	1.25
309	Moe Morhardt	4.00	2.00	1.25
310	Whitey Ford	50.00	25.00	12.50
311	Kubek Makes The Double Play(Tony Kubek)	12.00	6.00	3.50
312	Spahn Shows No-Hit Form(Warren Spahn)	18.00	7.50	4.50

313	Maris Blasts 61st(Roger Maris)	70.00	37.50	18.75
314	Colavito's Power(Rocky Colavito)	15.00	5.50	3.25
315	Ford Tosses a Curve(Whitey Ford)	25.00	10.00	6.00
316	Killebrew Sends One into Orbit(Harmon Killebrew)	20.00	10.00	6.00
317	Musial Plays 21st Season(Stan Musial)	20.00	8.75	5.25
318	The Switch Hitter Connect s(Mickey Mantle)	125.00	60.00	30.00
319	McCormick Shows His Stuff(Mike McCormick)	6.00	3.00	1.75
320	Hank Aaron	150.00	75.00	45.00
321	Lee Stange	4.00	2.00	1.25
322	Al Dark	4.00	2.00	1.25
323	Don Landrum	4.00	2.00	1.25
324	Joe McClain	4.00	2.00	1.25
325	Luis Aparicio	15.00	7.50	4.50
326	Tom Parsons	4.00	2.00	1.25
327	Ozzie Virgil	4.00	2.00	1.25
328	Ken Walters	4.00	2.00	1.25
329	Bob Bolin	4.00	2.00	1.25
330	Johnny Romano	4.00	2.00	1.25
331	Moe Drabowsky	4.00	2.00	1.25
332	Don Buddin	4.00	2.00	1.25
333	Frank Cipriani	4.00	2.00	1.25
334	Boston Red Sox Team	9.00	4.50	2.75
335	Bill Bruton	4.00	2.00	1.25
336	Billy Muffett	4.00	2.00	1.25
337	Jim Marshall	4.00	2.00	1.25
338	Billy Gardner	4.00	2.00	1.25
339	Jose Valdivielso	4.00	2.00	1.25
340	Don Drysdale	50.00	25.00	12.50
341	Mike Hershberger	4.00	2.00	1.25
342	Ed Rakow	4.00	2.00	1.25
343	Albie Pearson	4.00	2.00	1.25
344	Ed Bauta	4.00	2.00	1.25
345	Chuck Schilling	4.00	2.00	1.25
346	Jack Kralick	4.00	2.00	1.25
347	Chuck Hinton	4.00	2.00	1.25
348	Larry Burright	4.00	2.00	1.25
349	Paul Foytack	4.00	2.00	1.25
350	Frank Robinson	50.00	25.00	12.50
351	Braves' Backstops(Del Crandall, Joe Torre)	12.00	6.00	3.50
352	Frank Sullivan	4.00	2.00	1.25
353	Bill Mazeroski	20.00	10.00	6.00
354	Roman Mejias	4.00	2.00	1.25
355	Steve Barber	4.00	2.00	1.25
356	Tom Haller	4.00	2.00	1.25
357	Jerry Walker	4.00	2.00	1.25
358	Tommy Davis	4.00	2.00	1.25
359	Bobby Locke	4.00	2.00	1.25
360	Yogi Berra	80.00	40.00	20.00
361	Bob Hendley	4.00	2.00	1.25
362	Ty Cline	4.00	2.00	1.25
363	Bob Roselli	4.00	2.00	1.25
364	Ken Hunt	4.00	2.00	1.25
365	Charley Neal	4.00	2.00	1.25
366	Phil Regan	4.00	2.00	1.25
367	5th Checklist (353-429)	8.00	4.00	2.50
368	Bob Tillman	4.00	2.00	1.25
369	Ted Bowsfield	4.00	2.00	1.25
370	Ken Boyer	12.50	6.75	4.25
371	Earl Battey	4.00	2.00	1.25
372	Jack Curtis	4.00	2.00	1.25
373	Al Heist	4.00	2.00	1.25
374	Gene Mauch	4.00	2.00	1.25
375	Ron Fairly	4.00	2.00	1.25
376	Bud Daley	4.00	2.00	1.25
377	Johnny Orsino	4.00	2.00	1.25
378	Bennie Daniels	4.00	2.00	1.25
379	Chuck Essegian	4.00	2.00	1.25
380	Lou Burdette	4.00	2.00	1.25
381	Chico Cardenas	4.00	2.00	1.25
382	Dick Williams	4.00	2.00	1.25
383	Ray Sadecki	4.00	2.00	1.25
384	Kansas City Athletics Team	8.00	4.00	2.50
385	Early Wynn	12.00	6.00	3.50
386	Don Mincher	4.00	2.00	1.25
387	Lou Brock **RC**	130.00	60.00	30.00
388	Ryne Duren	4.00	2.00	1.25
389	Smoky Burgess	4.00	2.00	1.25
390	Orlando Cepeda (All-Star)	10.00	5.00	3.00
391	Bill Mazeroski (All-Star)	12.00	6.00	3.50
392	Ken Boyer (All-Star)	7.00	3.50	2.00
393	Roy McMillan (All-Star)	4.00	2.00	1.25
394	Hank Aaron (All-Star)	60.00	30.00	15.00
395	Willie Mays (All-Star)	45.00	25.00	12.50
396	Frank Robinson (All-Star)	17.50	6.75	4.00
397	John Roseboro (All-Star)	4.00	2.00	1.25
398	Don Drysdale (All-Star)	13.50	6.75	4.00
399	Warren Spahn (All-Star)	16.50	6.75	4.00
400	Elston Howard	15.00	7.50	4.50
401	AL & NL Homer Kings(Roger Maris, Orlando Cepeda)	50.00	30.00	15.00
402	Gino Cimoli	4.00	2.00	1.25
403	Chet Nichols	4.00	2.00	1.25
404	Tim Harkness	4.00	2.00	1.25
405	Jim Perry	4.00	2.00	1.25
406	Bob Taylor	4.00	2.00	1.25
407	Hank Aguirre	4.00	2.00	1.25
408	Gus Bell	4.00	2.00	1.25
409	Pittsburgh Pirates Team	11.00	5.50	3.25
410	Al Smith	4.00	2.00	1.25
411	Danny O'Connell	4.00	2.00	1.25
412	Charlie James	4.00	2.00	1.25
413	Matty Alou	4.00	2.00	1.25
414	Joe Gaines	4.00	2.00	1.25
415	Bill Virdon	4.00	2.00	1.25
416	Bob Scheffing	4.00	2.00	1.25
417	Joe Azcue	4.00	2.00	1.25
418	Andy Carey	4.00	2.00	1.25
419	Bob Bruce	4.00	2.00	1.25
420	Gus Triandos	4.00	2.00	1.25
421	Ken MacKenzie	4.00	2.00	1.25
422	Steve Bilko	4.00	2.00	1.25
423	Rival League Relief Aces(Roy Face, Hoyt Wilhelm)	9.00	4.50	2.75
424	Al McBean	4.00	2.00	1.25
425	Carl Yastrzemski	100.00	50.00	30.00
426	Bob Farley	4.00	2.00	1.25
427	Jake Wood	4.00	2.00	1.25
428	Joe Hicks	4.00	2.00	1.25
429	Bill O'Dell	4.00	2.00	1.25
430	Tony Kubek	15.00	7.50	4.50
431	Bob Rodgers **RC**	4.00	2.00	1.25
432	Jim Pendleton	4.00	2.00	1.25
433	Jim Archer	4.00	2.00	1.25
434	Clay Dalrymple	4.00	2.00	1.25
435	Larry Sherry	4.00	2.00	1.25
436	Felix Mantilla	4.00	2.00	1.25
437	Ray Moore	4.00	2.00	1.25
438	Dick Brown	4.00	2.00	1.25
439	Jerry Buchek	4.00	2.00	1.25
440	Joe Jay	4.00	2.00	1.25
441a	6th Series Checklist (430-506) (Large "CHECKLIST.")	9.00	4.50	2.75
441b	6th Series Checklist (430-506) (Small "CHECKLIST.")	9.00	4.50	2.75
442	Wes Stock	4.00	2.00	1.25
443	Del Crandall	4.00	2.00	1.25
444	Ted Wills	4.00	2.00	1.25
445	Vic Power	4.00	2.00	1.25
446	Don Elston	4.00	2.00	1.25
447	Willie Kirkland	7.00	3.50	2.00
448	Joe Gibbon	7.00	3.50	2.00
449	Jerry Adair	7.00	3.50	2.00
450	Jim O'Toole	7.00	3.50	2.00
451	Jose Tartabull **RC**	7.00	3.50	2.00
452	Earl Averill	7.00	3.50	2.00
453	Cal McLish	7.00	3.50	2.00
454	Floyd Robinson	7.00	3.50	2.00
455	Luis Arroyo	7.00	3.50	2.00
456	Joe Amalfitano	7.00	3.50	2.00
457	Lou Clinton	7.00	3.50	2.00
458a	Bob Buhl ("M" on cap)	17.50	8.75	5.25
458b	Bob Buhl (Plain cap.)	15.00	7.50	4.50
459	Ed Bailey	7.00	3.50	2.00
460	Jim Bunning	24.00	10.00	6.00
461	Ken Hubbs **RC**	15.00	7.50	4.50
462a	Willie Tasby ("W" on cap)	20.00	10.00	6.00
462b	Willie Tasby (Plain cap.)	16.00	8.00	4.75
463	Hank Bauer	13.00	4.50	2.75
464	Al Jackson **RC**	10.00	5.00	3.00
465	Cincinnati Reds Team	11.00	5.50	3.25
466	Norm Cash (All-Star)	13.50	6.75	4.00
467	Chuck Schilling (All-Star)	7.00	3.50	2.00
468	Brooks Robinson (All-Star)	15.00	7.50	4.50
469	Luis Aparicio (All-Star)	11.00	5.50	3.25
470	Al Kaline (All-Star)	20.00	10.00	6.00
471	Mickey Mantle (All-Star)	190.00	85.00	40.00
472	Rocky Colavito (All-Star)	12.00	6.00	3.50
473	Elston Howard (All-Star)	12.00	6.00	3.00
474	Frank Lary (All-Star)	7.00	3.50	2.00
475	Whitey Ford (All-Star)	15.00	7.50	4.50
476	Baltimore Orioles Team	12.50	6.25	3.75
477	Andre Rodgers	7.00	3.50	2.00
478	Don Zimmer	12.50	6.25	3.75
479	Joel Horlen **RC**	7.00	3.50	2.00
480	Harvey Kuenn	7.00	3.50	2.00
481	Vic Wertz	7.00	3.50	2.00
482	Sam Mele	7.00	3.50	2.00
483	Don McMahon	7.00	3.50	2.00
484	Dick Schofield	7.00	3.50	2.00
485	Pedro Ramos	7.00	3.50	2.00
486	Jim Gilliam	13.50	6.00	3.50
487	Jerry Lynch	7.00	3.50	2.00
488	Hal Brown	7.00	3.50	2.00
489	Julio Gotay	7.00	3.50	2.00
490	Clete Boyer	15.00	6.75	4.00
491	Leon Wagner	7.00	3.50	2.00
492	Hal Smith	7.00	3.50	2.00
493	Danny McDevitt	7.00	3.50	2.00
494	Sammy White	7.00	3.50	2.00
495	Don Cardwell	7.00	3.50	2.00
496	Wayne Causey	7.00	3.50	2.00
497	Ed Bouchee	7.00	3.50	2.00
498	Jim Donohue	7.00	3.50	2.00
499	Zoilo Versalles	7.00	3.50	2.00
500	Duke Snider	60.00	30.00	15.00
501	Claude Osteen	7.00	3.50	2.00
502	Hector Lopez	7.00	3.50	2.00
503	Danny Murtaugh	7.00	3.50	2.00
504	Eddie Bressoud	7.00	3.50	2.00
505	Juan Marichal	40.00	20.00	10.00
506	Charley Maxwell	7.00	3.50	2.00
507	Ernie Broglio	7.00	3.50	2.00
508	Gordy Coleman	7.00	3.50	2.00
509	Dave Giusti **RC**	7.00	3.50	2.00
510	Jim Lemon	7.00	3.50	2.00
511	Bubba Phillips	7.00	3.50	2.00
512	Mike Fornieles	7.00	3.50	2.00
513	Whitey Herzog	7.00	3.50	2.00
514	Sherm Lollar	7.00	3.50	2.00
515	Stan Williams	7.00	3.50	2.00
516a	7th Series Checklist (507-598) (Boxes are yellow.)	9.00	4.50	2.75
516b	7th Series Checklist (507-598) (Boxes are white.)	9.00	4.50	2.75
517	Dave Wickersham	7.00	3.50	2.00
518	Lee Maye	7.00	3.50	2.00
519	Bob Johnson	7.00	3.50	2.00
520	Bob Friend	7.00	3.50	2.00
521	Jacke Davis	7.00	3.50	2.00
522	Lindy McDaniel	7.00	3.50	2.00
523	Russ Nixon (SP)	15.00	7.50	4.50
524	Howie Nunn (SP)	15.00	7.50	4.50
525	George Thomas	10.00	5.00	3.00
526	Hal Woodeshick (SP)	15.00	7.50	4.50
527	Dick McAuliffe **RC**	10.00	5.00	3.00
528	Turk Lown	10.00	5.00	3.00
529	John Schaive (SP)	15.00	7.50	4.50
530	Bob Gibson (SP)	115.00	112.50	56.25
531	Bobby G. Smith	10.00	5.00	3.00
532	Dick Stigman	10.00	5.00	3.00
533	Charley Lau (SP)	15.00	7.50	4.50
534	Tony Gonzalez (SP)	15.00	7.50	4.50
535	Ed Roebuck	10.00	5.00	3.00
536	Dick Gernert	10.00	5.00	3.00
537	Cleveland Indians Team	20.00	10.00	6.00
538	Jack Sanford	10.00	5.00	3.00
539	Billy Moran	10.00	5.00	3.00
540	Jim Landis (SP)	15.00	7.50	4.50
541	Don Nottebart (SP)	15.00	7.50	4.50
542	Dave Philley	10.00	5.00	3.00
543	Bob Allen (SP)	15.00	7.50	4.50
544	Willie McCovey (SP)	95.00	50.00	30.00
545	Hoyt Wilhelm (SP)	50.00	25.00	12.50
546	Moe Thacker (SP)	15.00	7.50	4.50
547	Don Ferrarese	10.00	5.00	3.00
548	Bobby Del Greco	10.00	5.00	3.00
549	Bill Rigney (SP)	15.00	7.50	4.50
550	Art Mahaffey (SP)	15.00	7.50	4.50
551	Harry Bright	10.00	5.00	3.00
552	Chicago Cubs Team (SP)	50.00	25.00	12.50
553	Jim Coates	10.00	5.00	3.00
554	Bubba Morton (SP)	15.00	7.50	4.50
555	John Buzhardt (SP)	15.00	7.50	4.50
556	Al Spangler	10.00	5.00	3.00
557	Bob Anderson (SP)	15.00	7.50	4.50
558	John Goryl	10.00	5.00	3.00
559	Mike Higgins	10.00	5.00	3.00
560	Chuck Estrada (SP)	15.00	7.50	4.50
561	Gene Oliver (SP)	15.00	7.50	4.50
562	Bill Henry	10.00	5.00	3.00
563	Ken Aspromonte	10.00	5.00	3.00
564	Bob Grim	10.00	5.00	3.00
565	Jose Pagan	10.00	5.00	3.00
566	Marty Kutyna (SP)	15.00	7.50	4.50
567	Tracy Stallard (SP)	15.00	7.50	4.50
568	Jim Golden	10.00	5.00	3.00
569	Ed Sadowski (SP)	15.00	7.50	4.50
570	Bill Stafford	10.00	5.00	3.00
571	Billy Klaus (SP)	15.00	7.50	4.50
572	Bob Miller (SP)	15.00	7.50	4.50
573	Johnny Logan	10.00	5.00	3.00
574	Dean Stone	10.00	5.00	3.00
575	Red Schoendienst	35.00	17.00	8.00
576	Russ Kemmerer (SP)	15.00	7.50	4.50
577	Dave Nicholson (SP)	15.00	7.50	4.50
578	Jim Duffalo	10.00	5.00	3.00

		NM	E	VG
579	Jim Schaffer (SP)	15.00	7.50	4.50
580	Bill Monbouquette	10.00	5.00	3.00
581	Mel Roach	10.00	5.00	3.00
582	Ron Piche	10.00	5.00	3.00
583	Larry Osborne	10.00	5.00	3.00
584	Minnesota Twins Team (SP)	50.00	25.00	12.50
585	Glen Hobbie (SP)	15.00	7.50	4.50
586	Sammy Esposito (SP)	15.00	7.50	4.50
587	Frank Funk (SP)	15.00	7.50	4.50
588	Birdie Tebbetts	10.00	5.00	3.00
589	Bob Turley	20.00	8.75	5.25
590	Curt Flood	24.00	12.00	7.00
591	Rookie Parade Pitchers (Sam McDowell **RC**, Ron Nischwitz **RC**, Art Quirk, Dick Radatz **RC**, Ron Taylor **RC**)	75.00	37.50	18.75
592	Rookie Parade Pitchers (Bo Belinsky **RC**, Joe Bonikowski, Jim Bouton **RC**, Dan Pfister, Dave Stenhouse)	75.00	37.50	18.75
593	Rookie Parade Pitchers (Craig Anderson, Jack Hamilton **RC**, Jack Lamabe, Bob Moorhead, Bob Veale **RC**)	50.00	25.00	15.00
594	Rookie Parade Catchers (Doug Camilli **RC**, Doc Edwards **RC**, Don Pavletich **RC**, Ken Retzer **RC**, Bob Uecker **RC**)	75.00	37.50	18.75
595	Rookie Parade Infielders (Ed Charles **RC**, Marlin Coughtry, Bob Sadowski, Felix Torres)	35.00	17.00	9.00
596	Rookie Parade Infielders (Bernie Allen **RC**, Phil Linz **RC**, Joe Pepitone **RC**, Rich Rollins **RC**)	75.00	40.00	20.00
597	Rookie Parade Infielders (Rod Kanehl, Jim McKnight, Denis Menke **RC**, Amado Samuel)	45.00	20.00	12.00
598	Rookie Parade Outfielders (Howie Goss **RC**, Jim Hickman **RC**, Manny Jimenez **RC**, Al Luplow **RC**, Ed Olivares **RC**)	100.00	35.00	15.00

1962 Topps Baseball Bucks

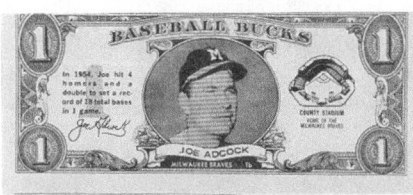

Issued in their own one-cent package, "Baseball Bucks" measure 4-1/8" x 1-3/4", were printed in black on green paper and designed to resemble dollar bills. The center player portrait has a banner underneath with the player's name. His home park is shown on the right and there is some biographical information at left. The back features a large denomination, with the player's league and team logo on either side. Poorly centered examples of this issue are the rule, rather than the exception. Sixty-two of the players appear on facsimile $1 notes. There are 24 $5 stars and 10 $10 superstars. Baseball Bucks are graded without regard to the vertical fold with which they were issued.

		NM	E	VG
Complete Set (96):		2,000	1,000	600.00
Common Player:		7.50	3.75	2.25
Wax Pack:		175.00		
(1)	Hank Aaron ($5)	50.00	25.00	15.00
(2)	Joe Adcock	7.50	3.75	2.25
(3)	George Altman	7.50	3.75	2.25
(4)	Jim Archer	7.50	3.75	2.25
(5)	Richie Ashburn ($5)	40.00	20.00	12.00
(6)	Ernie Banks ($10)	45.00	22.00	13.50
(7)	Earl Battey	7.50	3.75	2.25
(8)	Gus Bell	7.50	3.75	2.25
(9)	Yogi Berra ($5)	40.00	20.00	12.00
(10)	Ken Boyer ($10)	15.00	7.50	4.50
(11)	Jackie Brandt	7.50	3.75	2.25
(12)	Jim Bunning	15.00	7.50	4.50
(13)	Lou Burdette ($5)	7.50	3.75	2.25
(14)	Don Cardwell	7.50	3.75	2.25
(15)	Norm Cash ($5)	15.00	7.50	4.50
(16)	Orlando Cepeda ($5)	30.00	15.00	9.00
(17)	Roberto Clemente ($5)	200.00	100.00	60.00
(18)	Rocky Colavito ($5)	25.00	12.50	7.50
(19)	Chuck Cottier	7.50	3.75	2.25
(20)	Roger Craig	7.50	3.75	2.25
(21)	Bennie Daniels	7.50	3.75	2.25
(22)	Don Demeter	7.50	3.75	2.25
(23)	Don Drysdale	30.00	15.00	9.00
(24)	Chuck Estrada	7.50	3.75	2.25
(25)	Dick Farrell	7.50	3.75	2.25
(26)	Whitey Ford ($10)	40.00	20.00	12.00
(27)	Nellie Fox ($5)	30.00	15.00	9.00
(28)	Tito Francona	7.50	3.75	2.25
(29)	Bob Friend	7.50	3.75	2.25
(30)	Jim Gentile ($5)	7.50	3.75	2.25
(31)	Dick Gernert	7.50	3.75	2.25
(32)	Lenny Green	7.50	3.75	2.25
(33)	Dick Groat	7.50	3.75	2.25
(34)	Woody Held	7.50	3.75	2.25
(35)	Don Hoak	7.50	3.75	2.25
(36)	Gil Hodges ($5)	25.00	12.50	7.50
(37)	Frank Howard	10.00	5.00	3.00
(38)	Elston Howard	10.00	5.00	3.00
(39)	Dick Howser	7.50	3.75	2.25
(40)	Ken Hunt	7.50	3.75	2.25
(41)	Larry Jackson	7.50	3.75	2.25
(42)	Joe Jay	7.50	3.75	2.25
(43)	Al Kaline	30.00	15.00	9.00
(44)	Harmon Killebrew ($5)	40.00	20.00	12.00
(45)	Sandy Koufax ($5)	75.00	37.00	22.00
(46)	Harvey Kuenn	7.50	3.75	2.25
(47)	Jim Landis	7.50	3.75	2.25
(48)	Norm Larker	7.50	3.75	2.25
(49)	Frank Lary ($5)	7.50	3.75	2.25
(50)	Jerry Lumpe	7.50	3.75	2.25
(51)	Art Mahaffey	7.50	3.75	2.25
(52)	Frank Malzone	7.50	3.75	2.25
(53)	Felix Mantilla	7.50	3.75	2.25
(54)	Mickey Mantle ($10)	350.00	175.00	105.00
(55)	Roger Maris ($10)	45.00	22.00	13.50
(56)	Ed Mathews ($10)	35.00	17.50	10.50
(57)	Willie Mays ($10)	65.00	32.00	19.50
(58)	Ken McBride	7.50	3.75	2.25
(59)	Mike McCormick	7.50	3.75	2.25
(60)	Stu Miller	7.50	3.75	2.25
(61)	Minnie Minoso	10.00	5.00	3.00
(62)	Wally Moon ($5)	7.50	3.75	2.25
(63)	Stan Musial ($10)	60.00	30.00	18.00
(64)	Danny O'Connell	7.50	3.75	2.25
(65)	Jim O'Toole	7.50	3.75	2.25
(66)	Camilo Pascual ($5)	7.50	3.75	2.25
(67)	Jim Perry	7.50	3.75	2.25
(68)	Jimmy Piersall ($5)	12.00	6.00	3.50
(69)	Vada Pinson ($5)	12.00	6.00	3.50
(70)	Juan Pizarro	7.50	3.75	2.25
(71)	Johnny Podres	10.00	5.00	3.00
(72)	Vic Power ($5)	7.50	3.75	2.25
(73)	Bob Purkey	7.50	3.75	2.25
(74)	Pedro Ramos	7.50	3.75	2.25
(75)	Brooks Robinson ($5)	30.00	15.00	9.00
(76)	Floyd Robinson	7.50	3.75	2.25
(77)	Frank Robinson ($10)	35.00	17.50	10.50
(78)	Johnny Romano	7.50	3.75	2.25
(79)	Pete Runnels ($5)	7.50	3.75	2.25
(80)	Don Schwall	7.50	3.75	2.25
(81)	Bobby Shantz ($5)	7.50	3.75	2.25
(82)	Norm Siebern	7.50	3.75	2.25
(83)	Roy Sievers ($5)	7.50	3.75	2.25
(84)	Hal (W.) Smith	7.50	3.75	2.25
(85)	Warren Spahn ($10)	40.00	20.00	12.00
(86)	Dick Stuart	7.50	3.75	2.25
(87)	Tony Taylor	7.50	3.75	2.25
(88)	Lee Thomas	7.50	3.75	2.25
(89)	Gus Triandos	7.50	3.75	2.25
(90)	Leon Wagner	7.50	3.75	2.25
(91)	Jerry Walker	7.50	3.75	2.25
(92)	Bill White	7.50	3.75	2.25
(93)	Billy Williams	15.00	7.50	4.50
(94)	Gene Woodling	7.50	3.75	2.25
(95)	Early Wynn ($5)	15.00	7.50	4.50
(96)	Carl Yastrzemski	40.00	20.00	12.00

1962 Topps Foldees

This card states "foldee faces" rather than just the word foldee. Also, it reflects number "11", yet on the other side states #1 in a series of 12. This card is larger also, measuring 4 1/2" x 2 3/8"

(11)	Babe Ruth	25.00	12.50	7.50

1962 Topps Stamps

An artistic improvement over the somewhat drab Topps stamps of the previous year, the 1962 stamps, 1-3/8" x 1-7/8", had color player photographs set on red or yellow backgrounds. As in 1961, they were issued in two-stamp panels as insert with Topps baseball cards. A change from 1961 was the inclusion of team emblems in the set. A complete set consists of 201 stamps; Roy Sievers was originally portrayed on the wrong team - Athletics - and was later corrected to the Phillies.

		NM	E	VG
Complete Set (200):		800.00	400.00	240.00
Common Player:		3.00	1.50	.90
Stamp Album (Red):		60.00	30.00	18.00
(1)	Hank Aaron	15.00	7.50	4.50
(2)	Jerry Adair	3.00	1.50	.90
(3)	Joe Adcock	3.00	1.50	.90
(4)	Bob Allison	3.00	1.50	.90
(5)	Felipe Alou	4.00	2.00	1.25
(6)	George Altman	3.00	1.50	.90
(7)	Joe Amalfitano	3.00	1.50	.90
(8)	Ruben Amaro	3.00	1.50	.90
(9)	Luis Aparicio	6.00	3.00	1.75
(10)	Jim Archer	3.00	1.50	.90
(11)	Bob Aspromonte	3.00	1.50	.90
(12)	Ed Bailey	3.00	1.50	.90
(13)	Jack Baldschun	3.00	1.50	.90
(14)	Ernie Banks	9.00	4.50	2.75
(15)	Earl Battey	3.00	1.50	.90
(16)	Gus Bell	3.00	1.50	.90
(17)	Yogi Berra	12.00	6.00	3.50
(18)	Dick Bertell	3.00	1.50	.90
(19)	Steve Bilko	3.00	1.50	.90
(20)	Frank Bolling	3.00	1.50	.90
(21)	Steve Boros	3.00	1.50	.90
(22)	Ted Bowsfield	3.00	1.50	.90
(23)	Clete Boyer	3.00	1.50	.90
(24)	Ken Boyer	4.00	2.00	1.25
(25)	Jackie Brandt	3.00	1.50	.90
(26)	Bill Bruton	3.00	1.50	.90
(27)	Jim Bunning	6.00	3.00	1.75
(28)	Lou Burdette	3.00	1.50	.90
(29)	Smoky Burgess	3.00	1.50	.90
(30)	Johnny Callizon (Callison)	3.00	1.50	.90
(31)	Don Cardwell	3.00	1.50	.90
(32)	Camilo Carreon	3.00	1.50	.90
(33)	Norm Cash	4.00	2.00	1.25
(34)	Orlando Cepeda	6.00	3.00	1.75
(35)	Roberto Clemente	20.00	10.00	6.00
(36)	Ty Cline	3.00	1.50	.90
(37)	Rocky Colavito	6.00	3.00	1.75
(38)	Gordon Coleman	3.00	1.50	.90
(39)	Chuck Cottier	3.00	1.50	.90
(40)	Roger Craig	3.00	1.50	.90
(41)	Del Crandall	3.00	1.50	.90
(42)	Pete Daley	3.00	1.50	.90
(43)	Clay Dalrymple	3.00	1.50	.90
(44)	Bennie Daniels	3.00	1.50	.90
(45)	Jim Davenport	3.00	1.50	.90
(46)	Don Demeter	3.00	1.50	.90
(47)	Dick Donovan	3.00	1.50	.90
(48)	Don Drysdale	10.00	5.00	3.00
(49)	John Edwards	3.00	1.50	.90
(50)	Dick Ellsworth	3.00	1.50	.90
(51)	Chuck Estrada	3.00	1.50	.90
(52)	Roy Face	3.00	1.50	.90
(53)	Ron Fairly	3.00	1.50	.90
(54)	Dick Farrell	3.00	1.50	.90
(55)	Whitey Ford	12.00	6.00	3.50
(56)	Mike Fornieles	3.00	1.50	.90
(57)	Nellie Fox	7.00	3.50	2.00
(58)	Tito Francona	3.00	1.50	.90

(59)	Gene Freese	3.00	1.50	.90
(60)	Bob Friend	3.00	1.50	.90
(61)	Gary Geiger	3.00	1.50	.90
(62)	Jim Gentile	3.00	1.50	.90
(63)	Tony Gonzalez	3.00	1.50	.90
(64)	Lenny Green	3.00	1.50	.90
(65)	Dick Groat	3.00	1.50	.90
(66)	Ron Hansen	3.00	1.50	.90
(67)	Al Heist	3.00	1.50	.90
(68)	Woody Held	3.00	1.50	.90
(69)	Ray Herbert	3.00	1.50	.90
(70)	Chuck Hinton	3.00	1.50	.90
(71)	Don Hoak	3.00	1.50	.90
(72)	Glen Hobbie	3.00	1.50	.90
(73)	Gil Hodges	6.00	3.00	1.75
(74)	Jay Hook	3.00	1.50	.90
(75)	Elston Howard	4.00	2.00	1.25
(76)	Frank Howard	3.00	1.50	.90
(77)	Dick Howser	3.00	1.50	.90
(78)	Ken Hunt	3.00	1.50	.90
(79)	Larry Jackson	3.00	1.50	.90
(80)	Julian Javier	3.00	1.50	.90
(81)	Joe Jay	3.00	1.50	.90
(82)	Bob Johnson	3.00	1.50	.90
(83)	Sam Jones	3.00	1.50	.90
(84)	Al Kaline	9.00	4.50	2.75
(85)	Eddie Kasko	3.00	1.50	.90
(86)	Harmon Killebrew	10.00	5.00	3.00
(87)	Sandy Koufax	15.00	7.50	4.50
(88)	Jack Kralick	3.00	1.50	.90
(89)	Tony Kubek	4.00	2.00	1.25
(90)	Harvey Kuenn	3.00	1.50	.90
(91)	Jim Landis	3.00	1.50	.90
(92)	Hobie Landrith	3.00	1.50	.90
(93)	Frank Lary	3.00	1.50	.90
(94)	Barry Latman	3.00	1.50	.90
(95)	Jerry Lumpe	3.00	1.50	.90
(96)	Art Mahaffey	3.00	1.50	.90
(97)	Frank Malzone	3.00	1.50	.90
(98)	Felix Mantilla	3.00	1.50	.90
(99)	Mickey Mantle	50.00	25.00	15.00
(100)	Juan Marichal	6.00	3.00	1.75
(101)	Roger Maris	13.50	6.75	4.00
(102)	J.C. Martin	3.00	1.50	.90
(103)	Ed Mathews	9.00	4.50	2.75
(104)	Willie Mays	15.00	7.50	4.50
(105)	Bill Mazeroski	6.00	3.00	1.75
(106)	Ken McBride	3.00	1.50	.90
(107)	Tim McCarver	3.00	1.50	.90
(108)	Joe McClain	3.00	1.50	.90
(109)	Mike McCormick	3.00	1.50	.90
(110)	Lindy McDaniel	3.00	1.50	.90
(111)	Roy McMillan	3.00	1.50	.90
(112)	Bob L. Miller	3.00	1.50	.90
(113)	Stu Miller	3.00	1.50	.90
(114)	Minnie Minoso	6.00	3.00	1.75
(115)	Bill Monbouquette	3.00	1.50	.90
(116)	Wally Moon	3.00	1.50	.90
(117)	Don Mossi	3.00	1.50	.90
(118)	Stan Musial	15.00	7.50	4.50
(119)	Russ Nixon	3.00	1.50	.90
(120)	Danny O'Connell	3.00	1.50	.90
(121)	Jim O'Toole	3.00	1.50	.90
(122)	Milt Pappas	3.00	1.50	.90
(123)	Camilo Pascual	3.00	1.50	.90
(124)	Albie Pearson	3.00	1.50	.90
(125)	Jim Perry	3.00	1.50	.90
(126)	Bubba Phillips	3.00	1.50	.90
(127)	Jimmy Piersall	3.00	1.50	.90
(128)	Vada Pinson	3.00	1.50	.90
(129)	Juan Pizarro	3.00	1.50	.90
(130)	Johnny Podres	3.00	1.50	.90
(131)	Leo Posada	3.00	1.50	.90
(132)	Vic Power	3.00	1.50	.90
(133)	Bob Purkey	3.00	1.50	.90
(134)	Pedro Ramos	3.00	1.50	.90
(135)	Bobby Richardson	3.00	1.50	.90
(136)	Brooks Robinson	10.00	5.00	3.00
(137)	Floyd Robinson	3.00	1.50	.90
(138)	Frank Robinson	10.00	5.00	3.00
(139)	Bob Rodgers	3.00	1.50	.90
(140)	Johnny Romano	3.00	1.50	.90
(141)	John Roseboro	3.00	1.50	.90
(142)	Pete Runnels	3.00	1.50	.90
(143)	Ray Sadecki	3.00	1.50	.90
(144)	Ron Santo	3.00	1.50	.90
(145)	Chuck Schilling	3.00	1.50	.90
(146)	Barney Schultz	3.00	1.50	.90
(147)	Don Schwall	3.00	1.50	.90
(148)	Bobby Shantz	3.00	1.50	.90
(149)	Bob Shaw	3.00	1.50	.90
(150)	Norm Siebern	3.00	1.50	.90
(151)	Roy Sievers (Philadelphia)	3.00	1.50	.90
(152)	Bill Skowron	4.00	2.00	1.25
(153)	Hal (W.) Smith	3.00	1.50	.90
(154)	Duke Snider	12.00	6.00	3.50
(155)	Warren Spahn	9.00	4.50	2.75
(156)	Al Spangler	3.00	1.50	.90
(157)	Daryl Spencer	3.00	1.50	.90
(158)	Gene Stephens	3.00	1.50	.90
(159)	Dick Stuart	3.00	1.50	.90
(160)	Haywood Sullivan	3.00	1.50	.90
(161)	Tony Taylor	3.00	1.50	.90
(162)	George Thomas	3.00	1.50	.90
(163)	Lee Thomas	3.00	1.50	.90
(164)	Bob Tiefenauer	3.00	1.50	.90
(165)	Joe Torre	6.00	3.00	1.75
(166)	Gus Triandos	3.00	1.50	.90
(167)	Bill Tuttle	3.00	1.50	.90
(168)	Zoilo Versalles	3.00	1.50	.90
(169)	Bill Virdon	3.00	1.50	.90
(170)	Leon Wagner	3.00	1.50	.90
(171)	Jerry Walker	3.00	1.50	.90
(172)	Lee Walls	3.00	1.50	.90
(173)	Bill White	3.00	1.50	.90
(174)	Hoyt Wilhelm	4.00	2.00	1.25
(175)	Billy Williams	6.00	3.00	1.75
(176)	Jake Wood	3.00	1.50	.90
(177)	Gene Woodling	3.00	1.50	.90
(178)	Early Wynn	4.00	2.00	1.25
(179)	Carl Yastrzemski	12.00	6.00	3.50
(180)	Don Zimmer	3.00	1.50	.90
(181)	Baltimore Orioles Logo	3.00	1.50	.90
(182)	Boston Red Sox Logo	3.00	1.50	.90
(183)	Chicago Cubs Logo	3.00	1.50	.90
(184)	Chicago White Sox Logo	3.00	1.50	.90
(185)	Cincinnati Reds Logo	3.00	1.50	.90
(186)	Cleveland Indians Logo	3.00	1.50	.90
(187)	Detroit Tigers Logo	3.00	1.50	.90
(188)	Houston Colts Logo	3.00	1.50	.90
(189)	Kansas City Athletics Logo	3.00	1.50	.90
(190)	Los Angeles Angels Logo	3.00	1.50	.90
(191)	Los Angeles Dodgers Logo	3.00	1.50	.90
(192)	Milwaukee Braves Logo	3.00	1.50	.90
(193)	Minnesota Twins Logo	3.00	1.50	.90
(194)	New York Mets Logo	3.00	1.50	.90
(195)	New York Yankees Logo	6.00	3.00	1.75
(196)	Philadelphia Phillies Logo	3.00	1.50	.90
(197)	Pittsburgh Pirates Logo	3.00	1.50	.90
(198)	St. Louis Cardinals Logo	3.00	1.50	.90
(199)	San Francisco Giants Logo	3.00	1.50	.90
(200)	Washington Senators Logo	3.00	1.50	.90

1962 Topps Stamps Panels

Some advanced collectors pursue the 1962 Topps stamps in the form of the two-stamp panels in which they were issued. The 200 different stamps which make up the issue can be found on 245 different two-stamp panels, flanked at left by a smaller tab advertising the accompanying album. The unnumbered stamps are listed here alphabetically according to the name of the player or team which apears on the left end of the panel. Values shown are for full three-piece panels.

		NM	E	VG
	Complete Panel Set (245):	2,750	1,375	825.00
	Common Panel:	4.00	2.00	1.25
(1)	Hank Aaron/Ted Bowsfield	35.00	17.50	10.50
(2)	Jerry Adair/Tony Gonzalez	8.00	4.00	2.50
(3)	Joe Adcock/George Thomas	8.00	4.00	2.50
(4)	Bob Allison/Jim Davenport	8.00	4.00	2.50
(5)	Felipe Alou/Mickey Mantle	100.00	50.00	30.00
(6)	Felipe Alou/Chuck Schilling	9.00	4.50	2.75
(7)	George Altman/Rocky Colavito	10.00	5.00	3.00
(8)	George Altman/Don Schwall	8.00	4.00	2.50
(9)	Joe Amalfitano/Jim Gentile	8.00	4.00	2.50
(10)	Joe Amalfitano/Vic Power	8.00	4.00	2.50
(11)	Ruben Amaro/Carl Yastrzemski	30.00	15.00	9.00
(12)	Luis Aparicio/Dick Farrell	10.00	5.00	3.00
(13)	Luis Aparicio/Al Heist	10.00	5.00	3.00
(14)	Bob Aspromonte/Al Kaline	15.00	7.50	4.50
(15)	Ed Bailey/Jim Piersall	8.00	4.00	2.50
(16)	Ernie Banks/Milt Pappas	20.00	10.00	6.00
(17)	Earl Battey/Bob Clemente	35.00	17.50	10.50
(18)	Earl Battey/Ed Mathews	12.00	6.00	3.50
(19)	Gus Bell/Steve Boros	8.00	4.00	2.50
(20)	Gus Bell/Ty Cline	8.00	4.00	2.50
(21)	Yogi Berra/Roy Face	20.00	10.00	6.00
(22)	Yogi Berra/Jack Kralick	15.00	7.50	4.50
(23)	Dick Bertell/Hoyt Wilhelm	10.00	5.00	3.00
(24)	Dick Bertell/Don Zimmer	9.00	4.50	2.75
(25)	Steve Bilko/Ruben Amaro	8.00	4.00	2.50
(26)	Steve Bilko/Roy Sievers	8.00	4.00	2.50
(27)	Frank Bolling/Nellie Fox	10.00	5.00	3.00
(28)	Steve Boros/Art Mahaffey	8.00	4.00	2.50
(29)	Clete Boyer/Chuck Cottier	9.00	4.50	2.75
(30)	Ken Boyer/Bob Friend	9.00	4.50	2.75
(31)	Jackie Brandt/Frank Robinson	15.00	7.50	4.50
(32)	Bill Bruton/Ernie Banks	20.00	10.00	6.00
(33)	Bill Bruton/Jay Hook	8.00	4.00	2.50
(34)	Jim Bunning/Bob Miller	10.00	5.00	3.00
(35)	Jim Bunning/Jim O'Toole	10.00	5.00	3.00
(36)	Jim Bunning/Daryl Spencer	10.00	5.00	3.00
(37)	Lou Burdette/Ed Mathews	12.00	6.00	3.50
(38)	Lou Burdette/Willie Mays	35.00	17.50	10.50
(39)	Smoky Burgess/Bobby Richardson	9.00	4.50	2.75
(40)	Johnny Callizon (Callison)/Barry Latman	9.00	4.50	2.75
(41)	Johnny Callizon (Callison)/Frank Malzone	9.00	4.50	2.75
(42)	Johnny Callizon (Callison)/Willie Mays	35.00	17.50	10.50
(43)	Don Cardwell/Hoyt Wilhelm	10.00	5.00	3.00
(44)	Norm Cash/Dick Bertell	9.00	4.50	2.75
(45)	Norm Cash/Don Cardwell	9.00	4.50	2.75
(46)	Norm Cash/Dick Howser	9.00	4.50	2.75
(47)	Ty Cline/Art Mahaffey	8.00	4.00	2.50
(48)	Rocky Colavito/Sam Jones	10.00	5.00	3.00
(49)	Gordon Coleman/Pete Daley	8.00	4.00	2.50
(50)	Gordon Coleman/Danny O'Connell	8.00	4.00	2.50
(51)	Roger Craig/Ted Bowsfield	8.00	4.00	2.50
(52)	Roger Craig/Minnie Minoso	9.00	4.50	2.75
(53)	Del Crandall/Clete Boyer	9.00	4.50	2.75
(54)	Del Crandall/Ray Sadecki	8.00	4.00	2.50
(55)	Pete Daley/Bob Friend	8.00	4.00	2.50
(56)	Pete Daley/Mike McCormick	8.00	4.00	2.50
(57)	Clay Dalrymple/Woody Held	8.00	4.00	2.50
(58)	Clay Dalrymple/Pedro Ramos	8.00	4.00	2.50
(59)	Bennie Daniels/Jerry Walker	8.00	4.00	2.50
(60)	Jim Davenport/Harmon Killebrew	15.00	7.50	4.50
(61)	Don Demeter/Haywood Sullivan	8.00	4.00	2.50
(62)	Don Demeter/Gus Triandos	8.00	4.00	2.50
(63)	Don Demeter/Lee Walls	8.00	4.00	2.50
(64)	Dick Donovan/Jerry Adair	8.00	4.00	2.50
(65)	Dick Donovan/Jim Perry	8.00	4.00	2.50
(66)	Dick Donovan/Vada Pinson	9.00	4.50	2.75
(67)	John Edwards/Jerry Walker	8.00	4.00	2.50
(68)	Dick Ellsworth/Glen Hobbie	8.00	4.00	2.50
(69)	Dick Ellsworth/Pete Runnels	8.00	4.00	2.50
(70)	Chuck Estrada/Don Drysdale	12.00	6.00	3.50
(71)	Chuck Estrada/Al Kaline	15.00	7.50	4.50
(72)	Roy Face/Minnie Minoso	9.00	4.50	2.75
(73)	Ron Fairly/Jim Landis	8.00	4.00	2.50
(74)	Dick Farrell/Frank Lary	8.00	4.00	2.50
(75)	Whitey Ford/Joe Torre	15.00	7.50	4.50
(76)	Nellie Fox/Willie Mays	35.00	17.50	10.50
(77)	Tito Francona/Ken Boyer	9.00	4.50	2.75
(78)	Tito Francona/Bob Johnson	8.00	4.00	2.50
(79)	Gene Freese/Bob Allison	8.00	4.00	2.50
(80)	Gene Freese/Ernie Banks	15.00	7.50	4.50

(81)	Gary Geiger/Bobby Richardson	9.00	4.50	2.75
(82)	Jim Gentile/Hal W. Smith	8.00	4.00	2.50
(83)	Dick Groat/Joe McClain	8.00	4.00	2.50
(84)	Al Heist/Frank Lary	8.00	4.00	2.50
(85)	Woody Held/Orlando Cepeda	10.00	5.00	3.00
(86)	Ray Herbert/Frank Bolling	8.00	4.00	2.50
(87)	Ray Herbert/Eddie Kasko	8.00	4.00	2.50
(88)	Chuck Hinton/Dick Groat	8.00	4.00	2.50
(89)	Chuck Hinton/Stu Miller	8.00	4.00	2.50
(90)	Don Hoak/Bob Allison	8.00	4.00	2.50
(91)	Gil Hodges/Bennie Daniels	10.00	5.00	3.00
(92)	Gil Hodges/John Edwards	10.00	5.00	3.00
(93)	Elston Howard/Bob Clemente	35.00	17.50	10.50
(94)	Dick Howser/Don Zimmer	9.00	4.50	2.75
(95)	Ken Hunt/Lenny Green	8.00	4.00	2.50
(96)	Larry Jackson/Smoky Burgess	8.00	4.00	2.50
(97)	Larry Jackson/Gary Geiger	8.00	4.00	2.50
(98)	Joe Jay/Johnny Romano	8.00	4.00	2.50
(99)	Bob Johnson/Bob Friend	8.00	4.00	2.50
(100)	Al Kaline/Don Hoak	15.00	7.50	4.50
(101)	Eddie Kasko/Nellie Fox	10.00	5.00	3.00
(102)	Sandy Koufax/Joe Adcock	30.00	15.00	9.00
(103)	Sandy Koufax/Hobie Landrith	30.00	15.00	9.00
(104)	Sandy Koufax/Bob Shaw	30.00	15.00	9.00
(105)	Jack Kralick/Minnie Minoso	9.00	4.50	2.75
(106)	Harvey Kuenn/Ken Hunt	8.00	4.00	2.50
(107)	Havey Kuenn/Gene Woodling	8.00	4.00	2.50
(108)	Hobie Landrith/Mike Fornieles	8.00	4.00	2.50
(109)	Barry Latman/Tony Kubek	9.00	4.50	2.75
(110)	Barry Latman/Johnny Podres	8.00	4.00	2.50
(111)	Frank Malzone/Johnny Podres	8.00	4.00	2.50
(112)	Frank Malzone/Duke Snider	15.00	7.50	4.50
(113)	Felix Mantilla/Camilo Carreon	8.00	4.00	2.50
(114)	Mickey Mantle/Hank Aaron	125.00	62.00	37.00
(115)	Mickey Mantle/Dick Stuart	110.00	55.00	33.00
(116)	Juan Marichal/Bill Bruton	12.00	6.00	3.50
(117)	Juan Marichal/Gene Freese	12.00	6.00	3.50
(118)	Juan Marichal/Don Hoak	12.00	6.00	3.50
(119)	Roger Maris/Lou Burdette	20.00	10.00	6.00
(120)	Roger Maris/Nellie Fox	20.00	10.00	6.00
(121)	Roger Maris/Lee Thomas	20.00	10.00	6.00
(122)	J.C. Martin/Felix Mantilla	8.00	4.00	2.50
(123)	J.C. Martin/Barney Schultz	8.00	4.00	2.50
(124)	Willie Mays/Tony Kubek	35.00	17.50	10.50
(125)	Bill Mazeroski/Earl Battey	10.00	5.00	3.00
(126)	Bill Mazeroski/Elston Howard	10.00	5.00	3.00
(127)	Bill Mazeroski/Early Wynn	12.00	6.00	3.50
(128)	Ken McBride/Joe Torre	9.00	4.50	2.75
(129)	Tim McCarver/Bill Tuttle	9.00	4.50	2.75
(130)	Lindy McDaniel/Jim Piersall	8.00	4.00	2.50
(131)	Roy McMillan/Bob Allison	8.00	4.00	2.50
(132)	Roy McMillan/Albie Pearson	8.00	4.00	2.50
(133)	Roy McMillan/Leon Wagner	8.00	4.00	2.50
(134)	Bob Miller/Ron Hansen	8.00	4.00	2.50
(135)	Stu Miller/Joe McCain	8.00	4.00	2.50
(136)	Bill Monbouquette/Don Hoak	8.00	4.00	2.50
(137)	Bill Monbouquette/Joe Torre	9.00	4.50	2.75
(138)	Wally Moon/Frank Malzone	8.00	4.00	2.50
(139)	Wally Moon/Juan Pizarro	8.00	4.00	2.50
(140)	Wally Moon/Brooks Robinson	20.00	10.00	6.00
(141)	Don Mossi/Bill Bruton	8.00	4.00	2.50
(142)	Don Mossi/Johnny Podres	8.00	4.00	2.50
(143)	Don Mossi/Al Spangler	8.00	4.00	2.50
(144)	Stan Musial/Whitey Ford	30.00	15.00	9.00
(145)	Stan Musial/Joe Torre	30.00	15.00	9.00
(146)	Russ Nixon/Ed Bailey	8.00	4.00	2.50

(147)	Russ Nixon/Lindy McDaniel	8.00	4.00	2.50
(148)	Danny O'Connell/Mike McCormick	8.00	4.00	2.50
(149)	Jim O'Toole/Ron Hansen	8.00	4.00	2.50
(150)	Jim O'Toole/Gene Stephens	8.00	4.00	2.50
(151)	Camilo Pascual/Pete Daley	8.00	4.00	2.50
(152)	Camilo Pascual/Tim McCarver	9.00	4.50	2.75
(153)	Camilo Pascual/Bill Virdon	8.00	4.00	2.50
(154)	Albie Pearson/Julian Javier	8.00	4.00	2.50
(155)	Jim Perry/Frank Howard	8.00	4.00	2.50
(156)	Bubba Phillips/Don Drysdale	12.00	6.00	3.50
(157)	Vada Pinson/Tony Gonzalez	9.00	4.50	2.75
(158)	Vada Pinson/Frank Howard	9.00	4.50	2.75
(159)	Juan Pizarro/Jack Baldschun	8.00	4.00	2.50
(160)	Johnny Podres/Jim Archer	8.00	4.00	2.50
(161)	Leo Posada/Milt Pappas	8.00	4.00	2.50
(162)	Leo Posada/Johnny Romano	8.00	4.00	2.50
(163)	Vic Power/Hal W. Smith	8.00	4.00	2.50
(164)	Bob Purkey/Harmon Killebrew	15.00	7.50	4.50
(165)	Pedro Ramos/Orlando Cepeda	10.00	5.00	3.00
(166)	Brooks Robinson/Jack Baldschun	15.00	7.50	4.50
(167)	Brooks Robinson/Duke Snider	20.00	10.00	6.00
(168)	Floyd Robinson/Ron Fairly	8.00	4.00	2.50
(169)	Floyd Robinson/Tony Taylor	8.00	4.00	2.50
(170)	Bob Rodgers/Hank Aaron	35.00	17.50	10.50
(171)	Bob Rodgers/Roger Craig	8.00	4.00	2.50
(172)	Bob Rodgers/Johnny Romano	8.00	4.00	2.50
(173)	Johnny Romano/Minnie Minoso	9.00	4.50	2.75
(174)	John Roseboro/Bob Aspromonte	8.00	4.00	2.50
(175)	John Roseboro/Chuck Estrada	8.00	4.00	2.50
(176)	John Roseboro/Bubba Phillips	8.00	4.00	2.50
(177)	Ray Sadecki/Chuck Cottier	8.00	4.00	2.50
(178)	Ron Santo/Ernie Banks	20.00	10.00	6.00
(179)	Ron Santo/Joe Jay	9.00	4.50	2.75
(180)	Ron Santo/Leo Posada	9.00	4.50	2.75
(181)	Chuck Schilling/Hank Aaron	35.00	17.50	10.50
(182)	Chuck Schilling/Dick Stuart	8.00	4.00	2.50
(183)	Barney Schultz/Camilo Carreon	8.00	4.00	2.50
(184)	Don Schwall/Sam Jones	8.00	4.00	2.50
(185)	Bobby Shantz/Pete Runnels	8.00	4.00	2.50
(186)	Bob Shaw/Mike Fornieles	8.00	4.00	2.50
(187)	Bob Shaw/George Thomas	8.00	4.00	2.50
(188)	Norm Siebern/Dick Ellsworth	8.00	4.00	2.50
(189)	Norm Siebern/Bobby Shantz	8.00	4.00	2.50
(190)	Norm Siebern/Early Wynn	10.00	5.00	3.00
(191)	Roy Sievers/Carl Yastrzemski	30.00	15.00	9.00
(192)	Bill Skowron/Jim Davenport	9.00	4.50	2.75
(193)	Bill Skowron/Bob Purkey	9.00	4.50	2.75
(194)	Warren Spahn/Whitey Ford	20.00	10.00	6.00
(195)	Al Spangler/Jim Archer	8.00	4.00	2.50
(196)	Al Spangler/Jay Hook	8.00	4.00	2.50
(197)	Daryl Spencer/Gene Stephens	8.00	4.00	2.50
(198)	Haywood Sullivan/Jerry Lumpe	8.00	4.00	2.50
(199)	Haywood Sullivan/Billy Williams	10.00	5.00	3.00
(200)	Tony Taylor/Jim Landis	8.00	4.00	2.50
(201)	Lee Thomas/Ed Mathews	12.00	6.00	3.50
(202)	Bob Tiefenauer/Jackie Brandt	8.00	4.00	2.50

(203)	Bob Tiefenauer/Jake Wood	8.00	4.00	2.50
(204)	Gus Triandos/Billy Williams	10.00	5.00	3.00
(205)	Zoilo Versalles/Whitey Ford	12.50	6.25	3.75
(206)	Zoilo Versalles/Stan Musial	30.00	15.00	9.00
(207)	Zoilo Veraalles/Warren Spahn	12.00	6.00	3.50
(208)	Bill Virdon/Bob Friend	8.00	4.00	2.50
(209)	Bill Virdon/Bill Tuttle	8.00	4.00	2.50
(210)	Leon Wagner/Jim Davenport	8.00	4.00	2.50
(211)	Leon Wagner/Julian Javier	8.00	4.00	2.50
(212)	Lee Walls/Jerry Lumpe	8.00	4.00	2.50
(213)	Bill White/Al Kaline	15.00	7.50	4.50
(214)	Bill White/Ken McBride	8.00	4.00	2.50
(215)	Bill White/Bill Monbouquette	8.00	4.00	2.50
(216)	Jake Wood/Frank Robinson	12.00	6.00	3.50
(217)	Gene Woodling/Lenny Green	8.00	4.00	2.50
(218)	Early Wynn/Glen Hobbie	10.00	5.00	3.00
(219)	Early Wynn/Ed Mathews	15.00	7.50	4.50
(220)	Angels/Athletics	8.00	4.00	2.50
(221)	Angels/Colts	9.00	4.50	2.75
(222)	Angels/Orioles	8.00	4.00	2.50
(223)	Athletics/Mets	10.00	5.00	3.00
(224)	Athletics/Pirates	9.00	4.50	2.75
(225)	Cardinals/Indians	9.00	4.50	2.75
(226)	Colts/Mets	12.00	6.00	3.50
(227)	Colts/Twins	9.00	4.50	2.75
(228)	Cubs/Senators	9.00	4.50	2.75
(229)	Giants/Red Sox	9.00	4.50	2.75
(230)	Giants/Tigers	9.00	4.50	2.75
(231)	Giants/White Sox	12.00	6.00	3.50
(232)	Indians/Reds	9.00	4.50	2.75
(233)	Mets/Dodgers	10.00	5.00	3.00
(234)	Orioles/Pirates	9.00	4.50	2.75
(235)	Phillies/Senators	9.00	4.50	2.75
(236)	Red Sox/Braves	9.00	4.50	2.75
(237)	Red Sox/Phillies	9.00	4.50	2.75
(238)	Reds/Indians	9.00	4.50	2.75
(239)	Reds/Yankees	12.50	6.25	3.75
(240)	Tigers/Braves	9.00	4.50	2.75
(241)	Twins/Dodgers	12.50	6.25	3.75
(242)	White Sox/Cubs	10.00	5.00	3.00
(243)	White Sox/Phillies	10.00	5.00	3.00
(244)	Yankees/Cardinals	12.50	6.25	3.75
(245)	Yankees/Reds	12.50	6.25	3.75

1963 Topps

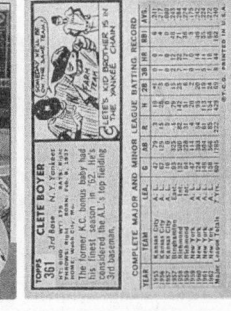

Although the number of cards dropped to 576, the 1963 Topps set is among the most popular of the 1960s. A color photo dominates the 2-1/2" x 3-1/2" card, but a colored circle at the bottom carries a black and white portrait as well. A colored band gives the player's name, team and position. The backs again feature career statistics and a cartoon, career summary and brief biographical details. The set is somewhat unlike those immediately preceding it in that there are fewer specialty cards. The major groupings are statistical leaders, World Series highlights and rookies. It is one rookie which makes the set special - Pete Rose. As one of the most avidly sought cards in history and a high-numbered card at that, the Rose rookie card accounts for much of the value of a complete set.

	NM	E	VG
Complete Set (576):	6,000	2,750	1,375
Common Player (1-446):	4.00	2.00	1.25
Common Player (447-576):	12.50	6.25	3.25

1	N.L. Batting Leaders(Hank Aaron, Bill White, Frank Robinson, Tommy Davis, Stan Musial)	45.00	20.00	10.00

#	Name			
2	A.L. Batting Leaders(Chuck Hinton, Mickey Mantle, Floyd Robinson, Pete Runnels, Norm Siebern)	40.00	20.00	10.00
3	N.L. Home Run Leaders(Hank Aaron, Ernie Banks, Orlando Cepeda, Willie Mays, Frank Robinson)	40.00	20.00	12.00
4	A.L. Home Run Leaders(Norm Cash, Rocky Colavito, Jim Gentile, Harmon Killebrew, Roger Maris, Leon Wagner)	21.00	10.00	6.00
5	N.L. E.R.A. Leaders(Don Drysdale, Bob Gibson, Sandy Koufax, Bob Shaw, Bob Purkey)	17.50	8.75	5.25
6	A.L. E.R.A. Leaders(Hank Aguirre, Dean Chance, Eddie Fisher, Whitey Ford, Robin Roberts)	10.00	5.00	3.00
7	N.L. Pitching Leaders(Don Drysdale, Joe Jay, Art Mahaffey, Billy O'Dell, Bob Purkey, Jack Sanford)	15.00	6.00	3.50
8	A.L. Pitching Leaders(Jim Bunning, Dick Donovan, Ray Herbert, Camilo Pascual, Ralph Terry)	10.00	5.00	3.00
9	N.L. Strikeout Leaders(Don Drysdale, Dick Farrell, Bob Gibson, Sandy Koufax, Billy O'Dell)	18.00	10.00	6.00
10	A.L. Strikeout Leaders(Jim Bunning, Jim Kaat, Camilo Pascual, Juan Pizarro, Ralph Terry)	9.00	4.50	2.75
11	Lee Walls	4.00	2.00	1.25
12	Steve Barber	4.00	2.00	1.25
13	Philadelphia Phillies Team	7.00	3.50	2.00
14	Pedro Ramos	4.00	2.00	1.25
15	Ken Hubbs	10.00	5.00	3.00
16	Al Smith	4.00	2.00	1.25
17	Ryne Duren	4.00	2.00	1.25
18	Buc Blasters(Smoky Burgess, Roberto Clemente, Bob Skinner, Dick Stuart)	65.00	37.50	18.75
19	Pete Burnside	4.00	2.00	1.25
20	Tony Kubek	12.50	6.25	3.75
21	Marty Keough	4.00	2.00	1.25
22	Curt Simmons	4.00	2.00	1.25
23	Ed Lopat	4.00	2.00	1.25
24	Bob Bruce	4.00	2.00	1.25
25	Al Kaline	50.00	25.00	12.50
26	Ray Moore	4.00	2.00	1.25
27	Choo Choo Coleman	4.00	2.00	1.25
28	Mike Fornieles	4.00	2.00	1.25
29a	1962 Rookie Stars(Sammy Ellis, Ray Culp, John Boozer RC, Jesse Gonder)	10.00	5.00	3.00
29b	1963 Rookie Stars(Sammy Ellis, Ray Culp RC, John Boozer, Jesse Gonder)	4.00	2.00	1.25
30	Harvey Kuenn	4.00	2.00	1.25
31	Cal Koonce	4.00	2.00	1.25
32	Tony Gonzalez	4.00	2.00	1.25
33	Bo Belinsky	4.00	2.00	1.25
34	Dick Schofield	4.00	2.00	1.25
35	John Buzhardt	4.00	2.00	1.25
36	Jerry Kindall	4.00	2.00	1.25
37	Jerry Lynch	4.00	2.00	1.25
38	Bud Daley	4.00	2.00	1.25
39	Los Angeles Angels Team	8.00	3.50	2.00
40	Vic Power	4.00	2.00	1.25
41	Charlie Lau	4.00	2.00	1.25
42	Stan Williams	4.00	2.00	1.25
43	Veteran Masters(Casey Stengel, Gene Woodling)	7.50	3.75	2.25
44	Terry Fox	4.00	2.00	1.25
45	Bob Aspromonte	4.00	2.00	1.25
46	Tommie Aaron RC	5.00	2.50	1.50
47	Don Lock	4.00	2.00	1.25
48	Birdie Tebbetts	4.00	2.00	1.25
49	Dal Maxvill RC	4.00	2.00	1.25
50	Bill Pierce	4.00	2.00	1.25
51	George Alusik	4.00	2.00	1.25
52	Chuck Schilling	4.00	2.00	1.25
53	Joe Moeller	4.00	2.00	1.25
54a	1962 Rookie Stars(Nelson Mathews RC, Harry Fanok RC, Jack Cullen RC, Dave DeBusschere RC)	15.00	7.50	4.50
54b	1963 Rookie Stars(Jack Cullen RC, Dave DeBusschere RC, Harry Fanok RC, Nelson Mathews RC)	8.00	4.00	2.50
55	Bill Virdon	4.00	2.00	1.25
56	Dennis Bennett	4.00	2.00	1.25
57	Billy Moran	4.00	2.00	1.25
58	Bob Will	4.00	2.00	1.25
59	Craig Anderson	4.00	2.00	1.25
60	Elston Howard	9.00	4.50	2.75
61	Ernie Bowman	4.00	2.00	1.25
62	Bob Hendley	4.00	2.00	1.25
63	Cincinnati Reds Team	10.00	5.00	3.00
64	Dick McAuliffe	4.00	2.00	1.25
65	Jackie Brandt	4.00	2.00	1.25
66	Mike Joyce	4.00	2.00	1.25
67	Ed Charles	4.00	2.00	1.25
68	Friendly Foes(Gil Hodges, Duke Snider)	20.00	10.00	6.00
69	Bud Zipfel	4.00	2.00	1.25
70	Jim O'Toole	4.00	2.00	1.25
71	Bobby Wine RC	4.00	2.00	1.25
72	Johnny Romano	4.00	2.00	1.25
73	Bobby Bragan	4.00	2.00	1.25
74	Denver Lemaster RC	4.00	2.00	1.25
75	Bob Allison	4.00	2.00	1.25
76	Earl Wilson	4.00	2.00	1.25
77	Al Spangler	4.00	2.00	1.25
78	Marv Throneberry	4.00	2.00	1.25
79	**1st Series Checklist (1-88)**	6.00	3.00	1.75
80	Jim Gilliam	6.00	3.00	1.75
81	Jimmie Schaffer	4.00	2.00	1.25
82	Ed Rakow	4.00	2.00	1.25
83	Charley James	4.00	2.00	1.25
84	Ron Kline	4.00	2.00	1.25
85	Tom Haller	4.00	2.00	1.25
86	Charley Maxwell	4.00	2.00	1.25
87	Bob Veale	4.00	2.00	1.25
88	Ron Hansen	4.00	2.00	1.25
89	Dick Stigman	4.00	2.00	1.25
90	Gordy Coleman	4.00	2.00	1.25
91	Dallas Green	4.00	2.00	1.25
92	Hector Lopez	4.00	2.00	1.25
93	Galen Cisco	4.00	2.00	1.25
94	Bob Schmidt	4.00	2.00	1.25
95	Larry Jackson	4.00	2.00	1.25
96	Lou Clinton	4.00	2.00	1.25
97	Bob Duliba	4.00	2.00	1.25
98	George Thomas	4.00	2.00	1.25
99	Jim Umbricht	4.00	2.00	1.25
100	Joe Cunningham	4.00	2.00	1.25
101	Joe Gibbon	4.00	2.00	1.25
102a	2nd Series Checklist (89-176) ("Checklist" in red on yellow.)	6.00	3.00	1.75
102b	2nd Series Checklist (89-176) ("Checklist" in white on red.)	10.00	5.00	3.00
103	Chuck Essegian	4.00	2.00	1.25
104	Lew Krausse	4.00	2.00	1.25
105	Ron Fairly	4.00	2.00	1.25
106	Bob Bolin	4.00	2.00	1.25
107	Jim Hickman	4.00	2.00	1.25
108	Hoyt Wilhelm	15.00	7.50	4.50
109	Lee Maye	4.00	2.00	1.25
110	Rich Rollins	4.00	2.00	1.25
111	Al Jackson	4.00	2.00	1.25
112	Dick Brown	4.00	2.00	1.25
113	Don Landrum (Photo actally Ron Santo.)		2.00	1.25
114	Dan Osinski	4.00	2.00	1.25
115	Carl Yastrzemski	40.00	20.00	12.00
116	Jim Brosnan	4.00	2.00	1.25
117	Jacke Davis	4.00	2.00	1.25
118	Sherm Lollar	4.00	2.00	1.25
119	Bob Lillis	4.00	2.00	1.25
120	Roger Maris	75.00	40.00	20.00
121	Jim Hannan	4.00	2.00	1.25
122	Julio Gotay	4.00	2.00	1.25
123	Frank Howard	4.00	2.00	1.25
124	Dick Howser	4.00	2.00	1.25
125	Robin Roberts	15.00	7.50	4.50
126	Bob Uecker	20.00	10.00	6.00
127	Bill Tuttle	4.00	2.00	1.25
128	Matty Alou	4.00	2.00	1.25
129	Gary Bell	4.00	2.00	1.25
130	Dick Groat	4.00	2.00	1.25
131	Washington Senators Team	8.00	3.50	2.00
132	Jack Hamilton	4.00	2.00	1.25
133	Gene Freese	4.00	2.00	1.25
134	Bob Scheffing	4.00	2.00	1.25
135	Richie Ashburn	15.00	7.50	4.50
136	Ike Delock	4.00	2.00	1.25
137	Mack Jones	4.00	2.00	1.25
138	Pride of N.L.(Willie Mays, Stan Musial)	60.00	30.00	18.00
139	Earl Averill	4.00	2.00	1.25
140	Frank Lary	4.00	2.00	1.25
141	Manny Mota RC	6.00	3.00	1.75
142	World Series Game 1 (Yanks' Ford Wins Series Opener)	11.00	5.50	3.25
143	World Series Game 2 (Sanford Flashes Shutout Magic)	5.00	2.50	1.50
144	World Series Game 3 (Maris Sparks Yankee Rally)	15.00	6.00	3.50
145	World Series Game 4 (Hiller Blasts Grand Slammer)	5.00	2.50	1.50
146	World Series Game 5 (Tresh's Homer Defeats Giants)	6.00	3.00	1.75
147	World Series Game 6 (Pierce Stars in 3-Hit Victory)	6.00	3.00	1.75
148	World Series Game 7 (Yanks Celebrate as Terry Wins)	7.00	3.50	2.00
149	Marv Breeding	4.00	2.00	1.25
150	Johnny Podres	6.00	3.00	1.75
151	Pittsburgh Pirates Team	12.00	5.00	3.00
152	Ron Nischwitz	4.00	2.00	1.25
153	Hal Smith	4.00	2.00	1.25
154	Walt Alston	7.50	3.75	2.25
155	Bill Stafford	4.00	2.00	1.25
156	Roy McMillan	4.00	2.00	1.25
157	Diego Segui RC	4.00	2.00	1.25
158	1963 Rookie Stars(Rogelio Alvarez, Tommy Harper RC, Dave Roberts, Bob Saverine)	6.00	3.00	1.75
159	Jim Pagliaroni	4.00	2.00	1.25
160	Juan Pizarro	4.00	2.00	1.25
161	Frank Torre	4.00	2.00	1.25
162	Minnesota Twins Team	8.00	3.50	2.00
163	Don Larsen	4.00	2.00	1.25
164	Bubba Morton	4.00	2.00	1.25
165	Jim Kaat	5.00	2.50	1.50
166	Johnny Keane	4.00	2.00	1.25
167	Jim Fregosi	4.00	2.00	1.25
168	Russ Nixon	4.00	2.00	1.25
169	1963 Rookie Stars(Dick Egan RC, Julio Navarro RC, Gaylord Perry, Tommie Sisk RC)	17.50	8.75	5.25
170	Joe Adcock	4.00	2.00	1.25
171	Steve Hamilton	4.00	2.00	1.25
172	Gene Oliver	4.00	2.00	1.25
173	Bombers' Best(Tom Tresh, Mickey Mantle, Bobby Richardson)	130.00	65.00	35.00
174	Larry Burright	4.00	2.00	1.25
175	Bob Buhl	4.00	2.00	1.25
176	Jim King	4.00	2.00	1.25
177	Bubba Phillips	4.00	2.00	1.25
178	Johnny Edwards	4.00	2.00	1.25
179	Ron Piche	4.00	2.00	1.25
180	Bill Skowron	10.00	5.00	3.00
181	Sammy Esposito	4.00	2.00	1.25
182	Albie Pearson	4.00	2.00	1.25
183	Joe Pepitone	10.00	5.00	3.00
184	Vern Law	4.00	2.00	1.25
185	Chuck Hiller	4.00	2.00	1.25
186	Jerry Zimmerman	4.00	2.00	1.25
187	Willie Kirkland	4.00	2.00	1.25
188	Eddie Bressoud	4.00	2.00	1.25
189	Dave Giusti	4.00	2.00	1.25
190	Minnie Minoso	6.00	3.00	1.75
191	3rd Series Checklist (177-264)	8.00	4.00	2.50
192	Clay Dalrymple	4.00	2.00	1.25
193	Andre Rodgers	4.00	2.00	1.25
194	Joe Nuxhall	4.00	2.00	1.25
195	Manny Jimenez	4.00	2.00	1.25
196	Doug Camilli	4.00	2.00	1.25
197	Roger Craig	4.00	2.00	1.25
198	Lenny Green	4.00	2.00	1.25
199	Joe Amalfitano	4.00	2.00	1.25
200	Mickey Mantle	500.00	200.00	120.00
201	Cecil Butler	4.00	2.00	1.25
202	Boston Red Sox Team	8.00	3.50	2.00

#	Player			
203	Chico Cardenas	4.00	2.00	1.25
204	Don Nottebart	4.00	2.00	1.25
205	Luis Aparicio	15.00	7.50	4.50
206	Ray Washburn	4.00	2.00	1.25
207	Ken Hunt	4.00	2.00	1.25
208	1963 Rookie Stars(Ron Herbel, John Miller, Ron Taylor, Wally Wolf)	4.00	2.00	1.25
209	Hobie Landrith	4.00	2.00	1.25
210	Sandy Koufax	150.00	75.00	37.50
211	Fred Whitfield	4.00	2.00	1.25
212	Glen Hobbie	4.00	2.00	1.25
213	Billy Hitchcock	4.00	2.00	1.25
214	Orlando Pena	4.00	2.00	1.25
215	Bob Skinner	4.00	2.00	1.25
216	Gene Conley	4.00	2.00	1.25
217	Joe Christopher	4.00	2.00	1.25
218	Tiger Twirlers(Jim Bunning, Frank Lary, Don Mossi)	7.50	3.75	2.25
219	Chuck Cottier	4.00	2.00	1.25
220	Camilo Pascual	4.00	2.00	1.25
221	Cookie Rojas RC	4.00	2.00	1.25
222	Chicago Cubs Team	8.00	3.50	2.00
223	Eddie Fisher	4.00	2.00	1.25
224	Mike Roarke	4.00	2.00	1.25
225	Joe Jay	4.00	2.00	1.25
226	Julian Javier	4.00	2.00	1.25
227	Jim Grant	4.00	2.00	1.25
228	1963 Rookie Stars(Max Alvis RC, Bob Bailey RC, Ed Kranepool RC, Tony Oliva RC)	60.00	30.00	18.00
229	Willie Davis	4.00	2.00	1.25
230	Pete Runnels	4.00	2.00	1.25
231	Eli Grba (Photo actually Ryne Duren.)	4.00	2.00	1.25
232	Frank Malzone	4.00	2.00	1.25
233	Casey Stengel	18.00	7.50	4.50
234	Dave Nicholson	4.00	2.00	1.25
235	Billy O'Dell	4.00	2.00	1.25
236	Bill Bryan	4.00	2.00	1.25
237	Jim Coates	4.00	2.00	1.25
238	Lou Johnson	4.00	2.00	1.25
239	Harvey Haddix	4.00	2.00	1.25
240	Rocky Colavito	17.50	8.75	5.25
241	Billy Smith	4.00	2.00	1.25
242	Power Plus(Hank Aaron, Ernie Banks)	60.00	30.00	15.00
243	Don Leppert	4.00	2.00	1.25
244	John Tsitouris	4.00	2.00	1.25
245	Gil Hodges	12.50	6.25	3.75
246	Lee Stange	4.00	2.00	1.25
247	New York Yankees Team	50.00	25.00	12.50
248	Tito Francona	4.00	2.00	1.25
249	Leo Burke	4.00	2.00	1.25
250	Stan Musial	100.00	50.00	25.00
251	Jack Lamabe	4.00	2.00	1.25
252	Ron Santo	13.50	6.75	4.00
253	1963 Rookie Stars(Len Gabrielson, Pete Jernigan, Deacon Jones, John Wojcik)	4.00	2.00	1.25
254	Mike Hershberger	4.00	2.00	1.25
255	Bob Shaw	4.00	2.00	1.25
256	Jerry Lumpe	4.00	2.00	1.25
257	Hank Aguirre	4.00	2.00	1.25
258	Alvin Dark	4.00	2.00	1.25
259	Johnny Logan	4.00	2.00	1.25
260	Jim Gentile	4.00	2.00	1.25
261	Bob Miller	4.00	2.00	1.25
262	Ellis Burton	4.00	2.00	1.25
263	Dave Stenhouse	4.00	2.00	1.25
264	Phil Linz	4.00	2.00	1.25
265	Vada Pinson	7.00	3.50	2.00
266	Bob Allen	4.00	2.00	1.25
267	Carl Sawatski	4.00	2.00	1.25
268	Don Demeter	4.00	2.00	1.25
269	Don Mincher	4.00	2.00	1.25
270	Felipe Alou	5.00	2.50	1.50
271	Dean Stone	4.00	2.00	1.25
272	Danny Murphy	4.00	2.00	1.25
273	Sammy Taylor	4.00	2.00	1.25
274	6th Series Checklist (265-352)	8.00	4.00	2.50
275	Ed Mathews	30.00	12.50	7.50
276	Barry Shetrone	4.00	2.00	1.25
277	Dick Farrell	4.00	2.00	1.25
278	Chico Fernandez	4.00	2.00	1.25
279	Wally Moon	4.00	2.00	1.25
280	Bob Rodgers	4.00	2.00	1.25
281	Tom Sturdivant	4.00	2.00	1.25
282	Bob Del Greco	4.00	2.00	1.25
283	Roy Sievers	4.00	2.00	1.25
284	Dave Sisler	4.00	2.00	1.25
285	Dick Stuart	4.00	2.00	1.25
286	Stu Miller	4.00	2.00	1.25
287	Dick Bertell	4.00	2.00	1.25
288	Chicago White Sox Team	10.00	4.00	2.50
289	Hal Brown	4.00	2.00	1.25
290	Bill White	4.00	2.00	1.25
291	Don Rudolph	4.00	2.00	1.25
292	Pumpsie Green	4.00	2.00	1.25
293	Bill Pleis	4.00	2.00	1.25
294	Bill Rigney	4.00	2.00	1.25
295	Ed Roebuck	4.00	2.00	1.25
296	Doc Edwards	4.00	2.00	1.25
297	Jim Golden	4.00	2.00	1.25
298	Don Dillard	4.00	2.00	1.25
299	1963 Rookie Stars(Tom Butters, Bob Dustal, Dave Morehead, Dan Schneider)	4.00	2.00	1.25
300	Willie Mays	145.00	70.00	35.00
301	Bill Fischer	4.00	2.00	1.25
302	Whitey Herzog	4.00	2.00	1.25
303	Earl Francis	4.00	2.00	1.25
304	Harry Bright	4.00	2.00	1.25
305	Don Hoak	4.00	2.00	1.25
306	Star Receivers(Earl Battey, Elston Howard)	5.00	2.50	1.50
307	Chet Nichols	4.00	2.00	1.25
308	Camilo Carreon	4.00	2.00	1.25
309	Jim Brewer	4.00	2.00	1.25
310	Tommy Davis	7.00	3.00	1.75
311	Joe McClain	4.00	2.00	1.25
312	Houston Colt .45s Team	13.50	6.75	4.00
313	Ernie Broglio	4.00	2.00	1.25
314	John Goryl	4.00	2.00	1.25
315	Ralph Terry	4.00	2.00	1.25
316	Norm Sherry	4.00	2.00	1.25
317	Sam McDowell	5.00	2.50	1.50
318	Gene Mauch	4.00	2.00	1.25
319	Joe Gaines	4.00	2.00	1.25
320	Warren Spahn	60.00	30.00	15.00
321	Gino Cimoli	4.00	2.00	1.25
322	Bob Turley	4.00	2.00	1.25
323	Bill Mazeroski	20.00	10.00	6.00
324	1963 Rookie Stars(Vic Davalillo RC, Phil Roof, Pete Ward RC, George Williams)	6.00	3.00	1.75
325	Jack Sanford	4.00	2.00	1.25
326	Hank Foiles	4.00	2.00	1.25
327	Paul Foytack	4.00	2.00	1.25
328	Dick Williams	4.00	2.00	1.25
329	Lindy McDaniel	4.00	2.00	1.25
330	Chuck Hinton	4.00	2.00	1.25
331	Series Foes(Bill Pierce, Bill Stafford)	10.00	5.00	3.00
332	Joel Horlen	4.00	2.00	1.25
333	Carl Warwick	4.00	2.00	1.25
334	Wynn Hawkins	4.00	2.00	1.25
335	Leon Wagner	4.00	2.00	1.25
336	Ed Bauta	4.00	2.00	1.25
337	Los Angeles Dodgers Team	18.00	7.50	4.50
338	Russ Kemmerer	4.00	2.00	1.25
339	Ted Bowsfield	4.00	2.00	1.25
340	Yogi Berra	100.00	50.00	25.00
341a	Jack Baldschun (White slash across body in inset photo.)	8.00	4.00	2.50
341b	Jack Baldschun (Slash repaired with red/ mottling.)	4.00	2.00	1.25
342	Gene Woodling	4.00	2.00	1.25
343	Johnny Pesky	4.00	2.00	1.25
344	Don Schwall	4.00	2.00	1.25
345	Brooks Robinson	55.00	30.00	15.00
346	Billy Hoeft	4.00	2.00	1.25
347	Joe Torre	17.50	8.75	5.25
348	Vic Wertz	4.00	2.00	1.25
349	Zoilo Versalles	4.00	2.00	1.25
350	Bob Purkey	4.00	2.00	1.25
351	Al Luplow	4.00	2.00	1.25
352	Ken Johnson	4.00	2.00	1.25
353	Billy Williams	20.00	10.00	6.00
354	Dom Zanni	4.00	2.00	1.25
355	Dean Chance	4.00	2.00	1.25
356	John Schaive	4.00	2.00	1.25
357	George Altman	4.00	2.00	1.25
358	Milt Pappas	4.00	2.00	1.25
359	Haywood Sullivan	4.00	2.00	1.25
360	Don Drysdale	45.00	25.00	12.50
361	Clete Boyer	9.00	4.50	2.75
362	5th Series Checklist (353-429)	9.00	4.50	2.75
363	Dick Radatz	4.00	2.00	1.25
364	Howie Goss	4.00	2.00	1.25
365	Jim Bunning	13.50	6.75	4.00
366	Tony Taylor	4.00	2.00	1.25
367	Tony Cloninger	4.00	2.00	1.25
368	Ed Bailey	4.00	2.00	1.25
369	Jim Lemon	4.00	2.00	1.25
370	Dick Donovan	4.00	2.00	1.25
371	Rod Kanehl	4.00	2.00	1.25
372	Don Lee	4.00	2.00	1.25
373	Jim Campbell	4.00	2.00	1.25
374	Claude Osteen	4.00	2.00	1.25
375	Ken Boyer	10.00	5.00	3.00
376	Johnnie Wyatt	4.00	2.00	1.25
377	Baltimore Orioles Team	10.00	4.50	2.75
378	Bill Henry	4.00	2.00	1.25
379	Bob Anderson	4.00	2.00	1.25
380	Ernie Banks	100.00	50.00	25.00
381	Frank Baumann	4.00	2.00	1.25
382	Ralph Houk	6.00	3.00	1.75
383	Pete Richert	4.00	2.00	1.25
384	Bob Tillman	4.00	2.00	1.25
385	Art Mahaffey	4.00	2.00	1.25
386	1963 Rookie Stars(John Bateman RC, Larry Bearnarth, Ed Kirkpatrick RC, Garry Roggenburk)	5.00	2.50	1.50
387	Al McBean	4.00	2.00	1.25
388	Jim Davenport	4.00	2.00	1.25
389	Frank Sullivan	4.00	2.00	1.25
390	Hank Aaron	165.00	80.00	50.00
391	Bill Dailey	4.00	2.00	1.25
392	Tribe Thumpers(Tito Francona, Johnny Romano)	4.50	2.25	1.25
393	Ken MacKenzie	4.00	2.00	1.25
394	Tim McCarver	9.00	4.50	2.75
395	Don McMahon	4.00	2.00	1.25
396	Joe Koppe	4.00	2.00	1.25
397	Kansas City Athletics Team	10.00	4.50	2.75
398	Boog Powell	12.50	6.25	3.75
399	Dick Ellsworth	4.00	2.00	1.25
400	Frank Robinson	55.00	30.00	15.00
401	Jim Bouton	12.00	6.00	3.50
402	Mickey Vernon	4.00	2.00	1.25
403	Ron Perranoski	4.00	2.00	1.25
404	Bob Oldis	4.00	2.00	1.25
405	Floyd Robinson	4.00	2.00	1.25
406	Howie Koplitz	4.00	2.00	1.25
407	1963 Rookie Stars(Larry Elliot, Frank Kostro, Chico Ruiz, Dick Simpson)	4.00	2.00	1.25
408	Billy Gardner	4.00	2.00	1.25
409	Roy Face	4.00	2.00	1.25
410	Earl Battey	4.00	2.00	1.25
411	Jim Constable	4.00	2.00	1.25
412	Dodgers' Big Three(Johnny Podres, Don Drysdale, Sandy Koufax)	50.00	25.00	12.50
413	Jerry Walker	4.00	2.00	1.25
414	Ty Cline	4.00	2.00	1.25
415	Bob Gibson	60.00	30.00	15.00
416	Alex Grammas	4.00	2.00	1.25
417	San Francisco Giants Team	10.00	4.50	2.75
418	Johnny Orsino	4.00	2.00	1.25
419	Tracy Stallard	4.00	2.00	1.25
420	Bobby Richardson	12.50	6.25	3.75
421	Tom Morgan	4.00	2.00	1.25
422	Fred Hutchinson	4.00	2.00	1.25
423	Ed Hobaugh	4.00	2.00	1.25
424	Charley Smith	4.00	2.00	1.25
425	Smoky Burgess	4.00	2.00	1.25
426	Barry Latman	4.00	2.00	1.25
427	Bernie Allen	4.00	2.00	1.25
428	Carl Boles	4.00	2.00	1.25
429	Lou Burdette	4.00	2.00	1.25
430	Norm Siebern	4.00	2.00	1.25
431a	6th Series Checklist (430-506) ("Checklist" in black on front.)	8.00	4.00	2.50
431b	6th Series Checklist (430-506) ("Checklist" in white.)	20.00	10.00	6.00
432	Roman Mejias	4.00	2.00	1.25
433	Denis Menke	4.00	2.00	1.25
434	Johnny Callison	4.00	2.00	1.25
435	Woody Held	4.00	2.00	1.25
436	Tim Harkness	4.00	2.00	1.25
437	Bill Bruton	4.00	2.00	1.25
438	Wes Stock	4.00	2.00	1.25
439	Don Zimmer	6.00	3.00	1.75
440	Juan Marichal	25.00	12.50	7.50
441	Lee Thomas	4.00	2.00	1.25
442	J.C. Hartman	4.00	2.00	1.25
443	Jim Piersall	7.00	3.50	2.00
444	Jim Maloney	4.00	2.00	1.25
445	Norm Cash	9.00	4.50	2.75
446	Whitey Ford	60.00	30.00	15.00
447	Felix Mantilla	12.50	6.25	3.25
448	Jack Kralick	12.50	6.25	3.25
449	Jose Tartabull	12.50	6.25	3.25

		NM	E	VG
450	Bob Friend	12.50	6.25	3.25
451	Cleveland Indians Team	20.00	10.00	6.00
452	Barney Schultz	12.50	6.25	3.25
453	Jake Wood	12.50	6.25	3.25
454a	Art Fowler (Card # on orange background.)	12.50	6.25	3.25
454b	Art Fowler (Card # on white background.)	30.00	15.00	9.00
455	Ruben Amaro	12.50	6.25	3.25
456	Jim Coker	12.50	6.25	3.25
457	Tex Clevenger	12.50	6.25	3.25
458	Al Lopez	20.00	10.00	6.00
459	Dick LeMay	12.50	6.25	3.25
460	Del Crandall	12.50	6.25	3.25
461	Norm Bass	12.50	6.25	3.25
462	Wally Post	12.50	6.25	3.25
463	Joe Schaffernoth	12.50	6.25	3.25
464	Ken Aspromonte	12.50	6.25	3.25
465	Chuck Estrada	12.50	6.25	3.25
466	1963 Rookie Stars(Bill Freehan RC, Tony Martinez, Nate Oliver, Jerry Robinson)	60.00	30.00	15.00
467	Phil Ortega	12.50	6.25	3.25
468	Carroll Hardy	12.50	6.25	3.25
469	Jay Hook	12.50	6.25	3.25
470	Tom Tresh (SP)	40.00	20.00	10.00
471	Ken Retzer	12.50	6.25	3.25
472	Lou Brock	75.00	37.50	18.75
473	New York Mets Team	75.00	37.50	18.75
474	Jack Fisher	12.50	6.25	3.25
475	Gus Triandos	12.50	6.25	3.25
476	Frank Funk	12.50	6.25	3.25
477	Donn Clendenon	12.50	6.25	3.25
478	Paul Brown	12.50	6.25	3.25
479	Ed Brinkman RC	12.50	6.25	3.25
480	Bill Monbouquette	12.50	6.25	3.25
481	Bob Taylor	12.50	6.25	3.25
482	Felix Torres	12.50	6.25	3.25
483	Jim Owens	12.50	6.25	3.25
484	Dale Long (SP)	15.00	7.50	4.50
485	Jim Landis	12.50	6.25	3.25
486	Ray Sadecki	12.50	6.25	3.25
487	John Roseboro	12.50	6.25	3.25
488	Jerry Adair	12.50	6.25	3.25
489	Paul Toth	12.50	6.25	3.25
490	Willie McCovey	80.00	40.00	24.00
491	Harry Craft	12.50	6.25	3.25
492	Dave Wickersham	12.50	6.25	3.25
493	Walt Bond	12.50	6.25	3.25
494	Phil Regan	12.50	6.25	3.25
495	Frank Thomas (SP)	15.00	7.50	4.50
496	1963 Rookie Stars(Carl Bouldin, Steve Dalkowski RC, Fred Newman RC, Jack Smith)	20.00	10.00	6.00
497	Bennie Daniels	12.50	6.25	3.25
498	Eddie Kasko	12.50	6.25	3.25
499	J.C. Martin	12.50	6.25	3.25
500	Harmon Killebrew (SP)	125.00	60.00	35.00
501	Joe Azcue	12.50	6.25	3.25
502	Daryl Spencer	12.50	6.25	3.25
503	Milwaukee Braves Team	20.00	10.00	6.00
504	Bob Johnson	12.50	6.25	3.25
505	Curt Flood	15.00	7.50	4.50
506	Gene Green	12.50	6.25	3.25
507	Roland Sheldon	12.50	6.25	3.25
508	Ted Savage	12.50	6.25	3.25
509a	7th Series Checklist (507-576) (Copyright centered.)	17.50	8.75	5.25
509b	7th Series Checklist (509-576) (Copyright to right.)	17.50	8.75	5.25
510	Ken McBride	12.50	6.25	3.25
511	Charlie Neal	12.50	6.25	3.25
512	Cal McLish	12.50	6.25	3.25
513	Gary Geiger	12.50	6.25	3.25
514	Larry Osborne	12.50	6.25	3.25
515	Don Elston	12.50	6.25	3.25
516	Purnal Goldy	12.50	6.25	3.25
517	Hal Woodeshick	12.50	6.25	3.25
518	Don Blasingame	12.50	6.25	3.25
519	Claude Raymond	12.50	6.25	3.25
520	Orlando Cepeda	30.00	15.00	9.00
521	Dan Pfister	12.50	6.25	3.25
522	1963 Rookie Stars(Mel Nelson, Gary Peters, Art Quirk, Jim Roland)	12.50	6.25	3.25
523	Bill Kunkel	12.50	6.25	3.25
524	St. Louis Cardinals Team	20.00	10.00	6.00
525	Nellie Fox	50.00	25.00	12.50
526	Dick Hall	12.50	6.25	3.25
527	Ed Sadowski	12.50	6.25	3.25
528	Carl Willey	12.50	6.25	3.25
529	Wes Covington	12.50	6.25	3.25
530	Don Mossi	12.50	6.25	3.25

		NM	E	VG
531	Sam Mele	12.50	6.25	3.25
532	Steve Boros	12.50	6.25	3.25
533	Bobby Shantz	12.50	6.25	3.25
534	Ken Walters	12.50	6.25	3.25
535	Jim Perry	12.50	6.25	3.25
536	Norm Larker	12.50	6.25	3.25
537	1963 Rookie Stars(Pedro Gonzalez RC, Ken McMullen RC, Pete Rose RC, Al Weis RC)	800.00	410.00	250.00
538	George Brunet	12.50	6.25	3.25
539	Wayne Causey	12.50	6.25	3.25
540	Bob Clemente	210.00	110.00	67.50
541	Ron Moeller	12.50	6.25	3.25
542	Lou Klimchock	12.50	6.25	3.25
543	Russ Snyder	12.50	6.25	3.25
544	1963 Rookie Stars(Duke Carmel RC, Bill Haas RC, Dick Phillips RC, Rusty Staub RC)	50.00	25.00	12.50
545	Jose Pagan	12.50	6.25	3.25
546	Hal Reniff	12.50	6.25	3.25
547	Gus Bell	12.50	6.25	3.25
548	Tom Satriano	12.50	6.25	3.25
549	1963 Rookie Stars(Marcelino Lopez RC, Pete Lovrich, Elmo Plaskett, Paul Ratliff)	13.00	6.50	3.25
550	Duke Snider	75.00	37.50	18.75
551	Billy Klaus	12.50	6.25	3.25
552	**Detroit Tigers Team**	50.00	25.00	12.50
553	1963 Rookie Stars(Brock Davis RC, Jim Gosger RC, John Herrnstein RC, Willie Stargell RC)	115.00	60.00	30.00
554	Hank Fischer	12.50	6.25	3.25
555	John Blanchard	15.00	7.50	3.75
556	Al Worthington	12.50	6.25	3.25
557	Cuno Barragan	12.50	6.25	3.25
558	1963 Rookie Stars(Bill Faul RC, Ron Hunt RC, Bob Lipski RC, Al Moran RC)	13.00	6.50	3.25
559	Danny Murtaugh	12.50	6.25	3.25
560	Ray Herbert	12.50	6.25	3.25
561	Mike de la Hoz	12.50	6.25	3.25
562	1963 Rookie Stars(Randy Cardinal RC, Dave McNally RC, Don Rowe RC, Ken Rowe RC)	25.00	12.50	7.50
563	Mike McCormick	12.50	6.25	3.25
564	George Banks	12.50	6.25	3.25
565	Larry Sherry	12.50	6.25	3.25
566	Cliff Cook	12.50	6.25	3.25
567	Jim Duffalo	12.50	6.25	3.25
568	Bob Sadowski	12.50	6.25	3.25
569	Luis Arroyo	12.50	6.25	3.25
570	Frank Bolling	12.50	6.25	3.25
571	Johnny Klippstein	12.50	6.25	3.25
572	Jack Spring	12.50	6.25	3.25
573	Coot Veal	12.50	6.25	3.25
574	Hal Kolstad	12.50	6.25	3.25
575	Don Cardwell	12.50	6.25	3.25
576	Johnny Temple	13.50	5.00	3.00

1963 Topps Famous Americans Stamps

Actually marketed as "Stamp Gum," this obscure test issue features 80 perforated stamps depicting great Americans from all walks of life, including two baseball players. The 2-9/16" x 1-3/8" stamps are printed in black, blue and yellow and combine a photographic portrait with a cartoon drawing. Centering is often a problem with these pieces. Only the baseball players are listed here.

		NM	E	VG
50	Babe Ruth	300.00	150.00	90.00
60	Lou Gehrig	250.00	125.00	75.00

1963 Topps Mickey Mantle Plaque

Advertised as a "mask" on high-number 1963 Topps wax wrappers, this is actually a plastic plaque. About 6" x 8", the plaque features a color picture of Mantle in embossed plastic with a faux wood frame, also embossed plastic, around it. A holed tab at top allows hanging.

	NM	E	VG
Mickey Mantle	3,500	1,750	1,050

1963 Topps Peel-Offs

Measuring 1-1/4" x 2-3/4", Topps Peel-Offs were an insert with 1963 Topps baseball cards. There are 46 players in the unnumbered set, each pictured in a color photo inside an oval with the player's name, team and position in a band below. The back of the Peel-Off is removable, leaving a sticky surface that made the Peel-Off a popular decorative item among youngsters of the day. Naturally, that makes them quite scarce today. The stickers can be found both blank-backed (much scarcer) and with instructions printed on the peel-off backing.

		NM	E	VG
Complete Set (46):		525.00	275.00	160.00
Common Player:		6.00	3.00	1.80
(1)	Hank Aaron	35.00	17.50	10.00
(2)	Luis Aparicio	12.50	6.25	3.75
(3)	Richie Ashburn	17.50	8.75	5.25
(4)	Bob Aspromonte	6.00	3.00	1.80
(5)	Ernie Banks	20.00	11.00	6.75
(6)	Ken Boyer	9.00	3.75	2.25
(7)	Jim Bunning	10.00	5.00	3.00
(8)	Johnny Callison	6.00	3.00	1.80
(9)	Orlando Cepeda	10.00	5.00	3.00
(10)	Roberto Clemente	50.00	25.00	15.00
(11)	Rocky Colavito	9.00	4.50	2.75
(12)	Tommy Davis	6.00	3.00	1.80
(13)	Dick Donovan	6.00	3.00	1.80
(14)	Don Drysdale	18.00	7.50	4.50
(15)	Dick Farrell	6.00	3.00	1.80
(16)	Jim Gentile	6.00	3.00	1.80
(17)	Ray Herbert	6.00	3.00	1.80
(18)	Chuck Hinton	6.00	3.00	1.80
(19)	Ken Hubbs	9.00	3.75	2.25
(20)	Al Jackson	6.00	3.00	1.80
(21)	Al Kaline	21.00	11.00	5.25
(22)	Harmon Killebrew	20.00	10.00	5.25
(23)	Sandy Koufax	40.00	20.00	12.00
(24)	Jerry Lumpe	6.00	3.00	1.80
(25)	Art Mahaffey	6.00	3.00	1.80
(26)	Mickey Mantle	100.00	50.00	30.00
(27)	Willie Mays	35.00	17.50	10.00
(28)	Bill Mazeroski	12.50	6.25	3.75
(29)	Bill Monbouquette	6.00	3.00	1.80
(30)	Stan Musial	35.00	17.50	10.00
(31)	Camilo Pascual	6.00	3.00	1.80
(32)	Bob Purkey	6.00	3.00	1.80
(33)	Bobby Richardson	10.00	4.50	2.75
(34)	Brooks Robinson	21.00	8.75	5.25
(35)	Floyd Robinson	6.00	3.00	1.80
(36)	Frank Robinson	21.00	8.75	5.25
(37)	Bob Rodgers	6.00	3.00	1.80
(38)	Johnny Romano	6.00	3.00	1.80
(39)	Jack Sanford	6.00	3.00	1.80
(40)	Norm Siebern	6.00	3.00	1.80
(41)	Warren Spahn	20.00	10.00	5.25
(42)	Dave Stenhouse	6.00	3.00	1.80
(43)	Ralph Terry	6.00	3.00	1.80

		NM	E	VG
(44)	Lee Thomas	6.00	3.00	1.80
(45)	Bill White	6.00	3.00	1.80
(46)	Carl Yastrzemski	24.00	12.00	7.00

1963 Topps Valentine Foldees

Featuring the artwork of 1960s cartoonist Jack Davis, this set of specialty cards had the left and right panels of the 4-1/2" x 2-3/8" pieces slit to allow either the top or the bottom half of the portrait to be folded over the central panel to create funny combinations. There were 55 cards in the series; Babe Ruth is the only baseball player included.

		NM	E	VG
	Complete Set (55):	150.00	75.00	45.00
6	Babe Ruth	25.00	12.50	7.50
34	Babe Ruth	25.00	12.50	7.50

1964 Topps

 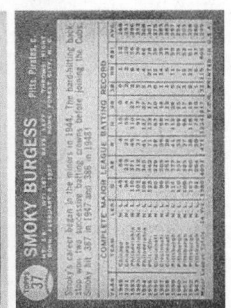

The 1964 Topps set is a 587-card issue of 2-1/2" x 3-1/2" cards which is considered by many as being among the company's best efforts. Card fronts feature a large color photo which blends into a top panel which contains the team name, while a panel below the picture carries the player's name and position. An interesting innovation on the back is a baseball quiz question which required the rubbing of a white panel to reveal the answer. As in 1963, specialty cards remained modest in number with a 12-card set of statistical leaders, a few multi-player cards, rookies and World Series highlights. An interesting card is an "In Memoriam" card for Ken Hubbs who was killed in an airplane crash.

		NM	E	VG
	Complete Set (587):	4,500	2,125	1,250
	Common Player (1-370):	3.50	1.75	1.00
	Common Player (371-522):	6.00	3.00	1.75
	Common Player (523-587):	9.00	4.50	2.75
1	N.L. E.R.A. Leaders(Dick Ellsworth, Bob Friend, Sandy Koufax)	30.00	12.50	6.25
2	A.L. E.R.A. Leaders(Camilo Pascual, Gary Peters, Juan Pizarro)	12.00	3.00	2.00
3	N.L. Pitching Leaders (Sandy Koufax, Jim Maloney, Juan Marichal, Warren Spahn)	35.00	17.00	8.00
4a	A.L. Pitching Leaders(Jim Bouton, Whitey Ford, Camilo Pascual) (Apostrophe after "Pitching" on back.)	24.00	12.00	7.00
4b	A.L. Pitching Leaders(Jim Bouton, Whitey Ford, Camilo Pascual) (No apostrophe.)	24.00	12.00	7.00
5	N.L. Strikeout Leaders (Don Drysdale, Sandy Koufax, Jim Maloney)	20.00	10.00	6.00
6	A.L. Strikeout Leaders (Jim Bunning, Camilo Pascual, Dick Stigman)	12.50	6.25	3.75
7	N.L. Batting Leaders (Hank Aaron, Roberto Clemente, Tommy Davis, Dick Groat)	21.00	10.00	6.00
8	A.L. Batting Leaders(Al Kaline, Rich Rollins, Carl Yastrzemski)	15.00	6.25	3.75
9	N.L. Home Run Leaders (Hank Aaron, Orlando Cepeda, Willie Mays, Willie McCovey)	35.00	17.00	8.00
10	A.L. Home Run Leaders (Bob Allison, Harmon Killebrew, Dick Stuart)	12.00	6.00	3.50
11	N.L. R.B.I. Leaders(Hank Aaron, Ken Boyer, Bill White)	12.50	6.25	3.75
12	A.L. R.B.I. Leaders (Al Kaline, Harmon Killebrew, Dick Stuart)	13.50	6.75	4.00
13	Hoyt Wilhelm	15.00	7.50	4.50
14	Dodgers Rookies (Dick Nen, Nick Willhite)	6.00	3.00	1.80
15	Zoilo Versalles	3.50	1.75	1.00
16	John Boozer	3.50	1.75	1.00
17	Willie Kirkland	3.50	1.75	1.00
18	Billy O'Dell	3.50	1.75	1.00
19	Don Wart	3.50	1.75	1.00
20	Bob Friend	3.50	1.75	1.00
21	Yogi Berra	40.00	20.00	12.00
22	Jerry Adair	3.50	1.75	1.00
23	Chris Zachary	3.50	1.75	1.00
24	Carl Sawatski	3.50	1.75	1.00
25	Bill Monbouquette	3.50	1.75	1.00
26	Gino Cimoli	3.50	1.75	1.00
27	New York Mets Team	9.00	3.75	2.25
28	Claude Osteen	3.50	1.75	1.00
29	Lou Brock	40.00	20.00	10.00
30	Ron Perranoski	3.50	1.75	1.00
31	Dave Nicholson	3.50	1.75	1.00
32	Dean Chance	3.50	1.75	1.00
33	Reds Rookies(Sammy Ellis, Mel Queen)	6.00	3.00	1.80
34	Jim Perry	3.50	1.75	1.00
35	Ed Mathews	25.00	12.00	6.00
36	Hal Reniff	3.50	1.75	1.00
37	Smoky Burgess	3.50	1.75	1.00
38	Jim Wynn **RC**	7.00	2.50	1.50
39	Hank Aguirre	3.50	1.75	1.00
40	Dick Groat	3.50	1.75	1.00
41	Friendly Foes(Willie McCovey, Leon Wagner)	15.00	7.50	4.50
42	Moe Drabowsky	3.50	1.75	1.00
43	Roy Sievers	3.50	1.75	1.00
44	Duke Carmel	3.50	1.75	1.00
45	Milt Pappas	3.50	1.75	1.00
46	Ed Brinkman	3.50	1.75	1.00
47	Giants Rookies(Jesus Alou **RC**, Ron Herbel)	9.00	4.50	2.75
48	Bob Perry	3.50	1.75	1.00
49	Bill Henry	3.50	1.75	1.00
50	Mickey Mantle	340.00	170.00	90.00
51	Pete Richert	3.50	1.75	1.00
52	Chuck Hinton	3.50	1.75	1.00
53	Denis Menke	3.50	1.75	1.00
54	Sam Mele	3.50	1.75	1.00
55	Ernie Banks	40.00	22.50	11.25
56	Hal Brown	3.50	1.75	1.00
57	Tim Harkness	3.50	1.75	1.00
58	Don Demeter	3.50	1.75	1.00
59	Ernie Broglio	3.50	1.75	1.00
60	Frank Malzone	3.50	1.75	1.00
61	Angel Backstops(Bob Rodgers, Ed Sadowski)	3.50	1.75	1.00
62	Ted Savage	3.50	1.75	1.00
63	Johnny Orsino	3.50	1.75	1.00
64	Ted Abernathy	3.50	1.75	1.00
65	Felipe Alou	4.50	2.25	1.25
66	Eddie Fisher	3.50	1.75	1.00
67	Detroit Tigers Team	9.00	4.50	2.75
68	Willie Davis	3.50	1.75	1.00
69	Clete Boyer	10.00	5.00	3.00
70	Joe Torre	12.00	6.00	3.50
71	Jack Spring	3.50	1.75	1.00
72	Chico Cardenas	3.50	1.75	1.00
73	Jimmie Hall **RC**	3.50	1.75	1.00
74	Pirates Rookies(Tom Butters, Bob Priddy)	6.00	3.00	1.80
75	Wayne Causey	3.50	1.75	1.00
76	1st Series Checklist (1-88)	5.00	2.50	1.50
77	Jerry Walker	3.50	1.75	1.00
78	Merritt Ranew	3.50	1.75	1.00
79	Bob Heffner	3.50	1.75	1.00
80	Vada Pinson	12.00	4.50	2.75
81	All-Star Vets(Nellie Fox, Harmon Killebrew)	17.50	6.25	3.75
82	Jim Davenport	3.50	1.75	1.00
83	Gus Triandos	3.50	1.75	1.00
84	Carl Willey	3.50	1.75	1.00
85	Pete Ward	3.50	1.75	1.00
86	Al Downing	3.50	1.75	1.00
87	St. Louis Cardinals Team	9.00	3.00	1.75
88	John Roseboro	3.50	1.75	1.00
89	Boog Powell	7.50	3.75	2.25
90	Earl Battey	3.50	1.75	1.00
91	Bob Bailey	3.50	1.75	1.00
92	Steve Ridzik	3.50	1.75	1.00
93	Gary Geiger	3.50	1.75	1.00
94	Braves Rookies(Jim Britton, Larry Maxie)	5.00	1.75	1.00
95	George Altman	3.50	1.75	1.00
96	Bob Buhl	3.50	1.75	1.00
97	Jim Fregosi	3.50	1.75	1.00
98	Bill Bruton	3.50	1.75	1.00
99	Al Stanek	3.50	1.75	1.00
100	Elston Howard	12.50	6.25	3.75
101	Walt Alston	6.00	3.00	1.75
102	2nd Series Checklist (89-176)	6.00	3.00	1.75
103	Curt Flood	5.00	2.50	1.50
104	Art Mahaffey	3.50	1.75	1.00
105	Woody Held	3.50	1.75	1.00
106	Joe Nuxhall	3.50	1.75	1.00
107	White Sox Rookies(Bruce Howard, Frank Kreutzer)	6.00	1.75	1.00
108	John Wyatt	3.50	1.75	1.00
109	Rusty Staub	10.00	5.00	3.00
110	Albie Pearson	3.50	1.75	1.00
111	Don Elston	3.50	1.75	1.00
112	Bob Tillman	3.50	1.75	1.00
113	Grover Powell	3.50	1.75	1.00
114	Don Lock	3.50	1.75	1.00
115	Frank Bolling	3.50	1.75	1.00
116	Twins Rookies(Tony Oliva, Jay Ward)	12.00	4.50	2.75
117	Earl Francis	3.50	1.75	1.00
118	John Blanchard	5.00	2.50	1.50
119	Gary Kolb	3.50	1.75	1.00
120	Don Drysdale	17.50	8.75	5.25
121	Pete Runnels	3.50	1.75	1.00
122	Don McMahon	3.50	1.75	1.00
123	Jose Pagan	3.50	1.75	1.00
124	Orlando Pena	3.50	1.75	1.00
125	Pete Rose	225.00	95.00	60.00
126	Russ Snyder	3.50	1.75	1.00
127	Angels Rookies(Aubrey Gatewood, Dick Simpson)	6.00	1.75	1.00
128	Mickey Lolich **RC**	12.50	6.25	3.75
129	Amado Samuel	3.50	1.75	1.00
130	Gary Peters	3.50	1.75	1.00
131	Steve Boros	3.50	1.75	1.00
132	Milwaukee Braves Team	9.00	3.00	1.75
133	Jim Grant	3.50	1.75	1.00
134	Don Zimmer	5.00	2.50	1.50
135	Johnny Callison	3.50	1.75	1.00
136	World Series Game 1 (Koufax Strikes Out 15)	30.00	15.00	9.00
137	World Series Game 2 (Davis Sparks Rally)	12.00	6.00	2.75
138	World Series Game 3 (L.A. Takes 3rd Straight)	15.00	7.50	4.75
139	World Series Game 4 (Sealing Yanks' Doom)	12.00	6.00	2.00
140	World Series (The Dodgers Celebrate)	12.00	6.00	2.00
141	Danny Murtaugh	3.50	1.75	1.00
142	John Bateman	3.50	1.75	1.00
143	Bubba Phillips	3.50	1.75	1.00
144	Al Worthington	3.50	1.75	1.00
145	Norm Siebern	3.50	1.75	1.00
146	Indians Rookies(Bob Chance **RC**, Tommy John **RC**)	17.50	8.75	5.25
147	Ray Sadecki	3.50	1.75	1.00
148	J.C. Martin	3.50	1.75	1.00
149	Paul Foytack	3.50	1.75	1.00

150	Willie Mays	100.00	50.00	30.00
151	K.C. Athletics Team	9.00	3.00	1.75
152	Denver Lemaster	3.50	1.75	1.00
153	Dick Williams	3.50	1.75	1.00
154	Dick Tracewski	3.50	1.75	1.00
155	Duke Snider	23.00	11.00	6.50
156	Bill Dailey	3.50	1.75	1.00
157	Gene Mauch	3.50	1.75	1.00
158	Ken Johnson	3.50	1.75	1.00
159	Charlie Dees	3.50	1.75	1.00
160	Ken Boyer	8.00	4.00	2.50
161	Dave McNally	3.50	1.75	1.00
162	Hitting Area(Vada Pinson, Dick Sisler)	6.00	2.50	1.50
163	Donn Clendenon	3.50	1.75	1.00
164	Bud Daley	3.50	1.75	1.00
165	Jerry Lumpe	3.50	1.75	1.00
166	Marty Keough	3.50	1.75	1.00
167	Senators Rookies(Mike Brumley **RC**, Lou Piniella **RC**)	27.50	13.50	8.25
168	Al Weis	3.50	1.75	1.00
169	Del Crandall	3.50	1.75	1.00
170	Dick Radatz	3.50	1.75	1.00
171	Ty Cline	3.50	1.75	1.00
172	Cleveland Indians Team	9.00	3.00	1.75
173	Ryne Duren	3.50	1.75	1.00
174	Doc Edwards	3.50	1.75	1.00
175	Billy Williams	17.50	8.75	5.25
176	Tracy Stallard	3.50	1.75	1.00
177	Harmon Killebrew	22.00	12.50	6.25
178	Hank Bauer	4.50	2.25	1.25
179	Carl Warwick	3.50	1.75	1.00
180	Tommy Davis	3.50	1.75	1.00
181	Dave Wickersham	3.50	1.75	1.00
182	Sox Sockers(Chuck Schilling, Carl Yastrzemski)	17.50	8.75	5.25
183	Ron Taylor	3.50	1.75	1.00
184	Al Luplow	3.50	1.75	1.00
185	Jim O'Toole	3.50	1.75	1.00
186	Roman Mejias	3.50	1.75	1.00
187	Ed Roebuck	3.50	1.75	1.00
188	3rd Series Checklist (177-264)	5.00	2.50	1.50
189	Bob Hendley	3.50	1.75	1.00
190	Bobby Richardson	17.50	8.25	4.75
191	Clay Dalrymple	3.50	1.75	1.00
192	Cubs Rookies(John Boccabella, Billy Cowan)	6.00	3.00	1.80
193	Jerry Lynch	3.50	1.75	1.00
194	John Goryl	3.50	1.75	1.00
195	Floyd Robinson	3.50	1.75	1.00
196	Jim Gentile	3.50	1.75	1.00
197	Frank Lary	3.50	1.75	1.00
198	Len Gabrielson	3.50	1.75	1.00
199	Joe Azcue	3.50	1.75	1.00
200	Sandy Koufax	115.00	62.50	31.25
201	Orioles Rookies(Sam Bowens, Wally Bunker **RC**)	6.00	3.00	1.80
202	Galen Cisco	3.50	1.75	1.00
203	John Kennedy	3.50	1.75	1.00
204	Matty Alou	3.50	1.75	1.00
205	Nellie Fox	12.50	6.25	3.75
206	Steve Hamilton	3.50	1.75	1.00
207	Fred Hutchinson	3.50	1.75	1.00
208	Wes Covington	3.50	1.75	1.00
209	Bob Allen	3.50	1.75	1.00
210	Carl Yastrzemski	45.00	23.00	12.00
211	Jim Coker	3.50	1.75	1.00
212	Pete Lovrich	3.50	1.75	1.00
213	Los Angeles Angels Team	9.00	3.00	1.75
214	Ken McMullen	3.50	1.75	1.00
215	Ray Herbert	3.50	1.75	1.00
216	Mike de la Hoz	3.50	1.75	1.00
217	Jim King	3.50	1.75	1.00
218	Hank Fischer	3.50	1.75	1.00
219	Young Aces(Jim Bouton, Al Downing)	12.00	6.00	4.00
220	Dick Ellsworth	3.50	1.75	1.00
221	Bob Saverine	3.50	1.75	1.00
222	Bill Pierce	3.50	1.75	1.00
223	George Banks	3.50	1.75	1.00
224	Tommie Sisk	3.50	1.75	1.00
225	Roger Maris	70.00	35.00	15.00
226	Colts Rookies(Gerald Grote **RC**, Larry Yellen)	6.00	2.50	1.50
227	Barry Latman	3.50	1.75	1.00
228	Felix Mantilla	3.50	1.75	1.00
229	Charley Lau	3.50	1.75	1.00
230	Brooks Robinson	37.50	18.00	10.00
231	Dick Calmus	3.50	1.75	1.00
232	Al Lopez	6.00	3.00	1.75
233	Hal Smith	3.50	1.75	1.00
234	Gary Bell	3.50	1.75	1.00
235	Ron Hunt	3.50	1.75	1.00
236	Bill Faul	3.50	1.75	1.00
237	Chicago Cubs Team	9.00	3.25	2.00
238	Roy McMillan	3.50	1.75	1.00
239	Herm Starrette	3.50	1.75	1.00
240	Bill White	3.50	1.75	1.00
241	Jim Owens	3.50	1.75	1.00
242	Harvey Kuenn	3.50	1.75	1.00
243	Phillies Rookies(Richie Allen **RC**, John Herrnstein)	17.50	8.75	5.25
244	Tony LaRussa **RC**	17.50	8.75	5.25
245	Dick Stigman	3.50	1.75	1.00
246	Manny Mota	3.50	1.75	1.00
247	Dave DeBusschere	6.00	2.50	1.50
248	Johnny Pesky	3.50	1.75	1.00
249	Doug Camilli	3.50	1.75	1.00
250	Al Kaline	35.00	20.00	10.00
251	Choo Choo Coleman	3.50	1.75	1.00
252	Ken Aspromonte	3.50	1.75	1.00
253	Wally Post	3.50	1.75	1.00
254	Don Hoak	3.50	1.75	1.00
255	Lee Thomas	3.50	1.75	1.00
256	Johnny Weekly	3.50	1.75	1.00
257	San Francisco Giants Team	9.00	4.50	1.75
258	Garry Roggenburk	3.50	1.75	1.00
259	Harry Bright	3.50	1.75	1.00
260	Frank Robinson	40.00	20.00	10.00
261	Jim Hannan	3.50	1.75	1.00
262	Cardinals Rookies(Harry Fanok, Mike Shannon **RC**)	10.00	4.50	2.75
263	Chuck Estrada	3.50	1.75	1.00
264	Jim Landis	3.50	1.75	1.00
265	Jim Bunning	17.50	8.25	4.75
266	Gene Freese	3.50	1.75	1.00
267	Wilbur Wood **RC**	5.00	2.50	1.50
268	Bill's Got It(Danny Murtaugh, Bill Virdon)	6.00	3.00	1.80
269	Ellis Burton	3.50	1.75	1.00
270	Rich Rollins	3.50	1.75	1.00
271	Bob Sadowski	3.50	1.75	1.00
272	Jake Wood	3.50	1.75	1.00
273	Mel Nelson	3.50	1.75	1.00
274	4th Series Checklist (265-352)	6.00	3.00	1.75
275	John Tsitouris	3.50	1.75	1.00
276	Jose Tartabull	3.50	1.75	1.00
277	Ken Retzer	3.50	1.75	1.00
278	Bobby Shantz	3.50	1.75	1.00
279	Joe Koppe	3.50	1.75	1.00
280	Juan Marichal	17.50	8.25	4.75
281	Yankees Rookies(Jake Gibbs, Tom Metcalf)	9.00	4.50	2.50
282	Bob Bruce	3.50	1.75	1.00
283	Tommy McCraw **RC**	3.50	1.75	1.00
284	Dick Schofield	3.50	1.75	1.00
285	Robin Roberts	12.50	6.25	3.75
286	Don Landrum	3.50	1.75	1.00
287	Red Sox Rookies(Tony Conigliaro **RC**, Bill Spanswick)	50.00	25.00	12.50
288	Al Moran	3.50	1.75	1.00
289	Frank Funk	3.50	1.75	1.00
290	Bob Allison	3.50	1.75	1.00
291	Phil Ortega	3.50	1.75	1.00
292	Mike Roarke	3.50	1.75	1.00
293	Phillies Team	9.00	4.50	2.75
294	Ken Hunt	3.50	1.75	1.00
295	Roger Craig	3.50	1.75	1.00
296	Ed Kirkpatrick	3.50	1.75	1.00
297	Ken MacKenzie	3.50	1.75	1.00
298	Harry Craft	3.50	1.75	1.00
299	Bill Stafford	3.50	1.75	1.00
300	Hank Aaron	110.00	55.00	30.00
301	Larry Brown	3.50	1.75	1.00
302	Dan Pfister	3.50	1.75	1.00
303	Jim Campbell	3.50	1.75	1.00
304	Bob Johnson	3.50	1.75	1.00
305	Jack Lamabe	3.50	1.75	1.00
306	Giant Gunners(Orlando Cepeda, Willie Mays)	35.00	20.00	10.00
307	Joe Gibbon	3.50	1.75	1.00
308	Gene Stephens	3.50	1.75	1.00
309	Paul Toth	3.50	1.75	1.00
310	Jim Gilliam	5.00	2.50	1.50
311	Tom Brown	3.50	1.75	1.00
312	Tigers Rookies(Fritz Fisher, Fred Gladding)	6.00	2.75	1.20
313	Chuck Hiller	3.50	1.75	1.00
314	Jerry Buchek	3.50	1.75	1.00
315	Bo Belinsky	3.50	1.75	1.00
316	Gene Oliver	3.50	1.75	1.00
317	Al Smith	3.50	1.75	1.00
318	Twins Team	9.00	4.00	2.75
319	Paul Brown	3.50	1.75	1.00
320	Rocky Colavito	15.50	7.25	4.75
321	Bob Lillis	3.50	1.75	1.00
322	George Brunet	3.50	1.75	1.00
323	John Buzhardt	3.50	1.75	1.00
324	Casey Stengel	20.00	10.25	5.75
325	Hector Lopez	3.50	1.75	1.00
326	Ron Brand	3.50	1.75	1.00
327	Don Blasingame	3.50	1.75	1.00
328	Bob Shaw	3.50	1.75	1.00
329	Russ Nixon	3.50	1.75	1.00
330	Tommy Harper	3.50	1.75	1.00
331	A.L. Bombers(Norm Cash, Al Kaline, Mickey Mantle, Roger Maris)	145.00	75.00	37.50
332	Ray Washburn	3.50	1.75	1.00
333	Billy Moran	3.50	1.75	1.00
334	Lew Krausse	3.50	1.75	1.00
335	Don Mossi	3.50	1.75	1.00
336	Andre Rodgers	3.50	1.75	1.00
337	Dodgers Rookies(Al Ferrara **RC**, Jeff Torborg **RC**)	7.00	3.00	1.75
338	Jack Kralick	3.50	1.75	1.00
339	Walt Bond	3.50	1.75	1.00
340	Joe Cunningham	3.50	1.75	1.00
341	Jim Roland	3.50	1.75	1.00
342	Willie Stargell	30.00	15.00	7.50
343	Senators Team	9.00	4.00	2.75
344	Phil Linz	3.50	1.75	1.00
345	Frank Thomas	3.50	1.75	1.00
346	Joe Jay	3.50	1.75	1.00
347	Bobby Wine	3.50	1.75	1.00
348	Ed Lopat	3.50	1.75	1.00
349	Art Fowler	3.50	1.75	1.00
350	Willie McCovey	20.00	10.00	6.00
351	Dan Schneider	3.50	1.75	1.00
352	Eddie Bressoud	3.50	1.75	1.00
353	Wally Moon	3.50	1.75	1.00
354	Dave Giusti	3.50	1.75	1.00
355	Vic Power	3.50	1.75	1.00
356	Reds Rookies(Bill McCool, Chico Ruiz)	6.00	2.75	1.50
357	Charley James	3.50	1.75	1.00
358	Ron Kline	3.50	1.75	1.00
359	Jim Schaffer	3.50	1.75	1.00
360	Joe Pepitone	4.50	2.25	1.25
361	Jay Hook	3.50	1.75	1.00
362	5th Series Checklist (353-429)	6.00	3.00	1.75
363	Dick McAuliffe	3.50	1.75	1.00
364	Joe Gaines	3.50	1.75	1.00
365	Cal McLish	3.50	1.75	1.00
366	Nelson Mathews	3.50	1.75	1.00
367	Fred Whitfield	3.50	1.75	1.00
368	White Sox Rookies(Fritz Ackley, Don Buford **RC**)	5.50	2.75	1.75
369	Jerry Zimmerman	3.50	1.75	1.00
370	Hal Woodeshick	3.50	1.75	1.00
371	Frank Howard	7.50	3.75	2.25
372	Howie Koplitz	6.00	3.00	1.75
373	Pittsburgh Pirates Team	14.00	6.50	4.25
374	Bobby Bolin	6.00	3.00	1.75
375	Ron Santo	20.00	10.00	6.00
376	Dave Morehead	6.00	3.00	1.75
377	Bob Skinner	6.00	3.00	1.75
378	Braves Rookies(Jack Smith, Woody Woodward **RC**)	7.00	3.00	1.75
379	Tony Gonzalez	6.00	3.00	1.75
380	Whitey Ford	40.00	20.00	10.00
381	Bob Taylor	6.00	3.00	1.75
382	Wes Stock	6.00	3.00	1.75
383	Bill Rigney	6.00	3.00	1.75
384	Ron Hansen	6.00	3.00	1.75
385	Curt Simmons	6.00	3.00	1.75
386	Lenny Green	6.00	3.00	1.75
387	Terry Fox	6.00	3.00	1.75
388	Athletics Rookies(John O'Donoghue, George Williams)	7.00	3.00	1.75
389	Jim Umbricht	6.00	3.00	1.75
390	Orlando Cepeda	17.50	8.75	5.25
391	Sam McDowell	6.00	3.00	1.75
392	Jim Pagliaroni	6.00	3.00	1.75
393	Casey Teaches(Ed Kranepool, Casey Stengel)	12.50	6.25	3.75
394	Bob Miller	6.00	3.00	1.75
395	Tom Tresh	13.50	6.75	4.00
396	Dennis Bennett	6.00	3.00	1.75
397	Chuck Cottier	6.00	3.00	1.75
398	Mets Rookies(Bill Haas, Dick Smith)	7.00	3.00	1.75
399	Jackie Brandt	6.00	3.00	1.75
400	Warren Spahn	35.00	17.50	8.75
401	Charlie Maxwell	6.00	3.00	1.75
402	Tom Sturdivant	6.00	3.00	1.75
403	Cincinnati Reds Team	12.00	6.00	3.00
404	Tony Martinez	6.00	3.00	1.75

No.	Player	NM	E	VG
405	Ken McBride	6.00	3.00	1.75
406	Al Spangler	6.00	3.00	1.75
407	Bill Freehan	6.00	3.00	1.75
408	Cubs Rookies(Fred Burdette, Jim Stewart)	7.00	3.00	1.75
409	Bill Fischer	6.00	3.00	1.75
410	Dick Stuart	6.00	3.00	1.75
411	Lee Walls	6.00	3.00	1.75
412	Ray Culp	6.00	3.00	1.75
413	Johnny Keane	6.00	3.00	1.75
414	Jack Sanford	6.00	3.00	1.75
415	Tony Kubek	12.50	6.25	3.75
416	Lee Maye	6.00	3.00	1.75
417	Don Cardwell	6.00	3.00	1.75
418	Orioles Rookies(Darold Knowles RC, Les Narum)	7.00	3.00	1.75
419	Ken Harrelson RC	9.00	4.50	2.75
420	Jim Maloney	6.00	3.00	1.75
421	Camilo Carreon	6.00	3.00	1.75
422	Jack Fisher	6.00	3.00	1.75
423	Tops in N.L.(Hank Aaron, Willie Mays)	125.00	62.50	31.50
424	Dick Bertell	6.00	3.00	1.75
425	Norm Cash	12.00	6.00	3.50
426	Bob Rodgers	6.00	3.00	1.75
427	Don Rudolph	6.00	3.00	1.75
428	Red Sox Rookies(Archie Skeen, Pete Smith)	7.00	3.00	1.75
429	Tim McCarver	12.50	6.25	3.75
430	Juan Pizarro	6.00	3.00	1.75
431	George Alusik	6.00	3.00	1.75
432	Ruben Amaro	6.00	3.00	1.75
433	New York Yankees Team	40.00	20.00	10.00
434	Don Nottebart	6.00	3.00	1.75
435	Vic Davalillo	6.00	3.00	1.75
436	Charlie Neal	6.00	3.00	1.75
437	Ed Bailey	6.00	3.00	1.75
438	6th Series Checklist (430-506)	11.00	5.50	3.25
439	Harvey Haddix	6.00	3.00	1.75
440	Bob Clemente	200.00	100.00	50.00
441	Bob Duliba	6.00	3.00	1.75
442	Pumpsie Green	6.00	3.00	1.75
443	Chuck Dressen	6.00	3.00	1.75
444	Larry Jackson	6.00	3.00	1.75
445	Bill Skowron	9.00	4.50	2.75
446	Julian Javier	6.00	3.00	1.75
447	Ted Bowsfield	6.00	3.00	1.75
448	Cookie Rojas	6.00	3.00	1.75
449	Deron Johnson	6.00	3.00	1.75
450	Steve Barber	6.00	3.00	1.75
451	Joe Amalfitano	6.00	3.00	1.75
452	Giants Rookies(Gil Garrido, Jim Hart RC)	8.50	3.75	2.25
453	Frank Baumann	6.00	3.00	1.75
454	Tommie Aaron	6.00	3.00	1.75
455	Bernie Allen	6.00	3.00	1.75
456	Dodgers Rookies(Wes Parker RC, John Werhas)	9.00	3.00	1.75
457	Jesse Gonder	6.00	3.00	1.75
458	Ralph Terry	6.00	3.00	1.75
459	Red Sox Rookies(Pete Charton, Dalton Jones)	7.00	3.00	1.75
460	Bob Gibson	30.00	15.00	7.50
461	George Thomas	6.00	3.00	1.75
462	Birdie Tebbetts	6.00	3.00	1.75
463	Don Leppert	6.00	3.00	1.75
464	Dallas Green	6.00	3.00	1.75
465	Mike Hershberger	6.00	3.00	1.75
466	Athletics Rookies(Dick Green RC, Aurelio Monteagudo)	7.00	3.00	1.75
467	Bob Aspromonte	6.00	3.00	1.75
468	Gaylord Perry	40.00	20.00	10.00
469	Cubs Rookies(Fred Norman, Sterling Slaughter)	7.00	3.00	1.75
470	Jim Bouton	10.00	5.00	3.00
471	Gates Brown RC	6.50	3.25	2.00
472	Vern Law	6.00	3.00	1.75
473	Baltimore Orioles Team	14.00	6.50	4.75
474	Larry Sherry	6.00	3.00	1.75
475	Ed Charles	6.00	3.00	1.75
476	Braves Rookies(Rico Carty RC, Dick Kelley)	10.00	4.50	2.75
477	Mike Joyce	6.00	3.00	1.75
478	Dick Howser	6.00	3.00	1.75
479	Cardinals Rookies(Dave Bakenhaster, Johnny Lewis)	6.00	3.00	1.75
480	Bob Purkey	6.00	3.00	1.75
481	Chuck Schilling	6.00	3.00	1.75
482	Phillies Rookies(John Briggs RC, Danny Cater RC)	7.00	3.00	1.75
483	Fred Valentine	6.00	3.00	1.75
484	Bill Pleis	6.00	3.00	1.75
485	Tom Haller	6.00	3.00	1.75
486	Bob Kennedy	6.00	3.00	1.75
487	Mike McCormick	6.00	3.00	1.75
488	Yankees Rookies(Bob Meyer, Pete Mikkelsen)	6.00	3.00	1.75
489	Julio Navarro	6.00	3.00	1.75
490	Ron Fairly	6.00	3.00	1.75
491	Ed Rakow	6.00	3.00	1.75
492	Colts Rookies(Jim Beauchamp, Mike White)	9.00	3.00	1.75
493	Don Lee	6.00	3.00	1.75
494	Al Jackson	6.00	3.00	1.75
495	Bill Virdon	6.00	3.00	1.75
496	Chicago White Sox Team	11.00	4.50	2.75
497	Jeoff Long	6.00	3.00	1.75
498	Dave Stenhouse	6.00	3.00	1.75
499	Indians Rookies(Chico Salmon, Gordon Seyfried)	7.00	3.00	1.75
500	Camilo Pascual	6.00	3.00	1.75
501	Bob Veale	6.00	3.00	1.75
502	Angels Rookies(Bobby Knoop RC, Bob Lee)	6.00	3.00	1.75
503	Earl Wilson	6.00	3.00	1.75
504	Claude Raymond	6.00	3.00	1.75
505	Stan Williams	6.00	3.00	1.75
506	Bobby Bragan	6.00	3.00	1.75
507	John Edwards	6.00	3.00	1.75
508	Diego Segui	7.00	3.00	1.75
509	Pirates Rookies(Gene Alley, Orlando McFarlane)	6.00	3.00	1.75
510	Lindy McDaniel	6.00	3.00	1.75
511	Lou Jackson	6.00	3.00	1.75
512	Tigers Rookies(Willie Horton RC, Joe Sparma RC)	22.50	11.00	6.75
513	Don Larsen	6.00	3.00	1.75
514	Jim Hickman	6.00	3.00	1.75
515	Johnny Romano	6.00	3.00	1.75
516	Twins Rookies(Jerry Arrigo, Dwight Siebler)	6.00	3.00	1.75
517a	7th Series Checklist (507-587) (Wrong numbering on back.)	15.00	7.50	4.50
517b	7th Series Checklist (507-587) (Correct numbering on back.)	11.00	5.50	3.25
518	Carl Bouldin	6.00	3.00	1.75
519	Charlie Smith	6.00	3.00	1.75
520	Jack Baldschun	6.00	3.00	1.75
521	Tom Satriano	6.00	3.00	1.75
522	Bobby Tiefenauer	6.00	3.00	1.75
523	Lou Burdette	10.00	4.50	2.75
524	Reds Rookies(Jim Dickson, Bobby Klaus)	11.00	4.50	2.75
525	Al McBean	9.00	4.50	2.75
526	Lou Clinton	9.00	4.50	2.75
527	Larry Bearnarth	9.00	4.50	2.75
528	Athletics Rookies(Dave Duncan RC, Tom Reynolds)	12.00	4.50	2.75
529	Al Dark	9.00	4.50	2.75
530	Leon Wagner	9.00	4.50	2.75
531	L.A. Dodgers Team	17.50	8.75	5.25
532	Twins Rookies(Bud Bloomfield, Joe Nossek)	9.00	4.50	2.75
533	Johnny Klippstein	9.00	4.50	2.75
534	Gus Bell	9.00	4.50	2.75
535	Phil Regan	9.00	4.50	2.75
536	Mets Rookies(Larry Elliot, John Stephenson)	11.00	4.50	2.75
537	Dan Osinski	9.00	4.50	2.75
538	Minnie Minoso	13.50	6.75	4.00
539	Roy Face	9.00	4.50	2.75
540	Luis Aparicio	35.00	17.50	10.00
541	Braves Rookies(Phil Niekro RC, Phil Roof)	75.00	37.50	18.75
542	Don Mincher	9.00	4.50	2.75
543	Bob Uecker	40.00	20.00	10.00
544	Colts Rookies(Steve Hertz, Joe Hoerner)	11.00	4.50	2.75
545	Max Alvis	9.00	4.50	2.75
546	Joe Christopher	9.00	4.50	2.75
547	Gil Hodges	15.00	7.50	4.50
548	N.L. Rookies(Wayne Schurr, Paul Speckenbach)	10.00	4.50	2.75
549	Joe Moeller	9.00	4.50	2.75
550	Ken Hubbs - In Memoriam	30.00	15.00	7.50
551	Billy Hoeft	9.00	4.50	2.75
552	Indians Rookies(Tom Kelley, Sonny Siebert RC)	12.00	5.50	3.25
553	Jim Brewer	9.00	4.50	2.75
554	Hank Foiles	9.00	4.50	2.75
555	Lee Stange	9.00	4.50	2.75
556	Mets Rookies(Steve Dillon, Ron Locke)	9.00	4.50	2.75
557	Leo Burke	9.00	4.50	2.75
558	Don Schwall	9.00	4.50	2.75
559	Dick Phillips	9.00	4.50	2.75
560	Dick Farrell	9.00	4.50	2.75
561	Phillies Rookies(Dave Bennett RC, Rick Wise RC)	11.00	5.50	3.25
562	Pedro Ramos	9.00	4.50	2.75
563	Dal Maxvill	9.00	4.50	2.75
564	A.L. Rookies(Joe McCabe, Jerry McNertney)	11.00	4.50	2.75
565	Stu Miller	9.00	4.50	2.75
566	Ed Kranepool	9.00	4.50	2.75
567	Jim Kaat	12.50	6.25	3.75
568	N.L. Rookies(Phil Gagliano, Cap Peterson)	12.00	4.50	2.75
569	Fred Newman	9.00	4.50	2.75
570	Bill Mazeroski	40.00	20.00	10.00
571	Gene Conley	9.00	4.50	2.75
572	A.L. Rookies(Dick Egan, Dave Gray)	10.00	4.50	2.75
573	Jim Duffalo	9.00	4.50	2.75
574	Manny Jimenez	9.00	4.50	2.75
575	Tony Cloninger	9.00	4.50	2.75
576	Mets Rookies(Jerry Hinsley, Bill Wakefield)	11.00	4.50	2.75
577	Gordy Coleman	9.00	4.50	2.75
578	Glen Hobbie	9.00	4.50	2.75
579	Boston Red Sox Team	17.50	8.75	5.25
580	Johnny Podres	11.00	5.50	3.25
581	Yankees Rookies(Pedro Gonzalez, Archie Moore)	12.00	4.50	2.75
582	Rod Kanehl	9.00	4.50	2.75
583	Tito Francona	9.00	4.50	2.75
584	Joel Horlen	9.00	4.50	2.75
585	Tony Taylor	9.00	4.50	2.75
586	Jim Piersall	10.00	5.00	3.00
587	Bennie Daniels	12.00	6.00	3.50

1964 Topps Coins

The 164 metal coins in this set were issued by Topps as inserts in the company's baseball card wax packs. The series is divided into two principal types, 120 "regular" coins and 44 All-Star coins. The 1 1/2" diameter coins feature a full-color background for the player photos in the "regular" series, while the players in the All-Star series are featured against plain red or blue backgrounds. There are two variations each of the Mantle, Causey and Hinton coins among the All-Star subset.

		NM	E	VG
	Complete Set (164):	1,125	550.00	325.00
	Common Player:	7.50	3.75	2.25
1	Don Zimmer	7.25	3.75	2.25
2	Jim Wynn	7.25	3.75	2.25
3	Johnny Orsino	7.25	3.75	2.25
4	Jim Bouton	9.00	3.75	2.25
5	Dick Groat	7.25	3.75	2.25
6	Leon Wagner	7.25	3.75	2.25
7	Frank Malzone	7.25	3.75	2.25
8	Steve Barber	7.25	3.75	2.25
9	Johnny Romano	7.25	3.75	2.25
10	Tom Tresh	9.00	3.75	2.25
11	Felipe Alou	7.25	3.75	2.25
12	Dick Stuart	7.25	3.75	2.25
13	Claude Osteen	7.25	3.75	2.25
14	Juan Pizarro	7.25	3.75	2.25
15	Donn Clendenon	7.25	3.75	2.25
16	Jimmie Hall	7.25	3.75	2.25
17	Larry Jackson	7.25	3.75	2.25
18	Brooks Robinson	17.50	7.50	4.50
19	Bob Allison	7.25	3.75	2.25
20	Ed Roebuck	7.25	3.75	2.25
21	Pete Ward	7.25	3.75	2.25
22	Willie McCovey	12.50	6.25	3.75
23	Elston Howard	9.00	3.50	2.00
24	Diego Segui	7.25	3.75	2.25

25	Ken Boyer	9.00	3.50	2.00
26	Carl Yastrzemski	20.00	10.00	6.00
27	Bill Mazeroski	12.50	6.25	3.75
28	Jerry Lumpe	7.25	3.75	2.25
29	Woody Held	7.25	3.75	2.25
30	Dick Radatz	7.25	3.75	2.25
31	Luis Aparicio	12.00	5.00	3.00
32	Dave Nicholson	7.25	3.75	2.25
33	Ed Mathews	15.00	7.50	4.50
34	Don Drysdale	15.00	7.50	4.50
35	Ray Culp	7.25	3.75	2.25
36	Juan Marichal	10.00	5.00	3.00
37	Frank Robinson	15.00	7.50	4.50
38	Chuck Hinton	7.25	3.75	2.25
39	Floyd Robinson	7.25	3.75	2.25
40	Tommy Harper	7.25	3.75	2.25
41	Ron Hansen	7.25	3.75	2.25
42	Ernie Banks	20.00	10.00	6.00
43	Jesse Gonder	7.25	3.75	2.25
44	Billy Williams	10.00	5.00	3.00
45	Vada Pinson	9.00	3.50	2.00
46	Rocky Colavito	9.00	4.50	2.75
47	Bill Monbouquette	7.25	3.75	2.25
48	Max Alvis	7.25	3.75	2.25
49	Norm Siebern	7.25	3.75	2.25
50	John Callison	7.25	3.75	2.25
51	Rich Rollins	7.25	3.75	2.25
52	Ken McBride	7.25	3.75	2.25
53	Don Lock	7.25	3.75	2.25
54	Ron Fairly	7.25	3.75	2.25
55	Roberto Clemente	30.00	15.00	9.00
56	Dick Ellsworth	7.25	3.75	2.25
57	Tommy Davis	7.25	3.75	2.25
58	Tony Gonzalez	7.25	3.75	2.25
59	Bob Gibson	15.00	7.50	4.50
60	Jim Maloney	7.25	3.75	2.25
61	Frank Howard	9.00	3.50	2.00
62	Jim Pagliaroni	7.25	3.75	2.25
63	Orlando Cepeda	10.00	5.00	3.00
64	Ron Perranoski	7.25	3.75	2.25
65	Curt Flood	7.25	3.75	2.25
66	Al McBean	7.25	3.75	2.25
67	Dean Chance	7.25	3.75	2.25
68	Ron Santo	10.00	3.75	2.25
69	Jack Baldschun	7.25	3.75	2.25
70	Milt Pappas	7.25	3.75	2.25
71	Gary Peters	7.25	3.75	2.25
72	Bobby Richardson	10.00	3.75	2.25
73	Lee Thomas	7.25	3.75	2.25
74	Hank Aguirre	7.25	3.75	2.25
75	Carl Willey	7.25	3.75	2.25
76	Camilo Pascual	7.25	3.75	2.25
77	Bob Friend	7.25	3.75	2.25
78	Bill White	7.25	3.75	2.25
79	Norm Cash	10.00	3.75	2.25
80	Willie Mays	35.00	15.00	9.00
81	Duke Carmel	7.25	3.75	2.25
82	Pete Rose	35.00	17.50	10.50
83	Hank Aaron	30.00	15.00	9.00
84	Bob Aspromonte	7.25	3.75	2.25
85	Jim O'Toole	7.25	3.75	2.25
86	Vic Davalillo	7.25	3.75	2.25
87	Bill Freehan	7.25	3.75	2.25
88	Warren Spahn	15.00	7.50	4.50
89	Ron Hunt	7.25	3.75	2.25
90	Denis Menke	7.25	3.75	2.25
91	Turk Farrell	7.25	3.75	2.25
92	Jim Hickman	7.25	3.75	2.25
93	Jim Bunning	12.00	4.50	2.75
94	Bob Hendley	7.25	3.75	2.25
95	Ernie Broglio	7.25	3.75	2.25
96	Rusty Staub	9.00	3.50	2.00
97	Lou Brock	12.00	5.00	3.00
98	Jim Fregosi	7.25	3.75	2.25
99	Jim Grant	7.25	3.75	2.25
100	Al Kaline	18.00	7.50	4.50
101	Earl Battey	7.25	3.75	2.25
102	Wayne Causey	7.25	3.75	2.25
103	Chuck Schilling	7.25	3.75	2.25
104	Boog Powell	10.00	3.75	2.25
105	Dave Wickersham	7.25	3.75	2.25
106	Sandy Koufax	30.00	15.00	9.00
107	John Bateman	7.25	3.75	2.25
108	Ed Brinkman	7.25	3.75	2.25
109	Al Downing	7.25	3.75	2.25
110	Joe Azcue	7.25	3.75	2.25
111	Albie Pearson	7.25	3.75	2.25
112	Harmon Killebrew	18.00	7.50	4.50
113	Tony Taylor	7.25	3.75	2.25
114	Alvin Jackson	7.25	3.75	2.25
115	Billy O'Dell	7.25	3.75	2.25
116	Don Demeter	7.25	3.75	2.25
117	Ed Charles	7.25	3.75	2.25
118	Joe Torre	10.00	3.75	2.25
119	Don Nottebart	7.25	3.75	2.25
120	Mickey Mantle	65.00	32.00	19.50
121	Joe Pepitone (All-Star)	9.00	3.75	2.25
122	Dick Stuart (All-Star)	7.25	3.75	2.25

123	Bobby Richardson (All-Star)	9.00	3.75	2.25
124	Jerry Lumpe (All-Star)	7.25	3.75	2.25
125	Brooks Robinson (All-Star)	13.50	6.25	3.75
126	Frank Malzone (All-Star)	7.25	3.75	2.25
127	Luis Aparicio (All-Star)	10.00	4.50	2.75
128	Jim Fregosi (All-Star)	7.25	3.75	2.25
129	Al Kaline (All-Star)	15.50	6.25	3.75
130	Leon Wagner (All-Star)	7.25	3.75	2.25
131a	Mickey Mantle (All-Star, lefthanded.)	50.00	22.00	13.50
131b	Mickey Mantle (All-Star, righthanded.)	55.00	25.00	15.00
132	Albie Pearson (All-Star)	7.25	3.75	2.25
133	Harmon Killebrew (All-Star)	15.50	6.25	3.75
134	Carl Yastrzemski (All-Star)	17.50	8.75	5.25
135	Elston Howard (All-Star)	9.00	3.50	2.00
136	Earl Battey (All-Star)	7.25	3.75	2.25
137	Camilo Pascual (All-Star)	7.25	3.75	2.25
138	Jim Bouton (All-Star)	9.00	3.50	2.00
139	Whitey Ford (All-Star)	16.00	7.50	4.50
140	Gary Peters (All-Star)	7.25	3.75	2.25
141	Bill White (All-Star)	7.25	3.75	2.25
142	Orlando Cepeda (All-Star)	10.00	4.50	2.75
143	Bill Mazeroski (All-Star)	10.00	5.00	3.00
144	Tony Taylor (All-Star)	7.25	3.75	2.25
145	Ken Boyer (All-Star)	9.00	3.50	2.00
146	Ron Santo (All-Star)	10.50	3.75	2.25
147	Dick Groat (All-Star)	7.25	3.75	2.25
148	Roy McMillan (All-Star)	7.25	3.75	2.25
149	Hank Aaron (All-Star)	27.50	13.50	8.25
150	Roberto Clemente (All-Star)	27.50	13.50	8.25
151	Willie Mays (All-Star)	27.50	13.50	8.25
152	Vada Pinson (All-Star)	9.00	3.50	2.00
153	Tommy Davis (All-Star)	7.25	3.75	2.25
154	Frank Robinson (All-Star)	13.50	6.25	3.75
155	Joe Torre (All-Star)	10.00	3.75	2.25
156	Tim McCarver (All-Star)	7.25	3.75	2.25
157	Juan Marichal (All-Star)	10.00	5.00	3.00
158	Jim Maloney (All-Star)	7.25	3.75	2.25
159	Sandy Koufax (All-Star)	27.50	13.50	8.25
160	Warren Spahn (All-Star)	12.50	6.25	3.75
161a	Wayne Causey (All-Star, N.L. on back.)	20.00	10.00	6.00
161b	Wayne Causey (All-Star, A.L. on back.)	7.25	3.75	2.25
162a	Chuck Hinton (All-Star, N.L. on back.)	20.00	10.00	6.00
162b	Chuck Hinton (All-Star, A.L. on back.)	7.25	3.75	2.25
163	Bob Aspromonte (All-Star)	7.25	3.75	2.25
164	Ron Hunt (All-Star)	7.25	3.75	2.25

1964 Topps Giants

Measuring 3-1/8" x 5-1/4" the Topps Giants were the company's first postcard-size issue. The cards feature large color photographs surrounded by white borders with a white baseball containing the player's name, position and team. Card backs carry another photo of the player surrounded by a newspaper-style explanation of the depicted career highlight. The 60-card set contains primarily stars which means it's an excellent place to find inexpensive cards of Hall of Famers. The '64 Giants were not printed in equal quantity and seven of the cards, including Sandy Koufax and Willie Mays, are significantly scarcer than the remainder of the set.

		NM	E	VG
Complete Set (60):		300.00	150.00	75.00
Common Player:		4.00	2.00	1.20
1	Gary Peters	4.00	2.00	1.20
2	Ken Johnson	4.00	2.00	1.20

3	Sandy Koufax (SP)	50.00	25.00	15.00
4	Bob Bailey	4.00	2.00	1.20
5	Milt Pappas	4.00	2.00	1.20
6	Ron Hunt	4.00	2.00	1.20
7	Whitey Ford	12.00	6.00	3.50
8	Roy McMillan	4.00	2.00	1.20
9	Rocky Colavito	6.00	3.00	1.75
10	Jim Bunning	10.00	5.00	3.700
11	Roberto Clemente	30.00	15.00	7.50
12	Al Kaline	12.00	6.00	3.50
13	Nellie Fox	10.00	5.00	3.00
14	Tony Gonzalez	4.00	2.00	1.20
15	Jim Gentile	4.00	2.00	1.20
16	Dean Chance	4.00	2.00	1.20
17	Dick Ellsworth	4.00	2.00	1.20
18	Jim Fregosi	4.00	2.00	1.20
19	Dick Groat	4.00	2.00	1.20
20	Chuck Hinton	4.00	2.00	1.20
21	Elston Howard	5.00	2.50	1.50
22	Dick Farrell	4.00	2.00	1.20
23	Albie Pearson	4.00	2.00	1.20
24	Frank Howard	4.00	2.00	1.25
25	Mickey Mantle	60.00	30.00	15.00
26	Joe Torre	7.50	3.75	2.50
27	Ed Brinkman	4.00	2.00	1.20
28	Bob Friend (SP)	15.00	7.25	4.75
29	Frank Robinson	12.00	6.00	3.50
30	Bill Freehan	4.00	2.00	1.20
31	Warren Spahn	12.00	6.00	3.50
32	Camilo Pascual	4.00	2.00	1.20
33	Pete Ward	4.00	2.00	1.20
34	Jim Maloney	4.00	2.00	1.20
35	Dave Wickersham	4.00	2.00	1.20
36	Johnny Callison	4.00	2.00	1.20
37	Juan Marichal	10.00	5.00	3.00
38	Harmon Killebrew	12.00	6.00	3.75
39	Luis Aparicio	10.00	5.00	3.00
40	Dick Radatz	4.00	2.00	1.20
41	Bob Gibson	7.00	3.50	2.00
42	Dick Stuart (SP)	15.00	7.50	4.50
43	Tommy Davis	4.00	2.00	1.20
44	Tony Oliva	5.50	3.75	2.00
45	Wayne Causey (SP)	15.00	7.50	4.50
46	Max Alvis	4.00	2.00	1.20
47	Galen Cisco (SP)	15.00	6.75	4.00
48	Carl Yastrzemski	12.00	4.50	2.75
49	Hank Aaron	35.00	17.50	8.75
50	Brooks Robinson	12.00	4.50	2.75
51	Willie Mays (SP)	50.00	25.00	12.50
52	Billy Williams	10.00	4.00	2.50
53	Juan Pizarro	4.00	2.00	1.20
54	Leon Wagner	4.00	2.00	1.20
55	Orlando Cepeda	10.00	3.50	2.00
56	Vada Pinson	5.00	1.75	1.00
57	Ken Boyer	6.00	1.75	1.00
58	Ron Santo	5.00	2.50	1.50
59	John Romano	4.00	2.00	1.20
60	Bill Skowron (SP)	40.00	20.00	12.00

1964 Topps Photo Tatoos

Apparently not content to leave the skin of American children without adornment, Topps jumped back into the tattoo field in 1964 with the release of a new series, measuring 1-9/16" x 3-1/2". The picture side for the 20 team tattoos gives the team logo and name.

		NM	E	VG
Complete Set (79):		3,000	1,500	900.00
Common Player:		15.00	7.50	4.50
Unopened Pack:		160.00		
(1)	Hank Aaron	135.00	65.00	40.00
(2)	Hank Aguirre	15.00	7.50	4.50
(3)	Max Alvis	15.00	7.50	4.50
(4)	Ernie Banks	80.00	40.00	24.00
(5)	Steve Barber	15.00	7.50	4.50
(6)	Ken Boyer	20.00	10.00	6.00
(7)	Johnny Callison	15.00	7.50	4.50
(8)	Norm Cash	20.00	10.00	6.00
(9)	Wayne Causey	15.00	7.50	4.50
(10)	Orlando Cepeda	50.00	25.00	15.00

(11)	Rocky Colavito	50.00	25.00	15.00
(12)	Ray Culp	15.00	7.50	4.50
(13)	Vic Davalillo (red and yellow back background)	15.00	7.50	4.50
(14)	Moe Drabowsky	15.00	7.50	4.50
(15)	Dick Ellsworth	15.00	7.50	4.50
(16)	Curt Flood	15.00	7.50	4.50
(17)	Bill Freehan	15.00	7.50	4.50
(18)	Jim Fregosi (red and yellow back background)	15.00	7.50	4.50
(19)	Bob Friend	15.00	7.50	4.50
(20)	Dick Groat	15.00	7.50	4.50
(21)	Woody Held	15.00	7.50	4.50
(22)	Frank Howard	20.00	10.00	6.00
(23)	Al Jackson	15.00	7.50	4.50
(24)	Larry Jackson	15.00	7.50	4.50
(25)	Ken Johnson	15.00	7.50	4.50
(26)	Al Kaline	60.00	30.00	18.00
(27)	Harmon Killebrew (Green background.)	60.00	30.00	18.00
(28)	Harmon Killebrew (Red background.)	60.00	30.00	18.00
(29)	Sandy Koufax (Horizontal band.)	135.00	65.00	40.00
(30)	Sandy Koufax (Diagonal band - red and yellow back background)	145.00	75.00	45.00
(31)	Don Lock	15.00	7.50	4.50
(32)	Frank Malzone	15.00	7.50	4.50
(33)	Mickey Mantle (Diagonal yellow band.)	325.00	160.00	100.00
(34a)	Mickey Mantle (Red triangle, back background red)	325.00	160.00	100.00
(34b)	Mickey Mantle (red triangle, back background yellow)	325.00	160.00	100.00
(35)	Eddie Mathews	60.00	30.00	18.00
(36)	Willie Mays (Yellow background encompasses head.)	135.00	65.00	40.00
(37)	Willie Mays (Yellow background ears-to-chin.)	135.00	65.00	40.00
(38)	Bill Mazeroski	60.00	30.00	18.00
(39)	Ken McBride	15.00	7.50	4.50
(40)	Bill Monbouquette	15.00	7.50	4.50
(41)	Dave Nicholson	15.00	7.50	4.50
(42)	Claude Osteen	15.00	7.50	4.50
(43)	Milt Pappas	15.00	7.50	4.50
(44)	Camilio Pascual	15.00	7.50	4.50
(45)	Albie Pearson	15.00	7.50	4.50
(46)	Ron Perranoski	15.00	7.50	4.50
(47)	Gary Peters	15.00	7.50	4.50
(48)	Boog Powell	20.00	10.00	6.00
(49)	Frank Robinson	60.00	30.00	18.00
(50)	John Romano	15.00	7.50	4.50
(51)	Norm Siebern	15.00	7.50	4.50
(52)	Warren Spahn	60.00	30.00	18.00
(53)	Dick Stuart	15.00	7.50	4.50
(54)	Lee Thomas	15.00	7.50	4.50
(55)	Joe Torre	25.00	12.50	7.50
(56)	Pete Ward (red and yellow wrappers)	15.00	7.50	4.50
(57)	Carlton Willey (red and yellow back background)	15.00	7.50	4.50
(58)	Billy Williams (red and yellow back background)	60.00	30.00	18.00
(59)	Carl Yastrzemski	75.00	37.50	22.50
(60)	Baltimore Orioles Logo	20.00	10.00	6.00
(61)	Boston Red Sox Logo	20.00	10.00	6.00
(62)	Chicago Cubs Logo	20.00	10.00	6.00
(63)	Chicago White Sox Logo	20.00	10.00	6.00
(64)	Cincinnati Reds Logo	20.00	10.00	6.00
(65)	Cleveland Indians Logo	20.00	10.00	6.00
(66)	Detroit Tigers Logo	20.00	10.00	6.00
(67)	Houston Colts Logo	25.00	12.50	7.50
(68)	Kansas City Athletics Logo (red and yellow back background)	20.00	10.00	6.00
(69)	Los Angeles Angels Logo	20.00	10.00	6.00
(70)	Los Angeles Dodgers Logo	20.00	10.00	6.00
(71)	Milwaukee Braves Logo	20.00	10.00	6.00
(72)	Minnesota Twins Logo	20.00	10.00	6.00
(73)	New York Mets Logo	25.00	12.50	7.50
(74)	New York Yankees Logo	25.00	12.50	7.50
(75)	Philadelphia Phillies Logo	20.00	10.00	6.00
(76)	Pittsburgh Pirates Logo	20.00	10.00	6.00
(77)	St. Louis Cardinals Logo	20.00	10.00	6.00
(78)	San Francisco Giants Logo	20.00	10.00	6.00
(79)	Washington Senators Logo	20.00	10.00	6.00

1964 Topps Rookie All-Star Banquet

Since 1959, Topps has sponsored a formal post-season banquet to honor its annual Rookie All-Star team. In 1964, the gum company deviated from the tradition dinner program by issuing a 36-card boxed set. Each of the cards is printed in black-and-white, with red or light blue graphic highlights. The first seven cards in the set feature Topps staff and baseball dignitaries involved in the selection of the rookie team. Cards #8-12 are composite photos of the 1959-63 Rookie All-Star team. Cards #13-34A showcase the '64 honorees. Each player's card is matched with a card from the team's public relations officer extolling the rookie's virtues. Each card in this unique dinner program measures 3" x 5-1/4" and is numbered as a "PAGE" in the lower-right corner.

		NM	E	VG
	Complete Boxed Set (36):	2,800	1,400	850.00
	Common Player:	17.50	8.75	5.25
1	Team Awards" Header Card	17.50	8.75	5.25
2	The Baseball World Votes(Tommy Davis, Jeff Torborg, Ron Santo, Billy Williams)	17.50	8.75	5.25
3	The Baseball World Votes (Six more clubhouse scenes.)	17.50	8.75	5.25
4	Election Committee (Photos of media and Hall of Famers Hank Greenberg and Fran Frisch.)	55.00	27.00	16.50
5	Election Committee (Photos of five media, Topps' VP Joel Shorin and Jackie Robinson.)	120.00	60.00	35.00
6	His Associates (Topps' Cy Berger, three others.)	17.50	8.75	5.25
7	Topps Salutes Joe Garagiola(Joe Garagiola)	95.00	45.00	25.00
8	The 1959 Topps Rookie All-Star Team(Willie McCovey, Pumpsie Green, Joe Koppe, Jim Baxes, Bobby Allison, Ron Fairly, Willie Tasby, John Romano, Jim Perry, Jim O'Toole)	225.00	110.00	65.00
9	The 1960 Topps Rookie All-Star Team(Jim Gentile, Julian Javier, Ron Hansen, Ron Santo, Tommy Davis, Frank Howard, Tony Curry, Jimmie Coker, Chuck Estrada, Dick Stigman)	225.00	110.00	65.00
10	The 1961 Topps Rookie All-Star Team(J.C. Martin, Jake Wood, Dick Howser, Charlie Smith, Billy Williams, Lee Thomas, Floyd Robinson, Joe Torre, Don Schwall, Jack Curtis)	185.00	90.00	55.00
11	The 1962 Topps Rookie All-Star Team(Fred Whitfield, Bernie Allen, Tom Tresh, Ed Charles, Manny Jiminez, Al Luplow, Boog Powell, Buck Rodgers, Dean Chance, Al Jackson)	185.00	90.00	55.00
12	The 1963 Topps Rookie All-Star Team(Pete Rose, Rusty Staub, Al Weis, Pete Ward, Jimmie Hall, Vic Davalillo, Tommy Harper, Jesse Gonder, Ray Culp, Gary Peters)	1,400	700.00	425.00
13	Card	17.50	8.75	5.25
14	Ed Uhas, Cleveland Indians PR	17.50	8.75	5.25
15	Bob Chance	135.00	65.00	40.00
16	Garry Schumacher, S.F. Giants PR	17.50	8.75	5.25
17	Hal Lanier	135.00	65.00	40.00
18	Larry Shenk, Phillies PR	17.50	8.75	5.25
19	Richie Allen	300.00	150.00	90.00
20	Jim Schaaf, Athletics PR	17.50	8.75	5.25
21	Bert Campaneris	160.00	80.00	45.00
22	Ernie Johnson, Braves PR	17.50	8.75	5.25
23	Rico Carty	160.00	80.00	45.00
24	Bill Crowley, Red Sox PR	17.50	8.75	5.25
25	Tony Conigliaro	345.00	175.00	100.00
26	Tom Mee, Twins PR	17.50	8.75	5.25
27	Tony Oliva	210.00	100.00	60.00
28	Burt Hawkins, Senators PR	17.50	8.75	5.25
29	Mike Brumley	135.00	65.00	40.00
30	Hank Zureick, Reds PR	17.50	8.75	5.25
31	Bill McCool	135.00	65.00	40.00
32	Rob Brown, Orioles PR	17.50	8.75	5.25
33	Wally Bunker	135.00	65.00	40.00
34	the Year" Header Card	17.50	8.75	5.25
34A	Luis Tiant (Minor League Player of the Year)	160.00	80.00	45.00
35	Rookie All-Star Trophy	17.50	8.75	5.25

1964 Topps Stand-Ups

These 2-1/2" x 3-1/2" cards were the first since the All-Star sets of 1951 to die-cut. This made it possible for a folded card to stand on display. The 77-cards in the set feature color photographs of the player with yellow and green backgrounds. Directions for folding are on the yellow top background, and when folded only the green background remains. Of the 77 cards, 55 were double-printed while 22 were single-printed, making them twice as scarce.

		NM	E	VG
	Complete Set (77):	3,500	1,750	1,050
	Common Player:	12.00	6.00	3.50
	Wax Pack (1):	600.00		
(1)	Hank Aaron	180.00	90.00	45.00
(2)	Hank Aguirre	12.00	6.00	3.50
(3)	George Altman	12.00	6.00	3.50
(4)	Max Alvis	12.00	6.00	3.50
(5)	Bob Aspromonte	12.00	6.00	3.50
(6)	Jack Baldschun (SP)	20.00	10.00	6.00
(7)	Ernie Banks	100.00	50.00	25.00
(8)	Steve Barber	12.00	6.00	3.50
(9)	Earl Battey	12.00	6.00	3.50
(10)	Ken Boyer	20.00	10.00	6.00
(11)	Ernie Broglio	12.00	6.00	3.50
(12)	Johnny Callison	12.00	6.00	3.50
(13)	Norm Cash (SP)	75.00	32.50	16.25
(14)	Wayne Causey	12.00	6.00	3.50
(15)	Orlando Cepeda	27.50	13.50	8.25
(16)	Ed Charles	12.00	6.00	3.50
(17)	Roberto Clemente	230.00	120.00	60.00
(18)	Donn Clendenon (SP)	20.00	10.00	6.00
(19)	Rocky Colavito	25.00	12.50	7.50
(20)	Ray Culp (SP)	20.00	10.00	6.00
(21)	Tommy Davis	12.00	6.00	3.50
(22)	Don Drysdale (SP)	140.00	70.00	35.00
(23)	Dick Ellsworth	12.00	6.00	3.50
(24)	Dick Farrell	12.00	6.00	3.50
(25)	Jim Fregosi	12.00	6.00	3.50
(26)	Bob Friend	12.00	6.00	3.50
(27)	Jim Gentile	12.00	6.00	3.50
(28)	Jesse Gonder (SP)	20.00	10.00	6.00

		NM	E	VG
(29)	Tony Gonzalez (SP)	20.00	10.00	6.00
(30)	Dick Groat	12.50	6.25	3.75
(31)	Woody Held	12.00	6.00	3.50
(32)	Chuck Hinton	12.00	6.00	3.50
(33)	Elston Howard	20.00	10.00	6.00
(34)	Frank Howard (SP)	27.50	13.50	8.25
(35)	Ron Hunt	12.00	6.00	3.50
(36)	Al Jackson	12.00	6.00	3.50
(37)	Ken Johnson	12.00	6.00	3.50
(38)	Al Kaline	100.00	50.00	25.00
(39)	Harmon Killebrew	100.00	50.00	25.00
(40)	Sandy Koufax	200.00	100.00	50.00
(41)	Don Lock (SP)	20.00	10.00	6.00
(42)	Jerry Lumpe (SP)	20.00	10.00	6.00
(43)	Jim Maloney	12.00	6.00	3.50
(44)	Frank Malzone	12.00	6.00	3.50
(45)	Mickey Mantle	550.00	275.00	137.50
(46)	Juan Marichal (SP)	120.00	60.00	30.00
(47)	Ed Mathews (SP)	150.00	75.00	37.50
(48)	Willie Mays	350.00	175.00	105.00
(49)	Bill Mazeroski	22.50	11.00	7.00
(50)	Ken McBride	12.00	6.00	3.50
(51)	Willie McCovey (SP)	120.00	60.00	30.00
(52)	Claude Osteen	12.00	6.00	3.50
(53)	Jim O'Toole	12.00	6.00	3.50
(54)	Camilo Pascual	12.00	6.00	3.50
(55)	Albie Pearson (SP)	20.00	10.00	6.00
(56)	Gary Peters	12.00	6.00	3.50
(57)	Vada Pinson	15.00	7.50	4.50
(58)	Juan Pizarro	12.00	6.00	3.50
(59)	Boog Powell	30.00	15.00	9.00
(60)	Bobby Richardson	30.00	15.00	9.00
(61)	Brooks Robinson	75.00	40.00	24.00
(62)	Floyd Robinson	12.00	6.00	3.50
(63)	Frank Robinson	75.00	40.00	24.00
(64)	Ed Roebuck (SP)	20.00	10.00	6.00
(65)	Rich Rollins	12.00	6.00	3.50
(66)	Johnny Romano	12.00	6.00	3.50
(67)	Ron Santo (SP)	50.00	25.00	12.50
(68)	Norm Siebern	12.00	6.00	3.50
(69)	Warren Spahn (SP)	130.00	65.00	40.00
(70)	Dick Stuart (SP)	20.00	10.00	6.00
(71)	Lee Thomas	12.00	6.00	3.50
(72)	Joe Torre	30.00	15.00	9.00
(73)	Pete Ward	12.00	6.00	3.50
(74)	Bill White (SP)	25.00	12.50	7.50
(75)	Billy Williams (SP)	120.00	60.00	30.00
(76)	Hal Woodeshick (SP)	75.00	40.00	24.00
(77)	Carl Yastrzemski (SP)	500.00	250.00	125.00

1965 Topps

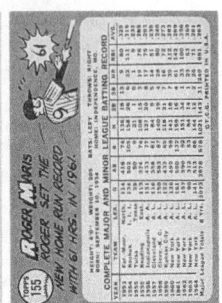

The 1965 Topps set features a large color photograph of the player surrounded by a colored, round-cornered frame and a white border. The bottom of the 2-1/2" x 3-1/2" cards includes a pennant with a color team logo and name over the left side of a rectangle which features the player's name and position. Backs feature statistics and, if space allowed, a cartoon and headline about the player. There are no multi-player cards in the 1965 set other than the usual team cards and World Series highlights. Rookie cards include team, as well as league groupings from two to four players per card. Also present in the 598-card set are statistical leaders. Certain cards in the high-number series (#523-598) were produced in lesser quantities than the rest of the series. Known as "short-prints," and valued somewhat higher than the other high numbers, they are indicated in the checklist by an (SP) after the player name.

	NM	E	VG
Complete Set (598):	4,000	2,000	1,200
Common Player (1-370):	3.00	1.50	.90
Common Player (371-598):	6.00	3.00	1.75

		NM	E	VG
1	A.L. Batting Leaders(Elston Howard, Tony Oliva, Brooks Robinson)	25.00	12.50	6.25
2	N.L. Batting Leaders(Hank Aaron, Rico Carty, Roberto Clemente)	25.00	10.00	5.00
3	A.L. Home Run Leaders(Harmon Killebrew, Mickey Mantle, Boog Powell)	50.00	25.00	15.00
4	N.L. Home Run Leaders(Johnny Callison, Orlando Cepeda, Jim Hart, Willie Mays, Billy Williams)	20.00	10.00	6.00
5	A.L. RBI Leaders(Harmon Killebrew, Mickey Mantle, Brooks Robinson, Dick Stuart)	35.00	17.50	10.00
6	N.L. RBI Leaders(Ken Boyer, Willie Mays, Ron Santo)	13.50	6.75	4.00
7	A.L. ERA Leaders(Dean Chance, Joel Horlen)	3.50	1.75	1.00
8	N.L. ERA Leaders(Don Drysdale, Sandy Koufax)	20.00	10.00	5.00
9	A.L. Pitching Leaders(Wally Bunker, Dean Chance, Gary Peters, Juan Pizarro, Dave Wickersham)	3.50	1.75	1.00
10	N.L. Pitching Leaders(Larry Jackson, Juan Marichal, Ray Sadecki)	4.50	2.25	1.25
11	A.L. Strikeout Leaders(Dean Chance, Al Downing, Camilo Pascual)	3.50	1.75	1.00
12	N.L. Strikeout Leaders(Don Drysdale, Bob Gibson, Bob Veale)	12.50	6.00	3.50
13	Pedro Ramos	3.00	1.50	.90
14	Len Gabrielson	3.00	1.50	.90
15	Robin Roberts	12.50	6.25	3.75
16	Astros Rookies(Sonny Jackson RC, Joe Morgan RC)	60.00	30.00	15.00
17	Johnny Romano	3.00	1.50	.90
18	Bill McCool	3.00	1.50	.90
19	Gates Brown	3.00	1.50	.90
20	Jim Bunning	15.00	7.50	4.50
21	Don Blasingame	3.00	1.50	.90
22	Charlie Smith	3.00	1.50	.90
23	Bob Tiefenauer	3.00	1.50	.90
24	Twins Team	7.50	3.75	2.25
25	Al McBean	3.00	1.50	.90
26	Bobby Knoop	3.00	1.50	.90
27	Dick Bertell	3.00	1.50	.90
28	Barney Schultz	3.00	1.50	.90
29	Felix Mantilla	3.00	1.50	.90
30	Jim Bouton	4.50	2.25	1.25
31	Mike White	3.00	1.50	.90
32	Herman Franks	3.00	1.50	.90
33	Jackie Brandt	3.00	1.50	.90
34	Cal Koonce	3.00	1.50	.90
35	Ed Charles	3.00	1.50	.90
36	Bobby Wine	3.00	1.50	.90
37	Fred Gladding	3.00	1.50	.90
38	Jim King	3.00	1.50	.90
39	Gerry Arrigo	3.00	1.50	.90
40	Frank Howard	4.50	2.25	1.25
41	White Sox Rookies(Bruce Howard, Marv Staehle)	3.00	1.50	.90
42	Earl Wilson	3.00	1.50	.90
43	Mike Shannon	3.00	1.50	.90
44	Wade Blasingame	3.00	1.50	.90
45	Roy McMillan	3.00	1.50	.90
46	Bob Lee	3.00	1.50	.90
47	Tommy Harper	3.00	1.50	.90
48	Claude Raymond	3.00	1.50	.90
49	Orioles Rookies(Curt Blefary RC, John Miller)	3.00	1.50	.90
50	Juan Marichal	13.50	6.75	4.00
51	Billy Bryan	3.00	1.50	.90
52	Ed Roebuck	3.00	1.50	.90
53	Dick McAuliffe	3.00	1.50	.90
54	Joe Gibbon	3.00	1.50	.90
55	Tony Conigliaro	18.00	9.00	5.50
56	Ron Kline	3.00	1.50	.90
57	Cards Team	7.50	3.75	2.25
58	Fred Talbot	3.00	1.50	.90
59	Nate Oliver	3.00	1.50	.90
60	Jim O'Toole	3.00	1.50	.90
61	Chris Cannizzaro	3.00	1.50	.90
62	Jim Katt (Kaat)	3.50	1.75	1.00
63	Ty Cline	3.00	1.50	.90
64	Lou Burdette	3.00	1.50	.90
65	Tony Kubek	11.00	5.50	3.25
66	Bill Rigney	3.00	1.50	.90
67	Harvey Haddix	3.00	1.50	.90
68	Del Crandall	3.00	1.50	.90
69	Bill Virdon	3.00	1.50	.90
70	Bill Skowron	3.50	1.75	1.00
71	John O'Donoghue	3.00	1.50	.90
72	Tony Gonzalez	3.00	1.50	.90
73	Dennis Ribant	3.00	1.50	.90
74	Red Sox Rookies(Rico Petrocelli RC, Jerry Stephenson)	15.00	6.75	4.00
75	Deron Johnson	3.00	1.50	.90
76	Sam McDowell	3.00	1.50	.90
77	Doug Camilli	3.00	1.50	.90
78	Dal Maxvill	3.00	1.50	.90
79a	1st Series Checklist (1-88) (61 is C. Cannizzaro)	3.50	1.75	1.00
79b	1st Series Checklist (1-88) (61 is Cannizzaro)	7.00	3.50	2.00
80	Turk Farrell	3.00	1.50	.90
81	Don Buford	3.00	1.50	.90
82	Braves Rookies(Santos Alomar RC, John Braun)	4.50	2.25	1.25
83	George Thomas	3.00	1.50	.90
84	Ron Herbel	3.00	1.50	.90
85	Willie Smith	3.00	1.50	.90
86	Les Narum	3.00	1.50	.90
87	Nelson Mathews	3.00	1.50	.90
88	Jack Lamabe	3.00	1.50	.90
89	Mike Hershberger	3.00	1.50	.90
90	Rich Rollins	3.00	1.50	.90
91	**Cubs Team**	7.50	3.75	2.25
92	Dick Howser	3.00	1.50	.90
93	Jack Fisher	3.00	1.50	.90
94	Charlie Lau	3.00	1.50	.90
95	Bill Mazeroski	12.50	6.25	3.75
96	Sonny Siebert	3.00	1.50	.90
97	Pedro Gonzalez	3.00	1.50	.90
98	Bob Miller	3.00	1.50	.90
99	Gil Hodges	9.00	4.50	2.75
100	Ken Boyer	7.50	2.25	1.25
101	Fred Newman	3.00	1.50	.90
102	Steve Boros	3.00	1.50	.90
103	Harvey Kuenn	3.00	1.50	.90
104	2nd Series Checklist (89-176)	4.00	2.00	1.25
105	Chico Salmon	3.00	1.50	.90
106	Gene Oliver	3.00	1.50	.90
107	Phillies Rookies(Pat Corrales RC, Costen Shockley)	4.00	2.00	1.25
108	Don Mincher	3.00	1.50	.90
109	Walt Bond	3.00	1.50	.90
110	Ron Santo	18.00	9.00	5.50
111	Lee Thomas	3.00	1.50	.90
112	Derrell Griffith	3.00	1.50	.90
113	Steve Barber	3.00	1.50	.90
114	Jim Hickman	3.00	1.50	.90
115	Bobby Richardson	20.00	10.00	5.00
116	Cardinals Rookies(Dave Dowling, Bob Tolan RC)	3.00	1.50	.90
117	Wes Stock	3.00	1.50	.90
118	Hal Lanier RC	3.00	1.50	.90
119	John Kennedy	3.00	1.50	.90
120	Frank Robinson	40.00	20.00	10.00
121	Gene Alley	3.00	1.50	.90
122	Bill Pleis	3.00	1.50	.90
123	Frank Thomas	3.00	1.50	.90
124	Tom Satriano	3.00	1.50	.90
125	Juan Pizarro	3.00	1.50	.90
126	Dodgers Team	7.50	3.75	2.25
127	Frank Lary	3.00	1.50	.90
128	Vic Davalillo	3.00	1.50	.90
129	Bennie Daniels	3.00	1.50	.90
130	Al Kaline	40.00	20.00	10.00
131	Johnny Keane	4.00	2.00	1.25
132	World Series Game 1 (Cards Take Opener)	10.00	5.00	3.00
133	World Series Game 2 (Stottlemyre Wins)	15.00	7.50	3.75
134	World Series Game 3 (Mantle's Clutch HR)	60.00	30.00	15.00
135	World Series Game 4 (Boyer's Grand-Slam)	15.00	7.00	4.00
136	World Series Game 5 (10th Inning Triumph)	7.00	3.50	2.00
137	World Series Game 6 (Bouton Wins Again)	10.00	5.00	3.00
138	World Series Game 7 (Gibson Wins Finale)	15.00	7.50	4.50
139	World Series (The Cards Celebrate)	9.00	4.50	2.75
140	Dean Chance	3.00	1.50	.90
141	Charlie James	3.00	1.50	.90
142	Bill Monbouquette	3.00	1.50	.90
143	Pirates Rookies(John Gelnar, Jerry May)	3.00	1.50	.90
144	Ed Kranepool	3.00	1.50	.90

145	Luis Tiant **RC**	20.00	10.00	5.00
146	Ron Hansen	3.00	1.50	.90
147	Dennis Bennett	3.00	1.50	.90
148	Willie Kirkland	3.00	1.50	.90
149	Wayne Schurr	3.00	1.50	.90
150	Brooks Robinson	35.00	18.00	10.00
151	Athletics Team	7.50	3.75	2.25
152	Phil Ortega	3.00	1.50	.90
153	Norm Cash	9.00	4.50	2.75
154	Bob Humphreys	3.00	1.50	.90
155	Roger Maris	50.00	25.00	15.00
156	Bob Sadowski	3.00	1.50	.90
157	Zoilo Versalles	3.00	1.50	.90
158	Dick Sisler	3.00	1.50	.90
159	Jim Duffalo	3.00	1.50	.90
160	Bob Clemente	170.00	85.00	40.00
161	Frank Baumann	3.00	1.50	.90
162	Russ Nixon	3.00	1.50	.90
163	John Briggs	3.00	1.50	.90
164	Al Spangler	3.00	1.50	.90
165	Dick Ellsworth	3.00	1.50	.90
166	Indians Rookies(Tommie Agee **RC**, George Culver)	9.00	4.50	2.75
167	Bill Wakefield	3.00	1.50	.90
168	Dick Green	3.00	1.50	.90
169	Dave Vineyard	3.00	1.50	.90
170	Hank Aaron	130.00	65.00	35.00
171	Jim Roland	3.00	1.50	.90
172	Jim Piersall	6.00	3.00	1.75
173	Tigers Team	8.00	4.00	2.50
174	Joe Jay	3.00	1.50	.90
175	Bob Aspromonte	3.00	1.50	.90
176	Willie McCovey	23.00	10.00	5.00
177	Pete Mikkelsen	3.00	1.50	.90
178	Dalton Jones	3.00	1.50	.90
179	Hal Woodeshick	3.00	1.50	.90
180	Bob Allison	3.00	1.50	.90
181	Senators Rookies(Don Loun, Joe McCabe)	3.00	1.50	.90
182	Mike de la Hoz	3.00	1.50	.90
183	Dave Nicholson	3.00	1.50	.90
184	John Boozer	3.00	1.50	.90
185	Max Alvis	3.00	1.50	.90
186	Billy Cowan	3.00	1.50	.90
187	Casey Stengel	12.50	6.25	3.75
188	Sam Bowens	3.00	1.50	.90
189	3rd Series Checklist (177-264)	6.50	3.25	2.00
190	Bill White	3.00	1.50	.90
191	Phil Regan	3.00	1.50	.90
192	Jim Coker	3.00	1.50	.90
193	Gaylord Perry	12.00	6.00	3.50
194	Angels Rookies(Bill Kelso, Rick Reichardt **RC**)	3.00	1.50	.90
195	Bob Veale	3.00	1.50	.90
196	Ron Fairly	3.00	1.50	.90
197	Diego Segui	3.00	1.50	.90
198	Smoky Burgess	3.00	1.50	.90
199	Bob Heffner	3.00	1.50	.90
200	Joe Torre	24.00	12.00	7.00
201	Twins Rookies(Cesar Tovar **RC**, Sandy Valdespino)	3.00	1.50	.90
202	Leo Burke	3.00	1.50	.90
203	Dallas Green	3.00	1.50	.90
204	Russ Snyder	3.00	1.50	.90
205	Warren Spahn	30.00	15.00	7.50
206	Willie Horton	3.00	1.50	.90
207	Pete Rose	130.00	65.00	35.00
208	Tommy John	6.00	3.00	1.75
209	Pirates Team	7.50	3.75	2.25
210	Jim Fregosi	3.00	1.50	.90
211	Steve Ridzik	3.00	1.50	.90
212	Ron Brand	3.00	1.50	.90
213	Jim Davenport	3.00	1.50	.90
214	Bob Purkey	3.00	1.50	.90
215	Pete Ward	3.00	1.50	.90
216	Al Worthington	3.00	1.50	.90
217	Walt Alston	9.00	4.50	2.75
218	Dick Schofield	3.00	1.50	.90
219	Bob Meyer	3.00	1.50	.90
220	Billy Williams	25.00	12.50	7.50
221	John Tsitouris	3.00	1.50	.90
222	Bob Tillman	3.00	1.50	.90
223	Dan Osinski	3.00	1.50	.90
224	Bob Chance	3.00	1.50	.90
225	Bo Belinsky	3.00	1.50	.90
226	Yankees Rookies(Jake Gibbs, Elvio Jimenez)	9.00	4.50	2.75
227	Bobby Klaus	3.00	1.50	.90
228	Jack Sanford	3.00	1.50	.90
229	Lou Clinton	3.00	1.50	.90
230	Ray Sadecki	3.00	1.50	.90
231	Jerry Adair	3.00	1.50	.90
232	Steve Blass **RC**	3.00	1.50	.90
233	Don Zimmer	6.00	3.00	1.75

234	White Sox Team	7.50	3.75	2.25
235	Chuck Hinton	3.00	1.50	.90
236	Dennis McLain **RC**	20.00	10.00	5.00
237	Bernie Allen	3.00	1.50	.90
238	Joe Moeller	3.00	1.50	.90
239	Doc Edwards	3.00	1.50	.90
240	Bob Bruce	3.00	1.50	.90
241	Mack Jones	3.00	1.50	.90
242	George Brunet	3.00	1.50	.90
243	Reds Rookies(Ted Davidson, Tommy Helms **RC**)	3.00	1.50	.90
244	Lindy McDaniel	3.00	1.50	.90
245	Joe Pepitone	15.00	7.00	4.00
246	Tom Butters	3.00	1.50	.90
247	Wally Moon	3.00	1.50	.90
248	Gus Triandos	3.00	1.50	.90
249	Dave McNally	3.00	1.50	.90
250	Willie Mays	135.00	65.00	45.00
251	Billy Herman	7.50	3.75	2.25
252	Pete Richert	3.00	1.50	.90
253	Danny Cater	3.00	1.50	.90
254	Roland Sheldon	3.00	1.50	.90
255	Camilo Pascual	3.00	1.50	.90
256	Tito Francona	3.00	1.50	.90
257	Jim Wynn	3.00	1.50	.90
258	Larry Bearnarth	3.00	1.50	.90
259	Tigers Rookies(Jim Northrup **RC**, Ray Oyler **RC**)	4.00	2.00	1.25
260	Don Drysdale	24.00	12.00	7.00
261	Duke Carmel	3.00	1.50	.90
262	Bud Daley	3.00	1.50	.90
263	Marty Keough	3.00	1.50	.90
264	Bob Buhl	3.00	1.50	.90
265	Jim Pagliaroni	3.00	1.50	.90
266	Bert Campaneris **RC**	15.00	7.50	4.50
267	**Senators Team**	7.50	3.75	2.25
268	Ken McBride	3.00	1.50	.90
269	Frank Bolling	3.00	1.50	.90
270	Milt Pappas	3.00	1.50	.90
271	Don Wert	3.00	1.50	.90
272	Chuck Schilling	3.00	1.50	.90
273	4th Series Checklist (265-352)	7.50	3.75	2.25
274	Lum Harris	3.00	1.50	.90
275	Dick Groat	3.00	1.50	.90
276	Hoyt Wilhelm	12.50	6.25	3.75
277	Johnny Lewis	3.00	1.50	.90
278	Ken Retzer	3.00	1.50	.90
279	Dick Tracewski	3.00	1.50	.90
280	Dick Stuart	3.00	1.50	.90
281	Bill Stafford	3.00	1.50	.90
282	Giants Rookies(Dick Estelle, Masanori Murakami **RC**)	20.00	10.00	6.00
283	Fred Whitfield	3.00	1.50	.90
284	Nick Willhite	3.00	1.50	.90
285	Ron Hunt	3.00	1.50	.90
286	Athletic Rookies(Jim Dickson, Aurelio Monteagudo)	3.00	1.50	.90
287	Gary Kolb	3.00	1.50	.90
288	Jack Hamilton	3.00	1.50	.90
289	Gordy Coleman	3.00	1.50	.90
290	Wally Bunker	3.00	1.50	.90
291	Jerry Lynch	3.00	1.50	.90
292	Larry Yellen	3.00	1.50	.90
293	Angels Team	7.50	3.75	2.25
294	Tim McCarver	8.00	4.00	2.50
295	Dick Radatz	3.00	1.50	.90
296	Tony Taylor	3.00	1.50	.90
297	Dave DeBusschere	4.00	2.00	1.25
298	Jim Stewart	3.00	1.50	.90
299	Jerry Zimmerman	3.00	1.50	.90
300	Sandy Koufax	120.00	60.00	35.00
301	Birdie Tebbetts	3.00	1.50	.90
302	Al Stanek	3.00	1.50	.90
303	Johnny Orsino	3.00	1.50	.90
304	Dave Stenhouse	3.00	1.50	.90
305	Rico Carty	3.00	1.50	.90
306	Bubba Phillips	3.00	1.50	.90
307	Barry Latman	3.00	1.50	.90
308	Mets Rookies(Cleon Jones **RC**, Tom Parsons)	8.00	4.00	2.50
309	Steve Hamilton	3.00	1.50	.90
310	Johnny Callison	3.00	1.50	.90
311	Orlando Pena	3.00	1.50	.90
312	Joe Nuxhall	3.00	1.50	.90
313	Jimmie Schaffer	3.00	1.50	.90
314	Sterling Slaughter	3.00	1.50	.90
315	Frank Malzone	3.00	1.50	.90
316	Reds Team	13.00	6.50	4.00
317	Don McMahon	3.00	1.50	.90
318	Matty Alou	3.00	1.50	.90
319	Ken McMullen	3.00	1.50	.90
320	Bob Gibson	33.00	16.00	8.50

321	Rusty Staub	7.50	3.75	2.25
322	Rick Wise	3.00	1.50	.90
323	Hank Bauer	3.00	1.50	.90
324	Bobby Locke	3.00	1.50	.90
325	Donn Clendenon	3.00	1.50	.90
326	Dwight Siebler	3.00	1.50	.90
327	Denis Menke	3.00	1.50	.90
328	Eddie Fisher	3.00	1.50	.90
329	Hawk Taylor	3.00	1.50	.90
330	Whitey Ford	50.00	25.00	12.50
331	Dodgers Rookies(Al Ferrara, John Purdin)	3.00	1.50	.90
332	Ted Abernathy	3.00	1.50	.90
333	Tommie Reynolds	3.00	1.50	.90
334	Vic Roznovsky	3.00	1.50	.90
335	Mickey Lolich	6.00	3.00	1.75
336	Woody Held	3.00	1.50	.90
337	Mike Cuellar	3.00	1.50	.90
338	Phillies Team	7.50	3.75	2.25
339	Ryne Duren	3.00	1.50	.90
340	Tony Oliva	15.00	7.50	4.50
341	Bobby Bolin	3.00	1.50	.90
342	Bob Rodgers	3.00	1.50	.90
343	Mike McCormick	3.00	1.50	.90
344	Wes Parker	3.00	1.50	.90
345	Floyd Robinson	3.00	1.50	.90
346	Bobby Bragan	3.00	1.50	.90
347	Roy Face	3.00	1.50	.90
348	George Banks	3.00	1.50	.90
349	Larry Miller	3.00	1.50	.90
350	Mickey Mantle	525.00	250.00	150.00
351	Jim Perry	3.00	1.50	.90
352	Alex Johnson **RC**	3.50	1.75	1.00
353	Jerry Lumpe	3.00	1.50	.90
354	Cubs Rookies(Billy Ott, Jack Warner)	3.00	1.50	.90
355	Vada Pinson	8.00	4.00	2.50
356	Bill Spanswick	3.00	1.50	.90
357	Carl Warwick	3.00	1.50	.90
358	Albie Pearson	3.00	1.50	.90
359	Ken Johnson	3.00	1.50	.90
360	Orlando Cepeda	21.00	10.00	6.00
361	5th Series Checklist (353-429)	9.00	4.50	2.75
362	Don Schwall	3.00	1.50	.90
363	Bob Johnson	3.00	1.50	.90
364	Galen Cisco	3.00	1.50	.90
365	Jim Gentile	3.00	1.50	.90
366	Dan Schneider	3.00	1.50	.90
367	Leon Wagner	3.00	1.50	.90
368	White Sox Rookies(Ken Berry **RC**, Joel Gibson)	3.00	1.50	.90
369	Phil Linz	3.00	1.50	.90
370	Tommy Davis	3.00	1.50	.90
371	Frank Kreutzer	7.50	3.75	2.25
372	Clay Dalrymple	7.50	3.75	2.25
373	Curt Simmons	7.50	3.75	2.25
374	Angels Rookies(Jose Cardenal **RC**, Dick Simpson)	9.00	4.50	2.75
375	Dave Wickersham	7.50	3.75	2.25
376	Jim Landis	7.50	3.75	2.25
377	Willie Stargell	20.00	10.00	6.00
378	Chuck Estrada	7.50	3.75	2.25
379	Giants Team	10.00	5.00	3.00
380	Rocky Colavito	15.00	6.00	3.50
381	Al Jackson	7.50	3.75	2.25
382	J.C. Martin	7.50	3.75	2.25
383	Felipe Alou	9.00	4.50	2.75
384	Johnny Klippstein	7.50	3.75	2.25
385	Carl Yastrzemski	40.00	20.00	10.00
386	Cubs Rookies(Paul Jaeckel, Fred Norman)	7.50	3.75	2.25
387	Johnny Podres	9.00	4.50	2.75
388	John Blanchard	7.50	3.75	2.25
389	Don Larsen	7.50	3.75	2.25
390	Bill Freehan	7.50	3.75	2.25
391	Mel McGaha	7.50	3.75	2.25
392	Bob Friend	7.50	3.75	2.25
393	Ed Kirkpatrick	7.50	3.75	2.25
394	Jim Hannan	7.50	3.75	2.25
395	Jim Hart	7.50	3.75	2.25
396	Frank Bertaina	7.50	3.75	2.25
397	Jerry Buchek	7.50	3.75	2.25
398	Reds Rookies(Dan Neville, Art Shamsky **RC**)	7.50	3.75	2.25
399	Ray Herbert	7.50	3.75	2.25
400	Harmon Killebrew	50.00	25.00	12.50
401	Carl Willey	7.50	3.75	2.25
402	Joe Amalfitano	7.50	3.75	2.25
403	Red Sox Team	10.00	5.00	3.00
404	Stan Williams	7.50	3.75	2.25
405	John Roseboro	7.50	3.75	2.25
406	Ralph Terry	7.50	3.75	2.25
407	Lee Maye	7.50	3.75	2.25
408	Larry Sherry	7.50	3.75	2.25

			NM	EX	VG
409	Astros Rookies(Jim Beauchamp, Larry Dierker RC)	12.00	4.50	2.75
410	Luis Aparicio	17.50	8.75	5.25
411	Roger Craig	7.50	3.75	2.25
412	Bob Bailey	7.50	3.75	2.25
413	Hal Reniff	7.50	3.75	2.25
414	Al Lopez	12.50	6.25	3.75
415	Curt Flood	12.50	6.25	3.75
416	Jim Brewer	7.50	3.75	2.25
417	Ed Brinkman	7.50	3.75	2.25
418	Johnny Edwards	7.50	3.75	2.25
419	Ruben Amaro	7.50	3.75	2.25
420	Larry Jackson	7.50	3.75	2.25
421	Twins Rookies(Gary Dotter, Jay Ward)	7.50	3.75	2.25
422	Aubrey Gatewood	7.50	3.75	2.25
423	Jesse Gonder	7.50	3.75	2.25
424	Gary Bell	7.50	3.75	2.25
425	Wayne Causey	7.50	3.75	2.25
426	Braves Team	10.00	5.00	3.00
427	Bob Saverine	7.50	3.75	2.25
428	Bob Shaw	7.50	3.75	2.25
429	Don Demeter	7.50	3.75	2.25
430	Gary Peters	7.50	3.75	2.25
431	Cardinals Rookies(Nelson Briles RC, Wayne Spiezio)	9.00	4.50	2.75
432	Jim Grant	7.50	3.75	2.25
433	John Bateman	7.50	3.75	2.25
434	Dave Morehead	7.50	3.75	2.25
435	Willie Davis	7.50	3.75	2.25
436	Don Elston	7.50	3.75	2.25
437	Chico Cardenas	7.50	3.75	2.25
438	Harry Walker	7.50	3.75	2.25
439	Moe Drabowsky	7.50	3.75	2.25
440	Tom Tresh	12.50	6.25	3.75
441	Denver Lemaster	7.50	3.75	2.25
442	Vic Power	7.50	3.75	2.25
443	6th Series Checklist (430-506)	9.00	4.50	2.75
444	Bob Hendley	7.50	3.75	2.25
445	Don Lock	7.50	3.75	2.25
446	Art Mahaffey	7.50	3.75	2.25
447	Julian Javier	7.50	3.75	2.25
448	Lee Stange	7.50	3.75	2.25
449	Mets Rookies(Jerry Hinsley, Gary Kroll)	7.50	3.75	2.25
450	Elston Howard	15.00	6.00	3.50
451	Jim Owens	7.50	3.75	2.25
452	Gary Geiger	7.50	3.75	2.25
453	Dodgers Rookies(Willie Crawford RC, John Werhas)	7.50	3.75	2.25
454	Ed Rakow	7.50	3.75	2.25
455	Norm Siebern	7.50	3.75	2.25
456	Bill Henry	7.50	3.75	2.25
457	Bob Kennedy	7.50	3.75	2.25
458	John Buzhardt	7.50	3.75	2.25
459	Frank Kostro	7.50	3.75	2.25
460	Richie Allen	25.00	12.50	6.25
461	Braves Rookies(Clay Carroll RC, Phil Niekro)	30.00	15.00	7.50
462	Lew Krausse (Photo actually Pete Lovrich.)	7.50	3.75	2.25
463	Manny Mota	7.50	3.75	2.25
464	Ron Piche	7.50	3.75	2.25
465	Tom Haller	7.50	3.75	2.25
466	Senators Rookies(Pete Craig, Dick Nen)	7.50	3.75	2.25
467	Ray Washburn	7.50	3.75	2.25
468	Larry Brown	7.50	3.75	2.25
469	Don Nottebart	7.50	3.75	2.25
470	Yogi Berra	50.00	25.00	15.00
471	Billy Hoeft	7.50	3.75	2.25
472	Don Pavletich	7.50	3.75	2.25
473	Orioles Rookies(Paul Blair RC, Dave Johnson RC)	12.50	6.25	3.75
474	Cookie Rojas	7.50	3.75	2.25
475	Clete Boyer	10.00	5.00	3.00
476	Billy O'Dell	7.50	3.75	2.25
477	Cardinals Rookies(Fritz Ackley RC, Steve Carlton RC)	160.00	80.00	48.00
478	Wilbur Wood	7.50	3.75	2.25
479	Ken Harrelson	7.50	3.75	2.25
480	Joel Horlen	7.50	3.75	2.25
481	Indians Team	10.00	5.00	3.00
482	Bob Priddy	7.50	3.75	2.25
483	George Smith	7.50	3.75	2.25
484	Ron Perranoski	7.50	3.75	2.25
485	Nellie Fox	15.00	7.50	4.50
486	Angels Rookies(Tom Egan, Pat Rogan)	7.50	3.75	2.25
487	Woody Woodward	7.50	3.75	2.25
488	Ted Wills	7.50	3.75	2.25
489	Gene Mauch	7.50	3.75	2.25
490	Earl Battey	7.50	3.75	2.25
491	Tracy Stallard	7.50	3.75	2.25
492	Gene Freese	7.50	3.75	2.25
493	Tigers Rookies(Bruce Brubaker, Bill Roman)	7.50	3.75	2.25
494	Jay Ritchie	7.50	3.75	2.25
495	Joe Christopher	7.50	3.75	2.25
496	Joe Cunningham	7.50	3.75	2.25
497	Giants Rookies(Ken Henderson RC, Jack Hiatt)	7.50	3.75	2.25
498	Gene Stephens	7.50	3.75	2.25
499	Stu Miller	7.50	3.75	2.25
500	Ed Mathews	40.00	20.00	12.00
501	Indians Rookies(Ralph Gagliano, Jim Rittwage)	7.50	3.75	2.25
502	Don Cardwell	7.50	3.75	2.25
503	Phil Gagliano	7.50	3.75	2.25
504	Jerry Grote	7.50	3.75	2.25
505	Ray Culp	7.50	3.75	2.25
506	Sam Mele	7.50	3.75	2.25
507	Sammy Ellis	7.50	3.75	2.25
508a	7th Series Checklist (507-598) (Large print on front.)	9.00	4.50	2.75
508b	7th Series Checklist (507-598) (Small print on front.)	9.00	4.50	2.75
509	Red Sox Rookies(Bob Guindon, Gerry Vezendy)	7.50	3.75	2.25
510	Ernie Banks	75.00	40.00	20.00
511	Ron Locke	7.50	3.75	2.25
512	Cap Peterson	7.50	3.75	2.25
513	Yankees Team	30.00	15.00	7.50
514	Joe Azcue	7.50	3.75	2.25
515	Vern Law	7.50	3.75	2.25
516	Al Weis	7.50	3.75	2.25
517	Angels Rookies(Paul Schaal, Jack Warner)	7.50	3.75	2.25
518	Ken Rowe	7.50	3.75	2.25
519	Bob Uecker	20.00	10.00	5.00
520	Tony Cloninger	7.50	3.75	2.25
521	Phillies Rookies(Dave Bennett, Morrie Stevens)	7.50	3.75	2.25
522	Hank Aguirre	7.50	3.75	2.25
523	Mike Brumley (SP)	9.00	4.50	2.75
524	Dave Giusti (SP)	9.00	4.50	2.75
525	Eddie Bressoud	7.50	3.75	2.25
526	Athletics Rookies(Catfish Hunter RC, Rene Lachemann RC, Skip Lockwood RC, Johnny Odom RC) (SP)	80.00	40.00	20.00
527	Jeff Torborg (SP)	9.00	4.50	2.75
528	George Altman	7.50	3.75	2.25
529	Jerry Fosnow (SP)	9.00	4.50	2.75
530	Jim Maloney	7.50	3.75	2.25
531	Chuck Hiller	7.50	3.75	2.25
532	Hector Lopez	9.00	4.50	2.75
533	Mets Rookies(Jim Bethke, Tug McGraw RC, Dan Napoleon, Ron Swoboda RC) (SP)	25.00	12.50	6.25
534	John Herrnstein	7.50	3.75	2.25
535	Jack Kralick (SP)	9.00	4.50	2.75
536	Andre Rodgers (SP)	9.00	4.50	2.75
537	Angels Rookies(Marcelino Lopez, Rudy May RC, Phil Roof)	9.00	4.50	2.75
538	Chuck Dressen (SP)	9.00	4.50	2.75
539	Herm Starrette	7.50	3.75	2.25
540	Lou Brock (SP)	33.00	12.50	6.25
541	White Sox Rookies(Greg Bollo, Bob Locker)	7.50	3.75	2.25
542	Lou Klimchock	7.50	3.75	2.25
543	Ed Connolly (SP)	9.00	4.50	2.75
544	Howie Reed	7.50	3.75	2.25
545	Jesus Alou (SP)	9.00	4.50	2.75
546	Indians Rookies(Ray Barker, Bill Davis, Mike Hedlund, Floyd Weaver)	7.50	3.75	2.25
547	Jake Wood (SP)	9.00	4.50	2.75
548	Dick Stigman	7.50	3.75	2.25
549	Cubs Rookies(Glenn Beckert RC, Roberto Pena)	12.00	6.00	3.50
550	Mel Stottlemyre RC (SP)	28.00	12.50	6.25
551	Mets Team (SP)	16.00	8.00	4.75
552	Julio Gotay	7.50	3.75	2.25
553	Houston Rookies(Dan Coombs, Jack McClure, Gene Ratliff)	7.50	3.75	2.25
554	Chico Ruiz (SP)	9.00	4.50	2.75
555	Jack Baldschun (SP)	9.00	4.50	2.75
556	Red Schoendienst (SP)	12.50	6.25	3.75
557	Jose Santiago	7.50	3.75	2.25
558	Tommie Sisk	7.50	3.75	2.25
559	Ed Bailey (SP)	9.00	4.50	2.75
560	Boog Powell (SP)	10.00	5.00	3.00
561	Dodgers Rookies(Dennis Daboll, Mike Kekich RC, Jim Lefebvre RC, Hector Valle)	12.00	6.00	3.50
562	Billy Moran	7.50	3.75	2.25
563	Julio Navarro	7.50	3.75	2.25
564	Mel Nelson	7.50	3.75	2.25
565	Ernie Broglio (SP)	9.00	4.50	2.75
566	Yankees Rookies(Gil Blanco, Art Lopez, Ross Moschitto) (SP)	13.00	5.00	3.00
567	Tommie Aaron	7.50	3.75	2.25
568	Ron Taylor (SP)	9.00	4.50	2.75
569	Gino Cimoli (SP)	9.00	4.50	2.75
570	Claude Osteen (SP)	12.00	4.50	2.75
571	Ossie Virgil (SP)	9.00	4.50	2.75
572	**Orioles team** (SP)	15.00	7.50	4.50
573	Red Sox Rookies(Jim Lonborg RC, Gerry Moses, Mike Ryan, Bill Schlesinger) (SP)	13.50	6.75	4.00
574	Roy Sievers	7.50	3.75	2.25
575	Jose Pagan	7.50	3.75	2.25
576	Terry Fox (SP)	9.00	4.50	2.75
577	A.L. Rookies(Jim Buschhorn, Darold Knowles, Richie Scheinblum) (SP)	9.00	4.50	2.75
578	Camilo Carreon (SP)	9.00	4.50	2.75
579	Dick Smith (SP)	9.00	4.50	2.75
580	Jimmie Hall (SP)	9.00	4.50	2.75
581	N.L. Rookies(Kevin Collins, Tony Perez RC, Dave Ricketts) (SP)	80.00	40.00	20.00
582	Bob Schmidt (SP)	9.00	4.50	2.75
583	Wes Covington (SP)	9.00	4.50	2.75
584	Harry Bright	7.50	3.75	2.25
585	Hank Fischer	7.50	3.75	2.25
586	Tommy McCraw (SP)	9.00	4.50	2.75
587	Joe Sparma	7.50	3.75	2.25
588	Lenny Green	7.50	3.75	2.25
589	Giants Rookies(Frank Linzy, Bob Schroder) (SP)	9.00	4.50	2.75
590	Johnnie Wyatt	7.50	3.75	2.25
591	Bob Skinner (SP)	9.00	4.50	2.75
592	Frank Bork (SP)	9.00	4.50	2.75
593	Tigers Rookies(Jackie Moore, John Sullivan) (SP)	9.00	4.50	2.75
594	Joe Gaines	7.50	3.75	2.25
595	Don Lee	7.50	3.75	2.25
596	Don Landrum (SP)	9.00	4.50	2.75
597	Twins Rookies(Joe Nossek, Dick Reese, John Sevcik)	7.00	3.50	2.00
598	Al Downing (SP)	25.00	6.00	3.00

1965 Topps Embossed

Inserted in regular packs, the 2-1/8" x 3-1/2" Topps Embossed cards feature a 3-D profile portrait on gold foil-like cardboard (some collectors report finding the cards with silver cardboard). The player's name, team and position are below the portrait - which is good, because most of the embossed portraits are otherwise unrecognizeable. There is a gold border with American League players framed in blue and National Leaguers in red.

	NM	E	VG
Complete Set (72):	400.00	140.00	60.00
Common Player:	4.00	1.50	.60

1	Carl Yastrzemski	15.00	5.25	2.25
2	Ron Fairly	4.00	1.50	.60
3	Max Alvis	4.00	1.50	.60
4	Jim Ray Hart	4.00	1.50	.60
5	Bill Skowron	5.00	1.75	.70
6	Ed Kranepool	4.00	1.50	.60
7	Tim McCarver	5.00	1.75	.70
8	Sandy Koufax	30.00	15.00	9.00
9	Donn Clendenon	4.00	1.50	.60
10	John Romano	4.00	1.50	.60
11	Mickey Mantle	70.00	35.00	12.00
12	Joe Torre	6.00	2.00	.90
13	Al Kaline	15.00	5.25	2.25
14	Al McBean	4.00	1.50	.60
15	Don Drysdale	11.00	3.50	1.50
16	Brooks Robinson	12.50	4.50	2.00
17	Jim Bunning	9.00	3.25	1.25
18	Gary Peters	4.00	1.50	.60
19	Roberto Clemente	40.00	14.00	6.00
20	Milt Pappas	4.00	1.50	.60
21	Wayne Causey	4.00	1.50	.60
22	Frank Robinson	12.50	4.50	2.00
23	Bill Mazeroski	9.00	3.25	1.25
24	Diego Segui	4.00	1.50	.60
25	Jim Bouton	4.00	1.50	.60
26	Ed Mathews	10.00	3.50	1.50
27	Willie Mays	25.00	9.00	4.00
28	Ron Santo	6.00	2.00	.90
29	Boog Powell	6.00	2.00	.90
30	Ken McBride	4.00	1.50	.60
31	Leon Wagner	4.00	1.50	.60
32	John Callison	4.00	1.50	.60
33	Zoilo Versalles	4.00	1.50	.60
34	Jack Baldschun	4.00	1.50	.60
35	Ron Hunt	4.00	1.50	.60
36	Richie Allen	6.00	2.00	.90
37	Frank Malzone	4.00	1.50	.60
38	Bob Allison	4.00	1.50	.60
39	Jim Fregosi	4.00	1.50	.60
40	Billy Williams	9.00	3.25	1.25
41	Bill Freehan	4.00	1.50	.60
42	Vada Pinson	5.00	1.75	.70
43	Bill White	4.00	1.50	.60
44	Roy McMillan	4.00	1.50	.60
45	Orlando Cepeda	9.00	3.25	1.25
46	Rocky Colavito	7.50	2.75	1.25
47	Ken Boyer	5.00	1.75	.70
48	Dick Radatz	4.00	1.50	.60
49	Tommy Davis	4.00	1.50	.60
50	Walt Bond	4.00	1.50	.60
51	John Orsino	4.00	1.50	.60
52	Joe Christopher	4.00	1.50	.60
53	Al Spangler	4.00	1.50	.60
54	Jim King	4.00	1.50	.60
55	Mickey Lolich	4.00	1.50	.60
56	Harmon Killebrew	10.00	3.50	1.50
57	Bob Shaw	4.00	1.50	.60
58	Ernie Banks	15.00	5.25	2.25
59	Hank Aaron	25.00	9.00	4.00
60	Chuck Hinton	4.00	1.50	.60
61	Bob Aspromonte	4.00	1.50	.60
62	Lee Maye	4.00	1.50	.60
63	Joe Cunningham	4.00	1.50	.60
64	Pete Ward	4.00	1.50	.60
65	Bobby Richardson	6.00	2.00	.90
66	Dean Chance	4.00	1.50	.60
67	Dick Ellsworth	4.00	1.50	.60
68	Jim Maloney	4.00	1.50	.60
69	Bob Gibson	9.00	3.25	1.25
70	Earl Battey	4.00	1.50	.60
71	Tony Kubek	5.00	1.75	.70
72	Jack Kralick	4.00	1.50	.60

1965 Topps Push-Pull

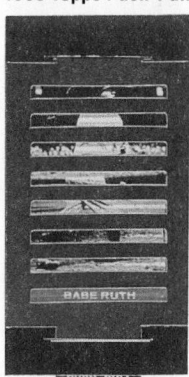

PUSH•PULL

Part of a 36-card set combining sports and non-sport subjects, the Push-Pull novelties have a louvered shutter attached to a tab at the bottom. When the tab is moved, from position to position, each of the underlying photos is revealed in turn. The cards measure 2-1/2" x 4-11/16". Backs are printed in black-and-white and contain biographical data. Three of the cards in the set feature baseball players.

	NM	E	VG
Complete Set (36):	3,650	1,800	1,050
(1) Lou Gehrig, Babe Ruth	500.00	250.00	150.00
(2) Casey Stengel Wins/ Loses	75.00	37.00	22.00
(3) Yogi Berra, Mickey Mantle	950.00	475.00	285.00

1965 Topps Transfers

Issued as strips of three players each as inserts in 1965, the Topps Transfers were 2" x 3" portraits of players. The transfers have blue or red bands at the top and bottom with the team name and position in the top band and the player's name in the bottom. As is so often the case, the superstars in the transfer set can be quite expensive, but like many of Topps non-card products, the common transfers are neither terribly expensive or popular today.

		NM	E	VG
Complete Set (72):		750.00	375.00	225.00
Common Player:		6.00	3.00	1.75
(1)	Hank Aaron	50.00	25.00	15.00
(2)	Richie Allen	12.00	6.00	3.50
(3)	Bob Allison	6.00	3.00	1.75
(4)	Max Alvis	6.00	3.00	1.75
(5)	Luis Aparicio	17.50	8.75	5.25
(6)	Bob Aspromonte	6.00	3.00	1.75
(7)	Walt Bond	6.00	3.00	1.75
(8)	Jim Bouton	9.00	4.50	2.75
(9)	Ken Boyer	10.00	5.00	3.00
(10)	Jim Bunning	17.50	8.75	5.25
(11)	John Callison	6.00	3.00	1.75
(12)	Rico Carty	6.00	3.00	1.75
(13)	Wayne Causey	6.00	3.00	1.75
(14)	Orlando Cepeda	17.50	8.75	5.25
(15)	Bob Chance	6.00	3.00	1.75
(16)	Dean Chance	6.00	3.00	1.75
(17)	Joe Christopher	6.00	3.00	1.75
(18)	Roberto Clemente	60.00	30.00	18.00
(19)	Rocky Colavito	15.00	7.50	4.50
(20)	Tony Conigliaro	10.00	5.00	3.00
(21)	Tommy Davis	6.00	3.00	1.75
(22)	Don Drysdale	17.50	8.75	5.25
(23)	Bill Freehan	6.00	3.00	1.75
(24)	Jim Fregosi	6.00	3.00	1.75
(25)	Bob Gibson	17.50	8.75	5.25
(26)	Dick Groat	6.00	3.00	1.75
(27)	Tom Haller	6.00	3.00	1.75
(28)	Chuck Hinton	6.00	3.00	1.75
(29)	Elston Howard	9.00	4.50	2.75
(30a)	Ron Hunt (shortstop)	9.00	4.50	2.75
(30b)	Ron Hunt (second base)	7.50	3.75	2.25
(31)	Al Jackson	6.00	3.00	1.75
(32)	Al Kaline	25.00	12.50	7.50
(33)	Harmon Killebrew	20.00	10.00	6.00
(34)	Jim King	6.00	3.00	1.75
(35)	Ron Kline	6.00	3.00	1.75
(36)	Bobby Knoop	6.00	3.00	1.75
(37)	Sandy Koufax	45.00	22.00	13.50
(38)	Ed Kranepool	6.00	3.00	1.75
(39)	Jim Maloney	6.00	3.00	1.75
(40)	Mickey Mantle	90.00	45.00	27.00
(41)	Juan Marichal	17.50	8.75	5.25
(42)	Lee Maye	6.00	3.00	1.75
(43)	Willie Mays	50.00	25.00	15.00
(44)	Bill Mazeroski	17.50	8.75	5.25
(45)	Tony Oliva	7.50	3.75	2.25
(46)	Jim O'Toole	6.00	3.00	1.75
(47)	Milt Pappas	6.00	3.00	1.75
(48)	Camilo Pascual	6.00	3.00	1.75
(49)	Gary Peters	6.00	3.00	1.75
(50)	Vada Pinson	6.00	3.00	1.75
(51)	Juan Pizarro	6.00	3.00	1.75
(52)	Boog Powell	10.00	5.00	3.00
(53)	Dick Radatz	6.00	3.00	1.75
(54)	Bobby Richardson	10.00	5.00	3.00
(55)	Brooks Robinson	20.00	10.00	6.00
(56)	Frank Robinson	20.00	10.00	6.00
(57)	Bob Rodgers	6.00	3.00	1.75
(58)	John Roseboro	6.00	3.00	1.75
(59)	Ron Santo	12.00	6.00	3.50
(60)	Diego Segui	6.00	3.00	1.75
(61)	Bill Skowron	9.00	4.50	2.75
(62)	Al Spangler	6.00	3.00	1.75
(63)	Dick Stuart	6.00	3.00	1.75
(64)	Luis Tiant	6.00	3.00	1.75
(65)	Joe Torre	12.00	6.00	3.50
(66)	Bob Veale	6.00	3.00	1.75
(67)	Leon Wagner	6.00	3.00	1.75
(68)	Pete Ward	6.00	3.00	1.75
(69)	Bill White	6.00	3.00	1.75
(70)	Dave Wickersham	6.00	3.00	1.75
(71)	Billy Williams	17.50	8.75	5.25
(72)	Carl Yastrzemski	25.00	12.50	7.50

1966 Topps

PETE ROSE   2nd base

In 1966, Topps produced another 598-card set. The 2-1/2" x 3-1/2" cards feature the traditional color photograph with a diagonal strip in the upper left-hand corner carrying the team name. A band at the bottom carries the player's name and position. Multi-player cards returned in 1966 after a year's hiatus. The statistical leader cards feature the categorical leader and two runners-up. Most team managers have cards as well. The 1966 set features a handful of cards found with or without a notice of the player's sale or trade to another team. Cards without the notice bring higher prices and are not included in the complete set prices. Some cards in the high series (#523-598) were short-printed - produced in lesser quantities than the rest of the series. They are valued somewhat higher than the others and are indicated in the checklist by an (SP) notation following the player name.

		NM	E	VG
Complete Set (598):		5,000	2,300	1,375
Common Player (1-370):		4.00	2.00	1.25
Common Player (371-446):		7.50	3.75	2.25
Common Player (447-522):		9.00	4.50	2.75
Common Player (523-598):		12.50	6.25	3.75
1	Willie Mays	240.00	125.00	62.50
2	Ted Abernathy	4.00	2.00	1.25
3	Sam Mele	4.00	2.00	1.25
4	Ray Culp	4.00	2.00	1.25
5	Jim Fregosi	4.00	2.00	1.25
6	Chuck Schilling	4.00	2.00	1.25
7	Tracy Stallard	4.00	2.00	1.25
8	Floyd Robinson	4.00	2.00	1.25
9	Clete Boyer	10.00	5.00	3.00
10	Tony Cloninger	4.00	2.00	1.25
11	Senators Rookies(Brant Alyea, Pete Craig)	4.00	2.00	1.25
12	John Tsitouris	4.00	2.00	1.25
13	Lou Johnson	4.00	2.00	1.25
14	Norm Siebern	4.00	2.00	1.25
15	Vern Law	4.00	2.00	1.25
16	Larry Brown	4.00	2.00	1.25
17	Johnny Stephenson	4.00	2.00	1.25
18	Roland Sheldon	4.00	2.00	1.25
19	Giants Team	7.50	3.75	2.25
20	Willie Horton	4.00	2.00	1.25
21	Don Nottebart	4.00	2.00	1.25
22	Joe Nossek	4.00	2.00	1.25
23	Jack Sanford	4.00	2.00	1.25
24	Don Kessinger **RC**	7.50	3.75	2.25
25	Pete Ward	4.00	2.00	1.25
26	Ray Sadecki	4.00	2.00	1.25
27	Orioles Rookies(Andy Etchebarren **RC**, Darold Knowles)	6.00	3.00	1.75
28	Phil Niekro	15.00	7.50	4.50
29	Mike Brumley	4.00	2.00	1.25
30	Pete Rose	80.00	40.00	20.00
31	Jack Cullen	4.00	2.00	1.25
32	Adolfo Phillips	4.00	2.00	1.25
33	Jim Pagliaroni	4.00	2.00	1.25

No.	Name			
34	1st Series Checklist (1-88)	7.50	3.75	2.25
35	Ron Swoboda	4.00	2.00	1.25
36	Jim Hunter	21.00	7.50	4.50
37	Billy Herman	6.00	3.00	1.75
38	Ron Nischwitz	4.00	2.00	1.25
39	Ken Henderson	4.00	2.00	1.25
40	Jim Grant	4.00	2.00	1.25
41	Don LeJohn	4.00	2.00	1.25
42	Aubrey Gatewood	4.00	2.00	1.25
43a	Don Landrum (No button on pants.)	4.00	2.00	1.25
43b	Don Landrum (Partial button on pants.)	6.00	3.00	1.75
43c	Don Landrum (Full button on pants.)	6.00	3.00	1.75
44	Indians Rookies(Bill Davis, Tom Kelley)	4.00	2.00	1.25
45	Jim Gentile	4.00	2.00	1.25
46	Howie Koplitz	4.00	2.00	1.25
47	J.C. Martin	4.00	2.00	1.25
48	Paul Blair	4.00	2.00	1.25
49	Woody Woodward	4.00	2.00	1.25
50	Mickey Mantle	325.00	130.00	80.00
51	Gordon Richardson	4.00	2.00	1.25
52	Power Plus(Johnny Callison, Wes Covington)	4.00	2.00	1.25
53	Bob Duliba	4.00	2.00	1.25
54	Jose Pagan	4.00	2.00	1.25
55	Ken Harrelson	4.00	2.00	1.25
56	Sandy Valdespino	4.00	2.00	1.25
57	Jim Lefebvre	4.00	2.00	1.25
58	Dave Wickersham	4.00	2.00	1.25
59	Reds Team	7.00	3.50	2.00
60	Curt Flood	7.50	3.60	2.25
61	Bob Bolin	4.00	2.00	1.25
62a	Merritt Ranew (No sold statement.)	20.00	10.00	6.00
62b	Merritt Ranew (With sold statement.)	4.00	2.00	1.25
63	Jim Stewart	4.00	2.00	1.25
64	Bob Bruce	4.00	2.00	1.25
65	Leon Wagner	4.00	2.00	1.25
66	Al Weis	4.00	2.00	1.25
67	Mets Rookies(Cleon Jones, Dick Selma)	4.00	2.00	1.25
68	Hal Reniff	4.00	2.00	1.25
69	Ken Hamlin	4.00	2.00	1.25
70	Carl Yastrzemski	25.00	12.50	6.25
71	Frank Carpin	4.00	2.00	1.25
72	Tony Perez	25.00	12.50	6.25
73	Jerry Zimmerman	4.00	2.00	1.25
74	Don Mossi	4.00	2.00	1.25
75	Tommy Davis	4.00	2.00	1.25
76	Red Schoendienst	7.50	3.75	2.25
77	Johnny Orsino	4.00	2.00	1.25
78	Frank Linzy	4.00	2.00	1.25
79	Joe Pepitone	8.00	4.00	2.50
80	Richie Allen	6.00	3.00	1.75
81	Ray Oyler	4.00	2.00	1.25
82	Bob Hendley	4.00	2.00	1.25
83	Albie Pearson	4.00	2.00	1.25
84	Braves Rookies(Jim Beauchamp, Dick Kelley)	4.00	2.00	1.25
85	Eddie Fisher	4.00	2.00	1.25
86	John Bateman	4.00	2.00	1.25
87	Dan Napoleon	4.00	2.00	1.25
88	Fred Whitfield	4.00	2.00	1.25
89	Ted Davidson	4.00	2.00	1.25
90	Luis Aparicio	15.00	7.50	4.50
91a	Bob Uecker (No trade statement.)	60.00	30.00	18.00
91b	Bob Uecker (With trade statement.)	20.00	10.00	6.00
92	Yankees Team	21.00	10.00	6.00
93	Jim Lonborg	4.00	2.00	1.25
94	Matty Alou	4.00	2.00	1.25
95	Pete Richert	4.00	2.00	1.25
96	Felipe Alou	6.00	3.00	1.75
97	Jim Merritt	4.00	2.00	1.25
98	Don Demeter	4.00	2.00	1.25
99	Buc Belters(Donn Clendenon, Willie Stargell)	8.00	4.00	2.50
100	Sandy Koufax	100.00	50.00	25.00
101a	2nd Series Checklist (89-176) (115 is Spahn)	12.50	6.25	3.75
101b	2nd Series Checklist (89-176) (115 is Henry)	7.50	3.75	2.25
102	Ed Kirkpatrick	4.00	2.00	1.25
103a	Dick Groat (No trade statement.)	21.00	10.00	6.00
103b	Dick Groat (With trade statement.)	4.00	2.00	1.25
104a	Alex Johnson (No trade statement.)	20.00	10.00	6.00
104b	Alex Johnson (With trade statement.)	4.00	2.00	1.25
105	Milt Pappas	4.00	2.00	1.25
106	Rusty Staub	6.00	3.00	1.75
107	Athletics Rookies(Larry Stahl, Ron Tompkins)	4.00	2.00	1.25
108	Bobby Klaus	4.00	2.00	1.25
109	Ralph Terry	4.00	2.00	1.25
110	Ernie Banks	33.00	15.00	9.00
111	Gary Peters	4.00	2.00	1.25
112	Manny Mota	4.00	2.00	1.25
113	Hank Aguirre	4.00	2.00	1.25
114	Jim Gosger	4.00	2.00	1.25
115	Bill Henry	4.00	2.00	1.25
116	Walt Alston	6.00	3.00	1.75
117	Jake Gibbs	4.00	2.00	1.25
118	Mike McCormick	4.00	2.00	1.25
119	Art Shamsky	4.00	2.00	1.25
120	Harmon Killebrew	23.00	12.00	6.00
121	Ray Herbert	4.00	2.00	1.25
122	Joe Gaines	4.00	2.00	1.25
123	Pirates Rookies(Frank Bork, Jerry May)	4.00	2.00	1.25
124	Tug McGraw	4.00	2.00	1.25
125	Lou Brock	28.00	14.00	8.00
126	Jim Palmer RC	85.00	40.00	24.00
127	Ken Berry	4.00	2.00	1.25
128	Jim Landis	4.00	2.00	1.25
129	Jack Kralick	4.00	2.00	1.25
130	Joe Torre	6.00	3.00	1.75
131	Angels Team	7.50	3.75	2.25
132	Orlando Cepeda	15.00	7.50	4.50
133	Don McMahon	4.00	2.00	1.25
134	Wes Parker	4.00	2.00	1.25
135	Dave Morehead	4.00	2.00	1.25
136	Woody Held	4.00	2.00	1.25
137	Pat Corrales	4.00	2.00	1.25
138	Roger Repoz	4.00	2.00	1.25
139	Cubs Rookies(Byron Browne, Don Young)	4.00	2.00	1.25
140	Jim Maloney	4.00	2.00	1.25
141	Tom McCraw	4.00	2.00	1.25
142	Don Dennis	4.00	2.00	1.25
143	Jose Tartabull	4.00	2.00	1.25
144	Don Schwall	4.00	2.00	1.25
145	Bill Freehan	4.00	2.00	1.25
146	George Altman	4.00	2.00	1.25
147	Lum Harris	4.00	2.00	1.25
148	Bob Johnson	4.00	2.00	1.25
149	Dick Nen	4.00	2.00	1.25
150	Rocky Colavito	12.00	6.00	3.50
151	Gary Wagner	4.00	2.00	1.25
152	Frank Malzone	4.00	2.00	1.25
153	Rico Carty	4.00	2.00	1.25
154	Chuck Hiller	4.00	2.00	1.25
155	Marcelino Lopez	4.00	2.00	1.25
156	D P Combo(Hal Lanier, Dick Schofield)	4.00	2.00	1.25
157	Rene Lachemann	4.00	2.00	1.25
158	Jim Brewer	4.00	2.00	1.25
159	Chico Ruiz	4.00	2.00	1.25
160	Whitey Ford	35.00	17.50	8.75
161a	Jerry Lumpe	4.00	2.00	1.25
161b	Jerry Lumpe (wedge missing from name plate on front)	4.00	2.00	1.25
162	Lee Maye	4.00	2.00	1.25
163	Tito Francona	4.00	2.00	1.25
164	White Sox Rookies(Tommie Agee, Marv Staehle)	4.00	2.00	1.25
165	Don Lock	4.00	2.00	1.25
166	Chris Krug	4.00	2.00	1.25
167	Boog Powell	6.00	3.00	1.75
168	Dan Osinski	4.00	2.00	1.25
169	Duke Sims	4.00	2.00	1.25
170	Cookie Rojas	4.00	2.00	1.25
171	Nick Willhite	4.00	2.00	1.25
172	Mets Team	6.00	3.00	1.75
173	Al Spangler	4.00	2.00	1.25
174	Ron Taylor	4.00	2.00	1.25
175	Bert Campaneris	4.00	2.00	1.25
176	Jim Davenport	4.00	2.00	1.25
177	Hector Lopez	4.00	2.00	1.25
178	Bob Tillman	4.00	2.00	1.25
179	Cardinals Rookies(Dennis Aust, Bob Tolan)	4.00	2.00	1.25
180	Vada Pinson	7.50	3.75	2.25
181	Al Worthington	4.00	2.00	1.25
182	Jerry Lynch	4.00	2.00	1.25
183a	3rd Series Checklist (177-264) (Large print on front.)	7.50	3.75	2.25
183b	3rd Series Checklist (177-264) (Small print on front.)	9.00	4.50	2.75
184	Denis Menke	4.00	2.00	1.25
185	Bob Buhl	4.00	2.00	1.25
186	Ruben Amaro	4.00	2.00	1.25
187	Chuck Dressen	4.00	2.00	1.25
188	Al Luplow	4.00	2.00	1.25
189	John Roseboro	4.00	2.00	1.25
190	Jimmie Hall	4.00	2.00	1.25
191	Darrell Sutherland	4.00	2.00	1.25
192	Vic Power	4.00	2.00	1.25
193	Dave McNally	4.00	2.00	1.25
194	Senators Team	6.00	3.00	1.75
195	Joe Morgan	30.00	12.50	7.50
196	Don Pavletich	4.00	2.00	1.25
197	Sonny Siebert	4.00	2.00	1.25
198	Mickey Stanley RC	6.00	3.00	1.75
199	Chisox Clubbers(Floyd Robinson, Johnny Romano, Bill Skowron)	6.00	3.00	1.75
200	Ed Mathews	20.00	10.00	6.00
201	Jim Dickson	4.00	2.00	1.25
202	Clay Dalrymple	4.00	2.00	1.25
203	Jose Santiago	4.00	2.00	1.25
204	Cubs Team	7.50	3.75	2.25
205	Tom Tresh	9.00	4.50	2.75
206	Alvin Jackson	4.00	2.00	1.25
207	Frank Quilici	4.00	2.00	1.25
208	Bob Miller	4.00	2.00	1.25
209	Tigers Rookies(Fritz Fisher, John Hiller RC)	4.00	2.00	1.25
210	Bill Mazeroski	17.50	8.75	5.25
211	Frank Kreutzer	4.00	2.00	1.25
212	Ed Kranepool	4.00	2.00	1.25
213	Fred Newman	4.00	2.00	1.25
214	Tommy Harper	4.00	2.00	1.25
215	N.L. Batting Leaders(Hank Aaron, Roberto Clemente, Willie Mays)	55.00	25.00	15.00
216	A.L. Batting Leaders(Vic Davalillo, Tony Oliva, Carl Yastrzemski)	21.00	10.00	4.75
217	N.L. Home Run Leaders(Willie Mays, Willie McCovey, Billy Williams)	22.50	10.00	3.75
218	A.L. Home Run Leaders(Norm Cash, Tony Conigliaro, Willie Horton)	12.50	6.25	3.75
219	N.L. RBI Leaders(Deron Johnson, Willie Mays, Frank Robinson)	15.00	7.50	3.75
220	A.L. RBI Leaders(Rocky Colavito, Willie Horton, Tony Oliva)	12.00	6.00	3.50
221	N.L. ERA Leaders(Sandy Koufax, Vern Law, Juan Marichal)	15.00	7.50	4.50
222	A.L. ERA Leaders(Eddie Fisher, Sam McDowell, Sonny Siebert)	6.00	3.00	1.75
223	N.L. Pitching Leaders(Tony Cloninger, Don Drysdale, Sandy Koufax)	16.00	8.00	4.75
224	A.L. Pitching Leaders(Jim Grant, Jim Kaat, Mel Stottlemyre)	9.00	4.50	2.75
225	N.L. Strikeout Leaders(Bob Gibson, Sandy Koufax, Bob Veale)	18.00	9.00	5.40
226	A.L. Strikeout Leaders(Mickey Lolich, Sam McDowell, Denny McLain, Sonny Siebert)	10.00	5.00	3.00
227	Russ Nixon	4.00	2.00	1.25
228	Larry Dierker	4.00	2.00	1.25
229	Hank Bauer	4.50	2.25	1.25
230	Johnny Callison	4.00	2.00	1.25
231	Floyd Weaver	4.00	2.00	1.25
232	Glenn Beckert	4.00	2.00	1.25
233	Dom Zanni	4.00	2.00	1.25
234	Yankees Rookies(Rich Beck, Roy White RC)	15.00	7.50	4.50
235	Don Cardwell	4.00	2.00	1.25
236	Mike Hershberger	4.00	2.00	1.25
237	Billy O'Dell	4.00	2.00	1.25
238	Dodgers Team	9.00	4.50	2.75
239	Orlando Pena	4.00	2.00	1.25
240	Earl Battey	4.00	2.00	1.25
241	Dennis Ribant	4.00	2.00	1.25
242	Jesus Alou	4.00	2.00	1.25
243	Nelson Briles	4.00	2.00	1.25
244	Astros Rookies(Chuck Harrison, Sonny Jackson)	4.00	2.00	1.25

245	John Buzhardt	4.00	2.00	1.25
246	Ed Bailey	4.00	2.00	1.25
247	Carl Warwick	4.00	2.00	1.25
248	Pete Mikkelsen	4.00	2.00	1.25
249	Bill Rigney	4.00	2.00	1.25
250	Sam Ellis	4.00	2.00	1.25
251	Ed Brinkman	4.00	2.00	1.25
252	Denver Lemaster	4.00	2.00	1.25
253	Don Wert	4.00	2.00	1.25
254	Phillies Rookies(Fergie Jenkins **RC**, Bill Sorrell)	68.00	34.00	18.00
255	Willie Stargell	20.00	10.00	6.00
256	Lew Krausse	4.00	2.00	1.25
257	Jeff Torborg	4.00	2.00	1.25
258	Dave Giusti	4.00	2.00	1.25
259	Red Sox Team	7.50	3.75	2.25
260	Bob Shaw	4.00	2.00	1.25
261	Ron Hansen	4.00	2.00	1.25
262	Jack Hamilton	4.00	2.00	1.25
263	Tom Egan	4.00	2.00	1.25
264	Twins Rookies(Andy Kosco, Ted Uhlaender)	4.00	2.00	1.25
265	Stu Miller	4.00	2.00	1.25
266	Pedro Gonzalez	4.00	2.00	1.25
267	Joe Sparma	4.00	2.00	1.25
268	John Blanchard	4.00	2.00	1.25
269	Don Heffner	4.00	2.00	1.25
270	Claude Osteen	4.00	2.00	1.25
271	Hal Lanier	4.00	2.00	1.25
272	Jack Baldschun	4.00	2.00	1.25
273	Astro Aces(Bob Aspromonte, Rusty Staub)	6.00	3.00	1.75
274	Buster Narum	4.00	2.00	1.25
275	Tim McCarver	10.00	5.00	3.00
276	Jim Bouton	6.00	3.00	1.75
277	George Thomas	4.00	2.00	1.25
278	Calvin Koonce	4.00	2.00	1.25
279a	4th Series Checklist (265-352) (Player's cap black.)	7.00	3.50	2.00
279b	4th Series Checklist (265-352) (Player's cap red.)	7.50	3.75	2.25
280	Bobby Knoop	4.00	2.00	1.25
281	Bruce Howard	4.00	2.00	1.25
282	Johnny Lewis	4.00	2.00	1.25
283	Jim Perry	4.00	2.00	1.25
284	Bobby Wine	4.00	2.00	1.25
285	Luis Tiant	4.00	2.00	1.25
286	Gary Geiger	4.00	2.00	1.25
287	Jack Aker	4.00	2.00	1.25
288	Dodgers Rookies(Bill Singer **RC**, Don Sutton **RC**)	60.00	30.00	15.00
289	Larry Sherry	4.00	2.00	1.25
290	Ron Santo	12.50	6.25	3.75
291	Moe Drabowsky	4.00	2.00	1.25
292	Jim Coker	4.00	2.00	1.25
293	Mike Shannon	4.00	2.00	1.25
294	Steve Ridzik	4.00	2.00	1.25
295	Jim Hart	4.00	2.00	1.25
296	Johnny Keane	4.00	2.00	1.25
297	Jim Owens	4.00	2.00	1.25
298	Rico Petrocelli	6.00	3.00	1.75
299	Lou Burdette	4.00	2.00	1.25
300	Bob Clemente	140.00	70.00	35.00
301	Greg Bollo	4.00	2.00	1.25
302	Ernie Bowman	4.00	2.00	1.25
303a	Indians Team (Dot between "PLACE" and "AMERICAN.")	6.00	3.00	1.75
303b	Indians Team (No dot.)	6.00	3.00	1.75
304	John Herrnstein	4.00	2.00	1.25
305	Camilo Pascual	4.00	2.00	1.25
306	Ty Cline	4.00	2.00	1.25
307	Clay Carroll	4.00	2.00	1.25
308	Tom Haller	4.00	2.00	1.25
309	Diego Segui	4.00	2.00	1.25
310	Frank Robinson	30.00	15.00	7.50
311	Reds Rookies(Tommy Helms, Dick Simpson)	4.00	2.00	1.25
312	Bob Saverine	4.00	2.00	1.25
313	Chris Zachary	4.00	2.00	1.25
314	Hector Valle	4.00	2.00	1.25
315	Norm Cash	11.00	5.50	3.25
316	Jack Fisher	4.00	2.00	1.25
317	Dalton Jones	4.00	2.00	1.25
318	Harry Walker	4.00	2.00	1.25
319	Gene Freese	4.00	2.00	1.25
320	Bob Gibson	30.00	15.00	9.00
321	Rick Reichardt	4.00	2.00	1.25
322	Bill Faul	4.00	2.00	1.25
323	Ray Barker	4.00	2.00	1.25
324	John Boozer	4.00	2.00	1.25
325	Vic Davalillo	4.00	2.00	1.25

326a	Braves Team (Dot between "PLACE" and "NATIONAL.")	7.50	3.75	2.25
326b	Braves Team (No dot.)	7.50	3.75	2.25
327	Bernie Allen	4.00	2.00	1.25
328	Jerry Grote	4.00	2.00	1.25
329	Pete Charton	4.00	2.00	1.25
330	Ron Fairly	4.00	2.00	1.25
331	Ron Herbel	4.00	2.00	1.25
332	Billy Bryan	4.00	2.00	1.25
333	Senators Rookies(Joe Coleman **RC**, Jim French)	4.00	2.00	1.25
334	Marty Keough	4.00	2.00	1.25
335	Juan Pizarro	4.00	2.00	1.25
336	Gene Alley	4.00	2.00	1.25
337	Fred Gladding	4.00	2.00	1.25
338	Dal Maxvill	4.00	2.00	1.25
339	Del Crandall	4.00	2.00	1.25
340	Dean Chance	4.00	2.00	1.25
341	Wes Westrum	4.00	2.00	1.25
342	Bob Humphreys	4.00	2.00	1.25
343	Joe Christopher	4.00	2.00	1.25
344	Steve Blass	4.00	2.00	1.25
345	Bob Allison	4.00	2.00	1.25
346	Mike de la Hoz	4.00	2.00	1.25
347	Phil Regan	4.00	2.00	1.25
348	**Orioles Team**	8.00	4.00	2.50
349	Cap Peterson	4.00	2.00	1.25
350	Mel Stottlemyre	6.00	3.00	1.75
351	Fred Valentine	4.00	2.00	1.25
352	Bob Aspromonte	4.00	2.00	1.25
353	Al McBean	4.00	2.00	1.25
354	Smoky Burgess	4.00	2.00	1.25
355	Wade Blasingame	4.00	2.00	1.25
356	Red Sox Rookies(Owen Johnson, Ken Sanders)	4.00	2.00	1.25
357	Gerry Arrigo	4.00	2.00	1.25
358	Charlie Smith	4.00	2.00	1.25
359	Johnny Briggs	4.00	2.00	1.25
360	Ron Hunt	4.00	2.00	1.25
361	Tom Satriano	4.00	2.00	1.25
362	Gates Brown	4.00	2.00	1.25
363	5th Series Checklist (353-429)	9.00	4.50	2.75
364	Nate Oliver	4.00	2.00	1.25
365	Roger Maris	60.00	30.00	18.00
366	Wayne Causey	4.00	2.00	1.25
367	Mel Nelson	4.00	2.00	1.25
368	Charlie Lau	4.00	2.00	1.25
369	Jim King	4.00	2.00	1.25
370	Chico Cardenas	4.00	2.00	1.25
371	Lee Stange	7.50	3.75	2.25
372	Harvey Kuenn	7.50	3.75	2.25
373	Giants Rookies(Dick Estelle, Jack Hiatt)	7.50	3.75	2.25
374	Bob Locker	7.50	3.75	2.25
375	Donn Clendenon	7.50	3.75	2.25
376	Paul Schaal	7.50	3.75	2.25
377	Turk Farrell	7.50	3.75	2.25
378	Dick Tracewski	7.50	3.75	2.25
379	Cards Team	10.00	5.00	3.00
380	Tony Conigliaro	12.50	6.25	3.75
381	Hank Fischer	7.50	3.75	2.25
382	Phil Roof	7.50	3.75	2.25
383	Jackie Brandt	7.50	3.75	2.25
384	Al Downing	7.50	3.75	2.25
385	Ken Boyer	10.00	5.00	3.00
386	Gil Hodges	11.00	5.50	3.25
387	Howie Reed	7.50	3.75	2.25
388	Don Mincher	7.50	3.75	2.25
389	Jim O'Toole	7.50	3.75	2.25
390	Brooks Robinson	40.00	20.00	10.00
391	Chuck Hinton	7.50	3.75	2.25
392	Cubs Rookies(Bill Hands **RC**, Randy Hundley **RC**)	12.00	6.00	3.50
393	George Brunet	7.50	3.75	2.25
394	Ron Brand	7.50	3.75	2.25
395	Len Gabrielson	7.50	3.75	2.25
396	Jerry Stephenson	7.50	3.75	2.25
397	Bill White	7.50	3.75	2.25
398	Danny Cater	7.50	3.75	2.25
399	Ray Washburn	7.50	3.75	2.25
400	Zoilo Versalles	7.50	3.75	2.25
401	Ken McMullen	7.50	3.75	2.25
402	Jim Hickman	7.50	3.75	2.25
403	Fred Talbot	7.50	3.75	2.25
404a	Pirates Team (Dot between "PLACE" and "NATIONAL.")	12.50	6.25	3.75
404b	Pirates Team (No dot.)	12.50	6.25	3.75
405	Elston Howard	9.00	4.50	2.75
406	Joe Jay	7.50	3.75	2.25
407	John Kennedy	7.50	3.75	2.25
408	Lee Thomas	7.50	3.75	2.25
409	Billy Hoeft	7.50	3.75	2.25
410	Al Kaline	40.00	20.00	10.00
411	Gene Mauch	7.50	3.75	2.25

412	Sam Bowens	7.50	3.75	2.25
413	John Romano	7.50	3.75	2.25
414	Dan Coombs	7.50	3.75	2.25
415	Max Alvis	7.50	3.75	2.25
416	Phil Ortega	7.50	3.75	2.25
417	Angels Rookies(Jim McGlothlin, Ed Sukla)	7.50	3.75	2.25
418	Phil Gagliano	7.50	3.75	2.25
419	Mike Ryan	7.50	3.75	2.25
420	Juan Marichal	15.00	7.50	3.75
421	Roy McMillan	7.50	3.75	2.25
422	Ed Charles	7.50	3.75	2.25
423	Ernie Broglio	7.50	3.75	2.25
424	Reds Rookies(Lee May **RC**, Darrell Osteen)	10.00	5.00	3.00
425	Bob Veale	7.50	3.75	2.25
426	White Sox Team	10.00	5.00	3.00
427	John Miller	7.50	3.75	2.25
428	Sandy Alomar	7.50	3.75	2.25
429	Bill Monbouquette	7.50	3.75	2.25
430	Don Drysdale	23.00	10.00	6.00
431	Walt Bond	7.50	3.75	2.25
432	Bob Heffner	7.50	3.75	2.25
433	Alvin Dark	7.50	3.75	2.25
434	Willie Kirkland	7.50	3.75	2.25
435	Jim Bunning	15.00	7.50	4.50
436	Julian Javier	7.50	3.75	2.25
437	Al Stanek	7.50	3.75	2.25
438	Willie Smith	7.50	3.75	2.25
439	Pedro Ramos	7.50	3.75	2.25
440	Deron Johnson	7.50	3.75	2.25
441	Tommie Sisk	7.50	3.75	2.25
442	Orioles Rookies(Ed Barnowski, Eddie Watt)	7.50	3.75	2.25
443	Bill Wakefield	7.50	3.75	2.25
444a	6th Series Checklist (430-506) (456 is R. Sox Rookies)	7.50	3.75	2.25
444b	6th Series Checklist (430-506) (456 is Red Sox Rookies)	9.00	4.50	2.75
445	Jim Kaat	9.00	4.50	2.75
446	Mack Jones	7.50	3.75	2.25
447	Dick Ellsworth (Photo actually Ken Hubbs.)	12.50	6.25	3.75
448	Eddie Stanky	9.00	4.50	2.75
449	Joe Moeller	9.00	4.50	2.75
450	Tony Oliva	15.00	7.50	4.50
451	Barry Latman	9.00	4.50	2.75
452	Joe Azcue	9.00	4.50	2.75
453	Ron Kline	9.00	4.50	2.75
454	Jerry Buchek	9.00	4.50	2.75
455	Mickey Lolich	9.00	4.50	2.75
456	Red Sox Rookies(Darrell Brandon, Joe Foy)	9.00	4.50	2.75
457	Joe Gibbon	9.00	4.50	2.75
458	Manny Jiminez (Jimenez)	9.00	4.50	2.75
459	Bill McCool	9.00	4.50	2.75
460	Curt Blefary	9.00	4.50	2.75
461	Roy Face	9.00	4.50	2.75
462	Bob Rodgers	9.00	4.50	2.75
463	**Phillies Team**	12.00	6.00	3.50
464	Larry Bearnarth	9.00	4.50	2.75
465	Don Buford	9.00	4.50	2.75
466	Ken Johnson	9.00	4.50	2.75
467	Vic Roznovsky	9.00	4.50	2.75
468	Johnny Podres	9.00	4.50	2.75
469	Yankees Rookies(Bobby Murcer **RC**, Dooley Womack)	30.00	15.00	7.50
470	Sam McDowell	9.00	4.50	2.75
471	Bob Skinner	9.00	4.50	2.75
472	Terry Fox	9.00	4.50	2.75
473	Rich Rollins	9.00	4.50	2.75
474	Dick Schofield	9.00	4.50	2.75
475	Dick Radatz	9.00	4.50	2.75
476	Bobby Bragan	9.00	4.50	2.75
477	Steve Barber	9.00	4.50	2.75
478	Tony Gonzalez	9.00	4.50	2.75
479	Jim Hannan	9.00	4.50	2.75
480	Dick Stuart	9.00	4.50	2.75
481	Bob Lee	9.00	4.50	2.75
482	Cubs Rookies(John Boccabella, Dave Dowling)	9.00	4.50	2.75
483	Joe Nuxhall	9.00	4.50	2.75
484	Wes Covington	9.00	4.50	2.75
485	Bob Bailey	9.00	4.50	2.75
486	Tommy John	9.00	4.50	2.75
487	Al Ferrara	9.00	4.50	2.75
488	George Banks	9.00	4.50	2.75
489	Curt Simmons	9.00	4.50	2.75
490	Bobby Richardson	20.00	10.00	5.00
491	Dennis Bennett	9.00	4.50	2.75
492	Athletics Team	12.00	6.00	3.50
493	Johnny Klippstein	9.00	4.50	2.75
494	Gordon Coleman	9.00	4.50	2.75
495	Dick McAuliffe	9.00	4.50	2.75

496	Lindy McDaniel	9.00	4.50	2.75
497	Chris Cannizzaro	9.00	4.50	2.75
498	Pirates Rookies(Woody Fryman RC, Luke Walker)	9.00	4.50	2.75
499	Wally Bunker	9.00	4.50	2.75
500	Hank Aaron	115.00	62.50	31.25
501	John O'Donoghue	9.00	4.50	2.75
502	Lenny Green	9.00	4.50	2.75
503	Steve Hamilton	9.00	4.50	2.75
504	Grady Hatton	9.00	4.50	2.75
505	Jose Cardenal	9.00	4.50	2.75
506	Bo Belinsky	9.00	4.50	2.75
507	John Edwards	9.00	4.50	2.75
508	Steve Hargan RC	9.00	4.50	2.75
509	Jake Wood	9.00	4.50	2.75
510	Hoyt Wilhelm	16.00	8.00	4.75
511	Giants Rookies(Bob Barton, Tito Fuentes RC)	9.00	4.50	2.75
512	Dick Stigman	9.00	4.50	2.75
513	Camilo Carreon	9.00	4.50	2.75
514	Hal Woodeshick	9.00	4.50	2.75
515	Frank Howard	9.00	4.50	2.75
516	Eddie Bressoud	9.00	4.50	2.75
517a	7th Series Checklist (507-598) (529 is W. Sox Rookies)	11.00	5.50	3.25
517b	7th Series Checklist (507-598) (529 is White Sox Rookies)	13.50	6.75	4.00
518	Braves Rookies(Herb Hippauf, Arnie Umbach)	9.00	4.50	2.75
519	Bob Friend	9.00	4.50	2.75
520	Jim Wynn	9.00	4.50	2.75
521	John Wyatt	9.00	4.50	2.75
522	Phil Linz	9.00	4.50	2.75
523	Bob Sadowski	12.50	6.25	3.75
524	Giants Rookies(Ollie Brown, Don Mason) (SP)	16.00	8.00	4.75
525	Gary Bell (SP)	16.00	8.00	4.75
526	Twins Team (SP)	75.00	37.50	18.75
527	Julio Navarro	12.50	6.25	3.75
528	Jesse Gonder (SP)	16.00	8.00	4.75
529	White Sox Rookies(Lee Elia RC, Dennis Higgins, Bill Voss)	12.50	6.25	3.75
530	Robin Roberts	40.00	20.00	10.00
531	Joe Cunningham	12.50	6.25	3.75
532	Aurelio Monteagudo (SP)	16.00	8.00	4.75
533	Jerry Adair (SP)	16.00	8.00	4.75
534	Mets Rookies(Dave Eilers, Rob Gardner)	12.50	6.25	3.75
535	Willie Davis (SP)	16.00	8.00	4.75
536	Dick Egan	12.50	6.25	3.75
537	Herman Franks	12.50	6.25	3.75
538	Bob Allen (SP)	16.00	8.00	4.75
539	Astros Rookies(Bill Heath, Carroll Sembera)	12.50	6.25	3.75
540	Denny McLain (SP)	50.00	25.00	15.00
541	Gene Oliver (SP)	16.00	8.00	4.75
542	George Smith	12.50	6.25	3.75
543	Roger Craig (SP)	16.00	8.00	4.75
544	Cardinals Rookies(Joe Hoerner, George Kernek, Jimmy Williams) (SP)	16.00	8.00	4.75
545	Dick Green (SP)	16.00	8.00	4.75
546	Dwight Siebler	12.50	6.25	3.75
547	Horace Clarke RC (SP)	45.00	22.50	11.25
548	Gary Kroll (SP)	16.00	8.00	4.75
549	Senators Rookies(Al Closter, Casey Cox)	12.50	6.25	3.75
550	Willie McCovey (SP)	95.00	50.00	25.00
551	Bob Purkey (SP)	16.00	8.00	4.75
552	Birdie Tebbetts (SP)	16.00	8.00	4.75
553	Major League Rookies(Pat Garrett, Jackie Warner)	12.50	6.25	3.75
554	Jim Northrup (SP)	16.00	8.00	4.75
555	Ron Perranoski (SP)	16.00	8.00	4.75
556	Mel Queen (SP)	16.00	8.00	4.75
557	Felix Mantilla (SP)	16.00	8.00	4.75
558	Red Sox Rookies(Guido Grilli, Pete Magrini, George Scott RC)	20.00	10.00	6.00
559	Roberto Pena (SP)	16.00	8.00	4.75
560	Joel Horlen	12.50	6.25	3.75
561	Choo Choo Coleman (SP)	25.00	12.50	6.25
562	Russ Snyder	12.50	6.25	3.75
563	Twins Rookies(Pete Cimino, Cesar Tovar)	12.50	6.25	3.75
564	Bob Chance (SP)	16.00	8.00	4.75
565	Jimmy Piersall (SP)	35.00	17.50	8.75
566	Mike Cuellar (SP)	16.00	8.00	4.75

567	Dick Howser (SP)	16.00	8.00	4.75
568	Athletics Rookies(Paul Lindblad, Ron Stone)	12.50	6.25	3.75
569	Orlando McFarlane (SP)	16.00	8.00	4.75
570	Art Mahaffey (SP)	16.00	8.00	4.75
571	Dave Roberts (SP)	16.00	8.00	4.75
572	Bob Priddy	12.50	6.25	3.75
573	Derrell Griffith	12.50	6.25	3.75
574	Mets Rookies(Bill Hepler, Bill Murphy)	12.50	6.25	3.75
575	Earl Wilson	12.50	6.25	3.75
576	Dave Nicholson (SP)	16.00	8.00	4.75
577	Jack Lamabe (SP)	16.00	8.00	4.75
578	Chi Chi Olivo (SP)	16.00	8.00	4.75
579	Orioles Rookies(Frank Bertaina, Gene Brabender, Dave Johnson)	20.00	10.00	5.00
580	Billy Williams (SP)	40.00	20.00	10.00
581	Tony Martinez	12.50	6.25	3.75
582	Garry Roggenburk	12.50	6.25	3.75
583	Tigers Team (SP)	75.00	37.50	22.50
584	Yankees Rookies(Frank Fernandez, Fritz Peterson RC)	15.00	7.50	4.50
585	Tony Taylor	12.50	6.25	3.75
586	Claude Raymond (SP)	18.00	8.00	4.75
587	Dick Bertell	12.50	6.25	3.75
588	Athletics Rookies(Chuck Dobson, Ken Suarez)	12.50	6.25	3.75
589	Lou Klimchock (SP)	16.00	8.00	4.75
590	Bill Skowron (SP)	35.00	15.00	7.50
591	N.L. Rookies(Grant Jackson RC, Bart Shirley) (SP)	16.00	8.00	4.75
592	Andre Rodgers	12.50	6.25	3.75
593	Doug Camilli (SP)	16.00	8.00	4.75
594	Chico Salmon	12.50	6.25	3.75
595	Larry Jackson	12.50	6.25	3.75
596	Astros Rookies(Nate Colbert RC, Greg Sims) (SP)	20.00	10.00	6.00
597	John Sullivan	12.50	6.25	3.75
598	Gaylord Perry (SP)	170.00	85.00	42.50

1966 Topps Comic Book Foldees

Comic book heroes and other fictional characters were the focus of this set of 44 "foldees." The pictures on the left and right ends of the 4-1/2" x 2-3/8" cards were cut through the middle to allow them to be folded over the central picture and each other to create funny combinations. Babe Ruth, in a rather generic drawing, is the only baseball player represented in the issue. A version of the set exists which carries a "T.G.C. PRINTED IN CANADA" copyright line; it is valued similarly.

		NM	E	VG
Complete Set (44):		100.00	50.00	30.00
12	Babe Ruth	20.00	10.00	7.25

1966 Topps Punch-Outs

Only a handful of surviving examples of this issue are known. It is believed they represent a prototype for the 1967 Topps Punch-Outs which were themselves issued only on a test basis. The cards are blank-backed, measuring about 2-1/2" x 4-5/8" and perforated at center to allow the American League and National League to be separated for game play. A team captain is pictured in black-and-white on each half of the card. The A.L. side has a red background with 35 yel-low baseballs to be punched out to determine game action. Background on the N.L. side is blue. Because of their rarity and lack of recent sales records, valuations for most pieces are not provided. This checklist is likely incomplete.

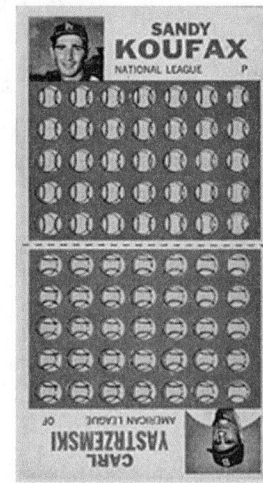

		NM
(1)	Ernie Banks, Mel Stottlemyre	
(2)	Johnny Callison, Jim Grant	
(3)	Donn Clendenon, Al Kaline	
(4)	Curt Flood, Bill Skowron	
(5)	Jim Ray Hart, Mickey Mantle	
(6)	Juan Marichal, Rich Rollins	
(7)	Sandy Koufax, Carl Yastrzemski (12/04 auction)	6,700
(8)	Roy McMillan, Frank Robinson (12/04 auction)	6,700
(9)	John Roseboro, Bobby Richardson	
(10)	Willie Stargell, Felix Mantilla	
(11)	Willie Mays, Tony Conigliaro	
(12)	Joe Torre, Harmon Killebrew	

1966 Topps Rub-Offs

Returning to a concept last tried in 1961, Topps tried an expanded version of Rub-Offs in 1966. Measuring 2-1/16" x 3", the Rub-Offs are in vertical format for the 100 players and horizontal for the 20 team pennants. The player Rub-Offs feature a color photo. Cutting procedures left well-centered examples in the distinct minority.

		NM	E	VG
Complete Set (120):		800.00	265.00	120.00
Common Player:		5.00	1.50	.75
(1)	Hank Aaron	30.00	11.00	5.00
(2)	Jerry Adair	5.00	1.50	.75
(3)	Richie Allen	6.00	2.00	.90
(4)	Jesus Alou	5.00	1.50	.75
(5)	Max Alvis	5.00	1.50	.75
(6)	Bob Aspromonte	5.00	1.50	.75
(7)	Ernie Banks	15.00	5.00	2.50
(8)	Earl Battey	5.00	1.50	.75
(9)	Curt Blefary	5.00	1.50	.75
(10)	Ken Boyer	6.00	2.00	.90
(11)	Bob Bruce	5.00	1.50	.75
(12)	Jim Bunning	10.00	3.50	1.50
(13)	Johnny Callison	5.00	1.50	.75
(14)	Bert Campaneris	5.00	1.50	.75
(15)	Jose Cardenal	5.00	1.50	.75
(16)	Dean Chance	5.00	1.50	.75
(17)	Ed Charles	5.00	1.50	.75
(18)	Bob Clemente	35.00	12.00	5.00
(19)	Tony Cloninger	5.00	1.50	.75
(20)	Rocky Colavito	6.00	2.00	.90
(21)	Tony Conigliaro	6.50	2.25	1.00
(22)	Vic Davilillo	5.00	1.50	.75

		NM	E	VG
(23)	Willie Davis	5.00	1.50	.75
(24)	Don Drysdale	10.00	3.50	1.50
(25)	Sammy Ellis	5.00	1.50	.75
(26)	Dick Ellsworth	5.00	1.50	.75
(27)	Ron Fairly	5.00	1.50	.75
(28)	Dick Farrell	5.00	1.50	.75
(29)	Eddie Fisher	5.00	1.50	.75
(30)	Jack Fisher	5.00	1.50	.75
(31)	Curt Flood	5.00	1.50	.75
(32)	Whitey Ford	15.00	5.25	2.25
(33)	Bill Freehan	5.00	1.50	.75
(34)	Jim Fregosi	5.00	1.50	.75
(35)	Bob Gibson	10.00	3.50	1.50
(36)	Jim Grant	5.00	1.50	.75
(37)	Jimmie Hall	5.00	1.50	.75
(38)	Ken Harrelson	5.00	1.50	.75
(39)	Jim Hart	5.00	1.50	.75
(40)	Joel Horlen	5.00	1.50	.75
(41)	Willie Horton	5.00	1.50	.75
(42)	Frank Howard	6.00	2.00	.90
(43)	Deron Johnson	5.00	1.50	.75
(44)	Al Kaline	12.50	4.50	2.00
(45)	Harmon Killebrew	10.00	3.50	1.50
(46)	Bobby Knoop	5.00	1.50	.75
(47)	Sandy Koufax	30.00	10.00	5.00
(48)	Ed Kranepool	5.00	1.50	.75
(49)	Gary Kroll	5.00	1.50	.75
(50)	Don Landrum	5.00	1.50	.75
(51)	Vernon Law	5.00	1.50	.75
(52)	Johnny Lewis	5.00	1.50	.75
(53)	Don Lock	5.00	1.50	.75
(54)	Mickey Lolich	5.00	1.50	.75
(55)	Jim Maloney	5.00	1.50	.75
(56)	Felix Mantilla	5.00	1.50	.75
(57)	Mickey Mantle	65.00	20.00	8.00
(58)	Juan Marichal	10.00	3.50	1.50
(59)	Ed Mathews	10.00	3.50	1.50
(60)	Willie Mays	30.00	10.00	5.00
(61)	Bill Mazeroski	10.00	3.50	1.50
(62)	Dick McAuliffe	5.00	1.50	.75
(63)	Tim McCarver	6.00	2.00	.90
(64)	Willie McCovey	10.00	3.50	1.50
(65)	Sammy McDowell	5.00	1.50	.75
(66)	Ken McMullen	5.00	1.50	.75
(67)	Denis Menke	5.00	1.50	.75
(68)	Bill Monbouquette	5.00	1.50	.75
(69)	Joe Morgan	10.00	3.50	1.50
(70)	Fred Newman	5.00	1.50	.75
(71)	John O'Donoghue	5.00	1.50	.75
(72)	Tony Oliva	6.00	2.00	.90
(73)	Johnny Orsino	5.00	1.50	.75
(74)	Phil Ortega	5.00	1.50	.75
(75)	Milt Pappas	5.00	1.50	.75
(76)	Dick Radatz	5.00	1.50	.75
(77)	Bobby Richardson	6.50	2.25	1.00
(78)	Pete Richert	5.00	1.50	.75
(79)	Brooks Robinson	12.50	4.50	2.00
(80)	Floyd Robinson	5.00	1.50	.75
(81)	Frank Robinson	12.50	4.50	2.00
(82)	Cookie Rojas	5.00	1.50	.75
(83)	Pete Rose	25.00	9.00	4.00
(84)	John Roseboro	5.00	1.50	.75
(85)	Ron Santo	6.50	2.25	1.00
(86)	Bill Skowron	5.00	1.75	.70
(87)	Willie Stargell	10.00	3.50	1.50
(88)	Mel Stottlemyre	5.00	1.50	.75
(89)	Dick Stuart	5.00	1.50	.75
(90)	Ron Swoboda	5.00	1.50	.75
(91)	Fred Talbot	5.00	1.50	.75
(92)	Ralph Terry	5.00	1.50	.75
(93)	Joe Torre	6.50	2.25	1.00
(94)	Tom Tresh	5.00	1.50	.75
(95)	Bob Veale	5.00	1.50	.75
(96)	Pete Ward	5.00	1.50	.75
(97)	Bill White	5.00	1.50	.75
(98)	Billy Williams	10.00	3.50	1.50
(99)	Jim Wynn	5.00	1.50	.75
(100)	Carl Yastrzemski	15.00	5.25	2.25
(101)	Angels Pennant	7.00	2.50	1.00
(102)	Astros Pennant	7.00	2.50	1.00
(103)	Athletics Pennant	7.00	2.50	1.00
(104)	Braves Pennant	7.00	2.50	1.00
(105)	Cards Pennant	7.00	2.50	1.00
(106)	Cubs Pennant	7.00	2.50	1.00
(107)	Dodgers Pennant	7.00	2.50	1.00
(108)	Giants Pennant	7.00	2.50	1.00
(109)	Indians Pennant	7.00	2.50	1.00
(110)	Mets Pennant	7.00	2.50	1.00
(111)	Orioles Pennant	7.00	2.50	1.00
(112)	Phillies Pennant	7.00	2.50	1.00
(113)	Pirates Pennant	7.00	2.50	1.00
(114)	Red Sox Pennant	7.00	2.50	1.00
(115)	Reds Pennant	7.00	2.50	1.00
(116)	Senators Pennant	7.00	2.50	1.00
(117)	Tigers Pennant	7.00	2.50	1.00
(118)	Twins Pennant	7.00	2.50	1.00
(119)	White Sox Pennant	7.00	2.50	1.00
(120)	Yankees Pennant	9.00	3.25	1.25

1967 Topps

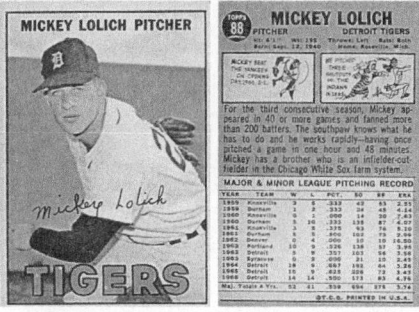

This 609-card set of 2-1/2" x 3-1/2" cards marked the largest set up to that time for Topps. Card fronts feature large color photographs bordered by white. The player's name and position are printed at the top with the team at the bottom. Across the front of the card with the exception of #254 (Milt Pappas) there is a facsimile autograph. The backs were the first to be done vertically, although they continued to carry familiar statistical and biographical information. The only subsets are statistical leaders and World Series highlights. Rookie cards are done by team or league with two players per card. The high numbers (#534-609) in '67 are quite scarce, and while it is known that some are even scarcer, by virtue of having been short-printed in relation to the rest of the series, there is no general agreement on which cards are involved. Cards in the high series which are generally believed to have been double-printed - and thus worth somewhat less than the other cards in the series - are indicated in the checklist by a (DP) notation following the player name.

		NM	E	VG
	Complete Set (609):	4,500	2,250	1,350
	Common Player (1-370):	3.00	1.50	.90
	Common Player (371-457):	6.00	2.00	1.25
	Common Player (458-533):	9.00	3.50	2.00
	Common Player (534-609):	18.00	6.00	3.50
1	The Champs(Hank Bauer, Brooks Robinson, Frank Robinson)	30.00	9.00	5.00
2	Jack Hamilton	3.00	1.50	.90
3	Duke Sims	3.00	1.50	.90
4	Hal Lanier	3.00	1.50	.90
5	Whitey Ford	28.00	15.00	7.50
6	Dick Simpson	3.00	1.50	.90
7	Don McMahon	3.00	1.50	.90
8	Chuck Harrison	3.00	1.50	.90
9	Ron Hansen	3.00	1.50	.90
10	Matty Alou	3.00	1.50	.90
11	Barry Moore	3.00	1.50	.90
12	Dodgers Rookies(Jimmy Campanis, Bill Singer)	3.00	1.50	.90
13	Joe Sparma	3.00	1.50	.90
14	Phil Linz	3.00	1.50	.90
15	Earl Battey	3.00	1.50	.90
16	Bill Hands	3.00	1.50	.90
17	Jim Gosger	3.00	1.50	.90
18	Gene Oliver	3.00	1.50	.90
19	Jim McGlothlin	3.00	1.50	.90
20	Orlando Cepeda	15.00	7.50	4.50
21	Dave Bristol	3.00	1.50	.90
22	Gene Brabender	3.00	1.50	.90
23	Larry Elliot	3.00	1.50	.90
24	Bob Allen	3.00	1.50	.90
25	Elston Howard	9.00	3.50	2.00
26a	Bob Priddy (No trade statement.)	25.00	12.50	6.25
26b	Bob Priddy (With trade statement.)	3.00	1.50	.90
27	Bob Saverine	3.00	1.50	.90
28	Barry Latman	3.00	1.50	.90
29	Tommy McCraw	3.00	1.50	.90
30	Al Kaline	24.00	12.00	7.00
31	Jim Brewer	3.00	1.50	.90
32	Bob Bailey	3.00	1.50	.90
33	Athletics Rookies(Sal Bando RC, Randy Schwartz)	4.00	2.00	1.25
34	Pete Cimino	3.00	1.50	.90
35	Rico Carty	3.00	1.50	.90
36	Bob Tillman	3.00	1.50	.90
37	Rick Wise	3.00	1.50	.90
38	Bob Johnson	3.00	1.50	.90
39	Curt Simmons	3.00	1.50	.90
40	Rick Reichardt	3.00	1.50	.90
41	Joe Hoerner	3.00	1.50	.90
42	Mets Team	12.00	6.00	3.50
43	Chico Salmon	3.00	1.50	.90
44	Joe Nuxhall	3.00	1.50	.90
45a	Roger Maris (Cards on front.)	50.00	25.00	12.50

		NM	E	VG
45b	Roger Maris (Yankees on front, blank-back proof.)	3,150	2,600	780.00
46	Lindy McDaniel	3.00	1.50	.90
47	Ken McMullen	3.00	1.50	.90
48	Bill Freehan	3.00	1.50	.90
49	Roy Face	3.00	1.50	.90
50	Tony Oliva	9.00	4.50	2.70
51	Astros Rookies(Dave Adlesh, Wes Bales)	3.00	1.50	.90
52	Dennis Higgins	3.00	1.50	.90
53	Clay Dalrymple	3.00	1.50	.90
54	Dick Green	3.00	1.50	.90
55	Don Drysdale	23.00	12.00	6.00
56	Jose Tartabull	3.00	1.50	.90
57	Pat Jarvis RC	3.00	1.50	.90
58a	Paul Schaal (Bat green above name.)	15.00	7.50	4.50
58b	Paul Schaal (Bat natural above name.)	3.00	1.50	.90
59	Ralph Terry	3.00	1.50	.90
60	Luis Aparicio	15.00	7.50	4.50
61	Gordy Coleman	3.00	1.50	.90
62a	1st Series Check List (1-109)(Frank Robinson) (Copyright symbol beneath T of Tribe.)	9.00	3.50	2.00
62b	1st Series Check List (1-109)(Frank Robinson) (Copyright symbol beneath r of Tribe.)	9.00	3.50	2.00
63	Cards Clubbers(Lou Brock, Curt Flood)	18.00	9.00	5.50
64	Fred Valentine	3.00	1.50	.90
65	Tom Haller	3.00	1.50	.90
66	Manny Mota	3.00	1.50	.90
67	Ken Berry	3.00	1.50	.90
68	Bob Buhl	3.00	1.50	.90
69	Vic Davalillo	3.00	1.50	.90
70	Ron Santo	10.00	5.00	3.00
71	Camilo Pascual	3.00	1.50	.90
72	Tigers Rookies(George Korince, John Matchick) (Korince photo actually James M. Brown.)	3.00	1.50	.90
73	Rusty Staub	5.00	1.50	.90
74	Wes Stock	3.00	1.50	.90
75	George Scott	3.00	1.50	.90
76	Jim Barbieri	3.00	1.50	.90
77	Dooley Womack	3.00	1.50	.90
78	Pat Corrales	3.00	1.50	.90
79	Bubba Morton	3.00	1.50	.90
80	Jim Maloney	3.00	1.50	.90
81	Eddie Stanky	3.00	1.50	.90
82	Steve Barber	3.00	1.50	.90
83	Ollie Brown	3.00	1.50	.90
84	Tommie Sisk	3.00	1.50	.90
85	Johnny Callison	3.00	1.50	.90
86a	Mike McCormick (No trade statement.)	30.00	15.00	9.00
86b	Mike McCormick (With trade statement.)	3.00	1.50	.90
87	George Altman	3.00	1.50	.90
88	Mickey Lolich	3.00	1.50	.90
89	Felix Millan RC	3.00	1.50	.90
90	Jim Nash	3.00	1.50	.90
91	Johnny Lewis	3.00	1.50	.90
92	Ray Washburn	3.00	1.50	.90
93	Yankees Rookies(Stan Bahnsen RC, Bobby Murcer RC)	18.00	9.00	5.50
94	Ron Fairly	3.00	1.50	.90
95	Sonny Siebert	3.00	1.50	.90
96	Art Shamsky	3.00	1.50	.90
97	Mike Cuellar	3.00	1.50	.90
98	Rich Rollins	3.00	1.50	.90
99	Lee Stange	3.00	1.50	.90
100	Frank Robinson	25.00	12.00	7.00
101	Ken Johnson	3.00	1.50	.90
102	Phillies Team	7.50	3.75	1.50
103a	2nd Series Check List (110-196)(Mickey Mantle) (170: Line after D)	25.00	12.50	7.50
103b	2nd Series Check List (110-196)(Mickey Mantle) (170: Period after D)	25.00	12.50	7.50
104	Minnie Rojas	3.00	1.50	.90
105	Ken Boyer	8.00	3.50	1.50
106	Randy Hundley	3.00	1.50	.90
107	Joel Horlen	3.00	1.50	.90
108	Alex Johnson	3.00	1.50	.90
109	Tribe Thumpers(Rocky Colavito, Leon Wagner)	12.00	6.00	2.75
110	Jack Aker	3.00	1.50	.90
111	John Kennedy	3.00	1.50	.90
112	Dave Wickersham	3.00	1.50	.90
113	Dave Nicholson	3.00	1.50	.90
114	Jack Baldschun	3.00	1.50	.90
115	Paul Casanova	3.00	1.50	.90

#	Player			
116	Herman Franks	3.00	1.50	.90
117a	Darrell Brandon	3.00	1.50	.90
117b	Darrell Brandon ("DI" appears above left elbow.)	3.00	1.50	.90
118	Bernie Allen	3.00	1.50	.90
119	Wade Blasingame	3.00	1.50	.90
120	Floyd Robinson	3.00	1.50	.90
121	Ed Bressoud	3.00	1.50	.90
122	George Brunet	3.00	1.50	.90
123	Pirates Rookies(Jim Price, Luke Walker)	3.00	1.50	.90
124	Jim Stewart	3.00	1.50	.90
125	Moe Drabowsky	3.00	1.50	.90
126	Tony Taylor	3.00	1.50	.90
127	John O'Donoghue	3.00	1.50	.90
128a	Ed Spiezio (Most of "SPIE" missing at top.)	75.00	37.50	22.50
128b	Ed Spiezio (Lettering all there.)	3.00	1.50	.90
129	Phil Roof	3.00	1.50	.90
130	Phil Regan	3.00	1.50	.90
131	Yankees Team	14.00	7.00	3.75
132	Ozzie Virgil	3.00	1.50	.90
133	Ron Kline	3.00	1.50	.90
134	Gates Brown	3.00	1.50	.90
135	Deron Johnson	3.00	1.50	.90
136	Carroll Sembera	3.00	1.50	.90
137	Twins Rookies(Ron Clark, Jim Ollom)	3.00	1.50	.90
138	Dick Kelley	3.00	1.50	.90
139	Dalton Jones	3.00	1.50	.90
140	Willie Stargell	21.00	10.00	6.00
141	John Miller	3.00	1.50	.90
142	Jackie Brandt	3.00	1.50	.90
143	Sox Sockers(Don Buford, Pete Ward)	3.00	1.50	.90
144	Bill Hepler	3.00	1.50	.90
145	Larry Brown	3.00	1.50	.90
146	Steve Carlton	40.00	20.00	10.00
147	Tom Egan	3.00	1.50	.90
148	Adolfo Phillips	3.00	1.50	.90
149a	Joe Moeller (White streak between "M" and cap.)	30.00	15.00	9.00
149b	Joe Moeller (No white streak.)	3.00	1.50	.90
150	Mickey Mantle	250.00	125.00	75.00
151	World Series Game 1 (Moe Mows Down 11)	7.00	3.00	1.75
152	World Series Game 2 (Palmer Blanks Dodgers)	12.00	5.50	3.25
153	World Series Game 3 (Blair's Homer Defeats L.A.)	7.00	3.00	1.75
154	World Series Game 4 (Orioles Win 4th Straight)	6.00	3.00	1.75
155	World Series (The Winners Celebrate)	7.50	3.75	2.25
156	Ron Herbel	3.00	1.50	.90
157	Danny Cater	3.00	1.50	.90
158	Jimmy Coker	3.00	1.50	.90
159	Bruce Howard	3.00	1.50	.90
160	Willie Davis	3.00	1.50	.90
161	Dick Williams	3.00	1.50	.90
162	Billy O'Dell	3.00	1.50	.90
163	Vic Roznovsky	3.00	1.50	.90
164	Dwight Siebler	3.00	1.50	.90
165	Cleon Jones	3.00	1.50	.90
166	Ed Mathews	24.00	12.00	7.00
167	Senators Rookies(Joe Coleman, Tim Cullen)	3.00	1.50	.90
168	Ray Culp	3.00	1.50	.90
169	Horace Clarke	3.00	1.50	.90
170	Dick McAuliffe	3.00	1.50	.90
171	Calvin Koonce	3.00	1.50	.90
172	Bill Heath	3.00	1.50	.90
173	Cards Team	7.00	2.50	1.50
174	Dick Radatz	3.00	1.50	.90
175	Bobby Knoop	3.00	1.50	.90
176	Sammy Ellis	3.00	1.50	.90
177	Tito Fuentes	3.00	1.50	.90
178	John Buzhardt	3.00	1.50	.90
179	Braves Rookies(Cecil Upshaw, Chas. Vaughan)	3.00	1.50	.90
180	Curt Blefary	3.00	1.50	.90
181	Terry Fox	3.00	1.50	.90
182	Ed Charles	3.00	1.50	.90
183	Jim Pagliaroni	3.00	1.50	.90
184	George Thomas	3.00	1.50	.90
185	Ken Holtzman RC	6.00	2.00	1.25
186	Mets Maulers(Ed Kranepool, Ron Swoboda)	7.00	3.75	2.00
187	Pedro Ramos	3.00	1.50	.90
188	Ken Harrelson	3.00	1.50	.90
189	Chuck Hinton	3.00	1.50	.90
190	Turk Farrell	3.00	1.50	.90
191a	3rd Series Check List (197-283)(Willie Mays) (214 is Dick Kelley)	10.00	4.50	2.75
191b	3rd Series Check List (197-283)(Willie Mays) (214 is Tom Kelley)	13.00	6.00	3.50
192	Fred Gladding	3.00	1.50	.90
193	Jose Cardenal	3.00	1.50	.90
194	Bob Allison	3.00	1.50	.90
195	Al Jackson	3.00	1.50	.90
196	Johnny Romano	3.00	1.50	.90
197	Ron Perranoski	3.00	1.50	.90
198	Chuck Hiller	3.00	1.50	.90
199	Billy Hitchcock	3.00	1.50	.90
200	Willie Mays	100.00	50.00	30.00
201	Hal Reniff	3.00	1.50	.90
202	Johnny Edwards	3.00	1.50	.90
203	Al McBean	3.00	1.50	.90
204	Orioles Rookies(Mike Epstein RC, Tom Phoebus)	3.00	1.50	.90
205	Dick Groat	3.00	1.50	.90
206	Dennis Bennett	3.00	1.50	.90
207	John Orsino	3.00	1.50	.90
208	Jack Lamabe	3.00	1.50	.90
209	Joe Nossek	3.00	1.50	.90
210	Bob Gibson	25.00	12.50	6.25
211	Twins Team	9.00	4.50	2.75
212	Chris Zachary	3.00	1.50	.90
213	Jay Johnstone RC	6.00	3.00	1.80
214	Tom Kelley	3.00	1.50	.90
215	Ernie Banks	30.00	12.50	7.50
216	Bengal Belters(Norm Cash, Al Kaline)	20.00	7.50	4.50
217	Rob Gardner	3.00	1.50	.90
218	Wes Parker	3.00	1.50	.90
219	Clay Carroll	3.00	1.50	.90
220	Jim Hart	3.00	1.50	.90
221	Woody Fryman	3.00	1.50	.90
222	Reds Rookies(Lee May, Darrell Osteen)	3.00	1.50	.90
223	Mike Ryan	3.00	1.50	.90
224	Walt Bond	3.00	1.50	.90
225	Mel Stottlemyre	4.00	2.00	1.25
226	Julian Javier	3.00	1.50	.90
227	Paul Lindblad	3.00	1.50	.90
228	Gil Hodges	10.00	4.50	2.75
229	Larry Jackson	3.00	1.50	.90
230	Boog Powell	9.00	4.00	2.50
231	John Bateman	3.00	1.50	.90
232	Don Buford	3.00	1.50	.90
233	A.L. ERA Leaders(Steve Hargan, Joel Horlen, Gary Peters)	5.00	1.50	.90
234	N.L. ERA Leaders(Mike Cuellar, Sandy Koufax, Juan Marichal)	13.00	6.00	3.50
235	A.L. Pitching Leaders(Jim Kaat, Denny McLain, Earl Wilson)	5.00	1.75	1.00
236	N.L. Pitching Leaders(Bob Gibson, Sandy Koufax, Juan Marichal, Gaylord Perry)	15.00	7.50	3.75
237	A.L. Strikeout Leaders(Jim Kaat, Sam McDowell, Earl Wilson)	5.00	1.75	1.00
238	N.L. Strikeout Leaders(Jim Bunning, Sandy Koufax, Bob Veale)	13.00	6.00	3.50
239	A.L. Batting Leaders(Al Kaline, Tony Oliva, Frank Robinson)	15.00	7.50	3.75
240	N.L. Batting Leaders(Felipe Alou, Matty Alou, Rico Carty)	11.00	5.50	3.25
241	A.L. RBI Leaders(Harmon Killebrew, Boog Powell, Frank Robinson)	14.00	5.50	3.25
242	N.L. RBI Leaders(Hank Aaron, Richie Allen, Bob Clemente)	20.00	7.50	3.75
243	A.L. Home Run Leaders(Harmon Killebrew, Boog Powell, Frank Robinson)	14.00	5.50	3.25
244	N.L. Home Run Leaders(Hank Aaron, Richie Allen, Willie Mays)	20.00	7.50	4.50
245	Curt Flood	8.00	2.50	1.50
246	Jim Perry	3.00	1.50	.90
247	Jerry Lumpe	3.00	1.50	.90
248	Gene Mauch	3.00	1.50	.90
249	Nick Willhite	3.00	1.50	.90
250	Hank Aaron	85.00	40.00	24.00
251	Woody Held	3.00	1.50	.90
252a	Bob Bolin (White streak between Bob and Bolin.)	60.00	30.00	18.00
252b	Bob Bolin (No white streak.)	3.00	1.50	.90
253	Indians Rookies(Bill Davis, Gus Gil)	3.00	1.50	.90
254	Milt Pappas	3.00	1.50	.90
255	Frank Howard	4.00	1.25	.70
256	Bob Hendley	3.00	1.50	.90
257	Charley Smith	3.00	1.50	.90
258	Lee Maye	3.00	1.50	.90
259	Don Dennis	3.00	1.50	.90
260	Jim Lefebvre	3.00	1.50	.90
261	John Wyatt	3.00	1.50	.90
262	Athletics Team	9.00	4.50	2.75
263	Hank Aguirre	3.00	1.50	.90
264	Ron Swoboda	3.00	1.50	.90
265	Lou Burdette	3.00	1.50	.90
266	Pitt Power(Donn Clendenon, Willie Stargell)	16.00	8.00	3.50
267	Don Schwall	3.00	1.50	.90
268	John Briggs	3.00	1.50	.90
269	Don Nottebart	3.00	1.50	.90
270	Zoilo Versalles	3.00	1.50	.90
271	Eddie Watt	3.00	1.50	.90
272	Cubs Rookies(Bill Connors, Dave Dowling)	3.00	1.50	.90
273	Dick Lines	3.00	1.50	.90
274	Bob Aspromonte	3.00	1.50	.90
275	Fred Whitfield	3.00	1.50	.90
276	Bruce Brubaker	3.00	1.50	.90
277	Steve Whitaker	3.00	1.50	.90
278	4th Series Check List (284-370) (Jim Kaat)	7.00	3.50	2.00
279	Frank Linzy	3.00	1.50	.90
280	Tony Conigliaro	12.00	4.50	2.75
281	Bob Rodgers	3.00	1.50	.90
282	Johnny Odom	3.00	1.50	.90
283	Gene Alley	3.00	1.50	.90
284	Johnny Podres	4.00	1.50	.90
285	Lou Brock	20.00	10.00	6.00
286	Wayne Causey	3.00	1.50	.90
287	Mets Rookies(Greg Goossen, Bart Shirley)	3.00	1.50	.90
288	Denver Lemaster	3.00	1.50	.90
289	Tom Tresh	8.00	3.00	1.75
290	Bill White	3.00	1.50	.90
291	Jim Hannan	3.00	1.50	.90
292	Don Pavletich	3.00	1.50	.90
293	Ed Kirkpatrick	3.00	1.50	.90
294	Walt Alston	9.00	3.50	2.00
295	Sam McDowell	3.00	.70	.90
296	Glenn Beckert	3.00	1.50	.90
297	Dave Morehead	3.00	1.50	.90
298	Ron Davis	3.00	1.50	.90
299	Norm Siebern	3.00	1.50	.90
300	Jim Kaat	6.00	2.00	1.25
301	Jesse Gonder	3.00	1.50	.90
302	Orioles Team	9.00	3.00	1.75
303	Gil Blanco	3.00	1.50	.90
304	Phil Gagliano	3.00	1.50	.90
305	Earl Wilson	3.00	1.50	.90
306	Bud Harrelson RC	9.00	3.50	2.00
307	Jim Beauchamp	3.00	1.50	.90
308	Al Downing	3.00	1.50	.90
309	Hurlers Beware(Richie Allen, Johnny Callison)	8.00	3.00	1.75
310	Gary Peters	3.00	1.50	.90
311	Ed Brinkman	3.00	1.50	.90
312	Don Mincher	3.00	1.50	.90
313	Bob Lee	3.00	1.50	.90
314	Red Sox Rookies(Mike Andrews RC, Reggie Smith RC)	13.00	6.00	3.50
315	Billy Williams	15.00	7.50	3.75
316	Jack Kralick	3.00	1.50	.90
317	Cesar Tovar	3.00	1.50	.90
318	Dave Giusti	3.00	1.50	.90
319	Paul Blair	3.00	1.50	.90
320	Gaylord Perry	15.00	7.50	4.50
321	Mayo Smith	3.00	1.50	.90
322	Jose Pagan	3.00	1.50	.90
323	Mike Hershberger	3.00	1.50	.90
324	Hal Woodeshick	3.00	1.50	.90
325	Chico Cardenas	3.00	1.50	.90
326	Bob Uecker	13.00	6.00	3.50
327	Angels Team	9.00	3.00	1.75
328	Clete Boyer	6.00	2.00	1.25
329	Charlie Lau	3.00	1.50	.90
330	Claude Osteen	3.00	1.50	.90
331	Joe Foy	3.00	1.50	.90
332	Jesus Alou	3.00	1.50	.90
333	Fergie Jenkins	15.00	5.00	2.50
334	Twin Terrors(Bob Allison, Harmon Killebrew)	20.00	7.50	4.50
335	Bob Veale	3.00	1.50	.90

336	Joe Azcue	3.00	1.50	.90
337	Joe Morgan	17.50	8.75	5.25
338	Bob Locker	3.00	1.50	.90
339	Chico Ruiz	3.00	1.50	.90
340	Joe Pepitone	6.00	2.00	1.25
341	Giants Rookies(Dick Dietz **RC**, Bill Sorrell)	3.00	1.50	.90
342	Hank Fischer	3.00	1.50	.90
343	Tom Satriano	3.00	1.50	.90
344	Ossie Chavarria	3.00	1.50	.90
345	Stu Miller	3.00	1.50	.90
346	Jim Hickman	3.00	1.50	.90
347	Grady Hatton	3.00	1.50	.90
348	Tug McGraw	4.00	1.50	.90
349	Bob Chance	3.00	1.50	.90
350	Joe Torre	10.00	3.50	2.00
351	Vern Law	3.00	1.50	.90
352	Ray Oyler	3.00	1.50	.90
353	Bill McCool	3.00	1.50	.90
354	Cubs Team	9.00	3.00	1.75
355	Carl Yastrzemski	55.00	30.00	15.00
356	Larry Jaster	3.00	1.50	.90
357	Bill Skowron	5.00	2.50	1.50
358	Ruben Amaro	3.00	1.50	.90
359	Dick Ellsworth	3.00	1.50	.90
360	Leon Wagner	3.00	1.50	.90
361	5th Series Check List (371-457) (Roberto Clemente)	12.00	4.50	2.75
362	Darold Knowles	3.00	1.50	.90
363	Dave Johnson	3.00	1.50	.90
364	Claude Raymond	3.00	1.50	.90
365	John Roseboro	3.00	1.50	.90
366	Andy Kosco	3.00	1.50	.90
367	Angels Rookies(Bill Kelso, Don Wallace)	3.00	1.50	.90
368	Jack Hiatt	3.00	1.50	.90
369	Jim Hunter	20.00	10.00	5.00
370	Tommy Davis	3.00	1.50	.90
371	Jim Lonborg	6.00	3.00	1.80
372	Mike de la Hoz	6.00	3.00	1.80
373	White Sox Rookies(Duane Josephson, Fred Klages)	6.00	3.00	1.80
374a	Mel Queen (Rule under stats totals nearly gone.)	6.00	3.00	1.80
374b	Mel Queen (Full rule.)	6.00	3.00	1.80
375	Jake Gibbs	6.00	3.00	1.80
376	Don Lock	6.00	3.00	1.80
377	Luis Tiant	6.00	3.00	1.80
378	Tigers Team	11.00	3.50	2.00
379	Jerry May	6.00	3.00	1.80
380	Dean Chance	6.00	3.00	1.80
381	Dick Schofield	6.00	3.00	1.80
382	Dave McNally	6.00	3.00	1.80
383	Ken Henderson	6.00	3.00	1.80
384	Cards Rookies(Jim Cosman, Dick Hughes)	6.00	3.00	1.80
385	Jim Fregosi	6.00	3.00	1.80
386	Dick Selma	6.00	3.00	1.80
387	Cap Peterson	6.00	3.00	1.80
388	Arnold Earley	6.00	3.00	1.80
389	Al Dark	6.00	3.00	1.80
390	Jim Wynn	6.00	3.00	1.80
391	Wilbur Wood	6.00	3.00	1.80
392	Tommy Harper	6.00	3.00	1.80
393	Jim Bouton	9.00	3.50	2.00
394	Jake Wood	6.00	3.00	1.80
395	Chris Short	6.00	3.00	1.80
396	Atlanta Aces (Tony Cloninger, Denis Menke)	9.00	3.50	2.00
397	Willie Smith	6.00	3.00	1.80
398	Jeff Torborg	6.00	3.00	1.80
399	Al Worthington	6.00	3.00	1.80
400	Roberto Clemente	115.00	62.50	31.80
401	Jim Coates	6.00	3.00	1.80
402a	Phillies Rookies (Grant Jackson, Billy Wilson) (Incomplete line under Wilson's stats.)	7.50	3.25	2.00
402b	Grant Jackson, Billy Wilson (Complete line.)	6.00	3.00	1.80
403	Dick Nen	6.00	3.00	1.80
404	Nelson Briles	6.00	3.00	1.80
405	Russ Snyder	6.00	3.00	1.80
406	Lee Elia	6.00	3.00	1.80
407	Reds Team	11.00	3.50	2.00
408	Jim Northrup	6.00	3.00	1.80
409	Ray Sadecki	6.00	3.00	1.80
410	Lou Johnson	6.00	3.00	1.80
411	Dick Howser	6.00	3.00	1.80
412	Astros Rookies(Norm Miller, Doug Rader **RC**)	7.50	2.50	1.50
413	Jerry Grote	6.00	3.00	1.80
414	Casey Cox	6.00	3.00	1.80
415	Sonny Jackson	6.00	3.00	1.80
416	Roger Repoz	6.00	3.00	1.80
417a	Bob Bruce (RBAVES on back.)	24.00	12.00	5.00
417b	Bob Bruce (Corrected)	6.00	3.00	1.80
418	Sam Mele	6.00	3.00	1.80
419	Don Kessinger	6.00	3.00	1.80
420	Denny McLain	9.00	3.50	2.00
421	Dal Maxvill	6.00	3.00	1.80
422	Hoyt Wilhelm	20.00	7.50	4.50
423	Fence Busters(Willie Mays, Willie McCovey)	28.00	12.50	7.50
424	Pedro Gonzalez	6.00	3.00	1.80
425	Pete Mikkelsen	6.00	3.00	1.80
426	Lou Clinton	6.00	3.00	1.80
427a	Ruben Gomez (Stats totals line nearly gone.)	12.00	6.00	3.50
427b	Ruben Gomez (Full stats totals line.)	6.00	3.00	1.80
428	Dodgers Rookies (Tom Hutton, Gene Michael **RC**)	8.00	3.00	1.75
429	Garry Roggenburk	6.00	3.00	1.80
430	Pete Rose	90.00	45.00	22.50
431	Ted Uhlaender	6.00	3.00	1.80
432	Jimmie Hall	6.00	3.00	1.80
433	Al Luplow	6.00	3.00	1.80
434	Eddie Fisher	6.00	3.00	1.80
435	Mack Jones	6.00	3.00	1.80
436	Pete Ward	6.00	3.00	1.80
437	Senators Team	11.00	3.50	2.00
438	Chuck Dobson	6.00	3.00	1.80
439	Byron Browne	6.00	3.00	1.80
440	Steve Hargan	6.00	3.00	1.80
441	Jim Davenport	6.00	3.00	1.80
442	Yankees Rookies (Bill Robinson **RC**, Joe Verbanic)	8.00	3.00	1.75
443	Tito Francona	6.00	3.00	1.80
444	George Smith	6.00	3.00	1.80
445	Don Sutton	20.00	7.50	4.50
446	Russ Nixon	6.00	3.00	1.80
447a	Bo Belinsky (1966 S.D. stats nearly gone)	8.00	3.00	1.75
447b	Bo Belinsky (Full 1966 S.D. stats line.)	6.00	3.00	1.80
448	Harry Walker	6.00	3.00	1.80
449	Orlando Pena	6.00	3.00	1.80
450	Richie Allen	12.00	6.00	3.50
451	Fred Newman	6.00	3.00	1.80
452	Ed Kranepool	6.00	3.00	1.80
453	Aurelio Monteagudo	6.00	3.00	1.80
454a	6th Series Check List (458-533)(Juan Marichal) (Left ear shows.)	10.00	4.50	2.75
454b	6th Series Check List (458-533)(Juan Marichal) (No left ear.)	12.00	6.00	3.50
455	Tommie Agee	6.00	3.00	1.80
456	Phil Niekro	20.00	7.50	4.50
457	Andy Etchebarren	6.00	3.00	1.80
458	Lee Thomas	9.00	4.50	2.70
459	Senators Rookies(Dick Bosman **RC**, Pete Craig)	9.00	4.50	2.70
460	Harmon Killebrew	60.00	30.00	15.00
461	Bob Miller	9.00	4.50	2.70
462	Bob Barton	9.00	4.50	2.70
463	Hill Aces(Sam McDowell, Sonny Siebert)	13.00	5.50	3.25
464	Dan Coombs	9.00	4.50	2.70
465	Willie Horton	9.00	4.50	2.70
466	Bobby Wine	9.00	4.50	2.70
467	Jim O'Toole	9.00	4.50	2.70
468	Ralph Houk	9.00	4.50	2.70
469	Len Gabrielson	9.00	4.50	2.70
470	Bob Shaw	9.00	4.50	2.70
471	Rene Lachemann	9.00	4.50	2.70
472	Pirates Rookies(John Gelnar, George Spriggs)	9.00	4.50	2.70
473	Jose Santiago	9.00	4.50	2.70
474	Bob Tolan	9.00	4.50	2.70
475	Jim Palmer	60.00	30.00	18.00
476	Tony Perez (SP)	40.00	20.00	12.70
477	Braves Team	14.00	5.50	3.25
478	Bob Humphreys	9.00	4.50	2.70
479	Gary Bell	9.00	4.50	2.70
480	Willie McCovey	30.00	15.00	7.50
481	Leo Durocher	18.00	9.00	3.50
482	Bill Monbouquette	9.00	4.50	2.70
483	Jim Landis	9.00	4.50	2.70
484	Jerry Adair	9.00	4.50	2.70
485	Tim McCarver	16.00	7.50	3.75
486	Twins Rookies(Rich Reese, Bill Whitby)	9.00	4.50	2.70
487	Tom Reynolds	9.00	4.50	2.70
488	Gerry Arrigo	9.00	4.50	2.70
489	Doug Clemens	9.00	4.50	2.70
490	Tony Cloninger	9.00	4.50	2.70
491	Sam Bowens	9.00	4.50	2.70
492	Pirates Team	20.00	10.00	3.75
493	Phil Ortega	9.00	4.50	2.70
494	Bill Rigney	9.00	4.50	2.70
495	Fritz Peterson	9.00	4.50	2.70
496	Orlando McFarlane	9.00	4.50	2.70
497	Ron Campbell	9.00	4.50	2.70
498	Larry Dierker	9.00	4.50	2.70
499	Indians Rookies(George Culver, Jose Vidal)	9.00	4.50	2.70
500	Juan Marichal	23.00	10.00	5.00
501	Jerry Zimmerman	9.00	4.50	2.70
502	Derrell Griffith	9.00	4.50	2.70
503	Dodgers Team	18.00	7.50	3.75
504	Orlando Martinez	9.00	4.50	2.70
505	Tommy Helms	9.00	4.50	2.70
506	Smoky Burgess	9.00	4.50	2.70
507	Orioles Rookies(Ed Barnowski, Larry Haney)	9.00	4.50	2.70
508	Dick Hall	9.00	4.50	2.70
509	Jim King	9.00	4.50	2.70
510	Bill Mazeroski	23.00	10.00	6.00
511	Don Wert	9.00	4.50	2.70
512	Red Schoendienst	18.00	7.50	4.50
513	Marcelino Lopez	9.00	4.50	2.70
514	John Werhas	9.00	4.50	2.70
515	Bert Campaneris	9.00	4.50	2.70
516	Giants Team	20.00	8.75	5.25
517	Fred Talbot	9.00	4.50	2.70
518	Denis Menke	9.00	4.50	2.70
519	Ted Davidson	9.00	4.50	2.70
520	Max Alvis	9.00	4.50	2.70
521	Bird Bombers(Curt Blefary, Boog Powell)	12.00	3.75	2.25
522	John Stephenson	9.00	4.50	2.70
523	Jim Merritt	9.00	4.50	2.70
524	Felix Mantilla	9.00	4.50	2.70
525	Ron Hunt	9.00	4.50	2.70
526	Tigers Rookies(Pat Dobson **RC**, George Korince)	12.00	5.50	3.25
527	Dennis Ribant	9.00	4.50	2.70
528	Rico Petrocelli	13.50	6.25	3.75
529	Gary Wagner	9.00	4.50	2.70
530	Felipe Alou	14.00	6.00	3.50
531	7th Series Check List (534-609)(Brooks Robinson)	14.00	6.00	3.50
532	Jim Hicks	9.00	4.50	2.70
533	Jack Fisher	9.00	4.50	2.70
534	Hank Bauer (DP)	12.00	4.00	2.50
535	Donn Clendenon	18.00	9.00	5.40
536	Cubs Rookies(Joe Niekro **RC**, Paul Popovich)	35.00	12.50	6.25
537	Chuck Estrada (DP)	12.00	4.00	2.50
538	J.C. Martin	12.00	9.00	5.40
539	Dick Egan (DP)	12.00	4.00	2.50
540	Norm Cash	50.00	25.00	12.50
541	Joe Gibbon	18.00	9.00	5.40
542	Athletics Rookies(Rick Monday **RC**, Tony Pierce) (DP)	13.50	6.25	3.75
543	Dan Schneider	18.00	9.00	5.40
544	Indians Team	20.00	10.00	5.00
545	Jim Grant	18.00	9.00	5.40
546	Woody Woodward	18.00	9.00	5.40
547	Red Sox Rookies(Russ Gibson, Bill Rohr) (DP)	12.00	4.00	2.50
548	Tony Gonzalez (DP)	12.00	4.00	2.50
549	Jack Sanford	18.00	9.00	5.40
550	Vada Pinson (DP)	18.00	9.00	5.40
551	Doug Camilli (DP)	8.00	4.00	2.50
552	Ted Savage	18.00	9.00	5.40
553	Yankees Rookies(Mike Hegan **RC**, Thad Tillotson)	38.00	15.00	7.50
554	Andre Rodgers (DP)	12.00	4.00	2.50
555	Don Cardwell	18.00	9.00	5.40
556	Al Weis (DP)	12.00	4.00	2.50
557	Al Ferrara	18.00	9.00	5.40
558	Orioles Rookies(Mark Belanger **RC**, Bill Dillman)	60.00	22.50	15.40
559	Dick Tracewski (DP)	12.00	4.00	2.50
560	Jim Bunning	55.00	22.50	11.25
561	Sandy Alomar	18.00	9.00	5.40
562	Steve Blass (DP)	12.00	4.00	2.50
563	Joe Adcock	25.00	12.00	6.50
564	Astros Rookies(Alonzo Harris, Aaron Pointer) (DP)	12.00	4.00	2.50
565	Lew Krausse	18.00	9.00	5.40
566	Gary Geiger (DP)	12.00	4.00	2.50
567	Steve Hamilton	18.00	9.00	5.40
568	John Sullivan	18.00	9.00	5.40
569	A.L. Rookies(Hank Allen **RC**, Rod Carew **RC**) (DP)	285.00	150.00	75.00
570	Maury Wills	65.00	25.00	12.50
571	Larry Sherry	18.00	9.00	5.40
572	Don Demeter	18.00	9.00	5.40

573	White Sox Team (Indians team stats on back)	23.00	10.00	5.00
574	Jerry Buchek	18.00	9.00	5.40
575	Dave Boswell **RC**	18.00	9.00	5.40
576	N.L. Rookies(Norm Gigon, Ramon Hernandez)	18.00	9.00	5.40
577	Bill Short	18.00	9.00	5.40
578	John Boccabella	18.00	9.00	5.40
579	Bill Henry	18.00	9.00	5.40
580	Rocky Colavito	125.00	75.00	37.50
581	Mets Rookies(Bill Denehy **RC**, Tom Seaver **RC**)	480.00	250.00	150.00
582	Jim Owens (DP)	8.00	4.00	2.50
583	Ray Barker	18.00	9.00	5.40
584	Jim Piersall	24.00	10.00	6.00
585	Wally Bunker	18.00	9.00	5.40
586	Manny Jimenez	18.00	9.00	5.40
587	N.L. Rookies(Don Shaw, Gary Sutherland)	18.00	9.00	5.40
588	Johnny Klippstein (DP)	12.00	4.00	2.50
589	Dave Ricketts (DP)	12.00	4.00	2.50
590	Pete Richert	18.00	9.00	5.40
591	Ty Cline	18.00	9.00	5.40
592	N.L. Rookies(Jim Shellenback, Ron Willis)	18.00	9.00	5.40
593	Wes Westrum	18.00	9.00	5.40
594	Dan Osinski	18.00	9.00	5.40
595	Cookie Rojas	18.00	9.00	5.40
596	Galen Cisco (DP)	12.00	4.00	2.50
597	Ted Abernathy	18.00	9.00	5.40
598	White Sox Rookies(Ed Stroud, Walt Williams)	18.00	9.00	5.40
599	Bob Duliba (DP)	12.00	4.00	2.50
600	Brooks Robinson (SP)	250.00	125.00	62.50
601	Bill Bryan (DP)	12.00	4.00	2.50
602	Juan Pizarro	18.00	9.00	5.40
603	Athletics Rookies(Tim Talton, Ramon Webster)	18.00	9.00	5.40
604	Red Sox Team	100.00	50.00	25.00
605	Mike Shannon	50.00	25.00	12.50
606	Ron Taylor	18.00	9.00	5.40
607	Mickey Stanley	25.00	12.50	7.50
608	Cubs Rookies(Rich Nye, John Upham) (DP)	12.00	4.00	2.50
609	Tommy John	80.00	40.00	20.00

1967 Topps Discs

Similar to the more common 28-piece set of 1968, this set of all-stars is known only in proof form, evidently intended to be pressed onto a pin-back button issue which never materialized. Printed on blank-backed silver foil about 2-3/8" square, the pieces have a 2-1/4" diameter center with color player portrait with name and position printed in black across the chest. Some pieces have a team name to the left and right of the player's picture. "JAPAN" is printed in tiny black letters at top-left, apparently intended to be folded under the rim of the button. The unnumbered discs are checklisted here alphabetically.

		NM	E	VG
	Complete Set (24):	15,000	7,500	3,750
	Common Player:	200.00	100.00	55.00
(1)	Hank Aaron (no cap)	2,000	1,000	500.00
(2)	Johnny Callison	200.00	100.00	55.00
(3)	Bert Campaneris	200.00	100.00	55.00
(4)	Leo Cardenas	200.00	100.00	55.00
(5)	Orlando Cepeda (no cap)	600.00	300.00	180.00
(6)	Roberto Clemente	2,150	1,075	555.00
(7)	Frank Howard	210.00	105.00	63.00
(8)	Cleon Jones	200.00	100.00	55.00
(9)	Bobby Knoop	200.00	100.00	55.00
(10)	Sandy Koufax	1,800	900.00	450.00
(11)	Mickey Mantle (OF)	4,000	2,000	1,000
(12)	Juan Marichal	600.00	300.00	180.00
(13)	Willie Mays	2,000	1,000	500.00
(14)	Sam McDowell	200.00	100.00	55.00
(15)	Denny McLain	225.00	105.00	63.00
(16)	Joe Morgan	600.00	300.00	180.00
(17)	Tony Oliva	200.00	100.00	55.00
(18)	Boog Powell	225.00	110.00	67.00
(19)	Brooks Robinson (facing left)	750.00	375.00	225.00
(20)	Frank Robinson	750.00	375.00	225.00
(21)	Johnny Romano	200.00	100.00	55.00

(22)	Ron Santo	225.00	105.00	63.00
(23)	Joe Torre	450.00	225.00	135.00
(24)	Carl Yastrzemski	750.00	375.00	225.00

1967 Topps Pin-Ups

The 5" x 7" "All Star Pin-ups" were wax pack inserts. They feature a full color picture with the player's name, position and team in a circle in one of the lower corners on the front. The numbered set consists of 32 players (generally big names). Because the large paper pin-ups had to be folded several times to fit into the wax packs, the factory-created folds are not considered when grading unless paper separations have developed along the seams. At least one of the pin-ups (Clemente) has been seen in an unnumbered version printed on better-quality sticker stock and not having fold lines.

		NM	E	VG
	Complete Set (32):	150.00	65.00	35.00
	Common Player:	2.00	.70	.30
1	Boog Powell	2.50	.90	.40
2	Bert Campaneris	2.00	.70	.30
3	Brooks Robinson	9.00	3.25	1.25
4	Tommie Agee	2.00	.70	.30
5	Carl Yastrzemski	9.00	3.25	1.25
6	Mickey Mantle	40.00	14.00	6.00
7	Frank Howard	2.50	.90	.40
8	Sam McDowell	2.00	.70	.30
9	Orlando Cepeda	6.00	2.00	.90
10	Chico Cardenas	2.00	.70	.30
11	Roberto Clemente	20.00	7.00	3.00
12	Willie Mays	15.00	5.25	2.25
13	Cleon Jones	2.00	.70	.30
14	John Callison	2.00	.70	.30
15	Hank Aaron	15.00	5.25	2.25
16	Don Drysdale	7.50	2.75	1.25
17	Bobby Knoop	2.00	.70	.30
18	Tony Oliva	2.50	.90	.40
19	Frank Robinson	9.00	3.25	1.25
20	Denny McLain	2.50	.90	.40
21	Al Kaline	9.00	3.25	1.25
22	Joe Pepitone	3.00	1.00	.45
23	Harmon Killebrew	7.50	2.75	1.25
24	Leon Wagner	2.00	.70	.30
25	Joe Morgan	7.50	2.75	1.25
26	Ron Santo	3.00	1.00	.45
27	Joe Torre	4.50	1.50	.70
28	Juan Marichal	6.00	2.00	.90
29	Matty Alou	2.00	.70	.30
30	Felipe Alou	2.00	.70	.30
31	Ron Hunt	2.00	.70	.30
32	Willie McCovey	7.50	2.75	1.25

1967 Topps Pirates Stickers

Considered a "test" issue, this 33-sticker set of 2-1/2" x 3-1/2" stickers is very similar to the Red Sox stickers which were produced the same year. Player stickers have a color picture (often just the player's head) and the player's name in large "comic book" letters. Besides the players, there are other topics such as "I Love the Pirates," "Bob Clemente for Mayor," and a number of similar sentiments. The stickers

have blank backs and are rather scarce.

		NM	E	VG
	Complete Set (33):	750.00	375.00	225.00
	Common Player:	15.00	7.50	4.50
1	Gene Alley	15.00	7.50	4.50
2	Matty Alou	15.00	7.50	4.50
3	Dennis Ribant	15.00	7.50	4.50
4	Steve Blass	15.00	7.50	4.50
5	Juan Pizarro	15.00	7.50	4.50
6	Bob Clemente	175.00	85.00	50.00
7	Donn Clendenon	15.00	7.50	4.50
8	Roy Face	15.00	7.50	4.50
9	Woody Fryman	15.00	7.50	4.50
10	Jesse Gonder	15.00	7.50	4.50
11	Vern Law	15.00	7.50	4.50
12	Al McBean	15.00	7.50	4.50
13	Jerry May	15.00	7.50	4.50
14	Bill Mazeroski	35.00	17.50	10.00
15	Pete Mikkelsen	15.00	7.50	4.50
16	Manny Mota	15.00	7.50	4.50
17	Billy O'Dell	15.00	7.50	4.50
18	Jose Pagan	15.00	7.50	4.50
19	Jim Pagliaroni	15.00	7.50	4.50
20	Johnny Pesky	15.00	7.50	4.50
21	Tommie Sisk	15.00	7.50	4.50
22	Willie Stargell	60.00	30.00	18.00
23	Bob Veale	15.00	7.50	4.50
24	Harry Walker	15.00	7.50	4.50
25	I Love The Pirates	20.00	10.00	6.00
26	Let's Go Pirates	20.00	10.00	6.00
27	Bob Clemente For Mayor	100.00	50.00	30.00
28	National League Batting Champion(Matty Alou)	15.00	7.50	4.50
29	Happiness Is A Pirate Win	20.00	10.00	6.00
30	Donn Clendenon Is My Hero	15.00	7.50	4.50
31	Pirates' Home Run Champion(Willie Stargell)	30.00	15.00	9.00
32	Pirates Logo	20.00	10.00	6.00
33	Pirates Pennant	25.00	12.50	7.50

1967 Topps Punch-Outs

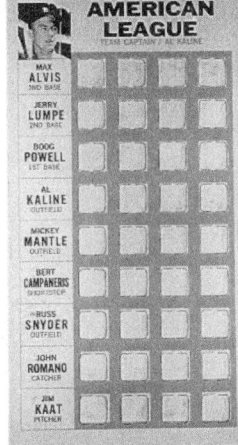

This test issue was reportedly released in the Maryland area in cello packs containing two perforated strips of three game cards each. Cards are printed in black, white and red and measure 2-1/2" x 4-2/3". Backs have instructions on how to play a baseball game by punching out the small squares on front. Only the "Team Captain" is pictured on the card. Each captain can be found with between one and four different lineups on his team, creating 196 different variations. The number of lineup variations for each captain is noted here. Some, though not all, of the cards of captains with different lineups have different photos at top. Among the more significant photo variations are Matty Alou, Roberto Clemente, Mickey Mantle and Frank Robinson. The unnumbered are listed here alphabetically. Previous checklists erroneously reported the existence of Punch-Outs of Bert Campaneris, Bob Gibson, Jerry Grote, Roy McMillan, and Brooks Robinson.

		NM	E	VG
	Complete Set (86):	20,000	10,000	6,000
	Common Player:	75.00	37.50	22.50
(1)	Hank Aaron- 2	1,500	750.00	450.00
(2)	Richie Allen - 3	125.00	65.00	35.00
(3)	Gene Alley - 2	90.00	45.00	27.50
(4)	Felipe Alou - 2	100.00	50.00	30.00
(5)	Matty Alou - 3	75.00	37.50	22.50
(6)	Max Alvis - 3	75.00	37.50	22.50
(7)	Luis Aparicio - 4	175.00	90.00	55.00

		NM	E	VG
(8)	Steve Barber - 2	90.00	45.00	27.50
(9)	Earl Battey - 3	75.00	37.50	22.50
(10)	Clete Boyer - 3	80.00	40.00	24.00
(11)	Ken Boyer - 3	80.00	40.00	24.00
(12)	Lou Brock - 2	250.00	125.00	75.00
(13)	Jim Bunning - 1	275.00	135.00	80.00
(14)	Johnny Callison - 2	90.00	45.00	27.50
(15)	Leo Cardenas - 3	75.00	37.50	22.50
(16)	Rico Carty - 2	90.00	45.00	27.50
(17)	Norm Cash - 3	80.00	40.00	24.00
(18)	Orlando Cepeda - 4	175.00	90.00	55.00
(19)	Ed Charles - 1	100.00	50.00	30.00
(20)	Roberto Clemente - 3	1,750	875.00	525.00
(21)	Don Clendenon - 2	90.00	45.00	27.50
(22)	Rocky Colavito - 1	200.00	100.00	50.00
(23)	Tony Conigliaro - 2	100.00	50.00	30.00
(24)	Willie Davis - 2	90.00	45.00	27.50
(25)	Johnny Edwards - 2	90.00	45.00	27.50
(26)	Andy Etchebarren - 2	90.00	45.00	27.50
(27)	Curt Flood - 2	90.00	45.00	27.50
(28)	Bill Freehan - 1	100.00	50.00	30.00
(29)	Jim Fregosi - 2	90.00	45.00	27.50
(30)	Dick Green - 3	75.00	37.50	22.50
(31)	Dick Groat - 3	80.00	40.00	24.00
(32)	Tom Haller - 2	90.00	45.00	27.50
(33)	Jim Ray Hart - 2	90.00	45.00	27.50
(34)	Mike Hershberger - 4	75.00	37.50	22.50
(35)	Elston Howard - 3	80.00	40.00	24.00
(36)	Frank Howard - 4	80.00	40.00	24.00
(37)	Ron Hunt - 3	75.00	37.50	22.50
(38)	Sonny Jackson - 1	100.00	50.00	30.00
(39)	Cleon Jones - 2	90.00	45.00	27.50
(40)	Jim Kaat - 2	100.00	50.00	30.00
(41)	Al Kaline - 2	250.00	125.00	75.00
(42)	Harmon Killebrew - 3	200.00	100.00	60.00
(43)	Bobby Knoop - 3	75.00	37.50	22.50
(44)	Sandy Koufax - 2	1,750	875.00	525.00
(45)	Ed Kranepool - 2	90.00	45.00	27.50
(46)	Jim Lefebvre - 2	90.00	45.00	27.50
(47)	Don Lock - 2	90.00	45.00	27.50
(48)	Jerry Lumpe - 1	100.00	50.00	30.00
(49)	Mickey Mantle - 2	2,500	1,250	750.00
(50)	Juan Marichal - 2	200.00	100.00	50.00
(51)	Willie Mays - 4	1,200	600.00	350.00
(52)	Bill Mazeroski - 2	225.00	115.00	65.00
(53)	Dick McAuliffe - 1	100.00	50.00	30.00
(54)	Tim McCarver - 3	80.00	40.00	24.00
(55)	Willie McCovey - 1	275.00	135.00	80.00
(56)	Denny McLain - 2	100.00	50.00	30.00
(57)	Denis Menke - 2	90.00	45.00	27.50
(58)	Joe Morgan - 2	225.00	115.00	65.00
(59)	Tony Oliva - 2	100.00	50.00	30.00
(60)	Joe Pepitone - 2	100.00	50.00	30.00
(61)	Gaylord Perry - 1	250.00	125.00	75.00
(62)	Vada Pinson - 2	100.00	50.00	30.00
(63)	Boog Powell - 4	80.00	40.00	24.00
(64)	Rick Reichardt - 1	100.00	50.00	30.00
(65)	Floyd Robinson - 1	100.00	50.00	30.00
(66)	Frank Robinson - 3	225.00	115.00	65.00
(67)	Johnny Romano - 4	75.00	37.50	22.50
(68)	Pete Rose - 2	1,750	875.00	525.00
(69)	John Roseboro - 1	100.00	50.00	30.00
(70)	Ron Santo - 2	150.00	75.00	45.00
(71)	Chico Salmon - 2	90.00	45.00	27.50
(72)	George Scott - 3	75.00	37.50	22.50
(73)	Sonny Siebert - 1	100.00	50.00	30.00
(74)	Russ Snyder - 3	75.00	37.50	22.50
(75)	Willie Stargell - 3	200.00	100.00	60.00
(76)	Mel Stottlemyre - 2	90.00	45.00	27.50
(77)	Joe Torre - 2	100.00	50.00	30.00
(78)	Cesar Tovar - 2	90.00	45.00	27.50
(79)	Tom Tresh - 2	90.00	45.00	27.50
(80)	Zoilo Versalles - 1	100.00	50.00	30.00
(81)	Leon Wagner - 2	90.00	45.00	27.50
(82)	Bill White - 3	75.00	37.50	22.50
(83)	Fred Whitfield - 3	75.00	37.50	22.50
(84)	Billy Williams - 2	225.00	115.00	65.00
(85)	Jimmy Wynn - 3	75.00	37.50	22.50
(86)	Carl Yastrzemski - 3	300.00	150.00	90.00

1967 Topps Red Sox Stickers

Like the 1967 Pirates Stickers, the Red Sox Stickers were part of the same test procedure. The Red Sox Stickers have the same 2-1/2" x 3-1/2" dimensions, color picture and large player's name on the front. A set is complete at 33 stickers. The majority are players, but themes such as "Let's Go Red Sox" are also included.

		NM	E	VG
Complete Set (33):		500.00	250.00	150.00
Common Player:		10.00	5.00	3.00
1	Dennis Bennett	10.00	5.00	3.00
2	Darrell Brandon	10.00	5.00	3.00
3	Tony Conigliaro	35.00	17.50	10.00
4	Don Demeter	10.00	5.00	3.00
5	Hank Fischer	10.00	5.00	3.00
6	Joe Foy	10.00	5.00	3.00
7	Mike Andrews	10.00	5.00	3.00
8	Dalton Jones	10.00	5.00	3.00
9	Jim Lonborg	10.00	5.00	3.00
10	Don McMahon	10.00	5.00	3.00
11	Dave Morehead	10.00	5.00	3.00
12	George Smith	10.00	5.00	3.00
13	Rico Petrocelli	15.00	7.50	4.50
14	Mike Ryan	10.00	5.00	3.00
15	Jose Santiago	10.00	5.00	3.00
16	George Scott	10.00	5.00	3.00
17	Sal Maglie	10.00	5.00	3.00
18	Reggie Smith	10.00	5.00	3.00
19	Lee Stange	10.00	5.00	3.00
20	Jerry Stephenson	10.00	5.00	3.00
21	Jose Tartabull	10.00	5.00	3.00
22	George Thomas	10.00	5.00	3.00
23	Bob Tillman	10.00	5.00	3.00
24	Johnnie Wyatt	10.00	5.00	3.00
25	Carl Yastrzemski	90.00	45.00	27.50
26	Dick Williams	10.00	5.00	3.00
27	I Love The Red Sox	12.50	6.25	3.75
28	Let's Go Red Sox	12.50	6.25	3.75
29	Carl Yastrzemski For Mayor	50.00	25.00	15.00
30	Tony Conigliaro Is My Hero	27.50	13.50	8.25
31	Happiness Is A Boston Win	12.50	6.25	3.75
32	Red Sox Logo	15.00	7.50	4.50
33	Red Sox Pennant	24.00	12.00	7.00

1967 Topps S.F. Giants Discs

One of several prototypes for pinback button sets which were never issued. Generally found in the form of a silver-foil cardboard square, about 2-3/8" a side, the 2-1/4" round center features color player photos or team booster slogans. The player's name and position are printed across his chest, the team name at top. At top-left is a tiny black "JAPAN." The unnumbered discs are checklisted here alphabetically.

		NM	E	VG
Complete Set (24):		9,000	4,500	2,200
Common Player:		200.00	100.00	60.00
(1)	Jesus Alou	200.00	100.00	60.00
(2)	Bob Bolin	200.00	100.00	60.00
(3)	Ollie Brown	200.00	100.00	60.00
(4)	Jim Davenport	200.00	100.00	60.00
(5)	Herman Franks	200.00	100.00	60.00
(6)	Len Gabrielson	200.00	100.00	60.00
(7)	Joe Gibbon	200.00	100.00	60.00
(8)	Tom Haller	200.00	100.00	60.00
(9)	Jim Ray Hart	200.00	100.00	60.00
(10)	Ron Herbel	200.00	100.00	60.00
(11)	Hal Lanier	200.00	100.00	60.00
(12)	Frank Linzy	200.00	100.00	60.00
(13)	Juan Marichal	975.00	460.00	275.00
(14)	Willie Mays	2,000	810.00	485.00
(15)	Willie McCovey	1,000	460.00	275.00
(16)	Lindy McDaniel	200.00	100.00	60.00
(17)	Gaylord Perry	900.00	410.00	245.00
(18)	Cap Peterson	200.00	100.00	60.00
(19)	Bob Priddy	200.00	100.00	60.00
(20)	Happiness is a Giant Win	115.00	57.00	34.00
(21)	I Love the Giants	115.00	57.00	34.00
(22)	Let's Go Giants	115.00	57.00	34.00
(23)	Willie Mays for Mayor (Willie Mays)	750.00	350.00	210.00
(24)	S.F. Giants Logo	115.00	57.00	34.00

1967 Topps Stand-Ups

Never actually issued, no more than a handful of each of these rare test issues have made their way into the hobby market. Designed so that the color photo of the player's head could be popped out of the black background and placed into a punch-out base to create a stand-up display, examples of these 3-1/8" x 5-1/4" cards can be found either on thick stock, die-cut around the portrait and with a die-cut stand, or as thin-stock proofs without the die-cutting. Blank-backed, there are 24 cards in the set, numbered on the front at bottom left.

		NM	E	VG
Complete Set, Thick (24):		75,000	37,500	22,500
Complete Set, Thin (24):		60,000	30,000	18,000
Common Player, Thick:		1,250	625.00	375.00
Common Player, Thin:		1,000	500.00	300.00
	THICK STOCK, DIE-CUT			
1	Pete Rose	4,750	2,375	1,425
2	Gary Peters	1,250	625.00	375.00
3	Frank Robinson	2,400	1,200	720.00
4	Jim Lonborg	1,250	625.00	375.00
5	Ron Swoboda	1,250	625.00	375.00
6	Harmon Killebrew	2,100	1,050	630.00
7	Roberto Clemente	8,500	4,250	2,550
8	Mickey Mantle	12,500	6,250	3,750
9	Jim Fregosi	1,250	625.00	375.00
10	Al Kaline	3,000	1,500	900.00
11	Don Drysdale	2,500	1,250	750.00
12	Dean Chance	1,250	625.00	375.00
13	Orlando Cepeda	1,750	875.00	525.00
14	Tim McCarver	1,400	700.00	420.00
15	Frank Howard	1,400	700.00	420.00
16	Max Alvis	1,250	625.00	375.00
17	Rusty Staub	1,400	700.00	420.00
18	Richie Allen	1,400	700.00	420.00
19	Willie Mays	8,500	4,250	2,550
20	Hank Aaron	8,500	4,250	2,550
21	Carl Yastrzemski	7,000	3,500	2,100
22	Ron Santo	1,600	800.00	480.00
23	Catfish Hunter	1,750	875.00	525.00
24	Jim Wynn	1,250	625.00	375.00
	THIN STOCK, PROOFS			
1	Pete Rose	3,750	1,875	1,125
2	Gary Peters	1,000	500.00	300.00
3	Frank Robinson	1,900	950.00	570.00
4	Jim Lonborg	1,000	500.00	300.00
5	Ron Swoboda	1,000	500.00	300.00
6	Harmon Killebrew	1,650	825.00	495.00
7	Roberto Clemente	6,500	3,250	1,950
8	Mickey Mantle	10,000	5,000	3,000
9	Jim Fregosi	1,000	500.00	300.00
10	Al Kaline	2,500	1,250	750.00
11	Don Drysdale	2,000	1,000	600.00
12	Dean Chance	1,000	500.00	300.00
13	Orlando Cepeda	1,400	700.00	420.00
14	Tim McCarver	1,100	550.00	330.00
15	Frank Howard	1,100	550.00	330.00
16	Max Alvis	1,000	500.00	300.00
17	Rusty Staub	1,100	550.00	330.00
18	Richie Allen	1,100	550.00	330.00
19	Willie Mays	7,000	3,500	2,100
20	Hank Aaron	7,000	3,500	2,100
21	Carl Yastrzemski	5,500	2,750	1,650
22	Ron Santo	1,350	650.00	350.00
23	Catfish Hunter	1,400	700.00	420.00
24	Jim Wynn	1,000	500.00	300.00

1967 Topps Who Am I?

A cartoon caption and goofy facial features were printed on the front of these 2-1/2" x 3-1/2" cards and were designed to be scratched off to reveal the portrait, name and claim to fame of the person beneath. This 44-card set includes all manner of U.S. and international historical figures, including four baseball players. Backs are printed in red and have a large question mark with several hints printed thereon. Unscratched cards are much rarer than scratched cards, though they carry only about a 50 percent premium.

	NM	E	VG
Complete Set (44):	850.00	425.00	250.00
Wax Pack:	350.00		
12 Babe Ruth	125.00	60.00	35.00
22 Mickey Mantle	225.00	110.00	65.00
33 Willie Mays	125.00	60.00	35.00
41 Sandy Koufax	125.00	60.00	35.00

1968 Tipps From Topps Book

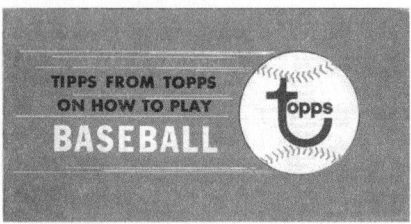

While the Bazooka brand is not referenced in this booklet, it presents the baseball playing tips that appeared on box backs of Bazooka gum. The player photo and cartoon tips are printed in blue in the interior pages of the 5-7/8" x 3" book. The front and back covers are black, white and green. The manner of distribution for this premium is not known.

	NM	E	VG
Tipps From Topps Book	150.00	75.00	45.00

1968 Topps

 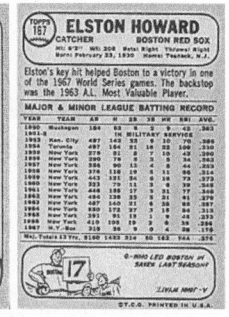

In 1968, Topps returned to a 598-card set of 2-1/2" x 3-1/2" cards. It is not, however, more of the same by way of appearance as the cards feature a color photograph on a background of what appears to be a burlap fabric. The player's name is below the photo but on the unusual background. A colored circle on the lower right carries the team and position. Backs were also changed, while retaining the vertical format introduced the previous year, with stats in the middle and cartoon at the bottom. The set features many of the old favorite subsets, including statistical leaders, World Series

highlights, multi-player cards, checklists, rookie cards and the return of All-Star cards. Most checklist cards are double-printed, once in the series preceding the series it lists and once within the series it lists; subtle variations between the pairs are listed where known. It is now believed that the Yellow Team variations of cards #49 and 66 originated in the Milton Bradley Win-A-Card board game.

	NM	E	VG
Complete Set (598):	3,000	1,500	900.00
Common Player (1-457):	2.00	1.00	.60
Common Player (458-598):	5.00	2.50	1.50
1 N.L. Batting Leaders(Matty Alou, Roberto Clemente, Tony Gonzalez)	20.00	7.50	3.75
2 A.L. Batting Leaders (Al Kaline, Frank Robinson, Carl Yastrzemski)	15.00	7.50	3.75
3 N.L. RBI Leaders(Hank Aaron, Orlando Cepeda, Roberto Clemente)	15.00	7.50	3.75
4 A.L. RBI Leaders (Harmon Killebrew, Frank Robinson, Carl Yastrzemski)	12.00	6.00	3.50
5 N.L. Home Run Leaders(Hank Aaron, Willie McCovey, Ron Santo, Jim Wynn)	24.00	10.00	6.00
6 A.L. Home Run Leaders (Frank Howard, Harmon Killebrew, Carl Yastrzemski)	14.00	6.00	3.50
7 N.L. ERA Leaders (Jim Bunning, Phil Niekro, Chris Short)	7.00	3.50	2.00
8 A.L. ERA Leaders (Joe Horlen, Gary Peters, Sonny Siebert)	2.00	1.00	.60
9 N.L. Pitching Leaders (Jim Bunning, Fergie Jenkins, Mike McCormick, Claude Osteen)	7.00	3.50	2.00
10a A.L. Pitching Leaders (Dean Chance, Jim Lonborg, Earl Wilson) ("Lonberg" on back.)	9.00	4.50	2.75
10b A.L. Pitching Leaders (Dean Chance, Jim Lonborg, Earl Wilson) ("Lonborg" on back.)	7.00	3.50	2.00
11 N.L. Strikeout Leaders (Jim Bunning, Fergie Jenkins, Gaylord Perry)	7.00	3.50	2.00
12 A.L. Strikeout Leaders (Dean Chance, Jim Lonborg, Sam McDowell)	7.00	3.50	2.00
13 Chuck Hartenstein	2.00	1.00	.60
14 Jerry McNertney	2.00	1.00	.60
15 Ron Hunt	2.00	1.00	.60
16 Indians Rookies (Lou Piniella, Richie Scheinblum)	5.00	2.50	1.50
17 Dick Hall	2.00	1.00	.60
18 Mike Hershberger	2.00	1.00	.60
19 Juan Pizarro	2.00	1.00	.60
20 Brooks Robinson	20.00	10.00	5.00
21 Ron Davis	2.00	1.00	.60
22 Pat Dobson	2.00	1.00	.60
23 Chico Cardenas	2.00	1.00	.60
24 Bobby Locke	2.00	1.00	.60
25 Julian Javier	2.00	1.00	.60
26 Darrell Brandon	2.00	1.00	.60
27 Gil Hodges	7.50	3.75	2.25
28 Ted Uhlaender	2.00	1.00	.60
29 Joe Verbanic	2.00	1.00	.60
30 Joe Torre	8.00	4.00	2.50
31 Ed Stroud	2.00	1.00	.60
32 Joe Gibbon	2.00	1.00	.60
33 Pete Ward	2.00	1.00	.60
34 Al Ferrara	2.00	1.00	.60
35 Steve Hargan	2.00	1.00	.60
36 Pirates Rookies (Bob Moose, Bob Robertson RC)	2.00	1.00	.60
37 Billy Williams	13.50	6.75	4.00
38 Tony Pierce	2.00	1.00	.60
39 Cookie Rojas	2.00	1.00	.60
40 Denny McLain	20.00	10.00	5.00
41 Julio Gotay	2.00	1.00	.60
42 Larry Haney	2.00	1.00	.60
43 Gary Bell	2.00	1.00	.60
44 Frank Kostro	2.00	1.00	.60
45 Tom Seaver	50.00	25.00	12.50
46 Dave Ricketts	2.00	1.00	.60
47 Ralph Houk	2.50	1.25	.70

	NM	E	VG
48 Ted Davidson	2.00	1.00	.60
49a Ed Brinkman (Yellow team.)	400.00	200.00	120.00
49b Ed Brinkman (White team.)	2.00	1.00	.60
50 Willie Mays	60.00	30.00	15.00
51 Bob Locker	2.00	1.00	.60
52 Hawk Taylor	2.00	1.00	.60
53 Gene Alley	2.00	1.00	.60
54 Stan Williams	2.00	1.00	.60
55 Felipe Alou	5.00	2.50	1.50
56 Orioles Rookies(Dave Leonhard, Dave May)	2.00	1.00	.60
57 Dan Schneider	2.00	1.00	.60
58 Ed Mathews	15.00	7.50	3.75
59 Don Lock	2.00	1.00	.60
60 Ken Holtzman	2.00	1.00	.60
61 Reggie Smith	2.00	1.00	.60
62 Chuck Dobson	2.00	1.00	.60
63 Dick Kenworthy	2.00	1.00	.60
64 Jim Merritt	2.00	1.00	.60
65 John Roseboro	2.00	1.00	.60
66a Casey Cox (Yellow team.)	50.00	25.00	15.00
66b Casey Cox (White team.)	2.00	1.00	.60
67 1st Series Check List (1-109)(Jim Kaat)	5.00	2.50	1.50
68 Ron Willis	2.00	1.00	.60
69 Tom Tresh	6.00	3.00	1.75
70 Bob Veale	2.00	1.00	.60
71 Vern Fuller	2.00	1.00	.60
72 Tommy John	5.00	2.50	1.50
73 Jim Hart	2.00	1.00	.60
74 Milt Pappas	2.00	1.00	.60
75 Don Mincher	2.00	1.00	.60
76 Braves Rookies(Jim Britton, Ron Reed RC)	2.00	1.00	.60
77 Don Wilson RC	2.00	1.00	.60
78 Jim Northrup	2.00	1.00	.60
79 Ted Kubiak	2.00	1.00	.60
80 Rod Carew	50.00	25.00	12.50
81 Larry Jackson	2.00	1.00	.60
82 Sam Bowens	2.00	1.00	.60
83 John Stephenson	2.00	1.00	.60
84 Bob Tolan	2.00	1.00	.60
85 Gaylord Perry	10.00	4.50	2.75
86 Willie Stargell	15.00	6.00	3.50
87 Dick Williams	2.00	1.00	.60
88 Phil Regan	2.00	1.00	.60
89 Jake Gibbs	2.00	1.00	.60
90 Vada Pinson	5.00	2.50	1.50
91 Jim Ollom	2.00	1.00	.60
92 Ed Kranepool	2.00	1.00	.60
93 Tony Cloninger	2.00	1.00	.60
94 Lee Maye	2.00	1.00	.60
95 Bob Aspromonte	2.00	1.00	.60
96 Senators Rookies (Frank Coggins, Dick Nold)	2.00	1.00	.60
97 Tom Phoebus	2.00	1.00	.60
98 Gary Sutherland	2.00	1.00	.60
99 Rocky Colavito	7.00	3.50	2.00
100 Bob Gibson	20.00	10.00	5.00
101 Glenn Beckert	2.00	1.00	.60
102 Jose Cardenal	2.00	1.00	.60
103 Don Sutton	9.00	4.50	2.75
104 Dick Dietz	2.00	1.00	.60
105 Al Downing	2.00	1.00	.60
106 Dalton Jones	2.00	1.00	.60
107 2nd Series Check List (110-196)(Juan Marichal)	5.00	2.50	1.50
108 Don Pavletich	2.00	1.00	.60
109 Bert Campaneris	2.00	1.00	.60
110 Hank Aaron	65.00	32.00	20.00
111 Rich Reese	2.00	1.00	.60
112 Woody Fryman	2.00	1.00	.60
113 Tigers Rookies(Tom Matchick, Daryl Patterson)	2.00	1.00	.60
114 Ron Swoboda	2.00	1.00	.60
115 Sam McDowell	2.00	1.00	.60
116 Ken McMullen	2.00	1.00	.60
117 Larry Jaster	2.00	1.00	.60
118 Mark Belanger	2.00	1.00	.60
119 Ted Savage	2.00	1.00	.60
120 Mel Stottlemyre	5.00	2.50	1.50
121 Jimmie Hall	2.00	1.00	.60
122 Gene Mauch	2.00	1.00	.60
123 Jose Santiago	2.00	1.00	.60
124 Nate Oliver	2.00	1.00	.60
125 Joe Horlen	2.00	1.00	.60
126 Bobby Etheridge	2.00	1.00	.60
127 Paul Lindblad	2.00	1.00	.60
128 Astros Rookies (Tom Dukes, Alonzo Harris)	2.00	1.00	.60
129 Mickey Stanley	2.00	1.00	.60
130 Tony Perez	15.00	5.00	3.00
131 Frank Bertaina	2.00	1.00	.60
132 Bud Harrelson	2.00	1.00	.60
133 Fred Whitfield	2.00	1.00	.60

#	Name			
134	Pat Jarvis	2.00	1.00	.60
135	Paul Blair	2.00	1.00	.60
136	Randy Hundley	2.00	1.00	.60
137	Twins Team	5.00	2.50	1.50
138	Ruben Amaro	2.00	1.00	.60
139	Chris Short	2.00	1.00	.60
140	Tony Conigliaro	5.00	2.50	1.50
141	Dal Maxvill	2.00	1.00	.60
142	White Sox Rookies(Buddy Bradford, Bill Voss)	2.00	1.00	.60
143	Pete Cimino	2.00	1.00	.60
144	Joe Morgan	12.00	6.00	3.50
145	Don Drysdale	15.00	7.50	4.50
146	Sal Bando	2.00	1.00	.60
147	Frank Linzy	2.00	1.00	.60
148	Dave Bristol	2.00	1.00	.60
149	Bob Saverine	2.00	1.00	.60
150	Roberto Clemente	90.00	50.00	25.00
151	World Series Game 1 (Brock Socks 4 Hits in Opener)	7.00	3.00	1.75
152	World Series Game 2 (Yaz Smashes Two Homers)	12.00	6.00	3.00
153	World Series Game 3 (Briles Cools Off Boston)	3.00	1.50	.90
154	World Series Game 4 (Gibson Hurls Shutout)	9.00	4.50	2.75
155	World Series Game 5 (Lonborg Wins Again)	6.00	3.00	1.75
156	World Series Game 6 (Petrocelli Socks Two Homers)	6.00	3.00	1.75
157	World Series Game 7 (St. Louis Wins It)	6.00	3.00	1.75
158	1967 World Series (The Cardinals Celebrate)	5.00	2.50	1.50
159	Don Kessinger	2.00	1.00	.60
160	Earl Wilson	2.00	1.00	.60
161	Norm Miller	2.00	1.00	.60
162	Cards Rookies(Hal Gilson, Mike Torrez RC)	2.00	1.00	.60
163	Gene Brabender	2.00	1.00	.60
164	Ramon Webster	2.00	1.00	.60
165	Tony Oliva	7.00	2.50	1.50
166	Claude Raymond	2.00	1.00	.60
167	Elston Howard	5.00	2.50	1.50
168	**Dodgers Team**	5.00	2.50	1.50
169	Bob Bolin	2.00	1.00	.60
170	Jim Fregosi	2.00	1.00	.60
171	Don Nottebart	2.00	1.00	.60
172	Walt Williams	2.00	1.00	.60
173	John Boozer	2.00	1.00	.60
174	Bob Tillman	2.00	1.00	.60
175	Maury Wills	2.00	1.00	.60
176	Bob Allen	2.00	1.00	.60
177	Mets Rookies (Jerry Koosman RC, Nolan Ryan RC)	500.00	245.00	150.00
178	Don Wert	2.00	1.00	.60
179	Bill Stoneman	2.00	1.00	.60
180	Curt Flood	3.00	1.50	.90
181	Jerry Zimmerman	2.00	1.00	.60
182	Dave Giusti	2.00	1.00	.60
183	Bob Kennedy	2.00	1.00	.60
184	Lou Johnson	2.00	1.00	.60
185	Tom Haller	2.00	1.00	.60
186	Eddie Watt	2.00	1.00	.60
187	Sonny Jackson	2.00	1.00	.60
188	Cap Peterson	2.00	1.00	.60
189	Bill Landis	2.00	1.00	.60
190	Bill White	2.00	1.00	.60
191	Dan Frisella	2.00	1.00	.60
192a	3rd Series Check List (197-283)(Carl Yastrzemski) ("To increase the..." on back.)	6.00	3.00	1.75
192b	3rd Series Check List (197-283)(Carl Yastrzemski) ("To increase your..." on back.)	6.00	3.00	1.75
193	Jack Hamilton	2.00	1.00	.60
194	Don Buford	2.00	1.00	.60
195	Joe Pepitone	5.00	2.50	1.50
196	Gary Nolan	2.00	1.00	.60
197	Larry Brown	2.00	1.00	.60
198	Roy Face	2.00	1.00	.60
199	A's Rookies (Darrell Osteen, Roberto Rodriguez)	2.00	1.00	.60
200	Orlando Cepeda	11.00	5.50	3.25
201	Mike Marshall RC	3.00	1.50	.90
202	Adolfo Phillips	2.00	1.00	.60
203	Dick Kelley	2.00	1.00	.60
204	Andy Etchebarren	2.00	1.00	.60
205	Juan Marichal	9.00	4.50	2.75
206	Cal Ermer	2.00	1.00	.60
207	Carroll Sembera	2.00	1.00	.60
208	Willie Davis	2.00	1.00	.60
209	Tim Cullen	2.00	1.00	.60
210	Gary Peters	2.00	1.00	.60
211	J.C. Martin	2.00	1.00	.60
212	Dave Morehead	2.00	1.00	.60
213	Chico Ruiz	2.00	1.00	.60
214	Yankees Rookies(Stan Bahnsen, Frank Fernandez)	2.00	1.00	.60
215	Jim Bunning	9.00	4.50	2.75
216	Bubba Morton	2.00	1.00	.60
217	Turk Farrell	2.00	1.00	.60
218	Ken Suarez	2.00	1.00	.60
219	Rob Gardner	2.00	1.00	.60
220	Harmon Killebrew	20.00	7.50	3.75
221	Braves Team	5.00	2.50	1.50
222	Jim Hardin	2.00	1.00	.60
223	Ollie Brown	2.00	1.00	.60
224	Jack Aker	2.00	1.00	.60
225	Richie Allen	6.00	3.00	1.75
226	Jimmie Price	2.00	1.00	.60
227	Joe Hoerner	2.00	1.00	.60
228	Dodgers Rookies (Jack Billingham RC, Jim Fairey)	2.00	1.00	.60
229	Fred Klages	2.00	1.00	.60
230	Pete Rose	50.00	25.00	12.50
231	Dave Baldwin	2.00	1.00	.60
232	Denis Menke	2.00	1.00	.60
233	George Scott	2.00	1.00	.60
234	Bill Monbouquette	2.00	1.00	.60
235	Ron Santo	15.00	7.50	4.50
236	Tug McGraw	2.00	1.00	.60
237	Alvin Dark	2.00	1.00	.60
238	Tom Satriano	2.00	1.00	.60
239	Bill Henry	2.00	1.00	.60
240	Al Kaline	35.00	18.00	10.00
241	Felix Millan	2.00	1.00	.60
242	Moe Drabowsky	2.00	1.00	.60
243	Rich Rollins	2.00	1.00	.60
244	John Donaldson	2.00	1.00	.60
245	Tony Gonzalez	2.00	1.00	.60
246	Fritz Peterson	2.00	1.00	.60
247	Reds Rookies (Johnny Bench RC, Ron Tompkins)	125.00	62.50	31.25
248	Fred Valentine	2.00	1.00	.60
249	Bill Singer	2.00	1.00	.60
250	Carl Yastrzemski	20.00	10.00	6.00
251	Manny Sanguillen RC	4.50	2.25	1.25
252	Angels Team	5.00	2.50	1.50
253	Dick Hughes	2.00	1.00	.60
254	Cleon Jones	2.00	1.00	.60
255	Dean Chance	2.00	1.00	.60
256	Norm Cash	7.00	3.50	2.00
257	Phil Niekro	9.00	4.50	2.75
258	Cubs Rookies (Jose Arcia, Bill Schlesinger)	2.00	1.00	.60
259	Ken Boyer	5.00	2.50	1.50
260	Jim Wynn	2.00	1.00	.60
261	Dave Duncan	2.00	1.00	.60
262	Rick Wise	2.00	1.00	.60
263	Horace Clarke	2.00	1.00	.60
264	Ted Abernathy	2.00	1.00	.60
265	Tommy Davis	2.00	1.00	.60
266	Paul Popovich	2.00	1.00	.60
267	Herman Franks	2.00	1.00	.60
268	Bob Humphreys	2.00	1.00	.60
269	Bob Tiefenauer	2.00	1.00	.60
270	Matty Alou	2.00	1.00	.60
271	Bobby Knoop	2.00	1.00	.60
272	Ray Culp	2.00	1.00	.60
273	Dave Johnson	2.00	1.00	.60
274	Mike Cuellar	2.00	1.00	.60
275	Tim McCarver	5.00	2.50	1.50
276	Jim Roland	2.00	1.00	.60
277	Jerry Buchek	2.00	1.00	.60
278a	4th Series Check List (284-370)(Orlando Cepeda) (Copyright at right.)	5.00	2.50	1.50
278b	4th Series Check List (284-370)(Orlando Cepeda) (Copyright at left.)	5.50	2.75	1.75
279	Bill Hands	2.00	1.00	.60
280	Mickey Mantle	315.00	125.00	75.00
281	Jim Campanis	2.00	1.00	.60
282	Rick Monday	2.00	1.00	.60
283	Mel Queen	2.00	1.00	.60
284	John Briggs	2.00	1.00	.60
285	Dick McAuliffe	2.00	1.00	.60
286	Cecil Upshaw	2.00	1.00	.60
287	White Sox Rookies (Mickey Abarbanel, Cisco Carlos)	2.00	1.00	.60
288	Dave Wickersham	2.00	1.00	.60
289	Woody Held	2.00	1.00	.60
290	Willie McCovey	18.00	7.50	3.75
291	Dick Lines	2.00	1.00	.60
292	Art Shamsky	2.00	1.00	.60
293	Bruce Howard	2.00	1.00	.60
294	Red Schoendienst	7.00	3.50	2.00
295	Sonny Siebert	2.00	1.00	.60
296	Byron Browne	2.00	1.00	.60
297	Russ Gibson	2.00	1.00	.60
298	Jim Brewer	2.00	1.00	.60
299	Gene Michael	2.00	1.00	.60
300	Rusty Staub	2.50	1.25	.70
301	Twins Rookies (George Mitterwald, Rick Renick)	2.00	1.00	.60
302	Gerry Arrigo	2.00	1.00	.60
303	Dick Green	2.00	1.00	.60
304	Sandy Valdespino	2.00	1.00	.60
305	Minnie Rojas	2.00	1.00	.60
306	Mike Ryan	2.00	1.00	.60
307	John Hiller	2.00	1.00	.60
308	Pirates Team	6.00	3.00	1.75
309	Ken Henderson	2.00	1.00	.60
310	Luis Aparicio	14.00	5.50	3.25
311	Jack Lamabe	2.00	1.00	.60
312	Curt Blefary	2.00	1.00	.60
313	Al Weis	2.00	1.00	.60
314	Red Sox Rookies (Bill Rohr, George Spriggs)	2.00	1.00	.60
315	Zoilo Versalles	2.00	1.00	.60
316	Steve Barber	2.00	1.00	.60
317	Ron Brand	2.00	1.00	.60
318	Chico Salmon	2.00	1.00	.60
319	George Culver	2.00	1.00	.60
320	Frank Howard	2.50	1.25	.70
321	Leo Durocher	6.00	3.00	1.75
322	Dave Boswell	2.00	1.00	.60
323	Deron Johnson	2.00	1.00	.60
324	Jim Nash	2.00	1.00	.60
325	Manny Mota	2.00	1.00	.60
326	Dennis Ribant	2.00	1.00	.60
327	Tony Taylor	2.00	1.00	.60
328	Angels Rookies (Chuck Vinson, Jim Weaver)	2.00	1.00	.60
329	Duane Josephson	2.00	1.00	.60
330	Roger Maris	40.00	20.00	12.00
331	Dan Osinski	2.00	1.00	.60
332	Doug Rader	2.00	1.00	.60
333	Ron Herbel	2.00	1.00	.60
334	Orioles Team	5.00	2.50	1.50
335	Bob Allison	2.00	1.00	.60
336	John Purdin	2.00	1.00	.60
337	Bill Robinson	2.00	1.00	.60
338	Bob Johnson	2.00	1.00	.60
339	Rich Nye	2.00	1.00	.60
340	Max Alvis	2.00	1.00	.60
341	Jim Lemon	2.00	1.00	.60
342	Ken Johnson	2.00	1.00	.60
343	Jim Gosger	2.00	1.00	.60
344	Donn Clendenon	2.00	1.00	.60
345	Bob Hendley	2.00	1.00	.60
346	Jerry Adair	2.00	1.00	.60
347	George Brunet	2.00	1.00	.60
348	Phillies Rookies (Larry Colton, Dick Thoenen)	2.00	1.00	.60
349	Ed Spiezio	2.00	1.00	.60
350	Hoyt Wilhelm	9.00	4.50	2.75
351	Bob Barton	2.00	1.00	.60
352	Jackie Hernandez	2.00	1.00	.60
353	Mack Jones	2.00	1.00	.60
354	Pete Richert	2.00	1.00	.60
355	Ernie Banks	24.00	10.00	6.00
356a	5th Series Check List (371-457)(Ken Holtzman) (Top of cap away from black circle.)	8.00	2.50	1.50
356b	5th Series Check List (371-457)(Ken Holtzman) (Top of cap near black circle.)	5.00	2.50	1.50
357	Len Gabrielson	2.00	1.00	.60
358	Mike Epstein	2.00	1.00	.60
359	Joe Moeller	2.00	1.00	.60
360	Willie Horton	2.00	1.00	.60
361	Harmon Killebrew (All-Star)	9.00	3.75	2.25
362	Orlando Cepeda (All-Star)	8.00	2.50	1.50
363	Rod Carew (All-Star)	9.00	3.25	2.00
364	Joe Morgan (All-Star)	8.00	3.00	1.75
365	Brooks Robinson (All-Star)	9.00	3.75	2.25
366	Ron Santo (All-Star)	8.00	2.50	1.50
367	Jim Fregosi (All-Star)	2.00	1.00	.60
368	Gene Alley (All-Star)	2.00	1.00	.60
369	Carl Yastrzemski (All-Star)	9.00	3.75	2.25
370	Hank Aaron (All-Star)	25.00	12.50	6.25
371	Tony Oliva (All-Star)	3.00	1.25	.70
372	Lou Brock (All-Star)	8.00	3.00	1.75
373	Frank Robinson (All-Star)	9.00	3.75	2.25
374	Roberto Clemente (All-Star)	25.00	12.50	6.25

375	Bill Freehan (All-Star)	2.00	1.00	.60
376	Tim McCarver (All-Star)	3.00	1.50	.90
377	Joe Horlen (All-Star)	2.00	1.00	.60
378	Bob Gibson (All-Star)	9.00	3.50	2.00
379	Gary Peters (All-Star)	2.00	1.00	.60
380	Ken Holtzman (All-Star)	2.00	1.00	.60
381	Boog Powell	3.00	1.50	.90
382	Ramon Hernandez	2.00	1.00	.60
383	Steve Whitaker	2.00	1.00	.60
384	Red Rookies (Bill Henry, Hal McRae **RC**)	6.00	3.00	1.75
385	Jim Hunter	10.00	5.00	3.00
386	Greg Goossen	2.00	1.00	.60
387	Joe Foy	2.00	1.00	.60
388	Ray Washburn	2.00	1.00	.60
389	Jay Johnstone	2.00	1.00	.60
390	Bill Mazeroski	10.00	5.00	3.00
391	Bob Priddy	2.00	1.00	.60
392	Grady Hatton	2.00	1.00	.60
393	Jim Perry	2.00	1.00	.60
394	Tommie Aaron	2.00	1.00	.60
395	Camilo Pascual	2.00	1.00	.60
396	Bobby Wine	2.00	1.00	.60
397	Vic Davalillo	2.00	1.00	.60
398	Jim Grant	2.00	1.00	.60
399	Ray Oyler	2.00	1.00	.60
400a	Mike McCormick (White team.)	600.00	300.00	180.00
400b	Mike McCormick (Yellow team.)	2.00	1.00	.60
401	Mets Team	5.00	2.50	1.50
402	Mike Hegan	2.00	1.00	.60
403	John Buzhardt	2.00	1.00	.60
404	Floyd Robinson	2.00	1.00	.60
405	Tommy Helms	2.00	1.00	.60
406	Dick Ellsworth	2.00	1.00	.60
407	Gary Kolb	2.00	1.00	.60
408	Steve Carlton	20.00	10.00	5.00
409	Orioles Rookies (Frank Peters, Ron Stone)	2.00	1.00	.60
410	Fergie Jenkins	10.00	5.00	3.00
411	Ron Hansen	2.00	1.00	.60
412	Clay Carroll	2.00	1.00	.60
413	Tommy McCraw	2.00	1.00	.60
414	Mickey Lolich	2.00	1.00	.60
415	Johnny Callison	2.00	1.00	.60
416	Bill Rigney	2.00	1.00	.60
417	Willie Crawford	2.00	1.00	.60
418	Eddie Fisher	2.00	1.00	.60
419	Jack Hiatt	2.00	1.00	.60
420	Cesar Tovar	2.00	1.00	.60
421	Ron Taylor	2.00	1.00	.60
422	Rene Lachemann	2.00	1.00	.60
423	Fred Gladding	2.00	1.00	.60
424	White Sox Team	5.00	2.50	1.50
425	Jim Maloney	2.00	1.00	.60
426	Hank Allen	2.00	1.00	.60
427	Dick Calmus	2.00	1.00	.60
428	Vic Roznovsky	2.00	1.00	.60
429	Tommie Sisk	2.00	1.00	.60
430	Rico Petrocelli	2.00	1.00	.60
431	Dooley Womack	2.00	1.00	.60
432	Indians Rookies (Bill Davis, Jose Vidal)	2.00	1.00	.60
433	Bob Rodgers	2.00	1.00	.60
434	Ricardo Joseph	2.00	1.00	.60
435	Ron Perranoski	2.00	1.00	.60
436	Hal Lanier	2.00	1.00	.60
437	Don Cardwell	2.00	1.00	.60
438	Lee Thomas	2.00	1.00	.60
439	Luman Harris	2.00	1.00	.60
440	Claude Osteen	2.00	1.00	.60
441	Alex Johnson	2.00	1.00	.60
442	Dick Bosman	2.00	1.00	.60
443	Joe Azcue	2.00	1.00	.60
444	Jack Fisher	2.00	1.00	.60
445	Mike Shannon	2.00	1.00	.60
446	Ron Kline	2.00	1.00	.60
447	Tigers Rookies (George Korince, Fred Lasher)	2.00	1.00	.60
448	Gary Wagner	2.00	1.00	.60
449	Gene Oliver	2.00	1.00	.60
450	Jim Kaat	2.50	1.25	.70
451	Al Spangler	2.00	1.00	.60
452	Jesus Alou	2.00	1.00	.60
453	Sammy Ellis	2.00	1.00	.60
454a	6th Series Check List (458-533)(Frank Robinson) (Neck chain shows.)	6.00	3.00	1.75
454b	6th Series Check List (458-533)(Frank Robinson) (No neck chain.)	6.00	3.00	1.75
455	Rico Carty	2.00	1.00	.60
456	John O'Donoghue	2.00	1.00	.60
457	Jim Lefebvre	2.00	1.00	.60
458	Lew Krausse	5.00	2.50	1.50

459	Dick Simpson	5.00	2.50	1.50
460	Jim Lonborg	5.00	2.50	1.50
461	Chuck Hiller	5.00	2.50	1.50
462	Barry Moore	5.00	2.50	1.50
463	Jimmie Schaffer	5.00	2.50	1.50
464	Don McMahon	5.00	2.50	1.50
465	Tommie Agee	5.00	2.50	1.50
466	Bill Dillman	5.00	2.50	1.50
467	Dick Howser	5.00	2.50	1.50
468	Larry Sherry	5.00	2.50	1.50
469	Ty Cline	5.00	2.50	1.50
470	Bill Freehan	5.00	2.50	1.50
471	Orlando Pena	5.00	2.50	1.50
472	Walt Alston	8.00	4.00	2.50
473	Al Worthington	5.00	2.50	1.50
474	Paul Schaal	5.00	2.50	1.50
475	Joe Niekro	5.00	2.50	1.50
476	Woody Woodward	5.00	2.50	1.50
477	Phillies Team	6.00	3.00	1.75
478	Dave McNally	5.00	2.50	1.50
479	Phil Gagliano	5.00	2.50	1.50
480	Manager's Dream (Chico Cardenas, Roberto Clemente, Tony Oliva)	65.00	35.00	20.00
481	John Wyatt	5.00	2.50	1.50
482	Jose Pagan	5.00	2.50	1.50
483	Darold Knowles	5.00	2.50	1.50
484	Phil Roof	5.00	2.50	1.50
485	Ken Berry	5.00	2.50	1.50
486	Cal Koonce	5.00	2.50	1.50
487	Lee May	5.00	2.50	1.50
488	Dick Tracewski	5.00	2.50	1.50
489	Wally Bunker	5.00	2.50	1.50
490	Super Stars (Harmon Killebrew, Mickey Mantle, Willie Mays)	140.00	70.00	35.00
491	Denny Lemaster	5.00	2.50	1.50
492	Jeff Torborg	5.00	2.50	1.50
493	Jim McGlothlin	5.00	2.50	1.50
494	Ray Sadecki	5.00	2.50	1.50
495	Leon Wagner	5.00	2.50	1.50
496	Steve Hamilton	5.00	2.50	1.50
497	Cards Team	6.00	3.00	1.75
498	Bill Bryan	5.00	2.50	1.50
499	Steve Blass	5.00	2.50	1.50
500	Frank Robinson	25.00	12.50	7.50
501	John Odom	5.00	2.50	1.50
502	Mike Andrews	5.00	2.50	1.50
503	Al Jackson	5.00	2.50	1.50
504	Russ Snyder	5.00	2.50	1.50
505	Joe Sparma	5.00	2.50	1.50
506	Clarence Jones	5.00	2.50	1.50
507	Wade Blasingame	5.00	2.50	1.50
508	Duke Sims	5.00	2.50	1.50
509	Dennis Higgins	5.00	2.50	1.50
510	Ron Fairly	5.00	2.50	1.50
511	Bill Kelso	5.00	2.50	1.50
512	Grant Jackson	5.00	2.50	1.50
513	Hank Bauer	5.00	2.50	1.50
514	Al McBean	5.00	2.50	1.50
515	Russ Nixon	5.00	2.50	1.50
516	Pete Mikkelsen	5.00	2.50	1.50
517	Diego Segui	5.00	2.50	1.50
518a	7th Series Check List (534-598)(Clete Boyer) (539 is Maj. L. Rookies)	6.00	3.00	1.75
518b	7th Series Check List (534-598)(Clete Boyer) (539 is Amer. L. Rookies)	10.00	5.00	3.00
519	Jerry Stephenson	5.00	2.50	1.50
520	Lou Brock	15.00	7.50	3.75
521	Don Shaw	5.00	2.50	1.50
522	Wayne Causey	5.00	2.50	1.50
523	John Tsitouris	5.00	2.50	1.50
524	Andy Kosco	5.00	2.50	1.50
525	Jim Davenport	5.00	2.50	1.50
526	Bill Denehy	5.00	2.50	1.50
527	Tito Francona	5.00	2.50	1.50
528	Tigers Team	48.00	22.50	11.25
529	Bruce Von Hoff	5.00	2.50	1.50
530	Bird Belters (Brooks Robinson, Frank Robinson)	23.00	12.50	6.25
531	Chuck Hinton	5.00	2.50	1.50
532	Luis Tiant	5.00	2.50	1.50
533	Wes Parker	5.00	2.50	1.50
534	Bob Miller	5.00	2.50	1.50
535	Danny Cater	5.00	2.50	1.50
536	Bill Short	5.00	2.50	1.50
537	Norm Siebern	5.00	2.50	1.50
538	Manny Jimenez	5.00	2.50	1.50
539	Major League Rookies (Mike Ferraro, Jim Ray)	5.00	2.50	1.50
540	Nelson Briles	5.00	2.50	1.50
541	Sandy Alomar	5.00	2.50	1.50
542	John Boccabella	5.00	2.50	1.50
543	Bob Lee	5.00	2.50	1.50

544	Mayo Smith	5.00	2.50	1.50
545	Lindy McDaniel	5.00	2.50	1.50
546	Roy White	4.50	2.25	1.25
547	Dan Coombs	5.00	2.50	1.50
548	Bernie Allen	5.00	2.50	1.50
549	Orioles Rookies (Curt Motton, Roger Nelson)	5.00	2.50	1.50
550	Clete Boyer	5.00	2.50	1.50
551	Darrell Sutherland	5.00	2.50	1.50
552	Ed Kirkpatrick	5.00	2.50	1.50
553	Hank Aguirre	5.00	2.50	1.50
554	A's Team	6.00	3.00	1.75
555	Jose Tartabull	5.00	2.50	1.50
556	Dick Selma	5.00	2.50	1.50
557	Frank Quilici	5.00	2.50	1.50
558	John Edwards	5.00	2.50	1.50
559	Pirates Rookies (Carl Taylor, Luke Walker)	5.00	2.50	1.50
560	Paul Casanova	5.00	2.50	1.50
561	Lee Elia	5.00	2.50	1.50
562	Jim Bouton	6.00	3.00	1.75
563	Ed Charles	5.00	2.50	1.50
564	Eddie Stanky	5.00	2.50	1.50
565	Larry Dierker	5.00	2.50	1.50
566	Ken Harrelson	5.00	2.50	1.50
567	Clay Dalrymple	5.00	2.50	1.50
568	Willie Smith	5.00	2.50	1.50
569	N.L. Rookies (Ivan Murrell, Les Rohr)	5.00	2.50	1.50
570	Rick Reichardt	5.00	2.50	1.50
571	Tony LaRussa	6.00	3.00	1.75
572	Don Bosch	5.00	2.50	1.50
573	Joe Coleman	5.00	2.50	1.50
574	Reds Team	7.50	3.75	2.25
575	Jim Palmer	35.00	17.50	8.75
576	Dave Adlesh	5.00	2.50	1.50
577	Fred Talbot	5.00	2.50	1.50
578	Orlando Martinez	5.00	2.50	1.50
579	N.L. Rookies (Larry Hisle **RC**, Mike Lum **RC**)	5.00	2.50	1.50
580	Bob Bailey	5.00	2.50	1.50
581	Garry Roggenburk	5.00	2.50	1.50
582	Jerry Grote	5.00	2.50	1.50
583	Gates Brown	6.00	3.00	1.75
584	Larry Shepard	5.00	2.50	1.50
585	Wilbur Wood	5.00	2.50	1.50
586	Jim Pagliaroni	5.00	2.50	1.50
587	Roger Repoz	5.00	2.50	1.50
588	Dick Schofield	5.00	2.50	1.50
589	Twins Rookies (Ron Clark, Moe Ogier)	5.00	2.50	1.50
590	Tommy Harper	5.00	2.50	1.50
591	Dick Nen	5.00	2.50	1.50
592	John Bateman	5.00	2.50	1.50
593	Lee Stange	5.00	2.50	1.50
594	Phil Linz	5.00	2.50	1.50
595	Phil Ortega	5.00	2.50	1.50
596	Charlie Smith	5.00	2.50	1.50
597	Bill McCool	5.00	2.50	1.50
598	Jerry May	10.00	5.00	2.50

1968 Topps "Batter Up" Game

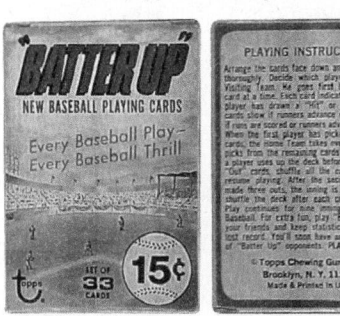

The same cards which were issued as pack inserts in 1968 Topps were sold in a much scarcer boxed-set form. Packaged in a colorful cardboard box with game rules on back, the set is labeled "Batter Up" and can be found in versions with 10 or 15 original retail price.

	NM	E	VG
Complete Boxed Set:	275.00	85.00	45.00

(See 1968 Topps Game for individual card checklist and values.)

1968 Topps 3-D

These very rare test-issue cards measure 2-1/4" x 3-1/2" with rounded corners and blank backs. They simulate a three-dimensional effect with backgrounds purposely blurred, in front of which is a sharp color player photograph. The outer layer is a thin coating of ribbed plastic. The special process gives the picture the illusion of depth when the card is moved or tilted. As this was done two years before Kellogg's began its 3-D cards, this test issue really was breaking new ground. Production and distribution were limited, making the cards very tough to find. Some cards, said to have been the first produced, are stamped on back with a notice from Visual Panographics of New York. "This is an experimental XOGRAPH card produced as a limited edition. Not for public circulation or distribution. Not for resale. To be returned to:".

		NM	E	VG
Common Player:		500.00	250.00	150.00
Wrapper:		900.00	450.00	275.00
(1)	Bob Clemente	12,000	6,000	3,600
(2)	Willie Davis	500.00	250.00	150.00
(3a)	Ron Fairly (Dugout in background)	500.00	250.00	150.00
(3a)	Ron Fairly (Dugout in background)	500.00	250.00	150.00
(4)	Curt Flood	750.00	370.00	220.00
(5)	Jim Lonborg	500.00	250.00	150.00
(6a)	Jim Maloney (Dugout in background)	750.00	370.00	220.00
(6a)	Jim Maloney (Dugout in background)	1,650	825.00	495.00
(6a)	Jim Maloney (Dugout in background)	5,000	2,500	1,500
(8)	Tony Perez	1,200	600.00	350.00
(9)	Boog Powell	750.00	375.00	225.00
(10)	Bill Robinson	500.00	250.00	150.00
(11)	Rusty Staub	1,200	600.00	350.00
(12)	Mel Stottlemyre	1,200	600.00	350.00
(13)	Ron Swoboda	500.00	250.00	150.00

1968 Topps 3-D Proofs

Three blank-backed proof cards are known to be associated with the 3-D issue. In the same format as the issued cards, the proofs have no player name and are lacking the circle with the team and position.

		NM	EX	VG
(1)	Tommy Davis (Mets)	1,500.	750.00	450.00
(2)	Rick Monday (A's)	1,500.	750.00	450.00
(3)	John O'Donogue (Reds)	1,500.	750.00	450.00

1968 Topps 3-D Prototype

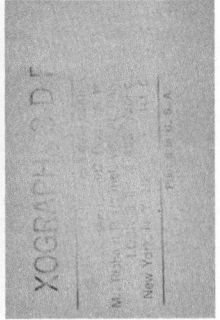

Apparently produced as a prototype for the 3-D cards which Topps issued as a test in 1968, this prototype card is 2-1/4" x 3-1/4" with square corners. The team name is in red block letters at top. The back carries a rubber-stamped notice which identifies the card as a "Xograph 3-D" product from New York City. Not all backs carry that stamp, however, with an authentic example of such turning up at the 2012 National Convention.

	NM	E	VG
Brooks Robinson	20,000	10,000	6,000

1968 Topps Action Stickers

Another of the many Topps test issues of the late 1960s, Action All-Star stickers were sold in a strip of three, with bubblegum, for 10 cents. The strip is comprised of three 3-1/4" x 5-1/4" panels, perforated at the joints for separation. The numbered central panel contains a large photo of a star player. The top and bottom panels each contain smaller pictures of three players. While there are 16 numbered center panels, only 12 of them are different; panels 13-16 are double-prints. Similarly, the triple-player panels at top and bottom of stickers 13-16 repeat panels from #1-4. Prices below are for stickers which have all three panels still joined. Individual panels are priced signicantly lower.

		NM	E	VG
Complete Set (16):		5,750	2,875	1,725
Common Panel:		130.00	65.00	45.00
1	Orlando Cepeda, Joe Horlen, Al Kaline, Bill Mazeroski, Claude Osteen, Mel Stottlemyre, Carl Yastrzemski	400.00	200.00	120.00
2	Don Drysdale, Harmon Killebrew, Mike McCormick, Tom Phoebus, George Scott, Ron Swoboda, Pete Ward	175.00	90.00	50.00
3	Hank Aaron, Paul Casanova, Jim Maloney, Joe Pepitone, Rick Reichardt, Frank Robinson, Tom Seaver	150.00	75.00	45.00
4	Bob Aspromonte, Johnny Callison, Dean Chance, Jim Lefebvre, Jim Lonborg, Frank Robinson, Ron Santo	200.00	100.00	60.00
5	Bert Campaneris, Al Downing, Willie Horton, Ed Kranepool, Willie Mays, Pete Rose, Ron Santo	500.00	250.00	150.00
6	Max Alvis, Ernie Banks, Al Kaline, Tim McCarver, Rusty Staub, Walt Williams, Carl Yastrzemski	400.00	200.00	120.00
7	Rod Carew, Tony Gonzalez, Steve Hargan, Mickey Mantle, Willie McCovey, Rick Monday, Billy Williams	1,750	875.00	525.00
8	Clete Boyer, Jim Bunning, Tony Conigliaro, Mike Cuellar, Joe Horlen, Ken McMullen, Don Mincher	130.00	65.00	45.00
9	Orlando Cepeda, Bob Clemente, Jim Fregosi, Harmon Killebrew, Willie Mays, Chris Short, Earl Wilson	400.00	200.00	120.00
10	Hank Aaron, Bob Gibson, Bud Harrelson, Jim Hunter, Mickey Mantle, Gary Peters, Vada Pinson	500.00	250.00	150.00
11	Don Drysdale, Bill Freehan, Frank Howard, Ferguson Jenkins, Tony Oliva, Bob Veale, Jim Wynn	300.00	150.00	90.00
12	Richie Allen, Bob Clemente, Sam McDowell, Jim McGlothlin, Tony Perez, Brooks Robinson, Joe Torre	1,150	575.00	325.00
13	Dean Chance, Don Drysdale, Jim Lefebvre, Tom Phoebus, Frank Robinson, George Scott, Carl Yastrzemski	400.00	200.00	120.00
14	Paul Casanova, Orlando Cepeda, Joe Horlen, Harmon Killebrew, Bill Mazeroski, Rick Reichardt, Tom Seaver	250.00	125.00	75.00
15	Bob Aspromonte, Johnny Callison, Jim Lonborg, Mike McCormick, Frank Robinson, Ron Swoboda, Pete Ward	175.00	90.00	50.00
16	Hank Aaron, Al Kaline, Jim Maloney, Claude Osteen, Joe Pepitone, Ron Santo, Mel Stottlemyre	300.00	150.00	90.00

1968 Topps Deckle Edge Proofs

While most Topps proofs are so rare as to preclude their listing in this catalog, the 1968 Deckle Edge test set is an exception. Usually found in the form of a 7-3/4" x 11" uncut sheet of nine black-and-white cards, single cards are sometimes encountered. The blank-backed sheet and cards can be found with the players' facsimile autographs printed in red, black or blue. Unnumbered cards are checklisted here alphabetically.

		NM	E	VG
Complete Set, Singles (9):		700.00	350.00	225.00
Uncut Sheet:		700.00	350.00	225.00
Common Player:		50.00	25.00	15.00
(1)	Dave Adlesh	50.00	25.00	15.00
(2)	Hank Aguire	50.00	25.00	15.00
(3)	Sandy Alomar	50.00	25.00	15.00

		NM	E	VG
(4)	Sonny Jackson	50.00	25.00	15.00
(5)	Bob Johnson	50.00	25.00	15.00
(6)	Claude Osteen	50.00	25.00	15.00
(7)	Juan Pizarro	50.00	25.00	15.00
(8)	Hal Woodeshick	50.00	25.00	15.00
(9)	Carl Yastrzemski	400.00	200.00	120.00

1968 Topps Discs

One of the scarcer Topps baseball collectibles, this set was apparently a never-completed test issue. These full-color, cardboard discs, which measure approximately 2-1/4" in diameter, were probably intended to be made into a pin set but production was never completed and no actual pins are known to exist. Uncut sheets of the player discs have been found. The discs include a player portrait photo with the name beneath and (usually) the city and team nickname along the sides.

		NM	E	VG
Complete Set (28):		12,800	6,400	4,000
Common Player:		200.00	100.00	60.00
(1)	Hank Aaron (w/cap)	1,000	500.00	300.00
(2)	Richie Allen	225.00	110.00	65.00
(3)	Gene Alley	200.00	100.00	60.00
(4)	Rod Carew	560.00	280.00	175.00
(5)	Orlando Cepeda (w/cap)	480.00	240.00	150.00
(6)	Dean Chance	200.00	100.00	60.00
(7)	Roberto Clemente	1,400	700.00	400.00
(8)	Tommy Davis	200.00	100.00	60.00
(9)	Bill Freehan	200.00	100.00	60.00
(10)	Jim Fregosi	200.00	100.00	60.00
(11)	Steve Hargan	200.00	100.00	60.00
(12)	Frank Howard	200.00	100.00	60.00
(13)	Al Kaline	560.00	280.00	175.00
(14)	Harmon Killebrew	560.00	280.00	175.00
(15)	Mickey Mantle (1B)	6,000	3,000	1,800
(16)	Willie Mays	1,000	500.00	300.00
(17)	Mike McCormick	200.00	100.00	60.00
(18)	Rick Monday	200.00	100.00	60.00
(19)	Claude Osteen	200.00	100.00	60.00
(20)	Gary Peters	200.00	100.00	60.00
(21)	Brooks Robinson (facing right)	560.00	280.00	175.00
(22)	Frank Robinson	560.00	280.00	175.00
(23)	Pete Rose	900.00	450.00	275.00
(24)	Ron Santo	250.00	125.00	75.00
(25)	Rusty Staub	220.00	110.00	70.00
(26)	Joe Torre	200.00	100.00	60.00
(27)	Bob Veale	200.00	100.00	60.00
(28)	Carl Yastrzemski	560.00	280.00	175.00

1968 Topps Game

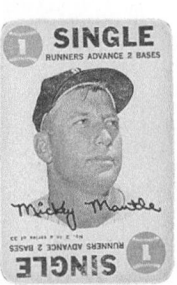 

A throwback to the Red and Blue Back sets of 1951, the 33-cards in the 1968 Topps Game set, inserted into packs of regular '68 Topps cards or purchases as a complete boxed set, enable the owner to play a game of baseball based on the game situations on each card. Also on the 2-1/4" x 3-1/4" cards was a color photograph of a player and his facsimile autograph. One redeeming social value of the set (assuming you're not mesmerized by the game) is that it affords an inexpensive way to get big-name cards as the set is loaded with stars, but not at all popular with collectors.

	NM	E	VG
Complete Set (33):	115.00	55.00	35.00
Common Player:	2.00	1.00	.60

		NM	E	VG
1	Mateo Alou	2.00	1.00	.60
2	Mickey Mantle	30.00	15.00	9.00
3	Carl Yastrzemski	10.00	5.00	3.00
4	Henry Aaron	12.00	6.00	3.50
5	Harmon Killebrew	9.00	4.50	2.75
6	Roberto Clemente	21.00	7.50	4.50
7	Frank Robinson	9.00	4.50	2.75
8	Willie Mays	12.00	6.00	3.50
9	Brooks Robinson	9.00	4.50	2.75
10	Tommy Davis	2.00	1.00	.60
11	Bill Freehan	2.00	1.00	.60
12	Claude Osteen	2.00	1.00	.60
13	Gary Peters	2.00	1.00	.60
14	Jim Lonborg	2.00	1.00	.60
15	Steve Hargan	2.00	1.00	.60
16	Dean Chance	2.00	1.00	.60
17	Mike McCormick	2.00	1.00	.60
18	Tim McCarver	3.00	1.50	.90
19	Ron Santo	6.00	3.00	1.75
20	Tony Gonzalez	2.00	1.00	.60
21	Frank Howard	3.00	1.50	.90
22	George Scott	2.00	1.00	.60
23	Rich Allen	6.00	3.00	1.75
24	Jim Wynn	2.00	1.00	.60
25	Gene Alley	2.00	1.00	.60
26	Rick Monday	2.00	1.00	.60
27	Al Kaline	9.00	4.50	2.75
28	Rusty Staub	3.00	1.50	.90
29	Rod Carew	9.00	4.50	2.75
30	Pete Rose	12.00	6.00	3.50
31	Joe Torre	6.00	3.00	1.75
32	Orlando Cepeda	6.00	3.00	1.75
33	Jim Fregosi	2.00	1.00	.60

1968 Topps Plaks

Among the scarcest Topps test issues of the late 1960s, the "All Star Baseball Plaks" were plastic busts of two dozen stars of the era which came packaged like model airplane parts. The busts had to be snapped off a sprue and could be inserted into a base which carried the player's name. Packed with the plastic plaks was one of two checklist cards which featured six color photos per side. The 2-1/8" x 4" checklist cards are popular with superstar collectors and are considerably easier to find today than the actual plaks. Wax packs of three plaks and two sticks of bubblegum were sold for a dime. Despite their appearance on the checklist cards, it is now believed that no plaks were issued of Gary Peters, Frank Robinson, Hank Aaron, Don Drysdale or Willie Mays.

		NM	E	VG
Complete Set (19):		15,000	7,500	4,500
Common Player:		250.00	125.00	75.00
(1)	Max Alvis	250.00	125.00	75.00
(2)	Dean Chance	250.00	125.00	75.00
(3)	Jim Fregosi	250.00	125.00	75.00
(4)	Frank Howard	350.00	175.00	105.00
(5)	Jim Hunter	625.00	312.50	187.50
(6)	Al Kaline	900.00	450.00	270.00
(7)	Harmon Killebrew	900.00	450.00	270.00
(8)	Jim Lonborg	250.00	125.00	75.00
(9a)	Mickey Mantle (Big nose)	3,500	1,750	1,050
(9b)	Mickey Mantle (Small nose)	3,500	1,750	1,050
(12)	Carl Yastrzemski	1,000	500.00	300.00
(14)	Richie Allen	350.00	175.00	105.00
(15)	Orlando Cepeda	900.00	450.00	270.00
(16)	Roberto Clemente	2,500	1,250	750.00
(17)	Tommy Davis	250.00	125.00	75.00
(20)	Tim McCarver	350.00	175.00	105.00
(21)	Ron Santo	350.00	175.00	105.00
(22)	Rusty Staub	350.00	175.00	105.00
(23)	Pete Rose	2,200	1,100	650.00
(24)	Jim Wynn	250.00	125.00	75.00
---	Checklist Card 1-12	1,600	800.00	480.00
---	Checklist Card 13-24	2,450	1,225	735.00

1968 Topps Posters

Yet another innovation from the creative minds at Topps appeared in 1968; a set of color player posters. Measuring 9-3/4" x 18-1/8," each poster was sold separately with its own piece of gum, rather than as an insert. The posters feature a large color photograph with a star at the bottom containing the player's name, position and team. There are 24 different posters which were folded numerous times to fit into the package they were sold in. Unless the paper has split at the folds, they are not considered in grading.

		NM	E	VG
Complete Set (24):		650.00	325.00	200.00
Common Player:		15.00	7.50	4.50
Unopened Pack:		175.00		
1	Dean Chance	15.00	7.50	4.50
2	Max Alvis	15.00	7.50	4.50
3	Frank Howard	17.50	8.75	5.25
4	Jim Fregosi	15.00	7.50	4.50
5	Catfish Hunter	20.00	10.00	6.00
6	Roberto Clemente	60.00	30.00	18.00
7	Don Drysdale	25.00	12.50	7.50
8	Jim Wynn	15.00	7.50	4.50
9	Al Kaline	25.00	12.50	7.50
10	Harmon Killebrew	25.00	12.50	7.50
11	Jim Lonborg	15.00	7.50	4.50
12	Orlando Cepeda	20.00	10.00	6.00
13	Gary Peters	15.00	7.50	4.50
14	Hank Aaron	50.00	25.00	15.00
15	Richie Allen	17.50	8.75	5.25
16	Carl Yastrzemski	30.00	15.00	9.00
17	Ron Swoboda	15.00	7.50	4.50
18	Mickey Mantle	80.00	40.00	24.00
19	Tim McCarver	15.00	7.50	4.50
20	Willie Mays	50.00	25.00	15.00
21	Ron Santo	17.50	8.75	5.25
22	Rusty Staub	17.50	8.75	5.25
23	Pete Rose	50.00	25.00	15.00
24	Frank Robinson	25.00	12.50	7.50

1968 Topps/Milton Bradley

As part of a Win-A-Card trading card board game, Milton Bradley contracted with Topps to print 132 special versions of its 1968 baseball cards, 1967 football cards and hot rod cards. The baseball cards can be differentiated from regular-issue 1968 Topps in that the yellow ink on back is much lighter and brighter than the dark yellow/gold ink usually found on back. Also, some of the card fronts will show evidence of the white-bordered football and hot rod cards at one or more edges. Collectors currently will pay only a small premium for the MB version, but that gap is likely to widen in the future.

		NM	E	VG
Complete (Baseball) Set (76):		600.00	300.00	180.00
Common Player:		6.00	3.00	1.80
7	N.L. ERA Leaders(Jim Bunning, Phil Niekro, Chris Short)	15.00	7.50	4.50
8	A.L. ERA Leaders(Joe Horlen, Gary Peters, Sonny Siebert)	6.00	3.00	1.80
10	A.L. Pitching Leaders (Dean Chance, Jim Lonborg, Earl Wilson)	18.00	8.50	3.75
13	Chuck Hartenstein	6.00	3.00	1.80
16	Indians Rookies (Lou Piniella, Richie Scheinblum)	10.00	5.00	3.00
17	Dick Hall	6.00	3.00	1.80
18	Mike Hershberger	6.00	3.00	1.80
19	Juan Pizarro	6.00	3.00	1.80

		NM	E	VG
20	Brooks Robinson	30.00	15.00	9.00
24	Bobby Locke	6.00	3.00	1.80
26	Darrell Brandon	6.00	3.00	1.80
34	Al Ferrara	6.00	3.00	1.80
36	Pirates Rookies (Bob Moose, Bob Robertson RC)	6.00	3.00	1.80
38	Tony Pierce	6.00	3.00	1.80
43	Gary Bell	6.00	3.00	1.80
44	Frank Kostro	6.00	3.00	1.80
45	Tom Seaver	45.00	23.00	12.00
48	Ted Davidson	6.00	3.00	1.80
49	Ed Brinkman (Yellow team.)	50.00	25.00	15.00
53	Gene Alley	6.00	3.00	1.80
57	Dan Schneider	6.00	3.00	1.80
58	Ed Mathews	24.00	12.00	7.00
60	Ken Holtzman	6.00	3.00	1.80
61	Reggie Smith	6.00	3.00	1.80
62	Chuck Dobson	6.00	3.00	1.80
64	Jim Merritt	6.00	3.00	1.80
66	Casey Cox (Yellow team.)	50.00	25.00	15.00
68	Ron Willis	6.00	3.00	1.80
72	Tommy John	9.00	4.50	2.70
74	Milt Pappas	6.00	3.00	1.80
77	Don Wilson RC	6.00	3.00	1.80
78	Jim Northrup	6.00	3.00	1.80
80	Rod Carew	30.00	14.75	8.25
81	Larry Jackson	6.00	3.00	1.80
85	Gaylord Perry	15.00	4.50	2.75
89	Jake Gibbs	6.00	3.00	1.80
94	Lee Maye	6.00	3.00	1.80
98	Gary Sutherland	6.00	3.00	1.80
99	Rocky Colavito	12.00	3.50	2.00
100	Bob Gibson	25.00	8.75	5.25
105	Al Downing	6.00	3.00	1.80
106	Dalton Jones	6.00	3.00	1.80
107	2nd Series Check List (110-196) (Juan Marichal)	4.00	2.00	1.25
108	Don Pavletich	6.00	3.00	1.80
110	Hank Aaron	65.00	32.00	18.00
112	Woody Fryman	6.00	3.00	1.80
113	Tigers Rookies (Tom Matchick, Daryl Patterson)	6.00	3.00	1.80
117	Larry Jaster	6.00	3.00	1.80
118	Mark Belanger	6.00	3.00	1.80
119	Ted Savage	6.00	3.00	1.80
120	Mel Stottlemyre	7.50	2.00	1.25
121	Jimmie Hall	6.00	3.00	1.80
124	Nate Oliver	6.00	3.00	1.80
127	Paul Lindblad	6.00	3.00	1.80
128	Astros Rookies (Tom Dukes, Alonzo Harris)	6.00	3.00	1.80
129	Mickey Stanley	6.00	3.00	1.80
136	Randy Hundley	6.00	3.00	1.80
139	Chris Short	6.00	3.00	1.80
143	Pete Cimino	6.00	3.00	1.80
146	Sal Bando	6.00	3.00	1.80
149	Bob Saverine	6.00	3.00	1.80
155	World Series Game 5 (Lonborg Wins Again)	12.00	6.00	3.50
156	World Series Game 6 (Petrocelli Socks Two Homers)	12.00	6.00	3.50
165	Tony Oliva	7.50	2.00	1.25
168	Dodgers Team	10.00	5.00	3.00
172	Walt Williams	6.00	3.00	1.80
175	Maury Wills	6.00	3.00	1.80
176	Bob Allen	6.00	3.00	1.80
177	Mets Rookies (Jerry Koosman RC, Nolan Ryan RC)	600.00	300.00	18.00
179	Bill Stoneman	6.00	3.00	1.80
180	Curt Flood	7.50	1.50	.90
185	Tom Haller	6.00	3.00	1.80
189	Bill Landis	6.00	3.00	1.80
191	Dan Frisella	6.00	3.00	1.80
193	Jack Hamilton	6.00	3.00	1.80
195	Joe Pepitone	9.00	4.50	2.70

1969 Topps

The 1969 Topps set broke yet another record for quantity as the issue is officially a whopping 664 cards. With substantial numbers of variations, the number of possible cards runs closer to 700. The design of the 2-1/2" x 3-1/2" cards in the set feature a color photo with the team name printed in block letters underneath. A circle contains the player's name and position. Card backs returned to a horizontal format. Despite the size of the set, it contains no team cards. It does, however, have multi-player cards, All-Stars, statistical leaders, and World Series highlights. Most significant among the varieties are white and yellow letter cards from the run of #'s 440-511. The complete set prices below do not include the scarcer and more expensive "white letter" variations.

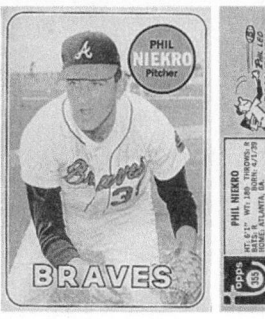

		NM	E	VG
	Complete Set (664):	3,150	1,550	925.00
	Common Player (1-588):	2.00	1.00	.60
	Common Player (589-664):	3.00	1.50	.90
1	A.L. Batting Leaders (Danny Cater, Tony Oliva, Carl Yastrzemski)	10.00	5.00	2.50
2	N.L. Batting Leaders (Felipe Alou, Matty Alou, Pete Rose)	18.00	7.50	4.50
3	A.L. RBI Leaders (Ken Harrelson, Frank Howard, Jim Northrup)	2.50	1.25	.75
4	N.L. RBI Leaders (Willie McCovey, Ron Santo, Billy Williams)	10.00	5.00	2.50
5	A.L. Home Run Leaders (Ken Harrelson, Willie Horton, Frank Howard)	6.00	3.00	1.75
6	N.L. Home Run Leaders (Richie Allen, Ernie Banks, Willie McCovey)	10.00	4.00	2.50
7	A.L. ERA Leaders (Sam McDowell, Dave McNally, Luis Tiant)	3.00	1.50	.90
8	N.L. ERA Leaders (Bobby Bolin, Bob Gibson, Bob Veale)	8.00	2.00	1.25
9	A.L. Pitching Leaders (Denny McLain, Dave McNally, Mel Stottlemyre, Luis Tiant)	4.00	2.00	1.25
10	N.L. Pitching Leaders (Bob Gibson, Fergie Jenkins, Juan Marichal)	8.00	2.50	1.50
11	A.L. Strikeout Leaders (Sam McDowell, Denny McLain, Luis Tiant)	3.00	1.50	.90
12	N.L. Strikeout Leaders (Bob Gibson, Fergie Jenkins, Bill Singer)	5.00	2.50	1.50
13	Mickey Stanley	2.00	1.00	.60
14	Al McBean	2.00	1.00	.60
15	Boog Powell	3.00	1.50	.90
16	Giants Rookies (Cesar Gutierrez, Rich Robertson)	2.00	1.00	.60
17	Mike Marshall	2.00	1.00	.60
18	Dick Schofield	2.00	1.00	.60
19	Ken Suarez	2.00	1.00	.60
20	Ernie Banks	25.00	12.50	7.50
21	Jose Santiago	2.00	1.00	.60
22	Jesus Alou	2.00	1.00	.60
23	Lew Krausse	2.00	1.00	.60
24	Walt Alston	4.00	2.00	1.25
25	Roy White	2.00	1.00	.60
26	Clay Carroll	2.00	1.00	.60
27	Bernie Allen	2.00	1.00	.60
28	Mike Ryan	2.00	1.00	.60
29	Dave Morehead	2.00	1.00	.60
30	Bob Allison	2.00	1.00	.60
31	Mets Rookies (Gary Gentry RC, Amos Otis RC)	3.00	1.50	.90
32	Sammy Ellis	2.00	1.00	.60
33	Wayne Causey	2.00	1.00	.60
34	Gary Peters	2.00	1.00	.60
35	Joe Morgan	12.00	5.00	3.00
36	Luke Walker	2.00	1.00	.60
37	Curt Motton	2.00	1.00	.60
38	Zoilo Versalles	2.00	1.00	.60
39	Dick Hughes	2.00	1.00	.60
40	Mayo Smith	2.00	1.00	.60
41	Bob Barton	2.00	1.00	.60
42	Tommy Harper	2.00	1.00	.60
43	Joe Niekro	2.00	1.00	.60
44	Danny Cater	2.00	1.00	.60
45	Maury Wills	2.00	1.00	.60

		NM	E	VG
46	Fritz Peterson	2.00	1.00	.60
47a	Paul Popovich (Emblem visible thru airbrush.)	15.00	7.50	4.50
47b	Paul Popovich (Helmet emblem completely airbrushed.)	2.00	1.00	.60
48	Brant Alyea	2.00	1.00	.60
49a	Royals Rookies (Steve Jones, Eliseo Rodriquez) (Rodriguez on front.)	15.00	7.50	4.50
49b	Royals Rookies (Steve Jones, Eliseo Rodriquez) (Rodriguez on front.)	2.00	1.00	.60
50	Roberto Clemente	65.00	30.00	15.00
51	Woody Fryman	2.00	1.00	.60
52	Mike Andrews	2.00	1.00	.60
53	Sonny Jackson	2.00	1.00	.60
54	Cisco Carlos	2.00	1.00	.60
55	Jerry Grote	2.00	1.00	.60
56	Rich Reese	2.00	1.00	.60
57	1st Series Check List (1-109) (Denny McLain)	4.00	2.00	1.25
58	Fred Gladding	2.00	1.00	.60
59	Jay Johnstone	2.00	1.00	.60
60	Nelson Briles	2.00	1.00	.60
61	Jimmie Hall	2.00	1.00	.60
62	Chico Salmon	2.00	1.00	.60
63	Jim Hickman	2.00	1.00	.60
64	Bill Monbouquette	2.00	1.00	.60
65	Willie Davis	2.00	1.00	.60
66	Orioles Rookies (Mike Adamson, Merv Rettenmund RC)	2.00	1.00	.60
67	Bill Stoneman	2.00	1.00	.60
68	Dave Duncan	2.00	1.00	.60
69	Steve Hamilton	2.00	1.00	.60
70	Tommy Helms	2.00	1.00	.60
71	Steve Whitaker	2.00	1.00	.60
72	Ron Taylor	2.00	1.00	.60
73	Johnny Briggs	2.00	1.00	.60
74	Preston Gomez	2.00	1.00	.60
75	Luis Aparicio	9.00	4.50	2.75
76	Norm Miller	2.00	1.00	.60
77a	Ron Perranoski (LA visible thru airbrush.)	10.00	5.00	2.50
77b	Ron Perranoski (Cap emblem completely airbrushed.)	2.00	1.00	.60
78	Tom Satriano	2.00	1.00	.60
79	Milt Pappas	2.00	1.00	.60
80	Norm Cash	6.00	3.00	1.75
81	Mel Queen	2.00	1.00	.60
82	Pirates Rookies (Rich Hebner RC, Al Oliver RC)	10.00	5.00	3.00
83	Mike Ferraro	2.00	1.00	.60
84	Bob Humphreys	2.00	1.00	.60
85	Lou Brock	20.00	10.00	6.00
86	Pete Richert	2.00	1.00	.60
87	Horace Clarke	2.00	1.00	.60
88	Rich Nye	2.00	1.00	.60
89	Russ Gibson	2.00	1.00	.60
90	Jerry Koosman	2.00	1.00	.60
91	Al Dark	2.00	1.00	.60
92	Jack Billingham	2.00	1.00	.60
93	Joe Foy	2.00	1.00	.60
94	Hank Aguirre	2.00	1.00	.60
95	Johnny Bench	85.00	40.00	25.00
96	Denver Lemaster	2.00	1.00	.60
97	Buddy Bradford	2.00	1.00	.60
98	Dave Giusti	2.00	1.00	.60
99a	Twins Rookies (Danny Morris, Graig Nettles RC) (Black loop above "Twins.")	20.00	6.75	4.00
99b	Twins Rookies (Danny Morris, Graig Nettles RC) (No black loop.)	18.00	9.00	5.50
100	Hank Aaron	60.00	30.00	15.00
101	Daryl Patterson	2.00	1.00	.60
102	Jim Davenport	2.00	1.00	.60
103	Roger Repoz	2.00	1.00	.60
104	Steve Blass	2.00	1.00	.60
105	Rick Monday	2.00	1.00	.60
106	Jim Hannan	2.00	1.00	.60
107a	2nd Series Check List (110-218) (Bob Gibson) (161 is Jim Purdin)	4.00	2.00	1.25
107b	2nd Series Check List (110-218) (Bob Gibson) (161 is John Purdin)	6.00	3.00	1.75
108	Tony Taylor	2.00	1.00	.60
109	Jim Lonborg	2.00	1.00	.60
110	Mike Shannon	2.00	1.00	.60
111	Johnny Morris	2.00	1.00	.60
112	J.C. Martin	2.00	1.00	.60

113	Dave May	2.00	1.00	.60
114	Yankees Rookies (Alan Closter, John Cumberland)	2.00	1.00	.60
115	Bill Hands	2.00	1.00	.60
116	Chuck Harrison	2.00	1.00	.60
117	Jim Fairey	2.00	1.00	.60
118	Stan Williams	2.00	1.00	.60
119	Doug Rader	2.00	1.00	.60
120	Pete Rose	48.00	20.00	10.00
121	Joe Grzenda	2.00	1.00	.60
122	Ron Fairly	2.00	1.00	.60
123	Wilbur Wood	2.00	1.00	.60
124	Hank Bauer	2.00	1.00	.60
125	Ray Sadecki	2.00	1.00	.60
126	Dick Tracewski	2.00	1.00	.60
127	Kevin Collins	2.00	1.00	.60
128	Tommie Aaron	2.00	1.00	.60
129	Bill McCool	2.00	1.00	.60
130	Carl Yastrzemski	38.00	15.50	8.50
131	Chris Cannizzaro	2.00	1.00	.60
132	Dave Baldwin	2.00	1.00	.60
133	Johnny Callison	2.00	1.00	.60
134	Jim Weaver	2.00	1.00	.60
135	Tommy Davis	2.00	1.00	.60
136	Cards Rookies (Steve Huntz, Mike Torrez)	2.00	1.00	.60
137	Wally Bunker	2.00	1.00	.60
138	John Bateman	2.00	1.00	.60
139	Andy Kosco	2.00	1.00	.60
140	Jim Lefebvre	2.00	1.00	.60
141	Bill Dillman	2.00	1.00	.60
142	Woody Woodward	2.00	1.00	.60
143	Joe Nossek	2.00	1.00	.60
144	Bob Hendley	2.00	1.00	.60
145	Max Alvis	2.00	1.00	.60
146	Jim Perry	2.00	1.00	.60
147	Leo Durocher	5.00	2.50	1.50
148	Lee Stange	2.00	1.00	.60
149	Ollie Brown	2.00	1.00	.60
150	Denny McLain	7.00	2.50	1.50
151a	Clay Dalrymple (Phillies)	15.00	7.50	3.75
151b	Clay Dalrymple (Orioles)	15.00	7.50	3.75
152	Tommie Sisk	2.00	1.00	.60
153	Ed Brinkman	2.00	1.00	.60
154	Jim Britton	2.00	1.00	.60
155	Pete Ward	2.00	1.00	.60
156	Astros Rookies(Hal Gilson, Leon McFadden)	2.00	1.00	.60
157	Bob Rodgers	2.00	1.00	.60
158	Joe Gibbon	2.00	1.00	.60
159	Jerry Adair	2.00	1.00	.60
160	Vada Pinson	3.00	1.50	.90
161	John Purdin	2.00	1.00	.60
162	World Series Game 1 (Gibson Fans 17; Sets New Record)	15.00	7.50	4.50
163	World Series Game 2 (Tiger Homers Deck The Cards)	6.00	3.00	1.75
164	World Series Game 3 (McCarver's Homer Puts St. Louis Ahead)	7.00	3.50	2.00
165	World Series Game 4 (Brock's Lead-Off HR Starts Cards' Romp)	7.00	3.50	2.00
166	World Series Game 5 (Kaline's Key Hit Sparks Tiger Rally)	7.00	3.50	2.00
167	World Series Game 6 (Tiger 10-Run Inning Ties Mark)	6.00	3.00	1.75
168	World Series Game 7 (Lolich Series Hero Outduels Gibson)	9.00	4.50	2.75
169	World Series (Tigers Celebrate Their Victory)	12.00	6.00	3.50
170	Frank Howard	3.00	1.50	.90
171	Glenn Beckert	2.00	1.00	.60
172	Jerry Stephenson	2.00	1.00	.60
173	White Sox Rookies (Bob Christian, Gerry Nyman)	2.00	1.00	.60
174	Grant Jackson	2.00	1.00	.60
175	Jim Bunning	8.00	4.00	2.50
176	Joe Azcue	2.00	1.00	.60
177	Ron Reed	2.00	1.00	.60
178	Ray Oyler	2.00	1.00	.60
179	Don Pavletich	2.00	1.00	.60
180	Willie Horton	2.00	1.00	.60
181	Mel Nelson	2.00	1.00	.60
182	Bill Rigney	2.00	1.00	.60
183	Don Shaw	2.00	1.00	.60
184	Roberto Pena	2.00	1.00	.60
185	Tom Phoebus	2.00	1.00	.60
186	John Edwards	2.00	1.00	.60
187	Leon Wagner	2.00	1.00	.60

188	Rick Wise	2.00	1.00	.60
189	Red Sox Rookies (Joe Lahoud, John Thibdeau)	2.00	1.00	.60
190	Willie Mays	80.00	40.00	20.00
191	Lindy McDaniel	2.00	1.00	.60
192	Jose Pagan	2.00	1.00	.60
193	Don Cardwell	2.00	1.00	.60
194	Ted Uhlaender	2.00	1.00	.60
195	John Odom	2.00	1.00	.60
196	Lum Harris	2.00	1.00	.60
197	Dick Selma	2.00	1.00	.60
198	Willie Smith	2.00	1.00	.60
199	Jim French	2.00	1.00	.60
200	Bob Gibson	15.00	7.50	4.50
201	Russ Snyder	2.00	1.00	.60
202	Don Wilson	2.00	1.00	.60
203	Dave Johnson	2.00	1.00	.60
204	Jack Hiatt	2.00	1.00	.60
205	Rick Reichardt	2.00	1.00	.60
206	Phillies Rookies(Larry Hisle, Barry L ersch)	2.00	1.00	.60
207	Roy Face	2.00	1.00	.60
208a	Donn Clendenon (Expos)	20.00	10.00	5.00
208b	Donn Clendenon (Houston)	2.00	1.00	.60
209	Larry Haney (Photo reversed.)	2.00	1.00	.60
210	Felix Millan	2.00	1.00	.60
211	Galen Cisco	2.00	1.00	.60
212	Tom Tresh	6.00	3.00	1.75
213	Gerry Arrigo	2.00	1.00	.60
214	3rd Series Check List (219-327)	4.00	2.00	1.25
215	Rico Petrocelli	2.00	1.00	.60
216	Don Sutton	11.00	4.00	2.50
217	John Donaldson	2.00	1.00	.60
218	John Roseboro	2.00	1.00	.60
219	Freddie Patek **RC**	2.00	1.00	.60
220	Sam McDowell	2.00	1.00	.60
221	Art Shamsky	2.00	1.00	.60
222	Duane Josephson	2.00	1.00	.60
223	Tom Dukes	2.00	1.00	.60
224	Angels Rookies (Bill Harrelson, Steve Kealey)	2.00	1.00	.60
225	Don Kessinger	2.00	1.00	.60
226	Bruce Howard	2.00	1.00	.60
227	Frank Johnson	2.00	1.00	.60
228	Dave Leonhard	2.00	1.00	.60
229	Don Lock	2.00	1.00	.60
230	Rusty Staub	3.00	1.50	.90
231	Pat Dobson	2.00	1.00	.60
232	Dave Ricketts	2.00	1.00	.60
233	Steve Barber	2.00	1.00	.60
234	Dave Bristol	2.00	1.00	.60
235	Jim Hunter	15.00	7.50	3.75
236	Manny Mota	2.00	1.00	.60
237	Bobby Cox **RC**	28.00	14.00	8.00
238	Ken Johnson	2.00	1.00	.60
239	Bob Taylor	2.00	1.00	.60
240	Ken Harrelson	2.00	1.00	.60
241	Jim Brewer	2.00	1.00	.60
242	Frank Kostro	2.00	1.00	.60
243	Ron Kline	2.00	1.00	.60
244	Indians Rookies (Ray Fosse **RC**, George Woodson)	3.50	1.75	1.00
245	Ed Charles	2.00	1.00	.60
246	Joe Coleman	2.00	1.00	.60
247	Gene Oliver	2.00	1.00	.60
248	Bob Priddy	2.00	1.00	.60
249	Ed Spiezio	2.00	1.00	.60
250	Frank Robinson	33.00	10.00	5.00
251	Ron Herbel	2.00	1.00	.60
252	Chuck Cottier	2.00	1.00	.60
253	Jerry Johnson	2.00	1.00	.60
254	Joe Schultz	2.00	1.00	.60
255	Steve Carlton	20.00	10.00	5.00
256	Gates Brown	2.00	1.00	.60
257	Jim Ray	2.00	1.00	.60
258	Jackie Hernandez	2.00	1.00	.60
259	Bill Short	2.00	1.00	.60
260	Reggie Jackson **RC**	225.00	110.00	67.00
261	Bob Johnson	2.00	1.00	.60
262	Mike Kekich	2.00	1.00	.60
263	Jerry May	2.00	1.00	.60
264	Bill Landis	2.00	1.00	.60
265	Chico Cardenas	2.00	1.00	.60
266	Dodgers Rookies (Alan Foster, Tom Hutton)	2.00	1.00	.60
267	Vicente Romo	2.00	1.00	.60
268	Al Spangler	2.00	1.00	.60
269	Al Weis	2.00	1.00	.60
270	Mickey Lolich	2.00	1.00	.60
271	Larry Stahl	2.00	1.00	.60
272	Ed Stroud	2.00	1.00	.60
273	Ron Willis	2.00	1.00	.60

274	Clyde King	2.00	1.00	.60
275	Vic Davalillo	2.00	1.00	.60
276	Gary Wagner	2.00	1.00	.60
277	Rod Hendricks **RC**	2.00	1.00	.60
278	Gary Geiger	2.00	1.00	.60
279	Roger Nelson	2.00	1.00	.60
280	Alex Johnson	2.00	1.00	.60
281	Ted Kubiak	2.00	1.00	.60
282	Pat Jarvis	2.00	1.00	.60
283	Sandy Alomar	2.00	1.00	.60
284	Expos Rookies (Jerry Robertson, Mike Wegener)	2.00	1.00	
285	Don Mincher	2.00	1.00	.60
286	Dock Ellis **RC**	3.00	1.50	.90
287	Jose Tartabull	2.00	1.00	.60
288	Ken Holtzman	2.00	1.00	.60
289	Bart Shirley	2.00	1.00	.60
290	Jim Kaat	4.00	1.50	.90
291	Vern Fuller	2.00	1.00	.60
292	Al Downing	2.00	1.00	.60
293	Dick Dietz	2.00	1.00	.60
294	Jim Lemon	2.00	1.00	.60
295	Tony Perez	14.00	6.00	3.00
296	Andy Messersmith **RC**	3.00	1.50	.90
297	Deron Johnson	2.00	1.00	.60
298	Dave Nicholson	2.00	1.00	.60
299	Mark Belanger	2.00	1.00	.60
300	Felipe Alou	4.00	2.00	1.25
301	Darrell Brandon	2.00	1.00	.60
302	Jim Pagliaroni	2.00	1.00	.60
303	Cal Koonce	2.00	1.00	.60
304	Padres Rookies (Bill Davis, Clarence Gaston **RC**)	4.00	2.00	1.25
305	Dick McAuliffe	2.00	1.00	.60
306	Jim Grant	2.00	1.00	.60
307	Gary Kolb	2.00	1.00	.60
308	Wade Blasingame	2.00	1.00	.60
309	Walt Williams	2.00	1.00	.60
310	Tom Haller	2.00	1.00	.60
311	Sparky Lyle **RC**	6.00	3.00	1.75
312	Lee Elia	2.00	1.00	.60
313	Bill Robinson	2.00	1.00	.60
314	4th Series Check List (328-425)(Don Drysdale)	5.00	2.50	1.50
315	Eddie Fisher	2.00	1.00	.60
316	Hal Lanier	2.00	1.00	.60
317	Bruce Look	2.00	1.00	.60
318	Jack Fisher	2.00	1.00	.60
319	Ken McMullen	2.00	1.00	.60
320	Dal Maxvill	2.00	1.00	.60
321	Jim McAndrew	2.00	1.00	.60
322	Jose Vidal	2.00	1.00	.60
323	Larry Miller	2.00	1.00	.60
324	Tigers Rookies (Les Cain, Dave Campbell)	2.00	1.00	.60
325	Jose Cardenal	2.00	1.00	.60
326	Gary Sutherland	2.00	1.00	.60
327	Willie Crawford	2.00	1.00	.60
328	Joe Horlen	2.00	1.00	.60
329	Rick Joseph	2.00	1.00	.60
330	Tony Conigliaro	6.00	3.00	1.75
331	Braves Rookies (Gil Garrido, Tom House **RC**)	2.00	1.00	.60
332	Fred Talbot	2.00	1.00	.60
333	Ivan Murrell	2.00	1.00	.60
334	Phil Roof	2.00	1.00	.60
335	Bill Mazeroski	10.00	5.00	3.00
336	Jim Roland	2.00	1.00	.60
337	Marty Martinez	2.00	1.00	.60
338	Del Unser **RC**	2.00	1.00	.60
339	Reds Rookies (Steve Mingori, Jose Pena)	2.00	1.00	.60
340	Dave McNally	2.00	1.00	.60
341	Dave Adlesh	2.00	1.00	.60
342	Bubba Morton	2.00	1.00	.60
343	Dan Frisella	2.00	1.00	.60
344	Tom Matchick	2.00	1.00	.60
345	Frank Linzy	2.00	1.00	.60
346	Wayne Comer	2.00	1.00	.60
347	Randy Hundley	2.00	1.00	.60
348	Steve Hargan	2.00	1.00	.60
349	Dick Williams	2.00	1.00	.60
350	Richie Allen	4.00	2.00	1.25
351	Carroll Sembera	2.00	1.00	.60
352	Paul Schaal	2.00	1.00	.60
353	Jeff Torborg	2.00	1.00	.60
354	Nate Oliver	2.00	1.00	.60
355	Phil Niekro	8.00	4.00	2.50
356	Frank Quilici	2.00	1.00	.60
357	Carl Taylor	2.00	1.00	.60
358	Athletics Rookies (George Lauzerique, Roberto Rodriguez)	2.00	1.00	.60
359	Dick Kelley	2.00	1.00	.60

#	Name			
360	Jim Wynn	2.00	1.00	.60
361	Gary Holman	2.00	1.00	.60
362	Jim Maloney	2.00	1.00	.60
363	Russ Nixon	2.00	1.00	.60
364	Tommie Agee	2.00	1.00	.60
365	Jim Fregosi	2.00	1.00	.60
366	Bo Belinsky	2.00	1.00	.60
367	Lou Johnson	2.00	1.00	.60
368	Vic Roznovsky	2.00	1.00	.60
369	Bob Skinner	2.00	1.00	.60
370	Juan Marichal	11.00	4.00	2.50
371	Sal Bando	2.00	1.00	.60
372	Adolfo Phillips	2.00	1.00	.60
373	Fred Lasher	2.00	1.00	.60
374	Bob Tillman	2.00	1.00	.60
375	Harmon Killebrew	20.00	10.00	6.00
376	Royals Rookies(Mike Fiore, Jim Rooker RC)	2.00	1.00	.60
377	Gary Bell	2.00	1.00	.60
378	Jose Herrera	2.00	1.00	.60
379	Ken Boyer	2.00	1.00	.60
380	Stan Bahnsen	2.00	1.00	.60
381	Ed Kranepool	2.00	1.00	.60
382	Pat Corrales	2.00	1.00	.60
383	Casey Cox	2.00	1.00	.60
384	Larry Shepard	2.00	1.00	.60
385	Orlando Cepeda	11.00	5.00	3.00
386	Jim McGlothlin	2.00	1.00	.60
387	Bobby Klaus	2.00	1.00	.60
388	Tom McCraw	2.00	1.00	.60
389	Dan Coombs	2.00	1.00	.60
390	Bill Freehan	2.00	1.00	.60
391	Ray Culp	2.00	1.00	.60
392	Bob Burda	2.00	1.00	.60
393	Gene Brabender	2.00	1.00	.60
394	Pilots Rookies (Lou Piniella, Marv Staehle)	4.00	2.00	1.25
395	Chris Short	2.00	1.00	.60
396	Jim Campanis	2.00	1.00	.60
397	Chuck Dobson	2.00	1.00	.60
398	Tito Francona	2.00	1.00	.60
399	Bob Bailey	2.00	1.00	.60
400	Don Drysdale	16.00	7.50	4.50
401	Jake Gibbs	2.00	1.00	.60
402	Ken Boswell	2.00	1.00	.60
403	Bob Miller	2.00	1.00	.60
404	Cubs Rookies (Vic LaRose, Gary Ross)	2.00	1.00	.60
405	Lee May	2.00	1.00	.60
406	Phil Ortega	2.00	1.00	.60
407	Tom Egan	2.00	1.00	.60
408	Nate Colbert	2.00	1.00	.60
409	Bob Moose	2.00	1.00	.60
410	Al Kaline	15.00	7.50	3.75
411	Larry Dierker	2.00	1.00	.60
412	5th Series Check List (426-512)(Mickey Mantle)	24.00	10.00	5.00
413	Roland Sheldon	2.00	1.00	.60
414	Duke Sims	2.00	1.00	.60
415	Ray Washburn	2.00	1.00	.60
416	Willie McCovey (All-Star)	9.00	3.50	2.00
417	Ken Harrelson (All-Star)	2.00	1.00	.60
418	Tommy Helms (All-Star)	2.00	1.00	.60
419	Rod Carew (All-Star)	9.00	4.00	2.50
420	Ron Santo (All-Star)	6.00	2.00	1.25
421	Brooks Robinson (All-Star)	10.00	4.50	2.75
422	Don Kessinger (All-Star)	2.00	1.00	.60
423	Bert Campaneris (All-Star)	2.00	1.00	.60
424	Pete Rose (All-Star)	30.00	12.50	6.25
425	Carl Yastrzemski (All-Star)	18.00	7.50	3.75
426	Curt Flood (All-Star)	3.00	1.50	.90
427	Tony Oliva (All-Star)	3.00	1.50	.90
428	Lou Brock (All-Star)	9.00	3.50	2.00
429	Willie Horton (All-Star)	2.00	1.00	.60
430	Johnny Bench (All-Star)	15.00	7.50	3.75
431	Bill Freehan (All-Star)	2.00	1.00	.60
432	Bob Gibson (All-Star)	9.00	4.00	2.50
433	Denny McLain (All-Star)	3.00	1.50	.90
434	Jerry Koosman (All-Star)	2.00	1.00	.60
435	Sam McDowell (All-Star)	2.00	1.00	.60
436	Gene Alley	2.00	1.00	.60
437	Luis Alcaraz	2.00	1.00	.60
438	Gary Waslewski	2.00	1.00	.60
439	White Sox Rookies (Ed Herrmann, Dan Lazar)	2.00	1.00	.60
440a	Willie McCovey (Last name in white.)	160.00	75.00	45.00
440b	Willie McCovey (Last name in yellow.)	20.00	7.50	3.75
441a	Dennis Higgins (Last name in white.)	60.00	30.00	18.00
441b	Dennis Higgins (Last name in yellow.)	2.00	1.00	.60
442	Ty Cline	2.00	1.00	.60
443	Don Wert	2.00	1.00	.60
444a	Joe Moeller (Last name in white.)	60.00	30.00	18.00
444b	Joe Moeller (Last name in yellow.)	2.00	1.00	.60
445	Bobby Knoop	2.00	1.00	.60
446	Claude Raymond	2.00	1.00	.60
447a	Ralph Houk (Last name in white.)	80.00	40.00	24.00
447b	Ralph Houk (Last name in yellow.)	5.00	2.50	1.50
448	Bob Tolan	2.00	1.00	.60
449	Paul Lindblad	2.00	1.00	.60
450	Billy Williams	20.00	7.50	3.75
451a	Rich Rollins (First name in white.)	60.00	30.00	18.00
451b	Rich Rollins (First name in yellow.)	2.00	1.00	.60
452a	Al Ferrara (First name in white.)	60.00	30.00	18.00
452b	Al Ferrara (First name in yellow.)	2.00	1.00	.60
453	Mike Cuellar	2.00	1.00	.60
454a	Phillies Rookies (Larry Colton, Don Money RC) (Names in white.)	60.00	30.00	18.00
454b	Phillies Rookies(Larry Colton, Don Money RC) (Names in yellow.)	2.00	1.00	.60
455	Sonny Siebert	2.00	1.00	.60
456	Bud Harrelson	2.00	1.00	.60
457	Dalton Jones	2.00	1.00	.60
458	Curt Blefary	2.00	1.00	.60
459	Dave Boswell	2.00	1.00	.60
460	Joe Torre	5.00	2.50	1.50
461a	Mike Epstein (Last name in white.)	60.00	30.00	18.00
461b	Mike Epstein (Last name in yellow.)	2.00	1.00	.60
462	Red Schoendienst	10.00	3.50	2.00
463	Dennis Ribant	2.00	1.00	.60
464a	Dave Marshall (Last name in white.)	60.00	30.00	18.00
464b	Dave Marshall (Last name in yellow.)	2.00	1.00	.60
465	Tommy John	4.00	2.00	1.25
466	John Boccabella	2.00	1.00	.60
467	Tom Reynolds	2.00	1.00	.60
468a	Pirates Rookies (Bruce Dal Canton, Bob Robertson) (Names in white.)	60.00	30.00	18.00
468b	Pirates Rookies (Bruce Dal Canton, Bob Robertson) (Names in yellow.)	2.00	1.00	.60
469	Chico Ruiz	2.00	1.00	.60
470a	Mel Stottlemyre (Last name in white.)	60.00	30.00	18.00
470b	Mel Stottlemyre (Last name in yellow.)	3.00	1.50	.90
471a	Ted Savage (Last name in white.)	60.00	30.00	18.00
471b	Ted Savage (Last name in yellow.)	2.00	1.00	.60
472	Jim Price	2.00	1.00	.60
473a	Jose Arcia (First name in white.)	60.00	30.00	18.00
473b	Jose Arcia (First name in yellow.)	2.00	1.00	.60
474	Tom Murphy	2.00	1.00	.60
475	Tim McCarver	3.00	1.50	.90
476a	Red Sox Rookies (Ken Brett RC, Gerry Moses) (Names in white.)	60.00	30.00	18.00
476b	Red Sox Rookies (Ken Brett RC, Gerry Moses) (Names in yellow.)	3.00	1.50	.90
477	Jeff James	2.00	1.00	.60
478	Don Buford	2.00	1.00	.60
479	Richie Scheinblum	2.00	1.00	.60
480	Tom Seaver	45.00	23.00	11.50
481	Bill Melton RC	2.00	1.00	.60
482a	Jim Gosger (First name in white.)	60.00	30.00	18.00
482b	Jim Gosger (First name in yellow.)	2.00	1.00	.60
483	Ted Abernathy	2.00	1.00	.60
484	Joe Gordon	10.00	5.00	3.00
485a	Gaylord Perry (Last name in white.)	100.00	45.00	27.50
485b	Gaylord Perry (Last name in yellow.)	16.00	8.00	4.50
486a	Paul Casanova (Last name in white.)	60.00	30.00	18.00
486b	Paul Casanova (Last name in yellow.)	2.00	1.00	.60
487	Denis Menke	2.00	1.00	.60
488	Joe Sparma	2.00	1.00	.60
489	Clete Boyer	3.00	1.50	.90
490	Matty Alou	2.00	1.00	.60
491a	Twins Rookies (Jerry Crider, George Mitterwald) (Names in white.)	60.00	30.00	18.00
491b	Twins Rookies(Jerry Crider, George Mitterwald) (Names in yellow.)	2.00	1.00	.60
492	Tony Cloninger	2.00	1.00	.60
493a	Wes Parker (Last name in white.)	60.00	30.00	18.00
493b	Wes Parker (Last name in yellow.)	2.00	1.00	.60
494	Ken Berry	2.00	1.00	.60
495	Bert Campaneris	2.00	1.00	.60
496	Larry Jaster	2.00	1.00	.60
497	Julian Javier	2.00	1.00	.60
498	Juan Pizarro	2.00	1.00	.60
499	Astros Rookies (Don Bryant, Steve Shea)	2.00	1.00	.60
500a	Mickey Mantle (Last name in white.)	2,000	800.00	425.00
500b	Mickey Mantle (Last name in yellow.)	275.00	125.00	75.00
501a	Tony Gonzalez (First name in white.)	60.00	30.00	18.00
501b	Tony Gonzalez (First name in yellow.)	2.00	1.00	.60
502	Minnie Rojas	2.00	1.00	.60
503	Larry Brown	2.00	1.00	.60
504	6th Series Check List (513-588)(Brooks Robinson)	7.00	3.50	2.00
505a	Bobby Bolin (Last name in white.)	60.00	30.00	18.00
505b	Bobby Bolin (Last name in yellow.)	2.00	1.00	.60
506	Paul Blair	2.00	1.00	.60
507	Cookie Rojas	2.00	1.00	.60
508	Moe Drabowsky	2.00	1.00	.60
509	Manny Sanguillen	2.00	1.00	.60
510	Rod Carew	30.00	15.00	7.50
511a	Diego Segui (First name in white.)	60.00	30.00	18.00
511b	Diego Segui (First name in yellow.)	2.00	1.00	.60
512	Cleon Jones	2.00	1.00	.60
513	Camilo Pascual	2.00	1.00	.60
514	Mike Lum	2.00	1.00	.60
515	Dick Green	2.00	1.00	.60
516	Earl Weaver	12.00	4.50	2.75
517	Mike McCormick	2.00	1.00	.60
518	Fred Whitfield	2.00	1.00	.60
519	Yankees Rookies (Len Boehmer, Gerry Kenney)	2.00	1.00	.60
520	Bob Veale	2.00	1.00	.60
521	George Thomas	2.00	1.00	.60
522	Joe Hoerner	2.00	1.00	.60
523	Bob Chance	2.00	1.00	.60
524	Expos Rookies (Jose Laboy, Floyd Wicker)	2.00	1.00	.60
525	Earl Wilson	2.00	1.00	.60
526	Hector Torres	2.00	1.00	.60
527	Al Lopez	6.00	3.00	1.75
528	Claude Osteen	2.00	1.00	.60
529	Ed Kirkpatrick	2.00	1.00	.60
530	Cesar Tovar	2.00	1.00	.60
531	Dick Farrell	2.00	1.00	.60
532	Bird Hill Aces (Mike Cuellar, Jim Hardin, Dave McNally, Tom Phoebus)	3.50	1.75	1.00
533	Nolan Ryan	190.00	95.00	60.00
534	Jerry McNertney	2.00	1.00	.60
535	Phil Regan	2.00	1.00	.60
536	Padres Rookies(Danny Breeden, Dave Roberts RC)	2.00	1.00	.60
537	Mike Paul	2.00	1.00	.60
538	Charlie Smith	2.00	1.00	.60
539	Ted Shows How(Mike Epstein, Ted Williams)	13.50	6.75	4.00
540	Curt Flood	3.00	1.50	.90
541	Joe Verbanic	2.00	1.00	.60
542	Bob Aspromonte	2.00	1.00	.60
543	Fred Newman	2.00	1.00	.60
544	Tigers Rookies (Mike Kilkenny, Ron Woods)	2.00	1.00	.60
545	Willie Stargell	12.00	6.00	3.00
546	Jim Nash	2.00	1.00	.60
547	Billy Martin	10.00	3.00	1.75
548	Bob Locker	2.00	1.00	.60
549	Ron Brand	2.00	1.00	.60
550	Brooks Robinson	23.00	12.50	7.50

551	Wayne Granger	2.00	1.00	.60
552	Dodgers Rookies (Ted Sizemore RC, Bill Sudakis RC)	3.00	1.50	.90
553	Ron Davis	2.00	1.00	.60
554	Frank Bertaina	2.00	1.00	.60
555	Jim Hart	2.00	1.00	.60
556	A's Stars (Sal Bando, Bert Campaneris, Danny Cater)	3.00	1.50	.90
557	Frank Fernandez	2.00	1.00	.60
558	Tom Burgmeier RC	2.00	1.00	.60
559	Cards Rookies(Joe Hague, Jim Hicks)	2.00	1.00	.60
560	Luis Tiant	2.00	1.00	.60
561	Ron Clark	2.00	1.00	.60
562	Bob Watson RC	4.00	2.00	1.25
563	Marty Pattin	2.00	1.00	.60
564	Gil Hodges	7.00	3.50	2.00
565	Hoyt Wilhelm	10.00	4.00	2.50
566	Ron Hansen	2.00	1.00	.60
567a	Pirates Rookies (Elvio Jimenez, Jim Shellenback) (No black outline around title letters.)	45.00	22.50	13.50
567b	Pirates Rookies (Elvio Jiminez, Jim Shellenback) (Title letters outlined in black.)	2.00	1.00	.60
568	Cecil Upshaw	2.00	1.00	.60
569	Billy Harris	2.00	1.00	.60
570	Ron Santo	20.00	7.50	3.75
571	Cap Peterson	2.00	1.00	.60
572	Giants Heroes (Juan Marichal, Willie McCovey)	13.00	4.50	2.75
573	Jim Palmer	10.00	5.00	2.50
574	George Scott	2.00	1.00	.60
575	Bill Singer	2.00	1.00	.60
576	Phillies Rookies (Ron Stone, Bill Wilson)	2.00	1.00	.60
577	Mike Hegan	2.00	1.00	.60
578	Don Bosch	2.00	1.00	.60
579	Dave Nelson RC	2.00	1.00	.60
580	Jim Northrup	2.00	1.00	.60
581	Gary Nolan	2.00	1.00	.60
582a	7th Series Check List (589-664)(Tony Oliva) (Red circle on back.)	4.50	2.25	1.25
582b	7th Series Check List (589-664)(Tony Oliva) (White circle on back.)	3.00	1.50	.90
583	Clyde Wright RC	2.00	1.00	.60
584	Don Mason	2.00	1.00	.60
585	Ron Swoboda	2.00	1.00	.60
586	Tim Cullen	2.00	1.00	.60
587	Joe Rudi RC	5.00	2.50	1.50
588	Bill White	3.00	1.50	.90
589	Joe Pepitone	6.00	3.00	1.75
590	Rico Carty	3.00	1.50	.90
591	Mike Hedlund	3.00	1.50	.90
592	Padres Rookies (Rafael Robles, Al Santorini)	3.00	1.50	.90
593	Don Nottebart	3.00	1.50	.90
594	Dooley Womack	3.00	1.50	.90
595	Lee Maye	3.00	1.50	.90
596	Chuck Hartenstein	3.00	1.50	.90
597	A.L. Rookies (Larry Burchart, Rollie Fingers RC, Bob Floyd)	40.00	17.50	8.75
598	Ruben Amaro	3.00	1.50	.90
599	John Boozer	3.00	1.50	.90
600	Tony Oliva	9.00	3.00	1.75
601	Tug McGraw	4.00	2.00	1.25
602	Cubs Rookies (Alec Distaso, Jim Qualls, Don Young)	3.00	1.50	.90
603	Joe Keough	3.00	1.50	.90
604	Bobby Etheridge	3.00	1.50	.90
605	Dick Ellsworth	3.00	1.50	.90
606	Gene Mauch	3.00	1.50	.90
607	Dick Bosman	3.00	1.50	.90
608	Dick Simpson	3.00	1.50	.90
609	Phil Gagliano	3.00	1.50	.90
610	Jim Hardin	3.00	1.50	.90
611	Braves Rookies (Bob Didier, Walt Hriniak, Gary Neibauer)	3.00	1.50	.90
612	Jack Aker	3.00	1.50	.90
613	Jim Beauchamp	3.00	1.50	.90
614	Astros Rookies (Tom Griffin, Skip Guinn)	3.00	1.50	.90
615	Len Gabrielson	3.00	1.50	.90
616	Don McMahon	3.00	1.50	.90
617	Jesse Gonder	3.00	1.50	.90
618	Ramon Webster	3.00	1.50	.90

619	Royals Rookies (Bill Butler, Pat Kelly RC, Juan Rios)	3.00	1.50	.90
620	Dean Chance	3.00	1.50	.90
621	Bill Voss	3.00	1.50	.90
622	Dan Osinski	3.00	1.50	.90
623	Hank Allen	3.00	1.50	.90
624	N.L. Rookies (Darrel Chaney, Duffy Dyer, Terry Harmon)	3.00	1.50	.90
625	Mack Jones	3.00	1.50	.90
626	Gene Michael	3.00	1.50	.90
627	George Stone	3.00	1.50	.90
628	Red Sox Rookies (Bill Conigliaro RC, Syd O'Brien, Fred Wenz)	4.00	2.00	1.25
629	Jack Hamilton	3.00	1.50	.90
630	Bobby Bonds RC	25.00	12.50	7.50
631	John Kennedy	3.00	1.50	.90
632	Jon Warden	3.00	1.50	.90
633	Harry Walker	3.00	1.50	.90
634	Andy Etchebarren	3.00	1.50	.90
635	George Culver	3.00	1.50	.90
636	Woodie Held	3.00	1.50	.90
637	Padres Rookies (Jerry DaVanon, Clay Kirby RC, Frank Reberger)	3.00	1.50	.90
638	Ed Sprague	3.00	1.50	.90
639	Barry Moore	3.00	1.50	.90
640	Fergie Jenkins	15.00	7.50	3.75
641	N.L. Rookies (Bobby Darwin, Tommy Dean, John Miller)	3.00	1.50	.90
642	John Hiller	3.00	1.50	.90
643	Billy Cowan	3.00	1.50	.90
644	Chuck Hinton	3.00	1.50	.90
645	George Brunet	3.00	1.50	.90
646	Expos Rookies (Dan McGinn, Carl Morton RC)	3.00	1.50	.90
647	Dave Wickersham	3.00	1.50	.90
648	Bobby Wine	3.00	1.50	.90
649	Al Jackson	3.00	1.50	.90
650	Ted Williams	25.00	12.50	6.25
651	Gus Gil	3.00	1.50	.90
652	Eddie Watt	3.00	1.50	.90
653	Aurelio Rodriguez RC (Photo actually batboy Leonard Garcia.)	6.00	3.00	1.75
654	White Sox Rookies (Carlos May RC, Rich Morales, Don Secrist)	3.50	1.75	1.00
655	Mike Hershberger	3.00	1.50	.90
656	Dan Schneider	3.00	1.50	.90
657	Bobby Murcer	6.00	3.00	1.75
658	A.L. Rookies (Bill Burbach, Tom Hall, Jim Miles)	3.00	1.50	.90
659	Johnny Podres	3.00	1.50	.90
660	Reggie Smith	3.00	1.50	.90
661	Jim Merritt	3.00	1.50	.90
662	Royals Rookies (Dick Drago, Bob Oliver, George Spriggs)	3.00	1.50	.90
663	Dick Radatz	4.50	2.25	1.25
664	Ron Hunt	13.50	3.00	1.00

1969 Topps 4-On-1 Mini Stickers

Another in the long line of Topps test issues, the 4-on-1s are 2-1/2" x 3-1/2" cards with blank backs featuring a quartet of miniature stickers in the design of the same cards from the 1969 Topps regular set. There are 25 different cards, for a total of 100 different stickers. As they are not common, Mint cards bring fairly strong prices on today's market. As the set was drawn from the 3rd Series of the regular cards, it includes some rookie stickers and World Series highlight stickers.

		NM	E	VG
Complete Set (25):		2,250	1,125	675.00
Common 4-in-1:		50.00	25.00	15.00
Unopened Pack:		375.00		
(1)	Jerry Adair, Willie Mays, Johnny Morris, Don Wilson	400.00	200.00	120.00
(2)	Tommie Aaron, Jim Britton, Donn Clendenon, Woody Woodward	50.00	25.00	15.00
(3)	Tommy Davis, Don Pavletich, Vada Pinson, World Series Game 4 (Lou Brock)	75.00	37.50	22.00
(4)	Max Alvis, Glenn Beckert, Ron Fairly, Rick Wise	50.00	25.00	15.00
(5)	Johnny Callison, Jim French, Lum Harris, Dick Selma	50.00	25.00	15.00
(6)	Bob Gibson, Larry Haney, Rick Reichardt, World Series Game 3 (Tim McCarver)	125.00	65.00	35.00
(7)	Wally Bunker, Don Cardwell, Joe Gibbon, Astros Rookies (Gilsen, McFadden)	50.00	25.00	15.00
(8)	Ollie Brown, Jim Bunning, Andy Kosco, Ron Reed	50.00	25.00	15.00
(9)	Bill Dillman, Jim Lefebvre, John Purdin, John Roseboro	50.00	25.00	15.00
(10)	Bill Hands, Chuck Harrison, Lindy McDaniel, Felix Millan	50.00	25.00	15.00
(11)	Jack Hiatt, Dave Johnson, Mel Nelson, Tommie Sisk	50.00	25.00	15.00
(12)	Clay Dalrymple, Leo Durocher, John Odom, Wilbur Wood	50.00	25.00	15.00
(13)	Hank Bauer, Kevin Collins, Ray Oyler, Russ Snyder	50.00	25.00	15.00
(14)	Gerry Arrigo, Jim Perry, Red Sox Rookies (Lahoud, Thibdeau), World Series Game 7 (Mickey Lolich)	50.00	25.00	15.00
(15)	Bill McCool, Roberto Pena, Doug Rader, World Series Game 2 (Willie Horton)	75.00	37.50	22.00
(16)	Ed Brinkman, Roy Face, Willie Horton, Bob Rodgers	50.00	25.00	15.00
(17)	Dave Baldwin, J.C. Martin, Dave May, Ray Sadecki	50.00	25.00	15.00
(18)	Jose Pagan, Tom Phoebus, Mike Shannon, World Series Game 1 (Bob Gibson)	50.00	25.00	15.00
(19)	Pete Rose, Lee Stange, Don Sutton, Ted Uhlaender	500.00	250.00	150.00
(20)	Joe Grzenda, Frank Howard, Dick Tracewski, Jim Weaver	50.00	25.00	15.00
(21)	Joe Azcue, Grant Jackson, Denny McLain, White Sox Rookies (Christman, Nyman)	50.00	25.00	15.00
(22)	John Edwards, Jim Fairey, Phillies Rookies, Stan Williams	50.00	25.00	15.00
(23)	John Bateman, Willie Smith, Leon Wagner, World Series Summary	50.00	25.00	15.00
(24)	Chris Cannizzaro, Bob Hendley, World Series Game 5 (Al Kaline), Yankees Rookies (Closter, Cumberland)	50.00	25.00	15.00
(25)	Joe Nossek, Rico Petrocelli, Carl Yastrzemski, Cardinals Rookies (Huntz, Torrez)	350.00	175.00	105.00

1969 Topps Bowie Kuhn

Following Kuhn's election as Commissioner in February 1969, Topps produced this special card, presumably for his personal use. In standard 2-1/2" x 3-1/2" format, but printed on thinner than usual card stock, the front has a photo of Kuhn's face composited with the drawing of a crowned baseball player sitting on top of the world. The horizontal back has a few personal data and a career summary.

 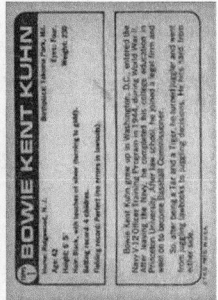

		NM	E	VG
1	Bowie Kuhn	90.00	45.00	27.50

1969 Topps Decals

Designed as an insert for 1969 regular issue card packs, these decals are virtually identical in format to the '69 cards. The 48 decals in the set measure 1" x 2-1/2", although they are mounted on white paper backing which measures 1-3/4" x 2-1/8." In March 2001, a hoard consisting of two original 10,000-piece rolls - 833 each of half the players in the set - was sold at auction. The players represented in that find are indicated in these listings with an asterisk.

		NM	E	VG
	Complete Set (48):	350.00	175.00	100.00
	Common Player:	4.00	2.00	1.25
(1)	Hank Aaron	25.00	12.50	7.50
(2)	Richie Allen	7.00	3.50	2.00
(3)	Felipe Alou	5.00	2.50	1.50
(4)	Matty Alou	4.00	2.00	1.25
(5)	Luis Aparicio	9.00	4.50	2.75
(6)	Bob Clemente	30.00	15.00	9.00
(7)	Donn Clendenon	4.00	2.00	1.25
(8)	Tommy Davis (*)	4.00	2.00	1.25
(9)	Don Drysdale (*)	10.00	5.00	3.00
(10)	Joe Foy (*)	4.00	2.00	1.25
(11)	Jim Fregosi	4.00	2.00	1.25
(12)	Bob Gibson (*)	10.00	5.00	3.00
(13)	Tony Gonzalez	4.00	2.00	1.25
(14)	Tom Haller	4.00	2.00	1.25
(15)	Ken Harrelson	4.00	2.00	1.25
(16)	Tommy Helms	4.00	2.00	1.25
(17)	Willie Horton (*)	4.00	2.00	1.25
(18)	Frank Howard	4.50	2.25	1.25
(19)	Reggie Jackson (*)	20.00	10.00	6.00
(20)	Fergie Jenkins	9.00	4.50	2.75
(21)	Harmon Killebrew (*)	10.00	5.00	3.00
(22)	Jerry Koosman (*)	4.00	2.00	1.25
(23)	Mickey Mantle	40.00	20.00	12.00
(24)	Willie Mays (*)	20.00	10.00	6.00
(25)	Tim McCarver	4.50	2.25	1.25
(26)	Willie McCovey	12.50	5.00	3.00
(27)	Sam McDowell (*)	4.00	2.00	1.25
(28)	Denny McLain (*)	4.00	2.00	1.25
(29)	Dave McNally (*)	4.00	2.00	1.25
(30)	Don Mincher	4.00	2.00	1.25
(31)	Rick Monday	4.00	2.00	1.25
(32)	Tony Oliva (*)	4.50	2.25	1.25
(33)	Camilo Pascual	4.00	2.00	1.25
(34)	Rick Reichardt (*)	4.00	2.00	1.25
(35)	Frank Robinson (*)	10.00	5.00	3.00
(36)	Pete Rose (*)	20.00	10.00	6.00
(37)	Ron Santo (*)	5.00	2.50	1.50
(38)	Tom Seaver (*)	12.00	6.00	3.50
(39)	Dick Selma (*)	4.00	2.00	1.25
(40)	Chris Short (*)	4.00	2.00	1.25
(41)	Rusty Staub	4.00	2.00	1.25
(42)	Mel Stottlemyre	4.00	2.00	1.25
(43)	Luis Tiant (*)	4.00	2.00	1.25
(44)	Pete Ward	4.00	2.00	1.25
(45)	Hoyt Wilhelm (*)	7.50	3.75	2.25
(46)	Maury Wills (*)	4.00	2.00	1.25
(47)	Jim Wynn (*)	4.00	2.00	1.25
(48)	Carl Yastrzemski (*)	12.00	6.00	3.50

1969 Topps Deckle Edge

These 2-1/4" x 3-1/4" cards take their name from their borders which have a scalloped effect. Fronts have a black-and-white player photo along with a blue facsimile autograph. Backs have the player's name and the card number in light blue ink in a small box at the bottom of the card. While there are only 33 numbered cards, there are actually 35 possible players; both Jim Wynn and Hoyt Wilhelm cards are found as #11 while cards of Joe Foy and Rusty Staub as #22. Straight-edged proof cards are sometimes found but these were never formally issued; they carry a premium.

		NM	E	VG
	Complete Set (33):	80.00	40.00	25.00
	Common Player:	1.00	.50	.30
	Proofs: 6-8X			
1	Brooks Robinson	9.00	4.50	2.75
2	Boog Powell	1.50	.70	.45
3	Ken Harrelson	1.00	.50	.30
4	Carl Yastrzemski	9.00	4.50	2.75
5	Jim Fregosi	1.00	.50	.30
6	Luis Aparicio	7.50	3.75	2.25
7	Luis Tiant	1.00	.50	.30
8	Denny McLain	1.00	.50	.30
9	Willie Horton	1.00	.50	.30
10	Bill Freehan	1.00	.50	.30
11a	Hoyt Wilhelm	6.00	3.00	1.75
11b	Jim Wynn	12.00	6.00	3.50
12	Rod Carew	7.50	3.75	2.25
13	Mel Stottlemyre	1.00	.50	.30
14	Rick Monday	1.00	.50	.30
15	Tommy Davis	1.00	.50	.30
16	Frank Howard	1.50	.70	.45
17	Felipe Alou	1.00	.50	.30
18	Don Kessinger	1.00	.50	.30
19	Ron Santo	2.00	1.00	.60
20	Tommy Helms	1.00	.50	.30
21	Pete Rose	15.00	7.50	4.50
22a	Rusty Staub	2.00	1.00	.60
22b	Joe Foy	9.00	4.50	2.75
23	Tom Haller	1.00	.50	.30
24	Maury Wills	1.00	.50	.30
25	Jerry Koosman	1.00	.50	.30
26	Richie Allen	3.00	1.50	.90
27	Roberto Clemente	20.00	10.00	6.00
28	Curt Flood	1.00	.50	.30
29	Bob Gibson	7.50	3.75	2.25
30	Al Ferrara	1.00	.50	.30
31	Willie McCovey	7.50	3.75	2.25
32	Juan Marichal	6.00	3.00	1.75
33	Willie Mays	15.00	7.50	4.50

1969 Topps Pack O' Fun Foldee

This foldee is larger than other versionas, measuring 5 1/4" x 3 1/8".

		NM	E	VG
(26)	Babe Ruth	25.00	12.50	7.50

1969 Topps Stamps

Topps continued to refine its efforts at baseball stamps in 1969 with the release of 240 player stamps, each measuring 1" x 1-7/16". Each stamp has a color photo along with the player's name, position and team. Unlike prior stamp issues, the 1969 stamps have 24 separate albums (one per team). The stamps were issued in strips of 12, many players appearing on two different strips.

	NM	E	VG
Complete Sheet Set (24):	200.00	100.00	60.00
Common Sheet:	5.00	2.50	1.50
Complete Stamp Album Set (24):	80.00	40.00	20.00
Single Stamp Album:	3.00	1.50	.90
Unopened Pack:	50.00		

		NM	E	VG
(1)	Tommie Agee, Sandy Alomar, Jose Cardenal, Dean Chance, Joe Foy, Jim Grant, Don Kessinger, Mickey Mantle, Jerry May, Bob Rodgers, Cookie Rojas, Gary Sutherland	55.00	27.50	16.50
(2)	Jesus Alou, Mike Andrews, Larry Brown, Moe Drabowsky, Alex Johnson, Lew Krausse, Jim Lefebvre, Dal Maxvill, John Odom, Claude Osteen, Rick Reichardt, Luis Tiant	5.00	2.50	1.50
(3)	Hank Aaron, Matty Alou, Max Alvis, Nelson Briles, Eddie Fisher, Bud Harrelson, Willie Horton, Randy Hundley, Larry Jaster, Jim Kaat, Gary Peters, Pete Ward	20.00	10.00	6.00
(4)	Don Buford, John Callison, Tommy Davis, Jackie Hernandez, Fergie Jenkins, Lee May, Denny McLain, Bob Oliver, Roberto Pena, Tony Perez, Joe Torre, Tom Tresh	7.50	3.75	2.25
(5)	Jim Bunning, Dean Chance, Joe Foy, Sonny Jackson, Don Kessinger, Rick Monday, Gaylord Perry, Roger Repoz, Cookie Rojas, Mel Stottlemyre, Leon Wagner, Jim Wynn	7.50	3.75	2.25
(6)	Felipe Alou, Gerry Arrigo, Bob Aspromonte, Gary Bell, Clay Dalrymple, Jim Fregosi, Tony Gonzalez, Duane Josephson, Dick McAuliffe, Tony Oliva, Brooks Robinson, Willie Stargell	20.00	10.00	6.00
(7)	Steve Barber, Donn Clendenon, Joe Coleman, Vic Davalillo, Russ Gibson, Jerry Grote, Tom Haller, Andy Kosco, Willie McCovey, Don Mincher, Joe Morgan, Don Wilson	7.50	3.75	2.25
(8)	George Brunet, Don Buford, John Callison, Danny Cater, Tommy Davis, Willie Davis, John Edwards, Jim Hart, Mickey Lolich, Willie Mays, Roberto Pena, Mickey Stanley	25.00	12.50	7.50
(9)	Ernie Banks, Glenn Beckert, Ken Berry, Horace Clarke, Roberto Clemente, Larry Dierker, Len Gabrielson, Jake Gibbs, Jerry Koosman, Sam McDowell, Tom Satriano, Bill Singer	25.00	12.50	7.50
(10)	Gene Alley, Lou Brock, Larry Brown, Moe Drabowsky, Frank Howard, Tommie John, Roger Nelson, Claude Osteen, Phil Regan, Rick Reichardt, Tony Taylor, Roy White	7.50	3.75	2.25
(11)	Bob Allison, John Bateman, Don Drysdale, Dave Johnson, Harmon Killebrew, Jim Maloney, Bill Mazeroski, Gerry McNertney, Ron Perranoski, Rico Petrocelli, Pete Rose, Billy Williams	35.00	17.50	10.50

(12) Bernie Allen (Senators), Jose Arcia, Stan Bahnsen, Sal Bando, Jim Davenport, Tito Francona, Dick Green, Ron Hunt, Mack Jones, Vada Pinson, George Scott, Don Wert — 5.00 2.50 1.50

(13) Gerry Arrigo, Bob Aspromonte, Joe Azcue, Curt Blefary, Orlando Cepeda, Bill Freehan, Jim Fregosi, Dave Giusti, Duane Josephson, Tim McCarver, Jose Santiago, Bob Tolan — 7.50 3.75 2.25

(14) Jerry Adair, Johnny Bench, Clete Boyer, John Briggs, Bert Campaneris, Woody Fryman, Ron Kline, Bobby Knoop, Ken McMullen, Adolfo Phillips, John Roseboro, Tom Seaver — 20.00 10.00 6.00

(15) Norm Cash, Ron Fairly, Bob Gibson, Bill Hands, Cleon Jones, Al Kaline, Paul Schaal, Mike Shannon, Duke Sims, Reggie Smith, Steve Whitaker, Carl Yastrzemski — 15.00 7.50 4.50

(16) Steve Barber, Paul Casanova, Dick Dietz, Russ Gibson, Jerry Grote, Tom Haller, Ed Kranepool, Juan Marichal, Denis Menke, Jim Nash, Bill Robinson, Frank Robinson — 15.00 7.50 4.50

(17) Bobby Bolin, Ollie Brown, Rod Carew, Mike Epstein, Bud Harrelson, Larry Jaster, Dave McNally, Willie Norton, Milt Pappas, Gary Peters, Paul Popovich, Stan Williams — 7.50 3.75 2.25

(18) Ted Abernathy, Bob Allison, Ed Brinkman, Don Drysdale, Jim Hardin, Julian Javier, Hal Lanier, Jim McGlothlin, Ron Perranoski, Rich Rollins, Ron Santo, Billy Williams — 15.00 7.50 4.50

(19) Richie Allen, Luis Aparicio, Wally Bunker, Curt Flood, Ken Harrelson, Jim Hunter, Denver Lemaster, Felix Millan, Jim Northrop (Northrup), Art Shamsky, Larry Stahl, Ted Uhlaender — 7.50 3.75 2.25

(20) Bob Bailey, Johnny Bench, Woody Fryman, Jim Hannan, Ron Kline, Al McBean, Camilo Pascual, Joe Pepitone, Doug Rader, Ron Reed, John Roseboro, Sonny Siebert — 7.50 3.75 2.25

(21) Jack Aker, Tommy Harper, Tommy Helms, Dennis Higgins, Jim Hunter, Don Lock, Lee Maye, Felix Millan, Jim Northrop (Northrup), Larry Stahl, Don Sutton, Zoilo Versalles — 7.50 3.75 2.25

(22) Norm Cash, Ed Charles, Joe Horlen, Pat Jarvis, Jim Lonborg, Manny Mota, Boog Powell, Dick Selma, Mike Shannon, Duke Sims, Steve Whitaker, Hoyt Wilhelm — 7.50 3.75 2.25

(23) Bernie Allen (Senator), Ray Culp, Al Ferrara, Tito Francona, Dick Green, Ron Hunt, Ray Oyler, Tom Phoebus, Rusty Staub, Bob Veale, Maury Wills, Wilbur Wood — 5.00 2.50 1.50

(24) Ernie Banks, Mark Belanger, Steve Blass, Horace Clarke, Bob Clemente, Larry Dierker, Dave Duncan, Chico Salmon, Chris Short, Ron Swoboda, Cesar Tovar, Rick Wise — 20.00 10.00 6.00

1969 Topps Super

These 2-1/4" x 3-1/4" cards are not the bigger "Super" cards which would be seen in following years. Rather, what enabled Topps to dub them "Super Baseball Cards" is their high-gloss finish which enhances the bright color photograph used on their fronts. The only other design element on the front is a facsimile autograph. The backs contain a box at the the bottom which carries the player's name, team, position, a copyright line and the card number. Another unusual feature is that the cards have rounded corners, although square-cornered proof cards are also known, completely printed on front and back.

		NM	E	VG
Complete Set (66):		6,000	3,000	1,800
Common Player:		20.00	10.00	6.00
Proofs: 2-3X				
1	Dave McNally	20.00	10.00	6.00
2	Frank Robinson	175.00	85.00	50.00
3	Brooks Robinson	175.00	85.00	50.00
4	Ken Harrelson	20.00	10.00	6.00
5	Carl Yastrzemski	250.00	125.00	75.00
6	Ray Culp	20.00	10.00	6.00
7	James Fregosi	20.00	10.00	6.00
8	Rick Reichardt	20.00	10.00	6.00
9	Vic Davalillo	20.00	10.00	6.00
10	Luis Aparicio	100.00	50.00	30.00
11	Pete Ward	20.00	10.00	6.00
12	Joe Horlen	20.00	10.00	6.00
13	Luis Tiant	20.00	10.00	6.00
14	Sam McDowell	20.00	10.00	6.00
15	Jose Cardenal	20.00	10.00	6.00
16	Willie Horton	20.00	10.00	6.00
17	Denny McLain	20.00	10.00	6.00
18	Bill Freehan	20.00	10.00	6.00
19	Harmon Killebrew	175.00	85.00	50.00
20	Tony Oliva	20.00	10.00	6.00
21	Dean Chance	20.00	10.00	6.00
22	Joe Foy	20.00	10.00	6.00
23	Roger Nelson	20.00	10.00	6.00
24	Mickey Mantle	1,100	550.00	350.00
25	Mel Stottlemyre	20.00	10.00	6.00
26	Roy White	20.00	10.00	6.00
27	Rick Monday	20.00	10.00	6.00
28	Reggie Jackson	400.00	200.00	120.00
29	Bert Campaneris	20.00	10.00	6.00
30	Frank Howard	20.00	10.00	6.00
31	Camilo Pascual	20.00	10.00	6.00
32	Tommy Davis	20.00	10.00	6.00
33	Don Mincher	20.00	10.00	6.00
34	Henry Aaron	400.00	200.00	120.00
35	Felipe Alou	20.00	10.00	6.00
36	Joe Torre	50.00	25.00	15.00
37	Fergie Jenkins	100.00	50.00	30.00
38	Ronald Santo	35.00	17.50	10.00
39	Billy Williams	100.00	50.00	30.00
40	Tommy Helms	20.00	10.00	6.00
41	Pete Rose	400.00	200.00	120.00
42	Joe Morgan	100.00	50.00	30.00
43	Jim Wynn	20.00	10.00	6.00
44	Curt Blefary	20.00	10.00	6.00
45	Willie Davis	20.00	10.00	6.00
46	Don Drysdale	135.00	65.00	40.00
47	Tom Haller	20.00	10.00	6.00
48	Rusty Staub	35.00	17.50	10.00
49	Maurice Wills	20.00	10.00	6.00
50	Cleon Jones	20.00	10.00	6.00
51	Jerry Koosman	20.00	10.00	6.00
52	Tom Seaver	175.00	87.00	52.00
53	Rich Allen	45.00	22.50	13.50
54	Chris Short	20.00	10.00	6.00
55	Cookie Rojas	20.00	10.00	6.00
56	Mateo Alou	20.00	10.00	6.00
57	Steve Blass	20.00	10.00	6.00
58	Roberto Clemente	500.00	250.00	150.00
59	Curt Flood	20.00	10.00	6.00
60	Bob Gibson	125.00	65.00	35.00
61	Tim McCarver	35.00	17.50	10.00
62	Dick Selma	20.00	10.00	6.00
63	Ollie Brown	20.00	10.00	6.00
64	Juan Marichal	100.00	50.00	30.00
65	Willie Mays	400.00	200.00	120.00
66	Willie McCovey	120.00	60.00	36.00

1969 Topps Team Posters

Picking up where the 1968 posters left off, the 1969 poster is larger at about 12" x 20". The posters each have a team focus with a large pennant carrying the team name, along with nine or 10 photos of players. Each of the photos has a facsimile autograph. The size of posters meant they had to be folded to fit in their packages. These original folds are not considered when grading, unless the paper has split on those seams.

		NM	E	VG
Complete Set (24):		2,250	1,125	675.00
Common Poster:		55.00	27.50	16.00
Unopened Pack:		190.00		
1	Detroit Tigers (Norm Cash, Bill Freehan, Willie Horton, Al Kaline, Mickey Lolich, Dick McAuliffe, Denny McLain, Jim Northrup, Mickey Stanley, Don Wert, Earl Wilson)	125.00	65.00	35.00
2	Atlanta Braves (Hank Aaron, Felipe Alou, Clete Boyer, Rico Carty, Tito Francona, Sonny Jackson, Pat Jarvis, Felix Millan, Phil Niekro, Milt Pappas, Joe Torre)	90.00	45.00	27.00
3	Boston Red Sox (Mike Andrews, Tony Conigliaro, Ray Culp, Russ Gibson, Ken Harrelson, Jim Lonborg, Rico Petrocelli, Jose Santiago, George Scott, Reggie Smith, Carl Yastrzemski)	100.00	50.00	30.00
4	Chicago Cubs (Ernie Banks, Glenn Beckert, Bill Hands, Jim Hickman, Ken Holtzman, Randy Hundley, Fergie Jenkins, Don Kessinger, Adolfo Phillips, Ron Santo, Billy Williams)	90.00	45.00	27.00
5	Baltimore Orioles (Mark Belanger, Paul Blair, Don Buford, Andy Etchebarren, Jim Hardin, Dave Johnson, Dave McNally, Tom Phoebus, Boog Powell, Brooks Robinson, Frank Robinson)	80.00	40.00	24.00
6	Houston Astros (Curt Blefary, Donn Clendenon, Larry Dierker, John Edwards, Denny Lemaster, Denis Menke, Norm Miller, Joe Morgan, Doug Rader, Don Wilson, Jim Wynn)	55.00	27.50	16.00

7	Kansas City Royals (Jerry Adair, Wally Bunker, Mike Fiore, Joe Foy, Jackie Hernandez, Pat Kelly, Dave Morehead, Roger Nelson, Dave Nicholson, Eliseo Rodriguez, Steve Whitaker)	55.00	27.50	16.00
8	Philadelphia Phillies (Richie Allen, Johnny Callison, Woody Fryman, Larry Hisle, Don Money, Cookie Rojas, Mike Ryan, Chris Short, Tony Taylor, Bill White, Rick Wise)	60.00	30.00	18.00
9	Seattle Pilots (Jack Aker, Steve Barber, Gary Bell, Tommy Davis, Jim Gosger, Tommy Harper, Gerry McNertney, Don Mincher, Ray Oyler, Rich Rollins, Chico Salmon)	150.00	75.00	45.00
10	Montreal Expos (Bob Bailey, John Bateman, Jack Billingham, Jim Grant, Larry Jaster, Mack Jones, Manny Mota, Rusty Staub, Gary Sutherland, Jim Williams, Maury Wills)	50.00	25.00	15.00
11	Chicago White Sox (Sandy Alomar, Luis Aparicio, Ken Berry, Buddy Bradford, Joe Horlen, Tommy John, Duane Josephson, Tom McCraw, Bill Melton, Pete Ward, Wilbur Wood)	55.00	27.50	16.00
12	San Diego Padres (Jose Arcia, Danny Breeden, Ollie Brown, Bill Davis, Ron Davis, Tony Gonzalez, Dick Kelley, Al McBean, Roberto Pena, Dick Selma, Ed Spiezio)	55.00	27.50	16.00
13	Cleveland Indians (Max Alvis, Joe Azcue, Jose Cardenal, Vern Fuller, Lou Johnson, Sam McDowell, Sonny Siebert, Duke Sims, Russ Snyder, Luis Tiant, Zoilo Versalles)	75.00	37.00	22.00
14	San Francisco Giants (Bobby Bolin, Jim Davenport, Dick Dietz, Jim Hart, Ron Hunt, Hal Lanier, Juan Marichal, Willie Mays, Willie McCovey, Gaylord Perry, Charlie Smith)	125.00	65.00	35.00
15	Minnesota Twins (Bob Allison, Chico Cardenas, Rod Carew, Dean Chance, Jim Kaat, Harmon Killebrew, Tony Oliva, Jim Perry, John Roseboro, Cesar Tovar, Ted Uhlaender)	100.00	50.00	30.00
16	Pittsburgh Pirates (Gene Alley, Matty Alou, Steve Blass, Jim Bunning, Bob Clemente, Rich Hebner, Jerry May, Bill Mazeroski, Bob Robertson, Willie Stargell, Bob Veale)	135.00	65.00	40.00
17	California Angels (Ruben Amaro, George Brunet, Bob Chance, Vic Davalillo, Jim Fregosi, Bobby Knoop, Jim McGlothlin, Rick Reichardt, Roger Repoz, Bob Rodgers, Hoyt Wilhelm)	60.00	30.00	18.00
18	St. Louis Cardinals (Nelson Briles, Lou Brock, Orlando Cepeda, Curt Flood, Bob Gibson, Julian Javier, Dal Maxvill, Tim McCarver, Vada Pinson, Mike Shannon, Ray Washburn)	75.00	37.50	22.00

19	New York Yankees (Stan Bahnsen, Horace Clarke, Bobby Cox, Jake Gibbs, Mickey Mantle, Joe Pepitone, Fritz Peterson, Bill Robinson, Mel Stottlemyre, Tom Tresh, Roy White)	165.00	82.00	49.00
20	Cincinnati Reds (Gerry Arrigo, Johnny Bench, Tommy Helms, Alex Johnson, Jim Maloney, Lee May, Gary Nolan, Tony Perez, Pete Rose, Bob Tolan, Woody Woodward)	110.00	55.00	33.00
21	Oakland Athletics (Sal Bando, Bert Campaneris, Danny Cater, Dick Green, Mike Hershberger, Jim Hunter, Reggie Jackson, Rick Monday, Jim Nash, John Odom, Jim Pagliaroni)	100.00	50.00	30.00
22	Los Angeles Dodgers (Willie Crawford, Willie Davis, Don Drysdale, Ron Fairly, Tom Haller, Andy Kosco, Jim Lefebvre, Claude Osteen, Paul Popovich, Bill Singer, Bill Sudakis)	80.00	40.00	24.00
23	Washington Senators (Bernie Allen, Brant Alyea, Ed Brinkman, Paul Casanova, Joe Coleman, Mike Epstein, Jim Hannan, Frank Howard, Ken McMullen, Camilo Pascual, Del Unser)	80.00	40.00	24.00
24	New York Mets (Tommie Agee, Ken Boswell, Ed Charles, Jerry Grote, Bud Harrelson, Cleon Jones, Jerry Koosman, Ed Kranepool, Jim McAndrew, Tom Seaver, Ron Swoboda)	150.00	75.00	45.00

1970 Topps

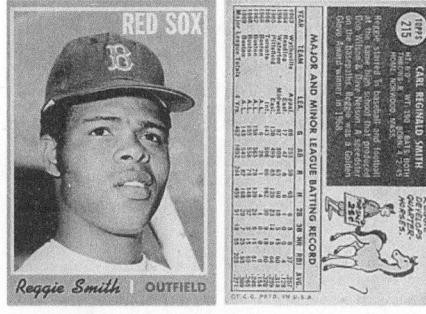

Topps established another set size record by coming out with 720 cards in 1970. The 2-1/2" x 3-1/2" cards have a color photo with a thin white frame. The photos have the player's team overprinted at the top, while the player's name in script and his position are at the bottom. A gray border surrounds the front. Card backs follow the normal design pattern, although they are more readable than some issues of the past. Team cards returned and were joined with many of the usual specialty cards. The World Series highlights were joined by cards with playoff highlights. Statistical leaders and All-Stars are also included in the set. High-numbered cards provide the most expensive cards in the set.

		NM	E	VG
	Complete Set (720):	2,400	1,200	725.00
	Common Player (1-546):	1.50	.75	.45
	Common Player (547-633):	4.00	2.00	1.00
	Common Player (634-720):	8.00	4.00	2.25
1	World Champions (Mets Team)	25.00	12.50	7.50
2	Diego Segui	1.50	.75	.45
3	Darrel Chaney	1.50	.75	.45
4	Tom Egan	1.50	.75	.45
5	Wes Parker	1.50	.75	.45
6	Grant Jackson	1.50	.75	.45
7	Indians Rookies(Gary Boyd, Russ Nagelson)	1.50	.75	.45
8	Jose Martinez	1.50	.75	.45

9	1st Series Check List (1-132)	8.00	4.00	2.50
10	Carl Yastrzemski	20.00	10.00	5.00
11	Nate Colbert	1.50	.75	.45
12	John Hiller	1.50	.75	.45
13	Jack Hiatt	1.50	.75	.45
14	Hank Allen	1.50	.75	.45
15	Larry Dierker	1.50	.75	.45
16	Charlie Metro	1.50	.75	.45
17	Hoyt Wilhelm	6.00	3.00	1.75
18	Carlos May	1.50	.75	.45
19	John Boccabella	1.50	.75	.45
20	Dave McNally	1.50	.75	.45
21	Athletics Rookies(Vida Blue RC, Gene Tenace RC)	5.00	2.50	1.25
22	Ray Washburn	1.50	.75	.45
23	Bill Robinson	1.50	.75	.45
24	Dick Selma	1.50	.75	.45
25	Cesar Tovar	1.50	.75	.45
26	Tug McGraw	1.50	.75	.45
27	Chuck Hinton	1.50	.75	.45
28	Billy Wilson	1.50	.75	.45
29	Sandy Alomar	1.50	.75	.45
30	Matty Alou	1.50	.75	.45
31	Marty Pattin	1.50	.75	.45
32	Harry Walker	1.50	.75	.45
33	Don Wert	1.50	.75	.45
34	Willie Crawford	1.50	.75	.45
35	Joe Horlen	1.50	.75	.45
36	Reds Rookies(Danny Breeden, Bernie Carbo RC)	1.50	.75	.45
37	Dick Drago	1.50	.75	.45
38	Mack Jones	1.50	.75	.45
39	Mike Nagy	1.50	.75	.45
40	Rich Allen	3.00	1.50	.90
41	George Lauzerique	1.50	.75	.45
42	Tito Fuentes	1.50	.75	.45
43	Jack Aker	1.50	.75	.45
44	Roberto Pena	1.50	.75	.45
45	Dave Johnson	1.50	.75	.45
46	Ken Rudolph	1.50	.75	.45
47	Bob Miller	1.50	.75	.45
48	Gill Garrido (Gil)	1.50	.75	.45
49	Tim Cullen	1.50	.75	.45
50	Tommie Agee	1.50	.75	.45
51	Bob Christian	1.50	.75	.45
52	Bruce Dal Canton	1.50	.75	.45
53	John Kennedy	1.50	.75	.45
54	Jeff Torborg	1.50	.75	.45
55	John Odom	1.50	.75	.45
56	Phillies Rookies(Joe Lis, Scott Reid)	1.50	.75	.45
57	Pat Kelly	1.50	.75	.45
58	Dave Marshall	1.50	.75	.45
59	Dick Ellsworth	1.50	.75	.45
60	Jim Wynn	1.50	.75	.45
61	N.L. Batting Leaders (Roberto Clemente, Cleon Jones, Pete Rose)	15.00	7.50	3.75
62	A.L. Batting Leaders(Rod Carew, Tony Oliva, Reggie Smith)	6.00	3.00	1.75
63	N.L. RBI Leaders(Willie McCovey, Tony Perez, Ron Santo)	5.00	2.50	1.50
64	A.L. RBI Leaders(Reggie Jackson, Harmon Killebrew, Boog Powell)	10.00	5.00	3.00
65	N.L. Home Run Leaders (Hank Aaron, Lee May, Willie McCovey)	10.00	5.00	3.00
66	A.L. Home Run Leaders (Frank Howard, Reggie Jackson, Harmon Killebrew)	8.00	4.00	2.50
67	N.L. ERA Leaders(Steve Carlton, Bob Gibson, Juan Marichal)	8.00	4.00	2.50
68	A.L. ERA Leaders(Dick Bosman, Mike Cuellar, Jim Palmer)	4.00	2.00	1.25
69	N.L. Pitching Leaders (Fergie Jenkins, Juan Marichal, Phil Niekro, Tom Seaver)	10.00	5.00	3.00
70	A.L. Pitching Leaders (Dave Boswell, Mike Cuellar, Dennis McLain, Dave McNally, Jim Perry, Mel Stottlemyre)	4.00	2.00	1.25
71	N.L. Strikeout Leaders (Bob Gibson, Fergie Jenkins, Bill Singer)	6.00	3.00	1.75

#	Player			
72	A.L. Strikeout Leaders (Mickey Lolich, Sam McDowell, Andy Messersmith)	4.00	2.00	1.25
73	Wayne Granger	1.50	.75	.45
74	Angels Rookies(Greg Washburn, Wally Wolf)	1.50	.75	.45
75	Jim Kaat	1.50	.75	.45
76	Carl Taylor	1.50	.75	.45
77	Frank Linzy	1.50	.75	.45
78	Joe Lahoud	1.50	.75	.45
79	Clay Kirby	1.50	.75	.45
80	Don Kessinger	1.50	.75	.45
81	Dave May	1.50	.75	.45
82	Frank Fernandez	1.50	.75	.45
83	Don Cardwell	1.50	.75	.45
84	Paul Casanova	1.50	.75	.45
85	Max Alvis	1.50	.75	.45
86	Lum Harris	1.50	.75	.45
87	Steve Renko	1.50	.75	.45
88	Pilots Rookies(Dick Baney, Miguel Fuentes)	1.50	.75	.45
89	Juan Rios	1.50	.75	.45
90	Tim McCarver	3.00	1.50	.90
91	Rich Morales	1.50	.75	.45
92	George Culver	1.50	.75	.45
93	Rick Renick	1.50	.75	.45
94	Fred Patek	1.50	.75	.45
95	Earl Wilson	1.50	.75	.45
96	Cards Rookies (Leron Lee, Jerry Reuss RC)	3.00	1.50	.90
97	Joe Moeller	1.50	.75	.45
98	Gates Brown	1.50	.75	.45
99	Bobby Pfeil	1.50	.75	.45
100	Mel Stottlemyre	1.50	.75	.45
101	Bobby Floyd	1.50	.75	.45
102	Joe Rudi	1.50	.75	.45
103	Frank Reberger	1.50	.75	.45
104	Gerry Moses	1.50	.75	.45
105	Tony Gonzalez	1.50	.75	.45
106	Darold Knowles	1.50	.75	.45
107	Bobby Etheridge	1.50	.75	.45
108	Tom Burgmeier	1.50	.75	.45
109	Expos Rookies(Garry Jestadt, Carl Morton)	1.50	.75	.45
110	Bob Moose	1.50	.75	.45
111	Mike Hegan	1.50	.75	.45
112	Dave Nelson	1.50	.75	.45
113	Jim Ray	1.50	.75	.45
114	Gene Michael	1.50	.75	.45
115	Alex Johnson	1.50	.75	.45
116	Sparky Lyle	1.50	.75	.45
117	Don Young	1.50	.75	.45
118	George Mitterwald	1.50	.75	.45
119	Chuck Taylor	1.50	.75	.45
120	Sal Bando	1.50	.75	.45
121	Orioles Rookies (Fred Beene, Terry Crowley RC)	1.50	.75	.45
122	George Stone	1.50	.75	.45
123	Don Gutteridge	1.50	.75	.45
124	Larry Jaster	1.50	.75	.45
125	Deron Johnson	1.50	.75	.45
126	Marty Martinez	1.50	.75	.45
127	Joe Coleman	1.50	.75	.45
128a	2nd Series Check List (133-263) (226 is R Perranoski)	5.00	2.50	1.50
128b	2nd Series Check List (133-263) (226 is R. Perranoski)	5.00	2.50	1.50
129	Jimmie Price	1.50	.75	.45
130	Ollie Brown	1.50	.75	.45
131	Dodgers Rookies (Ray Lamb, Bob Stinson)	1.50	.75	.45
132	Jim McGlothlin	1.50	.75	.45
133	Clay Carroll	1.50	.75	.45
134	Danny Walton	1.50	.75	.45
135	Dick Dietz	1.50	.75	.45
136	Steve Hargan	1.50	.75	.45
137	Art Shamsky	1.50	.75	.45
138	Joe Foy	1.50	.75	.45
139	Rich Nye	1.50	.75	.45
140	Reggie Jackson	50.00	25.00	12.50
141	Pirates Rookies (Dave Cash RC, Johnny Jeter)	1.50	.75	.45
142	Fritz Peterson	1.50	.75	.45
143	Phil Gagliano	1.50	.75	.45
144	Ray Culp	1.50	.75	.45
145	Rico Carty	1.50	.75	.45
146	Danny Murphy	1.50	.75	.45
147	Angel Hermoso	1.50	.75	.45
148	Earl Weaver	4.00	2.00	1.25
149	Billy Champion	1.50	.75	.45
150	Harmon Killebrew	10.00	5.00	3.00
151	Dave Roberts	1.50	.75	.45
152	Ike Brown	1.50	.75	.45
153	Gary Gentry	1.50	.75	.45

#	Player			
154	Senators Rookies (Jan Dukes, Jim Miles)	1.50	.75	.45
155	Denis Menke	1.50	.75	.45
156	Eddie Fisher	1.50	.75	.45
157	Manny Mota	1.50	.75	.45
158	Jerry McNertney	1.50	.75	.45
159	Tommy Helms	1.50	.75	.45
160	Phil Niekro	6.00	3.00	1.75
161	Richie Scheinblum	1.50	.75	.45
162	Jerry Johnson	1.50	.75	.45
163	Syd O'Brien	1.50	.75	.45
164	Ty Cline	1.50	.75	.45
165	Ed Kirkpatrick	1.50	.75	.45
166	Al Oliver	2.00	1.00	.60
167	Bill Burbach	1.50	.75	.45
168	Dave Watkins	1.50	.75	.45
169	Tom Hall	1.50	.75	.45
170	Billy Williams	8.00	4.00	2.50
171	Jim Nash	1.50	.75	.45
172	Braves Rookies(Ralph Garr RC, Garry Hill)	2.00	1.00	.60
173	Jim Hicks	1.50	.75	.45
174	Ted Sizemore	1.50	.75	.45
175	Dick Bosman	1.50	.75	.45
176	Jim Hart	1.50	.75	.45
177	Jim Northrup	1.50	.75	.45
178	Denny Lemaster	1.50	.75	.45
179	Ivan Murrell	1.50	.75	.45
180	Tommy John	2.00	1.00	.60
181	Sparky Anderson	6.00	3.00	1.75
182	Dick Hall	1.50	.75	.45
183	Jerry Grote	1.50	.75	.45
184	Ray Fosse	1.50	.75	.45
185	Don Mincher	1.50	.75	.45
186	Rick Joseph	1.50	.75	.45
187	Mike Hedlund	1.50	.75	.45
188	Manny Sanguillen	1.50	.75	.45
189	Yankees Rookies (Dave McDonald RC, Thurman Munson RC)	95.00	50.00	25.00
190	Joe Torre	6.00	3.00	1.75
191	Vicente Romo	1.50	.75	.45
192	Jim Qualls	1.50	.75	.45
193	Mike Wegener	1.50	.75	.45
194	Chuck Manuel	1.50	.75	.45
195	N.L.C.S. Game 1 (Seaver Wins Opener!)	8.00	5.00	3.00
196	N.L.C.S. Game 2 (Mets Show Muscle!)	6.00	3.00	1.75
197	N.L.C.S. Game 3 (Ryan Saves the Day!)	20.00	12.50	6.25
198	Mets Celebrate (We're Number One!)(Nolan Ryan)	15.00	7.50	4.50
199	A.L.C.S. Game 1 (Orioles Win A Squeaker!)	4.00	2.00	1.25
200	A.L.C.S. Game 2 (Powell Scores Winning Run!)	4.00	2.00	1.25
201	A.L.C.S. Game 3 (Birds Wrap It Up!)	6.00	3.00	1.80
202	Oriole Celebrate (Sweep Twins In Three!)	3.00	1.50	.90
203	Rudy May	1.50	.75	.45
204	Len Gabrielson	1.50	.75	.45
205	Bert Campaneris	1.50	.75	.45
206	Clete Boyer	1.50	.75	.45
207	Tigers Rookies(Norman McRae, Bob Reed)	1.50	.75	.45
208	Fred Gladding	1.50	.75	.45
209	Ken Suarez	1.50	.75	.45
210	Juan Marichal	6.00	3.00	1.75
211	Ted Williams	18.00	10.00	5.00
212	Al Santorini	1.50	.75	.45
213	Andy Etchebarren	1.50	.75	.45
214	Ken Boswell	1.50	.75	.45
215	Reggie Smith	1.50	.75	.45
216	Chuck Hartenstein	1.50	.75	.45
217	Ron Hansen	1.50	.75	.45
218	Ron Stone	1.50	.75	.45
219	Jerry Kenney	1.50	.75	.45
220	Steve Carlton	15.00	5.00	3.00
221	Ron Brand	1.50	.75	.45
222	Jim Rooker	1.50	.75	.45
223	Nate Oliver	1.50	.75	.45
224	Steve Barber	1.50	.75	.45
225	Lee May	1.50	.75	.45
226	Ron Perranoski	1.50	.75	.45
227	Astros Rookies (John Mayberry RC, Bob Watkins)	1.50	.75	.45
228	Aurelio Rodriguez	1.50	.75	.45
229	Rich Robertson	1.50	.75	.45
230	Brooks Robinson	18.00	7.50	3.75
231	Luis Tiant	1.50	.75	.45
232	Bob Didier	1.50	.75	.45
233	Lew Krausse	1.50	.75	.45
234	Tommy Dean	1.50	.75	.45
235	Mike Epstein	1.50	.75	.45

#	Player			
236	Bob Veale	1.50	.75	.45
237	Russ Gibson	1.50	.75	.45
238	Jose Laboy	1.50	.75	.45
239	Ken Berry	1.50	.75	.45
240	Fergie Jenkins	6.00	3.00	1.75
241	Royals Rookies (Al Fitzmorris, Scott Northey)	1.50	.75	.45
242	Walter Alston	4.00	2.00	1.25
243	Joe Sparma	1.50	.75	.45
244a	3rd Series Check List (264-372) (Red bat on front.)	6.00	3.00	1.75
244b	3rd Series Check List (264-372) (Brown bat on front.)	6.00	3.00	1.75
245	Leo Cardenas	1.50	.75	.45
246	Jim McAndrew	1.50	.75	.45
247	Lou Klimchock	1.50	.75	.45
248	Jesus Alou	1.50	.75	.45
249	Bob Locker	1.50	.75	.45
250	Willie McCovey	11.00	5.00	3.00
251	Dick Schofield	1.50	.75	.45
252	Lowell Palmer	1.50	.75	.45
253	Ron Woods	1.50	.75	.45
254	Camilo Pascual	1.50	.75	.45
255	Jim Spencer RC	1.50	.75	.45
256	Vic Davalillo	1.50	.75	.45
257	Dennis Higgins	1.50	.75	.45
258	Paul Popovich	1.50	.75	.45
259	Tommie Reynolds	1.50	.75	.45
260	Claude Osteen	1.50	.75	.45
261	Curt Motton	1.50	.75	.45
262	Padres Rookies(Jerry Morales, Jim Williams)	1.50	.75	.45
263	Duane Josephson	1.50	.75	.45
264	Rich Hebner	1.50	.75	.45
265	Randy Hundley	1.50	.75	.45
266	Wally Bunker	1.50	.75	.45
267	Twins Rookies(Herman Hill, Paul Ratliff)	1.50	.75	.45
268	Claude Raymond	1.50	.75	.45
269	Cesar Gutierrez	1.50	.75	.45
270	Chris Short	1.50	.75	.45
271	Greg Goossen	1.50	.75	.45
272	Hector Torres	1.50	.75	.45
273	Ralph Houk	4.00	2.00	1.25
274	Gerry Arrigo	1.50	.75	.45
275	Duke Sims	1.50	.75	.45
276	Ron Hunt	1.50	.75	.45
277	Paul Doyle	1.50	.75	.45
278	Tommie Aaron	1.50	.75	.45
279	Bill Lee RC	1.50	.75	.45
280	Donn Clendenon	1.50	.75	.45
281	Casey Cox	1.50	.75	.45
282	Steve Huntz	1.50	.75	.45
283	Angel Bravo	1.50	.75	.45
284	Jack Baldschun	1.50	.75	.45
285	Paul Blair	1.50	.75	.45
286	Dodgers Rookies (Bill Buckner RC, Jack Jenkins)	7.00	3.00	1.75
287	Fred Talbot	1.50	.75	.45
288	Larry Hisle	1.50	.75	.45
289	Gene Brabender	1.50	.75	.45
290	Rod Carew	14.00	5.00	3.00
291	Leo Durocher	4.00	2.00	1.25
292	Eddie Leon	1.50	.75	.45
293	Bob Bailey	1.50	.75	.45
294	Jose Azcue	1.50	.75	.45
295	Cecil Upshaw	1.50	.75	.45
296	Woody Woodward	1.50	.75	.45
297	Curt Blefary	1.50	.75	.45
298	Ken Henderson	1.50	.75	.45
299	Buddy Bradford	1.50	.75	.45
300	Tom Seaver	25.00	12.50	7.50
301	Chico Salmon	1.50	.75	.45
302	Jeff James	1.50	.75	.45
303a	Brant Ayea (ball in cartoon on back)	1.50	.75	.45
303b	Brant Ayea (no ball in cartoon)	1.50	.75	.45
304	Bill Russell RC	4.00	2.00	1.25
305	World Series Game 1 (Buford Belts Leadoff Homer!)	4.00	2.00	1.25
306	World Series Game 2 (Clendenon's HR Breaks Ice!)	4.00	2.00	1.25
307	World Series Game 3 (Agee's Catch Saves The Day!)	4.00	2.00	1.25
308	World Series Game 4 (Martin's Bunt Ends Deadlock!)	4.00	2.00	1.25
309	World Series Game 5 (Koosman Shuts The Door!)	6.00	2.00	1.25

310	World Series Celebration (Mets Whoop It Up!)	8.00	4.00	2.50
311	Dick Green	1.50	.75	.45
312	Mike Torrez	1.50	.75	.45
313	Mayo Smith	1.50	.75	.45
314	Bill McCool	1.50	.75	.45
315	Luis Aparicio	8.00	4.00	2.50
316	Skip Guinn	1.50	.75	.45
317	Red Sox Rookies (Luis Alvarado, Billy Conigliaro)	1.50	.75	.45
318	Willie Smith	1.50	.75	.45
319	Clayton Dalrymple	1.50	.75	.45
320	Jim Maloney	1.50	.75	.45
321	Lou Piniella	3.00	1.50	.90
322	Luke Walker	1.50	.75	.45
323	Wayne Comer	1.50	.75	.45
324	Tony Taylor	1.50	.75	.45
325	Dave Boswell	1.50	.75	.45
326	Bill Voss	1.50	.75	.45
327	Hal King	1.50	.75	.45
328	George Brunet	1.50	.75	.45
329	Chris Cannizzaro	1.50	.75	.45
330	Lou Brock	10.00	5.00	3.00
331	Chuck Dobson	1.50	.75	.45
332	Bobby Wine	1.50	.75	.45
333	Bobby Murcer	3.00	1.50	.90
334	Phil Regan	1.50	.75	.45
335	Bill Freehan	1.50	.75	.45
336	Del Unser	1.50	.75	.45
337	Mike McCormick	1.50	.75	.45
338	Paul Schaal	1.50	.75	.45
339	Johnny Edwards	1.50	.75	.45
340	Tony Conigliaro	4.00	2.00	1.25
341	Bill Sudakis	1.50	.75	.45
342	Wilbur Wood	1.50	.75	.45
343a	4th Series Check List (373-459) (Red bat on front.)	5.00	2.50	1.50
343b	4th Series Check List (373-459) (Brown bat on front.)	5.00	2.50	1.50
344	Marcelino Lopez	1.50	.75	.45
345	Al Ferrara	1.50	.75	.45
346	Red Schoendienst	7.00	2.00	1.25
347	Russ Snyder	1.50	.75	.45
348	Mets Rookies (Jesse Hudson, Mike Jorgensen)	1.50	.75	.45
349	Steve Hamilton	1.50	.75	.45
350	Roberto Clemente	60.00	30.00	15.00
351	Tom Murphy	1.50	.75	.45
352	Bob Barton	1.50	.75	.45
353	Stan Williams	1.50	.75	.45
354	Amos Otis	1.50	.75	.45
355	Doug Rader	1.50	.75	.45
356	Fred Lasher	1.50	.75	.45
357	Bob Burda	1.50	.75	.45
358	Pedro Borbon **RC**	1.50	.75	.45
359	Phil Roof	1.50	.75	.45
360	Curt Flood	2.00	1.00	.60
361	Ray Jarvis	1.50	.75	.45
362	Joe Hague	1.50	.75	.45
363	Tom Shopay	1.50	.75	.45
364	Dan McGinn	1.50	.75	.45
365	Zoilo Versalles	1.50	.75	.45
366	Barry Moore	1.50	.75	.45
367	Mike Lum	1.50	.75	.45
368	Ed Herrmann	1.50	.75	.45
369	Alan Foster	1.50	.75	.45
370	Tommy Harper	1.50	.75	.45
371	Rod Gaspar	1.50	.75	.45
372	Dave Giusti	1.50	.75	.45
373	Roy White	2.50	1.25	.75
374	Tommie Sisk	1.50	.75	.45
375	Johnny Callison	1.50	.75	.45
376	Lefty Phillips	1.50	.75	.45
377	Bill Butler	1.50	.75	.45
378	Jim Davenport	1.50	.75	.45
379	Tom Tischinski	1.50	.75	.45
380	Tony Perez	10.00	4.00	2.50
381	Athletics Rookies (Bobby Brooks, Mike Olivo)	1.50	.75	.45
382	Jack DiLauro	1.50	.75	.45
383	Mickey Stanley	1.50	.75	.45
384	Gary Neibauer	1.50	.75	.45
385	George Scott	1.50	.75	.45
386	Bill Dillman	1.50	.75	.45
387	Baltimore Orioles Team	3.00	1.50	.90
388	Byron Browne	1.50	.75	.45
389	Jim Shellenback	1.50	.75	.45
390	Willie Davis	1.50	.75	.45
391	Larry Brown	1.50	.75	.45
392	Walt Hriniak	1.50	.75	.45
393	John Gelnar	1.50	.75	.45
394	Gil Hodges	6.00	3.00	1.75
395	Walt Williams	1.50	.75	.45
396	Steve Blass	1.50	.75	.45

397	Roger Repoz	1.50	.75	.45
398	Bill Stoneman	1.50	.75	.45
399	New York Yankees Team	8.00	4.00	2.50
400	Denny McLain	1.50	.70	.45
401	Giants Rookies (John Harrell, Bernie Williams)	1.50	.75	.45
402	Ellie Rodriguez	1.50	.75	.45
403	Jim Bunning	6.00	3.00	1.75
404	Rich Reese	1.50	.75	.45
405	Bill Hands	1.50	.75	.45
406	Mike Andrews	1.50	.75	.45
407	Bob Watson	1.50	.75	.45
408	Paul Lindblad	1.50	.75	.45
409	Bob Tolan	1.50	.75	.45
410	Boog Powell	5.00	2.50	1.50
411	Los Angeles Dodgers Team	6.00	3.00	1.75
412	Larry Burchart	1.50	.75	.45
413	Sonny Jackson	1.50	.75	.45
414	Paul Edmondson	1.50	.75	.45
415	Julian Javier	1.50	.75	.45
416	Joe Verbanic	1.50	.75	.45
417	John Bateman	1.50	.75	.45
418	John Donaldson	1.50	.75	.45
419	Ron Taylor	1.50	.75	.45
420	Ken McMullen	1.50	.75	.45
421	Pat Dobson	1.50	.75	.45
422	Kansas City Royals Team	3.00	1.50	.90
423	Jerry May	1.50	.75	.45
424	Mike Kilkenny	1.50	.75	.45
425	Bobby Bonds	3.00	1.50	.90
426	Bill Rigney	1.50	.75	.45
427	Fred Norman	1.50	.75	.45
428	Don Buford	1.50	.75	.45
429	Cubs Rookies (Randy Bobb, Jim Cosman)	1.50	.75	.45
430	A. Messersmith	1.50	.75	.45
431	Ron Swoboda	1.50	.75	.45
432a	5th Series Check List (460-546) ("Baseball" on front in yellow.)	4.00	2.00	1.25
432b	5th Series Check List (460-546) ("Baseball" on front in white.)	4.00	2.00	1.25
433	Ron Bryant	1.50	.75	.45
434	Felipe Alou	2.50	1.25	.75
435	Nelson Briles	1.50	.75	.45
436	Philadelphia Phillies Team	3.00	1.50	.90
437	Danny Cater	1.50	.75	.45
438	Pat Jarvis	1.50	.75	.45
439	Lee Maye	1.50	.75	.45
440	Bill Mazeroski	8.00	4.00	2.50
441	John O'Donoghue	1.50	.75	.45
442	Gene Mauch	1.50	.75	.45
443	Al Jackson	1.50	.75	.45
444	White Sox Rookies (Bill Farmer, John Matias)	1.50	.75	.45
445	Vada Pinson	2.00	1.00	.60
446	Billy Grabarkewitz **RC**	1.50	.75	.45
447	Lee Stange	1.50	.75	.45
448	Houston Astros Team	3.00	1.50	.90
449	Jim Palmer	8.00	4.00	2.50
450	Willie McCovey (All-Star)	7.00	3.00	1.75
451	Boog Powell (All-Star)	2.00	1.00	.60
452	Felix Millan (All-Star)	1.50	.75	.45
453	Rod Carew (All-Star)	6.00	3.00	1.75
454	Ron Santo (All-Star)	3.00	1.50	.90
455	Brooks Robinson (All-Star)	8.00	3.00	1.75
456	Don Kessinger (All-Star)	1.50	.75	.45
457	Rico Petrocelli (All-Star)	1.50	.75	.45
458	Pete Rose (All-Star)	21.00	10.50	5.75
459	Reggie Jackson (All-Star)	10.00	5.00	3.00
460	Matty Alou (All-Star)	1.50	.75	.45
461	Carl Yastrzemski (All-Star)	10.00	5.00	3.00
462	Hank Aaron (All-Star)	25.00	12.50	7.50
463	Frank Robinson (All-Star)	8.00	4.00	2.50
464	Johnny Bench (All-Star)	15.00	7.50	3.75
465	Bill Freehan (All-Star)	1.50	.75	.45
466	Juan Marichal (All-Star)	6.00	3.00	1.75
467	Denny McLain (All-Star)	1.50	.70	.45
468	Jerry Koosman (All-Star)	1.50	.75	.45
469	Sam McDowell (All-Star)	1.50	.75	.45
470	Willie Stargell	10.00	5.00	3.00
471	Chris Zachary	1.50	.75	.45
472	Atlanta Braves Team	3.00	1.50	.90
473	Don Bryant	1.50	.75	.45
474	Dick Kelley	1.50	.75	.45
475	Dick McAuliffe	1.50	.75	.45
476	Don Shaw	1.50	.75	.45
477	Orioles Rookies (Roger Freed, Al Severinsen)	1.50	.75	.45
478	Bob Heise	1.50	.75	.45
479	Dick Woodson	1.50	.75	.45
480	Glenn Beckert	1.50	.75	.45
481	Jose Tartabull	1.50	.75	.45

482	Tom Hilgendorf	1.50	.75	.45
483	Gail Hopkins	1.50	.75	.45
484	Gary Nolan	1.50	.75	.45
485	Jay Johnstone	1.50	.75	.45
486	Terry Harmon	1.50	.75	.45
487	Cisco Carlos	1.50	.75	.45
488	J.C. Martin	1.50	.75	.45
489	Eddie Kasko	1.50	.75	.45
490	Bill Singer	1.50	.75	.45
491	Graig Nettles	3.00	2.00	.90
492	Astros Rookies (Keith Lampard, Scipio Spinks)	1.50	.75	.45
493	Lindy McDaniel	1.50	.75	.45
494	Larry Stahl	1.50	.75	.45
495	Dave Morehead	1.50	.75	.45
496	Steve Whitaker	1.50	.75	.45
497	Eddie Watt	1.50	.75	.45
498	Al Weis	1.50	.75	.45
499	Skip Lockwood	1.50	.75	.45
500	Hank Aaron	45.00	25.00	12.50
501	Chicago White Sox Team	3.00	1.50	.90
502	Rollie Fingers	11.00	4.00	2.50
503	Dal Maxvill	1.50	.75	.45
504	Don Pavletich	1.50	.75	.45
505	Ken Holtzman	1.50	.75	.45
506	Ed Stroud	1.50	.75	.45
507	Pat Corrales	1.50	.75	.45
508	Joe Niekro	1.50	.75	.45
509	Montreal Expos Team	3.00	1.50	.90
510	Tony Oliva	3.50	1.75	1.00
511	Joe Hoerner	1.50	.75	.45
512	Billy Harris	1.50	.75	.45
513	Preston Gomez	1.50	.75	.45
514	Steve Hovley	1.50	.75	.45
515	Don Wilson	1.50	.75	.45
516	Yankees Rookies (John Ellis, Jim Lyttle)	1.50	.75	.45
517	Joe Gibbon	1.50	.75	.45
518	Bill Melton	1.50	.75	.45
519	Don McMahon	1.50	.75	.45
520	Willie Horton	1.50	.75	.45
521	Cal Koonce	1.50	.75	.45
522	California Angels Team	3.00	1.50	.90
523	Jose Pena	1.50	.75	.45
524	Alvin Dark	1.50	.75	.45
525	Jerry Adair	1.50	.75	.45
526	Ron Herbel	1.50	.75	.45
527	Don Bosch	1.50	.75	.45
528	Elrod Hendricks	1.50	.75	.45
529	Bob Aspromonte	1.50	.75	.45
530	Bob Gibson	15.00	7.50	3.75
531	Ron Clark	1.50	.75	.45
532	Danny Murtaugh	1.50	.75	.45
533	Buzz Stephen	1.50	.75	.45
534	Minnesota Twins Team	3.00	1.50	.90
535	Andy Kosco	1.50	.75	.45
536	Mike Kekich	1.50	.75	.45
537	Joe Morgan	10.00	5.00	3.00
538	Bob Humphreys	1.50	.75	.45
539	Phillies Rookies (Larry Bowa **RC**, Dennis Doyle)	9.00	3.00	1.75
540	Gary Peters	1.50	.75	.45
541	Bill Heath	1.50	.75	.45
542a	6th Series Check List (547-633) (Gray bat on front.)	5.00	2.50	1.50
542b	6th Series Check List (547-633) (Brown bat on front.)	5.00	2.50	1.50
543	Clyde Wright	1.50	.75	.45
544	Cincinnati Reds Team	5.00	2.50	1.50
545	Ken Harrelson	1.50	.75	.45
546	Ron Reed	1.50	.75	.45
547	Rick Monday	4.00	2.00	1.25
548	Howie Reed	3.00	1.50	.90
549	St. Louis Cardinals Team	6.00	3.00	1.75
550	Frank Howard	5.00	2.50	1.50
551	Dock Ellis	4.00	2.00	1.25
552	Royals Rookies (Don O'Riley, Dennis Paepke, Fred Rico)	4.00	2.00	1.25
553	Jim Lefebvre	4.00	2.00	1.25
554	Tom Timmermann	4.00	2.00	1.25
555	Orlando Cepeda	15.00	7.50	3.75
556	Dave Bristol	4.00	2.00	1.25
557	Ed Kranepool	4.00	2.00	1.25
558	Vern Fuller	4.00	2.00	1.25
559	Tommy Davis	4.00	2.00	1.25
560	Gaylord Perry	8.00	4.00	2.50
561	Tom McCraw	4.00	2.00	1.25
562	Ted Abernathy	4.00	2.00	1.25
563	Boston Red Sox Team	8.00	4.00	2.50
564	Johnny Briggs	4.00	2.00	1.25
565	Jim Hunter	8.00	4.00	2.50
566	Gene Alley	4.00	2.00	1.25
567	Bob Oliver	4.00	2.00	1.25

568	Stan Bahnsen	4.00	2.00	1.25
569	Cookie Rojas	4.00	2.00	1.25
570	Jim Fregosi	5.00	2.50	1.50
571	Jim Brewer	4.00	2.00	1.25
572	Frank Quilici	4.00	2.00	1.25
573	Padres Rookies (Mike Corkins, Rafael Robles, Ron Slocum)	4.00	2.00	1.25
574	Bobby Bolin	4.00	2.00	1.25
575	Cleon Jones	4.00	2.00	1.25
576	Milt Pappas	4.00	2.00	1.25
577	Bernie Allen	4.00	2.00	1.25
578	Tom Griffin	4.00	2.00	1.25
579	Detroit Tigers Team	8.00	4.00	2.50
580	Pete Rose	50.00	25.00	15.00
581	Tom Satriano	4.00	2.00	1.25
582	Mike Paul	4.00	2.00	1.25
583	Hal Lanier	4.00	2.00	1.25
584	Al Downing	5.00	2.50	1.50
585	Rusty Staub	6.00	3.00	1.75
586	Rickey Clark	4.00	2.00	1.25
587	Jose Arcia	4.00	2.00	1.25
588a	7th Series Check List (634-720) (666 is Adolpho Phillips)	6.00	3.00	1.75
588b	7th Series Check List (634-720) (666 is Adolfo Phillips)	6.00	3.00	1.75
589	Joe Keough	4.00	2.00	1.25
590	Mike Cuellar	4.00	2.00	1.25
591	Mike Ryan	4.00	2.00	1.25
592	Daryl Patterson	4.00	2.00	1.25
593	Chicago Cubs Team	8.00	4.00	2.50
594	Jake Gibbs	4.00	2.00	1.25
595	Maury Wills	4.00	2.00	1.25
596	Mike Hershberger	4.00	2.00	1.25
597	Sonny Siebert	4.00	2.00	1.25
598	Joe Pepitone	5.00	2.50	1.50
599	Senators Rookies (Gene Martin, Dick Stelmaszek, Dick Such)	4.00	2.00	1.25
600	Willie Mays	70.00	40.00	20.00
601	Pete Richert	4.00	2.00	1.25
602	Ted Savage	4.00	2.00	1.25
603	Ray Oyler	4.00	2.00	1.25
604	Clarence Gaston	6.00	3.00	1.75
605	Rick Wise	4.00	2.00	1.25
606	Chico Ruiz	4.00	2.00	1.25
607	Gary Waslewski	4.00	2.00	1.25
608	Pittsburgh Pirates Team	8.00	4.00	2.50
609	Buck Martinez RC	6.00	3.00	1.75
610	Jerry Koosman	6.00	3.00	1.75
611	Norm Cash	6.00	3.00	1.75
612	Jim Hickman	4.00	2.00	1.25
613	Dave Baldwin	4.00	2.00	1.25
614	Mike Shannon	4.00	2.00	1.25
615	Mark Belanger	4.00	2.00	1.25
616	Jim Merritt	4.00	2.00	1.25
617	Jim French	4.00	2.00	1.25
618	Billy Wynne	4.00	2.00	1.25
619	Norm Miller	4.00	2.00	1.25
620	Jim Perry	4.00	2.00	1.25
621	Braves Rookies (Darrell Evans RC, Rick Kester, Mike McQueen)	10.00	5.00	3.00
622	Don Sutton	8.00	4.00	2.50
623	Horace Clarke	4.00	2.00	1.25
624	Clyde King	4.00	2.00	1.25
625	Dean Chance	4.00	2.00	1.25
626	Dave Ricketts	4.00	2.00	1.25
627	Gary Wagner	4.00	2.00	1.25
628	Wayne Garrett	4.00	2.00	1.25
629	Merv Rettenmund	4.00	2.00	1.25
630	Ernie Banks	45.00	25.00	12.50
631	Oakland Athletics Team	8.00	4.00	2.50
632	Gary Sutherland	4.00	2.00	1.25
633	Roger Nelson	4.00	2.00	1.25
634	Bud Harrelson	8.00	4.00	2.50
635	Bob Allison	8.00	4.00	2.50
636	Jim Stewart	8.00	4.00	2.50
637	Cleveland Indians Team	12.00	6.00	3.50
638	Frank Bertaina	8.00	4.00	2.50
639	Dave Campbell	8.00	4.00	2.50
640	Al Kaline	50.00	25.00	12.50
641	Al McBean	8.00	4.00	2.50
642	Angels Rookies (Greg Garrett, Gordon Lund, Jarvis Tatum)	8.00	4.00	2.50
643	Jose Pagan	8.00	4.00	2.50
644	Gerry Nyman	8.00	4.00	2.50
645	Don Money	8.00	4.00	2.50
646	Jim Britton	8.00	4.00	2.50
647	Tom Matchick	8.00	4.00	2.50
648	Larry Haney	8.00	4.00	2.50
649	Jimmie Hall	8.00	4.00	2.50
650	Sam McDowell	10.00	5.00	3.00
651	Jim Gosger	8.00	4.00	2.50
652	Rich Rollins	10.00	5.00	3.00

653	Moe Drabowsky	8.00	4.00	2.50
654	N.L. Rookies (Boots Day, Oscar Gamble RC, Angel Mangual)	10.00	5.00	3.00
655	John Roseboro	8.00	4.00	2.50
656	Jim Hardin	8.00	4.00	2.50
657	San Diego Padres Team	15.00	7.50	4.50
658	Ken Tatum	8.00	4.00	2.50
659	Pete Ward	8.00	4.00	2.50
660	Johnny Bench	60.00	30.00	18.00
661	Jerry Robertson	8.00	4.00	2.50
662	Frank Lucchesi	8.00	4.00	2.50
663	Tito Francona	8.00	4.00	2.50
664	Bob Robertson	8.00	4.00	2.50
665	Jim Lonborg	8.00	4.00	2.50
666	Adolfo Phillips	8.00	4.00	2.50
667	Bob Meyer	8.00	4.00	2.50
668	Bob Tillman	8.00	4.00	2.50
669	White Sox Rookies (Bart Johnson, Dan Lazar, Mickey Scott)	8.00	4.00	2.50
670	Ron Santo	20.00	10.00	5.00
671	Jim Campanis	10.00	5.00	3.00
672	Leon McFadden	8.00	4.00	2.50
673	Ted Uhlaender	8.00	4.00	2.50
674	Dave Leonhard	8.00	4.00	2.50
675	Jose Cardenal	10.00	5.00	3.00
676	Washington Senators Team	15.00	7.50	4.50
677	Woodie Fryman	8.00	4.00	2.50
678	Dave Duncan	15.00	7.50	4.50
679	Ray Sadecki	8.00	4.00	2.50
680	Rico Petrocelli	10.00	5.00	3.00
681	Bob Garibaldi	8.00	4.00	2.50
682	Dalton Jones	8.00	4.00	2.50
683	Reds Rookies (Vern Geishert, Hal McRae, Wayne Simpson)	10.00	5.00	3.00
684	Jack Fisher	8.00	4.00	2.50
685	Tom Haller	8.00	4.00	2.50
686	Jackie Hernandez	8.00	4.00	2.50
687	Bob Priddy	8.00	4.00	2.50
688	Ted Kubiak	8.00	4.00	2.50
689	Frank Tepedino	8.00	4.00	2.50
690	Ron Fairly	8.00	4.00	2.50
691	Joe Grzenda	8.00	4.00	2.50
692	Duffy Dyer	8.00	4.00	2.50
693	Bob Johnson	8.00	4.00	2.50
694	Gary Ross	8.00	4.00	2.50
695	Bobby Knoop	8.00	4.00	2.50
696	San Francisco Giants Team	12.00	6.00	3.00
697	Jim Hannan	8.00	4.00	2.50
698	Tom Tresh	10.00	5.00	3.00
699	Hank Aguirre	8.00	4.00	2.50
700	Frank Robinson	50.00	25.00	12.50
701	Jack Billingham	8.00	4.00	2.50
702	A.L. Rookies (Bob Johnson, Ron Klimkowski, Bill Zepp)	8.00	4.00	2.50
703	Lou Marone	8.00	4.00	2.50
704	Frank Baker	8.00	4.00	2.50
705	Tony Cloninger	8.00	4.00	2.50
706	John McNamara	8.00	4.00	2.50
707	Kevin Collins	8.00	4.00	2.50
708	Jose Santiago	8.00	4.00	2.50
709	Mike Fiore	8.00	4.00	2.50
710	Felix Millan	8.00	4.00	2.50
711	Ed Brinkman	8.00	4.00	2.50
712	Nolan Ryan	165.00	80.00	48.00
713	Seattle Pilots Team	20.00	10.00	6.00
714	Al Spangler	8.00	4.00	2.50
715	Mickey Lolich	8.00	4.00	2.50
716	Cards Rookies (Sal Campisi, Reggie Cleveland RC, Santiago Guzman)	10.00	5.00	3.00
717	Tom Phoebus	8.00	4.00	2.50
718	Ed Spiezio	8.00	4.00	2.50
719	Jim Roland	8.00	4.00	2.50
720	Rick Reichardt	12.00	5.00	2.50

1970 Topps Candy Lids

The 1970 Topps Candy Lids are a test issue that was utilized again in 1973. The set is made up of 24 lids that measure 1-7/8" in diameter and were the tops of small 1.1 oz. tubs of "Baseball Stars Candy." Unlike the 1973 versions, the 1970 lids have no border surrounding the full-color photos. Frank Howard, Tom Seaver and Carl Yastrzemski photos are found on the top (outside) of the candy lid.

		NM	E	VG
Complete Set (24):		2,800	1,400	840.00
Common Player:		40.00	20.00	12.00
(1)	Hank Aaron	350.00	175.00	105.00
(2)	Rich Allen	75.00	37.00	22.00
(3)	Luis Aparicio	140.00	70.00	42.00
(4)	Johnny Bench	225.00	110.00	67.00
(5)	Ollie Brown	40.00	20.00	12.00
(6)	Willie Davis	40.00	20.00	12.00
(7)	Jim Fregosi	40.00	20.00	12.00
(8)	Mike Hegan	40.00	20.00	12.00
(9)	Frank Howard	60.00	30.00	18.00
(10)	Reggie Jackson	275.00	135.00	82.00
(11)	Fergie Jenkins	130.00	65.00	39.00
(12)	Harmon Killebrew	175.00	87.00	52.00
(13)	Juan Marichal	140.00	70.00	42.00
(14)	Bill Mazeroski	140.00	70.00	42.00
(15)	Tim McCarver	60.00	30.00	18.00
(16)	Sam McDowell	40.00	20.00	12.00
(17)	Denny McLain	60.00	30.00	18.00
(18)	Lou Piniella	45.00	22.00	13.50
(19)	Frank Robinson	175.00	87.00	52.00
(20)	Tom Seaver	200.00	100.00	60.00
(21)	Rusty Staub	60.00	30.00	18.00
(22)	Mel Stottlemyre	40.00	20.00	12.00
(23)	Jim Wynn	40.00	20.00	12.00
(24)	Carl Yastrzemski	225.00	110.00	67.00

1970 Topps Cloth Stickers

The earliest and rarest of the Topps cloth sticker test issues, only 15 subjects are known, and only a single specimen apiece is known for many of them. In the same 2-1/2" x 3-1/2" size, and with the same design as the 1970 Topps baseball cards, the stickers are blank-backed. The stickers of Denny Lemaster, Dennis Higgins and Rich Nye use photos that are different from their '70 Topps cards. It is quite likely that the checklist presented here is incomplete. The stickers are unnumbered and are checklisted alphabetically.

		NM	E	VG
Common Player:		1,750	875.00	525.00
(1)	A.L. Playoff Game 2 (Boog Powell)	1,900	950.00	570.00
(2)	Bill Burbach	1,750	875.00	525.00
(3)	Gary Gentry	1,750	875.00	525.00
(4)	Tom Hall	1,750	875.00	525.00
(5)	Chuck Hartenstein	1,750	875.00	525.00
(6)	Dennis Higgins	1,750	875.00	525.00
(7)	Jose Laboy	1,750	875.00	525.00
(8)	Denny Lemaster	1,750	875.00	525.00
(9)	Juan Marichal	2,200	1,100	660.00
(10)	Willie McCovey	1,750	875.00	525.00
(11)	Jerry McNertney	1,750	875.00	525.00
(12)	Curt Motton	1,750	875.00	525.00
(13)	Ivan Murrell	1,750	875.00	525.00
(14)	N.L. Playoff Game 1 (Tom Seaver)	1,750	875.00	525.00
(15)	N.L. Playoff Game 3 (Nolan Ryan)	3,000	1,500	900.00
(16)	Phil Niekro	2,100	1,050	630.00
(17)	Jim Northrup	1,750	875.00	525.00
(18)	Rich Nye	1,750	875.00	525.00
(19)	Ron Perranoski	1,750	875.00	525.00
(20)	Al Santorini	1,750	875.00	525.00

1970 Topps Posters

Helping to ease a price increase, Topps included extremely fragile 8-11/16" x 9-5/8" posters in packs of regular cards. The posters feature color portraits and a smaller black and white "action" pose as well as the player's name, team and position at the top. Although there are Hall of Famers in the 24-poster set, all the top names are not represented. Folds from original packaging are not considered in grading unless they split the paper.

		NM	E	VG
Complete Set (24):		60.00	30.00	18.00
Common Player:		3.00	1.50	.90
1	Joe Horlen	3.00	1.50	.90
2	Phil Niekro	6.00	3.00	1.75
3	Willie Davis	3.00	1.50	.90
4	Lou Brock	7.00	3.50	2.00
5	Ron Santo	4.00	2.00	1.25
6	Ken Harrelson	3.00	1.50	.90
7	Willie McCovey	7.00	3.50	2.00
8	Rick Wise	3.00	1.50	.90
9	Andy Messersmith	3.00	1.50	.90
10	Ron Fairly	3.00	1.50	.90
11	Johnny Bench	10.00	5.00	3.00
12	Frank Robinson	10.00	5.00	3.00
13	Tommie Agee	3.00	1.50	.90
14	Roy White	3.00	1.50	.90
15	Larry Dierker	3.00	1.50	.90
16	Rod Carew	9.00	4.50	2.75
17	Don Mincher	3.00	1.50	.90
18	Ollie Brown	3.00	1.50	.90
19	Ed Kirkpatrick	3.00	1.50	.90
20	Reggie Smith	3.00	1.50	.90
21	Roberto Clemente	25.00	12.50	7.50
22	Frank Howard	3.00	1.50	.90
23	Bert Campaneris	3.00	1.50	.90
24	Denny McLain	3.00	1.50	.90

1970 Topps Scratch-Offs

Not having given up on the idea of a game which could be played with baseball cards, Topps provided a new game - the baseball scratch-off - in 1970. Unfolded, cards measure 3-3/8" x 5", and reveal a baseball game played by rubbing the black ink off playing squares to determine the "action." Fronts have a player picture as "captain," while backs have instructions and a scoreboard. Inserts with white centers are from 1970 while those with red centers are from 1971.

		NM	E	VG
Complete Set (24):		60.00	30.00	18.00
Common Player:		1.50	.75	.45
(1)	Hank Aaron	12.00	6.00	3.50
(2)	Rich Allen	2.50	1.25	.70
(3)	Luis Aparicio	3.50	1.75	1.00
(4)	Sal Bando	1.50	.75	.45
(5)	Glenn Beckert	1.50	.75	.45
(6)	Dick Bosman	1.50	.75	.45
(7)	Nate Colbert	1.50	.75	.45
(8)	Mike Hegan	1.50	.75	.45
(9)	Mack Jones	1.50	.75	.45
(10)	Al Kaline	4.50	2.25	1.25
(11)	Harmon Killebrew	4.50	2.25	1.25
(12)	Juan Marichal	3.50	1.75	1.00
(13)	Tim McCarver	2.50	1.25	.70
(14)	Sam McDowell	1.50	.75	.45
(15)	Claude Osteen	1.50	.75	.45
(16)	Tony Perez	3.50	1.75	1.00
(17)	Lou Piniella	1.50	.75	.45
(18)	Boog Powell	2.50	1.25	.70
(19)	Tom Seaver	4.50	2.25	1.25
(20)	Jim Spencer	1.50	.75	.45
(21)	Willie Stargell	3.50	1.75	1.00
(22)	Mel Stottlemyre	1.50	.75	.45
(23)	Jim Wynn	1.50	.75	.45
(24)	Carl Yastrzemski	6.00	3.00	1.75

1970 Topps Story Booklets

Measuring 2-1/2" x 3-7/16", the Topps Story Booklet was a 1970 regular pack insert. The booklet feature a photo, title and booklet number on the "cover." Inside are six pages of comic book story. The backs give a checklist of other available booklets. Not every star had a booklet as the set is only 24 in number.

		NM	E	VG
Complete Set (24):		65.00	32.50	20.00
Common Player:		1.50	.75	.45
1	Mike Cuellar	1.50	.75	.45
2	Rico Petrocelli	1.50	.75	.45
3	Jay Johnstone	1.50	.75	.45
4	Walt Williams	1.50	.75	.45
5	Vada Pinson	2.25	1.25	.70
6	Bill Freehan	1.50	.75	.45
7	Wally Bunker	1.50	.75	.45
8	Tony Oliva	2.25	1.25	.70
9	Bobby Murcer	2.00	1.00	.60
10	Reggie Jackson	9.00	4.50	2.75
11	Tommy Harper	1.50	.75	.45
12	Mike Epstein	1.50	.75	.45
13	Orlando Cepeda	4.00	2.00	1.25
14	Ernie Banks	7.00	3.50	2.00
15	Pete Rose	10.00	5.00	3.00
16	Denis Menke	1.50	.75	.45
17	Bill Singer	1.50	.75	.45
18	Rusty Staub	2.00	1.00	.60
19	Cleon Jones	1.50	.75	.45
20	Deron Johnson	1.50	.75	.45
21	Bob Moose	1.50	.75	.45
22	Bob Gibson	5.00	2.50	1.50
23	Al Ferrara	1.50	.75	.45
24	Willie Mays	10.00	5.00	3.00

1970 Topps Super

 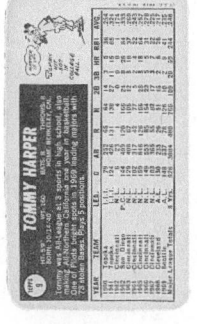

Representing a refinement of the concept begun in 1969, the 1970 Topps Supers had a new 3-1/8" x 5-1/4" size. Printed on thick stock with rounded corners, card fronts feature a borderless color photograph and facsimile autograph. Backs

are an enlarged version of the player's regular 1970 Topps card. Probably due to the press sheet configuration, eight of the 42 cards were short-printed. The most elusive is card #38 (Boog Powell). The set was more widely produced than was the case in 1969. Square-cornered proofs, either with blank or printed backs, are known, valued from 1X-2X the regular-card price.

		NM	E	VG
Complete Set (42):		250.00	125.00	75.00
Common Player:		4.00	2.00	1.25
Unopened Pack:		95.00		
Proofs: 1-2X				
1	Claude Osteen (SP)	10.00	5.00	3.00
2	Sal Bando (SP)	10.00	5.00	3.00
3	Luis Aparicio	9.00	4.50	2.75
4	Harmon Killebrew	15.00	7.50	4.50
5	Tom Seaver (SP)	25.00	12.50	7.50
6	Larry Dierker	4.00	2.00	1.25
7	Bill Freehan	4.00	2.00	1.25
8	Johnny Bench	20.00	10.00	6.00
9	Tommy Harper	4.00	2.00	1.25
10	Sam McDowell	4.00	2.00	1.25
11	Lou Brock	12.00	6.00	3.50
12	Roberto Clemente	40.00	20.00	12.00
13	Willie McCovey	12.00	6.00	3.50
14	Rico Petrocelli	4.00	2.00	1.25
15	Phil Niekro	9.00	4.50	2.75
16	Frank Howard	4.00	2.00	1.25
17	Denny McLain	4.00	2.00	1.25
18	Willie Mays	35.00	17.50	10.00
19	Willie Stargell	12.00	6.00	3.50
20	Joe Horlen	4.00	2.00	1.25
21	Ron Santo	6.00	3.00	1.75
22	Dick Bosman	4.00	2.00	1.25
23	Tim McCarver	5.00	2.50	1.50
24	Henry Aaron	35.00	17.50	10.00
25	Andy Messersmith	4.00	2.00	1.25
26	Tony Oliva	5.00	2.50	1.50
27	Mel Stottlemyre	4.00	2.00	1.25
28	Reggie Jackson	30.00	15.00	9.00
29	Carl Yastrzemski	20.00	10.00	6.00
30	James Fregosi	4.00	2.00	1.25
31	Vada Pinson	5.00	2.50	1.50
32	Lou Piniella	4.00	2.00	1.25
33	Robert Gibson	10.00	5.00	3.00
34	Pete Rose	35.00	17.50	10.00
35	Jim Wynn	4.00	2.00	1.25
36	Ollie Brown (SP)	10.00	5.00	3.00
37	Frank Robinson (SP)	35.00	17.50	10.00
38	Boog Powell (SP)	60.00	30.00	18.00
39	Willie Davis (SP)	10.00	5.00	3.00
40	Billy Williams (SP)	20.00	10.00	6.00
41	Rusty Staub	5.00	2.50	1.50
42	Tommie Agee	4.00	2.00	1.25

1971 Topps

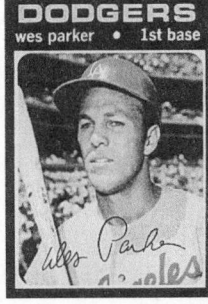 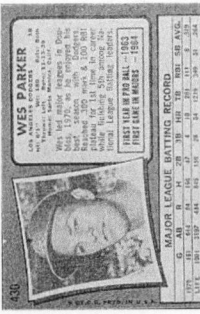

In 1971, Topps again increased the size of its set to 752 cards. These 2-1/2" x 3-1/2" cards feature a large color photo with a thin white frame. Above the picture, in the card's overall black border, is the player's name, team and position. A facsimile autograph completes the front. Backs feature a major change as a black-and-white "snapshot" of the player appears. Abbreviated statistics, a line giving the player's first pro and major league games and a short biography complete the back. Specialty cards in this issue are limited. There are statistical leaders as well as World Series and playoff highlights. High-number cards #644-752 are scarce, with about half of the cards being short-printed.

		NM	E	VG
Complete Set (752):		2,500	1,250	750.00
Common Player (1-523):		2.00	1.00	.60
Common Player (524-643):		4.00	2.00	1.00
Common Player (644-752):		6.00	3.00	1.75
1	World Champions (Orioles Team)	15.00	7.50	3.75
2	Dock Ellis	2.00	1.00	.60
3	Dick McAuliffe	2.00	1.00	.60

#	Player	Price 1	Price 2	Price 3
4	Vic Davalillo	2.00	1.00	.60
5	Thurman Munson	190.00	95.00	58.00
6	Ed Spiezio	2.00	1.00	.60
7	Jim Holt	2.00	1.00	.60
8	Mike McQueen	2.00	1.00	.60
9	George Scott	2.00	1.00	.60
10	Claude Osteen	2.00	1.00	.60
11	Elliott Maddox RC	2.00	1.00	.60
12	Johnny Callison	2.00	1.00	.60
13	White Sox Rookies (Charlie Brinkman, Dick Moloney)	2.00	1.00	.60
14	Dave Concepcion RC	15.00	7.50	4.50
15	Andy Messersmith	2.00	1.00	.60
16	Ken Singleton RC	4.00	2.00	1.25
17	Billy Sorrell	2.00	1.00	.60
18	Norm Miller	2.00	1.00	.60
19	Skip Pitlock	2.00	1.00	.60
20	Reggie Jackson	60.00	30.00	18.00
21	Dan McGinn	2.00	1.00	.60
22	Phil Roof	2.00	1.00	.60
23	Oscar Gamble	2.00	1.00	.60
24	Rich Hand	2.00	1.00	.60
25	Clarence Gaston	2.00	1.00	.60
26	Bert Blyleven RC	60.00	30.00	18.00
27	Pirates Rookies (Fred Cambria, Gene Clines)	2.00	1.00	.60
28	Ron Klimkowski	2.00	1.00	.60
29	Don Buford	2.00	1.00	.60
30	Phil Niekro	8.00	4.00	2.50
31	Eddie Kasko	2.00	1.00	.60
32	Jerry DaVanon	2.00	1.00	.60
33	Del Unser	2.00	1.00	.60
34	Sandy Vance	2.00	1.00	.60
35	Lou Piniella	4.00	2.00	1.25
36	Dean Chance	2.00	1.00	.60
37	Rich McKinney	2.00	1.00	.60
38	Jim Colborn RC	2.00	1.00	.60
39	Tigers Rookies (Gene Lamont, Lerrin LaGrow RC)	2.00	1.00	.60
40	Lee May	2.00	1.00	.60
41	Rick Austin	2.00	1.00	.60
42a	Boots Day (Stadium lights behind ear.)	8.00	4.00	2.50
42b	Boots Day (No stadium lights.)	8.00	4.00	2.50
43	Steve Kealey	2.00	1.00	.60
44	Johnny Edwards	2.00	1.00	.60
45	Jim Hunter	8.00	4.00	2.50
46	Dave Campbell	2.00	1.00	.60
47	Johnny Jeter	2.00	1.00	.60
48	Dave Baldwin	2.00	1.00	.60
49	Don Money	2.00	1.00	.60
50	Willie McCovey	10.00	5.00	3.00
51	Steve Kline	2.00	1.00	.60
52	Braves Rookies (Oscar Brown, Earl Williams RC)	2.00	1.00	.60
53	Paul Blair	2.00	1.00	.60
54	1st Series Checklist (1-132)	5.00	2.50	1.50
55	Steve Carlton	20.00	10.00	6.00
56	Duane Josephson	2.00	1.00	.60
57	Von Joshua	2.00	1.00	.60
58	Bill Lee	2.00	1.00	.60
59	Gene Mauch	2.00	1.00	.60
60	Dick Bosman	2.00	1.00	.60
61	A.L. Batting Leaders (Alex Johnson, Tony Oliva, Carl Yastrzemski)	8.00	4.00	2.50
62	N.L. Batting Leaders (Rico Carty, Manny Sanguillen, Joe Torre)	6.00	3.00	1.75
63	A.L. RBI Leaders (Tony Conigliaro, Frank Howard, Boog Powell)	6.00	3.00	1.75
64	N.L. RBI Leaders (Johnny Bench, Tony Perez, Billy Williams)	8.00	4.00	2.50
65	A.L. Home Run Leaders (Frank Howard, Harmon Killebrew, Carl Yastrzemski)	8.00	4.00	2.50
66	N.L. Home Run Leaders (Johnny Bench, Tony Perez, Billy Williams)	11.00	5.00	3.00
67	A.L. ERA Leaders (Jim Palmer, Diego Segui, Clyde Wright)	6.00	3.00	1.75
68	N.L. ERA Leaders (Tom Seaver, Wayne Simpson, Luke Walker)	6.00	3.00	1.75
69	A.L. Pitching Leaders (Mike Cuellar, Dave McNally, Jim Perry)	3.00	1.50	.90
70	N.L. Pitching Leaders (Bob Gibson, Fergie Jenkins, Gaylord Perry)	8.00	4.00	2.50
71	A.L. Strikeout Leaders (Bob Johnson, Mickey Lolich, Sam McDowell)	3.00	1.50	.90
72	N.L. Strikeout Leaders (Bob Gibson, Fergie Jenkins, Tom Seaver)	11.00	5.00	3.00
73	George Brunet	2.00	1.00	.60
74	Twins Rookies (Pete Hamm, Jim Nettles)	2.00	1.00	.60
75	Gary Nolan	2.00	1.00	.60
76	Ted Savage	2.00	1.00	.60
77	Mike Compton	2.00	1.00	.60
78	Jim Spencer	2.00	1.00	.60
79	Wade Blasingame	2.00	1.00	.60
80	Bill Melton	2.00	1.00	.60
81	Felix Millan	2.00	1.00	.60
82	Casey Cox	2.00	1.00	.60
83	Mets Rookies (Randy Bobb, Tim Foli RC)	2.00	1.00	.60
84	Marcel Lachemann	2.00	1.00	.60
85a	Billy Grabarkewitz (red sun)			
85b	Billy Grabarkewitz (white sun)	2.00	1.00	.60
86	Mike Kilkenny	2.00	1.00	.60
87	Jack Heidemann	2.00	1.00	.60
88	Hal King	2.00	1.00	.60
89	Ken Brett	2.00	1.00	.60
90	Joe Pepitone	2.00	1.00	.60
91	Bob Lemon	4.00	2.00	1.25
92	Fred Wenz	2.00	1.00	.60
93	Senators Rookies (Norm McRae, Denny Riddleberger)			
94	Don Hahn	2.00	1.00	.60
95	Luis Tiant	2.00	1.00	.60
96	Joe Hague	2.00	1.00	.60
97	Floyd Wicker	2.00	1.00	.60
98	Joe Decker	2.00	1.00	.60
99	Mark Belanger	2.00	1.00	.60
100	Pete Rose	80.00	40.00	20.00
101	Les Cain	2.00	1.00	.60
102	Astros Rookies (Ken Forsch RC, Larry Howard)	2.00	1.00	.60
103	Rich Severson	2.00	1.00	.60
104	Dan Frisella	2.00	1.00	.60
105	Tony Conigliaro	6.00	3.00	1.75
106	Tom Dukes	2.00	1.00	.60
107	Roy Foster	2.00	1.00	.60
108	John Cumberland	2.00	1.00	.60
109	Steve Hovley	2.00	1.00	.60
110	Bill Mazeroski	13.50	6.00	4.00
111	Yankees Rookies (Loyd Colson, Bobby Mitchell)	2.00	1.00	.60
112	Manny Mota	2.00	1.00	.60
113	Jerry Crider	2.00	1.00	.60
114	Billy Conigliaro	2.00	1.00	.60
115	Donn Clendenon	2.00	1.00	.60
116	Ken Sanders	2.00	1.00	.60
117	Ted Simmons RC	12.50	6.25	3.00
118	Cookie Rojas	2.00	1.00	.60
119	Frank Lucchesi	2.00	1.00	.60
120	Willie Horton	2.00	1.00	.60
121	Cubs Rookies (Jim Dunegan, Roe Skidmore)	2.00	1.00	.60
122	Eddie Watt	2.00	1.00	.60
123a	2nd Series Checklist (133-263) (Card # on right, orange helmet.)	5.00	2.50	1.50
123b	2nd Series Checklist (133-263) (Card # on right, red helmet.)	5.00	2.50	1.50
123c	2nd Series Checklist (133-263) (Card # centered.)	5.00	2.50	1.50
124	Don Gullett RC	2.00	1.00	.60
125	Ray Fosse	2.00	1.00	.60
126	Danny Coombs	2.00	1.00	.60
127	Danny Thompson RC	2.00	1.00	.60
128	Frank Johnson	2.00	1.00	.60
129	Aurelio Monteagudo	2.00	1.00	.60
130	Denis Menke	2.00	1.00	.60
131	Curt Blefary	2.00	1.00	.60
132	Jose Laboy	2.00	1.00	.60
133	Mickey Lolich	2.00	1.00	.60
134	Jose Arcia	2.00	1.00	.60
135	Rick Monday	2.00	1.00	.60
136	Duffy Dyer	2.00	1.00	.60
137	Marcelino Lopez	2.00	1.00	.60
138	Phillies Rookies (Joe Lis, Willie Montanez RC)	2.00	1.00	.60
139	Paul Casanova	2.00	1.00	.60
140	Gaylord Perry	8.00	4.00	2.50
141	Frank Quilici	2.00	1.00	.60
142	Mack Jones	2.00	1.00	.60
143	Steve Blass	2.00	1.00	.60
144a	Jackie Hernandez ('Pirates' in yellow)	2.00	1.00	.60
144b	Jackie Hernandez ('Pirates' in red)	2.00	1.00	.60
145	Bill Singer	2.00	1.00	.60
146	Ralph Houk	2.00	1.00	.60
147	Bob Priddy	2.00	1.00	.60
148	John Mayberry	2.00	1.00	.60
149	Mike Hershberger	2.00	1.00	.60
150	Sam McDowell	2.00	1.00	.60
151	Tommy Davis	2.00	1.00	.60
152	Angels Rookies (Lloyd Allen, Winston Llenas)	2.00	1.00	.60
153	Gary Ross	2.00	1.00	.60
154	Cesar Gutierrez	2.00	1.00	.60
155	Ken Henderson	2.00	1.00	.60
156	Bart Johnson	2.00	1.00	.60
157	Bob Bailey	2.00	1.00	.60
158	Jerry Reuss	2.00	1.00	.60
159	Jarvis Tatum	2.00	1.00	.60
160	Tom Seaver	25.00	12.50	7.50
161	Coins Checklist	4.00	2.00	1.25
162	Jack Billingham	2.00	1.00	.60
163	Buck Martinez	2.00	1.00	.60
164	Reds Rookies (Frank Duffy, Milt Wilcox RC)	2.00	1.00	.60
165	Cesar Tovar	2.00	1.00	.60
166	Joe Hoerner	2.00	1.00	.60
167	Tom Grieve	2.00	1.00	.60
168	Bruce Dal Canton	2.00	1.00	.60
169	Ed Herrmann	2.00	1.00	.60
170	Mike Cuellar	2.00	1.00	.60
171	Bobby Wine	2.00	1.00	.60
172	Duke Sims	2.00	1.00	.60
173	Gil Garrido	2.00	1.00	.60
174	Dave LaRoche RC	2.00	1.00	.60
175	Jim Hickman	2.00	1.00	.60
176	Red Sox Rookies (Doug Griffin, Bob Montgomery)	2.00	1.00	.60
177	Hal McRae	2.00	1.00	.60
178	Dave Duncan	2.00	1.00	.60
179	Mike Corkins	2.00	1.00	.60
180	Al Kaline	20.00	10.00	6.00
181	Hal Lanier	2.00	1.00	.60
182	Al Downing	2.00	1.00	.60
183	Gil Hodges	5.00	2.50	1.25
184	Stan Bahnsen	2.00	1.00	.60
185	Julian Javier	2.00	1.00	.60
186	Bob Spence	2.00	1.00	.60
187	Ted Abernathy	2.00	1.00	.60
188	Dodgers Rookies (Mike Strahler, Bob Valentine RC)	4.00	2.00	1.25
189	George Mitterwald	2.00	1.00	.60
190	Bob Tolan	2.00	1.00	.60
191	Mike Andrews	2.00	1.00	.60
192	Billy Wilson	2.00	1.00	.60
193	Bob Grich RC	5.00	2.50	1.50
194	Mike Lum	2.00	1.00	.60
195	A.L. Playoff Game 1 (Powell Muscles Twins!)	5.00	2.50	1.50
196	A.L. Playoff Game 2 (McNally Makes It Two Straight!)	3.00	1.50	.90
197	A.L. Playoff Game 3 (Palmer Mows 'Em Down!)	6.00	3.00	1.75
198	Orioles Celebrate! (A Team Effort!)	3.00	1.50	.90
199	N.L. Playoff Game 1 (Cline Pinch-Triple Decides It!)	3.00	1.50	.90
200	N.L. Playoff Game 2 (Tolan Scores For Third Time!)	3.00	1.50	.90
201	N.L. Playoff Game 3 (Cline Scores Winning Run!)	3.00	1.50	.90
202	Reds Celebrate! (World Series Bound!)	3.00	1.50	.90
203	Larry Gura RC	2.00	1.00	.60
204	Brewers Rookies (George Kopacz, Bernie Smith)	2.00	1.00	.60
205	Gerry Moses	2.00	1.00	.60
206a	3rd Series Checklist (264-393) (Orange helmet.)	6.00	3.00	1.75
206b	3rd Series Checklist (264-393) (Red helmet.)	6.00	3.00	1.75
207	Alan Foster	2.00	1.00	.60
208	Billy Martin	8.00	4.00	2.50
209	Steve Renko	2.00	1.00	.60
210	Rod Carew	15.00	7.50	4.50
211	Phil Hennigan	2.00	1.00	.60
212	Rich Hebner	2.00	1.00	.60
213	Frank Baker	2.00	1.00	.60
214	Al Ferrara	2.00	1.00	.60
215	Diego Segui	2.00	1.00	.60
216	Cards Rookies (Reggie Cleveland, Luis Melendez)	2.00	1.00	.60

No.	Player			
217	Ed Stroud	2.00	1.00	.60
218	Tony Cloninger	2.00	1.00	.60
219	Elrod Hendricks	2.00	1.00	.60
220	Ron Santo	8.00	4.00	2.50
221	Dave Morehead	2.00	1.00	.60
222	Bob Watson	2.00	1.00	.60
223	Cecil Upshaw	2.00	1.00	.60
224	Alan Gallagher	2.00	1.00	.60
225	Gary Peters	2.00	1.00	.60
226	Bill Russell	2.00	1.00	.60
227	Floyd Weaver	2.00	1.00	.60
228	Wayne Garrett	2.00	1.00	.60
229	Jim Hannan	2.00	1.00	.60
230	Willie Stargell	15.00	7.50	4.50
231	Indians Rookies(Vince Colbert, John Lowenstein RC)	2.00	1.00	.60
232	John Strohmayer	2.00	1.00	.60
233	Larry Bowa	2.00	1.00	.60
234	Jim Lyttle	2.00	1.00	.60
235	Nate Colbert	2.00	1.00	.60
236	Bob Humphreys	2.00	1.00	.60
237	Cesar Cedeno RC	6.00	3.00	1.75
238	Chuck Dobson	2.00	1.00	.60
239	Red Schoendienst	6.00	3.00	1.75
240	Clyde Wright	2.00	1.00	.60
241	Dave Nelson	2.00	1.00	.60
242	Jim Ray	2.00	1.00	.60
243	Carlos May	2.00	1.00	.60
244	Bob Tillman	2.00	1.00	.60
245	Jim Kaat	3.00	1.50	.90
246	Tony Taylor	2.00	1.00	.60
247	Royals Rookies(Jerry Cram, Paul Splittorff RC)	2.00	1.00	.60
248	Hoyt Wilhelm	8.00	4.00	2.50
249	Chico Salmon	2.00	1.00	.60
250	Johnny Bench	60.00	30.00	18.00
251	Frank Reberger	2.00	1.00	.60
252	Eddie Leon	2.00	1.00	.60
253	Bill Sudakis	2.00	1.00	.60
254	Cal Koonce	2.00	1.00	.60
255	Bob Robertson	2.00	1.00	.60
256	Tony Gonzalez	2.00	1.00	.60
257	Nelson Briles	2.00	1.00	.60
258	Dick Green	2.00	1.00	.60
259	Dave Marshall	2.00	1.00	.60
260	Tommy Harper	2.00	1.00	.60
261	Darold Knowles	2.00	1.00	.60
262	Padres Rookies(Dave Robinson, Jim Williams)	2.00	1.00	.60
263	John Ellis	2.00	1.00	.60
264	Joe Morgan	13.50	6.50	3.00
265a	Jim Northrup (Black "dot" at right of photo.)	2.00	1.00	.60
265b	Jim Northrup (Black "blob" at right of photo.)	2.00	1.00	.60
266	Bill Stoneman	2.00	1.00	.60
267	Rich Morales	2.00	1.00	.60
268	Phillies Team	4.00	2.00	1.25
269	Gail Hopkins	2.00	1.00	.60
270	Rico Carty	2.00	1.00	.60
271	Bill Zepp	2.00	1.00	.60
272	Tommy Helms	2.00	1.00	.60
273	Pete Richert	2.00	1.00	.60
274	Ron Slocum	2.00	1.00	.60
275	Vada Pinson	5.00	2.50	1.50
276	Giants Rookies(Mike Davison RC, George Foster RC)	10.00	5.00	2.50
277	Gary Waslewski	2.00	1.00	.60
278	Jerry Grote	2.00	1.00	.60
279	Lefty Phillips	2.00	1.00	.60
280	Fergie Jenkins	10.00	5.00	3.00
281	Danny Walton	2.00	1.00	.60
282	Jose Pagan	2.00	1.00	.60
283	Dick Such	2.00	1.00	.60
284	Jim Gosger	2.00	1.00	.60
285	Sal Bando	2.00	1.00	.60
286	Jerry McNertney	2.00	1.00	.60
287	Mike Fiore	2.00	1.00	.60
288	Joe Moeller	2.00	1.00	.60
289	White Sox Team	4.00	2.00	1.25
290	Tony Oliva	10.00	5.00	2.50
291	George Culver	2.00	1.00	.60
292	Jay Johnstone	2.00	1.00	.60
293	Pat Corrales	2.00	1.00	.60
294	Steve Dunning	2.00	1.00	.60
295	Bobby Bonds	4.00	2.00	1.25
296	Tom Timmermann	2.00	1.00	.60
297	Johnny Briggs	2.00	1.00	.60
298	Jim Nelson	2.00	1.00	.60
299	Ed Kirkpatrick	2.00	1.00	.60
300	Brooks Robinson	27.50	14.00	7.00
301	Earl Wilson	2.00	1.00	.60
302	Phil Gagliano	2.00	1.00	.60
303	Lindy McDaniel	2.00	1.00	.60
304	Ron Brand	2.00	1.00	.60
305	Reggie Smith	2.00	1.00	.60
306a	Jim Nash (Black blob, left center.)	4.00	2.00	1.25
306b	Jim Nash (Blob airbrushed away.)	2.00	1.00	.60
307	Don Wert	2.00	1.00	.60
308	Cards Team	3.00	1.50	.90
309	Dick Ellsworth	2.00	1.00	.60
310	Tommie Agee	2.00	1.00	.60
311	Lee Stange	2.00	1.00	.60
312	Harry Walker	2.00	1.00	.60
313	Tom Hall	2.00	1.00	.60
314	Jeff Torborg	2.00	1.00	.60
315	Ron Fairly	2.00	1.00	.60
316	Fred Scherman	2.00	1.00	.60
317	Athletics Rookies(Jim Driscoll, Angel Mangual)	2.00	1.00	.60
318	Rudy May	2.00	1.00	.60
319	Ty Cline	2.00	1.00	.60
320	Dave McNally	2.00	1.00	.60
321	Tom Matchick	2.00	1.00	.60
322	Jim Beauchamp	2.00	1.00	.60
323	Billy Champion	2.00	1.00	.60
324	Graig Nettles	4.00	2.00	1.25
325	Juan Marichal	8.00	4.00	2.50
326	Richie Scheinblum	2.00	1.00	.60
327	World Series Game 1 (Powell Homers To Opposite Field!)	3.00	1.50	.90
328	World Series Game 2 (Buford Goes 2-For-4!)	2.00	1.00	.60
329	World Series Game 3 (F. Robinson Shows Muscle!)	6.00	3.00	1.75
330	World Series Game 4 (Reds Stay Alive!)	2.00	1.00	.60
331	World Series Game 5 (B. Robinson Commits Robbery!)	8.00	4.00	2.50
332	World Series Celebration! (Convincing Performance!)	5.00	2.50	1.50
333	Clay Kirby	2.00	1.00	.60
334	Roberto Pena	2.00	1.00	.60
335	Jerry Koosman	2.00	1.00	.60
336	Tigers Team	4.00	2.00	1.25
337	Jesus Alou	2.00	1.00	.60
338	Gene Tenace	2.00	1.00	.60
339	Wayne Simpson	2.00	1.00	.60
340	Rico Petrocelli	2.00	1.00	.60
341	Steve Garvey RC	37.50	17.50	8.75
342	Frank Tepedino	2.00	1.00	.60
343	Pirates Rookies(Ed Acosta, Milt May RC)	2.00	1.00	.60
344	Ellie Rodriguez	2.00	1.00	.60
345	Joe Horlen	2.00	1.00	.60
346	Lum Harris	2.00	1.00	.60
347	Ted Uhlaender	2.00	1.00	.60
348	Fred Norman	2.00	1.00	.60
349	Rich Reese	2.00	1.00	.60
350	Billy Williams	11.00	5.50	3.00
351	Jim Shellenback	2.00	1.00	.60
352	Denny Doyle	2.00	1.00	.60
353	Carl Taylor	2.00	1.00	.60
354	Don McMahon	2.00	1.00	.60
355	Bud Harrelson	2.00	1.00	.60
356	Bob Locker	2.00	1.00	.60
357	Reds Team	4.00	2.00	1.25
358	Danny Cater	2.00	1.00	.60
359	Ron Reed	2.00	1.00	.60
360	Jim Fregosi	2.00	1.00	.60
361	Don Sutton	8.00	4.00	2.50
362	Orioles Rookies(Mike Adamson, Roger Freed)	2.00	1.00	.60
363	Mike Nagy	2.00	1.00	.60
364	Tommy Dean	2.00	1.00	.60
365	Bob Johnson	2.00	1.00	.60
366	Ron Stone	2.00	1.00	.60
367	Dalton Jones	2.00	1.00	.60
368	Bob Veale	2.00	1.00	.60
369a	4th Series Checklist (394-523) (Orange helmet.)	5.00	2.50	1.50
369b	4th Series Checklist (394-523) (Red helmet, black line above ear.)	6.00	3.00	1.75
369c	4th Series Checklist (394-523) (Red helmet, no line.)	6.00	3.00	1.75
370	Joe Torre	12.00	6.00	3.00
371	Jack Hiatt	2.00	1.00	.60
372	Lew Krausse	2.00	1.00	.60
373	Tom McCraw	2.00	1.00	.60
374	Clete Boyer	2.00	1.00	.60
375	Steve Hargan	2.00	1.00	.60
376	Expos Rookies(Clyde Mashore, Ernie McAnally)	2.00	1.00	.60
377	Greg Garrett	2.00	1.00	.60
378	Tito Fuentes	2.00	1.00	.60
379	Wayne Granger	2.00	1.00	.60
380	Ted Williams	12.00	6.00	3.50
381	Fred Gladding	2.00	1.00	.60
382	Jake Gibbs	2.00	1.00	.60
383	Rod Gaspar	2.00	1.00	.60
384	Rollie Fingers	8.00	4.00	2.50
385	Maury Wills	4.00	2.00	1.25
386	Red Sox Team	4.00	2.00	1.25
387	Ron Herbel	2.00	1.00	.60
388	Al Oliver	2.00	1.00	.60
389	Ed Brinkman	2.00	1.00	.60
390	Glenn Beckert	2.00	1.00	.60
391	Twins Rookies(Steve Brye, Cotton Nash)	2.00	1.00	.60
392	Grant Jackson	2.00	1.00	.60
393	Merv Rettenmund	2.00	1.00	.60
394	Clay Carroll	2.00	1.00	.60
395	Roy White	2.00	1.00	.60
396	Dick Schofield	2.00	1.00	.60
397	Alvin Dark	2.00	1.00	.60
398	Howie Reed	2.00	1.00	.60
399	Jim French	2.00	1.00	.60
400	Hank Aaron	50.00	25.00	15.00
401	Tom Murphy	2.00	1.00	.60
402	Dodgers Team	4.00	2.00	1.25
403	Joe Coleman	2.00	1.00	.60
404	Astros Rookies(Buddy Harris, Roger Metzger)	2.00	1.00	.60
405	Leo Cardenas	2.00	1.00	.60
406	Ray Sadecki	2.00	1.00	.60
407	Joe Rudi	2.00	1.00	.60
408	Rafael Robles	2.00	1.00	.60
409	Don Pavletich	2.00	1.00	.60
410	Ken Holtzman	2.00	1.00	.60
411	George Spriggs	2.00	1.00	.60
412	Jerry Johnson	2.00	1.00	.60
413	Pat Kelly	2.00	1.00	.60
414	Woodie Fryman	2.00	1.00	.60
415	Mike Hegan	2.00	1.00	.60
416	Gene Alley	2.00	1.00	.60
417	Dick Hall	2.00	1.00	.60
418	Adolfo Phillips	2.00	1.00	.60
419	Ron Hansen	2.00	1.00	.60
420	Jim Merritt	2.00	1.00	.60
421	John Stephenson	2.00	1.00	.60
422	Frank Bertaina	2.00	1.00	.60
423	Tigers Rookies(Tim Marting, Dennis Saunders)	2.00	1.00	.60
424	Roberto Rodriquez (Rodriguez)	2.00	1.00	.60
425	Doug Rader	2.00	1.00	.60
426	Chris Cannizzaro	2.00	1.00	.60
427	Bernie Allen	2.00	1.00	.60
428	Jim McAndrew	2.00	1.00	.60
429	Chuck Hinton	2.00	1.00	.60
430	Wes Parker	2.00	1.00	.60
431	Tom Burgmeier	2.00	1.00	.60
432	Bob Didier	2.00	1.00	.60
433	Skip Lockwood	2.00	1.00	.60
434	Gary Sutherland	2.00	1.00	.60
435	Jose Cardenal	2.00	1.00	.60
436	Wilbur Wood	2.00	1.00	.60
437	Danny Murtaugh	2.00	1.00	.60
438	Mike McCormick	2.00	1.00	.60
439	Phillies Rookies(Greg Luzinski RC, Scott Reid)	9.00	4.50	2.25
440	Bert Campaneris	2.00	1.00	.60
441	Milt Pappas	2.00	1.00	.60
442	Angels Team	4.00	2.00	1.25
443	Rich Robertson	2.00	1.00	.60
444	Jimmie Price	2.00	1.00	.60
445	Art Shamsky	2.00	1.00	.60
446	Bobby Bolin	2.00	1.00	.60
447	Cesar Geronimo RC	3.00	1.50	.90
448	Dave Roberts	2.00	1.00	.60
449	Brant Alyea	2.00	1.00	.60
450	Bob Gibson	15.00	7.50	4.50
451	Joe Keough	2.00	1.00	.60
452	John Boccabella	2.00	1.00	.60
453	Terry Crowley	2.00	1.00	.60
454	Mike Paul	2.00	1.00	.60
455	Don Kessinger	2.00	1.00	.60
456	Bob Meyer	2.00	1.00	.60
457	Willie Smith	2.00	1.00	.60
458	White Sox Rookies(Dave Lemonds, Ron Lolich)	2.00	1.00	.60
459	Jim Lefebvre	2.00	1.00	.60
460	Fritz Peterson	2.00	1.00	.60
461	Jim Hart	2.00	1.00	.60
462	**Senators Team**	5.00	2.50	1.50
463	Tom Kelley	2.00	1.00	.60
464	Aurelio Rodriguez	2.00	1.00	.60
465	Tim McCarver	6.00	3.00	1.75
466	Ken Berry	2.00	1.00	.60
467	Al Santorini	2.00	1.00	.60
468	Frank Fernandez	2.00	1.00	.60
469	Bob Aspromonte	2.00	1.00	.60

470	Bob Oliver	2.00	1.00	.60
471	Tom Griffin	2.00	1.00	.60
472	Ken Rudolph	2.00	1.00	.60
473	Gary Wagner	2.00	1.00	.60
474	Jim Fairey	2.00	1.00	.60
475	Ron Perranoski	2.00	1.00	.60
476	Dal Maxvill	2.00	1.00	.60
477	Earl Weaver	5.00	2.50	1.50
478	Bernie Carbo	2.00	1.00	.60
479	Dennis Higgins	2.00	1.00	.60
480	Manny Sanguillen	2.00	1.00	.60
481	Daryl Patterson	2.00	1.00	.60
482	**Padres Team**	5.00	2.50	1.50
483	Gene Michael	2.00	1.00	.60
484	Don Wilson	2.00	1.00	.60
485	Ken McMullen	2.00	1.00	.60
486	Steve Huntz	2.00	1.00	.60
487	Paul Schaal	2.00	1.00	.60
488	Jerry Stephenson	2.00	1.00	.60
489	Luis Alvarado	2.00	1.00	.60
490	Deron Johnson	2.00	1.00	.60
491	Jim Hardin	2.00	1.00	.60
492	Ken Boswell	2.00	1.00	.60
493	Dave May	2.00	1.00	.60
494	Braves Rookies(Ralph Garr, Rick Kester)	2.00	1.00	.60
495	Felipe Alou	3.00	1.50	.90
496	Woody Woodward	2.00	1.00	.60
497	Horacio Pina	2.00	1.00	.60
498	John Kennedy	2.00	1.00	.60
499	5th Series Checklist (524-643)	6.00	3.00	1.75
500	Jim Perry	2.00	1.00	.60
501	Andy Etchebarren	2.00	1.00	.60
502	**Cubs Team**	5.00	2.50	1.50
503	Gates Brown	2.00	1.00	.60
504	Ken Wright	2.00	1.00	.60
505	Ollie Brown	2.00	1.00	.60
506	Bobby Knoop	2.00	1.00	.60
507	George Stone	2.00	1.00	.60
508	Roger Repoz	2.00	1.00	.60
509	Jim Grant	2.00	1.00	.60
510	Ken Harrelson	2.00	1.00	.60
511	Chris Short	2.00	1.00	.60
512	Red Sox Rookies(Mike Garman, Dick Mills)	2.00	1.00	.60
513	Nolan Ryan	115.00	60.00	30.00
514	Ron Woods	2.00	1.00	.60
515	Carl Morton	2.00	1.00	.60
516	Ted Kubiak	2.00	1.00	.60
517	Charlie Fox	2.00	1.00	.60
518	Joe Grzenda	2.00	1.00	.60
519	Willie Crawford	2.00	1.00	.60
520	Tommy John	5.00	2.50	1.50
521	Leron Lee	2.00	1.00	.60
522	Twins Team	4.00	2.00	1.25
523	John Odom	2.00	1.00	.60
524	Mickey Stanley	4.00	2.00	1.25
525	Ernie Banks	48.00	25.00	12.50
526	Ray Jarvis	4.00	2.00	1.25
527	Cleon Jones	4.00	2.00	1.25
528	Wally Bunker	4.00	2.00	1.25
529	N.L. Rookies(Bill Buckner, Enzo Hernandez, Marty Perez)	6.00	3.00	1.75
530	Carl Yastrzemski	25.00	12.50	7.50
531	Mike Torrez	4.00	2.00	1.25
532	Bill Rigney	4.00	2.00	1.25
533	Mike Ryan	4.00	2.00	1.25
534	Luke Walker	4.00	2.00	1.25
535	Curt Flood	5.00	2.50	1.50
536	Claude Raymond	4.00	2.00	1.25
537	Tom Egan	4.00	2.00	1.25
538	Angel Bravo	4.00	2.00	1.25
539	Larry Brown	4.00	2.00	1.25
540	Larry Dierker	4.00	2.00	1.25
541	Bob Burda	4.00	2.00	1.25
542	Bob Miller	4.00	2.00	1.25
543	Yankees Team	8.00	4.00	2.50
544	Vida Blue	5.00	2.50	1.50
545	Dick Dietz	4.00	2.00	1.25
546	John Matias	4.00	2.00	1.25
547	Pat Dobson	4.00	2.00	1.25
548	Don Mason	4.00	2.00	1.25
549	Jim Brewer	4.00	2.00	1.25
550	Harmon Killebrew	23.00	12.50	8.00
551	Frank Linzy	4.00	2.00	1.25
552	Buddy Bradford	4.00	2.00	1.25
553	Kevin Collins	4.00	2.00	1.25
554	Lowell Palmer	4.00	2.00	1.25
555	Walt Williams	4.00	2.00	1.25
556	Jim McGlothlin	4.00	2.00	1.25
557	Tom Satriano	4.00	2.00	1.25
558	Hector Torres	4.00	2.00	1.25
559	A.L. Rookies(Terry Cox, Bill Gogolewski, Gary Jones)	4.00	2.00	1.25
560	Rusty Staub	5.00	2.50	1.50
561	Syd O'Brien	4.00	2.00	1.25
562	Dave Giusti	4.00	2.00	1.25
563	Giants Team	10.00	5.00	3.00
564	Al Fitzmorris	4.00	2.00	1.25
565	Jim Wynn	4.00	2.00	1.25
566	Tim Cullen	4.00	2.00	1.25
567	Walt Alston	6.00	3.00	1.75
568	Sal Campisi	4.00	2.00	1.25
569	Ivan Murrell	4.00	2.00	1.25
570	Jim Palmer	25.00	12.50	7.50
571	Ted Sizemore	4.00	2.00	1.25
572	Jerry Kenney	4.00	2.00	1.25
573	Ed Kranepool	4.00	2.00	1.25
574	Jim Bunning	12.00	6.00	3.00
575	Bill Freehan	4.00	2.00	1.25
576	Cubs Rookies(Brock Davis, Adrian Garrett, Garry Jestadt)	4.00	2.00	1.25
577	Jim Lonborg	4.00	2.00	1.25
578	Ron Hunt	4.00	2.00	1.25
579	Marty Pattin	4.00	2.00	1.25
580	Tony Perez	17.50	9.00	6.00
581	Roger Nelson	4.00	2.00	1.25
582	Dave Cash	4.00	2.00	1.25
583	Ron Cook	4.00	2.00	1.25
584	Indians Team	10.00	5.00	3.00
585	Willie Davis	4.00	2.00	1.25
586	Dick Woodson	4.00	2.00	1.25
587	Sonny Jackson	4.00	2.00	1.25
588	Tom Bradley	4.00	2.00	1.25
589	Bob Barton	4.00	2.00	1.25
590	Alex Johnson	4.00	2.00	1.25
591	Jackie Brown	4.00	2.00	1.25
592	Randy Hundley	4.00	2.00	1.25
593	Jack Aker	4.00	2.00	1.25
594	Cards Rookies(Bob Chlupsa, Al Hrabosky **RC**, Bob Stinson)	6.00	3.00	1.75
595	Dave Johnson	4.00	2.00	1.25
596	Mike Jorgensen	4.00	2.00	1.25
597	Ken Suarez	4.00	2.00	1.25
598	Rick Wise	4.00	2.00	1.25
599	Norm Cash	6.00	3.00	1.75
600	Willie Mays	100.00	50.00	30.00
601	Ken Tatum	4.00	2.00	1.25
602	Marty Martinez	4.00	2.00	1.25
603	**Pirates Team**	8.00	4.00	2.50
604	John Gelnar	4.00	2.00	1.25
605	Orlando Cepeda	13.50	7.00	3.50
606	Chuck Taylor	4.00	2.00	1.25
607	Paul Ratliff	4.00	2.00	1.25
608	Mike Wegener	4.00	2.00	1.25
609	Leo Durocher	8.00	4.00	2.50
610	Amos Otis	4.00	2.00	1.25
611	Tom Phoebus	4.00	2.00	1.25
612	Indians Rookies (Lou Camilli, Ted Ford, Steve Mingori)	4.00	2.00	1.25
613	Pedro Borbon	4.00	2.00	1.25
614	Billy Cowan	4.00	2.00	1.25
615	Mel Stottlemyre	6.00	3.00	1.75
616	Larry Hisle	4.00	2.00	1.25
617	Clay Dalrymple	4.00	2.00	1.25
618	Tug McGraw	4.00	2.00	1.25
619a	6th Series Checklist (644-752) (No copyright on back.)	5.00	2.50	1.50
619b	6th Series Checklist (644-752) (With copyright, no wavy line on helmet brim.)	4.00	2.00	1.25
619c	6th Series Checklist (644-752) (With copyright, wavy line on helmet brim.)	9.00	4.50	2.25
620	Frank Howard	5.00	2.50	1.50
621	Ron Bryant	4.00	2.00	1.25
622	Joe Lahoud	4.00	2.00	1.25
623	Pat Jarvis	4.00	2.00	1.25
624	Athletics Team	10.00	5.00	3.00
625	Lou Brock	25.00	12.50	7.50
626	Freddie Patek	4.00	2.00	1.25
627	Steve Hamilton	4.00	2.00	1.25
628	John Bateman	4.00	2.00	1.25
629	John Hiller	4.00	2.00	1.25
630	Roberto Clemente	115.00	55.00	30.00
631	Eddie Fisher	4.00	2.00	1.25
632	Darrel Chaney	4.00	2.00	1.25
633	A.L. Rookies (Bobby Brooks, Pete Koegel, Scott Northey)	4.00	2.00	1.25
634	Phil Regan	4.00	2.00	1.25
635	Bobby Murcer	15.00	7.50	4.50
636	Denny Lemaster	4.00	2.00	1.25
637	Dave Bristol	4.00	2.00	1.25
638	Stan Williams	4.00	2.00	1.25
639	Tom Haller	4.00	2.00	1.25
640	Frank Robinson	30.00	15.00	9.00
641	Mets Team	12.00	6.00	4.00
642	Jim Roland	4.00	2.00	1.25
643	Rick Reichardt	4.00	2.00	1.25
644	Jim Stewart (SP)	8.00	4.00	2.50
645	Jim Maloney (SP)	8.00	4.00	2.50
646	Bobby Floyd (SP)	8.00	4.00	2.50
647	Juan Pizarro	6.00	3.00	1.75
648	Mets Rookies (Rich Folkers, Ted Martinez, Jon Matlack **RC**) (SP)	20.00	10.00	6.00
649	Sparky Lyle (SP)	10.00	5.00	3.00
650	Rich Allen (SP)	30.00	15.00	9.00
651	Jerry Robertson (SP)	8.00	4.00	2.50
652	Braves Team	10.00	5.00	3.00
653	Russ Snyder (SP)	8.00	4.00	2.50
654	Don Shaw (SP)	8.00	4.00	2.50
655	Mike Epstein (SP)	8.00	4.00	2.50
656	Gerry Nyman (SP)	8.00	4.00	2.50
657	Jose Azcue	6.00	3.00	1.75
658	Paul Lindblad (SP)	8.00	4.00	2.50
659	Byron Browne (SP)	8.00	4.00	2.50
660	Ray Culp	6.00	3.00	1.75
661	Chuck Tanner (SP)	8.00	4.00	2.50
662	Mike Hedlund (SP)	8.00	4.00	2.50
663	Marv Staehle	6.00	3.00	1.75
664	Major League Rookies (Archie Reynolds, Bob Reynolds, Ken Reynolds) (SP)	8.00	4.00	2.50
665	Ron Swoboda (SP)	8.00	4.00	2.50
666	Gene Brabender (SP)	8.00	4.00	2.50
667	Pete Ward	6.00	3.00	1.75
668	Gary Neibauer	6.00	3.00	1.75
669	Ike Brown (SP)	8.00	4.00	2.50
670	Bill Hands	6.00	3.00	1.75
671	Bill Voss (SP)	8.00	4.00	2.50
672	Ed Crosby (SP)	8.00	4.00	2.50
673	Gerry Janeski (SP)	8.00	4.00	2.50
674	Expos Team	10.00	5.00	2.50
675	Dave Boswell	6.00	3.00	1.75
676	Tommie Reynolds	6.00	3.00	1.75
677	Jack DiLauro (SP)	8.00	4.00	2.50
678	George Thomas	6.00	3.00	1.75
679	Don O'Riley	6.00	3.00	1.75
680	Don Mincher (SP)	8.00	4.00	2.50
681	Bill Butler	6.00	3.00	1.75
682	Terry Harmon	6.00	3.00	1.75
683	Bill Burbach (SP)	8.00	4.00	2.50
684	Curt Motton	6.00	3.00	1.75
685	Moe Drabowsky	6.00	3.00	1.75
686	Chico Ruiz (SP)	8.00	4.00	2.50
687	Ron Taylor (SP)	8.00	4.00	2.50
688	Sparky Anderson (SP)	25.00	12.50	7.50
689	Frank Baker	6.00	3.00	1.75
690	Bob Moose	6.00	3.00	1.75
691	Bob Heise	6.00	3.00	1.75
692	A.L. Rookies(Hal Haydel, Rogelio Moret, Wayne Twitchell) (SP)	8.00	4.00	2.50
693	Jose Pena (SP)	8.00	4.00	2.50
694	Rick Renick (SP)	8.00	4.00	2.50
695	Joe Niekro	6.00	3.00	1.75
696	Jerry Morales	6.00	3.00	1.75
697	Rickey Clark (SP)	8.00	4.00	2.50
698	**Brewers Team** (SP)	15.00	7.50	3.75
699	Jim Britton	6.00	3.00	1.75
700	Boog Powell (SP)	20.00	10.00	6.00
701	Bob Garibaldi	6.00	3.00	1.75
702	Milt Ramirez	6.00	3.00	1.75
703	Mike Kekich	6.00	3.00	1.75
704	J.C. Martin (SP)	8.00	4.00	2.50
705	Dick Selma (SP)	8.00	4.00	2.50
706	Joe Foy (SP)	8.00	4.00	2.50
707	Fred Lasher	6.00	3.00	1.75
708	Russ Nagelson (SP)	8.00	4.00	2.50
709	Major League Rookies (Dusty Baker **RC**, Don Baylor **RC**, Tom Paciorek **RC**) (SP)	75.00	37.50	18.75
710	Sonny Siebert	6.00	3.00	1.75
711	Larry Stahl (SP)	8.00	4.00	2.50
712	Jose Martinez	6.00	3.00	1.75
713	Mike Marshall (SP)	8.00	4.00	2.50
714	Dick Williams (SP)	8.00	4.00	2.50
715	Horace Clarke (SP)	8.00	4.00	2.50
716	Dave Leonhard	6.00	3.00	1.75
717	Tommie Aaron (SP)	8.00	4.00	2.50
718	Billy Wynne	6.00	3.00	1.75
719	Jerry May (SP)	8.00	4.00	2.50
720	Matty Alou	6.00	3.00	1.75
721	John Morris	6.00	3.00	1.75
722	Astros Team (SP)	15.00	7.50	4.50
723	Vicente Romo (SP)	8.00	4.00	2.50
724	Tom Tischinski (SP)	8.00	4.00	2.50
725	Gary Gentry (SP)	8.00	4.00	2.50
726	Paul Popovich	6.00	3.00	1.75
727	Ray Lamb (SP)	8.00	4.00	2.50

		NM	E	VG
728	N.L. Rookies (Keith Lampard, Wayne Redmond, Bernie Williams)	6.00	3.00	1.75
729	Dick Billings	6.00	3.00	1.75
730	Jim Rooker	6.00	3.00	1.75
731	Jim Qualls (SP)	8.00	4.00	2.50
732	Bob Reed	6.00	3.00	1.75
733	Lee Maye (SP)	8.00	4.00	2.50
734	Rob Gardner (SP)	8.00	4.00	2.50
735	Mike Shannon (SP)	8.00	4.00	2.50
736	Mel Queen (SP)	8.00	4.00	2.50
737	Preston Gomez (SP)	8.00	4.00	2.50
738	Russ Gibson (SP)	8.00	4.00	2.50
739	Barry Lersch (SP)	8.00	4.00	2.50
740	Luis Aparicio (SP)	25.00	12.50	7.50
741	Skip Quinn	6.00	3.00	1.75
742	Kansas City Royals	10.00	5.00	3.00
743	John O'Donoghue (SP)	8.00	4.00	2.50
744	Chuck Manuel (SP)	8.00	4.00	2.50
745	Sandy Alomar (SP)	8.00	4.00	2.50
746	Andy Kosco	8.00	4.00	2.50
747	NL Rookies (Baylor Moore, Al Severinsen, Scipio Spinks)	8.00	4.00	2.50
748	John Purdin (SP)	8.00	4.00	2.50
749	Ken Szotkiewicz	6.00	3.00	1.75
750	Denny McClain (SP)	20.00	10.00	6.00
751	Al Weis (SP)	6.00	3.00	1.75
752	Dick Drago	10.00	5.00	3.00

1971 Topps All-Star Rookies Artist's Proofs

There exists only one set of these artist's proofs for a proposed set of All-Star Rookie cards. The standard-size card fronts are pasted onto 9-1/2" x 6-1/2" cardboard backing. It may have been intended that these be issued in card form for Topps' annual banquet. There is a player for each position on the 1970 All-Rookie Team, plus right- and left-handed pitchers. Players are listed here in alphabetical order.

		NM	E	VG
	Complete Set (10):	1,500	750.00	450.00
	Common Player:	200.00	100.00	60.00
(1)	Larry Bowa	350.00	175.00	105.00
(2)	Les Cain	200.00	100.00	60.00
(3)	Bernie Carbo	200.00	100.00	60.00
(4)	Dave Cash	200.00	100.00	60.00
(5)	Billy Conigliaro	200.00	100.00	60.00
(6)	John Ellis	200.00	100.00	60.00
(7)	Roy Foster	200.00	100.00	60.00
(8)	Alan Gallagher	200.00	100.00	60.00
(9)	Carl Morton	200.00	100.00	60.00
(10)	Thurman Munson	750.00	375.00	225.00

1971 Topps Coins

Measuring 1-1/2" in diameter, the latest edition of the Topps coins was a 153-piece set. The coins feature a color photograph surrounded by a colored band on the front. The band carries the player's name, team, position and several stars. Backs have a short biography, the coin number and encouragement to collect the entire set. Back colors differ, with #s 1-51 having a brass back, #s 52-102 chrome backs, and the rest have blue backs. Most of the stars of the period are included in the set.

		NM	E	VG

		NM	E	VG
	Complete Set (153):	500.00	250.00	150.00
	Common Player:	2.00	1.00	.60
1	Cito Gaston	2.00	1.00	.60
2	Dave Johnson	2.00	1.00	.60
3	Jim Bunning	8.00	4.00	2.50
4	Jim Spencer	2.00	1.00	.60
5	Felix Millan	2.00	1.00	.60
6	Gerry Moses	2.00	1.00	.60
7	Fergie Jenkins	8.00	4.00	2.50
8	Felipe Alou	2.50	1.25	.70
9	Jim McGlothlin	2.00	1.00	.60
10	Dick McAuliffe	2.00	1.00	.60
11	Joe Torre	5.00	2.50	1.50
12	Jim Perry	2.00	1.00	.60
13	Bobby Bonds	2.00	1.00	.60
14	Danny Cater	2.00	1.00	.60
15	Bill Mazeroski	8.00	4.00	2.50
16	Luis Aparicio	8.00	4.00	2.50
17	Doug Rader	2.00	1.00	.60
18	Vada Pinson	3.00	1.50	.90
19	John Bateman	2.00	1.00	.60
20	Lew Krausse	2.00	1.00	.60
21	Billy Grabarkewitz	2.00	1.00	.60
22	Frank Howard	2.00	1.00	.60
23	Jerry Koosman	2.00	1.00	.60
24	Rod Carew	10.00	5.00	3.00
25	Al Ferrara	2.00	1.00	.60
26	Dave McNally	2.00	1.00	.60
27	Jim Hickman	2.00	1.00	.60
28	Sandy Alomar	2.00	1.00	.60
29	Lee May	2.00	1.00	.60
30	Rico Petrocelli	2.00	1.00	.60
31	Don Money	2.00	1.00	.60
32	Jim Rooker	2.00	1.00	.60
33	Dick Dietz	2.00	1.00	.60
34	Roy White	2.00	1.00	.60
35	Carl Morton	2.00	1.00	.60
36	Walt Williams	2.00	1.00	.60
37	Phil Niekro	8.00	4.00	2.50
38	Bill Freehan	2.00	1.00	.60
39	Julian Javier	2.00	1.00	.60
40	Rick Monday	2.00	1.00	.60
41	Don Wilson	2.00	1.00	.60
42	Ray Fosse	2.00	1.00	.60
43	Art Shamsky	2.00	1.00	.60
44	Ted Savage	2.00	1.00	.60
45	Claude Osteen	2.00	1.00	.60
46	Ed Brinkman	2.00	1.00	.60
47	Matty Alou	2.00	1.00	.60
48	Bob Oliver	2.00	1.00	.60
49	Danny Coombs	2.00	1.00	.60
50	Frank Robinson	10.00	5.00	3.00
51	Randy Hundley	2.00	1.00	.60
52	Cesar Tovar	2.00	1.00	.60
53	Wayne Simpson	2.00	1.00	.60
54	Bobby Murcer	2.00	1.00	.60
55	Tony Taylor	2.00	1.00	.60
56	Tommy John	3.00	1.50	.90
57	Willie McCovey	9.00	4.50	2.75
58	Carl Yastrzemski	13.50	6.75	4.00
59	Bob Bailey	2.00	1.00	.60
60	Clyde Wright	2.00	1.00	.60
61	Orlando Cepeda	8.00	4.00	2.50
62	Al Kaline	10.00	5.00	3.00
63	Bob Gibson	9.00	4.50	2.75
64	Bert Campaneris	2.00	1.00	.60
65	Ted Sizemore	2.00	1.00	.60
66	Duke Sims	2.00	1.00	.60
67	Bud Harrelson	2.00	1.00	.60
68	Jerry McNertney	2.00	1.00	.60
69	Jim Wynn	2.00	1.00	.60
70	Dick Bosman	2.00	1.00	.60
71	Roberto Clemente	30.00	15.00	9.00
72	Rich Reese	2.00	1.00	.60
73	Gaylord Perry	8.00	4.00	2.50
74	Boog Powell	3.00	1.50	.90
75	Billy Williams	9.00	4.50	2.75
76	Bill Melton	2.00	1.00	.60
77	Nate Colbert	2.00	1.00	.60
78	Reggie Smith	2.00	1.00	.60
79	Deron Johnson	2.00	1.00	.60
80	Catfish Hunter	8.00	4.00	2.50
81	Bob Tolan	2.00	1.00	.60
82	Jim Northrup	2.00	1.00	.60
83	Ron Fairly	2.00	1.00	.60
84	Alex Johnson	2.00	1.00	.60
85	Pat Jarvis	2.00	1.00	.60
86	Sam McDowell	2.00	1.00	.60
87	Lou Brock	9.00	4.50	2.75
88	Danny Walton	2.00	1.00	.60
89	Denis Menke	2.00	1.00	.60
90	Jim Palmer	9.00	4.50	2.75
91	Tommie Agee	2.00	1.00	.60
92	Duane Josephson	2.00	1.00	.60
93	Willie Davis	2.00	1.00	.60
94	Mel Stottlemyre	2.00	1.00	.60
95	Ron Santo	5.00	2.50	1.50
96	Amos Otis	2.00	1.00	.60
97	Ken Henderson	2.00	1.00	.60
98	George Scott	2.00	1.00	.60
99	Dock Ellis	2.00	1.00	.60
100	Harmon Killebrew	10.00	5.00	3.00
101	Pete Rose	20.00	10.00	6.00
102	Rick Reichardt	2.00	1.00	.60
103	Cleon Jones	2.00	1.00	.60
104	Ron Perranoski	2.00	1.00	.60
105	Tony Perez	9.00	4.50	2.75
106	Mickey Lolich	2.00	1.00	.60
107	Tim McCarver	3.00	1.50	.90
108	Reggie Jackson	15.00	7.50	4.50
109	Chris Cannizzaro	2.00	1.00	.60
110	Steve Hargan	2.00	1.00	.60
111	Rusty Staub	3.00	1.50	.90
112	Andy Messersmith	2.00	1.00	.60
113	Rico Carty	2.00	1.00	.60
114	Brooks Robinson	10.00	5.00	3.00
115	Steve Carlton	9.00	4.50	2.75
116	Mike Hegan	2.00	1.00	.60
117	Joe Morgan	9.00	4.50	2.75
118	Thurman Munson	8.00	4.00	2.50
119	Don Kessinger	2.00	1.00	.60
120	Joe Horlen	2.00	1.00	.60
121	Wes Parker	2.00	1.00	.60
122	Sonny Siebert	2.00	1.00	.60
123	Willie Stargell	9.00	4.50	2.75
124	Ellie Rodriguez	2.00	1.00	.60
125	Juan Marichal	8.00	4.00	2.50
126	Mike Epstein	2.00	1.00	.60
127	Tom Seaver	10.00	5.00	3.00
128	Tony Oliva	3.00	1.50	.90
129	Jim Merritt	2.00	1.00	.60
130	Willie Horton	2.00	1.00	.60
131	Rick Wise	2.00	1.00	.60
132	Sal Bando	2.00	1.00	.60
133	Ollie Brown	2.00	1.00	.60
134	Ken Harrelson	2.00	1.00	.60
135	Mack Jones	2.00	1.00	.60
136	Jim Fregosi	2.00	1.00	.60
137	Hank Aaron	25.00	12.50	7.50
138	Fritz Peterson	2.00	1.00	.60
139	Joe Hague	2.00	1.00	.60
140	Tommy Harper	2.00	1.00	.60
141	Larry Dierker	2.00	1.00	.60
142	Tony Conigliaro	4.00	2.00	1.25
143	Glenn Beckert	2.00	1.00	.60
144	Carlos May	2.00	1.00	.60
145	Don Sutton	8.00	4.00	2.50
146	Paul Casanova	2.00	1.00	.60
147	Bob Moose	2.00	1.00	.60
148	Leo Cardenas	2.00	1.00	.60
149	Johnny Bench	10.00	5.00	3.00
150	Mike Cuellar	2.00	1.00	.60
151	Donn Clendenon	2.00	1.00	.60
152	Lou Piniella	3.00	1.50	.90
153	Willie Mays	25.00	12.50	7.50

1971 Topps Greatest Moments

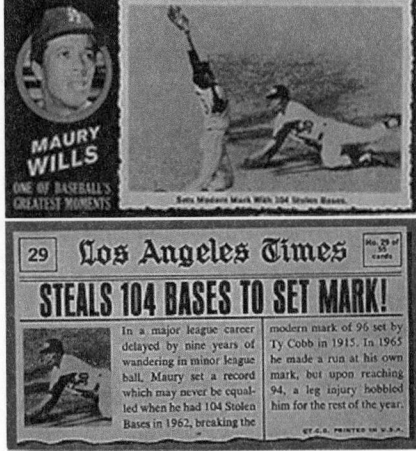

This 55-card set features highlights from the careers of top players of the day. The front of the 2-1/2" x 4-3/4" cards features a portrait photo of the player at left and deckle-edge action photo at right. There is a small headline on the white border of the action photo. The player's name and "One of Baseball's Greatest Moments" along with a black border complete the front. The back features a detail from the front photo and the story of the event. The newspaper style presentation includes the name of real newspapers. Relatively scarce, virtually every card in this set is a star or at least an above-average player. Because of their unusual size, 22 of the cards were double-printed, as indicated in the checklist here. Because of endemic centering problems there is a greater than usual value difference between NM and lower-grade cards.

	NM	E	VG
Complete Set (55):	4,500	2,250	1,350
Common Player:	45.00	25.00	10.00
1	Thurman Munson (DP)	400.00	200.00	100.00
2	Hoyt Wilhelm	75.00	37.50	22.50
3	Rico Carty	65.00	32.50	20.00
4	Carl Morton (DP)	45.00	25.00	6.00
5	Sal Bando (DP)	45.00	25.00	6.00
6	Bert Campaneris (DP)	45.00	25.00	6.00
7	Jim Kaat	70.00	35.00	20.00
8	Harmon Killebrew	300.00	125.00	65.00
9	Brooks Robinson	325.00	125.00	75.00
10	Jim Perry	45.00	22.50	13.50
11	Tony Oliva	125.00	62.50	310.00
12	Vada Pinson	125.00	62.50	310.00
13	Johnny Bench	300.00	150.00	90.00
14	Tony Perez	100.00	50.00	30.00
15	Pete Rose (DP)	200.00	75.00	45.00
16	Jim Fregosi (DP)	45.00	25.00	6.00
17	Alex Johnson (DP)	45.00	25.00	6.00
18	Clyde Wright (DP)	45.00	25.00	6.00
19	Al Kaline (DP)	100.00	50.00	30.00
20	Denny McLain	50.00	25.00	15.00
21	Jim Northrup	45.00	22.50	13.50
22	Bill Freehan	50.00	25.00	15.00
23	Mickey Lolich	60.00	30.00	18.00
24	Bob Gibson (DP)	75.00	37.50	22.50
25	Tim McCarver (DP)	35.00	17.50	10.00
26	Orlando Cepeda (DP)	45.00	22.50	13.50
27	Lou Brock (DP)	60.00	30.00	18.00
28	Nate Colbert (DP)	45.00	25.00	6.00
29	Maury Wills	50.00	25.00	15.00
30	Wes Parker	65.00	32.50	20.00
31	Jim Wynn	90.00	45.00	20.00
32	Larry Dierker	95.00	45.00	25.00
33	Bill Melton	60.00	30.00	18.00
34	Joe Morgan	75.00	37.50	22.50
35	Rusty Staub	150.00	75.00	35.00
36	Ernie Banks (DP)	135.00	65.00	32.00
37	Billy Williams	75.00	37.50	22.50
38	Lou Piniella	80.00	40.00	24.00
39	Rico Petrocelli (DP)	35.00	17.50	10.00
40	Carl Yastrzemski (DP)	95.00	47.50	210.00
41	Willie Mays (DP)	225.00	115.00	60.00
42	Tommy Harper	45.00	22.50	13.50
43	Jim Bunning (DP)	60.00	30.00	10.00
44	Fritz Peterson	60.00	30.00	18.00
45	Roy White	75.00	37.50	22.50
46	Bobby Murcer	165.00	80.00	50.00
47	Reggie Jackson	850.00	425.00	220.00
48	Frank Howard	60.00	30.00	18.00
49	Dick Bosman	50.00	25.00	15.00
50	Sam McDowell (DP)	45.00	12.50	10.00
51	Luis Aparicio (DP)	45.00	22.50	13.50
52	Willie McCovey (DP)	65.00	32.50	20.00
53	Joe Pepitone	250.00	125.00	60.00
54	Jerry Grote	140.00	70.00	35.00
55	Bud Harrelson	140.00	70.00	35.00

1971 Topps Scratch-Offs

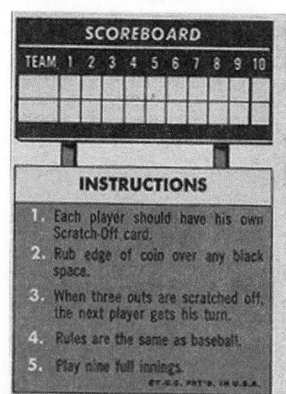

For a second year in 1971, Topps continued its scratch-off baseball card game with the same checklist of 24 players from the previous year. Unfolded, cards measure 3-3/8" x 5", and reveal a baseball game played by rubbing the black ink off squares to determine the "action." Fronts of the cards have a player picture as "captain," while backs have instructions and a scoreboard. Inserts with white centers are from 1970 while those with red centers are from 1971.

	NM	E	VG
Complete Set (24):	65.00	32.50	20.00

	Common Player:	1.50	.75	.45
(1)	Hank Aaron	7.50	3.75	2.25
(2)	Rich Allen	2.00	1.00	.60
(3)	Luis Aparicio	3.50	1.75	1.00
(4)	Sal Bando	1.50	.75	.45
(5)	Glenn Beckert	1.50	.75	.45
(6)	Dick Bosman	1.50	.75	.45
(7)	Nate Colbert	1.50	.75	.45
(8)	Mike Hegan	1.50	.75	.45
(9)	Mack Jones	1.50	.75	.45
(10)	Al Kaline	5.00	2.50	1.50
(11)	Harmon Killebrew	5.00	2.50	1.50
(12)	Juan Marichal	3.50	1.75	1.00
(13)	Tim McCarver	2.00	1.00	.60
(14)	Sam McDowell	1.50	.75	.45
(15)	Claude Osteen	1.50	.75	.45
(16)	Tony Perez	3.50	1.75	1.00
(17)	Lou Piniella	1.50	.75	.45
(18)	Boog Powell	2.00	1.00	.60
(19)	Tom Seaver	5.00	2.50	1.50
(20)	Jim Spencer	1.50	.75	.45
(21)	Willie Stargell	3.50	1.75	1.00
(22)	Mel Stottlemyre	1.50	.75	.45
(23)	Jim Wynn	1.50	.75	.45
(24)	Carl Yastrzemski	5.00	2.50	1.50

1971 Topps Super

 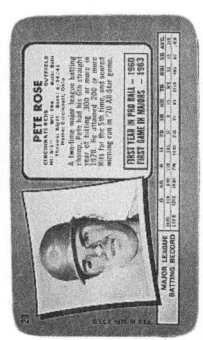

Topps continued to produce its special oversized cards in 1971. Measuring 3-1/8" x 5-1/4" with rounded corners, they feature a borderless color photograph with a facsimile autograph on front. Backs are basically enlargements of the player's regular Topps card. The set size was enlarged to 63 cards in 1971, so there are no short-printed cards as in 1970. Proof cards with square corners and blank backs, measuring about 3-3/8" x 5-1/2", are known.

	NM	E	VG
Complete Set (63):	300.00	150.00	90.00
Common Player:	3.00	1.50	.90
Wax Pack (3):	50.00		
Proofs: 1-2X			

1	Reggie Smith	3.00	1.50	.90
2	Gaylord Perry	7.50	3.75	2.25
3	Ted Savage	3.00	1.50	.90
4	Donn Clendenon	3.00	1.50	.90
5	Boog Powell	4.50	2.25	1.25
6	Tony Perez	7.50	3.75	2.25
7	Dick Bosman	3.00	1.50	.90
8	Alex Johnson	3.00	1.50	.90
9	Rusty Staub	3.50	1.75	1.00
10	Mel Stottlemyre	3.00	1.50	.90
11	Tony Oliva	4.00	2.00	1.25
12	Bill Freehan	3.00	1.50	.90
13	Fritz Peterson	3.00	1.50	.90
14	Wes Parker	3.00	1.50	.90
15	Cesar Cedeno	3.00	1.50	.90
16	Sam McDowell	3.00	1.50	.90
17	Frank Howard	3.00	1.50	.90
18	Dave McNally	3.00	1.50	.90
19	Rico Petrocelli	3.00	1.50	.90
20	Pete Rose	25.00	12.50	7.50
21	Luke Walker	3.00	1.50	.90
22	Nate Colbert	3.00	1.50	.90
23	Luis Aparicio	7.50	3.75	2.25
24	Jim Perry	3.00	1.50	.90
25	Louis Brock	9.00	4.50	2.75
26	Roy White	3.00	1.50	.90
27	Claude Osteen	3.00	1.50	.90
28	Carl W. Morton	3.00	1.50	.90
29	Rico Carty	3.00	1.50	.90
30	Larry Dierker	3.00	1.50	.90
31	Bert Campaneris	3.00	1.50	.90
32	Johnny Bench	10.00	5.00	3.00
33	Felix Millan	3.00	1.50	.90
34	Tim McCarver	3.50	1.75	1.00
35	Ronald Santo	6.00	3.00	1.75

36	Tommie Agee	3.00	1.50	.90
37	Roberto Clemente	40.00	20.00	12.00
38	Reggie Jackson	20.00	10.00	6.00
39	Clyde Wright	3.00	1.50	.90
40	Rich Allen	4.50	2.25	1.25
41	Curt Flood	3.50	1.75	1.00
42	Fergie Jenkins	7.50	3.75	2.25
43	Willie Stargell	9.00	4.50	2.75
44	Henry Aaron	25.00	12.50	7.50
45	Amos Otis	3.00	1.50	.90
46	Willie McCovey	9.00	4.50	2.75
47	William Melton	3.00	1.50	.90
48	Bob Gibson	9.00	4.50	2.75
49	Carl Yastrzemski	12.00	6.00	3.50
50	Glenn Beckert	3.00	1.50	.90
51	Ray Fosse	3.00	1.50	.90
52	Clarence Gaston	3.00	1.50	.90
53	Tom Seaver	10.00	5.00	3.00
54	Al Kaline	10.00	5.00	3.00
55	Jim Northrup	3.00	1.50	.90
56	Willie Mays	25.00	12.50	7.50
57	Sal Bando	3.00	1.50	.90
58	Deron Johnson	3.00	1.50	.90
59	Brooks Robinson	10.00	5.00	3.00
60	Harmon Killebrew	9.00	4.50	2.75
61	Joseph Torre	4.50	2.25	1.25
62	Lou Piniella	4.50	2.25	1.25
63	Tommy Harper	3.00	1.50	.90

1971 Topps Tattoos

Topps once again produced baseball tattoos in 1971. This time, the tattoos came in a variety of sizes, shapes and themes. The sheets of tattoos measure 3-1/2" x 14-1/4". Each sheet contains an assortment of tattoos in two sizes, 1-3/4" x 2-3/8", or 1-3/16" x 1-3/4". There are players, facsimile autographed baseballs, team pennants and assorted baseball cartoon figures carried on the 16 different sheets. Listings below are for complete sheets; with the exception of the biggest-name stars, individual tattoos have little or no collector value.

	NM	E	VG
Complete Sheet Set (16):	350.00	175.00	100.00
Common Sheet:	10.00	5.00	3.00
Unopened Pack:	25.00		

1	San Francisco Giants Pennant (Sal Bando, Dick Bosman, Nate Colbert, Cleon Jones, Juan Marichal)	25.00	12.50	7.50
2	New York Mets Pennant (Glenn Beckert, Tommy Harper, Ken Henderson, Fritz Peterson, Bob Robertson, Carl Yastrzemski)	35.00	17.50	10.00
3	Philadelphia Phillies Pennant (Orlando Cepeda, Jim Fregosi, Randy Hundley, Reggie Jackson, Jerry Koosman, Jim Palmer)	35.00	17.50	10.00
4	Sam McDowell Autograph (Dick Dietz, Cito Gaston, Dave Johnson, Sam McDowell, Gary Nolan, Amos Otis)	10.00	5.00	3.00

		NM	E	VG
5	L.A. Dodgers Pennant (Bill Grabarkewitz, Al Kaline, Lee May, Tom Murphy, Vada Pinson, Manny Sanguillen)	20.00	10.00	6.00
6	Harmon Killebrew Autograph (Luis Aparicio, Paul Blair, Chris Cannizzaro, Donn Clendenon, Larry Dieker, Harmon Killebrew)	25.00	12.50	7.50
7	Milwaukee Brewers Pennant (Rich Allen, Bert Campaneris, Don Money, Boog Powell, Ted Savage, Rusty Staub)	15.00	7.50	4.50
8	San Diego Padres Pennant (Leo Cardenas, Bill Hands, Frank Howard, Wes Parker, Reggie Smith, Willie Stargell)	10.00	5.00	3.00
9	Henry Aaron Autograph (Hank Aaron, Tommy Agee, Jim Hunter, Dick McAuliffe, Tony Perez, Lou Piniella)	35.00	17.50	10.00
10	Fergie Jenkins Autograph (Roberto Clemente, Tony Conigliaro, Fergie Jenkins, Thurman Munson, Gary Peters, Joe Torre)	50.00	25.00	15.00
11	Washington Senators Pennant (Johnny Bench, Rico Carty, Bill Mazeroski, Bob Oliver, Rico Petrocelli, Frank Robinson)	35.00	17.50	10.00
12	Houston Astros Pennant (Bill Freehan, Dave McNally, Felix Millan, Mel Stottlemyre, Bob Tolan, Billy Williams)	15.00	7.50	4.50
13	Willie McCovey Autograph (Ray Culp, Bud Harrelson, Mickey Lolich, Willie McCovey, Ron Santo, Roy White)	20.00	10.00	6.00
14	Tom Seaver Autograph (Bill Melton, Jim Perry, Pete Rose, Tom Seaver, Maury Wills, Clyde Wright)	45.00	22.00	13.50
15	St. Louis Cardinals Pennant (Rod Carew, Bob Gibson, Alex Johnson, Don Kessinger, Jim Merritt, Rick Monday)	20.00	10.00	6.00
16	Willie Mays Autograph (Larry Bowa, Mike Cuellar, Ray Fosse, Willie Mays, Carl Morton, Tony Oliva)	25.00	12.50	7.50

1972 Topps

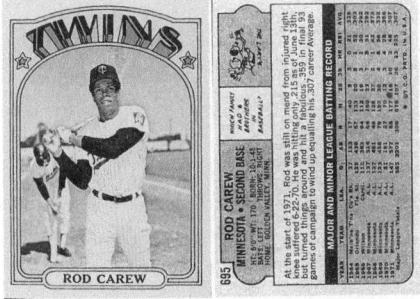

ROD CAREW

The largest Topps issue of its time appeared in 1972, with the set size reaching the 787 mark. The 2-1/2" x 3-1/2" cards are something special as well. Their fronts have a color photo which is shaped into an arch and surrounded by two different color borders, all of which is inside the overall white border. The player's name is in a white panel below the picture while the team name is above the picture in what might best be described as "superhero" type in a variety of colors. No mention of the player's position appears on the front. Cards backs are tame by comparison, featuring statistics and a trivia question. The set features a record number of specialty cards including more than six dozen "In Action" (shown as "IA" in checklists below) cards featuring action shots of popular players. There are the usual statistical leaders, playoff and World Series highlights. Other innovations are 16 "Boyhood Photo" cards which depict scrapbook black and white photos of 1972's top players, and a group of cards depicting the trophies which comprise baseball's major awards. Finally, a group of seven "Traded" cards was included which feature a large "Traded" across the front of the card.

	NM	E	VG
Complete Set (787):	1,500	750.00	450.00
Common Player (1-525):	1.50	.70	.45
Common Player (526-656):	4.00	2.00	1.00
Common Player (657-787):	12.00	6.00	3.00

		NM	E	VG
1	Pirates Team (World Champions)	8.00	4.00	2.50
2	Ray Culp	1.50	.70	.45
3	Bob Tolan	1.50	.70	.45
4	1st Series Checklist (1-132)	4.00	2.00	1.25
5	John Bateman	1.50	.70	.45
6	Fred Scherman	1.50	.70	.45
7	Enzo Hernandez	1.50	.70	.45
8	Ron Swoboda	1.50	.70	.45
9	Stan Williams	1.50	.70	.45
10	Amos Otis	1.50	.70	.45
11	Bobby Valentine	1.50	.70	.45
12	Jose Cardenal	1.50	.70	.45
13	Joe Grzenda	1.50	.70	.45
14	Phillies Rookies (Mike Anderson, Pete Koegel, Wayne Twitchell)	1.50	.70	.45
15	Walt Williams	1.50	.70	.45
16	Mike Jorgensen	1.50	.70	.45
17	Dave Duncan	1.50	.70	.45
18a	Juan Pizarro (Green under "C" and "S.")	7.50	3.75	2.25
18b	Juan Pizarro (Yellow under "C" and "S.")	1.50	.70	.45
19	Billy Cowan	1.50	.70	.45
20	Don Wilson	1.50	.70	.45
21	Braves Team	3.00	1.50	.90
22	Rob Gardner	1.50	.70	.45
23	Ted Kubiak	1.50	.70	.45
24	Ted Ford	1.50	.70	.45
25	Bill Singer	1.50	.70	.45
26	Andy Etchebarren	1.50	.70	.45
27	Bob Johnson	1.50	.70	.45
28	Twins Rookies (Steve Brye, Bob Gebhard, Hal Haydel)	1.50	.70	.45
29a	Bill Bonham (Green under "C" and "S.")	7.50	3.75	2.25
29b	Bill Bonham (Yellow under "C" and "S.")	1.50	.70	.45
30	Rico Petrocelli	1.50	.70	.45
31	Cleon Jones	1.50	.70	.45
32	Cleon Jones (In Action)	1.50	.70	.45
33	Billy Martin	6.00	3.00	1.75
34	Billy Martin (In Action)	2.00	1.00	.60
35	Jerry Johnson	1.50	.70	.45
36	Jerry Johnson (In Action)	1.50	.70	.45
37	Carl Yastrzemski	13.50	6.00	3.00
38	Carl Yastrzemski (In Action)	7.50	3.75	2.00
39	Bob Barton	1.50	.70	.45
40	Bob Barton (In Action)	1.50	.70	.45
41	Tommy Davis	1.50	.70	.45
42	Tommy Davis (In Action)	1.50	.70	.45
43	Rick Wise	1.50	.70	.45
44	Rick Wise (In Action)	1.50	.70	.45
45a	Glenn Beckert (Green under "C" and "S.")	7.50	3.75	2.25
45b	Glenn Beckert (Yellow under "C" and "S.")	1.50	.70	.45
46	Glenn Beckert (In Action)	1.50	.70	.45
47	John Ellis	1.50	.70	.45
48	John Ellis (In Action)	1.50	.70	.45
49	Willie Mays	50.00	25.00	12.50
50	Willie Mays (In Action)	20.00	10.00	6.00
51	Harmon Killebrew	8.00	4.00	2.50
52	Harmon Killebrew (In Action)	5.00	2.50	1.50
53	Bud Harrelson	1.50	.70	.45
54	Bud Harrelson (In Action)	1.50	.70	.45
55	Clyde Wright	1.50	.70	.45
56	Rich Chiles	1.50	.70	.45
57	Bob Oliver	1.50	.70	.45
58	Ernie McAnally	1.50	.70	.45
59	Fred Stanley RC	1.50	.70	.45
60	Manny Sanguillen	1.50	.70	.45
61	Cubs Rookies (Gene Hiser, Burt Hooton RC, Earl Stephenson)	1.50	.70	.45
62	Angel Mangual	1.50	.70	.45
63	Duke Sims	1.50	.70	.45
64	Pete Broberg	1.50	.70	.45
65	Cesar Cedeno	1.50	.70	.45
66	Ray Corbin	1.50	.70	.45
67	Red Schoendienst	4.00	2.00	1.25
68	Jim York	1.50	.70	.45
69	Roger Freed	1.50	.70	.45
70	Mike Cuellar	1.50	.70	.45
71	Angels Team	3.00	1.50	.90
72	Bruce Kison RC	1.50	.70	.45
73	Steve Huntz	1.50	.70	.45
74	Cecil Upshaw	1.50	.70	.45
75	Bert Campaneris	1.50	.70	.45
76	Don Carrithers	1.50	.70	.45
77	Ron Theobald	1.50	.70	.45
78	Steve Arlin	1.50	.70	.45
79	Red Sox Rookies (Cecil Cooper RC, Carlton Fisk RC, Mike Garman)	60.00	30.00	15.00
80	Tony Perez	6.00	3.00	1.75
81	Mike Hedlund	1.50	.70	.45
82	Ron Woods	1.50	.70	.45
83	Dalton Jones	1.50	.70	.45
84	Vince Colbert	1.50	.70	.45
85	N.L. Batting Leaders (Glenn Beckert, Ralph Garr, Joe Torre)	4.00	2.00	1.25
86	A.L. Batting Leaders (Bobby Murcer, Tony Oliva, Merv Rettenmund)	3.00	1.50	.90
87	N.L. R.B.I. Leaders (Hank Aaron, Willie Stargell, Joe Torre)	6.00	3.00	1.75
88	A.L. R.B.I. Leaders (Harmon Killebrew, Frank Robinson, Reggie Smith)	3.00	1.50	.90
89	N.L. Home Run Leaders (Hank Aaron, Lee May, Willie Stargell)	6.00	3.00	1.75
90	A.L. Home Run Leaders (Norm Cash, Reggie Jackson, Bill Melton)	5.00	2.50	1.25
91	N.L. E.R.A. Leaders (Dave Roberts (picture is Denny Coombs), Tom Seaver, Don Wilson)	2.50	1.25	.70
92	A.L. E.R.A. Leaders (Vida Blue, Jim Palmer, Wilbur Wood)	2.00	1.00	.60
93	N.L. Pitching Leaders (Steve Carlton, Al Downing, Fergie Jenkins, Tom Seaver)	4.00	2.00	1.25
94	A.L. Pitching Leaders (Vida Blue, Mickey Lolich, Wilbur Wood)	1.50	.70	.45
95	N.L. Strikeout Leaders (Fergie Jenkins, Tom Seaver, Bill Stoneman)	4.00	2.00	1.25
96	A.L. Strikeout Leaders (Vida Blue, Joe Coleman, Mickey Lolich)	1.50	.70	.45
97	Tom Kelley	1.50	.70	.45
98	Chuck Tanner	1.50	.70	.45
99	Ross Grimsley RC	1.50	.70	.45
100	Frank Robinson	12.00	8.00	4.75
101	Astros Rookies (Ray Busse, Bill Grief, J.R. Richard RC)	4.00	2.00	1.25
102	Lloyd Allen	1.50	.70	.45
103	2nd Series Checklist (133-263)	2.00	1.00	.60
104	Toby Harrah RC	1.50	.70	.45
105	Gary Gentry	1.50	.70	.45
106	Brewers Team	3.00	1.50	.90
107	Jose Cruz RC	3.00	1.50	.90
108	Gary Waslewski	1.50	.70	.45
109	Jerry May	1.50	.70	.45
110	Ron Hunt	1.50	.70	.45
111	Jim Grant	1.50	.70	.45
112	Greg Luzinski	1.50	.70	.45
113	Rogelio Moret	1.50	.70	.45
114	Bill Buckner	1.50	.70	.45
115	Jim Fregosi	1.50	.70	.45
116	Ed Farmer RC	1.50	.70	.45
117a	Cleo James (Green under "C" and "S.")	7.50	3.75	2.25
117b	Cleo James (Yellow under "C" and "S.")	1.50	.70	.45
118	Skip Lockwood	1.50	.70	.45
119	Marty Perez	1.50	.70	.45
120	Bill Freehan	1.50	.70	.45
121	Ed Sprague	1.50	.70	.45
122	Larry Biittner	1.50	.70	.45
123	Ed Acosta	1.50	.70	.45
124	Yankees Rookies (Alan Closter, Roger Hambright, Rusty Torres)	1.50	.70	.45
125	Dave Cash	1.50	.70	.45
126	Bart Johnson	1.50	.70	.45
127	Duffy Dyer	1.50	.70	.45
128	Eddie Watt	1.50	.70	.45
129	Charlie Fox	1.50	.70	.45
130	Bob Gibson	11.00	5.50	2.75

131	Jim Nettles	1.50	.70	.45
132	Joe Morgan	10.00	5.00	3.00
133	Joe Keough	1.50	.70	.45
134	Carl Morton	1.50	.70	.45
135	Vada Pinson	2.50	1.25	.70
136	Darrel Chaney	1.50	.70	.45
137	Dick Williams	1.50	.70	.45
138	Mike Kekich	1.50	.70	.45
139	Tim McCarver	3.00	1.50	.90
140	Pat Dobson	1.50	.70	.45
141	Mets Rookies (Buzz Capra, Jon Matlack, Leroy Stanton)	1.50	.70	.45
142	Chris Chambliss **RC**	3.00	1.50	.90
143	Garry Jestadt	1.50	.70	.45
144	Marty Pattin	1.50	.70	.45
145	Don Kessinger	1.50	.70	.45
146	Steve Kealey	1.50	.70	.45
147	Dave Kingman **RC**	6.00	3.00	1.75
148	Dick Billings	1.50	.70	.45
149	Gary Neibauer	1.50	.70	.45
150	Norm Cash	2.50	1.25	.70
151	Jim Brewer	1.50	.70	.45
152	Gene Clines	1.50	.70	.45
153	Rick Auerbach	1.50	.70	.45
154	Ted Simmons	4.00	2.00	1.25
155	Larry Dierker	1.50	.70	.45
156	Twins Team	3.00	1.50	.90
157	Don Gullett	1.50	.70	.45
158	Jerry Kenney	1.50	.70	.45
159	John Boccabella	1.50	.70	.45
160	Andy Messersmith	1.50	.70	.45
161	Brock Davis	1.50	.70	.45
162	Brewers Rookies (Jerry Bell, Darrell Porter **RC**, Bob Reynolds) (Bell and Porter photos transposed.)	1.50	.70	.45
163	Tug McGraw	1.50	.70	.45
164	Tug McGraw (In Action)	1.50	.70	.45
165	Chris Speier **RC**	1.50	.70	.45
166	Chris Speier (In Action)	1.50	.70	.45
167	Deron Johnson	1.50	.70	.45
168	Deron Johnson (In Action)	1.50	.70	.45
169	Vida Blue	4.00	2.00	1.25
170	Vida Blue (In Action)	2.00	1.00	.60
171	Darrell Evans	3.00	1.50	.90
172	Darrell Evans (In Action)	2.00	1.00	.60
173	Clay Kirby	1.50	.70	.45
174	Clay Kirby (In Action)	1.50	.70	.45
175	Tom Haller	1.50	.70	.45
176	Tom Haller (In Action)	1.50	.70	.45
177	Paul Schaal	1.50	.70	.45
178	Paul Schaal (In Action)	1.50	.70	.45
179	Dock Ellis	1.50	.70	.45
180	Dock Ellis (In Action)	1.50	.70	.45
181	Ed Kranepool	1.50	.70	.45
182	Ed Kranepool (In Action)	1.50	.70	.45
183	Bill Melton	1.50	.70	.45
184	Bill Melton (In Action)	1.50	.70	.45
185	Ron Bryant	1.50	.70	.45
186	Ron Bryant (In Action)	1.50	.70	.45
187	Gates Brown	1.50	.70	.45
188	Frank Lucchesi	1.50	.70	.45
189	Gene Tenace	1.50	.70	.45
190	Dave Giusti	1.50	.70	.45
191	Jeff Burroughs **RC**	3.00	1.50	.90
192	**Cubs Team**	4.00	2.00	1.25
193	Kurt Bevacqua **RC**	1.50	.70	.45
194	Fred Norman	1.50	.70	.45
195	Orlando Cepeda	8.00	4.00	2.50
196	Mel Queen	1.50	.70	.45
197	Johnny Briggs	1.50	.70	.45
198	Dodgers Rookies (Charlie Hough **RC**, Bob O'Brien, Mike Strahler)	5.00	2.50	1.50
199	Mike Fiore	1.50	.70	.45
200	Lou Brock	8.00	4.00	2.50
201	Phil Roof	1.50	.70	.45
202	Scipio Spinks	1.50	.70	.45
203	Ron Blomberg **RC**	2.50	1.25	.70
204	Tommy Helms	1.50	.70	.45
205	Dick Drago	1.50	.70	.45
206	Dal Maxvill	1.50	.70	.45
207	Tom Egan	1.50	.70	.45
208	Milt Pappas	1.50	.70	.45
209	Joe Rudi	1.50	.70	.45
210	Denny McLain	3.00	1.50	.90
211	Gary Sutherland	1.50	.70	.45
212	Grant Jackson	1.50	.70	.45
213	Angels Rookies (Art Kusnyer, Billy Parker, Tom Silverio)	1.50	.70	.45
214	Mike McQueen	1.50	.70	.45
215	Alex Johnson	1.50	.70	.45
216	Joe Niekro	1.50	.70	.45
217	Roger Metzger	1.50	.70	.45
218	Eddie Kasko	1.50	.70	.45
219	Rennie Stennett **RC**	1.50	.70	.45
220	Jim Perry	1.50	.70	.45

221	N.L. Playoffs (Bucs Champs)	4.00	2.00	1.25
222	A.L. Playoffs (Orioles Champs)	5.00	2.50	1.50
223	World Series Game 1	4.00	2.00	1.25
224	World Series Game 2	4.00	2.00	1.25
225	World Series Game 3	4.00	2.00	1.25
226	World Series Game 4 (Roberto Clemente)	12.50	6.25	3.50
227	World Series Game 5	4.00	2.00	1.25
228	World Series Game 6	4.00	2.00	1.25
229	World Series Game 7	4.00	2.00	1.25
230	Series Celebration (On Top of the World)	4.00	2.00	1.25
231	Casey Cox	1.50	.70	.45
232	Giants Rookies (Chris Arnold, Jim Barr, Dave Rader)	1.50	.70	.45
233	Jay Johnstone	1.50	.70	.45
234	Ron Taylor	1.50	.70	.45
235	Merv Rettenmund	1.50	.70	.45
236	Jim McGlothlin	1.50	.70	.45
237	Yankees Team	4.00	2.00	1.25
238	Leron Lee	1.50	.70	.45
239	Tom Timmermann	1.50	.70	.45
240	Rich Allen	3.00	1.50	.90
241	Rollie Fingers	6.00	3.00	1.75
242	Don Mincher	1.50	.70	.45
243	Frank Linzy	1.50	.70	.45
244	Steve Braun	1.50	.70	.45
245	Tommie Agee	1.50	.70	.45
246	Tom Burgmeier	1.50	.70	.45
247	Milt May	1.50	.70	.45
248	Tom Bradley	1.50	.70	.45
249	Harry Walker	1.50	.70	.45
250	Boog Powell	2.00	1.00	.60
251a	3rd Series Checklist (264-394) (Small print on front.)	3.00	1.50	.90
251b	3rd Series Checklist (264-394) (Large print on front.)	3.00	1.50	.90
252	Ken Reynolds	1.50	.70	.45
253	Sandy Alomar	1.50	.70	.45
254	Boots Day	1.50	.70	.45
255	Jim Lonborg	1.50	.70	.45
256	George Foster	2.50	1.25	.70
257	Tigers Rookies (Jim Foor, Tim Hosley, Paul Jata)	1.50	.70	.45
258	Randy Hundley	1.50	.70	.45
259	Sparky Lyle	1.50	.70	.45
260	Ralph Garr	1.50	.70	.45
261	Steve Mingori	1.50	.70	.45
262	Padres Team	3.00	1.50	.90
263	Felipe Alou	2.00	1.00	.60
264	Tommy John	2.00	1.00	.60
265	Wes Parker	1.50	.70	.45
266	Bobby Bolin	1.50	.70	.45
267	Dave Concepcion	2.00	1.00	.60
268	A's Rookies (Dwain Anderson, Chris Floethe)	1.50	.70	.45
269	Don Hahn	1.50	.70	.45
270	Jim Palmer	8.00	4.00	2.50
271	Ken Rudolph	1.50	.70	.45
272	Mickey Rivers **RC**	2.00	1.00	.60
273	Bobby Floyd	1.50	.70	.45
274	Al Severinsen	1.50	.70	.45
275	Cesar Tovar	1.50	.70	.45
276	Gene Mauch	1.50	.70	.45
277	Elliott Maddox	1.50	.70	.45
278	Dennis Higgins	1.50	.70	.45
279	Larry Brown	1.50	.70	.45
280	Willie McCovey	8.00	4.00	2.50
281	Bill Parsons	1.50	.70	.45
282	**Astros Team**	4.00	2.00	1.25
283	Darrell Brandon	1.50	.70	.45
284	Ike Brown	1.50	.70	.45
285	Gaylord Perry	6.00	3.00	1.75
286	Gene Alley	1.50	.70	.45
287	Jim Hardin	1.50	.70	.45
288	Johnny Jeter	1.50	.70	.45
289	Syd O'Brien	1.50	.70	.45
290	Sonny Siebert	1.50	.70	.45
291	Hal McRae	2.50	1.25	.70
292	Hal McRae (In Action)	1.50	.70	.45
293	Danny Frisella	1.50	.70	.45
294	Danny Frisella (In Action)	1.50	.70	.45
295	Dick Dietz	1.50	.70	.45
296	Dick Dietz (In Action)	1.50	.70	.45
297	Claude Osteen	1.50	.70	.45
298	Claude Osteen (In Action)	1.50	.70	.45
299	Hank Aaron	40.00	20.00	12.00
300	Hank Aaron (In Action)	25.00	12.50	7.50
301	George Mitterwald	1.50	.70	.45
302	George Mitterwald (In Action)	1.50	.70	.45
303	Joe Pepitone	2.00	1.00	.60
304	Joe Pepitone (In Action)	1.50	.70	.45
305	Ken Boswell	1.50	.70	.45
306	Ken Boswell (In Action)	1.50	.70	.45
307	Steve Renko	1.50	.70	.45
308	Steve Renko (In Action)	1.50	.70	.45

309	Roberto Clemente	40.00	20.00	12.00
310	Roberto Clemente (In Action)	24.00	12.00	7.50
311	Clay Carroll	1.50	.70	.45
312	Clay Carroll (In Action)	1.50	.70	.45
313	Luis Aparicio	6.00	3.00	1.75
314	Luis Aparicio (In Action)	4.00	2.00	1.25
315	Paul Splittorff	1.50	.70	.45
316	Cardinals Rookies (Jim Bibby **RC**, Santiago Guzman, Jorge Roque)	1.50	.70	.45
317	Rich Hand	1.50	.70	.45
318	Sonny Jackson	1.50	.70	.45
319	Aurelio Rodriguez	1.50	.70	.45
320	Steve Blass	1.50	.70	.45
321	Joe Lahoud	1.50	.70	.45
322	Jose Pena	1.50	.70	.45
323	Earl Weaver	5.00	2.50	1.50
324	Mike Ryan	1.50	.70	.45
325	Mel Stottlemyre	1.50	.70	.45
326	Pat Kelly	1.50	.70	.45
327	Steve Stone **RC**	3.00	1.50	.90
328	Red Sox Team	5.00	2.50	1.50
329	Roy Foster	1.50	.70	.45
330	Jim Hunter	6.00	3.00	1.75
331	Stan Swanson	1.50	.70	.45
332	Buck Martinez	1.50	.70	.45
333	Steve Barber	1.50	.70	.45
334	Rangers Rookies (Bill Fahey, Jim Mason, Tom Ragland)	1.50	.70	.45
335	Bill Hands	1.50	.70	.45
336	Marty Martinez	1.50	.70	.45
337	Mike Kilkenny	1.50	.70	.45
338	Bob Grich	1.50	.70	.45
339	Ron Cook	1.50	.70	.45
340	Roy White	1.50	.70	.45
341	Joe Torre (Boyhood Photo)	2.50	1.25	.70
342	Wilbur Wood (Boyhood Photo)	1.50	.70	.45
343	Willie Stargell (Boyhood Photo)	2.00	1.00	.60
344	Dave McNally (Boyhood Photo)	1.50	.70	.45
345	Rick Wise (Boyhood Photo)	1.50	.70	.45
346	Jim Fregosi (Boyhood Photo)	1.50	.70	.45
347	Tom Seaver (Boyhood Photo)	3.00	1.50	.90
348	Sal Bando (Boyhood Photo)	1.50	.70	.45
349	Al Fitzmorris	1.50	.70	.45
350	Frank Howard	2.00	1.00	.60
351	Braves Rookies (Jimmy Britton, Tom House, Rick Kester)	1.50	.70	.45
352	Dave LaRoche	1.50	.70	.45
353	Art Shamsky	1.50	.70	.45
354	Tom Murphy	1.50	.70	.45
355	Bob Watson	1.50	.70	.45
356	Gerry Moses	1.50	.70	.45
357	Woodie Fryman	1.50	.70	.45
358	Sparky Anderson	4.00	2.00	1.25
359	Don Pavletich	1.50	.70	.45
360	Dave Roberts	1.50	.70	.45
361	Mike Andrews	1.50	.70	.45
362	Mets Team	4.00	2.00	1.25
363	Ron Klimkowski	1.50	.70	.45
364	Johnny Callison	1.50	.70	.45
365	Dick Bosman	1.50	.70	.45
366	Jimmy Rosario	1.50	.70	.45
367	Ron Perranoski	1.50	.70	.45
368	Danny Thompson	1.50	.70	.45
369	Jim Lefebvre	1.50	.70	.45
370	Don Buford	1.50	.70	.45
371	Denny Lemaster	1.50	.70	.45
372	Royals Rookies (Lance Clemons, Monty Montgomery)	1.50	.70	.45
373	John Mayberry	1.50	.70	.45
374	Jack Heidemann	1.50	.70	.45
375	Reggie Cleveland	1.50	.70	.45
376	Andy Kosco	1.50	.70	.45
377	Terry Harmon	1.50	.70	.45
378	4th Series Checklist (395-525)	3.00	1.50	.90
379	Ken Berry	1.50	.70	.45
380	Earl Williams	1.50	.70	.45
381	White Sox Team	3.00	1.50	.90
382	Joe Gibbon	1.50	.70	.45
383	Brant Alyea	1.50	.70	.45
384	Dave Campbell	1.50	.70	.45
385	Mickey Stanley	1.50	.70	.45
386	Jim Colborn	1.50	.70	.45
387	Horace Clarke	1.50	.70	.45
388	Charlie Williams	1.50	.70	.45
389	Bill Rigney	1.50	.70	.45
390	Willie Davis	1.50	.70	.45
391	Ken Sanders	1.50	.70	.45
392	Pirates Rookies (Fred Cambria, Richie Zisk **RC**)	2.00	1.00	.60
393	Curt Motton	1.50	.70	.45
394	Ken Forsch	1.50	.70	.45

395	Matty Alou	1.50	.70	.45
396	Paul Lindblad	1.50	.70	.45
397	Phillies Team	4.00	2.00	1.25
398	Larry Hisle	2.00	1.00	.60
399	Milt Wilcox	1.50	.70	.45
400	Tony Oliva	3.00	1.50	.90
401	Jim Nash	1.50	.70	.45
402	Bobby Heise	1.50	.70	.45
403	John Cumberland	1.50	.70	.45
404	Jeff Torborg	1.50	.70	.45
405	Ron Fairly	1.50	.70	.45
406	George Hendrick **RC**	2.00	1.00	.60
407	Chuck Taylor	1.50	.70	.45
408	Jim Northrup	1.50	.70	.45
409	Frank Baker	1.50	.70	.45
410	Fergie Jenkins	6.00	3.00	1.75
411	Bob Montgomery	1.50	.70	.45
412	Dick Kelley	1.50	.70	.45
413	White Sox Rookies(Don Eddy, Dave Lemonds)	1.50	.70	.45
414	Bob Miller	1.50	.70	.45
415	Cookie Rojas	1.50	.70	.45
416	Johnny Edwards	1.50	.70	.45
417	Tom Hall	1.50	.70	.45
418	Tom Shopay	1.50	.70	.45
419	Jim Spencer	1.50	.70	.45
420	Steve Carlton	15.00	7.50	4.50
421	Ellie Rodriguez	1.50	.70	.45
422	Ray Lamb	1.50	.70	.45
423	Oscar Gamble	1.50	.70	.45
424	Bill Gogolewski	1.50	.70	.45
425	Ken Singleton	1.50	.70	.45
426	Ken Singleton (In Action)	1.50	.70	.45
427	Tito Fuentes	1.50	.70	.45
428	Tito Fuentes (In Action)	1.50	.70	.45
429	Bob Robertson	1.50	.70	.45
430	Bob Robertson (In Action)	1.50	.70	.45
431	Clarence Gaston	1.50	.70	.45
432	Clarence Gaston (In Action)	1.50	.70	.45
433	Johnny Bench	25.00	12.50	6.25
434	Johnny Bench (In Action)	15.00	7.50	3.75
435	Reggie Jackson	25.00	12.50	7.50
436	Reggie Jackson (In Action)	10.00	5.00	2.50
437	Maury Wills	1.50	.70	.45
438	Maury Wills (In Action)	1.50	.70	.45
439	Billy Williams	8.00	4.00	2.50
440	Billy Williams (In Action)	5.00	2.50	1.50
441	Thurman Munson	25.00	12.50	6.25
442	Thurman Munson (In Action)	10.00	5.00	3.00
443	Ken Henderson	1.50	.70	.45
444	Ken Henderson (In Action)	1.50	.70	.45
445	Tom Seaver	20.00	10.00	6.00
446	Tom Seaver (In Action)	10.00	5.00	2.50
447	Willie Stargell	15.00	7.50	4.50
448	Willie Stargell (In Action)	7.50	3.75	2.25
449	Bob Lemon	4.00	2.00	1.25
450	Mickey Lolich	1.50	.70	.45
451	Tony LaRussa	2.50	1.25	.70
452	Ed Herrmann	1.50	.70	.45
453	Barry Lersch	1.50	.70	.45
454	**A's Team**	4.00	2.00	1.25
455	Tommy Harper	1.50	.70	.45
456	Mark Belanger	1.50	.70	.45
457	Padres Rookies(Darcy Fast, Mike Ivie, Derrel Thomas **RC**)	1.50	.70	.45
458	Aurelio Monteagudo	1.50	.70	.45
459	Rick Renick	1.50	.70	.45
460	Al Downing	1.50	.70	.45
461	Tim Cullen	1.50	.70	.45
462	Rickey Clark	1.50	.70	.45
463	Bernie Carbo	1.50	.70	.45
464	Jim Roland	1.50	.70	.45
465	Gil Hodges	4.00	2.00	1.25
466	Norm Miller	1.50	.70	.45
467	Steve Kline	1.50	.70	.45
468	Richie Scheinblum	1.50	.70	.45
469	Ron Herbel	1.50	.70	.45
470	Ray Fosse	1.50	.70	.45
471	Luke Walker	1.50	.70	.45
472	Phil Gagliano	1.50	.70	.45
473	Dan McGinn	1.50	.70	.45
474	Orioles Rookies (Don Baylor, Roric Harrison **RC**, Johnny Oates **RC**)	10.00	5.00	3.00
475	Gary Nolan	1.50	.70	.45
476	Lee Richard	1.50	.70	.45
477	Tom Phoebus	1.50	.70	.45
478a	5th Series Checklist (526-656) (Small print on front.)	2.50	1.25	.70
478b	5th Series Checklist (526-656) (Large printing on front.)	2.50	1.25	.70
479	Don Shaw	1.50	.70	.45
480	Lee May	1.50	.70	.45
481	Billy Conigliaro	1.50	.70	.45
482	Joe Hoerner	1.50	.70	.45
483	Ken Suarez	1.50	.70	.45
484	Lum Harris	1.50	.70	.45
485	Phil Regan	1.50	.70	.45
486	John Lowenstein	1.50	.70	.45
487	Tigers Team	5.00	2.50	1.50
488	Mike Nagy	1.50	.70	.45
489	Expos Rookies(Terry Humphrey, Keith Lampard)	1.50	.70	.45
490	Dave McNally	1.50	.70	.45
491	Lou Piniella (Boyhood Photo)	1.50	.70	.45
492	Mel Stottlemyre (Boyhood Photo)	1.50	.70	.45
493	Bob Bailey (Boyhood Photo)	1.50	.70	.45
494	Willie Horton (Boyhood Photo)	1.50	.70	.45
495	Bill Melton (Boyhood Photo)	1.50	.70	.45
496	Bud Harrelson (Boyhood Photo)	1.50	.70	.45
497	Jim Perry (Boyhood Photo)	1.50	.70	.45
498	Brooks Robinson (Boyhood Photo)	4.00	2.00	1.25
499	Vicente Romo	1.50	.70	.45
500	Joe Torre	5.00	2.50	1.50
501	Pete Hamm	1.50	.70	.45
502	Jackie Hernandez	1.50	.70	.45
503	Gary Peters	1.50	.70	.45
504	Ed Spiezio	1.50	.70	.45
505	Mike Marshall	1.50	.70	.45
506	Indians Rookies(Terry Ley, Jim Moyer, Dick Tidrow **RC**)	1.50	.70	.45
507	Fred Gladding	1.50	.70	.45
508	Ellie Hendricks	1.50	.70	.45
509	Don McMahon	1.50	.70	.45
510	Ted Williams	20.00	10.00	5.00
511	Tony Taylor	1.50	.70	.45
512	Paul Popovich	1.50	.70	.45
513	Lindy McDaniel	1.50	.70	.45
514	Ted Sizemore	1.50	.70	.45
515	Bert Blyleven	12.50	6.25	3.75
516	Oscar Brown	1.50	.70	.45
517	Ken Brett	1.50	.70	.45
518	Wayne Garrett	1.50	.70	.45
519	Ted Abernathy	1.50	.70	.45
520	Larry Bowa	1.50	.70	.45
521	Alan Foster	1.50	.70	.45
522	Dodgers Team	4.00	2.00	1.25
523	Chuck Dobson	1.50	.70	.45
524	Reds Rookies(Ed Armbrister, Mel Behney)	1.50	.70	.45
525	Carlos May	1.50	.70	.45
526	Bob Bailey	4.00	2.00	1.00
527	Dave Leonhard	4.00	2.00	1.00
528	Ron Stone	4.00	2.00	1.00
529	Dave Nelson	4.00	2.00	1.00
530	Don Sutton	10.00	5.00	3.00
531	Freddie Patek	5.00	2.50	1.25
532	Fred Kendall	4.00	2.00	1.00
533	Ralph Houk	6.00	3.00	1.75
534	Jim Hickman	4.00	2.00	1.00
535	Ed Brinkman	4.00	2.00	1.00
536	Doug Rader	4.00	2.00	1.00
537	Bob Locker	4.00	2.00	1.00
538	Charlie Sands	4.00	2.00	1.00
539	Terry Forster **RC**	5.00	2.50	1.25
540	Felix Millan	4.00	2.00	1.00
541	Roger Repoz	4.00	2.00	1.00
542	Jack Billingham	4.00	2.00	1.00
543	Duane Josephson	4.00	2.00	1.00
544	Ted Martinez	4.00	2.00	1.00
545	Wayne Granger	4.00	2.00	1.00
546	Joe Hague	4.00	2.00	1.00
547	Indians Team	6.00	3.00	1.75
548	Frank Reberger	4.00	2.00	1.00
549	Dave May	4.00	2.00	1.00
550	Brooks Robinson	20.00	10.00	5.00
551	Ollie Brown	4.00	2.00	1.00
552	Ollie Brown (In Action)	4.00	2.00	1.00
553	Wilbur Wood	4.00	2.00	1.00
554	Wilbur Wood (In Action)	4.00	2.00	1.00
555	Ron Santo	8.00	4.00	2.50
556	Ron Santo (In Action)	5.00	2.50	1.25
557	John Odom	4.00	2.00	1.00
558	John Odom (In Action)	4.00	2.00	1.00
559	Pete Rose	35.00	17.50	10.50
560	Pete Rose (In Action)	20.00	10.00	5.00
561	Leo Cardenas	4.00	2.00	1.00
562	Leo Cardenas (In Action)	4.00	2.00	1.00
563	Ray Sadecki	4.00	2.00	1.00
564	Ray Sadecki (In Action)	4.00	2.00	1.00
565	Reggie Smith	4.00	2.00	1.00
566	Reggie Smith (In Action)	4.00	2.00	1.00
567	Juan Marichal	10.00	5.00	3.00
568	Juan Marichal (In Action)	5.00	2.50	1.50
569	Ed Kirkpatrick	4.00	2.00	1.00
570	Ed Kirkpatrick (In Action)	4.00	2.00	1.00
571	Nate Colbert	4.00	2.00	1.00
572	Nate Colbert (In Action)	4.00	2.00	1.00
573	Fritz Peterson	4.00	2.00	1.00
574	Fritz Peterson (In Action)	4.00	2.00	1.00
575	Al Oliver	5.00	2.50	1.25
576	Leo Durocher	5.00	2.50	1.50
577	Mike Paul	4.00	2.00	1.00
578	Billy Grabarkewitz	4.00	2.00	1.00
579	Doyle Alexander **RC**	5.00	2.50	1.25
580	Lou Piniella	5.00	2.50	1.50
581	Wade Blasingame	4.00	2.00	1.00
582	Expos Team	6.00	3.00	1.75
583	Darold Knowles	4.00	2.00	1.00
584	Jerry McNertney	4.00	2.00	1.00
585	George Scott	4.00	2.00	1.00
586	Denis Menke	4.00	2.00	1.00
587	Billy Wilson	4.00	2.00	1.00
588	Jim Holt	4.00	2.00	1.00
589	Hal Lanier	4.00	2.00	1.00
590	Graig Nettles	4.00	2.00	1.00
591	Paul Casanova	4.00	2.00	1.00
592	Lew Krausse	4.00	2.00	1.00
593	Rich Morales	4.00	2.00	1.00
594	Jim Beauchamp	4.00	2.00	1.00
595	Nolan Ryan	75.00	37.50	22.50
596	Manny Mota	4.00	2.00	1.00
597	Jim Magnuson	4.00	2.00	1.00
598	Hal King	4.00	2.00	1.00
599	Billy Champion	4.00	2.00	1.00
600	Al Kaline	20.00	10.00	5.00
601	George Stone	4.00	2.00	1.00
602	Dave Bristol	4.00	2.00	1.00
603	Jim Ray	4.00	2.00	1.00
604a	6th Series Checklist (657-787) (Copyright on right.)	6.00	3.00	1.75
604b	6th Series Checklist (657-787) (Copyright on left.)	6.00	3.00	1.75
605	Nelson Briles	4.00	2.00	1.00
606	Luis Melendez	4.00	2.00	1.00
607	Frank Duffy	4.00	2.00	1.00
608	Mike Corkins	4.00	2.00	1.00
609	Tom Grieve	4.00	2.00	1.00
610	Bill Stoneman	4.00	2.00	1.00
611	Rich Reese	4.00	2.00	1.00
612	Joe Decker	4.00	2.00	1.00
613	Mike Ferraro	4.00	2.00	1.00
614	Ted Uhlaender	4.00	2.00	1.00
615	Steve Hargan	4.00	2.00	1.00
616	Joe Ferguson **RC**	3.00	1.50	.90
617	**Royals Team**	6.00	3.00	1.75
618	Rich Robertson	4.00	2.00	1.00
619	Rich McKinney	4.00	2.00	1.00
620	Phil Niekro	10.00	5.00	3.00
621	Commissioners Award	4.00	2.00	1.00
622	Most Valuable Player Award	4.00	2.00	1.00
623	Cy Young Award	4.00	2.00	1.00
624	Minor League Player Of The Year Award	4.00	2.00	1.00
625	Rookie of the Year Award	4.00	2.00	1.00
626	Babe Ruth Award	4.00	2.00	1.00
627	Moe Drabowsky	4.00	2.00	1.00
628	Terry Crowley	4.00	2.00	1.00
629	Paul Doyle	4.00	2.00	1.00
630	Rich Hebner	4.00	2.00	1.00
631	John Strohmayer	4.00	2.00	1.00
632	Mike Hegan	4.00	2.00	1.00
633	Jack Hiatt	4.00	2.00	1.00
634	Dick Woodson	4.00	2.00	1.00
635	Don Money	4.00	2.00	1.00
636	Bill Lee	4.00	2.00	1.00
637	Preston Gomez	4.00	2.00	1.00
638	Ken Wright	4.00	2.00	1.00
639	J.C. Martin	4.00	2.00	1.00
640	Joe Coleman	4.00	2.00	1.00
641	Mike Lum	4.00	2.00	1.00
642	Denny Riddleberger	4.00	2.00	1.00
643	Russ Gibson	4.00	2.00	1.00
644	Bernie Allen	4.00	2.00	1.00
645	Jim Maloney	4.00	2.00	1.00
646	Chico Salmon	4.00	2.00	1.00
647	Bob Moose	4.00	2.00	1.00
648	Jim Lyttle	4.00	2.00	1.00
649	Pete Richert	4.00	2.00	1.00
650	Sal Bando	4.00	2.00	1.00
651	Reds Team	8.00	4.00	2.50
652	Marcelino Lopez	4.00	2.00	1.00
653	Jim Fairey	4.00	2.00	1.00
654	Horacio Pina	4.00	2.00	1.00
655	Jerry Grote	4.00	2.00	1.00
656	Rudy May	4.00	2.00	1.00
657	Bobby Wine	12.00	6.00	3.00
658	Steve Dunning	12.00	6.00	3.00
659	Bob Aspromonte	12.00	6.00	3.00
660	Paul Blair	12.00	6.00	3.00
661	Bill Virdon	12.00	6.00	3.00
662	Stan Bahnsen	12.00	6.00	3.00
663	Fran Healy	12.00	6.00	3.00
664	Bobby Knoop	12.00	6.00	3.00
665	Chris Short	12.00	6.00	3.00
666	Hector Torres	12.00	6.00	3.00
667	Ray Newman	12.00	6.00	3.00
668	Rangers Team	25.00	12.50	6.25

669	Willie Crawford	12.00	6.00	3.00
670	Ken Holtzman	12.00	6.00	3.00
671	Donn Clendenon	12.00	6.00	3.00
672	Archie Reynolds	12.00	6.00	3.00
673	Dave Marshall	12.00	6.00	3.00
674	John Kennedy	12.00	6.00	3.00
675	Pat Jarvis	12.00	6.00	3.00
676	Danny Cater	12.00	6.00	3.00
677	Ivan Murrell	12.00	6.00	3.00
678	Steve Luebber	12.00	6.00	3.00
679	Astros Rookies(Bob Fenwick, Bob Stinson)	12.00	6.00	3.00
680	Dave Johnson	12.00	6.00	3.00
681	Bobby Pfeil	12.00	6.00	3.00
682	Mike McCormick	12.00	6.00	3.00
683	Steve Hovley	12.00	6.00	3.00
684	Hal Breeden	12.00	6.00	3.00
685	Joe Horlen	12.00	6.00	3.00
686	Steve Garvey	25.00	12.50	7.50
687	Del Unser	12.00	6.00	3.00
688	Cardinals Team	15.00	7.50	3.75
689	Eddie Fisher	12.00	6.00	3.00
690	Willie Montanez	12.00	6.00	3.00
691	Curt Blefary	12.00	6.00	3.00
692	Curt Blefary (In Action)	12.00	6.00	3.00
693	Alan Gallagher	12.00	6.00	3.00
694	Alan Gallagher (In Action)	12.00	6.00	3.00
695	Rod Carew	50.00	25.00	15.00
696	Rod Carew (In Action)	25.00	12.50	7.50
697	Jerry Koosman	15.00	7.50	4.50
698	Jerry Koosman (In Action)	12.00	6.00	3.00
699	Bobby Murcer	13.00	6.50	3.75
700	Bobby Murcer (In Action)	12.00	6.00	3.00
701	Jose Pagan	12.00	6.00	3.00
702	Jose Pagan (In Action)	12.00	6.00	3.00
703	Doug Griffin	12.00	6.00	3.00
704	Doug Griffin (In Action)	12.00	6.00	3.00
705	Pat Corrales	12.00	6.00	3.00
706	Pat Corrales (In Action)	12.00	6.00	3.00
707	Tim Foli	12.00	6.00	3.00
708	Tim Foli (In Action)	12.00	6.00	3.00
709	Jim Kaat	15.00	7.50	4.50
710	Jim Kaat (In Action)	12.00	6.00	3.00
711	Bobby Bonds	12.00	6.00	3.00
712	Bobby Bonds (In Action)	12.00	6.00	3.00
713	Gene Michael	12.00	6.00	3.00
714	Gene Michael (In Action)	12.00	6.00	3.00
715	Mike Epstein	12.00	6.00	3.00
716	Jesus Alou	12.00	6.00	3.00
717	Bruce Dal Canton	12.00	6.00	3.00
718	Del Rice	12.00	6.00	3.00
719	Cesar Geronimo	12.00	6.00	3.00
720	Sam McDowell	12.00	6.00	3.00
721	Eddie Leon	12.00	6.00	3.00
722	Bill Sudakis	12.00	6.00	3.00
723	Al Santorini	12.00	6.00	3.00
724	A.L. Rookies(John Curtis, Rich Hinton, Mickey Scott)	12.00	6.00	3.00
725	Dick McAuliffe	12.00	6.00	3.00
726	Dick Selma	12.00	6.00	3.00
727	Jose Laboy	12.00	6.00	3.00
728	Gail Hopkins	12.00	6.00	3.00
729	Bob Veale	12.00	6.00	3.00
730	Rick Monday	12.00	6.00	3.00
731	Orioles Team	15.00	7.50	4.50
732	George Culver	12.00	6.00	3.00
733	Jim Hart	12.00	6.00	3.00
734	Bob Burda	12.00	6.00	3.00
735	Diego Segui	12.00	6.00	3.00
736	Bill Russell	12.00	6.00	3.00
737	Lenny Randle **RC**	12.00	6.00	3.00
738	Jim Merritt	12.00	6.00	3.00
739	Don Mason	12.00	6.00	3.00
740	Rico Carty	12.00	6.00	3.00
741	Major League Rookies (***Tom Hutton/John Milner/ Rick Minor***)	12.00	6.00	3.00
742	Jim Rooker	12.00	6.00	3.00
743	Cesar Gutierrez	12.00	6.00	3.00
744	Jim Slaton **RC**	12.00	6.00	3.00
745	Julian Javier	12.00	6.00	3.00
746	Lowell Palmer	12.00	6.00	3.00
747	Jim Stewart	13.00	6.50	3.75
748	Phil Hennigan	12.00	6.00	3.00
749	Walt Alston MG	15.00	7.50	4.50
750	Willie Horton	12.00	6.00	3.00
751	Steve Carlton (Traded)	25.00	12.50	8.00
752	Joe Morgan (Traded)	25.00	12.50	8.00
753	Denny McClain (Traded)	15.00	7.50	4.50
754	Frank Robinson (Traded)	25.00	12.50	8.00
755	Jim Fregosi (Traded)	15.00	7.50	4.50
756	Rick Wise (Traded)	12.00	6.00	3.00
757	Jose Cardenal (Traded)	12.00	6.00	3.00
758	Gil Garrido	12.00	6.00	3.00
759	Chris Cannizzaro	12.00	6.00	3.00
760	Bill Mazeroski	20.00	10.00	6.00
761	A.L./N.L. Rookies (***Ron Cey***, Ben Oglive, ***Bernie Williams***)	20.00	10.00	6.00
762	Wayne Simpson	12.00	6.00	3.00
763	Ron Hansen	12.00	6.00	3.00
764	Dusty Baker	17.50	8.75	5.00
765	Ken McMullen	12.00	6.00	3.00
766	Steve Hamilton	12.00	6.00	3.00
767	Tom McCraw	12.00	6.00	3.00
768	Denny Doyle	12.00	6.00	3.00
769	Jack Aker	12.00	6.00	3.00
770	Jim Wynn	12.00	6.00	3.00
771	San Francisco Giants	15.00	7.50	4.50
772	Ken Tatum	12.00	6.00	3.00
773	Ron Brand	12.00	6.00	3.00
774	Luis Alvarado	12.00	6.00	3.00
775	Jerry Reuss	12.00	6.00	3.00
776	Bill Voss	12.00	6.00	3.00
777	Hoyt Wilhelm	20.00	10.00	6.00
778	Twins Rookies (Vic Albury, ***Rick Dempsey***, Jim Strickland)	15.00	7.50	4.50
779	Tony Cloninger	12.00	6.00	3.00
780	Dick Green	12.00	6.00	3.00
781	Jim McAndrew	12.00	6.00	3.00
782	Larry Stahl	12.00	6.00	3.00
783	Les Cain	12.00	6.00	3.00
784	Ken Aspromonte	12.00	6.00	3.00
785	Vic Davalillo	12.00	6.00	3.00
786	Chuck Brinkman	12.00	6.00	3.00
787	Ron Reed	12.00	6.00	3.00

1972 Topps Candy Lid Test Issue

Between the production of its regular-issue candy lid sets of 1970 and 1973, Topps was working on another issue that survives today in proof form, either as uncropped squares or cut to the 1-7/8" diameter tabbed lid form meant to cover a plastic bucket of bubblegum nuggets. The 1972 proofs are very close to the 1973 issue in format; the principal difference is the player portrait does not have a solid-color border as on the 1973s, and that the pictures of Seaver and Yaz on the front are set against green, rather than orange, stars. The extent of the checklist is unknown.

		NM	E	VG
Complete Set (55):		12,000	6,000	3,600
Common Player:		100.00	50.00	30.00
(1)	Hank Aaron	900.00	450.00	275.00
(2)	Dick Allen	150.00	75.00	45.00
(3)	Dusty Baker	100.00	50.00	35.00
(4)	Sal Bando	100.00	50.00	30.00
(5)	Johnny Bench	450.00	225.00	135.00
(6)	Bobby Bonds	100.00	50.00	30.00
(7)	Dick Bosman	100.00	50.00	30.00
(8)	Lou Brock	250.00	125.00	75.00
(9)	Rod Carew	300.00	150.00	90.00
(10)	Steve Carlton	300.00	150.00	90.00
(11)	Nate Colbert	100.00	50.00	30.00
(12)	Willie Davis	100.00	50.00	30.00
(13)	Larry Dierker	100.00	50.00	30.00
(14)	Mike Epstein	100.00	50.00	30.00
(15)	Carlton Fisk	300.00	150.00	90.00
(16)	Tim Foli	100.00	50.00	30.00
(17)	Ray Fosse	100.00	50.00	30.00
(18)	Bill Freehan	100.00	50.00	30.00
(19)	Bob Gibson	300.00	150.00	90.00
(20)	Bud Harrelson	100.00	50.00	30.00
(21)	Catfish Hunter	250.00	125.00	75.00
(22)	Reggie Jackson	650.00	325.00	195.00
(23)	Fergie Jenkins	250.00	125.00	75.00
(24)	Al Kaline	350.00	175.00	100.00
(25)	Harmon Killebrew	350.00	175.00	100.00
(26)	Clay Kirby	100.00	50.00	30.00
(27)	Mickey Lolich	100.00	50.00	30.00
(28)	Greg Luzinski	100.00	50.00	30.00
(29)	Mike Marshall	100.00	50.00	30.00
(30)	Lee May	100.00	50.00	30.00
(31)	John Mayberry	100.00	50.00	30.00
(32)	Willie Mays	1,250	625.00	375.00
(33)	Willie McCovey	250.00	125.00	75.00
(34)	Thurman Munson	300.00	150.00	90.00
(35)	Bobby Murcer	150.00	75.00	45.00
(36)	Gary Nolan	100.00	50.00	30.00
(37)	Amos Otis	100.00	50.00	30.00
(38)	Jim Palmer	250.00	125.00	75.00
(39)	Gaylord Perry	250.00	125.00	75.00
(40)	Lou Piniella	150.00	75.00	45.00
(41)	Brooks Robinson	350.00	175.00	100.00
(42)	Frank Robinson	350.00	175.00	100.00
(43)	Ellie Rodriguez	100.00	50.00	30.00
(44)	Pete Rose	1,200	600.00	350.00
(45)	Nolan Ryan	2,500	1,250	750.00
(46)	Manny Sanguillen	100.00	50.00	30.00
(47)	George Scott	100.00	50.00	30.00
(48)	Tom Seaver	350.00	175.00	100.00
(49)	Chris Speier	100.00	50.00	30.00
(50)	Willie Stargell	250.00	125.00	75.00
(51)	Don Sutton	250.00	125.00	75.00
(52)	Joe Torre	150.00	75.00	45.00
(53)	Billy Williams	250.00	125.00	75.00
(54)	Wilbur Wood	100.00	50.00	30.00
(55)	Carl Yastrzemski	450.00	225.00	135.00

1972 Topps Cloth Stickers

Despite the fact they were never actually issued, examples of this test issue can readily be found within the hobby. The set of 33 contains stickers with designs identical to cards found in three contiguous rows of a regular Topps card sheet that year; thus the inclusion of a meaningless checklist card. Sometimes found in complete 33-sticker strips, or 132-piece sheets, individual stickers nominally measure 2-1/2" x 3-1/2," though dimensions vary according to the care with which they were cut. Stickers are unnumbered and blank-backed; most are found without the original paper backing as the glue used did not hold up well over the years. Eleven of the stickers are prone to miscutting and are identified with an (SP) in the checklist.

		NM	E	VG
Complete Set (33):		1,300	650.00	390.00
Common Player:		20.00	10.00	6.00
(1)	Hank Aaron	400.00	200.00	120.00
(2)	Luis Aparicio (In Action) (SP)	60.00	30.00	18.00
(3)	Ike Brown	20.00	10.00	6.00
(4)	Johnny Callison	20.00	10.00	6.00
(5)	Checklist 264-319	10.00	5.00	3.00
(6)	Roberto Clemente (In Action)	600.00	300.00	180.00
(7)	Dave Concepcion (SP)	40.00	20.00	12.00
(8)	Ron Cook	20.00	10.00	6.00
(9)	Willie Davis	20.00	10.00	6.00
(10)	Al Fitzmorris	20.00	10.00	6.00
(11)	Bobby Floyd	20.00	10.00	6.00
(12)	Roy Foster	20.00	10.00	6.00
(13)	Jim Fregosi (Boyhood Photo)	20.00	10.00	6.00
(14)	Danny Frisella (In Action)	20.00	10.00	6.00
(15)	Woody Fryman (SP)	25.00	12.50	7.50
(16)	Terry Harmon	20.00	10.00	6.00
(17)	Frank Howard (SP)	40.00	20.00	12.00
(18)	Ron Klimkowski	20.00	10.00	6.00
(19)	Joe Lahoud	20.00	10.00	6.00
(20)	Jim Lefebvre	20.00	10.00	6.00
(21)	Elliott Maddox	20.00	10.00	6.00
(22)	Marty Martinez	20.00	10.00	6.00
(23)	Willie McCovey (SP)	100.00	50.00	30.00
(24)	Hal McRae (SP)	30.00	15.00	9.00
(25)	Syd O'Brien (SP)	25.00	12.50	7.50
(26)	Red Sox team	25.00	12.50	7.50
(27)	Aurelio Rodriguez	20.00	10.00	6.00
(28)	Al Severinsen	20.00	10.00	6.00
(29)	Art Shamsky (SP)	25.00	12.50	7.50
(30)	Steve Stone (SP)	30.00	15.00	9.00
(31)	Stan Swanson (SP)	25.00	12.50	7.50
(32)	Bob Watson	20.00	10.00	6.00
(33)	Roy White (SP)	30.00	15.00	9.00

1972 Topps Posters

Issued as a separate set, rather than as a wax pack insert, these 9-7/16" x 18" posters feature a borderless full-color picture on the front with the player's name, team and position. Printed on very thin paper, the posters were folded for packaging, causing large creases that cannot be removed. Grading of these posters is done without regard to those packaging folds. Unfolded final production proofs are known.

		NM	E	VG
Complete Set (24):		700.00	350.00	200.00
Common Player:		12.00	6.00	3.50
Wax Pack:		50.00		
1	Dave McNally	12.00	6.00	3.50
2	Carl Yastrzemski	45.00	22.50	13.50
3	Bill Melton	12.00	6.00	3.50
4	Ray Fosse	12.00	6.00	3.50
5	Mickey Lolich	12.00	6.00	3.50
6	Amos Otis	12.00	6.00	3.50
7	Tony Oliva	15.00	7.50	4.50
8	Vida Blue	12.00	6.00	3.50
9	Hank Aaron	75.00	37.50	22.00
10	Fergie Jenkins	30.00	15.00	9.00
11	Pete Rose	75.00	37.50	22.00
12	Willie Davis	12.00	6.00	3.50
13	Tom Seaver	40.00	20.00	12.00
14	Rick Wise	12.00	6.00	3.50
15	Willie Stargell	30.00	15.00	9.00
16	Joe Torre	17.50	8.75	5.25
17	Willie Mays	75.00	37.50	22.00
18	Andy Messersmith	12.00	6.00	3.50
19	Wilbur Wood	12.00	6.00	3.50
20	Harmon Killebrew	35.00	17.50	10.00
21	Billy Williams	30.00	15.00	9.00
22	Bud Harrelson	12.00	6.00	3.50
23	Roberto Clemente	125.00	65.00	35.00
24	Willie McCovey	30.00	15.00	9.00

1973 Topps

Topps cut back to 660 cards in 1973. The set is interesting for it marks the last time cards were issued by series, a procedure which had produced many a scarce high number card over the years. These 2-1/2" x 3-1/2" cards have a color photo, accented by a silhouette of a player on the front, indicative of his position. Card backs are vertical for the first time since 1968, with the usual statistical and biographical information. Specialty cards begin with card number 1, which depicted Ruth, Mays and Aaron as the all-time home run leaders. It was followed by statistical leaders, although there also were additional all-time leader cards. Also present are playoff and World Series highlights. From the age-and-youth department, the 1973 Topps set has coaches and managers as well as more "Boyhood Photos."

		NM	E	VG
Complete Set (660):		975.00	500.00	300.00

Common Player (1-396):		.75	.40	.25
Common Player (397-528):		1.00	.50	.30
Common Player (529-660):		2.00	1.00	.60
Series 1/2/3 Wax Pack (10):		115.00		
Series 4 Wax Pack (10):		165.00		
Series 5 Wax Pack (10+1):		215.00		
1	All Time Home Run Leaders (Hank Aaron, Willie Mays, Babe Ruth)	35.00	17.50	8.75
2	Rich Hebner	.75	.40	.25
3	Jim Lonborg	.75	.40	.25
4	John Milner	.75	.40	.25
5	Ed Brinkman	.75	.40	.25
6	Mac Scarce	.75	.40	.25
7	Texas Rangers Team	1.00	.50	.30
8	Tom Hall	.75	.40	.25
9	Johnny Oates	.75	.40	.25
10	Don Sutton	3.00	1.50	.90
11	Chris Chambliss	.75	.40	.25
12a	Padres Mgr./Coaches (Dave Garcia, Johnny Podres, Bob Skinner, Whitey Wietelmann, Don Zimmer) (Coaches background brown.)	1.00	.50	.30
12b	Padres Mgr./Coaches (Dave Garcia, Johnny Podres, Bob Skinner, Whitey Wietelmann, Don Zimmer) (Coaches background orange.)	1.00	.50	.30
13	George Hendrick	.75	.40	.25
14	Sonny Siebert	.75	.40	.25
15	Ralph Garr	.75	.40	.25
16	Steve Braun	.75	.40	.25
17	Fred Gladding	.75	.40	.25
18	Leroy Stanton	.75	.40	.25
19	Tim Foli	.75	.40	.25
20a	Stan Bahnsen (Small gap in left border.)	1.00	.50	.30
20b	Stan Bahnsen (No gap.)	.75	.40	.25
21	Randy Hundley	.75	.40	.25
22	Ted Abernathy	.75	.40	.25
23	Dave Kingman	1.00	.50	.30
24	Al Santorini	.75	.40	.25
25	Roy White	.75	.40	.25
26	Pittsburgh Pirates Team	3.00	1.50	.75
27	Bill Gogolewski	.75	.40	.25
28	Hal McRae	.75	.40	.25
29	Tony Taylor	.75	.40	.25
30	Tug McGraw	.75	.40	.25
31a	Buddy Bell RC (Small gap in right border.)	6.00	3.00	1.75
31b	Buddy Bell RC (No gap.)	6.00	3.00	1.75
32	Fred Norman	.75	.40	.25
33	Jim Breazeale	.75	.40	.25
34	Pat Dobson	.75	.40	.25
35	Willie Davis	.75	.40	.25
36	Steve Barber	.75	.40	.25
37	Bill Robinson	.75	.40	.25
38	Mike Epstein	.75	.40	.25
39	Dave Roberts	.75	.40	.25
40	Reggie Smith	.75	.40	.25
41	Tom Walker	.75	.40	.25
42	Mike Andrews	.75	.40	.25
43	Randy Moffitt RC	.75	.40	.25
44	Rick Monday	.75	.40	.25
45	Ellie Rodriguez (Photo actually Paul Ratliff.)	.75	.40	.25
46	Lindy McDaniel	.75	.40	.25
47	Luis Melendez	.75	.40	.25
48	Paul Splittorff	.75	.40	.25
49a	Twins Mgr./Coaches (Vern Morgan, Frank Quilici, Bob Rodgers, Ralph Rowe, Al Worthington) (Coaches background brown.)	.75	.40	.25
49b	Twins Mgr./Coaches (Vern Morgan, Frank Quilici, Bob Rodgers, Ralph Rowe, Al Worthington) (Coaches background orange.)	.75	.40	.25
50	Roberto Clemente	40.00	20.00	12.00
51	Chuck Seelbach	.75	.40	.25
52	Denis Menke	.75	.40	.25
53	Steve Dunning	.75	.40	.25
54	Checklist 1-132	1.00	.50	.30
55	Jon Matlack	.75	.40	.25
56	Merv Rettenmund	.75	.40	.25
57	Derrel Thomas	.75	.40	.25
58	Mike Paul	.75	.40	.25
59	Steve Yeager RC	.75	.40	.25
60	Ken Holtzman	.75	.40	.25
61	Batting Leaders (Rod Carew, Billy Williams)	1.00	.50	.30

62	Home Run Leaders (Dick Allen, Johnny Bench)	1.00	.50	.30
63	Runs Batted In Leaders (Dick Allen, Johnny Bench)	1.00	.50	.30
64	Stolen Base Leaders (Lou Brock, Bert Campaneris)	1.00	.50	.30
65	Earned Run Average Leaders (Steve Carlton, Luis Tiant)	1.00	.50	.30
66	Victory Leaders (Steve Carlton, Gaylord Perry, Wilbur Wood)	1.00	.50	.30
67	Strikeout Leaders (Steve Carlton, Nolan Ryan)	20.00	10.00	6.00
68	Leading Firemen (Clay Carroll, Sparky Lyle)	.75	.40	.25
69	Phil Gagliano	.75	.40	.25
70	Milt Pappas	.75	.40	.25
71	Johnny Briggs	.75	.40	.25
72	Ron Reed	.75	.40	.25
73	Ed Herrmann	.75	.40	.25
74	Billy Champion	.75	.40	.25
75	Vada Pinson	1.00	.50	.30
76	Doug Rader	.75	.40	.25
77	Mike Torrez	.75	.40	.25
78	Richie Scheinblum	.75	.40	.25
79	Jim Willoughby	.75	.40	.25
80	Tony Oliva ("MINNSEOTA" on front is uncorrected error.)	1.00	.50	.30
81a	Cubs Mgr./Coaches (Hank Aguirre, Ernie Banks, Larry Jansen, Whitey Lockman, Pete Reiser) (Trees in coaches background.)	1.25	.60	.40
81b	Cubs Mgr./Coaches (Hank Aguirre, Ernie Banks, Larry Jansen, Whitey Lockman, Pete Reiser) (Solid orange background.)	1.25	.60	.40
82	Fritz Peterson	.75	.40	.25
83	Leron Lee	.75	.40	.25
84	Rollie Fingers	4.00	2.00	1.25
85	Ted Simmons	.75	.40	.25
86	Tom McCraw	.75	.40	.25
87	Ken Boswell	.75	.40	.25
88	Mickey Stanley	.75	.40	.25
89	Jack Billingham	.75	.40	.25
90	Brooks Robinson	12.50	6.25	3.75
91	Los Angeles Dodgers Team	2.00	1.00	.60
92	Jerry Bell	.75	.40	.25
93	Jesus Alou	.75	.40	.25
94	Dick Billings	.75	.40	.25
95	Steve Blass	.75	.40	.25
96	Doug Griffin	.75	.40	.25
97	Willie Montanez	.75	.40	.25
98	Dick Woodson	.75	.40	.25
99	Carl Taylor	.75	.40	.25
100	Hank Aaron	30.00	15.00	9.00
101	Ken Henderson	.75	.40	.25
102	Rudy May	.75	.40	.25
103	Celerino Sanchez	.75	.40	.25
104	Reggie Cleveland	.75	.40	.25
105	Carlos May	.75	.40	.25
106	Terry Humphrey	.75	.40	.25
107	Phil Hennigan	.75	.40	.25
108	Bill Russell	1.00	.50	.30
109	Doyle Alexander	.75	.40	.25
110	Bob Watson	.75	.40	.25
111	Dave Nelson	.75	.40	.25
112	Gary Ross	.75	.40	.25
113	Jerry Grote	.75	.40	.25
114	Lynn McGlothen	.75	.40	.25
115	Ron Santo	4.50	2.25	1.00
116a	Yankees Mgr./Coaches (Jim Hegan, Ralph Houk, Elston Howard, Dick Howser, Jim Turner) (Coaches background brown.)	2.00	1.00	.60
116b	Yankees Mgr./Coaches (Jim Hegan, Ralph Houk, Elston Howard, Dick Howser, Jim Turner) (Coaches background orange.)	2.00	1.00	.60
117	Ramon Hernandez	.75	.40	.25
118	John Mayberry	.75	.40	.25
119	Larry Bowa	1.50	.70	.45
120	Joe Coleman	.75	.40	.25
121	Dave Rader	.75	.40	.25
122	Jim Strickland	.75	.40	.25

No.	Player			
123	Sandy Alomar	.75	.40	.25
124	Jim Hardin	.75	.40	.25
125	Ron Fairly	.75	.40	.25
126	Jim Brewer	.75	.40	.25
127	Milwaukee Brewers Team	2.00	1.00	.60
128	Ted Sizemore	.75	.40	.25
129	Terry Forster	.75	.40	.25
130	Pete Rose	25.00	12.50	6.25
131a	Red Sox Mgr./Coaches (Doug Camilli, Eddie Kasko, Don Lenhardt, Eddie Popowski, Lee Stange) (Coaches background brown.)	.75	.40	.25
131b	Red Sox Mgr./Coaches (Doug Camilli, Eddie Kasko, Don Lenhardt, Eddie Popowski, Lee Stange) (Coaches background orange.)	.75	.40	.25
132	Matty Alou	.75	.40	.25
133	Dave Roberts	.75	.40	.25
134	Milt Wilcox	.75	.40	.25
135	Lee May	.75	.40	.25
136a	Orioles Mgr./Coaches (George Bamberger, Jim Frey, Billy Hunter, George Staller, Earl Weaver) (Coaches background brown.)	2.00	1.00	.60
136b	Orioles Mgr./Coaches (George Bamberger, Jim Frey, Billy Hunter, George Staller, Earl Weaver) (Coaches background orange.)	2.00	1.00	.60
137	Jim Beauchamp	.75	.40	.25
138	Horacio Pina	.75	.40	.25
139	Carmen Fanzone	.75	.40	.25
140	Lou Piniella	2.00	1.00	.60
141	Bruce Kison	.75	.40	.25
142	Thurman Munson	15.00	7.50	3.75
143	John Curtis	.75	.40	.25
144	Marty Perez	.75	.40	.25
145	Bobby Bonds	2.00	1.00	.60
146	Woodie Fryman	.75	.40	.25
147	Mike Anderson	.75	.40	.25
148	Dave Goltz RC	.75	.40	.25
149	Ron Hunt	.75	.40	.25
150	Wilbur Wood	1.50	.70	.45
151	Wes Parker	.75	.40	.25
152	Dave May	.75	.40	.25
153	Al Hrabosky	1.50	.70	.45
154	Jeff Torborg	.75	.40	.25
155	Sal Bando	.75	.40	.25
156	Cesar Geronimo	.75	.40	.25
157	Denny Riddleberger	.75	.40	.25
158	Houston Astros Team	2.00	1.00	.60
159	Clarence Gaston	.75	.40	.25
160	Jim Palmer	9.00	4.50	2.25
161	Ted Martinez	.75	.40	.25
162	Pete Broberg	.75	.40	.25
163	Vic Davalillo	.75	.40	.25
164	Monty Montgomery	.75	.40	.25
165	Luis Aparicio	4.00	2.00	1.25
166	Terry Harmon	.75	.40	.25
167	Steve Stone	1.00	.50	.30
168	Jim Northrup	.75	.40	.25
169	Ron Schueler	.75	.40	.25
170	Harmon Killebrew	5.00	2.50	1.25
171	Bernie Carbo	.75	.40	.25
172	Steve Kline	.75	.40	.25
173	Hal Breeden	.75	.40	.25
174	Rich Gossage RC	12.00	6.00	3.50
175	Frank Robinson	8.00	4.00	2.50
176	Chuck Taylor	.75	.40	.25
177	Bill Plummer	.75	.40	.25
178	Don Rose	.75	.40	.25
179a	A's Mgr./Coaches (Jerry Adair, Vern Hoscheit, Irv Noren, Wes Stock, Dick Williams) (Coaches background brown.)	1.00	.50	.30
179b	A's Mgr./Coaches (Jerry Adair, Vern Hoscheit, Irv Noren, Wes Stock, Dick Williams) (Coaches background orange, normal ears.)	1.00	.50	.30
179b	A's Mgr./Coaches (Jerry Adair, Vern Hoscheit, Irv Noren, Wes Stock, Dick Williams) (Coaches background orange, normal ears.)	1.00	.50	.30
179c	A's Mgr./Coaches (Jerry Adair, Vern Hoscheit, Irv Noren, Wes Stock, Dick Williams) (coaches background orange, cropped ears)	1.50	.50	.30
180	Fergie Jenkins	5.00	2.50	1.25
181	Jack Brohamer	.75	.40	.25
182	Mike Caldwell RC	.75	.40	.25
183	Don Buford	.75	.40	.25
184	Jerry Koosman	1.00	.50	.30
185	Jim Wynn	.75	.40	.25
186	Bill Fahey	.75	.40	.25
187	Luke Walker	.75	.40	.25
188	Cookie Rojas	.75	.40	.25
189	Greg Luzinski	1.50	.70	.45
190	Bob Gibson	10.00	5.00	2.50
191	Detroit Tigers Team	2.00	1.00	.60
192	Pat Jarvis	.75	.40	.25
193	Carlton Fisk	17.50	8.75	4.50
194	Jorge Orta RC	.75	.40	.25
195	Clay Carroll	.75	.40	.25
196	Ken McMullen	.75	.40	.25
197	Ed Goodson	.75	.40	.25
198	Horace Clarke	.75	.40	.25
199	Bert Blyleven	2.00	1.00	.50
200	Billy Williams	7.50	3.75	2.00
201	A.L. Playoffs (Hendrick Scores Winning Run.)	1.00	.50	.30
202	N.L. Playoffs (Foster's Run Decides It.)	1.00	.50	.30
203	World Series Game 1 (Tenace The Menace.)	1.00	.50	.30
204	World Series Game 2 (A's Make It Two Straight.)	1.00	.50	.30
205	World Series Game 3 (Reds Win Squeeker.)	1.00	.50	.30
206	World Series Game 4 (Tenace Singles In Ninth.)	1.00	.50	.30
207	World Series Game 5 (Odom Out At Plate.)	1.00	.50	.30
208	World Series Game 6 (Reds' Slugging Ties Series.)	4.00	2.00	1.25
209	World Series Game 7 (Campy Starts Winning Rally.)	1.00	.50	.30
210	A's Win! (World Champions.)	1.50	.70	.45
211	Balor Moore	.75	.40	.25
212	Joe Lahoud	.75	.40	.25
213	Steve Garvey	3.00	1.50	.90
214	Dave Hamilton	.75	.40	.25
215	Dusty Baker	1.00	.50	.30
216	Toby Harrah	.75	.40	.25
217	Don Wilson	.75	.40	.25
218	Aurelio Rodriguez	.75	.40	.25
219	St. Louis Cardinals Team	2.00	1.00	.60
220	Nolan Ryan	50.00	25.00	15.00
221	Fred Kendall	.75	.40	.25
222	Rob Gardner	.75	.40	.25
223	Bud Harrelson	.75	.40	.25
224	Bill Lee	.75	.40	.25
225	Al Oliver	1.00	.50	.30
226	Ray Fosse	.75	.40	.25
227	Wayne Twitchell	.75	.40	.25
228	Bobby Darwin	.75	.40	.25
229	Roric Harrison	.75	.40	.25
230	Joe Morgan	7.50	3.75	2.00
231	Bill Parsons	.75	.40	.25
232	Ken Singleton	.75	.40	.25
233	Ed Kirkpatrick	.75	.40	.25
234	Bill North RC	.75	.40	.25
235	Jim Hunter	6.00	3.00	1.50
236	Tito Fuentes	.75	.40	.25
237a	Braves Mgr./Coaches (Lew Burdette, Jim Busby, Roy Hartsfield, Eddie Mathews, Ken Silvestri) (Coaches background brown.)	1.00	.50	.30
237b	Braves Mgr./Coaches (Lew Burdette, Jim Busby, Roy Hartsfield, Eddie Mathews, Ken Silvestri) (Coaches background orange.)	1.00	.50	.30
238	Tony Muser	.75	.40	.25
239	Pete Richert	.75	.40	.25
240	Bobby Murcer	1.00	.50	.30
241	Dwain Anderson	.75	.40	.25
242	George Culver	.75	.40	.25
243	California Angels Team	2.00	1.00	.60
244	Ed Acosta	.75	.40	.25
245	Carl Yastrzemski	20.00	10.00	5.00
246	Ken Sanders	.75	.40	.25
247	Del Unser	.75	.40	.25
248	Jerry Johnson	.75	.40	.25
249	Larry Biittner	.75	.40	.25
250	Manny Sanguillen	.75	.40	.25
251	Roger Nelson	.75	.40	.25
252a	Giants Mgr./Coaches (Joe Amalfitano, Charlie Fox, Andy Gilbert, Don McMahon, John McNamara) (Coaches background brown.)	.75	.40	.25
252b	Giants Mgr./Coaches (Joe Amalfitano, Charlie Fox, Andy Gilbert, Don McMahon, John McNamara) (Coaches background orange.)	.75	.40	.25
253	Mark Belanger	.75	.40	.25
254	Bill Stoneman	.75	.40	.25
255	Reggie Jackson	15.00	7.50	3.75
256	Chris Zachary	.75	.40	.25
257a	Mets Mgr./Coaches (Yogi Berra, Roy McMillan, Joe Pignatano, Rube Walker, Eddie Yost) (Coaches background brown.)	2.00	1.00	.60
257b	Mets Mgr./Coaches (Yogi Berra, Roy McMillan, Joe Pignatano, Rube Walker, Eddie Yost) (Coaches background orange.)	2.00	1.00	.60
258	Tommy John	1.00	.50	.30
259	Jim Holt	.75	.40	.25
260	Gary Nolan	.75	.40	.25
261	Pat Kelly	.75	.40	.25
262	Jack Aker	.75	.40	.25
263	George Scott	.75	.40	.25
264	Checklist 133-264	1.00	.50	.30
265	Gene Michael	.75	.40	.25
266	Mike Lum	.75	.40	.25
267	Lloyd Allen	.75	.40	.25
268	Jerry Morales	.75	.40	.25
269	Tim McCarver	1.50	.70	.45
270	Luis Tiant	.75	.40	.25
271	Tom Hutton	.75	.40	.25
272	Ed Farmer	.75	.40	.25
273	Chris Speier	.75	.40	.25
274	Darold Knowles	.75	.40	.25
275	Tony Perez	6.00	3.00	1.50
276	Joe Lovitto	.75	.40	.25
277	Bob Miller	.75	.40	.25
278	Baltimore Orioles Team	3.00	1.50	.90
279	Mike Strahler	.75	.40	.25
280	Al Kaline	12.00	6.00	3.00
281	Mike Jorgensen	.75	.40	.25
282	Steve Hovley	.75	.40	.25
283	Ray Sadecki	.75	.40	.25
284	Glenn Borgmann	.75	.40	.25
285	Don Kessinger	.75	.40	.25
286	Frank Linzy	.75	.40	.25
287	Eddie Leon	.75	.40	.25
288	Gary Gentry	.75	.40	.25
289	Bob Oliver	.75	.40	.25
290	Cesar Cedeno	.75	.40	.25
291	Rogelio Moret	.75	.40	.25
292	Jose Cruz	.75	.40	.25
293	Bernie Allen	.75	.40	.25
294	Steve Arlin	.75	.40	.25
295	Bert Campaneris	.75	.40	.25
296	Reds Mgr./ Coaches (Sparky Anderson, Alex Grammas, Ted Kluszewski, George Scherger, Larry Shepard)	2.50	1.25	.70
297	Walt Williams	.75	.40	.25
298	Ron Bryant	.75	.40	.25
299	Ted Ford	.75	.40	.25
300	Steve Carlton	10.00	5.00	2.50
301	Billy Grabarkewitz	.75	.40	.25
302	Terry Crowley	.75	.40	.25
303	Nelson Briles	.75	.40	.25
304	Duke Sims	.75	.40	.25
305	Willie Mays	37.50	18.75	10.00
306	Tom Burgmeier	.75	.40	.25
307	Boots Day	.75	.40	.25
308	Skip Lockwood	.75	.40	.25
309	Paul Popovich	.75	.40	.25
310	Dick Allen	1.50	.70	.45
311	Joe Decker	.75	.40	.25
312	Oscar Brown	.75	.40	.25
313	Jim Ray	.75	.40	.25
314	Ron Swoboda	.75	.40	.25
315	John Odom	.75	.40	.25
316	San Diego Padres Team	2.00	1.00	.60
317	Danny Cater	.75	.40	.25

No.	Player			
318	Jim McGlothlin	.75	.40	.25
319	Jim Spencer	.75	.40	.25
320	Lou Brock	10.00	5.00	2.50
321	Rich Hinton	.75	.40	.25
322	Garry Maddox RC	1.00	.50	.30
323	Tigers Mgr./Coaches(Art Fowler, Billy Martin, Joe Schultz, Charlie Silvera, Dick Tracewski)	1.00	.50	.30
324	Al Downing	.75	.40	.25
325	Boog Powell	1.00	.50	.30
326	Darrell Brandon	.75	.40	.25
327	John Lowenstein	.75	.40	.25
328	Bill Bonham	.75	.40	.25
329	Ed Kranepool	.75	.40	.25
330	Rod Carew	10.00	5.00	2.50
331	Carl Morton	.75	.40	.25
332	John Felske RC	.75	.40	.25
333	Gene Clines	.75	.40	.25
334	Freddie Patek	.75	.40	.25
335	Bob Tolan	.75	.40	.25
336	Tom Bradley	.75	.40	.25
337	Dave Duncan	1.00	.50	.30
338	Checklist 265-396	1.00	.50	.30
339	Dick Tidrow	.75	.40	.25
340	Nate Colbert	.75	.40	.25
341	Jim Palmer (Boyhood Photo)	1.50	.70	.45
342	Sam McDowell (Boyhood Photo)	.75	.40	.25
343	Bobby Murcer (Boyhood Photo)	.75	.40	.25
344	Jim Hunter (Boyhood Photo)	1.50	.70	.45
345	Chris Speier (Boyhood Photo)	.75	.40	.25
346	Gaylord Perry (Boyhood Photo)	1.50	.70	.45
347	Kansas City Royals Team	2.00	1.00	.60
348	Rennie Stennett	.75	.40	.25
349	Dick McAuliffe	.75	.40	.25
350	Tom Seaver	12.50	6.25	3.00
351	Jimmy Stewart	.75	.40	.25
352	Don Stanhouse RC	.75	.40	.25
353	Steve Brye	.75	.40	.25
354	Billy Parker	.75	.40	.25
355	Mike Marshall	.75	.40	.25
356	White Sox Mgr./Coaches (Joe Lonnett, Jim Mahoney, Al Monchak, Johnny Sain, Chuck Tanner)	.75	.40	.25
357	Ross Grimsley	.75	.40	.25
358	Jim Nettles	.75	.40	.25
359	Cecil Upshaw	.75	.40	.25
360	Joe Rudi (Photo actually Gene Tenace.)	.75	.40	.25
361	Fran Healy	.75	.40	.25
362	Eddie Watt	.75	.40	.25
363	Jackie Hernandez	.75	.40	.25
364	Rick Wise	.75	.40	.25
365	Rico Petrocelli	.75	.40	.25
366	Brock Davis	.75	.40	.25
367	Burt Hooton	.75	.40	.25
368	Bill Buckner	1.00	.50	.30
369	Lerrin LaGrow	.75	.40	.25
370	Willie Stargell	8.00	4.00	2.00
371	Mike Kekich	.75	.40	.25
372	Oscar Gamble	.75	.40	.25
373	Clyde Wright	.75	.40	.25
374	Darrell Evans	1.00	.50	.30
375	Larry Dierker	.75	.40	.25
376	Frank Duffy	.75	.40	.25
377	Expos Mgr./Coaches (Dave Bristol, Larry Doby, Gene Mauch, Cal McLish, Jerry Zimmerman)	1.00	.50	.30
378	Lenny Randle	.75	.40	.25
379	Cy Acosta	.75	.40	.25
380	Johnny Bench	15.00	7.50	3.75
381	Vicente Romo	.75	.40	.25
382	Mike Hegan	.75	.40	.25
383	Diego Segui	.75	.40	.25
384	Don Baylor	3.00	1.50	.90
385	Jim Perry	.75	.40	.25
386	Don Money	.75	.40	.25
387	Jim Barr	.75	.40	.25
388	Ben Oglivie	.75	.40	.25
389	New York Mets Team	4.00	2.00	1.25
390	Mickey Lolich	.75	.40	.25
391	Lee Lacy RC	.75	.40	.25
392	Dick Drago	.75	.40	.25
393	Jose Cardenal	.75	.40	.25
394	Sparky Lyle	.75	.40	.25
395	Roger Metzger	.75	.40	.25
396	Grant Jackson	.75	.40	.25
397	Dave Cash	1.00	.50	.30
398	Rich Hand	1.00	.50	.30
399	George Foster	1.00	.50	.30
400	Gaylord Perry	7.00	3.50	1.75
401	Clyde Mashore	1.00	.50	.30
402	Jack Hiatt	1.00	.50	.30
403	Sonny Jackson	1.00	.50	.30
404	Chuck Brinkman	1.00	.50	.30
405	Cesar Tovar	1.00	.50	.30
406	Paul Lindblad	1.00	.50	.30
407	Felix Millan	1.00	.50	.30
408	Jim Colborn	1.00	.50	.30
409	Ivan Murrell	1.00	.50	.30
410	Willie McCovey	8.00	4.00	2.00
411	Ray Corbin	1.00	.50	.30
412	Manny Mota	1.00	.50	.30
413	Tom Timmermann	1.00	.50	.30
414	Ken Rudolph	1.00	.50	.30
415	Marty Pattin	1.00	.50	.30
416	Paul Schaal	1.00	.50	.30
417	Scipio Spinks	1.00	.50	.30
418	Bobby Grich	1.00	.50	.30
419	Casey Cox	1.00	.50	.30
420	Tommie Agee	1.00	.50	.30
421	Angels Mgr./Coaches (Tom Morgan, Salty Parker, Jimmie Reese, John Roseboro, Bobby Winkles)	1.50	.70	.45
422	Bob Robertson	1.00	.50	.30
423	Johnny Jeter	1.00	.50	.30
424	Denny Doyle	1.00	.50	.30
425	Alex Johnson	1.00	.50	.30
426a	Dave LaRoche (Pitcher's knee is missing on silouette on the bottom)	1.00	.50	.30
426b	Dave LaRoche (Pitcher's knee intact.)	1.00	.50	.30
427	Rick Auerbach	1.00	.50	.30
428	Wayne Simpson	1.00	.50	.30
429	Jim Fairey	1.00	.50	.30
430	Vida Blue	1.50	.70	.45
431	Gerry Moses	1.00	.50	.30
432	Dan Frisella	1.00	.50	.30
433	Willie Horton	1.00	.50	.30
434	San Francisco Giants Team	3.00	1.50	.90
435	Rico Carty	1.00	.50	.30
436	Jim McAndrew	1.00	.50	.30
437	John Kennedy	1.00	.50	.30
438	Enzo Hernandez	1.00	.50	.30
439	Eddie Fisher	1.00	.50	.30
440	Glenn Beckert	1.00	.50	.30
441	Gail Hopkins	1.00	.50	.30
442	Dick Dietz	1.00	.50	.30
443	Danny Thompson	1.00	.50	.30
444	Ken Brett	1.00	.50	.30
445	Ken Berry	1.00	.50	.30
446	Jerry Reuss	1.00	.50	.30
447	Joe Hague	1.00	.50	.30
448	John Hiller	1.00	.50	.30
449a	Indians Mgr./Coaches (Ken Aspromonte, Rocky Colavito, Joe Lutz, Warren Spahn) (Spahn's ear pointed.)	1.50	.70	.45
449b	Indians Mgr./Coaches (Ken Aspromonte, Rocky Colavito, Joe Lutz, Warren Spahn) (Spahn's ear round.)	2.00	1.00	.60
450	Joe Torre	4.00	2.00	1.00
451	John Vukovich	1.00	.50	.30
452	Paul Casanova	1.00	.50	.30
453	Checklist 397-528	1.25	.60	.40
454	Tom Haller	1.00	.50	.30
455	Bill Melton	1.00	.50	.30
456	Dick Green	1.00	.50	.30
457	John Strohmayer	1.00	.50	.30
458	Jim Mason	1.00	.50	.30
459	Jimmy Howarth	1.00	.50	.30
460	Bill Freehan	1.00	.50	.30
461	Mike Corkins	1.00	.50	.30
462	Ron Blomberg	1.00	.50	.30
463	Ken Tatum	1.00	.50	.30
464	Chicago Cubs Team	4.00	2.00	1.25
465	Dave Giusti	1.00	.50	.30
466	Jose Arcia	1.00	.50	.30
467	Mike Ryan	1.00	.50	.30
468	Tom Griffin	1.00	.50	.30
469	Dan Monzon	1.00	.50	.30
470	Mike Cuellar	1.00	.50	.30
471	All-Time Hit Leader (Ty Cobb)	8.00	4.00	2.00
472	All-Time Grand Slam Leader(Lou Gehrig)	12.00	6.00	3.50
473	All-Time Total Base Leader (Hank Aaron)	8.00	4.00	2.00
474	All-Time RBI Leader (Babe Ruth)	15.00	7.50	3.75
475	All-Time Batting Leader (Ty Cobb)	6.00	3.00	1.50
476	All-Time Shutout Leader (Walter Johnson)	3.00	1.50	.90
477	All-Time Victory Leader (Cy Young)	3.00	1.50	.90
478	All-Time Strikeout Leader (Walter Johnson)	3.00	1.50	.90
479	Hal Lanier	1.00	.50	.30
480	Juan Marichal	6.00	3.00	1.75
481	Chicago White Sox Team	3.00	1.50	.90
482	Rick Reuschel RC	2.00	1.00	.60
483	Dal Maxvill	1.00	.50	.30
484	Ernie McAnally	1.00	.50	.30
485	Norm Cash	1.50	.70	.45
486a	Phillies Mgr./Coaches (Carroll Berringer, Billy DeMars, Danny Ozark, Ray Rippelmeyer, Bobby Wine) (Coaches background brown-red.)	1.00	.50	.30
486b	Phillies Mgr./Coaches (Carroll Beringer, Billy DeMars, Danny Ozark, Ray Rippelmeyer, Bobby Wine) (Coaches background orange.)	1.00	.50	.30
487	Bruce Dal Canton	1.00	.50	.30
488	Dave Campbell	1.00	.50	.30
489	Jeff Burroughs	1.00	.50	.30
490	Claude Osteen	1.00	.50	.30
491	Bob Montgomery	1.00	.50	.30
492	Pedro Borbon	1.00	.50	.30
493	Duffy Dyer	1.00	.50	.30
494	Rich Morales	1.00	.50	.30
495	Tommy Helms	1.00	.50	.30
496	Ray Lamb	1.00	.50	.30
497	Cardinals Mgr./Coaches (Vern Benson, George Kissell, Red Schoendienst, Barney Schultz)	1.50	.70	.45
498	Graig Nettles	1.50	.70	.45
499	Bob Moose	1.00	.50	.30
500	Oakland A's Team	4.00	2.00	1.25
501	Larry Gura	1.00	.50	.30
502	Bobby Valentine	1.00	.50	.30
503	Phil Niekro	7.00	3.50	1.75
504a	Earl Williams (Small gap in each side border.)	1.00	.50	.30
504b	Earl Williams (No gaps in border.)	1.00	.50	.30
505	Bob Bailey	1.00	.50	.30
506	Bart Johnson	1.00	.50	.30
507	Darrel Chaney	1.00	.50	.30
508	Gates Brown	1.00	.50	.30
509	Jim Nash	1.00	.50	.30
510	Amos Otis	1.00	.50	.30
511	Sam McDowell	1.00	.50	.30
512	Dalton Jones	1.00	.50	.30
513	Dave Marshall	1.00	.50	.30
514	Jerry Kenney	1.00	.50	.30
515	Andy Messersmith	1.00	.50	.30
516	Danny Walton	1.00	.50	.30
517a	Pirates Mgr./Coaches (Don Leppert, Bill Mazeroski, Dave Ricketts, Bill Virdon, Mel Wright) (Coaches background brown.)	1.50	.70	.45
517b	Pirates Mgr./Coaches (Don Leppert, Bill Mazeroski, Dave Ricketts, Bill Virdon, Mel Wright) (Coaches background orange.)	1.50	.70	.45
518	Bob Veale	1.00	.50	.30
519	John Edwards	1.00	.50	.30
520	Mel Stottlemyre	1.25	.60	.40
521	Atlanta Braves Team	4.00	2.00	1.25
522	Leo Cardenas	1.00	.50	.30
523	Wayne Granger	1.00	.50	.30
524	Gene Tenace	1.00	.50	.30
525	Jim Fregosi	1.00	.50	.30
526	Ollie Brown	1.00	.50	.30
527	Dan McGinn	1.00	.50	.30
528	Paul Blair	1.00	.50	.30
529	Milt May	1.00	1.00	.60
530	Jim Kaat	4.00	2.00	1.25
531	Ron Woods	2.00	1.00	.60
532	Steve Mingori	2.00	1.00	.60
533	Larry Stahl	2.00	1.00	.60
534	Dave Lemonds	2.00	1.00	.60

535	John Callison	2.00	1.00	.60
536	Philadelphia Phillies Team	6.00	3.00	1.75
537	Bill Slayback	2.00	1.00	.60
538	Jim Hart	2.00	1.00	.60
539	Tom Murphy	2.00	1.00	.60
540	Cleon Jones	2.00	1.00	.60
541	Bob Bolin	2.00	1.00	.60
542	Pat Corrales	2.00	1.00	.60
543	Alan Foster	2.00	1.00	.60
544	Von Joshua	2.00	1.00	.60
545	Orlando Cepeda	8.00	4.00	2.25
546	Jim York	2.00	1.00	.60
547	Bobby Heise	2.00	1.00	.60
548	Don Durham	2.00	1.00	.60
549	Rangers Mgr./Coaches (Chuck Estrada, Whitey Herzog, Chuck Hiller, Jackie Moore)	2.00	1.00	.60
550	Dave Johnson	2.00	1.00	.60
551	Mike Kilkenny	2.00	1.00	.60
552	J.C. Martin	2.00	1.00	.60
553	Mickey Scott	2.00	1.00	.60
554	Dave Concepcion	2.00	1.00	.60
555	Bill Hands	2.00	1.00	.60
556	New York Yankees Team	8.00	4.00	2.00
557	Bernie Williams	2.00	1.00	.60
558	Jerry May	2.00	1.00	.60
559	Barry Lersch	2.00	1.00	.60
560	Frank Howard	3.00	1.50	.90
561	Jim Geddes	2.00	1.00	.60
562	Wayne Garrett	2.00	1.00	.60
563	Larry Haney	2.00	1.00	.60
564	Mike Thompson	2.00	1.00	.60
565	Jim Hickman	2.00	1.00	.60
566	Lew Krausse	2.00	1.00	.60
567	Bob Fenwick	2.00	1.00	.60
568	Ray Newman	2.00	1.00	.60
569	Dodgers Mgr./Coaches (Red Adams, Walt Alston, Monty Basgall, Jim Gilliam, Tom Lasorda)	5.00	2.50	1.50
570	Bill Singer	2.00	1.00	.60
571	Rusty Torres	2.00	1.00	.60
572	Gary Sutherland	2.00	1.00	.60
573	Fred Beene	2.00	1.00	.60
574	Bob Didier	2.00	1.00	.60
575	Dock Ellis	2.00	1.00	.60
576	Montreal Expos Team	5.00	2.50	1.50
577	Eric Soderholm RC	2.00	1.00	.60
578	Ken Wright	2.00	1.00	.60
579	Tom Grieve	2.00	1.00	.60
580	Joe Pepitone	2.00	1.00	.60
581	Steve Kealey	2.00	1.00	.60
582	Darrell Porter	2.00	1.00	.60
583	Bill Greif	2.00	1.00	.60
584	Chris Arnold	2.00	1.00	.60
585	Joe Niekro	2.00	1.00	.60
586	Bill Sudakis	2.00	1.00	.60
587	Rich McKinney	2.00	1.00	.60
588	Checklist 529-660	15.00	7.50	4.50
589	Ken Forsch	2.00	1.00	.60
590	Deron Johnson	2.00	1.00	.60
591	Mike Hedlund	2.00	1.00	.60
592	John Boccabella	2.00	1.00	.60
593	Royals Mgr./Coaches (Galen Cisco, Harry Dunlop, Charlie Lau, Jack McKeon)	2.00	1.00	.60
594	Vic Harris	2.00	1.00	.60
595	Don Gullett	2.00	1.00	.60
596	Boston Red Sox Team	5.00	2.50	1.50
597	Mickey Rivers	2.00	1.00	.60
598	Phil Roof	2.00	1.00	.60
599	Ed Crosby	2.00	1.00	.60
600	Dave McNally	2.00	1.00	.60
601	Rookie Catchers (George Pena, Sergio Robles, Rick Stelmaszek)	3.00	1.50	.90
602	Rookie Pitchers (Mel Behney, Ralph Garcia, Doug Rau RC)	3.00	1.50	.90
603	Rookie Third Basemen (Terry Hughes, Bill McNulty, Ken Reitz RC)	3.00	1.50	.90
604	Rookie Pitchers (Jesse Jefferson, Dennis O'Toole, Bob Strampe)	3.00	1.50	.90
605	Rookie First Basemen (Pat Bourque, Enos Cabell RC, Gonzalo Marquez)	3.00	1.50	.90
606	Rookie Outfielders (Gary Matthews RC, Tom Paciorek, Jorge Roque)	4.00	2.00	1.25

607	Rookie Shortstops (Ray Busse, Pepe Frias, Mario Guerrero)	3.00	1.50	.90
608	Rookie Pitchers (Steve Busby RC, Dick Colpaert, George Medich RC)	3.00	1.50	.90
609	Rookie Second Basemen (Larvell Blanks RC, Pedro Garcia RC, Dave Lopes RC)	5.00	2.50	1.50
610	Rookie Pitchers (Jimmy Freeman, Charlie Hough, Hank Webb)	4.00	2.00	1.25
611	Rookie Outfielders (Rich Coggins, Jim Wohlford, Richie Zisk)	3.00	1.50	.90
612	Rookie Pitchers (Steve Lawson, Bob Reynolds, Brent Strom)	3.00	1.50	.90
613	Rookie Catchers (Bob Boone RC, Mike Ivie, Skip Jutze)	12.00	6.00	3.00
614	Rookie Outfielders (Al Bumbry RC, Dwight Evans RC, Charlie Spikes)	20.00	10.00	6.00
615	Rookie Third Basemen (Ron Cey, John Hilton RC, Mike Schmidt RC)	160.00	80.00	40.00
616	Rookie Pitchers (Norm Angelini, Steve Blateric, Mike Garman)	3.00	1.50	.90
617	Rich Chiles	2.00	1.00	.60
618	Andy Etchebarren	2.00	1.00	.60
619	Billy Wilson	2.00	1.00	.60
620	Tommy Harper	2.00	1.00	.60
621	Joe Ferguson	2.00	1.00	.60
622	Larry Hisle	2.00	1.00	.60
623	Steve Renko	2.00	1.00	.60
624	Astros Mgr./Coaches (Leo Durocher, Preston Gomez, Grady Hatton, Hub Kittle, Jim Owens)	3.00	1.50	.90
625	Angel Mangual	2.00	1.00	.60
626	Bob Barton	2.00	1.00	.60
627	Luis Alvarado	2.00	1.00	.60
628	Jim Slaton	2.00	1.00	.60
629	Cleveland Indians Team	5.00	2.50	1.50
630	Denny McLain	6.00	3.00	1.75
631	Tom Matchick	2.00	1.00	.60
632	Dick Selma	2.00	1.00	.60
633	Ike Brown	2.00	1.00	.60
634	Alan Closter	2.00	1.00	.60
635	Gene Alley	2.00	1.00	.60
636	Rick Clark	2.00	1.00	.60
637	Norm Miller	2.00	1.00	.60
638	Ken Reynolds	2.00	1.00	.60
639	Willie Crawford	2.00	1.00	.60
640	Dick Bosman	2.00	1.00	.60
641	Cincinnati Reds Team	5.00	2.50	1.25
642	Jose Laboy	2.00	1.00	.60
643	Al Fitzmorris	2.00	1.00	.60
644	Jack Heidemann	2.00	1.00	.60
645	Bob Locker	2.00	1.00	.60
646	Brewers Mgr./Coaches (Del Crandall, Harvey Kuenn, Joe Nossek, Bob Shaw, Jim Walton)	2.00	1.00	.60
647	George Stone	2.00	1.00	.60
648	Tom Egan	2.00	1.00	.60
649	Rich Folkers	2.00	1.00	.60
650	Felipe Alou	4.00	2.00	1.25
651	Don Carrithers	2.00	1.00	.60
652	Ted Kubiak	2.00	1.00	.60
653	Joe Hoerner	2.00	1.00	.60
654	Minnesota Twins Team	4.00	2.00	1.25
655	Clay Kirby	2.00	1.00	.60
656	John Ellis	2.00	1.00	.60
657	Bob Johnson	2.00	1.00	.60
658	Elliott Maddox	2.00	1.00	.60
659	Jose Pagan	2.00	1.00	.60
660	Fred Scherman	2.00	1.00	.60

1973 Topps 1953 Reprints

Long before Topps reprinted virtually the entire 1953 set in its "Archives" program in 1991, selected cards from the '53 set had been reprinted in a rare eight-card issue. Some sources say the cards were produced as table favors at a Topps banquet, while at least one contemporary hobby periodical said they were sold on a test-issue basis in Brooklyn. It was said only 300 of the sets were made. Unlike the original cards in 2-5/8" x 3-3/4" format, the test issue cards are modern standard 2-1/2" x 3-1/2". Three of the players in the issue were misidentified. Card backs feature a career summary written as though in 1953; the backs are formatted differently than original 1953 Topps cards and are printed in black-and-white.

		NM	E	VG
	Complete Set (8):	750.00	375.00	225.00
	Common Player:	35.00	17.50	10.00
1	Satchell Paige	225.00	110.00	65.00
2	Jackie Robinson	300.00	150.00	90.00
3	Carl Furillo (Picture actually Bill Antonello.)	50.00	25.00	15.00
4	Al Rosen (Picture actually Jim Fridley.)	35.00	17.50	10.00
5	Hal Newhouser	40.00	20.00	12.00
6	Clyde McCullough (Picture actually Vic Janowicz.)	35.00	17.50	10.00
7	"Peanuts" Lowrey	35.00	17.50	10.00
8	Johnny Mize	85.00	42.50	25.00

1973 Topps Candy Lids

A bit out of the ordinary, the Topps Candy Lids were the top of a product called "Baseball Stars Bubble Gum." The bottom (inside) of the lids carry a color photo of a player with a ribbon containing the name, position and team. The lids are 1-7/8" in diameter. A total of 55 different lids were made, featuring most of the stars of the day.

		NM	E	VG
	Complete Set (55):	1,000	500.00	290.00
	Common Player:	8.00	4.00	2.50
	Unopened Tub:	175.00		
(1)	Hank Aaron	80.00	40.00	25.00
(2)	Dick Allen	10.00	5.00	3.00
(3)	Dusty Baker	8.00	4.00	2.50
(4)	Sal Bando	8.00	4.00	2.50
(5)	Johnny Bench	40.00	20.00	12.00
(6)	Bobby Bonds	8.00	4.00	2.50
(7)	Dick Bosman	8.00	4.00	2.50
(8)	Lou Brock	20.00	10.00	6.00
(9)	Rod Carew	32.00	16.00	9.50
(10)	Steve Carlton	32.00	16.00	9.50
(11)	Nate Colbert	8.00	4.00	2.50
(12)	Willie Davis	8.00	4.00	2.50
(13)	Larry Dierker	8.00	4.00	2.50
(14)	Mike Epstein	8.00	6.00	2.50
(15)	Carlton Fisk	20.00	10.00	6.00
(16)	Tim Foli	8.00	4.00	2.50
(17)	Ray Fosse	8.00	4.00	2.50
(18)	Bill Freehan	8.00	4.00	2.50
(19)	Bob Gibson	32.50	16.00	9.50
(20)	Bud Harrelson	8.00	4.00	2.50
(21)	Catfish Hunter	20.00	10.00	6.00
(22)	Reggie Jackson	52.00	26.00	15.50
(23)	Fergie Jenkins	20.00	10.00	6.00
(24)	Al Kaline	40.00	20.00	12.00
(25)	Harmon Killebrew	40.00	20.00	12.00
(26)	Clay Kirby	8.00	4.00	2.50
(27)	Mickey Lolich	8.00	4.00	2.50
(28)	Greg Luzinski	8.00	4.00	2.50
(29)	Mike Marshall	8.00	4.00	2.50
(30)	Lee May	8.00	4.00	2.50
(31)	John Mayberry	8.00	4.00	2.50
(32)	Willie Mays	80.00	40.00	25.00
(33)	Willie McCovey	20.00	10.00	6.00
(34)	Thurman Munson	32.50	16.00	9.50
(35)	Bobby Murcer	16.25	8.00	4.75
(36)	Gary Nolan	8.00	4.00	2.50
(37)	Amos Otis	8.00	4.00	2.50

(38)	Jim Palmer	20.00	10.00	6.00
(39)	Gaylord Perry	20.00	10.00	6.00
(40)	Lou Piniella	9.75	5.00	3.00
(41)	Brooks Robinson	40.00	20.00	12.00
(42)	Frank Robinson	40.00	20.00	12.00
(43)	Ellie Rodriguez	8.00	4.00	2.50
(44)	Pete Rose	65.00	32.50	19.50
(45)	Nolan Ryan	260.00	130.00	75.00
(46)	Manny Sanguillen	8.00	4.00	2.50
(47)	George Scott	8.00	4.00	2.50
(48)	Tom Seaver	32.50	16.00	9.50
(49)	Chris Speier	6.00	3.00	1.75
(50)	Willie Stargell	20.00	10.00	6.00
(51)	Don Sutton	20.00	10.00	6.00
(52)	Joe Torre	9.75	5.00	3.00
(53)	Billy Williams	20.00	10.00	6.00
(54)	Wilbur Wood	8.00	6.00	2.50
(55)	Carl Yastrzemski	45.50	22.75	13.50

1973 Topps Comics

Strictly a test issue, if ever publicly distributed at all (most are found without any folding which would have occurred had they actually been used to wrap a piece of bubblegum), the 24 players in the 1973 Topps Comics issue appear on 4-5/8" x 3-7/16" waxed paper wrappers. The inside of the wrapper combines a color photo and facsimile autograph with a comic-style presentation of the player's career highlights. The Comics share a checklist with the 1973 Topps Pin-Ups, virtually all star players.

		NM	E	VG
Complete Set (24):		13,500	6,750	4,050
Common Player:		200.00	100.00	60.00
(1)	Hank Aaron	1,100	550.00	330.00
(2)	Dick Allen	375.00	185.00	110.00
(3)	Johnny Bench	675.00	335.00	200.00
(4)	Steve Carlton	550.00	275.00	165.00
(5)	Nate Colbert	200.00	100.00	60.00
(6)	Willie Davis	200.00	100.00	60.00
(7)	Mike Epstein	200.00	100.00	60.00
(8)	Reggie Jackson	1,100	550.00	330.00
(9)	Harmon Killebrew	550.00	275.00	165.00
(10)	Mickey Lolich	200.00	100.00	60.00
(11)	Mike Marshall	200.00	100.00	60.00
(12)	Lee May	200.00	100.00	60.00
(13)	Willie McCovey	550.00	275.00	165.00
(14)	Bobby Murcer	300.00	150.00	90.00
(15)	Gaylord Perry	525.00	260.00	155.00
(16)	Lou Piniella	300.00	150.00	90.00
(17)	Brooks Robinson	900.00	450.00	270.00
(18)	Nolan Ryan	3,500	1,750	1,000
(19)	George Scott	200.00	100.00	60.00
(20)	Tom Seaver	750.00	375.00	225.00
(21)	Willie Stargell	550.00	275.00	165.00
(22)	Joe Torre	300.00	150.00	90.00
(23)	Billy Williams	525.00	260.00	155.00
(24)	Carl Yastrzemski	1,100	550.00	330.00

1973 Topps Pin-Ups

Another test issue of 1973, the 24 Topps Pin-Ups include the same basic format and the same checklist of star-caliber players as the Comics test issue of the same year. The

3-7/16" x 4-5/8" Pin-Ups are actually the inside of a wrapper for a piece of bubblegum. The color player photo features a decorative lozenge inserted at bottom with the player's name, team and position. There is also a facsimile autograph. Curiously, neither the Pin-Ups nor the Comics of 1973 bear team logos on the players' caps.

		NM	E	VG
Complete Set (24):		9,000	4,500	2,700
Common Player:		200.00	100.00	160.00
(1)	Hank Aaron	1,100	550.00	320.00
(2)	Dick Allen	300.00	150.00	90.00
(3)	Johnny Bench	800.00	400.00	240.00
(4)	Steve Carlton	700.00	350.00	200.00
(5)	Nate Colbert	200.00	100.00	60.00
(6)	Willie Davis	200.00	100.00	60.00
(7)	Mike Epstein	200.00	100.00	60.00
(8)	Reggie Jackson	1,100	550.00	320.00
(9)	Harmon Killebrew	750.00	375.00	225.00
(10)	Mickey Lolich	200.00	100.00	60.00
(11)	Mike Marshall	200.00	100.00	60.00
(12)	Lee May	200.00	100.00	60.00
(13)	Willie McCovey	750.00	375.00	225.00
(14)	Bobby Murcer	300.00	150.00	90.00
(15)	Gaylord Perry	700.00	350.00	200.00
(16)	Lou Piniella	300.00	150.00	90.00
(17)	Brooks Robinson	800.00	400.00	250.00
(18)	Nolan Ryan	1,200	600.00	400.00
(19)	George Scott	200.00	100.00	60.00
(20)	Tom Seaver	800.00	400.00	250.00
(21)	Willie Stargell	750.00	375.00	225.00
(22)	Joe Torre	375.00	185.00	120.00
(23)	Billy Williams	750.00	375.00	225.00
(24)	Carl Yastrzemski	875.00	440.00	275.00

1973 Topps Team Checklists

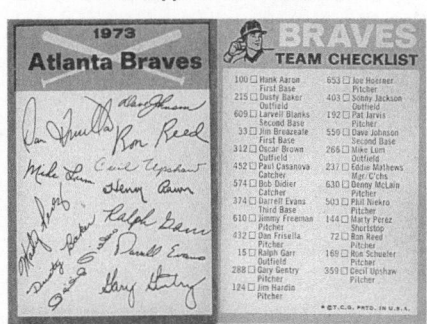

This is a 24-card unnumbered set of 2-1/2" x 3-1/2" cards that is generally believed to have been included with the high-numbered series in 1973, while also being made available in a mail-in offer. The front of the cards have the team name at the top and a white panel with various facsimile autographs takes up the rest of the space except for a blue border. Backs feature the team name and checklist. Relatively scarce, these somewhat mysterious cards are not included by many in their collections despite their obvious relationship to the regular set.

		NM	E	VG
Complete Set (24):		300.00	150.00	90.00
Common Checklist:		12.00	6.00	3.50
(1)	Atlanta Braves	12.00	6.00	3.50
(2)	Baltimore Orioles	12.00	6.00	3.50
(3)	Boston Red Sox	15.00	7.50	4.50
(4)	California Angels	12.00	6.00	3.50
(5)	Chicago Cubs	12.00	6.00	3.50
(6)	Chicago White Sox	12.00	6.00	3.50
(7)	Cincinnati Reds	15.00	7.50	4.50
(8)	Cleveland Indians	12.00	6.00	3.50
(9)	Detroit Tigers	15.00	7.50	4.50
(10)	Houston Astros	12.00	6.00	3.50
(11)	Kansas City Royals	12.00	6.00	3.50
(12)	Los Angeles Dodgers	12.00	6.00	3.50
(13)	Milwaukee Brewers	12.00	6.00	3.50
(14)	Minnesota Twins	12.00	6.00	3.50
(15)	Montreal Expos	12.00	6.00	3.50
(16)	New York Mets	15.00	7.50	4.50
(17)	New York Yankees	15.00	7.50	4.50
(18)	Oakland A's	15.00	9.00	5.50
(19)	Philadelphia Phillies	12.00	6.00	3.50
(20)	Pittsburgh Pirates	12.00	6.00	3.50
(21)	St. Louis Cardinals	12.00	6.00	3.50
(22)	San Diego Padres	12.00	6.00	3.50
(23)	San Francisco Giants	12.00	6.00	3.50
(24)	Texas Rangers	12.00	6.00	3.50

1974 Topps

Issued all at once at the beginning of the year, rather than by series throughout the baseball season as had been done since 1952, this 660-card '74 Topps set features a famous

group of error cards. At the time the cards were printed, it was uncertain whether the San Diego Padres would move to Washington, D.C., and by the time a decision was made some Padres cards had appeared with a "Washington, Nat'l League" designation on the front. A total of 15 cards were affected, and those with the Washington designation bring prices well in excess of regular cards of the same players (the Washington variations are not included in the complete set prices quoted below). The 2-1/2" x 3-1/2" cards feature color photos (frequently game-action shots) along with the player's name, team and position. Specialty cards abound, starting with a Hank Aaron tribute and running through the usual managers, statistical leaders, playoff and World Series highlights, multi-player rookie cards and All-Stars.

		NM	E	VG
Unopened Factory Set (704):		750.00		
Complete Set (660):		400.00	200.00	120.00
Common Player:		.40	.20	.10
Wax Pack (2):		9.00		
Wax Pack (8+1 - B.T.C.):		60.00		
Wax Box (36):		2,000		
Wax Pack (12+1 - B.T.C.):		75.00		
Wax Box (24):		1,875		
Cello Pack: (22):		115.00		
Rack Pack: (42):		250.00		
Vending Box (500):		925.00		
1	Hank Aaron (All-Time Home Run King)	40.00	7.50	4.00
2	Hank Aaron (Aaron Special 1954-57)	10.00	5.00	3.00
3	Hank Aaron (Aaron Special 1958-61)	10.00	5.00	3.00
4	Hank Aaron (Aaron Special 1962-65)	10.00	5.00	3.00
5	Hank Aaron (Aaron Special 1966-69)	10.00	5.00	3.00
6	Hank Aaron (Aaron Special 1970-73)	10.00	5.00	3.00
7	Jim Hunter	4.00	2.00	1.25
8	George Theodore	.40	.20	.10
9	Mickey Lolich	.40	.20	.09
10	Johnny Bench	15.00	9.00	5.50
11	Jim Bibby	.40	.20	.10
12	Dave May	.40	.20	.10
13	Tom Hilgendorf	.40	.20	.10
14	Paul Popovich	.40	.20	.10
15	Joe Torre	4.00	2.00	1.25
16	Baltimore Orioles Team	2.00	1.00	.60
17	Doug Bird	.40	.20	.10
18	Gary Thomasson	.40	.20	.10
19	Gerry Moses	.40	.20	.10
20	Nolan Ryan	25.00	15.00	9.00
21	Bob Gallagher	.40	.20	.10
22	Cy Acosta	.40	.20	.10
23	Craig Robinson	.40	.20	.10
24	John Hiller	.40	.20	.10
25	Ken Singleton	.40	.20	.10
26	Bill Campbell **RC**	.40	.20	.10
27	George Scott	.40	.20	.10
28	Manny Sanguillen	.40	.20	.10
29	Phil Niekro	4.00	2.00	1.25
30	Bobby Bonds	.40	.20	.09
31	Astros Mgr./Coaches (Roger Craig, Preston Gomez, Grady Hatton, Hub Kittle, Bob Lillis)	.40	.20	.09
32a	John Grubb (Washington)	3.00	1.50	.90
32b	John Grubb (San Diego)	.40	.20	.10
33	Don Newhauser	.40	.20	.10
34	Andy Kosco	.40	.20	.10
35	Gaylord Perry	4.00	2.00	1.25
36	St. Louis Cardinals Team	2.00	1.00	.60
37	Dave Sells	.40	.20	.10
38	Don Kessinger	.40	.20	.10
39	Ken Suarez	.40	.20	.10
40	Jim Palmer	6.00	3.00	1.75
41	Bobby Floyd	.40	.20	.10
42	Claude Osteen	.40	.20	.10
43	Jim Wynn	.40	.20	.10
44	Mel Stottlemyre	.75	.40	.25

45	Dave Johnson	.40	.20	.10
46	Pat Kelly	.40	.20	.10
47	Dick Ruthven **RC**	.40	.20	.10
48	Dick Sharon	.40	.20	.10
49	Steve Renko	.40	.20	.10
50	Rod Carew	6.00	3.00	1.75
51	Bobby Heise	.40	.20	.10
52	Al Oliver	.50	.25	.15
53a	Fred Kendall (Washington)	3.00	1.50	.90
53b	Fred Kendall (San Diego)	.40	.20	.10
54	Elias Sosa **RC**	.40	.20	.10
55	Frank Robinson	8.00	4.00	2.50
56	New York Mets Team	1.50	.70	.45
57	Darold Knowles	.40	.20	.10
58	Charlie Spikes	.40	.20	.10
59	Ross Grimsley	.40	.20	.10
60	Lou Brock	8.00	4.00	2.50
61	Luis Aparicio	4.00	2.00	1.25
62	Bob Locker	.40	.20	.10
63	Bill Sudakis	.40	.20	.10
64	Doug Rau	.40	.20	.10
65	Amos Otis	.40	.20	.10
66	Sparky Lyle	.40	.20	.10
67	Tommy Helms	.40	.20	.10
68	Grant Jackson	.40	.20	.10
69	Del Unser	.40	.20	.10
70	Dick Allen	.75	.40	.25
71	Danny Frisella	.40	.20	.10
72	Aurelio Rodriguez	.40	.20	.10
73	Mike Marshall	.40	.20	.10
74	Minnesota Twins Team	1.00	.50	.30
75	Jim Colborn	.40	.20	.10
76	Mickey Rivers	.40	.20	.10
77a	Rich Troedson (Washington)	3.00	1.50	.90
77b	Rich Troedson (San Diego)	.40	.20	.10
78	Giants Mgr./Coaches(Joe Amalfitano, Charlie Fox, Andy Gilbert, Don McMahon, John McNamara)	.40	.20	.10
79	Gene Tenace	.40	.20	.10
80	Tom Seaver	10.00	5.00	3.00
81	Frank Duffy	.40	.20	.10
82	Dave Giusti	.40	.20	.10
83	Orlando Cepeda	4.00	2.00	1.25
84	Rick Wise	.40	.20	.10
85	Joe Morgan	6.00	3.00	1.75
86	Joe Ferguson	.40	.20	.10
87	Fergie Jenkins	4.00	2.00	1.25
88	Freddie Patek	.40	.20	.10
89	Jackie Brown	.40	.20	.10
90	Bobby Murcer	.50	.25	.15
91	Ken Forsch	.40	.20	.10
92	Paul Blair	.40	.20	.10
93	Rod Gilbreath	.40	.20	.10
94	Detroit Tigers Team	1.00	.50	.30
95	Steve Carlton	8.00	4.00	2.50
96	Jerry Hairston Sr. **RC**	.40	.20	.10
97	Bob Bailey	.40	.20	.10
98	Bert Blyleven	6.00	3.00	1.75
99	Brewers Mgr./Coaches (Del Crandall, Harvey Kuenn, Joe Nossek, Jim Walton, Al Widmar)	.40	.20	.10
100	Willie Stargell	8.00	4.00	2.50
101	Bobby Valentine	.40	.20	.10
102a	Bill Greif (Washington)	3.00	1.50	.90
102b	Bill Greif (San Diego)	.40	.20	.10
103	Sal Bando	.40	.20	.10
104	Ron Bryant	.40	.20	.10
105	Carlton Fisk	10.00	5.00	3.00
106	Harry Parker	.40	.20	.10
107	Alex Johnson	.40	.20	.10
108	Al Hrabosky	.40	.20	.10
109	Bob Grich	.40	.20	.10
110	Billy Williams	5.00	2.50	1.50
111	Clay Carroll	.40	.20	.10
112	Dave Lopes	.40	.20	.10
113	Dick Drago	.40	.20	.10
114	California Angels Team	1.00	.50	.30
115	Willie Horton	.40	.20	.10
116	Jerry Reuss	.40	.20	.10
117	Ron Blomberg	.40	.20	.10
118	Bill Lee	.40	.20	.10
119	Phillies Mgr./Coaches (Carroll Beringer, Bill DeMars, Danny Ozark, Ray Rippelmeyer, Bobby Wine)	.40	.20	.10
120	Wilbur Wood	.40	.20	.10
121	Larry Lintz	.40	.20	.10
122	Jim Holt	.40	.20	.10
123	Nelson Briles	.40	.20	.10
124	Bob Coluccio	.40	.20	.10
125a	Nate Colbert (Washington)	3.00	1.50	.90
125b	Nate Colbert (San Diego)	.40	.20	.10
126	Checklist 1-132	.75	.40	.25
127	Tom Paciorek	.40	.20	.10

128	John Ellis	.40	.20	.10
129	Chris Speier	.40	.20	.10
130	Reggie Jackson	15.00	7.50	4.50
131	Bob Boone	1.50	.70	.45
132	Felix Millan	.40	.20	.10
133	David Clyde **RC**	.40	.20	.10
134	Denis Menke	.40	.20	.10
135	Roy White	.40	.20	.10
136	Rick Reuschel	.40	.20	.10
137	Al Bumbry	.40	.20	.10
138	Ed Brinkman	.40	.20	.10
139	Aurelio Monteagudo	.40	.20	.10
140	Darrell Evans	.75	.40	.25
141	Pat Bourque	.40	.20	.10
142	Pedro Garcia	.40	.20	.10
143	Dick Woodson	.40	.20	.10
144	Dodgers Mgr./Coaches (Red Adams, Walter Alston, Monty Basgall, Jim Gilliam, Tom Lasorda)	2.00	1.00	.60
145	Dock Ellis	.40	.20	.10
146	Ron Fairly	.40	.20	.10
147	Bart Johnson	.40	.20	.10
148a	Dave Hilton (Washington)	3.00	1.50	.90
148b	Dave Hilton (San Diego)	.40	.20	.10
149	Mac Scarce	.40	.20	.10
150	John Mayberry	.40	.20	.10
151	Diego Segui	.40	.20	.10
152	Oscar Gamble	.40	.20	.10
153	Jon Matlack	.40	.20	.10
154	Houston Astros Team	1.50	.70	.45
155	Bert Campaneris	.40	.20	.10
156	Randy Moffitt	.40	.20	.10
157	Vic Harris	.40	.20	.10
158	Jack Billingham	.40	.20	.10
159	Jim Ray Hart	.40	.20	.10
160	Brooks Robinson	6.00	3.00	1.75
161	Ray Burris **RC**	.50	.20	.10
162	Bill Freehan	.40	.20	.10
163	Ken Berry	.40	.20	.10
164	Tom House	.40	.20	.10
165	Willie Davis	.40	.20	.10
166	Royals Mgr./Coaches (Galen Cisco, Harry Dunlop, Charlie Lau, Jack McKeon)	.40	.20	.10
167	Luis Tiant	1.00	.50	.30
168	Danny Thompson	.40	.20	.10
169	Steve Rogers **RC**	.40	.20	.10
170	Bill Melton	.40	.20	.10
171	Eduardo Rodriguez	.40	.20	.10
172	Gene Clines	.40	.20	.10
173a	Randy Jones **RC** (Washington)	3.00	1.50	.90
173b	Randy Jones **RC** (San Diego)	.40	.20	.10
174	Bill Robinson	.40	.20	.10
175	Reggie Cleveland	.40	.20	.10
176	John Lowenstein	.40	.20	.10
177	Dave Roberts	.40	.20	.10
178	Garry Maddox	.40	.20	.10
179	Mets Mgr./Coaches(Yogi Berra, Roy McMillan, Joe Pignatano, Rube Walker, Eddie Yost)	1.50	.70	.45
180	Ken Holtzman	.40	.20	.10
181	Cesar Geronimo	.40	.20	.10
182	Lindy McDaniel	.40	.20	.10
183	Johnny Oates	.40	.20	.10
184	Texas Rangers Team	1.00	.50	.30
185	Jose Cardenal	.40	.20	.10
186	Fred Scherman	.40	.20	.10
187	Don Baylor	1.00	.50	.30
188	Rudy Meoli	.40	.20	.10
189	Jim Brewer	.40	.20	.10
190	Tony Oliva	1.50	.70	.45
191	Al Fitzmorris	.40	.20	.10
192	Mario Guerrero	.40	.20	.10
193	Tom Walker	.40	.20	.10
194	Darrell Porter	.40	.20	.10
195	Carlos May	.40	.20	.10
196	Jim Fregosi	.75	.40	.25
197a	Vicente Romo (Washington)	3.00	1.50	.90
197b	Vicente Romo (San Diego)	.40	.20	.10
198	Dave Cash	.40	.20	.10
199	Mike Kekich	.40	.20	.10
200	Cesar Cedeno	.40	.20	.10
201	Batting Leaders(Rod Carew, Pete Rose)	6.00	3.00	1.75
202	Home Run Leaders (Reggie Jackson, Willie Stargell)	4.00	2.00	1.25
203	RBI Leaders(Reggie Jackson, Willie Stargell)	4.00	2.00	1.25
204	Stolen Base Leaders(Lou Brock, Tommy Harper)	1.50	.70	.45
205	Victory Leaders(Ron Bryant, Wilbur Wood)	1.00	.50	.30

206	Earned Run Average Leaders(Jim Palmer, Tom Seaver)	2.00	1.00	.60
207	Strikeout Leaders(Nolan Ryan, Tom Seaver)	10.00	5.00	3.00
208	Leading Firemen(John Hiller, Mike Marshall)	1.00	.50	.30
209	Ted Sizemore	.40	.20	.10
210	Bill Singer	.40	.20	.10
211	Chicago Cubs Team	1.00	.50	.30
212	Rollie Fingers	4.00	2.00	1.25
213	Dave Rader	.40	.20	.10
214	Billy Grabarkewitz	.40	.20	.10
215	Al Kaline	9.00	4.50	2.75
216	Ray Sadecki	.40	.20	.10
217	Tim Foli	.40	.20	.10
218	Johnny Briggs	.40	.20	.10
219	Doug Griffin	.40	.20	.10
220	Don Sutton	4.00	2.00	1.25
221	White Sox Mgr./Coaches (Joe Lonnett, Jim Mahoney, Alex Monchak, Johnny Sain, Chuck Tanner)	.40	.20	.10
222	Ramon Hernandez	.40	.20	.10
223	Jeff Burroughs	.40	.20	.10
224	Roger Metzger	.40	.20	.10
225	Paul Splittorff	.40	.20	.10
226a	Washington Nat'l. Team	8.00	4.00	2.50
226b	San Diego Padres Team	7.50	3.75	2.25
227	Mike Lum	.40	.20	.10
228	Ted Kubiak	.40	.20	.10
229	Fritz Peterson	.40	.20	.10
230	Tony Perez	4.00	2.00	1.25
231	Dick Tidrow	.40	.20	.10
232	Steve Brye	.40	.20	.10
233	Jim Barr	.40	.20	.10
234	John Milner	.40	.20	.10
235	Dave McNally	.40	.20	.10
236	Cardinals Mgr./Coaches (Vern Benson, George Kissell, Johnny Lewis, Red Schoendienst, Barney Schultz)	.75	.40	.25
237	Ken Brett	.40	.20	.10
238	Fran Healy	.40	.20	.10
239	Bill Russell	.40	.20	.10
240	Joe Coleman	.40	.20	.10
241a	Glenn Beckert (Washington)	3.00	1.50	.90
241b	Glenn Beckert (San Diego)	.40	.20	.10
242	Bill Gogolewski	.40	.20	.10
243	Bob Oliver	.40	.20	.10
244	Carl Morton	.40	.20	.10
245	Cleon Jones	.40	.20	.10
246	Oakland A's Team	2.00	1.00	.60
247	Rick Miller	.40	.20	.10
248	Tom Hall	.40	.20	.10
249	George Mitterwald	.40	.20	.10
250a	Willie McCovey (Washington)	20.00	10.00	6.00
250b	Willie McCovey (San Diego)	15.00	7.50	4.50
251	Graig Nettles	1.50	.70	.45
252	Dave Parker **RC**	9.00	4.50	2.75
253	John Boccabella	.40	.20	.10
254	Stan Bahnsen	.40	.20	.10
255	Larry Bowa	1.00	.50	.30
256	Tom Griffin	.40	.20	.10
257	Buddy Bell	.40	.20	.10
258	Jerry Morales	.40	.20	.10
259	Bob Reynolds	.40	.20	.10
260	Ted Simmons	.75	.40	.25
261	Jerry Bell	.40	.20	.10
262	Ed Kirkpatrick	.40	.20	.10
263	Checklist 133-264	1.00	.50	.30
264	Joe Rudi	.40	.20	.10
265	Tug McGraw	.40	.20	.10
266	Jim Northrup	.40	.20	.10
267	Andy Messersmith	.40	.20	.10
268	Tom Grieve	.40	.20	.10
269	Bob Johnson	.40	.20	.10
270	Ron Santo	3.00	1.50	.90
271	Bill Hands	.40	.20	.10
272	Paul Casanova	.40	.20	.10
273	Checklist 265-396	.75	.40	.25
274	Fred Beene	.40	.20	.10
275	Ron Hunt	.40	.20	.10
276	Angels Mgr./Coaches (Tom Morgan, Salty Parker, Jimmie Reese, John Roseboro, Bobby Winkles)	.40	.20	.10
277	Gary Nolan	.40	.20	.10
278	Cookie Rojas	.40	.20	.10
279	Jim Crawford	.40	.20	.10
280	Carl Yastrzemski	10.00	5.00	3.00
281	San Francisco Giants Team	1.00	.50	.30
282	Doyle Alexander	.40	.20	.10
283	Mike Schmidt	15.00	7.50	4.50
284	Dave Duncan	.40	.20	.10

285	Reggie Smith	.40	.20	.10
286	Tony Muser	.40	.20	.10
287	Clay Kirby	.40	.20	.10
288	Gorman Thomas **RC**	2.00	1.00	.60
289	Rick Auerbach	.40	.20	.10
290	Vida Blue	1.00	.50	.30
291	Don Hahn	.40	.20	.10
292	Chuck Seelbach	.40	.20	.10
293	Milt May	.40	.20	.10
294	Steve Foucault	.40	.20	.10
295	Rick Monday	.40	.20	.10
296	Ray Corbin	.40	.20	.10
297	Hal Breeden	.40	.20	.10
298	Roric Harrison	.40	.20	.10
299	Gene Michael	.40	.20	.10
300	Pete Rose	20.00	10.00	6.00
301	Bob Montgomery	.40	.20	.10
302	Rudy May	.40	.20	.10
303	George Hendrick	.40	.20	.10
304	Don Wilson	.40	.20	.10
305	Tito Fuentes	.40	.20	.10
306	Orioles Mgr./Coaches (George Bamberger, Jim Frey, Billy Hunter, George Staller, Earl Weaver)	2.00	1.00	.60
307	Luis Melendez	.40	.20	.10
308	Bruce Dal Canton	.40	.20	.10
309a	Dave Roberts (Washington)	3.00	1.50	.90
309b	Dave Roberts (San Diego)	.40	.20	.10
310	Terry Forster	.40	.20	.10
311	Jerry Grote	.40	.20	.10
312	Deron Johnson	.40	.20	.10
313	Berry Lersch	.40	.20	.10
314	Milwaukee Brewers Team	1.00	.50	.30
315	Ron Cey	.50	.25	.15
316	Jim Perry	.40	.20	.10
317	Richie Zisk	.40	.20	.10
318	Jim Merritt	.40	.20	.10
319	Randy Hundley	.40	.20	.10
320	Dusty Baker	1.00	.50	.30
321	Steve Braun	.40	.20	.10
322	Ernie McAnally	.40	.20	.10
323	Richie Scheinblum	.40	.20	.10
324	Steve Kline	.40	.20	.10
325	Tommy Harper	.40	.20	.10
326	Reds Mgr./Coaches (Sparky Anderson, Alex Grammas, Ted Kluszewski, George Scherger, Larry Shepard)	2.00	1.00	.60
327	Tom Timmermann	.40	.20	.10
328	Skip Jutze	.40	.20	.10
329	Mark Belanger	.40	.20	.10
330	Juan Marichal	4.00	2.00	1.25
331	All-Star Catchers (Johnny Bench, Carlton Fisk)	4.00	2.00	1.25
332	All-Star First Basemen (Hank Aaron, Dick Allen)	6.00	3.00	1.75
333	All-Star Second Basemen (Rod Carew, Joe Morgan)	3.00	1.50	.90
334	All-Star Third Basemen (Brooks Robinson, Ron Santo)	2.00	1.00	.60
335	All-Star Shortstops (Bert Campaneris, Chris Speier)	1.00	.50	.30
336	All-Star Left Fielders (Bobby Murcer, Pete Rose)	5.00	2.50	1.50
337	All-Star Center Fielders (Cesar Cedeno, Amos Otis)	.75	.40	.25
338	All-Star Right Fielders (Reggie Jackson, Billy Williams)	4.00	2.00	1.25
339	All-Star Pitchers (Jim Hunter, Rick Wise)	2.00	1.00	.60
340	Thurman Munson	8.00	4.00	2.50
341	Dan Driessen **RC**	.40	.20	.10
342	Jim Lonborg	.40	.20	.10
343	Kansas City Royals Team	1.00	.50	.30
344	Mike Caldwell	.40	.20	.10
345	Bill North	.40	.20	.10
346	Ron Reed	.40	.20	.10
347	Sandy Alomar	.40	.20	.10
348	Pete Richert	.40	.20	.10
349	John Vukovich	.40	.20	.10
350	Bob Gibson	6.00	3.00	1.75
351	Dwight Evans	1.00	.50	.30
352	Bill Stoneman	.40	.20	.10
353	Rich Coggins	.40	.20	.10
354	Cubs Mgr./Coaches (Hank Aguirre, Whitey Lockman, Jim Marshall, J.C. Martin, Al Spangler)	.40	.20	.10
355	Dave Nelson	.40	.20	.10
356	Jerry Koosman	.40	.20	.10
357	Buddy Bradford	.40	.20	.10
358	Dal Maxvill	.40	.20	.10
359	Brent Strom	.40	.20	.10

360	Greg Luzinski	1.00	.50	.30
361	Don Carrithers	.40	.20	.10
362	Hal King	.40	.20	.10
363	New York Yankees Team	2.00	1.00	.60
364a	Clarence Gaston (Washington)	3.00	1.50	.90
364b	Clarence Gaston (San Diego)	.40	.20	.10
365	Steve Busby	.40	.20	.10
366	Larry Hisle	.40	.20	.10
367	Norm Cash	1.00	.50	.30
368	Manny Mota	.40	.20	.10
369	Paul Lindblad	.40	.20	.10
370	Bob Watson	.40	.20	.10
371	Jim Slaton	.40	.20	.10
372	Ken Reitz	.40	.20	.10
373	John Curtis	.40	.20	.10
374	Marty Perez	.40	.20	.10
375	Earl Williams	.40	.20	.10
376	Jorge Orta	.40	.20	.10
377	Ron Woods	.40	.20	.10
378	Burt Hooton	.40	.20	.10
379	Rangers Mgr./Coaches (Art Fowler, Frank Lucchesi, Billy Martin, Jackie Moore, Charlie Silvera)	.45	.25	.15
380	Bud Harrelson	.40	.20	.10
381	Charlie Sands	.40	.20	.10
382	Bob Moose	.40	.20	.10
383	Philadelphia Phillies Team	1.00	.50	.30
384	Chris Chambliss	.75	.40	.25
385	Don Gullett	.40	.20	.10
386	Gary Matthews	.40	.20	.10
387a	Rich Morales (Washington)	3.00	1.50	.90
387b	Rich Morales (San Diego)	.40	.20	.10
388	Phil Roof	.40	.20	.10
389	Gates Brown	.40	.20	.10
390	Lou Piniella	2.00	1.00	.60
391	Billy Champion	.40	.20	.10
392	Dick Green	.40	.20	.10
393	Orlando Pena	.40	.20	.10
394	Ken Henderson	.40	.20	.10
395	Doug Rader	.40	.20	.10
396	Tommy Davis	.40	.20	.10
397	George Stone	.40	.20	.10
398	Duke Sims	.40	.20	.10
399	Mike Paul	.40	.20	.10
400	Harmon Killebrew	6.00	3.00	1.75
401	Elliott Maddox	.40	.20	.10
402	Jim Rooker	.40	.20	.10
403	Red Sox Mgr./Coaches (Don Bryant, Darrell Johnson, Eddie Popowski, Lee Stange, Don Zimmer)	.40	.20	.10
404	Jim Howarth	.40	.20	.10
405	Ellie Rodriguez	.40	.20	.10
406	Steve Arlin	.40	.20	.10
407	Jim Wohlford	.40	.20	.10
408	Charlie Hough	1.00	.50	.30
409	Ike Brown	.40	.20	.10
410	Pedro Borbon	.40	.20	.10
411	Frank Baker	.40	.20	.10
412	Chuck Taylor	.40	.20	.10
413	Don Money	.40	.20	.10
414	Checklist 397-528	2.00	1.00	.60
415	Gary Gentry	.40	.20	.10
416	Chicago White Sox Team	1.00	.50	.30
417	Rich Folkers	.40	.20	.10
418	Walt Williams	.40	.20	.10
419	Wayne Twitchell	.40	.20	.10
420	Ray Fosse	.40	.20	.10
421	Dan Fife	.40	.20	.10
422	Gonzalo Marquez	.40	.20	.10
423	Fred Stanley	.40	.20	.10
424	Jim Beauchamp	.40	.20	.10
425	Pete Broberg	.40	.20	.10
426	Rennie Stennett	.40	.20	.10
427	Bobby Bolin	.40	.20	.10
428	Gary Sutherland	.40	.20	.10
429	Dick Lange	.40	.20	.10
430	Matty Alou	.40	.20	.10
431	Gene Garber **RC**	.40	.20	.10
432	Chris Arnold	.40	.20	.10
433	Lerrin LaGrow	.40	.20	.10
434	Ken McMullen	.40	.20	.10
435	Dave Concepcion	1.00	.50	.30
436	Don Hood	.40	.20	.10
437	Jim Lyttle	.40	.20	.10
438	Ed Herrmann	.40	.20	.10
439	Norm Miller	.40	.20	.10
440	Jim Kaat	1.50	.70	.45
441	Tom Ragland	.40	.20	.10
442	Alan Foster	.40	.20	.10
443	Tom Hutton	.40	.20	.10
444	Vic Davalillo	.40	.20	.10
445	George Medich	.40	.20	.10
446	Len Randle	.40	.20	.10

447	Twins Mgr./Coaches (Vern Morgan, Frank Quilici, Bob Rodgers, Ralph Rowe)	.40	.20	.10
448	Ron Hodges	.40	.20	.10
449	Tom McCraw	.40	.20	.10
450	Rich Hebner	.40	.20	.10
451	Tommy John	1.00	.50	.30
452	Gene Hiser	.40	.20	.10
453	Balor Moore	.40	.20	.10
454	Kurt Bevacqua	.40	.20	.10
455	Tom Bradley	.40	.20	.10
456	Dave Winfield **RC**	30.00	15.00	9.00
457	Chuck Goggin	.40	.20	.10
458	Jim Ray	.40	.20	.10
459	Cincinnati Reds Team	1.50	.70	.45
460	Boog Powell	1.00	.50	.30
461	John Odom	.40	.20	.10
462	Luis Alvarado	.40	.20	.10
463	Pat Dobson	.40	.20	.10
464	Jose Cruz	.40	.20	.10
465	Dick Bosman	.40	.20	.10
466	Dick Billings	.40	.20	.10
467	Winston Llenas	.40	.20	.10
468	Pepe Frias	.40	.20	.10
469	Joe Decker	.40	.20	.10
470	A.L. Playoffs (Reggie Jackson)	4.00	2.00	1.25
471	N.L. Playoffs (Jon Matlack)	.50	.25	.15
472	World Series Game 1 (Darold Knowles)	.50	.25	.15
473	World Series Game 2 (Willie Mays)	6.00	3.00	1.75
474	World Series Game 3	1.00	.50	.30
475	World Series Game 4	1.00	.50	.30
476	World Series Game 5	1.00	.50	.30
477	World Series Game 6 (Reggie Jackson)	4.00	2.00	1.25
478	World Series Game 7	1.50	.75	.45
479	A's Celebrate (Win 2nd Consecutive Championship!)	2.50	1.25	.75
480	Willie Crawford	.40	.20	.10
481	Jerry Terrell	.40	.20	.10
482	Bob Didier	.40	.20	.10
483	Atlanta Braves Team	1.00	.50	.30
484	Carmen Fanzone	.40	.20	.10
485	Felipe Alou	.50	.25	.15
486	Steve Stone	.40	.20	.10
487	Ted Martinez	.40	.20	.10
488	Andy Etchebarren	.40	.20	.10
489	Pirates Mgr./Coaches (Don Leppert, Bill Mazeroski, Danny Murtaugh, Don Osborn, Bob Skinner)	.75	.40	.25
490	Vada Pinson	1.00	.50	.30
491	Roger Nelson	.40	.20	.10
492	Mike Rogodzinski	.40	.20	.10
493	Joe Hoerner	.40	.20	.10
494	Ed Goodson	.40	.20	.10
495	Dick McAuliffe	.40	.20	.10
496	Tom Murphy	.40	.20	.10
497	Bobby Mitchell	.40	.20	.10
498	Pat Corrales	.40	.20	.10
499	Rusty Torres	.40	.20	.10
500	Lee May	.75	.40	.25
501	Eddie Leon	.40	.20	.10
502	Dave LaRoche	.40	.20	.10
503	Eric Soderholm	.40	.20	.10
504	Joe Niekro	.75	.40	.25
505	Bill Buckner	.75	.40	.25
506	Ed Farmer	.40	.20	.10
507	Larry Stahl	.40	.20	.10
508	Montreal Expos Team	1.00	.50	.30
509	Jesse Jefferson	.40	.20	.10
510	Wayne Garrett	.40	.20	.10
511	Toby Harrah	.40	.20	.10
512	Joe Lahoud	.40	.20	.10
513	Jim Campanis	.40	.20	.10
514	Paul Schaal	.40	.20	.10
515	Willie Montanez	.40	.20	.10
516	Horacio Pina	.40	.20	.10
517	Mike Hegan	.40	.20	.10
518	Derrel Thomas	.40	.20	.10
519	Bill Sharp	.40	.20	.10
520	Tim McCarver	1.50	.70	.45
521	Indians Mgr./Coaches (Ken Aspromonte, Clay Bryant, Tony Pacheco)	.40	.20	.10
522	J.R. Richard	1.00	.50	.30
523	Cecil Cooper	1.00	.50	.30
524	Bill Plummer	.40	.20	.10
525	Clyde Wright	.40	.20	.10
526	Frank Tepedino	.40	.20	.10
527	Bobby Darwin	.40	.20	.10
528	Bill Bonham	.40	.20	.10
529	Horace Clarke	.40	.20	.10
530	Mickey Stanley	.40	.20	.10

531	Expos Mgr./Coaches (Dave Bristol, Larry Doby, Gene Mauch, Cal McLish, Jerry Zimmerman)	.40	.20	.10
532	Skip Lockwood	.40	.20	.10
533	Mike Phillips	.40	.20	.10
534	Eddie Watt	.40	.20	.10
535	Bob Tolan	.40	.20	.10
536	Duffy Dyer	.40	.20	.10
537	Steve Mingori	.40	.20	.10
538	Cesar Tovar	.40	.20	.10
539	Lloyd Allen	.40	.20	.10
540	Bob Robertson	.40	.20	.10
541	Cleveland Indians Team	1.00	.50	.30
542	Rich Gossage	4.00	2.00	1.25
543	Danny Cater	.40	.20	.10
544	Ron Schueler	.40	.20	.10
545	Billy Conigliaro	.40	.20	.10
546	Mike Corkins	.40	.20	.10
547	Glenn Borgmann	.40	.20	.10
548	Sonny Siebert	.40	.20	.10
549	Mike Jorgensen	.40	.20	.10
550	Sam McDowell	.40	.20	.10
551	Von Joshua	.40	.20	.10
552	Denny Doyle	.40	.20	.10
553	Jim Willoughby	.40	.20	.10
554	Tim Johnson	.40	.20	.10
555	Woodie Fryman	.40	.20	.10
556	Dave Campbell	.40	.20	.10
557	Jim McGlothlin	.40	.20	.10
558	Bill Fahey	.40	.20	.10
559	Darrel Chaney	.40	.20	.10
560	Mike Cuellar	.40	.20	.10
561	Ed Kranepool	.40	.20	.10
562	Jack Aker	.40	.20	.10
563	Hal McRae	.75	.40	.25
564	Mike Ryan	.40	.20	.10
565	Milt Wilcox	.40	.20	.10
566	Jackie Hernandez	.40	.20	.10
567	Boston Red Sox Team	1.50	.75	.45
568	Mike Torrez	.40	.20	.10
569	Rick Dempsey	.40	.20	.10
570	Ralph Garr	.40	.20	.10
571	Rich Hand	.40	.20	.10
572	Enzo Hernandez	.40	.20	.10
573	Mike Adams	.40	.20	.10
574	Bill Parsons	.40	.20	.10
575	Steve Garvey	2.00	1.00	.60
576	Scipio Spinks	.40	.20	.10
577	Mike Sadek	.40	.20	.10
578	Ralph Houk	.75	.40	.25
579	Cecil Upshaw	.40	.20	.10
580	Jim Spencer	.40	.20	.10
581	Fred Norman	.40	.20	.10
582	Bucky Dent RC	2.00	1.00	.60
583	Marty Pattin	.40	.20	.10
584	Ken Rudolph	.40	.20	.10
585	Merv Rettenmund	.40	.20	.10
586	Jack Brohamer	.40	.20	.10
587	Larry Christenson RC	.40	.20	.10
588	Hal Lanier	.40	.20	.10
589	Boots Day	.40	.20	.10
590	Rogelio Moret	.40	.20	.10
591	Sonny Jackson	.40	.20	.10
592	Ed Bane	.40	.20	.10
593	Steve Yeager	.40	.20	.10
594	Leroy Stanton	.40	.20	.10
595	Steve Blass	.40	.20	.10
596	Rookie Pitchers(Wayne Garland RC, Fred Holdsworth, Mark Littell RC, Dick Pole)	.40	.20	.10
597	Rookie Shortstops(Dave Chalk, John Gamble, Pete Mackanin, Manny Trillo RC)	1.00	.50	.30
598	Rookie Outfielders (Dave Augustine RC, Ken Griffey RC, Steve Ontiveros RC, Jim Tyrone RC)	10.00	5.00	3.00
599a	Rookie Pitchers (Ron Diorio, Dave Freisleben, Frank Riccelli, Greg Shanahan) (Freisleben- Washington)	1.00	.50	.30
599b	Rookie Pitchers (Ron Diorio, Dave Freisleben, Frank Riccelli, Greg Shanahan) (Freisleben- San Diego large print.)	3.00	1.50	.90
599c	Rookie Pitchers (Ron Diorio, Dave Freisleben, Frank Riccelli, Greg Shanahan) (Freisleben- San Diego small print.)	5.00	2.50	1.50

600	Rookie Infielders (Ron Cash RC, Jim Cox RC, Bill Madlock RC, Reggie Sanders RC)	5.00	2.50	1.50
601	Rookie Outfielders(Ed Armbrister RC, Rich Bladt RC, Brian Downing RC, Bake McBride RC)	2.00	1.00	.60
602	Rookie Pitchers(Glenn Abbott, Rick Henninger, Craig Swan, Dan Vossler)	.75	.40	.25
603	Rookie Catchers(Barry Foote, Tom Lundstedt, Charlie Moore RC, Sergio Robles)	.75	.40	.25
604	Rookie Infielders(Terry Hughes RC, John Knox RC, Andy Thornton RC, Frank White RC)	4.00	2.00	1.25
605	Rookie Pitchers(Vic Albury RC, Ken Frailing RC, Kevin Kobel RC, Frank Tanana RC)	3.00	1.50	.90
606	Rookie Outfielders(Jim Fuller, Wilbur Howard, Tommy Smith, Otto Velez)	.75	.40	.25
607	Rookie Shortstops (Leo Foster, Tom Heintzelman, Dave Rosello, Frank Taveras RC)	.75	.40	.25
608a	Rookie Pitchers(Bob Apodaco, Dick Baney, John D'Acquisto, Mike Wallace) (Apodaca incorrect)	1.50	.75	.45
608b	Rookie Pitchers(Bob Apodaca, Dick Baney, John D'Acquisto, Mike Wallace) (Corrected)	.75	.40	.25
609	Rico Petrocelli	1.00	.50	.30
610	Dave Kingman	.75	.40	.25
611	Rick Stelmaszek	.40	.20	.10
612	Luke Walker	.40	.20	.10
613	Dan Monzon	.40	.20	.10
614	Adrian Devine	.40	.20	.10
615	Johnny Jeter	.40	.20	.10
616	Larry Gura	.40	.20	.10
617	Ted Ford	.40	.20	.10
618	Jim Mason	.40	.20	.10
619	Mike Anderson	.40	.20	.10
620	Al Downing	.40	.20	.10
621	Bernie Carbo	.40	.20	.10
622	Phil Gagliano	.40	.20	.10
623	Celerino Sanchez	.40	.20	.10
624	Bob Miller	.40	.20	.10
625	Ollie Brown	.40	.20	.10
626	Pittsburgh Pirates Team	1.00	.50	.30
627	Carl Taylor	.40	.20	.10
628	Ivan Murrell	.40	.20	.10
629	Rusty Staub	.75	.40	.25
630	Tommie Agee	.40	.20	.10
631	Steve Barber	.40	.20	.10
632	George Culver	.40	.20	.10
633	Dave Hamilton	.40	.20	.10
634	Braves Mgr./Coaches (Jim Busby, Eddie Mathews, Connie Ryan, Ken Silvestri, Herm Starrette)	2.00	1.00	.60
635	John Edwards	.40	.20	.10
636	Dave Goltz	.40	.20	.10
637	Checklist 529-660	1.00	.50	.30
638	Ken Sanders	.40	.20	.10
639	Joe Lovitto	.40	.20	.10
640	Milt Pappas	.40	.20	.10
641	Chuck Brinkman	.40	.20	.10
642	Terry Harmon	.40	.20	.10
643	Los Angeles Dodgers Team	2.50	1.25	.75
644	Wayne Granger	.40	.20	.10
645	Ken Boswell	.40	.20	.10
646	George Foster	.75	.40	.25
647	Juan Beniquez RC	.40	.20	.10
648	Terry Crowley	.40	.20	.10
649	Fernando Gonzalez	.40	.20	.10
650	Mike Epstein	.40	.20	.10
651	Leron Lee	.40	.20	.10
652	Gail Hopkins	.40	.20	.10
653	Mike Stinson	.40	.20	.10
654a	Jesus Alou (No position.)	4.00	2.00	1.25
654b	Jesus Alou ("Outfield")	.40	.20	.10
655	Mike Tyson	.40	.20	.10
656	Adrian Garrett	.40	.20	.10
657	Jim Shellenback	.40	.20	.10
658	Lee Lacy	.40	.20	.10
659	Joe Lis	.40	.20	.10
660	Larry Dierker	1.50	.70	.45

1974 Topps Action Emblem Cloth Stickers

This enigmatic Topps test issue has never found favor with collectors because no actual ballplayers are pictured. In fact, official team logos are not used either, negating the necessity of licensing from either Major League Baseball or the Players Association. The 2-1/2" x 3-1/2" cloth stickers were sold with a rub-off baseball game card in a Topps white test wrapper with a sticker describing them as "Topps Baseball Action Emblems Cloth Stickers." Each sticker features a generic ballplayer on front with a city (not team) name. At bottom is a pennant with another major league city named and a generic baseball symbol at its left. Backs are blank. This issue can be found in either a cloth sticker version or cardboard version. The cardboard pieces are worth about 4X the cloth type.

	NM	E	VG
Complete Set (24):	900.00	450.00	275.00
Common Sticker:	40.00	20.00	12.00
Wax Pack:	165.00		
Cardboard: 4X			

		NM	E	VG
(1)	Atlanta/Baltimore	40.00	20.00	12.00
(2)	Baltimore/Montreal	40.00	20.00	12.00
(3)	Boston/Oakland	40.00	20.00	12.00
(4)	California/St. Louis	40.00	20.00	12.00
(5)	Chicago/Houston	40.00	20.00	12.00
(6)	Chicago/Pittsburgh	40.00	20.00	12.00
(7)	Cincinnati/Minnesota	40.00	20.00	12.00
(8)	Cleveland/San Diego	40.00	20.00	12.00
(9)	Detroit/New York	40.00	20.00	12.00
(10)	Houston/Chicago	40.00	20.00	12.00
(11)	Kansas City/Philadelphia	40.00	20.00	12.00
(12)	Los Angeles/Milwaukee	40.00	20.00	12.00
(13)	Milwaukee/New York	40.00	20.00	12.00
(14)	Minnesota/California	40.00	20.00	12.00
(15)	Montreal/San Francisco	40.00	20.00	12.00
(16)	New York/Cincinnati	40.00	20.00	12.00
(17)	New York/Texas	40.00	20.00	12.00
(18)	Oakland/Boston	40.00	20.00	12.00
(19)	Philadelphia/Los Angeles	40.00	20.00	12.00
(20)	Pittsburgh/Cleveland	40.00	20.00	12.00
(21)	St. Louis/Kansas City	40.00	20.00	12.00
(22)	San Diego/Detroit	40.00	20.00	12.00
(23)	San Francisco/Chicago	40.00	20.00	12.00
(24)	Texas/Atlanta	40.00	20.00	12.00

1974 Topps Deckle Edge

These borderless 2-7/8" x 5" cards feature a black-and-white photograph with a blue facsimile autograph on the front. The backs have in handwritten script the player's name, team, position and the date and location of the picture. Below is a mock newspaper clipping providing a detail from the player's career. Backs can be found in either gray or white (somewhat scarcer). The cards take their names from their specially cut edges which give them a scalloped appearance. The 72-card set was a test issue and received rather limited distribution around Massachusetts. The cards were sold three per pack for five cents with a piece of gum, or in two-card pack with no gum. Proof versions with straight edges and white or gray backs are known; they are slightly larger, at about 3-1/8" x 5-1/4".

	NM	E	VG
Complete Set (72):	5,000	2,500	1,500
Common Player:	20.00	10.00	6.00
White Backs: 1.5X			
Proofs: .75-1X			
Wax Pack (5):	375.00		

		NM	E	VG
1	Amos Otis	20.00	10.00	6.00
2	Darrell Evans	20.00	10.00	6.00
3	Bob Gibson	110.00	55.00	33.00
4	David Nelson	20.00	10.00	6.00
5	Steve Carlton	110.00	55.00	33.00
6	Catfish Hunter	90.00	45.00	27.50
7	Thurman Munson	135.00	65.00	40.00
8	Bob Grich	20.00	10.00	6.00
9	Tom Seaver	150.00	75.00	45.00
10	Ted Simmons	20.00	10.00	6.00
11	Bobby Valentine	20.00	10.00	6.00

12	Don Sutton	90.00	45.00	27.50
13	Wilbur Wood	20.00	10.00	6.00
14	Doug Rader	20.00	10.00	6.00
15	Chris Chambliss	20.00	10.00	6.00
16	Pete Rose	295.00	150.00	90.00
17	John Hiller	20.00	10.00	6.00
18	Burt Hooton	20.00	10.00	6.00
19	Tim Foli	20.00	10.00	6.00
20	Lou Brock	100.00	50.00	30.00
21	Ron Bryant	20.00	10.00	6.00
22	Manuel Sanguillen	20.00	10.00	6.00
23	Bobby Tolan	20.00	10.00	6.00
24	Greg Luzinski	20.00	10.00	6.00
25	Brooks Robinson	150.00	75.00	45.00
26	Felix Millan	20.00	10.00	6.00
27	Luis Tiant	20.00	10.00	6.00
28	Willie McCovey	100.00	50.00	30.00
29	Chris Speier	20.00	10.00	6.00
30	George Scott	20.00	10.00	6.00
31	Willie Stargell	100.00	50.00	30.00
32	Rod Carew	120.00	60.00	36.00
33	Charlie Spikes	20.00	10.00	6.00
34	Nate Colbert	20.00	10.00	6.00
35	Richie Hebner	20.00	10.00	6.00
36	Bobby Bonds	20.00	10.00	6.00
37	Buddy Bell	20.00	10.00	6.00
38	Claude Osteen	20.00	10.00	6.00
39	Rich Allen	55.00	27.50	16.50
40	Bill Russell	20.00	10.00	6.00
41	Nolan Ryan	900.00	450.00	275.00
42	Willie Davis	20.00	10.00	6.00
43	Carl Yastrzemski	160.00	80.00	45.00
44	Jon Matlack	20.00	10.00	6.00
45	Jim Palmer	110.00	55.00	33.00
46	Bert Campaneris	20.00	10.00	6.00
47	Bert Blyleven	20.00	10.00	6.00
48	Jeff Burroughs	20.00	10.00	6.00
49	Jim Colborn	20.00	10.00	6.00
50	Dave Johnson	20.00	10.00	6.00
51	John Mayberry	20.00	10.00	6.00
52	Don Kessinger	20.00	10.00	6.00
53	Joe Coleman	20.00	10.00	6.00
54	Tony Perez	90.00	45.00	27.50
55	Jose Cardenal	20.00	10.00	6.00
56	Paul Splittorff	20.00	10.00	6.00
57	Henry Aaron	275.00	135.00	80.00
58	David May	20.00	10.00	6.00
59	Fergie Jenkins	90.00	45.00	27.50
60	Ron Blomberg	20.00	10.00	6.00
61	Reggie Jackson	175.00	85.00	50.00
62	Tony Oliva	40.00	20.00	12.00
63	Bobby Murcer	45.00	22.50	13.50
64	Carlton Fisk	100.00	50.00	30.00
65	Steve Rogers	20.00	10.00	6.00
66	Frank Robinson	150.00	75.00	45.00
67	Joe Ferguson	20.00	10.00	6.00
68	Bill Melton	20.00	10.00	6.00
69	Bob Watson	20.00	10.00	6.00
70	Larry Bowa	20.00	10.00	6.00
71	Johnny Bench	135.00	68.00	40.00
72	Willie Horton	20.00	10.00	6.00

1974 Topps Puzzles

One of many test issues by Topps in the mid-1970s, the 12-player jigsaw puzzle set was an innovation which never caught on with collectors. The 40-piece puzzles (4-3/4" x 7-1/2") feature color photos with a decorative lozenge at bottom naming the player, team and position. The 25-cent or 29-cent puzzles came in individual wrappers picturing Tom Seaver. Centering, particularly of the Ryan puzzle, is a plague with the puzzles, accounting for the greater than usual spread betwerrn NM and lower- grade values.

	NM	E	VG
Complete Set (12):	2,000	700.00	300.00
Common Player:	65.00	32.50	20.00
Wax Pack:	225.00		
Wrapper:	20.00		
(1) Hank Aaron	250.00	90.00	35.00

(2)	Dick Allen	65.00	25.00	12.00
(3)	Johnny Bench	125.00	44.00	18.50
(4)	Bobby Bonds	65.00	25.00	10.00
(5)	Bob Gibson	125.00	44.00	18.50
(6)	Reggie Jackson	200.00	70.00	30.00
(7)	Bobby Murcer	65.00	25.00	10.00
(8)	Jim Palmer	100.00	35.00	15.00
(9)	Nolan Ryan	650.00	225.00	100.00
(10)	Tom Seaver	125.00	44.00	18.50
(11)	Willie Stargell	100.00	35.00	15.00
(12)	Carl Yastrzemski	250.00	87.00	37.00

1974 Topps Stamps

Topps continued to market baseball stamps in 1974 through the release of 240 unnumbered stamps featuring color player portraits. The player's name, team and position are found in an oval at the bottom of the 1" x 1-1/2" stamps. The stamps, sold separately rather than issued as an insert, came in panels of 12. Two dozen team albums designed to hold 10 stamps were also issued.

		NM	E	VG
Complete Sheet Set (24):		90.00	45.00	25.00
Common Sheet:		2.00	1.00	.60
Complete Stamp Album Set (24):		300.00	150.00	90.00
Single Stamp Album:		5.00	2.50	1.50
(1)	Hank Aaron, Luis Aparicio, Bob Bailey, Johnny Bench, Ron Blomberg, Bob Boone, Lou Brock, Bud Harrelson, Randy Jones, Dave Rader, Nolan Ryan, Joe Torre	15.00	7.50	4.50
(2)	Buddy Bell, Steve Braun, Jerry Grote, Tommy Helms, Bill Lee, Mike Lum, Dave May, Brooks Robinson, Bill Russell, Del Unser, Wilbur Wood, Carl Yastrzemski	9.00	4.50	2.75
(3)	Jerry Bell, Jim Colborn, Toby Harrah, Ken Henderson, John Hiller, Randy Hundley, Don Kessinger, Jerry Koosman, Dave Lopes, Felix Millan, Thurman Munson, Ted Simmons	6.00	3.00	1.75
(4)	Jerry Bell, Bill Buckner, Jim Colborn, Ken Henderson, Don Kessinger, Felix Millan, George Mitterwald, Dave Roberts, Ted Simmons, Jim Slaton, Charlie Spikes, Paul Splittorff	2.00	1.00	.60
(5)	Glenn Beckert, Jim Bibby, Bill Buckner, Jim Lonborg, George Mitterwald, Dave Parker, Dave Roberts, Jim Slaton, Reggie Smith, Charlie Spikes, Paul Splittorff, Bob Watson	2.00	1.00	.60
(6)	Paul Blair, Bobby Bonds, Ed Brinkman, Norm Cash, Mike Epstein, Tommy Harper, Mike Marshall, Phil Niekro, Cookie Rojas, George Scott, Mel Stottlemyre, Jim Wynn	2.00	1.00	.60
(7)	Jack Billingham, Reggie Cleveland, Bobby Darwin, Dave Duncan, Tim Foli, Ed Goodson, Cleon Jones, Mickey Lolich, George Medich, John Milner, Rick Monday, Bobby Murcer	2.00	1.00	.60

(8)	Steve Carlton, Orlando Cepeda, Joe Decker, Reggie Jackson, Dave Johnson, John Mayberry, Bill Melton, Roger Metzger, Dave Nelson, Jerry Reuss, Jim Spencer, Bobby Valentine	10.00	5.00	3.00
(9)	Dan Driessen, Pedro Garcia, Grant Jackson, Al Kaline, Clay Kirby, Carlos May, Willie Montanez, Rogelio Moret, Jim Palmer, Doug Rader, J. R. Richard, Frank Robinson	7.50	3.75	2.25
(10)	Pedro Garcia, Ralph Garr, Wayne Garrett, Ron Hunt, Al Kaline, Fred Kendall, Carlos May, Jim Palmer, Doug Rader, Frank Robinson, Rick Wise, Richie Zisk	7.50	3.75	2.25
(11)	Dusty Baker, Larry Bowa, Steve Busby, Chris Chambliss, Dock Ellis, Cesar Geronimo, Fran Healy, Deron Johnson, Jorge Orta, Joe Rudi, Mickey Stanley, Rennie Stennett	2.00	1.00	.60
(12)	Bob Coluccio, Ray Corbin, John Ellis, Oscar Gamble, Dave Giusti, Bill Greif, Alex Johnson, Mike Jorgensen, Andy Messersmith, Bill Robinson, Elias Sosa, Willie Stargell	2.00	1.00	.60
(13)	Ron Bryant, Nate Colbert, Jose Cruz, Dan Driessen, Billy Grabarkewitz, Don Gullett, Willie Horton, Grant Jackson, Clay Kirby, Willie Montanez, Rogelio Moret, J. R. Richard	2.00	1.00	.60
(14)	Carlton Fisk, Bill Freehan, Bobby Grich, Vic Harris, George Hendrick, Ed Herrmann, Jim Holt, Ken Holtzman, Fergie Jenkins, Lou Piniella, Steve Rogers, Ken Singleton	5.00	2.50	1.50
(15)	Stan Bahnsen, Sal Bando, Mark Belanger, David Clyde, Willie Crawford, Burt Hooton, Jon Matlack, Tim McCarver, Joe Morgan, Gene Tenace, Dick Tidrow, Dave Winfield	7.50	3.75	2.25
(16)	Hank Aaron, Stan Bahnsen, Bob Bailey, Johnny Bench, Bob Boone, Jon Matlack, Tim McCarver, Joe Morgan, Dave Rader, Gene Tenace, Dick Tidrow, Joe Torre	10.00	5.00	3.00
(17)	John Boccabella, Frank Duffy, Darrell Evans, Sparky Lyle, Lee May, Don Money, Bill North, Ted Sizemore, Chris Speier, Wayne Twitchell, Billy Williams, Earl Williams	2.00	1.00	.60
(18)	John Boccabella, Bobby Darwin, Frank Duffy, Dave Duncan, Tim Foli, Cleon Jones, Mickey Lolich, Sparky Lyle, Lee May, Rick Monday, Bill North, Billy Williams	2.00	1.00	.60
(19)	Don Baylor, Vida Blue, Tom Bradley, Jose Cardenal, Ron Cey, Greg Luzinski, Johnny Oates, Tony Oliva, Al Oliver, Tony Perez, Darrell Porter, Roy White	3.00	1.50	.90
(20)	Pedro Borbon, Rod Carew, Roric Harrison, Jim Hunter, Ed Kirkpatrick, Garry Maddox, Gene Michael, Rick Miller, Claude Osteen, Amos Otis, Rich Reuschel, Mike Tyson	5.00	2.50	1.50

(21) Sandy Alomar, Bert
Campaneris, Dave
Concepcion, Tommy
Davis, Joe Ferguson, Tito
Fuentes, Jerry Morales,
Carl Morton, Gaylord
Perry, Vada Pinson, Dave
Roberts, Ellie Rodriguez 2.00 1.00 .60
(22) Dick Allen, Jeff Burroughs,
Joe Coleman, Terry
Forster, Bob Gibson,
Harmon Killebrew, Tug
McGraw, Bob Oliver,
Steve Renko, Pete Rose,
Luis Tiant, Otto Velez 12.00 6.00 3.50
(23) Johnny Briggs, Willie
Davis, Jim Fregosi, Rich
Hebner, Pat Kelly, Dave
Kingman, Willie McCovey,
Graig Nettles, Freddie
Patek, Marty Pattin,
Manny Sanguillen, Richie
Scheinblum 5.00 2.50 1.50
(24) Bert Blyleven, Nelson Briles,
Cesar Cedeno, Ron
Fairly, Johnny Grubb,
Dave McNally, Aurelio
Rodriguez, Ron Santo,
Tom Seaver, Bill Singer,
Bill Sudakis, Don Sutton 6.00 3.00 1.75

1974 Topps Team Checklists

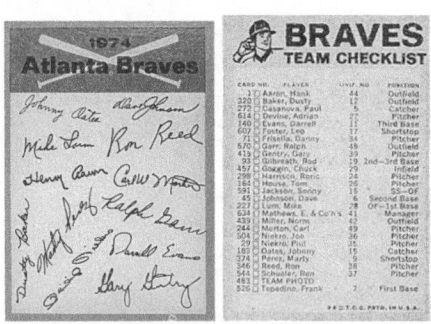

This set is a repeat of the 1973 set in the form of 24 unnumbered 2-1/2" x 3-1/2" checklist cards. Cards feature a team name on the front at the top with a white panel and a number of facsimile autographs below. Backs feature the team name and a checklist. The big difference between the 1973 and 1974 checklists is that the 1973s have blue borders while the 1974s have red borders. The 1974s were inserted into packages of the regular issue Topps cards and were also available in uncut sheet form as a wrapper redemption.

	NM	E	VG
Complete Set (24):	25.00	12.50	7.50
Common Checklist:	1.50	.75	.45
Uncut Sheet:	25.00	12.50	7.50

		NM	E	VG
(1)	Atlanta Braves	1.50	.75	.45
(2)	Baltimore Orioles	1.50	.75	.45
(3)	Boston Red Sox	1.50	.75	.45
(4)	California Angels	1.50	.75	.45
(5)	Chicago Cubs	1.50	.75	.45
(6)	Chicago White Sox	1.50	.75	.45
(7)	Cincinnati Reds	1.50	.75	.45
(8)	Cleveland Indians	1.50	.75	.45
(9)	Detroit Tigers	1.50	.75	.45
(10)	Houston Astros	1.50	.75	.45
(11)	Kansas City Royals	1.50	.75	.45
(12)	Los Angeles Dodgers	1.50	.75	.45
(13)	Milwaukee Brewers	1.50	.75	.45
(14)	Minnesota Twins	1.50	.75	.45
(15)	Montreal Expos	1.50	.75	.45
(16)	New York Mets	1.50	.75	.45
(17)	New York Yankees	1.50	.75	.45
(18)	Oakland A's	1.50	.75	.45
(19)	Philadelphia Phillies	1.50	.75	.45
(20)	Pittsburgh Pirates	1.50	.75	.45
(21)	St. Louis Cardinals	1.50	.75	.45
(22)	San Diego Padres	1.50	.75	.45
(23)	San Francisco Giants	1.50	.75	.45
(24)	Texas Rangers	1.50	.75	.45

1974 Topps Traded

Appearing late in the season, these 2-1/2" x 3-1/2" cards share the format of the regular-issue Topps cards. The major change is a large yellow panel with the word "Traded" in red, added below the player photo. Backs feature a "Baseball News" design that contains the details of the trade. Card numbers correspond to the player's regular card number in

1974 except that the suffix "T" is added. The set consists of 43 player cards and a checklist. In most cases, Topps did not obtain pictures of the players in their new uniforms. Instead, the Topps artists simply provided the needed changes to existing photos.

	NM	E	VG
Complete Set (44):	25.00	12.50	7.50
Common Player:	.50	.25	.15

		NM	E	VG
23T	Craig Robinson	.50	.25	.15
42T	Claude Osteen	.50	.25	.15
43T	Jim Wynn	.50	.25	.15
51T	Bobby Heise	.50	.25	.15
59T	Ross Grimsley	.50	.25	.15
62T	Bob Locker	.50	.25	.15
63T	Bill Sudakis	.50	.25	.15
73T	Mike Marshall	.50	.25	.15
123T	Nelson Briles	.50	.25	.15
139T	Aurelio Monteagudo	.50	.25	.15
151T	Diego Segui	.50	.25	.15
165T	Willie Davis	.50	.25	.15
175T	Reggie Cleveland	.50	.25	.15
182T	Lindy McDaniel	.50	.25	.15
186T	Fred Scherman	.50	.25	.15
249T	George Mitterwald	.50	.25	.15
262T	Ed Kirkpatrick	.50	.25	.15
269T	Bob Johnson	.50	.25	.15
270T	Ron Santo	3.00	1.50	.90
313T	Barry Lersch	.50	.25	.15
319T	Randy Hundley	.50	.25	.15
330T	Juan Marichal	4.00	2.00	1.25
348T	Pete Richert	.50	.25	.15
373T	John Curtis	.50	.25	.15
390T	Lou Piniella	2.00	1.00	.60
428T	Gary Sutherland	.50	.25	.15
454T	Kurt Bevacqua	.50	.25	.15
458T	Jim Ray	.50	.25	.15
485T	Felipe Alou	.75	.40	.25
486T	Steve Stone	.75	.40	.25
496T	Tom Murphy	.50	.25	.15
516T	Horacio Pina	.50	.25	.15
534T	Eddie Watt	.50	.25	.15
538T	Cesar Tovar	.50	.25	.15
544T	Ron Schueler	.50	.25	.15
579T	Cecil Upshaw	.50	.25	.15
585T	Merv Rettenmund	.50	.25	.15
612T	Luke Walker	.50	.25	.15
616T	Larry Gura	.50	.25	.15
618T	Jim Mason	.50	.25	.15
630T	Tommie Agee	.50	.25	.15
648T	Terry Crowley	.50	.25	.15
649T	Fernando Gonzalez	.50	.25	.15
----	Traded Checklist	.50	.25	.15

1975 Topps

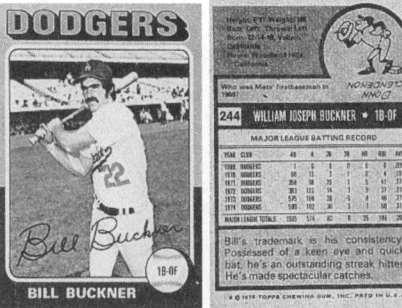

What was once seen as the strongest rookie card crop of any modern card set made this a collector favorite from the outset. Featuring the most colorful designs since 1972, cards feature large front photos with facsimile autographs. Red-and-green backs include a cartoon trivia fact and complete stats. A subset of 1951-74 MVP cards which reproduces or creates contemporary cards of past stars is one of several

special features of the set, as are a group of four-on-one rookie cards. While the cards were all issued at one time, the first 132 cards have been discovered to have been printed in somewhat lesser quantities than the rest of the issue. This scarcity is not noted among the mini-version of the set which was produced as a test issue. Team/manager cards are sometimes found on thinner, white cardboard stock; these are a special version produced for a mail-in offer.

	NM	E	VG
Complete Set (660):	550.00	275.00	165.00
Common Player:	.40	.20	.10
Mini Stars/Rookies: 1-1.5X			
Wax Pack (10):	40.00		
Wax Box (36):	2,400		
Cello Pack (18):	85.00		
Rack Pack (42):	190.00		
Vending Box (500):	1,350		

		NM	E	VG
1	Hank Aaron ('74 Highlights)	30.00	15.00	9.00
2	Lou Brock ('74 Highlights)	2.00	1.00	.60
3	Bob Gibson ('74 Highlights)	2.00	1.00	.60
4	Al Kaline ('74 Highlights)	4.00	2.00	1.25
5	Nolan Ryan ('74 Highlights)	12.00	6.00	3.50
6	Mike Marshall ('74 Highlights)	.40	.20	.10
7	Dick Bosman, Steve Busby, Nolan Ryan ('74 Highlights)	7.00	3.50	2.00
8	Rogelio Moret	.40	.20	.10
9	Frank Tepedino	.40	.20	.10
10	Willie Davis	.40	.20	.10
11	Bill Melton	.40	.20	.10
12	David Clyde	.40	.20	.10
13	Gene Locklear	.40	.20	.10
14	Milt Wilcox	.40	.20	.10
15	Jose Cardenal	.40	.20	.10
16	Frank Tanana	.40	.20	.10
17	Dave Concepcion	.75	.35	.25
18	Tigers team (Ralph Houk)	1.50	.70	.45
19	Jerry Koosman	.40	.20	.10
20	Thurman Munson	12.00	6.00	3.00
21	Rollie Fingers	3.00	1.50	.90
22	Dave Cash	.40	.20	.10
23	Bill Russell	.75	.40	.25
24	Al Fitzmorris	.40	.20	.10
25	Lee May	.75	.40	.25
26	Dave McNally	.40	.20	.10
27	Ken Reitz	.40	.20	.10
28	Tom Murphy	.40	.20	.10
29	Dave Parker	1.50	.70	.45
30	Bert Blyleven	4.00	2.00	1.25
31	Dave Rader	.40	.20	.10
32	Reggie Cleveland	.40	.20	.10
33	Dusty Baker	1.50	.70	.45
34	Steve Renko	.40	.20	.10
35	Ron Santo	2.00	1.00	.60
36	Joe Lovitto	.40	.20	.10
37	Dave Freisleben	.40	.20	.10
38	Buddy Bell	.75	.40	.25
39	Andy Thornton	.75	.40	.25
40	Bill Singer	.40	.20	.10
41	Cesar Geronimo	.40	.20	.10
42	Joe Coleman	.40	.20	.10
43	Cleon Jones	.40	.20	.10
44	Pat Dobson	.40	.20	.10
45	Joe Rudi	.40	.20	.10
46	Phillies Team (Danny Ozark)	1.50	.70	.45
47	Tommy John	1.50	.70	.45
48	Freddie Patek	.40	.20	.10
49	Larry Dierker	.75	.40	.25
50	Brooks Robinson	9.00	4.50	2.75
51	Bob Forsch RC	.75	.40	.25
52	Darrell Porter	.75	.40	.25
53	Dave Giusti	.40	.20	.10
54	Eric Soderholm	.40	.20	.10
55	Bobby Bonds	1.50	.70	.45
56	Rick Wise	.40	.20	.10
57	Dave Johnson	.75	.40	.25
58	Chuck Taylor	.40	.20	.10
59	Ken Henderson	.40	.20	.10
60	Fergie Jenkins	4.00	2.00	1.25
61	Dave Winfield	12.00	6.00	3.50
62	Fritz Peterson	.40	.20	.10
63	Steve Swisher	.40	.20	.10
64	Dave Chalk	.40	.20	.10
65	Don Gullett	.40	.20	.10
66	Willie Horton	.40	.20	.10
67	Tug McGraw	.40	.20	.10
68	Ron Blomberg	.40	.20	.10
69	John Odom	.40	.20	.10
70	Mike Schmidt	15.00	7.50	4.50
71	Charlie Hough	.75	.40	.25
72	Royals Team (Jack McKeon)	1.00	.50	.30

No.	Player			
73	J.R. Richard	.40	.20	.10
74	Mark Belanger	.40	.20	.10
75	Ted Simmons	1.00	.50	.30
76	Ed Sprague	.40	.20	.10
77	Richie Zisk	.40	.20	.10
78	Ray Corbin	.40	.20	.10
79	Gary Matthews	.40	.20	.10
80	Carlton Fisk	6.00	3.00	1.75
81	Ron Reed	.40	.20	.10
82	Pat Kelly	.40	.20	.10
83	Jim Merritt	.40	.20	.10
84	Enzo Hernandez	.40	.20	.10
85	Bill Bonham	.40	.20	.10
86	Joe Lis	.40	.20	.10
87	George Foster	1.00	.50	.30
88	Tom Egan	.40	.20	.10
89	Jim Ray	.40	.20	.10
90	Rusty Staub	1.00	.50	.30
91	Dick Green	.40	.20	.10
92	Cecil Upshaw	.40	.20	.10
93	Dave Lopes	1.00	.50	.30
94	Jim Lonborg	.75	.40	.25
95	John Mayberry	.75	.40	.25
96	Mike Cosgrove	.40	.20	.10
97	Earl Williams	.40	.20	.10
98	Rich Folkers	.40	.20	.10
99	Mike Hegan	.40	.20	.10
100	Willie Stargell	5.00	2.50	1.25
101	Expos Team(Gene Mauch)	1.00	.50	.30
102	Joe Decker	.40	.20	.10
103	Rick Miller	.40	.20	.10
104	Bill Madlock	.75	.40	.25
105	Buzz Capra	.40	.20	.10
106	Mike Hargrove RC	2.00	1.00	.60
107	Jim Barr	.40	.20	.10
108	Tom Hall	.40	.20	.10
109	George Hendrick	.40	.20	.10
110	Wilbur Wood	.40	.20	.10
111	Wayne Garrett	.40	.20	.10
112	Larry Hardy	.40	.20	.10
113	Elliott Maddox	.40	.20	.10
114	Dick Lange	.40	.20	.10
115	Joe Ferguson	.40	.20	.10
116	Lerrin LaGrow	.40	.20	.10
117	Orioles Team(Earl Weaver)	3.00	1.50	.90
118	Mike Anderson	.40	.20	.10
119	Tommy Helms	.40	.20	.10
120	Steve Busby (Photo actually Fran Healy.)	.40	.20	.10
121	Bill North	.40	.20	.10
122	Al Hrabosky	.75	.40	.25
123	Johnny Briggs	.40	.20	.10
124	Jerry Reuss	.75	.40	.25
125	Ken Singleton	.75	.40	.25
126	Checklist 1-132	2.00	1.00	.60
127	Glen Borgmann	.40	.20	.10
128	Bill Lee	.40	.20	.10
129	Rick Monday	.40	.20	.10
130	Phil Niekro	5.00	2.50	1.50
131	Toby Harrah	.40	.20	.10
132	Randy Moffitt	.40	.20	.10
133	Dan Driessen	.40	.20	.10
134	Ron Hodges	.40	.20	.10
135	Charlie Spikes	.40	.20	.10
136	Jim Mason	.40	.20	.10
137	Terry Forster	.40	.20	.10
138	Del Unser	.40	.20	.10
139	Horacio Pina	.40	.20	.10
140	Steve Garvey	2.00	1.00	.60
141	Mickey Stanley	.40	.20	.10
142	Bob Reynolds	.40	.20	.10
143	Cliff Johnson RC	.40	.20	.10
144	Jim Wohlford	.40	.20	.10
145	Ken Holtzman	.40	.20	.10
146	Padres Team(John McNamara)	1.00	.50	.30
147	Pedro Garcia	.40	.20	.10
148	Jim Rooker	.40	.20	.10
149	Tim Foli	.40	.20	.10
150	Bob Gibson	5.00	2.50	1.50
151	Steve Brye	.40	.20	.10
152	Mario Guerrero	.40	.20	.10
153	Rick Reuschel	.40	.20	.10
154	Mike Lum	.40	.20	.10
155	Jim Bibby	.40	.20	.10
156	Dave Kingman	1.00	.50	.30
157	Pedro Borbon	.40	.20	.10
158	Jerry Grote	.40	.20	.10
159	Steve Arlin	.40	.20	.10
160	Graig Nettles	1.00	.50	.30
161	Stan Bahnsen	.40	.20	.10
162	Willie Montanez	.40	.20	.10
163	Jim Brewer	.40	.20	.10
164	Mickey Rivers	.40	.20	.10
165	Doug Rader	.40	.20	.10
166	Woodie Fryman	.40	.20	.10
167	Rich Coggins	.40	.20	.10
168	Bill Greif	.40	.20	.10
169	Cookie Rojas	.40	.20	.10
170	Bert Campaneris	.40	.20	.10
171	Ed Kirkpatrick	.40	.20	.10
172	Red Sox Team(Darrell Johnson)	1.50	.70	.45
173	Steve Rogers	.40	.20	.10
174	Bake McBride	.40	.20	.10
175	Don Money	.40	.20	.10
176	Burt Hooton	.40	.20	.10
177	Vic Correll	.40	.20	.10
178	Cesar Tovar	.40	.20	.10
179	Tom Bradley	.40	.20	.10
180	Joe Morgan	7.00	3.50	2.00
181	Fred Beene	.40	.20	.10
182	Don Hahn	.40	.20	.10
183	Mel Stottlemyre	.40	.20	.10
184	Jorge Orta	.40	.20	.10
185	Steve Carlton	6.00	3.00	1.50
186	Willie Crawford	.40	.20	.10
187	Denny Doyle	.40	.20	.10
188	Tom Griffin	.40	.20	.10
189	1951-MVPs(Yogi Berra, Roy Campanella)	3.00	1.50	.90
190	1952-MVPs(Hank Sauer, Bobby Shantz)	1.00	.50	.30
191	1953-MVPs(Roy Campanella, Al Rosen)	1.50	.70	.45
192	1954-MVPs(Yogi Berra, Willie Mays)	4.00	2.00	1.25
193	1955-MVPs(Yogi Berra, Roy Campanella)	3.00	1.50	.90
194	1956-MVPs(Mickey Mantle, Don Newcombe)	7.00	3.50	2.00
195	1957-MVPs(Hank Aaron, Mickey Mantle)	9.00	4.50	2.75
196	1958-MVPs(Ernie Banks, Jackie Jensen)	2.50	1.25	.70
197	1959-MVPs(Ernie Banks, Nellie Fox)	2.00	1.00	.60
198	1960-MVPs(Dick Groat, Roger Maris)	1.50	.70	.45
199	1961-MVPs(Roger Maris, Frank Robinson)	2.00	1.00	.60
200	1962-MVPs(Mickey Mantle, Maury Wills)	7.00	3.50	2.00
201	1963-MVPs(Elston Howard, Sandy Koufax)	2.50	1.25	.70
202	1964-MVPs(Ken Boyer, Brooks Robinson)	1.00	.50	.30
203	1965-MVPs(Willie Mays, Zoilo Versalles)	2.00	1.00	.60
204	1966-MVPs(Roberto Clemente, Frank Robinson)	5.00	2.50	1.50
205	1967-MVPs(Orlando Cepeda, Carl Yastrzemski)	1.50	.70	.45
206	1968-MVPs(Bob Gibson, Denny McLain)	1.50	.70	.45
207	1969-MVPs(Harmon Killebrew, Willie McCovey)	2.00	1.00	.60
208	1970-MVPs(Johnny Bench, Boog Powell)	2.00	1.00	.60
209	1971-MVPs(Vida Blue, Joe Torre)	1.00	.50	.30
210	1972-MVPs(Rich Allen, Johnny Bench)	2.00	1.00	.60
211	1973-MVPs(Reggie Jackson, Pete Rose)	4.00	2.00	1.25
212	1974-MVPs(Jeff Burroughs, Steve Garvey)	1.00	.50	.30
213	Oscar Gamble	.40	.20	.10
214	Harry Parker	.40	.20	.10
215	Bobby Valentine	.40	.20	.10
216	Giants Team(Wes Westrum)	1.00	.50	.30
217	Lou Piniella	1.50	.70	.45
218	Jerry Johnson	.40	.20	.10
219	Ed Herrmann	.40	.20	.10
220	Don Sutton	3.00	1.50	.90
221	Aurelio Rodriguez (Rodriguez)	.40	.20	.10
222	Dan Spillner	.40	.20	.10
223	Robin Yount RC	50.00	25.00	15.00
224	Ramon Hernandez	.40	.20	.10
225	Bob Grich	.75	.40	.25
226	Bill Campbell	.40	.20	.10
227	Bob Watson	.40	.20	.10
228	George Brett RC	60.00	30.00	18.00
229	Barry Foote	.40	.20	.10
230	Jim Hunter	5.00	2.50	1.25
231	Mike Tyson	.40	.20	.10
232	Diego Segui	.40	.20	.10
233	Billy Grabarkewitz	.40	.20	.10
234	Tom Grieve	.40	.20	.10
235	Jack Billingham	.40	.20	.10
236	Angels Team(Dick Williams)	1.00	.50	.30
237	Carl Morton	.40	.20	.10
238	Dave Duncan	.75	.40	.25
239	George Stone	.40	.20	.10
240	Garry Maddox	.40	.20	.10
241	Dick Tidrow	.40	.20	.10
242	Jay Johnstone	.40	.20	.10
243	Jim Kaat	1.50	.70	.45
244	Bill Buckner	.75	.40	.25
245	Mickey Lolich	1.00	.50	.30
246	Cardinals Team(Red Schoendienst)	1.00	.50	.30
247	Enos Cabell	.40	.20	.10
248	Randy Jones	.40	.20	.10
249	Danny Thompson	.40	.20	.10
250	Ken Brett	.40	.20	.10
251	Fran Healy	.40	.20	.10
252	Fred Scherman	.40	.20	.10
253	Jesus Alou	.40	.20	.10
254	Mike Torrez	.40	.20	.10
255	Dwight Evans	1.00	.50	.30
256	Billy Champion	.40	.20	.10
257	Checklist 133-264	2.00	1.00	.60
258	Dave LaRoche	.40	.20	.10
259	Len Randle	.40	.20	.10
260	Johnny Bench	12.00	6.00	3.00
261	Andy Hassler	.40	.20	.10
262	Rowland Office	.40	.20	.10
263	Jim Perry	.40	.20	.10
264	John Milner	.40	.20	.10
265	Ron Bryant	.40	.20	.10
266	Sandy Alomar	.40	.20	.10
267	Dick Ruthven	.40	.20	.10
268	Hal McRae	.75	.40	.25
269	Doug Rau	.40	.20	.10
270	Ron Fairly	.40	.20	.10
271	Jerry Moses	.40	.20	.10
272	Lynn McGlothen	.40	.20	.10
273	Steve Braun	.40	.20	.10
274	Vicente Romo	.40	.20	.10
275	Paul Blair	.40	.20	.10
276	White Sox Team(Chuck Tanner)	1.00	.50	.30
277	Frank Taveras	.40	.20	.10
278	Paul Lindblad	.40	.20	.10
279	Milt May	.40	.20	.10
280	Carl Yastrzemski	10.00	5.00	3.00
281	Jim Slaton	.40	.20	.10
282	Jerry Morales	.40	.20	.10
283	Steve Foucault	.40	.20	.10
284	Ken Griffey	2.00	1.00	.60
285	Ellie Rodriguez	.40	.20	.10
286	Mike Jorgensen	.40	.20	.10
287	Roric Harrison	.40	.20	.10
288	Bruce Ellingsen	.40	.20	.10
289	Ken Rudolph	.40	.20	.10
290	Jon Matlack	.40	.20	.10
291	Bill Sudakis	.40	.20	.10
292	Ron Schueler	.40	.20	.10
293	Dick Sharon	.40	.20	.10
294	Geoff Zahn RC	.40	.20	.10
295	Vada Pinson	2.00	1.00	.60
296	Alan Foster	.40	.20	.10
297	Craig Kusick	.40	.20	.10
298	Johnny Grubb	.40	.20	.10
299	Bucky Dent	1.00	.50	.30
300	Reggie Jackson	12.00	6.00	3.50
301	Dave Roberts	.40	.20	.10
302	Rick Burleson RC	.75	.40	.25
303	Grant Jackson	.40	.20	.10
304	Pirates Team(Danny Murtaugh)	1.50	.70	.45
305	Jim Colborn	.40	.20	.10
306	Batting Leaders(Rod Carew, Ralph Garr)	1.50	.70	.45
307	Home Run Leaders(Dick Allen, Mike Schmidt)	3.00	1.50	.90
308	Runs Batted In Leaders(Johnny Bench, Jeff Burroughs)	1.50	.70	.45
309	Stolen Base Leaders(Lou Brock, Bill North)	1.50	.70	.45
310	Victory Leaders(Jim Hunter, Fergie Jenkins, Andy Messersmith, Phil Niekro)	1.50	.70	.45
311	Earned Run Average Leaders(Buzz Capra, Jim Hunter)	1.50	.70	.45
312	Strikeout Leaders(Steve Carlton, Nolan Ryan)	8.00	4.00	2.40
313	Leading Firemen(Terry Forster, Mike Marshall)	1.00	.50	.30

#	Name			
314	Buck Martinez	.40	.20	.10
315	Don Kessinger	.40	.20	.10
316	Jackie Brown	.40	.20	.10
317	Joe Lahoud	.40	.20	.10
318	Ernie McAnally	.40	.20	.10
319	Johnny Oates	.40	.20	.10
320	Pete Rose	20.00	10.00	6.00
321	Rudy May	.40	.20	.10
322	Ed Goodson	.40	.20	.10
323	Fred Holdsworth	.40	.20	.10
324	Ed Kranepool	.40	.20	.10
325	Tony Oliva	1.50	.70	.45
326	Wayne Twitchell	.40	.20	.10
327	Jerry Hairston Sr.	.40	.20	.10
328	Sonny Siebert	.40	.20	.10
329	Ted Kubiak	.40	.20	.10
330	Mike Marshall	.40	.20	.10
331	Indians Team(Frank Robinson)	1.50	.75	.45
332	Fred Kendall	.40	.20	.10
333	Dick Drago	.40	.20	.10
334	Greg Gross RC	.40	.20	.10
335	Jim Palmer	5.00	2.50	1.25
336	Rennie Stennett	.40	.20	.10
337	Kevin Kobel	.40	.20	.10
338	Rick Stelmaszek	.40	.20	.10
339	Jim Fregosi	1.00	.50	.30
340	Paul Splittorff	.40	.20	.10
341	Hal Breeden	.40	.20	.10
342	Leroy Stanton	.40	.20	.10
343	Danny Frisella	.40	.20	.10
344	Ben Oglivie	1.00	.50	.30
345	Clay Carroll	.40	.20	.10
346	Bobby Darwin	.40	.20	.10
347	Mike Caldwell	.40	.20	.10
348	Tony Muser	.40	.20	.10
349	Ray Sadecki	.40	.20	.10
350	Bobby Murcer	.75	.40	.25
351	Bob Boone	1.50	.70	.45
352	Darold Knowles	.40	.20	.10
353	Luis Melendez	.40	.20	.10
354	Dick Bosman	.40	.20	.10
355	Chris Cannizzaro	.40	.20	.10
356	Rico Petrocelli	.75	.40	.25
357	Ken Forsch	.40	.20	.10
358	Al Bumbry	.40	.20	.10
359	Paul Popovich	.40	.20	.10
360	George Scott	.40	.20	.10
361	Dodgers Team(Walter Alston)	1.50	.75	.45
362	Steve Hargan	.40	.20	.10
363	Carmen Fanzone	.40	.20	.10
364	Doug Bird	.40	.20	.10
365	Bob Bailey	.40	.20	.10
366	Ken Sanders	.40	.20	.10
367	Craig Robinson	.40	.20	.10
368	Vic Albury	.40	.20	.10
369	Merv Rettenmund	.40	.20	.10
370	Tom Seaver	10.00	5.00	3.00
371	Gates Brown	.40	.20	.10
372	John D'Acquisto	.40	.20	.10
373	Bill Sharp	.40	.20	.10
374	Eddie Watt	.40	.20	.10
375	Roy White	.45	.25	.15
376	Steve Yeager	.40	.20	.10
377	Tom Hilgendorf	.40	.20	.10
378	Derrel Thomas	.40	.20	.10
379	Bernie Carbo	.40	.20	.10
380	Sal Bando	.40	.20	.10
381	John Curtis	.40	.20	.10
382	Don Baylor	1.50	.70	.45
383	Jim York	.40	.20	.10
384	Brewers Team(Del Crandall)	1.50	.70	.45
385	Dock Ellis	.40	.20	.10
386	Checklist 265-396	2.00	1.00	.60
387	Jim Spencer	.40	.20	.10
388	Steve Stone	.75	.40	.25
389	Tony Solaita	.40	.20	.10
390	Ron Cey	1.00	.50	.30
391	Don DeMola	.40	.20	.10
392	Bruce Bochte	.40	.20	.10
393	Gary Gentry	.40	.20	.10
394	Larvell Blanks	.40	.20	.10
395	Bud Harrelson	.40	.20	.10
396	Fred Norman	.40	.20	.10
397	Bill Freehan	.75	.40	.25
398	Elias Sosa	.40	.20	.10
399	Terry Harmon	.40	.20	.10
400	Dick Allen	1.00	.50	.30
401	Mike Wallace	.40	.20	.10
402	Bob Tolan	.40	.20	.10
403	Tom Buskey	.40	.20	.10
404	Ted Sizemore	.40	.20	.10
405	John Montague	.40	.20	.10
406	Bob Gallagher	.40	.20	.10
407	Herb Washington RC	1.00	.50	.30
408	Clyde Wright	.40	.20	.10
409	Bob Robertson	.40	.20	.10
410	Mike Cueller (Cuellar)	.40	.20	.10
411	George Mitterwald	.40	.20	.10
412	Bill Hands	.40	.20	.10
413	Marty Pattin	.40	.20	.10
414	Manny Mota	.40	.20	.10
415	John Hiller	.40	.20	.10
416	Larry Lintz	.40	.20	.10
417	Skip Lockwood	.40	.20	.10
418	Leo Foster	.40	.20	.10
419	Dave Goltz	.40	.20	.10
420	Larry Bowa	1.50	.70	.45
421	Mets Team(Yogi Berra)	2.50	1.25	.70
422	Brian Downing	.40	.20	.10
423	Clay Kirby	.40	.20	.10
424	John Lowenstein	.40	.20	.10
425	Tito Fuentes	.40	.20	.10
426	George Medich	.40	.20	.10
427	Clarence Gaston	.40	.20	.10
428	Dave Hamilton	.40	.20	.10
429	Jim Dwyer RC	.40	.20	.10
430	Luis Tiant	1.00	.50	.30
431	Rod Gilbreath	.40	.20	.10
432	Ken Berry	.40	.20	.10
433	Larry Demery	.40	.20	.10
434	Bob Locker	.40	.20	.10
435	Dave Nelson	.40	.20	.10
436	Ken Frailing	.40	.20	.10
437	Al Cowens RC	.40	.20	.10
438	Don Carrithers	.40	.20	.10
439	Ed Brinkman	.40	.20	.10
440	Andy Messersmith	.40	.20	.10
441	Bobby Heise	.40	.20	.10
442	Maximino Leon	.40	.20	.10
443	Twins Team(Frank Quilici)	1.00	.50	.30
444	Gene Garber	.40	.20	.10
445	Felix Millan	.40	.20	.10
446	Bart Johnson	.40	.20	.10
447	Terry Crowley	.40	.20	.10
448	Frank Duffy	.40	.20	.10
449	Charlie Williams	.40	.20	.10
450	Willie McCovey	5.00	2.50	1.50
451	Rick Dempsey	.40	.20	.10
452	Angel Mangual	.40	.20	.10
453	Claude Osteen	.40	.20	.10
454	Doug Griffin	.40	.20	.10
455	Don Wilson	.40	.20	.10
456	Bob Coluccio	.40	.20	.10
457	Mario Mendoza	.40	.20	.10
458	Ross Grimsley	.40	.20	.10
459	A.L. Championships (Brooks Robinson)	1.00	.50	.30
460	N.L. Championships (Steve Garvey)	1.00	.50	.30
461	World Series Game 1(Reggie Jackson)	2.00	1.00	.60
462	World Series Game 2(Joe Ferguson)	.75	.40	.25
463	World Series Game 3(Rollie Fingers)	2.00	1.00	.60
464	World Series Game 4	.75	.40	.25
465	World Series Game 5	.75	.40	.25
466	A's Do It Again! (Win 3rd Straight World Series!)	1.50	.70	.45
467	Ed Halicki	.40	.20	.10
468	Bobby Mitchell	.40	.20	.10
469	Tom Dettore	.40	.20	.10
470	Jeff Burroughs	.40	.20	.10
471	Bob Stinson	.40	.20	.10
472	Bruce Dal Canton	.40	.20	.10
473	Ken McMullen	.40	.20	.10
474	Luke Walker	.40	.20	.10
475	Darrell Evans	1.00	.50	.30
476	Ed Figueroa RC	.40	.20	.10
477	Tom Hutton	.40	.20	.10
478	Tom Burgmeier	.40	.20	.10
479	Ken Boswell	.40	.20	.10
480	Carlos May	.40	.20	.10
481	Will McEnaney RC	.40	.20	.10
482	Tom McCraw	.40	.20	.10
483	Steve Ontiveros	.40	.20	.10
484	Glenn Beckert	.40	.20	.10
485	Sparky Lyle	.40	.20	.10
486	Ray Fosse	.40	.20	.10
487	Astros Team(Preston Gomez)	1.00	.50	.30
488	Bill Travers	.40	.20	.10
489	Cecil Cooper	1.00	.50	.30
490	Reggie Smith	.75	.40	.25
491	Doyle Alexander	.40	.20	.10
492	Rich Hebner	.40	.20	.10
493	Don Stanhouse	.40	.20	.10
494	Pete LaCock RC	.40	.20	.10
495	Nelson Briles	.40	.20	.10
496	Pepe Frias	.40	.20	.10
497	Jim Nettles	.40	.20	.10
498	Al Downing	.40	.20	.10
499	Marty Perez	.40	.20	.10
500	Nolan Ryan	43.00	22.00	13.00
501	Bill Robinson	.40	.20	.10
502	Pat Bourque	.40	.20	.10
503	Fred Stanley	.40	.20	.10
504	Buddy Bradford	.40	.20	.10
505	Chris Speier	.40	.20	.10
506	Leron Lee	.40	.20	.10
507	Tom Carroll	.40	.20	.10
508	Bob Hansen	.40	.20	.10
509	Dave Hilton	.40	.20	.10
510	Vida Blue	.75	.40	.25
511	Rangers Team(Billy Martin)	1.50	.75	.45
512	Larry Milbourne	.40	.20	.10
513	Dick Pole	.40	.20	.10
514	Jose Cruz	.40	.20	.10
515	Manny Sanguillen	.40	.20	.10
516	Don Hood	.40	.20	.10
517	Checklist 397-528	2.00	1.00	.60
518	Leo Cardenas	.40	.20	.10
519	Jim Todd	.40	.20	.10
520	Amos Otis	.40	.20	.10
521	Dennis Blair	.40	.20	.10
522	Gary Sutherland	.40	.20	.10
523	Tom Paciorek	.40	.20	.10
524	John Doherty	.40	.20	.10
525	Tom House	.40	.20	.10
526	Larry Hisle	.40	.20	.10
527	Mac Scarce	.40	.20	.10
528	Eddie Leon	.40	.20	.10
529	Gary Thomasson	.40	.20	.10
530	Gaylord Perry	3.00	1.50	.90
531	Reds Team(Sparky Anderson)	5.00	2.50	1.50
532	Gorman Thomas	.40	.20	.10
533	Rudy Meoli	.40	.20	.10
534	Alex Johnson	.40	.20	.10
535	Gene Tenace	.40	.20	.10
536	Bob Moose	.40	.20	.10
537	Tommy Harper	.40	.20	.10
538	Duffy Dyer	.40	.20	.10
539	Jesse Jefferson	.40	.20	.10
540	Lou Brock	5.00	2.50	1.50
541	Roger Metzger	.40	.20	.10
542	Pete Broberg	.40	.20	.10
543	Larry Biittner	.40	.20	.10
544	Steve Mingori	.40	.20	.10
545	Billy Williams	5.00	2.50	1.50
546	John Knox	.40	.20	.10
547	Von Joshua	.40	.20	.10
548	Charlie Sands	.40	.20	.10
549	Bill Butler	.40	.20	.10
550	Ralph Garr	.40	.20	.10
551	Larry Christenson	.40	.20	.10
552	Jack Brohamer	.40	.20	.10
553	John Boccabella	.40	.20	.10
554	Rich Gossage	1.50	.70	.45
555	Al Oliver	1.00	.50	.30
556	Tim Johnson	.40	.20	.10
557	Larry Gura	.40	.20	.10
558	Dave Roberts	.40	.20	.10
559	Bob Montgomery	.40	.20	.10
560	Tony Perez	5.00	2.50	1.25
561	A's Team(Alvin Dark)	1.00	.50	.30
562	Gary Nolan	.40	.20	.10
563	Wilbur Howard	.40	.20	.10
564	Tommy Davis	.40	.20	.10
565	Joe Torre	2.00	1.00	.60
566	Ray Burris	.40	.20	.10
567	Jim Sundberg RC	1.00	.50	.30
568	Dale Murray	.40	.20	.10
569	Frank White	.40	.20	.10
570	Jim Wynn	.40	.20	.10
571	Dave Lemanczyk	.40	.20	.10
572	Roger Nelson	.40	.20	.10
573	Orlando Pena	.40	.20	.10
574	Tony Taylor	.40	.20	.10
575	Gene Clines	.40	.20	.10
576	Phil Roof	.40	.20	.10
577	John Morris	.40	.20	.10
578	Dave Tomlin	.40	.20	.10
579	Skip Pitlock	.40	.20	.10
580	Frank Robinson	8.00	4.00	2.00
581	Darrel Chaney	.40	.20	.10
582	Eduardo Rodriguez	.40	.20	.10
583	Andy Etchebarren	.40	.20	.10
584	Mike Garman	.40	.20	.10
585	Chris Chambliss	.75	.40	.25
586	Tim McCarver	1.00	.50	.30
587	Chris Ward	.40	.20	.10
588	Rick Auerbach	.40	.20	.10
589	Braves Team(Clyde King)	1.00	.50	.30
590	Cesar Cedeno	.40	.20	.10
591	Glenn Abbott	.40	.20	.10
592	Balor Moore	.40	.20	.10
593	Gene Lamont	.40	.20	.10
594	Jim Fuller	.40	.20	.10
595	Joe Niekro	.40	.20	.10

596	Ollie Brown	.40	.20	.10
597	Winston Llenas	.40	.20	.10
598	Bruce Kison	.40	.20	.10
599	Nate Colbert	.40	.20	.10
600	Rod Carew	6.00	3.00	1.75
601	Juan Beniquez	.40	.20	.10
602	John Vukovich	.40	.20	.10
603	Lew Krausse	.40	.20	.10
604	Oscar Zamora	.40	.20	.10
605	John Ellis	.40	.20	.10
606	Bruce Miller	.40	.20	.10
607	Jim Holt	.40	.20	.10
608	Gene Michael	.40	.20	.10
609	Ellie Hendricks	.40	.20	.10
610	Ron Hunt	.40	.20	.10
611	Yankees Team(Bill Virdon)	2.00	1.00	.60
612	Terry Hughes	.40	.20	.10
613	Bill Parsons	.40	.20	.10
614	Rookie Pitchers(Jack Kucek, Dyar Miller, Vern Ruhle, Paul Siebert)	.40	.20	.10
615	Rookie Pitchers(Pat Darcy, Dennis Leonard **RC**, Tom Underwood **RC**, Hank Webb)	.40	.20	.10
616	Rookie Outfielders(Dave Augustine **RC**, Pepe Mangual **RC**, Jim Rice **RC**, John Scott **RC**)	30.00	15.00	9.00
617	Rookie Infielders(Mike Cubbage, Doug DeCinces **RC**, Reggie Sanders, Manny Trillo)	1.50	.70	.45
618	Rookie Pitchers(Jamie Easterly **RC**, Tom Johnson, Scott McGregor **RC**, Rick Rhoden **RC**)	2.00	1.00	.60
619	Rookie Outfielders(Benny Ayala, Nyls Nyman, Tommy Smith, Jerry Turner)	.40	.20	.10
620	Rookie Catchers-Outfielders(Gary Carter **RC**, Marc Hill **RC**, Danny Meyer **RC**, Leon Roberts **RC**)	17.50	8.75	5.25
621	Rookie Pitchers(John Denny **RC**, Rawly Eastwick **RC**, Jim Kern **RC**, Juan Veintidos)	.50	.25	.15
622	Rookie Outfielders(Ed Armbrister **RC**, Fred Lynn **RC**, Tom Poquette **RC**, Terry Whitfield **RC**)	7.00	3.50	2.00
623	Rookie Infielders(Phil Garner **RC**, Keith Hernandez **RC**, Bob Sheldon, Tom Veryzer **RC**)	10.00	5.00	2.50
624	Rookie Pitchers(Doug Konieczny, Gary Lavelle **RC**, Jim Otten, Eddie Solomon)	.40	.20	.10
625	Boog Powell	1.50	.75	.45
626	Larry Haney	.40	.20	.10
627	Tom Walker	.40	.20	.10
628	Ron LeFlore **RC**	.75	.40	.25
629	Joe Hoerner	.40	.20	.10
630	Greg Luzinski	1.00	.50	.30
631	Lee Lacy	.40	.20	.10
632	Morris Nettles	.40	.20	.10
633	Paul Casanova	.40	.20	.10
634	Cy Acosta	.40	.20	.10
635	Chuck Dobson	.40	.20	.10
636	Charlie Moore	.40	.20	.10
637	Ted Martinez	.40	.20	.10
638	Cubs Team(Jim Marshall)	1.50	.70	.45
639	Steve Kline	.40	.20	.10
640	Harmon Killebrew	8.00	4.00	2.50
641	Jim Northrup	.40	.20	.10
642	Mike Phillips	.40	.20	.10
643	Brent Strom	.40	.20	.10
644	Bill Fahey	.40	.20	.10
645	Danny Cater	.40	.20	.10
646	Checklist 529-660	1.00	.50	.30
647	Claudell Washington **RC**	.75	.40	.25
648	Dave Pagan	.40	.20	.10
649	Jack Heidemann	.40	.20	.10
650	Dave May	.40	.20	.10
651	John Morlan	.40	.20	.10
652	Lindy McDaniel	.40	.20	.10
653	Lee Richards	.40	.20	.10
654	Jerry Terrell	.40	.20	.10
655	Rico Carty	.40	.20	.10
656	Bill Plummer	.40	.20	.10

657	Bob Oliver	.40	.20	.10
658	Vic Harris	.40	.20	.10
659	Bob Apodaca	.40	.20	.10
660	Hank Aaron	25.00	12.50	7.50

1975 Topps Mini

This popular set was actually a test issue to see how collectors would react to cards which were 20 percent smaller than the standard 2-1/2" x 3-1/2". Other than their 2-1/4" x 3-1/8" size, they are exactly the same front and back as the regular-issue '75 Topps. The experimental cards were sold in Michigan and on the West Coast, where they were quickly gobbled up by collectors, dealers and speculators. While the minis for many years enjoyed a 2X premium over regular 1975 Topps values, that differential has shrunk in recent years.

	NM	E	VG
Complete Set (660):	450.00	210.00	125.00
Common Player:	.50	.25	.15
Wax Pack (10):	40.00		
Wax Box (36):	1,000		
Cello Pack (18):	100.00		
Cello Box (24)	1,750		
Rack Pack (42):	200.00		

(Stars and rookies valued 1X to 1.5X regular 1975 Topps.)

1975 Topps Team Checklist Sheet

Via a mail-in wrapper redemption, collectors could receive an uncut sheet of the 24 team photo/checklist cards from the 1975 Topps baseball set. Measuring about 10-1/2" x 20-1/8", the sheet could be cut into individual team cards of standard size. The sheet-cut cards differ from issued versions in that they have white backs and are printed on thinner stock than the pack-issued versions.

	NM	E	VG
Complete Sheet:	50.00	25.00	15.00

1976 Topps

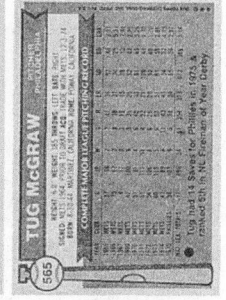

These 2-1/2" x 3-1/2" cards begin a design trend for Topps. The focus was more on the photo quality than in past years with a corresponding trend toward simplicity in the borders. The front of the cards has the player's name and team in two strips while his position is in the lower-left corner under a drawing of a player representing that position. The backs have a bat and ball with the card number on the left; statistics and personal information and career highlights on the right. The 660-card set features a number of specialty sets including record-setting performances, statistical leaders, playoff and World Series highlights, the Sporting News All-Time All-Stars and father and son combinations.

	NM	E	VG
Complete Set (660):	250.00	125.00	75.00
Common Player:	.40	.20	.10
Wax Pack (6):	30.00		
Wax Box (36 six-card):	1,200		

Wax Pack (10):	50.00			
Wax Box (36 10-card):	2,000			
Cello Pack (18):	60.00			
Cello Box (24):	1,950			
Rack Pack (42):	105.00			
Vending Box (500):	600.00			

1	Hank Aaron (Record Breaker)	20.00	10.00	5.00
2	Bobby Bonds (Record Breaker)	1.50	.70	.45
3	Mickey Lolich (Record Breaker)	.40	.20	.10
4	Dave Lopes (Record Breaker)	.40	.20	.10
5	Tom Seaver (Record Breaker)	3.00	1.50	.90
6	Rennie Stennett (Record Breaker)	.40	.20	.10
7	Jim Umbarger	.40	.20	.10
8	Tito Fuentes	.40	.20	.10
9	Paul Lindblad	.40	.20	.10
10	Lou Brock	6.50	2.50	1.50
11	Jim Hughes	.40	.20	.10
12	Richie Zisk	.40	.20	.10
13	Johnny Wockenfuss	.40	.20	.10
14	Gene Garber	.40	.20	.10
15	George Scott	.40	.20	.10
16	Bob Apodaca	.40	.20	.10
17	New York Yankees Team(Billy Martin)	1.50	.70	.45
18	Dale Murray	.40	.20	.10
19	George Brett	20.00	10.00	6.00
20	Bob Watson	.40	.20	.10
21	Dave LaRoche	.40	.20	.10
22	Bill Russell	1.00	.50	.30
23	Brian Downing	.40	.20	.10
24	Cesar Geronimo	.40	.20	.10
25	Mike Torrez	.40	.20	.10
26	Andy Thornton	.75	.40	.25
27	Ed Figueroa	.40	.20	.10
28	Dusty Baker	1.50	.70	.45
29	Rick Burleson	.40	.20	.10
30	John Montefusco **RC**	.40	.20	.10
31	Len Randle	.40	.20	.10
32	Danny Frisella	.40	.20	.10
33	Bill North	.40	.20	.10
34	Mike Garman	.40	.20	.10
35	Tony Oliva	1.00	.50	.30
36	Frank Taveras	.40	.20	.10
37	John Hiller	.40	.20	.10
38	Garry Maddox	.40	.20	.10
39	Pete Broberg	.40	.20	.10
40	Dave Kingman	.75	.40	.25
41	Tippy Martinez **RC**	.75	.40	.25
42	Barry Foote	.40	.20	.10
43	Paul Splittorff	.40	.20	.10
44	Doug Rader	.40	.20	.10
45	Boog Powell	.75	.40	.25
46	Los Angeles Dodgers Team(Walter Alston)	1.00	.50	.30
47	Jesse Jefferson	.40	.20	.10
48	Dave Concepcion	.40	.20	.10
49	Dave Duncan	.40	.20	.10
50	Fred Lynn	.75	.40	.25
51	Ray Burris	.40	.20	.10
52	Dave Chalk	.40	.20	.10
53	Mike Beard	.40	.20	.10
54	Dave Rader	.40	.20	.10
55	Gaylord Perry	3.00	1.50	.90
56	Bob Tolan	.40	.20	.10
57	Phil Garner	.40	.20	.10
58	Ron Reed	.40	.20	.10
59	Larry Hisle	.40	.20	.10
60	Jerry Reuss	.40	.20	.10
61	Ron LeFlore	.40	.20	.10
62	Johnny Oates	.40	.20	.10
63	Bobby Darwin	.40	.20	.10
64	Jerry Koosman	.40	.20	.10
65	Chris Chambliss	.40	.20	.10
66	Father & Son(Buddy Bell, Gus Bell)	.40	.20	.10
67	Father & Son(Bob Boone, Ray Boone)	.40	.20	.12
68	Father & Son(Joe Coleman, Joe Coleman, Jr.)	.40	.20	.10
69	Father & Son(Jim Hegan, Mike Hegan)	.40	.20	.10
70	Father & Son(Roy Smalley, III, Roy Smalley, Jr.)	.40	.20	.10
71	Steve Rogers	.40	.20	.10
72	Hal McRae	.40	.20	.10
73	Baltimore Orioles Team(Earl Weaver)	1.00	.50	.30
74	Oscar Gamble	.40	.20	.10
75	Larry Dierker	.40	.20	.10

#	Player			
76	Willie Crawford	.40	.20	.10
77	Pedro Borbon	.40	.20	.10
78	Cecil Cooper	.40	.20	.10
79	Jerry Morales	.40	.20	.10
80	Jim Kaat	.75	.40	.25
81	Darrell Evans	.75	.40	.25
82	Von Joshua	.40	.20	.10
83	Jim Spencer	.40	.20	.10
84	Brent Strom	.40	.20	.10
85	Mickey Rivers	.40	.20	.10
86	Mike Tyson	.40	.20	.10
87	Tom Burgmeier	.40	.20	.10
88	Duffy Dyer	.40	.20	.10
89	Vern Ruhle	.40	.20	.10
90	Sal Bando	.40	.20	.10
91	Tom Hutton	.40	.20	.10
92	Eduardo Rodriguez	.40	.20	.10
93	Mike Phillips	.40	.20	.10
94	Jim Dwyer	.40	.20	.10
95	Brooks Robinson	7.00	3.00	1.75
96	Doug Bird	.40	.20	.10
97	Wilbur Howard	.40	.20	.10
98	Dennis Eckersley RC	24.00	12.00	7.00
99	Lee Lacy	.40	.20	.10
100	Jim Hunter	4.00	2.00	1.00
101	Pete LaCock	.40	.20	.10
102	Jim Willoughby	.40	.20	.10
103	Biff Pocoroba	.40	.20	.10
104	Cincinnati Reds Team(Sparky Anderson)	1.00	.50	.30
105	Gary Lavelle	.40	.20	.10
106	Tom Grieve	.40	.20	.10
107	Dave Roberts	.40	.20	.10
108	Don Kirkwood	.40	.20	.10
109	Larry Lintz	.40	.20	.10
110	Carlos May	.40	.20	.10
111	Danny Thompson	.40	.20	.10
112	Kent Tekulve RC	.75	.40	.25
113	Gary Sutherland	.40	.20	.10
114	Jay Johnstone	.40	.20	.10
115	Ken Holtzman	.40	.20	.10
116	Charlie Moore	.40	.20	.10
117	Mike Jorgensen	.40	.20	.10
118	Boston Red Sox Team(Darrell Johnson)	1.00	.50	.30
119	Checklist 1-132	1.00	.50	.30
120	Rusty Staub	.75	.40	.25
121	Tony Solaita	.40	.20	.10
122	Mike Cosgrove	.40	.20	.10
123	Walt Williams	.40	.20	.10
124	Doug Rau	.40	.20	.10
125	Don Baylor	1.50	.70	.45
126	Tom Dettore	.40	.20	.10
127	Larvell Blanks	.40	.20	.10
128	Ken Griffey	1.00	.50	.30
129	Andy Etchebarren	.40	.20	.10
130	Luis Tiant	1.00	.50	.30
131	Bill Stein	.40	.20	.10
132	Don Hood	.40	.20	.10
133	Gary Matthews	.40	.20	.10
134	Mike Ivie	.40	.20	.10
135	Bake McBride	.40	.20	.10
136	Dave Goltz	.40	.20	.10
137	Bill Robinson	.40	.20	.10
138	Lerrin LaGrow	.40	.20	.10
139	Gorman Thomas	.75	.40	.25
140	Vida Blue	1.00	.50	.30
141	Larry Parrish RC	1.00	.50	.30
142	Dick Drago	.40	.20	.10
143	Jerry Grote	.40	.20	.10
144	Al Fitzmorris	.40	.20	.10
145	Larry Bowa	1.00	.50	.30
146	George Medich	.40	.20	.10
147	Houston Astros Team(Bill Virdon)	1.00	.50	.30
148	Stan Thomas	.40	.20	.10
149	Tommy Davis	.40	.20	.10
150	Steve Garvey	2.00	1.00	.60
151	Bill Bonham	.40	.20	.10
152	Leroy Stanton	.40	.20	.10
153	Buzz Capra	.40	.20	.10
154	Bucky Dent	.40	.20	.10
155	Jack Billingham	.40	.20	.10
156	Rico Carty	.40	.20	.10
157	Mike Caldwell	.40	.20	.10
158	Ken Reitz	.40	.20	.10
159	Jerry Terrell	.40	.20	.10
160	Dave Winfield	7.00	4.00	2.50
161	Bruce Kison	.40	.20	.10
162	Jack Pierce	.40	.20	.10
163	Jim Slaton	.40	.20	.10
164	Pepe Mangual	.40	.20	.10
165	Gene Tenace	.40	.20	.10
166	Skip Lockwood	.40	.20	.10
167	Freddie Patek	.40	.20	.10
168	Tom Hilgendorf	.40	.20	.10
169	Graig Nettles	.75	.40	.25
170	Rick Wise	.40	.20	.10
171	Greg Gross	.40	.20	.10
172	Texas Rangers Team(Frank Lucchesi)	1.00	.50	.30
173	Steve Swisher	.40	.20	.10
174	Charlie Hough	.75	.40	.25
175	Ken Singleton	.40	.20	.10
176	Dick Lange	.40	.20	.10
177	Marty Perez	.40	.20	.10
178	Tom Buskey	.40	.20	.10
179	George Foster	.75	.40	.25
180	Rich Gossage	1.00	.50	.30
181	Willie Montanez	.40	.20	.10
182	Harry Rasmussen	.40	.20	.10
183	Steve Braun	.40	.20	.10
184	Bill Greif	.40	.20	.10
185	Dave Parker	1.00	.50	.30
186	Tom Walker	.40	.20	.10
187	Pedro Garcia	.40	.20	.10
188	Fred Scherman	.40	.20	.10
189	Claudell Washington	.40	.20	.10
190	Jon Matlack	.40	.20	.10
191	N.L. Batting Leaders(Bill Madlock, Manny Sanguillen, Ted Simmons)	.75	.40	.25
192	A.L. Batting Leaders(Rod Carew, Fred Lynn, Thurman Munson)	1.00	.50	.30
193	N.L. Home Run Leaders(Dave Kingman, Greg Luzinski, Mike Schmidt)	2.00	1.00	.60
194	A.L. Home Run Leaders(Reggie Jackson, John Mayberry, George Scott)	2.00	1.00	.60
195	N.L. RBI Leaders(Johnny Bench, Greg Luzinski, Tony Perez)	1.00	.50	.30
196	A.L. RBI Leaders(Fred Lynn, John Mayberry, George Scott)	.40	.20	.10
197	N.L. Stolen Base Leaders(Lou Brock, Dave Lopes, Joe Morgan)	1.50	.70	.45
198	A.L. Stolen Base Leaders(Amos Otis, Mickey Rivers, Claudell Washington)	.40	.20	.10
199	N.L. Victory Leaders(Randy Jones, Andy Messersmith, Tom Seaver)	2.00	1.00	.60
200	A.L. Victory Leaders(Vida Blue, Jim Hunter, Jim Palmer)	1.00	.50	.30
201	N.L. ERA Leaders(Randy Jones, Andy Messersmith, Tom Seaver)	1.00	.50	.30
202	A.L. ERA Leaders(Dennis Eckersley, Jim Hunter, Jim Palmer)	2.00	1.00	.60
203	N.L. Strikeout Leaders(Andy Messersmith, John Montefusco, Tom Seaver)	1.50	.70	.45
204	A.L. Strikeout Leaders(Bert Blyleven, Gaylord Perry, Frank Tanana)	1.00	.50	.30
205	Major League Leading Firemen(Rich Gossage, Al Hrabosky)	.75	.40	.25
206	Manny Trillo	.40	.20	.10
207	Andy Hassler	.40	.20	.10
208	Mike Lum	.40	.20	.10
209	Alan Ashby	.40	.20	.10
210	Lee May	.40	.20	.10
211	Clay Carroll	.40	.20	.10
212	Pat Kelly	.40	.20	.10
213	Dave Heaverlo	.40	.20	.10
214	Eric Soderholm	.40	.20	.10
215	Reggie Smith	.40	.20	.10
216	Montreal Expos Team(Karl Kuehl)	1.00	.50	.30
217	Dave Freisleben	.40	.20	.10
218	John Knox	.40	.20	.10
219	Tom Murphy	.40	.20	.10
220	Manny Sanguillen	.40	.20	.10
221	Jim Todd	.40	.20	.10
222	Wayne Garrett	.40	.20	.10
223	Ollie Brown	.40	.20	.10
224	Jim York	.40	.20	.10
225	Roy White	.40	.20	.10
226	Jim Sundberg	.40	.20	.10
227	Oscar Zamora	.40	.20	.10
228	John Hale	.40	.20	.10
229	Jerry Remy RC	.40	.20	.10
230	Carl Yastrzemski	7.00	4.00	2.00
231	Tom House	.40	.20	.10
232	Frank Duffy	.40	.20	.10
233	Grant Jackson	.40	.20	.10
234	Mike Sadek	.40	.20	.10
235	Bert Blyleven	1.00	.50	.30
236	Kansas City Royals Team(Whitey Herzog)	1.00	.50	.30
237	Dave Hamilton	.40	.20	.10
238	Larry Biittner	.40	.20	.10
239	John Curtis	.40	.20	.10
240	Pete Rose	20.00	10.00	5.00
241	Hector Torres	.40	.20	.10
242	Dan Meyer	.40	.20	.10
243	Jim Rooker	.40	.20	.10
244	Bill Sharp	.40	.20	.10
245	Felix Millan	.40	.20	.10
246	Cesar Tovar	.40	.20	.10
247	Terry Harmon	.40	.20	.10
248	Dick Tidrow	.40	.20	.10
249	Cliff Johnson	.40	.20	.10
250	Fergie Jenkins	3.00	1.50	.90
251	Rick Monday	.40	.20	.10
252	Tim Nordbrook	.40	.20	.10
253	Bill Buckner	.75	.40	.25
254	Rudy Meoli	.40	.20	.10
255	Fritz Peterson	.40	.20	.10
256	Rowland Office	.40	.20	.10
257	Ross Grimsley	.40	.20	.10
258	Nyls Nyman	.40	.20	.10
259	Darrel Chaney	.40	.20	.10
260	Steve Busby	.40	.20	.10
261	Gary Thomasson	.40	.20	.10
262	Checklist 133-264	1.00	.50	.30
263	Lyman Bostock RC	.75	.40	.25
264	Steve Renko	.40	.20	.10
265	Willie Davis	.40	.20	.10
266	Alan Foster	.40	.20	.10
267	Aurelio Rodriguez	.40	.20	.10
268	Del Unser	.40	.20	.10
269	Rick Austin	.40	.20	.10
270	Willie Stargell	4.00	2.00	1.25
271	Jim Lonborg	.40	.20	.10
272	Rick Dempsey	.40	.20	.10
273	Joe Niekro	.40	.20	.10
274	Tommy Harper	.40	.20	.10
275	Rick Manning RC	.75	.40	.25
276	Mickey Scott	.40	.20	.10
277	Chicago Cubs Team(Jim Marshall)	1.00	.50	.30
278	Bernie Carbo	.40	.20	.10
279	Roy Howell	.40	.20	.10
280	Burt Hooton	.40	.20	.10
281	Dave May	.40	.20	.10
282	Dan Osborn	.40	.20	.10
283	Merv Rettenmund	.40	.20	.10
284	Steve Ontiveros	.40	.20	.10
285	Mike Cuellar	.40	.20	.10
286	Jim Wohlford	.40	.20	.10
287	Pete Mackanin	.40	.20	.10
288	Bill Campbell	.40	.20	.10
289	Enzo Hernandez	.40	.20	.10
290	Ted Simmons	.40	.20	.10
291	Ken Sanders	.40	.20	.10
292	Leon Roberts	.40	.20	.10
293	Bill Castro	.40	.20	.10
294	Ed Kirkpatrick	.40	.20	.10
295	Dave Cash	.40	.20	.10
296	Pat Dobson	.40	.20	.10
297	Roger Metzger	.40	.20	.10
298	Dick Bosman	.40	.20	.10
299	Champ Summers	.40	.20	.10
300	Johnny Bench	8.00	4.00	2.25
301	Jackie Brown	.40	.20	.10
302	Rick Miller	.40	.20	.10
303	Steve Foucault	.40	.20	.10
304	California Angels Team(Dick Williams)	1.00	.50	.30
305	Andy Messersmith	.40	.20	.10
306	Rod Gilbreath	.40	.20	.10
307	Al Bumbry	.40	.20	.10
308	Jim Barr	.40	.20	.10
309	Bill Melton	.40	.20	.10
310	Randy Jones	.40	.20	.10
311	Cookie Rojas	.40	.20	.10
312	Don Carrithers	.40	.20	.10
313	Dan Ford RC	.40	.20	.10
314	Ed Kranepool	.40	.20	.10
315	Al Hrabosky	.40	.20	.10
316	Robin Yount	8.00	4.00	2.50
317	John Candelaria RC	1.00	.50	.30
318	Bob Boone	.75	.40	.25

#	Player			
319	Larry Gura	.40	.20	.10
320	Willie Horton	.40	.20	.10
321	Jose Cruz	.75	.40	.25
322	Glenn Abbott	.40	.20	.10
323	Rob Sperring	.40	.20	.10
324	Jim Bibby	.40	.20	.10
325	Tony Perez	4.00	2.00	1.25
326	Dick Pole	.40	.20	.10
327	Dave Moates	.40	.20	.10
328	Carl Morton	.40	.20	.10
329	Joe Ferguson	.40	.20	.10
330	Nolan Ryan	20.00	10.50	6.50
331	San Diego Padres Team(John McNamara)	1.00	.50	.30
332	Charlie Williams	.40	.20	.10
333	Bob Coluccio	.40	.20	.10
334	Dennis Leonard	.40	.20	.10
335	Bob Grich	.75	.40	.25
336	Vic Albury	.40	.20	.10
337	Bud Harrelson	.40	.20	.10
338	Bob Bailey	.40	.20	.10
339	John Denny	.40	.20	.10
340	Jim Rice	5.00	1.50	.90
341	Lou Gehrig (All Time 1B)	9.00	5.00	3.00
342	Rogers Hornsby (All Time 2B)	2.50	1.25	.70
343	Pie Traynor (All Time 3B)	1.00	.50	.30
344	Honus Wagner (All Time SS)	5.00	2.50	1.50
345	Babe Ruth (All Time OF)	10.00	7.50	4.50
346	Ty Cobb (All Time OF)	9.00	5.00	3.00
347	Ted Williams (All Time OF)	8.00	5.00	3.00
348	Mickey Cochrane (All Time C)	1.00	.50	.30
349	Walter Johnson (All Time RHP)	4.00	2.00	1.25
350	Lefty Grove (All Time LHP)	1.00	.50	.30
351	Randy Hundley	.40	.20	.10
352	Dave Giusti	.40	.20	.10
353	Sixto Lezcano RC	.75	.40	.25
354	Ron Blomberg	.40	.20	.10
355	Steve Carlton	4.00	2.00	1.25
356	Ted Martinez	.40	.20	.10
357	Ken Forsch	.40	.20	.10
358	Buddy Bell	.40	.20	.10
359	Rick Reuschel	.40	.20	.10
360	Jeff Burroughs	.40	.20	.10
361	Detroit Tigers Team(Ralph Houk)	1.00	.50	.30
362	Will McEnaney	.40	.20	.10
363	Dave Collins RC	.40	.20	.12
364	Elias Sosa	.40	.20	.10
365	Carlton Fisk	5.00	2.50	1.50
366	Bobby Valentine	.40	.20	.10
367	Bruce Miller	.40	.20	.10
368	Wilbur Wood	.40	.20	.10
369	Frank White	.75	.40	.25
370	Ron Cey	.75	.40	.25
371	Ellie Hendricks	.40	.20	.10
372	Rick Baldwin	.40	.20	.10
373	Johnny Briggs	.40	.20	.10
374	Dan Warthen	.40	.20	.10
375	Ron Fairly	.40	.20	.10
376	Rich Hebner	.40	.20	.10
377	Mike Hegan	.40	.20	.10
378	Steve Stone	.40	.20	.10
379	Ken Boswell	.40	.20	.10
380	Bobby Bonds	1.00	.50	.30
381	Denny Doyle	.40	.20	.10
382	Matt Alexander	.40	.20	.10
383	John Ellis	.40	.20	.10
384	Philadelphia Phillies Team(Danny Ozark)	1.00	.50	.30
385	Mickey Lolich	.75	.40	.25
386	Ed Goodson	.40	.20	.10
387	Mike Miley	.40	.20	.10
388	Stan Perzanowski	.40	.20	.10
389	Glenn Adams	.40	.20	.10
390	Don Gullett	.40	.20	.10
391	Jerry Hairston Sr.	.40	.20	.10
392	Checklist 265-396	1.00	.50	.30
393	Paul Mitchell	.40	.20	.10
394	Fran Healy	.40	.20	.10
395	Jim Wynn	.40	.20	.10
396	Bill Lee	.40	.20	.10
397	Tim Foli	.40	.20	.10
398	Dave Tomlin	.40	.20	.10
399	Luis Melendez	.40	.20	.10
400	Rod Carew	5.00	2.50	1.50
401	Ken Brett	.40	.20	.10
402	Don Money	.40	.20	.10
403	Geoff Zahn	.40	.20	.10
404	Enos Cabell	.40	.20	.10
405	Rollie Fingers	3.00	1.50	.90
406	Ed Herrmann	.40	.20	.10
407	Tom Underwood	.40	.20	.10
408	Charlie Spikes	.40	.20	.10
409	Dave Lemanczyk	.40	.20	.10
410	Ralph Garr	.40	.20	.10
411	Bill Singer	.40	.20	.10
412	Toby Harrah	.40	.20	.10
413	Pete Varney	.40	.20	.10
414	Wayne Garland	.40	.20	.10
415	Vada Pinson	1.00	.50	.30
416	Tommy John	1.00	.50	.30
417	Gene Clines	.40	.20	.10
418	Jose Morales	.40	.20	.10
419	Reggie Cleveland	.40	.20	.10
420	Joe Morgan	4.00	2.00	1.25
421	Oakland A's Team	1.00	.50	.30
422	Johnny Grubb	.40	.20	.10
423	Ed Halicki	.40	.20	.10
424	Phil Roof	.40	.20	.10
425	Rennie Stennett	.40	.20	.10
426	Bob Forsch	.40	.20	.10
427	Kurt Bevacqua	.40	.20	.10
428	Jim Crawford	.40	.20	.10
429	Fred Stanley	.40	.20	.10
430	Jose Cardenal	.40	.20	.10
431	Dick Ruthven	.40	.20	.10
432	Tom Veryzer	.40	.20	.10
433	Rick Waits	.40	.20	.10
434	Morris Nettles	.40	.20	.10
435	Phil Niekro	3.00	1.50	.90
436	Bill Fahey	.40	.20	.10
437	Terry Forster	.40	.20	.10
438	Doug DeCinces	.40	.20	.10
439	Rick Rhoden	.40	.20	.10
440	John Mayberry	.40	.20	.10
441	Gary Carter	6.00	3.00	1.75
442	Hank Webb	.40	.20	.10
443	San Francisco Giants Team	1.00	.50	.30
444	Gary Nolan	.40	.20	.10
445	Rico Petrocelli	.40	.20	.10
446	Larry Haney	.40	.20	.10
447	Gene Locklear	.40	.20	.10
448	Tom Johnson	.40	.20	.10
449	Bob Robertson	.40	.20	.10
450	Jim Palmer	4.00	2.00	1.25
451	Buddy Bradford	.40	.20	.10
452	Tom Hausman	.40	.20	.10
453	Lou Piniella	1.50	.70	.45
454	Tom Griffin	.40	.20	.10
455	Dick Allen	.75	.40	.25
456	Joe Coleman	.40	.20	.10
457	Ed Crosby	.40	.20	.10
458	Earl Williams	.40	.20	.10
459	Jim Brewer	.40	.20	.10
460	Cesar Cedeno	.40	.20	.10
461	NL & AL Championships	.75	.40	.25
462	1975 World Series	.75	.40	.25
463	Steve Hargan	.40	.20	.10
464	Ken Henderson	.40	.20	.10
465	Mike Marshall	.40	.20	.10
466	Bob Stinson	.40	.20	.10
467	Woodie Fryman	.40	.20	.10
468	Jesus Alou	.40	.20	.10
469	Rawly Eastwick	.40	.20	.10
470	Bobby Murcer	.75	.40	.25
471	Jim Burton	.40	.20	.10
472	Bob Davis	.40	.20	.10
473	Paul Blair	.40	.20	.10
474	Ray Corbin	.40	.20	.10
475	Joe Rudi	.40	.20	.10
476	Bob Moose	.40	.20	.10
477	Cleveland Indians Team (Frank Robinson)	1.50	.70	.45
478	Lynn McGlothen	.40	.20	.10
479	Bobby Mitchell	.40	.20	.10
480	Mike Schmidt	12.00	6.00	3.00
481	Rudy May	.40	.20	.10
482	Tim Hosley	.40	.20	.10
483	Mickey Stanley	.40	.20	.10
484	Eric Raich	.40	.20	.10
485	Mike Hargrove	.40	.20	.10
486	Bruce Dal Canton	.40	.20	.10
487	Leron Lee	.40	.20	.10
488	Claude Osteen	.40	.20	.10
489	Skip Jutze	.40	.20	.10
490	Frank Tanana	.40	.20	.10
491	Terry Crowley	.40	.20	.10
492	Marty Pattin	.40	.20	.10
493	Derrel Thomas	.40	.20	.10
494	Craig Swan	.40	.20	.10
495	Nate Colbert	.40	.20	.10
496	Juan Beniquez	.40	.20	.10
497	Joe McIntosh	.40	.20	.10
498	Glenn Borgmann	.40	.20	.10
499	Mario Guerrero	.40	.20	.10
500	Reggie Jackson	10.00	5.00	3.00
501	Billy Champion	.40	.20	.10
502	Tim McCarver	1.00	.50	.30
503	Elliott Maddox	.40	.20	.10
504	Pittsburgh Pirates Team (Danny Murtaugh)	1.00	.50	.30
505	Mark Belanger	.40	.20	.10
506	George Mitterwald	.40	.20	.10
507	Ray Bare	.40	.20	.10
508	Duane Kuiper RC	.40	.20	.10
509	Bill Hands	.40	.20	.10
510	Amos Otis	.40	.20	.10
511	Jamie Easterly	.40	.20	.10
512	Ellie Rodriguez	.40	.20	.10
513	Bart Johnson	.40	.20	.10
514	Dan Driessen	.40	.20	.10
515	Steve Yeager	.40	.20	.10
516	Wayne Granger	.40	.20	.10
517	John Milner	.40	.20	.10
518	Doug Flynn RC	.40	.20	.10
519	Steve Brye	.40	.20	.10
520	Willie McCovey	4.00	2.00	1.25
521	Jim Colborn	.40	.20	.10
522	Ted Sizemore	.40	.20	.10
523	Bob Montgomery	.40	.20	.10
524	Pete Falcone	.40	.20	.10
525	Billy Williams	3.00	1.50	.75
526	Checklist 397-528	1.00	.50	.30
527	Mike Anderson	.40	.20	.10
528	Dock Ellis	.40	.20	.10
529	Deron Johnson	.40	.20	.10
530	Don Sutton	3.00	1.50	.90
531	New York Mets Team(Joe Frazier)	1.00	.50	.30
532	Milt May	.40	.20	.10
533	Lee Richard	.40	.20	.10
534	Stan Bahnsen	.40	.20	.10
535	Dave Nelson	.40	.20	.10
536	Mike Thompson	.40	.20	.10
537	Tony Muser	.40	.20	.10
538	Pat Darcy	.40	.20	.10
539	John Balaz	.40	.20	.10
540	Bill Freehan	.40	.20	.10
541	Steve Mingori	.40	.20	.10
542	Keith Hernandez	1.00	.50	.30
543	Wayne Twitchell	.40	.20	.10
544	Pepe Frias	.40	.20	.10
545	Sparky Lyle	.40	.20	.10
546	Dave Rosello	.40	.20	.10
547	Roric Harrison	.40	.20	.10
548	Manny Mota	.40	.20	.10
549	Randy Tate	.40	.20	.10
550	Hank Aaron	25.00	12.50	7.50
551	Jerry DaVanon	.40	.20	.10
552	Terry Humphrey	.40	.20	.10
553	Randy Moffitt	.40	.20	.10
554	Ray Fosse	.40	.20	.10
555	Dyar Miller	.40	.20	.10
556	Minnesota Twins Team(Gene Mauch)	1.00	.50	.30
557	Dan Spillner	.40	.20	.10
558	Clarence Gaston	.40	.20	.10
559	Clyde Wright	.40	.20	.10
560	Jorge Orta	.40	.20	.10
561	Tom Carroll	.40	.20	.10
562	Adrian Garrett	.40	.20	.10
563	Larry Demery	.40	.20	.10
564	Kurt Bevacqua (Bubble Gum Blowing Champ)	.40	.20	.10
565	Tug McGraw	.75	.40	.25
566	Ken McMullen	.40	.20	.10
567	George Stone	.40	.20	.10
568	Rob Andrews	.40	.20	.10
569	Nelson Briles	.40	.20	.10
570	George Hendrick	.40	.20	.10
571	Don DeMola	.40	.20	.10
572	Rich Coggins	.40	.20	.10
573	Bill Travers	.40	.20	.10
574	Don Kessinger	.40	.20	.10
575	Dwight Evans	.75	.40	.25
576	Maximino Leon	.40	.20	.10
577	Marc Hill	.40	.20	.10
578	Ted Kubiak	.40	.20	.10
579	Clay Kirby	.40	.20	.10
580	Bert Campaneris	.40	.20	.10
581	St. Louis Cardinals Team (Red Schoendienst)	1.50	.70	.45
582	Mike Kekich	.40	.20	.10
583	Tommy Helms	.40	.20	.10
584	Stan Wall	.40	.20	.10
585	Joe Torre	1.50	.70	.45
586	Ron Schueler	.40	.20	.10
587	Leo Cardenas	.40	.20	.10
588	Kevin Kobel	.40	.20	.10
589	Rookie Pitchers(Santo Alcala, Mike Flanagan RC, Joe Pactwa, Pablo Torrealba)	1.00	.50	.30

590	Rookie Outfielders(Henry Cruz, Chet Lemon **RC**, Ellis Valentine **RC**, Terry Whitfield)	.75	.40	.25
591	Rookie Pitchers(Steve Grilli, Craig Mitchell, Jose Sosa, George Throop)	.40	.20	.10
592	Rookie Infielders(Dave McKay **RC**, Willie Randolph **RC**, Jerry Royster **RC**, Roy Staiger **RC**)	6.00	3.00	1.75
593	Rookie Pitchers(Larry Anderson, Ken Crosby, Mark Littell, Butch Metzger **RC**)	.40	.20	.10
594	Rookie Catchers & Outfielders(Andy Merchant, Ed Ott, Royle Stillman, Jerry White)	.40	.20	.10
595	Rookie Pitchers(Steve Barr, Art DeFilippis, Randy Lerch, Sid Monge)	.40	.20	.10
596	Rookie Infielders(Lamar Johnson, Johnny LeMaster **RC**, Jerry Manuel, Craig Reynolds **RC**)	.40	.20	.10
597	Rookie Pitchers(Don Aase **RC**, Jack Kucek, Frank LaCorte, Mike Pazik)	.40	.20	.10
598	Rookie Outfielders (Hector Cruz, Jamie Quirk **RC**, Jerry Turner, Joe Wallis)	.40	.20	.10
599	Rookie Pitchers(Rob Dressler **RC**, Ron Guidry **RC**, Bob McClure **RC**, Pat Zachry **RC**)	7.00	3.50	1.50
600	Tom Seaver	8.00	4.00	2.50
601	Ken Rudolph	.40	.20	.10
602	Doug Konieczny	.40	.20	.10
603	Jim Holt	.40	.20	.10
604	Joe Lovitto	.40	.20	.10
605	Al Downing	.40	.20	.10
606	Milwaukee Brewers Team(Alex Grammas)	1.00	.50	.30
607	Rich Hinton	.40	.20	.10
608	Vic Correll	.40	.20	.10
609	Fred Norman	.40	.20	.10
610	Greg Luzinski	.75	.40	.25
611	Rich Folkers	.40	.20	.10
612	Joe Lahoud	.40	.20	.10
613	Tim Johnson	.40	.20	.10
614	Fernando Arroyo	.40	.20	.10
615	Mike Cubbage	.40	.20	.10
616	Buck Martinez	.40	.20	.10
617	Darold Knowles	.40	.20	.10
618	Jack Brohamer	.40	.20	.10
619	Bill Butler	.40	.20	.10
620	Al Oliver	.75	.40	.25
621	Tom Hall	.40	.20	.10
622	Rick Auerbach	.40	.20	.10
623	Bob Allietta	.40	.20	.10
624	Tony Taylor	.40	.20	.10
625	J.R. Richard	.40	.20	.10
626	Bob Sheldon	.40	.20	.10
627	Bill Plummer	.40	.20	.10
628	John D'Acquisto	.40	.20	.10
629	Sandy Alomar	.40	.20	.10
630	Chris Speier	.40	.20	.10
631	Atlanta Braves Team(Dave Bristol)	1.00	.50	.30
632	Rogelio Moret	.40	.20	.10
633	John Stearns **RC**	.40	.20	.10
634	Larry Christenson	.40	.20	.10
635	Jim Fregosi	.40	.20	.10
636	Joe Decker	.40	.20	.10
637	Bruce Bochte	.40	.20	.10
638	Doyle Alexander	.40	.20	.10
639	Fred Kendall	.40	.20	.10
640	Bill Madlock	.75	.40	.25
641	Tom Paciorek	.40	.20	.10
642	Dennis Blair	.40	.20	.10
643	Checklist 529-660	1.00	.50	.30
644	Tom Bradley	.40	.20	.10
645	Darrell Porter	.40	.20	.10
646	John Lowenstein	.40	.20	.10
647	Ramon Hernandez	.40	.20	.10
648	Al Cowens	.40	.20	.10
649	Dave Roberts	.40	.20	.10
650	Thurman Munson	8.00	4.00	2.00
651	John Odom	.40	.20	.10

652	Ed Armbrister	.40	.20	.10
653	Mike Norris **RC**	.40	.20	.10
654	Doug Griffin	.40	.20	.10
655	Mike Vail	.40	.20	.10
656	Chicago White Sox Team(Chuck Tanner)	1.00	.50	.30
657	Roy Smalley **RC**	.40	.20	.10
658	Jerry Johnson	.40	.20	.10
659	Ben Oglivie	.40	.20	.10
660	Dave Lopes	1.00	.50	.30

1976 Topps Cloth Sticker Prototypes

Apparently produced to test different materials for the cloth sticker set which would be issued the following year, these prototypes were never issued. Each of the players can be found on four different types of material. The blank-backed stickers feature the card fronts as they appeared in the regular 1976 issue. It is unknown whether other players were produced for the test.

		NM	E	VG
	Common Player:	30.00	15.00	9.00
(1a)	Bob Apodaca (Silk)	30.00	15.00	9.00
(1b)	Bob Apodaca (Thin felt.)	30.00	15.00	9.00
(1c)	Bob Apodaca (Textured felt.)	60.00	30.00	18.00
(1d)	Bob Apodaca (Thick felt.)	30.00	15.00	9.00
(2a)	Duffy Dyer (Silk)	30.00	15.00	9.00
(2b)	Duffy Dyer (Thin felt.)	30.00	15.00	9.00
(2c)	Duffy Dyer (Textured felt.)	60.00	30.00	18.00
(2d)	Duffy Dyer (Thick felt.)	30.00	15.00	9.00

1976 Topps Joe Garagiola

Topps produced this personal business card for long-time NBC announcer and former major leaguer Joe Garagiola. The front is in the format of a 1973 Topps card and has a color portrait. The back resembles the 1976 Topps card, is in black-and-white and provides contact information.

		NM	E	VG
1	Joe Garagiola	20.00	10.00	6.00

1976 Topps Team Checklist Sheet

Via a mail-in redemption (50¢ and a wrapper), collectors could receive an uncut sheet of the 24 team photo/checklist cards from the 1976 Topps baseball set. Measuring about 10-1/2" x 20-1/8", the sheet could be cut into individual team cards of standard size, though printed on stock that is lighter than pack-issued versions.

	NM	E	VG
Complete Sheet:	35.00	17.50	10.00

1976 Topps Traded

Similar to the Topps Traded set of 1974, the 2-1/2" x 3-1/2" cards feature photos of players traded after the printing deadline. The style of the cards is essentially the same as the regular issue, but with a large "Sports Extra" headline announcing the trade and its date. The backs continue in

newspaper style to detail the specifics of the trade. There are 43 player cards and one checklist in the set. Numbers remain the same as the player's regular card, with the addition of a "T" suffix.

 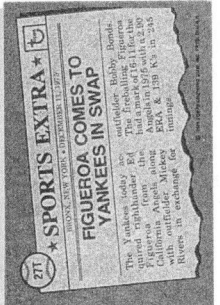

		NM	E	VG
Complete Set (44):		20.00	10.00	6.00
Common Player:		.75	.35	.20
27T	Ed Figueroa	.75	.35	.20
28T	Dusty Baker	1.25	.60	.40
44T	Doug Rader	.75	.35	.20
58T	Ron Reed	.75	.35	.20
74T	Oscar Gamble	.75	.35	.20
80T	Jim Kaat	.75	.35	.20
83T	Jim Spencer	.75	.35	.20
85T	Mickey Rivers	.75	.35	.20
99T	Lee Lacy	.75	.35	.20
120T	Rusty Staub	.75	.35	.20
127T	Larvell Blanks	.75	.35	.20
146T	George Medich	.75	.35	.20
158T	Ken Reitz	.75	.35	.20
208T	Mike Lum	.75	.35	.20
211T	Clay Carroll	.75	.35	.20
231T	Tom House	.75	.35	.20
250T	Fergie Jenkins	3.00	1.50	.90
259T	Darrel Chaney	.75	.35	.20
292T	Leon Roberts	.75	.35	.20
296T	Pat Dobson	.75	.35	.20
309T	Bill Melton	.75	.35	.20
338T	Bob Bailey	.75	.35	.20
380T	Bobby Bonds	.75	.35	.20
383T	John Ellis	.75	.35	.20
385T	Mickey Lolich	.75	.35	.20
401T	Ken Brett	.75	.35	.20
410T	Ralph Garr	.75	.35	.20
411T	Bill Singer	.75	.35	.20
428T	Jim Crawford	.75	.35	.20
434T	Morris Nettles	.75	.35	.20
464T	Ken Henderson	.75	.35	.20
497T	Joe McIntosh	.75	.35	.20
524T	Pete Falcone	.75	.35	.20
527T	Mike Anderson	.75	.35	.20
528T	Dock Ellis	.75	.35	.20
532T	Milt May	.75	.35	.20
554T	Ray Fosse	.75	.35	.20
579T	Clay Kirby	.75	.35	.20
583T	Tommy Helms	.75	.35	.20
592T	Willie Randolph	.75	.35	.20
618T	Jack Brohamer	.75	.35	.20
632T	Rogelio Moret	.75	.35	.20
649T	Dave Roberts	.75	.35	.20
----	Traded Checklist	.75	.35	.20

1976 Topps/Dynamite Magazine Panels

In at least one issue of its "Dynamite" kids' magazine, Scholastic Book Club teamed with Topps to insert a six-card panel of its 1976 baseball issue. Values shown are for just the uncut panel; complete magazines would bear a small premium.

		NM	E	VG
Complete Panel:		20.00	10.00	6.00
469	Rawly Eastwick			
471	Jim Burton			
474	Ray Corbin			
481	Rudy May			
482	Tim Hosley			
522	Ted Sizemore			

1977 Topps

The 1977 Topps Set is a 660-card effort featuring front designs dominated by a color photograph on which there is a facsimile autograph. Above the picture are the player's name, team and position. The backs of the 2-1/2" x 3-1/2" cards include personal and career statistics along with newspaper-style highlights and a cartoon. Specialty cards include statistical leaders, record performances, a new "Turn Back The Clock" feature which highlighted great past moments and a "Big League Brothers" feature.

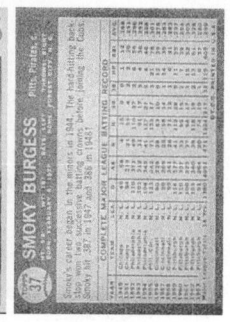

PIRATES

SMOKY BURGESS catcher

	NM	E	VG
Complete Set (660):	200.00	95.00	55.00
Common Player:	.25	.10	.06
Wax Pack (10):	22.50		
Wax Box (36):	675.00		
Cello Pack (18):	40.00		
Cello Box (24):	1,200		
Rack Pack (39):	65.00		
Rack Box (24):	2,000		
Vending Box (500):	350.00		

		NM	E	VG
1	Batting Leaders(George Brett, Bill Madlock)	6.00	3.00	1.75
2	Home Run Leaders(Graig Nettles, Mike Schmidt)	2.00	1.00	.60
3	RBI Leaders(George Foster, Lee May)	.75	.40	.25
4	Stolen Base Leaders(Dave Lopes, Bill North)	.50	.25	.15
5	Victory Leaders(Randy Jones, Jim Palmer)	1.00	.50	.30
6	Strikeout Leaders(Nolan Ryan, Tom Seaver)	10.00	5.00	3.00
7	ERA Leaders(John Denny, Mark Fidrych)	.50	.25	.15
8	Leading Firemen(Bill Campbell, Rawly Eastwick)	.25	.10	.06
9	Doug Rader	.25	.10	.06
10	Reggie Jackson	8.00	4.00	2.50
11	Rob Dressler	.25	.10	.06
12	Larry Haney	.25	.10	.06
13	Luis Gomez	.25	.10	.06
14	Tommy Smith	.25	.10	.06
15	Don Gullett	.25	.10	.06
16	Bob Jones	.25	.10	.06
17	Steve Stone	.25	.10	.06
18	Indians Team(Frank Robinson)	1.50	.70	.45
19	John D'Acquisto	.25	.10	.06
20	Graig Nettles	.75	.40	.25
21	Ken Forsch	.25	.10	.06
22	Bill Freehan	.25	.10	.06
23	Dan Driessen	.25	.10	.06
24	Carl Morton	.25	.10	.06
25	Dwight Evans	.75	.40	.25
26	Ray Sadecki	.25	.10	.06
27	Bill Buckner	.75	.40	.25
28	Woodie Fryman	.25	.10	.06
29	Bucky Dent	.50	.25	.15
30	Greg Luzinski	.50	.25	.15
31	Jim Todd	.25	.10	.06
32	Checklist 1-132	1.00	.50	.30
33	Wayne Garland	.25	.10	.06
34	Angels Team(Norm Sherry)	1.00	.50	.30
35	Rennie Stennett	.25	.10	.06
36	John Ellis	.25	.10	.06
37	Steve Hargan	.25	.10	.06
38	Craig Kusick	.25	.10	.06
39	Tom Griffin	.25	.10	.06
40	Bobby Murcer	.50	.25	.15
41	Jim Kern	.25	.10	.06
42	Jose Cruz	.25	.10	.06
43	Ray Bare	.25	.10	.06
44	Bud Harrelson	.25	.10	.06
45	Rawly Eastwick	.25	.10	.06
46	Buck Martinez	.25	.10	.06
47	Lynn McGlothen	.25	.10	.06
48	Tom Paciorek	.25	.10	.06
49	Grant Jackson	.25	.10	.06
50	Ron Cey	.50	.25	.15
51	Brewers Team(Alex Grammas)	1.00	.50	.30
52	Ellis Valentine	.25	.10	.06
53	Paul Mitchell	.25	.10	.06
54	Sandy Alomar	.25	.10	.06
55	Jeff Burroughs	.25	.10	.06
56	Rudy May	.25	.10	.06
57	Marc Hill	.25	.10	.06

		NM	E	VG
58	Chet Lemon	.25	.10	.06
59	Larry Christenson	.25	.10	.06
60	Jim Rice	2.00	1.00	.60
61	Manny Sanguillen	.25	.10	.06
62	Eric Raich	.25	.10	.06
63	Tito Fuentes	.25	.10	.06
64	Larry Biittner	.25	.10	.06
65	Skip Lockwood	.25	.10	.06
66	Roy Smalley	.25	.10	.06
67	Joaquin Andujar RC	.50	.25	.15
68	Bruce Bochte	.25	.10	.06
69	Jim Crawford	.25	.10	.06
70	Johnny Bench	8.00	4.00	2.00
71	Dock Ellis	.25	.10	.06
72	Mike Anderson	.25	.10	.06
73	Charlie Williams	.25	.10	.06
74	A's Team(Jack McKeon)	1.00	.50	.30
75	Dennis Leonard	.25	.10	.06
76	Tim Foli	.25	.10	.06
77	Dyar Miller	.25	.10	.06
78	Bob Davis	.25	.10	.06
79	Don Money	.25	.10	.06
80	Andy Messersmith	.25	.10	.06
81	Juan Beniquez	.25	.10	.06
82	Jim Rooker	.25	.10	.06
83	Kevin Bell	.25	.10	.06
84	Ollie Brown	.25	.10	.06
85	Duane Kuiper	.25	.10	.06
86	Pat Zachry	.25	.10	.06
87	Glenn Borgmann	.25	.10	.06
88	Stan Wall	.25	.10	.06
89	Butch Hobson RC	.25	.10	.06
90	Cesar Cedeno	.25	.10	.06
91	John Verhoeven	.25	.10	.06
92	Dave Rosello	.25	.10	.06
93	Tom Poquette	.25	.10	.06
94	Craig Swan	.25	.10	.06
95	Keith Hernandez	.75	.40	.25
96	Lou Piniella	.75	.40	.25
97	Dave Heaverlo	.25	.10	.06
98	Milt May	.25	.10	.06
99	Tom Hausman	.25	.10	.06
100	Joe Morgan	3.00	1.50	.90
101	Dick Bosman	.25	.10	.06
102	Jose Morales	.25	.10	.06
103	Mike Bacsik	.25	.10	.06
104	Omar Moreno RC	.50	.25	.15
105	Steve Yeager	.50	.25	.15
106	Mike Flanagan	.50	.25	.15
107	Bill Melton	.25	.10	.06
108	Alan Foster	.25	.10	.06
109	Jorge Orta	.25	.10	.06
110	Steve Carlton	4.00	2.00	1.25
111	Rico Petrocelli	.50	.25	.15
112	Bill Greif	.25	.10	.06
113	Blue Jays Mgr./Coaches (Roy Hartsfield, Don Leppert, Bob Miller, Jackie Moore, Harry Warner)	.75	.40	.25
114	Bruce Dal Canton	.25	.10	.06
115	Rick Manning	.25	.10	.06
116	Joe Niekro	.25	.10	.06
117	Frank White	.25	.10	.06
118	Rick Jones	.25	.10	.06
119	John Stearns	.25	.10	.06
120	Rod Carew	4.00	2.00	1.00
121	Gary Nolan	.25	.10	.06
122	Ben Oglivie	.25	.10	.06
123	Fred Stanley	.25	.10	.06
124	George Mitterwald	.25	.10	.06
125	Bill Travers	.25	.10	.06
126	Rod Gilbreath	.25	.10	.06
127	Ron Fairly	.25	.10	.06
128	Tommy John	.50	.25	.15
129	Mike Sadek	.25	.10	.06
130	Al Oliver	.75	.40	.25
131	Orlando Ramirez	.25	.10	.06
132	Chip Lang	.25	.10	.06
133	Ralph Garr	.25	.10	.06
134	Padres Team(John McNamara)	.75	.40	.25
135	Mark Belanger	.25	.10	.06
136	Jerry Mumphrey RC	.25	.10	.06
137	Jeff Terpko	.25	.10	.06
138	Bob Stinson	.25	.10	.06
139	Fred Norman	.25	.10	.06
140	Mike Schmidt	10.00	5.00	3.00
141	Mark Littell	.25	.10	.06
142	Steve Dillard	.25	.10	.06
143	Ed Herrmann	.25	.10	.06
144	Bruce Sutter RC	15.00	7.50	4.50
145	Tom Veryzer	.25	.10	.06
146	Dusty Baker	1.00	.50	.30
147	Jackie Brown	.25	.10	.06
148	Fran Healy	.25	.10	.06
149	Mike Cubbage	.25	.10	.06
150	Tom Seaver	6.00	3.00	1.75

		NM	E	VG
151	Johnnie LeMaster	.25	.10	.06
152	Gaylord Perry	2.50	1.25	.70
153	Ron Jackson	.25	.10	.06
154	Dave Giusti	.25	.10	.06
155	Joe Rudi	.25	.10	.06
156	Pete Mackanin	.25	.10	.06
157	Ken Brett	.25	.10	.06
158	Ted Kubiak	.25	.10	.06
159	Bernie Carbo	.25	.10	.06
160	Will McEnaney	.25	.10	.06
161	Garry Templeton RC	1.00	.50	.30
162	Mike Cuellar	.25	.10	.06
163	Dave Hilton	.25	.10	.06
164	Tug McGraw	.25	.10	.06
165	Jim Wynn	.25	.10	.06
166	Bill Campbell	.25	.10	.06
167	Rich Hebner	.25	.10	.06
168	Charlie Spikes	.25	.10	.06
169	Darold Knowles	.25	.10	.06
170	Thurman Munson	6.00	3.00	1.75
171	Ken Sanders	.25	.10	.06
172	John Milner	.25	.10	.06
173	Chuck Scrivener	.25	.10	.06
174	Nelson Briles	.25	.10	.06
175	Butch Wynegar RC	.25	.10	.06
176	Bob Robertson	.25	.10	.06
177	Bart Johnson	.25	.10	.06
178	Bombo Rivera	.25	.10	.06
179	Paul Hartzell	.25	.10	.06
180	Dave Lopes	.50	.25	.15
181	Ken McMullen	.25	.10	.06
182	Dan Spillner	.25	.10	.06
183	Cardinals Team(Vern Rapp)	1.00	.50	.30
184	Bo McLaughlin	.25	.10	.06
185	Sixto Lezcano	.25	.10	.06
186	Doug Flynn	.25	.10	.06
187	Dick Pole	.25	.10	.06
188	Bob Tolan	.25	.10	.06
189	Rick Dempsey	.25	.10	.06
190	Ray Burris	.25	.10	.06
191	Doug Griffin	.25	.10	.06
192	Clarence Gaston	.25	.10	.06
193	Larry Gura	.25	.10	.06
194	Gary Matthews	.25	.10	.06
195	Ed Figueroa	.25	.10	.06
196	Len Randle	.25	.10	.06
197	Ed Ott	.25	.10	.06
198	Wilbur Wood	.25	.10	.06
199	Pepe Frias	.25	.10	.06
200	Frank Tanana	.25	.10	.06
201	Ed Kranepool	.25	.10	.06
202	Tom Johnson	.25	.10	.06
203	Ed Armbrister	.25	.10	.06
204	Jeff Newman	.25	.10	.06
205	Pete Falcone	.25	.10	.06
206	Boog Powell	.75	.40	.25
207	Glenn Abbott	.25	.10	.06
208	Checklist 133-264	.75	.40	.25
209	Rob Andrews	.25	.10	.06
210	Fred Lynn	.50	.25	.15
211	Giants Team(Joe Altobelli)	.75	.40	.25
212	Jim Mason	.25	.10	.06
213	Maximino Leon	.25	.10	.06
214	Darrell Porter	.25	.10	.06
215	Butch Metzger	.25	.10	.06
216	Doug DeCinces	.25	.10	.06
217	Tom Underwood	.25	.10	.06
218	John Wathan RC	.25	.10	.06
219	Joe Coleman	.25	.10	.06
220	Chris Chambliss	.50	.25	.15
221	Bob Bailey	.25	.10	.06
222	Francisco Barrios	.25	.10	.06
223	Earl Williams	.25	.10	.06
224	Rusty Torres	.25	.10	.06
225	Bob Apodaca	.25	.10	.06
226	Leroy Stanton	.25	.10	.06
227	Joe Sambito RC	.25	.10	.06
228	Twins Team(Gene Mauch)	1.00	.50	.30
229	Don Kessinger	.25	.10	.06
230	Vida Blue	.25	.10	.06
231	George Brett (Record Breaker)	6.00	3.00	1.50
232	Minnie Minoso (Record Breaker)	.50	.25	.15
233	Jose Morales (Record Breaker)	.50	.25	.15
234	Nolan Ryan (Record Breaker)	12.00	6.00	3.00
235	Cecil Cooper	.25	.10	.06
236	Tom Buskey	.25	.10	.06
237	Gene Clines	.25	.10	.06
238	Tippy Martinez	.25	.10	.06
239	Bill Plummer	.25	.10	.06
240	Ron LeFlore	.25	.10	.06
241	Dave Tomlin	.25	.10	.06

#	Name			
242	Ken Henderson	.25	.10	.06
243	Ron Reed	.25	.10	.06
244	John Mayberry	.25	.10	.06
245	Rick Rhoden	.25	.10	.06
246	Mike Vail	.25	.10	.06
247	Chris Knapp	.25	.10	.06
248	Wilbur Howard	.25	.10	.06
249	Pete Redfern	.25	.10	.06
250	Bill Madlock	.50	.25	.15
251	Tony Muser	.25	.10	.06
252	Dale Murray	.25	.10	.06
253	John Hale	.25	.10	.06
254	Doyle Alexander	.25	.10	.06
255	George Scott	.25	.10	.06
256	Joe Hoerner	.25	.10	.06
257	Mike Miley	.25	.10	.06
258	Luis Tiant	.50	.25	.15
259	Mets Team(Joe Frazier)	1.00	.50	.30
260	J.R. Richard	.25	.10	.06
261	Phil Garner	.50	.25	.15
262	Al Cowens	.25	.10	.06
263	Mike Marshall	.25	.10	.06
264	Tom Hutton	.25	.10	.06
265	Mark Fidrych RC	5.00	2.50	1.50
266	Derrel Thomas	.25	.10	.06
267	Ray Fosse	.25	.10	.06
268	Rick Sawyer	.25	.10	.06
269	Joe Lis	.25	.10	.06
270	Dave Parker	.50	.25	.15
271	Terry Forster	.25	.10	.06
272	Lee Lacy	.25	.10	.06
273	Eric Soderholm	.25	.10	.06
274	Don Stanhouse	.25	.10	.06
275	Mike Hargrove	.25	.10	.06
276	A.L. Championship (Chambliss' Dramatic Homer Decides It)	.25	.13	.08
277	N.L. Championship (Reds Sweep Phillies 3 In Row)	3.00	1.50	.90
278	Danny Frisella	.25	.10	.06
279	Joe Wallis	.25	.10	.06
280	Jim Hunter	2.50	1.25	.70
281	Roy Staiger	.25	.10	.06
282	Sid Monge	.25	.10	.06
283	Jerry DaVanon	.25	.10	.06
284	Mike Norris	.25	.10	.06
285	Brooks Robinson	4.00	2.00	1.25
286	Johnny Grubb	.25	.10	.06
287	Reds Team(Sparky Anderson)	1.00	.50	.30
288	Bob Montgomery	.25	.10	.06
289	Gene Garber	.25	.10	.06
290	Amos Otis	.25	.10	.06
291	Jason Thompson RC	.25	.10	.06
292	Rogelio Moret	.25	.10	.06
293	Jack Brohamer	.25	.10	.06
294	George Medich	.25	.10	.06
295	Gary Carter	3.00	1.50	.90
296	Don Hood	.25	.10	.06
297	Ken Reitz	.25	.10	.06
298	Charlie Hough	.25	.10	.06
299	Otto Velez	.25	.10	.06
300	Jerry Koosman	.25	.10	.06
301	Toby Harrah	.25	.10	.06
302	Mike Garman	.25	.10	.06
303	Gene Tenace	.25	.10	.06
304	Jim Hughes	.25	.10	.06
305	Mickey Rivers	.25	.10	.06
306	Rick Waits	.25	.10	.06
307	Gary Sutherland	.25	.10	.06
308	Gene Pentz	.25	.10	.06
309	Red Sox Team (Don Zimmer)	1.50	.70	.45
310	Larry Bowa	.50	.25	.15
311	Vern Ruhle	.25	.10	.06
312	Rob Belloir	.25	.10	.06
313	Paul Blair	.25	.10	.06
314	Steve Mingori	.25	.10	.06
315	Dave Chalk	.25	.10	.06
316	Steve Rogers	.25	.10	.06
317	Kurt Bevacqua	.25	.10	.06
318	Duffy Dyer	.25	.10	.06
319	Rich Gossage	.75	.40	.25
320	Ken Griffey	.75	.40	.25
321	Dave Goltz	.25	.10	.06
322	Bill Russell	.50	.25	.15
323	Larry Lintz	.25	.10	.06
324	John Curtis	.25	.10	.06
325	Mike Ivie	.25	.10	.06
326	Jesse Jefferson	.25	.10	.06
327	Astros Team(Bill Virdon)	.75	.40	.25
328	Tommy Boggs	.25	.10	.06
329	Ron Hodges	.25	.10	.06
330	George Hendrick	.25	.10	.06
331	Jim Colborn	.25	.10	.06
332	Elliott Maddox	.25	.10	.06
333	Paul Reuschel	.25	.10	.06
334	Bill Stein	.25	.10	.06
335	Bill Robinson	.25	.10	.06
336	Denny Doyle	.25	.10	.06
337	Ron Schueler	.25	.10	.06
338	Dave Duncan	.25	.10	.06
339	Adrian Devine	.25	.10	.06
340	Hal McRae	.50	.25	.15
341	Joe Kerrigan	.25	.10	.06
342	Jerry Remy	.25	.10	.06
343	Ed Halicki	.25	.10	.06
344	Brian Downing	.25	.10	.06
345	Reggie Smith	.25	.10	.06
346	Bill Singer	.25	.10	.06
347	George Foster	.25	.10	.06
348	Brent Strom	.25	.10	.06
349	Jim Holt	.25	.10	.06
350	Larry Dierker	.25	.10	.06
351	Jim Sundberg	.25	.10	.06
352	Mike Phillips	.25	.10	.06
353	Stan Thomas	.25	.10	.06
354	Pirates Team(Chuck Tanner)	.75	.40	.25
355	Lou Brock	3.00	1.50	.90
356	Checklist 265-396	.75	.40	.25
357	Tim McCarver	.75	.40	.25
358	Tom House	.25	.10	.06
359	Willie Randolph	.75	.40	.25
360	Rick Monday	.25	.10	.06
361	Eduardo Rodriguez	.25	.10	.06
362	Tommy Davis	.25	.10	.06
363	Dave Roberts	.25	.10	.06
364	Vic Correll	.25	.10	.06
365	Mike Torrez	.25	.10	.06
366	Ted Sizemore	.25	.10	.06
367	Dave Hamilton	.25	.10	.06
368	Mike Jorgensen	.25	.10	.06
369	Terry Humphrey	.25	.10	.06
370	John Montefusco	.25	.10	.06
371	Royals Team(Whitey Herzog)	1.00	.50	.30
372	Rich Folkers	.25	.10	.06
373	Bert Campaneris	.25	.10	.06
374	Kent Tekulve	.25	.10	.06
375	Larry Hisle	.25	.10	.06
376	Nino Espinosa	.25	.10	.06
377	Dave McKay	.25	.10	.06
378	Jim Umbarger	.25	.10	.06
379	Larry Cox	.25	.10	.06
380	Lee May	.25	.10	.06
381	Bob Forsch	.25	.10	.06
382	Charlie Moore	.25	.10	.06
383	Stan Bahnsen	.25	.10	.06
384	Darrel Chaney	.25	.10	.06
385	Dave LaRoche	.25	.10	.06
386	Manny Mota	.25	.10	.06
387	Yankees Team(Billy Martin)	2.00	1.00	.60
388	Terry Harmon	.25	.10	.06
389	Ken Kravec	.25	.10	.06
390	Dave Winfield	3.00	1.50	.90
391	Dan Warthen	.25	.10	.06
392	Phil Roof	.25	.10	.06
393	John Lowenstein	.25	.10	.06
394	Bill Laxton	.25	.10	.06
395	Manny Trillo	.25	.10	.06
396	Tom Murphy	.25	.10	.06
397	Larry Herndon RC	.25	.10	.06
398	Tom Burgmeier	.25	.10	.06
399	Bruce Boisclair	.25	.10	.06
400	Steve Garvey	2.00	1.00	.60
401	Mickey Scott	.25	.10	.06
402	Tommy Helms	.25	.10	.06
403	Tom Grieve	.25	.10	.06
404	Eric Rasmussen	.25	.10	.06
405	Claudell Washington	.25	.10	.06
406	Tim Johnson	.25	.10	.06
407	Dave Freisleben	.25	.10	.06
408	Cesar Tovar	.25	.10	.06
409	Pete Broberg	.25	.10	.06
410	Willie Montanez	.25	.10	.06
411	World Series Games 1 & 2(Joe Morgan, Johnny Bench)	2.00	1.00	.60
412	World Series Games 3 & 4(Johnny Bench)	2.00	1.00	.60
413	World Series Summary	.75	.40	.25
414	Tommy Harper	.25	.10	.06
415	Jay Johnstone	.25	.10	.06
416	Chuck Hartenstein	.25	.10	.06
417	Wayne Garrett	.25	.10	.06
418	White Sox Team(Bob Lemon)	1.00	.50	.30
419	Steve Swisher	.25	.10	.06
420	Rusty Staub	.50	.25	.15
421	Doug Rau	.25	.10	.06
422	Freddie Patek	.25	.10	.06
423	Gary Lavelle	.25	.10	.06
424	Steve Brye	.25	.10	.06
425	Joe Torre	1.00	.50	.30
426	Dick Drago	.25	.10	.06
427	Dave Rader	.25	.10	.06
428	Rangers Team(Frank Lucchesi)	.75	.40	.25
429	Ken Boswell	.25	.10	.06
430	Fergie Jenkins	2.50	1.25	.70
431	Dave Collins	.25	.10	.06
432	Buzz Capra	.25	.10	.06
433	Nate Colbert (Turn Back The Clock)	.25	.10	.06
434	Carl Yastrzemski (Turn Back The Clock)	1.50	.70	.45
435	Maury Wills (Turn Back The Clock)	.50	.25	.15
436	Bob Keegan (Turn Back The Clock)	.25	.10	.06
437	Ralph Kiner (Turn Back The Clock)	.75	.40	.25
438	Marty Perez	.25	.10	.06
439	Gorman Thomas	.25	.10	.06
440	Jon Matlack	.25	.10	.06
441	Larvell Blanks	.25	.10	.06
442	Braves Team(Dave Bristol)	1.00	.50	.30
443	Lamar Johnson	.25	.10	.06
444	Wayne Twitchell	.25	.10	.06
445	Ken Singleton	.25	.10	.06
446	Bill Bonham	.25	.10	.06
447	Jerry Turner	.25	.10	.06
448	Ellie Rodriguez	.25	.10	.06
449	Al Fitzmorris	.25	.10	.06
450	Pete Rose	15.00	7.50	4.50
451	Checklist 397-528	1.00	.50	.30
452	Mike Caldwell	.25	.10	.06
453	Pedro Garcia	.25	.10	.06
454	Andy Etchebarren	.25	.10	.06
455	Rick Wise	.25	.10	.06
456	Leon Roberts	.25	.10	.06
457	Steve Luebber	.25	.10	.06
458	Leo Foster	.25	.10	.06
459	Steve Foucault	.25	.10	.06
460	Willie Stargell	4.00	2.00	1.25
461	Dick Tidrow	.25	.10	.06
462	Don Baylor	.30	.15	.10
463	Jamie Quirk	.25	.10	.06
464	Randy Moffitt	.25	.10	.06
465	Rico Carty	.25	.10	.06
466	Fred Holdsworth	.25	.10	.06
467	Phillies Team(Danny Ozark)	.50	.25	.15
468	Ramon Hernandez	.25	.10	.06
469	Pat Kelly	.25	.10	.06
470	Ted Simmons	.50	.25	.15
471	Del Unser	.25	.10	.06
472	Rookie Pitchers(Don Aase, Bob McClure, Gil Patterson (Photo is Sheldon Gill.), Dave Wehrmeister)	.25	.10	.06
473	Rookie Outfielders(Andre Dawson RC, Gene Richards RC, John Scott RC, Denny Walling RC)	25.00	10.00	5.00
474	Rookie Shortstops(Bob Bailor, Kiko Garcia, Craig Reynolds, Alex Taveras)	.25	.10	.06
475	Rookie Pitchers(Chris Batton, Rick Camp, Scott McGregor, Manny Sarmiento)	.25	.10	.06
476	Rookie Catchers(Gary Alexander RC, Rick Cerone RC, Dale Murphy RC, Kevin Pasley RC)	15.00	7.50	3.75
477	Rookie Infielders(Doug Ault, Rich Dauer RC, Orlando Gonzalez, Phil Mankowski)	.25	.10	.06
478	Rookie Pitchers(Jim Gideon, Leon Hooten, Dave Johnson, Mark Lemongello)	.25	.10	.06
479	Rookie Outfielders(Brian Asselstine, Wayne Gross RC, Sam Mejias, Alvis Woods)	.25	.10	.06
480	Carl Yastrzemski	6.00	3.00	1.75
481	Roger Metzger	.25	.10	.06
482	Tony Solaita	.25	.10	.06
483	Richie Zisk	.25	.10	.06
484	Burt Hooton	.25	.10	.06
485	Roy White	.25	.10	.06
486	Ed Bane	.25	.10	.06

#	Player	NM	E	VG
487	Rookie Pitchers(Larry Anderson, Ed Glynn, Joe Henderson, Greg Terlecky)	.25	.10	.06
488	Rookie Outfielders(Jack Clark **RC**, Ruppert Jones **RC**, Lee Mazzilli **RC**, Dan Thomas **RC**)	3.00	1.50	.90
489	Rookie Pitchers(Len Barker **RC**, Randy Lerch, Greg Minton **RC**, Mike Overy)	.75	.40	.25
490	Rookie Shortstops(Billy Almon **RC**, Mickey Klutts, Tommy McMillan, Mark Wagner)	.25	.10	.06
491	Rookie Pitchers(Mike Dupree **RC**, Dennis Martinez **RC**, Craig Mitchell **RC**, Bob Sykes **RC**)	3.00	1.50	.90
492	Rookie Outfielders(Tony Armas **RC**, Steve Kemp **RC**, Carlos Lopez **RC**, Gary Woods **RC**)	.75	.40	.25
493	Rookie Pitchers(Mike Krukow **RC**, Jim Otten, Gary Wheelock, Mike Willis)	.25	.10	.06
494	Rookie Infielders (Juan Bernhardt, Mike Champion, Jim Gantner **RC**, Bump Wills **RC**)	1.00	.50	.30
495	Al Hrabosky	.50	.25	.15
496	Gary Thomasson	.25	.10	.06
497	Clay Carroll	.25	.10	.06
498	Sal Bando	.25	.10	.06
499	Pablo Torrealba	.25	.10	.06
500	Dave Kingman	.75	.40	.25
501	Jim Bibby	.25	.10	.06
502	Randy Hundley	.25	.10	.06
503	Bill Lee	.25	.10	.06
504	Dodgers Team(Tom Lasorda)	1.50	.70	.45
505	Oscar Gamble	.50	.25	.15
506	Steve Grilli	.25	.10	.06
507	Mike Hegan	.25	.10	.06
508	Dave Pagan	.25	.10	.06
509	Cookie Rojas	.25	.10	.06
510	John Candelaria	.25	.10	.06
511	Bill Fahey	.25	.10	.06
512	Jack Billingham	.25	.10	.06
513	Jerry Terrell	.25	.10	.06
514	Cliff Johnson	.25	.10	.06
515	Chris Speier	.25	.10	.06
516	Bake McBride	.25	.10	.06
517	Pete Vuckovich **RC**	.50	.25	.15
518	Cubs Team(Herman Franks)	1.00	.50	.30
519	Don Kirkwood	.25	.10	.06
520	Garry Maddox	.50	.25	.15
521	Bob Grich	.25	.10	.06
522	Enzo Hernandez	.25	.10	.06
523	Rollie Fingers	2.50	1.25	.70
524	Rowland Office	.25	.10	.06
525	Dennis Eckersley	4.00	2.00	1.25
526	Larry Parrish	.25	.10	.06
527	Dan Meyer	.25	.10	.06
528	Bill Castro	.25	.10	.06
529	Jim Essian	.25	.10	.06
530	Rick Reuschel	.25	.10	.06
531	Lyman Bostock	.25	.10	.06
532	Jim Willoughby	.25	.10	.06
533	Mickey Stanley	.25	.10	.06
534	Paul Splittorff	.25	.10	.06
535	Cesar Geronimo	.25	.10	.06
536	Vic Albury	.25	.10	.06
537	Dave Roberts	.25	.10	.06
538	Frank Taveras	.25	.10	.06
539	Mike Wallace	.25	.10	.06
540	Bob Watson	.25	.10	.06
541	John Denny	.25	.10	.06
542	Frank Duffy	.25	.10	.06
543	Ron Blomberg	.25	.10	.06
544	Gary Ross	.25	.10	.06
545	Bob Boone	.25	.10	.06
546	Orioles Team(Earl Weaver)	1.50	.70	.45
547	Willie McCovey	3.00	1.50	.90
548	Joel Youngblood **RC**	.25	.10	.06
549	Jerry Royster	.25	.10	.06
550	Randy Jones	.25	.10	.06
551	Bill North	.25	.10	.06
552	Pepe Mangual	.25	.10	.06
553	Jack Heidemann	.25	.10	.06
554	Bruce Kimm	.25	.10	.06
555	Dan Ford	.25	.10	.06
556	Doug Bird	.25	.10	.06
557	Jerry White	.25	.10	.06
558	Elias Sosa	.25	.10	.06
559	Alan Bannister	.25	.10	.06
560	Dave Concepcion	.25	.10	.06
561	Pete LaCock	.25	.10	.06
562	Checklist 529-660	.75	.40	.25
563	Bruce Kison	.25	.10	.06
564	Alan Ashby	.25	.10	.06
565	Mickey Lolich	.50	.25	.15
566	Rick Miller	.25	.10	.06
567	Enos Cabell	.25	.10	.06
568	Carlos May	.25	.10	.06
569	Jim Lonborg	.25	.10	.06
570	Bobby Bonds	.75	.40	.25
571	Darrell Evans	.25	.10	.06
572	Ross Grimsley	.25	.10	.06
573	Joe Ferguson	.25	.10	.06
574	Aurelio Rodriguez	.25	.10	.06
575	Dick Ruthven	.25	.10	.06
576	Fred Kendall	.25	.10	.06
577	Jerry Augustine	.25	.10	.06
578	Bob Randall	.25	.10	.06
579	Don Carrithers	.25	.10	.06
580	George Brett	15.00	7.50	3.75
581	Pedro Borbon	.25	.10	.06
582	Ed Kirkpatrick	.25	.10	.06
583	Paul Lindblad	.25	.10	.06
584	Ed Goodson	.25	.10	.06
585	Rick Burleson	.25	.10	.06
586	Steve Renko	.25	.10	.06
587	Rick Baldwin	.25	.10	.06
588	Dave Moates	.25	.10	.06
589	Mike Cosgrove	.25	.10	.06
590	Buddy Bell	.25	.10	.06
591	Chris Arnold	.25	.10	.06
592	Dan Briggs	.25	.10	.06
593	Dennis Blair	.25	.10	.06
594	Biff Pocoroba	.25	.10	.06
595	John Hiller	.25	.10	.06
596	Jerry Martin **RC**	.25	.10	.06
597	Mariners Mgr./Coaches (Don Bryant, Jim Busby, Darrell Johnson, Vada Pinson, Wes Stock)	1.00	.50	.30
598	Sparky Lyle	.25	.10	.06
599	Mike Tyson	.25	.10	.06
600	Jim Palmer	3.00	1.50	.90
601	Mike Lum	.25	.10	.06
602	Andy Hassler	.25	.10	.06
603	Willie Davis	.25	.10	.06
604	Jim Slaton	.25	.10	.06
605	Felix Millan	.25	.10	.06
606	Steve Braun	.25	.10	.06
607	Larry Demery	.25	.10	.06
608	Roy Howell	.25	.10	.06
609	Jim Barr	.25	.10	.06
610	Jose Cardenal	.25	.10	.06
611	Dave Lemanczyk	.25	.10	.06
612	Barry Foote	.25	.10	.06
613	Reggie Cleveland	.25	.10	.06
614	Greg Gross	.25	.10	.06
615	Phil Niekro	2.50	1.25	.70
616	Tommy Sandt	.25	.10	.06
617	Bobby Darwin	.25	.10	.06
618	Pat Dobson	.25	.10	.06
619	Johnny Oates	.25	.10	.06
620	Don Sutton	2.50	1.25	.70
621	Tigers Team(Ralph Houk)	1.00	.50	.30
622	Jim Wohlford	.25	.10	.06
623	Jack Kucek	.25	.10	.06
624	Hector Cruz	.25	.10	.06
625	Ken Holtzman	.25	.10	.06
626	Al Bumbry	.25	.10	.06
627	Bob Myrick	.25	.10	.06
628	Mario Guerrero	.25	.10	.06
629	Bobby Valentine	.25	.10	.06
630	Bert Blyleven	3.00	1.50	.90
631	Big League Brothers (George Brett, Ken Brett)	5.00	2.50	1.50
632	Big League Brothers(Bob Forsch, Ken Forsch)	.25	.10	.06
633	Big League Brothers (Carlos May, Lee May)	.25	.10	.06
634	Big League Brothers(Paul Reuschel, Rick Reuschel) (Names switched.)	.25	.10	.06
635	Robin Yount	6.00	3.00	1.50
636	Santo Alcala	.25	.10	.06
637	Alex Johnson	.25	.10	.06
638	Jim Kaat	.50	.25	.15
639	Jerry Morales	.25	.10	.06
640	Carlton Fisk	4.00	2.00	1.25
641	Dan Larson	.25	.10	.06
642	Willie Crawford	.25	.10	.06
643	Mike Pazik	.25	.10	.06
644	Matt Alexander	.25	.10	.06
645	Jerry Reuss	.25	.10	.06
646	Andres Mora	.25	.10	.06
647	Expos Team(Dick Williams)	.75	.40	.25
648	Jim Spencer	.25	.10	.06
649	Dave Cash	.25	.10	.06
650	Nolan Ryan	30.00	15.00	7.50
651	Von Joshua	.25	.10	.06
652	Tom Walker	.25	.10	.06
653	Diego Segui	.25	.10	.06
654	Ron Pruitt	.25	.10	.06
655	Tony Perez	3.00	1.50	.90
656	Ron Guidry	1.00	.50	.30
657	Mick Kelleher	.25	.10	.06
658	Marty Pattin	.25	.10	.06
659	Merv Rettenmund	.25	.10	.06
660	Willie Horton	1.00	.50	.30

1977 Topps Cloth Stickers

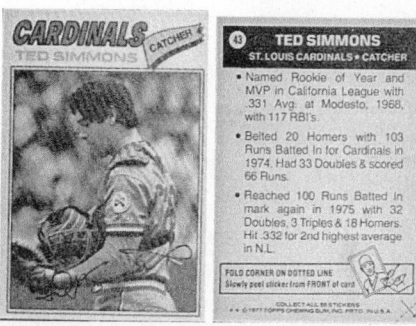

One of the few Topps specialty issues of the late 1970s, the 73-piece set of cloth stickers issued in 1977 includes 55 player stickers and 18 puzzle cards which could be joined to form a photo of the American League or National League All-Star teams. Issued as a separate issue, the 2-1/2" x 3-1/2" stickers have a paper backing which could be removed to allow the cloth to be adhered to a jacket, notebook, etc. Each player sticker can be found with one or two asterisks preceding the copyright line on back.

		NM	E	VG
Complete Set (73):		75.00	37.70	22.50
Common Player:		1.00	.50	.30
Wax Pack:		12.50		
Wax Box (36):		265.00		
1	Alan Ashby	1.00	.50	.30
2	Buddy Bell	1.00	.50	.30
3	Johnny Bench	5.00	2.50	1.50
4	Vida Blue	1.00	.50	.30
5	Bert Blyleven	3.00	.50	.30
6	Steve Braun	1.00	.50	.30
7	George Brett	8.00	4.00	2.50
8	Lou Brock	4.00	2.00	1.25
9	Jose Cardenal	1.00	.50	.30
10	Rod Carew	5.00	2.50	1.50
11	Steve Carlton	4.00	2.00	1.25
12	Dave Cash	1.00	.50	.30
13	Cesar Cedeno	1.00	.50	.30
14	Ron Cey	1.00	.50	.30
15	Mark Fidrych	2.50	1.25	.70
16	Dan Ford	1.00	.50	.30
17	Wayne Garland	1.00	.50	.30
18	Ralph Garr	1.00	.50	.30
19	Steve Garvey	2.00	1.00	.60
20	Mike Hargrove	1.00	.50	.30
21	Catfish Hunter	3.00	1.50	.90
22	Reggie Jackson	8.00	4.00	2.50
23	Randy Jones	1.00	.50	.30
24	Dave Kingman	1.00	.50	.30
25	Bill Madlock	1.00	.50	.30
26	Lee May	1.00	.50	.30
27	John Mayberry	1.00	.50	.30
28	Andy Messersmith	1.00	.50	.30
29	Willie Montanez	1.00	.50	.30
30	John Montefusco	1.00	.50	.30
31	Joe Morgan	4.00	2.00	1.25
32	Thurman Munson	4.00	2.00	1.25
33	Bobby Murcer	1.00	.50	.30
34	Al Oliver	1.00	.50	.30
35	Dave Pagan	1.00	.50	.30
36	Jim Palmer	4.00	2.00	1.25
37	Tony Perez	3.00	1.50	.90
38	Pete Rose	10.00	5.00	3.00
39	Joe Rudi	1.00	.50	.30
40	Nolan Ryan	20.00	10.00	6.00
41	Mike Schmidt	8.00	4.00	2.50
42	Tom Seaver	5.00	2.50	1.50

		NM	E	VG
43	Ted Simmons	1.00	.50	.30
44	Bill Singer	1.00	.50	.30
45	Willie Stargell	4.00	2.00	1.25
46	Rusty Staub	1.25	.60	.40
47	Don Sutton	3.00	1.50	.90
48	Luis Tiant	1.00	.50	.30
49	Bill Travers	1.00	.50	.30
50	Claudell Washington	1.00	.50	.30
51	Bob Watson	1.00	.50	.30
52	Dave Winfield	4.00	2.00	1.25
53	Carl Yastrzemski	7.00	3.50	2.00
54	Robin Yount	4.00	2.00	1.25
55	Richie Zisk	1.00	.50	.30
---	American League Nine-Piece Puzzle	6.00	3.00	1.75
---	National League Nine-Piece Puzzle	6.00	3.00	1.75

1977 Topps Proofs

Perhaps the most sought-after Topps proof card is the 1977 blank-back featuring Reggie Jackson in an Orioles uniform but designating his team as the Yankees, with whom he signed as a free agent prior to the 1977 season. Less well-known are a group of other players' cards that have uniform/team variations from the regularly issued versions. All of the handful of known examples were hand-cut from sheets. Backs are blank. a 66-card proof sheet including all 12 uniform/team variation proofs sold for $17,550 in a 4/10 auction.

	NM	E	VG
Don Baylor	350.00	175.00	100.00
Rollie Fingers	900.00	450.00	275.00
Al Fitzmorris	300.00	150.00	90.00
Wayne Garland	300.00	150.00	90.00
Bill Greif	200.00	100.00	60.00
Reggie Jackson	15,000		
Pat Kelly	300.00	150.00	90.00
Gary Matthews	450.00	225.00	135.00
Dan Meyer	300.00	150.00	90.00
Bill Singer	200.00	100.00	60.00
Steve Stone	350.00	175.00	100.00
Gene Tenace	425.00	210.00	125.00

1977 Topps Team Checklist Sheet

A redemption offer on packs of 1977 Topps cards offered an uncut sheet of the 26 team/checklist cards by mail. Besides the perforated team cards, the 10-1/2" x 22-1/2" sheet has a card offering collectors a card locker. The cards on the sheet are identical to the single team/checklist cards issued in packs, except they are printed on thinner card stock.

	NM	E	VG
Uncut Sheet	35.00	17.50	10.50

1977 Topps/Dynamite Magazine Panels

In at least two issues of its "Dynamite" kids' magazine, Scholastic Book Club teamed with Topps to insert a six-card panel of its 1977 baseball issue. Values shown are for just the uncut panel; complete magazines would bear a small premium.

		NM	E	VG
Complete Panel Set (2):		50.00	25.00	15.00
PANEL 1		25.00	12.50	7.50
215	Butch Metzger			
335	Bill Robinson			
599	Mike Tyson			
625	Ken Holtzman			
630	Bert Blyleven			
641	Dan Larson			
PANEL 2		30.00	15.00	9.00
242	Ken Henderson			
294	George Medich			
415	Jay Johnstone			
535	Cesar Geronimo			
580	George Brett			
626	Al Bumbry			

1978 Topps

 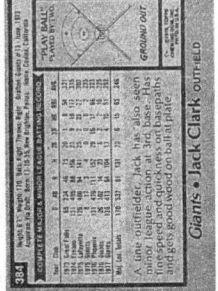

At 726 cards, this was the largest issue from Topps since 1972. In design, the color player photo is slightly larger than usual, with the player's name and team at the bottom. In the upper right-hand corner of the 2-1/2" x 3-1/2" cards, there is a small white baseball with the player's position. Most of the starting All-Stars from the previous year had a red, white and blue shield instead of the baseball. Backs feature statistics and a baseball situation which made a card game of baseball possible. Specialty cards include baseball records, statistical leaders and the World Series and playoffs. As one row of cards per sheet had to be double-printed to accommodate the 726-card set size, some cards are more common, yet that seems to have no serious impact on their prices.

		NM	E	VG
Complete Set (726):		185.00	100.00	45.00
Common Player:		.20	.10	.06
Wax Pack (14):		15.00		
Wax Box (36):		480.00		
Cello Pack (21):		25.00		
Cello Box (24):		600.00		
Rack Pack (39):		35.00		
Rack Box (24):		725.00		
Vending Box (500):		285.00		
1	Lou Brock (Record Breaker)	1.00	.50	.30
2	Sparky Lyle (Record Breaker)	.20	.10	.06
3	Willie McCovey (Record Breaker)	.50	.25	.15
4	Brooks Robinson (Record Breaker)	2.00	1.00	.60
5	Pete Rose (Record Breaker)	6.00	3.00	1.50
6	Nolan Ryan (Record Breaker)	12.50	7.50	3.75
7	Reggie Jackson (Record Breaker)	4.00	2.00	1.25
8	Mike Sadek	.20	.10	.06
9	Doug DeCinces	.20	.10	.06
10	Phil Niekro	3.00	1.50	.90
11	Rick Manning	.20	.10	.06
12	Don Aase	.20	.10	.06
13	Art Howe	.20	.10	.06
14	Lerrin LaGrow	.20	.10	.06
15	Tony Perez	4.00	2.00	1.25
16	Roy White	.20	.10	.06
17	Mike Krukow	.20	.10	.06
18	Bob Grich	.20	.10	.06
19	Darrell Porter	.20	.10	.06
20	Pete Rose	10.00	5.00	2.50
21	Steve Kemp	.20	.10	.06
22	Charlie Hough	.20	.10	.06
23a	Bump Wills (black circle between trophy and leg)	45.00	23.00	12.00
23b	Bump Wills (no circle)	.20	.10	.06
24	Don Money	.20	.10	.06
25	Jon Matlack	.20	.10	.06
26	Rich Hebner	.20	.10	.06
27	Geoff Zahn	.20	.10	.06
28	Ed Ott	.20	.10	.06
29	Bob Lacey	.20	.10	.06
30	George Hendrick	.20	.10	.06
31	Glenn Abbott	.20	.10	.06
32	Garry Templeton	.20	.10	.06
33	Dave Lemanczyk	.20	.10	.06
34	Willie McCovey	4.00	2.00	1.25
35	Sparky Lyle	.20	.10	.06
36	Eddie Murray **RC**	28.00	14.00	8.00
37	Rick Waits	.20	.10	.06
38	Willie Montanez	.20	.10	.06
39	Floyd Bannister **RC**	.45	.25	.14
40	Carl Yastrzemski	5.00	2.50	1.50
41	Burt Hooton	.20	.10	.06
42	Jorge Orta	.20	.10	.06
43	Bill Atkinson	.20	.10	.06
44	Toby Harrah	.20	.10	.06
45	Mark Fidrych	.30	.15	.09
46	Al Cowens	.20	.10	.06
47	Jack Billingham	.20	.10	.06
48	Don Baylor	.25	.13	.08
49	Ed Kranepool	.20	.10	.06
50	Rick Reuschel	.20	.10	.06
51	Charlie Moore	.20	.10	.06
52	Jim Lonborg	.20	.10	.06
53	Phil Garner	.20	.10	.06
54	Tom Johnson	.20	.10	.06
55	Mitchell Page	.20	.10	.06
56	Randy Jones	.20	.10	.06
57	Dan Meyer	.20	.10	.06
58	Bob Forsch	.20	.10	.06
59	Otto Velez	.20	.10	.06
60	Thurman Munson	5.00	2.50	1.25
61	Larvell Blanks	.20	.10	.06
62	Jim Barr	.20	.10	.06
63	Don Zimmer	.20	.10	.06
64	Gene Pentz	.20	.10	.06
65	Ken Singleton	.20	.10	.06
66	White Sox Team	.30	.15	.09
67	Claudell Washington	.20	.10	.06
68	Steve Foucault	.20	.10	.06
69	Mike Vail	.20	.10	.06
70	Rich Gossage	.20	.10	.06
71	Terry Humphrey	.20	.10	.06
72	Andre Dawson	5.00	1.50	.90
73	Andy Hassler	.20	.10	.06
74	Checklist 1-121	.20	.10	.06
75	Dick Ruthven	.20	.10	.06
76	Steve Ontiveros	.20	.10	.06
77	Ed Kirkpatrick	.20	.10	.06
78	Pablo Torrealba	.20	.10	.06
79	Darrell Johnson (DP)	.20	.10	.06
80	Ken Griffey	.20	.10	.06
81	Pete Redfern	.20	.10	.06
82	**Giants Team**	.30	.15	.09
83	Bob Montgomery	.20	.10	.06
84	Kent Tekulve	.20	.10	.06
85	Ron Fairly	.20	.10	.06
86	Dave Tomlin	.20	.10	.06
87	John Lowenstein	.20	.10	.06
88	Mike Phillips	.20	.10	.06
89	Ken Clay	.20	.10	.06
90	Larry Bowa	.20	.10	.06
91	Oscar Zamora	.20	.10	.06
92	Adrian Devine	.20	.10	.06
93	Bobby Cox	.40	.20	.12
94	Chuck Scrivener	.20	.10	.06
95	Jamie Quirk	.20	.10	.06
96	**Orioles Team**	.30	.15	.09
97	Stan Bahnsen	.20	.10	.06
98	Jim Essian	.20	.10	.06
99	Willie Hernandez **RC**	.30	.15	.09
100	George Brett	8.00	4.00	2.50
101	Sid Monge	.20	.10	.06
102	Matt Alexander	.20	.10	.06
103	Tom Murphy	.20	.10	.06
104	Lee Lacy	.20	.10	.06
105	Reggie Cleveland	.20	.10	.06
106	Bill Plummer	.20	.10	.06
107	Ed Halicki	.20	.10	.06
108	Von Joshua	.20	.10	.06
109	Joe Torre	.55	.30	.15
110	Richie Zisk	.20	.10	.06
111	Mike Tyson	.20	.10	.06
112	Astros Team	.30	.15	.09
113	Don Carrithers	.20	.10	.06
114	Paul Blair	.20	.10	.06
115	Gary Nolan	.20	.10	.06
116	Tucker Ashford	.20	.10	.06
117	John Montague	.20	.10	.06
118	Terry Harmon	.20	.10	.06
119	Denny Martinez	.20	.10	.06
120	Gary Carter	4.00	2.00	1.25
121	Alvis Woods	.20	.10	.06
122	Dennis Eckersley	3.00	2.00	1.25
123	Manny Trillo	.20	.10	.06

#	Player			
124	Dave Rozema **RC**	.20	.10	.06
125	George Scott	.20	.10	.06
126	Paul Moskau	.20	.10	.06
127	Chet Lemon	.20	.10	.06
128	Bill Russell	.20	.10	.06
129	Jim Colborn	.20	.10	.06
130	Jeff Burroughs	.20	.10	.06
131	Bert Blyleven	3.00	1.50	.90
132	Enos Cabell	.20	.10	.06
133	Jerry Augustine	.20	.10	.06
134	Steve Henderson **RC**	.20	.10	.06
135	Ron Guidry	.30	.15	.09
136	Ted Sizemore	.20	.10	.06
137	Craig Kusick	.20	.10	.06
138	Larry Demery	.20	.10	.06
139	Wayne Gross	.20	.10	.06
140	Rollie Fingers	3.00	1.50	.90
141	Ruppert Jones	.20	.10	.06
142	John Montefusco	.20	.10	.06
143	Keith Hernandez	.20	.10	.06
144	Jesse Jefferson	.20	.10	.06
145	Rick Monday	.20	.10	.06
146	Doyle Alexander	.20	.10	.06
147	Lee Mazzilli	.20	.10	.06
148	Andre Thornton	.20	.10	.06
149	Dale Murray	.20	.10	.06
150	Bobby Bonds	.20	.10	.06
151	Milt Wilcox	.20	.10	.06
152	Ivan DeJesus **RC**	.20	.10	.06
153	Steve Stone	.20	.10	.06
154	Cecil Cooper	.20	.10	.06
155	Butch Hobson	.20	.10	.06
156	Andy Messersmith	.20	.10	.06
157	Pete LaCock	.20	.10	.06
158	Joaquin Andujar	.20	.10	.06
159	Lou Piniella	.30	.15	.09
160	Jim Palmer	4.00	2.00	1.25
161	Bob Boone	.20	.10	.06
162	Paul Thormodsgard	.20	.10	.06
163	Bill North	.20	.10	.06
164	Bob Owchinko	.20	.10	.06
165	Rennie Stennett	.20	.10	.06
166	Carlos Lopez	.20	.10	.06
167	Tim Foli	.20	.10	.06
168	Reggie Smith	.20	.10	.06
169	Jerry Johnson	.20	.10	.06
170	Lou Brock	4.00	2.00	1.25
171	Pat Zachry	.20	.10	.06
172	Mike Hargrove	.20	.10	.06
173	Robin Yount	4.00	2.00	1.25
174	Wayne Garland	.20	.10	.06
175	Jerry Morales	.20	.10	.06
176	Milt May	.20	.10	.06
177	Gene Garber	.20	.10	.06
178	Dave Chalk	.20	.10	.06
179	Dick Tidrow	.20	.10	.06
180	Dave Concepcion	.20	.10	.06
181	Ken Forsch	.20	.10	.06
182	Jim Spencer	.20	.10	.06
183	Doug Bird	.20	.10	.06
184	Checklist 122-242	.20	.10	.06
185	Ellis Valentine	.20	.10	.06
186	Bob Stanley **RC**	.20	.10	.06
187	Jerry Royster	.20	.10	.06
188	Al Bumbry	.20	.10	.06
189	Tom Lasorda	.55	.30	.15
190	John Candelaria	.20	.10	.06
191	Rodney Scott	.20	.10	.06
192	Padres Team	.30	.15	.09
193	Rich Chiles	.20	.10	.06
194	Derrel Thomas	.20	.10	.06
195	Larry Dierker	.20	.10	.06
196	Bob Bailor	.20	.10	.06
197	Nino Espinosa	.20	.10	.06
198	Ron Pruitt	.20	.10	.06
199	Craig Reynolds	.20	.10	.06
200	Reggie Jackson	6.00	3.00	1.75
201	Batting Leaders (Rod Carew, Dave Parker)	.50	.25	.15
202	Home Run Leaders (George Foster, Jim Rice)	.25	.13	.08
203	RBI Leaders (George Foster, Larry Hisle)	.20	.10	.06
204	Stolen Base Leaders (Freddie Patek, Frank Taveras)	.20	.10	.06
205	Victory Leaders (Steve Carlton, Dave Goltz, Dennis Leonard, Jim Palmer)	.50	.25	.15
206	Strikeout Leaders (Phil Niekro, Nolan Ryan)	3.00	1.50	.90
207	ERA Leaders (John Candelaria, Frank Tanana)	.20	.10	.06
208	Leading Firemen (Bill Campbell, Rollie Fingers)	.25	.13	.08
209	Dock Ellis	.20	.10	.06
210	Jose Cardenal	.20	.10	.06
211	Earl Weaver (DP)	.50	.25	.15
212	Mike Caldwell	.20	.10	.06
213	Alan Bannister	.20	.10	.06
214	Angels Team	.30	.15	.09
215	Darrell Evans	.25	.13	.08
216	Mike Paxton	.20	.10	.06
217	Rod Gilbreath	.20	.10	.06
218	Marty Pattin	.20	.10	.06
219	Mike Cubbage	.20	.10	.06
220	Pedro Borbon	.20	.10	.06
221	Chris Speier	.20	.10	.06
222	Jerry Martin	.20	.10	.06
223	Bruce Kison	.20	.10	.06
224	Jerry Tabb	.20	.10	.06
225	Don Gullett	.20	.10	.06
226	Joe Ferguson	.20	.10	.06
227	Al Fitzmorris	.20	.10	.06
228	Manny Mota	.20	.10	.06
229	Leo Foster	.20	.10	.06
230	Al Hrabosky	.20	.10	.06
231	Wayne Nordhagen	.20	.10	.06
232	Mickey Stanley	.20	.10	.06
233	Dick Pole	.20	.10	.06
234	Herman Franks	.20	.10	.06
235	Tim McCarver	.30	.15	.09
236	Terry Whitfield	.20	.10	.06
237	Rich Dauer	.20	.10	.06
238	Juan Beniquez	.20	.10	.06
239	Dyar Miller	.20	.10	.06
240	Gene Tenace	.20	.10	.06
241	Pete Vuckovich	.20	.10	.06
242	Barry Bonnell	.20	.10	.06
243	Bob McClure	.20	.10	.06
244	Expos Team	.30	.15	.09
245	Rick Burleson	.20	.10	.06
246	Dan Driessen	.20	.10	.06
247	Larry Christenson	.20	.10	.06
248	Frank White	.20	.10	.06
249	Dave Goltz	.20	.10	.06
250	Graig Nettles	.25	.13	.08
251	Don Kirkwood	.20	.10	.06
252	Steve Swisher	.20	.10	.06
253	Jim Kern	.20	.10	.06
254	Dave Collins	.20	.10	.06
255	Jerry Reuss	.20	.10	.06
256	Joe Altobelli	.20	.10	.06
257	Hector Cruz	.20	.10	.06
258	John Hiller	.20	.10	.06
259	Dodgers Team	.50	.25	.15
260	Bert Campaneris	.20	.10	.06
261	Tim Hosley	.20	.10	.06
262	Rudy May	.20	.10	.06
263	Danny Walton	.20	.10	.06
264	Jamie Easterly	.20	.10	.06
265	Sal Bando	.20	.10	.06
266	Bob Shirley **RC**	.20	.10	.06
267	Doug Ault	.20	.10	.06
268	Gil Flores	.20	.10	.06
269	Wayne Twitchell	.20	.10	.06
270	Carlton Fisk	4.00	2.00	1.25
271	Randy Lerch	.20	.10	.06
272	Royle Stillman	.20	.10	.06
273	Fred Norman	.20	.10	.06
274	Freddie Patek	.20	.10	.06
275	Dan Ford	.20	.10	.06
276	Bill Bonham	.20	.10	.06
277	Bruce Boisclair	.20	.10	.06
278	Enrique Romo	.20	.10	.06
279	Bill Virdon	.20	.10	.06
280	Buddy Bell	.20	.10	.06
281	Eric Rasmussen	.20	.10	.06
282	Yankees Team	1.00	.50	.30
283	Omar Moreno	.20	.10	.06
284	Randy Moffitt	.20	.10	.06
285	Steve Yeager	.20	.10	.06
286	Ben Oglivie	.20	.10	.06
287	Kiko Garcia	.20	.10	.06
288	Dave Hamilton	.20	.10	.06
289	Checklist 243-363	.20	.10	.06
290	Willie Horton	.20	.10	.06
291	Gary Ross	.20	.10	.06
292	Gene Richard	.20	.10	.06
293	Mike Willis	.20	.10	.06
294	Larry Parrish	.20	.10	.06
295	Bill Lee	.20	.10	.06
296	Biff Pocoroba	.20	.10	.06
297	Warren Brusstar	.20	.10	.06
298	Tony Armas	.20	.10	.06
299	Whitey Herzog	.20	.10	.06
300	Joe Morgan	4.00	2.00	1.25
301	Buddy Schultz	.20	.10	.06
302	Cubs Team	.30	.15	.09
303	Sam Hinds	.20	.10	.06
304	John Milner	.20	.10	.06
305	Rico Carty	.20	.10	.06
306	Joe Niekro	.20	.10	.06
307	Glenn Borgmann	.20	.10	.06
308	Jim Rooker	.20	.10	.06
309	Cliff Johnson	.20	.10	.06
310	Don Sutton	3.00	1.50	.90
311	Jose Baez	.20	.10	.06
312	Greg Minton	.20	.10	.06
313	Andy Etchebarren	.20	.10	.06
314	Paul Lindblad	.20	.10	.06
315	Mark Belanger	.20	.10	.06
316	Henry Cruz	.20	.10	.06
317	Dave Johnson	.20	.10	.06
318	Tom Griffin	.20	.10	.06
319	Alan Ashby	.20	.10	.06
320	Fred Lynn	.20	.10	.06
321	Santo Alcala	.20	.10	.06
322	Tom Paciorek	.20	.10	.06
323	Jim Fregosi (DP)	.20	.10	.06
324	Vern Rapp	.20	.10	.06
325	Bruce Sutter	3.00	1.50	.90
326	Mike Lum	.20	.10	.06
327	Rick Langford	.20	.10	.06
328	Brewers Team	.30	.15	.09
329	John Verhoeven	.20	.10	.06
330	Bob Watson	.20	.10	.06
331	Mark Littell	.20	.10	.06
332	Duane Kuiper	.20	.10	.06
333	Jim Todd	.20	.10	.06
334	John Stearns	.20	.10	.06
335	Bucky Dent	.20	.10	.06
336	Steve Busby	.20	.10	.06
337	Tom Grieve	.20	.10	.06
338	Dave Heaverlo	.20	.10	.06
339	Mario Guerrero	.20	.10	.06
340	Bake McBride	.20	.10	.06
341	Mike Flanagan	.20	.10	.06
342	Aurelio Rodriguez	.20	.10	.06
343	John Wathan (DP)	.20	.10	.06
344	Sam Ewing	.20	.10	.06
345	Luis Tiant	.20	.10	.06
346	Larry Biittner	.20	.10	.06
347	Terry Forster	.20	.10	.06
348	Del Unser	.20	.10	.06
349	Rick Camp (DP)	.20	.10	.06
350	Steve Garvey	2.00	1.00	.60
351	Jeff Torborg	.20	.10	.06
352	Tony Scott	.20	.10	.06
353	Doug Bair	.20	.10	.06
354	Cesar Geronimo	.20	.10	.06
355	Bill Travers	.20	.10	.06
356	Mets Team	.60	.30	.20
357	Tom Poquette	.20	.10	.06
358	Mark Lemongello	.20	.10	.06
359	Marc Hill	.20	.10	.06
360	Mike Schmidt	8.00	4.00	2.00
361	Chris Knapp	.20	.10	.06
362	Dave May	.20	.10	.06
363	Bob Randall	.20	.10	.06
364	Jerry Turner	.20	.10	.06
365	Ed Figueroa	.20	.10	.06
366	Larry Milbourne (DP)	.20	.10	.06
367	Rick Dempsey	.20	.10	.06
368	Balor Moore	.20	.10	.06
369	Tim Nordbrook	.20	.10	.06
370	Rusty Staub	.25	.13	.08
371	Ray Burris	.20	.10	.06
372	Brian Asselstine	.20	.10	.06
373	Jim Willoughby	.20	.10	.06
374a	Jose Morales (Red stitching on position ball.)	.20	.10	.06
374b	Jose Morales (Black overprint on red stitching.)	.20	.10	.06
375	Tommy John	.30	.15	.09
376	Jim Wohlford	.20	.10	.06
377	Manny Sarmiento	.20	.10	.06
378	Bobby Winkles	.20	.10	.06
379	Skip Lockwood	.20	.10	.06
380	Ted Simmons	.20	.10	.06
381	Phillies Team	.35	.20	.11
382	Joe Lahoud	.20	.10	.06
383	Mario Mendoza	.20	.10	.06
384	Jack Clark	.30	.15	.09
385	Tito Fuentes	.20	.10	.06
386	Bob Gorinski	.20	.10	.06
387	Ken Holtzman	.20	.10	.06
388	Bill Fahey (DP)	.20	.10	.06
389	Julio Gonzalez	.20	.10	.06
390	Oscar Gamble	.20	.10	.06
391	Larry Haney	.20	.10	.06
392	Billy Almon	.20	.10	.06
393	Tippy Martinez	.20	.10	.06
394	Roy Howell	.20	.10	.06
395	Jim Hughes	.20	.10	.06
396	Bob Stinson	.20	.10	.06

#	Player			
397	Greg Gross	.20	.10	.06
398	Don Hood	.20	.10	.06
399	Pete Mackanin	.20	.10	.06
400	Nolan Ryan	25.00	12.50	6.25
401	Sparky Anderson	.55	.30	.15
402	Dave Campbell	.20	.10	.06
403	Bud Harrelson	.20	.10	.06
404	Tigers Team	.30	.15	.09
405	Rawly Eastwick	.20	.10	.06
406	Mike Jorgensen	.20	.10	.06
407	Odell Jones	.20	.10	.06
408	Joe Zdeb	.20	.10	.06
409	Ron Schueler	.20	.10	.06
410	Bill Madlock	.20	.10	.06
411	A.L. Championships (Yankees Rally To Defeat Royals)	.50	.25	.15
412	N.L. Championships (Dodgers Overpower Phillies In Four)	.50	.25	.15
413	World Series (Reggie & Yankees Reign Supreme)	2.00	1.00	.60
414	Darold Knowles (DP)	.20	.10	.06
415	Ray Fosse	.20	.10	.06
416	Jack Brohamer	.20	.10	.06
417	Mike Garman	.20	.10	.06
418	Tony Muser	.20	.10	.06
419	Jerry Garvin	.20	.10	.06
420	Greg Luzinski	.20	.10	.06
421	Junior Moore	.20	.10	.06
422	Steve Braun	.20	.10	.06
423	Dave Rosello	.20	.10	.06
424	**Red Sox Team**	.45	.25	.14
425	Steve Rogers	.20	.10	.06
426	Fred Kendall	.20	.10	.06
427	Mario Soto **RC**	.35	.20	.11
428	Joel Youngblood	.20	.10	.06
429	Mike Barlow	.20	.10	.06
430	Al Oliver	.30	.15	.09
431	Butch Metzger	.20	.10	.06
432	Terry Bulling	.20	.10	.06
433	Fernando Gonzalez	.20	.10	.06
434	Mike Norris	.20	.10	.06
435	Checklist 364-484	.20	.10	.06
436	Vic Harris (DP)	.20	.10	.06
437	Bo McLaughlin	.20	.10	.06
438	John Ellis	.20	.10	.06
439	Ken Kravec	.20	.10	.06
440	Dave Lopes	.20	.10	.06
441	Larry Gura	.20	.10	.06
442	Elliott Maddox	.20	.10	.06
443	Darrel Chaney	.20	.10	.06
444	Roy Hartsfield	.20	.10	.06
445	Mike Ivie	.20	.10	.06
446	Tug McGraw	.20	.10	.06
447	Leroy Stanton	.20	.10	.06
448	Bill Castro	.20	.10	.06
449	Tim Blackwell	.20	.10	.06
450	Tom Seaver	4.00	2.50	1.50
451	Twins Team	.30	.15	.09
452	Jerry Mumphrey	.20	.10	.06
453	Doug Flynn	.20	.10	.06
454	Dave LaRoche	.20	.10	.06
455	Bill Robinson	.20	.10	.06
456	Vern Ruhle	.20	.10	.06
457	Bob Bailey	.20	.10	.06
458	Jeff Newman	.20	.10	.06
459	Charlie Spikes	.20	.10	.06
460	Jim Hunter	3.00	1.50	.90
461	Rob Andrews	.20	.10	.06
462	Rogelio Moret	.20	.10	.06
463	Kevin Bell	.20	.10	.06
464	Jerry Grote	.20	.10	.06
465	Hal McRae	.20	.10	.06
466	Dennis Blair	.20	.10	.06
467	Alvin Dark	.20	.10	.06
468	Warren Cromartie **RC**	.20	.10	.06
469	Rick Cerone	.20	.10	.06
470	J.R. Richard	.20	.10	.06
471	Roy Smalley	.20	.10	.06
472	Ron Reed	.20	.10	.06
473	Bill Buckner	.20	.10	.06
474	Jim Slaton	.20	.10	.06
475	Gary Matthews	.20	.10	.06
476	Bill Stein	.20	.10	.06
477	Doug Capilla	.20	.10	.06
478	Jerry Remy	.20	.10	.06
479	Cardinals Team	.30	.15	.09
480	Ron LeFlore	.20	.10	.06
481	Jackson Todd	.20	.10	.06
482	Rick Miller	.20	.10	.06
483	Ken Macha	.20	.10	.06
484	Jim Norris	.20	.10	.06
485	Chris Chambliss	.20	.10	.06
486	John Curtis	.20	.10	.06
487	Jim Tyrone	.20	.10	.06
488	Dan Spillner	.20	.10	.06
489	Rudy Meoli	.20	.10	.06
490	Amos Otis	.20	.10	.06
491	Scott McGregor	.20	.10	.06
492	Jim Sundberg	.20	.10	.06
493	Steve Renko	.20	.10	.06
494	Chuck Tanner	.20	.10	.06
495	Dave Cash	.20	.10	.06
496	Jim Clancy **RC**	.20	.10	.06
497	Glenn Adams	.20	.10	.06
498	Joe Sambito	.20	.10	.06
499	Mariners Team	.30	.15	.09
500	George Foster	.20	.10	.06
501	Dave Roberts	.20	.10	.06
502	Pat Rockett	.20	.10	.06
503	Ike Hampton	.20	.10	.06
504	Roger Freed	.20	.10	.06
505	Felix Millan	.20	.10	.06
506	Ron Blomberg	.20	.10	.06
507	Willie Crawford	.20	.10	.06
508	Johnny Oates	.20	.10	.06
509	Brent Strom	.20	.10	.06
510	Willie Stargell	4.00	2.00	1.25
511	Frank Duffy	.20	.10	.06
512	Larry Herndon	.20	.10	.06
513	Barry Foote	.20	.10	.06
514	Rob Sperring	.20	.10	.06
515	Tim Corcoran	.20	.10	.06
516	Gary Beare	.20	.10	.06
517	Andres Mora	.20	.10	.06
518	Tommy Boggs (DP)	.20	.10	.06
519	Brian Downing	.20	.10	.06
520	Larry Hisle	.20	.10	.06
521	Steve Staggs	.20	.10	.06
522	Dick Williams	.20	.10	.06
523	Donnie Moore **RC**	.20	.10	.06
524	Bernie Carbo	.20	.10	.06
525	Jerry Terrell	.20	.10	.06
526	Reds Team	.45	.25	.14
527	Vic Correll	.20	.10	.06
528	Rob Picciolo	.20	.10	.06
529	Paul Hartzell	.20	.10	.06
530	Dave Winfield	4.00	2.00	1.25
531	Tom Underwood	.20	.10	.06
532	Skip Jutze	.20	.10	.06
533	Sandy Alomar	.20	.10	.06
534	Wilbur Howard	.20	.10	.06
535	Checklist 485-605	.20	.10	.06
536	Roric Harrison	.20	.10	.06
537	Bruce Bochte	.20	.10	.06
538	Johnnie LeMaster	.20	.10	.06
539	Vic Davalillo	.20	.10	.06
540	Steve Carlton	4.00	2.00	1.25
541	Larry Cox	.20	.10	.06
542	Tim Johnson	.20	.10	.06
543	Larry Harlow	.20	.10	.06
544	Len Randle	.20	.10	.06
545	Bill Campbell	.20	.10	.06
546	Ted Martinez	.20	.10	.06
547	John Scott	.20	.10	.06
548	Billy Hunter (DP)	.20	.10	.06
549	Joe Kerrigan	.20	.10	.06
550	John Mayberry	.20	.10	.06
551	Braves Team	.30	.15	.09
552	Francisco Barrios	.20	.10	.06
553	Terry Puhl **RC**	.25	.13	.08
554	Joe Coleman	.20	.10	.06
555	Butch Wynegar	.20	.10	.06
556	Ed Armbrister	.20	.10	.06
557	Tony Solaita	.20	.10	.06
558	Paul Mitchell	.20	.10	.06
559	Phil Mankowski	.20	.10	.06
560	Dave Parker	.20	.10	.06
561	Charlie Williams	.20	.10	.06
562	Glenn Burke	.20	.10	.06
563	Dave Rader	.20	.10	.06
564	Mick Kelleher	.20	.10	.06
565	Jerry Koosman	.20	.10	.06
566	Merv Rettenmund	.20	.10	.06
567	Dick Drago	.20	.10	.06
568	Tom Hutton	.20	.10	.06
569	Lary Sorensen **RC**	.20	.10	.06
570	Dave Kingman	.20	.10	.06
571	Buck Martinez	.20	.10	.06
572	Rick Wise	.20	.10	.06
573	Luis Gomez	.20	.10	.06
574	Bob Lemon	.50	.25	.15
575	Pat Dobson	.20	.10	.06
576	Sam Mejias	.20	.10	.06
577	A's Team	.30	.15	.09
578	Buzz Capra	.20	.10	.06
579	Rance Mulliniks **RC**	.25	.13	.08
580	Rod Carew	4.00	2.00	1.25
581	Lynn McGlothen	.20	.10	.06
582	Fran Healy	.20	.10	.06
583	George Medich	.20	.10	.06
584	John Hale	.20	.10	.06
585	Woodie Fryman	.20	.10	.06
586	Ed Goodson	.20	.10	.06
587	John Urrea	.20	.10	.06
588	Jim Mason	.20	.10	.06
589	Bob Knepper **RC**	.20	.10	.06
590	Bobby Murcer	.20	.10	.06
591	George Zeber	.20	.10	.06
592	Bob Apodaca	.20	.10	.06
593	Dave Skaggs	.20	.10	.06
594	Dave Freisleben	.20	.10	.06
595	Sixto Lezcano	.20	.10	.06
596	Gary Wheelock	.20	.10	.06
597	Steve Dillard	.20	.10	.06
598	Eddie Solomon	.20	.10	.06
599	Gary Woods	.20	.10	.06
600	Frank Tanana	.20	.10	.06
601	Gene Mauch	.20	.10	.06
602	Eric Soderholm	.20	.10	.06
603	Will McEnaney	.20	.10	.06
604	Earl Williams	.20	.10	.06
605	Rick Rhoden	.20	.10	.06
606	Pirates Team	.30	.15	.09
607	Fernando Arroyo	.20	.10	.06
608	Johnny Grubb	.20	.10	.06
609	John Denny	.20	.10	.06
610	Garry Maddox	.20	.10	.06
611	Pat Scanlon	.20	.10	.06
612	Ken Henderson	.20	.10	.06
613	Marty Perez	.20	.10	.06
614	Joe Wallis	.20	.10	.06
615	Clay Carroll	.20	.10	.06
616	Pat Kelly	.20	.10	.06
617	Joe Nolan	.20	.10	.06
618	Tommy Helms	.20	.10	.06
619	Thad Bosley **RC**	.20	.10	.06
620	Willie Randolph	.20	.10	.06
621	Craig Swan	.20	.10	.06
622	Champ Summers	.20	.10	.06
623	Eduardo Rodriguez	.20	.10	.06
624	Gary Alexander	.20	.10	.06
625	Jose Cruz	.20	.10	.06
626	Blue Jays Team	.30	.15	.09
627	Dave Johnson	.20	.10	.06
628	Ralph Garr	.20	.10	.06
629	Don Stanhouse	.20	.10	.06
630	Ron Cey	.20	.10	.06
631	Danny Ozark	.20	.10	.06
632	Rowland Office	.20	.10	.06
633	Tom Veryzer	.20	.10	.06
634	Len Barker	.20	.10	.06
635	Joe Rudi	.20	.10	.06
636	Jim Bibby	.20	.10	.06
637	Duffy Dyer	.20	.10	.06
638	Paul Splittorff	.20	.10	.06
639	Gene Clines	.20	.10	.06
640	Lee May	.20	.10	.06
641	Doug Rau	.20	.10	.06
642	Denny Doyle	.20	.10	.06
643	Tom House	.20	.10	.06
644	Jim Dwyer	.20	.10	.06
645	Mike Torrez	.20	.10	.06
646	Rick Auerbach	.20	.10	.06
647	Steve Dunning	.20	.10	.06
648	Gary Thomasson	.20	.10	.06
649	Moose Haas **RC**	.20	.10	.06
650	Cesar Cedeno	.20	.10	.06
651	Doug Rader	.20	.10	.06
652	Checklist 606-726	.20	.10	.06
653	Ron Hodges	.20	.10	.06
654	Pepe Frias	.20	.10	.06
655	Lyman Bostock	.20	.10	.06
656	Dave Garcia	.20	.10	.06
657	Bombo Rivera	.20	.10	.06
658	Manny Sanguillen	.20	.10	.06
659	Rangers Team	.30	.15	.09
660	Jason Thompson	.20	.10	.06
661	Grant Jackson	.20	.10	.06
662	Paul Dade	.20	.10	.06
663	Paul Reuschel	.20	.10	.06
664	Fred Stanley	.20	.10	.06
665	Dennis Leonard	.20	.10	.06
666	Billy Smith	.20	.10	.06
667	Jeff Byrd	.20	.10	.06
668	Dusty Baker	.35	.20	.11
669	Pete Falcone	.20	.10	.06
670	Jim Rice	4.00	2.00	1.20
671	Gary Lavelle	.20	.10	.06
672	Don Kessinger	.20	.10	.06
673	Steve Brye	.20	.10	.06
674	Ray Knight **RC**	1.00	.50	.30
675	Jay Johnstone	.20	.10	.06
676	Bob Myrick	.20	.10	.06
677	Ed Herrmann	.20	.10	.06
678	Tom Burgmeier	.20	.10	.06
679	Wayne Garrett	.20	.10	.06
680	Vida Blue	.20	.10	.06
681	Rob Belloir	.20	.10	.06
682	Ken Brett	.20	.10	.06
683	Mike Champion	.20	.10	.06
684	Ralph Houk	.20	.10	.06

685	Frank Taveras	.20	.10	.06
686	Gaylord Perry	3.00	1.50	.90
687	Julio Cruz RC	.25	.13	.08
688	George Mitterwald	.20	.10	.06
689	Indians Team	.30	.15	.09
690	Mickey Rivers	.20	.10	.06
691	Ross Grimsley	.20	.10	.06
692	Ken Reitz	.20	.10	.06
693	Lamar Johnson	.20	.10	.06
694	Elias Sosa	.20	.10	.06
695	Dwight Evans	.20	.10	.06
696	Steve Mingori	.20	.10	.06
697	Roger Metzger	.20	.10	.06
698	Juan Bernhardt	.20	.10	.06
699	Jackie Brown	.20	.10	.06
700	Johnny Bench	6.00	3.00	1.50
701	Rookie Pitchers(Tom Hume RC, Larry Landreth, Steve McCatty RC, Bruce Taylor)	.20	.10	.06
702	Rookie Catchers(Bill Nahorodny, Kevin Pasley, Rick Sweet, Don Werner)	.20	.10	.06
703	Rookie Pitchers(Larry Andersen RC, Tim Jones RC, Mickey Mahler RC, Jack Morris RC)	4.00	2.00	1.00
704	Rookie 2nd Basemen (Garth Iorg RC, Dave Oliver, Sam Perlozzo, Lou Whitaker RC)	6.00	3.00	1.50
705	Rookie Outfielders(Dave Bergman RC, Miguel Dilone, Clint Hurdle RC, Willie Norwood)	.20	.10	.06
706	Rookie 1st Basemen (Wayne Cage, Ted Cox, Pat Putnam RC, Dave Revering RC)	.20	.10	.06
707	Rookie Shortstops(Mickey Klutts RC, Paul Molitor RC, Alan Trammell RC, U.L. Washington RC)	30.00	15.00	9.00
708	Rookie Catchers(Bo Diaz RC, Dale Murphy, Lance Parrish RC, Ernie Whitt RC)	4.00	2.00	1.00
709	Rookie Pitchers(Steve Burke, Matt Keough RC, Lance Rautzhan, Dan Schatzeder RC)	.20	.10	.06
710	Rookie Outfielders(Dell Alston, Rick Bosetti, Mike Easler RC, Keith Smith)	.20	.10	.06
711	Rookie Pitchers(Cardell Camper, Dennis Lamp, Craig Mitchell, Roy Thomas)	.20	.10	.06
712	Bobby Valentine	.20	.10	.06
713	Bob Davis	.20	.10	.06
714	Mike Anderson	.20	.10	.06
715	Jim Kaat	.20	.10	.06
716	Clarence Gaston	.20	.10	.06
717	Nelson Briles	.20	.10	.06
718	Ron Jackson	.20	.10	.06
719	Randy Elliott	.20	.10	.06
720	Fergie Jenkins	3.00	1.50	.90
721	Billy Martin	.50	.25	.15
722	Pete Broberg	.20	.10	.06
723	Johnny Wockenfuss	.20	.10	.06
724	Royals Team	.30	.15	.09
725	Kurt Bevacqua	.20	.10	.06
726	Wilbur Wood	.20	.10	.06

1978 Topps Team Checklist Sheet

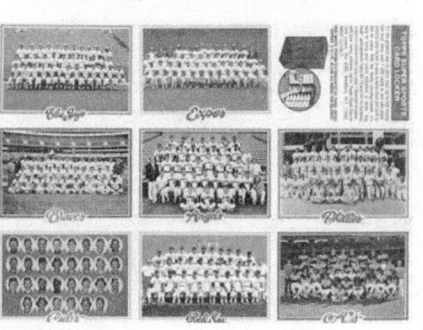

A redemption offer on packs of 1978 Topps cards offered an uncut sheet of the 26 team/checklist cards by mail. Besides the team cards, the 10-1/2" x 22-1/2" sheet has a card offering collectors card boxes. The cards on the sheet are identical to the single team/checklist cards issued in packs.

	NM	E	VG
Uncut Sheet	25.00	12.50	7.50

1978 Topps/Dynamite Magazine Panels

In issue No. 47 of its "Dynamite" kids' magazine, Scholastic Book Club teamed with Topps to insert a six-card panel of its 1978 baseball issue. Three such panels have been found thus far, one of which includes an Eddie Murray rookie. card. Values shown are for just the uncut panel; complete magazines would bear a small premium.

		NM	E	VG
Complete Panel Set (3):		60.00	30.00	18.00
	PANEL 1	40.00	20.00	12.00
36	Eddie Murray			
125	George Scott			
141	Ruppert Jones			
150	Bobby Bonds			
490	Amos Otis			
550	John Mayberry			
	PANEL 2	10.00	5.00	3.00
21	Steve Kemp			
168	Reggie Smith			
200	Reggie Jackson			
245	Rick Burleson			
332	Duane Kuiper			
440	Davey Lopes			
	PANEL 3	15.00	7.50	4.50
44	Toby Harrah			
120	Gary Carter			
130	Jeff Burroughs			
320	Fred Lynn			
335	Bucky Dent			
670	Jim Rice			

1978 Topps/Zest Soap

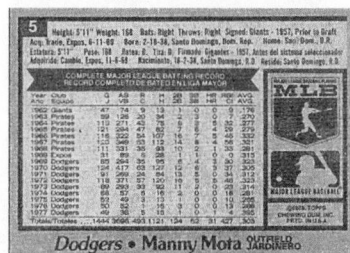

Produced by Topps for a Zest Soap promotion, the five cards in this set are almost identical to the regular issue, except the backs are printed in both Spanish and English, the game feature on back has been replaced by MLB and MLBPA logos and the card numbers are different. The cards measure 2-1/2" x 3-1/2". Because of the player selection and the bilingual backs, it seems obvious that this set was aimed at the Hispanic community. Cards were issued as complete sets in a cello package.

		NM/M	NM	E
Complete Set (5):		4.00		
Common Player:		.50		
1	Joaquin Andujar	2.00	1.00	.60

2	Bert Campaneris	4.50	2.25	1.25
3	Ed Figueroa	1.50	.70	.45
4	Willie Montanez	1.50	.70	.45
5	Manny Mota	4.50	2.25	1.25

1979 Topps

The size of this issue remained the same as in 1978 with 726 cards making their appearance. Actually, the 2-1/2" x 3-1/2" cards have a relatively minor design change from the previous year. The large color photo still dominates the front, with the player's name, team and position below it. The baseball with the player's position was moved to the lower left and the position replaced by a Topps logo. On the back, the printing color was changed and the game situation was replaced by a quiz called "Baseball Dates". Specialty cards include statistical leaders, major league records set during the season and eight cards devoted to career records. For the first time, rookies were arranged by teams under the heading of "Prospects." The key Ozzie Smith rookie card is usually seen with very poor centering.

	NM	E	VG
Complete Set (726):	140.00	75.00	37.50
Common Player:	.15	.08	.05
Wax Pack (12):	10.00		
Wax Box (36):	300.00		
Cello Pack (18):	12.50		
Cello Box (24):	325.00		
Super Cello Pack (28):	25.00		
Super Cello Box (24):	500.00		
Rack Pack (39):	25.00		
Rack Box (24):	480.00		
Vending Box (500):	165.00		

		NM	E	VG
1	Batting Leaders(Rod Carew, Dave Parker)	1.00	.50	.30
2	Home Run Leaders(George Foster, Jim Rice)	.15	.08	.05
3	RBI Leaders(George Foster, Jim Rice)	.15	.08	.05
4	Stolen Base Leaders(Ron LeFlore, Omar Moreno)	.15	.08	.05
5	Victory Leaders(Ron Guidry, Gaylord Perry)	.15	.08	.05
6	Strikeout Leaders(J.R. Richard, Nolan Ryan)	4.00	2.00	1.25
7	ERA Leaders(Ron Guidry, Craig Swan)	.15	.08	.05
8	Leading Firemen(Rollie Fingers, Rich Gossage)	.20	.10	.06
9	Dave Campbell	.15	.08	.05
10	Lee May	.15	.08	.05
11	Marc Hill	.15	.08	.05
12	Dick Drago	.15	.08	.05
13	Paul Dade	.15	.08	.05
14	Rafael Landestoy	.15	.08	.05
15	Ross Grimsley	.15	.08	.05
16	Fred Stanley	.15	.08	.05
17	Donnie Moore	.15	.08	.05
18	Tony Solaita	.15	.08	.05
19	Larry Gura	.15	.08	.05
20	Joe Morgan	3.00	1.50	.90
21	Kevin Kobel	.15	.08	.05
22	Mike Jorgensen	.15	.08	.05
23	Terry Forster	.15	.08	.05
24	Paul Molitor	8.00	4.00	2.00
25	Steve Carlton	3.00	1.50	.90
26	Jamie Quirk	.15	.08	.05
27	Dave Goltz	.15	.08	.05
28	Steve Brye	.15	.08	.05
29	Rick Langford	.15	.08	.05
30	Dave Winfield	3.00	1.50	.90
31	Tom House	.15	.08	.05
32	Jerry Mumphrey	.15	.08	.05
33	Dave Rozema	.15	.08	.05
34	Rob Andrews	.15	.08	.05
35	Ed Figueroa	.15	.08	.05
36	Alan Ashby	.15	.08	.05

#	Name			
37	Joe Kerrigan	.15	.08	.05
38	Bernie Carbo	.15	.08	.05
39	Dale Murphy	2.00	1.00	.60
40	Dennis Eckersley	2.50	1.25	.70
41	Twins Team(Gene Mauch)	.25	.13	.08
42	Ron Blomberg	.15	.08	.05
43	Wayne Twitchell	.15	.08	.05
44	Kurt Bevacqua	.15	.08	.05
45	Al Hrabosky	.15	.08	.05
46	Ron Hodges	.15	.08	.05
47	Fred Norman	.15	.08	.05
48	Merv Rettenmund	.15	.08	.05
49	Vern Ruhle	.15	.08	.05
50	Steve Garvey	1.50	.70	.45
51	Ray Fosse	.15	.08	.05
52	Randy Lerch	.15	.08	.05
53	Mick Kelleher	.15	.08	.05
54	Dell Alston	.15	.08	.05
55	Willie Stargell	3.00	1.50	.90
56	John Hale	.15	.08	.05
57	Eric Rasmussen	.15	.08	.05
58	Bob Randall	.15	.08	.05
59	John Denny	.15	.08	.05
60	Mickey Rivers	.15	.08	.05
61	Bo Diaz	.15	.08	.05
62	Randy Moffitt	.15	.08	.05
63	Jack Brohamer	.15	.08	.05
64	Tom Underwood	.15	.08	.05
65	Mark Belanger	.15	.08	.05
66	Tigers Team(Les Moss)	.25	.13	.08
67	Jim Mason	.15	.08	.05
68	Joe Niekro	.15	.08	.05
69	Elliott Maddox	.15	.08	.05
70	John Candelaria	.15	.08	.05
71	Brian Downing	.15	.08	.05
72	Steve Mingori	.15	.08	.05
73	Ken Henderson	.15	.08	.05
74	Shane Rawley RC	.15	.08	.05
75	Steve Yeager	.15	.08	.05
76	Warren Cromartie	.15	.08	.05
77	Dan Briggs	.15	.08	.05
78	Elias Sosa	.15	.08	.05
79	Ted Cox	.15	.08	.05
80	Jason Thompson	.15	.08	.05
81	Roger Erickson	.15	.08	.05
82	Mets Team(Joe Torre)	.75	.40	.25
83	Fred Kendall	.15	.08	.05
84	Greg Minton	.15	.08	.05
85	Gary Matthews	.15	.08	.05
86	Rodney Scott	.15	.08	.05
87	Pete Falcone	.15	.08	.05
88	Bob Molinaro	.15	.08	.05
89	Dick Tidrow	.15	.08	.05
90	Bob Boone	.15	.08	.05
91	Terry Crowley	.15	.08	.05
92	Jim Bibby	.15	.08	.05
93	Phil Mankowski	.15	.08	.05
94	Len Barker	.15	.08	.05
95	Robin Yount	4.00	2.00	1.00
96	Indians Team(Jeff Torborg)	.25	.13	.08
97	Sam Mejias	.15	.08	.05
98	Ray Burris	.15	.08	.05
99	John Wathan	.15	.08	.05
100	Tom Seaver	4.00	2.00	1.00
101	Roy Howell	.15	.08	.05
102	Mike Anderson	.15	.08	.05
103	Jim Todd	.15	.08	.05
104	Johnny Oates	.15	.08	.05
105	Rick Camp	.15	.08	.05
106	Frank Duffy	.15	.08	.05
107	Jesus Alou	.15	.08	.05
108	Eduardo Rodriguez	.15	.08	.05
109	Joel Youngblood	.15	.08	.05
110	Vida Blue	.15	.08	.05
111	Roger Freed	.15	.08	.05
112	Phillies Team(Danny Ozark)	.25	.13	.08
113	Pete Redfern	.15	.08	.05
114	Cliff Johnson	.15	.08	.05
115	Nolan Ryan	20.00	10.00	5.00
116	Ozzie Smith RC	60.00	30.00	15.00
117	Grant Jackson	.15	.08	.05
118	Bud Harrelson	.15	.08	.05
119	Don Stanhouse	.15	.08	.05
120	Jim Sundberg	.15	.08	.05
121	Checklist 1-121	.15	.08	.05
122	Mike Paxton	.15	.08	.05
123	Lou Whitaker	1.00	.50	.30
124	Dan Schatzeder	.15	.08	.05
125	Rick Burleson	.15	.08	.05
126	Doug Bair	.15	.08	.05
127	Thad Bosley	.15	.08	.05
128	Ted Martinez	.15	.08	.05
129	Marty Pattin	.15	.08	.05
130	Bob Watson	.15	.08	.05
131	Jim Clancy	.15	.08	.05

#	Name			
132	Rowland Office	.15	.08	.05
133	Bill Castro	.15	.08	.05
134	Alan Bannister	.15	.08	.05
135	Bobby Murcer	.15	.08	.05
136	Jim Kaat	.15	.08	.05
137	Larry Wolfe	.15	.08	.05
138	Mark Lee	.15	.08	.05
139	Luis Pujols	.15	.08	.05
140	Don Gullett	.15	.08	.05
141	Tom Paciorek	.15	.08	.05
142	Charlie Williams	.15	.08	.05
143	Tony Scott	.15	.08	.05
144	Sandy Alomar	.15	.08	.05
145	Rick Rhoden	.15	.08	.05
146	Duane Kuiper	.15	.08	.05
147	Dave Hamilton	.15	.08	.05
148	Bruce Boisclair	.15	.08	.05
149	Manny Sarmiento	.15	.08	.05
150	Wayne Cage	.15	.08	.05
151	John Hiller	.15	.08	.05
152	Rick Cerone	.15	.08	.05
153	Dennis Lamp	.15	.08	.05
154	Jim Gantner	.15	.08	.05
155	Dwight Evans	.15	.08	.05
156	Buddy Solomon	.15	.08	.05
157	U.L. Washington	.15	.08	.05
158	Joe Sambito	.15	.08	.05
159	Roy White	.15	.08	.05
160	Mike Flanagan	.15	.08	.05
161	Barry Foote	.15	.08	.05
162	Tom Johnson	.15	.08	.05
163	Glenn Burke	.15	.08	.05
164	Mickey Lolich	.15	.08	.05
165	Frank Taveras	.15	.08	.05
166	Leon Roberts	.15	.08	.05
167a	Roger Metzger (Solid vertical black line between first and last names, through "A" of "GIANTS.")	.50	.25	.15
167b	Roger Metzger (Partial black line.)	.25	.13	.08
167c	Roger Metzger (No black line.)	.15	.08	.05
168	Dave Freisleben	.15	.08	.05
169	Bill Nahorodny	.15	.08	.05
170	Don Sutton	2.50	1.25	.70
171	Gene Clines	.15	.08	.05
172	Mike Bruhert	.15	.08	.05
173	John Lowenstein	.15	.08	.05
174	Rick Auerbach	.15	.08	.05
175	George Hendrick	.15	.08	.05
176	Aurelio Rodriguez	.15	.08	.05
177	Ron Reed	.15	.08	.05
178	Alvis Woods	.15	.08	.05
179	Jim Beattie	.15	.08	.05
180	Larry Hisle	.15	.08	.05
181	Mike Garman	.15	.08	.05
182	Tim Johnson	.15	.08	.05
183	Paul Splittorff	.15	.08	.05
184	Darrel Chaney	.15	.08	.05
185	Mike Torrez	.15	.08	.05
186	Eric Soderholm	.15	.08	.05
187	Mark Lemongello	.15	.08	.05
188	Pat Kelly	.15	.08	.05
189	Eddie Whitson RC	.25	.13	.08
190	Ron Cey	.15	.08	.05
191	Mike Norris	.15	.08	.05
192	Cardinals Team(Ken Boyer)	.25	.13	.08
193	Glenn Adams	.15	.08	.05
194	Randy Jones	.15	.08	.05
195	Bill Madlock	.15	.08	.05
196	Steve Kemp	.15	.08	.05
197	Bob Apodaca	.15	.08	.05
198	Johnny Grubb	.15	.08	.05
199	Larry Milbourne	.15	.08	.05
200	Johnny Bench	4.00	2.00	1.00
201	Mike Edwards (Record Breaker)	.15	.08	.05
202	Ron Guidry (Record Breaker)	.15	.08	
203	J.R. Richard (Record Breaker)	.15	.08	.05
204	Pete Rose (Record Breaker)	1.00	.50	.30
205	John Stearns (Record Breaker)	.15	.08	
206	Sammy Stewart (Record Breaker)	.15	.08	.05
207	Dave Lemanczyk	.15	.08	.05
208	Clarence Gaston	.15	.08	.05
209	Reggie Cleveland	.15	.08	.05
210	Larry Bowa	.15	.08	.05
211	Denny Martinez	.15	.08	.05
212	Carney Lansford RC	.60	.30	.20
213	Bill Travers	.15	.08	.05

#	Name			
214	Red Sox Team(Don Zimmer)	.25	.13	.08
215	Willie McCovey	3.00	1.50	.90
216	Wilbur Wood	.15	.08	.05
217	Steve Dillard	.15	.08	.05
218	Dennis Leonard	.15	.08	.05
219	Roy Smalley	.15	.08	.05
220	Cesar Geronimo	.15	.08	.05
221	Jesse Jefferson	.15	.08	.05
222	Bob Beall	.15	.08	.05
223	Kent Tekulve	.15	.08	.05
224	Dave Revering	.15	.08	.05
225	Rich Gossage	.25	.13	.08
226	Ron Pruitt	.15	.08	.05
227	Steve Stone	.15	.08	.05
228	Vic Davalillo	.15	.08	.05
229	Doug Flynn	.15	.08	.05
230	Bob Forsch	.15	.08	.05
231	Johnny Wockenfuss	.15	.08	.05
232	Jimmy Sexton	.15	.08	.05
233	Paul Mitchell	.15	.08	.05
234	Toby Harrah	.15	.08	.05
235	Steve Rogers	.15	.08	.05
236	Jim Dwyer	.15	.08	.05
237	Billy Smith	.15	.08	.05
238	Balor Moore	.15	.08	.05
239	Willie Horton	.15	.08	.05
240	Rick Reuschel	.15	.08	.05
241	Checklist 122-242	.15	.08	.05
242	Pablo Torrealba	.15	.08	.05
243	Buck Martinez	.15	.08	.05
244	Pirates Team(Chuck Tanner)	.25	.13	.08
245	Jeff Burroughs	.15	.08	.05
246	Darrell Jackson	.15	.08	.05
247	Tucker Ashford	.15	.08	.05
248	Pete LaCock	.15	.08	.05
249	Paul Thormodsgard	.15	.08	.05
250	Willie Randolph	.15	.08	.05
251	Jack Morris	.40	.20	.12
252	Bob Stinson	.15	.08	.05
253	Rick Wise	.15	.08	.05
254	Luis Gomez	.15	.08	.05
255	Tommy John	.30	.15	.09
256	Mike Sadek	.15	.08	.05
257	Adrian Devine	.15	.08	.05
258	Mike Phillips	.15	.08	.05
259	Reds Team(Sparky Anderson)	.75	.40	.25
260	Richie Zisk	.15	.08	.05
261	Mario Guerrero	.15	.08	.05
262	Nelson Briles	.15	.08	.05
263	Oscar Gamble	.15	.08	.05
264	Don Robinson RC	.15	.08	.05
265	Don Money	.15	.08	.05
266	Jim Willoughby	.15	.08	.05
267	Joe Rudi	.15	.08	.05
268	Julio Gonzalez	.15	.08	.05
269	Woodie Fryman	.15	.08	.05
270	Butch Hobson	.15	.08	.05
271	Rawly Eastwick	.15	.08	.05
272	Tim Corcoran	.15	.08	.05
273	Jerry Terrell	.15	.08	.05
274	Willie Norwood	.15	.08	.05
275	Junior Moore	.15	.08	.05
276	Jim Colborn	.15	.08	.05
277	Tom Grieve	.15	.08	.05
278	Andy Messersmith	.15	.08	.05
279	Jerry Grote	.15	.08	.05
280	Andre Thornton	.15	.08	.05
281	Vic Correll	.15	.08	.05
282	Blue Jays Team(Roy Hartsfield)	.25	.13	.08
283	Ken Kravec	.15	.08	.05
284	Johnnie LeMaster	.15	.08	.05
285	Bobby Bonds	.15	.08	.05
286	Duffy Dyer	.15	.08	.05
287	Andres Mora	.15	.08	.05
288	Milt Wilcox	.15	.08	.05
289	Jose Cruz	.15	.08	.05
290	Dave Lopes	.15	.08	.05
291	Tom Griffin	.15	.08	.05
292	Don Reynolds	.15	.08	.05
293	Jerry Garvin	.15	.08	.05
294	Pepe Frias	.15	.08	.05
295	Mitchell Page	.15	.08	.05
296	Preston Hanna	.15	.08	.05
297	Ted Sizemore	.15	.08	.05
298	Rich Gale	.15	.08	.05
299	Steve Ontiveros	.15	.08	.05
300	Rod Carew	3.00	1.50	.90
301	Tom Hume	.15	.08	.05
302	Braves Team(Bobby Cox)	.45	.25	.14
303	Lary Sorensen	.15	.08	.05
304	Steve Swisher	.15	.08	.05
305	Willie Montanez	.15	.08	.05
306	Floyd Bannister	.15	.08	.05
307	Larvell Blanks	.15	.08	.05

No.	Player			
308	Bert Blyleven	2.00	1.00	.60
309	Ralph Garr	.15	.08	.05
310	Thurman Munson	4.00	2.50	1.50
311	Gary Lavelle	.15	.08	.05
312	Bob Robertson	.15	.08	.05
313	Dyar Miller	.15	.08	.05
314	Larry Harlow	.15	.08	.05
315	Jon Matlack	.15	.08	.05
316	Milt May	.15	.08	.05
317	Jose Cardenal	.15	.08	.05
318	Bob Welch RC	1.50	.70	.45
319	Wayne Garrett	.15	.08	.05
320	Carl Yastrzemski	4.00	2.00	1.00
321	Gaylord Perry	2.50	1.25	.70
322	Danny Goodwin	.15	.08	.05
323	Lynn McGlothen	.15	.08	.05
324	Mike Tyson	.15	.08	.05
325	Cecil Cooper	.15	.08	.05
326	Pedro Borbon	.15	.08	.05
327	Art Howe	.15	.08	.05
328	A's Team(Jack McKeon)	.25	.13	.08
329	Joe Coleman	.15	.08	.05
330	George Brett	6.00	4.00	2.00
331	Mickey Mahler	.15	.08	.05
332	Gary Alexander	.15	.08	.05
333	Chet Lemon	.15	.08	.05
334	Craig Swan	.15	.08	.05
335	Chris Chambliss	.15	.08	.05
336	Bobby Thompson	.15	.08	.05
337	John Montague	.15	.08	.05
338	Vic Harris	.15	.08	.05
339	Ron Jackson	.15	.08	.05
340	Jim Palmer	3.00	1.50	.90
341	Willie Upshaw RC	.20	.10	.06
342	Dave Roberts	.15	.08	.05
343	Ed Glynn	.15	.08	.05
344	Jerry Royster	.15	.08	.05
345	Tug McGraw	.15	.08	.05
346	Bill Buckner	.15	.08	.05
347	Doug Rau	.15	.08	.05
348	Andre Dawson	2.50	.70	.45
349	Jim Wright	.15	.08	.05
350	Garry Templeton	.15	.08	.05
351	Wayne Nordhagen	.15	.08	.05
352	Steve Renko	.15	.08	.05
353	Checklist 243-363	.15	.08	.05
354	Bill Bonham	.15	.08	.05
355	Lee Mazzilli	.15	.08	.05
356	Giants Team (Joe Altobelli)	.25	.13	.08
357	Jerry Augustine	.15	.08	.05
358	Alan Trammell	2.00	1.00	.60
359	Dan Spillner	.15	.08	.05
360	Amos Otis	.15	.08	.05
361	Tom Dixon	.15	.08	.05
362	Mike Cubbage	.15	.08	.05
363	Craig Skok	.15	.08	.05
364	Gene Richards	.15	.08	.05
365	Sparky Lyle	.15	.08	.05
366	Juan Bernhardt	.15	.08	.05
367	Dave Skaggs	.15	.08	.05
368	Don Aase	.15	.08	.05
369a	Bump Wills (Blue Jays)	2.00	1.00	.60
369b	Bump Wills (Rangers)	2.00	1.00	.60
370	Dave Kingman	.15	.08	.05
371	Jeff Holly	.15	.08	.05
372	Lamar Johnson	.15	.08	.05
373	Lance Rautzhan	.15	.08	.05
374	Ed Herrmann	.15	.08	.05
375	Bill Campbell	.15	.08	.05
376	Gorman Thomas	.15	.08	.05
377	Paul Moskau	.15	.08	.05
378	Rob Picciolo	.15	.08	.05
379	Dale Murray	.15	.08	.05
380	John Mayberry	.15	.08	.05
381	Astros Team(Bill Virdon)	.25	.13	.08
382	Jerry Martin	.15	.08	.05
383	Phil Garner	.15	.08	.05
384	Tommy Boggs	.15	.08	.05
385	Dan Ford	.15	.08	.05
386	Francisco Barrios	.15	.08	.05
387	Gary Thomasson	.15	.08	.05
388	Jack Billingham	.15	.08	.05
389	Joe Zdeb	.15	.08	.05
390	Rollie Fingers	2.50	1.25	.70
391	Al Oliver	.30	.15	.09
392	Doug Ault	.15	.08	.05
393	Scott McGregor	.15	.08	.05
394	Randy Stein	.15	.08	.05
395	Dave Cash	.15	.08	.05
396	Bill Plummer	.15	.08	.05
397	Sergio Ferrer	.15	.08	.05
398	Ivan DeJesus	.15	.08	.05
399	David Clyde	.15	.08	.05
400	Jim Rice	4.00	2.00	1.20
401	Ray Knight	.15	.08	.05
402	Paul Hartzell	.15	.08	.05
403	Tim Foli	.15	.08	.05
404	White Sox Team (Don Kessinger)	.25	.13	.08
405	Butch Wynegar	.15	.08	.05
406	Joe Wallis	.15	.08	.05
407	Pete Vuckovich	.15	.08	.05
408	Charlie Moore	.15	.08	.05
409	Willie Wilson RC	2.00	1.00	.60
410	Darrell Evans	.15	.08	.05
411	All-Time Hits Leaders(Ty Cobb, George Sisler)	.50	.25	.15
412	All-Time RBI Leaders (Hank Aaron, Hack Wilson)	.50	.25	.15
413	All-Time Home Run Leaders (Hank Aaron, Roger Maris)	4.50	2.25	1.25
414	All-Time Batting Average Leaders (Ty Cobb, Roger Hornsby)	.50	.25	.15
415	All-Time Stolen Bases Leader(Lou Brock)	.30	.15	.09
416	All-Time Wins Leaders (Jack Chesbro, Cy Young)	.25	.13	.08
417	All-Time Strikeout Leaders (Walter Johnson, Nolan Ryan)	4.50	2.25	1.25
418	All-Time ERA Leaders (Walter Johnson, Dutch Leonard)	.20	.10	.06
419	Dick Ruthven	.15	.08	.05
420	Ken Griffey	.15	.08	.05
421	Doug DeCinces	.15	.08	.05
422	Ruppert Jones	.15	.08	.05
423	Bob Montgomery	.15	.08	.05
424	Angels Team (Jim Fregosi)	.25	.13	.08
425	Rick Manning	.15	.08	.05
426	Chris Speier	.15	.08	.05
427	Andy Replogle	.15	.08	.05
428	Bobby Valentine	.15	.08	.05
429	John Urrea	.15	.08	.05
430	Dave Parker	.15	.08	.05
431	Glenn Borgmann	.15	.08	.05
432	Dave Heaverlo	.15	.08	.05
433	Larry Biittner	.15	.08	.05
434	Ken Clay	.15	.08	.05
435	Gene Tenace	.15	.08	.05
436	Hector Cruz	.15	.08	.05
437	Rick Williams	.15	.08	.05
438	Horace Speed	.15	.08	.05
439	Frank White	.15	.08	.05
440	Rusty Staub	.15	.08	.05
441	Lee Lacy	.15	.08	.05
442	Doyle Alexander	.15	.08	.05
443	Bruce Bochte	.15	.08	.05
444	Aurelio Lopez RC	.15	.08	.05
445	Steve Henderson	.15	.08	.05
446	Jim Lonborg	.15	.08	.05
447	Manny Sanguillen	.15	.08	.05
448	Moose Haas	.15	.08	.05
449	Bombo Rivera	.15	.08	.05
450	Dave Concepcion	.15	.08	.05
451	Royals Team (Whitey Herzog)	.25	.13	.08
452	Jerry Morales	.15	.08	.05
453	Chris Knapp	.15	.08	.05
454	Len Randle	.15	.08	.05
455	Bill Lee	.15	.08	.05
456	Chuck Baker	.15	.08	.05
457	Bruce Sutter	2.50	1.25	.70
458	Jim Essian	.15	.08	.05
459	Sid Monge	.15	.08	.05
460	Graig Nettles	.15	.08	.05
461	Jim Barr	.15	.08	.05
462	Otto Velez	.15	.08	.05
463	Steve Comer	.15	.08	.05
464	Joe Nolan	.15	.08	.05
465	Reggie Smith	.15	.08	.05
466	Mark Littell	.15	.08	.05
467	Don Kessinger	.15	.08	.05
468	Stan Bahnsen	.15	.08	.05
469	Lance Parrish	.30	.15	.09
470	Garry Maddox	.15	.08	.05
471	Joaquin Andujar	.15	.08	.05
472	Craig Kusick	.15	.08	.05
473	Dave Roberts	.15	.08	.05
474	Dick Davis	.15	.08	.05
475	Dan Driessen	.15	.08	.05
476	Tom Poquette	.15	.08	.05
477	Bob Grich	.15	.08	.05
478	Juan Beniquez	.15	.08	.05
479	Padres Team (Roger Craig)	.25	.13	.08
480	Fred Lynn	.15	.08	.05
481	Skip Lockwood	.15	.08	.05
482	Craig Reynolds	.15	.08	.05
483	Checklist 364-484	.15	.08	.05
484	Rick Waits	.15	.08	.05
485	Bucky Dent	.15	.08	.05
486	Bob Knepper	.15	.08	.05
487	Miguel Dilone	.15	.08	.05
488	Bob Owchinko	.15	.08	.05
489	Larry Cox (Photo actually Dave Rader.)	.15	.08	.05
490	Al Cowens	.15	.08	.05
491	Tippy Martinez	.15	.08	.05
492	Bob Bailor	.15	.08	.05
493	Larry Christenson	.15	.08	.05
494	Jerry White	.15	.08	.05
495	Tony Perez	2.00	1.00	.60
496	Barry Bonnell	.15	.08	.05
497	Glenn Abbott	.15	.08	.05
498	Rich Chiles	.15	.08	.05
499	Rangers Team (Pat Corrales)	.25	.13	.08
500	Ron Guidry	.20	.10	.06
501	Junior Kennedy	.15	.08	.05
502	Steve Braun	.15	.08	.05
503	Terry Humphrey	.15	.08	.05
504	Larry McWilliams RC	.15	.08	.05
505	Ed Kranepool	.15	.08	.05
506	John D'Acquisto	.15	.08	.05
507	Tony Armas	.15	.08	.05
508	Charlie Hough	.15	.08	.05
509	Mario Mendoza	.15	.08	.05
510	Ted Simmons	.15	.08	.05
511	Paul Reuschel	.15	.08	.05
512	Jack Clark	.15	.08	.05
513	Dave Johnson	.15	.08	.05
514	Mike Proly	.15	.08	.05
515	Enos Cabell	.15	.08	.05
516	Champ Summers	.15	.08	.05
517	Al Bumbry	.15	.08	.05
518	Jim Umbarger	.15	.08	.05
519	Ben Oglivie	.15	.08	.05
520	Gary Carter	3.00	1.50	.90
521	Sam Ewing	.15	.08	.05
522	Ken Holtzman	.15	.08	.05
523	John Milner	.15	.08	.05
524	Tom Burgmeier	.15	.08	.05
525	Freddie Patek	.15	.08	.05
526	Dodgers Team (Tom Lasorda)	.60	.30	.20
527	Lerrin LaGrow	.15	.08	.05
528	Wayne Gross	.15	.08	.05
529	Brian Asselstine	.15	.08	.05
530	Frank Tanana	.15	.08	.05
531	Fernando Gonzalez	.15	.08	.05
532	Buddy Schultz	.15	.08	.05
533	Leroy Stanton	.15	.08	.05
534	Ken Forsch	.15	.08	.05
535	Ellis Valentine	.15	.08	.05
536	Jerry Reuss	.15	.08	.05
537	Tom Veryzer	.15	.08	.05
538	Mike Ivie	.15	.08	.05
539	John Ellis	.15	.08	.05
540	Greg Luzinski	.15	.08	.05
541	Jim Slaton	.15	.08	.05
542	Rick Bosetti	.15	.08	.05
543	Kiko Garcia	.15	.08	.05
544	Fergie Jenkins	2.00	1.00	.60
545	John Stearns	.15	.08	.05
546	Bill Russell	.15	.08	.05
547	Clint Hurdle	.15	.08	.05
548	Enrique Romo	.15	.08	.05
549	Bob Bailey	.15	.08	.05
550	Sal Bando	.15	.08	.05
551	Cubs Team (Herman Franks)	.25	.13	.08
552	Jose Morales	.15	.08	.05
553	Denny Walling	.15	.08	.05
554	Matt Keough	.15	.08	.05
555	Biff Pocoroba	.15	.08	.05
556	Mike Lum	.15	.08	.05
557	Ken Brett	.15	.08	.05
558	Jay Johnstone	.15	.08	.05
559	Greg Pryor	.15	.08	.05
560	John Montefusco	.15	.08	.05
561	Ed Ott	.15	.08	.05
562	Dusty Baker	.20	.10	.06
563	Roy Thomas	.15	.08	.05
564	Jerry Turner	.15	.08	.05
565	Rico Carty	.15	.08	.05
566	Nino Espinosa	.15	.08	.05
567	Rich Hebner	.15	.08	.05
568	Carlos Lopez	.15	.08	.05
569	Bob Sykes	.15	.08	.05
570	Cesar Cedeno	.15	.08	.05
571	Darrell Porter	.15	.08	.05
572	Rod Gilbreath	.15	.08	.05
573	Jim Kern	.15	.08	.05
574	Claudell Washington	.15	.08	.05
575	Luis Tiant	.15	.08	.05
576	Mike Parrott	.15	.08	.05

577	Brewers Team(George Bamberger)	.25	.13	.08
578	Pete Broberg	.15	.08	.05
579	Greg Gross	.15	.08	.05
580	Ron Fairly	.15	.08	.05
581	Darold Knowles	.15	.08	.05
582	Paul Blair	.15	.08	.05
583	Julio Cruz	.15	.08	.05
584	Jim Rooker	.15	.08	.05
585	Hal McRae	.15	.08	.05
586	Bob Horner RC	1.00	.50	.30
587	Ken Reitz	.15	.08	.05
588	Tom Murphy	.15	.08	.05
589	Terry Whitfield	.15	.08	.05
590	J.R. Richard	.15	.08	.05
591	Mike Hargrove	.15	.08	.05
592	Mike Krukow	.15	.08	.05
593	Rick Dempsey	.15	.08	.05
594	Bob Shirley	.15	.08	.05
595	Phil Niekro	2.00	1.00	.60
596	Jim Wohlford	.15	.08	.05
597	Bob Stanley	.15	.08	.05
598	Mark Wagner	.15	.08	.05
599	Jim Spencer	.15	.08	.05
600	George Foster	.15	.08	.05
601	Dave LaRoche	.15	.08	.05
602	Checklist 485-605	.15	.08	.05
603	Rudy May	.15	.08	.05
604	Jeff Newman	.15	.08	.05
605	Rick Monday	.15	.08	.05
606	Expos Team(Dick Williams)	.25	.13	.08
607	Omar Moreno	.15	.08	.05
608	Dave McKay	.15	.08	.05
609	Silvio Martinez	.15	.08	.05
610	Mike Schmidt	6.00	3.00	1.75
611	Jim Norris	.15	.08	.05
612	Rick Honeycutt RC	.25	.13	.08
613	Mike Edwards	.15	.08	.05
614	Willie Hernandez	.15	.08	.05
615	Ken Singleton	.15	.08	.05
616	Billy Almon	.15	.08	.05
617	Terry Puhl	.15	.08	.05
618	Jerry Remy	.15	.08	.05
619	Ken Landreaux RC	.15	.08	.05
620	Bert Campaneris	.15	.08	.05
621	Pat Zachry	.15	.08	.05
622	Dave Collins	.15	.08	.05
623	Bob McClure	.15	.08	.05
624	Larry Herndon	.15	.08	.05
625	Mark Fidrych	.20	.10	.06
626	Yankees Team(Bob Lemon)	.60	.30	.20
627	Gary Serum	.15	.08	.05
628	Del Unser	.15	.08	.05
629	Gene Garber	.15	.08	.05
630	Bake McBride	.15	.08	.05
631	Jorge Orta	.15	.08	.05
632	Don Kirkwood	.15	.08	.05
633	Rob Wilfong	.15	.08	.05
634	Paul Lindblad	.15	.08	.05
635	Don Baylor	.30	.15	.09
636	Wayne Garland	.15	.08	.05
637	Bill Robinson	.15	.08	.05
638	Al Fitzmorris	.15	.08	.05
639	Manny Trillo	.15	.08	.05
640	Eddie Murray	9.00	5.00	2.50
641	Bobby Castillo RC	.15	.08	.05
642	Wilbur Howard	.15	.08	.05
643	Tom Hausman	.15	.08	.05
644	Manny Mota	.15	.08	.05
645	George Scott	.15	.08	.05
646	Rick Sweet	.15	.08	.05
647	Bob Lacey	.15	.08	.05
648	Lou Piniella	.25	.13	.08
649	John Curtis	.15	.08	.05
650	Pete Rose	10.00	5.00	2.50
651	Mike Caldwell	.15	.08	.05
652	Stan Papi	.15	.08	.05
653	Warren Brusstar	.15	.08	.05
654	Rick Miller	.15	.08	.05
655	Jerry Koosman	.15	.08	.05
656	Hosken Powell	.15	.08	.05
657	George Medich	.15	.08	.05
658	Taylor Duncan	.15	.08	.05
659	Mariners Team(Darrell Johnson)	.25	.13	.08
660	Ron LeFlore	.15	.08	.05
661	Bruce Kison	.15	.08	.05
662	Kevin Bell	.15	.08	.05
663	Mike Vail	.15	.08	.05
664	Doug Bird	.15	.08	.05
665	Lou Brock	3.00	1.50	.90
666	Rich Dauer	.15	.08	.05
667	Don Hood	.15	.08	.05
668	Bill North	.15	.08	.05
669	Checklist 606-726	.15	.08	.05
670	Jim Hunter	3.00	1.50	.90

671	Joe Ferguson	.15	.08	.05
672	Ed Halicki	.15	.08	.05
673	Tom Hutton	.15	.08	.05
674	Dave Tomlin	.15	.08	.05
675	Tim McCarver	.25	.13	.08
676	Johnny Sutton	.15	.08	.05
677	Larry Parrish	.15	.08	.05
678	Geoff Zahn	.15	.08	.05
679	Derrel Thomas	.15	.08	.05
680	Carlton Fisk	3.00	1.50	.90
681	John Henry Johnson RC	.15	.08	.05
682	Dave Chalk	.15	.08	.05
683	Dan Meyer	.15	.08	.05
684	Jamie Easterly	.15	.08	.05
685	Sixto Lezcano	.15	.08	.05
686	Ron Schueler	.15	.08	.05
687	Rennie Stennett	.15	.08	.05
688	Mike Willis	.15	.08	.05
689	Orioles Team(Earl Weaver)	.60	.30	.20
690	Buddy Bell	.15	.08	.05
691	Dock Ellis	.15	.08	.05
692	Mickey Stanley	.15	.08	.05
693	Dave Rader	.15	.08	.05
694	Burt Hooton	.15	.08	.05
695	Keith Hernandez	.15	.08	.05
696	Andy Hassler	.15	.08	.05
697	Dave Bergman	.15	.08	.05
698	Bill Stein	.15	.08	.05
699	Hal Dues	.15	.08	.05
700	Reggie Jackson	5.00	2.50	1.25
701	Orioles Prospects(Mark Corey, John Flinn, Sammy Stewart RC)	.15	.08	.05
702	Red Sox Prospects(Joel Finch, Garry Hancock, Allen Ripley)	.15	.08	.05
703	Angels Prospects(Jim Anderson, Dave Frost, Bob Slater)	.15	.08	.05
704	White Sox Prospects (Ross Baumgarten, Mike Colbern, Mike Squires RC)	.15	.08	.05
705	Indians Prospects(Alfredo Griffin RC, Tim Norrid, Dave Oliver)	.25	.13	.08
706	Tigers Prospects(Dave Stegman, Dave Tobik, Kip Young)	.15	.08	.05
707	Royals Prospects(Randy Bass, Jim Gaudet, Randy McGilberry)	.15	.08	.05
708	Brewers Prospects(Kevin Bass RC, Eddie Romero RC, Ned Yost)	.25	.13	.08
709	Twins Prospects(Sam Perlozzo, Rick Sofield, Kevin Stanfield)	.15	.08	.05
710	Yankees Prospects(Brian Doyle, Mike Heath RC, Dave Rajsich)	.20	.10	.06
711	A's Prospects(Dwayne Murphy RC, Bruce Robinson, Alan Wirth)	.15	.08	.05
712	Mariners Prospects(Bud Anderson, Greg Biercevicz, Byron McLaughlin)	.15	.08	.05
713	Rangers Prospects (Danny Darwin RC, Pat Putnam, Billy Sample RC)	.25	.13	.08
714	Blue Jays Prospect s(Victor Cruz, Pat Kelly, Ernie Whitt)	.15	.08	.05
715	Braves Prospects(Bruce Benedict RC, Glenn Hubbard RC, Larry Whisenton)	.25	.13	.08
716	Cubs Prospects(Dave Geisel, Karl Pagel, Scot Thompson RC)	.15	.08	.05
717	Reds Prospects(Mike LaCoss RC, Ron Oester RC, Harry Spilman RC)	.15	.08	.05
718	Astros Prospects(Bruce Bochy, Mike Fischlin, Don Pisker)	.15	.08	.05
719	Dodgers Prospects(Pedro Guerrero RC, Rudy Law RC, Joe Simpson)	1.50	.70	.45
720	Expos Prospects(Jerry Fry RC, Jerry Pirtle RC, Scott Sanderson RC)	.30	.15	.09
721	Mets Prospects(Juan Berenguer RC, Dwight Bernard, Dan Norman)	.15	.08	.05

722	Phillies Prospects(Jim Morrison RC, Lonnie Smith RC, Jim Wright RC)	.50	.25	.15
723	Pirates Prospects(Dale Berra RC, Eugenio Cotes, Ben Wiltbank)	.15	.08	.05
724	Cardinals Prospects(Tom Bruno, George Frazier RC, Terry Kennedy RC)	.20	.10	.06
725	Padres Prospects(Jim Beswick, Steve Mura, Broderick Perkins)	.15	.08	.05
726	Giants Prospects(Greg Johnston, Joe Strain, John Tamargo)	.15	.08	.05

1979 Topps Comics

Issued as the 3" x 3-3/4" wax wrapper for a five-cent piece of bubblegum, this "test" issue was bought up in great quantities by speculators and remains rather common. It is also inexpensive, because the comic-style player representations were not popular with collectors. The set is complete at 33 pieces. Each wax box contains only 11 different players. Original packaging folds are not considered in grading.

		NM	E	VG
Complete Set (33):		15.00	7.50	4.50
Common Player:		.25	.13	.08
Wax Box (72):		55.00		
1	Eddie Murray	1.50	.70	.45
2	Jim Rice	1.50	.90	.50
3	Carl Yastrzemski	1.50	.70	.45
4	Nolan Ryan	5.00	2.50	1.50
5	Chet Lemon	.25	.13	.08
6	Andre Thornton	.25	.13	.08
7	Rusty Staub	.25	.13	.08
8	Ron LeFlore	.25	.13	.08
9	George Brett	3.00	1.50	.90
10	Larry Hisle	.25	.13	.08
11	Rod Carew	1.50	.70	.45
12	Reggie Jackson	2.50	1.25	.70
13	Ron Guidry	.25	.13	.08
14	Mitchell Page	.25	.13	.08
15	Leon Roberts	.25	.13	.08
16	Al Oliver	.25	.13	.08
17	John Mayberry	.25	.13	.08
18	Bob Horner	.25	.13	.08
19	Phil Niekro	1.00	.50	.30
20	Dave Kingman	.25	.13	.08
21	John Bench	1.50	.70	.45
22	Tom Seaver	1.50	.70	.45
23	J.R. Richard	.25	.13	.08
24	Steve Garvey	.60	.30	.20
25	Reggie Smith	.25	.13	.08
26	Ross Grimsley	.25	.13	.08
27	Craig Swan	.25	.13	.08
28	Pete Rose	3.50	1.75	1.00
29	Dave Parker	.25	.13	.08
30	Ted Simmons	.25	.13	.08
31	Dave Winfield	1.50	.70	.45
32	Jack Clark	.25	.13	.08
33	Vida Blue	.25	.13	.08

1979 Topps Team Checklist Sheet

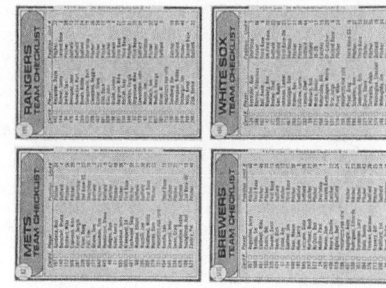

This uncut sheet of 26 team card/checklists was available via a mail-in offer. The sheet was mailed with two folds. The sheet cards are printed on lighter stock.

	NM	E	VG
Uncut Sheet:	20.00	10.00	6.00

1979 Topps/Dynamite Magazine Panels

In at least two issue of its "Dynamite" kids' magazine, Scholastic Book Club teamed with Topps to insert a six-card panel of its 1979 baseball issue. Complete magazines would bear a small premium.

		NM	E	VG
	Complete Panel:	20.00	10.00	6.00
2	Home Run Leaders(Jim Rice, George Foster)			
5	Victory Leaders(Ron Guidry, Gaylord Perry)			
6	Strikeout Leaders(Nolan Ryan, J.R. Richard)			
201	Mike Edwards (Record Breaker)			
202	Ron Guidry (Record Breaker)			
203	J.R. Richard (Record Breaker)			
	Complete Panel:	15.00	7.50	4.50
232	Jimmy Sexton			
292	Don Reynolds			
336	Bobby Thompson			
432	Dave Heaverlo			
532	Buddy Schultz			
539	John Ellis			

1980 Topps

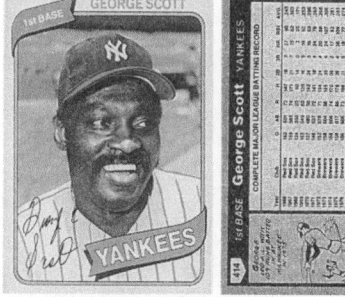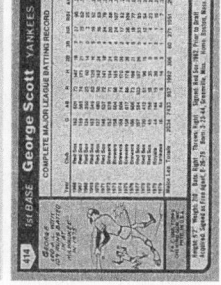

Again numbering 726 cards measuring 2-1/2" x 3-1/2", Topps did make some design changes in 1980. Fronts have the usual color picture with a facsimile autograph. The player's name appears above the picture, while his position is on a pennant at the upper left and his team on another pennant in the lower right. Backs no longer feature games, returning instead to statistics, personal information, a few headlines and a cartoon about the player. Specialty cards include statistical leaders, and previous season highlights. Many rookies again appear in team threesomes.

	NM	E	VG
Complete Set (726):	100.00	50.00	30.00
Common Player:	.15	.08	.05
Wax Pack (15):	10.00		

	Wax Box (36):	260.00		
	Cello Pack (25):	12.50		
	Cello Box (24):	275.00		
	Super Cello Pack (28):	14.00		
	Super Cello Box (24):	290.00		
	Rack Pack (42):	17.75		
	Rack Box (24):	360.00		
	Vending Box (500):	100.00		
1	Lou Brock, Carl Yastrzemski (Highlights)	1.00	.50	.30
2	Willie McCovey (Highlights)	.30	.15	.09
3	Manny Mota (Highlights)	.15	.08	.05
4	Pete Rose (Highlights)	2.00	1.00	.60
5	Garry Templeton (Highlights)	.15	.08	.05
6	Del Unser (Highlights)	.15	.08	.05
7	Mike Lum	.15	.08	.05
8	Craig Swan	.15	.08	.05
9a	Steve Braun (Name in yellow.)	200.00	100.00	60.00
9b	Steve Braun (Name in red.)	.15	.08	.05
10	Denny Martinez	.15	.08	.05
11	Jimmy Sexton	.15	.08	.05
12	John Curtis	.15	.08	.05
13	Ron Pruitt	.15	.08	.05
14	Dave Cash	.15	.08	.05
15	Bill Campbell	.15	.08	.05
16	Jerry Narron	.15	.08	.05
17	Bruce Sutter	2.00	1.00	.60
18	Ron Jackson	.15	.08	.05
19	Balor Moore	.15	.08	.05
20	Dan Ford	.15	.08	.05
21	Manny Sarmiento	.15	.08	.05
22	Pat Putnam	.15	.08	.05
23	Derrel Thomas	.15	.08	.05
24	Jim Slaton	.15	.08	.05
25	Lee Mazzilli	.15	.08	.05
26	Marty Pattin	.15	.08	.05
27	Del Unser	.15	.08	.05
28	Bruce Kison	.15	.08	.05
29	Mark Wagner	.15	.08	.05
30	Vida Blue	.15	.08	.05
31	Jay Johnstone	.15	.08	.05
32	Julio Cruz	.15	.08	.05
33	Tony Scott	.15	.08	.05
34	Jeff Newman	.15	.08	.05
35	Luis Tiant	.15	.08	.05
36	Rusty Torres	.15	.08	.05
37	Kiko Garcia	.15	.08	.05
38	Dan Spillner	.15	.08	.05
39	Rowland Office	.15	.08	.05
40	Carlton Fisk	2.50	1.25	.70
41	Rangers team(Pat Corrales)	.25	.13	.08
42	Dave Palmer RC	.15	.08	.05
43	Bombo Rivera	.15	.08	.05
44	Bill Fahey	.15	.08	.05
45	Frank White	.15	.08	.05
46	Rico Carty	.15	.08	.05
47	Bill Bonham	14.00		
48	Rick Miller	.15	.08	.05
49	Mario Guerrero	.15	.08	.05
50	J.R. Richard	.15	.08	.05
51	Joe Ferguson	.15	.08	.05
52	Warren Brusstar	.15	.08	.05
53	Ben Oglivie	.15	.08	.05
54	Dennis Lamp	.15	.08	.05
55	Bill Madlock	.15	.08	.05
56	Bobby Valentine	.15	.08	.05
57	Pete Vuckovich	.15	.08	.05
58	Doug Flynn	.15	.08	.05
59	Eddy Putman	.15	.08	.05
60	Bucky Dent	.20	.10	.06
61	Gary Serum	.15	.08	.05
62	Mike Ivie	.15	.08	.05
63	Bob Stanley	.15	.08	.05
64	Joe Nolan	.15	.08	.05
65	Al Bumbry	.15	.08	.05
66	Royals Team(Jim Frey)	.25	.13	.08
67	Doyle Alexander	.15	.08	.05
68	Larry Harlow	.15	.08	.05
69	Rick Williams	.15	.08	.05
70	Gary Carter	2.50	1.25	.70
71	John Milner	.15	.08	.05
72	Fred Howard	.15	.08	.05
73	Dave Collins	.15	.08	.05
74	Sid Monge	.15	.08	.05
75	Bill Russell	.15	.08	.05
76	John Stearns	.15	.08	.05
77	Dave Stieb RC	1.00	.50	.30
78	Ruppert Jones	.15	.08	.05
79	Bob Owchinko	.15	.08	.05
80	Ron LeFlore	.15	.08	.05
81	Ted Sizemore	.15	.08	.05
82	Astros Team(Bill Virdon)	.25	.13	.08
83	Steve Trout RC	.15	.08	.05
84	Gary Lavelle	.15	.08	.05
85	Ted Simmons	.15	.08	.05
86	Dave Hamilton	.15	.08	.05
87	Pepe Frias	.15	.08	.05
88	Ken Landreaux	.15	.08	.05
89	Don Hood	.15	.08	.05
90	Manny Trillo	.15	.08	.05
91	Rick Dempsey	.15	.08	.05
92	Rick Rhoden	.15	.08	.05
93	Dave Roberts	.15	.08	.05
94	Neil Allen RC	.15	.08	.05
95	Cecil Cooper	.15	.08	.05
96	A's Team(Jim Marshall)	.25	.13	.08
97	Bill Lee	.15	.08	.05
98	Jerry Terrell	.15	.08	.05
99	Victor Cruz	.15	.08	.05
100	Johnny Bench	3.00	1.50	.90
101	Aurelio Lopez	.15	.08	.05
102	Rich Dauer	.15	.08	.05
103	Bill Caudill RC	.15	.08	.05
104	Manny Mota	.15	.08	.05
105	Frank Tanana	.15	.08	.05
106	Jeff Leonard RC	.25	.13	.08
107	Francisco Barrios	.15	.08	.05
108	Bob Horner	.15	.08	.05
109	Bill Travers	.15	.08	.05
110	Fred Lynn	.15	.08	.05
111	Bob Knepper	.15	.08	.05
112	White Sox Team(Tony LaRussa)	.45	.25	.14
113	Geoff Zahn	.15	.08	.05
114	Juan Beniquez	.15	.08	.05
115	Sparky Lyle	.15	.08	.05
116	Larry Cox	.15	.08	.05
117	Dock Ellis	.15	.08	.05
118	Phil Garner	.15	.08	.05
119	Sammy Stewart	.15	.08	.05
120	Greg Luzinski	.15	.08	.05
121	Checklist 1-121	.15	.08	.05
122	Dave Rosello	.15	.08	.05
123	Lynn Jones	.15	.08	.05
124	Dave Lemanczyk	.15	.08	.05
125	Tony Perez	2.00	1.00	.60
126	Dave Tomlin	.15	.08	.05
127	Gary Thomasson	.15	.08	.05
128	Tom Burgmeier	.15	.08	.05
129	Craig Reynolds	.15	.08	.05
130	Amos Otis	.15	.08	.05
131	Paul Mitchell	.15	.08	.05
132	Biff Pocoroba	.15	.08	.05
133	Jerry Turner	.15	.08	.05
134	Matt Keough	.15	.08	.05
135	Bill Buckner	.15	.08	.05
136	Dick Ruthven	.15	.08	.05
137	John Castino RC	.15	.08	.05
138	Ross Baumgarten	.15	.08	.05
139	Dane Iorg RC	.15	.08	.05
140	Rich Gossage	.25	.13	.08
141	Gary Alexander	.15	.08	.05
142	Phil Huffman	.15	.08	.05
143	Bruce Bochte	.15	.08	.05
144	Steve Comer	.15	.08	.05
145	Darrell Evans	.15	.08	.05
146	Bob Welch	.15	.08	.05
147	Terry Puhl	.15	.08	.05
148	Manny Sanguillen	.15	.08	.05
149	Tom Hume	.15	.08	.05
150	Jason Thompson	.15	.08	.05
151	Tom Hausman	.15	.08	.05
152	John Fulgham	.15	.08	.05
153	Tim Blackwell	.15	.08	.05
154	Lary Sorensen	.15	.08	.05
155	Jerry Remy	.15	.08	.05
156	Tony Brizzolara	.15	.08	.05
157	Willie Wilson	.15	.08	.05
158	Rob Picciolo	.15	.08	.05
159	Ken Clay	.15	.08	.05
160	Eddie Murray	3.00	1.50	.90
161	Larry Christenson	.15	.08	.05
162	Bob Randall	.15	.08	.05
163	Steve Swisher	.15	.08	.05
164a	Greg Pryor (No name.)	200.00	100.00	60.00
164b	Greg Pryor (Name in blue.)	.15	.08	.05
165	Omar Moreno	.15	.08	.05
166	Glenn Abbott	.15	.08	.05
167	Jack Clark	.15	.08	.05
168	Rick Waits	.15	.08	.05
169	Luis Gomez	.15	.08	.05
170	Burt Hooton	.15	.08	.05
171	Fernando Gonzalez	.15	.08	.05
172	Ron Hodges	.15	.08	.05
173	John Henry Johnson	.15	.08	.05
174	Ray Knight	.15	.08	.05
175	Rick Reuschel	.15	.08	.05
176	Champ Summers	.15	.08	.05

No.	Player			
177	Dave Heaverlo	.15	.08	.05
178	Tim McCarver	.15	.08	.05
179	Ron Davis RC	.25	.13	.08
180	Warren Cromartie	.15	.08	.05
181	Moose Haas	.15	.08	.05
182	Ken Reitz	.15	.08	.05
183	Jim Anderson	.15	.08	.05
184	Steve Renko	.15	.08	.05
185	Hal McRae	.15	.08	.05
186	Junior Moore	.15	.08	.05
187	Alan Ashby	.15	.08	.05
188	Terry Crowley	.15	.08	.05
189	Kevin Kobel	.15	.08	.05
190	Buddy Bell	.15	.08	.05
191	Ted Martinez	.15	.08	.05
192	Braves Team(Bobby Cox)	.45	.25	.14
193	Dave Goltz	.15	.08	.05
194	Mike Easler	.15	.08	.05
195	John Montefusco	.15	.08	.05
196	Lance Parrish	.15	.08	.05
197	Byron McLaughlin	.15	.08	.05
198	Dell Alston	.15	.08	.05
199	Mike LaCoss	.15	.08	.05
200	Jim Rice	.30	.15	.09
201	Batting Leaders(Keith Hernandez, Fred Lynn)	.15	.08	.05
202	Home Run Leaders(Dave Kingman, Gorman Thomas)	.15	.08	.05
203	Runs Batted In Leaders(Don Baylor, Dave Winfield)	.35	.20	.11
204	Stolen Base Leaders(Omar Moreno, Willie Wilson)	.15	.08	.05
205	Victory Leaders(Mike Flanagan, Joe Niekro, Phil Niekro)	.25	.13	.08
206	Strikeout Leaders(J.R. Richard, Nolan Ryan)	3.50	1.75	1.00
207	ERA Leaders(Ron Guidry, J.R. Richard)	.25	.13	.08
208	Wayne Cage	.15	.08	.05
209	Von Joshua	.15	.08	.05
210	Steve Carlton	2.50	1.25	.70
211	Dave Skaggs	.15	.08	.05
212	Dave Roberts	.15	.08	.05
213	Mike Jorgensen	.15	.08	.05
214	Angels Team(Jim Fregosi)	.25	.13	.08
215	Sixto Lezcano	.15	.08	.05
216	Phil Mankowski	.15	.08	.05
217	Ed Halicki	.15	.08	.05
218	Jose Morales	.15	.08	.05
219	Steve Mingori	.15	.08	.05
220	Dave Concepcion	.15	.08	.05
221	Joe Cannon	.15	.08	.05
222	Ron Hassey RC	.25	.13	.08
223	Bob Sykes	.15	.08	.05
224	Willie Montanez	.15	.08	.05
225	Lou Piniella	.25	.13	.08
226	Bill Stein	.15	.08	.05
227	Len Barker	.15	.08	.05
228	Johnny Oates	.15	.08	.05
229	Jim Bibby	.15	.08	.05
230	Dave Winfield	2.50	1.25	.70
231	Steve McCatty	.15	.08	.05
232	Alan Trammell	.60	.30	.20
233	LaRue Washington	.15	.08	.05
234	Vern Ruhle	.15	.08	.05
235	Andre Dawson	2.50	1.50	.90
236	Marc Hill	.15	.08	.05
237	Scott McGregor	.15	.08	.05
238	Rob Wilfong	.15	.08	.05
239	Don Aase	.15	.08	.05
240	Dave Kingman	.15	.08	.05
241	Checklist 122-242	.15	.08	.05
242	Lamar Johnson	.15	.08	.05
243	Jerry Augustine	.15	.08	.05
244	Cardinals Team(Ken Boyer)	.25	.13	.08
245	Phil Niekro	2.00	1.00	.60
246	Tim Foli	.15	.08	.05
247	Frank Riccelli	.15	.08	.05
248	Jamie Quirk	.15	.08	.05
249	Jim Clancy	.15	.08	.05
250	Jim Kaat	.15	.08	.05
251	Kip Young	.15	.08	.05
252	Ted Cox	.15	.08	.05
253	John Montague	.15	.08	.05
254	Paul Dade	.15	.08	.05
255	Dusty Baker	.15	.08	.05
256	Roger Erickson	.15	.08	.05
257	Larry Herndon	.15	.08	.05
258	Paul Moskau	.15	.08	.05
259	Mets Team(Joe Torre)	.60	.30	.20
260	Al Oliver	.20	.10	.06
261	Dave Chalk	.15	.08	.05
262	Benny Ayala	.15	.08	.05
263	Dave LaRoche	.15	.08	.05
264	Bill Robinson	.15	.08	.05
265	Robin Yount	2.50	1.25	.70
266	Bernie Carbo	.15	.08	.05
267	Dan Schatzeder	.15	.08	.05
268	Rafael Landestoy	.15	.08	.05
269	Dave Tobik	.15	.08	.05
270	Mike Schmidt	4.50	2.25	1.25
271	Dick Drago	.15	.08	.05
272	Ralph Garr	.15	.08	.05
273	Eduardo Rodriguez	.15	.08	.05
274	Dale Murphy	1.50	.70	.45
275	Jerry Koosman	.15	.08	.05
276	Tom Veryzer	.15	.08	.05
277	Rick Bosetti	.15	.08	.05
278	Jim Spencer	.15	.08	.05
279	Rob Andrews	.15	.08	.05
280	Gaylord Perry	2.00	1.00	.60
281	Paul Blair	.15	.08	.05
282	Mariners Team(Darrell Johnson)	.25	.13	.08
283	John Ellis	.15	.08	.05
284	Larry Murray	.15	.08	.05
285	Don Baylor	.25	.13	.08
286	Darold Knowles	.15	.08	.05
287	John Lowenstein	.15	.08	.05
288	Dave Rozema	.15	.08	.05
289	Bruce Bochy	.15	.08	.05
290	Steve Garvey	1.00	.50	.30
291	Randy Scarbery	.15	.08	.05
292	Dale Berra	.15	.08	.05
293	Elias Sosa	.15	.08	.05
294	Charlie Spikes	.15	.08	.05
295	Larry Gura	.15	.08	.05
296	Dave Rader	.15	.08	.05
297	Tim Johnson	.15	.08	.05
298	Ken Holtzman	.15	.08	.05
299	Steve Henderson	.15	.08	.05
300	Ron Guidry	.25	.13	.08
301	Mike Edwards	.15	.08	.05
302	Dodgers Team(Tom Lasorda)	.60	.30	.20
303	Bill Castro	.15	.08	.05
304	Butch Wynegar	.15	.08	.05
305	Randy Jones	.15	.08	.05
306	Denny Walling	.15	.08	.05
307	Rick Honeycutt	.15	.08	.05
308	Mike Hargrove	.15	.08	.05
309	Larry McWilliams	.15	.08	.05
310	Dave Parker	.15	.08	.05
311	Roger Metzger	.15	.08	.05
312	Mike Barlow	.15	.08	.05
313	Johnny Grubb	.15	.08	.05
314	Tim Stoddard RC	.15	.08	.05
315	Steve Kemp	.15	.08	.05
316	Bob Lacey	.15	.08	.05
317	Mike Anderson	.15	.08	.05
318	Jerry Reuss	.15	.08	.05
319	Chris Speier	.15	.08	.05
320	Dennis Eckersley	2.00	1.00	.60
321	Keith Hernandez	.15	.08	.05
322	Claudell Washington	.15	.08	.05
323	Mick Kelleher	.15	.08	.05
324	Tom Underwood	.15	.08	.05
325	Dan Driessen	.15	.08	.05
326	Bo McLaughlin	.15	.08	.05
327	Ray Fosse	.15	.08	.05
328	Twins Team(Gene Mauch)	.25	.13	.08
329	Bert Roberge	.15	.08	.05
330	Al Cowens	.15	.08	.05
331	Rich Hebner	.15	.08	.05
332	Enrique Romo	.15	.08	.05
333	Jim Norris	.15	.08	.05
334	Jim Beattie	.15	.08	.05
335	Willie McCovey	2.50	1.25	.70
336	George Medich	.15	.08	.05
337	Carney Lansford	.15	.08	.05
338	Johnny Wockenfuss	.15	.08	.05
339	John D'Acquisto	.15	.08	.05
340	Ken Singleton	.15	.08	.05
341	Jim Essian	.15	.08	.05
342	Odell Jones	.15	.08	.05
343	Mike Vail	.15	.08	.05
344	Randy Lerch	.15	.08	.05
345	Larry Parrish	.15	.08	.05
346	Buddy Solomon	.15	.08	.05
347	Harry Chappas RC	.15	.08	.05
348	Checklist 243-363	.15	.08	.05
349	Jack Brohamer	.15	.08	.05
350	George Hendrick	.15	.08	.05
351	Bob Davis	.15	.08	.05
352	Dan Briggs	.15	.08	.05
353	Andy Hassler	.15	.08	.05
354	Rick Auerbach	.15	.08	.05
355	Gary Matthews	.15	.08	.05
356	Padres Team(Jerry Coleman)	.25	.13	.08
357	Bob McClure	.15	.08	.05
358	Lou Whitaker	.25	.13	.08
359	Randy Moffitt	.15	.08	.05
360	Darrell Porter	.15	.08	.05
361	Wayne Garland	.15	.08	.05
362	Danny Goodwin	.15	.08	.05
363	Wayne Gross	.15	.08	.05
364	Ray Burris	.15	.08	.05
365	Bobby Murcer	.25	.13	.08
366	Rob Dressler	.15	.08	.05
367	Billy Smith	.15	.08	.05
368	Willie Aikens RC	.20	.10	.06
369	Jim Kern	.15	.08	.05
370	Cesar Cedeno	.15	.08	.05
371	Jack Morris	.15	.08	.05
372	Joel Youngblood	.15	.08	.05
373	Dan Petry RC	.20	.10	.06
374	Jim Gantner	.15	.08	.05
375	Ross Grimsley	.15	.08	.05
376	Gary Allenson	.15	.08	.05
377	Junior Kennedy	.15	.08	.05
378	Jerry Mumphrey	.15	.08	.05
379	Kevin Bell	.15	.08	.05
380	Garry Maddox	.15	.08	.05
381	Cubs Team(Preston Gomez)	.25	.13	.08
382	Dave Freisleben	.15	.08	.05
383	Ed Ott	.15	.08	.05
384	Joey McLaughlin	.15	.08	.05
385	Enos Cabell	.15	.08	.05
386	Darrell Jackson	.15	.08	.05
387a	Fred Stanley (Name in yellow.)	200.00	100.00	60.00
387b	Fred Stanley (Name in red.)	.15	.08	.05
388	Mike Paxton	.15	.08	.05
389	Pete LaCock	.15	.08	.05
390	Fergie Jenkins	2.00	1.00	.60
391	Tony Armas	.15	.08	.05
392	Milt Wilcox	.15	.08	.05
393	Ozzie Smith	6.00	4.00	2.00
394	Reggie Cleveland	.15	.08	.05
395	Ellis Valentine	.15	.08	.05
396	Dan Meyer	.15	.08	.05
397	Roy Thomas	.15	.08	.05
398	Barry Foote	.15	.08	.05
399	Mike Proly	.15	.08	.05
400	George Foster	.15	.08	.05
401	Pete Falcone	.15	.08	.05
402	Merv Rettenmund	.15	.08	.05
403	Pete Redfern	.15	.08	.05
404	Orioles Team(Earl Weaver)	.60	.30	.20
405	Dwight Evans	.15	.08	.05
406	Paul Molitor	2.50	1.25	.70
407	Tony Solaita	.15	.08	.05
408	Bill North	.15	.08	.05
409	Paul Splittorff	.15	.08	.05
410	Bobby Bonds	.15	.08	.05
411	Frank LaCorte	.15	.08	.05
412	Thad Bosley	.15	.08	.05
413	Allen Ripley	.15	.08	.05
414	George Scott	.15	.08	.05
415	Bill Atkinson	.15	.08	.05
416	Tom Brookens RC	.15	.08	.05
417	Craig Chamberlain	.15	.08	.05
418	Roger Freed	.15	.08	.05
419	Vic Correll	.15	.08	.05
420	Butch Hobson	.15	.08	.05
421	Doug Bird	.15	.08	.05
422	Larry Milbourne	.15	.08	.05
423	Dave Frost	.15	.08	.05
424	Yankees Team(Dick Howser)	.45	.25	.14
425	Mark Belanger	.15	.08	.05
426	Grant Jackson	.15	.08	.05
427	Tom Hutton	.15	.08	.05
428	Pat Zachry	.15	.08	.05
429	Duane Kuiper	.15	.08	.05
430	Larry Hisle	.15	.08	.05
431	Mike Krukow	.15	.08	.05
432	Willie Norwood	.15	.08	.05
433	Rich Gale	.15	.08	.05
434	Johnnie LeMaster	.15	.08	.05
435	Don Gullett	.15	.08	.05
436	Billy Almon	.15	.08	.05
437	Joe Niekro	.15	.08	.05
438	Dave Revering	.15	.08	.05
439	Mike Phillips	.15	.08	.05
440	Don Sutton	2.00	1.00	.60
441	Eric Soderholm	.15	.08	.05
442	Jorge Orta	.15	.08	.05
443	Mike Parrott	.15	.08	.05
444	Alvis Woods	.15	.08	.05
445	Mark Fidrych	.25	.13	.08
446	Duffy Dyer	.15	.08	.05

#	Name			
447	Nino Espinosa	.15	.08	.05
448	Jim Wohlford	.15	.08	.05
449	Doug Bair	.15	.08	.05
450	George Brett	4.00	2.00	1.20
451	Indians Team (Dave Garcia)	.25	.13	.08
452	Steve Dillard	.15	.08	.05
453	Mike Bacsik	.15	.08	.05
454	Tom Donohue	.15	.08	.05
455	Mike Torrez	.15	.08	.05
456	Frank Taveras	.15	.08	.05
457	Bert Blyleven	1.00	.50	.30
458	Billy Sample	.15	.08	.05
459	Mickey Lolich	.15	.08	.05
460	Willie Randolph	.15	.08	.05
461	Dwayne Murphy	.15	.08	.05
462	Mike Sadek	.15	.08	.05
463	Jerry Royster	.15	.08	.05
464	John Denny	.15	.08	.05
465	Rick Monday	.15	.08	.05
466	Mike Squires	.15	.08	.05
467	Jesse Jefferson	.15	.08	.05
468	Aurelio Rodriguez	.15	.08	.05
469	Randy Niemann	.15	.08	.05
470	Bob Boone	.20	.10	.06
471	Hosken Powell	.15	.08	.05
472	Willie Hernandez	.15	.08	.05
473	Bump Wills	.15	.08	.05
474	Steve Busby	.15	.08	.05
475	Cesar Geronimo	.15	.08	.05
476	Bob Shirley	.15	.08	.05
477	Buck Martinez	.15	.08	.05
478	Gil Flores	.15	.08	.05
479	Expos Team (Dick Williams)	.25	.13	.08
480	Bob Watson	.15	.08	.05
481	Tom Paciorek	.15	.08	.05
482	Rickey Henderson **RC**	55.00	27.50	13.75
483	Bo Diaz	.15	.08	.05
484	Checklist 364-484	.15	.08	.05
485	Mickey Rivers	.15	.08	.05
486	Mike Tyson	.15	.08	.05
487	Wayne Nordhagen	.15	.08	.05
488	Roy Howell	.15	.08	.05
489	Preston Hanna	.15	.08	.05
490	Lee May	.15	.08	.05
491	Steve Mura	.15	.08	.05
492	Todd Cruz	.15	.08	.05
493	Jerry Martin	.15	.08	.05
494	Craig Minetto	.15	.08	.05
495	Bake McBride	.15	.08	.05
496	Silvio Martinez	.15	.08	.05
497	Jim Mason	.15	.08	.05
498	Danny Darwin	.15	.08	.05
499	Giants Team (Dave Bristol)	.25	.13	.08
500	Tom Seaver	2.00	1.50	.90
501	Rennie Stennett	.15	.08	.05
502	Rich Wortham	.15	.08	.05
503	Mike Cubbage	.15	.08	.05
504	Gene Garber	.15	.08	.05
505	Bert Campaneris	.15	.08	.05
506	Tom Buskey	.15	.08	.05
507	Leon Roberts	.15	.08	.05
508	U.L. Washington	.15	.08	.05
509	Ed Glynn	.15	.08	.05
510	Ron Cey	.15	.08	.05
511	Eric Wilkins	.15	.08	.05
512	Jose Cardenal	.15	.08	.05
513	Tom Dixon	.15	.08	.05
514	Steve Ontiveros	.15	.08	.05
515	Mike Caldwell	.15	.08	.05
516	Hector Cruz	.15	.08	.05
517	Don Stanhouse	.15	.08	.05
518	Nelson Norman	.15	.08	.05
519	Steve Nicosia	.15	.08	.05
520	Steve Rogers	.15	.08	.05
521	Ken Brett	.15	.08	.05
522	Jim Morrison	.15	.08	.05
523	Ken Henderson	.15	.08	.05
524	Jim Wright	.15	.08	.05
525	Clint Hurdle	.15	.08	.05
526	Phillies Team (Dallas Green)	.60	.30	.20
527	Doug Rau	.15	.08	.05
528	Adrian Devine	.15	.08	.05
529	Jim Barr	.15	.08	.05
530	Jim Sundberg	.15	.08	.05
531	Eric Rasmussen	.15	.08	.05
532	Willie Horton	.15	.08	.05
533	Checklist 485-605	.15	.08	.05
534	Andre Thornton	.15	.08	.05
535	Bob Forsch	.15	.08	.05
536	Lee Lacy	.15	.08	.05
537	Alex Trevino **RC**	.15	.08	.05
538	Joe Strain	.15	.08	.05
539	Rudy May	.15	.08	.05
540	Pete Rose	6.00	3.00	1.50
541	Miguel Dilone	.15	.08	.05
542	Joe Coleman	.15	.08	.05
543	Pat Kelly	.15	.08	.05
544	Rick Sutcliffe **RC**	2.00	1.00	.60
545	Jeff Burroughs	.15	.08	.05
546	Rick Langford	.15	.08	.05
547a	John Wathan (Name in yellow.)	200.00	100.00	60.00
547b	John Wathan (Name in red.)	.15	.08	.05
548	Dave Rajsich	.15	.08	.05
549	Larry Wolfe	.15	.08	.05
550	Ken Griffey	.15	.08	.05
551	Pirates Team (Chuck Tanner)	.25	.13	.08
552	Bill Nahorodny	.15	.08	.05
553	Dick Davis	.15	.08	.05
554	Art Howe	.15	.08	.05
555	Ed Figueroa	.15	.08	.05
556	Joe Rudi	.15	.08	.05
557	Mark Lee	.15	.08	.05
558	Alfredo Griffin	.15	.08	.05
559	Dale Murray	.15	.08	.05
560	Dave Lopes	.15	.08	.05
561	Eddie Whitson	.15	.08	.05
562	Joe Wallis	.15	.08	.05
563	Will McEnaney	.15	.08	.05
564	Rick Manning	.15	.08	.05
565	Dennis Leonard	.15	.08	.05
566	Bud Harrelson	.15	.08	.05
567	Skip Lockwood	.15	.08	.05
568	Gary Roenicke **RC**	.15	.08	.05
569	Terry Kennedy	.15	.08	.05
570	Roy Smalley	.15	.08	.05
571	Joe Sambito	.15	.08	.05
572	Jerry Morales	.15	.08	.05
573	Kent Tekulve	.15	.08	.05
574	Scot Thompson	.15	.08	.05
575	Ken Kravec	.15	.08	.05
576	Jim Dwyer	.15	.08	.05
577	Blue Jays Team (Bobby Mattick)	.25	.13	.08
578	Scott Sanderson	.15	.08	.05
579	Charlie Moore	.15	.08	.05
580	Nolan Ryan	14.00	7.50	3.75
581	Bob Bailor	.15	.08	.05
582	Brian Doyle	.15	.08	.05
583	Bob Stinson	.15	.08	.05
584	Kurt Bevacqua	.15	.08	.05
585	Al Hrabosky	.15	.08	.05
586	Mitchell Page	.15	.08	.05
587	Garry Templeton	.15	.08	.05
588	Greg Minton	.15	.08	.05
589	Chet Lemon	.15	.08	.05
590	Jim Palmer	2.50	1.25	.70
591	Rick Cerone	.15	.08	.05
592	Jon Matlack	.15	.08	.05
593	Jesus Alou	.15	.08	.05
594	Dick Tidrow	.15	.08	.05
595	Don Money	.15	.08	.05
596	Rick Matula	.15	.08	.05
597a	Tom Poquette (Name in yellow.)	200.00	100.00	60.00
597b	Tom Poquette (Name in red.)	.15	.08	.05
598	Fred Kendall	.15	.08	.05
599	Mike Norris	.15	.08	.05
600	Reggie Jackson	4.00	2.00	1.25
601	Buddy Schultz	.15	.08	.05
602	Brian Downing	.15	.08	.05
603	Jack Billingham	.15	.08	.05
604	Glenn Adams	.15	.08	.05
605	Terry Forster	.15	.08	.05
606	Reds Team (John McNamara)	.25	.13	.08
607	Woodie Fryman	.15	.08	.05
608	Alan Bannister	.15	.08	.05
609	Ron Reed	.15	.08	.05
610	Willie Stargell	2.50	1.25	.70
611	Jerry Garvin	.15	.08	.05
612	Cliff Johnson	.15	.08	.05
613	Randy Stein	.15	.08	.05
614	John Hiller	.15	.08	.05
615	Doug DeCinces	.15	.08	.05
616	Gene Richards	.15	.08	.05
617	Joaquin Andujar	.15	.08	.05
618	Bob Montgomery	.15	.08	.05
619	Sergio Ferrer	.15	.08	.05
620	Richie Zisk	.15	.08	.05
621	Bob Grich	.15	.08	.05
622	Mario Soto	.15	.08	.05
623	Gorman Thomas	.15	.08	.05
624	Lerrin LaGrow	.15	.08	.05
625	Chris Chambliss	.15	.08	.05
626	Tigers Team (Sparky Anderson)	.75	.40	.25
627	Pedro Borbon	.15	.08	.05
628	Doug Capilla	.15	.08	.05
629	Jim Todd	.15	.08	.05
630	Larry Bowa	.15	.08	.05
631	Mark Littell	.15	.08	.05
632	Barry Bonnell	.15	.08	.05
633	Bob Apodaca	.15	.08	.05
634	Glenn Borgmann	.15	.08	.05
635	John Candelaria	.15	.08	.05
636	Toby Harrah	.15	.08	.05
637	Joe Simpson	.15	.08	.05
638	Mark Clear **RC**	.15	.08	.05
639	Larry Biittner	.15	.08	.05
640	Mike Flanagan	.15	.08	.05
641	Ed Kranepool	.15	.08	.05
642	Ken Forsch	.15	.08	.05
643	John Mayberry	.15	.08	.05
644	Charlie Hough	.15	.08	.05
645	Rick Burleson	.15	.08	.05
646	Checklist 606-726	.15	.08	.05
647	Milt May	.15	.08	.05
648	Roy White	.15	.08	.05
649	Tom Griffin	.15	.08	.05
650	Joe Morgan	2.50	1.25	.70
651	Rollie Fingers	2.00	1.00	.60
652	Mario Mendoza	.15	.08	.05
653	Stan Bahnsen	.15	.08	.05
654	Bruce Boisclair	.15	.08	.05
655	Tug McGraw	.15	.08	.05
656	Larvell Blanks	.15	.08	.05
657	Dave Edwards	.15	.08	.05
658	Chris Knapp	.15	.08	.05
659	Brewers Team (George Bamberger)	.25	.13	.08
660	Rusty Staub	.15	.08	.05
661	Orioles Future Stars (Mark Corey, Dave Ford, Wayne Krenchicki)	.15	.08	.05
662	Red Sox Future Stars (Joel Finch, Mike O'Berry, Chuck Rainey)	.15	.08	.05
663	Angels Future Stars (Ralph Botting, Bob Clark, Dickie Thon **RC**)	.25	.13	.08
664	White Sox Future Stars (Mike Colbern, Guy Hoffman **RC**, Dewey Robinson)	.15	.08	.05
665	Indians Future Stars (Larry Andersen, Bobby Cuellar, Sandy Wihtol)	.15	.08	.05
666	Tigers Future Stars (Mike Chris, Al Greene, Bruce Robbins)	.15	.08	.05
667	Royals Future Stars (Renie Martin, Bill Paschall, Dan Quisenberry **RC**)	1.00	.50	.30
668	Brewers Future Stars (Danny Boitano, Willie Mueller, Lenn Sakata)	.15	.08	.05
669	Twins Future Stars (Dan Graham, Rick Sofield, Gary Ward **RC**)	.25	.13	.08
670	Yankees Future Stars (Bobby Brown, Brad Gulden, Darryl Jones)	.15	.08	.05
671	A's Future Stars (Derek Bryant, Brian Kingman, Mike Morgan **RC**)	.50	.25	.15
672	Mariners Future Stars (Charlie Beamon, Rodney Craig, Rafael Vasquez)	.15	.08	.05
673	Rangers Future Stars (Brian Allard, Jerry Don Gleaton, Greg Mahlberg)	.15	.08	.05
674	Blue Jays Future Stars (Butch Edge, Pat Kelly, Ted Wilborn)	.15	.08	.05
675	Braves Future Stars (Bruce Benedict, Larry Bradford, Eddie Miller)	.15	.08	.05
676	Cubs Future Stars (Dave Geisel, Steve Macko, Karl Pagel)	.15	.08	.05
677	Reds Future Stars (Art DeFreites, Frank Pastore **RC**, Harry Spilman)	.15	.08	.05
678	Astros Future Stars (Reggie Baldwin, Alan Knicely, Pete Ladd **RC**)	.15	.08	.05
679	Dodgers Future Stars (Joe Beckwith, Mickey Hatcher **RC**, Dave Patterson)	.25	.13	.08

680	Expos Future Stars(Tony Bernazard **RC**, Randy Miller, John Tamargo)	.15	.08	.05
681	Mets Future Stars(Dan Norman, Jesse Orosco **RC**, Mike Scott **RC**)	1.00	.50	.30
682	Phillies Future Stars (Ramon Aviles, Dickie Noles **RC**, Kevin Saucier)	.15	.08	.05
683	Pirates Future Stars (Dorian Boyland, Alberto Lois, Harry Saferight)	.15	.08	.05
684	Cardinals Future Stars (George Frazier, Tom Herr **RC**, Dan O'Brien)	.30	.15	.09
685	Padres Future Stars(Tim Flannery, Brian Greer, Jim Wilhelm)	.15	.08	.05
686	Giants Future Stars(Greg Johnston, Dennis Littlejohn, Phil Nastu)	.15	.08	.05
687	Mike Heath	.15	.08	.05
688	Steve Stone	.15	.08	.05
689	Red Sox Team(Don Zimmer)	.25	.13	.08
690	Tommy John	.25	.13	.08
691	Ivan DeJesus	.15	.08	.05
692	Rawly Eastwick	.15	.08	.05
693	Craig Kusick	.15	.08	.05
694	Jim Rooker	.15	.08	.05
695	Reggie Smith	.15	.08	.05
696	Julio Gonzalez	.15	.08	.05
697	David Clyde	.15	.08	.05
698	Oscar Gamble	.15	.08	.05
699	Floyd Bannister	.15	.08	.05
700	Rod Carew	2.50	1.25	.70
701	Ken Oberkfell **RC**	.15	.08	.05
702	Ed Farmer	.15	.08	.05
703	Otto Velez	.15	.08	.05
704	Gene Tenace	.15	.08	.05
705	Freddie Patek	.15	.08	.05
706	Tippy Martinez	.15	.08	.05
707	Elliott Maddox	.15	.08	.05
708	Bob Tolan	.15	.08	.05
709	Pat Underwood	.15	.08	.05
710	Graig Nettles	.25	.13	.08
711	Bob Galasso	.15	.08	.05
712	Rodney Scott	.15	.08	.05
713	Terry Whitfield	.15	.08	.05
714	Fred Norman	.15	.08	.05
715	Sal Bando	.15	.08	.05
716	Lynn McGlothen	.15	.08	.05
717	Mickey Klutts	.15	.08	.05
718	Greg Gross	.15	.08	.05
719	Don Robinson	.15	.08	.05
720	Carl Yastrzemski	3.00	1.50	.90
721	Paul Hartzell	.15	.08	.05
722	Jose Cruz	.15	.08	.05
723	Shane Rawley	.15	.08	.05
724	Jerry White	.15	.08	.05
725	Rick Wise	.15	.08	.05
726	Steve Yeager	.15	.08	.05

1980 Topps N.Y. Yankees Proof

One of the most popular proof cards of the era is this N.Y. Yankees team photo card with an inset photo of manager Billy Martin, who was fired in October, 1979, after punching a marshmellow salesman. By the time the cards were issued, Martin's name and photo had been replaced by rookie manager Dick Howser. The card is blank-backed and usually shows evidence of having been handcut from a proof sheet.

	NM	E	VG
N.Y. Yankees	200.00	100.00	60.00

1980 Topps Stickers Prototypes

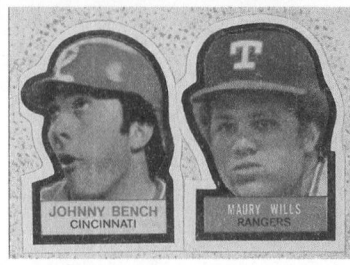

These appear to be prototypes for a Topp sticker issue that never materialized. In 3-1/2" x 2-1/2" format, the pieces have player picture pairs stuck onto a cardboard backing. Backs are blank. It is unknown if the listed examples, all of which are unique, comprise the entirety of the samples.

		NM	E	VG
Common Card:		125.00	60.00	35.00
(1)	Johnny Bench, Maury Wills	200.00	100.00	60.00
(2)	Nino Espinosa, Ron Cey	125.00	60.00	35.00
(3)	Dwight Evans, Carlton Fisk	150.00	75.00	45.00
(4)	Don (Ron) Guidry, Dave Parker	125.00	60.00	35.00
(5)	Reggie Jackson, J.R. Richard	200.00	100.00	60.00

1980 Topps Superstar 5x7 Photos

In actuality, these cards measure 4-7/8" x 6-7/8". These were another Topps "test" issue that was bought out almost entirely by speculators. The 60 cards have a color photo on the front and a blue ink facsimile autograph. Backs have the player's name, team, position and card number. The issue was printed on different cardboard stocks, with the first on thick cardboard with a white back and the second on thinner cardboard with a gray back. Prices below are for the more common gray backs; white backs are valued 2.5X-3X the figures shown, except for triple-print cards (indicated by "3P" in checklist), which are valued at about 7.5X the gray-back price in the white-back version. The white backs were test marketed in three-card cello packs in selected geographical areas.

		NM	E	VG
Complete Set, Gray Backs (60):		10.00	5.00	3.00
Complete Set, White Backs (60):		20.00	10.00	6.00
Common Player, Gray Back:		.25	.13	.08
Common Player, White Back:		.75	.40	.25
Wax Box (48):		10.00		
1	Willie Stargell	1.00	.50	.30
2	Mike Schmidt (3P)	1.50	.70	.45
3	Johnny Bench	1.00	.50	.30
4	Jim Palmer	.75	.40	.25
5	Jim Rice	1.00	.50	.30
6	Reggie Jackson (3P)	1.50	.70	.45
7	Ron Guidry	.45	.25	.14
8	Lee Mazzilli	.25	.13	.08
9	Don Baylor	.50	.25	.15
10	Fred Lynn	.25	.13	.08
11	Ken Singleton	.25	.13	.08
12	Rod Carew (3P)	.75	.40	.25
13	Steve Garvey (3P)	.50	.25	.15
14	George Brett (3P)	1.50	.70	.45
15	Tom Seaver	1.50	.70	.45
16	Dave Kingman	.25	.13	.08
17	Dave Parker (3P)	.25	.13	.08
18	Dave Winfield	1.00	.50	.30
19	Pete Rose	2.00	1.00	.60
20	Nolan Ryan	4.00	2.00	1.25
21	Graig Nettles	.25	.13	.08
22	Carl Yastrzemski	1.50	.70	.45
23	Tommy John	.40	.20	.12
24	George Foster	.25	.13	.08
25	J.R. Richard	.25	.13	.08
26	Keith Hernandez	.25	.13	.08
27	Bob Horner	.25	.13	.08
28	Eddie Murray	1.50	.70	.45
29	Steve Kemp	.25	.13	.08
30	Gorman Thomas	.25	.13	.08
31	Sixto Lezcano	.25	.13	.08
32	Bruce Sutter	1.00	.50	.30
33	Cecil Cooper	.25	.13	.08
34	Larry Bowa	.25	.13	.08
35	Al Oliver	.35	.20	.11
36	Ted Simmons	.25	.13	.08
37	Garry Templeton	.25	.13	.08
38	Jerry Koosman	.25	.13	.08
39	Darrell Porter	.25	.13	.08
40	Roy Smalley	.25	.13	.08
41	Craig Swan	.25	.13	.08
42	Jason Thompson	.25	.13	.08
43	Andre Thornton	.25	.13	.08
44	Rick Manning	.25	.13	.08
45	Kent Tekulve	.25	.13	.08
46	Phil Niekro	.75	.40	.25
47	Buddy Bell	.25	.13	.08
48	Randy Jones	.25	.13	.08
49	Brian Downing	.25	.13	.08
50	Amos Otis	.25	.13	.08
51	Rick Bosetti	.25	.13	.08
52	Gary Carter	.75	.40	.25
53	Larry Parrish	.25	.13	.08
54	Jack Clark	.25	.13	.08
55	Bruce Bochte	.25	.13	.08
56	Cesar Cedeno	.25	.13	.08
57	Chet Lemon	.25	.13	.08
58	Dave Revering	.25	.13	.08
59	Vida Blue	.25	.13	.08
60	Davey Lopes	.25	.13	.08

1980 Topps Team Checklist Sheet

This uncut sheet of 26 1980 Topps team cards was available via a mail-in offer. The sheet was mailed with two folds and includes an offer to picture yourself on a baseball card. The sheet cards are printed on lighter card stock.

	NM	E	VG
Uncut Sheet	15.00	7.50	4.50

1980 Topps Test Coins

These silver-dollar size (1-3/8" diameter) metal coins appear to have been a Topps test issue. The coins have a player portrait at center on obverse. On reverse center is player personal data and a Topps copyright line. Coins have been seen in compositions resembling bronze, silver and gold. Some of the coins have a hole at top.

	NM	E	VG
Rod Carew	150.00	75.00	45.00
Steve Garvey	150.00	75.00	45.00
Reggie Jackson	300.00	150.00	90.00

1953 Top Taste Bread Milwaukee Braves

This series of black-and-white mini-posters (8-1/2" x 11-1/4") depicts members of the 1953 Braves holding loaves of bread. They were probably intended for grocery store window or bakery aisle display. Backs are blank. It's unknown how many players are in the set. See also, Pictsweet Milwaukee Braves.

Common Player:	NM	E	VG
	150.00	75.00	45.00
(1) Lew Burdette	150.00	75.00	45.00
(2) George Crowe	150.00	75.00	45.00
(3) Andy Pafko	150.00	75.00	45.00
(4) Bucky Walters	150.00	75.00	45.00

1976 Towne Club discs

One of several regional sponsors of player disc sets in 1976 was the Towne Club Pop Centers chain. The discs are 3-3/8" diameter with a black-and-white player portrait photo in the center of the baseball design. A line of red stars is above, while the left and right panels feature one of several bright colors. Produced by Michael Schecter Associates under license from the Major League Baseball Players Association, the player photos have had uniform and cap logos removed. Backs are printed in red. The unnumbered checklist here is presented in alphabetical order.

	NM	E	VG
Complete Set (70):	50.00	25.00	15.00
Common Player:	1.00	.50	.30
(1) Henry Aaron	10.00	5.00	3.00
(2) Johnny Bench	5.00	2.50	1.50
(3) Vida Blue	1.00	.50	.30
(4) Larry Bowa	1.00	.50	.30
(5) Lou Brock	4.00	2.00	1.25
(6) Jeff Burroughs	1.00	.50	.30
(7) John Candelaria	1.00	.50	.30
(8) Jose Cardenal	1.00	.50	.30
(9) Rod Carew	4.00	2.00	1.25
(10) Steve Carlton	4.00	2.00	1.25
(11) Dave Cash	1.00	.50	.30
(12) Cesar Cedeno	1.00	.50	.30
(13) Ron Cey	1.00	.50	.30
(14) Carlton Fisk	4.00	2.00	1.25
(15) Tito Fuentes	1.00	.50	.30
(16) Steve Garvey	3.00	1.50	.90
(17) Ken Griffey	1.00	.50	.30
(18) Don Gullett	1.00	.50	.30
(19) Willie Horton	1.00	.50	.30
(20) Al Hrabosky	1.00	.50	.30
(21) Catfish Hunter	4.00	2.00	1.25
(22) Reggie Jackson (A's)	7.50	3.75	2.25
(23) Randy Jones	1.00	.50	.30
(24) Jim Kaat	1.00	.50	.30
(25) Don Kessinger	1.00	.50	.30
(26) Dave Kingman	1.00	.50	.30
(27) Jerry Koosman	1.00	.50	.30
(28) Mickey Lolich	1.00	.50	.30
(29) Greg Luzinski	1.00	.50	.30
(30) Fred Lynn	1.00	.50	.30
(31) Bill Madlock	1.00	.50	.30
(32) Carlos May	1.00	.50	.30
(33) John Mayberry	1.00	.50	.30
(34) Bake McBride	1.00	.50	.30
(35) Doc Medich	1.00	.50	.30
(36) Andy Messersmith	1.00	.50	.30
(37) Rick Monday	1.00	.50	.30
(38) John Montefusco	1.00	.50	.30
(39) Jerry Morales	1.00	.50	.30
(40) Joe Morgan	4.00	2.00	1.25
(41) Thurman Munson	5.00	2.50	1.50
(42) Bobby Murcer	1.00	.50	.30
(43) Al Oliver	1.00	.50	.30
(44) Jim Palmer	4.00	2.00	1.25
(45) Dave Parker	1.00	.50	.30
(46) Tony Perez	4.00	2.00	1.25
(47) Jerry Reuss	1.00	.50	.30
(48) Brooks Robinson	5.00	2.50	1.50
(49) Frank Robinson	5.00	2.50	1.50
(50) Steve Rogers	1.00	.50	.30
(51) Pete Rose	10.00	5.00	3.00
(52) Nolan Ryan	20.00	10.00	6.00
(53) Manny Sanguillen	1.00	.50	.30
(54) Mike Schmidt	7.50	3.75	2.25
(55) Tom Seaver	5.00	2.50	1.50
(56) Ted Simmons	1.00	.50	.30
(57) Reggie Smith	1.00	.50	.30
(58) Willie Stargell	4.00	2.00	1.25
(59) Rusty Staub	1.50	.70	.45
(60) Rennie Stennett	1.00	.50	.30
(61) Don Sutton	4.00	2.00	1.25
(62) Andy Thornton	1.00	.50	.30
(63) Luis Tiant	1.00	.50	.30
(64) Joe Torre	2.50	1.25	.70
(65) Mike Tyson	1.00	.50	.30
(66) Bob Watson	1.00	.50	.30
(67) Wilbur Wood	1.00	.50	.30
(68) Jimmy Wynn	1.00	.50	.30
(69) Carl Yastrzemski	6.00	3.00	1.75
(70) Richie Zisk	1.00	.50	.30

1910 Toy Town Post Office

Rather than a card issuer, this enigmatic rubber-stamp has been found on the backs of dozens of 1910-era baseball cards. Measuring 1/2" in diameter the seal is in purple ink. At center is a barred circle with "TOY TOWN" above and "POST OFFICE" below. The stamp was part of a Milton Bradley post office toy set and has been seen on different types of cards that eventually made their way into the hobby. On low-grade cards, the stamp neither greatly adds nor detracts from the value of the card on which it is placed.

(See individual card issuers for base values.)

1965 Trade Bloc Minnesota Twins

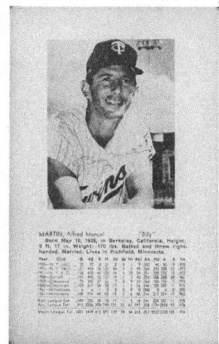

These cards were produced as part of a baseball game which was marketed at Metropolitan Stadium for $1. The blank-back cards measure 2-1/4" x 3-1/2" and are printed in either blue or sepia tones. Besides Twins players and staff, the set includes cards of various team souvenir items as well as old Met Stadium. Besides the player photo, cards include a facsimile autograph, stats and personal data. The unnumbered cards are checklisted here in alphabetical order.

	NM	E	VG
Complete Set (52):	1,200	600.00	350.00
Common Player:	30.00	15.00	9.00
Common Non-player Card:	10.00	5.00	3.00
(1) Bernard Allen	30.00	15.00	9.00
(2) Bob Allison	40.00	20.00	6.00
(3) Earl Battey	30.00	15.00	9.00
(4) Dave Boswell	30.00	15.00	9.00
(5) Gerald Fosnow	30.00	15.00	9.00
(6) James Grant	30.00	15.00	9.00
(7) Calvin Griffith	20.00	20.00	6.00
(8) Jimmie Hall	30.00	15.00	9.00
(9) Jim Kaat	50.00	15.00	7.50
(10) Harmon Killebrew	120.00	60.00	36.00
(11) Jerry Kindall	30.00	15.00	9.00
(12) Johnny Klippstein	30.00	15.00	9.00
(13) Frank Kostro	30.00	15.00	9.00
(14) James Lemon	30.00	15.00	9.00
(15) George "Doc" Lentz	30.00	15.00	9.00
(16) Alfred Martin (Billy)	30.00	15.00	9.00
(17) Sam Mele	30.00	15.00	9.00
(18) Donald Mincher	30.00	15.00	9.00
(19) Harold Naragon	30.00	15.00	9.00
(20) Melvin Nelson	30.00	15.00	9.00
(21) Joseph Nossek	30.00	15.00	9.00
(22) Pedro Oliva (Tony)	80.00	40.00	24.00
(23) Camilo Pascual	20.00	10.00	6.00
(24) James Perry	30.00	15.00	9.00
(25) Bill Pleis	30.00	15.00	9.00
(26) Richard Rollins	30.00	15.00	9.00
(27) John Sain	30.00	15.00	9.00
(28) John Sevcik	30.00	15.00	9.00
(29) Richard Stigman	30.00	15.00	9.00
(30) Sandy Valdespino	30.00	15.00	9.00
(31) Zoilo Versalles	50.00	25.00	7.50
(32) Allan Worthington	30.00	15.00	9.00
(33) Gerald Zimmerman	30.00	15.00	9.00
(34) Metropolitan Stadium	10.00	5.00	3.00
(35) L.A. Angels Logo	10.00	5.00	3.00
(36) K.C. Athletics Logo	10.00	5.00	3.00
(37) Cleveland Indians Logo	10.00	5.00	3.00
(38) Baltimore Orioles Logo	10.00	5.00	3.00
(39) Boston Red Sox Logo	10.00	5.00	3.00
(40) Washington Senators Logo	10.00	5.00	3.00
(41) Detroit Tigers Logo	10.00	5.00	3.00
(42) Minnesota Twins Logo	10.00	5.00	3.00
(43) Chicago White Sox Logo	10.00	5.00	3.00
(44) N.Y. Yankees Logo	10.00	5.00	3.00
(45) Twins Autographed Ball	10.00	5.00	3.00
(46) Twins Autographed Bat	10.00	5.00	3.00
(47) Twins Bobbin' Head Doll	10.00	5.00	3.00
(48) Twins Cap	10.00	5.00	3.00
(49) Twins Pennant	10.00	5.00	3.00
(50) Twins Scorebook	10.00	5.00	3.00
(51) Twins Warmup Jacket	10.00	5.00	3.00
(52) Twins Yearbook	10.00	5.00	3.00

1964 Transfer-ette Chicago Cubs Iron-ons

This novelty item features artist-rendered portraits of Cubs players which were designed to be transferred to t-shirts, notebook covers or other items via an iron-on process. Each package contains three sheets of nine images; one each in blue, black and red. The sheets are about 8-3/8" x 10-3/4" with each player image about 2-1/2" x 2-3/4". According to the packaging, other teams were planned, along with larger two-color player portraits.

	NM	E	VG
Complete Set:	50.00	25.00	15.00

BLACK SHEET
Ernie Banks
Dick Bertell
John Boccabella
Glen Hobbie
Calvin Koonce
Merritt Ranew
Andre Rodgers
Ron Santo
Jim Stewart
BLUE SHEET
Steve Boros
Lou Brock
Bob Buhl
Ellis Burton
Bill Cowan
Dick Ellsworth
Don Elston
Bob Kennedy
Jimmie Schaffer
RED SHEET
Tom Baker
Jim Brewer
Leo Burke
Larry Jackson
Don Landrum
Paul Toth
Jack Warner
Billy Williams
Chicago Cubs Logo

1964 Transfer-ette Chicago White Sox Iron-ons

This novelty item features artist-rendered portraits of White Sox players which were designed to be transferred to t-shirts, notebook covers or other items via an iron-on process. Each package contains three sheets of nine images; one each in blue, black and red. The sheets are about 8-3/8" x 10-3/4" with each player image about 2-1/2" x 2-3/4". According to the packaging, other teams were planned, along with larger two-color player portraits.

	NM	E	VG
Complete Set:	40.00	20.00	12.00

BLACK SHEET
Jim Brosnan
Don Buford

John Buzhardt
Joe Cunningham
Jim Golden
Joel Horlen
Charlie Maxwell
Dave Nicholson
Gene Stephens
BLUE SHEET
Fritz Ackley
Frank Bauman (Baumann)
Camilo Carreon
Dave DeBusschere
Ed Fisher
Mike Joyce
J.C. Martin
Tom McCraw
Hoyt Wilhelm
RED SHEET
Ron Hansen
Ray Herbert
Mike Hershberger
Jim Landis
Gary Peters
Floyd Robinson
Pete Ward
Al Weis
White Sox Logo

1969 Transogram

These 2-1/2" x 3-1/2" cards were printed on the back of toy baseball player statue boxes. The cards feature a color photo of the player surrounded by a rounded white border. Below the photo is the player's name in red and his team and other personal details all printed in black. The overall background is yellow. The cards were designed to be cut off the box, but collectors prefer to find the box intact and, better still, with the statue inside. While the cards themselves are not numbered, there is a number on each box's end flap, which is the order in which the cards are checklisted here. Three-player boxes were also sold.

		NM	E	VG
	CUT CARD OR STATUE			
(1)	Joe Azcue	12.50	6.25	3.75
(2)	Willie Horton	12.50	6.25	3.75
(3)	Luis Tiant	12.50	6.25	3.75
(4)	Denny McLain	12.50	6.25	3.75
(5)	Jose Cardenal	12.50	6.25	3.75
(6)	Al Kaline	30.00	15.00	9.00
(7)	Tony Oliva	15.00	7.50	4.50
(8)	Blue Moon Odom	12.50	6.25	3.75
(9)	Cesar Tovar	12.50	6.25	3.75
(10)	Rick Monday	12.50	6.25	3.75
(11)	Harmon Killebrew	25.00	12.50	7.50
(12)	Danny Cater	12.50	6.25	3.75
(13)	Brooks Robinson	35.00	17.50	10.00
(14)	Jim Fregosi	12.50	6.25	3.75
(15)	Dave McNally	12.50	6.25	3.75
(16)	Frank Robinson	35.00	17.50	10.00
(17)	Bobby Knoop	12.50	6.25	3.75
(18)	Rick Reichardt	12.50	6.25	3.75
(19)	Carl Yastrzemski	35.00	17.50	10.00
(20)	Pete Ward	12.50	6.25	3.75
(21)	Rico Petrocelli	12.50	6.25	3.75
(22)	Tommy John	15.00	7.50	4.50
(23)	Ken Harrelson	12.50	6.25	3.75
(24)	Luis Aparicio	25.00	12.50	7.50
(25)	Mike Epstein	12.50	6.25	3.75
(26)	Roy White	12.50	6.25	3.75
(27)	Camilo Pascual	12.50	6.25	3.75
(28)	Mel Stottlemyre	12.50	6.25	3.75
(29)	Frank Howard	15.00	7.50	4.50
(30)	Mickey Mantle	300.00	150.00	90.00
(31)	Lou Brock	25.00	12.50	7.50
(32)	Juan Marichal	25.00	12.50	7.50
(33)	Bob Gibson	25.00	12.50	7.50
(34)	Willie Mays	75.00	40.00	24.00
(35)	Tim McCarver	15.00	7.50	4.50
(36)	Willie McCovey	25.00	12.50	7.50
(37)	Don Wilson	12.50	6.25	3.75
(38)	Billy Williams	25.00	12.50	7.50

(39)	Dan Staub (Rusty)	15.00	7.50	4.50
(40)	Ernie Banks	45.00	22.50	13.50
(41)	Jim Wynn	12.50	6.25	3.75
(42)	Ron Santo	15.00	7.50	4.50
(43)	Tom Haller	12.50	6.25	3.75
(44)	Ron Swoboda	12.50	6.25	3.75
(45)	Willie Davis	12.50	6.25	3.75
(46)	Jerry Koosman	12.50	6.25	3.75
(47)	Jim Lefebvre	12.50	6.25	3.75
(48)	Tom Seaver	30.00	15.00	9.00
(49)	Joe Torre (Atlanta)	20.00	10.00	6.00
(50)	Tony Perez	25.00	12.50	7.50
(51)	Felipe Alou	12.50	6.25	3.75
(52)	Lee May	12.50	6.25	3.75
(53)	Hank Aaron	75.00	30.00	18.00
(54)	Pete Rose	75.00	30.00	18.00
(55)	Cookie Rojas	12.50	6.25	3.75
(56)	Roberto Clemente	125.00	65.00	39.00
(57)	Richie Allen	15.00	7.50	4.50
(58)	Matty Alou	12.50	6.25	3.75
(59)	Johnny Callison	12.50	6.25	3.75
(60)	Bill Mazeroski	25.00	12.50	7.50
	COMPLETE BOX W/STATUE			
(1)	Joe Azcue	85.00	42.50	25.00
(2)	Willie Horton	85.00	42.50	25.00
(3)	Luis Tiant	85.00	42.50	25.00
(4)	Denny McLain	85.00	42.50	25.00
(5)	Jose Cardenal	85.00	42.50	25.00
(6)	Al Kaline	175.00	85.00	50.00
(7)	Tony Oliva	100.00	50.00	30.00
(8)	Blue Moon Odom	85.00	42.50	25.00
(9)	Cesar Tovar	85.00	42.50	25.00
(10)	Rick Monday	85.00	42.50	25.00
(11)	Harmon Killebrew	200.00	100.00	60.00
(12)	Danny Cater	85.00	42.50	25.00
(13)	Brooks Robinson	250.00	125.00	75.00
(14)	Jim Fregosi	85.00	42.50	25.00
(15)	Dave McNally	85.00	42.50	25.00
(16)	Frank Robinson	250.00	125.00	75.00
(17)	Bobby Knoop	85.00	42.50	25.00
(18)	Rick Reichardt	85.00	42.50	25.00
(19)	Carl Yastrzemski	300.00	150.00	90.00
(20)	Pete Ward	85.00	42.50	25.00
(21)	Rico Petrocelli	85.00	42.50	25.00
(22)	Tommy John	120.00	60.00	36.00
(23)	Ken Harrelson	85.00	42.50	25.00
(24)	Luis Aparicio	175.00	85.00	50.00
(25)	Mike Epstein	85.00	42.50	25.00
(26)	Roy White	85.00	42.50	25.00
(27)	Camilo Pascual	85.00	42.50	25.00
(28)	Mel Stottlemyre	85.00	42.50	25.00
(29)	Frank Howard	100.00	50.00	30.00
(30)	Mickey Mantle	850.00	425.00	255.00
(31)	Lou Brock	175.00	85.00	50.00
(32)	Juan Marichal	175.00	85.00	50.00
(33)	Bob Gibson	175.00	85.00	50.00
(34)	Willie Mays	400.00	200.00	120.00
(35)	Tim McCarver	100.00	50.00	30.00
(36)	Willie McCovey	175.00	85.00	50.00
(37)	Don Wilson	85.00	42.50	25.00
(38)	Billy Williams	175.00	85.00	50.00
(39)	Dan Staub (Rusty)	120.00	60.00	36.00
(40)	Ernie Banks	350.00	175.00	100.00
(41)	Jim Wynn	85.00	42.50	25.00
(42)	Ron Santo	120.00	60.00	36.00
(43)	Tom Haller	85.00	42.50	25.00
(44)	Ron Swoboda	85.00	42.50	25.00
(45)	Willie Davis	85.00	42.50	25.00
(46)	Jerry Koosman	120.00	60.00	36.00
(47)	Jim Lefebvre	85.00	42.50	25.00
(48)	Tom Seaver	200.00	100.00	60.00
(49)	Joe Torre (Atlanta)	100.00	50.00	30.00
(50)	Tony Perez	175.00	85.00	50.00
(51)	Felipe Alou	100.00	50.00	30.00
(52)	Lee May	85.00	42.50	25.00
(53)	Hank Aaron	400.00	200.00	120.00
(54)	Pete Rose	400.00	200.00	120.00
(55)	Cookie Rojas	85.00	42.50	25.00
(56)	Roberto Clemente	450.00	225.00	135.00
(57)	Richie Allen	100.00	50.00	30.00
(58)	Matty Alou	85.00	42.50	25.00
(59)	Johnny Callison	85.00	42.50	25.00
(60)	Bill Mazeroski	175.00	85.00	50.00

1970 Transogram

The 1970 Transogram cards were found printed on boxes of three Transogram baseball player statues. The individual player cards are slightly larger than 1969's, at 2-9/16" x 3-1/2". The 30-card set has the same pictures as the 1969 set except for Joe Torre. All players in the '70 set were also in the '69 Transogram issue except for Reggie Jackson, Sam McDowell and Boog Powell. Each box contains a side panel with a series number and 1" x 1-1/4" portrait photos of the players in the series. Prices shown are for cards cut from the box.

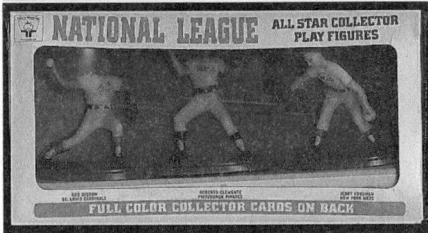

		NM	E	VG
Complete Set (30):		550.00	275.00	175.00
Complete Set, Boxes/Statues (10):		2,255	1,100	650.00
Common Player:		10.00	5.00	3.00
	Series 1 Boxed Set:	400.00	200.00	120.00
(1)	Pete Rose	50.00	25.00	15.00
(2)	Willie Mays	60.00	30.00	18.00
(3)	Cleon Jones	10.00	5.00	3.00
	Series 2 Boxed Set:	160.00	80.00	48.00
(4)	Ron Santo	15.00	7.50	4.50
(5)	Willie Davis	10.00	5.00	3.00
(6)	Willie McCovey	17.50	8.75	5.25
	Series 3 Boxed Set:	275.00	135.00	82.00
(7)	Juan Marichal	17.50	8.75	5.25
(8)	Joe Torre (St. Louis)	15.00	7.50	4.50
(9)	Ernie Banks	30.00	15.00	9.00
	Series 4 Boxed Set:	375.00	185.00	110.00
(10)	Hank Aaron	60.00	30.00	18.00
(11)	Jim Wynn	10.00	5.00	3.00
(12)	Tom Seaver	25.00	12.50	7.50
	Series 5 Boxed Set:	450.00	225.00	135.00
(13)	Bob Gibson	17.50	8.75	5.25
(14)	Roberto Clemente	100.00	50.00	30.00
(15)	Jerry Koosman	10.00	5.00	3.00
	Series 11 Boxed Set:	300.00	150.00	90.00
(16)	Denny McLain	12.50	6.25	3.75
(17)	Reggie Jackson	30.00	15.00	9.00
(18)	Boog Powell	15.00	7.50	4.50
	Series 12 Boxed Set:	175.00	87.00	52.00
(19)	Frank Robinson	25.00	12.50	7.50
(20)	Frank Howard	10.00	5.00	3.00
(21)	Rick Reichardt	10.00	5.00	3.00
	Series 13 Boxed Set:	225.00	110.00	67.00
(22)	Carl Yastrzemski	25.00	12.50	7.50
(23)	Tony Oliva	15.00	7.50	4.50
(24)	Mel Stottlemyre	10.00	5.00	3.00
	Series 14 Boxed Set:	180.00	90.00	54.00
(25)	Al Kaline	25.00	12.50	7.50
(26)	Jim Fregosi	10.00	5.00	3.00
(27)	Sam McDowell	10.00	5.00	3.00
	Series 15 Boxed Set:	180.00	90.00	54.00
(28)	Blue Moon Odom	10.00	5.00	3.00
(29)	Harmon Killebrew	25.00	12.50	7.50
(30)	Rico Petrocelli	10.00	5.00	3.00

1970 Transogram Mets

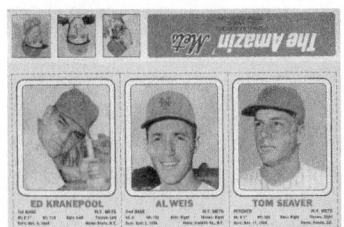

This Transogram set features members of the World Champion N.Y. Mets. Like the other 1970 Transograms, the issue was packaged in a three-statue cardboard box with cellophane front panel and cards printed on the back. Player cards are 2-9/16" x 3-1/2" and retain the basic format of Transogram cards of 1969-70: a color photo with player name in red and team, position and biographical details in black. Backs are blank. Values shown here are for cards cut from the box. Complete unopened boxes are worth 3-4X the figures shown.

	NM	E	VG

Complete Boxed Set (5):	1,400	700.00	425.00
Complete Panel Set (5):	650.00	325.00	200.00
Complete Card Set (15):	350.00	175.00	100.00
Common Player:	12.50	6.25	3.75
Series 21 Boxed Set	225.00	110.00	65.00
Series 21 Uncut Box/			
Panel	125.00	65.00	35.00
(1) Ed Kranepool	12.50	6.25	3.75
(2) Al Weis	12.50	6.25	3.75
(3) Tom Seaver	35.00	17.50	10.00
Series 22 Boxed Set	125.00	65.00	35.00
Series 22 Uncut Box/			
Panel	60.00	30.00	18.00
(4) Ken Boswell	12.50	6.25	3.75
(5) Jerry Koosman	12.50	6.25	3.75
(6) Jerry Grote	12.50	6.25	3.75
Series 23 Boxed Set	125.00	65.00	35.00
Series 23 Uncut Box/			
Panel	60.00	30.00	18.00
(7) Art Shamsky	12.50	6.25	3.75
(8) Gary Gentry	12.50	6.25	3.75
(9) Tommie Agee	12.50	6.25	3.75
Series 24 Boxed Set	685.00	340.00	200.00
Series 24 Uncut Box/			
Panel	350.00	175.00	100.00
(10) Nolan Ryan	225.00	110.00	65.00
(11) Tug McGraw	12.50	6.25	3.75
(12) Cleon Jones	12.50	6.25	3.75
Series 25 Boxed Set	150.00	75.00	45.00
Series 25 Uncut Box/			
Panel	60.00	30.00	18.00
(13) Ron Swoboda	12.50	6.25	3.75
(14) Bud Harrelson	12.50	6.25	3.75
(15) Donn Clendenon	12.50	6.25	3.75

1920s Otto Treulich & Son

 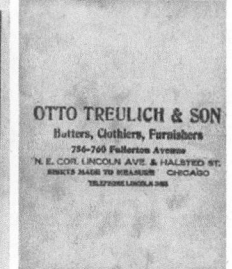

This promotional photocard was issued, according to the blue rubber-stamped advertising on back, by Chicago clothier Otto Treulich & Son. Front of the approximately 2-3/4" x 3-1/2" card has a black-and-white studio portrait of Cubs pitcher Grover Cleveland Alexander, dressed to the nines (presumably in the haberdashery of the sponsor), and bearing a facsimile autograph.

	NM	E	VG
Grover Alexander	400.00	200.00	120.00

1909 T.T.T. Cigarettes (T204)

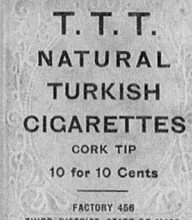 

This is one of two brands of cigarette advertising found on the backs of the ornate, gold-trimmed T204 cards. The initials stand for T.T. Tinayens, the Boston firm which also produced Ramly cigarettes, more commonly found mentioned on the cards' backs. In recent years collectors have begun paying a premium as high as 4-5X for the T.T.T. versions.

Premium: 4-5X

(See checklist under Ramly Cigarettes listing.)

1888 Rafael Tuck & Sons Artistic Series Baseball

This series of die-cut color lithographed player figures does not represent actual players, but rather generic figures in late 19th Century uniforms labeled with the names of vari-

ous major league teams of the era. The actual date of issue is unknown. The cardboard figures were issued in a sheet of 20 with duplicates. Individual figures vary in size with a typical piece about 1-1/2" wide and 2-3/4". Players are shown in batting, throwing and fielding poses. The set was lithographed in Germany and published in England by Rafael Tuck & Sons, a famous postcard publisher.

		NM	E	VG
Complete Set (10):		3,000	1,500	900.00
Common Card:		325.00	160.00	95.00
(1)	Baltimore	325.00	160.00	95.00
(2)	Boston	325.00	160.00	95.00
(3)	Brooklyn	325.00	160.00	95.00
(4)	Chicago	325.00	160.00	95.00
(5)	Detroit	325.00	160.00	95.00
(6)	Indianapolis	325.00	160.00	95.00
(7)	New York	325.00	160.00	95.00
(8)	Philadelphia	325.00	160.00	95.00
(9)	Pittsburgh	325.00	160.00	95.00
(10)	St. Louis	325.00	160.00	95.00

1925 Turf Cigarettes

"Sports Records" is the name of a two-series, 50-card issue by Turf Cigarettes. The last card in the set depicts George Sisler (though not named) on the front in a color action scene. Black-and-white back of the card describes Sisler's batting prowess. Like other British tobacco cards of the era, size is 2-5/8" x 1-3/8".

		NM	E	VG
50	Baseball(George Sisler)	125.00	45.00	25.00

1909-11 Ty Cobb Tobacco (T206)

Much rarer than the famed Honus Wagner card from the related cigarette card series known collectively as T206, the Ty Cobb brand tobacco back was known in only about half a dozen collections until June 1997 when a find of five lower-grade specimens was auctioned. Because T206 was generally collected by front design, rather than back, through most of the hobby's history, it has only been in recent years that the value of the "Ty Cobb-back" T206 has begun to approach the other great rarities of the series. The only front known with a Cobb tobacco back is the red-background portrait. Some of the extant examples appear to have been hand-cut from a sheet. In April 2002 a PSA-graded Good example sold at an auction for $18,055. Most recently, an SGC-graded card sold at an auction for $25,000 in May 2005, and another sold at an auction for $24,655 in November 2005.

SGC Fair NM 77,675, SGC Authentic 51,880

U

1906 Ullman Postcards

The designation of Giants' players as "World's Champions" dates this issue to 1906. The 3-1/2" x 5-1/2" cards have a black-and-white photo surrounded by a greenish or reddish-brown tone wooden-look frame with a plaque printed in the bottom border. Backs are printed in brown with typical postcard markings and include mention of "Ullman's 'Art Frame' Series." This checklist is likely not complete. The card of "Harry" (name actually Henry) Mathewson is the only known baseball card appearance of Christy's kid brother.

		NM	E	VG
Common Player:		2,100	1,050	600.00
(1)	Leon Ames	2,100	1,050	600.00
(2)	Mike Donlin	2,100	1,050	600.00
(3)	George Ferguson	2,100	1,050	600.00
(4)	Matty Fitzgerald	2,100	1,050	600.00
(5)	Billy Gilbert	2,100	1,050	600.00
(6)	Christy Matthewson (Mathewson)	9,800	5,000	3,000
(7)	Harry (Henry) Mathewson	1,200	600.00	360.00
(8)	Dan McGann (McGann on 1st Base.)	2,100	1,050	600.00
(9)	"Iron Arm" McGinnity	2,650	1,300	700.00
(10)	Manager McGraw	4,250	2,125	1,275
(11)	Strang and Bowerman(Sammy Strang, Frank Bowerman)	2,250	1,125	675.00
(12)	Hooks Wiltse	2,100	1,050	600.00
(13)	1906 National League Champion Chicago, Cubs			

1933 Uncle Jacks Candy

One of the lesser-known candy issues of the early 1930s was this New England regional set from Uncle Jacks, Inc., of Springfield, Mass., and Newport, R.I. The 1-7/8" x 2-7/8" blank-backed cards can be found printed in blue, red, purple or green duotone, and were sold in a see-through wax paper wrapper with a piece of candy and a coupon which could be redeemed (in quantities of 100) for a "league baseball" and a chance at a trip to the 1933 World Series. The set is among those listed in the American Card Catalog under the catchall number R317. The unnumbered cards are checklisted here alphabetically.

	NM	E	VG
Complete Set (30):	25,000	12,500	7,500
Common Player:	400.00	200.00	120.00

(1)	Earl Averill	1,000	500.00	300.00
(2)	James L. Bottomley	1,000	500.00	300.00
(3)	Ed Brandt	400.00	200.00	120.00
(4)	Ben Chapman	400.00	200.00	120.00
(5)	Gordon Cochrane	1,000	500.00	300.00
(6)	Joe Cronin	1,000	500.00	300.00
(7)	Hazen Cuyler	1,000	500.00	300.00
(8)	George Earnshaw	400.00	200.00	120.00
(9)	Wesley Ferrell	400.00	200.00	120.00
(10)	Jimmie Foxx	1,500	750.00	450.00
(11)	Frank Frisch	1,000	500.00	300.00
(12)	Burleigh Grimes	1,000	500.00	300.00
(13)	"Lefty" Grove	1,250	625.00	375.00
(14)	"Wild Bill" Hallahan	400.00	200.00	120.00
(15)	Leo Hartnett	1,000	500.00	300.00
(16)	"Babe" Herman	400.00	200.00	120.00
(17)	Rogers Hornsby	1,200	600.00	360.00
(18)	Charles Klein	1,000	500.00	300.00
(19)	Tony Lazzeri	1,000	500.00	300.00
(20)	Fred Lindstrom	1,000	500.00	300.00
(21)	Ted Lyons	1,000	500.00	300.00
(22)	"Pepper" Martin	650.00	325.00	200.00
(23)	Herb Pennock	1,000	500.00	300.00
(24)	"Babe" Ruth ("King of Swat")	4,000	2,000	1,200
(25)	Al Simmons	1,000	500.00	300.00
(26)	"Bill" Terry	1,000	500.00	300.00
(27)	"Dazzy" Vance	1,000	500.00	300.00
(28)	Lloyd Waner	1,000	500.00	300.00
(29)	Paul Waner	1,000	500.00	300.00
(30)	Hack Wilson	1,000	500.00	300.00

1958 Union 76 Sports Club Booklets

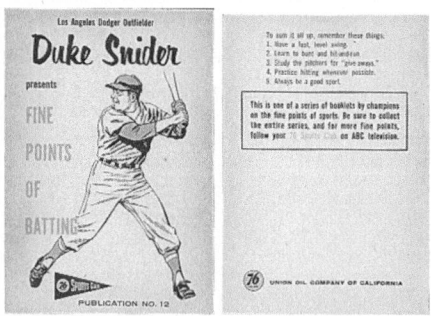

This series of sports instructional booklets was issued by Union Oil in conjunction with its Sports Club television program for youngsters. Besides seven baseball players, the series featured football, track, bowling, skiing, and other stars. The booklets are 12 pages and measure about 4" x 5-1/2". Fronts have a drawing of the player and are printed in Union Oil logo colors of orange and blue. The sports tips inside are well illustrated. Books are numbered on front.

		NM	E	VG
Complete (Baseball) Set (7):		320.00	160.00	90.00
Common Player:		30.00	15.00	9.00
12	Duke Snider	70.00	35.00	20.00
14	Bob Lemon	40.00	20.00	2.00
15	Red Schoendienst	40.00	20.00	2.00
20	Bill Rigney	30.00	15.00	9.00
38	Jackie Jensen	30.00	15.00	9.00
39	Warren Spahn	50.00	25.00	15.00
41	Ernie Banks	70.00	35.00	20.00

1980 Union Novelty N.Y. Yankees

The issue date cited in conjectural; the actual date of issue may have been several years later. This unauthorized collectors' issue purports to have been issued by Union Novelty Co., Los Angeles. The set features frequently-seen images of Yankees greats in a 3-1/2" x 5-1/2" black-and-white format. Cards are known in two styles. One version has printing on front with the player name(s), references to the team and a card number from within a series of 20. Backs of this type are identical, describing the card as "one in a collection of

nostalgic prints of famous athletes." The second type has nothing on front except the player photo. Backs of this style are arranged as a postcard. There is no price differential between the types.

		NM	EX	VG
Complete Set (20):		40.00	20.00	12.00
Common Card:		3.00	1.50	.90
1	Mickey Mantle	4.00	2.00	1.25
2	Mickey Mantle	4.00	2.00	1.25
3	Mickey Mantle	4.00	2.00	1.25
4	Mickey Mantle	4.00	2.00	1.25
5	Mickey Mantle	4.00	2.00	1.25
6	Mickey Mantle	4.00	2.00	1.25
7	Roger Maris & Mickey Mantle	3.00	1.50	.90
8	Mantle & Maris	3.00	1.50	.90
9	Lou Gehrig	4.00	2.00	1.25
10	Lou Gehrig & Joe DiMaggio	3.00	1.50	.90
11	DiMaggio and Bauer	3.00	1.50	.90
12	Joe DiMaggio	4.00	2.00	1.25
13	Joltin' Joe DiMaggio	4.00	2.00	1.25
14	"The Yankee Clipper" Joe DiMaggio	4.00	2.00	1.25
15	Roger Maris	3.00	1.50	.90
16	Whitey Ford	3.00	1.50	.90
17	Yogi Berra	3.00	1.50	.90
18	"The Iron Horse" Lou Gehrig	4.00	2.00	1.25
19	Phil Rizzuto	3.00	1.50	.90
20	Babe Ruth	4.00	2.00	1.25

1960 Union Oil Dodger Family Booklets

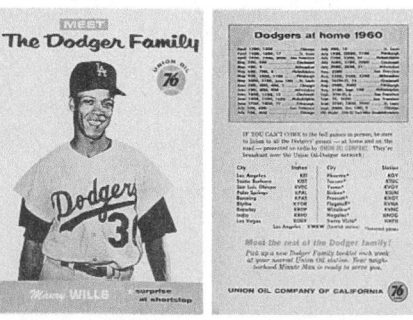

For its first major issue of Dodgers memorabilia, Union 76 gas stations in Southern California distributed a series of booklets profiling players and staff. Each 5-1/2" x 7-1/2" booklet has 16 black-and-white pages highlighted with red graphics. The covers have action poses with many other photos on the inside pages, along with a biography, personal information, career highlights, playing tips, etc. On back is a Dodgers schedule and Union 76 ad. The booklets were distributed on a one-per-week basis. They are listed here in alphabetical order.

		NM	E	VG
Complete Set (24):		300.00	150.00	90.00
Common Player:		12.00	6.00	3.50
(1)	Walter Alston	15.00	7.50	4.50
(2)	Roger Craig	12.00	6.00	3.50
(3)	Tom Davis	15.00	7.50	4.50
(4)	Don Demeter	12.00	6.00	3.50
(5)	Don Drysdale	15.00	7.50	4.50
(6)	Chuck Essegian	12.00	6.00	3.50
(7)	Jim Gilliam	15.00	7.50	4.50
(8)	Gil Hodges	12.00	6.00	3.50
(9)	Frank Howard	15.00	7.50	4.50
(10)	Sandy Koufax	80.00	40.00	24.00
(11)	Norm Larker	12.00	6.00	3.50
(12)	Wally Moon	12.00	6.00	3.50
(13)	Charlie Neal	12.00	6.00	3.50
(14)	Johnny Podres	12.00	6.00	3.50
(15)	Ed Roebuck	12.00	6.00	3.50
(16)	John Roseboro	12.00	6.00	3.50
(17)	Larry Sherry	12.00	6.00	3.50
(18)	Norm Sherry	12.00	6.00	3.50
(19)	Duke Snider	30.00	15.00	9.00
(20)	Stan Williams	12.00	6.00	3.50
(21)	Maury Wills	15.00	3.75	2.25
(22)	Coaches (Joe Becker, Bobby Bragan, Greg Mulleavy, Pete Reiser)	12.00	6.00	3.50
(23)	Jerry Doggett, Vin Scully (Announcers)	12.00	6.00	3.50

1961 Union Oil Dodger Family Booklets

For a second consecutive year, Union 76 gas stations in Southern California distributed a series of booklets profiling team members and staff. The 5-1/2" x 7-1/2" booklets have 16 black-and-white pages highlighted with red graphics. The

covers have large portraits while there are many photos on the inside pages, along with a biography, personal information, career highlights, playing tips, etc. On back is a Dodgers schedule and radio network information. The booklets were distributed on a one-per-week basis. They are listed here in alphabetical order.

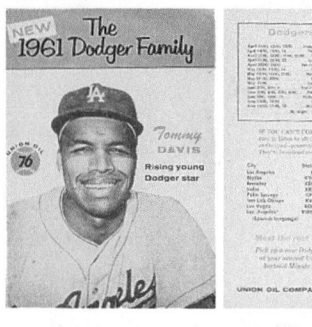

		NM	E	VG
Complete Set (24):		350.00	170.00	100.00
Common Player:		12.00	6.00	3.50
(1)	Walter Alston	15.00	7.50	4.50
(2)	Roger Craig	12.00	6.00	3.50
(3)	Tommy Davis	15.00	7.50	4.50
(4)	Willie Davis	15.00	7.50	4.50
(5)	Don Drysdale	30.00	15.00	9.00
(6)	Dick Farrell	12.00	6.00	3.50
(7)	Ron Fairly	12.00	6.00	3.50
(8)	Jim Gilliam	15.00	7.50	4.50
(9)	Gil Hodges	20.00	10.00	6.00
(10)	Frank Howard	15.00	7.50	4.50
(11)	Sandy Koufax	60.00	30.00	18.00
(12)	Norm Larker	12.00	6.00	3.50
(13)	Wally Moon	12.00	6.00	3.50
(14)	Charlie Neal	12.00	6.00	3.50
(15)	Ron Perranoski	12.00	6.00	3.50
(16)	Johnny Podres	12.00	6.00	3.50
(17)	John Roseboro	12.00	6.00	3.50
(18)	Larry Sherry	12.00	6.00	3.50
(19)	Norm Sherry	12.00	6.00	3.50
(20)	Duke Snider	30.00	15.00	9.00
(21)	Daryl Spencer	12.00	6.00	3.50
(22)	Stan Williams	12.00	6.00	3.50
(23)	Maury Wills	15.00	7.50	4.50
(24)	Jerry Doggett, Vin Scully (Announcers)	12.00	6.00	3.50

1962 Union Oil Dodgers Premium Pictures

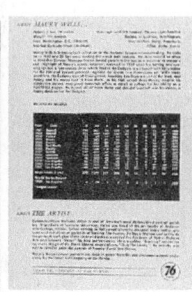

One of many premiums issued by Union Oil during the Dodgers' early years in Los Angeles, this set of player pictures is the most popular with collectors. The 8-1/2" x 11" pictures feature a large color pastel portrait of the player on front, along with a smaller action picture. The player's name is printed in the white border below. The artist's signature and a 1962 copyright are printed below the portrait. Backs are printed in black-and-white and include a career summary and complete minor and major league stats, a profile of sports artist Nicholas Volpe and an ad at bottom for Union Oil and its Union 76 brand of gasoline. The unnumbered pictures are checklisted here alphabetically. It was reported that 200,000 of each picture were produced.

		NM	E	VG
Complete Set (24):		225.00	115.00	70.00
Common Player:		8.00	4.00	2.50
(1)	Larry Burright	8.00	4.00	2.50
(2)	Doug Camilli	8.00	4.00	2.50
(3)	Andy Carey	8.00	4.00	2.50
(4)	Tom Davis	10.00	5.00	3.00
(5)	Willie Davis	10.00	5.00	3.00
(6)	Don Drysdale	20.00	10.00	6.00
(7)	Ron Fairly	8.00	4.00	2.50
(8)	Jim Gilliam	10.00	5.00	3.00
(9)	Tim Harkness	8.00	4.00	2.50
(10)	Frank Howard	10.00	5.00	3.00

		NM	E	VG
(11)	Sandy Koufax	40.00	20.00	12.00
(12)	Joe Moeller	8.00	4.00	2.50
(13)	Wally Moon	8.00	4.00	2.50
(14)	Ron Perranoski	8.00	4.00	2.50
(15)	Johnny Podres	8.00	4.00	2.50
(16)	Ed Roebuck	8.00	4.00	2.50
(17)	John Roseboro	8.00	4.00	2.50
(18)	Larry Sherry	8.00	4.00	2.50
(19)	Norm Sherry	8.00	4.00	2.50
(20)	Duke Snider	25.00	12.50	7.50
(21)	Daryl Spencer	8.00	4.00	2.50
(22)	Lee Walls	8.00	4.00	2.50
(23)	Stan Williams	8.00	4.00	2.50
(24)	Maury Wills	10.00	5.00	3.00

1964 Union Oil Dodgers Premium Pictures

 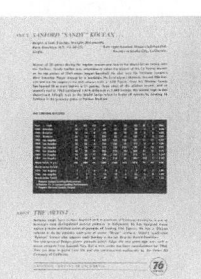

Paired pastel portraits, one in uniform and one in mufti, from sports artist Nicholas Volpe are featured on these large-format (8-1/2" x 11") premium pictures sponsored by Union Oil. The player's name is printed in the bottom border while the artist's signature is printed beneath the portraits. Backs are in black-and-white and feature personal data about the player and artist, complete minor and major league stats and Union Oil/Union 76 logos. The unnumbered pictures are checklisted here alphabetically.

		NM	E	VG
Complete Set (18):		165.00	80.00	50.00
Common Player:		8.00	4.00	2.50
(1)	Tommy Davis	10.00	5.00	3.00
(2)	Willie Davis	10.00	5.00	3.00
(3)	Don Drysdale	20.00	10.00	6.00
(4)	Ron Fairly	8.00	4.00	2.50
(5)	Jim Gilliam	10.00	5.00	3.00
(6)	Frank Howard	10.00	5.00	3.00
(7)	Sandy Koufax	35.00	17.50	10.00
(8)	Bob Miller	8.00	4.00	2.50
(9)	Joe Moeller	8.00	4.00	2.50
(10)	Wally Moon	8.00	4.00	2.50
(11)	Phil Ortega	8.00	4.00	2.50
(12)	Wes Parker	8.00	4.00	2.50
(13)	Ron Perranoski	8.00	4.00	2.50
(14)	John Podres	8.00	4.00	2.50
(15)	John Roseboro	8.00	4.00	2.50
(16)	Dick Tracewski	8.00	4.00	2.50
(17)	Lee Walls	8.00	4.00	2.50
(18)	Maury Wills	10.00	5.00	3.00

1969 Union Oil Dodgers Premium Pictures

These 8-1/2" x 11" cards were given to fans attending week night "Player Portrait Night" promotional games. The premiums are similar in format to earlier and later sets sponsored by Union Oil and created by sports artist Nicholas Volpe. Fronts have pastel player portraits and action drawings against a black background. Backs are in black-and-white and have player biographies, stats and a career summary, along with a word about the artist and an ad for Union Oil/Union 76. The unnumbered pictures are checklisted here alphabetically.

		NM	E	VG
Complete Set (13):		120.00	60.00	35.00
Common Player:		8.00	4.00	2.50
(1)	Walt Alston	10.00	5.00	3.00

		NM	E	VG
(2)	Jim Brewer	8.00	4.00	2.50
(3)	Willie Davis	10.00	5.00	3.00
(4)	Don Drysdale	20.00	10.00	6.00
(5)	Ron Fairly	8.00	4.00	2.50
(6)	Tom Haller	8.00	4.00	2.50
(7)	Jim Lefebvre	8.00	4.00	2.50
(8)	Claude Osteen	8.00	4.00	2.50
(9)	Wes Parker	8.00	4.00	2.50
(10)	Paul Popovich	8.00	4.00	2.50
(11)	Bill Singer	8.00	4.00	2.50
(12)	Bill Sudakis	8.00	4.00	2.50
(13)	Don Sutton	13.50	6.75	4.00

1968 Uniroyal Keds Cincinnati Reds

These 2-1/2" x 3-1/4" cards are printed in blue duotone on thin paper. Blank backed, they were intended to be put into an accompanying album. It is unknown whether this checklist is complete.

		NM	E	VG
Common Player:		20.00	10.00	6.00
(1)	Johnny Bench	40.00	20.00	12.00
(2)	Dave Bristol	20.00	10.00	6.00
(3)	Leo Cardenas	20.00	10.00	6.00
(4)	Tony Cloninger	20.00	10.00	6.00
(5)	Alex Johnson	20.00	10.00	6.00
(6)	Bob Johnson	20.00	10.00	6.00
(7)	Bob Lee	20.00	10.00	6.00
(8)	Jim Maloney	20.00	10.00	6.00
(9)	Lee May	20.00	10.00	6.00
(10)	Billy McCool	20.00	10.00	6.00
(11)	Vada Pinson	25.00	12.50	7.50
(12)	Pete Rose	150.00	75.00	45.00
(13)	Chico Ruiz	20.00	10.00	6.00
(14)	Fred Whitefield	20.00	10.00	6.00

1979 United Press International

Not widely circulated, and perhaps issued only as a proto-type, these cards feature a tiny (2" x 2-1/4" clear vinyl record attached to the back. Overall, the card is 2-3/4" x 5" and has on front a black-and-white or color photo with a UPI credit line in the very wide white border at bottom. The back is headed either "Sports Nostalgia" or "Great Moments in Sports." Player identification and career highlights are printed on back. The vinyl mini-record could be played on an ancient electronic entertainment device known as a turntable. Similar card/records were produced for other sports and historical highlights.

		NM	E	VG
Complete Set (9):		150.00	75.00	45.00
Common Player:		10.00	5.00	3.00
(1)	Hank Aaron (715th HR)	15.00	7.50	4.50
(2)	Joe DiMaggio (Hitting Streak Ends)	20.00	10.00	6.00
(3)	Lou Gehrig (Gehrig Day 7/4/39)	20.00	10.00	6.00
(4)	Mickey Mantle (Record HR)	25.00	12.50	7.50

		NM	E	VG
(5)	Stan Musial (3,000th Hit)	15.00	7.50	4.50
(6)	Babe Ruth (Famous Home Run)	20.00	10.00	6.00
(7)	Gene Tenace (Record HR)	10.00	5.00	3.00
(8)	Bobby Thomson (Famous HR)	12.00	6.00	3.50
(9)	Ted Williams (Last At-Bat)	15.00	7.50	4.50

1932 Universal Pictures Babe Ruth Premium

This 8" x 10" black-and-white photo was issued to promote what was advertised as a series of Babe Ruth shorts. The front pictures the movie star in a generic uniform with a fac-simile autograph. On back is advertising for the theater bill. It is likely the pictures were distributed blank-backed, allowing local theaters to have their advertising added.

	NM	E	VG
Babe Ruth	750.00	375.00	225.00

1925 Universal Toy & Novelty Brooklyn Dodgers (W504)

Printed on cheap paper in blue ink and intended to be cut apart into a team photo and 16 individual player cards, this set was originally issued on a 5-1/2" x 13" sheet. Single cut cards measure about 1-3/8" x 2-3/8", with the team picture about 5-1/2" x 3-1/2". Cards are blank-back. Cards are numbered in roughly alphabetical order beneath the photo, where the name, team, position and birth year are also printed.

		NM	E	VG
Complete Sheet:		1,800	900.00	540.00
Complete Set, Singles (17):		1,200	600.00	360.00
Common Player:		50.00	25.00	15.00
101	Edward W. Brown	50.00	25.00	15.00
102	John H. De Berry	50.00	25.00	15.00
103	William L. Doak	50.00	25.00	15.00
104	Wm. C. Ehrhardt (First name Welton.)	50.00	25.00	15.00
105	J.F. Fournier	50.00	25.00	15.00
106	T.H. Griffith	50.00	25.00	15.00
107	Burleigh A. Grimes	100.00	50.00	30.00
108	C.P. Hargreaves	50.00	25.00	15.00
109	Andrew A. High	50.00	25.00	15.00
110	Andy. H. Johnston (First name Jimmy.)	50.00	25.00	15.00
111	John Mitchell	50.00	25.00	15.00
112	"Tiny" Osborne	50.00	25.00	15.00
113	Milton Stock	50.00	25.00	15.00
114	James W. Taylor	50.00	25.00	15.00
115	"Dazzy" Vance	100.00	50.00	30.00
116	Zack D. Wheat	100.00	50.00	30.00
---	Brooklyn National League Team Photo	550.00	275.00	165.00

1925 Universal Toy & Novelty N.Y. Yankees (W504)

Printed on thick cardboard and intended to be cut apart into a team photo and 16 individual player cards, this set was originally issued on a 5-1/2" x 13" sheet. Single cut cards measure about 1-3/8" x 2-3/8", with the team picture about 5" x 3-1/2". Cards are blank-back. Player cards are numbered in alphabetical order beneath the photo, where the name, team, position and birth year are also printed.

		NM	E	VG
Complete Sheet:		4,000	2,000	1,200
Complete Set (17):		3,500	1,750	1,000
Common Player:		125.00	60.00	35.00
117	Bernard Bengough	125.00	60.00	35.00
118	Joseph Dugan	125.00	60.00	35.00
119	Waite Hoyt	200.00	100.00	60.00
120	Sam Jones	125.00	60.00	35.00
121	Robert Meusel	125.00	60.00	35.00
122	Walter C. Pipp	125.00	60.00	35.00
123	G.H. "Babe" Ruth	1,200	600.00	360.00
124	Wal. H. Schang	125.00	60.00	35.00
125	Robert J. Shawkey	125.00	60.00	35.00
126	Everett Scott	125.00	60.00	35.00
127	Urban Shocker	125.00	60.00	35.00
128	Aaron L. Ward	125.00	60.00	35.00
129	Lawton Witt	125.00	60.00	35.00
130	Carl Mays	140.00	70.00	42.00
131	Miller Huggins	200.00	100.00	60.00
132	Benj. Paschal	125.00	60.00	35.00
----	New York American League Team Photo	800.00	400.00	240.00

1925 Universal Toy & Novelty New York Giants (W504)

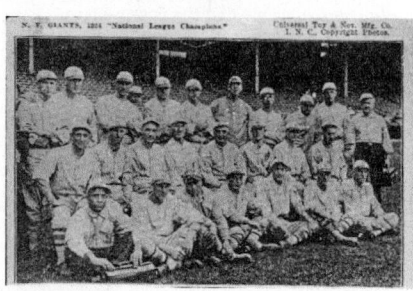

Printed on thick cardboard and intended to be cut apart into a team photo and 16 individual player cards, this set was originally issued on a 5-1/2" x 13" sheet. Single cut cards measure about 1-3/8" x 2-3/8", with the team picture about 5" x 3-1/2". Cards are blank-back. Player cards are numbered beneath the photo, where the name, team, position and birth year are also printed.

		NM	E	VG
Complete Sheet:		3,500	1,750	1,000
Complete Set (17):		3,000	1,500	900.00
Common Player:		125.00	60.00	35.00
133	Virgil Barnes	125.00	60.00	35.00
134	John N. Bentley	125.00	60.00	35.00
135	Frank Frisch	225.00	110.00	65.00
136	Harry Gowdy	125.00	60.00	35.00
137	Henry Groh	125.00	60.00	35.00
138	Travis Jackson	200.00	100.00	60.00
139	George Kelly	200.00	100.00	60.00
140	Emil Meusel	125.00	60.00	35.00
141	Hugh McQuillan	125.00	60.00	35.00
142	Arthur Nehf	125.00	60.00	35.00
143	Wilfred D. Ryan	125.00	60.00	35.00
144	Frank Snyder	125.00	60.00	35.00
145	Lewis R. Wilson	225.00	110.00	65.00
146	Ross Youngs	200.00	100.00	60.00
147	Hugh Jennings	200.00	100.00	60.00
148	John J. McGraw	200.00	100.00	60.00
---	New York National League Team Photo	400.00	200.00	120.00

1925 Universal Toy & Novelty Washington Senators (W504)

Printed on thick cardboard and intended to be cut apart into a team photo and 16 individual player cards, this set was originally issued on a 5-1/2" x 13" sheet. Single cut cards measure about 1-3/8" x 2-3/8", with the team picture about 5" x 3-1/2". Cards are blank-back. Player cards are numbered beneath the photo, where the name, team, position and birth year are also printed.

		NM	E	VG
Complete Sheet:				
Complete Set (17):				
Common Player:		50.00	25.00	15.00
149	Joe Judge	50.00	25.00	15.00
150	Wm. Hargrave	50.00	25.00	15.00
151	R. Peckinpaugh	50.00	25.00	15.00
152	O.L. Bluege	50.00	25.00	15.00
153	M.J. McNally	50.00	25.00	15.00
154	Sam Rice	200.00	100.00	60.00
155				
156				
157				
158				
159	Wm. Hargrave	50.00	25.00	15.00
160				
161				
162	Harold (Herold) Ruel	50.00	25.00	15.00
163				
164	George Mogridge	50.00	25.00	15.00
---	Washinton American League Team Photo	400.00	200.00	120.00

1933 U.S. Caramel (R328)

 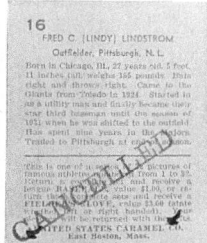

Produced by a Boston confectioner, this set is not limited to baseball, but is a set of 32 "Famous Athletes," of which 27 are baseball players. The 2-1/2" x 3" cards have a black-and-white picture on front with a red background and white border. Backs feature the player's name, position, team and league as well as a redemption ad and card number. The issue was among the last of the caramel card sets. The cards could be redeemed for a baseball and glove and were returned punch-cancelled and stamped. Card #16, short-printed to limit the number of prizes claimed, was first discovered in the late 1980s; only two examples are currently known.

		NM	E	VG
Common Player:		600.00	275.00	150.00
1	Edward T. (Eddie) Collins	1,000	450.00	250.00
2	Paul (Big Poison) Waner	1,000	450.00	250.00
3	Robert T. (Bobby) Jones (golfer)			
4	William (Bill) Terry	1,000	450.00	250.00
5	Earl B. Combs (Earle)	1,000	450.00	250.00
6	William (Bill) Dickey	1,000	450.00	250.00
7	Joseph (Joe) Cronin	1,000	450.00	250.00
8	Charles (Chick) Hafey	1,000	450.00	250.00
9	Gene Sarazen (golfer)			
10	Walter (Rabbit) Maranville	1,000	450.00	250.00
11	Rogers (Rajah) Hornsby	1,750	785.00	435.00
12	Gordon (Mickey) Cochrane	1,000	450.00	250.00
13	Lloyd (Little Poison) Waner	1,000	450.00	250.00
14	Tyrus (Ty) Cobb	3,000	1,350	750.00
15	Eugene (Gene) Tunney (boxer)			
16	Charles (Lindy) Lindstrom (2 known)	80,000		
17	Al. Simmons	1,000	450.00	250.00
18	Anthony (Tony) Lazzeri	1,000	450.00	250.00
19	Walter (Wally) Berger	600.00	275.00	150.00
20	Charles (Large Charlie) Ruffing	1,000	450.00	250.00
21	Charles (Chuck) Klein	1,000	450.00	250.00
22	John (Jack) Dempsey (boxer)			
23	James (Jimmy) Foxx	1,750	785.00	435.00
24	Frank J. (Lefty) O'Doul	750.00	335.00	185.00
25	Jack (Sailor Jack) Sharkey (boxer)			
26	Henry (Lou) Gehrig	6,000	2,700	1,500
27	Robert (Lefty) Grove	1,200	540.00	300.00
28	Edward Brant (Brandt)	600.00	275.00	150.00
29	George Earnshaw	600.00	275.00	150.00
30	Frank (Frankie) Frisch	1,000	450.00	250.00
31	Vernon (Lefty) Gomez	1,000	450.00	250.00
32	George (Babe) Ruth	7,500	3,250	1,900

1973 U.S. Playing Card Ruth/Gehrig

These decks of playing cards were produced for sale by the Smithsonian Institution in Washington, D.C. The 2-1/4" x 3-1/2" cards were sold as a pair. Backs have colorized pictures of the Yankees greats; Ruth on an orange background and Gehrig on red.

	NM	E	VG
Complete Set, Ruth (54):	25.00	12.50	7.50
Single Card, Ruth:	1.50	.75	.45
Complete Set, Gehrig (54):	15.00	7.50	4.50
Single Card, Gehrig:	.75	.40	.25

(A 50 percent premium attaches to a complete boxed pair of decks.)

1909-11 Uzit Cigarettes

Uzit is generally accepted as the second scarcest back advertiser (after Drum) found on T206. The typographic back is printed in light blue ink.

PREMIUMS
Commons: 35-45X
Hall of Famers: 6-8X

(See T206 for checklist.)

V

1938-39 Val Decker Packing Co. Cincinnati Reds Postcards

(See 1937-39 Orcajo Cincinnati Reds postcards for checklist and values.)

1950s-70s Van Heusen Advisory Staff Photos

Not a great deal is known about the distribution of these 8" x 10" black-and-white player photos. It is likely the checklist here is not complete. The photos are bordered in white with the player name at bottom. In one of the lower corners is the logo of the clothing manufacturer. This issue is differentiated from the Phillies photos because of the action poses and multi-team composition of the known examples.

		NM	E	VG
Common Player:		20.00	10.00	6.00
(1)	Hank Aaron (Braves, batting)	40.00	20.00	12.00
(2)	Paul Blair	20.00	10.00	6.00
(3)	Curt Blefary	20.00	10.00	6.00
(4)	Jerry Coleman (Yankees, throwing)	25.00	12.50	7.50
(5)	Tommy Davis (Dodgers, batting)	20.00	10.00	6.00
(6)	Dick Ellsworth (Phillies, portrait)	20.00	10.00	6.00
(7)	Tommy Davis (Dodgers, batting.)	20.00	10.00	6.00
(8)	Dick Hall (Phillies, portrait.)	20.00	10.00	6.00
(9)	Bob Hendley (Braves, follow-through.)	20.00	10.00	6.00
(10)	Chuck Hinton			
(11)	Don Lock (Phillies, upper body)	20.00	10.00	6.00
(12)	Jim Piersall	20.00	10.00	6.00
(13)	Cookie Rojas (Phillies, bat on shoulder)	20.00	10.00	6.00
	Cookie Rojas (Phillies, portrait)	20.00	10.00	6.00
(14)	Cookie Rojas (Phillies, bat on shoulder.)	20.00	10.00	6.00
(15)	Bill Skowron (Dodgers, full-length.)	25.00	12.50	7.50
	Joe Torre (Braves, portrait)	30.00	15.00	9.00
(16)	Maury Wills (Dodgers, batting)	25.00	12.50	7.50

1967 Van Heusen Phillies

Not a great deal is known about the distribution of these 8" x 10" black-and-white player portraits. It is possible the checklist here is not complete. The photos are bordered in white with the player name at bottom. At lower-right is the logo of the clothing manufacturer. This issue is differentiated from the Advisory Staff Photos because of the similitude of the portrait photos of the teammates.

		NM	E	VG
Common Player:		20.00	10.00	6.00
(1)	Bo Belinsky	20.00	10.00	6.00
(2)	Jim Bunning	35.00	17.50	10.50
(3)	Wes Covington	20.00	10.00	6.00
(4)	Dick Ellsworth	20.00	10.00	6.00
(5)	Dick Groat (portrait)	20.00	10.00	6.00
(6)	Chris Short	20.00	10.00	6.00
(7)	Bill White	20.00	10.00	6.00

1912 Vassar Sweaters

Star players of the day are pictured wearing the sponsor's product over their uniforms in this issue of 4" x 6-3/4" black-and-white cards. Player names are in the white border at bottom. It is not known whether this checklist is complete.

		NM	E	VG
Common Player:		1,250	625.00	375.00
(1)	Ty Cobb	5,000	2,500	1,500
(2)	Sam Crawford	1,750	875.00	525.00
(3)	Walter Johnson	2,750	1,375	825.00
(4)	Napoleon Lajoie	1,750	875.00	525.00
(5)	Smokey Joe Wood	1,250	625.00	375.00

1959 Venezuelan Topps

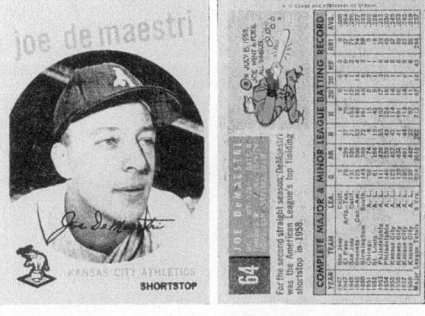

Beginning in 1959, Topps began marketing baseball cards in Venezuela, always a hotbed of baseball fandom. In most years, such as the debut set in 1959, the cards destined for the South American market represented a parallel of the first couple of series of Topps' regular U.S. issue. Print quality (usually lack of gloss on front) is the major difference between the two issues. Backs of some of the 1959 Venezuelan cards carry the credit line: "Impreso en Venezuela por Benco C.A." A reality of the Venezuelan cards is that they tend to survive in low-grade condition due to the local custom of gluing cards into albums and scrapbooks. After its 1959 issue, Topps produced Venezuelan cards only in the even-numbered years, except for 1967, until the last of the sets was issued in 1968.

		NM	E	VG
Complete Set (196):		10,000	4,000	2,400
Common Player:		45.00	18.00	11.00
1	Ford Frick	60.00	24.00	14.50
2	Eddie Yost	45.00	18.00	11.00
3	Don McMahon	45.00	18.00	11.00
4	Albie Pearson	45.00	18.00	11.00
5	Dick Donovan	45.00	18.00	11.00
6	Alex Grammas	45.00	18.00	11.00
7	Al Pilarcik	45.00	18.00	11.00
8	Phillies Team	75.00	30.00	18.00
9	Paul Giel	45.00	18.00	11.00
10	Mickey Mantle	2,000	550.00	350.00
11	Billy Hunter	45.00	18.00	11.00
12	Vern Law	45.00	18.00	11.00
13	Dick Gernert	45.00	18.00	11.00
14	Pete Whisenant	45.00	18.00	11.00
15	Dick Drott	45.00	18.00	11.00
16	Joe Pignatano	45.00	18.00	11.00
17	Danny's All-Stars (Ted Kluszewski, Danny Murtaugh, Frank Thomas)	50.00	20.00	12.00
18	Jack Urban	45.00	18.00	11.00
19	Ed Bressoud	45.00	18.00	11.00
20	Duke Snider	200.00	80.00	48.00
21	Connie Johnson	45.00	18.00	11.00
22	Al Smith	45.00	18.00	11.00
23	Murry Dickson	45.00	18.00	11.00
24	Red Wilson	45.00	18.00	11.00
25	Don Hoak	45.00	18.00	11.00
26	Chuck Stobbs	45.00	18.00	11.00
27	Andy Pafko	45.00	18.00	11.00
28	Red Worthington	45.00	18.00	11.00
29	Jim Bolger	45.00	18.00	11.00
30	Nellie Fox	100.00	40.00	24.00
31	Ken Lehman	45.00	18.00	11.00
32	Don Buddin	45.00	18.00	11.00
33	Ed Fitz Gerald	45.00	18.00	11.00
34	Pitchers Beware (Al Kaline, Charlie Maxwell)	90.00	36.00	22.00
35	Ted Kluszewski	60.00	24.00	14.50
36	Hank Aguirre	45.00	18.00	11.00
37	Gene Green	45.00	18.00	11.00
38	Morrie Martin	45.00	18.00	11.00
39	Ed Bouchee	45.00	18.00	11.00
40	Warren Spahn	125.00	50.00	30.00
41	Bob Martyn	45.00	18.00	11.00
42	Murray Wall	45.00	18.00	11.00
43	Steve Bilko	45.00	18.00	11.00
44	Vito Valentinetti	45.00	18.00	11.00
45	Andy Carey	45.00	18.00	11.00
46	Bill Henry	45.00	18.00	11.00
47	Jim Finigan	45.00	18.00	11.00
48	Orioles Team/Checklist 1-88	75.00	30.00	18.00
49	Bill Hall	45.00	18.00	11.00
50	Willie Mays	450.00	180.00	108.00
51	Rip Coleman	45.00	18.00	11.00
52	Coot Veal	45.00	18.00	11.00
53	Stan Williams	45.00	18.00	11.00
54	Mel Roach	45.00	18.00	11.00
55	Tom Brewer	45.00	18.00	11.00
56	Carl Sawatski	45.00	18.00	11.00
57	Al Cicotte	45.00	18.00	11.00
58	Eddie Miksis	45.00	18.00	11.00
59	Irv Noren	45.00	18.00	11.00
60	Bob Turley	45.00	18.00	11.00
61	Dick Brown	45.00	18.00	11.00
62	Tony Taylor	45.00	18.00	11.00
63	Jim Hearn	45.00	18.00	11.00
64	Joe DeMaestri	45.00	18.00	11.00
65	Frank Torre	45.00	18.00	11.00
66	Joe Ginsberg	45.00	18.00	11.00
67	Brooks Lawrence	45.00	18.00	11.00
68	Dick Schofield	45.00	18.00	11.00
69	Giants Team/Checklist 89-176	75.00	30.00	18.00
70	Harvey Kuenn	50.00	20.00	12.00
71	Don Bessent	45.00	18.00	11.00
72	Bill Renna	45.00	18.00	11.00
73	Ron Jackson	45.00	18.00	11.00
74	Directing the Power (Cookie Lavagetto, Jim Lemon, Roy Sievers)	45.00	18.00	11.00
75	Sam Jones	45.00	18.00	11.00
76	Bobby Richardson	50.00	20.00	12.00
77	John Goryl	45.00	18.00	11.00
78	Pedro Ramos	45.00	18.00	11.00
79	Harry Chiti	45.00	18.00	11.00
80	Minnie Minoso	55.00	22.00	13.00
81	Hal Jeffcoat	45.00	18.00	11.00
82	Bob Boyd	45.00	18.00	11.00
83	Bob Smith	45.00	18.00	11.00
84	Reno Bertoia	45.00	18.00	11.00
85	Harry Anderson	45.00	18.00	11.00
86	Bob Keegan	45.00	18.00	11.00
87	Danny O'Connell	45.00	18.00	11.00
88	Herb Score	45.00	18.00	11.00
89	Billy Gardner	45.00	18.00	11.00
90	Bill Skowron	55.00	22.00	13.00
91	Herb Moford	45.00	18.00	11.00
92	Dave Philley	45.00	18.00	11.00
93	Julio Becquer	45.00	18.00	11.00
94	White Sox Team	100.00	40.00	24.00
95	Carl Willey	45.00	18.00	11.00
96	Lou Berberet	45.00	18.00	11.00

97	Jerry Lynch	45.00	18.00	11.00
98	Arnie Portocarrero	45.00	18.00	11.00
99	Ted Kazanski	45.00	18.00	11.00
100	Bob Cerv	45.00	18.00	11.00
101	Alex Kellner	45.00	18.00	11.00
102	Felipe Alou	60.00	24.00	14.50
103	Billy Goodman	45.00	18.00	11.00
104	Del Rice	45.00	18.00	11.00
105	Lee Walls	45.00	18.00	11.00
106	Hal Woodeshick	45.00	18.00	11.00
107	Norm Larker	45.00	18.00	11.00
108	Zack Monroe	45.00	18.00	11.00
109	Bob Schmidt	45.00	18.00	11.00
110	George Witt	45.00	18.00	11.00
111	Redlegs Team/Checklist 89-176	75.00	30.00	18.00
112	Billy Consolo	45.00	18.00	11.00
113	Taylor Phillips	45.00	18.00	11.00
114	Earl Battey	45.00	18.00	11.00
115	Mickey Vernon	45.00	18.00	11.00
116	Bob Allison	45.00	18.00	11.00
117	John Blanchard	45.00	18.00	11.00
118	John Buzhardt	45.00	18.00	11.00
119	John Callison	45.00	18.00	11.00
120	Chuck Coles	45.00	18.00	11.00
121	Bob Conley	45.00	18.00	11.00
122	Bennie Daniels	45.00	18.00	11.00
123	Don Dillard	45.00	18.00	11.00
124	Dan Dobbek	45.00	18.00	11.00
125	Ron Fairly	45.00	18.00	11.00
126	Eddie Haas	45.00	18.00	11.00
127	Kent Hadley	45.00	18.00	11.00
128	Bob Hartman	45.00	18.00	11.00
129	Frank Herrera	45.00	18.00	11.00
130	Lou Jackson	45.00	18.00	11.00
131	Deron Johnson	50.00	20.00	12.00
132	Don Lee	45.00	18.00	11.00
133	Bob Lillis	45.00	18.00	11.00
134	Jim McDaniel	45.00	18.00	11.00
135	Gene Oliver	45.00	18.00	11.00
136	Jim O'Toole	45.00	18.00	11.00
137	Dick Ricketts	45.00	18.00	11.00
138	John Romano	45.00	18.00	11.00
139	Ed Sadowski	45.00	18.00	11.00
140	Charlie Secrest	45.00	18.00	11.00
141	Joe Shipley	45.00	18.00	11.00
142	Dick Stigman	45.00	18.00	11.00
143	Willie Tasby	45.00	18.00	11.00
144	Jerry Walker	45.00	18.00	11.00
145	Dom Zanni	45.00	18.00	11.00
146	Jerry Zimmerman	45.00	18.00	11.00
147	Cubs' Clubbers (Ernie Banks, Dale Long, Walt Moryn)	90.00	36.00	22.00
148	Mike McCormick	45.00	18.00	11.00
149	Jim Bunning	100.00	40.00	24.00
150	Stan Musial	400.00	160.00	100.00
151	Bob Malkmus	45.00	18.00	11.00
152	Johnny Klippstein	45.00	18.00	11.00
153	Jim Marshall	45.00	18.00	11.00
154	Ray Herbert	45.00	18.00	11.00
155	Enos Slaughter	90.00	36.00	22.00
156	Ace Hurlers(Billy Pierce, Robin Roberts)	65.00	26.00	15.50
157	Felix Mantilla	45.00	18.00	11.00
158	Walt Dropo	45.00	18.00	11.00
159	Bob Shaw	45.00	18.00	11.00
160	Dick Groat	45.00	18.00	11.00
161	Frank Baumann	45.00	18.00	11.00
162	Bobby G. Smith	45.00	18.00	11.00
163	Sandy Koufax	450.00	180.00	110.00
164	Johnny Groth	45.00	18.00	11.00
165	Bill Bruton	45.00	18.00	11.00
166	Destruction Crew (Rocky Colavito, Larry Doby, Minnie Minoso)	125.00	50.00	30.00
167	Duke Maas	45.00	18.00	11.00
168	Carroll Hardy	45.00	18.00	11.00
169	Ted Abernathy	45.00	18.00	11.00
170	Gene Woodling	45.00	18.00	11.00
171	Willard Schmidt	45.00	18.00	11.00
172	A's Team/Checklist 177-242	75.00	30.00	18.00
173	Bill Monbouquette	45.00	18.00	11.00
174	Jim Pendleton	45.00	18.00	11.00
175	Dick Farrell	45.00	18.00	11.00
176	Preston Ward	45.00	18.00	11.00
177	Johnny Briggs	45.00	18.00	11.00
178	Ruben Amaro	45.00	18.00	11.00
179	Don Rudolph	45.00	18.00	11.00
180	Yogi Berra	200.00	80.00	48.00
181	Bob Porterfield	45.00	18.00	11.00
182	Milt Graff	45.00	18.00	11.00
183	Stu Miller	45.00	18.00	11.00
184	Harvey Haddix	45.00	18.00	11.00
185	Jim Busby	45.00	18.00	11.00
186	Mudcat Grant	45.00	18.00	11.00
187	Bubba Phillips	45.00	18.00	11.00
188	Juan Pizarro	45.00	18.00	11.00
189	Neil Chrisley	45.00	18.00	11.00
190	Bill Virdon	45.00	18.00	11.00
191	Russ Kemmerer	45.00	18.00	11.00
192	Charley Beamon	45.00	18.00	11.00
193	Sammy Taylor	45.00	18.00	11.00
194	Jim Brosnan	45.00	18.00	11.00
195	Rip Repulski	45.00	18.00	11.00
196	Billy Moran	45.00	18.00	11.00

1960 Venezuelan Topps

Unlike its 1959 issue, which had a printed-in-Venezuela notice on the backs, Topps' 1960 issue for that South American market is virtually identical, front and back, to the company's U.S. product. The Venezuelan cards have less gloss on the front and the black ink on their backs is lighter. The Latin American version is a parallel of the first 198 cards from Topps' set. As usual with Latin American cards, low-grade examples are the norm due to the local collecting custom of pasting cards into albums and scrapbooks.

		NM	E	VG
	Complete Set (198):	7,900	3,150	1,900
	Common Player:	40.00	16.00	9.50
1	Early Wynn	95.00	30.00	20.00
2	Roman Mejias	40.00	16.00	9.50
3	Joe Adcock	40.00	16.00	9.50
4	Bob Purkey	40.00	16.00	9.50
5	Wally Moon	40.00	16.00	9.50
6	Lou Berberet	40.00	16.00	9.50
7	Master and Mentor(Willie Mays, Bill Rigney)	125.00	50.00	30.00
8	Bud Daley	40.00	16.00	9.50
9	Faye Throneberry	40.00	16.00	9.50
10	Ernie Banks	150.00	60.00	36.00
11	Norm Siebern	40.00	16.00	9.50
12	Milt Pappas	40.00	16.00	9.50
13	Wally Post	40.00	16.00	9.50
14	Jim Grant	40.00	16.00	9.50
15	Pete Runnels	40.00	16.00	9.50
16	Ernie Broglio	40.00	16.00	9.50
17	Johnny Callison	40.00	16.00	9.50
18	Dodgers Team/Checklist 1-88	100.00	40.00	24.00
19	Felix Mantilla	40.00	16.00	9.50
20	Roy Face	40.00	16.00	9.50
21	Dutch Dotterer	40.00	16.00	9.50
22	Rocky Bridges	40.00	16.00	9.50
23	Eddie Fisher	40.00	16.00	9.50
24	Dick Gray	40.00	16.00	9.50
25	Roy Sievers	40.00	16.00	9.50
26	Wayne Terwilliger	40.00	16.00	9.50
27	Dick Drott	40.00	16.00	9.50
28	Brooks Robinson	150.00	60.00	36.00
29	Clem Labine	40.00	16.00	9.50
30	Tito Francona	40.00	16.00	9.50
31	Sammy Esposito	40.00	16.00	9.50
32	Sophomore Stalwarts(Jim O'Toole, Vada Pinson)	40.00	16.00	9.50
33	Tom Morgan	40.00	16.00	9.50
34	Sparky Anderson	90.00	45.00	27.00
35	Whitey Ford	150.00	60.00	36.00
36	Russ Nixon	40.00	16.00	9.50
37	Bill Bruton	40.00	16.00	9.50
38	Jerry Casale	40.00	16.00	9.50
39	Earl Averill	40.00	16.00	9.50
40	Joe Cunningham	40.00	16.00	9.50
41	Barry Latman	40.00	16.00	9.50
42	Hobie Landrith	40.00	16.00	9.50
43	Senators Team/Checklist 1-88	75.00	30.00	18.00
44	Bobby Locke	40.00	16.00	9.50
45	Roy McMillan	40.00	16.00	9.50
46	Jack Fisher	40.00	16.00	9.50
47	Don Zimmer	40.00	16.00	9.50
48	Hal Smith	40.00	16.00	9.50
49	Curt Raydon	40.00	16.00	9.50
50	Al Kaline	150.00	60.00	36.00
51	Jim Coates	40.00	16.00	9.50
52	Dave Philley	40.00	16.00	9.50
53	Jackie Brandt	40.00	16.00	9.50
54	Mike Fornieles	40.00	16.00	9.50
55	Bill Mazeroski	90.00	45.00	27.00
56	Steve Korcheck	40.00	16.00	9.50
57	Win-Savers(Turk Lown, Gerry Staley)	40.00	16.00	9.50
58	Gino Cimoli	40.00	16.00	9.50
59	Juan Pizarro	40.00	16.00	9.50
60	Gus Triandos	40.00	16.00	9.50
61	Eddie Kasko	40.00	16.00	9.50
62	Roger Craig	40.00	16.00	9.50
63	George Strickland	40.00	16.00	9.50
64	Jack Meyer	40.00	16.00	9.50
65	Elston Howard	45.00	18.00	11.00
66	Bob Trowbridge	40.00	16.00	9.50
67	Jose Pagan	40.00	16.00	9.50
68	Dave Hillman	40.00	16.00	9.50
69	Billy Goodman	40.00	16.00	9.50
70	Lou Burdette	40.00	16.00	9.50
71	Marty Keough	40.00	16.00	9.50
72	Tigers Team/Checklist 89-176	75.00	30.00	18.00
73	Bob Gibson	100.00	40.00	24.00
74	Walt Moryn	40.00	16.00	9.50
75	Vic Power	40.00	16.00	9.50
76	Bill Fischer	40.00	16.00	9.50
77	Hank Foiles	40.00	16.00	9.50
78	Bob Grim	40.00	16.00	9.50
79	Walt Dropo	40.00	16.00	9.50
80	Johnny Antonelli	40.00	16.00	9.50
81	Russ Snyder	40.00	16.00	9.50
82	Ruben Gomez	40.00	16.00	9.50
83	Tony Kubek	40.00	16.00	9.50
84	Hal Smith	40.00	16.00	9.50
85	Frank Lary	40.00	16.00	9.50
86	Dick Gernert	40.00	16.00	9.50
87	John Romonosky	40.00	16.00	9.50
88	John Roseboro	40.00	16.00	9.50
89	Hal Brown	40.00	16.00	9.50
90	Bobby Avila	40.00	16.00	9.50
91	Bennie Daniels	40.00	16.00	9.50
92	Whitey Herzog	45.00	18.00	11.00
93	Art Schult	40.00	16.00	9.50
94	Leo Kiely	40.00	16.00	9.50
95	Frank Thomas	40.00	16.00	9.50
96	Ralph Terry	40.00	16.00	9.50
97	Ted Lepcio	40.00	16.00	9.50
98	Gordon Jones	40.00	16.00	9.50
99	Lenny Green	40.00	16.00	9.50
100	Nellie Fox	90.00	36.00	22.00
101	Bob Miller	40.00	16.00	9.50
102	Kent Hadley	40.00	16.00	9.50
103	Dick Farrell	40.00	16.00	9.50
104	Dick Schofield	40.00	16.00	9.50
105	Larry Sherry	40.00	16.00	9.50
106	Billy Gardner	40.00	16.00	9.50
107	Carl Willey	40.00	16.00	9.50
108	Pete Daley	40.00	16.00	9.50
109	Cletis Boyer	40.00	16.00	9.50
110	Cal McLish	40.00	16.00	9.50
111	Vic Wertz	40.00	16.00	9.50
112	Jack Harshman	40.00	16.00	9.50
113	Bob Skinner	40.00	16.00	9.50
114	Ken Aspromonte	40.00	16.00	9.50
115	Fork and Knuckler(Roy Face, Hoyt Wilhelm)	45.00	18.00	11.00
116	Jim Rivera	40.00	16.00	9.50
117	Tom Borland	40.00	16.00	9.50
118	Bob Bruce	40.00	16.00	9.50
119	Chico Cardenas	40.00	16.00	9.50
120	Duke Carmel	40.00	16.00	9.50
121	Camilo Carreon	40.00	16.00	9.50
122	Don Dillard	40.00	16.00	9.50
123	Dan Dobbek	40.00	16.00	9.50
124	Jim Donohue	40.00	16.00	9.50
125	Dick Ellsworth	40.00	16.00	9.50
126	Chuck Estrada	40.00	16.00	9.50
127	Ronnie Hansen	40.00	16.00	9.50
128	Bill Harris	40.00	16.00	9.50
129	Bob Hartman	40.00	16.00	9.50
130	Frank Herrera	40.00	16.00	9.50
131	Ed Hobaugh	40.00	16.00	9.50
132	Frank Howard	50.00	20.00	12.00
133	Manuel Javier	40.00	16.00	9.50
134	Deron Johnson	45.00	18.00	11.00
135	Ken Johnson	40.00	16.00	9.50
136	Jim Kaat	60.00	24.00	14.50
137	Lou Klimchock	40.00	16.00	9.50
138	Art Mahaffey	40.00	16.00	9.50
139	Carl Mathias	40.00	16.00	9.50
140	Julio Navarro	40.00	16.00	9.50
141	Jim Proctor	40.00	16.00	9.50
142	Bill Short	40.00	16.00	9.50
143	Al Spangler	40.00	16.00	9.50
144	Al Stieglitz	40.00	16.00	9.50
145	Jim Umbricht	40.00	16.00	9.50
146	Ted Wieand	40.00	16.00	9.50
147	Bob Will	40.00	16.00	9.50
148	Carl Yastrzemski	550.00	275.00	165.00
149	Bob Nieman	40.00	16.00	9.50
150	Billy Pierce	40.00	16.00	9.50
151	Giants Team/Checklist 177-264	75.00	30.00	18.00
152	Gail Harris	40.00	16.00	9.50
153	Bobby Thomson	40.00	16.00	9.50
154	Jim Davenport	40.00	16.00	9.50
155	Charlie Neal	40.00	16.00	9.50
156	Art Ceccarelli	40.00	16.00	9.50
157	Rocky Nelson	40.00	16.00	9.50
158	Wes Covington	40.00	16.00	9.50
159	Jim Piersall	45.00	18.00	11.00
160	Rival All-Stars(Ken Boyer, Mickey Mantle)	600.00	250.00	150.00
161	Ray Narleski	40.00	16.00	9.50

No.	Player	NM	E	VG
162	Sammy Taylor	40.00	16.00	9.50
163	Hector Lopez	40.00	16.00	9.50
164	Reds Team/Checklist 89-176	75.00	30.00	18.00
165	Jack Sanford	40.00	16.00	9.50
166	Chuck Essegian	40.00	16.00	9.50
167	Valmy Thomas	40.00	16.00	9.50
168	Alex Grammas	40.00	16.00	9.50
169	Jake Striker	40.00	16.00	9.50
170	Del Crandall	40.00	16.00	9.50
171	Johnny Groth	40.00	16.00	9.50
172	Willie Kirkland	40.00	16.00	9.50
173	Billy Martin	45.00	18.00	11.00
174	Indians Team/Checklist 89-176	75.00	30.00	18.00
175	Pedro Ramos	40.00	16.00	9.50
176	Vada Pinson	45.00	18.00	11.00
177	Johnny Kucks	40.00	16.00	9.50
178	Woody Held	40.00	16.00	9.50
179	Rip Coleman	40.00	16.00	9.50
180	Harry Simpson	40.00	16.00	9.50
181	Billy Loes	40.00	16.00	9.50
182	Glen Hobbie	40.00	16.00	9.50
183	Eli Grba	40.00	16.00	9.50
184	Gary Geiger	40.00	16.00	9.50
185	Jim Owens	40.00	16.00	9.50
186	Dave Sisler	40.00	16.00	9.50
187	Jay Hook	40.00	16.00	9.50
188	Dick Williams	40.00	16.00	9.50
189	Don McMahon	40.00	16.00	9.50
190	Gene Woodling	40.00	16.00	9.50
191	Johnny Klippstein	40.00	16.00	9.50
192	Danny O'Connell	40.00	16.00	9.50
193	Dick Hyde	40.00	16.00	9.50
194	Bobby Gene Smith	40.00	16.00	9.50
195	Lindy McDaniel	40.00	16.00	9.50
196	Andy Carey	40.00	16.00	9.50
197	Ron Kline	40.00	16.00	9.50
198	Jerry Lynch	40.00	16.00	9.50

1962 Venezuelan Topps

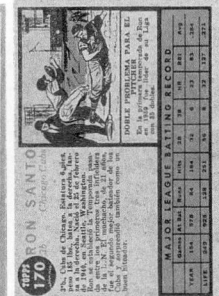

For the first time in its short history of producing baseball cards for the Venezuelan market, Topps in 1962 reprinted virtually the entire back of each card in Spanish (except the League Leaders cards #51-60). The player personal data, career summary and even the cartoon are En Espanol; only the stats are in English. There is no Topps credit or copyright line on the backs. Otherwise identical in format to the 1962 Topps North American issue, the Venezuelan set comprises the first 198 cards of the Topps issue, though cards #197 (Daryl Spencer) and 198 (Johnny Keane) have been replaced with two local Major Leaguers. Survivors of this issue tend to be in lower grades due to the common practice of gluing cards into albums or scrapbooks.

	NM	E	VG
Complete Set (198):	8,000	3,200	2,000
Common Player:	30.00	12.00	7.50

No.	Player	NM	E	VG
1	Roger Maris	750.00	300.00	185.00
2	Jim Brosnan	30.00	12.00	7.50
3	Pete Runnels	30.00	12.00	7.50
4	John DeMerit	30.00	12.00	7.50
5	Sandy Koufax	400.00	160.00	100.00
6	Marv Breeding	30.00	12.00	7.50
7	Frank Thomas	30.00	12.00	7.50
8	Ray Herbert	30.00	12.00	7.50
9	Jim Davenport	30.00	12.00	7.50
10	Roberto Clemente	550.00	220.00	135.00
11	Tom Morgan	30.00	12.00	7.50
12	Harry Craft	30.00	12.00	7.50
13	Dick Howser	30.00	12.00	7.50
14	Bill White	30.00	12.00	7.50
15	Dick Donovan	30.00	12.00	7.50
16	Darrell Johnson	30.00	12.00	7.50
17	Johnny Callison	30.00	12.00	7.50
18	Managers' Dream (Mickey Mantle, Willie Mays)	1,500	600.00	375.00
19	Ray Washburn	30.00	12.00	7.50
20	Rocky Colavito	60.00	24.00	15.00
21	Jim Kaat	30.00	12.00	7.50
22	Checklist 1-88	30.00	12.00	7.50
23	Norm Larker	30.00	12.00	7.50
24	Tigers team	90.00	36.00	22.00
25	Ernie Banks	175.00	70.00	45.00
26	Chris Cannizzaro	30.00	12.00	7.50
27	Chuck Cottier	30.00	12.00	7.50
28	Minnie Minoso	45.00	18.00	11.00
29	Casey Stengel	125.00	50.00	30.00
30	Eddie Mathews	125.00	50.00	30.00
31	Tom Tresh	40.00	16.00	10.00
32	John Roseboro	30.00	12.00	7.50
33	Don Larsen	30.00	12.00	7.50
34	Johnny Temple	30.00	12.00	7.50
35	Don Schwall	30.00	12.00	7.50
36	Don Leppert	30.00	12.00	7.50
37	Tribe Hill Trio (Barry Latman, Jim Perry, Dick Stigman)	30.00	12.00	7.50
38	Gene Stephens	30.00	12.00	7.50
39	Joe Koppe	30.00	12.00	7.50
40	Orlando Cepeda	65.00	25.00	15.00
41	Cliff Cook	30.00	12.00	7.50
42	Jim King	30.00	12.00	7.50
43	Dodgers team	125.00	50.00	30.00
44	Don Taussig	30.00	12.00	7.50
45	Brooks Robinson	200.00	80.00	50.00
46	Jack Baldschun	30.00	12.00	7.50
47	Bob Will	30.00	12.00	7.50
48	Ralph Terry	30.00	12.00	7.50
49	Hal Jones	30.00	12.00	7.50
50	Stan Musial	250.00	100.00	60.00
51	A.L. Batting Leaders (Norm Cash, Elston Howard, Al Kaline, Jim Piersall)	80.00	32.00	20.00
52	N.L. Batting Leaders (Ken Boyer, Roberto Clemente, Wally Moon, Vada Pinson)	225.00	90.00	55.00
53	A.L. Home Run Leaders (Jim Gentile, Harmon Killebrew, Mickey Mantle, Roger Maris)	400.00	160.00	100.00
54	N.L. Home Run Leaders (Orlando Cepeda, Willie Mays, Frank Robinson)	125.00	50.00	30.00
55	A.L. E.R.A. Leaders (Dick Donovan, Don Mossi, Milt Pappas, Bill Stafford)	30.00	12.00	7.50
56	N.L. E.R.A. Leaders (Mike McCormick, Jim O'Toole, Curt Simmons, Warren Spahn)	35.00	14.00	8.75
57	A.L. Win Leaders (Steve Barber, Jim Bunning, Whitey Ford, Frank Lary)	45.00	18.00	11.00
58	N.L. Win Leaders (Joe Jay, Jim O'Toole, Warren Spahn)	35.00	14.00	8.75
59	A.L. Strikeout Leaders (Jim Bunning, Whitey Ford, Camilo Pascual, Juan Pizzaro)	45.00	18.00	11.00
60	N.L. Strikeout Leaders (Don Drysdale, Sandy Koufax, Jim O'Toole, Stan Williams)	100.00	40.00	25.00
61	Cardinals Team	90.00	36.00	22.00
62	Steve Boros	30.00	12.00	7.50
63	Tony Cloninger	30.00	12.00	7.50
64	Russ Snyder	30.00	12.00	7.50
65	Bobby Richardson	40.00	16.00	10.00
66	Cuno Barragan (Barragan)	30.00	12.00	7.50
67	Harvey Haddix	30.00	12.00	7.50
68	Ken Hunt	30.00	12.00	7.50
69	Phil Ortega	30.00	12.00	7.50
70	Harmon Killebrew	125.00	50.00	30.00
71	Dick LeMay	30.00	12.00	7.50
72	Bob's Pupils (Steve Boros, Bob Scheffing, Jake Wood)	30.00	12.00	7.50
73	Nellie Fox	125.00	50.00	30.00
74	Bob Lillis	30.00	12.00	7.50
75	Milt Pappas	30.00	12.00	7.50
76	Howie Bedell	30.00	12.00	7.50
77	Tony Taylor	30.00	12.00	7.50
78	Gene Green	30.00	12.00	7.50
79	Ed Hobaugh	30.00	12.00	7.50
80	Vada Pinson	35.00	14.00	8.75
81	Jim Pagliaroni	30.00	12.00	7.50
82	Deron Johnson	30.00	12.00	7.50
83	Larry Jackson	30.00	12.00	7.50
84	Lenny Green	30.00	12.00	7.50
85	Gil Hodges	80.00	32.00	20.00
86	Donn Clendenon	30.00	12.00	7.50
87	Mike Roarke	30.00	12.00	7.50
88	Ralph Houk	30.00	12.00	7.50
89	Barney Schultz	30.00	12.00	7.50
90	Jim Piersall	30.00	12.00	7.50
91	J.C. Martin	30.00	12.00	7.50
92	Sam Jones	30.00	12.00	7.50
93	John Blanchard	30.00	12.00	7.50
94	Jay Hook	30.00	12.00	7.50
95	Don Hoak	30.00	12.00	7.50
96	Eli Grba	30.00	12.00	7.50
97	Tito Francona	30.00	12.00	7.50
98	Checklist 89-176	30.00	12.00	7.50
99	Boog Powell	75.00	30.00	18.50
100	Warren Spahn	125.00	50.00	30.00
101	Carroll Hardy	30.00	12.00	7.50
102	Al Schroll	30.00	12.00	7.50
103	Don Blasingame	30.00	12.00	7.50
104	Ted Savage	30.00	12.00	7.50
105	Don Mossi	30.00	12.00	7.50
106	Carl Sawatski	30.00	12.00	7.50
107	Mike McCormick	30.00	12.00	7.50
108	Willie Davis	30.00	12.00	7.50
109	Bob Shaw	30.00	12.00	7.50
110	Bill Skowron	35.00	14.00	8.75
111	Dallas Green	30.00	12.00	7.50
112	Hank Foiles	30.00	12.00	7.50
113	White Sox team	90.00	36.00	22.00
114	Howie Koplitz	30.00	12.00	7.50
115	Bob Skinner	30.00	12.00	7.50
116	Herb Score	30.00	12.00	7.50
117	Gary Geiger	30.00	12.00	7.50
118	Julian Javier	30.00	12.00	7.50
119	Danny Murphy	30.00	12.00	7.50
120	Bob Purkey	30.00	12.00	7.50
121	Billy Hitchcock	30.00	12.00	7.50
122	Norm Bass	30.00	12.00	7.50
123	Mike de la Hoz	30.00	12.00	7.50
124	Bill Pleis	30.00	12.00	7.50
125	Gene Woodling	30.00	12.00	7.50
126	Al Cicotte	30.00	12.00	7.50
127	Pride of the A's (Hank Bauer, Jerry Lumpe, Norm Siebern)	30.00	12.00	7.50
128	Art Fowler	30.00	12.00	7.50
129	Lee Walls	30.00	12.00	7.50
130	Frank Bolling	30.00	12.00	7.50
131	Pete Richert	30.00	12.00	7.50
132	Angels Team	90.00	36.00	22.00
133	Felipe Alou	45.00	18.00	11.00
134	Billy Hoeft	30.00	12.00	7.50
135	Babe as a Boy (Babe Ruth)	165.00	65.00	40.00
136	Babe Joins Yanks (Babe Ruth)	200.00	80.00	50.00
137	Babe and Mgr. Huggins (Babe Ruth)	165.00	65.00	40.00
138	The Famous Slugger (Babe Ruth)	200.00	80.00	50.00
139	Babe Hits 60 (Babe Ruth)	300.00	120.00	75.00
140	Gehrig and Ruth (Babe Ruth)	225.00	90.00	55.00
141	Twilight Years (Babe Ruth)	165.00	65.00	40.00
142	Coaching for the Dodgers (Babe Ruth)	165.00	65.00	40.00
143	Greatest Sports Hero (Babe Ruth)	165.00	65.00	40.00
144	Farewell Speech (Babe Ruth)	165.00	65.00	40.00
145	Barry Latman	30.00	12.00	7.50
146	Don Demeter	30.00	12.00	7.50
147	Bill Kunkel	30.00	12.00	7.50
148	Wally Post	30.00	12.00	7.50
149	Bob Duliba	30.00	12.00	7.50
150	Al Kaline	135.00	55.00	35.00
151	Johnny Klippstein	30.00	12.00	7.50
152	Mickey Vernon	30.00	12.00	7.50
153	Pumpsie Green	30.00	12.00	7.50
154	Lee Thomas	30.00	12.00	7.50
155	Stu Miller	30.00	12.00	7.50
156	Merritt Ranew	30.00	12.00	7.50
157	Wes Covington	30.00	12.00	7.50
158	Braves Team	90.00	36.00	22.00
159	Hal Reniff	30.00	12.00	7.50
160	Dick Stuart	30.00	12.00	7.50
161	Frank Baumann	30.00	12.00	7.50
162	Sammy Drake	30.00	12.00	7.50
163	Hot Corner Guardians (Cletis Boyer, Billy Gardner)	30.00	12.00	7.50
164	Hal Naragon	30.00	12.00	7.50

165	Jackie Brandt	30.00	12.00	7.50
166	Don Lee	30.00	12.00	7.50
167	Tim McCarver	125.00	50.00	30.00
168	Leo Posada	30.00	12.00	7.50
169	Bob Cerv	30.00	12.00	7.50
170	Ron Santo	40.00	16.00	10.00
171	Dave Sisler	30.00	12.00	7.50
172	Fred Hutchinson	30.00	12.00	7.50
173	Chico Fernandez	30.00	12.00	7.50
174	Carl Willey	30.00	12.00	7.50
175	Frank Howard	30.00	12.00	7.50
176	Eddie Yost	30.00	12.00	7.50
177	Bobby Shantz	30.00	12.00	7.50
178	Camilo Carreon	30.00	12.00	7.50
179	Tom Sturdivant	30.00	12.00	7.50
180	Bob Allison	30.00	12.00	7.50
181	Paul Brown	30.00	12.00	7.50
182	Bob Nieman	30.00	12.00	7.50
183	Roger Craig	30.00	12.00	7.50
184	Haywood Sullivan	30.00	12.00	7.50
185	Roland Sheldon	30.00	12.00	7.50
186	Mack Jones	30.00	12.00	7.50
187	Gene Conley	30.00	12.00	7.50
188	Chuck Hiller	30.00	12.00	7.50
189	Dick Hall	30.00	12.00	7.50
190	Wally Moon	30.00	12.00	7.50
191	Jim Brewer	30.00	12.00	7.50
192	Checklist 177-264	30.00	12.00	7.50
193	Eddie Kasko	30.00	12.00	7.50
194	Dean Chance	30.00	12.00	7.50
195	Joe Cunningham	30.00	12.00	7.50
196	Terry Fox	30.00	12.00	7.50
199	Elio Chacon	60.00	24.00	15.00
200	Luis Aparicio	250.00	100.00	62.00

1964 Venezuelan Topps

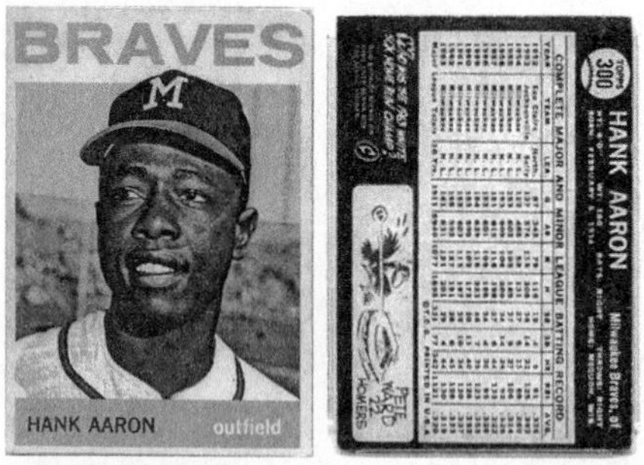

The first 370 cards of Topps' baseball set were issued in a parallel version for sale in Venezuela. Printed on thin cardboard with no front gloss, the cards are differentiated from the U.S. version by the use of a black border on back. Survivors of the issue are usually in low grade because of the common Latin American practice of collectors gluing the cards into the album that was available. Venezuelan Topps cards were often cut up to 1/8" smaller than their U.S. counterparts.

	NM	E	VG
Complete Set (370):	9,500	3,800	2,400
Common Player:	30.00	12.00	7.50
Album:	300.00	125.00	75.00

1	N.L. E.R.A. Leaders(Dick Ellsworth, Bob Friend, Sandy Koufax)	36.00	22.00	
2	A.L. E.R.A. Leaders(Camilo Pascual, Gary Peters, Juan Pizarro)	12.00	7.50	
3	N.L. Pitching Leaders(Sandy Koufax, Jim Maloney, Juan Marichal, Warren Spahn)	24.00	15.00	
4	A.L. Pitching Leaders(Jim Bouton, Whitey Ford, Camilo Pascual)	45.00	18.00	11.00
5	N.L. Strikeout Leaders(Don Drysdale, Sandy Koufax, Jim Maloney)	60.00	24.00	15.00
6	A.L. Strikeout Leaders(Jim Bunning, Camilo Pascual, Dick Stigman)	35.00	14.00	8.75
7	N.L. Batting Leaders(Hank Aaron, Roberto Clemente, Tommy Davis, Dick Groat)	100.00	40.00	25.00
8	A.L. Batting Leaders(Al Kaline, Rich Rollins, Carl Yastrzemski)	50.00	20.00	12.50
9	N.L. Home Run Leaders(Hank Aaron, Orlando Cepeda, Willie Mays, Willie McCovey)	75.00	30.00	18.50
10	A.L. Home Run Leaders (Bob Allison, Harmon Killebrew, Dick Stuart)	45.00	18.00	11.00
11	N.L. R.B.I. Leader s(Hank Aaron, Ken Boyer, Bill White)	50.00	20.00	12.50
12	A.L. R.B.I. Leaders(Al Kaline, Harmon Killebrew, Dick Stuart)	45.00	18.00	11.00
13	Hoyt Wilhelm	50.00	20.00	12.50
14	Dodgers Rookies(Dick Nen, Nick Willhite)	30.00	12.00	7.50
15	Zoilo Versalles	30.00	12.00	7.50
16	John Boozer	30.00	12.00	7.50
17	Willie Kirkland	30.00	12.00	7.50
18	Billy O'Dell	30.00	12.00	7.50
19	Don Wart	30.00	12.00	7.50
20	Bob Friend	30.00	12.00	7.50
21	Yogi Berra	100.00	40.00	25.00
22	Jerry Adair	30.00	12.00	7.50
23	Chris Zachary	30.00	12.00	7.50
24	Carl Sawatski	30.00	12.00	7.50
25	Bill Monbouquette	30.00	12.00	7.50
26	Gino Cimoli	30.00	12.00	7.50
27	Mets Team	65.00	26.00	16.00
28	Claude Osteen	30.00	12.00	7.50
29	Lou Brock	75.00	30.00	18.50
30	Ron Perranoski	30.00	12.00	7.50
31	Dave Nicholson	30.00	12.00	7.50
32	Dean Chance	30.00	12.00	7.50
33	Reds Rookies(Sammy Ellis, Mel Queen)	30.00	12.00	7.50
34	Jim Perry	30.00	12.00	7.50
35	Eddie Mathews	75.00	30.00	18.50
36	Hal Reniff	30.00	12.00	7.50
37	Smoky Burgess	30.00	12.00	7.50
38	Jim Wynn	30.00	12.00	7.50
39	Hank Aguirre	30.00	12.00	7.50
40	Dick Groat	30.00	12.00	7.50
41	Friendly Foes(Willie McCovey, Leon Wagner)	35.00	14.00	8.75
42	Moe Drabowsky	30.00	12.00	7.50
43	Roy Sievers	30.00	12.00	7.50
44	Duke Carmel	30.00	12.00	7.50
45	Milt Pappas	30.00	12.00	7.50
46	Ed Brinkman	30.00	12.00	7.50
47	Giants Rookies(Jesus Alou, Ron Herbel)	30.00	12.00	7.50
48	Bob Perry	30.00	12.00	7.50
49	Bill Henry	30.00	12.00	7.50
50	Mickey Mantle	1,800	720.00	450.00
51	Pete Richert	30.00	12.00	7.50
52	Chuck Hinton	30.00	12.00	7.50
53	Denis Menke	30.00	12.00	7.50
54	Sam Mele	30.00	12.00	7.50
55	Ernie Banks	75.00	30.00	18.50
56	Hal Brown	30.00	12.00	7.50
57	Tim Harkness	30.00	12.00	7.50
58	Don Demeter	30.00	12.00	7.50
59	Ernie Broglio	30.00	12.00	7.50
60	Frank Malzone	30.00	12.00	7.50
61	Angel Backstops(Bob Rodgers, Ed Sadowski)	30.00	12.00	7.50
62	Ted Savage	30.00	12.00	7.50
63	Johnny Orsino	30.00	12.00	7.50
64	Ted Abernathy	30.00	12.00	7.50
65	Felipe Alou	35.00	14.00	8.75
66	Eddie Fisher	30.00	12.00	7.50
67	Tigers Team	50.00	20.00	12.50
68	Willie Davis	30.00	12.00	7.50
69	Clete Boyer	35.00	14.00	8.75
70	Joe Torre	45.00	18.00	11.00
71	Jack Spring	30.00	12.00	7.50
72	Chico Cardenas	30.00	12.00	7.50
73	Jimmie Hall	30.00	12.00	7.50
74	Pirates Rookies(Tom Butters, Bob Priddy)	30.00	12.00	7.50
75	Wayne Causey	30.00	12.00	7.50
76	Checklist 1-88	30.00	12.00	7.50
77	Jerry Walker	30.00	12.00	7.50
78	Merritt Ranew	30.00	12.00	7.50
79	Bob Heffner	30.00	12.00	7.50
80	Vada Pinson	45.00	18.00	11.00
81	All-Star Vets(Nellie Fox, Harmon Killebrew)	50.00	20.00	12.50
82	Jim Davenport	30.00	12.00	7.50
83	Gus Triandos	30.00	12.00	7.50
84	Carl Willey	30.00	12.00	7.50
85	Pete Ward	30.00	12.00	7.50
86	Al Downing	30.00	12.00	7.50
87	Cardinals Team	100.00	40.00	25.00
88	John Roseboro	30.00	12.00	7.50
89	Boog Powell	35.00	14.00	8.75
90	Earl Battey	30.00	12.00	7.50
91	Bob Bailey	30.00	12.00	7.50
92	Steve Ridzik	30.00	12.00	7.50
93	Gary Geiger	30.00	12.00	7.50
94	Braves Rookies(Jim Britton, Larry Maxie)	30.00	12.00	7.50
95	George Altman	30.00	12.00	7.50
96	Bob Buhl	30.00	12.00	7.50
97	Jim Fregosi	30.00	12.00	7.50
98	Bill Bruton	30.00	12.00	7.50
99	Al Stanek	30.00	12.00	7.50
100	Elston Howard	35.00	14.00	8.75
101	Walt Alston	50.00	20.00	12.50
102	Checklist 89-176	30.00	12.00	7.50
103	Curt Flood	35.00	14.00	8.75
104	Art Mahaffey	30.00	12.00	7.50
105	Woody Held	30.00	12.00	7.50
106	Joe Nuxhall	30.00	12.00	7.50
107	White Sox Rookies (Bruce Howard, Frank Kreutzer)	30.00	12.00	7.50
108	John Wyatt	30.00	12.00	7.50
109	Rusty Staub	35.00	14.00	8.75
110	Albie Pearson	30.00	12.00	7.50
111	Don Elston	30.00	12.00	7.50
112	Bob Tillman	30.00	12.00	7.50
113	Grover Powell	30.00	12.00	7.50
114	Don Lock	30.00	12.00	7.50
115	Frank Bolling	30.00	12.00	7.50
116	Twins Rookies(Tony Oliva, Jay Ward)	45.00	18.00	11.00
117	Earl Francis	30.00	12.00	7.50
118	John Blanchard	30.00	12.00	7.50
119	Gary Kolb	30.00	12.00	7.50
120	Don Drysdale	75.00	30.00	18.50
121	Pete Runnels	30.00	12.00	7.50
122	Don McMahon	30.00	12.00	7.50
123	Jose Pagan	30.00	12.00	7.50
124	Orlando Pena	30.00	12.00	7.50
125	Pete Rose	450.00	180.00	110.00
126	Russ Snyder	30.00	12.00	7.50
127	Angels Rookies(Aubrey Gatewood, Dick Simpson)	30.00	12.00	7.50
128	Mickey Lolich	35.00	14.00	8.75
129	Amado Samuel	30.00	12.00	7.50
130	Gary Peters	30.00	12.00	7.50
131	Steve Boros	30.00	12.00	7.50
132	Braves Team	50.00	20.00	12.50
133	Jim Grant	30.00	12.00	7.50
134	Don Zimmer	30.00	12.00	7.50
135	Johnny Callison	30.00	12.00	7.50
136	World Series Game 1 (Koufax Strikes Out 15)	30.00	12.00	7.50
137	World Series Game 2 (Davis Sparks Rally)	30.00	12.00	7.50
138	World Series Game 3 (L.A. Takes 3rd Straight)	30.00	12.00	7.50
139	World Series Game 4 (Sealing Yanks' Doom)	30.00	12.00	7.50
140	World Series Summary (The Dodgers Celebrate)	30.00	12.00	7.50
141	Danny Murtaugh	30.00	12.00	7.50
142	John Bateman	30.00	12.00	7.50
143	Bubba Phillips	30.00	12.00	7.50
144	Al Worthington	30.00	12.00	7.50
145	Norm Siebern	30.00	12.00	7.50
146	Indians Rookies(Bob Chance, Tommy John)	50.00	20.00	12.50
147	Ray Sadecki	30.00	12.00	7.50
148	J.C. Martin	30.00	12.00	7.50
149	Paul Foytack	30.00	12.00	7.50
150	Willie Mays	375.00	150.00	94.00
151	Athletics Team	50.00	20.00	12.50
152	Denver Lemaster	30.00	12.00	7.50
153	Dick Williams	30.00	12.00	7.50
154	Dick Tracewski	30.00	12.00	7.50
155	Duke Snider	100.00	40.00	25.00
156	Bill Dailey	30.00	12.00	7.50
157	Gene Mauch	30.00	12.00	7.50
158	Ken Johnson	30.00	12.00	7.50
159	Charlie Dees	30.00	12.00	7.50
160	Ken Boyer	35.00	14.00	8.75
161	Dave McNally	30.00	12.00	7.50
162	Hitting Area(Vada Pinson, Dick Sisler)	30.00	12.00	7.50
163	Donn Clendenon	30.00	12.00	7.50
164	Bud Daley	30.00	12.00	7.50
165	Jerry Lumpe	30.00	12.00	7.50
166	Marty Keough	30.00	12.00	7.50
167	Senators Rookies(Mike Brumley, Lou Piniella)	60.00	24.00	15.00
168	Al Weis	30.00	12.00	7.50
169	Del Crandall	30.00	12.00	7.50
170	Dick Radatz	30.00	12.00	7.50
171	Ty Cline	30.00	12.00	7.50
172	Indians Team	50.00	20.00	12.50
173	Ryne Duren	30.00	12.00	7.50
174	Doc Edwards	30.00	12.00	7.50
175	Billy Williams	50.00	20.00	12.50
176	Tracy Stallard	30.00	12.00	7.50
177	Harmon Killebrew	75.00	30.00	18.50
178	Hank Bauer	30.00	12.00	7.50
179	Carl Warwick	30.00	12.00	7.50
180	Tommy Davis	30.00	12.00	7.50
181	Dave Wickersham	30.00	12.00	7.50
182	Sox Sockers(Chuck Schilling, Carl Yastrzemski)	50.00	20.00	12.50
183	Ron Taylor	30.00	12.00	7.50

184	Al Luplow	30.00	12.00	7.50
185	Jim O'Toole	30.00	12.00	7.50
186	Roman Mejias	30.00	12.00	7.50
187	Ed Roebuck	30.00	12.00	7.50
188	Checklist 177-264	30.00	12.00	7.50
189	Bob Hendley	30.00	12.00	7.50
190	Bobby Richardson	35.00	14.00	8.75
191	Clay Dalrymple	30.00	12.00	7.50
192	Cubs Rookies (John Boccabella, Billy Cowan)	30.00	12.00	7.50
193	Jerry Lynch	30.00	12.00	7.50
194	John Goryl	30.00	12.00	7.50
195	Floyd Robinson	30.00	12.00	7.50
196	Jim Gentile	30.00	12.00	7.50
197	Frank Lary	30.00	12.00	7.50
198	Len Gabrielson	30.00	12.00	7.50
199	Joe Azcue	30.00	12.00	7.50
200	Sandy Koufax	300.00	120.00	75.00
201	Orioles Rookies (Sam Bowens, Wally Bunker)	30.00	12.00	7.50
202	Galen Cisco	30.00	12.00	7.50
203	John Kennedy	30.00	12.00	7.50
204	Matty Alou	30.00	12.00	7.50
205	Nellie Fox	65.00	26.00	16.00
206	Steve Hamilton	30.00	12.00	7.50
207	Fred Hutchinson	30.00	12.00	7.50
208	Wes Covington	30.00	12.00	7.50
209	Bob Allen	30.00	12.00	7.50
210	Carl Yastrzemski	100.00	40.00	25.00
211	Jim Coker	30.00	12.00	7.50
212	Pete Lovrich	30.00	12.00	7.50
213	**Angels Team**	50.00	20.00	12.50
214	Ken McMullen	30.00	12.00	7.50
215	Ray Herbert	30.00	12.00	7.50
216	Mike de la Hoz	30.00	12.00	7.50
217	Jim King	30.00	12.00	7.50
218	Hank Fischer	30.00	12.00	7.50
219	Young Aces (Jim Bouton, Al Downing)	35.00	14.00	8.75
220	Dick Ellsworth	30.00	12.00	7.50
221	Bob Saverine	30.00	12.00	7.50
222	Bill Pierce	30.00	12.00	7.50
223	George Banks	30.00	12.00	7.50
224	Tommie Sisk	30.00	12.00	7.50
225	Roger Maris	300.00	120.00	75.00
226	Colts Rookies (Gerald Grote, Larry Yellen)	30.00	12.00	7.50
227	Barry Latman	30.00	12.00	7.50
228	Felix Mantilla	30.00	12.00	7.50
229	Charley Lau	30.00	12.00	7.50
230	Brooks Robinson	110.00	45.00	25.00
231	Dick Calmus	30.00	12.00	7.50
232	Al Lopez	50.00	20.00	12.50
233	Hal Smith	30.00	12.00	7.50
234	Gary Bell	30.00	12.00	7.50
235	Ron Hunt	30.00	12.00	7.50
236	Bill Faul	30.00	12.00	7.50
237	Cubs Team	50.00	20.00	12.50
238	Roy McMillan	30.00	12.00	7.50
239	Herm Starrette	30.00	12.00	7.50
240	Bill White	30.00	12.00	7.50
241	Jim Owens	30.00	12.00	7.50
242	Harvey Kuenn	30.00	12.00	7.50
243	Phillies Rookies (Richie Allen, John Herrnstein)	50.00	20.00	12.50
244	Tony LaRussa	35.00	14.00	8.75
245	Dick Stigman	30.00	12.00	7.50
246	Manny Mota	30.00	12.00	7.50
247	Dave DeBusschere	30.00	12.00	7.50
248	Johnny Pesky	30.00	12.00	7.50
249	Doug Camilli	30.00	12.00	7.50
250	Al Kaline	110.00	45.00	25.00
251	Choo Choo Coleman	30.00	12.00	7.50
252	Ken Aspromonte	30.00	12.00	7.50
253	Wally Post	30.00	12.00	7.50
254	Don Hoak	30.00	12.00	7.50
255	Lee Thomas	30.00	12.00	7.50
256	Johnny Weekly	30.00	12.00	7.50
257	Giants Team	50.00	20.00	12.50
258	Garry Roggenburk	30.00	12.00	7.50
259	Harry Bright	30.00	12.00	7.50
260	Frank Robinson	100.00	40.00	25.00
261	Jim Hannan	30.00	12.00	7.50
262	Cardinals Rookies(Harry Fanok, Mike Shannon)	35.00	14.00	8.75
263	Chuck Estrada	30.00	12.00	7.50
264	Jim Landis	30.00	12.00	7.50
265	Jim Bunning	50.00	20.00	12.50
266	Gene Freese	30.00	12.00	7.50
267	Wilbur Wood	30.00	12.00	7.50
268	Bill's Got It(Danny Murtaugh, Bill Virdon)	30.00	12.00	7.50
269	Ellis Burton	30.00	12.00	7.50
270	Rich Rollins	30.00	12.00	7.50
271	Bob Sadowski	30.00	12.00	7.50
272	Jake Wood	30.00	12.00	7.50
273	Mel Nelson	30.00	12.00	7.50
274	Checklist 265-352	30.00	12.00	7.50
275	John Tsitouris	30.00	12.00	7.50
276	Jose Tartabull	30.00	12.00	7.50
277	Ken Retzer	30.00	12.00	7.50
278	Bobby Shantz	30.00	12.00	7.50
279	Joe Koppe	30.00	12.00	7.50
280	Juan Marichal	65.00	26.00	16.00
281	Yankees Rookies(Jake Gibbs, Tom Metcalf)	30.00	12.00	7.50
282	Bob Bruce	30.00	12.00	7.50
283	Tommy McCraw	30.00	12.00	7.50
284	Dick Schofield	30.00	12.00	7.50
285	Robin Roberts	65.00	26.00	16.00
286	Don Landrum	30.00	12.00	7.50
287	Red Sox Rookies (Tony Conigliaro, Bill Spanswick)	35.00	14.00	8.75
288	Al Moran	30.00	12.00	7.50
289	Frank Funk	30.00	12.00	7.50
290	Bob Allison	30.00	12.00	7.50
291	Phil Ortega	30.00	12.00	7.50
292	Mike Roarke	30.00	12.00	7.50
293	**Phillies Team**	50.00	20.00	12.50
294	Ken Hunt	30.00	12.00	7.50
295	Roger Craig	30.00	12.00	7.50
296	Ed Kirkpatrick	30.00	12.00	7.50
297	Ken MacKenzie	30.00	12.00	7.50
298	Harry Craft	30.00	12.00	7.50
299	Bill Stafford	30.00	12.00	7.50
300	Hank Aaron	375.00	150.00	94.00
301	Larry Brown	30.00	12.00	7.50
302	Dan Pfister	30.00	12.00	7.50
303	Jim Campbell	30.00	12.00	7.50
304	Bob Johnson	30.00	12.00	7.50
305	Jack Lamabe	30.00	12.00	7.50
306	Giant Gunners (Orlando Cepeda, Willie Mays)	50.00	20.00	12.50
307	Joe Gibbon	30.00	12.00	7.50
308	Gene Stephens	30.00	12.00	7.50
309	Paul Toth	30.00	12.00	7.50
310	Jim Gilliam	30.00	12.00	7.50
311	Tom Brown	30.00	12.00	7.50
312	Tigers Rookies (Fritz Fisher, Fred Gladding)	30.00	12.00	7.50
313	Chuck Hiller	30.00	12.00	7.50
314	Jerry Buchek	30.00	12.00	7.50
315	Bo Belinsky	30.00	12.00	7.50
316	Gene Oliver	30.00	12.00	7.50
317	Al Smith	30.00	12.00	7.50
318	Twins Team	50.00	20.00	12.50
319	Paul Brown	30.00	12.00	7.50
320	Rocky Colavito	50.00	20.00	12.50
321	Bob Lillis	30.00	12.00	7.50
322	George Brunet	30.00	12.00	7.50
323	John Buzhardt	30.00	12.00	7.50
324	Casey Stengel	50.00	20.00	12.50
325	Hector Lopez	30.00	12.00	7.50
326	Ron Brand	30.00	12.00	7.50
327	Don Blasingame	30.00	12.00	7.50
328	Bob Shaw	30.00	12.00	7.50
329	Russ Nixon	30.00	12.00	7.50
330	Tommy Harper	30.00	12.00	7.50
331	A.L. Bombers (Norm Cash, Al Kaline, Mickey Mantle, Roger Maris)	600.00	240.00	150.00
332	Ray Washburn	30.00	12.00	7.50
333	Billy Moran	30.00	12.00	7.50
334	Lew Krausse	30.00	12.00	7.50
335	Don Mossi	30.00	12.00	7.50
336	Andre Rodgers	30.00	12.00	7.50
337	Dodgers Rookies (Al Ferrara, Jeff Torborg)	30.00	12.00	7.50
338	Jack Kralick	30.00	12.00	7.50
339	Walt Bond	30.00	12.00	7.50
340	Joe Cunningham	30.00	12.00	7.50
341	Jim Roland	30.00	12.00	7.50
342	Willie Stargell	65.00	26.00	16.00
343	Senators Team	50.00	20.00	12.50
344	Phil Linz	30.00	12.00	7.50
345	Frank Thomas	30.00	12.00	7.50
346	Joe Jay	30.00	12.00	7.50
347	Bobby Wine	30.00	12.00	7.50
348	Ed Lopat	30.00	12.00	7.50
349	Art Fowler	30.00	12.00	7.50
350	Willie McCovey	75.00	30.00	18.50
351	Dan Schneider	30.00	12.00	7.50
352	Eddie Bressoud	30.00	12.00	7.50
353	Wally Moon	30.00	12.00	7.50
354	Dave Giusti	30.00	12.00	7.50
355	Vic Power	30.00	12.00	7.50
356	Reds Rookies(Bill McCool, Chico Ruiz)	30.00	12.00	7.50
357	Charley James	30.00	12.00	7.50
358	Ron Kline	30.00	12.00	7.50
359	Jim Schaffer	30.00	12.00	7.50
360	Joe Pepitone	30.00	12.00	7.50
361	Jay Hook	30.00	12.00	7.50
362	Checklist 353-429	30.00	12.00	7.50
363	Dick McAuliffe	30.00	12.00	7.50
364	Joe Gaines	30.00	12.00	7.50
365	Cal McLish	30.00	12.00	7.50
366	Nelson Mathews	30.00	12.00	7.50
367	Fred Whitfield	30.00	12.00	7.50
368	White Sox Rookies(Fritz Ackley, Don Buford)	30.00	12.00	7.50
369	Jerry Zimmerman	30.00	12.00	7.50
370	Hal Woodeshick	30.00	12.00	7.50

1966 Venezuelan Topps

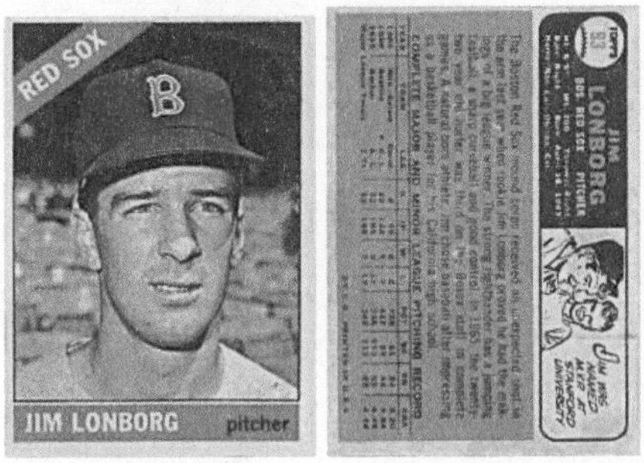

The first 370 cards on Topps' 1966 baseball set were reprinted for sale in the Venezuelan market. Identical in design to the Topps cards, they have no Spanish on them. The South American version is printed on darker cardboard that has virtually no gloss on front and bright orange-pink highlights on back. Low-grade cards are the norm for this and other Venezuelan issues as it is common collector practice south of the border to mount cards in scrapbooks and albums. The Venezuelan cards are often found up to 1/8" smaller than their U.S. counterparts.

		NM	E	VG
Complete Set (370):		8,000	3,250	2,000
Common Player:		30.00	12.00	7.50
1	Willie Mays	400.00	160.00	100.00
2	Ted Abernathy	30.00	12.00	7.50
3	Sam Mele	30.00	12.00	7.50
4	Ray Culp	30.00	12.00	7.50
5	Jim Fregosi	30.00	12.00	7.50
6	Chuck Schilling	30.00	12.00	7.50
7	Tracy Stallard	30.00	12.00	7.50
8	Floyd Robinson	30.00	12.00	7.50
9	Clete Boyer	35.00	14.00	8.75
10	Tony Cloninger	30.00	12.00	7.50
11	Senators Rookies (Brant Alyea, Pete Craig)	30.00	12.00	7.50
12	John Tsitouris	30.00	12.00	7.50
13	Lou Johnson	30.00	12.00	7.50
14	Norm Siebern	30.00	12.00	7.50
15	Vern Law	30.00	12.00	7.50
16	Larry Brown	30.00	12.00	7.50
17	Johnny Stephenson	30.00	12.00	7.50
18	Roland Sheldon	30.00	12.00	7.50
19	**Giants Team**	75.00	30.00	18.50
20	Willie Horton	30.00	12.00	7.50
21	Don Nottebart	30.00	12.00	7.50
22	Joe Nossek	30.00	12.00	7.50
23	Jack Sanford	30.00	12.00	7.50
24	Don Kessinger	30.00	12.00	7.50
25	Pete Ward	30.00	12.00	7.50
26	Ray Sadecki	30.00	12.00	7.50
27	Orioles Rookies (Andy Etchebarren, Darold Knowles)	30.00	12.00	7.50
28	Phil Niekro	100.00	40.00	25.00
29	Mike Brumley	30.00	12.00	7.50
30	Pete Rose	375.00	150.00	94.00
31	Jack Cullen	30.00	12.00	7.50
32	Adolfo Phillips	30.00	12.00	7.50
33	Jim Pagliaroni	30.00	12.00	7.50
34	Checklist 1-88	30.00	12.00	7.50
35	Ron Swoboda	30.00	12.00	7.50
36	Catfish Hunter	100.00	40.00	25.00
37	Billy Herman	90.00	36.00	22.00
38	Ron Nischwitz	30.00	12.00	7.50
39	Ken Henderson	30.00	12.00	7.50
40	Jim Grant	30.00	12.00	7.50
41	Don LeJohn	30.00	12.00	7.50
42	Aubrey Gatewood	30.00	12.00	7.50
43a	Don Landrum (No button on pants)	30.00	12.00	7.50
43b	Don Landrum (Partial button on pants)	30.00	12.00	7.50
43c	Don Landrum (Full button on pants)	30.00	12.00	7.50
44	Indians Rookies(Bill Davis, Tom Kelley)	30.00	12.00	7.50
45	Jim Gentile	30.00	12.00	7.50
46	Howie Koplitz	30.00	12.00	7.50
47	J.C. Martin	30.00	12.00	7.50
48	Paul Blair	30.00	12.00	7.50

#	Player			
49	Woody Woodward	30.00	12.00	7.50
50	Mickey Mantle	1,500	600.00	375.00
51	Gordon Richardson	30.00	12.00	7.50
52	Power Plus (Johnny Callison, Wes Covington)	30.00	12.00	7.50
53	Bob Duliba	30.00	12.00	7.50
54	Jose Pagan	30.00	12.00	7.50
55	Ken Harrelson	30.00	12.00	7.50
56	Sandy Valdespino	30.00	12.00	7.50
57	Jim Lefebvre	30.00	12.00	7.50
58	Dave Wickersham	30.00	12.00	7.50
59	Reds Team	75.00	30.00	18.50
60	Curt Flood	35.00	14.00	8.75
61	Bob Bolin	30.00	12.00	7.50
62a	Merritt Ranew (no sold statement)	40.00	16.00	9.50
63b	Merritt Ranew (with sold statement)	30.00	12.00	7.50
63	Jim Stewart	30.00	12.00	7.50
64	Bob Bruce	30.00	12.00	7.50
65	Leon Wagner	30.00	12.00	7.50
66	Al Weis	30.00	12.00	7.50
67	Mets Rookies (Cleon Jones, Dick Selma)	35.00	14.00	8.75
68	Hal Reniff	30.00	12.00	7.50
69	Ken Hamlin	30.00	12.00	7.50
70	Carl Yastrzemski	150.00	60.00	37.00
71	Frank Carpin	30.00	12.00	7.50
72	Tony Perez	150.00	60.00	37.00
73	Jerry Zimmerman	30.00	12.00	7.50
74	Don Mossi	30.00	12.00	7.50
75	Tommy Davis	30.00	12.00	7.50
76	Red Schoendienst	90.00	36.00	22.00
77	Johnny Orsino	30.00	12.00	7.50
78	Frank Linzy	30.00	12.00	7.50
79	Joe Pepitone	30.00	12.00	7.50
80	Richie Allen	45.00	18.00	11.00
81	Ray Oyler	30.00	12.00	7.50
82	Bob Hendley	30.00	12.00	7.50
83	Albie Pearson	30.00	12.00	7.50
84	Braves Rookies (Jim Beauchamp, Dick Kelley)	30.00	12.00	7.50
85	Eddie Fisher	30.00	12.00	7.50
86	John Bateman	30.00	12.00	7.50
87	Dan Napoleon	30.00	12.00	7.50
88	Fred Whitfield	30.00	12.00	7.50
89	Ted Davidson	30.00	12.00	7.50
90	Luis Aparicio	250.00	100.00	62.00
91a	Bob Uecker (No trade statement)	90.00	36.00	21.00
91b	Bob Uecker (With trade statement)	30.00	12.00	7.50
92	Yankees Team	125.00	50.00	30.00
93	Jim Lonborg	30.00	12.00	7.50
94	Matty Alou	30.00	12.00	7.50
95	Pete Richert	30.00	12.00	7.50
96	Felipe Alou	45.00	18.00	11.00
97	Jim Merritt	30.00	12.00	7.50
98	Don Demeter	30.00	12.00	7.50
99	Buc Belters (Donn Clendenon, Willie Stargell)	60.00	24.00	15.00
100	Sandy Koufax	300.00	120.00	75.00
101a	Checklist 89-176 (115 is Spahn)	40.00	16.00	9.00
101b	Checklist 89-176 (115 is Henry)	30.00	12.00	7.50
102	Ed Kirkpatrick	30.00	12.00	7.50
103a	Dick Groat (With trade statement)	30.00	12.00	7.50
103b	Dick Groat (No trade statement)	45.00	18.00	11.00
104a	Alex Johnson (No trade statement)	45.00	18.00	11.00
104b	Alex Johnson (With trade statement)	30.00	12.00	7.50
105	Milt Pappas	30.00	12.00	7.50
106	Rusty Staub	35.00	14.00	8.75
107	Athletics Rookies (Larry Stahl, Ron Tompkins)	30.00	12.00	7.50
108	Bobby Klaus	30.00	12.00	7.50
109	Ralph Terry	30.00	12.00	7.50
110	Ernie Banks	200.00	80.00	50.00
111	Gary Peters	30.00	12.00	7.50
112	Manny Mota	30.00	12.00	7.50
113	Hank Aguirre	30.00	12.00	7.50
114	Jim Gosger	30.00	12.00	7.50
115	Bill Henry	30.00	12.00	7.50
116	Walt Alston	90.00	36.00	22.00
117	Jake Gibbs	30.00	12.00	7.50
118	Mike McCormick	30.00	12.00	7.50
119	Art Shamsky	30.00	12.00	7.50
120	Harmon Killebrew	150.00	60.00	37.00
121	Ray Herbert	30.00	12.00	7.50
122	Joe Gaines	30.00	12.00	7.50
123	Pirates Rookies (Frank Bork, Jerry May)	30.00	12.00	7.50
124	Tug McGraw	30.00	12.00	7.50
125	Lou Brock	125.00	50.00	30.00
126	Jim Palmer	200.00	80.00	50.00
127	Ken Berry	30.00	12.00	7.50
128	Jim Landis	30.00	12.00	7.50
129	Jack Kralick	30.00	12.00	7.50
130	Joe Torre	45.00	18.00	11.00
131	Angels Team	75.00	30.00	18.50
132	Orlando Cepeda	100.00	40.00	25.00
133	Don McMahon	30.00	12.00	7.50
134	Wes Parker	30.00	12.00	7.50
135	Dave Morehead	30.00	12.00	7.50
136	Woody Held	30.00	12.00	7.50
137	Pat Corrales	30.00	12.00	7.50
138	Roger Repoz	30.00	12.00	7.50
139	Cubs Rookies (Byron Browne, Don Young)	30.00	12.00	7.50
140	Jim Maloney	30.00	12.00	7.50
141	Tom McCraw	30.00	12.00	7.50
142	Don Dennis	30.00	12.00	7.50
143	Jose Tartabull	30.00	12.00	7.50
144	Don Schwall	30.00	12.00	7.50
145	Bill Freehan	30.00	12.00	7.50
146	George Altman	30.00	12.00	7.50
147	Lum Harris	30.00	12.00	7.50
148	Bob Johnson	30.00	12.00	7.50
149	Dick Nen	30.00	12.00	7.50
150	Rocky Colavito	75.00	30.00	18.50
151	Gary Wagner	30.00	12.00	7.50
152	Frank Malzone	30.00	12.00	7.50
153	Rico Carty	30.00	12.00	7.50
154	Chuck Hiller	30.00	12.00	7.50
155	Marcelino Lopez	30.00	12.00	7.50
156	D P Combo (Hal Lanier, Dick Schofield)	30.00	12.00	7.50
157	Rene Lachemann	30.00	12.00	7.50
158	Jim Brewer	30.00	12.00	7.50
159	Chico Ruiz	30.00	12.00	7.50
160	Whitey Ford	150.00	60.00	37.00
161	Jerry Lumpe	30.00	12.00	7.50
162	Lee Maye	30.00	12.00	7.50
163	Tito Francona	30.00	12.00	7.50
164	White Sox Rookies (Tommie Agee, Marv Staehle)	30.00	12.00	7.50
165	Don Lock	30.00	12.00	7.50
166	Chris Krug	30.00	12.00	7.50
167	Boog Powell	45.00	18.00	11.00
168	Dan Osinski	30.00	12.00	7.50
169	Duke Sims	30.00	12.00	7.50
170	Cookie Rojas	30.00	12.00	7.50
171	Nick Willhite	30.00	12.00	7.50
172	Mets Team	150.00	60.00	37.00
173	Al Spangler	30.00	12.00	7.50
174	Ron Taylor	30.00	12.00	7.50
175	Bert Campaneris	45.00	18.00	11.00
176	Jim Davenport	30.00	12.00	7.50
177	Hector Lopez	30.00	12.00	7.50
178	Bob Tillman	30.00	12.00	7.50
179	Cardinals Rookies (Dennis Aust, Bob Tolan)	30.00	12.00	7.50
180	Vada Pinson	35.00	14.00	8.75
181	Al Worthington	30.00	12.00	7.50
182	Jerry Lynch	30.00	12.00	7.50
183a	Checklist 177-264 (Large print on front)	30.00	12.00	7.50
183b	Checklist 177-264 (Small print on front)	30.00	12.00	7.50
184	Denis Menke	30.00	12.00	7.50
185	Bob Buhl	30.00	12.00	7.50
186	Ruben Amaro	30.00	12.00	7.50
187	Chuck Dressen	30.00	12.00	7.50
188	Al Luplow	30.00	12.00	7.50
189	John Roseboro	30.00	12.00	7.50
190	Jimmie Hall	30.00	12.00	7.50
191	Darrell Sutherland	30.00	12.00	7.50
192	Vic Power	30.00	12.00	7.50
193	Dave McNally	30.00	12.00	7.50
194	Senators Team	75.00	30.00	18.50
195	Joe Morgan	125.00	50.00	30.00
196	Don Pavletich	30.00	12.00	7.50
197	Sonny Siebert	30.00	12.00	7.50
198	Mickey Stanley	30.00	12.00	7.50
199	Chisox Clubbers (Floyd Robinson, Johnny Romano, Bill Skowron)	30.00	12.00	7.50
200	Eddie Mathews	125.00	50.00	30.00
201	Jim Dickson	30.00	12.00	7.50
202	Clay Dalrymple	30.00	12.00	7.50
203	Jose Santiago	30.00	12.00	7.50
204	Cubs Team	90.00	36.00	22.00
205	Tom Tresh	30.00	12.00	7.50
206	Alvin Jackson	30.00	12.00	7.50
207	Frank Quilici	30.00	12.00	7.50
208	Bob Miller	30.00	12.00	7.50
209	Tigers Rookies (Fritz Fisher, John Hiller)	30.00	12.00	7.50
210	Bill Mazeroski	75.00	30.00	18.50
211	Frank Kreutzer	30.00	12.00	7.50
212	Ed Kranepool	30.00	12.00	7.50
213	Fred Newman	30.00	12.00	7.50
214	Tommy Harper	30.00	12.00	7.50
215	N.L. Batting Leaders (Hank Aaron, Roberto Clemente, Willie Mays)	300.00	120.00	75.00
216	A.L. Batting Leaders (Vic Davalillo, Tony Oliva, Carl Yastrzemski)	150.00	60.00	37.00
217	N.L. Home Run Leaders (Willie Mays, Willie McCovey, Billy Williams)	150.00	60.00	37.00
218	A.L. Home Run Leaders (Norm Cash, Tony Conigliaro, Willie Horton)	60.00	24.00	15.00
219	N.L. RBI Leaders (Deron Johnson, Willie Mays, Frank Robinson)	90.00	36.00	22.00
220	A.L. RBI Leaders (Rocky Colavito, Willie Horton, Tony Oliva)	60.00	24.00	15.00
221	N.L. ERA Leaders (Sandy Koufax, Vern Law, Juan Marichal)	90.00	36.00	22.00
222	A.L. ERA Leaders (Eddie Fisher, Sam McDowell, Sonny Siebert)	35.00	14.00	8.75
223	N.L. Pitching Leaders (Tony Cloninger, Don Drysdale, Sandy Koufax)	90.00	36.00	22.00
224	A.L. Pitching Leaders (Jim Grant, Jim Kaat, Mel Stottlemyre)	30.00	12.00	7.50
225	N.L. Strikeout Leaders (Bob Gibson, Sandy Koufax, Bob Veale)	90.00	36.00	22.00
226	A.L. Strikeout Leaders (Mickey Lolich, Sam McDowell, Denny McLain, Sonny Siebert)	45.00	18.00	11.00
227	Russ Nixon	30.00	12.00	7.50
228	Larry Dierker	30.00	12.00	7.50
229	Hank Bauer	30.00	12.00	7.50
230	Johnny Callison	30.00	12.00	7.50
231	Floyd Weaver	30.00	12.00	7.50
232	Glenn Beckert	30.00	12.00	7.50
233	Dom Zanni	30.00	12.00	7.50
234	Yankees Rookies (Rich Beck, Roy White)	35.00	14.00	8.75
235	Don Cardwell	30.00	12.00	7.50
236	Mike Hershberger	30.00	12.00	7.50
237	Billy O'Dell	30.00	12.00	7.50
238	Dodgers Team	100.00	40.00	25.00
239	Orlando Pena	30.00	12.00	7.50
240	Earl Battey	30.00	12.00	7.50
241	Dennis Ribant	30.00	12.00	7.50
242	Jesus Alou	30.00	12.00	7.50
243	Nelson Briles	30.00	12.00	7.50
244	Astros Rookies (Chuck Harrison, Sonny Jackson)	30.00	12.00	7.50
245	John Buzhardt	30.00	12.00	7.50
246	Ed Bailey	30.00	12.00	7.50
247	Carl Warwick	30.00	12.00	7.50
248	Pete Mikkelsen	30.00	12.00	7.50
249	Bill Rigney	30.00	12.00	7.50
250	Sam Ellis	30.00	12.00	7.50
251	Ed Brinkman	30.00	12.00	7.50
252	Denver Lemaster	30.00	12.00	7.50
253	Don Wert	30.00	12.00	7.50
254	Phillies Rookies (Fergie Jenkins, Bill Sorrell)	100.00	40.00	25.00
255	Willie Stargell	125.00	50.00	30.00
256	Lew Krausse	30.00	12.00	7.50
257	Jeff Torborg	30.00	12.00	7.50
258	Dave Giusti	30.00	12.00	7.50
259	Red Sox Team	75.00	30.00	18.50
260	Bob Shaw	30.00	12.00	7.50
261	Ron Hansen	30.00	12.00	7.50
262	Jack Hamilton	30.00	12.00	7.50
263	Tom Egan	30.00	12.00	7.50
264	Twins Rookies (Andy Kosco, Ted Uhlaender)	30.00	12.00	7.50
265	Stu Miller	30.00	12.00	7.50
266	Pedro Gonzalez	30.00	12.00	7.50
267	Joe Sparma	30.00	12.00	7.50
268	John Blanchard	30.00	12.00	7.50
269	Don Heffner	30.00	12.00	7.50
270	Claude Osteen	30.00	12.00	7.50
271	Hal Lanier	30.00	12.00	7.50
272	Jack Baldschun	30.00	12.00	7.50

273	Astro Aces (Bob Aspromonte, Rusty Staub)	30.00	12.00	7.50
274	Buster Narum	30.00	12.00	7.50
275	Tim McCarver	35.00	14.00	8.75
276	Jim Bouton	35.00	14.00	8.75
277	George Thomas	30.00	12.00	7.50
278	Calvin Koonce	30.00	12.00	7.50
279	Checklist 265-352	30.00	12.00	7.50
280	Bobby Knoop	30.00	12.00	7.50
281	Bruce Howard	30.00	12.00	7.50
282	Johnny Lewis	30.00	12.00	7.50
283	Jim Perry	30.00	12.00	7.50
284	Bobby Wine	30.00	12.00	7.50
285	Luis Tiant	45.00	18.00	11.00
286	Gary Geiger	30.00	12.00	7.50
287	Jack Aker	30.00	12.00	7.50
288	Dodgers Rookies(Bill Singer, Don Sutton)	125.00	50.00	30.00
289	Larry Sherry	30.00	12.00	7.50
290	Ron Santo	45.00	18.00	11.00
291	Moe Drabowsky	30.00	12.00	7.50
292	Jim Coker	30.00	12.00	7.50
293	Mike Shannon	30.00	12.00	7.50
294	Steve Ridzik	30.00	12.00	7.50
295	Jim Hart	30.00	12.00	7.50
296	Johnny Keane	30.00	12.00	7.50
297	Jim Owens	30.00	12.00	7.50
298	Rico Petrocelli	30.00	12.00	7.50
299	Lou Burdette	30.00	12.00	7.50
300	Roberto Clemente	650.00	260.00	160.00
301	Greg Bollo	30.00	12.00	7.50
302	Ernie Bowman	30.00	12.00	7.50
303a	Indians Team (Dot between "Place" and "American")	75.00	30.00	18.50
303b	Indians Team (no dot)	75.00	30.00	18.50
304	John Herrnstein	30.00	12.00	7.50
305	Camilo Pascual	30.00	12.00	7.50
306	Ty Cline	30.00	12.00	7.50
307	Clay Carroll	30.00	12.00	7.50
308	Tom Haller	30.00	12.00	7.50
309	Diego Segui	30.00	12.00	7.50
310	Frank Robinson	125.00	50.00	30.00
311	Reds Rookies(Tommy Helms, Dick Simpson)	30.00	12.00	7.50
312	Bob Saverine	30.00	12.00	7.50
313	Chris Zachary	30.00	12.00	7.50
314	Hector Valle	30.00	12.00	7.50
315	Norm Cash	30.00	12.00	7.50
316	Jack Fisher	30.00	12.00	7.50
317	Dalton Jones	30.00	12.00	7.50
318	Harry Walker	30.00	12.00	7.50
319	Gene Freese	30.00	12.00	7.50
320	Bob Gibson	125.00	50.00	30.00
321	Rick Reichardt	30.00	12.00	7.50
322	Bill Faul	30.00	12.00	7.50
323	Ray Barker	30.00	12.00	7.50
324	John Boozer	30.00	12.00	7.50
325	Vic Davalillo	100.00	40.00	25.00
326a	Braves Team (Dot between "Place" and "National")	75.00	30.00	18.50
326b	Braves Team (no dot)	75.00	30.00	18.50
327	Bernie Allen	30.00	12.00	7.50
328	Jerry Grote	30.00	12.00	7.50
329	Pete Charton	30.00	12.00	7.50
330	Ron Fairly	30.00	12.00	7.50
331	Ron Herbel	30.00	12.00	7.50
332	Billy Bryan	30.00	12.00	7.50
333	Senators Rookies(Joe Coleman, Jim French)	30.00	12.00	7.50
334	Marty Keough	30.00	12.00	7.50
335	Juan Pizarro	30.00	12.00	7.50
336	Gene Alley	30.00	12.00	7.50
337	Fred Gladding	30.00	12.00	7.50
338	Dal Maxvill	30.00	12.00	7.50
339	Del Crandall	30.00	12.00	7.50
340	Dean Chance	30.00	12.00	7.50
341	Wes Westrum	30.00	12.00	7.50
342	Bob Humphreys	30.00	12.00	7.50
343	Joe Christopher	30.00	12.00	7.50
344	Steve Blass	30.00	12.00	7.50
345	Bob Allison	30.00	12.00	7.50
346	Mike de la Hoz	30.00	12.00	7.50
347	Phil Regan	30.00	12.00	7.50
348	Orioles Team	125.00	50.00	30.00
349	Cap Peterson	30.00	12.00	7.50
350	Mel Stottlemyre	30.00	12.00	7.50
351	Fred Valentine	30.00	12.00	7.50
352	Bob Aspromonte	30.00	12.00	7.50
353	Al McBean	30.00	12.00	7.50
354	Smoky Burgess	30.00	12.00	7.50
355	Wade Blasingame	30.00	12.00	7.50
356	Red Sox Rookies(Owen Johnson, Ken Sanders)	30.00	12.00	7.50
357	Gerry Arrigo	30.00	12.00	7.50
358	Charlie Smith	30.00	12.00	7.50
359	Johnny Briggs	30.00	12.00	7.50
360	Ron Hunt	30.00	12.00	7.50
361	Tom Satriano	30.00	12.00	7.50
362	Gates Brown	30.00	12.00	7.50
363	Checklist 353-429	30.00	12.00	7.50
364	Nate Oliver	30.00	12.00	7.50
365	Roger Maris	200.00	80.00	50.00
366	Wayne Causey	30.00	12.00	7.50
367	Mel Nelson	30.00	12.00	7.50
368	Charlie Lau	30.00	12.00	7.50
369	Jim King	30.00	12.00	7.50
370	Chico Cardenas	30.00	12.00	7.50

1967 Venezuelan League

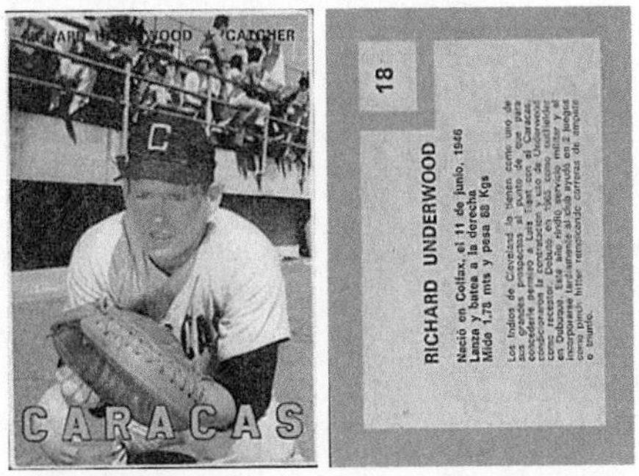

Three distinct series of baseball cards were issued in 1967 for sale in Venezuela, contiguously numbered. Cards #1-138 are players (including many future big leaguers) active in the country's Winter League. Cards are irregularly cut and somewhat smaller than the standard 2-1/2" x 3-1/2". Fronts have posed photos and a thin white border. The player name and position are at top in black, the team name is in large colored letters at bottom. Backs are printed horizontally in black on magenta with a few biographical bits and a one paragraph career summary. Like most of the Venezuelan cards of the era, these are crudely printed on cheap cardboard. Also like most Venezuelan cards, they are virtually impossible to find in any condition above Ex. Many are found with back damage due to having been glued into an album or scrapbook.

		NM	E	VG
	Complete Set (138):	3,500	1,750	1,000
	Common Player:	20.00	10.00	6.00
1	Regino Otero	40.00	20.00	12.00
2	Alejandro Carrasquel	20.00	10.00	6.00
3	Pompeyo Davilillo	25.00	12.50	7.50
4	Gonzalo Marquez	20.00	10.00	6.00
5	Octavio (Cookie) Rojas	35.00	17.50	10.50
6	Teodoro Obregon	20.00	10.00	6.00
7	Paul Schaal	25.00	12.50	7.50
8	Juan Francia	20.00	10.00	6.00
9	Luis Tiant	60.00	30.00	18.00
10	Jose Tartabull	30.00	15.00	9.00
11	Vic Davalillo	25.00	12.50	7.50
12	Cesar Tovar	25.00	12.50	7.50
13	Ron Klimkowski	20.00	10.00	6.00
14	Diego Segui	35.00	17.50	10.50
15	Luis Penalver	20.00	10.00	6.00
16	Urbano Lugo	20.00	10.00	6.00
17	Aurelio Monteagudo	20.00	10.00	6.00
18	Richard Underwood	25.00	12.50	7.50
19	Nelson Castellanos	20.00	10.00	6.00
20	Manuel Mendible	20.00	10.00	6.00
21	Fidel Garcia	40.00	20.00	12.00
22	Luis Cordoba	20.00	10.00	6.00
23	Jesus Padron	20.00	10.00	6.00
24	Lorenzo Fernandez	20.00	10.00	6.00
25	Leopoldo Tovar	20.00	10.00	6.00
26	Carlos Loreto	20.00	10.00	6.00
27	Oswaldo Blanco	20.00	10.00	6.00
28	Sid (Syd) O'Brien	20.00	10.00	6.00
29	Cesar Gutierrez	20.00	10.00	6.00
30	Luis Garcia	20.00	10.00	6.00
31	Fred Klages	20.00	10.00	6.00
32	Isaias Chavez	20.00	10.00	6.00
33	Walter Williams	25.00	12.50	7.50
34	Jim Hicks	20.00	10.00	6.00
35	Gustavo Sposito	20.00	10.00	6.00
36	Cisco Carlos	20.00	10.00	6.00
37	Jim Mooring	20.00	10.00	6.00
38	Alonso Olivares	20.00	10.00	6.00
39	Graciliano Parra	20.00	10.00	6.00
40	Merritt Ranew	20.00	10.00	6.00
41	Everest Contramaestre	20.00	10.00	6.00
42	Orlando Reyes	20.00	10.00	6.00
43	Edicto Arteaga	20.00	10.00	6.00
44	Francisco Diaz	20.00	10.00	6.00
45	Victor Colina	20.00	10.00	6.00
46a	Ramon Diaz	20.00	10.00	6.00
46b	Francisco Diaz (Blue back.)	20.00	10.00	6.00
47	Luis E. Aparicio	185.00	90.00	55.00
48	Reynaldo Cordeiro	60.00	30.00	18.00
49	Luis Aparicio, Sr.	25.00	12.50	7.50
50	Ramon Webster	20.00	10.00	6.00
51	Remigio Hermoso	20.00	10.00	6.00
52	Miguel de la Hoz	20.00	10.00	6.00
53	Enzo Hernandez	20.00	10.00	6.00
54	Ed Watt	20.00	10.00	6.00
55	Angel Bravo	20.00	10.00	6.00
56	Marv (Merv) Rettenmund	25.00	12.50	7.50
57	Jose Herrera	20.00	10.00	6.00
58	Tom Fisher	20.00	10.00	6.00
59	Jim Weaver	20.00	10.00	6.00
60a	Juan Quintana	20.00	10.00	6.00
60b	Frank Fernandez (Blue back.)	20.00	10.00	6.00
61	Hector Urbano	20.00	10.00	6.00
62	Hector Brito (Blue back.)	20.00	10.00	6.00
63	Jesus Romero	20.00	10.00	6.00
64	Carlos A. Moreno	20.00	10.00	6.00
65	Nestor Mendible	20.00	10.00	6.00
66	Armando Ortiz	20.00	10.00	6.00
67	Graciano Ravelo	20.00	10.00	6.00
68	Paul Knechtges	20.00	10.00	6.00
69	Marcelino Lopez	25.00	12.50	7.50
70	Wilfredo Calvino	25.00	12.50	7.50
71	Jesus Avila	20.00	10.00	6.00
72	Carlos Pascual	45.00	22.00	13.50
73	Bob Burda	20.00	10.00	6.00
74	Elio Chacon	20.00	10.00	6.00
75	Jacinto Hernandez	20.00	10.00	6.00
76	Jose M. Tovar	20.00	10.00	6.00
77	Bill Whitby	20.00	10.00	6.00
78	Enrique Izquierdo	20.00	10.00	6.00
79	Hilario Valdespino	30.00	15.00	9.00
80	John Lewis	20.00	10.00	6.00
81	Hector Martinez	40.00	20.00	12.00
82	Rene Paredes	20.00	10.00	6.00
83	Danny Morris	20.00	10.00	6.00
84	Pedro Ramos	25.00	12.50	7.50
85	Jose Ramon Lopez	20.00	10.00	6.00
86	Jesus Rizales	20.00	10.00	6.00
87	Winston Acosta	20.00	10.00	6.00
88	Pablo Bello	20.00	10.00	6.00
89	David Concepcion	200.00	100.00	60.00
90	Manuel Garcia	20.00	10.00	6.00
91	Anibal Longa	20.00	10.00	6.00
92	Francisco Moscoso	20.00	10.00	6.00
93	Mel McGaha	20.00	10.00	6.00
94	Aquiles Gomez	20.00	10.00	6.00
95	Alfonso Carrasquel (Blue back.)	40.00	20.00	12.00
96	Tom Murray	20.00	10.00	6.00
97	Gustavo Gil	20.00	10.00	6.00
98	Damaso Blanco	20.00	10.00	6.00
99	Alberto Cambero	20.00	10.00	6.00
100	Don Bryant	20.00	10.00	6.00
101	George Culver	20.00	10.00	6.00
102	Teolindo Acosta	20.00	10.00	6.00
103	Aaron Pointer	20.00	10.00	6.00
104	Ed Kirkpatrick	20.00	10.00	6.00
105	Luis Rodriguez	20.00	10.00	6.00
106	Mike Daniel	20.00	10.00	6.00
107	Cecilio Prieto (Blue back.)	20.00	10.00	6.00
108	Juan Quiroz	20.00	10.00	6.00
108	6.00			
109	Juan Campos	20.00	10.00	6.00
110	Freddy Rivero	20.00	10.00	6.00
111	Dick LeMay	20.00	10.00	6.00
112	Raul Ortega	20.00	10.00	6.00
113	Bruno Estaba	20.00	10.00	6.00
114	Evangelista Nunez	20.00	10.00	6.00
115a	Robert Munoz	20.00	10.00	6.00
115b	Alfonso Carrasquel (Red back.)	40.00	20.00	12.00
116	Tony Castanos	20.00	10.00	6.00
117	Domingo Barboza	20.00	10.00	6.00
118	Lucio Celis	20.00	10.00	6.00
119	Carlos Santeliz	20.00	10.00	6.00
120	Barton Shirley	25.00	12.50	7.50
121	Neudo Morales	20.00	10.00	6.00
122	Robert Cox	100.00	50.00	30.00
123	Cruz Amaya (Blue back.)	20.00	10.00	6.00
124	Jim Campanis	75.00	37.50	22.00
125	Dave Roberts	20.00	10.00	6.00
126	Gerry Crider	20.00	10.00	6.00
127	Domingo Carrasquel	20.00	10.00	6.00
128	Leo Marentette	20.00	10.00	6.00
129	Frank Kreutzer	20.00	10.00	6.00
130	Jim Dickson	20.00	10.00	6.00
131	Bob Oliver	20.00	10.00	6.00
132	Jose Bracho	20.00	10.00	6.00
133a	Pablo Torrealba	20.00	10.00	6.00
133b	Pablo Torrealba (Different picture.)	20.00	10.00	6.00
134	Iran Paz	20.00	10.00	6.00

135	Eliecer Bueno	20.00	10.00	6.00
136	Claudio Urdaneta	20.00	10.00	6.00
137	Faustino Zabala	20.00	10.00	6.00
138	Dario Chirinos	20.00	10.00	6.00

1967 Venezuelan Retirado

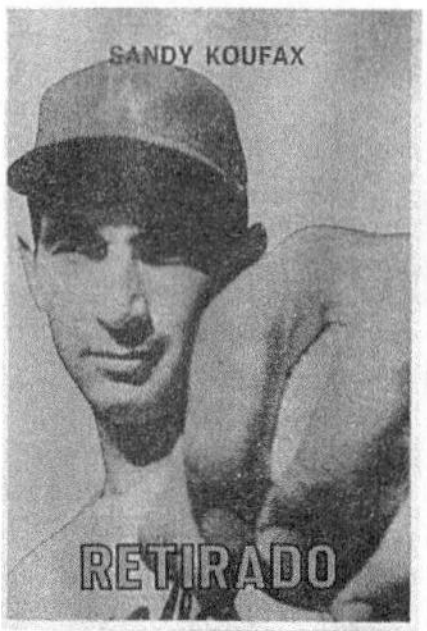

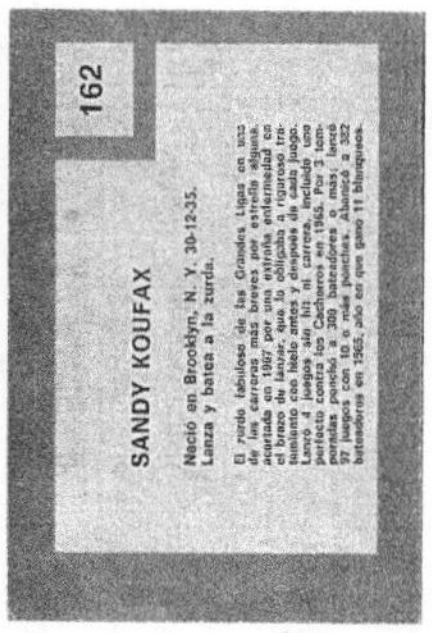

Three distinct series of baseball cards were issued in 1967 for sale in Venezuela, contiguously numbered. Cards #139-188 are former big league stars. The fronts of the roughly 2-1/2" x 3-1/2" Retirado cards have a blue background with the player's name in black at top and "RETIRADO" in red block letters at bottom. Player photos on the Retirado cards are sepia. Horizontal backs are printed in black on green with a bit of personal data and a career summary. Like most of the Venezuelan cards of the era, these are crudely printed on cheap cardboard. Also like most Venezuelan cards, they are virtually impossible to find in any condition above Ex. Many are found with back damage due to having been glued into an album or scrapbook.

		NM	E	VG
	Complete Set (50):	12,000	4,800	1,800
	Common Player:	250.00	100.00	37.00
139	Walter Johnson	750.00	300.00	110.00
140	Bill Dickey	300.00	120.00	45.00
141	Lou Gehrig	1,750	700.00	260.00
142	Rogers Hornsby	300.00	120.00	45.00
143	Honus Wagner	650.00	260.00	100.00
144	Pie Traynor	250.00	100.00	35.00
145	Joe DiMaggio	1,850	740.00	275.00
146	Ty Cobb	1,350	540.00	200.00
147	Babe Ruth	2,400	960.00	360.00
148	Ted Williams	1,000	400.00	150.00
149	Mel Ott	250.00	100.00	35.00
150	Cy Young	370.00	150.00	55.00
151	Christy Mathewson	750.00	300.00	110.00
152	Warren Spahn	300.00	120.00	45.00
153	Mickey Cochrane	250.00	100.00	35.00
154	George Sisler	250.00	100.00	35.00
155	Jimmy Collins	250.00	100.00	35.00
156	Tris Speaker	300.00	120.00	45.00
157	Stan Musial	700.00	280.00	100.00
158	Luke Appling	250.00	100.00	35.00
159	Nap Lajoie	250.00	100.00	35.00
160	Bill Terry	250.00	100.00	35.00
161	Bob Feller	370.00	150.00	55.00
162	Sandy Koufax	800.00	320.00	120.00
163	Jimmie Foxx	300.00	120.00	45.00
164	Joe Cronin	250.00	100.00	35.00
165	Frankie Frisch	250.00	100.00	35.00
166	Paul Waner	250.00	100.00	35.00
167	Lloyd Waner	250.00	100.00	35.00
168	Lefty Grove	250.00	100.00	35.00
169	Bobby Doerr	250.00	100.00	35.00
170	Al Simmons	250.00	100.00	35.00
171	Grover Alexander	350.00	140.00	50.00
172	Carl Hubbell	250.00	100.00	35.00
173	Mordecai Brown	250.00	100.00	35.00
174	Ted Lyons	250.00	100.00	35.00
175	Johnny Vander Meer	250.00	100.00	35.00
176	Alex Carrasquel	300.00	120.00	45.00
177	Satchel Paige	600.00	240.00	90.00
178	Whitey Ford	500.00	200.00	75.00
179	Yogi Berra	500.00	200.00	75.00
180	Roy Campanella	450.00	180.00	65.00
181	Alfonso Carrasquel	370.00	150.00	55.00
182	Johnny Mize	250.00	100.00	35.00
183	Ted Kluszewski (Photo actually Gene Bearden.)	300.00	120.00	45.00
184	Jackie Robinson	750.00	300.00	110.00
185	Bobby Avila	250.00	100.00	35.00
186	Phil Rizzuto	300.00	120.00	45.00
187	Minnie Minoso	300.00	120.00	45.00
188	Connie Marrero	250.00	100.00	35.00

1967 Venezuelan Topps

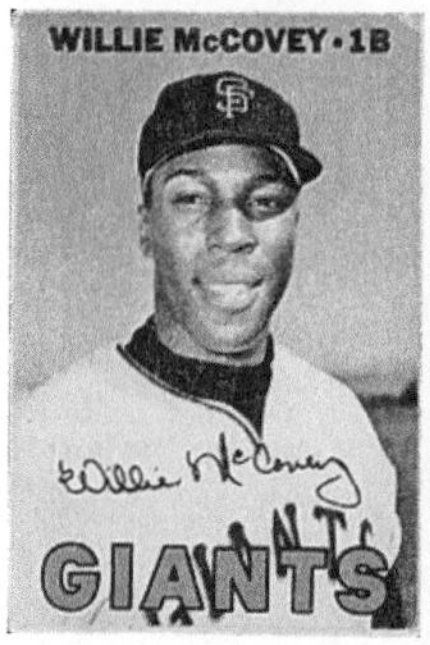

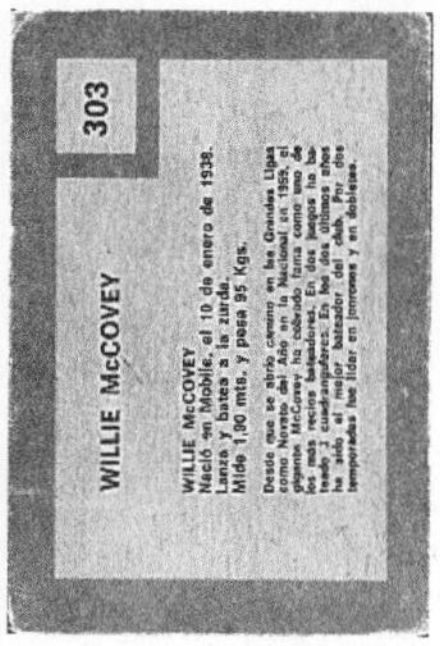

Cards numbered #189-338 in the 1967 Venezuelan issue feature then-current major leaguers. Card fronts are taken from Topps' 1967 baseball series, but are borderless, making them somewhat smaller than 2-1/2" x 3-1/2". Backs of the South American cards are horizontal and printed in black on blue and offer a few bits of personal data and a one-paragraph career summary. Like most Venezuelan cards of the era, these are crudely printed on cheap cardboard and seldom found in condition better than Ex. Many will show evidence on back of having been glued into an album or scrapbook.

		NM	E	VG
	Complete Set (150):	8,000	2,000	750.00
	Common Player:	35.00	14.00	5.25
189	Luis Aparicio	150.00	60.00	22.00
190	Vic Davalillo	35.00	14.00	5.25
191	Cesar Tovar	35.00	14.00	5.25
192	Mickey Mantle	1,500	600.00	225.00
193	Carl Yastrzemski	100.00	40.00	15.00
194	Frank Robinson	100.00	40.00	15.00
195	Willie Horton	35.00	14.00	5.25
196	Gary Peters	35.00	14.00	5.25
197	Bert Campaneris	40.00	16.00	6.00
198	Norm Cash	35.00	14.00	5.25
199	Boog Powell	35.00	14.00	5.25
200	George Scott	35.00	14.00	5.25
201	Frank Howard	35.00	14.00	5.25
202	Rick Reichardt	35.00	14.00	5.25
203	Jose Cardenal	35.00	14.00	5.25
204	Rico Petrocelli	35.00	14.00	5.25
205	Lew Krausse	35.00	14.00	5.25
206	Harmon Killebrew	100.00	40.00	15.00
207	Leon Wagner	35.00	14.00	5.25
208	Joe Foy	35.00	14.00	5.25
209	Joe Pepitone	40.00	16.00	6.00
210	Al Kaline	100.00	40.00	15.00
211	Brooks Robinson	100.00	40.00	15.00
212	Bill Freehan	35.00	14.00	5.25
213	Jim Lonborg	35.00	14.00	5.25
214a	Ed Mathews	100.00	40.00	15.00
214b	Jim Bunning (Should be #174.)	90.00	36.00	13.50
215	Dick Green	35.00	14.00	5.25
216	Tom Tresh	40.00	16.00	6.00
217	Dean Chance	35.00	14.00	5.25
218	Paul Blair	35.00	14.00	5.25
219	Larry Brown	35.00	14.00	5.25
220	Fred Valentine	35.00	14.00	5.25
221	Al Downing	35.00	14.00	5.25
222	Earl Battey	35.00	14.00	5.25
223	Don Mincher	35.00	14.00	5.25
224	Tommie Agee	35.00	14.00	5.25
225	Jim McGlothlin	35.00	14.00	5.25
226	Zoilo Versalles	35.00	14.00	5.25
227	Curt Blefary	35.00	14.00	5.25
228	Joel Horlen	35.00	14.00	5.25
229	Stu Miller	35.00	14.00	5.25
230	Tony Oliva	40.00	16.00	6.00
231	Paul Casanova	35.00	14.00	5.25
232	Orlando Pena	35.00	14.00	5.25
233	Ron Hansen	35.00	14.00	5.25
234	Earl Wilson	35.00	14.00	5.25
235	Ken Boyer	40.00	16.00	6.00
236	Jim Kaat	35.00	14.00	5.25
237	Dalton Jones	35.00	14.00	5.25
238	Pete Ward	35.00	14.00	5.25
239	Mickey Lolich	35.00	14.00	5.25
240	Jose Santiago	35.00	14.00	5.25
241	Dick McAuliffe	35.00	14.00	5.25
242	Mel Stottlemyre	35.00	14.00	5.25
243	Camilo Pascual	35.00	14.00	5.25
244	Jim Fregosi	35.00	14.00	5.25
245	Tony Conigliaro	40.00	16.00	6.00
246	Sonny Siebert	35.00	14.00	5.25
247	Jim Perry	35.00	14.00	5.25
248	Dave McNally	35.00	14.00	5.25
249	Fred Whitfield	35.00	14.00	5.25
250	Ken Berry	35.00	14.00	5.25
251	Jim Grant	35.00	14.00	5.25
252	Hank Aguirre	35.00	14.00	5.25
253	Don Wert	35.00	14.00	5.25
254	Wally Bunker	35.00	14.00	5.25
255	Elston Howard	40.00	16.00	6.00
256	Dave Johnson	35.00	14.00	5.25
257	Hoyt Wilhelm	75.00	30.00	11.00
258	Don Buford	35.00	14.00	5.25
259	Sam McDowell	35.00	14.00	5.25
260	Bobby Knoop	35.00	14.00	5.25
261	Denny McLain	35.00	14.00	5.25
262	Steve Hargan	35.00	14.00	5.25
263	Jim Nash	35.00	14.00	5.25
264	Jerry Adair	35.00	14.00	5.25
265	Tony Gonzalez	35.00	14.00	5.25
266	Mike Shannon	35.00	14.00	5.25
267	Bob Gibson	90.00	36.00	13.50
268	John Roseboro	35.00	14.00	5.25
269	Bob Aspromonte	35.00	14.00	5.25
270	Pete Rose	250.00	100.00	37.00
271	Rico Carty	40.00	16.00	6.00
272	Juan Pizarro	35.00	14.00	5.25
273	Willie Mays	250.00	100.00	37.00
274	Jim Bunning	90.00	36.00	13.50
275	Ernie Banks	100.00	40.00	15.00
276	Curt Flood	40.00	16.00	6.00
277	Mack Jones	35.00	14.00	5.25
278	Roberto Clemente	450.00	180.00	67.00
279	Sammy Ellis	35.00	14.00	5.25
280	Willie Stargell	90.00	36.00	13.50
281	Felipe Alou	40.00	16.00	6.00
282	Ed Kranepool	35.00	14.00	5.25
283	Nelson Briles	35.00	14.00	5.25
284	Hank Aaron	250.00	100.00	37.00
285	Vada Pinson	40.00	16.00	6.00
286	Jim LeFebvre	35.00	14.00	5.25
287	Hal Lanier	35.00	14.00	5.25
288	Ron Swoboda	35.00	14.00	5.25
289	Mike McCormick	35.00	14.00	5.25
290	Lou Johnson	35.00	14.00	5.25
291	Orlando Cepeda	90.00	36.00	13.50
292	Rusty Staub	40.00	16.00	6.00
293	Manny Mota	35.00	14.00	5.25
294	Tommy Harper	35.00	14.00	5.25
295	Don Drysdale	90.00	36.00	13.50
296	Mel Queen	35.00	14.00	5.25
297	Red Schoendienst	75.00	30.00	11.00
298	Matty Alou	35.00	14.00	5.25
299	Johnny Callison	35.00	14.00	5.25
300	Juan Marichal	90.00	36.00	13.50
301	Al McBean	35.00	14.00	5.25
302	Claude Osteen	35.00	14.00	5.25
303	Willie McCovey	90.00	36.00	13.50
304	Jim Owens	35.00	14.00	5.25
305	Chico Ruiz	35.00	14.00	5.25
306	Ferguson Jenkins	90.00	36.00	13.50
307	Lou Brock	90.00	36.00	13.50
308	Joe Morgan	90.00	36.00	13.50
309	Ron Santo	50.00	20.00	7.50
310	Chico Cardenas	35.00	14.00	5.25
311	Richie Allen	45.00	18.00	6.75
312	Gaylord Perry	75.00	30.00	11.00
313	Bill Mazeroski	75.00	30.00	11.00
314	Tony Taylor	35.00	14.00	5.25
315	Tommy Helms	35.00	14.00	5.25
316	Jim Wynn	35.00	14.00	5.25
317	Don Sutton	75.00	30.00	11.00
318	Mike Cuellar	45.00	18.00	6.75
319	Willie Davis	35.00	14.00	5.25
320	Julian Javier	35.00	14.00	5.25
321	Maury Wills	35.00	14.00	5.25
322	Gene Alley	35.00	14.00	5.25
323	Ray Sadecki	35.00	14.00	5.25
324	Joe Torre	45.00	18.00	6.75
325	Jim Maloney	35.00	14.00	5.25
326	Jim Davenport	35.00	14.00	5.25
327	Tony Perez	90.00	36.00	13.50
328	Roger Maris	100.00	40.00	15.00
329	Chris Short	35.00	14.00	5.25
330	Jesus Alou	35.00	14.00	5.25
331	Darron Johnson	35.00	14.00	5.25
332	Tommy Davis	35.00	14.00	5.25
333	Bob Veale	35.00	14.00	5.25
334	Bill McCool	35.00	14.00	5.25
335	Jim Hart	35.00	14.00	5.25
336	Roy Face	35.00	14.00	5.25
337	Billy Williams	75.00	30.00	11.00
338	Dick Groat	35.00	14.00	5.25

1968 Venezuelan Topps

The first 370 cards of Topps' 1968 baseball card set were reproduced in South America for sale in Venezuela. Besides being rather crudely printed on cheaper, non-gloss cardboard, the cards are virtually identical to the Topps U.S. version. The only difference is a tiny line of yellow type on back which reads: "Hecho en Venezuela - C.A. Litoven." Like most 1960s Venezuelan issues, these cards are seldom found in condition better than Excellent, and often with evidence on back of having been glued into an album or scrapbook. Venezuelan Topps cards are often found cut slightly smaller than the U.S. version, up to 1/8".

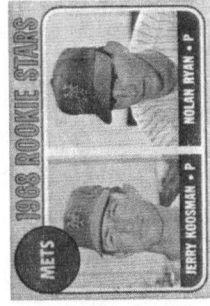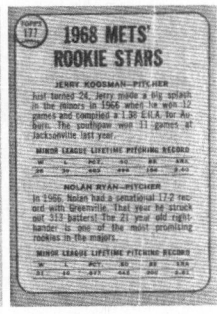

		NM	E	VG
	Complete Set (370):	25,000	10,000	6,250
	Common Player:	30.00	12.00	7.50
1	N.L. Batting Leaders(Matty Alou, Roberto Clemente, Tony Gonzalez)	80.00	32.00	20.00
2	A.L. Batting Leaders(Al Kaline, Frank Robinson, Carl Yastrzemski)	50.00	20.00	12.50
3	N.L. RBI Leaders(Hank Aaron, Orlando Cepeda, Roberto Clemente)	80.00	32.00	20.00
4	A.L. RBI Leaders (Harmon Killebrew, Frank Robinson, Carl Yastrzemski)	50.00	20.00	12.50
5	N.L. Home Run Leaders(Hank Aaron, Willie McCovey, Ron Santo, Jim Wynn)	60.00	24.00	15.00
6	A.L. Home Run Leaders (Frank Howard, Harmon Killebrew, Carl Yastrzemski)	50.00	20.00	12.50
7	N.L. ERA Leaders(Jim Bunning, Phil Niekro, Chris Short)	30.00	12.00	7.50
8	A.L. ERA Leaders(Joe Horlen, Gary Peters, Sonny Siebert)	30.00	12.00	7.50
9	N.L. Pitching Leaders (Jim Bunning, Fergie Jenkins, Mike McCormick, Claude Osteen)	30.00	12.00	7.50
10	A.L. Pitching Leaders (Dean Chance, Jim Lonborg, Earl Wilson)	30.00	12.00	7.50
11	N.L. Strikeout Leaders (Jim Bunning, Fergie Jenkins, Gaylord Perry)	30.00	12.00	7.50
12	A.L. Strikeout Leaders (Dean Chance, Jim Lonborg, Sam McDowell)	30.00	12.00	7.50
13	Chuck Hartenstein	30.00	12.00	7.50
14	Jerry McNertney	30.00	12.00	7.50
15	Ron Hunt	30.00	12.00	7.50
16	Indians Rookies(Lou Piniella, Richie Scheinblum)	40.00	16.00	10.00
17	Dick Hall	30.00	12.00	7.50
18	Mike Hershberger	30.00	12.00	7.50
19	Juan Pizarro	30.00	12.00	7.50
20	Brooks Robinson	120.00	48.00	30.00
21	Ron Davis	30.00	12.00	7.50
22	Pat Dobson	30.00	12.00	7.50
23	Chico Cardenas	30.00	12.00	7.50
24	Bobby Locke	30.00	12.00	7.50
25	Julian Javier	30.00	12.00	7.50
26	Darrell Brandon	30.00	12.00	7.50
27	Gil Hodges	50.00	20.00	12.50
28	Ted Uhlaender	30.00	12.00	7.50
29	Joe Verbanic	30.00	12.00	7.50
30	Joe Torre	40.00	16.00	10.00
31	Ed Stroud	30.00	12.00	7.50
32	Joe Gibbon	30.00	12.00	7.50
33	Pete Ward	30.00	12.00	7.50
34	Al Ferrara	30.00	12.00	7.50
35	Steve Hargan	30.00	12.00	7.50
36	Pirates Rookies(Bob Moose, Bob Robertson)	80.00	32.00	20.00
37	Billy Williams	80.00	32.00	20.00
38	Tony Pierce	30.00	12.00	7.50
39	Cookie Rojas	30.00	12.00	7.50
40	Denny McLain	40.00	16.00	10.00
41	Julio Gotay	30.00	12.00	7.50
42	Larry Haney	30.00	12.00	7.50
43	Gary Bell	30.00	12.00	7.50
44	Frank Kostro	30.00	12.00	7.50
45	Tom Seaver	120.00	48.00	30.00
46	Dave Ricketts	30.00	12.00	7.50
47	Ralph Houk	30.00	12.00	7.50
48	Ted Davidson	30.00	12.00	7.50
49	Ed Brinkman	30.00	12.00	7.50
50	Willie Mays	350.00	140.00	90.00
51	Bob Locker	30.00	12.00	7.50
52	Hawk Taylor	30.00	12.00	7.50
53	Gene Alley	30.00	12.00	7.50
54	Stan Williams	30.00	12.00	7.50
55	Felipe Alou	40.00	16.00	10.00
56	Orioles Rookies(Dave Leonhard, Dave May)	30.00	12.00	7.50
57	Dan Schneider	30.00	12.00	7.50
58	Eddie Mathews	120.00	48.00	30.00
59	Don Lock	30.00	12.00	7.50
60	Ken Holtzman	30.00	12.00	7.50
61	Reggie Smith	30.00	12.00	7.50
62	Chuck Dobson	30.00	12.00	7.50
63	Dick Kenworthy	30.00	12.00	7.50
64	Jim Merritt	30.00	12.00	7.50
65	John Roseboro	30.00	12.00	7.50
66	Casey Cox	30.00	12.00	7.50
67	Checklist 1-109(Jim Kaat)	30.00	12.00	7.50
68	Ron Willis	30.00	12.00	7.50
69	Tom Tresh	30.00	12.00	7.50
70	Bob Veale	30.00	12.00	7.50
71	Vern Fuller	30.00	12.00	7.50
72	Tommy John	30.00	12.00	7.50
73	Jim Hart	30.00	12.00	7.50
74	Milt Pappas	30.00	12.00	7.50
75	Don Mincher	30.00	12.00	7.50
76	Braves Rookies(Jim Britton, Ron Reed)	30.00	12.00	7.50
77	Don Wilson	30.00	12.00	7.50
78	Jim Northrup	30.00	12.00	7.50
79	Ted Kubiak	30.00	12.00	7.50
80	Rod Carew	120.00	48.00	30.00
81	Larry Jackson	30.00	12.00	7.50
82	Sam Bowens	30.00	12.00	7.50
83	John Stephenson	30.00	12.00	7.50
84	Bob Tolan	30.00	12.00	7.50
85	Gaylord Perry	80.00	32.00	20.00
86	Willie Stargell	100.00	40.00	25.00
87	Dick Williams	30.00	12.00	7.50
88	Phil Regan	30.00	12.00	7.50
89	Jake Gibbs	30.00	12.00	7.50
90	Vada Pinson	40.00	16.00	10.00
91	Jim Ollom	30.00	12.00	7.50
92	Ed Kranepool	30.00	12.00	7.50
93	Tony Cloninger	30.00	12.00	7.50
94	Lee Maye	30.00	12.00	7.50
95	Bob Aspromonte	30.00	12.00	7.50
96	Senators Rookies(Frank Coggins, Dick Nold)	30.00	12.00	7.50
97	Tom Phoebus	30.00	12.00	7.50
98	Gary Sutherland	30.00	12.00	7.50
99	Rocky Colavito	50.00	20.00	12.50
100	Bob Gibson	90.00	36.00	22.00
101	Glenn Beckert	30.00	12.00	7.50
102	Jose Cardenal	30.00	12.00	7.50
103	Don Sutton	80.00	32.00	20.00
104	Dick Dietz	30.00	12.00	7.50
105	Al Downing	30.00	12.00	7.50
106	Dalton Jones	30.00	12.00	7.50
107	Checklist 110-196(Juan Marichal)	30.00	12.00	7.50
108	Don Pavletich	30.00	12.00	7.50
109	Bert Campaneris	40.00	16.00	10.00
110	Hank Aaron	350.00	140.00	90.00
111	Rich Reese	30.00	12.00	7.50
112	Woody Fryman	30.00	12.00	7.50
113	Tigers Rookies(Tom Matchick, Daryl Patterson)	30.00	12.00	7.50
114	Ron Swoboda	30.00	12.00	7.50
115	Sam McDowell	30.00	12.00	7.50
116	Ken McMullen	30.00	12.00	7.50
117	Larry Jaster	30.00	12.00	7.50
118	Mark Belanger	30.00	12.00	7.50
119	Ted Savage	30.00	12.00	7.50
120	Mel Stottlemyre	30.00	12.00	7.50
121	Jimmie Hall	30.00	12.00	7.50
122	Gene Mauch	30.00	12.00	7.50
123	Jose Santiago	30.00	12.00	7.50
124	Nate Oliver	30.00	12.00	7.50
125	Joe Horlen	30.00	12.00	7.50
126	Bobby Etheridge	30.00	12.00	7.50
127	Paul Lindblad	30.00	12.00	7.50
128	Astros Rookies(Tom Dukes, Alonzo Harris)	30.00	12.00	7.50
129	Mickey Stanley	30.00	12.00	7.50
130	Tony Perez	90.00	36.00	22.00
131	Frank Bertaina	30.00	12.00	7.50
132	Bud Harrelson	30.00	12.00	7.50
133	Fred Whitfield	30.00	12.00	7.50
134	Pat Jarvis	30.00	12.00	7.50
135	Paul Blair	30.00	12.00	7.50
136	Randy Hundley	30.00	12.00	7.50
137	**Twins Team**	40.00	16.00	10.00
138	Ruben Amaro	30.00	12.00	7.50
139	Chris Short	30.00	12.00	7.50
140	Tony Conigliaro	40.00	16.00	10.00
141	Dal Maxvill	30.00	12.00	7.50
142	White Sox Rookies (Buddy Bradford, Bill Voss)	30.00	12.00	7.50
143	Pete Cimino	30.00	12.00	7.50
144	Joe Morgan	100.00	40.00	25.00
145	Don Drysdale	100.00	40.00	25.00
146	Sal Bando	30.00	12.00	7.50
147	Frank Linzy	30.00	12.00	7.50
148	Dave Bristol	30.00	12.00	7.50
149	Bob Saverine	30.00	12.00	7.50
150	Roberto Clemente	600.00	240.00	150.00
151	World Series Game 1 (Brock Socks 4 Hits in Opener)	30.00	12.00	7.50
152	World Series Game 2 (Yaz Smashes Two Homers)	40.00	16.00	10.00
153	World Series Game 3 (Briles Cools Off Boston)	30.00	12.00	7.50
154	World Series Game 4 (Gibson Hurls Shutout)	30.00	12.00	7.50
155	World Series Game 5 (Lonborg Wins Again)	30.00	12.00	7.50
156	World Series Game 6 (Petrocelli Socks Two Homers)	30.00	12.00	7.50
157	World Series Game 7 (St. Louis Wins It)	30.00	12.00	7.50
158	World Series Summary (The Cardinals Celebrate)	30.00	12.00	7.50
159	Don Kessinger	30.00	12.00	7.50
160	Earl Wilson	30.00	12.00	7.50
161	Norm Miller	30.00	12.00	7.50
162	Cardinals Rookies(Hal Gilson, Mike Torrez)	30.00	12.00	7.50
163	Gene Brabender	30.00	12.00	7.50
164	Ramon Webster	30.00	12.00	7.50
165	Tony Oliva	40.00	16.00	10.00
166	Claude Raymond	30.00	12.00	7.50
167	Elston Howard	30.00	12.00	7.50
168	Dodgers Team	50.00	20.00	12.50
169	Bob Bolin	30.00	12.00	7.50
170	Jim Fregosi	30.00	12.00	7.50
171	Don Nottebart	30.00	12.00	7.50
172	Walt Williams	30.00	12.00	7.50
173	John Boozer	30.00	12.00	7.50
174	Bob Tillman	30.00	12.00	7.50
175	Maury Wills	30.00	12.00	7.50
176	Bob Allen	30.00	12.00	7.50
177	Mets Rookies(Jerry Koosman **RC**, Nolan Ryan **RC**)	12,000	4,800	3,000
178	Don Wert	30.00	12.00	7.50
179	Bill Stoneman	30.00	12.00	7.50
180	Curt Flood	30.00	12.00	7.50
181	Jerry Zimmerman	30.00	12.00	7.50
182	Dave Giusti	30.00	12.00	7.50
183	Bob Kennedy	30.00	12.00	7.50
184	Lou Johnson	30.00	12.00	7.50
185	Tom Haller	30.00	12.00	7.50
186	Eddie Watt	30.00	12.00	7.50
187	Sonny Jackson	30.00	12.00	7.50
188	Cap Peterson	30.00	12.00	7.50
189	Bill Landis	30.00	12.00	7.50
190	Bill White	30.00	12.00	7.50
191	Dan Frisella	30.00	12.00	7.50
192	Checklist 197-283(Carl Yastrzemski)	40.00	16.00	10.00
193	Jack Hamilton	30.00	12.00	7.50
194	Don Buford	30.00	12.00	7.50
195	Joe Pepitone	30.00	12.00	7.50
196	Gary Nolan	30.00	12.00	7.50
197	Larry Brown	30.00	12.00	7.50
198	Roy Face	30.00	12.00	7.50
199	A's Rookies (Darrell Osteen, Roberto Rodriguez)	30.00	12.00	7.50
200	Orlando Cepeda	80.00	32.00	20.00
201	Mike Marshall	30.00	12.00	7.50
202	Adolfo Phillips	30.00	12.00	7.50
203	Dick Kelley	30.00	12.00	7.50
204	Andy Etchebarren	30.00	12.00	7.50
205	Juan Marichal	90.00	36.00	22.00
206	Cal Ermer	30.00	12.00	7.50
207	Carroll Sembera	30.00	12.00	7.50
208	Willie Davis	30.00	12.00	7.50
209	Tim Cullen	30.00	12.00	7.50
210	Gary Peters	30.00	12.00	7.50
211	J.C. Martin	30.00	12.00	7.50
212	Dave Morehead	30.00	12.00	7.50
213	Chico Ruiz	30.00	12.00	7.50

214	Yankees Rookies(Stan Bahnsen, Frank Fernandez)	30.00	12.00	7.50
215	Jim Bunning	90.00	36.00	22.00
216	Bubba Morton	30.00	12.00	7.50
217	Turk Farrell	30.00	12.00	7.50
218	Ken Suarez	30.00	12.00	7.50
219	Rob Gardner	30.00	12.00	7.50
220	Harmon Killebrew	120.00	48.00	30.00
221	Braves Team	40.00	16.00	10.00
222	Jim Hardin	30.00	12.00	7.50
223	Ollie Brown	30.00	12.00	7.50
224	Jack Aker	30.00	12.00	7.50
225	Richie Allen	40.00	16.00	10.00
226	Jimmie Price	30.00	12.00	7.50
227	Joe Hoerner	30.00	12.00	7.50
228	Dodgers Rookies(Jack Billingham, Jim Fairey)	30.00	12.00	7.50
229	Fred Klages	30.00	12.00	7.50
230	Pete Rose	350.00	140.00	90.00
231	Dave Baldwin	30.00	12.00	7.50
232	Denis Menke	30.00	12.00	7.50
233	George Scott	30.00	12.00	7.50
234	Bill Monbouquette	30.00	12.00	7.50
235	Ron Santo	50.00	20.00	12.50
236	Tug McGraw	30.00	12.00	7.50
237	Alvin Dark	30.00	12.00	7.50
238	Tom Satriano	30.00	12.00	7.50
239	Bill Henry	30.00	12.00	7.50
240	Al Kaline	120.00	48.00	30.00
241	Felix Millan	30.00	12.00	7.50
242	Moe Drabowsky	30.00	12.00	7.50
243	Rich Rollins	30.00	12.00	7.50
244	John Donaldson	30.00	12.00	7.50
245	Tony Gonzalez	30.00	12.00	7.50
246	Fritz Peterson	30.00	12.00	7.50
247	Reds Rookies(Johnny Bench, Ron Tompkins)	400.00	160.00	100.00
248	Fred Valentine	30.00	12.00	7.50
249	Bill Singer	30.00	12.00	7.50
250	Carl Yastrzemski	130.00	52.00	32.00
251	Manny Sanguillen	40.00	16.00	10.00
252	Angels Team	40.00	16.00	10.00
253	Dick Hughes	30.00	12.00	7.50
254	Cleon Jones	30.00	12.00	7.50
255	Dean Chance	30.00	12.00	7.50
256	Norm Cash	40.00	16.00	10.00
257	Phil Niekro	80.00	32.00	20.00
258	Cubs Rookies (Jose Arcia, Bill Schlesinger)	30.00	12.00	7.50
259	Ken Boyer	30.00	12.00	7.50
260	Jim Wynn	30.00	12.00	7.50
261	Dave Duncan	30.00	12.00	7.50
262	Rick Wise	30.00	12.00	7.50
263	Horace Clarke	30.00	12.00	7.50
264	Ted Abernathy	30.00	12.00	7.50
265	Tommy Davis	30.00	12.00	7.50
266	Paul Popovich	30.00	12.00	7.50
267	Herman Franks	30.00	12.00	7.50
268	Bob Humphreys	30.00	12.00	7.50
269	Bob Tiefenauer	30.00	12.00	7.50
270	Matty Alou	30.00	12.00	7.50
271	Bobby Knoop	30.00	12.00	7.50
272	Ray Culp	30.00	12.00	7.50
273	Dave Johnson	30.00	12.00	7.50
274	Mike Cuellar	30.00	12.00	7.50
275	Tim McCarver	30.00	12.00	7.50
276	Jim Roland	30.00	12.00	7.50
277	Jerry Buchek	30.00	12.00	7.50
278	Checklist 284-370 (Orlando Cepeda)	30.00	12.00	7.50
279	Bill Hands	30.00	12.00	7.50
280	Mickey Mantle	1,900	760.00	475.00
281	Jim Campanis	30.00	12.00	7.50
282	Rick Monday	30.00	12.00	7.50
283	Mel Queen	30.00	12.00	7.50
284	John Briggs	30.00	12.00	7.50
285	Dick McAuliffe	30.00	12.00	7.50
286	Cecil Upshaw	30.00	12.00	7.50
287	White Sox Rookies (Mickey Abarbanel, Cisco Carlos)	30.00	12.00	7.50
288	Dave Wickersham	30.00	12.00	7.50
289	Woody Held	30.00	12.00	7.50
290	Willie McCovey	120.00	48.00	30.00
291	Dick Lines	30.00	12.00	7.50
292	Art Shamsky	30.00	12.00	7.50
293	Bruce Howard	30.00	12.00	7.50
294	Red Schoendienst	80.00	32.00	20.00
295	Sonny Siebert	30.00	12.00	7.50
296	Byron Browne	30.00	12.00	7.50
297	Russ Gibson	30.00	12.00	7.50
298	Jim Brewer	30.00	12.00	7.50
299	Gene Michael	30.00	12.00	7.50
300	Rusty Staub	40.00	16.00	10.00
301	Twins Rookies(George Mitterwald, Rick Renick)	30.00	12.00	7.50
302	Gerry Arrigo	30.00	12.00	7.50
303	Dick Green	30.00	12.00	7.50
304	Sandy Valdespino	30.00	12.00	7.50
305	Minnie Rojas	30.00	12.00	7.50
306	Mike Ryan	30.00	12.00	7.50
307	John Hiller	30.00	12.00	7.50
308	Pirates Team	50.00	20.00	12.50
309	Ken Henderson	30.00	12.00	7.50
310	Luis Aparicio	150.00	60.00	37.00
311	Jack Lamabe	30.00	12.00	7.50
312	Curt Blefary	30.00	12.00	7.50
313	Al Weis	30.00	12.00	7.50
314	Red Sox Rookies(Bill Rohr, George Spriggs)	30.00	12.00	7.50
315	Zoilo Versalles	30.00	12.00	7.50
316	Steve Barber	30.00	12.00	7.50
317	Ron Brand	30.00	12.00	7.50
318	Chico Salmon	30.00	12.00	7.50
319	George Culver	30.00	12.00	7.50
320	Frank Howard	40.00	16.00	10.00
321	Leo Durocher	50.00	20.00	12.50
322	Dave Boswell	30.00	12.00	7.50
323	Deron Johnson	30.00	12.00	7.50
324	Jim Nash	30.00	12.00	7.50
325	Manny Mota	30.00	12.00	7.50
326	Dennis Ribant	30.00	12.00	7.50
327	Tony Taylor	30.00	12.00	7.50
328	Angels Rookies(Chuck Vinson, Jim Weaver)	30.00	12.00	7.50
329	Duane Josephson	30.00	12.00	7.50
330	Roger Maris	120.00	48.00	30.00
331	Dan Osinski	30.00	12.00	7.50
332	Doug Rader	30.00	12.00	7.50
333	Ron Herbel	30.00	12.00	7.50
334	**Orioles Team**	50.00	20.00	12.50
335	Bob Allison	30.00	12.00	7.50
336	John Purdin	30.00	12.00	7.50
337	Bill Robinson	30.00	12.00	7.50
338	Bob Johnson	30.00	12.00	7.50
339	Rich Nye	30.00	12.00	7.50
340	Max Alvis	30.00	12.00	7.50
341	Jim Lemon	30.00	12.00	7.50
342	Ken Johnson	30.00	12.00	7.50
343	Jim Gosger	30.00	12.00	7.50
344	Donn Clendenon	30.00	12.00	7.50
345	Bob Hendley	30.00	12.00	7.50
346	Jerry Adair	30.00	12.00	7.50
347	George Brunet	30.00	12.00	7.50
348	Phillies Rookies (Larry Colton, Dick Thoenen)	30.00	12.00	7.50
349	Ed Spiezio	30.00	12.00	7.50
350	Hoyt Wilhelm	80.00	32.00	20.00
351	Bob Barton	30.00	12.00	7.50
352	Jackie Hernandez	30.00	12.00	7.50
353	Mack Jones	30.00	12.00	7.50
354	Pete Richert	30.00	12.00	7.50
355	Ernie Banks	130.00	55.00	35.00
356	Checklist 371-457(Ken Holtzman)	30.00	12.00	7.50
357	Len Gabrielson	30.00	12.00	7.50
358	Mike Epstein	30.00	12.00	7.50
359	Joe Moeller	30.00	12.00	7.50
360	Willie Horton	30.00	12.00	7.50
361	Harmon Killebrew (All-Star)	50.00	20.00	12.50
362	Orlando Cepeda (All-Star)	40.00	16.00	10.00
363	Rod Carew (All-Star)	50.00	20.00	12.50
364	Joe Morgan (All-Star)	40.00	16.00	10.00
365	Brooks Robinson (All-Star)	50.00	20.00	12.50
366	Ron Santo (All-Star)	16.00	10.00	
367	Jim Fregosi (All-Star)	12.00	7.50	
368	Gene Alley (All-Star)	12.00	7.50	
369	Carl Yastrzemski (All-Star)	20.00	12.50	
370	Hank Aaron (All-Star)	100.00	62.00	

1970 Ovenca Venezuelan League

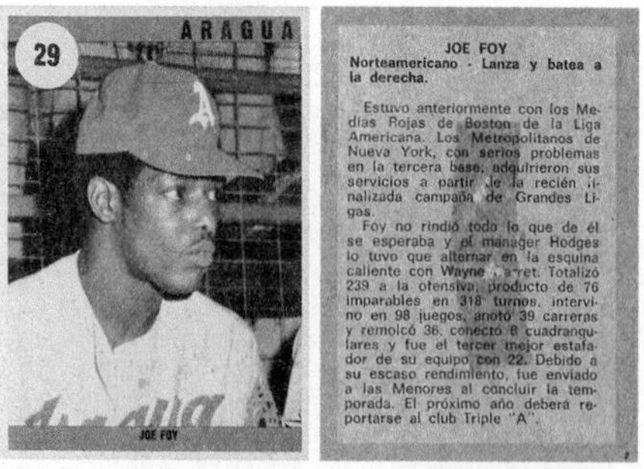

After partial parallels of Topps cards were produced off and on between 1959 and 1968, Venezuelan collectors and fans were offered a completely home-brewed baseball card issue for the 1970-71 winter league season. Similar in quality (i.e., less substantial card stock) to earlier sets, these were printed by Sport Grafico for Ovenca, though neither entity is mentioned on the cards. Slightly larger than 2-1/2" x 3-1/2", cards have large color photos with color stripes above and below bearing player and team name and card number. Backs are printed in black on blue with lengthy comments about the player and his career. Gaps in this checklist will be filled as information comes to light.

		NM	E	VG
	Complete Set (300):	2,250	1,100	650.00
	Common Player:	20.00	10.00	6.00
	Album:	200.00	100.00	60.00
1	Cesar Gutierrez	20.00	10.00	6.00
2	Elio Chacon	20.00	10.00	6.00
3	Luis Rodriguez	20.00	10.00	6.00
4	David Concepcion	75.00	37.50	22.00
5	Roberto Munoz	20.00	10.00	6.00
6	Jesus Rizales	20.00	10.00	6.00
7	Virgilio Mata	20.00	10.00	6.00
8	Manuel Garcia	30.00	15.00	9.00
9	Cesar Garrido	20.00	10.00	6.00
10	Alejandro Tovar	20.00	10.00	6.00
11	William Salazar	20.00	10.00	6.00
12	Jose Lopez	20.00	10.00	6.00
13	Romulo Castillo	20.00	10.00	6.00
14	Victor Jimenez	20.00	10.00	6.00
15	Jose Saiz	20.00	10.00	6.00
16	Wilfredo Calvino	20.00	10.00	6.00
17	Jesus Avila	20.00	10.00	6.00
18	Cruz Rodriguez	20.00	10.00	6.00
19	Julio Bracho	20.00	10.00	6.00
20	David Concepcion, Cesar Gutierrez	25.00	12.50	7.50
21	Double Play(David Concepcion)	25.00	12.50	7.50
22	Tigres de Aragua Logo	10.00	5.00	3.00
23	Orlando Tavares	20.00	10.00	6.00
24	David Concepcion (In Action)	30.00	15.00	9.00
25	Aragua Action	10.00	5.00	3.00
26	Aragua Action	10.00	5.00	3.00
27	Cesar Gutierrez	20.00	10.00	6.00
28	Play at Home	10.00	5.00	3.00
29	Joe Foy	20.00	10.00	6.00
30	Dennis Paepke	20.00	10.00	6.00
31	Fred Norman	20.00	10.00	6.00
32	John Purdin	20.00	10.00	6.00
33	Steve Huntz	20.00	10.00	6.00
34	Claide (Clyde) Mashore	20.00	10.00	6.00
35	Steve Mingori	20.00	10.00	6.00
36	Jim Breazeale	20.00	10.00	6.00
37	Charles Day	20.00	10.00	6.00
38	Bob Stinson	20.00	10.00	6.00
39	Phil Hennigan	20.00	10.00	6.00
40	Aragua Checklist (Wilfredo Calvino)	25.00	12.50	7.50
41	Faustino Zabala	20.00	10.00	6.00
42	Pablo Torrealba	20.00	10.00	6.00
43	Erasmo Diaz	20.00	10.00	6.00
44	Sebastian Martinez	20.00	10.00	6.00
45	Neudo Morales	20.00	10.00	6.00
46	Iran Paz	20.00	10.00	6.00
47	Franklyn Moreno	20.00	10.00	6.00
48	Claudio Urdaneta	20.00	10.00	6.00
49	Dario Chirinos	20.00	10.00	6.00
50	Domingo Carrasquel	20.00	10.00	6.00
51	Enrique Gonzalez	20.00	10.00	6.00
52	Ednio Gonzalez	20.00	10.00	6.00
53	Humberto Donquis	20.00	10.00	6.00
54	Antonio Ruiz	20.00	10.00	6.00
55	Efrain Urquiola	20.00	10.00	6.00
56	Tony Pacheco	20.00	10.00	6.00
57	Lucio Celis	20.00	10.00	6.00
58	Domingo Barboza	20.00	10.00	6.00
59	Faustino Zabala, Neudo Morales	15.00	7.50	4.50
60	Lara Action	10.00	5.00	3.00
61	Tony Pacheco, Lucio Celis, Domingo Barboza	15.00	7.50	4.50
62	Lara Team Logo	10.00	5.00	3.00
63	Alexis Corro	20.00	10.00	6.00
64	Lara Rookies in Action	10.00	5.00	3.00
65	Lara Play at First	10.00	5.00	3.00
66	Lara Play at Home	10.00	5.00	3.00
67	Lara Action	10.00	5.00	3.00
68	Jim Shellenback	20.00	10.00	6.00
69	Scipio Spinks	20.00	10.00	6.00
70	Ken Forsch	20.00	10.00	6.00
71	Oscar Zamora	20.00	10.00	6.00
72	Ronald Cook	20.00	10.00	6.00
73	Jackie Brown	20.00	10.00	6.00
74	Orlando Martinez	20.00	10.00	6.00
75	Bobby Watson	25.00	12.50	7.50
76	Jose Martinez	20.00	10.00	6.00
77	Roger Metzger	20.00	10.00	6.00
78	Tommy Reynolds	20.00	10.00	6.00
79	Cleo James	20.00	10.00	6.00
80	Lara Checkist(Tony Pacheco)	10.00	5.00	3.00

81	Gustavo Gil	20.00	10.00	6.00
82	Jesus Aristimuno	20.00	10.00	6.00
83	Armando Ortiz	20.00	10.00	6.00
84	Orlando Reyes	20.00	10.00	6.00
85	Damaso Blanco	20.00	10.00	6.00
86				
87	Victor Colina	20.00	10.00	6.00
88	Nelson Cana	20.00	10.00	6.00
89	Francisco Diaz	20.00	10.00	6.00
90	Edito Arteaga	20.00	10.00	6.00
91	Concepcion Escalona	20.00	10.00	6.00
92	Gilberto Marcano	20.00	10.00	6.00
93	Luis A. Serrano	20.00	10.00	6.00
94				
95	Raul Ortega	20.00	10.00	6.00
96	Carlos Patato Pascual	20.00	10.00	6.00
97	Leopold Tovar	20.00	10.00	6.00
98	Manuel Gonzalez	20.00	10.00	6.00
99	Magallanes Action	10.00	5.00	3.00
100	Comienza el Partido	20.00	10.00	6.00
101	Magallanes Rookies	15.00	7.50	4.50
102				
103	Marcano en la Lomita	15.00	7.50	4.50
104	Magallanes Fans	10.00	5.00	3.00
105	Magallanes Action	10.00	5.00	3.00
106				
107	Hal King, Jim Holt, Clarence Gaston, Herman Hill	15.00	7.50	4.50
108	Magallanes Caribbean Champions	10.00	5.00	3.00
109				
110	Herman Hill	20.00	10.00	6.00
111	Jim Holt	20.00	10.00	6.00
112	Orlando Pena	20.00	10.00	6.00
113	Magallanes Action	10.00	5.00	3.00
114	Hal King	20.00	10.00	6.00
115	Jorge Lauzerique	20.00	10.00	6.00
116	Rigoberto Mendoza	20.00	10.00	6.00
117	Allan (Alan) Closter	20.00	10.00	6.00
118	Clarence Gaston	25.00	12.50	7.50
119	John Morris	20.00	10.00	6.00
120	Patato Pascual, Unknown	15.00	7.50	4.50
121	Victor Davalillo	20.00	10.00	6.00
122	Cesar Tovar	20.00	10.00	6.00
123	Gonzalo Marquez	20.00	10.00	6.00
124	Luis Penalver	20.00	10.00	6.00
125	Alberto Cambero	20.00	10.00	6.00
126	Urbano Lugo	20.00	10.00	6.00
127	Juan Campos	20.00	10.00	6.00
128	William Castillo	20.00	10.00	6.00
129	Nelson Garcia	20.00	10.00	6.00
130	Ramon Guanchez	20.00	10.00	6.00
131	Jesus Marcano Trillo	40.00	20.00	12.00
132	Manuel Mendible	20.00	10.00	6.00
133	Teodoro Obregon	20.00	10.00	6.00
134	Jesus Padron	20.00	10.00	6.00
135	Ulises Urrieta	20.00	10.00	6.00
136	Antonio "Loco" Torres	20.00	10.00	6.00
137	Leopoldo Posada	20.00	10.00	6.00
138	Pompeyo Davilillo	20.00	10.00	6.00
139	Alonso Olivares	20.00	10.00	6.00
140	Cesar Tovar (In Action)	15.00	7.50	4.50
141	Caracas Rookies in Action	15.00	7.50	4.50
142				
143	Andres Barrios	20.00	10.00	6.00
144	Heriberto Morillo	20.00	10.00	6.00
145	Angel Cordova	20.00	10.00	6.00
146	Freddy Rivero	20.00	10.00	6.00
147	Rafael Velasquez	20.00	10.00	6.00
148	Camilo Pascual	30.00	15.00	9.00
149	Cesar Tovar, Vic Davalillo	20.00	10.00	6.00
150	Luis Tiant	30.00	15.00	9.00
151	Roberto Musulungo Hernandez	20.00	10.00	6.00
152	Kurt Devecqua (Bevacqua)	30.00	15.00	9.00
153	Cookie Rojas	30.00	15.00	9.00
154	Larry Howard	20.00	10.00	6.00
155	Rick Scheinblum	20.00	10.00	6.00
156	Diego Segui	25.00	12.50	7.50
157	Gregory Conger	20.00	10.00	6.00
158	Richard Falker (Falkner)	20.00	10.00	6.00
159	Ed Sprague	20.00	10.00	6.00
160	Zulia Checklist(Pompeyo Davilillo)	15.00	7.50	4.50
161	Luis Aparicio	75.00	37.00	22.00
162	Teolindo Acosta	20.00	10.00	6.00
163	Gustavo Sposito	20.00	10.00	6.00
164	Juan Francia	20.00	10.00	6.00
165	Graciliano Parra	20.00	10.00	6.00
166	Simon Salaya	20.00	10.00	6.00
167	Nelson Castellanos	20.00	10.00	6.00
168	Edgar Urbina	20.00	10.00	6.00
169	Luis Gonzalez	20.00	10.00	6.00
170	Olinto Rojas	20.00	10.00	6.00
171	Everest Contramaestre	20.00	10.00	6.00
172	Juan Quiroz	20.00	10.00	6.00
173	Juan Quintana	20.00	10.00	6.00
174	Hugo Bello	20.00	10.00	6.00
175	Jesus Llamozas	20.00	10.00	6.00
176	Luis Aparicio (Manager)	45.00	22.00	13.50
177	Luis Aparicio, Sr.	25.00	12.50	7.50
178	Antonio Brinez	20.00	10.00	6.00
179	Carlos Dickson Bell	20.00	10.00	6.00
180	Alfonso Carrasquel	30.00	15.00	9.00
181	**Zulia Action**	10.00	5.00	3.00
182	**Zulia Eagles Team Logo**	20.00	10.00	6.00
183	Nidio Sirit	20.00	10.00	6.00
184	**Zulia Action**	10.00	5.00	3.00
185	**Zulia Eagles Team Photo**	10.00	5.00	3.00
186	Bobby Cox (In Action)	20.00	10.00	6.00
187	**Zulia Play at Home**	10.00	5.00	3.00
188	Alfonso Carrasquel, Luis Aparicio	25.00	12.50	7.50
189	Teolindo Acosta, Gustavo Sposito	15.00	7.50	4.50
190	Leonardo Cardenas	20.00	10.00	6.00
191	Bart Johnson	20.00	10.00	6.00
192	Jerry Crider	20.00	10.00	6.00
193	Getty Janesky (Gerry Janeski)	20.00	10.00	6.00
194	John Matias	20.00	10.00	6.00
195	Walter Williams	25.00	12.50	7.50
196	Steve Hovley	20.00	10.00	6.00
197	Frank Fernandez	20.00	10.00	6.00
198	John Donaldson	20.00	10.00	6.00
199	Donald Eddy	20.00	10.00	6.00
200	Zulia Checklist (Luis Aparicio)	30.00	15.00	9.00
201	Jose Herrera	20.00	10.00	6.00
202	Aurelio Monteagudo	20.00	10.00	6.00
203	Remigio Hermoso	20.00	10.00	6.00
204	Angel Bravo	20.00	10.00	6.00
205	Enzo Hernandez	20.00	10.00	6.00
206	Oswaldo Blanco	20.00	10.00	6.00
207	Carlos Moreno	20.00	10.00	6.00
208	Adolfo Philips (Phillips)	20.00	10.00	6.00
209	Roberto Romero	20.00	10.00	6.00
210	Euclides Camejo	20.00	10.00	6.00
211	Oswaldo Troconis	20.00	10.00	6.00
212	Roberto Marcano	20.00	10.00	6.00
213	Victor Patino	20.00	10.00	6.00
214	Hector Urbano	20.00	10.00	6.00
215	Antonio Pipo Correa	20.00	10.00	6.00
216	Dave Garcia	25.00	12.50	7.50
217	Graciano Ravelo	20.00	10.00	6.00
218	Reinaldo Cordeiro	20.00	10.00	6.00
219	La Guaira Action	10.00	5.00	3.00
220	La Tropa Completa	20.00	10.00	6.00
221	Tomas Liscano Arias	20.00	10.00	6.00
222				
223	Jesus Romero	20.00	10.00	6.00
224	Julian Yanez	20.00	10.00	6.00
225	Enrique Gutierrez	20.00	10.00	6.00
226	Dionel Durand	20.00	10.00	6.00
227	Jose Gregorio Salas	20.00	10.00	6.00
228	Luis Camaleon Garcia	20.00	10.00	6.00
229	Alfredo Ortiz	20.00	10.00	6.00
230	Luis Contreras	20.00	10.00	6.00
231	Ed Spiezio	20.00	10.00	6.00
232	Paul Casanova	25.00	12.50	7.50
233	Mike Epstein	25.00	12.50	7.50
234	Casey Cox	20.00	10.00	6.00
235	Marcelino Lopez	20.00	10.00	6.00
236	Jerry Cram	20.00	10.00	6.00
237	Danny Coombs	20.00	10.00	6.00
238	Del Unser	20.00	10.00	6.00
239	Hector Brito	20.00	10.00	6.00
240	La Guaira Checklist	10.00	5.00	3.00
241	Larry Howard, Richie Scheinblum (In Action)	15.00	7.50	4.50
242	Ed Spiezio (In Action)	15.00	7.50	4.50
243	Clarence Gaston, Cesar Tovar (In Action)	15.00	7.50	4.50
244	Paul Casanova, Unknown	15.00	7.50	4.50
245	Vitico, Cesar Tovar	15.00	7.50	4.50
246	Pasion en el Juego	10.00	5.00	3.00
247	Luis Aparicio (In Action)	35.00	17.50	10.50
248	Angel Bravo (In Action)	15.00	7.50	4.50
249	Bobby Watson (In Action)	20.00	10.00	6.00
250	Alejandro "Palon" Carrasquel (Immortal)	25.00	12.50	7.50
251	Enrique Fonseca (Veteran)	20.00	10.00	6.00
252	Manuel Pollo Malpica (Immortal)	20.00	10.00	6.00
253	Emilio Cueche	20.00	10.00	6.00
254				
255	Felix "Tirahuequito" Machado (Veteran)			
256	Herberto Leal (Veteran)	20.00	10.00	6.00
257	Chucho Ramos (Veteran)	20.00	10.00	6.00
258	Julian Ladera (Veteran)	20.00	10.00	6.00
259	Carlos Ascanio (Veteran)	20.00	10.00	6.00
260	Jose Perez Colmenare (Immortal)	20.00	10.00	6.00
261	Isaias "Latigo" Chaves (Immortal)	20.00	10.00	6.00
262	Victor Garcia (Veteran)	20.00	10.00	6.00
263	Valentin Arevalo (Immortal)	20.00	10.00	6.00
264	Adolfredo Gonzalez (Veteran)	20.00	10.00	6.00
265	Hector Benitez Redondo (Veteran)	20.00	10.00	6.00
266	Ramon Fernandez (Veteran)	20.00	10.00	6.00
267	Guillermo Vento (Veteran)	20.00	10.00	6.00
268	Rafael Garcia Cedeno (Veteran)	20.00	10.00	6.00
269	Luis Oliveros (Veteran)	20.00	10.00	6.00
270	Luis Mono Zuloaga (Veteran)	20.00	10.00	6.00
271	Carlos Santeliz (Veteran)	20.00	10.00	6.00
272	Aureliano Patino	20.00	10.00	6.00
273	Rafael Olivares (Veteran)	20.00	10.00	6.00
274	Tarzan Contreras (Veteran)	20.00	10.00	6.00
275	Daniel Canonico	20.00	10.00	6.00
276	Babbino Fuenmayor (Veteran)	20.00	10.00	6.00
277	Rafael Galiz Tello (Veteran)	20.00	10.00	6.00
278	Pantaleon Espinoza	20.00	10.00	6.00
279	Miguel Sanabria (Veteran)	20.00	10.00	6.00
280				
281	Alfonso Carrasquel (Veteran)	40.00	20.00	12.00
282	Luis "Camaleon" Garcia (Veteran)	20.00	10.00	6.00
283	Balbino Inojosa (Veteran)	20.00	10.00	6.00
284	Humberto Popita Leal (Veteran)	20.00	10.00	6.00
285	Manuel Carrasquel (Veteran)	20.00	10.00	6.00
286	Ignacio Florez (Veteran)	20.00	10.00	6.00
287	Oscar Buzo Solorzino (Veteran)	20.00	10.00	6.00
288	Pelayo Chacon (Veteran)	20.00	10.00	6.00
289				
290	Micolas Berbesia (Veteran)	20.00	10.00	6.00
291	Julio Bracho (Veteran)	20.00	10.00	6.00
292	Dionisio Acosta (Veteran)	20.00	10.00	6.00
293	Gualberto Acosta (Veteran)	20.00	10.00	6.00
294	Winston Acosta (Veteran)	20.00	10.00	6.00
295	Jose Manuel Tovar (Veteran)	20.00	10.00	6.00
296	Carrao Bracho (Veteran)	20.00	10.00	6.00
297	Luis Romero Petit (Veteran)	20.00	10.00	6.00
298	Dalmiro Finol (Veteran)	20.00	10.00	6.00
299	Cerveceria Caracas Team Photo	20.00	10.00	6.00
300	Magallanes Campeones Nacionales Team	20.00	10.00	6.00

1972 Venezuelan Baseball Stamps

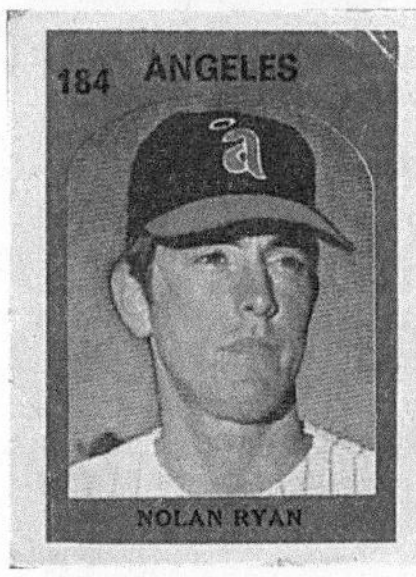

Utilizing most of the same photos as the 1972 Topps baseball cards, the 242 player stamps in this set feature only Major Leaguers, though with an overrepresentation of Hispanics, rather than the usual mix of U.S. and local talent. Stamps measure 2" x 2-9/16" and feature tombstone-shaped color photos at center, surrounded by a green background. The only printing is the player name, team name (in Spanish) and stamp number, all in black. A white border surrounds the whole. Backs are blank as the stamps were meant to be mounted in an album. Because stamps are seldom seen in higher grade, only a VG price is presented here. Stamps in Good should be valued at 50 percent of the price shown, and stamps grading Fair at 25 percent.

		NM	E	VG
Complete Set (242):		4,900	1,950	980.00
Common Player:		15.00	6.00	3.00
Album:		150.00	75.00	45.00
1	Vic Davalillo	50.00	20.00	10.00
2	Doug Griffin	15.00	6.00	3.00
3	Rod Carew	150.00	60.00	30.00
4	Joel Horlen	15.00	6.00	3.00
5	Jim Fregosi	15.00	6.00	3.00
6	Rod Carew ("en acion" - In Action)	100.00	40.00	20.00
7	Billy Champion	15.00	6.00	3.00
8	Ron Hansen	15.00	6.00	3.00
9	Bobby Murcer	15.00	6.00	3.00
10	Nellie Briles	15.00	6.00	3.00
11	Fred Patek	15.00	6.00	3.00
12	Mike Epstein	15.00	6.00	3.00
13	Dave Marshall	15.00	6.00	3.00
14	Steve Hargan	15.00	6.00	3.00
15	Duane Josephson	15.00	6.00	3.00
16	Steve Garvey	22.50	9.00	4.50
17	Eddie Fisher	15.00	6.00	3.00
18	Jack Aker	15.00	6.00	3.00
19	Ron Brand	15.00	6.00	3.00
20	Del Rice	15.00	6.00	3.00
21	Ollie Brown	15.00	6.00	3.00
22	Jamie McAndrew	15.00	6.00	3.00
23	Willie Horton	15.00	6.00	3.00
24	Eddie Leon	15.00	6.00	3.00
25	Steve Hovley	15.00	6.00	3.00
26	Moe Drabowsky	15.00	6.00	3.00
27	Dick Selma	15.00	6.00	3.00
28	Jim Lyttle	15.00	6.00	3.00
29	Sal Bando	15.00	6.00	3.00
30	Bill Lee	15.00	6.00	3.00
31	Al Kaline	150.00	60.00	30.00
32	Mike Lum	15.00	6.00	3.00
33	Les Cain	15.00	6.00	3.00
34	Richie Hebner	15.00	6.00	3.00
35	Donn Clendenon	15.00	6.00	3.00
36	Ralph Houk	15.00	6.00	3.00
37	Luis Melendez	15.00	6.00	3.00
38	Jim Hickman	15.00	6.00	3.00
39	Manny Mota	15.00	6.00	3.00
40	Bob Locker	15.00	6.00	3.00
41	Ron Santo	20.00	8.00	4.00
42	Tony Cloninger	15.00	6.00	3.00
43	Joe Ferguson	15.00	6.00	3.00
44	Mike McCormick	15.00	6.00	3.00
45	Bobby Wine	15.00	6.00	3.00
46	Preston Gomez	15.00	6.00	3.00
47	Pat Corrales (In Action)	15.00	6.00	3.00
48	Hector Torres	15.00	6.00	3.00
49	Fritz Peterson	15.00	6.00	3.00
50	Jim Rooker	15.00	6.00	3.00
51	Chris Short	15.00	6.00	3.00
52	Juan Marichal (In Action)	22.50	9.00	4.50
53	Teddy Martinez	15.00	6.00	3.00
54	Ken Aspromonte	15.00	6.00	3.00
55	Bobby Bonds	15.00	6.00	3.00
56	Rich Robertson	15.00	6.00	3.00
57	Nate Colbert (In Action)	15.00	6.00	3.00
58	Jose Pagan (In Action)	15.00	6.00	3.00
59	Curt Blefary (In Action)	15.00	6.00	3.00
60	Bill Mazeroski	100.00	40.00	20.00
61	John Odom	15.00	6.00	3.00
62	George Stone	15.00	6.00	3.00
63	Lew Krausse	15.00	6.00	3.00
64	Bobby Knoop	15.00	6.00	3.00
65	Pete Rose (In Action)	225.00	90.00	45.00
66	Steve Luebber	15.00	6.00	3.00
67	Bill Voss	15.00	6.00	3.00
68	Chico Salmon	15.00	6.00	3.00
69	Ivan Murrell	15.00	6.00	3.00
70	Gil Garrido	15.00	6.00	3.00
71	Terry Crowley	15.00	6.00	3.00
72	Bill Russell	15.00	6.00	3.00
73	Steve Dunning	15.00	6.00	3.00
74	Ray Sadecki (In Action)	15.00	6.00	3.00
75	Al Gallagher (In Action)	15.00	6.00	3.00
76	Cesar Gutierrez	15.00	6.00	3.00
77	John Kennedy	15.00	6.00	3.00
78	Joe Hague	15.00	6.00	3.00
79	Bruce Del Canton	15.00	6.00	3.00
80	Ken Holtzman	15.00	6.00	3.00
81	Rico Carty	15.00	6.00	3.00
82	Roger Repoz	15.00	6.00	3.00
83	Fran Healy	15.00	6.00	3.00
84	Al Gallagher	15.00	6.00	3.00
85	Rich McKinney	15.00	6.00	3.00
86	Lowell Palmer	15.00	6.00	3.00
87	Jose Cardenal	15.00	6.00	3.00
88	Ed Kirkpatrick (In Action)	15.00	6.00	3.00
89	Steve Carlton	150.00	60.00	30.00
90	Gail Hopkins	15.00	6.00	3.00
91	Reggie Smith	15.00	6.00	3.00
92	Denny Riddleberger	15.00	6.00	3.00
93	Don Sutton	60.00	24.00	12.00
94	Bob Moose	15.00	6.00	3.00
95	Joe Decker	15.00	6.00	3.00
96	Bill Wilson	15.00	6.00	3.00
97	Mike Ferraro	15.00	6.00	3.00
98	Jack Hiatt	15.00	6.00	3.00
99	Bill Grabarkewitz	15.00	6.00	3.00
100	Larry Stahl	15.00	6.00	3.00
101	Jim Slaton	15.00	6.00	3.00
102	Jim Wynn	15.00	6.00	3.00
103	Phil Niekro	60.00	24.00	12.00
104	Danny Cater	15.00	6.00	3.00
105	Ray Sadecki	15.00	6.00	3.00
106	Jack Billingham	15.00	6.00	3.00
107	Dave Nelson	15.00	6.00	3.00
108	Rudy May	15.00	6.00	3.00
109	Don Money	15.00	6.00	3.00
110	Diego Segui	15.00	6.00	3.00
111	Jose Pagan	15.00	6.00	3.00
112	John Strohmayer	15.00	6.00	3.00
113	Wade Blasingame	15.00	6.00	3.00
114	Ken Wright	15.00	6.00	3.00
115	Ken Tatum	15.00	6.00	3.00
116	Mike Paul	15.00	6.00	3.00
117	Tom McCraw	15.00	6.00	3.00
118	Bob Gibson	125.00	50.00	25.00
119	Al Santorini	15.00	6.00	3.00
120	Leo Cardenas	15.00	6.00	3.00
121	Jimmy Stewart	15.00	6.00	3.00
122	Willie Crawford	15.00	6.00	3.00
123	Bob Aspromonte	15.00	6.00	3.00
124	Frank Duffy	15.00	6.00	3.00
125	Hal Lanier	15.00	6.00	3.00
126	Nate Colbert	15.00	6.00	3.00
127	Russ Gibson	15.00	6.00	3.00
128	Cesar Geronimo	15.00	6.00	3.00
129	Pat Kelly	15.00	6.00	3.00
130	Horacio Pina	15.00	6.00	3.00
131	Charlie Brinkman	15.00	6.00	3.00
132	Bill Virdon	15.00	6.00	3.00
133	Hal McRae	15.00	6.00	3.00
134	Tony Oliva (In Action)	25.00	10.00	5.00
135	Gonzalo Marquez	15.00	6.00	3.00
136	Willie Montanez	15.00	6.00	3.00
137	Dick Green	15.00	6.00	3.00
138	Jim Ray	15.00	6.00	3.00
139	Denis Menke	15.00	6.00	3.00
140	Fred Kendall	15.00	6.00	3.00
141	Vida Blue	15.00	6.00	3.00
142	Tom Grieve	15.00	6.00	3.00
143	Ed Kirkpatrick (In Action)	15.00	6.00	3.00
144	George Scott	15.00	6.00	3.00
145	Hal Breeden	15.00	6.00	3.00
146	Ken McMullen	15.00	6.00	3.00
147	Jim Perry (In Action)	15.00	6.00	3.00
148	Wayne Granger	15.00	6.00	3.00
149	Mike Hegan	15.00	6.00	3.00
150	Al Oliver	20.00	8.00	4.00
151	Frank Robinson (In Action)	100.00	40.00	20.00
152	Paul Blair	15.00	6.00	3.00
153	Phil Hennigan	15.00	6.00	3.00
154	Ron Stone	15.00	6.00	3.00
155	Gene Michael	15.00	6.00	3.00
156	Jerry McNertney	15.00	6.00	3.00
157	Marcelino Lopez	15.00	6.00	3.00
158	Dave May	15.00	6.00	3.00
159	Jim Hart	15.00	6.00	3.00
160	Joe Coleman	15.00	6.00	3.00
161	Rick Reichardt	15.00	6.00	3.00
162	Ed Brinkman	15.00	6.00	3.00
163	Dick McAuliffe	15.00	6.00	3.00
164	Paul Doyle	15.00	6.00	3.00
165	Terry Forster	15.00	6.00	3.00
166	Steve Hamilton	15.00	6.00	3.00
167	Mike Corkins	15.00	6.00	3.00
168	Dave Concepcion	75.00	30.00	15.00
169	Bill Sudakis	15.00	6.00	3.00
170	Juan Marichal	100.00	40.00	20.00
171	Harmon Killebrew	150.00	60.00	30.00
172	Luis Tiant	20.00	8.00	4.00
173	Ted Uhlaender	15.00	6.00	3.00
174	Tim Foli	15.00	6.00	3.00
175	Luis Aparicio (In Action)	200.00	80.00	40.00
176	Bert Campaneris	15.00	6.00	3.00
177	Charlie Sands	15.00	6.00	3.00
178	Darold Knowles	15.00	6.00	3.00
179	Jerry Koosman	15.00	6.00	3.00
180	Leo Cardenas (In Action)	15.00	6.00	3.00
181	Luis Alvarado	15.00	6.00	3.00
182	Graig Nettles	17.50	7.00	3.50
183	Walter Alston	20.00	8.00	4.00
184	Nolan Ryan	550.00	220.00	110.00
185	Ed Sprague	15.00	6.00	3.00
186	Rich Reese	15.00	6.00	3.00
187	Pete Rose	300.00	120.00	60.00
188	Bernie Allen	15.00	6.00	3.00
189	Lou Piniella	17.50	7.00	3.50
190	Jerry Reuss	15.00	6.00	3.00
191	Bob Pfeil	15.00	6.00	3.00
192	Bob Burda	15.00	6.00	3.00
193	Walt Williams	15.00	6.00	3.00
194	Dusty Baker	17.50	7.00	3.50
195	Rich Morales	15.00	6.00	3.00
196	Bill Stoneman	15.00	6.00	3.00
197	Hal King	15.00	6.00	3.00
198	Julian Javier	15.00	6.00	3.00
199	Dave Mason	15.00	6.00	3.00
200	Bob Veale	15.00	6.00	3.00
201	Jim Beauchamp	15.00	6.00	3.00
202	Ron Santo (In Action)	17.50	7.00	3.50
203	Tom Seaver	150.00	60.00	30.00
204	Jim Merritt	15.00	6.00	3.00
205	Jerry Koosman (In Action)	15.00	6.00	3.00
206	Dick Woodson	15.00	6.00	3.00
207	Wayne Simpson	15.00	6.00	3.00
208	Jose Laboy	15.00	6.00	3.00
209	Sam McDowell	15.00	6.00	3.00
210	Bob Bailey	15.00	6.00	3.00
211	Jim Fairey	15.00	6.00	3.00
212	Felipe Alou	25.00	10.00	5.00
213	Dave Concepcion (In Action)	50.00	20.00	10.00
214	Wilbur Wood (In Action)	15.00	6.00	3.00
215	Enzo Hernandez	15.00	6.00	3.00
216	Ron Reed	15.00	6.00	3.00
217	Stan Bahnsen	15.00	6.00	3.00
218	Ollie Brown (In Action)	15.00	6.00	3.00
219	Pat Jarvis	15.00	6.00	3.00
220	Tim Foli (In Action)	15.00	6.00	3.00
221	Denny McLain	15.00	6.00	3.00
222	Jerry Grote	15.00	6.00	3.00
223	Davey Johnson	15.00	6.00	3.00
224	John Odom (In Action)	15.00	6.00	3.00
225	Paul Casanova	15.00	6.00	3.00
226	George Culver	15.00	6.00	3.00
227	Pat Corrales	15.00	6.00	3.00
228	Jim Kaat	15.00	6.00	3.00
229	Archie Reynolds	15.00	6.00	3.00
230	Frank Reberger	15.00	6.00	3.00
231	Carl Yastrzemski	150.00	60.00	30.00
232	Jim Holt	15.00	6.00	3.00
233	Lenny Randle	15.00	6.00	3.00
234	Doug Griffin (In Action)	15.00	6.00	3.00
235	Doug Rader	15.00	6.00	3.00
236	Jesus Alou	15.00	6.00	3.00
237	Wilbur Wood (In Action)	15.00	6.00	3.00
238	Jim Kaat (In Action)	15.00	6.00	3.00
239	Fritz Peterson (In Action)	15.00	6.00	3.00
240	Dennis Leonard	15.00	6.00	3.00
241	Brooks Robinson	150.00	60.00	30.00
242	Felix Millan	15.00	6.00	3.00

1972 Venezuelan League Stickers

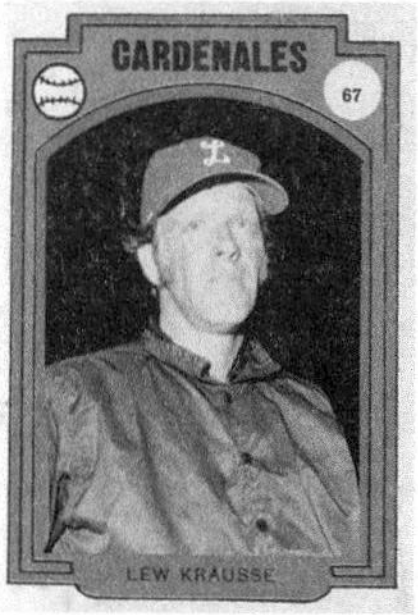

Issued in the winter league season of 1972-73, the Venezuelan League sticker set bears more than a passing similitude to the 1972 Topps baseball cards. The 2-1/2" x 3-1/2" stickers have tombstone-shaped photos framed in multi-colored borders with the team name at top and the player name in an oval cartouche at bottom. The sticker number is in a circle at top-right. Because they were intended to be mounted in an accompanying album, the backs are blank. Because so many of the stickers were once pasted into albums, and due to unfavorable climactic conditions, high-grade examples of Venezuelan stickers from the era are particularly scarce.

		NM	E	VG
Complete Set (249):		1,500	750.00	450.00
Common Player:		20.00	10.00	6.00
Album:		75.00	40.00	20.00
1	Dave Concepcion	30.00	15.00	9.00
2	Luis Rodriguez	25.00	12.50	7.50
3	Roberto Munoz	25.00	12.50	7.50
4	William Castillo	25.00	12.50	7.50
5	Jose Lopez	25.00	12.50	7.50
6	Armando Chacon	25.00	12.50	7.50
7	Juan Francia	25.00	12.50	7.50

8	Roric Harrison	25.00	12.50	7.50
9	Dave Concepcion, Escalona	30.00	15.00	9.00
10	Enrique Gutierrez	25.00	12.50	7.50
11	Luis Gonzalez	25.00	12.50	7.50
12	Jose Torres	25.00	12.50	7.50
13	William Salazar	25.00	12.50	7.50
14	Everest Contramaestre	25.00	12.50	7.50
15	Jesus Rizales	25.00	12.50	7.50
16	Ramon Velasquez	25.00	12.50	7.50
17	Rafael J. Velasquez	25.00	12.50	7.50
18	Jesus Loreto	25.00	12.50	7.50
19	Orlando Galindo	25.00	12.50	7.50
20	Jose Torres	25.00	12.50	7.50
21	Victor Jimenez	25.00	12.50	7.50
22	Hernan Silva	25.00	12.50	7.50
23	Leroy Stanton	25.00	12.50	7.50
24	Jesus Yanez	25.00	12.50	7.50
25	Orlando Tavares	25.00	12.50	7.50
26	Eddie Baez	25.00	12.50	7.50
27	Jim Frey	30.00	15.00	9.00
28	Eddie Watt	25.00	12.50	7.50
29	Aragua Team Logo	10.00	5.00	3.00
30	Carlos Orea	25.00	12.50	7.50
31	Rod Carew	75.00	37.00	22.00
32	Rod Carew, Enos Cabell	35.00	17.50	10.50
33	George Mitterwald	25.00	12.50	7.50
34	Enos Cabell	25.00	12.50	7.50
35	Eddy Baez	25.00	12.50	7.50
36	Teolindo Acosta	25.00	12.50	7.50
37	Ron Theobald	25.00	12.50	7.50
38	Milt Wilcox	30.00	15.00	9.00
39	Cesar Gutierrez	25.00	12.50	7.50
40	Ed Farmer	25.00	12.50	7.50
41	Dario Chirinos	25.00	12.50	7.50
42	Alberto Cambero	25.00	12.50	7.50
43	Eddy Diaz	25.00	12.50	7.50
44	Graciliano Parra	25.00	12.50	7.50
45	Bob Lee	25.00	12.50	7.50
46	Joe Keough	25.00	12.50	7.50
47	Dario Chirinos, Pablo Torrealba	25.00	12.50	7.50
48	Rafael Alvarez	25.00	12.50	7.50
49	Lucio Celis	25.00	12.50	7.50
50	Jose Martinez	25.00	12.50	7.50
51	Faustino Zabala	25.00	12.50	7.50
52	Jose Herrera	25.00	12.50	7.50
53	Monty Montgomery	25.00	12.50	7.50
54	Al Cowens	25.00	12.50	7.50
55	Lara Team	10.00	5.00	3.00
56	Luis Aparicio	60.00	30.00	18.00
57	Virgilio Mata	25.00	12.50	7.50
58	Franklin Moreno	25.00	12.50	7.50
59	Fidel Garcia	25.00	12.50	7.50
60	Victor Montilla	25.00	12.50	7.50
61	Bobby Mitchell	25.00	12.50	7.50
62	Pablo Torrealba	25.00	12.50	7.50
63	Joe Keough	25.00	12.50	7.50
64	Al Cowens	25.00	12.50	7.50
65	Dwight Evans	35.00	17.50	10.50
66	Rick Henninger	25.00	12.50	7.50
67	Lew Krausse	25.00	12.50	7.50
68	George Manz	25.00	12.50	7.50
69	John Lowenstein	25.00	12.50	7.50
70	Juan Quiroz	25.00	12.50	7.50
71	Sebastian Martinez	25.00	12.50	7.50
72	Claudio Urdaneta	25.00	12.50	7.50
73	Barry Raziano	25.00	12.50	7.50
74	Luis Aparicio	60.00	30.00	18.00
75	Lara Team Logo	10.00	5.00	3.00
76	Bobby Mitchell	25.00	12.50	7.50
77	Harold Hunter	25.00	12.50	7.50
78	Dick Pole	25.00	12.50	7.50
79	Carlos Davila	25.00	12.50	7.50
80	Enrique Gonzalez	25.00	12.50	7.50
81	Carlos Pascual	25.00	12.50	7.50
82	Edito Arteaga	25.00	12.50	7.50
83	William Fahey	25.00	12.50	7.50
84	Tomas Gonzalez	25.00	12.50	7.50
85	Rigoberto Mendoza	25.00	12.50	7.50
86	Rafael Jimenez	25.00	12.50	7.50
87	Jesus Aristimuno	25.00	12.50	7.50
88	Armando Ortiz	25.00	12.50	7.50
89	Bill Butler	25.00	12.50	7.50
90	Charles Day	25.00	12.50	7.50
91	Miguel Motolongo	25.00	12.50	7.50
92	Kurt Bavacqua (Bevacqua)	25.00	12.50	7.50
93	Esteban Padron	25.00	12.50	7.50
94	Angel Baez	25.00	12.50	7.50
95	Oscar Zamora	25.00	12.50	7.50
96	Manny Sarmiento	25.00	12.50	7.50
97	Nelson Canas	25.00	12.50	7.50
98	Victor Colina	25.00	12.50	7.50
99	Jerry Pirtle	25.00	12.50	7.50
100	Charles Day	25.00	12.50	7.50
101	Miguel Motolongo	25.00	12.50	7.50
102	Magallanes Group Photo	10.00	5.00	3.00
103	Jim Holt	25.00	12.50	7.50
104	Bob Darwin	25.00	12.50	7.50
105	Magallanes Team Logo	10.00	5.00	3.00
106	Oscar Del Busto	25.00	12.50	7.50
107	Jerry Jones	25.00	12.50	7.50
108	Eddie Leon	25.00	12.50	7.50
109	Armando Ortiz	25.00	12.50	7.50
110	Magallanes Team Photo	10.00	5.00	3.00
111	Magallanes Team Photo	10.00	5.00	3.00
112	Bob Darwin (Puzzle)	10.00	5.00	3.00
113	Bob Darwin	25.00	12.50	7.50
114	Rafael Cariel	25.00	12.50	7.50
115	Bob Darwin (Puzzle)	10.00	5.00	3.00
116	Bob Darwin (Puzzle)	10.00	5.00	3.00
117	Orlando Reyes	25.00	12.50	7.50
118	Edito Arteaga	25.00	12.50	7.50
119	Magallanes Roster (Carlos Pascual)	10.00	5.00	3.00
120	National Anthem	10.00	5.00	3.00
121	Barry Lersch	25.00	12.50	7.50
122	Elias Lugo	25.00	12.50	7.50
123	Simon Barreto	25.00	12.50	7.50
124	Manny Trillo	25.00	12.50	7.50
125	Joe Ferguson	25.00	12.50	7.50
126	Wilibaldo Quintana	25.00	12.50	7.50
127	Edgar Urbina	25.00	12.50	7.50
128	Nelson Garcia	25.00	12.50	7.50
129	Arguilio Freites	25.00	12.50	7.50
130	Carlos Rodriguez	25.00	12.50	7.50
131	Ozzie Virgil	25.00	12.50	7.50
132	Caracas Lions Team Logo	10.00	5.00	3.00
133	Virgilio Velasquez	25.00	12.50	7.50
134	Ed Sprague	25.00	12.50	7.50
135	Nelson Garcia	25.00	12.50	7.50
136	Jose Caldera	25.00	12.50	7.50
137	Antonio Armas	30.00	15.00	9.00
138	Dick Lange	25.00	12.50	7.50
139	Luis Sanz	25.00	12.50	7.50
140	Dave Lopez	25.00	12.50	7.50
141	Ulises Urrieta	25.00	12.50	7.50
142	Urbano Lugo	25.00	12.50	7.50
143	Bo Diaz	25.00	12.50	7.50
144	Andres Barrios	25.00	12.50	7.50
145	Victor Boll	25.00	12.50	7.50
146	Antonio Torres	25.00	12.50	7.50
147	Bert Campaneris	30.00	15.00	9.00
148	Carlos Alfonzo	25.00	12.50	7.50
149	Teodoro Obregon	25.00	12.50	7.50
150	Luis Penalver	25.00	12.50	7.50
151	Jose Ramon Jimenez	25.00	12.50	7.50
152	Cesar Tovar	25.00	12.50	7.50
153	Gonzalo Marquez	25.00	12.50	7.50
154	Dick Baney	25.00	12.50	7.50
155	Ed Armbrister	25.00	12.50	7.50
156	Ramon Webster	25.00	12.50	7.50
157	Francisco Navas	25.00	12.50	7.50
158	Hal McRae	25.00	12.50	7.50
159	Victor Davilillo	25.00	12.50	7.50
160	Geoff Zahn	25.00	12.50	7.50
161	Jesus Camacaro	25.00	12.50	7.50
162	Ruiz, Parra	25.00	12.50	7.50
163	Posada, Dick Billings	25.00	12.50	7.50
164	Tom Grieve	25.00	12.50	7.50
165	Tom Grieve	25.00	12.50	7.50
166	Dick Billings	25.00	12.50	7.50
167	Peter Broberg	25.00	12.50	7.50
168	Victor Fainette	25.00	12.50	7.50
169	Cruz Rodriguez	25.00	12.50	7.50
170	Oscar Gamble	25.00	12.50	7.50
171	Olinto Rojas	25.00	12.50	7.50
172	Nelson Paiva	25.00	12.50	7.50
173	Jackie Brown	25.00	12.50	7.50
174	Gustavo Sposito	25.00	12.50	7.50
175	Levy Ochoa	25.00	12.50	7.50
176	Larry Bittner (Biittner)	25.00	12.50	7.50
177	William Kirkpatrick	25.00	12.50	7.50
178	Nevil Romero	25.00	12.50	7.50
179	Eduardo Benitez	25.00	12.50	7.50
180	Heriberto Lemus	25.00	12.50	7.50
181	Toby Harrah	25.00	12.50	7.50
182	Alfonzo Collazo	25.00	12.50	7.50
183	Jesus Reyes	25.00	12.50	7.50
184	Hely Boscan	25.00	12.50	7.50
185	Mike (Mickey) Scott	25.00	12.50	7.50
186	Roberto Bracho	25.00	12.50	7.50
187	Walter William (Williams)	25.00	12.50	7.50
188	Nevil Romero	25.00	12.50	7.50
189	Jose Alfaro	25.00	12.50	7.50
190	Leonel Carrion	25.00	12.50	7.50
191	Jesus Padron	25.00	12.50	7.50
192	Posada, Chico Carrasquel	25.00	12.50	7.50
193	Domingo Barboza	25.00	12.50	7.50
194	Eduardo Benitez	25.00	12.50	7.50
195	Nidio Sirit	25.00	12.50	7.50
196	Jose Carrao Bracho	25.00	12.50	7.50
197	Levi Ochoa	25.00	12.50	7.50
198	Hely Boscan	25.00	12.50	7.50
199	Victor Fainette, Leonel Carrion	25.00	12.50	7.50
200	Luis Rivas	25.00	12.50	7.50
201	Luis Tiant	25.00	12.50	7.50
202	Graciano Ravelo	25.00	12.50	7.50
203	Hector Artiles	25.00	12.50	7.50
204	Enzo Hernandez	25.00	12.50	7.50
205	Remigio Hermoso	25.00	12.50	7.50
206	Hector Brito	25.00	12.50	7.50
207	Victor Patino	25.00	12.50	7.50
208	Romualdo Blanco	25.00	12.50	7.50
209	Antonio Carrera	25.00	12.50	7.50
210	Euclides Camejo	25.00	12.50	7.50
211	Carlos Moreno	25.00	12.50	7.50
212	Oswaldo Blanco	25.00	12.50	7.50
213	Jorge Padron	25.00	12.50	7.50
214	Manuel Garcia	25.00	12.50	7.50
215	La Guaira Group Photo	10.00	5.00	3.00
216	La Guaira Group Photo	10.00	5.00	3.00
217	Jose Salas	25.00	12.50	7.50
218	Luis Sanchez	25.00	12.50	7.50
219	Raul Velarde	25.00	12.50	7.50
220	Al Bumbry	25.00	12.50	7.50
221	**Group Photo**	10.00	5.00	3.00
222	Ivan Murrell	25.00	12.50	7.50
223	Jose Cardenal	25.00	12.50	7.50
224	**Group Photo**	10.00	5.00	3.00
225	**Group Photo**	10.00	5.00	3.00
226	Angel Bravo	25.00	12.50	7.50
227	Tom Murphy	25.00	12.50	7.50
228	Hector Urbano	25.00	12.50	7.50
229	Camilo Pascual	25.00	12.50	7.50
230	Pat Kelly	25.00	12.50	7.50
231	Robert Marcano	25.00	12.50	7.50
232	Paul Casanova	25.00	12.50	7.50
233	Preston Gomez	25.00	12.50	7.50
234	La Guaira Team Logo	10.00	5.00	3.00
235	Ken Forsch	25.00	12.50	7.50
236	Luis Tiant (Puzzle)	10.00	5.00	3.00
237	Luis Tiant (Puzzle)	10.00	5.00	3.00
238	Dionel Durand	25.00	12.50	7.50
239	Luis Tiant (Puzzle)	10.00	5.00	3.00
240	Luis Tiant (Puzzle)	10.00	5.00	3.00
241	Jim Rooker (Puzzle)	10.00	5.00	3.00
242	Jim Rooker (Puzzle)	10.00	5.00	3.00
243	William Parker	25.00	12.50	7.50
244	Jim Rooker (Puzzle)	10.00	5.00	3.00
245	Jim Rooker (Puzzle)	10.00	5.00	3.00
246	Jose Herrera	25.00	12.50	7.50
247	Aurelio Monteagudo	25.00	12.50	7.50
248	Ivan Murrell	25.00	12.50	7.50
249	Roster(Preston Gomez)	10.00	5.00	3.00

1973 Venezuelan League Stickers

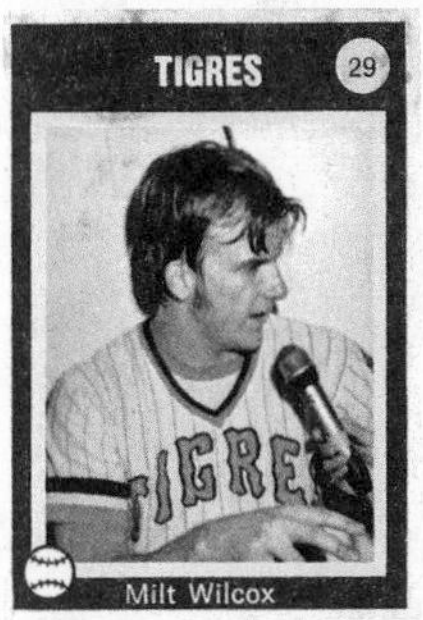

These stickers were made for collection in an album and as such are typically found in low grade and/or with evidence of once having been so mounted. Several gaps in the reported checklist require further research. Many former and future Major Leaguers are included in the issue. The basic player stickers have color photos surrounded by a multi-color border with the team name at top and the player name at bottom. Stickers are about 2-1/2" x 3-1/2" and numbered on front. A colorful album to house the set was also issued.

		NM	E	VG
	Common Player:	20.00	10.00	6.00
	Album:	75.00	40.00	25.00
1	Orlando Galindo	20.00	10.00	6.00
2	William Castillo	20.00	10.00	6.00
3	Everest Contramaestre	20.00	10.00	6.00
4	Luis Gonzalez	20.00	10.00	6.00
5	Jose Lopez	20.00	10.00	6.00
6	Cesar Orea	20.00	10.00	6.00
7	Luis H. Silva	20.00	10.00	6.00
8	Victor Jimenez	20.00	10.00	6.00
9	David Torres	20.00	10.00	6.00
10	Jose Torres	20.00	10.00	6.00
11	Ramon Velasquez	20.00	10.00	6.00

12	Jesus Avila	20.00	10.00	6.00
13	Carlos Loreto	20.00	10.00	6.00
14	Jesus Padron	20.00	10.00	6.00
15	Don Osborne	20.00	10.00	6.00
16	John Glass	20.00	10.00	6.00
17	Teolindo Acosta	20.00	10.00	6.00
18	Jim Todd	20.00	10.00	6.00
19	Roberto Munoz	20.00	10.00	6.00
20	Pete Lakock (LaCock)	20.00	10.00	6.00
21	Francisco Leandro	20.00	10.00	6.00
22	Jesus Rizales	20.00	10.00	6.00
23	Enos Cabell	25.00	12.50	7.50
24	Adrian Garret (Garrett)	20.00	10.00	6.00
25	Kurt Bavaqua (Bevacqua)	20.00	10.00	6.00
26	Jerry Moses	20.00	10.00	6.00
27	Jim Wiloughby (Willoughby)	20.00	10.00	6.00
28	Joel Youngblood	20.00	10.00	6.00
29	Milt Wilcox	25.00	12.50	7.50
30	Cesar Gutierrez	20.00	10.00	6.00
31	Efrain Urquiola	20.00	10.00	6.00
32	Carlos Pascual	20.00	10.00	6.00
33	Julio Bracho	20.00	10.00	6.00
34	Rafael Velasquez	20.00	10.00	6.00
35	Eddy Baez	20.00	10.00	6.00
36	Daniel Dubuc	20.00	10.00	6.00
37	Angel Leon	20.00	10.00	6.00
38	Angel Vargas	20.00	10.00	6.00
39	Motis Romero	20.00	10.00	6.00
40	Graciliano Parra	20.00	10.00	6.00
41	John Lowenstein	20.00	10.00	6.00
42	Nelson Garcia	20.00	10.00	6.00
43	Richard Burleson	25.00	12.50	7.50
44	Doug DeCinces	35.00	17.50	10.50
45	Eugene Martin	20.00	10.00	6.00
46	Jim Cox	20.00	10.00	6.00
47	Mike Adams	20.00	10.00	6.00
48	Richard Henninger	20.00	10.00	6.00
49	Sebastian Martinez	20.00	10.00	6.00
50	Lucio Celis	20.00	10.00	6.00
51	Alberto Cambero	20.00	10.00	6.00
52	Claudio Urdaneta	20.00	10.00	6.00
53	Victor Montilla	20.00	10.00	6.00
54	Pastor Perez	20.00	10.00	6.00
55	Enrique Gonzalez	20.00	10.00	6.00
56	Andres Barrios	20.00	10.00	6.00
57	Diego Herrera	20.00	10.00	6.00
58	Luis Aparicio	60.00	30.00	18.00
59	Teodoro Obregon	20.00	10.00	6.00
60	Dave Johnson	25.00	12.50	7.50
61	Roger Polanco	20.00	10.00	6.00
62	Ray Miller	20.00	10.00	6.00
63	Craig Caskey	20.00	10.00	6.00
64	David Wallace	20.00	10.00	6.00
65	**Lara Team Logo**	10.00	5.00	3.00
66	Herbert Hutson	20.00	10.00	6.00
67	Edgar Carusi	20.00	10.00	6.00
68	Luis Aponte	20.00	10.00	6.00
69	Joel Alcala	20.00	10.00	6.00
70	Dario Chirinos	20.00	10.00	6.00
71	Arnaldo Alvarado	20.00	10.00	6.00
72	Jose Bekis	20.00	10.00	6.00
73	Bill Moran	20.00	10.00	6.00
74	Steve McCartney	20.00	10.00	6.00
75	**Lara Action**	10.00	5.00	3.00
76	Rafael Alvarez	20.00	10.00	6.00
77	Juan Quiroz	20.00	10.00	6.00
78	Jim Rice	125.00	62.00	37.00
79	Ivan Murrel (Murrell)	20.00	10.00	6.00
80	James McKee	20.00	10.00	6.00
81	Rafael Cariel	20.00	10.00	6.00
82	George Theodore	20.00	10.00	6.00
83	Esteban Padron	20.00	10.00	6.00
84	Manuel Gonzalez	20.00	10.00	6.00
85	Edito Arteaga	20.00	10.00	6.00
86	Gus Gil	20.00	10.00	6.00
87	Oswaldo Olivares	20.00	10.00	6.00
88	Nelson Canas	20.00	10.00	6.00
89	Jesus Aristimuno	20.00	10.00	6.00
90	Orlando Reyes	20.00	10.00	6.00
91	Armando Ortiz	20.00	10.00	6.00
92	Gregorio Machado	20.00	10.00	6.00
93	Victor Colina	20.00	10.00	6.00
94	Alexis Ramirez	20.00	10.00	6.00
95	Jose Rios-Chiripa	20.00	10.00	6.00
96	Ed Napoleon	20.00	10.00	6.00
97	Bob Bailor	25.00	12.50	7.50
98	Dave Agustine (Augustine)	20.00	10.00	6.00
99	Bob Darwin	20.00	10.00	6.00
100	Gilberto Marcano	20.00	10.00	6.00
101	Jim Frey	25.00	12.50	7.50
102	Steve Braun	20.00	10.00	6.00
103	Don Hood	20.00	10.00	6.00
104	Mike Reinbach	20.00	10.00	6.00
105	Thomas Dettore	20.00	10.00	6.00
106	Wayne Garland	20.00	10.00	6.00
107	Mark Weens	20.00	10.00	6.00
108	Nelson Paiva	20.00	10.00	6.00
109	Manuel Sarmiento	20.00	10.00	6.00
110	Miguel Motolongo	20.00	10.00	6.00
111	Miguel Navas	20.00	10.00	6.00
112	Angel Baez	20.00	10.00	6.00
113	Raul Ortega	20.00	10.00	6.00
114	Humberto Montero	20.00	10.00	6.00
115	Tomas Gonzalez	20.00	10.00	6.00
116	Ruben Cabrera	20.00	10.00	6.00
117	Flores Bolivar	20.00	10.00	6.00
118	Felix Rodriguez	20.00	10.00	6.00
119	Ali Arape	20.00	10.00	6.00
120	Alexis Heredia	20.00	10.00	6.00
121	Arguilio Freites	20.00	10.00	6.00
122	Alfredo Ortiz	20.00	10.00	6.00
123	Simon Barreto	20.00	10.00	6.00
124	Urbano Lugo	20.00	10.00	6.00
125	Bo Diaz	20.00	10.00	6.00
126	Victor Boll	20.00	10.00	6.00
127	Jose Vinay Caldera	20.00	10.00	6.00
128	Leopoldo Tovar	20.00	10.00	6.00
129	Wilibaldo Quintana	20.00	10.00	6.00
130	Edgar Urbina	20.00	10.00	6.00
131	Ulises Urrieta	20.00	10.00	6.00
132	Antonio Torres	20.00	10.00	6.00
133	Luis Penalver	20.00	10.00	6.00
134	Heriberto Morillo	20.00	10.00	6.00
135	Tony Pacheco	20.00	10.00	6.00
136	Victor Davalillo	20.00	10.00	6.00
137	Jose Martinez	20.00	10.00	6.00
138	Jacinto Betancourt	20.00	10.00	6.00
139	Antonio Armas	40.00	20.00	12.00
140	Cesar Tovar	20.00	10.00	6.00
141	Jerry Johnson	20.00	10.00	6.00
142	Mike Anderson	20.00	10.00	6.00
143	Gonzalo Marquez	20.00	10.00	6.00
144	Peter Koegel	20.00	10.00	6.00
145	Pat Dobson	20.00	10.00	6.00
146	Craig Robinson	20.00	10.00	6.00
147	Luis Saez	20.00	10.00	6.00
148	Francisco Navas	20.00	10.00	6.00
149	Elias Lugo	20.00	10.00	6.00
150	Pablo Torrealba	20.00	10.00	6.00
151	Tom Grieve	20.00	10.00	6.00
152	Manny Trillo	40.00	20.00	12.00
153	Ed Sprague	20.00	10.00	6.00
154	Virgilio Velasquez	20.00	10.00	6.00
155	Dave Hamilton	20.00	10.00	6.00
156	Rafael Jimenez	20.00	10.00	6.00
157	Ubaldo Heredia	20.00	10.00	6.00
158	Rich Dempsey	30.00	15.00	9.00
159	Bill Parson (Parsons)	20.00	10.00	6.00
160	Caracas Leones	10.00	5.00	3.00
161	Gene Garber	25.00	12.50	7.50
162	Frank White	35.00	17.50	10.50
163	John Buck Martinez	20.00	10.00	6.00
164	Manuel Garcia	20.00	10.00	6.00
165	Jesus Padron	20.00	10.00	6.00
166	Oscar Gamble	25.00	12.50	7.50
167	Nelson Castellanos	20.00	10.00	6.00
168	Leo Posada	20.00	10.00	6.00
169	Eduardo Benitez	20.00	10.00	6.00
170	Luis Rivas	20.00	10.00	6.00
171	Alfonso Collazo	20.00	10.00	6.00
172	Levy Ochoa	20.00	10.00	6.00
173	Heriberto Lemus	20.00	10.00	6.00
174	Domingo Barboza	20.00	10.00	6.00
175	Jesus Reyes Barrios	20.00	10.00	6.00
176	Inal Fainete	20.00	10.00	6.00
177	Nidio Sirit	20.00	10.00	6.00
178	Nelson Paiva	20.00	10.00	6.00
179	Alfonso Carrasquel	35.00	17.50	10.50
180	Heli Boscan	20.00	10.00	6.00
181	Leonel Carrion	20.00	10.00	6.00
182	Jose Bracho	20.00	10.00	6.00
183	Gustavo Sposito	20.00	10.00	6.00
184	Iran Paz	20.00	10.00	6.00
185	Rich Reese	20.00	10.00	6.00
186	Al Cowans (Cowens)	25.00	12.50	7.50
187	Zulio Group Photo	10.00	5.00	3.00
188	Leo Posada, Alfonso Carrasquel	15.00	7.50	4.50
189	Octavio Rojas	20.00	10.00	6.00
190	Orlando Reyes	20.00	10.00	6.00
191	Mickey Scott	20.00	10.00	6.00
192	Harold King	20.00	10.00	6.00
193	Eduardo Acosta	20.00	10.00	6.00
194	Carlos Alfonso	20.00	10.00	6.00
195	Jose Lopez	20.00	10.00	6.00
196	Jerry Martin	20.00	10.00	6.00
197	Craig Kusick	20.00	10.00	6.00
198	Charles Murray	20.00	10.00	6.00
199	Alexis Corro	20.00	10.00	6.00
200	Jose Luis Alfaro	20.00	10.00	6.00
201	Juan Fco. Monasterio	20.00	10.00	6.00
202	Oscar Zamora	20.00	10.00	6.00
203	Ramon Moreno	20.00	10.00	6.00
204	Carlos Castillo	20.00	10.00	6.00
205	Ken Forsch	20.00	10.00	6.00
206	Leroy Stanton	20.00	10.00	6.00
207	Nevil Romero	20.00	10.00	6.00
208	Romualdo Blanco	20.00	10.00	6.00
209	Remigio Hermoso	20.00	10.00	6.00
210	Paul Casanova	20.00	10.00	6.00
211	Oswaldo Blanco	20.00	10.00	6.00
212	Oswaldo Troconis	20.00	10.00	6.00
213	Antonio Pipo Correa	20.00	10.00	6.00
214	Euclides Camejo	20.00	10.00	6.00
215	Dionel Duran	20.00	10.00	6.00
216	Hector Brito	20.00	10.00	6.00
217	Reinaldo Cordeiro	20.00	10.00	6.00
218	Jose Herrera	20.00	10.00	6.00
219	Hector Urbano	20.00	10.00	6.00
220	Jose Salas	20.00	10.00	6.00
221	Robert Marcano	20.00	10.00	6.00
222	Enzo Hernandez	20.00	10.00	6.00
223	Angel Bravo	20.00	10.00	6.00
224	Tomas Liscano	20.00	10.00	6.00
225	James Granford	20.00	10.00	6.00
226	Luis Salazar	20.00	10.00	6.00
227	Carlos Moreno	20.00	10.00	6.00
228	Manuel Malave	20.00	10.00	6.00
229	Al Bumbry	25.00	12.50	7.50
230	Luis Sanchez	20.00	10.00	6.00
231	Graziano Ravelo	20.00	10.00	6.00
232	La Guaira Tiburones Logo	10.00	5.00	3.00
233	John Jetter (Jeter)	20.00	10.00	6.00
234	Unknown			
235	Orlando Martinez	20.00	10.00	6.00
236	Tom Griffin	20.00	10.00	6.00
237	Lee Pitlock	20.00	10.00	6.00
238	Ray Burry	20.00	10.00	6.00
239	Preston Gomez	20.00	10.00	6.00
240	Aurelio Monteagudo	20.00	10.00	6.00
241	Carvajal/Bat Boy	20.00	10.00	6.00
242-249	Unknown			
250	Eduardo Benitez (a-t)	20.00	10.00	6.00
251	Ted (Tom) Heintzelman (b-t)	20.00	10.00	6.00
252	Ossie Virgil (c-t)	25.00	12.50	7.50
253	Alan Closter (d-t)	20.00	10.00	6.00
254	Carlos Avila (e-t)	20.00	10.00	6.00
255	David Concepcion (g-t)	40.00	20.00	12.00
256	Enrique Colina (h-t)	20.00	10.00	6.00
257	Damaso Blanco (a-n)	20.00	10.00	6.00
258	George Manz (a-c)	20.00	10.00	6.00
259	Peter MacKanin (b-c)	20.00	10.00	6.00
260	Neldy Castillo (c-c)	20.00	10.00	6.00
261	Leovanny Baez (a-z)	20.00	10.00	6.00
262	Mike Easler (b-z)	25.00	12.50	7.50
263	Peter Broberg (c-z)	20.00	10.00	6.00
264	Reggie Cleveland (d-z)	20.00	10.00	6.00
265	Stan Perzanowky (Perzanowski) (e-z)	20.00	10.00	6.00
266	Jerry Terrel (Terrell) (f-z)	20.00	10.00	6.00
267	Toby Harrah (h-z)	30.00	15.00	9.00
268	Franklyn Moreno (y-z)	20.00	10.00	6.00
269-275	Unknown			

1974 Venezuelan League Stickers

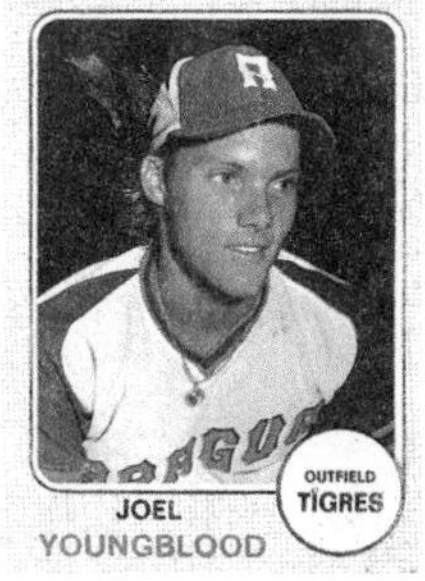

OUTFIELD
TIGRES
JOEL
YOUNGBLOOD

The 1974-75 winter league set of Venezuelan League stickers is a dead ringer for the 1968 Topps baseball cards. About 2-3/8" x 3-3/16", the stickers have photos framed in orange-mottled borders. The team name and position are in a circle at bottom, along with the player name in two colors. Because they were intended to be mounted in an accompanying album, the backs are blank. Because so many of the stickers were once pasted into albums, and due to unfavorable climactic conditions, high-grade examples of Venezuelan stickers from the era are particularly scarce.

	NM	E	VG
Complete Set (275):	1,500	750.00	450.00
Common Player:	20.00	10.00	6.00
Album:	75.00	40.00	25.00

1	Aragua Team Photo	10.00	5.00	3.00
2	Aragua Team Photo	10.00	5.00	3.00

3	Aragua Team Logo	10.00	5.00	3.00
4	Dave Concepcion	40.00	20.00	12.00
5	Ramon Velazquez	20.00	10.00	6.00
6	Carlos Orea	20.00	10.00	6.00
7	Francisco Leandro	20.00	10.00	6.00
8	Angel Hernandez	20.00	10.00	6.00
9	Armando Ortiz	20.00	10.00	6.00
10	Carlos Pascual	20.00	10.00	6.00
11	Argua Action	10.00	5.00	3.00
12	Milton Wilcox	25.00	12.50	7.50
13	Don Hood	20.00	10.00	6.00
14	Timothy Hosley	20.00	10.00	6.00
15	Teolindo Acosta	20.00	10.00	6.00
16	William Castillo	20.00	10.00	6.00
17	Aragua Action	10.00	5.00	3.00
18	Jesus Padron	20.00	10.00	6.00
19	Enos Cabell	25.00	12.50	7.50
20	Luis Silva	20.00	10.00	6.00
21	Aragua Action	10.00	5.00	3.00
22	Aragua Action	10.00	5.00	3.00
23	Joel Youngblood	25.00	12.50	7.50
24	Angel Vargas	20.00	10.00	6.00
25	Carlos Avila	20.00	10.00	6.00
26	Phil Gardner (Garner)	25.00	12.50	7.50
27	James Willoughby	20.00	10.00	6.00
28	Daniel Dubuc	20.00	10.00	6.00
29	Pancho	20.00	10.00	6.00
30	Aragua Action	10.00	5.00	3.00
31	Eastwick Rawlings (Rawly Eastwick)	25.00	12.50	7.50
32	David Torres	20.00	10.00	6.00
33	Robert Flynn	20.00	10.00	6.00
34	Duane Kuiper	25.00	12.50	7.50
35	Jesus Avila	20.00	10.00	6.00
36	Aragua Action	10.00	5.00	3.00
37	Aragua Action	10.00	5.00	3.00
38	Roberto Munoz	20.00	10.00	6.00
39	Eduardo Benitez	20.00	10.00	6.00
40	Aragua Action	10.00	5.00	3.00
41	Adrian Garret (Garrett)	20.00	10.00	6.00
42	Julio Bracho	20.00	10.00	6.00
43	Juan Quiroz	20.00	10.00	6.00
44	Angel Leon	20.00	10.00	6.00
45	Ossie Virgil	30.00	15.00	9.00
46	Lara Team Photo	10.00	5.00	3.00
47	Lara Team Photo	10.00	5.00	3.00
48	Lara Team Logo	10.00	5.00	3.00
49	Andres Barrios	20.00	10.00	6.00
50	Pastor Perez	20.00	10.00	6.00
51	Peter Koegel	20.00	10.00	6.00
52	Lara Action	10.00	5.00	3.00
53	Lowell Palmer	20.00	10.00	6.00
54	Alberto Cambero	20.00	10.00	6.00
55	Frank Snook	20.00	10.00	6.00
56	Steve McCartney	20.00	10.00	6.00
57	Lara Action	10.00	5.00	3.00
58	Dario Chirinos	20.00	10.00	6.00
59	Lara Action	10.00	5.00	3.00
60	Jim Cox	20.00	10.00	6.00
61	Terry Whitfield	20.00	10.00	6.00
62	Nelson Garcia	20.00	10.00	6.00
63	Lara Action	10.00	5.00	3.00
64	Sebastian Martinez	20.00	10.00	6.00
65	Lara Action	10.00	5.00	3.00
66	Rick Sawyer	20.00	10.00	6.00
67	Enrique Gonzalez	20.00	10.00	6.00
68	Tippy Martinez	30.00	15.00	9.00
69	Rafael Jimenez	20.00	10.00	6.00
70	Lara Action	10.00	5.00	3.00
71	Larvell Blanks	20.00	10.00	6.00
72	Franklin Tua	20.00	10.00	6.00
73	Craig Skok	20.00	10.00	6.00
74	Basilio Alvarado	20.00	10.00	6.00
75	Blas Arriechi	20.00	10.00	6.00
76	Dave Pagan	20.00	10.00	6.00
77	Roger Polanco	20.00	10.00	6.00
78	John Lowenstein	20.00	10.00	6.00
79	Francisco Leandro	20.00	10.00	6.00
80	Lucio Celis	20.00	10.00	6.00
81	Lara Action	10.00	5.00	3.00
82	Teodoro Obregon	20.00	10.00	6.00
83	Luis Aponte	20.00	10.00	6.00
84	Roberto Cox	40.00	20.00	12.00
85	Magallanes Team Photo	10.00	5.00	3.00
86	Magallanes Team Photo	10.00	5.00	3.00
87	Magallanes Team Logo	10.00	5.00	3.00
88	Oswaldo Olivares	20.00	10.00	6.00
89	Bob Bailor	25.00	12.50	7.50
90	Ali Arape	20.00	10.00	6.00
91	Jesus Aristimuno	20.00	10.00	6.00
92	Bob Andrews	20.00	10.00	6.00
93	Magallanes Action	10.00	5.00	3.00
94	Rick Stelmaszek	20.00	10.00	6.00
95	Damaso Blanco	20.00	10.00	6.00
96	Graciliano Parra	20.00	10.00	6.00
97	Merv Rettemund (Rettenmund)	25.00	12.50	7.50
98	Don Baylor	45.00	22.00	13.50
99	William Lister	20.00	10.00	6.00
100	Magallanes Action	10.00	5.00	3.00
101	Gregorio Machado	20.00	10.00	6.00
102	Doug Bair	20.00	10.00	6.00
103	Gilberto Marcano	20.00	10.00	6.00
104	Magallanes Action	10.00	5.00	3.00
105	Jim Sadowski	20.00	10.00	6.00
106	Miguel Nava	20.00	10.00	6.00
107	Ken (Kent) Tekulve	40.00	20.00	12.00
108	Wayne Garland	20.00	10.00	6.00
109	Magallanes Action	10.00	5.00	3.00
110	Alexis Ramirez	20.00	10.00	6.00
111	Dave Parker	60.00	30.00	18.00
112	Bob Veale	20.00	10.00	6.00
113	Manuel Sarmiento	20.00	10.00	6.00
114	Alberto Pedroza	20.00	10.00	6.00
115	Ruben Cabrera	20.00	10.00	6.00
116	Felix Rodriguez	20.00	10.00	6.00
117	Magallanes Action	10.00	5.00	3.00
118	Humberto Montero	20.00	10.00	6.00
119	Manuel Gonzalez	20.00	10.00	6.00
120	D. Flores	20.00	10.00	6.00
121	Jim Holt	20.00	10.00	6.00
122	Rafael Cariel	20.00	10.00	6.00
123	Magallanes Action	10.00	5.00	3.00
124	Deisi Bolivar	20.00	10.00	6.00
125	Edito Arteaga	20.00	10.00	6.00
126	Gustavo Gil	20.00	10.00	6.00
127	Larry Demeris (Demery)	20.00	10.00	6.00
128	Nelson Paiva	20.00	10.00	6.00
129	Steve Demeter	20.00	10.00	6.00
130	Caracas Leones Team Photo	10.00	5.00	3.00
131	Caracas Leones Team Photo	10.00	5.00	3.00
132	Caracas Leones Team Logo	10.00	5.00	3.00
133	Antonio Armas	40.00	20.00	12.00
134	Richard Dempsey	40.00	20.00	12.00
135	Toribio Garboza	20.00	10.00	6.00
136	Neldy Castillo	20.00	10.00	6.00
137	Ubaldo Heredia	20.00	10.00	6.00
138	Caracas Action	10.00	5.00	3.00
139	Jesus Marcano Trillo	40.00	20.00	12.00
140	Victor Albury	20.00	10.00	6.00
141	Uknown			
142	Peter Broberg	20.00	10.00	6.00
143	Alfredo Ortiz	20.00	10.00	6.00
144	Leopoldo Tovar	20.00	10.00	6.00
145	Caracas Action	10.00	5.00	3.00
146	Tom Buskey	20.00	10.00	6.00
147	Virgilio Velasquez	20.00	10.00	6.00
148	Cesar Tovar	20.00	10.00	6.00
149	Caracas Stadium	10.00	5.00	3.00
150	Don Stanhouse	20.00	10.00	6.00
151	Edgar Urbina	20.00	10.00	6.00
152	Pablo Torrealba	20.00	10.00	6.00
153	Jack Heidemann	20.00	10.00	6.00
154	Caracas Action	10.00	5.00	3.00
155	Luis Sanz	20.00	10.00	6.00
156	Gonzalo Marquez	20.00	10.00	6.00
157	Victor Davilillo	20.00	10.00	6.00
158	Bo Diaz	20.00	10.00	6.00
159	Caracas Action	10.00	5.00	3.00
160	Bill Butler	20.00	10.00	6.00
161	Elias Lugo	20.00	10.00	6.00
162	Tom Grieve	20.00	10.00	6.00
163	Caracas Action	10.00	5.00	3.00
164	Antonio Torres	20.00	10.00	6.00
165	Luis Penalver	20.00	10.00	6.00
166	Lenny Randle	20.00	10.00	6.00
167	Juan Gonzalez	20.00	10.00	6.00
168	Chuck Dobson	20.00	10.00	6.00
169	Urbano Lugo	20.00	10.00	6.00
170	Francisco Navas	20.00	10.00	6.00
171	Caracas Action	10.00	5.00	3.00
172	Jacinto Betancourt	20.00	10.00	6.00
173	Camilo Pascual	30.00	15.00	9.00
174	Frank White	30.00	15.00	9.00
175	Urbano Quintana	20.00	10.00	6.00
176	Jose Caldera	20.00	10.00	6.00
177	Caracas Action	10.00	5.00	3.00
178	Ulises Urrieta	20.00	10.00	6.00
179	Tomas Pacheco	20.00	10.00	6.00
180	La Guaira Tiburones Team Photo	10.00	5.00	3.00
181	La Guaira Tiburones Team Photo	10.00	5.00	3.00
182	La Guaira Tiburones Team Photo	10.00	5.00	3.00
183	Angel Bravo	20.00	10.00	6.00
184	Al Bumbry	25.00	12.50	7.50
185	Aurelio Monteagudo	20.00	10.00	6.00
186	Carlos Moreno	20.00	10.00	6.00
187	La Guaira Action	10.00	5.00	3.00
188	Hector Brito	20.00	10.00	6.00
189	Leroy Stanton	20.00	10.00	6.00
190	Romo Blanco	20.00	10.00	6.00
191	Marquina para Gorrias	10.00	5.00	3.00
192	Luis M. Sanchez	20.00	10.00	6.00
193	La Guaria Action	10.00	5.00	3.00
194	Jose Herrera	20.00	10.00	6.00
195	Victor Colina	20.00	10.00	6.00
196	Tiburones Team Bus	10.00	5.00	3.00
197	Jose Salas	20.00	10.00	6.00
198	La Guaira Action	10.00	5.00	3.00
199	Enzo Hernandez	20.00	10.00	6.00
200	Tomas Liscano	20.00	10.00	6.00
201	Paul Casanova	20.00	10.00	6.00
202	Machine	10.00	5.00	3.00
203	Graziano Ravelo	20.00	10.00	6.00
204	Ice Maker	10.00	5.00	3.00
205	Roland (Rowland) Office	20.00	10.00	6.00
206	Clubhouse	10.00	5.00	3.00
207	La Guaira Action	10.00	5.00	3.00
208	Dusty Baker	45.00	22.00	13.50
209	Replacements	10.00	5.00	3.00
210	Roric Harrison	20.00	10.00	6.00
211	Tom House	20.00	10.00	6.00
212	Jesus Aquino	20.00	10.00	6.00
213	Machine	10.00	5.00	3.00
214	La Guaira Action	10.00	5.00	3.00
215	Juan Monasterios	20.00	10.00	6.00
216	Angel Remigio Hermoso	20.00	10.00	6.00
217	Machine	10.00	5.00	3.00
218	Oswaldo Blanco	20.00	10.00	6.00
219	Infrared Light	10.00	5.00	3.00
220	Roberto Marcano	20.00	10.00	6.00
221	La Guaira Action	10.00	5.00	3.00
222	Jose Carvajal	20.00	10.00	6.00
223	Victor Patino	20.00	10.00	6.00
224	James Bird	20.00	10.00	6.00
225	La Guaira Action	10.00	5.00	3.00
226	Roland Sonny Jackson	25.00	12.50	7.50
227	Oscar Zamora	20.00	10.00	6.00
228	Antonio Pipo Correa	20.00	10.00	6.00
229	Manuel Malave	20.00	10.00	6.00
230	Nap Reyes	20.00	10.00	6.00
231	Zulia Aguilas Team Photo	10.00	5.00	3.00
232	Zluia Aguilas Team Photo	10.00	5.00	3.00
233	Zulia Aguilas Team Logo	10.00	5.00	3.00
234	Levy Ochoa	20.00	10.00	6.00
235	Billy Moran	20.00	10.00	6.00
236	Iran Paz	20.00	10.00	6.00
237	Alexis Corro	20.00	10.00	6.00
238	Zulia Action	10.00	5.00	3.00
239	Gus Sposito	20.00	10.00	6.00
240	Orlando Reyes	20.00	10.00	6.00
241	Carlos Alonso	20.00	10.00	6.00
242	Craig Kusick	20.00	10.00	6.00
243	Zulia Action	10.00	5.00	3.00
244	Domingo Barboza	20.00	10.00	6.00
245	Leonel Carrion	20.00	10.00	6.00
246	Jose Lopez	20.00	10.00	6.00
247	Bill Kirkpatrick	20.00	10.00	6.00
248	Alfonso Carrasquel	20.00	10.00	6.00
249	Richard Billings	20.00	10.00	6.00
250	Alfonzo Collazo	20.00	10.00	6.00
251	Orlando Ramirez	20.00	10.00	6.00
252	Ralph (Mickey) Scott	20.00	10.00	6.00
253	Luis Aparicio	60.00	30.00	18.00
254	Julio Bracho	20.00	10.00	6.00
255	Zulia Action	10.00	5.00	3.00
256	B. Jones	20.00	10.00	6.00
257	Heli Ramon Boscan	20.00	10.00	6.00
258	David Clyde	20.00	10.00	6.00
259	Cesar Gutierrez	20.00	10.00	6.00
260	Bob Randall	20.00	10.00	6.00
261	Jesus Reyes Barrios	20.00	10.00	6.00
262	Jose L. Alfaro	20.00	10.00	6.00
263	Claudio Urdaneta	20.00	10.00	6.00
264	Zulia Action	10.00	5.00	3.00
265	James Sundberg	30.00	15.00	9.00
266	Simon Barreto	20.00	10.00	6.00
267	Anthony Scott	20.00	10.00	6.00
268	Nidio Sirit	20.00	10.00	6.00
269	Zulia Action	10.00	5.00	3.00
270	Zulia Action	10.00	5.00	3.00
271	Leovanni Baez	20.00	10.00	6.00
272	Jefrey (Jeffrey) Terpko	20.00	10.00	6.00
273	Stan Perzanowski	20.00	10.00	6.00
274	Mike Easler	25.00	12.50	7.50
275	Jackie Moore	20.00	10.00	6.00

1976 Venezuelan League Stickers

The basic player stickers utizilize a design very similar to Topps' 1975 baseball cards, with player photos surrounded by a colorful border with the team name in large outline letters at top and the position is a baseball at bottom. Stickers are 2-3/8" x 3-3/16" and numbered on front. Like other Latin issues of the era, they are seldom available in high grade due to their intended useage and climactic conditions. Most of the stickers after #217 are specialty pieces with action photos, non-player subjects, multiple players, etc. A colorful album to house the set was also issued.

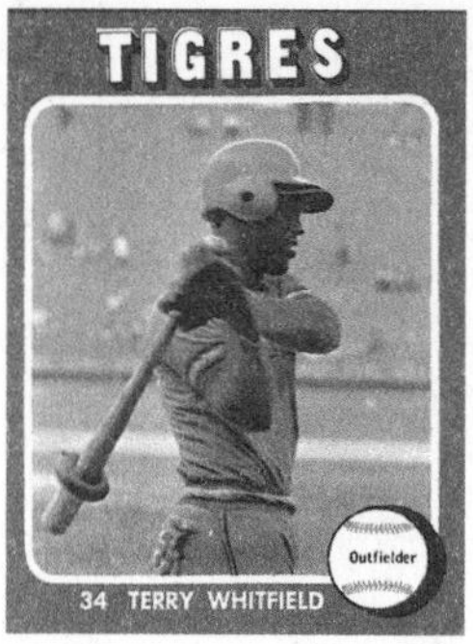

	NM	E	VG
Complete Set (330):	2,000	1,000	600.00
Common Player:	20.00	10.00	6.00
Album:	75.00	40.00	25.00

1	Ossie Virgil	30.00	15.00	9.00
2	Patato Pascual	20.00	10.00	6.00
3	Jesus Avila	20.00	10.00	6.00
4	Raul Ortega	20.00	10.00	6.00
5	Dave Concepcion	40.00	20.00	12.00
6	Jesus Araujo	20.00	10.00	6.00
7	Preston Hanna	20.00	10.00	6.00
8	Victor Davilillo	20.00	10.00	6.00
9	Jesus Padron	20.00	10.00	6.00
10	Joseph Sdeb (Zdeb)	20.00	10.00	6.00
11	Alfredo Ortiz	20.00	10.00	6.00
12	Teolindo Acosta	20.00	10.00	6.00
13	Cesar Tovar	20.00	10.00	6.00
14	Craig Kusick	20.00	10.00	6.00
15	Angel Hernandez	20.00	10.00	6.00
16	Roberto Munoz	20.00	10.00	6.00
17	Fred Andrews	20.00	10.00	6.00
18	Rafael Alvarez	20.00	10.00	6.00
19	Luis Aparicio	50.00	25.00	15.00
20	Jeffrey Newman	20.00	10.00	6.00
21	Tommy Sant (Sandt)	20.00	10.00	6.00
22	Simon Barreto	20.00	10.00	6.00
23	Willie Norwood	20.00	10.00	6.00
24	Juan Quiroz	20.00	10.00	6.00
25	Douglas Capilla	20.00	10.00	6.00
26	William Butler	20.00	10.00	6.00
27	William Castillo	20.00	10.00	6.00
28	Robert Maneely	20.00	10.00	6.00
29	Peter Bromberg (Broberg)	20.00	10.00	6.00
30	Jesse Jefferson	20.00	10.00	6.00
31	Carlos Avila	20.00	10.00	6.00
32	Aragua Action	10.00	5.00	3.00
33	Aragua Action	10.00	5.00	3.00
34	Terry Whitfield	20.00	10.00	6.00
35	Aragua Action	10.00	5.00	3.00
36	Gary Lance	20.00	10.00	6.00
37	Robert Cox	40.00	20.00	12.00
38	Leo Posada	20.00	10.00	6.00
39	Lucio Celis	20.00	10.00	6.00
40	Enrique Gonzalez	20.00	10.00	6.00
41	Jose Musiu Lopez	20.00	10.00	6.00
42	Jose Sandoval	20.00	10.00	6.00
43	Victor Correll	20.00	10.00	6.00
44	Pedro Lobaton	20.00	10.00	6.00
45	Jim Norris	20.00	10.00	6.00
46	Luis Aponte	20.00	10.00	6.00
47	Orlando Gonzalez	20.00	10.00	6.00
48	Edguardo Benitez	20.00	10.00	6.00
49	George Zeber	20.00	10.00	6.00
50	Carlos Rodriguez	20.00	10.00	6.00
51	Graig (Craig) Robinson	20.00	10.00	6.00
52	Hernan Silva	20.00	10.00	6.00
53	Bob Oliver	20.00	10.00	6.00
54	Jose Herrera	20.00	10.00	6.00
55	Pete Mackanin	20.00	10.00	6.00
56	Roger Polanco	20.00	10.00	6.00
57	Lara Stadium	10.00	5.00	3.00
58	Arnaldo Alvarado	20.00	10.00	6.00
59	Ron Selak	20.00	10.00	6.00
60	Nelson Canas	20.00	10.00	6.00
61	John Sutton	20.00	10.00	6.00
62	Nelson Garcia	20.00	10.00	6.00
63	Victor Patino	20.00	10.00	6.00
64	Francisco Navas	20.00	10.00	6.00
65	Robert Polinsky	20.00	10.00	6.00
66	Franklin Tua	20.00	10.00	6.00
67	Oscar Zamora	20.00	10.00	6.00
68	David Torres	20.00	10.00	6.00
69	Eddie Baez	20.00	10.00	6.00
70	Walter Williams	25.00	12.50	7.50
71	Cloyd Boyer	25.00	12.50	7.50
72	Carl (Garth?) Iorg	20.00	10.00	6.00
73	Pat Corrales	20.00	10.00	6.00
74	Alfonso Carrasquel	20.00	10.00	6.00
75	Antonio Torres	20.00	10.00	6.00
76	Camilo Pascual	30.00	15.00	9.00
77	Antonio Armas	40.00	20.00	12.00
78	Baudilio Diaz	20.00	10.00	6.00
79	Gary Beare	20.00	10.00	6.00
80	Steve Barr	20.00	10.00	6.00
81	Toribio Garboza	20.00	10.00	6.00
82	Mike Bassik (Bacsik)	20.00	10.00	6.00
83	Diego Segui	20.00	10.00	6.00
84	Jack Bastable	20.00	10.00	6.00
85	Ubaldo Heredia	20.00	10.00	6.00
86	Warren Cromartie	25.00	12.50	7.50
87	Elias Lugo	20.00	10.00	6.00
88	Mike (Mick) Kelleher	20.00	10.00	6.00
89	Marcano Trillo	40.00	20.00	12.00
90	Lenny Randle	20.00	10.00	6.00
91	Gonzalo Marquez	20.00	10.00	6.00
92	Jim Sadowski	20.00	10.00	6.00
93	Len Barker	25.00	12.50	7.50
94	Willi Quintana	20.00	10.00	6.00
95	Pablo Torrealba	20.00	10.00	6.00
96	Jim Hughes	20.00	10.00	6.00
97	Jose V. Caldera	20.00	10.00	6.00
98	Angel Vargas	20.00	10.00	6.00
99	Juan Gonzalez	20.00	10.00	6.00
100	Ulises Urrieta	20.00	10.00	6.00
101	Flores Bolivar	20.00	10.00	6.00
102	Robert Bowling	20.00	10.00	6.00
103	Rick Bladt	20.00	10.00	6.00
104	Luis Turner	20.00	10.00	6.00
105	Neldy Castillo	20.00	10.00	6.00
106	Adrian Garret (Garrett)	20.00	10.00	6.00
107	Bob Davis	20.00	10.00	6.00
108	La Guaira Action	10.00	5.00	3.00
109	Pompeyo Davalillo	20.00	10.00	6.00
110	Graciano Ravelo	20.00	10.00	6.00
111	Luis Lunar	20.00	10.00	6.00
112	Lester Morales	20.00	10.00	6.00
113	Enzo Hernandez	20.00	10.00	6.00
114	Aurelio Monteagudo	20.00	10.00	6.00
115	Angel Bravo	20.00	10.00	6.00
116	Carlos Moreno	20.00	10.00	6.00
117	Jose Cardenal	25.00	12.50	7.50
118	Rupert (Ruppert) Jones	20.00	10.00	6.00
119	Romo Blanco	20.00	10.00	6.00
120	Milton Ramirez	20.00	10.00	6.00
121	Antonio Correa	20.00	10.00	6.00
122	Clarence Gaston	25.00	12.50	7.50
123	Steve Lubber (Luebber)	20.00	10.00	6.00
124	Edwin Verhelst	20.00	10.00	6.00
125	Robert Johnson	20.00	10.00	6.00
126	Earl Bass	20.00	10.00	6.00
127	Jose Salas	20.00	10.00	6.00
128	Oswaldo Blanco	20.00	10.00	6.00
129	Steve Staag (Staggs)	20.00	10.00	6.00
130	Steve Patchin	20.00	10.00	6.00
131	Mike Kekish (Kekich)	20.00	10.00	6.00
132	Oswaldo Troconis	20.00	10.00	6.00
133	Dave May	20.00	10.00	6.00
134	Luis Salazar	20.00	10.00	6.00
135	Larry Gura	20.00	10.00	6.00
136	Rich Dauer	20.00	10.00	6.00
137	Pastor Perez	20.00	10.00	6.00
138	Paul Siebert	20.00	10.00	6.00
139	Luis M. Sanchez	20.00	10.00	6.00
140	Victor Colina	20.00	10.00	6.00
141	Adrian Devine	20.00	10.00	6.00
142	Robert Marcano	20.00	10.00	6.00
143	Juan Berenger (Berenguer)	25.00	12.50	7.50
144	Juan Monasterio	20.00	10.00	6.00
145	Donald Leppert	20.00	10.00	6.00
146	Gregorio Machado	20.00	10.00	6.00
147	Manuel Gonzalez	20.00	10.00	6.00
148	Wayne Granger	20.00	10.00	6.00
149	Remigio Hermoso	20.00	10.00	6.00
150	Rafael Cariel	20.00	10.00	6.00
151	Steve Dillard	20.00	10.00	6.00
152	Mitchell Page	20.00	10.00	6.00
153	Alexis Ramirez, Felix Rodriguez	15.00	7.50	4.50
154	Gary Wood	20.00	10.00	6.00
155	Ali Arape	20.00	10.00	6.00
156	Chris Batton	20.00	10.00	6.00
157	Gustavo Gil	20.00	10.00	6.00
158	Craig Reynolds	20.00	10.00	6.00
159	Jesus Aristimuno	20.00	10.00	6.00
160	Miguel Barreto	20.00	10.00	6.00
161	Alfonso Collazo	20.00	10.00	6.00
162	Steve Nicosia	20.00	10.00	6.00
163	Oswaldo Olivares	20.00	10.00	6.00
164	Robert Galasso	20.00	10.00	6.00
165	Alexis Ramirez	20.00	10.00	6.00
166	Craig Mitchell	20.00	10.00	6.00
167	Nelson Paiva	20.00	10.00	6.00
168	Ken Macha	20.00	10.00	6.00
169	Ruben Cabrera	20.00	10.00	6.00
170	Paul Reuschell (Reuschel)	20.00	10.00	6.00
171	Edito Arteaga	20.00	10.00	6.00
172	Olinto Rojas	20.00	10.00	6.00
173	Magallanes Action	10.00	5.00	3.00
174	Manny Sarmiento	20.00	10.00	6.00
175	Billy Moran	20.00	10.00	6.00
176	Eddie Watt	20.00	10.00	6.00
177	Michael Willis	20.00	10.00	6.00
178	Felix Rodriguez	20.00	10.00	6.00
179	James Easterly	20.00	10.00	6.00
180	Dave Parker	40.00	20.00	12.00
181	Luis Aparicio	50.00	25.00	15.00
182	Teodoro Obregon	20.00	10.00	6.00
183	Domingo Barboza	20.00	10.00	6.00
184	Not Issued, See #190			
185	Gilberto Marcano	20.00	10.00	6.00
186	Jose Alfaro	20.00	10.00	6.00
187	Jesus Reyes	20.00	10.00	6.00
188	Mike (Mickey) Scott	20.00	10.00	6.00
189	Carl Frost	20.00	10.00	6.00
190a	Norman Shiera	20.00	10.00	6.00
190b	Orlando Pena (See #184.)	20.00	10.00	6.00
191	Orlando Reyes	20.00	10.00	6.00
192	Milt Wilcox	25.00	12.50	7.50
193	Andrew Dyes	20.00	10.00	6.00
194	J. Hernandez	20.00	10.00	6.00
195	Dario Chirinos	20.00	10.00	6.00
196	Greg Shanahan	20.00	10.00	6.00
197	Gustavo Sposito	20.00	10.00	6.00
198	Sebastian Martinez	20.00	10.00	6.00
199	Leonel Carrion	20.00	10.00	6.00
200	Dennis Lawallyn (Lewallyn)	20.00	10.00	6.00
201	Charky (Charlie) Moore	20.00	10.00	6.00
202	Steve Mallory	20.00	10.00	6.00
203	Gary Martz	20.00	10.00	6.00
204	Lamar Johnson	20.00	10.00	6.00
205	Tim Johnson	20.00	10.00	6.00
206	Levy Ochoa	20.00	10.00	6.00
207	Bill Dancy	20.00	10.00	6.00
208	Antonio Garcia	20.00	10.00	6.00
209	Nidio Sirit	20.00	10.00	6.00
210	Norman Shiera	20.00	10.00	6.00
211	Not Issued, See #221			
212	Jesus Alfaro	20.00	10.00	6.00
213	Bobby Darwin	20.00	10.00	6.00
214	Zulia Action	10.00	5.00	3.00
215	Mike Seoane	20.00	10.00	6.00
216	Jim Gatner (Gantner)	20.00	10.00	6.00
217	Caracas Action	10.00	5.00	3.00
218	Caracas Action	10.00	5.00	3.00
219	Caracas Action	10.00	5.00	3.00
220	Caracas Action	10.00	5.00	3.00
221a	Caracas Action	10.00	5.00	3.00
221b	Joe Chourio (See #211.)	20.00	10.00	6.00
222	Lara Action	10.00	5.00	3.00
223	Ulises Urrieta, Antonio Armas, Manny Trillo	20.00	10.00	6.00
224	Magallanes Dugout	10.00	5.00	3.00
225	Remigio Hermoso, Gustavo Gil	15.00	7.50	4.50
226	Caracas Action	10.00	5.00	3.00
227	Manny Trillo, Dave Concepcion	20.00	10.00	6.00
228	Zulia Action	10.00	5.00	3.00
229	Caracas Pizarra Scoreboard	10.00	5.00	3.00
230	La Guaira Action	10.00	5.00	3.00
231	Caracas Action	10.00	5.00	3.00
232	La Guaira Action	10.00	5.00	3.00
233	Zulia Action	10.00	5.00	3.00
234	Caracas Publico	10.00	5.00	3.00
235	Magallanes Action	10.00	5.00	3.00
236	Aragua Action	10.00	5.00	3.00
237	La Guaira Action	10.00	5.00	3.00
238	La Guaira Action	10.00	5.00	3.00
239	La Guaira Action	10.00	5.00	3.00
240	La Guaira Action	10.00	5.00	3.00
241	Manny Trillo, Jose Cardenal	20.00	10.00	6.00
242	Pompeyo Davilillo, Lacheman	15.00	7.50	4.50
243	La Guaira Action	10.00	5.00	3.00
244	La Guaira Action	10.00	5.00	3.00
245	Action	10.00	5.00	3.00
246	Zulia Action	10.00	5.00	3.00
247	Zulia Action	10.00	5.00	3.00
248	Tim Johnson	20.00	10.00	6.00
249	La Guaira Action	10.00	5.00	3.00
250	La Guaira Action	10.00	5.00	3.00
251	La Guaira Action	10.00	5.00	3.00
252	La Guaira Action	10.00	5.00	3.00
253	La Guaira Action	10.00	5.00	3.00
254	La Guaira Action	10.00	5.00	3.00
255	La Guaira Action	10.00	5.00	3.00
256	La Guaira Action	10.00	5.00	3.00
257	Caracas Action	10.00	5.00	3.00
258	La Guaira Action	10.00	5.00	3.00
259	Zulia Action	10.00	5.00	3.00

260	Caracas Action	10.00	5.00	3.00
261	Caracas Action	10.00	5.00	3.00
262	La Guaira Clubhouse	10.00	5.00	3.00
263	La Guaira Clubhouse	10.00	5.00	3.00
264	La Guaira Clubhouse	10.00	5.00	3.00
265	La Guaira Clubhouse	10.00	5.00	3.00
266	La Guaira Action	10.00	5.00	3.00
267	La Guaira Action	10.00	5.00	3.00
268	La Guaira Action	10.00	5.00	3.00
269	Panoramica	10.00	5.00	3.00
270	Zulia Action	10.00	5.00	3.00
271	Aragua Puzzle	10.00	5.00	3.00
272	Aragua Puzzle	10.00	5.00	3.00
273	Aragua Puzzle	10.00	5.00	3.00
274	Aragua Puzzle	10.00	5.00	3.00
275	Aragua Puzzle	10.00	5.00	3.00
276	Aragua Puzzle	10.00	5.00	3.00
277	Aragua Puzzle	10.00	5.00	3.00
278	Aragua Puzzle	10.00	5.00	3.00
279	Aragua Puzzle	10.00	5.00	3.00
280	Lara Puzzle	10.00	5.00	3.00
281	Lara Puzzle	10.00	5.00	3.00
282	Lara Puzzle	10.00	5.00	3.00
283	Lara Puzzle	10.00	5.00	3.00
284	Lara Puzzle	10.00	5.00	3.00
285	Lara Puzzle	10.00	5.00	3.00
286	Lara Puzzle	10.00	5.00	3.00
287	Lara Puzzle	10.00	5.00	3.00
288	Lara Puzzle	10.00	5.00	3.00
289	Caracas Puzzle	10.00	5.00	3.00
290	Caracas Puzzle	10.00	5.00	3.00
291	Caracas Puzzle	10.00	5.00	3.00
292	Caracas Puzzle	10.00	5.00	3.00
293	Caracas Puzzle	10.00	5.00	3.00
294	Caracas Puzzle	10.00	5.00	3.00
295	Caracas Puzzle	10.00	5.00	3.00
296	Caracas Puzzle	10.00	5.00	3.00
297	Caracas Puzzle	10.00	5.00	3.00
298	La Guaira Puzzle	10.00	5.00	3.00
299	La Guaira Puzzle	10.00	5.00	3.00
300	La Guaira Puzzle	10.00	5.00	3.00
301	La Guaira Puzzle	10.00	5.00	3.00
302	La Guaira Puzzle	10.00	5.00	3.00
303	La Guaira Puzzle	10.00	5.00	3.00
304	La Guaira Puzzle	10.00	5.00	3.00
305	La Guaira Puzzle	10.00	5.00	3.00
306	La Guaira Puzzle	10.00	5.00	3.00
307	Magallanes Puzzle	10.00	5.00	3.00
308	Magallanes Puzzle	10.00	5.00	3.00
309	Magallanes Puzzle	10.00	5.00	3.00
310	Magallanes Puzzle	10.00	5.00	3.00
311	Magallanes Puzzle	10.00	5.00	3.00
312	Magallanes Puzzle	10.00	5.00	3.00
313	Magallanes Puzzle	10.00	5.00	3.00
314	Magallanes Puzzle	10.00	5.00	3.00
315	Magallanes Puzzle	10.00	5.00	3.00
316	Zulia Puzzle	10.00	5.00	3.00
317	Zulia Puzzle	10.00	5.00	3.00
318	Zulia Puzzle	10.00	5.00	3.00
319	Zulia Puzzle	10.00	5.00	3.00
320	Zulia Puzzle	10.00	5.00	3.00
321	Zulia Puzzle	10.00	5.00	3.00
322	Zulia Puzzle	10.00	5.00	3.00
323	Zulia Puzzle	10.00	5.00	3.00
324	Zulia Puzzle	10.00	5.00	3.00
325	Magallanes Navagantes Logo	10.00	5.00	3.00
326	Aragua Tigres Logo	10.00	5.00	3.00
327	Caracas Leones Logo	10.00	5.00	3.00
328	Zulia Aguilas Logo	10.00	5.00	3.00
329	Lara Cardenales Logo	10.00	5.00	3.00
330	La Guaira Tiburones Logo	10.00	5.00	3.00

1977 Venezuelan Baseball Stickers

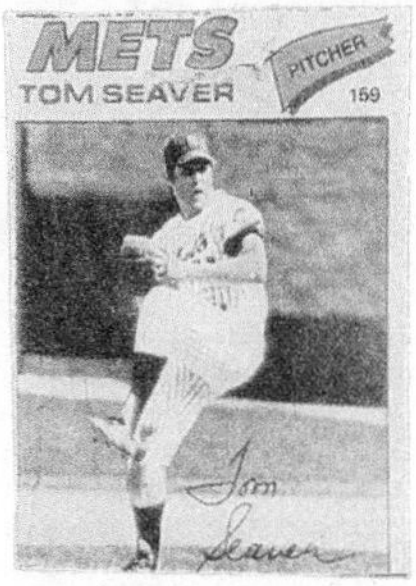

More than 400 pieces comprise this set of 2-3/8" x 3-1/8" blank-back stickers. The majority have color photos of winter league players with the team name, logo and position printed above, and the sticker number and name beneath the picture. There are many former and future Major League players in this group. A subset of some 50 stickers of American Major Leaguers is printed in reproduction of their 1977 Topps cards. Other stickers include group pictures, action photos, puzzle pieces, etc. The album issued to house the stickers has a player write-up in each space. Printed on very thin paper, and often removed from albums, these stickers are generally not found in condition above Very Good. For Good condition pieces, figure value at 50 percent of the prices shown here; stickers in Fair condition should be valued at 25 percent. Many of the stickers have player names misspelled.

	NM	E	VG
Complete Set (402):	4,000	1,600	800.00
Common Player:	15.00	6.00	3.00
Album:	125.00	50.00	25.00

1	Aragua Tigers Logo	15.00	6.00	3.00
2	Ozzie Virgil Sr.	20.00	8.00	4.00
3	Jesus Avila	15.00	6.00	3.00
4	Raul Ortega	15.00	6.00	3.00
5	Simon Barreto	15.00	6.00	3.00
6	Gustavo Quiroz	15.00	6.00	3.00
7	Jerry Cram	15.00	6.00	3.00
8	Pat Cristelli	15.00	6.00	3.00
9	Preston Hanna	15.00	6.00	3.00
10	Angel Hernandez	15.00	6.00	3.00
11	John M'Callen	15.00	6.00	3.00
12	Randy Miller	15.00	6.00	3.00
13	Dale Murray	15.00	6.00	3.00
14	Mike Nagy	15.00	6.00	3.00
15	Stan Perzanowski	15.00	6.00	3.00
16	Juan Quiroz	15.00	6.00	3.00
17	Graciano Parra	15.00	6.00	3.00
18	Larry Cox	15.00	6.00	3.00
19	Lenn Sakata	15.00	6.00	3.00
20	Lester Straker	15.00	6.00	3.00
21	Nelson Torres	15.00	6.00	3.00
22	Carlos Avila	15.00	6.00	3.00
23	Orlando Galindo	15.00	6.00	3.00
24	Dave Wagner	15.00	6.00	3.00
25	Dave Concepcion	60.00	24.00	12.00
26	Alfredo Ortiz	15.00	6.00	3.00
27	Mike Lum, Dave Concepcion, Larry Parrish	15.00	6.00	3.00
28	Jesus Padron	15.00	6.00	3.00
29	Larry Parrish	15.00	6.00	3.00
30	Rob Picciolo	15.00	6.00	3.00
31	Luis Rivas	15.00	6.00	3.00
32	Bob Slater	15.00	6.00	3.00
33	Larry Murray	15.00	6.00	3.00
34	Dave Soderholm	15.00	6.00	3.00
35	Luis Benitez	15.00	6.00	3.00
36	Cesar Tovar, Victor Davalillo	20.00	8.00	4.00
37	Luis Bravo	15.00	6.00	3.00
38	William Castillo	15.00	6.00	3.00
39	Terry Whitfield	15.00	6.00	3.00
40	Victor Davalillo	30.00	12.00	6.00
41	Mike Lum	15.00	6.00	3.00
42	Willie Norwood	15.00	6.00	3.00
43	Cesar Tovar	15.00	6.00	3.00
44	Joe Zdeb	15.00	6.00	3.00
45	Focion, Ozzie Virgil Sr.	15.00	6.00	3.00
46	Caracas Lions Logo	15.00	6.00	3.00
47	Felipe Alou	20.00	8.00	4.00
48	Alfonso Carrasquel (Chico)	35.00	14.00	7.00
49	Antonio Torres	15.00	6.00	3.00
50	Len Barker	15.00	6.00	3.00
51	Gary Beare	15.00	6.00	3.00
52	Cardell Camper	15.00	6.00	3.00
53	Juan Gonzalez	15.00	6.00	3.00
54	Paul Mirabella	15.00	6.00	3.00
55	Carney Lansford	15.00	6.00	3.00
56	Ubaldo Heredia	15.00	6.00	3.00
57	Elias Lugo	15.00	6.00	3.00
58	Oswaldo Troconis	15.00	6.00	3.00
59	Diego Segui	15.00	6.00	3.00
60	Lary Sorensen	15.00	6.00	3.00
61	Pablo Torrealba	15.00	6.00	3.00
62	Gustavo Bastardo	15.00	6.00	3.00
63	Luis Sanz	15.00	6.00	3.00
64	Steve Bowling	15.00	6.00	3.00
65	Tim Corcoran	15.00	6.00	3.00
66	Antonio Armas (Tony)	35.00	14.00	7.00
67	Toribio Garboza	15.00	6.00	3.00
68	Bob Molinaro	15.00	6.00	3.00
69	Willibaldo Quintana	15.00	6.00	3.00
70	Luis Turnes	15.00	6.00	3.00
71	Chuck Baker	15.00	6.00	3.00
72	Rob Belloir	15.00	6.00	3.00
73	Tom Brookens	15.00	6.00	3.00
74	Ron Hassey	15.00	6.00	3.00
75	Gonzalo Marquez	15.00	6.00	3.00
76	Bob Clark	15.00	6.00	3.00
77	Marcano Trillo (Manny)	30.00	12.00	6.00
78	Angel Vargas	15.00	6.00	3.00
79	Flores Bolivar	15.00	6.00	3.00
80	Baudilo Diaz (Bo)	15.00	6.00	3.00
81	Camilo Pascual	15.00	6.00	3.00
82	La Guaira Sharks Logo	15.00	6.00	3.00
83	Pompeyo Davalillo	17.50	7.00	3.50
84	Jose Martinez	15.00	6.00	3.00
85	Jim Willoughby	15.00	6.00	3.00
86	Romo Blanco	15.00	6.00	3.00
87	Mark Daly	15.00	6.00	3.00
88	Tom House	15.00	6.00	3.00
89	Danny Osborne	15.00	6.00	3.00
90	David Clyde	15.00	6.00	3.00
91	Luis Lunar	15.00	6.00	3.00
92	Randy McGilberry	15.00	6.00	3.00
93	Greg Minton	15.00	6.00	3.00
94	Aurelio Monteagudo	15.00	6.00	3.00
95	Carlos Moreno	15.00	6.00	3.00
96	Luis M. Sanchez	15.00	6.00	3.00
97	George Throop	15.00	6.00	3.00
98	Victor Colina	15.00	6.00	3.00
99	Edwin Verheist	15.00	6.00	3.00
100	John Wathan	15.00	6.00	3.00
101	Ruben Alcala	15.00	6.00	3.00
102	Ossie Blanco	15.00	6.00	3.00
103	Dave Cripe	15.00	6.00	3.00
104	Bob Marcano	15.00	6.00	3.00
105	Rudy Meoli	15.00	6.00	3.00
106	Pastor Perez	15.00	6.00	3.00
107	Milton Ramirez	15.00	6.00	3.00
108	Luis Salazar	15.00	6.00	3.00
109	Angel Bravo	15.00	6.00	3.00
110	Gene Clines	15.00	6.00	3.00
111	Jose Cardenal	15.00	6.00	3.00
112	Gabriel Ferrerc	15.00	6.00	3.00
113	Clint Hurdle	15.00	6.00	3.00
114	Juan Monasterio	15.00	6.00	3.00
115	Lester Morales	15.00	6.00	3.00
116	Carlos Hernandez	15.00	6.00	3.00
117	Nelo Lira	15.00	6.00	3.00
118	Raul Perez	15.00	6.00	3.00
119	Marcos Lunar	15.00	6.00	3.00
120	Franklin Moreno	15.00	6.00	3.00
121	Jerry Manuel	15.00	6.00	3.00
122	Ossie Blanco, Raul Perez	15.00	6.00	3.00
123	Tom McMillan	15.00	6.00	3.00
124	Roric Harrison	15.00	6.00	3.00
125	Tom Griffin	15.00	6.00	3.00
126	Juan Berenguer	15.00	6.00	3.00
127	Puzzle Piece (Reggie Jackson)	15.00	6.00	3.00
128	Puzzle Piece (Reggie Jackson)	15.00	6.00	3.00
129	Puzzle Piece (Reggie Jackson)	15.00	6.00	3.00
130	Puzzle Piece (Reggie Jackson)	15.00	6.00	3.00
131	Puzzle Piece (Reggie Jackson)	15.00	6.00	3.00
132	Puzzle Piece (Reggie Jackson)	15.00	6.00	3.00
133	Puzzle Piece (Reggie Jackson)	15.00	6.00	3.00
134	Puzzle Piece (Reggie Jackson)	15.00	6.00	3.00
135	Puzzle Piece (Reggie Jackson)	15.00	6.00	3.00
136	Reggie Jackson	325.00	130.00	65.00
137	Rod Carew	175.00	70.00	35.00
138	Dave Concepcion	90.00	36.00	18.00
139	Joe Morgan	125.00	50.00	25.00
140	Dave Parker	15.00	6.00	3.00
141	Carlton Fisk	125.00	50.00	25.00
142	Garry Maddox	15.00	6.00	3.00
143	George Foster	15.00	6.00	3.00
144	Fred Lynn	15.00	6.00	3.00
145	Lou Piniella	17.50	7.00	3.50
146	Mark Fidrych	15.00	6.00	3.00
147	Lou Brock	125.00	50.00	25.00
148	Mitchell Page	15.00	6.00	3.00
149	Sparky Lyle	15.00	6.00	3.00
150	Manny Sanguillen	15.00	6.00	3.00
151	Steve Carlton	125.00	50.00	25.00
152	Al Oliver	17.50	7.00	3.50
153	Davey Lopes	15.00	6.00	3.00
154	Johnny Bench	175.00	70.00	35.00
155	Richie Hebner	15.00	6.00	3.00
156	Cesar Cedeno	15.00	6.00	3.00
157	Manny Trillo	15.00	6.00	3.00
158	Nolan Ryan	1,500	600.00	300.00
159	Tom Seaver	175.00	70.00	35.00
160	Jim Palmer	125.00	50.00	25.00
161	Randy Jones	15.00	6.00	3.00
162	George Brett	325.00	130.00	65.00
163	Bill Madlock	15.00	6.00	3.00
164	Cesar Geronimo	15.00	6.00	3.00
165	Vida Blue	15.00	6.00	3.00
166	Tony Armas	35.00	14.00	7.00
167	Bill Campbell	15.00	6.00	3.00
168	Graig Nettles	15.00	6.00	3.00

169	Mike Schmidt	325.00	130.00	65.00
170	Willie Stargell	125.00	50.00	25.00
171	Ron Cey	15.00	6.00	3.00
172	Victor Davalillo	25.00	10.00	5.00
173	Pete Rose	375.00	150.00	75.00
174	Steve Yaeger	15.00	6.00	3.00
175	Frank Tanana	15.00	6.00	3.00
176	Carl Yastrzemski	175.00	70.00	35.00
177	Willie McCovey	125.00	50.00	25.00
178	Thurman Munson	125.00	50.00	25.00
179	Chris Chambliss	15.00	6.00	3.00
180	Bill Russell	15.00	6.00	3.00
181	Lara Cardinals Logo	15.00	6.00	3.00
182	Leo Posada	15.00	6.00	3.00
183	Lucio Celis	15.00	6.00	3.00
184	Enrique Gonzalez	15.00	6.00	3.00
185	Brian Abraham	15.00	6.00	3.00
186	Luis Aponte	15.00	6.00	3.00
187	Jose Lopez	15.00	6.00	3.00
188	Bobby Ramos	15.00	6.00	3.00
189	Tom Dixon	15.00	6.00	3.00
190	Gary Melson	15.00	6.00	3.00
191	Mark Budaska	15.00	6.00	3.00
192	Mark Fischlin	15.00	6.00	3.00
193	Garth Iorg	15.00	6.00	3.00
194	Mike Rowland	15.00	6.00	3.00
195	Dennis DeBarr	15.00	6.00	3.00
196	Gary Wilson	15.00	6.00	3.00
197	Dave McKay	15.00	6.00	3.00
198	Roberto Munoz	15.00	6.00	3.00
199	Roger Polanco	15.00	6.00	3.00
200	Pat Kelly	15.00	6.00	3.00
201	Hernan Silva	15.00	6.00	3.00
202	Francisco Navas	15.00	6.00	3.00
203	Pedro Lobaton	15.00	6.00	3.00
204	Pete Mackanin	15.00	6.00	3.00
205	Jose Caldera	15.00	6.00	3.00
206	Carlos Rodriguez (In Action)	15.00	6.00	3.00
207	Eddy Baez	15.00	6.00	3.00
208	Gary Metzeger	15.00	6.00	3.00
209	Rafael Sandoval	15.00	6.00	3.00
210	Arturo Sanchez	15.00	6.00	3.00
211	Franklin Tua	15.00	6.00	3.00
212	Teolindo Acosta	15.00	6.00	3.00
213	Arnaldo Alvarado	15.00	6.00	3.00
214	Orlando Gonzalez	15.00	6.00	3.00
215	Nelson Garcia	15.00	6.00	3.00
216	Terry Puhl	15.00	6.00	3.00
217	David Torres	15.00	6.00	3.00
218	Teolindo Acosta, Roberto Munoz	15.00	6.00	3.00
219	Terry Puhl, Mark Budaska	15.00	6.00	3.00
220	Gary Gray	15.00	6.00	3.00
221	Gustavo Gil	15.00	6.00	3.00
222	Epi Guerrero	15.00	6.00	3.00
223	Bobby Ramos, Enrique Gonzalez	15.00	6.00	3.00
224	Rick Sawyer	15.00	6.00	3.00
225	S. Byre	15.00	6.00	3.00
226	Magallanes Navigators Logo	15.00	6.00	3.00
227	Alex Monchak	15.00	6.00	3.00
228	Manuel Gonzalez	15.00	6.00	3.00
229	Olinto Rojas	15.00	6.00	3.00
230	Gregorio Machado	15.00	6.00	3.00
231	Ali Arape	15.00	6.00	3.00
232	Miguel Barreto	15.00	6.00	3.00
233	Manny Sarmiento	15.00	6.00	3.00
234	Jesus Aristimuno, Alexis Ramirez, Felix Rodriguez	15.00	6.00	3.00
235	Ed Glynn	15.00	6.00	3.00
236	Luis Jiminez	15.00	6.00	3.00
237	Bob Adams	15.00	6.00	3.00
238	Edito Arteaga	15.00	6.00	3.00
239	Rafael Cariel	15.00	6.00	3.00
240	Eddie Solomon	15.00	6.00	3.00
241	Rick Williams	15.00	6.00	3.00
242	Miguel Nava	15.00	6.00	3.00
243	Rod Scurry	15.00	6.00	3.00
244	Mike Eduards (Edwards)	15.00	6.00	3.00
245	Earl Stephenson	15.00	6.00	3.00
246	Alfonso Collazo	15.00	6.00	3.00
247	Ruben Cabrera	15.00	6.00	3.00
248	Alfredo Torres	15.00	6.00	3.00
249	John Valle	15.00	6.00	3.00
250	Jesus Aristimuno	15.00	6.00	3.00
251	Joe Cannon	15.00	6.00	3.00
252	John Pacella	15.00	6.00	3.00
253	Oswaldo Olivares	15.00	6.00	3.00
254	Gary Hargis	15.00	6.00	3.00
255	Nelson Paiva	15.00	6.00	3.00
256	Bob Oliver	15.00	6.00	3.00
257	Alexis Ramirez	15.00	6.00	3.00
258	Larry Wolfe	15.00	6.00	3.00
259	Don Boyland (Doe)	15.00	6.00	3.00
260	Mark Wagner	15.00	6.00	3.00
261	Jim Wright	15.00	6.00	3.00
262	Mitchell Page	15.00	6.00	3.00
263	Felix Rodriguez	15.00	6.00	3.00
264	Willie Aaron	15.00	6.00	3.00
265	Justo Massaro	15.00	6.00	3.00
266	Norm Angelini	15.00	6.00	3.00
267	Fred Breining	15.00	6.00	3.00
268	Bill Sample	15.00	6.00	3.00
269	Than Smith	15.00	6.00	3.00
270	Harry Doris (Dorish)	15.00	6.00	3.00
271	Zulia Eagles Logo	15.00	6.00	3.00
272	Luis Aparicio	35.00	14.00	7.00
273	Toni Taylor (Tony)	15.00	6.00	3.00
274	Teodoro Obregon	15.00	6.00	3.00
275	Gilberto Marcano	15.00	6.00	3.00
276	Jose Alfaro	15.00	6.00	3.00
277	Danny Boitano	15.00	6.00	3.00
278	Jesus Reyes	15.00	6.00	3.00
279	Johel Chourio	15.00	6.00	3.00
280	Scott Sanderson	15.00	6.00	3.00
281	Charles Kiffin	15.00	6.00	3.00
282	Bill Dancy	15.00	6.00	3.00
283	Tim Johnson	15.00	6.00	3.00
284	Norman Shiera	15.00	6.00	3.00
285	Lonnie Smith	15.00	6.00	3.00
286	Manny Seoane	15.00	6.00	3.00
287	David Wallace	15.00	6.00	3.00
288	Lareu Whashington (LaRue Washington)	15.00	6.00	3.00
289	Danny Warthen	15.00	6.00	3.00
290	Sebastian Martinez	15.00	6.00	3.00
291	Warren Brusstar	15.00	6.00	3.00
292	Steven Waterburry (Waterbury)	15.00	6.00	3.00
293	Gustavo Sposito	15.00	6.00	3.00
294	Billy Connors	15.00	6.00	3.00
295	Bod Reece (Bob)	15.00	6.00	3.00
296	Al Velasquez	15.00	6.00	3.00
297	Jesus Alfaro	15.00	6.00	3.00
298	Todd Cruz	15.00	6.00	3.00
299	Efren Chourio	15.00	6.00	3.00
300	Tim Norrid	15.00	6.00	3.00
301	Leonel Carrion	15.00	6.00	3.00
302	Dario Chirinos	15.00	6.00	3.00
303	Bobby Darwin	15.00	6.00	3.00
304	Levy Ochoa	15.00	6.00	3.00
305	Orlando Reyez (Reyes)	15.00	6.00	3.00
306	Antonio Garcia	15.00	6.00	3.00
307	Fred Andrews	15.00	6.00	3.00
308	Domingo Barboza	15.00	6.00	3.00
309	Emilio Rodriguez	15.00	6.00	3.00
310	Roger Brown (Rogers "Bobby")	15.00	6.00	3.00
311	Nelson Munoz	15.00	6.00	3.00
312	Unknown	15.00	6.00	3.00
313	Greg Pryor	15.00	6.00	3.00
314	Early Espina	15.00	6.00	3.00
315	Leonel Carrion, Dario Chirinos	15.00	6.00	3.00
316	Luis Aparicio	25.00	10.00	5.00
317	Alfonso Carrasquel (Chico)	20.00	8.00	4.00
318	Dave Concepcion	20.00	8.00	4.00
319	Antonio Armas (Tony)	20.00	8.00	4.00
320	Marcano Trillo (Manny)	20.00	8.00	4.00
321	Pablo Torrealba	15.00	6.00	3.00
322	Manny Sarmiento	15.00	6.00	3.00
323	Baudilo Diaz (Bo)	15.00	6.00	3.00
324	Victor Davalillo	15.00	6.00	3.00
325	Puzzle Piece(Dave Parker)	15.00	6.00	3.00
326	Puzzle Piece(Dave Parker)	15.00	6.00	3.00
327	Puzzle Piece(Dave Parker)	15.00	6.00	3.00
328	Puzzle Piece(Dave Parker)	15.00	6.00	3.00
329	Puzzle Piece(Dave Parker)	15.00	6.00	3.00
330	Puzzle Piece(Dave Parker)	15.00	6.00	3.00
331	Puzzle Piece(Dave Parker)	15.00	6.00	3.00
332	Puzzle Piece(Dave Parker)	15.00	6.00	3.00
333	Puzzle Piece(Dave Parker)	15.00	6.00	3.00
334	Dave Parker	15.00	6.00	3.00
335	Steve Bowling	15.00	6.00	3.00
336	Jose Herrera	15.00	6.00	3.00
337	Mitchell Page	15.00	6.00	3.00
338	Enos Cabell	15.00	6.00	3.00
339	Orlando Reyes	15.00	6.00	3.00
340	Felix Rodriguez	15.00	6.00	3.00
341	Baudilo Diaz (Bo)	15.00	6.00	3.00
342	Gonzalo Marquez	15.00	6.00	3.00
343	Mike Kelleher	15.00	6.00	3.00
344	Juan Monasterio	15.00	6.00	3.00
345	Diego Segui	15.00	6.00	3.00
346	Steve Lueber (Luebber)	15.00	6.00	3.00
347	Mike Scott	15.00	6.00	3.00
348	Angel Bravo	15.00	6.00	3.00
349	Terry Whitfield	15.00	6.00	3.00
350	Bob Oliver	15.00	6.00	3.00
351	Tim Jonhson (Johnson)	15.00	6.00	3.00
352	Gustavo Sposito	15.00	6.00	3.00
353	Jim Norris	15.00	6.00	3.00
354	Marcano Trillo (Manny)	20.00	8.00	4.00
355	Gary Woods	15.00	6.00	3.00
356	Felix Rodriguez	15.00	6.00	3.00
357	Dave May	15.00	6.00	3.00
358	Don Lepper (Leppert)	15.00	6.00	3.00
359	Magallanes Team Photo	15.00	6.00	3.00
360	Magallanes Team Photo	15.00	6.00	3.00
361	Action Photo	15.00	6.00	3.00
362	Action Photo	15.00	6.00	3.00
363	Antonio Torres, Leo Posada	15.00	6.00	3.00
364	Action Photo	15.00	6.00	3.00
365	Action Photo	15.00	6.00	3.00
366	Action Photo	15.00	6.00	3.00
367	Action Photo	15.00	6.00	3.00
368	Action Photo	15.00	6.00	3.00
369	Action Photo	15.00	6.00	3.00
370	Action Photo	15.00	6.00	3.00
371	Action Photo	15.00	6.00	3.00
372	Action Photo	15.00	6.00	3.00
373	Action Photo	15.00	6.00	3.00
374	Action Photo	15.00	6.00	3.00
375	Action Photo	15.00	6.00	3.00
376	Action Photo	15.00	6.00	3.00
377	Action Photo	15.00	6.00	3.00
378	Action Photo	15.00	6.00	3.00
399	Action Photo (Misnumbered)	15.00	6.00	3.00
380	Action Photo	15.00	6.00	3.00
381	Action Photo	15.00	6.00	3.00
382	Action Photo	15.00	6.00	3.00
383	Action Photo	15.00	6.00	3.00
384	Action Photo	15.00	6.00	3.00
385	Action Photo	15.00	6.00	3.00
386	Action Photo	15.00	6.00	3.00
387	Action Photo	15.00	6.00	3.00
388	Action Photo	15.00	6.00	3.00
389	Antonio Torres, Franklin Parra	15.00	6.00	3.00
390	Action Photo	15.00	6.00	3.00
391	Angel Bravo, Luis Aparicio	20.00	8.00	4.00
392	Action Photo	15.00	6.00	3.00
393	Action Photo	15.00	6.00	3.00
394	Action Photo	15.00	6.00	3.00
395	Action Photo	15.00	6.00	3.00
396	Action Photo	15.00	6.00	3.00
397	Action Photo	15.00	6.00	3.00
398	Action Photo	15.00	6.00	3.00
399	Action Photo	15.00	6.00	3.00
400	Action Photo	15.00	6.00	3.00
401	Action Photo	15.00	6.00	3.00
402	Tony Armas, Manny Trillo, Gonzalo Marquez	15.00	6.00	3.00

1952 Victoria

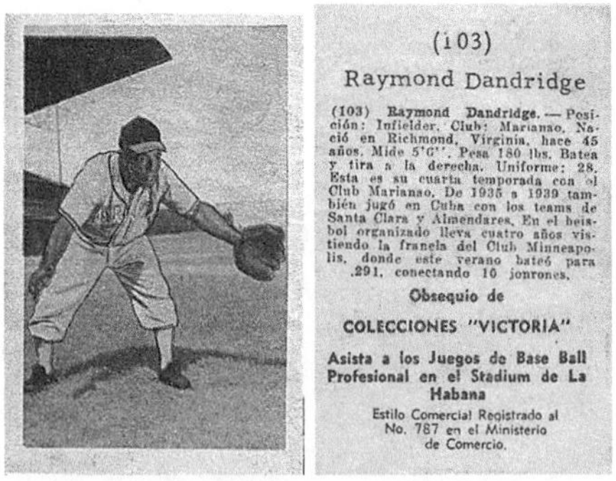

Produced during the 1952-53 Winter League season, these paper cards were formatted in the popular Latin American manner to be pasted into a colorful accompanying album. It is possible a principal venue for the set was the ballpark at Havana, since each card urges attendance at games there. The cards are printed on paper in a 2-1/8" x 3-1/8" size. Fronts have colorized photos with white borders, but no player identification. Backs are, of course, in Spanish and include a card number player personal data, career summary and a copyright notice. Besides local players, and former, current and future major league players, the set includes league umpires and broadcasters, etc. Names as presented in this checklist may not correspond exactly with those printed on card backs and may not be correct spellings of player names.

		NM	E	VG
Complete Set (168):		6,500	3,000	1,500
Common Player:		45.00	20.00	10.00
Album:		350.00	160.00	90.00
1	Amado Maestri (Umpire)	45.00	20.00	10.00
2	John Mullen (Umpire)	45.00	20.00	10.00
3	Havana Stadium	45.00	20.00	10.00
4	Bernardino Rodriguez (Umpire)	45.00	20.00	10.00
5	Raul Atan (Umpire)	45.00	20.00	10.00
6	Cuco Conde (Broadcaster)	45.00	20.00	10.00
7	Manolo de la Reguera (Broadcaster)	45.00	20.00	10.00
8	Rafael (Felo) Ramirez (Broadcaster)	60.00	30.00	20.00
9	Rafael Rubi (Broadcaster)	45.00	20.00	10.00
10	Gabino Delgado (Broadcaster)	45.00	20.00	10.00
11	Fernando Menendez (Broadcaster)	45.00	20.00	10.00
12	Buck Canel (Broadcaster)	50.00	25.00	15.00
13	Orlando Sanchez Diago (Broadcaster)	45.00	20.00	10.00
14	Pedro Galiana (Broadcaster)	45.00	20.00	10.00
15	Jess Losada (Broadcaster)	45.00	20.00	10.00
16	Juan Ealo (Broadcaster)	45.00	20.00	10.00
17	Rene Molina (Broadcaster)	45.00	20.00	10.00
18	Miguel A. Ruiz (Broadcaster)	45.00	20.00	10.00
19	Ruben Rodriguez (Broadcaster)	45.00	20.00	10.00
20	Havana Lions Pennant	30.00	15.00	9.00
21	Miguel Gonzalez	60.00	30.00	20.00
22	Tomas (Pipo) de la Noval	45.00	20.00	10.00
23	Salvador Hernandez	45.00	20.00	10.00
24	Manuel Garcia	45.00	20.00	10.00
25	Edilio Alfaro	45.00	20.00	10.00
26	Julio Navarro	45.00	20.00	10.00
27	Richard Rand	45.00	20.00	10.00
28	Andres Fleitas	45.00	20.00	10.00
29	Isaac Seoane	45.00	20.00	10.00
30	Jimmie Kerrigan	45.00	20.00	10.00
31	Robert Alexander	45.00	20.00	10.00
32	Charles Sipples	45.00	20.00	10.00
33	Adrian Zabala	45.00	20.00	10.00
34	Rogelio Martinez	45.00	20.00	10.00
35	Carlos Pascual	60.00	30.00	20.00
36	Mario Picone	45.00	20.00	10.00
37	Eusebio Perez (Silverio)	45.00	20.00	10.00
38	Julio Moreno	45.00	20.00	10.00
39	Gilberto Torres	45.00	20.00	10.00
40	Bert Haas	45.00	20.00	10.00
41	Johnny Jorgensen	45.00	20.00	10.00
42	Lou Klein	45.00	20.00	10.00
43	Damon Phillips	45.00	20.00	10.00
44	Orlando Varona	45.00	20.00	10.00
45	Jorge Lopez	45.00	20.00	10.00
46	Pedro Formenthal	60.00	30.00	20.00
47	Robert Usher	45.00	20.00	10.00
48	Edmundo (Sandy) Amoros	60.00	30.00	20.00
49	Alejandro Crespo	50.00	25.00	15.00
50	Oscar Sardinas	45.00	20.00	10.00
51	Almendares Pennant	30.00	15.00	9.00
52	Robert Bragan	50.00	25.00	15.00
53	Clemente (Sungo) Carreras	45.00	20.00	10.00
54	Rodolfo Fernandez	45.00	20.00	10.00
55	Manuel Fernandez	45.00	20.00	10.00
56	Orlando Echevarria	45.00	20.00	10.00
57	Charles Thompson	45.00	20.00	10.00
58	Oscar Fernandez	45.00	20.00	10.00
59	Hal Erickson	45.00	20.00	10.00
60	Conrado Marrero	50.00	25.00	15.00
61	Agapito Mayor	45.00	20.00	10.00
62	Octavio Rubert	45.00	20.00	10.00
63	Edward Roebuck	45.00	20.00	10.00
64	Duke Markell	50.00	20.00	10.00
65	Rene Massip	45.00	20.00	10.00
66	Pedro Naranjo	45.00	20.00	10.00
67	Roque Contreras	45.00	20.00	10.00
68	Wayne McLeland	45.00	20.00	10.00
69	Frank Kellert	45.00	20.00	10.00
70	Forrest Jacobs	50.00	25.00	15.00
71	Hector Rodriguez	50.00	25.00	15.00
72	Willy Miranda	50.00	25.00	15.00
73	Roberto Ortiz	50.00	25.00	15.00
74	Frank Carswell	45.00	20.00	10.00
75	Asdrubal Baro	45.00	20.00	10.00
76	Paul Smith	45.00	20.00	10.00
77	Antonio Napoles	45.00	20.00	10.00
78	Francisco Campos	45.00	20.00	10.00
79	Angel Scull	45.00	20.00	10.00
80	Raymond Coleman	45.00	20.00	10.00
81	Gino Cimolli (Cimoli)	50.00	25.00	15.00
82	Amado Ibanez	45.00	20.00	10.00
83	Avelino Canizarez	45.00	20.00	10.00
84	Conrado Perez	45.00	20.00	10.00
85	Marianao Pennant	30.00	15.00	9.00
86	Fermin Guerra	50.00	25.00	15.00
87	Jose Maria Fernandez	50.00	25.00	15.00
88	Jose (Joe) Olivares	45.00	20.00	10.00
89	Ramon Carneado	45.00	20.00	10.00
90	Alejandro (Baby) Fernandez	45.00	20.00	10.00
91	Emilio Cabrera	45.00	20.00	10.00
92	Sandalio Consuegra	50.00	25.00	15.00
93	Tomas Fine	45.00	20.00	10.00
94	Miguel Fornieles	50.00	25.00	15.00
95	Camilo Pascual	60.00	30.00	18.00
96	Miguel Lopez	45.00	20.00	10.00
97	Clarence Iott	50.00	25.00	15.00
98	Dale Matthewson	45.00	20.00	10.00
99	Hampton Coleman	50.00	25.00	15.00
100	Terris McDuffie	60.00	30.00	18.00
101	Raul Sanchez	45.00	20.00	10.00
102	Lorenzo Cabrera	45.00	20.00	10.00
103	Ray Dandridge	800.00	400.00	240.00
104	Silvio Garcia	45.00	20.00	10.00
105	Carlos De Souza	45.00	20.00	10.00
106	Oreste (Minnie) Minoso	100.00	50.00	30.00
107	Sebastian Basso	45.00	20.00	10.00
108	William Wilson	45.00	20.00	10.00
109	Hank Workman	50.00	25.00	15.00
110	Fernando Pedroso	45.00	20.00	10.00
111	Juan Antonio Vistuer	45.00	20.00	10.00
112	Hiram Gonzalez	45.00	20.00	10.00
113	Julio Becquer	45.00	20.00	10.00
114	Stan Rojek	45.00	20.00	10.00
115	Ramiro (Cuco) Vasquez	45.00	20.00	10.00
116	Juan Izaguirre	45.00	20.00	10.00
117	Cienfuegos Pennant	30.00	15.00	9.00
118	Billy Herman	110.00	55.00	35.00
119	Oscar Rodriguez	45.00	20.00	10.00
120	Julio Rojo	45.00	20.00	10.00
121	Pedro Pages	45.00	20.00	10.00
122	Felix Masud	45.00	20.00	10.00
123	Rafael Noble	50.00	25.00	15.00
124	Mario Diaz	45.00	20.00	10.00
125	Luis Aloma	45.00	20.00	10.00
126	Santiago Ulrich	45.00	20.00	10.00
127	Armando Roche	45.00	20.00	10.00
128	Raul Lopez	45.00	20.00	10.00
129	Armando Suarez	45.00	20.00	10.00
130	Vincente Lopez	45.00	20.00	10.00
131	Ernesto Morillas	45.00	20.00	10.00
132	Alfredo Ibanez	45.00	20.00	10.00
133	Allen J. Gettel	45.00	20.00	10.00
134	Ken Lehman	45.00	20.00	10.00
135	Pat Mc Clothin (McGlothin)	50.00	25.00	15.00
136	Rogenio Otero	45.00	20.00	10.00
137	Felipe Montemayor	45.00	20.00	10.00
138	Jack Cassini	50.00	25.00	15.00
139	Donald Zimmer	75.00	37.00	22.00
140	Robert Wilson	45.00	20.00	10.00
141	Humberto Fernandez	45.00	20.00	10.00
142	Pedro Ballester	45.00	20.00	10.00
143	Walt Morin (Moryn)	50.00	25.00	15.00
144	Roberto Fernandez	45.00	20.00	10.00
145	Claro Duany	60.00	30.00	18.00
146	Pablo Garcia	45.00	20.00	10.00
147	James Pendleton	50.00	25.00	15.00
148	Oscar Sierra	45.00	20.00	10.00
149	Adolfo Luque	80.00	40.00	25.00
150	Cando Lopez	45.00	20.00	10.00
151	Joe Black	100.00	50.00	30.00
152	Napoleon Reyes	60.00	30.00	18.00
153	Rafael (Villa) Cabrera	45.00	20.00	10.00
154	Charles (Red) Barrett	50.00	25.00	15.00
155	Fred Martin	45.00	20.00	10.00
156	Isidoro Leon	45.00	20.00	10.00
157	John Rutherford	50.00	20.00	10.00
158	Max Lanier	50.00	25.00	15.00
159	Julio Ramos	45.00	20.00	10.00
160	Manuel Hidalgo	45.00	20.00	10.00
161	Wilfredo Calvino	45.00	20.00	10.00
162	Joe Nakamura	60.00	30.00	20.00
163	Martiniano Garay	45.00	20.00	10.00
164	Fernando Rodriguez	45.00	20.00	10.00
165	Anibal Navarrette	45.00	20.00	10.00
166	Rafael Rivas	45.00	20.00	10.00
167	Wilfredo Salas	45.00	20.00	10.00
168	Jocko Thompson	45.00	20.00	10.00

1908 Victor Publishing Cy Young

Eschewing booze, women and gambling made Cy Young famous, according to this postcard issued by an Ohio company near the end of the pitcher's career. The 3-1/2" x 5-1/2" card has a large black-and-white photographic portrait at center with maroon and black illustrations emblematic of typical ballplayers' vices in the corners. The divided-back is printed in black with typical postcard markings.

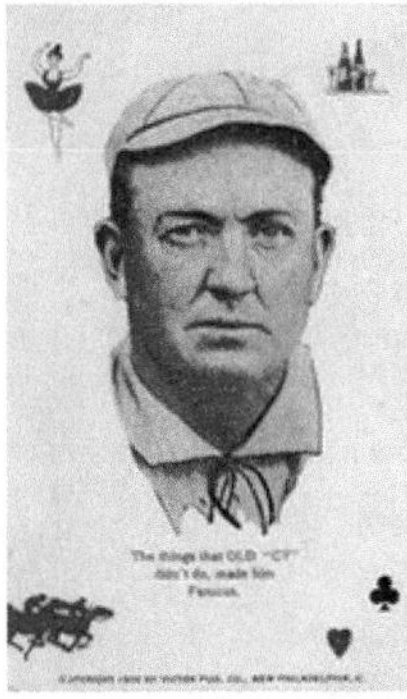

	NM	E	VG
Cy Young	450.00	225.00	135.00

1915 Victory Tobacco (T214)

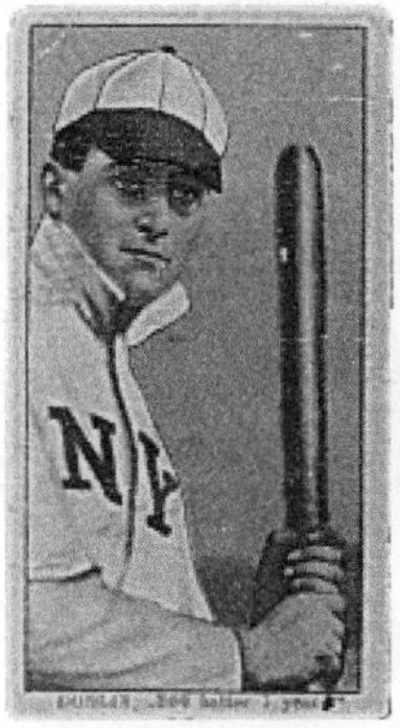

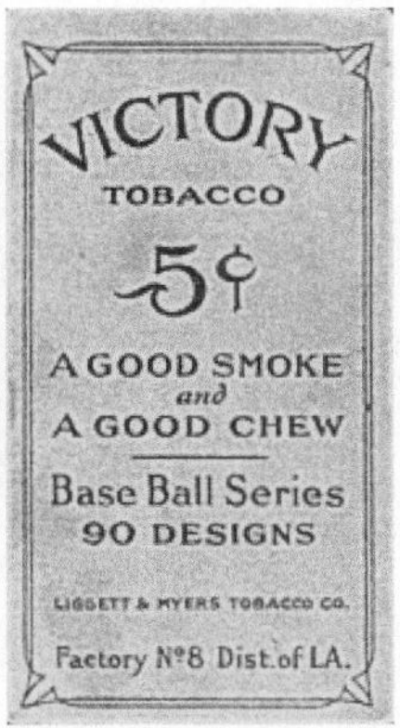

The T214 Victory set of 1915 is an obscure series of tobacco cards that is sometimes mistaken for the better-known T206 "White Border" set. The confusion is understandable because identical player poses were used for both sets. The Victory set can be easily identified, however, by the advertising for the Victory brand on the back of the cards. The set features players from the Federal League, both major leagues and at least one minor leaguer. While card backs advertise "90 Designs," fewer than 60 subjects have surfaced to date. The set had such limited distribution - apparently restricted to just the Louisiana area - and the cards are so rare that it may never be completely checklisted. Except for the advertising on the backs, the Victory cards are almost identical to the "Type 2" Coupon cards (T213), another obscure Louisiana tobacco set issued during the same period. Of the several tobacco sets issued in Louisana in the early part of the 20th Century, the T214 Victory cards are considered the most difficult to find. Gaps have been left in the numbering sequence to accommodate future additions.

		NM	E	VG
Common Player:		3,600	1,620	750.00
(1)	Red Ames	7,200	2,880	1,440
(2)	Chief Bender	14,400	5,760	2,880
(3)	Roger Bresnahan	14,400	5,760	2,880
(4)	Al Bridwell	7,200	2,880	1,440
(5)	Howie Camnitz	7,200	2,880	1,440
(6)	Hal Chase (Portrait)	10,200	4,080	2,040
(7)	Hal Chase (Throwing)	10,200	4,080	2,040
(8)	Ty Cobb (Portrait, red background.)	30,000	12,000	6,000
(9)	Doc Crandall	7,200	2,880	1,440
(10)	Birdie Cree	7,200	2,880	1,440
(11)	Josh Devore	7,200	2,880	1,440
(12)	Ray Demmitt	7,200	2,880	1,440
(13)	Mickey Doolan	7,200	2,880	1,440
(14)	Mike Donlin	7,200	2,880	1,440
(15)	Tom Downey	7,200	2,880	1,440
(16)	Larry Doyle	7,200	2,880	1,440
(17)	Kid Elberfeld	7,200	2,880	1,440
(18)	Johnny Evers	14,400	5,760	2,880
(19)	Russ Ford	7,200	2,880	1,440
(20)	Art Fromme	7,200	2,880	1,440
(21)	Chick Gandil	14,400	5,760	2,880
(22)	Rube Geyer	7,200	2,880	1,440
(23)	Clark Griffith	14,400	5,760	2,880
(24)	Bob Groom	7,200	2,880	1,440

(25)	Buck Herzog	7,200	2,880	1,440
(26)	Hughie Jennings	14,400	5,760	2,880
(27)	Walter Johnson (Hands at chest.)	18,000	7,200	3,600
(28)	Joe Kelley	14,400	5,760	2,880
(29)	Ed Konetchy	7,200	2,880	1,440
(30)	Nap Lajoie	14,400	5,760	2,880
(31)	Ed Lennox	7,200	2,880	1,440
(32)	Sherry Magee	7,200	2,880	1,440
(33)	Rube Marquard	14,400	5,760	2,880
(34)	John McGraw	14,400	5,760	2,880
(35)	George McQuillan	7,200	2,880	1,440
(36)	Chief Meyers (Catching)	7,200	2,880	1,440
(37)	Chief Meyers (Portrait)	7,200	2,880	1,440
(38)	George Mullin	7,200	2,880	1,440
(41)	Red Murray	7,200	2,880	1,440
(42)	Tom Needham	7,200	2,880	1,440
(43)	Rebel Oakes	7,200	2,880	1,440
(44)	Dode Paskert	7,200	2,880	1,440
(45)	Jack Quinn	7,200	2,880	1,440
(46)	Nap Rucker	7,200	2,880	1,440
(47)	Germany Schaefer	7,200	2,880	1,440
(48)	Wildfire Schulte	7,200	2,880	1,440
(49)	Frank Smith	7,200	2,880	1,440
(51)	Tris Speaker	16,200	6,480	3,240
(52)	George Stovall	7,200	2,880	1,440
(53)	Ed Summers	7,200	2,880	1,440
(54)	Bill Sweeney	7,200	2,880	1,440
(55)	Jeff Sweeney	7,200	2,880	1,440
(56)	Ira Thomas	7,200	2,880	1,440
(57)	Joe Tinker	14,400	5,760	2,880
(58)	Heinie Wagner	7,200	2,880	1,440
(59)	Zack Wheat	14,400	5,760	2,880
(60)	Kaiser Wilhelm	7,200	2,880	1,440
(61)	Hooks Wiltse	7,200	2,880	1,440

1929 Villa Theater Philadelphia A'S

These cards were issued in conjunction with a World Series promotion by a Philadelphia movie house. Fronts of the black-and-white 3-5/8" x 5-3/4" cards have player portraits with the player identified by name and position in the lower-right corner of the bottom order. On back is an ambiguously worded message promising a team-autographed ball will be given away at the Saturday matinee. It is unknown whether the five players on this checklist represent the complete issue.

		NM	E	VG
Common Player:		125.00	65.00	40.00
(1)	Eddie Collins	250.00	125.00	75.00
(2)	Jimmy Dykes	125.00	65.00	40.00
(3)	George "Mule" Haas	125.00	65.00	40.00
(4)	Edmund "Bing" Miller	125.00	65.00	40.00
(5)	Rube Walberg	125.00	65.00	40.00

1909-1912 Violet/Mint Chips (E254)

(See Colgan's Chips)

1886 Virginia Brights Black Stocking Nine (N48)

Issued during the late 1880s, though the attributed date is speculative, this series of cabinet-size (about 5" x 7-1/2") blank-back cards was available by sending in coupons found in Allen & Ginter's Virginia Brights brand cigarettes. Fronts have a sepia photo of Rubenesque women in baseball uniforms posed before a painted ballpark backdrop. In the bottom border is "BLACK STOCKING NINE. ALLEN & GINTER'S / Virginia Brights Cigarettes. / Crop of 1884 / HAND MADE CROP OF 1884." The beveled edges of the cabinet mount were originially gilt-trimmed.

	NM	E	VG
Common Card:	1,200	600.00	350.00

1887 Virginia Brights Polka Dot Nine

Issued during the late 1880s, though the attributed date is speculative, this series of cabinet-size (about 5" x 7-1/2") blank-back cards was available by sending in coupons found in Allen & Ginter's Virginia Brights brand cigarettes. Fronts have a sepia photo of women in baseball uniforms and polka-dot bandanas posed before a backdrop. In the top border of the yellow cardboard mount, printed in gold leaf, is "Virginia Brights / Cigarettes / CROP OF 1884". In a cartouche beneath the photo is "POLKA DOT NINE." Below that is "THE FULL SET OF THIS SERIES COMPRISES NINE DIFFERENT SUBJECTS. / REPRESENTING THE VARIOUS POSITIONS IN BASE BALL."

	NM	E	VG
Common Card:	1,100	540.00	330.00

1888 Virginia Brights Black Stocking Nine

Issued during the late 1880s, this series of cabinet-size (about 5" x 7-1/2") blank-back cards was available by sending in coupons found in Allen & Ginter's Virginia Brights brand cigarettes. Fronts have a sepia photo of Rubenesque women in a baseball uniform posed before a painted ballpark backdrop. The picture is framed by a fancy design. In the border above is "Virginia Brights / Cigarettes / Crop of 1884". Below the photo is the series title "Black Stocking Nine" and "The Full Set of this Series Comprises Nine Different / Subjects Representing the Various Positions in Base-Ball."

	NM	E	VG
Common Card:	2,400	1,200	725.00

1888 Virginia Brights Girl Baseball Players

(See 1888 Allen & Ginter Girl Baseball Players.)

1911-16 Virginia Extra Cigarettes (T216)

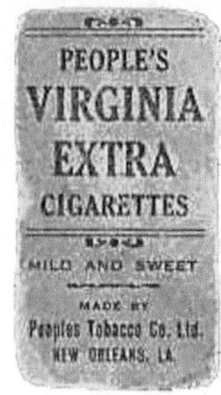 

The T216 baseball card set, issued by several brands of the Peoples Tobacco Co., is the last of the Louisana cigarette sets and the most confusing. Apparently issued over a period of several years between 1911 and 1916, the set employs the same pictures as several contemporary caramel and bakery sets. Cards measure a nominal 1-1/2" x 2-5/8", thought reasonable allowance must be made in consideration of original cutting methodology. Positive identification can be made by the back of the cards. The Peoples Tobacco cards carry advertising for one of three brands of cigarettes: Kotton, Mino or Virginia Extra. The Kotton brand is the most common, while the Virginia Extra and Mino backs command a premium. T216 cards are found in two types; one has a glossy front finish, while a second scarcer type is printed on a thin paper. The thin paper cards command an additional 15 percent premium. The cards represent players from the American, National and Federal Leagues.

		NM	E	VG
Common Player:		3,300	1,320	660.00
(1)	Jack Barry (Batting)	3,300	1,320	660.00
(2)	Jack Barry (Fielding)	3,300	1,320	660.00
(3)	Harry Bemis	3,300	1,320	660.00
(4a)	Chief Bender (Philadelphia, striped cap.)	8,800	3,520	1,760
(4b)	Chief Bender (Baltimore, striped cap.)	8,800	3,520	1,760
(5a)	Chief Bender (Philadelphia, white cap.)	8,800	3,520	1,760
(5b)	Chief Bender (Baltimore, white cap.)	8,800	3,520	1,760
(6)	Bill Bergen	3,300	1,320	660.00
(7a)	Bob Bescher (Cincinnati)	3,300	1,320	660.00
(7b)	Bob Bescher (St. Louis)	3,300	1,320	660.00
(8)	Roger Bresnahan	8,800	3,520	1,760
(9)	Al Bridwell (Batting)	3,300	1,320	660.00
(10a)	Al Bridwell (New York, sliding.)	3,300	1,320	660.00
(10b)	Al Bridwell (St. Louis, sliding.)	3,300	1,320	660.00
(11)	Donie Bush	3,300	1,320	660.00
(12)	Doc Casey	3,300	1,320	660.00
(13)	Frank Chance	8,800	3,520	1,760
(14a)	Hal Chase (New York, fielding.)	3,300	1,320	660.00
(14b)	Hal Chase (Buffalo, fielding.)	3,300	1,320	660.00
(15)	Hal Chase (Portrait)	3,300	1,320	660.00
(16a)	Ty Cobb (Detroit Am., standing.)	35,750	14,300	7,150
(16b)	Ty Cobb (Detroit Americans, standing.)	33,000	13,200	6,600
(17)	Ty Cobb (Detroit Americans, batting.)	33,000	13,200	6,600
(18a)	Eddie Collins (Phila. Am.)	8,800	3,520	1,760
(18b)	Eddie Collins (Phila. Amer.)	8,800	3,520	1,760
(19)	Eddie Collins (Chicago)	8,800	3,520	1,760
(20a)	Sam Crawford (Small print.)	8,800	3,520	1,760
(20b)	Sam Crawford (Large print.)	8,800	3,520	1,760
(21)	Harry Davis	3,300	1,320	660.00
(22)	Ray Demmitt	3,300	1,320	660.00
(23)	Art Devlin	3,300	1,320	660.00
(24a)	Wild Bill Donovan (Detroit)	3,300	1,320	660.00
(24b)	Wild Bill Donovan (New York)	3,300	1,320	660.00
(25a)	Red Dooin (Philadelphia)	3,300	1,320	660.00
(25b)	Red Dooin (Cincinnati)	3,300	1,320	660.00
(26a)	Mickey Doolan (Philadelphia)	3,300	1,320	660.00

(26b)	Mickey Doolan (Baltimore)	3,300	1,320	660.00
(27)	Patsy Dougherty	3,300	1,320	660.00
(28a)	Larry Doyle, Larry Doyle (N.Y. Nat'l, batting.)	3,300	1,320	660.00
(28b)	Larry Doyle (New York Nat'l, batting.)	3,300	1,320	660.00
(29)	Larry Doyle (Throwing)	3,300	1,320	660.00
(30)	Clyde Engle	3,300	1,320	660.00
(31a)	Johnny Evers (Chicago)	8,800	3,520	1,760
(31b)	Johnny Evers (Boston)	8,800	3,520	1,760
(32)	Art Fromme	3,300	1,320	660.00
(33a)	George Gibson (Pittsburg Nat'l, back view.)	3,300	1,320	660.00
(33b)	George Gibson (Pittsburgh Nat'l., back view.)	3,300	1,320	660.00
(34a)	George Gibson (Pittsburg Nat'l, front view.)	3,300	1,320	660.00
(34b)	George Gibson (Pittsburgh Nat'l., front view.)	3,300	1,320	660.00
(35a)	Topsy Hartsel (Phila. Am.)	3,300	1,320	660.00
(35b)	Topsy Hartsel (Phila. Amer.)	3,300	1,320	660.00
(36)	Roy Hartzell (Batting)	3,300	1,320	660.00
(37)	Roy Hartzell (Catching)	3,300	1,320	660.00
(38a)	Fred Jacklitsch (Philadelphia)	3,300	1,320	660.00
(38b)	Fred Jacklitsch (Baltimore)	3,300	1,320	660.00
(39a)	Hughie Jennings (Orange background.)	8,800	3,520	1,760
(39b)	Hughie Jennings (Red background.)	8,800	3,520	1,760
(40)	Red Kleinow	3,300	1,320	660.00
(41a)	Otto Knabe (Philadelphia)	3,300	1,320	660.00
(41b)	Otto Knabe (Baltimore)	3,300	1,320	660.00
(42)	Jack Knight	3,300	1,320	660.00
(43a)	Nap Lajoie (Philadelphia, fielding.)	13,750	5,500	2,750
(43b)	Nap Lajoie (Cleveland, fielding.)	13,750	5,500	2,750
(44)	Nap Lajoie (Portrait)	13,750	5,500	2,750
(45a)	Hans Lobert (Cincinnati)	3,300	1,320	660.00
(45b)	Hans Lobert (New York)	3,300	1,320	660.00
(46)	Sherry Magee	3,300	1,320	660.00
(47)	Rube Marquard	8,800	3,520	1,760
(48a)	Christy Matthewson (Mathewson) (Large print.)	33,000	13,200	6,600
(48b)	Christy Matthewson (Mathewson) (Small print.)	33,000	13,200	6,600
(49a)	John McGraw (Large print.)	8,800	3,520	1,760
(49b)	John McGraw (Small print.)	8,800	3,520	1,760
(50)	Larry McLean	3,300	1,320	660.00
(51)	George McQuillan	3,300	1,320	660.00
(52)	Dots Miller (Batting)	3,300	1,320	660.00
(53a)	Dots Miller (Pittsburg, fielding.)	3,300	1,320	660.00
(53b)	Dots Miller (St. Louis, fielding.)	3,300	1,320	660.00
(54a)	Danny Murphy (Philadelphia)	3,300	1,320	660.00
(54b)	Danny Murphy (Brooklyn)	3,300	1,320	660.00
(55)	Rebel Oakes	3,300	1,320	660.00
(56)	Bill O'Hara	3,300	1,320	660.00
(57)	Eddie Plank	8,800	3,520	1,760
(58a)	Germany Schaefer (Washington)	3,300	1,320	660.00
(58b)	Germany Schaefer (Newark)	3,300	1,320	660.00
(59)	Admiral Schlei	3,300	1,320	660.00
(60)	Boss Schmidt	3,300	1,320	660.00
(61)	Johnny Seigle	3,300	1,320	660.00
(62)	Dave Shean	3,300	1,320	660.00
(63)	Boss Smith (Schmidt)	3,300	1,320	660.00
(64)	Tris Speaker	16,500	6,600	3,300
(65)	Oscar Stanage	3,300	1,320	660.00
(66)	George Stovall	3,300	1,320	660.00
(67)	Jeff Sweeney	3,300	1,320	660.00
(68a)	Joe Tinker (Chicago Nat'l, batting.)	8,800	3,520	1,760
(68b)	Joe Tinker (Chicago Feds, batting.)	8,800	3,520	1,760
(69)	Joe Tinker (Portrait)	8,800	3,520	1,760
(70a)	Honus Wagner (Batting, S.S.)	33,000	13,200	6,600
(70b)	Honus Wagner (Batting, 2b.)	33,000	13,200	6,600
(71a)	Honus Wagner (Throwing, S.S.)	33,000	13,200	6,600
(71b)	Honus Wagner (Throwing, 2b.)	33,000	13,200	6,600
(72)	Hooks Wiltse	3,300	1,320	660.00
(73)	Cy Young	22,000	8,800	4,400
(74a)	Heinie Zimmerman (2b.)	3,300	1,320	660.00
(74b)	Heinie Zimmerman (3b.)	3,300	1,320	660.00

1949 Vis-Ed Cleveland Indian Magic Dials

Similar in concept to a Viewmaster, these hand-held "Magic Dial Big League Viewers" feature the members of the World Champion 1948 Cleveland Indians, plus Mickey Vernon, who joined the team in 1949, and, inexplicably, Pittsburgh Pirate Ralph Kiner. Each of the players is pictured on six single frames of 8 mm movie film (once in color, but now usually faded to sepia tones) mounted on a 2" cardboard circle within a red, white and blue 2-1/4" x 2" rectangular frame; the whole is held together by a metal rivet. The pictures can be viewed by turning the round cardboard dial. The dials came with a playing tips instructional pamphlet. Original price was 29 cents apiece.

		NM	E	VG
Complete Set (15):		1,200	600.00	350.00
Common Player:		75.00	37.00	22.00
(1)	Gene Bearden	75.00	37.00	22.00
(2)	Lou Boudreau (Batting)	125.00	62.00	37.00
(3)	Lou Boudreau (Double play.)	125.00	62.00	37.00
(4)	Lou Boudreau (Shortstop)	125.00	62.00	37.00
(5)	Larry Doby	125.00	62.00	37.00
(6)	Bob Feller	150.00	75.00	45.00
(7)	Joe Gordon (Double play.)	75.00	37.00	22.00
(8)	Joe Gordon (Second base.)	75.00	37.00	22.00
(9)	Jim Hegan	75.00	37.00	22.00
(10)	Ken Keltner	75.00	37.00	22.00
(11)	Ralph Kiner	125.00	62.00	37.00
(12)	Bob Lemon	125.00	62.00	37.00
(13)	Dale Mitchell	75.00	37.00	22.00
(14)	Satchel Paige	200.00	100.00	60.00
(15)	Mickey Vernon	75.00	37.00	22.00

1949 Vis-Ed Cleveland Indian Slide-cards

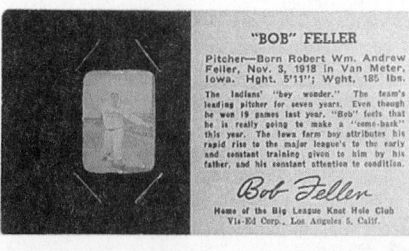

These unique novelties feature the members of the World Champion 1948 Cleveland Indians. The players are pictured on a single frame of 16mm film which has been inserted into slits cut on one end of the cardboard. The cardboard holders are dark blue and yellow, with blue printing. Fronts have player personal data, career highlights, the player's name in script and identification of the issuer. Backs have a list of "Magic Slides" which could be ordered for 33 cents each. It is likely that a slide-card exists for each of the players on that list, but only those which have been confirmed to date are checklisted here, in alphabetical order. Complete slide-cards measure 3-3/4" x 2". A plastic baseball-shaped viewer was sold with the slides.

		NM	E	VG
Common Player:		75.00	37.00	22.00
(1)	Lou Boudreau	90.00	45.00	27.00
(2)	Larry Doby	100.00	50.00	30.00
(3)	Bob Feller	125.00	62.00	37.00
(4)	Joe Gordon	75.00	37.00	22.00
(5)	Jim Hegan	75.00	37.00	22.00
(6)	Ken Keltner	75.00	37.00	22.00

1966 Volpe Tumblers

A number of teams co-operated in the production of base-ball player 12-oz. thermal tumblers which were distributed at local gas stations for a small sum and/or a minimum fuel purchase. The plastic tumblers have artwork portraits and smaller action pictures by Nicholas Volpe and facsimile autographs on colorful backgrounds. The glasses are 5-1/4" tall and 3" in diameter at the rim.

		NM	E	VG
Common Player:		20.00	10.00	6.00
	CINCINNATI REDS			
(1)	Chico Cardenas	20.00	10.00	6.00
(2)	Gordy Coleman	20.00	10.00	6.00
(3)	John Edwards	20.00	10.00	6.00
(4)	Sammy Ellis	20.00	10.00	6.00
(5)	Tommy Harper	20.00	10.00	6.00
(6)	Deron Johnson	20.00	10.00	6.00
(7)	Jim Maloney	20.00	10.00	6.00
(8)	Billy McCool	20.00	10.00	6.00
(9)	Joe Nuxhall	20.00	10.00	6.00
(10)	Jim O'Toole	20.00	10.00	6.00
(11)	Vada Pinson	30.00	15.00	9.00
(12)	Pete Rose	75.00	37.00	22.00
	CLEVELAND INDIANS			
(1)	Max Alvis	20.00	10.00	6.00
(2)	Joe Azcue	20.00	10.00	6.00
(3)	Larry Brown	20.00	10.00	6.00
(4)	Rocky Colavito	50.00	25.00	15.00
(5)	Vic Davalillo	20.00	10.00	6.00
(6)	Chuck Hinton	20.00	10.00	6.00
(7)	Dick Howser	20.00	10.00	6.00
(8)	Sam McDowell	20.00	10.00	6.00
(9)	Don McMahon	20.00	10.00	6.00
(10)	Sonny Siebert	20.00	10.00	6.00
(11)	Leon Wagner	20.00	10.00	6.00
(12)	Fred Whitfield	20.00	10.00	6.00
	NEW YORK METS			
(1)	Larry Bearnarth	20.00	10.00	6.00
(2)	Yogi Berra	50.00	25.00	15.00
(3)	Jack Fisher	20.00	10.00	6.00
(4)	Rob Gardner	20.00	10.00	6.00
(5)	Jim Hickman	20.00	10.00	6.00
(6)	Ron Hunt	20.00	10.00	6.00
(7)	Ed Kranepool	20.00	10.00	6.00
(8)	Johnny Lewis	20.00	10.00	6.00
(9)	Tug McGraw	20.00	10.00	6.00
(10)	Roy McMillan	20.00	10.00	6.00
(11)	Dick Stuart	20.00	10.00	6.00
(12)	Ron Swoboda	20.00	10.00	6.00
	DETROIT TIGERS			
(1)	Hank Aguirre	20.00	10.00	6.00
(2)	Norm Cash	30.00	15.00	9.00
(3)	Don Demeter	20.00	10.00	6.00
(4)	Bill Freehan	20.00	10.00	6.00
(5)	Willie Horton	20.00	10.00	6.00
(6)	Al Kaline	50.00	25.00	15.00
(7)	Mickey Lolich	20.00	10.00	6.00
(8)	Dick McAuliffe	20.00	10.00	6.00
(9)	Denny McLain	20.00	10.00	6.00
(10)	Joe Sparma	20.00	10.00	6.00
(11)	Don Wert	20.00	10.00	6.00
(12)	Dave Wickersham	20.00	10.00	6.00
	LOS ANGELES DODGERS			
(1)	Tommy Davis	20.00	10.00	6.00
(2)	Willie Davis	20.00	10.00	6.00
(3)	Don Drysdale	40.00	20.00	12.00
(4)	Ron Fairly	20.00	10.00	6.00
(5)	John Kennedy	20.00	10.00	6.00
(6)	Jim Lefebvre	20.00	10.00	6.00
(7)	Sandy Koufax	60.00	30.00	18.00
(8)	Claude Osteen	20.00	10.00	6.00
(9)	Wes Parker	20.00	10.00	6.00
(10)	Ron Perranoski	20.00	10.00	6.00
(11)	Johnny Roseboro	20.00	10.00	6.00
(12)	Maury Wills	20.00	10.00	6.00

1913 Voskamp's Coffee Pittsburgh Pirates

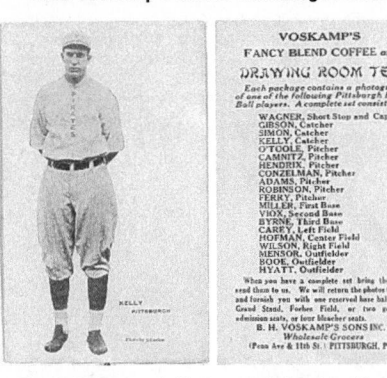

The 1913 Pittsburgh Pirates are featured in this set of cards given away in packages of coffee and tea and redeemable for seats at Pirates games. The 2-1/4" x 3-5/8" cards have black-and-white player photos on a plain white background, along with ID and a "Photo by Johnston" credit line. The black-and-white back has a checklist of the set and details of the ticket redemption program. Pose variations of the Hofman and O'Toole cards are reported to exist. The checklist for the unnumbered cards is presented here alphabetically. Because the set was issued just after the great tobacco card era, several of the Pirates in this set are not found on any other cards.

		NM	E	VG
Complete Set (20):		60,000	30,000	18,000
Common Player:		2,025	1,015	600.00
(1)	Babe Adams	2,025	1,015	600.00
(2)	Everitt Booe	2,025	1,015	600.00
(3)	Bobby Byrne	2,025	1,015	600.00
(4)	Howie Camnitz	2,025	1,015	600.00
(5)	Max Carey	3,000	1,500	900.00
(6)	Joe Conzelman	2,025	1,015	600.00
(7)	Jack Ferry	2,025	1,015	600.00
(8)	George Gibson	2,025	1,015	600.00
(9)	Claude Hendrix	2,025	1,015	600.00
(10)	Solly Hofman	2,025	1,015	600.00
(11)	Ham Hyatt	2,025	1,015	600.00
(12)	Bill Kelly	2,025	1,015	600.00
(13)	Ed Mensor	2,025	1,015	600.00
(14)	Dots Miller	2,025	1,015	600.00
(15)	Marty O'Toole	2,025	1,015	600.00
(16)	Hank Robinson	2,025	1,015	600.00
(17)	Mike Simon	2,025	1,015	600.00
(18)	Jim Viox	2,025	1,015	600.00
(19)	Honus Wagner	22,500	11,250	6,750
(20)	Owen Wilson	2,025	1,015	600.00

W

1922 W501

This "strip card" set, known as W501 in the American Card Catalog, is closely connected to the more popular E121 American Caramel set of 1921 and 1922. Because they were handcut from strips, measurements are relative, with well-cut cards typically about 1-7/8" to 2" by about 3-3/8". The W501 cards are numbered in the upper-right corner and have the notation "G-4-22" in the upper-left corner, apparently indicating the cards were issued in April of 1922.

		NM	E	VG
Complete Set (122):		37,500	19,000	11,500
Common Player:		125.00	65.00	40.00
1	Ed Rounnel (Rommel)	125.00	65.00	40.00
2	Urban Shocker	125.00	65.00	40.00
3	Dixie Davis	125.00	65.00	40.00
4	George Sisler	450.00	225.00	140.00
5	Bob Veach	125.00	65.00	40.00
6	Harry Heilman (Heilmann)	450.00	225.00	140.00
7a	Ira Falgstead (Name incorrect.)	125.00	65.00	40.00
7b	Ira Flagstead (Name correct.)	125.00	65.00	40.00
8	Ty Cobb	4,700	2,350	1,400
9	Oscar Vitt	125.00	65.00	40.00
10	Muddy Ruel	125.00	65.00	40.00
11	Derrill Pratt	125.00	65.00	40.00
12	Ed Gharrity	125.00	65.00	40.00
13	Joe Judge	125.00	65.00	40.00
14	Sam Rice	450.00	225.00	140.00
15	Clyde Milan	125.00	65.00	40.00
16	Joe Sewell	450.00	225.00	140.00
17	Walter Johnson	1,125	575.00	350.00
18	Jack McInnis	125.00	65.00	40.00
19	Tris Speaker	575.00	300.00	160.00
20	Jim Bagby Sr.	125.00	65.00	40.00
21	Stanley Coveleskie (Coveleski)	450.00	225.00	140.00
22	Bill Wambsganss	125.00	65.00	40.00
23	Walter Mails	125.00	65.00	40.00
24	Larry Gardner	125.00	65.00	40.00
25	Aaron Ward	125.00	65.00	40.00
26	Miller Huggins	450.00	225.00	140.00
27	Wally Schang	125.00	65.00	40.00
28	Tom Rogers	125.00	65.00	40.00
29	Carl Mays	150.00	75.00	45.00
30	Everett Scott	125.00	65.00	40.00
31	Robert Shawkey	125.00	65.00	40.00
32	Waite Hoyt	450.00	225.00	140.00
33	Mike McNally	125.00	65.00	40.00
34	Joe Bush	125.00	65.00	40.00
35	Bob Meusel	125.00	65.00	40.00
36	Elmer Miller	125.00	65.00	40.00
37	Dick Kerr	125.00	65.00	40.00
38	Eddie Collins	450.00	225.00	140.00
39	Kid Gleason	125.00	65.00	40.00
40	Johnny Mostil	125.00	65.00	40.00
41	Bib Falk (Bibb)	125.00	65.00	40.00
42	Clarence Hodge	125.00	65.00	40.00
43	Ray Schalk	450.00	225.00	140.00
44	Amos Strunk	125.00	65.00	40.00
45	Eddie Mulligan	125.00	65.00	40.00
46	Earl Sheely	125.00	65.00	40.00
47	Harry Hooper	450.00	225.00	140.00
48	Urban Faber	450.00	225.00	140.00
49	Babe Ruth	7,500	3,750	2,250
50	Ivy B. Wingo	125.00	65.00	40.00
51	Earle Neale	150.00	75.00	45.00
52	Jake Daubert	125.00	65.00	40.00
53	Ed Roush	450.00	225.00	140.00
54	Eppa J. Rixey	450.00	225.00	140.00
55	Elwood Martin	125.00	65.00	40.00
56	Bill Killifer (Killefer)	125.00	65.00	40.00
57	Charles Hollocher	125.00	65.00	40.00
58	Zeb Terry	125.00	65.00	40.00
59	G.C. Alexander	750.00	375.00	225.00
60	Turner Barber	125.00	65.00	40.00
61	John Rawlings	125.00	65.00	40.00
62	Frank Frisch	450.00	225.00	140.00
63	Pat Shea	125.00	65.00	40.00
64	Dave Bancroft	450.00	225.00	140.00
65	Cecil Causey	125.00	65.00	40.00
66	Frank Snyder	125.00	65.00	40.00
67	Heinie Groh	125.00	65.00	40.00
68	Ross Young (Youngs)	450.00	225.00	140.00
69	Fred Toney	125.00	65.00	40.00
70	Arthur Nehf	125.00	65.00	40.00
71	Earl Smith	125.00	65.00	40.00
72	George Kelly	450.00	225.00	140.00
73	John J. McGraw	450.00	225.00	140.00
74	Phil Douglas	125.00	65.00	40.00
75	Bill Ryan	125.00	65.00	40.00
76	Jess Haines	450.00	225.00	140.00
77	Milt Stock	125.00	65.00	40.00
78	William Doak	125.00	65.00	40.00
79	George Toporcer	125.00	65.00	40.00
80	Wilbur Cooper	125.00	65.00	40.00
81	George Whitted	125.00	65.00	40.00
82	Chas. Grimm	125.00	65.00	40.00
83	Rabbit Maranville	450.00	225.00	140.00
84	Babe Adams	125.00	65.00	40.00
85	Carson Bigbee	125.00	65.00	40.00
86	Max Carey	450.00	225.00	140.00
87	Whitey Glazner	125.00	65.00	40.00
88	George Gibson	125.00	65.00	40.00
89	Bill Southworth	125.00	65.00	40.00

		NM	E	VG
90	Hank Gowdy	125.00	65.00	40.00
91	Walter Holke	125.00	65.00	40.00
92	Joe Oeschger	125.00	65.00	40.00
93	Pete Kilduff	125.00	65.00	40.00
94	Hy Myers	125.00	65.00	40.00
95	Otto Miller	125.00	65.00	40.00
96	Wilbert Robinson	450.00	225.00	140.00
97	Zach Wheat	450.00	225.00	140.00
98	Walter Ruether	125.00	65.00	40.00
99	Curtis Walker	125.00	65.00	40.00
100	Fred Williams	125.00	65.00	40.00
101	Dave Danforth	125.00	65.00	40.00
102	Ed Rounnel (Rommel)	125.00	65.00	40.00
103	Carl Mays	150.00	75.00	45.00
104	Frank Frisch	450.00	225.00	140.00
105	Lou DeVormer	125.00	65.00	40.00
106	Tom Griffith	125.00	65.00	40.00
107	Harry Harper	125.00	65.00	40.00
108a	John Lavan	125.00	65.00	40.00
108b	John J. McGraw	450.00	225.00	140.00
109	Elmer Smith	125.00	65.00	40.00
110	George Dauss	125.00	65.00	40.00
111	Alexander Gaston	125.00	65.00	40.00
112	John Graney	125.00	65.00	40.00
113	Emil Muesel	125.00	65.00	40.00
114	Rogers Hornsby	625.00	300.00	180.00
115	Leslie Nunamaker	125.00	65.00	40.00
116	Steve O'Neill	125.00	65.00	40.00
117	Max Flack	125.00	65.00	40.00
118	Bill Southworth	125.00	65.00	40.00
119	Arthur Nehf	125.00	65.00	40.00
120	Chick Fewster	125.00	65.00	40.00

1928 W502

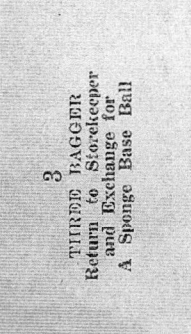

Issued in 1928, the manner of distribution for this set is unknown. Because some of the cards' backs indicate they were redeemable for prizes, they were most likely issued inside of a package of candy or similar product, or perhaps in an opaque envelope. The black-and-white cards measure about 1-3/8" x 2-1/2" and display the player's name at the bottom in capital letters preceded by a number in parentheses. The backs of the cards read either "One Bagger," "Three Bagger" or "Home Run." The listings here show two cards known to exist for numbers 38 and 40, which do not correspond to those numbers in 1931 W502. This raises the possibility there may have been a similar set issued in 1929 and/or 1930. The set carries the American Card Catalog designation W502.

		NM	E	VG
Complete Set (62):		13,500	5,400	2,700
Common Player:		75.00	30.00	15.00
1	Burleigh Grimes	150.00	60.00	30.00
2	Walter Reuther (Ruether)	75.00	30.00	15.00
3	Joe Dugan	75.00	30.00	15.00
4	Red Faber	150.00	60.00	30.00
5	Gabby Hartnett	150.00	60.00	30.00
6	Babe Ruth	4,500	1,800	900.00
7	Bob Meusel	75.00	30.00	15.00
8	Herb Pennock	150.00	60.00	30.00
9	George Burns (Photo is George J., not George H. Burns.)	75.00	30.00	15.00
10	Joe Sewell	150.00	60.00	30.00
11	George Uhle	75.00	30.00	15.00
12	Bob O'Farrell	75.00	30.00	15.00
13	Rogers Hornsby	350.00	175.00	105.00
14	"Pie" Traynor	150.00	60.00	30.00
15	Clarence Mitchell	75.00	30.00	15.00
16	Eppa Jepha Rixey	150.00	60.00	30.00
17	Carl Mays	90.00	35.00	17.50
18	Adolfo Luque	75.00	30.00	15.00
19	Dave Bancroft	150.00	60.00	30.00
20	George Kelly	150.00	60.00	30.00
21	Earl Combs (Earle)	150.00	60.00	30.00

		NM	E	VG
22	Harry Heilmann	150.00	60.00	30.00
23	Ray W. Schalk	150.00	60.00	30.00
24	Johnny Mostil	75.00	30.00	15.00
25	Hack Wilson (Photo actually Art Wilson.)	150.00	60.00	30.00
26	Lou Gehrig	2,000	1,000	600.00
27	Ty Cobb	2,000	1,000	600.00
28	Tris Speaker	200.00	80.00	40.00
29	Tony Lazzeri	150.00	60.00	30.00
30	Waite Hoyt	150.00	60.00	30.00
31	Sherwood Smith	75.00	30.00	15.00
32	Max Carey	150.00	60.00	30.00
33	Eugene Hargrave	75.00	30.00	15.00
34	Miguel L. Gonzales (Miguel A. Gonzalez)	75.00	30.00	15.00
35	Joe Judge	75.00	30.00	15.00
36	E.C. (Sam) Rice	150.00	60.00	30.00
37	Earl Sheely	75.00	30.00	15.00
38a	Sam Jones	75.00	30.00	15.00
38b	Emory E. Rigney	75.00	30.00	15.00
39	Bib A. Falk (Bibb)	75.00	30.00	15.00
40a	Nick Altrock	75.00	30.00	15.00
40b	Willie Kamm	75.00	30.00	15.00
41	Stanley Harris	150.00	60.00	30.00
42	John J. McGraw	150.00	60.00	30.00
43	Artie Nehf	75.00	30.00	15.00
44	Grover Alexander	250.00	100.00	50.00
45	Paul Waner	150.00	60.00	30.00
46	William H. Terry	150.00	60.00	30.00
47	Glenn Wright	75.00	30.00	15.00
48	Earl Smith	75.00	30.00	15.00
49	Leon (Goose) Goslin	150.00	60.00	30.00
50	Frank Frisch	150.00	60.00	30.00
51	Joe Harris	75.00	30.00	15.00
52	Fred (Cy) Williams	75.00	30.00	15.00
53	Eddie Roush	150.00	60.00	30.00
54	George Sisler	150.00	60.00	30.00
55	Ed Rommel	75.00	30.00	15.00
56	Rogers Peckinpaugh (Roger)	75.00	30.00	15.00
57	Stanley Coveleskie (Coveleski)	150.00	60.00	30.00
58	Lester Bell	75.00	30.00	15.00
59	Dave Bancroft	150.00	60.00	30.00
60	John P. McInnis	75.00	30.00	15.00

16	Jimmy Foxx	300.00	120.00	60.00
17	Nick Altrock	90.00	35.00	17.50
18	Charlie Grimm	90.00	35.00	17.50
19	Bill Terry	150.00	60.00	30.00
20	Clifton Heathcote	90.00	35.00	17.50
21	Burleigh Grimes	150.00	60.00	30.00
22	Red Faber	150.00	60.00	30.00
23	Gabby Hartnett	150.00	60.00	30.00
24	Earl (Earle) Combs	150.00	60.00	30.00
25	Hack Wilson	150.00	60.00	30.00
26	Stanley Harris	150.00	60.00	30.00
27	John J. McGraw	150.00	60.00	30.00
28	Paul Waner	150.00	60.00	30.00
29	Babe Ruth	4,500	1,800	900.00
30	Herb Pennock	150.00	60.00	30.00
31	Joe Sewell	150.00	60.00	30.00
32	Lou Gehrig	2,000	800.00	400.00
33	Tony Lazzeri	150.00	60.00	30.00
34	Waite Hoyt	150.00	60.00	30.00
35	Glenn Wright	90.00	35.00	17.50
36	Leon (Goose) Goslin	150.00	60.00	30.00
37	Frank Frisch	150.00	60.00	30.00
38	George Uhle	90.00	35.00	17.50
39	Bob O'Farrell	90.00	35.00	17.50
40	Rogers Hornsby	200.00	80.00	40.00
41	"Pie" Traynor	150.00	60.00	30.00
42	Clarence Mitchell	90.00	35.00	17.50
43	Sherwood Smith	90.00	35.00	17.50
44	Miguel A. Gonzalez	90.00	35.00	17.50
45	Joe Judge	90.00	35.00	17.50
46	Eppa Rixey	150.00	60.00	30.00
47	Adolfo Luque	90.00	35.00	17.50
48	E.C. (Sam) Rice	150.00	60.00	30.00
49	Earl Sheely	90.00	35.00	17.50
50	Sam Jones	90.00	35.00	17.50
51	Bib A. Falk	90.00	35.00	17.50
52	Willie Kamm	90.00	35.00	17.50
53	Roger Peckinpaugh	90.00	35.00	17.50
54	Lester Bell	90.00	35.00	17.50
55	L. Waner	150.00	60.00	30.00
56	Eugene Hargrave	90.00	35.00	17.50
57	Harry Heilmann	150.00	60.00	30.00
58	Earl Smith	90.00	35.00	17.50
59	Dave Bancroft	150.00	60.00	30.00
60	George Kelly	150.00	60.00	30.00

20	Carl Mays	375.00	150.00	75.00
21	Frank Frisch	900.00	360.00	180.00
22	Jess Barnes	350.00	140.00	70.00
23	Walter Johnson	1,500	600.00	300.00
24	Claude Jonnard	350.00	140.00	70.00
25	Dave Bancroft	900.00	360.00	180.00
26	Johnny Rawlings	350.00	140.00	70.00
27	"Pep" Young	350.00	140.00	70.00
28	Earl Smith	350.00	140.00	70.00
29	Willie Kamm	350.00	140.00	70.00
30	Art Fletcher	350.00	140.00	70.00
31	"Kid" Gleason	350.00	140.00	70.00
32	"Babe" Ruth	12,000	4,800	2,400
33	Guy Morton	350.00	140.00	70.00
34	Heinie Groh	350.00	140.00	70.00
35	Leon Cadore	350.00	140.00	70.00
36	Joe Tobin	350.00	140.00	70.00
37	"Rube" Marquard	900.00	360.00	180.00
38	Grover Alexander	1,200	480.00	240.00
39	George Burns	350.00	140.00	70.00
40	Joe Oeschger	350.00	140.00	70.00
41	"Chick" Shorten	350.00	140.00	70.00
42	Roger Hornsby (Rogers)	1,100	440.00	220.00
43	Adolfo Luque	350.00	140.00	70.00
44	Zack Wheat	900.00	360.00	180.00
45	Herb Pruett (Hub)	350.00	140.00	70.00
46	Rabbit Maranville	900.00	360.00	180.00
47	Jimmy Ring	350.00	140.00	70.00
48	Sherrod Smith	350.00	140.00	70.00
49	Lea Meadows (Lee)	350.00	140.00	70.00
50	Aaron Ward	350.00	140.00	70.00
51	Herb Pennock	900.00	360.00	180.00
52	Carlson Bigbee (Carson)	350.00	140.00	70.00
53	Max Carey	900.00	360.00	180.00
54	Charles Robertson	350.00	140.00	70.00
55	Urban Shocker	350.00	140.00	70.00
56	Dutch Ruether	350.00	140.00	70.00
57	Jake Daubert	350.00	140.00	70.00
58	Louis Guisto	350.00	140.00	70.00
59	Ivy Wingo	350.00	140.00	70.00
60	Bill Pertica	350.00	140.00	70.00
61	Luke Sewell	350.00	140.00	70.00
62	Hank Gowdy	350.00	140.00	70.00
63	Jack Scott	350.00	140.00	70.00
64	Stan Coveleskie (Coveleski)	900.00	360.00	180.00

1931 W502

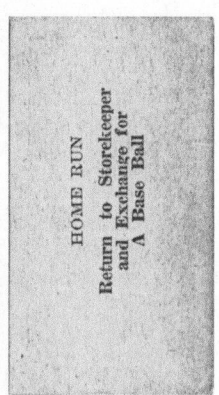

(46) EPPA RIXEY

HOME RUN
Return to Storekeeper
and Exchange for
A Base Ball

Issued in 1931, the manner of distribution for this set is unknown. Because some of the cards' backs indicate they were redeemable for prizes, they were most likely issued inside of a package of candy or similar product, or perhaps in an opaque envelope. The black-and-white cards measure about 1-3/8" x 2-1/2" and display the player's name at the bottom in capital letters preceded by a number in parentheses. The backs of the cards read either "One Bagger," "Three Bagger" or "Home Run." The set carries the American Card Catalog designation W502.

		NM	E	VG
Complete Set (60):		12,500	5,500	2,750
Common Player:		90.00	35.00	17.50
1	Muddy Ruel	90.00	35.00	17.50
2	John Grabowski	90.00	35.00	17.50
3	Mickey Cochrane	150.00	60.00	30.00
4	Bill Cissell	90.00	35.00	17.50
5	Carl Reynolds	90.00	35.00	17.50
6	Luke Sewell	90.00	35.00	17.50
7	Ted Lyons	150.00	60.00	30.00
8	Harvey Walker	90.00	35.00	17.50
9	Gerald Walker	90.00	35.00	17.50
10	Sam Byrd	90.00	35.00	17.50
11	Joe Vosmik	90.00	35.00	17.50
12	Dan MacFayden	90.00	35.00	17.50
13	William Dickey	150.00	60.00	30.00
14	Robert Grove	250.00	100.00	50.00
15	Al Simmons	150.00	60.00	30.00

1922 W503

Issued circa 1923, this 64-card set of blank-backed cards, measuring 1-3/4" x 2-3/4", feature black and white player photos surrounded by a white border. The player's name and team appear on the card, along with a card number in either the left or right bottom corner. There is no indication of the set's producer, although it is believed the cards were issued with candy or gum. The set carries a W503 American Card Catalog designation.

		NM	E	VG
Complete Set (64):		40,000	16,000	8,000
Common Player:		350.00	140.00	70.00
1	Joe Bush	350.00	140.00	70.00
2	Wally Schang	350.00	140.00	70.00
3	Dave Robertson	350.00	140.00	70.00
4	Wally Pipp	375.00	150.00	75.00
5	Bill Ryan	350.00	140.00	70.00
6	George Kelly	900.00	360.00	180.00
7	Frank Snyder	350.00	140.00	70.00
8	Jimmy O'Connell	350.00	140.00	70.00
9	Bill Cunningham	350.00	140.00	70.00
10	Norman McMillan	350.00	140.00	70.00
11	Waite Hoyt	900.00	360.00	180.00
12	Art Nehf	350.00	140.00	70.00
13	George Sisler	900.00	360.00	180.00
14	Al DeVormer	350.00	140.00	70.00
15	Casey Stengel	900.00	360.00	180.00
16	Ken Williams	350.00	140.00	70.00
17	Joe Dugan	350.00	140.00	70.00
18	"Irish" Meusel	350.00	140.00	70.00
19	Bob Meusel	350.00	140.00	70.00

1926 W511

1. BABE RUTH

Ruth is the only baseball player known in this set of athletic, cinematic and historical subjects. The approximately 1-1/2" x 2-1/2" black-and-white, blue-and-white, or maroon-and-white blank-backed card identifies the player, position and team typographically within the photo and has the card number and name in the bottom border. The card has been seen with numbers 1, 52 and 71, as well as unnumbered.

		NM	E	VG
1	Babe Ruth (Black-and-white.)	1,200	600.00	360.00
52	Babe Ruth (Blue duotone.)	1,200	600.00	360.00
71	Babe Ruth (Blue duotone.)	1,200	600.00	360.00
71	Babe Ruth (Maroon duotone.)	1,200	600.00	360.00
---	Babe Ruth ((Unnumbered, maroon.))	1,500	750.00	450.00

1926-27 W512

One of the many "strip card" sets of the period, the W512 set was initially issued in 1926 and includes 10 baseball players among its 50 cards. Also featured are boxers, golfers, tennis players, aviators, movie stars and other celebrities. The 1-3/8" x 2-1/4" cards feature crude color drawings of the subjects with their names below. A card number appears in the lower-left corner. Baseball players lead off the set and are numbered from 1 to 10. Like most strip cards, they have blank backs. At least four of the baseball player cards have been found in a second type, on which the team name is presented in a typewriter style font on the second line; these changes reflect player stat us as of 1927. Reprints of Ruth, Cobb, Johnson and Speaker are known.

3 "TY" COBB
Ex-Mgr. Detroit A.L.

	NM	E	VG
Common Player:	70.00	35.00	20.00
1 Dave Bancroft	100.00	50.00	30.00
2a Grover Alexander (Cubs)	240.00	120.00	70.00
2b Grover Alexander (Cardinals)	120.00	60.00	35.00
3a "Ty" Cobb	400.00	200.00	125.00
3b "Ty" Cobb (Ex-Mgr. Detroit A.L.)	450.00	225.00	140.00
4a Tris Speaker	120.00	60.00	30.00
4b Tris Speaker (Ex-Mgr. Cleveland A.L.)	120.00	60.00	30.00
5 Glen Wright (Glenn)	125.00	65.00	40.00
6 "Babe" Ruth	450.00	225.00	140.00
7a Everett Scott (Yankees)	100.00	50.00	30.00
7b Everett Scott (White Sox)	125.00	65.00	40.00
8a Frank Frisch (Giants)	100.00	50.00	30.00
8b Frank Frisch (Cardinals)	100.00	50.00	30.00
9a Rogers Hornsby (Cardinals)	120.00	60.00	35.00
9b Rogers Hornsby (Giants)	120.00	60.00	35.00
10 Dazzy Vance	100.00	50.00	30.00

1928 W513

69 Rube Benton
Giants Pitcher
New York National

This "strip card" set, issued in 1928 was actually a continuation of the W512 set issued two years earlier and is numbered starting with number 61 where the W512 set ended. The blank-backed cards measure 1-3/8" x 2-1/4" and display color drawings of the athletes, which include 14 boxers and the 26 baseball players listed here. The cards are numbered in the lower-left corner.

	NM	E	VG
Complete (Baseball) Set (26):	2,000	1,000	600.00
Common Player:	65.00	35.00	20.00
61 Eddie Roush	100.00	50.00	30.00
62 Waite Hoyt	100.00	50.00	30.00
63 "Gink" Hendrick	65.00	35.00	20.00
64 "Jumbo" Elliott	65.00	35.00	20.00
65 John Miljus	65.00	35.00	20.00
66 Jumping Joe Dugan	65.00	35.00	20.00
67 Smiling Bill Terry	100.00	50.00	30.00
68 Herb Pennock	100.00	50.00	30.00
69 Rube Benton	65.00	35.00	20.00
70 Paul Waner	100.00	50.00	30.00
71 Adolfo Luque	65.00	35.00	20.00
72 Burleigh Grimes	100.00	50.00	30.00
73 Lloyd Waner	100.00	50.00	30.00
74 Hack Wilson	100.00	50.00	30.00
75 Hal Carlson	65.00	35.00	20.00
76 L. Grantham	65.00	35.00	20.00
77 Wilcey Moore (Wilcy)	65.00	35.00	20.00

78 Jess Haines	100.00	50.00	30.00
79 Tony Lazzeri	100.00	50.00	30.00
80 Al DeVormer	65.00	35.00	20.00
81 Joe Harris	65.00	35.00	20.00
82 Pie Traynor	100.00	50.00	30.00
83 Mark Koenig	65.00	35.00	20.00
84 Babe Herman	75.00	40.00	25.00
85 George Harper	65.00	35.00	20.00
86 Earl Coombs (Earle Combs)	100.00	50.00	30.00

1920-21 W514

LEFTY WILLIAMS
PITCHER
CHICAGO "WHITE SOX" A. L.

Consisting of 120 cards, the W514 set is the largest of the various "strip card" issues of its era. Issued between 1920-1921, it is also one of the earliest and most widely-collected. The 1-3/8" x 2-1/2" cards feature color drawings of the players and display the card number in the lower-left corner. The player's name, position and team appear in the bottom border of the blank-backed cards. The set holds special interest for baseball historians because it includes seven of the eight Chicago "Black Sox" who were banned from baseball for their alleged role in throwing the 1919 World Series. The most famous of them, "Shoeless" Joe Jackson, makes his only strip card appearance in this set.

	NM	E	VG
Complete Set (124):	27,500	14,000	8,500
Common Player:	100.00	50.00	30.00
1 Ira Flagstead	100.00	50.00	30.00
2 Babe Ruth (HOME RUN KING)	2,400	1,200	750.00
3 Happy Felsch	1,500	750.00	450.00
4 Doc Lavan	100.00	50.00	30.00
5 Phil Douglas	100.00	50.00	30.00
6 Earle Neale	100.00	50.00	30.00
7 Leslie Nunamaker	100.00	50.00	30.00
8 Sam Jones	100.00	50.00	30.00
9 Claude Hendrix	100.00	50.00	30.00
10 Frank Schulte	100.00	50.00	30.00
11 Cactus Cravath	100.00	50.00	30.00
12 Pat Moran	100.00	50.00	30.00
13 Dick Rudolph	100.00	50.00	30.00
14 Arthur Fletcher	100.00	50.00	30.00
15 Joe Jackson	6,250	3,100	1,900
16 Bill Southworth	100.00	50.00	30.00
17 Ad Luque	100.00	50.00	30.00
18 Charlie Deal	100.00	50.00	30.00
19 Al Mamaux	100.00	50.00	30.00
20 Stuffy McInness (McInnis)	100.00	50.00	30.00
21a Rabbit Maranville (Braves)	250.00	125.00	75.00
21b Rabbit Maranville (Pirates)	250.00	125.00	75.00
22 Max Carey	250.00	125.00	75.00
23 Dick Kerr	100.00	50.00	30.00
24 George Burns	100.00	50.00	30.00
25 Eddie Collins	250.00	125.00	75.00
26 Steve O'Neil (O'Neill)	100.00	50.00	30.00
27 Bill Fisher	100.00	50.00	30.00
28 Rube Bressler	100.00	50.00	30.00
29 Bob Shawkey	100.00	50.00	30.00
30 Donie Bush	100.00	50.00	30.00
31 Chick Gandil	900.00	450.00	250.00
32 Ollie Zeider	100.00	50.00	30.00
33 Vean Gregg	100.00	50.00	30.00
34 Miller Huggins	250.00	125.00	75.00
35 Lefty Williams	1,000	500.00	300.00
36 Tub Spencer	100.00	50.00	30.00
37 Lew McCarty	100.00	50.00	30.00
38 Hod Eller	100.00	50.00	30.00
39 Joe Gedeon	100.00	50.00	30.00
40a Dave Bancroft (Quakers)	250.00	125.00	75.00
40b Dave Bancroft (Giants)	250.00	125.00	75.00
41 Clark Griffith	250.00	125.00	75.00
42 Wilbur Cooper	100.00	50.00	30.00

43 Ty Cobb	1,750	900.00	550.00
44 Roger Peckinpaugh	100.00	50.00	30.00
45 Nic Carter (Nick)	100.00	50.00	30.00
46 Heinie Groh	100.00	50.00	30.00
47a Bob Roth (Indians)	100.00	50.00	30.00
47b Bob Roth (Yankees)	100.00	50.00	30.00
48 Frank Davis	100.00	50.00	30.00
49 Leslie Mann	100.00	50.00	30.00
50 Fielder Jones	100.00	50.00	30.00
51 Bill Doak	100.00	50.00	30.00
52 John J. McGraw	250.00	125.00	75.00
53 Charles Hollocher	100.00	50.00	30.00
54 Babe Adams	100.00	50.00	30.00
55 Dode Paskert	100.00	50.00	30.00
56 Roger Hornsby (Rogers)	320.00	160.00	90.00
57 Max Rath	100.00	50.00	30.00
58 Jeff Pfeffer	100.00	50.00	30.00
59 Nick Cullop	100.00	50.00	30.00
60 Ray Schalk	250.00	125.00	75.00
61 Bill Jacobson	100.00	50.00	30.00
62 Nap Lajoie	280.00	140.00	80.00
63 George Gibson	100.00	50.00	30.00
64 Harry Hooper	250.00	125.00	75.00
65 Grover Alexander	375.00	190.00	120.00
66 Ping Bodie	100.00	50.00	30.00
67 Hank Gowdy	100.00	50.00	30.00
68 Jake Daubert	100.00	50.00	30.00
69 Red Faber	250.00	125.00	75.00
70 Ivan Olson	100.00	50.00	30.00
71 Pickles Dilhoefer	100.00	50.00	30.00
72 Christy Mathewson	1,100	550.00	325.00
73 Ira Wingo (Ivy)	100.00	50.00	30.00
74 Fred Merkle	100.00	50.00	30.00
75 Frank Baker	250.00	125.00	75.00
76 Bert Gallia	100.00	50.00	30.00
77 Milton Watson	100.00	50.00	30.00
78 Bert Shotten (Shotton)	100.00	50.00	30.00
79 Sam Rice	250.00	125.00	75.00
80 Dan Greiner	100.00	50.00	30.00
81 Larry Doyle	100.00	50.00	30.00
82 Eddie Cicotte	950.00	475.00	250.00
83 Hugo Bezdek	100.00	50.00	30.00
84 Wally Pipp	120.00	60.00	40.00
85 Eddie Rousch (Roush)	250.00	125.00	75.00
86 Slim Sallee	100.00	50.00	30.00
87 Bill Killifer (Killefer)	100.00	50.00	30.00
88 Bob Veach	100.00	50.00	30.00
89 Jim Burke	100.00	50.00	30.00
90 Everett Scott	100.00	50.00	30.00
91 Buck Weaver	1,400	700.00	420.00
92 George Whitted	100.00	50.00	30.00
93 Ed Konetchy	100.00	50.00	30.00
94 Walter Johnson	750.00	375.00	200.00
95 Sam Crawford	250.00	125.00	75.00
96 Fred Mitchell	100.00	50.00	30.00
97 Ira Thomas	100.00	50.00	30.00
98 Jimmy Ring	100.00	50.00	30.00
99 Wally Shange (Schang)	100.00	50.00	30.00
100 Benny Kauff	100.00	50.00	30.00
101 George Sisler	250.00	125.00	75.00
102 Tris Speaker	320.00	160.00	100.00
103 Carl Mays	120.00	60.00	40.00
104 Buck Herzog	100.00	50.00	30.00
105 Swede Risberg	3,500	1,750	1,100
106a Hugh Jennings (Tigers)	250.00	125.00	75.00
106b Hughie Jennings (Giants)	250.00	125.00	75.00
107 Pep Young	100.00	50.00	30.00
108 Walter Reuther (Ruether)	100.00	50.00	30.00
109 Joe Gharrity (Ed)	100.00	50.00	30.00
110 Zach Wheat	250.00	125.00	75.00
111 Jim Vaughn	100.00	50.00	30.00
112 Kid Gleason	100.00	50.00	30.00
113 Casey Stengel	250.00	125.00	75.00
114 Hal Chase	200.00	100.00	60.00
115 Oscar Stange (Stanage)	100.00	50.00	30.00
116 Larry Shean	100.00	50.00	30.00
117 Steve Pendergast	100.00	50.00	30.00
118 Larry Kopf	100.00	50.00	30.00
119 Charles (George) Whiteman	100.00	50.00	30.00
120 Jess Barnes	100.00	50.00	30.00

1923 W515-1

Cards in the 60-card "strip set" measure about 1-3/8" x 2-1/4" and feature color drawings. Backs are blank. The card number along with the player's name, position and team appear in the bottom border. Most cards also display a "U&U" copyright line, indicating that the photos on which the drawings were based were provided by Underwood & Underwood, a major news photo service of the day. The set has a heavy emphasis on New York players with 39 of the 60 cards depicting members of the Yankees, Dodgers or Giants. Babe Ruth appears on two cards and two other cards picture two players each.

representing International Feature Service/Company. Some cards can be found with part of a line of type at top that reads, "UNIVERSAL BASE BALL MATCHING CARDS."

		NM	E	VG
	Complete Set (60):	8,000	3,200	1,600
	Common Player:	50.00	20.00	10.00
1	Bill Cunningham	50.00	20.00	10.00
2	Al Mamaux	50.00	20.00	10.00
3	"Babe" Ruth	1,600	650.00	325.00
4	Dave Bancroft	100.00	40.00	20.00
5	Ed Rommel	50.00	20.00	10.00
6	"Babe" Adams	50.00	20.00	10.00
7	Clarence Walker	50.00	20.00	10.00
8	Waite Hoyt	100.00	40.00	20.00
9	Bob Shawkey	50.00	20.00	10.00
10	"Ty" Cobb	750.00	300.00	150.00
11	George Sisler	100.00	40.00	20.00
12	Jack Bentley	50.00	20.00	10.00
13	Jim O'Connell	50.00	20.00	10.00
14	Frank Frisch	100.00	40.00	20.00
15	Frank Baker	100.00	40.00	20.00
16	Burleigh Grimes	100.00	40.00	20.00
17	Wally Schang	50.00	20.00	10.00
18	Harry Heilman (Heilmann)	100.00	40.00	20.00
19	Aaron Ward	50.00	20.00	10.00
20	Carl Mays	60.00	24.00	12.00
21	The Meusel Bros.(Bob Meusel, Irish Meusel)	60.00	24.00	12.00
22	Arthur Nehf	50.00	20.00	10.00
23	Lee Meadows	50.00	20.00	10.00
24	"Casey" Stengel	100.00	40.00	20.00
25	Jack Scott	50.00	20.00	10.00
26	Kenneth Williams	50.00	20.00	10.00
27	Joe Bush	50.00	20.00	10.00
28	Tris Speaker	150.00	60.00	30.00
29	Ross Young (Youngs)	100.00	40.00	20.00
30	Joe Dugan	50.00	20.00	10.00
31	The Barnes Bros.(Jesse Barnes, Virgil Barnes)	60.00	24.00	12.00
32	George Kelly	100.00	40.00	20.00
33	Hugh McQuillen (McQuillan)	50.00	20.00	10.00
34	Hugh Jennings	100.00	40.00	20.00
35	Tom Griffith	50.00	20.00	10.00
36	Miller Huggins	100.00	40.00	20.00
37	"Whitey" Witt	50.00	20.00	10.00
38	Walter Johnson	400.00	160.00	80.00
39	"Wally" Pipp	50.00	20.00	10.00
40	"Dutch" Reuther (Ruether)	50.00	20.00	10.00
41	Jim Johnston	50.00	20.00	10.00
42	Willie Kamm	50.00	20.00	10.00
43	Sam Jones	50.00	20.00	10.00
44	Frank Snyder	50.00	20.00	10.00
45	John McGraw	100.00	40.00	20.00
46	Everett Scott	50.00	20.00	10.00
47	"Babe" Ruth	1,400	650.00	325.00
48	Urban Shocker	50.00	20.00	10.00
49	Grover Alexander	150.00	60.00	30.00
50	"Rabbit" Maranville	100.00	40.00	20.00
51	Ray Schalk	100.00	40.00	20.00
52	"Heinie" Groh	50.00	20.00	10.00
53	Wilbert Robinson	100.00	40.00	20.00
54	George Burns	50.00	20.00	10.00
55	Rogers Hornsby	150.00	60.00	30.00
56	Zack Wheat	100.00	40.00	20.00
57	Eddie Roush	100.00	40.00	20.00
58	Eddie Collins	100.00	40.00	20.00
59	Charlie Hollocher	50.00	20.00	10.00
60	Red Faber	100.00	40.00	20.00

1923 W515-2

A near duplicate of the W515-1 set in every respect except size, the W515-2 strip cards are larger in format, at about 1-1/2" x 2-1/2". Placement of the U&U copyright also differs between some players' cards in each set. Cards may be found with letters in the top border from the title, "THE LITTLE WONDER PICTURE SERIES."

		NM	E	VG
	Complete Set (60):	8,000	3,200	1,600
	Common Player:	50.00	25.00	15.00
1	Bill Cunningham	50.00	25.00	15.00
2	Al Mamaux	50.00	25.00	15.00
3	"Babe" Ruth	1,600	800.00	480.00
4	Dave Bancroft	100.00	50.00	30.00
5	Ed Rommel	50.00	25.00	15.00
6	"Babe" Adams	50.00	25.00	15.00
7	Clarence Walker	50.00	25.00	15.00
8	Waite Hoyt	100.00	50.00	30.00
9	Bob Shawkey	50.00	25.00	15.00
10	"Ty" Cobb	750.00	375.00	225.00
11	George Sisler	100.00	50.00	30.00
12	Jack Bentley	50.00	25.00	15.00
13	Jim O'Connell	50.00	25.00	15.00
14	Frank Frisch	100.00	50.00	30.00
15	Frank Baker	100.00	50.00	30.00
16	Burleigh Grimes	100.00	50.00	30.00
17	Wally Schang	50.00	25.00	15.00
18	Harry Heilman (Heilmann)	100.00	50.00	30.00
19	Aaron Ward	50.00	25.00	15.00
20	Carl Mays	60.00	30.00	18.00
21	The Meusel Bros.(Bob Meusel, Irish Meusel)	60.00	30.00	18.00
22	Arthur Nehf	50.00	25.00	15.00
23	Lee Meadows	50.00	25.00	15.00
24	"Casey" Stengel	100.00	50.00	30.00
25	Jack Scott	50.00	25.00	15.00
26	Kenneth Williams	50.00	25.00	15.00
27	Joe Bush	50.00	25.00	15.00
28	Tris Speaker	150.00	75.00	45.00
29	Ross Young (Youngs)	100.00	50.00	30.00
30	Joe Dugan	50.00	25.00	15.00
31	The Barnes Bros.(Jesse Barnes, Virgil Barnes)	60.00	30.00	18.00
32	George Kelly	100.00	50.00	30.00
33	Hugh McQuillen (McQuillan)	50.00	25.00	15.00
34	Hugh Jennings	100.00	50.00	30.00
35	Tom Griffith	50.00	25.00	15.00
36	Miller Huggins	100.00	50.00	30.00
37	"Whitey" Witt	50.00	25.00	15.00
38	Walter Johnson	400.00	200.00	120.00
39	"Wally" Pipp	50.00	25.00	15.00
40	"Dutch" Reuther (Ruether)	50.00	25.00	15.00
41	Jim Johnston	50.00	25.00	15.00
42	Willie Kamm	50.00	25.00	15.00
43	Sam Jones	50.00	25.00	15.00
44	Frank Snyder	50.00	25.00	15.00
45	John McGraw	100.00	50.00	30.00
46	Everett Scott	50.00	25.00	15.00
47	"Babe" Ruth	1,600	800.00	480.00
48	Urban Shocker	50.00	25.00	15.00
49	Grover Alexander	150.00	75.00	45.00
50	"Rabbit" Maranville	100.00	50.00	30.00
51	Ray Schalk	100.00	50.00	30.00
52	"Heinie" Groh	50.00	25.00	15.00
53	Wilbert Robinson	100.00	50.00	30.00
54	George Burns	50.00	25.00	15.00
55	Rogers Hornsby	150.00	75.00	45.00
56	Zack Wheat	100.00	50.00	30.00
57	Eddie Roush	100.00	50.00	30.00
58	Eddie Collins	100.00	50.00	30.00
59	Charlie Hollocher	50.00	25.00	15.00
60	Red Faber	100.00	50.00	30.00

1920 W516-1

This "strip card" set consists of 30 cards featuring colored drawings - either portraits or full-length action poses. The blank-backed cards measure 1-1/2" x 2-1/2". The player's name, position and team appear beneath the picture in hand-printed style. To the right of the name is the card number. The set can be identified by an "IFS" or "IFC" copyright symbol

		NM	E	VG
	Complete Set (30):	6,500	3,225	1,935
	Common Player:	50.00	25.00	10.00
1	Babe Ruth	4,000	1,250	600.00
2	Heinie Groh	50.00	25.00	10.00
3	Ping Bodie	50.00	25.00	10.00
4	Ray Shalk (Schalk)	100.00	40.00	20.00
5	Tris Speaker	150.00	60.00	30.00
6	Ty Cobb	750.00	300.00	150.00
7	Roger Hornsby (Rogers)	150.00	60.00	30.00
8	Walter Johnson	300.00	120.00	60.00
9	Grover Alexander	150.00	60.00	30.00
10	George Burns	50.00	25.00	10.00
11	Jimmy Ring	50.00	25.00	10.00
12	Jess Barnes	50.00	25.00	10.00
13	Larry Doyle	50.00	25.00	10.00
14	Arty Fletcher	50.00	25.00	10.00
15	Dick Rudolph	50.00	25.00	10.00
16	Benny Kauf (Kauff)	50.00	25.00	10.00
17	Art Nehf	50.00	25.00	10.00
18	Babe Adams	50.00	25.00	10.00
19	Will Cooper	50.00	25.00	10.00
20	R. Peckinpaugh	50.00	25.00	10.00
21	Eddie Cicotte	100.00	40.00	20.00
22	Hank Gowdy	50.00	25.00	10.00
23	Eddie Collins	100.00	40.00	20.00
24	Christy Mathewson	400.00	160.00	80.00
25	Clyde Milan	50.00	25.00	10.00
26	M. Kelley (should be G. Kelly)	100.00	40.00	20.00
27	Ed Hooper (Harry)	100.00	40.00	20.00
28	Pep. Young	50.00	25.00	10.00
29	Eddie Rousch (Roush)	100.00	40.00	20.00
30	Geo. Bancroft (Dave)	100.00	40.00	20.00

1920 W516-1-2

This set is a re-issue of the W516-1-1 set, with several changes: The pictures are reverse images of W516-1-1, and are printed only in black, red and yellow. Well cut, the blank-back cards measure a nominal 1-1/2" x 2-3/8". The cards display a backwards "IFC" copyright symbol.

		NM	E	VG
	Complete Set (30):	5,250	2,000	1,000
	Common Player:	50.00	25.00	10.00
1	Babe Ruth	2,000	1,000	600.00
2	Heinie Groh	50.00	25.00	10.00
3	Ping Bodie	50.00	25.00	10.00
4	Ray Shalk (Schalk)	100.00	40.00	20.00
5	Tris Speaker	150.00	60.00	30.00
6	Ty Cobb	750.00	300.00	150.00
7	Roger Hornsby (Rogers)	150.00	75.00	45.00
8	Walter Johnson	300.00	150.00	90.00
9	Grover Alexander	150.00	60.00	30.00
10	George Burns	50.00	25.00	10.00
11	Jimmy Ring	50.00	25.00	10.00
12	Jess Barnes	50.00	25.00	10.00
13	Larry Doyle	50.00	25.00	10.00
14	Arty Fletcher	50.00	25.00	10.00

		NM	E	VG
15	Dick Rudolph	50.00	25.00	10.00
16	Benny Kauf (Kauff)	50.00	25.00	10.00
17	Art Nehf	50.00	25.00	10.00
18	Babe Adams	50.00	25.00	10.00
19	Will Cooper	50.00	25.00	10.00
20	R. Peckinpaugh	50.00	25.00	10.00
21	Eddie Cicotte	100.00	50.00	30.00
22	Hank Gowdy	50.00	25.00	10.00
23	Eddie Collins	100.00	40.00	20.00
24	Christy Mathewson	400.00	200.00	120.00
25	Clyde Milan	50.00	25.00	10.00
26	M. Kelley (Should be G. Kelly.)	100.00	40.00	20.00
27	Ed Hooper (Harry)	100.00	40.00	20.00
28	Pep. Young	50.00	25.00	10.00
29	Eddie Rousch (Roush)	100.00	40.00	20.00
30	Geo. Bancroft (Dave)	100.00	40.00	20.00

1921 W516-2-1

PING BODIE Outfielder — HEINIE GROH Third Base — BABE RUTH Outfielder

This set is essentially a re-issue of the W516-1 set, with several changes: The pictures are reverse images of W516-1, and are printed o nly in red and blue. Cards have been renumbered and have player identification in typeset serifed style. The blank-backed cards measure about 1-1/2" x 2-3/8". The cards display a backwards "IFC" copyright symbol.

		NM	E	VG
	Complete Set (30):	4,500	1,800	900.00
	Common Player:	50.00	25.00	10.00
1	George Burns	50.00	25.00	10.00
2	Grover Alexander	150.00	60.00	30.00
3	Walter Johnson	250.00	100.00	50.00
4	Roger Hornsby (Rogers)	125.00	50.00	25.00
5	Ty Cobb	750.00	300.00	150.00
6	Tris Speaker	125.00	50.00	25.00
7	Ray Shalk (Schalk)	75.00	30.00	15.00
8	Ping Bodie	50.00	25.00	10.00
9	Heinie Groh	50.00	25.00	10.00
10	Babe Ruth	1,500	600.00	300.00
11	R. Peckinpaugh	50.00	25.00	10.00
12	Will. Cooper	50.00	25.00	10.00
13	Babe Adams	50.00	25.00	10.00
14	Art Nehf	50.00	25.00	10.00
15	Benny Kauf (Kauff)	50.00	25.00	10.00
16	Dick Rudolph	50.00	25.00	10.00
17	Arty. Fletcher	50.00	25.00	10.00
18	Larry Doyle	50.00	25.00	10.00
19	Jess Barnes	50.00	25.00	10.00
20	Jimmy Ring	50.00	25.00	10.00
21	George Bancroft (Dave)	75.00	30.00	15.00
22	Eddie Rousch (Roush)	75.00	30.00	15.00
23	Pep Young	50.00	25.00	10.00
24	Ed Hooper (Harry)	75.00	30.00	15.00
25	M. Kelley (Should be G. Kelly.)	75.00	30.00	15.00
26	Clyde Milan	50.00	25.00	10.00
27	Christy Mathewson	350.00	140.00	70.00
28	Eddie Collins	75.00	30.00	15.00
29	Hank Gowdy	50.00	25.00	10.00
30	Eddie Cicotte	125.00	50.00	25.00

1921 W516-2-2

BABE RUTH YANKS PITCHER.

This set is yet another variation in the W516 "family." In numbering it parallels W516-2-1, though the typography is in the same sans-serif font as W516-1. Like W516-2-1, the player pictures have been reversed. Well cut, the blank-backed cards measure a nominal 1-1/2" x 2-1/4". The cards display a backwards "IFC" copyright symbol in the picture portion.

		NM	E	VG
	Complete Set (30):	5,000	2,500	1,500
	Common Player:	50.00	25.00	10.00
1	George Burns	50.00	25.00	10.00
2	Grover Alexander	150.00	75.00	45.00
3	Walter Johnson	300.00	150.00	90.00
4	Roger Hornsby (Rogers)	125.00	62.00	37.00
5	Ty Cobb	750.00	375.00	225.00
6	Tris Speaker	125.00	62.00	37.00
7	Ray Shalk (Schalk)	75.00	37.50	22.50
8	Ping Bodie	50.00	25.00	10.00
9	Heinie Groh	50.00	25.00	10.00
10	Babe Ruth	2,000	1,000	600.00
11	R. Peckinpaugh	50.00	25.00	10.00
12	Will. Cooper	50.00	25.00	10.00
13	Babe Adams	50.00	25.00	10.00
14	Art Nehf	50.00	25.00	10.00
15	Benny Kauf (Kauff)	50.00	25.00	10.00
16	Dick Rudolph	50.00	25.00	10.00
17	Arty. Fletcher	50.00	25.00	10.00
18	Larry Doyle	50.00	25.00	10.00
19	Jess Barnes	50.00	25.00	10.00
20	Jimmy Ring	50.00	25.00	10.00
21	George Bancroft (Dave)	75.00	37.50	22.50
22	Eddie Rousch (Roush)	75.00	37.50	22.50
23	Pep Young	50.00	25.00	10.00
24	Ed Hooper (Harry)	75.00	37.50	22.50
25	M. Kelley (Should be G. Kelly.)	75.00	37.50	22.50
26	Clyde Milan	50.00	25.00	10.00
27	Christy Mathewson	400.00	200.00	120.00
28	Eddie Collins	75.00	37.50	22.50
29	Hank Gowdy	50.00	25.00	10.00
30	Eddie Cicotte	100.00	50.00	30.00

1921 W516-2-3

JESS BARNES Pitcher 19

This issue shares a checklist with W516-2-1, and is likewise printed only in red and blue, with typography in a serifed typeface. Unlike W516-2-1, however, the images on these cards are not reversed, as can easily be ascertained by looking at the copyright symbol and letters.

		NM	E	VG
	Complete Set (30):	5,000	2,500	1,500
	Common Player:			
1	George Burns	50.00	25.00	10.00
2	Grover Alexander	150.00	75.00	45.00
3	Walter Johnson	300.00	150.00	90.00
4	Roger Hornsby (Rogers)	125.00	62.00	37.00
5	Ty Cobb	750.00	375.00	225.00
6	Tris Speaker	125.00	62.00	37.00
7	Ray Shalk (Schalk)	75.00	30.00	15.00
8	Ping Bodie	50.00	25.00	10.00
9	Heinie Groh	50.00	25.00	10.00
10	Babe Ruth	2,000	1,000	600.00
11	R. Peckinpaugh	50.00	25.00	10.00
12	Will. Cooper	50.00	25.00	10.00
13	Babe Adams	50.00	25.00	10.00
14	Art Nehf	50.00	25.00	10.00
15	Benny Kauf (Kauff)	50.00	25.00	10.00
16	Dick Rudolph	50.00	25.00	10.00
17	Arty. Fletcher	50.00	25.00	10.00
18	Larry Doyle	50.00	25.00	10.00
19	Jess Barnes	50.00	25.00	10.00
20	Jimmy Ring	50.00	25.00	10.00
21	George Bancroft (Dave)	75.00	30.00	15.00
22	Eddie Rousch (Roush)	75.00	30.00	15.00
23	Pep Young	50.00	25.00	10.00
24	Ed Hooper (Harry)	75.00	30.00	15.00
25	M. Kelley (Should be G. Kelly.)	75.00	30.00	15.00

		NM	E	VG
26	Clyde Milan	50.00	25.00	10.00
27	Christy Mathewson	400.00	200.00	120.00
28	Eddie Collins	75.00	30.00	15.00
29	Hank Gowdy	50.00	25.00	10.00
30	Eddie Cicotte	100.00	50.00	30.00

1931 W517

The 54-player W517 set is an issue of 3" x 4" cards generally found in a sepia color, though other colors are known. The cards feature a player photo as well as his name and team. The card number appears in a small circle on the front, while the backs are blank. The set is heavy in stars of the period including two Babe Ruths (#4 and 20). The cards were sold in vertical strips of three cards; some cards are found with baseball plays in a line at top. Complete set prices do not include variations. The set was reprinted in three-card-strip format in 1997, with "W-517" printed in the lower-left corner of the reprints.

		NM	E	VG
	Complete Set (59):	15,000	7,500	4,400
	Common Player:	100.00	50.00	30.00
1	Earl Combs (Earle)	220.00	120.00	70.00
2	Pie Traynor	220.00	120.00	70.00
3	Eddie Rausch (Roush)	220.00	120.00	70.00
4	Babe Ruth (Throwing)	2,000	1,000	600.00
5a	Chalmer Cissell (Chicago)	100.00	50.00	30.00
5b	Chalmer Cissell (Cleveland)	100.00	50.00	30.00
6	Bill Sherdel	100.00	50.00	30.00
7	Bill Shore	100.00	50.00	30.00
8	Geo. Earnshaw	100.00	50.00	30.00
9	Bucky Harris	220.00	120.00	70.00
10	Charlie Klein	200.00	120.00	70.00
11a	Geo. Kelly (Reds)	100.00	50.00	30.00
11b	Geo. Kelly (Brooklyn)	175.00	90.00	50.00
12	Travis Jackson	220.00	120.00	70.00
13	Willie Kamm	100.00	50.00	30.00
14	Harry Heilman (Heilmann)	220.00	120.00	70.00
15	Grover Alexander	350.00	175.00	100.00
16	Frank Frisch	220.00	120.00	70.00
17	Jack Quinn	100.00	50.00	30.00
18	Cy Williams	100.00	50.00	30.00
19	Kiki Cuyler	220.00	120.00	70.00
20	Babe Ruth (Portrait)	2,400	1,200	750.00
21	Jimmie Foxx	475.00	250.00	150.00
22	Jimmy Dykes	100.00	50.00	30.00
23	Bill Terry	220.00	120.00	70.00
24	Freddy Lindstrom	220.00	120.00	70.00
25	Hughey Critz	100.00	50.00	30.00
26	Pete Donahue	100.00	50.00	30.00
27	Tony Lazzeri	220.00	120.00	70.00
28	Heine Manush (Heinie)	220.00	120.00	70.00
29a	Chick Hafey (Cardinals)	220.00	120.00	70.00
29b	Chick Hafey (Cincinnati)	220.00	120.00	70.00
30	Melvin Ott	275.00	140.00	80.00
31	Bing Miller	100.00	50.00	30.00
32	Geo. Haas	100.00	50.00	30.00
33a	Lefty O'Doul (Phillies)	125.00	65.00	40.00
33b	Lefty O'Doul (Brooklyn)	125.00	65.00	40.00
(34)	Paul Waner (No card number.)	220.00	120.00	70.00
34	Paul Waner (W/card number.)	220.00	120.00	70.00
35	Lou Gehrig	1,200	600.00	450.00
36	Dazzy Vance	220.00	120.00	70.00
37	Mickey Cochrane	220.00	120.00	70.00
38	Rogers Hornsby	300.00	150.00	90.00
39	Lefty Grove	260.00	130.00	80.00
40	Al Simmons	220.00	120.00	70.00
41	Rube Walberg	100.00	50.00	30.00
42	Hack Wilson	220.00	120.00	70.00
43	Art Shires	100.00	50.00	30.00
44	Sammy Hale	100.00	50.00	30.00
45	Ted Lyons	220.00	120.00	70.00
46	Joe Sewell	220.00	120.00	70.00
47	Goose Goslin	220.00	120.00	70.00
48	Lou Fonseca (Lew)	100.00	50.00	30.00

49	Bob Muesel (Meusel)	100.00	50.00	30.00
50	Lu Blue	100.00	50.00	30.00
51	Earl Averill	220.00	120.00	70.00
52	Eddy Collins (Eddie)	220.00	120.00	70.00
53	Joe Judge	100.00	50.00	30.00
54	Mickey Cochrane	220.00	120.00	70.00

1931 W517 Mini

Little is known about these smaller-format (1-3/4" x 2-3/4") versions of the W517 strip cards. They are identical in design to the more common 3" x 4" cards, although some, if not all, do not have the card number-in-circle found on regular W517s. It is presumed, though not confirmed, that all 54 of the regular versions can be found in the mini size, as well as several color variations.

PREMIUM: 2-3X

(See W517 for checklist and base card values.)

1920 W519 - Numbered 1

Cards in this 20-card "strip set" measure 1-1/2" x 2-1/2" and feature player drawings set against a brightly colored background. A card number appears in the lower-left corner followed by the player's name, printed in capital letters. The player drawings are all posed portraits, except for Joe Murphy and Ernie Kreuger, who are shown catching. Like all strip cards, the cards were sold in strips and have blank backs. The date of issue may be approximate.

		NM	E	VG
	Complete Set (20):	5,500	2,200	1,100
	Common Player:	100.00	40.00	20.00
1	Guy Morton	100.00	40.00	20.00
2	Rube Marquard	300.00	120.00	60.00
3	Gabby Cravath (Gavvy)	100.00	40.00	20.00
4	Ernie Krueger	100.00	40.00	20.00
5	Babe Ruth	2,400	960.00	480.00
6	George Sisler	300.00	120.00	60.00
7	Rube Benton	100.00	40.00	20.00
8	Jimmie Johnston	100.00	40.00	20.00
9	Wilbur Robinson (Wilbert)	300.00	120.00	60.00
10	Johnny Griffith	100.00	40.00	20.00
11	Frank Baker	300.00	120.00	60.00
12	Bob Veach	100.00	40.00	20.00
13	Jesse Barnes	100.00	40.00	20.00
14	Leon Cadore	100.00	40.00	20.00
15	Ray Schalk	300.00	120.00	60.00
16	Kid Gleasen (Gleason)	100.00	40.00	20.00
17	Joe Murphy	100.00	40.00	20.00
18	Frank Frisch	300.00	120.00	60.00
19	Eddie Collins	300.00	120.00	60.00
20	Wallie (Wally) Schang	100.00	40.00	20.00

1920 W519 - Numbered 2

A second type of numbered version of W519 exists on which the style of the card numbers differs as does, apparently, the numbering of the players. On Type 1 cards, the card number to the left of the player name is printed in the same heavy sans-serif style as the name. Type 2 cards have the number in a lighter typewriter-style font. While 10 Type 2 cards are currently confirmed to exist, it is expected the other 10 players from W519 were also issued.

		NM	E	VG
12	Joe Murphy	100.00	40.00	20.00
12	Bobby Veach	100.00	40.00	20.00
13	Jesse Barnes	100.00	40.00	20.00
13	Frank Frisch	300.00	120.00	60.00
14	Eddie Collins	300.00	120.00	60.00
16	Guy Morton	100.00	40.00	20.00
17	Rube Marquard	300.00	120.00	60.00
18	Gavvy Cravath	100.00	40.00	20.00
19	Ernie Kreuger	100.00	40.00	20.00
20a	Babe Ruth	2,400	960.00	480.00
20b	Wallie Schange (Wally Schang)	100.00	40.00	20.00

1920 W519 - Unnumbered

Cards in this 10-card set are identical in design and size (1-1/2" x 2-1/2") to the W519 Numbered set, except the player drawings are all set against a blue background and the cards are not numbered. With the lone exception of Eddie Ciotte, all of the subjects in the unnumbered set also appear in the numbered set.

		NM	E	VG
	Complete Set (10):	4,000	2,000	1,200
	Common Player:	100.00	50.00	30.00
(1)	Eddie Cicotte	400.00	200.00	120.00
(2)	Eddie Collins	300.00	150.00	90.00
(3)	Gabby Cravath (Gavvy)	100.00	50.00	30.00
(4)	Frank Frisch	300.00	150.00	90.00
(5)	Kid Gleasen (Gleason)	100.00	50.00	30.00
(6)	Ernie Kreuger	100.00	50.00	30.00
(7)	Rube Marquard	300.00	150.00	90.00
(8)	Guy Morton	100.00	50.00	30.00
(9)	Joe Murphy	100.00	50.00	30.00
(10)	Babe Ruth	2,200	1,100	650.00

1920 W520

Another "strip card" set issued circa 1920, cards in this set measure 1-3/8" x 2-1/4" and are numbered in the lower-right corner. The first nine cards in the set display portrait poses, while the rest are full-length action poses. Some of the poses in this set are the same as those in the W516 issue with the pictures reversed. The player's last name appears in the border beneath the picture. The cards are blank-backed.

		NM	E	VG
	Complete Set (20):	4,000	1,600	800.00
	Common Player:	50.00	20.00	10.00
1	Dave Bancroft	150.00	60.00	30.00
2	Christy Mathewson	400.00	160.00	80.00
3	Larry Doyle	50.00	20.00	10.00
4	Jess Barnes	50.00	20.00	10.00
5	Art Fletcher	50.00	20.00	10.00
6	Wilbur Cooper	50.00	20.00	10.00
7	Mike Gonzales (Gonzalez)	50.00	20.00	10.00
8	Zach Wheat	150.00	60.00	30.00
9	Tris Speaker	200.00	80.00	40.00
10	Benny Kauff	50.00	20.00	10.00
11	Zach Wheat	150.00	60.00	30.00
12	Phil Douglas	50.00	20.00	10.00
13	Babe Ruth	2,000	800.00	400.00
14	Stan Koveleski (Coveleski)	150.00	60.00	30.00
15	Goldie Rapp	50.00	20.00	10.00
16	Pol Perritt	50.00	20.00	10.00
17	Otto Miller	50.00	20.00	10.00
18	George Kelly	150.00	60.00	30.00
19	Mike Gonzales (Gonzalez)	50.00	20.00	10.00
20	Les Nunamaker	50.00	20.00	10.00

1921 W521

This issue is closely related to the W519 Numbered set. In fact, it uses the same color drawings as that set with the pictures reversed, resulting in a mirror-image of the W519 cards. The player poses and the numbering system are identical, as are the various background colors. The W521 cards are blank-backed and were sold in strips.

		NM	E	VG
	Complete Set (20):	3,000	1,200	600.00
	Common Player:	50.00	20.00	10.00
1	Guy Morton	50.00	20.00	10.00
2	Rube Marquard	150.00	60.00	30.00
3	Gabby Cravath (Gavvy)	50.00	20.00	10.00
4	Ernie Krueger	50.00	20.00	10.00
5	Babe Ruth	1,500	600.00	300.00
6	George Sisler	150.00	60.00	30.00
7	Rube Benton	50.00	20.00	10.00
8	Jimmie Johnston	50.00	20.00	10.00
9	Wilbur Robinson (Wilbert)	150.00	60.00	30.00
10	Johnny Griffith	50.00	20.00	10.00
11	Frank Baker	150.00	60.00	30.00
12	Bob Veach	50.00	20.00	10.00
13	Jesse Barnes	50.00	20.00	10.00
14	Leon Cadore	50.00	20.00	10.00
15	Ray Schalk	150.00	60.00	30.00
16	Kid Gleasen (Gleason)	50.00	20.00	10.00
17	Joe Murphy	50.00	20.00	10.00

18	Frank Frisch	150.00	60.00	30.00
19	Eddie Collins	150.00	60.00	30.00
20	Wallie (Wally) Schang	50.00	20.00	10.00

1920 W522

MIKE GONZALES

The 20 cards in this "strip card" set, issued circa 1920, are numbered from 31-50 and use the same players and drawings as the W520 set, issued about the same time. The cards measure 1-3/8" x 2-1/4" and are numbered in the lower left corner followed by the player's name. The cards have blank backs.

		NM	E	VG
Complete Set (20):		5,000	2,000	1,000
Common Player:		75.00	30.00	15.00
31	Benny Kauf (Kauff)	75.00	30.00	15.00
32	Tris Speaker	300.00	120.00	60.00
33	Zach Wheat	225.00	90.00	45.00
34	Mike Gonzales (Gonzalez)	75.00	30.00	15.00
35	Wilbur Cooper	75.00	30.00	15.00
36	Art Fletcher	75.00	30.00	15.00
37	Jess Barnes	75.00	30.00	15.00
38	Larry Doyle	75.00	30.00	15.00
39	Christy Mathewson	900.00	360.00	180.00
40	Dave Bancroft	225.00	90.00	45.00
41	Les Nunamaker	75.00	30.00	15.00
42	Mike Gonzales (Gonzalez)	75.00	30.00	15.00
43	George Kelly	225.00	90.00	45.00
44	Otto Miller	75.00	30.00	15.00
45	Pol Perritt	75.00	30.00	15.00
46	Goldie Rapp	75.00	30.00	15.00
47	Stan Koveleski (Coveleski)	225.00	90.00	45.00
48	Babe Ruth	2,250	900.00	450.00
49	Phil Douglas	75.00	30.00	15.00
50	Zach Wheat	225.00	90.00	45.00

1921 W551

JESS BARNES
"GIANTS" N. L.

Another "strip set" issued circa 1920, these 10 cards measure 1-3/8" x 2-1/4" and feature color drawings. The cards are unnumbered and blank-backed. Cards with typography in blue ink are modern reprints.

		NM	E	VG
Complete Set (10):		2,000	800.00	400.00
Complete Set, Uncut Strip:		2,500	1,000	500.00
Common Player:		50.00	20.00	10.00
(1)	Frank Baker	125.00	50.00	25.00
(2)	Dave Bancroft	125.00	50.00	25.00
(3)	Jess Barnes	50.00	20.00	10.00
(4)	Ty Cobb	400.00	160.00	80.00
(5)	Walter Johnson	175.00	70.00	35.00

(6)	Wally Pipp	50.00	20.00	10.00
(7)	Babe Ruth	1,100	450.00	225.00
(8)	George Sisler	125.00	50.00	25.00
(9)	Tris Speaker	150.00	60.00	30.00
(10)	Casey Stengel	125.00	50.00	25.00

1930 W554

This unidentified set of sepia, or less commonly, black-and-white cards features most of the era's stars in action poses. A facsimile autograph appears on the front of each of the blank-back 5" x 7" pictures. Cards can be found either with and/or without player name and, sometimes, team spelled out in all-capital letters in the bottom white border, with the position in upper- and lower-case between. The unnumbered pictures are checklisted here in alphabetical order. A version of the issue has been seen with advertising for "Big Prize" or Lucky Yo-Yo on the back, printed in red. Another known back stamp is a round black ad for "A. Bonemery / ICE CREAM / CONFECTIONERY."

		NM	E	VG
Complete Set (18):		4,000	2,000	900.00
Common Player:		60.00	25.00	12.50
(1)	Gordon S. (Mickey) Cochrane	100.00	40.00	20.00
(2)	Lewis A. Fonseca	60.00	25.00	12.50
(3)	Jimmy Foxx	200.00	80.00	40.00
(4)	Lou Gehrig	1,400	700.00	350.00
(5)	Burleigh Grimes	100.00	40.00	20.00
(6)	Robert M. Grove	125.00	50.00	25.00
(7)	Waite Hoyt	100.00	40.00	20.00
(8)	Joe Judge	60.00	25.00	12.50
(9)	Charles (Chuck) Klein	100.00	40.00	20.00
(10)	Douglas McWeeny	60.00	25.00	12.50
(11)	Frank O'Doul	75.00	30.00	15.00
(12)	Melvin Ott	125.00	50.00	25.00
(13)	Herbert Pennock	100.00	40.00	20.00
(14)	Eddie Rommel	60.00	25.00	12.50
(15)	Babe Ruth	1,200	480.00	240.00
(16)	Al Simmons	100.00	40.00	20.00
(17)	Lloyd Waner	100.00	40.00	20.00
(18)	Hack Wilson	125.00	50.00	25.00

1909-1910 W555

COBB, DETROIT AMER.

Designated as W555 in the American Card Catalog, the nearly square cards measure only 1-1/8" x 1-3-16" and feature a sepia-colored player photo. Sixty-six different cards have been discovered to date, but others may exist. A recent discovery indicates these cards were produced by Jay S. Meyer confectioners of Philly. The sets appear to be related to a series of contemporary candy cards (E93, E94, E97, and E98) because, with only two exceptions, the players and poses are the same. Recent discoveries also indicate the cards were issued four per box of Base Ball Snap Shots candy.

		NM	E	VG
Complete Set (67):		25,000	10,000	5,000
Common Player:		125.00	50.00	25.00
(1)	Red Ames	125.00	50.00	25.00
(2)	Jimmy Austin	125.00	50.00	25.00
(3)	Johnny Bates	125.00	50.00	25.00
(4)	Chief Bender	375.00	150.00	75.00

(5)	Bob Bescher	125.00	50.00	25.00
(6)	Joe Birmingham	125.00	50.00	25.00
(7)	Bill Bradley	125.00	50.00	25.00
(8)	Kitty Bransfield	125.00	50.00	25.00
(9)	Mordecai Brown	375.00	150.00	75.00
(10)	Bobby Byrne	125.00	50.00	25.00
(11)	Frank Chance	375.00	150.00	75.00
(12)	Hal Chase	375.00	150.00	75.00
(13)	Ed Cicotte	375.00	150.00	75.00
(14)	Fred Clarke	375.00	150.00	75.00
(15)	Ty Cobb	4,250	1,800	900.00
(16)	Eddie Collins (Dark uniform.)	375.00	150.00	75.00
(17)	Eddie Collins (Light uniform.)	375.00	150.00	75.00
(18)	Harry Coveleskie (Coveleski)	125.00	50.00	25.00
(19)	Sam Crawford	375.00	150.00	75.00
(20)	Harry Davis	125.00	50.00	25.00
(21)	Jim Delehanty (Delahanty)	125.00	50.00	25.00
(22)	Art Devlin	125.00	50.00	25.00
(23)	Josh Devore	125.00	50.00	25.00
(24)	Wild Bill Donovan	125.00	50.00	25.00
(25)	Red Dooin	125.00	50.00	25.00
(26)	Mickey Doolan	125.00	50.00	25.00
(27)	Bull Durham	125.00	50.00	25.00
(28)	Jimmy Dygert	125.00	50.00	25.00
(29)	Johnny Evers	375.00	150.00	75.00
(30)	Russ Ford	125.00	50.00	25.00
(31)	George Gibson	125.00	50.00	25.00
(32)	Clark Griffith	375.00	150.00	75.00
(33)	Topsy Hartsell (Hartsel)	125.00	50.00	25.00
(34)	Bill Heinchman (Hinchman)	125.00	50.00	25.00
(35)	Ira Hemphill	125.00	50.00	25.00
(36)	Hughie Jennings	375.00	150.00	75.00
(37)	Davy Jones	125.00	50.00	25.00
(38)	Addie Joss	500.00	200.00	100.00
(39)	Wee Willie Keeler	375.00	150.00	75.00
(40)	Red Kleinow	125.00	50.00	25.00
(41)	Nap Lajoie	375.00	150.00	75.00
(42)	Joe Lake	125.00	50.00	25.00
(43)	Tommy Leach	125.00	50.00	25.00
(44)	Harry Lord	125.00	50.00	25.00
(45)	Sherry Magee	125.00	50.00	25.00
(46)	Christy Mathewson	2,000	800.00	400.00
(47)	Amby McConnell	125.00	50.00	25.00
(48)	John McGraw	375.00	150.00	75.00
(49)	Chief Meyers	125.00	50.00	25.00
(50)	Earl Moore	125.00	50.00	25.00
(51)	Mike Mowery	125.00	50.00	25.00
(52)	George Mullin	125.00	50.00	25.00
(53)	Red Murray	125.00	50.00	25.00
(54)	Nichols	125.00	50.00	25.00
(55)	Jim Pastorious (Pastorius)	125.00	50.00	25.00
(56)	Deacon Phillippi (Phillippe)	125.00	50.00	25.00
(57)	Eddie Plank	375.00	150.00	75.00
(58)	Fred Snodgrass	125.00	50.00	25.00
(59)	Harry Steinfeldt	125.00	50.00	25.00
(60)	Joe Tinker	375.00	150.00	75.00
(61)	Hippo Vaughn	125.00	50.00	25.00
(62)	Honus Wagner	2,500	1,000	500.00
(63)	Rube Waddell	375.00	150.00	75.00
(64)	Hooks Wiltse	125.00	50.00	25.00
(65)	Cy Young (Standing, full name on front.)	1,500	600.00	300.00
(66)	Cy Young (Standing, last name on front.)	1,500	600.00	300.00
(67)	Cy Young (Portrait)	1,650	660.00	330.00

1927 W560

AL SIMMONS
Philadelphia Athletics

Although assigned a "W" number by the American Card Catalog, this is not a "strip card" issue in the same sense as most other "W" sets, although W560 cards are frequently found in uncut sheets of 16 cards. Cards measure a nominal

1-3/4" x 2-3/4" and are designed like a deck of playing cards, with the pictures on the various suits. The set includes aviators and other athletes in addition to baseball players. Cards can be found with designs printed in red or black, or less commonly with both and red and black on each card. Some players will also be found with different suit/value combinations.

		NM	E	VG
Complete Set, Sheets (64):		4,500	2,250	1,000
Complete (Baseball) Set (49):		3,000	1,500	900.00
Common Player:		25.00	12.50	7.50
(1)	Vic Aldridge	25.00	12.50	7.50
(2)	Lester Bell	25.00	12.50	7.50
(3)	Larry Benton	25.00	12.50	7.50
(4)	Max Bishop	25.00	12.50	7.50
(5)	Del Bissonette	25.00	12.50	7.50
(6)	Jim Bottomley	45.00	22.50	13.50
(7)	Guy Bush	25.00	12.50	7.50
(8)	W. Clark	25.00	12.50	7.50
(9)	Andy Cohen	25.00	12.50	7.50
(10)	Mickey Cochrane	45.00	22.50	13.50
(11)	Hugh Critz	25.00	12.50	7.50
(12)	Kiki Cuyler	45.00	22.50	13.50
(13)	Taylor Douthit	25.00	12.50	7.50
(14)	Fred Fitzsimmons	25.00	12.50	7.50
(15)	Jim Foxx	110.00	55.00	35.00
(16)	Lou Gehrig	600.00	300.00	180.00
(17)	Goose Goslin	45.00	22.50	13.50
(18)	Sam Gray	25.00	12.50	7.50
(19)	Lefty Grove	60.00	30.00	18.00
(20)	Jesse Haines	45.00	22.50	13.50
(21)	Babe Herman	30.00	15.00	9.00
(22)	Roger Hornsby (Rogers)	60.00	30.00	18.00
(23)	Waite Hoyt	45.00	22.50	13.50
(24)	Henry Johnson	25.00	12.50	7.50
(25)	Walter Johnson	150.00	75.00	45.00
(26)	Willie Kamm	25.00	12.50	7.50
(27)	Remy Kremer	25.00	12.50	7.50
(28)	Fred Lindstrom	45.00	22.50	13.50
(29)	Fred Maguire	25.00	12.50	7.50
(30)	Fred Marberry	25.00	12.50	7.50
(31)	Johnny Mostil	25.00	12.50	7.50
(32)	Buddy Myer	25.00	12.50	7.50
(33)	Herb Pennock	45.00	22.50	13.50
(34)	George Pipgras	25.00	12.50	7.50
(35)	Flint Rhem	25.00	12.50	7.50
(36)	Babe Ruth	700.00	350.00	210.00
(37)	Luke Sewell	25.00	12.50	7.50
(38)	Willie Sherdel	25.00	12.50	7.50
(39)	Al Simmons	45.00	22.50	13.50
(40)	Thomas Thevenow	25.00	12.50	7.50
(41)	Fresco Thompson	25.00	12.50	7.50
(42)	George Uhle	25.00	12.50	7.50
(43)	Dazzy Vance	45.00	22.50	13.50
(44)	Rube Walberg	25.00	12.50	7.50
(45)	Lloyd Waner	45.00	22.50	13.50
(46)	Paul Waner	45.00	22.50	13.50
(47)	Fred "Cy" Williams	25.00	12.50	7.50
(48)	Jim Wilson	25.00	12.50	7.50
(49)	Glen Wright (Glenn)	25.00	12.50	7.50

1928 W565

LOU GEHRIG
N.Y. YANKEES

Similar in concept to W560, the 50 cards comprising this set were printed on two 7" x 10-1/2" sheets of cheap cardboard, one in black-and-white and one in red-and-white, each with navy blue backs. Most of the cards in the issue are of movie stars, with a few boxers, ballplayers and other notables included. While most of the cards depict the person in the center of a playing card format, it is interesting to note that a full deck of cards cannot be made up by cutting the sheets. Individual cards are 1-1/4" x 2-1/8". Only the baseball players are listed here.

	NM	E	VG
Complete Set, Sheets (50):	800.00	400.00	240.00
Common Player:	75.00	37.50	22.50

(1)	Lou Gehrig	300.00	150.00	90.00
(2)	Harry Heilmann	75.00	37.50	22.50
(3)	Tony Lazzeri	75.00	37.50	22.50
(4)	Al Simmons	75.00	37.50	22.50

1923 W572

Jack Quinn
BOSTON A.L.

These cards, designated as W572 by the American Card Catalog, measure 1-5/16" x 2-1/2" and are blank-backed. Fronts feature black-and-white or sepia player photos. The set is closely related to the popular E120 American Caramel set issued in 1922 and, with the exception of Ty Cobb, it uses the same photos. The cards were originally issued as strips of 10, with baseball players and boxers often mixed. They are found on either a white, slick stock or a dark, coarser cardboard. The player's name on the front of the cards appears in script. All cards have on front a copyright symbol and one of several alphabetical combinations indicating the source of the photo. The baseball players from the set are checklisted here in alphabetical order.

		NM	E	VG
Complete (Baseball) Set (121):		22,500	11,225	5,700
Common Player:		125.00	65.00	40.00
(1)	Eddie Ainsmith	125.00	65.00	40.00
(2)	Vic Aldridge	125.00	65.00	40.00
(3)	Grover Alexander	400.00	195.00	120.00
(4)	Dave Bancroft	250.00	120.00	70.00
(5)	Walt Barbare	125.00	65.00	40.00
(6)	Jess Barnes	125.00	65.00	40.00
(7)	John Bassler	125.00	65.00	40.00
(8)	Lu Blue	125.00	65.00	40.00
(9)	Norman Boeckel	125.00	65.00	40.00
(10)	George Burns	125.00	65.00	40.00
(11)	Joe Bush	125.00	65.00	40.00
(12)	Leon Cadore	125.00	65.00	40.00
(13)	Virgil Cheevers (Cheeves)	125.00	65.00	40.00
(14)	Ty Cobb	5,500	2,250	1,000
(15)	Eddie Collins	250.00	120.00	70.00
(16)	John Collins	125.00	65.00	40.00
(17)	Wilbur Cooper	125.00	65.00	40.00
(18)	Stanley Coveleski	250.00	120.00	70.00
(19)	Walton Cruise	125.00	65.00	40.00
(20)	Dave Danforth	125.00	65.00	40.00
(21)	Jake Daubert	125.00	65.00	40.00
(22)	Hank DeBerry	125.00	65.00	40.00
(23)	Lou DeVormer	125.00	65.00	40.00
(24)	Bill Doak	125.00	65.00	40.00
(25)	Pete Donohue	125.00	65.00	40.00
(26)	Pat Duncan	125.00	65.00	40.00
(27)	Jimmy Dykes	125.00	65.00	40.00
(28)	Urban Faber	250.00	120.00	70.00
(29)	Bib Falk (Bibb)	125.00	65.00	40.00
(30)	Frank Frisch	250.00	120.00	70.00
(31)	C. Galloway	125.00	65.00	40.00
(32)	Ed Gharrity	125.00	65.00	40.00
(33)	Chas. Glazner	125.00	65.00	40.00
(34)	Hank Gowdy	125.00	65.00	40.00
(35)	Tom Griffith	125.00	65.00	40.00
(36)	Burleigh Grimes	250.00	120.00	70.00
(37)	Ray Grimes	125.00	65.00	40.00
(38)	Heinie Groh	125.00	65.00	40.00
(39)	Joe Harris	125.00	65.00	40.00
(40)	Stanley Harris	250.00	120.00	70.00
(41)	Joe Hauser	125.00	65.00	40.00
(42)	Harry Heilmann	250.00	120.00	70.00
(43)	Walter Henline	125.00	65.00	40.00
(44)	Chas. Hollocher	125.00	65.00	40.00
(45)	Harry Hooper	250.00	120.00	70.00
(46)	Rogers Hornsby	250.00	120.00	70.00
(47)	Waite Hoyt	250.00	120.00	70.00
(48)	Wilbur Hubbell	125.00	65.00	40.00
(49)	Wm. Jacobson	125.00	65.00	40.00
(50)	Chas. Jamieson	125.00	65.00	40.00
(51)	S. Johnson	125.00	65.00	40.00

(52)	Walter Johnson	750.00	375.00	240.00
(53)	Jimmy Johnston	125.00	65.00	40.00
(54)	Joe Judge	125.00	65.00	40.00
(55)	Geo. Kelly	250.00	120.00	70.00
(56)	Lee King	125.00	65.00	40.00
(57)	Larry Kopff (Kopf)	125.00	65.00	40.00
(58)	Geo. Leverette	125.00	65.00	40.00
(59)	Al Mamaux	125.00	65.00	40.00
(60)	"Rabbit" Maranville	250.00	120.00	70.00
(61)	"Rube" Marquard	250.00	120.00	70.00
(62)	Martin McManus	125.00	65.00	40.00
(63)	Lee Meadows	125.00	65.00	40.00
(64)	Mike Menosky	125.00	65.00	40.00
(65)	Bob Meusel	125.00	65.00	40.00
(66)	Emil Meusel	125.00	65.00	40.00
(67)	Geo. Mogridge	125.00	65.00	40.00
(68)	John Morrison	125.00	65.00	40.00
(69)	Johnny Mostil	125.00	65.00	40.00
(70)	Roliene Naylor	125.00	65.00	40.00
(71)	Art Nehf	125.00	65.00	40.00
(72)	Joe Oeschger	125.00	65.00	40.00
(73)	Bob O'Farrell	125.00	65.00	40.00
(74)	Steve O'Neill	125.00	65.00	40.00
(75)	Frank Parkinson	125.00	65.00	40.00
(76)	Ralph Perkins	125.00	65.00	40.00
(77)	H. Pillette	125.00	65.00	40.00
(78)	Ralph Pinelli	125.00	65.00	40.00
(79)	Wallie Pipp (Wally)	125.00	65.00	40.00
(80)	Ray Powell	125.00	65.00	40.00
(81)	Jack Quinn	125.00	65.00	40.00
(82)	Goldie Rapp	125.00	65.00	40.00
(83)	Walter Reuther (Ruether)	125.00	65.00	40.00
(84)	Sam Rice	250.00	120.00	70.00
(85)	Emory Rigney	125.00	65.00	40.00
(86)	Eppa Rixey	250.00	120.00	70.00
(87)	Ed Rommel	125.00	65.00	40.00
(88)	Eddie Roush	250.00	120.00	70.00
(89)	Babe Ruth	5,250	2,600	1,600
(90)	Ray Schalk	250.00	120.00	70.00
(91)	Wallie Schang (Wally)	125.00	65.00	40.00
(92)	Walter Schmidt	125.00	65.00	40.00
(93)	Joe Schultz	125.00	65.00	40.00
(94)	Hank Severeid	125.00	65.00	40.00
(95)	Joe Sewell	250.00	120.00	70.00
(96)	Bob Shawkey	125.00	65.00	40.00
(97)	Earl Sheely	125.00	65.00	40.00
(98)	Will Sherdel	125.00	65.00	40.00
(99)	Urban Shocker	50.00	25.00	15.00
(100)	George Sisler	250.00	120.00	70.00
(101)	Earl Smith	125.00	65.00	40.00
(102)	Elmer Smith	125.00	65.00	40.00
(103)	Jack Smith	125.00	65.00	40.00
(104)	Bill Southworth	125.00	65.00	40.00
(105)	Tris Speaker	450.00	120.00	75.00
(106)	Arnold Statz	125.00	65.00	40.00
(107)	Milton Stock	125.00	65.00	40.00
(108)	Jim Tierney	125.00	65.00	40.00
(109)	Harold Traynor	250.00	120.00	70.00
(110)	Geo. Uhle	125.00	65.00	40.00
(111)	Bob Veach	125.00	65.00	40.00
(112)	Clarence Walker	125.00	65.00	40.00
(113)	Curtis Walker	125.00	65.00	40.00
(114)	Bill Wambsganss	125.00	65.00	40.00
(115)	Aaron Ward	125.00	65.00	40.00
(116)	Zach Wheat	250.00	120.00	70.00
(117)	Fred Williams	125.00	65.00	40.00
(118)	Ken Williams	125.00	65.00	40.00
(119)	Ivy Wingo	125.00	65.00	40.00
(120)	Joe Wood	175.00	60.00	40.00
(121)	J.T. Zachary	125.00	65.00	40.00

1922 W573

DAVE (BEAUTY) BANCROFT
SHORT STOP, NEW YORK NATIONALS

These cards, identified as W573 in the American Card Catalog, are blank-backed, black-and-white versions of the popular E120 American Caramel set. These "strip cards," were sold in strips of 10 for a penny. The cards measure about 2-1/16" x 3-3/8", but allowances in width must be made because the cards were hand-cut from a horizontal strip. Some cards have been found with the advertising of various firms on back.

	NM	E	VG
Complete Set (240):	30,000	15,000	9,000
Common Player:	100.00	50.00	30.00

		NM	E	VG
(1)	Charles (Babe) Adams	100.00	50.00	30.00
(2)	Eddie Ainsmith	100.00	50.00	30.00
(3)	Vic Aldridge	100.00	50.00	30.00
(4)	Grover C. Alexander	400.00	200.00	120.00
(5)	Jim Bagby Sr.	100.00	50.00	30.00
(6)	Frank (Home Run) Baker	270.00	135.00	80.00
(7)	Dave (Beauty) Bancroft	270.00	80.00	135.00
(8)	Walt Barbare	100.00	50.00	30.00
(9)	Turner Barber	100.00	50.00	30.00
(10)	Jess Barnes	100.00	50.00	30.00
(11)	Clyde Barnhart	100.00	50.00	30.00
(12)	John Bassler	100.00	50.00	30.00
(13)	Will Bayne	100.00	50.00	30.00
(14)	Walter (Huck) Betts	100.00	50.00	30.00
(15)	Carson Bigbee	100.00	50.00	30.00
(16)	Lu Blue	100.00	50.00	30.00
(17)	Norman Boeckel	100.00	50.00	30.00
(18)	Sammy Bohne	100.00	50.00	30.00
(19)	George Burns	100.00	50.00	30.00
(20)	George Burns	100.00	50.00	30.00
(21)	"Bullet Joe" Bush	100.00	50.00	30.00
(22)	Leon Cadore	100.00	50.00	30.00
(23)	Marty Callaghan	100.00	50.00	30.00
(24)	Frank Calloway (Callaway)	100.00	50.00	30.00
(25)	Max Carey	270.00	135.00	80.00
(26)	Jimmy Caveney	100.00	50.00	30.00
(27)	Virgil Cheeves	100.00	50.00	30.00
(28)	Vern Clemons	100.00	50.00	30.00
(29)	Ty Cob (Cobb)	1,800	900.00	550.00
(30)	Bert Cole	100.00	50.00	30.00
(31)	Eddie Collins	270.00	135.00	80.00
(32)	John (Shano) Collins	100.00	50.00	30.00
(33)	T.P. (Pat) Collins	100.00	50.00	30.00
(34)	Wilbur Cooper	100.00	50.00	30.00
(35)	Harry Courtney	100.00	50.00	30.00
(36)	Stanley Coveleskie (Coveleski)	270.00	135.00	80.00
(37)	Elmer Cox	100.00	50.00	30.00
(38)	Sam Crane	100.00	50.00	30.00
(39)	Walton Cruise	100.00	50.00	30.00
(40)	Bill Cunningham	100.00	50.00	30.00
(41)	George Cutshaw	100.00	50.00	30.00
(42)	Dave Danforth	100.00	50.00	30.00
(43)	Jake Daubert	100.00	50.00	30.00
(44)	George Dauss	100.00	50.00	30.00
(45)	Frank (Dixie) Davis	100.00	50.00	30.00
(46)	Hank DeBerry	100.00	50.00	30.00
(47)	Albert Devormer (Lou DeVormer)	100.00	50.00	30.00
(48)	Bill Doak	100.00	50.00	30.00
(49)	Pete Donohue	100.00	50.00	30.00
(50)	"Shufflin" Phil Douglas	100.00	50.00	30.00
(51)	Joe Dugan	100.00	50.00	30.00
(52)	Louis (Pat) Duncan	100.00	50.00	30.00
(53)	Jimmy Dykes	100.00	50.00	30.00
(54)	Howard Ehmke	100.00	50.00	30.00
(55)	Frank Ellerbe	100.00	50.00	30.00
(56)	Urban (Red) Faber	270.00	135.00	80.00
(57)	Bib Falk (Bibb)	100.00	50.00	30.00
(58)	Dana Fillingim	100.00	50.00	30.00
(59)	Max Flack	100.00	50.00	30.00
(60)	Ira Flagstead	100.00	50.00	30.00
(61)	Art Fletcher	100.00	50.00	30.00
(62)	Horace Ford	100.00	50.00	30.00
(63)	Jack Fournier	100.00	50.00	30.00
(64)	Frank Frisch	270.00	135.00	80.00
(65)	Ollie Fuhrman	100.00	50.00	30.00
(66)	Clarance Galloway	100.00	50.00	30.00
(67)	Larry Gardner	100.00	50.00	30.00
(68)	Walter Gerber	100.00	50.00	30.00
(69)	Ed Gharrity	100.00	50.00	30.00
(70)	John Gillespie	100.00	50.00	30.00
(71)	Chas. (Whitey) Glazner	100.00	50.00	30.00
(72)	Johnny Gooch	100.00	50.00	30.00
(73)	Leon Goslin	270.00	135.00	80.00
(74)	Hank Gowdy	100.00	50.00	30.00
(75)	John Graney	100.00	50.00	30.00
(76)	Tom Griffith	100.00	50.00	30.00
(77)	Burleigh Grimes	270.00	135.00	80.00
(78)	Oscar Ray Grimes	100.00	50.00	30.00
(79)	Charlie Grimm	100.00	50.00	30.00
(80)	Heinie Groh	100.00	50.00	30.00
(81)	Jesse Haines	270.00	135.00	80.00
(82)	Earl Hamilton	100.00	50.00	30.00
(83)	Gene (Bubbles) Hargrave	100.00	50.00	30.00
(84)	Bryan Harris (Harriss)	100.00	50.00	30.00
(85)	Joe Harris	100.00	50.00	30.00
(86)	Stanley Harris	270.00	135.00	80.00
(87)	Chas. (Dowdy) Hartnett	270.00	135.00	80.00
(88)	Bob Hasty	100.00	50.00	30.00
(89)	Joe Hauser	100.00	50.00	30.00
(90)	Clif Heathcote	100.00	50.00	30.00
(91)	Harry Heilmann	270.00	135.00	80.00
(92)	Walter (Butch) Henline	100.00	50.00	30.00
(93)	Clarence (Shovel) Hodge	100.00	50.00	30.00
(94)	Walter Holke	100.00	50.00	30.00
(95)	Charles Hollocher	100.00	50.00	30.00
(96)	Harry Hooper	270.00	135.00	80.00
(97)	Rogers Hornsby	340.00	170.00	100.00
(98)	Waite Hoyt	270.00	135.00	80.00
(99)	Wilbur Hubbell (Wilbert)	100.00	50.00	30.00
(100)	Bernard (Bud) Hungling	100.00	50.00	30.00
(101)	Will Jacobson	75.00	37.50	22.50
(102)	Charlie Jamieson	100.00	50.00	30.00
(103)	Ernie Johnson	100.00	50.00	30.00
(104)	Sylvester Johnson	100.00	50.00	30.00
(105)	Walter Johnson	1,000	500.00	300.00
(106)	Jimmy Johnston	100.00	50.00	30.00
(107)	W.R. (Doc) Johnston	100.00	50.00	30.00
(108)	"Deacon" Sam Jones	100.00	50.00	30.00
(109)	Bob Jones	100.00	50.00	30.00
(110)	Percy Jones	100.00	50.00	30.00
(111)	Joe Judge	100.00	50.00	30.00
(112)	Ben Karr	100.00	50.00	30.00
(113)	Johnny Kelleher	100.00	50.00	30.00
(114)	George Kelly	270.00	135.00	80.00
(115)	Lee King	100.00	50.00	30.00
(116)	Wm (Larry) Kopff (Kopf)	100.00	50.00	30.00
(117)	Marty Krug	100.00	50.00	30.00
(118)	Johnny Lavan	100.00	50.00	30.00
(119)	Nemo Leibold	100.00	50.00	30.00
(120)	Roy Leslie	100.00	50.00	30.00
(121)	George Leverette (Leverett)	100.00	50.00	30.00
(122)	Adolfo Luque	100.00	50.00	30.00
(123)	Walter Mails	100.00	50.00	30.00
(124)	Al Mamaux	100.00	50.00	30.00
(125)	"Rabbit" Maranville	270.00	135.00	80.00
(126)	Cliff Markle	100.00	50.00	30.00
(127)	Richard (Rube) Marquard	270.00	135.00	80.00
(128)	Carl Mays	100.00	50.00	30.00
(129)	Hervey McClellan (Harvey)	100.00	50.00	30.00
(130)	Austin McHenry	100.00	50.00	30.00
(131)	"Stuffy" McInnis	100.00	50.00	30.00
(132)	Martin McManus	100.00	50.00	30.00
(133)	Mike McNally	100.00	50.00	30.00
(134)	Hugh McQuillan	100.00	50.00	30.00
(135)	Lee Meadows	100.00	50.00	30.00
(136)	Mike Menosky	100.00	50.00	30.00
(137)	Bob (Dutch) Meusel	100.00	50.00	30.00
(138)	Emil (Irish) Meusel	100.00	50.00	30.00
(139)	Clyde Milan	100.00	50.00	30.00
(140)	Edmund (Bing) Miller	100.00	50.00	30.00
(141)	Elmer Miller	100.00	50.00	30.00
(142)	Lawrence (Hack) Miller	100.00	50.00	30.00
(143)	Clarence Mitchell	100.00	50.00	30.00
(144)	George Mogridge	100.00	50.00	30.00
(145)	Roy Moore	100.00	50.00	30.00
(146)	John L. Mokan	100.00	50.00	30.00
(147)	John Morrison	100.00	50.00	30.00
(148)	Johnny Mostil	100.00	50.00	30.00
(149)	Elmer Myers	100.00	50.00	30.00
(150)	Hy Myers	100.00	50.00	30.00
(151)	Roliene Naylor (Roleine)	100.00	50.00	30.00
(152)	Earl "Greasy" Neale	100.00	50.00	30.00
(153)	Art Nehf	100.00	50.00	30.00
(154)	Les Nunamaker	100.00	50.00	30.00
(155)	Joe Oeschger	100.00	50.00	30.00
(156)	Bob O'Farrell	100.00	50.00	30.00
(157)	Ivan Olson	100.00	50.00	30.00
(158)	George O'Neil	100.00	50.00	30.00
(159)	Steve O'Neill	100.00	50.00	30.00
(160)	Frank Parkinson	100.00	50.00	30.00
(161)	Roger Peckinpaugh	100.00	50.00	30.00
(162)	Herb Pennock	270.00	135.00	80.00
(163)	Ralph (Cy) Perkins	100.00	50.00	30.00
(164)	Will Pertica	100.00	50.00	30.00
(165)	Jack Peters	100.00	50.00	30.00
(166)	Tom Phillips	100.00	50.00	30.00
(167)	Val Picinich	100.00	50.00	30.00
(168)	Herman Pillette	100.00	50.00	30.00
(169)	Ralph Pinelli	100.00	50.00	30.00
(170)	Wallie Pipp	100.00	50.00	30.00
(171)	Clark Pittenger (Clarke)	100.00	50.00	30.00
(172)	Raymond Powell	100.00	50.00	30.00
(173)	Derrill Pratt	100.00	50.00	30.00
(174)	Jack Quinn	100.00	50.00	30.00
(175)	Joe (Goldie) Rapp	100.00	50.00	30.00
(176)	John Rawlings	100.00	50.00	30.00
(177)	Walter (Dutch) Reuther (Ruether)	100.00	50.00	30.00
(178)	Sam Rice	270.00	135.00	80.00
(179)	Emory Rigney	100.00	50.00	30.00
(180)	Jimmy Ring	100.00	50.00	30.00
(181)	Eppa Rixey	270.00	135.00	80.00
(182)	Charles Robertson	100.00	50.00	30.00
(183)	Ed Rommel	100.00	50.00	30.00
(184)	Eddie Roush	270.00	135.00	80.00
(185)	Harold (Muddy) Ruel (Herold)	100.00	50.00	30.00
(186)	Babe Ruth	3,700	1,850	1,100
(187)	Ray Schalk	270.00	135.00	80.00
(188)	Wallie Schang	100.00	50.00	30.00
(189)	Ray Schmandt	100.00	50.00	30.00
(190)	Walter Schmidt	100.00	50.00	30.00
(191)	Joe Schultz	100.00	50.00	30.00
(192)	Everett Scott	100.00	50.00	30.00
(193)	Henry Severeid	100.00	50.00	30.00
(194)	Joe Sewell	270.00	135.00	80.00
(195)	Howard Shanks	100.00	50.00	30.00
(196)	Bob Shawkey	100.00	50.00	30.00
(197)	Earl Sheely	100.00	50.00	30.00
(198)	Will Sherdel	100.00	50.00	30.00
(199)	Ralph Shinners	100.00	50.00	30.00
(200)	Urban Shocker	100.00	50.00	30.00
(201)	Charles (Chick) Shorten	100.00	50.00	30.00
(202)	George Sisler	270.00	135.00	80.00
(203)	Earl Smith	100.00	50.00	30.00
(204)	Earl Smith	100.00	50.00	30.00
(205)	Elmer Smith	100.00	50.00	30.00
(206)	Jack Smith	100.00	50.00	30.00
(207)	Sherrod Smith	100.00	50.00	30.00
(208)	Colonel Snover	100.00	50.00	30.00
(209)	Frank Snyder	100.00	50.00	30.00
(210)	Al Sothoron	100.00	50.00	30.00
(211)	Bill Southworth	100.00	50.00	30.00
(212)	Tris Speaker	340.00	170.00	100.00
(213)	Arnold Statz	100.00	50.00	30.00
(214)	Milton Stock	100.00	50.00	30.00
(215)	Amos Strunk	100.00	50.00	30.00
(216)	Jim Tierney	100.00	50.00	30.00
(217)	John Tobin	100.00	50.00	30.00
(218)	Fred Toney	100.00	50.00	30.00
(219)	George Toporcer	100.00	50.00	30.00
(220)	Harold (Pie) Traynor	270.00	135.00	100.00
(221)	George Uhle	100.00	50.00	30.00
(222)	Elam Vangilder	100.00	50.00	30.00
(223)	Bob Veach	100.00	50.00	30.00
(224)	Clarence (Tillie) Walker	100.00	50.00	30.00
(225)	Curtis Walker	100.00	50.00	30.00
(226)	Al Walters	100.00	50.00	30.00
(227)	Bill Wambsganss	100.00	50.00	30.00
(228)	Aaron Ward	100.00	50.00	30.00
(229)	John Watson	100.00	50.00	30.00
(230)	Frank Welch	100.00	50.00	30.00
(231)	Zach Wheat	270.00	135.00	80.00
(232)	Fred (Cy) Williams	100.00	50.00	30.00
(233)	Kenneth Williams	100.00	50.00	30.00
(234)	Ivy Wingo	100.00	50.00	30.00
(235)	Joe Wood	100.00	50.00	30.00
(236)	Lawrence Woodall	100.00	50.00	30.00
(237)	Russell Wrightstone	100.00	50.00	30.00
(238)	Everett Yaryan	100.00	50.00	30.00
(239)	Ross Young (Youngs)	270.00	135.00	80.00
(240)	J.T. Zachary	100.00	50.00	30.00

1933 W574

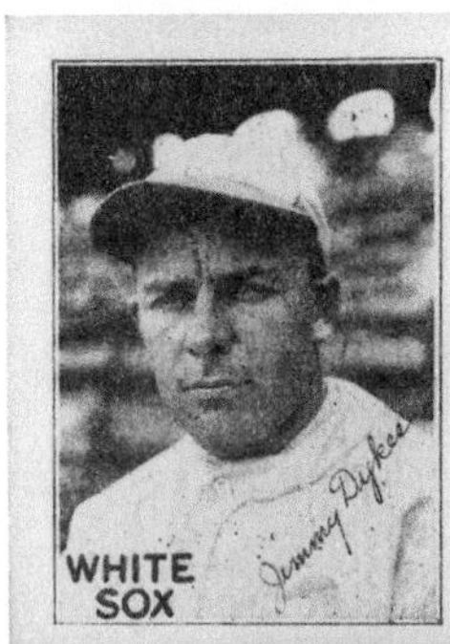

Cards in this set measure an unusual 2-1/4" x 2-7/8". They are unnumbered and are listed here in alphabetical order. The black-and-white photos have a facsimile autograph and team name at bottom.

	NM	E	VG
Complete Set (29):	3,750	1,900	1,100
Common Player:	75.00	40.00	25.00

		NM	E	VG
(1)	Dale Alexander	75.00	40.00	25.00
(2)	Ivy Paul Andrews	75.00	40.00	25.00
(3)	Luke Appling	320.00	160.00	100.00
(4)	Earl Averill	320.00	160.00	100.00
(5)	George Blaeholder	75.00	40.00	25.00
(6)	Irving Burns	75.00	40.00	25.00
(7)	Pat Caraway	75.00	40.00	25.00
(8)	Chalmer Cissell	75.00	40.00	25.00
(9)	Harry Davis	75.00	40.00	25.00

(10) Jimmy Dykes	75.00	40.00	25.00
(11) George Earnshaw	75.00	40.00	25.00
(12) Urban Faber	320.00	160.00	100.00
(13) Lewis Fonseca	75.00	40.00	25.00
(14) Jimmy Foxx	575.00	300.00	175.00
(15) Victor Frasier	75.00	40.00	25.00
(16) Robert Grove	450.00	225.00	150.00
(17) Frank Grube	75.00	40.00	25.00
(18) Irving Hadley	75.00	40.00	25.00
(19) Willie Kamm	75.00	40.00	25.00
(20) Bill Killefer	75.00	40.00	25.00
(21) Ralph Kress	75.00	40.00	25.00
(22) Fred Marberry	75.00	40.00	25.00
(23) Roger Peckinpaugh	75.00	40.00	25.00
(24) Frank Reiber	75.00	40.00	25.00
(25) Carl Reynolds	75.00	40.00	25.00
(26) Al Simmons	320.00	160.00	100.00
(27) Joe Vosmik	75.00	40.00	25.00
(28) Gerald Walker	75.00	40.00	25.00
(29) Whitlow Wyatt	75.00	40.00	25.00

1921-1922 W575-1

The known variations indicate this set was issued over a period of time, likely encompassing more than one calendar year or baseball season. Designated as W575 in the American Card Catalog, these "strip cards" are essentially blank-backed versions of the contemporary American Caramel E121 set, though the checklists do not exactly correspond. Ideally cut cards in W575-1 measure 2" x 3-1/4" and are printed in black-and-white. It is almost impossible to distinguish W575-1 cards from the blank-backed Koester's Bread Yankees and Giants cards issued to commemorate the 1921 "Subway" World Series. This checklist may not be complete. Gaps have been left among the assigned numbers to accommodate future additions.

	NM	E	VG
Common Player:	40.00	20.00	12.00
(1) Chas. "Babe" Adams	40.00	20.00	12.00
(2) G.C. Alexander	350.00	175.00	100.00
(3) Grover Alexander	350.00	175.00	100.00
(4) Jim Bagby Sr.	40.00	20.00	12.00
(5) J. Franklin Baker	175.00	85.00	50.00
(6) Frank Baker	175.00	85.00	50.00
(7) Dave Bancroft (Batting)	175.00	85.00	50.00
(8) Dave Bancroft (Fielding)	175.00	85.00	50.00
(9) Turner Barber	40.00	20.00	12.00
(10) Jesse Barnes	40.00	20.00	12.00
(11) Howard Berry	40.00	20.00	12.00
(12) L. Bigbee (Should be C.)	40.00	20.00	12.00
(13) Ping Bodie	40.00	20.00	12.00
(14) "Ed" Brown	40.00	20.00	12.00
(15) George Burns	40.00	20.00	12.00
(16) Geo. J. Burns	40.00	20.00	12.00
(17) "Bullet Joe" Bush	40.00	20.00	12.00
(18) Owen Bush	40.00	20.00	12.00
(19) Max Carey (Batting)	175.00	85.00	50.00
(20) Max Carey (Hands on hips.)	175.00	85.00	50.00
(21) Ty Cobb	2,000	1,000	600.00
(22) Eddie Collins	175.00	85.00	50.00
(23) "Rip" Collins	40.00	20.00	12.00
(24) Stanley Coveleskie (Coveleski)	175.00	85.00	50.00
(25) Bill Cunningham	40.00	20.00	12.00
(26a) Jake Daubert (1B.)	40.00	20.00	12.00
(26b) Jake Daubert (1st B.)	40.00	20.00	12.00
(28) George Dauss	40.00	20.00	12.00
(29) Dixie Davis	40.00	20.00	12.00
(30) Charles Deal (Dark uniform.)	40.00	20.00	12.00
(31) Charles Deal (Light uniform.)	40.00	20.00	12.00
(32) Lou DeVormer (Photo actually Emil "Irish" Meusel)	40.00	20.00	12.00
(33) William Doak	40.00	20.00	12.00
(34) Bill Donovan (Pitching)	40.00	20.00	12.00
(35) Bill Donovan (Portrait)	40.00	20.00	12.00
(36) Phil Douglas	40.00	20.00	12.00
(37a) Johnny Evers (Mgr.)	175.00	85.00	50.00
(37b) Johnny Evers (Manager)	175.00	85.00	50.00
(39) Urban Faber (Dark uniform.)	175.00	85.00	50.00
(40) Urban Faber (White uniform.)	175.00	85.00	50.00
(42) Bib Falk (Bibb)	40.00	20.00	12.00
(43) Alex Ferguson	40.00	20.00	12.00
(44) Wm. Fewster	40.00	20.00	12.00
(45) Ira Flagstead	40.00	20.00	12.00
(46) Art Fletcher	40.00	20.00	12.00
(47) Eddie Foster	40.00	20.00	12.00
(48) Frank Frisch	175.00	85.00	50.00
(49) W.L. Gardner	40.00	20.00	12.00
(50) Alexander Gaston	40.00	20.00	12.00
(51) E.P. Gharrity	40.00	20.00	12.00
(52) Chas. "Whitey" Glazner	40.00	20.00	12.00
(53) "Kid" Gleason	40.00	20.00	12.00
(54) "Mike" Gonzalez	40.00	20.00	12.00
(55) Hank Gowdy	40.00	20.00	12.00
(56a) John Graney (Util. o.f.)	40.00	20.00	12.00
(56b) John Graney (O.F.)	40.00	20.00	12.00
(57) Tom Griffith	40.00	20.00	12.00
(58) Chas. Grimm	40.00	20.00	12.00
(59a) Heinie Groh (Cincinnati)	40.00	20.00	12.00
(59b) Heinie Groh (New York)	40.00	20.00	12.00
(62) Jess Haines	175.00	85.00	50.00
(63) Harry Harper	40.00	20.00	12.00
(64) "Chicken" Hawks	40.00	20.00	12.00
(65) Harry Heilman (Heilmann) (Holding bat.)	175.00	85.00	50.00
(66) Harry Heilman (Heilmann) (Running)	175.00	85.00	50.00
(67) John Henry	40.00	20.00	12.00
(68) Clarence Hodge	40.00	20.00	12.00
(69) Fred Hoffman	40.00	20.00	12.00
(70a) Walter Holke (1st B., portrait)	40.00	20.00	12.00
(70b) Walter Holke (1B, portrait)	40.00	20.00	12.00
(71) Walter Holke (Throwing)	40.00	20.00	12.00
(72a) Charles Hollacher (Name incorrect.)	40.00	20.00	12.00
(72b) Charles Hollocher (Name correct.)	40.00	20.00	12.00
(73) Harry Hooper	175.00	85.00	50.00
(74a) Rogers Hornsby (2nd B.)	250.00	125.00	75.00
(74b) Rogers Hornsby (O.F.)	250.00	125.00	75.00
(75) Waite Hoyt	175.00	85.00	50.00
(76) Miller Huggins	175.00	85.00	50.00
(78) Wm. C. Jacobson	40.00	20.00	12.00
(79) Hugh Jennings	175.00	85.00	50.00
(80) Walter Johnson (Arms at chest.)	500.00	250.00	150.00
(81) Walter Johnson (Throwing)	500.00	250.00	150.00
(82) James Johnston	40.00	20.00	12.00
(84) Joe Judge (Batting)	40.00	20.00	12.00
(85) Joe Judge (Fielding)	40.00	20.00	12.00
(86a) George Kelly (1st B.)	175.00	85.00	50.00
(86b) George Kelly (1B.)	175.00	85.00	50.00
(88) Dick Kerr	40.00	20.00	12.00
(89) P.J. Kilduff	40.00	20.00	12.00
(90a) Bill Killefer	40.00	20.00	12.00
(90b) Bill Killifer (Killefer)	40.00	20.00	12.00
(92) John Lavan	40.00	20.00	12.00
(93) "Nemo" Leibold	40.00	20.00	12.00
(94) Duffy Lewis	40.00	20.00	12.00
(95) Walter Mails	40.00	20.00	12.00
(96) Al. Mamaux	40.00	20.00	12.00
(97) "Rabbit" Maranville	175.00	85.00	50.00
(98) Elwood Martin	40.00	20.00	12.00
(99a) Carl Mays (Name correct.)	40.00	20.00	12.00
(99b) Carl May (Mays)	40.00	20.00	12.00
(100) John McGraw (Mgr.)	175.00	85.00	50.00
(101) John McGraw (Manager)	175.00	85.00	50.00
(102) Jack McInnis	40.00	20.00	12.00
(103a) M.J. McNally (3B.)	40.00	20.00	12.00
(103b) M.J. McNally (3rd B.)	40.00	20.00	12.00
(104) Lee Meadows	40.00	20.00	12.00
(105) Emil Meusel	40.00	20.00	12.00
(106) R. Meusel	40.00	20.00	12.00
(107) Clyde Milan	40.00	20.00	12.00
(108) Elmer Miller	40.00	20.00	12.00
(109) Otto Miller	40.00	20.00	12.00
(110) John Mitchell (S.S.)	40.00	20.00	12.00
(111) John Mitchell (3rd B.)	40.00	20.00	12.00
(112) Guy Morton	40.00	20.00	12.00
(113) Johnny Mostil	40.00	20.00	12.00
(114) Eddie Mulligan	40.00	20.00	12.00
(115) Eddie Murphy	40.00	20.00	12.00
(116a) "Hy" Myers (C.F./O.F.)	40.00	20.00	12.00
(116b) Hy Myers (O.F.)	40.00	20.00	12.00
(117a) A.E. Neale	75.00	37.50	22.50
(117b) Earl Neale	75.00	37.00	22.00
(119) Arthur Nehf	40.00	20.00	12.00
(120) Joe Oeschger	40.00	20.00	12.00
(122) Chas. O'Leary	40.00	20.00	12.00
(123) Steve O'Neill	40.00	20.00	12.00
(124a) Roger Peckinbaugh (Name incorrect.)	40.00	20.00	12.00
(124b) Roger Peckinpaugh (Name correct.)	40.00	20.00	12.00
(125a) Jeff Pfeffer (Brooklyn)	40.00	20.00	12.00
(125b) Jeff Pfeffer (St. Louis)	40.00	20.00	12.00
(127) William Piercy	40.00	20.00	12.00
(128) Walter Pipp	40.00	20.00	12.00
(129) D.B. Pratt	40.00	20.00	12.00
(130) Jack Quinn	40.00	20.00	12.00
(131a) John Rawlings (2nd B.)	40.00	20.00	12.00
(131b) John Rawlings (2B.)	40.00	20.00	12.00
(133a) E.S. Rice (Name incorrect.)	175.00	85.00	50.00
(133b) E.C. Rice (Name correct.)	175.00	85.00	50.00
(134a) Eppa Rixey	175.00	85.00	50.00
(134b) Eppa Rixey, Jr.	175.00	85.00	50.00
(136) Wilbert Robinson	175.00	85.00	50.00
(137) Tom Rogers	40.00	20.00	12.00
(139) Ed Rounnel (Rommel)	40.00	20.00	12.00
(140) Robert Roth	40.00	20.00	12.00
(142a) Ed Roush (O.F.)	175.00	85.00	50.00
(142b) Ed Roush (C.F.)	175.00	85.00	50.00
(144) "Muddy" Ruel	40.00	20.00	12.00
(145) Walter Ruether	40.00	20.00	12.00
(146a) "Babe" Ruth (R.F.)	3,500	1,750	1,000
(146b) Babe Ruth (L.F.)	3,500	1,750	1,000
(147) "Babe" Ruth (W/man, bird.)	3,500	1,750	1,000
(148a) Bill Ryan	40.00	20.00	12.00
(148b) "Bill" Ryan	40.00	20.00	12.00
(149a) "Slim" Sallee (Ball in hand.)	40.00	20.00	12.00
(149b) "Slim" Sallee (No ball in hand.)	40.00	20.00	12.00
(151) Ray Schalk (Bunting)	175.00	85.00	50.00
(152) Ray Schalk (Catching)	175.00	85.00	50.00
(153a) Walter Schang	40.00	20.00	12.00
(153b) Wally Schang	40.00	20.00	12.00
(154a) Fred Schupp (Name incorrect.)	40.00	20.00	12.00
(154b) Ferd Schupp (Name correct.)	40.00	20.00	12.00
(155a) Everett Scott (Boston)	40.00	20.00	12.00
(155b) Everett Scott (New York)	40.00	20.00	12.00
(157) Hank Severeid	40.00	20.00	12.00
(159) Robert Shawkey	40.00	20.00	12.00
(160a) "Pat" Shea	40.00	20.00	12.00
(160b) Pat Shea	40.00	20.00	12.00
(161) Earl Sheely	40.00	20.00	12.00
(163) Urban Shocker	40.00	20.00	12.00
(165) George Sisler (Batting)	175.00	85.00	50.00
(166) George Sisler (Throwing)	175.00	85.00	50.00
(168) Earl Smith	40.00	20.00	12.00
(169) Elmer Smith	40.00	20.00	12.00
(170) J. Carlisle Smith	40.00	20.00	12.00
(171) Frank Snyder	40.00	20.00	12.00
(172) Bill Southworth	40.00	20.00	12.00
(173a) Tris Speaker (Large projection.)	250.00	125.00	75.00
(173b) Tris Speaker (Small projection.)	250.00	125.00	75.00
(175a) Charles Stengel (Batting)	175.00	85.00	50.00
(175b) Charles Stengel (Portrait)	175.00	85.00	50.00
(177) Milton Stock	40.00	20.00	12.00
(178a) Amos Strunk (C.F.)	40.00	20.00	12.00
(178b) Amos Strunk (O.F.)	40.00	20.00	12.00
(180a) Zeb Terry (Dark uniform, 2nd B.)	40.00	20.00	12.00
(180b) Zeb Terry (Dark uniform, 2B.)	40.00	20.00	12.00
(181) Zeb Terry (White uniform.)	40.00	20.00	12.00
(182) Chester Thomas	40.00	20.00	12.00
(183) Fred Toney (Both feet on ground.)	40.00	20.00	12.00
(184) Fred Toney (One foot in air.)	40.00	20.00	12.00
(185) George Toporcer	40.00	20.00	12.00
(186) George Tyler	40.00	20.00	12.00
(187) Jim Vaughn (Plain uniform.)	40.00	20.00	12.00
(188) Jim Vaughn (Striped uniform.)	40.00	20.00	12.00
(189) Bob Veach (Arm raised.)	40.00	20.00	12.00
(190) Bob Veach (Arms folded.)	40.00	20.00	12.00
(191a) Oscar Vitt (3rd B.)	40.00	20.00	12.00
(191b) Oscar Vitt (3B.)	40.00	20.00	12.00
(192) Curtis Walker	40.00	20.00	12.00
(193) W. Wambsganss	40.00	20.00	12.00
(194) Carl Weilman	40.00	20.00	12.00
(195) Zach Wheat	175.00	85.00	50.00
(196) George Whitted	40.00	20.00	12.00
(197) Fred Williams	40.00	20.00	12.00
(198) Ivy B. Wingo	40.00	20.00	12.00
(199) Lawton Witt	40.00	20.00	12.00
(200) Joe Wood	100.00	50.00	30.00
(202) Pep Young	40.00	20.00	12.00
(203) Ross Young (Youngs)	175.00	85.00	50.00

1922 W575-2

The blank-back, black-and-white cards in this set measure a nominal 2-1/8" x 3-3/8". Because of the design of the cards the set is sometimes called the "autograph on shoulder" series. Some cards have the player's position and team added to the name inscription. The cards were produced by Kromo Gravue Photo Co., Detroit, Mich., and sold as a boxed set.

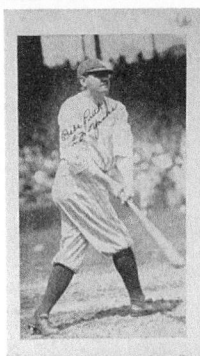

	NM	E	VG
Complete Set (40):	15,000	7,500	4,500
Common Player:	100.00	50.00	30.00
(1) Dave Bancroft	300.00	100.00	60.00
(2) Johnnie Bassler	100.00	50.00	30.00
(3) Joe Bush	100.00	50.00	30.00
(4) Ty Cobb	4,000	1,000	600.00
(5) Eddie Collins	300.00	100.00	60.00
(6) Stan Coveleskie (Coveleski)	300.00	100.00	60.00
(7) Jake Daubert	100.00	50.00	30.00
(8) Joe Dugan	100.00	50.00	30.00
(9) Red Faber	300.00	100.00	60.00
(10) Frank Frisch	300.00	100.00	60.00
(11) Walter H. Gerber	100.00	50.00	30.00
(12) Harry Heilmann	300.00	100.00	60.00
(13) Harry Hooper	300.00	100.00	60.00
(14) Rogers Hornsby	500.00	250.00	90.00
(15) Waite Hoyt	300.00	100.00	60.00
(16) Joe Judge	100.00	50.00	30.00
(17) Geo. Kelly	300.00	100.00	60.00
(18) Rabbit Maranville	300.00	100.00	60.00
(19) Rube Marquard	300.00	100.00	60.00
(20) Guy Morton	100.00	50.00	30.00
(21) Art Nehf	100.00	50.00	30.00
(22) Derrill B. Pratt	100.00	50.00	30.00
(23) Jimmy Ring	100.00	50.00	30.00
(24) Eppa Rixey	300.00	100.00	60.00
(25) Gene Robertson	100.00	50.00	30.00
(26) Ed Rommell (Rommel)	100.00	50.00	30.00
(27) Babe Ruth	3,500	1,750	1,050
(28) Wally Schang	100.00	50.00	30.00
(29) Everett Scott	100.00	50.00	30.00
(30) Henry Severeid	100.00	50.00	30.00
(31) Joe Sewell	300.00	100.00	60.00
(32) Geo. Sisler	300.00	100.00	60.00
(33) Tris Speaker	450.00	150.00	90.00
(34) (Riggs) Stephenson	100.00	50.00	30.00
(35) Zeb Terry	100.00	50.00	30.00
(36) Bobbie Veach	100.00	50.00	30.00
(37) Clarence Walker	100.00	50.00	30.00
(38) Johnnie Walker	100.00	50.00	30.00
(39) Zach Wheat	300.00	100.00	60.00
(40) Kenneth Williams	100.00	50.00	30.00

1925-31 W590

Originally unlisted in the American Card Catalog, this strip-card set was given the number W590 in later editions. It is part of a larger set cataloged as W580 which includes movie stars, boxers and other athletes. These cards measure approximately 1-3/8" x 2-1/2". Fronts have black-and-white player photos with a white border. In the bottom border is the player name, position, city and league or team nickname. Some cards can be found with a "Former" designation before the position. Several variations are known in team designations, indicating the set was probably reissued at least once between 1927-31. Backs are blank. Only the baseball players are listed here, in alphabetical order.

	NM	E	VG
Common Player:	100.00	50.00	30.00
(1a) Grover C. Alexander (Chicago N.L.)	450.00	150.00	90.00
(1b) Grover C. Alexander (House of David)	800.00	300.00	180.00
(2a) Dave Bancroft (Boston N.L.)	200.00	75.00	45.00
(2b) Dave Bancroft (New York N.L.)	200.00	75.00	45.00
(3a) Jess Barnes ("Pitcher" Boston N.L.)	100.00	50.00	30.00
(3b) Jess Barnes ("Former Pitcher" Boston N.L.)	100.00	50.00	30.00
(4) Ray Blades (St. Louis Cardinals)	100.00	50.00	30.00
(5) Pictbred Bluege (Ossie) (Third Baseman)	100.00	50.00	30.00
(6a) George Burns (New York N.L.)	100.00	50.00	30.00
(6b) George Burns (Philadelphia N.L.)	100.00	50.00	30.00
(7a) George Burns (Cleveland A.L. - 1st Baseman)	100.00	50.00	30.00
(7b) George Burns (Cleveland A.L. - Former 1st Baseman)	100.00	50.00	30.00
(8) Max Carey (Pittsburg N.L.)	200.00	75.00	45.00
(9a) Caveney (Jimmy)(Short Stop)	100.00	50.00	30.00
(9b) Caveney (Jimmy)(Former Short Stop)	100.00	50.00	30.00
(10) "Ty" Cobb	1,600	650.00	390.00
(11a) Eddie Collins (Chicago White Sox)	200.00	85.00	50.00
(11b) Eddie Collins (Philadelphia A.L.)	200.00	85.00	50.00
(12) George Dauss (Former Pitcher - Detroit)	100.00	50.00	30.00
(12a) George Dauss (Pitcher - Detroit)	100.00	50.00	30.00
(13) "Red" Faber	200.00	75.00	45.00
(14a) Frankie Frisch (New York N.L.)	200.00	85.00	50.00
(14b) Frank Frisch (St. Louis N.L.)	200.00	85.00	50.00
(15) Lou Gehrig (1st Baseman)	1,400	560.00	335.00
(17a) Hank Gowdy (Catcher)	100.00	50.00	30.00
(17b) Hank Gowdy (Former Catcher)	100.00	50.00	30.00
(18) Sam Gray	100.00	50.00	30.00
(19) Charley Grimm (Chicago N.L.)	100.00	50.00	30.00
(20) "Buckey" Harris (Manager, Washington A.L.)	200.00	75.00	45.00
(21a) Rogers Hornsby (St. Louis N.L.)	250.00	100.00	60.00
(21b) Rogers Hornsby (Boston N.L.)	250.00	100.00	60.00
(22) Travis Jackson (Short Stop, New York N.L.)	200.00	75.00	45.00
(23) Walter Johnson (Pitcher)	900.00	300.00	180.00
(24a) George Kelly (New York N.L.)	200.00	75.00	45.00
(24b) George Kelly (Chicago N.L.)	200.00	75.00	45.00
(25) Fred Lindstrom	200.00	75.00	45.00
(26a) Rabbit Maranville (Chicago N.L.)	200.00	75.00	45.00
(26b) Rabbit Maranville (Boston N.L.)	200.00	75.00	45.00
(27) Bob Meusel (Fielder, New York A.L.)	100.00	50.00	30.00
(28) Jack Quinn	100.00	50.00	30.00
(29) Eppa Rixey (Cincinnati N.L.)	200.00	75.00	45.00
(31) Eddie Rommel	100.00	50.00	30.00
(32) "Babe" Ruth (King of the Bat)	2,750	1,125	675.00
(33) Heinie Sand	100.00	50.00	30.00
(34) Geo. Sissler (Sisler)	200.00	75.00	45.00
(35) Earl Smith	100.00	50.00	30.00
(36a) Tris Speaker (Cleveland A.L.)	300.00	100.00	60.00
(36b) Tris Speaker (Manager, Newark)	300.00	100.00	60.00
(37) Roy Spencer	100.00	50.00	30.00
(38) Milton Stock	100.00	50.00	30.00
(39a) Phil Todt (Boston A.L.)	100.00	50.00	30.00
(39b) Phil Todt (Philadelphia A.L.)	100.00	50.00	30.00
(40) Dazzy Vance	200.00	75.00	45.00
(41) Zach Wheat (Brooklyn N.L.)	200.00	75.00	45.00
(42a) Kenneth Williams (St. Louis A.L.)	100.00	50.00	30.00
(42b) Kenneth Williams (Boston A.L.)	100.00	50.00	30.00
(43a) Ross Young (Youngs) (Right Fielder)	200.00	75.00	45.00
(43b) Ross Young (Youngs) (Former Right Fielder)	200.00	75.00	45.00

1921 W9316

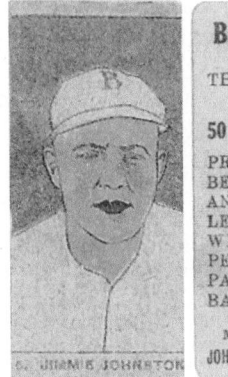

As crude as many of the strip cards of the era were, this issue is the worst. In the same blank-back format and size (about 1-1/2" x 2-1/2") as many contemporary strip cards, the set features 10 of the players from W519/W521. The artwork on these cards is very crudely done, almost child-like. The most striking feature about the pictures is the ruby red lips on the players. Unlisted in the American Card Catalog, this set was given the designation W9316 in John Stirling's Sports Card Catalog.

	NM	E	VG
Complete Set (10):	2,000	800.00	400.00
Common Player:	175.00	70.00	35.00
1 Bob Veach	175.00	70.00	35.00
2 Frank Baker	275.00	110.00	55.00
3 Wilbur (Wilbert) Robinson	275.00	110.00	55.00
4 Johnny Griffith	175.00	70.00	35.00
5 Jimmie Johnston	175.00	70.00	35.00
6 Wallie Schange (Wally Schang)	175.00	70.00	35.00
7 Leon Cadore	175.00	70.00	35.00
8 George Sisler	275.00	110.00	55.00
9 Ray Schalk	275.00	110.00	55.00
10 Jesse Barnes	175.00	70.00	35.00

1910 Hans Wagner Cigars

Circa 1910 the Freeman Cigar Co. apparently envisioned marketing a product named for the Pirates star shortstop. While it appears the cigar was never actually produced, various packaging elements have survived in proof examples. Most pieces are embossed and have a color lithograph which features a portrait of Wagner against a ballgame background. "HANS WAGNER" is in red and gold above. Usually found in the bottom border is "Title & Design Registered by Freeman Cigar Co." Collectors must be aware that various modern fantasy pieces purporting to be of the same genre exist in the market.

	NM	E	VG
Hans Wagner (7-1/4" x 6-1/2" box label)	12,500	6,250	3,750
Hans Wagner (4-1/2" octagonal label)	12,000	6,000	3,600
Hans Wagner (4-1/4" oval label)	12,500	6,250	3,750
Hans Wagner (3" cigar band)	1,600	800.00	480.00
Hans Wagner (Typographic box-side label.)	1,500	750.00	450.00

Hans Wagner
(Typographic box-top
label.) | 7,500 | 3,750 | 2,250

1880s John M. Ward Fan

The specific date of production for this ornate hand fan is unknown. Some examples show on their back an advertisement for "C. Philpot" of Springfield, Maine. The central portion of the fan is a round piece of heavy cardboard, about 7-3/4" in diameter, that features a color lithographic portrait of Ward on a baseball background. Around the picture is a peach-colored ribbon. A wooden handle is attached on back.

	NM	E	VG
John M. Ward	7,800	4,200	2,700

1934 Ward's Sporties Pins

The date of issue can only be approximated for this issue pf 1-1/4" diameter celluloid pin-back buttons. Ward's Sporties was evidently some kind of food product; at the center of each button is a black-and-white or blue-and-white portrait photo of a player with his name above and "Eats" below the picture. Printed around the photo portion in white on a red background is: "Good Sports Enjoy / WARD'S SPORTIES." Ward's bakeries issue several type of baseball cards and collectibles over the years, such as the 1947 Tip-Top bread cards. The checklist is in alphabetical order, and may not yet be complete.

	NM	E	VG
Complete Set (8):	3,000	1,500	900.00
Common Player:	325.00	160.00	100.00
(1) Dizzy Dean	1,000	500.00	300.00
(2) Jimmy Dykes	325.00	160.00	100.00
(3) Jimmie Foxx	1,000	500.00	300.00
(4) Frank Frisch	650.00	325.00	195.00
(5) Charlie Gehringer	650.00	325.00	195.00
(6) Charlie Grimm	325.00	160.00	100.00
(7) Schoolboy Rowe	325.00	160.00	100.00
(8) Jimmie Wilson	325.00	160.00	100.00

1916 Ware's

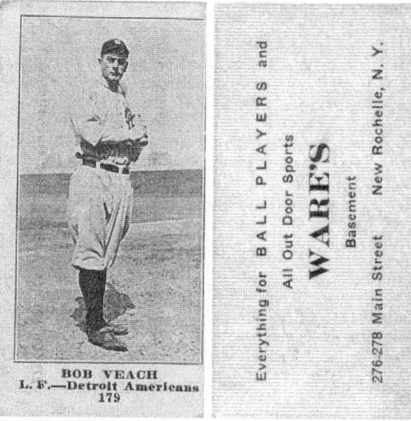

BOB VEACH
L. F.—Detroit Americans
179

Everything for BALL PLAYERS and
All Out Door Sports
WARE'S
Basement
276-278 Main Street   New Rochelle, N.Y.

One of several regional advertisers to use this 200-card set as a promotional medium was this New Rochelle, N.Y., store's sporting goods department. The checklist and relative value information are listed under 1916 M101-4 Blank Backs. Collectors can expect to pay a significant premium for individual cards to enhance a type card or superstar card collection. The American Card Catalog listed these 1-5/8" x 3" black-and-white cards as H801-9.

PREMIUMS:
Common Players: 2-4X
Hall of Famers: 1.5-2.5X

(See 1916 Sporting News M101-4 for checklist and price guide.)

1872 Warren Studio Boston Red Stockings Cabinets

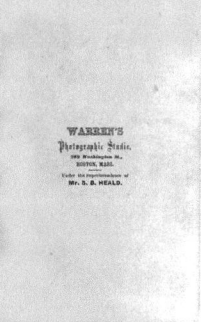

WARREN'S
Photographic Studio,
289 Washington St.,
BOSTON, MASS.
Under the Superintendence of
Mr. S. S. HEALD.

The champions from the premiere season of baseball's first professional league (some wearing their championship pins), are pictured on these cabinet cards. Members of the Boston Red Stockings were photographed in uniform at a local studio. The cards measure about 4-1/4" x 6-1/2" with sepia photos. In the bottom border is the name and address of the studio; information that is repeated on the otherwise blank back. Player identification is not found on the cards but can be deduced by studying contemporary team pictures.

	NM	E	VG
Common Player:	6,500	3,000	2,000
(1) Ross Barnes	9,000	4,000	2,500
(2) Dave Birdsall	6,500	3,000	2,000
(3) Charles Gould	6,500	3,000	2,000
(4) Andy Leonard	6,500	3,000	2,000
(5) Cal McVey	9,000	4,000	2,500
(6) Fraley Rogers	6,500	3,000	2,000
(7) John Ryan	6,500	3,000	2,000
(8) Harry Schafer	6,500	3,000	2,000
(9) Albert Spalding	42,000	9,000	5,400
(10) George Wright	30,000	9,000	5,400
(11) Harry Wright	30,000	9,000	5,400

1872 Warren Studio Boston Red Stockings CDVs

The champions from the premiere season of baseball's first professional league (some wearing their championship pins), are pictured on these cartes de visites depict. Members of the Boston Red Stockings were photographed at a local studio, most of them being pictured in coat-and-tie with only Harry Wright in uniform. The cards measure about 2-1/2" x 4-1/4" with sepia photos bordered in white. In the bottom border is the name and address of the studio; information which is repeated on the otherwise blank back. Player identification is not found on the cards but can be deduced by studying contemporary team pictures.

	NM	E	VG
Common Player:	4,500	3,000	2,000
(1) Ross Barnes	4,500	3,000	2,000
(2) Dave Birdsall	4,500	3,000	2,000
(3) Charlie Gould	4,500	3,000	2,000
(4) Andy Leonard	4,500	3,000	2,000
(5) Cal McVey	4,500	3,000	2,000
(6) Fraley Rogers	4,500	3,000	2,000
(7) John Ryan	4,500	3,000	2,000
(8) Harry Schafer	4,500	3,000	2,000
(9) Albert Spalding	15,000	7,500	3,750
(10) George Wright	10,000	5,000	3,000
(11) Harry Wright (Street clothes.)	10,000	5,000	3,000
(12) Harry Wright (Uniform)	10,000	5,000	3,000

1874 Warren Studio Boston Red Stockings Cabinets

The champions from the National Association Boston Red Stockings were photographed in uniform at a local studio.

The cards measure about 4-1/4" x 6-1/2" with sepia photos. In the bottom border is the name and address of the studio. Player identification is not found on the cards but can be deduced by studying contemporary team pictures.

	NM	E	VG
Common Player:	5,500	2,750	1,650
(1) Ross Barnes	8,250	2,750	1,650
(2) Tommy Beals	6,600	2,750	1,650
(3) George Hall	6,600	2,750	1,650
(4) Andy Leonard	5,500	2,750	1,650
(5) Cal McVey	8,250	2,750	1,650
(6) Harry Schafer	6,600	2,750	1,650

1931 Washington Senators Picture Pack

This set of souvenir pictures offers player photos in a black-and-white, blank-back format of about 6-1/8" x 9-1/2". Each picture has a white border and a facsimile player autograph.

	NM	E	VG
Complete Set (30):	800.00	400.00	240.00
Common Player:	25.00	12.50	7.50
(1) Nick Altrock	35.00	17.50	10.50
(2) Oswald Bluege	25.00	12.50	7.50
(3) Cliff Bolton	25.00	12.50	7.50
(4) Lloyd Brown	25.00	12.50	7.50
(5) Robert Burke	25.00	12.50	7.50
(6) Joe Cronin	50.00	25.00	15.00
(7) Alvin Crowder	25.00	12.50	7.50
(8) E.B. Eynon, Jr. (Secretary-Treasurer)	25.00	12.50	7.50
(9) Charles Fischer	25.00	12.50	7.50
(10) Edward Gharrity	25.00	12.50	7.50
(11) Clark Griffith	45.00	22.00	13.50
(12) Irving Hadley	25.00	12.50	7.50
(13) William Hargrave	25.00	12.50	7.50
(14) David Harris	25.00	12.50	7.50
(15) Jack Hayes	25.00	12.50	7.50
(16) Walter Johnson	125.00	62.00	37.00
(17) Sam Jones	25.00	12.50	7.50
(18) Baxter Jordan	25.00	12.50	7.50
(19) Joe Judge	25.00	12.50	7.50
(20) Joe Kuhel	25.00	12.50	7.50
(21) Henry Manush	50.00	25.00	15.00
(22) Fred Marberry	25.00	12.50	7.50
(23) Mike Martin	25.00	12.50	7.50
(24) Walter Masters	25.00	12.50	7.50
(25) Charles Myer	25.00	12.50	7.50
(26) Harry Rice	25.00	12.50	7.50
(27) Sam Rice	25.00	12.50	7.50
(28) Al Schacht	35.00	17.50	10.50
(29) Roy Spencer	25.00	12.50	7.50
(30) Sam West	25.00	12.50	7.50

1970 Washington Senators Traffic Safety

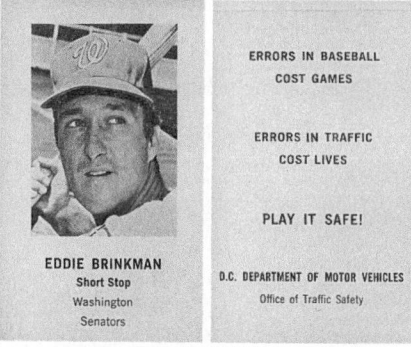

EDDIE BRINKMAN
Short Stop
Washington
Senators

ERRORS IN BASEBALL
COST GAMES

ERRORS IN TRAFFIC
COST LIVES

PLAY IT SAFE!

D.C. DEPARTMENT OF MOTOR VEHICLES
Office of Traffic Safety

Distributed in 1970 by the Washington, D.C. Department of Motor Vehicles, this issue promoting traffic safety was one of the first police sets. Featuring black-and-white player photos, the cards measure 2-1/2" x 3-7/8" and have large borders surrounding the pictures. The player's name and position are below; the team name appears in smaller type at the bottom. The set can be found on either pink card stock, used for the original print run, or on bright yellow stock, used for two subsequent printings. Aurelio Rodriguez, who joined the team after the season began, is known only in yellow; all other players can be found in both yellow and pink. The pink varieties carry a higher value. The backs of the cards offer traffic safety tips.

	NM	E	VG
Complete Set, Pink (10):	150.00	75.00	45.00
Common Player, Pink:	3.50	1.75	1.00
Complete Set, Yellow (11):	25.00	12.50	7.50
Common Player, Yellow:	2.50	1.25	.70
(1a) Dick Bosman (Pink)	3.50	1.75	1.00
(1b) Dick Bosman (Yellow)	2.50	1.25	.70
(2a) Eddie Brinkman (Pink)	3.50	1.75	1.00
(2b) Eddie Brinkman (Yellow)	2.50	1.25	.70
(3a) Paul Casanova (Pink)	3.50	1.75	1.00
(3b) Paul Casanova (Yellow)	2.50	1.25	.70
(4a) Mike Epstein (Pink)	3.50	1.75	1.00
(4b) Mike Epstein (Yellow)	2.50	1.25	.70
(5a) Frank Howard (Pink)	10.00	5.00	3.00
(5b) Frank Howard (Yellow)	7.50	3.75	2.25
(6a) Darold Knowles (Pink)	3.50	1.75	1.00
(6b) Darold Knowles (Yellow)	2.50	1.25	.70
(7a) Lee Maye (Pink)	3.50	1.75	1.00
(7b) Lee Maye (Yellow)	2.50	1.25	.70
(8a) Dave Nelson (Pink)(SP)	125.00	62.00	37.00
(8b) Dave Nelson (Yellow)	2.50	1.25	.70
(9) Aurelio Rodriguez (Yellow)(SP)	5.00	2.50	1.50
(10a) John Roseboro (Pink)	3.50	1.75	1.00
(10b) John Roseboro (Yellow)	2.50	1.25	.70
(11a) Ed Stroud (Pink)	3.50	1.75	1.00
(11b) Ed Stroud (Yellow)	2.50	1.25	.70

1971 Washington Senators Traffic Safety

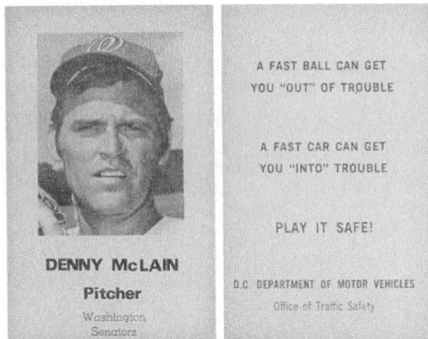

A FAST BALL CAN GET YOU "OUT" OF TROUBLE

A FAST CAR CAN GET YOU "INTO" TROUBLE

PLAY IT SAFE!

DENNY McLAIN
Pitcher
Washington Senators

D.C. DEPARTMENT OF MOTOR VEHICLES
Office of Traffic Safety

The 1971 Senators safety set was again issued by the Washington, D.C., Department of Motor Vehicles and was similar in design and size (2-1/2" x 3-7/8") to the previous year, except that it was printed on a pale yellow stock. The set, which features several new players, contains no scarce cards. The backs contain traffic safety messages.

	NM	E	VG
Complete Set (10):	12.50	6.25	3.75
Uncut Sheet:	12.50	6.25	3.75
Common Player:	1.00	.50	.30
(1) Dick Bosman	1.00	.50	.30
(2) Paul Casanova	1.00	.50	.30
(3) Tim Cullen	1.00	.50	.30
(4) Joe Foy	1.00	.50	.30
(5) Toby Harrah	1.00	.50	.30
(6) Frank Howard	2.50	1.25	.70
(7) Elliott Maddox	1.00	.50	.30
(8) Tom McCraw	1.00	.50	.30
(9) Denny McLain	3.00	1.50	.90
(10) Don Wert	.60	.30	.20

1910 Washington Times

Only American League players have so far been found in this issue by the Washington Times newspaper. The 2-9/16" x 3-9/16" cards have portrait or action photos of the players within a wide border. A white panel at bottom has the player name and team at left and "Washington Times Series" at right. All printing is in dark red. Backs are blank. The manner in which these cards were distributed is unknown, as is the extent of the checklist. The unnumbered cards are checklisted here in alphabetical order.

WALKER Washington
WASHINGTON TIMES SERIES

	NM	E	VG
Common Player:	2,500	1,250	750.00
(1) Ty Cobb	20,000	10,000	6,000
(2) Eddie Collins	7,500	3,750	2,250
(3) Wid Conroy	2,500	1,250	750.00
(4) Sam Crawford	7,500	3,750	2,250
(5) Harry Davis	2,500	1,250	750.00
(6) Bob Groom	2,500	1,250	750.00
(7) Nap Lajoie	7,500	3,750	2,250
(8) George McBride	2,500	1,250	750.00
(9) Clyde Milan	2,500	1,250	750.00
(10) Frank Oberlin	2,500	1,250	750.00
(11) Rube Oldring	2,500	1,250	750.00
(12) Freddie Parent (Freddy)	2,500	1,250	750.00
(13) Doc Reisling	2,500	1,250	750.00
(14) Gabby Street	2,500	1,250	750.00
(15) Lee Tannehill	2,500	1,250	750.00
(16) Bob Unglaub	2,500	1,250	750.00
(17) Dixie Walker	2,500	1,250	750.00
(18) Ed. Walsh	7,500	3,750	2,250
(19) Joe Wood	2,000	1,000	600.00
(20) Cy Young	12,500	6,250	3,750

1951 WBKB "Lucky Fan" Chicago Cubs

This series of black-and-white player glossies appears to have been a promotional giveaway from WBKB radio or television station in conjunction with Ben Bey's "Lucky Fan" club or contest. The 8-1/8" x 10" photos have a facsimile autograph on front. On back is a three-line rubber-stamped "COURTESY OF / BEN BEY "LUCKY FAN" / WBKB - CHICAGO." The checklist is arranged alphabetically.

	NM	E	VG
Complete Set (28):	900.00	450.00	270.00
Common Player:	40.00	20.00	12.00
(1) Frank Baumholtz	40.00	20.00	12.00
(2) Bob Borkowski	40.00	20.00	12.00
(3) Smoky Burgess	50.00	25.00	15.00
(4) Phil Cavarretta	40.00	20.00	12.00
(5) Chuck Connors	100.00	50.00	30.00
(6) Jack Cusick	40.00	20.00	12.00
(7) Bruce Edwards	40.00	20.00	12.00
(8) Dee Fondy	40.00	20.00	12.00
(9) Joe Hatten	40.00	20.00	12.00
(10) Gene Hermanski	40.00	20.00	12.00
(11) Frank Hiller	40.00	20.00	12.00
(12) Ransom Jackson	40.00	20.00	12.00
(13) Hal Jeffcoat	40.00	20.00	12.00
(14) Bob Kelly	40.00	20.00	12.00
(15) Johnny Klippstein	40.00	20.00	12.00
(16) Dutch Leonard	40.00	20.00	12.00
(17) Turk Lown	40.00	20.00	12.00
(18) Cal McLish	40.00	20.00	12.00
(19) Eddie Miksis	40.00	20.00	12.00
(20) Paul Minner	40.00	20.00	12.00
(21) Mickey Owen	40.00	20.00	12.00
(22) Andy Pafko	50.00	25.00	15.00
(23) Bob Ramazotti	40.00	20.00	12.00
(24) Bob Rush	40.00	20.00	12.00
(25) Hank Sauer	40.00	20.00	12.00
(26) Bob Schultz	40.00	20.00	12.00
(27) Bill Serena	40.00	20.00	12.00
(28) Roy Smalley	45.00	22.00	13.50

1911-14 Weber Bakery (D304)

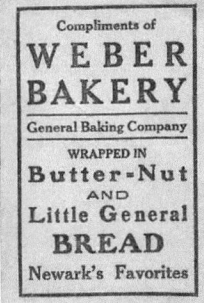

Compliments of
WEBER BAKERY
General Baking Company
WRAPPED IN
Butter-Nut
AND
Little General
BREAD
Newark's Favorites

RUBE MARQUARD, N.Y. NATL.

(See 1911-14 General Baking Co. for checklist and price information.)

1916 Weil Baking Co. (D329)

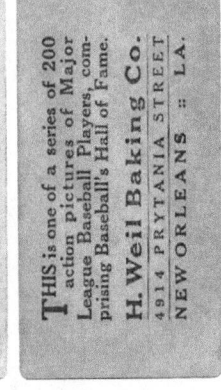

JOE JACKSON
L. F.—Chicago White Sox
87

THIS is one of a series of 200 action pictures of Major League Baseball Players, comprising Baseball's Hall of Fame.

H. Weil Baking Co.
4914 PRYTANIA STREET
NEW ORLEANS :: LA.

One of several issues by the New Orleans bakery, this 1-3/8" x 3" black-and-white set of 200 shares a checklist and relative values with the 1916 M101-4 Blank Backs set. Collectors can expect to pay a premium for a card with the Weil Baking ad on back to add to a type collection or superstar collection. The American Card Catalog lists this issue as D329.

		NM	E	VG
Complete Set (200):		77,000	38,500	23,100
Common Player:		195.00	100.00	50.00
1	Babe Adams	195.00	100.00	50.00
2	Sam Agnew	195.00	100.00	50.00
3	Eddie Ainsmith	195.00	100.00	50.00
4	Grover Alexander	880.00	455.00	230.00
5	Leon Ames	195.00	100.00	50.00
6	Jimmy Archer	195.00	100.00	50.00
7	Jimmy Austin	195.00	100.00	50.00
8	H.D. Baird	195.00	100.00	50.00
9	J. Franklin Baker	715.00	375.00	190.00
10	Dave Bancroft	715.00	375.00	190.00
11	Jack Barry	195.00	100.00	50.00
12	Zinn Beck	195.00	100.00	50.00
13	"Chief" Bender	715.00	375.00	190.00
14	Joe Benz	195.00	100.00	50.00
15	Bob Bescher	195.00	100.00	50.00
16	Al Betzel	195.00	100.00	50.00
17	Mordecai Brown	715.00	375.00	190.00
18	Eddie Burns	195.00	100.00	50.00
19	George Burns	195.00	100.00	50.00
20	Geo. J. Burns	195.00	100.00	50.00
21	Joe Bush	195.00	100.00	50.00
22	"Donie" Bush	195.00	100.00	50.00
23	Art Butler	195.00	100.00	50.00
24	Bobbie Byrne	195.00	100.00	50.00
25	Forrest Cady	195.00	100.00	50.00
26	Jimmy Callahan	195.00	100.00	50.00
27	Ray Caldwell	195.00	100.00	50.00
28	Max Carey	715.00	375.00	190.00
29	George Chalmers	195.00	100.00	50.00
30	Ray Chapman	195.00	100.00	50.00
31	Larry Cheney	195.00	100.00	50.00
32	Eddie Cicotte	1,000	375.00	190.00
33	Tom Clarke	195.00	100.00	50.00
34	Eddie Collins	715.00	375.00	190.00
35	"Shauno" Collins	195.00	100.00	50.00
36	Charles Comiskey	715.00	375.00	190.00
37	Joe Connolly	195.00	100.00	50.00
38	Ty Cobb	5,500	2,860	1,430
39	Harry Coveleskie (Coveleski)	195.00	100.00	50.00

40	Gavvy Cravath	195.00	100.00	50.00
41	Sam Crawford	715.00	375.00	190.00
42	Jean Dale	195.00	100.00	50.00
43	Jake Daubert	195.00	100.00	50.00
44	Charles Deal	195.00	100.00	50.00
45	Al Demaree	195.00	100.00	50.00
46	Josh Devore	195.00	100.00	50.00
47	William Doak	195.00	100.00	50.00
48	Bill Donovan	195.00	100.00	50.00
49	Charles Dooin	195.00	100.00	50.00
50	Mike Doolan	195.00	100.00	50.00
51	Larry Doyle	195.00	100.00	50.00
52	Jean Dubuc	195.00	100.00	50.00
53	Oscar Dugey	195.00	100.00	50.00
54	Johnny Evers	715.00	375.00	190.00
55	Urban Faber	715.00	375.00	190.00
56	"Hap" Felsch	2,000	860.00	430.00
57	Bill Fischer	195.00	100.00	50.00
58	Ray Fisher	195.00	100.00	50.00
59	Max Flack	195.00	100.00	50.00
60	Art Fletcher	195.00	100.00	50.00
61	Eddie Foster	195.00	100.00	50.00
62	Jacques Fournier	195.00	100.00	50.00
63	Del Gainer (Gainor)	195.00	100.00	50.00
64	"Chic" Gandil	715.00	375.00	190.00
65	Larry Gardner	195.00	100.00	50.00
66	Joe Gedeon	195.00	100.00	50.00
67	Gus Getz	195.00	100.00	50.00
68	Geo. Gibson	195.00	100.00	50.00
69	Wilbur Good	195.00	100.00	50.00
70	Hank Gowdy	195.00	100.00	50.00
71	John Graney	195.00	100.00	50.00
72	Clark Griffith	715.00	375.00	190.00
73	Tom Griffith	195.00	100.00	50.00
74	Heinie Groh	195.00	100.00	50.00
75	Earl Hamilton	195.00	100.00	50.00
76	Bob Harmon	195.00	100.00	50.00
77	Roy Hartzell	195.00	100.00	50.00
78	Claude Hendrix	195.00	100.00	50.00
79	Olaf Henriksen	195.00	100.00	50.00
80	John Henry	195.00	100.00	50.00
81	"Buck" Herzog	195.00	100.00	50.00
82	Hugh High	195.00	100.00	50.00
83	Dick Hoblitzell	195.00	100.00	50.00
84	Harry Hooper	715.00	375.00	190.00
85	Ivan Howard	195.00	100.00	50.00
86	Miller Huggins	715.00	375.00	190.00
87	Joe Jackson	20,000	7,150	3,575
88	William James	195.00	100.00	50.00
89	Harold Janvrin	195.00	100.00	50.00
90	Hugh Jennings	715.00	375.00	190.00
91	Walter Johnson	1,760	835.00	470.00
92	Fielder Jones	195.00	100.00	50.00
93	Joe Judge	195.00	100.00	50.00
94	Bennie Kauff	195.00	100.00	50.00
95	Wm. Killefer Jr.	195.00	100.00	50.00
96	Ed. Konetchy	195.00	100.00	50.00
97	Napoleon Lajoie	715.00	375.00	190.00
98	Jack Lapp	195.00	100.00	50.00
99	John Lavan	195.00	100.00	50.00
100	Jimmy Lavender	195.00	100.00	50.00
101	"Nemo" Leibold	195.00	100.00	50.00
102	H.B. Leonard	195.00	100.00	50.00
103	Duffy Lewis	250.00	125.00	75.00
104	Hans Lobert	195.00	100.00	50.00
105	Tom Long	195.00	100.00	50.00
106	Fred Luderus	195.00	100.00	50.00
107	Connie Mack	715.00	375.00	190.00
108	Lee Magee	195.00	100.00	50.00
109	Sherwood Magee	195.00	100.00	50.00
110	Al. Mamaux	195.00	100.00	50.00
111	Leslie Mann	195.00	100.00	50.00
112	"Rabbit" Maranville	715.00	375.00	190.00
113	Rube Marquard	715.00	375.00	190.00
114	J. Erskine Mayer	195.00	100.00	50.00
115	George McBride	195.00	100.00	50.00
116	John J. McGraw	715.00	375.00	190.00
117	Jack McInnis	195.00	100.00	50.00
118	Fred Merkle	195.00	100.00	50.00
119	Chief Meyers	195.00	100.00	50.00
120	Clyde Milan	195.00	100.00	50.00
121	John Miller	195.00	100.00	50.00
122	Otto Miller	195.00	100.00	50.00
123	Willie Mitchell	195.00	100.00	50.00
124	Fred Mollwitz	195.00	100.00	50.00
125	Pat Moran	195.00	100.00	50.00
126	Ray Morgan	195.00	100.00	50.00
127	Geo. Moriarty	195.00	100.00	50.00
128	Guy Morton	195.00	100.00	50.00
129	Mike Mowrey	195.00	100.00	50.00
130	Ed. Murphy	195.00	100.00	50.00
131	"Hy" Myers	195.00	100.00	50.00
132	J.A. Niehoff	195.00	100.00	50.00
133	Rube Oldring	195.00	100.00	50.00
134	Oliver O'Mara	195.00	100.00	50.00
135	Steve O'Neill	195.00	100.00	50.00
136	"Dode" Paskert	195.00	100.00	50.00
137	Roger Peckinpaugh	195.00	100.00	50.00
138	Walter Pipp	195.00	100.00	50.00
139	Derril Pratt (Derrill)	195.00	100.00	50.00
140	Pat Ragan	195.00	100.00	50.00
141	Bill Rariden	195.00	100.00	50.00
142	Eppa Rixey	715.00	375.00	190.00
143	Davey Robertson	195.00	100.00	50.00
144	Wilbert Robinson	715.00	375.00	190.00
145	Bob Roth	195.00	100.00	50.00
146	Ed. Roush	715.00	375.00	190.00
147	Clarence Rowland	195.00	100.00	50.00
148	"Nap" Rucker	195.00	100.00	50.00
149	Dick Rudolph	195.00	100.00	50.00
150	Reb Russell	195.00	100.00	50.00
151	Babe Ruth	27,500	14,300	7,150
152	Vic Saier	195.00	100.00	50.00
153	"Slim" Sallee	195.00	100.00	50.00
154	Ray Schalk	715.00	375.00	190.00
155	Walter Schang	195.00	100.00	50.00
156	Frank Schulte	195.00	100.00	50.00
157	Everett Scott	195.00	100.00	50.00
158	Jim Scott	195.00	100.00	50.00
159	Tom Seaton	195.00	100.00	50.00
160	Howard Shanks	195.00	100.00	50.00
161	Bob Shawkey	195.00	100.00	50.00
162	Ernie Shore	195.00	100.00	50.00
163	Burt Shotton	195.00	100.00	50.00
164	Geo. Sisler	715.00	375.00	190.00
165	J. Carlisle Smith	195.00	100.00	50.00
166	Fred Snodgrass	195.00	100.00	50.00
167	Geo. Stallings	195.00	100.00	50.00
168	Oscar Stanage	195.00	100.00	50.00
169	Charles Stengel	715.00	375.00	190.00
170	Milton Stock	195.00	100.00	50.00
171	Amos Strunk	195.00	100.00	50.00
172	Billy Sullivan	195.00	100.00	50.00
173	"Jeff" Tesreau	195.00	100.00	50.00
174	Joe Tinker	715.00	375.00	190.00
175	Fred Toney	195.00	100.00	50.00
176	Terry Turner	195.00	100.00	50.00
177	George Tyler	195.00	100.00	50.00
178	Jim Vaughn	195.00	100.00	50.00
179	Bob Veach	195.00	100.00	50.00
180	James Viox	195.00	100.00	50.00
181	Oscar Vitt	195.00	100.00	50.00
182	Hans Wagner	5,000	1,375	690.00
183	Clarence Walker	195.00	100.00	50.00
184	Ed. Walsh	715.00	375.00	190.00
185	W. Wambsganss (Photo actually Fritz Coumbe.)	195.00	100.00	50.00
186	Buck Weaver	1,320	690.00	340.00
187	Carl Weilman	195.00	100.00	50.00
188	Zach Wheat	715.00	375.00	190.00
189	Geo. Whitted	195.00	100.00	50.00
190	Fred Williams	195.00	100.00	50.00
191	Art Wilson	195.00	100.00	50.00
192	J. Owen Wilson	195.00	100.00	50.00
193	Ivy Wingo	195.00	100.00	50.00
194	"Mel" Wolfgang	195.00	100.00	50.00
195	Joe Wood	195.00	100.00	50.00
196	Steve Yerkes	195.00	100.00	50.00
197	"Pep" Young	195.00	100.00	50.00
198	Rollie Zeider	195.00	100.00	50.00
199	Heiny Zimmerman	195.00	100.00	50.00
200	Ed. Zwilling	195.00	100.00	50.00

1917 Weil Baking Co. (D328)

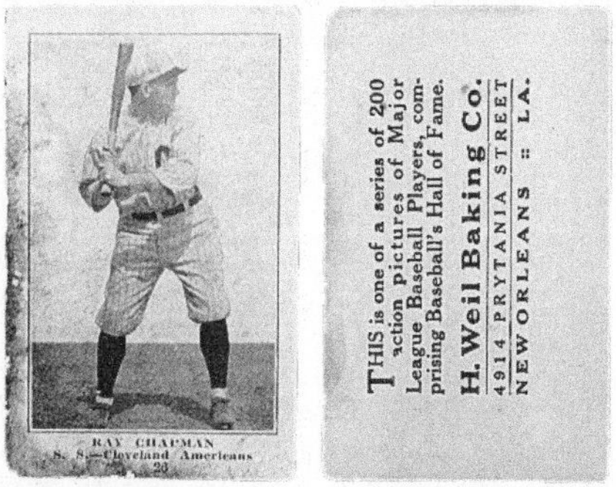
RAY CHAPMAN
THIS is one of a series of 200 action pictures of Major League Baseball Players, comprising Baseball's Hall of Fame.
H. Weil Baking Co.
4914 PRYTANIA STREET
NEW ORLEANS :: LA.

This set comprises one of several regional advertisers' use of the 200-card issue for promotional purposes. These cards are most often seen with the advertising of the Collins-McCarthy Candy Co. of San Francisco. Cards measure 2" x 3-1/4" and are printed in black-and-white. This set was listed as D328 in the American Card Catalog.

		NM	E	VG
	Complete Set (200):	140,000	70,000	42,500
	Common Player:	330.00	165.00	100.00
1	Sam Agnew	330.00	165.00	100.00
2	Grover Alexander	1,320	660.00	395.00
3	W.S. Alexander (W.E.)	330.00	165.00	100.00
4	Leon Ames	330.00	165.00	100.00
5	Fred Anderson	330.00	165.00	100.00
6	Ed Appleton	330.00	165.00	100.00
7	Jimmy Archer	330.00	165.00	100.00
8	Jimmy Austin	330.00	165.00	100.00
9	Jim Bagby Sr.	330.00	165.00	100.00
10	H.D. Baird	330.00	165.00	100.00
11	J. Franklin Baker	770.00	385.00	230.00
12	Dave Bancroft	770.00	385.00	230.00
13	Jack Barry	330.00	165.00	100.00
14	Joe Benz	330.00	165.00	100.00
15	Al Betzel	330.00	165.00	100.00
16	Ping Bodie	330.00	165.00	100.00
17	Joe Boehling	330.00	165.00	100.00
18	Eddie Burns	330.00	165.00	100.00
19	George Burns	330.00	165.00	100.00
20	Geo. J. Burns	330.00	165.00	100.00
21	Joe Bush	330.00	165.00	100.00
22	Owen Bush	330.00	165.00	100.00
23	Bobby Byrne	330.00	165.00	100.00
24	Forrest Cady	330.00	165.00	100.00
25	Max Carey	770.00	385.00	230.00
26	Ray Chapman	385.00	195.00	115.00
27	Larry Cheney	330.00	165.00	100.00
28	Eddie Cicotte	770.00	385.00	230.00
29	Tom Clarke	330.00	165.00	100.00
30	Ty Cobb	9,900	4,950	3,000
31	Eddie Collins	770.00	385.00	230.00
32	"Shauno" Collins (Shano)	330.00	165.00	100.00
33	Fred Coumbe	330.00	165.00	100.00
34	Harry Coveleskie (Coveleski)	330.00	165.00	100.00
35	Gavvy Cravath	330.00	165.00	100.00
36	Sam Crawford	770.00	385.00	230.00
37	Geo. Cutshaw	330.00	165.00	100.00
38	Jake Daubert	330.00	165.00	100.00
39	Geo. Dauss	330.00	165.00	100.00
40	Charles Deal	330.00	165.00	100.00
41	"Wheezer" Dell	330.00	165.00	100.00
42	William Doak	330.00	165.00	100.00
43	Bill Donovan	330.00	165.00	100.00
44	Larry Doyle	330.00	165.00	100.00
45	Johnny Evers	770.00	385.00	230.00
46	Urban Faber	770.00	385.00	230.00
47	"Hap" Felsch	1,650	825.00	495.00
48	Bill Fischer	330.00	165.00	100.00
49	Ray Fisher	330.00	165.00	100.00
50	Art Fletcher	330.00	165.00	100.00
51	Eddie Foster	330.00	165.00	100.00
52	Jacques Fournier	330.00	165.00	100.00
53	Del Gainer (Gainor)	330.00	165.00	100.00
54	Bert Gallia	330.00	165.00	100.00
55	"Chic" Gandil (Chick)	990.00	495.00	300.00
56	Larry Gardner	330.00	165.00	100.00
57	Joe Gedeon	330.00	165.00	100.00
58	Gus Getz	330.00	165.00	100.00
59	Frank Gilhooley	330.00	165.00	100.00
60	Wm. Gleason	330.00	165.00	100.00
61	M.A. Gonzales (Gonzalez)	330.00	165.00	100.00
62	Hank Gowdy	330.00	165.00	100.00
63	John Graney	330.00	165.00	100.00
64	Tom Griffith	330.00	165.00	100.00
65	Heinie Groh	330.00	165.00	100.00
66	Bob Groom	330.00	165.00	100.00
67	Louis Guisto	330.00	165.00	100.00
68	Earl Hamilton	330.00	165.00	100.00
69	Harry Harper	330.00	165.00	100.00
70	Grover Hartley	330.00	165.00	100.00
71	Harry Heilmann	770.00	385.00	230.00
72	Claude Hendrix	330.00	165.00	100.00
73	Olaf Henriksen	330.00	165.00	100.00
74	John Henry	330.00	165.00	100.00
75	"Buck" Herzog	330.00	165.00	100.00
76	Hugh High	330.00	165.00	100.00
77	Dick Hoblitzell	330.00	165.00	100.00
78	Walter Holke	330.00	165.00	100.00
79	Harry Hooper	770.00	385.00	230.00
80	Rogers Hornsby	1,320	660.00	395.00
81	Ivan Howard	330.00	165.00	100.00
82	Joe Jackson	27,500	13,750	8,250
83	Harold Janvrin	330.00	165.00	100.00
84	William James	330.00	165.00	100.00
85	C. Jamieson	330.00	165.00	100.00
86	Hugh Jennings	770.00	385.00	230.00
87	Walter Johnson	1,650	825.00	495.00
88	James Johnston	330.00	165.00	100.00
89	Fielder Jones	330.00	165.00	100.00
90	Joe Judge	330.00	165.00	100.00
91	Hans Lobert	330.00	165.00	100.00
92	Benny Kauff	330.00	165.00	100.00
93	Wm. Killefer Jr.	330.00	165.00	100.00
94	Ed. Konetchy	330.00	165.00	100.00
95	John Lavan	330.00	165.00	100.00
96	Jimmy Lavender	330.00	165.00	100.00
97	"Nemo" Leibold	330.00	165.00	100.00
98	H.B. Leonard	330.00	165.00	100.00

99	Duffy Lewis	330.00	165.00	100.00
100	Tom Long	330.00	165.00	100.00
101	Wm. Louden	330.00	165.00	100.00
102	Fred Luderus	330.00	165.00	100.00
103	Lee Magee	330.00	165.00	100.00
104	Sherwood Magee	330.00	165.00	100.00
105	Al Mamaux	330.00	165.00	100.00
106	Leslie Mann	330.00	165.00	100.00
107	"Rabbit" Maranville	770.00	385.00	230.00
108	Rube Marquard	770.00	385.00	230.00
109	Armando Marsans	330.00	165.00	100.00
110	J. Erskine Mayer	330.00	165.00	100.00
111	George McBride	330.00	165.00	100.00
112	Lew McCarty	330.00	165.00	100.00
113	John J. McGraw	770.00	385.00	230.00
114	Jack McInnis	330.00	165.00	100.00
115	Lee Meadows	330.00	165.00	100.00
116	Fred Merkle	330.00	165.00	100.00
117	"Chief" Meyers	330.00	165.00	100.00
118	Clyde Milan	330.00	165.00	100.00
119	Otto Miller	330.00	165.00	100.00
120	Clarence Mitchell	330.00	165.00	100.00
121	Ray Morgan	330.00	165.00	100.00
122	Guy Morton	330.00	165.00	100.00
123	"Mike" Mowrey	330.00	165.00	100.00
124	Elmer Myers	330.00	165.00	100.00
125	"Hy" Myers	330.00	165.00	100.00
126	A.E. Neale	385.00	195.00	115.00
127	Arthur Nehf	330.00	165.00	100.00
128	J.A. Niehoff	330.00	165.00	100.00
129	Steve O'Neill	330.00	165.00	100.00
130	"Dode" Paskert	330.00	165.00	100.00
131	Roger Peckinpaugh	330.00	165.00	100.00
132	"Pol" Perritt	330.00	165.00	100.00
133	"Jeff" Pfeffer	330.00	165.00	100.00
134	Walter Pipp	330.00	165.00	100.00
135	Derril Pratt (Derrill)	330.00	165.00	100.00
136	Bill Rariden	330.00	165.00	100.00
137	E.C. Rice	770.00	385.00	230.00
138	Wm. A. Ritter (Wm. H.)	330.00	165.00	100.00
139	Eppa Rixey	770.00	385.00	230.00
140	Davey Robertson	330.00	165.00	100.00
141	"Bob" Roth	330.00	165.00	100.00
142	Ed. Roush	770.00	385.00	230.00
143	Clarence Rowland	330.00	165.00	100.00
144	Dick Rudolph	330.00	165.00	100.00
145	William Rumler	330.00	165.00	100.00
146	Reb Russell	330.00	165.00	100.00
147	"Babe" Ruth	22,000	11,000	6,600
148	Vic Saier	330.00	165.00	100.00
149	"Slim" Sallee	330.00	165.00	100.00
150	Ray Schalk	770.00	385.00	230.00
151	Walter Schang	330.00	165.00	100.00
152	Frank Schulte	330.00	165.00	100.00
153	Ferd Schupp	330.00	165.00	100.00
154	Everett Scott	330.00	165.00	100.00
155	Hank Severeid	330.00	165.00	100.00
156	Howard Shanks	330.00	165.00	100.00
157	Bob Shawkey	330.00	165.00	100.00
158	Jas. Sheckard	330.00	165.00	100.00
159	Ernie Shore	330.00	165.00	100.00
160	C.H. Shorten	330.00	165.00	100.00
161	Burt Shotton	330.00	165.00	100.00
162	Geo. Sisler	770.00	385.00	230.00
163	Elmer Smith	330.00	165.00	100.00
164	J. Carlisle Smith	330.00	165.00	100.00
165	Fred Snodgrass	330.00	165.00	100.00
166	Tris Speaker	1,320	660.00	395.00
167	Oscar Stanage	330.00	165.00	100.00
168	Charles Stengel	770.00	385.00	230.00
169	Milton Stock	330.00	165.00	100.00
170	Amos Strunk	330.00	165.00	100.00
171	"Zeb" Terry	330.00	165.00	100.00
172	"Jeff" Tesreau	330.00	165.00	100.00
173	Chester Thomas	330.00	165.00	100.00
174	Fred Toney	330.00	165.00	100.00
175	Terry Turner	330.00	165.00	100.00
176	George Tyler	330.00	165.00	100.00
177	Jim Vaughn	330.00	165.00	100.00
178	Bob Veach	330.00	165.00	100.00
179	Oscar Vitt	330.00	165.00	100.00
180	Hans Wagner	7,700	3,850	2,300
181	Clarence Walker	330.00	165.00	100.00
182	Jim Walsh	330.00	165.00	100.00
183	Al Walters	330.00	165.00	100.00
184	W. Wambsganss	330.00	165.00	100.00
185	Buck Weaver	2,200	1,100	660.00
186	Carl Weilman	330.00	165.00	100.00
187	Zack Wheat	770.00	385.00	230.00
188	Geo. Whitted	330.00	165.00	100.00
189	Joe Wilhoit	330.00	165.00	100.00
190	Claude Williams	1,650	825.00	495.00
191	Fred Williams	330.00	165.00	100.00
192	Art Wilson	330.00	165.00	100.00
193	Lawton Witt	330.00	165.00	100.00
194	Joe Wood	495.00	250.00	150.00
195	William Wortman	330.00	165.00	100.00
196	Steve Yerkes	330.00	165.00	100.00
197	Earl Yingling	330.00	165.00	100.00
198	"Pep" (Ralph) Young	330.00	165.00	100.00
199	Rollie Zeider	330.00	165.00	100.00
200	Henry Zimmerman	330.00	165.00	100.00

1886 Welton Cigars N.Y. Giants (H812)

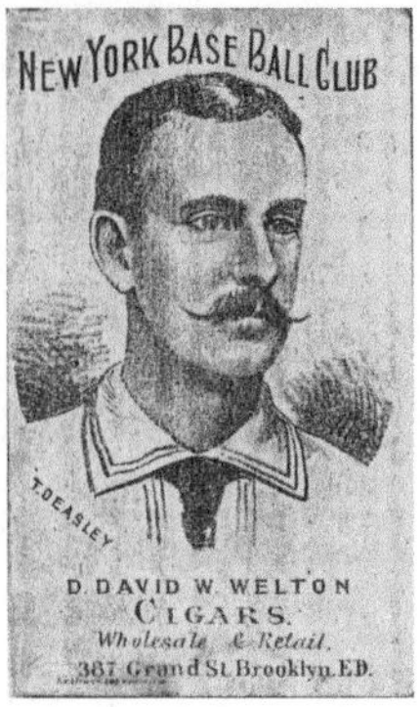

(See "1886 New York Base Ball Club" for checklist and values.)

1977 Wendy's Discs

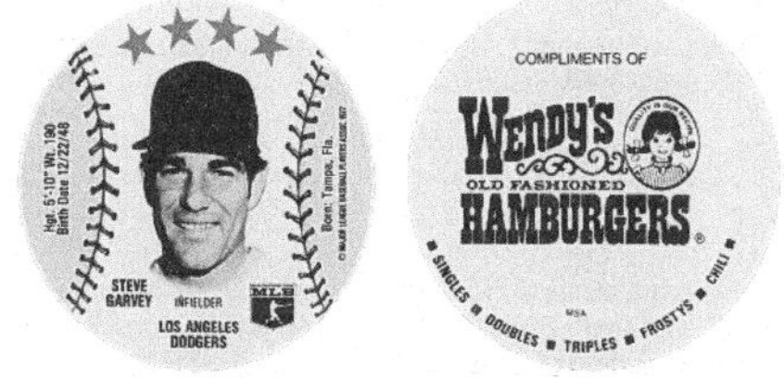

Virtually identical in format to the several locally sponsored disc sets of the previous year, these 3-3/8" diameter player discs were given away at participating stores in the fast-food hamburger chain. Discs once again feature black-and-white player portrait photos in the center of a baseball design. The left and right panels are in one of several bright colors. Licensed by the Players Association through Mike Schechter Associates, the player photos carry no uniform logos. Backs are printed in green. The unnumbered discs are checklisted here alphabetically.

		NM	E	VG
Complete Set (70):		325.00	165.00	100.00
Common Player:		3.00	1.50	.90
(1)	Sal Bando	3.00	1.50	.90
(2)	Buddy Bell	3.00	1.50	.90
(3)	Johnny Bench	20.00	10.00	6.00
(4)	Larry Bowa	3.00	1.50	.90
(5)	Steve Braun	3.00	1.50	.90
(6)	George Brett	30.00	15.00	9.00
(7)	Lou Brock	12.50	6.25	3.75
(8)	Jeff Burroughs	3.00	1.50	.90
(9)	Bert Campaneris	3.00	1.50	.90
(10)	John Candelaria	3.00	1.50	.90
(11)	Jose Cardenal	3.00	1.50	.90
(12)	Rod Carew	12.50	6.25	3.75
(13)	Steve Carlton	12.50	6.25	3.75
(14)	Dave Cash	3.00	1.50	.90
(15)	Cesar Cedeno	3.00	1.50	.90
(16)	Ron Cey	3.00	1.50	.90
(17)	Dave Concepcion	3.00	1.50	.90
(18)	Dennis Eckersley	12.50	6.25	3.75
(19)	Mark Fidrych	6.00	3.00	1.75
(20)	Rollie Fingers	12.50	6.25	3.75
(21)	Carlton Fisk	15.00	7.50	4.50
(22)	George Foster	3.00	1.50	.90
(23)	Wayne Garland	3.00	1.50	.90
(24)	Ralph Garr	3.00	1.50	.90
(25)	Steve Garvey	4.50	2.25	1.25
(26)	Cesar Geronimo	3.00	1.50	.90
(27)	Bobby Grich	3.00	1.50	.90
(28)	Ken Griffey Sr.	3.00	1.50	.90
(29)	Don Gullett	3.00	1.50	.90
(30)	Mike Hargrove	3.00	1.50	.90
(31)	Al Hrabosky	3.00	1.50	.90
(32)	Jim Hunter	12.50	6.25	3.75
(33)	Reggie Jackson	30.00	15.00	9.00
(34)	Randy Jones	3.00	1.50	.90
(35)	Dave Kingman	3.00	1.50	.90
(36)	Jerry Koosman	3.00	1.50	.90
(37)	Dave LaRoche	3.00	1.50	.90
(38)	Greg Luzinski	3.00	1.50	.90
(39)	Fred Lynn	3.00	1.50	.90
(40)	Bill Madlock	3.00	1.50	.90
(41)	Rick Manning	3.00	1.50	.90
(42)	Jon Matlock	3.00	1.50	.90
(43)	John Mayberry	3.00	1.50	.90
(44)	Hal McRae	3.00	1.50	.90
(45)	Andy Messersmith	3.00	1.50	.90
(46)	Rick Monday	3.00	1.50	.90
(47)	John Montefusco	3.00	1.50	.90
(48)	Joe Morgan	12.50	6.25	3.75
(49)	Thurman Munson	12.50	6.25	3.75
(50)	Bobby Murcer	3.00	1.50	.90
(51)	Bill North	3.00	1.50	.90
(52)	Jim Palmer	12.50	6.25	3.75
(53)	Tony Perez	12.50	6.25	3.75
(54)	Jerry Reuss	3.00	1.50	.90
(55)	Brooks Robinson	15.00	7.50	4.50
(56)	Pete Rose	55.00	27.50	16.50
(57)	Joe Rudi	3.00	1.50	.90
(58)	Nolan Ryan	65.00	32.50	20.00
(59)	Manny Sanguillen	3.00	1.50	.90
(60)	Mike Schmidt	35.00	18.00	12.00
(61)	Tom Seaver	15.00	7.50	4.50
(62)	Bill Singer	3.00	1.50	.90
(63)	Willie Stargell	12.50	6.25	3.75
(64)	Rusty Staub	4.00	2.00	1.25
(65)	Luis Tiant	3.00	1.50	.90
(66)	Bob Watson	3.00	1.50	.90
(67)	Butch Wynegar	3.00	1.50	.90
(68)	Carl Yastrzemski	18.00	10.00	6.00
(69)	Robin Yount	12.50	6.25	3.75
(70)	Richie Zisk	3.00	1.50	.90

1963 Western Oil Minnesota Twins

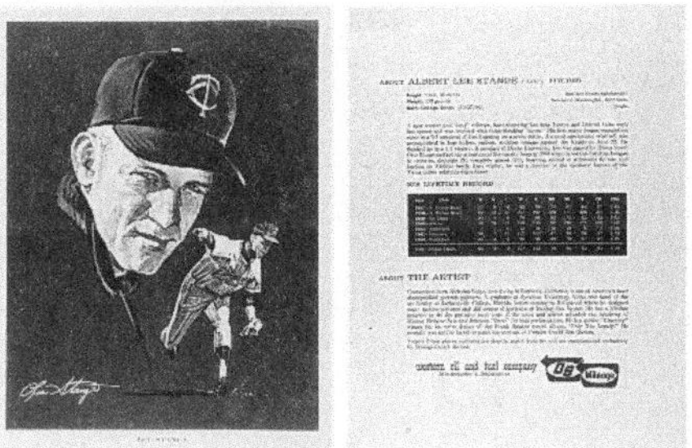

Issued by Mileage and DS gas stations, these 8-1/2" x 11" heavy paper portraits are the work of sports/entertainment artist Nicholas Volpe, who had done a similar series earlier for the Los Angeles Dodgers, and would do several more in the future for other baseball and NFL teams. The 1963 Twins issue features pastel portrait and action renderings against a black background on front. The player's name appears as a facsimile autograph in white on the painting and is printed in black in the white bottom border. Backs have biographical data and a career summary of the player at top. At center is a black box with complete major and minor league stats. At lower center is a biography of the artist, and, on most pictures, his portrait. The DS and Mileage logos of the Western Oil and Fuel Co. appear at bottom.

		NM	E	VG
Complete Set (24):		150.00	75.00	45.00
Common Player:		10.00	5.00	3.00
(1)	Bernie Allen	10.00	5.00	3.00
(2)	Bob Allison	15.00	7.50	4.50
(3)	George Banks	10.00	5.00	3.00
(4)	Earl Battey	12.50	6.25	3.75
(5)	Bill Dailey	10.00	5.00	3.00
(6)	John Goryl	10.00	5.00	3.00
(7)	Lenny Green	10.00	5.00	3.00
(8)	Jimmie Hall	10.00	5.00	3.00
(9)	Jim Kaat	15.00	7.50	4.50
(10)	Harmon Killebrew	30.00	15.00	9.00
(11)	Sam Mele	10.00	5.00	3.00
(12)	Don Mincher	10.00	5.00	3.00
(13)	Ray Moore	10.00	5.00	3.00
(14)	Camilo Pascual	12.50	6.25	3.75
(15)	Jim Perry	10.00	5.00	3.00
(16)	Bill Pleis	10.00	5.00	3.00
(17)	Vic Power	12.00	6.00	3.50
(18)	Garry Roggenburk	10.00	5.00	3.00
(19)	Jim Roland	10.00	5.00	3.00
(20)	Rich Rollins	10.00	5.00	3.00
(21)	Lee Stange	10.00	5.00	3.00
(22)	Dick Stigman	10.00	5.00	3.00
(23)	Zoilo Versalles	12.50	6.25	3.75
(24)	Jerry Zimmerman	10.00	5.00	3.00

1964 Western Oil Minnesota Twins

 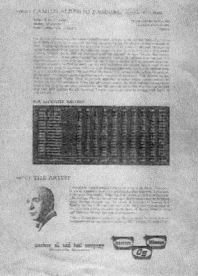

Identical in format to the previous year's issue, the 1964 set of Twins pictures features the use of a second portrait of the player in civilian dress rather than an action picture. The 1964 issue also has background of pastel colors, rather than all-black, and, on back, an oval/arrow logo for Western brand gas, along with the Mileage and DS logos.

		NM	E	VG
Complete Set (15):		120.00	60.00	35.00
Common Player:		10.00	5.00	3.00
(1)	Bernie Allen	10.00	5.00	3.00
(2)	Bob Allison	12.50	6.25	3.75
(3)	Earl Battey	12.50	6.25	3.75
(4)	Bill Dailey	10.00	5.00	3.00
(5)	Jimmie Hall	10.00	5.00	3.00
(6)	Jim Kaat	15.00	7.50	4.50
(7)	Harmon Killebrew	30.00	15.00	9.00
(8)	Don Mincher	10.00	5.00	3.00
(9)	Tony Oliva	25.00	12.50	7.50
(10)	Camilo Pascual	12.50	6.25	3.75
(11)	Bill Pleis	10.00	5.00	3.00
(12)	Jim Roland	10.00	5.00	3.00
(13)	Rich Rollins	10.00	5.00	3.00
(14)	Dick Stigman	10.00	5.00	3.00
(15)	Zoilo Versalles	12.50	6.25	3.75

1974 Weston Expos

This 10-card set features members of the Montreal Expos. Each full-color card measures 3-1/2" x 5-1/2" and includes a facsimile autograph in black ink with the player's name printed along the bottom. The backs are distinct because they are divided in half. The top of the card lists player data and 1973 statistics in English, while the bottom carries the same information in French. The cards are numbered according to the player's uniform number.

		NM	E	VG
Complete Set (10):		10.00	5.00	3.00
Common Player:		1.50	.75	.45
3	Bob Bailey	1.50	.75	.45
8	Boots Day	1.50	.75	.45
12	John Boccabella	1.50	.75	.45
16	Mike Jorgensen	1.50	.75	.45
18	Steve Renko	1.50	.75	.45
19	Tim Foli	1.50	.75	.45
21	Ernie McAnally	1.50	.75	.45
26	Bill Stoneman	1.50	.75	.45
29	Ken Singleton	1.50	.75	.45
33	Ron Hunt	1.50	.75	.45

1888 WG1 Base Ball Playing Cards

This little-known set of playing cards featuring drawings of real baseball players in action poses was issued in 1888 and includes members of the eight National League teams of the day. Each club is represented by nine players - one at each position - making the set complete at 72 cards. The cards measure 2-1/2" x 3-1/2" and have a blue-on-blue lathework pattern on back. The cards were sold as a boxed set. They were designed to resemble a deck of regular playing cards, and the various positions were all assigned the same denomination (for example, all of the pitchers were kings, catchers

were aces, etc.). There are no cards numbered either two, three, four or five; and rather than the typical hearts, clubs, diamonds and spades, each team represents a different "suit." The American Card Catalog designation is WG1.

		NM	E	VG
Complete Set (72):		90,000	35,000	17,500
Common Player:		900.00	360.00	180.00
Box:		5,000	2,500	1,500
(1)	Ed Andrews	900.00	360.00	180.00
(2)	Cap Anson	6,250	2,500	1,250
(3)	Charles Bassett	900.00	360.00	180.00
(4)	Charles Bastian	900.00	360.00	180.00
(5)	Charles Bennett	900.00	360.00	180.00
(6)	Henry Boyle	900.00	360.00	180.00
(7)	Dan Brouthers	3,000	1,200	600.00
(8)	Tom Brown	900.00	360.00	180.00
(9)	Tom Burns	900.00	360.00	180.00
(10)	Fred Carroll	900.00	360.00	180.00
(11)	Dan Casey	900.00	360.00	180.00
(12)	John Clarkson	3,000	1,200	600.00
(13)	Jack Clements	900.00	360.00	180.00
(14)	John Coleman	900.00	360.00	180.00
(15)	Roger Connor	3,000	1,200	600.00
(16)	Abner Dalrymple	900.00	360.00	180.00
(17)	Jerry Denny	900.00	360.00	180.00
(18)	Jim Donelly	900.00	360.00	180.00
(19)	Fred Dunlap	900.00	360.00	180.00
(20)	Dude Esterbrook	900.00	360.00	180.00
(21)	Buck Ewing	3,000	1,200	600.00
(22)	Sid Farrar	900.00	360.00	180.00
(23)	Silver Flint	900.00	360.00	180.00
(24)	Jim Fogarty	900.00	360.00	180.00
(25)	Elmer Foster	900.00	360.00	180.00
(26)	Pud Galvin	3,000	1,200	600.00
(27)	Charlie Getzein (Getzien)	900.00	360.00	180.00
(28)	Jack Glasscock	900.00	360.00	180.00
(29)	George Gore	900.00	360.00	180.00
(30)	Ned Hanlon	3,000	1,200	600.00
(31)	Paul Hines	900.00	360.00	180.00
(32)	Joe Hornung	900.00	360.00	180.00
(33)	Dummy Hoy	1,350	550.00	275.00
(34)	Arthur Irwin (Philadelphia)	900.00	360.00	180.00
(35)	John Irwin (Washington)	900.00	360.00	180.00
(36)	Dick Johnston	900.00	360.00	180.00
(37)	Tim Keefe	3,000	1,200	600.00
(38)	King Kelly	4,250	1,700	850.00
(39)	Willie Kuehne	900.00	360.00	180.00
(40)	Connie Mack	3,250	1,300	650.00
(41)	Al Maul	900.00	360.00	180.00
(42)	Al Meyers (Myers) (Washington)	900.00	360.00	180.00
(43)	George Meyers (Myers) (Indianapolis)	900.00	360.00	180.00
(44)	John Morrill	900.00	360.00	180.00
(45)	Joseph Mulvey	900.00	360.00	180.00
(46)	Billy Nash	900.00	360.00	180.00
(47)	Billy O'Brien	900.00	360.00	180.00
(48)	Orator Jim O'Rourke	3,000	1,200	600.00
(49)	Bob Pettit	900.00	360.00	180.00
(50)	Fred Pfeffer	900.00	360.00	180.00
(51)	Danny Richardson (New York)	900.00	360.00	180.00
(52)	Hardy Richardson (Detroit)	900.00	360.00	180.00
(53)	Jack Rowe	900.00	360.00	180.00
(54)	Jimmy Ryan	900.00	360.00	180.00
(55)	Emmett Seery	900.00	360.00	180.00
(56)	George Shoch	900.00	360.00	180.00
(57)	Otto Shomberg (Schomberg)	900.00	360.00	180.00
(58)	Pap Smith	900.00	360.00	180.00
(59)	Marty Sullivan	900.00	360.00	180.00
(60)	Billy Sunday	3,000	1,200	600.00
(61)	Ezra Sutton	900.00	360.00	180.00
(62)	Sam Thompson	3,000	1,200	600.00
(63)	Mike Tiernan	900.00	360.00	180.00
(64)	Larry Twitchell	900.00	360.00	180.00
(65)	Rip Van Haltren	900.00	360.00	180.00
(66)	John Ward	3,000	1,200	600.00
(67)	Deacon White	900.00	360.00	180.00
(68)	Jim Whitney	900.00	360.00	180.00
(69)	Ned Williamson	900.00	360.00	180.00
(70)	Walt Wilmot	900.00	360.00	180.00
(71)	Medoc Wise	900.00	360.00	180.00
(72)	George Wood	900.00	360.00	180.00

1932 Wheaties Babe Ruth Flip Book

This novelty item measures about 1-3/4" x 2-1/2" and is stapled at the bottom. When properly thumbed, the individual black-and-white pages inside present a simulated moving picture, "Babe Ruth Shows You How to Hit a Home Run". The covers feature orange and blue artwork.

	NM	E	VG
Babe Ruth	600.00	300.00	180.00

1933-1934 Wheaties

Sponsored by Wheaties via mail-in offers heard on baseball games on half a dozen radio stations, these black-and-white cards are blank-backed and feature posed action photo with facsimile autographs bordered in white. In a 3-1/4" x 5-3/8" format, they are similar in design to the later 1936 National Chicle "Fine Pens" (R313) and the Gold Medal Foods World Series (R313A) issue of 1934, though each of the photos found in this set are unique. To date, this likely incomplete checklist comprises on players from the Browns, Cardinals, Cubs, White Sox, Indians and the Des Moines Demons of the Western League.

		NM	E	VG
Common Player:				
(1)	Earl Averill	275.00	135.00	80.00
(2)	Geo. E. Blaeholder	45.00	22.50	13.50
(3)	Irving "Jack" Burns	45.00	22.50	13.50
(4)	Bruce Campbell	45.00	22.50	13.50
(5)	"Tex" Carleton	45.00	22.50	13.50
(6)	George Earnshaw	45.00	22.50	13.50
(7)	Red Faber	80.00	40.00	24.00
(8)	Fabian Gaffke	45.00	22.50	13.50
(9)	Odell Hale	180.00	90.00	55.00
(10)	Mel Harder	45.00	22.50	13.50
(11)	Roy Hudson	45.00	22.50	13.50
(12)	Chuck Klein	80.00	40.00	24.00
(13)	Jack Knott	45.00	22.50	13.50
(14)	Al Marchand	45.00	22.50	13.50
(15)	Ossie Orwoll	45.00	22.50	13.50
(16)	Al Simmons	80.00	40.00	24.00
(17)	Hal Trosky	45.00	22.50	13.50
(18)	Joe Vosmik	45.00	22.50	13.50
(19)	Bill Walker	45.00	22.50	13.50

1935 Wheaties - Series 1

This set of major leaguers (plus fictional sports hero Jack Armstrong) was issued on the back of Wheaties cereal boxes in 1935 and because of its design, is known as "Fancy Frame with Script Signature." The unnumbered cards measure 6" x 6-1/4" with frame, and 5" x 5-1/2" without the frame. The player photo is tinted blue, while the background is blue and orange. A facsimile autograph appears at the bottom of the photo. Illinois high school track star Herman "Jack" Waddlington posed for the photos of fictional Jack Armstrong "All-American Boy."

		NM	E	VG
Complete Set (27):		3,000	1,500	900.00
Common Player:		50.00	25.00	15.50
(1)	Jack Armstrong (Batting)	50.00	25.00	15.00
(2)	Jack Armstrong (Throwing)	50.00	25.00	15.00
(3)	Wally Berger	50.00	25.00	15.00
(4)	Tommy Bridges	50.00	25.00	15.00
(5)	Mickey Cochrane (Black hat.)	90.00	45.00	27.00
(6)	Michey Cochrane (White hat.)	425.00	210.00	125.00
(7)	James "Rip" Collins	50.00	25.00	15.00
(8)	Dizzy Dean	325.00	160.00	97.00
(9)	Dizzy Dean, Paul Dean	250.00	125.00	75.00
(10)	Paul Dean	55.00	27.50	16.50
(11)	William Delancey	50.00	25.00	15.00
(12)	"Jimmie" Foxx	190.00	95.00	60.00
(13)	Frank Frisch	75.00	37.50	22.00
(14)	Lou Gehrig	475.00	235.00	140.00
(15)	Goose Goslin	75.00	37.50	22.00
(16)	Lefty Grove	125.00	65.00	35.00
(17)	Carl Hubbell	85.00	40.00	25.00
(18)	Travis C. Jackson	75.00	37.50	22.00
(19)	"Chuck" Klein	75.00	37.50	22.00
(20)	Gus Mancuso	50.00	25.00	15.00
(21)	Pepper Martin (Batting)	55.00	27.50	16.50

		NM	E	VG
(22)	Pepper Martin (Portrait)	55.00	27.00	16.50
(23)	Joe Medwick	75.00	37.50	22.00
(24)	Melvin Ott	90.00	45.00	27.00
(25)	Harold Schumacher	50.00	25.00	15.00
(26)	Al Simmons	75.00	37.50	22.00
(27)	"Jo Jo" White	50.00	25.00	15.00

1936 Wheaties - Series 3

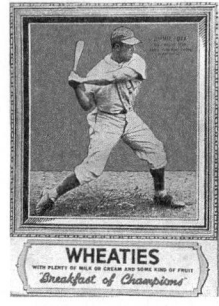

Consisting of 12 unnumbered cards, this set is similar in size (6" x 6-1/4" with frame) and design to the Wheaties of the previous year, but is known as "Fancy Frame with Printed Name and Data" because the cards also include a few printed words describing the player.

		NM	E	VG
Complete Set (12):		1,600	800.00	475.00
Common Player:		45.00	22.00	13.50
(1)	Earl Averill	60.00	30.00	18.00
(2)	Mickey Cochrane	60.00	30.00	18.00
(3)	Jimmy Foxx	200.00	100.00	60.00
(4)	Lou Gehrig	600.00	300.00	180.00
(5)	Hank Greenberg	175.00	90.00	50.00
(6)	"Gabby" Hartnett	60.00	30.00	18.00
(7)	Carl Hubbell	65.00	32.50	20.00
(8)	"Pepper" Martin	50.00	25.00	15.00
(9)	Van L. Mungo	45.00	22.50	13.50
(10)	"Buck" Newsom	45.00	22.50	13.50
(11)	"Arky" Vaughan	60.00	30.00	18.00
(12)	Jimmy Wilson	45.00	22.50	13.50

1936 Wheaties - Series 4

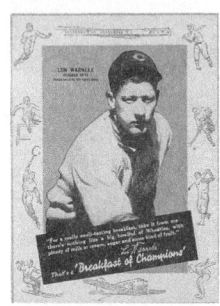

This larger size (8-1/2" x 6") card also made up the back of a Wheaties box, and because of its distinctive border which featured drawings of small athletic figures, it is referred to as "Thin Orange Border/Figures in Border." Twelve major leaguers are pictured in the unnumbered set. The photos are enclosed in a 4" x 6-1/2" box. Below the photo is an endorsement for Wheaties, the "Breakfast of Champions," and a facsimile autograph.

		NM	E	VG
Complete Set (12):		1,200	600.00	350.00
Common Player:		45.00	22.00	13.50
(1)	Curt Davis	45.00	22.50	13.50
(2)	Lou Gehrig	500.00	250.00	150.00
(3)	Charley Gehringer	75.00	37.50	22.00
(4)	Lefty Grove	165.00	85.00	50.00
(5)	Rollie Hemsley	45.00	22.50	13.50
(6)	Billy Herman	75.00	37.50	22.00
(7)	Joe Medwick	75.00	37.50	22.00
(8)	Mel Ott	80.00	40.00	25.00
(9)	Schoolboy Rowe	45.00	22.50	13.50
(10)	Arky Vaughan	75.00	37.50	22.00
(11)	Joe Vosmik	45.00	22.50	13.50
(12)	Lon Warneke	45.00	22.50	13.50

1936 Wheaties - Series 5

Often referred to as "How to Play Winning Baseball," this 12-card set features a large player photo surrounded by blue and white drawings that illustrate various playing tips. Different major leaguers offer advice on different aspects of the game. The cards again made up the back panel of a Wheaties box and measure 8-1/2" x 6-1/2". The cards are numbered from 1 through 12, and it is now believed that each can be found with or without a small number "28" followed by a letter from "A" through "L."

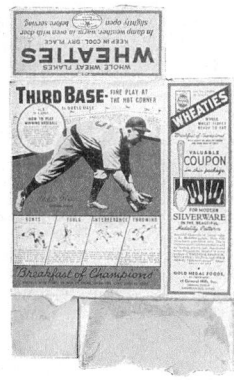

		NM	E	VG
Complete Set (12)		1,000	500.00	300.00
Common Player:		45.00	22.50	13.50
1	Lefty Gomez	85.00	45.00	25.00
2	Billy Herman	75.00	37.50	22.00
3	Luke Appling	75.00	37.50	22.00
4	Jimmie Foxx	90.00	45.00	27.00
5	Joe Medwick	75.00	37.50	22.00
6	Charles Gehringer	75.00	37.50	22.00
7a	Mel Ott (Tips in vertical sequence.)	95.00	45.00	25.00
7b	Mel Ott (Tips in two horizontal rows.)	95.00	45.00	25.00
8	Odell Hale	45.00	22.50	13.50
9	Bill Dickey	85.00	45.00	25.00
10	"Lefty" Grove	85.00	45.00	25.00
11	Carl Hubbell	80.00	40.00	25.00
12	Earl Averill	75.00	37.50	22.00

1936 Wheaties - Series UNC

These box-back cards were issued on single-serving packages of Wheaties that are marked, "Individual Service For Hotels Dining Cars Restaurants". The back panel measures about 2-3/4" x 4," and like many contemporary Wheaties box-back cards is printed in orange, white and blue. The player pictures and design of the single-serving box cards are similar to the central portions of the Wheaties cards cataloged as 1936 Series 4. Each of the five players known in the single-serving box series is also represented on Series 4, though it is not known whether the other eight players from Series 4 were also issued in the smaller size. Gaps have been left in the assigned numbers to accommodate future additions.

		NM	EX	VG
Common Player:		400.00	200.00	120.00
(2)	Lou Gehrig	2,000	1,000	600.00
(3)	Charley Gehringer	400.00	200.00	120.00
(4)	Lefty Grove	500.00	250.00	150.00
(7)	Joe Medwick	400.00	200.00	120.00
(8)	Mel Ott	500.00	250.00	150.00

1937 Wheaties - Series 14

Much reduced in size (2-5/8" x 3-7/8"), these unnumbered cards made up the back panels of single-serving size Wheaties boxes. The player photo (which is sometimes identical to the photos used in the larger series) is set against an orange or white background. The player's name appears in large capital letters with his position and team in smaller capitals. A facsimile autograph and Wheaties endorsement are also included. Some cards are also found with the number "29" followed by a letter.

		NM	E	VG
Complete Set (16):		4,000	2,000	1,200
Common Player:		200.00	100.00	60.00
(1)	"Zeke" Bonura	200.00	100.00	60.00
(2)	Tom Bridges	200.00	100.00	60.00
(3)	Dolph Camilli	200.00	100.00	60.00
(4)	Frank Demaree	200.00	100.00	60.00
(5)	Joe DiMaggio	750.00	375.00	225.00
(6)	Billy Herman	300.00	150.00	90.00
(7)	Carl Hubbell	350.00	175.00	105.00
(8)	Ernie Lombardi	300.00	150.00	90.00
(9)	"Pepper" Martin	250.00	125.00	75.00
(10)	Joe Moore	200.00	100.00	60.00
(11)	Van Mungo	200.00	100.00	60.00
(12)	Mel Ott	350.00	175.00	105.00
(13)	Raymond Radcliff	200.00	100.00	60.00
(14)	Cecil Travis	200.00	100.00	60.00
(15)	Harold Trosky	200.00	100.00	60.00
(16a)	"Arky" Vaughan (29L on card)	350.00	175.00	105.00
(16b)	"Arky" Vaughan (No 29L on card.)	350.00	175.00	105.00

1937 Wheaties - Series 6

Similar to the Series 5 set, this numbered, 12-card series is known as "How to Star in Baseball" and again includes a large player photo with small instructional drawings to illustrate playing tips. The cards measure 8-1/4" x 6" and include a facsimile autograph.

		NM	E	VG
Complete Set (12):		1,000	500.00	300.00
Common Player:		35.00	17.50	10.00
1	Bill Dickey	75.00	37.50	22.00
2	Red Ruffing	60.00	30.00	18.00
3	Zeke Bonura	35.00	17.50	10.00
4	Charlie Gehringer	60.00	30.00	18.00
5	"Arky" Vaughn (Vaughan)	60.00	30.00	18.00
6	Carl Hubbell	60.00	30.00	18.00
7	John Lewis	35.00	17.50	10.00
8	Heinie Manush	60.00	30.00	18.00
9	"Lefty" Grove	75.00	37.50	22.00
10	Billy Herman	60.00	30.00	18.00
11	Joe DiMaggio	400.00	200.00	120.00
12	Joe Medwick	60.00	30.00	18.00

1937 Wheaties - Series 7

This set of 6" x 8-1/4" panels contains several different card designs. One style (picturing Lombardi, Travis and Mungo) has a white background with an orange border and a large orange circle behind the player. Another design (showing Bonura, DiMaggio and Bridges) has the player outlined against a bright orange background with a Wheaties endorsement along the bottom. A third format (picturing Moore, Radcliff and Martin) has a distinctive red, white and blue border. And a fourth design (featuring Trosky, Demaree and Vaughan) has a tilted picture against an orange background framed in blue and white. The set also includes four Pacific Coast League Players (#29M-29P). The cards are numbered with a small "29" followed by a letter from "A" through "P."

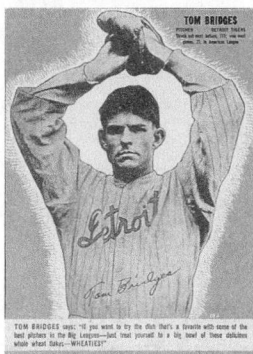

		NM	E	VG
Complete Set (16):		1,200	600.00	350.00
Common Player:		45.00	22.50	13.50
29A	"Zeke" Bonura	45.00	22.50	13.50
29B	Cecil Travis	45.00	22.50	13.50
29C	Frank Demaree	45.00	22.50	13.50
29D	Joe Moore	45.00	22.50	13.50
29E	Ernie Lombardi	60.00	30.00	18.00
29F	John L. "Pepper" Martin	50.00	25.00	15.00
29G	Harold Trosky	45.00	22.50	13.50
29H	Raymond Radcliff	45.00	22.50	13.50
29I	Joe DiMaggio	300.00	150.00	90.00
29J	Tom Bridges	45.00	22.50	13.50
29K	Van L. Mungo	45.00	22.50	13.50
29L	"Arky" Vaughn (Vaughan)	60.00	30.00	18.00
29M	Arnold Statz	100.00	50.00	30.00
29N	Wes Schulmerich	100.00	50.00	30.00
29O	Fred Mueller	100.00	50.00	30.00
29P	Gene Lillard	100.00	50.00	30.00

1937 Wheaties - Series 8

Another series printed on the back of Wheaties boxes in 1937, the eight cards in this set are unnumbered and measure 8-1/2" x 6". There are several different designs, but in all of them the player photo is surrounded by speckles of color, causing this series to be known as the "Speckled Orange, White and Blue" series. A facsimile autograph is included, along with brief printed 1936 season statistics.

		NM	E	VG
Complete Set (8):		1,300	650.00	400.00
Common Player:		120.00	60.00	36.00
(1)	Luke Appling	100.00	50.00	30.00
(2)	Earl Averill	100.00	50.00	30.00
(3)	Joe DiMaggio	450.00	225.00	135.00
(4)	Robert Feller	225.00	110.00	65.00
(5)	Chas. Gehringer	100.00	50.00	30.00
(6)	Lefty Grove	125.00	65.00	35.00
(7)	Carl Hubbell	125.00	65.00	35.00
(8)	Joe Medwick	100.00	50.00	30.00

1937 Wheaties - Series 9

This unnumbered set includes one player from each of the 16 major league teams and is generally referred to as the "Color Series." The cards measure 8-1/2" x 6" and were the back panels of Wheaties boxes. The player photos are shown inside or against large stars, circles, "V" shapes, rectangles and other geometric designs. A facsimile autograph and team designation are printed near the photo, while a Wheaties endorsement and a line of player stats appear along the bottom.

		NM	E	VG
Complete Set (16):		1,600	800.00	480.00
Common Player:		50.00	25.00	15.00
(1)	Zeke Bonura	50.00	25.00	15.00
(2)	Tom Bridges	50.00	25.00	15.00
(3)	Harland Clift (Harlond)	50.00	25.00	15.00
(4)	Kiki Cuyler	75.00	37.50	22.50
(5)	Joe DiMaggio	500.00	250.00	150.00
(6)	Robert Feller	175.00	85.00	50.00
(7)	Lefty Grove	100.00	50.00	30.00
(8)	Billy Herman	75.00	37.50	22.50
(9)	Carl Hubbell	90.00	45.00	27.50
(10)	Buck Jordan	50.00	25.00	15.00
(11)	"Pepper" Martin	60.00	30.00	18.00
(12)	John Moore	50.00	25.00	15.00
(13)	Wally Moses	50.00	25.00	15.00
(14)	Van L. Mungo	50.00	25.00	15.00
(15)	Cecil Travis	50.00	25.00	15.00
(16)	Arky Vaughan	75.00	37.50	22.50

1938 Wheaties - Series 10

One player from each major league team is included in this 16-card set, referred to as the "Biggest Thrills in Baseball" series. Measuring 8-1/2" x 6", each numbered card was the back panel of a Wheaties box and pictures a player along with a printed description of his biggest thrill in baseball and facsimile autograph. All 16 cards in this series have also been found on paper stock.

		NM	E	VG
Complete Set (16):		1,700	850.00	500.00
Common Player:		45.00	22.50	13.50
1	Bob Feller	160.00	80.00	45.00
2	Cecil Travis	45.00	22.50	13.50
3	Joe Medwick	65.00	32.50	20.00
4	Gerald Walker	45.00	22.50	13.50
5	Carl Hubbell	65.00	32.50	20.00
6	Bob Johnson	45.00	22.50	13.50
7	Beau Bell	45.00	22.50	13.50
8	Ernie Lombardi	65.00	32.50	20.00
9	Lefty Grove	80.00	40.00	24.00
10	Lou Fette	45.00	22.50	13.50
11	Joe DiMaggio	600.00	300.00	180.00
12	Pinky Whitney	45.00	22.50	13.50
13	Dizzy Dean	175.00	85.00	55.00
14	Charley Gehringer	65.00	32.50	20.00
15	Paul Waner	65.00	32.50	20.00
16	Dolf Camilli	45.00	22.50	13.50

1938 Wheaties - Series 11

Cards in this unnumbered, eight-card series measure 8-1/2" x 6" and show the players in street clothes either eating or getting ready to enjoy a bowl of Wheaties. Sometimes a waitress or other person also appears in the photo. The set is sometimes called the "Dress Clothes" or "Civies" series.

		NM	E	VG
Complete Set (8):		750.00	375.00	225.00
Common Player:		60.00	30.00	18.00
(1)	Lou Fette	60.00	30.00	18.00
(2)	Jimmie Foxx	145.00	75.00	45.00
(3)	Charlie Gehringer	115.00	55.00	35.00
(4)	Lefty Grove	115.00	55.00	35.00
(5)	Hank Greenberg, Roxie Lawson	175.00	90.00	54.00
(6)	Lee Grissom, Ernie Lombardi	85.00	40.00	25.00
(7)	Joe Medwick	85.00	40.00	25.00
(8)	Lon Warneke	60.00	30.00	18.00

1938 Wheaties - Series 15

Another set of small (2-5/8" x 3-7/8") cards, the photos in this unnumbered series made up the back panels of single-serving size Wheaties boxes. The panels have orange, blue and white backgrounds. Some of the photos are the same as those used in the larger Wheaties panels.

		NM	E	VG
Complete Set (11):		4,500	2,250	1,350
Common Player:		160.00	80.00	45.00
(1)	"Zeke" Bonura	160.00	80.00	45.00
(2)	Joe DiMaggio	1,300	650.00	390.00
(3)	Charles Gehringer (Batting)	400.00	200.00	120.00
(4)	Chas. Gehringer (Leaping)	400.00	200.00	120.00
(5)	Hank Greenberg	500.00	250.00	150.00
(6)	Lefty Grove	400.00	200.00	120.00
(7)	Carl Hubbell	325.00	160.00	97.00
(8)	John (Buddy) Lewis	160.00	80.00	45.00
(9)	Heinie Manush	300.00	150.00	90.00
(10)	Joe Medwick	300.00	150.00	90.00
(11)	Arky Vaughan	300.00	150.00	90.00

1939 Wheaties - Series 12

The nine cards in this numbered series, known as the "Personal Pointers" series, measure 8-1/4" x 6" and feature an instructional format similar to earlier Wheaties issues. The cards feature a player photo along with printed tips on various aspects of hitting and pitching.

	NM	E	VG
Complete Set (9):	1,500	750.00	450.00
Common Player:	100.00	50.00	30.00
1 Ernie Lombardi	160.00	80.00	45.00
2 Johnny Allen	100.00	50.00	30.00
3 Lefty Gomez	185.00	90.00	55.00
4 Bill Lee	100.00	50.00	30.00
5 Jimmie Foxx	250.00	125.00	75.00
6 Joe Medwick	160.00	80.00	45.00
7 Hank Greenberg	250.00	125.00	75.00
8 Mel Ott	185.00	90.00	55.00
9 Arky Vaughn (Vaughan)	160.00	80.00	45.00

1939 Wheaties - Series 13

Issued in baseball's centennial year of 1939, this set of eight 6" x 6-3/4" cards commemorates "100 Years of Baseball." Each of the numbered panels illustrates a significant event in baseball history.

	NM	E	VG
Complete Set (8):	650.00	325.00	200.00
Common Panel:	75.00	37.50	22.50
1 Design of First Diamond - 1838(Abner Doubleday)	75.00	37.50	22.50
2 Gets News of Nomination on Field - 1860(Abraham Lincoln)	125.00	62.50	37.50
3 Crowd Boos First Baseball Glove - 1869	75.00	37.50	22.50
4 Curve Ball Just an Illusion - 1877	75.00	37.50	22.50
5 Fencer's Mask is Pattern - 1877	75.00	37.50	22.50
6 Baseball Gets "All Dressed Up" - 1895	75.00	37.50	22.50
7 Modern Bludgeon Enters Game - 1895	75.00	37.50	22.50
8 "Casey at the Bat"	100.00	50.00	30.00

1940 Wheaties Champs of the USA

This set consists of 13 numbered panels (plus seven variations). Each pictures three athletes, including one, two or three baseball players; the others include football stars, golfers, skaters, racers, etc. The entire panel measures approximately 8-1/4" x 6", while the actual card measures approximately 6" square. Each athlete is pictured in what looks like a postage stamp with a serrated edge. A brief biography appears alongside the "stamp." Some variations are known

to exist among the first nine panels. The cards are numbered in the upper right corner.

	NM	E	VG
Complete Set (20):	1,400	700.00	425.00
Common Panel:	50.00	25.00	15.00
1A Bob Feller, Lynn Patrick, Charles "Red" Ruffing	135.00	67.00	40.00
1B Leo Durocher, Lynn Patrick, Charles "Red" Ruffing	90.00	45.00	27.00
2A Joe DiMaggio, Don Budge, Hank Greenberg	300.00	150.00	90.00
2B Joe DiMaggio, Mel Ott, Ellsworth Vines	200.00	100.00	60.00
3 Bernie Bierman, Bill Dickey, Jimmie Foxx	125.00	62.00	37.00
4 Morris Arnovich, Capt R.K. Baker, Earl "Dutch" Clark	50.00	25.00	15.00
5 Madison (Matty) Bell, Ab Jenkins, Joe Medwick	50.00	25.00	15.00
6A Ralph Guldahl, John Mize, Davey O'Brien	50.00	25.00	15.00
6B Bob Feller, John Mize, Rudy York	90.00	45.00	27.00
6C Ralph Guldahl, Gabby Hartnett, Davey O'Brien	50.00	25.00	15.00
7A Joe Cronin, Cecil Isbell, Byron Nelson	50.00	25.00	15.00
7B Joe Cronin, Hank Greenberg, Byron Nelson	75.00	37.00	22.00
7C Paul Derringer, Cecil Isbell, Byron Nelson	50.00	25.00	15.00
8A Ernie Lombardi, Jack Manders, George I. Myers	50.00	25.00	15.00
8B Paul Derringer, Ernie Lombardi, George I. Myers	50.00	25.00	15.00
9 Bob Bartlett, Captain R.C. Hanson, Terrell Jacobs	50.00	25.00	15.00
10 Lowell "Red" Dawson, Billy Herman, Adele Inge	50.00	25.00	15.00
11 Dolph Camilli, Antoinette Concello, Wallace Wade	50.00	25.00	15.00
12 Luke Appling, Stanley Hack, Hugh McManus	50.00	25.00	15.00
13 Felix Adler, Hal Trosky, Mabel Vinson	50.00	25.00	15.00

1941 Wheaties Champs of the USA

This eight-card series is actually a continuation of the previous year's Wheaties set, and the format is identical. The set begins with number 14, starting where the 1940 set ended.

	NM	E	VG
Complete Set (8):	800.00	400.00	240.00
Common Panel:	50.00	25.00	15.00
14 Felix Adler, Jimmie Foxx, Capt. R.G. Hanson	90.00	45.00	27.00
15 Bernie Bierman, Bob Feller, Jessie McLeod	90.00	45.00	27.00
16 Lowell "Red" Dawson, Hank Greenberg, J.W. Stoker	80.00	40.00	24.00
17 Antoinette Concello, Joe DiMaggio, Byron Nelson	300.00	150.00	90.00
18 Capt. R.L. Baker, Frank "Buck" McCormick, Harold "Pee Wee" Reese	90.00	45.00	27.00
19 William W. Robbins, Gene Sarazen, Gerald "Gee" Walker	50.00	25.00	15.00
20 Harry Danning, Barney McCosky, Bucky Walters	50.00	25.00	15.00
21 Joe "Flash" Gordon, Stan Hack, George I. Myers	50.00	25.00	15.00

1951 Wheaties

Printed as the backs of single-serving size boxes of Wheaties, the six-card 1951 set includes three baseball players and one football player, basketball player and golfer. Well-trimmed cards measure 2-1/2" x 3-1/4". The cards feature blue line drawings of the athletes with a facsimile autograph and descriptive title below. There is a wide white border. A small hoard of complete sets of unused boxes made its way into the hobby in the early 1990s. Complete boxes should be priced at 1.5X the values shown here.

	NM	E	VG
Complete Set (6):	600.00	300.00	180.00
Common Player:	85.00	42.00	25.00
(1) Bob Feller (Baseball)	100.00	50.00	30.00
(2) John Lujack (Football)	55.00	27.50	16.50
(3) George Mikan (Basketball)	110.00	55.00	35.00
(4) Stan Musial (Baseball)	150.00	75.00	45.00
(5) Sam Snead (Golfer)	65.00	32.50	20.00
(6) Ted Williams (Baseball)	200.00	100.00	60.00

1951 Wheaties Premium Photos

Whether or not these 5" x 7" black-and-white, blank-back photos were ever issued at all, or only on a test basis is unknown. Despite being unmarked, they are reliably attributed to General Mills, possibly intended for use as a Wheaties premium. The photos found on several of the pictures are the same pictures used on the box-back Wheaties cards of 1952. The pictures appear in most cases to be re-uses of team-issued images from photo packs and the like. Player names are in the bottom border in capital letters. Each picture has a small alpha-numeric identifier in the lower-right corner. The scope of the issue is unknown as several letters in the sequence are missing. The letter shown in this checklist is preceded in each case by "A8491."

	NM	E	VG
Complete Baseball Set (8):	2,600	1,300	775.00
Common Player:	66.00	33.00	20.00
A Stan Musial	325.00	160.00	95.00
C Richie Ashburn	120.00	60.00	36.00
D Bob Feller	120.00	60.00	36.00
E Al Rosen	65.00	32.50	20.00
F Larry (Yogi) Berra	175.00	85.00	50.00
G Mickey Mantle	1,600	800.00	480.00
H Betty Schalow (Ice skater)	15.00	7.50	4.50
J Bob Lemon	65.00	32.50	20.00
K Roy Campanella	150.00	75.00	45.00

1952 Wheaties

BOB FELLER
PITCHER, CLEVELAND INDIANS

These 2" x 2-3/4" cards appeared on the back of the popular cereal boxes. Actually, sports figures had been appearing on the backs of the boxes for many years, but in 1952, of the 30 athletes depicted, 10 were baseball players. That means there are 20 baseball cards, as each player appears in both a portrait and an action drawing. The cards have a blue line drawing on an orange background with a white border. The player's name, team, and position appear at the bottom. The cards have rounded corners, but are often found poorly cut from the boxes. This set was extensively counterfeited circa 2002, which had a chilling effect on values of cards not professionally graded by a major certification company.

		NM	E	VG
Complete (Baseball) Set (20):		650.00	325.00	195.00
Common Player:		20.00	10.00	6.00
(1)	Larry "Yogi" Berra (Portrait)	50.00	25.00	15.00
(2)	Larry "Yogi" Berra (Action)	50.00	25.00	15.00
(3)	Roy Campanella (Portrait)	50.00	25.00	15.00
(4)	Roy Campanella (Action)	50.00	25.00	15.00
(5)	Bob Feller (Portrait)	30.00	15.00	9.00
(6)	Bob Feller (Action)	30.00	15.00	9.00
(7)	George Kell (Portrait)	25.00	12.50	7.50
(8)	George Kell (Action)	25.00	12.50	7.50
(9)	Ralph Kiner (Portrait)	25.00	12.50	7.50
(10)	Ralph Kiner (Action)	25.00	12.50	7.50
(11)	Bob Lemon (Portrait)	25.00	12.50	7.50
(12)	Bob Lemon (Action)	25.00	12.50	7.50
(13)	Stan Musial (Portrait)	60.00	30.00	18.00
(14)	Stan Musial (Action)	60.00	30.00	18.00
(15)	Phil Rizzuto (Portrait)	30.00	15.00	9.00
(16)	Phil Rizzuto (Action)	30.00	15.00	9.00
(17)	Elwin "Preacher" Roe (Portrait)	20.00	10.00	6.00
(18)	Elwin "Preacher" Roe (Action)	20.00	10.00	6.00
(19)	Ted Williams (Portrait)	100.00	50.00	30.00
(20)	Ted Williams (Action)	100.00	50.00	30.00

1952 Wheaties Tin Trays

This unique cereal box premium took the shape of a 4-7/8" x 5-1/8" tin tray which was glued to the back of Wheaties boxes. A cream-colored border surrounded the 3" x 4" color photo debossed at center. A black facsimile autograph appears across the photo. At top a small hole was punched for hanging the plaque. Backs were blank, and are often found with glue and paper residue on the gold-tone metal. Most of the plates have acquired numerous scratches and dings over the years, making true Near Mint examples very scarce. The unnumbered trays are checklisted alphabetically. A George Kell tray was long believed to exist but has never been verified.

	NM	E	VG
Complete Set (4):	1,200	600.00	350.00
Common Player:	50.00	25.00	15.00

(1)	Ralph Kiner	50.00	25.00	15.00
(2)	Stan Musial	125.00	65.00	35.00
(3)	Phil Rizzuto	90.00	45.00	27.00
(4)	Jackie Robinson	2,000	1,000	600.00

1964 Wheaties Stamps

This General Mills' promotion included 50 player stamps and a 48-page orange album called "Wheaties Major League All-Star Baseball Player Stamp Album." The 2-1/2" x 2-3/4" stamps have a color player photo at center with a facsimile autograph and surrounded by a white border. Backs are blank. The unnumbered set is checklisted here in alphabetical order.

		NM	E	VG
Complete Set (50):		325.00	160.00	95.00
Complete Set, In Album:		125.00	65.00	35.00
Common Player:		4.00	2.00	1.25
Album:		40.00	20.00	12.00
(1)	Hank Aaron	30.00	15.00	9.00
(2)	Bob Allison	4.00	2.00	1.25
(3)	Luis Aparicio	7.50	3.75	2.25
(4)	Ed Bailey	4.00	2.00	1.25
(5)	Steve Barber	4.00	2.00	1.25
(6)	Earl Battey	4.00	2.00	1.25
(7)	Jim Bouton	5.00	2.50	1.50
(8)	Ken Boyer	5.00	2.50	1.50
(9)	Jim Bunning	15.00	7.50	4.50
(10)	Orlando Cepeda	10.00	5.00	3.00
(11)	Roberto Clemente	45.00	22.50	13.50
(12)	Ray Culp	4.00	2.00	1.25
(13)	Tommy Davis	4.00	2.00	1.25
(14)	John Edwards	4.00	2.00	1.25
(15)	Whitey Ford	20.00	10.00	6.00
(16)	Nellie Fox	10.00	5.00	3.00
(17)	Bob Friend	4.00	2.00	1.25
(18)	Jim Gilliam	5.00	2.50	1.50
(19)	Jim Grant	4.00	2.00	1.25
(20)	Dick Groat	4.00	2.00	1.25
(21)	Elston Howard	5.00	2.50	1.50
(22)	Larry Jackson	4.00	2.00	1.25
(23)	Julian Javier	4.00	2.00	1.25
(24)	Al Kaline	12.50	6.25	3.75
(25)	Harmon Killebrew	12.50	6.25	3.75
(26)	Don Leppert	4.00	2.00	1.25
(27)	Frank Malzone	4.00	2.00	1.25
(28)	Juan Marichal	7.50	3.75	2.25
(29)	Willie Mays	30.00	15.00	9.00
(30)	Ken McBride	4.00	2.00	1.25
(31)	Willie McCovey	10.00	5.00	3.00
(32)	Jim O'Toole	4.00	2.00	1.25
(33)	Albie Pearson	4.00	2.00	1.25
(34)	Joe Pepitone	5.00	2.50	1.50
(35)	Ron Perranoski	4.00	2.00	1.25
(36)	Juan Pizarro	4.00	2.00	1.25
(37)	Dick Radatz	4.00	2.00	1.25
(38)	Bobby Richardson	6.00	3.00	1.75
(39)	Brooks Robinson	12.50	6.25	3.75
(40)	Ron Santo	6.00	3.00	1.75
(41)	Norm Siebern	4.00	2.00	1.25
(42)	Duke Snider	20.00	10.00	6.00
(43)	Warren Spahn	12.50	6.25	3.75
(44)	Joe Torre	12.00	6.00	3.50
(45)	Tom Tresh	5.00	2.50	1.50
(46)	Zoilo Versalles (Versalles)	4.00	2.00	1.25
(47)	Leon Wagner	4.00	2.00	1.25
(48)	Bill White	4.00	2.00	1.25
(49)	Hal Woodeshick	4.00	2.00	1.25
(50)	Carl Yastrzemski	25.00	13.00	8.00

1937 WHIO-Sy Burick Cincinnati Reds Postcards

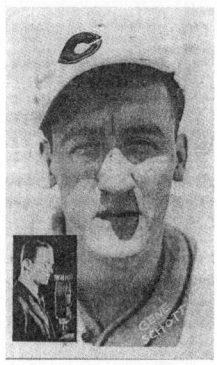

(See 1937-39 Orcajo Cincinnati Reds postcards for checklist, values.)

1889 C.S. White & Co. Boston N.L.

C.S. White & Co.

M. J. KELLY,
CAPTAIN
BOSTON BASE BALL CLUB

(See 1889 Number 7 Cigars for checklist and value information.)

1921 White's Bakery Baltimore Orioles

LEFTY GROVES
Pitcher
Baltimore Orioles
1921

This team set of the 1921 International League champions was advertised as being issued on a one-per-day basis in wrapped loaves of White's Big Tip-Top bread, a Baltimore product. Printed on thin card stock, the sepia-toned cards measure about 3-1/4" x 5-1/2". The unnumbered cards are checklisted here alphabetically, with gaps left in the assigned numbering to accommodate possible future additions. The team and card set included many former and future major leaguers, most notably Hall of Fame pitcher Lefty Grove.

		NM	EX	VG
Common Player:		2,400.		1,200.
(1)	James Aitcheson	2,400.		1,200.
(3)	Max Bishop	2,400.		1,200.
(5)	Rufus Clarke	2,400.		1,200.
(6)	Duck Davis	2,400.		1,200.
(7)	Jack Dunn	2,750.		1,375.
(8)	Ben Egan	2,400.		1,200.
(10)	Harry Frank	2,400.		1,200.
(11)	Lefty" Groves (Grove)	30,000		15,000.
(12)	Bill Holden	2,400.		1,200.
(13)	Merwin Jacobson	2,400.		1,200.
(14)	Wade Lefler	2,400.		1,200.

(15)	R. (Rudy) Kneisch	2,400	1,200
(16)	Otis Lawry	2,400	1,200
(17)	Jimmy Lyston	2,400	1,200
(18)	Fritz Maisel	2,400	1,200
(19)	Lefty Matthews	2,400	1,200
(20)	Jimmy Murphy	2,400	1,200
(21)	Jack Ogden	2,400	1,200
(22)	Jim Sullivan	2,400	1,200

1977 Wiffle Insert Discs

Similar in concept and format to the many contemporary MSA baseball player disc sets, the pieces inserted within Wiffle brand baseball, softball and bat boxes differ in that they are smaller, at 2-3/8" diameter, and feature a larger checklist. The discs feature black-and-white player portrait photos in the center of a baseball design. The left and right panels are in one of several bright colors. Licensed by the players' association through Mike Schechter Associates, the player photos carry no uniform logos. Backs are printed in black and orange. The unnumbered discs are checklisted here alphabetically.

		NM	E	VG
Complete Set (80):		325.00	160.00	100.00
Common Player:		2.50	1.25	.70
(1)	Sal Bando	2.50	1.25	.70
(2)	Buddy Bell	2.50	1.25	.70
(3)	Johnny Bench	7.50	3.75	2.25
(4)	Vida Blue	2.50	1.25	.70
(5)	Bert Blyleven	3.00	1.50	.90
(6)	Bobby Bonds	2.50	1.25	.70
(7)	George Brett	9.00	4.50	2.70
(8)	Lou Brock	6.00	3.00	1.75
(9)	Bill Buckner	2.50	1.25	.70
(10)	Ray Burris	2.50	1.25	.70
(11)	Jeff Burroughs	2.50	1.25	.70
(12)	Bert Campaneris	2.50	1.25	.70
(13)	Rod Carew	6.00	3.00	1.75
(14)	Steve Carlton	6.00	3.00	1.75
(15)	Dave Cash	2.50	1.25	.70
(16)	Cesar Cedeno	2.50	1.25	.70
(17)	Ron Cey	2.50	1.25	.70
(18)	Chris Chambliss	2.50	1.25	.70
(19)	Dave Concepcion	2.50	1.25	.70
(20)	Dennis Eckersley	6.00	3.00	1.75
(21)	Mark Fidrych	3.50	1.75	1.00
(22)	Rollie Fingers	6.00	3.00	1.75
(23)	Carlton Fisk	6.00	3.00	1.75
(24)	George Foster	2.50	1.25	.70
(25)	Wayne Garland	2.50	1.25	.70
(26)	Ralph Garr	2.50	1.25	.70
(27)	Steve Garvey	5.00	2.50	1.50
(28)	Don Gullett	2.50	1.25	.70
(29)	Larry Hisle	2.50	1.25	.70
(30)	Al Hrabosky	2.50	1.25	.70
(31)	Catfish Hunter	6.00	3.00	1.75
(32)	Reggie Jackson	9.00	4.50	2.70
(33)	Randy Jones	2.50	1.25	.70
(34)	Dave Kingman	2.50	1.25	.70
(35)	Jerry Koosman	2.50	1.25	.70
(36)	Ed Kranepool	2.50	1.25	.70
(37)	Ron LeFlore	2.50	1.25	.70
(38)	Sixto Lezcano	2.50	1.25	.70
(39)	Davey Lopes	2.50	1.25	.70
(40)	Greg Luzinski	2.50	1.25	.70
(41)	Fred Lynn	2.50	1.25	.70
(42)	Garry Maddox	2.50	1.25	.70
(43)	Jon Matlock	2.50	1.25	.70
(44)	Gary Matthews	2.50	1.25	.70
(45)	Lee May	2.50	1.25	.70
(46)	John Mayberry	2.50	1.25	.70
(47)	Bake McBride	2.50	1.25	.70
(48)	Tug McGraw	2.50	1.25	.70
(49)	Hal McRae	2.50	1.25	.70
(50)	Andy Messersmith	2.50	1.25	.70
(51)	Randy Moffitt	2.50	1.25	.70
(52)	John Montefusco	2.50	1.25	.70
(53)	Joe Morgan	6.00	3.00	1.75
(54)	Thurman Munson	6.00	3.00	1.75
(55)	Graig Nettles	2.50	1.25	.70
(56)	Al Oliver	2.50	1.25	.70
(57)	Jorge Orta	2.50	1.25	.70
(58)	Jim Palmer	6.00	3.00	1.75
(59)	Dave Parker	2.50	1.25	.70
(60)	Tony Perez	6.00	3.00	1.75
(61)	Gaylord Perry	6.00	3.00	1.75
(62)	Jim Rice	3.00	1.50	.90
(63)	Steve Rogers	2.50	1.25	.70
(64)	Pete Rose	15.00	7.50	4.50
(65)	Joe Rudi	2.50	1.25	.70
(66)	Nolan Ryan	30.00	15.00	9.00
(67)	Manny Sanguillen	2.50	1.25	.70
(68)	Mike Schmidt	9.00	4.50	2.70
(69)	Tom Seaver	7.50	3.75	2.25
(70)	Ted Simmons	2.50	1.25	.70
(71)	Reggie Smith	2.50	1.25	.70
(72)	Willie Stargell	6.00	3.00	1.75
(73)	Rusty Staub	2.50	1.25	.70
(74)	Frank Tanana	2.50	1.25	.70
(75)	Gene Tenace	2.50	1.25	.70
(76)	Luis Tiant	2.50	1.25	.70
(77)	Manny Trillo	2.50	1.25	.70
(78)	Bob Watson	2.50	1.25	.70
(79)	Carl Yastrzemski	7.50	3.75	2.25
(80)	Richie Zisk	2.50	1.25	.70

1978 Wiffle Box-Side Discs

Similar in concept and format to the many contemporary MSA baseball player disc sets, the pieces printed on the sides of Wiffle-brand baseball boxes differ in that they are smaller, at 2-3/8" diameter, and feature a larger checklist. The discs feature black-and-white player portrait photos in the center of a baseball design. The left and right panels are in one of several bright colors. Licensed by the players' association through Mike Schechter Associates, the player photos carry no uniform logos. Backs are printed in black and orange. The unnumbered discs are checklisted here alphabetically.

		NM	E	VG
Complete Set (88):		325.00	160.00	100.00
Common Player:		2.50	1.25	.70
(1)	Sal Bando	2.50	1.25	.70
(2)	Buddy Bell	2.50	1.25	.70
(3)	Johnny Bench	7.50	3.75	2.25
(4)	Vida Blue	2.50	1.25	.70
(5)	Bert Blyleven	3.00	1.50	.90
(6)	Bobby Bonds	2.50	1.25	.70
(7)	George Brett	9.00	6.00	3.50
(8)	Lou Brock	6.00	3.00	1.75
(9)	Bill Buckner	2.50	1.25	.70
(10)	Ray Burris	2.50	1.25	.70
(11)	Jeff Burroughs	2.50	1.25	.70
(12)	Bert Campaneris	2.50	1.25	.70
(13)	John Candelaria	2.50	1.25	.70
(14)	Jose Cardenal	2.50	1.25	.70
(15)	Rod Carew	6.00	3.00	1.75
(16)	Steve Carlton	6.00	3.00	1.75
(17)	Dave Cash	2.50	1.25	.70
(18)	Cesar Cedeno	2.50	1.25	.70
(19)	Ron Cey	2.50	1.25	.70
(20)	Chris Chambliss	2.50	1.25	.70
(21)	Dave Concepcion	2.50	1.25	.70
(22)	Dennis Eckersley	6.00	3.00	1.75
(23)	Mark Fidrych	3.50	1.75	1.00
(24)	Rollie Fingers	6.00	3.00	1.75
(25)	Carlton Fisk	6.00	3.00	1.75
(26)	George Foster	2.50	1.25	.70
(27)	Wayne Garland	2.50	1.25	.70
(28)	Ralph Garr	2.50	1.25	.70
(29)	Steve Garvey	5.00	2.50	1.50
(30)	Don Gullett	2.50	1.25	.70
(31)	Larry Hisle	2.50	1.25	.70
(32)	Al Hrabosky	2.50	1.25	.70
(33)	Catfish Hunter	6.00	3.00	1.75
(34)	Reggie Jackson	9.00	6.00	3.50
(35)	Randy Jones	2.50	1.25	.70
(36)	Von Joshua	2.50	1.25	.70
(37)	Dave Kingman	2.50	1.25	.70
(38)	Jerry Koosman	2.50	1.25	.70
(39)	Ed Kranepool	2.50	1.25	.70
(40)	Ron LeFlore	2.50	1.25	.70
(41)	Sixto Lezcano	2.50	1.25	.70
(42)	Davey Lopes	2.50	1.25	.70
(43)	Greg Luzinski	2.50	1.25	.70
(44)	Fred Lynn	2.50	1.25	.70
(45)	Garry Maddox	2.50	1.25	.70
(46)	Jon Matlock	2.50	1.25	.70
(47)	Gary Matthews	2.50	1.25	.70
(48)	Lee May	2.50	1.25	.70
(49)	John Mayberry	2.50	1.25	.70
(50)	Bake McBride	2.50	1.25	.70
(51)	Tug McGraw	2.50	1.25	.70
(52)	Hal McRae	2.50	1.25	.70
(53)	Andy Messersmith	2.50	1.25	.70
(54)	Randy Moffitt	2.50	1.25	.70
(55)	John Montefusco	2.50	1.25	.70
(56)	Joe Morgan	6.00	3.00	1.75
(57)	Thurman Munson	6.00	3.00	1.75
(58)	Graig Nettles	2.50	1.25	.70
(59)	Bill North	2.50	1.25	.70
(60)	Al Oliver	2.50	1.25	.70
(61)	Jorge Orta	2.50	1.25	.70
(62)	Jim Palmer	6.00	3.00	1.75
(63)	Dave Parker	2.50	1.25	.70
(64)	Tony Perez	6.00	3.00	1.75
(65)	Gaylord Perry	6.00	3.00	1.75
(66)	Jim Rice	3.00	1.50	.90
(67)	Ellie Rodriguez	2.50	1.25	.70
(68)	Steve Rogers	2.50	1.25	.70
(69)	Pete Rose	15.00	7.50	4.50
(70)	Joe Rudi	2.50	1.25	.70
(71)	Nolan Ryan	30.00	15.00	9.00
(72)	Manny Sanguillen	2.50	1.25	.70
(73)	Mike Schmidt	9.00	6.00	3.50
(74)	Tom Seaver	7.50	3.75	2.25
(75)	Ted Simmons	2.50	1.25	.70
(76)	Reggie Smith	2.50	1.25	.70
(77)	Jim Spencer	2.50	1.25	.70
(78)	Willie Stargell	6.00	3.00	1.75
(79)	Rusty Staub	2.50	1.25	.70
(80)	Rennie Stennett	2.50	1.25	.70
(81)	Frank Tanana	2.50	1.25	.70
(82)	Gene Tenace	2.50	1.25	.70
(83)	Luis Tiant	2.50	1.25	.70
(84)	Manny Trillo	2.50	1.25	.70
(85)	Bob Watson	2.50	1.25	.70
(86)	Butch Wynegar	2.50	1.25	.70
(87)	Carl Yastrzemski	7.50	3.75	2.25
(88)	Richie Zisk	2.50	1.25	.70

1922 Willard's Chocolates Premium

Details on distribution of this 7-1/8" x 11-1/4" premium are unclear, likely involving some sort of wrapper or coupon redemption. The blank-back piece has a central photo of Babe Ruth in action. A facsimile autograph appears in a panel at bottom.

	NM	E	VG
Babe Ruth	4,000	2,000	1,200

1923 Willard's Chocolate (V100)

Issued circa 1923, this set was produced by the Willard Chocolate Co. of Canada and features sepia-toned photographs on cards measuring about 2" x 3-1/4". The cards are blank-backed and feature the player's name in script on the front, along with a tiny credit line: "Photo by International."

The set is complete at 180 cards and nearly one-fourth of the photos used in the set are identical to the better known E120 American Caramel set. The Willard set is identified as V100 in the American Card Catalog.

		NM	E	VG
Complete Set (180):		80,000	40,000	24,000
Common Player:		100.00	50.00	30.00
(1)	Chas. B. Adams	100.00	50.00	30.00
(2)	Grover C. Alexander	400.00	200.00	125.00
(3)	J.P. Austin	100.00	50.00	30.00
(4)	J.C. Bagby Sr.	100.00	50.00	30.00
(5)	J. Franklin Baker	300.00	150.00	90.00
(6)	David J. Bancroft	300.00	150.00	90.00
(7)	Turner Barber	100.00	50.00	30.00
(8)	Jesse L. Barnes	100.00	50.00	30.00
(9)	J.C. Bassler	100.00	50.00	30.00
(10)	L.A. Blue	100.00	50.00	30.00
(11)	Norman D. Boeckel	100.00	50.00	30.00
(12)	F.L. Brazil (Brazill)	100.00	50.00	30.00
(13)	G.H. Burns	100.00	50.00	30.00
(14)	Geo. J. Burns	100.00	50.00	30.00
(15)	Leon Cadore	100.00	50.00	30.00
(16)	Max G. Carey	300.00	150.00	90.00
(17)	Harold G. Carlson	100.00	50.00	30.00
(18)	Lloyd R Christenberry (Christenbury)	100.00	50.00	30.00
(19)	Vernon J. Clemons	100.00	50.00	30.00
(20)	T.R. Cobb	2,400	1,200	750.00
(21)	Bert Cole	100.00	50.00	30.00
(22)	John F. Collins	100.00	50.00	30.00
(23)	S. Coveleskie (Coveleski)	300.00	150.00	90.00
(24)	Walton E. Cruise	100.00	50.00	30.00
(25)	G.W. Cutshaw	100.00	50.00	30.00
(26)	Jacob E. Daubert	100.00	50.00	30.00
(27)	Geo. Dauss	100.00	50.00	30.00
(28)	F.T. Davis	100.00	50.00	30.00
(29)	Chas. A. Deal	100.00	50.00	30.00
(30)	William L. Doak	100.00	50.00	30.00
(31)	William E. Donovan	100.00	50.00	30.00
(32)	Hugh Duffy	300.00	150.00	90.00
(33)	J.A. Dugan	100.00	50.00	30.00
(34)	Louis B. Duncan	100.00	50.00	30.00
(35)	James Dykes	100.00	50.00	30.00
(36)	H.J. Ehmke	100.00	50.00	30.00
(37)	F.R. Ellerbe	100.00	50.00	30.00
(38)	E.G. Erickson	100.00	50.00	30.00
(39)	John J. Evers	300.00	150.00	90.00
(40)	U.C. Faber	300.00	150.00	90.00
(41)	B.A. Falk	100.00	50.00	30.00
(42)	Max Flack	100.00	50.00	30.00
(43)	Lee Fohl	100.00	50.00	30.00
(44)	Jacques F. Fournier	100.00	50.00	30.00
(45)	Frank F. Frisch	300.00	150.00	90.00
(46)	C.E. Galloway	100.00	50.00	30.00
(47)	W.C. Gardner	100.00	50.00	30.00
(48)	E.P. Gharrity	100.00	50.00	30.00
(49)	Geo. Gibson	100.00	50.00	30.00
(50)	Wm. Gleason	100.00	50.00	30.00
(51)	William Gleason	100.00	50.00	30.00
(52)	Henry M. Gowdy	100.00	50.00	30.00
(53)	I.M. Griffin	100.00	50.00	30.00
(54)	Tom Griffith	100.00	50.00	30.00
(55)	Burleigh A. Grimes	300.00	150.00	90.00
(56)	Charles J. Grimm	100.00	50.00	30.00
(57)	Jesse J. Haines	300.00	150.00	90.00
(58)	S.R. Harris	300.00	150.00	90.00
(59)	W.B. Harris	100.00	50.00	30.00
(60)	R.K. Hasty	100.00	50.00	30.00
(61)	H.E. Heilman (Heilmann)	300.00	150.00	90.00
(62)	Walter J. Henline	100.00	50.00	30.00
(63)	Walter L. Holke	100.00	50.00	30.00
(64)	Charles J. Hollocher	100.00	50.00	30.00
(65)	H.B. Hooper	300.00	150.00	90.00
(66)	Rogers Hornsby	400.00	200.00	125.00
(67)	W.C. Hoyt	300.00	150.00	90.00
(68)	Miller Huggins	300.00	150.00	90.00
(69)	W.C. Jacobsen (Jacobson)	100.00	50.00	30.00
(70)	C.D. Jamieson	100.00	50.00	30.00
(71)	Ernest Johnson	100.00	50.00	30.00
(72)	W.P. Johnson	3,000	1,500	900.00
(73)	James H. Johnston	100.00	50.00	30.00
(74)	R.W. Jones	100.00	50.00	30.00
(75)	Samuel Pond Jones	100.00	50.00	30.00
(76)	J.I. Judge	100.00	50.00	30.00
(77)	James W. Keenan	100.00	50.00	30.00
(78)	Geo. L. Kelly	300.00	150.00	90.00
(79)	Peter J. Kilduff	100.00	50.00	30.00
(80)	William Killefer	100.00	50.00	30.00
(81)	Lee King	100.00	50.00	30.00
(82)	Ray Kolp	100.00	50.00	30.00
(83)	John Lavan	100.00	50.00	30.00
(84)	H.L. Leibold	100.00	50.00	30.00
(85)	Connie Mack	600.00	300.00	180.00
(86)	J.W. Mails	100.00	50.00	30.00
(87)	Walter J. Maranville	300.00	150.00	90.00
(88)	Richard W. Marquard	300.00	150.00	90.00
(89)	C.W. Mays	100.00	50.00	30.00
(90)	Geo. F. McBride	100.00	50.00	30.00
(91)	H.M. McClellan	100.00	50.00	30.00
(92)	John J. McGraw	300.00	150.00	90.00
(93)	Austin B. McHenry	100.00	50.00	30.00
(94)	J. McInnis	100.00	50.00	30.00
(95)	Douglas McWeeney (McWeeny)	100.00	50.00	30.00
(96)	M. Menosky	100.00	50.00	30.00
(97)	Emil F. Meusel	100.00	50.00	30.00
(98)	R. Meusel	100.00	50.00	30.00
(99)	Henry W. Meyers	100.00	50.00	30.00
(100)	J.C. Milan	100.00	50.00	30.00
(101)	John K. Miljus	100.00	50.00	30.00
(102)	Edmund J. Miller	100.00	50.00	30.00
(103)	Elmer Miller	100.00	50.00	30.00
(104)	Otto L. Miller	100.00	50.00	30.00
(105)	Fred Mitchell	100.00	50.00	30.00
(106)	Geo. Mogridge	100.00	50.00	30.00
(107)	Patrick J. Moran	100.00	50.00	30.00
(108)	John D. Morrison	100.00	50.00	30.00
(109)	J.A. Mostil	100.00	50.00	30.00
(110)	Clarence F. Mueller	100.00	50.00	30.00
(111)	A. Earle Neale	100.00	50.00	30.00
(112)	Joseph Oeschger	100.00	50.00	30.00
(113)	Robert J. O'Farrell	100.00	50.00	30.00
(114)	J.C. Oldham	100.00	50.00	30.00
(115)	I.M. Olson	100.00	50.00	30.00
(116)	Geo. M. O'Neil	100.00	50.00	30.00
(117)	S.F. O'Neill	100.00	50.00	30.00
(118)	Frank J. Parkinson	100.00	50.00	30.00
(119)	Geo. H. Paskert	100.00	50.00	30.00
(120)	R.T. Peckinpaugh	100.00	50.00	30.00
(121)	H.J. Pennock	300.00	150.00	90.00
(122)	Ralph Perkins	100.00	50.00	30.00
(123)	Edw. J. Pfeffer	100.00	50.00	30.00
(124)	W.C. Pipp	100.00	50.00	30.00
(125)	Charles Elmer Ponder	100.00	50.00	30.00
(126)	Raymond R. Powell	100.00	50.00	30.00
(127)	D.B. Pratt	100.00	50.00	30.00
(128)	Joseph Rapp	100.00	50.00	30.00
(129)	John H. Rawlings	100.00	50.00	30.00
(130)	E.S. Rice (Should be E.C.)	300.00	150.00	90.00
(131)	Branch Rickey	600.00	300.00	180.00
(132)	James J. Ring	100.00	50.00	30.00
(133)	Eppa J. Rixey	300.00	150.00	90.00
(134)	Davis A. Robertson	100.00	50.00	30.00
(135)	Edwin Rommel	100.00	50.00	30.00
(136)	Edd J. Roush	300.00	150.00	90.00
(137)	Harold Ruel (Herold)	100.00	50.00	30.00
(138)	Allen Russell	100.00	50.00	30.00
(139)	G.H. Ruth	4,500	2,250	1,400
(140)	Wilfred D. Ryan	100.00	50.00	30.00
(141)	Henry F. Sallee	100.00	50.00	30.00
(142)	W.H. Schang	100.00	50.00	30.00
(143)	Raymond H. Schmandt	100.00	50.00	30.00
(144)	Everett Scott	100.00	50.00	30.00
(145)	Henry Severeid	100.00	50.00	30.00
(146)	Jos. W. Sewell	300.00	150.00	90.00
(147)	Howard S. Shanks	100.00	50.00	30.00
(148)	E.H. Sheely	100.00	50.00	30.00
(149)	Ralph Shinners	100.00	50.00	30.00
(150)	U.J. Shocker	100.00	50.00	30.00
(151)	G.H. Sisler	300.00	150.00	90.00
(152)	Earl L. Smith	100.00	50.00	30.00
(153)	Earl S. Smith	100.00	50.00	30.00
(154)	Geo. A. Smith	100.00	50.00	30.00
(155)	J.W. Smith	100.00	50.00	30.00
(156)	Tris E. Speaker	750.00	375.00	225.00
(157)	Arnold Staatz (Statz)	100.00	50.00	30.00
(158)	J.R. Stephenson	100.00	50.00	30.00
(159)	Milton J. Stock	100.00	50.00	30.00
(160)	John L. Sullivan	100.00	50.00	30.00
(161)	H.F. Tormahlen	100.00	50.00	30.00
(162)	Jas. A. Tierney	100.00	50.00	30.00
(163)	J.T. Tobin	100.00	50.00	30.00
(164)	Jas. L. Vaughn	100.00	50.00	30.00
(165)	R.H. Veach	100.00	50.00	30.00
(166)	C.W. Walker	100.00	50.00	30.00
(167)	A.L. Ward	100.00	50.00	30.00
(168)	Zack D. Wheat	300.00	150.00	90.00
(169)	George B. Whitted	100.00	50.00	30.00
(170)	Irvin K. Wilhelm	100.00	50.00	30.00
(171)	Roy H. Wilkinson	100.00	50.00	30.00
(172)	Fred C. Williams	100.00	50.00	30.00
(173)	K.R. Williams	100.00	50.00	30.00
(174)	Sam'l W. Wilson	100.00	50.00	30.00
(175)	Ivy B. Wingo	100.00	50.00	30.00
(176)	L.W. Witt	100.00	50.00	30.00
(177)	Joseph Wood	200.00	100.00	60.00
(178)	E. Yaryan	100.00	50.00	30.00
(179)	R.S. Young	100.00	50.00	30.00
(180)	Ross Young (Youngs)	300.00	150.00	90.00

1924 Willard's Chocolate Sports Champions (V122)

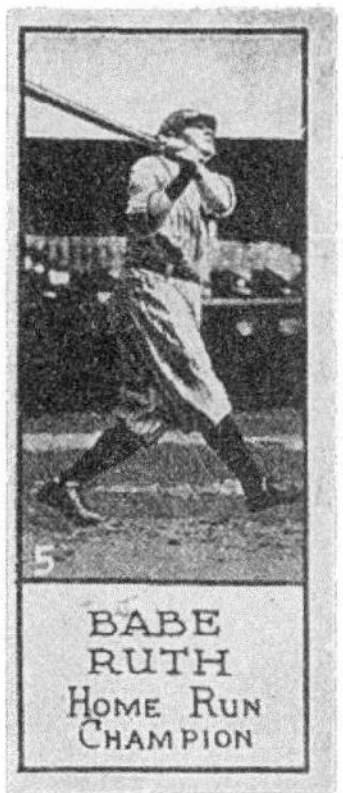

Three baseball players are featured among this 56-card Canadian set. The black-and-white cards are printed on thin paper measuring 1-3/8" x 3-3/8". Backs are blank. The set features male and female athletes from many different sports, with a distinct Canadian flavor. The candy company was headquartered in Toronto.

		NM	E	VG
2	Eddie Collins	600.00	300.00	180.00
5	Babe Ruth	3,250	1,625	975.00
39	Ty Cobb	2,250	1,125	675.00

1889 E.R. Williams Card Game

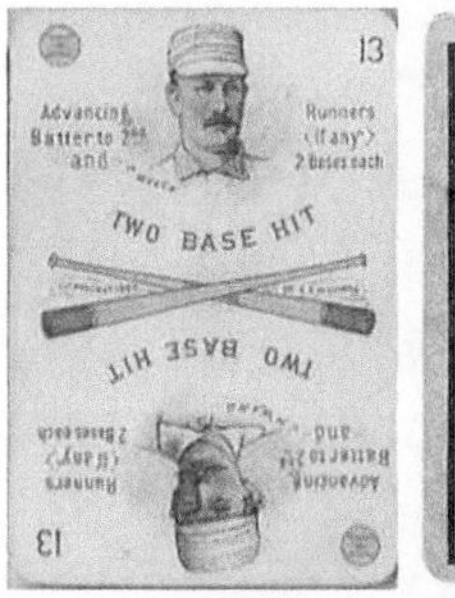

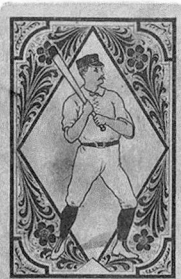

This set of 52 playing cards came packed in its own box that advertised the set as the "Egerton R. Williams Popular Indoor Base Ball Game." Designed to look like a conventional deck of playing cards, the set included various players from the National League and the American Association. Although the set contains 52 cards (like a typical deck of playing cards) only 19 actually feature color drawings of players. Each of these cards pictures two different players (one at the top and a second at the bottom, separated by sepia-colored crossed bats in the middle), resulting in 38 different players. The remaining 33 cards in the deck are strictly game cards showing a specific baseball play (such as "Batter Out on Fly" or "Two Base Hit," etc.). The cards have green-tinted backs and measure 2-7/16" x 3-1/2". Each one carries an 1889 copyright line by E.R. Williams.

		NM	E	VG
Complete Boxed Set:		24,000	12,000	7,250
Common Player Card:		600.00	300.00	225.00
Common Game Action Card:		110.00	55.00	30.00
(1)	Cap Anson, Buck Ewing	2,400	1,200	720.00
(2)	Dan Brouthers, Arlie Latham	900.00	450.00	275.00
(3)	Charles Buffinton, Bob Carruthers	600.00	300.00	225.00
(4)	Hick Carpenter, Cliff Carroll	600.00	300.00	225.00
(5)	Charles Comiskey, Roger Connor	1,200	600.00	360.00
(6)	Pop Corkhill, Jim Fogarty	600.00	300.00	225.00
(7)	John Clarkson, Tim Keefe	1,200	600.00	360.00
(8)	Jerry Denny, Mike Tiernan	600.00	300.00	225.00
(9)	Dave Foutz, King Kelly	2,200	1,100	660.00
(10)	Pud Galvin, Dave Orr	900.00	450.00	275.00
(11)	Jack Glasscock, Tommy Tucker	600.00	300.00	225.00
(12)	Mike Griffin, Ed McKean	600.00	300.00	225.00
(13)	Dummy Hoy, Long John Reilley (Reilly)	900.00	450.00	275.00
(14)	Arthur Irwin, Ned Williamson	600.00	300.00	225.00
(15)	Silver King, John Tener	900.00	450.00	275.00

		NM	E	VG
(16)	Al Myers, Cub Stricker	600.00	300.00	225.00
(17)	Fred Pfeffer, Chicken Wolf	600.00	300.00	225.00
(18)	Tom Ramsey, Gus Weyhing	600.00	300.00	225.00
(19)	John Ward, Curt Welch	1,000	500.00	300.00

1908 R.C. Williams Cy Young Postcard

A mature Cy Young, about age 42, is pictured on this postcard bearing the imprint of R.C. Williams. No other contemporary cards with this imprint have been reported.

	NM	E	VG
Cy Young	800.00	400.00	240.00

1911 Williams Baking Philadelphia A's (D359)

 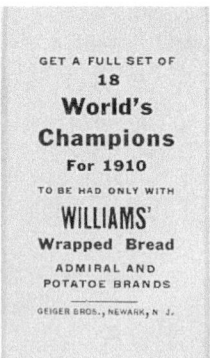

This Philadelphia Athletics team set is among the scarcest early 20th Century baking company issues. It commemorates the A's 1910 Championship season, and, except for pitcher Jack Coombs, the checklist includes nearly all key members of the club, including manager Connie Mack. The cards are the standard size for the era, 1-1/2" x 2-5/8". Fronts feature a player portrait set against a colored background. The player's name and the word "Athletics" appear at the bottom, while "World's Champions 1910" is printed along the top. Backs of the cards advertise the set as the "Athletics Series." Collectors should be aware that the same checklist was used for a similar Athletics set issued by Rochester Baking and Cullivan's Fireside tobacco (T208) and also that blank-backed versions are also known to exist, cataloged as E104 in the American Card Catalog.

		NM	E	VG
Complete Set (18):		85,000	35,000	17,000
Common Player:		3,200	1,600	800.00
(1)	Home Run Baker	7,750	3,500	1,750
(2)	Jack Barry	3,200	1,600	800.00
(3)	Chief Bender	7,750	3,500	1,750
(4)	Eddie Collins	7,750	3,500	1,750
(5)	Harry Davis	6,000	3,000	1,500
(6)	Jimmy Dygert	3,200	1,600	800.00
(7)	Topsy Hartsel	3,200	1,600	800.00
(8)	Harry Krause	3,200	1,600	800.00
(9)	Jack Lapp	3,200	1,600	800.00
(10)	Paddy Livingston	3,200	1,600	800.00
(11)	Bris Lord	3,200	1,600	800.00
(12)	Connie Mack	14,000	7,900	4,575
(13)	Cy Morgan	3,200	1,600	800.00
(14)	Danny Murphy	6,000	3,000	1,500
(15)	Rube Oldring	3,200	1,600	800.00
(16)	Eddie Plank	16,000	7,900	4,575
(17)	Amos Strunk	3,200	1,600	800.00
(18a)	Ira Thomas (1910 at top)	3,200	1,600	800.00
(18b)	Ira Thomas (1910 at right)	3,200	1,600	800.00

1910 Williams Caramels (E103)

This 30-card set issued by the Williams Caramel Co. of Oxford, Pa., in 1910 can be differentiated from other similar sets because it was printed on a thin paper stock rather than cardboard. Measuring approximately 1-3/4" x 2-5/8", each card features a player portrait set against a red background. The bottom of the card lists the player's last name, position and team; beneath that is the line, "The Williams Caramel Co. Oxford Pa." Nearly all of the photos in the set, which is designated E103 by the ACC, are identical to those in the M116 Sporting Life set.

		NM	E	VG
Complete Set (30):		156,000	60,000	30,000
Common Player:		1,175	475.00	225.00
(1)	Chas. Bender	5,400	2,150	1,100
(2)	Roger Bresnahan	5,400	2,150	1,100
(3)	Mordecai Brown	5,400	2,150	1,100
(4)	Frank Chance	5,400	2,150	1,100
(5)	Hal Chase	4,000	1,450	700.00
(6)	Ty Cobb	45,000	18,000	9,000
(7)	Edward Collins	5,400	2,150	1,100
(8)	Sam Crawford	5,400	2,150	1,100
(9)	Harry Davis	1,175	475.00	225.00
(10)	Arthur Devlin	1,175	475.00	225.00
(11)	William Donovan	1,175	475.00	225.00
(12)	Chas. Dooin	1,175	475.00	225.00
(13)	L. Doyle	1,175	475.00	225.00
(14)	John Ewing	1,175	475.00	225.00
(15)	George Gibson	1,175	475.00	225.00
(16)	Hugh Jennings	5,400	2,150	1,100
(17)	David Jones	1,175	475.00	225.00
(18)	Tim Jordan	1,175	475.00	225.00
(19)	N. Lajoie	5,400	2,150	1,100
(20)	Thomas Leach	1,175	475.00	225.00
(21)	Harry Lord	1,175	475.00	225.00
(22)	Chris. Mathewson	18,000	7,200	3,600
(23)	John McLean	1,175	475.00	225.00
(24)	Geo. W. McQuillan	1,175	475.00	225.00
(25)	Pastorius	1,175	475.00	225.00
(26)	N. Rucker	1,175	475.00	225.00
(27)	Fred Tenny (Tenney)	1,175	475.00	225.00
(28)	Ira Thomas	1,175	475.00	225.00
(29)	Hans Wagner	35,000	14,400	7,200
(30)	Robert Wood	1,175	475.00	225.00

1950s-70s Wilson Advisory Staff Photos

Advisory staff photos were a promotional item which debuted in the early 1950s, flourished in the 1960s and died in the early 1970s. Generally 8" x 10" (sometimes a little larger), these black-and-white (a few later were color) glossy photos picture players who had contracted with a major baseball equipment company to endorse and use their product. Usually the product - most often a glove - was prominently displayed in the photo. The pictures were often displayed in the windows of sporting goods stores or the walls of sports departments and were sometimes made available to customers. Because the companies tended to stick with players over the years, some photos were reissued, sometimes with and sometimes without a change of team, pose or style. The photos are checklisted here in alphabetical order. A pose description is given where known. It is unlikely this list is complete. Gaps have been left in the assigned numbering to accommodate future additions. In general, Wilson advisory staff photos feature the player name and a line of type indicating the player's status as an advisory staffer in the bottom border.

		NM	E	VG
Common Player:		14.00	7.00	4.00
(1)	Bob Allison (Twins, full-length.)	20.00	10.00	6.00
(2)	Felipe Alou (Braves, neck-to-cap.)	25.00	12.50	7.50
(3)	Felipe Alou (Braves, upper body.)	25.00	12.50	7.50
(4)	Max Alvis (Indians, hands on knees.)	20.00	10.00	6.00
(5)	Max Alvis (Indians, upper body.)	20.00	10.00	6.00
(6)	Luis Aparicio (White Sox, horizontal, fielding.)	50.00	25.00	15.00
(7)	Luis Aparicio (White Sox, fielding, full-length.)	40.00	20.00	12.00
(8)	Luis Aparicio (Orioles, full-length.)	50.00	25.00	15.00
(9)	Gerry Arrigo (Reds, full-length pitching.)	20.00	10.00	6.00
(10)	Ernie Banks (Batting)	75.00	37.00	22.00
(11)	Ernie Banks (Horizontal, fielding.)	60.00	30.00	18.00
(12)	Glenn Beckert (Cubs, fielding, ball in hand.)	25.00	12.50	7.50
(13)	Glenn Beckert (Cubs, fielding, no ball.)	25.00	12.50	7.50
(14)	Paul Blair (Orioles, full-length.)	25.00	12.50	7.50
(15)	Don Blasingame (Cardinals, belt-up.)	20.00	10.00	6.00
(16)	Bob Bolin (Giants, pitching follow-through.)	20.00	10.00	6.00
(17)	Dave Boswell (Twins, full-length.)	20.00	10.00	6.00
(18)	Dave Boswell (Twins, waist-up, stretch position.)	20.00	10.00	6.00
(19)	Jackie Brandt (Orioles, full-length.)	20.00	10.00	6.00
(20)	Smoky Burgess (Pirates, sitting on step w/ three bats.)	20.00	10.00	6.00
(21)	Rico Carty (Milwaukee Braves, batting.)	20.00	10.00	6.00
(22)	Rico Carty (Milwaukee Braves, dugout step.)	20.00	10.00	6.00
(23)	Rico Carty (Atlanta Braves, batting.)	20.00	10.00	6.00
(24)	Paul Casanova (Senators, catching crouch.)	20.00	10.00	6.00
(25)	Norm Cash (Tigers, batting, waist-up.)	25.00	12.50	7.50
(26)	Orlando Cepeda (Braves, batting.)	30.00	15.00	9.00
(27)	Orlando Cepeda (Cardinals, dugout step.)	25.00	12.50	7.50
(28)	Orlando Cepeda (Cardinals, fielding.)	25.00	12.50	7.50
(29)	Jim Davenport (Giants, fielding.)	20.00	10.00	6.00
(30)	Vic Davalillo (Indians, upper body.)	20.00	10.00	6.00
(31)	Willie Davis (Dodgers, full-length.)	20.00	10.00	6.00
(32)	Chuck Dobson (A's, full-length.)	20.00	10.00	6.00
(35)	"Moe" Drabowsky (Cubs, thighs-up.)	20.00	10.00	6.00
(36)	Don Drysdale (L.A. Dodgers, follow-through.)	25.00	12.50	7.50
(37)	Dick Ellsworth (Cubs, pitching follow-through.)	20.00	10.00	6.00
(38)	Dick Ellsworth (Phillies, full-length.)	20.00	10.00	6.00
(39)	Del Ennis (Cardinals, kneeling.)	20.00	10.00	6.00
(40)	Bob Feller (Seated, glove on knee.)	120.00	60.00	36.00
(41)	Nellie Fox (White Sox, chest-up.)	35.00	17.50	10.50
(42)	Nellie Fox (White Sox, fielding grounder.)	50.00	25.00	15.00
(43)	Nelson Fox (White Sox, seated.)	50.00	25.00	15.00
(44)	Nelson Fox (Colt .45s, batting.)	50.00	25.00	15.00
(45)	Bill Freehan (Catching crouch.)	20.00	10.00	6.00
(46)	Bill Freehan (Two pictures.)	20.00	10.00	6.00
(47)	Phil Gagliano (Cardinals, fielding, photo actually Ed Spiezio.)	25.00	12.50	7.50
(48)	Jim Gentile (Orioles, batting, chest-up.)	20.00	10.00	6.00
(49)	Vernon "Lefty" Gomez (w/ glasses.)	25.00	12.50	7.50

(50)	Lefty Gomez (No glasses.)	25.00	12.50	7.50
(51)	Jim Hall (Angels, fielding.)	25.00	12.50	7.50
(52a)	Don Hoak (Pirates, full-length, waist up.)	20.00	10.00	6.00
(52b)	Don Hoak (Pirates, waist up.)	20.00	10.00	6.00
(53)	Gil Hodges (L.A. Dodgers, belt-up batting.)	50.00	25.00	15.00
(54)	Willie Horton (Tigers, full-length.)	20.00	10.00	6.00
(55)	Bruce Howard (White Sox, pitching follow-through.)	20.00	10.00	6.00
(56)	Jim Hunter (K.C. A's, beginning wind-up.)	25.00	12.50	7.50
(57)	Jim Hunter (Oakland A's, full-length, photo actuallyChuck Dobson.)	25.00	12.50	7.50
(58)	Mack Jones (Reds, full-length.)	20.00	10.00	6.00
(59)	Duane Josephson (White Sox, catching crouch.)	20.00	10.00	6.00
(61)	Jim Kaat (Twins, upper body.)	25.00	12.50	7.50
(62)	Al Kaline (Full-length, batting.)	75.00	37.00	22.00
(63)	Al Kaline (Upper body, batting.)	75.00	37.00	22.00
(64)	Al Kaline (Upper body, hands on knees.)	75.00	37.00	22.00
(65)	Al Kaline (Upper body.)	75.00	37.00	22.00
(66)	Al Kaline (Upper body, looking right.)	75.00	37.00	22.00
(67)	Harmon Killebrew (Twins, upper body, batting.)	50.00	25.00	15.00
(68)	Harmon Killebrew (Twins, batting, looking front.)	50.00	25.00	15.00
(69)	Harmon Killebrew (Twins, kneeling.)	50.00	25.00	15.00
(70)	Cal Koonce (Cubs, pitching follow-through.)	20.00	10.00	6.00
(71)	Harvey Kuenn (Tigers, batting.)	25.00	12.50	7.50
(72)	Harvey Kuenn (Tigers, upper body.)	25.00	12.50	7.50
(73)	Hal Lanier (Giants, throwing.)	20.00	10.00	6.00
(74)	Juan Marichal (Giants, upper body.)	25.00	12.50	7.50
(75)	Billy Martin (Reds fielding)	60.00	30.00	18.00
(75)	Willie McCovey (Giants, batting.)	25.00	12.50	7.50
(76)	Sam McDowell (Indians, seated, no cap.)	25.00	12.50	7.50
(77)	Dennis McLain (Tigers, hands at chest.)	25.00	12.50	7.50
(78)	Roy McMillan (Braves, batting.)	20.00	10.00	6.00
(79)	Roy McMillan (Reds, belt-up.)	20.00	10.00	6.00
(81)	Denis Menke (Braves, fielding.)	20.00	10.00	6.00
(82)	Denis Menke (Braves, upper body.)	20.00	10.00	6.00
(83)	Don Mincher (Angels, full-length.)	20.00	10.00	6.00
(84)	Joe Morgan (Astros, batting.)	40.00	20.00	12.00
(85)	Joe Morgan (Astros, fielding.)	40.00	20.00	12.00
(86)	Jim Nash (A's, pitching.)	20.00	10.00	6.00
(87)	Rich Nye (Cubs, pitching.)	20.00	10.00	6.00
(88)	John Odom (Kansas City A's, pitching.)	20.00	10.00	6.00
(89)	John Odom (Oakland A's, belt-up pose.)	20.00	10.00	6.00
(90)	John Orsino (Orioles, kneeling.)	20.00	10.00	6.00
(91)	Jim O'Toole (Reds, upper body, warm-up jacket.)	20.00	10.00	6.00
(92)	Jim O'Toole (White Sox, upper body.)	20.00	10.00	6.00
(93)	Ray Oyler (Tigers, fielding.)	20.00	10.00	6.00
(94)	Milt Pappas (Orioles, pitching, full-length.)	20.00	10.00	6.00
(95)	Milt Pappas (Orioles, pitching, knees-up.)	20.00	10.00	6.00
(96)	Don Pavletich (Reds, full-length.)	20.00	10.00	6.00
(97)	Don Pavletich (Reds, squatting.)	20.00	10.00	6.00

(98)	Albie Pearson (Angels, glove under left arm.)	20.00	10.00	6.00
(99)	Ron Perranoski (Dodgers, upper body.)	20.00	10.00	6.00
(100)	Ron Perranoski (Twins, belt-up from side.)	25.00	12.50	7.50
(101)	Ron Perranoski (Twins, pitching.)	20.00	10.00	6.00
(102)	Gaylord Perry (Giants, pitching.)	25.00	12.50	7.50
(103)	Billy Pierce (White Sox, knees-up.)	25.00	12.50	7.50
(104)	Bob Purkey (Reds, waist-up.)	20.00	10.00	6.00
(105)	Doug Rader (Astros, fielding.)	20.00	10.00	6.00
(106)	Dick Radatz (Radatz) (Red Sox, upper body.))	20.00	10.00	6.00
(107)	Dick Radatz (Red Sox, upper body.)	20.00	10.00	6.00
(108)	Pete Runnels (Red Sox, kneeling on deck.)	25.00	12.50	7.50
(109)	Ron Santo (Cubs, fielding.)	25.00	12.50	7.50
(110)	George Scott (Red Sox, upper body.)	20.00	10.00	6.00
(111)	Larry Sherry (Dodgers, full-length.)	20.00	10.00	6.00
(112)	Chris Short (Phillies, upper body.)	20.00	10.00	6.00
(113)	Hal Smith (Pirates, batting.)	25.00	12.50	7.50
(114)	Mickey Stanley (Tigers, full-length.)	20.00	10.00	6.00
(115)	Tony Taylor (Phillies, bat on shoulder.)	20.00	10.00	6.00
(116)	Frank Thomas (Pirates, waist-up.)	20.00	10.00	6.00
(117)	Frank Thomas (Cubs, batting.)	20.00	10.00	6.00
(119)	Jeff Torborg (Dodgers, holding mask.)	20.00	10.00	6.00
(121)	Al Weis (White Sox, ready to throw.)	20.00	10.00	6.00
(122)	Al Weis (Mets, fielding.)	20.00	10.00	6.00
(123)	Ted Williams (Batting)	125.00	62.00	37.00
(125)	Bobby Wine (Phillies, ready to throw.)	20.00	10.00	6.00
(126)	Rick Wise (Phillies, upper body.)	20.00	10.00	6.00
(128)	Woody Woodward (Reds, belt-to-cap.)	25.00	12.50	7.50
(130)	Early Wynn (White Sox, full-length.)	25.00	12.50	7.50
(131)	Jim Wynn (Colt .45s, batting, upper body.)	20.00	10.00	6.00
(132)	Jim Wynn (Astros, batting, full-length.)	20.00	10.00	6.00
(133)	Don Zimmer (Cubs, waist-up batting.)	20.00	10.00	6.00

1961 Wilson Advisory Staff Cards

Similar in format to the contemporary 8x10" photos, these 2-3/4" x 4" cards have black-and-white player poses on front, prominently displaying a Wilson glove. In the white bottom border is: "Member-Advisory Staff, Wilson Sporting Goods Co." A blue facsimile autograph is printed across the picture. Backs are blank. The checklist, presented here alphabetically, may not be complete.

		NM	E	VG
Common Player:		10.00	5.00	3.00
(1)	Dick Ellsworth	10.00	5.00	3.00
(2)	Don Hoak	12.00	6.00	3.50
(3)	Harvey Kuenn	12.00	6.00	3.50
(4)	Roy McMillan	10.00	5.00	3.00

(5)	Jim Piersall	12.00	6.00	3.50
(6)	Ron Santo	16.00	8.00	4.75

1954 Wilson Franks

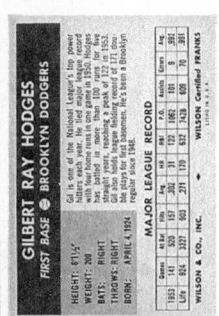

		NM	EX	VG
Complete Set (20):		30,000	12,000	6,000
Common Player:		600.00	200.00	75.00
Advertising Poster:		7,500	3,500	2,000
(1)	Roy Campanella	2,400	900.00	450.00
(2)	Del Ennis	600.00	200.00	75.00
(3)	Carl Erskine	675.00	275.00	135.00
(4)	Ferris Fain	600.00	200.00	75.00
(5)	Bob Feller	2,250	500.00	250.00
(6)	Nelson Fox	1,800	500.00	250.00
(7)	Johnny Groth	750.00	300.00	150.00
(8)	Stan Hack	1,100	440.00	220.00
(9)	Gil Hodges	1,750	800.00	350.00
(10)	Ray Jablonski	600.00	200.00	75.00
(11)	Harvey Kuenn	900.00	360.00	180.00
(12)	Roy McMillan	600.00	200.00	75.00
(13)	Andy Pafko	600.00	200.00	75.00
(14)	Paul Richards	900.00	360.00	180.00
(15)	Hank Sauer	900.00	360.00	180.00
(16)	Red Schoendienst	1,400	400.00	200.00
(17)	Enos Slaughter	1,550	425.00	200.00
(18)	Vern Stephens	600.00	200.00	75.00
(19)	Sammy White	600.00	200.00	75.00
(20)	Ted Williams	17,500	6,500	3,500

1955 Wilson Franks Baseball Books

A year after issuing its 20-card set of baseball cards as package inserts, Wilson Meats created a series of four Baseball Books ("for boys") and four Fun Books ("for girls") that were inserted into packages of Wilson Certified Franks. The comic-style books were 16 pages in a size of about 4-1/2" x 3-1/2", printed on low-grade paper. The front cover has a large comic book-style portrait of the player on a yellow background with a stylized baseball diamond. The inside pages have baseball tips presented in comic book illustrations.

		NM	EX	VG
Complete Set (4):				
Common Player:		400.00	200.00	125.00
1	Pointers on Pitching(Bob Feller)	600.00	300.00	180.00
2	Batting and Fielding Secrets (player unknown)	1,250	625.00	400.00
3	Playing the Infield(Harvey Kuenn)	400.00	200.00	125.00
4	Hot to Catch(Sammy White)	400.00	200.00	125.00

1961 Wilson Meats L.A.Dodgers/Angels

It is likely these 5-1/2" x 8-1/2" photos were prepared for promotional appearances by players on behalf of the meat company. The player name and sometimes team name appears at the bottom of the photo and the sponsor's message appears at bottom, "Courtesy of WILSON & CO., Inc., Fine Meat Products." Backs are blank. The pictures are often found with player autographs, another indicator of their use at personal appearances.

		NM	E	VG
		60.00	30.00	18.00
(1)	Ron Fairly	60.00	30.00	18.00
(2)	Gil Hodges	125.00	65.00	39.00
(3)	Frank Howard	75.00	37.00	23.00
(4)	Ted Kluszewski	90.00	45.00	27.00
(5)	Ron Perranowski	60.00	30.00	18.00
(6)	John Roseboro	60.00	30.00	18.00

1977 Wilson Sporting Goods Mini-Posters

REGGIE JACKSON

Though unmarked as such, these 6" x 9" cards are a promotion from Wilson. The blank-back cards have a color action photo with white borders and a facsimile autograph.

		NM	E	VG
Complete Set (10):		200.00	100.00	60.00
Common Player:		10.00	5.00	3.00
(1)	Johnny Bench	35.00	17.50	10.50
(2)	George Brett	50.00	25.00	15.00
(3)	Rod Carew	30.00	15.00	9.00
(4)	Dave Concepcion	10.00	5.00	3.00
(5)	Steve Garvey	15.00	7.50	4.50
(6)	Reggie Jackson	40.00	20.00	12.00
(7)	Greg Luzinski	10.00	5.00	3.00
(8)	Pete Rose	75.00	37.00	22.00
(9)	Mike Schmidt	40.00	20.00	12.00
(10)	Tom Seaver	40.00	17.50	10.50

1955-1958 Don Wingfield Washington Nationals Postcards

JOSE VALDIVELSO
WASHINGTON NATIONALS
Photo By ~ Don Wingfield
Griffith Stadium
Washington, D. C.

This series of 3-1/2" x 5-1/2" black-and-white glossy postcards provided Nationals' players with a vehicle for accommodating fan requests. Player portraits or action poses are bordered in white with three (or in the case of Valdivielso, five) lines of type at bottom identifying the player, team and copyright holder. Most have "Photo Post Card" at top on back and "Devolite Peerless" in the stamp box. The unnumbered cards are checklisted here in alphabetical order.

		NM	E	VG
Complete Set (12):		1,800	900.00	550.00
Common Player:		150.00	75.00	45.00
(1)	Jim Busby	150.00	75.00	45.00
(2)	Chuck Dressen	150.00	75.00	45.00
(3)	Ed Fitz Gerald	150.00	75.00	45.00
(4)	Jim Lemon	175.00	85.00	55.00
(5)	Bob Porterfield	150.00	75.00	45.00
(6)	Pete Runnels	150.00	75.00	45.00
(7)	Roy Sievers	175.00	85.00	55.00
(8)	Chuck Stobbs	150.00	75.00	45.00
(9)	Dean Stone	150.00	75.00	45.00
(10)	Jose Valdivelso (Valdivielso)	175.00	85.00	55.00

(11)	Mickey Vernon	175.00	85.00	55.00
(12)	Ed Yost	150.00	75.00	45.00

1957-1959 Don Wingfield Photocards

These black-and-white glossy photocards are usually blank-back, evidently for use as in-person handouts, rather than by mail. In 3-1/2" x 5-1/2" size, the player photos are bordered in white with an especially wide white bottom border for affixing an autograph. Other than the autograph which may appear, the player is not identified on the card. Wingfield's name may appear in white letters in the lower-right corner of the photo, may be on a credit line on back or may not appear at all.

		NM	E	VG
Common Player:		50.00	25.00	15.00
(1)	Ted Abernathy	50.00	25.00	15.00
(2)	Bobby Allison	50.00	25.00	15.00
(3)	Tex Clevenger	50.00	25.00	15.00
(4)	Russ Kemmerer	50.00	25.00	15.00
(5)	Harmon Killebrew	100.00	50.00	30.00
(6)	Bob Usher	50.00	25.00	15.00
(7)	Hal Woodeshick	50.00	25.00	15.00

1960s Don Wingfield Postcards - b/w

A second type of player photo postcards was produced by Alexandria, Va., photographer Don Wingfield beginning around 1960. Also black-and-white, the 3-1/2" x 5-1/2" cards have (usually) borderless poses on front with no extraneous graphics. Backs have standard postcard indicia plus (on most cards) the player name and team and a copyright line with Wingfield's name and address. At top on back is "Post Card," with "Place Stamp Here" in the postage box. Washington Senators players dominate the checklist which also includes stars of other teams. The autograph on the pictured card was added by the player after printing and is not part of the design. The currently known checklist is presented here alphabetically.

		NM	E	VG
Common Player:		50.00	25.00	15.00
(1)	Bob Allison	55.00	27.50	16.50
(2)	Ernie Banks	100.00	50.00	30.00
(3)	Earl Battey (Batting, chest to cap.)	50.00	25.00	15.00
(4)	Earl Battey (Kneeling w/bat.)	50.00	25.00	15.00
(5)	Norm Cash	60.00	30.00	18.00
(6)	Jim Coates	50.00	25.00	15.00
(7)	Rocky Colavito	60.00	30.00	18.00
(8)	Chuck Cottier	50.00	25.00	15.00
(9)	Bennie Daniels	50.00	25.00	15.00
(10)	Dan Dobbek	50.00	25.00	15.00
(11)	Nellie Fox	60.00	30.00	18.00
(12)	Jim Gentile	50.00	25.00	15.00
(13)	Gene Green	50.00	25.00	15.00
(14)	Steve Hamilton	50.00	25.00	15.00
(15)	Ken Hamlin	50.00	25.00	15.00

(16a)	Rudy Hernandez (Postcard back.)	50.00	25.00	15.00
(16b)	Rudy Hernandez (Restuarant ad on back.)	60.00	30.00	18.00
(17)	Ed Hobaugh	50.00	25.00	15.00
(18)	Elston Howard	60.00	30.00	18.00
(19)	Bob Johnson	50.00	25.00	15.00
(20)	Russ Kemmerer	50.00	25.00	15.00
(21)	Harmon Killebrew	100.00	50.00	30.00
(22)	Dale Long	50.00	25.00	15.00
(23)	Mickey Mantle	325.00	160.00	100.00
(24)	Roger Maris	200.00	100.00	60.00
(25)	Willie Mays	250.00	125.00	75.00
(26)	Stan Musial	200.00	100.00	60.00
(27)	Claude Osteen	50.00	25.00	15.00
(28)	Ken Retzer	50.00	25.00	15.00
(29)	Brooks Robinson	100.00	50.00	30.00
(30)	Don Rudolph	50.00	25.00	15.00
(31)	Bill Skowron	60.00	30.00	18.00
(32)	Dave Stenhouse	50.00	25.00	15.00
(33)	Jose Valdivielso	50.00	25.00	15.00
(34)	Gene Woodling	50.00	25.00	15.00
(35)	Bud Zipfel	50.00	25.00	15.00

1960s Don Wingfield Postcards - color

Similar in format to the contemporary series of black-and-white player photo postcards, only a single player is known to have been issued in color by Alexandria, Va., photographer Don Wingfield. The card is 3-1/2" x 5-1/2" with standard postcard indicia on back.

	NM	E	VG
C14711 Harmon Killebrew	110.00	55.00	33.00

1951-53 Wisconsin's Athletic Hall of Fame Postcards

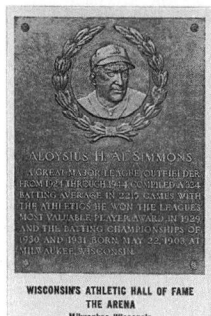

This set of black-and-white postcards reproduces the plaques of athletes in the state's Hall of Fame, as displayed in Milwaukee's Arena during the 1950s. Backs have typical postcard markings.

		NM	E	VG
Complete Set (12):		150.00	75.00	45.00
Common Player:		10.00	5.00	3.00
(1)	Addie Joss	20.00	10.00	6.00
(2)	Alvin Kraenzlein (Track)	10.00	5.00	3.00
(3)	"Strangler" Lewis (Wrestling)	12.50	6.25	3.75
(4)	George McBride	10.00	5.00	3.00
(5)	Ralph Metcalfe (Track)	10.00	5.00	3.00
(6)	Ernie Nevers	20.00	10.00	6.00
(7)	"Kid" Nichols	20.00	10.00	6.00
(8)	"Pa" O'Dea (Football)	10.00	5.00	3.00
(9)	Dave Schreiner (Football)	10.00	5.00	3.00
(10)	Al Simmons	20.00	10.00	6.00
(11)	Billy Sullivan	12.50	6.25	3.75
(12)	Bob Zuppke (Basketball)	10.00	5.00	3.00

1922 Witmor Candy Co.

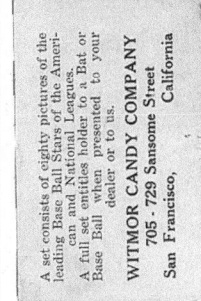

WALTER JOHNSON
P.—Washington Americans

Two types of Witmor issues are known, both of which utilize the format of the 1921-22 W575-1 blank-back strip cards. Printed in black-and-white and measuring about 2" x 3-1/4" the two types of Witmor issues are differentiated by the ads on back for the San Francisco candy company. One type has the advertising in a horizontal format, the other has the advertising in a vertical design. Values of Witmor Candy cards carry a premium over the more common blank-back versions. The extent to which the Witmors and W575-1 share a checklist, particularly the latter's variations, is unknown.

PREMIUMS:
Common Players: 3-4X
Hall of Famers: 3-4X

(See 1921-22 W575-1 for checklist and value information.)

1907 Wolverine News Co. Detroit Tigers

HERMAN SCHAEFER

This series of postcards depicts members of the A.L. champ Tigers. The 3-5/16" x 5-5/16" black-and-white cards have posed or posed action photos on front, with a narrow white border at bottom carrying player identification. Backs are standard postcard format with a credit line to Wolverine News Co.

		NM	E	VG
	Complete Set (20):	24,000	12,000	7,200
	Common Player:	200.00	100.00	60.00
(1)	Ty Cobb (Batting)	9,000	4,500	2,700
(2)	Ty Cobb (Portrait)	12,000	5,250	3,000
(3)	Bill Coughlin	200.00	100.00	60.00
(4)	Sam Crawford (Bunting)	500.00	250.00	75.00
(5)	Sam Crawford (Chest-to-cap portrait.)	500.00	250.00	75.00
(6)	"Wild Bill" Donovan (Pitching)	200.00	100.00	60.00
(7)	"Wild Bill" Donovan ("at the Water Wagon")	300.00	75.00	45.00
(8)	Jerry Downs	200.00	100.00	60.00
(9)	Hughie Jennings (Manager)	250.00	125.00	75.00
(10)	Hughie Jennings (On the Coaching line.)	600.00	300.00	90.00
(11)	Davy Jones	200.00	100.00	60.00
(12)	Ed Killian	200.00	100.00	60.00
(13)	George Mullin	200.00	100.00	60.00
(14)	Charlie O'Leary	200.00	100.00	60.00
(15)	Fred Payne	200.00	100.00	60.00
(16)	Claude Rossman	200.00	100.00	60.00
(17)	Herman Schaefer	200.00	100.00	60.00
(18)	Herman Schaefer, Charley O'Leary	200.00	100.00	60.00
(19)	Charlie Schmidt	200.00	100.00	60.00
(20)	Eddie Siever	200.00	100.00	60.00

1886 J. Wood Studio N.Y. Giants Cabinets

Members of the 1886 N.Y. Giants were immortalized in this series of 4-1/4" x 6-7/8" studio cabinets. The sepia portraits are bordered in gold. The photos were likely available singly from the studio or as a complete set, with an advertising frontpiece and a 6-9/16" x 4-3/16" composite photo. It is interesting to note that on one version of the composite card, baseball caps were artificially added to the portraits. The photos became the basis for the same players' cards in several late 1880s card series.

		NM	E	VG
	Common Player:	10,000	5,000	3,000
(1)	Roger Connor	25,000	7,500	4,500
(2)	Larry Corcoran	10,000	5,000	3,000
(3)	Pat Deasley	10,000	5,000	3,000
(4)	Mike Dorgan	10,000	5,000	3,000
(5)	Dude Esterbrook	10,000	5,000	3,000
(6)	Buck Ewing	35,000	7,500	4,500
(7)	Joe Gerhardt	10,000	5,000	3,000
(8)	Pete Gillespie	10,000	5,000	3,000
(9)	Tim Keefe	25,000	7,500	4,500
(10)	Jim Mutrie	10,000	5,000	3,000
(11)	Jim O'Rourke	30,000	7,500	4,500
(12)	Danny Richardson	10,000	5,000	3,000
(13)	John Ward	30,000	7,500	4,500
(14)	Mickey Welch	25,000	7,500	4,500
(15)	N.Y. Giants Team Composite (No caps.)	25,000	10,000	6,000
(16)	N.Y. Giants Team Composite (With caps.)	25,000	10,000	6,000

1886 J. Wood Studio N.Y. Metropolitans Cabinets

Nattily attired in dress shirts and sporty dotted ties, members of the 1886 N.Y. Metropolitans of the American Association were immortalized in this series of 4-1/2" x 6-1/2" studio cabinets. The vignetted sepia portraits are framed in gold. The photos became the basis for the same players' cards in the "dotted tie" subset of the 1887 Old Judge cigarette card issue, indicating that more of the cabinet-size photos may yet be added to this checklist.

	NM	E	VG
Common Player:	12,500	6,250	3,750
Jos. Crotty	12,500	6,250	3,750
E.L. Cushman	12,500	6,250	3,750
E.E. Foster	12,500	6,250	3,750
Al. Mays	12,500	6,250	3,750
Jas. Roseman	12,500	6,250	3,750

1921 Wool's American-Maid Bread

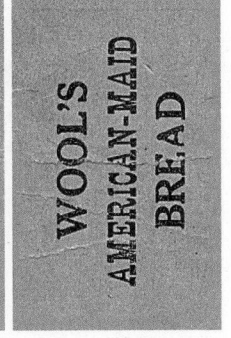

TY COBB
DETROIT A.L.

WOOL'S AMERICAN-MAID BREAD

This seldom-seen variation of the W551 strip-card set appears to have been locally overprinted at an unknown location for use as a bread purchase premium. It is presumed the same checklist for W551 can be found with the Wool's back advertising. If ideally cut from the strip, the cards would measure 1-3/8" x 2-1/4". They feature color drawings and are unnumbered.

	NM	E	VG
Complete Set (10):	6,000	3,000	1,800
Common Player:	250.00	125.00	65.00

		NM	E	VG
(1)	Frank Baker	600.00	300.00	150.00
(2)	Dave Bancroft	600.00	300.00	150.00
(3)	Jess Barnes	250.00	125.00	75.00
(4)	Ty Cobb	2,400	1,200	600.00
(5)	Walter Johnson	900.00	450.00	225.00
(6)	Wally Pipp	300.00	150.00	90.00
(7)	Babe Ruth	2,750	1,375	750.00
(8)	George Sisler	600.00	400.00	120.00
(9)	Tris Speaker	750.00	375.00	180.00
(10)	Casey Stengel	450.00	225.00	135.00

1933 Worch Cigar

This set of unnumbered postcard-size (3-7/16" x 5-7/16") cards, utilizing photos from the Minneapolis Star and St. Paul Dispatch newspapers, was used as a promotion by Worch Cigar Co. of St. Paul, Minn. Although there is no advertising for Worch Cigars on the cards themselves, the cards were mailed in envelopes bearing the Worch name. The cards feature portrait or posed action photos. Player identification, which may be full name or last name, with or without team, may be found in several different styles, either printed on the background, or in a white or black box. Sometimes a photo credit is also present. Many pictures have the top of the background whited out.

		NM	E	VG
	Common Player:	175.00	90.00	55.00
(1)	Sparky Adams	175.00	90.00	55.00
(2)	Dale Alexander	175.00	90.00	55.00
(3)	Ivy Paul Andrews	175.00	90.00	55.00
(4a)	Earl Averill (Cleveland)	600.00	300.00	150.00
(4b)	Earl Averill (No team designation.)	600.00	300.00	150.00
(5)	Richard Bartell	175.00	90.00	55.00
(6)	Herman Bell	175.00	90.00	55.00
(7)	Walter Berger	175.00	90.00	55.00
(8)	Huck Betts	175.00	90.00	55.00
(9)	Max Bishop	175.00	90.00	55.00
(10)	Jim Bottomley	600.00	300.00	150.00
(11a)	Tom Bridges (Name and team in box.)	175.00	90.00	55.00
(11b)	Tom Bridges (No box.)	175.00	90.00	55.00
(12)	Clint Brown	175.00	90.00	55.00
(13a)	Donie Bush	175.00	90.00	55.00
(13b)	Donie Bush	175.00	90.00	55.00
(14a)	Max Carey (Brooklyn)	600.00	300.00	150.00
(14b)	Max Carey (No team designation.)	600.00	300.00	150.00
(15)	Tex Carlton	175.00	90.00	55.00
(16)	Ben Chapman	175.00	90.00	55.00
(17)	Chalmer Cissell	175.00	90.00	55.00
(18)	Mickey Cochrane	600.00	300.00	150.00
(19)	Ripper Collins	175.00	90.00	55.00
(20)	Earle Combs	600.00	300.00	150.00
(21)	Adam Comorosky	175.00	90.00	55.00
(22)	Estel Crabtree	175.00	90.00	55.00
(23)	Rodger Cramer (Roger)	175.00	90.00	55.00
(24)	Pat Crawford	175.00	90.00	55.00
(25)	Hugh Critz	175.00	90.00	55.00
(26a)	Joe Cronin (Name and team in box.)	600.00	300.00	150.00
(26b)	Joe Cronin (No box.)	600.00	300.00	150.00
(27)	Frank Crosetti	150.00	67.00	37.00
(28)	Alvin Crowder	175.00	90.00	55.00
(29a)	Tony Cuccinello (Photo background.)	175.00	90.00	55.00
(29b)	Tony Cuccinello (Blank background.)	175.00	90.00	55.00
(30)	KiKi Cuyler	600.00	300.00	150.00
(31)	Geo. Davis	175.00	90.00	55.00
(32)	Dizzy Dean	1,200	600.00	300.00
(33)	Wm. Dickey	450.00	200.00	110.00
(34)	Leo Durocher	600.00	300.00	150.00
(35)	James Dykes	175.00	90.00	55.00
(36)	George Earnshaw	175.00	90.00	55.00
(37)	Woody English	175.00	90.00	55.00
(38a)	Richard Ferrell (Name and team in box.)	600.00	300.00	150.00

(38b)	Richard Ferrell (No box.)	600.00	300.00	150.00
(39a)	Wesley Ferrell (Name and team in box.)	175.00	90.00	55.00
(39b)	Wesley Ferrell (No box.)	175.00	90.00	55.00
(40)	Fred Fitzsimmons	175.00	90.00	55.00
(41)	Lew Fonseca	175.00	90.00	55.00
(42)	Bob Fothergill	175.00	90.00	55.00
(43)	James Foxx	1,200	600.00	300.00
(44)	Fred Frankhouse	175.00	90.00	55.00
(45)	Frank Frisch	600.00	300.00	150.00
(46a)	Leon Gaslin (Name incorrect.)	600.00	300.00	150.00
(46b)	Leon Goslin (Name correct.)	600.00	300.00	150.00
(47)	Lou Gehrig	3,000	1,500	750.00
(48)	Charles Gehringer	600.00	300.00	150.00
(49)	George Gibson	175.00	90.00	55.00
(50)	Vernon Gomez	600.00	300.00	150.00
(51)	George Grantham	175.00	90.00	55.00
(52)	Grimes The Lord Of Burleigh (Burleigh Grimes)	600.00	300.00	150.00
(53)	Charlie Grimm	175.00	90.00	55.00
(54)	Robt. Grove	900.00	450.00	225.00
(55)	Frank Grube	175.00	90.00	55.00
(56)	Chic Hafey (Chick)	600.00	300.00	150.00
(57)	Jess Haines	600.00	300.00	150.00
(58)	Bill Hallahan	175.00	90.00	55.00
(59)	Mel Harder	175.00	90.00	55.00
(60)	Dave Harris	175.00	90.00	55.00
(61a)	Gabby Hartnett (Small projection.)	600.00	300.00	150.00
(61b)	Gabby Hartnett (Large projection.)	600.00	300.00	150.00
(62)	George Hass (Haas)	175.00	90.00	55.00
(63)	Ray Hayworth	175.00	90.00	55.00
(64)	Harvey Hendrick	175.00	90.00	55.00
(65)	Dutch Henry	175.00	90.00	55.00
(66)	"Babe" Herman	150.00	67.00	37.00
(67)	Bill Herman	600.00	300.00	150.00
(68)	Frank Higgins	175.00	90.00	55.00
(69)	Oral Hildebrand	175.00	90.00	55.00
(70)	"Shanty" Hogan	175.00	90.00	55.00
(71)	Roger Hornsby (Rogers)	900.00	450.00	225.00
(72)	Carl Hubbell	450.00	200.00	110.00
(73)	Travis Jackson	600.00	300.00	150.00
(74)	Hank Johnson	175.00	90.00	55.00
(75)	Syl Johnson	175.00	90.00	55.00
(76)	Smead Jolley	175.00	90.00	55.00
(77)	Wm. Kamm	175.00	90.00	55.00
(78)	Wes Kingdon	175.00	90.00	55.00
(79a)	Charles Klein (Philadelphia, N.L.)	600.00	300.00	150.00
(79b)	Charles Klein (Chicago, N.L.)	600.00	300.00	150.00
(80)	Jos. Kuhel	175.00	90.00	55.00
(81a)	Tony Lazzeri (Name and team in box.)	600.00	300.00	150.00
(81b)	Tony Lazzeri (No box.)	600.00	300.00	150.00
(82)	Sam Leslie	175.00	90.00	55.00
(83)	Ernie Lombardi	600.00	300.00	150.00
(84)	Al Lopez	600.00	300.00	150.00
(85)	Red Lucas	175.00	90.00	55.00
(86)	Adolfo Luque	175.00	90.00	22.00
(87)	Ted Lyons	600.00	300.00	150.00
(88)	Connie Mack	600.00	300.00	150.00
(89)	Gus Mancuso	175.00	90.00	55.00
(90)	Henry Manush	600.00	300.00	150.00
(91)	Fred Marberry	175.00	90.00	55.00
(92)	Pepper Martin	200.00	90.00	50.00
(93)	Wm. McKechnie	600.00	300.00	150.00
(94)	Joe Medwick	600.00	300.00	150.00
(95)	Jim Mooney	175.00	90.00	55.00
(96)	Joe Moore	175.00	90.00	55.00
(97)	Joe Mowry	175.00	90.00	55.00
(98)	Van Mungo	175.00	90.00	55.00
(99)	Buddy Myer	175.00	90.00	55.00
(100)	"Lefty" O'Doul	200.00	90.00	50.00
(101)	Bob O'Farrell	175.00	90.00	55.00
(102)	Ernie Orsatti	175.00	90.00	55.00
(103)	Melvin Ott	750.00	375.00	200.00
(104)	Roy Parmelee	175.00	90.00	55.00
(105)	Homer Peel	175.00	90.00	55.00
(106)	George Pipgras	175.00	90.00	55.00
(107)	Harry Rice	175.00	90.00	55.00
(108)	Paul Richards	175.00	90.00	55.00
(109)	Eppa Rixey	600.00	300.00	150.00
(110)	Charles Ruffing	600.00	300.00	150.00
(111)	Jack Russell	175.00	90.00	55.00
(112)	Babe Ruth	52,000	3,000	1,500
(113)	"Blondy" Ryan	175.00	90.00	55.00
(114)	Wilfred Ryan	175.00	90.00	55.00
(115)	Fred Schulte	175.00	90.00	55.00
(116)	Hal Schumacher	175.00	90.00	55.00
(117a)	Luke Sewel (Sewell) (Name and team in box.))	175.00	90.00	55.00
(117b)	Luke Sewel (Sewell) (No box.)	175.00	90.00	55.00

(118)	Al Simmons	600.00	300.00	150.00
(119)	Ray Spencer	175.00	90.00	55.00
(120)	Casey Stengel	600.00	300.00	150.00
(121)	Riggs Stephenson	175.00	90.00	55.00
(122)	Walter Stewart	175.00	90.00	55.00
(123)	John Stone	175.00	90.00	55.00
(124)	Gabby Street	175.00	90.00	55.00
(125)	Gus Suhr	175.00	90.00	55.00
(126)	Evar Swanson	175.00	90.00	55.00
(127)	Dan Taylor	175.00	90.00	55.00
(128)	Bill Terry	600.00	300.00	150.00
(129)	Al Todd	175.00	90.00	55.00
(130)	Pie Traynor	600.00	300.00	150.00
(131)	William Urbanski	175.00	90.00	55.00
(132)	Dazzy Vance	600.00	300.00	150.00
(133)	Lloyd (Floyd) Vaughan	600.00	300.00	150.00
(134)	Johnny Vergez	175.00	90.00	55.00
(135)	George Walberg	175.00	90.00	55.00
(136)	Bill Walker	175.00	90.00	55.00
(137)	Gerald Walker	175.00	90.00	55.00
(138a)	Lloyd Waner (Photo background.)	600.00	300.00	150.00
(138b)	Lloyd Waner (Blank background.)	600.00	300.00	150.00
(139a)	Paul Waner (Photo background.)	600.00	300.00	150.00
(139b)	Paul Waner (Blank background, small projection.)	600.00	300.00	150.00
(139c)	Lloyd Waner (Blank background, large projection.)	600.00	300.00	150.00
(140)	Lon Warneke	175.00	90.00	55.00
(141)	George Watkins	175.00	90.00	55.00
(142)	Monte Weaver	175.00	90.00	55.00
(143)	Sam West	175.00	90.00	55.00
(144)	Earl Whitehill	175.00	90.00	55.00
(145)	Hack Wilson	600.00	300.00	150.00
(146)	Jimmy Wilson	175.00	90.00	55.00

1933 World Wide Gum (Canadian Goudey, V353)

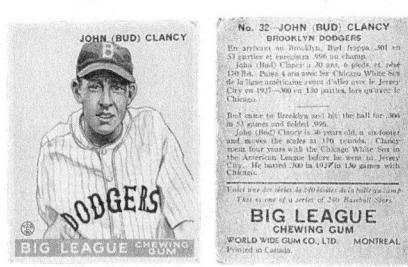

Also known as "Canadian Goudeys," this 94-card set drew heavily on its U.S. contemporary. Card fronts are identical to the '33 Goudeys and the backs are nearly so. The first 52 cards in the set carry the same card numbers as their American counterparts, while cards #53-94 have different numbers than the U.S. version. Card backs can be found printed entirely in English, or in English and French; the former being somewhat scarcer. Cards measure approximately 2-3/8" x 2-7/8".

		NM	E	VG
Complete Set (94):		20,000	10,000	6,000
Common Player:		60.00	30.00	18.00
1	Benny Bengough	550.00	60.00	20.00
2	Arthur (Dazzy) Vance	250.00	110.00	60.00
3	Hugh Critz	60.00	30.00	18.00
4	Henry (Heinie) Schuble	60.00	30.00	18.00
5	Floyd (Babe) Herman	110.00	50.00	25.00
6	Jimmy Dykes	60.00	30.00	18.00
7	Ted Lyons	250.00	110.00	60.00
8	Roy Johnson	60.00	30.00	18.00
9	Dave Harris	60.00	30.00	18.00
10	Glenn Myatt	60.00	30.00	18.00
11	Billy Rogell	60.00	30.00	18.00
12	George Pipgras	60.00	30.00	18.00
13	Lafayette Thompson	60.00	30.00	18.00
14	Henry Johnson	60.00	30.00	18.00
15	Victor Sorrell	60.00	30.00	18.00
16	George Blaeholder	60.00	30.00	18.00
17	Watson Clark	60.00	30.00	18.00
18	Herold (Muddy) Ruel	60.00	30.00	18.00
19	Bill Dickey	275.00	125.00	70.00
20	Bill Terry	250.00	110.00	60.00
21	Phil Collins	60.00	30.00	18.00
22	Harold (Pie) Traynor	250.00	110.00	60.00
23	Hazen (Ki-Ki) Cuyler	250.00	110.00	60.00
24	Horace Ford	60.00	30.00	18.00
25	Paul Waner	250.00	110.00	60.00
26	Chalmer Cissell	60.00	30.00	18.00
27	George Connally	60.00	30.00	18.00
28	Dick Bartell	60.00	30.00	18.00
29	Jimmy Foxx	350.00	155.00	85.00

30	Frank Hogan	60.00	30.00	18.00
31	Tony Lazzeri	250.00	110.00	60.00
32	John (Bud) Clancy	60.00	30.00	18.00
33	Ralph Kress	60.00	30.00	18.00
34	Bob O'Farrell	60.00	30.00	18.00
35	Al Simmons	250.00	110.00	60.00
36	Tommy Thevenow	60.00	30.00	18.00
37	Jimmy Wilson	60.00	30.00	18.00
38	Fred Brickell	60.00	30.00	18.00
39	Mark Koenig	60.00	30.00	18.00
40	Taylor Douthit	60.00	30.00	18.00
41	Gus Mancuso	60.00	30.00	18.00
42	Eddie Collins	250.00	110.00	60.00
43	Lew Fonseca	60.00	30.00	18.00
44	Jim Bottomley	250.00	110.00	60.00
45	Larry Benton	60.00	30.00	18.00
46	Ethan Allen	60.00	30.00	18.00
47	Henry "Heinie" Manush	250.00	110.00	60.00
48	Marty McManus	60.00	30.00	18.00
49	Frank Frisch	250.00	110.00	60.00
50	Ed Brandt	60.00	30.00	18.00
51	Charlie Grimm	60.00	30.00	18.00
52	Andy Cohen	60.00	30.00	18.00
53	Jack Quinn	60.00	30.00	18.00
54	Urban (Red) Faber	250.00	110.00	60.00
55	Lou Gehrig	2,100	950.00	525.00
56	John Welch	60.00	30.00	18.00
57	Bill Walker	60.00	30.00	18.00
58	Frank (Lefty) O'Doul	90.00	40.00	22.50
59	Edmund (Bing) Miller	60.00	30.00	18.00
60	Waite Hoyt	250.00	110.00	60.00
61	Max Bishop	60.00	30.00	18.00
62	"Pepper" Martin	90.00	40.00	22.50
63	Joe Cronin	250.00	110.00	60.00
64	Burleigh Grimes	250.00	110.00	60.00
65	Milton Gaston	60.00	30.00	18.00
66	George Grantham	60.00	30.00	18.00
67	Guy Bush	60.00	30.00	18.00
68	Willie Kamm	60.00	30.00	18.00
69	Gordon (Mickey) Cochrane	250.00	110.00	60.00
70	Adam Comorosky	60.00	30.00	18.00
71	Alvin Crowder	60.00	30.00	18.00
72	Willis Hudlin	60.00	30.00	18.00
73	Eddie Farrell	60.00	30.00	18.00
74	Leo Durocher	250.00	110.00	60.00
75	Walter Stewart	60.00	30.00	18.00
76	George Walberg	60.00	30.00	18.00
77	Glenn Wright	60.00	30.00	18.00
78	Charles (Buddy) Myer	60.00	30.00	18.00
79	James (Zack) Taylor	60.00	30.00	18.00
80	George Herman (Babe) Ruth	4,000	1,800	1,000
81	D'Arcy (Jake) Flowers	60.00	30.00	18.00
82	Ray Kolp	60.00	30.00	18.00
83	Oswald Bluege	60.00	30.00	18.00
84	Morris (Moe) Berg	600.00	275.00	150.00
85	Jimmy Foxx	400.00	180.00	100.00
86	Sam Byrd	60.00	30.00	11.00
87	Danny Mcfayden (McFayden)	60.00	30.00	18.00
88	Joe Judge	60.00	30.00	18.00
89	Joe Sewell	250.00	110.00	60.00
90	Lloyd Waner	250.00	110.00	60.00
91	Luke Sewell	60.00	30.00	18.00
92	Leo Mangum	60.00	30.00	18.00
93	George Herman (Babe) Ruth	3,600	1,625	900.00
94	Al Spohrer	60.00	30.00	18.00

1934 World Wide Gum (Canadian Goudey, V354)

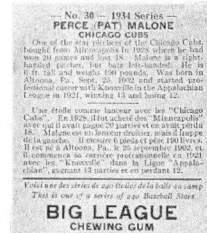

Again a near-clone of the American issue, the '34 "Canadian Goudeys" feature the same number (96) and size (2-3/8" x 2-7/8") of cards. Player selection is considerably different, however. Cards #1-48 feature the same front design as the '33 World Wide/Goudey sets. Cards #49-96 have the "Lou Gehrig says..." graphic on the front. Unlike the 1933 cards, backs are only found with bi-lingual text.

		NM	E	VG
Complete Set (96):		19,000	8,500	4,500
Common Player:		75.00	35.00	20.00
1	Rogers Hornsby	900.00	400.00	250.00

2	Eddie Morgan	75.00	35.00	20.00
3	Valentine J. (Val) Picinich	75.00	35.00	20.00
4	Rabbit Maranville	250.00	120.00	75.00
5	Flint Rhem	75.00	35.00	20.00
6	Jim Elliott	75.00	35.00	20.00
7	Fred (Red) Lucas	75.00	35.00	20.00
8	Fred Marberry	75.00	35.00	20.00
9	Clifton Heathcote	75.00	35.00	20.00
10	Bernie Friberg	75.00	35.00	20.00
11	Elwood (Woody) English	75.00	35.00	20.00
12	Carl Reynolds	75.00	35.00	20.00
13	Ray Benge	75.00	35.00	20.00
14	Ben Cantwell	75.00	35.00	20.00
15	Irvin (Bump) Hadley	75.00	35.00	20.00
16	Herb Pennock	250.00	120.00	75.00
17	Fred Lindstrom	250.00	120.00	75.00
18	Edgar (Sam) Rice	250.00	120.00	75.00
19	Fred Frankhouse	75.00	35.00	20.00
20	Fred Fitzsimmons	75.00	35.00	20.00
21	Earl Coombs (Earle Combs)	250.00	120.00	75.00
22	George Uhle	75.00	35.00	20.00
23	Richard Coffman	75.00	35.00	20.00
24	Travis C. Jackson	250.00	120.00	75.00
25	Robert J. Burke	75.00	35.00	20.00
26	Randy Moore	75.00	35.00	20.00
27	John Henry (Heinie) Sand	75.00	35.00	20.00
28	George Herman (Babe) Ruth	4,200	2,000	1,600
29	Tris Speaker	300.00	145.00	90.00
30	Perce (Pat) Malone	75.00	35.00	20.00
31	Sam Jones	75.00	35.00	20.00
32	Eppa Rixey	250.00	120.00	75.00
33	Floyd (Pete) Scott	75.00	35.00	20.00
34	Pete Jablonowski	75.00	35.00	20.00
35	Clyde Manion	75.00	35.00	20.00
36	Dibrell Williams	75.00	35.00	20.00
37	Glenn Spencer	75.00	35.00	20.00
38	Ray Kremer	75.00	35.00	20.00
39	Phil Todt	75.00	35.00	20.00
40	Russell Rollings	75.00	35.00	20.00
41	Earl Clark	75.00	35.00	20.00
42	Jess Petty	75.00	35.00	20.00
43	Frank O'Rourke	75.00	35.00	20.00
44	Jesse Haines	250.00	120.00	75.00
45	Horace Lisenbee	75.00	35.00	20.00
46	Owen Carroll	75.00	35.00	20.00
47	Tom Zachary	75.00	35.00	20.00
48	Charlie Ruffing	250.00	120.00	75.00
49	Ray Benge	75.00	35.00	20.00
50	Elwood (Woody) English	75.00	35.00	20.00
51	Ben Chapman	75.00	35.00	20.00
52	Joe Kuhel	75.00	35.00	20.00
53	Bill Terry	250.00	120.00	75.00
54	Robert (Lefty) Grove	550.00	225.00	135.00
55	Jerome (Dizzy) Dean	450.00	220.00	140.00
56	Charles (Chuck) Klein	250.00	120.00	75.00
57	Charley Gehringer	250.00	120.00	75.00
58	Jimmy Foxx	650.00	325.00	195.00
59	Gordon (Mickey) Cochrane	250.00	120.00	75.00
60	Willie Kamm	75.00	35.00	20.00
61	Charlie Grimm	75.00	35.00	20.00
62	Ed Brandt	75.00	35.00	20.00
63	Tony Piet	75.00	35.00	20.00
64	Frank Frisch	250.00	120.00	75.00
65	Alvin Crowder	75.00	35.00	20.00
66	Frank Hogan	75.00	35.00	20.00
67	Paul Waner	250.00	120.00	75.00
68	Henry (Heinie) Manush	250.00	120.00	75.00
69	Leo Durocher	250.00	120.00	75.00
70	Floyd Vaughan	250.00	120.00	75.00
71	Carl Hubbell	275.00	135.00	85.00
72	Hugh Critz	75.00	35.00	20.00
73	John (Blondy) Ryan	75.00	35.00	20.00
74	Roger Cramer	75.00	35.00	20.00
75	Baxter Jordan	75.00	35.00	20.00
76	Ed Coleman	75.00	35.00	20.00
77	Julius Solters	75.00	35.00	20.00
78	Charles (Chick) Hafey	250.00	120.00	75.00
79	Larry French	75.00	35.00	20.00
80	Frank (Don) Hurst	75.00	35.00	20.00
81	Gerald Walker	75.00	35.00	20.00
82	Ernie Lombardi	250.00	120.00	75.00
83	Walter (Huck) Betts	75.00	35.00	20.00
84	Luke Appling	250.00	120.00	75.00
85	John Frederick	75.00	35.00	20.00
86	Fred Walker	75.00	35.00	20.00
87	Tom Bridges	75.00	35.00	20.00
88	Dick Porter	75.00	35.00	20.00
89	John Stone	75.00	35.00	20.00
90	James (Tex) Carleton	75.00	35.00	20.00
91	Joe Stripp	75.00	35.00	20.00
92	Lou Gehrig	2,500	1,225	775.00
93	George Earnshaw	75.00	35.00	20.00
94	Oscar Melillo	75.00	35.00	20.00
95	Oral Hildebrand	75.00	35.00	20.00
96	John Allen	75.00	35.00	20.00

1936 World Wide Gum (Canadian Goudey, V355)

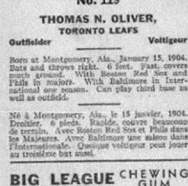

No. 119
THOMAS N. OLIVER,
TORONTO LEAFS

Outfielder   Voltigeur

Born at Montgomery, Ala., January 15, 1904.
Bats and throws right. 6 feet. Fast, covers
much ground. With Boston Red Sox and
Phils in majors. With Baltimore in International one season. Can play third base as
well as outfield.

Né à Montgomery, Ala., le 15 janvier, 1904.
Droitier. 6 pieds. Rapide, couvre beaucoup
de terrain. Avec Boston Red Sox et Phils dans
les Majeures. Avec Baltimore une saison dans
l'Internationale. Quelque voltigeur peut jouer
au troisième but aussi.

BIG LEAGUE CHEWING GUM

World Wide Gum Co. Ltd. Granby, Que.
Printed in Canada.

No. 119 TOM OLIVER

This black and white Canadian set was issued by World
Wide Gum in 1936. The cards measure approximately 2-1/2"
x 2-7/8", and the set includes both portrait and action photos.
The card number and player's name (appearing in all capital
letters) are printed inside a white box below the photo.

		NM	E	VG
Complete Set (135):		47,500	23,750	14,250
Common Player:		175.00	85.00	40.00
1	Jimmy Dykes	475.00	90.00	40.00
2	Paul Waner	250.00	125.00	75.00
3	Cy Blanton	175.00	85.00	40.00
4	Sam Leslie	175.00	85.00	40.00
5	Johnny Louis Vergez	175.00	85.00	40.00
6	Arky Vaughan	250.00	125.00	75.00
7	Bill Terry	250.00	125.00	75.00
8	Joe Moore	175.00	85.00	40.00
9	Gus Mancuso	175.00	85.00	40.00
10	Fred Marberry	175.00	85.00	40.00
11	George Selkirk	175.00	85.00	40.00
12	Spud Davis	175.00	85.00	40.00
13	Chuck Klein	250.00	125.00	75.00
14	Fred Fitzsimmons	175.00	85.00	40.00
15	Bill Delancey	175.00	85.00	40.00
16	Billy Herman	250.00	125.00	75.00
17	George Davis	175.00	85.00	40.00
18	Rip Collins	175.00	85.00	40.00
19	Dizzy Dean	750.00	325.00	120.00
20	Roy Parmelee	175.00	85.00	40.00
21	Vic Sorrell	175.00	85.00	40.00
22	Harry Danning	175.00	85.00	40.00
23	Hal Schumacher	175.00	85.00	40.00
24	Cy Perkins	175.00	85.00	40.00
25	Speedy Durocher	250.00	125.00	75.00
26	Glenn Myatt	175.00	85.00	40.00
27	Bob Seeds	175.00	85.00	40.00
28	Jimmy Ripple	175.00	85.00	40.00
29	Al Schacht	175.00	85.00	40.00
30	Pete Fox	175.00	85.00	40.00
31	Del Baker	175.00	85.00	40.00
32	Flea Clifton	175.00	85.00	40.00
33	Tommy Bridges	175.00	85.00	40.00
34	Bill Dickey	250.00	115.00	65.00
35	Wally Berger	175.00	85.00	40.00
36	Slick Castleman	175.00	85.00	40.00
37	Dick Bartell	175.00	85.00	40.00
38	Red Rolfe	175.00	85.00	40.00
39	Waite Hoyt	250.00	125.00	75.00
40	Wes Ferrell	175.00	85.00	40.00
41	Hank Greenberg	800.00	400.00	180.00
42	Charlie Gehringer	250.00	125.00	75.00
43	Goose Goslin	250.00	125.00	75.00
44	Schoolboy Rowe	175.00	85.00	40.00
45	Mickey Cochrane	250.00	125.00	75.00
46	Joe Cronin	250.00	125.00	75.00
47	Jimmie Foxx	750.00	350.00	125.00
48	Jerry Walker	175.00	85.00	40.00
49	Charlie Gelbert	175.00	85.00	40.00
50	Roy Hayworth (Ray)	175.00	85.00	40.00
51	Joe DiMaggio	20,000	10,000	4,500
52	Billy Rogell	175.00	85.00	40.00
53	Joe McCarthy	250.00	125.00	75.00
54	Phil Cavaretta (Cavarretta)	175.00	85.00	40.00
55	Kiki Cuyler	250.00	125.00	75.00
56	Lefty Gomez	250.00	125.00	75.00
57	Gabby Hartnett	250.00	125.00	75.00
58	Johnny Marcum	175.00	85.00	40.00
59	Burgess Whitehead	175.00	85.00	40.00
60	Whitey Whitehill	175.00	85.00	40.00
61	Buckey Walters	175.00	85.00	40.00
62	Luke Sewell	175.00	85.00	40.00
63	Joey Kuhel	175.00	85.00	40.00
64	Lou Finney	175.00	85.00	40.00
65	Fred Lindstrom	250.00	125.00	75.00
66	Paul Derringer	175.00	85.00	40.00
67	Steve O'Neil (O'Neill)	175.00	85.00	40.00
68	Mule Haas	175.00	85.00	40.00
69	Freck Owen	175.00	85.00	40.00
70	Wild Bill Hallahan	175.00	85.00	40.00
71	Bill Urbanski	175.00	85.00	40.00
72	Dan Taylor	175.00	85.00	40.00

73	Heinie Manush	250.00	125.00	75.00
74	Jo-Jo White	175.00	85.00	40.00
75	Mickey Medwick (Ducky)	250.00	125.00	75.00
76	Joe Vosmik	175.00	85.00	40.00
77	Al Simmons	250.00	125.00	75.00
78	Shag Shaughnessy	175.00	85.00	40.00
79	Harry Smythe	175.00	85.00	40.00
80	Benny Tate	175.00	85.00	40.00
81	Billy Rhiel	175.00	85.00	40.00
82	Lauri Myllykangas	175.00	85.00	40.00
83	Ben Sankey	175.00	85.00	40.00
84	Crip Polli	175.00	85.00	40.00
85	Jim Bottomley	250.00	125.00	75.00
86	William Clark	175.00	85.00	40.00
87	Ossie Bluege	175.00	85.00	40.00
88	Lefty Grove	550.00	225.00	65.00
89	Charlie Grimm	175.00	85.00	40.00
90	Ben Chapman	175.00	85.00	40.00
91	Frank Crosetti	175.00	60.00	40.00
92	John Pomorski	175.00	85.00	40.00
93	Jesse Haines	250.00	125.00	75.00
94	Chick Hafey	250.00	125.00	75.00
95	Tony Piet	175.00	85.00	40.00
96	Lou Gehrig	4,000	2,000	1,400
97	Bill Jurges	175.00	85.00	40.00
98	Smead Jolley	175.00	85.00	40.00
99	Jimmy Wilson	175.00	85.00	40.00
100	Lonnie Warneke	175.00	85.00	40.00
101	Lefty Tamulis	175.00	85.00	40.00
102	Charlie Ruffing	250.00	125.00	75.00
103	Earl Grace	175.00	85.00	40.00
104	Rox Lawson	175.00	85.00	40.00
105	Stan Hack	175.00	85.00	40.00
106	August Galan	175.00	85.00	40.00
107	Frank Frisch	250.00	125.00	75.00
108	Bill McKechnie	250.00	125.00	75.00
109	Bill Lee	175.00	85.00	40.00
110	Connie Mack	250.00	125.00	75.00
111	Frank Reiber	175.00	85.00	40.00
112	Zeke Bonura	175.00	85.00	40.00
113	Luke Appling	250.00	125.00	75.00
114	Monte Pearson	175.00	85.00	40.00
115	Bob O'Farrell	175.00	85.00	40.00
116	Marvin Duke	175.00	85.00	40.00
117	Paul Florence	175.00	85.00	40.00
118	John Berley	175.00	85.00	40.00
119	Tom Oliver	175.00	85.00	40.00
120	Norman Kies	175.00	85.00	40.00
121	Hal King	175.00	85.00	40.00
122	Tom Abernathy	175.00	85.00	40.00
123	Phil Hensick	175.00	85.00	40.00
124	Roy Schalk (Ray)	250.00	125.00	75.00
125	Paul Dunlap	175.00	85.00	40.00
126	Benny Bates	175.00	85.00	40.00
127	George Puccinelli	175.00	85.00	40.00
128	Stevie Stevenson	175.00	85.00	40.00
129	Rabbit Maranville	250.00	125.00	75.00
130	Bucky Harris	250.00	125.00	75.00
131	Al Lopez	250.00	125.00	75.00
132	Buddy Myer	175.00	85.00	40.00
133	Cliff Bolton	175.00	85.00	40.00
134	Estel Crabtree	175.00	85.00	40.00
135	Phil Weintraub	2,400	1,200	600.00

1939 World Wide Gum (Canadian Goudey, V351)

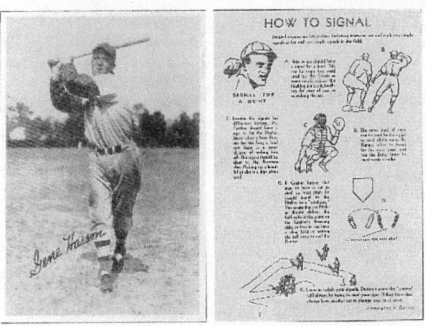

These premium pictures are analogous to the R303-A issue in the U.S. The 4" x 5-3/4" pictures were given away with
the purchase of World Wide gum. The pictures are printed in
sepia on cream-colored paper. Fronts have a bordered photo
with facsimile autograph. Backs have a "How to . . ." baseball
playing tip illustrated with drawings. Backs of the Canadian
version differ from the U.S. pieces in the absence of a border
line around the playing tip, and the use of a "Lithographed in
Canada" notice at lower-right. The unnumbered pictures are
checklisted here in alphabetical order.

	NM	E	VG
Complete Set (25):	11,000	5,500	3,250
Common Player:	200.00	100.00	60.00

(1)	Morris Arnovich	200.00	100.00	60.00
(2)	Sam Bell	260.00	130.00	70.00
(3)	Zeke Bonura	200.00	100.00	60.00
(4)	Earl Caldwell	200.00	100.00	60.00
(5)	Flea Clifton	200.00	100.00	60.00
(6)	Frank Crosetti	280.00	140.00	60.00
(7)	Harry Danning	200.00	100.00	60.00
(8)	Jerome Herman Dean	575.00	300.00	180.00
(9)	Emile De Jonghe	260.00	130.00	70.00
(10)	Paul Derringer	200.00	100.00	60.00
(11)	Joe DiMaggio	2,100	1,050	550.00
(12)	Vince DiMaggio	200.00	100.00	60.00
(13)	Charlie Gehringer	450.00	225.00	105.00
(14)	Gene Hasson	260.00	130.00	70.00
(15)	Tommy Henrich	300.00	150.00	90.00
(16)	Fred Hutchinson	200.00	100.00	60.00
(17)	Phil Marchildon	200.00	100.00	60.00
(18)	Mike Meola	200.00	100.00	60.00
(19)	Arnold Moser	260.00	130.00	70.00
(20)	Frank Pytlak	200.00	100.00	60.00
(21)	Frank Reiber	200.00	100.00	60.00
(22)	Lee Rogers	200.00	100.00	60.00
(23)	Cecil Travis	200.00	100.00	60.00
(24)	Hal Trosky	200.00	100.00	60.00
(25)	Ted Williams	3,000	1,500	900.00

1975 WTMJ Milwaukee Brewers Broadcasters

To promote its schedule of radio and television broadcasts of Brewers baseball, WTMJ issued this set of broadcaster and schedule cards to potential sponsors. The standard 2-1/2" x 3-1/2" cards are printed in team colors of blue and gold. The on-air talent cards have portraits and facsimile autographs on front, with career summaries on back. The schedule cards have game-action photos on front along with the slogan, "Brewers 75: It's Gonna' Be A Whole New Ballgame!" The cards were distributed in a wax pack with gum.

		NM	E	VG
Complete Set (7):		50.00	25.00	15.00
Common Card:		5.00	2.50	1.50
1	Jim Irwin	8.00	4.00	2.50
2	Gary Bender	8.00	4.00	2.50
3	Bob Uecker	25.00	12.50	7.50
4	Merle Harmon	8.00	4.00	2.50
(5)	TV Schedule	5.00	2.50	1.50
(6)	Radio Schedule, Part 1	5.00	2.50	1.50
(7)	Radio Schedule, Part 2	5.00	2.50	1.50

1910 W-UNC Strip Cards

MATHEWSON, N.Y.

Considerably earlier than most known strip cards, these pieces were cut from a notebook cover. The known players point to a 1910 issue date. Crudely printed on flimsy stock, the cards feature familiar colorized portraits of players on brightly colored backgrounds. The format is about 1-3/8" x 2-3/8" and some cards have evidence of a 1-16th" yellow strip around the outside of the black border. Player name and city are printed in the white border at bottom. Backs are blank. The unnumbered cards are listed here in alphabetical order, though the checklist may or may not be complete.

		NM	E	VG
Common Player:		450.00	180.00	90.00
(1)	Babe Adams	450.00	180.00	90.00
(2)	Chief Bender	900.00	450.00	225.00
(3)	Roger Bresnahan	900.00	450.00	225.00
(4)	Donie Bush	450.00	180.00	90.00
(5)	Bobby Byrne	450.00	180.00	90.00
(6)	Bill Carrigan	450.00	180.00	90.00
(7)	Frank Chance	900.00	450.00	225.00
(8)	Hal Chase	450.00	180.00	90.00
(9)	Ty Cobb	4,125	1,100	550.00
(10)	Willis Cole	450.00	180.00	90.00
(11)	Eddie Collins	900.00	450.00	225.00
(12)	Jack Coombs	450.00	180.00	90.00
(13)	Sam Crawford	900.00	450.00	225.00
(14)	Johnny Evers	900.00	450.00	225.00
(15)	Solly Hoffman	450.00	180.00	90.00
(16)	Hughie Jennings	900.00	450.00	225.00

(17)	Walter Johnston			
	(Johnson)	2,250	600.00	300.00
(18)	Johnny Kling	450.00	180.00	90.00
(19)	Ed Konetchy	450.00	180.00	90.00
(20)	Harry Lord	450.00	180.00	90.00
(21)	Sherry Magee	450.00	180.00	90.00
(22)	Christy Mathewson	2,400	1,200	600.00
(23)	Mike Mitchell	450.00	180.00	90.00
(24)	Tris Speaker	1,150	600.00	225.00
(25)	Oscar Stanage	450.00	180.00	90.00
(26)	Honus Wagner	3,000	1,500	600.00

1911 W-UNC Strip Cards

Based on the selection of confirmed subjects, 1911 seems to be the best approximation for the issue date of this black-and-white, blank-backed strip card set. Similar in format and even typography to the set identified as 1915 W-UNC Strip Cards, the cards in this set were probably issued in a nominal 1-5/8" x 2" size, although significant differences in size are seen on the few known examples, possibly due to the manner in which they were cut. Fronts of the individual player cards have posed action photos with a black frame and bordered in white. Player identification is at bottom. The checklist here is certainly incomplete.

	VG
Catcher Irwin (Emil Erwin)	1,600.
Hans Lobert	1,600.
Christy Mathewson	4,500.
Philadelphia A's composite	2,250.

1912 W-UNC Strip Cards

The attributed issue date is speculative, based on the limited known roster. In much the same size and format as W555, these small (photo image area is 1-3/8" x 1-1/2") blank-back cards appear to have been cut off a box or other packaging and may actually be candy cards. Black-and-white photos are framed in dark green with the player's last name in white capital letters below.

		NM	E	VG
Common Player:		2,000	800.00	400.00
(1)	Jack Barry	2,000	800.00	400.00
(2)	Brown	2,000	800.00	400.00
(3)	Bill Carrigan	2,000	800.00	400.00
(4)	Larry Doyle	2,000	800.00	400.00
(5)	Tommy Leach	2,000	800.00	400.00
(6)	Oscar Stanage	2,000	800.00	400.00
(7)	Honus Wagner	9,000	4,500	2,700
(8)	Cy Young	6,500	2,600	1,300

1915 W-UNC Strip Cards

Utilizing many photos familiar to collectors from contemporary card sets, including pictures that were several years old at the time of issue, this appears to be a strip-card issue whose scarcity has caused it to elude cataloging efforts heretofore. Cards are printed in black-and-white, blank-backed and are nominally 1-3/4" x 2-3/4". Player or photo identification appears in the bottom border, or at right on horizontally formatted cards.

Walter Johnson, Wash.Amer.

		NM	E	VG
Common Player:		500.00	250.00	150.00
(1)	Ty Cobb	6,500	2,600	1,300
(2)	Sam Crawford	1,500	700.00	350.00
(3)	Jake Daubert	500.00	225.00	110.00
(4)	Larry Doyle	500.00	200.00	100.00
(5)	Johnny Evers	1,500	600.00	300.00
(6)	Joe Jackson	16,000	6,400	3,200
(7)	Walter Johnson	2,500	1,000	500.00
(8)	Neopolean (Napoleon)			
	Lajoie	2,000	900.00	450.00
(9)	Sherwood Magee	500.00	200.00	100.00
(10)	Fred Maisel	500.00	200.00	100.00
(11)	Walter (Rabbit) Maranville	1,500	600.00	300.00
(12)	Rube Marquard	1,500	600.00	300.00
(13)	Christy Mathewson	2,750	1,100	550.00
(14)	Phila. Athletics, Champ.	750.00	300.00	150.00
(15)	Eddie Plank	2,250	1,100	550.00
(16)	Ready for the Wallop			
	(Honus Wagner, Roger			
	Bresnahan)	1,500	600.00	300.00
(17)	"Demon Dave" Robertson	500.00	225.00	120.00
(18)	Nap Rucker	500.00	200.00	100.00
(19)	Jake Stahl	500.00	225.00	120.00
(20)	Jim Thorpe	15,000	7,500	3,750
(21)	Hans Wagner	3,500	1,400	700.00
(22)	Joe Wood	600.00	240.00	120.00
(23)	Heiny Zimmerman	500.00	225.00	120.00

1918-20 W-UNC "Big Head" Strip Cards

Given the known player content and the fact that no team designations are printed on the cards, it is impossible to more accurately date this blank-back strip card issue. The 1-3/8" x 2-1/2" cards have color artwork of the players in full-body poses. The pictures are unusual in that the players' heads are out of proportion to the rest of the body. Whether the portraits were meant to be accurate portrayals is conjecture. Player names given here are as printed on the cards.

		NM	E	VG
Complete Set (20):		16,000	6,400	3,200
Common Player:		500.00	350.00	150.00
(1)	Jim Bagby Sr.	500.00	350.00	150.00
(2)	Home Run Baker	800.00	475.00	300.00
(3)	Dave Bancroft	800.00	475.00	300.00
(4)	Ping Bodie	500.00	350.00	150.00
(5)	Geo. Burns	500.00	350.00	150.00
(6)	Leon Cadore	500.00	350.00	150.00
(7)	Ty Cobb	4,000	2,500	1,250
(8)	Larry Doyle	500.00	350.00	150.00
(9)	Hinie Groh	500.00	350.00	150.00
(10)	R. Hornsby	2,000	1,000	750.00
(11)	Johnston (Walter			
	Johnson)	1,500	850.00	500.00
(12)	Joe Judge	500.00	350.00	150.00
(13)	Eddy Konetchy	500.00	350.00	150.00
(14)	Carl Mays	500.00	350.00	150.00

		NM	E	VG
(15)	Zeb Milan	500.00	350.00	150.00
(16)	Sam Rice	800.00	475.00	300.00
(17)	Babe Ruth	14,000	8,000	3,000
(18)	Ray Schalk	800.00	475.00	300.00
(19)	Wally Schang	500.00	350.00	150.00
(20)	Geo. Sisler	1,500	850.00	500.00

1920s W-UNC Playing Strip Cards (2)

Because only three players have thus far been check-listed from this set, it is not possible to more precisely date this issue. Likely printed on a sheet similar to other playing card/strip card sets of the era, the individual cards are about 1-1/2" x 2-1/2", printed in either red (hearts, diamonds) or black (clubs, spades), with a player photo at center. Backs are blank.

VALUES UNDETERMINED

6C	Bob Meusel
9S	Tris Speaker
AD	Babe Ruth

1921 W-UNC Self-Developing Strip Cards

The technology of a self-developing photographic base-ball card was popularized in the early 1930s by Ray-O-Print and again in the late late 1940s and early 1950s by Topps, but appears to have been pioneered circa 1921 by an unknown company which produced this series. Individual cards measure between 1-1/16" and 1-3/16" in width and 1-13/16" in depth. In black-and-white, they feature action poses on a dark background with the player name and team in white. A white border surrounds the picture. Backs are blank. The unnumbered cards are checklisted here alphabetically, though the list is probably incomplete.

		NM	E	VG
Common Player:		100.00	40.00	20.00
(1)	Grover Alexander	450.00	180.00	90.00
(2)	Ty Cobb	2,000	800.00	400.00
(3)	Eddie Collins	300.00	120.00	60.00
(4)	Jake Daubert	100.00	40.00	20.00
(5)	Red Faber	250.00	100.00	50.00
(6)	Max Flack	100.00	40.00	20.00
(7)	"Roger (Rogers) Hornsby"	350.00	140.00	70.00
(8)	Doc Johnston	100.00	40.00	20.00
(9)	Walter Johnston (Johnson)	900.00	360.00	180.00
(10)	Bill Killifer (Killefer)	100.00	40.00	20.00
(11)	Steve O'Neill	100.00	40.00	20.00
(12)	Derrill Pratt	100.00	40.00	20.00
(13)	"Babe" Ruth	3,500	1,400	700.00
(14)	Wallie Schang	100.00	40.00	20.00

1926 W-UNC Strip Cards

Ruth is the only baseball player known in this set of athletic, cinematic and historical subjects. The approximately 1-1/2" x 2-1/2" black-and-white, blue-and-white, or maroon-and-white blank-backed card identifies the player, position and team typographically within the photo and has the card number and name in the bottom border. The card has been seen with numbers 1, 52 and 71, as well as unnumbered.

		NM	E	VG
1	Babe Ruth (Black-and-white.)	800.00	400.00	240.00
52	Babe Ruth (Blue duotone.)	800.00	400.00	240.00
71	Babe Ruth (Blue duotone.)	800.00	400.00	240.00
71	Babe Ruth (Maroon duotone.)	800.00	400.00	240.00
---	Babe Ruth ((Unnumbered, maroon.))	1,100	550.00	330.00

1929 W-UNC Playing Strip Cards (1)

Recent discoveries indicate that this issue was produced by Universal Toy & Novelty circa 1929. Likely printed on a sheet similar to other playing card/strip card sets of the era, the individual cards are about 1-1/2" x 2-1/2". The front has a crude black-and-white drawing of the player inside a suit-shaped design on a red (clubs or spades) or black (hearts and diamonds) background. Back is blank.

		NM	E	VG
4C	Walter Hoyt	250.00	125.00	75.00
6C	Shanty Hogan	150.00	75.00	45.00
7S	Doug McWeeny	150.00	75.00	45.00
5H	Lou Gehrig	600.00	300.00	180.00
5D	Babe Ruth	750.00	370.00	220.00

1931 W-UNC Strip Cards

(14) ROBERT GROVE

This issue is virtually identical in format to the various 1928-1931 issues cataloged as W502, York Caramel, Yuengling Ice Cream, etc. The black-and-white, cards measure about 1-3/8" (give or take a 1/16") x 2-1/2". Player photos are bordered in white with the name printed in capital letters at bottom. At bottom-left is a card number in parentheses. This issue's checklist is identical to the 1931 W502, the only difference being these cards have blank backs.

		NM	E	VG
Complete Set (60):		12,500	5,000	2,500
Common Player:		75.00	30.00	15.00
1	Muddy Ruel	75.00	30.00	15.00
2	John Grabowski	75.00	30.00	15.00
3	Mickey Cochrane	150.00	60.00	30.00
4	Bill Cissell	75.00	30.00	15.00
5	Carl Reynolds	75.00	30.00	15.00
6	Luke Sewell	75.00	30.00	15.00
7	Ted Lyons	150.00	60.00	30.00
8	Harvey Walker	75.00	30.00	15.00
9	Gerald Walker	75.00	30.00	15.00
10	Sam Byrd	75.00	30.00	15.00
11	Joe Vosmik	75.00	30.00	15.00
12	Dan MacFayden	75.00	30.00	15.00
13	William Dickey	150.00	60.00	30.00
14	Robert Grove	300.00	120.00	60.00
15	Al Simmons	150.00	60.00	30.00
16	Jimmy Foxx	300.00	120.00	60.00
17	Nick Altrock	75.00	30.00	15.00
18	Charlie Grimm	75.00	30.00	15.00
19	Bill Terry	150.00	60.00	30.00
20	Clifton Heathcote	75.00	30.00	15.00
21	Burleigh Grimes	150.00	60.00	30.00
22	Red Faber	150.00	60.00	30.00
23	Gabby Hartnett	150.00	60.00	30.00
24	Earl (Earle) Combs	150.00	60.00	30.00
25	Hack Wilson	150.00	60.00	30.00

		NM	E	VG
26	Stanley Harris	150.00	60.00	30.00
27	John J. McGraw	150.00	60.00	30.00
28	Paul Waner	150.00	60.00	30.00
29	Babe Ruth	4,000	1,600	800.00
30	Herb Pennock	150.00	60.00	30.00
31	Joe Sewell	150.00	60.00	30.00
32	Lou Gehrig	2,000	800.00	400.00
33	Tony Lazzeri	150.00	60.00	30.00
34	Waite Hoyt	150.00	60.00	30.00
35	Glenn Wright	75.00	30.00	15.00
36	Leon (Goose) Goslin	150.00	60.00	30.00
37	Frank Frisch	150.00	60.00	30.00
38	George Uhle	75.00	30.00	15.00
39	Bob O'Farrell	75.00	30.00	15.00
40	Rogers Hornsby	200.00	80.00	40.00
41	"Pie" Traynor	150.00	60.00	30.00
42	Clarence Mitchell	75.00	30.00	15.00
43	Sherwood Smith	75.00	30.00	15.00
44	Miguel A. Gonzalez	75.00	30.00	15.00
45	Joe Judge	75.00	30.00	15.00
46	Eppa Rixey	150.00	60.00	30.00
47	Adolfo Luque	75.00	30.00	15.00
48	E.C. (Sam) Rice	150.00	60.00	30.00
49	Earl Sheely	75.00	30.00	15.00
50	Sam Jones	75.00	30.00	15.00
51	Bib A. Falk	75.00	30.00	15.00
52	Willie Kamm	75.00	30.00	15.00
53	Roger Peckinpaugh	75.00	30.00	15.00
54	Lester Bell	75.00	30.00	15.00
55	L. Waner	150.00	60.00	30.00
56	Eugene Hargrave	75.00	30.00	15.00
57	Harry Heilmann	150.00	60.00	30.00
58	Earl Smith	75.00	30.00	15.00
59	Dave Bancroft	150.00	60.00	30.00
60	George Kelly	150.00	60.00	30.00

Y

1972 The Yawkey Red Sox

Boston Red Sox players of the 1930s are featured in this collectors' issue. The issue date given is only a guess. The 2-1/2" x 3-1/2" cards have black-and-whie player photos with brown borders and black graphics. Backs are also in black-and-white with personal data, a career summary and a promotion for the Red Sox long-time charity, The Jimmy Fund. The unnumbered cards are listed here alphabetically.

		NM	E	VG
Complete Set (45):		45.00	22.50	13.50
Common Player:		3.00	1.50	.90
(1)	Mel Almada	4.50	2.25	1.25
(2)	Morris "Moe" Berg	9.00	4.50	2.75
(3)	Max Bishop	3.00	1.50	.90
(4)	Doc Bowers	3.00	1.50	.90
(5)	Joe Cascarella	3.00	1.50	.90
(6)	Ben Chapman	3.00	1.50	.90
(7)	Bill Cissell	3.00	1.50	.90
(8)	Dusty Cooke	3.00	1.50	.90
(9)	Doc Cramer	3.00	1.50	.90
(10)	Joe Cronin	4.50	2.25	1.25
(11)	George Dickey	3.00	1.50	.90
(12)	Emerson Dickman	3.00	1.50	.90
(13)	Bobby Doerr	4.50	2.25	1.25
(14)	Rick Ferrell	4.50	2.25	1.25
(15)	Wes Ferrell	3.00	1.50	.90
(16)	Jimmie Foxx	7.50	3.75	2.25
(17)	Joe Gonzales	3.00	1.50	.90
(18)	Lefty Grove	6.00	3.00	1.75
(19)	Bucky Harris	4.50	2.25	1.25
(20)	Jim Henry	3.00	1.50	.90

		NM	E	VG
(21)	Pinky Higgins	3.00	1.50	.90
(22)	Lefty Hockette	3.00	1.50	.90
(23)	Roy Johnson	3.00	1.50	.90
(24)	John Kroner	3.00	1.50	.90
(25)	Heinie Manush	4.50	2.25	1.25
(26)	Archie McKain	3.00	1.50	.90
(27)	Eric McNair	3.00	1.50	.90
(28)	Oscar Melillo	3.00	1.50	.90
(29)	Bing Miller	3.00	1.50	.90
(30)	Joe Mulligan	3.00	1.50	.90
(31)	Bobo Newsom	3.00	1.50	.90
(32)	Ted Olson	3.00	1.50	.90
(33)	Fritz Ostermueller	3.00	1.50	.90
(34)	George Pipgras	3.00	1.50	.90
(35)	Dusty Rhodes	3.00	1.50	.90
(36)	Walt Ripley	3.00	1.50	.90
(37)	Buck Rogers	3.00	1.50	.90
(38)	Jack Russell	3.00	1.50	.90
(39)	Tommy Thomas	3.00	1.50	.90
(40)	Hy Vandenberg	3.00	1.50	.90
(41)	Rube Walberg	3.00	1.50	.90
(42)	Johnny Welch	3.00	1.50	.90
(43)	Bill Werber	3.00	1.50	.90
(44)	Dib Williams	3.00	1.50	.90
(45)	Black Jack Wilson	3.00	1.50	.90

1959 Yoo-Hoo

Issued as a promotion for Yoo-Hoo chocolate flavored soft drink (it's a New York thing), this issue features five New York Yankees players. The black-and-white blank-backed cards measure 2-7/16" x 5-1/8", including a tab at the bottom which could be redeemed for various prizes. The top of the card features a posed spring training photo and includes a fac-simile autograph and "Me for Yoo-Hoo" slogan. Prices shown here are for complete cards; cards without tabs would be val-ued at one-half of these figures. A Mickey Mantle advertising piece in larger size is often collected as an adjunct to the set, but no card of Mantle was issued. The Berra card is consider-ably scarcer than the others.

		NM	E	VG
Complete Set, W/Tabs (5):		4,500	2,250	1,350
Complete Set, No Tabs (5):		1,350	675.00	415.00
Common Player, W/Tab:		800.00	400.00	240.00
Common Player, No Tab:				
WITH TAB				
(1)	Yogi Berra	1,200	600.00	360.00
(2)	Whitey Ford	1,200	600.00	360.00
(3)	Tony Kubek	800.00	400.00	240.00
(4)	Gil McDougald	800.00	400.00	240.00
(5)	Bill Skowron	800.00	400.00	240.00
NO TAB				
(1)	Yogi Berra	300.00	150.00	90.00
(2)	Whitey Ford	300.00	150.00	90.00
(3)	Tony Kubek	250.00	125.00	75.00
(4)	Gil McDougald	250.00	125.00	75.00
(5)	Bill Skowron	250.00	125.00	75.00

1959 Yoo-Hoo Bottle Caps

These lids for the chocolate soft drink feature black-and-white player portraits with the player name across the chest

and "ME FOR" above with "YOO-HOO" below. Caps come in two styles, the older pry-off style and a later, larger screw-top.

	NM	E	VG
Common Player:	200.00	100.00	60.00
Screw-Tops: +25 Percent			
(1a) Yogi Berra (portrait)	400.00	200.00	120.00
(1b) Yogi Berra (drinking Yoo-Hoo)	400.00	200.00	120.00
(2a) Whitey Ford (cap straight)	400.00	200.00	120.00
(2b) Whitey Ford (cap tilted)	400.00	200.00	120.00
(3) Tony Kubek	200.00	100.00	60.00
(4a) Mickey Mantle (large portrait)	800.00	400.00	250.00
(4b) Mickey Mantle (small portrait, name under YOO-HOO)	800.00	400.00	250.00
(5) Gil McDougald	200.00	100.00	60.00
(6) Bobby Richardson (screw top)	200.00	100.00	60.00
(7) Moose Skowron	200.00	100.00	60.00

1959 Yoo-Hoo Mickey Mantle

In a different format than the other contemporary Yoo-Hoo Yankees cards, the manner of original distribution of this card is unclear. The 2-5/8" x 3-5/8" black-and-white card has a portrait photo and endorsement for the product on front. Back is blank.

	NM	E	VG
Mickey Mantle	3,750	1,800	1,200

1964 Yoo-Hoo Counter Sign

Seven N.Y. Yankees and Bill Skowron in a Senators' cap are pictured on this 11" x 14" easel-back counter display for the chocolate soft drink. Printed in brown, yellow and white, the sign has a hand holding a bottle in front of each player's portrait.

	NM	E	VG
Yogi Berra, Whitey Ford, Elston Howard, Mickey Mantle, Joe Pepitone, Bobby Richardson, Moose Skowron, Tom Tresh	1,650	800.00	480.00

1927 York Caramel Type 1 (E210)

Issued in 1927 by the York Caramel Co. of York, Pa., these black-and-white cards are among the last of the caramel is-sues. Measuring 1-3/8" x 2-1/2", they are similar in appear-ance to earlier candy and tobacco cards. Fronts have the player's name in capital letters beneath the photo preceded by a number in parentheses. The back also lists the player's name in capital letters, along with a brief phrase describing him and the line, "This is one of a series of sixty of the most prominent stars in baseball." The bottom of the cards reads "York Caramel Co. York, Pa." The set includes several varia-tions and is designated in the ACC as E210. It is closely relat-ed to the W502 set of the same year. Cards can be found on

white or gray card stock. Type 1 cards can be differentiated from Type 2s by the orientation of the back printing. On Type 1 cards, the player name on back is at right when a normally-viewed front is turned over.

		NM	E	VG
Complete Set (60):		40,000	16,000	8,000
Common Player:		250.00	100.00	50.00
1	Burleigh Grimes	500.00	200.00	100.00
2	Walter Reuther (Ruether)	500.00	200.00	100.00
3	Joe Duggan (Dugan)	250.00	100.00	50.00
4	Red Faber	500.00	200.00	100.00
5	Gabby Hartnett	500.00	200.00	100.00
6	Babe Ruth	15,000	4,800	2,400
7	Bob Meusel	250.00	100.00	50.00
8a	Herb Pennock (Team name on jersey.)	500.00	200.00	100.00
8b	Herb Pennock (No team name.)	500.00	200.00	100.00
9	George Burns	250.00	100.00	50.00
10	Joe Sewell	500.00	200.00	100.00
11	George Uhle	250.00	100.00	50.00
12a	Bob O'Farrel (O'Farrell) (Team name on jersey.))	250.00	100.00	50.00
12b	Bob O'Farrel (O'Farrell) (No team name.))	250.00	100.00	50.00
13	Rogers Hornsby	600.00	240.00	120.00
14	Pie Traynor	500.00	200.00	100.00
15	Clarence Mitchell	250.00	100.00	50.00
16	Eppa Jepha Rixey (Jeptha)	500.00	200.00	100.00
17	Carl Mays	250.00	100.00	50.00
18	Adolph Luque (Adolfo)	250.00	100.00	50.00
19	Dave Bancroft	500.00	200.00	100.00
20	George Kelly	500.00	200.00	100.00
21	Ira Flagstead	250.00	100.00	50.00
22	Harry Heilmann	500.00	200.00	100.00
23	Raymond W. Shalk (Schalk)	500.00	200.00	100.00
24	Johnny Mostil	250.00	100.00	50.00
25	Hack Wilson (Photo actually Art Wilson.)	500.00	200.00	100.00
26	Tom Zachary	250.00	100.00	50.00
27	Ty Cobb	5,500	2,750	1,650
28	Tris Speaker	675.00	375.00	225.00
29	Ralph Perkins	250.00	100.00	50.00
30	Jess Haines	500.00	200.00	100.00
31	Sherwood Smith (Photo actually Jack Coombs.)	250.00	100.00	50.00
32	Max Carey	500.00	200.00	100.00
33	Eugene Hargraves (Hargrave)	250.00	100.00	50.00
34	Miguel L. Gonzales (Miguel A. Gonzalez)	250.00	100.00	50.00
35a	Clifton Heathcot (Heathcote)(Team name on jersey.))	250.00	100.00	50.00
35b	Clifton Heathcot (Heathcote)(No team name.))	250.00	100.00	50.00
35c	Clifton Heathcote (Correct spelling.) (Team Name on jersey.))	250.00	100.00	50.00
36	E.C. (Sam) Rice	500.00	200.00	100.00
37	Earl Sheely	250.00	100.00	50.00
38a	Emory E. Rigney (Team name on jersey.)	250.00	100.00	50.00
38b	Emory E. Rigney (No team name.)	250.00	100.00	50.00
39	Bib A. Falk (Bibb)	250.00	100.00	50.00
40	Nick Altrock	250.00	100.00	50.00
41	Stanley Harris	500.00	200.00	100.00
42	John J. McGraw	500.00	200.00	100.00
43	Wilbert Robinson	500.00	200.00	100.00
44	Grover Alexander	750.00	300.00	150.00
45	Walter Johnson	1,000	400.00	200.00
46	William H. Terry (Photo actually Zeb Terry.)	500.00	200.00	100.00
47	Edward Collins	500.00	200.00	100.00
48	Marty McManus	250.00	100.00	50.00
49	Leon (Goose) Goslin	500.00	200.00	100.00
50	Frank Frisch	500.00	200.00	100.00
51	Jimmie Dykes	250.00	100.00	50.00
52	Fred (Cy) Williams	250.00	100.00	50.00
53	Eddie Roush	500.00	200.00	100.00
54	George Sisler	500.00	200.00	100.00
55	Ed Rommel	250.00	100.00	50.00
56a	Rogers Peckinpaugh (Roger)(Card number upside-down.))	250.00	100.00	50.00
56b	Rogers Peckinpaugh (Roger)(Card number corrected.))	250.00	100.00	50.00
57	Stanley Coveleskie (Coveleski)	500.00	200.00	100.00

		NM	E	VG
58	Clarence Gallaway (Galloway)	250.00	100.00	50.00
59	Bob Shawkey	250.00	100.00	50.00
60	John P. McInnis	250.00	100.00	50.00

1927 York Caramel Type 2 (E210)

Type 2 York Caramels are in the same size and format as the Type 1 cards. They can be differentiated from Type 1 cards by the orientation of the back printing. On Type 2 cards, the player name appears at left when a normally-held card is turned over. Type 2 cards are all printed on white stock. Some players and photos were changed, and the descriptive lines about the players were changed on most cards.

		NM	E	VG
Complete Set (60):		45,000	18,000	9,000
Common Player:		250.00	100.00	50.00
1	Burleigh Grimes	500.00	200.00	100.00
2	Walter Reuther (Ruether)	250.00	100.00	50.00
3	Joe Dugan	250.00	100.00	50.00
4	Red Faber	500.00	200.00	100.00
5	Gabby Hartnett	500.00	200.00	100.00
6	Babe Ruth	12,000	4,800	2,400
7	Bob Meusel	250.00	100.00	50.00
8	Herb Pennock (Profile)	500.00	200.00	100.00
9	George Burns	250.00	100.00	50.00
10	Joe Sewell	500.00	200.00	100.00
11	George Uhle	250.00	100.00	50.00
12	Bob O'Farrell	250.00	100.00	50.00
13	Rogers Hornsby	600.00	240.00	120.00
14	Pie Traynor	500.00	200.00	100.00
15	Clarence Mitchell	250.00	100.00	50.00
16	Eppa Rixey	500.00	200.00	100.00
17	Carl Mays	250.00	100.00	50.00
18	Adolfo Luque	250.00	100.00	50.00
19	Dave Bancroft	500.00	200.00	100.00
20	George Kelly	500.00	200.00	100.00
21	Earle Combs	500.00	200.00	100.00
22	Harry Heilmann	500.00	200.00	100.00
23	Ray W. Schalk	500.00	200.00	100.00
24	Johnny Mostil	250.00	100.00	50.00
25	Hack Wilson	500.00	200.00	100.00
26	Lou Gehrig	10,000	2,600	1,300
27	Ty Cobb	6,500	2,600	1,300
28	Tris Speaker	600.00	240.00	120.00
29	Tony Lazzeri	500.00	200.00	100.00
30	Waite Hoyt	500.00	200.00	100.00
31	Sherwood Smith (Photo actually Jack Coombs.)	250.00	100.00	50.00
32	Max Carey	500.00	200.00	100.00
33	Eugene Hargrave (Hargraves)	250.00	100.00	50.00
34	Miguel L. Gonzales (Miguel A. Gonzalez)	250.00	100.00	50.00
35	Joe Judge	250.00	100.00	50.00
36	E.C. (Sam) Rice	500.00	200.00	100.00
37	Earl Sheely	250.00	100.00	50.00
38	Sam Jones	250.00	100.00	50.00
39	Bib (Bibb) A. Falk	250.00	100.00	50.00
40	Willie Kamm	250.00	100.00	50.00
41	Stanley Harris	500.00	200.00	100.00
42	John J. McGraw	500.00	200.00	100.00
43	Artie Nehf	250.00	100.00	50.00
44	Grover Alexander	750.00	300.00	150.00
45	Paul Waner	500.00	200.00	100.00
46	William H. Terry (Photo actually Zeb Terry.)	500.00	200.00	100.00
47	Glenn Wright	250.00	100.00	50.00
48	Earl Smith	250.00	100.00	50.00
49	Leon (Goose) Goslin	500.00	200.00	100.00
50	Frank Frisch	500.00	200.00	100.00
51	Joe Harris	250.00	100.00	50.00
52	Fred (Cy) Williams	250.00	100.00	50.00
53	Eddie Roush	500.00	200.00	100.00
54	George Sisler	500.00	200.00	100.00
55	Ed Rommel	250.00	100.00	50.00
56	Rogers Peckinpaugh (Roger)	250.00	100.00	50.00
57	Stanley Coveleskie (Coveleski)	500.00	200.00	100.00
58	Lester Bell	250.00	100.00	50.00
59	L. Waner	500.00	200.00	100.00
60	John P. McInnis	250.00	100.00	50.00

1917 Youth's Companion Stamps

The date attributed is speculative. This set of poster-stamps was issued to promote a Boston-based weekly magazine. Although the set is not named, the left-handed pitcher depicted is identical to a known photo of Rube Marquard. The 1-7/8" x 2-1/2" stamp is, of course, blank-backed and is part of a set which featured other sporting activities, hobbys and topics suitable for young readers.

	NM	E	VG
Rube Marquard	200.00	100.00	60.00

1928 Yuengling's Ice Cream (F50)

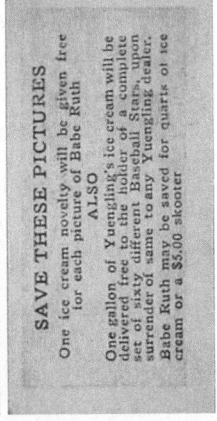

Issued in 1928, the Yuengling's Ice Cream issue consists of 60 black-and-white cards measuring 1-3/8" x 2-1/2". The photos are similar to those used in the E210 and W502 sets. Other ice cream companies such as Harrington's and Tharp's produced nearly identical cards. Two types of cards are seen, though whether either or both can be found for all players is unknown. Besides typographical placement differences on front, the back of one type mentions a "$5.00 skooter" as a redemption, while the other type has no mention of the toy. Collectors could redeem an entire set of Yuengling's cards for a gallon of ice cream. Yuengling's, located in Pottsville, Pa., was a brewery that converted its product line to ice cream during Prohibition.

		NM	E	VG
Complete Set (60):		40,000	20,000	12,000
Common Player:		200.00	100.00	60.00
1	Burleigh Grimes	500.00	200.00	100.00
2	Walter Reuther (Ruether)	200.00	100.00	60.00
3	Joe Dugan	200.00	100.00	60.00
4	Red Faber	500.00	200.00	100.00
5	Gabby Hartnett	500.00	200.00	100.00
6	Babe Ruth	9,000	4,500	2,400
7	Bob Meusel	200.00	100.00	60.00
8	Herb Pennock	500.00	200.00	100.00
9	George Burns	200.00	100.00	60.00
10	Joe Sewell	500.00	200.00	100.00
11	George Uhle	200.00	100.00	60.00
12	Bob O'Farrell	200.00	100.00	60.00
13	Rogers Hornsby	600.00	240.00	120.00
14	"Pie" Traynor	500.00	200.00	100.00
15	Clarence Mitchell	200.00	100.00	60.00
16	Eppa Jepha Rixey	500.00	200.00	100.00
17	Carl Mays	200.00	100.00	60.00
18	Adolfo Luque	200.00	100.00	60.00
19	Dave Bancroft	500.00	200.00	100.00
20	George Kelly	500.00	200.00	100.00
21	Earl (Earle) Combs	500.00	200.00	100.00
22	Harry Heilmann	500.00	200.00	100.00
23	Ray W. Schalk	500.00	200.00	100.00
24	Johnny Mostil	200.00	100.00	60.00
25	Hack Wilson	500.00	200.00	100.00
26	Lou Gehrig	4,000	2,000	1,200
27	Ty Cobb	5,500	2,600	1,300
28	Tris Speaker	600.00	240.00	120.00
29	Tony Lazzeri	500.00	200.00	100.00
30	Waite Hoyt	500.00	200.00	100.00
31	Sherwood Smith	200.00	100.00	60.00
32	Max Carey	500.00	200.00	100.00
33	Eugene Hargrave	200.00	100.00	60.00
34	Miguel L. Gonzales (Miguel A. Gonzalez)	200.00	100.00	60.00
35	Joe Judge	200.00	100.00	60.00

		NM	E	VG
36	E.C. (Sam) Rice	500.00	200.00	100.00
37	Earl Sheely	200.00	100.00	60.00
38	Sam Jones	200.00	100.00	60.00
39	Bib (Bibb) A. Falk	200.00	100.00	60.00
40	Willie Kamm	200.00	100.00	60.00
41	Stanley Harris	500.00	200.00	100.00
42	John J. McGraw	500.00	200.00	100.00
43	Artie Nehf	200.00	100.00	60.00
44	Grover Alexander	750.00	300.00	160.00
45	Paul Waner	500.00	200.00	100.00
46	William H. Terry	500.00	200.00	100.00
47	Glenn Wright	200.00	100.00	60.00
48	Earl Smith	200.00	100.00	60.00
49	Leon (Goose) Goslin	500.00	200.00	100.00
50	Frank Frisch	500.00	200.00	100.00
51	Joe Harris	200.00	100.00	60.00
52	Fred (Cy) Williams	200.00	100.00	60.00
53	Eddie Roush	500.00	200.00	100.00
54	George Sisler	500.00	200.00	100.00
55	Ed. Rommel	200.00	100.00	60.00
56	Rogers Peckinpaugh (Roger)	200.00	100.00	60.00
57	Stanley Coveleskie (Coveleski)	500.00	200.00	100.00
58	Lester Bell	200.00	100.00	60.00
59	L. Waner	500.00	200.00	100.00
60	John P. McInnis	200.00	100.00	60.00

1888 Yum Yum Tobacco (N403)

An extremely rare series of tobacco cards, this set was issued in 1888 by August Beck & Co., Chicago. The cards vary slightly in size but average 1-3/8" x 2-3/4". They were distributed in packages of the company's Yum Yum smoking and chewing tobacco and are found in two distinct types: photographic portraits and full-length action drawings copied from photos used in the Old Judge sets of the same period. In both types, the player's name and position appear in capital letters below the photo, while the very bottom of the card states: "Smoke and Chew 'Yum Yum' Tobacco. A. Beck & Co. Chicago, Ill." Players from all eight National League clubs, plus Brooklyn of the American Association, are included in the set. The checklist here has gaps left to accommodate future additions.

		NM	E	VG
Common Player:		9,000	5,000	3,500
(3)	Cap Anson (Portrait)	45,000	22,500	13,500
(4)	Cap Anson (Batting)	23,750	11,250	6,750
(7)	Lady Baldwin (Left arm extended.)	9,750	4,875	2,925
(11)	Dan Brouthers (Batting)	18,000	9,000	5,400
(13)	Willard "California" Brown	9,750	4,875	2,925
(15)	Charles Buffington (Buffinton)	9,750	4,875	2,925
(17)	Tom Burns (Portrait)	16,500	8,250	4,950
(18)	Tom Burns (With bat.)	9,750	4,875	2,925
(21)	John Clarkson (Portrait)	30,000	15,000	9,000
(22)	John Clarkson (Throwing, arm back.)	18,000	9,000	5,400
(25)	John Coleman (Portrait)	16,500	8,250	4,950
(27)	Roger Connor (Batting)	18,000	9,000	5,400
(28)	Roger Connor (Portrait)	30,000	15,000	9,000
(30)	Larry Corcoran (Portrait)	16,500	8,250	4,950
(34)	Tom Daily (Daly) (Portrait) (Photo actually Billy Sunday.))	17,250	8,625	5,175
(36)	Tom Deasley (Portrait)	16,500	8,250	4,950
(39)	Mike Dorgan (Portrait)	16,500	8,250	4,950
(40)	Dude Esterbrook (Portrait)	16,500	8,250	4,950
(41)	Buck Ewing (Portrait)	30,000	15,000	9,000
(42)	Buck Ewing (With bat.)	18,000	9,000	5,400
(45)	Silver Flint (Portrait)	16,500	8,250	4,950
(47)	Jim Fogarty (Throwing)	9,750	4,875	2,925

(49)	Pud Galvin (Ball in hands at chest.)	18,000	9,000	5,400
(51)	Joe Gerhardt	16,500	8,250	4,950
(53)	Charlie Getzein (Getzien) (Holding ball.))	9,750	4,875	2,925
(55)	Pete Gillespie (Portrait)	16,500	8,250	4,950
(57)	Jack Glasscock	9,750	4,875	2,925
(59)	George Gore (Leaning on bat.)	9,750	4,875	2,925
(61)	Ed Greer (Portrait)	16,500	8,250	4,950
(65)	Tim Keefe (Pitching)	18,000	9,000	5,400
(66)	Tim Keefe (Portrait)	30,000	15,000	9,000
(67)	King Kelly (Batting)	18,000	9,000	5,400
(68)	King Kelly (Photo, standing by urn.)	45,000	22,500	13,500
(70)	Gus Krock (Portrait)	16,500	8,250	4,950
(72)	Connie Mack	18,000	9,000	5,400
(74)	Kid Madden (Ball in raised right hand.)	9,750	4,875	2,925
(76)	Doggie Miller (Leaning on bat.)	9,750	4,875	2,925
(78)	John Morrill (Leaning on bat.)	9,750	4,875	2,925
(80)	James Mutrie (Portrait)	16,500	8,250	4,950
(82)	Billy Nash (Holding bat.)	9,750	4,875	2,925
(84)	Jim O'Rourke (Portrait)	30,000	15,000	9,000
(85)	Jim O'Rourke (With bat.)	18,000	9,000	5,400
(87)	Fred Pfeffer (Bat on shoulder.)	9,750	4,875	2,925
(90)	Danny Richardson (Portrait)	16,500	8,250	4,950
(92)	Chief Roseman (Portrait)	16,500	8,250	4,950
(94)	Jimmy Ryan (Portrait)	16,500	8,250	4,950
(95)	Jimmy Ryan (Throwing)	9,750	4,875	2,925
(97)	Bill Sowders (Ball in hands at chest.)	9,750	4,875	2,925
(100)	Marty Sullivan (Portrait)	16,500	8,250	4,950
(102)	Billy Sunday (Fielding)	18,000	9,000	5,400
(103)	Billy Sunday (Portrait) (Photo actually Mark Baldwin.))	18,000	9,000	5,400
(105)	Ezra Sutton (Batting)	9,750	4,875	2,925
(110)	Mike Tiernan (Portrait)	16,500	8,250	4,950
(111)	Mike Tiernan (With bat.)	9,750	4,875	2,925
(115)	Rip Van Haltren (Photo not Van Haltren.)	16,500	8,250	4,950
(119)	John Ward (Portrait)	30,000	15,000	9,000
(123)	Mickey Welch (Ball in hands at chest.)	18,000	9,000	5,400
(124)	Mickey Welch (Portrait)	30,000	15,000	9,000
(125)	Mickey Welch (Right arm extended.)	18,000	9,000	5,400
(129)	Jim Whitney (Throwing)	9,750	4,875	2,925
(133)	George Wood (Throwing, arm behind head.)	9,750	4,875	2,925

Z

1954-1955 Zipcards Baltimore Orioles

Given the homemade appearance of these cards, it must be surmised that they were an early collectors' issue. It is possible they date from as early as 1956, only a few years after the Orioles joined the American League. Cards are found in three formats. One type measures about 2" x 2-5/8" (all measurements are approximate due to the hand-cut nature of the cards) and is printed on thin yellow cardboard. They feature a chest-to-cap black-and-white circular player photo at center. A second type is about 2-3/4" x 3-5/8", black-and-white, with square portrait or posed action photos and "BALTIMORE" at top in what appears to be a picture of an embossed plastic Dymo label maker strip. The third type is also about 2-3/4" x 3-5/8" and is similar in design to the Dymo-lable format, except "Baltimore" is printed at top in a serifed italic typeface. All cards are blank-backed. Where known, the type of each card is indicated on this checklist by "RP" (round photo), "DL" (Dymo-label) or "SI" (serifed italic). It is possible this checklist is incomplete.

	NM	E	VG
Common Player:	30.00	15.00	9.00
54-01 Jimmie Dykes	30.00	15.00	9.00
54-02 Tom Oliver	30.00	15.00	9.00
54-03 Frank Skaff	30.00	15.00	9.00
54-04 Eddie Waitkuss (Waitkus) (DL)	30.00	15.00	9.00
54-05 Chuck Diering (DL)	30.00	15.00	9.00
54-06 Chick Chakales (RP)	30.00	15.00	9.00
54-07 Marlin Stuart (RP)	30.00	15.00	9.00
54-08 Jim Brideweser (RP)	30.00	15.00	9.00
54-09 Chico Garcia (RP)	30.00	15.00	9.00
54-10 Jim Fridley (RP)	30.00	15.00	9.00
54-11 Billy O'Dell (DL)	30.00	15.00	9.00
54-12 Unknown			
54-13 Joe Durham (DL)	30.00	15.00	9.00
55-01 Wayne Causey (RP)	30.00	15.00	9.00
55-02 Jim Dyck	30.00	15.00	9.00
55-03 Hoot Evers (SI)	30.00	15.00	9.00
55-04 Tom Gastall (RP)	30.00	15.00	9.00
55-05 Bob Hale (RP)	30.00	15.00	9.00
55-06 Bob Kennedy (SI)	30.00	15.00	9.00
55-07 Don Leppert (SI)	30.00	15.00	9.00
55-08 Les Moss (SI)	30.00	15.00	9.00
55-09 Bob Nelson (RP)	30.00	15.00	9.00
55-10 Dave Philley (RP)	30.00	15.00	9.00
55-11 Unknown			
55-12 Unknown			
55-13 Art Schallock (RP)	30.00	15.00	9.00
55-14 Bobby Young (SI)	30.00	15.00	9.00
55-15 Unknown			
55-16 Lum Harris	30.00	15.00	9.00

1977 Zip'z discs

Virtually identical in format to the several locally sponsored disc sets of the previous year, these 3-3/8" diameter player discs were given away at the sponsor's sundae bars around the cvountry. Some are found with a black rubber-stamp on back of the specific Zip's location. Discs once again feature black-and-white player portrait photos in the center of a baseball design. The left and right panels are in one of several bright colors. Licensed by the players' association through Mike Schechter Associates, the player photos carry no uniform logos. Backs are printed in reddish-orange. The unnumbered discs are checklisted here alphabetically.

		NM	E	VG
Complete Set (70):		120.00	60.00	35.00
Common Player:		2.00	1.00	.60
(1)	Sal Bando	2.00	1.00	.60
(2)	Buddy Bell	2.00	1.00	.60
(3)	Johnny Bench	7.50	3.75	2.25
(4)	Larry Bowa	2.00	1.00	.60
(5)	Steve Braun	2.00	1.00	.60
(6)	George Brett	15.00	7.50	4.50
(7)	Lou Brock	6.00	3.00	1.75
(8)	Jeff Burroughs	2.00	1.00	.60
(9)	Bert Campaneris	2.00	1.00	.60
(10)	John Candelaria	2.00	1.00	.60
(11)	Jose Cardenal	2.00	1.00	.60
(12)	Rod Carew	6.00	3.00	1.75
(13)	Steve Carlton	6.00	3.00	1.75
(14)	Dave Cash	2.00	1.00	.60
(15)	Cesar Cedeno	2.00	1.00	.60
(16)	Ron Cey	2.00	1.00	.60
(17)	Dave Concepcion	2.00	1.00	.60
(18)	Dennis Eckersley	6.00	3.00	1.75
(19)	Mark Fidrych	3.00	1.50	.90
(20)	Rollie Fingers	6.00	3.00	1.75
(21)	Carlton Fisk	6.00	3.00	1.75
(22)	George Foster	2.00	1.00	.60
(23)	Wayne Garland	2.00	1.00	.60
(24)	Ralph Garr	2.00	1.00	.60
(25)	Steve Garvey	5.00	2.50	1.50
(26)	Cesar Geronimo	2.00	1.00	.60
(27)	Bobby Grich	2.00	1.00	.60
(28)	Ken Griffey Sr.	2.00	1.00	.60
(29)	Don Gullett	2.00	1.00	.60
(30)	Mike Hargrove	2.00	1.00	.60
(31)	Al Hrabosky	2.00	1.00	.60
(32)	Jim Hunter	6.00	3.00	1.75
(33)	Reggie Jackson	12.00	6.00	3.50
(34)	Randy Jones	2.00	1.00	.60
(35)	Dave Kingman	2.00	1.00	.60
(36)	Jerry Koosman	2.00	1.00	.60
(37)	Dave LaRoche	2.00	1.00	.60
(38)	Greg Luzinski	2.00	1.00	.60
(39)	Fred Lynn	2.00	1.00	.60
(40)	Bill Madlock	2.00	1.00	.60
(41)	Rick Manning	2.00	1.00	.60
(42)	Jon Matlock	2.00	1.00	.60
(43)	John Mayberry	2.00	1.00	.60
(44)	Hal McRae	2.00	1.00	.60
(45)	Andy Messersmith	2.00	1.00	.60
(46)	Rick Monday	2.00	1.00	.60
(47)	John Montefusco	2.00	1.00	.60
(48)	Joe Morgan	6.00	3.00	1.75
(49)	Thurman Munson	5.00	2.50	1.50
(50)	Bobby Murcer	2.00	1.00	.60
(51)	Bill North	2.00	1.00	.60
(52)	Jim Palmer	6.00	3.00	1.75
(53)	Tony Perez	6.00	3.00	1.75
(54)	Jerry Reuss	2.00	1.00	.60
(55)	Brooks Robinson	7.50	3.75	2.25
(56)	Pete Rose	25.00	12.50	7.50
(57)	Joe Rudi	2.00	1.00	.60
(58)	Nolan Ryan	35.00	17.50	10.00
(59)	Manny Sanguillen	2.00	1.00	.60
(60)	Mike Schmidt	15.00	7.50	4.50
(61)	Tom Seaver	7.50	3.75	2.25
(62)	Bill Singer	2.00	1.00	.60
(63)	Willie Stargell	6.00	3.00	1.75
(64)	Rusty Staub	2.00	1.00	.60
(65)	Luis Tiant	2.00	1.00	.60
(66)	Bob Watson	2.00	1.00	.60
(67)	Butch Wynegar	2.00	1.00	.60
(68)	Carl Yastrzemski	10.00	5.00	3.00
(69)	Robin Yount	6.00	3.00	1.75
(70)	Richie Zisk	2.00	1.00	.60

1950s Bill Zuber's Restaurant

 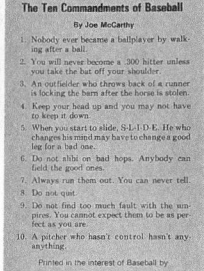

These 3-1/2" x 5-1/2" black-and-white cards were produced as a promotional item for an Iowa restaurant owned by the former big league pitcher (1936-47). The semi-gloss front has a portrait and facsimile autograph. One type has an advertising message at left and the inscription, "Good Hitting." On back are printed Joe McCarthy's "Ten Commandments of Baseball." A second type has the inscription, "Sincerest Wishes," with a postcard-style back featuring an advertising message in the top-left corner.

		NM	E	VG
(1)	Bill Zuber (Ten Commandments back.)	8.00	4.00	2.50
(2)	Bill Zuber (Postcard back.)	8.00	4.00	2.50

MINOR LEAGUE (1867-1969)

Prior to 1970 virtually all minor league baseball cards were issued as single cards rather than the complete sets. Like contemporary major league cards they were usually intended as premiums given away with the purchase of goos and services.

The listings which follow offer individual card prices in three grades of preservation to allow accurate valuations of superstar and other special interest cards, along with cards that were short-printed or otherwise are scarce.

A

1959 APCO Meat Packing Co. San Antonio Missions

The extent of this issue, as well as its distribution are not known. The 3-1/2" x 4-1/2" black-and-white cards may have been packaged with meat products and/or given away at the ballpark. The team was Class AA affiliate of the Chicago Cubs.

		NM	EX	VG
Common Player:		50.00	25.00	15.00
(1)	Russell Gragg	50.00	25.00	15.00
(2)	Mike Lutz	50.00	25.00	15.00
	(In Corpus Christi uniform.)			

1960 Armour Meats Denver Bears

Ten cards from this Class AA farm team of the Detroit Tigers have been checklisted, with others possibly to be discovered. The black-and-white blank-backed cards measure 2-1/2" x 3-1/4" and were issued with a coupon attached to the right side. The unnumbered cards are checklisted here alphabetically.

		NM	EX	VG
Complete Set (10):		650.00	325.00	195.00
Common Player:		75.00	37.00	22.00
(1)	George Alusik	75.00	37.00	22.00
(2)	Tony Bartirome	75.00	37.00	22.00
(3)	Edward J. Donnelly	75.00	37.00	22.00
(4)	James R. McDaniel	75.00	37.00	22.00
(5)	Charlie Metro	75.00	37.00	22.00
(6)	Harry Perkowski	75.00	37.00	22.00
(7)	Vernon E. Rapp	75.00	37.00	22.00
(8)	James Stump	75.00	37.00	22.00
(9)	Ozzie Virgil	75.00	37.00	22.00
(10)	Robert Walz	75.00	37.00	22.00

1940 Associated Stations San Francisco Seals

This album and sticker set was created as a premium by a Northern California gas company. Individual stickers were given away each week at participating service stations. The blank-backed, 1-3/4" x 2-5/8" stickers have the player's name in a black strip at the bottom. Pages in the accompanying 3-1/2" x 6" album have space for an autograph and a few career highlights for each player. The checklist is presented in page order of the album.

	NM	EX	VG
Complete Set (26):	500.00	250.00	125.00

Common Player:		20.00	10.00	6.00
Album:		100.00	50.00	30.00
(1)	"Lefty" O'Doul	40.00	20.00	12.00
(2)	Sam Gibson	20.00	10.00	6.00
(3)	Brooks Holder	20.00	10.00	6.00
(4)	Ted Norbert	20.00	10.00	6.00
(5)	Win Ballou	20.00	10.00	6.00
(6)	Al Wright	20.00	10.00	6.00
(7)	Al Epperly	20.00	10.00	6.00
(8)	Orville Jorgens	20.00	10.00	6.00
(9)	Larry Powell	20.00	10.00	6.00
(10)	Joe Sprinz	20.00	10.00	6.00
(11)	Harvey Storey	20.00	10.00	6.00
(12)	Jack Burns	20.00	10.00	6.00
(13)	Bob Price	20.00	10.00	6.00
(14)	Larry Guay	20.00	10.00	6.00
(15)	Frank Dasso	20.00	10.00	6.00
(16)	Eddie Stutz	20.00	10.00	6.00
(17)	John Barrett	20.00	10.00	6.00
(18)	Eddie Botelho	20.00	10.00	6.00
(19)	Ferris Fain	30.00	15.00	9.00
(20)	Larry Woodall	20.00	10.00	6.00
(21)	Ted Jennings	20.00	10.00	6.00
(22)	Jack Warner	20.00	10.00	6.00
(23)	Wil Leonard	20.00	10.00	6.00
(24)	Gene Kiley	20.00	10.00	6.00
(25)	Bob Jensen	20.00	10.00	6.00
(26)	Wilfrid Le Febvre	20.00	10.00	6.00

1952 Atlanta Crackers Souvenir Pictures Album

Rather than a set of individual baseball cards, the Class AA Southern Association farm club of the Boston Braves issued this souvenir picture album depicting players (including future major leaguers like Chuck Tanner, Art Fowler and Carl Wiley), staff and media. About 8-1/8" x 7-1/2", the album has embossed metallic light blue covers and dark blue graphics. Inside are eight black-and-white pages with three card-like images per page. The pictures are in about the same size and format as Globe Printing's contemporary minor league baseball card team sets.

	NM	EX	VG
Complete Souvenir Book:	400.00	200.00	120.00
1952 Atlanta Crackers	.00	.00	.00

1910 A.W.H./A.W.A. Caramels Virginia League (E222)

 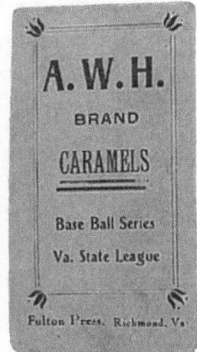

This rare set of cards picturing players from the Virginia League was issued by the A.W.H. (or A.W.A.) Caramel Co. in 1910. The cards measure 1-1/2" x 2-3/4" and feature player portraits in either red, black, brown or blue duotones. Examples of 12 different cards have been found. The front of the card displays the player's last name and team below his photo. The back states "A.W.H. (or A.W.A.) Brand Caramels" in large letters with "Base Ball Series/Va. State League" below. At least four variations in back typography and borders are known.

		EX	VG
Complete Set (12):		130,000	65,000
Common Player:		11,000	6,500
(1)	Tom Guiheen	11,000	6,500
(2)	Buck Hooker	11,000	6,500
(3)	Ison	11,000	6,500
(4)	Lipe	11,000	6,500
(5)	McCauley	11,000	6,500
(6)	Otey	11,000	6,500
(7)	Revelle	11,000	6,500
(8)	Ryan	11,000	6,500
(9)	Shaughnessy	11,000	6,500
(10)	Sieber	11,000	6,500
(11)	Smith	11,000	6,500
(12)	Titman	11,000	6,500

B

1910 Baltimore News Orioles

The Eastern League Baltimore Orioles are featured in this set of schedule cards issued by a local newspaper. Cards measure 2-3/4" x 3-1/2" and feature player photographs on front, with a wide border. Player name, position, team and league are printed at the bottom of the photo. Backs have both the "Home" and "Abroad" schedule for the team, along with ads at top and bottom for the newspaper. All printing on front is in red-and-white; backs are in black-and-white. The checklist here is likely incomplete.

		NM	EX	VG
Common Player:		1,200	600.00	350.00
(1)	Byers	1,200	600.00	350.00
(2)	Jim Egan	1,200	600.00	350.00
(3)	Maisel	1,200	600.00	350.00
(4)	Malloy	1,200	600.00	350.00
(5)	Jimmy Murray	1,200	600.00	350.00

1914 Baltimore News Orioles

The International League Baltimore Orioles are one of two teams featured (along with the city's Federal League team) in this set of newspaper promotional cards. The 2-5/8" x 3-5/8" cards are monochrome printed in either blue or red with wide borders on front framing full-length action poses on which the background has been erased in favor of artificial shadows. Player name, position and league are printed on front. Backs have a "HOME" and "ABROAD" schedule with an ad for the paper at top and a line at bottom which reads, "This Card is Given to," with space for a signature. At least one card, a Babe Ruth, has been seen with "Compliments Baltimore International League" replacing the newspaper ad at top. Only the minor league Orioles players are listed here, the Terrapins cards are listed in the major league section of this catalog. This checklist is almost certainly incomplete.

		NM	EX	VG
Common Player:		3,000	1,500	900.00
(1)	Neal Ball	3,000	1,500	900.00
(2)	Ensign Cottrell	3,000	1,500	900.00
(3)	Birdie Cree	3,000	1,500	900.00
(4)	Bert Daniels	3,000	1,500	900.00
(5)	Davidson	3,000	1,500	900.00
(6)	Jack Dunn	4,500	2,250	1,350
(7)	Gleichmann	3,000	1,500	900.00
(8)	Allen Russell (Allan)	3,000	1,500	900.00
(10)	Babe Ruth ((Blue PSA VG-EX sold in 5/06 auction for $244,000. Red PSA Poor-Fair sold in 4/06 auction for $150,800. Red SGC VG sold in 5/08 auction for $517,000. Red PSA Poor-Fair sold in 5/09 auction for $152,750.)			
(11)	Ernie Shore	3,000	1,500	900.00

		NM	EX	VG
(12)	George Twombley (Twombly)	3,000	1,500	900.00
(13)	Orioles Team w/Ruth (Slabbed authentic sold in 5/08 auction for $52,875.)			

1952 Baltimore Orioles Team Issue

ROY WEATHERLY

While most of the company's issues were for minor league teams in the lower classifications, Globe Printing of San Jose, Calif., also produced a set for the International League Baltimore Orioles. Similar to the company's other issues, the black-and-white cards measure 2-1/4" x 3-3/8". Reliable reports indicate that individual cards were given away with ice cream purchases at the ballpark. The checklist here is obviously incomplete. In 1952 the O's were the top farm club of the Philadelphia Phillies.

		NM	EX	VG
Common Player:		75.00	37.50	22.50
(1)	Al Cihocki	75.00	37.50	22.50
(2)	Blix Donnelly	75.00	37.50	22.50
(3)	Bob Greenwood	75.00	37.50	22.50
(4)	Don Heffner	75.00	37.50	22.50
(5)	Russ Kerns	75.00	37.50	22.50
(6)	Howie Moss	75.00	37.50	22.50
(7)	Dee Phillips	75.00	37.50	22.50
(8)	Jerry Scala	75.00	37.50	22.50
(9)	Danny Schell	75.00	37.50	22.50
(10)	Paul Stuffel	75.00	37.50	22.50
(11)	Roy Weatherly	75.00	37.50	22.50

1923 Baltimore Shirt Co. Kansas City Blues

LENA BLACKBURNE

Kansas City's Pennant Winning 1923 BLUES 1923 Compliments Baltimore 4 Stores KANSAS CITY, MO.

This unusual souvenir of the American Association Champion K.C. Blues is in the form of a 48" x 3-5/8" accordian-fold packet. Individual 1-7/8" x 3-1/4" black-and-white photos of the players are glued onto the black backing paper. Because the photos are rather easily removed, they may be encountered as singles. The players are checklisted here as they originally appeared, from left to right, on the foldout. There is no advertising on the individual pictures, just on the outer covers.

		NM	EX	VG
Complete Foldout:		1,000	500.00	300.00
Complete Set, Singles:		750.00	375.00	225.00
Common Player:		50.00	25.00	15.00
(1)	Wilbur Good	50.00	25.00	15.00
(2)	Bill Skiff	50.00	25.00	15.00
(3)	Lew McCarty	50.00	25.00	15.00
(4)	Dudley Branom	50.00	25.00	15.00
(5)	Lena Blackburne	55.00	27.50	16.50
(6)	Walter Hammond	50.00	25.00	15.00
(7)	Glen Wright (Glenn)	60.00	30.00	18.00
(8)	Geo. Armstrong	50.00	25.00	15.00
(9)	Beals Becker	50.00	25.00	15.00
(10)	"Dutch" Zwilling	50.00	25.00	15.00
(11)	Pete Scott	50.00	25.00	15.00
(12)	"Bunny" Brief	50.00	25.00	15.00
(13)	Jimmie Zinn	50.00	25.00	15.00
(14)	Ferd Schupp	50.00	25.00	15.00
(15)	Roy Wilkinson	50.00	25.00	15.00
(16)	Ray Caldwell	50.00	25.00	15.00
(17)	Joe Dawson	50.00	25.00	15.00
(18)	John Saladna	50.00	25.00	15.00
(19)	Herb Thormahlen	50.00	25.00	15.00
(20)	"Nick" Carter	50.00	25.00	15.00
(21)	George Muehlebach (President)	50.00	25.00	15.00

1909 Bastian Gum Pin

It is unknown whether other members of the championship 1909 Rochester Bronchos of the Eastern League were honored on these black-and-white pinback celluloid buttons or only their manager. The pin measures about 1-1/4" in diameter and as originally issued had a paper insert in back crediting it to Bastian Bros. Gum.

	NM	EX	VG
John H. Ganzel	150.00	75.00	45.00

1961 Bee Hive Starch Toronto Maple Leafs

BEE HIVE PLAYER PHOTO

DAVE POPE, outfielder - 1961

This 24-card set features players of the Toronto Maple Leafs, an independent team in the International League which featured future Hall of Fame Manager Sparky Anderson as its second baseman. The black-and-white cards are printed on thin, blank-backed stock and measure approximately 2-1/2" x 3-1/4". As the cards are not numbered, the checklist below is presented alphabetically.

		NM	EX	VG
Complete Set (24):		2,400	1,200	725.00
Common Player:		90.00	45.00	25.00
(1)	George Anderson	450.00	225.00	135.00
(2)	Fritzie Brickell	90.00	45.00	25.00
(3)	Ellis Burton	90.00	45.00	25.00
(4)	Bob Chakales	90.00	45.00	25.00
(5)	Rip Coleman	90.00	45.00	25.00
(6)	Steve Demeter	90.00	45.00	25.00
(7)	Joe Hannah	90.00	45.00	25.00
(8)	Earl Hersh	90.00	45.00	25.00
(9)	Lou Jackson	90.00	45.00	25.00
(10)	Ken Johnson	90.00	45.00	25.00
(11)	Lou Johnson	90.00	45.00	25.00
(12)	John Lipon	90.00	45.00	25.00
(13)	Carl Mathias	90.00	45.00	25.00
(14)	Bill Moran	90.00	45.00	25.00
(15)	Ron Negray	90.00	45.00	25.00
(16)	Herb Plews	90.00	45.00	25.00
(17)	Dave Pope	90.00	45.00	25.00
(18)	Steve Ridzik	90.00	45.00	25.00
(19)	Raul Sanchez	90.00	45.00	25.00
(20)	Pat Scantlebury	90.00	45.00	25.00
(21)	Bill Smith	90.00	45.00	25.00
(22)	Bob Smith	90.00	45.00	25.00
(23)	Chuck Tanner	125.00	65.00	35.00
(24)	Tim Thompson	90.00	45.00	25.00

1911 Big Eater Sacramento Solons

BYRAM SAC'TO HE EATS "BIG EATER"

This very rare set was issued circa 1911 and includes only members of the Pacific Coast League Sacramento Solons. The black-and-white cards measure 2-1/8" x 4" and feature action photos. The lower part of the card contains a three-line caption that includes the player's last name, team designation (abbreviated to "Sac'to"), and the promotional line: "He Eats 'Big Eater.'" Although the exact origin is undetermined, it is believed that "Big Eaters" were a candy novelty.

		NM	EX	VG
Complete Set (20):		150,000	75,000	45,000
Common Player:		7,750	3,875	2,325
(1)	Frank Arellanes	7,750	3,875	2,325
(2)	Spider Baum	7,750	3,875	2,325
(3)	Herb Byram	7,750	3,875	2,325
(4)	Babe Danzig	7,750	3,875	2,325
(5)	Jack Fitzgerald	7,750	3,875	2,325
(6)	George Gaddy	7,750	3,875	2,325
(7)	Al Heister	7,750	3,875	2,325
(8)	Ben Hunt	7,750	3,875	2,325
(9)	Butch Kerns	7,750	3,875	2,325
(10)	Mickey LaLonge	7,750	3,875	2,325
(11)	Dutch Lerchen	7,750	3,875	2,325
(12)	Jimmy Lewis	7,750	3,875	2,325
(13)	Chris Mahoney	7,750	3,875	2,325
(14)	Dick Nebinger	7,750	3,875	2,325
(15)	Patsy O'Rourke	7,750	3,875	2,325
(16)	Jimmy Shinn	7,750	3,875	2,325
(17)	Chester Thomas	7,750	3,875	2,325
(18)	Fuller Thompson	7,750	3,875	2,325
(19)	Frank Thornton	7,750	3,875	2,325
(20)	Deacon Van Buren	7,750	3,875	2,325

1950 Big League Stars (V362)

Chuck Connors
MONTREAL ROYALS
Infielder
Born at Brooklyn, N.Y., on April 10, 1921. Bats left. Throws left. 6'5". 210 lbs. Hit .319, 20 homers and batted in 108 runs with Royals in 1949.

Champ intérieur
Né à Brooklyn, N.Y., le 10 avril 1921. Frappe de la gauche, lance de la gauche. 6'5". 210 livres. Frappa .319, 20 coups de circuit et participa à 108 buts avec les Royaux en 1949.

BIG LEAGUE STARS — No. 2

International League players are featured in this 48-card set. Measuring 3-1/4" x 2-5/8", the blank-backed cards are printed in blue-on-white with English and French stats and biographical data.

		NM	EX	VG
Complete Set (48):		4,500	2,750	1,200
Common Player:		90.00	40.00	25.00
1	Rocky Bridges	100.00	50.00	30.00
2	Chuck Connors	750.00	370.00	220.00
3	Jake Wade	90.00	40.00	25.00
4	Al Cihocki	90.00	40.00	25.00
5	John Simmons	90.00	40.00	25.00
6	Frank Trechock	90.00	40.00	25.00
7	Steve Lembo	90.00	40.00	25.00
8	Johnny Welaj	90.00	40.00	25.00
9	Seymour Block	90.00	40.00	25.00
10	Pat McGlothlin	90.00	40.00	25.00
11	Bryan Stephens	90.00	40.00	25.00
12	Clarence Podbielan	90.00	40.00	25.00
13	Clem Hausmann	90.00	40.00	25.00
14	Turk Lown	90.00	40.00	25.00
15	Joe Payne	90.00	40.00	25.00
16	Coacker Triplett (Coaker)	90.00	40.00	25.00
17	Nick Strincevich	90.00	40.00	25.00
18	Charlie Thompson	90.00	40.00	25.00
19	Erick Silverman	90.00	40.00	25.00
20	George Schmees	90.00	40.00	25.00
21	George Binks	90.00	40.00	25.00
22	Gino Cimoli	100.00	50.00	30.00
23	Marty Tabacheck	90.00	40.00	25.00
24	Al Gionfriddo	100.00	50.00	30.00
25	Ronnie Lee	90.00	40.00	25.00
26	Clyde King	90.00	40.00	25.00
27	Harry Heslet	90.00	40.00	25.00
28	Jerry Scala	90.00	40.00	25.00
29	Boris Woyt	90.00	40.00	25.00
30	Jack Collum	90.00	40.00	25.00
31	Chet Laabs	90.00	40.00	25.00
32	Carden Gillwater	90.00	40.00	25.00
33	Irving Medlinger	90.00	40.00	25.00
34	Toby Atwell	90.00	40.00	25.00
35	Charlie Marshall	90.00	40.00	25.00
36	Johnny Mayo	90.00	40.00	25.00
37	Gene Markland	90.00	40.00	25.00
38	Russ Kerns	90.00	40.00	25.00
39	Jim Prendergast	90.00	40.00	25.00
40	Lou Welaj	90.00	40.00	25.00
41	Clyde Kluttz	90.00	40.00	25.00
42	Bill Glynn	90.00	40.00	25.00
43	Don Richmond	90.00	40.00	25.00
44	Hank Biasatti	90.00	40.00	25.00
45	Tom Lasorda	600.00	300.00	180.00
46	Al Roberge	90.00	40.00	25.00
47	George Byam	90.00	40.00	25.00
48	Dutch Mele	90.00	40.00	25.00

1910 Bishop & Co. P.C.L. Teams (E221)

A very rare issue, this series of team pictures of clubs in the Pacific Coast League was distributed by Bishop & Co. of Los Angeles in 1910. The team photos were printed on a thin, newsprint-type paper that measures an elongated 10" x 2-3/4". Although there were six teams in the PCL at the time, only five clubs have been found - the sixth team, Sacramento, was apparently never issued. The cards indicate that they were issued with five-cent packages of Bishop's Milk Chocolate and that the photos were taken by the Los Angeles Examiner. The black-and-white team photos are found with red, blue, yellow, purple, or green background.

	NM	EX	VG
Complete Set (5):	50,000	25,000	15,000
Common Team:	11,000	5,500	3,250
(1) Los Angeles	11,000	5,500	3,250
(2) Oakland	11,000	5,500	3,250
(3) Portland	11,000	5,500	3,250
(4) San Francisco	12,500	6,250	3,750
(5) Vernon	11,000	5,500	3,250

1910 Bishop & Co. P.C.L. (E99)

 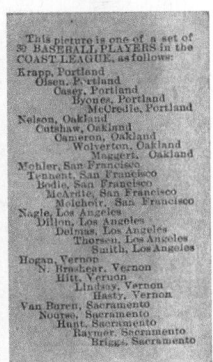

Hap. Hogan, c. Vernon

The first of two obscure sets produced by the Los Angeles candy maker Bishop & Co., this 30-card set was issued in 1910 and depicts players from the Pacific Coast League, showing five players from each of the six teams. The cards measure approximately 1-1/2" x 2-3/4" and feature black-and-white player photos with colored backgrounds (green, blue, purple, yellow, or rarely, black). The player's last name, position and team appear along the bottom. The backs of the cards contain the complete checklist in groups of five, according to team, with each name indented slightly more than the name above. Cards in the 1910 set do not contain the name "Bishop & Company, California" along the bottom on the back.

	NM	EX	VG
Complete Set (30):	60,000	30,000	18,000
Common Player:	2,000	1,000	600.00
(1) Bodie	2,000	1,000	600.00
(2) N. Brashear	2,000	1,000	600.00
(3) Briggs	2,000	1,000	600.00
(4) Byones (Byrnes)	2,000	1,000	600.00
(5) Cameron	2,000	1,000	600.00
(6) Casey	2,000	1,000	600.00
(7) Cutshaw	2,000	1,000	600.00
(8) Delmas	2,000	1,000	600.00
(9) Dillon	2,000	1,000	600.00
(10) Hasty	2,000	1,000	600.00
(11) Hitt	2,000	1,000	600.00
(12) Hap. Hogan	2,000	1,000	600.00
(13) Hunt	2,000	1,000	600.00
(14) Krapp	2,000	1,000	600.00
(15) John Lindsay	2,000	1,000	600.00
(16) Maggert	2,000	1,000	600.00
(17) McArdle	2,000	1,000	600.00
(18) McCredie (McCreedie)	2,000	1,000	600.00
(19) Melchior	2,000	1,000	600.00
(20) Mohler	2,000	1,000	600.00
(21) Nagle	2,000	1,000	600.00
(22) Nelson	2,000	1,000	600.00
(23) Nourse	2,000	1,000	600.00
(24) Olsen	2,000	1,000	600.00
(25) Raymer	2,000	1,000	600.00
(26) Smith	2,000	1,000	600.00
(27) Tennent (Tennant)	2,000	1,000	600.00
(28) Thorsen	2,000	1,000	600.00
(29) Van Buren	2,000	1,000	600.00
(30) Wolverton	2,000	1,000	600.00

1911 Bishop & Co. P.C.L. Type I (E100)

This set was issued by the confectioner Bishop & Co. of Los Angeles, which had produced a similar set a year earlier. Both sets showcased star players from the Pacific Coast League. The cards measure approximately 1-1/2" x 2-3/4" and feature black-and-white photos with a background of green, blue, yellow, purple or red. The backs contain the complete checklist of the set, listing the players in groups of five by team, with one line indented slightly more than the previous

one. In addition to the checklist, the 1911 set can be differentiated from the previous year because the line "Bishop & Company, California" appears along the bottom.

 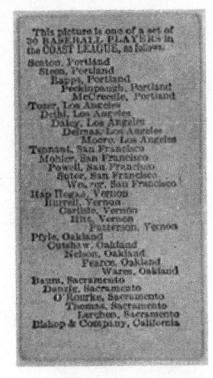

P. O'Rourke, 2b Sacramento

	NM	EX	VG
Complete Set (30):	75,000	37,000	22,000
Common Player:	2,200	1,100	650.00
(1) Spider Baum	2,200	1,100	650.00
(2) Burrell	2,200	1,100	650.00
(3) Carlisle	2,200	1,100	650.00
(4) Cutshaw	2,200	1,100	650.00
(5) Pete Daley	2,200	1,100	650.00
(6) Danzig	2,200	1,100	650.00
(7) Delhi	2,200	1,100	650.00
(8) Delmas	2,200	1,100	650.00
(9) Hitt	2,200	1,100	650.00
(10) Hap Hogan	2,200	1,100	650.00
(Actually Walter Bray.)			
(11) Lerchen	2,200	1,100	650.00
(12) McCreddie (McCreedie)	2,200	1,100	650.00
(13) Mohler	2,200	1,100	650.00
(14) Moore	2,200	1,100	650.00
(15) Slim Nelson	2,200	1,100	650.00
(16) P. O'Rourke	2,200	1,100	650.00
(17) Patterson	2,200	1,100	650.00
(18) Bunny Pearce	2,200	1,100	650.00
(19) Peckinpaugh	2,200	1,100	650.00
(20) Monte Pfyle (Pfyl)	2,200	1,100	650.00
(21) Powell	2,200	1,100	650.00
(22) Rapps	2,200	1,100	650.00
(23) Seaton	2,200	1,100	650.00
(24) Steen	2,200	1,100	650.00
(25) Sutor (Suter)	2,200	1,100	650.00
(26) Tennant	2,200	1,100	650.00
(27) Thomas	2,200	1,100	650.00
(28) Tozer	2,200	1,100	650.00
(29) Clyde Wares	2,200	1,100	650.00
(30) Weaver	15,000	7,500	4,500

1911 Bishop & Co. P.C.L. Type II (E100)

Sutor, p., Frisco.

Currently little over half of the checklist of Bishop & Co. (E100) has been found in a second version. These cards have thus far been seen only with green and orange backgrounds, are blank-backed, have larger, reversed negatives, cropping of the photos and have caption differences.

	NM	EX	VG
Common Player:	2,750	1,350	825.00
(1) Burrell	2,750	1,350	825.00
(2) Danzig	2,750	1,350	825.00
(3) Delhi	2,750	1,350	825.00
(4) Hitt	2,750	1,350	825.00
(5) Lerchen	2,750	1,350	825.00
(6) McCreddie (McCreedie)	2,750	1,350	825.00
(7) Slim Nelson	2,750	1,350	825.00
(8) P. O'Rourke	2,750	1,350	825.00
(9) Patterson	2,750	1,350	825.00
(10) Bunny Pearce	2,750	1,350	825.00
(11) Monte Pfyle	2,750	1,350	825.00
(12) Rapps	2,750	1,350	825.00
(13) Seaton	2,750	1,350	825.00
(14) Steen	2,750	1,350	825.00
(15) Sutot (Suter)	2,750	1,350	825.00
(16) Tennant	2,750	1,350	825.00
(17) Weaver	17,500	8,750	5,250

1954 Blossom Dairy Charleston Senators

The Class AAA farm team of the Chicago White Sox is featured in this team set sponsored by a Charleston, W. Va., dairy. The 2-1/4" x 3-3/16" black-and-white cards are either a late issue by Globe Printing (which issued many minor league sets from 1951-52) or were patterned after the Globe issues, right down to the issue of an album to house the cards. A white box is superimposed over the posed action photos and contains the player and sponsor identification. Cards are blank-backed.

	NM	EX	VG
Complete Set (22):	2,200	1,100	650.00
Common Player:	100.00	50.00	30.00
Album:	150.00	75.00	45.00
(1) Al Baro	100.00	50.00	30.00
(2) Joe Becker	100.00	50.00	30.00
(3) Joe Carroll	100.00	50.00	30.00
(4) Gerald "Red" Fahr	100.00	50.00	30.00
(5) Dick Fowler	100.00	50.00	30.00
(6) Alex Garbowski	100.00	50.00	30.00
(7) Gordon Goldsberry	100.00	50.00	30.00
(8) Ross Grimsley	100.00	50.00	30.00
(9) Sam Hairston	125.00	65.00	35.00
(10) Phil Haugstad	100.00	50.00	30.00
(11) Tom Hurd	100.00	50.00	30.00
(12) Bill Killinger	100.00	50.00	30.00
(13) John Kropf	100.00	50.00	30.00
(14) Bob Masser	100.00	50.00	30.00
(15) Danny Menendez	100.00	50.00	30.00
(16) Bill Paolisso	100.00	50.00	30.00
(17) Bill Pope	100.00	50.00	30.00
(18) Lou Sleater	100.00	50.00	30.00
(19) Dick Strahs	100.00	50.00	30.00
(20) Joe Torpey	100.00	50.00	30.00
(21) Bill Voiselle	100.00	50.00	30.00
(22) Al Ware	100.00	50.00	30.00

1958 Bond Bread Buffalo Bisons

 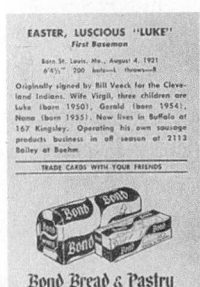

Nine members of the International League affiliate of the Kansas City Athletics are featured in this set. The 2-1/2" x 3-1/2" cards are printed on very thin cardboard. Fronts have a black-and-white player photo, the player's name and position, and an ad for a TV Western. Card backs are printed in red and blue and include a few biographical details and a career summary, along with an illustrated ad.

	NM	EX	VG
Complete Set (9):	350.00	175.00	100.00
Common Player:	40.00	20.00	12.00
(1) Al Aber	40.00	20.00	12.00
(2) Joe Caffie	40.00	20.00	12.00
(3) Phil Cavaretta	40.00	20.00	12.00
(4) Rip Coleman	40.00	20.00	12.00
(5) Luke Easter	60.00	30.00	18.00
(6) Ken Johnson	40.00	20.00	12.00
(7) Lou Ortiz	40.00	20.00	12.00
(8) Jack Phillips	40.00	20.00	12.00
(9) Jim Small	40.00	20.00	12.00

1949 Bowman Pacific Coast League

 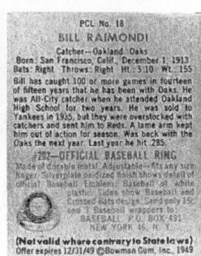

One of the scarcest issues of the postwar period, the 1949 Bowman PCL set was issued only on the West Coast. Like the 1949 Bowman regular issue, the cards contain black-and-white photos overprinted with various pastel colors. Thirty-six cards, which measure 2-1/16" x 2-1/2", make up the set. It is believed that the cards may have been issued only in sheets and not sold in gum packs. Consequently, many cards are found which display evidence of having been cut with a scissors.

		NM	EX	VG
Complete Set (36):		15,000	7,500	4,500
Common Player:		500.00	240.00	145.00
1	Lee Anthony	500.00	240.00	145.00
2	George Metkovich	500.00	240.00	145.00
3	Ralph Hodgin	500.00	240.00	145.00
4	George Woods	500.00	240.00	145.00
5	Xavier Rescigno	500.00	240.00	145.00
6	Mickey Grasso	500.00	240.00	145.00
7	Johnny Rucker	500.00	240.00	145.00
8	Jack Brewer	500.00	240.00	145.00
9	Dom D'Allessandro	500.00	240.00	145.00
10	Charlie Gassaway	500.00	240.00	145.00
11	Tony Freitas	500.00	240.00	145.00
12	Gordon Maltzberger	500.00	240.00	145.00
13	John Jensen	500.00	240.00	145.00
14	Joyner White	500.00	240.00	145.00
15	Harvey Storey	500.00	240.00	145.00
16	Dick Lajeski	500.00	240.00	145.00
17	Albie Glossop	500.00	240.00	145.00
18	Bill Raimondi	500.00	240.00	145.00
19	Ken Holcombe	500.00	240.00	145.00
20	Don Ross	500.00	240.00	145.00
21	Pete Coscarart	500.00	240.00	145.00
22	Tony York	500.00	240.00	145.00
23	Jake Mooty	500.00	240.00	145.00
24	Charles Adams	500.00	240.00	145.00
25	Les Scarsella	500.00	240.00	145.00
26	Joe Marty	500.00	240.00	145.00
27	Frank Kelleher	500.00	240.00	145.00
28	Lee Handley	500.00	240.00	145.00
29	Herman Besse	500.00	240.00	145.00
30	John Lazor	500.00	240.00	145.00
31	Eddie Malone	500.00	240.00	145.00
32	Maurice Van Robays	500.00	240.00	145.00
33	Jim Tabor	500.00	240.00	145.00
34	Gene Handley	500.00	240.00	145.00
35	Tom Seats	500.00	240.00	145.00
36	Ora Burnett	500.00	240.00	145.00

1933 Buffalo Bisons Jigsaw Puzzles

Produced as a stadium promotional giveaway, this set consists of 19 player puzzles and one for Hall of Fame Manager Ray Schalk. Each of the 11" x 14", 200-piece, black-and-white puzzles was produced in an edition of 10,000. Puzzles carried a red serial number, and certain numbers could be redeemed for tickets and other prizes. The known puzzles are checklisted below in alphabetical order.

		NM	EX	VG
Complete Set (15):		5,000	2,500	1,500
Common Player:		335.00	165.00	100.00
(1)	Joe Bartulis	335.00	165.00	100.00
(2)	Joe Bloomer	335.00	165.00	100.00
(3)	Ollie Carnegie	335.00	165.00	100.00
(4)	Clyde "Buck" Crouse	335.00	165.00	100.00
(5)	Harry Danning	335.00	165.00	100.00
(6)	Gilbert English	335.00	165.00	100.00
(7)	Fred Fussell	335.00	165.00	100.00
(8)	Bob Gould	335.00	165.00	100.00
(9)	Len Koenecke	335.00	165.00	100.00
(10)	Ray Lucas	335.00	165.00	100.00
(11)	Clarence Mueller	335.00	165.00	100.00

(12)	Ray Schalk	500.00	250.00	150.00
(13)	Jack Smith	335.00	165.00	100.00
(14)	Roy Tarr	335.00	165.00	100.00
(15)	Johnny Wilson	335.00	165.00	100.00

1934 Buffalo Bisons Team Issue

Apparently a team issue, these 4" x 7-1/16" black-and-white blank-backed cards feature posed action photos with white borders and a facsimile autograph. The player's full name and position are printed in the bottom border, along with a career summary. This checklist is probably incomplete though the exact scope of the issue is unknown.

		NM	EX	VG
Common Player:		400.00	200.00	120.00
(1)	Kenneth L. Ash	400.00	200.00	120.00
(2)	Harold "Ace" Elliott	400.00	200.00	120.00
(3)	Gregory T. Mulleavy	400.00	200.00	120.00
(4)	Irving M. Plummer	400.00	200.00	120.00

1940 Buffalo Bisons Team Issue

FRED HUTCHINSON, Pitcher

Many former and future big leaguers are included in this set of black-and-white, 2" x 3", cards. Fronts picture the players in poses at old Offerman Stadium. The player's name and position are printed in the white border at bottom. Backs have a career summary and highlights. The unnumbered cards are checklisted here alphabetically.

		NM	EX	VG
Complete Set (24):		9,000	4,500	2,700
Common Player:		400.00	200.00	120.00
(1)	Ollie Carnegie	400.00	200.00	120.00
(2)	Dan Carnevale	400.00	200.00	120.00
(3)	Earl Cook	400.00	200.00	120.00
(4)	Les Fleming	400.00	200.00	120.00
(5)	Floyd Giebel	400.00	200.00	120.00
(6)	Jimmy Hutch	400.00	200.00	120.00
(7)	Fred Hutchinson	400.00	200.00	120.00
(8)	Art Jacobs	400.00	200.00	120.00
(9)	John Kroner	400.00	200.00	120.00
(10)	Sal Maglie	600.00	300.00	180.00
(11)	Joe Martin	400.00	200.00	120.00
(12)	Clyde McCullough	400.00	200.00	120.00
(13)	Greg Mulleavy	400.00	200.00	120.00
(14)	Pat Mullin	400.00	200.00	120.00
(15)	Hank Nowak	400.00	200.00	120.00
(16)	Steve O'Neil	400.00	200.00	120.00
(17)	Jimmy Outlaw	400.00	200.00	120.00
(18)	Joe Rogalski	400.00	200.00	120.00
(19)	Les Scarsella	400.00	200.00	120.00
(20)	Mayo Smith	400.00	200.00	120.00
(21)	Floyd Stromme	400.00	200.00	120.00
(22)	Jim Trexler	400.00	200.00	120.00
(23)	Hal White	400.00	200.00	120.00
(24)	Frank Zubik	400.00	200.00	120.00

1947 Buffalo Bisons Team Issue

Despite some anomalies among the players checklisted thus far, this appears to have been a 1947 team-issued set of 8" a 10" black-and-white player photographs. Fronts include player identification in the form of a facsimile autograph. Backs are blank.

		NM	EX	VG
Common Player:		30.00	15.00	9.00
(1)	Johnny Bero	30.00	15.00	9.00
(2)	Hank Biasatti	30.00	15.00	9.00
(3)	Eddie Boland	30.00	15.00	9.00
(4)	Ray Coleman	30.00	15.00	9.00
(5)	Zeb "Red" Eaton	30.00	15.00	9.00

(6)	Lonny Frey	30.00	15.00	9.00
(8)	Freddie Hancock	30.00	15.00	9.00
(9)	Gabby Hartnett	65.00	32.00	19.50
(10)	Clem Hausman	30.00	15.00	9.00
(11)	Manuel Hidalgo	30.00	15.00	9.00
(12)	Chet Laabs	30.00	15.00	9.00
(14)	Johnny McHale	30.00	15.00	9.00
(15)	Edward Mierkowicz	30.00	15.00	9.00
(16)	Eddie Mordarski	30.00	15.00	9.00
(17)	Hank Perry	30.00	15.00	9.00
(18)	Billy Pierce, Ted Gray	45.00	22.00	13.50
(19)	Bill Radulovich	30.00	15.00	9.00
(21)	Earl Rapp, Clint Conatser, Anse Moore, Coaker Triplett	30.00	15.00	9.00
(22)	Vic Wertz	40.00	20.00	12.00

1950 Bush & Hancock/Oak Hall Roanoke Red Sox

These blank-back, black-and-white cards have a portrait photo on front surrounded by a white border. Beneath the photo is a credit line and space for an autograph. Cards exist in 3-1/2" x 5" size with sponsor's credit reading "Compliments of Bush & Hancock," and in 4" x 6" format with sponsor's credit reading, "Compliments of Oak Hall." It is not known whether the checklist presented here is complete. Roanoke was a Class B Piedmont League farm club.

		NM	EX	VG
Common Player:		50.00	25.00	15.00
(1)	Tom Casey	50.00	25.00	15.00
(2)	George Contratto	50.00	25.00	15.00
(3)	Ike Delock	65.00	32.50	20.00
(4)	Red Marion	50.00	25.00	15.00
(5)	Rod Morgan	50.00	25.00	15.00
(6)	Julio Ondani	50.00	25.00	15.00
(7)	Joe Reedy	50.00	25.00	15.00
(8)	Johnny Sehrt	50.00	25.00	15.00
(9)	Sammy White	65.00	32.50	20.00
(10)	Bob Wilson	50.00	25.00	15.00

C

1943 Centennial Flour Seattle Rainiers

 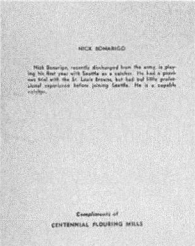

The 25 cards in this 4" x 5" black-and-white set feature players of the Pacific Coast League Seattle Rainiers. Identical in format to the set issued in 1944, the '43s can be identified by the lines of type at the bottom of the card back reading, "Compliments of/CENTENNIAL FLOURING MILLS."

		NM	EX	VG
Complete Set (25):		1,100	550.00	325.00
Common Player:		60.00	30.00	18.00
(1)	John Babich	60.00	30.00	18.00
(2)	Nick Bonarigo (Buonarigo)	60.00	30.00	18.00
(3)	Eddie Carnett	60.00	30.00	18.00
(4)	Lloyd Christopher	60.00	30.00	18.00
(5)	Joe Demoran	60.00	30.00	18.00
(6)	Joe Dobbins	60.00	30.00	18.00
(7)	Glenn Elliott	60.00	30.00	18.00
(8)	Carl Fischer	60.00	30.00	18.00
(9)	Leonard Gabrielson	60.00	30.00	18.00
(10)	Stanley Gray	60.00	30.00	18.00
(11)	Dick Gyselman	60.00	30.00	18.00
(12)	Jim Jewell	60.00	30.00	18.00
(13)	Syl Johnson	60.00	30.00	18.00
(14)	Pete Jonas	60.00	30.00	18.00
(15)	Bill Kats	60.00	30.00	18.00

		NM	EX	VG
(16)	Lynn King	60.00	30.00	18.00
(17)	Bill Lawrence	60.00	30.00	18.00
(18)	Clarence Marshall	60.00	30.00	18.00
(19)	Bill Matheson	60.00	30.00	18.00
(20)	Ford Mullen	60.00	30.00	18.00
(21)	Bill Skiff	60.00	30.00	18.00
(22)	Byron Speece	60.00	30.00	18.00
(23)	Hal Sueme	60.00	30.00	18.00
(24)	Hal Turpin	60.00	30.00	18.00
(25)	John Yelovic	60.00	30.00	18.00

1944 Centennial Flour Seattle Rainiers

Identical in format to the previous year's issue, the 25 black-and-white 4" x 5" cards issued in 1944 can be differentiated from the 1943 set by the two lines of type at the bottom of each card's back. In the 1944 set, it reads, "Compliments of/CENTENNIAL HOTCAKE AND WAFFLE FLOUR."

		NM	EX	VG
Complete Set (25):		1,350	675.00	400.00
Common Player:		60.00	30.00	18.00
(1)	John Babich	60.00	30.00	18.00
(2)	Paul Carpenter	60.00	30.00	18.00
(3)	Lloyd Christopher	60.00	30.00	18.00
(4)	Joe Demoran	60.00	30.00	18.00
(5)	Joe Dobbins	60.00	30.00	18.00
(6)	Glenn Elliott	60.00	30.00	18.00
(7)	Carl Fischer	60.00	30.00	18.00
(8)	Bob Garbould (Gorbould)	60.00	30.00	18.00
(9)	Stanley Gray	60.00	30.00	18.00
(10)	Dick Gyselman	60.00	30.00	18.00
(11)	Gene Holt	60.00	30.00	18.00
(12)	Roy Johnson	60.00	30.00	18.00
(13)	Syl Johnson	60.00	30.00	18.00
(14)	Al Libke	60.00	30.00	18.00
(15)	Bill Lyman	60.00	30.00	18.00
(16)	Bill Matheson	60.00	30.00	18.00
(17)	Jack McClure	60.00	30.00	18.00
(18)	Jimmy Ripple	60.00	30.00	18.00
(19)	Bill Skiff	60.00	30.00	18.00
(20)	Byron Speece	60.00	30.00	18.00
(21)	Hal Sueme	60.00	30.00	18.00
(22)	Frank Tincup	60.00	30.00	18.00
(23)	Jack Treece	60.00	30.00	18.00
(24)	Hal Turpin	60.00	30.00	18.00
(25)	Sicks Stadium	65.00	32.50	20.00

1945 Centennial Flour Seattle Rainiers

 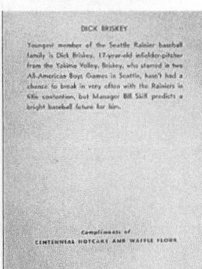

The 27 blue-and-white or black-and-white cards in the third consecutive issue for this Pacific Coast League team are distinguished from the two previous issues by the borderless photo on the front and the fact that the name and team are printed in a black bar at the bottom. The set can be distinguished from the 1947 issue by virtue of the fact that the player biography on back is not surrounded by a frame. The cards measure slightly narrower but longer than the 1943-44 issues, at 3-7/8" x 5-1/8".

		NM	EX	VG
Complete Set (27):		1,500	750.00	450.00
Common Player:		60.00	30.00	18.00
(1)	Charley Aleno	60.00	30.00	18.00
(2)	Dick Briskey	60.00	30.00	18.00
(3)	John Carpenter	60.00	30.00	18.00
(4)	Joe Demoran	60.00	30.00	18.00
(5)	Joe Dobbins	60.00	30.00	18.00
(6)	Glenn Elliott	60.00	30.00	18.00
(7)	Bob Finley	60.00	30.00	18.00
(8)	Carl Fischer	60.00	30.00	18.00
(9)	Keith Frazier	60.00	30.00	18.00
(10)	Johnny Gill	60.00	30.00	18.00
(11)	Bob Gorbould	60.00	30.00	18.00
(12)	Chet Johnson	60.00	30.00	18.00
(13)	Syl Johnson	60.00	30.00	18.00
(14)	Bill Kats	60.00	30.00	18.00
(15)	Billy Lyman	60.00	30.00	18.00
(16)	Bill Matheson	60.00	30.00	18.00
(17)	George McDonald	60.00	30.00	18.00
(18)	Ted Norbert	60.00	30.00	18.00
(19)	Alex Palica	60.00	30.00	18.00
(20)	Joe Passero	60.00	30.00	18.00
(21)	Hal Patchett	60.00	30.00	18.00
(22)	Bill Skiff	60.00	30.00	18.00
(23)	Byron Speece	60.00	30.00	18.00
(24)	Hal Sueme	60.00	30.00	18.00
(25)	Eddie Taylor	60.00	30.00	18.00
(26)	Hal Turpin	60.00	30.00	18.00
(27)	Jack Whipple	60.00	30.00	18.00

1947 Centennial Flour Seattle Rainiers

 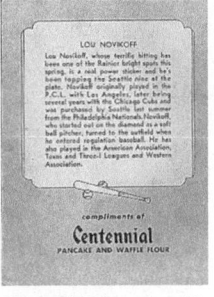

After a lapse of one year, Centennial Flour returned to issue a final black-and-white 32-card set for 1947. Identical in size (3-7/8" x 5-1/8") and front format to the 1945 issue, the '47s can be identified by the white framed box on back containing the player's biography.

		NM	EX	VG
Complete Set (32):		1,100	550.00	325.00
Common Player:		50.00	25.00	15.00
(1)	Dick Barrett	50.00	25.00	15.00
(2)	Joe Buzas	50.00	25.00	15.00
(3)	Paul Carpenter	50.00	25.00	15.00
(4)	Rex Cecil	50.00	25.00	15.00
(5)	Tony Criscola	50.00	25.00	15.00
(6)	Walter Dubiel	50.00	25.00	15.00
(7)	Doug Ford	50.00	25.00	15.00
(8)	Rollie Hemsley	50.00	25.00	15.00
(9)	Jim Hill	50.00	25.00	15.00
(10)	Jim Hopper	50.00	25.00	15.00
(11)	Sigmund Jakucki	50.00	25.00	15.00
(12)	Bob Johnson	60.00	30.00	18.00
(13)	Pete Jonas	50.00	25.00	15.00
(14)	Joe Kaney	50.00	25.00	15.00
(15)	Hillis Layne	50.00	25.00	15.00
(16)	Lou Novikoff	50.00	25.00	15.00
(17)	Johnny O'Neil	50.00	25.00	15.00
(18)	John Orphal	50.00	25.00	15.00
(19)	Ike Pearson	50.00	25.00	15.00
(20)	Bill Posedel	50.00	25.00	15.00
(21)	Don Pulford	50.00	25.00	15.00
(22)	Tom Reis	50.00	25.00	15.00
(23)	Charley Ripple	50.00	25.00	15.00
(24)	Mickey Rocco	50.00	25.00	15.00
(25)	Johnny Rucker	50.00	25.00	15.00
(26)	Earl Sheely	50.00	25.00	15.00
(27)	Bob Stagg	50.00	25.00	15.00
(28)	Hal Sueme	50.00	25.00	15.00
(29)	Eddie Taylor	50.00	25.00	15.00
(30)	Ed Vanni	50.00	25.00	15.00
(31)	JoJo White	50.00	25.00	15.00
(32)	Tony York	50.00	25.00	15.00

1957-58 Chattanooga Lookouts Team Issue

Based on the known and certainly incomplete checklist seen thus far, this issue of 8" x 10" black-and-white, blank-back player photos can only be generally attributed to year of issue. With a credit line to Moss Photo Service of New York City, the pictures feature action poses of the players taken in historic Engel Stadium. Facsimile autographs are pre-printed on the front. During the late 1950s the Lookouts were the top farm club of the Washington Senators.

		NM	EX	VG
Common Player:		30.00	15.00	9.00
(1)	Bobby Brown	30.00	15.00	9.00
(2)	Hal Griggs	30.00	15.00	9.00
(2)	Harmon Killebrew	200.00	100.00	60.00
(3)	Jesse Levan	30.00	15.00	9.00
(3)	Ernie Oravetz	30.00	15.00	9.00
(4)	Stan Roseboro	30.00	15.00	9.00
(5)	Bunky Stewart	30.00	15.00	9.00

1967 Chevron/Uniroyal Vancouver Mounties

These 2" x 3" black-and-white cards were distributed by local gas stations and picture members of the top farm club of the Kansas City A's. Backs are printed in red and black on white.

		NM	EX	VG
Complete Set (27):		4,500	2,250	1,300
Common Player:		200.00	100.00	60.00
(1)	Sal Bando	350.00	175.00	105.00
(2)	Frank Bastrire (Trainer)	200.00	100.00	60.00
(3)	Ossie Chavarria	200.00	100.00	60.00
(4)	Jim Dickson	200.00	100.00	60.00
(5)	John Donaldson	200.00	100.00	60.00
(6)	Jim Driscoll	200.00	100.00	60.00
(7)	Bob Duliba	200.00	100.00	60.00
(8)	Bill Edgerton	200.00	100.00	60.00
(9)	Larry Elliot	200.00	100.00	60.00
(10)	Ernie Foli	200.00	100.00	60.00
(11)	Joe Gaines	200.00	100.00	60.00
(12)	Vern Handrahan	200.00	100.00	60.00
(13)	Jim Hughes	200.00	100.00	60.00
(14)	Woody Huyke	200.00	100.00	60.00
(15)	Rene Lachemann	225.00	110.00	67.00
(16)	Bob Meyer	200.00	100.00	60.00
(17)	Wayne Norton	200.00	100.00	60.00
(18)	Gerry Reimer	200.00	100.00	60.00
(19)	Roberto Rodriguez	200.00	100.00	60.00
(20)	Ken Sanders	200.00	100.00	60.00
(21)	Randy Schwartz	200.00	100.00	60.00
(22)	Diego Segui	275.00	135.00	82.00
(23)	Paul Seitz	200.00	100.00	60.00
(24)	Ron Tompkins	200.00	100.00	60.00
(25)	Mickey Vernon	350.00	175.00	105.00
(26)	Jim Ward	200.00	100.00	60.00
(27)	Don Yingling	200.00	100.00	60.00

1909 Clement Bros. Bread (D380-1)

This set features only players of the Rochester Bronchos team in the Eastern League. According to the bakery ad on back, the cards were distributed one per loaf of bread. The 1-1/2" x 2-3/4" cards feature a player photo on front in an oval frame against a white background. The player's last name, position and "Rochester" are printed beneath.

		NM	EX	VG
Complete Set (8):		25,000	12,500	7,500
Common Player:		5,000	2,500	1,500
(1)	Groat Anderson	5,000	2,500	1,500
(2)	Emil Batch	5,000	2,500	1,500
(3)	John Butler	5,000	2,500	1,500
(4)	Ed Holly	5,000	2,500	1,500
(5)	Jim Holmes	5,000	2,500	1,500
(6)	George McConnell	5,000	2,500	1,500
(7)	Fred Osborn	5,000	2,500	1,500
(8)	Harry Partee	5,000	2,500	1,500

1910 Clement Bros. Bread (D380)

For the second of two annual issues, the bakery added an unknown number of major league players' cards to those of six of the hometeam Rochester club of the Eastern League. While the backs remained identical to the previous issue, featuring advertising for the bakery's bread and pies, the fronts adopted the standard format of the era, black-and-white player photos surrounded by a white border, with the player's last name, position and city printed at bottom. Size remained 1-1/2" x 2-3/4".

		NM	EX	VG
Common Player:		5,750	2,850	1,700
(1)	Whitey Alperman	5,750	2,850	1,700
(2)	Bill Bailey	5,750	2,850	1,700
(3)	Walter Blair	5,750	2,850	1,700
(4)	Hal Chase	6,500	3,200	1,950
(5)	Ty Cobb	40,000	25,000	15,000
(6)	Eddie Collins	15,000	10,000	6,000
(7)	Roy Hartzell	5,750	2,850	1,700
(8)	Harry Howell	5,750	2,850	1,700
(9)	Addie Joss	15,000	10,000	6,000
(10)	Ditus Lagoe	5,750	2,850	1,700
(11)	George McConnell	5,750	2,850	1,700
(12)	George Mullin	5,750	2,850	1,700
(13)	Fred Osborn	5,750	2,850	1,700
(14)	Harry Patee	5,750	2,850	1,700
(15)	Pat Ragan	5,750	2,850	1,700
(16)	Oscar Stanage	5,750	2,850	1,700
(17)	George Stone	5,750	2,850	1,700
(18)	Ed Summers	5,750	2,850	1,700
(19)	Joe Tinker	15,000	10,000	6,000
(20)	Bert Tooley	5,750	2,850	1,700
(21)	Heinie Zimmerman	5,750	2,850	1,700

1953 Coca-Cola Galveston White Caps

This set appears to have been an issue of the Globe Printing Co., which produced many lower-minors team sets in the years preceding, or it may just share the format. The 2-1/4" x 3-3/8" cards have borderless black-and-white photos on front and blank backs. In a white box near the bottom of the picture is the player name and "Compliments of / Coca-Cola Bottling Co." Galveston was champion of the 1953 Class B Gulf Coast League and not affiliated with any major league team.

		NM	EX	VG
Complete Set (16):		1,000	500.00	300.00
Common Player:		75.00	37.50	22.00
(1)	Ed Bohnslav	75.00	37.50	22.00
(2)	Mike Conovan	75.00	37.50	22.00
(3)	Pop Faucett	75.00	37.50	22.00
(4)	Bobby Flis	75.00	37.50	22.00
(5)	Stan Goletz	75.00	37.50	22.00
(6)	Jerry Kleinsmith	75.00	37.50	22.00
(7)	Charlie Lehrmann	75.00	37.50	22.00
(8)	Jim Logan	75.00	37.50	22.00
(9)	Bob Miller	75.00	37.50	22.00
(10)	Tom Moore	75.00	37.50	22.00
(11)	Bob Pugatch	75.00	37.50	22.00
(12)	Bob Ramsey	75.00	37.50	22.00
(13)	Hank Robinson	75.00	37.50	22.00
(14)	Charlie Schmidt	75.00	37.50	22.00
(15)	Barnie White	75.00	37.50	22.00
(16)	Hank Yzquierdo (Izquierdo)	75.00	37.50	22.00

1952 Colorado Springs Sky Sox Team Issue

From the Class A Western League runners-up, this is one of many minor league sets issued in the early 1950s by the Globe Printing Co., of San Jose, Calif. The '52 Sky Sox were a farm team of the Chicago White Sox. Players included former Negro Leaguers and future major leaguers Connie Johnson and Sam Hairston, plus bonus-baby bust Gus Keriazakos. Cards are about 2-1/4" x 3-1/4", printed in black-and-white with blank backs. An album with die-cut pages to allow the corners of the cards to be slipped in was also available. Cards were likely given away one or two at a time at home games.

		NM	EX	VG
Complete Set (19):		1,200	600.00	360.00
Common Player:		60.00	30.00	18.00
Album:		100.00	50.00	30.00
(1)	Jerry Crosby	60.00	30.00	18.00
(2)	Vic Fucci	60.00	30.00	18.00
(3)	Don Gutteridge	60.00	30.00	18.00
(4)	Sam Hairston	90.00	45.00	27.00
(5)	Al Jacinto	60.00	30.00	18.00
(6)	Connie Johnson	75.00	37.50	22.00
(7)	Bob Kellogg	60.00	30.00	18.00
(8)	Gus Keriazakos	60.00	30.00	18.00
(9)	Ken Landenberger	60.00	30.00	18.00
(10)	George Noga	60.00	30.00	18.00
(11)	Floyd Penfold	60.00	30.00	18.00
(12)	Bill Pope	60.00	30.00	18.00
(13)	J.W. Porter	60.00	30.00	18.00
(14)	Bill (Red) Rose	60.00	30.00	18.00
(15)	Don Rudolph	60.00	30.00	18.00
(16)	Andy Skurski	60.00	30.00	18.00
(17)	Dick Strahs	60.00	30.00	18.00
(18)	Bill Wells	60.00	30.00	18.00
(19)	Dick Welteroth	60.00	30.00	18.00

1952 Columbus Cardinals Team Issue

This set of cards was a product of the Globe Printing Co. of San Jose, Calif. The cards were given away at Golden Park during the 1952 season. The cards measure 2-1/8" x 3-3/8" and have black-and-white photos of players with the player's name in a white box in the bottom-left corner of the photograph. The backs are blank. The cards are unnumbered and listed in alphabetical order, although this checklist may not be complete. The team was a Class A South Atlantic League affiliate of the St. Louis Cardinals.

		NM	EX	VG
Complete Set (17):		1,000	500.00	300.00
Common Player:		60.00	30.00	18.00
(1)	Chief Bender	60.00	30.00	18.00
(2)	Bob Betancourt	60.00	30.00	18.00
(3)	Tom Burgess	60.00	30.00	18.00
(4)	Jack Byers	60.00	30.00	18.00
(5)	Mike Curnan	60.00	30.00	18.00
(6)	Gil Daley	60.00	30.00	18.00
(7)	Bill Harris	60.00	30.00	18.00
(8)	Ev Joyner	60.00	30.00	18.00
(9)	Bob Kerce	60.00	30.00	18.00
(10)	Ted Lewandowski	60.00	30.00	18.00
(11)	John Mackey	60.00	30.00	18.00
(12)	Bill Paolisso	60.00	30.00	18.00
(13)	Dennis Reeder	60.00	30.00	18.00
(14)	Whit Ulrich	60.00	30.00	18.00
(15)	Norman Shope	60.00	30.00	18.00
(16)	Don Swartz	60.00	30.00	18.00
(17)	Len Wile	60.00	30.00	18.00

1955 Columbus Jets Photos

A top farm club of the Kansas City A's in 1955 the Columbus (Ohio) Jets issued these black-and-white glossy photocards. In 3-5/8" x 5-5/8" format, the cards have a facsimile autograph on front. It is possible that the checklist presented here in alphabetical order of the unnumbered cards may be incomplete.

		NM	EX	VG
Complete Set (21):		900.00	450.00	275.00
Common Player:		45.00	22.50	13.50
(1)	Hal Bevan	45.00	22.50	13.50
(2)	Paul Burris	45.00	22.50	13.50
(3)	Ted Del Guercio	45.00	22.50	13.50
(4)	Carl Duser	45.00	22.50	13.50
(5)	Charlie Haag	45.00	22.50	13.50
(6)	Forrest "Spook" Jacobs	60.00	30.00	18.00
(7)	Dick Kryhoski	45.00	22.50	13.50
(8)	Mike Kume	45.00	22.50	13.50
(9)	Al Lakeman	45.00	22.50	13.50
(10)	Jackie Mayo	45.00	22.50	13.50
(11)	Jim Miller	45.00	22.50	13.50
(12)	Al Pinkston	50.00	25.00	15.00
(13)	Al Romberger	45.00	22.50	13.50
(14)	Bill Stewart	45.00	22.50	13.50
(15)	Russ Sullivan	45.00	22.50	13.50
(16)	"Jake" Thies	45.00	22.50	13.50
(17)	Bob Trice	45.00	22.50	13.50
(18)	Ozzie VanBrabant	45.00	22.50	13.50
(19)	Frank Verdi	45.00	22.50	13.50
(20)	Leroy Wheat	45.00	22.50	13.50
(21)	Spider Wilhelm	45.00	22.50	13.50

1957 Columbus Jets Postcards

In 1957, the Columbus (Ohio) Jets began a long association as a top farm team of the Pittsburgh Pirates. That year, the team issued this set of postcards. The black-and-white glossy cards measure 3-9/16" x 5-1/2" and have the player name and position overprinted in black block letters near the bottom of the photo. Backs have postcard indicia and a notice of printing by the Howard Photo Service of New York City. The unnumbered cards are presented here alphabetically but it is unknown whether this checklist is complete at 20.

		NM	EX	VG
Complete Set (20):		900.00	450.00	275.00
Common Player:		45.00	22.50	13.50
(1)	Dick Barone	45.00	22.50	13.50
(2)	Ron Blackburn	45.00	22.50	13.50
(3)	Jackie Brown	45.00	22.50	13.50
(4)	Ed Burtschy	45.00	22.50	13.50
(5)	Whammy Douglas	50.00	25.00	15.00
(6)	Howie Goss	45.00	22.50	13.50
(7)	Al Grunwald	45.00	22.50	13.50
(8)	Gail Henley	45.00	22.50	13.50
(9)	Don Kildoo	45.00	22.50	13.50
(10)	Danny Kravitz	45.00	22.50	13.50
(11)	Bob Kuzava	45.00	22.50	13.50
(12)	Johnny Lipon	45.00	22.50	13.50
(13)	Cholly Naranjo	45.00	22.50	13.50
(14)	Eddie O'Brien	60.00	30.00	18.00
(15)	Frank Oceak	45.00	22.50	13.50
(16)	Harding Peterson	60.00	30.00	18.00
(17)	John Powers	45.00	22.50	13.50
(18)	James Rice	45.00	22.50	13.50
(19)	Russ Sullivan	45.00	22.50	13.50
(20)	Ken Toothman	45.00	22.50	13.50

1958 Columbus Jets Photos

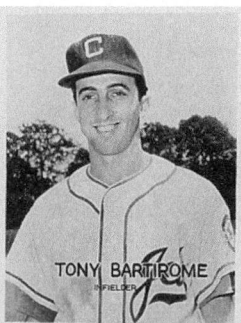

In format similar to the postcard issue of the previous year, and sharing some of the same pictures, this set of photocards is smaller, at 4" x 5", and is blank-backed. It is unknown whether the alphabetical checklist of the unnumbered cards presented here is complete.

		NM	EX	VG
Complete Set (17):		650.00	325.00	200.00
Common Player:		40.00	20.00	12.00
(1)	Gair Allie	40.00	20.00	12.00
(2)	Luis Arroyo	40.00	20.00	12.00
(3)	Tony Bartirome	45.00	22.50	13.50
(4)	Jim Baumer	40.00	20.00	12.00
(5)	Bill Causion	40.00	20.00	12.00
(6)	Whammy Douglas	40.00	20.00	12.00
(7)	Joe Gibbon	40.00	20.00	12.00
(8)	Howie Goss	40.00	20.00	12.00
(9)	Spook Jacobs	50.00	25.00	15.00
(10)	Clyde King	40.00	20.00	12.00
(11)	Cholly Naranjo	40.00	20.00	12.00
(12)	George O'Donnell	40.00	20.00	12.00
(13)	Laurin Pepper	40.00	20.00	12.00
(14)	Dick Rand	40.00	20.00	12.00
(15)	Leo Rodriguez	40.00	20.00	12.00
(16)	Don Rowe	40.00	20.00	12.00
(17)	Art Swanson	40.00	20.00	12.00

1910 Contentnea First Series (T209)

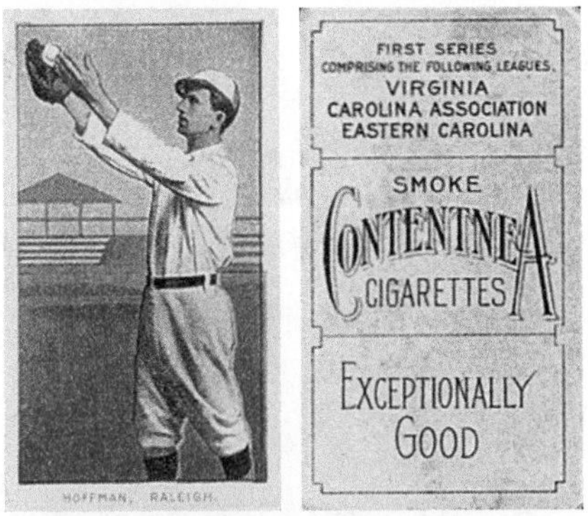
HOFFMAN, RALEIGH
FIRST SERIES
COMPRISING THE FOLLOWING LEAGUES.
VIRGINIA
CAROLINA ASSOCIATION
EASTERN CAROLINA
SMOKE
CONTENTNEA
CIGARETTES
EXCEPTIONALLY
GOOD

The 1910 Contentnea minor league set actually consists of two distinctively different series, both featuring players from the Virginia League, Carolina Association and Eastern Carolina League. The cards were distributed in packages of Contentnea cigarettes. The first series, featuring color photographs, consists of just 16 cards, each measuring 1-9/16" x 2-11/16". The front of the card has the player's last name and team printed at the bottom, while the back identifies the card as "First Series" and carries an advertisement for Contentnea cigarettes. Many first series cards are also found with rubber-stamped "Factory No. 12, 4th Dist. N.C." on back. The second series, belived to have been issued later in 1910, is a massive 221-card set consisting of black-and- white player photos. The cards in this series are slightly larger, measuring 1-5/8" x 2-3/4". They carry the words "Photo Series" on the back, along with the cigarette advertisement. Only a handful of the players in the Contentnea set ever advanced to the major leagues and the set contains no major stars. Subsequently, it generally holds interest only to collectors who specialize in the old southern minor leagues.

		NM	EX	VG
Complete Set (16):		27,500	13,500	8,250
Common Player:		1,850	925.00	555.00
(1)	Armstrong	1,850	925.00	555.00
(2)	Booles	1,850	925.00	555.00
(3)	Bourquise (Bourquoise)	1,850	925.00	555.00
(4)	Cooper	1,850	925.00	555.00
(5)	Cowell	1,850	925.00	555.00
(6)	Crockett	1,850	925.00	555.00
(7)	Fullenwider	1,850	925.00	555.00
(8)	Gilmore	1,850	925.00	555.00
(9)	Hoffman	1,850	925.00	555.00
(10)	Lane	1,850	925.00	555.00
(11)	Martin	1,850	925.00	555.00
(12)	McGeehan	1,850	925.00	555.00
(13)	Pope	1,850	925.00	555.00
(14)	Sisson	1,850	925.00	555.00
(15)	Stubbe	1,850	925.00	555.00
(16)	Walsh	1,850	925.00	555.00

1910 Contentnea Photo Series (T209)

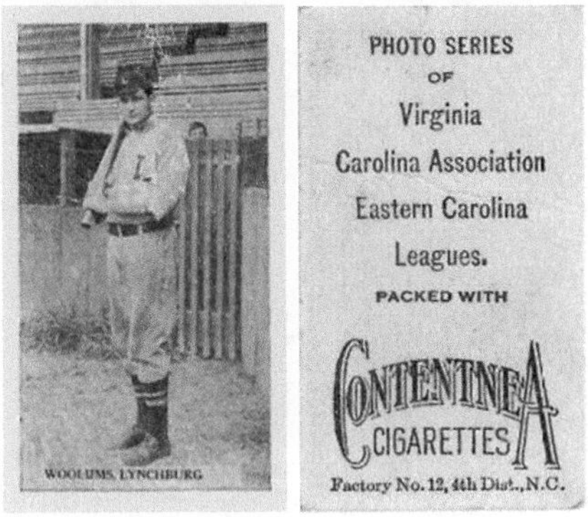
WOOLUMS, LYNCHBURG
PHOTO SERIES
OF
Virginia
Carolina Association
Eastern Carolina
Leagues.
PACKED WITH
CONTENTNEA
CIGARETTES
Factory No. 12, 4th Dist., N.C.

		NM	EX	VG
Common Player:		675.00	340.00	200.00
(1)	Abercrombie	675.00	340.00	200.00
(2)	Andrada	675.00	340.00	200.00
(3a)	Armstrong, Norfolk	675.00	340.00	200.00
(3b)	Armstrong, Wilson	675.00	340.00	200.00
(4)	Averett	675.00	340.00	200.00
(5)	Baker	675.00	340.00	200.00
(6)	Banner (Bonner)	675.00	340.00	200.00
(7)	Bausewein (Bansewein)	675.00	340.00	200.00
(8)	Beatty	675.00	340.00	200.00
(9)	Bentley	675.00	340.00	200.00
(10)	Beusse	675.00	340.00	200.00
(11)	Biel	675.00	340.00	200.00
(12)	Bigbie (Raleigh)	675.00	340.00	200.00
(13)	Bigbie (Richmond)	675.00	340.00	200.00
(14)	Blackstone	675.00	340.00	200.00
(15)	Bonner	675.00	340.00	200.00
(16)	Bourquin	675.00	340.00	200.00
(17)	Bowen	675.00	340.00	200.00
(18)	Boyle	675.00	340.00	200.00
(19)	Brandon	675.00	340.00	200.00
(20)	Brazelle (Brazell)	675.00	340.00	200.00
(21)	Brent	675.00	340.00	200.00
(22)	Brown	675.00	340.00	200.00
(23)	Busch	675.00	340.00	200.00
(24)	Bussey	675.00	340.00	200.00
(25)	Byrd	675.00	340.00	200.00
(26)	Cafalu (Cefalu)	675.00	340.00	200.00
(27)	Callahan	675.00	340.00	200.00
(28)	Chandler	675.00	340.00	200.00
(29)	Clapp	675.00	340.00	200.00
(30)	Clark (Clarke)	675.00	340.00	200.00
(31)	Clemens	675.00	340.00	200.00
(32)	Clunk	675.00	340.00	200.00
(33)	Cooper	675.00	340.00	200.00
(34)	Corbett	675.00	340.00	200.00
(35)	Cote	675.00	340.00	200.00
(36)	Coutts	675.00	340.00	200.00
(37)	Cowan (Cowen)	675.00	340.00	200.00
(38)	Cowells (Cowell)	675.00	340.00	200.00
(39)	Creagan (Cregan)	675.00	340.00	200.00
(40)	Crockett	675.00	340.00	200.00
(41)	Lave Cross	675.00	340.00	200.00
(42)	Dailey	675.00	340.00	200.00
(43)	C. Derrck (Derrick)	675.00	340.00	200.00
(44)	F. Derrick	675.00	340.00	200.00
(45)	Doak (Greensboro)	675.00	340.00	200.00
(46)	Doak (Wilmington)	675.00	340.00	200.00
(47)	Dobard	675.00	340.00	200.00
(48)	Dobson	675.00	340.00	200.00
(49)	Doyle	675.00	340.00	200.00
(50)	Drumm	675.00	340.00	200.00
(51)	Duvie	675.00	340.00	200.00
(52)	Ebinger	675.00	340.00	200.00
(53)	Eldridge	675.00	340.00	200.00
(54)	Evans	675.00	340.00	200.00
(55)	Fairbanks	675.00	340.00	200.00
(56)	Farmer	675.00	340.00	200.00
(57)	Ferrell	675.00	340.00	200.00
(58)	Fisher	675.00	340.00	200.00
(59)	Flowers	675.00	340.00	200.00
(60)	Fogarty	675.00	340.00	200.00
(61)	Foltz	675.00	340.00	200.00
(62)	Foreman	675.00	340.00	200.00
(63)	Forque	675.00	340.00	200.00
(64)	Francis	675.00	340.00	200.00
(65)	Fulton	675.00	340.00	200.00
(66)	Galvin	675.00	340.00	200.00
(67)	Gardin	675.00	340.00	200.00
(68)	Garman	675.00	340.00	200.00
(69)	Gastmeyer	675.00	340.00	200.00
(70)	Gaston	675.00	340.00	200.00
(71)	Gates	675.00	340.00	200.00
(72)	Gehring	675.00	340.00	200.00
(73)	Gillespie	675.00	340.00	200.00
(74)	Gorham	675.00	340.00	200.00
(75)	Griffin (Danville)	675.00	340.00	200.00
(76)	Griffin (Lynchburg)	675.00	340.00	200.00
(77)	Guiheen	675.00	340.00	200.00
(78)	Gunderson	675.00	340.00	200.00
(79)	Hale	675.00	340.00	200.00
(80)	Halland (Holland)	675.00	340.00	200.00
(81)	Hamilton	675.00	340.00	200.00
(82)	Hammersley	675.00	340.00	200.00
(83)	Handiboe	675.00	340.00	200.00
(84)	Hannifen (Hannifan)	675.00	340.00	200.00
(85)	Hargrave	675.00	340.00	200.00
(86)	Harrington	675.00	340.00	200.00
(87)	Harris	675.00	340.00	200.00
(88)	Hart	675.00	340.00	200.00
(89)	Hartley	675.00	340.00	200.00
(90)	Hawkins	675.00	340.00	200.00
(91)	Hearne (Hearn)	675.00	340.00	200.00
(92)	Hicks	675.00	340.00	200.00
(93)	Hobbs	675.00	340.00	200.00
(94)	Hoffman	675.00	340.00	200.00
(95)	Hooker	675.00	340.00	200.00
(96)	Howard	675.00	340.00	200.00
(97)	Howedel (Howedell)	675.00	340.00	200.00
(98)	Hudson	675.00	340.00	200.00
(99)	Humphrey	675.00	340.00	200.00
(100)	Hyames	600.00	300.00	175.00
(101)	Irvine	675.00	340.00	200.00
(102)	Irving	675.00	340.00	200.00
(103)	Jackson (Greensboro)	675.00	340.00	200.00
(104)	Jackson (Spartanburg)	675.00	340.00	200.00
(105)	Jenkins (Greenville)	675.00	340.00	200.00
(106)	Jenkins (Roanoke)	675.00	340.00	200.00
(107)	Jobson	675.00	340.00	200.00
(108)	Johnson	675.00	340.00	200.00
(109)	Keating	675.00	340.00	200.00
(110)	Kelley	675.00	340.00	200.00
(111)	Kelly (Anderson)	675.00	340.00	200.00
(112)	Kelly (Goldsboro)	675.00	340.00	200.00
(113)	"King" Kelly	675.00	340.00	200.00
(114)	King	675.00	340.00	200.00
(115)	Kite	675.00	340.00	200.00
(116)	Kunkle	675.00	340.00	200.00
(117)	Landgraff	675.00	340.00	200.00
(118)	Lane	675.00	340.00	200.00
(119)	Lathrop	675.00	340.00	200.00
(120)	Lavoia	675.00	340.00	200.00
(121)	Levy	675.00	340.00	200.00
(122)	Lloyd	675.00	340.00	200.00
(123)	Loval (Laval)	675.00	340.00	200.00
(124)	Lucia	675.00	340.00	200.00
(125)	Luyster	675.00	340.00	200.00
(126)	MacConachie	675.00	340.00	200.00
(127)	Malcolm	675.00	340.00	200.00
(128)	Martin	675.00	340.00	200.00
(129)	Mayberry	675.00	340.00	200.00
(130)	A. McCarthy	675.00	340.00	200.00
(131)	J. McCarthy	675.00	340.00	200.00
(132)	McCormick	675.00	340.00	200.00
(133)	McFarland	675.00	340.00	200.00
(134)	McFarlin	675.00	340.00	200.00
(135)	C. McGeehan	675.00	340.00	200.00
(136)	Dan McGeehan	675.00	340.00	200.00
(137)	McHugh	675.00	340.00	200.00
(138)	McKeavitt (McKevitt)	675.00	340.00	200.00
(139)	Merchant	675.00	340.00	200.00
(140)	Midkiff	675.00	340.00	200.00
(141)	Miller	675.00	340.00	200.00
(142)	Missitt	675.00	340.00	200.00
(143)	Morgan	675.00	340.00	200.00
(144)	Morrissey (Morrisey)	675.00	340.00	200.00
(145)	Mullany (Mullaney)	675.00	340.00	200.00
(146)	Mullinix	675.00	340.00	200.00
(147)	Mundell	600.00	300.00	175.00
(148)	Munsen (Munson)	675.00	340.00	200.00
(149)	Murdock (Murdoch)	675.00	340.00	200.00
(150)	Newton	675.00	340.00	200.00
(151)	Noojin	675.00	340.00	200.00
(152)	Novak	675.00	340.00	200.00
(153)	Ochs	675.00	340.00	200.00
(154)	Painter	675.00	340.00	200.00
(155)	Peloguin	675.00	340.00	200.00
(156)	Phealean (Phelan)	675.00	340.00	200.00
(157)	Phoenix	675.00	340.00	200.00
(158)	Powell	675.00	340.00	200.00
(159)	Presley (Pressley), Pritchard	800.00	400.00	200.00
(160)	Priest	675.00	340.00	200.00
(161)	Prim	675.00	340.00	200.00
(162)	Pritchard	675.00	340.00	200.00
(163)	Rawe (Rowe)	675.00	340.00	200.00
(164)	Redfern (Redfearn)	675.00	340.00	200.00
(165)	Reggy	675.00	340.00	200.00
(166)	Richardson	675.00	340.00	200.00
(167)	Rickard	675.00	340.00	200.00
(168)	Rickert	675.00	340.00	200.00
(169)	Ridgeway (Ridgway)	675.00	340.00	200.00
(170)	Roth	675.00	340.00	200.00
(171)	Salve	675.00	340.00	200.00
(172)	Schmidt	675.00	340.00	200.00
(173)	Schrader	675.00	340.00	200.00
(174)	Schumaker	675.00	340.00	200.00
(175)	Sexton	675.00	340.00	200.00
(176)	Shanghnessy (Shaughnessy)	675.00	340.00	200.00
(177)	Sharp	675.00	340.00	200.00
(178)	Shaw	675.00	340.00	200.00
(179)	Simmons	675.00	340.00	200.00
(180)	A. Smith	675.00	340.00	200.00
(181)	D. Smith	675.00	340.00	200.00
(182)	Smith (Portsmouth)	675.00	340.00	200.00
(183)	Spratt	675.00	340.00	200.00
(184)	Springs	675.00	340.00	200.00
(185)	Stewart	675.00	340.00	200.00
(186)	Stoehr	675.00	340.00	200.00
(187)	Stouch	675.00	340.00	200.00
(188)	Sullivan	675.00	340.00	200.00
(189)	Swindell	675.00	340.00	200.00
(190)	Taxis	675.00	340.00	200.00
(191)	Templin	600.00	300.00	175.00
(192)	Thompson	675.00	340.00	200.00
(193)	B.E. Thompson (Dressed as Uncle Sam.)	2,500	1,250	750.00
(194)	Tiedeman	675.00	340.00	200.00
(195)	Titman	675.00	340.00	200.00
(196)	Toner	675.00	340.00	200.00
(197)	Turner	675.00	340.00	200.00
(198)	Tydeman	675.00	340.00	200.00
(199)	Vail	675.00	340.00	200.00
(200)	Verbout	675.00	340.00	200.00
(201)	Vickery	675.00	340.00	200.00
(202)	Walker (Norfolk)	675.00	340.00	200.00
(203)	Walker (Spartanburg)	675.00	340.00	200.00
(204)	Wallace	675.00	340.00	200.00
(205)	Walsh	675.00	340.00	200.00
(206)	Walters	675.00	340.00	200.00
(207)	Waters	675.00	340.00	200.00
(208)	Waymack	675.00	340.00	200.00
(209)	Webb	675.00	340.00	200.00
(210)	Wehrell	675.00	340.00	200.00
(211)	Weldon	675.00	340.00	200.00
(212)	Welsher	675.00	340.00	200.00
(213)	Westlake	675.00	340.00	200.00
(214)	Williams	675.00	340.00	200.00
(215)	Willis	675.00	340.00	200.00
(216)	Wingo	675.00	340.00	200.00
(217)	Wolf	600.00	300.00	150.00
(218)	Wood	675.00	340.00	200.00
(219)	Woolums	675.00	340.00	200.00
(220)	Workman	675.00	340.00	200.00
(221)	Wright	600.00	300.00	150.00
(222)	Wynne	675.00	340.00	200.00

1924 Crescent Ice Cream Hanbury

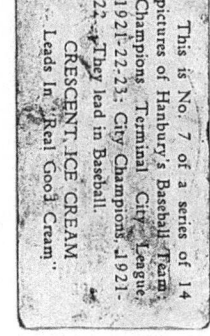

7—Art Morse
Short Stop

This is No. 7 of a series of 14 pictures of Hanbury's Baseball Team. Champions Terminal City League. 1921-22-23; City Champions 1921. 22—They lead in Baseball. CRESCENT ICE CREAM. Leads in "Real Good Cream."

Rather than a professional minor league team, this Canadian set features members of an amateur or semi-pro team sponsored by the Hanbury Sawmill in the Vancouver, B.C., Terminal Amateur League. The 2-1/4" x 1-5/8" black-and-white cards have a player portrait photo in an oval on front, with identification and card number below. On back is an identically worded summation of the team's recent seasons' championships, the card number, and an ad for the sponsor. Some cards are found with backs promoting the issue and announcing prizes.

		NM	EX	VG
Complete Set (14):		4,000	1,350	800.00
Common Player:		300.00	150.00	90.00
1	Jack Lester (Mascot)	300.00	150.00	90.00
2	Frank Coyle	300.00	150.00	90.00
3	Fred Inch	300.00	150.00	90.00
4	Robt. Mills	300.00	150.00	90.00
5	John Daniels (Capt.)	300.00	150.00	90.00
6	Doug. May	300.00	150.00	90.00
7	Art Morse	300.00	150.00	90.00
8	Chas. Stevenson	300.00	150.00	90.00
9	Tom Raftery	300.00	150.00	90.00
10	Frank Williams	300.00	150.00	90.00
11	Unknown	300.00	150.00	90.00
12	Don Stewart	300.00	150.00	90.00
13	Roy Goodall	300.00	150.00	90.00
14	Cecil Kimberley	300.00	150.00	90.00

1940 Crowley's Milk Binghamton Triplets

Members of the Binghamton, N.Y., Eastern League team are known in this set of 3" x 5" cards. Some have been seen with stamped postcard backs. Blue-and-white player photos are framed by a red rendition of a ballpark scene on the front of the unnumbered cards. Each card has a facsimile autograph ostensibly written by the pictured player. It is unknown whether the checklist below is complete. Several of the players later appeared with the N.Y. Yankees and other teams.

		NM	EX	VG
Complete Set (18):		6,000	3,000	1,800
Common Player:		550.00	275.00	165.00
(1)	Jimmy Adlam	550.00	275.00	165.00
(2)	Russ Bergman	550.00	275.00	165.00
(3)	Bruno Betzel	550.00	275.00	165.00
(4)	Bill Bevens	550.00	275.00	165.00
(5)	Johnny Bianco	550.00	275.00	165.00
(6)	Fred Collins	550.00	275.00	165.00
(7)	Vince DeBiassi	550.00	275.00	165.00
(8)	Jack Graham	550.00	275.00	165.00
(9)	Randy Gumpert	550.00	275.00	165.00
(10)	Al Gurske	550.00	275.00	165.00
(11)	Mike Milosevich	550.00	275.00	165.00
(12)	Billie O'Donnell (Trainer)	550.00	275.00	165.00
(13)	Earl Reid	550.00	275.00	165.00
(14)	Aaron Robinson	550.00	275.00	165.00
(15)	Frankie Silvanic	550.00	275.00	165.00
(16)	Pete Suder	550.00	275.00	165.00
(17)	Ray Volps	550.00	275.00	165.00
(18)	Herb White	550.00	275.00	165.00

D

1952 Dallas Eagles Team Issue

A Class AA Texas League farm team of the Cleveland Indians, the Eagles were one of the higher minor league teams chronicled by Globe Printing in its series of 2-1/4" x 3-3/8" blank-back, black-and-white cards sets of the early 1950s. The checklist here is not complete. This set differs from most Globe issues in the use of white borders around the photos on front. The checklist here may not be complete.

		NM	EX	VG
Common Player:		75.00	37.50	22.50
(1)	Ralph Albers	75.00	37.50	22.50
(2)	Dick Aylward	75.00	37.50	22.50
(3)	Jodie Beeler	75.00	37.50	22.50
(4)	Bob Bundy	75.00	37.50	22.50
(5)	Johnny Creel	75.00	37.50	22.50
(6)	Bob Cullins	75.00	37.50	22.50
(7)	Hal Erickson	75.00	37.50	22.50
(8)	Dave Hoskins	75.00	37.50	22.50
(9)	Bud Hutson	75.00	37.50	22.50
(10)	Edward Knoblauch	75.00	37.50	22.50
(11)	Walt Lanfranconi	75.00	37.50	22.50
(12)	Joe Kotrany	75.00	37.50	22.50
(13)	Joe Macko	75.00	37.50	22.50
(14)	Alan Maul	75.00	37.50	22.50
(15)	Peter Mazar	75.00	37.50	22.50
(16)	Dutch Meyer	75.00	37.50	22.50
(17)	Don Mossi	90.00	45.00	27.00
(18)	Clyde Perry	75.00	37.50	22.50
(19)	Ray Peters	75.00	37.50	22.50
(20)	Harry Sullivan	75.00	37.50	22.50
(21)	Frank Tomay	75.00	37.50	22.50
(22)	Edward Varhely	75.00	37.50	22.50

1959 Darigold Farms Spokane Indians

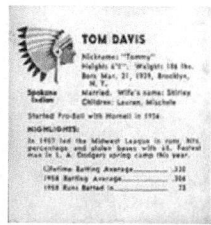

The unnumbered cards in this set were glued to milk cartons by a folded tab at the top of each card. The basic card measures 2-1/2" x 2-3/8", with a 2-1/2" x 2-1/8" tab. Black-and-white player photos are set against colored backgrounds of yellow (1-8), red (9-16) and blue (17-22). Player biographical details and stats are printed in black on the back. Values shown are for cards without the superfluous tabs.

		NM	EX	VG
Complete Set (22):		4,500	2,250	1,350
Common Player:		200.00	100.00	60.00
(1)	Facundo Barragan	200.00	100.00	60.00
(2)	Steve Bilko	225.00	110.00	65.00
(3)	Bobby Bragan	225.00	110.00	65.00
(4)	Chuck Churn	200.00	100.00	60.00
(5)	Tom Davis	450.00	225.00	135.00
(6)	Dom Domenichelli	200.00	100.00	60.00
(7)	Bob Giallombardo	200.00	100.00	60.00
(8)	Connie Grob	200.00	100.00	60.00
(9)	Fred Hatfield	200.00	100.00	60.00
(10)	Bob Lillis	225.00	110.00	65.00
(11)	Lloyd Merritt	200.00	100.00	60.00
(12)	Larry Miller	200.00	100.00	60.00
(13)	Chris Nicolosi	200.00	100.00	60.00
(14)	Allen Norris	200.00	100.00	60.00
(15)	Phil Ortega	200.00	100.00	60.00
(16)	Phillips Paine	200.00	100.00	60.00
(17)	Bill Parsons	200.00	100.00	60.00
(18)	Hisel Patrick	200.00	100.00	60.00
(19)	Tony Roig	200.00	100.00	60.00
(20)	Tom Saffell	200.00	100.00	60.00
(21)	Norm Sherry	250.00	125.00	75.00
(22)	Ben Wade	200.00	100.00	60.00

1960 Darigold Farms Spokane Indians

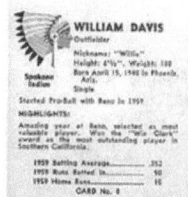

For its second annual baseball card set, the dairy added two cards and numbered the issue on the back. Card fronts were black-and-white photos against colored backgrounds of yellow (1-8), green (9-16) and red (17-24). A facsimile autograph appears on the front as well. The basic card measures 2-

3/8" x 2-11/16", with a folded 2-3/8" x 2-1/16" tab at the top, by which the card was glued to a milk carton. Backs are black-and-white. Values shown are for cards without the superfluous tab.

		NM	EX	VG
Complete Set (24):		4,500	2,250	1,350
Common Player:		145.00	75.00	40.00
1	Chris Nicolosi	145.00	75.00	40.00
2	Jim Pagliaroni	145.00	75.00	40.00
3	Roy Smalley	145.00	75.00	40.00
4	Bill Bethel	145.00	75.00	40.00
5	Joe Liscio	145.00	75.00	40.00
6	Curt Roberts	145.00	75.00	40.00
7	Ed Palmquist	145.00	75.00	40.00
8	Willie Davis	300.00	150.00	90.00
9	Bob Giallombardo	145.00	75.00	40.00
10	Pedro Gomez	145.00	75.00	40.00
11	Mel Nelson	145.00	75.00	40.00
12	Charley Smith	145.00	75.00	40.00
13	Clarence Churn	145.00	75.00	40.00
14	Ramon Conde	145.00	75.00	40.00
15	George O'Donnell	145.00	75.00	40.00
16	Tony Roig	145.00	75.00	40.00
17	Frank Howard	450.00	225.00	135.00
18	Billy Harris	145.00	75.00	40.00
19	Mike Brumley	145.00	75.00	40.00
20	Earl Robinson	145.00	75.00	40.00
21	Ron Fairly	400.00	200.00	120.00
22	Joe Frazier	145.00	75.00	40.00
23	Allen Norris	145.00	75.00	40.00
24	Ford Young	145.00	75.00	40.00

E

1928 Pacific Coast League Exhibits

This regional series of 32 cards pictures players from the six California teams in the Pacific Coast League. Like the 1928 major league Exhibits, the PCL cards have a blue tint and are not numbered. They are blank-backed and measure 3-3/8" x 5-3/8". The set includes several misspellings. Cards are occasionally found with a corner clipped, the card corner to be used as a coupon with redemption value.

		NM	EX	VG
Complete Set (32):		26,250	13,125	7,875
Common Player:		750.00	375.00	225.00
1	Buzz Arlett	1,200	600.00	360.00
2	Earl Averill	3,150	1,575	945.00
3	Carl Berger (Walter)	1,200	600.00	360.00
4	"Ping" Bodie	1,050	525.00	315.00
5	Carl Dittmar	750.00	375.00	225.00
6	Jack Fenton	750.00	375.00	225.00
7	Neal "Mickey" Finn (Cornelius)	750.00	375.00	225.00
8	Ray French	750.00	375.00	225.00
9	Tony Governor	750.00	375.00	225.00
10	"Truck" Hannah	750.00	375.00	225.00
11	Mickey Heath	750.00	375.00	225.00
12	Wally Hood	750.00	375.00	225.00
13	"Fuzzy" Hufft	750.00	375.00	225.00
14	Smead Jolly (Smead Jolley)	900.00	450.00	270.00
15	Bobby "Ducky" Jones	750.00	375.00	225.00
16	Rudy Kallio	750.00	375.00	225.00
17	Ray Keating	750.00	375.00	225.00
18	Johnny Kerr	750.00	375.00	225.00
19	Harry Krause	750.00	375.00	225.00
20	Lynford H. Larry (Lary)	750.00	375.00	225.00
21	Dudley Lee	750.00	375.00	225.00
22	Walter "Duster" Mails	750.00	375.00	225.00
23	Jimmy Reese	750.00	370.00	220.00
24	"Dusty" Rhodes	750.00	375.00	225.00
25	Hal Rhyne	750.00	375.00	225.00
26	Hank Severied (Severeid)	750.00	375.00	225.00
27	Earl Sheely	750.00	375.00	225.00
28	Frank Shellenback	750.00	375.00	225.00
29	Gordon Slade	750.00	375.00	225.00
30	Hollis Thurston	750.00	375.00	225.00
31	"Babe" Twombly	750.00	375.00	225.00
32	Earl "Tex" Weathersby	750.00	375.00	225.00

1953 Montreal Royals Exhibits

Twenty-four Montreal Royals, including many future Brooklyn and L.A. Dodgers and Hall of Fame managers Walt Alston and Tommy Lasorda, were included in a 64-card Canadian issue by Exhibit Supply Co., of Chicago. The cards are slightly smaller, at 3-1/4" x 5-1/4", than standard Exhibits and printed - blank-backed - on gray stock. Numbered on front, cards of the Montreal players can be found in either blue or reddish-brown tint. Only the Royals players from the issue are checklisted here.

	NM	EX	VG
Complete Set (24):	450.00	225.00	135.00
Common Player:	15.00	7.50	4.50
33 Don Hoak	25.00	12.50	7.50
34 Bob Alexander	15.00	7.50	4.50
35 John Simmons	15.00	7.50	4.50
36 Steve Lembo	15.00	7.50	4.50
37 Norm Larker	20.00	10.00	6.00
38 Bob Ludwick	15.00	7.50	4.50
39 Walt Moryn	20.00	10.00	6.00
40 Charlie Thompson	15.00	7.50	4.50
41 Ed Roebuck	20.00	10.00	6.00
42 Russell Rose	15.00	7.50	4.50
43 Edmundo (Sandy) Amoros	25.00	12.50	7.50
44 Bob Milliken	15.00	7.50	4.50
45 Art Fabbro	15.00	7.50	4.50
46 Spook Jacobs	15.00	7.50	4.50
47 Carmen Mauro	15.00	7.50	4.50
48 Walter Fiala	15.00	7.50	4.50
49 Rocky Nelson	15.00	7.50	4.50
50 Tom La Sorda (Lasorda)	60.00	30.00	18.00
51 Ronnie Lee	15.00	7.50	4.50
52 Hampton Coleman	15.00	7.50	4.50
53 Frank Marchio	15.00	7.50	4.50
54 William Sampson	15.00	7.50	4.50
55 Gil Mills	15.00	7.50	4.50
56 Al Ronning	15.00	7.50	4.50
61 Walt Alston	40.00	20.00	12.00

F

1953 Fargo-Moorhead Twins Team Issue

This set of team-issued cards includes the first of future home-run king Roger Maris (spelled Maras in the traditional family manner). The cards are about 3-1/4" x 5-5/16" with a white border surrounding a black-and-white posed photo. Player identification is in three lines of white type at lower-left. Backs are blank, except some cards which bear a rubber-stamped promotional message from the "Red River Scenes" newspaper. The unnumbered cards are checklisted here in alphabetical order. Three of the players are known in two or more poses.

	NM	EX	VG
Complete Set (21):	3,500	1,750	1,000
Common Player:	60.00	30.00	18.00
(1) Zeke Bonura	60.00	30.00	18.00
(2) Bob Borovicka	60.00	30.00	18.00
(3) Ken Braeseke	60.00	30.00	18.00
(4) Joe Camacho	60.00	30.00	18.00
(5) Galen Fiss	60.00	30.00	18.00
(6) Frank Gravino	60.00	30.00	18.00
(Batting follow-through.)			
(7) Frank Gravino (Hands on hips.)	60.00	30.00	18.00
(8) Frank Gravino (Hands on knees.)	60.00	30.00	18.00

(9) Santo Luberto/Fldg	60.00	30.00	18.00
(10) Roger Maras/Fldg	1,250	625.00	375.00
(11) Roger Maras/Btg	1,250	625.00	375.00
(12) Jerry Mehlish (Mehlisch)	60.00	30.00	18.00
(13) Bob Melton	60.00	30.00	18.00
(14) Ray Mendoza	60.00	30.00	18.00
(Stretching at 1B, ball in glove.)			
(15) Ray Mendoza	60.00	30.00	18.00
(Stretching at 1B, no ball.)			
(16) John Morse	60.00	30.00	18.00
(17) Don Nance	60.00	30.00	18.00
(18) Ray Seif	60.00	30.00	18.00
(19) Will Sirois	60.00	30.00	18.00
(20) Dick Wegner	60.00	30.00	18.00
(21) Don Wolf	60.00	30.00	18.00

1966 Foremost Milk St. Petersburg Cardinals

GEORGE "Sparky" ANDERSON
ST. PETERSBURG CARDINALS 1966

This 20-card black-and-white set includes players and the manager, Sparky Anderson, of the Florida State League farm club of the St. Louis Cardinals. The unnumbered, blank-backed cards measure 3-1/2" x 5-1/2".

	NM	EX	VG
Complete Set (20):	50.00	25.00	15.00
Common Player:	2.50	1.25	.75
(1) George "Sparky" Anderson	17.50	8.75	5.25
(2) Dave Bakenhaster	2.50	1.25	.75
(3) Leonard Boyer	4.00	2.00	1.25
(4) Ron Braddock	2.50	1.25	.75
(5) Thomas "Chip" Coulter	2.50	1.25	.75
(6) Ernest "Sweet Pea" Davis	2.50	1.25	.75
(7) Phil Knuckles	2.50	1.25	.75
(8) Doug Lukens	2.50	1.25	.75
(9) Terry Milani	2.50	1.25	.75
(10) Tim Morgan	2.50	1.25	.75
(11) Harry Parker	2.50	1.25	.75
(12) Jerry Robertson	2.50	1.25	.75
(13) Francisco Rodriguez	2.50	1.25	.75
(14) John "Sonny" Ruberto	2.50	1.25	.75
(15) Charlie Stewart	2.50	1.25	.75
(16) Gary L. Stone	2.50	1.25	.75
(17) Charles "Tim" Thompson	2.50	1.25	.75
(18) Jose Villar	2.50	1.25	.75
(19) Archie L. Wade	2.50	1.25	.75
(20) Jim Williamson	2.50	1.25	.75

1921 Frederick Foto Service

This issue comprises a mix of Pacific Coast League and Major League players. Because Frederick Foto was located in Sacramento, a preponderance of the minor leaguers are Sacramento Senators. The method of the cards' distribution is unknkown. The cards are black-and-white glossy photographs glued to a cardboard backing. The photos are bordered in white with top and bottom borders considerably wider than those on the sides. About 1-3/16" x 2-5/8", the cards have blank backs. On front is the player's last name and city, printed in a hand-lettered style. Most cards have a "Frerredick / Foto." credit in the same style. Other cards have a banner-and-circle "Foto / Frederick / Service logo." It is likely this checklist is not complete. Gaps have been left in the assigned numbering for future additions.

	NM	EX	VG
Common Player:	750.00	375.00	225.00
(1) Agnew	750.00	375.00	225.00
(2) Alexander	750.00	375.00	225.00
(3) Cady	750.00	375.00	225.00
(4) Ike Caveny (Caveney)	750.00	375.00	225.00

(6) Compton, with bat	750.00	375.00	225.00
(7) Compton, with glove	750.00	375.00	225.00
(8) Les Cook/btg	750.00	375.00	225.00
(9) Les Cook/Fldg	750.00	375.00	225.00
(10) Carroll Canfield	750.00	375.00	225.00
(11) Brick Eldred	750.00	375.00	225.00
(12) Rowdy Elliott	750.00	375.00	225.00
(13) Tony Faeth	750.00	375.00	225.00
(14) Paul Fittery	750.00	375.00	225.00
(15) Gedeon	750.00	375.00	225.00
(16) Griffith	750.00	375.00	225.00
(17) Charlie Hollocher	750.00	375.00	225.00
(18) Jones	750.00	375.00	225.00
(19) Willie Kamm	750.00	375.00	225.00
(21) Manny Kopp, bat at waist level	750.00	375.00	225.00
(22) Manny Kopp, bat on shoulder	750.00	375.00	225.00
(23) Earl Kuntz (Kunz)	750.00	375.00	225.00
(24) Duster Mails (Arms at sides.)	750.00	375.00	225.00
(25) Duster Mails (Hands at chest.)	750.00	375.00	225.00
(26) Duster Mails (Follow-through.)	750.00	375.00	225.00
(27) Duster Mails (Wind-up.)	750.00	375.00	225.00
(29) Patsy McGaffigan, bat at waist level	750.00	375.00	225.00
(30) Patsy McGaffigan, bat on shoulder	750.00	375.00	225.00
(31) Roxie Middleton	750.00	375.00	225.00
(32) Hack Miller	900.00	450.00	270.00
(33) Mollwitz	750.00	375.00	225.00
(34) Dick Niehaus	750.00	375.00	225.00
(35) Billy Orr (Batting)	750.00	375.00	225.00
(36) Billy Orr (Hands on knees.)	750.00	375.00	225.00
(37) Dode Paskert	750.00	375.00	225.00
(38) Ken Penner (Right foot off ground.)	750.00	375.00	225.00
(39) Ken Penner (Right foot on ground.)	750.00	375.00	225.00
(40) Charlie Pick	750.00	375.00	225.00
(41) Babe Pinelli	1,000	500.00	300.00
(42) Bill Prough	750.00	375.00	225.00
(43) Addison Read	750.00	375.00	225.00
Reuther	750.00	375.00	225.00
(44) Bill Rodgers	750.00	375.00	225.00
(45) Pete Rose	750.00	375.00	225.00
(46) Babe Ruth	40,000	20,000	12,000
(47) Buddy Ryan (Holding bat, 3/4 length.)	750.00	375.00	225.00
(48) Buddy Ryan (Holding bat, full-length.)	750.00	375.00	225.00
(49) Buddy Ryan (Swinging bat.)	750.00	375.00	225.00
(50) Bobby Schang	750.00	375.00	225.00
(51) Les Sheehan	750.00	375.00	225.00
(52) Shore	750.00	375.00	225.00
(53) Stumpf	750.00	375.00	225.00
(54) Tobin	750.00	375.00	225.00
(60) Kettle Wirts (Chicago)	750.00	375.00	225.00
(61) Kettle Wirts (Dallas)	750.00	375.00	225.00
(62) Archie Yelle	750.00	375.00	225.00
Unidentified player, arms folded.	750.00	375.00	225.00
Unidentified player, batting follow-through.	750.00	375.00	225.00

1951 Fresno Cardinals Team Issue

These 2-1/4" x 3-3/8" black-and-white, unnumbered, blank-backed cards were one of many minor league team sets issued by Globe Printing of San Jose, Calif., in the early 1950s. Cards were usually given away at the ballpark on a one-per-week or one-per-homestand basis, accounting for the rarity of surviving sets. The team was a California League (Class C) affiliate of the St. Louis Cardinals.

	NM	EX	VG
Complete Set (17):	1,000	500.00	300.00
Common Player:	60.00	30.00	18.00
(1) Hal Atkinson	60.00	30.00	18.00
(2) Larry Barton	60.00	30.00	18.00
(3) Charlie Brooks	60.00	30.00	18.00
(4) Bill Burton	60.00	30.00	18.00
(5) Ray Herrera	60.00	30.00	18.00
(6) Earl Jones	60.00	30.00	18.00
(7) Jim King	60.00	30.00	18.00
(8) Whitey Lageman	60.00	30.00	18.00
(9) Wally Lamers	60.00	30.00	18.00
(10) John McNamara	75.00	37.00	22.00
(11) Gerry Mertz	60.00	30.00	18.00
(12) Frank Olasin	60.00	30.00	18.00
(13) Howie Phillips	60.00	30.00	18.00
(14) Jack Ramsey	60.00	30.00	18.00
(15) Tony Stathos	60.00	30.00	18.00
(16) Whit Ulrich	60.00	30.00	18.00
(17) Pete Younie	60.00	30.00	18.00

1952 Frostade

(See 1952 Parkhurst.)

1954 Fruiterie Saint Louis Tommy Lasorda

The date of issue attributed is only a best guess. It is also unknown how many other Montreal Royals players may be found in this issue. Printed in black-and-white on fairly thick 5-1/2" x 7" cardboard, this card features a portrait photo of the Royals' pitcher and future Hall of Fame manager along with a facsimile autograph on the borderless front. Rubber-stamped at top of the otherwise blank back is: "Fruiterie / Saint Louis De Franos / 515 RUE ROY PL. 1729," presumably identification of a Montreal business which distributed the card.

	NM	EX	VG
Tommy Lasorda	100.00	50.00	30.00

G

1911 Gilmartin Printing Co. S.F. Seals

These extremely scarce cards were issued as a premium by the Gilmartin Printing Co. of San Francisco and feature only members of the city's PCL Seals team. The 5" x 7" cards have full-length posed portraits of the players at center, printed in a blue-green tone and surrounded by a wide white border. The player's name, position team and year are scripted in the lower-left corner of the photo. Backs are blank. This checklist is known to be incomplete. Some cards have the sponsor's imprint below the photo.

		NM	EX	VG
Common Player:		4,500	2,200	1,350
(1)	Claude Berry	4,500	2,200	1,350
(2)	Frank Browning	4,500	2,200	1,350
(6)	Willard Meikle	4,500	2,200	1,350
(7)	Frank Miller	4,500	2,200	1,350
(9)	Harry Sutor	4,500	2,200	1,350
(10)	Tom Tennant	4,500	2,200	1,350
(12)	Geo. Weaver	11,000	5,500	3,250

1956-57 Gil's Drive-Ins Seattle Rainiers

By presenting any nine of these pictures to either of GIL'S DRIVE-INS you will receive FREE an 8"x 10" player picture of your choice and you still keep your nine small pictures.

Two locations to serve you

GIL'S DRIVE-IN

4406 Rainier Avenue
1 mile south of Sicks' Stadium
—and—
3500 Avalon Way
35th S. W. and Avalon Way
West Seattle

(See 1956-57 Seattle Popcorn for checklist and values.)

1951-1954 Globe Printing

The team-issue card sets and souvenir picture albums listed in previous editions under the heading of Globe Printing are now found alphabetically by team name as per this list:

1951 Fresno Cardinals
1951 San Jose Red Sox
1952 Atlanta Crackers
1952 Baltimore Orioles
1952 Colorado Springs Sky Sox
1952 Columbus Cardinals
1952 Dallas Eagles
1952 Ft. Worth Cats
1952 Great Falls Electrics
1952 Jamestown Falcons
1952 Miami Beach Flamingos
1952 Ogden Reds
1952 Oshkosh Giants
1952 Ponca City Dodgers/KOM Mgrs.
1952 San Diego Padres
1952 Shawnee Hawks
1952-1953 Sioux City Soos
1952 Stockton Ports (Knowles)
1952 Syracuse Chiefs
1952 Ventura Braves
1953 Galveston White Caps (Coca-Cola)
1954 Charleston Senators (Blossom Dairy)
1954 Lewiston Broncs (Veltex)
1954 Sacramento Solons
1954 Sioux City Soos
1954 Stock Ports (MD)

1943 Golden Quality Ice Cream Wilkes-Barre Barons

This rare war-time minor league issue depicts the Hall of Fame manager, Tony Lazzeri, and players on the Class A Eastern League Barons. The 4" x 5" black-and-white cards have facsimile player autographs. Printed in the bottom border at left are the team and year; at right is "Compliments of Golden Quality Ice Cream Co."

		NM	EX	VG
Complete Set (6):		600.00	300.00	180.00
Common Player:		75.00	37.50	22.50
(1)	Alex Damalitron	75.00	37.50	22.50
(2)	Tony Lazzeri (Bat on shoulder.)	175.00	90.00	55.00
(3)	Tony Lazzeri (Hands on knees.)	175.00	90.00	55.00
(4)	Jim McDonnell	75.00	37.50	22.50
(5)	Joe Pennington	75.00	37.50	22.50
(6)	Ned Tryon	75.00	37.50	22.50

1957 Golden State Dairy S.F. Seals Stickers

There are 23 stickers known in this set, featuring the last minor league team in San Francisco. Virtually every player who appeared in more than 10 games for the Seals that season is included in the set. The stickers measure approximately 2" x 2-1/2", are printed in black-and-white, and blank-backed. A 3-1/2" x 6" album to house the stickers was also issued, with biographical data and space for an autograph on each player's page. The stickers are checklisted here alphabetically, as the stickers are unnumbered.

		NM	EX	VG
Complete Set (23):		550.00	275.00	165.00
Common Player:		25.00	12.50	7.50
Album:		150.00	75.00	45.00
(1)	William "Bill" Abernathie	25.00	12.50	7.50
(2)	Kenneth "Chip" Aspromonte	25.00	12.50	7.50
(3)	Harry "Fritz" Dorish	25.00	12.50	7.50
(4)	Joe "Flash" Gordon	25.00	12.50	7.50
(5)	Grady Hatton Jr.	25.00	12.50	7.50
(6)	Thomas "Tommy" Hurd	25.00	12.50	7.50
(7)	Frank Kellert	25.00	12.50	7.50
(8)	Richard "Marty" Keough	25.00	12.50	7.50
(9)	Leo "Black Cat" Kiely	25.00	12.50	7.50
(10)	Harry William Malmberg	25.00	12.50	7.50
(11)	John McCall	25.00	12.50	7.50
(12)	Albert "Albie" Pearson	40.00	20.00	12.00
(13)	Jack Phillips	25.00	12.50	7.50
(14)	William "Bill" Renna	25.00	12.50	7.50
(15)	Edward "Ed" Sadowski	25.00	12.50	7.50
(16)	Robert W. Smith	25.00	12.50	7.50
(17)	Jack Spring	25.00	12.50	7.50
(18)	Jospeh H. Tanner	25.00	12.50	7.50
(19)	Salvador "Sal" Taormina	25.00	12.50	7.50
(20)	Maynard "Bert" Thiel	25.00	12.50	7.50
(21)	Anthony "Nini" Tornay	25.00	12.50	7.50
(22)	Thomas "Tommy" Umphlett	25.00	12.50	7.50
(23)	Glenn "Cap" Wright	25.00	12.50	7.50

1943 Grand Studio Milwaukee Brewers

It's unknown how these blank-backed, black-and-white, 3-1/2" x 5-1/2" pictures were distributed. The only identification is "PHOTO BY GRAND STUDIO" in the lower-right corner. It's likely the pictures were sold as a set at Borchert Field.

		NM	EX	VG
Complete Set (22):		1,000	500.00	300.00
Common Player:		60.00	30.00	20.00
(1)	Joe Berry	60.00	30.00	20.00
(2)	Bob Bowman	60.00	30.00	20.00
(3)	Earl Caldwell	60.00	30.00	20.00
(4)	Grey Clarke	60.00	30.00	20.00
(5)	Merv Conner	60.00	30.00	20.00
(6)	Paul Erickson	60.00	30.00	20.00
(7)	Charlie Grimm	80.00	40.00	25.00
(8)	Hank Helf	60.00	30.00	20.00
(9)	Don Johnson	60.00	30.00	20.00
(10)	Wes Livengood	60.00	30.00	20.00
(11)	Hershell Martin	60.00	30.00	20.00
(12)	Tommy Nelson	60.00	30.00	20.00
(13)	Ted Norbert	60.00	30.00	20.00
(14)	Bill Norman	60.00	30.00	20.00
(15)	Henry Oana	125.00	65.00	40.00
(16)	Jimmy Pruett	60.00	30.00	20.00
(17)	Bill Sahlin	60.00	30.00	20.00
(18)	Frank Secroy	60.00	30.00	20.00
(19)	Red Smith	60.00	30.00	20.00
(20)	Charles Sproull	60.00	30.00	20.00
(21)	Hugh Todd	60.00	30.00	20.00
(22)	Tony York	60.00	30.00	20.00

1944 Grand Studio Milwaukee Brewers

Future Hall of Fame manager Casey Stengel is featured in the second of three annual team-issued photocard sets. The 3-1/2" x 5-1/2" cards have black-and-white portrait photos with facsimile autographs, bordered in white. Backs are blank.

	NM	EX	VG
Complete Set (26):	900.00	450.00	275.00
Common Player:	50.00	25.00	15.00
(1) Julio Acosta	50.00	25.00	15.00
(2) Heinz Becker	50.00	25.00	15.00
(3) George Binks	50.00	25.00	15.00
(4) Bob Bowman	50.00	25.00	15.00
(5) Earl Caldwell	50.00	25.00	15.00
(6) Dick Culler	50.00	25.00	15.00
(7) Roy Easterwood	50.00	25.00	15.00
(8) Jack Farmer	50.00	25.00	15.00
(9) Charles Gassaway	50.00	25.00	15.00
(10) Dick Hearn	50.00	25.00	15.00
(11) Don Hendrickson	50.00	25.00	15.00
(12) Ed Levy	50.00	25.00	15.00
(13) Hershel Martin	50.00	25.00	15.00
(14) Bill Nagel	50.00	25.00	15.00
(15) Tommy Nelson	50.00	25.00	15.00
(16) Bill Norman	50.00	25.00	15.00
(17) Hal Peck	50.00	25.00	15.00
(18) Jimmy Pruett	50.00	25.00	15.00
(19) Ken Raddant	50.00	25.00	15.00
(20) Owen Scheetz	50.00	25.00	15.00
(21) Eddie Scheive	50.00	25.00	15.00
(22) Frank Secory	50.00	25.00	15.00
(23) Red Smith	50.00	25.00	15.00
(24) Floyd Speer	50.00	25.00	15.00
(25) Charlie Sproull	50.00	25.00	15.00
(26) Casey Stengel	300.00	150.00	90.00

1945 Grand Studio Milwaukee Brewers

The format remained unchanged for the last of three annual team-issued photocard sets. The 3-1/2" x 5-1/2" cards have black-and-white portrait photos with facsimile autographs, bordered in white. Backs are blank.

	NM	EX	VG
Complete Set (16):	625.00	300.00	175.00
Common Player:	50.00	25.00	15.00
(1) Julio Acosta	50.00	25.00	15.00
(2) Arky Biggs	50.00	25.00	15.00
(3) Bill Burgo	50.00	25.00	15.00
(4) Nick Cullop	50.00	25.00	15.00
(5) Wendell "Peaches" Davis	50.00	25.00	15.00
(6) Otto Denning	50.00	25.00	15.00
(7) Lew Flick	50.00	25.00	15.00
(8) Don Hendrickson	50.00	25.00	15.00
(9) Ed Kobersky	50.00	25.00	15.00
(10) Carl Lindquist	50.00	25.00	15.00
(11) Jack McGillen	50.00	25.00	15.00
(12) Gene Nance	50.00	25.00	15.00
(13) Bill Norman	50.00	25.00	15.00
(14) Joe Rullo	50.00	25.00	15.00
(15) Owen Scheetz	50.00	25.00	15.00
(16) Floyd Speer	50.00	25.00	15.00

1952 Great Falls Electrics Team Issue

Formatted like the other known minor league issues from Globe Printing of San Jose, Calif., in the early 1950s, this set chronicles the 1952 version of the Class C (Pioneer League) Great Falls (Montana) Electrics, a farm club of the Brooklyn Dodgers. The blank-backed cards are black-and-white and measure about 2-1/4" x 3-3/8". An album was issued with the cards.

	NM	EX	VG
Complete Set (16):	800.00	400.00	240.00
Common Player:	60.00	30.00	18.00
(1) Don Bricker	60.00	30.00	18.00
(2) Larry Hampshire	60.00	30.00	18.00
(3) Ernie Jordan	60.00	30.00	18.00
(4) Lou Landini	60.00	30.00	18.00
(5) Danny Lastres	60.00	30.00	18.00
(6) Joe Oliffe	60.00	30.00	18.00
(7) Len Payne	60.00	30.00	18.00
(8) Lou Rochelli	60.00	30.00	18.00
(9) Earl Silverthorn	60.00	30.00	18.00
(10) Eddie Serrano	60.00	30.00	18.00
(11) Rick Small	60.00	30.00	18.00
(12) Dick Smith	60.00	30.00	18.00
(13) Hal Snyder	60.00	30.00	18.00
(14) Armando Suarez	60.00	30.00	18.00
(15) Emy Unzicker	60.00	30.00	18.00
Album:	100.00	50.00	30.00

1888 Gypsy Queen California League

Until further specimens are reported, the attributed date of issue is speculative between about 1887-89. Undiscovered until 1998 was the fact that Gypsy Queen, a cigarette manufactured by Goodwin & Co. (Old Judge, etc.) had issued minor league cards, presumably of the relatively new California League. Like some contemporary issues, the card is a stiff piece of cardboard with a sepia-toned player photo glued to it. Size is about 1-1/2" x 2-1/2". As of November 2001, only one card was known from this issue. In Fair to Good condition it was sold at auction for $80,273, then a record price for any 19th Century card.

(1) Jas McDonald

H

1949 Hage's Dairy

Hage's Dairy of California began a three-year run of regional baseball cards featuring Pacific Coast League players in 1949. The cards were distributed inside popcorn boxes at the concession stand in Lane Field Park, home of the P.C.L. San Diego Padres. The 1949 set, like the following two years, was printed on thin stock measuring on average 2-5/8" x 3-1/8". The checklist includes several different poses for some of the players. Cards were continually being added or withdrawn to reflect roster changes on the minor league clubs. The Hage's sets were dominated by San Diego players, but also included representatives from the seven other P.C.L. teams. The 1949 cards can be found in four different tints: sepia, green, blue, and black-and-white. The unnumbered cards have blank backs or advertising messages on back. The player's name and team appear inside a box on the front of the card, and the 1949 cards can be dated by the large (quarter-inch) type used for the team names, which are sometimes referred to by city and other times by nickname.

	NM	EX	VG
Complete Set (107):	40,000	20,000	10,000
Common Player:	400.00	200.00	100.00
(1) "Buster" Adams	400.00	200.00	100.00
(2) "Red" Adams	400.00	200.00	100.00
(3) Lee Anthony	400.00	200.00	100.00
(4) Rinaldo Ardizoia	400.00	200.00	100.00
(5) Del Baker	400.00	200.00	100.00
(6) Ed Basinski	400.00	200.00	100.00
(7) Jim Baxes	400.00	200.00	100.00
(8) H. Becker	400.00	200.00	100.00
(9) Herman Besse	400.00	200.00	100.00
(10) Tom Bridges	400.00	200.00	100.00
(11) Gene Brocker	400.00	200.00	100.00
(12) Ralph Buxton	400.00	200.00	100.00
(13) Mickey Burnett	400.00	200.00	100.00
(14) Dain Clay/Pose	400.00	200.00	100.00
(15) Dain Clay/Btg	400.00	200.00	100.00
(16) Dain Corriden, Jim Reese	475.00	235.00	120.00
(17) Pete Coscarart	400.00	200.00	100.00
(18) Dom Dallessandro	400.00	200.00	100.00
(19) Con Dempsey	400.00	200.00	100.00
(20) Vince DiBiasi	400.00	200.00	100.00
(21) Luke Easter (Batting stance.)	600.00	300.00	150.00
(22) Luke Easter (Batting follow through.)	600.00	300.00	150.00
(23) Ed Fernandez	400.00	200.00	100.00
(24) Les Fleming	400.00	200.00	100.00
(25) Jess Flores	400.00	200.00	100.00
(26) Cecil Garriott	400.00	200.00	100.00
(27) Charles Gassaway	400.00	200.00	100.00
(28) Johnny Gorsica	400.00	200.00	100.00
(29) Mickey Grasso	400.00	200.00	100.00
(30) Will Hafey/Pitching	400.00	200.00	100.00
(31) Will Hafey/Pose	400.00	200.00	100.00
(32) "Jeep" Handley	400.00	200.00	100.00
(33) "Bucky" Harris/Portrait	600.00	300.00	150.00
(34) "Bucky" Harris/Shouting	600.00	300.00	150.00
(35) Roy Helser	400.00	200.00	100.00
(36) Lloyd Hittle	400.00	200.00	100.00
(37) Ralph Hodgin	400.00	200.00	100.00
(38) Leroy Jarvis	400.00	200.00	100.00
(39) John Jensen	400.00	200.00	100.00
(40) Al Jurisich	400.00	200.00	100.00
(41) Herb Karpel	600.00	300.00	150.00
(42) Frank Kelleher	400.00	200.00	100.00
(43) Bill Kelly	400.00	200.00	100.00
(44) Bob Kelly	400.00	200.00	100.00
(45) Frank Kerr	400.00	200.00	100.00
(46) Thomas Kipp	400.00	200.00	100.00
(47) Al Lien	400.00	200.00	100.00
(48) Lyman Linde/Pose	400.00	200.00	100.00
(49) Lyman Linde/Pitching	400.00	200.00	100.00
(50) Dennis Luby	400.00	200.00	100.00
(51) "Red" Lynn	400.00	200.00	100.00
(52) Pat Malone	400.00	200.00	100.00
(53) Billy Martin	1,250	625.00	375.00
(54) Joe Marty	400.00	200.00	100.00
(55) Cliff Melton	400.00	200.00	100.00
(56) Steve Mesner	400.00	200.00	100.00
(57) Leon Mohr	400.00	200.00	100.00
(58) "Butch" Moran	400.00	200.00	100.00
(59) Glen Moulder	400.00	200.00	100.00
(60) Steve Nagy	400.00	200.00	100.00
(61) Roy Nicely	400.00	200.00	100.00
(62) Walt Nothe	400.00	200.00	100.00
(63) John O'Neill	400.00	200.00	100.00
(64) "Pluto" Oliver	400.00	200.00	100.00
(65) Al Olsen/Pose	400.00	200.00	100.00
(66) Al Olsen/Throwing	400.00	200.00	100.00
(67) John Ostrowski	400.00	200.00	100.00
(68) Roy Partee	400.00	200.00	100.00
(69) Bill Raimondi	400.00	200.00	100.00
(70) Bill Ramsey	400.00	200.00	100.00
(71) Len Ratto	400.00	200.00	100.00
(72) Xavier Rescigno	400.00	200.00	100.00
(73) John Ritchey/Btg	400.00	200.00	100.00
(74) John Ritchey/Catching	400.00	200.00	100.00
(75) Mickey Rocco	400.00	200.00	100.00
(76) John Rucker	400.00	200.00	100.00
(77) Clarence Russell	400.00	200.00	100.00
(78) Jack Salverson	400.00	200.00	100.00
(79) Charlie Schanz	400.00	200.00	125.00
(80) Bill Schuster	400.00	200.00	100.00
(81) Tom Seats	400.00	200.00	100.00
(82) Neil Sheridan	400.00	200.00	100.00
(83) Vince Shupe	400.00	200.00	100.00
(84) Joe Sprinz	400.00	200.00	100.00
(85) Chuck Stevens	400.00	200.00	100.00
(86) Harvey Storey	400.00	200.00	100.00
(87) Jim Tabor (Sacramento)	400.00	200.00	100.00
(88) Jim Tabor (Seattle)	400.00	200.00	100.00
(89) "Junior" Thompson	400.00	200.00	100.00
(90) Arky Vaughn	625.00	310.00	175.00
(91) Jackie Warner	400.00	200.00	100.00
(92) Jim Warner	400.00	200.00	100.00
(93) Dick Wenner	400.00	200.00	100.00
(94) Max West/Pose	400.00	200.00	100.00
(95) Max West (Batting swing.)	400.00	200.00	100.00
(96) Max West (Batting follow-through.)	400.00	200.00	100.00
(97) Hank Weyse	400.00	200.00	100.00
(98) "Fuzzy" White	400.00	200.00	100.00
(99) Jo Jo White	400.00	200.00	100.00
(100) Artie Wilson	400.00	200.00	100.00
(101) Bill Wilson	400.00	200.00	100.00
(102) Bobbie Wilson/Pose	400.00	200.00	100.00
(103) Bobbie Wilson/Fldg	400.00	200.00	100.00
(104) "Pinky" Woods	400.00	200.00	100.00
(105) Tony York	400.00	200.00	100.00
(106) Del Young	400.00	200.00	100.00
(107) Frank Zak	400.00	200.00	100.00

1950 Hage's Dairy

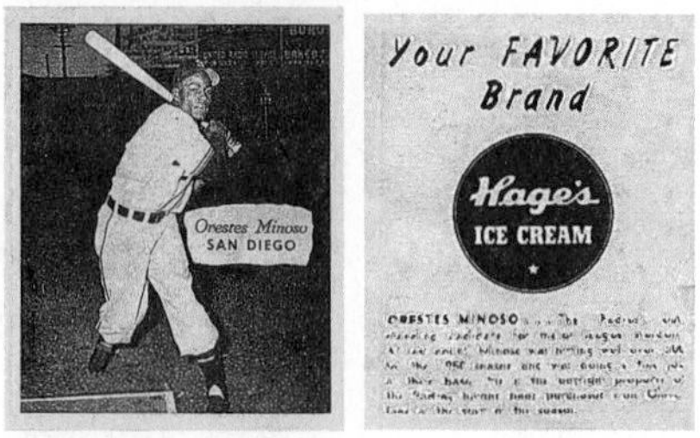

The 1950 P.C.L. set from Hage's Dairy was similar in design and size (about 2-5/8" x 3-1/8") to the previous year and was again distributed in popcorn boxes at San Diego's Lane Field. The 1950 cards are in black-and-white with most backs containing an advertisement for Hage's Milk, Ice Cream or Ice Cream Bars. Some backs are blank. The advertising backs also contain the player's name and either brief 1949 statistics or career highlights at bottom. Many players were issued in more than one pose. Again, Padres dominate the unnumbered set with lesser representation from the other P.C.L. clubs. For the 1950 edition all team names are referred to by city (no nicknames) and the typeface is smaller. Gaps have been left in the assigned numbering to accommodate future additions to the checklist.

		NM	EX	VG
Complete Set (128):		45,000	22,500	13,500
Common Player:		375.00	185.00	110.00
(1)	"Buster" Adams/Kneeling	375.00	185.00	110.00
(2a)	"Buster" Adams (Batting follow-through, with inscription.)	375.00	185.00	110.00
(2b)	"Buster" Adams (Batting follow-through, no inscription.)	375.00	185.00	110.00
(2c)	"Buster" Adams (Batting follow-through, body to left.)	375.00	185.00	110.00
(3a)	"Buster" Adams (Batting stance, caption box touching waist.)	375.00	185.00	110.00
(3b)	"Buster" Adams (Batting stance, caption box not touching waist.)	375.00	185.00	110.00
(4)	"Red" Adams	375.00	185.00	110.00
(5)	Dewey Adkins (Photo actually Albie Glossop.)	375.00	185.00	110.00
(6)	Rinaldo Ardizoia	375.00	185.00	110.00
(7)	Jose Bache	375.00	185.00	110.00
(8a)	Del Baker, Jim Reese (Bat visible at lower right.)	375.00	185.00	110.00
(8b)	Del Baker, Jim Reese (No bat visible.)	375.00	185.00	110.00
(9)	George Bamberger	375.00	185.00	110.00
(10)	Richard Barrett	375.00	185.00	110.00
(11)	Frank Baumholtz	375.00	185.00	110.00
(12)	Henry Behrman	375.00	185.00	110.00
(13)	Bill Bevens	375.00	185.00	110.00
(14)	Ernie Bickhaus	375.00	185.00	110.00
(15)	Bill Burgher/Pose	375.00	185.00	110.00
(16)	Bill Burgher/Catching	375.00	185.00	110.00
(17)	Mark Christman	375.00	185.00	110.00
(18)	Clint Conatser	375.00	185.00	110.00
(19)	Herb Conyers/Fldg	375.00	185.00	110.00
(20)	Herb Conyers/Btg	375.00	185.00	110.00
(21)	Jim Davis	375.00	185.00	110.00
(22)	Ted Del Guercio	375.00	185.00	110.00
(23)	Vince DiBiasi	375.00	185.00	110.00
(24)	Jess Dobernic	375.00	185.00	110.00
(25)	"Red" Embree/Pose	375.00	185.00	110.00
(26)	"Red" Embree/Pitching	375.00	185.00	110.00
(27)	Elbie Fletcher	375.00	185.00	110.00
(28)	Guy Fletcher	375.00	185.00	110.00
(30)	Tony Freitas	375.00	185.00	110.00
(31)	Denny Galehouse	375.00	185.00	110.00
(32)	Jack Graham/Pose (Looking to left.)	375.00	185.00	110.00
(33)	Jack Graham/Pose (Looking straight ahead.)	375.00	185.00	110.00
(34)	Jack Graham (Batting swing.)	375.00	185.00	110.00
(35)	Jack Graham (Batting stance.)	375.00	185.00	110.00
(36)	Orval Grove	375.00	185.00	110.00
(37)	Lee Handley	375.00	185.00	110.00
(38)	Ralph Hodgin	375.00	185.00	110.00
(39)	Don Johnson	375.00	185.00	110.00
(40)	Al Jurisich/Pose	375.00	185.00	110.00
(41)	Al Jurisich (Pitching wind-up.)	375.00	185.00	110.00
(42)	Al Jurisich (Pitching follow-through.)	375.00	185.00	110.00
(43)	Bill Kelly	375.00	185.00	110.00
(44)	Frank Kerr	375.00	185.00	110.00
(45)	Tom Kipp/Pose	375.00	185.00	110.00
(46)	Tom Kipp/Pitching	375.00	185.00	110.00
(47)	Mel Knezovich	375.00	185.00	110.00
(48)	Red Kress	375.00	185.00	110.00
(49)	Dario Lodigiani	375.00	185.00	110.00
(50)	Dennis Luby/Pose	375.00	185.00	110.00
(51)	Dennis Luby/Fldg	375.00	185.00	110.00
(52)	Al Lyons	375.00	185.00	110.00
(53)	Clarence Maddern	375.00	185.00	110.00
(54)	Joe Marty	375.00	185.00	110.00
(55)	Bob McCall	375.00	185.00	110.00
(56)	Cal McIrvin	375.00	185.00	110.00
(57)	Orestes Minoso (Batting follow-through.)	850.00	425.00	250.00
(58)	Orestes Minoso/Bunting	850.00	425.00	250.00
(59)	Leon Mohr	375.00	185.00	110.00
(60)	Dee Moore/Btg	375.00	185.00	110.00
(61)	Dee Moore/Catching	375.00	185.00	110.00
(62)	Jim Moran	375.00	185.00	110.00
(63)	Glen Moulder	375.00	185.00	110.00
(64)	Milt Neilsen/Pose	375.00	185.00	110.00
(65)	Milt Neilsen/Btg	375.00	185.00	110.00
(66)	Milt Neilsen/Throwing	375.00	185.00	110.00
(67)	Rube Novotney	375.00	185.00	110.00
(68)	Al Olsen	375.00	185.00	110.00
(69)	Manny Perez	375.00	185.00	110.00
(70)	Bill Raemondi (Raimondi)	375.00	185.00	110.00
(71)	Len Ratto	375.00	185.00	110.00
(72)	Mickey Rocco	375.00	185.00	110.00
(73)	Marv Rotblatt	375.00	185.00	110.00
(74)	Lynwood Rowe/Pose	400.00	200.00	120.00
(75)	Lynwood Rowe/Pitching	400.00	200.00	120.00
(76)	Clarence Russell	375.00	185.00	110.00
(77)	Hal Saltzman (Pitching follow-through.)	375.00	185.00	110.00
(78)	Hal Saltzman (Pitching wind-up.)	375.00	185.00	110.00
(79)	Hal Saltzman (Pitching, leg in air.)	375.00	185.00	110.00
(81)	Mike Sandlock	375.00	185.00	110.00
(82)	Bob Savage/Pose	375.00	185.00	110.00
(83)	Bob Savage/Pitching	375.00	185.00	110.00
(84)	Charlie Schanz	375.00	185.00	110.00
(85)	Bill Schuster	375.00	185.00	110.00
(86)	Neill Sheridan	375.00	185.00	110.00
(87)	Harry Simpson (Batting swing.)	525.00	260.00	150.00
(88)	Harry Simpson (Batting stance.)	525.00	260.00	150.00
(89)	Harry Simpson (Batting stance, close up.)	525.00	260.00	150.00
(90)	Harry Simpson (Batting follow-through.)	525.00	260.00	150.00
(91)	Elmer Singleton	375.00	185.00	110.00
(92)	Al Smith/Pose	375.00	185.00	110.00
(93)	Al Smith (Batting stance.)	375.00	185.00	110.00
(94)	Al Smith/Fldg	375.00	185.00	110.00
(95)	Alphonse Smith (Glove above knee.)	375.00	185.00	110.00
(96)	Alphonse Smith (Glove below knee.)	375.00	185.00	110.00
(97)	Steve Souchock	375.00	185.00	110.00
(98)	Jim Steiner	375.00	185.00	110.00
(99)	Harvey Storey (Batting stance.)	375.00	185.00	110.00
(100)	Harvey Storey (Swinging bat.)	375.00	185.00	110.00
(101)	Harvey Storey/Throwing	375.00	185.00	110.00
(102)	Harvey Storey/Fldg (Ball in glove.)	375.00	185.00	110.00
(103)	Max Surkont	375.00	185.00	110.00
(104)	Jim Tabor	375.00	185.00	110.00
(105)	Forrest Thompson	375.00	185.00	110.00
(106)	Mike Tresh/Pose	375.00	185.00	110.00
(107)	Mike Tresh/Catching	375.00	185.00	110.00
(108)	Ben Wade	375.00	185.00	110.00
(109)	Kenny Washington	375.00	185.00	110.00
(110)	Bill Waters/Pose	375.00	185.00	110.00
(111)	Bill Waters/Pitching	375.00	185.00	110.00
(112)	Roy Welmaker/Pose	375.00	185.00	110.00
(113)	Roy Welmaker/Pitching	375.00	185.00	110.00
(114)	Max West/Pose	375.00	185.00	110.00
(115)	Max West (Batting stance.)	375.00	185.00	110.00
(116)	Max West/Kneeling	375.00	185.00	110.00
(117)	Max West (Batting follow-through.)	375.00	185.00	110.00
(118)	Al White	375.00	185.00	110.00
(119)	"Whitey" Wietelmann/Pose	375.00	185.00	110.00
(120)	"Whitey" Wietelmann/Bunting	375.00	185.00	110.00
(121)	"Whitey" Wietelmann (Batting stance.)	375.00	185.00	110.00
(122)	"Whitey" Wietelmann/Throwing	375.00	185.00	110.00
(123)	Bobbie Wilson	375.00	185.00	110.00
(124)	Bobby Wilson	375.00	185.00	110.00
(125)	Roy Zimmerman	375.00	185.00	110.00
(126)	George Zuverink	375.00	185.00	110.00

1951 Hage's Dairy

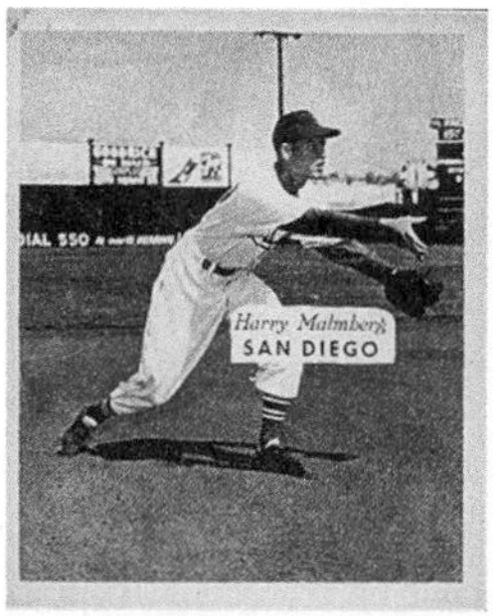

The final year of the Hage's P.C.L. issues saw the set reduced to 53 different unnumbered cards, all but 12 of them Padres. Among them are seven cards of Cleveland Indians players, which were issued during an exhibition series with the major league club, and six cards picturing members of the Hollywood Stars. No other P.C.L. teams are represented. The cards maintained the same size and style of the previous two years but were printed in more color tints, including blue, green, burgundy, gold, gray and sepia (but not black-and-white). The 1951 cards have blank backs and were again distributed in popcorn boxes at the San Diego stadium. The 1951 cards are the most common of the three sets issued by Hage's Dairy. The Indians and Stars players were issued in lesser quantities than the Padres, however, and command a higher value.

		NM	EX	VG
Complete Set (54):		18,000	9,000	5,500
Common Player:		300.00	150.00	90.00
(1)	"Buster" Adams	300.00	150.00	90.00
(2)	Del Baker	300.00	150.00	90.00
(3)	Ray Boone	850.00	425.00	250.00
(4)	Russ Christopher	300.00	150.00	90.00
(5)	Allie Clark	850.00	425.00	250.00
(6)	Herb Conyers	300.00	150.00	90.00
(7)	Luke Easter	850.00	420.00	250.00
(8)	"Red" Embree/Pitching (Foot in air.)	300.00	150.00	90.00
(9)	"Red" Embree/Pitching (Hands up.)	300.00	150.00	90.00
(10)	Jess Flores	850.00	425.00	250.00
(11)	Murray Franklin	300.00	150.00	90.00
(12)	Jack Graham/Portrait	300.00	150.00	90.00
(13)	Jack Graham/Btg	300.00	150.00	90.00
(14)	Gene Handley	300.00	150.00	90.00
(15)	Charles Harris	300.00	150.00	90.00
(16)	Sam Jones/Pitching (Hands back.)	300.00	150.00	90.00
(17)	Sam Jones/Pitching (Hands up.)	300.00	150.00	90.00
(18)	Sam Jones/Pitching (Leg in air.)	300.00	150.00	90.00
(19)	Al Jurisich	300.00	150.00	90.00
(20)	Frank Kerr/Btg	300.00	150.00	90.00
(21)	Frank Kerr/Catching	300.00	150.00	90.00
(22)	Dick Kinaman	300.00	150.00	90.00
(23)	Clarence Maddern/Btg	300.00	150.00	90.00
(24)	Clarence Maddern/Fldg	300.00	150.00	90.00
(25)	Harry Malmberg/Bunting	300.00	150.00	90.00
(26)	Harry Malmberg (Batting follow-through.)	300.00	150.00	90.00
(27)	Harry Malmberg/Fldg	300.00	150.00	90.00
(28)	Gordon Maltzberger	300.00	150.00	90.00
(29)	Al Olsen (Cleveland)	850.00	425.00	250.00
(30)	Al Olsen (San Diego)	300.00	150.00	90.00
(31)	Jimmy Reese (Clapping)	350.00	175.00	100.00
(32)	Jimmy Reese (Hands on knees.)	350.00	175.00	100.00
(33)	Al Rosen	900.00	450.00	270.00
(34)	Joe Rowell	300.00	150.00	90.00
(35)	Mike Sandlock	300.00	150.00	90.00
(36)	George Schmees	300.00	150.00	90.00
(37)	Harry Simpson	300.00	150.00	90.00
(38)	Charlie Sipple	300.00	150.00	90.00
(39)	Harvey Storey (Batting follow-through.)	300.00	150.00	90.00
(40)	Harvey Storey (Batting stance.)	300.00	150.00	90.00
(41)	Harvey Storey/Fldg	300.00	150.00	90.00
(42)	Jack Tobin	300.00	150.00	90.00
(43)	Frank Tornay	300.00	150.00	90.00
(44)	Thurman Tucker	300.00	150.00	90.00
(45)	Ben Wade	300.00	150.00	90.00
(46)	Roy Welmaker	300.00	150.00	90.00
(47)	Leroy Wheat	300.00	150.00	90.00
(48)	Don White	300.00	150.00	90.00
(49)	"Whitey" Wietelman/Btg	300.00	150.00	90.00
(50)	"Whitey" Wietelman/Fldg	300.00	150.00	90.00
(51)	Bobby Wilson/Btg	300.00	150.00	90.00
(52)	Bobby Wilson/Fldg	300.00	150.00	90.00
(53)	Tony York	300.00	150.00	90.00
(54)	George Zuverink	850.00	425.00	250.00

1886 Hancock's Syracuse Stars

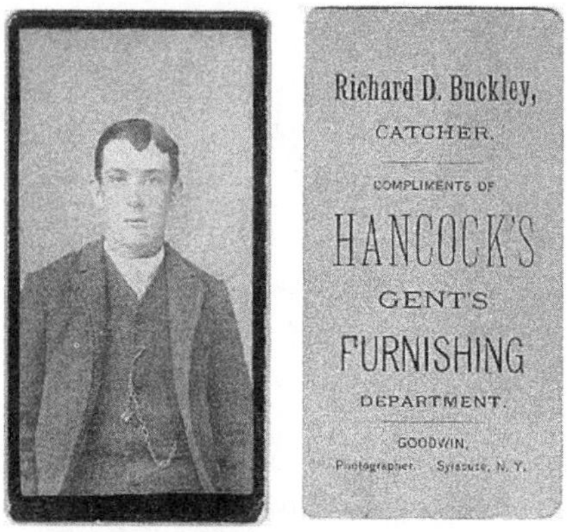

Currently representing the earliest known minor league baseball cards is this issue by a Syracuse department store's menswear department. The 1-5/8" x 3-3/16" cards feature sepia photos glued to a stiff black cardboard backing with a gilt edge. The photos show the players in suits, presumably from the sponsor's racks. Backs have the player name and position printed at top. At center is an ad for Hancock's. At bottom is a credit line to "Goodwin" as photographer. Each card is currently known in only a single example. It is possible other players of the International League Stars may yet be discovered.

Values Undetermined

(1)	Richard D. Buckley
(2)	Douglas Crothers (SGC-graded EX sold in 2009 auction for $16,335.)
(3)	Philip H. Tomney

1960 Henry House Wieners Seattle Rainiers

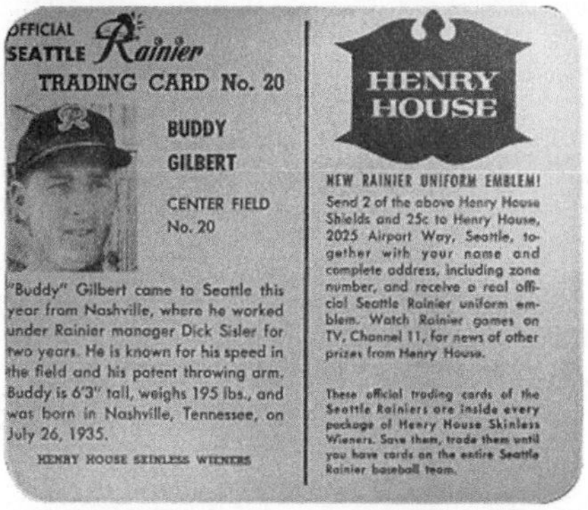
OFFICIAL SEATTLE Rainier
TRADING CARD No. 20
BUDDY GILBERT
CENTER FIELD No. 20
"Buddy" Gilbert came to Seattle this year from Nashville, where he worked under Rainier manager Dick Sisler for two years. He is known for his speed in the field and his potent throwing arm. Buddy is 6'3" tall, weighs 195 lbs., and was born in Nashville, Tennessee, on July 26, 1935.
HENRY HOUSE SKINLESS WIENERS
HENRY HOUSE
NEW RAINIER UNIFORM EMBLEM!
Send 2 of the above Henry House Shields and 25c to Henry House, 2025 Airport Way, Seattle, together with your name and complete address, including zone number, and receive a real official Seattle Rainier uniform emblem. Watch Rainier games on TV, Channel 11, for news of other prizes from Henry House.
These official trading cards of the Seattle Rainiers are inside every package of Henry House Skinless Wieners. Save them, trade them until you have cards on the entire Seattle Rainier baseball team.

Eighteen different cards are known in this hot dog set; most players played major league baseball prior to their appearance with the Pacific Coast League Seattle Rainiers in 1960. Printed in red, the 4-1/2" x 3-3/4" cards are skip-numbered by player uniform number.

		NM	EX	VG
Complete Set (18):		5,500	2,750	1,600
Common Player:		300.00	150.00	90.00
2	Harry Malmberg	300.00	150.00	90.00
3	Francisco Obregon	300.00	150.00	90.00
4	Johnny O'Brien	375.00	185.00	110.00
5	Gordon Coleman	300.00	150.00	90.00
6	Bill Hain	300.00	150.00	90.00
8	Dick Sisler	300.00	150.00	90.00
9	Jerry Zimmerman	300.00	150.00	90.00
10	Hal Bevan	300.00	150.00	90.00
14	Rudy Regaldo	300.00	150.00	90.00
15	Paul Pettit	300.00	150.00	90.00
20	Buddy Gilbert	300.00	150.00	90.00
21	Erv Palica	300.00	150.00	90.00
22	Joe Taylor	300.00	150.00	90.00
25	Bill Kennedy	300.00	150.00	90.00
26	Dave Stenhouse	300.00	150.00	90.00
28	Ray Ripplemeyer	300.00	150.00	90.00
30	Charlie Beamon	300.00	150.00	90.00
33	Don Rudolph	300.00	150.00	90.00

1888 S.F. Hess California League (N321)

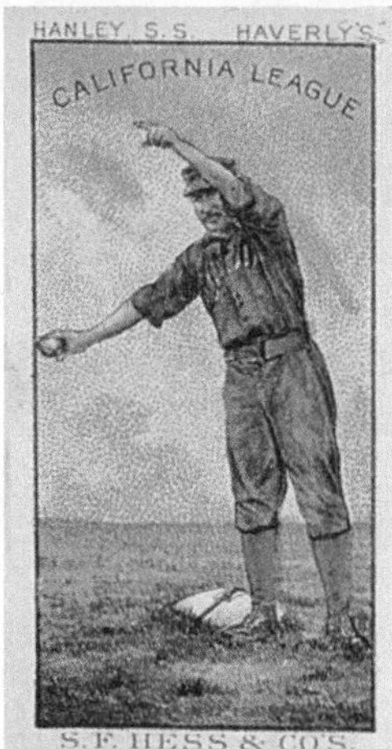
HANLEY S.S. HAVERLY'S
CALIFORNIA LEAGUE
S.F. HESS & CO'S.
CREOLE CIGARETTES.

One of several tobacco card sets produced by S.F. Hess & Co. of Rochester, this rare 40-card issue features players from the California League. The cards measure 2-7/8" x 1-1/2" and feature color drawings of players. The player's name and team are printed along the top margin of the card, while the words "S.F. Hess and Co.'s/Creole Cigarettes" appear at the bottom. "California League" is also printed in large capital letters above the player drawing, while the 1888 copyright date appears below. There are 35 players (including one umpire) in the set, and five players are pictured on two cards each, resulting in 40 different cards. One example each of 30 of the cards have been discovered printed on thin paper stock, though the exact nature of that version is undetermined; currently values are about equal to the regular-issue version.

		NM	EX	VG
Common Player:		5,400	3,000	2,250
(1)	Eddie Bennett	5,400	3,000	2,250
(2)	George Borchers	5,400	3,000	2,250
(3)	Tom Buckley	5,400	3,000	2,250
(4)	Turk Burke/Btg	5,400	3,000	2,250
(5)	Turk Burke (Ready to pitch.)	5,400	3,000	2,250
(6)	Frank Carroll	5,400	3,000	2,250
(7)	John Donohue	5,400	3,000	2,250
(8)	Jack Donovan	5,400	3,000	2,250
(9)	Michael Finn	5,400	3,000	2,250
(10)	Jim Gagus	5,400	3,000	2,250
(11)	William Gurnett			
(12)	George Hanley	5,400	3,000	2,250
(13)	Pop Hardie (C., wearing mask.)	5,400	3,000	2,250
(14)	Pop Hardie (C.F., with bat.)	5,400	3,000	2,250
(15)	Jack Hayes	5,400	3,000	2,250
(16)	Jack Lawton	5,400	3,000	2,250
(17)	Rube Levy	5,400	3,000	2,250
(18)	Daniel Long	5,400	3,000	2,250
(19)	Tom McCord	5,400	3,000	2,250
(20)	Peter Meegan	5,400	3,000	2,250
(21)	Henry Moore	5,400	3,000	2,250
(22)	James Mullee	5,400	3,000	2,250
(23)	Billy Newhert	5,400	3,000	2,250
(24)	Joseph Noonan	5,400	3,000	2,250
(25)	Harry O'Day	5,400	3,000	2,250
(26)	Hip Perrier	5,400	3,000	2,250
(27)	Thomas Powers/Catching (1st B.)	5,400	3,000	2,250
(28)	Thomas Powers (1st B. & Capt., with bat)	5,400	3,000	2,250
(29)	Jack Ryan	5,400	3,000	2,250
(30)	Charles Selna	5,400	3,000	2,250
(31)	Joseph Shea	5,400	3,000	2,250
(32)	Jack Sheridan/Umpire	5,400	3,000	2,250
(33)	"Big" Smith	5,400	3,000	2,250
(34)	Hugh Smith	5,400	3,000	2,250
(35)	John Smith	5,400	3,000	2,250
(36)	Leonard Stockwell/Throwing	5,400	3,000	2,250
(37)	Leonard Stockwell (With bat.)	5,400	3,000	2,250
(38)	Charles Sweeney	5,400	3,000	2,250
(39)	Pop Swett	5,400	3,000	2,250
(40)	Milton Whitehead	5,400	3,000	2,250

1888 S.F. Hess California League (N338-1)

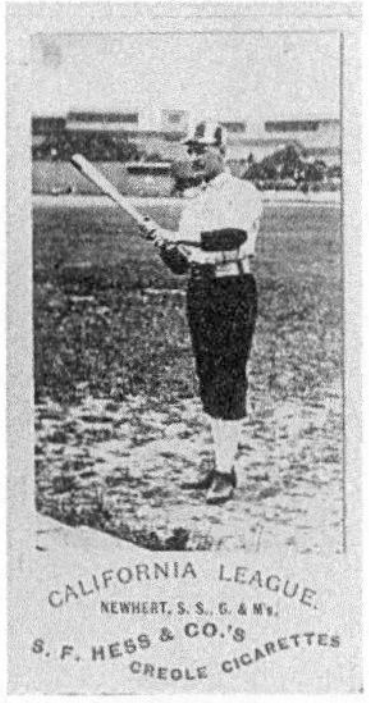
CALIFORNIA LEAGUE
S. F. HESS & CO.'S
CREOLE CIGARETTES

This tobacco card set picturing players from the California League is one of the rarest of all 19th Century issues. Issued in the late 1880s by S.F. Hess & Co. of Rochester, these 2-7/8" x 1-1/2" cards are so rare that only several examples are known to exist. Some of the photos in the N338-1 set are identical to the drawings in the N321 set, issued by S.F. Hess in 1888. The N338-1 cards are found with the words "California League" printed in an arc either above or below the player photo. The player's name appears below the photo. At the bottom of the card the words "S.F. Hess & Co.'s Creole Cigarettes" are printed in a rolling style.

		NM	EX	VG
Common Player:		18,000	9,000	5,250
(1)	Borsher	18,000	9,000	5,250
(2)	Buckley	18,000	9,000	5,250
(3)	Carroll	18,000	9,000	5,250
(4)	Ebright	18,000	9,000	5,250
(5)	Gagur (Gagus)	18,000	9,000	5,250
(6)	Incell	18,000	9,000	5,250
(7)	Lawton	18,000	9,000	5,250
(8)	Levy/Throwing	18,000	9,000	5,250
(9)	Levy (With bat.)	18,000	9,000	5,250
(10)	McDonald	18,000	9,000	5,250
(11)	McGinty	20,250	10,125	6,075
(12)	Meegan	18,000	9,000	5,250
(13)	Newhert	18,000	9,000	5,250
(14)	Noonan	18,000	9,000	5,250
(15)	Perrier	18,000	9,000	5,250
(16)	Perrier, H. Smith	18,000	9,000	5,250
(17)	Ryan	18,000	9,000	5,250
(18)	J. Smith, N. Smith	18,000	9,000	5,250
(19)	Sweeney	18,000	9,000	5,250

1888 S.F. Hess Newsboys League (N333)

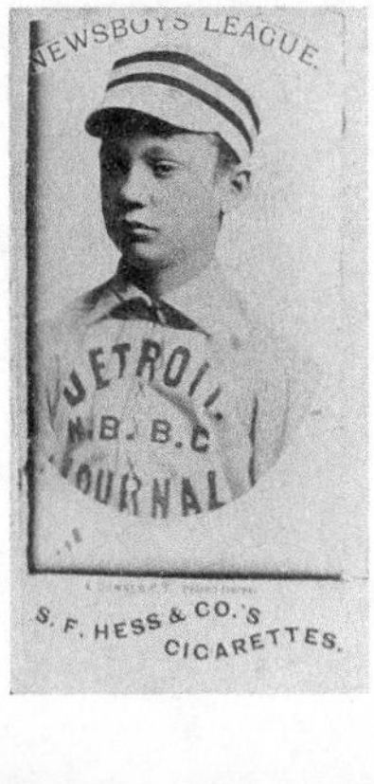
NEWSBOYS LEAGUE
DETROIT
N.B.B.C
JOURNAL
S. F. HESS & CO.'S
CIGARETTES.

Although not picturing professional baseball players, these cards issued by S.F. Hess and Co. have a baseball theme. Cards measure 1-1/2" x 2-7/8" and feature pictures of "newsies" from papers in eight different cities (Rochester, Cleveland, Philadelphia, Boston, Albany, Detroit, New York and Syracuse). The boys are pictured in a photographs wearing baseball uniforms, often bearing the name of their newspaper. The boy's name, position and newspaper are printed below, while the words "Newsboys League" appears in capital letters at the top of the card. No identification is provided for the four Philadelphia newsboys, so a photo description is provided in the checklist that follows. Gaps have been left in the assigned numbering for future additions.

		NM	EX	VG
Common Player:		2,400	1,200	725.00
(1)	R.J. Bell	2,400	1,200	725.00
(2)	Bibby (Boston Globe)	2,400	1,200	725.00
(3)	Binden	2,400	1,200	725.00
(4)	Bowen	2,400	1,200	725.00
(5)	Boyle	2,400	1,200	725.00
(6)	Britcher	2,400	1,200	725.00
(7)	Caine	2,400	1,200	725.00
(8)	I. Cohen	2,400	1,200	725.00
(9)	R. Cohen	2,400	1,200	725.00
(10)	Collins (Boston Globe)	2,400	1,200	725.00
(11)	Cross	2,400	1,200	725.00
(12)	F. Cuddy	2,400	1,200	725.00
(13)	E. Daisey	2,400	1,200	725.00
(14)	Davis	2,400	1,200	725.00
(15)	B. Dinsmore	2,400	1,200	725.00
(16)	Donovan	2,400	1,200	725.00
(17)	A. Downer	2,400	1,200	725.00
(18)	Drory (Boston Globe)	2,400	1,200	725.00
(19)	Fanelly	2,400	1,200	725.00
(20)	J. Flood	2,400	1,200	725.00
(21)	C. Gallagher	2,400	1,200	725.00
(22)	M.H. Gallagher	2,400	1,200	725.00
(23)	D. Galligher	2,400	1,200	725.00
(24)	J. Galligher	2,400	1,200	725.00
(25)	Haskins	2,400	1,200	725.00
(26)	Herze	2,400	1,200	725.00
(27)	Holmes (Press & Knickerbocker)	2,400	1,200	725.00
(28)	F. Horan	2,400	1,200	725.00
(29)	Hosler	2,400	1,200	725.00
(30)	Hyde (Boston Globe)	2,400	1,200	725.00
(31)	Keilty	2,400	1,200	725.00
(32)	C. Kellogg	2,400	1,200	725.00
(33)	Mahoney (Rochester Post-Express)	2,400	1,200	725.00
(34)	Mayer	2,400	1,200	725.00
(35)	McCourt (Boston Globe)	2,400	1,200	725.00
(36)	I. McDonald	2,400	1,200	725.00
(37)	McDowell (Rochester)	2,400	1,200	725.00
(38)	McGrady	2,400	1,200	725.00
(39)	O'Brien	2,400	1,200	725.00
(41)	E.C. Murphy	2,400	1,200	725.00
(42)	Sabin	2,400	1,200	725.00
(43)	Shedd	2,400	1,200	725.00
(44)	R. Sheehan	2,400	1,200	725.00
(45)	W. Smith (Syracuse Herald)	2,400	1,200	725.00
(46)	Talbot	2,400	1,200	725.00
(47)	Walsh	2,400	1,200	725.00
(48)	Whitman	2,400	1,200	725.00
(49)	Yeomans	2,400	1,200	725.00
(50)	Cleveland Newsboy (In cap, facing right.)	2,400	1,200	725.00
(51)	Philadelphia Newsboy (Hair parted on right side.)	2,400	1,200	725.00
(52)	Philadelphia Newsboy (Hair parted on left side.)	2,400	1,200	725.00
(53)	Philadelphia Newsboy (No part in hair.)	2,400	1,200	725.00
(54)	Philadelphia Newsboy (Head shaved.)	2,400	1,200	725.00

1949 Hollywood Stars Team Issue

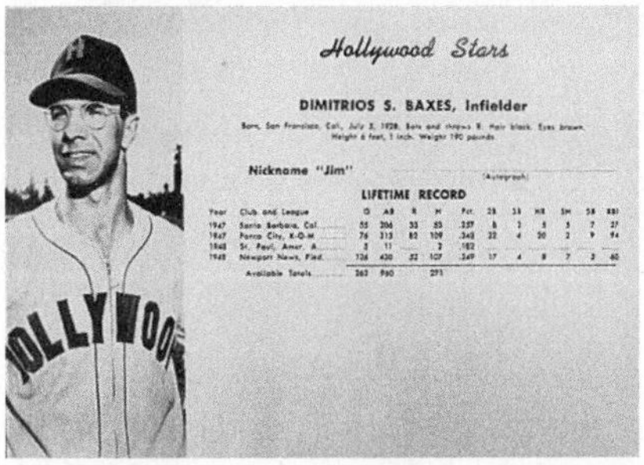
Hollywood Stars
DIMITRIOS S. BAXES, Infielder
Nickname "Jim"
LIFETIME RECORD

A team issue probably related to similar 1948-49 cards produced by Pacific Coast League cross-town rivals the L.A. Angels, these cards were likely produced by the publisher of the teams' yearbooks and sold at stadium souvenir stands. The cards are blank-backed, printed in black-and-white on thin semi-gloss cardboard, measuring 7-1/16" x 4-7/8". Portrait or posed action photos appear at left with complete major and minor league stats at right. A space for an autograph appears beneath the player's biographical data. The unnumbered cards are checklisted here in alphabetical order.

		NM	EX	VG
Complete Set (24):		500.00	250.00	150.00
Common Player:		25.00	12.50	7.50
(1)	Jim Baxes	25.00	12.50	7.50
(2)	George Fallon	25.00	12.50	7.50
(3)	John Fitzpatrick	25.00	12.50	7.50
(4)	George Genovese	25.00	12.50	7.50

		NM	EX	VG
(5)	Herb Gorman	75.00	37.50	22.50
(6)	Gene Handley	25.00	12.50	7.50
(7)	Fred Haney	25.00	12.50	7.50
(8)	Jim Hughes	25.00	12.50	7.50
(9)	Frank Kelleher	25.00	12.50	7.50
(10)	Gordy Maltzberger	25.00	12.50	7.50
(11)	Glen Moulder	25.00	12.50	7.50
(12)	Irv Noren	25.00	12.50	7.50
(13)	Ed Oliver	25.00	12.50	7.50
(14)	Karl Olsen	25.00	12.50	7.50
(15)	John O'Neil	25.00	12.50	7.50
(16)	Jack Paepke	25.00	12.50	7.50
(17)	Willard Ramsdell	25.00	12.50	7.50
(18)	Jack Salveson	25.00	12.50	7.50
(19)	Mike Sandlock	25.00	12.50	7.50
(20)	Art Shallock	25.00	12.50	7.50
(21)	Andy Skurski	25.00	12.50	7.50
(22)	Chuck Stevens	25.00	12.50	7.50
(23)	Al Unser	25.00	12.50	7.50
(24)	George Woods	25.00	12.50	7.50

1950 Hollywood Stars Team Issue

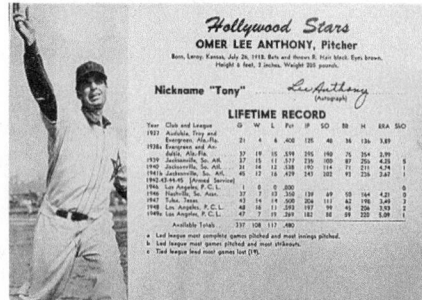

Virtually identical in format to the previous year's issue, the 1950 set differs principally in the inclusion of a facsimile autograph on front. In 1950, the Hollywood Stars were the PCL affiliate of the Brooklyn Dodgers. Both sets were listed in "The American Card Catalog" as W720.

		NM	EX	VG
Complete Set (32):		850.00	425.00	250.00
Common Player:		25.00	12.50	7.50
(1)	Lee Anthony	25.00	12.50	7.50
(2)	Bill Antonello	25.00	12.50	7.50
(3)	Dick Barrett	25.00	12.50	7.50
(4)	Jim Baxes	25.00	12.50	7.50
(5)	Clint Conatser	25.00	12.50	7.50
(6)	Cliff Dapper	25.00	12.50	7.50
(7)	George Fallon	25.00	12.50	7.50
(8)	John Fitzpatrick	25.00	12.50	7.50
(9)	Murray Franklin	75.00	37.50	22.50
(10)	Herb Gorman	75.00	37.50	22.50
(11)	Gene Handley	25.00	12.50	7.50
(12)	Fred Haney	25.00	12.50	7.50
(13)	Clarence Hicks	25.00	12.50	7.50
(14)	Herb Karpel	200.00	100.00	60.00
(15)	Frank Kelleher	25.00	12.50	7.50
(16)	Ken Lehman	25.00	12.50	7.50
(17)	Johnny Lindell	25.00	12.50	7.50
(18)	Gordy Maltzberger	25.00	12.50	7.50
(19)	Dan Menendez	25.00	12.50	7.50
(20)	Pershing Mondroff	25.00	12.50	7.50
(21)	Glen Moulder	25.00	12.50	7.50
(22)	John O'Neil	25.00	12.50	7.50
(23)	Jack Paepke	25.00	12.50	7.50
(24)	Jean Roy	25.00	12.50	7.50
(25)	Jack Salveson	25.00	12.50	7.50
(26)	Mike Sandlock	25.00	12.50	7.50
(27)	Ed Saver	25.00	12.50	7.50
(28)	George Schmees	25.00	12.50	7.50
(29)	Art Shallock	25.00	12.50	7.50
(30)	Chuck Stevens	25.00	12.50	7.50
(31)	Ben Wade	25.00	12.50	7.50
(32)	George Woods	25.00	12.50	7.50

1957 Hollywood Stars Team Issue

Presumably issued by the team, which had a working relationship with the Pittsburgh Pirates, this 23-card set features black-and-white blank-backed photos in a 4-1/8" x 6-

3/16" format. Each picture has a facsimile autograph printed in black across the front. The unnumbered cards are checklisted here alphabetically.

		NM	EX	VG
Complete Set (23):		900.00	450.00	275.00
Common Player:		40.00	20.00	12.00
(1)	Jim Baumer	40.00	20.00	12.00
(2)	Carlos Bernier	40.00	20.00	12.00
(3)	Bill Causion	40.00	20.00	12.00
(4)	Chuck Churn	40.00	20.00	12.00
(5)	Bennie Daniels	40.00	20.00	12.00
(6)	Joe Duhem	40.00	20.00	12.00
(7)	John Fitzpatrick	40.00	20.00	12.00
(8)	Bob Garber	40.00	20.00	12.00
(9)	Bill Hall	40.00	20.00	12.00
(10)	Forrest "Spook" Jacobs	50.00	25.00	15.00
(11)	Clyde King	40.00	20.00	12.00
(12)	Nick Koback	40.00	20.00	12.00
(13)	Pete Naton	40.00	20.00	12.00
(14)	George O'Donnell	40.00	20.00	12.00
(15)	Paul Pettit	40.00	20.00	12.00
(16)	Curt Raydon	40.00	20.00	12.00
(17)	Leo Rodriguez	40.00	20.00	12.00
(18)	Don Rowe	40.00	20.00	12.00
(19)	Dick Smith	40.00	20.00	12.00
(20)	R.C. Stevens	40.00	20.00	12.00
(21)	Ben Wade	40.00	20.00	12.00
(22)	Fred Waters	40.00	20.00	12.00
(23)	George Witt	40.00	20.00	12.00

1912 Home Run Kisses (E136)

This 90-card set of Pacific Coast League players was produced in 1912 by the San Francisco candy company of Collins-McCarthy. Each card measures about 2-1/4" x 4-3/16" and features sepia-toned player photos surrounded by an ornate frame. The front of the card has the words "Home Run Kisses" above the player's name. Some cards found are blank-backed, but others exist with a back that advises "Save Home Run Kisses Pictures for Valuable Premiums" along with other details of the Collins-McCarthy promotion. A third type of back exists with an advertising logo for "BARDELL / SEPIA/ SAN FRANCISCO." Redeemed cards were punch-cancelled, often with a heart-shaped hole.

		NM	EX	VG
Complete Set (90):		90,000	45,000	27,000
Common Player:		1,000	500.00	300.00
(1)	Ables	1,000	500.00	300.00
(2)	Agnew	1,000	500.00	300.00
(3)	Altman	1,000	500.00	300.00
(4)	Frank Arrelanes (Arellanes)	1,000	500.00	300.00
(5)	Auer	1,000	500.00	300.00
(6)	Bancroft	6,500	3,250	1,950
(7)	Bayless	1,000	500.00	300.00
(8)	Berry	1,000	500.00	300.00
(9)	Boles	1,000	500.00	300.00
(10)	Brashear	1,000	500.00	300.00
(11)	Brooks (Los Angeles)	1,000	500.00	300.00
(12)	Brooks (Oakland)	1,000	500.00	300.00
(13)	Brown	1,000	500.00	300.00
(14)	Burrell	1,000	500.00	300.00
(15)	Butler	1,000	500.00	300.00
(16)	Carlisle	1,000	500.00	300.00
(17)	Carson	1,000	500.00	300.00
(18)	Castleton	1,000	500.00	300.00
(19)	Chadbourne	1,000	500.00	300.00
(20)	Check	1,000	500.00	300.00
(21)	Core	1,000	500.00	300.00
(22)	Corhan	1,000	500.00	300.00
(23)	Coy	1,000	500.00	300.00
(24)	Daley	1,000	500.00	300.00
(25)	Dillon	1,000	500.00	300.00
(26)	Doane	1,000	500.00	300.00
(27)	Driscoll	1,000	500.00	300.00
(28)	Fisher	1,000	500.00	300.00
(29)	Flater	1,000	500.00	300.00
(30)	Gaddy	1,000	500.00	300.00
(31)	Gregg	1,000	500.00	300.00
(32)	Gregory	1,000	500.00	300.00
(33)	Harkness	1,000	500.00	300.00
(34)	Heitmuller	1,000	500.00	300.00
(35)	Henley	1,000	500.00	300.00
(36)	Hiester	1,000	500.00	300.00
(37)	Hoffman	1,000	500.00	300.00
(38)	Hogan	1,000	500.00	300.00
(39)	Hosp	1,000	500.00	300.00
(40)	Howley	1,000	500.00	300.00
(41)	Ireland	1,000	500.00	300.00
(42)	Johnson	1,000	500.00	300.00
(43)	Kane	1,000	500.00	300.00
(44)	Klawitter	1,000	500.00	300.00
(45)	Kreitz	1,000	500.00	300.00
(46)	Krueger	1,000	500.00	300.00
(47)	Leard	1,000	500.00	300.00
(48)	Leverencz	1,000	500.00	300.00
(49)	Lewis	1,000	500.00	300.00
(50)	Bill Lindsay	1,000	500.00	300.00
(51)	Litschi	1,000	500.00	300.00
(52)	Lober	1,000	500.00	300.00
(53)	Malarkey	1,000	500.00	300.00
(54)	Martinoni	1,000	500.00	300.00
(55)	McArdle	1,000	500.00	300.00
(56)	McCorry	1,000	500.00	300.00
(57)	McDowell	1,000	500.00	300.00
(58)	McIver	1,000	500.00	300.00
(59)	Metzger	1,000	500.00	300.00
(60)	Miller	1,000	500.00	300.00
(61)	Mundorf	1,000	500.00	300.00
(62)	Nagle	1,000	500.00	300.00
(63)	Noyes	1,000	500.00	300.00
(64)	Olmstead	1,000	500.00	300.00
(65)	O'Rourke	1,000	500.00	300.00
(66)	Page	1,000	500.00	300.00
(67)	Parkins	1,000	500.00	300.00
(68)	Patterson (Oakland)	1,000	500.00	300.00
(69)	Patterson (Vernon)	1,000	500.00	300.00
(70)	Pernoll	1,000	500.00	300.00
(71)	Powell	1,000	500.00	300.00
(72)	Price	1,000	500.00	300.00
(73)	Raftery	1,000	500.00	300.00
(74)	Raleigh	1,000	500.00	300.00
(75)	Rogers	1,000	500.00	300.00
(76)	Schmidt	1,000	500.00	300.00
(77)	Schwenk	1,000	500.00	300.00
(78)	Sheehan	1,000	500.00	300.00
(79)	Shinn	1,000	500.00	300.00
(80)	Slagle	1,000	500.00	300.00
(81)	Smith	1,000	500.00	300.00
(82)	Stone	1,000	500.00	300.00
(83)	Swain	1,000	500.00	300.00
(84)	Taylor	1,000	500.00	300.00
(85)	Tiedeman	1,000	500.00	300.00
(86)	Toner	1,000	500.00	300.00
(87)	Tozer	1,000	500.00	300.00
(88)	Van Buren	1,000	500.00	300.00
(89)	Williams	1,000	500.00	300.00
(90)	Zacher	1,000	500.00	300.00

1940 Hughes Frozen Confections Sacramento Solons

 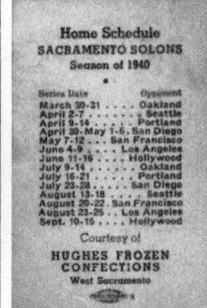

These borderless 2" x 3" black-and-white cards of the Sacramento Solons can be found in two versions, either blank-backed or with the 1940 Solons Pacific Coast League schedule printed on back. Fronts featured action poses with a facsimile autograph.

		NM	EX	VG
Complete Set (20):		8,250	4,125	2,475
Common Player:		450.00	220.00	135.00
(1)	Mel Almada	450.00	220.00	135.00
(2)	Frank Asbell	450.00	220.00	135.00
(3)	Larry Barton	450.00	220.00	135.00
(4)	Robert Blattner	450.00	220.00	135.00
(5)	Bennie Borgmann	450.00	220.00	135.00
(6)	Tony Freitas	450.00	220.00	135.00
(7)	Art Garibaldi	450.00	220.00	135.00
(8)	Jim Grilk	450.00	220.00	135.00
(9)	Gene Handley	450.00	220.00	135.00
(10)	Oscar Judd	450.00	220.00	135.00
(11)	Lynn King	450.00	220.00	135.00
(12)	Norbert Kleinke	450.00	220.00	135.00
(13)	Max Marshall	450.00	220.00	135.00
(14)	William McLaughlin	450.00	220.00	135.00
(15)	Bruce Ogrodowski	450.00	220.00	135.00
(16)	Franich Riel	450.00	220.00	135.00
(17)	Bill Schmidt	450.00	220.00	135.00
(18)	Melvin Wasley	450.00	220.00	135.00
(19)	Chet Wieczorek	450.00	220.00	135.00
(20)	Deb Williams	450.00	220.00	135.00

1957 Hygrade Meats Seattle Rainiers

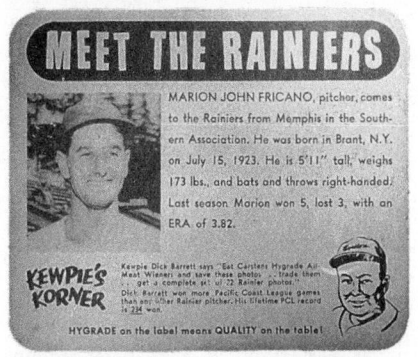

While the front of the cards mentions a complete set of 22 cards, only a dozen have been checklisted to date. The round-cornered cards measure 4-1/2" x 3-3/4" and are printed in red on white. Backs are blank. The cards feature only players of the Pacific Coast League Seattle Rainiers. The cards are unnumbered.

		NM	EX	VG
Common Player:		400.00	200.00	120.00
(1)	Dick Aylward	400.00	200.00	120.00
(2)	Bob Balcena	400.00	200.00	120.00
(3)	Jim Dyck	400.00	200.00	120.00
(4)	Marion Fricano	400.00	200.00	120.00
(5)	Bill Glynn	400.00	200.00	120.00
(6)	Larry Jansen	400.00	200.00	120.00
(7)	Bill Kennedy	400.00	200.00	120.00
(8)	Jack Lohrke	400.00	200.00	120.00
(9)	Frank O'Doul	800.00	400.00	240.00
(10)	Ray Orteig	400.00	200.00	120.00
(11)	Joe Taylor	400.00	200.00	120.00
(12)	Morrie (Maury) Wills	800.00	400.00	240.00

I

1912 Imperial Tobacco (C46)

This minor league set, issued in 1912 by the Imperial Tobacco Co., is the only tobacco baseball set issued in Canada. Designated as C46 in the American Card Catalog, each sepia-toned card measures 1-1/2" x 2-5/8" and features a distinctive card design that pictures the player inside an oval surrounded by a simulated woodgrain background featuring a bat, ball and glove in the borders. The player's last name appears in capital letters in a panel beneath the oval. (An exception is the card of James Murray, whose caption includes both first and last names.) The backs include the player's name and team at the top, followed by a brief biography. The 90 subjects in the set are members of the eight teams in the Eastern League (Rochester, Toronto, Buffalo, Newark, Providence, Baltimore, Montreal and Jersey City), even though the card backs refer to it as the International League. The set contains many players with major league experience, including Hall of Famers Joe Kelley and Joe "Iron Man" McGinnity.

		NM	EX	VG
Complete Set (90):		13,000	4,290	1,690
Common Player:		150.00	50.00	20.00
1	William O'Hara	180.00	60.00	30.00
2	James McGinley	160.00	55.00	27.00
3	"Frenchy" LeClaire	150.00	50.00	20.00
4	John White	150.00	50.00	20.00
5	James Murray	150.00	50.00	20.00
6	Joe Ward	150.00	50.00	20.00
7	Whitey Alperman	150.00	50.00	20.00
8	"Natty" Nattress	150.00	50.00	20.00
9	Fred Sline	150.00	50.00	20.00
10	Royal Rock	150.00	50.00	20.00
11	Ray Demmitt	150.00	50.00	20.00
12	"Butcher Boy" Schmidt	150.00	50.00	20.00
13	Samuel Frock	150.00	50.00	20.00
14	Fred Burchell	150.00	50.00	20.00
15	Jack Kelley	150.00	50.00	20.00
16	Frank Barberich	150.00	50.00	20.00
17	Frank Corridon	150.00	50.00	20.00
18	"Doc" Adkins	150.00	50.00	20.00
19	Jack Dunn	150.00	50.00	20.00
20	James Walsh	150.00	50.00	20.00
21	Charles Hanford	150.00	50.00	20.00
22	Dick Rudolph	150.00	50.00	20.00
23	Curt Elston	150.00	50.00	20.00
24	Charles Silton (Sitton)	150.00	50.00	20.00
25	Charlie French	150.00	50.00	20.00
26	John Ganzel	150.00	50.00	20.00
27	Joe Kelley	850.00	280.00	110.00
28	Benny Meyers	150.00	50.00	20.00
29	George Schirm	150.00	50.00	20.00
30	William Purtell	150.00	50.00	20.00
31	Bayard Sharpe	150.00	50.00	20.00
32	Tony Smith	150.00	50.00	20.00
33	John Lush	150.00	50.00	20.00
34	William Collins	150.00	50.00	20.00
35	Art Phelan	150.00	50.00	20.00
36	Edward Phelps	150.00	50.00	20.00
37	"Rube" Vickers	150.00	50.00	20.00
38	Cy Seymour	150.00	50.00	20.00
39	"Shadow" Carroll	150.00	50.00	20.00
40	Jake Gettman	150.00	50.00	20.00
41	Luther Taylor	400.00	130.00	52.00
42	Walter Justis	150.00	50.00	20.00
43	Robert Fisher	150.00	50.00	20.00
44	Fred Parent	150.00	50.00	20.00
45	James Dygert	150.00	50.00	20.00
46	Johnnie Butler	150.00	50.00	20.00
47	Fred Mitchell	150.00	50.00	20.00
48	Heinie Batch	150.00	50.00	20.00
49	Michael Corcoran	150.00	50.00	20.00
50	Edward Doescher	150.00	50.00	20.00
51	George Wheeler	150.00	50.00	20.00
52	Elijah Jones	150.00	50.00	20.00
53	Fred Truesdale	150.00	50.00	20.00
54	Fred Beebe	150.00	50.00	20.00
55	Louis Brockett	150.00	50.00	20.00
56	Robt. Wells	150.00	50.00	20.00
57	"Lew" McAllister	150.00	50.00	20.00
58	Ralph Stroud	150.00	50.00	20.00
59	James Manser	150.00	50.00	20.00
60	Jim Holmes	150.00	50.00	20.00
61	Rube Dessau	150.00	50.00	20.00
62	Fred Jacklitsch	150.00	50.00	20.00
63	Stanley Graham	150.00	50.00	20.00
64	Noah Henline	150.00	50.00	20.00
65	"Chick" Gandil	1,300	430.00	170.00
66	Tom Hughes	150.00	50.00	20.00
67	Joseph Delehanty	150.00	50.00	20.00
68	Geo. Pierce	150.00	50.00	20.00
69	Bob Gaunt (Gantt)	150.00	50.00	20.00
70	Edward Fitzpatrick	150.00	50.00	20.00
71	Wyatt Lee	150.00	50.00	20.00
72	John Kissinger	150.00	50.00	20.00
73	William Malarkey	150.00	50.00	20.00
74	William Byers	150.00	50.00	20.00
75	George Simmons	150.00	50.00	20.00
76	Daniel Moeller	150.00	50.00	20.00
77	Joseph McGinnity	850.00	280.00	110.00
78	Alex Hardy	150.00	50.00	20.00
79	Bob Holmes	150.00	50.00	20.00
80	William Baxter	150.00	50.00	20.00
81	Edward Spencer	150.00	50.00	20.00
82	Bradley Kocher	150.00	50.00	20.00
83	Robert Shaw	150.00	50.00	20.00
84	Joseph Yeager	150.00	50.00	20.00
85	Anthony Carlo	150.00	50.00	20.00
86	William Abstein	150.00	50.00	20.00
87	Tim Jordan	150.00	50.00	20.00
88	Dick Breen	150.00	50.00	20.00
89	Tom McCarty	150.00	50.00	46.00
90	Ed Curtis	160.00	55.00	25.00

1923 Indianapolis Indians Foldout

Twenty-one players and staff are featured in this black-and-white accordion-fold souvenir. Each of the cards measures about 2" x 3".

	NM	EX	VG
Complete Foldout:	650.00	325.00	195.00
(Checklist not available.)			

1950 Indianapolis Indians Team Issue

Action poses are featured in this set of team-issue 8" x 10" black-and-white glossy photos. Players are identified by a facsimile autograph on front. It is unknown whether the checklist is complete. The Indians were the Class AAA American Association affiliate of the Pittsburgh Pirates in 1950.

		NM	EX	VG
Common Player:		30.00	15.00	9.00
(1)	Monty Basgall	30.00	15.00	9.00
(2)	Ted Beard	30.00	15.00	9.00
(3)	Gus Bell	40.00	20.00	12.00
(4)	Eddie Bockman	30.00	15.00	9.00
(5)	Dale Coogan	30.00	15.00	9.00
(6)	"Del" Dallessandro	30.00	15.00	9.00
(7)	Nanny Fernandez	30.00	15.00	9.00
(8)	Eddy Fitz Gerald	30.00	15.00	9.00
(9)	Al Grunwald	30.00	15.00	9.00
(10)	Frank Kalin	30.00	15.00	9.00
(11)	Paul LaPalme	30.00	15.00	9.00
(12)	Royce Lint	30.00	15.00	9.00
(13)	Al Lopez	45.00	22.00	13.50
(14)	Forrest Main	30.00	15.00	9.00
(15)	Danny O'Connell	30.00	15.00	9.00
(16)	Frank Papish	30.00	15.00	9.00
(17)	Eddie Stevens	30.00	15.00	9.00
(18)	Leo Wells	30.00	15.00	9.00

J

1952 Jamestown Falcons Team Issue

CHARLEY LAU

This Class D farm club of the Detroit Tigers won the 1952 Pony (Pennsylvania-Ontario-New York) League playoffs. Like other issues of Globe Printing, the roughly 2-1/4" x 3-3/8" cards are black-and-white with blank backs and the player name in a white strip at bottom-front. A light green album slotted to hold the cards is known for this issue.

		NM	EX	VG
Complete Set (18):		800.00	400.00	240.00
Common Player:		60.00	30.00	18.00
Album:		100.00	50.00	30.00
(1)	Dick Barr	60.00	30.00	18.00
(2)	Jerry Davie	60.00	30.00	18.00
(3)	John Fickinger	60.00	30.00	18.00
(4)	Paul Franks	60.00	30.00	18.00
(5)	Red Gookin	60.00	30.00	18.00
(6)	Bill Harbour	60.00	30.00	18.00
(7)	Dick Hatfield	60.00	30.00	18.00
(8)	Charley Lau	90.00	45.00	30.00
(9)	Dick Lisiecki	60.00	30.00	18.00
(10)	Tony Lupien	60.00	30.00	18.00
(11)	Joe Melago	60.00	30.00	18.00
(12)	Claude Mitschele	60.00	30.00	18.00
(13)	Bob Neebling	60.00	30.00	18.00
(14)	Fran Oneto	60.00	30.00	18.00
(15)	George Risley	60.00	30.00	18.00
(16)	Bob Szabo	60.00	30.00	18.00
(17)	Ken Walters	60.00	30.00	18.00
(18)	Gabby Witucki	60.00	30.00	18.00

1909 Walter Johnson "Weiser Wonder" Postcards

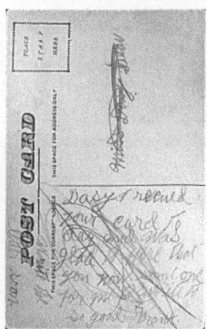

This issue-date(s) on these postcards are conjectural. Two distinct styles are known using versions of the same full-length portrait of Johnson in a studio standing on an ornate rug in front of a curtain depicting drapes, urn, etc. Johnson is wearing the uniform of the Weiser (Idaho) semi-pro team for whom he pitched prior to beginning his Hall of Fame career with the Washington Senators in 1907. The earlier of the cards utilizes the undivided-back postcard format which was current only until 1908. It is printed in sepia tones and identifies Johnson as the "Weiser Wonder" in a line of white type at the bottom. A later version, on a post-1908 divided-back postcard, is printed in bluetone. The card identifies him in a white strip at bottom. It is likely one or both of these cards continued to be produced or at least available after Johnson became a major league star. Both cards are in standard 3-1/2" x 5-1/2" format.

	NM	EX	VG
Walter Johnson (Bluetone)	6,000	3,000	1,800
Walter Johnson (Sepia)	6,000	3,000	1,800

1967 Jones Dairy Buffalo Bison All-Stars

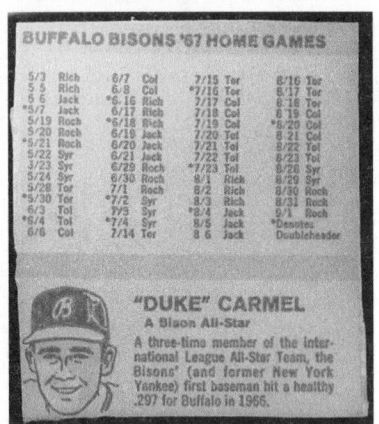

Apparently printed as part of a milk carton, only a single player is known for this issue. Printed in red and yellow, the piece includes a 1967 team home schedule, a player drawing and career highlights in a 2-3/4" x 3-1/8" format. Other players may yet surface.

		NM	EX	VG
(1)	"Duke" Carmel	80.00	40.00	25.00

K

1962 Kahn's Wieners Atlanta Crackers

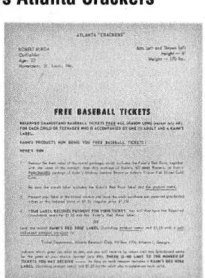

Kahn's made a single foray into the minor league market in 1962 with a separate 24-card set of Atlanta Crackers. The cards feature the same basic format, 3-1/4" x 4", borderless black-and-white photos with a Kahn's ad message in a white panel below the picture, as the major league issue. The backs are slightly different, having a free ticket offer in place of the player stats. Atlanta was the top farm club of the St. Louis Cardinals in 1962. The most famous alumnus in the set is Tim McCarver.

		NM	EX	VG
	Complete Set (24):	2,000	1,000	600.00
	Common Player:	80.00	40.00	24.00
(1)	James (Jimmy) Edward Beauchamp	80.00	40.00	24.00
(2)	Gerald Peter Buchek	80.00	40.00	24.00
(3)	Robert Burda	80.00	40.00	24.00
(4)	Hal Deitz	80.00	40.00	24.00
(5)	Robert John Duliba	80.00	40.00	24.00
(6)	Harry Michael Fanok	80.00	40.00	24.00
(7)	Phil Gagliano	80.00	40.00	24.00
(8)	John Glenn	80.00	40.00	24.00
(9)	Leroy Gregory	80.00	40.00	24.00
(10)	Richard (Dick) Henry Hughes	80.00	40.00	24.00
(11)	John Charles Kucks, Jr.	80.00	40.00	24.00
(12)	Johnny Joe Lewis	80.00	40.00	24.00
(13)	James (Mac - Timmie) Timothy McCarver	175.00	87.50	52.50
(14)	Robert F. Milliken	80.00	40.00	24.00
(15)	Joe Morgan	80.00	40.00	24.00
(16)	Ronald Charles Plaza	80.00	40.00	24.00
(17)	Bob Sadowski	80.00	40.00	24.00
(18)	Jim Saul	80.00	40.00	24.00
(19)	Willard Schmidt	80.00	40.00	24.00
(20)	Joe Schultz	80.00	40.00	24.00
(21)	Thomas Michael (Mike) Shannon	125.00	62.50	37.50
(22)	Paul Louis Toth	80.00	40.00	24.00
(23)	Andrew Lou Vickery	80.00	40.00	24.00
(24)	Fred Dwight Whitfield	80.00	40.00	24.00

1939 Kimball Automobile Trois-Rivieres Photocards

This set of 18 postcards and an accompanying envelope features the player of the Trois-Rivieres (Three Rivers) club of the Quebec Provincial League. Until 1940, the six-team QPL was not a part of organized baseball's minor league system. Several of the players were either former or future minor leaguers within OB. Paul "Pepper" Martin in the set is not the

Pepper Martin of the contemporary, Gas House Gang St. Louis Cardinals. The black-and-white cards are about post-card-size and blank-backed, printed on sturdy card stock.

		NM	EX	VG
	Complete Set (18):	1,350	675.00	400.00
	Common Player:	90.00	45.00	25.00
(1)	George Andrews	90.00	45.00	25.00
(2)	Norm Bell	90.00	45.00	25.00
(3)	Henry Block	90.00	45.00	25.00
(4)	Addie Copple	90.00	45.00	25.00
(5)	Phil Corrigan	90.00	45.00	25.00
(6)	Joe Dickinson	90.00	45.00	25.00
(7)	Bill Hoffner	90.00	45.00	25.00
(8)	Jack Leroy	90.00	45.00	25.00
(9)	Leo Maloney	90.00	45.00	25.00
(10)	Martin	90.00	45.00	25.00
(11)	McGurk	90.00	45.00	25.00
(12)	Connie O'Leary	90.00	45.00	25.00
(13)	James Pickens	90.00	45.00	25.00
(14)	Dutch Prather	90.00	45.00	25.00
(15)	Jamie Skelton	90.00	45.00	25.00
(16)	Byron Speece	90.00	45.00	25.00
(17)	Gene Sullivan	90.00	45.00	25.00
(18)	Grover Wearshing	90.00	45.00	25.00

1952 Knowles Service Stations Stockton Ports

Contemporary, and sharing a format with the many Globe minor league issues of the early '50s, this set of Stockton Ports (Class C California League) cards carries the advertising of Knowles Service Stations. The blank-backed, black-and-white cards measure 2-1/4" x 3-1/2" and are unnumbered. Among the players is a Japanese national whose card is in strong demand.

		NM	EX	VG
	Complete Set (11):	1,000	500.00	300.00
	Common Player:	90.00	45.00	25.00
	Album:	150.00	75.00	45.00
(1)	Wayne Clary	90.00	45.00	25.00
(2)	Harry Clements	90.00	45.00	25.00
(3)	John Crocco	90.00	45.00	25.00
(4)	Tony Freitas	90.00	45.00	25.00
(5)	Fibber Hirayama	250.00	125.00	75.00
(6)	Dave Mann	90.00	45.00	25.00
(7)	Larry Mann	90.00	45.00	25.00
(8)	Hank Moreno	90.00	45.00	25.00
(9)	Frank Romero	90.00	45.00	25.00
(10)	Chuck Thomas	90.00	45.00	25.00
(11)	Bud Watkins	90.00	45.00	25.00

1922-23 Kolb's Mothers' Bread Pins (PB4)

Over a two-year period, Kolb's bakery sponsored a series of pins featuring members of the Reading (Pa.) Aces of the International League. The pins are 7/8" in diameter with black-and-white portraits on a white background. The player name (last name only, usually) and position are indicated beneath the photo. Above the photo, in red, is the sponsor's identification. The pins issued in 1922 have "MOTHERS'" in all capital letters; the 1923 pins have "Mothers'" in upper and lower case.

		NM	EX	VG
	Complete Set (32):	1,700	850.00	500.00
	Common Player:	125.00	65.00	40.00
(1)	Spencer Abbott	125.00	65.00	40.00
(2)	Charlie Babington	125.00	65.00	40.00

(3)	Bill Barrett	125.00	65.00	40.00
(4)	R. Bates	125.00	65.00	40.00
(5)	Chief Bender	200.00	100.00	60.00
(6)	Myrl Brown	125.00	65.00	40.00
(7)	Fred Carts	125.00	65.00	40.00
(8)	Nig Clarke	125.00	65.00	40.00
(9)	Tom Connelly	125.00	65.00	40.00
(10)	Gus Getz	125.00	65.00	40.00
(11)	Frank Gilhooley	125.00	65.00	40.00
(12)	Ray Gordonier	125.00	65.00	40.00
(13)	Hinkey Haines	150.00	75.00	45.00
(14)	Francis Karpp	125.00	65.00	40.00
(15)	Joseph Kelley	125.00	65.00	40.00
(16)	Andrew Kotch	125.00	65.00	40.00
(17)	William Lightner	125.00	65.00	40.00
(18)	Byrd Lynn	125.00	65.00	40.00
(19)	Al Mamaux	125.00	65.00	40.00
(20)	Martin	125.00	65.00	40.00
(21)	Ralph Miller	125.00	65.00	40.00
(22)	Otto Pahlman	125.00	65.00	40.00
(23)	Sam Post	125.00	65.00	40.00
(24)	Al Schact	150.00	75.00	45.00
(25)	John Scott	125.00	65.00	40.00
(26)	Walt Smallwood	125.00	65.00	40.00
(27)	Ross Swartz	125.00	65.00	40.00
(28)	Fred Thomas	125.00	65.00	40.00
(29)	Myles Thomas	125.00	65.00	40.00
(30)	Walt Tragesser	125.00	65.00	40.00
(31)	Washburn	125.00	65.00	40.00
(32)	Walter Wolfe	125.00	65.00	40.00

L

1952 La Patrie Album Sportif

Ballplayers from Montreal of the International League and several of the teams from the Class C Provincial (Quebec) League were featured in a series of colorized photos printed in the Sunday rotogravure section of "La Patrie" newspaper. The photos are approximately 11" x 15-3/8" with red left and bottom trim and a vertical blue stripe at far left. Player information is printed in black and is in French. A number of the players went on to stardom with the Brooklyn and/or Los Angeles Dodgers.

		NM	EX	VG
	Complete Set (18):	650.00	325.00	175.00
	Common Player:	25.00	12.50	7.50
(1)	Bob Alexander	25.00	12.50	7.50
(2)	Hampton Coleman	25.00	12.50	7.50
(3)	Walter Fiala	25.00	12.50	7.50
(4)	Jim Gilliams (Gilliam)	45.00	22.50	13.50
(5)	Tom Hackett	25.00	12.50	7.50
(6)	Don Hoak	35.00	17.50	10.00
(7)	Herbie Lash	25.00	12.50	7.50
(8)	Tommy Lasorda	150.00	75.00	45.00
(9)	Mal Mallette	25.00	12.50	7.50
(10)	Georges Maranda (Aug. 17)	25.00	12.50	7.50
(11)	Carmen Mauro	25.00	12.50	7.50
(12)	Solly Mohn	25.00	12.50	7.50
(13)	Jacques Monette	25.00	12.50	7.50
(14)	Johnny Podres	75.00	37.50	22.50
(15)	Ed Roebuck	25.00	12.50	7.50
(16)	Charlie Thompson	25.00	12.50	7.50
(17)	Don Thompson	25.00	12.50	7.50
(18)	John Wingo	25.00	12.50	7.50

1928-1932 La Presse Baseball Rotos

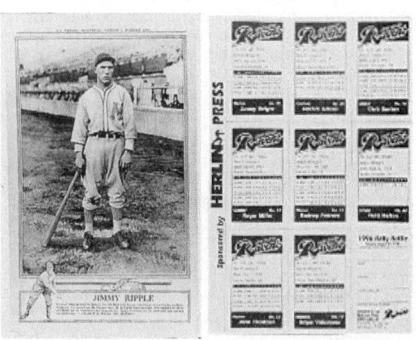

Players from Montreal's team in the International League (and occasionally other major and minor league teams' stars) were featured in a series of photos between 1928-32 in the Saturday rotogravure section of Montreal's "La Presse" newspaper. The format remained fairly consistent over the years. Large hand-tinted player photos were featured on the approximately 11" x 17-3/4" pages, with writeup in French below. On back was whatever features and ads happened to appear on the following page. The known baseball player list is presented here in chronological order. Other athletes were also featured in the issue, but are not listed here. Gaps have been left in the numbering to better accommodate future additions to this list.

		NM	EX	VG
Common Player:		60.00	30.00	20.00
	1928	.00	.00	.00
(2)	Aldrick Gaudette (May 19)	60.00	30.00	20.00
(4)	Robert Shawkey (June 2)	80.00	40.00	24.00
(5)	Lachine team photo, portraits of starting nine (June 9)	60.00	30.00	20.00
(6)	Roy Buckalew, Frank Dunagan, Chester Fowler, Thomas Gulley, Peter Radwan, Richard Smith (June 16)	60.00	30.00	20.00
(7)	Seymour Edward Bailey (June 23)	60.00	30.00	20.00
(8)	Wilson F. Fewster (June 30)	60.00	30.00	20.00
(10)	Tom Daly (July 14)	60.00	30.00	20.00
(14)	Red Holt (Aug. 11)	60.00	30.00	20.00
(17)	George Herman Ruth (Oct. 13)	750.00	375.00	225.00
(20)	Johnny Prud'homme (Nov. 3)	60.00	30.00	20.00
	1929			
(2)	Walter Paul Gautreau (April 13)	60.00	30.00	20.00
(4)	Herb Thormahlen (April 27)	60.00	30.00	20.00
(9)	Elon Hogsett (July 13)	60.00	30.00	20.00
(12)	Robert M. "Lefty" Grove (Oct. 19)	200.00	100.00	60.00
(15)	Philadelphia A's Stars (Mickey Cochrane, Jimmie Foxx, Connie Mack, Al Simmons, Rube Walberg, Bing Miller) (Nov. 16)	90.00	45.00	27.00
	1930			
(3)	Martin Griffin, John Pomorski, Arthur Smith, Herb Thormahlen (May 31)	60.00	30.00	20.00
(4)	James Calleran, Edward Conley, Lee Head, Jimmy Ripple (June 7)	60.00	30.00	20.00
(7)	Del Bissonette (June 28)	60.00	30.00	20.00
(9)	Joe Hauser (July 12)	75.00	37.00	22.00
(14)	Gowell Sylvester Claset (Sept. 13)	60.00	30.00	20.00
(17)	Hack Wilson (Oct. 11)	200.00	100.00	60.00
	1931			
(2)	Chuck Klein (May 30)	175.00	87.00	52.00
(3)	Jocko Conlan (June 6)	100.00	50.00	30.00
(5)	Lee Head (June 20)	60.00	30.00	20.00
(7)	Jimmy Ripple (July 4)	60.00	30.00	20.00
(9)	Sol Mishkin (July 18)	60.00	30.00	20.00
(11)	Walter Brown (Aug. 15)	60.00	30.00	20.00
(15)	Johnny Allen, Frank Barnes, Guy Cantrell, Ken Strong (Nov. 14)	60.00	30.00	20.00
(16)	John Pepper Martin (Nov. 21)	80.00	40.00	24.00
	1932			
(2)	Johnny Grabowski (May 28)	60.00	30.00	20.00
(3)	Charles Sullivan (June 4)	60.00	30.00	20.00
(5)	Walter "Doc" Gautreau (June 18)	60.00	30.00	20.00
(6)	John Clancy (June 25)	60.00	30.00	20.00
(7)	Buck Walters (July 2)	75.00	37.00	22.00
(8)	Bill McAfee (July 9)	60.00	30.00	20.00
(9)	George Puccinelli (July 16)	60.00	30.00	20.00
(11)	Buck Crouse (Aug. 6)	60.00	30.00	20.00
(12)	Ollie Carnegie (Aug. 13)	60.00	30.00	20.00
(13)	Leo Mangum (Aug. 20)	60.00	30.00	20.00
(17)	Roy Parmelee (Nov. 19)	60.00	30.00	20.00
	(Dates of issue not confirmed.)			
	Dan Howley	60.00	30.00	20.00

1952 Laval Dairy Provincial League

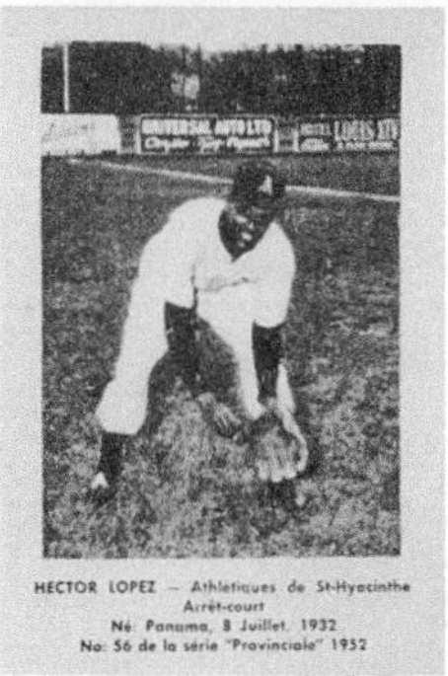
HECTOR LOPEZ — Athlétiques de St-Hyacinthe
Arrêt-court
Né Panama, 8 Juillet, 1932
No: 56 de la série "Provinciale" 1952

This scarce Canadian minor league issue includes only players from the Class C Provincial League, centered in Quebec. The black-and-white cards are blank-backed and measure 1-3/4" x 2-1/2". The player name, position, date and place of birth and card number is in French. Teams represented in the set are Quebec (Braves), St. Jean (Pirates), Three Rivers (Independent), Drummondville (Senators), Granby (Phillies) and Ste. Hyacinthe (Philadelphia A's).

		NM	EX	VG
Complete Set (114):		8,000	4,000	2,500
Common Player:		70.00	35.00	20.00
1	Georges McQuinn	70.00	35.00	20.00
2	Cliff Statham	70.00	35.00	20.00
3	Frank Wilson	70.00	35.00	20.00
4	Frank Neri	70.00	35.00	20.00
5	Georges Maranda	70.00	35.00	20.00
6	Richard "Dick" Cordeiro	70.00	35.00	20.00
7	Roger McCardell	70.00	35.00	20.00
8	Joseph Janiak	70.00	35.00	20.00
9	Herbert Shankman	70.00	35.00	20.00
10	Joe Subbiondo	70.00	35.00	20.00
11	Jack Brenner	70.00	35.00	20.00
12	Donald Buchanan	70.00	35.00	20.00
13	Robert Smith	70.00	35.00	20.00
14	Raymond League	70.00	35.00	20.00
15	Mike Fandozzi	70.00	35.00	20.00
16	Dick Moler	70.00	35.00	20.00
17	Edward Bazydio	70.00	35.00	20.00
18	Danny Mazurek	70.00	35.00	20.00
19	Edwin Charles	70.00	35.00	20.00
20	Jack Nullaney	70.00	35.00	20.00
21	Bob Bolan	70.00	35.00	20.00
22	Bob Long	70.00	35.00	20.00
23	Cleo Lewright	70.00	35.00	20.00
24	Herb Taylor	70.00	35.00	20.00
25	Frankie Gaeta	70.00	35.00	20.00
26	Bill Truitt	70.00	35.00	20.00
27	Jean Prats	70.00	35.00	20.00
28	Tex Taylor	70.00	35.00	20.00
29	Ron Delbianco	70.00	35.00	20.00
30	Joe DiLorenzo	70.00	35.00	20.00
31	Johnny Paszek	70.00	35.00	20.00
32	Ken Suess	70.00	35.00	20.00
33	Harry Sims	70.00	35.00	20.00
34	William Jackson	70.00	35.00	20.00
35	Jerry Mayers	70.00	35.00	20.00
36	Gordon Maltzberger	70.00	35.00	20.00
37	Gerry Cabana	70.00	35.00	20.00
38	Gary Rutkey	70.00	35.00	20.00
39	Ken Hatcher	70.00	35.00	20.00
40	Vincent Cosenza	70.00	35.00	20.00
41	Edward Yaeger	70.00	35.00	20.00
42	Jimmy Orr	70.00	35.00	20.00
43	Johnny Di Matino	70.00	35.00	20.00
44	Lenny Wisneski	70.00	35.00	20.00
45	Pete Caniglia	70.00	35.00	20.00
46	Guy Coleman	70.00	35.00	20.00
47	Herb Fleischer	70.00	35.00	20.00
48	Charles Yahrling	70.00	35.00	20.00
49	Roger Bedard	70.00	35.00	20.00
50	Al Barillari	70.00	35.00	20.00
51	Hugh Mulcahy	100.00	50.00	30.00
52	Vincent Canepa	70.00	35.00	20.00
53	Bob Loranger	70.00	35.00	20.00
54	Georges Carpentier	70.00	35.00	20.00
55	Bill Hamilton	70.00	35.00	20.00
56	Hector Lopez	130.00	70.00	40.00
57	Joel Taylor	70.00	35.00	20.00
58	Alonzo Brathwaite	200.00	10.00	60.00
59	Carl McQuillen	70.00	35.00	20.00
60	Robert Trice	70.00	35.00	20.00
61	John Dworak	70.00	35.00	20.00
62	Al Pinkston	100.00	50.00	30.00
63	William Shannon	70.00	35.00	20.00
64	Stanley Wotychowisz	70.00	35.00	20.00
65	Roger Herbert	70.00	35.00	20.00
66	Troy Spencer	70.00	35.00	20.00
67	Johnny Rohan	70.00	35.00	20.00
68	John Sosh	70.00	35.00	20.00
69	Ramon Mason	70.00	35.00	20.00
70	Tom Smith	70.00	35.00	20.00
71	Douglas McBean	70.00	35.00	20.00
72	Bill Babik	70.00	35.00	20.00
73	Dante Cozzi	70.00	35.00	20.00
74	Melville Doxtater	70.00	35.00	20.00
75	William Gilray	70.00	35.00	20.00
76	Armando Diaz	70.00	35.00	20.00
77	Ackroyd Smith	70.00	35.00	20.00
78	Germain Pizarro	70.00	35.00	20.00
79	Jim Heap	70.00	35.00	20.00
80	Herbert Crompton	70.00	35.00	20.00
81	Howard Bodell	70.00	35.00	20.00
82	Andre Schreiser	70.00	35.00	20.00
83	John Wingo	70.00	35.00	20.00
84	Salvatore Arduini	70.00	35.00	20.00
85	Fred Pallito	70.00	35.00	20.00
86	Aaron Osofsky	70.00	35.00	20.00
87	Jack DiGrace	70.00	35.00	20.00
88	Alphonso Chico Girard (Gerrard)	70.00	35.00	20.00
89	Manuel Trabous	70.00	35.00	20.00
90	Tom Barnes	70.00	35.00	20.00
91	Humberto Robinson	70.00	35.00	20.00
92	Jack Bukowatz	70.00	35.00	20.00
93	Marco Mainini	70.00	35.00	20.00
94	Claude St. Vincent	70.00	35.00	20.00
95	Fernand Brosseau	70.00	35.00	20.00
96	John Malangone	70.00	35.00	20.00
97	Pierre Nantel	70.00	35.00	20.00
98	Donald Stevens	70.00	35.00	20.00
99	Jim Prappas	70.00	35.00	20.00
100	Richard Fitzgerald	70.00	35.00	20.00
101	Yves Aubin	70.00	35.00	20.00
102	Frank Novosel	70.00	35.00	20.00
103	Tony Campos	70.00	35.00	20.00
104	Gelso Oviedo	70.00	35.00	20.00
105	Guly Becker	70.00	35.00	20.00
106	Aurelio Ala	70.00	35.00	20.00
107	Orlando Andux	70.00	35.00	20.00
108	Tom Hackett	70.00	35.00	20.00
109	Guillame Vargas	70.00	35.00	20.00
110	Fransisco Salfran	70.00	35.00	20.00
111	Jean-Marc Blais	70.00	35.00	20.00
112	Vince Pizzitola	70.00	35.00	20.00
113	John Olsen	70.00	35.00	20.00
114	Jacques Monette	70.00	35.00	20.00

1948 Los Angeles Angels Team Issue

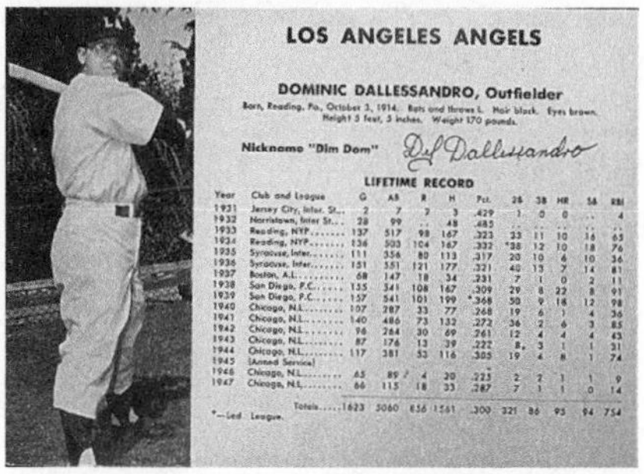
LOS ANGELES ANGELS
DOMINIC DALLESSANDRO, Outfielder
Nickname "Dim Dom"
LIFETIME RECORD

A team-issued set sold in a paper envelope for $1 at the ballpark, these cards were produced by the same firm which published the team's yearbook, Pacific Coast Sports Publishing Co., of Los Angeles. The blank-backed cards measure 6-3/4" x 4-3/4" and are printed in black-and-white on thin cardboard with a semi-gloss front surface. Cards feature a facsimile player autograph on front, along with a posed action or portrait photo and complete major and minor league stats. The cards are listed in the American Card Catalog, along with the subsequent year's issue, as W725. Many of the players on this Pacific Coast League team were former or future Chicago Cubs. The unnumbered cards are checklisted here alphabetically.

		NM	EX	VG
Complete Set (26):		650.00	325.00	200.00
Common Player:		30.00	15.00	9.00
(1)	Cliff Aberson	30.00	15.00	9.00
(2)	Red Adams	30.00	15.00	9.00
(3)	John Adkins	30.00	15.00	9.00
(4)	Lee Anthony	30.00	15.00	9.00
(5)	Russ Bauers	30.00	15.00	9.00
(6)	Ora Burnett	30.00	15.00	9.00
(7)	Donald Carlsen	30.00	15.00	9.00
(8)	Dom Dallessandro	30.00	15.00	9.00
(9)	Cecil Garriott	30.00	15.00	9.00
(10)	Paul Gillespie	30.00	15.00	9.00
(11)	Al Glossop	30.00	15.00	9.00
(12)	Tom Hafey	30.00	15.00	9.00
(13)	Don Johnson	30.00	15.00	9.00
(14)	Bill Kelly	30.00	15.00	9.00
(15)	Hal Kleine	30.00	15.00	9.00
(16)	Walt Lanfranconi	30.00	15.00	9.00
(17)	Ed Lukon	30.00	15.00	9.00
(18)	Red Lynn	30.00	15.00	9.00
(19)	Eddie Malone	30.00	15.00	9.00
(20)	Len Merullo	30.00	15.00	9.00
(21)	Ralph Novotney	30.00	15.00	9.00
(22)	John Ostrowski	30.00	15.00	9.00
(23)	John Sanford	30.00	15.00	9.00
(24)	Ed Sauer	30.00	15.00	9.00
(25)	Bill Schuster	30.00	15.00	9.00
(26)	John Warner	30.00	15.00	9.00

1949 Los Angeles Angels Team Issue

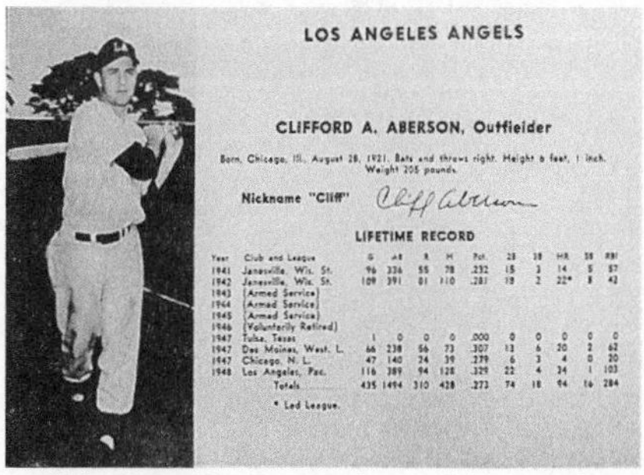
LOS ANGELES ANGELS
CLIFFORD A. ABERSON, Outfielder
Nickname "Cliff"
LIFETIME RECORD

Little changed in the second year of this team issue. Cards remained at 6-3/4" x 4-3/4" in format, printed black-and-white on semi-gloss cardboard with a blank back. Many of the players (and even some of the photos) were repeated from the previous year. The unnumbered cards are checklisted here in alphabetical order.

		NM	EX	VG
Complete Set (39):		1,000	500.00	300.00
Common Player:		30.00	15.00	9.00
(1)	Cliff Aberson	30.00	15.00	9.00
(2)	Donald Alfano	30.00	15.00	9.00
(3)	Quentin Altizer	30.00	15.00	9.00
(4)	Lee Anthony	30.00	15.00	9.00
(5)	Nels Burbrink	30.00	15.00	9.00
(6)	Smoky Burgess	75.00	37.50	22.00
(7)	Don Carlsen	30.00	15.00	9.00
(8)	Joe Damato	30.00	15.00	9.00
(9)	Bill Emmerich	30.00	15.00	9.00
(10)	Ken Gables	30.00	15.00	9.00
(11)	Cecil Garriott	30.00	15.00	9.00
(12)	Al Glossop	30.00	15.00	9.00
(13)	Gordon Goldsberry	30.00	15.00	9.00
(14)	Frank Gustine	30.00	15.00	9.00
(15)	Lee Handley	30.00	15.00	9.00
(16)	Alan Ihde	30.00	15.00	9.00
(17)	Bob Kelley (Announcer)	30.00	15.00	9.00
(18)	Bill Kelly	30.00	15.00	9.00
(19)	Bob Kelly	30.00	15.00	9.00

		NM	EX	VG
(20)	Walt Lanfranconi	30.00	15.00	9.00
(21)	Red Lynn	30.00	15.00	9.00
(22)	Clarence Maddern	30.00	15.00	9.00
(23)	Eddie Malone	30.00	15.00	9.00
(24)	Carmen Mauro	30.00	15.00	9.00
(25)	Booker McDaniels	75.00	37.50	22.00
(26)	Cal McLish	50.00	25.00	15.00
(27)	Butch Moran	30.00	15.00	9.00
(28)	Ralph Novotney	30.00	15.00	9.00
(29)	John Ostrowski	30.00	15.00	9.00
(30)	Bobby Rhawn	30.00	15.00	9.00
(31)	Bill Schuster	30.00	15.00	9.00
(32)	Pat Seerey	30.00	15.00	9.00
(33)	Bryan Stephens	30.00	15.00	9.00
(34)	Bob Sturgeon	30.00	15.00	9.00
(35)	Wayne Terwilliger	45.00	22.00	13.50
(36)	Gordon Van Dyke	30.00	15.00	9.00
(37)	John Warner	30.00	15.00	9.00
(38)	Don Watkins	30.00	15.00	9.00
(39)	Trainers, Bat Boys	30.00	15.00	9.00
	(Dickie Evans, Joe Liscio, Dave Flores, Billy Lund)			

1930-31 Lucke Badge & Button Baltimore Orioles Pins

These 7/8" diameter celluloid pinback buttons were produced by the Baltimore novelty firm of Lucke Badge & Button Co. Issued to honor fan favorites on their "Day," the buttons have black-and-white portrait photos at center, surrounded by a white rim. At top is the player name, at bottom is the team name and year. A paper label inside the back of the button identifies the maker and includes a union label.

	NM	EX	VG
Joe Hauser (1930)	300.00	150.00	90.00
Don Heffner (1931)	200.00	100.00	60.00

M

1910 Mascot Gum Pins

Only players from the Eastern League champion Rochester Bronchos are known on these 7/8" diameter pinback buttons. Fronts have a black-and-white player photo on a blue background with the player's last name at left and "ROCHESTER" at right. A paper insert on the reverse advertises "Ball Player's Buttons Free With Mascot Gum." This checklist may not be complete.

		NM	EX	VG
Common Player:		300.00	150.00	90.00
(1)	Alperman	300.00	150.00	90.00
(2)	Anderson	300.00	150.00	90.00
(3)	Heinie Batch	300.00	150.00	90.00
(4)	Blair	300.00	150.00	90.00
(5)	Holmes	300.00	150.00	90.00
(6)	Lafitte	300.00	150.00	90.00
(7)	Manning	300.00	150.00	90.00
(8)	McConnell	300.00	150.00	90.00
(9)	Moeller	300.00	150.00	90.00
(10)	Moran	300.00	150.00	90.00
(11)	Osborn	300.00	150.00	90.00
(12)	Don Carlos Ragon (Ragan)	300.00	150.00	90.00
(13)	Savidge	300.00	150.00	90.00
(14)	Simmons	300.00	150.00	90.00
(15)	Spencer	300.00	150.00	90.00
(16)	Tooley	300.00	150.00	90.00
(17)	Ward	300.00	150.00	90.00

1952 May Co. Chuck Stevens Premium

The date given is speculative, about midway through the player's term with the Hollywood Stars of the Pacific Coast League. The 4-1/2" x 6" blank-backed black-and-white card features a portrait of what the caption at bottom calls the "popular first baseman." The caption also calls the piece a "MAY CO. 'Back To School' Party Souvenir Photo." The cards are often found bearing the player's autograph, presumably obtained at the event.

	NM	EX	VG
Chuck Stevens	75.00	40.00	25.00

1960s-70s J.D. McCarthy Postcards

For details of J.D. McCarthy's prolific body of black-and-white player postcards, see the introductory material in the vintage major league section.

Common Player: $1-3

SPOKANE INDIANS
(1)	Roy Hartsfield

TOLEDO MUD HENS
(1)	Loren Babe
(2)	Stan Bahnsen
(3)	Bill Bethea
(4)	Joe Cherry
(5)	Horace Clark
(6)	Wayne Comer
(7)	Jack Cullen (2)
(8)	Jack Curtis (2)
(9)	Gil Downs
(10)	Joe Faraci
(11)	Frank Fernandez
(12)	Mike Ferraro
(13)	Mickey Harrington
(14)	Mike Hegan
(15)	Jim Horsford (2)
(16)	Dick Hughes
(17)	Elvio Jiminez (2)
(18)	Robert Lasko
(19)	Artie Lopez
(20)	Roy Majtyka
(21)	Tom Martz
(22)	Ed Merritt (2)
(23)	Archie Moore (2)
(24)	Al Moran
(25)	Bobby Murcer
(26)	Tony Przybycien
(27)	Bill Roman
(28)	Bob Schmidt (2)
(29)	Tom Shafer
(30)	Billy Shantz
(31)	Shantz-Senger-Babe
(32)	Bob Tiefenauer
(33)	Paul Toth (2)
(34)	Andrew Vickery
(35)	Jerry Walker
(36)	Don Wallace
(37)	Dooley Womack

1954 MD Super Service Sacramento Solons

This issue features only players of the Pacific Coast League Sacramento Solons. The unnumbered cards are printed in black-and-white and carry an ad for a local gas station. The borderless, blank-backed cards measure 2-1/8" x 3-3/8".

	NM	EX	VG
Complete Set (6):	1,200	600.00	360.00

		NM	EX	VG
Common Player:		200.00	100.00	60.00
(1)	Joe Brovia	200.00	100.00	60.00
(2)	Al Cicotte	200.00	100.00	60.00
(3)	Nippy Jones	200.00	100.00	60.00
(4)	Richie Meyers	200.00	100.00	60.00
(5)	Hank Schenz	200.00	100.00	60.00
(6)	Bud Sheeley	200.00	100.00	60.00

1952 Miami Beach Flamingos Team Issue

These 2-1/4" x 3-3/8" black-and-white, unnumbered, blank-backed cards were one of many minor league team sets issued by Globe Printing of San Jose, Calif., in the early 1950s. Cards were usually given away at the ballpark on a one-per-week or one-per-homestand basis, accounting for the rarity of surviving sets. An embossed album slotted to accommodate the cards was also issued. The Flamingos were an unaffiliated team in the Class B Florida International League.

		NM	EX	VG
Complete Set (25):		1,000	500.00	300.00
Common Player:		60.00	30.00	18.00
Album:		100.00	50.00	30.00
(1)	Billy Barrett	60.00	30.00	18.00
(2)	Art Bosch	60.00	30.00	18.00
(3)	Jack Caro	60.00	30.00	18.00
(4)	Chuck Ehlman	60.00	30.00	18.00
(5)	Oscar Garmendia	60.00	30.00	18.00
(6)	George Handy	60.00	30.00	18.00
(7)	Clark Henry	60.00	30.00	18.00
(8)	Dario Jiminez	60.00	30.00	18.00
(9)	Jesse Levan	60.00	30.00	18.00
(10)	Bobby Lyons	60.00	30.00	18.00
(11)	Pepper Martin	125.00	62.00	37.00
(12)	Dick McMillin	60.00	30.00	18.00
(13)	Pete Morant	60.00	30.00	18.00
(14)	Chico Morilla	60.00	30.00	18.00
(15)	Ken Munroe	60.00	30.00	18.00
(16)	Walt Nothe	60.00	30.00	18.00
(17)	Marshall O'Coine	60.00	30.00	18.00
(18)	Whitey Platt	60.00	30.00	18.00
(19)	Johnny Podgajny	60.00	30.00	18.00
(20)	Knobby Rosa	60.00	30.00	18.00
(21)	Harry Raulerson	60.00	30.00	18.00
(22)	Mort Smith	60.00	30.00	18.00
(23)	Tommy Venn	60.00	30.00	18.00
(24)	George Wehmeyer	60.00	30.00	18.00
(25)	Ray Williams	60.00	30.00	18.00

1963 Milwaukee Sausage Seattle Rainiers

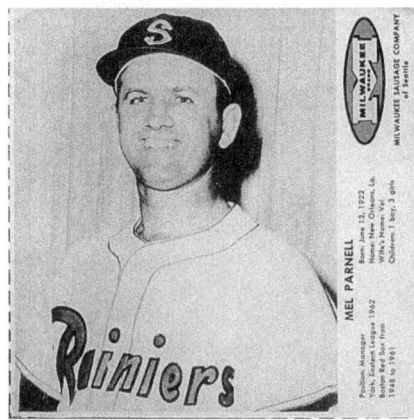

Inserted into meat packages by a Seattle sausage company, the 11 cards known in this set are all Seattle Rainiers players, several of whom had big league experience. Cards measure approximately 4-1/4"-square and are printed in blue, red and yellow. The unnumbered cards are checklisted in alphabetical order.

		NM	EX	VG
Complete Set (11):		7,500	3,750	2,250
Common Player:		750.00	375.00	225.00
(1)	Dave Hall	750.00	375.00	225.00
(2)	Bill Harrell	750.00	375.00	225.00
(3)	Pete Jernigan	750.00	375.00	225.00

		NM	EX	VG
(4)	Bill McLeod	750.00	375.00	225.00
(5)	Mel Parnell	825.00	420.00	250.00
(6)	Elmer Singleton	750.00	375.00	225.00
(7)	Archie Skeen	750.00	375.00	225.00
(8)	Paul Smith	750.00	375.00	225.00
(9)	Pete Smith	750.00	375.00	225.00
(10)	Bill Spanswick	750.00	375.00	225.00
(11)	George Spencer	750.00	375.00	225.00

1909 Minneapolis Tribune/St. Paul Pioneer Press Mirrors

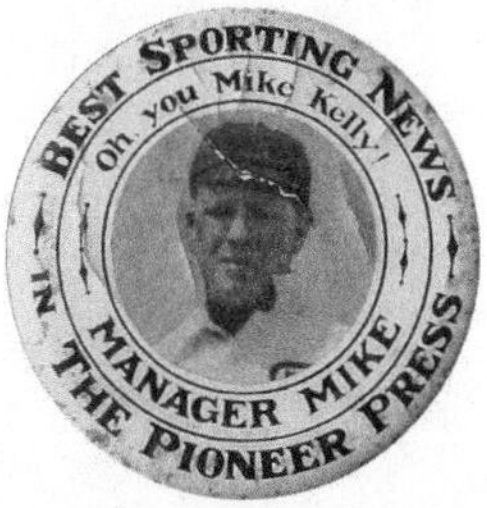

From the few players known, it is apparent these mirrors were issued in 1909 by two of the Twin Cities' daily newspapers. Each mirror is 2-1/8" diameter with a celluloid back. At center is a black-and-white player photo. All typography is in b/w, as well. A pair of concentric circles around the photo contain the player's name and a short description of his prowess. Olmstead's reads, "Unhittable in the Pinches"; Carisch's reads, "Nails 'em to the Cross Every Time." The outer circle contains an ad for the newspaper. This checklist is probably incomplete.

		NM	EX	VG
Common Player:		600.00	300.00	180.00
(1)	Fred Carisch	600.00	300.00	180.00
(2)	Michael Kelly	600.00	300.00	180.00
(3)	Fred Olmstead	600.00	300.00	180.00

1911 Mono Cigarettes (T217)

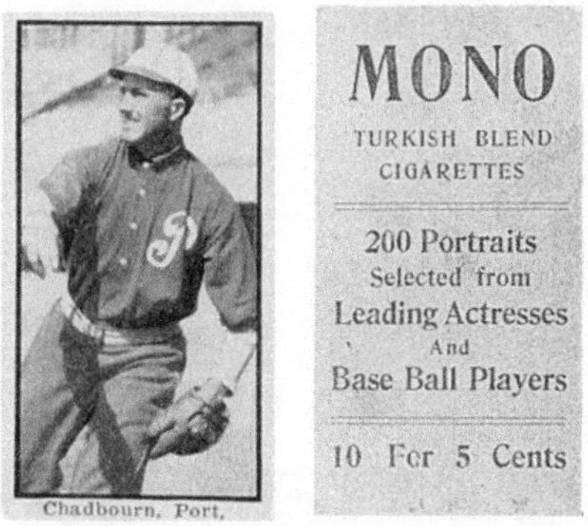

As was common with many tobacco issues of the period, the T217 set - distributed on the West Coast by Mono Cigarettes - feature both baseball players and "Leading Actresses." The 23 baseball players in the Mono set are all from the Pacific Coast League. Two of the players (Delhi and Hughie Smith) are shown in two poses, resulting in a total of 25 different cards. The players are pictured in black-and-white photos on a card that measures approximately 1-1/2" x 2-5/8", the standard size of a tobacco card. The player's name and team appear at the bottom, while the back of the card carries an advertisement for Mono Cigarettes. The Mono set, which can be dated to the 1909-1911 period, is among the rarest of all tobacco cards.

		NM	EX	VG
Complete Set (25):		90,000	45,000	27,000
Common Player:		3,750	1,875	900
(1)	Aiken	3,750	1,875	900
(2)	Curtis Bernard	3,750	1,875	900
(3)	L. Burrell	3,750	1,875	900
(4)	Chadbourn	3,750	1,875	900
(5)	R. Couchman	3,750	1,875	900
(6)	Elmer Criger	3,750	1,875	900
(7)	Pete Daley	3,750	1,875	900
(8)	W. Delhi (Glove at chest level.)	3,750	1,875	900
(9)	W. Delhi (Glove at shoulder level.)	3,750	1,875	900
(10)	Bert Delmas	3,750	1,875	900
(11)	Ivan Howard	3,750	1,875	900
(12)	Kitty Knight	3,750	1,875	900
(13)	Gene Knapp (Krapp)	3,750	1,875	900
(14)	Metzger	3,750	1,875	900
(15)	Carl Mitze	3,750	1,875	900
(16)	J. O'Rourke	3,750	1,875	900
(17)	R. Peckinpaugh	3,750	1,875	900
(18)	Walter Schmidt	3,750	1,875	900
(19)	Hughie Smith (Batting)	3,750	1,875	900
(20)	Hughie Smith (Fielding)	3,750	1,875	900
(21)	Wm. Stein	3,750	1,875	900
(22)	Elmer Thorsen	3,750	1,875	900
(23)	Oscar Vitt	3,750	1,875	900
(24)	Clyde Wares	3,750	1,875	900
(25)	Geo. Wheeler	3,750	1,875	900

1961 Jeffrey W. Morey Postcards

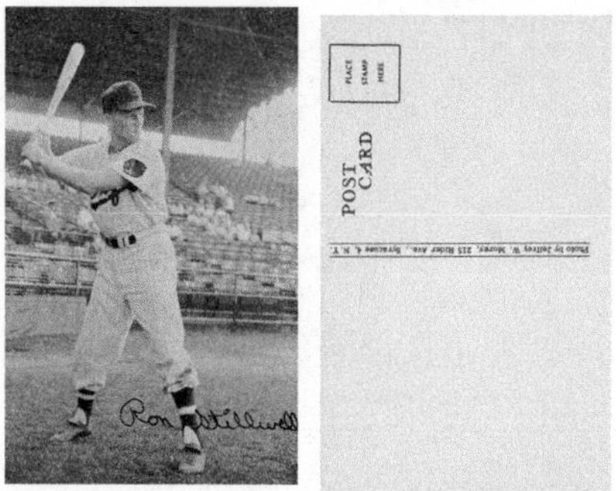

This set of 3-1/2" x 5-1/2", black-and-white postcards was produced to accomodate fan mail requests by two players each from the Columbus Clippers and Syracuse Chiefs. Fronts have a facsimile autograph. Divided-postcard backs have a credit line to the photographer and standard postcard markings.

		NM	EX	VG
Complete Set (4):		125.00	65.00	37.50
Common Player:		35.00	17.50	10.50
(1)	Larry Elliot	35.00	17.50	10.50
(2)	Don Rowe	35.00	17.50	10.50
(3)	Ted Sadowski	35.00	17.50	10.50
(4)	Ron Stillwell	35.00	17.50	10.50

1947 Morley Studios Team Cards

Besides issuing individual player cards of the Tacoma team, Morley Studios also issued postcard-size pictures of the teams in the Class B Western International League of 1947. The 3-1/2" x 5-1/2" cards are blank-backed and carry a "Morley Studios / 1947" imprint on front.

		NM	EX	VG
Complete Set (8):		600.00	300.00	180.00
Common Player:		75.00	37.50	22.50
(1)	Bremerton Bluejackets	75.00	37.50	22.50
(2)	Salem Senators	75.00	37.50	22.50
(3)	Spokane Indians	75.00	37.50	22.50
(4)	Tacoma Tigers	75.00	37.50	22.50
(5)	Vancouver Capilanos	75.00	37.50	22.50
(6)	Victoria Athletics	75.00	37.50	22.50
(7)	Yakima Stars	75.00	37.50	22.50
(8)	Wenatchee Chiefs	75.00	37.50	22.50

1947 Morley Studios Tacoma Tigers

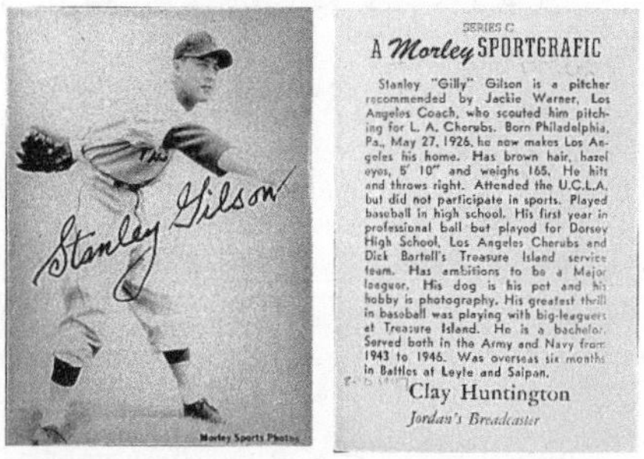

This set of Tacoma Tigers (Western International League) features borderless black-and-white posed action photos with a facsimile autograph on front. A "Morley Sports Photos" or "Morley Studios" credit line appears at the bottom. Backs of the first seven cards are blank, while the others feature player biographies credited to "Jordan's (bread sponsor) Broadcaster" Clay Huntington and a Series A through F designation (though some cards lack the letter code). The unnumbered cards measure 2-1/2" x 3-1/2".

		NM	EX	VG
Complete Set (28):		3,500	1,750	1,000
Common Player:		125.00	65.00	40.00
	Blank-Backed	.00	.00	.00
(1)	Hank Bartolomei	125.00	65.00	40.00
(2)	Rod Belcher (Broadcaster)	125.00	65.00	40.00
(3)	Tip Berg (Trainer)	125.00	65.00	40.00
(4)	Gene Clough	125.00	65.00	40.00
(5)	Clay Huntington (Broadcaster)	125.00	65.00	40.00
(6)	Donald Mooney (Bat boy.)	125.00	65.00	40.00
(7)	Buck Tinsley	125.00	65.00	40.00
	Series A	.00	.00	.00
(8)	Richard A. Greco	125.00	65.00	40.00
(9)	Cy Greenlaw	125.00	65.00	40.00
(10)	Bob Joratz	125.00	65.00	40.00
(11)	Earl Kuper	125.00	65.00	40.00
	Series B	.00	.00	.00
(12)	Neil Clifford	125.00	65.00	40.00
(13)	Red Harvel	125.00	65.00	40.00
(14)	Julian Morgan	125.00	65.00	40.00
(15)	Pete Tedeschi	125.00	65.00	40.00
	Series C	.00	.00	.00
(16)	Stanley Gilson	125.00	65.00	40.00
(17)	Harry Nygard	125.00	65.00	40.00
(18)	Cleve Ramsey	125.00	65.00	40.00
(19)	Pete Sabutis	125.00	65.00	40.00
	Series D	.00	.00	.00
(20)	Mitch Chetkovich	125.00	65.00	40.00
(21)	Leroy Paton	125.00	65.00	40.00
(22)	Carl Shaply	125.00	65.00	40.00
(23)	Glenn Stetter	125.00	65.00	40.00
	Series E	.00	.00	.00
(24)	Bob Hedington	125.00	65.00	40.00
(25)	Ed Keehan	125.00	65.00	40.00
(26)	Gordon Walden	125.00	65.00	40.00
	Series F	.00	.00	.00
(27)	Maury Donovan	125.00	65.00	40.00
(28)	Guy Miller	125.00	65.00	40.00

1952 Mother's Cookies

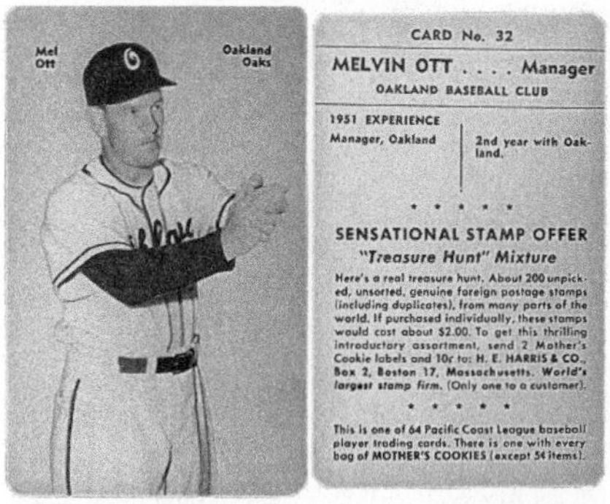

This is one of the most popular regional minor league sets ever issued. Cards of Pacific Coast League players were included in packages of cookies. Distribution was limited to the West Coast. The 64 cards feature full color photos on a colored background, with player name and team. The cards measure 2-13/16" x 3-1/2", though the cards' rounded corners cause some variation in listed size. Card backs feature a very brief player statistic, card numbers and an offer for purchasing postage stamps. Five cards (11, 16, 29, 37 and 43) are considered scarce, while card #4 (Chuck Connors) is the most popular.

		NM	EX	VG
Complete Set (64):		4,500	2,100	1,250
Common Player:		60.00	30.00	20.00
1a	Johnny Lindell (Regular back.)	80.00	40.00	25.00
1b	Johnny Lindell ('52 Hollywood schedule on back)	80.00	40.00	25.00
2	Jim Davis	60.00	30.00	20.00
3	Al Gettle (Gettel)	60.00	30.00	20.00
4	Chuck Connors	600.00	300.00	200.00
5	Joe Grace	60.00	30.00	20.00
6	Eddie Basinski	60.00	30.00	20.00
7a	Gene Handley (Regular back.)	60.00	30.00	20.00
7b	Gene Handley (Schedule back.)	60.00	30.00	20.00
8	Walt Judnich	60.00	30.00	20.00
9	Jim Marshall	60.00	30.00	20.00
10	Max West	60.00	30.00	20.00
11	Bill MacCawley	120.00	60.00	35.00
12	Moreno Peiretti	60.00	30.00	20.00
13a	Fred Haney (Regular back.)	75.00	37.50	22.50
13b	Fred Haney ('52 Hollywood schedule on back)	75.00	37.50	22.50
14	Earl Johnson	60.00	30.00	20.00
15	Dave Dahle	60.00	30.00	20.00
16	Bob Talbot	120.00	60.00	35.00
17	Smokey Singleton	60.00	30.00	20.00
18	Frank Austin	60.00	30.00	20.00
19	Joe Gordon	90.00	45.00	27.50
20	Joe Marty	60.00	30.00	20.00
21	Bob Gillespie	60.00	30.00	20.00
22	Red Embree	60.00	30.00	20.00
23a	Lefty Olsen (Brown belt.)	60.00	30.00	20.00
23b	Lefty Olsen (Black belt.)	90.00	45.00	27.50
24a	Whitey Wietelmann (Large photo, much of bat missing.)	60.00	30.00	20.00
24b	Whitey Wietelmann (Small photo, more bat shows.)	60.00	30.00	20.00
25	Frank O'Doul	100.00	50.00	30.00
26	Memo Luna	60.00	30.00	20.00
27	John Davis	60.00	30.00	20.00
28	Dick Faber	60.00	30.00	20.00
29	Buddy Peterson	225.00	110.00	67.00
30	Hank Schenz	60.00	30.00	20.00
31	Tookie Gilbert	60.00	30.00	20.00
32	Mel Ott	200.00	100.00	60.00
33	Sam Chapman	60.00	30.00	20.00
34a	John Ragni (Outfielder)	60.00	30.00	20.00
34b	John Ragni (Pitcher)	100.00	50.00	30.00
35	Dick Cole	60.00	30.00	20.00
36	Tom Saffell	60.00	30.00	20.00
37	Roy Welmaker	120.00	60.00	35.00
38	Lou Stringer	60.00	30.00	20.00
39a	Chuck Stevens (Team on back Hollywood.)	60.00	30.00	20.00
39b	Chuck Stevens (Team on back Seattle.)	60.00	30.00	20.00
39c	Chuck Stevens (No team on back.)	60.00	30.00	20.00
40	Artie Wilson	90.00	45.00	30.00
41	Charlie Schanz	60.00	30.00	20.00
42	Al Lyons	60.00	30.00	20.00
43	Joe Erautt	300.00	150.00	90.00
44	Clarence Maddern	60.00	30.00	20.00
45	Gene Baker	60.00	30.00	20.00
46	Tom Heath	60.00	30.00	20.00
47	Al Lien	60.00	30.00	20.00
48	Bill Reeder	60.00	30.00	20.00
49	Bob Thurman	60.00	30.00	20.00
50	Ray Orteig	60.00	30.00	20.00

		NM	EX	VG
51	Joe Brovia	60.00	30.00	20.00
52	Jim Russell	60.00	30.00	20.00
53	Fred Sanford	60.00	30.00	20.00
54	Jim Gladd	60.00	30.00	20.00
55	Clay Hopper	60.00	30.00	20.00
56	Bill Glynn	60.00	30.00	20.00
57	Mike McCormick	60.00	30.00	20.00
58	Richie Myers	60.00	30.00	20.00
59	Vinnie Smith	60.00	30.00	20.00
60a	Stan Hack (Brown belt.)	80.00	40.00	25.00
60b	Stan Hack (Black belt.)	80.00	40.00	25.00
61	Bob Spicer	60.00	30.00	20.00
62	Jack Hollis	60.00	30.00	20.00
63	Ed Chandler	60.00	30.00	20.00
64	Bill Moisan	85.00	45.00	25.00

1953 Mother's Cookies

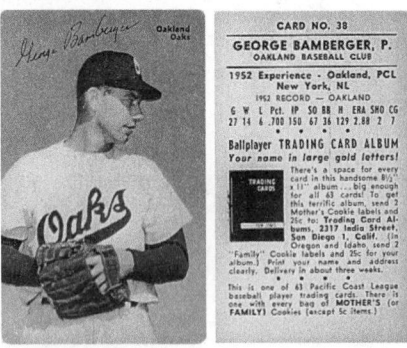

The 1953 Mother's Cookies cards are again 2-3/16" x 3-1/2", with rounded corners. There are 63 players from Pacific Coast League teams included. The full-color fronts have facsimile autographs rather than printed player names, and card backs offer a trading card album. Cards are generally more plentiful than in the 1952 set, with 11 of the cards apparently double printed.

		NM	EX	VG
Complete Set (63):		1,725	850.00	525.00
Common Player:		30.00	15.00	9.00
Album:		125.00	65.00	40.00
1	Lee Winter	35.00	17.50	10.00
2	Joe Ostrowski	30.00	15.00	9.00
3	Will Ramsdell	30.00	15.00	9.00
4	Bobby Bragan	40.00	20.00	12.00
5	Fletcher Robbe	30.00	15.00	9.00
6	Aaron Robinson	30.00	15.00	9.00
7	Augie Galan	30.00	15.00	9.00
8	Buddy Peterson	30.00	15.00	9.00
9	Frank Lefty O'Doul	65.00	32.50	20.00
10	Walt Pocekay	30.00	15.00	9.00
11	Nini Tornay	30.00	15.00	9.00
12	Jim Moran	30.00	15.00	9.00
13	George Schmees	30.00	15.00	9.00
14	Al Widmar	30.00	15.00	9.00
15	Ritchie Myers	30.00	15.00	9.00
16	Bill Howerton	30.00	15.00	9.00
17	Chuck Stevens	30.00	15.00	9.00
18	Joe Brovia	30.00	15.00	9.00
19	Max West	30.00	15.00	9.00
20	Eddie Malone	30.00	15.00	9.00
21	Gene Handley	30.00	15.00	9.00
22	William D. McCawley	30.00	15.00	9.00
23	Bill Sweeney	30.00	15.00	9.00
24	Tom Alston	30.00	15.00	9.00
25	George Vico	30.00	15.00	9.00
26	Hank Arft	30.00	15.00	9.00
27	Al Benton	30.00	15.00	9.00
28	"Pete" Milne	30.00	15.00	9.00
29	Jim Gladd	30.00	15.00	9.00
30	Earl Rapp	35.00	17.50	10.00
31	Ray Orteig	30.00	15.00	9.00
32	Eddie Basinski	30.00	15.00	9.00
33	Reno Cheso	30.00	15.00	9.00
34	Clarence Maddern	30.00	15.00	9.00
35	Marino Pieretti	30.00	15.00	9.00
36	Bill Raimondi	30.00	15.00	9.00
37	Frank Kelleher	30.00	15.00	9.00
38	George Bamberger	35.00	17.50	10.00
39	Dick Smith	30.00	15.00	9.00
40	Charley Schanz	30.00	15.00	9.00
41	John Van Cuyk	30.00	15.00	9.00
42	Lloyd Hittle	30.00	15.00	9.00
43	Tommy Heath	30.00	15.00	9.00
44	Frank Kalin	30.00	15.00	9.00
45	Jack Tobin	30.00	15.00	9.00
46	Jim Davis	30.00	15.00	9.00
47	Claude Christie	30.00	15.00	9.00
48	Elvin Tappe	30.00	15.00	9.00
49	Stan Hack	60.00	30.00	18.00
50	Fred Richards	30.00	15.00	9.00
51	Clay Hopper	30.00	15.00	9.00
52	Roy Welmaker	30.00	15.00	9.00
53	Red Adams	30.00	15.00	9.00
54	Piper Davis	60.00	30.00	18.00
55	Spider Jorgensen	30.00	15.00	9.00
56	Lee Walls	30.00	15.00	9.00
57	Jack Phillips	30.00	15.00	9.00
58	Red Lynn	30.00	15.00	9.00
59	Eddie Beckman	30.00	15.00	9.00
60	Gene Desautels	30.00	15.00	9.00
61	Bob Dillinger	30.00	15.00	9.00
62	Al Federoff	55.00	27.50	16.50
63	Bill Boemler	30.00	15.00	9.00

1920 Mrs. Sherlock's Bread Pins

Members of the Toledo Mud Hens of the American Association are featured on this set of pins sponsored by Mrs. Sherlock's Bread. The 7/8" celluloid pins have a player portrait in black-and-white at center, with his name and position indicated below. At top, in either red or black type is, "Mrs. Sherlock's Home Made Bread." Backs credit manufacture to Bastian Bros. of Rochester, N.Y., "Mfr's of ribbon metal and celluloid novelties." The unnumbered pins are checklisted here alphabetically.

		NM	EX	VG
Complete Set (19):		850.00	425.00	250.00
Common Player:		60.00	30.00	18.00
(1)	Brady	60.00	30.00	18.00
(2)	Roger Bresnahan	90.00	45.00	27.00
(3)	Jean Dubuc	60.00	30.00	18.00
(4)	Dyer	60.00	30.00	18.00
(5)	Fox	60.00	30.00	18.00
(6)	Ham Hyatt	60.00	30.00	18.00
(7)	Jones	60.00	30.00	18.00
(8)	Joe Kelly	60.00	30.00	18.00
(9)	M. Kelly	60.00	30.00	18.00
(10)	Art Kores	60.00	30.00	18.00
(11)	McColl	60.00	30.00	18.00
(12)	Norm McNeill (McNeil)	60.00	30.00	18.00
(13)	Middleton	60.00	30.00	18.00
(14)	Murphy	60.00	30.00	18.00
(15)	Nelson	60.00	30.00	18.00
(16)	Dutch Stryker	60.00	30.00	18.00
(17)	Thompson	60.00	30.00	18.00
(18)	Al Wickland	60.00	30.00	18.00
(19)	Joe Wilhoit	60.00	30.00	18.00

1922 Mrs. Sherlock's Bread Pins (PB5)

Members of the Toledo Mud Hens of the American Association are featured on this set of pins sponsored by Mrs. Sherlock's Bread. The 5/8" celluloid pins have a player portrait in brown or green at center, with name and position indicated below. At top, in either brown or green type is, "Eat Mrs. Sherlock's Bread." The pins are numbered at lower-left.

		NM	EX	VG
Complete Set (21):		900.00	450.00	275.00
Common Player:		60.00	30.00	18.00
1	Roger Bresnahan	90.00	45.00	27.00
2	Brad Kocher	60.00	30.00	18.00
3	Hill	60.00	30.00	18.00
4	Huber	60.00	30.00	18.00
5	Doc Ayers	60.00	30.00	18.00
6	Parks	60.00	30.00	18.00
7	Giard	60.00	30.00	18.00
8	Grimes	60.00	30.00	18.00
9	McCullough	60.00	30.00	18.00
10	Shoup	60.00	30.00	18.00
11	Al Wickland	60.00	30.00	18.00
12	Baker	60.00	30.00	18.00
13	Schauffle	60.00	30.00	18.00
14	Wright	60.00	30.00	18.00
15	Lamar	60.00	30.00	18.00
16	Sallee	60.00	30.00	18.00
17	Fred Luderus	60.00	30.00	18.00
18	Walgomat	60.00	30.00	18.00
19	Ed Konetchy	60.00	30.00	18.00
20	O'Neill	60.00	30.00	18.00
21	Hugh Bedient	60.00	30.00	18.00

1933 Mrs. Sherlock's Bread Pins

Members of the Toledo Mud Hens of the American Association are featured on this set of pins sponsored by Mrs. Sherlock's Bread. The 7/8" celluloid pins have a player portrait in black-and-white at center, with his name and position indicated below. At top, in red type, is "Mrs. Sherlock's Home Made Bread" in two lines. The unnumbered pins are checklisted here alphabetically.

		NM	EX	VG
Complete Set (18):		800.00	400.00	240.00
Common Player:		50.00	25.00	15.00
(1)	LeRoy Bachman	50.00	25.00	15.00
(2)	George Detore	50.00	25.00	15.00
(3)	Frank Doljack	50.00	25.00	15.00
(4)	Milt Galatzer	50.00	25.00	15.00
(5)	Walter Henline	50.00	25.00	15.00
(6)	Roxie Lawson	50.00	25.00	15.00
(7)	Thornton Lee	50.00	25.00	15.00
(8)	Ed Montague	50.00	25.00	15.00
(9)	Steve O'Neill	50.00	25.00	15.00
(10)	Monte Pearson	50.00	25.00	15.00
(11)	Bob Reis	50.00	25.00	15.00
(12)	Scott	50.00	25.00	15.00
(13)	Bill Sweeney	50.00	25.00	15.00
(14)	Hal Trosky	50.00	25.00	15.00
(15)	Pete Turgeon	50.00	25.00	15.00
(16)	Forrest Twogood	50.00	25.00	15.00
(17)	Max West	50.00	25.00	15.00
(18)	Ralph Winegarner	50.00	25.00	15.00

1956 Mutual Savings Dick Stuart

Possibly issued in conjunction with an autograph appearance at the bank, Dick Stuart is pictured on this black-and-white postcard-sized photocard as an outfielder for the Western League Lincoln Chiefs in 1956, the season in which he hit 66 home runs.

	NM	EX	VG
Dick Stuart	100.00	50.00	30.00

N

1960 National Bank of Washington Tacoma Giants

These 3" x 5" unnumbered cards have color photos on front and are usually found with black-and-white backs with the bank's advertising. Uncut sheets of the cards were sold at Cheney Stadium in Tacoma either blank-backed or with a message from the Tacoma Athletic Commission. Only members of the Pacific Coast League Tacoma Giants are included in the set. The set contains the first card issued of Hall of Fame pitcher Juan Marichal. Unfortunately, fellow Hall of Famer Willie McCovey, who played in 17 games for Tacoma in 1960, is not included in the set.

		NM	EX	VG
Complete Set (21):		1,700	850.00	500.00
Common Player:		60.00	30.00	18.00
(1)	Matty Alou	75.00	37.00	22.00
(2)	Ossie Alvarez	60.00	30.00	18.00
(3)	Don Choate	60.00	30.00	18.00
(4)	Red Davis	60.00	30.00	18.00
(5)	Bob Farley	60.00	30.00	18.00
(6)	Eddie Fisher	60.00	30.00	18.00
(7)	Tom Haller	60.00	30.00	18.00
(8)	Sherman Jones	60.00	30.00	18.00

		NM	EX	VG
(9)	Juan Marichal	400.00	200.00	120.00
(10)	Ray Monzant	60.00	30.00	18.00
(11)	Danny O'Connell	60.00	30.00	18.00
(12)	Jose Pagan	60.00	30.00	18.00
(13)	Bob Perry	60.00	30.00	18.00
(14)	Dick Phillips	60.00	30.00	18.00
(15)	Bobby Prescott	60.00	30.00	18.00
(16)	Marshall Renfroe	60.00	30.00	18.00
(17)	Frank Reveira	60.00	30.00	18.00
(18)	Dusty Rhodes	35.00	17.50	10.00
(19)	Sal Taormina	60.00	30.00	18.00
(20)	Verle Tiefenthaler	60.00	30.00	18.00
(21)	Dom Zanni	60.00	30.00	18.00

1961 National Bank of Washington Tacoma Giants

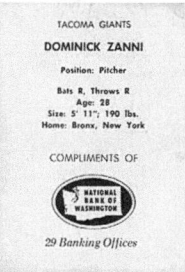

These 3" x 4" cards feature borderless sepia photos on the front. Backs have a sponsor's ad and a few player stats printed in dark blue. The unnumbered cards are checklisted here in alphabetical order.

		NM	EX	VG
Complete Set (21):		800.00	400.00	240.00
Common Player:		30.00	15.00	10.00
(1)	Rafael Alomar	40.00	20.00	12.00
(2)	Ernie Bowman	30.00	15.00	10.00
(3)	Bud Byerly	30.00	15.00	10.00
(4)	Ray Daviault	30.00	15.00	10.00
(5)	Red Davis	30.00	15.00	10.00
(6)	Bob Farley	30.00	15.00	10.00
(7)	Gil Garrido	30.00	15.00	10.00
(8)	John Goetz	30.00	15.00	10.00
(9)	Bill Hain	30.00	15.00	10.00
(10)	Ronald Herbel	30.00	15.00	10.00
(11)	Lynn Lovenguth	30.00	15.00	10.00
(12)	Georges H. Maranda	30.00	15.00	10.00
(13)	Manuel Mota	100.00	50.00	30.00
(14)	John Orsino	30.00	15.00	10.00
(15)	Bob Perry	30.00	15.00	10.00
(16)	Gaylord Perry	175.00	90.00	55.00
(17)	Dick Phillips	30.00	15.00	10.00
(18)	Frank Reveira	30.00	15.00	10.00
(19)	Dusty Rhodes	40.00	20.00	12.00
(20)	Verle Tiefenthaler	30.00	15.00	10.00
(21)	Dom Zanni	30.00	15.00	10.00

1907 Newark Evening World Supplements

The Newark Sailors of the Class A Eastern League are featured in this set of supplements from a local newspaper. The 7-1/2" x 10-15/16" pieces are printed in either sepia or black-and-white. An ornate border surrounds a player pose on a plain background. In a box beneath is player identification. Backs are blank. The unnumbered supplements are checklisted here in alphabetical order, though the list may not yet be complete.

		NM	EX	VG
Common Player:		400.00	200.00	120.00
(1)	William Carrick	400.00	200.00	120.00
(2)	James Cockman	400.00	200.00	120.00
(3)	Clyde Engle	400.00	200.00	120.00
(4)	James Jones	400.00	200.00	120.00
(5)	Paul Krichell	400.00	200.00	120.00
(6)	Henry LaBelle	400.00	200.00	120.00
(7)	William Mahling	400.00	200.00	120.00
(8)	Chas. McCafferty	400.00	200.00	120.00
(9)	Thomas McCarthy	400.00	200.00	120.00
(10)	James Mullen (Mullin)	400.00	200.00	120.00
(11)	Al Pardee	400.00	200.00	120.00
(12)	Bayard Sharpe	400.00	200.00	120.00

		NM	EX	VG
(13)	John E. Shea	400.00	200.00	120.00
(14)	Oscar Stanage	400.00	200.00	120.00
(15)	Elmer Zacher	400.00	200.00	120.00

1950 Oak Hall Roanoke Red Sox

(See 1950 Bush & Hancock Roanoke Red Sox.)

1913 Oakland Oaks Team Issue

Stylistically similar to contemporary Zeenuts cards, little is known about this series. The blank-back, approximately 2" x 3-5/8" cards have full-length sepiatone player poses on a sepiatone background. The player's last name and city are printed in all caps in two lines at bottom. It is unknown whether the cards on the list comprise a complete set. Their manner of distribution is likewise unknown, they may have been a strip card issue or a candy insert.

		NM	EX	VG
Common Player:		2,400	1,200	700.00
(1)	Ody Abbott	2,400	1,200	700.00
(2)	Harry Ables	2,400	1,200	700.00
(3)	Jesse Becker	2,400	1,200	700.00
(4)	W.W. Cook	2,400	1,200	700.00
(5)	Bert Coy	2,400	1,200	700.00
(6)	Rube Gardner	2,400	1,200	700.00
(7)	Howard Gregory	2,400	1,200	700.00
(8)	Gus Hetling	2,400	1,200	700.00
(9)	Jack Killilay	2,400	1,200	700.00
(10)	Bill Leard	2,400	1,200	700.00
(11)	John Malarkey	2,400	1,200	700.00
(12)	Carl Mitze	2,400	1,200	700.00
(13)	John Ness	2,400	1,200	700.00
(14)	Henry Olmstead	2,400	1,200	700.00
(15)	Cy Parkin	2,400	1,200	700.00
(16)	W.J. Pearce	2,400	1,200	700.00
(17)	Heine Pernoll	2,400	1,200	700.00
(18)	Ashley Pope	2,400	1,200	700.00
(19)	George Schirm	2,400	1,200	700.00
(20)	Elmer Zacher	2,400	1,200	700.00

1909 Obak (T212)

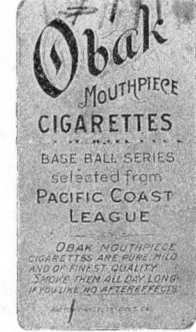

Produced annually from 1909 to 1911, the Obak cards were actually three separate and distinct sets, but they were all grouped together under a single T212 designation in the American Card Catalog. The Obak sets are closely related in style to the more popular T206 "White Border" set issued over the same three-year period, and, in fact, were produced by the California branch of the same American Tobacco Co. conglomerate. The Obaks are the standard tobacco card size, about 1-1/2" x 2-5/8", and feature a colored lithograph, along with the player's name and team, on the front of the card. The year of issue can easily be determined by examing the back. The 1909 issue has blue printing with the name "Obak" appearing in an "Old English" type style. For 1910 the type face was changed to straight block letters; and in 1911 the backs were printed in red and include a brief biography and player statistics. The 1909 edition featured only

teams from the Pacific Coast League. Cards can be found with backs that do or do not have a border around the text, though neither version appears to be scarcer than the other. Many 1909 Obaks with the "no-frame" back design show evidence of having been cut by hand from sheets, rather than machine-cut.

		NM	EX	VG
Complete Set (76):		45,000	27,500	11,000
Common Player:		650.00	325.00	195.00
(1)	Baum	650.00	325.00	195.00
(2)	Beall	650.00	325.00	195.00
(3)	Bernard	650.00	325.00	195.00
(4)	Berry	650.00	325.00	195.00
(5)	Bodie	650.00	325.00	195.00
(6)	Boyce	650.00	325.00	195.00
(7)	Brackenridge	650.00	325.00	195.00
(8)	N. Brashear	650.00	325.00	195.00
(9)	Breen	650.00	325.00	195.00
(10)	Brown	650.00	325.00	195.00
(11)	D. Brown	650.00	325.00	195.00
(12)	Browning	650.00	325.00	195.00
(13)	Byrnes	650.00	325.00	195.00
(14)	Cameron	650.00	325.00	195.00
(15)	Carroll	650.00	325.00	195.00
(16)	Carson	650.00	325.00	195.00
(17)	Christian	650.00	325.00	195.00
(18)	Coy	650.00	325.00	195.00
(19)	Delmas	650.00	325.00	195.00
(20)	Dillon	650.00	325.00	195.00
(21)	Eagan	650.00	325.00	195.00
(22)	Easterly (Eastley)	650.00	325.00	195.00
(23)	Ehman	650.00	325.00	195.00
(24)	Fisher	650.00	325.00	195.00
(25)	Fitzgerald	650.00	325.00	195.00
(26)	Flannagan	650.00	325.00	195.00
(27)	Gandil	7,500	3,700	2,200
(28)	Garrett	650.00	325.00	195.00
(29)	Graham	650.00	325.00	195.00
(30)	Graney	650.00	325.00	195.00
(31)	Griffin	650.00	325.00	195.00
(32)	Guyn	650.00	325.00	195.00
(33)	Haley	650.00	325.00	195.00
(34)	Harkins	650.00	325.00	195.00
(35)	Henley	650.00	325.00	195.00
(36)	Hitt	650.00	325.00	195.00
(37)	Hogan	650.00	325.00	195.00
(38)	W. Hogan	650.00	325.00	195.00
(39)	Howard	650.00	325.00	195.00
(40)	Howse	650.00	325.00	195.00
(41)	Jansing	650.00	325.00	195.00
(42)	LaLonge	650.00	325.00	195.00
(43)	C. Lewis	650.00	325.00	195.00
(44)	D. Lewis	650.00	325.00	195.00
(45)	J. Lewis	650.00	325.00	195.00
(46)	Martinke	650.00	325.00	195.00
(47)	McArdle	650.00	325.00	195.00
(48)	McCredie	650.00	325.00	195.00
(49)	McKune	650.00	325.00	195.00
(50)	Melchior	650.00	325.00	195.00
(51)	Mohler	650.00	325.00	195.00
(52)	Mott	650.00	325.00	195.00
(53)	Mundorff	650.00	325.00	195.00
(54)	Murphy	650.00	325.00	195.00
(55)	Nagle	650.00	325.00	195.00
(56)	Nelson	650.00	325.00	195.00
(57)	Olson	650.00	325.00	195.00
(58)	Ornsdorff	650.00	325.00	195.00
(59)	Ort	650.00	325.00	195.00
(60)	Ragan	650.00	325.00	195.00
(61)	Raymer	650.00	325.00	195.00
(62)	Reidy	650.00	325.00	195.00
(63)	Ryan	650.00	325.00	195.00
(64)	Shinn	650.00	325.00	195.00
(65)	Smith	650.00	325.00	195.00
(66)	Speas	650.00	325.00	195.00
(67)	Stoval (Stovall)	650.00	325.00	195.00
(68)	Tennant	650.00	325.00	195.00
(69)	Whalen	650.00	325.00	195.00
(70)	Wheeler	650.00	325.00	195.00
(71)	Wiggs	650.00	325.00	195.00
(72)	Willett	650.00	325.00	195.00
(73)	J. Williams	650.00	325.00	195.00
(74)	R. Williams	650.00	325.00	195.00
(75)	Willis	650.00	325.00	195.00
(76)	Zeider	650.00	325.00	195.00

1910 Obak 150 Subjects (T212)

The most common, yet most complex, of the three annual T212 baseball card issues from Obak Cigarettes is the 1910 edition. Besides players from the six Pacific Coast League teams, cards were also issued for the four-team Northwestern

League. This change caused the addition of a league abbreviation, along with the player's last name and city on front. Backs are again printed in blue, but utilize a less ornate typography than the 1909 cards. The 1910 Obak set is formatted similar to the more popular T206 "White Border" set issued at the same time "back East," and, in fact, was produced by the California branch of the same American Tobacco Company conglomerate. Obaks are the standard tobacco-card size, about 1-1/2" x 2-5/8", featuring a color lithograph on front. The 1910 issue comprises two major types, one which mentions "150 SUBJECTS," on back, the other specifying "175 SUBJECTS." Forty player cards, all from the PCL, are known to exist in both 150- and 175-subject versions, the former being much scarcer. Many of the 150-subject cards can be found with significant picture variations, such as missing team names on jerseys, plain versus striped caps, different background colors or different picture cropping. Unique to the 1910 Obaks is a selection of 35 different advertising slogans which are found on back between the boxed text elements. How many of the slogans can be found on each player's cards is unknown; some are seen on only a handful of different players' cards while others are found on dozens.

		NM	EX	VG
Complete Set (40):		25,000	13,000	5,500
Common Player:		600.00	320.00	125.00
(1)	Charlie Armbuster (Ambruster)	600.00	320.00	125.00
(2)	Claude Berry	600.00	320.00	125.00
(3)	John Brackenridge	600.00	320.00	125.00
(4)	N. Brashear (Norman)	600.00	320.00	125.00
(5)	Hap Briggs	600.00	320.00	125.00
(6)	Don Cameron	600.00	320.00	125.00
(7)	Bert Coy	600.00	320.00	125.00
(8)	Elmer Criger	600.00	320.00	125.00
(9)	Babe Danzig	600.00	320.00	125.00
(10)	Cap Dillon	600.00	320.00	125.00
(11)	Bill Fisher	600.00	320.00	125.00
(12)	Ed Griffin	600.00	320.00	125.00
(13)	Cack Henley	600.00	320.00	125.00
(14)	Al Hiester	600.00	320.00	125.00
(15)	Happy Hogan	600.00	320.00	125.00
(16)	Ivan Howard	600.00	320.00	125.00
(17)	Gene Krapp	600.00	320.00	125.00
(18)	Mickey LaLonge	600.00	320.00	125.00
(19)	George Manush	600.00	320.00	125.00
(20)	Roy McArdle	600.00	320.00	125.00
(21)	Walt McCredie	600.00	320.00	125.00
(22)	Henry Melchoir	600.00	320.00	125.00
(23)	Kid Mohler	600.00	320.00	125.00
(24)	Walter Moser	600.00	320.00	125.00
(25)	Howard Mundorf	600.00	320.00	125.00
(26)	Howard Murphy	600.00	320.00	125.00
(27)	George Ort	600.00	320.00	125.00
(28)	Hank Perry	600.00	320.00	125.00
(29)	Bill Rapps	600.00	320.00	125.00
(30)	H. Smith (Hugh)	600.00	320.00	125.00
(31)	J. Smith (Jud)	600.00	320.00	125.00
(32)	Bill Steen	600.00	320.00	125.00
(33)	Harry Stewart	600.00	320.00	125.00
(34)	Pinky Swander	600.00	320.00	125.00
(35)	Lefty Tonnesen (Tonneson)	600.00	320.00	125.00
(36)	Jimmy Whalen	600.00	320.00	125.00
(37)	Roy Willett	600.00	320.00	125.00
(38)	Jimmy Williams	600.00	320.00	125.00
(39)	Ralph Willis	600.00	320.00	125.00
(40)	Harry Wolverton	600.00	320.00	125.00

1910 Obak 175 Subjects (T212)

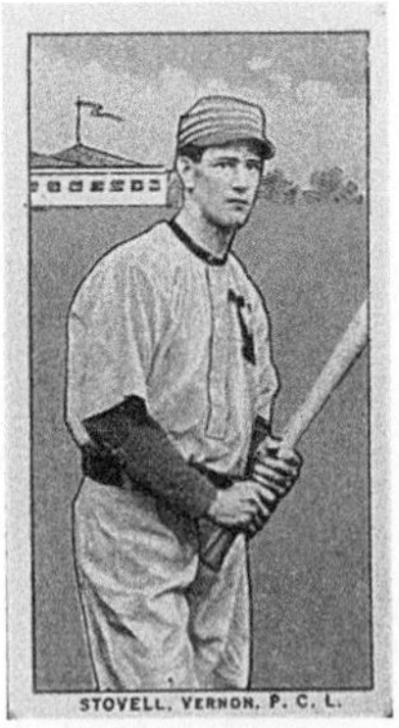
STOVELL, VERNON, P. C. L.

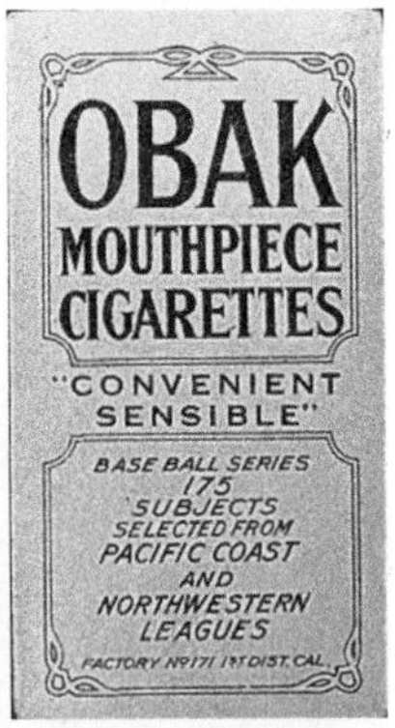
OBAK
MOUTHPIECE
CIGARETTES
"CONVENIENT SENSIBLE"
BASE BALL SERIES 175 SUBJECTS SELECTED FROM PACIFIC COAST AND NORTHWESTERN LEAGUES

The most common, yet most complex, of the three annual T212 baseball card issues from Obak Cigarettes is the 1910 edition. Besides players from the six Pacific Coast League teams, cards were also issued for the four-team Northwestern League. This change caused the addition of a league abbreviation, along with the player's last name and city on front. Backs are again printed in blue, but utilize a less ornate typography than the 1909 cards. The 1910 Obak set is formatted similar to the more popular T206 "White Border" set issued at the same time "back East," and, in fact, was produced by the California branch of the same American Tobacco Co. conglomerate. Obaks are the standard tobacco-card size, about 1-1/2" x 2-5/8", featuring a color lithograph on front. The 1910 issue comprises two major types, one which mentions "150 SUBJECTS," on back, the other specifying "175 SUBJECTS." Forty player cards, all from the PCL, are known to exist in both 150- and 175-subject versions, the former being much scarcer. Many of the 150-subject cards can be found with significant picture variations, such as missing team names on jerseys, plain versus striped caps, different background colors or different picture cropping. Unique to the 1910 Obaks is a selection of 35 different advertising slogans which are found on back between the boxed text elements. How many of the slogans can be found on each player's cards is unknown; some are seen on only a handful of different players' cards while others are found on dozens.

		NM	EX	VG
Complete Set (175):		38,000	20,000	9,000
Common Player:		275.00	140.00	65.00
(1)	Agnew	275.00	140.00	65.00
(2)	Akin	275.00	140.00	65.00
(3)	Ames	275.00	140.00	65.00
(4)	Annis	275.00	140.00	65.00
(5)	Armbuster (Armbruster)	275.00	140.00	65.00
(6)	Baker	275.00	140.00	65.00
(7)	Bassey	275.00	140.00	65.00
(8)	Baum	275.00	140.00	65.00
	Beall (Now believed not to exist.)	275.00	140.00	65.00
(9)	Bennett	275.00	140.00	65.00
(10)	Bernard	275.00	140.00	65.00
(11)	Berry	275.00	140.00	65.00
(12)	Blankenship	275.00	140.00	65.00
(13)	Boardman	275.00	140.00	65.00
(14)	Bodie	275.00	140.00	65.00
(15)	Bonner	275.00	140.00	65.00
(16)	Brackenridge	275.00	140.00	65.00
(17)	N. Brashear	275.00	140.00	65.00
(18)	R. Brashear	275.00	140.00	65.00
(19)	Breen	275.00	140.00	65.00
(20)	Briggs	275.00	140.00	65.00
(21)	Brinker	275.00	140.00	65.00
(22)	Briswalter	275.00	140.00	65.00
(23)	Brooks	275.00	140.00	65.00
(24)	Brown (Sacramento)	275.00	140.00	65.00
(25)	Brown (Vernon)	275.00	140.00	65.00
(26)	D. Brown	275.00	140.00	65.00
(27)	Browning	275.00	140.00	65.00
(28)	Burrell	275.00	140.00	65.00
(29)	Byrd	275.00	140.00	65.00
(30)	Byrnes	275.00	140.00	65.00
(31)	Cameron	275.00	140.00	65.00
(32)	Capron	275.00	140.00	65.00
(33)	Carlisle	275.00	140.00	65.00
(34)	Carroll	275.00	140.00	65.00
(35)	Cartwright	275.00	140.00	65.00
(36)	Casey	275.00	140.00	65.00
(37)	Caslleton (Castleton)	400.00	200.00	100.00
(38)	Chenault	275.00	140.00	65.00
(39)	Christian	275.00	140.00	65.00
(40)	Coleman	275.00	140.00	65.00
(41)	Cooney	275.00	140.00	65.00
(42)	Coy	275.00	140.00	65.00
(43)	Criger	275.00	140.00	65.00
(44)	Custer	275.00	140.00	65.00
(45)	Cutshaw	275.00	140.00	65.00
(46)	Daley	275.00	140.00	65.00
(47)	Danzig	275.00	140.00	65.00
(48)	Daringer	275.00	140.00	65.00
(49)	Davis	275.00	140.00	65.00
(50)	Delhi	275.00	140.00	65.00
(51)	Delmas	275.00	140.00	65.00
(52)	Dillon	275.00	140.00	65.00
(53)	Dretchko	275.00	140.00	65.00
(54)	Eastley	275.00	140.00	65.00
(55)	Erickson	275.00	140.00	65.00
(56)	Flannagan	275.00	140.00	65.00
(57)	Fisher (Portland)	275.00	140.00	65.00
(58)	Fisher (Vernon)	275.00	140.00	65.00
(59)	Fitzgerald	275.00	140.00	65.00
(60)	Flood	275.00	140.00	65.00
(61)	Fournier	275.00	140.00	65.00
(62)	Frisk	275.00	140.00	65.00
(63)	Gaddy	275.00	140.00	65.00
(64)	Gardner	275.00	140.00	65.00
(65)	Garrett	275.00	140.00	65.00
(66)	Greggs (Gregg)	275.00	140.00	65.00
(67)	Griffin	275.00	140.00	65.00
(68)	Gurney	275.00	140.00	65.00
(69)	Hall (Seattle)	275.00	140.00	65.00
(70)	Hall (Tacoma)	275.00	140.00	65.00
(71)	Harkins	275.00	140.00	65.00
(72)	Hartman	275.00	140.00	65.00
(73)	Hendrix	275.00	140.00	65.00
(74)	Henley	275.00	140.00	65.00
(75)	Hensling	275.00	140.00	65.00
(76)	Hetling	275.00	140.00	65.00
(77)	Hickey	275.00	140.00	65.00
(78)	Hiester	275.00	140.00	65.00
(79)	Hitt	275.00	140.00	65.00
(80)	Hogan (Oakland)	275.00	140.00	65.00
(81)	Hogan (Vernon)	275.00	140.00	65.00
(82)	Hollis	275.00	140.00	65.00
(83)	Holm	275.00	140.00	65.00
(84)	Howard	275.00	140.00	65.00
(85)	Hunt	275.00	140.00	65.00
(86)	James	275.00	140.00	65.00
(87)	Jansing	275.00	140.00	65.00
(88)	Jensen	275.00	140.00	65.00
(89)	Johnston	275.00	140.00	65.00
(90)	Keener	275.00	140.00	65.00
(91)	Killilay	275.00	140.00	65.00
(92)	Kippert	275.00	140.00	65.00
(93)	Klein	275.00	140.00	65.00
(94)	Krapp	275.00	140.00	65.00
(95)	Kusel	275.00	140.00	65.00
(96)	LaLonge	275.00	140.00	65.00
(97)	Lewis	275.00	140.00	65.00
(98)	J. Lewis	275.00	140.00	65.00
(99)	John Lindsay	275.00	140.00	65.00
(100)	Lively	275.00	140.00	65.00
(101)	Lynch	275.00	140.00	65.00
(102)	Manush	275.00	140.00	65.00
(103)	Martinke	275.00	140.00	65.00
(104)	McArdle	275.00	140.00	65.00
(105)	McCredie	275.00	140.00	65.00
(106)	Melchior	275.00	140.00	65.00
(107)	Miller (San Francisco)	275.00	140.00	65.00
(108)	Miller (Seattle)	275.00	140.00	65.00
(109)	Mitze	275.00	140.00	65.00
(110)	Mohler	275.00	140.00	65.00
(111)	Moser	275.00	140.00	65.00
(112)	Mott	275.00	140.00	65.00
(113)	Mundorff (Mundorf)	275.00	140.00	65.00
(114)	Murphy	275.00	140.00	65.00
(115)	Nagle	275.00	140.00	65.00
(116)	Nelson	275.00	140.00	65.00
(117)	Netzel	275.00	140.00	65.00
(118)	Nourse	275.00	140.00	65.00
(119)	Nordyke	275.00	140.00	65.00
(120)	Olson	275.00	140.00	65.00
(121)	Orendorff (Orsnsdorff)	275.00	140.00	65.00
(122)	Ort	275.00	140.00	65.00
(123)	Ostdiek	275.00	140.00	65.00
(124)	Pennington	275.00	140.00	65.00
(125)	Perrine	275.00	140.00	65.00
(126)	Perry	275.00	140.00	65.00
(127)	Persons	275.00	140.00	65.00
(128)	Rapps	275.00	140.00	65.00
(129)	Raymer	275.00	140.00	65.00
(130)	Raymond	275.00	140.00	65.00
(131)	Rockenfield	275.00	140.00	65.00
(132)	Roth	275.00	140.00	65.00
(133)	D. Ryan	275.00	140.00	65.00
(134)	J. Ryan	275.00	140.00	65.00
(135)	Scharnweber	275.00	140.00	65.00
(136)	Schmutz	275.00	140.00	65.00
(137)	Seaton (Portland)	275.00	140.00	65.00
(138)	Seaton (Seattle)	275.00	140.00	65.00
(139)	Shafer	275.00	140.00	65.00
(140)	Shaw	275.00	140.00	65.00
(141)	Shea	275.00	140.00	65.00
(142)	Shinn	275.00	140.00	65.00
(143)	Smith	275.00	140.00	65.00
(144)	H. Smith	275.00	140.00	65.00
(145)	J. Smith	275.00	140.00	65.00
(146)	Speas	275.00	140.00	65.00
(147)	Spiesman	275.00	140.00	65.00
(148)	Starkell	275.00	140.00	65.00
(149)	Steen	275.00	140.00	65.00
(150)	Stevens	275.00	140.00	65.00
(151)	Stewart	275.00	140.00	65.00
(152)	Stovell (Stovall)	275.00	140.00	65.00
(153)	Streib	275.00	140.00	65.00
(154)	Sugden	275.00	140.00	65.00
(155)	Sutor (Suter)	275.00	140.00	65.00
(156)	Swain	275.00	140.00	65.00
(157)	Swander	275.00	140.00	65.00
(158)	Tennant	275.00	140.00	65.00
(159)	Thomas	275.00	140.00	65.00
(160)	Thompson	275.00	140.00	65.00
(161)	Thorsen	275.00	140.00	65.00
(162)	Tonnesen (Tonneson)	275.00	140.00	65.00
(163)	Tozer	275.00	140.00	65.00
(164)	Van Buren	275.00	140.00	65.00
(165)	Vitt	275.00	140.00	65.00
(166)	Wares	275.00	140.00	65.00
(167)	Waring	275.00	140.00	65.00
(168)	Warren	275.00	140.00	65.00
(169)	Weed	275.00	140.00	65.00
(170)	Whalen	275.00	140.00	65.00
(171)	Willett	275.00	140.00	65.00
(172)	Williams	275.00	140.00	65.00
(173)	Willis	275.00	140.00	65.00
(174)	Wolverton	275.00	140.00	65.00
(175)	Zackert	275.00	140.00	65.00

1911 Obak (T212)

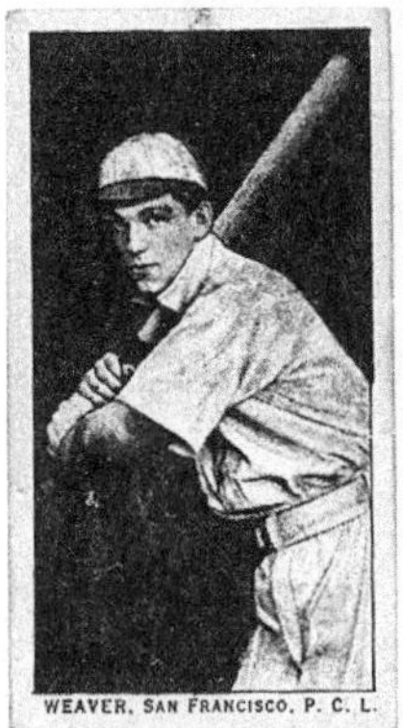
WEAVER, SAN FRANCISCO, P. C. L.

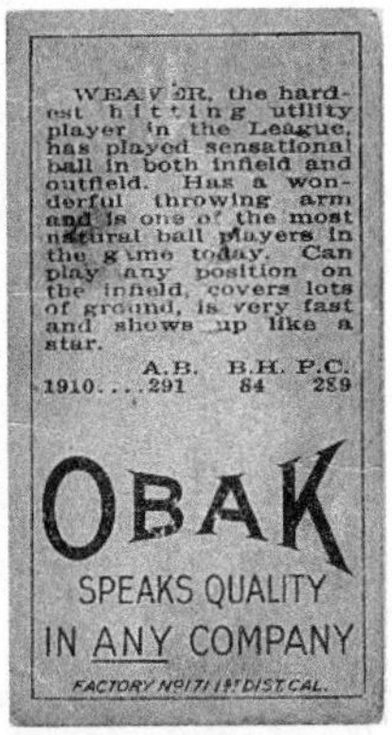
WEAVER, the hardest hitting utility player in the League, has played sensational ball in both infield and outfield. Has a wonderful throwing arm and is one of the most natural ball players in the game today. Can play any position on the infield, covers lots of ground, is very fast and shows up like a star.
A.B. B.H. P.C.
1910....291 84 289
OBAK
SPEAKS QUALITY
IN ANY COMPANY

The last of the three annual T212 baseball card issues from Obak Cigarettes is the 1911 edition, again featuring players from the six Pacific Coast League teams and the four-team Northwestern League. Often using the same chromolithographic picture on front as the 1910 cards, the 1911s are easily distinguished by the use of red, rather than blue, printing on back. Also new to the 1911s was the addition of a sentence or two about the player and, on most cards, recent years' statistics, an innovation also seen on the contemporary T205 cards "back East." In fact the Obaks were produced by the California branch of the same American Tobacco Company conglomerate. Obaks are the standard tobacco card size, about 1-1/2" x 2-5/8".

		NM	EX	VG
Complete Set (175):		45,000	22,500	13,500
Common Player:		275.00	138.00	68.00
(1)	Abbott	275.00	138.00	68.00

(2)	Ables	275.00	138.00	68.00
(3)	Adams	275.00	138.00	68.00
(4)	Agnew	275.00	138.00	68.00
(5)	Akin	275.00	138.00	68.00
(6)	Annis	275.00	138.00	68.00
(7)	Arrelanes (Arellanes)	275.00	138.00	68.00
(8)	Barry	275.00	138.00	68.00
(9)	Bassey	275.00	138.00	68.00
(10)	Baum	275.00	138.00	68.00
(11)	Bennett	275.00	138.00	68.00
(12)	Bernard	275.00	138.00	68.00
(13)	Berry	275.00	138.00	68.00
(14)	Bloomfield	275.00	138.00	68.00
(15)	Bonner	275.00	138.00	68.00
(16)	Brackenridge	275.00	138.00	68.00
(17)	Brashear	275.00	138.00	68.00
(18)	R. Brashear	275.00	138.00	68.00
(19)	Brinker	275.00	138.00	68.00
(20)	Brown	275.00	138.00	68.00
(21)	Browning	275.00	138.00	68.00
(22)	Bues	275.00	138.00	68.00
(23)	Burrell	275.00	138.00	68.00
(24)	Burns	275.00	138.00	68.00
(25)	Butler	275.00	138.00	68.00
(26)	Byram	275.00	138.00	68.00
(27)	Carlisle	275.00	138.00	68.00
(28)	Carson	275.00	138.00	68.00
(29)	Cartwright	275.00	138.00	68.00
(30)	Casey	275.00	138.00	68.00
(31)	Castleton	325.00	138.00	68.00
(32)	Chadbourne	275.00	138.00	68.00
(33)	Christian	275.00	138.00	68.00
(34)	Coleman	275.00	138.00	68.00
(35)	Cooney	275.00	138.00	68.00
(36)	Coy	275.00	138.00	68.00
(37)	Criger	275.00	138.00	68.00
(38)	Crukshank	275.00	138.00	68.00
(39)	Cutshaw	275.00	138.00	68.00
(40)	Daley	275.00	138.00	68.00
(41)	Danzig	275.00	138.00	68.00
(42)	Dashwood	275.00	138.00	68.00
(43)	Davis	275.00	138.00	68.00
(44)	Delhi	275.00	138.00	68.00
(45)	Delmas	275.00	138.00	68.00
(46)	Dillon	275.00	138.00	68.00
(47)	Engel	275.00	138.00	68.00
(48)	Erickson	275.00	138.00	68.00
(49)	Fitzgerald	275.00	138.00	68.00
(50)	Flater	275.00	138.00	68.00
(51)	Frisk	275.00	138.00	68.00
(52)	Fullerton	275.00	138.00	68.00
(53)	Garrett	275.00	138.00	68.00
(54)	Goodman	275.00	138.00	68.00
(55)	Gordon	275.00	138.00	68.00
(56)	Grindle	275.00	138.00	68.00
(57)	Hall	275.00	138.00	68.00
(58)	Harris	275.00	138.00	68.00
(59)	Hasty	275.00	138.00	68.00
(60)	Henderson	275.00	138.00	68.00
(61)	Henley	275.00	138.00	68.00
(62)	Hetling	275.00	138.00	68.00
(63)	Hiester	275.00	138.00	68.00
(64)	Higgins	275.00	138.00	68.00
(65)	Hitt	275.00	138.00	68.00
(66)	Hoffman	275.00	138.00	68.00
(67)	Hogan	275.00	138.00	68.00
(68)	Holm	275.00	138.00	68.00
(69)	Householder	275.00	138.00	68.00
(70)	Hosp	275.00	138.00	68.00
(71)	Howard	275.00	138.00	68.00
(72)	Hunt	275.00	138.00	68.00
(73)	James	275.00	138.00	68.00
(74)	Jensen	275.00	138.00	68.00
(75)	Kading	275.00	138.00	68.00
(76)	Kane	275.00	138.00	68.00
(77)	Kippert	275.00	138.00	68.00
(78)	Knight	275.00	138.00	68.00
(79)	Koestner	275.00	138.00	68.00
(80)	Krueger	275.00	138.00	68.00
(81)	Kuhn	275.00	138.00	68.00
(82)	LaLonge	275.00	138.00	68.00
(83)	Lamline	275.00	138.00	68.00
(84)	Leard	275.00	138.00	68.00
(85)	Lerchen	275.00	138.00	68.00
(86)	Lewis	275.00	138.00	68.00
(87)	Madden	275.00	138.00	68.00
(88)	Maggert	275.00	138.00	68.00
(89)	Mahoney	275.00	138.00	68.00
(90)	McArdle	275.00	138.00	68.00
(91)	McCredie	275.00	138.00	68.00
(92)	McDonnell	275.00	138.00	68.00
(93)	Meikle	275.00	138.00	68.00
(94)	Melchior	275.00	138.00	68.00
(95)	Mensor	550.00	275.00	165.00
(96)	Metzger	275.00	138.00	68.00
(97)	Miller (Oakland)	275.00	138.00	68.00
(98)	Miller (San Francisco)	275.00	138.00	68.00
(99)	Ten Million	3,000	1,500	750.00
(100)	Mitze	275.00	138.00	68.00
(101)	Mohler	275.00	138.00	68.00
(102)	Moore	275.00	138.00	68.00
(103)	Morse	275.00	138.00	68.00
(104)	Moskiman	275.00	138.00	68.00
(105)	Mundorff	275.00	138.00	68.00
(106)	Murray	275.00	138.00	68.00
(107)	Netzel	275.00	138.00	68.00
(108)	Nordyke	275.00	138.00	68.00
(109)	Nourse	275.00	138.00	68.00
(110)	O'Rourke	275.00	138.00	68.00
(111)	Ostdiek	275.00	138.00	68.00
(112)	Patterson	275.00	138.00	68.00
(113)	Pearce	275.00	138.00	68.00
(114)	Peckinpaugh	475.00	235.00	140.00
(115)	Pernoll	275.00	138.00	68.00
(116)	Pfyl	275.00	138.00	68.00
(117)	Powell	275.00	138.00	68.00
(118)	Raleigh	275.00	138.00	68.00
(119)	Rapps	275.00	138.00	68.00
(120)	Raymer	275.00	138.00	68.00
(121)	Raymond	275.00	138.00	68.00
(122)	Reddick	275.00	138.00	68.00
(123)	Roche	275.00	138.00	68.00
(124)	Rockenfield	275.00	138.00	68.00
(125)	Rogers	275.00	138.00	68.00
(126)	Ross	275.00	138.00	68.00
(127)	Ryan	275.00	138.00	68.00
(128)	J. Ryan	275.00	138.00	68.00
(129)	Scharnweber	275.00	138.00	68.00
(130)	Schmidt	275.00	138.00	68.00
(131)	Schmutz	275.00	138.00	68.00
(132)	Seaton (Portland)	275.00	138.00	68.00
(133)	Seaton (Seattle)	275.00	138.00	68.00
(134)	Shaw	275.00	138.00	68.00
(135)	Shea	275.00	138.00	68.00
(136)	Sheehan (Portland)	275.00	138.00	68.00
(137)	Sheehan (Vernon)	275.00	138.00	68.00
(138)	Shinn	275.00	138.00	68.00
(139)	Skeels	275.00	138.00	68.00
(140)	H. Smith	275.00	138.00	68.00
(141)	Speas	275.00	138.00	68.00
(142)	Spencer	275.00	138.00	68.00
(143)	Spiesman	275.00	138.00	68.00
(144)	Starkel	275.00	138.00	68.00
(145)	Steen	275.00	138.00	68.00
(146)	Stewart	275.00	138.00	68.00
(147)	Stinson	275.00	138.00	68.00
(148)	Stovall	275.00	138.00	68.00
(149)	Strand	275.00	138.00	68.00
(150)	Sutor (Suter)	275.00	138.00	68.00
(151)	Swain	275.00	138.00	68.00
(152)	Tennant	275.00	138.00	68.00
(153)	Thomas (Sacramento)	275.00	138.00	68.00
(154)	Thomas (Victoria)	275.00	138.00	68.00
(155)	Thompson	275.00	138.00	68.00
(156)	Thornton	275.00	138.00	68.00
(157)	Thorsen	275.00	138.00	68.00
(158)	Tiedeman	275.00	138.00	68.00
(159)	Tozer	275.00	138.00	68.00
(160)	Van Buren	275.00	138.00	68.00
(161)	Vitt	275.00	138.00	68.00
(162)	Ward	275.00	138.00	68.00
(163)	Wares	275.00	138.00	68.00
(164)	Warren	275.00	138.00	68.00
(165)	Weaver	9,750	4,875	2,925
(166)	Weed	275.00	138.00	68.00
(167)	Wheeler	275.00	138.00	68.00
(168)	Wiggs	275.00	138.00	68.00
(169)	Willett	275.00	138.00	68.00
(170)	Williams	275.00	138.00	68.00
(171)	Wolverton	275.00	138.00	68.00
(172)	Zacher	275.00	138.00	68.00
(173)	Zackert	275.00	138.00	68.00
(174)	Zamlock	275.00	138.00	68.00
(175)	Zimmerman	275.00	138.00	68.00

1911 Obak Cabinets (T4)

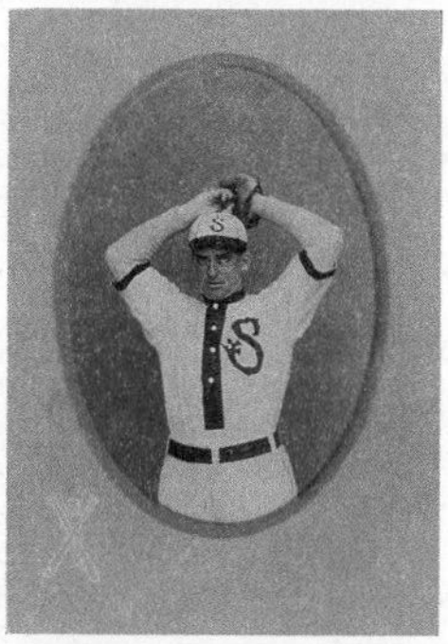

Among the scarcest of all the 20th Century tobacco issues, the T4 Obak Premiums are cabinet-sized cards distributed in conjunction with the better-known Obak T212 card set of players from the Northwestern and Pacific Coast Leagues. The Obak Premiums measure about 5" x 7" and are printed on a cardboard-like paper. The cards featured a black-and-white player photo inside a 3-1/2" x 5" oval. There is no printing on the front of the card to identify the player or indicate the manufacturer. The backs are blank. In most cases the photos used for the premiums are identical to the T212 pictures, except for some cropping differences. Under the Obak mail-in promotion, 50 coupons from cigarette packages were required to obtain just one premium card, which explains their extreme scarcity today. All 175 players pictured in the T212 set were theoretically available as premium cards, but to date many remain undiscovered. Only those cards that have been confirmed to survive are listed with a value here. Most of the Obak premiums that exist in original condition contain a number, written in pencil on the back of the card, that corresponds to the checklist printed on the coupon. A large group of the cabinets, most of which had been cut down to just the oval portrait, was offered in a September 2002 auction.

		NM	EX	VG
Common Player:		6,750	3,500	2,200
	LOS ANGELES			
1	H. Smith	5,750	2,875	1,725
2	Tozer	5,750	2,875	1,725
3	Howard	5,750	2,875	1,725
4	Daley	5,750	2,875	1,725
5	Bernard			
6	Dillon	5,750	2,875	1,725
7	Delmas			
8	Delhi	5,750	2,875	1,725
9	Criger			
10	Thorsen	5,750	2,875	1,725
11	Agnew			
12	Akin			
13	Metzger			
14	Abbott			
15	Wheeler	5,750	2,875	1,725
16	Moore			
17	Grindle			
	OAKLAND			
18	Wolverton			
19	Mitze	5,750	2,875	1,725
20	Wares			
21	Cutshaw	5,750	2,875	1,725
22	Christian	5,750	2,875	1,725
23	Wiggs			
24	Maggert	5,750	2,875	1,725
25	Pfyl			
26	Pearce			
27	Hetling			
28	Hoffman			
29	Pernoll	5,750	2,875	1,725
30	Coy			
31	Tiedeman	5,750	2,875	1,725
32	Knight	.00	.00	.00
33	Flater	5,750	2,875	1,725
34	Zacher	5,750	2,875	1,725
35	Ables	5,750	2,875	1,725
36	Miller			
	PORTLAND (PCL)			
37	Ryan	5,750	2,875	1,725
38	Rapps	5,750	2,875	1,725
39	McCredie			
40	Seaton			
41	Steen			
42	Chadbourne	5,750	2,875	1,725
43	Krueger			
44	Sheehan			
45	Roger Peckinpaugh	5,750	2,875	1,725
46	Bill Rodgers	5,750	2,875	1,725
47	Murray			
48	Fullerton			
49	Kuhn	5,750	2,875	1,725
50	Koestner			
51	Henderson			
52	Barry			
	SACRAMENTO			
53	LaLonge			
54	Heister			
55	Hunt			
56	Van Buren			
57	Fitzgerald	5,750	2,875	1,725
58	Danzig	5,750	2,875	1,725
59	Baum	5,750	2,875	1,725
60	Shinn	5,750	2,875	1,725
61	Nourse			
62	O'Rourke			
63	Lerchen			
64	Thornton			
65	Thomas	5,750	2,875	1,725
66	Thompson			
67	Byram			
68	Frank Arrelanes (Arellanes)			
69	Mahoney			
	SAN FRANCISCO			
70	McArdle			
71	Melchior	5,750	2,875	1,725
72	Vitt	5,750	2,875	1,725
73	Henley			
74	Berry	5,750	2,875	1,725
75	Miller	5,750	2,875	1,725
76	Tennant	5,750	2,875	1,725
77	Mohler	5,750	2,875	1,725
78	Shaw			
79	Sutor	5,750	2,875	1,725
80	Browning	5,750	2,875	1,725
81	Ryan	5,750	2,875	1,725
82	Powell	5,750	2,875	1,725
83	Schmidt	5,750	2,875	1,725
84	Meikle	5,750	2,875	1,725
85	Madden	5,750	2,875	1,725
86	Buck Weaver (VG-EX example auctioned in 2005 for $26,435.)			
87	Moskiman	5,750	2,875	1,725
88	Zamlock	5,750	2,875	1,725
	VERNON			
89	Brown			
90	Hogan			
91	Brashear			
92	Carlisle	5,750	2,875	1,725
93	Burrell	5,750	2,875	1,725
94	Brackenridge	5,750	2,875	1,725
95	Hitt			
96	Willett	5,750	2,875	1,725
97	Stewart	5,750	2,875	1,725
98	Carson	5,750	2,875	1,725
99	Raleigh	5,750	2,875	1,725
100	Ham Patterson	5,750	2,875	1,725
101	Hosp			
102	Sheehan			
103	Castleton			
104	Ross			
105	Stinson	5,750	2,875	1,725
106	McDonnell	5,750	2,875	1,725
107	Kane	5,750	2,875	1,725
	PORTLAND (NWL)			
108	Harris			
109	Garrett			
110	Stovall			
111	Mundorff	5,750	2,875	1,725
112	Lamline			
113	Bloomfield			
114	Williams			
115	Mensor			
116	Casey			
117	Speas			
	SPOKANE			
118	Netzel			

		NM	EX	VG
119	Strand			
120	Hasty			
121	Zimmerman			
122	Cooney			
123	Frisk			
124	Nordyke			
125	Kippert			
126	Bonner			
127	Ostdiek			
128	Cartwright			
129	Holm			
TACOMA				
130	Higgins			
131	Warren			
132	Morse			
133	Burns			
134	Gordon			
135	Bassey			
136	Rockenfield			
137	Coleman			
138	Schmutz			
139	Hall			
140	Annis	5,750	2,875	1,725
VANCOUVER				
141	Engel			
142	Brashear			
143	Adams			
144	Spiesman			
145	Brinker			
146	Bennett			
147	James			
148	Lewis			
149	Scharnweber			
150	Swain			
151	Jensen			
152	Erickson			
VICTORIA				
153	Roche			
154	Davis			
155	Goodman			
156	Ward			
157	Reddick			
158	Householder	5,750	2,875	1,725
159	Dashwood	5,750	2,875	1,725
160	Starkel			
161	Thomas			
162	Ten Million			
163	Raymer			
SEATTLE				
164	Bues			
165	Crukshank			
166	Kading			
167	Spencer	5,750	2,875	1,725
168	Leard			
169	Seaton			
170	Shea			
171	Butler			
172	Skeels			
173	Weed			
174	Raymond	5,750	2,875	1,725
175	Zackert			

1911 Obak Coupon

About 3" x 3", this coupon was found in each box of Obak cigarettes. Printed in green on white, the coupon has a list of the cabinet cards which could be obtained by redeeming 50 of the coupons.

	NM	EX	VG
Obak Coupon	100.00	50.00	30.00

1908 Offerman Buffalo Bisons Postcards

Virtually identical in format to the Major League player post-cards issued by American League Publishing Co., Cleveland, these cards carry the imprint of F.J. Offerman and depict Buffalo Bisons players of the Eastern League. The 3-1/2" x 4-1/2" black-and-white cards have a large posed action photo on a white background with a vignetted oval portrait at top. Player information and stats are printed below. The back has typical postcard markings. It is unknown whether this checklist is complete.

		NM	EX	VG
Common Player:		700.00	350.00	210.00
(1)	James Archer	700.00	350.00	210.00
(2)	James Cleary	700.00	350.00	210.00
(3)	Larry Hesterfer	700.00	350.00	210.00
(4)	Hunter Hill	700.00	350.00	210.00
(5)	William H. Keister	700.00	350.00	210.00
(6)	Charles Kisinger	700.00	350.00	210.00
(7)	Lewis Knapp	700.00	350.00	210.00
(8)	Lew McAllister	700.00	350.00	210.00
(9)	George N. McConnell	700.00	350.00	210.00
(10)	William J. Milligan	700.00	350.00	210.00
(11)	James Murray	700.00	350.00	210.00
(12)	William Nattress	700.00	350.00	210.00
(13)	Ralph Parrot	700.00	350.00	210.00
(14)	John B. Ryan	700.00	350.00	210.00
(15)	George Schirm	700.00	350.00	210.00
(16)	George Smith	700.00	350.00	210.00
(17)	John H. Vowinkle	700.00	350.00	210.00
(18)	John White	700.00	350.00	210.00
(19)	Merton Whitney	700.00	350.00	210.00

1952 Ogden Reds Team Issue

These 2-1/4" x 3-3/8" black-and-white, unnumbered, blank-backed cards were one of many minor league team sets issued by Globe Printing of San Jose, Calif., in the early 1950s. Cards were usually given away at the ballpark on a one-per-week or one-per-homestand basis, accounting for the rarity of surviving sets. The O-Reds were a Class C Pioneer League farm club of the Cincinnati Reds.

		NM	EX	VG
Complete Set (18):		800.00	400.00	240.00
Common Player:		60.00	30.00	18.00
Album:		100.00	50.00	30.00
(1)	Ralph Birkofer	60.00	30.00	18.00
(2)	William A. Bowman	60.00	30.00	18.00
(3)	David Bristol	60.00	30.00	18.00
(4)	Vincent E. Capece	60.00	30.00	18.00
(5)	Gerald Davis	60.00	30.00	18.00
(6)	Ralph Dollinger	60.00	30.00	18.00
(7)	Robert E. Durnbaugh	60.00	30.00	18.00
(8)	Raymond Estes	60.00	30.00	18.00
(9)	Robert J. Flowers	60.00	30.00	18.00
(10)	Nunzio Izzo	60.00	30.00	18.00
(11)	Howard E. Leister	60.00	30.00	18.00
(12)	Steve Mesner	60.00	30.00	18.00
(13)	Dee C. Moore	60.00	30.00	18.00
(14)	Augie Navarro (Announcer)	60.00	30.00	18.00
(15)	John Omerza	60.00	30.00	18.00
(16)	James W. St. Claire	60.00	30.00	18.00
(17)	Grady N. Watts	60.00	30.00	18.00
(18)	Carl M. Wells	60.00	30.00	18.00

1955 Old Homestead Franks Des Moines Bruins

A very rare minor league issue, this set features players of the Class A Western League farm team of the Chicago Cubs. Many of the players were future major leaguers. Cards measure about 2-1/2" x 3-3/4" and have black-and-white portrait photos of the players with a facsimile autograph across

the jersey. A black strip at the bottom of the card has the player and team name, and the position. Backs have an ad for the issuing hot dog company.

		NM	EX	VG
Complete Set (21):		5,000	2,500	1,500
Common Player:		250.00	125.00	75.00
(1)	Bob Andersoon	250.00	125.00	75.00
(2)	Ray Bellino	250.00	125.00	75.00
(3)	Don Biebel	250.00	125.00	75.00
(4)	Bobby Cooke	250.00	125.00	75.00
(5)	Dave Cunningham	250.00	125.00	75.00
(6)	Bert Flammini	250.00	125.00	75.00
(7)	Gene Fodge	250.00	125.00	75.00
(8)	Eddie Haas	250.00	125.00	75.00
(9)	Paul Hoffmeister	250.00	125.00	75.00
(10)	Pepper Martin	350.00	175.00	100.00
(11)	Jim McDaniel	250.00	125.00	75.00
(12)	Bob McKee	250.00	125.00	75.00
(13)	Paul Menking	250.00	125.00	75.00
(14)	Vern Morgan	250.00	125.00	75.00
(15)	Joe Pearson	250.00	125.00	75.00
(16)	John Pramesa	250.00	125.00	75.00
(17)	Joe Stanka	250.00	125.00	75.00
(18)	Jim Stoddard	250.00	125.00	75.00
(19)	Bob Thorpe	250.00	125.00	75.00
(20)	Burdy Thurlby	250.00	125.00	75.00
(21)	Don Watkins	250.00	125.00	75.00

1959 O'Keefe Ale Montreal Royals

This set of large (3" x 4") player stamps was issued in conjunction with an album as a promotion by O'Keefe Ale in Quebec. The pictures are black-and-white with player identification in the bottom border. Backs are blank and the edges are perforated. Many former Brooklyn Dodgers are included in the issue. The unnumbered stamps are listed here in alphabetical order.

		NM	EX	VG
Complete Set (24):		900.00	450.00	275.00
Common Player:		30.00	15.00	9.00
Album:		200.00	100.00	60.00
(1)	Edmundo Amoros	45.00	22.50	13.50
(2)	Bob Aspromonte	35.00	17.50	10.00
(3)	Batters Records	12.50	6.25	3.75
(4)	Babe Birrer	30.00	15.00	9.00
(5)	Clay Bryant	30.00	15.00	9.00
(6)	Mike Brumley	30.00	15.00	9.00
(7)	Yvon Dunn (Trainer)	20.00	10.00	6.00
(8)	Bill George	30.00	15.00	9.00
(9)	Mike Goliat	30.00	15.00	9.00
(10)	John Gray	30.00	15.00	9.00
(11)	Billy Harris	30.00	15.00	9.00
(12)	Jim Koranda	30.00	15.00	9.00
(13)	Paul LaPalme	30.00	15.00	9.00
(14)	Tom Lasorda	200.00	100.00	60.00
(15)	Bob Lennon	30.00	15.00	9.00
(16)	Clyde Parris	30.00	15.00	9.00
(17)	Pitchers Records	12.50	6.25	3.75
(18)	Ed Rakow	30.00	15.00	9.00
(19)	Curt Roberts	30.00	15.00	9.00
(20)	Freddy Rodriguez	30.00	15.00	9.00
(21)	Harry Schwegman	30.00	15.00	9.00
(22)	Angel Scull	30.00	15.00	9.00
(23)	Dick Teed	30.00	15.00	9.00
(24)	Rene Valdes (Valdez)	30.00	15.00	9.00

1910 Old Mill Cigarettes Series 1 (S. Atlantic League)

Because of their distinctive red borders, this 1910 minor league tobacco issue is often called the Red Border set by collectors. It's ACC designation is T210. A massive set, it consists of some 640 cards, each measuring 1-1/2" x 2-5/8". Fronts feature a glossy black-and-white photo, while the backs carry an ad for Old Mill Cigarettes. Each of the eight series is devoted to a different minor league. Series 1 features players from the South Atlantic League; Series 2 pictures players from the Virginia League; Series 3 is devoted to the Texas League; Series 4 features the Virginia Valley League; Series 5 pictures players from the Carolina Associations; Series 6 spotlights the Blue Grass League; Series 7 is devoted to the Eastern Carolina League; and Series 8 show players from the Southern Association. The various series are identified by a number along the top on the back of the cards. Collectors generally agree that Series 8 cards, which are often found irregularly sized due to hand-cutting from original sheets, are the scarcest of the series. The relative scarcity of the various series is reflected in the prices listed. Collectors should be aware that some Series 3 cards (Texas League) can be found with orange, rather than red, borders - apparently because not enough red ink was used during part of the print run.

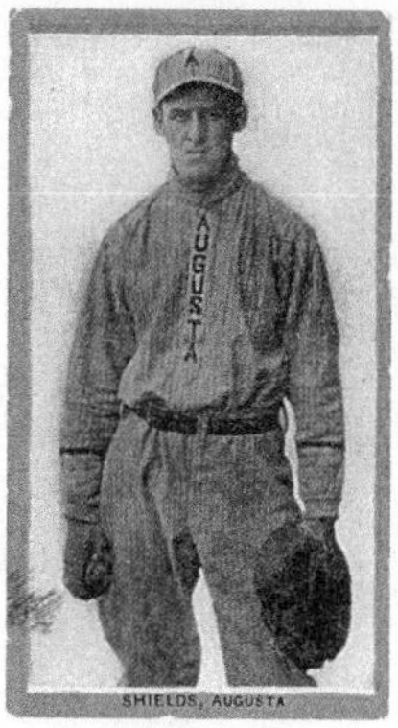

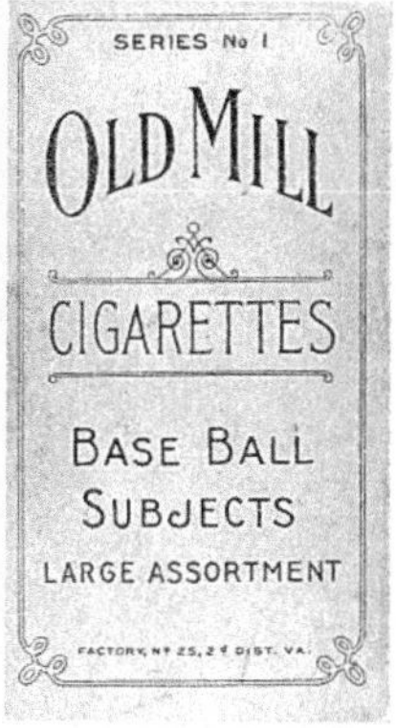

	NM	EX	VG
Common Player:	325.00	140.00	80.00
(1) Bagwell	325.00	140.00	80.00
(2) Balenti	325.00	140.00	80.00
(3) Becker	325.00	140.00	80.00
(4) Bensen	325.00	140.00	80.00
(5) Benton	325.00	140.00	80.00
(6) Bierkortte	325.00	140.00	80.00
(7) Bierman	325.00	140.00	80.00
(8) (William) Breitenstein	325.00	140.00	80.00
(9) Bremmerhof	325.00	140.00	80.00
(10) Carter	325.00	140.00	80.00
(11) Cavender	325.00	140.00	80.00
(12) Collins	325.00	140.00	80.00
(13) DeFraites	325.00	140.00	80.00
(14) Dudley	325.00	140.00	80.00
(15) Dwyer	325.00	140.00	80.00
(16) Edwards	325.00	140.00	80.00
(17) Enbanks	325.00	140.00	80.00
(18) Eubank	325.00	140.00	80.00
(19) Fox	325.00	140.00	80.00
(20) Hannifan	325.00	140.00	80.00
(21) Hartley	325.00	140.00	80.00
(22) Hauser	325.00	140.00	80.00
(23) Hille	325.00	140.00	80.00
(24) Howard	325.00	140.00	80.00
(25) Hoyt	325.00	140.00	80.00
(26) Huber	325.00	140.00	80.00
(27) Ison	325.00	140.00	80.00
(28) Jones	325.00	140.00	80.00
(29) Kalkhoff	325.00	140.00	80.00
(30) Krebs	325.00	140.00	80.00
(31) Lawrence	325.00	140.00	80.00
(32) Lee (Jacksonville)	325.00	140.00	80.00
(33) Lee (Macon)	325.00	140.00	80.00
(34) Lewis (Columbia)	325.00	140.00	80.00
(35) Lewis (Columbus)	325.00	140.00	80.00
(36) Lipe (Batting)	325.00	140.00	80.00
(37) Lipe (Portrait)	325.00	140.00	80.00
(38) Long	325.00	140.00	80.00
(39) Magoon	325.00	140.00	80.00
(40) Manion	325.00	140.00	80.00
(41) Marshall	325.00	140.00	80.00
(42) Martin	325.00	140.00	80.00
(43) Martina	325.00	140.00	80.00
(44) Massing	325.00	140.00	80.00
(45) McLeod	325.00	140.00	80.00
(46) McMahon	325.00	140.00	80.00
(47) Morse	325.00	140.00	80.00
(48) Mullane	325.00	140.00	80.00
(49) Mulldowney	325.00	140.00	80.00
(50) Murch	325.00	140.00	80.00
(51) Norcum	325.00	140.00	80.00
(52) Pelkey	325.00	140.00	80.00
(53) Petit	325.00	140.00	80.00
(54) Pierce	325.00	140.00	80.00
(55) Pope	325.00	140.00	80.00
(56) Radebaugh	325.00	140.00	80.00
(57) Raynolds	325.00	140.00	80.00
(58) Reagan	325.00	140.00	80.00
(59) Redfern (Redfearn)	325.00	140.00	80.00
(60) Reynolds	325.00	140.00	80.00
(61) Schulz	325.00	140.00	80.00
(62) Schulze	325.00	140.00	80.00
(63) Schwietzka	325.00	140.00	80.00
(64) Shields	325.00	140.00	80.00
(65) Sisson	325.00	140.00	80.00
(66) Smith	325.00	140.00	80.00
(67) Sweeney	325.00	140.00	80.00
(68) Taffee	325.00	140.00	80.00
(69) Toren	325.00	140.00	80.00
(70) Viola	325.00	140.00	80.00
(71) Wagner	325.00	140.00	80.00
(72) Wahl	325.00	140.00	80.00
(73) Weems	325.00	140.00	80.00
(74) Wells	325.00	140.00	80.00
(75) Wohlleben	325.00	140.00	80.00

1910 Old Mill Cigarettes Series 2 (Virginia League)

	NM	EX	VG
Common Player:	325.00	165.00	100.00
(1) Andrada	325.00	165.00	100.00
(2) Archer	325.00	165.00	100.00
(3) Baker	325.00	165.00	100.00
(4) Beham	325.00	165.00	100.00
(5) Bonner	325.00	165.00	100.00
(6) Bowen	325.00	165.00	100.00
(7) Brandon	325.00	165.00	100.00
(8) Breivogel	325.00	165.00	100.00
(9) Brooks	325.00	165.00	100.00
(10) Brown	325.00	165.00	100.00
(11) Busch	325.00	165.00	100.00
(12) Bussey	325.00	165.00	100.00
(13) Cefalu	325.00	165.00	100.00
(14) Chandler	325.00	165.00	100.00
(15) Clarke	325.00	165.00	100.00
(16) Clunk	325.00	165.00	100.00
(17) Cote	325.00	165.00	100.00
(18) Cowan	325.00	165.00	100.00
(19) Decker	325.00	165.00	100.00
(20) Doyle	325.00	165.00	100.00
(21) Eddowes	325.00	165.00	100.00
(22) Fisher	325.00	165.00	100.00
(23) Fox	325.00	165.00	100.00
(24) Foxen	325.00	165.00	100.00
(25) Gaston	325.00	165.00	100.00
(26) Gehring	325.00	165.00	100.00
(27) Griffin (Danville)	325.00	165.00	100.00
(28) Griffin (Lynchburg)	325.00	165.00	100.00
(29) Hale	325.00	165.00	100.00
(30) Hamilton	325.00	165.00	100.00
(31) Hanks	325.00	165.00	100.00
(32) Hannafin	325.00	165.00	100.00
(33) Hoffman	325.00	165.00	100.00
(34) Holland	325.00	165.00	100.00
(35) Hooker	325.00	165.00	100.00
(36) Irving	325.00	165.00	100.00
(37) Jackson (Lynchburg)	325.00	165.00	100.00
(38) Jackson (Norfolk)	325.00	165.00	100.00
(39) Jackson (Portsmouth)	325.00	165.00	100.00
(40) Jackson (Richmond)	325.00	165.00	100.00
(41) Jenkins	325.00	165.00	100.00
(42) Keifel	325.00	165.00	100.00
(43) Kirkpatrick	325.00	165.00	100.00
(44) Kunkel	325.00	165.00	100.00
(45) Landgraff	325.00	165.00	100.00
(46) Larkins	325.00	165.00	100.00
(47) Laughlin	325.00	165.00	100.00
(48) Lawlor	325.00	165.00	100.00
(49) Levy	325.00	165.00	100.00
(50) Lloyd	325.00	165.00	100.00
(51) Loos	325.00	165.00	100.00
(52) Lovell	325.00	165.00	100.00
(53) Lucia	325.00	165.00	100.00
(54) MacConachie	325.00	165.00	100.00
(55) Mayberry	325.00	165.00	100.00
(56) McFarland	325.00	165.00	100.00
(57) Messitt	325.00	165.00	100.00
(58) Michel	325.00	165.00	100.00
(59) Mullaney	325.00	165.00	100.00
(60) Munson	325.00	165.00	100.00
(61) Neuton	325.00	165.00	100.00
(62) Nimmo	325.00	165.00	100.00
(63) Norris	325.00	165.00	100.00
(64) Peterson	325.00	165.00	100.00
(65) Powell	325.00	165.00	100.00
(66) Pressly (Pressley)	325.00	165.00	100.00
(67) Pritchard	325.00	165.00	100.00
(68) Revelle	325.00	165.00	100.00
(69) Rowe	325.00	165.00	100.00
(70) Schmidt	325.00	165.00	100.00
(71) Schrader	325.00	165.00	100.00
(72) Sharp	325.00	165.00	100.00
(73) Shaw	325.00	165.00	100.00
(74) Smith (Lynchburg, batting.)	325.00	165.00	100.00
(75) Smith (Lynchburg, catching.)	325.00	165.00	100.00
(76) Smith (Portsmouth)	325.00	165.00	100.00
(77) Spicer	325.00	165.00	100.00
(78) Titman	325.00	165.00	100.00
(79) Toner	325.00	165.00	100.00
(80) Tydeman	325.00	165.00	100.00
(81) Vail	325.00	165.00	100.00
(82) Verbout	325.00	165.00	100.00
(83) Walker	325.00	165.00	100.00
(84) Wallace	325.00	165.00	100.00
(85) Waymack	325.00	165.00	100.00
(86) Woolums	325.00	165.00	100.00
(87) Zimmerman	325.00	165.00	100.00

1910 Old Mill Cigarettes Series 3 (Texas League)

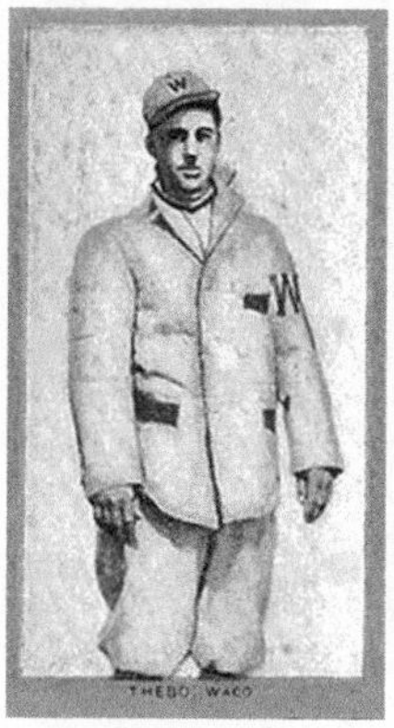

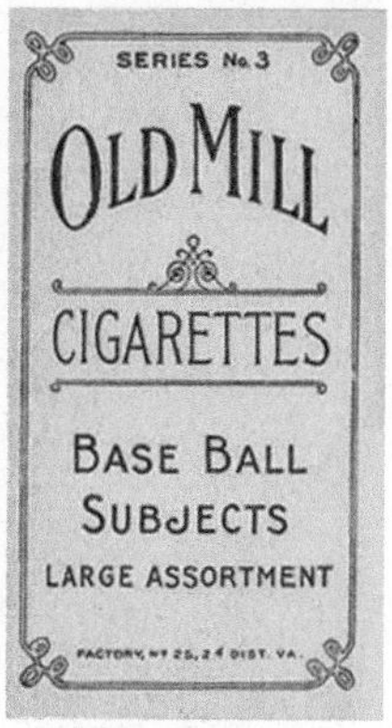

	NM	EX	VG
Common Player:	325.00	165.00	100.00
(1) Alexander	325.00	165.00	100.00
(2) Ash	325.00	165.00	100.00
(3) Bandy	325.00	165.00	100.00
(4) Barenkemp	325.00	165.00	100.00
(5) Belew	325.00	165.00	100.00
(6) Bell	325.00	165.00	100.00
(7) Bennett	325.00	165.00	100.00
(8) Berick	325.00	165.00	100.00
(9) Billiard	325.00	165.00	100.00
(10) Blanding	325.00	165.00	100.00
(11) Blue	325.00	165.00	100.00
(12) Burch	325.00	165.00	100.00
(13) Burk	325.00	165.00	100.00
(14) Carlin	325.00	165.00	100.00
(15) Conaway	325.00	165.00	100.00
(16) Corkhill	325.00	165.00	100.00
(17) Cowan	325.00	165.00	100.00
(18) Coyle	325.00	165.00	100.00
(19) Crable	325.00	165.00	100.00
(20) Curry	325.00	165.00	100.00
(21) Dale	325.00	165.00	100.00
(22) Davis	325.00	165.00	100.00
(23) Deardorff	325.00	165.00	100.00
(24) Donnelley	325.00	165.00	100.00
(25) Doyle	325.00	165.00	100.00
(26) Druke	325.00	165.00	100.00
(27) Dugey	325.00	165.00	100.00
(28) Ens	325.00	165.00	100.00
(29) Evans	325.00	165.00	100.00
(30) Fillman	325.00	165.00	100.00
(31) Firestine	325.00	165.00	100.00
(32) Francis	325.00	165.00	100.00
(33) Galloway	325.00	165.00	100.00
(34) Gardner	325.00	165.00	100.00
(35) Gear	325.00	165.00	100.00
(36) Glawe	325.00	165.00	100.00
(37) Gordon	325.00	165.00	100.00
(38) Gowdy	325.00	165.00	100.00
(39) Harbison	325.00	165.00	100.00
(40) Harper	325.00	165.00	100.00
(41) Hicks	325.00	165.00	100.00
(42) Hill	325.00	165.00	100.00
(43) Hinninger	325.00	165.00	100.00
(44) Hirsch	325.00	165.00	100.00
(45) Hise	325.00	165.00	100.00
(46) Hooks	325.00	165.00	100.00
(47) Hornsby	325.00	165.00	100.00
(48) Howell	325.00	165.00	100.00
(49) Johnston	325.00	165.00	100.00
(50) Jolley	325.00	165.00	100.00
(51) Jones	325.00	165.00	100.00
(52) Kaphan	325.00	165.00	100.00
(53) Kipp	325.00	165.00	100.00
(54) Leidy	325.00	165.00	100.00
(55) Malloy	325.00	165.00	100.00
(56) Maloney	325.00	165.00	100.00
(57) Meagher	325.00	165.00	100.00
(58) Merritt	325.00	165.00	100.00
(59) McKay	325.00	165.00	100.00
(60) Mills	325.00	165.00	100.00
(61) Morris	325.00	165.00	100.00
(62) Mullen	325.00	165.00	100.00
(63) Munsell	325.00	165.00	100.00
(64) Nagel	325.00	165.00	100.00
(65) Northen	325.00	165.00	100.00
(66) Ogle	325.00	165.00	100.00
(67) Onslow	325.00	165.00	100.00
(68) Pendleton	325.00	165.00	100.00
(69) Powell	325.00	165.00	100.00
(70) Riley	325.00	165.00	100.00
(71) Robertson	325.00	165.00	100.00
(72) Rose	325.00	165.00	100.00
(73) Salazor	325.00	165.00	100.00
(74) Shindel	325.00	165.00	100.00
(75) Shontz	325.00	165.00	100.00
(76) Slaven	325.00	165.00	100.00
(77) Smith (Bat over shoulder.)	325.00	165.00	100.00
(78) Smith (Bat at hip level.)	325.00	165.00	100.00
(79) Spangler	325.00	165.00	100.00
(80) Stadeli	325.00	165.00	100.00
(81) Stinson	325.00	165.00	100.00
(82) Storch	325.00	165.00	100.00
(83) Stringer	325.00	165.00	100.00
(84) Tesreau	325.00	165.00	100.00
(85) Thebo	325.00	165.00	100.00
(86) Tullas	325.00	165.00	100.00
(87) Walsh	325.00	165.00	100.00
(88) Watson	325.00	165.00	100.00
(89) Weber	325.00	165.00	100.00
(90) Weeks	325.00	165.00	100.00
(91) Wertherford	325.00	165.00	100.00
(92) Wickenhofer	325.00	165.00	100.00
(93) Williams	325.00	165.00	100.00
(94) Woodburn	325.00	165.00	100.00
(95) Yantz	325.00	165.00	100.00

1910 Old Mill Cigarettes Series 4 (Va. Valley Leag.)

	NM	EX	VG
Common Player:	400.00	175.00	100.00
(1) Aylor	400.00	175.00	100.00
(2) Benney	400.00	175.00	100.00
(3) Best	400.00	175.00	100.00
(4) Bonno	400.00	175.00	100.00
(5) Brown	400.00	175.00	100.00
(6) Brumfield	400.00	175.00	100.00
(7) Campbell	400.00	175.00	100.00
(8) Canepa	400.00	175.00	100.00
(9) Carney	400.00	175.00	100.00
(10) Carter	400.00	175.00	100.00
(11) Cochrane	400.00	175.00	100.00
(12) Coller	400.00	175.00	100.00
(13) Connolly	400.00	175.00	100.00
(14) Davis	400.00	175.00	100.00
(15) Donnell	400.00	175.00	100.00
(16) Doshmer	400.00	175.00	100.00
(17) Dougherty	400.00	175.00	100.00
(18) Erlewein	400.00	175.00	100.00
(19) Farrell	400.00	175.00	100.00
(20) Geary	400.00	175.00	100.00

(21)	Halterman	400.00	175.00	100.00
(22)	Headly	400.00	175.00	100.00
(23)	Hollis	400.00	175.00	100.00
(24)	Hunter	400.00	175.00	100.00
(25)	Johnson	400.00	175.00	100.00
(26)	Kane	400.00	175.00	100.00
(27)	Kuehn	400.00	175.00	100.00
(28)	Leonard	400.00	175.00	100.00
(29)	Lux	400.00	175.00	100.00
(30)	McClain	400.00	175.00	100.00
(31)	Mollenkamp	400.00	175.00	100.00
(32)	Moore	400.00	175.00	100.00
(33)	Moye	400.00	175.00	100.00
(34)	O'Connor	400.00	175.00	100.00
(35)	Orcutt	400.00	175.00	100.00
(36)	Pick	400.00	175.00	100.00
(37)	Pickels	400.00	175.00	100.00
(38)	Schafer	400.00	175.00	100.00
(39)	Seaman	400.00	175.00	100.00
(40)	Spicer	400.00	175.00	100.00
(41)	Stanley	400.00	175.00	100.00
(42)	Stockum	400.00	175.00	100.00
(43)	Titlow	400.00	175.00	100.00
(44)	Waldron	400.00	175.00	100.00
(45)	Wills	400.00	175.00	100.00
(46)	Witter	400.00	175.00	100.00
(47)	Womach	400.00	175.00	100.00
(48)	Young	400.00	175.00	100.00
(49)	Zurlage	400.00	175.00	100.00

1910 Old Mill Cigarettes Series 5 (Carolina Assn.)

		NM	EX	VG
Common Player:		400.00	175.00	100.00
(1)	Abercrombie	400.00	175.00	100.00
(2)	Averett	400.00	175.00	100.00
(3)	Bansewein	400.00	175.00	100.00
(4)	Bentley	400.00	175.00	100.00
(5)	C.G. Beusse	400.00	175.00	100.00
(6)	Fred Beusse	400.00	175.00	100.00
(7)	Bigbie	400.00	175.00	100.00
(8)	Bivens	400.00	175.00	100.00
(9)	Blackstone	400.00	175.00	100.00
(10)	Brannon	400.00	175.00	100.00
(11)	Brazell	400.00	175.00	100.00
(12)	Brent	400.00	175.00	100.00
(13)	Bullock	400.00	175.00	100.00
(14)	Cashion	400.00	175.00	100.00
(15)	Corbett (3/4 length view)	400.00	175.00	100.00
(16)	Corbett (Full length view.)	400.00	175.00	100.00
(17)	Coutts	400.00	175.00	100.00
(18)	Lave Cross	400.00	175.00	100.00
(19)	Crouch	400.00	175.00	100.00
(20)	C.L. Derrick	400.00	175.00	100.00
(21)	F.B. Derrick	400.00	175.00	100.00
(22)	Dobard	400.00	175.00	100.00
(23)	Drumm	400.00	175.00	100.00
(24)	Duvie	400.00	175.00	100.00
(25)	Ehrhardt	400.00	175.00	100.00
(26)	Eldridge	400.00	175.00	100.00
(27)	Fairbanks	400.00	175.00	100.00
(28)	Farmer	400.00	175.00	100.00
(29)	Ferrell	400.00	175.00	100.00
(30)	Finn	400.00	175.00	100.00
(31)	Flowers	400.00	175.00	100.00
(32)	Fogarty	400.00	175.00	100.00
(33)	Francisco	400.00	175.00	100.00
(34)	Gardin	400.00	175.00	100.00
(35)	Gilmore	400.00	175.00	100.00
(36)	Gorham	400.00	175.00	100.00
(37)	Gorman	400.00	175.00	100.00
(38)	Guss	400.00	175.00	100.00
(39)	Hammersley	400.00	175.00	100.00
(40)	Hargrave	400.00	175.00	100.00
(41)	Harrington	400.00	175.00	100.00
(42)	Harris	400.00	175.00	100.00
(43)	Hartley	400.00	175.00	100.00
(44)	Hayes	400.00	175.00	100.00
(45)	Hicks	400.00	175.00	100.00
(46)	Humphrey	400.00	175.00	100.00
(47)	Jackson	400.00	175.00	100.00
(48)	James	400.00	175.00	100.00
(49)	Jenkins	400.00	175.00	100.00
(50)	Johnston	400.00	175.00	100.00
(51)	Kelly	400.00	175.00	100.00
(52)	Laval	400.00	175.00	100.00
(53)	Lothrop	400.00	175.00	100.00
(54)	MacConachie	400.00	175.00	100.00
(55)	Mangum	400.00	175.00	100.00
(56)	A. McCarthy	400.00	175.00	100.00
(57)	J. McCarthy	400.00	175.00	100.00
(58)	McEnroe	400.00	175.00	100.00
(59)	McFarlin	400.00	175.00	100.00
(60)	McHugh	400.00	175.00	100.00
(61)	McKevitt	400.00	175.00	100.00
(62)	Midkiff	400.00	175.00	100.00
(63)	Moore	400.00	175.00	100.00
(64)	Noojin	400.00	175.00	100.00
(65)	Ochs	400.00	175.00	100.00
(66)	Painter	400.00	175.00	100.00
(67)	Redfern (Redfearn)	400.00	175.00	100.00
(68)	Reis	400.00	175.00	100.00
(69)	Rickard	400.00	175.00	100.00
(70)	Roth (Batting)	400.00	175.00	100.00
(71)	Roth (Fielding)	400.00	175.00	100.00
(72)	Smith	400.00	175.00	100.00
(73)	Springs	400.00	175.00	100.00
(74)	Stouch	400.00	175.00	100.00
(75)	Taxis	400.00	175.00	100.00
(76)	Templin	400.00	175.00	100.00
(77)	Thrasher	400.00	175.00	100.00
(78)	Trammell	400.00	175.00	100.00
(79)	Walker	400.00	175.00	100.00
(80)	Walters	400.00	175.00	100.00
(81)	Wehrell	400.00	175.00	100.00
(82)	Weldon	400.00	175.00	100.00
(83)	Williams	400.00	175.00	100.00
(84)	Wingo	400.00	175.00	100.00
(85)	Workman	400.00	175.00	100.00
(86)	Wynne	400.00	175.00	100.00
(87)	Wysong	400.00	175.00	100.00

1910 Old Mill Cigarettes Series 6 (Blue Grass Leag.)

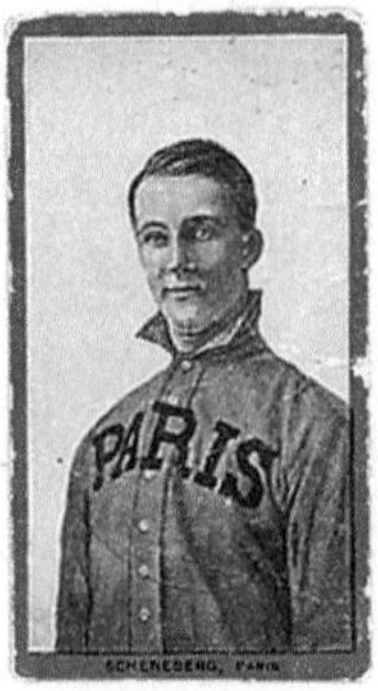

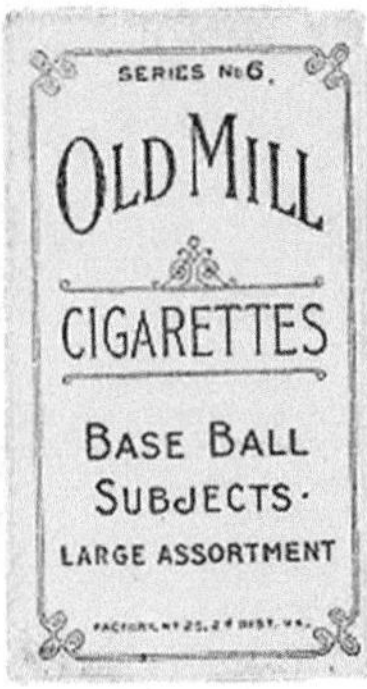

		NM	EX	VG
Common Player:		600.00	250.00	150.00
(1)	Angermeier (Fielding)	600.00	250.00	150.00
(2)	Angermeir (Portrait)	600.00	250.00	150.00
(3)	Atwell	600.00	250.00	150.00
(4)	Badger	600.00	250.00	150.00
(5)	Barnett	600.00	250.00	150.00
(6)	Barney	600.00	250.00	150.00
(7)	Beard	600.00	250.00	150.00
(8)	Bohannon	600.00	250.00	150.00
(9)	Callahan	600.00	250.00	150.00
(10)	Chapman	600.00	250.00	150.00
(11)	Chase	600.00	250.00	150.00
(12)	Coleman	600.00	250.00	150.00
(13)	Cornell (Frankfort)	600.00	250.00	150.00
(14)	Cornell (Winchester)	600.00	250.00	150.00
(15)	Creager	600.00	250.00	150.00
(16)	Dailey	600.00	250.00	150.00
(17)	Edington	600.00	250.00	150.00
(18)	Elgin	600.00	250.00	150.00
(19)	Ellis	600.00	250.00	150.00
(20)	Everden	600.00	250.00	150.00
(21)	Gisler	600.00	250.00	150.00
(22)	Goodman	600.00	250.00	150.00
(23)	Goostree (Hands behind back.)	600.00	250.00	150.00
(24)	Goostree (Leaning on bat.)	600.00	250.00	150.00
(25)	Haines	600.00	250.00	150.00
(26)	Harold	600.00	250.00	150.00
(27)	Heveron	600.00	250.00	150.00
(28)	Hicks	600.00	250.00	150.00
(29)	Hoffmann	600.00	250.00	150.00
(30)	Horn	600.00	250.00	150.00
(31)	Kaiser	600.00	250.00	150.00
(32)	Keifel	600.00	250.00	150.00
(33)	Kimbrough	600.00	250.00	150.00
(34)	Kircher (Shelbyville)	600.00	250.00	150.00
(35)	Kircher (Winchester)	600.00	250.00	150.00
(36)	Kuhlman (3/4 length)	600.00	250.00	150.00
(37)	Kuhlmann (Portrait)	600.00	250.00	150.00
(38)	L'Heureux	600.00	250.00	150.00
(39)	McIlvain	600.00	250.00	150.00
(40)	McKernan	600.00	250.00	150.00
(41)	Meyers	600.00	250.00	150.00
(42)	Moloney	600.00	250.00	150.00
(43)	Mullin	600.00	250.00	150.00
(44)	Olson	600.00	250.00	150.00
(45)	Oyler	600.00	250.00	150.00
(46)	Reed	600.00	250.00	150.00
(47)	Ross	600.00	250.00	150.00
(48)	Scheneberg (Fielding)	600.00	250.00	150.00
(49)	Scheneberg (Portrait)	600.00	250.00	150.00
(50)	Schultz	600.00	250.00	150.00
(51)	Scott	600.00	250.00	150.00
(52)	Sinex	600.00	250.00	150.00
(53)	Stengel		25,000	17,500
(54)	Thoss	600.00	250.00	150.00
(55)	Tilford	600.00	250.00	150.00
(56)	Toney	600.00	250.00	150.00
(57)	Van Landingham (Valladingham) (Lexington)	600.00	250.00	150.00
(58)	Van Landingham (Valladingham) (Shelbyville)	600.00	250.00	150.00
(59)	Viox	600.00	250.00	150.00
(60)	Walden	600.00	250.00	150.00
(61)	Whitaker	600.00	250.00	150.00
(62)	Wills	600.00	250.00	150.00
(63)	Womble	600.00	250.00	150.00
(64)	Wright	600.00	250.00	150.00
(65)	Yaeger	600.00	250.00	150.00
(66)	Yancey	600.00	250.00	150.00

1910 Old Mill Cigarettes Series 7 (E. Carolina League)

		NM	EX	VG
Common Player:		450.00	200.00	125.00
(1)	Armstrong	450.00	200.00	125.00
(2)	Beatty	450.00	200.00	125.00
(3)	Biel	450.00	200.00	125.00
(4)	Bonner	450.00	200.00	125.00
(5)	Brandt	450.00	200.00	125.00
(6)	Brown	450.00	200.00	125.00
(7)	Cantwell	450.00	200.00	125.00
(8)	Carrol	450.00	200.00	125.00
(9)	Cooney	450.00	200.00	125.00
(10)	Cooper	450.00	200.00	125.00
(11)	Cowell	450.00	200.00	125.00
(12)	Creager (Cregan)	450.00	200.00	125.00
(13)	Crockett	450.00	200.00	125.00
(14)	Dailey	450.00	200.00	125.00
(15)	Dobbs	450.00	200.00	125.00
(16)	Dussault	450.00	200.00	125.00
(17)	Dwyer	450.00	200.00	125.00
(18)	Evans	450.00	200.00	125.00
(19)	Forgue	450.00	200.00	125.00
(20)	Fulton	450.00	200.00	125.00
(21)	Galvin	450.00	200.00	125.00
(22)	Gastmeyer (Batting)	450.00	200.00	125.00
(23)	Gastmeyer (Fielding)	450.00	200.00	125.00
(24)	Gates	450.00	200.00	125.00
(25)	Gillespie	450.00	200.00	125.00
(26)	Griffin	450.00	200.00	125.00
(27)	Gunderson	450.00	200.00	125.00
(28)	Ham	450.00	200.00	125.00
(29)	Handibe (Handiboe)	450.00	200.00	125.00
(30)	Hart	450.00	200.00	125.00
(31)	Hartley	450.00	200.00	125.00
(32)	Hobbs	450.00	200.00	125.00
(33)	Hyames	450.00	200.00	125.00
(34)	Irving	450.00	200.00	125.00
(35)	Kaiser	450.00	200.00	125.00
(36)	Kelley	450.00	200.00	125.00
(37)	Kelly	450.00	200.00	125.00
(38)	Kelly (Mascot, Goldsboro.)	750.00	370.00	220.00
(39)	Luyster	450.00	200.00	125.00
(40)	MacDonald	450.00	200.00	125.00
(41)	Malcolm	450.00	200.00	125.00
(42)	J. Erskine Mayer	500.00	250.00	125.00
(43)	McCormac (McCormick)	450.00	200.00	125.00
(44)	McGeeham (McGeehan)	450.00	200.00	125.00
(45)	Merchant	450.00	200.00	125.00
(46)	Mills	450.00	200.00	125.00
(47)	Morgan	450.00	200.00	125.00
(48)	Morris	450.00	200.00	125.00
(49)	Munson	450.00	200.00	125.00
(50)	Newman	450.00	200.00	125.00
(51)	Noval (Novak)	450.00	200.00	125.00
(52)	O'Halloran	450.00	200.00	125.00
(53)	Phelan	450.00	200.00	125.00
(54)	Prim	450.00	200.00	125.00
(55)	Reeves	450.00	200.00	125.00
(56)	Richardson	450.00	200.00	125.00
(57)	Schumaker	450.00	200.00	125.00
(58)	Sharp	450.00	200.00	125.00
(59)	Sherrill	450.00	200.00	125.00
(60)	Simmons	450.00	200.00	125.00
(61)	Steinbach	450.00	200.00	125.00
(62)	Stoehr	450.00	200.00	125.00
(63)	Taylor	450.00	200.00	125.00
(64)	Webb	450.00	200.00	125.00
(65)	Whelan	450.00	200.00	125.00
(66)	Wolf	450.00	200.00	125.00
(67)	Wright	450.00	200.00	125.00

1910 Old Mill Cigarettes Series 8 (Southern Assn.)

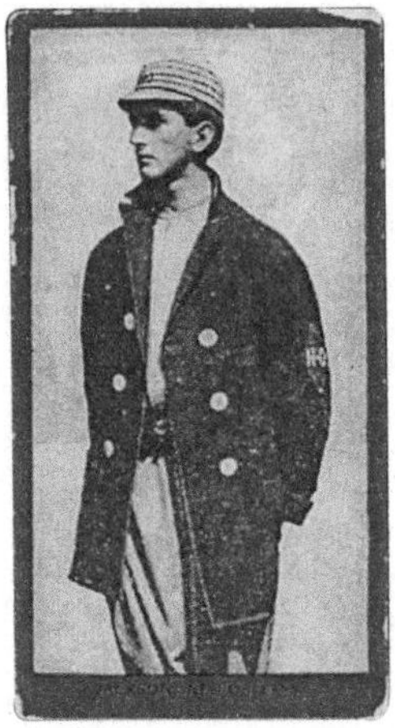

		NM	EX	VG
Common Player:		750.00	370.00	220.00
(1)	Allen (Memphis)	750.00	370.00	220.00
(2)	Allen (Mobile)	750.00	370.00	220.00
(3)	Anderson	750.00	370.00	220.00
(4)	Babb	750.00	370.00	220.00
(5)	Bartley	750.00	370.00	220.00
(6)	Bauer	750.00	370.00	220.00
(7)	Bay	750.00	370.00	220.00
(8)	Bayliss	750.00	370.00	220.00
(9)	Berger	750.00	370.00	220.00
(10)	Bernhard	750.00	370.00	220.00
(11)	Bitroff	750.00	370.00	220.00
(12)	Breitenstein	750.00	370.00	220.00
(13)	Bronkie	750.00	370.00	220.00
(14)	Brooks	750.00	370.00	220.00
(15)	Burnett	750.00	370.00	220.00
(16)	Cafalu	750.00	370.00	220.00
(17)	Carson	750.00	370.00	220.00
(18)	Case	750.00	370.00	220.00
(19)	Chappelle	750.00	370.00	220.00
(20)	Cohen	750.00	370.00	220.00
(21)	Collins	750.00	370.00	220.00
(22)	Crandall	750.00	370.00	220.00
(23)	Cross	750.00	370.00	220.00

		NM	EX	VG
(24)	Jud. Daly	750.00	370.00	220.00
(25)	Davis	750.00	370.00	220.00
(26)	Demaree	750.00	370.00	220.00
(27)	DeMontreville	750.00	370.00	220.00
(28)	E. DeMontreville	750.00	370.00	220.00
(29)	Dick	750.00	370.00	220.00
(30)	Dobbs	750.00	370.00	220.00
(31)	Dudley	750.00	370.00	220.00
(32)	Dunn	750.00	370.00	220.00
(33)	Elliot	750.00	370.00	220.00
(34)	Emery	750.00	370.00	220.00
(35)	Erloff	750.00	370.00	220.00
(36)	Farrell	750.00	370.00	220.00
(37)	Fisher	750.00	370.00	220.00
(38)	Fleharty	750.00	370.00	220.00
(39)	Flood	750.00	370.00	220.00
(40)	Foster	750.00	370.00	220.00
(41)	Fritz	750.00	370.00	220.00
(42)	Greminger	750.00	370.00	220.00
(43)	Gribbon	750.00	370.00	220.00
(44)	Griffin	750.00	370.00	220.00
(45)	Gygli	750.00	370.00	220.00
(46)	Hanks	750.00	370.00	220.00
(47)	Hart	750.00	370.00	220.00
(48)	Hess	750.00	370.00	220.00
(49)	Hickman	750.00	370.00	220.00
(50)	Hohnhorst	750.00	370.00	220.00
(51)	Huelsman	750.00	370.00	220.00
(52)	Jackson (PSA 2 auctioned 5/10 for $111,625			
(53)	Jordan	750.00	370.00	220.00
(54)	Kane	750.00	370.00	220.00
(55)	Kelly	750.00	370.00	220.00
(56)	Kerwin	750.00	370.00	220.00
(57)	Keupper	750.00	370.00	220.00
(58)	LaFitte	750.00	370.00	220.00
(59)	Larsen	750.00	370.00	220.00
(60)	Bill Lindsay	750.00	370.00	220.00
(61)	Lynch	750.00	370.00	220.00
(62)	Manuel	750.00	370.00	220.00
(63)	Manush	750.00	370.00	220.00
(64)	Marcan	750.00	370.00	220.00
(65)	Maxwell	750.00	370.00	220.00
(66)	McBride	750.00	370.00	220.00
(67)	McCreery	750.00	370.00	220.00
(68)	McGilvray	750.00	370.00	220.00
(69)	McLaurin	750.00	370.00	220.00
(70)	McTigue	750.00	370.00	220.00
(71)	Miller (Chattanooga)	750.00	370.00	220.00
(72)	Miller (Montgomery)	750.00	370.00	220.00
(73)	Molesworth	750.00	370.00	220.00
(74)	Moran	750.00	370.00	220.00
(75)	Newton	750.00	370.00	220.00
(76)	Nolley	750.00	370.00	220.00
(77)	Osteen	750.00	370.00	220.00
(78)	Ower	750.00	370.00	220.00
(79)	Paige	750.00	370.00	220.00
(80)	Patterson	750.00	370.00	220.00
(81)	Pepe	750.00	370.00	220.00
(82)	Perdue	750.00	370.00	220.00
(83)	Peters	750.00	370.00	220.00
(84)	Phillips	750.00	370.00	220.00
(85)	Pratt	750.00	370.00	220.00
(86)	Rementer	750.00	370.00	220.00
(87)	Rhodes	750.00	370.00	220.00
(88)	Rhoton	750.00	370.00	220.00
(89)	Robertson	750.00	370.00	220.00
(90)	Rogers	750.00	370.00	220.00
(91)	Rohe	750.00	370.00	220.00
(92)	Seabough (Seabaugh)	750.00	370.00	220.00
(93)	Seitz	750.00	370.00	220.00
(94)	Schlitzer	750.00	370.00	220.00
(95)	Schopp	750.00	370.00	220.00
(96)	Siegle	750.00	370.00	220.00
(97)	Smith (Montgomery)	750.00	370.00	220.00
(98)	Sid. Smith (Atlanta)	750.00	370.00	220.00
(99)	Steele	750.00	370.00	220.00
(100)	Swacina	750.00	370.00	220.00
(101)	Sweeney	750.00	370.00	220.00
(102)	Thomas (Fielding)	750.00	370.00	220.00
(103)	Thomas (Portrait)	750.00	370.00	220.00
(104)	Vinson	750.00	370.00	220.00
(105)	Wagner (Birmingham)	750.00	370.00	220.00
(106)	Wagner (Mobile)	750.00	370.00	220.00
(107)	Walker	750.00	370.00	220.00
(108)	Wanner	750.00	370.00	220.00
(109)	Welf	750.00	370.00	220.00
(110)	Whiteman	750.00	370.00	220.00
(111)	Whitney	750.00	370.00	220.00
(112)	Wilder	750.00	370.00	220.00
(113)	Wiseman	750.00	370.00	220.00
(114)	Yerkes	750.00	370.00	220.00

1910 Old Mill Cabinets (H801-7)

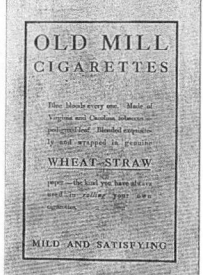

Similar in size and style to the more popular T3 Turkey Red cabinet cards of the same period, the Old Mill cabinets are much scarcer and picture fewer players. Issued in 1910 as a premium by Old Mill Cigarettes, these minor league cards measure approximately 5-3/8" x 7-5/8". Unlike the Turkey Reds, which feature full-color lithographs, the Old Mill cabinet cards picture the players in black-and-white photos surrounded by a wide tan border. The player's last name is printed in black in the lower-left corner, while his team designation appears in the lower-right. Backs carry an advertisement for Old Mill. There are currently 34 known subjects in the set. The Old Mill cabinet cards carry the ACC designation H801-7. Gaps have been left in the numbering to accomodate future additions to this checklist.

		NM	EX	VG
	Common Player:	7,500	3,750	2,250
(1)	Armstrong	7,500	3,750	2,250
(2)	Bentley	7,500	3,750	2,250
(3)	Bonner	7,500	3,750	2,250
(4)	Bowen	7,500	3,750	2,250
(5)	Brazille (Brazell)	7,500	3,750	2,250
(6)	Bush (Busch)	7,500	3,750	2,250
(7)	Bussey	7,500	3,750	2,250
(8)	Cross	7,500	3,750	2,250
(9)	Derrick	7,500	3,750	2,250
(10)	Doane	7,500	3,750	2,250
(11)	Doyle	7,500	3,750	2,250
(12)	Fox	7,500	3,750	2,250
(13)	Galvin	7,500	3,750	2,250
(14)	Griffin	7,500	3,750	2,250
(15)	Hearn	7,500	3,750	2,250
(16)	Hobbs	7,500	3,750	2,250
(17)	Hooker	7,500	3,750	2,250
(18)	Kirkpatrick	7,500	3,750	2,250
(19)	Laughlin	7,500	3,750	2,250
(20)	Luyster	7,500	3,750	2,250
(21)	McKevitt	7,500	3,750	2,250
(22)	Munson	7,500	3,750	2,250
(23)	Noojn (Noojin)	7,500	3,750	2,250
(24)	O'Halloran	7,500	3,750	2,250
(25)	Pressly	7,500	3,750	2,250
(26)	Revelle	7,500	3,750	2,250
(27)	Richardson	7,500	3,750	2,250
(28)	Rickard	7,500	3,750	2,250
(29)	Simmons	7,500	3,750	2,250
(30)	A. Smith	7,500	3,750	2,250
(31)	Spratt	7,500	3,750	2,250
(32)	Titman	7,500	3,750	2,250
(33)	Walters	7,500	3,750	2,250
(34)	Wallace	7,500	3,750	2,250
(35)	Weherell (Wehrell)	7,500	3,750	2,250
(36)	Ivey Wingo	7,500	3,750	2,250
(37)	Woolums	7,500	3,750	2,250

1949 Omaha Cardinals Player Picture Book

JIM BARKLEY, Outfield

While not baseball cards, this team booklet served the same purpose - providing fans with pictures of the local Western League (Class A) affiliate of the St. Louis Cardinals. It's also possible that individual player pages of the book have made their way into card collections over the years. The booklet is 5" x 3-1/4" in size, with 20 pages of photos and semi-gloss front and back covers, stapled together at the spine. The front has printed in red: "OMAHA CARDINALS / BASEBALL TEAM / 1949." Each inside page has back-to-back black-and-white photos with identification beneath. The pairings are checklisted here in the order in which they appear in the booklet.

	NM	EX	VG
Complete Booklet:	350.00	175.00	100.00

(1-2)	Ced Durst, Russ Kerns
(3-4)	Nick Adzick, Bob Rausch
(5-6)	Ed Nietopski, Fran Haus
(7-8)	Fritz Marolewski, Bernie Creger
(9-10)	Vaughn Hazen, Sid Langston
(11-12)	Bob Reash, Jim Barkley
(13-14)	Marty Garlock, Hank Williams
(15-16)	Lou Ciola, Joe Presko
(17-18)	Dave Thomas, Bob Mahoney
(19-20)	Stadium Photo (Dick Bokelmann)

1956 Omaha Cardinals Picture-Pak

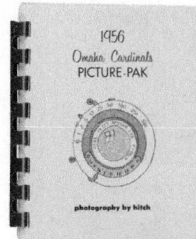

Evidently a concession stand souvenir, this "Picture-Pak" is a comb-bound set of 3-1/2" x 4-3/8" black-and-white player portraits. Each picture is printed on semi-gloss cardboard with a white facsimile autograph.

		NM	EX	VG
	Complete Book:	400.00	150.00	90.00
(1)	Tom Alston			
(2)	Alberto Baro			
(3)	Nels Burbrink			
(4)	Tom Cheney			
(5)	Ray Coleman			
(6)	Jim Command			
(7)	Chuck Harmon			
(8)	Walt Lammons			
(9)	Stan Jok			
(10)	Gordon Jones			
(11)	Johnny Keane			
(12)	Marty Kutyna			
(13)	Ed Mayer			
(14)	Herb Moford			
(15)	Mo Mozzali			
(16)	Jim Pearce			
(17)	Charlie Peete			
(18)	Danny Schell			
(19)	Dick Schofield			
(20)	Barney Schultz			
(21)	Wally Shannon			
(22)	Glen Stabelfeld			

1957 Omaha Cardinals Picture-Pak

These 3-3/8" x 4-3/8" black-and-white, blank-back photos were sold in a team picture pack. Fronts have a facsimile autograph. The unnumbered cards are checklisted here in alphabetical order.

		NM	EX	VG
	Complete Set (25):	800.00	400.00	240.00
	Common Player:	35.00	17.50	10.00
(1)	Frank Barnes	35.00	17.50	10.00
(2)	Bill Bergesch	35.00	17.50	10.00
(3)	Dick Brown	35.00	17.50	10.00
(4)	Tom Cheney	35.00	17.50	10.00
(5)	Nels Chittum	35.00	17.50	10.00
(6)	Jim Command	35.00	17.50	10.00
(7)	Chuck Diering	35.00	17.50	10.00
(8)	Sherry Dixon	35.00	17.50	10.00
(9)	Bob Durnbaugh	35.00	17.50	10.00
(10)	Glen Gorbous	35.00	17.50	10.00
(11)	Johnny Keane	35.00	17.50	10.00
(12)	Jim King	35.00	17.50	10.00
(13)	Paul Kippels	35.00	17.50	10.00
(14)	Don Lassetter	35.00	17.50	10.00
(15)	Don Liddle	35.00	17.50	10.00
(16)	Lou Limmer	35.00	17.50	10.00
(17)	Boyd Linker	35.00	17.50	10.00
(18)	Bob Mabe	35.00	17.50	10.00
(19)	Herb Moford	35.00	17.50	10.00
(20)	Rance Pless	35.00	17.50	10.00
(21)	Kelton Russell	35.00	17.50	10.00
(22)	Barney Schultz	35.00	17.50	10.00
(23)	Milt Smith	35.00	17.50	10.00
(24)	Glen Stabelfeld	35.00	17.50	10.00
(25)	Header Card	35.00	17.50	10.00

1958 Omaha Cardinals Picture-Pak

This rare late-1950s minor league issue contains the first card of Hall of Fame pitcher Bob Gibson. Probably sold as a complete set in format similar to major league picture packs of the era, there are 23 player cards and a header card. Cards measure 3-3/8" x 4-3/8", have a black-and-white player picture and facsimile autograph. They are blank-backed. The checklist of the unnumbered cards is printed here in alphabetical order.

		NM	EX	VG
Complete Set (24):		1,500	750.00	450.00
Common Player:		40.00	20.00	12.00
(1)	Tony Alomar	60.00	30.00	18.00
(2)	Dave Benedict	40.00	20.00	12.00
(3)	Bill Bergesch	40.00	20.00	12.00
(4)	Bob Blaylock	40.00	20.00	12.00
(5)	Prentice "Pidge" Browne	40.00	20.00	12.00
(6)	Chris Cannizzaro	40.00	20.00	12.00
(7)	Nels Chittum	40.00	20.00	12.00
(8)	Don Choate	40.00	20.00	12.00
(9)	Phil Clark	40.00	20.00	12.00
(10)	Jim Frey	75.00	37.50	22.50
(11)	Bob Gibson	500.00	250.00	150.00
(12)	Ev Joyner	40.00	20.00	12.00
(13)	Johnny Keane	40.00	20.00	12.00
(14)	Paul Kippels	40.00	20.00	12.00
(15)	Boyd Linker	40.00	20.00	12.00
(16)	Bob Mabe	40.00	20.00	12.00
(17)	Bernard Mateosky	40.00	20.00	12.00
(18)	Ronnie Plaza	40.00	20.00	12.00
(19)	Bill Queen	40.00	20.00	12.00
(20)	Bill Smith	40.00	20.00	12.00
(21)	Bobby G. Smith	40.00	20.00	12.00
(22)	Lee Tate	40.00	20.00	12.00
(23)	Benny Valenzuela	40.00	20.00	12.00
(24)	Header card	40.00	20.00	12.00

1962 Omaha Dodgers

This unnumbered black-and-white set measures 3-3/8" x 4-1/4" and is blank-backed. It was produced by photographer/collector Mel Bailey in an edition of 1,000 sets, sold for 50 cents by mail and at the stadium concession stand. Cards bear a facsimile autograph.

		NM	EX	VG
Complete Set (22):		175.00	90.00	50.00
Common Player:		12.50	6.25	3.75
(1)	Joe Altobelli	12.50	6.25	3.75
(2)	Jim Barbieri	12.50	6.25	3.75
(3)	Scott Breeden	12.50	6.25	3.75
(4)	Mike Brumley	12.50	6.25	3.75
(5)	Jose Cesar	12.50	6.25	3.75
(6)	Bill Hunter	12.50	6.25	3.75
(7)	Don LeJohn	12.50	6.25	3.75
(8)	Jack Lutz	12.50	6.25	3.75
(9)	Ken McMullen	12.50	6.25	3.75
(10)	Danny Ozark	12.50	6.25	3.75
(11)	Curt Roberts	12.50	6.25	3.75
(12)	Ernie Rodriguez	12.50	6.25	3.75
(13)	Dick Scarbrough	12.50	6.25	3.75
(14)	Bart Shirley	12.50	6.25	3.75
(15)	Dick Smith	12.50	6.25	3.75
(16)	Jack Smith	12.50	6.25	3.75
(17)	Nate Smith	12.50	6.25	3.75
(18)	Gene Snyder	12.50	6.25	3.75
(19)	Burbon Wheeler	12.50	6.25	3.75
(20)	Nick Wilhite (Willhite)	12.50	6.25	3.75
(21)	Jim Williams	12.50	6.25	3.75
(22)	Larry Williams	12.50	6.25	3.75

1952 Oshkosh Giants Team Issue

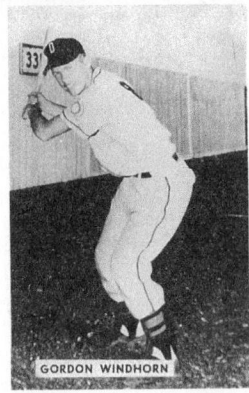

GORDON WINDHORN

These 2-1/4" x 3-3/8" black-and-white, unnumbered, blank-backed cards were one of many minor league team sets issued by Globe Printing of San Jose, Calif., in the early 1950s. Cards were usually given away at the ballpark on a one-per-week or one-per-homestand basis, accounting for the rarity of surviving sets. The O-Giants were the Wisconsin State League affiliate of the N.Y. Giants. For a Class D team, a surprising number of the Oshkosh players graduated to the major leagues.

		NM	EX	VG
Complete Set (19):		1,000	500.00	300.00
Common Player:		60.00	30.00	18.00
Album:		100.00	50.00	30.00
(1)	Dan Banaszak	60.00	30.00	18.00
(2)	Paul Bentley	60.00	30.00	18.00
(3)	Joe Berke	60.00	30.00	18.00
(4)	Joe DeBellis	60.00	30.00	18.00
(5)	Ron Edwards	60.00	30.00	18.00
(6)	Dave Garcia	60.00	30.00	18.00
(7)	Weldon Grimesley	60.00	30.00	18.00
(8)	Cam Lewis	60.00	30.00	18.00
(9)	Paul McAuley	60.00	30.00	18.00
(10)	Don Mills	60.00	30.00	18.00
(11)	Ed Opich	60.00	30.00	18.00
(12)	John Practico	60.00	30.00	18.00
(13)	Rob R. Schmidt	60.00	30.00	18.00
(14)	Rob W. Schmidt	60.00	30.00	18.00
(15)	Frank Szekula	60.00	30.00	18.00
(16)	Victor Vick	60.00	30.00	18.00
(17)	Donald Wall	60.00	30.00	18.00
(18)	Ken Whitehead	60.00	30.00	18.00
(19)	Gordon Windhorn	60.00	30.00	18.00

P

1911 Pacific Coast Biscuit (D310)

 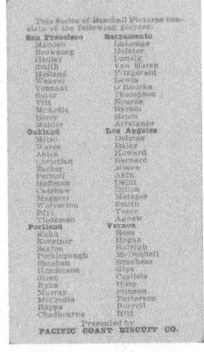

A dozen players each from six Pacific Coast League teams are represented in this set. Cards are about 2-1/2" x 4-1/4" with either black-and-white or sepia pictures on front. Backs have a checklist arranged by team. Some cards are found stamped on the back by Aldon Candy Co., Portland, Ore.

		NM	EX	VG
Complete Set (72):		135,000	67,500	40,500
Common Player:		1,700	850.00	500.00
(1)	Ables	1,700	850.00	500.00
(2)	Agnew	1,700	850.00	500.00
(3)	Akin	1,700	850.00	500.00
(4)	Frank Arrelanes (Arellanes)	1,700	850.00	500.00
(5)	Baum	1,700	850.00	500.00
(6)	Bernard	1,700	850.00	500.00
(7)	Berry	1,700	850.00	500.00
(8)	Brashear	1,700	850.00	500.00
(9)	Browning	1,700	850.00	500.00
(10)	Burrell	1,700	850.00	500.00
(11)	Byram	1,700	850.00	500.00
(12)	Carlisle	1,700	850.00	500.00
(13)	Chadbourne	1,700	850.00	500.00
(14)	Christian	1,700	850.00	500.00
(15)	Cutshaw	1,700	850.00	500.00
(16)	Daley	1,700	850.00	500.00
(17)	Danzig	1,700	850.00	500.00
(18)	Delhi	1,700	850.00	500.00
(19)	Delmas	1,700	850.00	500.00
(20)	Dillon	1,700	850.00	500.00
(21)	Fitzgerald	1,700	850.00	500.00
(22)	Gipe	1,700	850.00	500.00
(23)	Heister	1,700	850.00	500.00
(24)	Henderson	1,700	850.00	500.00
(25)	Henley	1,700	850.00	500.00
(26)	Hitt	1,700	850.00	500.00
(27)	Hoffman	1,700	850.00	500.00
(28)	Hogan	1,700	850.00	500.00
(29)	Holland	1,700	850.00	500.00
(30)	Hosp	1,700	850.00	500.00
(31)	Howard	1,700	850.00	500.00
(32)	Kostner	1,700	850.00	500.00
(33)	Kuhn	1,700	850.00	500.00
(34)	LaLonge	1,700	850.00	500.00
(35)	Lewis	1,700	850.00	500.00
(36)	Maddern	1,700	850.00	500.00
(37)	Maggert	1,700	850.00	500.00
(38)	McArdle	1,700	850.00	500.00
(39)	McCredie	1,700	850.00	500.00
(40)	McDonnell	1,700	850.00	500.00
(41)	Metzger	1,700	850.00	500.00
(42)	Mitze	1,700	850.00	500.00
(43)	Mohler	1,700	850.00	500.00
(44)	Moore	1,700	850.00	500.00
(45)	Murray	1,700	850.00	500.00
(46)	Nourse	1,700	850.00	500.00
(47)	O'Rourke	1,700	850.00	500.00
(48)	Patterson	1,700	850.00	500.00
(49)	Peckinpaugh	2,100	1,050	625.00
(50)	Pernoll	1,700	850.00	500.00
(51)	Pfyl	1,700	850.00	500.00
(52)	Raleigh	1,700	850.00	500.00
(53)	Rapps	1,700	850.00	500.00
(54)	Ross	1,700	850.00	500.00
(55)	Ryan	1,700	850.00	500.00
(56)	Seaton	1,700	850.00	500.00
(57)	Sheehan	1,700	850.00	500.00
(58)	A. Smith	1,700	850.00	500.00
(59)	H. Smith	1,700	850.00	500.00
(60)	Steen	1,700	850.00	500.00
(61)	Stinson	1,700	850.00	500.00
(62)	Sutor	1,700	850.00	500.00
(63)	Tennant	1,700	850.00	500.00
(64)	Thompson	1,700	850.00	500.00
(65)	Tiedeman	1,700	850.00	500.00
(66)	Tozer	1,700	850.00	500.00
(67)	Van Buren	1,700	850.00	500.00
(68)	Witt	1,700	850.00	500.00
(69)	Wares	1,700	850.00	500.00
(70)	Weaver	18,000	9,000	5,500
(71)	Wolverton	1,700	850.00	500.00
(72)	Zacher	1,700	850.00	500.00

1911 Pacific Coast Biscuit (D311)

A dozen players each from six Pacific Coast League teams are represented in this set. Cards are about 1-1/2" x 2-5/8" with pastel colored pictures on front. Backs have a checklist arranged by team.

		NM	EX	VG
Complete Set (72):		125,000	62,500	37,500
Common Player:		1,700	850.00	510.00
(1)	Agnew	1,700	850.00	510.00
(2)	Akin	1,700	850.00	510.00
(3)	Frank Arrelanes (Arellanes)	1,700	850.00	510.00
(4)	Baum	1,700	850.00	510.00
(5)	Bernard	1,700	850.00	510.00
(6)	Berry	1,700	850.00	510.00
(7)	Brashear	1,700	850.00	510.00
(8)	Brown	1,700	850.00	510.00
(9)	Browning	1,700	850.00	510.00
(10)	Burrell	1,700	850.00	510.00
(11)	Byram	1,700	850.00	510.00
(12)	Castleton	1,700	850.00	510.00
(13)	Chadbourne	1,700	850.00	510.00
(14)	Christian	1,700	850.00	510.00
(15)	Cutshaw	1,700	850.00	510.00
(16)	Daley	1,700	850.00	510.00
(17)	Danzig	1,700	850.00	510.00
(18)	Delhi	1,700	850.00	510.00
(19)	Delmas	1,700	850.00	510.00
(20)	Dillon	1,700	850.00	510.00
(21)	Fitzgerald	1,700	850.00	510.00
(22)	Gipe	1,700	850.00	510.00
(23)	Gregory	1,700	850.00	510.00
(24)	Harkness	1,700	850.00	510.00
(25)	Heister	1,700	850.00	510.00
(26)	Henderson	1,700	850.00	510.00
(27)	Hoffman	1,700	850.00	510.00
(28)	Hogan	1,700	850.00	510.00
(29)	Holland	1,700	850.00	510.00
(30)	Hosp	1,700	850.00	510.00
(31)	Howard	1,700	850.00	510.00
(32)	Kuhn	1,700	850.00	510.00
(33)	LaLonge	1,700	850.00	510.00
(34)	Lewis	1,700	850.00	510.00
(35)	Maggert	1,700	850.00	510.00
(36)	McArdle	1,700	850.00	510.00
(37)	McCredie	1,700	850.00	510.00
(38)	McDonnell	1,700	850.00	510.00
(39)	Meikle	1,700	850.00	510.00
(40)	Melchior	1,700	850.00	510.00
(41)	Metzger	1,700	850.00	510.00
(42)	Mitze	1,700	850.00	510.00
(43)	Mohler	1,700	850.00	510.00
(44)	Moore	1,700	850.00	510.00
(45)	Murray	1,700	850.00	510.00
(46)	Nourse	1,700	850.00	510.00
(47)	O'Rourke	1,700	850.00	510.00
(48)	Patterson	1,700	850.00	510.00

(49)	Pearce	1,700	850.00	500.00
(50)	Peckinpaugh	2,000	1,000	600.00
(51)	Pernoll	1,700	850.00	510.00
(52)	Pfyl	1,700	850.00	510.00
(53)	Raleigh	1,700	850.00	510.00
(54)	Rapps	1,700	850.00	510.00
(55)	Ryan	1,700	850.00	510.00
(56)	Schmidt	1,700	850.00	510.00
(57)	Seaton	1,700	850.00	510.00
(58)	Sheehan	1,700	850.00	510.00
(59)	A. Smith	1,700	850.00	510.00
(60)	H. Smith	1,700	850.00	510.00
(61)	Stamfield	1,700	850.00	510.00
(62)	Steen	1,700	850.00	510.00
(63)	Stinson	1,700	850.00	510.00
(64)	Sutor	1,700	850.00	510.00
(65)	Tennant	1,700	850.00	510.00
(66)	Thompson	1,700	850.00	510.00
(67)	Tiedeman	1,700	850.00	510.00
(68)	Tozer	1,700	850.00	510.00
(69)	Van Buren	1,700	850.00	510.00
(70)	Vitt	1,700	850.00	510.00
(71)	Wares	1,700	850.00	510.00
(72)	Wolverton	1,700	850.00	510.00

1943-47 Parade Sportive

Over a period of years in the mid-1940s, Montreal sports radio personality Paul Stuart's Parade Sportive program issued a series of baseball player pictures of Montreal Royals and, occasionally, other International League stars. The pictures were issued in 5" x 9-1/2" and 7" x 10" black-and-white, blank-back format. Each picture carries the name of the radio station on which Stuart's program was broadcast, along with an ad at the bottom for one of his sponsors. The unnumbered pictures are listed here alphabetically; it is unknown whether this list constitutes the complete issue.

		NM	EX	VG
Common Player:		30.00	15.00	9.00
(1)	Jack Banta	30.00	15.00	9.00
(2)	Stan Briard	30.00	15.00	9.00
(3)	Les Burge	30.00	15.00	9.00
(4)	Paul Calvert	30.00	15.00	9.00
(5)	Al Campanis	45.00	22.50	13.50
(6)	Red Durrett	30.00	15.00	9.00
(7)	Herman Franks	30.00	15.00	9.00
(8)	John Gabbard	30.00	15.00	9.00
(9)	Roland Gladu	30.00	15.00	9.00
(10)	Ray Hathaway	30.00	15.00	9.00
(11)	Clay Hopper	30.00	15.00	9.00
(12)	John Jorgensen	30.00	15.00	9.00
(13)	Paul "Pepper" Martin	30.00	15.00	9.00
(14)	Steve Nagy	30.00	15.00	9.00
(15)	Roy Portlow (Partlow)	40.00	20.00	12.00
(16)	Marv Rackley	30.00	15.00	9.00
(17)	Jackie Robinson	300.00	150.00	90.00
(18)	Jean-Pierre Roy	30.00	15.00	9.00
(19)	1944 Montreal Royals Team Photo	50.00	25.00	15.00
(20)	1945 Montreal Royals Team Photo (CLUB MONTREAL (ROYAUX) 1945)	60.00	30.00	18.00
(21)	1945 Montreal Royals Team Photo (Les "Royaux" 1945)	60.00	30.00	18.00
(22)	1946 Montreal Royals Team Photo	200.00	100.00	60.00
(23)	Stan Briard, Roland Gladu, Jean-Pierre Roy	30.00	15.00	9.00
(24)	Checklist (Paul Stuart)	30.00	15.00	9.00

1952 Parkhurst

Produced by a Canadian competitor to Kool-Aid, this 100-card set features players from three International League teams, the Toronto Maple Leafs, Montreal Royals and Ottawa Athletics, along with cards featuring baseball playing tips and quizzes. Measuring 2" x 2-1/2", the cards feature black-and-white player photos on front. Backs are printed in red and have a few biographical details, 1951 stats and an ad for Frostade.

		NM	EX	VG
Complete Set (100):		2,400	1,200	725.00
Common Player (1-25, 49-100):		25.00	12.50	7.50
Common Card (26-48):		15.00	7.50	4.50
1	Joe Becker	80.00	35.00	9.00
2	Aaron Silverman	75.00	37.50	22.50
3	Bobby Rhawn	25.00	12.50	7.50
4	Russ Bauers	25.00	12.50	7.50
5	Bill Jennings	25.00	12.50	7.50
6	Grover Bowers	25.00	12.50	7.50
7	Vic Lombardi	25.00	12.50	7.50
8	Billy DeMars	25.00	12.50	7.50
9	Frank Colman	25.00	12.50	7.50
10	Charley Grant	25.00	12.50	7.50
11	Irving Medlinger	25.00	12.50	7.50
12	Burke McLaughlin	25.00	12.50	7.50
13	Lew Morton	25.00	12.50	7.50
14	Red Barrett	25.00	12.50	7.50
15	Leon Foulk	25.00	12.50	7.50
16	Neil Sheridan	25.00	12.50	7.50
17	Ferrell Anderson	25.00	12.50	7.50
18	Roy Shore	25.00	12.50	7.50
19	Duke Markell	75.00	37.50	22.50
20	Bobby Balcena	25.00	12.50	7.50
21	Wilmer Fields	25.00	12.50	7.50
22	Charlie White	25.00	12.50	7.50
23	Red Fahr	25.00	12.50	7.50
24	Jose Bracho	25.00	12.50	7.50
25	Ed Stevens	25.00	12.50	7.50
26	Maple Leaf Stadium	25.00	12.50	7.50
27	Throwing Home	15.00	7.50	4.50
28	Regulation Baseball Diamond	15.00	7.50	4.50
29	Gripping the Bat	15.00	7.50	4.50
30	Hiding the Pitch	15.00	7.50	4.50
31	Catcher's Stance	15.00	7.50	4.50
32	Quiz: "How long does..."	15.00	7.50	4.50
33	Finger and Arm Exercises	15.00	7.50	4.50
34	First Baseman	15.00	7.50	4.50
35	Pitcher's Stance	15.00	7.50	4.50
36	Swinging Bats	15.00	7.50	4.50
37	Quiz: "Can a player advance..."	15.00	7.50	4.50
38	Watch the Ball	15.00	7.50	4.50
39	Quiz: "Can a team..."	15.00	7.50	4.50
40	Quiz: "Can a player put ..."	15.00	7.50	4.50
41	How to Bunt	15.00	7.50	4.50
42	Wrist Snap	15.00	7.50	4.50
43	Pitching Practice	15.00	7.50	4.50
44	Stealing Bases	15.00	7.50	4.50
45	Pitching 1	15.00	7.50	4.50
46	Pitching 2	15.00	7.50	4.50
47	Signals	15.00	7.50	4.50
48	Regulation baseballs	15.00	7.50	4.50
49	Al Ronning	25.00	12.50	7.50
50	Bill Lane	25.00	12.50	7.50
51	Will Sampson	25.00	12.50	7.50
52	Charlie Thompson	25.00	12.50	7.50
53	Ezra McGlothin	25.00	12.50	7.50
54	Spook Jacobs	30.00	15.00	9.00
55	Art Fabbro	25.00	12.50	7.50
56	Jim Hughes	25.00	12.50	7.50
57	Don Hoak	30.00	15.00	9.00
58	Tommy Lasorda	100.00	50.00	30.00
59	Gil Mills	25.00	12.50	7.50
60	Malcolm Mallette	25.00	12.50	7.50
61	Rocky Nelson	25.00	12.50	7.50
62	John Simmons	25.00	12.50	7.50
63	Bob Alexander	25.00	12.50	7.50
64	Dan Bankhead	35.00	17.50	10.00
65	Solomon Coleman	25.00	12.50	7.50
66	Walt Alston	100.00	50.00	30.00
67	Walt Fiala	25.00	12.50	7.50
68	Jim Gilliam	65.00	32.00	19.50
69	Jim Pendleton	25.00	12.50	7.50
70	Gino Cimoli	30.00	15.00	9.00
71	Carmen Mauro	25.00	12.50	7.50
72	Walt Moryn	25.00	12.50	7.50
73	Jim Romano	25.00	12.50	7.50
74	Joe Lutz	25.00	12.50	7.50
75	Ed Roebuck	25.00	12.50	7.50
76	Johnny Podres	65.00	32.00	19.50
77	Walter Novik	25.00	12.50	7.50
78	Lefty Gohl	25.00	12.50	7.50
79	Tom Kirk	25.00	12.50	7.50
80	Bob Betz	25.00	12.50	7.50
81	Bill Hockenbury	25.00	12.50	7.50
82	Al Rubeling	25.00	12.50	7.50
83	Julius Watlington	25.00	12.50	7.50
84	Frank Fanovich	25.00	12.50	7.50
85	Hank Foiles	25.00	12.50	7.50
86	Lou Limmer	25.00	12.50	7.50
87	Ed Hrabcsak	25.00	12.50	7.50
88	Bob Gardner	25.00	12.50	7.50
89	John Metkovich	25.00	12.50	7.50
90	Jean-Pierre Roy	25.00	12.50	7.50
91	Frank Skaff	25.00	12.50	7.50
92	Harry Desert	25.00	12.50	7.50
93	Stan Jok	25.00	12.50	7.50
94	Russ Swingle	25.00	12.50	7.50
95	Bob Wellman	25.00	12.50	7.50
96	John Conway	25.00	12.50	7.50
97	George Maskovich	25.00	12.50	7.50
98	Charlie Bishop	25.00	12.50	7.50
99	Joe Murray	25.00	12.50	7.50
100	Mike Kume	25.00	12.50	7.50

1935 Pebble Beach Clothiers

This series of black-and-white postcards includes only members of the three Bay area Pacific Coast League teams - the Oakland Oaks, Mission Reds and San Francisco Seals. The 3-1/2" x 5-3/8" cards have player identification at left in the bottom white border. The logotype of the clothier which sponsored the issue is at lower-right. The cards - each authentically autographed - were distributed by an area radio station. Backs have typical postcard indicia. This checklist may not be complete.

		NM	EX	VG
Common Player:		750.00	375.00	225.00
(1)	Leroy Anton	750.00	375.00	225.00
(2)	Joe DiMaggio	7,500	3,750	2,250
(3)	Wee Ludolph	750.00	375.00	225.00
(4)	Walter "The Great" Mails	750.00	375.00	225.00
(5)	Lefty O'Doul	3,650	1,825	1,100
(6)	Gabby Street	1,200	600.00	360.00
(7)	Oscar Vitt	900.00	450.00	270.00

1962 Pepsi-Cola Tulsa Oilers

 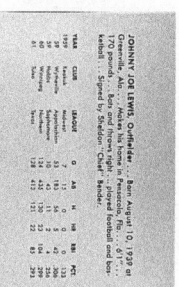

The Texas League farm club of the St. Louis Cardinals is featured in this issue of sepia-colored 2-1/2" x 3-1/2" cards issued regionally by Pepsi. The unnumbered cards are checklisted here alphabetically.

		NM	EX	VG
Complete Set (24):		275.00	135.00	80.00
Common Player:		12.00	6.00	3.50
(1)	Bob Blaylock	12.00	6.00	3.50
(2)	Bud Bloomfield	12.00	6.00	3.50
(3)	Dick Hughes	12.00	6.00	3.50
(4)	Gary Kolb	12.00	6.00	3.50
(5)	Chris Krug	12.00	6.00	3.50
(6)	Hank Kuhlmann	12.00	6.00	3.50
(7)	Whitey Kurowski	12.00	6.00	3.50
(8)	Johnny Joe Lewis	12.00	6.00	3.50
(9)	Elmer Lindsey	12.00	6.00	3.50
(10)	Jeoff Long	12.00	6.00	3.50
(11)	Pepper Martin	15.00	7.50	4.50
(12)	Jerry Marx	12.00	6.00	3.50
(13)	Weldon Maudin	12.00	6.00	3.50
(14)	Dal Maxvill	15.00	7.50	4.50
(15)	Bill McNamee	12.00	6.00	3.50
(16)	Joe Patterson	12.00	6.00	3.50
(17)	Gordon Richardson	12.00	6.00	3.50
(18)	Daryl Robertson	12.00	6.00	3.50
(19)	Tom Schwaner	12.00	6.00	3.50
(20)	Joe Shipley	12.00	6.00	3.50
(21)	Jon Smith	12.00	6.00	3.50
(22)	Clint Stark	12.00	6.00	3.50
(23)	Terry Tucker	12.00	6.00	3.50
(24)	Bill Wakefield	12.00	6.00	3.50

1963 Pepsi-Cola Tulsa Oilers

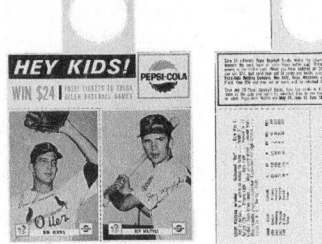

These 2-1/2" x 3-1/2", unnumbered, cards were issued in two-card panels with a holed top panel to hang on bottles. Each player's name could also be found under the cork liner of the bottle caps and when all 24 cards and caps were collected, a $24 prize could be collected. It must be assumed that some player caps were short-printed.

		NM	EX	VG
Complete Set, Singles (24):		75.00	37.50	22.50
Complete Set, Panels (12):		90.00	45.00	27.50
Common Player:		4.00	2.00	1.25
(1)	Dennis Aust	4.00	2.00	1.25
(2)	Jimmy Beauchamp	4.00	2.00	1.25
(3)	"Bud" Bloomfield	4.00	2.00	1.25
(4)	Felix de Leon	4.00	2.00	1.25
(5)	Don Dennis	4.00	2.00	1.25
(6)	Lamar Drummonds	4.00	2.00	1.25
(7)	Tom Hilgendorf	4.00	2.00	1.25
(8)	Gary Kolb	4.00	2.00	1.25
(9)	Chris Krug	4.00	2.00	1.25
(10)	"Bee" Lindsey	4.00	2.00	1.25
(11)	Roy Majtyka	4.00	2.00	1.25
(12)	Pepper Martin	7.50	3.75	2.25
(13)	Jerry Marx	4.00	2.00	1.25
(14)	"Hunkey" Mauldin	4.00	2.00	1.25
(15)	Joe Patterson	4.00	2.00	1.25
(16)	Grover Resinger	4.00	2.00	1.25
(17)	Gordon Richardson	4.00	2.00	1.25
(18)	Jon Smith	4.00	2.00	1.25
(19)	Chuck Taylor	4.00	2.00	1.25
(20)	Terry Tucker (Batboy)	4.00	2.00	1.25
(21)	Lou Vickery	4.00	2.00	1.25
(22)	Bill Wakefield	4.00	2.00	1.25
(23)	Harry Watts	4.00	2.00	1.25
(24)	Jerry Wild	4.00	2.00	1.25

1964 Pepsi-Cola Tulsa Oiler Autograph Cards

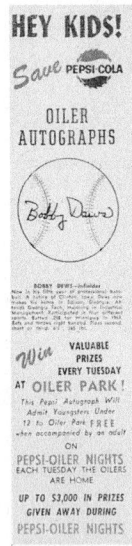

These unusual baseball cards - they don't have pictures! - were one of several 1960s issues by Pepsi in conjunction with the Tulsa Oilers. Apparently carton stuffers (they measure 2-3/16" x 9"), the cards provided free children's admission on special Pepsi-Oiler nights. The cards are printed in red, white and blue and have short player biographies under the baseball containing the facsimile autograph. The unnumbered cards are listed here in alphabetical order.

		NM	EX	VG
Complete Set (8):		30.00	15.00	9.00
Common Player:		5.00	2.50	1.50
(1)	Bob Blaylock	5.00	2.50	1.50
(2)	Nelson Briles	5.00	2.50	1.50
(3)	Bobby Dews	5.00	2.50	1.50
(4)	Roy Majtyka	5.00	2.50	1.50
(5)	Otto Meischner	5.00	2.50	1.50
(6)	Rogers Robinson	5.00	2.50	1.50
(7)	Jerry Wild	5.00	2.50	1.50
(8)	Lou Vickery	5.00	2.50	1.50

1966 Pepsi-Cola Tulsa Oilers

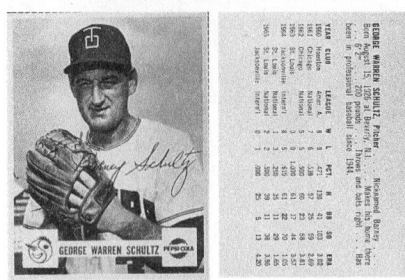

These 2-1/2" x 3-1/2" unnumbered cards were issued in two-card panels. Four cards were double-printed, each appearing on two different panels. Each player's name could also be found under the cork liner of the bottle caps and when all 24 cards and caps were collected, a $24 prize could be collected. It must be assumed that some player cards or caps were short-printed.

		NM	EX	VG
Complete Set (24):		175.00	90.00	55.00
Complete Panel Set (16):		225.00	115.00	70.00
Common Player:		10.00	5.00	3.00
Common Panel:		15.00	7.50	4.50
(1)	Florian Ackley	10.00	5.00	3.00
(2)	Dennis Aust	10.00	5.00	3.00
(3)	Elio Chacon (DP)	10.00	5.00	3.00
(4)	James Cosman	10.00	5.00	3.00
(5)	Mack Creager	10.00	5.00	3.00
(6)	Robert Dews (DP)	10.00	5.00	3.00
(7)	Harold Gilson	10.00	5.00	3.00
(8)	Larry Jaster	10.00	5.00	3.00
(9)	Alex Johnson	10.00	5.00	3.00
(10)	George Kernek (DP)	10.00	5.00	3.00
(11)	Jose Laboy	10.00	5.00	3.00
(12)	Richard LeMay	10.00	5.00	3.00
(13)	Charles Metro	10.00	5.00	3.00
(14)	David Pavlesic	10.00	5.00	3.00
(15)	Robert Pfeil	10.00	5.00	3.00
(16)	Ronald Piche	10.00	5.00	3.00
(17)	Robert Radovich	10.00	5.00	3.00
(18)	David Ricketts (DP)	10.00	5.00	3.00
(19)	Theodore Savage	10.00	5.00	3.00
(20)	George Schultz	10.00	5.00	3.00
(21)	Edward Spiezio	10.00	5.00	3.00
(22)	Clint Stark	10.00	5.00	3.00
(23)	Robert Tolan	10.00	5.00	3.00
(24)	Walter Williams	10.00	5.00	3.00

1956 Portland Beaver All-Star Pins

Stars of the Pacific Coast League Portland Beavers, all former and/or future major leaguers, are featured on these 1" black-and-white celluloid pins.

		NM	EX	VG
Complete Set (8):		1,300	650.00	375.00
Common Player:		175.00	90.00	55.00
(1)	Jim Baxes	175.00	90.00	55.00
(2)	Bob Borkowski	175.00	90.00	55.00
(3)	Sam Calderone	175.00	90.00	55.00
(4)	Jack Littrell	175.00	90.00	55.00
(5)	Luis Marquez	175.00	90.00	55.00
(6)	Ed Mickelson	175.00	90.00	55.00
(7)	Tom Saffell	175.00	90.00	55.00
(8)	Rene Valdez	175.00	90.00	55.00

R

1958 Ralph's Thriftway Seattle Rainiers

(See 1958 Seattle Popcorn for checklist and values.)

1968 Red Barn Memphis Blues

A regional issue from a Memphis chain of fast-food restaurants, these 2-1/2" x 3-3/4" cards feature members of the New York Mets' Class AA farm team. Cards have a blue-tinted player photo within an orange barn design. Player information is printed below. Backs are blank. The cards are checklisted here by uniform number.

		NM	EX	VG
Complete Set (8):		600.00	300.00	180.00
Common Player:		75.00	37.50	22.50
3	Mike "Spider" Jorgensen	75.00	37.50	22.50
6	Joe Moock	75.00	37.50	22.50
9	Rod Gaspar	75.00	37.50	22.50
16	Barry "Chief" Raziano	75.00	37.50	22.50
17	Curtis "Bubba" Brown	75.00	37.50	22.50
18	Roger Stevens	75.00	37.50	22.50
19	Ron Paul	75.00	37.50	22.50
24	Steve "Teddy" Christopher	75.00	37.50	22.50

1910 Red Sun (T211)

The 1910 minor league tobacco set issued by Red Sun Cigarettes features 75 players from the Southern Association. The Red Sun issue is similar in size and style to the massive 640-card Old Mill set (T210) issued the same year. Cards in both sets measure 1-1/2" x 2-5/8" and feature glossy black-and-white player photos. Unlike the Old Mill set, however, the Red Sun cards have a green border surrounding the photograph and a bright red and white advertisement for Red Sun cigarettes on the back. A line at the bottom promotes the cards as "First Series 1 to 75," implying that additional sets would follow, but apparently none ever did. Each of the 75 subjects in the Red Sun set was also pictured in Series Eight of the Old Mill set. Because of the "Glossy" nature of the photographs, cards in both the Old Mill and Red Sun sets are susceptible to cracking, making condition and proper grading of these cards especially important to collectors.

		NM	EX	VG
Complete Set (75):		160,000	80,000	47,500
Common Player:		2,150	1,075	645.00
(1)	Allen	2,150	1,075	645.00
(2)	Anderson	2,150	1,075	645.00
(3)	Babb	2,150	1,075	645.00
(4)	Bartley	2,150	1,075	645.00
(5)	Bay	2,150	1,075	645.00
(6)	Bayliss	2,150	1,075	645.00
(7)	Berger	2,150	1,075	645.00
(8)	Bernard	2,150	1,075	645.00
(9)	Bitroff	2,150	1,075	645.00
(10)	Breitenstein	2,150	1,075	645.00
(11)	Bronkie	2,150	1,075	645.00
(12)	Brooks	2,150	1,075	645.00
(13)	Cafalu	2,150	1,075	645.00
(14)	Case	2,150	1,075	645.00
(15)	Chappelle	2,150	1,075	645.00
(16)	Cohen	2,150	1,075	645.00
(17)	Cross	2,150	1,075	645.00
(18)	Jud. Daly	2,150	1,075	645.00
(19)	Davis	2,150	1,075	645.00
(20)	DeMontreville	2,150	1,075	645.00
(21)	E. DeMontreville	2,150	1,075	645.00
(22)	Dick	2,150	1,075	645.00
(23)	Dunn	2,150	1,075	645.00
(24)	Erloff	2,150	1,075	645.00
(25)	Fisher	2,150	1,075	645.00
(26)	Flood	2,150	1,075	645.00
(27)	Foster	2,150	1,075	645.00
(28)	Fritz	2,150	1,075	645.00
(29)	Greminger	2,150	1,075	645.00
(30)	Gribbon	2,150	1,075	645.00
(31)	Griffin	2,150	1,075	645.00
(32)	Gygli	2,150	1,075	645.00
(33)	Hanks	2,150	1,075	645.00
(34)	Hart	2,150	1,075	645.00
(35)	Hess	2,150	1,075	645.00
(36)	Hickman	2,150	1,075	645.00
(37)	Hohnhorst	2,150	1,075	645.00
(38)	Huelsman	2,150	1,075	645.00
(39)	Jordan	2,150	1,075	645.00
(40)	Kane	2,150	1,075	645.00
(41)	Kelly	2,150	1,075	645.00
(42)	Kerwin	2,150	1,075	645.00
(43)	Keupper	2,150	1,075	645.00
(44)	LaFitte	2,150	1,075	645.00
(45)	Bill Lindsay	2,150	1,075	645.00
(46)	Lynch	2,150	1,075	645.00
(47)	Manush	2,150	1,075	645.00
(48)	McCreery	2,150	1,075	645.00
(49)	Miller	2,150	1,075	645.00
(50)	Molesworth	2,150	1,075	645.00
(51)	Moran	2,150	1,075	645.00
(52)	Nolley	2,150	1,075	645.00
(53)	Paige	2,150	1,075	645.00
(54)	Pepe	2,150	1,075	645.00
(55)	Perdue	2,150	1,075	645.00
(56)	Pratt	2,150	1,075	645.00
(57)	Rhoton	2,150	1,075	645.00
(58)	Robertson	2,150	1,075	645.00
(59)	Rogers	2,150	1,075	645.00

		NM	EX	VG
(60)	Rohe	2,150	1,075	645.00
(61)	Seabaugh	2,150	1,075	645.00
(62)	Seitz	2,150	1,075	645.00
(63)	Siegle	2,150	1,075	645.00
(64)	Smith	2,150	1,075	645.00
(65)	Sid. Smith	2,150	1,075	645.00
(66)	Steele	2,150	1,075	645.00
(67)	Swacina	2,150	1,075	645.00
(68)	Sweeney	2,150	1,075	645.00
(69)	Thomas	2,150	1,075	645.00
(70)	Vinson	2,150	1,075	645.00
(71)	Wagner	2,150	1,075	645.00
(72)	Walker	2,150	1,075	645.00
(73)	Welf	2,150	1,075	645.00
(74)	Wilder	2,150	1,075	645.00
(75)	Wiseman	2,150	1,075	645.00

1945 Remar Bread Oakland Oaks

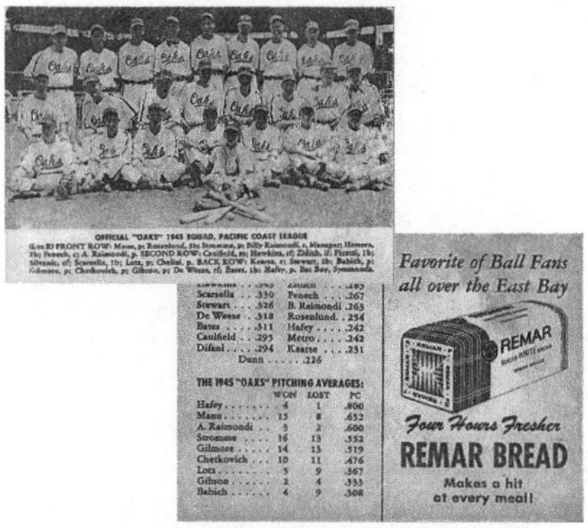
OFFICIAL "OAKS" 1945 SQUAD, PACIFIC COAST LEAGUE
Scarsella . . . .330 Fenech 267
Stewart . . . .326 B. Raimondi .263
De Weese . .318 Rosenlund. . .254
Bates . . . . .311 Hafey 242
Caulfield . . .295 Metro 242
Difani . . . . .294 Kearse 231
Dunn 226
THE 1945 "OAKS" PITCHING AVERAGES:
WON LOST PC
Hafey . . . . . . 4 1 .800
Mann . . . . . . 15 8 .652
A. Raimondi . . 3 2 .600
Stromme . . . . 16 13 .552
Gilmore . . . . . 14 13 .519
Chetkovich . . . 10 11 .476
Lotz . . . . 5 9 .367
Gibson . . . . . . 2 4 .333
Babich . . . . . . 4 9 .308
Favorite of Ball Fans all over the East Bay
REMAR
Four Hours Fresher
REMAR BREAD
Makes a hit at every meal!

This 4-7/8" x 3-5/8" card features on front a black-and-white team photo, borderless at the top and sides. In the white strip at bottom, the players are identified. The back is printed in black with red highlights and presents the season stats for batting average and pitchers' won-lost percentage. At right is a picture of a loaf of the sponsor's bread. At present, only two examples of this card are known to exist.

	NM	EX	VG
Oakland Oaks Team Photo	2,500	1,250	750.00

1946 Remar Bread Oakland Oaks

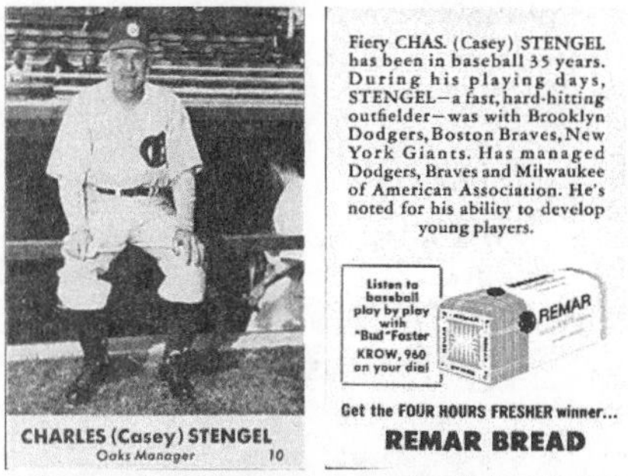
CHARLES (Casey) STENGEL
Oaks Manager 10
Fiery CHAS. (Casey) STENGEL has been in baseball 35 years. During his playing days, STENGEL—a fast, hard-hitting outfielder—was with Brooklyn Dodgers, Boston Braves, New York Giants. Has managed Dodgers, Braves and Milwaukee of American Association. He's noted for his ability to develop young players.
Listen to baseball play by play with "Bud" Foster KROW, 960 on your dial
REMAR
Get the FOUR HOURS FRESHER winner...
REMAR BREAD

Remar Baking Co. issued several baseball card sets in the northern California area from 1946-1950, all picturing members of the Oakland Oaks of the Pacific Coast League. The 1946 set consists of 23 cards (five unnumbered, 18 numbered). Measuring 2" x 3", the cards were printed on heavy paper and feature black and white photos with the player's name, team and position at the bottom. The backs contain a brief write-up plus an ad for Remar Bread printed in red. The cards were distributed one per week. The first five cards were unnumbered. The rest of the set is numbered on the front, but begins with number "5," rather than "6."

		NM	EX	VG
Complete Set (23):		600.00	300.00	180.00
Common Player:		25.00	12.50	7.50
5	Hershell Martin (Hershel)	25.00	12.50	7.50
6	Bill Hart	25.00	12.50	7.50
7	Charlie Gassaway	25.00	12.50	7.50
8	Wally Westlake	25.00	12.50	7.50
9	Mickey Burnett	25.00	12.50	7.50
10	Charles (Casey) Stengel	110.00	55.00	35.00
11	Charlie Metro	25.00	12.50	7.50
12	Tom Hafey	25.00	12.50	7.50
13	Tony Sabol	25.00	12.50	7.50
14	Ed Kearse	25.00	12.50	7.50
15	Bud Foster (Announcer)	25.00	12.50	7.50
16	Johnny Price	25.00	12.50	7.50
17	Gene Bearden	25.00	12.50	7.50
18	Floyd Speer	25.00	12.50	7.50
19	Bryan Stephens	25.00	12.50	7.50
20	Rinaldo (Rugger) Ardizoia	25.00	12.50	7.50
21	Ralph Buxton	25.00	12.50	7.50
22	Ambrose (Bo) Palica	25.00	12.50	7.50
----	Brooks Holder	25.00	12.50	7.50
----	Henry (Cotton) Pippen	25.00	12.50	7.50
----	Billy Raimondi	90.00	45.00	27.50
----	Les Scarsella	25.00	12.50	7.50
----	Glen (Gabby) Stewart	25.00	12.50	7.50

1947 Remar Bread Oakland Oaks

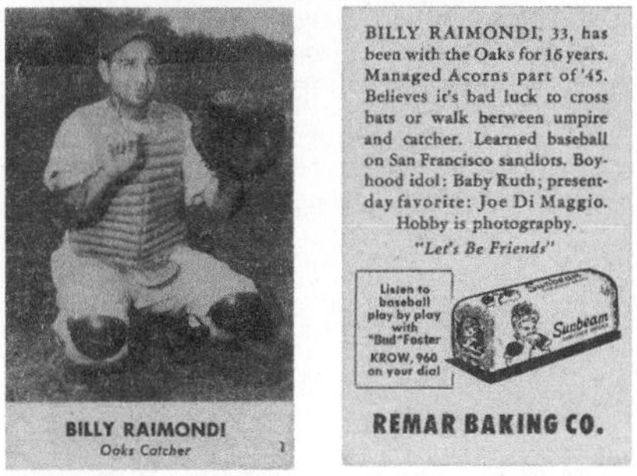
BILLY RAIMONDI
Oaks Catcher 1
BILLY RAIMONDI, 33, has been with the Oaks for 16 years. Managed Acorns part of '45. Believes it's bad luck to cross bats or walk between umpire and catcher. Learned baseball on San Francisco sandlots. Boyhood idol: Baby Ruth; present-day favorite: Joe Di Maggio. Hobby is photography.
"Let's Be Friends"
Listen to baseball play by play with "Bud" Foster KROW, 960 on your dial
Sunbeam
REMAR BAKING CO.

Remar's second set consisted of 25 numbered cards, again measuring 2" x 3". The cards are nearly identical to the previous year's set, except the loaf of bread on the back is printed in blue, rather than red.

		NM	EX	VG
Complete Set (25):		600.00	300.00	180.00
Common Player:		25.00	12.50	7.50
1	Billy Raimondi	25.00	12.50	7.50
2	Les Scarsella	25.00	12.50	7.50
3	Brooks Holder	25.00	12.50	7.50
4	Charlie Gassaway	25.00	12.50	7.50
5	Mickey Burnett	25.00	12.50	7.50
6	Ralph Buxton	25.00	12.50	7.50
7	Ed Kearse	25.00	12.50	7.50
8	Charles (Casey) Stengel	75.00	37.50	22.50
9	Bud Foster (Announcer)	25.00	12.50	7.50
10	Ambrose (Bo) Palica	25.00	12.50	7.50
11	Tom Hafey	25.00	12.50	7.50
12	Hershel Martin	25.00	12.50	7.50
13	Henry (Cotton) Pippen	25.00	12.50	7.50
14	Floyd Speer	25.00	12.50	7.50
15	Tony Sabol	25.00	12.50	7.50
16	Will Hafey	25.00	12.50	7.50
17	Ray Hamrick	25.00	12.50	7.50
18	Maurice Van Robays	25.00	12.50	7.50
19	Dario Lodigiani	25.00	12.50	7.50
20	Mel (Dizz) Duezabou	25.00	12.50	7.50
21	Damon Hayes	25.00	12.50	7.50
22	Gene Lillard	25.00	12.50	7.50
23	Aldon Wilkie	25.00	12.50	7.50
24	Dewey Soriano	25.00	12.50	7.50
25	Glen Crawford	25.00	12.50	7.50

1948 Remar/Sunbeam Bread Oakland Oaks

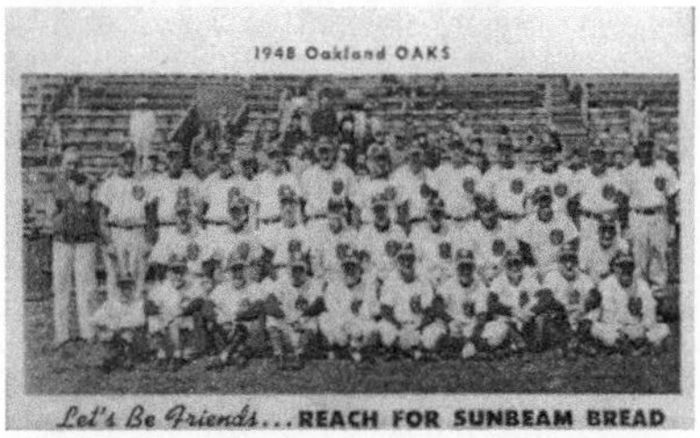
1948 Oakland OAKS
Let's Be Friends... REACH FOR SUNBEAM BREAD

One of the great minor league rarities, only two examples of this 3-1/4" x 5-1/2" black-and-white team photo card are known.

	NM	EX	VG
1948 Oakland Oaks Team Photo	4,000	2,000	1,200

1949 Remar Bread Oakland Oaks

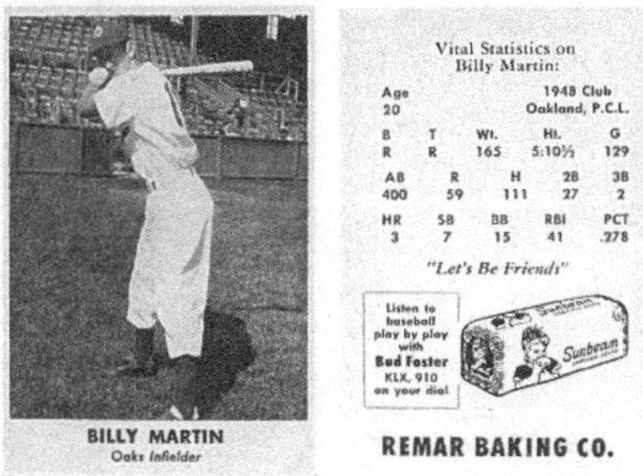
BILLY MARTIN
Oaks Infielder
Vital Statistics on Billy Martin:
Age 20
1948 Club Oakland, P.C.L.
B R T R Wt. 165 Ht. 5:10½ G 129
AB 400 R 59 H 111 2B 27 3B 2
HR 3 SB 7 BB 15 RBI 41 PCT .278
"Let's Be Friends"
Listen to baseball play by play with Bud Foster KLX, 910 on your dial
Sunbeam
REMAR BAKING CO.

The 1949 Remar Bread issue was increased to 32 cards, again measuring 2" x 3". Unlike the two earlier sets, photos in the 1949 Remar set are surrounded by a thin, white border and are unnumbered. The player's name, team and position appear below the black and white photo. The backs are printed in blue and include the player's 1948 statistics and the distinctive loaf of bread.

		NM	EX	VG
Complete Set (32):		700.00	350.00	210.00
Common Player:		20.00	10.00	6.00
(1)	Ralph Buxton	20.00	10.00	6.00
(2)	Milo Candini	20.00	10.00	6.00
(3)	Rex Cecil	20.00	10.00	6.00
(4)	Loyd Christopher (Lloyd)	20.00	10.00	6.00
(5)	Charles Dressen	20.00	10.00	6.00
(6)	Mel Duezabou	20.00	10.00	6.00
(7)	Bud Foster (Sportscaster)	20.00	10.00	6.00
(8)	Charlie Gassaway	20.00	10.00	6.00
(9)	Ray Hamrick	20.00	10.00	6.00
(10)	Jack Jensen	25.00	12.50	7.50
(11)	Earl Jones	20.00	10.00	6.00
(12)	George Kelly	60.00	30.00	18.00
(13)	Frank Kerr	20.00	10.00	6.00
(14)	Richard Kryhoski	20.00	10.00	6.00
(15)	Harry Lavagetto	20.00	10.00	6.00
(16)	Dario Lodigiani	20.00	10.00	6.00
(17)	Billy Martin	100.00	50.00	30.00
(18)	George Metkovich	20.00	10.00	6.00
(19)	Frank Nelson	20.00	10.00	6.00
(20)	Don Padgett	20.00	10.00	6.00
(21)	Alonzo Perry	40.00	20.00	12.00
(22)	Bill Raimondi	20.00	10.00	6.00
(23)	Earl Rapp	20.00	10.00	6.00
(24)	Eddie Samcoff	20.00	10.00	6.00
(25)	Les Scarsella	20.00	10.00	6.00
(26)	Forest Thompson (Forrest)	20.00	10.00	6.00
(27)	Earl Toolson	20.00	10.00	6.00
(28)	Lou Tost	20.00	10.00	6.00
(29)	Maurice Van Robays	20.00	10.00	6.00
(30)	Jim Wallace	20.00	10.00	6.00
(31)	Arthur Lee Wilson	40.00	20.00	12.00
(32)	Parnell Woods	40.00	20.00	12.00

1950 Remar Bread Oakland Oaks

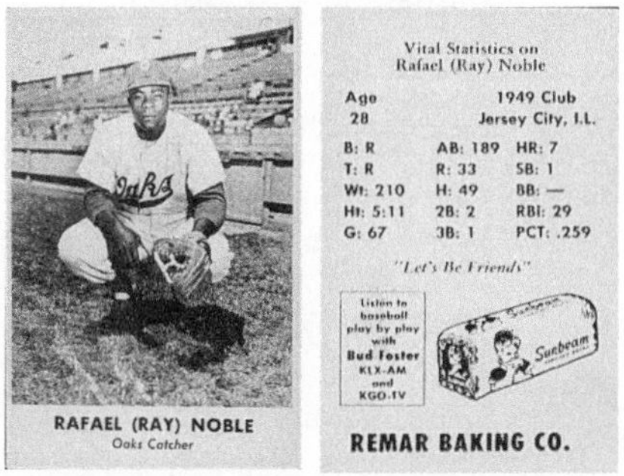
RAFAEL (RAY) NOBLE
Oaks Catcher
Vital Statistics on Rafael (Ray) Noble
Age 28
1949 Club Jersey City, I.L.
B: R AB: 189 HR: 7
T: R R: 33 SB: 1
Wt: 210 H: 49 BB: —
Ht: 5:11 2B: 2 RBI: 29
G: 67 3B: 1 PCT: .259
"Let's Be Friends"
Listen to baseball play by play with Bud Foster KLX-AM and KGO-TV
Sunbeam
REMAR BAKING CO.

The most common of the Remar Bread issues, the 1950 set contains 27 unnumbered cards, again measuring 2" x 3" and featuring members of the Oakland Oaks. The cards are nearly identical to the previous year's set but can be differentiated by the 1949 statistics on the back.

		NM	EX	VG
Complete Set (27):		500.00	250.00	150.00
Common Player:		20.00	10.00	6.00
(1)	George Bamberger	20.00	10.00	6.00
(2)	Hank Behrman	20.00	10.00	6.00
(3)	Loyd Christopher (Lloyd)	20.00	10.00	6.00
(4)	Chuck Dressen	20.00	10.00	6.00
(5)	Mel Duezabou	20.00	10.00	6.00
(6)	Augie Galan	20.00	10.00	6.00
(7)	Charlie Gassaway	20.00	10.00	6.00
(8)	Allen Gettel	20.00	10.00	6.00
(9)	Ernie W. Groth	20.00	10.00	6.00
(10)	Ray Hamrick	20.00	10.00	6.00
(11)	Earl Harrist	20.00	10.00	6.00
(12)	Billy Herman	60.00	30.00	18.00
(13)	Bob Hofman	20.00	10.00	6.00
(14)	George Kelly	60.00	30.00	18.00
(15)	Harry Lavagetto	20.00	10.00	6.00
(16)	Eddie Malone	20.00	10.00	6.00
(17)	George Metkovich	20.00	10.00	6.00
(18)	Frank Nelson	20.00	10.00	6.00
(19)	Rafael (Ray) Noble	20.00	10.00	6.00
(20)	Don Padgett	20.00	10.00	6.00
(21)	Earl Rapp	20.00	10.00	6.00
(22)	Clyde Shoun	20.00	10.00	6.00
(23)	Forrest Thompson	20.00	10.00	6.00
(24)	Louis Tost	20.00	10.00	6.00
(25)	Dick Wakefield	20.00	10.00	6.00
(26)	Artie Wilson	40.00	20.00	12.00
(27)	Roy Zimmerman	20.00	10.00	6.00

1958 Richmond Virginians Team Issue

This set of black-and-white cards features members of the N.Y. Yankees' top farm club in posed action photos with a stadium background. Issued on a pair of 8-1/2" x 10" sheets, single cards measure about 2-1/8" x 3" including the white borders around the picture. The player name is in a white strip within the photo. Backs have only the player name and a two-line credit at bottom to Galeski Photo Finishing.

		NM	EX	VG
Complete Set (21):		1,200	600.00	360.00
Common Player:		60.00	30.00	18.00
(1)	Billy Bethel	60.00	30.00	18.00
(2)	Cletis Boyer	90.00	45.00	27.50
(3)	Wade Browning	60.00	30.00	18.00
(4)	Bob Chakales	60.00	30.00	18.00
(5)	Jim Coates	60.00	30.00	18.00
(6)	Jim Command	60.00	30.00	18.00
(7)	Bobby Deakin	60.00	30.00	18.00
(8)	Bob Del Greco	60.00	30.00	18.00
(9)	John Jaciuk	60.00	30.00	18.00
(10)	John James	60.00	30.00	18.00
(11)	Deron Johnson	75.00	37.50	22.50
(12)	Len Johnston	60.00	30.00	18.00
(13)	Bob Kline	60.00	30.00	18.00
(14)	Ed Lopat	80.00	40.00	24.00

		NM	EX	VG
(15)	Bob Oldis	60.00	30.00	18.00
(16)	Wilson Parsons	60.00	30.00	18.00
(17)	Rance Pless	60.00	30.00	18.00
(18)	Jim Post	60.00	30.00	18.00
(19)	Danny Schell	60.00	30.00	18.00
(20)	Gerry Thomas	60.00	30.00	18.00
(21)	Bob Weisler	60.00	30.00	18.00

1959 Richmond Virginians

Photos of half a dozen local favorites of the International League Richmond Virginians were featured on ticket stubs during the 1959 season. The black-and-white player portions of the stub measure 2" x 3" and are blank-backed. The unnumbered cards are listed here alphabetically. Richmond was a farm club of the N.Y. Yankees.

		NM	EX	VG
Complete Set (6):		1,200	625.00	375.00
Common Player:		90.00	45.00	25.00
(1)	Clete Boyer	300.00	150.00	90.00
(2)	Jim Coates	200.00	100.00	60.00
(3)	Eli Grba	200.00	100.00	60.00
(4)	John James	200.00	100.00	60.00
(5)	Dick Sanders	200.00	100.00	60.00
(6)	Bill Short	200.00	100.00	60.00

1960 Richmond Virginians

Jerry Thomas
MADISON HEIGHTS, VA.

In 1960, the Richmond Virginians of the International League continued the practice of using player photos on their game tickets. Black-and-white with a blank-back, the player portions of the tickets can be found in two sizes. Unnumbered cards are checklisted here alphabetically. The Richmond team was a farm club of the N.Y. Yankees.

		NM	EX	VG
Complete Set (6):		1,750	875.00	525.00
Common Player:		300.00	150.00	90.00
SMALL SIZE (2" x 2-3/4")		.00	.00	.00
(1)	Bob Martyn	300.00	150.00	90.00
(2)	Jack Reed	300.00	150.00	90.00
LARGE SIZE (2-3/8" x 2-7/8")		.00	.00	.00
(1)	Tony Asaro	300.00	150.00	90.00
(2)	Bill Shantz	300.00	150.00	90.00
(3)	Jerry Thomas	300.00	150.00	90.00
(4)	Bob Weisler	300.00	150.00	90.00

1966 Royal Crown Cola Columbus Yankees

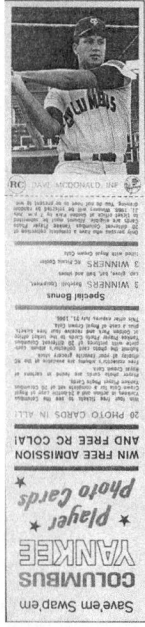

This set of 20 cards was distributed in eight packs of Royal Crown Cola, then based in Columbus, Ga. They were part of a strip measuring 2-1/4" wide. The first 3" of the 9-1/2" strip has a black-and-white photo of the player with his name,

position and other biographical data, along with an RC logo in blue and red. The bottom of the strip has a promotion sponsored by the ball club and RC, offering a case of cola for turning in a complete set in an album provided for the cards. Those who turned in the cards were also eligible to win baseball equipment or picnic coolers in a giveaway at a July 31 game that year. Most cards have the advertisement removed. Strips that include the advertisement should be valued at 1.5X of values shown. The cards are unnumbered and listed in alphabetical order.

		NM	EX	VG
Complete Set (20):		800.00	400.00	240.00
Common Player:		40.00	20.00	12.00
Album:		800.00	400.00	240.00
(1)	Gil Blanco	40.00	20.00	12.00
(2)	Ronnie Boyer	50.00	25.00	15.00
(3)	Jim Brenneman	40.00	20.00	12.00
(4)	Butch Cretara	40.00	20.00	12.00
(5)	Bill Henry	40.00	20.00	12.00
(6)	Joe Jeran	40.00	20.00	12.00
(7)	Jerry Kenney	40.00	20.00	12.00
(8)	Ronnie Kirk	40.00	20.00	12.00
(9)	Tom Kowalski	40.00	20.00	12.00
(10)	Jim Marrujo	40.00	20.00	12.00
(11)	Dave McDonald	40.00	20.00	12.00
(12)	Ed Merritt	40.00	20.00	12.00
(13)	Jim Palma	40.00	20.00	12.00
(14)	Cecil Perkins	40.00	20.00	12.00
(15)	Jack Reed	40.00	20.00	12.00
(16)	Ellie Rodriguez	60.00	30.00	18.00
(17)	John Schroeppel	40.00	20.00	12.00
(18)	Dave Truelock	40.00	20.00	12.00
(19)	Steve Whitaker	40.00	20.00	12.00
(20)	Earl Willoughby	40.00	20.00	12.00

S

1952 San Diego Padres Team Issue

LONNIE SUMMERS

The Padres were one of the highest classification minor league teams for which Globe Printing produced baseball cards in the early 1950s. Like other sets from the San Jose, Calif., printer, the 2-1/8" x 3-3/8" cards are black-and-white, blank-backed and feature the player's name on a white strip on front. Because the Padres are quite often found as a team set, it's likely they were not distributed a card at a time as seems to have been the case with other sets. In 1952, the team was in the Open Classification Pacific Coast League.

		NM	EX	VG
Complete Set (18):		1,000	500.00	300.00
Common Player:		60.00	30.00	18.00
(1)	Al Benton	60.00	30.00	18.00
(2)	Dain Clay	60.00	30.00	18.00
(3)	John Davis	125.00	62.00	37.00
(4)	Dick Faber	60.00	30.00	18.00
(5)	Ben Flowers	60.00	30.00	18.00
(6)	Murray Franklin	60.00	30.00	18.00
(7)	Herb Gorman	90.00	45.00	27.50
(8)	Jack Graham	60.00	30.00	18.00
(9)	Memo Luna	60.00	30.00	18.00
(10)	Lefty O'Doul (Seated, light background.)	125.00	62.00	37.00
(11)	Lefty O'Doul (Standing, dark background.)	125.00	62.00	37.00
(12)	Al Olsen	60.00	30.00	18.00
(13)	Jimmie Reese	100.00	50.00	30.00
(14)	Al Richter	60.00	30.00	18.00
(15)	Jack Salveson	60.00	30.00	18.00
(16)	Lou Stringer	60.00	30.00	18.00
(17)	Lonnie Summers	60.00	30.00	18.00
(18)	Jack Tobin	60.00	30.00	18.00

1950 San Francisco Seals Popcorn

These 3-1/4" x 4-1/2" black-and-white cards were issued with the purchase of caramel corn at Sicks Stadium.

		NM	EX	VG
Complete Set (13):		700.00	350.00	210.00
Common Player:		60.00	30.00	17.50
(1)	Dick Briskey	60.00	30.00	17.50
(2)	Ralph Buxton	60.00	30.00	17.50
(3)	Harry Feldman	60.00	30.00	17.50
(4)	Chet Johnson	60.00	30.00	17.50
(5)	Al Lien	60.00	30.00	17.50
(6)	Dario Lodigiani	60.00	30.00	17.50
(7)	Cliff Melton	60.00	30.00	17.50
(8)	Roy Nicely	60.00	30.00	17.50
(9)	Roy Partee	60.00	30.00	17.50
(10)	Manny Perez	60.00	30.00	17.50
(11)	Neill Sheridan	60.00	30.00	17.50
(12)	Elmer Singleton	60.00	30.00	17.50
(13)	Jack Tobin	60.00	30.00	17.50

1953 San Francisco Seals Team Issue

This set of 25 cards was sold at Seals Stadium and by mail for 25 cents. Fronts of the 4" x 5" black-and-white cards contain a player photo with facsimile autograph. The player's name, team and position are printed in the white bottom border. Backs of the unnumbered cards are blank. Melton is a rare short-print which has been reprinted.

		NM	EX	VG
Complete Set (25):		600.00	300.00	180.00
Common Player:		30.00	15.00	9.00
(1)	Bill Boemler	30.00	15.00	9.00
(2)	Bill Bradford	30.00	15.00	9.00
(3)	Reno Cheso	30.00	15.00	9.00
(4)	Harlond Clift	30.00	15.00	9.00
(5)	Walt Clough	30.00	15.00	9.00
(6)	Cliff Coggin	30.00	15.00	9.00
(7)	Tommy Heath	30.00	15.00	9.00
(8)	Leo Hughes (Trainer)	30.00	15.00	9.00
(9)	Frank Kalin	30.00	15.00	9.00
(10)	Al Lien	30.00	15.00	9.00
(11)	Al Lyons	30.00	15.00	9.00
(12)	John McCall	30.00	15.00	9.00
(13)	Bill McCawley	30.00	15.00	9.00
(14)	Dave Melton (SP)	200.00	100.00	60.00
(15)	Jim Moran	30.00	15.00	9.00
(16)	Bob Muncrief	30.00	15.00	9.00
(17)	Leo Righetti	30.00	15.00	9.00
(18)	Ted Shandor	30.00	15.00	9.00
(19)	Elmer Singleton	30.00	15.00	9.00
(20)	Lou Stringer	30.00	15.00	9.00
(21)	Sal Taormina	30.00	15.00	9.00
(22)	Will Tiesiera	30.00	15.00	9.00
(23)	Nini Tornay	30.00	15.00	9.00
(24)	George Vico	30.00	15.00	9.00
(25)	Jerry Zuvela	30.00	15.00	9.00

1951 San Jose Red Sox Team Issue

MARVIN OWEN

These 2-1/4" x 3-3/8" black-and-white, unnumbered, blank-backed cards were one of many minor league team sets issued by Globe Printing of San Jose, Calif., in the early 1950s. Cards were usually given away at the ballpark on a one-per-week or one-per-homestand basis, accounting for the rarity of surviving sets. The team was a Class C farm club for the Boston Red Sox in the California League. An album exists for the set, but curiously, it is dated 1952.

		NM	EX	VG
Complete Set (18):		1,000	500.00	300.00
Common Player:		60.00	30.00	18.00
(1)	Ken Aspromonte	75.00	37.00	22.00
(2)	Joe Buck	60.00	30.00	18.00
(3)	Harold Buckwalter	60.00	30.00	18.00
(4)	Al Curtis	60.00	30.00	18.00
(5)	Marvin Eyre	60.00	30.00	18.00
(6)	Jack Heinen	60.00	30.00	18.00
(7)	John Kinney	60.00	30.00	18.00
(8)	Walt Lucas	60.00	30.00	18.00
(9)	Syl McNinch	60.00	30.00	18.00
(10)	Stan McWilliams	60.00	30.00	18.00
(11)	Marvin Owen	60.00	30.00	18.00
(12)	Dick Piedrotti	60.00	30.00	18.00
(13)	Al Schroll	60.00	30.00	18.00

		NM	EX	VG
(14)	Ed Sobczak	60.00	30.00	18.00
(15)	Joe Stephenson	60.00	30.00	18.00
(16)	George Storti	60.00	30.00	18.00
(17)	Allan Van Alstyne	60.00	30.00	18.00
(18)	Floyd Warr	60.00	30.00	18.00

1963 Scheible Press Rochester Red Wings

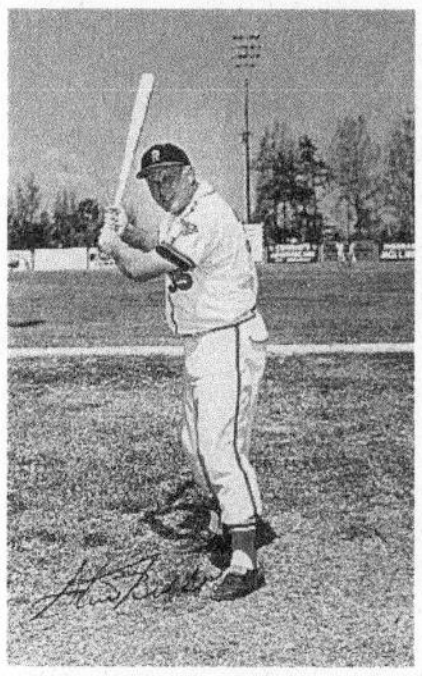

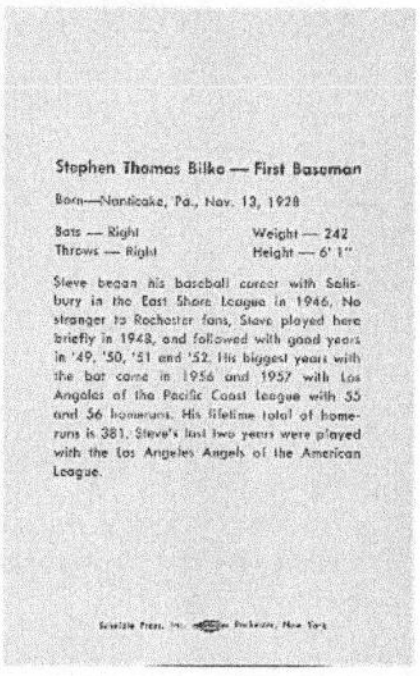
Stephen Thomas Bilko — First Baseman

Born—Nanticoke, Pa., Nov. 13, 1928

Bats — Right   Weight — 242
Throws — Right   Height — 6' 1"

Steve began his baseball career with Salisbury in the East Shore League in 1946. No stranger to Rochester fans, Steve played here briefly in 1948, and followed with good years in '49, '50, '51 and '52. His biggest years with the bat came in 1956 and 1957 with Los Angeles of the Pacific Coast League with 55 and 56 homeruns. His lifetime total of homeruns is 381. Steve's last two years were played with the Los Angeles Angels of the American League.

Apparently sold as a stadium concession stand item in a paper and cellophane envelope, the full-color 3-13/16" x 5-7/8" cards are found printed on either a heavy paper stock or thin cardboard stock, each with identical black-and-white back. Two blank-backed cards in slightly larger (4" x 5-7/8") format are checklisted here, although their relationship to the other photos is unknown. The '63 Red Wings were the International League affiliate of the Baltimore Orioles.

		NM	EX	VG
Complete Set (11):		250.00	125.00	75.00
Common Player:		20.00	10.00	6.00
(1)	Joe Altobelli	25.00	12.50	7.50
(2)	Steve Bilko	20.00	10.00	6.00
(3)	Sam E. Bowens	20.00	10.00	6.00
(4)	Don Brummer	20.00	10.00	6.00
(5)	Nelson Chittum (Cardboard only.)	20.00	10.00	6.00
(6a)	Luke Easter (Small format.)	40.00	20.00	12.00
(6b)	Luke Easter (Large format.)	75.00	40.00	25.00
(7)	Darrell Johnson, Chris Krug (Paper only.)	25.00	12.50	7.50
(8)	Ron Kabbes (Large format.)	20.00	10.00	6.00
(9)	Fred Valentine	20.00	10.00	6.00
(10)	Ozzie Virgil	20.00	10.00	6.00
(11)	Ray Youngdahl	20.00	10.00	6.00

1954-1968 Seattle Rainiers/Angels Popcorn

One of the longest-running minor league baseball card promotions was the 1954-68 Seattle popcorn cards. The principal sponsor was Centennial Mills, which had issued cards in the 1940s. Similar in format throughout their period of issue, the cards are 2" x 3" in size, black-and-white, usually featuring portrait photos on the front with the player's name or name and position below. In some years the cards were printed on semi-glossy stock. Some years' card backs are blank, in other years, backs feature ads for various local businesses; in a few years, cards could be found with both blank and printed backs. Many photo and spelling variations are known throughout the series; most are noted in the appropriate checklists. The unnumbered cards are checklisted alphabetically. It is possible a few stragglers will be added to these checklists in the future. In most years a group of 20 cards was released early in the year, supplemented later in the season as roster changes dictated. The cards were given away with the purchase of a box of popcorn sold at Seattle's Sicks stadium. During the card-issuing era, Seattle was an independent team in the Pacific Coast League in 1954-55. From 1956-60 they were a top farm team in the Reds system. They were a Red Sox affiliate from 1961-64, before tying up with the California Angels in 1965.

(Consult checklists for attribution of blank-back cards.)

1954 Seattle Rainiers Popcorn

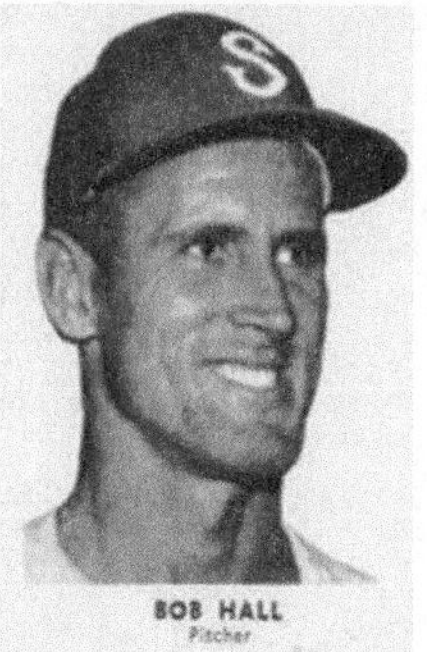

(Blank-back. Most players photographed in dark cap with light "S.")

		NM	EX	VG
Complete Set (26):		2,500	1,250	750.00
Common Player:		110.00	55.00	35.00
(1)	Gene Bearden	110.00	55.00	35.00
(2)	Al Brightman	110.00	55.00	35.00
(3)	Jack Burkowatz	110.00	55.00	35.00
(4)	Tommy Byrne (Photo reversed, backwards "S" on cap.)	110.00	55.00	35.00
(5)	Joe Erautt	110.00	55.00	35.00
(6)	Bill Evans	110.00	55.00	35.00
(7)	Van Fletcher	110.00	55.00	35.00
(8)	Bob Hall	110.00	55.00	35.00
(9)	Pete Hernandez	110.00	55.00	35.00
(10)	Lloyd Jenney	110.00	55.00	35.00
(11)	Joe Joshua	110.00	55.00	35.00
(12)	Vern Kindsfather	110.00	55.00	35.00
(13)	Tom Lovrich	110.00	55.00	35.00
(14)	Clarence Maddern	110.00	55.00	35.00
(15)	Don Mallott	110.00	55.00	35.00
(16)	Loren Meyers	110.00	55.00	35.00
(17)	Steve Nagy	110.00	55.00	35.00
(18)	Ray Orteig	110.00	55.00	35.00
(19)	Gerry Priddy	110.00	55.00	35.00
(20)	George Schmees	110.00	55.00	35.00
(21)	Bill Schuster	110.00	55.00	35.00
(22)	Leo Thomas	110.00	55.00	35.00
(23)	Jack Tobin	110.00	55.00	35.00
(24)	Al Widmer	110.00	55.00	35.00
(25)	Artie Wilson	175.00	85.00	50.00
(26)	Al Zarilla	110.00	55.00	35.00

1955 Seattle Rainiers Popcorn

(Blank-back. All players wearing light caps with "R" logo.)

		NM	EX	VG
Complete Set (22):		2,000	1,000	600.00
Common Player:		110.00	55.00	35.00
(1)	Bob Balcena	110.00	55.00	35.00
(2)	Monty Basgall	110.00	55.00	35.00
(3)	Ewell Blackwell	135.00	65.00	40.00
(4)	Bill Brenner	110.00	55.00	35.00
(5)	Jack Burkowatz	110.00	55.00	35.00
(6)	Van Fletcher	110.00	55.00	35.00
(7)	Joe Ginsberg	110.00	55.00	35.00
(8)	Jehosie Heard	110.00	55.00	35.00
(9)	Fred Hutchinson	110.00	55.00	35.00
(10)	Larry Jansen	110.00	55.00	35.00
(11)	Bob Kelly	110.00	55.00	35.00
(12)	Bill Kennedy	110.00	55.00	35.00
(13)	Lou Kretlow	110.00	55.00	35.00
(14)	Rocco Krsnich	110.00	55.00	35.00
(15)	Carmen Mauro	110.00	55.00	35.00
(16)	John Oldham	110.00	55.00	35.00
(17)	George Schmees	110.00	55.00	35.00
(18)	Elmer Singleton	110.00	55.00	35.00
(19)	Alan Strange	110.00	55.00	35.00
(20)	Gene Verble	110.00	55.00	35.00
(21)	Marv Williams	110.00	55.00	35.00
(22)	Harvey Zernia	110.00	55.00	35.00

1956 Seattle Rainiers Popcorn

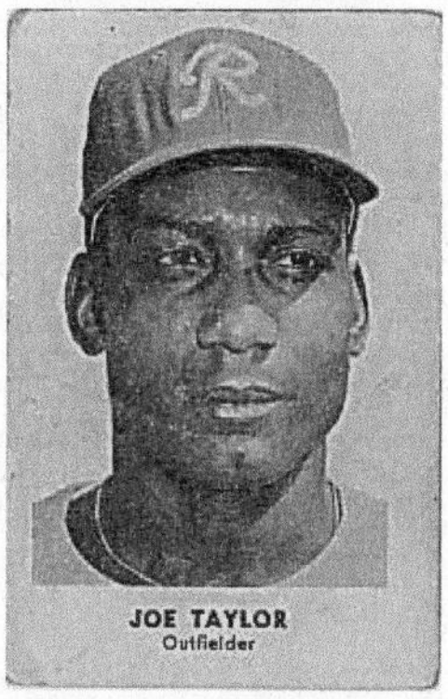

(Blank-back or Gil's Drive-Ins (two locations) ad on back. Players wearing light cap with white "R.")

		NM	EX	VG
Complete Set (27):		2,500	1,250	750.00
Common Player:		110.00	55.00	35.00
(1)	Fred Baczewski	110.00	55.00	35.00
(2)	Bob Balcena	110.00	55.00	35.00
(3)	Bill Brenner	110.00	55.00	35.00
(4)	Sherry Dixon	110.00	55.00	35.00
(5)	Don Fracchia	110.00	55.00	35.00
(6)	Bill Glynn	110.00	55.00	35.00
(7)	Larry Jansen	110.00	55.00	35.00
(8)	Howie Judson	110.00	55.00	35.00
(9)	Bill Kennedy	110.00	55.00	35.00
(10)	Jack Lohrke	110.00	55.00	35.00
(11)	Vic Lombardi	110.00	55.00	35.00
(12)	Carmen Mauro	110.00	55.00	35.00
(13)	Ray Orteig	110.00	55.00	35.00
(14)	Bud Podbielan	110.00	55.00	35.00
(15)	Leo Righetti	110.00	55.00	35.00
(16)	Jim Robertson	110.00	55.00	35.00
(17)	Art Shallock (Schallock)	110.00	55.00	35.00
(18)	Art Schult	110.00	55.00	35.00
(19)	Luke Sewell	135.00	65.00	40.00
(20)	Elmer Singleton	110.00	55.00	35.00
(21a)	Milt Smith (Action)	110.00	55.00	35.00
(21b)	Milt Smith (Portrait)	110.00	55.00	35.00
(22)	Vern Stephens	110.00	55.00	35.00
(23)	Alan Strange	110.00	55.00	35.00
(24)	Joe Taylor	110.00	55.00	35.00
(25)	Artie Wilson	175.00	85.00	50.00
(26)	Harvey Zernia	110.00	55.00	35.00

1957 Seattle Rainiers Popcorn

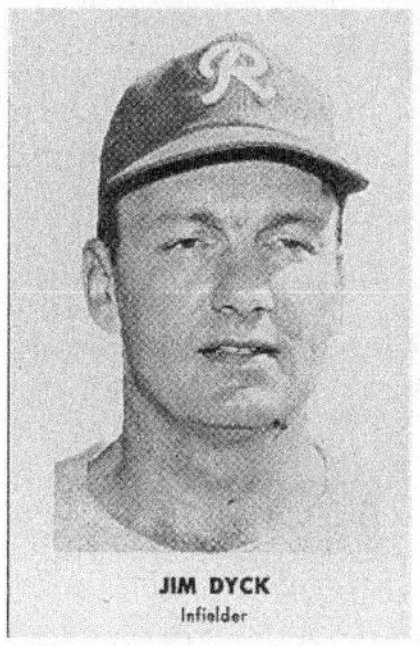

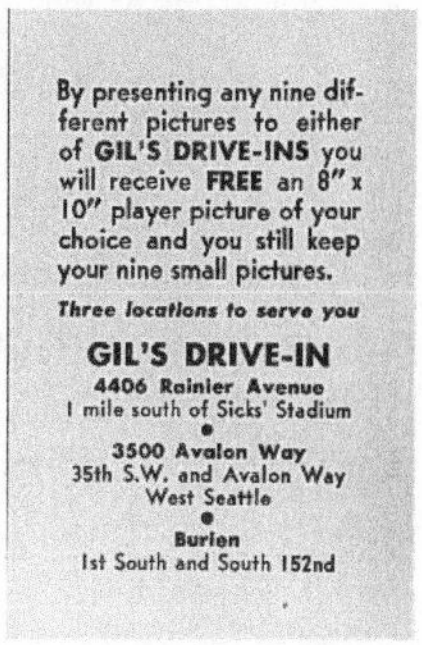
By presenting any nine different pictures to either of GIL'S DRIVE-INS you will receive FREE an 8" x 10" player picture of your choice and you still keep your nine small pictures.

Three locations to serve you

GIL'S DRIVE-IN

4406 Rainier Avenue
1 mile south of Sicks' Stadium

3500 Avalon Way
35th S.W. and Avalon Way
West Seattle

Burien
1st South and South 152nd

(Blank-back or Gil's Drive-Ins (three locations) ad on back. Players wearing lighter caps with white "R." No base on letter "T" on outfielders or pitchers cards.)

		NM	EX	VG
Complete Set (24):		2,000	1,000	600.00
Common Player:		100.00	50.00	30.00
(1)	Dick Aylward	100.00	50.00	30.00
(2)	Bob Balcena	100.00	50.00	30.00
(3)	Eddie Basinki	100.00	50.00	30.00
(4)	Hal Bevan	100.00	50.00	30.00
(5)	Joe Black	125.00	65.00	35.00
(6)	Juan Delis	100.00	50.00	30.00
(7)	Jim Dyck	100.00	50.00	30.00
(8)	Marion Fricano	100.00	50.00	30.00
(9)	Bill Glynn	100.00	50.00	30.00
(10)	Larry Jansen	100.00	50.00	30.00
(11)	Howie Judson	100.00	50.00	30.00
(12)	Bill Kennedy	100.00	50.00	30.00
(13)	Jack Lohrke	100.00	50.00	30.00
(14)	Carmen Mauro	100.00	50.00	30.00
(15)	George Munger	100.00	50.00	30.00
(16)	Lefty O'Doul	150.00	75.00	45.00
(17)	Ray Orteig	100.00	50.00	30.00
(18)	Duane Pillette	100.00	50.00	30.00
(19)	Bud Podbielan	100.00	50.00	30.00
(20)	Charley Rabe	100.00	50.00	30.00
(21)	Leo Righetti	100.00	50.00	30.00
(22)	Joe Taylor	100.00	50.00	30.00
(23)	Edo Vanni	100.00	50.00	30.00
(24)	Morrie Wills (Maury)	250.00	125.00	75.00

1958 Seattle Rainiers Popcorn

(All cards have Ralph's Thriftway Market ad on back.)

		NM	EX	VG
Complete Set (19):		1,250	625.00	375.00
Common Player:		75.00	35.00	20.00
(1)	Bob Balcena	75.00	35.00	20.00
(2)	Ed Basinki	75.00	35.00	20.00
(3)	Hal Bevan	75.00	35.00	20.00
(4)	Jack Bloomfield	75.00	35.00	20.00
(5)	Juan Delis	75.00	35.00	20.00
(6)	Dutch Dotterer	75.00	35.00	20.00
(7)	Jim Dyck	75.00	35.00	20.00
(8)	Al Federoff	90.00	45.00	27.50
(9)	Art Fowler	75.00	35.00	20.00
(10)	Bill Kennedy	75.00	35.00	20.00
(11)	Marty Kutyna	75.00	35.00	20.00
(12)	Ray Orteig	75.00	35.00	20.00
(13)	Duane Pillette	75.00	35.00	20.00
(14)	Vada Pinson	225.00	110.00	70.00
(15)	Connie Ryan	75.00	35.00	20.00
(16)	Phil Shartzer	75.00	35.00	20.00
(17)	Max Surkont	75.00	35.00	20.00
(18)	Gale Wade	75.00	35.00	20.00
(19)	Ted Wieand	75.00	35.00	20.00

1959 Seattle Rainiers Popcorn

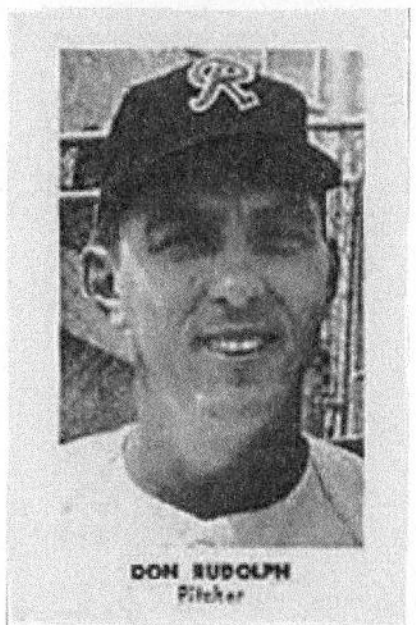

(Blank-back. First printing cards have players in lighter cap with white "R." Second printing cards have darker caps with shadow around "R.")

		NM	EX	VG
Complete Set (37):		2,500	1,250	750.00
Common Player:		75.00	35.00	20.00
(1)	Bobby Adams	75.00	35.00	20.00
(2)	Frank Amaya	75.00	35.00	20.00
(3)	Hal Bevan	75.00	35.00	20.00
(4)	Jack Bloomfield	75.00	35.00	20.00
(5)	Clarence Churn	75.00	35.00	20.00
(6)	Jack Dittmer	75.00	35.00	20.00

(7)	Jim Dyck	75.00	35.00	20.00
(8)	Dee Fondy	75.00	35.00	20.00
(9)	Mark Freeman	75.00	35.00	20.00
(10)	Dick Hanlon	75.00	35.00	20.00
(11)	Carroll Hardy	75.00	35.00	20.00
(12)	Bobby Henrich	75.00	35.00	20.00
(13)	Jay Hook	75.00	35.00	20.00
(14)	Fred Hutchinson	75.00	35.00	20.00
(15)	Jake Jenkins	75.00	35.00	20.00
(16)	Eddie Kazak	75.00	35.00	20.00
(17)	Bill Kennedy	75.00	35.00	20.00
(18)	Harry Lowrey	75.00	35.00	20.00
(19a)	Harry Malmbeg (Malmberg)	75.00	35.00	20.00
(19b)	Harry Malmberg	75.00	35.00	20.00
(20)	Bob Mape (Mabe)	75.00	35.00	20.00
(21)	Darrell Martin	75.00	35.00	20.00
(22)	John McCall	75.00	35.00	20.00
(23)	Claude Osteen	75.00	35.00	20.00
(24)	Paul Pettit	75.00	35.00	20.00
(25)	Charley Rabe	75.00	35.00	20.00
(26)	Rudy Regalado	75.00	35.00	20.00
(27)	Eric Rodin	75.00	35.00	20.00
(28)	Don Rudolph	75.00	35.00	20.00
(29)	Lou Skizas	75.00	35.00	20.00
(30)	Dave Stenhouse	75.00	35.00	20.00
(31)	Alan Strange	75.00	35.00	20.00
(32)	Max Surkont	75.00	35.00	20.00
(33)	Ted Tappe	75.00	35.00	20.00
(34)	Elmer Valo	75.00	35.00	20.00
(35)	Gale Wade	75.00	35.00	20.00
(36)	Bill Wight	75.00	35.00	20.00
(37)	Ed Winceniak	75.00	35.00	20.00

1960 Seattle Rainiers Popcorn

JOHNNY O'BRIEN
Infielder

(Blank-back. All players posed against outfield fence wearing dark caps with shadowed "R.")

		NM	EX	VG
Complete Set (18):		1,200	600.00	350.00
Common Player:		75.00	35.00	20.00
(1)	Charlie Beamon	75.00	35.00	20.00
(2)	Hal Bevan	75.00	35.00	20.00
(3)	Whammy Douglas	75.00	35.00	20.00
(4)	Buddy Gilbert	75.00	35.00	20.00
(5)	Hal Jeffcoat	75.00	35.00	20.00
(6)	Leigh Lawrence	75.00	35.00	20.00
(7)	Darrell Martin	75.00	35.00	20.00
(8)	Francisco Obregon	75.00	35.00	20.00
(9)	Johnny O'Brien	90.00	45.00	27.50
(10)	Paul Pettitt	75.00	35.00	20.00
(11)	Ray Rippelmeyer (Ripplemeyer)	75.00	35.00	20.00
(12)	Don Rudolph	75.00	35.00	20.00
(13)	Willard Schmidt	75.00	35.00	20.00
(14)	Dick Sisler	75.00	35.00	20.00
(15)	Lou Skizas	75.00	35.00	20.00
(16)	Joe Taylor	75.00	35.00	20.00
(17)	Bob Thurman	75.00	35.00	20.00
(18)	Gerald Zimmerman	75.00	35.00	20.00

1961 Seattle Rainiers Popcorn

JOHN TILLMAN
Infielder

(Blank-back. New uniforms: dark cap with stylized "S," "Rainiers" on chest. Many players have both portrait and action poses. Tough to distinguish from 1962 set; names on '61s are more compact, bold than on '62 which has taller, lighter names.)

		NM	EX	VG
Complete Set (29):		2,000	1,000	600.00
Common Player:		75.00	35.00	20.00
(1)	Galen Cisco	75.00	35.00	20.00
(2)	Marlan Coughtry/Btg	75.00	35.00	20.00

(3)	Marlin Coughtry/Portrait	75.00	35.00	20.00
(4)	Pete Cronin	75.00	35.00	20.00
(5)	Arnold Earley	75.00	35.00	20.00
(6)	Bob Heffner/Pitching	75.00	35.00	20.00
(7)	Bob Heffner/Portrait	75.00	35.00	20.00
(8)	Curt Jensen/Action	75.00	35.00	20.00
(9)	Curt Jensen/Portrait	75.00	35.00	20.00
(10)	Harry Malmberg/Coach	75.00	35.00	20.00
(11)	Harry Malmberg (Player-coach.)	75.00	35.00	20.00
(12)	Dave Mann	75.00	35.00	20.00
(13)	Darrell Martin	75.00	35.00	20.00
(14)	Erv Palica/Pitching	75.00	35.00	20.00
(15)	Ervin Palica/Portrait	75.00	35.00	20.00
(16)	Johnny Pesky/Action	90.00	45.00	27.50
(17)	Johnny Pesky/Portrait	90.00	45.00	27.50
(18)	Dick Radatz	100.00	50.00	30.00
(19)	Ted Schreiber/Btg	75.00	35.00	20.00
(20)	Ted Shreiber/Portrait	75.00	35.00	20.00
(21)	Paul Smith/Action	75.00	35.00	20.00
(22)	Paul Smith/Portrait	75.00	35.00	20.00
(23)	John Tillman/Infielder	75.00	35.00	20.00
(24)	Bob Tillman/Catcher	75.00	35.00	20.00
(25)	Bo Toft	75.00	35.00	20.00
(26)	Tom Umphlett/Action	75.00	35.00	20.00
(27)	Tom Umphlett/Portrait	75.00	35.00	20.00
(28)	Earl Wilson	75.00	35.00	20.00
(29)	Ken Wolfe	75.00	35.00	20.00

1962 Seattle Rainiers Popcorn

BILLY HARRELL

(Blank-back. Nearly identical to '61s except for player name. On 1961 cards, name is compact and bold; on '62s the name is taller, lighter. Some photos repeated from 1961.)

		NM	EX	VG
Complete Set (19):		1,250	625.00	375.00
Common Player:		75.00	35.00	20.00
(1)	Dave Hall	75.00	35.00	20.00
(2)	Billy Harrell	75.00	35.00	20.00
(3)	Curt Jensen (Jenson)	75.00	35.00	20.00
(4)	Stew MacDonald	75.00	35.00	20.00
(5)	Bill MacLeod	75.00	35.00	20.00
(6)	Dave Mann (Action)	75.00	35.00	20.00
(7)	Dave Mann (Portrait)	75.00	35.00	20.00
(8)	Dave Morehead	75.00	35.00	20.00
(9)	John Pesky	90.00	45.00	27.50
(10)	Ted Schreiber (Second baseman.)	75.00	35.00	20.00
(11)	Ted Schreiber (Infielder)	75.00	35.00	20.00
(12)	Elmer Singleton	75.00	35.00	20.00
(13)	Archie Skeen	75.00	35.00	20.00
(14)	Pete Smith	75.00	35.00	20.00
(15)	George Spencer	75.00	35.00	20.00
(16)	Bo Toft (1961 photo)	75.00	35.00	20.00
(17)	Bo Toft (New photo.)	75.00	35.00	20.00
(18)	Tom Umphlett	75.00	35.00	20.00
(19)	Ken Wolfe	75.00	35.00	20.00

1963 Seattle Rainiers Popcorn

(Blank-back. No positions stated on cards except for manager and coach. Impossible to differentiate 1963 issue from 1964 except by player selection.)

		NM	EX	VG
Complete Set (15):		800.00	400.00	240.00
Common Player:		60.00	30.00	17.50
(1)	Don Gile	60.00	30.00	17.50
(2)	Dave Hall	60.00	30.00	17.50
(3)	Billy Harrell	60.00	30.00	17.50
(4)	Pete Jernigan	60.00	30.00	17.50
(5)	Stan Johnson	60.00	30.00	17.50
(6)	Dalton Jones	60.00	30.00	17.50
(7)	Mel Parnell	60.00	30.00	17.50
(8)	Joe Pedrazzini	60.00	30.00	17.50
(9)	Elmer Singleton	60.00	30.00	17.50
(10)	Archie Skeen	60.00	30.00	17.50
(11)	Rac Slider	60.00	30.00	17.50
(12)	Pete Smith	60.00	30.00	17.50
(13)	Bill Spanswick	60.00	30.00	17.50
(14)	George Spencer	60.00	30.00	17.50
(15)	Wilbur Wood	90.00	45.00	27.50

1964 Seattle Rainiers Popcorn

EARL AVERILL

(Blank-back. Impossible to differentiate between 1963 and 1964 issues except by player selection.)

		NM	EX	VG
Complete Set (18):		1,000	500.00	300.00
Common Player:		60.00	30.00	17.50
(1)	Earl Averill	60.00	30.00	17.50
(2)	Billy Gardner	60.00	30.00	17.50
(3)	Russ Gibson	60.00	30.00	17.50
(4)	Guido Grilli	60.00	30.00	17.50
(5)	Bob Guindon	60.00	30.00	17.50
(6)	Billy Harrell	60.00	30.00	17.50
(7)	Fred Holmes	60.00	30.00	17.50
(8)	Stan Johnson	60.00	30.00	17.50
(9)	Hal Kolstad	60.00	30.00	17.50
(10)	Felix Maldonado	60.00	30.00	17.50
(11)	Gary Modrell	60.00	30.00	17.50
(12)	Merlin Nippert	60.00	30.00	17.50
(13)	Rico Petrocelli	100.00	50.00	30.00
(14)	Jay Ritchie	60.00	30.00	17.50
(15)	Barry Shetrone	60.00	30.00	17.50
(16)	Pete Smith	60.00	30.00	17.50
(17)	Bill Tuttle	60.00	30.00	17.50
(18)	Edo Vanni	60.00	30.00	17.50

1965 Seattle Angels Popcorn

(Back has cartoon angel batting. Several cards, issued prior to the season, have blank-backs.)

		NM	EX	VG
Complete Set (22):		600.00	300.00	180.00
Common Player:		30.00	15.00	9.00
(1)	Earl Averill	30.00	15.00	9.00
(2)	Tom Burgmeier	30.00	15.00	9.00
(3)	Bob Guindon	30.00	15.00	9.00
(4)	Jack Hernandez	30.00	15.00	9.00
(5)	Fred Holmes	30.00	15.00	9.00
(6)	Ed Kirkpatrick	30.00	15.00	9.00
(7)	Hal Kolstad	30.00	15.00	9.00
(8)	Joe Koppe	30.00	15.00	9.00
(9)	Les Kuhnz	30.00	15.00	9.00
(10)	Bob Lemon	60.00	30.00	17.50
(11)	Bobby Locke	30.00	15.00	9.00
(12)	Jim McGlothlin	30.00	15.00	9.00
(13a)	Bob Radovich (Blank-back.)	30.00	15.00	9.00
(13b)	Bob Radovich (Ad-back.)	30.00	15.00	9.00
(14)	Merritt Ranew	30.00	15.00	9.00
(15)	Jimmie Reese (Blank-back.)	45.00	22.50	13.50
(16a)	Rick Reichardt (Blank-back.)	30.00	15.00	9.00
(16b)	Rick Reichardt (Ad-back.)	30.00	15.00	9.00
(17)	Tom Satriano	30.00	15.00	9.00
(18)	Dick Simpson	30.00	15.00	9.00
(19)	Jack Spring (Blank-back.)	30.00	15.00	9.00
(20)	Ed Sukla	30.00	15.00	9.00
(21)	Jackie Warner	30.00	15.00	9.00
(22)	Stan Williams	30.00	15.00	9.00

1966 Seattle Angels Popcorn

JIM CAMPANIS

SEATTLE ANGELS
GAMES BROADCAST ON
KVI RADIO 570
Presented by
CHEVRON DEALERS
STANDARD STATIONS
WESTERN AIRLINES
HOUSEHOLD FINANCE CORP.
WHEATIES, BREAKFAST OF CHAMPIONS

(Cartoon angel pitching on back, first "Presented by" advertiser at bottom is Chevron Dealers.)

		NM	EX	VG
Complete Set (29):		900.00	450.00	275.00
Common Player:		30.00	15.00	9.00
(1)	Del Bates	30.00	15.00	9.00
(2)	Tom Burgmeier	30.00	15.00	9.00
(3)	Jim Campanis	40.00	20.00	12.00
(4)	Jim Coates	30.00	15.00	9.00
(5)	Tony Cortopassi	30.00	15.00	9.00
(6)	Chuck Estrada	30.00	15.00	9.00
(7)	Ray Hernandez	30.00	15.00	9.00
(8)	Jay Johnstone	50.00	25.00	15.00

		NM	EX	VG
(9)	Bill Kelso	30.00	15.00	9.00
(10)	Vic LaRose	30.00	15.00	9.00
(11)	Bobby Locke	30.00	15.00	9.00
(12)	Rudy May	30.00	15.00	9.00
(13)	Andy Messersmith	50.00	25.00	15.00
(14)	Bubba Morton	30.00	15.00	9.00
(15)	Cotton Nash	30.00	15.00	9.00
(16)	John Olerud	50.00	25.00	15.00
(17)	Marty Pattin	30.00	15.00	9.00
(18)	Merritt Ranew	30.00	15.00	9.00
(19)	Minnie Rojas	30.00	15.00	9.00
(20)	George Rubio	30.00	15.00	9.00
(21)	Al Spangler	30.00	15.00	9.00
(22)	Ed Sukla	30.00	15.00	9.00
(23)	Felix Torres	30.00	15.00	9.00
(24)	Hector Torres	30.00	15.00	9.00
(25)	Ken Turner	30.00	15.00	9.00
(26)	Chuck Vinson	30.00	15.00	9.00
(27)	Don Wallace	30.00	15.00	9.00
(28)	Jack D. Warner	30.00	15.00	9.00
(29)	Mike White	30.00	15.00	9.00

1967 Seattle Angels Popcorn

(Cartoon angel pitching on back, first "Presented by" advertiser is Western Airlines.)

		NM	EX	VG
Complete Set (19):		500.00	250.00	150.00
Common Player:		30.00	15.00	9.00
(1)	George Banks	30.00	15.00	9.00
(2)	Tom Burgmeier	30.00	15.00	9.00
(3)	Jim Coates	30.00	15.00	9.00
(4)	Chuck Cottier	30.00	15.00	9.00
(5)	Tony Curry	30.00	15.00	9.00
(6)	Vern Geishert	30.00	15.00	9.00
(7)	Jesse Hickman	30.00	15.00	9.00
(8)	Bill Kelso	30.00	15.00	9.00
(9)	Ed Kirkpatrick	30.00	15.00	9.00
(10)	Chris Krug	30.00	15.00	9.00
(11)	Bobby Locke	30.00	15.00	9.00
(12)	Bill Murphy	30.00	15.00	9.00
(13)	Marty Pattin	30.00	15.00	9.00
(14)	Merritt Ranew	30.00	15.00	9.00
(15)	Bob Sadowski	30.00	15.00	9.00
(16)	Ed Sukla	30.00	15.00	9.00
(17)	Hector Torres	30.00	15.00	9.00
(18)	Chuck Vinson	30.00	15.00	9.00
(19)	Don Wallace	30.00	15.00	9.00

1968 Seattle Angels Popcorn

JARVIS TATUM

(Blank-back.)

		NM	EX	VG
Complete Set (18):		500.00	250.00	150.00
Common Player:		30.00	15.00	9.00
(1)	Ethan Blackaby	30.00	15.00	9.00
(2)	Jim Coates	30.00	15.00	9.00
(3)	Tom Egan	30.00	15.00	9.00
(4)	Larry Elliott (Elliot)	30.00	15.00	9.00
(5)	Jim Engelhardt	30.00	15.00	9.00
(6)	Gus Gil	30.00	15.00	9.00
(7)	Bill Harrelson	30.00	15.00	9.00
(8)	Steve Hovley	30.00	15.00	9.00
(9)	Jim Mahoney	30.00	15.00	9.00
(10)	Mickey McGuire	30.00	15.00	9.00
(11)	Joe Overton	30.00	15.00	9.00
(12)	Marty Pattin	30.00	15.00	9.00
(13)	Larry Sherry	30.00	15.00	9.00
(14)	Marv Staehle	30.00	15.00	9.00
(15)	Ed Sukla	30.00	15.00	9.00
(16)	Jarvis Tatum	30.00	15.00	9.00
(17)	Hawk Taylor	30.00	15.00	9.00
(18)	Chuck Vinson	30.00	15.00	9.00

1952 Shawnee Hawks Team Issue

LOYD McPHERSON

Formatted like the other known minor league issues from Globe Printing of San Jose, Calif., this set chronicles the 1952 version of the Class D (Sooner State League) Shawnee (Okla.) Hawks. The blank-backed cards are black-and-white and measure about 2-1/4" x 3-3/8". The checklist here is incomplete, the set probably having been originally issued with about 18 cards.

		NM	EX	VG
Common Player:		60.00	30.00	18.00
(1)	Russell Bland (Blanco)	60.00	30.00	18.00
(2)	Perry Haddock	60.00	30.00	18.00
(3)	Jim Kenaga	60.00	30.00	18.00
(4)	Hal Long	60.00	30.00	18.00
(5)	Loyd McPherson	60.00	30.00	18.00
(6)	Rolando Olmo	60.00	30.00	18.00
(7)	Dave Rolette	60.00	30.00	18.00
(8)	Hank Salazar	60.00	30.00	18.00

1960 Shopsy's Frankfurters Toronto Maple Leafs

SHOPSY'S PLAYER PHOTO

BILL SMITH - Trainer 1960

Only the Toronto Maple Leafs of the International League - including many former and future major leaguers - are included in this set. The cards are about 2-1/4" x 3-1/4", blank-back and printed in black-and-white. The unnumbered cards are checklisted here alphabetically.

		NM	EX	VG
Complete Set (23):		2,000	1,000	600.00
Common Player:		90.00	45.00	30.00
Album:		100.00	50.00	30.00
(1)	George Anderson (Sparky)	150.00	75.00	45.00
(2)	Bob Chakales	90.00	45.00	30.00
(3)	Al Cicotte	90.00	45.00	30.00
(4)	Rip Coleman	90.00	45.00	30.00
(5)	Steve Demeter	90.00	45.00	30.00
(6)	Don Dillard	90.00	45.00	30.00
(7)	Frank Funk	90.00	45.00	30.00
(8)	Russ Heman	90.00	45.00	30.00
(9)	Earl Hersh	90.00	45.00	30.00
(10)	Allen Jones	90.00	45.00	30.00
(11)	Jim King	90.00	45.00	30.00
(12)	Jack Kubiszyn	90.00	45.00	30.00
(13)	Mel McGaha	90.00	45.00	30.00
(14)	Bill Moran	90.00	45.00	30.00
(15)	Ron Negray	90.00	45.00	30.00
(16)	Herb Plews	90.00	45.00	30.00
(17)	Steve Ridzik	90.00	45.00	30.00
(18)	Pat Scantlebury	90.00	45.00	30.00
(19)	Bill Smith (Trainer)	90.00	45.00	30.00
(20)	Bob Smith	90.00	45.00	30.00
(21)	Tim Thompson	90.00	45.00	30.00
(22)	Jack Waters	90.00	45.00	30.00
(23)	Archie Wilson	90.00	45.00	30.00

1947 Signal Gasoline Pacific Coast League

Lou NOVIKOFF — SLUGGING SEATTLE STAR

Lourie Novikoff . . .
Seattle Outfielder
Nickname, "Nova"
Throws right, bats right
Height—5' 10"
Weight—180 lbs.

FOLLOW THE RAINIERS WITH
Leo Lassen
Signal's ACE SPORTSCASTER
KRSC DIAL 1150

FOR BETTER CAR PERFORMANCE
REMEMBER . . .
It takes Extra Quality to Go Farther

. . . and SIGNAL is the Famous "GO FARTHER" Gasoline

Five of the eight PCL teams participated in this baseball card promotion, giving away cards of hometeam players. Because of vagaries of local distribution, some teams, notably Sacramento and Seattle, are scarcer than others, and there are specific player rarities among other teams. The black-and-white cards are 5-9/16" x 3-1/2" and feature on the front a drawing of the player and several personal or career highlights in cartoon form. The artwork was done by former N.Y. Giants pitcher Al Demaree. On the backs are player biographical details, an ad for Signal Gas and an ad for the co-sponsoring radio station in each locale. Cards are unnumbered.

	NM	EX	VG
Complete Set (89):	7,000	3,500	2,100

(Team sets listed below.)

1947 Signal Gasoline Hollywood Stars

		NM	EX	VG
Complete Set (20):		1,200	600.00	350.00
Common Player:		50.00	25.00	15.00
(1)	Ed Albosta	50.00	25.00	15.00
(2)	Carl Cox	50.00	25.00	15.00
(3)	Frank Dasso	50.00	25.00	15.00
(4)	Tod Davis	50.00	25.00	15.00
(5)	Jim Delsing	50.00	25.00	15.00
(6)	Jimmy Dykes	50.00	25.00	15.00
(7)	Paul Gregory	50.00	25.00	15.00
(8)	Fred Haney	50.00	25.00	15.00
(9)	Frank Kelleher	50.00	25.00	15.00
(10)	Joe Krakauskas	50.00	25.00	15.00
(11)	Al Libke	50.00	25.00	15.00
(12)	Tony Lupien	50.00	25.00	15.00
(13)	Xaiver Rescigno	50.00	25.00	15.00
(14)	Jack Sherman	50.00	25.00	15.00
(15)	Andy Skurski	50.00	25.00	15.00
(16)	Glen (Glenn) Stewart	50.00	25.00	15.00
(17)	Al Unser	50.00	25.00	15.00
(18)	Fred Vaughn	50.00	25.00	15.00
(19)	Woody Williams	250.00	125.00	75.00
(20)	Dutch (Gus) Zernial	75.00	37.00	22.00

1947 Signal Gasoline Los Angeles Angels

		NM	EX	VG
Complete Set (18):		700.00	350.00	210.00
Common Player:		40.00	20.00	12.00
(1)	Red Adams	40.00	20.00	12.00
(2)	Larry Barton	40.00	20.00	12.00
(3)	Cliff Chambers	40.00	20.00	12.00
(4)	Lloyd Christopher	40.00	20.00	12.00
(5)	Cece Garriott	40.00	20.00	12.00
(6)	Al Glossop	40.00	20.00	12.00
(7)	Bill Kelly	40.00	20.00	12.00
(8)	Red Lynn	40.00	20.00	12.00
(9)	Eddie Malone	40.00	20.00	12.00
(10)	Dutch McCall	40.00	20.00	12.00
(11)	Don Osborne	40.00	20.00	12.00
(12)	John Ostrowski	40.00	20.00	12.00
(13)	Reggie Otero	40.00	20.00	12.00
(14)	Ray Prim	40.00	20.00	12.00
(15)	Ed Sauer	40.00	20.00	12.00
(16)	Bill Schuster	40.00	20.00	12.00
(17)	Tuck Stainback	40.00	20.00	12.00
(18)	Lou Stringer	40.00	20.00	12.00

1947 Signal Gasoline Oakland Oaks

		NM	EX	VG
Complete Set (19):		800.00	400.00	240.00
Common Player:		40.00	20.00	12.00
(1)	Vic Buccola	40.00	20.00	12.00
(2)	Mickey Burnett	40.00	20.00	12.00
(3)	Ralph Buxton	40.00	20.00	12.00
(4)	Vince DiMaggio	95.00	47.00	28.00
(5)	Dizz Duezabou	40.00	20.00	12.00
(6)	Bud Foster	40.00	20.00	12.00
(7)	Sherriff Gassaway	40.00	20.00	12.00
(8)	Tom Hafey	40.00	20.00	12.00
(9)	Brooks Holder	40.00	20.00	12.00
(10)	Gene Lillard	40.00	20.00	12.00
(11)	Dario Lodigiani	40.00	20.00	12.00
(12)	Hershel Martin	40.00	20.00	12.00
(13)	Cotton Pippen	40.00	20.00	12.00
(14)	Billy Raimondi	40.00	20.00	12.00
(15)	Tony Sabol	40.00	20.00	12.00
(16)	Les Scarsella	40.00	20.00	12.00
(17)	Floyd Speer	40.00	20.00	12.00
(18)	Casey Stengel	100.00	50.00	30.00
(19)	Maurice Van Robays	40.00	20.00	12.00

1947 Signal Gasoline Sacramento Solons

		NM	EX	VG
Complete Set (16):		2,000	1,000	600.00
Common Player:		60.00	30.00	18.00
(1)	Bud Beasley	60.00	30.00	18.00
(2)	Frank Dasso	60.00	30.00	18.00
(3)	Ed Fitzgerald (Fitz Gerald)	60.00	30.00	18.00
(4)	Guy Fletcher	60.00	30.00	18.00
(5)	Tony Freitas	60.00	30.00	18.00
(6)	Red Mann	60.00	30.00	18.00
(7)	Joe Marty	60.00	30.00	18.00
(8)	Steve Mesner	60.00	30.00	18.00
(9)	Bill Ramsey	60.00	30.00	18.00
(10)	Charley Ripple	250.00	125.00	75.00
(11)	John Rizzo	250.00	125.00	75.00
(12)	Al Smith	250.00	125.00	75.00
(13)	Ronnie Smith	250.00	125.00	75.00
(14)	Tommy Thompson	250.00	125.00	75.00
(15)	Jim Warner	115.00	55.00	35.00
(16)	Ed Zipay	115.00	55.00	35.00

1947 Signal Gasoline Seattle Rainiers

	NM	EX	VG
Complete Set (16):	1,750	875.00	525.00
Common Player:	75.00	37.00	22.00
(1) Kewpie Barrett	100.00	50.00	30.00
(2) Herman Besse	100.00	50.00	30.00
(3) Guy Fletcher	100.00	50.00	30.00
(4) Jack Jakucki	100.00	50.00	30.00
(5) Bob Johnson	100.00	50.00	30.00
(6) Pete Jonas	275.00	135.00	82.00
(7) Hillis Layne	100.00	50.00	30.00
(8) Red Mann	100.00	50.00	30.00
(9) Lou Novikoff	100.00	50.00	30.00
(10) John O'Neill	100.00	50.00	30.00
(11) Bill Ramsey	100.00	50.00	30.00
(12) Mickey Rocco	100.00	50.00	30.00
(13) George Scharein	100.00	50.00	30.00
(14) Hal Sueme	100.00	50.00	30.00
(15) Jo Jo White	100.00	50.00	30.00
(16) Tony York	100.00	50.00	30.00

1948 Signal Gasoline Oakland Oaks

Issued by Signal Oil in the Oakland area in 1948, this 24-card set features members of the Oakland Oaks of the Pacific Coast League. The unnumbered cards, measuring 2-3/8" x 3-1/2", were given away at gas stations. The front consists of a color photo, while the backs (printed in either blue or black) contain a brief player write-up along with a Signal Oil ad and logo.

	NM	EX	VG
Complete Set (24):	900.00	450.00	275.00
Common Player:	40.00	20.00	12.00
(1) John C. Babich	40.00	20.00	12.00
(2) Ralph Buxton	40.00	20.00	12.00
(3) Loyd E. Christopher (Lloyd)	40.00	20.00	12.00
(4) Merrill Russell Combs	40.00	20.00	12.00
(5) Melvin E. Deuzabou	40.00	20.00	12.00
(6) Nicholas ("Nick") Etten	40.00	20.00	12.00
(7) Bud Foster (Announcer)	40.00	20.00	12.00
(8) Charles Gassaway	40.00	20.00	12.00
(9) Will Hafey	40.00	20.00	12.00
(10) Ray Hamrick	40.00	20.00	12.00
(11) Brooks Richard Holder	40.00	20.00	12.00
(12) Earl Jones	40.00	20.00	12.00
(13) Harry "Cookie" Lavagetto	40.00	20.00	12.00
(14) Robert E. Lillard	40.00	20.00	12.00
(15) Dario Lodigiani	40.00	20.00	12.00
(16) Ernie Lombardi	75.00	37.50	22.50
(17a) Alfred Manuel Martin (Born 1921.)	65.00	32.50	20.00
(17b) Alfred Manuel Martin (Born 1928.)	75.00	37.50	22.50
(18) George Michael Metkovich	40.00	20.00	12.00
(19) William L. Raimondi	40.00	20.00	12.00
(20) Les George Scarsella	40.00	20.00	12.00
(21) Floyd Vernie Speer	40.00	20.00	12.00
(22) Charles "Casey" Stengel	115.00	57.00	34.00
(23) Maurice Van Robays	40.00	20.00	12.00
(24) Aldon Jay Wilkie	40.00	20.00	12.00

1951 Sioux City Soos Postcards

These black-and-white team-issued postcards feature on their fronts posed full-length photos of members of the Class A Western League farm team of the New York Giants. In standard 3-1/2" x 5-1/2" size, the cards have a wide border at bottom which has the team name, the year and a logo featuring an ear of corn. Backs have typical postcard indicia. Players are not identified anywhere on the cards. It is presumed this checklist is incomplete.

	NM	EX	VG
Common Player:	60.00	30.00	18.00
(1) Ray Berns	60.00	30.00	18.00
(2) Ed Bressoud	60.00	30.00	18.00
(3) Mario Picone	60.00	30.00	18.00
(4) Bob Reid	60.00	30.00	18.00

1952-1953 Sioux City Soos Team Issue

From the Class A Western League, this is one of many minor league team sets issued in the early 1950s by Globe Printing of San Jose, Calif. The early 1950s Soos were a farm team of the New York Giants. Cards are about 2-1/4" x 3-3/8", printed in black-and-white with blank backs. It appears as if the Soos were the only team to have issued cards in both 1952 and 1953, since some cards are known with players unique to each season as well as cards of players who were with Sioux City in both 1952 and 1953.

	NM	EX	VG
Complete Set (29):	1,500	750.00	450.00
Common Player:	60.00	30.00	18.00
Album:	100.00	50.00	30.00
1952			
(1) Ray Berns	60.00	30.00	18.00
(2) Eddie Bressoud	60.00	30.00	18.00
(3) Irv Burton	60.00	30.00	18.00
(4) Bob Easterbrook	60.00	30.00	18.00
(5) George Erath	60.00	30.00	18.00
(6) Don Fracchia	60.00	30.00	18.00
(7) Dick Hamlin	60.00	30.00	18.00
(8) Gail Harris	60.00	30.00	18.00
(9) Chico Ibanez	60.00	30.00	18.00
(10) Bob Lee	60.00	30.00	18.00
(11) Bill McMillan	60.00	30.00	18.00
(12) Dick Messner	60.00	30.00	18.00
(13) Roy Pardue	60.00	30.00	18.00
(14) Mario Picone	60.00	30.00	18.00
(15) Jim Singleton	60.00	30.00	18.00
(16) John Uber	60.00	30.00	18.00
(17) Ernie Yelen	60.00	30.00	18.00
1952/1953			
(18) Bob Giddings	60.00	30.00	18.00
(19) Ray Johnson	60.00	30.00	18.00
(20) Denny Landry (Bat boy.)	60.00	30.00	18.00
(21) Vince LaSala	60.00	30.00	18.00
(22) Ray Mueller	60.00	30.00	18.00
1953			
(23) Dick Getter	60.00	30.00	18.00
(24) Dick Hamlin	60.00	30.00	18.00
(25) Jake Jenkins	60.00	30.00	18.00
(26) Jim Jones	60.00	30.00	18.00
(27) Bob Myers	60.00	30.00	18.00
(28) Clyde Stevens	60.00	30.00	18.00
(29) Joe Stupak	60.00	30.00	18.00

1954 Sioux City Soos Souvenir Pictures Album

Rather than a set of individual baseball cards, the Class A Western League farm club of the New York Giants issued this souvenir picture album depicting players (including future major league star and N.L. president Bill White), staff and media. About 8-1/8" x 7-1/2", the album has embossed metallic gold covers and orange graphics. Inside are eight black-and-white pages with three card-like images per page. The pictures are in about the same size and format as Globe Printing's contemporary minor league baseball card team sets.

	NM	EX	VG
Complete Souvenir Book:	300.00	150.00	90.00
1954 Sioux City Soos			

1947 Smith's Oakland Oaks

This regional set of Oakland Oaks (Pacific Coast League) cards was issued in 1947 by Smith's Clothing stores and is numbered in the lower right corner. The card fronts include a black and white photo with the player's name, team and position below. The backs carry a brief player write-up and an advertisement for Smith's Clothing. The cards measure 2" x 3". The Max Marshall card was apparently short-printed and is much scarcer than the rest of the set.

	NM	EX	VG
Complete Set (25):	800.00	400.00	240.00
Common Player:	25.00	12.50	7.50
1 Charles (Casey) Stengel	125.00	65.00	35.00
2 Billy Raimondi	25.00	12.50	7.50
3 Les Scarsella	25.00	12.50	7.50
4 Brooks Holder	25.00	12.50	7.50
5 Ray Hamrick	25.00	12.50	7.50
6 Gene Lillard	25.00	12.50	7.50
7 Maurice Van Robays	25.00	12.50	7.50
8 Charlie (Sheriff) Gassaway	25.00	12.50	7.50
9 Henry (Cotton) Pippen	25.00	12.50	7.50
10 James Arnold	25.00	12.50	7.50
11 Ralph (Buck) Buxton	25.00	12.50	7.50
12 Ambrose (Bo) Palica	25.00	12.50	7.50
13 Tony Sabol	25.00	12.50	7.50
14 Ed Kearse	25.00	12.50	7.50
15 Bill Hart	25.00	12.50	7.50
16 Donald (Snuffy) Smith	25.00	12.50	7.50
17 Oral (Mickey) Burnett	25.00	12.50	7.50
18 Tom Hafey	25.00	12.50	7.50
19 Will Hafey	25.00	12.50	7.50
20 Paul Gillespie	25.00	12.50	7.50
21 Damon Hayes	25.00	12.50	7.50
22 Max Marshall	350.00	175.00	100.00
23 Mel (Dizz) Duezabou	25.00	12.50	7.50
24 Mel Reeves	25.00	12.50	7.50
25 Joe Faria	25.00	12.50	7.50

1948 Smith's Oakland Oaks

The 1948 Smith's Clothing issue was another 25-card regional set featuring members of the Oakland Oaks of the Pacific Coast League. Almost identical to the 1947 Smith's issue, the black and white cards again measure 2" x 3" but were printed on heavier, glossy stock. The player's name, team and position appear below the photo with the card number in the lower right corner. The back has a brief player write-up and an ad for Smith's clothing.

	NM	EX	VG
Complete Set (25):	700.00	350.00	210.00
Common Player:	25.00	12.50	7.50
1 Billy Raimondi	25.00	12.50	7.50
2 Brooks Holder	25.00	12.50	7.50
3 Will Hafey	25.00	12.50	7.50
4 Nick Etten	25.00	12.50	7.50
5 Lloyd Christopher	25.00	12.50	7.50
6 Les Scarsella	25.00	12.50	7.50
7 Ray Hamrick	25.00	12.50	7.50
8 Gene Lillard	25.00	12.50	7.50
9 Maurice Van Robays	25.00	12.50	7.50
10 Charlie Gassaway	25.00	12.50	7.50
11 Ralph (Buck) Buxton	25.00	12.50	7.50
12 Tom Hafey	25.00	12.50	7.50
13 Damon Hayes	25.00	12.50	7.50
14 Mel (Dizz) Duezabou	25.00	12.50	7.50
15 Dario Lodigiani	25.00	12.50	7.50
16 Vic Buccola	25.00	12.50	7.50
17 Billy Martin	90.00	45.00	27.00
18 Floyd Speer	25.00	12.50	7.50
19 Eddie Samcoff	25.00	12.50	7.50

		NM	EX	VG
20	Charles (Casey) Stengel	90.00	45.00	27.00
21	Lloyd Hittle	25.00	12.50	7.50
22	Johnny Babich	25.00	12.50	7.50
23	Merrill Combs	25.00	12.50	7.50
24	Eddie Murphy	25.00	12.50	7.50
25	Bob Klinger	25.00	12.50	7.50

1948 Sommer & Kaufmann San Francisco Seals

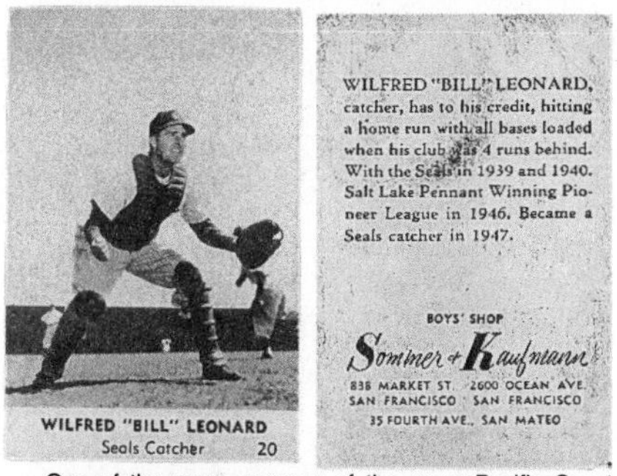
WILFRED "BILL" LEONARD
Seals Catcher 20
WILFRED "BILL" LEONARD, catcher, has to his credit, hitting a home run with all bases loaded when his club was 4 runs behind. With the Seals in 1939 and 1940. Salt Lake Pennant Winning Pioneer League in 1946. Became a Seals catcher in 1947.
BOYS' SHOP
Sommer & Kaufmann
838 MARKET ST. 2600 OCEAN AVE.
SAN FRANCISCO SAN FRANCISCO
35 FOURTH AVE., SAN MATEO

One of the more common of the many Pacific Coast League issues of the late 1940s, this emission from the San Francisco boys' clothier features 30 black-and-white 2" x 3" cards. Fronts have a player photo, name, position and card number. Backs have a few biographical details and stats, along with an ad. The 1948 issue can be differentiated from the 1949 issue by the words "BOYS SHOP" above the company logo on back.

		NM	EX	VG
Complete Set (30):		1,500	750.00	450.00
Common Player:		60.00	30.00	18.50
1	Lefty O'Doul	100.00	50.00	30.00
2	Jack Brewer	60.00	30.00	18.50
3	Con Dempsey	60.00	30.00	18.50
4	Tommy Fine	60.00	30.00	18.50
5	Kenneth Gables	60.00	30.00	18.50
6	Robert Joyce	60.00	30.00	18.50
7	Al Lien	60.00	30.00	18.50
8	Cliff Melton	60.00	30.00	18.50
9	Frank Shofner	60.00	30.00	18.50
10	Don Trower	60.00	30.00	18.50
11	Joe Brovia	60.00	30.00	18.50
12	Dino Paul Restelli	60.00	30.00	18.50
13	Gene Woodling	75.00	37.00	22.00
14	Ben Guintini	60.00	30.00	18.50
15	Felix Mackiewicz	60.00	30.00	18.50
16	John Patrick Tobin	60.00	30.00	18.50
17	Manuel Perez	60.00	30.00	18.50
18	Bill Werle	60.00	30.00	18.50
19	Homer Howell	60.00	30.00	18.50
20	Wilfred Leonard	60.00	30.00	18.50
21	Bruce Ogrodowski	60.00	30.00	18.50
22	Dick Lajeskie	60.00	30.00	18.50
23	Hugh Luby	60.00	30.00	18.50
24	Roy Nicely	60.00	30.00	18.50
25	Ray Orteig	60.00	30.00	18.50
26	Michael Rocco	60.00	30.00	18.50
27	Del Young	60.00	30.00	18.50
28	Joe Sprinz	60.00	30.00	18.50
29	Doc Hughes	60.00	30.00	18.50
30	Batboys (Don Rode, Albert Boro, Charlie Barnes)	60.00	30.00	18.50

1949 Sommer & Kaufmann San Francisco Seals

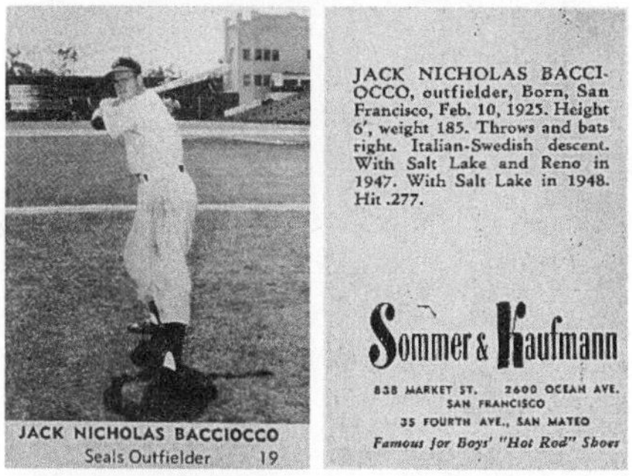
JACK NICHOLAS BACCIOCCO
Seals Outfielder 19
JACK NICHOLAS BACCIOCCO, outfielder, Born, San Francisco, Feb. 10, 1925. Height 6', weight 185. Throws and bats right. Italian-Swedish descent. With Salt Lake and Reno in 1947. With Salt Lake in 1948. Hit .277.
Sommer & Kaufmann
838 MARKET ST. 2600 OCEAN AVE.
SAN FRANCISCO
35 FOURTH AVE., SAN MATEO
Famous for Boys' "Hot Rod" Shoes

Twenty-eight black-and-white cards numbered 1-29 (#24 unknown) make up the second and final card issue of the "Frisco area clothier." Measuring 2" x 3", the cards are nearly identical to the '48 issue. The '49s can be identified by the mention of "Hot Rod" shoes on the back. Fronts feature a borderless player photo with a panel at the bottom giving name, position and card number. Backs have the ad for the boy's shop and a brief biographical player sketch.

		NM	EX	VG
Complete Set (29):		2,000	1,000	600.00
Common Player:		75.00	37.00	22.00
1	Lefty O'Doul	100.00	50.00	30.00
2	Jack Brewer	75.00	37.00	22.00
3	Kenneth Gables	75.00	37.00	22.00
4	Con Dempsey	75.00	37.00	22.00
5	Al Lien	75.00	37.00	22.00
6	Cliff Melton	75.00	37.00	22.00
7	Steve Nagy	75.00	37.00	22.00
8	Manny Perez	75.00	37.00	22.00
9	Roy Jarvis	75.00	37.00	22.00
10	Roy Partee	75.00	37.00	22.00
11	Reno Cheso	75.00	37.00	22.00
12	Dick Lajeskie	75.00	37.00	22.00
13	Roy Nicely	75.00	37.00	22.00
14	Mickey Rocco	75.00	37.00	22.00
15	Frank Shofner	75.00	37.00	22.00
16	Richard Holder	75.00	37.00	22.00
17	Dino Restelli	75.00	37.00	22.00
18	Floyd J. "Arky" Vaughan	150.00	75.00	45.00
19	Jackie Bacciocco	75.00	37.00	22.00
20	Bob Drilling	75.00	37.00	22.00
21	Del Young	75.00	37.00	22.00
22	Joe Sprinz	75.00	37.00	22.00
23	Doc Hughes	75.00	37.00	22.00
24	Unknown	75.00	37.00	22.00
25	Bert Singleton	75.00	37.00	22.00
26	John Brocker	75.00	37.00	22.00
27	Jack Tobin	75.00	37.00	22.00
28	Walt Judnich	75.00	37.00	22.00
29	Hal Feldman	75.00	37.00	22.00

1909 Spargo Hartford Senators Postcards

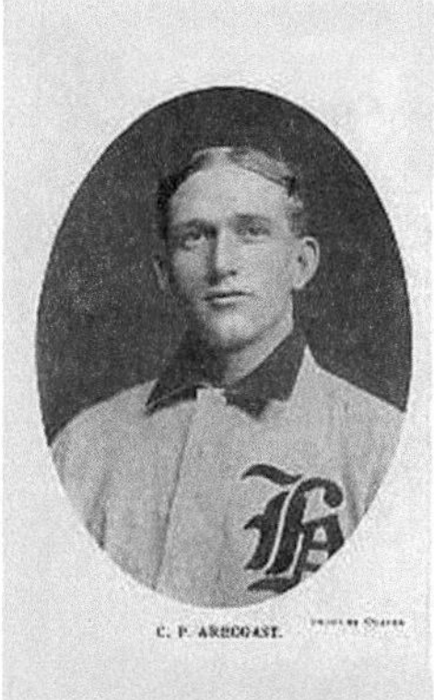
C. P. ARBOGAST.

Members on the Connecticut League (Class B) champion Hartford Senators are pictured on these black-and-white postcards. Player portraits are featured in an oval on front with identication below. A photo credit to "Oliver" is provided. The typically formatted back has a credit line for the publisher, A.W. Spargo. It is likely other members of the team exist on cards yet to be reported.

		NM	EX	VG
Common Player:		700.00	350.00	200.00
(1)	C.P. Arbogast	700.00	350.00	200.00
(2)	Tom J. Connery	700.00	350.00	200.00
(3)	Ray L. Fisher	700.00	350.00	200.00
(4)	C.A. Wadleigh	700.00	350.00	200.00

1867 Sterey Photographers Troy Haymakers

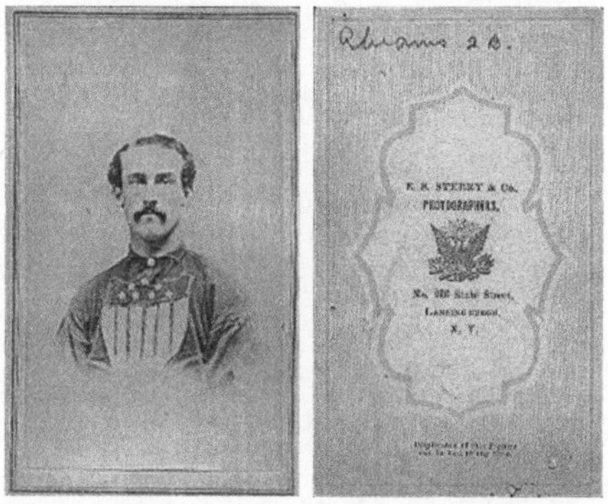

Pre-dating the use of baseball cards as promotional premiums for other products, this issue comprises cartes de visites of members of the Troy Haymakers, one of the powerhouse "amateur" teams in the days prior to the 1871 formation of the National Association, the first professional baseball league. The approximately 2-1/2" x 4" cards have black-and-white player portrait photos glued to a heavy cardboard backing which on its reverse carries in blue the advertising of E.S. Sterey & Co., Photographers, of Lansingburgh, N.Y. The players are not identified on the cards except for the names and, sometimes, positions pencilled on back. While many CDVs of individual players of the era, along with team poses and composites, are known, this issue is important because it represents one of the first efforts to create a "team set." It is likely cards of other Troy players were issued and may surface someday.

NM EX VG

(Only a single card is known for each player, each has been certified by SGC as "Fair".)

(1)	Abrams
(2)	Bill Craver
(3)	Steve King
(4)	Bub McAtee
(5)	Peter McKeon
(6)	McQuide

1933 St. Paul Daily News

(See 1933 Worch Cigar American Association.)

1946 Sunbeam Bread Sacramento Solons

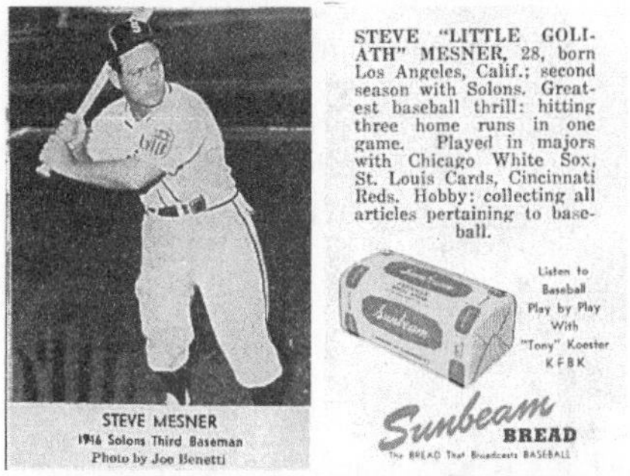
STEVE "LITTLE GOLIATH" MESNER, 28, born Los Angeles, Calif.; second season with Solons. Greatest baseball thrill: hitting three home runs in one game. Played in majors with Chicago White Sox, St. Louis Cards, Cincinnati Reds. Hobby: collecting all articles pertaining to baseball.
Listen to Baseball Play by Play With "Tony" Koester KFBK
STEVE MESNER
1946 Solons Third Baseman
Photo by Joe Benetti
Sunbeam BREAD

The 21 unnumbered cards in this Pacific Coast League team set are printed with black-and-white fronts containing a borderless player photo with a panel beneath containing name, position and a photo credit. Backs are printed in blue, red and yellow and contain a brief career summary and an ad for the bread brand. Each card can be found with two versions of the ad on back. One has a smaller loaf of bread and the word "Sunbeam" in blue, the other has a larger picture and "Sunbeam" in red. The cards measure approximately 2" x 3". Players are checklisted here in alphabetical order.

		NM	EX	VG
Complete Set (21):		900.00	450.00	240.00
Common Player:		75.00	35.00	20.00
(1)	Bud Beasley	75.00	35.00	20.00
(2)	Jack Calvey	75.00	35.00	20.00
(3)	Gene Corbett	75.00	35.00	20.00
(4)	Bill Conroy	75.00	35.00	20.00
(5)	Guy Fletcher	75.00	35.00	20.00
(6)	Tony Freitas	75.00	35.00	20.00
(7)	Ted Greenhalgh	75.00	35.00	20.00
(8)	Al Jarlett	75.00	35.00	20.00
(9)	Jesse Landrum	75.00	35.00	20.00
(10)	Gene Lillard	75.00	35.00	20.00
(11)	Garth Mann	75.00	35.00	20.00
(12)	Lilo Marcucci	75.00	35.00	20.00
(13)	Joe Marty (SP)	225.00	110.00	65.00
(14)	Steve Mesner	75.00	35.00	20.00
(15)	Herm Pillette	75.00	35.00	20.00
(16)	Earl Sheely	75.00	35.00	20.00
(17)	Al Smith	75.00	35.00	20.00
(18)	Gerald Staley	75.00	35.00	20.00
(19)	Averett Thompson	75.00	35.00	20.00
(20)	Jo Jo White	75.00	35.00	20.00
(21)	Bud Zipay	75.00	35.00	20.00

1947 Sunbeam Bread Sacramento Solons

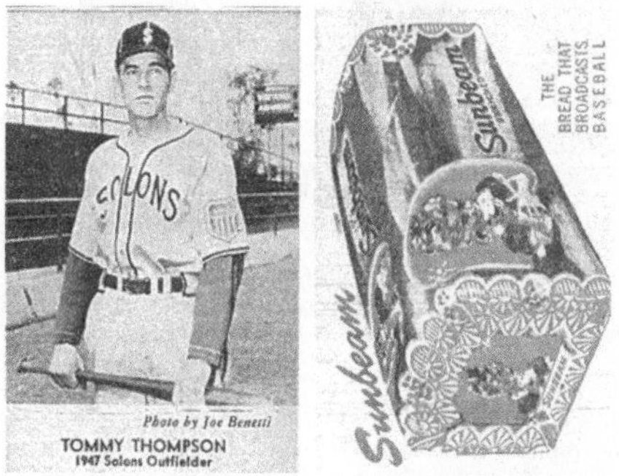
Photo by Joe Benetti
TOMMY THOMPSON
1947 Solons Outfielder
Sunbeam
THE BREAD THAT BROADCASTS BASEBALL

Similar in format to the 1946 issue, the 26 cards in the '47 set again featured black-and-white player photos on front, with a panel beneath giving player name, position and photo credit. Backs of the 2" x 3" cards had a color depiction of a loaf of the sponsoring company's bread. The unnumbered cards are alphabetically checklisted here.

		NM	EX	VG
Complete Set (26):		1,250	625.00	375.00
Common Player:		50.00	25.00	15.00
(1)	Gene Babbit	50.00	25.00	15.00
(2)	Bob Barthelson	50.00	25.00	15.00
(3)	Bud Beasley	50.00	25.00	15.00
(4)	Chuck Cronin	50.00	25.00	15.00
(5)	Eddie Fernandes	50.00	25.00	15.00
(6)	Ed Fitz Gerald	50.00	25.00	15.00
(7)	Guy Fletcher	50.00	25.00	15.00
(8)	Tony Freitas	50.00	25.00	15.00
(9)	Garth Mann	50.00	25.00	15.00
(10)	Joe Marty	50.00	25.00	15.00
(11)	Lou McCollum	50.00	25.00	15.00
(12)	Steve Mesner	50.00	25.00	15.00
(13)	Frank Nelson	50.00	25.00	15.00
(14)	Tommy Nelson	50.00	25.00	15.00
(15)	Joe Orengo	50.00	25.00	15.00
(16)	Hugh Orphan	50.00	25.00	15.00
(17)	Nick Pesut	50.00	25.00	15.00
(18)	Bill Ramsey	50.00	25.00	15.00
(19)	Johnny Rizzo	50.00	25.00	15.00
(20)	Mike Schemer	250.00	125.00	75.00

		NM	EX	VG
(21)	Al Smith	50.00	25.00	15.00
(22)	Tommy Thompson	50.00	25.00	15.00
(23)	Jim Warner	50.00	25.00	15.00
(24)	Mel Wasley	50.00	25.00	15.00
(25)	Leo Wells	50.00	25.00	15.00
(26)	Eddie Zipay	50.00	25.00	15.00

1949 Sunbeam/Pureta Sacramento Solons

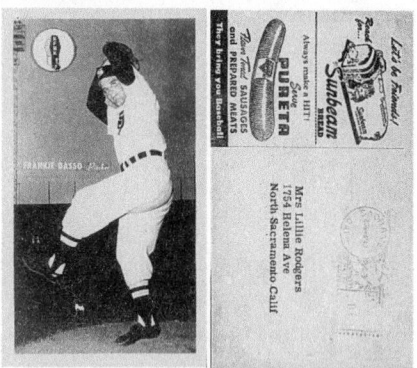

Players of the Pacific Coast League's Sacramento Solons were featured in this postcard-size (3-1/4" x 5-1/2") set. Fronts featured black-and-white player photos and the logo of the team's radio broadcaster. Backs feature ads for Sunbeam Bread and Pureta meats.

		NM	EX	VG
Complete Set (12):		2,000	1,000	600.00
Common Player:		250.00	125.00	80.00
(1)	Del Baker	250.00	125.00	80.00
(2)	Frankie Dasso	250.00	125.00	80.00
(3)	Walt Dropo	325.00	160.00	100.00
(4)	Bob Gillespie	250.00	125.00	80.00
(5)	Joe Grace	250.00	125.00	80.00
(6)	Ralph Hodgin	250.00	125.00	80.00
(7)	Freddie Marsh	250.00	125.00	80.00
(8)	Joe Marty	250.00	125.00	80.00
(9)	Len Ratto	250.00	125.00	80.00
(10)	Jim Tabor	250.00	125.00	80.00
(11)	Al White	250.00	125.00	80.00
(12)	Bill Wilson	250.00	125.00	80.00

1949 Sunbeam Bread Stockton Ports

These 2" x 3" unnumbered cards can be found printed in either black-and-white or blue tinted. The Ports were the Class C California League farm club of the Chicago White Sox.

		NM	EX	VG
Complete Set (12):		3,000	1,500	900.00
Common Player:		275.00	135.00	85.00
(1)	Nino Bongiovanni	275.00	135.00	85.00
(2)	Lou Bronzan	275.00	135.00	85.00
(3)	Jimmie Brown	275.00	135.00	85.00
(4)	Rocco Cardinale	275.00	135.00	85.00
(5)	Harry Clements	275.00	135.00	85.00
(6)	Norm Grabar	275.00	135.00	85.00
(7)	Bud Guldborg	275.00	135.00	85.00
(8)	Carl Hoberg	275.00	135.00	85.00
(9)	Eddie Murphy	275.00	135.00	85.00
(10)	Sandy Sandel	275.00	135.00	85.00
(11)	Dick Stone	275.00	135.00	85.00
(12)	Matt Zidich	275.00	135.00	85.00

1950 Sunbeam Bread Stockton Ports

SHORT-STOP – ROBERT LOUIS STEVENS, 21, single, native of Stockton. Graduate Edison High. 1947: baseball, football, basketball. Attended Stockton College. Played football. Bats right and throws right. A local boy making good. Signed to first professional contract by Ports, Spring of '49; starting his second season.

REACH FOR SUNBEAM BREAD PIES PASTRIES

ROBERT LOUIS STEVENS short-stop

Gravem-Inglis Baking Co.

These 2" x 3" unnumbered cards are printed in black-and-white. The Ports were an unaffiliated team in the Class C California League.

		NM	EX	VG
Complete Set (13):		1,800	900.00	550.00
Common Player:		150.00	75.00	45.00
(1)	Richard L. Adams	150.00	75.00	45.00
(2)	James Edward Brown	150.00	75.00	45.00
(3)	Harry Clements	150.00	75.00	45.00
(4)	John Burton Goldborg	150.00	75.00	45.00
(5)	Gerald Lee Haines	150.00	75.00	45.00
(6)	Alfred Michael Heist	150.00	75.00	45.00
(7)	Don Masterson	150.00	75.00	45.00
(8)	Lauren Hugh Monroe	150.00	75.00	45.00
(9)	Frank E. Murray	150.00	75.00	45.00
(10)	Lauren Keith Simon Jr.	150.00	75.00	45.00
(11)	George Anthony Stanich	150.00	75.00	45.00
(12)	Robert Louis Stevens	150.00	75.00	45.00
(13)	Harold Lee Zurcher	150.00	75.00	45.00

1962 Supertest Toronto Maple Leafs

The extent of the checklist for this issue is unknown. It is assumed the cards were given away with gasoline purchases. Printed on thick, porous paper in a 5-1/2" x 8-1/2" format, the cards have a black-and-white photo, facsimile autograph and sponsor's logo on front. Backs are blank.

		NM	EX	VG
Common Player:		60.00	30.00	18.00
(1)	Chuck Dressen	75.00	37.50	22.50
(2)	Russ Heman	60.00	30.00	18.00

1952 Syracuse Chiefs Team Issue

Like the other contemporary issues of Globe Printing, the cards of the '52 Chiefs (International League, unaffiliated) share a blank-back, black-and-white format. Player names are in black in a white strip on front. Cards measure about 2-1/4" x 3-3/8". The checklist here is incomplete.

		NM	EX	VG
Common Player:		60.00	30.00	18.00
(1)	Bruno Betzel	60.00	30.00	18.00
(2)	Johnny Blatnick	60.00	30.00	18.00
(3)	Charles Eisenmann	60.00	30.00	18.00
(4)	Myron Hayworth	60.00	30.00	18.00
(5)	John Welaj	60.00	30.00	18.00

T

1966 Toledo Mud Hens Team Issue

(3-1/4" x 5-1/2") (Unnumbered)

		NM	EX	VG
Complete Set (25):		1,000	500.00	300.00
Common Player:		40.00	20.00	12.00
(1)	Loren Babe	40.00	20.00	12.00
(2)	Stan Bahnsen	40.00	20.00	12.00
(3)	Bill Bethea	40.00	20.00	12.00
(4)	Wayne Comer	40.00	20.00	12.00
(5)	Jack Cullen	40.00	20.00	12.00
(6)	Jack Curtis	40.00	20.00	12.00
(7)	Gil Downs	40.00	20.00	12.00
(8)	Joe Faroci	40.00	20.00	12.00
(9)	Frank Fernandez	40.00	20.00	12.00
(10)	Mike Ferraro	40.00	20.00	12.00
(11)	Doc Foley	40.00	20.00	12.00
(12)	Mike Hegan	40.00	20.00	12.00
(13)	Jim Horsford	40.00	20.00	12.00
(14)	Dick Hughes	40.00	20.00	12.00
(15)	Elvio Jiminez	40.00	20.00	12.00
(16)	Bob Lasko	40.00	20.00	12.00
(17)	Jim Merritt	40.00	20.00	12.00
(18)	Archie Moore	40.00	20.00	12.00
(19)	Bobby Murcer	90.00	45.00	27.00
(20)	Tony Preybycian	40.00	20.00	12.00
(21)	Bob Schmidt	40.00	20.00	12.00
(22)	Charlie Senger, Loren Babe, Bill Shantz	40.00	20.00	12.00
(23)	Bill Shantz	40.00	20.00	12.00
(24)	Paul Toth	40.00	20.00	12.00
(25)	Jerry Walker	40.00	20.00	12.00

1964 True Ade / WGR Buffalo Bisons

Members of the International League Buffalo Bisons, Class AAA farm club of the N.Y. Mets are featured in this set of contest cards. Persons who assembled a complete nine-player set could redeem the cards for ballgame tickets. The cards were found in cartons of Tru Ade beverage. The blank-back cards are printed in red and about 1-1/4" x 6-1/2" overall. At bottom is a player photo with his name and position above, and team below, separated by a dotted line from the upper portion of the card which has contest details and logos of the sponsoring beverage company and WGR radio. The player portion of the card measures about 1-1/4" x 1-1/4". It is evident that at least nine players were issued in the set, possibly with some short-printed; this checklist is, therefore, incomplete. The unnumbered cards are listed here in alphabetical order.

		NM	EX	VG
Common Player:		150.00	75.00	45.00
(1)	Ed Bauta	150.00	75.00	45.00
(2)	Choo Choo Coleman	200.00	100.00	60.00
(3)	Pumpsie Green	300.00	150.00	90.00
(4)	Cleon Jones	200.00	100.00	60.00

1960 Tulsa Oilers Team Issue

This team issue by the St. Louis Cardinals' farm club consists of a dozen black-and-white player photos. Players are identified by a facsimile autograph on front. Backs of the approximately 4-1/8" x 5" photos are blank.

		NM	EX	VG
Complete Set (18):		350.00	175.00	100.00
Common Player:		20.00	10.00	6.00
(1)	Jim Beauchamp	15.00	7.50	4.50
(2)	Bob Blaylock	20.00	10.00	6.00
(3)	Artie Burnett	20.00	10.00	6.00
(4)	Bill Carpenter	20.00	10.00	6.00
(5)	Julio Gotay	20.00	10.00	6.00
(6)	Jim Hickman	20.00	10.00	6.00
(7)	Ray Katt	20.00	10.00	6.00
(8)	Harry Keister	20.00	10.00	6.00
(9)	Fred Koenig	20.00	10.00	6.00
(10)	Gordon Richardson	20.00	10.00	6.00
(11)	Rich Rogers	20.00	10.00	6.00
(12)	Lynn Rube	20.00	10.00	6.00
(13)	Jim Schaffer	20.00	10.00	6.00
(14)	Clint Stark	20.00	10.00	6.00
(15)	Ted Thiem	20.00	10.00	6.00
(16)	Dixie Walker	20.00	10.00	6.00
(17)	Harry Watts	20.00	10.00	6.00
(18)	Fred Whitfield	20.00	10.00	6.00

1888-1889 Uhlman St. Paul Cabinets

While this cabinet-card issue utilizes the same format (about 4-1/4" x 6-1/2") and the same Goodwin & Co. copyright photos found on contemporary Old Judge cards, they are, according to advertising on the bottom, the product of Uhlman (presumably a studio) in St. Joseph, Mo. All cards known to date depict members of the St. Paul Apostles of the newly formed Western Association.

		NM	EX	VG
Common Player:		1,300	650.00	400.00
(1)	Cal Broughton	1,300	650.00	400.00
(2)	Scrappy Carroll	1,300	650.00	400.00
(3)	George Treadway	1,300	650.00	400.00
(4)	A.M. Tuckerman	1,300	650.00	400.00
(5)	Milton West	1,300	650.00	400.00

1958 Union Oil Sacramento Solons

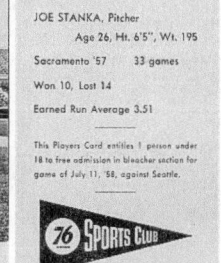

Ten members of the independent Pacific Coast League team were included in a black-and-white card set distributed at Union 76 gas stations in that locale. Fronts feature borderless player photos with a wide white strip at the bottom on which is printed the player, team name and the position. Backs have brief stats, a "76 Sports Club" pennant and information about a specific game for which the card can be exchanged for admission by a child. Cards measure approximately 2-1/2" x 3-1/4".

		NM	EX	VG
Complete Set (10):		500.00	250.00	150.00
Common Player:		50.00	25.00	15.00
(1)	Marshall Bridges	65.00	32.00	19.50
(2)	Dick Cole	50.00	25.00	15.00
(3)	Jim Greengrass	50.00	25.00	15.00
(4)	Al Heist	50.00	25.00	15.00
(5)	Nippy Jones	50.00	25.00	15.00
(6)	Carlos Paula	50.00	25.00	15.00
(7)	Kal Segrist	50.00	25.00	15.00
(8)	Sibbi Sisti	50.00	25.00	15.00
(9)	Joe Stanka	80.00	40.00	24.00
(10)	Bud Watkins	50.00	25.00	15.00

1960 Union Oil Seattle Rainiers

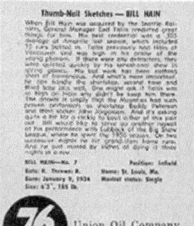

Given away at Union 76 gas stations in the Seattle area, this set of nine full-color cards measure approximately 3-1/8" x 4". Backs have brief biographical data, a career summary and a large Union 76 logo. The cards are skip-numbered.

		NM	EX	VG
Complete Set (9):		200.00	100.00	60.00
Common Player:		12.00	6.00	3.50
4	Francisco Obregon	20.00	10.00	6.00
6	Drew Gilbert	12.00	6.00	3.50
7	Bill Hain	12.00	6.00	3.50
10	Ray Ripplemeyer	100.00	50.00	30.00
13	Joe Taylor	12.00	6.00	3.50
15	Lou Skizas	12.00	6.00	3.50
17	Don Rudolph	12.00	6.00	3.50
19	Gordy Coleman	15.00	7.50	4.50
22	Hal Beven	12.00	6.00	3.50

1961 Union Oil Pacific Coast League

The last of three Union Oil PCL issues, the 67 cards in this set feature sepia-toned borderless photos on front in a 3" to 3-1/8" x 4" format. Backs are printed in blue and feature biographical data, a career summary, and ads by the issuing oil company and participating radio station co-sponsors. Six of the eight teams in the '61 PCL are featured, with Salt Lake City and Vancouver not participating in the promotion. Presumably because of smaller print runs, the cards distributed in Hawaii and Spokane bring a premium price. Hall of Fame pitcher Gaylord Perry is featured on his first baseball card in this set. Only the Tacoma cards are numbered and they are skip-numbered.

(Team sets listed below.)

1961 Union Oil Hawaii Islanders

		NM	EX	VG
Complete Set (10):		450.00	225.00	135.00
Common Player:		60.00	30.00	18.00
(1)	Ray Jablonski	60.00	30.00	18.00
(2)	Jim McManus	60.00	30.00	18.00
(3)	George Prescott	75.00	37.50	22.50
(4)	Diego Segui	60.00	30.00	18.00
(5)	Rachel Slider	60.00	30.00	18.00
(6)	Jim Small	60.00	30.00	18.00
(7)	Milt Smith	60.00	30.00	18.00
(8)	Dave Thies	60.00	30.00	18.00
(9)	Jay Ward	60.00	30.00	18.00
(10)	Bill Werle	60.00	30.00	18.00

1961 Union Oil Portland Beavers

		NM	EX	VG
Complete Set (13):		150.00	75.00	45.00
Common Player:		12.00	6.00	3.50
(1)	Ed Bauta	12.00	6.00	3.50
(2)	Vern Benson	12.00	6.00	3.50
(3)	Jerry Buchek	12.00	6.00	3.50
(4)	Bob Burda	12.00	6.00	3.50
(5)	Duke Carmel	12.00	6.00	3.50
(6)	Don Choate	12.00	6.00	3.50
(7)	Phil Gagliano	12.00	6.00	3.50
(8)	Jim Hickman	12.00	6.00	3.50
(9)	Ray Katt	12.00	6.00	3.50
(10)	Mel Nelson	12.00	6.00	3.50
(11)	Jim Shaffer	12.00	6.00	3.50
(12)	Mike Shannon	17.50	8.75	5.25
(13)	Clint Stark	12.00	6.00	3.50

1961 Union Oil San Diego Padres

		NM	EX	VG
Complete Set (12):		175.00	90.00	45.00
Common Player:		12.00	6.00	3.50
(1)	Dick Barone	12.00	6.00	3.50
(2)	Jim Bolger	12.00	6.00	3.50
(3)	Kent Hadley	12.00	6.00	3.50
(4)	Mike Hershberger	15.00	7.50	4.50

(5)	Stan Johnson	12.00	6.00	3.50
(6)	Dick Lines	12.00	6.00	3.50
(7)	Jim Napier	12.00	6.00	3.50
(8)	Tony Roig	12.00	6.00	3.50
(9)	Herb Score	40.00	20.00	12.00
(10)	Harry Simpson	20.00	10.00	6.00
(11)	Joe Taylor	12.00	6.00	3.50
(12)	Ben Wade	12.00	6.00	3.50

1961 Union Oil Seattle Rainiers

		NM	EX	VG
Complete Set (11):		100.00	50.00	30.00
Common Player:		10.00	5.00	3.00
(1)	Galen Cisco	10.00	5.00	3.00
(2)	Lou Clinton	10.00	5.00	3.00
(3)	Marlan Coughtry	10.00	5.00	3.00
(4)	Harry Malmberg	10.00	5.00	3.00
(5)	Dave Mann	10.00	5.00	3.00
(6)	Derrell Martin	10.00	5.00	3.00
(7)	Erv Palica	10.00	5.00	3.00
(8)	John Pesky	15.00	7.50	4.50
(9)	Bob Tillman	10.00	5.00	3.00
(10)	Marv Toft	10.00	5.00	3.00
(11)	Tom Umphlett	10.00	5.00	3.00

1961 Union Oil Spokane Indians

		NM	EX	VG
Complete Set (11):		450.00	225.00	135.00
Common Player:		35.00	17.50	10.00
(1)	Doug Camilli	35.00	17.50	10.00
(2)	Ramon Conde	35.00	17.50	10.00
(3)	Bob Giallombardo	35.00	17.50	10.00
(4)	Mike Goliat	35.00	17.50	10.00
(5)	Preston Gomez (SP)	135.00	67.00	40.00
(6)	Rod Graber	35.00	17.50	10.00
(7)	Tim Harkness	35.00	17.50	10.00
(8)	Jim Harwell	35.00	17.50	10.00
(9)	Howie Reed	35.00	17.50	10.00
(10)	Curt Roberts	35.00	17.50	10.00
(11)	Rene Valdes (Valdez)	35.00	17.50	10.00

1961 Union Oil Tacoma Giants

		NM	EX	VG
Complete Set (10):		200.00	100.00	60.00
Common Player:		15.00	7.50	4.50
10	Red Davis	15.00	7.50	4.50
12	Dick Phillips	15.00	7.50	4.50
17	Gil Garrido	15.00	7.50	4.50
20	Georges Maranda	15.00	7.50	4.50
25	John Orsino	15.00	7.50	4.50
26	Dusty Rhodes	20.00	10.00	6.00
28	Ron Herbel	15.00	7.50	4.50
29	Gaylord Perry	60.00	30.00	18.00
30	Rafael Alomar	20.00	10.00	6.00
34	Bob Farley	15.00	7.50	4.50

1961 Union Oil Taiyo Whales

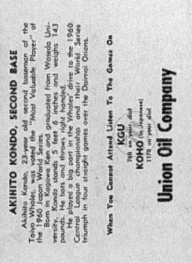

This three-card set was produced in conjunction with an exhibition series played in October 1961, between the Taiyo Whales of Japan's Central League, and the Hawaii Islanders, a Class AAA Pacific Cost League farm club of the K.C. Athletics. The player cards measure just over 3" x 4", while the team photo card is 5" x 3-3/4". Cards are black-and-white and have some player biography and ads for Union Oil Co., and the English - and Japanese - language radio stations that carried the games.

		NM	EX	VG
Complete Set (3):		175.00	87.00	52.00
(1)	Akihito Kondo	50.00	25.00	15.00
(2)	Gentaro Shimada	50.00	25.00	15.00
(3)	Taiyo Whales Team	90.00	45.00	27.00

V

1951 Vancouver Capilanos Popcorn Issue

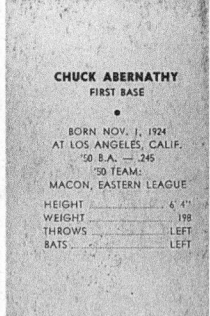

CHUCK ABERNATHY
FIRST BASE
★
BORN NOV. 1, 1924
AT LOS ANGELES, CALIF.
'50 B.A. — .245
'50 TEAM:
MACON, EASTERN LEAGUE
HEIGHT .... 6' 4"
WEIGHT 198
THROWS .... LEFT
BATS .... LEFT

These cards measure 1-7/8" x 2-7/8", are printed in black-and-white and have 1950 stats on back. Names may appear in slightly different form than checklisted here. The Caps played in the Class B Western International League and were not affiliated with any major league club.

		NM	EX	VG
Complete Set (24):		4,000	2,000	1,200
Common Player:		200.00	100.00	60.00
(1)	Chuck Abernathy	200.00	100.00	60.00
(2)	Jerry Barta	200.00	100.00	60.00
(3)	Bud Beasley	200.00	100.00	60.00
(4)	Gordy Brunswick	200.00	100.00	60.00
(5)	Reno Cheso	200.00	100.00	60.00
(6)	Ken Chorlton	200.00	100.00	60.00
(7)	Carl Gunnarson	200.00	100.00	60.00
(8)	Pete Hernandez	200.00	100.00	60.00
(9)	Vern Kindsfather	200.00	100.00	60.00
(10)	Bobby McGuire	200.00	100.00	60.00
(11)	Bob McLean	200.00	100.00	60.00
(12)	Charlie Mead	200.00	100.00	60.00
(13)	Jimmy Moore	200.00	100.00	60.00
(14)	George Nicholas	200.00	100.00	60.00
(15)	John Ritchey	200.00	100.00	60.00
(16)	Sandy Robertson	200.00	100.00	60.00
(17)	Bill Schuster	200.00	100.00	60.00
(18)	Dick Sinovic	200.00	100.00	60.00
(19)	Ron Smith	200.00	100.00	60.00
(20)	Bob Snyder	200.00	100.00	60.00
(21)	Don Tisnerat	200.00	100.00	60.00
(22)	Ray Tran	200.00	100.00	60.00
(23)	Reg Wallis (Trainer)	200.00	100.00	60.00
(24)	Bill Whyte	200.00	100.00	60.00

1952 Vancouver Capilanos Popcorn Issue

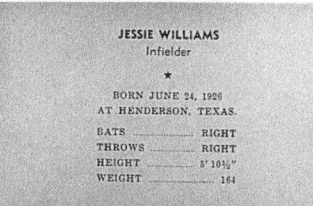

JESSIE WILLIAMS
Infielder
★
BORN JUNE 24, 1926
AT HENDERSON, TEXAS
BATS .... RIGHT
THROWS .... RIGHT
HEIGHT .... 5' 10½"
WEIGHT 164

These cards measure 2" x 3-1/8", are printed in black-and-white and have 1951 stats on back. Names may appear in slightly different form than checklisted here. The Caps played in the Class A Western International League and were not affiliated with any major league club.

		NM	EX	VG
Complete Set (20):		3,500	1,750	1,000
Common Player:		200.00	100.00	60.00
(1)	Gordie Brunswick	200.00	100.00	60.00
(2)	Bob Duretto	200.00	100.00	60.00
(3)	Van Fletcher	200.00	100.00	60.00
(4)	John Guldborg	200.00	100.00	60.00
(5)	Paul Jones	200.00	100.00	60.00
(6)	Eddie Locke	200.00	100.00	60.00
(7)	Tom Lovrich	200.00	100.00	60.00
(8)	Jimmy Moore	200.00	100.00	60.00
(9)	George Nicholas	200.00	100.00	60.00
(10a)	John Ritchey	200.00	100.00	60.00
(10b)	Johnny Ritchie	200.00	100.00	60.00
(11)	Bill Schuster	200.00	100.00	60.00
(12)	Bob Snyder	200.00	100.00	60.00
(13)	Len Tran	200.00	100.00	60.00
(14)	Ray Tran	200.00	100.00	60.00
(15)	Edo Vanni	200.00	100.00	60.00
(16)	Jim Wert	200.00	100.00	60.00
(17)	Bill Whyte	200.00	100.00	60.00
(18)	Jessie Williams (Batting)	200.00	100.00	60.00
(19)	Jesse Williams (Fielding)	200.00	100.00	60.00

1953 Vancouver Capilanos Popcorn Issue

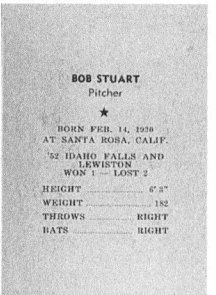

BOB STUART
Pitcher
★
BORN FEB. 14, 1930
AT SANTA ROSA, CALIF.
'52 IDAHO FALLS AND
LEWISTON
WON 1 — LOST 2
HEIGHT .... 6'3"
WEIGHT 182
THROWS .... RIGHT
BATS .... RIGHT

These cards measure 2-3/16" x 3-3/16", are printed in black-and-white and have 1952 stats on back. Names may appear in slightly different form than checklisted here. The Caps played in the Class A Western International League and were not affiliated with any major league club.

		NM	EX	VG
Complete Set (18):		3,000	1,500	900.00
Common Player:		200.00	100.00	60.00
(1)	Dick Briskey	200.00	100.00	60.00
(2)	Jack Bukowatz	200.00	100.00	60.00
(3)	Ken Chorlton	200.00	100.00	60.00
(4)	Van Fletcher	200.00	100.00	60.00
(5)	John Guldborg	200.00	100.00	60.00
(6)	Carl Gunnerson	200.00	100.00	60.00
(7)	Jim Hedgecock	200.00	100.00	60.00
(8)	Gordon Hernandez	200.00	100.00	60.00
(9)	Pete Hernandez	200.00	100.00	60.00
(10)	Jim Leavitt	200.00	100.00	60.00
(11)	Rod MacKay	200.00	100.00	60.00
(12)	Frank Mascaro	200.00	100.00	60.00
(13)	Lonnie Myers	200.00	100.00	60.00
(14)	Rod Owen	200.00	100.00	60.00
(15)	Harvey Storey	200.00	100.00	60.00
(16)	Bob Stuart	200.00	100.00	60.00
(17)	Dale Thomason	200.00	100.00	60.00
(18)	Jim Wert	200.00	100.00	60.00

1954 Vancouver Capilanos Popcorn Issue

K. CHORLTON

These cards measure 2-3/16" x 3-5/16" and are printed in black-and-white. Names may appear in slightly different form than checklisted here. The Caps were the 1954 champs of the Class A Western International League and were not affiliated with any major league club.

		NM	EX	VG
Complete Set (15):		2,500	1,250	750.00
Common Player:		200.00	100.00	60.00
(1)	Bill Brenner	200.00	100.00	60.00
(2)	Ken Chorlton	200.00	100.00	60.00
(3)	Jim Clarke (Clark)	200.00	100.00	60.00
(4)	John Cordell	200.00	100.00	60.00
(5)	Bob Duretto	200.00	100.00	60.00
(6)	Dick Greco	200.00	100.00	60.00
(7)	Arnie Hallgren	200.00	100.00	60.00
(8)	Danny Holden	200.00	100.00	60.00
(9)	Rod McKay	200.00	100.00	60.00
(10)	George Nicholas	200.00	100.00	60.00
(11)	Nick Pesut	200.00	100.00	60.00
(12)	Ken Richardson	200.00	100.00	60.00
(13)	Bob Roberts	200.00	100.00	60.00
(14)	Bob Wellman	200.00	100.00	60.00
(15)	Marvin Williams	200.00	100.00	60.00

1954 Veltex Lewiston Broncs

LARRY BARTON
Compliments of your
VELTEX DEALER

It is evident from the format of the card and of the accompanying album that this is a product of Globe Printing, which produced many minor league sets in the early 1950s. What makes this set of the 1954 Class A (Western International League) affiliate of the Baltimore Orioles unusual among Globe issues is the mention of a sponsor. The blank-back, black-and-white cards measure 2-3/16" x 3-3/8". The checklist below is obviously incomplete.

		NM	EX	VG
Common player:		60.00	30.00	18.00
Album:		150.00	75.00	45.00
(1)	Larry Barton	60.00	30.00	18.00

1952 Ventura Braves Team Issue

These 2-1/4" x 3-3/8" black-and-white, unnumbered, blank-backed cards were one of many minor league team sets issued by Globe Printing of San Jose, Calif., in the early 1950s. Cards were usually given away at the ballpark on a one-per-week or one-per-homestand basis, accounting for the rarity of surviving complete sets. It is known that 18 V-Braves were issued in this set, though only 14 have been checklisted to date. The team was a Class C California League farm club of the Boston Braves.

		NM	EX	VG
Common Player:		60.00	30.00	18.00
Album:		100.00	50.00	30.00
(1)	Al Aguilar	60.00	30.00	18.00
(2)	Bud Belardi	60.00	30.00	18.00
(3)	Frank Followell	60.00	30.00	18.00
(4)	Glenn Hittner	60.00	30.00	18.00
(5)	Lee Kast	60.00	30.00	18.00
(6)	Richie Morse	60.00	30.00	18.00
(7)	Frank Nubin	60.00	30.00	18.00
(8)	George Owen	60.00	30.00	18.00
(9)	Manny Perez	60.00	30.00	18.00
(10)	Jose Perez	60.00	30.00	18.00
(11)	Harley Resh	60.00	30.00	18.00
(12)	Jack Schlarb	60.00	30.00	18.00
(13)	Bob Sturgeon	60.00	30.00	18.00
(14)	Billy Wells	60.00	30.00	18.00

W

1911 Western Playground Association

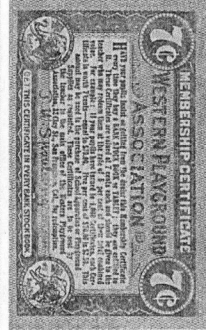

Stars from around the Pacific Coast League are featured on this rare and unusual issue. The 2-1/4" x 3-1/2" cards have a front design similar to contemporary Zeenuts cards: A dark brown border surrounding a sepia posed action picture (which appears to be a heavily retouched photo). Printed in white at left or right are "WESTERN PLAYGROUND ASSOCIATION / P.C. (or sometimes 'P.S.') LEAGUE" and the player's last name. Backs are a "Membership Certificate" indicating the cards could be redeemed for five percent of their seven-cent "face value" toward the purchase of school playground apparatus or supplies. The cards were received with the purchase of "Bank Stock" brand composition books.

	NM	EX	VG
Common Player:	9,000	4,500	2,700

(1)	Claude Berry	9,000	4,500	2,700
(2)	Roy Brashear	9,000	4,500	2,700
(3)	Herb Byram	9,000	4,500	2,700
(4)	Walt Carlisle	9,000	4,500	2,700
(5)	Roy Caslleton (Castleton)	9,000	4,500	2,700
(6)	Chet Chadborne (Chadbourne)	9,000	4,500	2,700
(7)	Tyler Christian	9,000	4,500	2,700
(8)	Bert Coy	9,000	4,500	2,700
(9)	Pete Daley	9,000	4,500	2,700
(10)	Pop Dillon	9,000	4,500	2,700
(11)	Joe French	9,000	4,500	2,700
(12)	Howie Gregory	9,000	4,500	2,700
(13)	Spec Harkness	9,000	4,500	2,700
(14)	Heinie Heitmuller	9,000	4,500	2,700
(15)	Ben Henderson	9,000	4,500	2,700
(16)	Cack Henley	9,000	4,500	2,700
(17)	Izzy Hoffman	9,000	4,500	2,700
(18)	Happy Hogan	9,000	4,500	2,700
(19)	Johnny Kane	9,000	4,500	2,700
(20)	Jimmy Lewis	9,000	4,500	2,700
(21)	Tom Madden	9,000	4,500	2,700
(22)	Chris Mahoney	9,000	4,500	2,700
(23)	George Metzger	9,000	4,500	2,700
(24)	Fred Miller	9,000	4,500	2,700
(25)	Kid Mohler	9,000	4,500	2,700
(26)	Walter Nagle	9,000	4,500	2,700
(27)	Patsy O'Rourke	9,000	4,500	2,700
(28)	Ham Patterson	9,000	4,500	2,700
(29)	Roger Peckinpaugh	9,000	4,500	2,700
(30)	Bill Rapps	9,000	4,500	2,700
(31)	Bill Rogers (Rodgers)	9,000	4,500	2,700
(32)	Buddy Ryan	9,000	4,500	2,700
(33)	Walter Schmitt (Schmidt)	9,000	4,500	2,700
(34)	Tom Seaton	9,000	4,500	2,700
(35)	Jerry Sheehan	9,000	4,500	2,700
(36)	Harry Stewart	9,000	4,500	2,700
(37)	George Stinson	9,000	4,500	2,700
(38)	Harry Suter (Sutor)	9,000	4,500	2,700
(39)	Harry Wolverton	9,000	4,500	2,700
(40)	Elmer Zacher	9,000	4,500	2,700

1932 Wheaties Minneapolis Millers

Because of their similarity to the 1933 issue which carried Wheaties advertising on the back, these postcard-size photos of the 1932 Millers are believed to also have been issued by the Minneapolis-based cereal company. The 3-7/16" x 5-7/16" cards have black-and-white portraits or posed action photos on front, along with a facsimile autograph. Backs are blank.

		NM	EX	VG
	Complete Set (24):	1,350	700.00	400.00
	Common Player:	60.00	30.00	20.00
(1)	J.C. "Rube" Benton	60.00	30.00	20.00
(2)	Donie Bush	60.00	30.00	20.00
(3)	Andy Cohen	70.00	35.00	20.00
(4)	"Pea Ridge" Day	60.00	30.00	20.00
(5)	Ray Fitzgerald	60.00	30.00	20.00
(6)	F.P. "Babe" Ganzel	60.00	30.00	20.00
(7)	Wes Griffin	60.00	30.00	20.00
(8)	Spencer Harris	60.00	30.00	20.00
(9)	Joe Hauser	120.00	60.00	40.00
(10)	Frank J. "Dutch" Henry	60.00	30.00	20.00
(11)	Phil Hensick	60.00	30.00	20.00
(12)	Bunker Hill	60.00	30.00	20.00
(13)	Joe Mowry	60.00	30.00	20.00
(14)	Jess Petty	60.00	30.00	20.00
(15)	Paul Richards	70.00	35.00	20.00
(16)	Bill Rodda	60.00	30.00	20.00
(17)	Harry Rose	60.00	30.00	20.00
(18)	Art Ruble	60.00	30.00	20.00
(19)	"Rosy" Ryan	60.00	30.00	20.00
(20)	Al Sheehan	60.00	30.00	20.00
(21)	Ed Sicking	60.00	30.00	20.00
(22)	Ernie Smith	60.00	30.00	20.00
(23)	Hy Van Denberg	60.00	30.00	20.00
(24)	E.R. Vangilder	60.00	30.00	20.00

1933 Wheaties Minneapolis Millers

Prior to printing their first major league baseball cards on the backs of cereal boxes in 1935, Wheaties sponsored a minor league set for the hometown Minneapolis Millers in 1933. The 4" x 5-3/4" cards have a sepia-toned posed action photo on front, along with a facsimile autograph. The player's name, position, team and year are printed in the bottom border. The postcard back, printed in black-and-white, has a drawing of a Wheaties box and an ad for the cereal. All unmailed examples seen to date have a purple rubber-stamped "VOID" in the postage box at top. The unnumbered cards are checklisted here alphabetically.

		NM	EX	VG
	Complete Set (24):	2,250	1,125	650.00
	Common Player:	90.00	45.00	27.00
(1)	Dave Bancroft	150.00	75.00	45.00
(2)	Rube Benton	90.00	45.00	27.00
(3)	Andy Cohen	150.00	75.00	45.00
(4)	Bob Fothergill	90.00	45.00	27.00
(5)	"Babe" Ganzel	90.00	45.00	27.00
(6)	Joe Glenn	90.00	45.00	27.00
(7)	Wes Griffin	90.00	45.00	27.00
(8)	Jack Hallet	90.00	45.00	27.00
(9)	Jerry Harrington (Announcer)	90.00	45.00	27.00
(10)	Spencer Harris	100.00	50.00	30.00
(11)	Joe Hauser	200.00	100.00	60.00
(12)	Butch Henline	90.00	45.00	27.00
(13)	Walter Hilcher	90.00	45.00	27.00
(14)	Dutch Holland	90.00	45.00	27.00
(15)	Harry Holsclaw	90.00	45.00	27.00
(16)	Wes Kingdon	90.00	45.00	27.00
(17)	George Murray	90.00	45.00	27.00
(18)	Leo Norris	90.00	45.00	27.00
(19)	Jess Petty	90.00	45.00	27.00
(20)	Art Ruble	90.00	45.00	27.00
(21)	Al Sheehan (Announcer)	90.00	45.00	27.00
(22)	Ernie Smith	90.00	45.00	27.00
(23)	Wally Tauscher	90.00	45.00	27.00
(24)	Hy VanDenburg	90.00	45.00	27.00

1933 Wheaties Seattle Indians

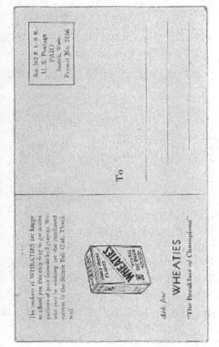

Prior to printing their first major league baseball cards on the backs of cereal boxes in 1935, Wheaties sponsored a minor league set for the Seattle Indians in 1933. The 4-1/8" x 7" cards have a sepia-toned posed portrait or action photo on front, along with a facsimile autograph. The player's name, position, team and year are printed in the bottom border. The postcard back, printed in black-and-white, has a drawing of a Wheaties box and an ad for the cereal. The unnumbered cards are checklisted here alphabetically; it is likely this list is incomplete.

		NM	EX	VG
	Common Player:	450.00	225.00	135.00
(1)	George Burns	600.00	300.00	180.00
(2)	Joe Coscarart	450.00	225.00	135.00
(3)	Leo Lassen ((Broadcaster))	450.00	225.00	135.00
(4)	Bill Radonits	450.00	225.00	135.00
(5)	"Junk" Walters	450.00	225.00	135.00

1912 Whitehead & Hoag P.C.L. Pins

A paper insert originally in the back of these pins identifies the maker as Whitehead & Hoag of San Francisco. The 7/8" diameter celluloid pins are printed in either black or blue on a white background. A player portrait photo is at center, with his last name below. Above is the city of his team and the Pacific Coast League initials. Listed in the "American Card Catalog" as PM5, the unnumbered pins are checklisted here alphabetically; it's possible additional pins in the issue remain to be reported. All pins seen are Oakland players except McCredie, Shehann, Rapp, and Seaton (Portland) as well as Berry (San Fransisco).

		NM	EX	VG
	Complete Set (26):	15,000	7,500	4,500
	Common Player:	600.00	300.00	180.00
(1)	Harry Ables	600.00	300.00	180.00
(2)	Claude Berry	600.00	300.00	180.00
(3)	Tyler Christian	600.00	300.00	180.00
(4)	Al Cook	600.00	300.00	180.00
(5)	Bert Coy	600.00	300.00	180.00
(6)	Jack Flater	600.00	300.00	180.00
(7)	Howie Gregory	600.00	300.00	180.00
(8)	Joe Hamilton	600.00	300.00	180.00
(9)	Gus Hetling	600.00	300.00	180.00
(10a)	Hille	600.00	300.00	180.00
(10b)	Mgr. Hille	600.00	300.00	180.00
(11)	Izzy Hoffman	600.00	300.00	180.00
(12)	Bill Leard	600.00	300.00	180.00
(13)	Bill Malarkey	600.00	300.00	180.00
(14)	Elmer Martinoni	600.00	300.00	180.00
(15)	Walter McCredie	600.00	300.00	180.00
(16)	Honus Mitze	600.00	300.00	180.00
(17)	Cy Parkins	600.00	300.00	180.00
(18)	Ashley Pope	600.00	300.00	180.00
(19)	Bill Rapp (Rapps)	600.00	300.00	180.00
(20)	Tom Seaton	600.00	300.00	180.00
(21a)	Bud Sharpe	600.00	300.00	180.00
(21b)	Mgr. Sharpe	600.00	300.00	180.00
(22)	Tommy Sheehan	600.00	300.00	180.00
(23)	Smith	600.00	300.00	180.00
(24)	John Tiedeman (Tiedemann)	600.00	300.00	180.00
(25)	Eddie Wilkinson	600.00	300.00	180.00
(26)	Elmer Zacher	600.00	300.00	180.00

1919 Winkelman's Quaker Bread Pins

This issue of 1-1/4" diameter celluloid pinback buttons features members of the Memphis Chickasaws in black-and-white portraits on a pale yellow background, surrounded by an orange border with the sponsor's advertising. A large turtle is pictured at bottom. Currently only three players are known, though it is likely more were issued.

		NM	EX	VG
	Common Player:	1,300	650.00	400.00
(1)	Baerwald	1,300	650.00	400.00
(2)	Carey	1,300	650.00	400.00
(3)	Bob Coulson	1,300	650.00	400.00

1933-35 Worch Cigar American Association

Though the issuer is not identified anywhere on these blank-backed, 3-7/16" x 5-7/16" black-and-white cards (though some are found with a box on front crediting the photo to the St. Paul Daily News, or the Minneapolis Star or Journal), the individual player photos were available as premiums for redemption of cigar bands by the Worch Cigar Co., of St. Paul, Minn. The issue is similar in format to the major league cards of the same era, and indeed the cards were offered together. Most collectors prefer to chase either the major leaguers or the minor leaguers independently, so they are cataloged in that fashion. The set encompasses players from the 1932-35 Minneapolis Millers, the 1933 St. Paul Saints and a handful from the Columbus Redbirds, Kansas City Blues and a few other teams. The unnumbered cards are checklisted below alphabetically. Player identification is presented in several different styles and may include just the last name or also the first name. Several players are known in more than one pose. The checklist here is likely incomplete.

		NM	EX	VG
Common Player:		90.00	45.00	27.00
(1)	Dave Bancroft	200.00	100.00	60.00
(2)	Clyde Beck	90.00	45.00	27.00
(3)	Rube Benton	90.00	45.00	27.00
(4)	W. Berger	90.00	45.00	27.00
(5)	Brannon	90.00	45.00	27.00
(6)	Spurgeon Chandler	90.00	45.00	27.00
(7)	Tiny Chaplin	90.00	45.00	27.00
(8)	Andy Cohen	90.00	45.00	27.00
(9)	Nick Cullop	90.00	45.00	27.00
(10)	Bob Fenner	90.00	45.00	27.00
(11)	Fischall	90.00	45.00	27.00
(12)	Gaffke	90.00	45.00	27.00
(13)	Foster Ganzel	90.00	45.00	27.00
(14)	Foster Ganzel	90.00	45.00	27.00
(15)	Louis Garland	90.00	45.00	27.00
(16)	Johnny Gill	90.00	45.00	27.00
(17)	Joe Glenn	90.00	45.00	27.00
(18)	Angelo Guiliani	90.00	45.00	27.00
(19)	Pinky Hargrave	90.00	45.00	27.00
(20)	Slim Harriss	90.00	45.00	27.00
(21)	Spencer Harris (bating, front view)	90.00	45.00	27.00
(22)	Spencer Harris (bating, side view)	90.00	45.00	27.00
(23)	Joe Hauser	150.00	75.00	45.00
(24)	Walter Henline	90.00	45.00	27.00
(25)	Phil Hensick	90.00	45.00	27.00
(26)	Walter Hilcher	90.00	45.00	27.00
(27)	Jesse Hill	90.00	45.00	27.00
(28)	Dutch Holland (batting, facng left)	90.00	45.00	27.00
(29)	Dutch Holland (batting, facing right)	90.00	45.00	27.00
(30)	Harry Holsclaw	90.00	45.00	27.00
(31)	Meredith Hopkins	90.00	45.00	27.00
(32)	Irvine Jeffries	90.00	45.00	27.00
(33)	Monk Joyner	90.00	45.00	27.00
(34)	Fred Koster	90.00	45.00	27.00
(35)	Walter Mails	90.00	45.00	27.00
(36)	Chuck Marrow	90.00	45.00	27.00
(37)	Emmett McCann	90.00	45.00	27.00
(38)	Marty McManus	90.00	45.00	27.00
(39)	Joe Mowry	90.00	45.00	27.00
(40)	Les Munns	90.00	45.00	27.00
(41)	George Murray	90.00	45.00	27.00
(42)	Floyd Newkirk	90.00	45.00	27.00
(43)	Leo Norris	90.00	45.00	27.00
(44)	Frank Packard	90.00	45.00	27.00
(45)	Ben Paschal	90.00	45.00	27.00
(46a)	Jess Petty/Throwing (Right foot off ground.)	90.00	45.00	27.00
(46b)	Jess Petty	90.00	45.00	27.00
(47)	Ray Radcliff	90.00	45.00	27.00
(48)	Larry Rosenthal	90.00	45.00	27.00
(49a)	Art Ruble	90.00	45.00	27.00
(49b)	Art Ruble	90.00	45.00	27.00
(50)	Art Shires	90.00	45.00	27.00
(51a)	Ernest Smith	90.00	45.00	27.00
(52b)	Ernest Smith	90.00	45.00	27.00
(53)	Ray Starr	90.00	45.00	27.00
(54)	Monty Stratton	300.00	150.00	90.00
(55)	Walter Tauscher	90.00	45.00	27.00
(56)	Myles Thomas	90.00	45.00	27.00
(57)	Phil Todt	90.00	45.00	27.00
(58)	Gene Trow	90.00	45.00	27.00
(59	Hy Van Denburg	90.00	45.00	27.00
(60)	Elam Van Gilder	90.00	45.00	27.00
(61)	Charles Wilson	90.00	45.00	27.00
(62)	Ab. Wright	90.00	45.00	27.00
(63)	Emil Yde	90.00	45.00	27.00
(64)	Russ Young	90.00	45.00	27.00

Z

1911 Zeenut Pacific Coast League

Produced annually for 28 years, these Pacific Coast League cards were the longest-running and most popular baseball issues ever to appear on the West Coast. Issued by the Collins-McCarthy Candy Co. (later known as the Collins-Hencke Candy Co. and then simply the Collins Candy Co.) of San Francisco, Zeenut cards were inserted in boxes of the company's products: Zeenuts, Ruf-Neks and Home Run Kisses. All Zeenut cards issued from 1913 through 1937 had an approximately half-inch coupon at the bottom that could be redeemed for various prizes. Since most of these coupons were removed (and many not too carefully) Zeenuts are difficult to find in top condition today, and only a very small percentage survived with the coupon intact. (The sizes listed in the following descriptions are for cards without coupons.) Over the 28-year span, it is estimated that nearly 3,700 different cards were issued as part of the Zeenuts series, but new discoveries are still being made, and the checklist continues to grow. It is sometimes difficult to differentiate one year from another after 1930. Because it is so rare to find Zeenuts cards with the coupon still attached, values listed are for cards without the coupon. Cards with the coupon still intact will generally command a significant premium. The first Zeenut cards measure about 2-1/8" x 4" and feature a sepia-toned photo on a brown background surrounded by an off-white border. The backs of the cards are blank. Although the 1911 cards did not include the coupon bottom, some cards have been found with punch holes, indicating they may have also been used for redemptions. A total of 122 different players have been found.

		NM	EX	VG
Common Player:		350.00	175.00	105.00
(1)	Abbott	350.00	175.00	105.00
(2)	Ables	350.00	175.00	105.00
(3a)	Agnew (Large pose.)	350.00	175.00	105.00
(3b)	Agnew (Small pose.)	350.00	175.00	105.00
(4a)	Akin (Large pose.)	350.00	175.00	105.00
(4b)	Akin (Small pose.)	350.00	175.00	105.00
(5)	Frank Arellanes	350.00	175.00	105.00
(6a)	Arlett (Large pose.)	350.00	175.00	105.00
(6b)	Arlett (Middle size pose.)	350.00	175.00	105.00
(6c)	Arlett (Small pose.)	350.00	175.00	105.00
(7)	Barry	350.00	175.00	105.00
(8)	Baum	350.00	175.00	105.00
(9)	Bernard	350.00	175.00	105.00
(10)	Berry	350.00	175.00	105.00
(11)	Bohen (Card is not known in high grade.)		5,000	2,500
(12)	Brackenridge	350.00	175.00	105.00
(13)	Brashear	350.00	175.00	105.00
(14a)	Brown (Large pose.)	350.00	175.00	105.00
(14b)	Brown (Small pose.)	350.00	175.00	105.00
(15)	Browning	350.00	175.00	105.00
(16a)	Burrell (Large pose.)	350.00	175.00	105.00
(16b)	Burrell (Small pose.)	350.00	175.00	105.00
(17)	Byram	350.00	175.00	105.00
(18)	Carlisle	350.00	175.00	105.00
(19)	Carman	350.00	175.00	105.00
(20a)	Carson (Large pose.)	350.00	175.00	105.00
(20b)	Carson (Middle size pose.)	350.00	175.00	105.00
(20c)	Carson (Small pose.)	350.00	175.00	105.00
(21)	Castleton	350.00	175.00	105.00
(22)	Chadbourne	350.00	175.00	105.00
(23)	Christian	350.00	175.00	105.00
(24)	Couchman	350.00	175.00	105.00
(25)	Coy	350.00	175.00	105.00
(26)	Criger	350.00	175.00	105.00
(27)	Cutshaw	350.00	175.00	105.00
(28)	Daley	350.00	175.00	105.00
(29)	Danzig	350.00	175.00	105.00
(30)	Delhi	350.00	175.00	105.00
(31a)	Delmas (Large pose.)	350.00	175.00	105.00
(31b)	Delmas (Small pose.)	350.00	175.00	105.00
(32)	Dillon	350.00	175.00	105.00
(33a)	Discoll (Name incorrect.)	350.00	175.00	105.00
(33b)	Driscoll (Name correct.)	350.00	175.00	105.00
(34)	Dulin	350.00	175.00	105.00
(35)	Fanning	350.00	175.00	105.00
(36)	Fitzgerald	350.00	175.00	105.00
(37)	Flater	350.00	175.00	105.00
(38)	French	350.00	175.00	105.00
(39)	Fullerton	350.00	175.00	105.00
(40)	Gleason	350.00	175.00	105.00
(41)	Gregory	350.00	175.00	105.00
(42)	Halla	825.00	430.00	260.00
(43)	Harkness	350.00	175.00	105.00
(44a)	Heitmuller (Large pose.)	650.00	325.00	195.00
(44b)	Heitmuller (Small pose.)	350.00	175.00	105.00
(45)	Henley	350.00	175.00	105.00
(46)	Hetling	350.00	175.00	105.00
(47)	Hiester	350.00	175.00	105.00
(48a)	Hitt (Large pose.)	350.00	175.00	105.00
(48b)	Hitt (Small pose.)	350.00	175.00	105.00
(50)	Hoffman	350.00	175.00	105.00
(51)	Hogan	350.00	175.00	105.00
(52a)	Holland (Large pose.)	350.00	175.00	105.00
(52b)	Holland (Small pose.)	350.00	175.00	105.00
(53)	Hosp	350.00	175.00	105.00
(54a)	Howard (Large pose.)	350.00	175.00	105.00
(54b)	Howard (Small pose.)	350.00	175.00	105.00
(55)	Kane	350.00	175.00	105.00
(56)	Kerns	350.00	175.00	105.00
(57)	Kilroy	350.00	175.00	105.00
(58)	Knight	350.00	175.00	105.00
(59)	Koestner	350.00	175.00	105.00
(60)	Krueger	350.00	175.00	105.00
(61)	Kuhn	350.00	175.00	105.00
(62)	LaLonge	350.00	175.00	105.00
(63)	Lerchen	350.00	175.00	105.00
(64)	Leverenz	350.00	175.00	105.00
(65)	Lewis	350.00	175.00	105.00
(66)	Bill Lindsay	350.00	175.00	105.00
(67)	Lober	350.00	175.00	105.00
(68)	Madden	350.00	175.00	105.00
(69)	Maggert	350.00	175.00	105.00
(70)	Mahoney	350.00	175.00	105.00
(71)	Martinoni	350.00	175.00	105.00
(72)	McArdle	350.00	175.00	105.00
(73)	McCredie	350.00	175.00	105.00
(74)	McDonnell	350.00	175.00	105.00
(75a)	McKune (Large pose.)	350.00	175.00	105.00
(75b)	McKune (Middle size pose.)	350.00	175.00	105.00
(75c)	McKune (Small pose.)	350.00	175.00	105.00
(76)	Meikle	350.00	175.00	105.00
(77)	Melchior	350.00	175.00	105.00
(78)	Metzger	350.00	175.00	105.00
(79)	Miller	350.00	175.00	105.00
(80)	Mitze	350.00	175.00	105.00
(81)	Mohler	350.00	175.00	105.00
(82a)	Moore (Large pose.)	350.00	175.00	105.00
(82b)	Moore (Small pose.)	350.00	175.00	105.00
(83a)	Moskiman (Lettering size large.)	350.00	175.00	105.00
(83b)	Moskiman (Lettering size small.)	350.00	175.00	105.00
(84)	Murray	350.00	175.00	105.00
(85)	Naylor	350.00	175.00	105.00
(86)	Nebinger	350.00	175.00	105.00
(87)	Nourse	350.00	175.00	105.00
(88a)	Noyes (Large pose.)	350.00	175.00	105.00
(88b)	Noyes (Small pose.)	350.00	175.00	105.00
(89)	O'Rourke	350.00	175.00	105.00
(90)	Patterson (Oakland)	350.00	175.00	105.00
(91)	Patterson (Vernon)	350.00	175.00	105.00
(92)	Pearce	350.00	175.00	105.00
(93)	Peckinpaugh	750.00	375.00	225.00
(94)	Pernoll	350.00	175.00	105.00
(95)	Pfyl	350.00	175.00	105.00
(96)	Powell	350.00	175.00	105.00
(97a)	Raleigh (Large pose.)	350.00	175.00	105.00
(97b)	Raleigh (Small pose.)	350.00	175.00	105.00
(98)	Rapps	350.00	175.00	105.00
(99)	Rodgers	350.00	175.00	105.00
(100a)	Ryan (Portland, box around name and team.)	450.00	225.00	150.00
(100b)	Ryan (Portland, no box around name and team.)	350.00	175.00	105.00
(101)	Ryan (San Francisco)	350.00	175.00	105.00
(102)	Seaton	350.00	175.00	105.00
(103)	Shaw	350.00	175.00	105.00
(104)	Sheehan	350.00	175.00	105.00
(105)	Shinn	350.00	175.00	105.00
106a	Smith (Los Angeles, large pose.)	350.00	175.00	105.00
(106b)	Smith (Los Angeles, small pose.)	350.00	175.00	105.00
(107a)	Smith (San Francisco, large pose.)	350.00	175.00	105.00
(107b)	Smith (San Francisco, small pose.)	350.00	175.00	105.00
(108)	Steen	350.00	175.00	105.00
(109)	Stewart	350.00	175.00	105.00
(110a)	Stinson (Large pose.)	350.00	175.00	105.00
(110b)	Stinson (Small pose.)	350.00	175.00	105.00
(111)	Sutor (Suter)	350.00	175.00	105.00
(112)	Tennant	350.00	175.00	105.00
(113)	Thomas	350.00	175.00	105.00
(114)	Thompson	350.00	175.00	105.00
(115)	Thornton	350.00	175.00	105.00
(116)	Tiedeman	350.00	175.00	105.00
(117)	Van Buren	350.00	175.00	105.00
(118)	Vitt	350.00	175.00	105.00
(119)	Wares	350.00	175.00	105.00
(120)	Buck Weaver	14,000	5,500	3,500
(121)	Wolverton	350.00	175.00	105.00
(122)	Zacher	350.00	175.00	105.00
(123)	Zamloch	350.00	175.00	105.00

1912 Zeenut Pacific Coast League

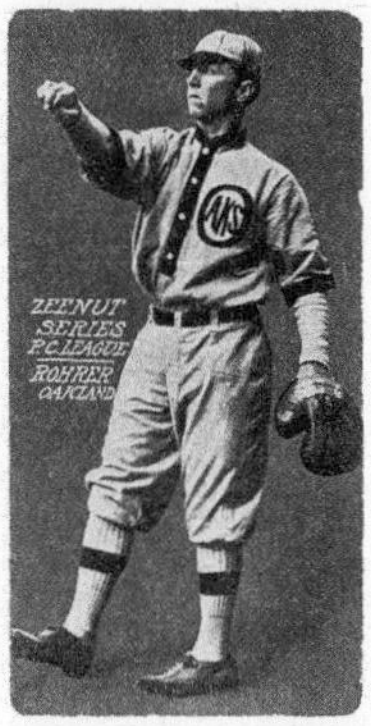

The second series of Zeenut cards measure about 2-1/8" x 4-1/16" and featured sepia-toned photographs on a brown background with no border. Most cards have blank backs, but some have been found with printing advising collectors to "Save Zeenut pictures for valuable premiums," or with one of two sizes of a Bardell logo. The checklist consists of 158 subjects, but more cards are still being discovered. Zeenut cards which were redeemed for prizes will exhibit a hole-punch cancellation, often heart-shaped.

		NM	EX	VG
Common Player:		125.00	65.00	45.00
(1)	Abbott	125.00	65.00	45.00
(2)	Ables	125.00	65.00	45.00
(3)	Agnew	125.00	65.00	45.00
(4)	Altman	125.00	65.00	45.00
(5)	Frank Arellanes	125.00	65.00	45.00
(6)	Auer	125.00	65.00	45.00
(7)	Baker (Horizontal pose.)	125.00	65.00	45.00
(8)	Baker (Vertical pose.)	125.00	65.00	45.00
(9)	Bancroft	3,000	1,500	900.00
(10)	Baum	125.00	65.00	45.00
(11)	Bayless	125.00	65.00	45.00
(12)	Berger	125.00	65.00	45.00
(13)	Berry	125.00	65.00	45.00
(14)	Bohen	125.00	65.00	45.00
(15)	Boles	125.00	65.00	45.00
(16)	Bonner	125.00	65.00	45.00
(17)	Boone	125.00	65.00	45.00
(18)	Brackenridge	125.00	65.00	45.00
(19)	Brashear	125.00	65.00	45.00
(20)	Breen	125.00	65.00	45.00
(21)	Brooks (Los Angeles)	125.00	65.00	45.00
(22)	Brooks (Oakland)	125.00	65.00	45.00
(23)	Brown	125.00	65.00	45.00
(24)	Burch	125.00	65.00	45.00
(25)	Burrell	125.00	65.00	45.00
(26)	Butcher	125.00	65.00	45.00
(27)	Butler	125.00	65.00	45.00
(28)	Byram	125.00	65.00	45.00
(29)	Carlisle	125.00	65.00	45.00
(30)	Carson	125.00	65.00	45.00
(31)	Castleton	125.00	65.00	45.00
(32)	Chadbourne	125.00	65.00	45.00
(33)	Chech	125.00	65.00	45.00
(34)	Cheek	125.00	65.00	45.00
(35)	Christian	125.00	65.00	45.00
(36)	Cook	125.00	65.00	45.00
(37)	Core	125.00	65.00	45.00
(38)	Corhan	125.00	65.00	45.00
(39)	Coy	125.00	65.00	45.00
(40)	Daley	125.00	65.00	45.00
(41)	Delhi	125.00	65.00	45.00
(42)	Dillon	125.00	65.00	45.00
(43)	Doane	125.00	65.00	45.00
(44)	Driscoll	125.00	65.00	45.00
(45)	Durbin	125.00	65.00	45.00
(46)	Fanning	125.00	65.00	45.00
(47)	Felts	125.00	65.00	45.00
(48)	Fisher	125.00	65.00	45.00
(49)	Fitzgerald	125.00	65.00	45.00
(50)	Flater	125.00	65.00	45.00
(51)	Frick	125.00	65.00	45.00
(52)	Gaddy	125.00	65.00	45.00
(53)	Gedeon	125.00	65.00	45.00
(54)	Gilligan	125.00	65.00	45.00
(55)	Girot	125.00	65.00	45.00
(56)	Gray	125.00	65.00	45.00
(57)	Gregg	125.00	65.00	45.00
(58)	Gregory	125.00	65.00	45.00
(59)	Halla	125.00	65.00	45.00
(60)	Hamilton (Oakland)	125.00	65.00	45.00
(61)	Hamilton (San Francisco)	125.00	65.00	45.00
(62)	Harkness	125.00	65.00	45.00
(63)	Hartley	125.00	65.00	45.00
(64)	Heitmuller	125.00	65.00	45.00
(65)	Henley	125.00	65.00	45.00
(66)	Hetling (Glove open.)	125.00	65.00	45.00
(67)	Hetling (Glove closed.)	125.00	65.00	45.00
(68)	Hiester	125.00	65.00	45.00
(69)	Higginbottom	125.00	65.00	45.00
(70)	Hitt	125.00	65.00	45.00
(71)	Hoffman	125.00	65.00	45.00
(72)	Hogan	125.00	65.00	45.00
(73)	Hosp	125.00	65.00	45.00
(74)	Howard	125.00	65.00	45.00
(75)	Howley	125.00	65.00	45.00
(76)	Ireland	125.00	65.00	45.00
(77)	Jackson	125.00	65.00	45.00
(78)	Johnson	125.00	65.00	45.00
(79)	Kane	125.00	65.00	45.00
(80)	Killilay	125.00	65.00	45.00
(81)	Klawitter	125.00	65.00	45.00
(82)	Knight	125.00	65.00	45.00
(83)	Koestner ("P" visible.)	125.00	65.00	45.00
(84)	Koestner (No "P" visible.)	125.00	65.00	45.00
(85)	Kreitz	125.00	65.00	45.00
(86)	Krueger	125.00	65.00	45.00
(87)	LaLonge	125.00	65.00	45.00
(88)	Leard	125.00	65.00	45.00
(89)	Leverenz	125.00	65.00	45.00
(90)	Lewis	125.00	65.00	45.00
(91)	Bill Lindsay	125.00	65.00	45.00
(92)	Litschi	125.00	65.00	45.00
(93)	Lober	125.00	65.00	45.00
(94)	Madden	125.00	65.00	45.00
(95)	Mahoney	125.00	65.00	45.00
(96)	Malarkey	125.00	65.00	45.00
(97)	Martinoni	125.00	65.00	45.00
(98)	McArdle	125.00	65.00	45.00
(99)	McAvoy	125.00	65.00	45.00
(100)	McCorrey	125.00	65.00	45.00
(101)	McCredie	125.00	65.00	45.00
(102)	McDonald	125.00	65.00	45.00
(103)	McDowell	125.00	65.00	45.00
(104)	McIver	125.00	65.00	45.00
(105)	Meikle	125.00	65.00	45.00
(106)	Metzger	125.00	65.00	45.00
(107)	Miller (Sacramento)	125.00	65.00	45.00
(108)	Miller (San Francisco)	125.00	65.00	45.00
(109)	Mitze	125.00	65.00	45.00
(110)	Mohler	125.00	65.00	45.00
(111)	Moore	125.00	65.00	45.00
(112)	Mundorf (Batting)	125.00	65.00	45.00
(113)	Mundorf (Fielding)	125.00	65.00	45.00
(114)	Nagle	125.00	65.00	45.00
(115)	Noyes	125.00	65.00	45.00
(116)	O'Rourke	125.00	65.00	45.00
(117)	Olmstead	125.00	65.00	45.00
(118)	Orr	125.00	65.00	45.00
(119)	Page	125.00	65.00	45.00
(120)	Parkins	125.00	65.00	45.00
(121)	Patterson (Oakland)	125.00	65.00	45.00
(122)	Patterson (Vernon)	125.00	65.00	45.00
(123)	Pernol	125.00	65.00	45.00
(124)	Pope	125.00	65.00	45.00
(125)	Powell	125.00	65.00	45.00
(126)	Price	125.00	65.00	45.00
(127)	Raftery	125.00	65.00	45.00
(128)	Raleigh	125.00	65.00	45.00
(129)	Rapps ("P" visible.)	125.00	65.00	45.00
(130)	Rapps (No "P" visible.)	125.00	65.00	45.00
(131)	Reidy	125.00	65.00	45.00
(132)	Rodgers	125.00	65.00	45.00
(133)	Rohrer	125.00	65.00	45.00
(134)	Schmidt	125.00	65.00	45.00
(135)	Schwenk	125.00	65.00	45.00
(136)	Sharpe	125.00	65.00	45.00
(137)	Sheehan	125.00	65.00	45.00
(138)	Shinn	125.00	65.00	45.00
(139)	Slagle	125.00	65.00	45.00
(140)	Smith	125.00	65.00	45.00
(141)	Stewart	125.00	65.00	45.00
(142)	Stinson	125.00	65.00	45.00
(143)	Stone	125.00	65.00	45.00
(144)	Sullivan	125.00	65.00	45.00
(145)	Swain	125.00	65.00	45.00
(146)	Taylor	125.00	65.00	45.00
(147)	Temple	125.00	65.00	45.00
(148)	Tiedeman	125.00	65.00	45.00
(149)	Toner	125.00	65.00	45.00
(150)	Tozer	125.00	65.00	45.00
(151)	Van Buren	125.00	65.00	45.00
(152)	Wagner	125.00	65.00	45.00
(153)	Whalen	125.00	65.00	45.00
(154)	Williams (Sacramento)	125.00	65.00	45.00
(155)	Williams (San Francisco)	125.00	65.00	45.00
(156)	Joe Williams	125.00	65.00	45.00
(157)	Wuffli	125.00	65.00	45.00
(158)	Zacher	125.00	65.00	45.00
(159)	Zimmerman	125.00	65.00	45.00

1913 Zeenut Pacific Coast League

The 1913 Zeenut cards measure about 2" x 3-3/4" without the coupon, and feature black-and-white photos on a white, borderless background. To date, 146 different poses have been found. The backs are blank.

		NM	EX	VG
Common Player:		125.00	65.00	45.00
(1)	Abbott	125.00	65.00	45.00
(2)	Ables	125.00	65.00	45.00
(3)	Frank Arelanes (Arellanes)	125.00	65.00	45.00
(4)	Arlett	125.00	65.00	45.00
(5)	Baker	125.00	65.00	45.00
(6)	Baum	125.00	65.00	45.00
(7)	Bayless	125.00	65.00	45.00
(8)	Becker	125.00	65.00	45.00
(9)	Berry	125.00	65.00	45.00
(10)	Bliss	125.00	65.00	45.00
(11)	Boles	125.00	65.00	45.00
(12)	Brackenridge	125.00	65.00	45.00
(13)	Brashear	125.00	65.00	45.00
(14)	Brooks	125.00	65.00	45.00
(15)	Byrnes	125.00	65.00	45.00
(16)	Cadreau	125.00	65.00	45.00
(17)	Carlisle	125.00	65.00	45.00
(18)	Carson	125.00	65.00	45.00
(19)	Cartwright	125.00	65.00	45.00
(20)	Chadbourne	125.00	65.00	45.00
(21)	Charles	125.00	65.00	45.00
(22)	Cheek	125.00	65.00	45.00
(23)	Christian	125.00	65.00	45.00
(24)	Clarke	125.00	65.00	45.00
(25)	Clemons	125.00	65.00	45.00
(26)	Cook	125.00	65.00	45.00
(27)	Corhan	125.00	65.00	45.00
(28)	Coy	125.00	65.00	45.00
(29)	Crabb	125.00	65.00	45.00
(30)	Crisp	125.00	65.00	45.00
(31)	Derrick	125.00	65.00	45.00
(32)	DeCanniere	125.00	65.00	45.00
(33)	Dillon	125.00	65.00	45.00
(34)	Doane	125.00	65.00	45.00
(35)	Douglass	125.00	65.00	45.00
(36)	Downs	125.00	65.00	45.00
(37)	Driscoll	125.00	65.00	45.00
(38)	Drucke	125.00	65.00	45.00
(39)	Elliott	125.00	65.00	45.00
(40)	Ellis	125.00	65.00	45.00
(41)	Fanning	125.00	65.00	45.00
(42)	Fisher	125.00	65.00	45.00
(43)	Fitzgerald	125.00	65.00	45.00
(44)	Gardner	125.00	65.00	45.00
(45)	Gill	125.00	65.00	45.00
(46)	Goodwin	125.00	65.00	45.00
(47a)	Gregory (Large pose.)	125.00	65.00	45.00
(47b)	Gregory (Small pose.)	125.00	65.00	45.00
(48)	Grey	125.00	65.00	45.00
(49)	Guest	125.00	65.00	45.00
(50)	Hagerman	125.00	65.00	45.00
(51)	Halla	125.00	65.00	45.00
(52)	Hallinan	125.00	65.00	45.00
(53)	Harry Heilmann	6,000	4,000	2,000
(54)	Henley	125.00	65.00	45.00
(55)	Hetling	125.00	65.00	45.00
(56)	Higginbotham	125.00	65.00	45.00
(57)	Hitt	125.00	65.00	45.00
(58)	Hoffman	125.00	65.00	45.00
(59)	Hogan (San Francisco)	125.00	65.00	45.00
(60)	Hogan (Vernon)	125.00	65.00	45.00
(61)	Hosp	125.00	65.00	45.00
(62)	Howard (Los Angeles)	125.00	65.00	45.00
(63)	Howard (San Francisco)	125.00	65.00	45.00
(64)	Hughes	125.00	65.00	45.00
(65)	Jackson	125.00	65.00	45.00
(66)	James	125.00	65.00	45.00
(67)	Johnson	125.00	65.00	45.00
(68)	Johnston	125.00	65.00	45.00
(69)	Kane	125.00	65.00	45.00
(70)	Kaylor	125.00	65.00	45.00
(71)	Kenworthy	125.00	65.00	45.00
(72)	Killilay	125.00	65.00	45.00
(73)	Klawitter	125.00	65.00	45.00
(74)	Koestner	125.00	65.00	45.00
(75)	Kores	125.00	65.00	45.00
(76)	Krapp	125.00	65.00	45.00
(77)	Kreitz	125.00	65.00	45.00
(78)	Krause	125.00	65.00	45.00
(79)	Krueger	125.00	65.00	45.00
(80)	Leard	125.00	65.00	45.00
(81)	Leifield	125.00	65.00	45.00
(82)	Lewis	125.00	65.00	45.00
(83)	Bill Lindsay	125.00	65.00	45.00
(84)	Litschi	125.00	65.00	45.00
(85)	Lively	125.00	65.00	45.00
(86)	Lober	125.00	65.00	45.00
(87)	Lohman	125.00	65.00	45.00
(88)	Maggart	125.00	65.00	45.00
(89)	Malarky	125.00	65.00	45.00
(90)	McArdle	125.00	65.00	45.00
(91)	McCarl	125.00	65.00	45.00
(92)	McCormick	125.00	65.00	45.00
(93)	McCorry	125.00	65.00	45.00
(94)	McCredie	125.00	65.00	45.00
(95)	McDonnell	125.00	65.00	45.00
(96)	Meloan	125.00	65.00	45.00
(97)	Metzger	125.00	65.00	45.00
(98)	Miller	125.00	65.00	45.00
(99)	Mitze	125.00	65.00	45.00
(100)	Moore	125.00	65.00	45.00
(101)	Moran	125.00	65.00	45.00
(102)	Mundorf	125.00	65.00	45.00
(103)	Munsell	125.00	65.00	45.00
(104)	Ness	125.00	65.00	45.00
(105)	O'Rourke	125.00	65.00	45.00
(106)	Overall	125.00	65.00	45.00
(107)	Page	125.00	65.00	45.00
(108)	Parkin	125.00	65.00	45.00
(109)	Patterson	125.00	65.00	45.00
(110)	Pearce	125.00	65.00	45.00
(111)	Pernoll	125.00	65.00	45.00
(112)	Perritt	125.00	65.00	45.00
(113)	Pope	125.00	65.00	45.00
(114)	Pruitt	125.00	65.00	45.00
(115)	Raleigh	125.00	65.00	45.00
(116)	Reitmyer	125.00	65.00	45.00
(117)	Riordan	125.00	65.00	45.00
(118)	Rodgers	125.00	65.00	45.00
(119)	Rogers	125.00	65.00	45.00

(120)	Rohrer	125.00	65.00	45.00
(121)	Ryan	125.00	65.00	45.00
(122)	Schaller	125.00	65.00	45.00
(123)	Schirm	125.00	65.00	45.00
(124)	Schmidt	125.00	65.00	45.00
(125)	Schulz	125.00	65.00	45.00
(126)	Sepulveda	125.00	65.00	45.00
(127)	Shinn	125.00	65.00	45.00
(128)	Spenger	125.00	65.00	45.00
(129)	Stanley	125.00	65.00	45.00
(130)	Stanridge	125.00	65.00	45.00
(131)	Stark	125.00	65.00	45.00
(132)	Sterritt	125.00	65.00	45.00
(133)	Stroud	125.00	65.00	45.00
(134)	Tennant	125.00	65.00	45.00
(135)	Thomas	125.00	65.00	45.00
(136)	Todd	125.00	65.00	45.00
(137)	Tonneman	125.00	65.00	45.00
(138)	Tozer	125.00	65.00	45.00
(139)	Van Buren	125.00	65.00	45.00
(140)	Wagner	125.00	65.00	45.00
(141)	West	125.00	65.00	45.00
(142)	Williams	125.00	65.00	45.00
(143)	Wolverton	125.00	65.00	45.00
(144)	Wotell	125.00	65.00	45.00
(145)	Wuffli	125.00	65.00	45.00
(146)	Young	125.00	65.00	45.00
(147)	Zacher	125.00	65.00	45.00
(148)	Zimmerman	125.00	65.00	45.00

1914 Zeenut Pacific Coast League

The 1914 Zeenut cards measure about 2" x 4-1/16" without the coupon, and feature black-and-white photos on a gray, borderless background. To date, 146 different poses have been found. The backs are blank.

		NM	EX	VG
Common Player:		100.00	50.00	30.00
(1)	Ables	100.00	50.00	30.00
(2)	Abstein	100.00	50.00	30.00
(3)	Alexander	100.00	50.00	30.00
(4)	Arbogast	100.00	50.00	30.00
(5)	Arlett	100.00	50.00	30.00
(6)	Frank Arrelanes (Arellanes)	100.00	50.00	30.00
(7)	Bancroft	1,000	700.00	300.00
(8)	Barham	100.00	50.00	30.00
(9)	Barrenkamp	100.00	50.00	30.00
(10)	Barton	100.00	50.00	30.00
(11)	Baum	100.00	50.00	30.00
(12)	Bayless	100.00	50.00	30.00
(13a)	Bliss (Large pose.)	100.00	50.00	30.00
(13b)	Bliss (Small pose.)	100.00	50.00	30.00
(14)	Boles	100.00	50.00	30.00
(15)	Borton	100.00	50.00	30.00
(16)	Brashear	100.00	50.00	30.00
(17)	Brenegan	100.00	50.00	30.00
(18)	Brooks	100.00	50.00	30.00
(19)	Brown	100.00	50.00	30.00
(20)	Butler	100.00	50.00	30.00
(21)	Jacinto Calvo	900.00	600.00	250.00
(22)	Carlisle	100.00	50.00	30.00
(23)	Cartwright	100.00	50.00	30.00
(24)	Charles	100.00	50.00	30.00
(25)	Chech	100.00	50.00	30.00
(26)	Christian	100.00	50.00	30.00
(27)	Clarke	100.00	50.00	30.00
(28)	Colligan	100.00	50.00	30.00
(29)	Cook	100.00	50.00	30.00
(31)	Coy	100.00	50.00	30.00
(32)	Crabb	100.00	50.00	30.00
(33)	Davis	100.00	50.00	30.00
(34)	Derrick	100.00	50.00	30.00
(35)	Devlin	100.00	50.00	30.00
(36)	DeCannier	100.00	50.00	30.00
(37)	Dillon	100.00	50.00	30.00
(38)	Doane	100.00	50.00	30.00
(39)	Downs	100.00	50.00	30.00
(40)	Ehmke	100.00	50.00	30.00
(41)	Elliott	100.00	50.00	30.00
(42)	Ellis	100.00	50.00	30.00
(43)	Evans	100.00	50.00	30.00
(44)	Fanning	100.00	50.00	30.00
(45)	Fisher	100.00	50.00	30.00
(46)	Fitzgerald	100.00	50.00	30.00
(47)	Fleharty	100.00	50.00	30.00
(48)	Frambach	100.00	50.00	30.00
(49)	Gardner	100.00	50.00	30.00
(50)	Gedeon	100.00	50.00	30.00
(51)	Geyer	100.00	50.00	30.00
(52)	Gianini	100.00	50.00	30.00
(53)	Gregory	100.00	50.00	30.00
(54)	Guest	100.00	50.00	30.00
(55)	Hallinan	100.00	50.00	30.00
(56)	Hannah	100.00	50.00	30.00
(57)	Harkness (Batting)	100.00	50.00	30.00
(58)	Haworth (Batting)	100.00	50.00	30.00
(59)	Haworth (Catching)	100.00	50.00	30.00
(60)	Henderson	100.00	50.00	30.00
(61)	Henley	100.00	50.00	30.00
(62)	Hern	100.00	50.00	30.00
(63)	Hettling	100.00	50.00	30.00
(64)	Higginbotham	100.00	50.00	30.00
(65)	Hitt	100.00	50.00	30.00
(66)	Hogan	100.00	50.00	30.00
(67a)	Hosp (Large pose.)	100.00	50.00	30.00
(67b)	Hosp (Small pose.)	100.00	50.00	30.00
(68)	Howard	100.00	50.00	30.00
(69)	Hughes (Los Angeles)	100.00	50.00	30.00
(70)	Hughes (San Francisco)	100.00	50.00	30.00
(71)	Johnson	100.00	50.00	30.00
(72)	Kane	100.00	50.00	30.00
(73)	Kaylor	100.00	50.00	30.00
(74)	Killilay	100.00	50.00	30.00
(75)	Klawitter	100.00	50.00	30.00
(76)	Klepfler	100.00	50.00	30.00
(77)	Kores	100.00	50.00	30.00
(78)	Kramer	100.00	50.00	30.00
(79)	Krause	100.00	50.00	30.00
(80a)	Leard (Large pose.)	100.00	50.00	30.00
(80b)	Leard (Small pose.)	100.00	50.00	30.00
(81)	Liefeld	100.00	50.00	30.00
(82)	Litschi	100.00	50.00	30.00
(83)	Lober	100.00	50.00	30.00
(84)	Loomis	100.00	50.00	30.00
(85)	Love	100.00	50.00	30.00
(86)	Lynn	100.00	50.00	30.00
(87)	Maggart	100.00	50.00	30.00
(88)	Malarkey	100.00	50.00	30.00
(89)	Martinoni	100.00	50.00	30.00
(90)	McArdle	100.00	50.00	30.00
(91)	McCredie	100.00	50.00	30.00
(92)	McDonald	100.00	50.00	30.00
(93)	Meek	100.00	50.00	30.00
(94)	Meloan	100.00	50.00	30.00
(95)	Menges	100.00	50.00	30.00
(96)	Metzger	100.00	50.00	30.00
(97)	Middleton	100.00	50.00	30.00
(98)	Mitze	100.00	50.00	30.00
(99)	Mohler	100.00	50.00	30.00
(100)	Moore	100.00	50.00	30.00
(101)	Moran	100.00	50.00	30.00
(102)	Mundorf	100.00	50.00	30.00
(103)	Murphy	100.00	50.00	30.00
(104)	Musser	100.00	50.00	30.00
(105)	Ness	100.00	50.00	30.00
(106)	O'Leary	100.00	50.00	30.00
(107)	Orr	100.00	50.00	30.00
(108)	Page	100.00	50.00	30.00
(109)	Pape	100.00	50.00	30.00
(110)	Parkin	100.00	50.00	30.00
(111a)	Peet (Large pose.)	100.00	50.00	30.00
(111b)	Peet (Small pose.)	100.00	50.00	30.00
(112)	Perkins	100.00	50.00	30.00
(113)	Pernoll	100.00	50.00	30.00
(114)	Perritt	100.00	50.00	30.00
(115)	Powell	100.00	50.00	30.00
(116)	Prough	100.00	50.00	30.00
(117)	Pruiett	100.00	50.00	30.00
(118)	Quinlan	100.00	50.00	30.00
(119a)	Raney (Incorrect spelling.)	100.00	50.00	30.00
(119b)	Ramey (Correct spelling.)	100.00	50.00	30.00
(120)	Rieger	100.00	50.00	30.00
(121)	Rodgers	100.00	50.00	30.00
(122)	Rogers	100.00	50.00	30.00
(123)	Rohrer	100.00	50.00	30.00
(124)	Ryan	100.00	50.00	30.00
(125)	Ryan	100.00	50.00	30.00
(126)	Sawyer	100.00	50.00	30.00
(127)	Schaller	100.00	50.00	30.00
(128	Schmidt	100.00	50.00	30.00
(129)	Sepulveda	100.00	50.00	30.00
(130)	Shinn	100.00	50.00	30.00
(131)	Slagle	100.00	50.00	30.00
(132)	Speas	100.00	50.00	30.00
(133)	Stanridge	100.00	50.00	30.00
(134)	Stroud	100.00	50.00	30.00
(135)	Tennant	100.00	50.00	30.00
(136	Tobin	100.00	50.00	30.00
(137)	Tozer	100.00	50.00	30.00
(138)	Van Buren	100.00	50.00	30.00
(139)	West	100.00	50.00	30.00
(140)	White	100.00	50.00	30.00
(141)	Wolter	100.00	50.00	30.00
(142)	Wolverton	100.00	50.00	30.00
(143)	Yantz	100.00	50.00	30.00
(144)	Young	100.00	50.00	30.00
(145)	Zacher	100.00	50.00	30.00
(146)	Zumwalt	100.00	50.00	30.00

1915 Zeenut Pacific Coast League

The 1915 Zeenut cards are dated on the front, making identification very easy. They measure about 2" x 3-3/4" without the coupon and feature a black-and-white photo on a light background. To date 141 different cards are known to exist. This year is among the toughest of all Zeenuts to find.

		NM	EX	VG
Common Player:		100.00	45.00	25.00
With Coupon:		900.00	400.00	240.00
(1)	Ables	100.00	45.00	25.00
(2)	Abstein	100.00	45.00	25.00
(3)	Alcock	100.00	45.00	25.00
(4)	Arbogast	100.00	45.00	25.00
(5)	Baerwald	100.00	45.00	25.00
(6)	Barbour	100.00	45.00	25.00
(7)	Bates	100.00	45.00	25.00
(8)	Baum	100.00	45.00	25.00
(9)	Bayless	100.00	45.00	25.00
(10)	Beatty	100.00	45.00	25.00
(11)	Beer	100.00	45.00	25.00
(12)	Benham	100.00	45.00	25.00
(13)	Berger	100.00	45.00	25.00
(14)	Beumiller	100.00	45.00	25.00
(15)	Blankenship	100.00	45.00	25.00
(16)	Block	100.00	45.00	25.00
(17)	Bodie	100.00	45.00	25.00
(18)	Boles	100.00	45.00	25.00
(19)	Boyd	100.00	45.00	25.00
(20)	Bromley	100.00	45.00	25.00
(21)	Brown	100.00	45.00	25.00
(22)	Burns	300.00	135.00	75.00
(23)	Carlisle	100.00	45.00	25.00
(24)	Carrisch	100.00	45.00	25.00
(25)	Charles	100.00	45.00	25.00
(26)	Chech	100.00	45.00	25.00
(27)	Christian	100.00	45.00	25.00
(28)	Clarke	100.00	45.00	25.00
(29)	Couch	100.00	45.00	25.00
(30)	Stan Covaleski (Coveleski)	2,000	1,200	600.00
(31)	Daniels	100.00	45.00	25.00
(32)	Davis	100.00	45.00	25.00
(33)	DeCanniere	100.00	45.00	25.00
(34)	Dent	100.00	45.00	25.00
(35)	Derrick	100.00	45.00	25.00
(36)	Dillon	100.00	45.00	25.00
(37)	Doane	100.00	45.00	25.00
(38)	Downs	100.00	45.00	25.00
(39)	Elliott	100.00	45.00	25.00
(40)	F. Elliott	100.00	45.00	25.00
(41)	Ellis	100.00	45.00	25.00
(42)	Evans	100.00	45.00	25.00
(43)	Fanning	100.00	45.00	25.00
(44)	Faye	100.00	45.00	25.00
(45)	Fisher	100.00	45.00	25.00
(46)	Fittery	100.00	45.00	25.00
(47)	Fitzgerald	100.00	45.00	25.00
(48)	Fromme	100.00	45.00	25.00
(49)	Gardiner	100.00	45.00	25.00
(50)	Gedeon	100.00	45.00	25.00
(51)	Gleischmann	100.00	45.00	25.00
(52)	Gregory	100.00	45.00	25.00
(53)	Guest	100.00	45.00	25.00
(54)	Hall	100.00	45.00	25.00
(55)	Halla	100.00	45.00	25.00
(56)	Hallinan	100.00	45.00	25.00
(57)	Hannah	100.00	45.00	25.00
(58)	Harper	100.00	45.00	25.00
(59)	Harry Heilmann	1,500	800.00	400.00
(60)	Henley	100.00	45.00	25.00
(61)	Hetling	100.00	45.00	25.00
(62)	Higginbotham	100.00	45.00	25.00
(63)	Hilliard	100.00	45.00	25.00
(64)	Hitt (Winding up.)	100.00	45.00	25.00
(65)	Hitt (Throwing)	100.00	45.00	25.00
(66)	Hogan	100.00	45.00	25.00
(67)	Hosp	100.00	45.00	25.00
(68)	Howard	100.00	45.00	25.00
(69)	Hughes	100.00	45.00	25.00
(70)	Johnson	100.00	45.00	25.00
(71)	Jones	100.00	45.00	25.00
(72)	Kahler	100.00	45.00	25.00
(73)	Kane	100.00	45.00	25.00
(74)	Karr	100.00	45.00	25.00
(75)	Killilay	100.00	45.00	25.00
(76)	Klawitter	100.00	45.00	25.00
(77)	Koerner	100.00	45.00	25.00
(78)	Krause	100.00	45.00	25.00
(79)	Kuhn	100.00	45.00	25.00
(80)	LaRoy	100.00	45.00	25.00
(81)	Leard	100.00	45.00	25.00

		NM	EX	VG
(82)	Bill Lindsay	100.00	45.00	25.00
(83)	Litschi	100.00	45.00	25.00
(84)	Lober	100.00	45.00	25.00
(85)	Love	100.00	45.00	25.00
(86)	Lush	100.00	45.00	25.00
(87)	Maggart	100.00	45.00	25.00
(88)	Malarkey	100.00	45.00	25.00
(89)	Manda	100.00	45.00	25.00
(90)	Marcan	100.00	45.00	25.00
(91)	Martinoni	100.00	45.00	25.00
(92)	McAvoy	100.00	45.00	25.00
(93)	McCredie	100.00	45.00	25.00
(94)	McDonell	100.00	45.00	25.00
(95)	Fred McMullen (McMullin)	9,500	4,750	2,850
(96)	Meek	100.00	45.00	25.00
(97)	Meloan	100.00	45.00	25.00
(98)	Metzger	100.00	45.00	25.00
(99)	Middleton	100.00	45.00	25.00
(100)	Mitchell	100.00	45.00	25.00
(101)	Mitze	100.00	45.00	25.00
(102)	Morgan	100.00	45.00	25.00
(103)	Mundorff	100.00	45.00	25.00
(104)	Murphy	100.00	45.00	25.00
(105)	Ness	100.00	45.00	25.00
(106)	Nutt	100.00	45.00	25.00
(107)	Orr	100.00	45.00	25.00
(108)	Pernoll	100.00	45.00	25.00
(109)	Perritt	100.00	45.00	25.00
(110)	Piercey	100.00	45.00	25.00
(111)	Price	100.00	45.00	25.00
(112)	Prough	100.00	45.00	25.00
(113)	Prueitt	100.00	45.00	25.00
(114)	Purtell	100.00	45.00	25.00
(115)	Reed	100.00	45.00	25.00
(116)	Reisigl	100.00	45.00	25.00
(117)	Remneas	100.00	45.00	25.00
(118)	Swede Risberg	5,500	2,500	1,500
(119)	Rohrer	100.00	45.00	25.00
(120)	Russell	100.00	45.00	25.00
(121)	Ryan (Los Angeles)	100.00	45.00	25.00
(122)	Ryan	100.00	45.00	25.00
(123)	Schaller	100.00	45.00	25.00
(124)	Schmidt	100.00	45.00	25.00
(125)	Scoggins	100.00	45.00	25.00
(126)	Sepulveda	100.00	45.00	25.00
(127)	Shinn	100.00	45.00	25.00
(128)	Smith	100.00	45.00	25.00
(129)	Speas	100.00	45.00	25.00
(130)	Spencer	100.00	45.00	25.00
(132)	Tennant	100.00	45.00	25.00
(133)	Terry	100.00	45.00	25.00
(134)	Tobin	100.00	45.00	25.00
(135)	West	100.00	45.00	25.00
(136)	White	100.00	45.00	25.00
(137)	Claude Williams	5,500	2,500	1,500
(138)	Johnny Williams	250.00	110.00	65.00
(139)	Wolter	100.00	45.00	25.00
(140)	Wolverton	100.00	45.00	25.00
(141)	Zacher	100.00	45.00	25.00

1916 Zeenut Pacific Coast League

The 1916 Zeenuts measure about 2" x 3-3/4" without the coupon and are dated on the front (some cards were misdated 1915 however). The card fronts feature black-and-white photos on a blue background. There are 144 known subjects. The 1916 series is among the more difficult.

		NM	EX	VG
Common Player:		100.00	50.00	30.00
(1)	Autrey	100.00	50.00	30.00
(2)	Barbeau	100.00	50.00	30.00
(3)	Barry	100.00	50.00	30.00
(4)	Bassler	100.00	50.00	30.00
(5)	Bates	100.00	50.00	30.00
(6)	Baum	100.00	50.00	30.00
(7)	Bayless	100.00	50.00	30.00
(8)	Beer	100.00	50.00	30.00
(9)	Berg	100.00	50.00	30.00
(10)	Berger	100.00	50.00	30.00
(11)	Blankenship	100.00	50.00	30.00
(12)	Block	100.00	50.00	30.00
(13)	Bodie	150.00	80.00	40.00
(14)	Bohne	350.00	200.00	150.00
(15)	Boles	100.00	50.00	30.00
(16)	Boyd	100.00	50.00	30.00
(17)	Brief	100.00	50.00	30.00
(18)	Brooks	100.00	50.00	30.00
(19)	Brown	100.00	50.00	30.00
(20)	Butler	100.00	50.00	30.00
(21)	Callahan	100.00	50.00	30.00
(22)	Carrisch	100.00	50.00	30.00
(23)	Frank Chance	2,000	1,200	600.00
(24)	Jimmy Claxton	15,000	9,500	7,000
(25)	Coffey	100.00	50.00	30.00
(26)	Cook	100.00	50.00	30.00
(27)	Corbett	100.00	50.00	30.00
(28)	Couch	100.00	50.00	30.00
(29)	Crandall	100.00	50.00	30.00
(30)	Dalton	100.00	50.00	30.00
(31)	Davis	100.00	50.00	30.00
(32)	Derrick	100.00	50.00	30.00
(33)	Doane	100.00	50.00	30.00
(34)	Downs	100.00	50.00	30.00
(35)	Dugan	100.00	50.00	30.00
(36)	Eldred	100.00	50.00	30.00
(37)	F. Elliott	100.00	50.00	30.00
(38)	H. Elliott	100.00	50.00	30.00
(39)	Ellis	100.00	50.00	30.00
(40)	Erickson	100.00	50.00	30.00
(41)	Fanning	100.00	50.00	30.00
(42)	Fisher	100.00	50.00	30.00
(43)	Fittery	100.00	50.00	30.00
(44)	Fitzgerald	100.00	50.00	30.00
(45)	Fromme	100.00	50.00	30.00
(46)	Galloway	100.00	50.00	30.00
(47)	Gardner	100.00	50.00	30.00
(48)	Gay	100.00	50.00	30.00
(49)	Gleischmann	100.00	50.00	30.00
(50)	Griffith	100.00	50.00	30.00
(51)	Griggs	100.00	50.00	30.00
(52)	Guisto	100.00	50.00	30.00
(53)	Hagerman	100.00	50.00	30.00
(54)	Hall	100.00	50.00	30.00
(55)	Hallinan	100.00	50.00	30.00
(56)	Hannah	100.00	50.00	30.00
(57)	Harstadt	100.00	50.00	30.00
(58)	Haworth	100.00	50.00	30.00
(59)	Hess	100.00	50.00	30.00
(60)	Higginbotham	100.00	50.00	30.00
(61)	Hitt	100.00	50.00	30.00
(62)	Hogg	100.00	50.00	30.00
(63)	Hollocher	100.00	50.00	30.00
(64)	Horstman	100.00	50.00	30.00
(65)	Houck	100.00	50.00	30.00
(66)	Howard	100.00	50.00	30.00
(67)	Hughes	100.00	50.00	30.00
(68)	E. Johnston	100.00	50.00	30.00
(69)	G. Johnston	100.00	50.00	30.00
(70)	Jones	100.00	50.00	30.00
(71)	Kahler	100.00	50.00	30.00
(72)	Kane	100.00	50.00	30.00
(73)	Kelly	100.00	50.00	30.00
(74)	Kenworthy	100.00	50.00	30.00
(75)	Klawitter	100.00	50.00	30.00
(76)	Klein	100.00	50.00	30.00
(77)	Koerner	100.00	50.00	30.00
(78)	Krause	100.00	50.00	30.00
(79)	Kuhn	100.00	50.00	30.00
(80)	Lane	100.00	50.00	30.00
(81)	Larsen	100.00	50.00	30.00
(82)	Lush	100.00	50.00	30.00
(83)	Machold	100.00	50.00	30.00
(84)	Maggert	100.00	50.00	30.00
(85)	Manser	100.00	50.00	30.00
(86)	Martin	100.00	50.00	30.00
(87)	Mattick	100.00	50.00	30.00
(88)	McCredie	100.00	50.00	30.00
(89)	McGaffigan	100.00	50.00	30.00
(90)	McLarry	100.00	50.00	30.00
(91)	Menges	100.00	50.00	30.00
(92)	Middleton	100.00	50.00	30.00
(93)	Mitchell	100.00	50.00	30.00
(94)	Mitze	100.00	50.00	30.00
(95)	Munsell	100.00	50.00	30.00
(96)	Murphy	100.00	50.00	30.00
(97)	Nixon	100.00	50.00	30.00
(98)	Noyes	100.00	50.00	30.00
(99)	Nutt	100.00	50.00	30.00
(100)	O'Brien	100.00	50.00	30.00
(101)	Oldham	100.00	50.00	30.00
(102)	Orr	100.00	50.00	30.00
(103)	Patterson	100.00	50.00	30.00
(104)	Perritt	100.00	50.00	30.00
(105)	Prough	100.00	50.00	30.00
(106)	Prueitt	100.00	50.00	30.00
(107)	Quinlan	100.00	50.00	30.00
(108)	Quinn (Portland)	100.00	50.00	30.00
(109)	Quinn (Vernon)	100.00	50.00	30.00
(110)	Rader	100.00	50.00	30.00
(111)	Randall	100.00	50.00	30.00
(112)	Rath	100.00	50.00	30.00
(113)	Reisegl	100.00	50.00	30.00
(114)	Reuther (Ruether)	100.00	50.00	30.00
(115)	Swede Risberg	5,000	2,000	1,250
(116)	Roche	100.00	50.00	30.00
(117)	Ryan	100.00	50.00	30.00
(118)	Ryan	100.00	50.00	30.00
(119)	Scoggins	100.00	50.00	30.00
(120)	Sepulveda	100.00	50.00	30.00
(121)	Schaller	100.00	50.00	30.00
(122)	Sheehan	100.00	50.00	30.00
(123)	Shinn	100.00	50.00	30.00
(124)	Smith	100.00	50.00	30.00
(125)	Sothoron	100.00	50.00	30.00
(126)	Southworth	100.00	50.00	30.00
(127)	Speas	100.00	50.00	30.00
(128)	Spencer	100.00	50.00	30.00
(129)	Standridge	100.00	50.00	30.00
(130)	Steen	100.00	50.00	30.00
(131)	Stumpf	100.00	50.00	30.00
(132)	Vann	100.00	50.00	30.00
(133)	Vaughn	100.00	50.00	30.00
(134)	Ward	100.00	50.00	30.00
(135)	Whalling	100.00	50.00	30.00
(136)	Wilie	100.00	50.00	30.00
(137)	Williams	100.00	50.00	30.00
(138)	Wolverton	100.00	50.00	30.00
(139)	Wuffli	100.00	50.00	30.00
(140)	Zabel	100.00	50.00	30.00
(141)	Zacher	100.00	50.00	30.00
(142)	Zimmerman	100.00	50.00	30.00

1917 Zeenut Pacific Coast League

The 1917 Zeenuts measure about 1-3/4" x 3-3/4" and feature black-and-white photos on a light background. They are dated on the front and have blank backs. An advertising poster has been found listing 119 players (two pose variations brings the total to 121), but to date, six players on the list have not been found.

		NM	EX	VG
Common Player:		90.00	45.00	30.00
(1)	Arlett	90.00	45.00	30.00
(2)	Frank Arrelanes (Arellanes)	90.00	45.00	30.00
(3)	Baker (Catching)	90.00	45.00	30.00
(4)	Baker (Throwing)	90.00	45.00	30.00
(5)	Baldwin	90.00	45.00	30.00
(6)	Bassler	90.00	45.00	30.00
(7)	Baum	90.00	45.00	30.00
(8)	Beer	90.00	45.00	30.00
(9)	Bernhard	90.00	45.00	30.00
(10)	Bliss	90.00	45.00	30.00
(11)	Boles	90.00	45.00	30.00
(12)	Brenton	90.00	45.00	30.00
(13)	Brief	90.00	45.00	30.00
(14)	Brown	90.00	45.00	30.00
(15)	Burns	200.00	150.00	75.00
(16)	Callahan	90.00	45.00	30.00
(17)	Callan	90.00	45.00	30.00
(18)	Jacinto Calvo	700.00	400.00	200.00
(19)	Chadbourne	90.00	45.00	30.00
(20)	Frank Chance	1,800	1,000	500.00
(21)	Coltrin	90.00	45.00	30.00
(22)	Connifer	90.00	45.00	30.00
(23)	Corhan	90.00	45.00	30.00
(24)	Crandall (Los Angeles)	90.00	45.00	30.00
(25)	Crandall (Salt Lake)	90.00	45.00	30.00
(26)	Cress	90.00	45.00	30.00
(27)	Davis	90.00	45.00	30.00
(28)	DeCanniere	90.00	45.00	30.00
(29)	Doane	90.00	45.00	30.00
(30)	Dougan	90.00	45.00	30.00
(31)	Dougherty	90.00	45.00	30.00
(32)	Downs	90.00	45.00	30.00
(33)	Dubuc	90.00	45.00	30.00
(34)	Ellis	90.00	45.00	30.00
(35)	Erickson	90.00	45.00	30.00
(36)	Evans	90.00	45.00	30.00
(37)	Farmer	90.00	45.00	30.00
(38)	Fincher	90.00	45.00	30.00
(39)	Fisher	90.00	45.00	30.00
(40)	Fitzgerald	90.00	45.00	30.00
(41)	Fournier	90.00	45.00	30.00
(42)	Fromme	90.00	45.00	30.00
(43)	Galloway	90.00	45.00	30.00
(44)	Gislason	90.00	45.00	30.00
(45)	Goodbred	90.00	45.00	30.00
(46)	Griggs	90.00	45.00	30.00
(47)	Groehling	90.00	45.00	30.00
(48)	Hall (Los Angeles)	90.00	45.00	30.00
(49)	Hall (San Francisco)	90.00	45.00	30.00
(50)	Hannah	90.00	45.00	30.00
(51)	Harstad	90.00	45.00	30.00
(52)	Helfrich	90.00	45.00	30.00
(53)	Hess	90.00	45.00	30.00
(54)	Hitt	90.00	45.00	30.00
(55)	Hoff	90.00	45.00	30.00
(56)	Hollacher	90.00	45.00	30.00
(57)	Hollywood	90.00	45.00	30.00
(58)	Houck	90.00	45.00	30.00
(59)	Howard	90.00	45.00	30.00
(60)	Hughes	90.00	45.00	30.00
(61)	Johnson	90.00	45.00	30.00
(62)	Kilhullen	90.00	45.00	30.00
(63)	Killiffer (Killefer)	90.00	45.00	30.00
(64)	Koerner	90.00	45.00	30.00
(65)	Krause	90.00	45.00	30.00
(66)	Lane	90.00	45.00	30.00
(67)	Lapan	90.00	45.00	30.00
(68)	Leake	90.00	45.00	30.00
(69)	Lee	90.00	45.00	30.00
(70)	Leverenz	90.00	45.00	30.00
(71)	Maggert	90.00	45.00	30.00
(72)	Maisel	90.00	45.00	30.00
(73)	Mattick	90.00	45.00	30.00
(74)	McCreedie	90.00	45.00	30.00
(75)	McLarry	90.00	45.00	30.00

		NM	EX	VG
(76)	Mensor	500.00	250.00	150.00
(77)	Emil "Irish" Meusel	200.00	100.00	70.00
(78)	Middleton	90.00	45.00	30.00
(79)	Miller (Batting)	90.00	45.00	30.00
(80)	Miller (Throwing)	90.00	45.00	30.00
(81)	Mitchell	90.00	45.00	30.00
(82)	Mitze	90.00	45.00	30.00
(83)	Murphy	90.00	45.00	30.00
(84)	Murray	90.00	45.00	30.00
(85)	O'Brien	90.00	45.00	30.00
(86)	O'Mara	90.00	45.00	30.00
(87)	Oldham	90.00	45.00	30.00
(88)	Orr	90.00	45.00	30.00
(89)	Penelli	90.00	45.00	30.00
(90)	Penner	90.00	45.00	30.00
(91)	Pick	90.00	45.00	30.00
(92)	Prough	90.00	45.00	30.00
(93)	Pruiett	90.00	45.00	30.00
(94)	Quinlan	90.00	45.00	30.00
(95)	Quinn	90.00	45.00	30.00
(96)	Rath	90.00	45.00	30.00
(97)	Roche	90.00	45.00	30.00
(98)	Ryan (Los Angeles)	90.00	45.00	30.00
(99)	Ryan (Salt Lake)	90.00	45.00	30.00
(100)	Schaller	90.00	45.00	30.00
(101)	Schinkle	90.00	45.00	30.00
(102)	Schultz	90.00	45.00	30.00
(103)	Sheehan	90.00	45.00	30.00
(104)	Sheeley	90.00	45.00	30.00
(105)	Shinn	90.00	45.00	30.00
(106)	Siglin	90.00	45.00	30.00
(107)	Simon	90.00	45.00	30.00
(108)	Smith	90.00	45.00	30.00
(109)	Snyder	90.00	45.00	30.00
(110)	Stanridge	90.00	45.00	30.00
(111)	Steen	90.00	45.00	30.00
(112)	Stovall	90.00	45.00	30.00
(113)	Stumpf	90.00	45.00	30.00
(114)	Sullivan	90.00	45.00	30.00
(115)	Terry	90.00	45.00	30.00
(116)	Tobin	90.00	45.00	30.00
(117)	Valencia	90.00	45.00	30.00
(118)	Vaughn	90.00	45.00	30.00
(119)	Whalling	90.00	45.00	30.00
(120)	Wilie	90.00	45.00	30.00
(121)	Wolverton	90.00	45.00	30.00

1918 Zeenut Pacific Coast League

The 1918 Zeenuts are among the most distinctive because of the red borders surrounding the photos. They measure about 1-13/16" x 3-5/8" and are among the more difficult years to find.

		NM	EX	VG
Common Player:		250.00	120.00	60.00
With Coupon:		800.00	400.00	240.00
(1)	Alcock	250.00	120.00	60.00
(2)	Arkenburg	250.00	120.00	60.00
(3)	A. Arlett	250.00	120.00	60.00
(4)	Baum	250.00	120.00	60.00
(5)	Boles	250.00	120.00	60.00
(6)	Borton	250.00	120.00	60.00
(7)	Brenton	250.00	120.00	60.00
(8)	Bromley	250.00	120.00	60.00
(9)	Brooks	250.00	120.00	60.00
(10)	Brown	250.00	120.00	60.00
(11)	Caldera	250.00	120.00	60.00
(12)	Camm (Kamm)	250.00	120.00	60.00
(13)	Chadbourne	250.00	120.00	60.00
(14)	Chappell	250.00	120.00	60.00
(15)	Codington	250.00	120.00	60.00
(16)	Conwright	250.00	120.00	60.00
(17)	Cooper	250.00	120.00	60.00
(18)	Cox	250.00	120.00	60.00
(19)	Crandall (Los Angeles)	250.00	120.00	60.00
(20)	Crandall (Salt Lake)	250.00	120.00	60.00
(21)	Crawford	4,000	3,000	2,000
(22)	Croll	250.00	120.00	60.00
(23)	Davis	250.00	120.00	60.00
(24)	DeVormer	250.00	120.00	60.00
(25)	Dobbs	250.00	120.00	60.00
(26)	Downs	250.00	120.00	60.00
(27)	Dubuc	250.00	120.00	60.00
(28)	Dunn	250.00	120.00	60.00
(29)	Easterly	250.00	120.00	60.00
(30)	Eldred	250.00	120.00	60.00
(31)	Elliot	250.00	120.00	60.00
(32)	Ellis	250.00	120.00	60.00
(33)	Essick	250.00	120.00	60.00
(34)	Farmer	250.00	120.00	60.00
(35)	Fisher	250.00	120.00	60.00
(36)	Fittery	250.00	120.00	60.00
(37)	Forsythe	250.00	120.00	60.00
(38)	Fournier	250.00	120.00	60.00
(39)	Fromme	250.00	120.00	60.00
(40)	Gardner (Oakland)	250.00	120.00	60.00
(41)	Gardner (Sacramento)	250.00	120.00	60.00
(42)	Goldie	250.00	120.00	60.00
(43)	Griggs	250.00	120.00	60.00
(44)	Hawkes	250.00	120.00	60.00
(45)	Hollander	250.00	120.00	60.00
(46)	Hosp	250.00	120.00	60.00
(47)	Howard	250.00	120.00	60.00
(48)	Hummel	250.00	120.00	60.00
(49)	Hunter	250.00	120.00	60.00
(50)	Johnson	250.00	120.00	60.00
(51)	G. Johnson	250.00	120.00	60.00
(52)	Kantlehner	250.00	120.00	60.00
(53)	Killefer	250.00	120.00	60.00
(54)	Koerner	250.00	120.00	60.00
(55)	Konnick	250.00	120.00	60.00
(56)	Kremer	250.00	120.00	60.00
(57)	Lapan	250.00	120.00	60.00
(58)	Leake	250.00	120.00	60.00
(59)	Leathers	250.00	120.00	60.00
(60)	Leifer	250.00	120.00	60.00
(61)	Leverenz	250.00	120.00	60.00
(62)	Llewlyn	250.00	120.00	60.00
(63)	Martin	250.00	120.00	60.00
(64)	McCabe	250.00	120.00	60.00
(65)	McCredie	250.00	120.00	60.00
(66)	McKee	250.00	120.00	60.00
(67)	McNulty	250.00	120.00	60.00
(68)	Mensor	700.00	400.00	200.00
(69)	Middleton	250.00	120.00	60.00
(70)	Miller (Oakland)	250.00	120.00	60.00
(71)	Miller (Salt Lake)	250.00	120.00	60.00
(72)	J. Mitchell	250.00	120.00	60.00
(73)	R. Mitchell	250.00	120.00	60.00
(74)	Mitze	250.00	120.00	60.00
(75)	Moore	250.00	120.00	60.00
(76)	Morton	250.00	120.00	60.00
(77)	Murray	250.00	120.00	60.00
(78)	O'Doul	3,000	2,000	1,000
(79)	Orr	250.00	120.00	60.00
(80)	Pepe	250.00	120.00	60.00
(81)	Pertica	250.00	120.00	60.00
(82)	Phillips	250.00	120.00	60.00
(83)	Pick	250.00	120.00	60.00
(84)	Pinelli	250.00	120.00	60.00
(85)	Prentice	250.00	120.00	60.00
(86)	Prough	250.00	120.00	60.00
(87)	Quinlan	250.00	120.00	60.00
(88)	Ritchie	250.00	120.00	60.00
(89)	Rogers	250.00	120.00	60.00
(90)	Ryan	250.00	120.00	60.00
(91)	Sand	250.00	120.00	60.00
(92)	Shader	250.00	120.00	60.00
(93)	Sheely	250.00	120.00	60.00
(94)	Siglin	250.00	120.00	60.00
(95)	Smale	250.00	120.00	60.00
(96)	Smith (Salt Lake City)	250.00	120.00	60.00
(97)	Smith (San Francisco)	250.00	120.00	60.00
(98)	Stanbridge	250.00	120.00	60.00
(99)	Terry	250.00	120.00	60.00
(100)	Valencia	250.00	120.00	60.00
(101)	West	250.00	120.00	60.00
(102)	Wilie	250.00	120.00	60.00
(103)	Williams	250.00	120.00	60.00
(104)	Wisterzill	250.00	120.00	60.00

1919 Zeenut Pacific Coast League

The 1919 Zeenuts cards are dated on the front and measure about 1-3/4" x 3-5/8". They featured borderless, sepia-toned photos. To date, 144 subjects exist in the series.

		NM	EX	VG
Common Player:		100.00	50.00	30.00
(1)	Ally	100.00	50.00	30.00
(2)	Fatty Arbuckle	6,000	4,000	2,000
(3)	A. Arlett	100.00	50.00	30.00
(4)	R. Arlett	100.00	50.00	30.00
(5)	Baker	100.00	50.00	30.00
(6)	Baldwin	100.00	50.00	30.00
(7)	Baum	100.00	50.00	30.00
(8)	Beck	100.00	50.00	30.00
(9)	Bigbee	100.00	50.00	30.00
(10)	Blue	100.00	50.00	30.00
(11)	Bohne	300.00	200.00	100.00
(12)	Boles	100.00	50.00	30.00
(13)	Borton	100.00	50.00	30.00
(14)	Bowman	100.00	50.00	30.00
(15)	Brooks	100.00	50.00	30.00
(16)	Brown	100.00	50.00	30.00
(17)	Byler	100.00	50.00	30.00
(18)	Caldera	100.00	50.00	30.00
(19)	Cavaney	100.00	50.00	30.00
(20)	Chadbourne	100.00	50.00	30.00
(21)	Chech	100.00	50.00	30.00
(22)	Church	100.00	50.00	30.00
(23)	Clymer	100.00	50.00	30.00
(24)	Coleman	100.00	50.00	30.00
(25)	Compton	100.00	50.00	30.00
(26)	Conkwright	100.00	50.00	30.00
(27)	Connolly	100.00	50.00	30.00
(28)	Cook	100.00	50.00	30.00
(29)	Cooper (Los Angeles)	100.00	50.00	30.00
(30)	Cooper (Oakland)	100.00	50.00	30.00
(31)	Cooper (Portland)	100.00	50.00	30.00
(32)	Corhan	100.00	50.00	30.00
(33)	Couch	100.00	50.00	30.00
(34)	Cox	100.00	50.00	30.00
(35)	Crandall (Los Angeles)	100.00	50.00	30.00
(36)	Crandall (San Francisco)	100.00	50.00	30.00
(37)	Crespi	100.00	50.00	30.00
(38)	Croll	100.00	50.00	30.00
(39)	Cunningham	100.00	50.00	30.00
(40)	Dawson	100.00	50.00	30.00
(41)	Dell	100.00	50.00	30.00
(42)	DeVormer	100.00	50.00	30.00
(43)	Paddy Driscoll	125.00	65.00	39.00
(44)	Eastley	100.00	50.00	30.00
(45)	Edington	100.00	50.00	30.00
(46)	Eldred	100.00	50.00	30.00
(47)	Elliott	100.00	50.00	30.00
(48)	Ellis	100.00	50.00	30.00
(49)	Essick	100.00	50.00	30.00
(50)	Fabrique	100.00	50.00	30.00
(51)	Falkenberg	100.00	50.00	30.00
(52)	Fallentine	100.00	50.00	30.00
(53)	Finneran	100.00	50.00	30.00
(54)	Fisher (Sacramento)	100.00	50.00	30.00
(55)	Fisher (Vernon)	100.00	50.00	30.00
(56)	Fitzgerald	100.00	50.00	30.00
(57)	Flannigan	100.00	50.00	30.00
(58)	Fournier	100.00	50.00	30.00
(59)	French	100.00	50.00	30.00
(60)	Fromme	100.00	50.00	30.00
(61)	Gibson	100.00	50.00	30.00
(62)	Griggs	100.00	50.00	30.00
(63)	Haney	100.00	50.00	30.00
(64)	Harper	100.00	50.00	30.00
(65)	Henkle	100.00	50.00	30.00
(66)	Herr	100.00	50.00	30.00
(67)	Hickey	100.00	50.00	30.00
(68)	High	100.00	50.00	30.00
(69)	Holling	100.00	50.00	30.00
(70)	Hosp	100.00	50.00	30.00
(71)	Houck	100.00	50.00	30.00
(72)	Howard	100.00	50.00	30.00
(73)	Kamm	100.00	50.00	30.00
(74)	Kenworthy	100.00	50.00	30.00
(75)	Killefer	100.00	50.00	30.00
(76)	King	100.00	50.00	30.00
(77)	Koehler	100.00	50.00	30.00
(78)	Koerner	100.00	50.00	30.00
(79)	Kramer (Oakland)	100.00	50.00	30.00
(80)	Kramer (San Francisco)	100.00	50.00	30.00
(81)	Land	100.00	50.00	30.00
(82)	Lane	100.00	50.00	30.00
(83)	Lapan	100.00	50.00	30.00
(84)	Larkin	100.00	50.00	30.00
(85)	Lee	100.00	50.00	30.00
(86)	Long	100.00	50.00	30.00
(87)	Mails	100.00	50.00	30.00
(88)	Mains	100.00	50.00	30.00
(89)	Maisel	100.00	50.00	30.00
(90)	Mathes	100.00	50.00	30.00
(91)	McCredie	100.00	50.00	30.00
(92)	McGaffigan	100.00	50.00	30.00
(93)	McHenry	100.00	50.00	30.00
(94)	McNulty	100.00	50.00	30.00
(95)	Meusel	100.00	50.00	30.00
(96)	Middleton	100.00	50.00	30.00
(97)	Mitchell	100.00	50.00	30.00
(98)	Mitze	100.00	50.00	30.00
(99)	Mulory	100.00	50.00	30.00
(100)	Murphy	100.00	50.00	30.00
(101)	Murray	100.00	50.00	30.00
(102)	Niehoff (Los Angeles)	100.00	50.00	30.00
(103)	Niehoff (Seattle)	100.00	50.00	30.00
(104)	Norse	100.00	50.00	30.00
(105)	Oldham	100.00	50.00	30.00
(106)	Orr	100.00	50.00	30.00
(107)	Penner	100.00	50.00	30.00
(108)	Pennington	100.00	50.00	30.00
(109)	Piercy	100.00	50.00	30.00
(110)	Pinelli	150.00	75.00	45.00
(111)	C. Prough	100.00	50.00	30.00
(112)	Rader	100.00	50.00	30.00
(113)	Reiger	100.00	50.00	30.00
(114)	Ritchie	100.00	50.00	30.00
(115)	Roach	100.00	50.00	30.00
(116)	Rodgers	100.00	50.00	30.00
(117)	Rumler	100.00	50.00	30.00
(118)	Sands	100.00	50.00	30.00
(119)	Schick	100.00	50.00	30.00
(120)	Schultz	100.00	50.00	30.00
(121)	Scott	100.00	50.00	30.00
(122)	Seaton	100.00	50.00	30.00
(123)	Sheely	100.00	50.00	30.00
(124)	Siglin	100.00	50.00	30.00
(125)	Smith	100.00	50.00	30.00
(126)	Bill Smith	100.00	50.00	30.00
(127)	Snell	100.00	50.00	30.00
(128)	Spangler	100.00	50.00	30.00
(129)	Speas	100.00	50.00	30.00
(130)	Spencer	100.00	50.00	30.00

(131) Starasenich	100.00	50.00	30.00
(132) Stumpf	100.00	50.00	30.00
(133) Sutherland	100.00	50.00	30.00
(134) Dazzy Vance	800.00	600.00	400.00
(135) Walker	100.00	50.00	30.00
(136) Walsh	100.00	50.00	30.00
(137) Ware	100.00	50.00	30.00
(138) Weaver	100.00	50.00	30.00
(139) Westerzil	100.00	50.00	30.00
(140) Wilhoit	100.00	50.00	30.00
(141) Wilie	100.00	50.00	30.00
(142) Willets	100.00	50.00	30.00
(143) Zamloch	100.00	50.00	30.00
(144) Zweifel	100.00	50.00	30.00

1920 Zeenut Pacific Coast League

The 1920 Zeenuts cards were dated on the front and measure about 1-3/4" x 3-5/8". They featured borderless, sepia-toned photos. To date, 151 have been found for 1920.

	NM	EX	VG
Common Player:	90.00	45.00	30.00
(1) Adams	90.00	45.00	30.00
(2) Agnew	90.00	45.00	30.00
(3) Alcock	90.00	45.00	30.00
(4) Aldrige	90.00	45.00	30.00
(5) Andrews	90.00	45.00	30.00
(6) Anfinson	90.00	45.00	30.00
(7) A. Arlett	90.00	45.00	30.00
(8) R. Arlett	90.00	45.00	30.00
(9) Baker	90.00	45.00	30.00
(10) Baldwin	90.00	45.00	30.00
(11) Bassler	90.00	45.00	30.00
(12) Baum	90.00	45.00	30.00
(13) Blue	90.00	45.00	30.00
(14) Bohne	300.00	200.00	100.00
(15) Brenton	90.00	45.00	30.00
(16) Bromley (Dark hat.)	90.00	45.00	30.00
(17) Bromley (Light hat.)	90.00	45.00	30.00
(18) Brown	90.00	45.00	30.00
(19) Butler	90.00	45.00	30.00
(20) Caveney	90.00	45.00	30.00
(21) Chadbourne	90.00	45.00	30.00
(22) Compton	90.00	45.00	30.00
(23) Connolly	90.00	45.00	30.00
(24) Cook	90.00	45.00	30.00
(25) Corhan	90.00	45.00	30.00
(26) Cox	90.00	45.00	30.00
(27) K. Crandall	90.00	45.00	30.00
(28) O. Crandall	90.00	45.00	30.00
(29) Crawford	2,000	1,200	600.00
(30) Cullop	90.00	45.00	30.00
(31) Cunningham	90.00	45.00	30.00
(32) DeVitalis	90.00	45.00	30.00
(33) DeVormer	90.00	45.00	30.00
(34) Dooley	90.00	45.00	30.00
(35) Dorman	90.00	45.00	30.00
(36) Dumovich	90.00	45.00	30.00
(37) Dylar	90.00	45.00	30.00
(38) Edington	90.00	45.00	30.00
(39) Eldred	90.00	45.00	30.00
(40) Ellis	90.00	45.00	30.00
(41) Essick	90.00	45.00	30.00
(42) Fisher	90.00	45.00	30.00
(43) Fitzgerald	90.00	45.00	30.00
(44) Fromme	90.00	45.00	30.00
(45) Gardner	90.00	45.00	30.00
(46) Ginglardi	90.00	45.00	30.00
(47) Gough	90.00	45.00	30.00
(48) Griggs	90.00	45.00	30.00
(49) Guisto	90.00	45.00	30.00
(50) Hamilton	90.00	45.00	30.00
(51) Hanicy	90.00	45.00	30.00
(52) Hartford	90.00	45.00	30.00
(53) High	90.00	45.00	30.00
(54) Hill	90.00	45.00	30.00
(55) Hodges	90.00	45.00	30.00
(56) Howard	90.00	45.00	30.00
(57) James	90.00	45.00	30.00
(58) Jenkins	90.00	45.00	30.00
(59) Johnson (Portland)	90.00	45.00	30.00
(60) Johnson (Salt Lake)	90.00	45.00	30.00
(61) Jones	90.00	45.00	30.00
(62) Juney	90.00	45.00	30.00
(63) Kallio	90.00	45.00	30.00
(64) Kamm	90.00	45.00	30.00
(65) Keating	90.00	45.00	30.00
(66) Kenworthy	90.00	45.00	30.00
(67) Killeen	90.00	45.00	30.00
(68) Killefer	90.00	45.00	30.00
(69) Kingdon	90.00	45.00	30.00
(70) Knight	90.00	45.00	30.00
(71) Koehler	90.00	45.00	30.00
(72) Koerner	90.00	45.00	30.00
(73) Kopp	90.00	45.00	30.00
(74) Kremer	90.00	45.00	30.00
(75) Krug	90.00	45.00	30.00
(76) Kunz	90.00	45.00	30.00
(77) Lambert	90.00	45.00	30.00
(78) Lane	90.00	45.00	30.00
(79) Larkin	90.00	45.00	30.00
(80) Leverenz	90.00	45.00	30.00
(81) Long	90.00	45.00	30.00
(82) Love	90.00	45.00	30.00
(83) Maggart	90.00	45.00	30.00
(84) Mails	90.00	45.00	30.00
(85) Maisel	90.00	45.00	30.00
(86) Matterson	90.00	45.00	30.00
(87) Matteson	90.00	45.00	30.00
(88) McAuley	90.00	45.00	30.00
(89) McCredie	90.00	45.00	30.00
(90) McGaffigan	90.00	45.00	30.00
(91) McHenry	90.00	45.00	30.00
(92) McQuaid	90.00	45.00	30.00
(93) Miller	90.00	45.00	30.00
(94) Mitchell	90.00	45.00	30.00
(95) J. Mitchell	90.00	45.00	30.00
(96) Mitchell	90.00	45.00	30.00
(97) Mitze	90.00	45.00	30.00
(98) Moffitt	90.00	45.00	30.00
(99) Mollwitz	90.00	45.00	30.00
(100) Morse	90.00	45.00	30.00
(101) Mulligan	90.00	45.00	30.00
(102) Murphy	90.00	45.00	30.00
(103) Niehoff	90.00	45.00	30.00
(104) Nixon	90.00	45.00	30.00
(105) O'Shaughnessy	90.00	45.00	30.00
(106) Orr	90.00	45.00	30.00
(107) Paull	90.00	45.00	30.00
(108) Penner	90.00	45.00	30.00
(109) Pertica	90.00	45.00	30.00
(110) Peterson	90.00	45.00	30.00
(111) Polson	90.00	45.00	30.00
(112) Prough	90.00	45.00	30.00
(113) Reagan	90.00	45.00	30.00
(114) Reiger	90.00	45.00	30.00
(115) Reilly	90.00	45.00	30.00
(116) Rheinhart	90.00	45.00	30.00
(117) Rodgers	90.00	45.00	30.00
(118) Ross	90.00	45.00	30.00
(119) Rumler	90.00	45.00	30.00
(120) Russell	90.00	45.00	30.00
(121) Sands	90.00	45.00	30.00
(122) Schaller	90.00	45.00	30.00
(123) Schang	90.00	45.00	30.00
(124) Schellenback	90.00	45.00	30.00
(125) Schick	90.00	45.00	30.00
(126) Schorr	90.00	45.00	30.00
(127) Schroeder	90.00	45.00	30.00
(128) Scott	90.00	45.00	30.00
(129) Seaton	90.00	45.00	30.00
(130) Sheely	90.00	45.00	30.00
(131) Siebold	90.00	45.00	30.00
(132) Siglin	90.00	45.00	30.00
(133) Smith	90.00	45.00	30.00
(134) G. Smith	90.00	45.00	30.00
(135) Spellman	90.00	45.00	30.00
(136) Spranger	90.00	45.00	30.00
(137) Stroud	90.00	45.00	30.00
(138) Stumpf	90.00	45.00	30.00
(139) Sullivan	90.00	45.00	30.00
(140) Sutherland	90.00	45.00	30.00
(141) Thurston (Dark hat.)	90.00	45.00	30.00
(142) Thurston (Light hat.)	90.00	45.00	30.00
(143) Walsh	90.00	45.00	30.00
(144) Wares	90.00	45.00	30.00
(145) Weaver	90.00	45.00	30.00
(146) Willie	90.00	45.00	30.00
(147) Winn	90.00	45.00	30.00
(148) Wisterzill	90.00	45.00	30.00
(149) Worth	90.00	45.00	30.00
(150) Yelle	90.00	45.00	30.00
(151) Zamlock	90.00	45.00	30.00
(152) Zeider	90.00	45.00	30.00

1921 Zeenut Pacific Coast League

The 1921 Zeenuts cards were dated on the front and measure about 1-3/4" x 3-11/16". They featured borderless, sepia-toned photos. To date, 168 different subjects have been discovered for 1921 (even though a promotional flier indicates 180 players).

	NM	EX	VG
Common Player:	75.00	40.00	25.00
With Coupon:	1,200	500.00	300.00
(1) Adams	75.00	40.00	25.00
(2) Alcock	75.00	40.00	25.00
(3) Aldridge	75.00	40.00	25.00
(4) Alton	75.00	40.00	25.00
(5) Anfinson	75.00	40.00	25.00
(6) Arlett	75.00	40.00	25.00
(7) Baker	75.00	40.00	25.00
(8) Baldwin	75.00	40.00	25.00
(9) Bates	75.00	40.00	25.00
(10) Berry	75.00	40.00	25.00
(11) Blacholder	75.00	40.00	25.00
(12) Blossom	75.00	40.00	25.00
(13) Bourg	75.00	40.00	25.00
(14) Brinley	75.00	40.00	25.00
(15) Bromley	75.00	40.00	25.00
(16) Brown	75.00	40.00	25.00
(17) Brubaker	75.00	40.00	25.00
(18) Butler	75.00	40.00	25.00
(19) Byler	75.00	40.00	25.00
(20) Carroll	75.00	40.00	25.00
(21) Casey	75.00	40.00	25.00
(22) Cather	75.00	40.00	25.00
(23) Caveney	75.00	40.00	25.00
(24) Chadbourne	75.00	40.00	25.00
(25) Compton	75.00	40.00	25.00
(26) Connel	75.00	40.00	25.00
(27) Cook	75.00	40.00	25.00
(28) Cooper	75.00	40.00	25.00
(29) Couch	75.00	40.00	25.00
(30) Cox	75.00	40.00	25.00
(31) Crandall	75.00	40.00	25.00
(32) Cravath	75.00	40.00	25.00
(33) Crawford	2,000	1,200	600.00
(34) Crumpler	75.00	40.00	25.00
(35) Cunningham	75.00	40.00	25.00
(36) Daley	75.00	40.00	25.00
(37) Dell	75.00	40.00	25.00
(38) Demaree	75.00	40.00	25.00
(39) Douglas	75.00	40.00	25.00
(40) Dumovich	75.00	40.00	25.00
(41) Elliott	75.00	40.00	25.00
(42) Ellis	75.00	40.00	25.00
(43) Ellison	75.00	40.00	25.00
(44) Essick	75.00	40.00	25.00
(45) Faeth	75.00	40.00	25.00
(46) Fisher	75.00	40.00	25.00
(47) Fittery	75.00	40.00	25.00
(48) Fitzgerald	75.00	40.00	25.00
(49) Flaherty	75.00	40.00	25.00
(50) Francis	75.00	40.00	25.00
(51) French	75.00	40.00	25.00
(52) Fromme	75.00	40.00	25.00
(53) Gardner	75.00	40.00	25.00
(54) Geary	75.00	40.00	25.00
(55) Gennin	75.00	40.00	25.00
(56) Gorman	75.00	40.00	25.00
(57) Gould	75.00	40.00	25.00
(58) Griggs	75.00	40.00	25.00
(59) Hale	75.00	40.00	25.00
(60) Hannah	75.00	40.00	25.00
(61) Hansen	75.00	40.00	25.00
(62) Hesse	75.00	40.00	25.00
(63) High	75.00	40.00	25.00
(64) Hughes	75.00	40.00	25.00
(65) Hyatt	75.00	40.00	25.00
(66) Jackson	75.00	40.00	25.00
(67) Jacobs	75.00	40.00	25.00
(68) Jacobs	75.00	40.00	25.00
(69) Jenkins	75.00	40.00	25.00
(70) Johnson	75.00	40.00	25.00
(71) Jones	75.00	40.00	25.00
(72) Jourden	75.00	40.00	25.00
(73) Kallio	75.00	40.00	25.00
(74) Kamm	75.00	40.00	25.00
(75) Kearns	75.00	40.00	25.00
(76) Kelly	75.00	40.00	25.00
(77) Kersten	75.00	40.00	25.00
(78) Kifer	75.00	40.00	25.00
(79) Killefer	75.00	40.00	25.00
(80) King	75.00	40.00	25.00
(81) Kingdon	75.00	40.00	25.00
(82) Knight	75.00	40.00	25.00
(83) Koehler	75.00	40.00	25.00
(84) Kopp	75.00	40.00	25.00
(85) Krause	75.00	40.00	25.00
(86) Kremer	75.00	40.00	25.00
(87) Krug	75.00	40.00	25.00
(88) Kunz	75.00	40.00	25.00
(89) Lane	75.00	40.00	25.00
(90) Leverenz	75.00	40.00	25.00
(91) Lewis	75.00	40.00	25.00
(92) Lindimore	75.00	40.00	25.00
(93) Love	75.00	40.00	25.00
(94) Ludolph	75.00	40.00	25.00
(95) Lynn	75.00	40.00	25.00
(96) Lyons	75.00	40.00	25.00
(97) McAuley	75.00	40.00	25.00
(98) McCredie	75.00	40.00	25.00
(99) McGaffigan	75.00	40.00	25.00
(100) McGraw	75.00	40.00	25.00
(101) McQuaid	75.00	40.00	25.00
(102) Merritt	75.00	40.00	25.00
(103) Middleton	75.00	40.00	25.00
(104) Miller	75.00	40.00	25.00
(105) Mitchell	75.00	40.00	25.00
(106) Mitze	75.00	40.00	25.00
(107) Mollwitz	75.00	40.00	25.00
(108) Morse	75.00	40.00	25.00

		NM	EX	VG
(109)	Murphy (Seattle)	75.00	40.00	25.00
(110)	Murphy (Vernon)	75.00	40.00	25.00
(111)	Mustain	75.00	40.00	25.00
(112)	Nickels	75.00	40.00	25.00
(113)	Niehaus	75.00	40.00	25.00
(114)	Niehoff	75.00	40.00	25.00
(115)	Nofziger	75.00	40.00	25.00
(116)	O'Connell	75.00	40.00	25.00
(117)	O'Doul	800.00	600.00	400.00
(118)	O'Malia	75.00	40.00	25.00
(119)	Oldring	75.00	40.00	25.00
(120)	Oliver	75.00	40.00	25.00
(121)	Orr	75.00	40.00	25.00
(122)	Paton	75.00	40.00	25.00
(123)	Penner	75.00	40.00	25.00
(124)	Pick	75.00	40.00	25.00
(125)	Pillette	75.00	40.00	25.00
(126)	Pinelli	75.00	40.00	25.00
(127)	Polson	75.00	40.00	25.00
(128)	Poole	75.00	40.00	25.00
(129)	Prough	75.00	40.00	25.00
(130)	Rath	75.00	40.00	25.00
(131)	Read	75.00	40.00	25.00
(132)	Reinhardt	75.00	40.00	25.00
(133)	Rieger	75.00	40.00	25.00
(134)	Rogers	75.00	40.00	25.00
(135)	Rose (Sacramento)	75.00	40.00	25.00
(136)	Rose (Salt Lake)	75.00	40.00	25.00
(137)	Ross (Portland)	75.00	40.00	25.00
(138)	Ross (Sacramento)	75.00	40.00	25.00
(139)	Ryan	75.00	40.00	25.00
(140)	Sand	75.00	40.00	25.00
(141)	Schick	75.00	40.00	25.00
(142)	Schneider	75.00	40.00	25.00
(143)	Scott	75.00	40.00	25.00
(144)	Shang	75.00	40.00	25.00
(145)	Sheehan	75.00	40.00	25.00
(146)	Shore	75.00	40.00	25.00
(147)	Shorr	75.00	40.00	25.00
(148)	Shultis	75.00	40.00	25.00
(149)	Siebold	75.00	40.00	25.00
(150)	Siglin	75.00	40.00	25.00
(151)	Smallwood	75.00	40.00	25.00
(152)	Smith	75.00	40.00	25.00
(153)	Spencer	75.00	40.00	25.00
(154)	Stanage	75.00	40.00	25.00
(155)	Statz	75.00	40.00	25.00
(156)	Stumph	75.00	40.00	25.00
(157)	Thomas	75.00	40.00	25.00
(158)	Thurston	75.00	40.00	25.00
(159)	Tyrrell	75.00	40.00	25.00
(160)	Van Osdoll	75.00	40.00	25.00
(161)	Walsh	75.00	40.00	25.00
(162)	White	75.00	40.00	25.00
(163)	Wilhoit	75.00	40.00	25.00
(164)	Wilie	75.00	40.00	25.00
(165)	Winn	75.00	40.00	25.00
(166)	Wolfer	75.00	40.00	25.00
(167)	Yelle	75.00	40.00	25.00
(168)	Young	75.00	40.00	25.00
(169)	Zeider	75.00	40.00	25.00

1922 Zeenut Pacific Coast League

The 1922 Zeenuts are dated on the front, measure about 1-13/16" x 3-9/16" and feature black-and-white photos with sepia highlights. There are 162 subjects, and four of them (Koehler, Williams, Gregg and Schneider) have been found with variations in color tones.

		NM	EX	VG
Common Player:		75.00	40.00	25.00
(1)	J. Adams	75.00	40.00	25.00
(2)	S. Adams	75.00	40.00	25.00
(3)	Agnew	75.00	40.00	25.00
(4)	Anfinson	75.00	40.00	25.00
(5)	Arlett	75.00	40.00	25.00
(6)	Baldwin	75.00	40.00	25.00
(7)	Barney	75.00	40.00	25.00
(8)	Bell	75.00	40.00	25.00
(9)	Blaeholder	75.00	40.00	25.00
(10)	Bodie	75.00	40.00	25.00
(11)	Brenton	75.00	40.00	25.00
(12)	Bromley	75.00	40.00	25.00
(13)	Brovold	75.00	40.00	25.00
(14)	Brown	75.00	40.00	25.00
(15)	Brubaker	75.00	40.00	25.00
(16)	Burger	75.00	40.00	25.00
(17)	Byler	75.00	40.00	25.00
(18)	Canfield	75.00	40.00	25.00
(19)	Carroll	75.00	40.00	25.00
(20)	Cartwright	75.00	40.00	25.00
(21)	Chadbourne	75.00	40.00	25.00
(22)	Compton	75.00	40.00	25.00
(23)	Connolly	75.00	40.00	25.00
(24)	Cook	75.00	40.00	25.00
(25)	Cooper	75.00	40.00	25.00
(26)	Coumbe	75.00	40.00	25.00
(27)	Cox	75.00	40.00	25.00
(28)	Crandall	75.00	40.00	25.00
(29)	Crumpler	75.00	40.00	25.00
(30)	Cueto	600.00	400.00	200.00
(31)	Dailey	75.00	40.00	25.00
(32)	Daly	75.00	40.00	25.00
(33)	Deal	75.00	40.00	25.00
(34)	Dell	75.00	40.00	25.00
(35)	Doyle	75.00	40.00	25.00
(36)	Dumovich	75.00	40.00	25.00
(37)	Eldred	75.00	40.00	25.00
(38)	Eller	75.00	40.00	25.00
(39)	Elliott	75.00	40.00	25.00
(40)	Ellison	75.00	40.00	25.00
(41)	Essick	75.00	40.00	25.00
(42)	Finneran	75.00	40.00	25.00
(43)	Fittery	75.00	40.00	25.00
(44)	Fitzgerald	75.00	40.00	25.00
(45)	Freeman	75.00	40.00	25.00
(46)	French	75.00	40.00	25.00
(47)	Gardner	75.00	40.00	25.00
(48)	Geary	75.00	40.00	25.00
(49)	Gibson	75.00	40.00	25.00
(50)	Gilder	75.00	40.00	25.00
(51)	Gould	75.00	40.00	25.00
(52)	Gregg	75.00	40.00	25.00
(53)	Gressett	75.00	40.00	25.00
(54)	Griggs	75.00	40.00	25.00
(55)	Hampton	75.00	40.00	25.00
(56)	Hannah	75.00	40.00	25.00
(57)	Hawks	75.00	40.00	25.00
(58)	Henke	75.00	40.00	25.00
(59)	High (Portland)	75.00	40.00	25.00
(60)	High (Vernon)	75.00	40.00	25.00
(61)	Houck	75.00	40.00	25.00
(62)	Howard	75.00	40.00	25.00
(63)	Hughes	75.00	40.00	25.00
(64)	Hyatt	75.00	40.00	25.00
(65)	Jacobs	75.00	40.00	25.00
(66)	James	75.00	40.00	25.00
(67)	Jenkins	75.00	40.00	25.00
(68)	Jones	75.00	40.00	25.00
(69)	Kallio	75.00	40.00	25.00
(70)	Kamm	75.00	40.00	25.00
(71)	Keiser	75.00	40.00	25.00
(72)	Kelly	75.00	40.00	25.00
(73)	Kenworthy	75.00	40.00	25.00
(74)	Kilduff	75.00	40.00	25.00
(75)	Killefer	75.00	40.00	25.00
(76)	Killhullen	75.00	40.00	25.00
(77)	King	75.00	40.00	25.00
(78)	Knight	75.00	40.00	25.00
(79)	Koehler	75.00	40.00	25.00
(80)	Kremer	75.00	40.00	25.00
(81)	Kunz	75.00	40.00	25.00
(82)	Lafayette	75.00	40.00	25.00
(83)	Lane	75.00	40.00	25.00
(84)	Tony Lazzeri	3,000	1,500	900.00
(85)	Lefevre	75.00	40.00	25.00
(86)	D. Lewis	75.00	40.00	25.00
(87)	S. Lewis	75.00	40.00	25.00
(88)	Lindimore	75.00	40.00	25.00
(89)	Locker	75.00	40.00	25.00
(90)	Lyons	75.00	40.00	25.00
(91)	Mack	75.00	40.00	25.00
(92)	Marriott	75.00	40.00	25.00
(93)	May	75.00	40.00	25.00
(94)	McAuley	75.00	40.00	25.00
(95)	McCabe	75.00	40.00	25.00
(96)	McCann	75.00	40.00	25.00
(97)	McCredie	75.00	40.00	25.00
(98)	McNeely	75.00	40.00	25.00
(99)	McQuaid	75.00	40.00	25.00
(100)	Miller	75.00	40.00	25.00
(101)	Mitchell	75.00	40.00	25.00
(102)	Mitze	75.00	40.00	25.00
(103)	Mollwitz	75.00	40.00	25.00
(104)	Monahan	75.00	40.00	25.00
(105)	Murphy (Seattle)	75.00	40.00	25.00
(106)	Murphy (Vernon)	75.00	40.00	25.00
(107)	Niehaus	75.00	40.00	25.00
(108)	O'Connell	75.00	40.00	25.00
(109)	Orr	75.00	40.00	25.00
(110)	Owen	75.00	40.00	25.00
(111)	Pearce	75.00	40.00	25.00
(112)	Pick	75.00	40.00	25.00
(113)	Ponder	75.00	40.00	25.00
(114)	Poole	75.00	40.00	25.00
(115)	Prough	75.00	40.00	25.00
(116)	Read	75.00	40.00	25.00
(117)	Richardson	75.00	40.00	25.00
(118)	Rieger	75.00	40.00	25.00
(119)	Ritchie	75.00	40.00	25.00
(120)	Ross	75.00	40.00	25.00
(121)	Ryan	75.00	40.00	25.00
(122)	Sand	75.00	40.00	25.00
(123)	Sargent	75.00	40.00	25.00
(124)	Sawyer	75.00	40.00	25.00
(125)	Schang	75.00	40.00	25.00
(126)	Schick	75.00	40.00	25.00
(127)	Schneider	75.00	40.00	25.00
(128)	Schorr	75.00	40.00	25.00
(129)	Schulte (Oakland)	75.00	40.00	25.00
(130)	Schulte (Seattle)	75.00	40.00	25.00
(131)	Scott	75.00	40.00	25.00
(132)	See	75.00	40.00	25.00
(133)	Shea	75.00	40.00	25.00
(134)	Sheehan	75.00	40.00	25.00
(135)	Siglin	75.00	40.00	25.00
(136)	Smith	75.00	40.00	25.00
(137)	Soria	75.00	40.00	25.00
(138)	Spencer	75.00	40.00	25.00
(139)	Stanage	75.00	40.00	25.00
(140)	Strand	75.00	40.00	25.00
(141)	Stumpf	75.00	40.00	25.00
(142)	Sullivan	75.00	40.00	25.00
(143)	Sutherland	75.00	40.00	25.00
(144)	Thomas	75.00	40.00	25.00
(145)	Jim Thorpe	30,000	17,500	9,500
(146)	Thurston	75.00	40.00	25.00
(147)	Tobin	75.00	40.00	25.00
(148)	Turner	75.00	40.00	25.00
(149)	Twombly	75.00	40.00	25.00
(150)	Valla	75.00	40.00	25.00
(151)	Vargas	75.00	40.00	25.00
(152)	Viveros	75.00	40.00	25.00
(153)	Wallace	75.00	40.00	25.00
(154)	Walsh	75.00	40.00	25.00
(155)	Wells	75.00	40.00	25.00
(156)	Westersil	75.00	40.00	25.00
(157)	Wheat	75.00	40.00	25.00
(158)	Wilhoit	75.00	40.00	25.00
(159)	Wilie	75.00	40.00	25.00
(160)	Williams	75.00	40.00	25.00
(161)	Yelle	75.00	40.00	25.00
(162)	Zeider	75.00	40.00	25.00

1923 Zeenut Pacific Coast League

This is the only year that Zeenuts cards were issued in two different sizes. Cards in the "regular" series measure about 1-7/8" x 3-1/2", feature black-and-white photos and are dated 1923. A second series, containing just 24 cards (all San Francisco and Oakland players), are sepia-toned re-issues of the 1922 series with a "1923" date and measure about 1/16" longer. The re-issued cards have coupons with an expiration date of April 1, 1923. The dated cards have coupons with an expiration date of April 1, 1924.

		NM	EX	VG
Common Player:		75.00	40.00	25.00
With Coupon:		1,000	500.00	300.00
(1)	Agnew (1923 photo)	75.00	40.00	25.00
(2)	Agnew (1922 photo re-dated)	75.00	40.00	25.00
(3)	Alten	75.00	40.00	25.00
(4)	Anderson	75.00	40.00	25.00
(5)	Anfinson	75.00	40.00	25.00
(6)	Arlett	75.00	40.00	25.00
(7)	Baker	75.00	40.00	25.00
(8)	Baldwin	75.00	40.00	25.00
(9)	Barney	75.00	40.00	25.00
(10)	Blake	75.00	40.00	25.00
(11)	Bodie	75.00	40.00	25.00
(12)	Brazil	75.00	40.00	25.00
(13)	Brenton	75.00	40.00	25.00
(14)	Brown (Oakland)	75.00	40.00	25.00
(15)	Brown (Sacramento)	75.00	40.00	25.00
(16)	Brubaker	75.00	40.00	25.00
(17)	Buckley	75.00	40.00	25.00
(18)	Canfield	75.00	40.00	25.00
(19)	Carroll	75.00	40.00	25.00
(20)	Cather	75.00	40.00	25.00
(21)	Chadbourne	75.00	40.00	25.00
(22)	Charvez	75.00	40.00	25.00
(23)	Cochrane	75.00	40.00	25.00
(24)	Colwell	75.00	40.00	25.00
(25)	Compton	75.00	40.00	25.00
(26)	Cook	75.00	40.00	25.00
(27)	Cooper (1923 photo)	75.00	40.00	25.00
(28)	Cooper (1922 photo re-date)	75.00	40.00	25.00
(29)	Coumbe	75.00	40.00	25.00
(30)	Courtney	75.00	40.00	25.00
(31)	Crandall	75.00	40.00	25.00
(32)	Crane	75.00	40.00	25.00
(33)	Crowder	75.00	40.00	25.00
(34)	Crumpler	75.00	40.00	25.00
(35)	Daly (Los Angeles)	75.00	40.00	25.00
(36)	Daly (Portland)	75.00	40.00	25.00
(37)	Deal	75.00	40.00	25.00
(38)	Doyle	75.00	40.00	25.00
(39)	Duchalsky	75.00	40.00	25.00
(40)	Eckert	75.00	40.00	25.00
(41)	Eldred	75.00	40.00	25.00
(42)	Eley	75.00	40.00	25.00
(43)	Eller	75.00	40.00	25.00
(44)	Ellison (1923 photo)	75.00	40.00	25.00
(45)	Ellison (1922 photo re-dated)	75.00	40.00	25.00
(46)	Essick	75.00	40.00	25.00
(47)	Fittery	75.00	40.00	25.00
(48)	Flashkamper	75.00	40.00	25.00
(49)	Frederick	75.00	40.00	25.00

(50)	French	75.00	40.00	25.00
(51)	Geary (1923 photo)	75.00	40.00	25.00
(52)	Geary (1922 photo re-dated)	75.00	40.00	25.00
(53)	Gilder	75.00	40.00	25.00
(54)	Golvin	75.00	40.00	25.00
(55)	Gorman	75.00	40.00	25.00
(56)	Gould	75.00	40.00	25.00
(57)	Gressett	75.00	40.00	25.00
(58)	Griggs	75.00	40.00	25.00
(59)	Hannah (Los Angeles)	75.00	40.00	25.00
(60)	Hannah (Vernon)	75.00	40.00	25.00
(61)	Hemingway	75.00	40.00	25.00
(62)	Hendryx	75.00	40.00	25.00
(63)	High	75.00	40.00	25.00
(64)	H. High	75.00	40.00	25.00
(65)	Hodge	75.00	40.00	25.00
(66)	Hood	75.00	40.00	25.00
(67)	Houghs	75.00	40.00	25.00
(68)	Howard (1923 photo)	75.00	40.00	25.00
(69)	Howard (1922 photo re-date)	75.00	40.00	25.00
(70)	Del Howard	75.00	40.00	25.00
(71)	Jacobs	75.00	40.00	25.00
(72)	James	75.00	40.00	25.00
(73)	Johnson	75.00	40.00	25.00
(74)	Johnston	75.00	40.00	25.00
(75)	Jolly (Jolley)	75.00	40.00	25.00
(76)	Jones (Los Angeles)	75.00	40.00	25.00
(77)	Jones (Oakland)	75.00	40.00	25.00
(78)	Jones (Portland)	75.00	40.00	25.00
(79)	Kallio	75.00	40.00	25.00
(80)	Kearns	75.00	40.00	25.00
(81)	Keiser	75.00	40.00	25.00
(82)	Keller	75.00	40.00	25.00
(83)	Kelly (San Francisco)	75.00	40.00	25.00
(84)	Kelly (Seattle)	75.00	40.00	25.00
(85)	Kenna	75.00	40.00	25.00
(86)	Kilduff	75.00	40.00	25.00
(87)	Killifer	75.00	40.00	25.00
(88)	King	75.00	40.00	25.00
(89)	Knight (1923 photo)	75.00	40.00	25.00
(90)	Knight (1922 photo re-dated)	75.00	40.00	25.00
(91)	Koehler	75.00	40.00	25.00
(92)	Kopp	75.00	40.00	25.00
(93)	Krause	75.00	40.00	25.00
(94)	Kremer	75.00	40.00	25.00
(95)	Krug	75.00	40.00	25.00
(96)	Lafayette (1923 photo)	75.00	40.00	25.00
(97)	Lafayette (1922 photo re-dated)	75.00	40.00	25.00
(98)	Lane	75.00	40.00	25.00
(99)	Lefevre	75.00	40.00	25.00
(100)	Leslie	75.00	40.00	25.00
(101)	Levere	75.00	40.00	25.00
(102)	Leverenz	75.00	40.00	25.00
(103)	Lewis	75.00	40.00	25.00
(104)	Lindimore	75.00	40.00	25.00
(105)	Locker	75.00	40.00	25.00
(106)	Lyons	75.00	40.00	25.00
(107)	Maderas	75.00	40.00	25.00
(108)	Mails	75.00	40.00	25.00
(109)	Marriott	75.00	40.00	25.00
(110)	Matzen	75.00	40.00	25.00
(111)	McAuley	75.00	40.00	25.00
(112)	McAuliffe	75.00	40.00	25.00
(113)	McCabe (Los Angeles)	75.00	40.00	25.00
(114)	McCabe (Salt Lake)	75.00	40.00	25.00
(115)	McCann	75.00	40.00	25.00
(116)	McGaffigan	75.00	40.00	25.00
(117)	McGinnis	75.00	40.00	25.00
(118)	McNeilly	75.00	40.00	25.00
(119)	McWeeney	75.00	40.00	25.00
(120)	Middleton	75.00	40.00	25.00
(121)	Miller	75.00	40.00	25.00
(122)	Mitchell (1923 photo)	75.00	40.00	25.00
(123)	Mitchell (1922 photo re-date)	75.00	40.00	25.00
(124)	Mitze	75.00	40.00	25.00
(125)	Mulligan	75.00	40.00	25.00
(126)	Murchio	75.00	40.00	25.00
(127)	D. Murphy	75.00	40.00	25.00
(128)	R. Murphy	75.00	40.00	25.00
(129)	Noack	75.00	40.00	25.00
(130)	O'Brien	75.00	40.00	25.00
(131)	Onslow	75.00	40.00	25.00
(132)	Orr	75.00	40.00	25.00
(133)	Pearce	75.00	40.00	25.00
(134)	Penner	75.00	40.00	25.00
(135)	Peters	75.00	40.00	25.00
(136)	Pick	75.00	40.00	25.00
(137)	Pigg	75.00	40.00	25.00
(138)	Plummer	75.00	40.00	25.00
(139)	Ponder	75.00	40.00	25.00
(140)	Poole	75.00	40.00	25.00
(141)	Ramage	75.00	40.00	25.00
(142)	Read (1923 photo)	75.00	40.00	25.00
(143)	Read (1922 photo re-dated)	75.00	40.00	25.00
(144)	Rhyne	75.00	40.00	25.00
(145)	Ritchie	75.00	40.00	25.00
(146)	Robertson	75.00	40.00	25.00
(147)	Rohwer (Sacramento)	75.00	40.00	25.00
(148)	Rohwer (Seattle)	75.00	40.00	25.00
(149)	Ryan	75.00	40.00	25.00
(150)	Sawyer	75.00	40.00	25.00
(151)	Schang	75.00	40.00	25.00
(152)	Schneider	75.00	40.00	25.00
(153)	Schroeder	75.00	40.00	25.00
(154)	Scott	75.00	40.00	25.00
(155)	See	75.00	40.00	25.00
(156)	Shea	75.00	40.00	25.00
(157)	M. Shea	75.00	40.00	25.00
(158)	Spec Shea	75.00	40.00	25.00
(159)	Sheehan	75.00	40.00	25.00
(160)	Shellenback	75.00	40.00	25.00
(161)	Siglin	75.00	40.00	25.00
(162)	Singleton	75.00	40.00	25.00
(163)	Smith	75.00	40.00	25.00
(164)	M.H. Smith	75.00	40.00	25.00
(165)	Stanton	75.00	40.00	25.00
(166)	Strand	75.00	40.00	25.00
(167)	Stumpf	75.00	40.00	25.00
(168)	Sutherland	75.00	40.00	25.00
(169)	Tesar	75.00	40.00	25.00
(170)	Thomas (Los Angeles)	75.00	40.00	25.00
(171)	Thomas (Oakland)	75.00	40.00	25.00
(172)	Tobin	75.00	40.00	25.00
(173)	Twombly	75.00	40.00	25.00
(174)	Valla	75.00	40.00	25.00
(175)	Vargas	75.00	40.00	25.00
(176)	Vitt	75.00	40.00	25.00
(177)	Wallace	75.00	40.00	25.00
(178)	Walsh (San Francisco)	75.00	40.00	25.00
(179)	Walsh (Seattle)	75.00	40.00	25.00
(180)	Paul Waner	1,500	800.00	500.00
(181)	Wells (Oakland)	75.00	40.00	25.00
(182)	Wells (San Francisco)	75.00	40.00	25.00
(183)	Welsh	75.00	40.00	25.00
(184)	Wilhoit	75.00	40.00	25.00
(185)	Wilie (1923 photo)	75.00	40.00	25.00
(186)	Wilie (1922 photo re-dated)	75.00	40.00	25.00
(187)	Williams	75.00	40.00	25.00
(188)	Witzel	75.00	40.00	25.00
(189)	Wolfer	75.00	40.00	25.00
(190)	Wolverton	75.00	40.00	25.00
(191)	Yarrison	75.00	40.00	25.00
(192)	Yaryan	75.00	40.00	25.00
(193)	Yelle (1923 photo)	75.00	40.00	25.00
(194)	Yelle (1922 photo re-dated)	75.00	40.00	25.00
(195)	Moses Yellowhorse	1,800	900.00	550.00
(196)	Zeider	75.00	40.00	25.00

1924 Zeenut Pacific Coast League

Zeenut cards in 1924 measure about 1-3/4" x 3-7/16" and display the date on the front. The cards include a full photographic background. There are 144 subjects known.

		NM	EX	VG
	Common Player:	75.00	40.00	25.00
(1)	Adams	125.00	65.00	40.00
(2)	Agnew	75.00	40.00	25.00
(3)	Arlett	75.00	40.00	25.00
(4)	Baker	75.00	40.00	25.00
(5)	E. Baldwin	75.00	40.00	25.00
(6)	T. Baldwin	75.00	40.00	25.00
(7)	Beck	75.00	40.00	25.00
(8)	Benton	75.00	40.00	25.00
(9)	Bernard	75.00	40.00	25.00
(10)	Bigbee	75.00	40.00	25.00
(11)	Billings	75.00	40.00	25.00
(12)	Blakesly	75.00	40.00	25.00
(13)	Brady	75.00	40.00	25.00
(14)	Brazil	75.00	40.00	25.00
(15)	Brown	75.00	40.00	25.00
(16)	Brubaker	75.00	40.00	25.00
(17)	Buckley	75.00	40.00	25.00
(18)	Burger	75.00	40.00	25.00
(19)	Byler	75.00	40.00	25.00
(20)	Cadore	75.00	40.00	25.00
(21)	Cather	75.00	40.00	25.00
(22)	Chadbourne	75.00	40.00	25.00
(23)	Christian	75.00	40.00	25.00
(24)	Mickey Cochrane (Portland)	2,500	1,250	750.00
(25)	Cochrane (Sacramento)	75.00	40.00	25.00
(26)	Cooper	75.00	40.00	25.00
(27)	Coumbe	75.00	40.00	25.00
(28)	Cox	75.00	40.00	25.00
(29)	Crandall	75.00	40.00	25.00
(30)	Daly	75.00	40.00	25.00
(31)	Deal	75.00	40.00	25.00
(32)	Distel	75.00	40.00	25.00
(33)	Durst	75.00	40.00	25.00
(34)	Eckert	75.00	40.00	25.00
(35)	Eldred	75.00	40.00	25.00
(36)	Ellison	75.00	40.00	25.00
(37)	Essick	75.00	40.00	25.00
(38)	Flashkamper	75.00	40.00	25.00
(39)	Foster	75.00	40.00	25.00
(40)	Fredericks	75.00	40.00	25.00
(41)	Geary	75.00	40.00	25.00
(42)	Goebel	75.00	40.00	25.00
(43)	Golvin	75.00	40.00	25.00
(44)	Gorman	75.00	40.00	25.00
(45)	Gould	75.00	40.00	25.00
(46)	Gressett	75.00	40.00	25.00
(47)	Griffin (San Francisco)	75.00	40.00	25.00
(48)	Griffin (Vernon)	75.00	40.00	25.00
(49)	Guisto	75.00	40.00	25.00
(50)	Gunther	75.00	40.00	25.00
(51)	Hall	75.00	40.00	25.00
(52)	Hannah	75.00	40.00	25.00
(53)	Hendryx	75.00	40.00	25.00
(54)	High	75.00	40.00	25.00
(55)	Hodge	75.00	40.00	25.00
(56)	Hood	75.00	40.00	25.00
(57)	Ivan Howard	75.00	40.00	25.00
(58)	Hughes (Los Angeles)	75.00	40.00	25.00
(59)	Hughes (Sacramento)	75.00	40.00	25.00
(60)	Jacobs	75.00	40.00	25.00
(61)	James	75.00	40.00	25.00
(62)	Jenkins	75.00	40.00	25.00
(63)	Johnson	75.00	40.00	25.00
(64)	Jones	75.00	40.00	25.00
(65)	Keck	75.00	40.00	25.00
(66)	Kelley	75.00	40.00	25.00
(67)	Kenworthy	75.00	40.00	25.00
(68)	Kilduff	75.00	40.00	25.00
(69)	Killifer	75.00	40.00	25.00
(70)	Kimmick	75.00	40.00	25.00
(71)	Kopp	75.00	40.00	25.00
(72)	Krause	75.00	40.00	25.00
(73)	Krug	75.00	40.00	25.00
(74)	Kunz	75.00	40.00	25.00
(75)	Lafayette	75.00	40.00	25.00
(76)	Lennon	75.00	40.00	25.00
(77)	Leptich	75.00	40.00	25.00
(78)	Leslie	75.00	40.00	25.00
(79)	Leverenz	75.00	40.00	25.00
(80)	Lewis	75.00	40.00	25.00
(81)	Maderas	75.00	40.00	25.00
(82)	Mails	75.00	40.00	25.00
(83)	McAuley	75.00	40.00	25.00
(84)	McCann	75.00	40.00	25.00
(85)	McDowell	75.00	40.00	25.00
(86)	McNeely	75.00	40.00	25.00
(87)	Menosky	75.00	40.00	25.00
(88)	Meyers	75.00	40.00	25.00
(89)	Miller	75.00	40.00	25.00
(90)	Mitchell	75.00	40.00	25.00
(91)	Mulligan	75.00	40.00	25.00
(92)	D. Murphy	75.00	40.00	25.00
(93)	R. Murphy	75.00	40.00	25.00
(94)	Osborne	75.00	40.00	25.00
(95)	Paynter	75.00	40.00	25.00
(96)	Penner	75.00	40.00	25.00
(97)	Peters (Sacramento)	75.00	40.00	25.00
(98)	Peters (Salt Lake)	75.00	40.00	25.00
(99)	Pick	75.00	40.00	25.00
(100)	Pillette	75.00	40.00	25.00
(101)	Poole	75.00	40.00	25.00
(102)	Prough	75.00	40.00	25.00
(103)	Querry	75.00	40.00	25.00
(104)	Read	75.00	40.00	25.00
(105)	Rhyne	75.00	40.00	25.00
(106)	Ritchie	75.00	40.00	25.00
(107)	Root	75.00	40.00	25.00
(108)	Rowher	75.00	40.00	25.00
(109)	Schang	75.00	40.00	25.00
(110)	Schneider	75.00	40.00	25.00
(111)	Schorr	75.00	40.00	25.00
(112)	Schroeder	75.00	40.00	25.00
(113)	Scott	75.00	40.00	25.00
(114)	Sellers	75.00	40.00	25.00
(115)	"Speck" Shay	75.00	40.00	25.00
(116)	Shea (Sacramento)	75.00	40.00	25.00
(117)	Shea (San Francisco)	75.00	40.00	25.00
(118)	Shellenback	75.00	40.00	25.00
(119)	Siebold	75.00	40.00	25.00
(120)	Siglin	75.00	40.00	25.00
(121)	Slade	75.00	40.00	25.00
(122)	Smith (Sacramento)	75.00	40.00	25.00
(123)	Smith (San Francisco)	75.00	40.00	25.00
(124)	Stanton	75.00	40.00	25.00
(125)	Tanner	75.00	40.00	25.00
(126)	Twomley	75.00	40.00	25.00
(127)	Valla	75.00	40.00	25.00
(128)	Vargas	75.00	40.00	25.00
(129)	Vines	75.00	40.00	25.00
(130)	Vitt	75.00	40.00	25.00
(131)	Wallace	75.00	40.00	25.00
(132)	Walsh	75.00	40.00	25.00
(133)	Paul Waner	1,200	600.00	350.00
(134)	Warner (Fielding)	75.00	40.00	25.00
(135)	Warner (Throwing)	75.00	40.00	25.00
(136)	Welsh	75.00	40.00	25.00
(137)	Wetzel	75.00	40.00	25.00
(138)	Whalen	75.00	40.00	25.00
(139)	Wilhoit	75.00	40.00	25.00
(140)	Williams (San Francisco)	75.00	40.00	25.00
(141)	Williams (Seattle)	75.00	40.00	25.00
(142)	Wolfer	75.00	40.00	25.00
(143)	Yelle	75.00	40.00	25.00
(144)	Moses Yellowhorse	1,000	500.00	300.00

1925 Zeenut Pacific Coast League

Zeenut cards in 1925 measure about 1-3/4" x 3-7/16" and display the date on the front. The cards include a full photographic background. There are 162 subjects known for 1925.

		NM	EX	VG
Common Player:		75.00	40.00	25.00
With Coupon:		450.00	225.00	140.00
(1)	Adeylatte	75.00	40.00	25.00
(2)	Agnew	75.00	40.00	25.00
(3)	Arlett	75.00	40.00	25.00
(4)	Bagby	75.00	40.00	25.00
(5)	Bahr	75.00	40.00	25.00
(6)	Baker	75.00	40.00	25.00
(7)	E. Baldwin	75.00	40.00	25.00
(8)	Barfoot	75.00	40.00	25.00
(9)	Beck	75.00	40.00	25.00
(10)	Becker	75.00	40.00	25.00
(11)	Blakesley	75.00	40.00	25.00
(12)	Boehler	75.00	40.00	25.00
(13)	Brady	75.00	40.00	25.00
(14)	Brandt	75.00	40.00	25.00
(15)	Bratcher	75.00	40.00	25.00
(16)	Brazil	75.00	40.00	25.00
(17)	Brower	75.00	40.00	25.00
(18)	Brown	75.00	40.00	25.00
(19)	Brubaker	75.00	40.00	25.00
(20)	Bryan	75.00	40.00	25.00
(21)	Canfield	75.00	40.00	25.00
(22)	W. Canfield	75.00	40.00	25.00
(23)	Cather	75.00	40.00	25.00
(24)	Chavez	75.00	40.00	25.00
(25)	Christain	75.00	40.00	25.00
(26)	Cochrane	75.00	40.00	25.00
(27)	Connolly	75.00	40.00	25.00
(28)	Cook	75.00	40.00	25.00
(29)	Cooper	75.00	40.00	25.00
(30)	Coumbe	75.00	40.00	25.00
(31)	Crandall	75.00	40.00	25.00
(32)	Crane	75.00	40.00	25.00
(33)	Crockett	75.00	40.00	25.00
(34)	Crosby	75.00	40.00	25.00
(35)	Cutshaw	75.00	40.00	25.00
(36)	Daly	75.00	40.00	25.00
(37)	Davis	75.00	40.00	25.00
(38)	Deal	75.00	40.00	25.00
(39)	Delaney	75.00	40.00	25.00
(40)	Dempsey	75.00	40.00	25.00
(41)	Dumovich	75.00	40.00	25.00
(42)	Eckert	75.00	40.00	25.00
(43)	Eldred	75.00	40.00	25.00
(44)	Elliott	75.00	40.00	25.00
(45)	Ellison	75.00	40.00	25.00
(46)	Emmer	75.00	40.00	25.00
(47)	Ennis	75.00	40.00	25.00
(48)	Essick	75.00	40.00	25.00
(49)	Finn	75.00	40.00	25.00
(50)	Flowers	75.00	40.00	25.00
(51)	Frederick	75.00	40.00	25.00
(52)	Fussell	75.00	40.00	25.00
(53)	Geary	75.00	40.00	25.00
(54)	Gorman	75.00	40.00	25.00
(55)	Griffin (San Francisco)	75.00	40.00	25.00
(56)	Griffin (Vernon)	75.00	40.00	25.00
(57)	Grimes	75.00	40.00	25.00
(58)	Guisto	75.00	40.00	25.00
(59)	Hannah	75.00	40.00	25.00
(60)	Haughy	75.00	40.00	25.00
(61)	Hemingway	75.00	40.00	25.00
(62)	Hendryx	75.00	40.00	25.00
(63)	Herman	200.00	100.00	50.00
(64)	High	75.00	40.00	25.00
(65)	Hoffman	75.00	40.00	25.00
(66)	Hood	75.00	40.00	25.00
(67)	Horan	75.00	40.00	25.00
(68)	Horton	75.00	40.00	25.00
(69)	Howard	75.00	40.00	25.00
(70)	Hughes	75.00	40.00	25.00
(71)	Hulvey	75.00	40.00	25.00
(72)	Hunnefield	75.00	40.00	25.00
(73)	Jacobs	75.00	40.00	25.00
(74)	James	75.00	40.00	25.00
(75)	Keating	75.00	40.00	25.00
(76)	Keefe	75.00	40.00	25.00
(77)	Kelly	75.00	40.00	25.00
(78)	Kilduff	75.00	40.00	25.00
(79)	Kohler	75.00	40.00	25.00
(80)	Kopp	75.00	40.00	25.00
(81)	Krause	75.00	40.00	25.00
(82)	Krug	75.00	40.00	25.00
(83)	Kunz	75.00	40.00	25.00
(84)	Lafayette	75.00	40.00	25.00
(85)	Tony Lazzeri	450.00	250.00	175.00
(86)	Leslie	75.00	40.00	25.00
(87)	Leverenz	75.00	40.00	25.00
(88)	Duffy Lewis	75.00	40.00	25.00
(89)	Lindemore	75.00	40.00	25.00
(90)	Ludolph	75.00	40.00	25.00
(91)	Makin	75.00	40.00	25.00
(92)	Martin (Sacramento)	75.00	40.00	25.00
(93)	Martin (Portland)	75.00	40.00	25.00
(94)	McCabe	75.00	40.00	25.00
(95)	McCann	75.00	40.00	25.00
(96)	McCarren	75.00	40.00	25.00
(97)	McDonald	75.00	40.00	25.00
(98)	McGinnis (Portland)	75.00	40.00	25.00
(99)	McGinnis (Sacramento)	75.00	40.00	25.00
(100)	McLaughlin	75.00	40.00	25.00
(101)	Milstead	75.00	40.00	25.00
(102)	Mitchell	75.00	40.00	25.00
(103)	Moudy	75.00	40.00	25.00
(104)	Mulcahy	75.00	40.00	25.00
(105)	Mulligan	75.00	40.00	25.00
(106)	Lefty O'Doul	450.00	250.00	175.00
(107)	O'Neil	75.00	40.00	25.00
(108)	Ortman	75.00	40.00	25.00
(109)	Pailey	75.00	40.00	25.00
(110)	Paynter	75.00	40.00	25.00
(111)	Peery	75.00	40.00	25.00
(112)	Penner	75.00	40.00	25.00
(113)	Pfeffer	75.00	40.00	25.00
(114)	Phillips	75.00	40.00	25.00
(115)	Pickering	75.00	40.00	25.00
(116)	Piercy	75.00	40.00	25.00
(117)	Pillette	75.00	40.00	25.00
(118)	Plummer	75.00	40.00	25.00
(119)	Ponder	75.00	40.00	25.00
(120)	Pruett	75.00	40.00	25.00
(121)	Rawlings	75.00	40.00	25.00
(122)	Read	75.00	40.00	25.00
(123)	Jimmy Reese	300.00	200.00	100.00
(124)	Rhyne	75.00	40.00	25.00
(125)	Riconda	75.00	40.00	25.00
(126)	Ritchie	75.00	40.00	25.00
(127)	Rohwer	75.00	40.00	25.00
(128)	Rowland	75.00	40.00	25.00
(129)	Ryan	75.00	40.00	25.00
(130)	Sandberg	75.00	40.00	25.00
(131)	Schang	75.00	40.00	25.00
(132)	Shea	75.00	40.00	25.00
(133)	M. Shea	75.00	40.00	25.00
(134)	Shellenbach	75.00	40.00	25.00
(135)	Sherling	75.00	40.00	25.00
(136)	Siglin	75.00	40.00	25.00
(137)	Slade	75.00	40.00	25.00
(138)	Spencer	75.00	40.00	25.00
(139)	Steward	75.00	40.00	25.00
(140)	Stivers	75.00	40.00	25.00
(141)	Suhr	75.00	40.00	25.00
(142)	Sutherland	75.00	40.00	25.00
(143)	Thomas (Portland)	75.00	40.00	25.00
(144)	Thomas (Vernon)	75.00	40.00	25.00
(145)	Thompson	75.00	40.00	25.00
(146)	Tobin	75.00	40.00	25.00
(147)	Twombly	75.00	40.00	25.00
(148)	Valla	75.00	40.00	25.00
(149)	Vinci	75.00	40.00	25.00
(150)	O. Vitt	75.00	40.00	25.00
(151)	Wachenfeld	75.00	40.00	25.00
(152)	Paul Waner	1,200	600.00	350.00
(153)	Lloyd Waner	1,200	600.00	360.00
(154)	Warner	75.00	40.00	25.00
(155)	Watson	75.00	40.00	25.00
(156)	Weinert	75.00	40.00	25.00
(157)	Whaley	75.00	40.00	25.00
(158)	Whitney	75.00	40.00	25.00
(159)	Williams	75.00	40.00	25.00
(160)	Winters	75.00	40.00	25.00
(161)	Wolfer	75.00	40.00	25.00
(162)	Woodring	75.00	40.00	25.00
(163)	Yeargin	75.00	40.00	25.00
(164)	Yelle	75.00	40.00	25.00

1926 Zeenut Pacific Coast League

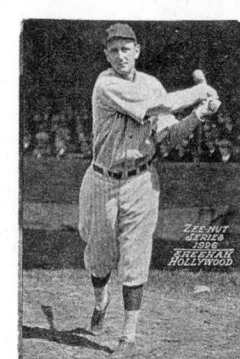

Except for their slightly smaller size (1-3/4" x 3-7/16"), the 1926 Zeenut cards are nearly identical to the previous two years. Considered more difficult than other Zeenuts series of this era, the 1926 set consists of more than 170 known subjects.

		NM	EX	VG
Common Player:		60.00	30.00	20.00
With Coupon:		450.00	225.00	140.00
(1)	Agnew	60.00	30.00	20.00
(2)	Allen	60.00	30.00	20.00
(3)	Alley	60.00	30.00	20.00
(4)	Averill	1,500	750.00	450.00
(5)	Bagwell	60.00	30.00	20.00
(6)	Baker	60.00	30.00	20.00
(7)	T. Baldwin	60.00	30.00	20.00
(8)	Berry	60.00	30.00	20.00
(9)	Bool	60.00	30.00	20.00
(10)	Boone	60.00	30.00	20.00
(11)	Boyd	60.00	30.00	20.00
(12)	Brady	60.00	30.00	20.00
(13)	Brazil	60.00	30.00	20.00
(14)	Brower	60.00	30.00	20.00
(15)	Brubaker	60.00	30.00	20.00
(16)	Bryan	60.00	30.00	20.00
(17)	Burns	60.00	30.00	20.00
(18)	C. Canfield	60.00	30.00	20.00
(19)	W. Canfield	60.00	30.00	20.00
(20)	Carson	60.00	30.00	20.00
(21)	Christian	60.00	30.00	20.00
(22)	Cole	60.00	30.00	20.00
(23)	Connolly	60.00	30.00	20.00
(24)	Cook	60.00	30.00	20.00
(25)	Couch	60.00	30.00	20.00
(26)	Coumbe	60.00	30.00	20.00
(27)	Crockett	60.00	30.00	20.00
(28)	Cunningham	60.00	30.00	20.00
(29)	Cutshaw	60.00	30.00	20.00
(30)	Daglia	60.00	30.00	20.00
(31)	Danning	60.00	30.00	20.00
(32)	Davis	60.00	30.00	20.00
(33)	Delaney	60.00	30.00	20.00
(34)	Eckert	60.00	30.00	20.00
(35)	Eldred	60.00	30.00	20.00
(36)	Elliott	60.00	30.00	20.00
(37)	Ellison	60.00	30.00	20.00
(38)	Ellsworth	60.00	30.00	20.00
(39)	Elsh	60.00	30.00	20.00
(40)	Fenton	60.00	30.00	20.00
(41)	Finn	60.00	30.00	20.00
(42)	Flashkamper	60.00	30.00	20.00
(43)	Fowler	60.00	30.00	20.00
(44)	Frederick	60.00	30.00	20.00
(45)	Freeman	60.00	30.00	20.00
(46)	French	60.00	30.00	20.00
(47)	Garrison	60.00	30.00	20.00
(48)	Geary	60.00	30.00	20.00
(49)	Gillespie	60.00	30.00	20.00
(50)	Glazner	60.00	30.00	20.00
(51)	Gould	60.00	30.00	20.00
(52)	Governor	60.00	30.00	20.00
(53)	Griffin (Missions)	60.00	30.00	20.00
(54)	Griffin (San Francisco)	60.00	30.00	20.00
(55)	Guisto	60.00	30.00	20.00
(56)	Hamilton	60.00	30.00	20.00
(57)	Hannah	60.00	30.00	20.00
(58)	Hansen	60.00	30.00	20.00
(59)	Hasty	60.00	30.00	20.00
(60)	Hemingway	60.00	30.00	20.00
(61)	Hendryx	60.00	30.00	20.00
(62)	Hickok	60.00	30.00	20.00
(63)	Hillis	60.00	30.00	20.00
(64)	Hoffman	60.00	30.00	20.00
(65)	Hollerson	60.00	30.00	20.00
(66)	Holmes	60.00	30.00	20.00
(67)	Hood	60.00	30.00	20.00
(68)	Howard	60.00	30.00	20.00
(69)	Hufft	60.00	30.00	20.00
(70)	Hughes	60.00	30.00	20.00
(71)	Hulvey	60.00	30.00	20.00
(72)	Hurst	60.00	30.00	20.00
(73)	R. Jacobs	60.00	30.00	20.00
(74)	Jahn	60.00	30.00	20.00
(75)	Jenkins	60.00	30.00	20.00
(76)	Johnson	60.00	30.00	20.00
(77)	Jolly (Jolley)	100.00	50.00	30.00
(78)	Jones	60.00	30.00	20.00
(79)	Kallio	60.00	30.00	20.00
(80)	Keating	60.00	30.00	20.00
(81)	Kerr (Hollywood)	60.00	30.00	20.00
(82)	Kerr (San Francisco)	60.00	30.00	20.00
(83)	Kilduff	60.00	30.00	20.00
(84)	Killifer	60.00	30.00	20.00
(85)	Knight	60.00	30.00	20.00
(86)	Koehler	60.00	30.00	20.00
(87)	Kopp	60.00	30.00	20.00
(88)	Krause	60.00	30.00	20.00
(89)	Krug	60.00	30.00	20.00
(90)	Kunz	60.00	30.00	20.00
(91)	Lafayette	60.00	30.00	20.00
(92)	Lane	60.00	30.00	20.00
(93)	Lang	60.00	30.00	20.00
(94)	Lary	60.00	30.00	20.00
(95)	Leslie	60.00	30.00	20.00
(96)	Lindemore	60.00	30.00	20.00
(97)	Ludolph	60.00	30.00	20.00
(98)	Makin	60.00	30.00	20.00
(99)	Mangum	60.00	30.00	20.00
(100)	Martin	60.00	30.00	20.00
(101)	McCredie	60.00	30.00	20.00
(102)	McDowell	60.00	30.00	20.00
(103)	McKenry	60.00	30.00	20.00
(104)	McLoughlin	60.00	30.00	20.00
(105)	McNally	60.00	30.00	20.00
(106)	McPhee	60.00	30.00	20.00
(107)	Meeker	60.00	30.00	20.00
(108)	Metz	60.00	30.00	20.00
(109)	Miller	60.00	30.00	20.00
(110)	Mitchell (Los Angeles)	60.00	30.00	20.00
(111)	Mitchell (San Francisco)	60.00	30.00	20.00
(112)	Monroe	60.00	30.00	20.00
(113)	Moudy	60.00	30.00	20.00
(114)	Mulcahy	60.00	30.00	20.00
(115)	Mulligan	60.00	30.00	20.00
(116)	Murphy	60.00	30.00	20.00
(117)	Lefty O'Doul	600.00	300.00	180.00
(118)	O'Neill	60.00	30.00	20.00
(119)	Oeschger	60.00	30.00	20.00
(120)	Oliver	60.00	30.00	20.00
(121)	Ortman	60.00	30.00	20.00
(122)	Osborn	60.00	30.00	20.00
(123)	Paynter	60.00	30.00	20.00
(124)	Peters	60.00	30.00	20.00
(125)	Pfahler	60.00	30.00	20.00
(126)	Pillette	60.00	30.00	20.00
(127)	Plummer	60.00	30.00	20.00
(128)	Prothro	60.00	30.00	20.00
(129)	Pruett	60.00	30.00	20.00
(130)	Rachac	60.00	30.00	20.00
(131)	Ramsey	60.00	30.00	20.00
(132)	Rathjen	60.00	30.00	20.00
(133)	Read	60.00	30.00	20.00
(134)	Redman	60.00	30.00	20.00
(135)	Jimmy Reese	60.00	30.00	20.00
(136)	Rodda	60.00	30.00	20.00
(137)	Rohwer	60.00	30.00	20.00
(138)	Ryan	60.00	30.00	20.00
(139)	Sandberg	60.00	30.00	20.00
(140)	Sanders	60.00	30.00	20.00
(141)	E. Shea	60.00	30.00	20.00
(142)	M. Shea	60.00	30.00	20.00
(143)	Sheehan	60.00	30.00	20.00
(144)	Shellenbach	60.00	30.00	20.00
(145)	Sherlock	60.00	30.00	20.00
(146)	Siglin	60.00	30.00	20.00
(147)	Slade	60.00	30.00	20.00
(148)	E. Smith	60.00	30.00	20.00
(149)	M. Smith	60.00	30.00	20.00
(150)	Staley	60.00	30.00	20.00

		NM	EX	VG
(151)	Statz	120.00	60.00	40.00
(152)	Stroud	60.00	30.00	20.00
(153)	Stuart	60.00	30.00	20.00
(154)	Suhr	60.00	30.00	20.00
(155)	Swanson	60.00	30.00	20.00
(156)	Sweeney	60.00	30.00	20.00
(157)	Tadevich	60.00	30.00	20.00
(158)	Thomas	60.00	30.00	20.00
(159)	Thompson	60.00	30.00	20.00
(160)	Tobin	60.00	30.00	20.00
(161)	Valla	60.00	30.00	20.00
(162)	Vargas	60.00	30.00	20.00
(163)	Vinci	60.00	30.00	20.00
(164)	Walters	60.00	30.00	20.00
(165)	Lloyd Waner	1,600.	800.00	480.00
(166)	Weis	60.00	30.00	20.00
(167)	Whitney	60.00	30.00	20.00
(168)	Williams	60.00	30.00	20.00
(169)	Wright	60.00	30.00	20.00
(170)	Yelle	60.00	30.00	20.00
(171)	Zaeffel	60.00	30.00	20.00
(172)	Zoellers	60.00	30.00	20.00

1927 Zeenut Pacific Coast League

The 1927 Zeenuts are about the same size (1-3/4" x 3-3/8") and color as the 1926 issue, except the year is expressed in just two digits (27), a practice that continued through 1930. There are 144 subjects known.

		NM	EX	VG
Common Player:		60.00	30.00	20.00
With Coupon:		450.00	225.00	140.00
(1)	Agnew	60.00	30.00	20.00
(2)	Arlett	60.00	30.00	20.00
(3)	Averill	900.00	450.00	270.00
(4)	Backer	60.00	30.00	20.00
(5)	Bagwell	60.00	30.00	20.00
(6)	Baker	60.00	30.00	20.00
(7)	D. Baker	60.00	30.00	20.00
(8)	Ballenger	60.00	30.00	20.00
(9)	Baumgartner	60.00	30.00	20.00
(10)	Bigbee	60.00	30.00	20.00
(11)	Boehler	60.00	30.00	20.00
(12)	Bool	60.00	30.00	20.00
(13)	Borreani	60.00	30.00	20.00
(14)	Brady	60.00	30.00	20.00
(15)	Bratcher	60.00	30.00	20.00
(16)	Brett	60.00	30.00	20.00
(17)	Brown	60.00	30.00	20.00
(18)	Brubaker	60.00	30.00	20.00
(19)	Bryan	60.00	30.00	20.00
(20)	Callaghan	60.00	30.00	20.00
(21)	Caveney	60.00	30.00	20.00
(22)	Christian	60.00	30.00	20.00
(23)	Cissell	60.00	30.00	20.00
(24)	Cook	60.00	30.00	20.00
(25)	Cooper (Oakland)	60.00	30.00	20.00
(26)	Cooper (Sacramento)	60.00	30.00	20.00
(27)	Cox	60.00	30.00	20.00
(28)	Cunningham	60.00	30.00	20.00
(29)	Daglia	60.00	30.00	20.00
(30)	Dickerman	60.00	30.00	20.00
(31)	Dumovitch	60.00	30.00	20.00
(32)	Eckert	60.00	30.00	20.00
(33)	Eldred	60.00	30.00	20.00
(34)	Ellison	60.00	30.00	20.00
(35)	Fenton	60.00	30.00	20.00
(36)	Finn	60.00	30.00	20.00
(37)	Fischer	60.00	30.00	20.00
(38)	Frederick	60.00	30.00	20.00
(39)	French	60.00	30.00	20.00
(40)	Fullerton	60.00	30.00	20.00
(41)	Geary	60.00	30.00	20.00
(42)	Gillespie	60.00	30.00	20.00
(43)	Gooch	60.00	30.00	20.00
(44)	Gould	60.00	30.00	20.00
(45)	Governor	60.00	30.00	20.00
(46)	Guisto	60.00	30.00	20.00
(47)	Hannah	60.00	30.00	20.00
(48)	Hasty	60.00	30.00	20.00
(49)	Hemingway	60.00	30.00	20.00
(50)	Hoffman	60.00	30.00	20.00
(51)	Hood	60.00	30.00	20.00
(52)	Hooper	900.00	450.00	270.00
(53)	Hudgens	60.00	30.00	20.00
(54)	Hufft	60.00	30.00	20.00
(55)	Hughes	60.00	30.00	20.00
(56)	Jahn	60.00	30.00	20.00
(57)	Johnson (Portland)	60.00	30.00	20.00
(58)	Johnson (Seals)	60.00	30.00	20.00
(59)	Jolly (Jolley)	90.00	45.00	30.00
(60)	Jones	60.00	30.00	20.00
(61)	Kallio	60.00	30.00	20.00
(62)	Keating	60.00	30.00	20.00
(63)	Keefe	60.00	30.00	20.00
(64)	Killifer	60.00	30.00	20.00
(65)	Kimmick	60.00	30.00	20.00
(66)	Kinney	60.00	30.00	20.00
(67)	Knight	60.00	30.00	20.00
(68)	Koehler	60.00	30.00	20.00
(69)	Kopp	60.00	30.00	20.00
(70)	Krause	60.00	30.00	20.00
(71)	Krug	60.00	30.00	20.00
(72)	Kunz	60.00	30.00	20.00
(73)	Lary	60.00	30.00	20.00
(74)	Leard	60.00	30.00	20.00
(75)	Lingrel	60.00	30.00	20.00
(76)	Ludolph	60.00	30.00	20.00
(77)	Mails	60.00	30.00	20.00
(78)	Makin	60.00	30.00	20.00
(79)	Martin	60.00	30.00	20.00
(80)	May	60.00	30.00	20.00
(81)	McCabe	60.00	30.00	20.00
(82)	McCurdy	60.00	30.00	20.00
(83)	McDaniel	60.00	30.00	20.00
(84)	McGee	60.00	30.00	20.00
(85)	McLaughlin	60.00	30.00	20.00
(86)	McMurtry	60.00	30.00	20.00
(87)	Metz	60.00	30.00	20.00
(88)	Miljus	60.00	30.00	20.00
(89)	Mitchell	60.00	30.00	20.00
(90)	Monroe	60.00	30.00	20.00
(91)	Moudy	60.00	30.00	20.00
(92)	Mulligan	60.00	30.00	20.00
(93)	Murphy	60.00	30.00	20.00
(94)	O'Brien	60.00	30.00	20.00
(95)	Lefty O'Doul	600.00	300.00	180.00
(96)	Oliver	60.00	30.00	20.00
(97)	Osborn	60.00	30.00	20.00
(98)	Parker (Missions, batting.)	60.00	30.00	20.00
(99)	Parker (Missions, throwing.)	60.00	30.00	20.00
(100)	Parker (Portland)	60.00	30.00	20.00
(101)	Peters	60.00	30.00	20.00
(102)	Pillette	60.00	30.00	20.00
(103)	Ponder	60.00	30.00	20.00
(104)	Prothro	120.00	60.00	40.00
(105)	Rachac	60.00	30.00	20.00
(106)	Ramsey	60.00	30.00	20.00
(107)	Read	60.00	30.00	20.00
(108)	Jimmy Reese	375.00	190.00	120.00
(109)	Rodda	60.00	30.00	20.00
(110)	Rohwer	60.00	30.00	20.00
(111)	Rose	60.00	30.00	20.00
(112)	Ryan	60.00	30.00	20.00
(113)	Sandberg	60.00	30.00	20.00
(114)	Sanders	60.00	30.00	20.00
(115)	Severeid	60.00	30.00	20.00
(116)	Shea	60.00	30.00	20.00
(117)	Sheehan (Hollywood)	60.00	30.00	20.00
(118)	Sheehan (Seals)	60.00	30.00	20.00
(119)	Sherlock	60.00	30.00	20.00
(120a)	Shinners (Date is "1927.")	60.00	30.00	20.00
(120b)	Shinners (Date is "27.")	60.00	30.00	20.00
(121)	Singleton	60.00	30.00	20.00
(122)	Slade	60.00	30.00	20.00
(123)	E. Smith	60.00	30.00	20.00
(124)	Sparks	60.00	30.00	20.00
(125)	Stokes	60.00	30.00	20.00
(126)	J. Storti	60.00	30.00	20.00
(127)	L. Storti	60.00	30.00	20.00
(128)	Strand	60.00	30.00	20.00
(129)	Suhr	60.00	30.00	20.00
(130)	Sunseri	60.00	30.00	20.00
(131)	Swanson	60.00	30.00	20.00
(132)	Tierney	60.00	30.00	20.00
(133)	Valla	60.00	30.00	20.00
(134)	Vargas	60.00	30.00	20.00
(135)	Vitt	60.00	30.00	20.00
(136)	Weinert	60.00	30.00	20.00
(137)	Weis	60.00	30.00	20.00
(138)	Wendell	60.00	30.00	20.00
(139)	Whitney	60.00	30.00	20.00
(140)	Williams	60.00	30.00	20.00
(141)	Guy Williams	60.00	30.00	20.00
(142)	Woodson	60.00	30.00	20.00
(143)	Wright	60.00	30.00	20.00
(144)	Yelle	60.00	30.00	20.00

1928 Zeenut Pacific Coast League

Zeenut cards from 1928 through 1930 maintain the same format as the 1927 series. Measuring about 1-3/4" x 3-3/8", the 1928 series consists of 168 known subjects.

		NM	EX	VG
Common Player:		60.00	30.00	20.00
With Coupo n		800.00	400.00	240.00
(1)	Agnew	60.00	30.00	20.00
(2)	Earl Averill	900.00	450.00	270.00
(3)	Backer	60.00	30.00	20.00
(4)	Baker	60.00	30.00	20.00
(5)	Baldwin	60.00	30.00	20.00
(6)	Barfoot	60.00	30.00	20.00
(7)	Bassler	60.00	30.00	20.00
(8)	Berger	60.00	30.00	20.00
(9)	Bigbee (Los Angeles)	60.00	30.00	20.00
(10)	Bigbee (Portland)	60.00	30.00	20.00
(11)	Bodie	60.00	30.00	20.00
(12)	Boehler	60.00	30.00	20.00
(13)	Bool	60.00	30.00	20.00
(14)	Boone	60.00	30.00	20.00
(15)	Borreani	60.00	30.00	20.00
(16)	Bratcher	60.00	30.00	20.00
(17)	Brenzel	60.00	30.00	20.00
(18)	Brubaker	60.00	30.00	20.00
(19)	Bryan	60.00	30.00	20.00
(20)	Burkett	60.00	30.00	20.00
(21)	Camilli	60.00	30.00	20.00
(22)	W. Canfield	60.00	30.00	20.00
(23)	Caveney	60.00	30.00	20.00
(24)	Syd Cohen	775.00	385.00	230.00
(25)	Cook	60.00	30.00	20.00
(26)	Cooper	60.00	30.00	20.00
(27)	Craghead	60.00	30.00	20.00
(28)	Crosetti	300.00	150.00	90.00
(29)	Cunningham	60.00	30.00	20.00
(30)	Daglia	60.00	30.00	20.00
(31)	Davis	60.00	30.00	20.00
(32)	Dean	60.00	30.00	20.00
(33)	Dittmar	60.00	30.00	20.00
(34)	Donovan	60.00	30.00	20.00
(35)	Downs	60.00	30.00	20.00
(36)	Duff	60.00	30.00	20.00
(37)	Eckert	60.00	30.00	20.00
(38)	Eldred	60.00	30.00	20.00
(39)	Ellsworth	60.00	30.00	20.00
(40)	Fenton	60.00	30.00	20.00
(41)	Finn	60.00	30.00	20.00
(42)	Fitterer	60.00	30.00	20.00
(43)	Flynn	60.00	30.00	20.00
(44)	Frazier	60.00	30.00	20.00
(45)	French (Portland)	60.00	30.00	20.00
(46)	French (Sacramento)	60.00	30.00	20.00
(47)	Fullerton	60.00	30.00	20.00
(48)	Gabler	60.00	30.00	20.00
(49)	Gomes	60.00	30.00	20.00
(50)	Gooch	60.00	30.00	20.00
(51)	Gould	60.00	30.00	20.00
(52)	Governor	60.00	30.00	20.00
(53)	Graham ("S" on uniform.)	60.00	30.00	20.00
(54)	Graham (No "S" on uniform.)	60.00	30.00	20.00
(55)	Guisto	60.00	30.00	20.00
(56)	Hannah	60.00	30.00	20.00
(57)	Hansen	60.00	30.00	20.00
(58)	Harris	60.00	30.00	20.00
(59)	Hasty	60.00	30.00	20.00
(60)	Heath	60.00	30.00	20.00
(61)	Hoffman	60.00	30.00	20.00
(62)	Holling	60.00	30.00	20.00
(63)	Hood	60.00	30.00	20.00
(64)	House	60.00	30.00	20.00
(65)	Howard	60.00	30.00	20.00
(66)	Hudgens	60.00	30.00	20.00
(67)	Hufft	60.00	30.00	20.00
(68)	Hughes	60.00	30.00	20.00
(69)	Hulvey	60.00	30.00	20.00
(70)	Jacobs	60.00	30.00	20.00
(71)	Johnson (Portland)	60.00	30.00	20.00
(72)	Johnson (San Francisco)	60.00	30.00	20.00
(73)	Jolley	90.00	45.00	30.00
(74)	Jones (Batting)	60.00	30.00	20.00
(75)	Jones (Throwing)	60.00	30.00	20.00
(76)	Kallio	60.00	30.00	20.00
(77)	Keating	60.00	30.00	20.00
(78)	Keefe	60.00	30.00	20.00
(79)	Keesey	60.00	30.00	20.00
(80)	Kerr	60.00	30.00	20.00
(81)	Killifer	60.00	30.00	20.00
(82)	Kinney	60.00	30.00	20.00
(83)	Knight	60.00	30.00	20.00
(84)	Knothe	60.00	30.00	20.00
(85)	Koehler	60.00	30.00	20.00
(86)	Kopp	60.00	30.00	20.00
(87)	Krause	60.00	30.00	20.00
(88)	Krug	60.00	30.00	20.00
(89)	Lary	60.00	30.00	20.00
(90)	LeBourveau	60.00	30.00	20.00
(91)	Lee	60.00	30.00	20.00
(92)	Ernie Lombardi	1,350	700.00	400.00
(93)	Mails	60.00	30.00	20.00
(94)	Martin (Missions)	60.00	30.00	20.00
(95)	Martin (Seattle)	60.00	30.00	20.00
(96)	May	60.00	30.00	20.00
(97)	McCabe	60.00	30.00	20.00
(98)	McCrea	60.00	30.00	20.00
(99)	McDaniel	60.00	30.00	20.00
(100)	McLaughlin	60.00	30.00	20.00
(101)	McNulty	60.00	30.00	20.00
(102)	Mellano	60.00	30.00	20.00
(103)	Irish Muesel (Meusel)	60.00	30.00	20.00
(104)	Middleton	60.00	30.00	20.00
(105)	Sol Mishkin	400.00	200.00	120.00
(106)	Mitchell	60.00	30.00	20.00
(107)	Monroe	60.00	30.00	20.00
(108)	Moudy	60.00	30.00	20.00
(109)	Mulcahy	60.00	30.00	20.00
(110)	Muller	60.00	30.00	20.00

(111)	Mulligan	60.00	30.00	20.00
(112)	W. Murphy	60.00	30.00	20.00
(113)	Nance	60.00	30.00	20.00
(114)	Nelson	60.00	30.00	20.00
(115)	Osborn	60.00	30.00	20.00
(116)	Osborne	60.00	30.00	20.00
(117)	Parker	60.00	30.00	20.00
(118)	Peters	60.00	30.00	20.00
(119)	Pillette	60.00	30.00	20.00
(120)	Pinelli	60.00	30.00	20.00
(121)	Plitt	60.00	30.00	20.00
(122)	Ponder	60.00	30.00	20.00
(123)	Rachac	60.00	30.00	20.00
(124)	Read	60.00	30.00	20.00
(125)	Reed	60.00	30.00	20.00
(126)	Jimmy Reese	375.00	190.00	120.00
(127)	Rego	60.00	30.00	20.00
(128)	Rhodes	60.00	30.00	20.00
(129)	Rhyne	60.00	30.00	20.00
(130)	Rodda	60.00	30.00	20.00
(131)	Rohwer	60.00	30.00	20.00
(132)	Rose	60.00	30.00	20.00
(133)	Roth	60.00	30.00	20.00
(134)	Ruble	60.00	30.00	20.00
(135)	Ryan	60.00	30.00	20.00
(136)	Sandberg	60.00	30.00	20.00
(137)	Schulmerich	60.00	30.00	20.00
(138)	Severeid	60.00	30.00	20.00
(139)	Shea	60.00	30.00	20.00
(140)	Sheely	60.00	30.00	20.00
(141)	Shellenback	60.00	30.00	20.00
(142)	Sherlock	60.00	30.00	20.00
(143)	Sigafoos	60.00	30.00	20.00
(144)	Singleton	60.00	30.00	20.00
(145)	Slade	60.00	30.00	20.00
(146)	Smith	60.00	30.00	20.00
(147)	Sprinz	60.00	30.00	20.00
(148)	Staley	60.00	30.00	20.00
(149)	Suhr	60.00	30.00	20.00
(150)	Sunseri	60.00	30.00	20.00
(151)	Swanson	60.00	30.00	20.00
(152)	Sweeney	60.00	30.00	20.00
(153)	Teachout	60.00	30.00	20.00
(154)	Twombly	60.00	30.00	20.00
(155)	Vargas	60.00	30.00	20.00
(156)	Vinci	60.00	30.00	20.00
(157)	Vitt	60.00	30.00	20.00
(158)	Warhop	60.00	30.00	20.00
(159)	Weathersby	60.00	30.00	20.00
(160)	Weiss	60.00	30.00	20.00
(161)	Welch	60.00	30.00	20.00
(162)	Wera	60.00	30.00	20.00
(163)	Wetzel	60.00	30.00	20.00
(164)	Whitney	60.00	30.00	20.00
(165)	Williams	60.00	30.00	20.00
(166)	Wilson	60.00	30.00	20.00
(167)	Wolfer	60.00	30.00	20.00
(168)	Yerkes	60.00	30.00	20.00

1929 Zeenut Pacific Coast League

Zeenut cards from 1928 through 1930 maintain the same format as the 1927 series. Measuring about 1-3/4" x 3-1/2", the 1929 series consists of 168 known subjects.

		NM	EX	VG
Common Player:		60.00	30.00	20.00
With Coupon:		600.00	300.00	180.00
(1)	Albert	60.00	30.00	20.00
(2)	Almada	150.00	75.00	40.00
(3)	Anderson	60.00	30.00	20.00
(4)	Anton	60.00	30.00	20.00
(5)	Backer	60.00	30.00	20.00
(6)	Baker	60.00	30.00	20.00
(7)	Baldwin	60.00	30.00	20.00
(8)	Barbee	60.00	30.00	20.00
(9)	Barfoot	60.00	30.00	20.00
(10)	Bassler	60.00	30.00	20.00
(11)	Bates	60.00	30.00	20.00
(12)	Berger	60.00	30.00	20.00
(13)	Boehler	60.00	30.00	20.00
(14)	Boone	60.00	30.00	20.00
(15)	Borreani	60.00	30.00	20.00
(16)	Brenzel	60.00	30.00	20.00
(17)	Brooks	60.00	30.00	20.00
(18)	Brubaker	60.00	30.00	20.00
(19)	Bryan	60.00	30.00	20.00
(20)	Burke	60.00	30.00	20.00
(21)	Burkett	60.00	30.00	20.00
(22)	Burns	60.00	30.00	20.00
(23)	Bush	60.00	30.00	20.00
(24)	Butler	60.00	30.00	20.00
(25)	Camilli	60.00	30.00	20.00
(26)	Carlyle (Hollywood)	60.00	30.00	20.00
(27)	Carlyle	60.00	30.00	20.00
(28)	Cascarella	60.00	30.00	20.00
(29)	Caveney	60.00	30.00	20.00
(30)	Childs	60.00	30.00	20.00
(31)	Christensen	60.00	30.00	20.00
(32)	Cole	60.00	30.00	20.00
(33)	Collard	60.00	30.00	20.00
(34)	Cooper	60.00	30.00	20.00
(35)	Couch	60.00	30.00	20.00
(36)	Cox	60.00	30.00	20.00
(37)	Craghead	60.00	30.00	20.00
(38)	Crandall	60.00	30.00	20.00
(39)	Cronin	60.00	30.00	20.00
(40)	Crosetti	150.00	75.00	40.00
(41)	Daglia	60.00	30.00	20.00
(42)	Davis	60.00	30.00	20.00
(43)	Dean	60.00	30.00	20.00
(44)	Dittmar	60.00	30.00	20.00
(45)	Donovan	60.00	30.00	20.00
(46)	Dumovich	60.00	30.00	20.00
(47)	Eckardt	60.00	30.00	20.00
(48)	Ellsworth	60.00	30.00	20.00
(49)	Fenton	60.00	30.00	20.00
(50)	Finn	60.00	30.00	20.00
(51)	Fisch	60.00	30.00	20.00
(52)	Flynn	60.00	30.00	20.00
(53)	Frazier	60.00	30.00	20.00
(54)	Freitas	60.00	30.00	20.00
(55)	French	60.00	30.00	20.00
(56)	Gabler	60.00	30.00	20.00
(57)	Glynn	60.00	30.00	20.00
(58)	Lefty Gomez	1,800	900.00	550.00
(59)	Gould	60.00	30.00	20.00
(60)	Governor	60.00	30.00	20.00
(61)	Graham	60.00	30.00	20.00
(62)	Hand	60.00	30.00	20.00
(63)	Hannah	60.00	30.00	20.00
(64)	Harris	60.00	30.00	20.00
(65)	Heath	60.00	30.00	20.00
(66)	Heatherly	60.00	30.00	20.00
(67)	Hepting	60.00	30.00	20.00
(68)	Hillis	60.00	30.00	20.00
(69)	Hoffman	60.00	30.00	20.00
(70)	Holling	60.00	30.00	20.00
(71)	Hood	60.00	30.00	20.00
(72)	House	60.00	30.00	20.00
(73)	Howard	60.00	30.00	20.00
(74)	Hubbell	60.00	30.00	20.00
(75)	Hufft	60.00	30.00	20.00
(76)	Hurst	60.00	30.00	20.00
(77)	Jacobs (Los Angeles)	60.00	30.00	20.00
(78)	Jacobs (San Francisco)	60.00	30.00	20.00
(79)	Jahn	60.00	30.00	20.00
(80)	Jeffcoat	60.00	30.00	20.00
(81)	Johnson	60.00	30.00	20.00
(82)	Jolley	90.00	45.00	30.00
(83)	Gordon Jones (San Francisco)	60.00	30.00	20.00
(84)	Jones	60.00	30.00	20.00
(85)	Kallio	60.00	30.00	20.00
(86)	Kasich	60.00	30.00	20.00
(87)	Keane	60.00	30.00	20.00
(88)	Keating	60.00	30.00	20.00
(89)	Keesey	60.00	30.00	20.00
(90)	Killifer	60.00	30.00	20.00
(91)	Knight	60.00	30.00	20.00
(92)	Knothe	60.00	30.00	20.00
(93)	Knott	60.00	30.00	20.00
(94)	Koehler	60.00	30.00	20.00
(95)	Krasovich	60.00	30.00	20.00
(96)	Krause	60.00	30.00	20.00
(97)	Krug (Hollywood)	60.00	30.00	20.00
(98)	Krug (Los Angeles)	60.00	30.00	20.00
(99)	Kunz	60.00	30.00	20.00
(100)	Langford	60.00	30.00	20.00
(101)	Lee	60.00	30.00	20.00
(102)	Ernie Lombardi	900.00	450.00	275.00
(103)	Mahaffey	60.00	30.00	20.00
(104)	Mails	60.00	30.00	20.00
(105)	Maloney	60.00	30.00	20.00
(106)	McCabe	60.00	30.00	20.00
(107)	McDaniel	60.00	30.00	20.00
(108)	McEvoy	60.00	30.00	20.00
(109)	McIssacs	60.00	30.00	20.00
(110)	McQuaid	60.00	30.00	20.00
(111)	Miller	60.00	30.00	20.00
(112)	Monroe	60.00	30.00	20.00
(113)	Muller	60.00	30.00	20.00
(114)	Mulligan	60.00	30.00	20.00
(115)	Nance	60.00	30.00	20.00
(116)	Nelson	60.00	30.00	20.00
(117)	Nevers	60.00	30.00	20.00
(118)	Oana	700.00	350.00	200.00
(119)	Olney	60.00	30.00	20.00
(120)	Ortman	60.00	30.00	20.00
(121)	Osborne	60.00	30.00	20.00
(122)	Ostenberg	60.00	30.00	20.00
(123)	Peters	60.00	30.00	20.00
(124)	Pillette	60.00	30.00	20.00
(125)	Pinelli	60.00	30.00	20.00
(126)	Pipgras	60.00	30.00	20.00
(127)	Plitt	60.00	30.00	20.00
(128)	Polvogt	60.00	30.00	20.00
(129)	Rachac	60.00	30.00	20.00
(130)	Read	60.00	30.00	20.00
(131)	Reed	60.00	30.00	20.00
(132)	Jimmy Reese	300.00	150.00	90.00
(133)	Rego	60.00	30.00	20.00
(134)	Ritter	60.00	30.00	20.00
(135)	Roberts	60.00	30.00	20.00
(136)	Rodda	60.00	30.00	20.00
(137)	Rodgers	60.00	30.00	20.00
(138)	Rohwer	60.00	30.00	20.00
(139)	Rollings	60.00	30.00	20.00
(140)	Rumler	60.00	30.00	20.00
(141)	Ryan	60.00	30.00	20.00
(142)	Sandberg	60.00	30.00	20.00
(143)	Schino	60.00	30.00	20.00
(144)	Schmidt	60.00	30.00	20.00
(145)	Schulmerich	60.00	30.00	20.00
(146)	Scott	60.00	30.00	20.00
(147)	Severeid	60.00	30.00	20.00
(148)	Shanklin	60.00	30.00	20.00
(149)	Sherlock	60.00	30.00	20.00
(150)	Slade	60.00	30.00	20.00
(151)	Staley	60.00	30.00	20.00
(152)	Statz	90.00	45.00	30.00
(153)	Steinecke	60.00	30.00	20.00
(154)	Suhr	60.00	30.00	20.00
(155)	Taylor	60.00	30.00	20.00
(156)	Thurston	60.00	30.00	20.00
(157)	Tierney	60.00	30.00	20.00
(158)	Tolson	60.00	30.00	20.00
(159)	Tomlin	60.00	30.00	20.00
(160)	Vergez	60.00	30.00	20.00
(161)	Vinci	60.00	30.00	20.00
(162)	Volkman	60.00	30.00	20.00
(163)	Walsh	60.00	30.00	20.00
(164)	Warren	60.00	30.00	20.00
(165)	Webb	60.00	30.00	20.00
(166)	Weustling	60.00	30.00	20.00
(167)	Williams	60.00	30.00	20.00
(168)	Wingo	60.00	30.00	20.00

1930 Zeenut Pacific Coast League

Zeenut cards from 1928 through 1930 maintain the same format as the 1927 series. Measuring about 1-13/16" x 3-1/2", the 1930 series consists of 186 known subjects. There are some lettering variations in the series. Most coupons carry an expiration date of April 1, 1931, but some coupons have no expiration date stated.

		NM	EX	VG
Common Player:		60.00	30.00	20.00
With Coupon		350.00	175.00	100.00
(1)	Allington	60.00	30.00	20.00
(2)	Almada	75.00	40.00	25.00
(3)	Andrews	60.00	30.00	20.00
(4)	Anton	60.00	30.00	20.00
(5)	Arlett	60.00	30.00	20.00
(6)	Backer	60.00	30.00	20.00
(7)	Baecht	60.00	30.00	20.00
(8)	Baker	60.00	30.00	20.00
(9)	Baldwin	60.00	30.00	20.00
(10)	Ballou	60.00	30.00	20.00
(11)	Barbee	60.00	30.00	20.00
(12)	Barfoot	60.00	30.00	20.00
(13)	Bassler	60.00	30.00	20.00
(14)	Bates	60.00	30.00	20.00
(15)	Beck	60.00	30.00	20.00
(16)	Boone	60.00	30.00	20.00
(17)	Bowman	60.00	30.00	20.00
(18)	Brannon	60.00	30.00	20.00
(19)	Brenzel	60.00	30.00	20.00
(20)	Brown	60.00	30.00	20.00
(21)	Brubaker	60.00	30.00	20.00
(22)	Brucker	60.00	30.00	20.00
(23)	Bryan	60.00	30.00	20.00
(24)	Burkett	60.00	30.00	20.00
(25)	Burns	60.00	30.00	20.00
(26)	Butler	60.00	30.00	20.00
(27)	Camilli	60.00	30.00	20.00
(28)	Carlyle	60.00	30.00	20.00
(29)	Caster	60.00	30.00	20.00
(30)	Caveney	60.00	30.00	20.00
(31)	Chamberlain	60.00	30.00	20.00
(32)	Chatham	60.00	30.00	20.00
(33)	Childs	60.00	30.00	20.00
(34)	Christensen	60.00	30.00	20.00
(35)	Church	60.00	30.00	20.00
(36)	Cole	60.00	30.00	20.00
(37)	Coleman	60.00	30.00	20.00
(38)	Collins	60.00	30.00	20.00
(39)	Coscarart	60.00	30.00	20.00
(40)	Cox	60.00	30.00	20.00
(41)	Coyle	60.00	30.00	20.00
(42)	Craghead	60.00	30.00	20.00
(43)	Cronin	60.00	30.00	20.00
(44)	Crosetti	150.00	75.00	45.00
(45)	Daglia	60.00	30.00	20.00
(46)	Davis	60.00	30.00	20.00
(47)	Dean	60.00	30.00	20.00
(48)	DeViveiros	60.00	30.00	20.00
(49)	Dittmar	60.00	30.00	20.00
(50)	Donovan	60.00	30.00	20.00
(51)	Douglas	60.00	30.00	20.00
(52)	Dumovich	60.00	30.00	20.00
(53)	Edwards	60.00	30.00	20.00
(54)	Ellsworth	60.00	30.00	20.00

(55)	Falk	60.00	30.00	20.00
(56)	Fisch	60.00	30.00	20.00
(57)	Flynn	60.00	30.00	20.00
(58)	Freitas	60.00	30.00	20.00
(59)	French (Portland)	60.00	30.00	20.00
(60)	French (Sacramento)	60.00	30.00	20.00
(61)	Gabler	60.00	30.00	20.00
(62)	Gaston	60.00	30.00	20.00
(63)	Gazella	60.00	30.00	20.00
(64)	Gould	60.00	30.00	20.00
(65)	Governor	60.00	30.00	20.00
(66)	Green	60.00	30.00	20.00
(67)	Griffin	60.00	30.00	20.00
(68)	Haney	60.00	30.00	20.00
(69)	Hannah	60.00	30.00	20.00
(70)	Harper	60.00	30.00	20.00
(71)	Heath	60.00	30.00	20.00
(72)	Hillis	60.00	30.00	20.00
(73)	Hoag	60.00	30.00	20.00
(74)	Hoffman	60.00	30.00	20.00
(75)	Holland	60.00	30.00	20.00
(76)	Hollerson	60.00	30.00	20.00
(77)	Holling	60.00	30.00	20.00
(78)	Hood	60.00	30.00	20.00
(79)	Horn	60.00	30.00	20.00
(80)	House	60.00	30.00	20.00
(81)	Hubbell	60.00	30.00	20.00
(82)	Hufft	60.00	30.00	20.00
(83)	Hurst	60.00	30.00	20.00
(84)	Jacobs (Los Angeles)	60.00	30.00	20.00
(85)	Jacobs (Oakland)	60.00	30.00	20.00
(86)	Jacobs	60.00	30.00	20.00
(87)	Jahn	60.00	30.00	20.00
(88)	Jeffcoat	60.00	30.00	20.00
(89)	Johns	60.00	30.00	20.00
(90)	Johnson (Portland)	60.00	30.00	20.00
(91)	Johnson (Seattle)	60.00	30.00	20.00
(92)	Joiner	60.00	30.00	20.00
(93)	Kallio	60.00	30.00	20.00
(94)	Kasich	60.00	30.00	20.00
(95)	Keating	60.00	30.00	20.00
(96)	Kelly	60.00	30.00	20.00
(97)	Killifer	60.00	30.00	20.00
(98)	Knight	60.00	30.00	20.00
(99)	Knothe	60.00	30.00	20.00
(100)	Koehler	60.00	30.00	20.00
(101)	Kunz	60.00	30.00	20.00
(102)	Lamanski	60.00	30.00	20.00
(103)	Lawrence	60.00	30.00	20.00
(104)	Lee	60.00	30.00	20.00
(105)	Leishman	60.00	30.00	20.00
(106)	Lelivelt	60.00	30.00	20.00
(107)	Lieber	60.00	30.00	20.00
(108)	Ernie Lombardi	700.00	350.00	200.00
(109)	Mails	60.00	30.00	20.00
(110)	Maloney	60.00	30.00	20.00
(111)	Martin	60.00	30.00	20.00
(112)	McDougal	60.00	30.00	20.00
(113)	McLaughlin	60.00	30.00	20.00
(114)	McQuaide	60.00	30.00	20.00
(115)	Mellana	60.00	30.00	20.00
(116)	Miljus ("S" on uniform.)	60.00	30.00	20.00
(117)	Miljus ("Seals" on uniform.)	60.00	30.00	20.00
(118)	Monroe	60.00	30.00	20.00
(119)	Montgomery	60.00	30.00	20.00
(120)	Moore	60.00	30.00	20.00
(121)	Mulana	60.00	30.00	20.00
(122)	Muller	60.00	30.00	20.00
(123)	Mulligan	60.00	30.00	20.00
(124)	Nelson	60.00	30.00	20.00
(125)	Nevers	450.00	225.00	150.00
(126)	Odell	60.00	30.00	20.00
(127)	Olney	60.00	30.00	20.00
(128)	Osborne	60.00	30.00	20.00
(129)	Page	60.00	30.00	20.00
(130)	Palmisano	60.00	30.00	20.00
(131)	Parker	60.00	30.00	20.00
(132)	Pasedel	60.00	30.00	20.00
(133)	Pearson	60.00	30.00	20.00
(134)	Penebskey	60.00	30.00	20.00
(135)	Perry	60.00	30.00	20.00
(136)	Peters	60.00	30.00	20.00
(137)	Petterson	60.00	30.00	20.00
(138)	H. Pillette	60.00	30.00	20.00
(139)	T. Pillette	60.00	30.00	20.00
(140)	Pinelli	60.00	30.00	20.00
(141)	Pipgrass	60.00	30.00	20.00
(142)	Porter	60.00	30.00	20.00
(143)	Powles	60.00	30.00	20.00
(144)	Read	60.00	30.00	20.00
(145)	Reed	60.00	30.00	20.00
(146)	Rehg	60.00	30.00	20.00
(147)	Ricci	60.00	30.00	20.00
(148)	Roberts	60.00	30.00	20.00
(149)	Rodda	60.00	30.00	20.00
(150)	Rohwer	60.00	30.00	20.00
(151)	Rosenberg	2,250	1,100	675.00
(152)	Rumler	60.00	30.00	20.00
(153)	Ryan	60.00	30.00	20.00
(154)	Schino	60.00	30.00	20.00
(155)	Severeid	60.00	30.00	20.00
(156)	Shanklin	60.00	30.00	20.00
(157)	Sheely	60.00	30.00	20.00
(158)	Sigafoos	60.00	30.00	20.00
(159)	Statz	90.00	45.00	30.00
(160)	Steinbacker	60.00	30.00	20.00
(161)	Stevenson	60.00	30.00	20.00
(162)	Sulik	60.00	30.00	20.00
(163)	Taylor	60.00	30.00	20.00
(164)	Thomas (Sacramento)	60.00	30.00	20.00
(165)	Thomas (San Francisco)	60.00	30.00	20.00
(166)	Trembly	60.00	30.00	20.00
(167)	Turner	60.00	30.00	20.00
(168)	Turpin	60.00	30.00	20.00
(169)	Uhalt	60.00	30.00	20.00
(170)	Vergez	60.00	30.00	20.00
(171)	Vinci	60.00	30.00	20.00
(172)	Vitt	60.00	30.00	20.00
(173)	Wallgren	60.00	30.00	20.00
(174)	Walsh	60.00	30.00	20.00
(175)	Ward	60.00	30.00	20.00
(176)	Warren	60.00	30.00	20.00
(177)	Webb	60.00	30.00	20.00
(178)	Wetzell	60.00	30.00	20.00
(179)	F. Wetzel	60.00	30.00	20.00
(180)	Williams	60.00	30.00	20.00
(181)	Wilson	60.00	30.00	20.00
(182)	Wingo	60.00	30.00	20.00
(183)	Wirts	60.00	30.00	20.00
(184)	Woodall	60.00	30.00	20.00
(185)	Zamlack	60.00	30.00	20.00
(186)	Zinn	60.00	30.00	20.00

1931 Zeenut Pacific Coast League

COAST LEAGUE
CAMILLI
SACRAMENTO
CUT COUPON HERE
GOOD FOR VALUABLE PREMIUMS
ASK YOUR DEALER FOR LIST
This offer expires April 1st, 1932

Beginning in 1931, Zeenuts cards were no longer dated on the front, and cards without the coupon are very difficult to date. The words "Zeenuts Series" were also dropped from the front and replaced with the words "Coast League." Zeenut cards in 1931 measure 1-3/4" x 3-1/2".

		NM	EX	VG
Common Player:		60.00	30.00	20.00
With Coupon:		800.00	400.00	240.00
(1)	Abbott	60.00	30.00	20.00
(2)	Andrews	60.00	30.00	20.00
(3)	Anton	60.00	30.00	20.00
(4)	Backer	60.00	30.00	20.00
(5)	Baker	60.00	30.00	20.00
(6)	Baldwin	60.00	30.00	20.00
(7)	Barbee	60.00	30.00	20.00
(8)	Barton	60.00	30.00	20.00
(9)	Bassler	60.00	30.00	20.00
(10)	Berger (Missions)	60.00	30.00	20.00
(11)	Berger (Portland)	60.00	30.00	20.00
(12)	Biggs	60.00	30.00	20.00
(13)	Bowman	60.00	30.00	20.00
(14)	Brenzel	60.00	30.00	20.00
(15)	Bryan	60.00	30.00	20.00
(16)	Burns	60.00	30.00	20.00
(17)	Camilli	60.00	30.00	20.00
(18)	Campbell	60.00	30.00	20.00
(19)	Carlyle	60.00	30.00	20.00
(20)	Caveney	60.00	30.00	20.00
(21)	Chesterfield	60.00	30.00	20.00
(22)	Cole	60.00	30.00	20.00
(23)	Coleman	60.00	30.00	20.00
(24)	Coscarart	60.00	30.00	20.00
(25)	Crosetti	300.00	150.00	90.00
(26)	Davis	60.00	30.00	20.00
(27)	DeBerry	60.00	30.00	20.00
(28)	Demaree	60.00	30.00	20.00
(29)	Dean	60.00	30.00	20.00
(30)	Delaney	60.00	30.00	20.00
(31)	Dondero	60.00	30.00	20.00
(32)	Donovan	60.00	30.00	20.00
(33)	Douglas	60.00	30.00	20.00
(34)	Ellsworth	60.00	30.00	20.00
(35)	Farrell	60.00	30.00	20.00
(36)	Fenton	60.00	30.00	20.00
(37)	Fitzpatrick	60.00	30.00	20.00
(38)	Flagstead	60.00	30.00	20.00
(39)	Flynn	60.00	30.00	20.00
(40)	Frazier	60.00	30.00	20.00
(41)	Freitas	60.00	30.00	20.00
(42)	French	60.00	30.00	20.00
(43)	Fullerton	60.00	30.00	20.00
(44)	Gabler	60.00	30.00	20.00
(45)	Gazella	60.00	30.00	20.00
(46)	Hale	60.00	30.00	20.00
(47)	Hamilton	60.00	30.00	20.00
(48)	Haney	60.00	30.00	20.00
(49)	Hannah	60.00	30.00	20.00
(50)	Harper	60.00	30.00	20.00
(51)	Henderson	60.00	30.00	20.00
(52)	Herrmann	60.00	30.00	20.00
(53)	Hoffman	60.00	30.00	20.00
(54)	Holland	60.00	30.00	20.00
(55)	Holling	60.00	30.00	20.00
(56)	Hubbell	60.00	30.00	20.00
(57)	Hufft	60.00	30.00	20.00
(58)	Hurst	60.00	30.00	20.00
(59)	Jacobs	60.00	30.00	20.00
(60)	Kallio	60.00	30.00	20.00
(61)	Keating	60.00	30.00	20.00
(62)	Keesey	60.00	30.00	20.00
(63)	Knothe	60.00	30.00	20.00
(64)	Knott	60.00	30.00	20.00
(65)	Kohler	60.00	30.00	20.00
(66)	Lamanski	60.00	30.00	20.00
(67)	Lee	60.00	30.00	20.00
(68)	Lelivelt	60.00	30.00	20.00
(69)	Lieber	60.00	30.00	20.00
(70)	Lipanovic	60.00	30.00	20.00
(71)	McDonald	60.00	30.00	20.00
(72)	McDougall	60.00	30.00	20.00
(73)	McLaughlin	60.00	30.00	20.00
(74)	Monroe	60.00	30.00	20.00
(75)	Moss	60.00	30.00	20.00
(76)	Mulligan	60.00	30.00	20.00
(77)	Ortman	60.00	30.00	20.00
(78)	Orwoll	60.00	30.00	20.00
(79)	Parker	60.00	30.00	20.00
(80)	Penebskey	60.00	30.00	20.00
(81)	H. Pillette	60.00	30.00	20.00
(82)	T. Pillette	60.00	30.00	20.00
(83)	Pinelli	60.00	30.00	20.00
(84)	Pool	60.00	30.00	20.00
(85)	Posedel	60.00	30.00	20.00
(86)	Powers	60.00	30.00	20.00
(87)	Read	60.00	30.00	20.00
(88)	Andy Reese	60.00	30.00	20.00
(89)	Rhiel	60.00	30.00	20.00
(90)	Ricci	60.00	30.00	20.00
(91)	Rohwer	60.00	30.00	20.00
(92)	Ryan	60.00	30.00	20.00
(93)	Schino	60.00	30.00	20.00
(94)	Schulte	60.00	30.00	20.00
(95)	Severeid	60.00	30.00	20.00
(96)	Sharpe	60.00	30.00	20.00
(97)	Shellenback	60.00	30.00	20.00
(98)	Simas	60.00	30.00	20.00
(99)	Steinbacker	60.00	30.00	20.00
(100)	Summa	60.00	30.00	20.00
(101)	Tubbs	60.00	30.00	20.00
(102)	Turner	60.00	30.00	20.00
(103)	Turpin	60.00	30.00	20.00
(104)	Uhalt	60.00	30.00	20.00
(105)	Vinci	60.00	30.00	20.00
(106)	Vitt	60.00	30.00	20.00
(107)	Wade	60.00	30.00	20.00
(108)	Walsh	60.00	30.00	20.00
(109)	Walters	60.00	30.00	20.00
(110)	Wera	60.00	30.00	20.00
(111)	Wetzel	60.00	30.00	20.00
(112)	Williams (Portland)	60.00	30.00	20.00
(113)	Williams (San Francisco)	60.00	30.00	20.00
(114)	Wingo	60.00	30.00	20.00
(115)	Wirts	60.00	30.00	20.00
(116)	Wise	60.00	30.00	20.00
(117)	Woodall	60.00	30.00	20.00
(118)	Yerkes	60.00	30.00	20.00
(119)	Zamlock	60.00	30.00	20.00
(120)	Zinn	60.00	30.00	20.00

1932 Zeenut Pacific Coast League

Coast
League
OANA
San Francisco

Beginning in 1931, Zeenuts cards were no longer dated on the front, and cards without the coupon are very difficult to date. The words "Zeenuts Series" were dropped from the front and replaced with "Coast League." Zeenut cards in 1932 measure 1-3/4" x 3-1/2".

		NM	EX	VG
Common Player:		60.00	30.00	20.00
With Coupon:		600.00	300.00	180.00
(1)	Abbott	60.00	30.00	20.00
(2)	Almada	75.00	40.00	25.00
(3)	Anton	60.00	30.00	20.00
(4)	Babich	60.00	30.00	20.00
(5)	Backer	60.00	30.00	20.00
(6)	Baker	60.00	30.00	20.00
(7)	Ballou	60.00	30.00	20.00
(8)	Bassler	60.00	30.00	20.00
(9)	Berger	60.00	30.00	20.00
(10)	Blackerby	60.00	30.00	20.00
(11)	Bordagaray	60.00	30.00	20.00
(12)	Brannon	60.00	30.00	20.00
(13)	Briggs	60.00	30.00	20.00
(14)	Brubaker	60.00	30.00	20.00
(15)	Callaghan	60.00	30.00	20.00
(16)	Camilli	60.00	30.00	20.00
(17)	Campbell	60.00	30.00	20.00
(18)	Carlyle	60.00	30.00	20.00
(19)	Caster	60.00	30.00	20.00

(20)	Caveney	60.00	30.00	20.00
(21)	Chamberlain	60.00	30.00	20.00
(22)	Cole	60.00	30.00	20.00
(23)	Collard	60.00	30.00	20.00
(24)	Cook	60.00	30.00	20.00
(25)	Coscarart	60.00	30.00	20.00
(26)	Cox	60.00	30.00	20.00
(27)	Cronin	60.00	30.00	20.00
(28)	Daglia	60.00	30.00	20.00
(29)	Dahlgren	70.00	35.00	20.00
(30)	Davis	60.00	30.00	20.00
(31)	Dean	60.00	30.00	20.00
(32)	Delaney	60.00	30.00	20.00
(33)	Demaree	60.00	30.00	20.00
(34)	Devine	60.00	30.00	20.00
(35)	DeViveiros	60.00	30.00	20.00
(36)	Dittmar	60.00	30.00	20.00
(37)	Donovan	60.00	30.00	20.00
(38)	Ellsworth	60.00	30.00	20.00
(39)	Fitzpatrick	60.00	30.00	20.00
(40)	Frazier	60.00	30.00	20.00
(41)	Freitas	60.00	30.00	20.00
(42)	Garibaldi	60.00	30.00	20.00
(43)	Gaston	60.00	30.00	20.00
(44)	Gazella	60.00	30.00	20.00
(45)	Gillick	60.00	30.00	20.00
(46)	Hafey	60.00	30.00	20.00
(47)	Haney	60.00	30.00	20.00
(48)	Hannah	60.00	30.00	20.00
(49)	Henderson	60.00	30.00	20.00
(50)	Herrmann	60.00	30.00	20.00
(51)	Hipps	60.00	30.00	20.00
(52)	Hofman	60.00	30.00	20.00
(53)	Holland	60.00	30.00	20.00
(54)	House	60.00	30.00	20.00
(55)	Hufft	60.00	30.00	20.00
(56)	Hunt	60.00	30.00	20.00
(57)	Hurst	60.00	30.00	20.00
(58)	Jacobs	60.00	30.00	20.00
(59)	Johns	60.00	30.00	20.00
(60)	Johnson (Missions)	60.00	30.00	20.00
(61)	Johnson (Portland)	60.00	30.00	20.00
(62)	Johnson (Seattle)	60.00	30.00	20.00
(63)	Joiner	60.00	30.00	20.00
(64)	Kallio	60.00	30.00	20.00
(65)	Kasich	60.00	30.00	20.00
(66)	Keesey	60.00	30.00	20.00
(67)	Kelly	60.00	30.00	20.00
(68)	Koehler	60.00	30.00	20.00
(69)	Lee	60.00	30.00	20.00
(70)	Lieber	60.00	30.00	20.00
(71)	Mailho	60.00	30.00	20.00
(72)	Martin (Oakland)	60.00	30.00	20.00
(73)	Martin (San Francisco)	60.00	30.00	20.00
(74)	McNeely	60.00	30.00	20.00
(75)	Miljus	60.00	30.00	20.00
(76)	Monroe	60.00	30.00	20.00
(77)	Mosolf	60.00	30.00	20.00
(78)	Moss	60.00	30.00	20.00
(79)	Muller	60.00	30.00	20.00
(80)	Mulligan	60.00	30.00	20.00
(81)	Oana	550.00	275.00	175.00
(82)	Osborn	60.00	30.00	20.00
(83)	Page	60.00	30.00	20.00
(84)	Penebsky	60.00	30.00	20.00
(85)	H. Pillette	60.00	30.00	20.00
(86)	Pinelli	75.00	40.00	25.00
(87)	Poole	60.00	30.00	20.00
(88)	Quellich	60.00	30.00	20.00
(89)	Read	60.00	30.00	20.00
(90)	Ricci	60.00	30.00	20.00
(91)	Salvo	60.00	30.00	20.00
(92)	Sankey	60.00	30.00	20.00
(93)	Sheehan	60.00	30.00	20.00
(94)	Shellenback	60.00	30.00	20.00
(95)	Sherlock (Hollywood)	60.00	30.00	20.00
(96)	Sherlock (Missions)	60.00	30.00	20.00
(97)	Shores	60.00	30.00	20.00
(98)	Simas	60.00	30.00	20.00
(99)	Statz	90.00	45.00	30.00
(100)	Steinbacker	60.00	30.00	20.00
(101)	Sulik	60.00	30.00	20.00
(102)	Summa	60.00	30.00	20.00
(103)	Thomas	60.00	30.00	20.00
(104)	Uhalt	60.00	30.00	20.00
(105)	Vinci	60.00	30.00	20.00
(106)	Vitt	60.00	30.00	20.00
(107)	Walsh (Missions)	60.00	30.00	20.00
(108)	Walsh (Oakland)	60.00	30.00	20.00
(109)	Walters	60.00	30.00	20.00
(110)	Ward	60.00	30.00	20.00
(111)	Welsh	60.00	30.00	20.00
(112)	Wera	60.00	30.00	20.00
(113)	Williams	60.00	30.00	20.00
(114)	Willoughby	60.00	30.00	20.00
(115)	Wirts	60.00	30.00	20.00
(116)	Wise	60.00	30.00	20.00
(117)	Woodall	60.00	30.00	20.00
(118)	Yde	60.00	30.00	20.00
(119)	Zahniser	60.00	30.00	20.00
(120)	Zamloch	60.00	30.00	20.00

1933 Zeenut Pacific Coast League (Sepia)

This is the most confusing era for Zeenut cards. The cards of 1933-36 are nearly identical, displaying the words, "Coast League" in a small rectangle with rounded corners, along with the player's name and team. The photos are black-and-white (except 1933 Zeenuts have also been found with sepia photos). Because no date appears on the photos, cards from these years are impossible to tell apart without the coupon bottom that lists an expiration date. To date over 161 subjects have been found, with some known to exist in all four years. There are cases where the exact same photo was used from one year to the next (sometimes with minor cropping differences). All cards of Joe and Vince DiMaggio have their last name misspelled "DeMaggio." Cards of all years measure about 1-3/4" x 3-1/2" with coupon.

		NM	EX	VG
Common Player:		60.00	30.00	20.00
With Coupon:		400.00	200.00	120.00
(1)	L. Almada	75.00	40.00	25.00
(2)	Anton	60.00	30.00	20.00
(3)	Bassler	60.00	30.00	20.00
(4)	Bonnelly	60.00	30.00	20.00
(5)	Bordagary	60.00	30.00	20.00
(6)	Bottarini	60.00	30.00	20.00
(7)	Brannan	60.00	30.00	20.00
(8)	Brubaker	60.00	30.00	20.00
(9)	Bryan	60.00	30.00	20.00
(10)	Burns	60.00	30.00	20.00
(11)	Camilli	60.00	30.00	20.00
(12)	Chozen	60.00	30.00	20.00
(13)	Cole	60.00	30.00	20.00
(14)	Cronin	60.00	30.00	20.00
(15)	Dahlgren	60.00	30.00	20.00
(16)	Donovan	60.00	30.00	20.00
(17)	Douglas	60.00	30.00	20.00
(18)	Flynn	60.00	30.00	20.00
(19)	French	60.00	30.00	20.00
(20)	Frietas	60.00	30.00	20.00
(21)	Galan	60.00	30.00	20.00
(22)	Hofmann	60.00	30.00	20.00
(23)	Kelman	60.00	30.00	20.00
(24)	Lelivelt	60.00	30.00	20.00
(25)	Ludolph	60.00	30.00	20.00
(26)	McDonald	60.00	30.00	20.00
(27)	McNeely	60.00	30.00	20.00
(28)	McQuaid	60.00	30.00	20.00
(29)	Moncrief	60.00	30.00	20.00
(30)	Nelson	60.00	30.00	20.00
(31)	Osborne	60.00	30.00	20.00
(32)	Petersen	60.00	30.00	20.00
(33)	Reeves	60.00	30.00	20.00
(34)	Scott	60.00	30.00	20.00
(35)	Shellenback	60.00	30.00	20.00
(36)	J. Sherlock	60.00	30.00	20.00
(37)	V. Sherlock	60.00	30.00	20.00
(38)	Steinbacker	60.00	30.00	20.00
(39)	Stine	60.00	30.00	20.00
(40)	Strange	60.00	30.00	20.00
(41)	Sulik	60.00	30.00	20.00
(42)	Sweetland	60.00	30.00	20.00
(43)	Uhalt	60.00	30.00	20.00
(44)	Vinci	60.00	30.00	20.00
(45)	Vitt	60.00	30.00	20.00
(46)	Wetzel	60.00	30.00	20.00
(47)	Woodall	60.00	30.00	20.00
(48)	Zinn	60.00	30.00	20.00

1933-36 Zeenut Pacific Coast League (Black-and-White)

		NM	EX	VG
Common Player:		60.00	30.00	20.00
With Coupon:		750.00	375.00	225.00
(1a)	Almada (Large pose.)	75.00	40.00	25.00
(1b)	Almada (Small pose.)	75.00	40.00	25.00
(2a)	Anton (Large pose.)	60.00	30.00	20.00
(2b)	Anton (Small pose.)	60.00	30.00	20.00
(3)	Babich	60.00	30.00	20.00
(4)	Backer	60.00	30.00	20.00
(5)	Ballou (Black stockings.)	60.00	30.00	20.00
(6a)	Ballou (Stockings with band, large pose.)	60.00	30.00	20.00
(6b)	Ballou (Stockings with band, small pose.)	60.00	30.00	20.00
(7)	Barath	60.00	30.00	20.00
(8)	Beck	60.00	30.00	20.00
(9)	C. Beck	60.00	30.00	20.00
(10)	W. Beck	60.00	30.00	20.00
(11)	Becker	60.00	30.00	20.00
(12)	Biongovanni	60.00	30.00	20.00
(13)	Blackerby	60.00	30.00	20.00
(14)	Blakely	60.00	30.00	20.00
(15)	Borja (Sacramento)	60.00	30.00	20.00
(16)	Borja (Seals)	60.00	30.00	20.00
(17)	Brundin	60.00	30.00	20.00
(18)	Carlyle	60.00	30.00	20.00
(19a)	Caveney (Name incorrect.)	60.00	30.00	20.00
(19b)	Cavaney (Name correct.)	60.00	30.00	20.00
(20)	Chelini	60.00	30.00	20.00
(21)	Cole (With glove.)	60.00	30.00	20.00
(22)	Cole (No glove.)	60.00	30.00	20.00
(23)	Connors	60.00	30.00	20.00
(24)	Coscarart (Missions)	60.00	30.00	20.00
(25)	Coscarart (Seattle)	60.00	30.00	20.00
(26)	Cox	60.00	30.00	20.00
(27)	Davis	60.00	30.00	20.00
(28)	J. DeMaggio (DiMaggio) (Batting)	20,000	10,000	6,000
(29)	J. DeMaggio (DiMaggio) (Throwing)	20,000	10,000	6,000
(30)	V. DeMaggio (DiMaggio)	1,000	500.00	300.00
(31)	DeViveiros	60.00	30.00	20.00
(32)	Densmore	60.00	30.00	20.00
(33)	Dittmar	60.00	30.00	20.00
(34)	Donovan	60.00	30.00	20.00
(35)	Douglas (Oakland)	60.00	30.00	20.00
(36)	Douglas (Seals)	60.00	30.00	20.00
(37a)	Duggan (Large pose.)	60.00	30.00	20.00
(37b)	Duggan (Small pose.)	60.00	30.00	20.00
(38)	Durst	60.00	30.00	20.00
(39a)	Eckhardt (Large pose.)	60.00	30.00	20.00
(39b)	Eckhardt (Small pose.)	60.00	30.00	20.00
(40)	Ellsworth	60.00	30.00	20.00
(41)	Fenton	60.00	30.00	20.00
(42)	Fitzpatrick	60.00	30.00	20.00
(43)	Francovich	60.00	30.00	20.00
(44)	Funk	60.00	30.00	20.00
(45a)	Garibaldi (Large pose.)	60.00	30.00	20.00
(45b)	Garibaldi (Small pose.)	60.00	30.00	20.00
(46)	Gibson (Black sleeves.)	60.00	30.00	20.00
(47)	Gibson (White sleeves.)	60.00	30.00	20.00
(48)	Gira	60.00	30.00	20.00
(49)	Glaister	60.00	30.00	20.00
(50)	Graves	60.00	30.00	20.00
(51a)	Hafey (Missions, large pose.)	60.00	30.00	20.00
(51b)	Hafey (Missions, middle-size pose.)	60.00	30.00	20.00
(51c)	Hafey (Missions, small pose.)	60.00	30.00	20.00
(52)	Hafey (Sacramento)	60.00	30.00	20.00
(53)	Haid (Oakland)	60.00	30.00	20.00
(54)	Haid (Seattle)	60.00	30.00	20.00
(55)	Haney	60.00	30.00	20.00
(56a)	Hartwig (Sacramento, large pose.)	60.00	30.00	20.00
(56b)	Hartwig (Sacramento, small pose.)	60.00	30.00	20.00
(57)	Hartwig (Seals)	60.00	30.00	20.00
(58)	Henderson	60.00	30.00	20.00
(59)	Herrmann	60.00	30.00	20.00
(60)	B. Holder	60.00	30.00	20.00
(61)	Holland	60.00	30.00	20.00
(62)	Horne	60.00	30.00	20.00
(63)	House	60.00	30.00	20.00
(64)	Hunt	60.00	30.00	20.00
(65)	A.E. Jacobs	60.00	30.00	20.00
(66)	Johns	60.00	30.00	20.00
(67)	D. Johnson	60.00	30.00	20.00
(68)	L. Johnson	60.00	30.00	20.00
(69)	Joiner	60.00	30.00	20.00
(70)	Jolley	90.00	45.00	30.00
(71)	Joost	60.00	30.00	20.00
(72)	Jorgensen	60.00	30.00	20.00
(73)	Kallio	60.00	30.00	20.00
(74)	Kamm	60.00	30.00	20.00
(75)	Kampouris	60.00	30.00	20.00
(76)	E. Kelly (Oakland)	60.00	30.00	20.00
(77)	E. Kelly (Seattle)	60.00	30.00	20.00
(78)	Kenna	60.00	30.00	20.00
(79)	Kintana	60.00	30.00	20.00
(80)	Lahman	60.00	30.00	20.00
(81)	Lieber	60.00	30.00	20.00
(82)	Ludolph	60.00	30.00	20.00
(83)	Mailho	60.00	30.00	20.00
(84a)	Mails (Large pose.)	60.00	30.00	20.00
(84b)	Mails (Small pose.)	60.00	30.00	20.00
(85)	Marty (Black sleeves.)	60.00	30.00	20.00
(86)	Marty (White sleeves.)	60.00	30.00	20.00
(87)	Massuci (Batting follow-through.)	60.00	30.00	20.00
(88)	Masucci (Different pose.)	60.00	30.00	20.00
(89a)	McEvoy (Large pose.)	60.00	30.00	20.00
(89b)	McEvoy (Small pose.)	60.00	30.00	20.00
(90)	McIsaacs	60.00	30.00	20.00
(91)	McMullen (Oakland)	60.00	30.00	20.00
(92)	McMullen (Seals)	60.00	30.00	20.00
(93)	Mitchell	60.00	30.00	20.00
(94a)	Monzo (Large pose.)	60.00	30.00	20.00
(94b)	Monzo (Small pose.)	60.00	30.00	20.00
(95)	Mort (Throwing)	60.00	30.00	20.00
(96)	Mort (Batting)	60.00	30.00	20.00
(97a)	Muller (Oakland, large pose.)	60.00	30.00	20.00
(97b)	Muller (Oakland, small pose.)	60.00	30.00	20.00
(98)	Muller (Seattle)	60.00	30.00	20.00
(99)	Mulligan (Hands showing.)	60.00	30.00	20.00
(100)	Mulligan (Hands not showing.)	60.00	30.00	20.00

(101)	Newkirk	60.00	30.00	20.00
(102)	Nicholas	60.00	30.00	20.00
(103)	Nitcholas	60.00	30.00	20.00
(103a)	Norbert (Large pose.)	60.00	30.00	20.00
(103b)	Norbert (Small pose.)	60.00	30.00	20.00
(105)	O'Doul (Black sleeves.)	675.00	350.00	200.00
(106)	O'Doul (White sleeves.)	675.00	350.00	200.00
(107)	Oglesby	60.00	30.00	20.00
(108)	Ostenberg	60.00	30.00	20.00
(109)	Outen (Throwing)	60.00	30.00	20.00
(110)	Outen (Batting)	60.00	30.00	20.00
(111)	Page (Hollywood)	60.00	30.00	20.00
(112)	Page (Seattle)	60.00	30.00	20.00
(113)	Palmisano	60.00	30.00	20.00
(114)	Parker	60.00	30.00	20.00
(115)	Phebus	60.00	30.00	20.00
(116)	T. Pillette	60.00	30.00	20.00
(117)	Pool	60.00	30.00	20.00
(118)	Powers	60.00	30.00	20.00
(119)	Quellich	60.00	30.00	20.00
(120)	Radonitz	60.00	30.00	20.00
(121a)	Raimondi (Large pose.)	60.00	30.00	20.00
(121b)	Raimondi (Small pose.)	60.00	30.00	20.00
(122a)	Jimmy Reese (Large pose.)	300.00	200.00	100.00
(122b)	Jimmy Reese (Small pose.)	300.00	200.00	100.00
(123)	Rego	60.00	30.00	20.00
(124)	Rhyne (Front)	60.00	30.00	20.00
(125)	Rosenberg	60.00	30.00	20.00
(126)	Salinsen	60.00	30.00	20.00
(127)	Salkeld	60.00	30.00	20.00
(128)	Salvo	60.00	30.00	20.00
(129)	Sever	60.00	30.00	20.00
(130)	Sheehan (Black sleeves.)	60.00	30.00	20.00
(131)	Sheehan (White sleeves.)	60.00	30.00	20.00
(132a)	Sheely (Large pose.)	60.00	30.00	20.00
(132b)	Sheely (Small pose.)	60.00	30.00	20.00
(134)	Sprinz	60.00	30.00	20.00
(135)	Starritt	60.00	30.00	20.00
(136)	Statz	90.00	45.00	30.00
(137a)	Steinbacker (Large pose.)	60.00	30.00	20.00
(137b)	Steinbacker (Small pose.)	60.00	30.00	20.00
(138)	Stewart	60.00	30.00	20.00
(139)	Stitzel (Los Angeles)	60.00	30.00	20.00
(140)	Stitzel (Missions)	60.00	30.00	20.00
(141)	Stitzel (Seals)	60.00	30.00	20.00
(142)	Stoneham	60.00	30.00	20.00
(143)	Street	60.00	30.00	20.00
(144)	Stroner	60.00	30.00	20.00
(145)	Stutz	60.00	30.00	20.00
(146)	Sulik	60.00	30.00	20.00
(147a)	Thurston (Mission)	60.00	30.00	20.00
(147b)	Thurston (Missions)	60.00	30.00	20.00
(148)	Vitt (Hollywood)	60.00	30.00	20.00
(149)	Vitt (Oakland)	60.00	30.00	20.00
(150)	Wallgren	60.00	30.00	20.00
(151)	Walsh	60.00	30.00	20.00
(152)	Walters	60.00	30.00	20.00
(153)	West	60.00	30.00	20.00
(154a)	Wirts (Large pose.)	60.00	30.00	20.00
(154b)	Wirts (Small pose.)	60.00	30.00	20.00
(155)	Woodall (Batting)	60.00	30.00	20.00
(156)	Woodall (Throwing)	60.00	30.00	20.00
(157)	Wright (Facing to front.)	60.00	30.00	20.00
(158)	Wright (Facing to left.)	60.00	30.00	20.00
(159)	Zinn	60.00	30.00	20.00

1937-38 Zeenut Pacific Coast League

The 1937 and 1938 Zeenuts are similar to the 1933-1936 issues, except the black rectangle containing the player's name and team has square (rather than rounded) corners. Again, it is difficult to distinguish between the two years. In 1938, Zeenuts eliminated the coupon bottom and began including a separate coupon in the candy package along with the baseball card. The final two years of the Zeenuts issues, the 1937 and 1938 cards, are among the more difficult to find. With coupon, the 1937 cards measure about 1-5/8" x 3-7/16". The coupon-less 1938 cards measure about 1-3/4" x 2-13/16".

		NM	EX	VG
Common Player:		60.00	25.00	15.00
With Coupon:		400.00	200.00	120.00
(1)	Annunzio	60.00	25.00	15.00
(2)	Baker	60.00	25.00	15.00
(3)	Ballou	60.00	25.00	15.00
(4)	C. Beck	60.00	25.00	15.00
(5)	W. Beck	60.00	25.00	15.00
(6)	Bolin	60.00	25.00	15.00
(7)	Bongiavanni	60.00	25.00	15.00
(8)	Boss	60.00	25.00	15.00
(9)	Carson	60.00	25.00	15.00
(10)	Clabaugh	60.00	25.00	15.00
(11)	Clifford	60.00	25.00	15.00
(12)	B. Cole	60.00	25.00	15.00
(13)	Coscarart	60.00	25.00	15.00
(14)	Cronin	60.00	25.00	15.00
(15)	Cullop	60.00	25.00	15.00
(16)	Daglia	60.00	25.00	15.00
(17)	D. DeMaggio (DiMaggio)	1,600	800.00	500.00
(18)	Douglas	60.00	25.00	15.00
(19)	Frankovich	60.00	25.00	15.00
(20)	Frazier	60.00	25.00	15.00
(21)	Fredericks	60.00	25.00	15.00
(22)	Freitas	60.00	25.00	15.00
(23)	Gabrielson (Oakland)	60.00	25.00	15.00
(24)	Gabrielson (Seattle)	60.00	25.00	15.00
(25)	Garibaldi	60.00	25.00	15.00
(26)	Gibson	60.00	25.00	15.00
(27)	Gill	60.00	25.00	15.00
(28)	Graves	60.00	25.00	15.00
(29)	Guay	60.00	25.00	15.00
(30)	Gudat	60.00	25.00	15.00
(31)	Haid	60.00	25.00	15.00
(32)	Hannah	60.00	25.00	15.00
(33)	Hawkins	60.00	25.00	15.00
(34)	Herrmann	60.00	25.00	15.00
(35)	Holder	60.00	25.00	15.00
(36)	Jennings	60.00	25.00	15.00
(37)	Judnich	60.00	25.00	15.00
(38)	Klinger	60.00	25.00	15.00
(39)	Koenig	60.00	25.00	15.00
(40)	Koupal	60.00	25.00	15.00
(41)	Koy	60.00	25.00	15.00

(42)	Lamanski	60.00	25.00	15.00
(43)	Leishman (Oakland)	60.00	25.00	15.00
(44)	Leishman (Seattle)	60.00	25.00	15.00
(45)	G. Lillard	60.00	25.00	15.00
(46)	Mann	60.00	25.00	15.00
(47)	Marble (Hollywood)	60.00	25.00	15.00
(49)	Miller	60.00	25.00	15.00
(50)	Mills	60.00	25.00	15.00
(51)	Monzo	60.00	25.00	15.00
(52)	B. Mort (Hollywood)	60.00	25.00	15.00
(53)	B. Mort (Missions)	60.00	25.00	15.00
(54)	Muller	60.00	25.00	15.00
(55)	Murray	60.00	25.00	15.00
(56)	Newsome	60.00	25.00	15.00
(57)	Nitcholas	60.00	25.00	15.00
(58)	Olds	60.00	25.00	15.00
(59)	Orengo	60.00	25.00	15.00
(60)	Osborne	60.00	25.00	15.00
(61)	Outen	60.00	25.00	15.00
(62)	C. Outen (Hollywood)	60.00	25.00	15.00
(63)	C. Outen (Missions)	60.00	25.00	15.00
(64)	Pippin	60.00	25.00	15.00
(65)	Powell	60.00	25.00	15.00
(66)	Radonitz	60.00	25.00	15.00
(67)	Raimondi (Oakland)	60.00	25.00	15.00
(68)	Raimondi (San Francisco)	60.00	25.00	15.00
(69)	A. Raimondi	60.00	25.00	15.00
(70)	W. Raimondi	60.00	25.00	15.00
(71)	Rhyne	60.00	25.00	15.00
(72)	Rosenberg (Missions)	1,200	600.00	360.00
(73)	Rosenberg (Portland)	1,200	600.00	360.00
(74)	Sawyer	60.00	25.00	15.00
(75)	Seats	60.00	25.00	15.00
(76)	Sheehan (Oakland)	60.00	25.00	15.00
(77)	Sheehan (San Francisco)	60.00	25.00	15.00
(78)	Shores	60.00	25.00	15.00
(79)	Slade (Hollywood)	60.00	25.00	15.00
(80)	Slade (Missions)	60.00	25.00	15.00
(81)	Sprinz (Missions)	60.00	25.00	15.00
(82)	Sprinz (San Francisco)	60.00	25.00	15.00
(83)	Statz	75.00	37.50	22.50
(84)	Storey	60.00	25.00	15.00
(85)	Stringfellow	60.00	25.00	15.00
(86)	Stutz	60.00	25.00	15.00
(87)	Sweeney	60.00	25.00	15.00
(88)	Thomson	60.00	25.00	15.00
(89)	Tost (Hollywood)	60.00	25.00	15.00
(90)	Tost (Missions)	60.00	25.00	15.00
(91)	Ulrich	60.00	25.00	15.00
(92)	Vergez	60.00	25.00	15.00
(93)	Vezelich	60.00	25.00	15.00
(94)	Vitter (Hollywood)	60.00	25.00	15.00
(95)	Vitter (San Francisco)	60.00	25.00	15.00
(96)	West	60.00	25.00	15.00
(97)	Wilson	60.00	25.00	15.00
(98)	Woodall	60.00	25.00	15.00
(99)	Wright	60.00	25.00	15.00

Alphabetical Index

Chronological Index